12 -DEC

HARRAP'S
Paperback

French-English
Dictionary

Dictionnaire
Anglais-Français

HARRAP'S
Paperback

French-English Dictionary

Dictionnaire Anglais-Français

Edited by Helen Knox

HARRAP
London

Distributed in the United States by
PRENTICE HALL
New York

First published as
Harrap's Concise French and English Dictionary
in 1984

First published in this edition
in Great Britain
by HARRAP BOOKS Ltd
Chelsea House, 26 Market Square, Bromley, Kent BR1 1NA

ISBN 0 245-54411-9
In the United States, ISBN 0-13-383043-8

Library of Congress Cataloging-in-Publication Data

Harrap's concise French and English dictionary / edited by
Patricia Forbes and Muriel Holland Smith: completely
revised and edited by Helen Knox.
p.   cm.
"First published in Great Britain, 1984" — T.p. verso
ISBN 0-13-383035-7 : $16.95 (U.S. : est.). — ISBN 0-13-
383050 (vinyl) : $12.95 (U.S. : est.). — ISBN 0-13-383043-8
(pbk.) : $7.95 (U.S. : est.)
1. French language—Dictionaries—English. 2. English
language—Dictionaries—French.
I. Forbes, Patricia II. Smith, Muriel Holland III. Knox,
Helen. IV. Title: Concise French and English dictionary.
PC2640.H27 1990
443'.21—dc20
89-26638
CIP

Printed and bound in Great Britain
by Cox & Wyman Limited, Reading

Preface

This dictionary is a completely revised and considerably enlarged version of *Harrap's Concise French and English Dictionary* originally compiled by the late R. P. Jago and published in 1949, and revised and edited by Patricia Forbes and Muriel Holland Smith in 1978. The aim of the present edition is to provide the user, whether student, businessman or tourist with an up-to-date practical work of reference giving translations of modern English and French vocabulary. The word list, especially in the French–English part, has been greatly extended to include words which have appeared since 1978 and some of the more common scientific, technical and computer vocabulary. The user will also find many more Americanisms. As with all Harrap dictionaries, care has been taken to include a great number of examples to show the various uses of the more important words. British English spellings have been used throughout the dictionary, but American differences in spelling are given in the text. The user's attention is also drawn to a new and useful device: where an English word such as **sweet** has an American equivalent, the Americanism is given in brackets, e.g. **sweet** *n* (*NAm:* = **candy**). Similarly, under **candy** the user will find the English equivalent (*Br* = **sweet**).

The phonetics of both French and English words, and Americanisms where applicable, are given according to the International Phonetic Association, with some modifications. A table of phonetic symbols is given at the beginning of each part of the dictionary.

The layout of the dictionary has been considerably modified: redundant punctuation has been deleted and all headwords and derivatives are printed in a larger, clearer typeface, allowing for easier reference. In order to save space and include as many examples as possible, when a headword appears in an example in exactly the same form, it is represented by the initial, e.g. **fail** *vi* **to f. in one's duty**, manquer à son devoir.

The section 'How to use the dictionary' gives a detailed guide to the layout.

In the English–French part, nouns, verbs, adjectives and adverbs which have the same form are shown together under one headword with the divisions **I., II., III.** etc. e.g. **part I.** *n*, **II.** *adv*, **III.** *v*. Where an article is shorter and contains fewer sections, the divisions **1., 2., 3.** etc. have been used, e.g. **pain 1.** *n* **2.** *vtr*. Derivatives are listed under the main headword and are shown in full with a stress mark, e.g. **identify** *vtr* **1.** identifier ... **i'dentical** *a* identique. **identifi'cation** *n* identification *f*. If a derivative is pronounced somewhat differently from the main headword, the phonetics are given, e.g. **immobile** [i'moubail] *a* ... **immobili'zation** [-bilai-] *n* ...

In the French–English part all derivatives are written in full and given a translation, e.g. **faible** *a* feeble, weak. **faiblement** *adv* feebly, weakly. All French nouns and verbs are entered as separate headwords and are followed by their derivatives (where applicable), e.g. **fidèle** and **fidèlement** are shown together under **fidélité**, **accommodant** is under **accommoder**. Where a word is both adjective and noun, it will be found under the word from which it derives, e.g. **accidenté, -ée** *a & n* is under **accident** *nm*.

Irregular plurals of nouns, irregular feminine forms of adjectives and irregular conjugations of verbs are indicated in both parts, and on the English–French part irregular comparatives and superlatives of adjectives are also shown. The user is advised to consult the French or English headword for information on irregular forms.

Common abbreviations, which have previously been listed at the end of each part of the dictionary are now included in the text in their alphabetical place. Thus, **FF** *abbr* **1**. *frères* **2**. *Franc français* will be found after **février** and before **fi**.

The production of this edition could not have been achieved without the assistance of the large team of compilers, proofreaders and advisers who took part in the revision work. I should like to thank them for their efforts and valuable help. Grateful thanks are also due to the printers who coped so efficiently with an often difficult manuscript.

The Editor
London, 1984

Préface

Ce dictionnaire est une version entièrement refondue et considérablement augmentée du *Harrap's Concise French and English Dictionary* élaboré par M. R. P. Jago, aujourd'hui disparu, et publié en 1949 puis revu et mis au point par Patricia Forbes et Muriel Holland Smith en 1978. La présente édition a pour objet de mettre à la disposition de son utilisateur – étudiant, homme d'affaires ou touriste – un ouvrage de référence pratique et à jour donnant les traductions du vocabulaire moderne anglais et français. Le vocabulaire, particulièrement celui de la partie français–anglais, a été considérablement enrichi et inclut des mot apparus depuis 1978, ainsi que les mots scientifiques, techniques, notamment d'informatique, les plus usuels. L'utilisateur trouvera également un plus grand nombre d'américanismes. Comme tous les dictionnaires Harrap, cet ouvrage donne un grand nombre d'exemples qui illustrent les diverses utilisations des mots les plus importants.

L'orthographe des mots anglais respecte l'usage britannique, mais les variantes américaines sont signalées. Nous attirons l'attention de l'utilisateur sur un principe de présentation à la fois nouveau et utile: lorsqu'un mot anglais tel que **sweet** n possède un équivalent américain, l'américanisme est donné entre parenthèses; ex. **sweet** n (*NAm:* = **candy**). Inversement, au mot **candy** l'utilisateur trouvera l'équivalent britannique (*Br* = **sweet**).

La transcription phonétique des mots français et anglais, et des américanismes le cas échéant, respecte les signes de l'Association Phonétique Internationale, mais avec quelques modifications. Un tableau des signes phonétiques est donné au début de chaque partie.

La présentation du dictionnaire a été considérablement modifiée: la ponctuation non indispensable a été supprimée et tous les mots-vedettes et leurs dérivés sont imprimés dans un corps plus gros et plus clair, ce qui facilite la consultation. Pour gagner de la place et donner le plus grand nombre d'exemples, la règle suivante a été adoptée: lorsqu'un mot-vedette figure exactement sous la même forme dans un exemple, il est représenté par sa première lettre; ex. **fail** *vi* **to f. in one's duty**, manquer à son devoir.
   La rubrique intitulée 'Comment utiliser le dictionnaire' donne une explication détaillée de la présentation.

   Dans la partie anglais–français, les noms, verbes, adjectifs et adverbes ayant la même forme sont groupés sous le même mot-vedette et séparés par les sous-titres I., II., III. etc.; ex. **part** I. *n*, II. *adv*, III. *v*. Lorsqu'un article est plus court et comporte moins de parties, les sous-titres 1., 2., 3. etc. sont utilisés, ex. **pain** 1. *n* 2. *vtr*. Les dérivés suivent le mot-vedette et sont écrits en toutes lettres avec indication de l'accentuation; ex. **identify** *vtr* 1. identifier ... **i'dentical** *a* identique. **identifi'cation** *n* identification *f*. Si la prononciation d'un dérivé est légèrement différente de celle du mot-vedette, la différence phonétique est signalée; ex. **immobile** (i'moubail) *a* ... **immobili'zation** [-bilai-] *n* ...
   Dans la partie français–anglais, tous les dérivés sont écrits intégralement avec leur traduction; ex. **faible** *a* feeble, weak. **faiblement** *adv* feebly, weakly. Tous les noms et verbes français sont indiqués sous la forme de mots-vedettes et suivis de leurs dérivés (s'il y a lieu); ex. **fidèle** et **fidèlement** sont indiqués ensemble sous **fidélité**, et **accommodant** sous **accommoder**.
   Lorsqu'un mot est à la fois adjectif et nom, il apparaît sous le mot dont il dérive; ainsi, **accidenté, -ée** *a & n* figure sous **accident** *nm*.

Les pluriels irréguliers des noms, les formes féminines irrégulières des adjectifs, et les conjugaisons irrégulières des verbes sont indiqués dans les deux parties, et dans la partie anglais–français, les comparatifs et superlatifs irréguliers des adjectifs sont également indiqués. Pour les formes irrégulières, l'utilisateur est prié de consulter le mot-vedette français ou anglais.

Les abréviations courantes, qui dans l'édition précédente étaient données à la fin de chaque partie du dictionnaire, sont désormais mises à leur place alphabétique dans le texte. Ainsi, **FF** *abbr* **1.** *frères* **2.** *Franc français* est placé entre **février** et **fi**.

La présente édition n'aurait pu voir le jour sans la contribution d'un grand nombre de collaborateurs: rédacteurs, correcteurs et conseillers. Je tiens à les remercier de leurs efforts et de leur aide précieuse. Je remercie également l'imprimeur qui a su exploiter si efficacement un manuscrit souvent difficile à suivre.

La rédactrice
Londres, 1984

Abbreviations used in the dictionary
Abréviations utilisées dans le dictionnaire

a	*adjective*	adjectif
A:	*archaism*	désuet
abbr	*abbreviation*	abréviation
acc	*accusative*	accusatif
adj	*adjective*	adjectif
adj phr	*adjectival phrase*	locution adjective
Adm:	*administration; civil service*	administration
adv	*adverb*	adverbe
adv phr	*adverbial phrase*	locution adverbiale
Aer:	*aeronautics*	aéronautique
Agr:	*agriculture*	agriculture
Anat:	*anatomy*	anatomie
approx	*approximately*	sens approché
Arach:	*arachnida*	arachnides
Arch:	*architecture*	architecture
Archeol:	*archaeology*	archéologie
Arms:	*arms; armaments*	armes, armements
Art:	*art*	beaux-arts
Artil:	*artillery*	artillerie
Astr:	*astronomy*	astronomie
Astrol:	*astrology*	astrologie
AtomPh:	*nuclear physics*	sciences nucléaires
Austr:	*Australia; Australian, Australianism*	Australie; australien, expression australienne
Aut:	*motoring; automobile industry*	automobilisme, industrie automobile
aux	*auxiliary*	auxiliaire
Av:	*aviation; aircraft*	aviation; avions
B:	*Bible; biblical*	Bible; biblique
Bank:	*banking*	opérations bancaires
Belg:	*Belgium; Belgian*	Belgique; belge
BHist:	*Bible history*	histoire sainte
Bill:	*billiards*	jeu de billard
BioCh:	*biochemistry*	biochimie
Biol:	*biology*	biologie
Bookb:	*bookbinding*	reliure
Book-k:	*book-keeping*	comptabilité
Bootm:	*boot and shoe industry*	industrie de la chaussure
Bot:	*botany*	botanique
Box:	*boxing*	boxe
Br	*British*	britannique
Breed:	*breeding*	élevage
Can:	*Canada; Canadian(ism)*	Canada; canadien, canadianisme
Cards:	*card games*	jeux de cartes
Carp:	*carpentry*	charpenterie; menuiserie du bâtiment
Cer:	*ceramics*	céramique
Ch:	*chemistry*	chimie
Chess:	*chess*	jeu d'échecs
Cin:	*cinema*	cinéma
CivE:	*civil engineering*	génie civil
Cl:	*clothing*	vêtements
Cmptr:	*computers; data processing*	ordinateurs; informatique
cogn acc	*cognate accusative*	accusatif de l'objet interne
coll	*collective*	collectif
comp	*comparative*	comparatif
condit	*conditional*	conditionnel
conj	*conjunction*	conjonction
conj like	*conjugated like*	se conjugue comme
Const:	*construction, building industry*	industrie du bâtiment
Corr:	*correspondence, letters*	correspondance, lettres
Cr:	*cricket*	cricket
Crust:	*crustacea*	crustacés
Cu:	*culinary; cooking*	culinaire; cuisine
Cust:	*customs*	douane
Cy:	*bicycles; cycling*	bicyclettes; cyclisme
Danc:	*dancing*	danse
dat	*dative*	datif
def	*(i) definite (ii) defective (verb)*	(i) défini (ii) (verbe) défectif
dem	*demonstrative*	demonstratif
Dent:	*dentistry*	art dentaire
Dipl:	*diplomacy; diplomatic*	diplomatie; diplomatique
DomEc:	*domestic economy; household equipment*	économie domestique; équipment ménager
Dressm:	*dressmaking*	couture (mode)
Dy:	*dyeing*	teinture
Ecc:	*ecclesiastical*	église et clergé
eg	*for example*	par exemple
El:	*electricity; electrical*	électricité, électrique
Elcs:	*electronics*	électronique
Eng	*England, English*	Angleterre, anglais
Engr:	*engraving*	gravure
Ent:	*entomology*	entomologie
Equit:	*equitation; riding*	équitation
esp	*especially*	surtout
etc		
*(etc, **etc**)*	*et cetera*	et caetera
Ethn:	*ethnology*	ethnologie
Exp:	*explosives*	explosifs
f	*feminine*	féminin
F:	*colloquial(ism)*	familier, style de la conversation
Fb:	*(Association) football*	football

PolEc:	*political economy; economics*	économie politique		*Swim:*	*swimming*	natation
poss	*possessive*	possessif		*Tail:*	*tailoring*	mode masculin
Post:	*postal services*	postes et télécommunications		*Tchn:*	*technical*	terme technique, terme de métier
pp	*past participle*	participe passé		*Ten:*	*tennis*	tennis
pr	*present (tense)*	présent (de l'indicatif)		*Tex:*	*textiles; textile industry*	industries textiles
pref	*prefix*	préfixe		*Th:*	*theatre, theatrical*	théâtre
prep	*preposition*	préposition		*Theol:*	*theology*	théologie
prep phr	*prepositional phrase*	locution prépositive		*thg*	*thing(s)*	(chose(s))
Prn	*proper name*	nom propre		*Tls:*	*tools*	outils
pron	*pronoun*	pronom		*Toil:*	*toilet, makeup*	toilette; maquillage
Prov	*proverb*	proverbe		*Toys:*	*toys*	jouets
prp	*present participle*	participe présent		*Tp:*	*transport*	transports
Psy:	*psychology*	psychologie		*Turf:*	*turf, horse racing*	turf, courses
Psychics:	*psychics*	métapsychisme		*TV:*	*television*	télévision
pt	*past tense*	passé défini		*Typ:*	*typography*	typographie
Publ:	*publishing*	édition		*Typw:*	*typing; typewriters*	dactylographie; machines à écrire
Pyr:	*pyrotechnics*	pyrotechnie				
				US:	*United States; American*	États-Unis; américain
qch (**qch**)	*(something)*	quelque chose		*usu*	*usually*	d'ordinaire
qn (**qn**)	*(someone)*	quelqu'un		*usu with sg const*	*usually with singular construction*	verbe généralement au singulier
qv	*which see*	se rapporter à ce mot				
				v	*verb*	verbe
Rac:	*racing*	courses		**v.**	*(you)*	vous
Rad:	*radar*	radar		*V:*	*vulgar: not in polite use*	trivial
Rail:	*railways*	chemins de fer		*var*	*variable*	variable
RCCh:	*Roman Catholic Church*	Église catholique		*Veh:*	*vehicles*	véhicules
Rec:	*tape recorders; record players*	magnétophones; tourne-disques		*Ven:*	*venery; hunting*	chasse
rel	*relative*	relatif		*Vet:*	*veterinary science*	art vétérinaire
Rel:	*religion(s)*	religion(s)		*vi*	*intransitive verb*	verbe intransitif
Rept:	*reptiles*	reptiles		*v ind tr*	*indirectly transitive verb*	verbe transitif indirect
Rtm:	*registered trademark*	marque déposée		*Vit:*	*viticulture*	viticulture
Rugby Fb·	*Rugby*	rugby		*vpr*	*pronominal verb*	verbe pronominal
				vtr	*transitive verb*	verbe transitif
Sch:	*schools and universities; students' (slang, etc)*	écoles; universités; (argot, etc) scolaire		*Wr:*	*wrestling*	lutte
Scot:	*Scotland; Scottish*	Écosse; écossais		*WTel:*	*wireless telegraphy & telephony; radio*	téléphonie et télégraphie sans fils; radio
Scout:	*scout and guide movements*	scoutisme				
Sculp:	*sculpture*	sculpture		*Y:*	*yachting*	yachting
sg, sing	*singular*	singulier				
Ski:	*skiing*	le ski		*Z:*	*zoology; mammals*	zoologie; mammifères
Sma:	*small arms*	armes portatives				
s.o. (**s.o.**)	*someone*	(quelqu'un)		=	*nearest equivalent (of an institution, an office, etc, when systems vary in the different countries)*	équivalent le plus proche (d'un terme désignant une institution, une charge, etc, dans les cas où les systèmes varient dans les différents pays)
Sp:	*sport*	sport				
Space:	*astronautics; space travel*	astronautique; voyages interplanétaires				
St Exch:	*Stock Exchange*	terme de Bourse				
sth (**sth**)	*something*	(quelque chose)				
Surg:	*surg:*	chirurgie				
Surv:	*surveying*	géodésie et levé de plans				
SwFr:	*Swiss French*	mot utilisé en Suisse				

xii

PART ONE

ENGLISH−FRENCH

Table of Phonetic Symbols

Consonants and semiconsonants

[p]   pat [pæt]; top [tɔp]

[b]   but [bʌt]; tab [tæb]

[m]   mat [mæt]; ram [ræm]; prism ['prizm]

[f]   fat [fæt]; laugh [lɑːf]; rough [rʌf]; elephant ['elifənt]

[v]   vat [væt]; avail [ə'veil]; rave [reiv]

[t]   tap [tæp]; pat [pæt]; trap [træp]

[d]   dab [dæb]; madder ['mædər]; build [bild]

[n]   no, know [nou]; ban [bæn]; gnat [næt]

[s]   sat [sæt]; scene [siːn]; mouse [maus]; ice [ais]; psychology [sai'kɔlədʒi]

[θ]   thatch [θætʃ]; ether ['iːθər]; faith [feiθ]; breath [breθ]

[z]   zinc [ziŋk]; buzz [bʌz]; houses ['hauziz]; business ['biznis]

[ð]   that [ðæt]; there [ðɛər]; mother ['mʌðər]; breathe [briːð]

[l]   lad [læd]; all [ɔːl]; table ['teibl]

[ʃ]   sham [ʃæm]; dish [diʃ]; sugar ['ʃugər]; ocean ['ouʃ(ə)n]; nation ['neiʃ(ə)n]; machine [mə'ʃiːn]

[tʃ]   chat [tʃæt]; search [səːrtʃ]; chisel ['tʃizl]; thatch [θætʃ]; rich [ritʃ]

[ʒ]   pleasure ['pleʒər]; vision ['viʒn]; beige [beiʒ]

[dʒ]   jam [dʒæm]; jail, gaol [dʒeil]; gem [dʒem]; gin [dʒin]; rage [reidʒ]; edge [edʒ]; badger ['bædʒər]

[k]   cat [kæt]; kitten ['kitn]; choir ['kwaiər]; cue, queue [kjuː]; arctic ['ɑːktik]; exercise ['eksəsaiz]

[g]   to [gou]; ghost [goust]; guard [gɑːd]; again [ə'gen]; egg [eg]; exist [eg'zist]; hungry ['hʌŋgri]

[h]   hat [hæt]; cohere [kou'hiər]

[x]   loch [lɔx]

[ŋ]   bang [bæŋ]; sing [siŋ]; singer ['siŋər]; anchor ['æŋkər]; anger ['æŋgər]; link [liŋk]

[r]   rat [ræt]; arise [ə'raiz]; brain [brein]

[r]   (*sounded only when a final* r *is carried on to the next word*) far [fɑːr]; sailor ['seilər]; finger ['fiŋgər]

[j]   yam [jæm]; yet [jet]; youth [juːθ]

[w]   wall [wɔːl]; await [ə'weit]; quite [kwait]

[(h)w]   what [(h)wɔt]; why [(h)wai]

Vowels and vowel combinations

[iː]   bee [biː]; fever ['fiːvər]; see, sea [siː]; release [ri'liːs]

[iə]   beer, bier [biər]; appear [ə'piər]; really ['riəli]

[i]   bit [bit]; added ['ædid]; drastic ['dræstik]; sieve [siv]

[e]   bet [bet]; leopard ['lepəd]; menace ['menəs]; said [sed]

[ei]   date [deit]; day [dei]; rain, rein, reign [rein]

[ɛə]   bear, bare [bɛər]; there, their [ðɛər]

[æ]   bat [bæt]; add [æd]

[ai]   aisle, isle [ail]; height [hait]; life [laif]; fly [flai]; beside [bi'said]

[ɑː]   art [ɑːt]; ask [ɑːsk]; car [kɑːr]; father ['fɑːðər]

[au]   fowl, foul [faul]; house [haus]; cow [kau]

[ɔ]   wad [wɔd]; wash [wɔʃ]; lot [lɔt]

[ɔː]   all [ɔːl]; haul [hɔːl]; saw [sɔː]; caught, court [kɔːt]; short [ʃɔːt]; wart [wɔːt]; thought [θɔːt]

[ɔi]   boil [bɔil]; toy [tɔi]; oyster ['ɔistər]; loyal ['lɔiəl]

[ou]   low [lou]; soap [soup]; rope [roup]; road, rode [roud]; sew, so, sow (*verb*) [sou]

[uː]   shoe [ʃuː]; prove [pruːv]; threw, through [θruː]; frugal ['fruːgl]; (*slightly shorter*) room [ru(ː)m]

[juː]   few [fjuː]; huge [hjuːdʒ]; humour ['hjuːmər]

[(j)uː]   suit [s(j)uːt]; suicide ['s(j)uːisaid]

[(j)uə]   lurid ['l(j)uərid]; lure [l(j)uər]

[u]   put [put]; wool [wul]; wood, would [wud]; full [ful]

[ju]   incubate ['inkjubeit]; duplicity [dju'plisiti]

[uə]   poor [puər]; sure [ʃuər]

[ʌ]   cut [kʌt]; sun, son [sʌn]; cover ['kʌvər]; rough [rʌf]

[əː]   curl [kəːl]; herb [həːb]; learn [ləːn]

[ə]   decency ['diːsənsi]; obey [ə'bei] amend [ə'mend]; delicate ['delikət]

A

A, a¹ [ei] *n* **1.** (la lettre) A, a *m*; **he knows the book from A to Z,** il connaît le livre à fond; **A1,** *NAm: also* **A number 1,** de première qualité; (*house number*) **51a, 51 bis;** *Sch:* **A levels** = baccalauréat *m*, *F:* bac *m*; *Aut:* **the A3** = la (route) nationale 3, la N3 [entrwɑ] **2.** *Mus:* la *m* **3. A bomb,** bombe A.

a² *before vowel* **an** [ə, ən *stressed* ei, æn] *indef art* **1.** un, une; **a man,** un homme; **an apple,** une pomme; **an M.P.** [ən'em'piː] = un député **2.** (*def art in Fr*) (*a*) **to have a red nose,** avoir le nez rouge (*b*) **to have a taste for sth,** avoir le goût de qch (*c*) (*generalizing*) **a woman takes life too seriously,** les femmes prennent la vie trop au sérieux **3.** (*distributive*) **two pounds a kilo,** deux livres le kilo; **fifty francs a head,** cinquante francs par tête, par personne; **three times a week,** trois fois par semaine; **50 kilometres an hour,** 50 kilomètres à l'heure **4. it gives me an appetite,** cela me donne de l'appétit **5.** (*a*) (= *a certain*) **I know a Doctor Hugo,** je connais un certain docteur Hugo; **in a sense,** dans un certain sens (*b*) (= *the same*) **to eat two at a time,** en manger deux à la fois; **to come in two at a time,** entrer deux par deux; **to be of a size,** être de la même grandeur, de (la) même taille (*c*) (= *a single*) **I haven't understood a word,** je n'ai pas compris un seul mot; **not a penny,** pas un sou **6.** (*omitted in Fr*) (*a*) **he's a doctor,** il est médecin (*b*) (*before nouns in apposition*) **Caen, a town in Normandy,** Caen, ville de Normandie (*c*) **to make a fortune,** faire fortune; **to have a right to sth,** avoir droit à qch (*d*) **what a man!** quel homme! **what a pity!** quel dommage! (*e*) **in a taxi,** en taxi; **to live like a lord,** vivre comme un prince; **to sell at a loss,** vendre à perte.

AA *abbr* **1.** *Automobile Association* **2.** *Alcoholics Anonymous.*

aback [ə'bæk] *adv* **to be taken a.,** être, rester, déconcerté, interdit.

abacus ['æbəkəs] *n* abaque *m;* boulier-compteur *m.*

abalone [æbə'louni] *n* (*pl* **abalone**) *Moll:* ormeau *m.*

abandon [ə'bændən] **1.** *n* **with gay a.,** avec désinvolture **2.** *vtr* abandonner; délaisser (sa famille); renoncer à (un projet); **to a. ship,** abandonner le navire.

abase [ə'beis] *vtr Lit:* abaisser, humilier (qn); **to a. oneself,** s'abaisser, s'humilier.

abashed [ə'bæʃt] *a* déconcerté; confus, interdit.

abate [ə'beit] *vi* (*of storm*) diminuer, se calmer, s'apaiser; (*of flood*) baisser; (*of wind*) se modérer, tomber. **a'batement** *n* diminution *f*, apaisement *m;* **noise a. campaign,** campagne contre le bruit.

abattoir ['æbətwɑːr] *n* abattoir *m.*

abbess ['æbes] *n* abbesse *f.*

abbey ['æbi] *n* **1.** abbaye *f* **2. a.** (**church**), (église) abbatiale (*f*).

abbot ['æbət] *n* abbé *m* (d'un monastère).

abbreviate [ə'briːvieit] *vtr* abréger (un nom, un livre). **abbrevi'ation** *n* abréviation *f.*

ABC ['eibiː'siː] *n* abc *m*, ABC *m.*

abdicate ['æbdikeit] *vtr & i* abdiquer (un trône); renoncer à (un droit, une responsabilité). **abdi'cation** *n* abdication *f;* renonciation *f.*

abdomen ['æbdəmen] *n* abdomen *m*; bas-ventre *m.* **ab'dominal** *a* abdominal, -aux.

abduct [æb'dʌkt] *vtr* enlever, kidnapper (qn). **ab'duction** *n* enlèvement *m*, kidnapping *m.* **ab'ductor** *n* ravisseur, -euse; kidnappeur, -euse.

aberration [æbə'reiʃn] *n* **1.** aberration *f*, déviation *f* **2. mental a.,** aberration; égarement *m* de l'esprit; confusion mentale.

abet [ə'bet] *vtr* (**abetted**) **to a. s.o. in a crime,** encourager qn à un crime; **to aid and a. s.o.,** être le complice de qn. **a'betting** *n* (**aiding and**) **a.,** complicité *f.*

abeyance [ə'beiəns] *n* suspension *f* (d'une loi); **in a.,** en suspens.

abhor [əb'hɔːr] *vtr* détester; avoir (qn, qch) en horreur. **ab'horrence** *n* horreur *f* (of, de). **ab'horrent** *a* odieux, répugnant (to, à).

abide [ə'baid] **1.** *vi* **to a. by,** tenir (sa promesse); se conformer à (une règle) **2.** *vtr* **I can't a. him,** je ne peux pas le sentir.

ability [ə'biliti] *n* (*pl* **abilities**) **1.** capacité *f*, pouvoir *m* (de faire qch) **2.** habileté *f*, capacité; compétence *f;* **to do sth to the best of one's a.,** faire qch de son mieux; **a man of great a.,** un homme très doué.

abject ['æbdʒekt] *a* **1.** abject; misérable; **a. poverty,** misère *f* **2.** (*of apology*) servile. **'abjectly** *adv* **1.** misérablement **2.** avec servilité.

ablaze [ə'bleiz] *adv & a* en feu, en flammes; **to be a.,** flamber; **a. with light,** resplendissant de lumière; **a. with anger,** fou de colère.

able ['eibl] *a* **1.** (*a*) capable, compétent, habile (*b*) **to be a. to do sth** (i) savoir, être capable de, faire qch (ii) pouvoir, être à même de, faire qch; **a. to pay,** en mesure de payer **2. a. piece of work,** travail bien fait. **'able-'bodied** *a* (homme) fort, robuste; *Mil:* valide; *Nau:* **a.(-bodied) seaman,** matelot de deuxième classe. **'ably** *adv* habilement; avec compétence.

ablutions [ə'bluːʃnz] *npl* ablutions *f.*

abnormal [æb'nɔːml] *a* anormal, -aux. **abnor'mality** *n* (*pl* **-ties**) **1.** caractère anormal (de qch) **2.** anomalie *f;* difformité *f.* **ab'normally** *adv* anormalement.

aboard [ə'bɔːd] **1.** *adv* à bord; **to go a.,** monter à bord; s'embarquer; **all a.!** (i) *Nau:* embarquez! à bord! (ii) *Rail: etc:* en voiture! **2.** *prep a.* (*a*) **ship,** à bord d'un navire; **a. a train, an aircraft,** dans un train, un avion; à bord d'un avion.

abode [ə'boud] *n Lit:* demeure *f;* *Jur:* **of no fixed a.,** sans domicile fixe.

abolish [ə'bɔliʃ] *vtr* abolir, supprimer (un usage, un abus); abroger (une loi). **abo'lition** *n* abolition *f*; suppression *f*.

abominable [ə'bɔminəbl] *a* abominable. **a'bominably** *adv* abominablement.

abominate [ə'bɔmineit] *vtr* abominer; avoir (qch) en abomination, en horreur. **abomi'nation** *n* abomination *f*.

aborigine [æbə'ridʒini] *n* aborigène *mf*. **abo-'riginal** *a & n* aborigène (*mf*).

abort [ə'bɔːt] *vtr & i* (faire) avorter. **abortion** *n* 1. avortement *m*; **to have an a.**, (se faire) avorter 2. œuvre mal venue. **a'bortionist** *n* avorteur, -euse. **a'bortive** *a* avorté, manqué.

abound [ə'baund] *vi* abonder (**in, with, en**).

about [ə'baut] *adv & prep* 1. (*a*) autour (de) (*b*) de côté et d'autre; **to wander a.**, errer, se promener, par-ci par-là; **don't leave those papers lying a.**, ne laissez pas traîner ces papiers; **there's a great deal of flu a.**, il y a beaucoup de grippe actuellement (*c*) **there's sth unusual a. him**, il y a chez lui quelque chose d'inhabituel 2. *Nau:* **ready a.!** paré à virer! *Mil:* **a. turn!** *US:* **a. face!** demi-tour! 3. environ, presque; **there are a. thirty**, il y en a une trentaine; **that's a. right**, c'est à peu près cela; **it's a. time** (i) il est presque temps (ii) *Iron:* il est grand temps! **he came a. three o'clock**, il est venu vers trois heures 4. au sujet de; **to enquire a. sth**, se renseigner sur qch; **to quarrel a. nothing**, se disputer à propos de rien; **what's it all a.?** de quoi s'agit-il? **to speak a. sth**, parler de qch; **what did he say a. it?** qu'est-ce qu'il en a dit? **how a., what a., a game of chess?** si on faisait une partie d'échecs? **what a. my bath?** et mon bain? 5. (*a*) **to be a. to do sth**, être sur le point de faire qch (*b*) **this is how I go a. it**, voici comment je m'y prends; **while you're a. it**, pendant que vous y êtes. **a'bout-'face, a'bout-'turn** *n* demi-tour *m*; *Fig:* volte-face *f*.

above [ə'bʌv] *adv & prep* 1. au-dessus (de) (*a*) **the water reached a. their knees**, l'eau leur montait jusqu'au-dessus des genoux (*b*) **to hover a. the town**, planer au-dessus de la ville; **a voice from a.**, une voix d'en haut; **view from a.**, vue plongeante (*c*) **his voice was heard a. the din**, on entendait sa voix pardessus le tumulte (*d*) **he is a. me in rank**, il est mon supérieur hiérarchique; **you must show yourself a. prejudice**, il faut être au-dessus des préjugés; **to live a. one's means**, vivre au-delà de ses moyens; **the flat a.**, l'appartement du dessus; **temperature a. normal**, température supérieure à la normale; **that's a. me**, cela me dépasse; **a. all**, surtout; **to get a. oneself**, faire le suffisant 2. (*in book*) **see paragraph a.**, voir le paragraphe ci-dessus, plus haut 3. (*of pers*) **to be a. (all) suspicion**, être au-dessus de tout soupçon; **he is a. (doing) that**, il se respecte trop pour faire cela 4. **a. twenty**, plus de vingt. **it was all a.**, c'était tout à fait correct, de règle. **a'bove-'mentioned, a'bove-'named** *a* sus-mentionné, susdit.

abrasion [ə'breiʒn] *n* (*a*) frottement *m*; abrasion *f* (*b*) *Med:* éraflure *f*, écorchure *f* (de la peau). **a'brasive** *a* (*of pers*) contrariant; (*of manner*) énervant; (*of voice*) caustique; *Tchn:* abrasif, -ive.

abreast [ə'brest] *adv* (*a*) de front; *Navy: Av:* **(in) line**

a., en ligne de front (*b*) **to walk two a.**, marcher par deux, par rangs de deux; **to be a. of the times**, être de son temps; **to keep wages a. of the cost of living**, maintenir les salaires au niveau du coût de la vie.

abridge [ə'bridʒ] *vtr* abréger (un ouvrage); raccourcir (un chapitre); **abridged edition**, édition abrégée; **abrégé** *m*. **a'bridg(e)ment** *n* (*a*) abrégement *m* (*b*) abrégé.

abroad [ə'brɔːd] *adv* 1. à l'étranger; **to live a.**, vivre à l'étranger; **to return from a.**, revenir de l'étranger 2. au loin; de tous côtés; **the news got a.**, la nouvelle s'est répandue.

abrupt [ə'brʌpt] *a* (départ, caractère) brusque; (départ) précipité; (ton) cassant; (style) heurté, saccadé; (*of slope*) raide, abrupt. **a'bruptly** *adv* (*a*) (sortir) brusquement; (répondre) avec brusquerie (*b*) (monter) en pente raide. **a'bruptness** *n* (*a*) brusquerie *f*; précipitation *f* (d'un départ) (*b*) raideur *f* (d'une pente).

abscess ['æbses] *n* abcès *m*.

abscond ['æb'skɔnd] *vi* s'enfuir, s'évader (**from,** de).

absence ['æbsəns] *n* 1. absence *f*; *Jur:* **sentenced in (his, her) a.**, condamné(e) par contumace 2. manque *m*, défaut *m* (de qch); **in the a. of any information**, faute de, à défaut de, renseignements 3. **a. of mind**, distraction *f*.

absent I. *a* ['æbsənt] absent; (air) distrait; *Mil: etc:* **a. without leave**, porté absent, manquant. II. *vpr* [æb'sent] **to a. oneself**, s'absenter. **absen'tee** *n* absent, -ente; manquant, -ante (à l'appel). **absen'teeism** *n* absentéisme *m*. **'absent'minded** *a* distrait. **'absent'mindedly** *adv* distraitement. **'absent'mindedness** *n* distraction *f*.

absolute ['æbsəluːt] *a* (*a*) absolu; **a. power**, pouvoir absolu, illimité; **a. majority**, majorité absolue (*b*) *F:* **he's an a. idiot**, c'est un parfait imbécile; **it's an a. scandal**, c'est un véritable scandale. **'absolutely** *adv* absolument; **you're a. right!** vous avez tout à fait raison!

absolution [æbsə'luːʃn] *n* absolution *f*.

absolve [əb'zɔlv] *vtr* 1. absoudre (s.o. **of** a sin, qn d'un péché) 2. affranchir, délier (s.o. **from** a vow, qn d'un vœu).

absorb [əb'sɔːb] *vtr* 1. (*a*) absorber (un liquide) (*b*) amortir (un choc) 2. (*of pers*) **to become absorbed in sth**, s'absorber dans qch; **he was absorbed in his business**, ses affaires l'absorbaient; **absorbed in his books**, plongé dans ses livres. **ab'sorbency** *n* capacité d'absorption. **ab'sorbent** *a & n* absorbant (*m*). **ab'sorber** *n* **shock a.**, amortisseur *m*. **absorption** *n* 1. absorption *f* 2. amortissement *m* (de chocs).

abstain [əb'stein] *vi* s'abstenir (**from,** de).

abstemious [əb'stiːmiəs] *a* sobre, tempérant. **ab-'stemiously** *adv* sobrement; frugalement. **ab-'stemiousness** *n* sobriété *f*.

abstention [əb'stenʃn] *n* abstention *f*.

abstinence ['æbstinəns] *n* abstinence *f*.

abstract I. *a & n* ['æbstrækt] abstrait (*m*); **a. painting**, peinture abstraite. II. *n* ['æbstrækt] (*a*) résumé *m*; abrégé *m*, précis *m*; relevé *m* (d'un compte) (*b*) peinture, sculpture, abstraite (*c*) **in the a.**, dans l'abstrait *m*. III. *vtr* [æb'strækt] 1. soustraire, dérober (**sth from s.o.**, qch à qn); détourner (de l'argent) 2.

résumer (un texte). **ab'stracted** *a* distrait. **ab'-
stractedly** *adv* distraitement. **ab'straction** *n*
1. soustraction *f* (de documents) 2. abstraction *f*.
abstruse [æb'stru:s] *a* abstrus.
absurd [əb'sɔːd] *a* absurde; déraisonnable; **it's a.!**
c'est idiot! **ab'surdity** *n* absurdité *f*. **ab'surdly**
adv absurdement.
abundant [ə'bʌndənt] *a* abondant. **a'bundance**
n abondance *f*; **in a.,** en abondance. **a'bundantly**
adv abondamment; à foison; **it is a. plain that,** il est
manifeste que.
abuse I. *n* [ə'bju:s] 1. abus *m* 2. insultes *fpl*, injures
fpl. **II.** *vtr* [ə'bju:z] 1. abuser de (son autorité) 2.
maltraiter (qn) 3. (*a*) médire de (qn) (*b*) injurier (qn);
dire des injures à (qn). **a'busive** *a* (propos) injurieux; (homme) grossier. **a'busively** *adv* grossièrement.
abut [ə'bʌt] *vi* (**abutted**) **to a. on, against, sth,** s'appuyer, buter, contre, qch.
abysmal [ə'bizml] *a* 1. sans fond; **a. ignorance,**
ignorance profonde, extrême 2. *F:* atroce, abominable.
abyss [ə'bis] *n* abîme *m*; gouffre *m*.
AC *abbr El:* alternating current.
acacia [ə'keiʃə] *n Bot:* acacia *m*.
academic [ækə'demik] 1. *a* (*a*) académique; (sujet)
théorique **a. discussion,** discussion abstraite (*b*) (carrière, année) universitaire 2. *n* universitaire *mf*.
academy [ə'kædəmi] *n* (*pl* **academies**) académie
f; esp Scot: Sch: = lycée *m*; collège *m*; **the Royal
A. (of Arts),** l'Académie royale des Beaux-Arts (de
Londres) = le Salon; **a. of music,** conservatoire *m*;
military a., école *f* militaire; fencing a., salle *f* d'e-
scrime. **acade'mician** *n* académicien, -ienne.
accede [æk'si:d] *vi* 1. **to a. to the throne,** monter sur
le trône. 2. **to a. to a request,** donner son adhésion à
une demande.
accelerate [æk'seləreit] 1. *vtr* accélérer; précipiter
(les événements); activer (un travail) 2. *vi Aut:* accélérer; (*of motion*) s'accélérer. **acce'ration** *n*
accélération *f*. **ac'celerator** *n* accélérateur *m*.
accent I. *n* ['æksənt] accent *m*; **to have a German a.,**
avoir l'accent allemand; **fashion with the a. on youth,**
mode qui met l'accent sur la jeunesse. **II.** *vtr*
[æk'sent] accentuer (un mot).
accentuate [æk'sentjueit] *vtr* accentuer, appuyer
sur (un mot); faire ressortir (un détail). **ac-
centu'ation** *n* accentuation *f*.
accept [ək'sept] *vtr* accepter (un cadeau); admettre
(les excuses de qn); **the accepted custom,** l'usage
admis; **accepted opinion,** idées reçues, l'opinion courante. **ac'ceptable** *a* acceptable; **your cheque was
most a.,** votre chèque est arrivé fort à propos. **ac-
'ceptance** *n* acceptation *f*; accueil *m* favorable
(de qch); réception *f* (d'un article commandé).
access ['ækses] *n* 1. accès *m*, abord *m; PN: Aut:* **a.
only,** entrée interdite sauf aux riverains; **a. road,**
route d'accès; **to have a. to s.o.,** sth, avoir accès
auprès de qn, à qch 2. accès (de fièvre, de colère).
accessi'bility *n* accessibilité *f*. **ac'cessible** *a*
accessible.
accession [æk'seʃn] *n* accession *f*; **a. to the throne,**
avènement *m* au trône; (*in library*) **accessions,** additions *f*.

accessory [æk'sesəri] 1. *a* accessoire (to,
à) 2. *n* (*pl* **accessories**) accessoire *m* 3. *n & a* **a. to a
crime,** complice *mf* d'un crime.
accident ['æksidənt] *n* accident *m*; **by a.,** (i) (laisser
tomber qch) accidentellement (ii) (se rencontrer)
par hasard; **fatal a.,** accident mortel; fatalité *f*; **the
victims of an a.,** les accidentés *m*; **a. insurance,** assu-
rance-accident *f*. **acci'dental** *a* accidentel, fortuit; **a. meeting,** rencontre de hasard. **acci-
'dentally** *adv* (i) accidentellement (ii) par
hasard. **'accident-prone** *a* prédisposé aux accidents.
acclaim [ə'kleim] 1. *vtr* acclamer 2. *n* acclamation *f*.
acclimatize, *NAm:* **acclimate** [ə'klaimətaiz,
ə'klaimeit] *vtr* acclimater; **to become acclimatized,**
s'acclimater. **acclimati'zation,** *NAm:* **accli-
mation** *n* acclimatation *f*.
accolade ['ækəleid] *n* approbation *f*, éloge *m*.
accommodate [ə'kɔmədeit] *vtr* 1. (*a*) adapter,
ajuster (**to sth,** à qch) (*b*) concilier (des opinions) 2.
to a. s.o. with sth, fournir qch à qn; **to a. s.o. with a
loan,** faire un prêt à qn 3. loger, recevoir (tant de
personnes); **the restaurant can a. 100 people,** il y a
assez de place dans le restaurant pour 100 personnes. **a'ccommodating** *a* (*of pers*) complaisant,
accommodant, obligeant. **accommo'dation** *n*
(*a*) ajustement *m*, adaptation *f* (**to,** à); **to come to an
a.,** arriver à un compromis; s'arranger (à l'amiable)
(*b*) (*NAm: usu* **accommodations**) logement *m*; **we have
no sleeping a.,** nous n'avons pas de chambres; **did
you have good a. in France?** étiez-vous bien logés en
France? **a. address,** adresse de convention; *Rail: US:*
a. (train), (train *m*) omnibus *m*.
accompany [ə'kʌmpəni] *vtr* 1.
accompagner; **to be accompanied by s.o.,** être
accompagné de qn 2. *Mus:* accompagner (qn) (**on
the piano,** au piano). **a'ccompaniment** *n* accompagnement *m*. **a'ccompanist** *n Mus:* accompagnateur, -trice.
accomplice [ə'kʌmplis] *n* complice *mf*.
accomplish [ə'kʌmpliʃ] *vtr* accomplir, achever, exécuter, venir à bout de (qch); effectuer (un voyage);
to a. one's aim, atteindre son but. **a'ccom-
plished** *a* (musicien) accompli, achevé. **a'ccom-
plishment** *n* 1. accomplissement *m* (d'une tâche)
2. *usu pl* talents *m* (d'agrément).
accord [ə'kɔːd] 1. *n* (*a*) accord *m*, consentement *m*;
with one a., d'un commun accord (*b*) **to do sth of
ones' own a.,** faire qch de son plein gré 2. (*a*) *vi*
s'accorder (*b*) *vtr* accorder (to, à). **a'ccordance** *n*
accord *m*; **in a. with your instructions,** conformément
à vos ordres; **in a. with the truth,** conforme à la
vérité. **a'ccording** *adv used in prep phr* (*a*) **a. to
the instructions,** selon, suivant, les ordres; **a. to age,**
par rang d'âge; **a. to plan,** conformément au plan
(*b*) **a. to him,** d'après lui; à l'en croire; **a. to that,**
d'après cela. **a'ccordingly** *adv* 1. **to act a.,** agir
en conséquence 2. en conséquence, donc; **a. I wrote
to him,** je lui ai donc écrit.
accordion [ə'kɔːdiən] *n* accordéon *m*.
accost [ə'kɔst] *vtr* accoster, aborder.
account [ə'kaunt] I. *n* 1. (*a*) compte *m*; **bank a.,**
compte en banque; **current a.,** *NAm:* **checking a.,**
compte courant; **deposit a.,** compte d'épargne; **sav-**

ings a., compte d'épargne; **to open an a.,** ouvrir un compte; **accounts (department) (of a firm),** (service *m* de) la comptabilité (d'une entreprise); **to keep the accounts,** tenir les comptes; **to pay a sum on a.,** payer un acompte, verser des arrhes; **to have an a.,** *NAm:* **a charge a., with s.o.,** avoir un compte chez qn; **put it on my a.,** mettez-le sur, à, mon compte; **expense a.,** indemnité *f* pour frais professionnels (*b*) (*statement*) exposé *m*; **expense a.,** note *f* de frais (*c*) to **turn sth to a.,** tirer parti de qch; mettre qch à profit (*d*) **to call s.o. to a.,** demander une explication à qn; **he gave a good a. of himself,** il s'en est bien tiré **2.** (*a*) (**person**) **of some a.,** (personne) qui compte; **of no a.,** insignifiant; sans importance; peu important; **to take sth into a.,** tenir compte de qch (*b*) **on a. of s.o., sth,** à cause de qn, qch; **I was nervous on his a.,** j'avais peur pour lui; **on every a.,** sous tous les rapports; **on no a., not on any a.,** en aucun cas (*c*) **to act on one's own a.,** agir de sa propre initiative **3.** récit *m* (d'un fait); exposé; *Journ:* compte-rendu *m*; **to give an a. of sth,** faire le récit de qch; **by all accounts,** au dire de tout le monde. **II.** *vtr & ind tr* **to a. for sth,** rendre compte de (sa conduite); expliquer (une circonstance); **I can't a. for it,** je n'y comprends rien; (*after accident*) **three people have still not been accounted for,** trois personnes n'ont pas encore été retrouvées; **there's no accounting for tastes,** chacun (à) son goût. **accountable** *a* responsable (**for,** de; **to,** envers). **a'ccountancy** *n* (*a*) comptabilité (*b*) profession *f* de comptable. **a'ccountant** *n* comptable *mf*; **chartered a.,** *NAm:* **certified public a.** = expert-comptable *m*. **a'ccounting** *n* comptabilité.

accredit [ə'kredit] *vtr* accréditer (un ambassadeur) (**to a government,** auprès d'un gouvernement). **a'ccredited** *a* (*of pers*) accrédité, autorisé.

accrue [ə'kru:] *vi* **1.** (*of money*) revenir (**to s.o.,** à qn) **2.** *Fin:* (*of interest*) s'accumuler; **accrued interest,** intérêt couru.

accumulate [ə'kju:mjuleit] **1.** *vtr* accumuler, amasser (une fortune). **2.** *vi* s'accumuler, s'amonceler, s'entasser. **accumu'lation** *n* accumulation *f*, amoncellement *m*; monceau *m*, tas *m*. **a'ccumulative** *a* qui s'accumule. **a'ccumulator** *n El:* accumulateur *m*, *F:* accu *m*.

accurate ['ækjurət] *a* exact, juste, précis; (traduction) fidèle. **'accuracy** *n* exactitude *f*; justesse *f*; précision *f*. **'accurately** *adv* exactement, avec précision.

accuse [ə'kju:z] *vtr* accuser (s.o. of sth, qn de qch). **accu'sation** *n* accusation *f*. **a'ccusative** *a & n* *Gram:* accusatif (*m*). **a'ccused** *Jur:* **the a.,** le, la, prévenu(e); l'accusé(e). **a'ccuser** *n* accusateur, -trice. **a'ccusing** *a* accusateur, -trice. **a'ccusingly** *adv* d'une manière accusatrice.

accustom [ə'kʌstəm] *vtr* accoutumer, habituer (s.o. to sth, qn à qch). **a'ccustomed** *a* **1. to be a. to sth, to doing sth,** être habitué, accoutumé, à qch, à faire qch; **to get a. to sth, to doing sth,** s'habituer, s'accoutumer, à qch, à faire qch **2.** habituel, coutumier; d'usage.

ace [eis] *n* **1.** (*a*) (*of cards, etc*) as *m*; **within an a. of sth,** à deux doigts de qch (*b*) *Ten:* (**service**) **a.,** ace *m* **2.** *Sp: etc:* **a. driver,** as du volant.

acerbity [ə'sɔ:biti] *n* acerbité *f*.

acetate ['æsiteit] *n* *Ch:* acétate *m*.

acetic [ə'si:tik] *a* *Ch:* acétique; **a. acid,** acide acétique.

acetone ['æsitoun] *n* acétone *f*.

acetylene [ə'setili:n] *n* *Ch:* acétylène *m*; **a. welding,** soudure autogène.

ache [eik] **I.** *n* mal *m*, douleur *f*; **stomach a.,** mal de ventre; **I've got stomach a.,** j'ai mal au ventre. **II.** *vi* (*a*) **my head aches,** j'ai mal à la tête; **my back's aching,** mon dos me fait mal; **it makes my heart a.,** cela me serre le cœur (*b*) **he was aching to join in,** il brûlait d'y prendre part. **'aching** *a* douloureux; (dent) qui (vous) fait mal.

achieve [ə'tʃi:v] *vtr* **1.** accomplir (un exploit); réaliser (une entreprise) **2.** acquérir (de l'honneur) **3.** atteindre, parvenir à (un but); **he'll never a. anything,** il n'arrivera jamais à rien. **a'chievement** *n* **1.** accomplissement *m*, réalisation *f* (d'une ambition) **2.** exploit *m*.

Achilles [ə'kili:z] *Prnm* Achille; *Fig:* **Achilles' heel,** point faible (de qn).

acid ['æsid] **1.** *a* (*a*) acide; **a. drops,** bonbons acidulés (*b*) (*of character*) revêche, aigre; (*of remark*) acide **2.** *n* (*a*) acide *m*; *Fig:* **a test,** épreuve décisive (*b*) *F:* (= L.S.D.) acide. **a'cidity** *n* acidité *f*; aigreur *f* (d'une réponse).

acknowledge [ək'nɔlidʒ] *vtr* **1.** reconnaître (**as,** pour); avouer (qch); **to a. defeat,** s'avouer vaincu **2.** répondre à (un salut); **to a. (receipt of) a letter,** accuser réception d'une lettre. **ack'nowledg(e)-ment** *n* (*a*) reconnaissance *f* (d'une erreur); aveu *m* (d'une faute) (*b*) reçu *m* (d'un paiement); **a. of receipt,** accusé *m* de réception (d'une lettre) (*c*) *pl* (*in preface*) remerciements *mpl*.

acne ['ækni] *n* *Med:* acné *f*.

acolyte ['ækəlait] *n* acolyte *m*.

acorn ['eikɔ:n] *n* *Bot:* gland *m* (du chêne).

acoustic [ə'ku:stik] **1.** *a* acoustique **2.** *npl* **acoustics,** acoustique *f*.

acquaint [ə'kweint] *vtr* **1. to a. s.o. with sth,** informer qn de qch; faire savoir qch à qn; **to a. s.o. with the facts,** mettre qn au courant **2.** (*a*) **to be acquainted with s.o.,** connaître qn (*b*) **to become acquainted with s.o.,** faire la connaissance de qn; **to become acquainted with the facts,** prendre connaissance des faits. **a'cquaintance** *n* **1.** connaissance *f* (**with,** de); **to make s.o.'s a.,** faire la connaissance de qn **2.** (*pers*) connaissance.

acquiesce [ækwi'es] *vi* acquiescer, donner son assentiment (**in,** à). **acqui'escence** *n* assentiment *m*. **acqui'escent** *a* consentant.

acquire [ə'kwaiər] *vtr* acquérir (qch); prendre (une habitude); **to a. a taste for sth,** prendre goût à qch; **acquired taste,** goût qui s'acquiert.

acquisition [ækwi'ziʃn] *n* acquisition *f*. **a'cquisitive** *a* âpre au gain.

acquit [ə'kwit] *vtr* (**acquitted**) **1.** acquitter (un accusé); **to a. s.o. of sth,** absoudre qn de qch **2. he acquitted himself well,** il s'en est bien tiré. **a'cquittal** *n* acquittement *m* (d'un accusé).

acre ['eikər] *n* *Meas:* acre *f* (= 0, 4 hectare); *approx* = demi-hectare *m*. **acreage** *n* superficie *f* (en mesures agraires).

acrid ['ækrid] *a* 1. (goût, fumée) âcre 2. (style) mordant; (critique) acerbe.

acrimonious [ækri'mouniəs] *a* acrimonieux; (*of woman*) acariâtre; **the discussion became a.**, la discussion s'est envenimée. **acri'moniously** *adv* avec acrimonie. **'acrimony** *n* acrimonie *f*; aigreur *f*.

acrobat ['ækrəbæt] *n* acrobate *mf*. **acro'batic** *a* acrobatique. **acrobatics** *npl* acrobatie(s) *f* (*pl*).

acronym ['ækrənim] *n* sigle *m*.

across [ə'krɔs] *adv & prep* en travers (de) 1. (*a*) **to walk a.** (**a street**), traverser (une rue); **to run a.**, traverser en courant; **to go a. a bridge**, franchir, passer (sur), un pont; **to get sth a. to s.o.**, faire comprendre qch à qn (*b*) **to lay sth a.** (**sth**), mettre qch en travers (de qch) (*c*) **to come, run, a. s.o.**, rencontrer qn (par hasard) 2. (*a*) **the distance a.**, la distance en largeur; **the river is a kilometre a.**, le fleuve a un kilomètre de large (*b*) **he lives a. the street** (**from us**), il habite de l'autre côté de la rue, en face (de chez nous) (*c*) (*in crosswords*) horizontalement.

acrylic [ə'krilik] *a & n* acrylique (*m*).

act [ækt] I. *n* 1. acte *m*; (*a*) **a. of kindness**, acte de bonté (*b*) **A. of Parliament**, loi *f*, décret *m* 2. action *f*; **an a. of folly**, une folie; **to catch s.o. in the a.**, prendre qn sur le fait; **caught in the a.**, pris en flagrant délit 3. *Th:* (*a*) acte (d'une pièce); numéro *m* (dans un cirque) (*b*) **to put on an a.**, jouer la comédie; **to get in on the a.**, s'ingérer dans l'affaire. II. *v* 1. *vtr* (*a*) *Th:* jouer (une pièce); tenir (un rôle); **to a. the fool**, faire l'imbécile (*b*) **he was only acting**, il faisait semblant 2. *vi* agir (*a*) **I acted for the best**, j'ai fait pour le mieux; **to a. for, on behalf of, s.o.**, agir au nom de qn; représenter qn; **to a. as secretary to s.o.**, servir, faire office, de secrétaire à qn; **to a. upon advice**, suivre un conseil (*b*) **the engine acts as a brake**, le moteur fait fonction de frein (*c*) *Th: Cin:* jouer (*d*) (*of pers, machine*) **to a. up**, faire des siennes. **'acting** I. *a* par intérim; suppléant; intérimaire, provisoire. II. *n* 1. action *f* 2. (*a*) jeu *m* (d'un acteur) (*b*) **she's done some a.**, elle a fait du théâtre (*c*) **it's only a.**, c'est de la comédie.

action ['ækʃn] *n* 1. action *f*; **industrial a.**, grève *f*; **to take a.**, agir; **to suit the a. to the word**, joindre le geste à la parole; **to put a plan into a.**, mettre un projet à exécution; **out of a.**, hors de service, détraqué, en panne 2. (*deed*) action, acte *m*, fait *m* 3. *Th:* action (d'une pièce) 4. (*a*) action, gestes *mpl* (d'un joueur) (*b*) mécanisme *m* (d'une montre) 5. *Jur:* **a. at law**, procès *m*; **to bring an a. against s.o.**, intenter une action à, contre, qn 6. action, engagement *m*; **to go into a.**, engager le combat; **killed in a.**, tué à l'ennemi. **'actionable** *a Jur:* (action) qui expose (qn) à des poursuites.

active ['æktiv] *a* 1. actif; alerte; (cerveau) éveillé; (volcan) en activité; **a. imagination**, imagination vive 2. **to take an a. part in sth**, prendre une part active à qch; *Mil:* **to be on the a. list**, être en situation d'activité; **on a. service**, en campagne. **'activate** *vtr* activer. **'activist** *n* activiste *mf*. **ac'tivity** *n* activité *f*; mouvement *m* (de la rue).

actor ['æktər] *n* acteur *m*, comédien *m*.

actress ['æktrəs] *n* actrice *f*, comédienne *f*.

actual ['æktjuəl] *a* réel, véritable; **it's an a. fact, an a.**

case, c'est un fait positif, un cas concret. **actu'ality** *n* réalité *f*. **'actually** *adv* réellement, véritablement; effectivement; en fait; **he a. said no**, il est allé (même) jusqu'à dire non.

actuate ['æktjueit] *vtr* 1. mettre en action, actionner (une machine) 2. animer, faire agir (qn).

acumen ['ækjumən] *n* finesse *f* (d'esprit); perspicacité *f* (en affaires).

acupuncture ['ækjupʌŋkʃə] *n* acuponcture *f*, acupuncture *f*. **'acupuncturist** *n* acuponcteur *m*, acupuncteur *m*.

acute [ə'kju:t] *a* 1. (angle, accent) aigu; (manque) grave; **a. pain, disease**, douleur, maladie, aiguë 2. (*a*) (*of hearing*) fin (*b*) (esprit) fin, pénétrant. **a'cutely** *adv* (*a*) (souffrir) vivement, intensément (*b*) (observer) avec perspicacité, avec finesse.

ad [æd] *n F: see* **advertisement**.

AD *abbr anno domini*, après Jésus-Christ.

Adam ['ædəm] *Prnm* Adam; *Anat:* **A.'s apple**, pomme *f* d'Adam.

adamant ['ædəmənt] *a* inflexible.

adapt [ə'dæpt] 1. *vtr* adapter, ajuster, accommoder (**sth to sth**, qch à qch); remanier (une œuvre) 2. *vi* s'adapter. **adapta'bility** *n* faculté *f* d'adaptation. **a'daptable** *a* adaptable; **he's very a.**, il s'arrange de tout. **adap'tation** *n* adaptation *f*. **a'dapter, adaptor** *n* 1. adaptateur, -trice 2. *El:* adapt(at)eur *m*.

add [æd] 1. *vtr* ajouter, joindre (**to**, à); **added to which**, ajoutez que; **he added that**, il ajouta que 2. *vi* **to a. to sth**, ajouter à, augmenter (qch) 3. *vtr* **to a. (together)**, additionner, totaliser (des chiffres). **'adding machine** *n* machine *f* à calculer. **'add 'up** *vtr & i* additionner (des chiffres); *F:* **it doesn't a. up**, cela n'a ni rime ni raison.

adder ['ædər] *n* vipère *f*.

addict ['ædikt] *n* intoxiqué, -ée; *F:* fanatique *mf* (de football); **drug a.**, toxicomane *mf*. **a'ddicted** *a* adonné (**to**, à). **a'ddiction** *n* manie *f* (**to**, de); **drug a.**, toxicomanie *f*. **a'ddictive** *a* (drogue) qui crée une dépendance.

addition [ə'diʃn] *n* addition *f*; **additions to the staff**, adjonction *f*, additions, au personnel; **in a.**, en plus, en outre; de plus; par surcroît. **a'dditional** *a* supplémentaire, additionnel; **an a. reason**, une raison de plus. **a'dditionally** *adv* en plus, en outre. **a'dditive** *n* additif *m*.

address [ə'dres, *NAm:* 'ædres] I. *n*. 1. adresse *f* (d'une lettre); **a. book**, carnet, répertoire, d'adresses 2. discours *m*, allocution *f* 3. formes *fpl*, titres *m* de politesse. II. *vtr* 1. mettre, écrire, l'adresse sur (une lettre); **a letter addressed to my mother**, une lettre adressée à ma mère 2. (*a*) adresser (des reproches) (**to s.o.**, à qn) (*b*) s'adresser, adresser la parole, à (qn); haranguer (une assemblée); **he addressed me as "comrade"**, il m'a appelé "camarade" 3. *Golf:* viser (la balle). **addre'ssee** *n* destinataire *mf*.

adduce [ə'dju:s] *vtr* alléguer, apporter (des preuves); citer (une autorité).

adenoids ['ædənɔidz] *npl Med:* végétations *f* (adénoïdes).

adept ['ædept] 1. *a* **to be a. at doing sth**, être expert, habile, à qch 2. *n* expert *m* (**in, at**, en).

adequate ['ædikwət] *a* suffisant; approprié (**for**, à);

(*of pers*) compétent. 'a**dequately** *adv* suffisamment.

adhere [əd'hiər] *vi* 1. (*of thg*) adhérer, se coller 2. (*of pers*) (*a*) **to a. to a party**, adhérer à un parti (*b*) **to a. to**, persister dans (sa décision); tenir (une promesse). a**d'herence** *n* 1. (*of thg*) adhérence *f* (**to**, à) 2. (*of pers*) adhésion *f* (**to a party**, à un parti). a**d'herent** *a & n* adhérent, -ente.

adhesion [əd'hiːʒn] *n* adhérence *f* (**to**, à); adhérence au sol (des pneus). a**d'hesive** [-'hiːz-] 1. *a* adhésif, collant; **a. tape**, ruban adhésif; *NAm:* sparadrap *m; Med:* **a. plaster**, sparadrap 2. *n* adhésif *m*, colle *f*.

ad infinitum ['ædinfi'naitəm] *Lt adv phr* à l'infini.

adjacent [ə'dʒeisənt] *a* (angle, terrain) adjacent; attenant; (terrain) avoisinant.

adjective ['ædʒiktiv] *n Gram:* adjectif *m*. a**djec-** '**tival** *a* adjectif.

adjoin [ə'dʒɔin] 1. *vtr* avoisiner (un lieu); toucher à, être contigu à (qch) 2. *vi* **the two houses a.**, les deux maisons sont contiguës. a**'djoining** *a* contigu; avoisinant; **the a. room**, la pièce voisine.

adjourn [ə'dʒəːn] 1. *vtr* ajourner, renvoyer à un autre jour 2. *vi* (*a*) (*of meeting*) (i) s'ajourner (**until**, à) (ii) lever la séance (*b*) **to a. to the sitting room**, passer au salon. a**'djournment** *n* (*a*) ajournement *m*, suspension *f* (d'une séance) (*b*) renvoi *m*, remise *f* (d'une affaire).

adjudicate [ə'dʒuːdikeit] *vtr & i* juger, décider (une affaire). **adjudi'cation** *n* jugement *m*, décision *f*, arrêt *m*. a**'djudicator** *n* arbitre *m*; juge *m*; (*in competitions, etc.*) membre *m* du jury.

adjunct ['ædʒʌŋkt] *n* accessoire *m* (**of**, de).

adjust [ə'dʒʌst] *vtr & i* 1. arranger (une affaire); régler (un différend) 2. (*a*) ajuster (qch à qch); **to a. (oneself) to sth**, s'adapter à qch (*b*) régler (une montre) (*c*) rajuster (sa cravate). a**'djustable** *a* (siège) réglable. a**'djustment** *n* règlement *m* (d'un différend); réglage *m* (d'un mécanisme); adaptation *f* (d'une personne).

adjutant ['ædʒətənt] *n Mil:* (i) capitaine adjudant major (ii) officier adjoint.

ad lib ['æd'lib] *F: adv phr* à volonté; (manger) à discrétion.

ad-lib 1. *vtr & i* (**ad-libbed**) improviser 2. *a* improvisé.

adman, -men ['ædmæn, -men] *n F:* publicitaire *m*.

admin ['ædmin] *n F:* administration *f*.

administer [əd'ministər] *vtr* administrer (un pays); gérer (des biens); **to a. justice**, dispenser, rendre, la justice; **to a. an oath to s.o.**, faire prêter serment à qn. **adminis'tration** *n* administration *f*; gestion *f*; *esp NAm:* **the A.**, l'Administration, le gouvernement. a**d'ministrative** *a* administratif. a**d'ministrator** *n* administrateur, -trice; gestionnaire *mf*.

admiral ['ædmərəl] *n* 1. (i) amiral *m*, -aux (ii) vice-amiral *m* d'escadre 2. *Ent:* **red a.**, vulcain *m*. 'A**d-miralty (the)** *n Hist:* = le ministère de la Marine; l'Amirauté *f*.

admire [əd'maiər] *vtr* admirer. **admirable** *a* admirable. '**admirably** *adv* admirablement. **admi'ra-tion** *n* admiration *f*. a**d'mirer** *n* admirateur, -trice. a**d'miring** *a* (regard) admiratif. a**d'mir-ingly** *adv* avec admiration.

admission [əd'miʃn] *n* 1. admission *f*, accès *m* (à une école); **a. free**, entrée gratuite; **to gain a.**, se faire admettre (dans un endroit) 2. confession *f* (d'un crime); aveu *m*; **by, on, one's own a.**, de son propre aveu. a**d'missible** *a* (projet) acceptable; *Jur:* (témoignage) recevable.

admit [əd'mit] *v* (**admitted**) 1. *vtr* (*a*) admettre (qn à qch); laisser entrer (qn); **a. bearer**, laissez passer (*b*) admettre (des excuses); reconnaître (sa faute); **to a. one's guilt**, s'avouer coupable 2. (*a*) *v ind tr* **it admits of no doubt**, cela ne permet aucun doute (*b*) **to a. to (having done) sth**, reconnaître (avoir fait) qch. a**d'-mittance** *n* permission *f* d'entrer; admission *f*; entrée *f* (**to**, dans); accès *m* (**to**, à, auprès de); *PN:* **no a.**, entrée interdite. a**d'mitted** *a* (usage) admis. a**d'mittedly** *adv* de l'aveu général; **a. he is a thief**, c'est un voleur, j'en conviens.

admonish [əd'mɔniʃ] *vtr* admonester, reprendre (qn). **admo'nition** *n* réprimande *f*, remontrance *f*.

ad nauseam [æd'nɔːziæm] *Lt adv phr* à n'en plus finir.

ado [ə'duː] *n* **without further a., without (any) more a.**, sans plus de façon; **much a. about nothing**, beaucoup de bruit pour rien.

adolescence [ædə'lesns] *n* adolescence *f*. **ado-'lescent** *a & n* adolescent, -ente.

adopt [ə'dɔpt] *vtr* adopter; choisir, embrasser (une carrière); prendre (un ton). a**'dopted** *a* adopté; (fils) adoptif; **a. country**, pays d'adoption. a**'dop-tion** *n* adoption *f*; choix *m* (d'une carrière). a**'dop-tive** *a* (père, enfant) adoptif.

adore [ə'dɔːr] *vtr* adorer. a**'dorable** *a* adorable. a**'dorably** *adv* adorablement, à ravir. **ado'ra-tion** *n* adoration *f*. a**'doringly** *adv* avec adoration.

adorn [ə'dɔːn] *vtr* orner, parer (**with**, de). a**'dorn-ment** *n* ornement *m*, parure *f*.

adrenalin [ə'drenəlin] *n* adrénaline *f*.

Adriatic (Sea) (the) [ɔːdiːeidri'ætik('siː)] *a & n Geog:* (la mer) Adriatique.

adrift [ə'drift] *adv* (*of boat*) à la dérive; **to turn, cast, a.**, abandonner (un bateau) à la dérive; *Fig:* abandonner, renvoyer (qn); **to come a.**, (i) (*of rope*) se détacher (ii) (*of plan*) aller à la dérive; tomber à l'eau.

adroit [ə'drɔit] *a* adroit; habile. a**'droitly** *adv* adroitement, habilement. a**'droitness** *n* adresse *f*, dextérité *f*.

adulation [ædju'leiʃn] *n* adulation *f*.

adult ['ædʌlt] *a & n* adulte (*mf*).

adulterate [ə'dʌltəreit] *vtr* frelater (un aliment). **adulte'ration** *n* frelatage *m*.

adulterer, *f* -eress [ə'dʌltərər, -əres] *n* adultère *mf*. a**'dulterous** *a* adultère. a**'dultery** *n* adultère *m*.

advance [əd'vɑːns] I. *n* 1. avance *f*; marche *f* en avant; **a. booking**, place retenue à l'avance; **a. notice**, préavis *m; Mil:* **a. guard**, avant-garde *f*; **to arrive in a.**, arriver en avance; **to pay in a.**, payer d'avance; **to book in a.**, retenir (une place) à l'avance; **two hours in a.**, deux heures à l'avance 2. avancement *m*, progrès *m* (des sciences) 3. **to make advances to s.o.**, faire des avances à qn 4. *Com:* (*a*) avance (de fonds); **a. on securities,** prêt *m* sur titres (*b*) (*at auction*) **any a.?** qui dit mieux? **II.** *v* **1.** *vtr* (*a*) avancer (le pied, l'heure d'un paiement, une opinion) (*b*) faire avancer, progresser (les sciences) (*c*) **to a. s.o. money,** avancer de l'argent à qn **2.** *vi* s'avancer (**towards,** vers) (*a*) progresser; **the work is advancing,** le travail avance, fait des progrès, progresse (*b*) (*of employee*) recevoir de l'avancement. **ad′vanced** *a* (*a*) avancé (*b*) **a. mathematics,** mathématiques supérieures; *Sch:* **a. level** = baccalauréat *m, F:* bac *m* (*c*) **the season is (well) a.,** c'est la fin de la saison. **ad′vancement** *n* avancement (d'une carrière); progrès (de la science).

advantage [əd′vɑːntidʒ] *n* avantage *m;* **to take a. of,** profiter de (qch); exploiter (qn); **to turn sth. to a.,** tirer parti de qch; **to show sth off to a.,** faire valoir qch; **it would be to your a. to do it,** vous auriez intérêt à le faire. **advan′tageous** *a* avantageux (**to,** pour); profitable; utile.

advent [′ædvənt] *n* **1.** *Ecc:* (*a*) avènement *m* (du Messie) (*b*) **A.,** l'Avent *m* **2.** arrivée *f;* venue *f.*

adventure [əd′ventʃər] *n* aventure *f;* **a. story,** histoire d'aventures. **ad′venturer** *n* aventurier, -ière. **ad′venturous** *a* aventureux; (projet) hasardeux, risqué.

adverb [′ædvəːb] *n Gram:* adverbe *m.* **ad′verbial** *a* adverbial.

adversary [′ædvəsəri] *n* (*pl* **adversaries**) adversaire *mf.*

adverse [′ædvəːs] *a* (*a*) contraire, opposé (**to,** à) (*b*) (effet) défavorable. **ad′versity** *n* adversité *f.*

advert [′ædvəːt] *n F: see* **advertisement.**

advertise [′ædvətaiz] *vtr & i* faire de la réclame, de la publicité (pour un produit, un événement); afficher (une vente); **to a. in the paper,** mettre une annonce dans le journal. **ad′vertisement** *n* (*a*) publicité, réclame; *TV: etc:* spot *m* publicitaire (*b*) (*in newspaper*) annonce; **to put an a. in the paper,** mettre une annonce dans le journal (*c*) (*on wall*) affiche *f.* ′**advertiser** *n* annonceur *m.* ′**advertising** *n* publicité, réclame; (*in newspaper*) annonces *fpl;* **a. agency,** agence publicitaire, de publicité.

advice [əd′vais] *n* (*no pl*) (*a*) conseil(s) *m(pl),* avis *m;* **piece of a.,** conseil; **to ask s.o. for (his) a.,** demander conseil à qn (*b*) *Com:* avis; **a. note,** lettre d'avis.

advise [əd′vaiz] *vtr* (*a*) conseiller (qn); **to a. s.o. to do sth.,** conseiller à qn de faire qch (*b*) recommander (qch) (à qn) (*c*) **to a. against sth.,** déconseiller qch (*d*) **to a. s.o. of sth,** aviser qn de qch. **advisa′bility** *n* opportunité *f.* **ad′visable** *a* recommandable, recommandé, à conseiller. **ad′visedly** *adv* en connaissance de cause. **ad′viser** *n* conseiller, -ère. **ad′visory** *a* consultatif.

advocate I. *n* [′ædvəkət] **1.** avocat, -ate; défenseur *m,* partisan, -ane (d'une cause) **2.** *Jur: Scot:* avocat. **II.** *vtr* [′ædvəkeit] préconiser, recommander.

Aegean (Sea) (the) [ðiːiˈdʒiən(siː)] *a & n Geog:* (la mer) Egée.

aegis [′iːdʒis] *n* **under the a. of,** sous l'égide de.

aeon [′iːən] *n* éternité *f.*

aerate [′ɛəreit] *vtr* aérer.

aerial [′ɛəriəl] **1.** *a* aérien **2.** *n* (*NAm:* = **antenna**) antenne *f.*

aero- [′ɛərou-] *pref* aéro-. **aero′batics** *npl* acro-

baties aériennes; voltige *f.* **ae′robics** *npl* aérobic *m.* ′**aerodrome** *n* aérodrome *m.* **aerody′namics** *npl* aérodynamique *f.* ′**aerofoil** *n Av:* plan *m* à profil d'aile. **aero′nautic(al)** *a* aéronautique. **aero′nautics** *npl* aéronautique *f.* ′**aeroplane** *n* avion *m.* ′**aerosol** *n* aérosol *m;* bombe *f.* ′**aerospace** *n* aérospatiale *f.*

aesthete [′iːsθiːt] *n* esthète *mf.* **aes′thetic** *a* esthétique. **aes′thetically** *adv* esthétiquement.

afar [əˈfɑːr] *adv* au loin; **from a.,** de loin.

affable [′æfəbl] *a* affable. **affa′bility** *n* affabilité *f.* ′**affably** *adv* avec affabilité.

affair [əˈfɛər] *n* affaire *f;* **that's my a.,** ça, c'est mon affaire; **cela ne vous regarde pas;** (**love**) **a.,** affaire de cœur; **to have an a. with s.o.,** avoir une liaison avec qn; **in the present state of affairs,** du train où vont les choses.

affect¹ [əˈfekt] *vtr* (*a*) affecter (une manière); simuler (l'indifférence); **to a. stupidity,** faire l'idiot (*b*) aimer, avoir une préférence pour (qch). **affec′tation** *n* affectation *f.* **a′ffected**¹ *a* (*a*) affecté, maniéré (*b*) (*of emotion*) simulé. **a′ffectedly** *adv* avec affectation.

affect² *vtr* **1.** atteindre, toucher; affecter (un organe); influer sur (qch); altérer (la santé); **it affects me personally,** cela me touche personnellement **2.** affecter, affliger, toucher (qn); **nothing affects him,** rien ne l'émeut. **a′ffected**² *a* (*a*) atteint (d'une maladie) (*b*) ému, touché. **a′ffection** *n* affection *f,* attachement *m;* tendresse *f.* **a′ffectionate** *a* affectueux. **a′ffectionately** *adv* affectueusement.

affidavit [æfiˈdeivit] *n Jur:* déclaration *f* par écrit et sous serment.

affiliate [əˈfilieit] *vtr* affilier; **to be, become, affiliated,** s'affilier; **affiliated company,** filiale *f.* **affili′ation** *n* affiliation *f;* attaches *fpl* (politiques).

affinity [əˈfiniti] *n* (*a*) affinité *f* (*b*) attrait *m,* attraction *f* (**for, to,** pour).

affirm [əˈfəːm] *vtr* affirmer, soutenir (**that,** que). **affir′mation** *n* affirmation *f.* **a′ffirmative** **1.** *a* affirmatif **2.** *n* **to answer in the a.,** répondre par l'affirmative *f.* **a′ffirmatively** *adv* affirmativement.

afflict [əˈflikt] *vtr* affliger (**with,** de); désoler. **a′ffliction** *n* affliction *f;* calamité *f.*

affluence [′æfluəns] *n* richesse *f.* ′**affluent** *a* riche; **a. society,** société d'abondance.

afford [əˈfɔːd] *vtr* (*usu with* **can**) (*a*) avoir les moyens (de faire qch); **I can't a. it,** je ne peux pas me l'offrir (*b*) **can you a. the time?** disposez-vous du temps (nécessaire)? **I can't a. to be away for two weeks,** je ne peux pas me permettre une absence de deux semaines; **I can a. to wait,** je peux attendre.

afforestation [əfɔrisˈteiʃn] *n* (re)boisement *m.*

affray [əˈfrei] *n Jur:* bagarre *f.*

affront [əˈfrʌnt] **I.** *n* affront *m,* offense *f.* **II.** *vtr* offenser, faire un affront à (qn).

Afghanistan [æfgæniˈstɑːn] *Prn Geog:* Afghanistan *m.* ′**Afghan** *a & n* Afghan, -e.

afield [əˈfiːld] *adv* **far a.,** très loin.

afloat [əˈflout] *adv & a* (navire) à flot; sur l'eau; (vie) en mer; (servir) sur mer; (*of pers*) **to keep a.,** (i) surnager (ii) *Fig:* se maintenir à flot.

afoot [əˈfut] *adv* **a plan is a. to,** on envisage un projet pour; **there's something a.**, il se prépare quelque chose.

afraid [ə'freid] *a* **to be a. of s.o., sth**, avoir peur de qn, qch; **craindre** qn, qch; **don't be a.**, n'ayez pas peur; **ne craignez rien; to be a. to do, of doing, sth**, avoir peur, craindre, de faire qch; ne pas oser faire qch; **I'm a. he will die**, j'ai peur, je crains, qu'il ne meure; **I'm a. we're going to be late**, j'ai bien peur que nous allons arriver en retard; **I'm a. so, not**, j'ai bien peur que oui, que non; **I'm a. he's out**, je regrette, (je suis) désolé, mais il est sorti.

afresh [ə'freʃ] *adv* de, à, nouveau; **to start a.**, recommencer.

Africa ['æfrikə] *Prn Geog:* Afrique *f.* **'African** *a & n* africain, -aine.

Afrikaans [æfri'kɑ:ns] *n Ling:* afrika(a)ns *m.* **Afri'kaner** *a & n* afrikaner (*mf*).

Afro ['æfrou] *a* **A. (hairstyle)**, (coiffure) afro.

aft [ɑ:ft] *adv Nau: Av:* sur, à, vers, l'arrière.

after ['ɑ:ftər] I. *adv* **après 1.** (*order*) **to come a.**, venir après, à la suite (de qn, qch); **you speak first, I'll speak a.**, parlez d'abord, je parlerai ensuite **2.** (*time*) **I heard of it a.**, je l'ai appris plus tard; **he was ill for months a.**, il en est resté malade pendant des mois; **soon a.**, bientôt après; **the week a.**, la semaine d'après, la semaine suivante; **the day a.**, le lendemain. II. *prep* **1.** **a.**près; (*place*) **to walk, run, a. s.o.**, marcher, courir, après qn; **close the door a. you, please**, fermez la porte derrière vous, s'il vous plaît; **the police are a. you**, la police est à vos trousses; **what's he a.?** (i) qu'est-ce qu'il a en tête? (ii) qu'est-ce qu'il cherche? **I see what you're a.**, je vois où vous voulez en venir **2.** (*time*) **a. dinner**, après le dîner; **a.-dinner speech**, discours d'après dîner; **on and a. the 15th**, à partir du quinze; **a. hours**, après le travail, la fermeture; **the day a. tomorrow**, après-demain; **a. all**, après tout, enfin; **it is a. five (o'clock)**, il est cinq heures passées, il est plus de cinq heures; *NAm:* **twenty a. four**, quatre heures vingt; **he read page a. page**, il a lu page sur page **3.** (*order*) **a. you**, après vous; (*at meal*) servez-vous d'abord; **one a. the other**, l'un après l'autre; (entrer) à la file, en file **4.** (*manner*) **a. Turner**, d'après, à la manière de, Turner. III. *conj* (*a*) après que + *ind* **I came a. he had gone**, je suis venu après qu'il fut parti (*b*) après + *infin* **a. I'd seen him I went out**, après l'avoir vu je suis sorti. **'afterbirth** *n* placenta *m.* **'aftercare** *n* surveillance *f* (de convalescents, de délinquants); postcure *f* (de convalescents). **'after(-)effect(s)** *n* (*pl*) suite(s) *f*(*pl*), répercussion(s) *f*(*pl*) (d'un événement); contrecoup *m*; séquelles *fpl* (d'une maladie, d'un événement). **'afterlife** *n* **1.** vie *f* après la mort **2. in a.**, plus tard dans la vie. **'aftermath** *n* suites, répercussion(s), séquelles (d'un événement). **'afternoon** *n* après-midi *m or f inv;* **good a.!** (*on meeting*) bonjour! (*on leaving*) au revoir; **at half past three in the a.**, à trois heures et demie de l'après-midi; **he comes in the afternoon(s)**, il vient l'après-midi; **we're leaving on Thursday a.**, on part jeudi après-midi. **after'noons** *adv NAm:* (pendant) l'après-midi. **'afters** *npl Cu: F:* dessert *m.* **'after-sales (service)** *n* service *m* après-vente. **'after-shave (lotion)** *n* lotion *f* après-rasage. **'aftertaste** *n* arrière-goût *m.* **'afterthought** *n* ré-flexion *f* après coup; **to add sth as an a.**, ajouter qch après coup. **'afterwards** *adv* après, plus tard, ensuite.

again [ə'gen, *occ* ə'gein] *adv* (*often translated by vb with pref* re-) **to begin a.**, recommencer; **to do sth a.**, refaire qch; **to come down, up, a.**, redescendre, remonter **1.** (*a*) de nouveau, encore; **once a.**, encore une fois; une fois de plus; **here we are a.!** nous revoilà! **don't do it a.!** ne recommencez pas, plus! **never a.**, plus jamais; **a. and a., time and (time) a.**, maintes et maintes fois; **now and a.**, de temps en temps; **as large a.**, deux fois aussi grand (*b*) **to send sth back a.**, renvoyer qch; **to come a.**, revenir; *F:* **come a.?** pardon? (*c*) **what's his name a.?** comment s'appelle-t-il déjà? **2.** (*a*) de plus, d'ailleurs (*b*) (then) **a., (and) a.**, d'autre part.

against [ə'genst, *occ* ə'geinst] *prep* (*a*) contre; **she was a. the idea**, elle s'opposait à l'idée; **a. the rules**, contraire aux règlements; **to go a. nature**, aller à l'encontre de la nature (*b*) **to come up a. sth**, (se) heurter contre qch; **leaning a. the wall**, appuyé contre le mur, adossé au mur; **to show up a. a background**, se détacher sur un fond (*c*) **my rights (as) a. the Government**, mes droits vis-à-vis du gouvernement; **three deaths this year (as) a. ten in 1980**, trois morts cette année contre dix en 1980.

agate ['ægət] *n Miner:* agate *f.*

age [eidʒ] I. *n* **1.** (*a*) âge *m;* **what a. is he? what's his a.?** quel âge a-t-il? **he's twenty years of a.**, il a vingt ans; il est âgé de vingt ans; **he doesn't look his a.**, il ne paraît pas son âge; **to be under a.**, être mineur; **to come of a.**, atteindre sa majorité; **to be of a.**, être majeur; **a. limit**, limite *f* d'âge; **to come into the 15–20 a. group**, faire partie du groupe des 15 à 20 ans (*b*) (**old**) **a.**, vieillesse *f* **2.** (*a*) âge, époque *f*, siècle *m;* **the atomic a.**, l'ère *f* atomique (*b*) *F:* **it's ages since I saw him, I haven't seen him for ages**, il y a une éternité que je ne l'ai vu. II. *vi & tr* vieillir. **aged** I. ['eidʒid] **1.** *a* âgé, vieux **2.** *npl* **the a.**, les personnes âgées; les vieux. II. [eidʒd] *a* **1. a. twenty (years)**, âgé de vingt ans **2. I found him greatly a.**, je l'ai trouvé bien vieilli. **'ageing** *NAm: also* **'aging 1.** *a* vieillissant **2.** *n* vieillissement *m.* **'ageless** *a* toujours jeune. **'age-old** *a* séculaire.

agency ['eidʒənsi] *n* (*pl* agencies) **1.** action *f;* **through s.o.'s a.**, par l'intermédiaire, l'entremise, de qn **2.** *Com:* agence *f*, bureau *m;* **travel a.**, agence de tourisme.

agenda [ə'dʒendə] *n* ordre *m* du jour.

agent ['eidʒənt] *n* agent *m; Com:* représentant *m;* concessionnaire *m;* **travel a.**, agent de tourisme.

agglomeration [əgləmə'reiʃn] *n* agglomération *f.*

aggravate ['ægrəveit] *vtr* **1.** aggraver; envenimer (une querelle); augmenter (la douleur) **2.** *F:* agacer, exaspérer (qn). **'aggravating** *a F:* agaçant, exaspérant. **aggra'vation** *n* (*a*) aggravation *f* (*b*) *F:* agacement *m*, exaspération *f.*

aggregate ['ægrigət] **1.** *a* global **2.** *n* (*a*) ensemble *m*, total *m;* **in the a.**, en somme, dans l'ensemble (*b*) *CivE:* granulat *m.*

aggression [ə'greʃn] *n* agression *f.* **a'ggressive** *a* agressif. **a'ggressively** *adv* d'une manière agressive; agressivement. **a'ggressor** *n* agresseur *m.*

aggrieved [ə'gri:vd] *a* chagriné; blessé.

aggro ['ægrou] *n* (*no pl*) *F:* (*a*) agressivité *f* (*b*) bagarre(s) *f* (*pl*), grabuge *m*.

aghast [ə'gɑ:st] *a* consterné (**at,** de); sidéré.

agile ['ædʒail] *a* agile. **a'gility** *n* agilité *f*.

agitate ['ædʒiteit] **1.** *vtr* agiter **2.** *vi* faire de l'agitation (**for, against,** pour, contre). **'agitated** *a* agité; ému; troublé. **agi'tation** *n* **1.** agitation *f*; (*of pers*) émotion *f*; trouble *m* **2.** agitation (politique). **'agitator** *n* agitateur, -trice.

agnostic [æg'nɔstik] *a & n* agnostique (*mf*).

ago [ə'gou] *adv* **ten years a.,** il y a dix ans; **a little while a.,** tout à l'heure; tantôt; **long a.,** il y a longtemps; **as long a. as 1840,** déjà en 1840.

agog [ə'gɔg] *adv & a* **to be** (**all**) **a. to do sth,** être impatient de faire qch; **the whole town was a.,** toute la ville était en émoi.

agonize ['ægənaiz] *vi* se faire beaucoup de souci (**over sth,** pour qch). **'agonized** *a* (cri) d'angoisse. **'agonizing** *a* (*of pain*) atroce; (*of spectacle*) navrant; (*of decision*) angoissant; **a. cry,** cri déchirant.

agony ['ægəni] *n* (*pl* **agonies**) **1.** angoisse *f*; **to suffer agonies,** être au supplice; **to be in a.,** souffrir de douleurs atroces; **in an a. of fear,** saisi d'une peur atroce; *Journ: F:* **a. column,** courrier *m* du cœur **2.** (**death**) **a.,** agonie *f*.

agoraphobia [ægərə'foubiə] *nf* agoraphobie *f*.

agrarian [ə'grɛəriən] *a* (mesure, loi) agraire.

agree [ə'gri:] **I.** *vtr* accepter (une condition); se mettre d'accord sur (un prix); **agreed!** d'accord! entendu! **agreed place,** endroit convenu; **unless otherwise agreed,** sauf arrangement contraire. **II.** *vi* **1.** (*a*) **to a. to sth,** consentir à, accepter, qch; **to a. to do sth,** accepter, convenir de, consentir à, faire qch; **to a. to differ,** différer à l'amiable; **I a. that he was wrong,** j'admets qu'il s'est trompé (*b*) **to a. with s.o. about sth,** être du même avis que qn, être d'accord avec qn, sur qch; **I entirely a. with you,** je suis entièrement de votre avis; **I don't a. with this theory,** je n'accepte pas cette théorie (*c*) (*of two or more people*) s'accorder, être d'accord, se mettre d'accord (**about, on,** sur; **to do,** pour faire); s'entendre bien; **to a. on, about, a price,** convenir d'un prix **2.** (*of thgs*) (*a*) s'accorder, concorder (ensemble) (*b*) **the climate does not a. with him,** le climat ne lui convient pas, ne lui va pas; **mussels don't a. with me,** les moules ne me réussissent pas (*c*) *Gram:* s'accorder. **a'greeable** *a* agréable; **to be a. to sth, to doing sth,** consentir à qch, à faire qch. **a'greeably** *adv* agréablement. **a'greement** *n* **1.** convention *f* (de salaires); contrat *m* **2. to be in a. with s.o.,** être d'accord avec qn; **to come to an a. with s.o.,** se mettre d'accord avec qn; **by mutual a.,** de gré à gré; à l'amiable **3.** *Gram:* accord *m* (**with,** avec).

agriculture ['ægrikʌltʃər] *n* agriculture *f*. **agri'cultural** *a* agricole; **a. engineer,** ingénieur agronome; **a. college,** école d'agriculture. **agri'culturalist** *n* (*farmer*) agriculteur *m*; (*scientist*) agronome *mf*.

agronomy [ə'grɔnəmi] *n* agronomie *f*.

aground [ə'graund] *adv Nau:* échoué; **to run a.,** (s')échouer.

ahead [ə'hed] *adv* **1.** *Nau:* **full speed a.!** en avant toute! **2.** en avant (**of,** de); **go straight a.,** allez tout

droit (devant vous); **go a.!** allez-y! vas-y! **to get a.,** (i) prendre de l'avance (**of s.o.,** sur qn); devancer, dépasser (**of s.o.,** qn) (ii) *Fig:* avancer (dans sa carrière); réussir (dans la vie); **to be two hours a. of s.o.,** avoir deux heures d'avance sur qn; **to think, plan, look, a.,** penser à l'avenir; **to be a. of one's time,** être en avance sur son temps; **we arrived a. of time,** nous sommes arrivés en avance, avant l'heure.

ahoy [ə'hɔi] *int Nau:* **ship a.!** oh(é) du navire!

aid [eid] **I.** *n* **1.** aide *f*, assistance *f*, secours *m*; **with the a. of,** avec l'aide de (qn); à l'aide de (qch); **collection in a. of the deaf,** quête au profit des sourds; *F:* **what's** (**all**) **this in a. of?** c'est en quel honneur? **2. aids,** aides; **hearing a.,** audiophone *m*; *Sch:* **audiovisual aids,** matériel audio-visuel. **II.** *vtr* **1.** aider, assister (qn); venir à l'aide de (qn); *Jur:* **to a. and abet s.o.,** être le complice de qn **2.** contribuer à (la guérison).

aide [eid] *n* (*pers*) aide *mf*; assistant, -ante.

ailment ['eilmənt] *n* mal *m*, *pl* maux; maladie (légère). **'ailing** *a* souffrant.

aim [eim] **I.** *n* **1. to miss one's a.,** manquer son coup, son but; **to take a.** (**at s.o., sth**), viser (qn, qch) **2.** but; **his a. was to,** il avait pour but de; **with the a. of doing sth,** dans le but, le dessein, de faire qch. **II.** *vtr & i* **1.** (*a*) lancer (une pierre), porter (un coup) (**at,** à) (*b*) **to a. a gun at s.o.,** tirer sur, à s.o. **with a gun,** viser qn avec un fusil; braquer un fusil sur qn; **measure aimed against, at, us,** mesure dirigée contre nous **2. to a. at,** viser (qch); poursuivre (un but); **to a. at doing sth,** viser, aspirer, à faire qch; **to a. to do sth,** avoir l'intention de faire qch. **'aimless** *a*, **'aimlessly** *adv* sans but.

air [ɛər] **I.** *n* **1.** (*a*) air *m*; **to go out for a breath of** (**fresh**) **a., for some a.,** sortir prendre l'air; *Fig:* **to walk on a.,** être aux anges; **there's sth in the air,** il se prépare qch; *F:* **I can't live on a.,** je ne vis pas de l'air du temps (*b*) **to travel by a.,** voyager par avion; **high up in the a.,** très haut dans le ciel, dans les airs; **to throw sth** (**up**) **in(to) the a.,** jeter qch en l'air; *F:* (*of pers*) **to go up in the a.,** exploser (de colère); **it's all in the a. as yet,** ce ne sont encore que des projets en l'air (*c*) *WTel: etc:* **to be on the a.,** (i) (*of pers*) parler à la radio, à la télévision (ii) (*of programme*) être radiodiffusé; passer sur les antennes (iii) (*of station*) émettre **2.** *Mus:* air **3.** air; **with an amused a.,** d'un air amusé; **to put on airs** (**and graces**), prendre de grands airs. **II.** *vtr* **1.** aérer (une pièce, du linge) **2.** exposer (ses griefs); faire parade de (ses connaissances). **'airbase** *n* base aérienne. **'airbed** *n* matelas *m* pneumatique. **'airborne** *a* aéroporté; **the plane got a.,** l'avion a décollé. **'airbrake** *n* (*a*) *Aut:* frein *m* à air comprimé (*b*) *Av:* aérofrein *m*. **'air-conditioned** *a* climatisé. **'air-conditioner** *n* climatiseur *m*. **'air conditioning** *n* climatisation *f*. **'air-cooled** *a* refroidi par l'air; (moteur) à refroidissement par air. **'aircraft** *n inv in pl* avion *m*. **'aircraft carrier** *n* porte-avions *m inv*. **'aircraftman, -men** *n* soldat *m* de la RAF. **'aircraftwoman, -women** *n* femme *f* soldat de la WRAF. **'aircrew** *n* équipage *m* (d'un avion). **'airdrome** *n NAm:* (*Brit:* = **aerodrome**) aérodrome *m*. **'airdrop 1.** *n* largage *m* (de charges) **2.** *vtr* (**airdropped**) larguer (des charges). **'airfield** *n* terrain *m* d'aviation. **'air force** *n* armée *f* de l'air; forces aériennes. **'air freight** *n* transport *m* par air; **by a. freight,** par avion. **'air-freight** *vtr* transporter par avion. **'air gun** *n* fusil *m* à air comprimé. **'air hostess** *n* hôtesse *f* de l'air. **'airily** *adv* d'un ton cavalier; avec désinvolture. **'airing** *n* ventilation *f*, aération *f* (d'une pièce); **a. cupboard,** armoire chauffante. **'airless** *a* (*of room*) privé d'air, renfermé; (*of weather*) sans vent. **'airlift** 1. *n* pont aérien 2. *vtr* transporter par avion. **'airline** *n* compagnie, ligne, aérienne. **'airliner** *n* avion de ligne. **'airlock** *n* (*in spacecraft*) sas *m*; (*in pipe*) bouchon *m* d'air. **'airmail** *n* service postal aérien; **by a.,** par avion. **'airman, -men** (*a*) aviateur *m* (*b*) soldat (d'une armée de l'air). **'air 'marshal** *n* général *m* de corps (d'une armée de l'air). **'airplane** *n NAm:* (*Brit:* = **aeroplane**) avion. **'airport** *n* aéroport *m*. **'air raid** *n* attaque aérienne; raid (aérien). **'airship** *n* dirigeable *m*. **'airshow** *n* salon *m* de l'aéronautique; meeting *m* d'aviation. **'airsick** *a* to be a., avoir le mal de l'air. **'airsickness** *n* mal de l'air. **'airspeed** *n Av:* vitesse *f*. **'airstrip** *n* piste *f* d'atterrissage. **'air terminal** *n* aérogare *f*. **'airtight** *n* étanche (à l'air); hermétique. **'air-to-air** *a* (missile) air-air *inv.* **'air traffic con'trol** *n* contrôle de la navigation aérienne. **'air traffic con'troller** *n* contrôleur, -euse, de la navigation aérienne; aiguilleur *m* du ciel. **'airway** *n* route, voie, aérienne. **'airwoman, -women** *n* (*a*) aviatrice *f* (*b*) femme soldat (d'une armée de l'air). **'airworthiness** *n* navigabilité *f*. **'airworthy** *a* (avion) muni d'un certificat de navigabilité. **airy** *a* (**-ier, -iest**) (*a*) (*of room*) bien aéré (*b*) (*of promise*) vain, en l'air; (*of conduct*) insouciant, désinvolte. **'airy-'fairy** *a F:* farfelu.

aisle [ail] *n* nef latérale (d'une église); passage *m* (entre bancs); couloir central (d'autobus).

ajar [ə'dʒɑːr] *adv & a* (*of door*) entrouvert.

akimbo [ə'kimbou] *adv* **with arms a.,** les (deux) poings sur les hanches.

akin [ə'kin] *a* **a. to,** qui ressemble à; **feeling a. to fear,** sentiment voisin, qui tient, de l'effroi.

alabaster [ælə'bɑːstər] *n* albâtre *m*.

alacrity [ə'lækriti] *n* empressement *m*.

alarm [ə'lɑːm] **I.** *n* 1. alarme *f*, alerte *f*; **to raise, give, the a.,** donner l'alarme, l'alerte; **false a.,** fausse alerte; **a. signal,** signal d'alarme; **a. bell,** cloche d'alarme; tocsin *m* 2. **a.** (**clock**), réveil *m*, réveille-matin *m inv* 3. avertisseur *m* (d'incendie). **II.** *vtr* 1. alarmer 2. (*frighten*) effrayer; **to be alarmed at sth,** s'alarmer, s'effrayer, de qch. **a'larming** *a* alarmant. **a'larmist** *a & n* alarmiste (*mf*).

alas [ə'læs] *int* hélas!

Albania [æl'beiniə] *Prn Geog:* Albanie *f*. **Al-'banian** *a & n* albanais, -aise.

albatros [ælbətros] *n* albatros *m*.

albeit [ɔːl'biːit] *conj Lit:* quoique, bien que + *sub.*

albino [æl'biːnou] *n* albinos *mf*.

album [ælbəm] *n* album *m*.

alcohol [ælkəhɔl] *n* alcool *m*. **alco'holic** 1. *a* alcoolique; **a. drink,** boisson alcoolisée 2. *n* (*pers*) alcoolique *mf*. **'alcoholism** *n* alcoolisme *m*.

alcove [ælkouv] *n* alcôve *f*, niche *f*, enfoncement *m* (dans un mur).

alder [ɔːldər] *n Bot:* au(l)ne *m*.

alderman [ˈːldəmən] *n* (*pl* **aldermen**) = conseiller, -ère, municipal(e) (d'une grande ville).

ale [eil] *n* bière; **pale a.,** bière blonde.

alert [ə'ləːt] 1. *a* (*a*) vigilant, éveillé (*b*) alerte, actif, vif 2. *n* alerte *f*; **to be on the a.,** être sur le qui-vive, en état d'alerte 3. *vtr* alerter. **a'lertness** *n* 1. vigilance *f*; promptitude *f* (**in doing sth.,** à faire qch) 2. vivacité *f*.

alfalfa [æl'fælfə] *n Bot:* luzerne *f*.

alfresco [æl'freskou] *a & adv* en plein air.

algae [ældʒiː] *npl Bot:* algues *f*.

algebra [ældʒibrə] *n* algèbre *f*. **alge'braic** *a* algébrique.

Algeria [æl'dʒiəriə] *Prn Geog:* Algérie *f*. **Al'gerian** *a & n* algérien, -ienne. **Al'giers** *Prn Geog:* Alger *m*.

alias [eiliəs] 1. *adv* alias, autrement dit 2. *n* (*pl* **aliases** [-iz]) faux nom, nom d'emprunt.

alibi [ælibai] *n* alibi *m*.

alien [eiliən] *a & n* étranger, -ère. **'alienate** *vtr* (s')aliéner (qn). **alie'nation** *n* aliénation *f*.

alight[1] [ə'lait] *vi* 1. descendre (**from a train,** d'un train). 2. (*of bird*) se poser.

alight[2] *a* allumé; en feu; **to set sth a.,** mettre le feu à qch; **to catch a.,** s'allumer, prendre feu.

align [ə'lain] 1. *vtr* aligner 2. *vi* s'aligner. **a'lignment** *n* alignement *m*.

alike [ə'laik] 1. *a* semblable, pareil; **to be, look, a.,** se ressembler; **all things are a. to him,** tout lui est égal 2. *adv* de la même manière; **dressed a.,** habillés de même; **winter and summer a.,** été comme hiver.

alimentary [æli'mentəri] *a* alimentaire; *Anat:* **a. canal,** tube digestif.

alimony [ælimoni] *n Jur:* pension *f* alimentaire.

alive [ə'laiv] *a* 1. vivant, en vie; **to be burnt a.,** être brûlé vif; **it's good to be a.!** il fait bon vivre! **dead or a.,** mort ou vif; **no man a.,** personne au monde; **to keep a.,** maintenir (qn) en vie; garder (un souvenir); *F:* **to be a. and kicking,** être plein de vie 2. **to be a. to sth,** se rendre compte, avoir conscience, de qch 3. (*of pers*) (i) remuant (ii) à l'esprit éveillé; **look a.!** remuez-vous! 4. **to be a. with,** (i) (*of cheese*) grouiller de (vers) (ii) fourmiller de (monde).

alkali [ælkəlai] *n Ch:* base *f*. **'alkaline** *a* basique.

all [ɔːl] 1. *a & pron* tout, tous; *f* toute, toutes (*a*) **a. France,** toute la France; **a. men,** tous les hommes; **a. (of) the others,** tous les autres; **a. day,** (pendant) toute la journée; **a. his life,** toute sa vie; **a. the way,** tout le long du chemin; **is that a. the luggage you're taking?** c'est tout ce que vous emportez de bagages? **a. those books are his,** tous ces livres(-là) sont à lui; **he ate it a., a. of it,** il a tout mangé; **take it a., prenez** (le) tout; **I'll take a. four,** je prendrai tous les quatre; **a. that,** tout cela, tout ça; **you're not as ill as a. that,** tu n'es pas (aus)si malade que ça; **for a. his wealth,** en dépit de, malgré, sa fortune; **at a. hours,** à toute heure (*b*) *pron* **we a. love him,** nous l'aimons tous; **we are a. agreed,** nous sommes tous d'accord; **a. of us,** nous tous; *Fb: etc:* **five a.,** cinq à cinq; *Ten:* **fifteen a.,** quinze partout (*c*) *pron* **a. that I did,** tout ce que j'ai fait; **a. that happens,** tout ce qui arrive;

that's a., c'est tout; voilà tout; **if that's a.**, si ce n'est que cela; **it was a. I could do not to laugh,** je me tenais à quatre pour ne pas rire; **for a. I know,** autant que je sache; **once and for a.,** une fois pour toutes; **most of a.**, surtout **2.** *adv* tout; **dressed a. in black,** habillé tout en, de, noir; **she is a. alone,** elle est toute seule; **she is a. for accepting,** elle est tout en faveur d'accepter; **to be the better,** tant mieux; **a. the more,** d'autant plus; **a. the faster,** d'autant plus vite; **a. at once** (i) (*suddenly*) tout à coup, soudain (ii) (*together*) tout d'un coup; **that's a. very well but,** tout cela est bel et bien mais; **to go a. out,** ne pas s'épargner (**to do sth,** pour faire qch); *F*: **he's not a. there,** il est un peu simple d'esprit; **to be a. in,** être épuisé, éreinté; **I didn't speak at a.,** je n'ai pas parlé du tout; **not at a.** (i) pas du tout (ii) (*when thanked*) je vous en prie; (**taking it**) **a. in a.,** à tout prendre **3.** *n* tout *m*; totalité *f*; **his a.,** tout ce qu'il a. 'all-'clear *n* (signal *m* de) fin *f* d'alerte. 'all-em-'bracing *a* (*of knowledge*) vaste. 'all-im'port-ant *a* de la plus haute importance. 'all-in *a* (prix) tout compris; **a.-in wrestling,** catch *m*. 'all-night *a* qui dure toute la nuit; **a.-n. service,** permanence *f* de nuit. 'all-'out *a* (*effort*) suprême, maximum; (*strike*) total. 'all-'powerful *a* tout-puissant. 'all-'purpose *a* universel; à tout faire. 'all-'round *a* (athlète) complet. 'all-'rounder *n* athlète complet, -ète; **he's a good a.-r.,** il est fort en tout. 'all-'star *a* (spectacle) joué exclusivement par des vedettes. 'all-'time *a* (record) sans précédent.

allay [ə'lei] *vtr* apaiser; calmer, dissiper (des doutes).

allege [ə'ledʒ] *vtr* alléguer, prétendre (**that,** que); prétexter (un rendez-vous). **alle'gation** *n* allégation *f*. **a'lleged** *a* (motif) allégué; (voleur) présumé. **a'llegedly** *adv* prétendument.

allegiance [ə'li:dʒəns] *n* fidélité *f* (**to,** à); **oath of a.,** serment d'allégeance.

allegory ['æligəri] *n* (*pl* allegories) allégorie *f*. **alle-'gorical** *a* allégorique.

allergy ['ælədʒi] *n* (*pl* allergies) allergie *f*. **a'llergic** *a* allergique (**to,** à).

alleviate [ə'li:vieit] *vtr* alléger, soulager (la douleur); adoucir (le chagrin). **allevi'ation** *n* allégement *m*.

alley ['æli] *n* (*in town*) ruelle *f*; passage *m*; **a. cat,** chat de gouttière.

alliance [ə'laiəns] *n* alliance *f*.

allied ['ælaid] *a* **1.** allié (**to, with,** à, avec) **2.** du même ordre; de la même famille; (industrie) connexe.

alligator ['æligeitər] *n Rept*: alligator *m*.

alliteration [ælitə'reiʃn] *n* allitération *f*.

allocate ['æləkeit] *vtr* allouer, assigner (qch à qn); affecter (une somme); attribuer (des fonctions). **allo'cation** *n*. allocation *f*; affectation *f* (d'une somme); attribution *f* (de fonctions).

allot [ə'lɔt] *vtr* (**allotted**) attribuer, assigner (qch à qn). **a'llotment** *n* **1.** attribution *f* (de qch à qn) **2.** (*a*) portion *f* (*b*) terrain loué pour la culture de légumes.

allow [ə'lau] *vtr* **1.** admettre (une requête) **2.** (*a*) (*permit*) permettre (qch à qn); **to a. s.o. to do sth,** permettre à qn de, autoriser qn à, faire qch; **passengers are not allowed on the bridge,** la passerelle est

interdite aux passagers (*b*) **to a. oneself to be deceived,** se laisser tromper **3.** (*a*) accorder (un délai), consentir (une remise) (**to,** à) (*b*) *vi* **to a. for,** tenir compte de (qch); prévoir (des difficultés). **a'llow-able** *a* (témoignage) admissible; (dépense) déductible. **a'llowance** *n* **1.** pension *f* (alimentaire); rente *f*; (*of food*) ration *f*; **travelling a.,** indemnité *f* de déplacement; *Adm*: **family a.,** allocation(s) familiale(s); *Fin*: **personal a.,** abattement personnel (sur l'impôt) **2.** *Com*: remise *f*, rabais *m* **3. to make allowance(s) for sth,** tenir compte de qch.

alloy ['ælɔi] *n* alliage *m*.

allspice ['ɔːlspais] *n Bot*: poivre *m* de la Jamaïque.

allude [ə'l(j)uːd] *vi* **to a. to,** faire allusion à.

allure [ə'ljuər] **1.** *vtr* attirer **2.** *n* attrait *m*, charme *m*. **a'lluring** *a* attrayant, séduisant.

allusion [ə'luːʒn] *n* allusion *f*.

alluvial [ə'luːviəl] *a Geol*: (terrain) alluvial.

ally I. *vtr* [ə'lai] **to a. oneself to, with,** s'allier à, avec. **II.** *n* **ally** ['ælai] (*pl* **allies**) allié, -ée.

almanac ['ɔːlmənæk] *n* almanach *m*.

almighty [ɔːl'maiti] **1.** *a* tout-puissant; *F*: **an a. din,** un bruit de tous les diables **2.** *n* **the A.,** le Tout-Puissant.

almond ['ɑːmənd] *n* **1.** amande *f*; **a. paste,** pâte d'amandes **2. a. (tree),** amandier *m*.

almost ['ɔːlmoust] *adv* presque; à peu près; **it's a. noon,** il est bientôt, près de, midi; **he a. fell,** il a failli tomber.

alms [ɑːmz] *npl* aumône *f*; **to give a. to s.o.,** faire l'aumône à qn. **'almshouse** *n* hospice *m*.

aloft [ə'lɔft] *adv* (*a*) *Nau*: dans la mâture (*b*) en haut; en l'air.

alone [ə'loun] *a* **1.** seul; **I did it a.,** je l'ai fait tout seul; **I want to speak to you a.,** je voudrais vous parler seul à seul **2. to leave a.,** (i) laisser (qn, qch) tranquille (ii) laisser (qn) faire (iii) ne pas se mêler de (qch); **too tired to walk, let a. run,** trop fatigué pour marcher, encore moins courir.

along [ə'lɔŋ] **1.** *prep* le long de; **to go a. a street,** suivre une rue; **trees a. the river,** arbres au bord de la rivière **2.** *adv* (*a*) **to go a.,** avancer; continuer son chemin; **come a.!** venez donc! **come a. now!** allons donc! **he'll be a. soon,** il va bientôt arriver (*b*) (*time*) **all a.,** depuis, dès, le début (*c*) **take me a. with you,** emmène-moi avec toi. **along'side** *adv & prep* à côté (de); *Nau*: **to come a. (the quay),** accoster (le quai); (*of ships*) **to lie a. (of) each other,** être bord à bord.

aloof [ə'luːf] *adv & a* (se tenir) à l'écart; (se montrer) distant. **a'loofness** *n* réserve *f*.

aloud [ə'laud] *adv* à haute voix; (tout) haut.

alphabet ['ælfəbet] *n* alphabet *m*. **alphabetical** *a* alphabétique. **alpha'betically** *adv* alphabétiquement.

Alps (the) [ði:'ælps] *Prn pl Geog*: les Alpes *f*. **'alpine** *a* (club) alpin; (paysage) alpestre.

already [ɔːl'redi] *adv* déjà.

Alsatian [æl'seiʃn] **1.** *a & n Geog*: alsacien, -ienne **2.** *n* (*dog*) berger allemand.

also ['ɔːlsou] *adv* aussi; également; **not only, but a.,** non seulement, mais aussi. **'also-ran** *n* (*a*) *Turf*: cheval non classé (*b*) *F*: (*pers*) non-valeur *f*.

altar ['ɔːltər] *n* autel *m*.

alter ['ɔːltər] **1.** vtr changer, modifier; retoucher (un vêtement); remanier (un texte) **2.** vi changer. **alte'ration** n changement m, modification f; retouche f (aux vêtements); remaniement m (d'un texte); révision f (d'un horaire).

altercation [ɔːltəˈkeiʃn] n altercation f.

alternate I. a [ɔːlˈtəːnət] alternatif; **on a.** days, tous les deux jours. **II.** v ['ɔːltəneit] **1.** vtr faire alterner (deux choses) **2.** vi alterner (**with**, avec). **al'ternately** adv alternativement; tour à tour. **'alternating** a alternant; El: (courant) alternatif. **'alternator** n El: alternateur m.

alternative [ɔːlˈtəːnətiv] **1.** a alternatif; **a. proposal,** contre-proposition f **2.** n alternative f; **there's no a.,** il n'y a pas de choix, d'autre solution. **al'ternatively** adv avec l'alternative de; ou bien.

although [ɔːlˈðou] conj bien que, quoique + sub.

altimeter ['æltimiːtər] n Av: altimètre m.

altitude ['æltitjuːd] n altitude f; **at a.,** en altitude.

alto ['æltou] n Mus: **1.** alto m **2.** (a) (male) hautecontre f (b) (female) contralto m.

altogether [ɔːltəˈgeðər] **1.** adv a (wholly) entièrement, tout à fait (b) (on the whole) somme toute; **taking things a.,** à tout prendre (c) **how much a.?** combien en tout? **2.** n F: **in the a.,** tout nu.

altruist ['æltruist] n altruiste mf. **altru'istic** a altruiste.

aluminium [ælju'miniəm] n NAm: **aluminum** [əˈluːminəm] n aluminium m.

alumnus [əˈlʌmnəs] n (pl alumni) NAm: ancien(ne) élève, ancien(ne) étudiant(e).

always ['ɔːlweiz] adv toujours.

am [æm] see **be**.

a.m. ['eiˈem] abbr ante meridiem, avant midi; **nine a.m.,** neuf heures du matin.

amalgam [əˈmælgəm] n amalgame m. **amalgamate 1.** vtr amalgamer; fusionner **2.** vi s'amalgamer; fusionner. **amalga'mation** n amalgamation f; fusion f.

amass [əˈmæs] vtr amasser; accumuler.

amateur ['æmətər] n amateur m; **a. painter,** peintre amateur; **a. work,** travail d'amateur. **'amateurish** a (travail d')amateur.

amaze [əˈmeiz] vtr confondre, stupéfier. **a'mazed** a confondu, stupéfait (**at sth,** de qch). **a'mazement** n stupéfaction f; stupeur f. **a'mazing** a stupéfiant; étonnant; F: formidable. **a'mazingly** adv étonnamment; (réussir) à merveille.

Amazon (the) [ðiːˈæməzən] Prn l'Amazone f.

ambassador [æmˈbæsədər] n ambassadeur m, f ambassadrice. **ambassadress** n ambassadrice f.

amber ['æmbər] n ambre m; **a.(-coloured),** ambré; Aut: **a. light,** feu orange.

ambidextrous [æmbiˈdekstrəs] a ambidextre.

ambiguous [æmˈbigjuəs] a **1.** ambigu, -uë; équivoque **2.** (résultat) incertain. **ambi'guity** n ambiguïté f. **am'biguously** adv de manière ambiguë, équivoque.

ambition [æmˈbiʃn] n ambition f. **am'bitious** a ambitieux; **to be a. to do sth,** ambitionner de faire qch. **am'bitiously** adv ambitieusement.

ambivalent [æmˈbivələnt] a ambivalent.

amble ['æmbl] vi **to a. (along),** aller, marcher, d'un pas tranquille.

ambulance ['æmbjuləns] n ambulance f; **a. man,** ambulancier m.

ambush ['æmbuʃ] **I.** n (pl ambushes) embuscade f; guet-apens m; **to lie in a.,** être en embuscade. **II.** vtr faire tomber (qn) dans une embuscade.

ameliorate [əˈmiːliəreit] **1.** vtr améliorer **2.** vi s'améliorer. **amelio'ration** n amélioration f.

amen [ɑːˈmen] int amen.

amenable [əˈmiːnəbl] a soumis (à la discipline); docile (aux conseils); **a. to reason,** raisonnable.

amend [əˈmend] vtr amender, modifier (un projet de loi); corriger (un texte). **a'mendment** n modification f, Pol: amendement m. **a'mends** npl **to make a.,** faire amende honorable; **to make a. to s.o. for sth,** dédommager qn de qch.

amenity [əˈmiːniti] n (pl amenities) **1.** agrément m (d'un lieu); (in hospital) **a. bed,** chambre privée (payante) **2.** pl agréments, aménagements mpl (d'un hôtel).

America [əˈmerikə] Prn Amérique f; **North, South, A.,** Amérique du Nord, du Sud. **A'merican** a & n américain, -aine; **A. Indian,** Amérindien, -ienne.

amethyst ['æmiθist] n améthyste f.

amiable ['eimiəbl] a aimable (to, envers). **ami-a'bility** n amabilité f (to, envers). **'amiably** adv aimablement.

amicable ['æmikəbl] a amical; (arrangement) à l'amiable. **'amicably** adv amicalement; (arranger qch) à l'amiable.

amid(st) [əˈmid(st)] prep au milieu de; parmi.

amiss [əˈmis] adv & a **1. to take sth a.,** prendre qch de travers, en mauvaise part **2. that won't come a.,** cela n'arrive pas mal à propos; **something's a.,** il y a qch qui cloche.

ammeter ['æmitər] n ampèremètre m.

ammonia [əˈmouniə] n Ch: (a) (gaz m) ammoniac m (b) (liquid) ammoniaque f.

ammunition [æmjuˈniʃn] n munitions fpl.

amnesia [æmˈniːziə] n Med: amnésie f.

amnesty ['æmnisti] n (pl amnesties) amnistie f.

amoeba, NAm: also **ameba** [əˈmiːbə] n (pl amoebas, -bae) amibe f. **amoebic,** NAm: also **amebic** a amibien.

amok [əˈmɔk] adv **to run a.,** devenir comme fou; s'emporter.

among(st) [əˈmʌŋ(st)] prep parmi, entre (a) **sitting a. her children,** assise au milieu de ses enfants (b) **a. friends,** entre amis; **a. yourselves, a. you,** entre vous; **to count s.o. a. one's friends,** compter qn au nombre de ses amis.

amoral [eiˈmɔrəl] a amoral, -aux.

amorous ['æmərəs] a amoureux. **'amorously** adv amoureusement; avec amour.

amorphous [əˈmɔːfəs] a amorphe.

amount [əˈmaunt] **I.** n **1.** somme f; montant m, total m (d'une facture); quantité f; **any a. of money,** énormément d'argent. **II.** vi **1.** (of money) s'élever, (se) monter (to, à); **I don't know what my debts a. to,** j'ignore le montant de mes dettes **2. that amounts to the same thing,** cela revient au même; **his words a. to a refusal,** ses paroles sont l'équivalent d'un refus; **he'll never a. to much,** il ne fera jamais grand-chose.

amp [æmp] n (a) = **ampere** (b) = **amplifier.**

ampere ['æmpɛər] *n Meas:* ampère *m.*

ampersand ['æmpəsænd] *n Typ:* et commercial.

amphetamine [æm'fetəmin] *n* amphétamine.

amphibian [æm'fibiən] *a & n* **1.** *Z:* amphibie *(m)* **2.** *Mil:* (véhicule *m*) amphibie. **am'phibious** *a* amphibie.

amphitheatre, *NAm:* **-theater** ['æmfiθiətər] *n* amphithéâtre *m; Geol:* cirque *m* (de montagnes).

ample ['æmpl] *a (a)* (vêtement) ample; **a. resources,** d'abondantes, de grosses, ressources *(b)* **you have a. time,** vous avez largement le temps. **'amply** *adv* amplement.

amplify ['æmplifai] *vtr* **(amplified)** amplifier (le son); **to a.** (on) **a story,** amplifier, ajouter des détails à, un récit. **'amplifier** *n El:* amplificateur *m.*

amputate ['æmpjuteit] *vtr* amputer; **his leg was amputated,** il a été amputé de la jambe. **ampu'tation** *n* amputation *f.*

amuck [ə'mʌk] *adv see* **amok.**

amuse [ə'mjuːz] *vtr (a)* amuser, faire rire (qn); **to be amused at, by, sth,** être amusé de qch (*b*) amuser, divertir, distraire (qn); **to a. oneself,** s'amuser, se divertir **(by doing sth,** à faire qch; **with sth,** avec qch); **to be amused by sth,** trouver qch amusant; **how can I keep them amused?** comment puis-je les occuper? **a'musement** *n* amusement *m (a)* **smile of a.,** sourire amusé (*b*) divertissement *m,* distraction *f;* **a. park,** parc d'attractions. **a'musing** *a* amusant; divertissant. **a'musingly** *adv* d'une manière amusante.

an [æn, ən] *indef art see* **a².**

anachronism [ə'nækrənizm] *n* anachronisme *m.* **anach'ronistic** *a* anachronique.

an(a)emia [ə'niːmiə] *n* anémie *f.* **a'n(a)emic** *a* anémique.

an(a)esthetic [ænis'θetik] *a & n* anesthésique *(m).* **an(a)esthetist** [ə'niːsθətist] *n* anesthésiste *mf.*

anagram ['ænəgræm] *n* anagramme *f.*

anal ['einl] *a Anat:* anal, -aux.

analgesic [ænəl'giːzik] *a & n Med:* analgésique *(m).*

analog ['ænəlɒg] *n* **a. computer,** calculateur analogique.

analogous [ə'næləgəs] *a* analogue (**to, with,** à).

analogy [ə'nælədʒi] *n (pl* **analogies)** analogie *f* (**to, with,** avec). **ana'logical** *a* analogique.

analyse, *NAm:* **analyze** ['ænəlaiz] *vtr* analyser; faire l'analyse de (qch); *Psy:* psychanalyser. **a'nalysis, -es** *n* analyse *f; Psy:* psychanalyse *f.* **'analyst** *n* analyste *mf; Psy:* (psych)analyste *mf.* **ana'lytic(al)** *a* analytique.

anarchy ['ænəki] *n* anarchie *f.* **a'narchic(al)** *a* anarchique. **'anarchist** *n* anarchiste *mf.*

anathema [ə'næθəmə] *n* anathème *m;* **those ideas are (an) a. to him,** il a ces idées en horreur.

anatomy [ə'nætəmi] *n (pl* **anatomies)** anatomie *f.* **ana'tomical** *a* anatomique.

ancestor ['ænsestər] *n* ancêtre *m;* aïeul *m, pl* aïeux. **an'cestral** *a* ancestral, héréditaire; **his a. home,** la maison de ses ancêtres. **'ancestry** *n* **1.** ascendance *f;* race *f;* lignée *f* **2.** *coll* ancêtres *mpl;* aïeux *mpl.*

anchor ['æŋkər] **I.** *n* ancre *f;* **at a.,** à l'ancre. **II.** *v* **1.** *vtr* mouiller (un navire); *Fig:* ancrer **2.** *vi* jeter l'ancre; mouiller. **'anchorage** *n (a)* ancrage *m,* mouillage *m (b)* droits *mpl* d'ancrage. **'anchorman, -men** *n WTel: TV:* présentateur, -trice, d'une émission.

anchovy ['æntʃəvi] *n (pl* **anchovies)** anchois *m.*

ancient ['einʃənt] *a (a)* ancien; (monument) historique *(b)* **the a. world,** le monde antique; *n* **the ancients,** les anciens *(c) (of pers)* très vieux.

ancillary [æn'siləri] *a* subordonné (**to,** à); accessoire; *(in hospital)* (personnel) non médical.

and [ænd, ənd] *conj* **1.** *(a)* et; **a knife a. fork,** un couteau et une fourchette *(b)* **two hundred a. two,** deux cent deux; **four a. a half,** quatre et demi; **four a. three quarters,** quatre trois quarts; **an hour a. twenty minutes,** une heure vingt minutes *(c)* **ham a. eggs,** œufs au jambon; **now a. then,** de temps en temps *(d)* **better a. better,** de mieux en mieux; **smaller a. smaller,** de plus en plus petit; **a. so on, a. so forth,** et ainsi de suite **2.** *(a)* **he could read a. write,** il savait lire et écrire *(b)* **wait a. see,** attendez voir; **try a. help me,** essayez de m'aider.

Andes (the) [ðiː'ændiːz] *Prnpl Geog:* les Andes *f.*

Andorra [æn'dɔrə] *Prn Geog:* (la République d')Andorre *f.*

anecdote ['ænikdout] *n* anecdote *f.*

anemone [ə'neməni] *n Bot:* anémone *f.*

angel ['eindʒəl] *n* ange *m; F:* **be an a. and make the beds,** tu serais un ange, un amour, si tu faisais les lits. **angelic** [æn'dzelik] *a* angélique. **an'gelica** *n Bot: Cu:* angélique *f.*

anger ['æŋgər] **1.** *n* colère *f;* emportement *m;* **in a.,** sous le coup de la colère **2.** *vtr* mettre (qn) en colère.

angle¹ ['æŋgl] **1.** *n (a)* angle *m;* **at an a. of 45°,** qui forme un angle de 45°; **at an a.,** en biais *(b)* angle, point *m* de vue; **from every a.,** sous tous les angles **2.** *vtr (a)* mettre (qch) de biais *(b)* présenter (des faits) sous un certain angle.

angle² *vi* pêcher à la ligne; **to a. for,** pêcher (la truite); quêter (une invitation). **'angler** *n* pêcheur, -euse, à la ligne. **'angling** *n* pêche *f* à la ligne.

Anglican ['æŋglikən] *a & n Ecc:* anglican, -ane; **the A. Church,** l'Église anglicane.

anglicism ['æŋglisizm] *n* anglicisme *m.* **'anglicize** *vtr* angliciser.

Anglo-Saxon ['æŋglou'sæksn] **1.** *a & n* anglo-saxon, -onne **2.** *n Ling:* anglo-saxon *m.*

angora [æŋ'gɔːrə] *n (a)* **a. (goat, rabbit),** (chèvre *f,* lapin *m)* angora *m (b) Tex:* (tissu *m)* angora.

angry ['æŋgri] *a* (**-ier, -iest**) *(a) (of pers)* en colère, fâché (**with s.o. about sth,** contre qn de qch); **to get a.,** se mettre en colère, se fâcher; **to make s.o. a.,** mettre qn en colère, fâcher qn; **a. voices,** voix irritées *(b) (of wound)* enflammé; *(of sky)* à l'orage. **'angrily** *adv* en colère, avec colère.

anguish ['æŋgwiʃ] *n (no pl)* angoisse *f;* douleur *f;* **in a.,** au supplice. **'anguished** *a* angoissé.

angular ['æŋgulər] *a* anguleux.

animal ['æniməl] *a & n* animal, -aux *(m);* **a. life,** la vie animale.

animate 1. ['ænimət] *a* animé **2.** ['ænimeit] *vtr* animer; encourager, stimuler. **'animated** *a* animé; **to become a.,** s'animer; *Cin:* **a. cartoons,** dessins animés. **ani'mation** *n* animation *f;* vivacité *f;* entrain *m.* **'animator** *n* animateur, -trice.

animosity [æni'mɔsiti] *n* animosité *f*.

aniseed ['ænisi:d] *n* (graine *f* d')anis *m*.

ankle ['æŋkl] *n* cheville *f*; **a. socks**, socquettes *fpl*. **'anklebone** *n* astragale *m*.

annals ['ænəlz] *npl* annales *fpl*.

annex [ə'neks] *vtr* annexer (**sth to sth**, qch à qch). **annex'ation** *n* annexion *f* (**of**, de). **'annex(e)** *n* annexe *f*.

annihilate [ə'naiəleit] *vtr* anéantir (une armée); annihiler (un argument). **annihi'lation** *n* anéantissement *m*.

anniversary [æni'vəːsəri] *n* (*pl* **anniversaries**) anniversaire *m*; **wedding a.**, anniversaire de mariage.

annotate ['ænəteit] *vtr* annoter. **anno'tation** *n* annotation *f*.

announce [ə'nauns] *vtr* annoncer (qn, qch); faire part de (la naissance). **a'nnouncement** *n* annonce *f*, avis *m*; (*of birth, marriage*) faire-part *m*. **a'nnouncer** *n* WTel: TV: speaker *m*, speakerine *f*.

annoy [ə'nɔi] *vtr* (*a*) contrarier (qn) (*b*) agacer, fâcher, énerver (qn). **a'nnoyance** *n* (*a*) contrariété *f*; **look of a.**, air contrarié (*b*) désagrément *m*, ennui *m*. **a'nnoyed** *a* contrarié, fâché; **to get a. with s.o. about sth**, se fâcher contre qn à cause de qch. **a'nnoying** *a* contrariant, ennuyeux; agaçant, énervant, fâcheux.

annual ['ænjuəl] 1. *a* annuel 2. *n* (*a*) Bot: plante annuelle (*b*) (*book*) annuaire *m*; tous les ans. **'annually** *adv* annuellement.

annuity [ə'njuiti] *n* (*pl* **annuities**) rente (annuelle); **life a.**, rente viagère.

annul [ə'nʌl] *vtr* (**annulled**) annuler; abroger (une loi). **a'nnulment** *n* annulation *f*; abrogation *f*.

anode ['ænoud] *n* El: anode *f*.

anomaly [ə'nɔməli] *n* (*pl* **anomalies**) anomalie *f*. **a'nomalous** *a* anormal, -aux.

anonymous [ə'nɔniməs] *a* anonyme. **ano'nymity** *n* anonymat *m*. **a'nonymously** *adv* anonymement.

anorak ['ænəræk] *n* Cost: anorak *m*.

anorexia [ænɔ'reksiə] *n* Med: anorexie *f*; **a. nervosa**, anorexie mentale.

another [ə'nʌðər] *a & pron* 1. (*an additional*) encore (un(e)); **in a. ten years**, dans dix ans d'ici; **without a. word**, sans un mot de plus 2. (*a*) (*similar*) un(e) autre, un(e) second(e); **he's a. Mussolini**, c'est un second Mussolini 3. (*a different*) un(e) autre; **that is** (quite) **a. matter**, c'est (tout) autre chose; **we'll do it a. time**, on le fera une autre fois; F: **tell me a.!** c'est pas vrai! 4. (*a*) **science is one thing, art is a.**, la science est une chose, l'art en est une autre; **one way or a.**, d'une façon ou d'une autre (*b*) (*reciprocal*) **one a.**, l'un l'autre, les uns les autres; **near one a.**, l'un près de l'autre; **love one a.**, aimez-vous les uns les autres; **they adore one a.**, ils s'adorent; **to help one a.**, s'entraider.

answer ['ɑːnsər] I. *n* 1. réponse *f* (à une question); réplique *f* (à une critique); **he has an a. to everything**, il a réponse à tout; **in a. to your letter**, en réponse à votre lettre 2. solution *f* (d'un problème). II. *vtr & i* répondre (à qn, à une lettre, au téléphone); **to a. for s.o.**, répondre de qn; se porter garant de qn; **he has a lot to a. for**, il est responsable de bien des choses;

to a. back, répliquer; **don't a. back!** pas de réplique! **to a. the door**, aller ouvrir (la porte); **to a.** (**to**) **a description**, répondre à un signalement; **that will a. the purpose**, cela fera l'affaire. **'answerable** *a* responsable (**to s.o. for sth**, envers qn de qch); **to be a. to an authority**, relever d'une autorité; **he's a. to nobody**, il ne doit de comptes à personne.

ant [ænt] *n* fourmi *f*. **'anteater** *n* fourmilier *m*. **'anthill** *n* fourmilière *f*.

antagonize [æn'tægənaiz] *vtr* éveiller l'antagonisme, l'hostilité, de (qn); contrarier (qn). **an'tagonism** *n* antagonisme *m*, opposition *f*. **antago'nistic** *a* opposé, hostile (**to**, à).

Antarctic [æn'tɑːktik] *a & n* antarctique (*m*). **An'tarctica** *n* Antarctique *m*.

ante- ['ænti-] *pref* anté-; pré-; *occ* anti-. **ante'cedent** 1. *a* antécédent, antérieur (**to**, à) 2. *n* antécédent *m*. **'antedate** *vtr* antidater (un document); précéder (un événement). **antedi'luvian** *a*. antédiluvien. **ante'natal** *a* prénatal, -als. **'anteroom** *n* antichambre *f*.

antelope ['æntiloup] *n* Z: antilope *f*.

antenna, -ae [æn'tenə, -iː] *n* antenne *f*.

anthem ['ænθəm] *n* 1. Ecc Mus: motet *m* 2. **national a.**, hymne national.

anthology [æn'θɔlədʒi] *n* (*pl* **anthologies**) anthologie *f*.

anthracite ['ænθrəsait] *n* Min: anthracite *m*.

anthropology [ænθrə'pɔlədʒi] *n* anthropologie *f*. **anthropo'logical** *a* anthropologique. **an'thropologist** *n* anthropologue *mf*, anthropologiste *mf*.

anti- ['ænti-] *pref* anti-, contre-; F: **I'm a bit a.** (**unions**), je suis un peu contre (les syndicats). **anti'aircraft** *a* (canon) antiaérien. **antibi'otic** *a & n* antibiotique (*m*). **'antibody** *n* anticorps *m*. **anti'climax** *n* retour *m* à l'ordinaire; déception *f*. **anti'clockwise** (*NAm:* = **counterclockwise**) *a & adv* dans le sens inverse des aiguilles d'une montre. **anticonsti'tutional** *a* anticonstitutionnel. **anti'cyclone** *n* anticyclone *m*. **'antidote** *n* antidote *m*, contrepoison *m*. **'antifreeze** *n* Aut: antigel *m inv*. **anti'histamine** *n* Med: antihistaminique *m*. **anti'nuclear** *a* antinucléaire, antiatomique. **anti'perspirant** *n* antiperspirant *m*. **antise'mitic** *a* antisémitique. **anti'septic** *a & n* antiseptique (*m*). **anti-'skid** *a* antidérapant. **anti'social** *a* antisocial. **anti-'tank** *a* (engin) antichar. **anti'theft** *a* (dispositif) antivol *inv*.

anticipate [æn'tisipeit] 1. *vtr* (*a*) anticiper sur (les événements); savourer (un plaisir) d'avance (*b*) escompter (un résultat) (*c*) prévenir; devancer (qn); **to a. s.o.'s wishes**, aller au-devant des désirs de qn (*d*) prévoir, envisager (une difficulté) 2. *vi* s'attendre (**that**, à ce que). **antici'pation** *n* anticipation *f*; **in a. of**, en prévision de. **anticipatory** *a* anticipé.

antics ['æntiks] *npl* bouffonneries *fpl*; gambades *fpl*; cabrioles *fpl*.

antipathy [æn'tipəθi] *n* antipathie *f* (**to**, pour). **antipa'thetic** *a* antipathique (**to**, à).

antipodes (**the**) [ðiːæn'tipədiːz] *npl* antipodes *mpl*.

antiquary ['æntikwəri] *n* (*pl* **antiquaries**) antiquaire *mf.* anti'quarian 1. *a* d'antiquaire 2. *n* antiquaire *mf*; **a. bookseller,** libraire spécialisé(e) dans les vieilles éditions.

antique [æn'ti:k] 1. *a* antique; ancien; **a. furniture,** meubles d'époque 2. *n* objet *m* d'art; *pl* antiquités *fpl*; **a. dealer,** antiquaire *mf*; **a. shop,** magasin d'antiquités. 'antiquated [-kweitid] *a* vieilli, vieillot; *(of ideas)* vieux jeu. an'tiquity [-kwiti] *n* antiquité *f*.

antirrhinum [ænti'rainəm] *n Bot:* muflier *m*, gueule-de-loup *f*.

antithesis, -es [æn'tiθisis, -i:z] *n* 1. antithèse *f* (to, of, de) 2. opposé *m*, contraire *m* (de).

antler ['æntlər] *n* andouiller *m*; *pl* bois *mpl*.

antonym ['æntənim] *n* antonyme *m*.

anus ['einəs] *n (pl* anuses) *Anat:* anus *m*.

anvil ['ænvil] *n Metalw:* enclume *f*.

anxiety [æŋ'zaiəti] *n (a)* inquiétude *f*; **deep a.,** angoisse *f*, anxiété *f (b)* sollicitude *f* (pour la sécurité de qn) *(c)* désir *m* (de plaire).

anxious ['æŋkʃəs] *a* 1. *(a) (of pers)* inquiet, soucieux (**about,** sur, de, au sujet de); *(homme, regard)* anxieux; **very a.,** angoissé; **he is a. about her health,** sa santé le préoccupe *(b) (of thg)* inquiétant; *(moment)* d'anxiété 2. désireux; **to be a. to do sth,** tenir beaucoup à faire qch; désirer vivement faire qch; être impatient, anxieux, de faire qch. 'anxiously *adv* 1. *(a)* avec inquiétude *(b)* anxieusement 2. avec sollicitude 3. avec impatience.

any ['eni] I. *a & pron* 1. **have you a. milk, margarine, eggs?** avez-vous du lait, de la margarine, des œufs? **have you got a.?** en avez-vous? **have you got a. more milk, eggs?** avez-vous encore du lait, d'autres œufs? **if a. of them should see him,** si aucun d'entre eux le voyait; **there are few if a.,** il y en a peu ou pas (du tout) 2. **I can't find a.,** je n'en trouve pas; **he hasn't a. money,** il n'a pas d'argent; **he hasn't a. reason to complain,** il n'a aucune raison de se plaindre; **it is difficult to find a. explanation for it,** il est difficile d'en trouver aucune explication 3. *(a)* n'importe (le)quel; **come a. day (you like),** venez n'importe quel jour; **a. doctor will tell you that,** n'importe quel médecin vous le dira; **that may happen a. day,** cela peut arriver d'un jour à l'autre; **take a. two cards,** prenez deux cartes quelconques *(b)* **at a. hour of the day,** à toute heure de la journée. II. *adv* **I don't see him a. more,** je ne le vois plus; **I cannot go a. further,** je ne peux pas aller plus loin; **is he a. better?** est-ce qu'il va un peu mieux?

anybody ['enibɒdi], anyone ['eniwʌn] *n & pron* 1. quelqu'un; *(with implied negation)* personne; **can you see a.?** voyez-vous quelqu'un? **does a. dare to say so?** y a-t-il personne qui ose le dire? 2. **not a., ne . . .** personne; **there was hardly a.,** il n'y avait presque personne 3. n'importe qui; tout le monde; **a. will tell you so,** le premier venu vous le dira; **a. would think he was mad,** on le croirait fou; **a. who had seen him,** quiconque l'aurait vu; **a. but me,** tout autre que moi; **bring along a. you like,** amenez qui vous voudrez; **I haven't met a. else,** je n'ai rencontré personne d'autre 4. **is he a.?** est-il quelqu'un?

anyhow ['enihau] *adv* 1. **to do sth a.,** faire qch n'importe comment 2. en tout cas, de toute façon; **a. you can try,** vous pouvez toujours essayer.

anyplace ['enipleis] *adv NAm:* = anywhere.

anything ['eniθiŋ] *pron & n* 1. quelque chose; *(with implied negation)* rien; **can I do a. for you?** est-ce que je peux vous aider? **is there a. more pleasant than that?** est-il rien de plus agréable que cela? **if a. should happen to him,** s'il lui arrivait quelque malheur 2. **not a.,** ne . . . rien; **hardly a.,** presque rien 3. *(no matter what)* n'importe quoi; tout; **he eats a.,** il mange de tout; **a. you like,** tout ce que vous voudrez; **he is a. but mad,** il n'est rien moins que fou; **a. but!** loin de là! 4. *adv phr (intensive) F:* **to work like a.,** travailler comme un fou; **it's raining like a.,** il pleut à torrents; **as easy as a.,** facile comme tout, comme bonjour.

anyway ['eniwei] *adv* = anyhow 2.

anywhere ['eniwɛər] *adv* 1. n'importe où; **can you see it a.?** peux-tu le voir quelque part? **a. you like,** où vous voudrez; **a. else,** (partout) ailleurs 2. **not a.,** nulle part.

aorta [ei'ɔ:tə] *n Anat:* aorte *f*.

apart [ə'pɑ:t] *adv* 1. *(a)* **to stand a.,** être séparé, se tenir à l'écart (**from,** de); **born two years a.,** nés à deux ans d'intervalle *(b)* **to keep a.,** séparer; tenir séparé; **to stand with one's feet a.,** se tenir les jambes écartées; **they are a kilometre a.,** ils sont à un kilomètre l'un de l'autre; **lines ten centimetres a.,** lignes espacées de dix centimètres; **you can't tell them a.,** on ne peut pas les distinguer l'un de l'autre; **they consider themselves in a class a.,** ils se considèrent au-dessus des autres 2. **to take a.,** démonter (une machine); **to come a.,** *(of clothes)* se découdre; *(of seam)* se défaire; *(of two objects)* se détacher; *(of object)* tomber en morceaux 3. **a. from him,** à part lui; sauf lui; **a. from the fact that,** outre que; **joking a.,** plaisanterie à part.

apartheid [ə'pɑ:teit, -tait] *n* apartheid *m*.

apartment [ə'pɑ:tmənt] *n (a)* pièce *f (b) usu pl O:* logement *m*; **furnished apartments,** chambres meublées; meublé *m (c) NAm:* appartement *m*; **a. block, house,** immeuble *m*.

apathy ['æpəθi] *n* apathie *f*, indifférence *f*. apa'thetic *a* apathique.

ape [eip] I. *n Z:* (grand) singe (sans queue). II. *vtr* singer; imiter; mimer (qn).

aperitif [ə'peritif] *n* apéritif *m*.

aperture ['æpətjuər] *n* ouverture *f*.

apex ['eipeks] *n* sommet *m* (d'un triangle).

aphid ['eifid] *n (pl* aphids), aphis ['eifis] *n (pl* aphides) *Ent:* aphis *m*; puceron *m*.

aphrodisiac [æfrou'diziæk] *n* aphrodisiaque *m*.

apiary ['eipiəri] *n (pl* apiaries) rucher *m*.

apiculture ['eipikʌltʃər] *n* apiculture *f*.

apiece [ə'pi:s] *adv* chacun; **to cost five francs a.,** coûter cinq francs (la) pièce; **to receive a present a.,** recevoir chacun un cadeau.

aplomb [ə'plɔm] *n* aplomb *m*.

apocalypse [ə'pɔkəlips] *n* apocalypse *f*. apoca'lyptic *a* apocalyptique.

apocryphal [ə'pɔkrifəl] *a* apocryphe.

apologetic [əpɔlə'dʒetik] *a* (ton) d'excuse; **to be a.,** s'excuser (**about,** de). apolo'getically *adv* pour s'excuser; en s'excusant.

apologize [ə'pɔlədʒaiz] *vi* **to a. to s.o. for sth, for having done sth,** s'excuser de qch, d'avoir fait qch, auprès de qn. a'pology n excuses fpl; F: an a. for a dinner, un semblant de dîner.

apoplexy ['æpəpleksi] n apoplexie f. apo'pletic a apoplectique; a. fit, attaque d'apoplexie.

apostle [ə'posl] n apôtre m; the Apostles' Creed, le Symbole des Apôtres.

apostrophe [ə'pɔstrəfi] n apostrophe f.

appal [ə'pɔ:l] vtr (appalled) consterner; épouvanter (qn); we are appalled at the idea, l'idée nous frappe d'horreur. a'ppalling a épouvantable, effroyable. a'ppallingly adv épouvantablement, effroyablement.

apparatus [æpə'reitəs] n coll appareil m; dispositif m; Gym: agrès mpl.

apparent [ə'pærənt] a (a) apparent, manifeste, évident (b) (of emotion) prétendu; his a. indifference, son air d'indifférence. a'pparently adv apparemment; a. this is true, il paraît que c'est vrai.

apparition [æpə'riʃn] n apparition f.

appeal [ə'pi:l] I. n 1. appel m (a) a. for calm, for help, appel au calme, au secours; to make an a. to s.o.'s generosity, faire appel à la générosité de qn (b) Jur: Court of A., cour d'appel; to lodge an a., se pourvoir en appel; acquitted on a., acquitté en seconde instance 2. appel (for a cause, en faveur d'une cause) 3. attrait m, charme m. II. vi 1. to a. to, faire appel à (qn, la générosité de qn); to a. to s.o. for help, mercy, demander (le) secours, demander grâce, à qn; I a. to you to go, je vous supplie de partir 2. Jur: etc: faire opposition (against, à); appeler (against a judgement, d'un jugement); en appeler (to, à) 3. to a. to s.o., attirer qn; that doesn't a. to me, cela ne me dit rien. a'ppealing a (regard) suppliant; (ton) émouvant; (personnalité) sympathique. a'ppealingly adv d'un ton, d'un regard, suppliant.

appear [ə'piər] vi 1. paraître, apparaître; se montrer 2. (a) se présenter; Jur: comparaître (before, devant); to a. for s.o., représenter qn; (of counsel) plaider pour qn (b) to a. on the stage, entrer en scène; that was when I appeared on the scene, c'est à ce moment que je suis arrivé (c) (of book) paraître 3. (seem) to a. sad, paraître triste, avoir l'air triste; you a. to have forgotten, il semble que vous ayez oublié; vous semblez avoir oublié; so it appears, il paraît que oui. a'ppearance n 1. (a) apparition f; entrée f (en scène); to put in an a., (i) paraître, se montrer (ii) faire acte de présence; to make a first a., faire ses débuts (b) comparution f (devant un tribunal) (c) parution f (d'un livre) 2. apparence f, air m, aspect m; (of pers) mine f; to, by, from, all appearances, selon toute apparence; don't judge by appearances, ne jugez pas selon les apparences.

appease [ə'pi:z] vtr apaiser. a'ppeasement n apaisement m.

append [ə'pend] vtr attacher, joindre (qch à qch); apposer (sa signature); ajouter (des notes marginales). a'ppendage n appendice m; accessoire m.

appendix [ə'pendiks] n (a) (pl appendixes) Anat: appendice m (b) (pl appendices) appendice (d'un livre); annexe f (d'un rapport). appendi'citis [-'saitis] n appendicite f.

appetite ['æpitait] n appétit m; to have a good a.,

avoir bon appétit. 'appetizer n (a) (drink) apéritif m (b) (food) amuse-gueule m inv. 'appetizing a appétissant.

applaud [ə'plɔ:d] vtr applaudir; approuver (une décision). a'pplause n applaudissements mpl.

apple ['æpl] n pomme f; eating a., pomme à couteau; baking a., cooking a., pomme à cuire; Cu: a. pie = tarte aux pommes; in a. pie order, en ordre parfait; a. pie bed, lit en portefeuille; a. (tree), pommier m; she's the a. of his eye, il la soigne comme la prunelle de ses yeux.

appliance [ə'plaiəns] n appareil m (électroménager); dispositif m; engin m.

apply [ə'plai] vtr & i (applied) 1. (a) appliquer (sth to sth, qch sur qch); to a. the brakes, serrer le frein, freiner (b) this applies to you, ceci s'applique à vous (c) to a. oneself, to a. one's mind, to sth, s'appliquer à qch 2. to a. to s.o., s'adresser, recourir, à qn (pour avoir qch); to a. for a job, poser sa candidature à, demander, solliciter, un emploi. 'applicable a applicable, approprié (to, à). 'applicant n 1. candidat, -ate (à un emploi) 2. Jur: demandeur, -eresse. appli'cation n 1. application f (de qch sur qch) 2. assiduité f, application 3. demande f (d'emploi); candidature f (à un poste); a. form, formulaire de demande; on a., sur demande; tickets on a. to the theatre, s'adresser au théâtre pour avoir des billets. 'applicator n applicateur m ap'plied a a. mathematics, a. science, mathématiques appliquées; sciences expérimentales.

appoint [ə'pɔint] vtr 1. nommer (s.o. to sth, qn à qch); to a. s.o. ambassador, nommer qn ambassadeur 2. fixer (l'heure); arrêter (un jour); at the a. time, à l'heure dite, convenue; well a. house, maison bien installée, équipée. a'ppointment n 1. rendez-vous m inv; to make an a. with s.o., se donner rendez-vous, prendre rendez-vous avec qn; have you got an a.? avez-vous pris rendez-vous? to meet by a., se rencontrer sur rendez-vous 2. (a) nomination f (à un emploi); (of shop) by a. to Her Majesty = fournisseur attitré de sa Majesté (b) emploi m; poste m; Journ: appointments (vacant) = offres fpl d'emploi.

apposite ['æpəzit] a à propos.

appraise [ə'preiz] vtr estimer, évaluer (qch); expertiser (les dégâts), etc). a'ppraisal n évaluation f, estimation f; expertise f (des dégâts).

appreciate [ə'pri:ʃieit] 1. vtr apprécier; se rendre compte de (la difficulté, etc); être sensible à, reconnaissant de (la gentillesse de qn) 2. vi (of goods) augmenter de valeur, de prix. a'ppreciable a appréciable; (changement) sensible. a'ppreciably adv sensiblement. appreci'ation n 1. appréciation f (de la situation); estimation f, évaluation f 2. critique f (d'un livre) 3. hausse f (de valeur). a'ppreciative a (jugement) élogieux; (of pers) reconnaissant (of, de); sensible (of, à); appréciateur. a'ppreciatively adv avec reconnaissance; (écouter) avec satisfaction.

apprehend [æpri'hend] vtr appréhender, arrêter (qn) appre'hension n 1. appréhension f 2. arrestation f (de qn). appre'hensive a timide, craintif. appre'hensively adv avec appréhension.

apprentice [ə'prentis] n apprenti, -ie; a. carpenter,

apprenti menuisier. **a′pprenticed** *a* en apprentissage (**to s.o.**, chez qn). **a′pprenticeship** *n* apprentissage *m*.

appro [′æprou] *n Com: F:* **on a.**, à l'essai.

approach [ə′prout∫] I. *n* (*pl* **approaches**) 1. approche *f*; abord *m*; **his a. to the problem**, sa façon d'aborder le problème; **to make approaches to s.o.**, faire des avances à qn 2. voie *f* d'accès; *usu pl* approches, abords (d'une ville). II. *v* 1. *vi* (s')approcher 2. *vtr* (*a*) s'approcher de (qn, qch); aborder, approcher (qn); approcher de (qch) (*b*) aborder, s'attaquer à (une question). **a′pproachable** *a* accessible; (*of pers*) abordable, approchable, d'un abord facile. **a′pproaching** *a* approchant; (voiture) qui vient en sens inverse; (départ) prochain.

approbation [æprə′bei∫n] *n* 1. approbation *f*; assentiment *m* 2. jugement *m* favorable; **smile of a.**, sourire approbateur.

appropriate I. [ə′prouprieit] *vtr* s'approprier (qch); s'emparer de (qch). II. [ə′proupriət] *a* propre, convenable, approprié (**to, for**, à); (observation) juste, à propos; (nom) bien choisi. **a′ppropriately** *adv* convenablement; à propos. **appropri′ation** *n* 1. appropriation *f* 2. affection *f* (de fonds) 3. *Pol:* crédit *m* (budgétaire).

approve [ə′pru:v] 1. *vtr* approuver; sanctionner (une action); ratifier (une décision); agréer (un contrat) 2. *vi* **to a. of sth**, approuver qch; **I don't a. of your friends**, vos amis ne me plaisent pas; **he doesn't a. of our playing football**, il n'approuve pas que nous jouions au football. **a′pproval** *n* approbation *f*; **to nod a.**, faire un signe de tête approbateur; *Com:* **on a.**, sous, à, condition; à l'essai. **a′pproving** *a* approbateur, -trice. **a′pprovingly** *adv* d'un air approbateur.

approximate 1. [ə′prɔksimət] *a* (calcul) approximatif 2. [ə′prɔksimeit] *vi* approcher, se rapprocher (**to**, de). **a′pproximately** *adv* approximativement. **approxi′mation** *n* approximation *f*.

apricot [′eiprikɔt] *n* 1. abricot *m* 2. **a.** (tree), abricotier *m*.

April [′eipril] *n* avril *m*; **A. Fool's Day**, le premier avril; **to play an A. Fool's Day trick on s.o.**, faire un poisson d'avril à qn.

apron [eiprən] *n* tablier *m*; *Av:* aire *f* de stationnement; **tied to one's mother's apron strings**, pendu aux jupons de sa mère; *Th:* **a. (stage)**, avant-scène *f*.

apropos [æprə′pou] *a & adv* à propos (**of**, de).

apse [æps] *n Arch:* abside *f*.

apt [æpt] *a* 1. (mot) juste; (choix de mots) heureux 2. **a. to do sth** (*a*) (*of pers*) enclin, porté, à faire qch; **to be a. to do sth**, avoir tendance à faire qch (*b*) (*of thg*) sujet à, susceptible de, faire qch 3. (élève) intelligent, doué. **′aptitude** *n* aptitude *f* (**for**, à, pour). **′aptly** *adv* avec justesse; à propos. **′aptness** *n* justesse *f*, à-propos *m* (d'une observation).

aqualung [′ækwəlʌŋ] *n* scaphandre *m* autonome.

aquamarine [ækwəmə′ri:n] *n* aigue-marine *f*.

aquaplane [′ækwəplein] *vi* 1. *Sp:* faire de l'aquaplane 2. *Aut:* faire de l'aquaplaning, de l'aquaplanage.

aquarium [ə′kwεəriəm] *n* aquarium *m*.

Aquarius [ə′kwεəriəs] *Prn Astr:* le Verseau.

aquatic [ə′kwætik] *a* (plante) aquatique; (sport) nautique).

aqueduct [′ækwidʌkt] *n* aqueduc *m*.

aquiline [′ækwilain] *a* aquilin.

Arab [′ærəb] *a & n* arabe (*mf*). **A′rabian** *a* arabe, d'Arabie; **the A. Nights**, les Mille et une Nuits. **′Arabic** 1. *a* (chiffre) arabe 2. *n Ling:* arabe *m*.

arable [′ærəbl] *a* (terre) arable, labourable.

arbitrate [′a:bitreit] *vtr & i* arbitrer. **′arbitrarily** *adv* arbitrairement. **′arbitrary** *a* arbitraire. **arbi′tration** *n* arbitrage *m*; **to go to a.**, soumettre une question à l'arbitrage. **′arbitrator** *n* arbitre *m*.

arc [a:k] *n* arc *m*; **a. lamp**, lampe à arc; **a. welding**, soudure à arc.

arcade [a:′keid] *n* (*a*) galerie marchande (*b*) arcade(s) *f(pl)* (le long d'un mur).

arcane [a:′kein] *a Lit:* mystérieux.

arch[1] [a:t∫] I. *v* 1. *vtr* arquer, cambrer, cintrer; **to a. one's back**, se cambrer; creuser la taille; (*of cat*) **to a. its back**, faire le dos rond 2. *vi* former une voûte (over, au-dessus de). II. *n* (*pl* **arches**) 1. voûte *f*, arc *m*; arceau *m* (d'une voûte); arche *f* (d'un pont) 2. *Anat:* arcade sourcilière; cambrure *f* (du pied); **to have fallen arches**, avoir les pieds plats. **′archway** *n* voûte *f* (d'entrée); portail *m* (d'une église).

arch[2] *a* espiègle; coquin.

arch- [a:t∫] *pref* **a. enemy**, grand adversaire; **a. villain**, scélérat achevé.

arch(a)eology [a:ki′ɔlədʒi] *n* archéologie *f*. **arch(a)eo′logical** *a* archéologique. **arch(a)e′ologist** *n* archéologue *mf*.

archaic [a:′keiik] *a* archaïque.

archangel [′a:keindʒəl] *n* archange *m*.

archbishop [a:t∫′bi∫əp] *n* archevêque *m*.

archer [′a:t∫ə] *n* archer *m*. **′archery** *n* tir *m* à l'arc.

archetype [′a:kitaip] archétype *m*.

archipelago [a:ki′peləgou] *n* archipel *m*.

architect [′a:kitekt] *n* architecte *m*. **′architecture** *n* architecture *f*.

archives [′a:kaivz] *npl* archives *fpl*. **archivist** [′a:kivist] *n* archiviste *mf*.

Arctic [′a:ktic] 1. *a* (cercle) arctique; (temps) glacial 2. *n* Arctique *m*.

ardent [′a:dənt] *a* ardent; passionné. **′ardently** *adv* ardemment; avec ardeur.

ardour, *NAm:* **ardor** [′a:dər] *n* ardeur *f*.

arduous [′a:djuəs] *a* ardu, pénible; (travail laborieux. **′arduously** *adv* péniblement. **′arduousness** *n* difficulté *f*.

are [a:r] *see* **be**.

area [′εəriə] *n* 1. aire *f*, superficie *f*; surface *f* 2. région *f*; territoire *m*; quartier *m* (d'une ville); secteur *m* (économique); domaine *m* (de connaissances); **industrial a.**, zone industrielle; (*in room*) **dining a.**, coin *m* salle à manger; coin-repas *m inv*; **a. of agreement**, terrain *m* d'entente.

arena [ə′ri:nə] *n* arène *f*.

Argentina [a:dʒən′ti:nə] *Prn Geog:* Argentine *f*. **Argen′tinian** *a & n Geog:* Argentine *f*. **′Argentine** *a & n Geog:* 1. **the A. (Republic)**, la République Argentine, l'Argentine *f* 2. argentin, -ine.

argue [′a:gju:] 1. *vi* (*a*) se disputer (**with s.o. about sth**, avec qn à propos de qch) (*b*) discuter (**about**, sur, de); raisonner, argumenter (**about**, sur); plaider (for, against, pour, contre); to a. that, soutenir que 2. *vtr* discuter, débattre (une question); to a. the toss, discutailler. 'arguable *a* (*a*) (opinion) soutenable, défendable (*b*) (fait) contestable, discutable. 'arguably *adv* this is a. the best, on peut soutenir que celui-ci soit le meilleur. 'argument *n* 1. dispute *f*, discussion *f*; to have an a. with s.o., se disputer avec qn (about sth, à propos de qch) 2. (*a*) discussion, débat *m* (*b*) argument *m* (for, against, en faveur de, contre); for a.'s sake, à titre d'exemple. argu'mentative *a* chicaneur.

argy-bargy ['ɑːdʒi'bɑːdʒi] *n F:* chamaillerie *f*.

aria ['ɑːriə] *n Mus:* aria *f*.

arid ['ærid] *a* aride. a'ridity *n* aridité *f*.

Aries ['ɛəriːz] *Prn Astr:* le Bélier.

arise [ə'raiz] *vi* (arose; arisen) 1. (*of thg*) (*a*) s'élever, surgir, survenir (*of difficulty*) se présenter; (*of question*) se poser; should the occasion a., le cas échéant (*b*) émaner, provenir, résulter (from, de) 2. *A: & Lit:* (*of pers*) se lever.

aristocrat ['æristəkræt] *n* aristocrate *mf*. ari'stocracy *n* aristocratie *f*. aristo'cratic *a* aristocratique.

arithmetic [ə'riθmətik] *n* arithmétique *f*; calcul *m*; mental a., calcul mental. arith'metical *a* arithmétique.

ark [ɑːk] *n* arche *f*; Noah's A., l'arche de Noé.

arm¹ [ɑːm] *n* 1. bras *m*; with a basket over, on, one's a., un panier au bras; a. in a., bras dessus bras dessous; she took my a., elle m'a pris le bras; to put one's a. round s.o., entourer qn de son bras; at a.'s length, à bout de bras; à distance; with open arms, à bras ouverts 2. manche *f* (de robe); bras (de fauteuil, de mer); accoudoir *m* (de fauteuil); fléau *m* (de balance). 'armband *n* brassard *m*. 'armchair *n* fauteuil *m*; a. critic, critique en chambre. 'armful *n* brassée *f*; by the a., à pleins bras. 'armhole *n Cl:* emmanchure *f*. 'armpit *n* aisselle *f*.

arm² I. *v* 1. *vtr* armer (qn) 2. *vi* to a (oneself), s'armer (against, contre). II. *n* 1. *usu pl* arme(s) *f*(*pl*); to be up in arms (i) s'armer (against, contre) (ii) *Fig:* être en révolte ouverte, protester (about, contre); the arms race, la course aux armements 2. (coat of) arms, armoiries *fpl*. 'armaments *npl* armements *mpl*. 'armature *n Biol:* armure *f*; *El: Const:* armature *f*. armed *a* armé (with, de); the a. forces, les forces armées. 'armour, *NAm:* 'armor *n* armure *f*; a. (plate, plating), blindage *m* (d'un véhicule); cuirasse *f* (d'un navire). 'armoured, 'armour-'plated, *NAm:* 'armored, 'armor-'plated *a* (véhicule) blindé; (navire) cuirassé. 'armoury, *NAm:* 'armory (*a*) magasin *m* d'armes (*b*) *NAm:* fabrique *f* d'armes. 'army *n* armée *f*; to be in the a., être dans l'armée; être militaire; the Salvation A., l'Armée du Salut.

armistice ['ɑːmistis] *n* armistice *m*.

aroma [ə'roumə] *n* arôme *m*. aro'matic *a* aromatique.

arose [ə'rouz] *see* arise.

around [ə'raund] 1. *adv* autour, à l'entour; all a., tout autour, de tous côtés; the woods a., les bois d'alentour; to wander a., errer, rôder; there was nobody a., il n'y avait personne; *F:* a. here, dans ces parages; *F:* he's been a., il a roulé sa bosse 2. *prep*

autour de; it cost a. five pounds, cela a coûté environ, à peu près, cinq livres.

arouse [ə'rauz] *vtr* 1. (*a*) réveiller (qn) (*b*) stimuler (qn) 2. éveiller, exciter, provoquer (un sentiment).

arrange [ə'reindʒ] 1. *vtr* arranger (*a*) aménager (as, en); disposer (des fleurs); mettre en ordre (des livres); ranger (des meubles) (*b*) *Mus:* adapter (un morceau) (for, pour) (*c*) fixer (une date); organiser (un concert); the meeting arranged for Thursday, la réunion prévue pour jeudi; it was arranged that, il a été convenu que 2. *vi* to a. (with s.o.) to do sth, s'arranger (avec qn) pour faire qch; convenir de faire qch; to a. for sth. to be done, prendre des dispositions pour que qch se fasse. a'rrangement *n* 1. (*a*) arrangement *m*, aménagement *m* (d'une maison); to make arrangements for sth, prendre des dispositions, faire des préparatifs, pour qch; flower a., (i) art *m* de disposer les fleurs (ii) composition florale 2. accord *m*, entente *f* (avec qn); price by a., prix à débattre.

array [ə'rei] *n* étalage *m*.

arrears [ə'riəz] *npl* arriéré *m*; rent in a., loyer arriéré; to get into a., s'arriérer.

arrest [ə'rest] I. *n* (*a*) arrestation *f*; under a., en état d'arrestation (*b*) arrêt *m*, suspension *f* (du progrès); cardiac a., arrêt du cœur. II. *vtr* arrêter (un mouvement, un malfaiteur); fixer (l'attention). a'rresting *a* (spectacle) frappant, impressionnant.

arrive [ə'raiv] *vi* 1. (*a*) arriver (at, in, à, dans) (*b*) réussir (dans la vie) 2. to a. at, arriver, aboutir, à (une conclusion); fixer (un prix). a'rrival *n* arrivée *f*; *Com:* arrivage *m* (de marchandises); new a., nouveau venu.

arrogant ['ærəgənt] *a* arrogant. 'arrogance *n* arrogance *f*.

arrow ['ærou] *n* flèche *f*.

arse [ɑːs] *n P:* cul *m*.

arsenal ['ɑːsənl] *n* arsenal *m*, -aux.

arsenic ['ɑːsnik] *n* arsenic *m*.

arson ['ɑːsn] *n* incendie *m* volontaire. 'arsonist *n* incendiaire *mf*.

art [ɑːt] *n* art *m*; work of a., œuvre d'art; the (fine) arts, les beaux-arts; arts and crafts, artisanat *m*; a. exhibition, exposition d'art; a. school, école des beaux-arts; *Sch:* faculty of arts, faculté des lettres. 'artful *a* rusé, astucieux; malin. 'artfully *adv* astucieusement. 'artfulness *n* astuce *f*.

artefact ['ɑːtifækt] *n* objet façonné.

arteriosclerosis [ɑː'tiəriousklə'rousis] *n Med:* artériosclérose *f*.

artery ['ɑːtəri] *n* (*pl* arteries) artère *f*. ar'terial *a* 1. *Anat:* artériel. 2. a. road, grande voie de communication; grande route.

artesian [ɑː'tiːziən] *a* a. well, puits artésien.

arthritis [ɑː'θraitis] *n Med:* arthrite *f*; rheumatoid a., rhumatisme *m* articulaire. ar'thritic *a* arthritique.

artichoke ['ɑːtitʃouk] *n* 1. (globe) a., artichaut *m* 2. Jerusalem a., topinambour *m*.

article ['ɑːtikl] *n* article *m*; objet *m*; clause *f* (d'un contrat); articles of association, contrat *m* de société; a. of clothing, vêtement *m*.

articulate I. [ɑː'tikjuleit] *vtr & i* articuler (un mot); articulated lorry, semi-remorque *f*. II. [ɑː'tikjulət] *a*

(langage) articulé; (pers) qui s'exprime bien. **ar-'ticulation** *n* articulation *f*.
artifact ['ɑːtifækt] *n* objet façonné.
artifice ['ɑːtifis] *n* 1. artifice *m* 2. adresse *f*.
artificial [ɑːti'fiʃl] *a* 1. artificiel 2. (style) factice; (pers) qui manque de naturel. **arti'ficially** *adv* artificiellement.
artillery [ɑː'tiləri] *n* artillerie *f*.
artisan [ɑːti'zæn] *n* artisan *m*; ouvrier qualifié.
artist ['ɑːtist] *n* artiste *mf*. **ar'tiste** *n Th:* artiste *mf*; **he's an a.,** il est peintre. **ar'tistic** *a* artistique. **ar'tistically** *adv* artistiquement; avec art. **'artistry** *n* art *m*.
as [əz, *stressed* æz] I. *adv* 1. aussi, si; **as tall as,** aussi grand que; **not as tall as,** pas si, pas aussi, grand que 2. **I worked as hard as I could,** j'ai travaillé tant que j'ai pu 3. **as from the 15th,** à partir du 15; **as for, as regards, as to,** quant à. II. *conj & adv* 1. (*degree*) que; **twice as big as,** deux fois plus grand que; **by day as well as by night,** de jour comme de nuit; **as pale as death,** pâle comme la mort 2. (*concessive*) **ignorant as he is,** tout ignorant qu'il est; **be that as it may,** quoi qu'il en soit; **search as I might,** j'avais beau chercher 3. (*manner*) (*a*) comme; **do as you like,** faites comme vous voudrez; **leave it as it is,** laissez-le tel quel, tel qu'il est; **as it is,** les choses étant ainsi; **as often happens,** comme il, ainsi qu'il, arrive souvent; **mother is well, as are the children** (*b*) to consider s.o. **as a friend,** considérer qn comme un ami; **as an old friend,** en tant que vieil ami; **to treat s.o. as a stranger,** traiter qn en étranger; **he was often ill as a child,** enfant, il était souvent malade; *Th:* **X as Hamlet,** X dans le rôle de Hamlet 4. (*time*) comme; (*a*) **one day as,** un jour que (*b*) **as he grew older,** en vieillissant 5. (*reason*) **as you're not ready,** comme, puisque, vous n'êtes pas prêt 6. (*result*) **he's not so foolish as to believe it,** il n'est pas assez stupide pour le croire. III. *rel pron* **animals such as the lion,** animaux tels que, comme, le lion.
asbestos [æs'bestəs, æz-] *n* amiante *m*. **asbes-'tosis** *n Med:* asbestose *f*.
ascend [ə'send] 1. *vi* monter 2. *vtr* monter sur (le trône); gravir (une colline); remonter (un fleuve). **a'scendancy** *n* ascendant *m* (**over,** sur). **a'scendant** *n* to be in the a., avoir de l'ascendant *m*. **a'scension** (*a*) *n* ascension *f* (*b*) *Prn Geog:* A. (Island), (l'île *f* de) l'Ascension. **a'scent** *n* (*a*) ascension (*b*) montée *f*; pente *f*.
ascertain [æsə'tein] *vtr* constater (un fait); s'assurer, s'informer, de (la vérité de qch).
ascetic [ə'setik] 1. *a* ascétique 2. *n* ascète *mf*. **a'sceticism** *n* ascétisme *m*.
ascribe [ə'skraib] *vtr* attribuer, imputer (**to,** à). **a'scribable** *a* attribuable, imputable.
aseptic [ei'septik] *a Med:* aseptique.
asexual [ei'seksjuəl] *a* asexué.
ash¹ [æʃ] *n* **a.** (tree), frêne *m*.
ash² *n* (*pl* **ashes**) cendre(s) *f(pl)*; **to reduce to ashes,** réduire en cendres; *Ecc:* A. Wednesday, mercredi des Cendres. **'ash-'blond(e)** *a* blond cendré *inv*. **'ashcan** *NAm:* n boîte *f* à ordures; poubelle *f*. **'ashen** *a* (visage) blême. **'ashtray** *n* cendrier *m*.
ashamed [ə'ʃeimd] *a* honteux, confus; **to be a. of**

s.o., sth, avoir honte de qn, qch; **I'm a. of you,** vous me faites honte; **you ought to be a. of yourself,** vous devriez avoir honte.
ashore [ə'ʃɔːr] *adv Nau:* à terre; **to put (passengers) a.,** débarquer (des passagers).
Asia ['eiʃə] *Prn Geog:* Asie *f*. **'Asian** 1. *a* asiatique 2. *n* Asiatique *mf*, Asiate *mf*. **Asi'atic** *a & n* asiatique *mf*.
aside [ə'said] 1. *adv* de côté; à l'écart; **to put sth a.,** écarter qch; mettre qch de côté; **to take s.o. a.,** prendre qn à part; **to stand a.,** (i) se tenir à l'écart (ii) se ranger; **putting that a.,** à part cela 2. *n Th:* aparté *m*; **in an a.,** en aparté.
asinine ['æsinain] *a* stupide, idiot.
ask [ɑːsk] *vtr & i* (**asked** [ɑːskt]) demander 1. **to a. s.o. a question,** poser une question à qn; **a. him his name,** demandez-lui son nom; **a. a policeman,** adressez-vous à un agent (de police); *F:* **a. me another!** je n'ai pas la moindre idée; **if you a. me,** à mon avis 2. (*a*) **to a. s.o. a favour,** demander une faveur à qn (*b*) **to a. £60 for sth,** demander £60 pour qch 3. (*a*) **to a. s.o. to do sth,** demander à faire qch; **he asked to go out,** il a demandé s'il pouvait sortir (*b*) **to a. s.o. to do sth,** demander à qn de faire qch 4. (*a*) **to a. about sth.,** se renseigner sur qch; **to a. s.o. about sth,** interroger qn sur qch (*b*) **to a. after s.o.,** demander des nouvelles de qn 5. (*a*) **to a. for s.o.,** demander à voir qn (*b*) **to a. for sth.,** demander qch; **to a. for sth back,** redemander un objet prêté 6. **to a. s.o. to lunch,** inviter qn à déjeuner; **to a. s.o. back,** rendre une invitation à qn. **'asking** *n* **it's yours for the a.,** il n'y a qu'à le demander; **a. price,** prix demandé.
askance [ə'skæns] *adv* **to look a. at s.o., sth,** regarder qn, qch, de travers, avec méfiance.
askew [ə'skjuː] *adv* de biais, de travers.
asleep [ə'sliːp] *adv & a* endormi 1. **to be a.,** dormir; **to fall a.,** s'endormir 2. **my foot's a.,** j'ai le pied engourdi.
asparagus [əs'pærəgəs] *n coll* asperges *fpl*.
aspect ['æspekt] *n* 1. exposition *f*, orientation *f*; **house with a south-facing a.,** maison exposée au midi 2. aspect *m*; **from all aspects,** sous tous les aspects.
asperity [æs'periti] *n* (*a*) âpreté *f* (d'un reproche) (*b*) rigueur *f* (du climat).
aspersion [əs'pɜːʃn] *n* calomnie *f*; **to cast aspersions on s.o., sth,** dénigrer qn, qch.
asphalt ['æsfælt] *n* asphalte *m*; **a. road,** route asphaltée.
asphyxia [æs'fiksiə] *n* asphyxie *f*. **as'phyxiate** 1. *vtr* asphyxier 2. *vi* s'asphyxier. **asphyxi'ation** *n* asphyxie.
aspirate ['æspərət] *Ling:* 1. *a* aspiré 2. *n* (*a*) (lettre) aspirée *f* (*b*) (la lettre) h.
aspire [ə'spaiər] *vi* aspirer (**to sth,** à qch). **aspi'ration** *n* aspiration *f*. **a'spiring** *a* ambitieux.
aspirin ['æsp(ə)rin] *n Pharm:* aspirine *f*.
ass [æs] *n* (*pl* **asses**) 1. âne, *f* ânesse 2. *F:* idiot, -ote; âne; **to make an a. of oneself,** faire l'idiot, l'imbécile.
assailant [ə'seilənt] *n* assaillant, -ante; agresseur *m*.
assassin [ə'sæsin] *n* assassin *m*. **a'ssassinate** *vtr* assassiner. **assassi'nation** *n* assassinat *m*.
assault [ə'sɔːlt] I. *vtr* 1. attaquer, donner l'assaut à (une ville) 2. attaquer, agresser (qn); *Jur:* (*sexually*) violenter (une femme); **to be assaulted,** être victime

assemble 20 atheism

d'une agression. **II.** n (a) Mil: assaut m; **a. course,** (i) parcours du combattant (ii) piste d'assaut (b) attaque f, agression f; Jur: **a. and battery,** coups mpl et blessures fpl.

assemble [ə'sembl] **1.** vtr (a) assembler (des objets); réunir (des personnes) (b) monter (une machine) **2.** vi s'assembler; se rassembler. **a'ssembly** n **1.** assemblée f; **in open a.,** en séance publique **2.** réunion f (de personnes); Sch: rassemblement m **3.** assemblage m, montage m (d'une machine); Ind: **a. line,** chaîne de montage.

assent [ə'sent] **I.** vi donner son assentiment (to, à). **II.** n assentiment m.

assert [ə'sə:t] vtr (a) revendiquer, faire valoir (ses droits); imposer (son autorité); **to a. oneself,** s'imposer (b) protester de (son innocence); affirmer, soutenir (that, que). **a'ssertion** n assertion f; affirmation f. **a'ssertive** a autoritaire.

assess [ə'ses] vtr (a) répartir, établir (un impôt) (b) estimer (la valeur de qch); évaluer (qch); juger de (la qualité) (c) taxer (une propriété). **a'ssessment** n **1.** (a) répartition f (d'un impôt) (b) estimation f (de la valeur de qch); évaluation f (de dégâts); jugement m (de la qualité) (c) imposition f (d'une propriété); Jur: fixation f (de dommages-intérêts) **2.** (amount) cote f. **a'ssessor** n expert m; Adm: contrôleur, -euse (de contributions).

asset ['æset] n (a) pl Fin: actif m, avoir m; Jur: **personal assets,** biens mpl meubles (b) avantage m.

assiduous [ə'sidjuəs] a assidu. **assi'duity** n assiduité f **(in doing sth.,** à faire qch). **a'ssiduously** adv assidûment.

assign [ə'sain] vtr **1.** assigner (qch à qn); attribuer (un sens) **(to a word,** à un mot) **2.** céder, transférer (une propriété) **(to s.o.,** à qn) **3.** nommer (qn) **(to a job,** à une tâche). **assignation** [æsig'neifn] n rendez-vous m inv. **a'ssignment** n tâche assignée.

assimilate [ə'simileit] vtr assimiler **(to,** à). **assimi-'lation** n assimilation f **(to, with,** à).

assist [ə'sist] vtr aider (qn) **(to do, in doing sth,** à faire qch). **a'ssistance** n aide f, secours m; Adm: assistance f; **to come to s.o.'s a.,** venir à l'aide de qn; **can I be of any a.?** puis-je vous aider? **a'ssistant 1.** a adjoint, auxiliaire; **a. manager,** sous-directeur, -trice; Sch: **a. master, mistress,** professeur m (de lycée) **2.** n aide mf; assistant, -ante (de laboratoire); **(shop) a.,** vendeur, -euse.

assizes [ə'saiziz] npl Jur: assises fpl.

associate I. [ə'soufieit] vtr & i (s')associer **(with, s.o., sth,** avec, à, qn, qch); **to a. with s.o.,** fréquenter qn. **II.** [ə'soufiət] **1.** a associé **2.** n (a) associé, -ée; membre correspondant (d'une académie) (b) camarade mf. **associ'ation** n association f; **a. football,** football (association).

assorted [ə'sɔ:tid] a assorti; (of sweets, etc.) varié; **well a., ill a.,** bien, mal, assorti. **a'ssortment** n assortiment m.

assume [ə'sju:m] vtr **1.** prendre; se donner, affecter (un air); assumer (une charge); se charger d'(un devoir); prendre en main (la direction de qch); s'attribuer, s'approprier (un droit); adopter (un nom) **2.** présumer, supposer (qch); **assuming (that),** en supposant, en admettant, que + sub; **let us a. that,** supposons que + sub. **a'ssumed** a supposé, feint,

faux; **a. name,** nom d'emprunt. **a'ssumption** n **1.** Ecc: Assomption f (de la Vierge) **2. a. of office,** entrée f en fonctions **3.** supposition f, hypothèse f **4.** affectation f (de vertu).

assure [ə'fuər] vtr assurer. **a'ssurance** n assurance f; **to give s.o. one's a. that,** assurer qn, promettre formellement à qn, que; **life a.,** assurance-vie f. **a'ssured** a & n assuré(e). **a'ssuredly** adv assurément.

aster ['æstər] n Bot: aster m.

asterisk ['æstərisk] n astérisque m.

astern [ə'stə:n] adv Nau: à, sur, l'arrière; **full speed a.!** en arrière toute!

asteroid ['æstərɔid] n astéroïde m.

asthma ['æs(θ)mə] n asthme m. **asth'matic** a & n asthmatique (mf).

astigmatism [æ'stigmətizm] n astigmatisme m. **astig'matic** a & n astigmate (mf).

astonish [ə'stɔnif] vtr étonner, surprendre; **to be astonished to see sth,** s'étonner de voir qch; **to look astonished,** avoir l'air étonné, surpris. **a'stonishing** a étonnant, surprenant. **a'stonishingly** adv étonnamment. **a'stonishment** n étonnement m; (grande) surprise; **look of a.,** regard étonné.

astound [ə'staund] vtr confondre; stupéfier. **a'stounding** a abasourdissant.

astray [ə'strei] a & adv égaré; **to go a.,** s'égarer; **to lead s.o. a.,** détourner qn de la bonne voie.

astride [ə'straid] adv & prep à califourchon; **a. a chair,** à cheval sur une chaise.

astringent [ə'strind'ʒənt] a & n astringent (m).

astrology [ə'strɔlədʒi] n astrologie f. **a'strologer** n astrologue mf. **astro'logical** a astrologique.

astronaut ['æstrɔnɔ:t] n astronaute mf.

astronomy [ə'strɔnəmi] n astronomie f. **a'stronomer** n astronome m. **astro'nomic(al)** a astronomique.

astrophysics [æstrou'fiziks] n (usu with sing const) astrophysique f.

astute [ə'stju:t] a fin, avisé, astucieux. **a'stutely** adv avec finesse; astucieusement. **a'stuteness** n finesse f, astuce f.

asylum [ə'sailəm] n asile m.

asymmetrical [eisi'metrikl] a asymétrique.

at [æt] prep **1.** (a) à; **at school,** à l'école; **at the table,** à la table; **at hand,** sous la main; **at sea,** en mer (b) **at home,** à la maison, chez soi; **at the hairdresser's,** chez le coiffeur (c) **at the window,** à, devant, près de, la fenêtre **2. at six o'clock,** à six heures; **at present,** à présent; **two at a time,** deux par deux, deux à la fois; **at night,** la nuit **3. at two francs a kilo,** (à) deux francs le kilo; **at fifty kilometres an hour,** à cinquante kilomètres à l'heure **4. at my request,** sur ma demande; **at all events,** en tout cas; **not at all,** pas du tout **5. good at maths,** fort en maths; **good at games,** sportif, -ive **6.** (a) **to look at sth.,** regarder qch; **surprised at sth,** étonné de qch (b) **to laugh at s.o.,** se moquer de qn (c) **at work,** au travail; **she's at it again!** voilà qu'elle recommence! **while we are at it,** pendant que nous y sommes (d) F: **she's always (on) at him,** elle s'en prend toujours à lui.

ate [et, NAm: eit] see **eat.**

atheism ['eiθiizm] n athéisme m. **'atheist** n athée mf.

Athens [ˈæθənz] *Prn* Athènes *f.* **A'thenian** [əˈθiːnjən] *a & n* athénien, -ienne.

athlete [ˈæθliːt] *n* athlète *mf*; *Med:* **a.'s foot**, mycose *f.* **ath'letic** *a* athlétique; **he's very a.**, il est très sportif. **ath'letics** *npl* athlétisme *m*, *NAm:* sports *mpl*; **a. club**, club d'athlétisme.

Atlantic [ətˈlæntik] *a & n* the A. **(Ocean)**, l'océan *m* Atlantique, l'Atlantique *m*.

atlas [ˈætləs] *n* atlas *m*.

atmosphere [ˈætməsfiər] *n* atmosphère *f*. **atmos'pheric** *a* atmosphérique. **atmos'pherics** *npl WTel:* parasites *mpl*.

atoll [ˈætɔl] *n* atoll *m*.

atom [ˈætəm] *n* atome *m*; **a. bomb**, bombe atomique; **smashed to atoms**, réduit en miettes; **not an a.** of commonsense, pas un grain de bon sens. **a'tomic** *a* atomique. **'atomize** *vtr* atomiser. **'atomizer** *n* atomiseur *m*.

atone [əˈtoun] *vi* to a. for, expier, réparer (une faute). **a'tonement** *n* expiation *f*, réparation *f* (for a fault, d'une faute).

atrocious [əˈtroʊʃəs] *a* atroce. **a'trociously** *adv* atrocement. **a'trocity** *n* atrocité *f*.

atrophy [ˈætrəfi] **I.** *n* atrophie *f*. **II.** *vi* (atrophied) s'atrophier.

attach [əˈtætʃ] **1.** *vtr* attacher; fixer (un fil); annexer (un document); **to a. oneself to**, se joindre à (un groupe); **to a. importance to**, attacher de l'importance à; **to be attached to s.o.**, s'attacher, être attaché, à qn **2.** *vi* s'attacher. **a'ttaché** *n* attaché, -ée; **a. case**, mallette *f*, porte-documents *m inv*, attaché-case *m*. **a'ttachment** *n* **1.** (*affection*) attachement *m* **2.** accessoire *m* (d'une machine).

attack [əˈtæk] **I.** *vtr* attaquer; s'attaquer à (un problème). **II.** *n* **1.** attaque *f*; assaut *m* **2.** *Med:* attaque; crise *f* (de nerfs); accès *m* (de fièvre). **a'ttacker** *n* attaquant, -ante; agresseur *m*.

attain [əˈtein] *vtr & i* arriver à, parvenir à (un grand âge); acquérir (des connaissances); **to a. (to)**, atteindre (à) (la perfection). **a'ttainable** *a* accessible (by s.o., à qn); à la portée (by s.o., de qn). **a'ttainment** *n* **1.** réalisation *f* (d'une ambition) **2.** *usu pl* connaissance(s) *f(pl)*; talent(s) *(m)pl*.

attempt [əˈtempt] **I.** *n* tentative *f*, essai *m*, effort *m*; **first a.**, coup *m* d'essai; **to make an a. to do sth**, essayer de faire qch; **to succeed at the first a.**, réussir du premier coup; **to give up the a.**, y renoncer; **a. on s.o.'s life**, attentat *m* contre qn. **II.** *vtr* (a) **to a. to do sth**, essayer, tenter, tâcher, de faire qch (b) tenter (l'impossible); entreprendre (un travail); **attempted murder**, tentative de meurtre.

attend [əˈtend] **1.** *vtr* (a) assister à (une réunion); aller à (l'église); suivre (un cours); **the lectures are well attended**, les cours sont très suivis (b) (of doctor) soigner (un malade) **2.** *vi* (a) y assister (b) faire attention (to, à) (c) **to a. to**, s'occuper de (qn, qch); servir (un client). **a'ttendance** *n* **1.** (of doctor) **a. on s.o.**, visites *fpl* à qn; **to be in a.**, être de service **2.** (a) présence *f* (à une réunion); **regular a.**, assiduité *f*; **school a.**, fréquentation *f* scolaire (b) (people) assistance *f*. **a'ttendant 1.** *n* surveillant, -ante; (in museum) gardien, -ienne; *pl* suite *f* (d'un prince) **2.** *a* (symptôme) concomitant; (problème) qui accompagne (qch).

attention [əˈtenʃn] **1.** *n* (a) attention *f*; **to turn one's a. to**, porter son attention sur; **to pay a.**, faire attention (to, à); **to attract a.**, se faire remarquer; attirer l'attention (de qn); **for the a. of**, à l'attention de (b) soins *mpl*, entretien *m* (to sth, de qch) **2.** *int Mil:* **a.!** garde-à-vous! **to, at, a.**, au garde-à-vous. **a'ttentive** *a* **1.** attentif (to, à); soucieux (to, de) **2.** prévenant (to s.o., envers qn). **a'ttentively** *adv* attentivement. **a'ttentiveness** *n* attention.

attenuate [əˈtenjueit] *vtr* atténuer.

attest [əˈtest] *vtr* attester. **atte'station** *n* attestation *f*.

attic [ˈætik] *n* grenier *m*; **a. room**, mansarde *f*.

attitude [ˈætitjuːd] *n* attitude *f*; **a. of mind**, état *m* d'esprit.

attorney [əˈtəːni] *n* **1.** *NAm:* avoué *m*; **district a.** = procureur *m* de la République **2.** **A. General** = procureur général **3.** procureur, fondé *m* de pouvoir; **power of a.**, procuration *f*.

attract [əˈtrækt] *vtr* attirer (to, à, vers). **a'ttraction** *n* attraction *f* (to, towards, vers); attrait *m*; charme *m*. **a'ttractive** *a* attrayant, attirant; (prix) intéressant. **a'ttractively** *adv* d'une manière attrayante. **a'ttractiveness** *n* attrait, charme.

attribute I. *vtr* [əˈtribjuːt] attribuer, imputer (to, à). **II.** *n* [ˈætribjuːt] attribut *m*. **a'ttributable** *a* attribuable, imputable (to, à). **attri'bution** *n* attribution *f*. **a'ttributive** *a* attributif; *Gram:* qualicatif.

attrition [əˈtriʃn] *n* usure *f* par le frottement; **war of a.**, guerre d'usure.

attune [əˈtjuːn] *vtr* exercer, accoutumer (to, à).

aubergine [ˈoubəʒiːn] *n* aubergine *f*.

auburn [ˈɔːbən] *a* (of hair) châtain roux; auburn *inv*.

auction [ˈɔːkʃn] **I.** *n* **a. (sale)**, vente *f* aux enchères; (vente à la) criée *f*; **to put sth up for a.**, mettre qch aux enchères; **a. room**, salle des ventes. **II.** *vtr* vendre (qch) aux enchères. **auctio'neer** *n* commissaire-priseur *m*.

audacious [ɔːˈdeiʃəs] *a* audacieux. **au'daciously** *adv* avec audace. **au'dacity** *n* audace *f*.

audible [ˈɔːdibl] *a* perceptible (à l'oreille); distinct, audible; **he was scarcely a.**, on l'entendait à peine. **audi'bility** *n* audibilité *f*. **'audibly** *adv* distinctement.

audience [ˈɔːdjəns] *n* **1.** (interview) audience *f* **2.** assistance *f*; *Th:* spectateurs *mpl*, auditoire *m*, public *m*; (at concert, conference) auditeurs *mpl*; **the whole audience**, toute la salle.

audio [ˈɔːdiou] *a* sonore; **a. typist**, dactylo audio-magnéto. **audio-'visual** *a* audio-visuel, -elle.

audit [ˈɔːdit] **I.** *n* vérification *f* (de comptes). **II.** *vtr* vérifier (des comptes). **'auditor** *n* expert-comptable *m*; vérificateur *m* de comptes.

audition [ɔːˈdiʃn] **1.** *n* audition *f*, séance *f* d'essai **2.** *vtr & i* auditionner.

auditorium [ɔːdiˈtɔːriəm] *n* salle *f*.

augment [ɔːgˈment] *vtr & i* augmenter (with, by, de). **augmen'tation** *n* augmentation *f*.

augur [ˈɔːgər] *vi* **to a. well, ill, for**, être de bon, de mauvais, augure, pour.

August¹ [ˈɔːgəst] *n* août *m*; **in A.**, en août; **au mois d'août**; **(on) the fifth of A.**, (on) A. the fifth, le cinq août.

august² [ɔː'gʌst] *a* auguste.

aunt [ɑːnt] *n* tante *f*; **A. Sally**, (i) = jeu *m* de massacre (ii) objet *m* de dérision. **'auntie, 'aunty** *n F:* tata *f*, tantine *f*.

au pair [ou'peər] *a & n* **au p. (girl)**, étudiante au pair.

aura ['ɔːrə] *n* aura *f* (de qn); atmosphère *f* (d'un endroit).

auricle ['ɔːrikl] *a Anat:* auricule *f* (de l'oreille).

aurora [ɔː'rɔːrə] *n* **a. borealis**, aurore boréale.

auspices ['ɔːspisiz] *npl* auspices *mpl*; **under the a. of,** sous les auspices de. **au'spicious** *a* propice, favorable; de bon augure. **au'spiciously** *adv* sous d'heureux auspices; favorablement.

Aussie ['ɔzi] *a & n F:* = **australian.**

austere [ɔːs'tiər] *a* austère. **au'sterely** *adv.* austèrement. **aus'terity** *n* austérité *f*; **time of a.,** période de restrictions.

Australia [ɔ'streiliə] *Prn Geog:* Australie *f.* **Au'stralian** *a & n* australien, -ienne.

Austria ['ɔstriə] *Prn Geog:* Autriche *f.* **'Austrian** *a & n* autrichien, -ienne.

authentic [ɔː'θentik] *a* authentique. **au'thentically** *adv* authentiquement. **au'thenticate** *vtr* 1. établir l'authenticité de (qch) 2. *Jur:* authentifier (un acte). **authen'ticity** [-'tisiti] *n* authenticité *f.*

author ['ɔːθər] *n* auteur *m.*

authorize ['ɔːθəraiz] *vtr* autoriser (qch; **s.o. to do sth,** qn à faire qch). **authori'tarian** *a* autoritaire. **au'thoritative** *a* 1. (caractère) autoritaire; (ton) d'autorité 2. (document) qui fait autorité; **a. source,** source autorisée. **au'thoritatively** *adv* 1. d'une manière autoritaire 2. avec autorité. **au'thority** *n* 1. autorité *f*; **to have a. over s.o.,** avoir autorité sur qn; **who's in a. here?** qui commande ici? 2. autorisation *f* **(to do sth,** de faire qch); **on one's own a.,** de sa propre autorité 3. *(of pers, book)* **to be an a. on sth,** faire autorité en matière de qch; **on good a.,** de bonne source 4. service (administratif); **the authorities,** les autorités, l'administration *f.* **authori'zation** *n* autorisation *f* **(to do,** de faire). **'authorized** *a* autorisé; *Adm:* (prix) homologué; **the A. Version,** la traduction anglaise de la Bible de 1611.

autistic [ɔː'tistik] *a Med:* autistique.

auto- ['ɔːtou] *pref* auto-. **'auto** *n NAm: F:* voiture *f.* **autobio'graphical** *a* autobiographique. **autobi'ography** *n* autobiographie *f.* **au'tocracy** *n* autocratie *f.* **'autocrat** *n* autocrate *m.* **auto'cratic** *a* autocratique. **'autograph** I. *n* autographe *m.* II. *vtr* signer, dédicacer (un livre). **'automat** *n NAm:* restaurant *m* à distributeurs automatiques. **'automated** *a* automatisé. **auto'-matic** 1. *a.* automatique 2. *(a)* (gun) automatique *m (b)* voiture (avec boîte de vitesse) automatique. **auto'matically** *adv* automatiquement. **auto-'mation** *n* automatisation *f.* **au'tomaton** *n* automate *m.* **'automobile** *n NAm:* auto(mobile) *f*, voiture. **auto'motive** *a* automoteur; (industrie) automobile. **au'tonomous** *a* autonome. **au-'tonomy** *n* autonomie *f.* **'autopsy** *n* autopsie *f.* **autosu'ggestion** *n* autosuggestion *f.*

autumn ['ɔːtəm] *n (NAm:* = **fall)** automne *m*; **in a.,** en automne. **au'tumnal** *a* automnal; d'automne.

auxiliary [ɔːg'ziliəri] *a & n* auxiliaire *(mf).*

avail [ə'veil] I. *vtr & i* **to a. oneself of (sth),** se servir, user, profiter, de (qch); saisir (une occasion). II. *n* **it's of no a.,** c'est inutile; cela ne sert à rien; **to no a.,** sans (grand) résultat. **availa'bility** *n* disponibilité *f.* **a'vailable** *a* disponible; *(of pers)* libre, accessible; **to try every a. means,** essayer (par) tous les moyens possibles.

avalanche ['ævəlɑːnʃ] *n* avalanche *f.*

avarice ['ævəris] *n* avarice *f.* **ava'ricious** *a* avare.

avenge [ə'vendʒ] *vtr* venger; **to a. oneself,** se venger **(on,** de). **a'venger** *n* vengeur, -eresse. **a'venging** *a* vengeur, -eresse.

avenue ['ævənjuː] *n (a)* avenue *f (b) Fig:* voie *f* (qui amène à qch).

average ['ævəridʒ] I. *n* moyenne *f*; **on (an) a.,** en moyenne; **above, below, a.,** au-dessus, au-dessous, de la moyenne. II. *a* moyen. III. *vtr & i* établir, faire, la moyenne (des chiffres, etc); atteindre une moyenne de (six, etc); **he averages eight hours' work a day,** il travaille en moyenne huit heures par jour.

averse [ə'vɜːs] *a* opposé **(to,** à); **to be a. to sth,** répugner à qch; **he's not a. to a glass of beer,** il prend volontiers un verre de bière. **a'version** *n* 1. aversion *f*, répugnance *f*; **to take an a. to s.o.,** prendre qn, qch, en grippe 2. objet *m* d'aversion; **my pet a.,** ma bête noire.

avert [ə'vɜːt] *vtr* détourner (les yeux) **(from,** de); écarter, prévenir (un danger).

aviary ['eiviəri] *n (pl* **aviaries)** volière *f.*

aviation [eivi'eiʃn] *n* aviation *f.* **'aviator** *n* aviateur, -trice. **avi'onics** *npl* avionique *f.*

avid ['ævid] *a* avide **(for,** de). **a'vidity** *n* avidité *f.* **'avidly** *adv* avidement.

avocado [ævə'kɑːdou] *n* **a. (pear),** avocat *m.*

avoid [ə'void] *vtr* éviter (qn, qch; **doing sth,** de faire qch); se soustraire à (l'impôt); **to a. s.o.'s eyes,** fuir le regard de qn. **a'voidable** *a* évitable. **a'voidance** *n* action *f* d'éviter; **her a. of me,** son soin à m'éviter; **tax a.,** évasion fiscale.

avoirdupois [ævədə'poiz] *n (a)* poids *m* du commerce *(b) esp NAm: F:* embonpoint *m.*

avow [ə'vau] *vtr* avouer. **a'vowal** *n* aveu *m.* **a'vowed** *a* (ennemi) déclaré; (athée) avoué. **a'vowedly** *adv* ouvertement, franchement.

await [ə'weit] *vtr* attendre; *Com:* **awaiting your instructions,** dans l'attente de vos instructions; **parcels awaiting delivery,** colis en souffrance.

awake [ə'weik] I. *v* **(awoke, awoken)** 1. *vi (a)* s'éveiller, se réveiller *(b)* **to a. to (sth),** se rendre compte, prendre conscience, de (qch) 2. *vtr* éveiller, réveiller. II. *a (a)* éveillé, réveillé; **I was a.,** je ne dormais pas; **wide a.,** bien éveillé; **to keep a.,** veiller; **to keep s.o. a.,** tenir qn éveillé *(b)* en éveil, attentif; **to be a. to (sth),** avoir conscience de (qch). **a'waken** *vtr & i* = **awake** I. **a'wakening** *n* réveil *m*; **rude a.,** amère désillusion.

award [ə'wɔːd] I. *vtr* adjuger, décerner (un prix); conférer (des honneurs); accorder (une augmentation de salaire); attribuer (des dommages-intérêts). II. *n* prix, récompense *f.* **a'warding** *n* décernement *m* (d'un prix).

aware [ə'weər] *a* conscient, avisé, informé **(of sth,** de qch); **to be a. of sth,** avoir connaissance, avoir conscience, être au courant, de qch; savoir, ne pas ignorer, qch; **not that I'm a. of,** pas que je sache; **to become a. of sth,** prendre connaissance de, apprendre, qch. **a'wareness** n conscience f (de qch).

awash [ə'wɔʃ] a inondé (**with,** de).

away [ə'wei] adv 1. (*in compound verbs*) **to go a.,** partir, s'en aller; **the ball rolled a.,** la balle a roulé plus loin; **to run a.,** s'enfuir; **to take sth a.,** emporter qch; **put that knife a.!** range, pose, ce couteau! **to melt a.,** fondre; **to fritter a.,** gaspiller (son argent) 2. (*continuity*) **to work a.,** continuer à travailler; **to do sth right a.,** faire qch tout de suite 3. (*a*) loin (**from,** de); au loin; **far a.,** dans le lointain; au loin; **five kilometres a.,** à (une distance de) cinq kilomètres; **a. with you!** allez-vous-en! (*b*) **when he is a.,** quand il n'est pas là; **when I have to be a.,** lorsque je dois m'absenter; **a. (from work)** absent; *Sp:* **a. match,** match à l'extérieur.

awe [ɔː] I. n crainte f; respect m; **to be, stand, in a. of s.o.,** (i) craindre, redouter, qn (ii) être intimidé par qn. II. vtr intimider (qn); inspirer un respect mêlé de crainte à (qn). **'awe-inspiring, awesome** a impressionnant, imposant; (spectacle) grandiose. **'awe-struck** a 1. frappé d'une terreur mystérieuse 2. intimidé. **'awful** a 1. terrible, terrifiant 2. F: terrible; affreux; effroyable; **what a. weather!** quel temps de chien! **a. din,** bruit terrible. **'awfully** adv F: terriblement; **I'm a. sorry,** je regrette infiniment, énormément; **a. funny,** très drôle; drôle comme tout.

awhile [ə'wail] adv pendant quelque temps; un moment; **wait a.,** attendez un peu.

awkward ['ɔːkwəd] a 1. gauche, maladroit; **the a. age,** l'âge ingrat 2. (*of pers, smile*) embarrassé, gêné 3. (*of situation*) fâcheux, gênant; délicat; mauvais (moment) 4. incommode, peu commode; (virage) difficile; **he's an a. customer,** c'est un homme difficile; il n'est pas commode. **'awkwardly** adv 1. gauchement, maladroitement 2. d'une manière embarrassée. **'awkwardness** n 1. (*a*) gaucherie f; maladresse f; (*b*) manque m de grâce 2. embarras m 3. inconvénient m (d'une situation).

awl [ɔːl] n Tls: alène f, poinçon m, perçoir m.

awning ['ɔːniŋ] n banne f (de magasin); auvent m (de tente); marquise f (de théâtre); vélum m; Nau: tente f.

awoke, awoken [ə'wouk, ə'woukən] see **awake**.

awry [ə'rai] adv & a de travers; (*of plans*) **to go a.,** aller tout de travers.

axe, NAm: also **ax** [æks] I. n (pl **axes**) hache f; Fig: **to have an a. to grind,** agir dans un but intéressé. II. vtr réduire (les dépenses); abandonner (un projet); renvoyer (qn).

axiom ['æksiəm] n axiome m. **axio'matic** a axiomatique; **it's a.,** c'est évident.

axis ['æksis] n (pl **axes**) axe m.

axle ['æksl] n 1. a. (tree), essieu m; Aut: **rear a.,** essieu, pont m, arrière; **a. box,** boîte de l'essieu; **a. pin,** clavette d'essieu 2. arbre m, axe m (d'une roue).

ay(e) [ai] 1. adv Dial: oui 2. n (*in voting*) **ayes and noes,** voix fpl pour et contre.

azalea [ə'zeiliə] n Bot: azalée f.

Azores (the) [ðiə'zɔːz] Prnpl les Açores fpl.

azure ['æʒər, 'eizjər] 1. n azur m 2. a (ciel) d'azur.

B

B, b [biː] *n* **1.** (*a*) (la lettre) B, b *m* (*b*) (*in numbering*) **51b,** 51 (i) bis (ii) ter (*c*) **B road** = route secondaire **2.** *Mus:* si *m*.

BA *abbr Bachelor of Arts.*

babble ['bæbl] **I.** *n* **1.** babillage *m* **2.** bavardage *m* **3.** gazouillement *m* (d'un ruisseau). **II.** *v* **1.** *vi* (*a*) babiller (*b*) bavarder (*c*) (*of stream*) gazouiller **2.** *vtr* bafouiller. **'babbling** *a* (ruisseau) gazouillant.

babe [beib] *n* (*a*) *Lit:* petit(e) enfant (*b*) *esp NAm: F:* **hi, b.!** salut chéri(e), ma petite, mon petit!

babel ['beibəl] *n* brouhaha *m* (de conversation).

baboon [bə'buːn] *n Z:* babouin *m*.

baby ['beibi] *n* (*pl* **babies**) (*a*) bébé *m*; **b. of the family,** benjamin(e); *F:* **to be left holding the b.,** avoir l'affaire sur les bras, payer les pots cassés; **b. clothes,** vêtements de bébé; layette *f*; *NAm:* **b. carriage** (*Br* = **pram**) voiture d'enfant; **b. boy, girl,** petit garçon, petite fille; **b. elephant,** bébé éléphant, **b. monkey,** bébé singe; **b. face,** visage poupin; **b. grand (piano),** (piano *m*) demi-queue *m*; *esp NAm:* **hi, b.!** salut, chéri(e)! (*b*) **that's your b.,** ça, c'est ton affaire! débrouille-toi! **'babyish** *a* puéril; d'enfant. **'baby-sit** *vi* (**baby-sat**), garder les bébés; faire du baby-sitting. **'baby-sitter** *n* baby-sitter *mf*. **'baby-sitting** *n* baby-sitting.

bachelor ['bætʃələr] *n* **1.** célibataire *m*; garçon *m*; **b. girl,** célibataire *f*; **b. flat,** garçonnière *f* **2.** *Sch:* **B. of Arts, of Science** = licencié(e) ès lettres, ès sciences.

bacillus [bə'siləs] *n* (*pl* **bacilli**) *Biol:* bacille *m*.

back [bæk] **I.** *n* **1.** (*a*) dos *m*; **to fall on one's b.,** tomber à la renverse; **to do sth. behind s.o.'s b.,** faire qch derrière le dos, à l'insu, de qn; **to be glad to see the b. of s.o.,** être content de voir partir qn; **to put s.o.'s b. up,** mettre qn en colère; **b. to b.,** dos à dos; adossés; **b. to front,** sens devant derrière; **with one's b. to the wall,** (i) adossé au mur (ii) *Fig:* réduit à la dernière extrémité; poussé au pied du mur; **to put one's b. into it,** s'y mettre énergiquement (*b*) les reins *m*; **to break one's b.,** se casser la colonne vertébrale; **to break the b. of the work,** faire le plus gros du travail **2.** dos (d'un livre); verso *m* (d'une page); fin *f* (d'un livre); dossier *m* (d'une chaise); revers *m* (de la main); envers *m*, revers (d'une médaille); derrière *m* (de la tête); arrière *m* (d'une maison, d'une voiture); **he knows London like the b. of his hand,** il connaît Londres comme (le fond de) sa poche; **let's go round (to) the b.,** allons à l'arrière; **the dress fastens at the b.,** la robe se ferme dans le dos; **idea at the b. of one's mind,** idée (de) derrière la tête; arrière-pensée *f* 3. (*a*) *Fb:* arrière (*b*) fond *m* (d'une salle, de la scène, d'un tiroir); *F:* **to live at the b. of beyond,** habiter un trou perdu. **II.** *a* (*a*) (siège, roue) arrière; (porte, jardin) de derrière; *Fig:* **to get in by the b. door,** entrer par la petite porte; **b. room,** pièce qui donne sur l'arrière; **b. streets,** (i) petites rues (ii) bas quartiers (d'une ville); *Fig:* **to take a b. seat,** passer

au second plan; *F:* **b.-seat driver,** personne qui donne des conseils au conducteur (*b*) **b. rent,** arriéré(s) *m(pl)* de loyer; **b. pay,** rappel *m* de traitement; **b. number,** vieux numéro (d'un magazine). **III.** *adv* **1.** (*place*) (*a*) en arrière; **stand b.!** rangez-vous! **house standing b. from the road,** maison en retrait; (*b*) **to hit b.,** rendre coup pour coup; **to call s.o. b.,** rappeler qn; **to come b.,** revenir, rentrer; **he's b.,** il est de retour; **as soon as I get b.,** dès mon retour **2.** (*time*) **a few years b.,** il y a quelques années; **as far b. as 1939, b. in 1939,** déjà en 1939; dès 1939. **IV.** *v* **1.** *vi* reculer; *Aut:* faire marche arrière; **to b. into a lane,** entrer en marche arrière dans un chemin **2.** *vtr* (*a*) soutenir (qn); financer (qn, *Th:* une pièce) (*b*) parier, miser, sur (un cheval); jouer (un cheval) (*c*) **to b. a car out of a garage,** sortir une voiture d'un garage en marche arrière (*d*) renforcer (une carte). **'backache** *n* mal *m* de reins. **'back a'way** *vi* reculer (**from,** devant). **'back'bencher** *n* *Pol:* député *m* sans portefeuille. **'backbite** *vi* critiquer. **'backbiting** *n* médisance *f*. **'backbone** *n* (*a*) colonne vertébrale; (*of fish*) grande arête; **English to the b.,** anglais jusqu'au bout des ongles; **to be the b. of a movement,** mener un mouvement (*b*) force *f* de caractère; **he's got no b.,** c'est un emplâtre. **'backbreaking** *a* (travail) éreintant. **'backchat** *n* *F:* impertinence *f*, réplique *f*. **'backcloth** *n* toile *f* de fond. **'backcomb** *vtr* crêper (les cheveux). **'back'date** *vtr* antidater (un chèque); (*increase*) **backdated to 1st July,** (augmentation) avec effet rétroactif au 1er juillet. **'back'down** *vi* admettre qu'on a tort; en rabattre. **'backdrop** *n* = **backcloth**. **'backer** *n* partisan, -ane; *Com: Fin:* commanditaire *m*. **'back'fire 1.** *vi* (*a*) (*of engine*) pétarader; avoir des retours (de flamme) (*b*) (*of plan*) rater **2.** *n* (*of engine*) pétarade *f*; retour *m* (de flamme). **'back'gammon** *n* tric-trac *m*. **'background** *n* (*a*) fond, arrière-plan *m*; **in the b.,** dans le fond; à l'arrière-plan; **against a dark b.,** sur (un) fond sombre; **to stay in the b.,** s'effacer; se tenir à l'écart; **b. music,** (i) *Th: Cin:* fond sonore (ii) musique de fond (*b*) (*of pers*) (i) origines *fpl*; milieu (social) formation *f* (iii) *esp Med:* antécédents *mpl* (*c*) contexte *m* (d'un événement); données *fpl* de base (d'un problème); **b. reading,** lectures générales (sur un sujet). **'backhand** *n* & *n Ten: etc:* b. (stroke), (coup *m* en) revers *m*. **'back'handed** *a* (*a*) *Ten: etc:* (coup) en revers (*b*) (compliment) équivoque. **back'hander** *n* *F:* (*a*) revers (*b*) pot-de-vin *m*. **'back'in** *vi* entrer (i) (*in car*) en marche arrière (ii) (*on foot*) à reculons. **'backing** *n* (*a*) renforcement (d'une carte) (*b*) soutien *m* (d'un projet) (*c*) *Mus:* accompagnement *m*. **'backlash** *n* contrecoup *m* (d'un événement). **'backless** *a* (robe) sans dos. **'backlog** *n* (*a*) arriéré (de travail) (*b*) *NAm:* réserve *f*. **'back'onto** *vtr* (*of house*) donner sur. **'back 'out** vi (a) sortir (i) (in car) en marche arrière (ii) (on foot) à reculons (b) F: manquer à sa promesse; se dédire (of sth, de qch). **'back-pack** n sac m à dos. **'backpacking** n NAm: tourisme m à pied. **'back-'pedal** vi (-pedalled) (a) pédaler à l'envers (b) faire marche arrière. **'back-'side** n F: derrière. **'back'stage** adv & a dans les coulisses. **'back'stairs** npl escalier m de service; Fig: b. gossip, propos d'antichambre. **'back-stroke** n nage f sur le dos. **'backtrack** vi (a) revenir sur ses pas (b) faire marche arrière. **'back up 1.** vtr (a) soutenir (b) faire reculer (une voiture) **2.** vi reculer; Aut: faire marche arrière. **'backup** n (a) soutien (b) réserve. **'backward 1.** a (mouvement) en arrière; (enfant) arriéré; (of pers) lent, peu empressé (**in doing sth,** à faire qch) **2.** adv = BACKWARDS. **'backwardness** n (a) arriération mentale (b) lenteur f, hésitation f (**in doing sth,** à faire qch). **'backwards** adv (a) en arrière; (tomber) à la renverse; (marcher) à reculons; **to walk b. and forwards,** se promener de long en large; aller et venir (b) (connaître qch) parfaitement. **'backwater** n (a) bras m de décharge (d'une rivière) (b) coin m paisible; Pej: trou perdu. **'backwoods** npl NAm: forêts f de l'intérieur. **back'yard** n (a) arrière-cour f (b) NAm: jardin m de derrière.

bacon ['beikən] n lard m; bacon m; **egg and b.,** œufs au jambon; F: **to save one's b.,** sauver sa peau; F: **to bring home the b.,** (i) pourvoir aux besoins de la famille (ii) décrocher la timbale.

bacteria [bæk'tiəriə] npl bactéries fpl. **bacteri-o'logical** a bactériologique. **bacteri'ologist** n bactériologiste mf. **bacteri'ology** n bactériologie f.

bad [bæd] **I.** a (comp worse; sup worst) (a) mauvais; (of pers) méchant; (of coin) faux; (of rotting food) avarié; (of teeth) (i) (rotten) carié (ii) (unsightly) vilain; gros (rhume); violent (mal de tête); (accident, faute) grave; (coup) mal visé; **b. language,** gros mots; (of food) **to go b.,** se gâter, s'avarier; **it's a b. business!** c'est une mauvaise affaire! **things are b.,** les affaires vont mal; **it wouldn't be a b. thing if,** on ne ferait pas mal de; **he speaks b. French,** il parle mal le français; **to be b. at** (lying, etc), ne pas savoir (mentir, etc); **he's b. at maths,** il n'est pas fort en maths; **not at all b.,** pas mal du tout; **not so b.,** pas si mal; **not too b.,** pas trop mal; F: **(that's, it's) too b.!** c'est trop fort! c'est bien dommage! **he's not b.** (-looking), not b. to look at, il n'est pas mal (fichu); **from b. to worse,** de mal en pis; **to be b.** for, ne rien valoir à (qn), pour (qch); **it's b. for the health,** c'est mauvais pour la santé; **to feel b. about sth,** avoir du remords au sujet de, regretter, qch (b) (ill) **I feel b.,** je ne me sens pas bien; je me sens mal; **she's very b. today,** elle est très mal aujourd'hui; **she's got a b. finger,** elle a mal au doigt; **b. leg,** jambe malade. **II.** adv esp NAm: F: = **badly. 'baddie,** **-y** n F: méchant m. **'badly** adv (comp worse; superl worst) **1.** mal; **to do b.,** mal réussir; **things are going b.,** les choses vont mal; **to be b. off,** être dans la gêne; **to be b. off for sth,** manquer de qch; **he took it b.,** il a mal pris la chose **2.** (blessé) gravement, grièvement; Sp: etc: (battu) à plate(s) couture(s); **the b. disabled,** les grands infirmes **3. to want sth b.,** avoir grande

envie de qch; **to need sth b.,** avoir bien, grand, besoin de qch. **'badness** n **1.** mauvaise qualité **2.** (of pers) méchanceté f. **'bad-'tempered** a (of pers) **to be b.-t.,** (i) (generally) avoir mauvais caractère (ii) (at the moment) être de mauvaise humeur.

bade [bæd] see bid I.

badge [bædʒ] n **1.** (showing rank, occupation, membership) insigne m, f, médaille f; (bearing slogan, joke) badge m, macaron m **2.** signe distinctif.

badger ['bædʒər] **1.** n Z: blaireau m **2.** vtr harceler, tourmenter, tracasser (qn).

badminton ['bædmintən] n badminton m.

baffle ['bæfl] vtr (a) confondre, déconcerter, dérouter (qn); (b) déjouer (un complot). **'baffling** a déconcertant.

bag [bæg] **I.** n **1.** (a) sac m; pl (for journey) bagages mpl; (diplomatic) b., valise f (diplomatique); paper b., sac en papier; shopping b., cabas m; (with) b. and baggage, avec armes et bagages; bags under the eyes, poches sous les yeux; F: there's bags of it, il y en a des tas (b) Ven: tableau (de chasse); F: in the b., dans le sac **2.** P: old b., vieille chipie. **II.** v (bagged) **1.** vi (of trousers) goder (aux genoux); (of garment) bouffer. **2.** vtr tuer (du gibier); F: empocher, s'emparer de (qch); bags I go first! c'est moi le premier! **'bagful** n plein sac. **'baggy** a (-ier, -iest) (vêtement) (trop) ample; (pantalon) flottant, bouffant. **'bagpipes** npl cornemuse f.

baggage ['bægidʒ] n **1.** bagages mpl; Av: b. handler, bagagiste m; NAm: Rail: b. car, fourgon m; NAm: b. room, consigne f **2.** Mil: matériel m (d'une armée).

Bahamas (the) [bə'hɑ:məz] Prn Geog: les Bahamas f.

bail¹ [beil] **I.** n Jur: caution f; (out) on b., en liberté provisoire (sous caution); to go, stand, b. for s.o., se porter garant de qn. **II.** vtr **to b. s.o. (out),** (i) Jur: se porter caution pour (obtenir la mise en liberté provisoire de) qn (ii) Fig: tirer qn d'affaire.

bail² [beil] **1.** vtr **to b. out,** écoper (un bateau); vider (l'eau) **2.** vi NAm: = BALE OUT.

bailiff ['beilif] n **1.** agent m de poursuites; huissier m. **2.** régisseur m (d'un domaine).

bairn [beə(r)n] n Scot: enfant.

bait [beit] **I.** n Fish: appât m; amorce f; Fig: appât, leurre m; **to rise to, to swallow, the b.,** mordre à l'hameçon. **II.** vtr **1.** amorcer (un hameçon) **2.** harceler (qn, un animal).

baize [beiz] n Tex: feutrine f; green b., tapis vert.

bake [beik] **1.** vtr cuire, faire cuire (au four) **2.** vi (of bread) cuire (au four). **'baker** n boulanger, -ère; b.'s wife, boulangère; b.'s (shop), boulangerie f. **'bakery** n boulangerie. **'baking 1.** n cuisson f (du pain); b. dish, plat allant au four; b. sheet, tray, plaque f (à gâteaux); b. powder, levure artificielle **2.** a & adv F: it's b. (hot) in there! on cuit là-dedans!

balaclava [bælə'klɑ:və] n Cl: b. (helmet), passe-montagne m; cagoule f.

balance ['bæləns] **I.** n **1.** (scales) balance f; **to hang in the b.,** rester en balance. **2.** équilibre m; **to keep, lose, one's b.,** garder, perdre, l'équilibre; off b., mal équilibré; **b. of power,** équilibre des pouvoirs. **3.** Com: solde m (d'un compte); b. in hand, solde créditeur; débit b., b. due, solde débiteur; Fin: b. of payments, balance des paiements; b. of trade, balance

commerciale; **b. sheet,** bilan *m; Fig:* **to strike a b.,**
tenir la balance égale **(between,** entre); **on b.,** à tout
prendre. **II.** *v* 1. *vtr (a)* balancer, peser (les conséquences) *(b)* mettre, maintenir (un objet) en équilibre; équilibrer (des forces); faire contrepoids à (qch)
(c) Fin: Com: balancer, solder (un compte); équilibrer (le budget); régler (les livres) 2. *vi* être, rester, en
équilibre. **'balanced** *a* équilibré. **'balancing** *n*
(a) mise *f* en équilibre; *Ant:* **wheel b.,** équilibrage *m*
des roues; **b. act,** tours d'équilibre; acrobaties *fpl (b)*
règlement *m* des comptes.

balcony ['bælkəni] *n (pl* **balconies)** *(a)* balcon *m (b)*
Th: fauteuils *mpl* de deuxième galerie.

bald [bɔːld] *a* **(-er, -est)** 1. *(a) (of pers)* chauve; **to be**
going b., commencer à perdre les, ses, cheveux; **b.**
patch, tonsure *f (b)* (pneu) lisse 2. *(of style)* plat,
sec; **b. statement of fact,** simple exposition des faits.
'bald-'headed *a* chauve. **'baldly** *adv* plate-
ment. **'baldness** *n* 1. calvitie *f* 2. *(of style)* sécheresse *f.*

balderdash ['bɔːldədæʃ] *n F:* balivernes *fpl.*

bale¹ [beil] *n Com:* balle *f,* ballot *m.*

bale² *vi Av:* **to b. out,** sauter en parachute.

Balearic [bæli'ærik] *a Geog:* **the B. Islands,** les îles *f*
Baléares.

baleful ['beilful] *a* sinistre.

balk [bɔːk] 1. *vtr* contrarier (les desseins de qn) 2. *vi*
regimber **(at,** devant); rechigner **(at (doing) sth,** à
(faire) qch).

Balkans (the) [ðə'bɔːlkənz] *Prn pl Geog:* les Balkans *m;* les États *m* balkaniques.

ball¹ [bɔːl] *n* boule *f* (de croquet); balle *f* (de tennis);
ballon *m* (de football); bille *f* (de billard); pelote *f,*
peloton *m* (de laine); **b. of the foot,** plante *f* du pied;
b. bearing(s), roulement *m* à billes; **to keep the b.**
rolling, soutenir la conversation, le jeu; **to start the**
b. rolling, commencer; mettre le jeu en train; *F:* **to**
be on the b., connaître son affaire; **to play b.,** (i) jouer
à la balle, *NAm:* au base-ball (ii) *F:* coopérer; **the b.**
is in your court, (c'est) à vous (de jouer) 2. *pl V: (a)*
testicules *mpl,* couilles *fpl (b)* bêtises *fpl;* conneries
fpl. **'ballboy, -girl** *n Ten:* ramasseur, -euse, de
balles. **'ballcock** *n* robinet *m* à flotteur. **'ball-**
point *n b.* (pen), stylo *m* (à) bille.

ball² *n* bal *m; P:* **to have a b.,** se marrer. **'ballroom**
n salle *f* de bal; **b. dancing,** danse de salon.

ballad ['bæləd] *n Mus:* romance *f; Lit:* ballade *f.*

ballast ['bæləst] *n Nau: etc:* lest *m.*

ballet ['bælei] *n* ballet *m;* danse *f* classique; **b. dancer,**
danseur, -euse, de ballet. **ballerina** [bælə'riːnə] *n*
ballerine *f.*

ballistic [bə'listik] *a* balistique. **ba'llistics** *npl*
balistique *f.*

balloon [bə'luːn] *n* ballon *m.* **ba'llooning** *n*
ascension *f* en ballon. **ba'llooonist** *n* aéronaute
mf.

ballot ['bælət] **I.** *n (a)* tour *m* de scrutin; **to vote by**
b., voter au scrutin *(b)* scrutin *m,* vote *m;* **b. paper,**
bulletin de vote; **b. box,** urne *f* (de scrutin). **II.** *vi*
voter au scrutin.

ballyhoo [bæli'huː] *n P:* 1. grosse réclame; battage *m*
2. baratin *m.*

balmy ['bɑːmi] *a (a)* (temps) d'une douceur délicieuse
(b) F: idiot, toqué.

balsa ['bɔːlsə] *n b.* **(wood),** balsa *m.*

balsam ['bɔːlsəm] *n* baume *m;* **friar's b.,** baume de
benjoin.

Baltic ['bɔːltik] *a & n* (port) balte; **the B. (Sea),** la
(mer) Baltique.

balustrade [bælə'streid] *n* balustrade *f.*

bamboo [bæm'buː] *n* bambou *m.*

bamboozle [bæm'buːzl] *vtr* tromper, mystifier, refaire, embobeliner (qn).

ban [bæn] 1. *n (a)* proscription *f;* interdiction *f* (d'un
film) *(b)* interdit *m* 2. *vtr* **(banned)** interdire; *Jur:*
mettre (un livre) à l'index; **to be banned (from driv-**
ing), se faire retirer son permis (de conduire). **'ban-**
ning *n* = **ban** 1. *(a).*

banal [bə'nɑːl] *a* banal, -aux; ordinaire. **ba'nality** *n*
banalité *f.*

banana [bə'nɑːnə] *n* banane *f;* **b. (tree),** bananier *m.*

band¹ [bænd] *n* bande *f;* ruban *m* (d'un chapeau);
elastic, rubber, b., élastique *m.* **'bandsaw** *n* scie *f*
à ruban.

band² *n* 1. bande *f,* troupe *f;* compagnie *f* 2. *Mus:*
orchestre *m; Mil:* musique *f;* **brass b.,** fanfare *f.*
'bandmaster *n* chef *m* de musique. **'bands-**
man, -men *n* musicien *m.* **'bandstand** *n*
kiosque *m* à musique. **'band to'gether** *vi* se
réunir en bande; se solidariser. **'bandwagon** *n* **to**
jump on the b., se mettre dans le mouvement.

bandage ['bændidʒ] **I.** *n Med:* bandage *m;* bande *f;*
(for wound) pansement *m; (over eyes)* bandeau *m;*
elastic b., crêpe *b.,* bande Velpeau. **II.** *vtr* **to b. (up),**
bander; mettre un pansement sur (une blessure).

b. & b. *abbr* bed and breakfast.

bandit ['bændit] *n* bandit *m,* brigand *m.*

bandy¹ ['bændi] *vtr* **(bandied)** (se) renvoyer (des
paroles); échanger (des plaisanteries). **'bandy**
a'bout *vtr* répandre (une nouvelle); parler, discuter, de (qch).

bandy² *a (of pers)* bancal; *(of legs)* arqué. **'bandy-**
'legged *a* bancal.

bane [bein] *n* **it's the b. of my life,** cela m'empoisonne
l'existence.

bang [bæŋ] **I.** *n* coup (violent); détonation *f* (de fusil);
claquement *m* (de porte); *Av:* bang *m* (supersonique); **to go off with a b.,** détoner. **II.** *v* 1. *vi (a)*
to b. at, on, the door, donner de grands coups dans
la porte; **to b. on the table with one's fist,** frapper la
table du poing *(b) (of door)* claquer, battre 2. *vtr (a)*
frapper (violemment); (faire) claquer (une porte) *(b)*
(se) cogner (la tête) **(on, against,** à, contre). **III.** *int*
pan! boum! **IV.** *adv F:* **to go b.,** éclater; **b. in the**
middle, en plein milieu; **to arrive b. on time,** arriver
pile; **it's b. on!** c'est au poil! **'bang a'bout** *vi* faire
du bruit. **'bang 'into** *vtr* (se) cogner à, contre;
heurter; bousculer (qn). **'banger** *n F: (a)* saucisse
f (b) (car) **(old) b.,** (vieille) bagnole, (vieux) tacot.

bangle ['bæŋgl] *n* bracelet *m.*

banish ['bæniʃ] *vtr* bannir; exiler (qn) **'banish-**
ment *n* bannissement *m,* exil *m.*

banister(s) ['bænistər, -əz] *n(pl)* rampe *f* (d'escalier).

banjo ['bændʒou] *n Mus:* banjo *m.*

bank¹ [bæŋk] **I.** *n* 1. *(a)* talus *m; CivE:* remblai *m (b)*
banc *m* (de sable) *(c)* digue *f* 2. bord *m,* rive *f,* rivage
m (d'une rivière); berge *f* (d'un canal); **left b.,** rive

gauche. **II.** *v* 1. *vtr* **to b. (up),** endiguer (une rivière); relever (un virage); remblayer (une route); amonceler (de la terre); couvrir (un feu) 2. *vi* (*a*) (*of snow*) s'entasser, s'amonceler (*b*) *Av:* virer (sur l'aile).

bank² I. *n* banque *f*; **merchant b.,** banque d'affaires; **b. account,** compte en banque; **b. clerk,** employé(e) de banque; **b. book,** livret de banque. **II.** *v* 1. *vtr* déposer (de l'argent) en banque. 2. *vi* avoir un compte en banque (**with,** à). **'bankbook** *n* livret *m* de banque. **'banker** *n* banquier *m.* **'banking** *n* 1. affaires *fpl* de banque. 2. profession *f* de banquier. **'banknote** *n* billet *m* de banque. **'bank 'on** *vtr* compter sur. **'bankrupt** 1. *a & n* failli(e); **to go b.,** faire faillite; **to be b.,** être en faillite 2. *vtr* (*a*) mettre en faillite (*b*) ruiner. **'bankruptcy** *n* faillite *f.*

bank³ *n* rang *m* (d'avirons, de touches).

banner ['bænər] *n* bannière *f*, étendard *m*; *Journ:* **b. headline,** manchette *f.*

bannister(s) ['bænistər, -əz] *n*(*pl*) *see* **banister(s).**

banns [bænz] *npl* bans *m* (de mariage).

banquet ['bæŋkwit] *n* banquet *m*; festin *m.*

bantam ['bæntəm] *n* coq nain, poule naine. **'bantamweight** *n Box:* poids *m* coq.

banter ['bæntər] *n* badinage *m*; raillerie *f.*

bap [bæp] *n* petit pain rond au lait.

baptize [bæp'taiz] *vtr* baptiser. **'baptism** *n* baptême *m.* **'Baptist** *n* baptiste *mf.*

bar [bɑːr] I. *n* 1. (*a*) barre *f*; tablette *f* (de chocolat); lingot *m* (d'or); pain *m* (de savon); élément *m* (d'un feu électrique) (*b*) *pl* barreaux *m* (d'une cage); **behind bars,** sous les verrous (*c*) (*in harbour*) barre (de sable) 2. empêchement *m*, obstacle *m*; **colour b.,** ségrégation raciale. 3. *Jur:* (*a*) barre (des accusés); **the prisoner at the b.,** l'accusé(e) (*b*) barreau (des avocats); **to be called to the b.,** être reçu au barreau 4. bar *m*; (*in station*) buvette *f*; comptoir *m* (dans un bar) 5. *Mus:* mesure *f.* **II.** *vtr* (**barred**) 1. (*a*) barrer (la route, la porte) (*b*) exclure (qn) 2. défendre, interdire (qch). **III.** *prep.* excepté, sauf; **b. none,** sans exception. **'barmaid** *n* serveuse *f* (dans un bar). **'barman, -men** *n* barman *m.* **'barring** *prep see* **bar III.**

barb [bɑːb] *n* (*a*) barbillon *m*, dardillon *m* (d'un hameçon) (*b*) picot *m* (de barbelé). **barbed** *a* **b. wire,** (fil de fer) barbelé *m.*

Barbados [bɑː'beidɔs] *Prn Geog:* Barbade *f.*

barbarian [bɑː'beəriən] *n* barbare *mf.* **bar'baric** [-'bærik] *a* barbare. **bar'barity** *n* barbarie *f.* **'barbarous** *a* barbare. **'barbarously** *adv* cruellement.

barbecue ['bɑːbikjuː] 1. *n* barbecue *m* 2. *vtr* griller au barbecue.

barber ['bɑːbər] *n* coiffeur *m* pour hommes; **barber's pole,** enseigne *f* de barbier. **barber's,** *NAm:* **'barbershop** *n* salon *m* de coiffure pour hommes.

barbiturate [bɑː'bitjurət] *n* barbiturique *m.*

bard [bɑːd] *n Lit:* poète *m*; **the B. (of Avon)** = SHAKESPEARE.

bare ['beər] I. *a* 1. nu; dénudé; (paysage) nu; (arbre) dépouillé; (placard) vide; **to lay b.,** mettre à nu; exposer; *El:* **b. wire,** fil dénudé; **with his b. hands,** à mains nues; **on the b. earth, floor,** sur la dure; **the**

b. facts, le fait brutal 2. (majorité) faible; **to earn a b. living,** gagner tout juste de quoi vivre; **b. necessities,** juste ce qu'il faut pour vivre; **b. minimum,** strict minimum. **II.** *vtr* mettre à nu; montrer (les dents); se découvrir (la tête). **'bareback** *adv* (monter) à nu, à cru. **'barefaced** *a* (mensonge) éhonté. **'barefoot** 1. *adv* nu-pieds 2. *a* aux pieds nus. **'bare'headed** *a & adv* nu-tête, tête nue. **'barely** *adv* à peine; tout juste. **'bareness** *n* nudité *f*, dénuement *m.*

bargain ['bɑːgin] 1. *n* (*a*) marché *m*, affaire *f*; **into the b.,** par-dessus le marché; **it's a b.!** c'est convenu! (*b*) occasion *f*; **b. price,** prix exceptionnel, avantageux; **b. hunter,** chercheur, -euse, d'occasions; **b. sale,** (vente *f* de) soldes *mpl*; **b. counter,** rayon des soldes **it's a real b.!** c'est une occasion! 2. *vi* (*a*) négocier, marchander (**with s.o.,** avec qn); **I didn't b. for that!** je ne m'attendais pas à cela! **he got more than he bargained for,** il a eu du fil à retordre. **'bargaining** *n* marchandage *m*; **collective b.,** convention collective.

barge [bɑːdʒ] 1. *n* chaland *m*, péniche *f*; barque *f* (de cérémonie) 2. *vi* marcher lourdement. **bar'gee,** *NAm:* **'bargeman, -men** *n* marinier *m.* **'barge 'in** *vi* (*a*) entrer comme un ouragan (*b*) intervenir (mal à propos). **'barge 'into** *vtr* (*a*) faire irruption dans (une pièce) (*b*) interrompre (une conversation) (*c*) = BANG INTO. **'bargepole** *n* gaffe *f*; *F:* **I wouldn't touch it with a b.,** je ne veux rien avoir à faire avec ça.

baritone ['bæritoun] *a & n Mus:* **b. (voice),** (voix *f* de) baryton *m.*

barium ['beəriəm] *n Ch:* baryum *m*; *Med:* **b. meal,** sulfate de baryum.

bark¹ [bɑːk] I. *n* écorce *f* (d'arbre). II. *vtr* **to b. one's shins,** s'érafler les tibias.

bark² 1. *n* (*of dog*) aboiement *m*; (*of fox*) glapissement *m*; **his b. is worse than his bite,** il fait plus de bruit que de mal 2. *vi* (*a*) (*of dog*) aboyer (**at,** après, contre); (*of fox*) glapir; *Fig:* **to b. up the wrong tree,** suivre une fausse piste. **'barker** *n* (*at fair*) aboyeur *m.* **'barking** *n* aboiement(s) *m*(*pl*). **'bark 'out** *vtr* donner (un ordre) d'un ton sec.

barley ['bɑːli] *n* orge *f*; **b. sugar,** sucre *m* d'orge; **b. water,** tisane *f* d'orge.

barmy ['bɑːmi] *a* (-**ier, -iest**) *F:* idiot, toqué.

barn [bɑːn] *n* grange *f*; *esp NAm:* étable *f*, écurie *f*; **b. dance,** danses folkloriques. **'barnyard** *n* basse-cour *f.*

barnacle ['bɑːnəkl] *n Crust:* anatife *m*; bernache *f*, bernacle *f.*

barometer [bə'rɔmitər] *n* baromètre *m.*

baron ['bærən] *n* baron *m.* **'baroness** *n* baronne *f.* **'baronet** *n* baronnet *m.* **ba'ronial** *a* seigneurial.

barrack ['bærək] *vtr* chahuter, huer (qn). **'barrackroom** *n* chambrée *f*; **b. language,** propos de corps de garde. **'barracks** *npl* caserne *f*; **confined to b.,** consigné (au quartier).

barrage ['bærɑːʒ] *n* 1. barrage *m* (d'un fleuve) 2. (*a*) *Mil:* tir *m* de barrage (*b*) torrent *m*, flot *m*, feu roulant (de questions).

barrel ['bærəl] *n* 1. tonneau *m*, barrique *f*, fût *m* (de vin); baril *m* (de pétrole); caque *f* (de harengs); *Fig:*

over **a b.**, dans le pétrin 2. cylindre *m*; canon *m* (de fusil); **b. organ**, orgue *m* de Barbarie.

barren ['bærən] *a* stérile, improductif; (terre) aride. '**barrenness** *n* stérilité *f*.

barricade ['bærikeid] 1. *n* barricade *f* 2. *vtr* barricader.

barrier ['bæriər] *n* barrière *f*; (*at station*) portillon *m*; obstacle *m* (au progrès); **sound b.**, mur *m* du son.

barrister ['bæristər] *n* avocat *m*.

barrow ['bærou] *n* brouette *f* (de jardinier); diable *m* (de porteur); baladeuse *f*, voiture *f* à bras (de marchand); **b. boy**, marchand des quatre saisons.

barter ['bɑːtər] 1. *n* échange *m*; troc *m* 2. *vtr* échanger, troquer (**for**, contre). '**barter a'way** *vtr* vendre (sa liberté).

basalt ['bæsɔːlt] *n* basalte *m*.

base [beis] 1. *n* base *f*; pied *m* (d'arbre); socle *m* (de lampe) 2. *vtr* baser, fonder (**on**, sur); (*of pers, company*) **to be based at**, être basé à; **to b. oneself on sth**, se baser, se fonder, sur qch 3. *a* bas; indigne; (motif, métal) vil. '**baseball** *n* base-ball *m*. '**baseboard** *n* *NAm*: (*Br* = **skirting (board**)) plinthe *f*. '**baseless** *a* sans fondement. '**baseline** *n* *Ten*: ligne *f* de fond. '**basely** *adv* bassement. '**basement** *n* sous-sol *m*. '**baseness** *n* bassesse *f*.

bash [bæʃ] *F*: 1. *n* coup *m*; (*of pan, car, hat*) **to have had a b.**, être bosselé, cabossé; (*of pers*) **to have a b. at sth**, essayer (de faire) qch; tenter le coup 2. *vtr* cogner (à, sur); cabosser (un chapeau). '**bash a'bout** *vtr* assommer (qn). '**bash 'down**, '**in** *vtr* défoncer (une porte).

bashful ['bæʃful] *a* timide. '**bashfully** *adv* timidement. '**bashfulness** *n* timidité *f*.

basic ['beisik] *a* (principe) fondamental; (vocabulaire, salaire) de base. '**basically** *adv* au fond; fondamentalement. '**basics** *npl* éléments (essentiels).

basil ['bæzl] *n* *Bot*: basilic *m*.

basilica [bə'zilikə] *n* basilique *f*.

basin ['beisn] *n* 1. bassin *m*; (*for food*) bol *m*; (*for washing*) bassine *f*, cuvette *f*; (*plumbed in*) lavabo *m*; (*of fountain*) vasque *f* 2. bassin (d'un fleuve).

basis ['beisis] *n* (*pl* **bases**) base *f*; fondement *m*; **on the b. of**, à partir de.

bask [bɑːsk] *vi* (*a*) se chauffer, faire le lézard (au soleil) (*b*) jouir (**in**, de).

basket ['bɑːskit] *n* corbeille *f*; panier *m*; cabas *m*; **shopping b.**, panier à provisions. '**basketball** *n* basket(-ball) *m*. '**basketchair** *n* chaise *f* en rotin, en osier. '**basketmaker** *n* vannier *m*. '**basketwork** *n* vannerie *f*.

Basle [bɑːl] *Prn Geog*: Bâle *f*.

Basque [bæsk] *a* & *n* basque (*mf*).

bass¹ [bæs] *n* (*no pl*) *Ich*: (*a*) **sea b.**, serran *m* (*b*) bar *m*.

bass² [beis] *a* & *n* (*pl* **basses**) *Mus*: basse *f*; **b. voice**, voix de basse; **b. key**, clef de fa.

bassoon [bə'suːn] *n* *Mus*: basson *m*. **ba'ssoonist** *n* basson *m*.

bastard ['bɑːstəd] (*a*) *a* & *n* bâtard, -e (*b*) *n* *P*: salaud *m*; **lucky b.!** veinard!

baste [beist] *vtr* (*a*) *Cu*: arroser (un rôti) (*b*) *esp NAm*: (*Br* = **tack**) *Needlew*: bâtir.

bat¹ [bæt] *n* *Z*: chauve-souris *f*; *F*: **to have bats in the belfry**, avoir une araignée au plafond.

bat² I. *n* 1. batte *f* (de cricket); *Fig*: **off one's own b.**, de sa propre initiative 2. raquette *f* (de ping-pong). II. *v* (**batted**) 1. *vi* manier la batte; *Cr*: être au guichet 2. *vtr* frapper (une balle) (avec une batte); *F*: **he didn't b. an eyelid**, il n'a pas sourcillé. '**batsman**, -**men** *n* *Cr*: batteur *m*.

batch [bætʃ] *n* (*pl* **batches**) fournée *f* (de pain); paquet *m* (de lettres); lot *m* (de marchandises).

bated ['beitid] *a* **with b. breath**, à voix basse; (attendre) en retenant son souffle.

bath [bɑːθ] I. *n* (*pl* **baths**) 1. bain *m*; **to have, take, a b.**, prendre un bain; (**public**) **baths**, bains (publics); (**swimming**) **bath(s)**, piscine *f*; **b. salts**, sels de bain; **b. towel**, serviette de bain 2. (*NAm:* = **tub**) baignoire *f*. II. *v* 1. *vtr* baigner, donner un bain à (qn) 2. *vi* prendre un bain. '**bathmat** *n* tapis *m* de bain. '**bathrobe** *n* peignoir *m*. '**bathroom** *n* salle *f* de bains. '**bathtub** *n* *esp NAm*: (*Br* = **bath**) baignoire.

bathe [beið] I. *v* 1. *vtr* baigner; laver (une plaie); **bathed in**, baigné de (larmes, sang); **bathed in sweat**, en nage 2. *vi* (*a*) se baigner (*b*) *NAm*: prendre un bain. II. *n* bain *m* (de mer, de rivière); baignade *f*; **to go for a b.**, (aller) se baigner. '**bather** *n* baigneur, -euse. '**bathing** *n* bains *mpl* (de mer, de rivière); baignades *fpl*; **b. costume, suit**, maillot *m* (de bain); **b. trunks**, slip *m* (de bain); **b. cap**, bonnet de bain.

batik [bə'tiːk] *n* batik *m*.

baton ['bætən] *n* bâton *m*; (*in relay race*) témoin *m*.

battalion [bə'tæljən] *n* bataillon *m*.

batten ['bætn] *n* latte *f*.

batter ['bætər] I. *n* *Cu*: pâte *f* lisse; pâte à frire; (*for pancakes*) pâte à crêpes. II. *v* 1. *vtr* battre; maltraiter (un enfant) 2. *vi* **to b. at the door**, frapper avec violence à la porte. '**batter 'down** *vtr* défoncer (une porte). '**battered** *a* (meuble) délabré; (chapeau) cabossé; (visage) meurtri; (enfant) (cruellement) maltraité, (enfant) martyr; (femme) battue.

battery ['bætəri] *n* (*pl* **batteries**) 1. *Artil: etc*: batterie *f* 2. (*a*) *El*: pile *f*; accumulateur(s) *m*(*pl*); (**car**) **b.**, batterie (*b*) *Husb*: (*for hens*) batterie 3. *Jur*: **assault and b.**, coups *mpl* et blessures *fpl*.

battle ['bætl] I. *n* 1. bataille *f*; combat *m*; **b. cry**, cri de guerre; **b. cruiser**, croiseur de combat; **b. dress**, tenue de campagne; **to fight a, give, b.**, livrer bataille; **that's half the b.**, c'est bataille à moitié gagnée; **b. royal**, bataille en règle. II. *vi* se battre; lutter (**against**, contre). '**battleaxe**, *NAm*: -**ax** *n* (*a*) hâche *f* d'armes (*b*) *F*: (*woman*) virago *f*. '**battlefield** *n* champ *m* de bataille. '**battlements** *npl* (*a*) (*wall*) créneaux *mpl* (*b*) (*roof*) rempart *m*. '**battleship** *n* cuirassé *m*.

bauble ['bɔːbl] *n* babiole *f*.

baulk [bɔːk] *v* = **balk**.

bauxite ['bɔːksait] *n* *Miner*: bauxite *f*.

bawl [bɔːl] *vtr* & *i* **to b. (out)**, brailler. '**bawl 'out** *vtr* *esp NAm*: *F*: engueuler (qn).

bay¹ [bei] *n* *Bot*: laurier (commun); laurier-sauce *m*, *pl* lauriers-sauce; **b. tree**, laurier; *Cu*: **b. leaf**, feuille de laurier.

bay² *n* *Geog*: baie *f*.

bay³ *n* 1. travée *f* (d'un mur) 2. (*a*) enfoncement *m*; baie *f*; (*b*) **sick b.**, infirmerie *f*; *Aut*: **parking b.**, place f de stationnement; *Com:* **loading b.,** quai *m* de chargement; **b. window,** fenêtre en saillie.

bay⁴ 1. *vi* (*of dog*) aboyer **2.** *n* **to be at b.,** être aux abois; **to keep at b.,** tenir en échec.

bay⁵ *a & n* (cheval) bai (*m*).

bayonet ['beiənit] *n Mil:* baïonnette *f.*

bazaar [bə'zɑːr] *n* **1.** bazar *m* (oriental) **2.** vente *f* de charité.

BBC *abbr British Broadcasting Corporation.*

BC *abbr before Christ,* avant Jésus-Christ.

be [biː] *vi* (was, *pl* were; been) être **1.** (*a*) **Mary is pretty, Mary's pretty,** Marie est jolie; **seeing is believing,** voir c'est croire; **isn't he lucky!** il en a de la chance! (*b*) **he is, he's, an Englishman,** il est anglais, c'est un Anglais; **if I were you,** à votre place, si j'étais vous (*c*) **three and two are five,** trois et deux font cinq **2.** (*a*) **I was at the meeting,** j'ai assisté à la réunion; **I don't know where I am,** (i) je ne sais pas où (i) je suis (ii) j'en suis (*b*) **how are you?** comment allez-vous? (*c*) **how much is that?** combien cela coûte-t-il? cela fait combien? **how far is it to London?** combien y a-t-il d'ici à Londres? (*d*) **when is the concert?** quand le concert aura-t-il lieu? **Christmas is on a Sunday this year,** Noël tombe un dimanche cette année; **to-day is, it's, the sixth of May,** c'est, nous sommes (aujourd'hui) le six mai; **tomorrow is Friday,** c'est demain vendredi **3.** (*a*) (*of pers*) **to be** (= *feel*) **cold, afraid,** avoir froid, peur (*b*) **to be twenty (years old),** avoir vingt ans **4.** (*a*) **that may be,** cela se peut; **so be it!** soit! **everything must remain (just) as it is,** tout doit rester tel quel; **be that as it may,** quoi qu'il en soit (*b*) *impers* **there is, there are,** il y a; **what is there to see?** qu'est-ce qu'il y a à voir? **there will be dancing,** on dansera; **there were 10 cats,** il y avait 10 chats; **there were six, a dozen, of us,** nous étions six, une douzaine **5. I have been to see David,** j'ai été, je suis allé, voir David; **I have been to the museum,** j'ai visité le musée; **where have you been?** d'où venez-vous? **has anyone been?** est-il venu quelqu'un? **6.** *impers* (*a*) **it is six o'clock,** il est six heures; **it is late,** il est tard; **it is a fortnight since I saw him,** il y a quinze jours que je ne l'ai vu (*b*) **it's fine, cold,** il fait beau (temps), il fait froid (*c*) **it is said,** on dit; **it's for you to decide,** c'est à vous de décider; **what is it?** (i) qu'est-ce que c'est? (ii) que voulez-vous? (iii) qu'est-ce qu'il y a? **as it were,** pour ainsi dire **7.** (*aux*) (*a*) **I am, was, doing sth,** je fais, faisais, qch; **he was working,** il était en train de travailler; **they are always laughing,** ils sont toujours à rire; **I've (just) been writing,** je viens d'écrire; **I've been waiting for a long time,** j'attends depuis longtemps (*b*) (*passive*) **he was killed,** il a été tué; on l'a tué; **he is allowed, not allowed, to smoke,** on lui permet, il lui est défendu, de fumer; **he is to be pitied,** il est à plaindre; **what's to be done?** que faire? (*c*) (*denoting future*) **I am to see him tomorrow,** je dois le voir demain; **he was never to see them again,** il ne devait plus les revoir (*d*) (*necessity, duty*) **you are not to go,** il vous est interdit, défendu, d'y aller; vous ne devez pas y aller **8. are you happy?—yes, I am,** êtes-vous heureux?—mais oui! oui, je le suis; **he's back—is he?** il est de retour—vraiment? **so you're back, are you?** alors vous voilà de retour? **isn't it lovely? it's lovely, isn't it?** c'est beau, n'est-ce pas? **'be-all** *n* the be-al-

and end-all, le but suprême. **'being** *n* **1.** existence *f*; **to bring into b.,** réaliser (un projet); **to come into b.,** prendre naissance, forme; **it is still in b.,** cela existe toujours **2.** être *m* (*a*) **all my b.,** tout mon être (*b*) **a human b.,** un être humain.

beach [biːtʃ] *n* (*pl* beaches) plage *f*; grève *f*; rivage *m*; **b. ball,** ballon de plage. **'beachcomber** *n* batteur *m* de grève. **'beachhead** *n* tête *f* de pont. **'beachwear** *n* (*no pl*) vêtements *mpl* de plage.

beacon ['biːkən] *n* **1.** feu *m* (d'alarme) **2.** phare *m*; balise *f*; *Aut:* **Belisha b.,** sphère orange lumineuse (indiquant un passage clouté).

bead [biːd] *n* perle *f*; goutte *f*; grain *m* (de chapelet); **(string of) beads,** collier *m.* **'beady** *a* (yeux) en vrille.

beagle ['biːgl] *n* (*dog*) beagle *m.*

beak [biːk] *n* (*of bird*) bec *m*; *F:* (*of pers*) nez crochu.

beaker ['biːkər] *n* gobelet *m*; *Ch:* vase *m.*

beam [biːm] **I.** *n* **1.** (*a*) poutre *f* solive *f* (*b*) fléau *m* (d'une balance) **2.** (*of ship*) **on her b. ends,** accoté; *F:* (*of pers*) **on one's b. ends,** à bout de ressources **3.** (*a*) rayon *m*, trait *m* (de lumière); faisceau *m* (de phare) (*b*) large sourire *m* (de joie) (*c*) *Elcs:* faisceau; *Av:* axe balisé (d'atterrissage); *F:* **to be off b.,** dérailler. **II.** *v* **1.** *vi* (*of the sun, of pers*) rayonner; (*of face, pers*) s'épanouir **2.** *vtr WTel:* transmettre par ondes dirigées. **'beaming** *a* rayonnant; (soleil, visage, sourire) radieux.

bean [biːn] *n* haricot *m*; grain *m* (de café); **green, French,** *NAm:* **string, beans,** haricots verts; **broad b.,** fève *f*; **runner b.,** haricot d'Espagne; **baked beans,** haricots blancs (en conserve) à la sauce tomate; *F:* **full of beans,** plein d'entrain; **he hasn't a b.,** il n'a pas le sou.

bear¹ ['beər] *n* **1.** ours *m*; **she-b.,** ourse *f*; **b. cub,** ourson *m*; *Astr:* **the Great B.,** la Grande Ourse; *Fig:* **b. garden,** pétaudière *f*; **like a b. with a sore head,** d'une humeur massacrante **2.** *St. Exch:* baissier *m.*

bear² *vtr & i* (bore [bɔːr]; borne [bɔːn]) (*a*) porter (un fardeau, un nom) (*b*) supporter (la douleur, la vue de qch); soutenir (un poids); **I can't b. it any longer,** je n'en peux plus; **I can't b. (the sight of) him,** je ne peux pas le sentir, le souffrir (*c*) **to b. (to the) right,** prendre, obliquer, à droite (*d*) **to bring one's mind to b. on sth,** porter son attention sur qch; **to bring sth to b. on,** exercer (une pression) sur; apporter, consacrer (son énergie) à (*e*) donner naissance à (un enfant); *Fin:* porter (intérêt); **she has borne him a son,** elle lui a donné un fils. **'bearable** *a* supportable. **'bear 'down** *vi* appuyer avec force (on, sur). **'bear 'down 'on** *vtr* (= *approach*) (*of pers, vehicle*) foncer sur. **'bearer** *n* porteur, -euse; titulaire *mf* (d'un passeport); *Fin:* **b. bond,** obligation au porteur. **'bearing** *n* (*a*) (*of pers*) port *m*, maintien *m* (*b*) *Tchn:* palier *m*; roulement *m*; coussinet *m* (*c*) (*compass*) **b.,** relèvement *m* (au compas); **to take a ship's bearings,** faire le point; *Fig:* **to get one's bearings,** se repérer, s'orienter; **to lose one's bearings,** se désorienter; perdre le nord (*d*) portée *f* (d'un argument); **it has no b. on,** cela n'a aucun rapport avec. **'bear 'out** *vtr* confirmer, justifier, corroborer (une assertion). **'bear 'up** *vi* faire face (under, à); **b. up!** courage! **how are you?—bearing up,**

comment ça va?—je me défends. **'bear 'with** *vtr* supporter (qch); **b. w. me,** patientez un peu.

beard [biəd] *n* barbe *f*; **to have a b.,** porter la barbe. **'bearded** *a* barbu. **'beardless** *a* imberbe; sans barbe.

beast [bi:st] *n* **1.** bête *f*; *pl Agr:* bétail *m*, bestiaux *mpl* **2.** (*pers*) animal *m*, brute *f*; chameau *m*. **'beastly** *a* (*a*) brutal (*b*) *F:* dégoûtant, infect; **what b. weather!** quel sale temps!

beat [bi:t] **I.** *vtr & i* (**beat; beaten**) **1.** battre; **to b. on, at, the door,** frapper à, donner de grands coups dans, la porte; **to b. a drum,** battre du tambour; **to b. a retreat,** battre la retraite; **to b. time,** battre la mesure; **off the beaten track,** hors des sentiers battus; (*endroit*) écarté; **to b. about the bush,** tourner autour du pot; **I won't b. about the bush,** je n'irai pas par quatre chemins; *P:* **b. it!** fiche le camp! **2.** (*a*) battre, vaincre (qn, un record); *F:* **it beats me,** cela me dépasse; **that beats everything!** ça c'est le comble! (*b*) devancer (qn). **II.** *n* **1.** (*a*) battement *m* (du cœur) (*b*) *Mus:* mesure *f*, temps *m* **2.** ronde *f* (d'un agent de police). **III.** *a F:* (**dead**) **b.,** éreinté; (complètement) crevé. **'beat 'back** *vtr* repousser (qn); rabattre (les flammes). **'beat 'down 1.** *vtr* (*a*) défoncer (une porte) (*b*) rabattre (un prix); faire baisser le prix à (qn); marchander avec (qn) **2.** *vi* (*of sun*) donner, taper (**on,** sur). **'beater** *n* (*for carpets*) tapette *f*; (*for eggs*) fouet *m*, batteur *m*. **'beat 'in** *vtr* défoncer (une porte). **'beating** *n* **1.** battement (du cœur) **2.** (*a*) coups *mpl*; rossée *f*; (*b*) défaite *f*. **'beat 'off** *vtr* repousser (une attaque). **'beat 'out** *vtr* (*a*) battre (le fer); marteler (l'or) (*b*) marquer (un rhythme) (*c*) *F:* **to b. s.o.'s brains out,** assommer qn. **'beat 'up** *vtr* rouer (qn) de coups; tabasser (qn).

beatify [bi(:)'ætifai] *vtr Ecc:* béatifier. **beatifi'cation** *n* béatification *f*.

beautiful ['bju:tiful] *a* beau, belle; magnifique. **beau'tician** *n* esthéticien, -ienne. **'beautifully** *adv* admirablement, parfaitement; à merveille. **'beautify** *vtr* embellir. **'beauty** *n* beauté *f*; **b. treatment,** soins de beauté; **b. specialist,** esthéticien, -ienne; **b. salon, parlour,** institut de beauté; **b. spot** (i) coin, site, pittoresque (ii) (*on skin*) grain de beauté; *F:* **that's the b. of it,** c'est là le plus beau de l'affaire; *F:* **isn't it a b.?** c'est beau, n'est-ce pas?

beaver ['bi:vər] *n Z:* castor *m*.

becalmed [bi'ka:md] *a* encalminé.

became [bi'keim] *see* **become.**

because [bi'kɔz] *conj* parce que. **be'cause of** *prep phr* à cause de.

beck [bek] *n* **to be at s.o.'s b. and call,** obéir à qn au doigt et à l'œil.

beckon ['bekən] *vtr & i* faire signe ((**to**) s.o., à qn); appeler (qn) du doigt, de la main.

become [bi'kʌm] *vi* (**became** [bi'keim]; **become**) (*a*) devenir; **to b. a priest,** se faire prêtre; **to b. accustomed to,** s'accoutumer à (*b*) **what's b. of him?** qu'est-il devenu? **be'coming** *a* (*of clothes*) seyant; (*of behaviour*) bienséant; **her dress is very b.,** sa robe lui va très bien.

bed [bed] *n* **1.** lit *m*; **to go to b.,** se coucher; *F:* **to go to b. with s.o.,** coucher avec qn; **to get into b.,** se mettre au lit; **to be in b.,** être couché; (*through illness*) garder

le lit; **to get out of b.,** se lever; **to get out of b. on the wrong side,** se lever du pied gauche; **to put a child to b.,** coucher un enfant; **to make a b.,** faire un lit; **b. and breakfast,** (i) chambre *f* avec petit déjeuner (ii) (*sign*) = chambres *fpl*; **b. jacket,** liseuse *f*; **b. linen,** literie *f*; **b. wetting,** incontinence nocturne **2.** (*a*) lit (d'une rivière); fond *m* (de la mer); banc *m* (d'huîtres (*b*) (*in garden*) planche *f*, carré *m*; (**flower**) **b.,** parterre *m*; (*border*) plate-bande *f* (*c*) *Geol:* couche *f*; *Miner:* gisement *m*. **'bedbug** *n* punaise *f*. **'bedclothes** *npl* couvertures *fpl* et draps *mpl* de lit; literie. **'bedcover** *n* = **'bedspread.** **'bedding** *n* **1.** (*a*) = **bedclothes** (*b*) (*for animals*) litière *f* **2. b. (out),** repiquage *m* (**de plants,** plantes à repiquer. **'bed 'down 1.** *vtr* faire la litière à (un animal); coucher (qn) **2.** *vi* (*of pers*) (se) coucher. **'bedfellow** *n* **they make strange bedfellows,** c'est une association inattendue. **'bedhead** *n* tête *f* de lit. **'bed 'out** *vtr* repiquer (des plantes). **'bedpan** *n* bassin *m* de lit. **'bedpost** *n* colonne *f* de lit. **'bedridden** *a* cloué au lit. **'bedrock** *n* (*a*) *Geol:* roche *f* de fond (*b*) fondement *m* (de sa croyance); **to get down to b.,** descendre au fond des choses. **'bedroom** *n* chambre à coucher. **'bedside** *n* chevet *m*; **b. rug,** descente de lit; **b. lamp,** lampe de chevet; **b. table,** table de nuit; **b. manner,** comportement (d'un médecin) au chevet du malade. **bed-'sitter, bed'sittingroom,** *F:* **'bed'sit** *n* studio *m*; chambre meublée. **'bedsore** *n* escarre *f*. **'bedspread** *n* couvre-lit *m*, dessus-de-lit *m*. **'bedstead** *n* bois *m* de lit. **'bedtime** *n* heure *f* du coucher; **it's past my b.,** je devrais être déjà couché; **b. story,** histoire pour endormir un enfant.

bedevil [bi'devl] *vtr* ensorceler. **be'devilled** *a* ensorcelé.

bedlam ['bedləm] *n* chahut *m*; charivari *m*.

bedraggled [bi'drægld] *a* débraillé; trempé.

bee [bi:] *n* abeille *f*; *F:* **to have a b. in one's bonnet,** avoir une idée fixe. **'beehive** *n* ruche *f*. **'beekeeper** *n* apiculteur, -trice. **'beekeeping** *n* apiculture *f*. **'beeline** *n F:* **to make a b. for,** aller droit vers. **'beeswax** *n* cire *f* d'abeilles.

beech [bi:tʃ] *n* (*pl* **beeches**) hêtre *m*; **copper b.,** hêtre rouge. **'beechnut** *n* faîne *f*.

beef [bi:f] **1.** *n* (*a*) (*no pl*) *Cu:* bœuf *m*; **roast b.,** rôti *m* de bœuf; rosbif *m* (*b*) (*pl* **beefs**) plainte *f*. **2.** *vi F:* rouspéter (**about,** contre). **'beefburger** *n* hamburger *m*. **'beefeater** *n* hallebardier *m* (de la Tour de Londres). **'beefsteak** *n Cu:* bifteck *m*. **'beefy** *a* (**-ier, -est**) *F:* costaud.

been [bi:n] *see* **be.**

beer [biər] *n coll* bière *f*. **'beermat** *n* dessous *m* de verre (en carton).

beet [bi:t] *n* betterave *f*; **sugar b.,** betterave à sucre; **b. sugar,** sucre de betterave. **'beetroot** *n* (*NAm:* = **beet**) betterave (potagère).

beetle ['bi:tl] *n Ent:* coléoptère *m*; scarabée *m*; **black b.,** cafard *m*; blatte *f*.

befall [bi'fɔ:l] *vtr & i* (*conj like* FALL; *used only in 3rd pers*) *Lit:* arriver, survenir (à qn).

befit [bi'fit] *vtr* (**befitted**) (*used only in 3rd pers*) *Lit:* convenir à (qn, qch).

before [bi'fɔːr] **1.** *adv* (*a*) **this page and the one b.,** cette page et la précédente (*b*) (*time*) auparavant,

avant; **the day b.**, le jour précédent, la veille; **the evening b.**, la veille au soir; **the year b.**, l'année d'avant, un an auparavant; il y a un an; **I have seen him b.**, je l'ai déjà vu; **I have never seen him b.**, je ne l'ai jamais vu (de ma vie); **go on as b.**, faites comme par le passé 2. *prep* (*a*) (*place*) devant; **b. my eyes**, sous mes yeux (*b*) (*time*) avant; **b. long**, avant longtemps, avant peu; **it ought to have been done b. now**, ce devrait être déjà fait; **b. answering**, avant de répondre (*c*) (*order*) **b. everything else**, avant tout 3. *conj* (*a*) **come and see me b. you leave**, venez me voir avant de partir, avant votre départ (*b*) **he will die b. he will steal**, il préfère mourir plutôt que de voler. **be′forehand** *adv* à l'avance, d'avance; au préalable.

befriend [bi′frend] *vtr* se montrer l'ami de (qn).

beg [beg] *vtr & i* (**begged**) 1. mendier; (*of thg*) **to sit up and b.**, faire le beau; (*of thg*) **to go begging**, ne pas trouver d'amateurs 2. solliciter (une faveur) (**of s.o.**, de qn); **to b. s.o. to do sth**, supplier qn de faire qch; **to b. for mercy**, demander grâce; **I b. your pardon**, je vous demande pardon; **I b. (of) you!** je vous en prie! **to b. the question**, faire une pétition de principe. **beggar** 1. *n* mendiant, -ante; *Prov:* **beggars can't be choosers**, ne choisit pas qui emprunte; *F:* **poor b.!** pauvre diable *m*; **lucky b.!** veinard, -arde! 2. *vtr* **to b. description**, défier toute description. **′beggarly** *a* minable, misérable; (salaire) dérisoire.

begin [bi′gin] *vtr & i* (**began** [bi′gæn]; **begun** [bi′gʌn]) commencer (**to do, doing**, à, de, faire; **by doing, with**, par); se mettre (à faire); entamer (qch); débuter; **the day began well**, la journée s'annonçait bien; **he soon began to complain**, il n'a pas tardé à se plaindre; **he began early**, il s'y est mis de bonne heure; **to b. with**, (tout) d'abord; pour commencer; **to b. again**, recommencer. **be′ginner** *n* débutant, -ante. **be′ginning** *n* commencement *m*; début *m*; origine *f*; **at, in, the b.**, au commencement, au début; *Sch:* **b. of term**, rentrée *f* des classes.

begonia [bi′gounjə] *n Bot:* bégonia *m*.

begrudge [bi′grʌdʒ] *vtr see* **grudge** 2.

behalf [bi′hɑːf] *n* **on b. of s.o.**, au nom de qn; de la part de qn; (agir) pour qn; (plaider) en faveur de qn; (s'inquiéter) au sujet de qn.

behave [bi′heiv] *vi* (*a*) se conduire, se comporter; **to b. (oneself) (well)**, se conduire bien; bien agir (**towards s.o.**, envers qn); **b. yourself!** sois sage! tienstoi bien! (*b*) (*of machine*) (bien) marcher. **be′haved** *a* **well(-)b.**, sage, poli; qui se conduit bien; **badly(-)b.**, qui se conduit mal. **be′haviour** *NAm:* **be′havior** *n* comportement *m*, conduite *f*; maintien *m* (**towards s.o.**, envers qn); **to be on one's best b.**, se surveiller.

behead [bi′hed] *vtr* décapiter (qn).

behind [bi′haind] 1. *adv* (venir) derrière; (rester) en arrière; **from b.**, par derrière; **to be b. with one's work**, être en retard dans son travail 2. *prep.* (*a*) derrière (*b*) *Fig:* **what's b. all this?** qu'y a-t-il derrière tout cela? **to be b.** s.o., soutenir qn (*c*) (*not so advanced*) en arrière de, en retard sur 3. *n F:* derrière *m.* **be′hindhand** *adv & a* en arrière, en retard (**with**, pour).

behold [bi′hould] *vtr* (**beheld**) *Lit:* voir; apercevoir;

imp **b.!** voyez! **be′holder** *n* spectateur, -trice; témoin *m*.

beige [beiʒ] *a & n* beige (*m*).

belated [bi′leitid] *a* (*of pers*) attardé, en retard; (*of greetings*) tardif; *adv* un peu tard; trop tard. **be′latedly** *adv* tardivement.

belch [beltʃ] I. *v* 1. *vi* faire un renvoi; *F:* roter 2. *vtr* **to b. (forth)**, vomir (des flammes). II. *n* (*pl* **belches**) renvoi *m*; *F:* rot *m*.

beleaguered [bi′liːgəd] *a* assiégé.

belfry [′belfri] *n* (*pl* **belfries**) beffroi *m*, clocher *m*.

Belgium [′beldʒəm] *Prn Geog:* Belgique *f*. **′Belgian** *a & n* belge (*mf*).

believe [bi′liːv] 1. *vtr* croire; **I b. (that) I'm right**, je crois avoir raison; **I b. not**, je crois que non; **I b. so**, je crois que oui; **he is believed to be in Rome**, on le croit à Rome; **if he's to be believed**, à l'en croire 2. *vi* croire (**in God**, en Dieu; **in ghosts**, aux revenants; **in s.o.'s word**, à la parole de qn); avoir confiance (**in s.o.**, en qn); être partisan (**in a method**, d'une méthode). **be′lief** *f* croyance *f* (**in God**, en Dieu; **in ghosts**, aux revenants); conviction *f*; **beyond b.**, incroyable; **it is my b. that**, je suis convaincu que. **be′lievable** *a* croyable. **be′liever** *n* croyant, -ante; **to be a great b. in**, croire à; être partisan de; être convaincu de l'efficacité de (qch).

belittle [bi′litl] *vtr* rabaisser, déprécier.

bell [bel] *n* cloche *f*; (*smaller*) clochette *f*; (*small and round*) grelot *m*; (*in house*) sonnette *f*; (*on bicycle*) timbre *m*; (*electric*) sonnerie *f*; **b. ringer**, sonneur *m*. **′bellboy**, *NAm:* **-hop** *n* groom *m* (d'hôtel); chasseur *m.* **′bellpush** *n* bouton *m* (de sonnerie).

belle [bel] *n* beauté *f*; reine *f* (du bal).

belligerent [be′lidʒərənt] *a & n* belligérant(e). **be′lligerence** *n* belligérance *f*.

bellow [′belou] I. *v* 1. *vi* beugler, mugir; hurler 2. *vtr* **to b. (out)**, hurler; beugler. II. *n* beuglement *m*, mugissement *m*; hurlement *m*.

bellows [′belouz] *npl* 1. (**pair of**) **b.**, soufflet *m* (pour le feu) 2. soufflerie *f* (d'un orgue).

belly [′beli] *n* (*pl* **bellies**) ventre *m*; **b. dance**, danse du ventre; **b. laugh**, gros rire franc; *Av:* **b. landing**, atterrissage sur le ventre; *Cu:* **b. (of) pork**, poitrine *f* de porc. **′bellyache** 1. *n* mal *m* de ventre 2. *vi P:* ronchonner, rouspéter. **′bellyflop** *n Swim: F:* **to do a b.**, faire un plat. **′bellyful** *n P:* **to have had a b.**, en avoir plein le dos.

belong [bi′lɔŋ] *vi* 1. appartenir (**to**, à); **that book belongs to me**, ce livre m'appartient, est à moi 2. (*be appropriate*) être propre (à qch); **to b. together**, aller ensemble 3. être membre, faire partie (**to a club**, d'un club); **put it back where it belongs**, remettez-le à sa place; **to feel that one belongs, doesn't b.**, se sentir chez soi, isolé. **be′longings** *npl* affaires *fpl*, effets *mpl*; **personal belongings**, objets personnels.

beloved 1. [bi′lʌvd] *a* **b. by all**, aimé de tous 2. [bi′lʌvid] *a & n* bien-aimé(e).

below [bi′lou] 1. *adv* en bas; au-dessous, en-dessous; **here b. (on earth)**, ici-bas; **voices from b.**, voix qui viennent d'en bas; **the people (in the flat) b.**, les gens du dessous; **the passage quoted b.**, le passage cité (i) ci-dessous (ii) ci-après 2. *prep* au-dessous de; sous (la surface); en contre-bas de (la rue); en aval de (la ville).

belt [belt] I. n 1. ceinture f; Aut: Av: **seat b., safety b.,** ceinture de sécurité; **to hit s.o. below the b.,** donner à qn un coup bas; (judo) **to be a brown b.,** être ceinture marron 2. (on machine) courroie f 3. région f (de maïs); Adm: **green b.,** zone verte. II. vtr F: flanquer une raclée à (qn). **'belt a'long, 'down, 'up,** etc vtr & i F: aller, descendre, monter, etc, à toute vitesse. **'belt 'out** vtr F: brailler (une chanson). **'belt 'up** vi F: la boucler.

bemoan [bi'moun] vtr pleurer (qch), se lamenter de (qch).

bemused [bi'mju:zd] a hébété; abasourdi.

bench [ben(t)ʃ] n (pl benches) 1. banc m; banquette f; gradin m (de stade); Jur: **to be on the b.,** (i) être magistrat (ii) siéger au tribunal 2. (in workshop) établi m.

bend [bend] I. n 1. (of pipe) coude m; (of arm) pli m; (of road) virage m; PN: **bends for 5 kilometres,** virages sur 5 kilomètres; **round the b.,** (i) juste après le coin (ii) F: (of pers) fou, cinglé 2. Med: **the bends,** la maladie des caissons. II. v (bent) 1. vtr courber, plier (le bras); fléchir (le genou); **to b. out of shape,** fausser; **to b. the rules,** faire une entorse aux règlements 2. vi (of branch) plier; (of pers) se courber; se pencher (over s.o., sth, sur qn, qch); **the road bends (round) to the right,** la route fait une courbe à droite. **'bend 'back(wards)** 1. vtr replier 2. vi (of pers) se pencher en arrière. **'bend 'down** vi (of pers) se baisser; se courber. **'bend 'forward** vi (of pers) se pencher en avant. **'bend 'over** 1. vtr replier 2. vi (of pers) se pencher; **to b. o. backwards to do sth,** se mettre en quatre pour faire qch.

beneath [bi'ni:θ] 1. adv au-dessous, en-dessous; en bas 2. prep au-dessous de; sous; **it's b. him,** c'est indigne de lui.

benediction [beni'dikʃn] n bénédiction f.

benefactor [benifæktər] n bienfaiteur m. **'benefactress** n bienfaitrice f.

beneficent [bi'nefisənt] a 1. bienfaisant 2. salutaire.

beneficial [beni'fiʃl] a salutaire; avantageux.

beneficiary [beni'fiʃəri] n bénéficiaire mf.

benefit ['benifit] I. n 1. avantage m, profit m; bienfait m; **for the b. of his health,** dans l'intérêt de sa santé; **to give s.o. the b. of the doubt,** laisser à qn le bénéfice du doute 2. Adm: indemnité f, allocation f; prestation f; **unemployment, maternity, b.,** allocation de chômage, de maternité; **child b.,** allocation(s) familiale(s) 3. b. (performance, match), représentation f, match m, au bénéfice de qn. II. v 1. vi profiter (from, by, de) 2. vtr profiter à.

benevolence [bi'nevələns] n bienveillance f. **be'nevolent** a bienveillant (to, envers); **b. society,** association de bienfaisance.

benign [bi'nain] a bénin.

bent [bent] I. a 1. (a) courbé, plié; (dos) voûté; (b) faussé, fléchi; (châssis) tordu (c) P: malhonnête; (gardien) véreux (d) P: homosexuel 2. **b. on doing sth,** déterminé, résolu, à faire qch. II. n penchant m, inclination f, dispositions f(pl) (for, pour).

benzene ['benzi:n] n Ch: benzène m. **benzine** ['benzi:n, ben'zi:n] n Ch: benzine f.

bequeath [bi'kwi:ð] vtr léguer (to, à). **be'quest** n legs m; (in museum) fonds m.

bereave [bi'ri:v] vtr (bereft or bereaved) priver (s.o. of sth, qn de qch). **be'reaved** 1. a en deuil 2. n(pl) famille f du mort. **be'reavement** n perte f (d'un parent); deuil m.

beret ['berei] n béret m.

Berlin [bəː'lin] Prn Geog: Berlin; **East, West, B.,** Berlin Est, Ouest.

Bermuda [bə'mju:də] Prn Geog: Bermudes fpl; Cl: **B. shorts,** npl bermudas, bermuda m.

berry ['beri] n (pl berries) Bot: baie f.

berserk [bə'zɜːk] a **to go b.,** devenir fou furieux.

berth [bəːθ] 1. n (a) (for ship) poste m de mouillage, d'amarrage; **to give a wide b.,** éviter (qn, qch) (b) Nau: Rail: couchette f 2. v (a) vtr amarrer (un navire) (b) vi (of ship) mouiller.

beset [bi'set] vtr (beset; besetting) Lit: 1. assaillir (qn); **b. with dangers,** entouré de dangers 2. **b. by doubts,** assailli de doutes. **be'setting** a obsédant.

beside [bi'said] prep à côté, auprès, de; **that is b. the point,** c'est en dehors du sujet; cela n'a rien à voir avec l'affaire; **to be b. oneself,** être hors de soi; **b. oneself with joy,** fou de joie.

besides [bi'saidz] 1. adv (a) en outre, en plus; **nothing b.,** rien de plus (b) d'ailleurs; du reste; et en outre 2. prep (= in addition to) en plus de, sans compter; (= other than) excepté, hormis; **others b. him,** d'autres que lui.

besiege [bi'si:dʒ] vtr assiéger.

bespoke [bi'spouk] a (vêtement) (fait) sur commande, sur mesure; (tailleur) à façon.

best [best] 1. a & n (a) (le) meilleur, (la) meilleure (in, de); le mieux; (at wedding) **b. man,** garçon d'honneur; **my b. dress,** ma plus belle robe; **with the b. of them,** comme pas un; **the b. of it is that,** le plus beau de l'affaire, c'est que; **to know what is b. for s.o.,** savoir ce qui convient le mieux à qn; **the b. thing would be, it would be b., to,** le mieux serait de; **I think it (would be) b. to,** je crois qu'il vaudrait mieux; **to do one's b.,** faire de son mieux, faire (tout) son possible; **he did his b. to smile,** il s'est efforcé de sourire; **to be at one's b.,** être en forme; **to be looking (at) one's b.,** être en beauté; **to have the b. of it,** l'emporter; **the b. part of an hour, of a year,** une heure ou peu s'en faut; la plus grande partie de l'année; **all the b.! the b. of luck!** bonne chance! **to make the b. of a bad job,** faire contre mauvaise fortune bon cœur; **to play the b. of three (games),** jouer au meilleur de trois (b) **at (the) b.,** au mieux; **he's not very friendly at the b. of times,** il n'est pas particulièrement sympathique; **to act for the b.,** agir pour le mieux; **to the b. of my ability,** de mon mieux; **to the b. of my belief, knowledge,** autant que je sache 2. adv (a) (the) b., le mieux; **as b. I could,** de mon mieux; **you know b.,** c'est vous le mieux placé pour en juger; **do as you think b.,** faites comme bon vous semble(ra) (b) **the b. dressed man,** l'homme le mieux habillé; **the b. known actor,** l'acteur le plus connu. **best'seller** n best-seller m.

bestial ['bestjəl] a bestial. **besti'ality** n bestialité f.

bet [bet] I. n pari m. II. vtr i (bet; betting) parier; **to b. on a horse,** jouer un cheval; **to b. s.o. that,** parier à qn que; F: **(I) b. (you) I will!** chiche (que je le fais)! **'better** n parieur, -euse. **'betting** n paris mpl;

the b. is 20 to 1, la cote est (à) 20 contre 1; b. shop = bureau du pari mutuel.

betray [bi'trei] *vtr* 1. trahir 2. révéler, laisser voir (son ignorance); livrer (un secret). **be'trayal** *n* trahison *f*.

betrothal [bi'trouðəl] *n Lit:* fiançailles *fpl*.

better ['betər] I. *a, n, & adv* 1. *a* meilleur; b. **than** average, supérieur à la moyenne; he's no b. **than**, il ne vaut pas mieux que; he's a b. man **than** you, il vaut plus que vous; you're b. **(at it) than** me, tu le fais, tu t'y connais, mieux que moi; I had hoped for **b. things**, j'avais espéré mieux; the b. **part of the day, of an hour**, la plus grande partie de la journée; une heure ou peu s'en faut 2. *a & n* mieux; **that's b.**, voilà qui est mieux; **it couldn't be b.**, c'est on ne peut mieux; **all the b., so much the b.**, tant mieux; to **get b.**, s'améliorer; (*after illness*) se remettre; **the weather is b.**, il fait meilleur; to **be b. (in health)**, aller mieux; **change for the b.**, changement en mieux; to **get the b. of s.o.**, l'emporter sur qn; **you'll be all the b. for it**, vous vous en trouverez d'autant mieux 3. *adv* (*a*) mieux; **b. and b.**, de mieux en mieux; to **think b. of it**, se raviser; *F:* to **go one b. than s.o.**, damer le pion à qn; **b. still**, mieux encore; **you'd b. stay**, il vaut mieux que vous restiez; vous feriez bien de rester; **we'd b. be going**, il est temps de rentrer (*b*) **b. dressed**, mieux habillé; **b. known**, plus connu; **b. off**, plus riche; he's b. **off where he is**, il est bien mieux là où il est. II. *vtr* (*a*) améliorer; to b. **oneself**, améliorer sa condition (*b*) dépasser (un exploit).

between [bi'twi:n] 1. *prep* entre; **no one can come b. us**, personne ne peut nous séparer; **b. now and Monday**, d'ici (à) lundi; **they did it b. them**, ils l'ont fait à eux; **the two of them**, à eux deux; b. **you and me, b. ourselves**, entre nous 2. *adv* (in) **b.**, entre les deux; dans l'intervalle.

bevel ['bevəl] 1. *n* (*a*) biseau *m* (*b*) *Tls:* fausse équerre 2. *vtr* (**bevelled**) biseauter.

beverage ['bevəridʒ] *n* boisson *f*.

bevy ['bevi] *n* (*pl* **bevies**) bande *f*, troupe *f*.

beware [bi'wɛər] *vi & tr* (*only in inf & imp*) se méfier (**of**, de); se garder (**of**, de; **of doing**, de faire); b.**!** prenez garde (**of**, à qch)! *PN:* b. **of the dog** = attention, chien méchant; b. **of pickpockets**, attention aux pickpockets.

bewilder [bi'wildər] *vtr* désorienter, dérouter (qn); ahurir (qn). **be'wildered** *a* désorienté, dérouté; ahuri. **be'wildering** *a* déroutant; ahurissant. **be'wilderment** *n* trouble *m*; ahurissement *m*.

bewitch [bi'witʃ] *vtr* ensorceler; *Fig:* charmer. **be-'witching** *a* ravissant.

beyond [bi'jɔnd] 1. *adv* au(-)delà, par(-)delà, plus loin 2. *prep* (*a*) au delà de, par delà; au-dessus de (ses moyens); **it's b. me**, cela me dépasse; **b. doubt**, hors de doute; **b. belief**, incroyable; **that's b. a joke**, cela dépasse les bornes (de la plaisanterie) (*b*) **and b. that**, et à part cela.

biannual [bi'ænjuəl] *a* semestriel.

bias ['baiəs] *n* 1. *Needlew:* (**cut**) **on the b.**, (tissu) (coupé) dans le biais; **b. binding**, (ruban *m* en) biais 2. parti pris (**towards, against**, pour, contre). **'bias(s)ed** *a* partial.

bib [bib] *n* bavoir *m*, bavette *f* (d'enfant).

Bible ['baibl] *n* Bible *f*. **biblical** ['biblikl] *a* biblique.

bibliography [bibli'ɔgrəfi] *n* bibliographie *f*. **bi-bli'ographer** *n* bibliographe *mf*. **'bibliophile** *n* bibliophile *mf*.

bicarbonate [bai'kɑ:bənit] *n* b. (**of soda**), bicarbonate *m* de soude.

bicentenary [baisen'ti:nəri], **bicentennial** [bisen'teniəl] *a & n* bicentenaire (*m*).

biceps ['baiseps] *n Anat:* biceps *m*.

bicker ['bikər] *vi* se quereller, se chamailler.

bicycle ['baisikl] *n* bicyclette *f*; vélo *m*; to **ride a b.**, faire de la bicyclette, du vélo.

bid [bid] I. *n* (*a*) offre *f*; (*at auction*) enchère *f*; to **make a b. for sth**, (i) (*at auction*) faire une enchère pour qch (ii) *Fig:* viser (à) qch; **escape b.**, tentative *f* d'évasion (*b*) *Cards:* appel *m*; demande *f*; **no b.!** parole! II. *vtr & i* 1. (**bade, bid; bidden, bid**) *A: & Lit:* (*a*) to b. **s.o. goodbye**, dire au revoir à qn; to b. **s.o. welcome**, souhaiter la bienvenue à qn (*b*) commander (**s.o. to do sth**, à qn de faire qch) 2. (**bid**) (*a*) (*at auction*) to b. **£10 for sth**, faire une offre de £10 pour qch; to b. **for power**, viser au, le pouvoir (*b*) *Cards:* demander, appeler. **'bidder** *n* enchérisseur *m*; **the highest b.**, le plus offrant. **'bidding** *n* 1. to **do s.o.'s b.**, exécuter les ordres de qn 2. enchères *fpl*; *Cards:* **the b. is closed**, l'enchère est faite.

bide [baid] *vtr only used in* to b. **one's time**, attendre son heure, attendre le bon moment.

bidet ['bi:dei] *n* bidet *m*.

biennial [bai'enjəl] *a & n* biennal; *Bot:* b. (**plant**), plante bisannuelle.

bier [biər] *n* civière *f*.

biff [bif] *vtr F:* flanquer une baffe à.

bifocals [bai'foukəlz] *npl* verres *mpl* à double foyer.

big [big] (**bigger; biggest**) 1. *a* (*large*) grand; (*bulky*) gros; b. **man** (i) homme grand, de grande taille (ii) gros homme (iii) homme grand, marquant; b. **brother**, frère aîné; to **grow big(ger)**, grandir; grossir; *ICE:* b. **end**, tête *f* de bielle; (*for circus*) b. **top**, chapiteau *m*; (*at fairground*) b. **dipper** (*NAm:* = **roller coaster**), montagnes *fpl* russes; b. **drop in prices**, forte baisse de prix; to **earn b. money**, gagner gros; b. **business**, les grosses affaires; *Iron: F:* b. **deal!** la belle affaire! *F:* b. **noise, shot, gun**, gros bonnet; *F:* b. **name**, grand nom, grand personnage (du théâtre, etc); *F:* to **be in the b. time**, être arrivé (au sommet de l'échelle); *F:* to **have b. ideas**, voir grand; *F:* to **look b.**, faire l'important; *F:* he's **too b. for his boots**, il se croit sorti de la cuisse de Jupiter; *Iron: F:* **that's b. of you!** grand merci! 2. *adv* to **talk, act, b.**, faire l'important; to **think b.**, voir grand. **'bighead** *n F:* crâneur, -euse. **'big'headed** *a F:* crâneur. **'bigwig** *n F:* (*pers*) gros bonnet.

bigamy ['bigəmi] *n* bigamie *f*. **'bigamist** *n* bigame *mf*. **'bigamous** *a* bigame.

bigot ['bigət] *n Rel:* bigot, -ote; *Pol:* fanatique *mf*. **'bigoted** *a Rel:* bigot; *Pol:* fanatique. **'bigotry** *n Rel:* bigoterie *f*; *Pol:* fanatisme *m*.

bike [baik] *n F:* (= BICYCLE) vélo *m*, bécane *f*.

bikini [bi'ki:ni] *n* bikini *m*.

bilateral [bai'lætərəl] *a* bilatéral.

bilberry ['bilbəri] *n* (*pl* **bilberries**) *Bot:* airelle *f*; myrtille *f*.

bile [bail] *n* bile *f*. **'bilious** ['bil-] *a* bilieux; b. **attack**, crise de foie; to **feel b.**, avoir la nausée.

bilge [bildʒ] *n Nau:* **b.** (**water**), eau *f* de cale; *F:* **to talk b.**, dire des bêtises *f*.

bilingual [bai'lingwəl] *a* bilingue.

bill¹ [bil] **1.** *n* bec *m* (d'oiseau) **2.** *vi* **to b. and coo**, (*of birds*) roucouler; (*of pers*) faire des mamours.

bill² **1.** *n* (*a*) facture *f*; (*in restaurant*) addition *f*; (*in hotel*) note *f* (*b*) *NAm:* billet *m* (de banque) (*c*) *Fin:* **b. of exchange**, lettre *f* de change (*d*) affiche *f*; placard *m*; **stick no bills!** défense d'afficher! **that will fill, fit, the b.**, cela fera l'affaire (*e*) **b. of fare**, carte *f* du jour; menu *m*; **b. of sale**, acte *m* de vente (*f*) *Parl:* projet *m* de loi; déclaration *f* (de droits) **2.** *vtr* (*a*) envoyer une facture à (qn) (**for**, pour) (*b*) *Th:* afficher. **'billboard** *n* panneau *m* d'affichage. **'billfold** *n NAm:* (*Br* = **wallet**) portefeuille *m.* **'billhook** *n Tls:* vouge *m*; serpe *f.* **'billposter, -sticker** *n* colleur *m* d'affiches.

billet ['bilit] *Mil:* **1.** *vtr* loger (des troupes) (**on s.o.**, chez qn) **2.** *n* logement *m*, cantonnement *m.*

billiard ['biljəd] *n* **billiards**, (jeu *m* de) billard *m*; **b. ball**, bille *f* (de billard); **b. room**, (salle de) billiard; **b. table**, billard.

billion ['biljən] *n* (*NAm:* = **trillion**) billion *m* (10¹²); *NAm:* milliard *m* (10⁹).

billow ['bilou] *vi* (*of sea*) se soulever; (*of flag*) ondoyer.

billygoat ['biligout] *n* bouc *m.*

bin [bin] *n* coffre *m*; huche *f*; casier *m* (à bouteilles); (**rubbish**) **b.**, boîte *f* à ordures; poubelle *f.*

binary ['bainəri] *a* binaire.

bind [baind] **1.** *vtr* (**bound** [baund]) (*a*) **to b.** (**together, on**), lier; attacher; **to b. s.o.**, ligoter qn; **bound hand and foot**, pieds et poings liés; **to b. sth** (**down**) (**on**)**to sth**, attacher qch à qch; **to b.** (**up**), bander (une blessure) (*b*) relier (un livre) (*c*) border (un tapis) (*d*) lier, engager (qn); obliger (qn) (**to do**, à faire) **2.** *n F:* scie *f.* **'binder** *n* **1.** (*pers*) relieur, -euse (de livres) **2.** (*thg*) (*a*) *Agr:* lieuse *f* (de gerbes) (*b*) classeur *m* (pour papiers). **'bindery** *n* atelier *m* de reliure. **'binding** **1.** *a* obligatoire (**on s.o.**, pour qn); (contrat) qui lie (qn) **2.** *n* reliure *f* (de livre); fixation *f* (de ski); bordure *f* (de couture). **'bind 'over** *vtr Jur:* **to b. s.o. o. to keep the peace**, exiger de qn sous caution qu'il ne se livrera à aucune voie de fait; **to be bound over**, être sommé par un magistrat d'observer une bonne conduite. **'bindweed** *n Bot:* liseron *m.*

binge [bindʒ] *n F:* **to go on a b.**, faire la bombe.

bingo ['bingou] *n* loto (joué collectivement).

binoculars [bi'nɔkjuləz] *npl* jumelles *fpl.*

bio- ['baiou-] *pref* bio-. **biochemist** [baiou'kemist] *n* biochimiste *mf.* **bio'chemistry** *n* biochimie *f.* **biode'gradable** *a* biodégradable. **bi'ographer** *n* biographe *mf.* **bio'graphical** *a* biographique. **bi'ography** *n* biographie *f.* **bio'logical** *a* biologique. **bi'ologist** *n* biologiste *mf.* **bi'ology** *n* biologie *f.* **bi'onic** *a* bionique. **bionics** *npl* bionique *f.* **'biopsy** *n* biopsie *f.*

biped ['baiped] *n* bipède *m.*

biplane ['baiplein] *n Av:* biplan *m.*

birch [bəːtʃ] *n* (*pl* **birches**) **1.** *Bot:* bouleau *m*; **silver b.**, bouleau blanc **2. b.** (**rod**), verge *f.*

bird [bəːd] *n* **1.** oiseau *m*; **b.'s-eye view** (i) vue à vol d'oiseau (ii) *F:* résumé *m* (d'une situation); *Prov:* **a**

b. in the hand is worth two in the bush, un tiens vaut mieux que deux tu l'auras; *F:* **to give s.o. the b.**, (i) envoyer promener qn (ii) *Th:* siffler qn **2.** *F:* (*a*) individu *m*, type *m* (*b*) jeune fille *f*, nana *f.* **'birdbrained** *a F:* à tête de linotte. **'birdcage** *n* cage *f* à oiseaux. **'birdwatcher** *n* ornithologue *mf.*

biro ['baiərou] *n Rtm:* (marque de) stylo *m* à bille.

birth [bəːθ] *n* **1.** naissance *f*; (*childbirth*) accouchement *m*; **by b.**, de naissance; **b. certificate**, acte de naissance; **b. control**, contrôle des naissances; **b. rate**, natalité *f.* **2. to give b.**, donner naissance (**to**, à); (*of animal*) mettre bas. **'birthday** *n* anniversaire *m*; *F:* **in one's b. suit**, dans le costume d'Adam. **'birthmark** *n* envie *f*; tache *f* de vin. **'birthplace** *n* lieu *m* de naissance. **'birthright** *n* droit *m* de naissance.

Biscay ['biskei] *Prn Geog:* **the Bay of B.**, le golfe de Gascogne.

biscuit ['biskit] *n* (*a*) (*NAm:* = **cookie**) biscuit *m*; petit gâteau sec (*b*) *NAm:* (*Br* = **scone**) petit pain (au lait).

bisect [bai'sekt] *vtr* couper, diviser (en deux parties égales).

bisexual [bai'seksjuəl] *a* bis(s)exué, bis(s)exuel.

bishop ['biʃəp] *n* **1.** *Ecc:* évêque *m.* **2.** *Chess:* fou *m.* **'bishopric** *n* évêché *m.*

bison ['baisn] *n* (*inv in pl*) *Z:* bison *m.*

bit¹ [bit] *n* **1.** mors *m* (d'une bride); **to take the b. between one's teeth**, prendre le mors aux dents **2.** *Tls:* mèche *f* (de vilebrequin).

bit² *n* **1.** morceau *m*; bout *m* (de papier); brin *m* (de paille); **in bits**, en morceaux; **to come to bits**, tomber en morceaux; se désagréger; *F:* **my bits and pieces**, mes (petites) affaires; *F:* **to do one's b.**, y mettre du sien; *Th:* **b. part**, rôle de figurant **2.** (*a*) **a b.** (**of**), un peu (de); **a little b.**, un petit peu; **he's a b. late**, il est un peu en retard; **he's a b. of a liar**, il est un peu menteur; **wait a b.!** attendez un peu! **after a b.**, au bout de quelques minutes; **a good b. older**, sensiblement plus âgé; **b. by b.**, peu à peu; **not a b.** (**of it**) pas du tout! **it's not a b. of use!** cela ne sert absolument à rien! (*b*) **a b. of news**, une nouvelle; **a b. of luck**, une chance.

bit³ *n Cmptr:* bit *m.*

bit⁴ *see* **bite.**

bitch [bitʃ] **1.** *n* (*pl* **bitches**) chienne *f* (*b*) *P:* garce *f* **2.** *vi F:* rouspéter (**about**, contre). **'bitchy** *a P:* garce, vache.

bite [bait] **I.** *n* **1.** morsure *f*; (*of insect*) piqûre *f*; *Fish:* touche *f* **2.** bouchée *f*; *F:* morceau *m*; **I haven't had a b.** (**to eat**) **all day**, je n'ai rien mangé de la journée. **II.** *vtr & i* (**bit; bitten**) mordre; (*of insect*) piquer; **to b. one's nails, one's lip**, se ronger les ongles; se mordre la lèvre; *Prov:* **once bitten twice shy**, chat échaudé craint l'eau froide; **to be bitten with a desire to do sth**, brûler de faire qch; **to b. off more than one can chew**, tenter qch au-dessus de ses forces; *F:* **to b. s.o.'s head off**, rembarrer qn. **'biting** *a* mordant; (vent) cinglant; (froid) perçant.

bitter ['bitər] **1.** *a* (goût) amer; (vin) acerbe; (vent) mordant, cinglant; (froid) glacial; (ennemi) acharné; (ton) âpre; (remords) cuisant; **b. experience**, expérience cruelle; **to the b. end**, jusqu'au bout **2.** *n* (*a*) bière anglaise (*b*) *pl* bitter *m.* **'bitterly** *adv* amèrement, avec amertume; cruellement (déçu); **it was b. cold,** il faisait un froid de loup. **'bitterness** n amertume f. **'bittersweet** a aigre-doux.

bittern ['bitə(:)n] n Orn: butor m.

bitumen ['bitjumin] n bitume m. **bi'tuminous** a bitumineux.

bivouac ['bivuæk] n Mil: bivouac m.

biweekly [bai'wi:kli] a 1. de tous les quinze jours 2. bihebdomadaire.

bizarre [bi'zɑ:r] a bizarre.

blab [blæb] (**blabbed**) **1.** vi (a) parler indiscrètement; F: vendre la mèche (b) F: jaser **2.** vtr **to b. out,** divulguer (un secret).

black [blæk] **1.** a (-er, -est) noir; **b. and blue,** meurtri; couvert de bleus; **b. eyes,** œil poché; **b. pudding,** boudin m; **b. magic,** magie noire; **(accident) b. spot,** point noir; **to give s.o. a b. look,** regarder qn d'un air furieux; **b. day,** jour sombre; **things are looking b.,** les affaires prennent une mauvaise tournure **2.** n (a) noir m; **to wear, be dressed in, b.,** porter du noir, être habillé de noir; **b.(-)and(-)white television,** téléviseur (en) noir et blanc; **I have his consent in b. and white,** j'ai son consentement par écrit (b) (pers) Noir, -e (c) **in the b.,** (of bank account) (of pers) solvable **3.** vtr (a) noircir; cirer (des chaussures) (b) pocher (l'œil à qn) (c) Ind: boycotter. **'blackball** vtr blackbouler. **'blackberry** n mûre f; **b. bush,** ronce f, mûrier m. **'blackbird** n merle m. **'blackboard** n tableau noir. **'blackcurrant** n cassis m. **'blacken** vtr noircir. **'blackfly** n mouche noire. **'blackhead** n (on skin) point noir. **'blackleg** n Ind: (NAm: = scab) jaune m. **'blacklist 1.** n liste noire **2.** vtr mettre sur la liste noire. **'blackmail 1.** n chantage m **2.** vtr faire chanter (qn). **'blackmailer** n maître-chanteur m. **'blackness** n noirceur f; obscurité f. **'blackout** n (a) (during war) black-out m (b) panne f d'électricité (c) (of pers) évanouissement m (d) black-out (sur une nouvelle). **'black 'out 1.** vtr faire le black-out dans (une maison) **2.** vi s'évanouir. **'blacksmith** n forgeron m; maréchal-ferrant m.

bladder ['blædər] n vessie f; vésicule f.

blade [bleid] n **1.** brin m (d'herbe) **2.** lame f (de couteau); couperet m (de guillotine) **3.** pale f (d'aviron, d'hélice); fer m (de bêche).

blame [bleim] **1.** n (a) responsabilité f; faute f; **to put the b. for sth on s.o.,** rejeter sur qn la responsabilité de qch (b) blâme m; reproche(s) m(pl) **2.** vtr (a) **to b. s.o. for sth, b. sth on s.o.,** rejeter sur qn la responsabilité de qch; **he's to b.,** c'est (de) sa faute; **you've only yourself to b.,** vous l'avez voulu; **to b. sth for an accident,** attribuer un accident à qch (b) **to b. s.o. for sth,** reprocher qch à qn, blâmer qn de qch; **I'm in no way to b.,** je n'ai rien à me reprocher. **'blameless** a irréprochable. **'blameworthy** a blâmable.

blanch [blɑ:ntʃ] **1.** vtr blanchir (des légumes); monder (des amandes). **2.** vi (of pers) blêmir, pâlir.

blancmange [blə'mɔnʒ] n Cu: blanc-manger m.

bland [blænd] a doux; (of pers) affable.

blandishments ['blændiʃmənts] npl flatteries fpl.

blank [blæŋk] **1.** a (-er, -est) (a) blanc; (chèque) en blanc; (mur) aveugle; (cartouche) à blanc; **b. space,** espace vide; blanc m; **b. verse,** vers blancs (b) (regard) sans expression; (existence) vide; **my mind went b.,** je me sentais la tête vide; **to look b.,** avoir l'air ahuri, déconcerté (c) (découragement) profond; (refus) absolu **2.** n (a) blanc; (espace m) vide m; trou m (de mémoire); **to leave blanks,** laisser des blancs; **my mind's a b.,** j'ai la tête vide (b) cartouche f à blanc (c) esp NAm: (Br = form) formulaire m, formule f; Fig: **to draw a b.,** échouer, faire chou blanc. **'blankly** adv (regarder) (i) d'un air ahuri (ii) sans expression.

blanket ['blæŋkit] n couverture f; couche f (de neige); nappe f (de brume); **electric b.,** couverture chauffante; **b. agreement,** accord général.

blare ['blɛər] **1.** n son (éclatant) **2.** vi (of trumpet) sonner; (of music) retentir. **'blare 'out** vtr & i (faire) retentir.

blarney ['blɑ:ni] n cajolerie f, boniments mpl.

blasé ['blɑ:zei] a blasé.

blaspheme [blæs'fi:m] vi & tr blasphémer. **blas'phemer** n blasphémateur, -trice; **'blasphemous** [-fəməs] a (of pers) blasphémateur; (of words) blasphématoire. **'blasphemously** adv avec impiété. **'blasphemy** [-fəmi] n blasphème m.

blast [blɑ:st] **1.** n (a) coup m de vent; rafale f; jet m (de vapeur) (b) **b. on the whistle, on the siren,** coup de sifflet, de sirène; **(at) full b.,** en pleine activité; (travailler) d'arrache-pied (c) souffle m (d'une explosion); explosion **2.** vtr (a) faire sauter (b) ruiner, détruire (des espérances) **3.** int F: **b. (it)!** flûte (alors)! **'blasted** a F: sacré. **'blasting** n Min: travail m aux explosifs; PN: **beware of b.!** attention aux coups de mine! **'blast-off** n décollage m (d'une fusée). **'blast 'off** vi Space: décoller.

blatant ['bleitənt] a (mensonge) flagrant; (mépris) criant.

blaze¹ [bleiz] **1.** n (a) flamme(s) f(pl); flambée f; feu m; flamboiement m (du soleil); éclat m (de couleurs, de colère) (b) F: **to run like blazes,** courir comme un dératé; **go to blazes!** allez au diable! **2.** vi (of fire) flamber; (of sun) flamboyer; (of jewels) étinceler. **'blazing** a (a) en feu; enflammé; (feu) ardent; (soleil) flambant (b) F: (of pers) **b. row,** dispute violente.

blaze² vtr **to b. a trail,** frayer un chemin.

blazer ['bleizər] n Cl: blazer m.

bleach [bli:tʃ] **1.** n décolorant m; **(household) b.,** (eau f de) javel f **2.** vtr blanchir; décolorer; (s')oxygéner (les cheveux).

bleak [bli:k] a (-er, -est) (a) (terrain) exposé au vent (b) (temps) triste et froid; (vent) glacial (c) (avenir) morne; (sourire) pâle, glacé. **'bleakly** adv d'un air morne; tristement.

bleary ['bliəri] a (of eyes) trouble, larmoyant, chassieux. **'bleary-eyed** a aux yeux troubles, larmoyants, chassieux.

bleat [bli:t] **1.** n bêlement m **2.** vi (a) bêler (b) F: se plaindre (**about,** de).

bleed [bli:d] v (**bled**) **1.** vtr saigner; **to b. s.o. white,** saigner qn à blanc. **2.** v.i. saigner; perdre du sang; **his nose is bleeding,** il saigne du nez. **'bleeding 1.** a saignant **2.** n écoulement m de sang; saignement m (de nez).

bleep [bli:p] **1.** n bip(-bip) m **2.** (a) vi faire bip (b) *vtr* **to b. s.o.**, rechercher qn par dispositif d'appel. **'bleeper** *n* récepteur d'appel, de poche.

blemish ['blemiʃ] *n* tache *f*; défaut *m*; (*on reputation*) tare *f*, souillure *f*.

blend [blend] **1.** *n* mélange *m*; coupage *m* (de vins); alliance *f* (de qualités); fusion *f* (d'idées) **2.** *v* (*a*) *vtr* mélanger (**with**, à, avec); joindre (**with**, à); couper (des vins); allier, marier, fondre (des couleurs) (*b*) *vi* se mélanger (**with**, à, avec); se (con)fondre (**into**, en); (*of colours*) s'allier, se marier (**with**, a); (*of parties*) fusionner. **'blender** *n* DomEc: mixeur *m*. **'blend 'in 1.** *vtr* mélanger (du beurre) **2.** *vi* (*of colours*) s'allier, se marier (**with**, à).

bless [bles] *vtr* bénir; **to be blessed with good health**, jouir d'une bonne santé; **b. my soul!** mon Dieu! **well, I'm blessed!** par exemple! **b. you!** (i) que Dieu vous bénisse! (ii) (*when s.o. sneezes*) à vos souhaits! **blessed** ['blesid] *a* (*a*) (martyr) bienheureux; **the B. Virgin**, la Sainte Vierge (*b*) *F:* fichu (contretemps); **the whole b. day**, toute la sainte journée; **every b. day**, tous les jours que Dieu fait. **'blessing** *n* (*a*) bénédiction *f*; *pl* grâces *fpl* (de Dieu) (*b*) *usu pl* avantages *mpl*, bienfaits *mpl* (de la civilisation); **b. in disguise**, bienfait inattendu.

blew [blu:] *see* **blow**[1]

blight [blait] **1.** *n* (*a*) (*on plants*) rouille *f*; (*on cereals*) charbon *m*; (*on trees*) cloque *f* (*b*) influence *f* néfaste; fléau *m* **2.** *vtr* rouiller (des plantes); flétrir (des espérances). **'blighter** *n* F: individu *m*, type *m*; **lucky b.!** veinard, -arde!

blimey ['blaimi] *int* P: mince alors!

blind[1] [blaind] **1.** *a* (*a*) aveugle; **b. man, woman**, aveugle *mf*; **b. man's buff**, colin-maillard *m*; **b. in one eye**, borgne; **b. as a bat**, myope comme une taupe; **to turn a b. eye to sth**, fermer les yeux sur qch; **to be b. to sth**, ne pas voir qch (*b*) (virage) masqué; **b. spot**, (i) *Aut: etc:* angle mort (ii) *Fig:* côté faible; **b. alley**, impasse *f*; *F:* **b. date**, rendez-vous avec qn qu'on ne connaît pas; *F:* **he didn't take a b. bit of notice**, il n'a pas fait la moindre attention (*c*) *Av:* (vol) sans visibilité **2.** *n* **the b.**, les aveugles *m*; **it's (a case of) the b. leading the b.**, c'est un aveugle qui en conduit un autre **3.** *adv* (*a*) *Av:* (voler) sans visibilité (*b*) *F:* **b. drunk**, soûl, bourré **4.** *vtr* aveugler. **'blindfold 1.** *n* bandeau *m* **2.** *vtr* bander les yeux à, de (qn) **3.** *a* & *adv* les yeux bandés. **'blinding** *a* aveuglant; (mal de tête) fou. **'blindly** *adv* aveuglément; en aveugle; à l'aveuglette. **'blindness** *n* (*a*) cécité *f* (*b*) *Fig:* aveuglement *m*; **b. to sth**, refus *m* de reconnaître qch.

blind[2] *n* **1.** store *m*; **roller b.**, store sur rouleau; **Venetian b.**, store vénitien. **2.** masque *m*, feinte *f*.

blink [blink] **1.** *n* (*a*) clign(ot)ement *m* (des yeux) (*b*) F: (*of TV, machine*) **on the b.**, qui fait des siennes **2.** *vi* & *tr* **to b.** (one's eyes), clign(ot)er (des yeux). **'blinkers** *npl* œillères *fpl*. **'blinking** *a* F: sacré; **b. idiot!** espèce d'idiot!

blip [blip] *n* Rad: spot *m* (sur l'écran); top *m* d'écho.

bliss [blis] *n* béatitude *f*, félicité *f*. **'blissful** *a* (bien)-heureux; **b. days**, jours sereins. **'blissfully** *adv* **b. happy**, au comble du bonheur.

blister ['blistər] **1** *n* (*on skin*) ampoule *f*, cloque *f*; (*on paint*) boursouflure *f* **2.** *v* (*a*) *vtr* faire venir une ampoule à (la peau); boursoufler (la peinture) (*b*) *vi*

(*of skin*) se couvrir d'ampoules; (*of paint*) se boursoufler, cloquer.

blithe [blaið] *a* joyeux, allègre. **blithely** *adv* joyeusement, allègrement.

blithering ['bliðəriŋ] *a* F: sacré.

blitz [blits] **1.** *n* bombardement *m* aérien; *Hist:* blitz *m*; *F:* **to have a b. on sth**, s'attaquer à qch **2.** *vtr* bombarder.

blizzard ['blizəd] *n* tempête *f* de neige.

bloated ['bloutid] *a* boursouflé, gonflé, bouffi; (*from overeating*) gavé.

bloater ['bloutər] *n* (hareng) bouffi.

blob [blɔb] *n* tache *f*; pâté *m* (d'encre).

bloc [blɔk] *n* Pol: bloc *m*.

block [blɔk] **1.** *n* (*a*) bloc *m* (de pierre); bille *f*, tronçon *m* (de bois); tablette *f* (de chocolat); billot *m* (de boucher); Toy: cube *m*; P: **to knock s.o.'s b. off**, casser la gueule à qn; **in b. letters, capitals**, en majuscules d'imprimerie (*b*) pâté *m* (de maisons); **b. of flats**, immeuble *m* (d'appartements); **office b.**, immeuble de bureaux; **school b.**, groupe *m* scolaire; *NAm:* **two blocks away**, à deux rues d'ici (*c*) *Austr:* lot *m* (de terrains) (*d*) *Fin:* tranche *f* (d'actions); **b. booking**, location (de places) en bloc (*e*) encombrement *m*, embouteillage *m*; (*in pipe*) obstruction *f*; *Psy:* blocage (mental) (*f*) **b. and tackle**, palan *m* **2.** *vtr* bloquer, obstruer; boucher (un tuyau); gêner (la circulation); *PN:* **road blocked**, rue barrée; **to b. s.o.'s way**, barrer le passage à qn. **blo'ckade 1.** *n* blocus *m* **2.** *vtr* bloquer (un port). **'blockage** *n* obstruction *f* (d'un tuyau); embouteillage (dans une rue). **'blockbuster** *n* F: spectacle *m*, livre *m*, etc, à grand succès. **'blockhead** *n* F: idiot, -ote. **'block 'in, 'out** *vtr* ébaucher (un projet). **'block 'up** *vtr* bloquer, obstruer; boucher (un tuyau); murer, condamner (une porte).

bloke [blouk] *n* F: type *m*.

blond, f blonde [blɔnd] *a* & *n* blond, -e.

blood [blʌd] *n* sang *m*; **it makes my b. boil, run cold**, cela me fait bouillir, me fige, me glace, le sang; **bad b.**, animosité *f*, rancune *f*; *Equ:* **new b.**, sang frais; **b. money**, prix du sang; **b. sports**, la chasse; **b. blister**, pinçon *m*; **b. orange**, (orange) sanguine *f*; **b. pressure**, tension artérielle; **to have high, low, b. pressure**, faire de l'hypertension, de l'hypotension; **b. vessel**, vaisseau sanguin; **b. donor**, donneur, -euse, de sang; **b. group**, groupe sanguin; **it's, it runs, in the b.**, il a cela dans le sang; **blue b.**, sang bleu, noble; **b. is thicker than water**, nous sommes unis par la force du sang. **'bloodbath** *n* carnage *m*. **'bloodcurdling** *a* qui vous fige le sang. **'bloodhound** *n* limier *m*. **'bloodless** *a* (*a*) anémié (*b*) (victoire) sans effusion de sang. **'blood-'red** *a* rouge sang *inv*. **'bloodshed** *n* effusion *f* de sang. **'bloodshot** *a* (œil) injecté de sang; (*of eye*) **to become b.**, s'injecter. **'bloodstain** *n* tache *f* de sang. **'bloodstained** *a* taché de sang; ensanglanté. **'bloodstock** *n* (chevaux *mpl*) pur-sang *m inv*. **'bloodstream** *n* sang *m*. **'bloodthirsty** *a* sanguinaire. **'bloody 1.** *a* (**-ier, -iest**) taché de sang; ensanglanté; (combat) sanglant; (nez) en sang **2.** *P:* (*a*) *a* sacré (menteur) (*b*) *adv* vachement; **what b. awful weather!** quel fichu temps! **it's a b. nuisance!** c'est drôlement emmerdant! **bloody-'minded** *a* *P:* vache; **he's b.-m.**, c'est un mauvais coucheur.

bloom [blu:m] 1. n (a) fleur f; **in (full) b.**, éclos, épanoui; en pleine fleur; en pleine floraison (b) velouté m, duvet m (d'un fruit) 2. vi fleurir, être en fleur. **'bloomer** n F: gaffe f. **'bloomers** npl Cl: culotte bouffante. **'blooming** a (a) en fleur (b) (of pers) florissant; resplendissant (with, de) (c) F: sacré, fichu.

blossom ['blɔsəm] 1. n fleur(s) f(pl); **orange b.**, fleur d'oranger 2. vi fleurir; **to b. (out)**, s'épanouir.

blot [blɔt] 1. n tache f; pâté m (d'encre) 2. vtr (blotted) (a) tacher; (of ink) faire des pâtés sur (qch); F: **to b. one's copybook**, ternir sa réputation (b) sécher (l'encre, la page). **'blot 'out** vtr (a) effacer (un souvenir) (b) (of fog) masquer (l'horizon). **'blotter** n (a) buvard m (b) NAm: registre m. **'blotting 'paper** n (papier) buvard.

blotch [blɔtʃ] n (pl blotches) tache f. **'blotchy** a (teint) couperosé, couvert de rougeurs.

blotto ['blɔtou] a F: soûl, bourré.

blouse [blauz] n Cl: chemisier m; corsage m.

blow¹ [blou] v (blew [blu:]; blown) 1 vi (a) (of wind) souffler; **the wind's blowing**, il fait du vent; **it's blowing a gale**, le vent souffle en tempête; **the door blew open**, le vent a ouvert la porte; **to b. on one's fingers**, souffler dans, sur, ses doigts (b) (of horn) sonner; **a whistle blew**, il y a eu un coup de sifflet (c) (of fuse) sauter; (of lightbulb) être grillé 2. vtr (a) (of wind) chasser (la pluie); pousser (un navire) (b) envoyer (un baiser); **to b. one's nose**, se moucher (c) donner un coup de (sifflet); jouer, sonner, de (la trompette); F: **to b. one's own trumpet**, chanter ses propres louanges (d) faire (des bulles); souffler (le verre) (e) faire sauter (un plomb); griller (une lampe); F: **to b. one's top**, sortir de ses gonds (f) F: gaspiller (de l'argent); louper (une occasion) (g) F: **b. him, the expense!** tant pis pour toi, pour la dépense! **b. it!** flûte (alors)! **'blow a'way** 1. vtr (of wind) chasser (les nuages); emporter (des papiers) 2. vi (of papers) s'envoler. **'blow 'down** 1. vtr (of wind) abattre, renverser (un arbre) 2. vi (of tree) être abattu par le vent. **'blow-dry** 1. vtr (blow-dried) **to b.-d. s.o.'s hair**, faire un brushing à qn. 2. n brushing m. **blowed** a F: well, **I'm b.!** ça, par exemple! **'blower** n F: téléphone m. **'blowfly** n mouche f à viande. **'blowhole** n évent m (de baleine). **'blow 'in** vi F: arriver à l'improviste. **'blowlamp** n (NAm: = blowtorch) lampe f à souder; chalumeau m. **'blow 'off** 1. vtr souffler (la poussière); (of wind) emporter (un chapeau) 2. vi (of hat) s'envoler. **'blow 'out** 1. vtr (a) souffler, éteindre (une bougie) (b) gonfler (les joues) (c) **to b. s.o.'s brains o.**, brûler la cervelle à qn 2. vi (of candle) s'éteindre; (of tyre) éclater; (of paper) s'envoler (of the window, par la fenêtre). **'blow-out** n (a) éclatement m (de pneu) (b) P: gueuleton m. **'blow 'over** (a) vi & tr (se) renverser (b) vi (of storm) se calmer; (of scandal) passer. **'blowtorch** n NAm: = blowlamp. **'blow 'up** 1. vi (explode) sauter, exploser, éclater; (of pers) éclater (de colère) 2. vtr (a) faire sauter, faire exploser (b) gonfler (un pneu) (c) agrandir (une photo); exagérer (un événement). **'blow-up** n Phot: agrandissement m. **'blowy** a venteux.

blow² n coup m; (with fist) coup de poing; **at, with,**

one **b.**, du premier coup; **to come to blows**, en venir aux mains. **'blow-by-blow** a (récit) détaillé.

blowzy ['blauzi] a F: (of woman) vulgaire; débraillé.

blubber¹ ['blʌbər] 1. n graisse f de baleine 2. vi pleurer bruyamment.

bludgeon ['blʌdʒən] 1. n matraque f 2. vtr matraquer (qn). **'bludgeon 'into** vtr forcer (qn) (doing, à faire).

blue [blu:] 1. a (a) bleu; Med: **b. baby**, enfant bleu; F: **to feel b.**, avoir le cafard; F: **I've told you till I'm b. in the face**, je me tue à te le dire (b) (plaisanterie) obscène; (film) porno 2. n (a) bleu m; **out of the b.**, (événement) imprévu; (arriver) à l'improviste (b) **the blues** (i) Mus: le blues (ii) F: le cafard 3. vtr F: gaspiller (de l'argent). **'bluebell** n jacinthe f des bois. **'blueberry** n Bot: airelle f, myrtille f. **'bluebottle** n mouche f à viande. **'blue-eyed** a aux yeux bleus; F: **b.-e. boy**, petit chou-chou. **'blueprint** n plan (détaillé). **'bluestocking** n (woman) bas-bleu m.

bluff¹ [blʌf] 1. a (a) (of cliff) escarpé, à pic (b) (of pers) carré; brusque; un peu bourru 2. n cap m à pic; à-pic m.

bluff² 1. n bluff m; **to call s.o.'s b.**, relever le défi de qn 2. vtr & i bluffer.

blunder ['blʌndər] 1. n bévue f, gaffe f 2. vi (a) faire une bévue, une gaffe (b) **to b. into s.o.**, se heurter contre qn; **to b. through**, s'en tirer tant bien que mal. **'blundering** a maladroit.

blunt [blʌnt] 1. a (-er, -est) (a) (couteau) émoussé; (instrument) épointé (b) (of pers) brusque, carré; (fait) brutal 2. vtr émousser (un couteau); épointer (une aiguille). **'bluntly** adv brusquement, carrément; brutalement. **'bluntness** n 1. manque m de tranchant (d'un couteau) 2. brusquerie f; franc-parler m.

blur [blə:r] 1. n brouillard m, flou m 2. vtr (blurred) brouiller, troubler, estomper; **eyes blurred with tears**, yeux voilés de larmes.

blurb [blə:b] n baratin m publicitaire.

blurt [blə:t] vtr **to b. out**, lâcher, laisser échapper (un mot, un secret).

blush [blʌʃ] 1. n (pl blushes) rougeur f (de honte) 2. vi rougir. **'blusher** n rouge m (à joues). **'blushing** a rougissant.

bluster ['blʌstər] vi (a) (of wind) souffler en rafales; (b) (of pers) parler haut et sans ménagement; fulminer. **'blustery** a (jour) de grand vent; (vent) violent.

BO abbr body odour, odeur corporelle.

boa ['bouə] n Z: boa m.

boar [bɔ:r] n Z: verrat m; **wild b.**, sanglier m.

board [bɔ:d] 1. n (a) planche f; **across the b.**, pour tout le monde; général (b) carton m (c) tableau m (de jeu) (d) nourriture f, pension f; **full b.**, pension complète; **b. and lodging**, bed and b., chambre f avec pension; le vivre et le couvert; **with b. and lodging**, logé et nourri (e) **b. of inquiry**, commission f d'enquête; **b. of examiners**, jury m (d'examen); Com: **b. (of directors)**, conseil m d'administration f; **b. meeting**, réunion du conseil (f) Nau: Av: **on b.**, à bord; **to go on b.**, monter à bord; (of plans) **to go by the b.**, être abandonné 2. v (a) vi être en pension (with, chez) (b) vtr (i) couvrir (une fenêtre) de planches (ii) monter à bord d'(un navire, un avion); monter dans (un train, un autobus). **'boarder** n pensionnaire mf; Sch: interne mf. **'boarding** n b. **card,** carte d'embarquement; b. **house,** pension (de famille); b. **school,** pensionnat m, internat m. **'boardroom** n salle f de réunion (du conseil d'administration). **'boardwalk** n NAm: chemin formé de planches.

boast [boust] 1. n vantardise f 2. v (a) vi se vanter (**about, of,** de); **that's nothing to b. about,** il n'y a pas là de quoi être fier; **without wishing to b.,** sans vanité (b) vtr (être fier de) posséder. **'boaster** n vantard, -arde. **'boastful** a vantard. **'boastfulness,** **'boasting** n vantardise.

boat [bout] n (a) bateau m; canot m; barque f (de pêcheur); embarcation f; navire m; **by b.,** en bateau; **to go by b.,** prendre le bateau; **to be all in the same** b., être tous dans le même cas; b. **builder,** constructeur de canots, de bateaux; b. **race,** course à l'aviron; b. **train,** train du bateau (b) **gravy, sauce,** b., saucière f. **'boater** n (hat) canotier m. **'boat-hook** n gaffe f. **'boathouse** n hangar m à bateaux. **'boating** n canotage m. **'boatswain** ['bousn] n maître m d'équipage.

bob[1] [bob] n (a) coiffure f à la Jeanne d'Arc (b) b.(**sleigh**), b.(**sled**), bob(sleigh) m.

bob[2] vi (**bobbed**) s'agiter; **to b. up,** surgir brusquement; revenir à la surface; **to b. up and down in the water,** danser sur l'eau.

bob[3] n F: A: shilling m.

bobbin ['bobin] n bobine f.

bobby ['bobi] n F: agent m de police, flic m; NAm: b. **pin** (Br = **hairgrip**), pince f à cheveux.

bodice ['bodis] n corsage m (d'une robe).

body ['bodi] n (pl **bodies**) (a) corps m; (**dead**) b., cadavre m; **over my dead b.!** à mon corps défendant! **main b.,** gros m (d'une armée); **legislative b.,** corps législatif; **public b.,** corporation f; **large b. of people,** foule nombreuse; **to come in a b.,** venir en masse (b) carrosserie f (de voiture); fuselage m (d'avion); corps (de bâtiment, de document); nerf f (d'église). **'bodily** 1. a corporel (besoin) matériel; (douleur) physique 2. adv à bras-le-corps. **'bodybuilding** n culturisme m. **'bodyguard** n garde(s) m(pl) du corps. **'bodywork** n Aut: carrosserie.

boffin ['bofin] n F: savant m; inventeur m scientifique.

bog [bog] 1. n (a) fondrière f; marécage m; (peat) tourbière f (b) P: cabinets mpl. **'bog 'down** vtr **to get bogged d.,** s'embourber, s'enliser. **'boggy** a marécageux; tourbeux.

bogey ['bougi] n 1. spectre m; épouvantail m 2. Golf: un coup au-dessus de la normale. **'bogeyman** n croque-mitaine m.

boggle ['bogl] vi rechigner (**at sth,** devant qch.; **at doing sth,** à faire qch); **the mind boggles,** cela confond l'imagination.

bogie ['bougi] n Rail: bog(g)ie m.

bogus ['bougas] a faux, f fausse; feint, simulé.

boil[1] [boil] n Med: furoncle m.

boil[2] 1. n (of water) **to come to, to go off, the b.,** commencer à, cesser de, bouillir; **to bring to the b.,** faire bouillir; amener à ébullition; **to be on, off, the b.,** bouillir, ne plus bouillir 2. v (a) vi bouillir; (violently) bouillonner; **to b. fast, gently,** bouillir à gros,

à petits, bouillons; **the pan has, the potatoes have, boiled dry,** l'eau de la casserole, des pommes de terre, s'est complètement évaporée (b) vtr faire bouillir; (faire) cuire à l'eau; **boiled water,** eau bouillie; **boiled egg,** œuf à la coque. **'boil a'way** vi s'évaporer. **'boil 'down** 1. vtr faire réduire (une sauce); condenser (un récit) 2. vi (a) (of food) réduire (b) F: se résumer, revenir (to, à). **'boiler** n chaudière f; b. **suit,** bleu(s) m(pl) de chauffe. **'boiling** 1. n b. **point,** point d'ébullition 2. a bouillant 3. a & adv F: b. (**hot**), tout bouillant; **it's b. (hot) in there!** on cuit là-dedans! **'boil 'over** vi déborder; (of milk) se sauver. **'boil 'up** 1. vtr faire bouillir (du potage) 2. vi (of trouble) surgir, monter.

boisterous ['boistərəs] a bruyant, turbulent; tapageur; (temps) violent. **'boisterously** adv bruyamment.

bold [bould] a (-**er,** -**est**) (a) hardi; audacieux; (regard) confiant (b) impudent; effronté; **as b. as brass,** d'un air effronté (c) (style) hardi; (trait) accusé; (contour) net; (dessin) vigoureux; (coloris) vif; puissant (relief); Typ: (caractère) gras. **'boldly** adv (a) hardiment; audacieusement; (affirmer) avec confiance (b) effrontément (c) (peindre) avec hardiesse; (se détacher) nettement. **'boldness** n (a) hardiesse f; audace f (b) effronterie f (c) hardiesse (de style); netteté f (d'un trait); vigueur f (d'un dessin); vivacité f (d'un coloris).

bollard ['bolɑːd] n borne f.

bollocks ['boləks] npl V: see **ball**[1] 2.

Bolshevik ['bolʃəvik] a & n bolchevik (mf). **'bolshie, -y** a F: vache; **he's very b.,** c'est un mauvais coucheur.

bolster ['boulstər] n traversin m. **'bolster ('up)** vtr soutenir.

bolt [boult] I. n 1. éclair m; coup m de foudre; Fig: b. **from the blue,** événement imprévu; coup de tonnerre 2. verrou m (de porte); pêne m (de serrure); culasse f mobile (de fusil) 3. (fastener) boulon m; cheville f 4. fuite f; **to make a b. for,** s'élancer, se précipiter, vers; **to make a b. for it,** décamper, filer. II. v 1. vi (of pers) décamper; (of horse) s'emballer 2. vtr (a) verrouiller (une porte) (b) boulonner, cheviller (c) gober, bouffer (son dîner). III. adv b. **upright,** tout droit; droit comme un piquet.

bomb [bom] 1. n bombe f; **atom b.,** bombe atomique; **letter, car, parcel, b.,** lettre, voiture, piégée; paquet piégé; b. **disposal,** désamorçage m (et enlèvement m de bombes non éclatées); F: **to go like a b.,** (i) (of car) rouler à toute vitesse; gazer (ii) marcher à merveille; F: **to cost a b.,** coûter les yeux de la tête 2. vtr bombarder. **bom'bard** vtr bombarder. **bom'-bardment** n bombardement m. **'bomber** n (a) (aircraft) bombardier m (b) (pers) plastiqueur m. **'bombing** n bombardement m; plasticage m. **'bombproof** a (abri) blindé. **'bombshell** n Fig: coup m de tonnerre. **'bombsite** n terrain m vague (où une bombe a rasé les bâtiments).

bombastic [bom'bæstik] a grandiloquent.

bona fide [bouna'faidi] a & adv de bonne foi; (of offer) sérieux. **bona 'fides** n bonne foi.

bonanza [bə'nænzə] n filon m; mine f d'or.

bond [bond] 1. n (a) lien m; attache f (b) adhérence f (c) engagement m, contrat m (d) Fin: bon m; titre *m*; **premium b.**, bon à lots (*e*) *Com:* (*of goods*) **in b.**, à l'entrepôt **2.** *vtr* coller; liaisonner (des pierres). **'bondage** *n* esclavage *m*. **'bonded** *a* (marchandises) en dépôt; **b. warehouse**, entrepôt de la douane.

bone [boun] **1.** *n* (*a*) os *m*; arête *f* (de poisson); **off the b.**, (poulet) désossé, sans os; *Fig:* **frozen to the b.**, glacé jusqu'à la moelle (des os); **b. dry**, absolument sec; **b. idle, lazy**, paresseux comme une couleuvre; **I feel it in my bones**, j'en ai le pressentiment; **to make no bones about doing sth**, ne pas hésiter à faire qch; **b. of contention**, pomme *f* de discorde; *F:* **to have a b. to pick with s.o.**, se plaindre de qch à qn; **b. china**, porcelaine tendre (*b*) *pl* ossements *mpl* (de mort) **2.** *vtr* désosser (la viande); ôter les arêtes d'(un poisson). **'bonehead** *n P:* imbécile *mf*. **'boneless** *a* désossé, sans os; (poisson) sans arêtes. **'bonemeal** *n* engrais *m* (d'os). **'boneshaker** *n F:* vieille (i) bécane (ii) guimbarde. **'bony** *a* (-**ier**, -**iest**) (*a*) osseux (*b*) (*of pers, limb*) décharné (*c*) (*of meat*) plein d'os; (*of fish*) plein d'arêtes.

bonfire ['bɔnfaiər] *n* feu *m* (i) de joie (ii) de jardin.

bonkers ['bɔŋkəz] *a F:* fou, cinglé.

bonnet ['bɔnit] *n* (*a*) *Cl:* bonnet *m* (*b*) *Aut:* (*NAm:* = **hood**) capot *m*.

bonus ['bounəs] *n* (*pl* **bonuses**) prime *f*; gratification *f*; **cost of living b.**, indemnité *f* de vie chère; **noclaim(s) b.**, bonification *f* pour non-sinistre; *F:* bonus *m*.

boo [bu:] **1.** *int* hou! *F:* **he wouldn't say b. to a goose**, c'est un timide **2.** *n* huées *fpl* **3.** *vtr & i* huer. **'booing** *n* huées.

boob [bu:b] *F:* **1.** *n* (*a*) gaffe *f* (*b*) **boobs**, nénés *mpl* **2.** *vi* faire une gaffe.

booby ['bu:bi] *n* (*pl* **boobies**) *F:* nigaud, -aude; **b. prize**, prix décerné (par plaisanterie) au dernier, au perdant; **b. trap**, piège *m*. **'booby-trap** *vtr* (**booby-trapped**) piéger.

book [buk] **I. n 1.** livre *m*; *F:* bouquin *m*; carnet *m* (de notes, de billets); pochette *f* (d'allumettes); **school b.**, livre de classe; **exercise b.**, cahier *m*; (**tele**)-**phone b.**, annuaire *m* (du téléphone); **b. club**, club du livre; **b. learning**, connaissances livresques **2.** livret *m* (d'un opéra) **3.** registre *m*; **account b.**, livre de comptes; **to be in s.o.'s good, bad, books**, être bien, mal, vu de qn; **to bring s.o. to b. for sth**, forcer qn à rendre compte de qch; *esp Rac:* **to make a b.**, faire un livre. **II. v. 1.** *vtr* (*a*) inscrire, enregistrer (une commande) (*b*) *F:* (*of policeman*) donner une contravention, un procès-verbal, un P-V, à (qn) (*c*) retenir, réserver (une chambre); louer (une place); prendre (un billet); (*of hotel*) **fully booked**, complet; (*of pers*) **booked (up)**, pris **2.** *vi* (i) réserver (ii) prendre, une place, un billet. **'bookable** *a* qui peut être retenu, réservé. **'bookbinder** *n* relieur, -euse. **'bookbinding** *n* reliure *f*. **'bookcase** *n Furn:* bibliothèque *f*. **'bookie** *n F:* book(maker) *m*. **'book 'in 1.** *vtr* réserver une chambre à (qn) **2.** *vi* (*a*) prendre une chambre (*b*) (*on arrival*) s'inscrire (au registre). **'booking** *n* (*a*) enregistrement *m*, inscription *f* (*b*) *Th:* etc: réservation *f* (de places); **b. clerk**, employé, -ée, du guichet; **b. office**, guichet. **'bookish** *a* (*of pers*) studieux; (connaissance) liv-

resque. **'bookkeeper** *n* teneur *m* de livres. **'bookkeeping** *n* tenue *f* de(s) livres. *f*. **'booklet** *n* brochure *f*. **'bookmaker** *n* bookmaker. **'bookmark(er)** *n* signet *m*. **'bookmobile** *n* (*Br* = **mobile library**) *NAm:* bibliobus *m*. **'bookseller** *n* libraire *mf*. **'bookshelf**, *pl* -**shelves** *n* rayon *m* (de bibliothèque). **'bookshop** *n* (*NAm:* = **bookstore**) librairie *f*. **'bookstall**, **'bookstand** *n* (*a*) étalage *m* de livres (*b*) (*NAm:* = **newsstand**) kiosque *m* à journaux; bibliothèque *f* (de gare). **'bookstore** *n NAm:* = **bookshop**. **'bookworm** *n* liseur, -euse, acharné, -ée; *F:* bouquineur, -euse.

boom[1] [bu:m] *n* **1.** (*at harbour mouth*) barrage *m* **2.** bout-dehors *m* (de foc); flèche *f* (de grue); perche *f* (de microphone).

boom[2] **1.** *n* (*a*) grondement *m* (du canon); mugissement *m* (du vent); ronflement *m* (de l'orgue); bang *m* (supersonique) (*b*) *Com:* hausse *f* rapide; boom *m*; vague *f* de prospérité; **b. town**, ville en plein essor **2.** *vi* (*a*) gronder, mugir; (*of organ*) ronfler; (*of voice*) retentir (*b*) *Com:* être en hausse; (*of business*) bien marcher, être en plein essor. **'boom 'out 1.** *vtr* dire (qch) d'une voix retentissante **2.** *vi* retentir.

boomerang ['bu:məræŋ] **1.** *n* boomerang *m* **2.** *vi* faire boumerang.

boon [bu:n] **1.** *n* bienfait *m*, avantage *m* **2.** *a* **b. companion**, gai companion.

boor ['buər] *n* rustre *m*. **'boorish** *a* rustre, grossier. **'boorishly** *adv* en rustre; grossièrement. **'boorishness** *n* grossièreté *f*; manque *m* de savoir-vivre.

boost [bu:st] **1.** *n* **to give (s.o., sth) a b.** = **boost 2.** (*a*), (*b*), (*c*) **2.** *vtr* (*a*) soulever (qn) par derrière (*b*) relancer (une industrie); augmenter (la productivité); relever (le moral) (*c*) faire de la réclame pour (*d*) *El:* survolter. **'booster** *n* (*a*) *El:* survolteur *m* (*b*) *Med:* **b. (dose)**, (dose *f* de) rappel *m* (*c*) **b. (rocket)**, fusée *f* de démarrage.

boot [bu:t] **1.** *n* (*a*) (**ankle) b.**, bottine *f*; bottillon *m*; chaussure montante; (**knee) b.**, botte *f*; (**laced) b.**, brodequin *m*; **the b. is on the other foot**, c'est tout (juste) le contraire; *F:* **to get the b.**, être mis à la porte; *F:* **to put the b. in**, flanquer des coups de pied à qn (qui est déjà terrassé) (*b*) *Aut:* (*NAm:* = **trunk**) coffre *m* **2.** *vtr F:* (*a*) donner un coup de pied à (*b*) **to b. s.o. (out)**, mettre, flanquer, qn à la porte. **boo'tee** *n* chausson *m* (de bébé). **'bootlace** *n* lacet *m* (de chaussure).

booth [bu:ð] *n* baraque *f* (de marché); cabine *f* (téléphonique); **polling b.**, isoloir *m*.

booty ['bu:ti] *n* butin *m*.

booze [bu:z] **1.** *n* (*no pl*) *F:* boisson (alcoolisée); alcool *m*; **there's no b.**, il n'y a rien à boire **2.** *vi F:* boire; picoler. **'boozer** *n F:* (*a*) ivrogne *mf* (*b*) bistrot *m*. **'booze-up** *n F:* beuverie *f*. **'boozy** *a F:* (soirée) où l'on boit beaucoup.

boracic [bə'ræsik] *a* borique.

border ['bɔ:dər] **1.** *n* (*a*) bord *m* (d'un lac); lisière *f* (d'un bois); marge *f* (d'un chemin); frontière *f* (d'un pays); **b. town**, ville frontière (*b*) (*edging*) bordure *f* **2.** *vtr* border. **'bordering** *a* contigu, voisin, limitrophe. **'borderland** *n* pays frontière. **'borderline** *n* ligne *f* de séparation; limite(s) *f* (*pl*); **b. case,**

cas limite. 'border 'on (*also* u'pon) *vtr* toucher (à); être limitrophe, voisin, de; friser (la folie).

bore¹ [bɔːr] 1. *n* calibre *m* (d'un fusil, d'un tuyau) 2. *vtr & i* forer (un puits); percer, creuser (un trou); faire un sondage (pour trouver des minerais). 'bore-hole *n Min:* trou *m* de sonde.

bore² 1. *n* (*pers*) raseur, -euse; (*thg*) ennui *m*, corvée *f*; *F:* scie *f* 2. *vtr* ennuyer, *F:* raser, assommer (qn); **to be bored stiff, bored to tears,** s'ennuyer à mourir. 'boredom *n* ennui. 'boring *a* ennuyeux; *F:* rasant.

bore³ *n* (*in river*) mascaret *m*.

bore⁴ *see* bear².

born [bɔːn] *a* to be b., naître; **he was b. in 1950,** il est né en 1950; **b. in London,** né(e) à Londres; **French-b.,** français de naissance; **a Londoner b. and bred,** un vrai Londonien de Londres; **a b. poet,** un poète né; *F:* **a b. fool,** un parfait idiot; *F:* **I wasn't b. yesterday,** je ne suis pas né d'hier; *F:* **in all my b. days,** de toute ma vie.

borne [bɔːn] *see* bear².

borough ['bʌrə] *n* ville *f*; municipalité *f*.

borrow ['bɔrou] *vtr* emprunter (from, à). 'borrower *n* emprunteur, -euse. 'borrowing *n* emprunt *m*.

borstal ['bɔːstl] *n* maison *f* de redressement.

bos'n ['bousn] *n* = bosun.

bosom ['buzəm] *n* sein *m*; poitrine *f*; (*of woman*) seins *mpl*; **in the b. of,** au sein de; **b. friend,** ami intime.

boss¹ [bɔs] *F:* 1. *n* (*pl* bosses) patron, -onne; chef *m* 2. *vtr* mener, diriger. 'boss a'bout, a'round *vtr F:* mener (qn) par le bout du nez; régenter. 'bossy *a F:* autoritaire.

boss² *a F:* **to make a b. shot (at sth),** rater son coup. 'boss-eyed *a F:* qui louche.

bosun ['bousn] *n Nau:* maître *m* d'équipage.

botany ['bɔtəni] *n* botanique *f*. bo'tanical *a* botanique. 'botanist *n* botaniste *mf*.

botch [bɔtʃ] *vtr F:* to b. (up), (i) bousiller, saboter (un travail) (ii) rafistoler.

both [bouθ] 1. *a. & pron* tous (les) deux, toutes (les) deux; l'un(e) et l'autre; **b. (of them) are dead,** ils sont morts tous (les) deux; **to hold sth in b. hands,** tenir qch à deux mains; **on b. sides,** des deux côtés; **b. alike,** l'un comme l'autre 2. *adv* **b. you and I,** (et) vous et moi; **she b. attracts and repels me,** elle m'attire et me repousse à la fois.

bother ['bɔðər] 1. *v* (*a*) *vtr* gêner, ennuyer, déranger, tracasser, *F:* embêter (qn); **don't b. me!** laissez-moi tranquille! *F:* **I can't be bothered,** ça m'embête; *F:* **I can't be bothered to do it,** j'ai la flemme de le faire; *F:* **I'm not bothered (about it)!** ça m'est bien égal! **b. (it)!** zut (alors)! (*b*) *vi* s'inquiéter (about, de); s'occuper (with, de); se donner la peine (to do, de faire); **don't b. to bring a mac,** ce n'est pas la peine de prendre un imper 2. *n* ennui *m*; *F:* embêtement *m*.

bottle ['bɔtl] 1. *n* bouteille *f*; (*small*) flacon *m*; (*wide-mouthed*) bocal *m*; can(n)ette *f* (de bière); **(baby's) b.,** biberon *m*; **hot water b.,** bouillotte *f*; **b. opener,** ouvre-bouteille(s) *m*; décapsuleur *m*; **wine b.,** bouteille à vin; **b. of wine,** bouteille de vin; **b. party,** réunion où chacun apporte à boire; *F:* **to hit the b.,** (se mettre à) boire (beaucoup) 2. *vtr* mettre (du vin) en bouteilles; mettre (des fruits) en bocaux.

'bottlebrush *n* goupillon *m*. 'bottled *a* (vin) en bouteille; (bière) en can(n)ette; (fruits) en bocal. 'bottle-fed *a* nourri au biberon. 'bottle-green *a* vert bouteille. 'bottleneck *n* 1. goulot *m* (de bouteille) 2. (*a*) rétrécissement *m* de la chaussée (*b*) embouteillage *m*, bouchon *m* 3. (*in production*) goulot d'étranglement. 'bottle 'up *vtr* étouffer (ses sentiments); ravaler, refouler (sa colère). 'bottling *n* mise *f* en bouteille(s), en bocaux.

bottom ['bɔtəm] 1. *n* bas *m* (d'une colline, d'un escalier, d'une page); fond *m* (d'un puits, d'une boîte, de la mer); dessous *m* (d'un verre); (*of pers*) derrière *m*; **at the b. of the garden,** au fond du jardin; **at the b. of the page,** au, en, bas de la page; **at the b. of the list,** en fin de liste; **he's at the b. of the class,** c'est le dernier de la classe; **from the b. of one's heart,** du fond de son cœur; *Fig:* **to be at the b. of sth,** être (i) (*of pers*) l'instigateur (ii) la cause, de qch; **to knock the b. out of an argument,** démolir un argument; **the b. has fallen out of the market,** le marché s'est effondré; *P:* **bottoms up!** cul sec! 2. *a* du, en, bas; inférieur; *Aut:* **b. gear,** première vitesse. 'bottomless *a* sans fond; inépuisable. 'bottom 'out *vi* être au plus bas.

bough [bau] *n* branche *f*, rameau *m*.

bought [bɔːt] *see* buy².

boulder ['bouldər] *n* grosse pierre (roulée).

bounce [bauns] 1. *n* 1. rebond *m* (d'une balle); **on the b.,** au bond 2. (*of pers*) vitalité *f*, énergie *f*. II. *v* 1. *vi* (*a*) (*of ball*) rebondir (*b*) (*of pers.*) **to b. in,** entrer en coup de vent (*c*) *F:* (*of cheque*) être sans provision 2. *vtr* faire rebondir. 'bouncer *n F:* videur *m*. 'bouncing *a* (ballon) rebondissant; (bébé) resplendissant (de vie et de santé). 'bouncy *a* (balle) qui rebondit bien; (*of pers*) dynamique.

bound¹ 1. *n usu pl* limite(s) *f* (*pl*), bornes *fpl*; **out of bounds,** défendu (aux élèves); **to go beyond the bounds of reason,** dépasser les bornes de la raison; **to keep within bounds,** rester dans la juste mesure 2. *vtr* limiter, borner.

bound² 1. *n* bond *m*, saut *m* 2. *vi* bondir, sauter.

bound³ *see* bind 1. *a* 1. (*a*) lié (*b*) (livre) relié (*c*) **to be b. up with,** se relier à; (*of pers*) **to be b. up in sth,** se préoccuper de qch 2. (*a*) **to be b. to do sth,** être obligé, tenu, de faire qch; devoir faire qch; *F:* **I'll be b.!** j'en suis sûr! (*b*) **he's b. to come,** il ne peut pas manquer de venir; **it's b. to rain,** il pleuvra sûrement; **it's b. to happen,** c'est fatal.

bound⁴ *a* **b. for,** en partance, en route, pour; **b. for home, homeward b.,** sur le chemin du retour.

boundary ['baundəri] *n* (*pl* boundaries) limite *f*, bornes *fpl*; frontière *f*.

bounty ['baunti] *n* (*a*) générosité *f* (*b*) (*pl* bounties) gratification *f* (à un employé); prime *f*. 'bountiful *a* bienfaisant; généreux.

bouquet [bu'kei] *n* bouquet *m*.

bourbon ['bɔːbən] *n NAm:* whisky *m* de maïs.

bourgeois ['buəʒwaː] *a* bourgeois.

bout [baut] *n* (*a*) *Sp:* tour *m*, reprise *f*; *Box:* combat *m*; *Wr: Fenc:* assaut *m* (*b*) accès *m* (de fièvre); période *f* (d'activité).

boutique [buː'tiːk] *n* (*a*) boutique *f* (de modes) (*b*) (*in store*) rayon *m* (des jeunes).

bovine ['bouvain] **1.** *a* bovin **2.** *npl* Z: les bovins.

bow¹ [bou] *n* (*a*) arc *m*; **to have two strings to one's b.**, avoir deux cordes à son arc; **b. window**, fenêtre en saillie (*b*) Mus: archet *m* (de violon) (*c*) nœud *m* (de ruban); **b. tie**, nœud papillon. **'bow-legged** *a* bancal.

bow² [bau] **1.** *n* salut *m*; révérence *f*; inclination *f* de tête; **to take a b.**, saluer **2.** *v* (*a*) *vi* (*of performer*) saluer; **to b. (down)**, s'incliner (**to**, devant); baisser la tête; **to b. and scrape**, faire des salamalecs (*b*) *vtr* incliner, baisser (la tête); fléchir (le genou); courber, voûter (le dos). **'bow 'out** *vi* se retirer.

bow³ [bau] *n* (*often pl*) (*of ship*) avant *m*.

bowels ['bauəlz] *npl* intestins *mpl*; entrailles *fpl* (de la terre).

bowl¹ [boul] *n* (*for food*) bol *m*, coupe *f*; (*for washing*) bassine *f*, cuvette *f*.

bowl² [boul] **I.** *n* boule *f*; (*game of*) **bowls**, (i) (*outdoor*) (jeu *m* de) boules *fpl* (ii) (*indoor*) bowling *m*. **II.** *v* **1.** *vtr* (*a*) rouler, faire courir (un cerceau) (*b*) lancer, rouler (une boule) (*c*) Cr: (i) servir (la balle) (ii) renverser le guichet à (qn) **2.** *vi* (*a*) jouer aux boules, au bowling (*b*) Cr: servir la balle. **'bowl a'long** *vi* rouler rapidement. **'bowler** *n* (*a*) joueur, -euse, de boules, de bowling; Cr: lanceur, -euse (*b*) **b. (hat)**, (chapeau *m*) melon *m*. **'bowling** *n* (*outdoor*) (jeu de) boules; (*indoor*) bowling; **b. green**, terrain de boules; **b. alley**, bowling. **'bowl 'over** *vtr* (*a*) renverser (*b*) déconcerter, bouleverser (qn).

box¹ [bɔks] *n coll Bot:* buis *m*. **'boxwood** *n* (bois *m* de) buis.

box² **1.** *n* (*pl* boxes) (*a*) boîte *f*; (*large*) coffre *m*; (*small*) coffret *m*; (*large wooden*) caisse *f*; (*cardboard*) carton *m*; F: télé(vision) *f*; (*post office*) **b. number**, numéro de boîte postale; **b. office**, bureau de location; guichet *m*; Av: **black b.**, boîte noire (*b*) Th: loge *f* (*c*) (*for horse* (i) (*in stable*) box *m* (ii) Veh: van *m* (*d*) Jur: barre *f* (des témoins); banc *m* (des jurés) **2.** *vtr* mettre en boîte. **'box 'in** *vtr* enfermer. **'Boxing Day** *n* le lendemain de Noël. **'boxroom** *n* débarras *m*.

box³ **I.** *n* **b. on the ear**, gifle *f*. **II.** *v* **1.** *vtr* (*a*) boxer (qn) (*b*) **to b. s.o.'s ears**, gifler qn **2.** *vi* boxer, faire de la boxe. **'boxer** *n* (*a*) boxeur *m* (*b*) (*dog*) boxer *m*. **'boxing** *n* boxe; **b. gloves, match**, gants, match, de boxe.

boy [bɔi] *n* (*a*) garçon *m*; F: gamin *m*, gosse *m*; **an English b.**, un jeune Anglais; **when I was a b.**, quand j'étais petit; F: **my dear b.!** mon cher (ami)! *esp* NAm: F: **oh b.!** mince! (*b*) Sch: élève *m*; **old b.**, ancien élève (*c*) fils *m*. **'boyfriend** *n* petit ami. **'boyhood** *n* enfance *f*, adolescence *f*. **'boyish** *a* puéril, enfantin, d'enfant; gamin; (manières) de garçon.

boycott ['bɔikɔt] **1.** *vtr* boycotter **2.** *n* (*also* **'boycotting**) boycottage *m*.

BR *abbr* British Rail.

bra [brɑ:] *n* soutien-gorge *m*; (*strapless*) bustier *m*.

brace [breis] **1.** *n* (*a*) Const: etc: attache *f*, lien *m*; entretoise *f* (*b*) appareil *m* dentaire (*c*) *pl* Cl: (NAm: = **suspenders**) bretelles *fpl* (*d*) paire *f* (de perdrix, de faisans) (*e*) Tls: **b. (and bit)**, vilebrequin *m* **2.** *vtr* (*a*) ancrer (un mur); armer (une poutre) (*b*) appuyer (le pied), s'arc-bouter (du pied) (**against**, contre); **to**

b. oneself, b. up, se raidir; **b. yourself for the shock!** tiens-toi bien! prépare-toi à recevoir la nouvelle! **'bracing** *a* (air, climat) vivifiant, tonifiant.

bracelet ['breislit] *n* bracelet *m*.

bracken ['brækən] *n* fougère *f*.

bracket ['brækit] **1.** *n* (*a*) support *m*; Arch: corbeau *m*; (*b*) applique *f* (pour lampe) (*c*) Typ: etc: (*round*) parenthèse *f*; (*square*) crochet *m*; (*linking different lines*) accolade *f* (*d*) tranche *f* (de revenus) **2.** *vtr* (*a*) mettre entre parenthèses, entre crochets (*b*) réunir par une accolade (*c*) **to b. (together)**, relier, rapprocher.

brackish ['brækiʃ] *a* (*of water*) saumâtre.

bradawl ['brædɔːl] *n* Tls: poinçon *m*.

brag [bræg] *vi* (**bragged**) se vanter. **'bragging** **1.** *a* vantard **2.** *n* vantardise *f*.

braid [breid] **1.** *n* galon *m*, ganse *f*; **gold b.**, galon d'or (*b*) *esp* NAm: (Br = **plait**) tresse *f* **2.** *vtr esp* NAm: (Br = **plait**) tresser.

braille [breil] *n* braille *m*; **b. type**, caractères braille.

brain [brein] **1.** *n* (*a*) cerveau *m*; Anat: *usu pl* cervelle *f*; F: **to have an idea, a tune, on the b.**, être obsédé par une idée, un air; **he hasn't got much b.**, F: **a lot of brains**, il n'est pas très intelligent; **to rack, cudgel, one's brains**, se creuser la cervelle; **b. disease**, maladie cérébrale; **b. drain**, drainage des cerveaux; **brains**, NAm: **b., trust**, brain-trust *m* (*b*) F: (*pers*) cerveau **2.** *vtr* F: assommer (qn). **'brainchild** *n* idée originale. **'brainless** *a* stupide. **'brainstorm** *n* (*a*) Med: transport *m* au cerveau (*b*) NAm: = **brainwave**. **'brainwash** *vtr* faire un lavage de cerveau à (qn). **'brainwashing** *n* lavage de cerveau. **'brainwave** *n* F: (NAm: = **brainstorm**) idée *f* de génie. **'brainy** *a* (*-ier, -iest*) F: intelligent, calé.

braise [breiz] *vtr* Cu: braiser; cuire à l'étouffée; **braised beef**, bœuf en daube.

brake [breik] **1.** *n* frein *m*; **b. fluid**, liquide pour freins; **b. light**, stop *m* **2.** *vtr & i* freiner. **'braking** *n* freinage *m*; **b. distance**, distance de freinage, d'arrêt.

bramble ['bræmbl] *n* ronce *f*.

bran [bræn] *n* son *m*.

branch [brɑ:ntʃ] **1.** *n* (*pl* **branches**) (*a*) branche *f*; rameau *m*; (*of river*) bras *m*; (*of road, railway*) embranchement *m*; Rail: **b. line**, ligne d'embranchement (*b*) Com: **b. (office)**, succursale *f*, filiale *f* **2.** *vi* **to b. (off)**, se ramifier; (*of 'road*) bifurquer. **'branch out** *vi* étendre ses activités (**into**, à).

brand [brænd] **1.** *n* tison *m* (*b*) fer *m* à marquer (*c*) marque (faite avec un fer à marquer) (*d*) Com: marque (de fabrique); **b. image**, image de marque; **b. name**, nom de marque; **his own b. of humour**, un sens de l'humour bien à lui **2.** *vtr* (*a*) marquer (au fer chaud) (*b*) noter, stigmatiser (**as a liar**, comme menteur). **'branded** *a* (*a*) marqué à chaud (*b*) (produits) de marque. **'branding iron** *n* fer à marquer. **'brand-new** *a* tout (flambant) neuf.

brandish ['brændiʃ] *vtr* brandir.

brandy ['brændi] *n* cognac *m*; eau-de-vie *f* (de prunes, etc); **b. and soda**, fine *f* à l'eau.

brash [bræʃ] *a* effronté; exubérant.

brass [brɑ:s] *n coll* (*a*) cuivre *m* (jaune); laiton *m*; **b. plate**, plaque de cuivre; F: **b. hat**, officier d'état-major; F: **the top b.**, les grosses légumes; F: **to get down to b. tacks**, en venir aux faits (*b*) Mus: **the b.**, les cuivres; **b. band,** fanfare *f* (*c*) (*pl* **brasses**) (*in church*) plaque tombale en cuivre; **b. rubbing,** frottis d'une plaque tombale en cuivre (*d*) *P:* argent *m,* fric *m* (*e*) *P:* toupet *m,* culot *m.* **'brassy** *a* (*a*) cuivré (*b*) (*of pers*) effronté.

brassière ['bræziər] *n* soutien-gorge *m;* (*strapless*) bustier *m.*

brat [bræt] *n usu Pej:* gosse *mf,* mioche *mf.*

bravado [brə'vɑːdou] *n* bravade *f.*

brave [breiv] 1. *a* (-er, -est) courageux, brave 2. *vtr* braver; défier. **'bravely** *adv* courageusement. **'bravery** *n* courage *m.*

bravo [brɑː'vou] *int* bravo!

bravura [brə'vjuərə] *n* bravoure *f.*

brawl [brɔːl] 1. *n* rixe *f,* bagarre *f* 2. *vi* se bagarrer, se chamailler.

brawn [brɔːn] *n* (*a*) muscles *mpl* (*b*) *Cu:* fromage *m* de tête. **'brawny** *a* (-ier, -iest) (bras) musculeux; (*of pers*) musclé, *F:* costaud.

bray [brei] 1. *n* braiement *m* 2. *vi* braire.

brazen ['breizn] 1. *a* (*a*) *Lit:* d'airain (*b*) **b.(-faced),** effronté, impudent 2. *vtr* **to b. it out,** payer d'effronterie.

Brazil [brə'zil] *Prn Geog:* Brésil *m;* **B. nut,** noix du Brésil. **Bra'zilian** *a & n* brésilien, -ienne.

breach [briːtʃ] *n* (*pl* **breaches**) (*a*) infraction *f,* manquement *m* (au devoir); violation *f* (d'une loi); abus *m* (de confiance); rupture *f* (de contrat); **b. of the peace,** attentat *m* contre l'ordre public; **b. of promise,** violation de promesse de mariage·(*b*) brouille *f,* rupture (entre amis) (*c*) brèche *f* (dans un mur).

bread [bred] *n coll* (*a*) pain *m;* **b. and butter** (i) pain beurré (ii) *Fig:* gagne-pain *m;* **writing is his b. and butter,** il gagne sa croûte à écrire; **slice, piece, of b. and butter,** tartine beurrée, de beurre; **b. sauce,** sauce à la mie de pain; **he knows which side his b. is buttered,** il sait où est son avantage (*b*) *P:* argent *m,* galette *f.* **'bread-and-butter** *a* (lettre) de remerciement. **'breadbasket** *n* corbeille *f* à pain. **'breadbin** *n* boîte *f,* huche *f,* à pain. **'breadboard** *n* planche *f* à pain. **'breadcrumbs** *npl* miettes *fpl* de pain; *Cu:* chapelure *f.* **'breadknife, -knives** *n* couteau *m* à pain. **'breadline** *n* **on the b.,** sans argent, sur la paille. **'breadwinner** *n* soutien *m* de famille.

breadth [bredθ] *n* largeur *f;* **the wood is two metres in b.,** le bois a deux mètres de large.

break [breik] I. *n* (*a*) cassure *f,* brisure *f;* rupture *f;* fracture *f* (d'un os); trouée *f,* brèche *f* (dans une haie); éclaircie *f* (dans un ciel nuageux); *WTel: TV:* coupure *f,* interruption *f* (dans une émission); **b. in the weather,** changement *m* de temps; **b. of day,** point *m* du jour; *F:* **to make a b. for it,** s'évader (*b*) (moment *m* de) repos *m;* répit *m;* (*on journey*) arrêt *m; Sch:* (i) récréation *f* (entre les classes) (ii) vacances *fpl;* **coffee, tea, b.** = pause-café *f;* **lunch b.,** heure *f* du déjeuner; **an hour's b.,** un battement d'une heure; **without a b.,** sans relâche; *NAm:* **give me a b.!** arrête de m'embêter! (*c*) *F:* chance *f;* **to have a lucky b.,** avoir de la veine; **give me a b.,** laissez-moi essayer (encore une fois). II. *v* (**broke; broken**) 1. *vtr* (*a*) casser, briser, rompre; entamer (la peau); battre (un record); *Av:* franchir (le mur du son); *Ten:* gagner (le service de qn); **to b. one's arm,**

se casser le bras; **to b. open,** enfoncer (une porte); forcer (un coffre-fort); **to b. ranks, the ice, the silence, a charm,** rompre les rangs, la glace, le silence, un charme; **to b. new ground,** faire œuvre de pionnier; **to b. one's journey,** s'arrêter en route; interrompre son voyage; *Ind:* **to b. a strike,** briser un grève (*b*) dresser (un cheval); briser (qn, la résistance); abattre (le courage); ruiner (qn, la santé de qn); amortir (une chute); *Cards: etc:* faire sauter (la banque); **to b. s.o.'s heart,** briser le cœur à qn; to **b. s.o. of a habit,** corriger qn d'une habitude (*c*) violer, ne pas observer (une loi); manquer à (sa parole); rompre (un contrat) (*d*) apprendre (qch à qn); **to b. cover,** déboucher; **to b. wind,** lâcher un vent, *F:* péter 2. *vi* (*a*) (se) casser; se briser; se rompre; (*of wave*) déferler; (*of voice*) (i) (*at puberty*) muer (ii) (*with emotion*) s'altérer; (*of heart*) se briser; (*of weather*) changer; (*of clouds*) se disperser; (*of pers under interrogation*) s'effondrer; **to b. open,** s'ouvrir; **to b. even,** rentrer dans ses frais; **to b. with,** rompre avec (*b*) (*of day*) poindre; (*of storm, news*) éclater; **to b. free, loose,** se dégager; s'évader; s'affranchir. **'breakable** *a* cassable; fragile. **'breakables** *npl* objets *mpl* fragiles. **'breakage** *n* rupture; bris *m;* **to pay for breakages,** payer la casse. **'break a'way** 1. *vtr* détacher (**from,** de) 2. *vi* se détacher (**from,** de); s'échapper. **'breakaway** *n* abandon *m;* sécession *f;* **b. group,** groupe dissident, rebelle. **'break 'down** 1. *vtr* (*a*) abattre, démolir (un mur); défoncer, enfoncer (une porte); briser (la résistance); vaincre (toute opposition) (*b*) décomposer (une substance, une idée); faire le détail d'(un compte) 2. *vi* (*a*) (*of plan*) échouer; (*of argument, resistance*) s'effondrer (*b*) (*of pers*) (i) faire une dépression nerveuse (ii) ne plus pouvoir se contenir (iii) éclater en sanglots (*c*) (*of car, etc*) tomber en panne. **'breakdown** *n* (*a*) rupture (de négociations); arrêt complet (dans un service) (*b*) (**nervous**) **b.,** dépression nerveuse (*c*) (*of car, etc*) panne *f;* **b. truck,** dépanneuse *f;* **b. service,** service de dépannage (*d*) décomposition *f* (d'une substance, d'une idée); analyse *f* (d'un argument); répartition *f* (de la population par âge) **'breaker** *n* (*a*) brisant *m* (*b*) (*pers*) casseur, -euse; **to send a car to the b.'s (yard),** mettre une voiture à la casse. **'breakfast** 1. *n* petit déjeuner; **to have b.,** prendre le, son, petit déjeuner; **b. cup (and saucer),** déjeuner 2. *vi* prendre le, son, petit déjeuner. **'break 'in** 1. *vtr* (*a*) défoncer, enfoncer (une porte) (*b*) dresser (un cheval); accoutumer (qn) (**to,** à) 2. *vi* (*a*) intervenir; **to b. in on** (**s.o. a conversation**), interrompre (qn, une conversation) (*b*) (*of burglar*) s'introduire par effraction. **'break-in** *n* cambriolage *m;* effraction *f.* **'breaking** *n* bris; rupture; fracture (d'un os); interruption (d'un voyage); **at b. point,** (i) au point de rupture (ii) (*of s.o.'s patience*) à bout; *Jur:* **b. and entering,** (entrée *f* par) effraction. **'break 'into** *vtr* (*a*) s'introduire par effraction dans, cambrioler (une maison); forcer (une caisse) (*b*) interrompre (une conversation); **to b. into laughter,** éclater de rire; **to b. into song, into a trot,** se mettre à chanter, à trotter (*c*) entamer (des provisions, un billet de banque). **'breakneck** *a* **at b. speed,** à une vitesse folle. **'break 'off** 1. *vtr* (*a*) casser, rompre; détacher (*b*) interrompre, abandonner (son travail); rompre (des négociations, des fiançailles); **to b. off relations with s.o.**, rompre avec qn 2. *vi* (*a*) se détacher (net) (*b*) s'arrêter. 'break 'out *vi* (*a*) (*of war*) éclater; **to b. out in a sweat**, se mettre à suer; **to b. out in spots**, se couvrir de boutons (*b*) s'échapper, s'évader. 'breakout *n* évasion *f* (de prison). 'break 'through *vtr & i* enfoncer (une barrière); se frayer un chemin (à travers la foule); (*of sun*) percer (les nuages); (*of troops, science*) faire une percée (dans les défenses de l'ennemi, dans une barrière); *Av:* franchir (le mur du son). 'breakthrough *n* percée. 'break 'up 1. *vtr* mettre en morceaux; briser; démolir (un bâtiment); ameublir (le sol); désagréger (la surface d'une chaussée); démembrer (un empire); disperser (une foule); détruire (un mariage); rompre (une coalition); **to b. up a fight**, séparer les combattants 2. *vi* (*of ship, empire, group*) se disjoindre; (*of ice*) débâcler; (*of road surface*) se désagréger; (*of meeting*) se séparer; (*of crowd, clouds*) se disperser; (*of marriage*) s'en aller à vau-l'eau; (*of weather*) se gâter; *Sch:* **we b. up on the 4th**, les vacances commencent le 4. 'breakup *n* (*a*) démembrement *m* (d'un empire); dissolution *f* (d'une assemblée); rupture (d'un mariage) (*b*) morcellement *m* (d'un terrain). 'breakwater *n* brise-lames *m inv.*

breast [brest] *n* (*a*) (*of woman*) sein *m* (*b*) poitrine *f*; *Cu:* blanc *m* (de poulet); **to make a clean b. of it**, tout avouer; *Cl:* **b. pocket**, poche de poitrine. 'breast-feed *vtr* (-fed) allaiter (au sein). 'breast-feeding *n* allaitement *m* (au sein). 'breaststroke *n Swim:* brasse *f.*

breath [breθ] *n* haleine *f*, souffle *m*; **not a b. of air, wind**, pas un souffle d'air; **to have bad b.**, avoir (une) mauvaise haleine; **to draw b.**, respirer; **to take a deep b.**, respirer profondément; **all in the same b.**, d'un seul coup; **to hold, catch, one's b.**, retenir son souffle; **to get one's b. back**, reprendre haleine; **to waste one's b.**, perdre ses paroles; **out of b.**, hors d'haleine, à bout de souffle; **to be short of b.**, avoir le souffle court; **to take s.o.'s b. away**, couper le souffle à qn; **to speak under one's b.**, parler à voix basse. 'breathalyse *vtr* donner l'alcoo(l)test à (qn). 'breathalyser *n* alcoo(l)test *m*. 'breathless *a* hors d'haleine, essoufflé; haletant; (poursuite) à perdre haleine; (silence) angoissant. 'breathlessly *adv* en haletant. 'breathtaking *a* à vous couper le souffle.

breathe [bri:ð] 1. *vi* respirer; souffler 2. *vtr* respirer; laisser échapper (un soupir); **don't b. a word of it!** n'en soufflez (pas un) mot! 'breathe 'in *vtr & i* aspirer. 'breathe 'out *vtr & i* expirer. 'breather *n F:* moment *m* de repos; **give me a b.!** laisse-moi souffler! **to go out for a b.**, sortir prendre l'air, un bol d'air. 'breathing *n* respiration *f*; souffle *m*; heavy **b.**, respiration bruyante; **b. apparatus**, appareil respiratoire; **b. space**, le temps de souffler; (moment *m* de) répit *m.*

bred [bred] *see* breed.

breeches ['britʃiz] *npl Cl:* culotte *f.*

breed [bri:d] I. *v* (bred) 1. *vtr* (*a*) élever (du bétail); faire l'élevage de; **country-bred**, élevé à la campagne (*b*) faire naître, engendrer (le crime) 2. *vi* multiplier, se reproduire. II. *n* race *f.* 'breeder *n* (*a*) éleveur,

-euse (d'animaux) (*b*) *AtomPh:* **b. reactor**, réacteur (auto)générateur. 'breeding *n* 1. (*a*) reproduction *f* (*b*) élevage *m* (d'animaux) 2. éducation *f*; (**good**) **b.**, savoir-vivre *m.*

breeze [bri:z] 1. *n* brise *f*; **stiff b.**, vent frais 2. *vi F:* **to b. in, out**, entrer, sortir, en coup de vent. 'breezily *adv* jovialement, avec désinvolture. 'breeziness *n* (*of pers*) jovialité *f*, désinvolture *f.* 'breezy *a* (*a*) (endroit) exposé au vent; (jour) de grand vent (*b*) (*of pers*) jovial, désinvolte.

breezeblock ['bri:zblɔk] *n Const:* parpaing *m.*

Breton ['bretən] *a & n* breton, -onne.

breviary ['bri:viəri] *n* (*pl* **breviaries**) *Ecc:* bréviaire *m.*

brevity ['breviti] *n* brièveté *f*, concision *f.*

brew [bru:] 1. *n* infusion *f* (de thé) 2. *v* (*a*) *vtr* brasser (la bière); faire infuser, préparer (le thé) (*b*) *vi* (*of beer*) fermenter; (*of tea*) infuser; **there's a storm brewing**, un orage se prépare; **there's sth brewing**, il se trame qch; il y a qch dans l'air. 'brewer *n* brasseur *m.* 'brewery *n* brasserie *f.* 'brewing *n* brassage *m.* 'brew 'up *vi F:* préparer le thé.

briar ['braiər] *n see* brier

bribe [braib] 1. *n* pot-de-vin *m* 2. *vtr* soudoyer, acheter (qn); suborner (un témoin). 'bribery *n* corruption *f.*

bric-a-brac ['brikəbræk] *n* (*no pl*) bric-à-brac *m.*

brick [brik] *n* brique *f*; *Toy:* (*NAm:* = **block**) cube *m*; *F:* **to drop a b.**, faire une gaffe; *F:* **he came down on me like a ton of bricks**, il m'est tombé dessus sur le dos; **b. wall**, mur en briques; *F:* **to beat one's head against a b. wall**, se buter à l'impossible; perdre son temps. 'brickbat *n F:* insulte *f*; invective *f.* 'brick-built *a* en brique(s). 'bricklayer *n* maçon *m* en briques. 'brick 'up *vtr* murer (une fenêtre). 'brick-'red *a* (rouge) brique *inv.* 'brickwork *n* briquetage *m.* 'brickworks *npl* briqueterie *f.*

bride *nf*, **bridegroom** *nm* ['braid(gru:m)] (*before marriage*) fiancée, -é; (*after marriage*) nouvelle mariée, nouveau marié; **the b. and (bride)groom**, les fiancés; les nouveaux mariés. 'bridal *a* nuptial; de noce(s); (voile) de mariée; (appartement) pour jeunes mariés. 'bridesmaid *n* demoiselle *f* d'honneur. 'bride-to-be *n* future mariée.

bridge¹ [bridʒ] 1. *n* (*a*) pont *m* (*b*) (*on ship*) passerelle *f* (de commandement) (*c*) dos *m*, arête *f* (du nez) (*d*) *Dent:* bridge *m* 2. *vtr* construire un pont sur (une rivière); **to b. a gap**, combler une lacune; **bridging loan**, crédit de relais. 'bridgehead *n Mil:* tête *f* de pont.

bridge² *n Cards:* bridge *m.*

bridle ['braidl] I. *n* bride *f*; **b. path**, piste cavalière. II. *v* 1. *vtr* (*a*) brider (un cheval) (*b*) mettre un frein à (sa langue) 2. *vi* redresser la tête; se rengorger.

brief [bri:f] 1. *a* bref; court; concis; **in b., to be b.**, bref; en deux mots 2. *n* (*a*) *Jur:* dossier *m*; *Fig:* **I hold no b. for him**, ce n'est pas moi qui vais plaider sa cause (*b*) instructions *fpl* (*c*) *pl Cl:* slip *m* 3. *vtr* (*a*) confier une cause à (un avocat) (*b*) donner des instructions à (qn); informer (qn) (**on**, de). 'briefcase *n* serviette *f.* 'briefing *n* instructions; briefing *m.* 'briefly *adv* brièvement; en peu de mots. 'briefness *n* brièveté *f*; concision *f.*

brier ['braiər] n Bot: (a) églantier m (b) ronce f, rosier m sauvage (c) **b. (pipe),** pipe de bruyère.

brigade [bri'geid] n brigade f. **briga'dier** n général m de brigade.

brigand ['brigənd] n brigand m, bandit m.

bright [brait] **1.** a (-er, -est) (a) (of star, metal, eyes) brillant; (of light, colour) vif; (of sunshine, colour) éclatant; (of eyes) lumineux; (of weather) clair; **b. intervals,** éclaircies fpl; **to get brighter,** s'éclaircir; **to look on the b. side (of things),** prendre les choses par le bon côté (b) (of pers) vif, animé (c) (of pers) intelligent, éveillé; **b. idea,** idée lumineuse **2.** adv **b. and early,** de bonne heure. **'brighten ('up)** (a) vtr faire briller, faire reluire; aviver (une couleur); égayer (une pièce) (b) vi (of face) s'éclairer; (of weather) s'éclaircir; (of pers) s'animer. **'brightly** adv avec éclat; (sourire) gaiement. **'brightness** n éclat m; clarté f; (of pers) vivacité f.

brilliant ['briljənt] a éclatant; (of star, pers, career) brillant; **b. idea,** idée lumineuse. **'brilliance** n éclat m; brillant m. **'brilliantly** adv avec éclat; (jouer) brillamment.

brim [brim] **1.** n bord m **2.** vi (brimmed) **to b. (over),** déborder. **'brimful** a plein jusqu'au bord; Fig: débordant.

brine [brain] n eau salée; Cu: saumure f. **'briny** a saumâtre, salé.

bring [briŋ] vtr (brought [brɔːt]) amener (qn); apporter (qch); **to b. tears to s.o.'s eyes,** faire venir les larmes aux yeux de qn; **to b. s.o. luck,** porter bonheur à qn; Jur: **to b. an action against s.o.,** intenter un procès à qn; **you've brought it on yourself,** vous l'avez voulu; vous vous l'êtes attiré; **to b. sth to s.o.'s attention,** attirer l'attention de qn sur qch; **to b. sth to an end,** mettre fin à qch; **to b. oneself to do sth.,** se résoudre (à contre-cœur) à faire qch. **'bring a'bout** vtr (a) amener, causer, occasionner; provoquer (un accident); opérer (un changement). **'bring a'long** vtr amener (qn); apporter (qch). **'bring 'back** vtr rapporter (qch); ramener (qn); rappeler (des souvenirs); rétablir (la discipline). **'bring 'down** vtr (a) abattre (un arbre); faire tomber (des fruits, un gouvernement); (of enemy) descendre (un avion); (of pilot) faire atterrir (un avion); terrasser (un adversaire); Th: F: **to b. the house d.,** faire crouler la salle (sous les applaudissements) (b) faire descendre (qn); descendre (qch); faire baisser (un prix); abaisser (la température); réduire (la natalité, une enflure). **'bring 'forward** vtr (a) avancer (qch); faire avancer (qn); produire (un témoin); Book-k: reporter (une somme) (b) avancer (une réunion). **'bring 'in** vtr (a) introduire, faire entrer (qn); rentrer (qch); introduire, lancer (une mode); faire intervenir (un expert); Fin: **to b. in interest,** rapporter (b) déposer (un projet de loi); (of jury) rendre (un verdict). **'bring 'off** vtr réussir (un coup); mener à bien (une affaire). **'bring 'on** vtr produire, occasionner, provoquer (une maladie); (of sun) faire pousser (des plantes); Th: amener (qn), apporter (qch), sur la scène. **'bring 'out** vtr (a) sortir (qch); faire sortir (qn); faire ressortir (le sens de qch); faire valoir (une couleur) (b) publier, faire paraître (un livre). **'bring 'over** vtr = **bring round** (a) & (c). **'bring 'round** vtr (a) apporter (qch), amener

(qn) (b) ranimer (qn) (c) convertir (qn) **(to, à)** (d) (r)amener (la conversation) **(to, sur).** **'bring to-'gether** vtr (a) réunir; **to b. t. (again),** réconcilier (deux personnes) (b) **to b. t. two people,** favoriser la collaboration de deux personnes. **'bring 'up** vtr (a) monter (qch); faire monter (qn) (b) vomir, rendre (son repas) (c) approcher (une chaise) **(to, de); to be brought up short by sth,** buter contre qch; s'arrêter pile devant qch; **to be brought up before a magistrate,** comparaître devant un magistrat (d) élever (des enfants); **well, badly, brought up,** bien, mal, élevé (e) soulever (une question); mettre (une question) sur le tapis.

brink [briŋk] n bord m; **on the b. of sth,** au bord, Fig: à deux doigts, de qch. **'brinkmanship** n politique f du bord de l'abîme.

brisk [brisk] a (-er, -est) (a) vif, actif, animé; (promenade) à bon pas; (vent) frais; **at a b. pace,** à vive allure (b) (commerce) actif; **business is b.,** les affaires marchent. **'briskly** adv vivement; avec entrain. **'briskness** n vivacité f, animation f, entrain m; fraîcheur f (du vent); activité f (des affaires).

brisket ['briskit] n Cu: poitrine f de bœuf.

bristle ['brisl] **1.** n soie f; poil m (de brosse, de barbe) **2.** vi **to b. (up),** se hérisser **(with, de); bristling with,** hérissé de. **'bristly** a hérissé; (menton) couvert de poils.

Britain ['britən] Prn Geog: **(Great) B.,** Grande-Bretagne f. **'British 1.** a britannique; de (la) Grande-Bretagne; F: anglais; **the B. Isles,** les îles britanniques **2.** npl **the B.,** les Britanniques m; F: les Anglais m. **'Britisher** n NAm: = **Briton.** **'Briton** n Britannique mf.

Brittany ['britəni] Prn Bretagne f.

brittle ['britl] a fragile, cassant.

broach [broutʃ] vtr entamer (un sujet de conversation).

broad [brɔːd] **1.** a (-er, -est) (a) large; **in b. daylight,** en plein jour; **it's as b. as it's long,** cela revient au même; **b. outline,** aperçu (général) (b) (accent) prononcé (c) (of joke) gros **2.** n esp NAm: femme f, nana f. **'broadcast I.** n émission f. **II.** v (broadcast) **1.** vtr (a) répandre (une nouvelle) (b) WTel: TV: (radio)diffuser; téléviser **2.** vi (a) (of pers) parler à la radio; paraître à la télévision (b) (of station) émettre. **III.** a (radio) diffusé; télévisé. **'broadcaster** n radioreporter m; présentateur, -trice; speaker, -erine. **'broadcasting** n radiodiffusion f; télévision; (programmes) émissions fpl. **'broaden** vtr & i (s')élargir **'broadly** adv **b. (speaking),** d'une façon générale; généralement (parlant). **'broad'minded** a **to be b.,** avoir l'esprit large. **'broad'mindedness** n largeur f d'esprit. **'broad-'shouldered** a large d'épaules. **'broadside** n bordée f.

brocade [bra'keid] n Tex: brocart m.

broccoli ['brɔkəli] n Hort: brocoli m.

brochure ['brouʃər] n brochure f, dépliant m.

brogue¹ [broug] n chaussure f de marche.

brogue² n accent irlandais.

broil [brɔil] NAm: vtr & i griller. **'broiler** n poulet m (à rôtir).

broke [brouk] (a) v see **break II** (b) a F: **(stony, flat) b.,** sans le sou, fauché, à sec.

broken ['broukən] 1. *v see* **break II** 2. *a* (*a*) cassé, brisé, rompu; (terrain) accidenté; (chemin) raboteux, défoncé; (sommeil) interrompu, agité; **in a b. voice**, d'une voix entrecoupée; **in b. French**, en mauvais français (*b*) (cœur) brisé; (mariage) en ruine(s); (homme) ruiné, abattu; **b. home**, foyer détruit (*c*) (*of promise*) violé, manqué. **'broken-'down** *a* cassé; (voiture) en panne; (moteur) détraqué; (meuble) délabré. **broken-'hearted** *a* au cœur brisé.

broker ['broukər] *n* courtier *m*; agent *m* (de change, d'assurance).

brolly ['brɔli] *n* (*pl* **brollies**) *F:* parapluie *m*; pépin *m*.

bromide ['broumaid] *n* (*a*) *Ch:* bromure *m* (*b*) banalité *f*; lieu commun; cliché *m*.

bronchial ['brɔŋkiəl] *a* bronchique; **b. tubes**, bronches *fpl*. **bron'chitis** *n* bronchite *f*.

bronze [brɔnz] 1. *n coll* bronze *m* 2. *a* de, en, bronze 3. *vtr & i* (se) bronzer (au soleil).

brooch [broutʃ] *n* (*pl* **brooches**) broche *f*.

brood [bru:d] 1. *n* couvée *f*, nichée *f* 2. *vi* (*a*) (*of hen*) couver (*b*) (*of pers*) broyer du noir. **'brood 'over, 'on, a 'bout** *vtr* remâcher (le passé); ruminer (une idée). **'broody** *a* (*a*) (poule) couveuse; (*of pers*) qui désire des enfants (*b*) (*of pers*) distrait, rêveur.

brook [bruk] *n* ruisseau *m*.

broom [bru:m] *n* 1. *Bot:* genêt *m* 2. balai *m*; *Fig:* **new b.**, (apport *m* de) sang frais. **'broomstick** *n* manche *m* à balai.

broth [brɔθ] *n Cu:* bouillon *m*, potage *m*.

brothel ['brɔθl] *n* bordel *m*.

brother ['brʌðər] *n* frère *m*; confrère *m* (d'une société); *Pol:* camarade *m*. **'brotherhood** *n* fraternité *f*; *Ecc:* confrérie *f*. **'brother-in-law** *n* beau-frère *m*. **'brotherly** *a* fraternel, de frères.

brought [brɔːt] *see* **bring**.

brow [brau] *n* (*a*) (*eyebrow*) arcade sourcilière; sourcil *m* (*b*) (*forehead*) front *m* (*c*) haut *m* (de colline); bord *m* (de précipice). **'browbeat** *vtr* (-beat; -beaten) intimider (qn).

brown [braun] I. *a* (*a*) brun; marron *inv*; (*of hair*) châtain; **b. bread**, pain bis; **b. paper**, papier d'emballage; **b. sugar**, cassonade *f* (*b*) bruni (par le soleil), bronzé. II. *n* brun *m*; marron *m*. III. *v* 1. *vtr* brunir; *Cu:* (faire) rissoler (la viande); faire dorer (des légumes); faire roussir (une sauce) 2. *vi* se brunir; *Cu:* roussir. **'brownie** *n* (*a*) *Scout:* jeannette *f* (*b*) *NAm: Cu:* petit gâteau au chocolat. **'brownish** *a* brunâtre. **'brown 'off** *vtr F:* décourager (qn); **to be browned off**, avoir le cafard; en avoir ras le bol.

browse [brauz] *vi* (*of animals*) brouter; (*of pers*) feuilleter des livres; **I'm just browsing**, je ne fais que regarder.

bruise [bru:z] 1. *n* meurtrissure *f*; bleu *m* 2. *vtr* meurtrir; **to b. one's arm**, se meurtrir le bras, se faire un bleu au bras. **'bruiser** *n F:* costaud *m*.

brunch [brʌntʃ] *n F:* petit déjeuner et déjeuner combinés.

brunette [bru:'net] *a & n* (*of woman*) brune (*f*), brunette (*f*).

brunt [brʌnt] *n* choc *m*; **to bear the b. of sth**, soutenir le plus fort, le poids, de qch.

brush [brʌʃ] 1. *n* (*a*) (*no pl*) broussailles *fpl* (*b*) (*pl* **brushes**) brosse *f*; (*for paint*) pinceau *m*; (*broom*)

balai *m*; **(hand) b.**, balayette *f* (*c*) queue *f* (de renard) (*d*) coup *m* de brosse (à un vêtement) (*e*) rencontre *f*, échauffourée *f* (avec l'ennemi); accrochage *m* 2. *vtr* (*a*) brosser (un vêtement, les cheveux); se brosser (les cheveux, les dents); balayer (le plancher) (*b*) frôler, effleurer, raser (une surface). **'brush a'gainst** *vtr* frôler, effleurer. **'brush a'side** *vtr* écarter. **'brush a'way** *vtr* enlever (qch) à coups de brosse, de balai; essuyer (des larmes); écarter (des difficultés). **'brush 'down** *vtr* donner un coup de brosse à; brosser (un cheval). **'brushed** *a* (nylon) gratté. **'brush 'off** 1. *vtr* (*a*) enlever (qch) à coups de brosse, de balai (*b*) envoyer promener (qn) 2. *vi* (*of mud*) s'enlever à coups de brosse. **'brush-off** *n F:* **to give s.o. the b.-o.**, envoyer promener qn. **'brush 'past** *vtr & i* frôler (qn, qch) en passant. **'brush 'up** *vtr & i* balayer (qch); ramasser (qch) avec une brosse, un balai; **to b. up (on) a subject**, se remettre à, repasser, un sujet. **'brushwood** *n* broussailles. **'brushwork** *n* touche *f* (d'un peintre).

brusque [bru:sk] *a* brusque; (ton) rude, bourru. **'brusquely** *adv* avec brusquerie. **'brusqueness** *n* brusquerie *f*.

Brussels ['brʌslz] *Prn Geog:* Bruxelles *f*; **B. sprouts**, choux *mpl* de Bruxelles.

brute [bru:t] 1. *n* brute *f*; *F:* **b. of a job**, travail de chien 2. *a* (*of beast*) brut; (*of force*) brutal; **by b. force**, de vive force. **'brutal** *a* brutal. **bru'tality** *n* brutalité *f*. **'brutally** *adv* brutalement. **'brutish** *a* de brute; bestial.

BSc *abbr Bachelor of Science.*

bubble ['bʌbl] 1. *n* bulle *f* (d'air, de savon); bouillon *m* (de liquide bouillant); **b. bath**, bain moussant 2. *vi* bouillonner; (*of wine*) pétiller; **to b. over**, déborder. **'bubbly** 1. *a* (vin) pétillant 2. *n F:* champagne *m*.

buck [bʌk] I. *n* (*a*) mâle *m* (du lapin); *esp* daim *m*, chevreuil *m*; *F:* **b. teeth**, dents de lièvre (*b*) *esp NAm: F:* dollar *m* (*c*) *F:* **to pass the b.**, mettre l'affaire sur le dos d'un autre 2. *v* (*a*) *vi* (*of horse*) faire un saut (*b*) *vtr F:* s'opposer à (un projet). **'buck 'up 1.** *vtr* remonter (le courage de) (qn) 2. *vi* (*a*) reprendre courage (*b*) se dépêcher.

bucket ['bʌkit] *n* 1. seau *m*; *Aut:* **b. seat**, baquet *m* 2. **b. shop**, agence *f* de voyages à prix réduits. **'bucket 'down** *vi F:* pleuvoir à verse, à seaux. **'bucketful** *n* plein seau.

buckle ['bʌkl] I. *n* boucle *f*. II. *v* 1. *vtr* (*a*) boucler (une ceinture) (*b*) gauchir; voiler (une roue) 2. *vi* (*a*) (*of belt*) se boucler (*b*) (*of metal*) (se) gondoler, gauchir; (*of wheel*) se voiler. **'buckle 'down** *vi* s'y mettre; s'appliquer (**to**, à).

buckram ['bʌkrəm] *n Tex:* bougran *m*.

buckwheat ['bʌkwi:t] *n* sarrasin *m*; blé noir.

bud [bʌd] 1. *n* bourgeon *m*; bouton *m* (de fleur); **to come into b.**, bourgeonner 2. *vi* (**budded**) bourgeonner. **'budding** *a* (*a*) (arbre) bourgeonnant; (fleur) en bouton (*b*) (artiste) en herbe; (*of passion*) naissant.

Buddhism ['budizm] *n* bouddhisme *m*. **'Buddhist** 1. *a & n* bouddhiste 2. *a* bouddhique.

buddy ['bʌdi] *n esp NAm: F:* copain, -ine.

budge [bʌdʒ] 1. *vi* bouger; *Fig:* céder 2. *vtr* faire bouger; *Fig:* faire céder.

budgerigar ['bʌdʒəriga:r] *n Orn:* perruche *f.*

budget ['bʌdʒit] **1.** *n* budget *m*; *Bank:* **b. account,** compte-crédit *m* 2. *v* (*a*) *vi* ménager son argent; **to b. for sth,** inscrire qch au budget (*b*) *vtr* budgétiser.

budgie ['bʌdʒi] *n Orn: F:* perruche *f.*

buff [bʌf] **1.** *a & n* (couleur *f*) chamois *m inv* 2. *n F:* (*a*) **in the b.,** tout nu, à poil (*b*) entousiaste *mf* 3. *vtr* polir.

buffalo ['bʌfəlou, -ouz] *n* (*pl* **buffalo, buffaloes**) *Z:* buffle *m.*

buffer ['bʌfər] *n* tampon *m*; *Rail:* (*in station*) butoir *m*; *Pol:* **b. state,** état tampon.

buffet¹ ['bʌfit] *vtr* **to b.** (**about**), (*of waves*) ballotter, battre; (*of wind*) secouer.

buffet² ['bufei] *n* buffet *m*; **b. lunch,** lunch *m*; *Rail:* **b. car,** voiture-buffet *f.*

buffoon [bə'fu:n] *n* bouffon *m*. **bu'ffoonery** *n* bouffonnerie *fpl.*

bug [bʌg] **1.** *n* (*a*) punaise *f* (*b*) *F:* insecte *m*; (petite) bestiole (*c*) *F:* microbe *m*, virus *m* (*d*) *F:* micro clandestin 2. *vtr* (**bugged**) *F:* (*a*) installer un micro clandestin dans (une pièce) (*b*) ennuyer, emmerder (qn). **'bugbear** *n* cauchemar *m*; bête noire. **'bugger** *P:* **1.** *n* salaud *m* 2. *int* merde! **'buggy** *n* (*pl* **-ies**) (*a*) buggy *m*, jeep *m* (*b*) *esp NAm:* poussette *f* (d'enfant)

bugle ['bju:gl] *n* clairon *m*. **'bugler** *n* clairon.

build [bild] **1.** *n* (*of pers*) carrure *f*; taille *f* 2. *vtr* (**built**) bâtir (une maison); construire (un navire, une route); **built of stone,** construit de, en, pierre. **'builder** *n* entrepreneur *m* (en bâtiment); (*employee*) manœuvre *m*; ouvrier *m*; constructeur *m* (de navires). **'building** *n* construction *f*; bâtiment *m*; (*offices, flats*) immeuble *m*; **public b.,** édifice public; **b. land, plot,** terrain à bâtir; **b.** (**trade**), le bâtiment; **b. society** = (i) société immobilière (ii) caisse *f* d'épargne-logement. **'build 'in(to)** *vtr* encastrer (un placard); incorporer (des problèmes). **'build 'on** *vtr* ajouter. **'build 'up** (*a*) *vtr* bâtir (une fortune); développer (ses affaires, ses forces, ses muscles); échafauder (un système); se faire (une réputation); se créer (une clientèle); (*of food*) donner des forces; **this area has been built up,** on a beaucoup construit par ici (*b*) *vi* s'accumuler, s'accroître; (*of traffic*) devenir très dense. **'build-up** *n* accumulation *f*, augmentation *f*; *Mil:* mise *f* sur pied. **'built-in** *a* (placard) encastré; (problème) inhérent. **'built-up** *a* **b.-up area,** agglomération (urbaine).

bulb [bʌlb] *n* (*a*) *Bot:* bulbe *m*, oignon *m* (*b*) *El:* ampoule *f*. **'bulbous** *a* bulbeux.

Bulgaria [bʌl'gɛəriə] *Prn Geog:* Bulgarie *f*. **Bul'garian** *a & n* bulgare (*mf*).

bulge [bʌldʒ] **1.** *n* bombement *m*, renflement *m*; ventre *m* (d'une cruche); hernie *f* (d'un pneu); poussée *f* (de la natalité) 2. *vi* **to b.** (**out**), bomber; faire saillie. **'bulging** *a* (front) bombé; (œil) protubérant; (sac) bourré (**with**, de).

bulk [bʌlk] *n* grandeur *f*, grosseur *f*, volume *m*; **the** (**great**) **b. of,** la masse, la plupart (des hommes); la plus grande partie de (l'argent); **in b.,** en gros; en vrac; **b. buying,** achat en grande quantité. **'bulkhead** *n NArch: etc:* cloison *f*. **'bulky** *a* (**-ier, -iest**) volumineux, encombrant; gros; (livre) épais.

bull [bul] *n* (*a*) taureau *m* (*b*) **b.** (**elephant**), (éléphant *m*) mâle *m* (*c*) *St Exch:* haussier *m*. **'bulldog** *n* bouledogue *m*; **b. clip,** pince *f* (à dessin). **'bulldoze** *vtr* déblayer (un terrain) au bulldozer. **'bulldozer** *n* bulldozer *m*. **'bullfight** *n* course *f* de taureaux; corrida *f*. **'bullfighter** *n* matador *m*. **'bullfinch** *n* (*pl* **-es**) *Orn:* bouvreuil *m*. **'bullfrog** *n* grenouille *f* taureau. **'bullock** *n* bœuf *m*; (*young*) bouvillon *m*. **'bullring** *n* arène *f* (pour les courses de taureaux). **'bull's-eye** *n* noir *m* (d'une cible); **to hit the b.-e.,** faire mouche; mettre dans le mille.

bullet ['bulit] *n* balle *f*. **'bullet-headed** *a* à tête ronde. **'bulletproof** *a* (gilet) pare-balles *inv*.

bulletin ['bulitin] *n* bulletin *m*; **news b.,** bulletin d'informations; *TV:* actualités *fpl.*

bullion ['buljən] *n* or *m*, argent *m*, en lingots.

bully ['buli] **1.** *n* (*pl* **bullies**) brute *f* 2. *vtr* intimider; brutaliser (qn). **'bullying 1.** *a* brutal 2 *n* intimidation *f*; brutalité *f.*

bulrush ['bulrʌʃ] *n* (*pl* **bulrushes**) jonc *m* (des marais).

bulwark ['bulwək] *n* rempart *m.*

bum [bʌm] *P:* **1.** *n* (*a*) derrière *m* (*b*) (*pers*) clochard *m*; fainéant *m* 2. *vtr* (**bummed**) **to b. sth off** s.o., taper qn de qch; **to b. a lift, a meal, off** s.o., se faire emmener en voiture, se faire inviter, par qn. **'bum a'round** *vi* fainéanter.

bumblebee ['bʌmblbi:] *n Ent:* bourdon *m.*

bumf [bʌmf] *n F:* paperasserie(s) *f*(*pl*).

bump [bʌmp] **1.** *n* (*a*) choc (sourd); heurt *m*; secousse *f*, cahot *m* (*b*) bosse *f* 2. *v* (*a*) *vtr* **to b.** (**into**), heurter; se heurter, se cogner, à, contre; buter contre (qch); entrer en collision avec (qch); bousculer (qn); **to b. one's head on sth,** se cogner la tête à qch; *F:* **to b. into** s.o., rencontrer qn par hasard (*b*) *vtr & i* (*of two thgs, pers*) **to b.** (**into one another**), se heurter (*c*) *vi* cahoter. **'bumper** *n* (*a*) *Aut:* pare-chocs *m inv* (*b*) **b. crop,** récolte exceptionnelle. **'bump 'off** *vtr P:* assassiner, supprimer (qn). **'bump 'up** *vtr F:* faire monter (un prix). **'bumpy** *a* (**-ier, -iest**) (chemin) cahoteux, inégal.

bumptious ['bʌmpʃəs] *a* suffisant.

bun [bʌn] (*a*) *Cu:* petit pain au lait (*b*) (cheveux enroulés en) chignon *m.*

bunch [bʌntʃ] *n* (*pl* **bunches**) (*a*) bouquet *m* (de fleurs); touffe *f* (d'herbes); grappe *f* (de raisin); botte *f* (de radis); régime *m* (de bananes); trousseau *m* (de clefs); *Hairdr:* *pl* couettes *fpl* (*b*) *F:* groupe *m* (de personnes); **the best of the b.,** le meilleur de la bande. **'bunch 'up** *vi* se serrer, s'entasser.

bundle ['bʌndl] **1.** *n* paquet *m* (de linge); ballot *m* (de marchandises); liasse *f* (de papiers); fagot *m* (de bois); botte *f* (d'asperges); *F:* **b. of nerves,** paquet de nerfs 2. *vtr* (*a*) **to b. up,** empaqueter (qch); mettre (qch) en paquet (*b*) fourrer (qch) (**into, dans**); **to b. s.o. out, off,** faire sortir, se débarrasser de, qn à la hâte, sans cérémonie.

bung [bʌŋ] **1.** *n* bonde *f* 2. *vtr F:* mettre, fourrer (qch). **'bung 'up** *vtr F:* boucher.

bungalow ['bʌŋgəlou] *n* bungalow *m.*

bungle ['bʌŋgl] *vtr* bousiller, gâcher. **'bungler** *n* bousilleur, -euse. **'bungling 1.** *a* maladroit 2. *n* bousillage *m*, gâchis *m.*

bunion ['bʌnjən] *n Med:* oignon *m.*

bunk [bʌŋk] *n* (*a*) couchette *f* (*b*) **b. beds, bunks,** lits superposés (c) P: **to do a b.,** filer, ficher le camp (d) P: (also **'bunkum**) blague(s) f(pl); bêtises fpl. **'bunker** n (a) (i) (in ship) soute f, (ii) (in garden) coffre m (à charbon) (b) Golf: bunker m (c) Mil: blockhaus m.

bunny ['bʌni] n (pl **bunnies**) F: **b. (rabbit),** Jeannot lapin m; **b. girl,** employée de boîte de nuit habillée en lapin.

bunting ['bʌntiŋ] n 1. (no pl) drapeaux mpl, pavillons mpl; pavoisement m 2. Orn: bruant m.

buoy [bɔi] 1. n bouée f; balise flottante 2. vtr to b. (up), faire flotter; Fig: soutenir. **'buoyancy** n (a) (of object) flottabilité f; (of liquid) poussée f (b) (of pers) entrain m. **'buoyant** a (a) (of object) flottable (b) (of pers) plein d'entrain; optimiste; (démarche) élastique; Com: (marché) animé.

burble ['bəːbl] vi (a) murmurer (des sons inarticulés) (b) débiter des sottises.

burden ['bəːdn] 1. n fardeau m, charge f; poids m (des impôts); **to be a b. to s.o.,** être à charge à qn; **b. of proof,** charge de la preuve; **beast of b.,** bête de somme 2. vtr charger, alourdir, accabler (**s.o. with sth,** qn de qch).

bureau ['bjuərou] n (pl **bureaux**) 1. Furn: (a) bureau m; secrétaire m (b) NAm: (Br = **chest of drawers**) commode f 2. (a) (office) bureau (de renseignements) (b) (department) service m (du gouvernement). **bu'reaucracy** n bureaucratie f. **'bureaucrat** n bureaucrate mf. **bureau'cratic** a bureaucratique.

burger ['bəːgər] n Cu: F: hamburger m.

burglar ['bəːglər] n cambrioleur, -euse; **b. alarm,** alarme antivol. **'burglarize** vtr NAm: cambrioler. **'burglary** n cambriolage m. **'burgle** vtr cambrioler.

Burgundy ['bəːgəndi] 1. Prn Bourgogne f 2. n **b.,** (vin m de) bourgogne m.

burial ['beriəl] n enterrement m; **b. ground,** cimetière m.

burlesque [bəː'lesk] n burlesque m; parodie f.

burly ['bəːli] a (-ier, -iest) (of pers) solidement bâti.

burn [bəːn] 1. n brûlure f 2. vtr & i (**burnt, burned**) brûler; **to b. one's fingers,** se brûler les doigts; F: **to b. one's boats,** brûler ses vaisseaux; F: **to b. the midnight oil,** travailler tard dans la nuit; **burnt to a cinder,** réduit en cendres; (rôti) carbonisé; **burnt to death,** mort carbonisé; **all the lights were burning,** toutes les lumières étaient allumées. **'burn 'down** 1. vtr brûler, incendier 2. vi (a) être brûlé, incendié (b) (of fire) baisser. **'burner** n (of gas cooker) brûleur m; Bunsen **b.,** bec m Bunsen. **'burning** 1. a (bâtiment) en feu, incendié; (charbon) allumé; (désir) ardent; **b. pain,** douleur cuisante; **b. question,** question brûlante 2. n incendie m (d'une maison); **there's a smell of b.,** ça sent le brûlé. **'burn 'off** vtr brûler. **'burn 'out** 1. vtr (a) brûler, incendier, l'intérieur de (la maison) (b) El: griller 2. vi (a) (of fire) s'éteindre (b) El: sauter. **'burn 'up** 1. vtr brûler, consumer 2. vi (of fire) flamber; (of rocket) brûler.

burp [bəːp] P: 1. n renvoi m; rot m 2. vi faire un renvoi, un rot; roter.

burrow ['bʌrou] 1. n terrier m 2. v (a) vtr creuser (un trou) (b) vi fouir la terre.

burr [bəːr] n 1. Bot: teigne f (de bardane) 2. (on trees) broussin m.

bursar ['bəːsər] n Sch: économe mf; intendant, -ante. **'bursary** n bourse f (d'études).

burst [bəːst] 1. n éclatement m, explosion f; jet m, jaillissement m (de flamme); rafale f (de tir); éclat m (de rire); élan m (d'éloquence); salve f (d'applaudissements); poussée f (d'activité); pointe f (de vitesse); F: tuyau (d'eau) crevé 2. v (**burst**) (a) vi éclater; (of boiler) sauter; (of tyre) crever; **to b. in, out,** entrer, sortir, en coup de vent; **to b. in on,** interrompre; **to b. into, out of, a room,** entrer dans une,· sortir d'une, pièce en coup de vent; **to b. into laughter, b. out laughing,** éclater, pouffer, de rire; **to b. into tears, b. out crying,** fondre en larmes; **to b. into song, b. out singing,** se mettre à chanter; **to b. into flames,** s'enflammer; **to be bursting at the seams,** (i) (of dress) se découdre (ii) F: (of building) être plein à éclater, à craquer; **to be bursting with health, with pride,** déborder de santé, crever d'orgueil; **to be bursting to do sth,** brûler, mourir d'envie, de faire qch (b) vtr faire éclater; crever (un ballon); rompre (ses liens); faire sauter (une chaudière); se rompre (un vaisseau sanguin); (of river) **to b. its banks,** rompre ses berges. **'burst 'open** 1. vtr ouvrir avec violence 2. vi s'ouvrir tout d'un coup.

bury ['beri] vtr (**buried**) enterrer, inhumer, ensevelir, (at sea) immerger (un mort); enfouir (un trésor); enfoncer (les mains dans ses poches); **to b. one's face in one's hands,** se cacher la figure dans les mains; Fig: **to b. one's head in the sand,** pratiquer la politique de l'autruche; **to b. oneself in the country,** s'enterrer à la campagne; **to b. oneself in one's studies,** se plonger dans l'étude; F: **to b. the hatchet,** enterrer la hache de guerre.

bus [bʌs] 1. n (pl **buses,** NAm: **busses**) autobus m, F: bus m; (in country) autocar m, F: car m; **b. stop,** arrêt d'autobus; **b. shelter,** abribus m 2. vtr (**bus(s)ed**) transporter par autobus. **'busman** n **to take a busman's holiday,** faire du métier en guise de congé.

bush [buʃ] n 1. (pl **bushes**) (a) buisson m (b) fourré m, taillis m 2. (Africa, Austr:) **the b.,** la brousse. **'bushed** a F: fatigué, rompu, crevé. **'bushy** a touffu; broussailleux.

business ['biznis] n 1. affaire f; besogne f; **it's my b. to,** c'est à moi de; **it's none of your b.,** cela ne vous regarde pas; **to make it one's b. to do sth,** prendre sur soi de faire qch; **it's a sorry b.,** c'est une triste affaire 2. (a) les affaires; **b. is b.,** les affaires sont les affaires; **to go into b.,** entrer dans les affaires; **to do b. with s.o.,** faire des affaires avec qn; **on b.,** pour affaires; **b. hours,** heures d'ouverture; **b. studies,** études commerciales (b) (pl **businesses**) (fonds m de) commerce m. **'businesslike** a (of pers) capable, pratique; (of manner) sérieux. **'businessman, -woman** n (pl **-men, -women**) homme m, femme f, d'affaires.

busker ['bʌskər] n musicien, -ienne, ambulant(e), des rues.

bust[1] [bʌst] n (a) Sculp: buste m (b) poitrine f.

bust[2] vtr (**bust**) F: casser; **to go b.,** faire faillite. **'bust 'up** vtr F: rompre, briser. **'bust-up** n F: querelle f; brouille f.

bustle ['bʌsl] 1. vi **to b. (about),** s'activer, s'affairer

2. *n* remue-ménage *m*. **'bustling** *a* affairé; empressé; animé.

busy ['bizi] **1.** *a* (**ier, -iest**) (*a*) affairé; occupé; actif; (jour) chargé; (moment) de grande activité; **b. street,** rue passante, animée; **to be b. doing sth,** s'occuper, être occupé, à faire qch; être en train de faire qch; **to keep oneself b.,** s'activer, s'occuper (*b*) *esp NAm: Tp:* (*of line*) occupé **2.** *vpr* **to b. oneself with,** s'occuper à, de. **'busily** *adv* activement; avec empressement. **'busybody** *n* officieux, -euse.

but [bʌt] **1.** *conj* mais **2.** *adv* ne . . . que; seulement; **he is nothing b. a student,** ce n'est qu'un étudiant; **one can b. try,** on peut toujours essayer **3.** *conj or prep* (= *except*) (*a*) sauf, excepté; **anything b. that,** tout plutôt que cela; **anyone b. him,** n'importe qui d'autre que lui; **he's anything b. a hero,** il n'est aucunement un héros; **there's nothing for it b. to obey,** il n'y a qu'à obéir; **the last b. one,** l'avant-dernier (*b*) **b. for,** sans; **b. for that,** à part cela **4.** *n* mais *m*.

butane ['bjuːteɪn] *n Ch:* butane *m*.

butcher ['butʃər] **1.** *n* boucher *m*; **b.'s (shop),** boucherie *f* **2.** *vtr* abattre (un animal); égorger, massacrer. **'butchery** *n* boucherie *f*.

butler ['bʌtlər] *n* maître *m* d'hôtel.

butt[1] [bʌt] *n* (gros) tonneau; barrique *f*.

butt[2] [bʌt] *n* (*a*) **b. (end),** (gros) bout; souche *f* (d'arbre); mégot *m* (de cigarette, de cigare) (*b*) crosse *f* (de fusil).

butt[3] *n* (*a*) *pl Sma:* champ *m* de tir (*b*) but *m*; (*of pers*) souffre-douleur *m inv*; **to be a b. for sth,** être en butte à qch.

butt[4] **1.** *n* coup *m* de tête; coup de corne **2.** *vtr* donner un coup de tête, de corne à. **'butt 'in** *vi* intervenir (sans façon) (**on,** dans); interrompre.

butter ['bʌtər] **1.** *n* beurre *m*; **b. bean,** haricot beurre; **b. dish,** beurrier *m*; **b. knife,** couteau à beurre **2.** *vtr* beurrer. **'buttercup** *n Bot:* bouton *m* d'or. **'butterfingers** *n F:* maladroit, -e. **'butterfly** *n* (*pl* **-ies**) (*a*) *Ent:* papillon *m*; *F:* **to have butterflies (in one's stomach),** avoir la tremblote (*b*) *Swim:* **b. (stroke),** brasse *f* papillon. **'buttermilk** *n* babeurre *m*. **'butterscotch** *n* caramel (dur) au beurre. **'butter 'up** *vtr F:* flatter (qn).

buttock ['bʌtək] *n* fesse *f*; **the buttocks,** le derrière, les fesses.

button ['bʌtn] **1.** *n* bouton *m*; pastille *f* (de chocolat); **tummy, belly, b.,** nombril *m*; **b. mushroom,** (petit) champignon de Paris **2.** *vtr & i* **to b. (up),** (se) boutonner; **buttoned up,** taciturne, renfermé (*b*) *Swim:* **button-hole 1.** *n* boutonnière *f*; **to wear a b.,** porter une fleur à sa boutonnière **2.** *vtr F:* retenir, agrafer (qn). **'button-through** *a F:* (robe) qui se boutonne devant.

buttress ['bʌtrɪs] **1.** *n* (*pl* **buttresses**) contrefort *m*; **flying b.,** arc-boutant *m* **2.** *vtr* arc-bouter; étayer.

buxom ['bʌksəm] *a* (*of woman*) rondelet, potelé.

buy [bai] **1.** *n* achat *m*; affaire *f* **2.** *vtr* (**bought**) (*a*) acheter (**sth from s.o.,** qch à qn); **sth for s.o.,** qch à, pour, qn); **to b. off, up,** acheter (*b*) *P:* croire, gober (une histoire peu probable). **'buy 'back** *vtr* racheter. **'buyer** *n* acheteur, -euse. **'buy 'out** *vtr* désintéresser (un associé).

buzz [bʌz] **I.** *n* (*pl* **buzzes**) (*a*) bourdonnement *m*; brouhaha *m* (de conversations); *W.Tel:* (bruits *m* de) friture *f* (*b*) *F:* coup *m* de fil. **II.** *v* **1.** *vi* (*a*) bourdonner (*b*) **to b. (for s.o.),** sonner (qn) **2.** *vtr* (*a*) sonner (qn) (*b*) *F:* passer un coup de fil à (qn) (*c*) *F:* (*of aircraft*) harceler; frôler (le sol). **'buzzer** *n* sirène *f*; sonnerie *f*. **'buzzing** *n* bourdonnement *m*. **'buzz 'off** *vi P:* s'en aller, décamper.

buzzard ['bʌzəd] *n Orn:* buse *f*.

by [bai] **1.** *prep* (*a*) (*near*) (au)près de, à côté de; **by the sea,** au bord de la mer; (**all) by oneself,** (tout) seul; **he always keeps his gun by him,** il a toujours son revolver sous la main (*b*) par; **by car,** en voiture; **by train,** par le, en, train; **by land and sea,** par terre et par mer; **to be punished by s.o.,** être puni par qn; **to have a child by s.o.,** avoir un enfant de qn; **made by hand,** fait (à la) main; **known by the name of X,** connu sous le nom d'X; **by force,** de force; **by mistake,** par (suite d'une) erreur; **three metres by two,** trois mètres sur deux; *F:* **by the way,** à propos (*c*) **by doing that you will offend him,** en faisant cela vous l'offenserez; **what do you gain by doing that?** que gagnez-vous à faire cela? (*d*) **by law,** conformément à la loi; **to judge by appearances,** juger sur les apparences; **by my watch,** à ma montre; **by the kilo,** au kilo (*e*) **by degrees,** par degrés; **one by one,** un à un; **longer by two metres,** plus long de deux mètres (*f*) **by day,** de jour, le jour; **by Monday,** d'ici lundi; **by three o'clock,** avant trois heures; **he ought to be here by now,** il devrait être déjà ici (*g*) **I know him by sight,** je le connais de vue **2.** *adv* près; **close by,** tout près; **(taking it) by and large,** à tout prendre; généralement; **to put sth by,** mettre qch de côté; **to pass by,** passer; **by and by,** tout à l'heure; bientôt. **'by-election** *n* élection partielle. **'bygone 1.** *a* in **b. days,** autrefois **2.** *npl* **let bygones be bygones,** oublions le passé. **'by(-)law** *n* (*NAm:* = **ordinance**) arrêté *m* municipal. **'bypass 1.** *n* route *f* de contournement, d'évitement **2.** *vtr* contourner, éviter. **'by-product** *n* sous-produit *m*; dérivé *m*. **'byroad** *n* = **byway**. **'bystander** *n* assistant, -ante; spectateur, -trice. **'byway** *n* chemin vicinal. **'byword** *n* synonyme *m* (**for,** de).

bye [bai] *n* (*a*) *Cr:* balle passée (*b*) *Sp:* (*of player*) **to have a b.,** être exempt (d'un match).

bye(-bye) ['bai(bai)] *int F:* au revoir! salut! (*child's language*) **to go to bye-byes,** aller au dodo.

byte [bait] *n Cmptr:* multiplet *m*.

C

C, c [siː] n (a) (la lettre) C, c m (b) Mus: ut m, do m; **in C,** en do.

c, ca abbr circa, environ.

cab [kæb] n (a) taxi m (b) cabine f (de camion). **'cabby,** NAm: **'cabdriver** n chauffeur m de taxi.

cabaret ['kæbərei] n spectacle m (de cabaret).

cabbage ['kæbidʒ] n chou m; **c. lettuce,** laitue pommée; F: **since his accident he's become a c.,** depuis son accident il est devenu incapable de rien faire, il est complètement paralysé.

cabin ['kæbin] n (a) cabane f; case f (b) Nau: Av: cabine f; **c. cruiser,** yacht de croisière (à moteur).

cabinet ['kæbinət] n (a) meuble m (à tiroirs); (with glass doors) vitrine f; **filing c.,** classeur m, fichier m (b) Pol: cabinet m; conseil m des ministres; **c. minister,** ministre d'état; membre du cabinet (ministériel). **'cabinet-maker** n ébéniste m.

cable ['keibl] **1.** n (a) câble m; **c. television,** télédistribution f; **c. car,** funiculaire m; téléphérique m (b) Telecom: (also **'cablegram**) câblogramme m, câble **2.** vtr & i câbler.

caboodle [kə'buːdl] n F: **the whole c.,** tout le bataclan.

cache [kæʃ] n (a) cachette f (b) dépôt caché (d'armes).

cackle ['kækl] **1.** n (of hen) caquet m; (of pers) ricanement m; rire saccadé **2.** vi (of hen) caqueter; (of pers) ricaner.

cactus ['kæktəs] n (pl **cacti**) Bot: cactus m.

cadaverous [kə'dævərəs] a cadavéreux.

caddie ['kædi] n Golf: caddie m.

caddy ['kædi] n (pl **caddies**) (tea) c., boîte f à thé.

cadence ['keidəns] n cadence f.

cadenza [kə'denzə] n Mus: cadence f.

cadet [kə'det] n élève m (i) d'une école militaire (ii) de la préparation militaire.

cadge [kædʒ] vtr & i écornifler; quémander; **to c. sth from s.o.,** taper qn de qch. **'cadger** n tapeur, -euse; écornifleur, -euse.

cadmium ['kædmiəm] n Miner: cadmium.

caesarean, -ian, NAm: **cesarean, -ian** [si'zɛəriən] a & n Med: **c. (section),** césarienne f.

café ['kæfei] n café-restaurant) m. **cafeteria** [kæfə'tiəriə] n cafétéria f.

caffeine ['kæfiːn] n caféine f.

caftan ['kæftæn] n Cost: caf(e)tan m.

cage [keidʒ] **1.** n (a) cage f; **c. bird,** oiseau de volière (b) cabine f (d'ascenseur) **2.** vtr **to c. (in, up),** mettre en cage. **'cagey** a (**cagier, cagiest**) F: défiant; réservé; **to be c. about one's age,** ne pas vouloir avouer son âge.

cahoots [kə'huːts] npl F: **in c.,** de mèche (with, avec).

cairn ['kɛən] n cairn m.

Cairo ['kaiərou] Prn Geog: le Caire.

cajole [kə'dʒoul] vtr cajoler; enjôler. **ca'jolery** n cajolerie(s) f(pl).

cake [keik] **1.** n (a) gâteau m; pâtisserie f; **c. shop,** pâtisserie; **it's selling like hot cakes,** cela se vend comme des petits pains; F: **that takes the c.!** c'est le comble, c'est le bouquet! F: **it's a piece of c.,** c'est simple comme bonjour (b) pain m (de savon); tablette f (de chocolat) **2.** vi faire croûte; (of blood, etc) se cailler; **caked with mud,** plaqué de boue.

calamine ['kæləmain] n **c. lotion,** lotion calmante à la calamine.

calamity [kə'læmiti] n (pl **calamities**) calamité f. **ca'lamitous** a désastreux.

calcium ['kælsiəm] n calcium m.

calculate ['kælkjuleit] vtr & i calculer; évaluer; estimer; faire un calcul; **words calculated to reassure us,** paroles propres à nous rassurer. **'calculated** a délibéré; calculé. **'calculating** a calculateur; **c. machine,** machine à calculer. **calcu'lation** n calcul. **'calculator** n calculatrice f. **'calculus** n (pl **-culi**) calcul m.

calendar ['kælindər] n calendrier m; **c. year,** année civile.

calf¹ [kɑːf] n (pl **calves**) veau m; **cow in c.,** vache pleine; **elephant c.,** éléphanteau m.

calf² n (pl **calves**) mollet m (de la jambe).

calibre, NAm: **caliber** ['kælibər] n calibre m. **'calibrate** vtr calibrer. **cali'bration** n calibrage m.

calico ['kælikou] n Tex: calicot m.

calipers ['kælipəz] npl NAm: see **callipers**.

call [kɔːl] **I.** n (a) appel m; cri m; **c. for help,** appel au secours; Th: (**curtain**) **c.,** rappel m; **within c.,** à portée de voix; **to give s.o. a c.,** (i) appeler (ii) réveiller, qn; **to be on c.,** être de service; **to have no c. for sth,** ne pas avoir besoin de qch (b) (**telephone**) **c.,** coup m de téléphone, F: de fil; Adm: communication f; **to make a (phone) c.,** téléphoner; **c. sign,** indicatif d'appel; **c. girl,** call-girl f (c) visite f; **to make a c. on s.o.,** rendre visite à qn; Nau: **port of c.,** port d'escale (d) demande f (d'argent); Fin: appel de fonds. **II.** v **1.** vtr (a) appeler (qn); crier (qch); héler (un taxi); téléphoner à (qn); faire venir (un médecin); convoquer (une assemblée); réveiller (qn) (b) **to be called, to c. oneself,** s'appeler; **to c. s.o. names,** injurier (qn); **to c. s.o. a liar,** traiter qn de menteur; **let's c. it £5,** disons, mettons, £5 **2.** vi (a) appeler; crier; **to c. to s.o.,** appeler, héler, qn; Tp: **who's calling?** c'est de la part de qui? (b) **to c. at s.o.'s house,** (i) rendre visite à qn (ii) passer chez qn; **has anyone called?** est-il venu qn? (c) (of ship) faire escale (à un port); (of train) s'arrêter (à une gare). **'call 'back 1.** vtr & i rappeler (qn) **2.** vi repasser. **'callbox** n cabine f (téléphonique). **'callboy** n (a) Th: avertisseur m (b) NAm: chasseur m (d'hôtel). **'caller** n visiteur, -euse; Tp: demandeur, -euse. **'call for** vtr

(a) appeler, faire venir (qn); demander, exiger (une explication); **to c. for help,** crier au secours (b) venir prendre, venir chercher. **'call 'in 1.** vtr (a) appeler, faire venir (qn); faire appel à (un spécialiste) (b) retirer (qch) de la circulation **2.** vi passer (**at, on,** chez). **'calling** n vocation f. **'call 'off** vtr (a) décommander (une grève); annuler (un rendez-vous) (b) rappeler (un chien). **'call on** vtr rendre visite à (qn); **to c. on s.o. for sth,** demander qch à qn. **'call 'out 1.** vtr appeler, faire venir (qn); donner l'ordre de grève à (des ouvriers) **2.** vi appeler; crier; **to c. out to s.o.,** appeler, héler, qn. **'call 'up 1.** vtr (a) évoquer (des souvenirs) (b) Mil: mobiliser (qn) **2.** vtr & i esp NAm: téléphoner à (qn). **'call-up** n Mil: appel (sous les drapeaux); mobilisation f. **'call 'upon** vtr **to c. u. s.o. for sth,** demander qch à qn.

calligraphy [kə'ligrəfi] n calligraphie f.

callipers ['kælipəz] npl (a) compas m (de calibre) (b) Med: attelle-étrier f; étrier m.

callous ['kæləs] a (of pers) insensible, endurci. **'callously** adv sans pitié, sans cœur.

callus ['kæləs] n (pl **calluses**) durillon m.

calm [kɑːm] **1.** a calme, tranquille **2.** n (also **calmness**) calme m; tranquillité f **3.** vtr & i **to c. (down),** (se) calmer, (s')apaiser. **'calmly** adv calmement, avec calme.

calorie ['kæləri] n calorie f. **calo'rific** a calorifique.

calumny ['kæləmni] n calomnie f.

calve [kɑːv] vi vêler. **'calves** npl see **calf.**

calyx ['keiliks] n (pl **-yxes, -yces**) Bot: calice m.

cam [kæm] n Mec: came f. **'camshaft** n Mec: arbre m à came(s).

camber ['kæmbər] **1.** n bombement m (d'une route) **2.** vtr bomber (une chaussée).

Cambodia [kæm'boudiə] Prn Hist: Geog: Cambodge m.

came [keim] see **come.**

camel ['kæməl] n (a) chameau m; **c. (hair) coat,** manteau m en poil de chameau (b) (colour) fauve m.

camellia [kə'miːliə] n Bot: camélia m.

cameo ['kæmiou] n camée m.

camera ['kæmərə] n appareil m (photographique); cine, film, NAm: movie, **c.,** caméra f. **'cameraman,** n (pl **-men**) cameraman m; cadreur m.

camomile ['kæməmail] n Bot: camomille f.

camouflage ['kæməflɑːʒ] **1.** n camouflage m **2.** vtr camoufler.

camp[1] [kæmp] **1.** n camp m; campement m; **c. bed,** lit de camp; **camp(ing) chair,** chaise pliante; Fig: **c. follower,** partisan, -ane **2.** vi **to c. (out),** camper; faire du camping. **'camper** n **1.** campeur, -euse **2.** NAm: camionnette f de camping. **'campfire** n feu m de camp. **'camping** n camping; **c. equipment,** matériel de camping; **c. stove,** camping -gaz m. **'campsite** n (terrain m de) camping.

camp[2] a homosexuel; tapette.

campaign [kæm'pein] **1.** n campagne f **2.** vi faire (une) campagne, des campagnes. **cam'paigner** n militant, -ante.

camphor ['kæmfər] n camphre m. **'camphorated** a **c. oil,** huile camphrée.

campion ['kæmpiən] n Bot: lychnide f.

campus ['kæmpəs] n campus m.

can[1] [kæn] **1.** n (a) bidon m (d'huile); **watering c.,** arrosoir m; NAm: trash, garbage, **c.** (Br = dustbin), boîte f à ordures; poubelle f (b) boîte (de conserve, de bière) **2.** vtr (**canned**) mettre (des aliments) en boîte, en conserve. **'canned** a (a) (aliment) en conserve, en boîte (b) (of music) enregistré (c) P: ivre.

can[2] modal aux v (pres **can,** neg **cannot, can't;** pret: **could,** neg **could not, couldn't**) **1.** pouvoir; I **c. do it,** je peux le faire; **c. I help you?** puis-je vous aider? I **cannot allow that,** je ne saurais permettre cela; **as soon as I c.,** aussitôt que je pourrai; **all he c., could,** de son mieux; **that cannot be,** cela ne se peut pas; **what c. it be?** qu'est-ce que cela peut être? **it could be that,** il est possible que; **what c. he want?** qu'est-ce qu'il peut bien vouloir? **she's as pleased as c. be,** elle est on ne peut plus contente **2.** savoir; I **c. swim,** je sais nager **3.** (permission = may) **when c. I move in?** quand pourrai-je emménager? **4.** (not translated) I **c. see, hear, feel, nothing,** je ne vois, n'entends, ne sens, rien **5.** **you c. but try,** vous pouvez toujours essayer.

Canada ['kænədə] Prn Geog: Canada m. **Ca'nadian** a & n canadien, -ienne.

canal [kə'næl] n canal m.

canary [kə'nɛəri] n (pl **canaries**) (a) Orn: canari m, serin m (b) **c. (yellow),** jaune m canari.

cancel ['kænsəl] vtr (**cancelled**) annuler; résilier; biffer (un mot); supprimer (un train); décommander (une réunion); oblitérer (un timbre); Mth: éliminer. **cance'llation** n annulation f; résiliation f; oblitération f. **'cancel 'out** vtr & i **to c. (each other) o.,** s'annuler.

cancer ['kænsər] n (a) cancer m (du poumon, du sein, etc); **c. patient,** cancéreux, -euse; **c. specialist,** cancérologue mf (b) Astr: Cancer. **'cancerous** a cancéreux.

candelabra [kændə'lɑːbrə] n candélabre m.

candid ['kændid] a franc, sincère. **'candidly** adv franchement, sincèrement.

candidate ['kændidət] n candidat, -e, aspirant, -e, prétendant, -e (**for sth,** à qch). **'candidacy, 'candidature** n candidature f.

candied ['kændid] a Comest: confit.

candle ['kændl] n (wax) bougie f; (tallow) chandelle f; (in church) cierge m; F: **to burn the c. at both ends,** brûler la chandelle par les deux bouts; F: **he can't hold a c. to you,** il ne vous arrive pas à la cheville. **'candlelight** n lumière f de chandelle; **by c.,** à la chandelle. **'Candlemas** n Ecc: la Chandeleur. **'candlestick** n chandelier m; bougeoir m. **'candlewick** n Tex: chenille f (de coton).

candour, NAm: **candor** ['kændər] n franchise f.

candy ['kændi] n esp NAm: bonbon(s) m(pl); **c. store** (Br = **sweet shop**), confiserie f; **cotton c.,** n barbe f à papa. **'candyfloss** n Br barbe à papa. **'candy-striped** a pékiné.

cane [kein] **1.** n canne f; jonc m; rotin m; **c. furniture,** meubles en rotin; **raspberry c.,** tige f de framboisier; **sugar c.,** canne à sucre; **c. sugar,** sucre de canne **2.** vtr donner des coups de canne à (qn). **'caning** n Sch: correction f.

canine ['keinain] **1.** a canin **2.** n canine f.

canister ['kænistər] n boîte f (en fer blanc).

canker ['kæŋkər] *n* gale *f* (du chien); chancre *m*.

cannibal ['kænibəl] *n & a* cannibale (*mf*). **'cannibalism** *n* cannibalisme *m*. **'cannibalize** *vtr* démonter (un moteur) pour utiliser les pièces détachées.

cannabis ['kænəbis] *n* cannabis *m*.

cannon ['kænən] **I.** *n* canon *m*; **c. fodder,** chair à canon. **II.** *vi* **(cannoned) to c. into s.o., sth,** se heurter contre qn, qch. **'cannonball** *n* boulet *m* de canon.

cannot ['kænɔt] *see* **can.**

canny ['kæni] *a* (**-ier, -iest**) *esp Scot:* prudent, circonspect. **'cannily** *adv* avec prudence, avec circonspection.

canoe [kə'nu:] **1.** *n* canoë *m*; *FrC:* canot *m*; **dugout c.,** pirogue *f* **2.** *vi* (**canoed**) faire du canoë. **ca'noeist** *n* canoéiste *mf*.

canon ['kænən] *n* (*a*) canon *m*; **c. law,** droit canon (*b*) (*pers*) chanoine *m*. **canoni'zation** *n* canonisation *f*. **'canonize** *vtr* canoniser.

canoodle [kə'nu:dl] *vi F:* se faire des mamours.

canopy ['kænəpi] *n* dais *m*; baldaquin *m* (de lit); (*over doorway*) auvent *m*.

cant [kænt] *n* (*a*) jargon *m*; argot *m* (*b*) langage *m* hypocrite.

can't [kɑ:nt] *see* **can.**

Cantab. ['kæntæb] *abbr Cantabrigiensis,* de l'Université de Cambridge.

cantaloup(e) [kæntəlu:p] *n Hort:* cantaloup *m*.

cantankerous [kæn'tæŋkərəs] *a* revêche, acariâtre; hargneux; querelleur.

cantata [kæn'tɑ:tə] *n Mus:* cantate *f*.

canteen [kæn'ti:n] *n* (*a*) cantine *f* (*b*) **c. of cutlery,** ménagère *f*.

canter ['kæntər] **1.** *n* petit galop **2.** *vi* aller au petit galop.

Canterbury ['kæntəbəri] *Prn* Cantorbéry *m*; *Bot:* **C. bell,** campanule *f* (à grosses fleurs).

cantilever ['kæntili:vər] *n* **c. bridge,** pont cantilever.

canvas ['kænvəs] *n* (grosse) toile *f*; **under c.,** sous la tente; *Nau:* sous voile.

canvass ['kænvəs] **1.** *vtr* (*a*) solliciter (des suffrages); prospecter (la clientèle); *Pol:* faire une tournée électorale dans (une ville); **to c. s.o.,** solliciter la voix de qn (*b*) examiner minutieusement (une question) **2.** *vi* faire une tournée électorale. **'canvasser** *n Pol:* agent électoral; *Com:* démarcheur, -euse. **'canvassing** *n* sollicitation *f* (de suffrages); démarchage *m*.

canyon ['kænjən] *n* cañon *m*, canyon *m*.

cap [kæp] **1.** *n* (*a*) bonnet *m*; (*with peak*) casquette *f*; toque *f* (de magistrat, de jockey); *Mil:* (*hard*) képi *m*; (*soft*) calot *m*; *Sch:* **c. and gown,** costume *m* académique; *Sp:* **to have three caps,** avoir joué trois fois dans l'équipe nationale; *F:* **c. in hand,** chapeau bas (*b*) chapeau *m* (de protection); capuchon *m* (de stylo); capsule *f* (de bouteille); bouchon *m* (d'objectif); (*contraceptive*) (**Dutch**) **c.,** diaphragme *m* (*c*) *Toys:* amorce *f* **2.** *vtr* (**capped**) (*a*) coiffer; capsuler (une bouteille); (*of clouds*) couronner (une montagne) (*b*) (*outdo*) surpasser; renchérir sur; **that caps it all!** ça c'est le bouquet! (*c*) *Sp:* nommer (qn) à l'équipe nationale.

capable ['keipəbl] *a* (*a*) capable, compétent (*b*) susceptible. **capa'bility** *n* capacité *f* (**for, de**). **'capably** *adv* avec compétence.

capacity [kə'pæsiti] *n* (*a*) capacité *f*; contenance *f* (d'un tonneau); *Ind:* rendement *m*; **seating c.,** nombre *m* de places (assises); **filled to c.,** (salle) comble (*b*) aptitude *f* (**for, à**); capacité; **in the c. of,** en qualité *f* de; **in one's official c.,** dans l'exercice de ses fonctions; **in a private, advisory, c.,** à titre privé, consultatif. **ca'pacious** *a* vaste, ample. **ca'pacitor** *n Elcs:* condensateur *m*.

cape¹ [keip] *n Cl:* pèlerine *f*; cape *f*.

cape² *n* cap *m*. **'Cape 'Town** *Prn Geog:* le Cap.

caper¹ ['keipər] *n Cu:* câpre *f*.

caper² **1.** *n* (*a*) cabriole *f* (*b*) *F:* farce *f* **2.** *vi* **to c. (about),** faire des cabrioles; gambader.

capillary [kə'piləri] *a & n* capillaire (*m*).

capital ['kæpitl] **1.** *a* capital; (lettre) majuscule **2.** *n* (*a*) (*city*) capitale *f* (*b*) majuscule *f* (*c*) *Fin:* capital *m*; fonds *m*(*pl*); **to make c. out of sth,** profiter de qch; **c. assets,** actif immobilisé; **c. goods,** biens d'équipement; **c. expenditure,** mise de fonds; **c. gains tax,** impôt sur les plus-values (*d*) *Arch:* chapiteau *m* **3.** *int* excellent! **'capitalism** *n* capitalisme *m*. **'capitalist** *a & n* capitaliste (*mf*). **capitali'zation** *n* capitalisation *f*. **'capitalize** *vtr & i* capitaliser. **'capitalize 'on** *vtr* tourner (qch) à son avantage.

capitulate [kə'pitjuleit] *vi* capituler. **capitu'lation** *n* capitulation *f*.

capon ['keipən] *n Cu:* chapon *m*.

caprice [kə'pri:s] *n* caprice *m*. **ca'pricious** *a* capricieux. **ca'priciously** *adv* capricieusement.

Capricorn ['kæprikɔ:n] *n Astr:* Capricorne *m*.

capsicum ['kæpsikəm] *n Comest:* (*sweet*) poivron *m*; (*hot*) piment *m*.

capsize [kæp'saiz] *vi & tr* (faire) chavirer.

capstan ['kæpstən] *n* cabestan *m*.

capsule ['kæpsju:l] *n* capsule *f*.

captain ['kæptin] **1.** *n* capitaine *m*; chef *m*; *Av:* commandant *m* (de bord) **2.** *vtr* commander (un navire); conduire (une expédition); diriger; *Sp:* être le capitaine de (l'équipe). **'captaincy** *n* grade *m* de capitaine; commandement *m* (d'une équipe).

caption ['kæpʃən] *n* (*under illustration*) légende *f*; (*heading*) en-tête *m*; *Cin:* sous-titre *m*.

captivate ['kæptiveit] *vtr* captiver; charmer.

captive ['kæptiv] **1.** *a* captif **2.** *n* captif, -ive; prisonnier, -ière. **cap'tivity** *n* captivité *f*.

capture ['kæptʃər] **1.** *n* capture *f* **2.** *vtr* capturer (un navire, un malfaiteur), prendre (une ville) (**from,** à); s'emparer de (qn); captiver (l'attention); saisir (une ressemblance); *Com:* **to c. the market,** accaparer la vente. **'captor** *n* celui, celle, qui fait qn prisonnier; (*unlawful*) ravisseur, -euse.

car [kɑ:r] *n* (*NAm:* = **automobile**) voiture *f*; auto-(mobile) *f*; *Rail: NAm:* voiture, wagon *m*. **'car-park** *n* parking *m*. **'carport** *n* abri-garage *m*. **'carsick** *a* **to be c.,** avoir le mal de voiture, de la route. **'carwash** *n* lave-auto *m*.

carafe [kə'ræf] *n* carafe *f*.

caramel ['kærəməl] *n Cu:* caramel *m*.

carat ['kærət] *n Meas:* carat *m*; **eighteen-c. gold,** or à dix-huit carats.

caravan ['kærəvæn] *n* (*a*) caravane *f* (*b*) (*NAm:* = **trailer**) caravane (de camping); **gipsy c.,** roulotte *f*; **c. site,** camping *m* (pour caravanes). **'caravanning** *n* camping en caravane.

caraway ['kærəwei] *n Cu:* carvi *m*, cumin *m*.
carbohydrate [ka:bou'haidreit] *n Ch:* hydrate *m* de carbone.
carbolic [ka:'bɔlik] *a Ch:* phénique; (savon) phéniqué; **c. acid,** phénol *m*.
carbon ['ka:bən] *n* carbone *m*; **c. dioxide,** gaz *m* carbonique; **c. monoxide,** oxyde *m* de carbone; **c. dating,** datation au carbone; *Typew:* **c. (paper),** (papier *m*) carbone; **c. (copy),** double *m.* 'car**bon**ate *n* carbonate *m.* car'**bonic** *a* carbonique. car**bo'niferous** *a* carbonifère. 'carbonize *vtr* carboniser.
carborundum [ka:bə'rʌndəm] *n* carborundum *m.*
carboy ['ka:bɔi] *n* bonbonne *f.*
carbuncle ['ka:bʌŋkl] *n* (*a*) escarboucle *f* (*b*) *Med:* furoncle *m.*
carburettor, -er, *NAm:* **-etor** [ka:bə'retər, -bju-, *NAm:* 'ka:bəreitər] *n* carburateur *m.*
carcase, -cass ['ka:kəs] *n* carcasse *f*; *F:* corps *m.*
carcinogen [ka:'sinədʒen] *n* substance *f* cancérigène, cancérogène.
card [ka:d] *n* (*a*) carte *f*; **playing c.,** carte à jouer; **index c.,** fiche *f*; **c. index,** fichier *m*; **banker's c.,** cheque (guarantee) **c.,** carte (de garantie) bancaire; **credit,** *esp NAm:* **charge, c.,** carte de crédit; **a game of cards,** une partie de cartes; **c. game,** jeu de cartes; **c. table,** table de jeu; *Fig:* **to play one's cards right,** bien jouer son jeu; **to put one's cards on the table,** mettre cartes sur table; *F:* **it's quite on the cards,** il est bien possible; *F:* **to get one's cards,** être renvoyé (*b*) *F:* (*pers*) original, -e. 'cardboard *n* carton *m*; **c. box,** (boîte en) carton. 'card-carrying *a* **c.-c. member,** membre affilié. 'cardsharp(er) *n* tricheur, -euse.
cardiac ['ka:diæk] *a* cardiaque.
cardigan ['ka:digən] *n Cl:* cardigan *m.*
cardinal ['ka:dinl] *a & n* cardinal (*m*).
cardiology [ka:di'ɔlədʒi] *n* cardiologie *f.* 'cardiogram *n Med:* cardiogramme *m.* cardi'ologist *n* cardiologue *mf.*
care ['keər] **1.** *n* (*a*) souci *m*; inquiétude *f* (*b*) soin(s) *m*(*pl*); attention *f*; ménagement *m*; *Jur:* **without due c.,** avec négligence; **to take c. of,** prendre soin, s'occuper, de; **to take c. in doing sth,** apporter du soin à faire qch; **to take c. not to do sth,** se garder de faire qch; **take c.!** faites attention! prenez garde! **to take c. of oneself, one's health,** se soigner, se ménager; **he can take c. of himself,** il sait se débrouiller; **that matter will take c. of itself,** cela s'arrangera tout seul; (*on parcel*) **with c.,** fragile (*c*) soin(s), charge *f*; *pl* responsabilités *fpl* (d'État); (*on letter*) **c. of Mrs X,** aux bons soins de, chez, Mme X; *Adm:* **in c.,** (enfant) assisté; **to put sth in s.o.'s c.,** confier qch à, aux soins de, qn **2.** *vi* (*a*) se soucier, se préoccuper (**about,** de); **I don't c.!** I couldn't c. less! ça m'est égal! peu m'importe! *F:* je m'en fiche! **what do I c.?** **who cares?** qu'est-ce que cela peut bien (me) faire? **for all I c.,** pour tout ce que ça me fait; **that's all he cares about,** il n'y a que cela qui l'intéresse (*b*) vouloir, aimer (**to do,** faire); **if you c. to,** si cela vous plaît de. 'care 'for *vtr* (*a*) aimer; **I don't c. f. this music,** cette musique ne me dit rien (*b*) soigner (qn); **well cared for,** (air) soigné. 'carefree *a* insouciant; sans souci. 'careful *a* (*a*) soigneux; (travail) attentif, soigné; **be c.!** faites attention! **be c. you don't fall,** fais attention de ne pas tomber (*b*) prudent, circonspect; **c. with money,** regardant. 'carefully *adv* (*a*) soigneusement (*b*) prudemment. 'carefulness *n* (*a*) soin *m*, attention *f* (*b*) prudence *f.* 'careless *a* qui manque de soin; sans soin; négligent; **c. mistake,** faute d'inattention. 'carelessly *adv* (*a*) avec insouciance (*b*) négligemment; sans soin. 'carelessness *n* (*a*) insouciance *f* (*b*) manque *m* de soin; négligence *f.* 'caretaker *n* concierge *mf* (de maison); gardien, -ienne (d'immeuble, de musée); **c. government,** gouvernement intérimaire. 'careworn *a* rongé par les soucis. 'caring *a* compatissant.
career [kə'riər] **1.** *n* carrière *f*; **c. girl,** femme qui veut faire (une) carrière; **c. diplomat,** diplomate de carrière; *Sch:* **careers master, mistress,** orienteur, -euse, professionnel(le) **2.** *vi* **to c. (along),** aller à toute vitesse.
caress [kə'res] **1.** *n* (*pl* **caresses**) caresse *f* **2.** *vtr* caresser.
cargo ['ka:gou] *n* (*pl* **cargoes**) cargaison *f*; chargement *m*; **c. boat,** cargo *m.*
Caribbean [kæri'bi:ən] *a & n* the C. (Sea), la mer des Antilles, des Caraïbes; **the C. Islands,** les Antilles *f.*
caribou ['kæribu:] *n Z:* caribou *m.*
caricature ['kærikətjuər] **1.** *n* caricature *f* **2.** *vtr* caricaturer. 'caricaturist *n* caricaturiste *mf.*
caries ['keəri:z] *n Med:* carie *f.*
carmine ['ka:main] *a & n* carmin (*m inv*).
carnage ['ka:nidʒ] *n* carnage *m.*
carnal ['ka:nl] *a* charnel; sensuel; sexuel; (péchés) de la chair.
carnation [ka:'neiʃn] *n Bot:* œillet *m.*
carnival ['ka:nivəl] *n* carnaval *m*, *pl* -als.
carnivore ['ka:nivɔ:r] *n* carnivore *m*, carnassier *m.* car'nivorous *a* carnivore, carnassier.
carol ['kærəl] *n* (**Christmas**) **c.,** (chant *m* de) noël *m.*
carouse [kə'rauz] *vi* faire la fête, *F:* la bombe.
carousel [kærə'sel] *n* (*a*) *NAm:* (*Br* = **roundabout**) manège *m* (de foire) (*b*) (*conveyer*) carrousel *m.*
carp[1] [ka:p] *n inv Ich:* carpe *f.*
carp[2] *vi* grogner; trouver à redire (**at,** à). 'carping **1.** *a* malveillant **2.** *n* censure *f.*
carpenter ['ka:pintər] *n* charpentier *m*; menuisier *m* (en bâtiments). 'carpentry *n* charpenterie *f*; (grosse) menuiserie.
carpet ['ka:pit] **1.** *n* tapis *m*; (*fitted*) moquette *f*; **c. sweeper,** balai mécanique; *F:* (*of pers*) **to be on the c.,** être sur la sellette **2.** *vtr* recouvrir d'un tapis, d'une moquette. 'carpeting *n* moquette.
carriage ['kæridʒ] *n* (*a*) port *m*, transport *m*; *Com:* **c. free,** franco; franc de port; **c. paid,** (en) port payé (*b*) (*of pers*) port, maintien *m* (*c*) (**horse and**) **c.,** voiture *f*; équipage *m*; **c. and pair,** voiture à deux chevaux (*d*) *Rail:* (*NAm:* = **coach**) voiture, wagon *m* (*e*) chariot *m* (d'une machine à écrire). 'carriageway *n* chaussée *f*; **dual c.,** route *f* à quatre voies.
carrier ['kæriər] *n* **1.** (*a*) porteur, -euse (*b*) *Com:* transporteur *m*; camionneur *m*; **c. pigeon,** pigeon voyageur **2.** support *m*; (*on bicycle, etc*) portebagages *m inv*; **c. (bag),** (grand) sac (en plastique, en papier) **3.** (**aircraft**) **c.,** porte-avions *m inv*; (**troop**)

c., (avion *m* de) transport *m* de troupes; **personnel c.**, véhicule *m* de transport de troupes.

carrion ['kæriən] *n* charogne *f*; **c. crow**, corneille noire.

carrot ['kærət] *n Hort:* carotte *f.* '**carroty** *a* (cheveux) carotte *inv.*

carry ['kæri] *v* (carried) 1. *vtr* (*a*) porter; transporter (des marchandises); emporter (un souvenir); (*of bus, wires*) conduire (qn, le son); (*of pipes*) amener (l'eau); (*of pillar*) supporter (le poids); **to c. oneself well**, se tenir bien; **to c. all before one**, triompher sur toute la ligne; **to c. one's hearers with one**, entraîner son auditoire; *F:* **to c. the can**, payer les pots cassés (*b*) (faire) adopter (une proposition) (*c*) (*of shop*) tenir (un article) (*d*) *Mth:* retenir; **two down, c. one**, je pose deux et je retiens un 2. *vi* (*of voice*) porter. '**carry a'long** *vtr* emporter, entraîner. '**carry a'way** *vtr* emporter; enlever; *Fig:* **to be, get, carried a.**, être entraîné, enlevé (par une émotion); se laisser emporter; *F:* s'emballer. '**carrycot** *n* porte-bébé *m inv.* '**carry 'forward** *vtr* reporter. '**carryings-on** *npl F:* histoire(s) *f(pl).* '**carry 'off** *vtr* emporter (qch); emmener, enlever (qn); remporter (le prix). '**carry 'on** 1. *vtr* poursuivre; continuer; exercer (un métier); entretenir (une correspondance); soutenir (une conversation) 2. *vi* (*a*) continuer; persévérer, persister (*b*) *F:* faire une scène; **don't c. on like that!** ne vous emballez pas comme ça! (*c*) *F:* avoir une liaison (**with**, avec). '**carry-on** *n F:* histoire(s). '**carry 'out** *vtr* (*a*) emporter, sortir (*b*) mettre à exécution, effectuer; exécuter (un programme); s'acquitter de (la tâche); appliquer (une loi). '**carry-out** *n Scot: & NAm:* repas *m* à emporter; plats cuisinés à emporter. '**carry 'over** *vtr* reporter. '**carry 'through** *vtr* mener à bonne fin.

cart [kɑːt] 1. *n* charrette *f*; **c. track**, chemin charretier; *Fig:* **to put the c. before the horse**, mettre la charrue devant les bœufs; *F:* **to be in the c.**, être dans de beaux draps 2. *vtr* charrier; transporter; *F:* **to c. (about)**, trimbaler. '**carthorse** *n* cheval *m* de trait. '**cartload** *n* charretée *f.* '**cartwheel** *n* roue *f* de charrette; *Gym:* **to turn cartwheels**, faire la roue.

cartilage ['kɑːtilidʒ] *n* cartilage *m.*

cartographer [kɑː'tɔɡrəfər] *n* cartographe *mf.*

carton ['kɑːtən] *n* (boîte *f* en) carton; pot *m* (de crème); cartouche *f* (de cigarettes).

cartoon [kɑː'tuːn] *n* (*a*) *Art:* carton *m* (*b*) *Journ:* dessin *m* humoristique; **strip c.**, bande(s) dessinée(s) (*c*) *Cin:* dessin animé. **car'toonist** *n* dessinateur, -trice (humoristique, de dessins animés); *Journ:* caricaturiste *mf.*

cartridge ['kɑːtridʒ] *n* cartouche *f*; *Phot:* chargeur *m*; **c. paper**, papier fort, à cartouche.

carve [kɑːv] *vtr* (*a*) sculpter, graver, ciseler (du marbre, du bois) (*b*) découper (la viande). '**carver** *n* 1. (*a*) sculpteur *m* (sur bois) (*b*) découpeur, -euse (de la viande) 2. (*a*) couteau *m* à découper (*b*) fauteuil *m* de table (à bras). '**carve 'up** *vtr* (*a*) découper (la viande); démembrer (un pays) (*b*) *P:* donner des coups de couteau à (qn). '**carving** *n* (*a*) *Art:* sculpture *f*; gravure *f*, ciselure *f* (*b*) découpage *m* (de la viande); **c. knife, fork**, couteau, fourchette, à découper.

cascade [kæs'keid] 1. *n* chute *f* d'eau; cascade *f* 2. *vi* tomber en cascade.

case¹ [keis] *n* (*a*) cas *m*; **if that's the c.**, s'il en est ainsi; **that's often the c.**, cela arrive souvent; **it's a c. of**, il s'agit de; **in c. of**, en cas de; **in c. he isn't there**, au cas, dans le cas, où il n'y serait pas; **in that c.**, en ce cas, dans ce cas-là; **in any c.**, en tout cas; **just in c.**, à tout hasard; **in most cases**, dans la plupart des cas; **as the c. may be**, selon le cas; **c. history**, antécédents *mpl* (de qn); **c. load**, (nombre *m* de) dossiers *mpl* (d'un médecin, etc) (*b*) *Jur:* cause *f*, affaire *f*; procès *m*; **the c. for the Crown**, l'accusation *f* (*c*) arguments *mpl* (**for, against**, en faveur de, contre) (*d*) *F:* (*pers*) original, -e. '**casebook** *n* dossier (médical). '**case-hardened** *a* (*of pers*) endurci. '**casework** *n* (*of social worker*) traitement individuel.

case² *n* (*a*) (*suitcase*) valise *f* (*b*) caisse *f* (de marchandises) (*c*) étui *m* (à lunettes, à cigarettes); coffret *m*, écrin *m* (pour bijoux); boîte *f* (de violon); (**display**) **c.**, vitrine *f*; *Typ:* **lower c.**, bas *m* de casse. '**casement** ('**window**') *n* fenêtre *f* à battant; croisée *f.*

cash [kæʃ] 1. *n no pl* espèce(s) *f(pl)*; argent (comptant); **to be short of c.**, être à sec; **c. down**, argent (au) comptant; **to pay c. (down)**, payer comptant, *F:* cash; **c. (in hand)**, encaisse *f*; **in c.**, en espèces; **c. price**, prix (au) comptant; **c. on delivery**, paiement à la livraison; **c. with order**, envoi contre remboursement; **c. box, desk**, caisse *f*; **c. register**, caisse (enregistreuse); **c. crop**, culture commerciale; **c. and carry**, supermarché de demi-gros; **c. flow**, cash-flow *m* 2. *vtr* toucher, encaisser; **to c. a cheque**, toucher un chèque. '**ca'shier** 1. *n* caissier, -ière 2. *vtr* casser (un officier). '**cash 'in 'on** *vtr* tirer profit de.

cashew [kæ'ʃuː] *n* **c. (nut)**, (noix *f* de) cajou *m.*

cashmere ['kæʃmiər] *n* cachemire *m.*

casino, *pl* -**os** [kə'siːnou, -ouz] *n* casino *m.*

cask [kɑːsk] *n* barrique *f*, fût *m*, tonneau *m.*

casket ['kɑːskit] *n* (*a*) coffret *m* (*b*) *NAm:* (*Br* = **coffin**) cercueil *m.*

casserole ['kæsəroul] 1. *n* (*a*) cocotte *f* (*b*) ragoût *m* (en cocotte) 2. *vtr* faire cuire en cocotte.

cassette [kæ'set] *n* (*a*) *Phot:* chargeur *m* (*b*) (*for tape recorder*) cassette *f.*

cassock ['kæsək] *n Ecc:* soutane *f.*

cast [kɑːst] 1. *n* (*a*) coup *m* (de dés); *Fish:* lancer *m* (de la ligne) (*b*) moule *m*; (**plaster**) **c.**, (moulage *m* au) plâtre (*c*) tournure *f* (d'esprit); **c. of features**, physionomie *f*; **to have a c. in one's eye**, avoir une tendance à loucher (*d*) *Th:* distribution *f* (des rôles); troupe *f* 2. *vtr* (**cast**) (*a*) jeter, lancer; projeter (une ombre); (*of snake*) **to c. its skin**, muer (*b*); **to c. one's vote**, donner sa voix, voter (**for**, pour) (*c*) fondre (du métal); mouler (un cylindre); couler (une statue); **c. iron**, (fer *m* de) fonte *f* (*d*) *Th:* distribuer les rôles de (la pièce); **to c. s.o. as**, assigner à qn le rôle de. '**cast a'bout, a'round, 'for** *vtr* chercher. '**cast a'side** *vtr* se défaire de. '**cast a'way** *vtr* **to be c. a.**, faire naufrage. '**castaway** *n* naufragé, -ée. '**casting** 1. *a* **c. vote**, voix prépondérante 2. *n* (*a*) moulage, fonte (*b*) pièce de fonte, pièce coulée (*c*) *Th:* distribution (des rôles). '**cast-'iron** *a* (*a*) (poêle) de, en, fonte (*b*) (alibi) irréfutable.

'cast'off 1. *vtr* rejeter; se défaire de 2. *vtr & i* (a) *Nau:* larguer les amarres (d'un bateau) (b) *Knit:* arrêter (les mailles). 'cast-off clothes, 'cast-offs *npl* vêtements *mpl* de rebut. 'cast 'on *vtr & i Knit:* monter (des mailles).

castanets [kæstə'nets] *npl* castagnettes *fpl*.

caste [kɑːst] *n* caste *f*.

caster ['kɑːstər] *n* = castor.

castigate ['kæstigeit] *vtr* châtier, corriger (qn); critiquer sévèrement (qch).

castle ['kɑːsl] 1. *n* (a) château (fort) (b) *Chess:* tour *f* 2. *vtr & i Chess:* roquer.

castor ['kɑːstər] *n* (a) saupoudroir *m*; c. sugar, sucre en poudre; c. oil, huile de ricin (b) roulette *f* (de fauteuil).

castrate [kæ'streit] *vtr* châtrer.

casual ['kæʒjuəl] *a* (a) fortuit, accidentel; (commentaire) fait en passant (b) (travail) intermittent; (main-d'œuvre) temporaire (c) insouciant; désinvolte (d) (vêtements) sport *inv.* 'casually *adv* (a) fortuitement, par hasard, en passant (b) négligemment; avec désinvolture. 'casuals *npl* chaussures *fpl*, vêtements *mpl*, sport.

casualty ['kæʒjuəlti] *n* (*pl* casualties) (a) accident *m* (de personne); c. department, service des urgences (d'un hôpital) (b) victime *f* (d'un accident); blessé, -ée; accidenté, -ée (c) *Mil:* casualties, pertes *fpl*.

cat [kæt] *n* 1. (a) chat *m*; chatte *f*; *Z:* the (great) cats, les grands félins; c. burglar, monte-en-l'air *m inv*; *F:* to be like a c. on hot bricks, être sur des épines; *F:* to let the c. out of the bag, vendre la mèche; they quarrel like c. and dog, ils s'entendent comme chien et chat; *F:* it's raining cats and dogs, il pleut à torrents; *F:* it's not big enough to swing a c. (in), c'est grand comme un mouchoir de poche; *F:* to put the c. among the pigeons, enfermer le loup dans la bergerie (b) *F:* (of woman) chipie *f.* 'cat-and-'mouse *a* to play a c.-a.-m. game with s.o., jouer avec qn comme un chat avec une souris. 'catcall *n Th:* sifflet *m.* 'catfish *n* poisson-chat *m.* 'catgut *n Mus:* (corde *f* de) boyau *m*; *Surg:* catgut *m.* 'catkin *n Bot:* chaton *m.* 'catnap *n F:* (petit) somme, sieste *f.* 'cat's-eye *n* (*in road*) cataphote *m.* 'catsuit *n Cl:* combinaison *f* (de danse). 'catty *a* (-ier, -iest) *F:* (*esp of woman*) méchant; rosse; c. remark, rosserie *f.* 'catwalk *n* passerelle *f.*

cataclysm ['kætəklizm] *n* cataclysme *m.*

catacombs ['kætəkuːmz] *npl* catacombes *f.*

catalogue, *NAm:* catalog ['kætəlɔg] 1. *n* catalogue *m*, liste *f* 2. *vtr* cataloguer.

catalyst ['kætəlist] *n* catalyseur *m.*

catamaran [kætəmə'ræn] *n Nau:* catamaran *m.*

catapult ['kætəpʌlt] 1. *n* lance-pierre(s) *m inv*; fronde *f*; *Av:* catapulte *f* (de lancement) 2. *vtr Av:* catapulter (un avion).

cataract ['kætərækt] *n* cataracte *f.*

catarrh [kə'tɑːr] *n Med:* catarrhe *m.*

catastrophe [kə'tæstrəfi] *n* catastrophe *f.* cata-'strophic *a* catastrophique.

catch [kætʃ] I. *n* (a) prise *f*; *Fish:* pêche *f* (b) (*pl* catches) (*on door*) loquet *m* (c) attrape *f*; c. question, colle *f.* II. *v* (caught [kɔːt]) 1. *vtr* (a) attraper, prendre; saisir; avoir; ne pas manquer (le train); you

won't c. me doing that again! on ne m'y reprendra plus; to c. s.o. doing sth, surprendre qn à faire qch; we were caught in the storm, l'orage nous a surpris; to c. one's sleeve on a nail, accrocher sa manche à un clou; to c. one's foot on sth, se prendre le pied dans qch (b) saisir, percevoir, entendre (un bruit); rencontrer (le regard de qn); attirer (l'attention de qn); frapper (la vue); to c. s.o.'s eye, attirer l'attention de qn (c) attraper (une maladie) 2. *vi* (*of sleeve*) s'accrocher (on, à); (*of fire*) prendre; *Cu:* (*of milk*) attacher. 'catch 'at *vtr* essayer de saisir; s'accrocher à. 'catching *a* (*of illness*) contagieux, infectieux; (*of tune*) entraînant. 'catchment ('area) *n* réseau *m* de ramassage (d'écoliers). 'catch 'on *vi* (a) (*of fashion*) prendre; réussir (b) comprendre, *F:* piger. 'catch 'out *vtr* prendre (qn) sur le fait, en faute. 'catchphrase *n* = catchword. 'catch 'up 1. *vtr* rattraper (qn) 2. *vi* (a) se rattraper; se remettre au courant (with, on, the news, des nouvelles); to c. up with s.o., rattraper qn. 'catchword *n* scie *f*, rengaine *f*; slogan *m.* 'catchy *a* (air) entraînant.

catechize ['kætikaiz] *vtr* catéchiser. 'catechism *n* catéchisme *m.*

category ['kætigəri] *n* (*pl* categories) catégorie *f.* cate'goric(al) *a* catégorique. cate'gorically *adv* catégoriquement. 'categorize *vtr* classer par catégories.

cater ['keitər] *vi* s'occuper de la restauration (for, de, pour). 'caterer *n* restaurateur *m*; traiteur *m.* 'cater 'for *vtr* pourvoir à (un goût); s'adresser à (qn). 'catering *n* restauration; approvisionnement *m.*

caterpillar ['kætəpilər] *n* chenille *f*; c. tractor, autochenille *f*; tracteur à chenilles.

caterwaul ['kætəwɔːl] *vi* miauler; crier.

cathedral [kə'θiːdrəl] *n* cathédrale *f*; c. city, ville épiscopale, évêché *m.*

catheter ['kæθitər] *n Med:* sonde (creuse).

cathode ['kæθoud] *n Elcs:* cathode *f*; c. ray tube, tube cathodique.

catholic ['kæθəlik] 1. *a* (a) universel (b) tolérant; (esprit) large; (goût) éclectique 2. *a & n Ecc:* catholique (*mf*). ca'tholicism [-isizm] *n* catholicisme *m.*

cattle ['kætl] *n coll inv* bétail *m*; bestiaux *mpl*; beef c., bœufs de boucherie; c. shed, étable *f*; c. breeding, élevage du bétail; *PN:* c. crossing, passage de troupeaux; c. show, comice agricole. 'cattlecake *n* tourteau *m.*

Caucasian [kɔː'keiʒən, -zjən] 1. *a Geog:* (a) caucasien (b) *Ethn:* de race blanche 2. *n* (a) *Geog:* caucasien, -ienne (b) *Ethn:* blanc *m*, blanche *f.*

caucus ['kɔːkəs] *n Pol:* comité électoral.

caught [kɔːt] *see* catch.

cauldron ['kɔːldrən] *n* chaudron *m.*

cauliflower ['kɔliflauər] *n* chou-fleur *m*; c. cheese, chou-fleur au gratin.

cause [kɔːz] 1. *n* cause *f*; raison *f*; c. and effect, la cause et l'effet; to be the c. of sth, être (la) cause de qch; to have good c. for doing sth, avoir de bonnes raisons pour faire qch; and with good c., et pour cause; c. for complaint, sujet *m* de plainte; in the c. of justice, pour (la cause de) la justice 2. *vtr* (a) causer, occasionner (un malheur); provoquer (un incendie) (b) **to c. s.o. to do sth,** faire faire qch à qn.

causeway ['kɔːzwei] *n* chaussée *f*; levée *f*.

caustic ['kɔːstik] *a* caustique; (esprit) mordant. 'caustically *adv* d'un ton mordant.

cauterize ['kɔːtəraiz] *vtr* cautériser. **cauteri'zation** *n* cautérisation *f*.

caution ['kɔːʃən] **1.** *n* (a) précaution *f*, prévoyance *f*, prudence *f*; circonspection *f* (b) avis *m*, avertissement *m* (c) réprimande *f* **2.** *vtr* (a) avertir (qn) (b) menacer (qn) de poursuites à la prochaine occasion. 'cautionary *a* (conte) moral. 'cautious *a* circonspect, prudent. 'cautiously *adv* prudemment. 'cautiousness *n* prudence *f*.

cavalcade [kævəl'keid] *n* cavalcade *f*.

cavalier [kævə'liər] *a & n* cavalier (*m*).

cavalry ['kævəlri] *n* cavalerie *f*.

cave [keiv] *n* caverne *f*, grotte *f*; **c. art,** art rupestre. 'cave 'in *vi* s'effondrer; céder. 'caveman *pl* -men *n* homme *m* des cavernes. 'caving *n* spéléologie *f*.

cavern ['kævən] *n* caverne *f*; grotte *f*. 'cavernous *a* caverneux.

caviar(e) ['kævia:r] *n* caviar *m*.

cavil ['kævil] *vi* (**cavilled**) chicaner, ergoter.

cavity ['kæviti] *n* cavité *f*; creux *m*; trou *m*; **c. wall,** mur double.

cavort [kə'vɔːt] *vi* faire des cabrioles.

caw [kɔː] *vi* croasser.

cayenne ['keien] *n* *Cu:* **c. (pepper),** poivre *m* de Cayenne.

CB *abbr* *WTel:* *citizens' band.*

cc *abbr* *cubic centimetre(s).*

cease [siːs] *vtr & i* cesser (**doing sth,** de faire qch); **to c. fire,** cesser le feu. 'ceasefire *n* cessez-le-feu *m* *inv.* 'ceaseless *a* incessant; sans arrêt. 'ceaselessly *adv* sans cesse; sans arrêt.

cedar ['siːdər] *n* *Bot:* cèdre *m*.

cede [siːd] *vtr* céder.

cedilla [si'dilə] *n* cédille *f*.

ceiling ['siːliŋ] *n* plafond *m*; **output has reached its c.,** la production plafonne.

celebrate ['selibreit] *vtr* célébrer; commémorer, fêter (un événement). 'celebrated *a* célèbre (**for,** par); renommé (**for,** pour). **cele'bration** *n* (a) célébration *f* (b) réunion *f* pour fêter qch; *F:* **this calls for a c.,** il faut arroser ça. **ce'lebrity** *n* célébrité *f*.

celeriac [sə'leriæk] *n* *Hort:* céleri-rave *m*.

celery ['seləri] *n* *Hort:* céleri *m*.

celestial [sə'lestiəl] *a* céleste.

celibate ['selibət] *a & n* célibataire (*mf*). 'celibacy *n* célibat *m*.

cell [sel] *n* cellule *f*; *El:* élément *m* (de pile); **dry c.,** pile sèche. 'cellular *a* cellulaire; (couverture) en maille aérée. 'celluloid *n* celluloïd *m*. 'cellulite *n* cellulite *f*. 'cellulose *n* cellulose *f*.

cellar ['selər] *n* cave *f*.

cello ['tʃelou] *n* (*pl* **cellos**) violoncelle *m*. 'cellist *n* violoncelliste *mf*.

cellophane ['seləfein] *n* *Rtm:* cellophane *f*.

Celsius ['selsiəs] *Prn* Celsius *inv.*

Celt [kelt] *n* *Ethn:* celte *mf*. 'Celtic *a* celtique; celte.

cement [si'ment] **1.** *n* ciment *m*; **c. mixer,** bétonnière *f* **2.** *vtr* cimenter.

cemetery ['semətri] *n* (*pl* **cemeteries**) cimetière *m*.

cenotaph ['senətɑːf] *n* cénotaphe *m*.

censer ['sensər] *n* *Ecc:* encensoir *m*.

censor ['sensər] **1.** *n* censeur *m*; censure *f* (militaire, etc) **2.** *vtr* censurer; interdire; passer (une lettre) par le contrôle. 'censorship *n* censure.

censure ['senʃər] **1.** *n* blâme *m*; **vote of c.,** motion de censure **2.** *vtr* blâmer.

census ['sensəs] *n* (*pl* **censuses**) recensement *m*.

cent [sent] *n* (a) cent *m*; **I haven't got a c.,** je n'ai pas le sou (b) **per c.,** pour cent. **cente'narian** *a & n* centenaire (*mf*). **cen'tenary , cen'tennial** *a & n* centenaire (*m*). 'centigrade *a* centigrade. 'centimetre, *NAm:* 'centimeter *n* centimètre *m*. 'centipede *n* mille-pattes *m* *inv.*

center ['sentər] *n* *NAm:* = **centre.**

central ['sentrəl] *a* central; **c. heating,** chauffage central. 'centralize *vtr & i* (se) centraliser. 'centrally *adv* au centre; **c. heated,** avec chauffage central.

centre, *NAm:* **center** ['sentər] **1.** *n* centre *m*; milieu *m*; **in the c.,** au centre; **c. of gravity,** centre de gravité; **city c.,** centre (de la) ville; **c. arch,** arche centrale; *Fb:* **c. forward,** avant-centre *m*; **c. half,** demi-centre; *Pol:* **c. party,** parti du centre **2.** *vtr* centrer; concentrer (son affection) (**on,** sur). 'centre 'on, *F:* 'round *vtr* se concentrer sur, autour de.

centrifugal [sentri'fjuːgəl] *a* centrifuge. 'centrifuge *n* centrifugeuse *f*.

century ['sentʃəri] *n* (*pl* **centuries**) (a) siècle *m*; **in the twentieth c.,** au vingtième siècle (b) *Cr:* centaine *f*.

ceramic [sə'ræmik] *a* céramique; (carreau) de céramique. **ce'ramics** *npl* céramique *f*.

cereal ['siəriəl] *n* céréale *f*.

ceremony ['seriməni] *n* (*pl* **ceremonies**) cérémonie *f*; **without c.,** sans cérémonie(s), sans façon; **to stand on c.,** faire des cérémonies, des façons. **cere'monial 1.** *a* de cérémonie **2.** *n* cérémonial *m*. **cere'monially** *adv* en grande cérémonie. **cere'monious** *a* cérémonieux. **cere'moniously** *adv* avec cérémonie.

cert [sɜːt] *n* *F:* **it's a dead c.,** c'est une certitude (absolue), une affaire sûre; c'est couru.

certain ['sɜːtən] *a* (a) certain; **to be c. of sth,** être certain, sûr, de qch; **I'm almost c. of it,** j'en suis presque sûr; j'en ai la presque certitude; **to know sth for c.,** être bien sûr de qch; **to make, be, c. of sth,** s'assurer (de) qch; **I'm c. he'll come,** je suis sûr, certain, qu'il viendra (b) **there are c. things,** il y a certaines choses; **c. people,** (de) certaines personnes, certains *mpl*; **a c. Mr Martin,** un certain M. Martin. 'certainly *adv* (a) certainement; assurément; à coup sûr (b) assurément; parfaitement; sans faute; **c.!** bien sûr! **c. not!** bien sûr que non! 'certainty *n* certitude *f*; chose certaine.

certificate [sə'tifikit] *n* certificat *m*; attestation *f*; *Fin:* certificat d'actions; *Sch:* diplôme *m*, brevet *m*; **birth, death, c.,** acte de naissance, de décès; **savings c.,** bon m d'épargne. 'certifiable *a* que l'on peut certifier; *F:* (*of pers*) fou à lier. **cer'tificated** *a* diplômé. 'certify **1.** *vtr* (a) certifier, déclarer, attester; constater (un décès); *F:* **you should be certified!** t'es fou, dingue! (b) authentiquer, homologuer, légaliser (un document); *NAm:*

certified mail (*Br* = **registered post**), envoi en re- commandé (*c*) *Sch:* diplômer, breveter (qn) **2.** *vi* attester (**to sth,** qch). **'certitude** *n* certitude *f*.

cervix ['sə:viks] *n* (*pl* **cervixes**) *Anat:* col *m* de l'utérus. **'cervical, cer'vical** *a* cervical; **c. smear,** frottis cervical.

cesarean, -ian [si'zeəriən] *a* & *n NAm:* = **caes- arean, -ian.**

cessation [se'seiʃən] *n* cessation *f*; arrêt *m*.

cesspit, cesspool ['sespit, -pu:l] *n* fosse *f* d'ai- sances.

Chad [tʃæd] *Prn Geog:* Tchad *m*.

chafe [tʃeif] **1.** *vtr* (*a*) frictionner; user; écorcher (la peau) (*b*) échauffer (en frottant) **2.** *vi* (*a*) s'user (par le frottement); (*of skin*) s'écorcher (*b*) s'énerver, s'ir- riter (**at,** de). **'chafing 'dish** *n DomEc:* réchaud *m* de table.

chaff [tʃɑ:f] **1.** *n* (*a*) balle *f* (du grain) (*b*) *Agr:* menue paille **2.** *vtr* railler (qn).

chaffinch ['tʃæfintʃ] *n* (*pl* **chaffinches**) *Orn:* pinson *m*.

chagrin ['ʃægrin] *n* chagrin *m*, dépit *m*.

chain [tʃein] **1.** *n* chaîne *f*; suite *f*, série *f* (d'événe- ments); **in chains,** (prisonnier) enchaîné; (*in WC*) **to pull the c.,** tirer la chasse d'eau; **c. store,** magasin à succursales (multiples); **c. reaction,** réaction en chaîne; **c. letter,** chaîne; **c. smoker,** fumeur, -euse, à la file, invétéré(e) **2.** *vtr* attacher, retenir, par une chaîne; enchaîner; mettre (un chien) à la chaîne. **'chainsaw** *n* scie *f* à chaînette; tronçonneuse *f*. **'chain-smoke** *vtr* & *i* fumer (des cigarettes) à la file.

chair ['tʃeər] *n* chaise *f*; siège *m*; (*with arms*) fauteuil *m*; *Sch:* chaire (de professeur de faculté); **to take a c.,** s'asseoir; **to be in the c.,** occuper le fauteuil (pré- sidentiel); présider; **to take the c.,** prendre la prési- dence; **c. lift,** télésiège *m*. **'chairman** (*pl* -**men**), **-person** *n* président, -ente; **Mr C., Madam C.,** M. le Président, Mme la Présidente. **'chairmanship** *n* présidence *f*. **'chairwoman** *n* (*pl* -**women**) présidente.

chalet ['ʃælei] *n* chalet *m*.

chalice ['tʃælis] *n Ecc:* calice *m*.

chalk [tʃɔ:k] **1.** *n* craie *f*; **French c.,** craie de tailleur; *F:* **they're as different as c. and cheese,** c'est le jour et la nuit; *F:* **not by a long c.,** tant s'en faut **2.** *vtr* marquer, écrire, à la craie. **'chalk 'up** *vtr F:* rem- porter (une victoire); **c. it up (to me),** mettez-le sur mon compte. **'chalky** *a* crayeux.

challenge ['tʃælindʒ] **1.** *n* (*a*) défi *m*; sommation *f* (d'une sentinelle); *Sp:* challenge *m*; **this work is a real c. to me,** ce travail est une vraie gageure pour moi **2.** *vtr* (*a*) défier; provoquer (qn au combat) (*b*) (*of sentry*) faire une sommation à (qn) (*c*) disputer, mettre en question (la parole de qn); contester (un droit); *Jur:* récuser (un juré). **'challenger** *n* pro- vocateur, - trice; *Sp:* challengeur *m*. **'challenging** *a* (discours) provocateur; (air) de défi.

chamber ['tʃeimbər] *n* (*a*) salle *f*; *Adm:* **C. of Com- merce,** chambre *f* de commerce; **c. music,** musique de chambre; **c. (pot),** pot *m* de chambre (*b*) **cham- bers,** cabinet *m*, étude *f* (d'un avocat). **'chamber- maid** *n* femme *f* de chambre.

chameleon [kə'mi:liən] *n Rept:* caméléon *m*.

chamfer ['ʃæmfər] *n* biseau *m*, chanfrein *m*.

chammy ['ʃæmi] *n* c. **(leather),** (peau *f* de) chamois *m*.

chamois *n* (*a*) *Z:* ['ʃæmwɑ:] chamois *m* (*b*) ['ʃæmi] **c. (leather),** (peau *f* de) chamois.

champ [tʃæmp] **1.** *n F:* champion, -ionne **2.** *vtr* & *i* mâcher, mâchonner; **to c. (at) the bit,** ronger le frein.

champagne [ʃæm'pein] *n* champagne *m*.

champion ['tʃæmpiən] **1.** *n* champion, -onne; **a c. gymnast,** un champion de la gymnastique **2.** *vtr* soutenir, défendre. **'championship** *n* défense *f* (d'une cause); *Sp:* championnat *m*.

chance [tʃɑ:ns] **1.** *n* (*a*) hasard *m*; sort *m*; **by c., by any c.,** par hasard; **to leave nothing to c.,** ne rien laisser au hasard (*b*) chance(s) *f* (*pl*); **the chances are that,** il y a fort à parier que; **to take a c.,** courir un risque; **I'm not taking any chances,** je ne veux rien risquer, laisser au hasard; **to have an eye to the main c.,** veiller à ses propres intérêts (*c*) occasion *f*; **to have, stand, a c.,** avoir des chances de succès **2.** *a* fortuit, accidentel; (rencontre) de hasard **3.** *v* (*a*) *vi* **to c. to do sth,** faire qch par hasard (*b*) *vtr* risquer; *F:* **to c. it,** risquer le coup. **'chance (up)'on** *vtr* rencontrer (qn), trouver (qch), par hasard. **'chancy** *a F:* incertain; risqué.

chancel ['tʃɑ:nsəl] *n EccArch:* chœur *m*.

chancellor ['tʃɑ:nsələr] *n* chancelier *m*; **C. of the Exchequer,** Chancelier de l'Échiquier.

chandelier [ʃændə'liər] *n* lustre *m*.

change ['tʃeindʒ] **I.** *n* (*a*) changement *m*; revirement *m* (d'opinion); **c. for the better, for the worse,** change- ment en mieux, en mal; **to make a c.,** effectuer un changement (**in,** à); **it makes a c.,** ça change un peu; **for a c.,** pour changer; **gear c.,** changement de vitesse; **c. of clothes,** vêtements de rechange; **the c. (of life),** le retour d'âge (*b*) monnaie *f*; **small, loose, c.,** petite monnaie; **to give s.o. (the) c. for, of, £5,** faire à qn la monnaie de cinq livres; *F:* **he won't get much c. out of me,** il perdra ses peines avec moi. **II.** *v* **1.** *vtr* (*a*) changer; relever (la garde); **to c. one thing into another,** changer une chose en une autre; **to c. one's mind, tune,** changer d'avis, de ton; **to c. the subject,** changer de sujet; parler d'autre chose; **to c. one's clothes, to get changed,** *vi* **to c.,** changer de vêtements; se changer; **to c. gear, colour, trains,** changer de vitesse, de couleur, de train (*b*) échanger (sth for sth, qch contre qch); **to c. places (with s.o.),** changer de place (avec qn) (*c*) changer (des chèques de voyage, un billet de banque étranger) (**into,** en); faire la monnaie (d'un billet de banque) **2.** *vi* (se) changer (**into,** en); **to c. for the better,** changer en mieux; *Trans:* **all c.!** tout le monde descend! **'changeable** *a* (*of pers*) changeant; (*of weather*) variable. **'change 'down** *vi Aut:* rétrograder. **'changeless** *a* immuable. **'change 'over** *vi* passer (**from, to,** de, à). **'changeover** *n* change- ment; relève *f* (de la garde). **'change 'up** *vi Aut:* monter les vitesses. **'changing** **1.** *a* changeant; (expression) mobile **2.** *n* changement; relève *f* (de la garde); **c. room,** vestiaire *m*.

channel ['tʃænl] **1.** *n* (*a*) lit *m* (d'une rivière) (*b*) passe *f*, chenal *m* (d'un port); *Geog:* détroit *m*, canal *m*; **the (English) C.,** la Manche; **the C. Islands,** les îles Anglo-Normandes (*c*) canal, conduit *m* (d'un liquide); **rigole** *f* (d'écoulement); **voie** *f* (diplomatique, etc); **official channels**, filière administrative; **channels of communication**, artères *fpl* (d'un pays) (*d*) *TV:* chaîne *f* 2. *vtr* **(channelled)** canaliser.

chant [tʃɑːnt] 1. *n* (*a*) *Mus:* chant *m; Ecc:* psalmodie *f* (*b*) (*of crowd*) chant scandé 2. *vtr & i* (*a*) *Ecc:* psalmodier (*b*) (*of crowd*) scander, entonner (des slogans).

chaos [ˈkeiɔs] *n* chaos *m*. **chaˈotic** *a* chaotique. **chaˈotically** *adv* sans ordre.

chap¹ [tʃæp] 1. *n* gerçure *f*, crevasse *f* 2. *vi* **(chapped)** se gercer, se crevasser.

chap² *n F:* garçon *m*, homme *m*; type *m*, individu *m*; **old c.**, mon vieux.

chapel [ˈtʃæpl] *n* (*a*) chapelle *f* (*b*) temple *m* (nonconformiste).

chaperon(e) [ˈʃæpəroun] 1. *n* chaperon *m* 2. *vtr* chaperonner (une jeune fille).

chaplain [ˈtʃæplin] *n* aumônier *m*; chapelain *m*.

chapter [ˈtʃæptər] *n* chapitre *m*; **to give c. and verse**, citer ses autorités; **a c. of accidents**, une suite de malheurs. **ˈchapterhouse** *n* salle *f* capitulaire.

char¹ [tʃɑːr] *vtr & i* **(charred)** (se) carboniser.

char² *F:* 1. *n* (*also* **-lady, -woman**) femme *f* de ménage 2. *vi* faire des ménages.

char³ *n P:* thé *m*; **a cup of c.**, une tasse de thé.

character [ˈkærɪktər] *n* (*a*) caractère *m*; **books of that c.**, livres de ce genre; **to be in c. with sth**, s'accorder, s'harmoniser, avec qch; **work that lacks c.**, œuvre qui manque de cachet; **man of (strong) c.**, homme de caractère, de volonté; **to be in, out of, c.**, s'accorder bien, ne pas s'accorder, avec le caractère de qn; **c. actor**, acteur de genre (*b*) personnage *m* (de roman); **suspicious c.**, individu *m*, type *m*, louche; *F:* **he's a c.**, c'est un original, un numéro. **characteˈristic** 1. *a* caractéristique; **this attitude is c. of him**, cette attitude le caractérise 2. *n* caractéristique *f*. **characteˈristically** *adv* d'une manière caractéristique. **characteriˈzation** *n* caractérisation *f*. **ˈcharacterize** *vtr* caractériser. **ˈcharacterless** *a* sans caractère.

charade [ʃəˈrɑːd] *n* charade *f*.

charcoal [ˈtʃɑːkoul] *n* charbon *m* (de bois); *Art:* fusain *m*; **c. drawing**, (dessin *m* au) fusain; **c. grey**, (gris) anthracite *inv*.

chard [tʃɑːd] *n Hort: Cu:* **Swiss c.**, bette *f*, blette *f*.

charge [tʃɑːdʒ] I. *n* (*a*) *Mil: Exp: El:* charge *f* (*b*) **frais** *mpl*, prix *m*; **list of charges**, tarif *m*; **bank charges**, frais de banque; **delivery c., c. for delivery**, (frais de) port *m*; **admission c.**, droit *m* d'entrée; **no c. for admission**, entrée gratuite; **extra c.**, supplément *m*; **at a c. of £5 a day**, moyennant cinq livres par jour; **free of c.**, à titre gratuit, à titre gracieux; **c. account**, compte crédit d'achats (*c*) (*duty*) charge; fonction *f*; garde *f*; soin *m*; **to take c. of**, se charger, prendre soin, de; prendre en charge; in **s.o.'s c.**, à la garde de qn; **to be in c. of**, être responsable de; **to leave s.o. in c. of**, confier à qn la garde de; **person in c.**, administrateur, -trice (**of**, de); responsable *mf*; préposé, -ée (*d*) personne, chose, confiée à la garde de qn (*e*) *Jur:* charge; inculpation *f*; **to bring a c. against s.o.**, porter une accusation, porter plainte, contre qn. II. *v* 1. *vtr* (*a*) charger (un fusil, un accumulateur) (*b*) *Jur:* **to c. s.o. with**, charger, inculper,

qn de (*c*) prendre, demander (un prix); prélever (une commission); **they charged me £20 for the room**, ils m'ont fait payer la chambre vingt livres; **c. it to my account**, mettez-le sur mon compte 2. *vtr & i Mil:* charger 3. *vi* (*a*) se précipiter, s'élancer; **to c. in, out**, entrer, sortir, en coup de vent (*b*) (*of battery*) se recharger. **ˈcharger** *n* chargeur *m* (d'accumulateur).

chariot [ˈtʃæriət] *n* char *m*.

charisma [kæˈrizmə] *n* charisme *m*. **charisˈmatic** *a* charismatique.

charity [ˈtʃæriti] *n* (*a*) charité *f*; **out of c.**, par charité; *Prov:* **c. begins at home**, charité bien ordonnée commence par soi-même (*b*) charité, aumônes *fpl*; bienfaisance *f* (*c*) (*society*) œuvre *f* charitable, de bienfaisance, de charité. **ˈcharitable** *a* charitable; (œuvre) de bienfaisance. **ˈcharitably** *adv* charitablement.

charm [tʃɑːm] 1. *n* (*a*) charme *m*; **it works like a c.**, ça marche à merveille (*b*) (**lucky**) **c.**, breloque *f*; amulette *f*, porte-bonheur *m inv* 2. *vtr* charmer. **ˈcharming** *a* charmant. **ˈcharmingly** *adv* d'une façon charmante.

chart [tʃɑːt] 1. *n* (*a*) carte (marine) (*b*) *Stat:* graphique *m*, diagramme *m*; tableau *m*; **organisation c.**, organigramme *m; Med:* **temperature c.**, feuille *f* de température; *F:* **the (pop) charts**, le palmarès, le hit-parade 2. *vtr* dresser la carte d'(une côte, etc); porter sur une carte, sur une feuille, sur un graphique; suivre (les progrès de qn).

charter [ˈtʃɑːtər] *n* (*a*) charte *f* (d'une ville); statuts *mpl* (d'une société); privilège *m* (d'une banque) (*b*) affrètement *m* (d'un navire, d'un avion); **c. aircraft**, charter *m*; **c. flight**, (vol) charter 2. *vtr* affréter (un navire, un avion); **chartered aircraft**, charter.

chary [ˈtʃɛəri] *a* prudent, circonspect; **to be c. of doing sth**, hésiter à faire qch; **c. of praise**, avare de louanges.

chase [tʃeis] 1. *n* chasse *f*, poursuite *f*; **to give c. to**, donner la chasse à; in **c. of**, à la poursuite de; **to go on a wild goose c.**, courir après la lune 2. *vtr* poursuivre; donner la chasse à. **ˈchase ˈafter** *vtr* courir après. **ˈchase aˈway, out** *vtr* chasser. **ˈchase ˈup** *vtr F:* presser (qn); activer (une affaire).

chasm [ˈkæzəm] *n* gouffre *m*; abîme *m*.

chassis [ˈʃæsi] *n* (*inv in pl*) *Aut:* châssis *m*.

chaste [tʃeist] *a* (*of pers*) chaste; pudique; (*of style*) pur, sobre. **ˈchastely** *adv* chastement; sobrement. **ˈchastity** *n* chasteté *f*.

chasten [ˈtʃeisn] *vtr* châtier; assagir, rabattre l'orgueil de (qn). **ˈchastening** *a* (pensée) qui assagit.

chastise [tʃæsˈtaiz] *vtr* châtier; corriger. **chasˈtisement** *n* châtiment *m*; correction *f*.

chat [tʃæt] 1. *n* causerie *f*, causette *f*; **to have a c. with s.o.**, bavarder avec qn; *TV: WTel:* **c. show**, émission de bavardages 2. *vi* **(chatted)** causer, bavarder. **ˈchatty** *a F:* (*of pers*) bavard; (*of letter*) plein de bavardages. **ˈchat ˈup** *vtr F:* baratiner.

chatter [ˈtʃætər] 1. *n* (*of birds*) jacassement *m*; (*of pers*) bavardage *m*; (*of teeth*) claquement *m* 2. *vi* (*of birds*) jacasser; (*of pers*) bavarder, jaser; (*of teeth*) claquer. **ˈchatterbox** *n* grand(e) bavard(e); moulin *m* à paroles.

chauffeur [ˈʃoufər, ʃouˈfəːr] *n* chauffeur *m*.

chauvinism ['ʃouvinizm] *n* chauvinisme *m*. **'chauvinist** *n* chauvin, -ine; **male c.**, phallocrate *m*.

cheap [tʃi:p] **1.** *a* (*a*) (à) bon marché; pas cher; **cheaper**, (à) meilleur marché, moins cher; **dirt c.**, pour rien; **it's c. and nasty**, c'est de la camelote; **c. rate**, tarif réduit; **on the c.**, à peu de frais (*b*) de peu de valeur; (humour) superficiel **2.** *adv* (à) bon marché; (pour) pas cher. **'cheapen** *vtr* baisser le prix de; **to c. oneself**, se déprécier. **'cheaply** *adv* = **cheap 2**. **'cheapness** *n* bas prix; bon marché; *Fig:* médiocrité *f*.

cheat [tʃi:t] **1.** *n* trompeur, -euse (par habitude); escroc *m*; (*at games*) tricheur, -euse **2.** *v* (*a*) *vtr* tromper; frauder; **to c. s.o. out of sth**, escroquer qch à qn (*b*) *vi* (*at games*) tricher. **'cheating** *n* tromperie *f*; fourberie *f*; (*at games*) tricherie *f*.

check¹ [tʃek] **1.** *n* (*a*) *Chess:* échec *m*; **c.!** échec au roi! (*b*) revers *m*, obstacle *m* (*c*) arrêt *m*; frein *m*; **to keep in c.**, tenir en échec (*d*) contrôle *m*, vérification *f*; **to keep a c. on**, contrôler (*e*) ticket *m*; bulletin *m* (de bagages); *esp NAm:* addition *f*, note *f*; (*f*) *NAm:* (*Br* = **cheque**) chèque *m* **2.** *vtr* (*a*) *Chess:* mettre (le roi) en échec (*b*) arrêter; enrayer; refouler, retenir (sa colère); réprimer (une passion) (*c*) vérifier; contrôler (*d*) réprimander (qn). **'checkbook** *n* *NAm:* (*Br* = **chequebook**) carnet *m* de chèques. **'checker** *n* contrôleur, -euse; *NAm:* (*in supermarket*) caissier, -ière. **'check 'in** *vi* s'inscrire (à un hôtel); *Av:* se présenter à l'enregistrement **2.** *vtr* enregistrer. **'check-in** *n* *esp Av:* **c.-in (desk)**, (guichet *m* d')enregistrement *m*. **'checklist** *n* liste *f* de contrôle. **'checkmate 1.** *n* *Chess:* échec *m* et mat *m*; *Fig:* défaite *f* **2.** *vtr Chess:* faire échec et mat à (qn); *Fig:* contrecarrer. **'check 'off** *vtr* pointer, cocher. **'check 'on** *vtr* vérifier. **'check 'out 1.** *vi* (*a*) régler sa note (à l'hôtel) (*b*) (*of facts*) se recouper **2.** *vtr* (*a*) retirer (ses bagages) (de la consigne) (*b*) vérifier. **'check-out** *n* (*in supermarket*) caisse *f*; **c.-o. assistant**, caissier, -ière. **'check 'over** *vtr* vérifier; contrôler. **'checkpoint** *n* contrôle. **'checkroom** *n* *NAm:* (*Br* = **left luggage office**) consigne. **'check 'up ('on)** *vtr & i* vérifier. **'checkup** *n* examen médical complet; **to give s.o. a c.**, faire le bilan de santé de qn.

check² *n* *Tex:* carreau *m*; **c. material**, tissu à carreaux. **'checked** *a* (tissu) à carreaux. **'checkerboard** *n* (*Br* = **draught-board**) damier *m*. **'checkered** *a* *NAm:* = **chequered**. **'checkers** *npl* *NAm:* (*Br* = **draughts**) (jeu *m* de) dames *fpl*.

cheek [tʃi:k] **1.** *n* (*a*) joue *f*; **c. by jowl with s.o.**, côte à côte avec qn; **c. to c.**, joue contre joue (*b*) *F:* toupet *m*, culot *m*; **what a c.!** quel culot! **2.** *vtr F:* faire l'insolent avec (qn). **'cheekbone** *n* pommette *f*. **'cheekily** *adv* d'une manière insolente, effrontée. **'cheeky** *a F:* insolent, effronté.

cheep [tʃi:p] (*of bird*) **1.** *n* piaulement *m* **2.** *vi* piauler.

cheer [tʃiər] **I.** *n* hourra *m*; **cheers**, acclamations *fpl*, bravos *mpl*; **three cheers for**, un ban pour; *F:* **cheers!** (i) (*when drinking*) à la vôtre! à la tienne! (ii) à bientôt! (iii) merci! **II.** *v* **1.** *vtr* (*a*) **to c. (up)**, égayer, remonter, relever le moral de (qn) (*b*) acclamer, applaudir **2.** *vi* applaudir; pousser des hourras. **'cheerful** *a* gai; de bonne humeur; (*of expres-*

sion) riant. **'cheerfully** *adv* gaiement; allègrement. **'cheerfulness** *n* gaieté *f*; bonne humeur. **'cheerily** *adv* gaiement. **'cheering 1.** *a* (*of news, etc*) encourageant **2.** *n* hourras *mpl*, acclamations. **cheeri'o** *int F:* à bientôt! **'cheerleader** *n* meneur, -euse, de ban. **'cheerless** *a* morne, triste, sombre. **'cheer 'up** *vi* reprendre courage; **c. up!** courage! **'cheery** *a* joyeux, gai.

cheese [tʃi:z] *n* fromage *m*; **c. straws**, allumettes au fromage; *Phot:* **say c.!** souriez! **'cheeseboard** *n* plateau *m* à, de, fromage(s). **'cheeseburger** *n* hamburger recouvert d'une tranche de fromage. **'cheesecake** *n* tarte *f* au fromage blanc. **'cheesecloth** *n* gaze *f*. **'cheesed 'off** *a F:* **to be c. o.**, en avoir marre (**with**, de). **'cheeseparing** *n* **c. (economy)**, économies *fpl* de bouts de chandelle.

cheetah ['tʃi:tə] *n* *Z:* guépard *m*.

chef [ʃef] *n* chef *m* (de cuisine).

chemical ['kemikl] **1.** *a* chimique **2.** *n* produit *m* chimique.

chemist ['kemist] *n* (*a*) chimiste *mf* (*b*) (*NAm:* = **druggist**) pharmacien, -ienne; **c.'s (shop)** (*NAm:* = **drugstore**), pharmacie *f*. **'chemistry** *n* chimie *f*.

cheque [tʃek] *n* (*NAm:* = **check**) chèque *m*; **to pay by c.**, payer par chèque. **'chequebook** *n* (*NAm:* = **checkbook**) carnet *m* de chèques.

chequerboard, *NAm:* **checkerboard** ['tʃekəbɔːd] *n* damier *m*. **'chequered**, *NAm:* **'checkered** *a* (*a*) (tissu) à carreaux, en damier (*b*) varié; (*of career*) mouvementé.

cherish ['tʃeriʃ] *vtr* chérir; bercer, caresser (un espoir); nourrir (une idée); **cherished**, très cher.

cherry ['tʃeri] *n* cerise *f*; **c. pie**, tarte aux cerises; **c. brandy**, cherry(-brandy) *m*; **c. orchard**, cerisaie *f*; **c. (tree)**, cerisier *m*; **c. (red)**, (rouge) cerise *inv*. **'cherrystone** *n* noyau *m* de cerise.

cherub ['tʃerəb] *n* chérubin *m*. **che'rubic** *a* de chérubin, d'ange.

chervil ['tʃɜːvil] *n* *Bot:* cerfeuil *m*.

chess [tʃes] *n* (jeu *m* d')échecs *mpl*; **to play c.**, jouer aux échecs. **'chessboard** *n* échiquier *m*. **'chessmen** *npl* pièces *f* (du jeu d'échecs).

chest [tʃest] *n* (*a*) coffre *m*, caisse *f*; **c. of drawers** (*NAm:* = **bureau**), commode *f* (*b*) *Anat:* poitrine *f*; **cold on the c.**, rhume de poitrine; **to have a weak c.**, être bronchitique; *Fig:* **to get it off one's c.**, dire ce qu'on a sur le cœur. **'chesty** *a* (*of pers*) bronchitique; (toux) de poitrine.

chestnut ['tʃesnʌt] **1.** *n* (*a*) châtaigne *f*; marron *m*; **horse c.**, marron d'Inde; **c. (tree)**, châtaignier *m*; marronnier *m*; **horse c. (tree)**, marronnier d'Inde (*b*) *F:* vieille plaisanterie **2.** *a* (*colour*) châtain; (cheval) alezan.

chew [tʃuː] *vtr* mâcher, mastiquer; **chewing gum**, chewing-gum *m*. **'chew 'over** *vtr* méditer sur; ruminer. **'chewy** *a* difficile à mâcher.

chic [ʃiːk] *a & n* chic (*m*) *inv*.

chick [tʃik] *n* poussin *m*. **'chickpea** *n* *Bot:* pois *m* chiche. **'chickweed** *n* *Bot:* mouron *m* des oiseaux.

chicken ['tʃikin] *n* poulet *m*; **spring c.**, poussin *m*; **c. liver**, foie de volaille; *Prov:* **don't count your chickens before they're hatched**, il ne faut pas vendre la peau de l'ours avant de l'avoir tué; *F:* **she's no c.**, elle n'est plus toute jeune. **'chickenfeed** *n F:* petite monnaie; gnognote *f.* **'chicken 'out** *vi F:* flancher. **'chickenpox** *n Med:* varicelle *f.*

chicory ['tʃikəri] *n Bot: (in coffee)* chicorée *f;* (*as vegetable*) endive *f.*

chief [tʃiːf] **1.** *n* chef *m;* patron *m;* **in c.,** en chef **2.** *a* principal; premier; (ingénieur) en chef; (hôte) d'honneur. **'chiefly** *adv* surtout; principalement. **'chieftain** *n* chef de clan.

chiffon ['ʃifɔn] *n Tex:* mousseline *f* de soie.

chihuahua [tʃi'wa:wa] *n (dog)* chihuahua *m.*

chilblain ['tʃilblein] *n* engelure *f.*

child [tʃaild] *n (pl* **children)** enfant *mf;* petit, -e; **from a c.,** dès son enfance; **that's c.'s play,** c'est un jeu d'enfant; **c. welfare,** protection de l'enfance; **children's books,** livres pour enfants. **'childbirth** *n* accouchement *m;* **in c.,** en couches *fpl.* **'childhood** *n* enfance *f;* **in one's second c.,** retombé en enfance. **'childish** *a* enfantin, d'enfant; *Pej:* puéril; **don't be c.!** ne fais pas l'enfant! **'childishly** *adv* comme un enfant. **'childishness** *n Pej:* enfantillage *m,* puérilité *f.* **'childless** *a* sans enfant(s). **'childlike** *a* d'enfant; enfantin; naïf.

Chile ['tʃili] *Prn Geog:* Chili *m.* **'Chilean** *a & n* Chilien, -ienne.

chill [tʃil] **1.** *n (a) Med:* **to catch a c.,** prendre froid, un refroidissement *(b)* frisson *m* (de crainte); **to cast a c. over,** jeter un froid sur *(c)* froideur *f;* **there's a c. in the air,** il fait un peu frais; **to take the c. off,** dégourdir, tiédir (l'eau), chambrer (le vin) **2.** *a* froid **3.** *vtr* refroidir, glacer; réfrigérer, frigorifier (la viande); mettre au frais (du vin); **chilled to the bone,** transi (de froid). **'chilliness** *n* froid *m,* fraîcheur *f; Fig:* froideur *f.* **'chilling** *a* glacial; (récit) à vous glacer le sang. **'chilly** *a* froid; (temps) frais; (regard) glacial; *(of pers)* **to feel c.,** avoir froid.

chilli, *NAm:* **chili** ['tʃili] *n Cu:* piment *m* (rouge).

chime [tʃaim] **1.** *n* carillon *m* **2.** *vi & tr* carillonner; *(of clock)* sonner (les heures).

chimney ['tʃimni] *n* cheminée *f.* **'chimneybreast** *n* manteau *m* de (la) cheminée. **'chimneypot** *n* tuyau *m* de cheminée. **'chimneystack** *n (a)* souche *f* (de cheminée) *(b)* cheminée (d'usine). **'chimneysweep** *n* ramoneur *m.*

chimpanzee, *F:* **chimp** [tʃimpæn'zi:, tʃimp] *n* chimpanzé *m.*

chin [tʃin] *n* menton *m.*

China ['tʃainə] **1.** *Prn Geog:* Chine *f;* **People's Republic of C.,** République populaire de Chine **2.** *n no pl* porcelaine *f;* **c. cup,** tasse de, en, porcelaine. **Chi'nese** *a & n* chinois, -e; **C. People's Republic,** République populaire de Chine.

chink¹ [tʃiŋk] *n* fente *f,* crevasse *f* (dans un mur); entrebâillement *m* (de la porte).

chink² **1.** *n* tintement *m* **2.** *vtr & i* (faire) tinter.

Chink³ *n P: Pej:* Chinois, -e; Chinetoque *mf.*

chintz [tʃints] *n Tex:* chintz *m,* perse *f.*

chip [tʃip] **I.** *n (a)* éclat *m;* copeau *m* (de bois); fragment *m* (de pierre); écaille *f* (d'émail); *Cu: pl (NAm: = French fries)* (pommes *fpl* de terre) frites *fpl; NAm:* **(potato) chips** (*Br =* **crisps),** (pommes) chips *mpl; F:* **to have a c. on one's shoulder,** être aigri; se sentir méprisé; *F:* **he's a c. off the old block,** c'est

bien le fils de son père *(b)* ébréchure *f* (d'assiette); écornure *f (c) Gaming:* jeton *m (d) Elcs:* microplaquette *f,* puce *f,* pastille *f.* **II.** *v.* **(chipped) 1.** *vtr (a)* tailler (par éclats); *Cu:* **chipped potatoes** (*NAm:* **French fried potatoes),** pommes (de terre) frites *(b)* ébrécher (une tasse); écorner (un meuble); écailler (de l'émail) **2.** *vi* s'ébrécher, s'écailler. **'chip a'way 1.** *vtr* enlever des morceaux de (peinture) **2.** *vi* s'écailler. **'chipboard** *n* bois aggloméré; *NAm:* carton gris. **'chip 'in** *vi F: (a)* intervenir *(b)* payer sa part. **'chippings** *npl* éclats *mpl;* copeaux *mpl* (de bois); *PN:* **loose c.,** gravillons *mpl.*

chipmunk ['tʃipmʌŋk] *n Z:* tamia *m* rayé.

chipolata [tʃipə'la:tə] *n Comest:* chipolata *f.*

chiropodist [ki'rɔpədist] *n* pédicure *mf.* **chi'ropody** *n* pédicurie *f;* soins *mpl* du pied.

chiropractor ['kaiəroupræktər] *n* chiropraticien, -ienne.

chirp, chirrup [tʃə:p, 'tʃirəp] *vi (of bird)* pépier, gazouiller; *(of grasshopper)* chanter. **'chirpy** *a F:* gai; d'humeur gaie.

chisel ['tʃizl] **1.** *n* ciseau *m;* **(cold) c.,** burin *m* **2.** *vtr* **(chiselled)** ciseler; buriner.

chit¹ [tʃit] *n* **c. of a girl,** gamine *f.*

chit² *(a)* lettre *f;* petit mot *(b)* note *f.*

chitchat ['tʃittʃæt] *n F:* bavardages *mpl.*

chivalrous ['ʃivəlrəs] *a* chevaleresque; courtois. **'chivalry** *n (a) Hist:* chevalerie *f (b)* conduite *f* chevaleresque; courtoisie *f.*

chives [tʃaivz] *npl Bot:* ciboulette *f.*

chiv(v)y ['tʃivi] *vtr F:* poursuivre, chasser; harceler.

chlorate ['klɔ:reit] *n Ch:* chlorate *m.*

chloride ['klɔ:raid] *n Ch:* chlorure *m.*

chlorine ['klɔ:ri:n] *n Ch:* chlore *m.* **'chlorinate** *vtr* javelliser (l'eau); *Ch:* chlor(ur)er.

chloroform ['klɔrəfɔ:m] *n* chloroforme *m.*

chlorophyll ['klɔrəfil] *n Ch:* chlorophylle *f.*

choc-ice ['tʃɔkais] *n* esquimau *m.*

chock [tʃɔk] *n* cale *f.* **'chock-a-'block, 'chock-'full** *a F:* plein à craquer; bondé.

chocolate ['tʃɔklət] **1.** *n* chocolat *m;* **c. egg,** œuf en chocolat **2.** *a (de couleur)* chocolat *inv.*

choice [tʃɔis] **1.** *n* choix *m;* **big, wide, c.,** grand choix; **to make one's c.,** faire son choix; choisir; **you have no c. in the matter,** vous n'avez pas le choix; **Hobson's c.,** choix qui ne laisse pas d'alternative; **from c.,** de préférence **2.** *a* (mot) bien choisi; (article) de choix.

choir ['kwaiər] *n* chœur *m.* **'choirboy** *n* jeune choriste *m.* **'choirmaster** *n* maître *m* de chapelle.

choke [tʃouk] **I.** *v* **1.** *vtr (a)* étouffer, suffoquer (qn) *(b)* **to c. (up),** obstruer, boucher **(with,** de) **2.** *vi* étouffer, suffoquer **(with,** de); s'étrangler **(on,** avec). **II.** *n (a) Aut:* starter *m (b) Bot:* foin *m* (d'artichaut). **'choke 'back** *vtr* refouler. **'choker** *n* collier *m* (de chien).

cholera ['kɔlərə] *n Med:* choléra *m.*

cholesterol [kɔ'lestərɔl] *n Med:* cholestérol *m.*

choose [tʃu:z] *vtr & i* **(chose** [tʃouz] **chosen** ['tʃouzn]) *(a)* choisir; faire son choix; adopter (une méthode) **there's nothing to c. between them,** l'un vaut l'autre; ils se valent; **the chosen people,** les élus; **a few well chosen words,** quelques paroles (bien) choisies (b) décider; **when I c.**, quand je voudrai; **I do as I c.**, je fais comme il me plaît. **'choos(e)y** a F: difficile (**about,** sur).

chop [tʃɔp] **1.** n (a) coup m (de hache, de couperet); F: **to get the c.**, être mis à la porte (b) Cu: côtelette f **2.** vtr (**chopped**) (a) couper; fendre; Cu: hacher; **chopping board,** planche à hacher (b) **to c. and change,** changer d'avis comme une girouette. **'chop 'down** vtr abattre (un arbre). **'chop 'off** vtr trancher, couper. **'chopper** n (a) hachoir m, couperet m (b) F: hélicoptère m. **'choppy** a (of sea) agité. **'chopsticks** npl baguettes fpl. **'chop 'up** vtr couper en morceaux; Cu: hacher (menu).

choral ['kɔːrəl] a choral; **c. society,** chorale f. **cho-'ral(e)** n choral m.

chord [kɔːd] n Mus: accord m; Fig: **to strike a c.**, faire vibrer la corde sensible.

chore [tʃɔːr] n corvée f; travail quotidien (du ménage); **to do the chores,** faire le ménage.

choreography [kɔriˈɔɡrəfi] n chorégraphie f. **cho-re'ographer** n chorégraphe mf.

chorister ['kɔristər] n choriste mf.

chortle ['ʃɔːtl] **I.** n gloussement m (de joie). **II.** vi glousser (de joie).

chorus ['kɔːrəs] n (a) chœur m; **c. of praise,** concert m de louanges; **in c.,** en chœur; **c. girl,** girl f (b) refrain m (d'une chanson); **to join in the c.,** chanter le refrain en chœur.

chose, chosen [tʃouz, 'tʃouzn] see **choose**.

chowder ['tʃaudər] n Cu: NAm: soupe f de poisson, de coquillages.

Christ [kraist] Prn le Christ; Jésus-Christ m.

christen ['krisn] vtr baptiser. **'christening** n baptême m.

Christian ['kristiən] a & n chrétien, -ienne; **C. name,** nom de baptême, prénom m; **C. Scientist,** scientiste chrétien. **Christi'anity** n christianisme m.

Christmas ['krisməs] n Noël m; **at C.,** à Noël; **merry C.!** joyeux Noël! **C. card, tree,** carte, arbre, de Noël; **C. Day,** le jour de Noël; **C. Eve,** la veille de Noël; **C. stocking** = sabot de Noël; **Father C.,** le père Noël.

chrome [kroum] n chrome m; **c. steel,** acier chromé; **c. yellow,** jaune de chrome. **'chromium** n chrome; **c. plating,** chromage m. **'chromium-'plated** a chromé.

chromosome ['krouməsoum] n Biol: chromosome m.

chronic ['krɔnik] a (a) Med: chronique; **c. ill health,** invalidité f (b) F: affreux. **'chronically** adv chroniquement.

chronicle ['krɔnikl] **1.** n chronique f; suite f (d'évènements) **2.** vtr faire la chronique de. **'chronicler** n chroniqueur, -euse.

chronological [krɔnəˈlɔdʒikl] a chronologique; **in c. order,** par ordre chronologique. **chrono-'logically** adv chronologiquement. **chro'nometer** n chronomètre m.

chrysalis ['krisəlis] n (pl **chrysalises**) chrysalide f.

chrysanthemum [kriˈsænθiməm] n Bot: chrysanthème m.

chubby ['tʃʌbi] a (**-ier, -iest**) potelé; (visage) joufflu.

chuck¹ [tʃʌk] vtr F: (a) jeter, lancer, balancer (b) **to c. (in, up),** lâcher, plaquer (qn, son emploi). **'chuck a'way** vtr F: jeter; se débarrasser de. **'chuck 'out**

vtr F: jeter; flanquer (qn) à la porte, vider (qn). **'chucker-'out** n F: videur m.

chuck² n (a) Cu: **c. (steak),** paleron m de bœuf (b) Tls: mandrin m.

chuckle ['tʃʌkl] **1.** n petit rire; gloussement m **2.** vi rire tout bas, glousser.

chug [tʃʌg] vi (**chugged**) (of machine) souffler; haleter.

chum [tʃʌm] n F: copain m, copine f.

chump [tʃʌmp] n (a) Cu: **c. chop,** côtelette d'agneau (coupée entre le gigot et le carré) (b) F: nigaud m.

chunk [tʃʌŋk] n gros morceau; quignon m (de pain).

church [tʃəːtʃ] n (pl **churches**) église f; temple (protestant); **to go into, enter, the C.,** entrer dans les ordres; **to go to c.,** aller à l'église, à l'office, à la messe; **c. hall,** salle paroissiale. **'churchgoer** n pratiquant, -ante. **'church'warden** n marguillier m. **'churchyard** n cimetière m.

churlish ['tʃəːliʃ] a (a) grossier (b) hargneux, grincheux. **'churlishness** n (a) grossièreté f (b) tempérament hargneux.

churn [tʃəːn] **1.** n (a) (machine) baratte f (b) bidon m (à lait) **2.** vtr baratter (la crème); battre (le beurre); **to c. (up),** brasser (l'eau). **'churn 'out** vtr produire à la chaîne.

chute [ʃuːt] n glissière f, déversoir m; Sp: piste f (pour toboggans).

chutney ['tʃʌtni] n condiment m (aux fruits).

CIA abbr NAm: Central Intelligence Agency.

CID abbr Criminal Investigation Department.

cicada [siˈkaːdə] n cigale f.

cider ['saidər] n cidre m.

cigar [siˈɡaːr] n cigare m.

cigarette [siɡəˈret] n cigarette f; **c. case,** étui m à cigarettes, porte-cigarettes m inv; **c. holder,** fume-cigarette m inv; **c. paper,** papier à cigarettes.

cinch [sintʃ] n F: **it's a c.,** c'est facile.

cinder ['sindər] n cendre f. **'cindertrack** n cendrée f.

Cinderella [sindəˈrelə] Prnf Lit: Cendrillon; Fig: parent m pauvre.

cinema ['sinimə] n cinéma m. **'cine(-)camera** n caméra f. **'cine(-)film** n film m (cinématographique). **'cine(-)pro'jector** n projecteur m de cinéma.

cinnamon ['sinəmən] n cannelle f.

cipher ['saifər] n (a) zéro m; **he's a mere c.,** c'est un zéro (b) chiffre m; **in c.,** en chiffre.

circa ['səːkə] prep environ.

circle ['səːkl] **1.** n (a) cercle m; NAm: **traffic c.** (Br = **roundabout**), rond-point m; **to run round in circles,** tourner en rond; **to stand in a c.,** faire cercle; **to come full c.,** revenir à son point de départ; **in certain circles,** dans certains milieux (b) Th: **dress c.,** (premier) balcon; **upper c.,** seconde galerie **2.** (a) vtr entourer; faire le tour de (qch); **to c. (round),** tourner autour de (b) vi **to c. (round),** décrire des cercles. **'circular** a & n (lettre) circulaire (f). **'circularize** vtr envoyer des circulaires (to, à). **'circulate** vtr & i (faire) circuler. **circu'lation** n circulation f; tirage m (d'un journal); Fin: roulement m (de fonds); **to put into c.,** mettre en circulation.

circuit ['səːkit] n circuit m; tour m; tournée f (de

juge); **to make a c. of,** faire le tour de; *Jur:* **to go on c.,** aller en tournée; *El:* **c. breaker,** coupe-circuit *m inv;* disjoncteur *m;* **closed c. television,** télévision en circuit fermé. **circuitous** [səˈkjuitəs] *a* (chemin) détourné; (moyen) indirect.

circumcise [ˈsɔːkəmsaiz] *vtr* circoncire. **circum-ˈcision** *n* circoncision *f.*

circumference [səˈkʌmfərəns] *n* circonférence *f;* **in c.,** de circonférence.

circumflex [ˈsɔːkəmfleks] *a & n* **c.** (accent), accent *m* circonflexe.

circumscribe [ˈsɔːkəmskraib] *vtr* circonscrire; limiter (des pouvoirs). **circumˈscription** *n* (a) restriction *f* (b) circonscription *f.*

circumspect [ˈsɔːkəmspekt] *a* circonspect. **circumˈspection** *n* circonspection *f.*

circumstances [ˈsɔːkəmstənsiz] *npl* circonstances *fpl;* **in, under, the c.,** dans ces circonstances; **under no c., not under any c.,** en aucun cas; **under similar c.,** en pareille occasion; **that depends on c.,** c'est selon; **if his c. allow,** si ses moyens le permettent; **in easy c.,** dans l'aisance. **circumˈstantial** *a* (a) circonstanciel; **c. evidence,** preuves indirectes (b) (rapport) circonstancié.

circumvent [sɔːkəmˈvent] *vtr* circonvenir.

circus [ˈsɔːkəs] *n* (*pl* **circuses**) cirque *m.*

cirrhosis [siˈrousis] *n Med:* cirrhose *f.*

cistern [ˈsistən] *n* réservoir *m* à eau; citerne *f;* (*of WC*) (réservoir de) chasse *f* d'eau.

citadel [ˈsitədel] *n* citadelle *f.*

cite [sait] *vtr* citer. **ciˈtation** *n* citation *f.*

citizen [ˈsitizən] *n* citoyen, -enne; **citizens' band (radio),** (radio de la) citizen band. **ˈcitizenship** *n* droit *m* de cité; citoyenneté *f;* nationalité *f;* **good c.,** civisme *m.*

citrus [ˈsitrəs] *n Bot:* citrus *m;* **c. fruit(s),** agrumes *mpl.* **ˈcitric** *a* citrique.

city [ˈsiti] *n* (*pl* **cities**) (a) (grande) ville; **the C.,** la Cité de Londres; **he's in the C.,** il est dans la finance; *Journ:* **C. page,** rubrique financière (b) ville épiscopale; **c. hall,** hôtel de ville.

civet [ˈsivit] *n Z:* civette *f.*

civic [ˈsivik] **1.** *a* civique; **c. authorities,** autorités municipales; **c. centre,** centre municipal **2.** *npl Sch:* **civics,** instruction *f* civique.

civil [ˈsivl] *a* (a) civil; **c. liberties, rights,** libertés, droits, civiques; **c. war,** guerre civile; **c. defence,** protection civile; **c. servant,** fonctionnaire *mf;* **c. service,** administration (civile) (b) poli, civil. **ciˈvilian** *a & n* civil (*mf*); **in c. life,** dans le civil. **ciˈvility** *n* civilité *f.* **civiliˈzation** *n* civilisation *f.* **ˈcivilize** *vtr* civiliser. **ˈcivilized** *a* civilisé. **ˈcivilly** *adv* poliment.

clad [klæd] *see* **clothe.** **ˈcladding** *n* revêtement *m.*

claim [kleim] **1.** *n* (a) demande *f;* revendication *f* (de salaire); réclamation *f* (b) droit *m,* titre *m,* prétention *f* (to, à); **to lay c. to sth,** prétendre à, s'attribuer, qch; **to put in a c.,** faire valoir ses droits (c) *Jur:* réclamation; **to put in a c. for damages,** demander une indemnité; réclamer des dommages-intérêts *m; Ins:* **to put in a c.,** réclamer l'indemnité (d'assurance); **I have many claims on my time,** mon temps est presque entièrement pris (d) concession (minière)

2. *vtr* (a) réclamer, revendiquer (un droit); demander (de l'attention) (b) prétendre, affirmer, soutenir (que) (c) reprendre (ses bagages) (à la consigne). **ˈclaimant** *n* prétendant, -ante; revendicateur, -trice; demandeur, -eresse (d'allocations).

clairvoyant [kleəˈvɔiənt] **1.** *a* doué de seconde vue **2.** *n* voyant, -ante. **clairˈvoyance** *n* voyance *f.*

clam [klæm] *n Moll:* clam *m;* palourde *f.* **ˈclam ˈup** *vi* (**clammed**) *F:* se taire.

clamber [ˈklæmbər] *vi* grimper; **to c. over a wall,** escalader un mur.

clammy [ˈklæmi] *a* (*of skin*) (froid et) moite; (*of weather*) (froid et) humide.

clamour, *NAm:* **clamor** [ˈklæmər] **1.** *n* clameur *f;* cris *mpl;* vociférations *fpl* **2.** *vi* vociférer; **to c. for sth,** réclamer qch à grands cris. **ˈclamorous** *a* (*of crowd*) bruyant; vociférant.

clamp [klæmp] **1.** *n* crampon *m;* agrafe *f; Carp:* valet *m* (d'établi), serre-joint(s) *m; Surg:* clamp *m* **2.** *vtr* agrafer; brider; fixer. **ˈclamp(-)down** *n* limitation *f* (on, de). **ˈclamp ˈdown** *on vtr* serrer la vis à (qn); mettre fin à, supprimer (un abus).

clan [klæn] *n* clan *m.* **ˈclannish** *a* (*of pers*) qui a l'esprit de clan; (groupe) fermé. **ˈclansman, -men** *n* membre *m* d'un clan.

clandestine [klænˈdestin] *a* clandestin.

clang [klæŋ] **1.** *n* son *m* métallique; bruit retentissant **2.** *vi* retentir, résonner. **ˈclanger** *n F:* **to drop a c.,** faire une gaffe.

clank [klæŋk] **1.** *n* bruit métallique; cliquetis *m* **2.** *vtr & i* (faire) cliqueter.

clap [klæp] **I.** *n* **1.** (a) battement *m* (de la main); **to give s.o. a c.,** applaudir qn (b) tape *f,* coup *m* (de la main); **c. of thunder,** coup de tonnerre. **II.** *v* (**clapped**) **1.** *vtr* (a) **to c. one's hands,** battre des mains; **to c. s.o. on the back,** donner à qn une tape dans le dos (b) applaudir (c) mettre; appuyer, enfoncer ((on)to, sur, à); **to c. s.o. in prison,** fourrer qn en prison; *F:* **to c. eyes on,** voir **2.** *vi* applaudir. **ˈclapped(-out)** *a F:* foutu, fourbu. **ˈclapper** *n* battant *m* (de cloche). **ˈclapperboard** *n Cin:* claquette *f* (de synchronisation). **ˈclapping** *n* battement *m* des mains; applaudissements *mpl.* **ˈclaptrap** *n F:* boniment *m.*

claret [ˈklærət] *n* bordeaux *m* (rouge).

clarify [ˈklærifai] *vtr* clarifier. **clarifiˈcation** *n* clarification *f;* mise *f* au point.

clarinet [klæriˈnet] *n* clarinette *f.* **clariˈnettist** *n* clarinettiste *mf.*

clarity [ˈklæriti] *n* clarté *f.*

clash [klæʃ] **1.** *n* (*pl* **clashes**) (a) fracas *m,* choc *m* (métallique); résonnement *m* (de cloches) (b) conflit *m* (d'opinions); heurt *m* (d'intérêts); (*between mobs*) échauffourée *f* (c) discordance *f* (de couleurs) **2.** *vi* (*of swords*) s'entrechoquer; (*of cymbals*) résonner; (*of opinions*) s'opposer, être en désaccord; (*of interests*) se heurter; (*of colours*) jurer; **the dates c.,** les deux rendez-vous tombent le même jour.

clasp [klɑːsp] **1.** *n* fermeture *f* (de coffret); fermoir *m* (de sac, de collier) **2.** *vtr* serrer, étreindre; **to c. s.o.'s hand,** serrer la main à qn; **to c. one's hands,** joindre les mains. **ˈclaspknife** *n* (*pl* **-knives**) couteau pliant.

class [klɑːs] **1.** *n* (*pl* **classes**) (a) classe *f;* sorte *f,* genre *m*, ordre *m*; type *m* (de navires); c. **struggle**, lutte des classes; **French** c., classe de français; **evening classes**, cours *m* du soir; **in a c. of its own**, unique, sans pareil; *Sch:* **first c. honours degree** = licence avec mention très bien (*b*) *NAm:* promotion *f* 2. *vtr* classer. 'class-'conscious *a* **to be c.-c.**, avoir une conscience de classe. 'classification *n* classification *f*. 'classified *a* (*a*) *Journ:* c. **ad**, petite annonce (*b*) (document) secret. 'classify *vtr* classifier. 'classless *a* sans classe(s). 'classmate *n* camarade *mf* de classe. 'classroom *n* (salle *f* de) classe. 'classy *a F:* bon genre; chic.

classic ['klæsik] *a & n* classique (*mf*); *Sch:* **classics**, les humanités *fpl*; le latin et le grec. 'classical *a* classique.

clatter ['klætər] 1. *n* bruit *m* (de vaisselle); fracas *m*; vacarme *m* 2. *vi* faire du bruit; résonner; **to c. down** descendre bruyamment.

clause [klɔːz] *n* (*a*) clause *f*, article *m*; (*of will*) disposition *f* (*b*) *Gram:* membre *m* de phrase; proposition *f*.

claustrophobia [klɔːstrə'foubiə] *n Med:* claustrophobie *f*. claustro'phobic *a* (*of pers*) claustrophobe; (*endroit*) claustrophobique.

clavicle ['klævikl] *n Anat:* clavicule *f*.

claw [klɔː] 1. *n* griffe *f* (de félin); serre *f* (d'oiseau de proie); pince *f* (de homard); c. **hammer**, marteau à panne fendue 2. *vtr* griffer, égratigner; déchirer avec ses griffes. 'claw 'at *vtr* s'accrocher à, agripper. 'claw 'back *vtr* récupérer (une somme).

clay [klei] *n* argile *f*; (terre *f*) glaise *f*.

clean [kliːn] 1. *a* (-er, -est) (*a*) propre, net; (papier) blanc; (permis de conduire) vierge; *F:* **keep it c.!** pas de grossièretés *f!* c. **break**, cassure nette, franche; **the doctor gave me a c. bill of health**, le docteur m'a trouvé en pleine forme; *F:* **to come c.**, tout avouer (*b*) (boxeur) loyal 2. *adv* tout à fait; **I c. forgot**, j'ai complètement oublié; **they got c. away**, ils ont décampé sans laisser de traces; **to cut c. through sth**, couper qch de part en part 3. *n* **to give sth a c.**, nettoyer qch 4. *vtr* nettoyer; faire (une chambre); **to c. one's teeth**, se laver, se brosser, les dents; **to c. one's nails**, se curer les ongles. 'clean-'cut *a* (*a*) net, bien défini (*b*) (*of pers*) propre et soigné. 'cleaner *n* 1. (*pers*) (*a*) femme *f* de ménage (*b*) (**dry**) c., teinturier, -ière; (**dry**) **cleaner's**, teinturerie *f*; pressing *m*; *F:* **to take s.o. to the cleaners**, nettoyer qn 2. (*a*) appareil *m* à nettoyer (*b*) (**household**) c., produit *m* d'entretien; (*for stains*) détachant *m*. 'cleaning *n* nettoyage *m*; nettoiement *m* (des rues); (*of house*) ménage *m*; c. **lady**, femme de ménage; (**household**) c. **materials**, produits *mpl* d'entretien. 'clean-'limbed *a* bien découplé. cleanliness ['klenlinəs], 'cleanness *n* propreté *f*; netteté *f*. cleanly 1. *adv* ['kliːnli] proprement, nettement 2. *a* ['klenli] propre. 'clean 'out *vtr* nettoyer. 'clean-'shaven *a* sans barbe (ni moustache); rasé de près. 'clean 'up *vtr & i* nettoyer.

cleanse [klenz] *vtr* curer (un égout); laver (une plaie); démaquiller (le visage); purifier (l'âme). 'cleanser, 'cleansing 'cream, 'cleansing 'lotion *n* démaquillant *m*.

clear ['kliər] I. *a* (-er, -est) (*a*) clair, limpide; net; (verre) transparent; c. **soup**, bouillon *m*; **on a c. day**, par temps clair; **as c. as day**, clair comme le jour; c. **conscience**, conscience nette (*b*) (signe) certain, évident; c. **case of bribery**, cas de corruption manifeste; **to make one's meaning, oneself, c.**, se faire comprendre; **things are becoming clear(er)**, les choses commencent à s'éclaircir; c. **thinker**, esprit lucide; **to be c. about sth**, être convaincu de qch; c. **profit**, bénéfice clair et net; c. **loss**, perte sèche; c. **majority**, majorité absolue; **three c. days**, trois jours francs (*c*) libre, dégagé (**of**, de); **all c.!** fin d'alerte; **the coast is c.**, le champ est libre. II. *adv* (*a*) **loud and c.**, haut et clair (*b*) **to steer, keep, c. of s.o., sth**, éviter qn, qch; **to stand c.**, s'écarter; **stand c. of the doors!** dégagez les portes! **to get, be, c. of**, s'éloigner de. III. *n* **to be in the c.**, être au-dessus de tout soupçon. IV. *v* 1. *vtr* (*a*) éclaircir; clarifier (un liquide); dépurer (le sang); **to c. the air**, (i) donner de l'air (ii) mettre les choses au point; **to c. one's throat**, s'éclaircir la voix, se racler la gorge; **to c. one's head**, s'éclaircir les idées; **to c. one's conscience**, décharger sa conscience (*b*) innocenter, disculper (qn) (**of a charge**, d'une accusation); **to c. oneself**, se disculper (*c*) dégager, désencombrer (une route); déblayer, défricher (un terrain); (faire) évacuer, débarrasser (une salle); débarrasser (une table); déboucher (un tuyau); *Fig:* **to c. the decks**, déblayer le terrain; **to c. a way for s.o.**, ouvrir un passage à qn; **to c. one's plate**, faire assiette nette (*d*) *Com: Fin:* solder, liquider (des marchandises, un compte); *PN:* **to c.**, en solde (*e*) franchir (une barrière); (*of ship*) quitter (le port) (*f*) s'acquitter d'(une dette); compenser (un chèque) (*g*) expédier (un navire); dédouaner (des marchandises); demander, donner, l'autorisation de (qch) (*h*) gagner, faire un bénéfice net de (10%, £100); **I cleared £100 on that deal**, cette affaire m'a rapporté £100 2. *vi* (*of weather*) s'éclaircir; se lever; (*of mist*) se dissiper; (*of sky*) se dégager. 'clearance *n* (*a*) = clearing 1. **slum** c., élimination *f* des taudis; c. **sale**, (vente *f* de) soldes *mpl* (*b*) autorisation *f* (de vol); contrôle *m* (de sécurité) (*c*) espace *m* (libre); jeu *m*. 'clear a'way 1. *vtr* enlever, écarter 2. *vi* desservir. 'clear-'cut *a* net. 'clear-'headed *a* qui voit juste; perspicace. 'clearing *n* 1. (*a*) clarification *f* (d'un liquide) (*b*) dégagement *m*, désencombrement *m* (d'une route); enlèvement *m* (de débris); déblaiement *m*, défrichement *m* (d'un terrain); évacuation *f* (d'une salle); débouchement *m* (d'un tuyau) (*c*) *Com: Fin:* liquidation *f*, solde *m* (de marchandises, d'un compte) (*d*) franchissement *m* (d'une barrière) (*e*) acquittement *m* (d'une dette); compensation *f* (d'un chèque); c. **bank**, banque de clearing; c. **house**, (i) *Bank:* chambre de compensation (ii) agence centrale (de renseignements (*f*) expédition *f* (d'un navire); dédouanement *m* (de marchandises) 2. (*in forest*) clairière *f*. 'clearly *adv* (voir) clair; (distinguer) clairement, nettement; (comprendre) bien; évidemment. 'clearness *n* clarté *f*; netteté *f*. 'clear 'off 1. *vtr* enlever (des objets); débarrasser (la table) 2. *vi F:* filer, décamper, vider les lieux. 'clear 'out 1. *vtr* nettoyer; vider (une armoire); débarrasser, (faire) évacuer (une pièce); enlever, jeter (des débris) 2. *vi F:* = clear off 2. 'clear-'sighted *a Fig:* clairvoyant.

'clear 'up 1. *vtr* (*a*) (re)mettre (une pièce) en ordre; ranger (ses affaires) (*b*) éclaircir (un mystère); dissiper (un malentendu) 2. *vi* (*a*) ranger (*b*) (*of weather*) s'éclaircir (*c*) (*of illness, problem*) disparaître. 'clearway *n* route *f* à stationnement interdit.

cleavage ['kliːvidʒ] *n* (*a*) fissure *f* (*b*) naissance *f* des seins. 'cleaver *n* couperet *m*.

clef [klef] *n Mus:* clef *f*; bass, treble, c., clef de fa, de sol.

cleft [kleft] 1. *n* fente *f* 2. *a Fig:* c. stick, impasse *f*; *Med:* c. palate, palais fendu.

clematis ['klemətis] *n Bot:* clématite *f*.

clement ['klemənt] *a* clément. 'clemency *n* clémence *f*.

clementine ['klemənti:n] *n* clémentine *f*.

clench [klentʃ] *vtr* serrer (les dents, le poing); with clenched fists, les poings serrés.

clergy ['klɜːdʒi] *n coll* clergé *m*. 'clergyman *n* (*pl* -men) ecclésiastique *m*.

cleric ['klerik] *n* ecclésiastique *m*. 'clerical *a* (*a*) clérical; du clergé (*b*) (travail) de bureau; (faute) de copiste.

clerk [klɑːk, *NAm:* klɜːk] *n* (*a*) employé, -ée (de bureau); commis *m*; clerc *m* (de notaire); bank c., employé de banque; c. of works, conducteur *m* des travaux; *Jur:* c. of the court, greffier *m* (du tribunal (*b*) *NAm:* vendeur, -euse.

clever ['klevər] *a* (-er, -est) (*a*) habile (at, à); intelligent; c. with one's hands, adroit de ses mains; that's not very c., ça c'est pas malin; c. at maths, fort en maths; he was too c. for us, il nous a roulés (*b*) (dispositif) ingénieux; (ouvrage) bien fait; (argument) astucieux. 'cleverly *adv* habilement, adroitement; avec intelligence; ingénieusement. 'cleverness *n* habileté *f*; intelligence *f*; ingéniosité *f*.

cliché ['kliːʃei] *n* cliché *m*.

click [klik] 1. *n* bruit sec; (dé)clic *m*; claquement *m* (de langue) 2. *v* (*a*) *vi* cliqueter; claquer; (*of door*) to c. shut, se fermer avec un bruit sec; *F:* it suddenly clicked (with him), tout à coup il a compris, pigé (*b*) *vtr* faire claquer (les talons, la langue). 'clicking *n* cliquetis *m*.

client ['klaiənt] *n* client, -ente. clientele [kliːɒn'tel] *n* clientèle *f*.

cliff [klif] *n* falaise *f*. 'cliffhanger *n* récit *m*, concours *m*, etc, à suspense.

climate ['klaimət] *n* climat *m*. cli'matic *a* (zone) climatique.

climax ['klaimæks] *n* (*pl* climaxes) point culminant; apogée *m*; *Physiol:* orgasme *m*.

climb [klaim] 1. *n* ascension *f*; montée *f*; côte *f*; stiff c., grimpée *f*; *Sp:* hill c., course de côte; *Av:* rate of c., vitesse ascensionnelle. 2. *vtr & i* to c. (up), monter, gravir; grimper (un escalier); grimper à (un arbre); monter à (une échelle); escalader (une falaise); faire l'ascension (d'une montagne); (*of aircraft*) prendre de l'altitude; (*of road*) aller en montant; to c. over a wall, escalader un mur; to c. on the roof, monter sur le toit; to c. down a ladder, descendre d'une échelle; to c. out of a hole, se hisser hors d'un trou; to c. into, monter dans (son lit, un avion). 'climb 'down *vi* (*a*) descendre (*b*) *F:* en rabattre. 'climber *n* (*a*) grimpeur, -euse; alpiniste *mf*; (social) c., arriviste *mf* (*b*) plante grimpante. 'climbing *n*

escalade *f*; montée *f*; (mountain) c., alpinisme *m*; c. frame, cage à grimper.

clinch [klintʃ] 1. *n* (*pl* clinches) (*a*) (*of fighters*) in a c., corps à corps (*b*) *F:* étreinte *f* (d'amoureux) 2. *vtr* conclure (un marché); confirmer (un argument); that clinches it! cela me décide!

cling [kliŋ] *vi* (clung [klʌŋ]) (*a*) s'attacher, s'accrocher, se cramponner (to, à); se serrer, se coller (to s.o., contre qn); to c. together, to one another, se tenir étroitement enlacés (*b*) adhérer (to, à).

clinic ['klinik] *n* clinique *f*. 'clinical *a* (*a*) clinique; (thermomètre) médical (*b*) impartial.

clink [kliŋk] 1. *n* (*a*) tintement *m*; choc *m* (de verres) (*b*) *P:* prison *f*, taule *f* 2. *vtr & i* (faire) tinter; to c. glasses (with s.o.), trinquer (avec qn). 'clinker *n* 1. brique *f* à four 2. mâchefer *m* (de forge); escarbilles *fpl*.

clip¹ [klip] 1. *n* pince *f* (à cheveux); attache *f*; *Jewel:* clip *m*; *MecE:* collier *m*; *Sma:* chargeur *m*; (paper) c., trombone *m*; bicycle clips, pinces à pantalon 2. *vtr* (clipped) attacher (avec une pince). 'clipboard *n* planchette *f* (porte-papiers). 'clip-on *a* qui s'attache avec une pince.

clip² 1. *n* (*a*) extrait *m* (de film); *F:* c. joint, boîte de nuit où l'on reçoit le coup de fusil (*b*) *F:* taloche *f* 2. *vtr* (clipped) (*a*) tondre (un mouton); couper, tailler (une haie); poinçonner (un billet); to c. (out), découper (une photo) (*b*) *F:* flanquer une taloche à (qn). 'clipped *a* (*of speech*) saccadé. 'clipper *n ANau:* clipper *m*. 'clippers *npl* (*for hair*) tondeuse *f*; (*for hedge*) sécateur *m*; (*for nails*) pince *f* à ongles. 'clipping *n* coupure *f* (de journal); rognure *f* (d'ongle).

clique [kliːk] *n* coterie *f*, clique *f*. 'cliqu(e)y, 'cliquish *a* qui a l'esprit de clique.

cloak [klouk] 1. *n* cape *f*; manteau *m* 2. *vtr* masquer, voiler. 'cloak-and-'dagger *a* (roman) de cape et d'épée. 'cloakroom *n* (*a*) vestiaire *m* (*b*) toilettes *fpl*.

clock [klɒk] 1. *n* (*a*) (large) horloge *f*; (smaller) pendule *f*; grandfather c., horloge de parquet; carriage c., pendulette *f*; speaking c., horloge parlante; it's two o'c., il est deux heures; to work round the c., travailler vingt-quatre heures sur vingt-quatre; one hour by the c., une heure d'horloge; c. golf, jeu de l'horloge; c. radio, radio-réveil *m* (*b*) compteur *m* (de voiture, de taxi) 2. *v* (*a*) *vtr* chronométrer (un coureur) (*b*) *vi Ind:* to c. in, out, on, off, pointer à l'arrivée, à la sortie. 'clock 'up *vtr* faire (100 km). 'clock-watcher *n* employé, -ée, qui ne pense qu'à l'heure de sortie. 'clockwise *a & adv* dans le sens des aiguilles d'une montre. 'clockwork *n* mouvement *m* d'horlogerie; c. train, train mécanique; like c., comme sur des roulettes.

clog [klɒg] 1. *n* sabot *m* 2. *vtr & i* (clogged) to c. (up), (se) boucher.

cloister ['klɒistər] I. *n* cloître *m*. II. *vtr* cloîtrer; cloistered life, vie cloîtrée.

clone [kloun] *n Biol:* clone *m*.

close¹ [klous] 1. *a* (-er, -est) (*a*) près, proche (to, de); (rapport) étroit; (ami) intime; (traduction) fidèle; c. resemblance, ressemblance exacte; at c. quarters, de près; *F:* that was a c. call, shave, thing, nous l'avons échappé belle (*b*) (grain) fin; (*of texture*) serré; (*of* investigation) minutieux, attentif; (of attention) soutenu; to keep (a) c. watch on s.o., surveiller qn de près (c) (of weather) lourd; it's very c. in here, cela manque d'air, cela sent le renfermé, ici (d) (concours) à forces égales, vivement contesté; c. finish, arrivée serrée (e) (of pers) peu communicatif, réservé (f) (of pers) avare, regardant (g) c. season, chasse, pêche, fermée 2. adv étroitement; près, de près; to follow c. behind s.o., suivre qn de près; to stand c. together, se tenir serrés; c. at hand, c. by, tout près, tout proche; c. by, to, (tout) près de; c. to, on, 50 cars, presque 50 voitures; c. to the ground, au ras du sol; to be c. on fifty, friser la cinquantaine; to come closer (together), se rapprocher 3. n (a) enceinte f (de cathédrale) (b) impasse f. 'close-'cropped a coupé ras. 'close-'fitting a (vêtement) ajusté, collant. 'close-'knit a très lié (ensemble). 'closely adv étroitement (gardé); très (lié); (ressembler) exactement; (examiner) de près, attentivement; we are c. related, nous sommes proches parents. 'closeness n (a) proximité f, rapprochement m; intimité f (d'amitié) (b) exactitude f (d'une ressemblance); fidélité f (d'une traduction) (c) manque m d'air; lourdeur f (du temps). 'close-'set a (yeux) rapprochés. 'close-up n Cin: gros plan.

close² [klouz] I. n fin f; conclusion f; to draw to a c., tirer à sa fin. II. v 1. vtr (a) fermer; barrer (une rue); road closed to traffic, route interdite à la circulation (b) conclure, terminer; fermer (un débat); lever (une séance); arrêter, clore (un compte); to c. the ranks, serrer les rangs 2. vi (a) (se) fermer; se refermer (b) finir; (se) terminer; to c. round s.o., encercler qn; to c. with s.o., conclure le marché avec qn. closed a fermé; (of road) barré; (tuyau) bouché; PN: fermé; Th: relâche; behind c. doors, à huis clos; Ind: c. shop, atelier qui n'admet pas de travailleurs non-syndiqués; c. circuit television, télévision en circuit fermé; Fig: c. book, sujet en lequel on est complètement ignorant. 'close 'down vtr & i fermer (un magasin); TV: WTel: terminer l'émission. 'close-down n fermeture f (d'un magasin); WTel: TV: fin d'émission. 'close 'in 1. vtr clôturer 2. vi (of night) tomber; (of days) raccourcir; to c. in on s.o., cerner qn de près. 'close 'up 1. vtr boucher; (re)fermer (complètement); serrer (les rangs) 2. vi (a) se refermer (b) se serrer. 'closing 1. n fermeture (d'une usine); clôture f (d'un compte); early c. day, jour où les magasins sont fermés l'après-midi; c. time, heure de (la) fermeture; StExch: c. prices, derniers cours 2. a qui (se) ferme; final, dernier.

closet ['klozit] 1. n NAm: (Br = wardrobe) armoire f, placard m, penderie f 2. vtr to be closeted with s.o., être enfermé en tête-à-tête avec qn.

clot [klot] 1. n (a) caillot m (de sang); c. on the brain, embolie cérébrale (b) F: idiot, -ote, imbécile mf 2. vtr (clotted) coaguler; figer; clotted cream, crème caillée.

cloth [klɔθ] 1. n (a) tissu m; étoffe f; (of wool) drap m; (of linen, cotton) toile f; (on furniture) tapis m; Bookb: c. binding, reliure toile f; linge m; torchon m; lavette f; (for floors) serpillière f (c) nappe f.

clothe [klouð] vtr (re)vêtir, habiller (in, with, de). clothes npl (a) vêtements mpl; to put on, take off,

one's c., s'habiller, se déshabiller; with one's c. on, off, tout habillé, déshabillé; c. brush, brosse à habits; c. horse, séchoir m (à linge); (dirty) c. basket, panier à linge (b) couvertures fpl et draps mpl (de lit). 'clothesline n corde f à linge. 'clothespeg, NAm: -pin n pince f à linge. 'clothing n vêtements; habillement m; article of c., vêtement; the c. trade, l'industrie du vêtement.

cloud [klaud] 1. n nuage m; nuée f (d'insectes); Fig: to have one's head in the clouds, être dans les nuages; to be on c. nine, être aux anges; to be under a c., être (i) l'objet de soupçons (ii) en défaveur; c. cuckoo land, pays de cocagne 2. v (a) vtr couvrir, obscurcir (le ciel); embuer (une vitre); rendre trouble (un liquide); clouded sky, ciel couvert (de nuages); to c. the issue, embrouiller la question (b) vi to c. (over), se couvrir; s'assombrir. 'cloudburst n trombe f d'eau. 'cloudiness n aspect nuageux (du ciel). 'cloudless a (ciel) sans nuages. 'cloudy a (temps, ciel) couvert, nuageux; (liquide) trouble.

clout [klaut] F: 1. n (a) taloche f (b) influence f, piston m 2. vtr flanquer une taloche à (qn).

clove [klouv] n clou m de girofle; c. of garlic, gousse f d'ail.

cloven ['klouvn] a c. hoof, pied fourchu, sabot fendu.

clover ['klouvər] n Bot: trèfle m; F: to be in c., être comme un coq en pâte. 'cloverleaf n (a) feuille f de trèfle (b) c. (intersection), croisement m en trèfle.

clown [klaun] 1. n clown m; Pej: bouffon m 2. vi faire le clown. 'clowning n bouffonnerie f, pitrerie f.

cloy [klɔi] vi (of food, sweets) rassasier; écœurer. 'cloying a rassasiant, écœurant.

club [klʌb] 1. n (a) massue f, gourdin m (b) Golf: club m, crosse f (c) Cards: trèfle m (d) club (de tennis); cercle m (littéraire); youth c., foyer m de jeunes; book c., club du livre; c. sandwich, sandwich double (à trois tranches de pain); F: join the c.! (et) moi aussi! 2. vtr (clubbed) frapper (qn) avec une massue; matraquer (qn); assommer (qn) de coups de massue. 'clubfoot n pied-bot m. 'clubhouse n pavillon m. 'club to'gether vi se cotiser (to, pour).

cluck [klʌk] 1. n gloussement m 2. vi glousser.

clue [klu:] n indication f, indice m; (of crossword) définition f; to find the c. to sth., trouver la clef de qch; to give s.o. a c., mettre qn sur la voie, sur la piste; F: I haven't a c., je n'en ai pas la moindre idée. 'clueless a F: qui ne sait rien de rien. 'clue 'up vtr F: renseigner (qn); to be clued up, être à la page.

clump [klʌmp] 1. n groupe m, bouquet m (d'arbres); massif m (d'arbustes); touffe f (de fleurs) 2. vi to c. (about), marcher lourdement.

clumsy ['klʌmzi] a (-ier, -iest) maladroit, gauche; (of shape) lourd. 'clumsily adv maladroitement, gauchement. 'clumsiness n maladresse f, gaucherie f.

clung [klʌŋ] see cling.

clunk [klʌŋk] n bruit sourd (métallique).

cluster ['klʌstər] 1. n bouquet m (de fleurs); grappe f (de raisin); groupe m (d'arbres); nœud m (de diamants); amas *m* (d'étoiles) **2.** *vi* se grouper, se rassembler (**round,** autour de).

clutch [klʌtʃ] **1.** *n* (*pl* **clutches**) (*a*) **to be in, fall into, s.o.'s clutches,** être, tomber, sous les griffes de qn; **to make a c. at sth,** essayer de saisir qch (*b*) *Aut:* embrayage *m*; **to let in, let out, the c.,** embrayer, débrayer; **c. plate,** disque d'embrayage **2.** *vtr* **to c. (at),** (essayer de) saisir; serrer; s'agripper, se cramponner, à; *Fig:* **to c. at straws,** se raccrocher à n'importe quoi.

clutter [ʹklʌtər] **1.** *n* encombrement *m*, pagaille *f*, confusion *f*; **in a c.,** en désordre **2.** *vtr* **to c. (up),** encombrer (**with,** de).

cm *abbr* centimetre.

CND *abbr Campaign for Nuclear Disarmament,* Comité de désarmement nucléaire, CDN.

Co *abbr company.*

c/o *abbr care of.*

coach [koutʃ] **1.** *n* (*pl* **coaches**) (*a*) (*horse-drawn*) carrosse *f*; *Aut:* (auto)car *m*; **c. tour,** excursion en car; *Rail:* voiture *f*, wagon *m* (*b*) répétiteur, -trice; *Sp:* entraîneur *m* **2.** *vtr* donner des leçons particulières à (qn); *Sp:* entraîner (qn).

coagulate [kouʹægjuleit] *vtr & i* (se) coaguler. **coaguʹlation** *n* coagulation *f*.

coal [koul] *n* charbon *m*; houille *f*; **c. gas,** gaz de houille; *Fig:* **to haul s.o. over the coals,** laver la tête à qn; **c. merchant,** marchand de charbon. **ʹcoalface** *n* front *m* de taille. **ʹcoalfield** *n* bassin houiller. **ʹcoalman** *n* (*pl* **-men**) marchand *m* de charbon. **ʹcoalmine** *n* mine *f* de charbon; houillère *f.* **ʹcoalminer** *n* mineur *m.* **ʹcoalmining** *n* exploitation *f* de la houille; charbonnage *m*; industrie houillère.

coalesce [kouəʹles] *vi* s'unir; se fondre.

coalition [kouəʹliʃn] *n* coalition *f.*

coarse [kɔːs] *a* (**-r, -est**) grossier; vulgaire; (rire, tissu) gros; (peau) rude. **ʹcoarsely** *adv* grossièrement. **ʹcoarseness** *n* grossièreté *f*; grosseur *m* de fil (d'un tissu).

coast [koust] **1.** *n* côte *f*; rivage *m*, littoral *m*; **from c. to c.,** d'une mer à l'autre **2.** *vi* **to c. along, down,** rouler, descendre, en roue libre. **ʹcoastal** *a* côtier. **ʹcoaster** *n* (*a*) *Nau:* caboteur *m* (*b*) dessous *m* de bouteille, de verre. **ʹcoastguard** *n* garde-côte *m.* **ʹcoastline** *n* littoral.

coat [kout] **1.** *n* (*a*) (*short*) veste *f*; veston *m*; (*long*) manteau *m*; **c. of arms,** armoiries *fpl* (*b*) poil *m* (de chien); robe *f* (de cheval); pelage *m* (de loup) (*c*) couche *f* (de peinture) **2.** *vtr* enduire (**with,** de); revêtir, armer (un câble); *Cu:* enrober, napper (de chocolat). **ʹcoathanger** *n* cintre *m.* **ʹcoating** *n* couche. **ʹcoatrack** *n* portemanteau *m.*

coax [kouks] *vtr* enjôler; encourager (**into,** à). **ʹcoaxing 1.** *a* cajoleur **2.** *n* cajolerie *f.*

cob [kɔb] *n* épi *m* (de maïs).

cobalt [ʹkoubɔːlt] *n Ch:* cobalt *m.*

cobber [ʹkɔbər] *n Austr: F:* copain, -ine.

cobble(stone) [ʹkɔbl(stoun)] *n* pavé *m*, caillou *m* (de chaussée). **ʹcobbled** *a* pavé.

cobbler [ʹkɔblər] *n* cordonnier *m.*

cobra [ʹkoubrə] *n Rept:* cobra *m.*

cobweb [ʹkɔbweb] *n* toile *f* d'araignée.

cocaine [kouʹkein] *n Pharm:* cocaïne *f.*

cock [kɔk] **1.** *n* (*a*) coq *m*; *F:* **c. and bull story,** histoire à dormir debout (*b*) **c. (bird),** oiseau *m* mâle (*c*) robinet *m* (*d*) *Sma:* chien *m* (de fusil); **to go off at half c.,** mal démarrer (*e*) *V:* pénis *m* **2.** *vtr* dresser (les oreilles); armer (un fusil). **coʹckade** *n* cocarde *f.* **ʹcock-a-doodle-ʹdoo** *int* cocorico! **ʹcock-a-ʹhoop** *a F:* triomphant; fier comme Artaban. **cockaʹtoo** *n Orn:* cacatoès *m.* **ʹcockcrow** *n* **at c.,** au (premier) chant du coq. **ʹcocked** *a* (chapeau) à cornes; *F:* **to knock s.o. into a c. hat,** battre qn à plates coutures. **ʹcocker** *n* **c. (spaniel),** cocker *m.* **ʹcockerel** *n* jeune coq. **ʹcockeyed** *a F:* de travers, de traviole; (project) absurde. **ʹcockpit** *n* poste *m* (i) (*in aircraft*) de pilotage (ii) (*in racing car*) du pilote. **ʹcockroach** *n* (*pl* **-es**) *Ent:* cafard *m*, blatte *f.* **ʹcockscomb** *n* crête *f* de coq. **ʹcocksure,** *F:* **ʹcocky** *a* sûr de soi; suffisant. **ʹcocktail** *n* (*a*) (*drink*) cocktail *m*; **prawn c.,** crevettes à la mayonnaise; **fruit c.,** salade *f* de fruits; **c. lounge, cabinet,** bar *m*; **c. party,** cocktail (*b*) **Molotov c.,** cocktail Molotov.

cockle [ʹkɔkl] *n Moll:* coque *f*; *Fig:* **it warmed the cockles of my heart,** cela m'a réchauffé.

cockney [ʹkɔkni] *a & n* cockney *mf*, londonien, -ienne.

cocoa [ʹkoukou] *n* cacao *m.*

coconut [ʹkoukənʌt] *n* noix *f* de coco; **c. shy,** jeu de massacre; **c. palm,** cocotier *m*; **c. matting,** natte en fibres (de coco).

cocoon [kəʹkuːn] *n Ent:* cocon *m.*

cod(fish) [ʹkɔd(fiʃ)] *n* morue *f*; (*fresh*) cabillaud *m*; **salt c.,** morue salée; **c. liver oil,** huile de foie de morue. **ʹcodswallop** *n F:* bêtises *fpl*; bidon *m.*

COD *abbr cash on delivery.*

coddle [ʹkɔdl] *vtr* (*a*) faire cuire (des œufs) en cocotte (*b*) dorloter (qn).

code [koud] **1.** *n* (*a*) code *m*; **Highway C.,** code de la route (*b*) (*secret*) code, chiffre *m*; **c. word,** mot convenu; **to write a message in c.,** chiffrer un message; **in c.,** en chiffre(s) (*c*) *Tp:* indicatif *m*; **postal c.,** *NAm:* **zip c.,** code postal **2.** *vtr* coder; chiffrer. **ʹcoding** *n* codage *m*, chiffrement *m* (d'un message).

codeine [ʹkoudiːn] *n Pharm:* codéine *f.*

codicil [ʹkɔdisil] *n* codicille *m.*

co-director [ʹkoudaiʹrektər] *n* codirecteur, -trice; coadministrateur, -trice.

co-driver [ʹkoudraivər] *n Rac:* copilote *m.*

coed [ʹkouʹed] *F:* **1.** *a* (école) mixte **2.** *n NAm:* élève *f* d'une école mixte. **coeduʹcation** *n* enseignement *m* mixte. **coeduʹcational** *a* (école) mixte.

coefficient [kouiʹfiʃənt] *n* coefficient *m.*

coerce [kouʹəːs] *vtr* contraindre (**s.o. into doing sth,** qn à faire qch). **coʹercion** *n* contrainte *f.*

coexist [kouigʹzist] *vi* coexister (**with,** avec). **coexistence** [kouigʹzistəns] *n* coexistence *f.*

C of E *abbr Church of England.*

coffee [ʹkɔfi] *n* café *m*; **c. bar,** café; **black c.,** café noir; **white c.,** café au lait; (café) crème *m*; **c. table,** table (basse) de salon; **c.-table book,** livre de grand format illustré en couleur. **ʹcoffeepot** *n* cafetière *f.*

coffer [ʹkɔfər] *n* coffre *m.*

coffin [ʹkɔfin] *n* (*NAm:* = **casket**) cercueil *m.*

cog [ˈkɔg] *n* dent *f* (d'une roue dentée); *Fig:* **c. in the machine,** rien qu'un rouage de la machine. **'cogwheel** *n* roue dentée.

cogent [ˈkoudʒənt] *a* (argument) irrésistible; (motif) puissant; (raison) valable. **'cogently** *adv* avec force.

cogitate [ˈkɔdʒiteit] **1.** *vi* méditer (**on,** sur) **2.** *vtr* projeter (un plan).

cognac [ˈkɔnjæk] *n* cognac *m*.

cohabit [kouˈhæbit] *vi* cohabiter.

cohere [kouˈhiər] *vi* (*of whole, of parts*) se tenir ensemble; s'agglomérer; (*of argument*) se suivre (logiquement). **co'herence** *n* cohérence *f*. **co'herent** *a* cohérent; (*of thinker*) qui a de la suite dans les idées. **co'herently** *adv* d'une manière cohérente. **co'hesion** *n* cohésion *f*. **co'hesive** *a* cohésif.

coil [kɔil] **1.** *n* rouleau *m*; (re)pli *m* (d'un cordage); anneau *m* (d'un serpent); tourbillon *m* (de fumée); chignon *m* (de cheveux); (*contraceptive*) stérilet *m*; *El:* enroulement *m*, bobine *f* **2.** *v* (*a*) *vtr* (en)rouler (*b*) *vi* (*of river*) serpenter; (*of snake*) **to c. (itself) up,** s'enrouler.

coin [kɔin] **1.** *n* pièce *f* (de monnaie) **2.** *vtr* (*a*) **to c. money,** (i) frapper de la monnaie (ii) *Fig:* faire des affaires d'or (*b*) inventer (un mot); *F:* **to c. a phrase,** pour ainsi dire. **'coinage** *n* (*a*) système *m* monétaire (*b*) monnaie(s) *f* (*pl*). **'coin-op** *n F:* laverie *f* automatique. **'coin-'operated** *a* automatique.

coincide [kouinˈsaid] *vi* coïncider (**with,** avec). **co'incidence** *n* coïncidence *f*. **coinci'dental** *a* de coïncidence.

coke [kouk] *n* (*a*) (*coal*) coke *m* (*b*) *Rtm:* (*drink*) coca *m* (*c*) *P:* (*drug*) coco *f*.

colander [ˈkʌləndər] *n DomEc:* passoire *f*.

cold [kould] **1.** *a* froid; **as c. as ice,** glacé; (*of weather*) **it's c.,** il fait froid; (*of pers*) **to be, feel, c.,** avoir froid; **my feet are c.,** j'ai froid aux pieds; j'ai les pieds froids; *F:* **to have c. feet,** avoir la frousse; **to get, grow, cold(er),** (se) refroidir; *F:* **out c.,** sans connaissance; **c. front,** front froid; **c. cream,** cold-cream *m*; *Cu:* **c. meat(s),** *NAm:* **c. cuts** = assiette anglaise; **c. store,** chambre frigorifique; **c. storage,** conservation par le froid; *Fig:* **to put sth into c. storage,** mettre qch en veilleuse; **in c. blood,** de sang-froid; **c. comfort,** piètre consolation; **c. war,** guerre froide; **to give s.o. the c. shoulder,** tourner le dos à qn; **that leaves me c.,** cela ne me fait ni chaud ni froid **2.** *n* (*a*) froid *m*; **to feel the c.,** être frileux; *Fig:* **out in the c.,** à l'écart (*b*) *Med:* rhume *m*; **bad c.,** gros rhume; **c. in the head,** rhume de cerveau; **to have a c.,** être enrhumé; **to catch, get, (a) c.,** s'enrhumer; attraper, prendre, froid; **they all had colds,** ils étaient tous enrhumés; **c. sore,** herpès *m*. **'cold-'blooded** *a* (animal) à sang froid; (*of pers*) froid; insensible; (*of action*) prémédité; délibéré. **'cold-'hearted** *a* au cœur froid. **'coldly** *adv* froidement; avec froideur. **'coldness** *n* froideur *f*.

coleslaw [ˈkoulslɔː] *n* salade *f* de chou cru.

colic [ˈkɔlik] *n Med:* colique(s) *f*(*pl*).

colitis [kɔˈlaitis] *n Med:* colite *f*.

collaborate [kəˈlæbəreit] *vi* collaborer (**with,** avec). **collabo'ration** *n* collaboration *f*. **co'llaborator** *n* collaborateur, -trice.

collapse [kəˈlæps] **1.** *n* écroulement *m*, effondrement *m*; débâcle *f* (d'un pays); chute *f* (de prix); *Med:* collapsus *m* **2.** *v* (*a*) *vi* s'écrouler; s'effondrer; (*of pers*) s'affaisser (*b*) *vtr* plier. **co'llapsible** *a* pliant; démontable; escamotable.

collar [ˈkɔlər] **1.** *n* col *m*; (*detachable*) faux col; collerette *f* (de dentelle); collier *m* (de chien); *Tchn:* collier, bague *f*; **to seize s.o. by the c.,** saisir qn au collet **2.** *vtr F:* attraper, pincer (qn). **'collarbone** *n* clavicule *f*.

collate [kɔˈleit] *vtr* collationner; comparer. **co'llation** *n* collation *f*.

collateral [kɔˈlætərəl] *a* collatéral; (fait) concomitant; (raison) accessoire; *Fin:* **c. security,** *n* **c.,** nantissement *m* subsidiaire.

colleague [ˈkɔliːg] *n* collègue *mf*; confrère *m*.

collect [kəˈlekt] **1.** *vtr* (*a*) rassembler; réunir; recueillir, ramasser, assembler (des documents); percevoir (des impôts); encaisser (de l'argent); **to c. oneself,** se reprendre; **to c. one's thoughts,** se recueillir (*b*) passer prendre (qn); aller chercher (ses bagages) (*c*) collectionner (des timbres) **2.** *vi* (*a*) (*of people*) s'assembler, se rassembler; (*of thgs*) s'amasser (*b*) faire la quête (**for,** pour) **3.** *adv NAm: Tp:* **to call c.,** téléphoner en PCV. **co'llected** *a* recueilli. **co'llection** *n* **1.** (*action*) (*a*) rassemblement *m*; recouvrement *m* (d'une somme); perception *f* (des impôts); levée *f* (des lettres); enlèvement *m* (des ordures) (*b*) *Ecc: etc:* quête *f*, collecte *f* (**for,** pour) (*c*) amas *m*, assemblage *m* (d'objets divers); collection *f* (de timbres, etc); recueil *m* (de poèmes). **co'llective** *a* collectif; **c. bargaining** = convention collective. **co'llectively** *adv* collectivement. **co'llector** *n* collectionneur, -euse (de timbres); **(tax) c.,** percepteur *m* (des contributions directes); receveur *m* (des contributions indirectes); **ticket c.,** contrôleur *m*.

college [ˈkɔlidʒ] *n* collège *m*; **when I was at c.,** quand j'étais en faculté; **military c.,** école *f* militaire; **c. of education, teacher training c.** = école normale; **c. of further education** = centre *m* d'enseignement postscolaire; centre de formation permanente, continue; **agricultural c.** = institut *m* agronomique.

collide [kəˈlaid] *vi* se heurter; entrer en collision; **to c. with,** heurter; entrer en collision avec. **co'llision** *n* collision *f*; (*of ships*) abordage *m*; **c. course,** cap de collision.

collie [ˈkɔli] *n* colley *m*.

collier [ˈkɔljər] *n* mineur *m* (de charbon). **'colliery** *n* mine *f* (de charbon); houillère *f*.

colloquial [kəˈloukwiəl] *a* familier; de (la) conversation; (français) parlé. **co'lloquialism** *n* expression familière. **co'lloquially** *adv* familièrement.

collusion [kəˈluːʒn] *n* collusion *f*; **to act in c. with s.o.,** agir de complicité avec qn.

cologne [kəˈloun] *n Toil:* eau *f* de Cologne.

colon [ˈkoulən] *n* (*a*) deux-points *m* (*b*) *Anat:* côlon *m*.

colonel [ˈkɔːnl] *n* colonel *m*.

colonnade [kɔləˈneid] *n* colonnade *f*.

colony [ˈkɔləni] *n* colonie *f*. **colonial** *a* & *n* colonial(e). **co'lonialism** *n* colonialisme *m*. **co'lonialist** *a* & *n* colonialiste (*mf*). **'colonist** *n* colon *m.* **coloni'zation** *n* colonisation *f.* **'colonize** *vtr* coloniser.

Colorado [kɔlə'rɑːdou] *Prn Geog:* Colorado *m; Ent:* **C. beetle,** doryphore *m.*

colossus [kə'lɔsəs] *n* (*pl* **colossi**) colosse *m.* **co'lossal** *a* colossal. **co'lossally** *adv* colossalement.

colour, *NAm:* **color** ['kʌlər] **1.** *n* (*a*) couleur *f;* **what c. is it?** de quelle couleur est-ce? **local c.,** couleur locale; **c. scheme,** disposition des coloris; **to see sth in its true colours,** voir qch sous son vrai jour; *F:* **to see the c. of s.o.'s money,** voir la couleur de l'argent de qn; **c. photo, TV,** photo, télévision, en couleur; (*of pers*) **high c.,** vivacité de teint; **to lose c.,** se décolorer; (*of pers*) pâlir; perdre ses couleurs; *F:* **to be off c.,** ne pas être dans son assiette; **c. problem,** problème du racisme, des races de couleur; **c. bar,** discrimination raciale (*b*) *pl Mil: etc:* couleurs; drapeau *m; Nau:* pavillon *m;* **to pass (an examination) with flying colours,** passer haut la main; **to show oneself in one's true colours,** se révéler tel qu'on est **2.** *v* (*a*) *vtr* colorier; colorier; **to c. sth blue,** colorer qch en bleu (*b*) *vi* (*of pers*) rougir. **'colour-blind,** *NAm:* **'color-** *a* daltonien. **'colour-blindness,** *NAm:* **'color-** *n* daltonisme *m.* **'coloured,** *NAm:* **'colored 1.** *a* coloré; colorié; (photo) en couleur; (personne) de couleur; **highly c.,** coloré; haut en couleur; **flesh-c.,** couleur (de) chair; **violet-c.,** couleur de violette **2.** *n* personne *f* de couleur. **'colourful,** *NAm:* **'color-** *a* coloré; (style) pittoresque; **c. character,** original, -ale. **'colouring,** *NAm:* **'color-** *n* coloration *f;* (*of pers*) teint *m.* **'colourless** *a* sans couleur; incolore.

colt [koult] *n* (*a*) poulain *m* (*b*) *Sp:* débutant, -ante.

column ['kɔləm] *n* colonne *f;* **spinal c.,** colonne vertébrale; *Av:* **control c.,** levier *m* de commande; *Journ:* **theatrical c.,** rubrique *f* des théâtres. **'columnist** *n* journaliste *mf.*

coma ['koumə] *n Med:* coma *m;* **in a c.,** dans le coma. **'comatose** *a* comateux.

comb [koum] **1.** *n* (*a*) peigne *m* (*b*) crête *f* (de coq) **2.** *vtr* (*a*) peigner; **to c. one's hair,** se peigner (*b*) (*of police, etc*) ratisser. **'comb 'out** *vtr* démêler (les cheveux).

combat ['kɔmbæt] **1.** *n* combat *m* **2.** *vtr & i* combattre (**with, against,** contre). **'combatant** *a & n* combattant, -ante.

combine 1. *n* ['kɔmbain] *Fin:* cartel *m,* trust *m; Agr:* **c. (harvester),** moissonneuse-batteuse *f* **2.** *v* [kəm-'bain] (*a*) *vtr* combiner; allier (**with,** à); (ré)unir; **to c. business with pleasure,** joindre l'utile à l'agréable (*b*) *vi* (*of people*) s'unir, s'associer, se liguer (**against,** contre); (*of workers*) se syndiquer; (*of parties, firms*) fusionner; (*of events*) concourir; *Ch:* se combiner. **combi'nation** *n* (*a*) association *f* (de personnes) (*b*) combinaison *f;* concours *m* (de circonstances) (*c*) chiffre *m* (de la serrure d'un coffre-fort); **c. lock,** serrure à combinaison (*d*) (**motorcycle) c.,** (motocyclette *f* à) side-car *m.* **com'bined** *a* combiné; (travail) fait en collaboration; (effort) réuni, conjugué; *Mil:* **c. operation(s),** opération interalliée combinée; opération interalliées.

combustion [kəm'bʌstʃən] *n* combustion *f.* **com'bustible** *a & n* combustible (*m*).

come [kʌm] *vi* (*pt* **came** [keim]; *pp* **come**) (*a*) venir; arriver; **he comes this way every week,** il passe par ici tous les huit jours; **here he comes!** le voilà qui arrive! **c. here!** viens ici! **coming!** j'arrive! **to c. for,** venir chercher; **c. with me,** viens avec moi; **c. and see me soon,** venez me voir bientôt; **I've c. to see you,** je viens vous voir; **he's c. a long way,** (i) il arrive de loin (ii) *Fig:* il a fait du chemin; **to c. and go,** aller et venir; **to take things as they c.,** prendre les choses comme elles viennent; **c. what may,** quoi qu'il arrive; **in years to c.,** dans les temps à venir; **c. (c.) now!** allons! voyons! *F:* **he had it coming to him,** il l'avait bien mérité; cela lui pendait au nez; *F:* **c. again?** comment? *F:* **c. summer,** en été (*b*) **that comes on page 20,** cela se trouve à la page 20; **it comes in six colours,** cela existe en six couleurs; **how does the door c. to be open?** comment se fait-il que la porte soit ouverte? *F:* **how c.?** comment (ça)? **that comes easy to him,** cela lui est facile; **to c. expensive,** coûter, revenir, cher; **to c. apart, undone,** se défaire; se décoller; se détacher; **now (that) I c. to think of it,** (maintenant) que j'y songe; **I've c. to believe that,** j'en suis venu à croire que (*c*) **what will c. of it?** qu'en résultera-t-il? **nothing much came of it,** il n'en est pas sorti grand-chose; **no good will c. of it,** cela tournera mal; **that's what comes of fooling around,** voilà ce qui arrive quand on fait l'idiot; (*of pers*) **to c. from a good family,** être d'une bonne famille (*d*) *P:* jouir. **'come a'bout** *vi* arriver; **how did it c. a. that?** comment se fait-il que? + *sub.* **'come a'cross 1.** *vtr* trouver par hasard; tomber sur **2.** *vi* traverser; *Fig:* **to c. a. well, badly,** faire bonne, mauvaise, impression. **'come 'after** *vtr & i* suivre. **'come a'long** *vi* (*a*) venir; arriver; **c. a.!** allons-(y)! dépêche-toi! (*b*) faire des progrès; (*of plant*) (bien) venir. **'come 'at** *vtr* (*of adversary*) s'avancer vers (qn). **'come a'way** *vi* partir (**from,** de); (*of handle*) se détacher; **c. a. from there!** ôte-toi de là! **'come 'back** *vi* (*a*) revenir; **to c. b. to what I was saying,** pour en revenir à ce que je disais (*b*) répliquer (**at s.o.,** à qn). **'comeback** *n* (*a*) retour *m* (en vogue, au pouvoir, à la scène) (*b*) réplique *f.* **'come be'fore** *vtr* (*a*) précéder (*b*) = **come up 2.** (*e*). **'come be'tween** *vtr* (venir) se mettre entre. **'come 'by 1.** *vi* passer **2.** *vtr* obtenir, recevoir. **'come 'down 1.** *vtr & i* descendre **2.** *vi* (*of aircraft*) atterrir; (*of rain*) tomber; (*of prices*) baisser; (*of houses*) être démoli; **to c. d. on the side of,** se décider en faveur de; **to c. d. on s.o.,** tomber sur (le dos à) qn; **to c. d. with a cold,** attraper la grippe. **'comedown** *n F:* humiliation *f;* douche *f.* **'come 'forward** *vi* (*a*) s'avancer (**as,** comme) se présenter (**as,** comme). **'come 'in** *vi* entrer; arriver; (*of tide*) monter; (*of money*) rentrer; **to c. in handy, useful,** tomber bien; être utile; servir à quelque chose; **to c. in for sth,** recevoir qch; *F:* **where do I c. in?** et moi, n'y suis-je pour rien? **'come 'into** *vtr* (*a*) entrer dans (une pièce); **to c. i. the world,** venir au monde; **to say the first thing that comes i. one's head,** dire la première chose qui vous passe par la tête, qui vous vient à l'esprit (*b*) hériter de (l'argent). **'come 'off 1.** *vtr & i* (*a*) tomber (d'un cheval); *F:* **c. o. it!** en voilà assez! la barbe! (*b*) (*of stain, button*) partir, se détacher (d'un vêtement) **2.** *vi* (*of event*) avoir lieu; (*of plan*) réussir, se réaliser (*b*) (*of pers*) s'en tirer, s'en sortir (c) P: (of pers) jouir. 'come 'on 1. vi (a) = come along (b) Th: (of actor) entrer en scène (c) (of rain, illness) commencer; it came on to rain, il s'est mis à pleuvoir; I've got a cold coming on, je m'enrhume 2. vtr = come across 1. 'come 'out vi (a) sortir (of, de); (of thg) partir; (of sun, book) paraître; (of stain) s'enlever, s'en aller; (of colour) déteindre; (of facts) se faire jour; (of calculation) se résoudre, tomber juste; (of total) to c. o. at, se monter à; Sch: to c. o. top, être reçu premier; to c. o. in a rash, avoir une éruption de boutons; the photo didn't c. o. (well), la photo n'est pas bonne; F: to c. o. with a remark, lâcher une observation (b) to c. o. (on strike), se mettre en grève (c) se prononcer (against, for, contre, pour). 'come 'over 1. vi venir, arriver (from, de); to c. o. to s.o.'s way of thinking, se mettre, se ranger, du parti de qn; to c. o. ill, faint, F: funny, être pris d'un malaise; to c. o. well, badly, faire bonne, mauvaise, impression 2. vtr (of feeling) gagner (qn); what's c. o. you? qu'est-ce qui vous prend? 'come r n first c., premier venu, première venue; open to all comers, ouvert à tout venant, à tous venants. 'come 'round vi (a) faire le tour, un détour (by, par) (b) venir; c. r. and see me on Saturday, viens me voir samedi (c) (of festival) revenir (every 10 years, tous les 10 ans) (d) (of pers) reprendre connaissance, revenir à soi (e) se reprendre; he'll c. r., il en reviendra; to c. r. to s.o.'s way of thinking, se mettre, se ranger, du parti de qn. 'come 'through 1. vtr traverser 2. vtr & i se tirer (indemne) (de qch); survivre (à une maladie) 3. vi (of message) arriver. 'come 'to vtr & i (a) = come round (d); to c. to one's senses, (i) = come round (d) (ii) revenir à la raison (b) how much does it c.? cela fait combien? the dinner came to £20, le dîner est revenu à £20; what are things coming to? où allons-nous? it comes to the same thing, cela revient au même; if it comes to that, (i) à ce compte-là (ii) s'il faut bien en arriver là; F: c. to that, pendant que j'y suis; à propos; when it comes to politics, pour ce qui est de la politique; the idea came to me that, il m'est venu à l'esprit que; suddenly it came to me, tout d'un coup (i) je m'en suis souvenu (ii) j'ai eu une idée. 'come 'under vtr tomber sous (l'influence de qn); être compris, se classer sous (une rubrique). 'come 'up 1. vtr & i monter; the water came up to their knees, l'eau leur venait (jusqu')aux genoux; she already comes up to my shoulder, elle m'arrive déjà à l'épaule 2. vi (a) s'approcher (to, de); to c. up against, rencontrer, se heurter à; entrer en conflit avec (b) (of plants) sortir (de terre); pousser (c) (of question) se présenter, être soulevé; to c. up (for discussion), venir sur le tapis; something's c. up, il s'est passé quelque chose; F: to c. up with, trouver (une solution) (d) to c. up to, égaler; to c. up to s.o.'s expectations, répondre à l'attente de qn (e) Jur: etc: (of pers) comparaître (before, devant); (of case) être entendu (before, par) (f) (of diver) revenir à la surface. 'come up 'on vtr = come across 1. come-'uppance n F: to get one's c.-u., n'avoir que ce qu'on a mérité. 'coming 1. a (of year) qui vient, prochain, à venir; (of generation) futur; F: (of pers) d'avenir 2. n venue f; arrivée f; c. and going, va-et-vient m; comings and goings, allées et venues.

comedy ['kɔmədi] n comédie f. co'median [kə'mi:diən] n (acteur m) comique m. comedi-'enne n actrice f comique.

comet ['kɔmit] n comète f.

comfort ['kʌmfət] 1. n (a) consolation f; réconfort m; soulagement m; to take c., se consoler (from, de) (b) confort m; bien-être m; pl commodités fpl; I like c., j'aime mes aises; every modern c., tout le confort moderne; to live in c., vivre dans l'aisance f; NAm: c. station, W-C mpl 2. vtr consoler, soulager (qn). 'comfortable a confortable; agréable; (revenu) suffisant; to make oneself c., se mettre à son aise; it's so c. here, on est bien, il fait si bon, ici. 'comfortably adv confortablement; agréablement; (vivre) dans l'aisance; to be c. off, être à l'aise. 'comforter n 1. (pers) consolateur, -trice; Job's c., ami, -ie, de Job 2. (a) (scarf) cache-nez m inv (b) NAm: couverture matelassée; (stuffed with feathers) édredon m. 'comforting a réconfortant; (paroles) de consolation. 'comfortless a sans confort, désolé. 'comfy a F: confortable; (of pers) bien.

comic ['kɔmik] 1. a comique; c. strip, bande dessinée 2. n (a) (pers) comique m (b) journal m de bandes dessinées. 'comical a comique. 'comically adv comiquement.

comma ['kɔmə] n virgule f; inverted commas, guillemets mpl.

command [kə'mɑ:nd] 1. n (a) ordre m, commandement m; at s.o.'s c., sur les ordres de qn; Th: c. performance, représentation commandée par le souverain; under the c. of, sous le commandement de; word of c., commandement; to be in c. of, avoir le commandement de, commander (b) connaissance f, maîtrise f (d'une langue); to have a c. of several languages, posséder plusieurs langues; the money at my c., les fonds à ma disposition 2. vtr & i ordonner, commander (s.o. to do sth, à qn de faire qch); commander (un régiment); avoir (qch) à sa disposition; forcer (l'attention); inspirer (le respect); to c. a high price, se vendre très cher. commandant [kɔmən'dænt] n commandant m. comman'deer vtr réquisitionner n Mil: commandant m; chef m (de section); Nau: capitaine m de frégate; c. in chief, commandant en chef. co'mmanding a (officier) commandant; (ton) d'autorité, de commandement; (air) imposant; (of position) dominant. co'mmandment n commandement m. co'mmando n Mil: commando m.

commemorate [kə'meməreit] vtr commémorer. commemo'ration n commémoration f. co'memorative a commémoratif.

commence [kə'mens] vtr & i commencer (à, de, faire qch). co'mmencement n (a) commencement m, début m (b) Sch: NAm: (Br = graduation) cérémonie f de la remise des diplômes.

commend [kə'mend] vtr (a) recommander; confier (qch à qn) (b) louer (for, de). co'mmendable a louable, recommandable. co'mmendably adv d'une manière louable. commen'dation n éloge m; recommandation f.

commensurate [kə'menʃərət] a proportionné (with, à).

comment ['kɔment] 1. n commentaire m; observation f; critique f; no c., sans commentaire 2. vi faire observer (that, que); to c. on, commenter (un texte), critiquer (la conduite de qn), faire des observations sur. **'commentary** n commentaire m; (of event) reportage m. **'commentate** vi esp Sp: faire le reportage (**on**, de). **'commentator** n TV: WTel: Sp: reporter m; Pol: commentateur, -trice.

commerce ['kɔmə:s] n commerce m; affaires fpl. **co'mmercial 1.** a commercial **2.** n. TV: WTel: émission f publicitaire. **commerciali'zation** n commercialisation f. **co'mmercialize** vtr commercialiser. **co'mmercially** adv commercialement.

commie ['kɔmi] a & n F: communiste (mf); coco mf inv.

commiserate [kə'mizəreit] vi témoigner de la commisération (**with**, à). **commise'ration** n commisération f.

commissar [kɔmi'sɑ:r] n commissaire m (du peuple). **commi'ssariat** n commissariat m.

commission [kə'miʃn] **1.** n (a) commission f; Com: **on c.**, à la commission; **in c.**, (navire) en commission; (avion) en service; **out of c.**, (voiture) en panne; (ascenseur) hors service (b) Mil: brevet m (d'officier); **to get one's c.**, être nommé officier; **to resign one's c.**, démissionner (c) (to artist) commande f **2.** vtr (a) charger (qn) (**to do**, de faire); Mil: nommer (qn) officier (b) commander (un tableau). **commissio'naire** n commissionnaire m (d'hôtel). **co'mmissioner** n membre m d'une commission, commissaire m; **c. of police** = préfet m de police; **c. for oaths**, solicitor qui reçoit des déclarations sous serment.

commit [kə'mit] vtr (**committed**) (a) remettre, confier (**to s.o., s.o.'s care**, à qn, aux soins de qn); **to c. sth to memory**, apprendre qch par cœur; **to c. s.o. (to prison)**, envoyer qn en prison; **to c. s.o. for trial**, mettre qn en accusation; **to c. oneself**, s'engager; **to be committed to**, être engagé à; **without committing myself**, sans me compromettre (b) commettre (un crime). **co'mmitment** n (usu pl) engagement(s) m(pl); obligation(s) f(pl). **co'mmittal** n (a) mise f en terre (d'un cadavre) (b) Jur: internement m.

committee [kə'miti] n comité m; commission f, management c., conseil m d'administration; **to be on a c.**, faire partie d'un comité; **c. meeting**, réunion de comité.

commodious [kə'moudiəs] a spacieux.

commodity [kə'mɔditi] n marchandise f; denrée f; **basic commodities**, produits m de base.

commodore ['kɔmədɔ:r] n (a) Nau: chef m de division; MilAv: **air c.**, général m de brigade (b) capitaine m (d'un yacht-club).

common ['kɔmən] **1.** a (**-er, -est**) (a) commun (**to**, à); (mur) mitoyen; **c. land**, champs communs; **c. law**, droit coutumier; **c. knowledge**, connaissance générale, opinion courante; **C. Market**, Marché commun (b) ordinaire; (événement) fréquent, qui arrive souvent; (nom) vulgaire (d'une plante); **c. honesty**, la probité la plus élémentaire, simple; **in c. use**, d'usage courant; **c. or garden**, commun; **c. people**, gens du peuple; plèbe f (c) (of pers, manners) vulgaire; trivial **2.** n (a) terrain communal (b) **to have sth in c. (with s.o.)**, avoir qch en commun (avec qn); **they have nothing in c.**, ils n'ont rien de commun. **'commoner** n roturier, -ière. **'common-law** a

(époux) de droit coutumier. **'commonly** adv communément, ordinairement; généralement. **'commonplace 1.** n lieu commun **2.** a banal. **'commonroom** n salle f (i) commune (ii) des professeurs. **'commons** npl **the (House of) C.**, la Chambre des Communes, les Communes fpl. **common'sense** n sens commun, bon sens; **c. attitude**, attitude pleine de bon sens. **'Commonwealth (the)** n le Commonwealth (britannique).

commotion [kə'mouʃn] n agitation f; commotion f; confusion f.

commune 1. n ['kɔmju:n] commune f; communauté f (de hippies) **2.** vi [kə'mju:n] converser (**with s.o.**, avec qn); communier (avec la nature). **'communal** a commun; communautaire.

communicate [kə'mju:nikeit] vtr & i communiquer (avec); entrer en rapport (avec); faire connaître (une nouvelle à qn). **co'mmunicable** a Med: transmissible. **co'mmunicant** n Ecc: communiant, -ante. **communi'cation** n communication f; Rail: **c. cord**, corde de signal d'alarme; **radio c.**, liaison f par radio. **co'mmunicative** a communicatif. **co'mmunion** n communion f. **co'mmuniqué** n communiqué m.

communism ['kɔmjunizm] n communisme m; **'communist** a & n communiste (mf).

community [kə'mju:niti] n (pl **communities**) communauté f; **c. centre**, centre civique, social; **c. singing**, chansons populaires reprises en chœur par l'assistance.

commute [kə'mju:t] **1.** vtr (a) Jur: commuer (une peine) (b) échanger (**into**, pour) **2.** vi faire un trajet journalier; faire la navette. **co'mmuter** n banlieusard, carde; personne qui fait la navette; **c. belt**, (grande) banlieue.

compact¹ ['kɔmpækt] n convention f, pacte m, accord m.

compact² 1. a [kəm'pækt] compact; serré, tassé **2.** n ['kɔmpækt] (a) poudrier m (de sac à main) (b) NAm: Aut: voiture compacte (c) accord m, convention f.

companion [kəm'pænjən] n **1.** compagnon, f compagne; (employee) dame f de compagnie **2.** (a) manuel m (b) pendant m (d'un objet d'art). **com'panionable** a sociable; agréable. **com'panionship** n compagnie f. **com'panionway** n Nau: escalier m des cabines.

company ['kʌmpəni] n (pl **companies**) (a) compagnie f; **to keep s.o. c.**, tenir compagnie à qn; **to part c. (with s.o.)**, se séparer (de qn); **he's very good c.**, c'est un compagnon agréable; Prov: **two's c., three's a crowd**, deux s'amusent, trois s'embêtent; **to get into bad c.**, faire de mauvaises fréquentations; Com: **joint stock c.**, société par actions; **Smith and Company**, Smith et Compagnie (b) invités mpl; **we've got c. to dinner**, nous avons du monde à dîner (c) Th: troupe f; Nau: **ship's c.**, équipage m.

compare [kəm'peər] **1.** n **beyond c.**, sans comparaison; sans pareil **2.** v (a) vtr comparer (**to, with**, à, avec); confronter (des textes); (**as**) **compared with**, en comparaison de; Fig: **to c. notes**, échanger ses impressions avec qn (b) vi être comparable (**with**, à); **to c. favourably with**, ne le céder en rien à qn. **comparable** ['kɔmpərəbl] a comparable (**with, to**, à). **com'parative** a comparatif; (coût) relatif; (of *study*) comparé; **he's a c. stranger**, je ne le connais guère. **com'paratively** *adv* comparativement; relativement. **com'parison** *n* comparaison *f*; **in c. with**, en comparaison de; **by c. with**, par comparaison à; **there is no c. between them**, ils ne peuvent être comparés.

compartment [kəm'pɑːtmənt] *n* compartiment *m*.

compass ['kʌmpəs] *n* (*pl* **compasses**) (*a*) *Mth:* **(pair of) compasses**, compas *m* (*b*) *Nav:* boussole *f* (de poche); compas (de mer); *Fig:* étendue *f*.

compassion [kəm'pæʃn] *n* compassion *f*. **com'passionate** *a* compatissant **(to(wards)**, envers); *ps.* **leave**, permission exceptionnelle (pour raisons familiales). **com'passionately** *adv* avec compassion.

compatible [kəm'pætibl] *a* compatible (**with**, avec). **compati'bility** *n* compatibilité *f*.

compatriot [kəm'pætriət] *n* compatriote *mf*.

compel [kəm'pel] *vtr* (**compelled**) contraindre (**s.o. to do.**, qn à faire); **he compels respect**, il impose le respect. **com'pelling** *a* irrésistible.

compendium [kəm'pendiəm] *n* (*a*) abrégé *m* (*b*) malle *f* (de jeux).

compensate ['kɔmpənseit] **1.** *vtr* compenser; **to c. s.o. for sth**, dédommager (qn de qch) **2.** *vi* **to c. for sth**, racheter, compenser, qch. **compen'sation** *n* compensation *f*; dédommagement *m*.

compère ['kɔmpeər] **1.** *n* animateur, -trice **2.** *vtr* animer (un spectacle).

compete [kəm'piːt] *vi* concourir; **to c. with s.o.**, faire concurrence à qn; **to c. with s.o. for a prize**, disputer un prix à qn.

competent ['kɔmpitənt] *a* compétent (**to do**, pour faire);. capable. **'competence** *n* compétence *f*; capacité *f*. **'competently** *adv* avec compétence.

competition [kɔmpə'tiʃn] *n* (*a*) compétition *f*; concurrence *f*; **in c. with**, en concurrence avec (*b*) compétition, concours *m*. **com'petitive** *a* (esprit) de concurrence; (prix) concurrentiel; **c. examination**, concours. **com'petitor** *n* concurrent, -ente.

compile [kəm'pail] *vtr* compiler; dresser (un catalogue); composer (un recueil). **compi'lation** *n* compilation *f*. **com'piler** *n* compilateur, -trice.

complacent [kəm'pleisnt] *a* content de soi-même; (air) suffisant. **com'placency** *n* contentement *m* de soi-même; suffisance *f*. **com'placently** *adv* avec suffisance.

complain [kəm'plein] *vi* se plaindre (**of, about,** de; **that**, que); **I have nothing to c. about**, je n'ai pas à me plaindre. **com'plaint** *n* (*a*) plainte *f*; réclamation *f*; **to make, lodge, a c. against s.o.**, porter plainte contre qn (*b*) sujet *m* de plainte; grief *m* (*c*) maladie *f*; mal *m*.

complement ['kɔmplimənt] **1.** *n* (*a*) **(full) c.**, effectif (complet) (*b*) complément *m* **2.** *vtr* être le complément de; compléter. **comple'mentary** *a* complémentaire.

complete [kəm'pliːt] **1.** *a* (*a*) complet; entier; total; *F:* **he's a c. idiot!** c'est un parfait idiot! (*b*) terminé; achevé **2.** *vtr* (*a*) compléter; achever, terminer; accomplir (*b*) remplir (une formule). **com'pletely** *adv* complètement. **com'pleteness** *n* état complet. **com'pletion** *n* achèvement *m*; **near c.**, près d'être achevé; **on c. (of contract)**, dès la signature du contrat.

complex ['kɔmpleks] **1.** *a* complexe **2.** *n* (*pl* **complexes**) complexe *m* (industriel, d'infériorité). **com'plexity** *n* complexité *f*.

complexion [kəm'plekʃn] *n* teint *m*; *Fig:* **that puts a different c. on the matter**, voilà qui change la situation.

complicate ['kɔmplikeit] *vtr* compliquer. **'complicated** *a* compliqué. **compli'cation** *n* complication *f*.

complicity [kəm'plisiti] *n* complicité *f* (**in,** à).

compliment **1.** *n* ['kɔmplimənt] compliment *m*; **to pay s.o. a c.**, faire un compliment à qn; **to send one's compliments to s.o.**, se rappeler au bon souvenir de qn; (*on book*) **with compliments**, hommages *mpl* (de l'éditeur, etc) **2.** *vtr* ['kɔmpliment] complimenter, féliciter (qn) (**on, de**, sur). **compli'mentary** *a* (*a*) flatteur (*b*) (exemplaire) à titre gracieux; (billet) de faveur.

comply [kəm'plai] *vi* (**complied**) **to c. with**, se conformer à; observer, obéir à (une règle); accéder à (une demande). **com'pliance** *n* soumission *f* (**with**, à); **in c. with**, conformément à. **com'pliant** *a* accommodant.

component [kəm'pounənt] **1.** *a* constituant **2.** *n* composante *f* (de force, d'une idée); *Elcs: etc:* composant *m*; *Ind:* pièce (détachée).

compose [kəm'pouz] *vtr* composer; **to be composed of**, se composer de; **to c. oneself**, se calmer. **com'posed** *a* calme, tranquille. **com'poser** *n* compositeur, -trice. **compo'sition** *n* composition *f*; (*compound*) composé *m*; *Sch:* rédaction *f*. **com'positor** [-'pozitər] *n* *Typ:* compositeur *m*. **com'posure** [-'pouʒər] *n* sang-froid *m*; calme *m*.

compos mentis ['kɔmpos'mentis] *Lt phr* sain d'esprit.

compost ['kɔmpost] *n* compost *m*; terreau *m*.

compound **1.** ['kɔmpaund] (*a*) *a* composé; *Med:* (*of fracture*) compliqué; (nombre) complexe; *Fin:* **c. interest**, intérêts composés (*b*) *n* composé *m*; *Gram:* **c. word**, mot composé; *Const:* enceinte *f* **2.** *vtr* [kəm'paund] (*a*) combiner (des éléments) (*b*) aggraver (un problème).

comprehend [kɔmpri'hend] *vtr* comprendre. **compre'hensible** *a* compréhensible. **compre'hension** *n* compréhension *f*. **compre'hensive** **1.** *a* compréhensif; (*of knowledge*) étendu; (exposé) détaillé, complet; *Ins:* **fully c.**, (police) tous risques; **c. school** = collège *m* d'enseignement secondaire, CES *m* **2.** *n* = **c. school**.

compress **1.** *n* ['kɔmpres] *Med:* compresse *f* **2.** *vtr* [kəm'pres] comprimer; condenser (un discours); concentrer (son style). **com'pression** *n* compression *f*; concentration *f* (du style). **com'pressor** *n* compresseur *m*.

comprise [kəm'praiz] *vtr* comprendre; constituer.

compromise ['kɔmprəmaiz] **1.** *n* compromis *m* **2.** *v* (*a*) *vtr* compromettre (*b*) *vi* transiger; accepter un compromis. **'compromising** *a* compromettant.

compulsion [kəm'pʌlʃn] *n* contrainte *f*; **under c.**, par, sous la, contrainte. **com'pulsive** *a* (fumeur) invétéré. **com'pulsively** *adv* par besoin. **com'pulsorily** *adv* obligatoirement. **com'pulsory** *a* obligatoire.

compunction [kəm'pʌŋkʃn] *n* remords *m*; **without c.**, sans scrupule.

compute [kəm'pju:t] *vtr* calculer. **compu'tation** *n* calcul *m*. **com'puter** *n* ordinateur *m*; **c. science**, informatique *f*; **c. scientist**, informaticien, -ienne. **computeri'zation** *n* automatisation *f* (électronique); informatisation *f*. **com'puterize** *vtr* informatiser. **com'puting** *n* informatique.

comrade ['kɔmreid] *n* camarade *mf*; **c. in arms**, compagnon, *f* compagne, d'armes. **'comradeship** *n* camaraderie *f*.

con¹ [kɔn] *F*: 1. *n* **c. (trick)**, escroquerie *f*; **c. man**, escroc *m* 2. *vtr* (**conned**) escroquer; **I've been conned**, on m'a eu.

con² *n* *F*: **the pros and cons**, le pour et le contre.

concave ['kɔnkeiv] *a* concave.

conceal [kən'si:l] *vtr* cacher (**from**, à); dissimuler (la vérité); tenir secret (un projet); **concealed lighting**, éclairage indirect. **con'cealment** *n* dissimulation *f*; **in c.**, en cachette.

concede [kən'si:d] *vtr* concéder; **to c. defeat**, s'avouer vaincu.

conceit [kən'si:t] *n* vanité *f*, suffisance *f*. **con'ceited** *a* suffisant, vaniteux. **con'ceitedly** *adv* avec vanité, avec suffisance.

conceive [kən'si:v] *vtr* & *i* **to c. (of)**, concevoir; comprendre. **con'ceivable** *a* concevable. **con'ceivably** *adv* **he may c. have done it**, il est concevable qu'il l'ait fait.

concentrate ['kɔnsəntreit] 1. *n* concentré *m* 2. *v* (*a*) *vtr* concentrer (*b*) *vi* se concentrer (**on**, sur); s'appliquer (**on doing**, à faire). **concen'tration** *n* concentration *f*; **c. camp**, camp de concentration. **con'centric** *a* concentrique.

concept ['kɔnsept] *n* concept *m*; idée générale; notion *f*. **con'ception** *n* conception *f*.

concern [kən'sɔ:n] 1. *n* (*a*) intérêt *m* (**in**, dans); **it's no c. of his**, cela ne le regarde pas; il n'a rien à y voir (*b*) souci *m*, inquiétude *f* (**about**, à l'égard de); **to show c.**, se montrer inquiet (**about**, de qch, au sujet de qn) (*c*) *Com*: entreprise *f*; fonds *m* de commerce; affaire *f* 2. *vtr* (*a*) concerner, regarder; intéresser; **that does not c. me**, cela ne me regarde pas, n'est pas mon affaire; **to whom it may c.**, à qui de droit; **as far as I'm concerned**, en ce qui me concerne, quant à moi; **to c. oneself with, to be concerned in**, s'intéresser à, s'occuper de; **the persons concerned**, les intéressés; **the department concerned**, le service compétent (*b*) **to be concerned**, s'inquiéter, être inquiet (**about**, de qch, au sujet de qn). **con'cerned** *a* inquiet, soucieux. **con'cerning** *prep* concernant, en ce qui concerne.

concert ['kɔnsət] *n* concert *m*; **c. performer**, concertiste *mf*; **c. hall**, salle de concert; *Fig*: **in c. (with)**, de concert (avec). **con'certed** *a* concerté.

concertina [kɔnsə'ti:nə] 1. *n* concertina *m* 2. *vi* (*of vehicle*) se télescoper.

concerto [kən'tʃɛətou] *n* concerto *m*.

concession [kən'seʃn] *n* concession *f*; *Com*: réduction *f* (de prix). **con'cessionary** *a* concessionnaire; (tarif) réduit.

conch [kɔntʃ] *n* (*pl* **conches**) *Moll*: conque *f*.

conciliate [kən'silieit] *vtr* concilier; réconcilier. **concili'ation** *n* conciliation *f*; **c. service**, conseil d'arbitrage. **con'ciliatory** *a* conciliant; (procédure) conciliatoire; (esprit) de conciliation.

concise [kən'sais] *a* concis; (dictionnaire) abrégé. **con'cisely** *adv* avec concision. **con'ciseness**, **con'cision** *n* concision *f*.

conclave ['kɔnkleiv] *n* *RCCh*: conclave *m*; réunion *f* (à huis clos).

conclude [kən'klu:d] *vtr* & *i* conclure; (se) terminer. **con'cluding** *a* final. **con'clusion** *n* conclusion *f*; **in c.**, pour conclure; **to come to the c. that**, conclure que. **con'clusive** *a* concluant; (*of test*) probant. **con'clusively** *adv* d'une manière concluante.

concoct [kən'kɔkt] *vtr* combiner; confectionner (un plat); inventer (un projet). **con'coction** *n* mixture *f*.

concord ['kɔnkɔ:d] *n* concorde *f*; entente *f*. **con'cordance** *n* concordance *f*; index *m*.

concourse ['kɔnkɔ:s] *n* (*a*) foule *f* (de personnes) (*b*) hall *m* (de gare).

concrete ['kɔnkri:t] 1. *a*. concret; pratique 2. *n* béton *m*; **c. mixer**, bétonnière *f* 3. *vtr* bétonner. **'concreting** *n* bétonnage *m*.

concubine ['kɔnkjubain] *nf* concubine.

concur [kən'kɔ:r] *vi* (**concurred**) (*a*) (*of events*) coïncider, concourir (*b*) être d'accord (**with s.o.**, avec qn). **concurrence** [kən'kʌrəns] *n* (*a*) concours *m* (de circonstances) (*b*) (*of pers*) accord *m*. **con'current** *a* simultané. **con'currently** *adv* simultanément; *Jur*: **the sentences to run c.**, avec confusion des peines.

concussed [kən'kʌst] *a* commotionné. **con'cussion** *n* commotion (cérébrale).

condemn [kən'dem] *vtr* (*a*) condamner; **to c. to death**, condamner à mort; **condemned man**, condamné *m*; **condemned cell**, cellule des condamnés (*b*) déclarer inutilisable; *Mil*: réformer (du matériel). **condem'nation** *n* condamnation *f*.

condense [kən'dens] *vtr* & *i* (se) condenser; **condensed milk**, lait condensé, concentré. **conden'sation** *n* condensation *f*. **con'denser** *n* *Mch*: condenseur *m*; *El*: condensateur *m*.

condescend [kɔndi'send] *vi* condescendre (à faire). **conde'scending** *a* condescendant; **to be c.**, se montrer condescendant (**to s.o.**, envers qn). **conde'scendingly** *adv* avec condescendance. **conde'scension** *n* condescendance *f* (**to**, envers).

condiment ['kɔndimənt] *n* condiment *m*.

condition [kən'diʃn] 1. *n* condition *f*; **on c. that**, à condition que, de; **under these conditions**, dans ces conditions; **physical c.**, état *m* physique; **in (good) c.**, (i) (*of thg*) en bon état (ii) (*of pers*) en (bonne) forme; **in bad c.**, **out of c.**, (i) (*of thg*) en mauvais état (ii) (*of pers*) pas en forme; **factory working conditions**, conditions de travail à l'usine; **weather conditions**, conditions atmosphériques 2. *vtr* conditionner. **con'ditional** *a* & *n* conditionnel (*m*); **c. on**, dépendant de. **con'ditionally** *adv* conditionnellement. **con'ditioner** *n* (hair) **c.**, lotion *f* capillaire.

condolences [kən'doulənsiz] *npl* condoléances *fpl*.

condom ['kɔndəm] *n* préservatif *m*.

condominium [kɔndou'miniəm] *n* *NAm*: immeuble *m* en copropriété.

condone [kən'doun] *vtr* trouver des excuses pour (qch); pardonner (une action); racheter.

conducive [kən'djuːsiv] *a* **c. to,** favourable, qui contribue, à.

conduct 1. ['kɔndʌkt] *n* conduite *f* **2.** [kən'dʌkt] *vtr* conduire; mener, gérer (des affaires); diriger (un orchestre); **conducted tour,** visite guidée; **to c. one-self,** se conduire. **con'duction** *n* conduction *f*. **con'ductor** *n* **1.** *(a)* chef *m* d'orchestre *(b)* *(f* **conductress)** receveur, -euse (d'autobus); *NAm:* Rail: chef de train **2.** conducteur *m* (de chaleur).

cone [koun] *n (a)* cône *m (b)* cornet *m* (de glace).

confab ['kɔnfæb] *n F:* causerie *f*.

confectionery [kən'fekʃnəri] *n* confiserie *f*; pâtisserie *f*. **con'fectioner** *n* confiseur, -euse; pâtissier, -ière.

confederate 1. [kən'fedərət] *(a) a & n* confédéré(e) *(b) n Jur:* complice *mf* **2.** [kən'fedəreit] *vtr & i* (se) confédérer. **con'federacy, confede'ration** *n* confédération *f*.

confer [kən'fɔːr] *v* **(conferred)** *(a) vtr* conférer **(on,** à) *(b) vi* conférer **(on, about,** de). **'conference** ['kɔnfərəns] *n* conférence *f*; congrès *m*; **in c.,** en conférence; **press c.,** conférence de presse.

confess [kən'fes] **1.** *vtr* confesser; avouer (une faute) **2.** *vi* faire des aveux; **to c. (to a crime),** avouer (un crime); *Ecc:* **to c. (oneself),** se confesser. **con'fession** *n* confession *f*; aveu *m*; *Ecc:* **to go to c.,** aller à confesse *f*; **to make one's c.,** faire sa confession, se confesser. **con'fessional** *n Ecc:* confessional *m*. **con'fessor** *n* confesseur *m*.

confetti [kən'feti] *n* confetti(s) *m(pl)*.

confide [kən'faid] *vtr* confier. **'confidant, -ante** *n* confident, -ente. **con'fide 'in** *vtr* se confier à (qn). **'confidence** *n (a)* confiance *f* **(in, en); to have every c. in,** avoir une confiance totale en; **vote of no c.,** motion de censure *(b)* assurance *f*; confiance (en soi-même) *(c)* confidence *f*; **in c.,** en confidence; **in strict c.,** à titre essentiellement confidentiel; **c. trick,** escroquerie *f*; **c. man,** escroc *m*. **'confident** *a* assuré; sûr **(of,** de); persuadé **(that,** que). **confi'dential** *a* confidentiel; (homme) de confiance; (secrétaire) particulier. **confi-'dentially** *adv* en confidence; confidentiellement. **'confidently** *adv* avec confiance. **con'fiding** *a* confiant.

confine [kən'fain] *vtr (a)* enfermer, emprisonner (qn); **to be confined to bed,** être obligé de garder le lit *(b)* limiter, borner; **to c. oneself to doing sth,** se borner, se limiter, à faire qch; **to c. oneself to facts,** s'en tenir aux faits; **confined space,** espace étroit. **con'finement** *n (a)* emprisonnement *m*; réclusion *f*; **in solitary c.,** au régime cellulaire *(b) (of woman)* couches *fpl*, accouchement *m*.

confirm [kən'fɔːm] *vtr* confirmer; (r)affermir (son pouvoir); fortifier (une résolution); ratifier (un prix); **confirming my letter,** en confirmation de ma lettre. **confir'mation** *n* confirmation *f*; (r)affermissement *m* (de l'autorité de qn). **con'firmed** *a* (fumeur) invétéré; (ivrogne) incorrigible; (célibataire) endurci.

confiscate ['kɔnfiskeit] *vtr* confisquer **(from s.o.,** à qn). **confis'cation** *n* confiscation *f*.

conflagration [kɔnflə'greiʃn] *n* incendie *m*.

conflict 1. *n* ['kɔnflikt] conflit *m* **2.** *vi* [kən'flikt] être en conflit, en contradiction **(with,** avec). **con'flict-**ing *a* incompatible; opposé; **c. evidence,** témoignages discordants.

confluence ['kɔnfluəns] *n Geog:* confluent *m*.

conform [kən'fɔːm] *vi* se conformer **(to, with,** à); obéir **(to,** à). **confor'mation** *n* conformation *f*. **con'formist** *a & n* conformiste *(mf)*. **con'for-mity** *n* conformité **(to, with,** à); **in c. with,** conformément à.

confound [kən'faund] *vtr* confondre; *F:* **c. you!** au diable! **c. it!** zut! **you confounded idiot!** espèce d'idiot!

confront [kən'frʌnt] *vtr* affronter, faire face à (un danger, etc); **to c. s.o. with sth,** confronter qn avec qch. **confron'tation** *n* confrontation *f*; affrontement *m* (d'un danger, etc).

confuse [kən'fjuːz] *vtr (a)* confondre; mêler, brouiller (qch) *(b)* embrouiller *(c)* troubler. **con'fused** *a* confus; (projet) embrouillé; **to get, be, c.,** se confondre; s'embrouiller; se troubler. **con'fusedly** [-idli] *adv* confusément; d'un air confus. **con'fusing** *a* déroutant; **it's very c.,** on s'y perd. **con'fusion** *n* confusion *f*.

congeal [kən'dʒiːl] *vtr & i* (se) figer.

congenial [kən'dʒiːniəl] *a* agréable; *(of pers)* sympathique, aimable. **con'genially** *adv* agréablement.

congenital [kən'dʒenitl] *a* congénital.

conger ['kɔŋgər] *n Ich:* **c. (eel),** congre *m*.

congested [kən'dʒestid] *a (a) Med:* congestionné *(b) (of street, etc)* encombré, embouteillé; *(of city, etc)* surpeuplé. **con'gestion** *n (a) Med:* congestion *f (b)* encombrement *m* (de rue, de circulation); surpeuplement *m* (de ville).

conglomeration [kənglɔmə'reiʃn] *n* collection *f*.

congratulate [kən'grætjuleit] *vtr* féliciter (on, de). **congratu'lations** *npl* félicitations *fpl*. **con-gratu'latory** *a* (lettre) de félicitation(s).

congregate ['kɔŋgrigeit] *vi* se rassembler, s'assembler. **congre'gation** *n (in church)* assistance *f*; assemblée *f* (des fidèles).

congress ['kɔŋgres] *n* congrès *m*; confédération *f* (de syndicats); *Parl: (in Fr and US:)* Congrès (du Sénat et de la Chambre). **con'gressional** *a esp NAm: Pol:* du Congrès. **'congressman, -men** *n NAm: Pol:* membre *m* du Congrès.

conical ['kɔnikl] *a* conique.

conifer ['kɔnifər] *n Bot:* conifère *m*. **co'niferous** [kə'nifərəs] *a Bot:* conifère.

conjecture [kən'dʒektʃər] **1.** *n* conjecture *f*; supposition *f* **2.** *vtr & i* conjecturer; supposer. **con'jec-tural** *a* conjectural.

conjugal ['kɔndʒugəl] *a* conjugal.

conjugate ['kɔndʒugeit] *vtr & i* (se) conjuguer. **con-ju'gation** *n* conjugaison *f*.

conjunction [kən'dʒʌŋkʃn] *n* conjonction *f*; **in c. with,** conjointement avec.

conjunctivitis [kəndʒʌŋkti'vaitis] *n Med:* conjonctivite *f*.

conjuncture [kən'dʒʌŋktʃər] *n* conjoncture *f*.

conjure 1. *vtr* (faire) sortir (un lapin, un œuf) **2.** *vi* faire des tours de passe-passe; **a name to c. with,** un nom tout-puissant. **'conjurer, -or** *n* prestidigitateur, -trice. **'conjure 'up** *vtr* évoquer. **'conjuring** *n* prestidigitation *f*; **c. trick,** tour de passe-passe.

conk [kɔŋk] *n F:* nez *m*; pif *m*. **'conk 'out** *vi F:* tomber en panne.

conker ['kɔŋkər] *n F:* marron *m* (d'Inde).

connect [kə'nekt] **1.** *vtr* (*a*) (re)lier, (ré)unir, rattacher, raccorder; (**with, to, à**); *Tp:* mettre en communication; *El:* **to c. (up)**, connecter; **connected by telephone**, relié par téléphone; *El:* **connected to the mains**, branché sur le secteur; **connecting rooms**, chambres communicantes; *Aut:* **connecting rod**, bielle *f* (*b*) associer (**with sth**, avec, à, qch); **to be connected with**, avoir des rapports avec; être allié à (une famille) **2.** *vi* se (re)lier, se réunir; se raccorder; *Rail: etc:* faire correspondance (**with**, avec). **co'nnected** *a* connexe; lié; (*of pers*) **well connected**, bien apparenté. **co'nnecter, -or** *n* raccord *m*. **co'nnection** *n* rapport *m*, liaison *f*; connexion *f*; lien *m* (de famille, etc); *El:* contact *m*; *Tp:* communication *f*; *Rail: etc:* correspondance *f*; (*object*) raccord *m*; **in c. with**, à propos de; **in this c.**, à ce propos; **in another c.**, d'autre part; **to form a c. with**, établir des rapports, des relations *f*, avec.

connive [kə'naiv] *vi* **to c. at**, fermer les yeux sur. **co'nnivance** *n* connivence *f*; complicité *f*; **with s.o.'s c.**, d'intelligence avec qn.

connoisseur [kɔnə'sə:r] *n* connaisseur *mf*, *occ* -euse (**of, en**).

conquer ['kɔŋkər] *vtr* conquérir; vaincre; surmonter (des difficultés). **'conquering** *a* conquérant; victorieux; (héros) triomphant. **'conqueror** *n* conquérant *m* (d'un pays); vainqueur *m*. **'conquest** *n* conquête *f*.

conscience ['kɔnʃəns] *n* conscience *f*; **to have a clear, an easy, c.**, avoir la conscience tranquille; **to have a guilty c.**, avoir mauvaise conscience; se sentir coupable; **to have sth on one's c.**, avoir qch sur la conscience; **in all c.**, tout bien considéré. **'conscience-stricken** *a* pris de remords. **consci'entious** *a* consciencieux; **c. objector**, objecteur de conscience. **consci'entiously** *adv* consciencieusement. **consci'entiousness** *n* conscience.

conscious ['kɔnʃəs] *a* conscient; **to be c. of**, avoir conscience de; **to become c. of**, s'apercevoir de; *Med:* **to become c.**, reprendre connaissance. **'consciously** *adv* consciemment. **'consciousness** *n* conscience *f*; *Med:* connaissance *f*; **to lose, regain, c.**, perdre, reprendre, connaissance.

conscript 1. *n* ['kɔnskript] conscrit *m* **2.** *vtr* [kən'skript] enrôler (par conscription). **con'scription** *n* conscription *f*.

consecrate ['kɔnsikreit] *vtr* consacrer. **conse'cration** *n* consécration *f*; sacre *m* (d'un roi).

consecutive [kən'sekjutiv] *a* consécutif; **on three c. days**, trois jours de suite. **con'secutively** *adv* consécutivement.

consensus [kən'sensəs] *n* consensus *m* (d'opinion); unanimité *f*, accord *m*.

consent [kən'sent] **1.** *n* consentement *m*; assentiment *m*; **by common c.**, d'un commun accord; **age of c.**, âge nubile **2.** *vi* consentir; **I c.**, j'y consens; **consenting adults**, adultes consentants.

consequence ['kɔnsikwəns] *n* conséquence *f*; suites *fpl*; **in c.**, par conséquent; **in c. of**, par suite de; **it's of no c.**, cela n'a pas d'importance, ne fait rien.

'consequent *a* résultant (**upon**, de). **conse'quential** *a* conséquent. **'consequently** *adv & conj* par conséquent.

conserve [kən'sə:v] *vtr* conserver, préserver. **con'servancy, conser'vation** *n* conservation *f*; protection *f* (de l'environnement). **conser'vationist** *n* partisan, -ane, de la protection de l'environnement. **con'servatism** *n* conservatisme *m*. **con'servative 1.** *a* prudent; orthodoxe; **at a c. estimate**, au bas mot **2.** *a & n Pol:* conservateur, -trice. **con'servatory** *n* (*a*) *Hort:* serre *f* (*b*) (*also* **conservatoire**) conservatoire *m* (de musique).

consider [kən'sidər] *vtr* (*a*) considérer (une question); envisager (une possibilité); réfléchir, songer, à; **I will c. it**, j'y réfléchirai; **considered opinion**, opinion réfléchie; **all things considered**, tout bien considéré (*b*) prendre (une offre) en considération; étudier, examiner (une proposition); avoir égard à (la sensibilité de qn); tenir compte de (la difficulté); regarder à (la dépense); **I c. him crazy**, je le considère comme fou; **to c. oneself happy**, s'estimer heureux; **to c. that**, estimer que. **con'siderable** *a* considérable. **con'siderably** *adv* considérablement. **con'siderate** *a* prévenant, plein d'égards (**towards, pour, envers**). **con'siderately** *adv* avec prévenance. **conside'ration** *n* considération *f*; **to take sth into c.**, tenir compte de qch; **taking everything into c.**, tout bien considéré; **after due c.**, après mûre réflexion; **question under c.**, question à l'examen, à l'étude; **it is of no c.**, cela n'a pas d'importance, n'entre pas en ligne de compte; **for a c.**, moyennant paiement. **con'sidering** *prep* étant donné, vu; *F:* **it's not so bad c.**, somme toute ce n'est pas si mal.

consign [kən'sain] *vtr* (*a*) expédier (des marchandises) (*b*) remettre (**to**, à). **consi'gnee** *n* consignataire *mf*. **con'signment** *n* (*sent*) envoi *m*; (*arrived*) arrivage *m*.

consist [kən'sist] *vi* **to c. of**, consister en, dans (qch). **con'sistency** *n* consistance *f*. **con'sistent** *a* conséquent; logique; **ideas that are not c.**, idées qui ne se tiennent pas; **c. with**, compatible, d'accord, avec. **con'sistently** *adv* avec logique; (arriver) régulièrement; **c. with**, conformément à.

console 1. *n* ['kɔnsoul] *Elcs:* pupitre *m* (de commande) **2.** *vtr* [kən'soul] consoler (**for**, de). **con'solation** *n* consolation *f*; **c. prize**, prix de consolation. **con'soling** *a* consolant; consolateur.

consolidate [kən'sɔlideit] *vtr* consolider, (r)affermir. **consoli'dation** *n* consolidation *f*.

consonant ['kɔnsənənt] *n Ling:* consonne *f*.

consort 1. *n* ['kɔnsɔ:t] époux, -ouse; **prince c.**, prince consort **2.** *vi* [kən'sɔ:t] s'associer, frayer, avec (qn); fréquenter (qn).

consortium [kən'sɔ:tiəm] *n* consortium *m*.

conspicuous [kən'spikjuəs] *a* manifeste; (bien) en évidence; (fait) remarquable, frappant; (monument) voyant; (bravoure) insigne; **to be c.**, attirer les regards; **to be c. by one's absence**, briller par son absence; **to make oneself c.**, se faire remarquer. **con'spicuously** *adv* manifestement; visiblement; bien en évidence.

conspire [kən'spaiər] *vi* conspirer (**against**, contre; **to do**, à faire); comploter (**to do**, de faire). **con'spiracy** *n* conspiration *f*, conjuration *f*. **con-**

'spirator n conspirateur, -trice; conjuré,-ée.
conspira'torial a de conspirateur.

constable ['kʌnstəbl] n agent m de police; approx =
gendarme m; chief c. = commissaire m de police
divisionnaire. constabulary [kən'stæbjuləri] n
police f; gendarmerie f.

constant ['kɔnstənt] a (a) constant; stable; invariable (b) (bruit) incessant, continu (c) (ami) loyal,
fidèle. 'constancy n constance f. 'constantly
adv constamment.

constellation [kɔnstə'leiʃn] n constellation f.

consternation [kɔnstə'neiʃn] n consternation f;
look of c., regard consterné.

constipate ['kɔnstipeit] vtr constiper. 'constipated a constipé. consti'pation n constipation f.

constituent [kən'stitjuənt] 1. a constituant, constitutif 2. n (a) élément constitutif; composant m (b)
électeur, -trice (d'une circonscription électorale).
con'stituency n circonscription électorale.

constitute ['kɔnstitjuːt] vtr constituer. consti'tution n constitution f. consti'tutional 1. a
constitutionnel; Med: diathésique 2. n (petite)
promenade. consti'tutionally adv constitu-
tionnellement; Med: par tempérament.

constrained [kən'streind] a contraint (to do, de
faire); (sourire) forcé; (air) gêné. con'straint n
contrainte f.

constrict [kən'strikt] vtr resserrer; étrangler; serrer
(le corps). con'striction n resserrement m, étranglement m; Med: constriction f.

construct [kən'strʌkt] vtr construire; bâtir. con-
'struction n construction f; under c., in course of
c., en construction; to put a wrong c. on sth, mal
interpréter qch. con'structive a constructif;
(esprit) créateur. con'structor n constructeur m.

construe [kən'struː] vtr interpréter.

consul ['kɔnsəl] n consul m. 'consular a consulaire.
'consulate n consulat m.

consult [kən'sʌlt] 1. vtr consulter (about, sur) 2. vi
to c. (together), délibérer (with, avec); se consulter.
con'sultant n médecin consultant; Ind: etc:
expert-conseil m; c. engineer, ingénieur-conseil m.
consul'tation n consultation f. con'sultative
a consultatif. con'sulting a (heures, cabinet) de
consultation; c. engineer, ingénieur-conseil.

consume [kən'sjuːm] vtr consommer; (of fire) consumer; (of pers) to be consumed with, by, brûler de
(désir); être rongé de (jalousie). con'sumer n
consommateur, -trice; abonné, -ée (du gaz); c. goods,
biens de consommation; c. society, société de consommation. con'suming a dévorant.

consummate 1. a [kən'sʌmət] (artiste) consommé,
achevé 2. vtr ['kɔnsəmeit] consommer. consu'm-
mation n consommation f.

consumption [kən'sʌmpʃn] n (a) consommation f
(b) Med: A: phtisie f.

contact ['kɔntækt] 1. n (a) contact m; to be in c.
with s.o., être en contact, en rapport, avec qn; c.
lens, verre, lentille, de contact (b) usu pl F: (pers)
relation f 2. vtr contacter, se mettre en contact, en
rapport, avec (qn).

contagion [kən'teidʒən] n contagion f. con-
'tagious a contagieux.

contain [kən'tein] vtr contenir; to c. oneself, se maî-

triser; to c. one's laughter, s'empêcher de rire. con-
'tainer n récipient m; contenant m; Rail: etc: conteneur m; c. ship, porte-conteneurs m inv. con-
'tainerize vtr conteneuriser.

contaminate [kən'tæmineit] vtr contaminer. con-
tami'nation n contamination f.

contemplate ['kɔntempleit] vtr contempler; prévoir; envisager, projeter (sth, qch; doing sth, de faire
qch). contem'plation n contemplation f. con-
'templative a contemplatif.

contemporary [kən'tempərəri] a & n contempo-
rain(e) (with, de).

contempt [kən'tempt] n mépris m; dédain m; to hold
in c., mépriser; beneath c., tout ce qu'il y a de plus
méprisable; Jur: c. of court, outrage m au tribunal.
con'temptible a méprisable. con'temp-
tuous a dédaigneux (of, de); méprisant; (geste) de
mépris. con'temptuously adv avec mépris.

contend [kən'tend] vtr & i combattre, lutter (with,
against, contre); disputer (with s.o. for sth, qch avec
qn); to c. that, prétendre, soutenir, affirmer, que +
ind. con'tender n concurrent, -ente. con'ten-
tion n (a) dispute f (b) affirmation f; my c. is that,
je soutiens que. con'tentious a (of pers) querelleur; (of issue) disputé.

content¹ ['kɔntent] n contenu m; teneur f (en or);
titre m (d'alcool); contents, contenu (d'une bouteille,
d'une lettre); (of book) (table of) contents, table f
des matières; high protein c., riche en protéine.

content² [kən'tent] 1. a contentement m 2. a content, satisfait (with, de); to be c. with, se contenter
de; he's quite c. to, il ne demande pas mieux que de
3. vtr contenter; to c. oneself with (doing) sth., se
contenter de (faire) qch. con'tented a content
(with, de). con'tentedly adv avec contentement;
(vivre) content. con'tentedness, con'tent-
ment n contentement.

contest 1. n ['kɔntest] (a) combat m, lutte f (b) concours m 2. vtr [kən'test] contester (un fait); disputer
(un poste). con'testant n concurrent, -ente.

context ['kɔntekst] n contexte m; in the c. of, dans le
contexte de.

continent ['kɔntinənt] n continent m; (on) the C.,
(en) Europe (continentale). conti'nental a continental; (pays, habitant) de l'Europe (continentale);
c. breakfast, café complet; c. quilt, couette f.

contingency [kən'tindʒənsi] n éventualité f; cas
imprévu; to be prepared for every c., parer à toute
éventualité, à l'imprévu; c. plans, plans d'urgence.
con'tingent 1. a contingent; éventuel; to be c.
(up)on, dépendre de 2. n contingent m.

continue [kən'tinjuː] 1. vtr continuer (to do, à, de,
faire); poursuivre (son travail); reprendre (une conversation); to be continued, à suivre; to c. in office,
garder sa charge 2. vi (se) continuer; se prolonger;
(se) poursuivre. con'tinual a continuel. con-
'tinually adv continuellement; sans cesse, sans
arrêt. con'tinuance n continuation f; durée f.
continu'ation n continuation; prolongement
(d'un mur); suite f (d'une histoire). conti'nuity n
continuité f; Cin: etc: c. girl, script-girl f, script(e) f.
con'tinuous a continu; Cin: etc: (spectacle)
permanent. con'tinuously adv sans interruption.

contort [kən'tɔːt] *vtr* tordre; **face contorted with pain**, visage contracté, crispé, par la douleur. **con'tortion** *n* contorsion *f.* **con'tortionist** *n* contorsionniste *mf.*

contour ['kɔntuər] *n* contour *m*; profil *m*; (*on map*) **c. (line)**, courbe *f* de niveau.

contraband ['kɔntrəbænd] *n* contrebande *f.*

contraception [kɔntrə'sepʃən] *n* contraception *f.* **contra'ceptive** *a & n* contraceptif (*m*).

contract 1. *n* ['kɔntrækt] contrat *m*; acte *m* (de vente); **to enter into a c.**, passer un contrat (**with**, avec); **to put work out to c.**, mettre un travail à l'entreprise; *Cards:* **c. bridge**, bridge contrat **2.** *v* [kən'trækt] (*a*) *vtr & i* (se) contracter; (se) crisper (les traits); (se) rétrécir (*b*) *vtr* contracter (une obligation, etc); **to c. to do sth**, entreprendre de faire qch. **con'tract 'in** *vi* s'engager par contrat préalable. **con'traction** *n* contraction *f.* **con'tractor** *n* entrepreneur *m.* **con'tract 'out** *vi* renoncer par contrat préalable (**of**, à). **con'tractual** *a* contractuel.

contradict [kɔntrə'dikt] *vtr* contredire; démentir. **contra'diction** *n* contradiction *f*; **c. in terms**, contradiction dans les termes. **contra'dictory** *a* contradictoire.

contralto [kən'træltou] *n Mus:* contralto *m.*

contraption [kən'træpʃn] *n F:* dispositif *m*, machin *m*, truc *m.*

contrary ['kɔntrəri] **1.** *a* (*a*) contraire (**to**, à); opposé (à), en opposition (avec); **c. to nature**, contre (la) nature (*b*) [kən'treəri] contrariant **2.** *n* contraire *m*; **on the c.**, au contraire; **unless you hear to the c.**, à moins d'avis contraire **3.** *adv* contrairement (**to**, à); en opposition (**to**, à, avec). **contrariness** [kən'treərinis] *n* esprit *m* de contradiction.

contrast 1. *n* ['kɔntrɑːst] contraste *m* (**between**, entre); **in c. with**, to, par contraste avec **2.** *v* [kən'trɑːst] (*a*) *vtr* contraster, mettre en contraste (**with**, avec) (*b*) *vi* contraster, faire contraste (**with**, avec). **con'trasting** *a* opposé; (*of colours*) contrasté.

contravene [kɔntrə'viːn] *vtr* enfreindre. **contra'vention** *n* contravention *f*, infraction *f* (**of**, à).

contribute [kən'tribjuːt] *vtr & i* contribuer (**to**, à); collaborer (à un journal); aider (au succès); payer sa part; cotiser (à un club, pour un cadeau). **contri'bution** *n* contribution *f*; cotisation *f*; article (écrit pour un journal). **con'tributor** *n* collaborateur, -trice. **con'tributory** *a* **to be a c. cause of sth**, contribuer à qch.

contrite ['kɔntrait] *a* contrit; repentant. **contrition** [kən'triʃn] *n* contrition *f.*

contrive [kən'traiv] *vtr* inventer, combiner; **to c. to do sth**, trouver moyen de faire qch. **con'trivance** *n* appareil *m*; dispositif *m*; engin *m*; truc *m.* **con'trived** *a* forcé, qui manque de naturel.

control [kən'troul] **1.** *n* (*a*) contrôle *m*; autorité *f* (**over**, sur); maîtrise *f*; **circumstances beyond our c.**, circonstances indépendantes de notre volonté; **to lose c. of sth**, perdre le contrôle de qch; **to lose c. of oneself**, ne plus être maître de soi; **under c.**, bien en main; **everything's under c.**, tout est fin prêt; **under government**, sous le contrôle du gouvernement; **to bring under c.**, maîtriser; **to be in c.**, commander; **the car went out of c.**, le conducteur a perdu le contrôle de sa voiture; **(foreign) exchange c.**, réglementation *f* du trafic des changes; **birth c.**, contrôle des naissances (*b*) commande *f*; manœuvre *f*; *pl* gouvernes *fpl* (d'un avion); **at the controls**, aux commandes; *Elcs:* **volume c.**, (bouton *m* de) réglage *m* de volume; *Av:* **c. tower**, tour de contrôle (*c*) (*in experiment*) cas *m* témoin **2.** *vtr* **(controlled)** diriger; régler; réglementer (la circulation); maîtriser, gouverner (ses sentiments); contrôler (ses réactions, une région); enrayer (l'inflation); **to c. oneself**, se maîtriser, se dominer, se contrôler. **con'troller** *n* contrôleur, -euse; *Av:* **air traffic c.**, aiguilleur *m* du ciel. **con'trolling** *a* dirigeant; *Com:* **c. interest**, participation majoritaire.

controversial [kɔntrə'vəːʃl] *a* (*of question*) controversé, controversable; discutable; (*of pers*) discuté. **'controversy, -'trov-** *n* controverse *f.*

contusion [kən'tjuːʒn] *n* contusion *f.*

conundrum [kə'nʌndrəm] *n* devinette *f*; énigme *f.*

conurbation [kɔnəː'beiʃn] *n* conurbation *f.*

convalesce [kɔnvə'les] *vi* être en convalescence; relever de maladie. **conva'lescence** *n* convalescence *f.* **conva'lescent** *a & n* convalescent, -ente.

convection [kən'vekʃn] *n* convection *f.* **con'vector** *n* **c. (heater)**, radiateur *m* à convection.

convene [kən'viːn] **1.** *vtr* convoquer **2.** *vi* s'assembler. **con'vener** *n* membre *m* (d'un syndicat) qui convoque les réunions.

convenience [kən'viːniəns] *n* (*a*) commodité *f*; convenance *f*; **at your c.**, à votre bon plaisir; **at your earliest c.**, dans les meilleurs délais; **c. foods**, aliments minute; **all modern conveniences**, tout le confort moderne (*b*) W.-C. *mpl.* **con'venient** *a* commode; (*of time*) opportun; (*of house*) bien situé; **if it's c. to you**, si cela vous convient, ne vous dérange pas; **si vous n'y voyez pas d'inconvénient. con'veniently** *adv* à propos.

convent ['kɔnvənt] *n* couvent *m* (de femmes).

convention [kən'venʃn] *n* (*a*) convention *f* (*b*) usage *m*; *pl* convenances *fpl.* **con'ventional** *a* conventionnel; classique. **con'ventionally** *adv* conventionnellement.

converge [kən'vəːdʒ] *vi* converger (**on**, sur). **con'vergence** *n* convergence *f.* **con'vergent, con'verging** *a* convergent.

conversant [kən'vəːsənt] *a* **c. with**, versé dans, au courant de, compétent en.

converse¹ [kən'vəːs] *vi* converser; parler. **conver'sation** *n* conversation *f*; entretien *m.* **conver'sational** *a* (style) de (la) conversation. **conver'sationalist** *n* **to be a good c.**, avoir de la conversation. **conver'sationally** *adv* sur le ton de la conversation.

converse² ['kɔnvəːs] *a & n* inverse (*m*). **con'versely** *adv* inversement.

convert 1. *n* ['kɔnvəːt] converti, -ie **2.** *vtr* [kən'vəːt] convertir (**to**, à; **into**, en); aménager (une maison); *Rugby Fb:* transformer (un essai). **con'version** *n* conversion *f* (**to**, à; **into**, en); aménagement *m* (d'une maison); *Rugby Fb:* transformation *f* (d'un essai). **con'verter** *n* convertisseur *m.* **converti'bility** *n* convertibilité *f.* **con'vertible 1.** *a* convertible (**into**, en) **2.** *n Aut:* décapotable *f*, cabriolet *m.*

convex ['kɔnveks] *a* convexe.

convey [kən'vei] *vtr* transporter, porter; (a)mener; transmettre (le son); communiquer, faire comprendre (sa pensée). **con'veyance** *n* (*a*) transport *m* (*b*) véhicule *m*. **con'veyancing** *n Jur*: rédaction *f* des actes de cession. **con'veyor** *n* (*machine*) transporteur *m*; c. (belt), tapis roulant; convoyeur *m*.

convict 1. *n* ['kɔnvikt] détenu, -ue; *esp Hist*: forçat *m*, bagnard *m* 2. *vtr* [kən'vikt] to c. s.o. (of a crime), reconnaître qn coupable (d'un crime). **con'viction** *n* (*a*) condamnation *f* (d'un criminel) (*b*) conviction *f*; persuasion *f*; to carry c., convaincre.

convince [kən'vins] *vtr* convaincre, persuader (**s.o. of sth,** qn de qch). **con'vincing** *a* convaincant; persuasif. **con'vincingly** *adv* d'une façon convaincante.

convivial [kən'viviəl] *a* gai.

convoke [kən'vouk] *vtr* convoquer. **convo'cation** *n* (*a*) convocation *f* (d'une assemblée) (*b*) assemblée *f*.

convoluted [kɔnvə'luːtid] *a* (*of leaf*) convoluté; (*of argument*) contourné.

convolvulus [kən'vɔlvjuləs] *n Bot*: volubilis *m*; liseron *m*.

convoy ['kɔnvɔi] 1. *n* convoi *m*; **in c.,** en convoi 2. *vtr Mil*: *Navy*: convoyer, escorter.

convulse [kən'vʌls] *vtr* bouleverser (la vie de qn); ébranler (la terre); **to be convulsed with laughter,** se tordre de rire; **face convulsed with terror,** visage convulsé, décomposé, par la terreur. **con'vulsion** *n* convulsion *f*; **to be in convulsions (of laughter),** se tordre de rire. **con'vulsive** *a* convulsif.

coo [kuː] *vi* roucouler; (*of baby*) gazouiller. **'cooing** *n* roucoulement *m*.

cook [kuk] 1. *n* cuisinier, -ière 2. *v* (*a*) *vtr* (faire) cuire; *F*: to c. the books, truquer les comptes (*b*) *vi* (*of food*) cuire; (*of pers*) faire la cuisine; cuisiner; *F*: what's cooking? qu'est-ce qui se passe? **'cookbook** *n NAm*: (*Br* = **cookery book**) livre *m* de cuisine. **'cooker** *n* (*a*) cuisinière *f* (*b*) pomme *f* à cuire. **'cookery** *n* cuisine; **c. book,** livre de cuisine. **'cookie** *n NAm*: (*Br* = **biscuit**) biscuit *m*, petit gâteau sec. **'cooking** *n* (*a*) cuisson *f*; **c. apple,** pomme *f* à cuire (*b*) cuisine; **c. utensils,** batterie de cuisine. **'cookout** *n NAm*: (*Br* = **barbecue**) barbecue *m*.

cool [kuːl] 1. *a* (**-er, -est**) (*a*) frais, *f* fraîche; (*of drink*) rafraîchissant; (*of pers*) calme; (*of pers, reception*) froid; **it's c.,** il fait frais; **it's getting cool(er),** le temps se rafraîchit; **to be kept in a c. place,** tenir, garder, au frais; (*of pers*) **to keep c.,** garder son sang-froid; **keep c.!** du calme! **c. as a cucumber,** avec un sang-froid imperturbable (*b*) *F*: effronté; **he's a c. customer,** quel toupet! **a c. thousand,** la jolie somme de mille livres 2. *n* **in the c. of the evening,** dans la fraîcheur du soir; *F*: **to keep, lose, one's c.,** garder, perdre, son sang-froid 3. *adv F*: **to play it c.,** être décontracté 4. *vtr & i* (se) rafraîchir, (se) refroidir; **to c. one's heels,** faire le pied de grue. **'cool 'down** *vtr & i* (se) rafraîchir; (se) refroidir (*after anger*) (se) calmer. **'cooler** *n* (*a*) glacière *f*; refroidisseur *m* (*b*) *P*: prison *f*, taule *f*. **'cooling** 1. *a* rafraîchissant 2. *n* rafraîchissement *m*; refroidissement *m*;

Ind: **c.-off period,** période de réflexion (entre négociations). **'coolly** *adv* (*a*) (recevoir qn) froidement (*b*) (agir) avec sang-froid, calmement (*c*) *F*: effrontément. **'coolness** *n* (*a*) fraîcheur *f* (de l'air) (*b*) calme, sang-froid *m* (*c*) froideur *f* (d'un accueil) (*d*) *F*: toupet *m*.

coop [kuːp] *n* poulailler *m*, cage *f* à poules. **'coop 'up** *vtr* claquemurer, enfermer.

cooperate [kou'ɔpəreit] *vi* coopérer (**with s.o. in sth,** avec qn à qch). **coope'ration** *n* coopération *f*, concours *m* (in, à). **co'operative** 1. *a* coopératif 2. *n F*: **co-op,** coopérative *f*.

co-opt [kou'ɔpt] *vtr* coopter (qn).

coordinate 1. *n* [kou'ɔːdinət] *Mth*: coordonnée *f*; *Cl*: *pl* coordonnés *mpl* 2. *vtr* [kou'ɔːdineit] coordonner. **coordi'nation** *n* coordination *f*. **co'ordinator** *n* coordinateur, -trice.

coot [kuːt] *n Orn*: foulque *f*.

cop [kɔp] *F*: 1. *n* (*a*) (= policeman) flic *m* (*b*) **it's not much c.,** ça ne vaut pas grand-chose 2. *vtr* (**copped**) attraper; **you'll c. it!** tu vas prendre qch!

cope [koup] *vi* se débrouiller; **to c. with,** s'occuper, se charger de, faire face à.

co-pilot ['koupailət] *n Av*: copilote *m*.

copious ['koupjəs] *a* copieux, abondant. **'copiously** *adv* copieusement; abondamment.

copper ['kɔpər] *n* (*a*) cuivre *m*; **c.(-coloured),** cuivré (*b*) *F*: copper(s), petite monnaie (*c*) *F*: (= policeman) flic *m*. **'copperplate** *n* **c. (handwriting),** écriture moulée.

coppice ['kɔpis] *n*, **copse** [kɔps] *n* taillis *m*.

copulate ['kɔpjuleit] *vi* copuler. **copu'lation** *n* copulation *f*.

copy ['kɔpi] 1. *n* (*pl* **copies**) (*a*) copie *f* (*b*) exemplaire *m* (d'un livre); numéro *m* (d'un journal) (*c*) *Journ*: (sujet *m* d')article *m* 2. *vtr* copier (**from,** sur). **'copier** *n* duplicateur *m*. **'copybook** *n* cahier *m*. **'copycat** *n F*: copieur, -euse; singe *m*. **'copy 'out** *vtr* copier. **'copyright** *n* droit *m* d'auteur; copyright *m*. **'copywriter** *n* concepteur-rédacteur, conceptrice-rédactrice, publicitaire.

coquettish [kə'ketiʃ] *a* coquet; provocant.

coral ['kɔrəl] 1. *n* corail *m* 2. *a* (récif) corallien; (île, collier) de corail; **c.(-coloured),** (couleur) (de) corail *inv*.

cord [kɔːd] *n* (*a*) corde *f*; cordon *m*; ficelle *f*; **vocal cords,** cordes vocales; **umbilical c.,** cordon ombilical; **spinal c.,** moelle épinière (*b*) *Tex*: = **corduroy** (*c*) *pl F*: pantalon *m* en velours côtelé.

cordial ['kɔːdiəl] 1. *a* cordial 2. *n* cordial *m*, sirop *m*. **cordi'ality** *n* cordialité *f*. **'cordially** *adv* cordialement.

cordon ['kɔːdən] *n* cordon *m*. **'cordon 'off** *vtr* isoler (une rue) (par un cordon de police, etc).

corduroy ['kɔːdərɔi] *n Tex*: velours côtelé, à côtes.

core [kɔːr] 1. *n* centre *m*; cœur *m* (de pile atomique, etc); trognon *m* (de pomme, etc); noyau *m* (d'ordinateur, etc); *Min*: **c. (sample),** carotte *f*; *Pol*: *etc*: **hard c.,** noyau (d'opposants); *Fig*: **to the c.,** jusqu'à la moelle des os 2. *vtr* vider (une pomme). **'corer** *n* (**apple**) **c.,** vide-pomme *m*.

corgi ['kɔːgi] *n* (chien *m*) corgi *m*.

coriander [kɔri'ændər] *n Bot*: coriandre *f*.

cork [kɔːk] 1. *n* (*a*) liège *m*; **c. oak,** chêne-liège *m* (*b*) bouchon *m*; **to take the c. out of a bottle,** déboucher une bouteille 2. *vtr* **to c. (up),** boucher (une bouteille). **'corked** *a* (vin) qui sent le bouchon. **'cork-screw** *n* tire-bouchon *m*.

cormorant ['kɔːmərənt] *n Orn:* cormoran *m*.

corn¹ [kɔːn] *n* grain(s) *m(pl)*, blé(s) *m(pl)*; *esp NAm:* maïs *m*; **c. on the cob,** épi de maïs; **c. oil,** huile de maïs. **'corncob** *n* épi *m* de maïs. **'cornflakes** *npl* flocons *mpl* de maïs; cornflakes *mpl.* **'cornflour,** *NAm:* **'cornstarch** *n* farine *f* de maïs; *Rtm:* maïzena *f.* **'cornflower** *n Bot:* bl(e)uet *m*. **'corny** *a* (-ier, -iest) *F:* banal; *(of joke)* usé.

corn² *n* cor *m* (au pied); *F:* **to tread on s.o.'s corns,** froisser qn; **c. plaster,** coricide *m*.

cornea ['kɔːniə] *n Anat:* cornée *f* (de l'œil).

corned beef [kɔːnd'biːf] *n* corned-beef *m*.

corner ['kɔːnər] 1. *n* coin *m*; angle *m* (de rue, etc); *Aut:* tournant *m*, virage *m*; *Com:* monopole *m* **(on, de); c. cupboard,** armoire de coin; encoignure *f*; **c. shop,** magasin du coin; **to search every c. of the house,** chercher dans tous les coins et recoins de la maison; **out of the c. of one's eye,** du coin de l'œil; **(a)round the c.,** (i) après le coin, en tournant le coin (ii) tout près (iii) *(of future event)* qui approche; **to drive s.o. into a c.,** acculer, coincer, qn; **in a tight c.,** dans une mauvaise passe 2. *v (a) vtr* acculer, coincer (qn); accaparer (le marché) *(b) vi Aut:* prendre un virage. **'cornerstone** *n* pierre *f* angulaire.

cornet ['kɔːnit] *n (a) Mus:* cornet *m* (à pistons) *(b)* cornet (de glace).

cornice ['kɔːnis] *n* corniche *f*.

Cornwall ['kɔːnwəl] *Prn* (le comté de) Cornouailles *f.* **'Cornish** *a* cornouaillais.

corolla [kə'rɔlə] *n Bot:* corolle *f*.

coronary ['kɔrənəri] *a & n Anat:* (artère) coronaire; *Med:* **c. (thrombosis),** infarctus *m* (du myocarde); thrombose *f*.

coronation [kɔrə'neiʃn] *n* couronnement *m*, sacre *m* (d'un roi).

coroner ['kɔrənər] *n Jur:* coroner *m* (officier civil chargé d'instruire en cas de mort violente ou subite).

coronet ['kɔrənit] *n (a) (for noble)* (petite) couronne *(b) (for woman)* diadème *m*.

corporal¹ ['kɔːpərəl] *n Mil:* *(of infantry)* caporal *m*; *(of cavalry, artillery)* brigadier *m*; *MilAv:* caporal-chef *m*.

corporal² *a (châtiment)* corporel.

corporate ['kɔːpərət] *a* constitué (en corps); *(of responsibility)* collectif; **body c., c. body,** corps constitué. **corpo'ration** *n (a) Com:* société enregistrée *(b)* conseil municipal.

corps [kɔːr] *n* corps *m* (diplomatique); **Army air c.,** corps d'armée aérienne.

corpse [kɔːps] *n* cadavre *m*; corps (mort).

corpulent ['kɔːpjulənt] *a* corpulent. **'corpulence** *n* corpulence *f*.

corpuscle ['kɔːpʌsl] *n* corpuscule *m*; **blood corpuscles,** globules sanguins.

correct [kə'rekt] 1. *vtr* corriger (une faute); rectifier (une erreur); reprendre (qn) 2. *a* correct, exact; *(réponse)* juste; *(conduite)* conforme à l'usage; **he's quite c.,** il a tout à fait raison. **co'rrection** *n* correction *f*; rectification *f* (d'une erreur). **co'rrec-**

tive *a* correctif. **co'rrectly** *adv* correctement. **co'rrectness** *n* correction; exactitude *f*, justesse *f*.

correlate ['kɔrəleit] 1. *vi* être en corrélation (with, avec) 2. *vtr* mettre en corrélation (with, avec). **corre'lation** *n* corrélation *f*.

correspond [kɔri'spɔnd] *vi (a)* correspondre, être conforme (with, to, à) *(b)* correspondre (with s.o., avec qn); **they c.,** ils s'écrivent. **corre'spondence** *n* correspondance *f*; *(letters)* courrier *m*; **c. course,** cours par correspondance. **corre'spondent** *n* correspondant, -ante; *Journ:* **special c.,** envoyé spécial. **corre'sponding** *a* correspondant; conforme (to, à). **corre'spondingly** *adv* également.

corridor ['kɔridɔːr] *n* couloir *m*; corridor *m*; **c. train,** train à couloir.

corroborate [kə'rɔbəreit] *vtr* corroborer. **corrob-o'ration** *n* corroboration *f*.

corrode [kə'roud] *vtr & i* (se) corroder. **co'rrosion** *n* corrosion *f*. **co'rrosive** *a & n* corrosif *(m)*.

corrugated ['kɔrugeitid] *a (carton)* ondulé; **c. iron,** tôle ondulée.

corrupt [kə'rʌpt] 1. *a* corrompu; vénal; **c. practices,** tractations malhonnêtes; trafic d'influence 2. *vtr* corrompre. **co'rruption, co'rruptness** *n* corruption *f*.

corset ['kɔːsit] *n Cl:* corset *m*.

Corsica ['kɔːsikə] *Prn Geog:* Corse *f.* **'Corsican** *a & n* corse *(mf)*.

cortex ['kɔːteks] *n (pl* cortices) *Bot: Anat:* cortex *m*.

cortisone ['kɔːtizoun] *n* cortisone *f*.

cos [kɔs] *n* **c. (lettuce),** (laitue) romaine *(f)*.

cosh [kɔʃ] 1. *n (pl* coshes) *F:* matraque *f* 2. *vtr* matraquer, assommer (qn).

cosmetic [kɔz'metik] 1. *a* cosmétique 2. *n* produit *m* de beauté; cosmétique *m*.

cosmic ['kɔzmik] *a* cosmique.

cosmonaut ['kɔzmənɔːt] *n* cosmonaute *mf*.

cosmopolitan [kɔzmə'pɔlitən] *a & n* cosmopolite *(mf)*.

cosmos ['kɔzmɔs] *n* cosmos *m*.

cosset ['kɔsit] *vtr* dorloter, choyer.

cost [kɔst] 1. *n* coût *m*; frais *mpl*; **c. of living,** coût de la vie; **at the c. of one's life,** au prix de sa vie; **at all costs,** à tout prix; **whatever the c.,** coûte que coûte; **to my c.,** à mes dépens *mpl*; **at enormous c.,** au prix de dépenses *fpl* énormes; **at c. (price),** au prix coûtant; *Jur:* **ordered to pay costs,** condamné aux frais (d'instance), aux dépens 2. *v (a) vtr & i (cost)* coûter; **it c. him 50 francs,** cela lui revient à 50 francs; **whatever it costs,** coûte que coûte *(b) vtr (costed)* établir le prix de revient de (qch). **cost-e'ffective** *a* rentable. **'costing** *n* établissement du prix de revient. **'costliness** *n* haut prix; cherté *f.* **'costly** *a* (-ier, -iest) *(a)* de grand prix; de luxe *(b)* coûteux.

co-star ['kou'stɑːr] *Cin: etc:* 1. *n* partenaire *mf* 2. *vi (co-starred)* partager la vedette (with, avec).

costermonger ['kɔstəmʌngər] *n* marchant, -ande, des quatre saisons.

costume ['kɔstjuːm] *n* costume *m*; **swimming, bathing, c.,** maillot *m* (de bain); **c. jewellery,** bijoux de fantaisie; **c. ball,** bal travesti, costumé.

cosy, *NAm:* cozy ['kəuzi] 1. *a* (-ier, -iest) chaud, confortable; (lit) douillet; (*of pers*) bien au chaud; **it's c. here,** il fait bon ici 2. *n* **tea, egg, c.,** couvre-théière *m*, -œuf *m.* 'cosily *adv* confortablement; douillettement. 'cosiness *n* chaleur agréable.

cot [kɔt] *n* lit *m* d'enfant.

cottage ['kɔtidʒ] *n* petite maison à la campagne; cottage *m*; (*thatched*) chaumière *f*; (*for holidays*) villa *f*; **c. industry,** industrie artisanale; **c. hospital,** petit hôpital de médecine générale (où on ne traite pas les cas sérieux); **c. cheese,** fromage blanc (maigre); **c. pie** = hachis parmentier.

cotton ['kɔtn] *n* (*a*) coton *m*; **c. goods,** cotonnades *fpl*; **c. wool,** ouate *f*, coton hydrophile; **c. mill,** filature de coton; **c. dress,** robe en, de, coton (*b*) (fil *m* de) coton. 'cotton 'on *vi F:* **to c. on to sth,** piger qch.

couch [kautʃ] 1. *n* (*pl* couches) canapé *m*, divan *m* 2. *vtr* formuler, exprimer.

couchette [ku:'ʃet] *n Rail:* couchette *f*.

cough [kɔf] 1. *n* toux *f*; **to have a c.,** tousser; **c. drop, mixture,** pastille, sirop, pour, contre, la toux 2. *vi* tousser. 'coughing *n* **fit of c., c. fit,** accès *m*, quinte *f*, de toux. 'cough 'up *vtr & i* cracher.

could [kud] *see* can.

council ['kaunsl] *n* conseil *m*; **district c.** = conseil municipal; **county c.** = conseil départemental; **c. house, flat** = habitation *f* à loyer modéré, HLM; **c. estate,** groupe de HLM (*b*) *Ecc:* concile *m.* 'councillor *n* conseiller, -ère.

counsel ['kaunsl] 1. *n* (*a*) conseil *m*; **to take c. with s.o.,** consulter qn; **to keep one's (own) c.,** garder ses projets pour soi (*b*) *Jur:* avocat, -ate; **c. for the defence,** avocat de la défense 2. *vtr* conseiller (**s.o. to do,** à qn de faire). 'counsellor *n* (*a*) conseiller, -ère (*b*) *NAm: Jur:* avocat, -ate.

count¹ [kaunt] 1. *n* (*a*) compte *m*; dépouillement *m* (du scrutin); (*of people*) dénombrement *m*; **to keep c. of,** tenir le compte de; **to lose c.,** perdre le compte; **blood c.,** numération *f* globulaire; **to be out for the c.,** être (mis) knock-out, K-O (*b*) *Jur:* chef *m* (d'accusation); **on the first c.,** au premier chef 2. *v* (*a*) *vtr* compter; dénombrer (des personnes); **to c. the votes,** dépouiller le scrutin; **to c. the cost,** calculer la dépense; **to c. oneself lucky, one's blessings,** s'estimer heureux; **counting, not counting, the dog,** y compris, sans compter, le chien (*b*) *vi* compter; **counting from tomorrow,** à compter de demain; **he doesn't c.,** il ne compte pas, il n'a pas d'importance; **every minute counts,** il n'y a pas une minute à perdre; **to c. as,** compter comme, pour; **to c. against s.o.,** porter préjudice à qn. 'countdown *n* compte à rebours. 'count 'in *vtr F:* compter; **c. me in!** je suis partant! 'countinghouse *n* comptabilité *f.* 'countless *a* innombrable. 'count 'on *vtr* compter sur; **to c. on doing sth,** compter faire qch. 'count 'out *vtr* (*a*) compter (des billets, etc) un à un (*b*) *Box:* mettre knock-out (*c*) *F:* ne pas compter sur (qn). 'count u'pon *vtr* = count on.

count² *n* comte *m.* 'countess *n* comtesse *f.*

countenance ['kauntinəns] 1. *n* (*a*) visage *m*; figure *f*; **to keep one's c.,** ne pas se laisser décontenancer 2. *vtr* autoriser, approuver.

counter¹ ['kauntər] *n* (*a*) (*device*) compteur *m*; Geiger **c.,** compteur Geiger (*b*) *Games:* fiche *f*; jeton *m* (*c*) (*in bank*) guichet *m*; (*in shop*) comptoir *m*; **over the c.,** (acheter un médicament) sans ordonnance; *Fig:* **under the c.,** en cachette.

counter² 1. *a & adv* contraire, opposé (**to,** à); en sens inverse; à contresens; **c. to,** à l'encontre de 2. *v* (*a*) *vtr* parer, bloquer (un coup); contrecarrer (*b*) *vi* riposter. counte'ract *vtr* neutraliser; parer à (un résultat). 'counterattack 1. *n* contre-attaque *f* 2. *vtr & i* contre-attaquer. counter'balance *vtr* contrebalancer, faire contrepoids à. counter-'clockwise *a & adv NAm:* (*Br* = anticlockwise) en sens inverse des aiguilles d'une montre. counter'espionage, counterin'telligence *n* contre-espionnage *m.* 'counterfeit [-fit] 1. *a & n* faux (*m*) 2. *vtr* contrefaire. 'counterfoil *n* souche *f*, talon *m* (de chèque, etc). 'countermand *vtr* annuler, révoquer (un ordre). 'countermeasure *n* contre-mesure *f.* countero'ffensive *n* contre-offensive *f.* 'counterpane *n* couvre-lit *m*, dessus-de-lit *m.* 'counterpart *n* contrepartie *f*; (*pers*) homologue *mf.* 'counterpoint *n Mus:* contrepoint *m.* 'counterpoise *vtr* = counterbalance. counterpro'ductive *a* qui a des effets contraires; improductif. counterrevo'lution *n* contre-révolution *f.* counterrevo'lutionary *a* contre-révolutionnaire. 'countersign *vtr* contresigner. 'countersink *vtr* (-sank; -sunk) noyer (la tête d'une vis).

country ['kʌntri] *n* (*pl* countries) (*a*) pays *m*; région *f*; terrain *m*; (*native country*) patrie *f*; *Pol:* **to go to the c.** = procéder aux élections législatives (*b*) (*as opposed to town*) campagne *f*; (*as opposed to the capital*) province *f*; **in the c.,** à la campagne; **c. life,** vie, de, à la, campagne; **c. house,** maison de campagne; résidence *f* secondaire; **c. cousin,** cousin de province; **c. and western (music),** country music *f.* 'countryman, -men, -woman, -women *n* (*a*) (fellow) **c.,** compatriote *mf* (*b*) campagnard, -arde. 'countryside *n* paysage *m*; campagne; pays *m.*

county ['kaunti] *n* (*pl* counties) comté *m* (= département *m*); **c. town,** chef-lieu *m* (de comté).

coup [ku:] *n* (*pl* coups [ku:z]) coup (i) audacieux (ii) d'état.

coupé ['ku:pei] *n Aut: sports* **c.,** coupé *m* sport.

couple ['kʌpl] 1. *n* couple *m*; **to work in couples,** se mettre à deux pour travailler; **in a c. of minutes,** dans un instant; **married c.,** (deux) époux *mpl*; **young c.,** jeunes mariés 2. *vtr* atteler (des wagons; etc); accoupler (deux animaux); **coupled with,** joint à. 'couplet *n* distique *m.* 'coupling *n* (*device*) attelage *m.*

coupon ['ku:pɔn] *n* coupon *m*; (*offering reduction*) bon *m*; (*during rationing*) ticket *m* (de pain, etc); (*for football pools*) formulaire *m*; **reply c.,** coupon-réponse *m.*

courage ['kʌridʒ] *n* courage *m* (**to do sth,** de faire qch); **to have the c. of one's convictions,** avoir le courage de ses opinions. courageous [kə'reidʒəs] *a* courageux. cou'rageously *adv* courageusement.

courgette [kuə'ʒet] *n Hort:* courgette *f.*

courier ['kuriər] n courrier m, messager m; (of tourist party) guide m; accompagnateur, -trice.

course [kɔːs] 1. n (a) cours m; route f; direction f; marche f (d'un astre); courant m (des affaires); NAm: Av: cap m; **in the c. of time**, à la longue; **in the c. of the conversation**, au cours de la conversation; **in the ordinary c. (of things)**, normalement; **in c. of construction**, en cours de construction; **to let things take their c.**, laisser faire; **c. of action**, ligne f de conduite; **to take a c. of action**, prendre un parti; **the only c. open to me**, ma seule ressource; **to be on c.**, être sur la bonne voie; **to be off c.**, faire fausse route; **of c.**, bien sûr; bien entendu; naturellement; certainement; **of c. not!** bien sûr que non! (b) Sch: cours; Publ: méthode f (de français); **to take a c.**, suivre un cours (c) série f (de piqûres); Med: c. (**of treatment**), traitement m (d) Cu: plat m (e) champ m (de courses); terrain m (de golf) 2. vi (of liquid) couler fort.

court [kɔːt] 1. n (a) cour (royale); **to hold c.**, se faire faire la cour; **c. shoe**, escarpin m; Cards: **c. card**, figure f (b) Jur: cour; tribunal m; **c. of appeal**, cour d'appel; **c. of inquiry**, commission f d'enquête; **to take s.o. to c.**, poursuivre qn (en justice); **to settle out of c.**, s'arranger à l'amiable (c) Sp: terrain m (de squash, etc); Ten: court m, tennis m 2. vtr courtiser, faire la cour à (une femme); rechercher (des applaudissements); aller au-devant (du danger); **courting couple**, couple d'amoureux. **'courthouse** n esp NAm: palais m de justice; tribunal. **'courtier** n courtisan m. **court-'martial** 1. n conseil m de guerre 2. vtr (**-martialled**) faire passer (qn en conseil de guerre. **'courtroom** n salle f du tribunal. **'courtship** n cour (faite à une femme). **'courtyard** n cour.

courteous ['kɔːtiəs] a courtois, poli (**to**, envers). **'courteously** adv courtoisement. **'courtesy** n courtoisie f, politesse f; **by c. of**, avec la gracieuse permission de; **c. title**, titre de courtoisie; **c. bus** = minibus mis à la libre disposition des clients d'un hôtel; Aut: **c. light**, plafonnier m.

cousin ['kʌzn] n cousin, -ine.

cove [kouv] n anse f; petite baie.

covenant ['kʌvənənt] n Jur: convention f, contrat m; (**deed of) c.**, pacte m 2. vtr promettre, accorder, par contrat.

Coventry ['kɔvəntri] Prn F: **to send s.o. to c.**, mettre qn en quarantaine.

cover ['kʌvər] 1. n (a) couverture f (de lit, de livre etc); enveloppe f (de lettre, de pneu); fourreau m (de parapluie); bâche f (pour une voiture); couvercle m (de casserole); Mec: carter m (pour une machine); (**loose) c.**, housse f; **to read a book from c. to c.**, lire un livre d'un bout à l'autre; **under separate c.**, sous pli séparé; **c. girl**, cover-girl f; (in restaurant) **c. charge**, couvert m (b) abri m; **to take c.**, s'abriter, s'embusquer; se mettre à l'abri; **under c.**, à l'abri, à couvert; **under c. of darkness**, à la faveur de la nuit (c) Ins: couverture; **full c.**, garantie totale; **c. note**, lettre de couverture 2. vtr (a) couvrir (**with**, de); recouvrir; **to c. oneself**, se couvrir (b) couvrir, parcourir (une distance); **to c. a great deal of ground**, faire beaucoup de chemin (c) dissimuler, couvrir (sa confusion, etc); **to c. one's tracks**, couvrir sa marche (d) **to c. s.o. with a revolver**, braquer un revolver sur

qn (e) comprendre, englober, embrasser (les faits, etc); **to c. all eventualities**, parer à toute éventualité (f) couvrir (ses dépenses); rentrer dans (ses frais); **£10 should c. it**, £10 devraient y suffire, en être assez (g) Ins: couvrir (un risque); **he is covered against fire**, son assurance couvre le risque d'incendie; il est assuré contre les incendies (h) Journ: couvrir (un événement) (i) Games: marquer (un adversaire). **'coverage** n Journ: couverture (d'un événement); **news c.**, informations fpl. **'coverall(s)** n(pl) esp NAm: (Br = **overall(s)**) bleu(s) m(pl) (de travail). **'covering** 1. a (of letter) explicatif; Mil: (tir) de soutien 2. n couverture; enveloppe. **'coverlet** n couvre-lit m, -pied(s) m. **'cover 'up** 1. vtr (re)couvrir; cacher; dissimuler (la vérité) 2. vi se couvrir; **to c. up for s.o.**, couvrir qn. **'cover-up** n dissimulation f; étouffement m (d'un scandale). **covert** ['kʌvət, NAm: 'kouv-] a caché, secret.

covet ['kʌvət] vtr convoiter. **'covetous** a avide; (regard) de convoitise. **'covetously** adv avec convoitise, avidement.

cow [kau] 1. n vache f; (of elephant, seal) femelle f; P: (woman) garce f, bique f; F: **till the cows come home**, jusqu'à la semaine des quatre jeudis 2. vtr intimider, dompter. **'cowboy** n cow-boy m. **'cowhand, -herd, -man** n vacher m, bouvier m. **'cowhide** n (peau f de) vache. **'cowshed** n étable f. **'cowslip** n Bot: coucou m.

coward ['kauəd] n lâche mf. **'cowardice** n lâcheté f. **'cowardly** a lâche.

cower ['kauər] vi se blottir, se tapir.

cowl [kaul] n capuchon m.

cox [kɔks] Row: 1. n (pl **coxes**) barreur m 2. vtr barrer.

coy [kɔi] a timide; qui fait la sainte nitouche. **'coyly** adv timidement. **'coyness** n timidité f.

crab [kræb] n crabe m; **c. apple**, pomme sauvage. **'crabbed** a (écriture) en pattes de mouche. **'crabby** a grincheux.

crack [kræk] I. n (a) claquement m (de fouet); détonation f, coup sec; craquement m (de branches); **c. on the head**, coup violent sur la tête; F: **to have a c. at sth**, essayer de faire qch (b) fente f, fissure f (in wall) lézarde f; (in pottery) fêlure f; (in ground) crevasse f; (in varnish) craquelure f; entrebâillement m (d'une porte); **at the c. of dawn**, au point du jour (c) F: plaisanterie f; vanne f. II. a (régiment) d'élite; **c. shot**, fin tireur; tireur d'élite; **c. player**, as m, crack m. III. v 1. vtr (a) faire claquer (un fouet); se cogner (la tête); **to c. s.o. over the head**, assommer qn (b) fêler (un verre); fracturer (un os); lézarder, crevasser (un mur); casser (une noix); F: **to c. a bottle** (**with s.o.**), ouvrir une bouteille (avec qn) (c) résoudre (un problème); décrypter (un chiffre); percer (un coffre-fort) (d) F: faire (une plaisanterie) 2. vi (a) craquer; (of whip) claquer (b) se fêler; se fissurer; (of wall) se lézarder; F: **to get cracking**, s'y mettre; **get cracking!** grouille-toi! **'crackbrained**, F: **'cracked**, **'crackers** a fou; cinglé, toqué, timbré, loufoque. **'crack 'down 'on** vtr mettre le frein à (qch); devenir plus strict avec (qn). **'cracker** n (a) biscuit non sucré (b) pétard m; (Christmas) **c.**, diablotin m. **'crackpot** a & n fou, f folle; cinglé. **'crack 'up** F: (a) vi (of pers) flancher, s'effondrer, craquer (b) *vtr* it's not all it's cracked up to be, ce n'est pas tout ce qu'on en dit.

crackle ['krækl] **1.** *n* craquement *m* (de feuilles); crépitement *m* (d'un feu); grésillement *m*; *WTel:* friture *f* **2.** *vi* (*of leaves*) craquer; (*of fire*) crépiter, pétiller; (*of frying*) grésiller. **'crackling** *n* (*a*) = **crackle 1.** (*b*) *Cu:* couenne *f* (de rôti de porc).

cradle ['kreidl] **1.** *n* berceau *m*; support *m* (de téléphone); *Const:* pont volant **2.** *vtr* bercer (un enfant); tenir (qch) délicatement.

craft [krɑːft] *n* (*a*) ruse *f*; fourberie *f* (*b*) métier (manuel); profession *f* (*c*) *inv* embarcation *f*. **'craftily** *adv* astucieusement. **'craftiness** *n* ruse, astuce *f*. **'craftsman, -men** *n* (*a*) artisan *m*; ouvrier qualifié; homme *m* de métier (*b*) artiste *m* dans son métier. **'craftsmanship** *n* (connaissance *f* du) métier; **wonderful piece of c.,** chef-d'œuvre merveilleux. **'crafty** *a* (-ier, -iest) astucieux, rusé; (*of pers*) malin.

crag [kræg] *n* rocher escarpé, à pic. **'craggy** *a* (rocher) escarpé; (visage) taillé à la serpe.

cram [kræm] *v* (crammed) **1.** *vtr* (*a*) fourrer (sth into sth, qch dans qch); bourrer (with, de); entasser (des passagers); enfoncer (son chapeau) (*b*) *Sch:* chauffer (un candidat) **2.** *vi* s'entasser (into, dans); to c. (for an exam), bachoter. **'cram-'full** *a* bondé; bourré. **'crammers** *n Sch: F:* boîte *f* à bachot.

cramp [kræmp] **1.** *n* crampe *f* **2.** *vtr* gêner; to c. s.o.'s style, priver qn de ses moyens. **cramped** *a* à l'étroit; (couloir) resserré; (style) contraint; c. writing, pattes *fpl* de mouches. **'crampon** *n* crampon *m* à glace.

cranberry ['krænbəri] *n Bot:* canneberge *f*.

crane [krein] **1.** *n Orn: Mec:* grue *f* **2.** *vtr & i* to c. (one's neck) forward, allonger le cou.

cranium ['kreiniəm] *n* crâne *m*.

crank [kræŋk] **1.** *n* (*a*) *MecE:* manivelle *f* (*b*) *F:* (*pers*) excentrique *mf* **2.** *vtr* to c. (up), lancer (un moteur) à la manivelle. **'crankcase** *n* carter *m* (d'un moteur). **'crankshaft** *n* vilebrequin *m*. **'cranky** *a* excentrique.

cranny ['kræni] *n* nooks and crannies, coins et recoins *mpl*.

crap [kræp] *n V:* merde *f*.

crash [kræʃ] **I.** *n* (*pl* crashes) (*a*) fracas *m*; coup *m* (de tonnerre); c.! patatras! (*b*) *Com:* débâcle *f*; *Fin:* krach *m* (*c*) (car, plane) c., accident *m* (de voiture, d'avion); c. helmet, casque (protecteur); c. barrier, glissière *f* (de sécurité); *Av:* c. landing, atterrissage en catastrophe; c. course, cours accéléré; c. diet, régime choc. **II.** *v* **1.** *vtr* to c. one's car, avoir un accident avec sa voiture **2.** *vi* (*a*) éclater, tomber, avec fracas; (*of aircraft*) s'écraser (au sol); (*of car*) to c. into a tree, percuter (contre), entrer dans, un arbre; (*of vehicles*) to c. into one another, se tamponner (*b*) (*of business*) s'effondrer. **'crashing** *a F:* c. bore, personne assommante; scie *f*. **'crash-'land** *vi* atterrir en catastrophe.

crass [kræs] *a* grossier; (ignorance) crasse.

crate [kreit] *n* caisse *f* (à claire-voie); cageot *m*.

crater ['kreitər] *n* cratère *m*; (*from bomb*) entonnoir *m*.

cravat [krə'væt] *n Cl:* foulard *m*.

crave [kreiv] *vi* to c. (for) sth, désirer ardemment qch. **'craving** *n* désir ardent; besoin *m* (d'alcool).

crawl [krɔːl] **1.** *n* (*a*) at a c., très lentement (*b*) *Swim:* crawl *m* **2.** *vi* (*a*) ramper; aller à quatre pattes; se traîner; (*of car*) avancer très lentement; *F:* to c. to s.o., s'aplatir devant qn (*b*) to be crawling with vermin, grouiller de vermine; it makes my flesh c., cela me donne la chair de poule. **'crawler** *n F:* (*pers*) lèche-bottes *mf inv*; *Aut:* c. lane, voie pour véhicules lents.

crayfish ['kreifiʃ] *n* (*inv in pl*) (*freshwater*) écrevisse *f*; (*saltwater*) langouste *f*.

crayon ['kreiən] *n* crayon *m* de couleur; *Art:* pastel *m*.

craze [kreiz] *n* manie *f* (for, de); engouement *m* (for, pour); it's the latest c., cela fait fureur. **'crazed** *a* fou; affolé (with, de); *Cer:* craquelé. **'crazily** *adv* follement. **'craziness** *n* folie *f*. **'crazy** *a* (-ier, -iest) fou; toqué; affolé (with, de); (angle) bizarre; to drive s.o. c., rendre qn fou; *F:* like c., comme un fou; c. paving, dallage irrégulier.

creak [kriːk] **1.** *n* grincement *m*; (*of shoes*) craquement *m* **2.** *vi* grincer; (*of shoes*) craquer. **'creaky** *a* qui grince; qui craque.

cream [kriːm] **1.** *n* crème *f*; c. cheese, fromage blanc (gras); c. of asparagus soup, crème d'asperges; c. (coloured), crème *inv* **2.** *vtr* écrémer (le lait); *Cu:* travailler, battre, du beurre en crème; creamed potatoes, purée *f* de pommes de terre. **'creamery** *n* (*a*) (*shop*) crémerie *f* (*b*) laiterie (industrielle). **'cream 'off** *vtr* écrémer (le lait); prélever (la meilleure partie de qch). **'creamy** *a* (-ier, -iest) crémeux.

crease [kriːs] **1.** *n* (faux) pli **2.** *v* (*a*) *vtr* plisser; (*accidentally*) chiffonner, froisser (*b*) *vi* prendre un faux pli, se froisser.

create [kriː'eit] **1.** *vtr* créer; faire, produire (un objet, une impression) **2.** *vi F:* faire une scène. **cre'ation** *n* création *f*; the latest c., la dernière mode. **cre-'ative** *a* créateur; (*of pers*) créatif. **crea'tivity** *n* créativité *f*. **cre'ator** *n* créateur, -trice.

creature ['kriːtʃər] *n* créature *f*; être *m*; animal *m*, bête *f*; c. of habit, esclave *mf* de ses habitudes; c. comforts, aisance matérielle.

crèche [kreiʃ] *n* crèche *f*; pouponnière *f*.

credence ['kriːdəns] *n* croyance *f*; to give c. to sth, ajouter foi à qch.

credentials [kri'denʃlz] *npl* pièce(s) *f*(*pl*) d'identité; (*of diplomat*) lettres *fpl* de créance.

credible ['kredibl] *a* croyable; (*of pers*) digne de foi. **credi'bility** *n* crédibilité *f*; c. gap, perte de confiance; divergence *f*.

credit ['kredit] **1.** *n* (*a*) croyance *f*; to give c. to a rumour, ajouter foi à un bruit (*b*) crédit *m*, influence *f* (with s.o., auprès de qn); mérite *m*, honneur *m*; to take c. for sth, s'attribuer le mérite de qch; to give s.o. c. for sth, attribuer à qn le mérite de qch; I gave him c. for more sense, je lui supposais plus de jugement; it does him c., cela lui fait honneur; to his c., à son honneur; to be a c. to s.o., faire honneur à qn; *Cin:* c. titles, credits, générique *m* (*c*) *Com:* crédit; to give s.o. c., faire crédit à qn; on c., à crédit; c. balance, solde créditeur; c. side, avoir *m*; actif *m*; c. note, note de crédit; c. rating, (degré de) solvabilité *f* (*d*) *Sch:* unité *f* de valeur **2.** *vtr* (*a*) ajouter foi à, croire (*b*) attribuer (une qualité à qn); I credited you with more sense, je vous supposais plus de jugement; **to be credited with having done sth,** passer pour avoir fait qch (b) Com: créditer (**with,** de). '**creditable** a estimable, honorable. '**creditably** adv honorablement. '**creditor** n créancier,-ière.

credulous ['kredjuləs] a crédule. **cre'dulity,** '**credulousness** n crédulité f. '**credulously** adv crédulement; avec crédulité.

creed [kri:d] n credo m inv.

creek [kri:k] n crique f, anse f; F: **to be up the c.,** être dans le pétrin.

creel [kri:l] n Fish: panier m de pêche.

creep [kri:p] **1.** n F: (a) saligaud, -aude (b) pl **to give s.o. the creeps,** donner la chair de poule à qn **2.** vi (**crept**) ramper; (of pers) se glisser; **to c. in,** entrer à pas de loup; **to c. up to sth,** avancer très lentement jusqu'à qch; **to c. up on s.o.,** surprendre qn; (of feeling) **to c. over s.o.,** gagner qn; **to make s.o.'s flesh c.,** donner la chair de poule à qn. '**creeper** n (a) Bot: plante rampante; **Virginia c.,** vigne f vierge (b) pl NAm: Cl: barboteuse f. '**creepy** a F: qui donne la chair de poule. **creepy-'crawly** n F: (petite) bestiole.

cremate [kri'meit] vtr incinérer (un mort). **cre'mation** n incinération f, crémation f (des morts). **crematorium** [kremə'tɔ:riəm] n (pl **-toria**) (four m) crématoire (m); crématorium m.

creosote ['kri:əsout] **1.** n créosote f **2.** vtr créosoter (le bois).

crêpe [kreip] n crêpe m; **c. paper,** papier crêpe; **c. bandage,** bande Velpeau; **c.(-rubber) soles,** semelles (de) crêpe.

crept [krept] see **creep.**

crescent ['kresnt] n (a) croissant m; **c. moon,** croissant de lune (b) rue f en arc de cercle.

cress [kres] n Bot: cresson m.

crest [krest] n (a) crête f (de coq); cimier m (de heaume) (b) (of hill) crête, sommet m, arête f (c) armoiries fpl. '**crestfallen** a (of pers) abattu, découragé; déconfit.

cretin ['kretin] n crétin, -ine. '**cretinous** a crétin.

crevasse [krə'væs] n crevasse f (glaciaire).

crevice ['krevis] n fente f; lézarde f; fissure f.

crew [kru:] **1.** n Nau: équipage m; Row: etc: équipe f; Pej: bande f, troupe f; **sorry c.,** triste engeance f; **c. cut,** (coupe de) cheveux en brosse; Cl: **c. neck,** col ras **2.** vi **to c. for s.o.,** servir d'équipier à qn.

crib [krib] **1.** n (a) mangeoire f, râtelier m (b) lit m d'enfant; Ecc: crèche f (c) Sch: F: traduction f (d'auteur), corrigé m (de thème) (employés subrepticement) **2.** vtr & i (**cribbed**) Sch: F: copier (**off, from,** sur).

crick [krik] **1.** n **c. in the neck,** torticolis m; **c. in the back,** tour m de reins **2.** vtr **to c. one's neck, one's back,** se donner un torticolis, un tour de reins.

cricket¹ ['krikit] n Ent: grillon m; cricri m.

cricket² n Games: cricket m; **that's not c.,** cela ne se fait pas, ce n'est pas de jeu. '**cricketer** n joueur, -euse, de cricket.

cried [kraid] see **cry 2.**

crime [kraim] n crime m; (minor) délit m; '**criminal 1.** a criminel; **C. Investigation Department** = Police f judiciaire; **c. lawyer,** avocat au criminel; F: **it's c.!** c'est un crime! **2.** n criminel, -elle. **crimi-**

'**nologist** n criminologiste mf. **crimi'nology** n criminologie f.

crimson ['krimzn] a & n cramoisi (m).

cringe [krindʒ] vi (a) ramper (**before,** devant) (b) se tapir; se dérober. '**cringing** a (geste) craintif; (conduite) servile.

crinkle ['kriŋkl] **1.** vtr froisser, chiffonner **2.** vi se froisser, se chiffonner. '**crinkly** a (papier) gaufré; (of skin) ridé.

cripple ['kripl] **1.** n estropié, -ée; boiteux, -euse; infirme mf **2.** vtr (a) estropier (qn); **crippled with rheumatism,** perclus de rhumatismes (b) disloquer (une machine); désemparer (un navire); paralyser (l'industrie).

crisis ['kraisis] n (pl **crises**) crise f.

crisp [krisp] **1.** a (biscuit) croustillant; (légume) croquant; (style) nerveux; (ton) tranchant, cassant; (air) vif **2.** n (**potato**) **crisps** (NAm: = (**potato**) **chips**), (pommes) chips mpl. '**crispbread** n biscotte f (scandinave). '**crisply** adv (dire) d'un ton tranchant. '**crispness** n (a) qualité croustillante (d'un biscuit) (b) netteté f (de style) (c) froid vif (de l'air). '**crispy** a croustillant, croquant.

crisscross ['kriskrɔs] **1.** n entrecroisement m **2.** a entrecroisé **3.** vtr & i (s')entrecroiser.

criterion [krai'tiəriən] n (pl **criteria**) critère m.

critic ['kritik] n (a) critique m (littéraire, de cinéma, etc) (b) censeur m (de la conduite d'autrui). '**critical** a critique; **to be c. of,** critiquer. '**critically** adv en critique, d'un œil critique; **c. ill,** dangereusement malade. '**criticism** n critique f. '**criticize** vtr critiquer. **cri'tique** n critique f.

croak [krouk] **1.** n (of frog) coassement m; (of raven) croassement m; (of pers) voix f rauque **2.** v (a) vi (of frog) coasser; (of raven) croasser; (of pers) parler d'une voix rauque (b) vtr dire d'une voix rauque.

crochet ['krouʃei] **1.** n (travail m au) crochet **2.** v (**crocheted** ['krouʃeid]) (a) vtr faire (qch) au crochet; (b) vi faire du crochet.

crock [krɔk] n (a) cruche f; (b) tesson m (de poterie) (c) F: (car) tacot m (d) F: (pers) croulant m. '**crockery** n vaisselle f; (earthenware) poterie f; (china) faïence f.

crocodile ['krɔkədail] n (a) Amph: crocodile m (b) file f (d'enfants).

crocus ['kroukəs] n (pl **crocuses**) Bot: crocus m.

crony ['krouni] n (pl **cronies**) (vieux) copain, (vieille) copine.

crook [kruk] **1.** n (a) houlette f (de berger); crosse f (d'évêque) (b) angle m; courbure f; coude m (c) F: escroc m **2.** vtr courber. **crooked** ['krukid] a (a) tordu; tortueux; de travers (b) malhonnête. '**crookedness** [-id-] n (a) irrégularité f (b) malhonnêteté f.

croon [kru:n] vtr & i chantonner. '**crooner** n chanteur, -euse, de charme.

crop [krɔp] **1.** n (a) jabot m (d'un oiseau) (b) manche m (de fouet); **riding c.,** cravache f (c) culture f; récolte f, moisson f; **the crops,** la récolte **2.** vtr (**cropped**) (a) tondre, couper ras (les cheveux) (b) (of animal) brouter (l'herbe). '**cropper** n F: **to come a c.,** ramasser une pelle. '**crop 'up** vi F: se présenter, surgir.

croquet ['kroukei] n (jeu m de) croquet m.

cross [krɔs] **I.** n (pl **crosses**) **1.** croix f; **the Red C.,** la crotch 82 cry

Croix rouge 2. (a) croisement m (de races); mélange m (between, de) (b) hybride m 3. Dressm: cut on the c., coupé dans le biais. II. v 1. vtr (a) croiser (les jambes); F: to keep one's fingers crossed, toucher du bois; Tp: crossed line, ligne embrouillée; mauvaise communication (b) Ecc: to c. oneself, se signer; F: c. my heart (and hope to die)! croix de bois (croix de fer)! (c) barrer (un chèque) (d) traverser (la rue); passer (sur) (un pont); franchir (le seuil); to c. one's mind, se présenter à l'esprit de qn (e) contrecarrer (les desseins de qn) (f) croiser (des animaux) 2. vi (a) (of roads) se croiser (b) to c. (over), traverser, passer (d'un lieu à un autre); to c. from Calais to Dover, faire la traversée de Calais à Douvres. III. a (a) transversal; they are at c. purposes, il y a un malentendu (entre eux) (b) (of pers) de mauvaise humeur; fâché; to get c., se fâcher (with, contre); to be c. with s.o., en vouloir à qn. 'crossbreed n hybride. 'cross-check 1. n contre-épreuve f 2. vtr contre-vérifier. 'cross-'country a & n c.-c. (race), cross(-country) m. cross-exami'nation n contre-interrogatoire m. cross-ex'amine vtr (a) Jur: interroger (qn) contradictoirement (b) soumettre (qn) à un interrogatoire serré. 'cross-eyed a qui louche. 'crossfire n feu croisé. 'cross-grained a F: (of pers) revêche, grincheux. 'crossing n (a) traversée f (de la mer); passage m (d'un fleuve) (b) croisement m (de rues); carrefour m; pedestrian, zebra, c. (NAm: = crosswalk) passage pour piétons; passage clouté; Rail: level, NAm: grade, c., passage à niveau. 'cross-'legged a & adv les jambes croisées. 'crossly adv avec (mauvaise) humeur. 'cross 'off, 'out vtr rayer, barrer. 'crosspatch n F: grincheux, -euse. 'crossply a & n c. (tyre), (pneu) diagonal. cross-'question vtr soumettre (qn) à un interrogatoire serré. 'cross-'reference n renvoi m. 'crossroad(s) n(pl) carrefour m. 'cross-section n Biol: coupe transversale; Fig: tranche f (de la population). 'crosswalk n NAm: = pedestrian crossing. 'crosswind n vent m de travers. 'crosswise adv en travers. 'cross-word n c. (puzzle), mots croisés.

crotch ['krɔtʃ] n (pl crotches) fourche f; (of trousers) entre(-) jambes m.

crotchet ['krɔtʃit] n Mus: (NAm: = quarter note) noire f. 'crotchety a revêche, grincheux, grognon.

crouch [krautʃ] vi se tapir; s'accroupir.

crow¹ [krou] n Orn: corneille f; corbeau m; as the c. flies, à vol d'oiseau; NAm: to eat c. (Br = to eat humble pie) s'humilier; (on face) c.'s feet, pattes d'oie; Nau: crow's nest, nid de pie. 'crowbar n pince f à levier.

crow² 1. n chant m (de coq) 2. vi (of cock) chanter; (of pers) chanter victoire (over, sur); (of baby) gazouiller.

crowd [kraud] 1. n foule f; Pej: bande f (de gens); Cin: figurants mpl; in a c., in crowds, en foule; c. scene, scène de masses fpl 2. v (a) vtr entasser; serrer (b) vi to c. (together), se presser en foule, s'entasser, se serrer. 'crowded a (of room, etc) bondé; encombré (with, de); we're too c. here, il y a trop de

monde ici; on est vraiment tassé. 'crowd 'out vtr ne pas laisser de place à.

crown [kraun] 1. n (a) couronne f; c. prince, prince héritier; c. jewels, joyaux de la Couronne; Jur: C. court = tribunal de grande instance (b) sommet m, haut m (de la tête); (of hat) forme f; (of tree) cime f; (of roof) faîte m; Dent: couronne; (of road) axe m; (of bottle) c. cap, capsule f (métallique) 2. vtr couronner; P: flanquer un de ces coups sur la tête de (qn); to c. s.o. king, couronner qn roi; F: to c. it all! pour comble de malheur! 'crowning 1. a suprême 2. n couronnement m.

crucial ['kru:ʃl] a crucial; décisif, critique.

crucifix ['kru:sifiks] n (pl crucifixes) crucifix m. cruci'fixion n crucifixion f. 'crucify vtr crucifier.

crude [kru:d] a (pétrole) brut; (outil) primitif; (of colour) cru; (of manners) grossier. 'crudely adv crûment; grossièrement. 'crudeness, 'crudity n crudité f (d'expression, de couleurs); grossièreté f (de manières).

cruel ['kruəl] a (crueller, cruellest) cruel. 'cruelly adv cruellement. 'cruelty n cruauté f (to, envers).

cruet ['kru:it] n DomEc: huilier m.

cruise [kru:z] 1. n croisière f 2. vi Nau: croiser; (of vehicle) rouler à la vitesse de croisière; (of taxi) marauder; (of vehicle) cruising speed, vitesse de croisière. 'cruiser n Nau: croiseur m; (cabin) c., yacht m de plaisance (à moteur).

crumb [krʌm] n miette f; (opposed to crust) mie f; Fig: brin m (de consolation). 'crumble 1. vtr émietter (du pain); effriter (de la terre) 2. vi (of bread) s'émietter; (of earth) s'effriter, s'ébouler; (of masonry) s'écrouler; (of empire) s'effondrer. 'crumbly a friable. 'crummy a (-ier, -iest) F: minable.

crumpet ['krʌmpit] n Cu: sorte de crêpe épaisse, sans sucre (servie grillée et beurrée); F: a nice bit of c., une jolie pépée.

crumple ['krʌmpl] vtr & i (se) friper; (se) froisser; (se) chiffonner.

crunch [krʌntʃ] 1. n (pl crunches) craquement m, crissement m; F: when it comes to the c., au moment critique 2. v (a) vtr (with teeth) croquer; (with foot) écraser; (grind) broyer (b) vi craquer; crisser. 'crunchy a croquant.

crusade [kru:'seid] 1. n croisade f 2. vi (a) Hist: aller en croisade (b) mener une campagne. cru'sader n (a) Hist: croisé m (b) champion, -onne (for, de).

crush [krʌʃ] I. n foule f, bousculade f; c. barrier, barrière pour contenir la foule; F: to have a c. on s.o., avoir un béguin pour qn; (drink) lemon c., citron pressé. II. v 1. vtr (a) écraser; broyer; concasser (des pierres); fourrer (into, dans); crushed together, entassés (b) froisser (une robe) 2. vi se presser en foule; s'entasser. 'crushing a écrasant.

crust [krʌst] n croûte f; écorce f (terrestre); couche f de rouille). 'crusty a (pain) croustillant; (of pers) hargneux, bourru.

crustacean [krʌ'steiʃn] n crustacé m.

crutch [krʌtʃ] n (pl crutches) (a) béquille f; Fig: soutien m (b) = crotch.

crux [krʌks] n point capital, crucial (d'une discussion); nœud m (de la question).

cry [krai] 1. n (pl cries) (a) cri m; to give a c., pousser

un cri; *Fig*: **it's a far c. from,** il y a loin de (*b*) **to have a good c.,** bien pleurer **2.** *vtr & i* (**cried**) (*a*) crier; s'écrier; **to c.** (**out**), pousser un cri, des cris; **to c. for help,** crier au secours; **"that's not true!" he cried,** "c'est faux!" s'écria-t-il (*b*) pleurer (**over,** sur; **for joy,** de joie); **to c. one's eyes out,** pleurer comme un veau; **to c. oneself to sleep,** s'endormir à force de pleurer; **he laughed till he cried,** il a ri jusqu'aux larmes. **'cry 'down** *vtr* déprécier. **'crying 1.** *a* (*a*) (enfant) qui pleure (*b*) (*of injustice*) criant, flagrant; (besoin) pressant; **it's a c. shame!** c'est une honte! **2.** *n* (*a*) cri(*s*) *m*(*pl*) (*b*) larmes *fpl*. **'cry 'off** *vi* se dédire. **'cry 'out 'for** *vtr* réclamer.

crypt [kript] *n* crypte *f*.

cryptic ['kriptik] *a* (silence) énigmatique. **'cryptically** *adv* énigmatique.

crystal ['kristl] *n* cristal *m*; *NAm*: verre *m* de montre; **c. ball,** boule de cristal. **crystal-'clear** *a* clair comme le jour. **'crystal-gazing** *n* divination *f* par la boule de cristal. **'crystalline** *a* cristallin. **crystalli'zation** *n* cristallisation *f*. **'crystallize** *vtr & i* (se) cristalliser; **crystallized fruit,** fruits confits, fruits candis. **crysta- 'llography** *n* cristallographie *f*.

CSE *abbr Certificate of Secondary Education.*

cub [kʌb] *n* petit *m* (d'un animal); *Scout*: louveteau *m*; (*fox*) renardeau *m*; (*bear*) ourson *m*; (*lion*) lionceau *m*; **wolf c.,** louveteau.

Cuba ['kju:bə] *Prn Geog*: Cuba *m*; **in C.,** à Cuba. **'Cuban** *a & n* Cubain, -aine.

cubbyhole ['kʌbihoul] *n* cachette *f*.

cube [kju:b] **1.** *n* cube *m*; *Cu*: dé *m* (de viande); *Mth*: **c. root,** racine cubique **2.** *vtr Mth*: cuber; *Cu*: couper en dés. **'cubic** *a* cubique; **c. metre,** mètre cube; **c. capacity,** volume *m*. **'cubism** *n Art*: cubisme *m*. **'cubist** *n* cubiste (*mf*).

cubicle ['kju:bikl] *n* alcôve *f*, box *m* (d'un dortoir); cabine *f* (d'une piscine).

cuckoo ['kuku:] **1.** *n Orn*: coucou *m*; **c. clock,** (pendule à) coucou **2.** *a F*: niais, cinglé, loufoque.

cucumber ['kju:kʌmbər] *n* concombre *m*.

cud [kʌd] *n* **to chew the c.,** ruminer.

cuddle ['kʌdl] **1.** *vtr* serrer (qn) doucement dans ses bras; câliner **2.** *vi* **to c.** (**up**), se pelotonner (**to,** contre). **'cuddly** *a F*: qui invite aux caresses; **c. toy,** jouet en peluche.

cudgel ['kʌdʒl] **1.** *n* gourdin *m*; *Fig*: **to take up the cudgels for,** prendre fait et cause pour **2.** *vtr* (**cudgelled**) donner des coups de bâton à; *Fig*: se creuser (la cervelle).

cue¹ [kju:] *n Th*: réplique *f*; *Fig*: indication *f*; **to give s.o. his c.,** donner la réplique à qn; **to take one's c. from s.o.,** prendre exemple sur qn. **'cue 'in** *vtr* donner (i) *Th*: la réplique (ii) *TV*: une indication, à (qn).

cue² *n* queue *f* (de billard).

cuff¹ [kʌf] *n* manchette *f* (de chemise); poignet *m*; *NAm*: (*Br* = **turnup**) revers *m* de pantalon; *Fig*: **off the c.,** impromptu. **'cufflinks** *npl* boutons *mpl* de manchette.

cuff² **1.** *n* taloche *f*, calotte *f* **2.** *vtr* talocher.

cul-de-sac ['kʌldəsæk] *n* impasse *f*; voie *f* sans issue.

culinary ['kʌlinəri] *a* culinaire.

cull [kʌl] **1.** *n* élimination *f* (d'animaux) **2.** *vtr* éliminer (des animaux).

culminate ['kʌlmineit] *vi* **to c. in,** se terminer en, par; **culminating point,** point culminant. **culmi'nation** *n* point culminant; apogée *m* (de la gloire).

culottes [k(j)u'lɔts] *npl Cl*: jupe-culotte *f*.

culpable ['kʌlpəbl] *a* coupable.

culprit ['kʌlprit] *n* coupable *mf*.

cult [kʌlt] *n* culte *m*; **c. figure,** idole *f*.

cultivate ['kʌltiveit] *vtr* cultiver. **'cultivated** *a* cultivé. **culti'vation** *n* culture *f*. **'cultivator** *n* (*pers*) cultivateur, -trice; (*tool*) cultivateur; (*machine*) motoculteur *m*.

culture ['kʌltʃər] *n* culture *f*. **'cultural** *a* culturel; *Agr*: cultural. **'cultured** *a* cultivé; (perle) de culture.

cumbersome ['kʌmbəsəm] *a* encombrant.

cumin ['kju:min] *n Bot*: cumin *m*.

cumulative ['kju:mjulətiv] *a* cumulatif.

cunning ['kʌniŋ] **1.** *n* ruse *f*, astuce *f* **2.** *a* rusé; malin; astucieux; (dispositif) ingénieux. **'cunningly** *adv* avec ruse.

cup [kʌp] **1.** *n* tasse *f*; (*trophy*) coupe *f*; (*of brassiere*) bonnet *m*; **c. of tea,** tasse de thé; **coffee c.,** tasse à café; *F*: **that's not everybody's c. of tea,** ce n'est pas au goût de tout le monde; *Fb*: **c. tie,** match éliminatoire; **c. final,** finale du championnat, de coupe **2.** *vtr* (**cupped**) mettre (les mains) (**round,** autour de). **'cupful** *n* (pleine) tasse. **'cuppa** *n P*: tasse de thé.

cupboard ['kʌbəd] *n* placard *m*, armoire *f*; **c. love,** amour intéressé.

cupidity [kju:'piditi] *n* cupidité *f*.

cupola ['kju:pələ] *n Arch*: coupole *f*, dôme *m*.

curate ['kjuərət] *n Ecc*: vicaire *m*.

curator [kjuə'reitər] *n* conservateur *m* (de musée).

curb [kə:b] **1.** *n* (*a*) mors *m* (d'un cheval); **to put a c. on one's spending,** mettre un frein à ses dépenses (*b*) *NAm*: (*also* **'curbstone**) (*Br* = **kerb(stone)**) bordure *f* (de trottoir) **2.** *vtr* réprimer, refréner (sa colère); modérer (son impatience).

curd [kə:d] *n* **curd(s),** lait caillé; **c. cheese,** fromage blanc (maigre); **lemon c.,** crème *f* de citron.

curdle ['kə:dl] *vtr & i* (*of milk*) (se) cailler; (*of blood*) (se) figer.

cure ['kjuər] **1.** *n* (*a*) guérison *f* (*b*) cure *f*; remède *m* **2.** *vtr* (*a*) guérir (qn) (**of,** de); remédier à (un mal); **to be cured,** se guérir (**of,** de) (*b*) saler, fumer (la viande); saurer (des harengs); *Leath*: saler (des peaux). **'curable** *a* guérissable. **'curative** *a* curatif. **'cure-all** *n* panacée *f*.

curfew ['kə:fju:] *n* couvre-feu *m*.

curio ['kjuəriou] *n* curiosité *f*; bibelot *m*.

curiosity [kjuəri'ositi] *n* curiosité *f*. **'curious** *a* (*a*) curieux (*b*) (*strange*) curieux, singulier. **'curiously** *adv* (*a*) avec curiosité (*b*) (*strangely*) curieusement.

curl [kə:l] **1.** *n* boucle *f* (de cheveux); spirale *f* (de fumée); (*of hair*) **in curls,** bouclé, frisé; **with a c. of the lip,** avec une moue dédaigneuse **2.** *v* (*a*) *vtr & i* boucler, friser (les cheveux); **curling tongs,** fer à friser (*b*) *vi* (*of paper, leaf*) se recroqueviller; (*of smoke*) s'élever en spirales. **'curler** *n Hairdr*: bigoudi *m*. **'curl 'up** *vi* se mettre en boule, en rond; se pelotonner. **'curly** *a* (**-ier, -iest**) bouclé, frisé; (*of* *lettuce*) frisé. 'curly-haired *a* aux cheveux bouclés, frisés.

curlew ['kəːlju] *n* Orn: courlis *m*.

currant ['kʌrənt] *n* (*a*) groseille *f*; c. bush, groseillier *m* (*b*) raisin sec, de Corinthe; c. bun, petit pain aux raisins.

currency ['kʌrənsi] *n* unité *f* monétaire (d'un pays); monnaie *f*; foreign c., devise, monnaie, étrangère; hard c., devise forte; (*of idea*) to gain c., s'accréditer.

current ['kʌrənt] 1. *n* courant *m*; Fig: cours *m* (des événements) 2. *a* courant, en cours; actuel; Bank: c. account, compte courant; (*of magazine*) c. number, dernier numéro; in c. use, d'usage courant; c. events, actualités *fpl*. 'currently *adv* actuellement.

curriculum [kə'rikjuləm] *n* programme *m* d'études; c. vitae, curriculum vitae *m*.

curry¹ ['kʌri] *n* Cu: curry *m*. 'curried *a* au curry.

curry² *vtr* étriller (un cheval); to c. favour with s.o., s'insinuer dans les bonnes grâces de qn. 'curry-comb *n* étrille *f*.

curse [kəːs] 1. *n* (*a*) malédiction *f*; F: (*of woman*) to have the c., avoir ses règles (*b*) imprécation *f*; juron *m* (*c*) fléau *m* 2. *v* (*a*) *vtr* maudire; cursed with, affligé de (*b*) *vi* sacrer, jurer. 'cursed [-sid] *a* maudit; F: sacré.

cursor ['kəːsər] *n* curseur *m*.

cursory ['kəːsəri] *a* superficiel; (coup d'œil) rapide. 'cursorily *adv* rapidement; à la hâte.

curt [kəːt] *a* brusque; sec; (ton) cassant. 'curtly *adv* sèchement; d'un ton cassant.

curtail [kəː'teil] *vtr* abréger, écourter (un article); diminuer (l'autorité de qn); restreindre, réduire (ses dépenses).

curtain ['kəːtn] 1. *n* rideau *m*; Pol: iron c., Th: safety c., rideau de fer; Th: c. call, rappel *m*; c. raiser, lever *m* de rideau 2. *vtr* garnir de rideaux. 'curtain 'off *vtr* cacher, diviser, par un rideau.

curts(e)y ['kəːtsi] 1. *n* révérence *f* 2. *vi* faire une révérence (to, à).

curve [kəːv] 1. *n* courbe *f*; (*of arch*) voussure *f*; (*in road*) tournant *m*, virage *m*; (*of plank*) cambrure *f*; *pl* (*of woman*) rondeurs *fpl* 2. *v* (*a*) *vtr* courber, cintrer (*b*) *vi* se courber; faire, décrire, une courbe. cur'vaceous *a* F: (femme) bien roulée. curvature ['kəːvətʃər] *n* courbure *f*; déviation *f* (de la colonne vertébrale). curved *a* courbé, courbe.

cushion ['kuʃən] 1. *n* coussin *m* 2. *vtr* garnir (un siège) de coussins; Fig: amortir (un coup).

cushy ['kuʃi] *a* (-ier, -iest) F: (emploi) facile, pépère; c. number, bonne planque.

cussedness ['kʌsidnis] *n* F: perversité *f*; out of sheer c., par esprit *m* de contradiction.

custard ['kʌstəd] *n* Cu: crème anglaise; baked c., flan *m*; c. pie, tarte à la crème.

custody ['kʌstədi] *n* (*a*) garde *f*; in safe c., sous bonne garde (*b*) emprisonnement *m*; détention *f*; to take s.o. into c., arrêter qn; to be in c., être en détention préventive. cus'todian *n* gardien, -ienne; conservateur, -trice (d'un monument).

custom ['kʌstəm] *n* (*a*) coutume *f*, usage *m*, habitude *f* (*b*) Adm: customs, douane *f*; customs officer, douanier *m*; customs duty, droits de douane; to go through (the) customs, passer la douane (*c*) Com: (*of shop*) clientèle *f*; to lose c., perdre des clients *mpl*.

'customary *a* habituel, coutumier; d'usage. 'custom-'built, -made *a* fait sur commande; hors série. 'customer *n* client, -ente; F: a queer c., un drôle de type; ugly c., sale type. 'customize *vtr* faire sur commande; personnaliser.

cut [kʌt] 1. *n* (*a*) coupure *f* (au doigt, El: de courant, dans un film); coupe *f* (des cheveux, d'un vêtement; Journ: dans un article, Cards: des cartes); entaille *f* (au menton); Surg: incision *f*; taille *f* (d'un diamant); (*route*) short c., raccourci *m* (*b*) coup *m* (de couteau, etc); Fig: c. and thrust, jeu *m* d'attaques et de ripostes; F: a c. above s.o., supérieur à qn (*c*) réduction *f* (in, de); wage cuts, réductions de salaires (*d*) morceau *m* (de viande); F: to get one's c., avoir sa part de gâteau 2. *a* coupé; (prix) réduit; c. glass, cristal taillé; Cl: well c., de bonne coupe; Fig: c. and dried, prévu; (avis) tout fait 3. *vtr & i* (cut; cut) (*a*) couper; tailler; trancher; faucher (les foins); tondre (le gazon); faire (une dent); Surg: inciser; to c. one's finger, se couper au, le, doigt; to c. one's nails, se couper les ongles; to have one's hair c., se faire couper les cheveux; to c. s.o.'s throat, couper la gorge à qn; Fig: to c. one's own throat, travailler à sa propre ruine; to c. s.o. to the quick, piquer qn au vif; cloth that cuts easily, tissu qui se coupe facilement; atmosphere you could c. with a knife, atmosphère très tendue; Fig: that cuts both ways, c'est un argument à double tranchant; to c. in(to) four, (se) couper en quatre; to c. into, entamer (un gâteau); inciser (l'écorce); intervenir dans (une conversation) (*b*) réduire, baisser (des prix); couper (les nombres); abréger, raccourcir (un discours); faire des coupures dans (un film); to c. one's losses, faire la part du feu; Aut: to c. a corner, prendre un virage à la corde; Fig: to c. corners, faire des économies (de temps); F: to c. and run, filer; to c. short, écourter (une visite); couper la parole à (qn); to c. a long story short, bref; Cin: c.! coupez! (*c*) Cin: procéder au montage (d'un film) (*d*) creuser (un canal); graver (des caractères); Rec: faire (un disque); to c. one's way through a wood, se frayer un chemin à travers un bois; to c. across the fields, couper à travers champs (*e*) Cards: couper (les cartes); to c. for deal, tirer pour la donne (*f*) F: manquer exprès à (un rendez-vous); Sch: sécher (un cours); to c. s.o. dead, faire semblant de ne pas voir qn. 'cut a'way *vtr* couper, ôter. 'cutaway *n* NAm: Cl: (Br = morning coat) jaquette *f*. 'cut 'back *vtr* tailler, élaguer (un arbre); baisser (des prix); to c. b. (on), diminuer (la production). 'cutback *n* réduction (in, de). 'cut 'down *vtr* (*a*) couper, abattre (un arbre); faucher (qn) (*b*) abréger (un discours); élaguer (une pièce de théâtre); to c. d. (on), couper, réduire (les dépenses); to c. d. (on) drinking, boire moins. 'cut 'in *vi* se mêler à la conversation; Aut: (*after overtaking*) se rabattre trop vite; to c. in on s.o., couper la route à qn. 'cut 'off *vtr* couper; trancher (la tête à qn); (*of pers*) to feel c. o., se sentir isolé; Tp: I've been c. o., on m'a coupé; to c. s.o. o. without a penny, déshériter qn. 'cut 'out 1. *vtr* (*a*) couper; enlever; découper (un article de journal); tailler (un vêtement); (*of pers*) to be c. o. for sth, to do sth, être fait, taillé, pour qch; être de taille à faire qch; to have one's work c. o., avoir de quoi faire; avoir du

pain sur la planche (b) supprimer (qch); **to c. o.
smoking,** arrêter de fumer; *F:* **c. it o.!** ça suffit! **2.** *vi
(of engine)* caler. **'cut-'price** *a* (article) au rabais;
(magasin) de demi-gros. **'cutter** *n* (a) (*pers*) cou-
peur, -euse; tailleur *m* (de pierres); *Cin:* monteur,
-euse (b) *Tls:* coupoir *m*; lame *f* (c) *Nau:* vedette *f*;
Navy: canot *m.* **'cut-throat 1.** *a & n* **c. (razor),**
rasoir *m* à manche **2.** *n* (*pers*) assassin *m* **3.** *a (of
competition)* acharné. **'cutting 1.** *a* (a) coupant,
tranchant; (*of tool*) **c. edge,** tranchant *m* (b) (*of
wind*) cinglant, glacial; (*of remark*) mordant, cinglant; (*of criticism*) incisif **2.** *n* (a) coupe *f*; taille *f*
(d'un diamant); *Cin:* montage *m*; **c. room,** salle de
montage (b) coupure *f* (de journal); *Hort:* bouture *f*
(c) *Rail: etc:* tranchée *f.* **'cut 'up 1.** *vtr* couper;
découper (un poulet); hacher (des légumes); *F:* **to be
very c. up,** être profondément affecté (**about,** par) **2.**
vi F: **to c. up rough,** se mettre en colère.
cute [kju:t] *a esp NAm:* mignon, coquet; gentil.
cuticle ['kju:tikl] *n* peau *f* (à la base de l'ongle);
cuticule *f*; **c. remover,** crème de manucure.
cutlery ['kʌtləri] *n* coutellerie *f*; couverts *mpl.*
cutlet ['kʌtlət] *n Cu:* (a) côtelette *f* (b) croquette *f* de
viande.
cuttlefish ['kʌtlfiʃ] *n* seiche *f.* **'cuttlebone** *n* os
m de seiche.

cwt *abbr* hundredweight.
cyanide ['saiənaid] *n Ch:* cyanure *m.*
cyclamen ['sikləmən] *n Bot:* cyclamen *m.*
cycle ['saikl] **1.** *n* (a) cycle *m* (d'événements) (b)
bicyclette *f*, vélo *m*; **c. track,** piste cyclable; **c. racing,**
courses cyclistes; **c. racing track,** vélodrome *m* **2.** *vi*
faire de la bicyclette, du vélo; aller à bicyclette, en
vélo. **'cyclical** *a (of movement)* cyclique. **'cycling** *n* cyclisme *m.* **'cyclist** *n* cycliste *mf*; **racing
c.,** coureur, -euse, cycliste.
cyclone ['saikloun] *n Meteor:* cyclone *m.*
cygnet ['signət] *n Orn:* jeune cygne *m.*
cylinder ['silindər] *n* cylindre *m*; *ICE:* **c. head,**
culasse *f.* **cy'lindrical** *a* cylindrique.
cymbal ['simbəl] *n Mus:* cymbale *f.*
cynic ['sinik] *n* cynique *mf.* **'cynical** *a* cynique.
'cynically *adv* cyniquement. **'cynicism** *n*
cynisme *m.*
cypress ['saiprəs] *n* (*pl* **cypresses**) *Bot:* cyprès *m.*
Cyprus ['saiprəs] *Prn Geog:* Chypre *f.* **'Cypriot** *a*
& n c(h)ypriote (*mf*).
cyst [sist] *n Med:* kyste *m.* **cy'stitis** *n* cystite *f.*
Czechoslovakia [tʃekəslə'vækiə] *Prn Geog:*
Tchécoslovaquie *f.* **Czech** *a & n* tchèque (*mf*).
Czecho'slovak, **-'vakian** *a & n* tchécoslovaque (*mf*).

D

D, d [di:] n (a) (la lettre) D, d, m (b) Mus: ré m.
DA abbr NAm: district attorney.
dab¹ [dæb] **1.** n (a) coup léger (b) petite tache (de peinture); touche f (de couleur); petit morceau (de beurre); P: **dabs**, empreintes digitales **2.** a & n F: to be a d. **(hand)** at sth, être calé, un crack, en qch **3.** vtr **(dabbed)** donner un petit coup à; tamponner; to **d. one's eyes**, se tamponner les yeux.
dab² n Ich: limande f.
dabble ['dæbl] vi barboter (dans l'eau); to **d. in politics**, se mêler un peu de la politique; to **d. on the stock exchange**, boursicoter.
dachshund ['dækshund] n teckel m.
dad [dæd], **daddy** ['dædi] n F: papa m. **daddy-'longlegs** n Ent: tipule f, faucheux m; F: cousin m.
daffodil ['dæfədil] n Bot: jonquille f.
daft [dɑːft] a F: idiot, bête, stupide; toqué, cinglé; **don't be d.**, ne fais pas l'imbécile.
dagger ['dægər] n poignard m, dague f; Typ: croix f; to **be at daggers drawn**, être à couteaux tirés **(with s.o.**, avec qn); to **look daggers at s.o.**, foudroyer qn du regard.
dago ['deigou] n Pej: F: métèque m.
dahlia ['deiliə] n Bot: dahlia m.
daily ['deili] **1.** a journalier, quotidien; **d. (help)**, femme f de ménage; **d. (paper)**, (pl **dailies**) quotidien m **2.** adv quotidiennement; tous les jours; journellement.
dainty ['deinti] a (-ier, -iest) (of food) friand, délicat; (of pers) délicat, gentil; (awkward) difficile. **'daintily** adv délicatement. **'daintiness** n délicatesse f; raffinement m.
dairy ['dɛəri] n (pl **dairies**) laiterie f; (shop) crémerie f; **d. produce**, produits laitiers; **d. cattle**, vaches laitières; **d. farming**, industrie laitière. **'dairyman** n (pl -men) Com: laitier m; crémier m.
dais ['deiis] n estrade f (d'honneur).
daisy ['deizi] n (pl **daisies**) Bot: (wild) pâquerette f; (cultivated) marguerite f.
dale [deil] n vallée f; vallon m.
dam [dæm] **1.** n barrage m **2.** vtr **(dammed)** to **d. (up)**, endiguer, construire un barrage sur (un cours d'eau, un lac).
damage ['dæmidʒ] **1.** n (a) dommage(s) m(pl), dégâts mpl; avarie(s) f(pl); **there's no great d. done**, il n'y a pas grand mal; F: **what's the d.?** ça fait combien? (b) préjudice m, tort m (c) pl Jur: dommages-intérêts mpl **2.** vtr (a) endommager; avarier; abîmer; to **be damaged**, souffrir (b) faire du tort, nuire, à. **'damaging** a préjudiciable, nuisible.
dame [deim] n (title) dame f; (in pantomime) vieille femme comique (jouée par un homme); NAm: F: femme f, nana f.
dammit ['dæmit] int F: zut! mince! **it was as near as d.**, il était moins une.

damn [dæm] **1.** n F: **I don't give, care, a d.**, je m'en fiche; je m'en moque comme de l'an 40 **2.** a & adv (also **damned**) F: (a) a sacré; **you d. fool!** espèce d'idiot! **he's a d. nuisance**, qu'il est embêtant! (b) adv vachement, diablement; **it's d. hot!** il fait rudement chaud! **he does d. all**, il ne fiche rien **3.** int d. **(it)!** zut! mince! **4.** vtr condamner (un livre); éreinter (un auteur); perdre, ruiner (qn, un projet); Theol: damner; F: **well I'll be damned!** ça alors! **d. him!** que le diable l'emporte! qu'il aille se faire fiche! **damnable** ['dæmnəbl] a F: maudit. **'damnably** adv vachement, diablement. **dam'nation 1.** n Theol: damnation (éternelle) **2.** int F: zut! mince! **'damnedest** n F: to **do one's d.**, faire tout son possible **(to**, pour). **'damning** a (fait) accablant.
damp [dæmp] **1.** n humidité f; **d. course**, couche isolante **2.** vtr mouiller; humecter; refroidir (le courage de qn); étouffer (un feu); to **d. s.o.'s spirits**, décourager (qn) **3.** a humide; (of skin) moite. **'dampen** vtr = **damp 2.** **'damper** n registre m (de foyer); Mec: El: etc: amortisseur m; Fig: to **put a d. on**, jeter un froid sur. **'dampness** n humidité f; (of skin) moiteur f. **'damp-proof** a imperméable; **d.-p. course**, couche isolante.
damson ['dæmzən] n prune f de Damas.
dance [dɑːns] **1.** n danse f; Fig: to **lead s.o. a merry d.**, donner du fil à retordre à qn; **d. hall**, dancing m (b) bal m; soirée dansante **2.** vtr & i danser; to **d. with s.o.**, faire danser qn; to **d. for joy**, danser de joie; to **d. attendance on s.o.**, faire l'empressé auprès de qn. **'danceband** n orchestre m de (musique de) danse. **'dancer** n danseur, -euse. **'dancing** n danse f; **country, folk, d.**, danse folklorique.
dandelion ['dændilaiən] n Bot: pissenlit m.
dandruff ['dændrʌf] n pellicules fpl (du cuir chevelu).
dandy ['dændi] n (pl **dandies**) dandy m.
Dane [dein] n Danois, -oise. **'Danish** a & n danois (m).
danger ['deindʒər] n danger m; to **be in d.**, être en danger; courir un danger; **out of d.**, hors de danger; Med: **on the d. list**, gravement malade; to **be in d. of**, courir le risque de; (of building) to **be in d. of collapsing**, menacer ruine; PN: **d., road up**, attention (aux) travaux; **d. money**, prime de risque. **'dangerous** a dangereux; périlleux; (maladie) grave. **'dangerously** adv dangereusement; gravement (malade).
dangle ['dæŋgl] **1.** vi pendiller, pendre; **with legs dangling**, les jambes ballantes **2.** vtr balancer; Fig: faire miroiter (un espoir).
dank [dæŋk] a humide (et froid).
dapper ['dæpər] a (esp of a man) pimpant.
dare ['dɛər] **1.** n défi m; **for a d.**, pour relever un défi **2.** vtr (3rd sg pr **dare**; pt **dared, dare**) oser; **how d.**

you! vous avez cette audace! **I d.** say, sans doute; c'est bien possible; **I d. say that,** je suppose que; **to d. to do sth,** oser faire qch; **to d. s.o. to do sth,** défier qn de faire qch; **I d. you!** chiche! **'daredevil** *n* casse-cou *m inv.* **'daring 1.** *a* audacieux, hardi; téméraire **2.** *n* audace *f,* hardiesse *f;* témérité *f.* **'daringly** *adv* audacieusement.

dark [dɑːk] **1.** *a* (*a*) sombre, obscur, noir; **it's d.,** il fait nuit, il fait noir; **it's going d.,** il commence à faire nuit; **the sky is getting d.,** le ciel s'assombrit; **d. glasses,** lunettes noires (*b*) (*of colour*) foncé, sombre; **d. blue dresses,** robes bleu foncé (*c*) (*of pers*) brun; (*of complexion*) basané (*d*) (*pensée*) sombre, triste; (*dessein*) noir; **to look on the d. side of things,** voir tout en noir (*e*) mystérieux; **to keep sth d.,** tenir qch secret; *Fig:* **he's a d. horse,** on ne sait rien de lui; *Hist:* **the D. Ages,** le haut moyen âge **2.** *n* obscurité *f;* ténèbres *fpl;* **to be afraid of the d.,** avoir peur du noir; **after d.,** après la tombée de la nuit; **in the d.,** (i) dans le noir (ii) *Fig:* (laissé) dans l'ignorance. **'darken** *vtr & i* (s')obscurcir; (s')assombrir; foncer. **'darkly** *adv* obscurément; d'un ton, air, menaçant. **'darkness** *n* obscurité. **'darkroom** *n Phot:* cabinet noir. **'dark-'skinned** *a* à peau brune; *Ethn:* (gens) de couleur.

darling ['dɑːliŋ] *n & a* favori, -ite; bien-aimé, -ée; **my d.!** mon chéri! ma chérie! **she's a little d.!** c'est un petit amour! **the d. of the people,** l'idole *f* du peuple; **d. little place,** endroit charmant, adorable.

darn [dɑːn] **1.** *n* reprise *f* **2.** *vtr* repriser; **darning needle,** aiguille à repriser.

dart [dɑːt] **1.** *n* (*a*) fléchette *f;* (*game of*) **darts,** (jeu *m* de) fléchettes (*b*) *Dressm:* pince *f* (*c*) **to make a d. across the road,** se précipiter à travers la rue **2.** *v* (*a*) *vi* se précipiter, s'élancer (**across the road,** à travers la rue); **to d. in, out,** entrer, sortir, comme une flèche (*b*) *vtr* lancer (un regard). **'dartboard** *n* cible *f.*

dash [dæʃ] **1.** *n* (*a*) *Cu: etc:* soupçon *m,* goutte *f* (de cognac); pointe *f* (de vanille); tache *f,* touche *f* (de couleur) (*b*) *Typ:* tiret *m;* (*in Morse*) trait *m* (*c*) course *f* à toute vitesse; **to make a d. forward,** s'élancer; **to make a d. at sth,** se précipiter sur qch; **to make a d. for it,** (essayer de) s'enfuir (*d*) (*of pers*) élan *m,* entrain *m* (*e*) *esp NAm: Sp:* sprint *m* **2.** *v* (*a*) *vtr* heurter violemment; jeter (par terre); anéantir (les espoirs de qn); abattre (le courage de qn); **to d. sth to pieces,** fracasser qch; *F:* **d. (it)!** zut! (*b*) *vi* (*of waves*) se heurter; **to be dashed to pieces,** se fracasser; (*of pers*) **to d. at,** se précipiter sur; **to d. in, out,** entrer, sortir, en coup de vent; **I must d.!** il faut que je me sauve, que je file! **'dashboard** *n Aut:* tableau *m* de bord. **'dashing** *a* (*of pers*) plein d'élan; fringant. **'dash 'off 1.** *vtr* écrire en vitesse **2.** *vi* partir à toute vitesse.

data ['deitə] *npl* données *fpl.* **d. processing,** (i) traitement de l'information *f* (ii) (*science*) informatique *f.*

date¹ [deit] *n Bot:* datte *f;* **d. palm,** dattier *m.*

date² **1.** *n* (*a*) date *f;* (*on coins*) millésime *m;* **d. of birth,** date de naissance; **what's the d. today?** quelle est la date aujourd'hui? **the d. today is the first,** nous sommes aujourd'hui le premier; **what is the d. of this paper?** de quand est ce journal? **up to d.,** (i) à jour (**with one's work,** dans son travail); au courant (**with the latest developments,** des derniers dé-

veloppements) (ii) (*modern*) à la page; **out of d.,** démodé; (*billet*) périmé; **to d.,** à ce jour (*b*) *F:* rendez-vous *m* (*c*) *esp NAm: F:* ami, -ie (avec qui on a fixé un rendez-vous). **II.** *v* **1.** *vtr* (*a*) dater (une lettre); composer (un billet) (*b*) assigner une date à (un tableau); **her clothes d. her,** ses vêtements trahissent son âge (*c*) *esp NAm: F:* sortir avec (qn) **2.** *vi* dater. **'date 'back to, 'date 'from** *vtr* remonter à, dater de. **'dated** *a* démodé; qui commence à dater. **'dateless** *a* sans date. **'dateline** *n* ligne *f* de changement de date.

daub [dɔːb] **1.** *n* barbouillage *m* **2.** *vtr* barbouiller.

daughter ['dɔːtər] *n* fille *f.* **'daughter-in-law** *n* belle-fille *f, pl* belles-filles; bru *f.*

daunt [dɔːnt] *vtr* intimider; **nothing daunted,** aucunement intimidé. **'daunting** *a* (*of pers*) intimidant; (*of task*) rebutant. **'dauntless** *a* intrépide.

dawdle ['dɔːdl] *vi* flâner; traîn(ass)er. **'dawdler** *n* flâneur, -euse; traînard, -arde. **'dawdling** *n* flânerie *f.*

dawn [dɔːn] **1.** *n* aube *f; esp Fig:* aurore *f;* **at d.,** au point du jour **2.** *vi* (*of day*) poindre; se lever; **at last it dawned on me that,** enfin il m'est venu à l'esprit que; **the truth dawned on him,** il a compris la vérité.

day [dei] *n* jour *m;* (*as a day's work*) journée *f;* **it's a fine d.,** il fait beau aujourd'hui; **to work d. and night,** travailler nuit et jour; **all d. (long),** toute la journée; **to be paid by the d.,** être payé à la journée; **twice a d.,** deux fois par jour; **six years to the d.,** six ans jour pour jour; **the d. before, after (sth),** la veille, le lendemain (de qch); **two days before, after (sth),** l'avant-veille *f,* le surlendemain (de qch); **the d. before yesterday,** avant-hier *m;* **the d. after tomorrow,** après-demain *m;* **the d. (that, when),** le jour où; **(on) that d.,** ce jour-là; **every other d.,** tous les deux jours; **d. after d., d. in d. out,** jour après jour; **d. by d.,** jour par jour; **from d. to d.,** de jour en jour; **to live from d. to d.,** vivre au jour le jour; **he's sixty if he's a d.,** il a soixante ans bien sonnés; *F:* **let's call it a d.,** ça suffit pour aujourd'hui; *F:* **that'll be the d.!** ce sera la semaine des quatre jeudis! **d. nursery,** crèche *f;* **d. school,** externat *m;* **d. boy, girl,** externe *mf;* **to be on (the) d. shift, on days,** être de jour; **d. return (ticket),** (billet *m* d')aller et retour *m* valable pour la journée; **to travel by d.,** voyager le, de, jour; **what d. (of the week) is it?** quel jour (de la semaine) sommes-nous (aujourd'hui)? **he may arrive any d. (now),** il peut arriver d'un jour à l'autre; **one d., one of these days,** un jour (ou l'autre); un de ces jours; **one d. when, as,** un jour que; **the other d.,** l'autre jour; **d. off,** jour de congé; **the good old days,** le bon vieux temps; **in days gone by,** autrefois; **in those days,** à cette époque; **in my d., de mon temps; in my young days,** du temps de ma jeunesse; **in days to come,** dans les temps à venir; **these days,** de nos jours; **to this d.,** encore aujourd'hui; **to have had its d.,** avoir fait son temps. **'daybed** *n* lit *m* de repos. **'daybreak** *n* **at d.,** au point du jour. **'daydream 1.** *n* rêv(ass)erie *f* **2.** *vi* rêv(ass)er. **'daylight** *n* (*a*) (lumière *f* de) jour; **in (the) d., by d.,** à la lumière du jour; **in broad d.,** en plein jour; au grand jour; *Fig:* **to (begin to) see d.,** (commencer à) voir clair; *F:* **it's d. robbery!** c'est du vol manifeste! *F:* **to beat the living daylights out of s.o.,** battre qn comme plâtre (*b*) point du jour. **'daytime** n jour, journée; **in the d.,** pendant la journée; de jour; **d. flights,** vols de jour. **'day-to-'day** a journalier; de tous les jours.

daze [deiz] **1.** n **in a d.,** étourdi; hébété **2.** vtr (of blow) étourdir; (of drug) hébéter.

dazzle ['dæzl] vtr éblouir, aveugler. **'dazzling** a éblouissant, aveuglant; éclatant.

deacon, -ess ['di:kən, -is] n Ecc: diacre m, diaconesse f.

dead [ded] **1.** a mort; (doigt) engourdi; (charbon) éteint; **he's d.,** il est mort; **the d. man, woman,** le mort, la morte; Rail: **d. man's handle,** homme-mort m; **to drop (down) d.,** tomber mort; **stone d.,** raide mort; **d. as a doornail,** mort et bien mort; **d. and buried,** mort et enterré; **d. to the world,** profondément endormi; sans connaissance; (of limb) **to go d.,** s'engourdir; Tp: **the line went d.,** on a coupé la communication; Fig: **this has become a d. letter,** ceci est tombé en désuétude; Fig: **d. wood,** personnel inutile; **d. period,** période d'inactivité; **d. centre,** en plein milieu; **d. end,** impasse f; **to come to a d. stop,** s'arrêter net, pile; **d. calm,** calme plat; **d. silence,** silence de mort **2.** n (a) pl **the d.,** les morts m; **d. march,** marche funèbre (b) **at d. of night,** au plus profond de la nuit; **in the d. of winter,** au plus fort de l'hiver **3.** adv absolument; **d. drunk,** ivre mort; **d. tired,** F: beat, éreinté, claqué; **d. slow,** aussi lentement que possible; PN: au pas; **to stop d.,** s'arrêter net; **to arrive d. on time,** arriver pile; **to be d. (set) against,** être absolument opposé à. **'dead-(-and)-a'live** a (endroit) mort, triste. **'dead-'beat** n esp NAm: clochard m; hippy m. **'deaden** vtr amortir (un coup); étouffer, assourdir (un bruit); émousser (les sens); calmer (les nerfs). **'dead-'end** a (emploi) sans avenir. **'deadline** n date f limite; heure f limite. **'deadlock** n impasse f. **'deadly 1.** a mortel; (of weapon) meurtrier; (combat) à mort; (péché) capital; (silence) de mort! **in d. earnest,** tout à fait sérieux (b) ennuyeux, rasant **2.** adv mortellement; comme la mort; **d. dull,** rasant. **'deadpan** a F: (visage) figé; pince-sans-rire inv. **'dead-'weight** n poids mort.

deaf [def] **1.** a sourd; **d. in one ear,** sourd d'une oreille; **d. and dumb,** sourd-muet; **d. as a (door)post,** sourd comme un pot; **to turn a d. ear (to),** faire la sourde oreille (à) **2.** npl **the d.,** les sourds m. **'deaf-aid** n appareil m acoustique. **'deafen** vtr (temporarily) assourdir; (permanently) rendre sourd. **'deafening** a assourdissant. **'deaf-'mute** n sourd-muet, f sourde-muette. **'deafness** n surdité f.

deal[1] [di:l] n & adv **a good, great, d.,** beaucoup (of, de); **that's saying a good d.,** ce n'est pas peu dire; **I think a great d. of him,** je l'estime beaucoup; **he is a good d. better,** il va beaucoup mieux.

deal[2] **1.** n (a) Cards: donne f; **whose d. is it?** à qui de donner? (b) Com: affaire f; marché m; coup m (de Bourse); transaction f (au comptant); **it's a d.!** d'accord! **to give s.o. a fair, a raw, d.,** agir équitablement, injustement, envers qn **2.** v (dealt) (a) vtr **to d. (out),** distribuer (qch) (to, among, entre); **to d. out justice,** rendre la justice; **to d. s.o. a blow,** porter un coup à qn (b) vi **to d. with,** traiter, négocier, avec (qn); se fournir chez (qn); avoir affaire à (qn); traiter de,

s'occuper de (qch); venir à bout d'(un problème); **I know how to d. with him,** je sais comment m'y prendre avec lui; **difficult man to d. with,** homme pas commode; Com: **to d. in timber,** faire le commerce du bois **3.** vtr & i Cards: donner (les cartes). **'dealer** n (a) Cards: donneur m (b) Com: négociant m (**in, en); distributeur m (in, de); marchand, -ande (in, de); Aut: stockiste m. **'dealing(s)** n(pl) relations f (avec); Pej: menées fpl.

dean [di:n] n Ecc: Sch: doyen m.

dear ['diər] **1.** a (a) cher (**to,** à); (in letter) **D. Madam,** Madame, Mademoiselle; **D. Sir,** Monsieur; **D. Mr Smith,** cher Monsieur; F: **d. little child,** enfant adorable (b) (expensive) cher, coûteux **2.** n cher, f chère; chéri, -ie; **my d.,** mon cher ami; mon petit (chou); **you're a d.!** tu es un amour! **be a d.,** sois gentil **3.** adv (vendre, payer) cher **4.** int **d. me!** mon Dieu! **oh d.!** (i) oh là là! (ii) (annoyance) zut! **'dearly** adv cher; **to love s.o. d.,** aimer tendrement, être très attaché à qn; **I should d. love to go,** j'aimerais beaucoup y aller.

dearth [də:θ] n disette f, pénurie f.

death [deθ] n mort f; Adm: décès m; **to be at d.'s door,** être à l'article de la mort; **to put s.o. to d.,** mettre qn à mort; **to drink oneself to d.,** se tuer à force de boire; **to be in at the d.,** assister au dénouement (d'une affaire); F: **to look like d. (warmed up),** avoir un air de déterré; **to die a violent d.,** mourir de mort violente; F: **he'll be the d. of me,** il me fera mourir; F: **to catch one's d. (of cold),** attraper la crève; F: **to be sick to d. of sth,** en avoir marre, ras le bol, de qch; Journ: **deaths,** nécrologie f; **d. mask,** masque mortuaire; **d. wish,** pulsion de mort; **d. duty,** NAm: **d. tax,** droit de succession; **d. warrant,** ordre d'exécution. **'deathbed** n lit m de mort. **'death-blow** n coup mortel, fatal. **'deathly 1.** a de mort; cadavérique **2.** adv comme la mort; **d. pale,** d'une pâleur mortelle. **'death's-head** n tête f de mort. **'deathtrap** n endroit, véhicule, dangereux.

debar [di'ba:r] vtr (debarred) **to d. s.o. from sth,** exclure qn de qch; **to d. s.o. from doing sth,** interdire à qn de faire qch.

debase [di'beis] vtr avilir, dégrader (qn); déprécier, altérer (la monnaie).

debate [di'beit] **1.** n débat m; discussion f **2.** v (a) vtr débattre, discuter, agiter (une question) (b) vi discuter (**with s.o. on sth,** avec qn sur qch); **debating society,** société de débats contradictoires. **de'batable** a contestable, discutable.

debauch [di'bɔ:tʃ] vtr débaucher, corrompre (qn). **de'bauched** a débauché, corrompu. **de-'bauchery** n débauche f.

debility [di'biliti] n Med: débilité f.

debit ['debit] **1.** n débit m; doit m; **d. balance,** solde débiteur; **direct d.,** prélèvement m bancaire automatique **2.** vtr débiter (un compte); **to d. s.o. with a sum,** porter une somme au débit de qn; débiter qn d'une somme.

debonair [debə'neər] a jovial.

debrief [di'bri:f] **1.** n (also de'briefing) rapport m (de fin de mission) **2.** vtr & i faire (faire) un rapport de fin de mission (à qn).

debris ['debri:] n débris mpl; détritus mpl.

debt [det] n dette f; créance f; **bad debts,** mauvaises créances; **to be in d.**, être endetté; avoir des dettes; **to be out of d.**, ne plus avoir de dettes; **to get into d.**, s'endetter; faire des dettes; **to be no longer in s.o.'s d.**, être quitte envers qn; *Fig:* ne plus être redevable à qn (**for**, de); **d. collector**, agent de recouvrement. **'debtor** n débiteur, -trice.

debunk [di:'bʌŋk] *vtr F:* déboulonner (qn); démentir (qch); démystifier.

début ['deibju:] *n esp Th:* début *m*.

decade ['dekeid] *n* décennie *f*.

decadence ['dekədəns] *n* décadence *f*. **'decadent**, *a* décadent.

decaffeinated [di:'kæfi:neitid] *a* (café) décaféiné.

decamp [di'kæmp] *vi F:* décamper, filer.

decant [di'kænt] *vtr* décanter. **de'canter** *n* carafe *f*.

decapitate [di'kæpiteit] *vtr* décapiter (qn).

decay [di'kei] **1.** *n* décadence *f* (d'un pays); délabrement *m* (d'un bâtiment); pourriture *f* (du bois); carie *f* (des dents); **senile d.**, affaiblissement *m* sénile; (*of house*) **to fall into d.**, tomber en ruine **2.** *vi* pourrir; (*of nation*) tomber en décadence; (*of house*) tomber en ruine; se délabrer; (*of empire*) décliner; (*of teeth*) se carier. **de'cayed** *a* pourri; (*of building*) en ruine; (*of tooth*) carié. **de'caying** *a* en pourriture; (dent) qui se carie.

decease [di'si:s] *n Adm:* décès *m*. **de'ceased 1.** *a* décédé **2.** *n* défunt, défunte.

deceit [di'si:t] *n* tromperie *f*. **de'ceitful** *a* trompeur, faux; (regard) mensonger. **de'ceitfully** *adv* faussement, avec duplicité. **de'ceitfulness** *n* fausseté *f*.

deceive [di'si:v] *vtr* tromper, abuser.

decelerate [di:'seləreit] *vi & tr* ralentir.

December [di'sembər] *n* décembre *m*.

decent ['di:snt] *a* (*a*) bienséant, convenable; décent; *F:* **are you d.?** es-tu habillé? (*b*) *F:* passable; assez bon; **the food is quite d.**, la nourriture n'est pas mal (*c*) *F:* **a d. (sort of) chap**, un bon type; **that's very d. of you**, c'est très chic de ta part. **'decency** *n* décence *f*; **common d.**, les convenances (sociales); **(sense of) d.**, pudeur *f*. **'decently** *adv* décemment, convenablement.

decentralize [di:'sentrəlaiz] *vtr* décentraliser. **decentrali'zation** *n* décentralisation *f*.

deception [di'sepʃn] *n* tromperie *f*; supercherie *f*; fraude *f*. **de'ceptive** *a* trompeur. **de'ceptively** *adv* **he's d. quiet**, il a un air tranquille bien trompeur. **de'ceptiveness** *n* caractère trompeur.

decibel ['desibel] *n* décibel *m*.

decide [di'said] **1.** *vtr* (*a*) décider; trancher (une question); juger (un différend); **to d. s.o. to do sth**, décider qn à faire qch (*b*) décider de (l'avenir de qn); **nothing has been decided yet**, il n'y a encore rien de décidé; **I have decided what I shall do**, mon parti est pris **2.** *vi* se décider (**on**, à; **in favour of**, en faveur de); **to d. to do sth**, décider de, se décider à, faire qch; **to d. on a day**, fixer un jour. **de'cided** *a* (*a*) décidé; (avis) arrêté; (ton) net, résolu; (refus) catégorique (*b*) (succès) incontestable; (changement) marqué. **de'cidedly** *adv* (*a*) résolument, avec décision (*b*) incontestablement. **de'cider** *n* facteur, *Sp:* but, décisif; *Games:* belle *f*. **de'ciding** *a* décisif; **d. game**, la belle.

deciduous [di'sidjuəs] *a Bot:* (arbre) à feuilles caduques.

decimal ['desiməl] **1.** *a* décimal; **d. point** = virgule *f*; **to five d. places**, jusqu'à la cinquième décimale **2.** *n* décimale *f*. **decimali'zation** *n* décimalisation *f*.

decimate ['desimeit] *vtr* décimer.

decipher [di'saifər] *vtr* déchiffrer.

decision [di'siʒn] *n* décision *f*; *Jur:* arrêt *m*; **to come to a d.**, arriver à une décision; se décider. **de'cisive** [di'saisiv] *a* (*a*) décisif; (*of experiment*) concluant (*b*) (*of pers, manner*) décidé; (ton) tranchant, net. **de'cisively** *adv* d'une façon décidée.

deck [dek] **1.** *n* (*a*) (*of ship*) pont *m*; (*of bus*) **top d.**, impériale *f* (*b*) *Rec:* platine *f* (*c*) *esp NAm:* jeu *m* (de cartes). **2.** *vtr* **to d. (out)**, parer (**with**, de). **'deckchair** *n* transatlantique *m*; fauteuil *m* relax(e).

declaim [di'kleim] *vtr & i* déclamer.

declare [di'klεər] *vtr & i* déclarer; **to d. war**, déclarer la guerre (**on, against**, à); *Cust:* **have you anything to d.?** avez-vous quelque chose à déclarer? **to d. oneself**, se déclarer. **declaration** [deklə'reiʃn] déclaration *f*.

declension [di'klenʃn] *n* déclinaison *f*.

decline [di'klain] **1.** *n* déclin *m*; baisse *f* (de prix); **to be on the d.**, décliner; (*of prices*) être en baisse **2.** *v* (*a*) *vtr* décliner; refuser (*b*) *vi* décliner; (*of prices*) être en baisse; (*refuse*) s'excuser; refuser (**to do**, de faire). **de'clining** *a* **in one's d. years**, au déclin de la vie.

decode [di:'koud] *vtr* décoder.

decoke ['di:'kouk] *Aut: F:* **1.** *n* décalaminage *m* (du moteur) **2.** *vtr* décalaminer.

decolonize [di:'kɔlənaiz] *vtr* décoloniser.

decompose [di:kəm'pouz] *vi & tr* (se) décomposer. **decompo'sition** *n* décomposition *f*.

decompression [di:kəm'preʃn] *n* décompression *f*; **d. chamber**, chambre de décompression; **d. sickness**, maladie des caissons.

decongestant [di:kən'dʒestənt] *n Med:* décongestif *m*.

decontaminate [di:kən'tæmineit] *vtr* décontaminer.

décor ['deikɔːr] *n Th:* décor *m*.

decorate ['dekəreit] *vtr* (*a*) décorer, orner (**with**, de); peindre et tapisser (un appartement) (*b*) décorer (un soldat). **deco'ration** *n* (*a*) (action) (*also* '**decorating**) décoration *f* (*b*) (state) (*also* '**decorating**) décor *m* (d'un appartement) (*c*) (*medal*) décoration. **'decorative** *a* décoratif. **'decorator** *n* décorateur, -trice.

decorum [di'kɔːrəm] *n* décorum *m*. **'decorous** *a* convenable; bienséant.

decoy 1. *n* (*pl* **decoys**) ['di:kɔi] (*bird*) appeau *m*; (*pers*) compère *m* **2.** *vtr* [di'kɔi] attirer (qn) (**into a trap**, dans un piège).

decrease 1. *n* ['di:kri:s] diminution *f*, décroissance *f*; baisse *f* (**in price**, de prix); **d. in speed**, ralentissement *m* **2.** *vtr & i* [di'kri:s] diminuer; décroître; baisser. **de'creasing** *a* décroissant. **de'creasingly** *adv* de moins en moins.

decree [di'kri:] **1.** *n Adm:* décret *m*, édit *m*; *Jur:* décision *f*, arrêté *m*, arrêt *m*, jugement *m*; (*divorce*) **d. absolute, nisi**, jugement irrévocable, provisoire **2.** *vtr* décréter, ordonner.

decrepit [di'krepit] *a* (*of pers*) décrépit; (*of house*) qui tombe en ruine, délabré. **de'crepitude** *n* décrépitude *f*; (*of house*) délabrement *m*.

decry [di'krai] *vtr* décrier, dénigrer.

dedicate ['dedikeit] *vtr* 1. (*a*) consacrer, dédier (une église); **to d.** oneself, one's life, to sth, se vouer, se consacrer, à qch (*b*) dédier (un livre) (**to**, à). **dedi'cation** *n* (*a*) consécration *f* (d'une église) (*b*) dédicace *f* (d'un livre) (*c*) (*of pers*) dévouement *m*.

deduce [di'dju:s] *vtr* déduire, conclure.

deduct [di'dʌkt] *vtr* déduire (**from**, de); **to d. 5% from salaries**, faire une retenue de 5% sur les salaires. **de'ductible** *a* déductible. **de'duction** *n* (*a*) (*conclusion*) déduction *f* (*b*) déduction; (*of pay*) retenue (**from**, sur).

deed [di:d] *n* (*a*) action *f*, acte *m*; **outstanding d.**, exploit *m*; **in d.**, en fait (*b*) *Jur:* acte (notarié); **by d. poll**, légalement.

deep [di:p] 1. *a* (*a*) profond; **to be ten metres d.**, avoir dix mètres de profondeur; **d. in thought**, plongé dans ses pensées (*b*) (soupir, sommeil, désespoir) profond; **d. concern**, vive préoccupation (*c*) (placard) large; **four d.**, sur quatre rangs (*d*) (*of colour*) foncé, sombre; (*of sound*) grave (*e*) (*of pers*) malin 2. *adv* profondément 3. *n* the **d.**, (les grands fonds de) l'océan *m*. **'deepen** 1. *vtr* approfondir, creuser (un puits); augmenter, rendre plus intense (un sentiment); foncer (une couleur); rendre (un son) plus grave 2. *vi* devenir plus profond; (*of colour*) devenir plus foncé; (*of sound*) devenir plus grave; (*of shadows*) s'épaissir. **'deep-'freeze** 1. *n* congélateur *m* 2. *vtr* surgeler. **'deep-'fry** *vtr Cu:* faire frire en friteuse. **'deeply** *adv* profondément; **d. moved**, vivement affecté; *Fig:* **to go d. into sth**, approfondir qch. **'deepness** *n* profondeur *f*; gravité *f* (d'un son). **'deep-'rooted**, **-'seated** *a* profond; profondément enraciné; (conviction) intime; (préjugé) tenace. **'deep-'sea** *a* (animal) pélagique; (*of fishing*) hauturier. **'deep-'set** *a* (yeux) enfoncés.

deer ['diər] *n inv* (**red**) **d.**, cerf *m*; (**fallow**) **d.**, daim *m*; (**roe**) **d.**, chevreuil *m*. **'deerskin** *n* peau *f* de daim. **'deerstalker** *n* chapeau *m* de chasse (à la Sherlock Holmes).

deface [di'feis] *vtr* dégrader; mutiler.

defamatory [di'fæmətri] *a* diffamatoire; diffamant. **defa'mation** *n* diffamation *f*.

default [di'fɔ:lt] 1. *n Jur:* défaut *m*; **in d. of**, à défaut de; *Sp:* **by d.**, à forfait 2. *vi* manquer à ses engagements. **de'faulter** *n* délinquant, -ante.

defeat [di'fi:t] 1. *n* défaite *f*; renversement *m*, échec *m* (d'un projet) 2. *vtr* battre, vaincre (une armée); renverser, mettre en minorité (un gouvernement); faire échouer (un projet); **to d. the object**, aller à l'encontre du but proposé. **de'featist** *n* défaitiste *mf*.

defect 1. *n* ['di:fekt] défaut *m*; imperfection *f*; vice *m* (de construction); tare *f* 2. *vi* [di'fekt] faire défection; passer à l'ennemi. **de'fection** *n* défection *f*. **de'fective** *a* défectueux; imparfait; (freins) mauvais; (mémoire) infidèle; (enfant) anormal. **de'fector** *n* transfuge *mf*.

defence, *NAm:* **defense** [di'fens] *n* défense *f*;

protection *f*; justification *f* (d'un argument); *Mil: pl* ouvrages *mpl* de défense; *Jur:* counsel for the **d.**, défenseur *m*; **witness for the d.**, témoin à décharge; **in his d.**, à sa décharge. **de'fenceless**, *NAm:* **de'fenseless** *a* sans défense. **de'fensive** 1. *a* défensif 2. *n* **to be on the d.**, se tenir sur la défensive.

defend [di'fend] *vtr* défendre, protéger (**from**, against, contre); justifier (une opinion). **de'fendant** *n Jur:* défendeur, -eresse; (*in criminal case*) accusé, -ée. **de'fender** *n* défenseur *m*. **de'fending** *a Sp:* (champion) en titre.

defer [di'fə:r] *vtr* (**deferred**) différer, remettre, ajourner; renvoyer (une affaire); reculer (un paiement); reporter (qch à plus tard); suspendre (un jugement). **de'ferment** *n* ajournement *m*; renvoi *m*.

defer [di'fə:r] *vi* déférer (**to**, à). **'deference** *n* déférence *f*. **defe'rential** *a* (ton) de déférence; (*of pers*) plein de déférence. **defe'rentially** *adv* avec déférence.

defiance [di'faiəns] *n* défi *m*; **in d. of**, au mépris de. **de'fiant** *a* (air) de défi; provocant; intraitable. **de'fiantly** *adv* d'un air de défi.

deficiency [di'fiʃənsi] *n* (*pl* **deficiencies**) (*a*) manque *m*, insuffisance *f*, défaut *m*; *Med:* carence *f* (de vitamines); déficience *f* (du foie); **d. disease**, maladie de carence (*b*) défaut, imperfection *f*. **de'ficient** *a* insuffisant; **to be d. in sth**, manquer de qch.

deficit ['defisit] *n Com: Fin:* déficit *m*.

defile ['di:fail] *n Geog:* défilé *m*.

defile ['di:fail] *vtr* souiller, salir.

define [di'fain] *vtr* définir; préciser (son attitude); déterminer (l'étendue de qch); formuler (ses pensées); délimiter (des pouvoirs); **well defined outlines**, contours nettement dessinés. **definite** ['definit] *a* défini; bien déterminé; précis; (réponse) catégorique; (commande) ferme; **it's d.** (**that**) **he'll come**, il est certain qu'il viendra; *Gram:* **d. article**, article défini. **'definitely** *adv* décidément; nettement; catégoriquement; **d.!** bien sûr (que oui)! **he'll d. come**, il est certain qu'il viendra. **defi'nition** *n* définition *f*; netteté *f* (du son). **de'finitive** *a* définitif.

deflate [di'fleit] *vtr* dégonfler; remettre (qn) à sa place; *Fin:* amener la déflation de (la monnaie). **de'flation** *n* dégonflement *m*; *Fin:* déflation *f*. **de'flationary** *a Fin:* déflationniste.

deflect [di'flekt] 1. *vtr* (faire) dévier; détourner 2. *vi* dévier. **de'flection** *n* déflexion *f*.

deform [di'fɔ:m] *vtr* déformer. **de'formed** *a* difforme; contrefait. **de'formity** *n* difformité *f*.

defraud [di'frɔ:d] *vtr* frauder (le fisc); **to d. s.o. of sth**, escroquer qch à qn.

defray [di'frei] *vtr* couvrir (les frais); **to d. s.o.'s expenses**, défrayer qn.

defrost [di:'frost] *vtr* dégivrer (un réfrigérateur); décongeler (des aliments).

deft [deft] *a* adroit, habile. **'deftly** *adv* adroitement. **'deftness** *n* adresse *f*.

defunct [di'fʌŋkt] *a* défunt; décédé.

defuse [di:'fju:z] *vtr* désamorcer.

defy [di'fai] *vtr* défier, braver; mettre (qn) au défi; résister à (une attaque).

degenerate 1. *vi* [di'dʒenəreit] dégénérer (**into**, en)

2. *a* & *n* [di'dʒenərət] dégénéré, -ée. **de'generacy,
degene'ration** *n* dégénérescence *f*.

degrade [di'greid] *vtr* dégrader; avilir. **degradation** [degrə'deiʃn] *n* avilissement *m*. **de'grading**
a avilissant, dégradant.

degree [di'gri:] *n* (*a*) degré *m*; **to some d., to a certain
d.,** à un certain degré; jusqu'à un certain point; **in
the highest d.,** au plus haut degré; **in some d.,** dans
une certaine mesure; **by degrees,** par degrés; petit à
petit; **d. of humidity,** titre *m* d'eau (*b*) *Sch:* grade *m*
(universitaire); licence *f* (ès lettres, d'anglais); **to have
a d.,** avoir sa licence.

dehumanize [di:'hju:mənaiz] *vtr* déshumaniser.

dehydrate [di:hai'dreit] *vtr* déshydrater. **dehy-
'dration** *n* déshydratation *f*.

de-ice [di:'ais] *vtr* dégivrer. **de-'icer** *n* dégivreur
m. **'de-'icing** *n* dégivrage *m*.

deign [dein] *vi* **to d. to do sth,** daigner faire qch.

dejected [di'dʒektid] *a* abattu, découragé. **de-
'jectedly** *adv* d'un air découragé. **de'jection** *n*
découragement *m*.

delay [di'lei] **1.** *n* délai *m*; retard *m*; **without further
d.,** sans plus tarder **2.** *v* (*a*) *vtr* retarder; remettre
(une affaire); retenir (qn); différer (un paiement)
entraver (le progrès); **delayed-action fuse,** détonateur
à retardement (*b*) *vi* s'attarder, tarder ((**in**) doing sth,
à faire qch). **de'laying** *a* dilatoire.

delegate **1.** *n* ['deligət] délégué, -ée **2.** *vtr* ['deligeit]
déléguer. **dele'gation** *n* délégation *f*.

delete [di'li:t] *vtr* effacer, rayer. **de'letion** *n* rature
f; suppression *f*.

deliberate **1.** *a* [di'libərət] (*a*) délibéré; réfléchi;
prémédité, voulu; calculé (*b*) (pas) mesuré, lent **2.**
vtr & *i* [di'libəreit] délibérer ((**on**) sth, de, sur, qch).
de'liberately *adv* (*a*) à dessein; exprès (*b*) posément, délibérément. **delibe'ration** *n* délibération
f; réflexion *f*; with d., posément, après réflexion.

delicacy ['delikəsi] *n* (*pl* **delicacies**) (*a*) délicatesse *f*
(*b*) mets délicat. **'delicate** *a* délicat. **'delicately**
adv délicatement; avec délicatesse. **delica'tessen**
n épicerie fine; charcuterie *f*.

delicious [di'liʃəs] *a* délicieux; exquis. **de'liciously** *adv* délicieusement.

delight [di'lait] **1.** *n* (*a*) joie *f*; **much to the d. of,** à la
grande joie, au grand plaisir, de (*b*) (thg or pers)
délice *m*, délices *fpl*; plaisir **2.** *v* (*a*) *vtr* enchanter,
ravir, réjouir (*b*) *vi* **to d. in** (doing) sth, se délecter à
(faire) qch. **de'lighted** *a* enchanté, ravi (**with, at,**
de; **to do sth,** de faire qch); **I shall be d.!** avec grand
plaisir! **de'lightful** *a* délicieux, ravissant; charmant. **de'lightfully** *adv* délicieusement; à ravir.

delinquency [di'liŋkwənsi] *n* délinquance *f*. **de-
'linquent** *a* & *n* délinquant, -ante.

delirious [di'liriəs] *a* délirant; (malade) en délire; **to
be d.,** délirer; *Med:* être en délire. **de'liriously**
adv **d. happy,** délirant de joie. **de'lirium** *n* délire
m.

deliver [di'livər] *vtr* (*a*) remettre (un paquet); livrer
(des marchandises); distribuer (des lettres); **to d. a
message,** faire une commission (*b*) délivrer, sauver
(*c*) porter, donner (un coup); lancer (une attaque)
(*d*) faire, prononcer (un discours) (*e*) mettre au
monde (un enfant). **de'liverance** *n* délivrance *f*.
de'liverer *n* sauveur *m*. **de'livery** *n* (*a*) livraison

f (d'un paquet); distribution *f* (de lettres); **d. note,**
bulletin de livraison; **d. man,** livreur *m* (*b*) diction *f*,
débit *m* (d'un orateur) (*c*) accouchement *m* (d'un
enfant).

delta ['deltə] *n* delta *m*; **d. wing aircraft,** avion aux
ailes (en) delta.

delude [di'lu:d] *vtr* tromper (qn); duper (qn); en faire
accroire à (qn); **to d. oneself,** se faire des illusions.
de'lusion *n* illusion *f*; **to be under a d.,** se faire
des illusions.

deluge ['delju:dʒ] **1.** *n* déluge *m*; avalanche *f* (de
lettres) **2.** *vtr* inonder (**with,** de).

delve [delv] *vi* fouiller (**into,** dans).

demand [di'ma:nd] **1.** *n* (*a*) demande *f*, réclamation *f*,
revendication *f*; *pl* exigences *fpl*, nécessités *fpl*; **to
make many demands on s.o.,** exiger beaucoup de qn;
Com: **d. (note),** avertissement *m*; **on d.,** sur demande
(*b*) *Com:* **supply and d.,** l'offre et la demande; **to be
in d.,** être demandé **2.** *vtr* réclamer (qch à qn); exiger
(qch de qn; que + *sub*); revendiquer; (*of thg*) demander. **de'manding** *a* exigeant; (travail) astreignant.

demarcation [di'ma:'keiʃn] *n* démarcation *f*; *Ind:*
d. dispute, conflit d'attributions.

demean [di'mi:n] *vtr* abaisser; **to d. oneself,** s'a-
baisser.

demeanour, *NAm:* **-or** [di'mi:nər] *n* attitude *f*;
maintien *m*.

demented [di'mentid] *a* fou; dément.

demerara [demə'reərə] *n* **d. (sugar),** cassonade *f*.

demijohn ['demidʒɔn] *n* dame-jeanne *f*.

demilitarize [di:'militəraiz] *vtr* démilitariser.

demise [di'maiz] *n* décès *m*, mort *f*.

demister [di:'mistər] *n* *Aut:* (dispositif *m*) antibuée
(*m*).

demo ['demou] *n* *F:* manif *f*.

demobilize [di:'moubilaiz], *F:* **demob** [di:'mɔb]
(**demobbed**) *vtr* démobiliser. **demobili'zation** *F:*
de'mob *n* démobilisation *f*.

democracy [di'mɔkrəsi] *n* (*pl* **democracies**) démocratie *f*; **people's d.,** démocratie populaire. **'democrat** *n* démocrate *mf*. **demo'cratic** *a* démocratique; (parti) démocrate. **demo'cratically**
adv démocratiquement.

demography [di'mɔgrəfi] *n* démographie *f*.

demolish [di'mɔliʃ] *vtr* démolir; *F:* dévorer (un
gâteau). **demo'lition** *n* démolition *f*.

demon ['di:mən] *n* démon *m*. **demoniac** [di'moun-
iæk], **demoniacal** [di:mə'naiəkl], **demonic**
[di'mɔnik] *a* démoniaque.

demonstrate ['demənstreit] **1.** *vtr* démontrer (une
vérité); décrire, expliquer (un système); *Com:* faire
la démonstration d'(un appareil) **2.** *vi* *Pol:* manifester. **'demonstrable** *a* démontrable. **'de-
monstrably** *adv* manifestement. **demon-
'stration** *n* démonstration *f*; *Pol:* manifestation
f; **d. model,** modèle de démonstration. **de'mon-
strative** *a* démonstratif. **de'monstratively**
adv avec effusion. **'demonstrator** *n* démonstrateur, -trice; *Sch:* préparateur, -trice; *Pol:*
manifestant, -ante.

demoralize [di'mɔrəlaiz] *vtr* démoraliser. **de-
morali'zation** *n* démoralisation *f*.

demote [di'mout] *vtr* rétrograder.

demur [di'mɔːr] vi (**demurred**) soulever des objections (at, contre).

demure [di'mjuər] a posé, modeste. **de′murely** adv d'un air posé; modestement.

den [den] n tanière f, repaire m (de bêtes, de voleurs); F: cabinet m de travail.

denationalize [diː'næʃnəlaiz] vtr dénationaliser.

denial [di'naiəl] n refus m (d'un droit); déni m (de justice); démenti m (de la vérité); dénégation f.

denier ['deniər] n **15 d. stocking**, bas (de) 15 deniers mpl.

denigrate ['denigreit] vtr dénigrer.

denim ['denim] n Tex: (toile f de) jean m; (thicker) treillis m; pl Cl: (i) (blue-)jean(s) m(pl) (ii) bleus mpl (de travail); **d. skirt**, jupe en jean.

Denmark ['denmɑːk] Prn Geog: Danemark m.

denomination [dinɔmi'neiʃn] n (a) dénomination f (b) Rel: culte m, confession f (c) catégorie f; (of coin) valeur f. **de′nominator** n Mth: **common d.**, dénominateur commun.

denote [di'nout] vtr dénoter; signifier.

denounce [di'nauns] vtr dénoncer; s'élever contre (un abus); **to d. s.o. as an impostor**, taxer qn d'imposture.

dense [dens] a (a) dense; épais; (of crowd) compact (b) stupide, bête. **′densely** adv **d. wooded**, couvert de forêts épaisses; **d. populated**, très peuplé. **′density** n densité f.

dent [dent] **1.** n bosse f, bosselure f **2.** vtr bosseler, bossuer, cabosser.

dentist ['dentist] n dentiste mf. **′dental** a dentaire; **d. surgeon**, chirurgien dentiste. **′dentifrice** n dentifrice m. **′dentistry** n médecine f dentaire. **′denture(s)** n(pl) dentier m.

denude [di'njuːd] vtr dénuder.

denunciation [dinʌnsi'eiʃn] n dénonciation f; accusation publique.

deny [di'nai] vtr (a) nier (un fait); démentir (une nouvelle); **I don't d. it**, je n'en disconviens pas; **there is no denying the fact**, c'est un fait indéniable (b) **to d. s.o. sth**, refuser qch à qn; **to d. oneself sth**, se priver de qch.

deodorant [diː'oudərənt] n désodorisant m, déodorant m.

depart [di'pɑːt] vi s'en aller, partir; **to d. from**, quitter (un endroit); s'écarter (d'une règle). **de′parted 1.** a (of glory) passé, évanoui; (of pers) mort, défunt **2.** n défunt, -unte. **de′parture** n (a) départ m; **d. lounge**, salle de départ (b) exception f (**from**, à); **new d.**, nouvelle tendance.

department [di'pɑːtmənt] n (a) département m; service m (b) (in shop) rayon m; comptoir m; **d. store**, grand magasin (c) ministère m. **depart′mental** a (chef') de service.

depend [di'pend] vi dépendre (**on**, de); **that depends entirely on you**, cela ne tient qu'à vous; **that depends, it all depends**, cela dépend; F: c'est selon; **to d. (up)on s.o.**, compter sur qn; **d. (up)on it**, comptez là-dessus. **de′pendable** a (of pers) digne de confiance; (of news) sûr; (machine) fiable. **de′pendant** n personne f à charge; pl charges fpl de famille. **de′pendence** n dépendance f (**on**, de). **de′pendency** n dépendance. **de′pendent 1.** a dépendant (**on**, de) **2.** a & n d. (**person**), (personne f) à charge.

depict [di'pikt] vtr dépeindre; représenter.

depilatory [di'pilətəri] a & n dépilatoire (m).

deplete [di'pliːt] vtr épuiser; réduire. **de′pletion** n épuisement m; réduction f.

deplore [di'plɔːr] vtr déplorer; regretter vivement. **de′plorable** a déplorable. **de′plorably** adv déplorablement.

deploy [di'plɔi] vtr déployer. **de′ployment** n déploiement m.

depopulate [diː'pɔpjuleit] vtr dépeupler. **depopu′lation** n dépeuplement m; dépopulation f; **rural d.**, exode rural.

deport [di'pɔːt] vtr expulser (un étranger); déporter (un condamné). **depor′tation** n expulsion f; déportation f.

deportment [di'pɔːtmənt] n maintien m.

depose [di'pouz] vtr déposer. **depo′sition** n déposition f.

deposit [di'pɔzit] **1.** n (a) dépôt m (d'argent); (partial payment) acompte m, arrhes fpl; Com: (on bottle) consigne f, caution f; Pol: (of candidate) cautionnement m; **bank d.**, dépôt en banque; **d. account**, compte d'épargne; **to pay a d.**, verser des arrhes (b) dépôt; gisement m (de minerai); **to form a d.**, se déposer **2.** vtr déposer. **de′positor** n déposant, -ante (en banque). **de′pository** n dépôt.

deprave [di'preiv] vtr dépraver, corrompre. **depravity** [-′præv-] n dépravation f.

deprecate ['deprəkeit] vtr désapprouver. **′deprecating** a désapprobateur. **depre′cation** n désapprobation f.

depreciate [di'priːʃieit] vtr & i (se) déprécier. **depreci′ation** n dépréciation f.

depress [di'pres] vtr (a) abaisser (qch); appuyer sur (un bouton); (faire) baisser (les prix) (b) déprimer, décourager (qn). **de′pressed** a (a) (of pers) déprimé; **to feel d.**, avoir le cafard b (of region) touché par la crise. **de′pressing** a déprimant, décourageant. **de′pressingly** adv d'une manière déprimante. **de′pression** n (a) abaissement m (d'un bouton) (b) dépression f; crise f (économique); marasme m (des affaires).

deprive [di'praiv] vtr priver; **to d. oneself**, se priver. **de′prived** a (enfant) déshérité. **depri′vation** n privation f.

dept abbr department.

depth [depθ] n profondeur f; fond m, hauteur f (de l'eau); épaisseur f (d'une couche); gravité f (d'un son); largeur f (d'un placard); intensité f (de coloris); **to get out of one's d.**, (i) perdre pied (ii) sortir de sa compétence; **in d.**, en profondeur; **in the depth(s) of**, au plus fort de (l'hiver); au plus profond de (la nuit); dans le plus profond (désespoir); **d. charge**, grenade sous-marine.

depute [di'pjuːt] vtr déléguer; députer (qn). **depu′tation** n députation f, délégation f. **′deputize** vi **to d. for s.o.**, remplacer, assurer l'intérim de, qn. **′deputy** n fondé m de pouvoir; substitut m, suppléant, -ante; délégué, -ée (d'un fonctionnaire); Pol: député m; **d. mayor**, adjoint, -ointe (au maire).

derail [di'reil] vtr faire dérailler (un train). **de′railment** n déraillement m.

derange [di'reindʒ] vtr (a) déranger le cerveau de (qn); **he, his mind, is deranged,** c'est un détraqué; il a l'esprit dérangé (b) dérégler, détraquer (une machine).

derelict ['derilikt] a abandonné; (tombé) en ruine(s). **dere'liction** n négligence f (**of duty,** dans le service).

derestricted [di:ri'striktid] a Aut: (route) sans limitation de vitesse.

deride [di'raid] vtr tourner en dérision. **de'rision** [di'riʒn] n dérision f; **object of d.,** objet de risée f. **de'risive, de'risory** a (rire) moqueur; (offre) dérisoire. **de'risively** adv d'un ton de dérision.

derive [di'raiv] vtr & i tirer (son origine) (**from sth,** de qch); trouver (du plaisir) (**from sth,** de qch); puiser (une idée **(from s.o.,** chez qn); **word derived from Latin,** mot qui vient du latin; **to be derived, to d., from,** dériver, (pro)venir, de. **deri'vation** n dérivation f. **de'rivative** [di'ri-] a & n dérivé (m); (ouvrage m) sans originalité.

dermatitis [də:mə'taitis] n dermatite f. **derma'tologist** n dermatologue mf. **derma'tology** n dermatologie f.

derogatory [di'rɔgətəri] a (of remark) désobligeant, qui abaisse (qn); (sens) péjoratif.

derrick ['derik] n Nau: mât m de charge; Petr: derrick m; tour f de forage.

derv [də:v] n gas-oil m.

descale [di:'skeil] vtr détartrer.

descend [di'send] 1. vi (a) descendre; (of darkness) tomber; **to d. to s.o.'s level, to doing sth,** s'abaisser au niveau de qn, à faire qch; **to d. on s.o.,** (i) (of thieves) s'abattre sur qn (ii) (of visitors) faire irruption chez qn (b) (of property) passer (**from, to,** de, en, à); **to be descended from s.o.,** descendre de qn 2. vtr descendre (un escalier). **de'scendant** n descendant, -ante. **de'scent** n (a) descente f (b) descendance f, famille f.

describe [di'skraib] vtr décrire; dépeindre; **to d. s.o. as,** qualifier qn de. **des'cription** n description f; Adm: signalement m; **beyond d.,** indescriptible; **people of this d.,** des gens de cette sorte, espèce. **des'criptive** a descriptif.

desecrate ['desikreit] vtr profaner, souiller.

desegregate [di:'segrigeit] vtr mettre fin à la ségrégation raciale dans (une école).

desert[1] [di'zə:t] n usu pl mérite(s) m(pl); **to get one's deserts,** avoir ce que l'on mérite.

desert[2] ['dezət] 1. a (plante) désertique; **d. island,** île déserte; **d. boot,** chaussure montante 2. n désert m.

desert[3] [di'zə:t] vtr & i déserter; abandonner (qn). **de'serted** a (of pers) abandonné; (of place) désert. **de'serter** n déserteur m. **de'sertion** n désertion f; abandon m (de qn).

deserve [di'zə:v] vtr mériter (de faire; que + sub); être digne de. **deservedly** [di'zə:vidli] adv à juste titre; à bon droit. **de'serving** a (of pers) méritant; (of action) méritoire.

desiccate ['desikeit] vtr dessécher.

design [di'zain] 1. n (a) dessein m, intention f, projet m; pl visées fpl; **by d.,** à dessein (b) dessin m (d'ornement); Needlew: etc: modèle m, motif m (c) plan m (d'un roman); dessin, étude f, avant-projet m (d'une machine); **car of the latest d.,** voiture dernier modèle

(d) (subject) esthétique (industrielle) 2. vtr concevoir; préparer (un projet); créer (une robe); dessiner (un tissu); **designed for,** destiné à. **de'signer** n dessinateur, -trice; décorateur, -trice (de théâtre, d'intérieurs); esthéticien, -ienne (industriel, -elle). **de'signing** 1. a intrigant 2. n esthétique (industrielle).

designate 1. ['dezigneit] vtr désigner, nommer (qn à une fonction) 2. a ['dezignət] désigné. **desig'nation** n désignation f.

desire [di'zaiər] 1. n désir m (**for, to,** de); **to have a d. to do sth,** avoir envie de faire qch 2. vtr désirer; avoir envie de (qch); **it leaves much to be desired,** cela laisse beaucoup à désirer. **de'sirable** a désirable; souhaitable; (of property) beau. **de'sirous** a désireux (**of,** de).

desk [desk] n Sch: pupitre m; (office) bureau m; (in shop) caisse f; (in hotel) réception f. **'deskwork** n travail m de bureau.

desolate ['desələt] a désolé; (lieu) désert; (of pers) affligé; (cri) de désolation. **'desolated** a désolé. **'desolately** adv d'un air désolé. **deso'lation** n désolation f; dévastation f (d'un pays).

despair [di'spεər] 1. n désespoir m; **in d.,** au désespoir; **to drive s.o. to d.,** réduire qn au désespoir 2. vi (se) désespérer (**of,** de). **de'spairing** a désespéré. **de'spairingly** adv désespérément; avec désespoir.

despatch [di'spætʃ] n & v = **dispatch.**

desperate ['despərət] a désespéré; (combat) acharné; **d. man,** désespéré; **to be d. for sth,** avoir grand besoin de qch; **to do something d.,** faire un malheur. **'desperately** adv désespérément; gravement (malade); éperdument (amoureux). **despe'ration** n **in d.,** au désespoir; **to drive s.o. to d.,** pousser qn à bout.

despicable [di'spikəbl, 'desp-] a méprisable. **de'spicably, 'desp-** adv bassement.

despise [di'spaiz] vtr mépriser; dédaigner.

despite [di'spait] prep malgré; en dépit de.

despondency [di'spɔndənsi] n découragement m, abattement m. **de'spondent** a découragé, abattu. **de'spondently** adv d'un air découragé, abattu.

despot ['despɔt] n despote m; tyran m. **de'spotic** a despotique; (of pers) despote. **de'spotically** adv despotiquement. **'despotism** n despotisme m.

dessert [di'zə:t] n dessert m; **d. plate,** assiette à dessert; **d. wine,** vin de liqueur. **de'ssertspoon** n cuiller f à dessert.

destination [desti'neiʃn] n destination f.

destine ['destin] vtr destiner (**for,** à). **'destiny** n destin m, destinée f; sort m.

destitute ['destitju:t] a (a) dépourvu, dénué (**of,** de) (b) indigent; sans ressources; **utterly d.,** dans la misère. **desti'tution** n dénuement m, indigence f; misère f.

destroy [di'strɔi] vtr détruire; anéantir; tuer, abattre (une bête). **de'stroyer** n (pers) destructeur, -trice; Nau: contre-torpilleur m. **de'struction** n destruction f; ravages mpl (du feu). **de'structive** a destructeur; (effet) destructif; **d. child,** brise-tout m. **de'structiveness** n pouvoir destructeur (d'une bombe); (of pers) penchant m à détruire. **de'structor** n incinérateur m (à ordures).

desultory ['desəltri] *a* décousu; sans suite; (lectures) sans méthode.

detach [di'tætʃ] *vtr* détacher (**from**, de). **de'tachable** *a* détachable, amovible. **de'tached** *a* détaché; (*of pers*) désintéressé; (air) indifférent; **d. house**, maison séparée; pavillon *m*. **de'tachment** *n* (*a*) détachement *m* (*b*) (*removal*) séparation *f*.

detail ['di:teil, NAm: di'teil] 1. *n* (*a*) détail *m*; **in d.**, en détail; **in every d.**, dans le moindre détail; **to go into detail(s)**, entrer dans les détails (*b*) Mil: détachement *m* 2. *vtr* (*a*) raconter en détail; énumérer (les faits); détailler (*b*) Mil: détacher. **'detailed, NAm: de'tailed** *a* détaillé.

detain [di'tein] *vtr* détenir (qn en prison); retenir (qn); empêcher (qn) de partir.

detect [di'tekt] *vtr* découvrir (un coupable); déceler (un crime); détecter (une fuite de gaz). **de'tection** *n* découverte *f*; détection *f*; **to escape d.**, se dérober aux recherches; (*of mistake*) passer inaperçu. **de'tective** *n* agent *m* de la Sûreté; **private d.**, détective (privé); **d. story**, roman policier. **de'tector** *n* détecteur *m* (de fumée).

detention [di'tenʃn] *n* détention *f* (en prison); Sch: retenue *f*; **to give a pupil a d.**, consigner, F: coller, un élève.

deter [di'tə:r] *vtr* (**deterred**) détourner, décourager (**s.o. from doing**, qn de faire).

detergent [di'tə:dʒənt] *a & n* détergent (*m*); lessive *f*; lave-vaisselle *m inv*.

deteriorate [di'tiəriəreit] *vi* se détériorer; dégénérer. **deterio'ration** *n* détérioration *f*; dégénération *f*.

determine [di'tə:min] *vtr & i* déterminer, fixer (une date); délimiter (une frontière); constater (la nature de qch); décider (une question); décider de (l'avenir de qn); **to d. to do sth**, se déterminer, se décider, à faire qch. **determi'nation** *n* détermination *f*. **de'termined** *a* (*of pers*) déterminé, résolu (**to do sth**, à faire qch).

deterrent [di'terənt] *n* arme *f* de dissuasion; **to act as a d.**, exercer un effet préventif.

detest [di'test] *vtr* détester. **de'testable** *a* détestable. **de'testably** *adv* détestablement. **dete'station** *n* haine *f*.

dethrone [di'θroun] *vtr* détrôner (un roi).

detonate ['detəneit] *vtr & i* (faire) détoner; (faire) sauter. **deto'nation** *n* détonation *f*. **'detonator** *n* détonateur *m*.

detour ['di:tuər] *n* détour *m*; déviation *f*.

detract [di'trækt] *vi* **to d. from**, diminuer.

detriment ['detrimənt] *n* détriment *m*, préjudice *m*; **to the d. of**, au détriment de; **without d. to**, sans nuire à. **detri'mental** *a* nuisible (**to**, à).

deuce [dju:s] *n* (*a*) Cards: etc: deux *m* (*b*) Ten: égalité *f* (à quarante); quarante partout.

devalue [di:'vælju:] *vtr* dévaluer (une monnaie). **devalu'ation** *n* dévaluation *f*.

devastate ['devəsteit] *vtr* dévaster, ravager; foudroyer (qn). **'devastating** *a* (*of storm*) dévastateur; (raisonnement) accablant; (charme) irrésistible; (choc) foudroyant. **'devastatingly** *adv* **d. beautiful**, d'une beauté incomparable. **deva'station** *n* dévastation *f*.

develop [di'veləp] 1. *vtr* développer; exploiter, mettre en valeur (une région); construire sur (un terrain); contracter (une maladie); manifester (une tendance) 2. *vi* se développer; se manifester; (*of crisis*) se produire. **de'veloper** *n* (*a*) (*pers*) promoteur *m* (*b*) Phot: révélateur *m*. **de'veloping** 1. *a* (pays) en voie de développement 2. *n* développement *m*; exploitation *f* (d'une région). **de'velopment** *n* (*a*) développement; exploitation (d'une région) (*b*) (*built-up area*) lotissement *m* (*c*) **a new d.**, un fait nouveau; **to await further developments**, attendre la suite des événements.

deviate ['di:vieit] *vi* dévier, s'écarter. **'deviant** *a & n* déviant(e) (*mf*). **devi'ation** *n* déviation *f* (**from**, de); écart *m* (de la norme).

device [di'vais] *n* (*a*) dispositif *m*, appareil *m*; mécanisme *m* (*b*) expédient *m*; **to leave s.o. to his own devices**, laisser qn seul (*c*) Her: emblème *m*, devise *f*.

devil ['devl] *n* (*a*) diable *m*; F: **he's a d.!** (*of child*) c'est un petit démon! (*of man*) il est terrible! F: **poor d.!** pauvre diable! F: **silly d.**, espèce d'idiot! **be a d.**, laisse-toi tenter; **to play d.'s advocate**, se faire l'avocat du diable; **to be between the d. and the deep blue sea**, être entre l'enclume et le marteau; **talk of the d.!** quand on parle du loup (on en voit la queue); F: **go to the d.!** va au diable! (*b*) F: **what the d. are you doing?** que diable faites-vous là? **how the d.?** comment diable? **to work like the d.**, travailler comme un forçat; **to have the, a, d. of a job**, avoir un mal de chien (**to do sth**, à faire qch); **there'll be the d. to pay**, ça nous coûtera cher. **'devilish** *a* diabolique. **'devilled, NAm: -viled** *a* Cu: fortement épicé, poivré; au curry. **'devil-may-care** *a* insouciant. **'devilment, 'devilry** *n* méchanceté *f*; espièglerie *f*.

devious ['di:viəs] *a* détourné, tortueux; (*of pers*) retors. **'deviously** *adv* d'une façon détournée.

devise [di'vaiz] *vtr* inventer, imaginer (un appareil); combiner, tramer (un complot).

devoid [di'void] *a* dénué, dépourvu (**of**, de).

devolution [di:və'lu:ʃn] *n* Pol: décentralisation *f*.

devolve [di'vɒlv] *vi* **to d. on**, revenir, incomber, à.

devote [di'vout] *vtr* consacrer, vouer; **to d. oneself to**, se consacrer, se vouer, s'adonner à. **de'voted** *a* dévoué, attaché. **de'votedly** *adv* avec dévouement. **de'votion** *n* dévouement *m*; dévotion *f* (à Dieu). **de'votional** *a* de dévotion.

devour [di'vauər] *vtr* dévorer. **de'vouring** *a* dévorant.

devout [di'vaut] *a* dévot, pieux; (*of wish*) fervent, sincère. **de'voutly** *adv* avec dévotion; (espérer) sincèrement.

dew [dju:] *n* rosée *f*. **'dewdrop** *n* goutte *f* de rosée. **'dewy-'eyed** *a* aux yeux brillants (de larmes).

dexterity [dek'steriti] *n* dextérité *f*; habileté *f*. **'dext(e)rous** *a* adroit, habile (**in doing**, à faire). **'dext(e)rously** *adv* avec dextérité.

DHSS *abbr* Department of Health and Social Security.

diabetes [daiə'bi:ti:z] *n* Med: diabète *m*. **diabetic** [-'betik] *a & n* diabétique (*mf*).

diabolical [daiə'bɒlikl] *a* diabolique; F: atroce, infernal. **dia'bolically** *adv* diaboliquement.

diagnose ['daiəgnouz] *vtr* diagnostiquer. **diag'nosis** *n* (*pl* -oses) Med: diagnostic *m*.

diagonal [dai'ægənl] 1. *a* diagonal 2. *n* diagonale *f*. **di'agonally** *adv* diagonalement, en diagonale.

diagram 95 dig

diagram ['daiəgræm] *n* diagramme *m*, schéma *m*; graphique *m* (de température).

dial ['daiəl] **1.** *n* cadran *m* **2.** *vtr & i* (**dialled**) *Tp:* composer, faire (un numéro); **to d. 999**, appeler Police Secours; **to d. Paris (direct)**, avoir Paris par l'automatique; **dialling tone**, tonalité *f*; **dialling code**, indicatif *m*.

dialect ['daiəlekt] *n* dialecte *m*; **local d.**, patois *m*; **d. word**, mot dialectal.

dialogue ['daiələɔg] *n* dialogue *m*.

dialysis [dai'ælisis] *n* (*pl* **dialyses**) dialyse *f*; **kidney d.**, dialyse péritonéale.

diameter [dai'æmitər] *n* diamètre *m*; **it's 60 cm in d.**, il a 60 cm de diamètre. **dia'metrical** *a* diamétral. **dia'metrically** *adv* diamétralement.

diamond ['daiəmənd] **1.** *n* (*a*) diamant *m*; **d. merchant**, diamantaire *m*; *F:* **rough d.**, personne *f* aux dehors grossiers mais bon enfant; **d. jubilee**, fête du soixantième anniversaire (*b*) (*shape*) losange *m*; *Cards:* carreau *m*; *Sp:* terrain *m* de baseball **2.** *a* (bague) de diamant(s). **'diamond-shaped** *a* en losange.

diaper ['daiəpər] *n NAm:* couche *f* (de bébé).

diaphragm ['daiəfræm] *n* diaphragme *m*.

diarr(o)ea [daiə'riːə] *n Med:* diarrhée *f*.

diary ['daiəri] *n* (*pl* **diaries**) (*a*) journal *m* (intime) (*b*) (*for engagements*) agenda *m*. **'diarist** *n* auteur *m* d'un journal (intime).

dice [dais] **1.** *npl* (*pl* of **die**¹ (*a*)) *Games:* dé *mpl* **2.** *vtr Cu:* couper en dés. **'dice 'with** *vtr* **to d. w. death**, risquer sa vie. **'dicey** *a F:* risqué.

dickens ['dikinz] *n F:* **what the d. are you doing?** que diable fais-tu?

dicky ['diki] *a F:* branlant; **he has a d. heart**, il a le cœur fragile, malade.

dictate [dik'teit] **1.** *vtr* dicter (une lettre) **2.** *vi* faire la loi (**to s.o.**, à qn); **I won't be dictated to**, on ne me donne pas d'ordres. **dic'tates** *npl* ordres *mpl.* **dic-'tation** *n* dictée *f.* **dic'tator** *n* dictateur *m.* **dicta'torial** *a* dictatorial. **dicta'torially** *adv* dictatorialement. **dic'tatorship** *n* dictature *f.*

diction ['dikʃn] *n* diction *f.*

dictionary ['dikʃnəri] *n* (*pl* **dictionaries**) dictionnaire *m.*

did [did] *see* **do**¹ II.

diddle ['didl] *vtr F:* escroquer, rouler (qn).

die¹ [dai] *n* (*a*) (*pl* **dice**) *Games:* dé *m* (*b*) *Num:* (in minting) coin *m*; *Metalw:* matrice *f.* **'die-casting** *n* moulage *m* en coquille.

die² *vi* (**died**) mourir; (*of animals*) crever; *F:* (*of engine*) caler; **to be dying**, mourir; être à l'agonie; **he died yesterday**, il est mort hier; **to d. a natural death**, mourir de mort naturelle; **to d. a hero's death**, mourir en héros; **old superstitions d. hard**, les vieilles superstitions ont la vie dure; **never say d.!** il ne faut jamais désespérer; **I nearly died (laughing)**, je mourais de rire; **I'm dying of thirst, for a drink**, je meurs de soif; **to be dying to do sth**, mourir, brûler, d'envie de faire qch; **his secret died with him**, il a emporté son secret dans le tombeau. **'die a'way** *vi* (*of sound*) s'éteindre. **'die 'back** *vi* (*of plant*) se faner. **'die 'down** *vi* (*of fire*) baisser; (*of wind*) tomber; (*of excitement*) se calmer. **'diehard** *n* réactionnaire *mf.* **'die 'off**

vi mourir les uns après les autres. **'die 'out** *vi* disparaître; (*of family*) s'éteindre.

diesel ['diːzəl] *n* (*a*) **d. (engine)**, (i) (locomotive *f*) diesel *m* (ii) (moteur *m*) diesel (*b*) **d. (oil)**, gas-oil *m.*

diet ['daiət] **1.** *n* (*a*) alimentation *f*, nourriture *f* (*b*) régime *m*; **to go, be, on a d.**, se mettre, être, au régime **2.** *vi* se mettre, être, au régime. **'dietary** *a* diététique. **die'tetics** *npl* diététique *f.* **die'tician** *n* diététicien, -ienne.

diff [dif] *n F: Aut:* différentiel *m.*

differ ['difər] *vi* différer, être différent (**from**, de); (*of two people*) **to d. about sth**, ne pas s'accorder sur qch; **to agree to d.**, garder chacun son opinion.

difference ['difrəns] *n* (*a*) différence *f* (**in**, de; **between**, entre); **to tell the d. between**, connaître la différence entre; **I don't quite see the d.**, je ne saisis pas la nuance; **it makes no d.**, cela ne fait rien; **it makes no d. to me**, cela m'est égal; **that makes all the d.**, voilà qui change tout; **but with a d.**, mais pas comme les autres; **to split the d.**, partager la différence (*b*) **d. (of opinion)**, différence d'opinions; différend *m*; **settle your differences**, mettez-vous d'accord. **'different** *a* (*a*) différent (**from, to, de**); **quite d.**, pas comme les autres; **that's quite a d. matter**, ça, c'est une autre affaire; **he does it to be d.**, il le fait pour se faire remarquer (*b*) **d. kinds of**, différentes, diverses, espèces de. **diffe'rential 1.** *a* différentiel **2.** *n* (*a*) écart *m* (de salaires); **wage differentials**, hiérarchie salariale (*b*) *Aut:* différentiel *m.* **diffe'rentiate 1.** *vtr* différencier (**from**, de) **2.** *vi* faire la différence (**between**, entre). **'differently** *adv* différemment; **he speaks d. from you**, il ne parle pas de la même manière, il parle autrement, que vous.

difficult ['difikəlt] *a* difficile; **it is d. to believe that**, on a peine à croire que; **to get on with**, (personne) difficile à vivre. **'difficulty** *n* (*a*) difficulté *f*; **to have d. (in) doing sth**, avoir de la difficulté, du mal, à faire qch; **d. in breathing**, gêne *f* dans la respiration; **the d. is to**, le difficile, c'est de; **I see no d. about it**, je n'y vois pas d'obstacle, d'inconvénient; **to make difficulties**, faire des difficultés (*b*) embarras *m*, ennui *m*; **to be in d.**, être dans l'embarras; **financial difficulties**, ennuis d'argent; **to get into difficulties**, se créer des ennuis.

diffidence ['difidəns] *n* manque *m* d'assurance. **'diffident** *a* qui manque d'assurance; (sourire) timide; **I was d. about speaking to him**, j'hésitais à lui parler. **'diffidently** *adv* timidement; en hésitant.

diffuse 1. *vtr & i* [di'fjuːz] (se) diffuser **2.** *a* [di'fjuːs] diffus. **di'ffusion** *n* diffusion *f.*

dig [dig] **1.** *n* (*a*) coup *m* de coude (**in the ribs**, dans les côtes); *Fig:* allusion *f* (critique), coup de patte (**at s.o.**, à qn); **that's a d. at you**, c'est une pierre dans votre jardin (*b*) *Archeol:* fouille(s) *f*(*pl*) **2.** *v* (**digging; dug** [dʌg]) (*a*) *vtr* bêcher, retourner (la terre); arracher (des pommes de terre); creuser (un trou); enfoncer (**sth into sth**, qch dans qch); donner un coup de coude à (qn) (**in the ribs**, dans les côtes); *P:* **I d. that!** ça me plaît, ça me botte! (*b*) *vi* faire des fouilles (archéologiques). **'dig 'for** *vtr Min:* faire des fouilles pour extraire (de l'or). **'digger** *n* (*a*) (*pers*) bêcheur *m* (*b*) (*machine*) excavateur *m*, pelleteuse *f.* **'dig 'in 1.** *vtr* enterrer (le fumier); enfoncer (un couteau); *Fig:* **to d. one's heels in,** s'entêter 2. *vi* (a) *Mil:* se retrancher (b) *F:* manger, bouffer; **d. in!** vas-y, mange! **'dig 'into** *vtr* (a) enfoncer (un couteau) dans (b) fouiller dans (c) *F:* attaquer (un repas). **'dig 'out** *vtr* déterrer; extraire. **digs** *npl F:* logement *m*; **to live in d.,** loger en garni. **'dig 'up** *vtr* déraciner (une plante); mettre à jour (un trésor); piocher (la terre); déterrer (un cadavre); *F:* dénicher.

digest 1. *n* ['daidʒest] sommaire *m*; *Journ:* digest *m* 2. *vtr* [dai'dʒest] digérer. **di'gestible** *a* digestible. **di'gestion** *n* digestion *f*. **di'gestive** *a* & *n* digestif; **d. (biscuit),** sablé *m*.

digit ['didʒit] *n* (a) doigt *m*; orteil *m* (b) chiffre *m*. **'digital** *a* (ordinateur) numérique; **d. watch,** montre (à affichage) numérique, montre digitale.

dignify ['dignifai] *vtr* donner de la dignité à. **'dignified** *a* plein de dignité; (air) digne. **'dignitary** *n* (*pl* **-ies**) dignitaire *m*. **'dignity** *n* dignité *f*; **beneath his d.,** au-dessous de lui.

digress [dai'gres] *vi* faire une digression (**from,** de); s'écarter (du sujet). **di'gression** *n* digression *f*, écart *m* (du sujet).

dike [daik] *n* digue *f*, levée *f*.

dilapidated [di'læpideitid] *a* délabré. **dilapidation** *n* délabrement *m*.

dilate [dai'leit] *vtr* & *i* (*of eyes, etc*) (se) dilater. **di'lation** *n* dilatation *f*.

dilatory ['dilətəri] *a* (*of pers*) lent (à agir); (réponse) dilatoire.

dilemma [d(a)i'lemə] *n* dilemme *m*; **in, on the horns of, a d.,** pris dans un dilemme.

diligence ['dilidʒəns] *n* assiduité *f*, zèle *m*. **'diligent** *a* assidu, appliqué. **'diligently** *adv* avec assiduité.

dill [dil] *n Bot:* aneth *m*; fenouil *m*.

dillydally ['dilidæli] *vi F:* traîner, traînasser; lambiner; (se) baguenauder.

dilute [dai'lju:t] *vtr* diluer; couper (le vin); atténuer (une doctrine); délayer (une couleur). **di'lution** *n* dilution *f*.

dim [dim] 1. *a* (*of light, sight*) faible; (*of room*) sombre; (*of shape*) obscur; (*of memory*) vague; *F:* (*of pers*) stupide, bête; **to grow d.,** (*of light, sight*) baisser; (*of memory*) s'effacer; *F:* **to take a d. view of,** avoir une piètre opinion de 2. *v* (**dimmed**) (a) *vtr* obscurcir (la vue); mettre (une lampe) en veilleuse; ternir (la beauté); troubler (la mémoire) (b) *vi* (*of light, sight*) baisser; (*of outlines*) s'effacer. **'dimly** *adv* faiblement; vaguement. **'dimmer** *n El:* **d. (switch),** interrupteur *m* à gradation de lumière. **'dimness** *n* faiblesse *f* (d'éclairage); obscurité *f* (d'une salle); imprécision *f* (d'un souvenir); *F:* (*of pers*) stupidité *f*. **'dimwit** *n F:* idiot, -ote. **'dim-'witted** *a F:* idiot.

dime [daim] *n NAm:* pièce *f* de dix cents.

dimension [dai'menʃn] *n* dimension *f*.

diminish [di'miniʃ] *vtr* & *i* diminuer. **di'minishing** *a* qui diminue; **d. returns,** rendements décroissants. **di'minutive** 1. *a* & *n Gram:* diminutif (*m*) 2. *a* tout petit; minuscule.

dimple ['dimpl] *n* fossette *f*.

din [din] *n* tapage *m*, vacarme *m*; *esp Sch:* chahut *m*; **what a d.!** quel boucan! **'din 'into** *vtr* **to d. sth i. s.o.,** seriner qch à qn.

dine [dain] *vi* dîner; **to d. out,** dîner en ville, chez des amis; **dining room,** salle à manger; *Rail:* **dining car,** wagon-restaurant *m*. **'diner** *n* 1. (*pers*) dîneur, -euse 2. *NAm:* (a) *Rail:* wagon-restaurant (b) petit restaurant, café *m*.

dinghy ['dingi] *n* (*pl* **dinghies**) youyou *m*; **rubber d.,** canot *m* pneumatique.

dingy ['dindʒi] *a* (**-ier, -iest**) miteux; défraîchi; (*of colour*) terne; sale. **'dinginess** *n* aspect miteux.

dinner ['dinər] *n* dîner *m*; (*lunch*) déjeuner *m*; **public d.,** banquet *m*; **school d.,** repas *m* scolaire; **to be having d.,** to be at the d. table, être à table; **d. jacket** (*NAm:* = **tuxedo**), smoking *m*; **to have, give, a d. party,** avoir, inviter, du monde à dîner; **to go out for, to, d.,** dîner en ville, au restaurant, chez des amis; **d. service,** service de table; **d. time,** l'heure du dîner.

dinosaur ['dainəsɔ:r] *n* dinosaure *m*.

dint [dint] *n* **by d. of,** à force de.

diocese ['daiəsis] *n Ecc:* diocèse *m*. **diocesan** [dai'ɔsisən] *a* diocésain.

dioxide [dai'ɔksaid] *n Ch:* dioxyde *m*.

dip [dip] I. *n* (a) *F:* baignade *f*; **I'm going for a d.,** je vais me baigner (b) inclinaison *f* (du terrain) (c) (**sheep**) **d.,** bain *m* parasiticide (pour moutons) (d) *Cu:* hors-d'œuvre *m* (au fromage); mousse *f* (au poisson). II. *v* (**dipped**) 1. *vtr* (a) plonger; (*into liquid*) tremper; immerger (un métal); baigner (des moutons) (b) baisser (qch); *Aut:* **to d. the headlights,** se mettre en code 2. *vi* plonger; (*of sun, road*) baisser; **to d. into,** feuilleter (un livre); puiser dans (sa poche). **dipped** *a* (phares) code. **'dipper** *n* (a) *DomEc:* louche *f* (b) (*at fairground*) **big d.,** montagnes *fpl* russes (c) *Aut:* **d. (switch)** (*also* **'dipswitch**), basculeur *m* de phares. **'dipstick** *n Aut:* jauge *f* (de niveau) d'huile.

Dip.Ed. *abbr Diploma in Education.*

diphtheria [dif'θiəriə] *n Med:* diphtérie *f*.

diploma [di'ploumə] *n* diplôme *m*.

diplomacy [di'plouməsi] *n* diplomatie *f*. **'diplomat** *n*, **di'plomatist** *n* diplomate *m*. **diplo'matic** *a* diplomatique; (*of pers*) diplomate; **the d. service,** la diplomatie; la carrière. **diplo'matically** *adv* diplomatiquement.

dipsomania [dipsou'meiniə] *n* dipsomanie *f*. **dipso'maniac** *n* dipsomane *mf*.

dire ['daiər] *a* désastreux, affreux; néfaste; **d. necessity,** dure nécessité; **in d. straits,** dans la plus grande détresse.

direct [d(a)i'rekt] 1. *vtr* (a) adresser (une lettre) (**to,** à) (b) conduire (ses affaires); diriger, gérer (une entreprise); guider (qn); attirer (l'attention de qn) (**to,** sur); orienter (ses efforts) (**towards,** vers); *Th: Cin:* mettre (une pièce) en scène; **could you d. me to the station?** pourriez-vous m'indiquer le chemin de la gare? **to d. s.o. to do sth,** ordonner à qn de faire qch; **as directed,** selon les instructions 2. *a* (a) direct; (réponse) catégorique; (*of cause*) immédiat; *El:* (courant) continu; **d. taxation,** contributions directes; *Gram:* **d. object,** complément direct; **to be a d. descendant of s.o.,** descendre de qn en ligne directe; **d. hit,** coup au but (b) (*of pers*) franc 3. *adv* (aller) directement, tout droit; *Tp:* (obtenir un numéro) par l'automatique. **di'rective** *n* directive *f*.

di'rectly 1. adv (a) (aller) directement; (tout) droit; (descendre de qn) en ligne directe (b) absolument; diamétralement (opposé); juste (en face) (c) (parler) franchement (d) (of time) tout de suite, tout à l'heure **2.** conj F: aussitôt que, dès que. **di'rectness** n franchise f.

direction [d(a)i'rekʃn] n (a) direction f, administration f (d'une société) (b) direction, sens m; **in every d.**, en tous sens; **in the d. of**, dans la direction de; **in the opposite d.**, en sens inverse; **you're looking in the wrong d.**, vous ne regardez pas du bon côté; **sense of d.**, sens de l'orientation f; WTel: **d. finder**, radiogoniomètre m (c) usu pl instruction(s) f(pl); **directions for use**, mode m d'emploi; Th: **stage directions**, indications fpl scéniques. **di'rectional** a directionnel.

director [d(a)i'rektər] n directeur, trice (d'une société); gérant, -ante (d'une entreprise); administrateur, -trice; Th: Cin: metteur m en scène; **D. of Public Prosecutions**, approx = chef m de parquet. **di'rectorate** n (conseil m d')administration f. **di'rectory** n (pl -ies) répertoire m (d'adresses); guide m des rues; Tp: annuaire m (des téléphones); Rtm: Bottin m; **d. inquiries**, (service m des) renseignements mpl.

dirge [də:dʒ] n chant m funèbre.

dirt [də:t] n saleté f; boue f; crotte f; (on skin) crasse f; ordure(s) f(pl) (de chien); (of material) to **show the d.**, être salissant; **to treat s.o. like d.**, traiter qn comme un chien; NAm: **d. farmer**, exploitant agricole; **d. road**, chemin de terre; Sp: **d. track**, cendrée f; F: **d. cheap**, à vil prix. **'dirtily** adv salement. **'dirtiness** n saleté f, malpropreté f. **'dirty 1.** a (a) sale; malpropre; crasseux; crotté; (of valves, etc) encrassé; **d. work**, (i) travail salissant (ii) Fig: grosse, sale, besogne; **to get d.**, (se) salir (b) (esprit) cochon; (mot) grossier; **d. old man**, vieux cochon; **d. story**, saleté f; **d. trick**, vilain, sale, tour; F: **to do the d. on s.o.**, jouer un sale coup à qn; F: **to give s.o. a d. look**, regarder qn d'un sale œil **2.** vtr & i (se) salir.

disability [disə'biliti] n (pl disabilities) incapacité f; (physical) infirmité f; Adm: **d. allowance**, pension d'invalidité f. **dis'able** vtr mettre (qn) hors de combat, (une machine) hors de service; estropier (qn). **dis'abled 1.** a infirme; impotent; Adm: invalide **2.** npl **the d.**, les infirmes m; les impotents m; Adm: les invalides m. **dis'ablement** n invalidité.

disadvantage [disəd'vɑ:ntidʒ] n désavantage m; inconvénient m; **at a d.**, au dépourvu; désavantagé; sous un jour désavantageux. **disad'vantaged** a désavantagé. **disadvan'tageous** a désavantageux (to, à).

disagree [disə'gri:] vi (a) être en désaccord, ne pas être d'accord (with, avec); (of figures) ne pas concorder; **to d. with s.o.**, ne pas être du même avis que qn; **I d.**, je ne suis pas de cet avis (b) (quarrel) se brouiller (with s.o., avec qn) (c) (of climate) ne pas convenir (with s.o., à qn); **pork disagrees with him**, il digère mal le porc. **disa'greeable** a désagréable; (of incident) fâcheux; (of pers) désobligeant. **disa'greeably** adv désagréablement. **disa'greement** n (a) (between statements) différence f (b) dé-

saccord m (**with s.o. about sth**, avec qn sur qch); brouille f.

disallow [disə'lau] vtr rejeter; Fb: annuler.

disappear [disə'piər] vi disparaître; **he disappeared in(to) the crowd**, il s'est perdu dans la foule. **disa'ppearance** n disparition f.

disappoint [disə'point] vtr décevoir; désappointer (qn); (after promising) manquer de parole à (qn). **disa'ppointed** a déçu; **I'm d. with, in, you**, vous m'avez déçu. **disa'ppointing** a décevant. **disa'ppointment** n déception f; déboire m.

disapprove [disə'pru:v] vi **to d. of**, désapprouver. **disa'pproval** n désapprobation f; **look of d.**, regard désapprobateur. **disa'pprovingly** adv avec désapprobation.

disarm [dis'ɑ:m] vtr & i désarmer. **dis'armament** n désarmement m. **dis'arming** a désarmant. **dis'armingly** adv **he was d. frank**, il montrait une franchise désarmante.

disarrange [disə'reindʒ] vtr mettre en désordre; déranger.

disarray [disə'rei] n **in d.**, en désordre m; (of troops) en déroute f; (of thoughts) en grand désarroi.

disassociate [disə'souʃieit] vtr dissocier.

disaster [di'zɑ:stər] n désastre m; catastrophe f (de chemin de fer); (by fire, flood) sinistre m; **d. area**, région sinistrée. **di'sastrous** a désastreux. **di'sastrously** adv désastreusement.

disband [dis'bænd] vtr licencier (des troupes); dissoudre (un comité).

disbelieve [disbi'li:v] vtr ne pas croire (à). **disbe'lief** n incrédulité f. **disbe'liever** n incrédule mf.

disc [disk] n disque m; (of cardboard) rondelle f; **identity d.**, plaque f d'identité; **d. jockey**, disc-jockey m; Med: **slipped d.**, hernie discale; Aut: **d. brake**, frein à disque.

discard [dis'kɑ:d] vtr mettre de côté; se défaire de; abandonner (un projet); Cards: se défausser d'(une couleur).

discern [di'sə:n] vtr distinguer, discerner. **di'scernible** a perceptible. **di'scerning** a plein de discernement; (esprit) pénétrant; (goût) délicat. **di'scernment** n discernement m.

discharge 1. n ['distʃɑ:dʒ] (a) décharge f; échappement m (de gaz); déversement m (d'eau); exercice m (d'une fonction); renvoi m (d'un employé); mise f en liberté, libération f (d'un prisonnier) (b) El: décharge; Med: pertes fpl **2.** v [dis'tʃɑ:dʒ] (a) vtr décharger; projecter (de la fumée); déverser (de l'eau); s'acquitter de (sa fonction); congédier (un employé); Mil: réformer (qn); libérer, relaxer (un prisonnier); renvoyer (un malade guéri); réhabiliter (un banqueroutier); **he was discharged from hospital yesterday**, il est sorti de l'hôpital hier (b) vi (of wound) suppurer; (of river) se jeter (**into**, dans).

disciple [di'saipl] n disciple m.

discipline ['disiplin] **1.** n discipline f **2.** vtr discipliner. **discipli'narian** n personne stricte en matière de discipline. **disci'plinary** a disciplinaire.

disclaim [dis'kleim] vtr désavouer. **dis'claimer** n désaveu m.

disclose [dis'klouz] vtr révéler, divulguer. **dis'closure** n révélation f, divulgation f.

disco ['diskou] *n F:* discothèque *f.*

discolour, *NAm:* **-or** [dis'kʌlər] *vtr & i* (se) décolorer. **discolo(u)ration** *n* décoloration *f.*

discomfiture [dis'kʌmfitʃər] *n* embarras *m.*

discomfort [dis'kʌmfət] *n (a)* manque *m* de confort *(b)* malaise *m*, gêne *f.*

disconcert [diskən'sə:t] *vtr* déconcerter. **discon'certing** *a* déconcertant. **discon'certingly** *adv* d'une manière déconcertante.

disconnect [diskə'nekt] *vtr* séparer, détacher, disjoindre; décrocher (des wagons); *El:* débrancher (une radio); couper (l'eau, *Tp:* la ligne). **disco'nnected** *a* détaché; *El:* débranché; *Tp:* coupé; *(of speech)* décousu, sans suite.

disconsolate [dis'kɔnsələt] *a* inconsolable; désolé. **dis'consolately** *adv* d'un air désolé.

discontent [diskən'tent] *n* mécontentement *m.* **discon'tented** *a* mécontent (**with,** de).

discontinue [diskən'tinju:] **1.** *vtr* cesser **2.** *vi* discontinuer, cesser. **discon'tinuous** *a* discontinu.

discord ['diskɔ:d] *n* discorde *f*, désaccord *m*; *Mus:* (i) dissonance *f* (ii) accord dissonant. **dis'cordant** *a* discordant; *Mus:* dissonant.

discotheque ['diskoutek] *n* discothèque *f.*

discount 1. *n* ['diskaunt] remise *f*, rabais *m*; escompte *m*; ristourne *f*; **to give a d.,** faire une remise (**on,** sur) (**at (a) d.,** au rabais; **d. for cash,** escompte au comptant; **d. store, (ware)house,** magasin de demi-gros **2.** *vtr* [dis'kaunt] *(a)* ne pas tenir compte de; faire peu de cas de (l'avis de qn) *(b) Fin:* escompter (un effet).

discourage [dis'kʌridʒ] *vtr* décourager; abattre (qn); **to become discouraged,** se décourager. **dis'couragement** *n (act)* désapprobation *f*, dissuasion *f*; *(state)* découragement *m.* **dis'couraging** *a* décourageant.

discourteous [dis'kə:tiəs] *a* impoli; discourtois. **dis'courteously** *adv* impoliment. **dis'courtesy** *n* impolitesse *f.*

discover [dis'kʌvər] *vtr* découvrir; dénicher; s'apercevoir, se rendre compte (**that,** que). **dis'coverer** *n* découvreur *m.* **dis'covery** *n* découverte *f*; *(find)* trouvaille *f*; **voyage of d.,** voyage d'exploration *f.*

discredit [dis'kredit] **1.** *n (a)* doute *m (b)* discrédit *m* **2.** *vtr (a)* ne pas croire, mettre en doute (une rumeur) *(b)* discréditer. **dis'creditable** *a* peu digne, peu honorable.

discreet [dis'kri:t] *a* discret. **dis'creetly** *adv* discrètement. **dis'cretion** *n* discrétion *f*; **I shall use my d.,** je ferai comme bon me semblera; **age of d.,** âge de raison; **at s.o.'s d.,** à la discrétion de qn; **d. is the better part of valour,** l'essentiel du courage c'est la prudence. **dis'cretionary** *a* discrétionnaire.

discrepancy [dis'krepənsi] *n* désaccord *m*; divergence *f* (de témoignage).

discrete [dis'kri:t] *a Tchn:* discret.

discriminate [dis'krimineit] **1.** *vtr* distinguer (**from,** de) **2.** *vi* distinguer, établir une distinction (**between,** entre); **to d. in favour of s.o.,** faire des distinctions en faveur de qn. **dis'criminating** *a (of pers)* plein de discernement; judicieux; (acheteur) avisé; (goût) fin; *Adm:* (tarif) différentiel. **discrimi'nation** *n (a)* discernement *m*; jugement *m*; **man of d.,** homme judicieux *(b)* distinction *f*, discrimination *f.*

discus ['diskəs] *n Sp:* disque *m.*

discuss [dis'kʌs] *vtr* discuter, débattre (un problème); délibérer (une question); parler, discuter, de (qn). **dis'cussion** *n* discussion *f*; **under d.,** en discussion.

disdain [dis'dein] **1.** *n* dédain *m* **2.** *vtr* dédaigner. **dis'dainful** *a* dédaigneux. **dis'dainfully** *adv* dédaigneusement.

disease [di'zi:z] *n* maladie *f.* **di'seased** *a* malade.

disembark [disem'ba:k] *vtr & i* débarquer. **disembar'kation** *n* débarquement *m.*

disembodied [disim'bɔdid] *a* désincarné.

disenchantment [disin'tʃɑ:ntmənt] *n* désenchantement *m*; désillusion *f.* **disen'chantea** *a* désenchanté; désillusionné.

disengage [disin'geidʒ] *vtr* dégager; *MecE:* débrayer. **disen'gaged** *a* libre, inoccupé.

disentangle [disin'tæŋgl] *vtr* démêler; débrouiller; dénouer (une intrigue).

disfavour, *NAm:* **-or** [dis'feivər] *n* défaveur *f* (**with s.o.,** auprès de qn); **to fall into d.,** tomber en disgrâce.

disfigure [dis'figər] *vtr* défigurer. **dis'figurement** *n* défigurement *m.*

disgorge [dis'gɔ:dʒ] *vtr* dégorger; rendre.

disgrace [dis'greis] **1.** *n (a)* disgrâce *f*; **in d.,** en disgrâce, en pénitence *f (b)* honte *f*, déshonneur *m*; **to be a d. to one's family,** être la honte de sa famille **2.** *vtr* déshonorer; **to d. oneself,** se conduire indignement. **dis'graced** *a (of pers)* disgracié. **dis'graceful** *a* honteux; scandaleux. **dis'gracefully** *adv* honteusement; scandaleusement.

disgruntled [dis'grʌntld] *a* contrarié, mécontent (**at,** de); (humeur) maussade.

disguise [dis'gaiz] **1.** *n* déguisement *m*; **in d.,** déguisé **2.** *vtr* déguiser (**as,** en); masquer (une odeur); dissimuler (ses sentiments); **there is no disguising the fact that,** il faut avouer que.

disgust [dis'gʌst] **1.** *n* dégoût *m* (**at, for,** pour); **in d.,** écœuré, dégoûté **2.** *vtr* dégoûter; écœurer (qn). **dis'gusted** *a* dégoûté, écœuré (**at, by, de, par**). **dis'gusting** *a* dégoûtant; répugnant; écœurant.

dish [diʃ] **1.** *n (a)* plat *m* (à poisson); *Tchn:* récipient *m*; *Phot:* cuvette *f*; **vegetable d.,** légumier *m*; **to wash, do, the dishes,** faire la vaisselle *(b)* plat (de viande); mets *m* **2.** *vtr F:* ruiner. **'dishcloth** *n* torchon *m* (à laver la vaisselle); lavette *f.* **'dish 'out** *vtr (a)* servir (des légumes) *(b) F:* distribuer. **'dishpan** *n NAm:* (*Br =* **washing up bowl**) bassine *f* (à vaisselle). **'dish 'up** *vtr (a)* mettre sur un plat, servir (de la viande) *(b) F:* sortir tout un tas (d'excuses). **'dishwasher** *n* lave-vaisselle *m.* **'dishwater** *n* eau *f* de vaisselle; *F:* (*tasteless coffee*) lavasse *f.* **'dishy** *a F:* beau, sexy.

dishearten [dis'ha:tn] *vtr* décourager, abattre; **to be disheartened,** se décourager. **dis'heartening** *a* décourageant.

dishevelled [di'ʃevəld] *a* échevelé; (vêtements) en désordre, froissés.

dishonest [dis'ɔnist] *a* malhonnête; peu honnête. **dis'honestly** *adv* malhonnêtement. **dis'honesty** *n* malhonnêteté *f.*

dishonour, *NAm:* **-or** [dis'ɔnər] **1.** *n* déshonneur *m* **2.** *vtr* déshonorer; manquer à (sa parole); **dis-**

honoured cheque, chèque impayé. **dis'honour-able,** *NAm:* **-orable** *a* (*of pers*) sans honneur; (*of action*) honteux. **dis'honourably,** *NAm:* **-orably** *adv* avec déshonneur.

disillusion [disi'lu:ʒn] 1. *n* désillusion *f* 2. *vtr* désillusionner, désabuser, désenchanter. **disi'llusionment** *n* désillusionnement *m*.

disincentive [disin'sentiv] *n* facteur décourageant, qui décourage (le travail).

disinclination [disinkli'neiʃn] *n* répugnance *f*, aversion *f* (**for,** à, pour). **disin'clined** *a* peu disposé, peu enclin (**to do,** à faire).

disinfect [disin'fekt] *vtr* désinfecter. **disin'fect-ant** *a* & *n* désinfectant (*m*). **disin'fection** *n* désinfection *f*.

disingenuous [disin'dʒenjuəs] *a* peu sincère, sans franchise; déloyal; faux.

disinherit [disin'herit] *vtr* déshériter.

disintegrate [dis'intigreit] *vtr & i* (se) désintégrer. **disinte'gration** *n* désintégration *f*.

disinterested [dis'intristid] *a* (*a*) (*unbiased*) désintéressé (*b*) (*uninterested*) indifférent. **dis-'interestedly** *adv* avec (i) désintéressement (ii) indifférence.

disjointed [dis'dʒɔintid] *a* (discours sans suite; (style) décousu.

disk [disk] *n NAm:* = **disc.**

dislike [dis'laik] 1. *n* aversion *f*, répugnance *f* (**to, of, for,** pour); **to take a d. to,** prendre en grippe 2. *vtr* ne pas aimer; détester; **I don't d. him,** il ne me déplaît pas.

dislocate ['disləkeit] *vtr* (*a*) *Med:* disloquer, luxer, déboîter (un membre); **to d. one's shoulder,** se disloquer l'épaule; **to d. one's jaw,** se décrocher la mâchoire (*b*) désorganiser (des affaires); bouleverser (un projet). **dislo'cation** *n* (*a*) *Med:* dislocation *f*, luxation *f*, déboîtement *m* (d'un membre) (*b*) désorganisation *f* (des affaires); bouleversement *m* (d'un projet).

dislodge [dis'lɔdʒ] *vtr* déloger; détacher; **to become dislodged,** se détacher.

disloyalty [dis'lɔiəlti] *n* infidélité *f*, déloyauté *f*. **dis'loyal** *a* infidèle; déloyal. **dis'loyally** *adv* infidèlement, déloyalement.

dismal ['dizml] *a* sombre; lugubre; (échec) lamentable. **'dismally** *adv* lugubrement; (échouer) lamentablement.

dismantle [dis'mæntl] *vtr* démonter.

dismay [dis'mei] 1. *n* consternation *f*; **in d.,** (d'un air) consterné 2. *vtr* consterner.

dismember [dis'membər] *vtr* démembrer.

dismiss [dis'mis] *vtr* (*a*) congédier, licencier, renvoyer (un employé); destituer (un fonctionnaire) (*b*) congédier (qn); dissoudre (une assemblée); *Mil:* faire rompre les rangs aux (troupes); **d.!** rompez (les rangs)! (*c*) chasser (qch de ses pensées); quitter, abandonner (un sujet de conversation); écarter (une proposition); *Jur:* rejeter (une demande); **to d. a charge, a case,** rendre une ordonnance de non-lieu, une fin de non-recevoir. **dis'missal** *n* congédiement *m*, licenciement *m*, renvoi *m* (d'un employé); destitution *f* (d'un fonctionnaire); rejet *m* (d'une demande).

dismount [dis'maunt] 1. *vi* descendre (de cheval, de

vélo); mettre pied à terre 2. *vtr* démonter (un cavalier).

disobey [disə'bei] *vtr* désobéir à. **diso'bedience** *n* désobéissance *f* (**to,** à); **civil d.,** résistance passive. **diso'bedient** *a* désobéissant (**to,** à).

disobliging [disə'blaidʒiŋ] *a* désobligeant.

disorder [dis'ɔ:dər] *n* (*a*) désordre *m*, confusion *f*; dérangement *m* (**in, de**); **in d.,** en désordre (*b*) (*riot*) désordre(s) *m(pl)* (*c*) *Med:* troubles *mpl*, affection *f* (de digestion). **dis'ordered** *a* en désordre; (combat) désordonné; *Med:* (foie) malade. **dis'orderly** *a* en désordre; (*of pers, behaviour*) désordonné; (*of mob*) turbulent, tumultueux.

disorganize [dis'ɔ:gənaiz] *vtr* désorganiser; **to become disorganized,** se désorganiser. **disorgani'zation** *n* désorganisation *f*.

disorientate, *esp NAm:* **disorient** [dis-'ɔ:riənt(eit)] *vtr* désorienter.

disown [dis'oun] *vtr* désavouer (qch); renier (qn).

disparage [dis'pæridʒ] *vtr* dénigrer. **dis'parage-ment** *n* dénigrement *m*. **dis'paraging** *a* (terme) de dénigrement; (*of remark*) désobligeant, peu flatteur. **dis'paragingly** *adv* **to speak d. of s.o.,** parler de qn en termes peu flatteurs.

disparate ['dispərət] *a* disparate.

dispassionate [dis'pæʃənət] *a* (*a*) calme (*b*) impartial. **dis'passionately** *adv* (*a*) avec calme (*b*) impartialement.

dispatch [di'spætʃ] 1. *n* (*pl* **dispatches**) (*a*) expédition *f* (de qch); envoi *m*; *Com:* **d. note,** bulletin d'expédition (*b*) dépêche *f*; *Mil:* **mentioned in dispatches,** cité à l'ordre *m* du jour; *Adm:* **d. box,** boîte à documents; **d. rider,** estafette *f* (*c*) promptitude *f* 2. *vtr* (*a*) expédier; envoyer; dépêcher (un courrier) (*b*) tuer, achever (une bête).

dispel [dis'pel] *vtr* (**dispelled**) chasser, dissiper.

dispense [dis'pens] *vtr* dispenser, distribuer (des aumônes); administrer (la justice); *Pharm:* préparer (des médicaments); exécuter (une ordonnance); **dispensing chemist,** pharmacien, -ienne (diplômé(e)). **dis'pense 'with** *vtr* se passer de. **dis'pensary** *n* (*a*) pharmacie *f* (d'hôpital) (*b*) officine *f* (de pharmacie). **dispen'sation** *n* dispense *f* (**from, de**). **dis'penser** *n* (*a*) pharmacien, -ienne (*b*) (*machine*) distributeur *m* (de lessive); **cash d.,** distributeur de billets.

disperse [dis'pə:s] *vtr & i* (se) disperser; (se) dissiper. **dis'persal** *n*, **dis'persion** *n* dispersion *f*.

dispirited [di'spiritid] *a* découragé, abattu.

displace [dis'pleis] *vtr* (*a*) déplacer; **displaced person,** personne déplacée (*b*) remplacer (**by,** par). **dis-'placement** *n* (*a*) déplacement *m* (*b*) remplacement *m* (**by,** par).

display [di'splei] 1. *n* (*a*) étalage *m* (de marchandises); manifestation *f* (de colère); déploiement *m* (de force, d'amabilité); *Elcs:* affichage *m* (de données); **air d.,** fête *f* aéronautique; **d. window, case,** vitrine *f*; **d. cabinet, unit,** présentoir *m* (*b*) (*ostentation*) étalage (de luxe); parade *f*, apparat *m* 2. *vtr* (*a*) étaler, exposer (des marchandises); afficher (un avis); manifester (un sentiment); faire preuve de (courage); faire parade de (ses bijoux) (*b*) *Elcs:* afficher, visualiser (des données).

displease [dis'pli:z] *vtr* déplaire à (qn); contrarier,

mécontenter (qn); **displeased at, with,** mécontent de.
dis'pleasing a déplaisant, désagréable (to, à).
displeasure [dis'pleʒər] n mécontentement m; déplaisir m.
dispose [dis'pouz] vtr (a) disposer, arranger (b) disposer (s.o. **to do sth,** qn à faire qch). **dis'posable** a (a) (revenue, etc) disponible (b) (serviette) à jeter; (emballage) perdu. **dis'posal** n (a) enlèvement m (d'ordures); désamorçage m (d'une bombe); **(waste) d. unit,** broyeur m (d'ordures) (b) **at s.o.'s d.,** à la disposition de qn; **to have sth at one's d.,** disposer de qch. **dis'posed** a disposé; **well d. to(wards),** bien disposé à, bien intentionné envers. **dis'pose 'of** vtr se débarrasser de; tuer, expédier (qn); régler (une affaire); Com: écouler (des marchandises); céder (son fonds); **to be disposed of,** à vendre.
dispo'sition n (a) (arrangement) disposition f (b) (of pers) caractère m, naturel m (c) inclination f, penchant m, tendance f **(to,** à).
dispossess [dispə'zes] vtr déposséder **(of,** de).
disproportionate [dispra'pɔ:ʃənət] a disproportionné **(to,** à). **dispro'portionately** adv d'une façon disproportionnée.
disprove [dis'pru:v] vtr réfuter; démontrer la fausseté d'(une déclaration).
dispute [dis'pju:t] **1.** n (a) contestation f, débat m; **the matter in, under, d.,** l'affaire dont il s'agit; l'affaire contestée, Jur: en litige; **beyond d.,** incontestable (b) querelle f, dispute f; Jur: litige m; Ind: conflit m (du travail) **2.** v (a) vi se disputer; **to d. with s.o. about sth,** débattre qch avec qn (b) vtr contester (une affirmation). **dis'putable** a contestable.
disqualify [dis'kwɔlifai] vtr rendre incapable **(from (doing), sth,** de faire qch); Sp: disqualifier (qn); **to d. s.o. from driving,** retirer le permis de conduire à qn. **disqualifi'cation** n (cause f d')incapacité f; Sp: etc: disqualification f.
disquieting [dis'kwaiətiŋ] a inquiétant.
disregard [disri'ga:d] **1.** n indifférence f **(for,** à) **2.** vtr ne tenir aucun compte de; négliger; passer outre à (une interdiction).
disrepair [disri'pɛər] n délabrement m; **to fall into d.,** se délabrer; tomber en ruine(s); **in (a state of) d.,** délabré.
disrepute [disri'pju:t] n déshonneur m; **to bring sth into d.,** discréditer qch. **disreputable** [dis'repjutəbl] a (of action) honteux; (of pers) de mauvaise réputation; (of clothes) minable; (quartier) mal famé.
disrespect [disri'spekt] n manque m de respect **(for,** envers). **disre'spectful** a irrespectueux, irrévérencieux. **disre'spectfully** adv sans respect.
disrupt [dis'rʌpt] vtr désorganiser (une administration); interrompre (une réunion); perturber (les services publics). **dis'ruption** n interruption f; perturbation f. **dis'ruptive** a perturbateur; (élève) turbulent.
dissatisfaction ['disætis'fækʃn] n mécontentement m **(with, at,** de). **dis'satisfied** a mécontent **(with, at,** de).
dissect [di'sekt] vtr disséquer. **di'ssection** n dissection f.
dissemble [di'sembl] vtr & i dissimuler.

disseminate [di'semineit] vtr disséminer.
dissension [di'senʃn] n dissension f.
dissent [di'sent] **1.** n dissentiment m; Ecc: dissidence f **2.** vi différer **(from s.o. about sth,** de qn sur qch); Ecc: être dissident. **di'ssenter** n dissident, -ente.
dissertation [disə'teiʃn] n dissertation f.
disservice [di'sɔ:vis] n mauvais service (rendu); **to do s.o. a d.,** rendre un mauvais service à qn.
dissident ['disidənt] a & n dissident, -ente. **'dissidence** n dissidence f.
dissimilar [di'similər] a dissemblable **(to,** à, de); différent **(to,** de).
dissimulate [di'simjuleit] vtr & i dissimuler. **dissimu'lation** n dissimulation f.
dissipate ['disipeit] vtr disperser; gaspiller (une fortune). **'dissipated** a (of pers) dissipé, débauché; (of life) désordonné. **dissi'pation** n (a) dissipation f; gaspillage m (d'une fortune) (b) (of pers) débauche f.
dissociate [di'souʃieit] vtr dissocier **(from,** de); **to d. oneself,** se désolidariser **(from,** de). **dissoci'ation** n dissociation f.
dissolute ['disəlu:t] a dissolu; (of pers) débauché; **to lead a d. life,** vivre dans la débauche.
dissolve [di'zɔlv] **1.** vtr (faire) dissoudre **2.** vi se dissoudre; fondre; **to d. into tears,** fondre en larmes. **disso'lution** n dissolution f.
dissuade [di'sweid] vtr **to d. s.o. from doing sth,** dissuader qn de faire qch. **di'ssuasion** n dissuasion f.
distance ['distəns] n distance f; **at a d. of 10 km,** à une distance de 10 km; **it's within walking d.,** on peut y aller à pied; **seen from a d.,** vu de loin; **in the d.,** dans le lointain, au loin; **to keep s.o. at a d.,** tenir qn à distance; **to keep one's d.,** garder ses distances. **'distant** a (a) éloigné; lointain; **to have a d. view of sth,** voir qch de loin; **in the d. future,** dans un avenir lointain (b) (of pers) réservé, froid, distant. **'distantly** adv (a) (vu) de loin; **d. related,** d'une parenté éloignée (b) (observer) avec réserve; froidement.
distaste [dis'teist] n dégoût m **(for,** de); répugnance f **(for,** pour). **dis'tasteful** a désagréable; déplaisant **(to,** à).
distemper¹ [dis'tempər] **1.** n détrempe f, badigeon m **2.** vtr badigeonner (un mur).
distemper² n maladie f des jeunes chiens.
distend [dis'tend] vtr & i (se) distendre.
distil [di'stil] vtr (distilled) distiller. **dis'tiller** n distillateur m. **dis'tillery** n distillerie f.
distinct [di'stiŋkt] a (a) distinct, différent **(from,** de); **to keep two things d.,** distinguer entre deux choses (b) distinct, net; (souvenir) clair, précis; (ordre) formel; (of smell) marqué. **dis'tinction** n distinction f **(between,** entre); **to gain d.,** se distinguer; Sch: **with d.,** (reçu) avec mention f. **dis'tinctive** a distinctif. **dis'tinctly** adv (a) distinctement, clairement; **I told him d.,** je le lui ai dit expressément (b) indéniablement, décidément.
distinguish [di'stiŋgwiʃ] **1.** vtr (a) distinguer, discerner (b) distinguer, différencier **(from,** de); **to d. oneself by,** se distinguer, se signaler, par; **distinguishing mark,** signe distinctif, (on passport) particulier **2.** vi faire une distinction **(between,** entre).

distort 101 do

di'stinguishable *a* (a) perceptible; reconnaissable (b) qui se distingue (from, de). di'stinguished *a* distingué; (écrivain) de distinction; (personnage) de marque.

distort [di'stɔːt] *vtr* déformer; tordre; (of anger) décomposer (le visage); fausser, dénaturer (les faits); distorted ideas, idées biscornues. di'stortion *n* distorsion *f*; déformation *f*; altération *f* (des traits).

distract [di'strækt] *vtr* distraire (from, de). di'stracted *a* affolé, éperdu. di'stractedly *adv* comme un fou; éperdument. di'stracting *a* qui distrait l'attention; qui dérange. di'straction *n* (a) distraction *f*; divertissement *m*; interruption *f* (b) affolement *m*; to drive s.o. to d., rendre qn fou; to love s.o. to d., aimer qn éperdument.

distraught [di'strɔːt] *a* angoissé; affolé.

distress [dis'tres] 1. *n* (a) détresse *f*; angoisse *f*; bouleversement *m*; (poverty) misère *f*; in d., dans la peine (b) détresse, embarras *m*; in d., (navire) en détresse, en perdition; d. signal, signal de détresse 2. *vtr* faire de la peine à, affliger, chagriner (qn). dis'tressed *a* affligé, désolé; bouleversé. dis'tressing *a* affligeant, pénible.

distribute [dis'tribjuːt] *vtr* distribuer; répartir. distri'bution *n* distribution *f*; répartition *f*. di'stributive *a* distributif. di'stributor *n* (a) distributeur, -trice (b) Com: concessionnaire *mf* (d'un produit) (c) El: distributeur *m*; Aut: delco *m* (Rtm).

district ['distrikt] *n* région *f*; territoire *m*; (in town) quartier *m*; (in city) arrondissement *m*; Adm: district *m*, secteur *m*; circonscription électorale; Com: d. manager, directeur régional; d. nurse, infirmière visiteuse.

distrust [dis'trʌst] 1. *n* méfiance *f*; défiance *f* 2. *vtr* se méfier, se défier, de. dis'trustful *a* méfiant, défiant (of, de).

disturb [di'stɜːb] *vtr* déranger; troubler (qn, de l'eau); inquiéter (qn); agiter, remuer (une surface); please don't d. yourself! ne vous dérangez pas! di'sturbance *n* trouble(s) *m(pl)*; dérangement *m* (de qn); bruit *m*, tapage *m*; émeute *f*; to cause, create, a d., troubler l'ordre public. di'sturbing *a* inquiétant, troublant.

disuse [dis'juːs] *n* désuétude *f*; to fall into d., tomber en désuétude. dis'used *a* hors d'usage; (of church) désaffecté; (of mine) abandonné.

ditch [ditʃ] 1. *n* (pl ditches) fossé *m*; rigole *f* (d'écoulement) 2. *v* (a) *vtr* F: se débarrasser de; abandonner (b) *vtr* & *i* to d. (an aircraft), faire un amerrissage forcé; amerrir.

dither ['diðər] F: 1. *n* to be all of a d., être tout agité, dans tous ses états 2. *vi* hésiter; stop dithering! décide-toi!

ditto ['ditou] *n* idem; de même.

divan [di'væn] *n* (a) divan *m* (b) d. (bed), divan-lit *m*, pl divans-lits; lit *m* divan.

dive [daiv] 1. *n* (a) plongeon *m*; (of submarine) plongée *f*; (of aircraft) piqué *m* (b) F: bouge *m* 2. *vi* (pt dived, NAm: dove [douv]) plonger (into, dans); (of aircraft) piquer, descendre en piqué; to d. head first, piquer une tête (into, dans); to d. for pearls, pêcher des perles; to d. into a doorway, se précipiter dans une entrée; diving bell, cloche à plonger;

diving suit, scaphandre *m*. 'dive-bomb *vtr* attaquer en piqué. 'dive-bombing *n* attaque *f* en piqué. 'diver *n* (a) plongeur *m* (b) scaphandrier *m*. 'divingboard *n* plongeoir *m*.

diverge [dai'vɜːdʒ] *vi* diverger, s'écarter. di'vergence *n* divergence *f*. di'vergent, di'verging *a* divergent.

diverse [dai'vɜːs] *a* divers, différent; varié. diversifi'cation *n* diversification *f*. di'versify *vi* diversifier. di'versity *n* diversité *f*.

diversion [dai'vɜːʃn] *n* (a) déviation *f* (de la circulation); détournement *m* (d'une route); dérivation *f* (d'un cours d'eau, El: du courant) (b) diversion *f* (de l'esprit); to create a d., faire diversion (c) divertissement *m*, distraction *f*. di'versionary *a* destiné à faire diversion; Mil: (manœuvre) de diversion.

divert [d(a)i'vɜːt] *vtr* (a) détourner; écarter (un coup); dévier (la circulation); dériver (un cours d'eau); dérouter (un navire); distraire (l'attention de qn) (b) divertir, amuser.

divide [di'vaid] I. *n* ligne *f* de partage. II. *v* 1. *vtr* (a) diviser (into, en; by, par) (b) partager, répartir (among, entre); we d. the work among us, nous nous partageons le travail (c) séparer (from, de) (d) désunir (une famille) 2. *vi* se diviser, se partager (into, en); (of road) bifurquer; Parl: aller aux voix; 3 divides into 9, neuf est divisible par trois. di'vided *a* divisé; partagé; (peuple) désuni; Cl: d. skirt, jupe-culotte *f*. 'dividend *n* dividende *m*. di'viding *a* (ligne) de démarcation; (mur) mitoyen.

divine[1] [di'vain] *a* (a) divin (b) F: beau, admirable; (endroit) charmant. di'vinely *adv* divinement. di'vinity [-'viniti] *n* (a) divinité *f*; dieu *m* (b) Sch: théologie *f*.

divine[2] *vtr* deviner (l'avenir); prédire. di'viner *n* water d., radiesthésiste *mf*; sourcier, -ière. di'vining *n* water d., radiesthésie *f*; d. rod, baguette de sourcier.

division [di'viʒn] *n* (a) division *f*; partage *m* (into, en); répartition *f* (b) Parl: vote *m*. di'visible [di'vizibl] *a* divisible (by, par). di'visive [di'vaisiv] *a* qui sème le désaccord. di'visor *n* Mth: diviseur *m*.

divorce [di'vɔːs] 1. *n* divorce *m* 2. *vtr* divorcer d'avec (qn); isoler, séparer (deux idées); he wants to get divorced, il veut divorcer. divor'cee [-'siː] *n* divorcé, -ée.

divulge [d(a)i'vʌldʒ] *vtr* divulguer.

DIY *abbr* do-it-yourself, bricolage *m*.

dizziness ['dizinis] *n* étourdissement *m*, vertige(s) *m(pl)*. 'dizzily *adv* (marcher) avec une sensation de vertige; (monter) vertigineusement. 'dizzy *a* (-ier, -iest) pris de vertige; (of height, speed) vertigineux; to feel d., avoir le vertige; to make s.o. d., donner le vertige à, étourdir, qn.

DJ *abbr* (a) dinner jacket (b) disc jockey.

do[1] [duː] *v* (does; did; done) I. *n* F: (a) soirée *f*; réception *f* (b) it's a poor do! c'est plutôt minable! come on, fair dos! dis donc, sois juste! (c) the dos and don'ts, ce qui se fait et ce qui ne se fait pas. II. *vtr* 1. faire; to do again, refaire; I won't do it again, je ne le ferai plus; what do you do (for a living)? qu'est-ce que vous faites (dans la vie)? he did brilliantly at his exam, il a réussi brillamment (son examen); Sch:

he's doing medicine, il fait (de) la médecine; the car was doing sixty, la voiture faisait du soixante; are you doing anything tomorrow? avez-vous quelque chose en vue pour demain? what are you doing? (i) qu'est-ce que vous faites? (ii) que devenez-vous? to do 10 years (in prison), faire 10 ans de prison; it isn't the done thing, it isn't done, cela ne se fait pas; I shall do nothing of the sort, no such thing, je n'en ferai rien; what's to be done? que faire? what can I do for you? en quoi puis-je vous être utile? to do sth for s.o., rendre (un) service à qn; F: this music does nothing for me, cette musique ne me dit rien; it can't be done, cela n'est pas possible; well done! bravo! très bien! F: that's done it! ça y est! she did nothing but cry, elle n'a fait que pleurer; F: nothing doing! rien à faire! ça ne prend pas! 2. (a) faire (une chambre, un calcul, les cheveux à qn); to do s.o.'s, one's, hair, coiffer qn, se coiffer (b) (faire) cuire (la viande); well done, (steak) bien cuit; done to a turn, (cuit) à point (c) F: visiter, faire (un musée) (d) F: (cheat) escroquer, rouler, avoir (qn); to do s.o. out of sth, soutirer qch à qn, refaire qn de qch (e) F: (of police) prendre, épingler (qn); to be, get, done for speeding, se faire paumer pour excès de vitesse (f) F: they do you very well here, on mange très bien ici; to do oneself well, faire bonne chère 3. (a) (after a bargain made) done! entendu! d'accord! (b) to have done, avoir fini; the work is done, le travail est fait, fini (c) how do you do? enchanté (de faire votre connaissance); to be doing well, aller bien; how are you doing? comment ça va? he's a young man who will do well, c'est un garçon qui réussira 4. (suffice) that will do, (i) c'est bien (ii) cela suffit; en voilà assez! this room will do for the office, cette pièce ira bien comme bureau; that won't do, cela ne fera pas l'affaire, n'ira pas du tout; that will do me, cela fera mon affaire. III. verb substitute 1. why do you act as you do? pourquoi agir comme vous le faites? as their fathers did, comme (le faisaient) leurs pères; he writes better than I do, il écrit mieux que moi 2. may I open these letters?—please do, puis-je ouvrir ces lettres?—je vous en prie! did you see him?—I did, l'avez-vous vu?—oui (je l'ai vu); I like coffee; do you? j'aime le café; et vous? you like him, don't you? vous l'aimez, n'est-ce pas? you do love me, don't you? tu m'aimes pas vrai? don't! ne faites pas cela! 3. you like Paris? so do I, vous aimez Paris? moi aussi; neither do I, moi non plus. IV. v aux 1. (emphasis) he 'did go, il y est bien allé; why don't you work?—I 'do work! pourquoi ne travaillez-vous pas?—mais si, je travaille! 'did he really, indeed? non vraiment? il a fait ça? 'do sit down, asseyez-vous donc! 'do shut up! voulez-vous bien vous taire! 2. (actual form in questions and negative statements) do you see him? le voyez-vous? (est-ce que) vous le voyez? we do not know, nous ne le savons pas; don't do it! n'en faites rien! he didn't laugh, il n'a pas ri. do a'way 'with vtr supprimer; abolir (un usage). 'do 'by vtr F: to do well by s.o., bien agir envers qn; he's (been) hard done by, on s'est très mal conduit envers lui. 'doer n F: personne active, dynamique. 'do 'for vtr (a) F: faire le ménage de (qn) (b) P: tuer, faire son affaire à (qn); F: done f., (i) perdu, fichu (ii) (tired) éreinté (c) what will you do f. food? qu'est-ce que

vous allez faire pour avoir de quoi manger? 'do-'gooder n F: Pej: faiseur, -euse, de bonnes œuvres. 'do 'in vtr P: tuer, faire son affaire à (qn); F: done in, éreinté, crevé. 'doing n this is her d., c'est elle qui a fait cela; that takes some d., ce n'est pas facile; cela ne se fait pas en un tour de main. 'doings F: 1. n machin m, truc m 2. npl faits mpl et gestes mpl (de qn); allées fpl et venues fpl (chez qn). do-it-your'self n bricolage m; do-it-y. enthusiast, bricoleur, - euse, passionné(e). 'do 'out vtr faire, nettoyer (à fond) (une pièce). 'do 'up vtr (a) faire, ficeler (un paquet); emballer (des marchandises); fermer, boutonner, agrafer (un vêtement) (b) remettre (qch) à neuf; réparer; to do oneself up, se faire beau. 'do 'with vtr (a) what have you done w. my pen? qu'est-ce que tu as fait de mon stylo? she didn't know what to do w. herself, elle ne savait pas quoi faire (b) I don't want (to have) anything to do w. him, je ne veux pas avoir affaire à lui; to have nothing to do w., n'être pour rien dans, ne rien à voir avec, ne rien faire à (qch); it's (something) to do w. computers, il s'agit des ordinateurs; he's had a lot to do w. it, il y est pour beaucoup (c) it's all over and done w., c'est fini, tout ça! (d) I could do w. a cup of tea, je prendrais bien une tasse de thé (e) F: I can't do w. him, it, je ne peux pas le supporter. 'do with'out vtr se passer de.

do² [dou] n Mus: do m, ut m.

doc [dɔk] n F: docteur m, médecin m; toubib m.

docile ['dousail] a docile. do'cility n docilité f.

dock¹ [dɔk] n Bot: patience f.

dock² vtr couper (la queue à un chien); diminuer (un salaire); retenir, faire une retenue d'(une somme) (from, sur).

dock³ 1. n bassin m (d'un port); pl docks mpl; dry d., cale sèche; ship in dry d., navire en radoub m; F: (of car) in d., en réparation f 2. vtr & i (faire) entrer au bassin, aux docks; Space: (s')arrimer. 'docker n docker m. 'docking n mise f, entrée f, au bassin, aux docks; Space: arrimage m. 'dockyard n chantier naval; naval d., arsenal m maritime.

dock⁴ n Jur: banc m des accusés, des prévenus.

docket ['dɔkit] n étiquette f, fiche f; récépissé m (de douane).

doctor ['dɔktər] 1. n (a) Sch: docteur m (of Laws, en droit; of Science, ès sciences) (b) Med: docteur, médecin m; woman d., femme médecin, docteur; she's a d., elle est médecin 2. vtr (a) soigner (un malade) (b) châtrer (un animal) (c) falsifier, truquer (des comptes); frelater (du vin).

doctrine ['dɔktrin] n doctrine f. doctri'naire a doctrinaire. doc'trinal a doctrinal.

document 1. n ['dɔkjumənt] document m; pl dossier m (d'une affaire); d. case, porte-documents m 2. vtr [-ment] documenter. docu'mentary a & n (pl documentaries) documentaire (m). documen'tation n documentation f.

dodder ['dɔdər] vi F: trembloter; marcher d'un pas branlant. 'dodderer n F: gâteux, -euse. 'doddering, 'doddery a F: tremblant, branlant; (of pers) gâteux, gaga.

dodge [dɔdʒ] 1. n (a) Sp: etc: esquive f (b) F: ruse f, truc m 2. v (a) vi se jeter de côté; sauter (behind, derrière) (b) vtr esquiver (un coup); éviter; escamoter (une difficulté). 'dodgem n F: d. (car), auto tamponneuse. 'dodgy a (-ier, -iest) F: risqué; (of situation) épineux, délicat; (of chair) branlant.

doe [dou] n (of deer) biche f; (of tame rabbit) lapine f; (of wild rabbit, hare) hase f. 'doeskin n peau f de daim.

DOE abbr Department of the Environment.

does [dʌz, dəz] see do¹ II.

dog [dɔg] 1. n chien, f chienne; guard d., chien de garde; F: lucky d.! veinard! P: dirty d., sale type m; d. racing, F: the dogs, courses fpl de lévriers; F: to go to the dogs, gâcher sa vie; (of business) aller à la ruine; d. show, exposition canine; d. biscuit, biscuit pour chiens; d. collar, (i) collier de chien (ii) F: faux col (d'ecclésiastique); F: to lead a d.'s life, mener une vie de chien; F: not to have a d.'s chance, ne pas avoir l'ombre d'une chance; it's a case of d. eat d., c'est un cas où les loups se mangent entre eux; F: dressed up like a d.'s dinner, vachement bien fringué 2. vtr (dogged) suivre (qn) à la piste; to d. s.o.'s footsteps, talonner qn; dogged by, poursuivi par (la malchance). 'dog-eared a (é)corné. 'dogfight n F: combat aérien (entre chasseurs). dogged ['dɔgid] a obstiné; résolu; tenace. 'doggedly adv avec ténacité; opiniâtrement. 'doggedness n obstination f; courage m tenace. 'doggo adv F: to lie d., rester coi; faire le mort. 'doggone(d) a NAm: F: sacré. 'doggy, -ie n (pl -gies) F: chien; toutou m. 'dog(gy)-paddle (i) n nage f (ii) vi nager, à la chien. 'doghouse n F: in the d., en disgrâce, mal en cour. 'dogleg n coude m (dans un chemin). 'dogsbody n (pl -ies) F: factotum m, bonne f à tout faire. 'dog-'tired a F: éreinté, claqué.

doggerel ['dɔgərəl] n vers mpl de mirliton.

dogma ['dɔgmə] n dogme m. dog'matic a dogmatique; autoritaire. dog'matically adv d'un ton autoritaire.

doh [dou] n Mus: do m, ut m.

doldrums ['dɔldrəmz] npl F: to be in the d., avoir le cafard; (of business) être dans le marasme.

dole [doul] n indemnité f de chômage; to go on the d., s'inscrire au chômage. 'dole out vtr distribuer au compte-gouttes.

doleful ['doulful] a lugubre; (cri) douloureux; (of pers) triste. 'dolefully adv lugubrement; tristement.

doll ['dɔl] n poupée f; to play with dolls, jouer à la poupée; d.'s house, NAm: 'dollhouse n maison f de poupée. 'doll 'up vtr to d. oneself up, se pomponner, se faire beau. 'dolly n F: (a) poupée (b) d. (bird), jeune fille; belle poupée.

dollar ['dɔlər] n dollar m; F: you can bet your bottom d., tu peux parier tout ce que tu veux, jusqu'à ton dernier sou.

dollop ['dɔləp] n F: gros morceau (de beurre); (bonne) cuillerée (de crème).

dolphin ['dɔlfin] n Z: dauphin m.

dolt [doult] n lourdaud, -aude.

domain [də'mein] n domaine m.

dome [doum] n dôme m.

domestic [də'mestik] a (vie) de famille; (affaires) de ménage; (femme) d'intérieur; (commerce, vol) intérieur; (animal) domestique; d. (servant), domestique mf, employé, -ée, de maison; d. science, (i) arts ménagers (ii) enseignement ménager. do'mesticate vtr domestiquer (un animal). do'mesticated a (animal) domestiqué; (of pers) d'intérieur; to be d., aimer la vie d'intérieur. dome'sticity n (attachment m à la) vie de famille.

domiciled ['dɔmisaild] a domicilié (at, à).

dominate ['dɔmineit] vtr & i dominer. 'dominance n prédominance f (d'un pays). 'dominant 1. a dominant; (pouvoir) dominateur 2. n Mus: dominante f. domi'nation n domination f.

domineer [dɔmi'niər] vi se montrer autoritaire; to d. over s.o., tyranniser qn. domi'neering a dominateur, autoritaire.

dominion [də'minjən] n (a) domination f, autorité f, empire m (over, sur) (b) dominion m.

domino ['dɔminou] n (pl dominoes) domino m; to play dominoes, jouer aux dominos.

don [dɔn] n = professeur m (d'université). 'donnish a (air) pédant.

donate [dou'neit] vtr faire (un) don de. do'nation n don m; (action) donation f.

done [dʌn] see do¹ II.

donkey ['dɔŋki] n âne, f ânesse; baudet m; d. jacket, grande veste de laine (d'ouvrier); F: to talk the hind leg(s) off a d., être bavard comme une pie; F: I haven't seen him for d.'s years, il y a une éternité que je ne l'ai vu. 'donkeywork n F: (plus) gros m d'un travail.

donor ['dounər] n donateur, -trice; Med: blood d., donneur, -euse (de sang).

don't-know [dount'nou] n F: there were 5 d.-knows, il y avait 5 "sans opinion".

doodle ['du:dl] vi griffonner (distraitement).

doom [du:m] 1. n (a) destin m (funeste); sort (malheureux) (b) perte f, ruine f 2. vtr condamner (to, à); doomed man, homme perdu (d'avance); doomed to failure, voué à l'échec. 'doomsday n (jour m du) jugement dernier; F: till d., indéfiniment.

door [dɔər] n porte f; (of train, car) portière f; two doors away, deux portes plus loin; out of doors, (au-)dehors; en plein air. 'doorbell n sonnette f. 'doorkeeper n portier m; concierge mf (d'immeuble). 'doorknob n poignée f. 'doorman n (pl -men) portier. 'doormat n paillasson m (d'entrée); F: (of pers) chiffe molle. 'doorstep n seuil m, pas m de la porte; F: grosse tranche de pain. 'doorstop n (to keep door open) cale f; (to protect wall) butoir m. 'door-to-door a .d.-to-d. selling, porte à porte m; to be a d.-to-d. salesman, faire du porte à porte. 'doorway n (encadrement m de la) porte; in the d., sur le pas de, à, la porte.

dope [doup] F: 1. n (a) drogue f; esp Rac: dopant m, doping m (b) renseignement m, tuyau m; to get the d., se faire tuyauter (c) (pers) crétin, -ine; nouille f 2. vtr doper (qn, un cheval); verser une drogue dans (une boisson). 'dop(e)y a F: (a) drogué; (à moitié) endormi (b) abruti; stupide.

dormant ['dɔ:mənt] a (of passions) assoupi, endormi; (volcan) en repos, en sommeil; Biol: dormant; (of law) inapplique; to lie d., être en sommeil.

dormer ['dɔ:mər] n d. (window), lucarne f.

dormitory ['dɔ:mətri] n dortoir m; d. town, ville dortoir, cité dortoir.

dormouse ['dɔːmaus, -mais] n (pl **doormice**) loir m.
dose [dous] 1. n (a) dose f (de médicament) (b) F: attaque f (de grippe) 2. vtr administrer, donner, un médicament à (qn). '**dosage** n posologie f (d'un médicament).
doss [dɔs] vi coucher à l'asile de nuit. '**doss 'down** vi P: se coucher, se pieuter. '**dosser** n P: clochard, -arde. '**dosshouse** n asile m de nuit.
dossier ['dɔsiei, -iər] n dossier m.
dot [dɔt] 1. n point m; Tex: (polka) d., pois m; F: **on the d.**, à l'heure (pile) 2. vtr (dotted) mettre un point sur (un i); **dotted line**, ligne pointillée; pointillé m; **hillside dotted with houses**, coteau parsemé de villas. '**dotty** a F: fou, toqué.
dote [dout] vi to d. (up)on s.o., aimer qn à la folie. '**dotage** n gâtisme m; **in one's d.**, gâteux. '**doting** a qui aime à la folie.
double ['dʌbl] 1. a double; (porte) à deux battants; (chambre) pour deux personnes; **d. chin**, double menton; **d. boiler, saucepan**, bain-marie m; **d. whisky**, double whisky; **d. bed**, grand lit; lit pour 2 personnes; **d. cream**, crème (fraîche) épaisse; **with a d. meaning**, à deux, double, sens; **to reach d. figures**, atteindre les deux chiffres; **to play a d. game**, jouer un double jeu; **"all" is spelt "a, d. l"**, "all" s'écrit "a, deux l"; **my phone number is three d. four two**, mon numéro de téléphone est trente-quatre quarante-deux; F: **to do a d. take**, y regarder de nouveau; **d. the number**, le double; deux fois autant; **I'm d. your age**, je suis deux fois plus âgé que vous 2. adv (courbé) en deux, (voir) double 3. n (a) double m; Gaming: **d. or quits**, quitte ou double; Ten: **mixed doubles**, double mixte; **men's doubles**, double messieurs; **at the d.**, au pas de course (b) double; (pers) sosie m; Cin: doublure f 4. vtr & i (a) doubler; Cards: (at bridge) contrer; Th: **to d. parts**, jouer deux rôles (b) plier en deux, replier. '**double 'back** 1. vtr replier 2. vi revenir sur ses pas; (of road) faire un brusque crochet. '**double-'barrelled** a (fusil) à deux coups; F: (nom) à rallonge.
double 'bass n Mus: contrebasse f. '**double-'breasted** a (veston) croisé. '**double-'check** vtr revérifier. '**double-'cross** vtr F: tromper, refaire (qn). '**double-'decker** n (a) autobus m à impériale (b) sandwich m double.
double-de'clutch vi Aut: faire un double débrayage. '**double-'edged** a à deux tranchants. '**double-'glazed** a (fenêtre) à double vitrage. **double-'glazing** n double vitrage m; doubles fenêtres fpl. '**double-'jointed** a désarticulé. '**double 'over** 1. vtr replier 2. vi se plier, se courber (en deux); se tordre (**with laughter**, de rire). **double-'park** vi stationner en double file. **double-'parking** n stationnement m en double file. '**double-'quick** a & adv F: **d.-q., in d.-q. time**, (i) au pas gymnastique (ii) en moins de rien. '**double 'up** vi (a) se plier, se courber (en deux); **to d. up with laughter**, se tordre de rire (b) partager une chambre (**with s.o.**, avec qn). '**doubly** adv doublement; **to be d. careful**, redoubler de prudence.
doubt [daut] 1. n doute m; **in d.**, (of pers) dans le doute; (of thg) en doute; **when in d.**, dans le doute; **to have (one's) doubts about sth**, avoir des doutes

sur qch; **to cast d. on sth**, mettre qch en doute; **to d. whether**, douter que + sub; **it's beyond d.**, c'est hors de doute, il n'y a pas de doute; **no d.**, sans doute; **without (a) d.**, sans aucun doute 2. vtr & i douter de (qn, qch); **to d. whether, if**, douter que; **I d. it**, j'en doute. '**doubtful** a (of thg) douteux; (of pers) indécis, incertain; (caractère) suspect, louche, équivoque; **in d. taste**, d'un goût douteux; **it is d. whether**, il est douteux que; **I was d. about speaking**, j'hésitais à parler; **to be d. about**, avoir des doutes sur. '**doubtfully** adv d'un air de doute; en hésitant. '**doubting** a incrédule. '**doubtless** adv sans doute; très probablement.
dough [dou] n (a) pâte f (à pain) (b) F: argent m, fric m. '**doughnut** n Cu: beignet m.
dove[1] [dʌv] n colombe f. '**dovecot** n colombier m. '**dovetail** 1. n Carp: queue-d'aronde f 2. v (a) vtr assembler à queue-d'aronde (b) vi se joindre, se raccorder.
dove[2] [douv] see **dive** 2.
Dover ['douvər] Prn Geog: Douvres f; **the Straits of D.**, le Pas de Calais.
dowdy ['daudi] a sans élégance. '**dowdiness** n manque m d'élégance.
down[1] [daun] n duvet m. '**downy** 1. a duveteux, duveté; (fruit) velouté 2. n F: (quilt) couette f.
down[2] [daun] 1. adv (a) (direction) vers le bas; (de haut) en bas; (crosswords) verticalement; **to go d.**, descendre; **to fall d.**, tomber (i) (from a height) à terre (ii) (from a standing position) par terre; **cash d.**, argent comptant; **d. with the traitors!** à bas les traîtres! (to dog) (lie) **d.!** couché! **to come d. to earth**, redescendre sur terre (b) (position) **d. (below)**, en bas, en contrebas; **d. there**, là-bas; **d. here**, ici; **further d.**, plus bas; **he isn't d. yet**, il n'est pas encore descendu; **to have gone, to be, d. with flu**, être grippé; F: **d. under**, aux antipodes; **the blinds were d.**, les stores étaient baissés; **face d.**, face en dessous; **head d.**, la tête en bas; **the sun is d.**, le soleil est couché; (of price) **bread is d.**, le prix du pain a baissé; **your tyres are d.**, vos pneus sont dégonflés; **to hit a man when he's d.**, frapper un homme à terre; **to put sth d.**, (i) poser (ii) écrire, qch; **he's £5 d.**, il a un déficit de £5; **to be 10 points d.**, être en retard de 10 points; **d. to recent times**, jusqu'à présent; **d. to here**, jusqu'ici; F: **to be d. on s.o.**, en vouloir à qn; **to feel, be, d.**, avoir le cafard; **d. in the mouth**, découragé, abattu 2. prep **to slide d. the wall**, se laisser couler le long du mur; **her hair hangs d. her back**, les cheveux lui pendent dans le dos; **to go d. the street**, descendre la rue; **d. (the) river**, en aval; **to fall d. the stairs**, tomber en bas de l'escalier; **d. town**, en ville 3. a (train) descendant; D: **payment**, acompte m 4. n F: **to have a d. on s.o.**, en vouloir à qn, avoir une dent contre qn; **the ups and downs of life**, les hauts et bas mpl de la vie 5. vtr terrasser, abattre (qn); descendre (un avion); **to d. tools**, (i) cesser de travailler (ii) se mettre en grève; **to d. a drink**, s'envoyer un verre. '**down-and-'out** 1. a sans le sou 2. n clochard m, sans-le-sou m. '**down-at-'heel** a (soulier) éculé; (of pers) miteux. '**downbeat** n Mus: temps frappé. '**downcast** a abattu, déprimé; (regard) baissé. '**downfall** n chute f; (of pers) ruine f. '**downgrade** 1. n **on the d.**, sur le déclin 2. vtr

rétrograder (qn); déclasser (qch). '**down**-'**hearted** *a* découragé; déprimé. **down'hill** *adv* to go d., (i) (*of road*) aller en descendant; (*of car*) descendre (la côte) (ii) *Fig:* être sur le déclin; (*of business*) péricliter. '**downpipe** *n* tuyau *m* de descente. '**downpour** *n* forte pluie, averse *f*. '**downright 1.** *adv* (*a*) tout à fait, complètement (*b*) nettement, carrément; (refuser) catégoriquement **2.** *a* (*of pers, language*) direct, franc (*b*) absolu, complet; (mensonge) éclatant; (refus) catégorique. **down'stairs 1.** *adv* en bas, au rez-de-chaussée; **to go d.**, descendre (l'escalier) **2.** *a* (pièces) d'en bas, du rez-de-chaussée. '**downstream** *adv* en aval. '**down-to-'earth** *a* terre-à-terre. '**down-town** *a & adv esp NAm:* en ville; **d. (sector)**, centre (commercial) (d'une ville). '**downward** *a* (mouvement) descendant, en bas; (tendance) à la baisse. '**downwards** *adv* (de haut) en bas; vers le bas; en descendant; **face d.**, face en dessous. '**downwind** *a & adv* vent arrière.

downs [daunz] *npl* collines *fpl* crayeuses.

dowry ['dauəri] *n* (*pl* **dowries**) dot *f*.

doz *abbr* dozen, douzaine.

doze [douz] **1.** *n* (petit) somme **2.** *vi* sommeiller; **to d. off**, s'assoupir. '**dozy** *a* somnolent; *F:* stupide.

dozen ['dʌzn] *n* douzaine *f*; **half a d.**, une demi-douzaine; **six d. bottles**, six douzaines de bouteilles; **baker's d.**, treize à la douzaine; *F:* **to talk nineteen to the d.**, avoir la langue bien pendue; **dozens of people**, des douzaines, beaucoup, de gens.

DPP *abbr* Director of Public Prosecutions.

Dr *abbr* doctor.

drab [dræb] *a* terne; gris; brun; beige.

draconian [drə'kouniən] *a* draconien.

draft [drɑːft] **1.** *n* (*a*) ébauche *f* (d'un ouvrage); brouillon *m* (d'une lettre); plan *m*, tracé *m* (*b*) *Bank:* traite *f* (*c*) *esp Mil:* détachement *m*, contingent *m* (d'hommes) (*d*) *NAm: Mil:* conscription *f*; **d. dodger**, réfractaire *m* (*e*) *NAm:* = **draught 2.** *vtr* (*a*) rédiger (un acte); faire le brouillon d'(une lettre) (*b*) détacher (des troupes); désigner, affecter (qn) (**to a job**, à un poste) (*c*) *NAm: Mil:* appeler (des conscrits) sous les drapeaux.

drag [dræg] **I.** *n* (*a*) (*for dredging*) drague *f*; (*for retrieving lost object*) araignée *f*; *Fish:* seine *f*, drège *f*; *Agr:* herse *f*; *Aut:* **d. race**, concours d'accélération (*b*) *Av: etc:* traînée *f*, résistance *f* (à l'avancement) (*c*) *F:* (*of pers*) raseur, -euse; (*of thg*) ennui *m*, scie *f*; **what a d.!** quelle barbe! (*d*) *F:* travesti *m*; **in d.**, en travesti (*e*) *P:* bouffée *f* (de cigarette). **II.** *v* (**dragged**) **1.** *vtr* (*a*) **to d. (about, along)**, traîner, entraîner, tirer; **to d. one's feet**, (i) traîner les pieds (ii) *F:* (*also* **to d. one's heels**) montrer peu d'empressement (à faire qch) (*b*) draguer (un étang) **2.** *vi* traîner (à terre); (*of lawsuit*) traîner en longueur; *Nau:* (*of anchor*) chasser. '**drag a'way** *vtr* entraîner, emmener, arracher, de force. '**drag 'down** *vtr* entraîner en bas. '**drag 'in** *vtr* faire entrer, amener, de force. '**drag-net** *n* drague, seine, drège. '**drag 'on** *vi* s'éterniser. '**drag 'out** *vtr* **to d. s.o. out of bed**, tirer qn de son lit; **to d. the truth out of s.o.**, arracher la vérité à qn. '**drag 'up** *vtr F:* (*a*) déterrer (une vieille histoire) (*b*) mal élever (qn).

dragon ['drægən] *n* dragon *m*. '**dragonfly** *n* (*pl* -**flies**) libellule *f*.

dragoon [drə'guːn] *vtr* **to d. s.o. into doing sth**, contraindre qn à faire qch.

drain [drein] **1.** *n* (*a*) (*open*) canal *m* (de décharge); rigole *f*; (*piped*) égout *m*; tuyau *m* d'écoulement; canalisation *f* sanitaire (d'une maison); *F:* **to throw money down the d.**, jeter son argent par les fenêtres (*b*) perte *f*, fuite *f* (d'énergie); épuisement *m* (de ressources) **2.** *v* **to d. (off, away)** (*a*) *vtr* évacuer, faire couler(de l'eau); (faire) égoutter (une bouteille, des légumes); vider (un verre, un étang); assécher, drainer (un terrain); *Aut:* vidanger (l'huile, le carter); (*b*) *vi* (*of water*) s'écouler; (*of thg*) s'égoutter. '**drainage** *n* (*a*) écoulement *m* (de l'eau); assèchement *m*, drainage *m* (du terrain) (*b*) système *m* d'égouts; **main d.**, tout-à-l'égout *m inv*. '**draining** *n* = **drainage** (*a*); **d. board** (*also* '**drainer**) égouttoir *m*. '**drainpipe** *n* tuyau d'écoulement.

drake [dreik] *n* canard *m* mâle.

drama ['drɑːmə] *n* drame *m*; art *m* dramatique; théâtre *m*. **dramatic** [drə'mætik] *a* dramatique; (effet) théâtral. **dra'matically** *adv* dramatiquement. **dra'matics** *npl* théâtre. '**dramatist** *n* auteur *m* dramatique. **dramati'zation** *n* adaptation *f* (d'un roman) à la scène. '**dramatize** *vtr* dramatiser; adapter (un roman) à la scène.

drank [dræŋk] *see* **drink 2.**

drape [dreip] *vtr* draper, tendre (**with**, **in**, de). '**draper** *n* marchand, -ande, de tissus, de nouveautés; **d.'s (shop)** (*also* '**drapery** (*NAm:* = **dry goods (store)**), (magasin *m* de) tissus *mpl*, nouveautés *fpl*.

drastic ['dræstik] *a* énergique, rigoureux, draconien. '**drastically** *adv* énergiquement, rigoureusement.

drat [dræt] *int F:* **d. (it)!** zut! mince (alors)! '**dratted** *a F:* sacré.

draught, NAm: draft [drɑːft] *n* (*a*) courant *m* d'air; (*of chimney*) tirage *m*; **d. beer, beer on d.**, bière à la pression; **d. excluder**, bourrelet *m* (de porte); **d. horse**, cheval de trait (*b*) (*drinking*) trait *m*, coup *m* (de vin) (*c*) *Nau:* tirant *m* d'eau (d'un navire) (*d*) **draughts** (*NAm:* = **checkers**) (jeu *m* de) dames *fpl*. '**draughtboard** *n* (*NAm:* = **checkerboard**) damier *m*. '**draughtproof** *a* calfeutré. '**draughtsman** *n* (*pl* -**men**) dessinateur, -trice. '**draughtsmanship** *n* (*a*) art *m* du dessin industriel (*b*) talent *m* de dessinateur. '**draughty** *a* (-**ier**, -**iest**) plein de courants d'air; exposé à tous les vents.

draw [drɔː] **I.** *n* (*a*) tirage *m*; *F:* **to be quick on the d.**, avoir la gâchette facile (*b*) tirage au sort; loterie *f*; tombola *f*; **that's the luck of the d.**, c'est la vie! (*c*) attraction *f*; clou *m* (de la fête) (*d*) *Sp:* partie nulle; match nul. **II.** *v* (**drew; drawn**) **1.** *vtr* (*a*) tirer; baisser (un store); remorquer (une caravane) (*b*) (*take in*) aspirer (de l'air) (*c*) (*attract*) attirer (une foule); **to d. s.o. into the conversation**, faire entrer qn dans la conversation; **to be drawn into doing sth**, se laisser entraîner à faire qch (*d*) tirer, retirer, ôter (**sth from sth**, qch de qch); arracher (un clou, une dent); **to d. (lots) for sth**, tirer qch au sort (*e*) puiser (de l'eau); toucher (de l'argent); vider (une volaille); **to d. blood,** faire saigner qn; **he refused to be drawn,** il a refusé de se commettre (*f*) dessiner; tracer (un plan); tirer (une ligne); dresser (une carte); faire (un portrait); *Fig:* **I d. the line at that,** je n'accepte pas cela (*g*) *Sp:* **to d. (a game),** faire match nul, partie nulle (**with,** avec) (*h*) établir (une comparaison) **2.** *vi* (*a*) **to d. near (to s.o.),** s'approcher (de qn); **to d. to one side,** se ranger, s'écarter; (*of train*) **to d. into a station,** entrer en gare; **to d. round (the table),** s'assembler (autour d'une table); **to d. to an end,** tirer, toucher, à sa fin; **to d. level with s.o.,** arriver à la hauteur de qn (*b*) (*of chimney*) tirer; (*of pump*) aspirer; (*of tea*) infuser (*c*) dessiner. **'draw a'long** *vtr* tirer, traîner, entraîner. **'draw a'part** *vi* s'écarter. **'draw a'side 1.** *vtr* (*a*) détourner, écarter (qch) (*b*) tirer, prendre (qn) à l'écart **2.** *vi* s'écarter; se ranger. **'draw 'back 1.** *vtr* (*a*) tirer en arrière; retirer (la main) (*b*) tirer, ouvrir (les rideaux) **2.** *vi* (se) reculer; se retirer en arrière. **'drawback** *n* inconvénient *m*, désavantage *m*. **'drawbridge** *n* pont-levis *m*. **'draw 'down** *vtr* baisser (les stores). **'drawer** *n* tiroir *m*; **chest of drawers,** commode *f*; **bottom d.** (*NAm:* **hope chest**), trousseau *m*. **'draw 'in 1.** *vtr* (*a*) (*of cat*) rentrer, rétracter (ses griffes) (*b*) aspirer (l'air) **2.** *vi* (*a*) **the days are drawing in,** les jours diminuent, raccourcissent (*b*) (*of car*) se ranger (le long du trottoir). **'drawing** *n* (*a*) dessin *m*; **rough d.,** ébauche *f*, croquis *m*; **d. board,** planche à dessin; *Fig:* **still on the d. board,** encore à l'étude; **d. paper,** papier à dessin; **d. pin** (*NAm:* = **thumbtack**), punaise *f*; **d. room,** salon *m* (*b*) **d. (for) (lots),** tirage (au sort). **drawn** *a* (*a*) (visage) tiré (*b*) (combat) indécis; *Sp:* (match) nul. **'draw 'off** *vtr* retirer (ses gants); soutirer (un liquide). **'draw 'on 1.** *vi* s'avancer; **night was drawing on,** la nuit approchait **2.** *vtr* (*a*) prendre, tirer, sur (ses économies) (*b*) s'inspirer de (ses expériences). **'draw 'out** *vtr* (*a*) sortir, retirer; arracher (un clou) (*b*) faire parler (qn) (*c*) étirer (le fer); prolonger; tirer (une affaire) en longueur; **long-drawn-out story,** récit prolongé. **'drawstring** *n* cordon *m*. **'draw 'up 1.** *vtr* (*a*) **to d. oneself up (to one's full height),** se (re)dresser (*b*) approcher (une chaise) (**to the table,** de la table); aligner (des troupes) (*c*) dresser, rédiger (un document); établir (un compte) **2.** *vi* (*of car*) s'arrêter; (*at kerb*) se ranger (le long du trottoir).

drawl [drɔːl] **1.** *n* voix traînante **2.** *v* (*a*) *vi* parler (*b*) *vtr* dire (qch) d'une voix traînante.

dread [dred] **1.** *n* crainte *f*, terreur *f*, épouvante *f*; effroi *m* **2.** *vtr* redouter, craindre. **'dreadful** *a* (*a*) terrible, redoutable (*b*) atroce, épouvantable; **it's d.,** c'est affreux. **'dreadfully** *adv* terriblement, horriblement; affreusement; *F:* **I'm d. sorry,** je regrette infiniment.

dream [driːm] **1.** *n* rêve *m*; **to have a d.,** faire un rêve; **sweet dreams!** faites de beaux rêves! **to see sth in a d.,** voir qch en songe; (*of pers*) **to be in a d.,** être dans les nuages; rêvasser; *F:* **d. car,** voiture de rêve; **my d. car,** la voiture de mes rêves **2.** *vtr & i* (**dreamed** *or* **dreamt** [dremt]) rêver (**of, about,** de); (*daydream*) rêvasser; **I shouldn't d. of doing it,** jamais je ne m'aviserais de faire cela; **no one would have dreamt**

of that, personne n'aurait songé à cela. **'dreamer** *n* rêveur, -euse. **'dreamily** *adv* d'un air rêveur. **'dreaming** *n* rêves *mpl.* **'dreamy** *a* (**-ier, -iest**) (*a*) rêveur (*b*) *F:* charmant, chouette.

dreary ['driəri] *a* (**-ier, -iest**) triste, morne; (discours) ennuyeux; (régime) monotone. **'drearily** *adv* tristement. **'dreariness** *n* tristesse *f*; aspect *m* morne.

dredge[1] [dredʒ] *vtr & i* draguer; **to d. for sth,** draguer à la recherche de qch. **'dredge**[1] *n* (*a*) (*pers, ship*) dragueur *m* (*b*) (*machine*) drague *f*. **'dredge 'up** *vtr* draguer (un objet); *F:* déterrer (un sujet). **'dredging** *n* dragage *m*.

dredge[2] *vtr Cu:* saupoudrer (**with,** de). **'dredger**[2] *n DomEc:* saupoudroir *m* (à farine); saupoudreuse *f* (à sucre).

dregs [dregz] *npl* lie *f* (de vin).

drench [drentʃ] *vtr* tremper, mouiller (**with,** de); **drenched to the skin,** trempé jusqu'aux os. **'drenching** *a* **d. rain,** pluie battante.

Dresden ['drezdən] *Prn* **D. china,** porcelaine *f* de Saxe.

dress [dres] **1.** *n* (*a*) tenue *f*; costume *m*; habit(s) *m*(*pl*); **evening d.,** tenue de soirée; *Mil:* **(full) d. uniform,** uniforme de cérémonie; *Th:* **d. circle,** (premier) balcon; **d. rehearsal,** répétition générale (*b*) (*woman's garment*) robe *f* **2.** *vtr* (*a*) habiller (qn) (**in, de, en**); **well, badly, dressed,** bien, mal, habillé; **to be dressed for,** être en tenue de (*b*) orner, parer (**with,** de); *Com:* faire (la vitrine) (*c*) *Mil:* aligner (des troupes) (*d*) *Med:* panser (une blessure) (*e*) dresser, tailler (des pierres); *Cu:* apprêter, accommoder (un mets); parer (de la viande); assaisonner (une salade) **3.** *vpr & i* **to d. (oneself),** s'habiller (**in, de, en**) **4.** *vi Mil:* (*of troops*) s'aligner. **'dresser** *n* **1.** (*pers*) *Th:* habilleur, -euse; *Ind:* apprêteur, -euse; **window d.,** étalagiste *mf* **2.** *Furn:* (*a*) buffet *m*; vaisselier *m* (*b*) *esp NAm:* (*Br* = **dressing table**) coiffeuse *f.* **'dressing** *n* habillement *m*; **d. gown,** robe de chambre; peignoir *m*; **d. room,** (i) (*in house*) cabinet de toilette; dressing-room *m* (ii) *Th:* loge *f* (d'acteur); **d. table,** (*NAm:* = **dresser**) coiffeuse; *F:* **to give s.o. a d. down,** semoncer qn (*b*) *Cu:* (**salad**) **d.,** assaisonnement *m* (pour la salade); **French d.,** vinaigrette *f* (*c*) *Med:* pansement *m.* **'dressmaker** *n* couturier, -ière. **'dressmaking** *n* couture *f.* **'dress 'up 1.** *vi* **to d. up, get dressed up,** se faire beau, belle (*b*) (*disguise*) se mettre en travesti; se déguiser (**as, en**) **2.** *vtr* (*a*) habiller (*b*) déguiser, costumer (qn) (**as, en**). **'dressy** *a* (**-ier, -iest**) chic, élégant; (trop) habillé.

drew [druː] *see* **draw** II.

dribble ['dribl] **I.** *n* filet *m* (de liquide). **II.** *v* **1.** *vi* (*a*) (*of liquid*) tomber goutte à goutte (*b*) (*of pers*) baver **2.** *vtr & i Fb:* dribbler (le ballon). **'driblet** *n* (*a*) gouttelette *f* (d'eau) (*b*) petite quantité. **'dribs and 'drabs** *npl* **in d. a. d.,** petit à petit.

dried [draid] (*a*) *v see* **dry** II. (*b*) *a* séché; (fruit) sec; (œufs) en poudre.

drier ['draiər] *n* = **dryer.**

drift [drift] **1.** *n* (*a*) mouvement *m*; **continental d.,** dérive *f* des continents; **d. ice,** glaces flottantes (*b*) direction *f*, sens *m* (d'un courant) (*c*) cours *m*, marche *f* (des événements) (*d*) tendance *f*, portée *f* (de questions) (*e*) amoncellement *m* (de neige);

congère f 2. vi (a) dériver; aller à la dérive; (of ship) être en dérive; (of aircraft) déporter; **to let oneself d.,** se laisser aller; (of two pers) **to d. apart,** se séparer peu à peu; se perdre de vue (b) (of snow) s'amonceler (c) (of events) tendre (vers un but). **'drifter** n personne f qui se laisse aller. **'driftwood** n bois flottant, flotté.

drill¹ [dril] **1.** n (a) (bit) foret m, mèche f (b) perceuse f (électrique); Dent: fraise f, F: roulette f; CivE: foreuse f; **pneumatic d.,** marteau-piqueur m (à air comprimé) (c) Mil: etc: exercice(s) m(pl); F: **what's the d.?** qu'est-ce qu'il faut faire? **2.** vtr & i (a) forer; percer; Dent: fraiser; **to d. for oil,** forer pour rechercher du pétrole (b) (faire) faire l'exercice, des exercices (à qn).

drill² n Tex: coutil m; treillis m.

drily ['draili] adv = **dryly.**

drink [driŋk] **1.** n (a) boisson f; **food and d.,** le boire et le manger; **to give s.o. a d.,** donner à boire à qn; faire boire qn; offrir à boire à qn; **to have a d.,** boire quelque chose; **to have a d. of water,** boire un verre d'eau (b) (alcoholic) boisson; (in bar) consommation f; **to have a d.,** prendre quelque chose; prendre, boire, un verre; **come round for a d., for drinks,** venez prendre l'apéritif m; **d. problem,** alcoolisme m; problème d'alcoolisme; **to take to d.,** s'adonner à la boisson; boire; **to be the worse for d.,** avoir trop bu (c) F: la mer **2.** vtr & i (drank; drunk) boire; manger (du potage); **will you have something to d.?** voulez-vous boire, prendre, quelque chose? **to d. to s.o., to s.o.'s health,** boire à la santé de qn; **then he started to d.,** à ce moment-là il a commencé à boire. **'drinkable** a (vin) buvable; (eau) potable. **'drinker** n buveur, -euse. **'drink 'in** vtr boire (de l'eau, des paroles de qn). **'drinking** n alcoolisme m; ivrognerie f; **d. trough,** abreuvoir m; **d. water,** eau potable; **d. fountain,** fontaine publique; (in factory) poste d'eau potable. **'drink 'up** vtr & i achever de boire; vider (un verre). **drunk 1.** a ivre; soûl; Fig: enivré (with, de, par); **to get d.,** se soûler; s'enivrer; **d. as a lord,** soûl comme un Polonais; Jur: **d. and disorderly** = en état d'ivresse manifeste dans un lieu public **2.** n ivrogne m; homme, femme, ivre. **'drunkard** n ivrogne; alcoolique mf. **'drunken** a (état) d'ivresse; (homme) ivrogne, ivre; (querelle) d'ivrognes; Jur: **d. driving,** conduite en état d'ébriété. **'drunkenly** adv comme un ivrogne. **'drunkenness** n ivresse f; (habit) ivrognerie f.

drip [drip] **1.** n (a) bruit m de l'eau qui goutte; goutte f (b) Med: goutte-à-goutte m inv; perfusion f (c) F: (pers) nouille f **2.** v (dripped) (a) vi dégoutter, s'égoutter; tomber goutte à goutte; dégouliner; (of tap) goutter; (of walls) suinter; **dripping with sweat,** ruisselant de sueur (b) vtr laisser tomber goutte à goutte. **'drip-'dry** a (chemise) ne nécessitant aucun repassage. **'drip-'feed** vtr (drip-fed) Med: nourrir par perfusion. **'dripping 1.** a ruisselant; (robinet) qui goutte; **d. (wet),** trempé **2.** n (a) égouttement m (b) Cu: graisse f de rôti.

drive [draiv] **I** n (a) promenade f en voiture; **it's an hour's d. (away),** c'est à une heure de voiture (b) battue f (de gibier) (c) MecE: (mouvement m de) propulsion f; transmission f; actionnement m; Aut: **lefthand d.,** conduite f à gauche; **direct d.,** prise

directe; **front-wheel d.,** traction f avant (d) Golf: Ten: drive m (e) (of pers) dynamisme m, énergie f; **to have lots of d.,** être très dynamique (f) offensive f (contre un abus); campagne f (de vente) (g) Psy: pulsion (sexuelle) (h) allée f; (to large house) avenue f (i) tournoi m (de bridge). **II.** v (drove, driven) **1.** vtr (a) chasser (devant soi); conduire (le bétail); rabattre (le gibier) (b) (of pers) faire marcher (une machine); conduire (une voiture, qn); piloter (une voiture de course); **to d. s.o. (back) home,** reconduire, ramener, qn chez lui (en voiture) (c) pousser (qn à une action); contraindre (qn à faire qch); **he was driven to it,** on lui a forcé la main; **to d. s.o. mad, out of his mind,** rendre qn fou (d) surcharger (qn) de travail, exploiter (qn); **to d. oneself too hard,** se surmener (e) enfoncer (un clou); percer (un tunnel); **to d. a bargain,** conclure un marché (f) Golf: Ten: driver (g) MecE: actionner, commander (une machine). **2.** vi (a) **to d. (along the road),** rouler (sur la route); **to d. to London,** aller en voiture à Londres; **to d. on the right,** circuler à droite; **can you d.?** savez-vous conduire? **who was driving?** qui était au volant? **'drive a'long 1.** vtr chasser **2.** vi rouler (en voiture). **'drive at** vtr **what are you driving at?** où voulez-vous en venir? **'drive a'way 1.** vtr chasser, éloigner, repousser **2.** vi partir en voiture; démarrer. **'drive 'back 1.** vtr (a) repousser, faire reculer (b) reconduire, ramener (qn) en voiture **2.** vi rentrer, revenir, en voiture. **'drive 'in 1.** vtr enfoncer (un clou); visser (une vis) **2.** vi entrer (en voiture). **'drive-in** n & a **d.-in** (cinema, restaurant, bank), cinéma m, restaurant, banque f, accessible en voiture; drive-in m inv. **'drive 'off** vi partir en voiture; démarrer. **'drive 'on** vi continuer sa route. **'drive 'out 1.** vi sortir en voiture **2.** vtr chasser. **'drive 'over 1.** vtr écraser **2.** vi se rendre (chez qn) en voiture. **'driver** n conducteur, -trice; chauffeur m (de taxi); **racing d.,** coureur, -euse, automobile; NAm: **d.'s license** (Br = **driving licence**), permis m de conduire. **'driveshaft** n Aut: arbre m de transmission. **'drive 'through** vtr passer par (une ville) en voiture. **'drive 'up** vi s'approcher; s'arrêter. **'driveway** n allée f. **'driving 1.** a **d. force,** force motrice; **d. rain,** pluie fouettée par le vent, battante **2.** n conduite f (d'une voiture); **d. school,** auto-école f; **d. licence** (NAm: = **driver's license),** permis de conduire; **to pass one's d. test,** avoir son permis (de conduire).

drivel ['drivl] n radotage m; balivernes fpl.

drizzle ['drizl] **1.** n bruine f, crachin m **2.** vi bruiner, crachiner. **'drizzly** a bruineux.

dromedary ['drɔmədəri] n dromadaire m.

drone [droun] **1.** n (a) Ent: abeille f mâle; faux-bourdon m (b) fainéant, -ante (c) bourdonnement m (d'insectes); ronronnement m, vrombissement m (d'un moteur); débit m monotone (d'une voix) **2.** vi (of insect) bourdonner; (of engine) ronronner, vrombir; (of pers) **to d. on, away,** parler d'une voix monotone.

drool [dru:l] vi baver; Fig: **to d. over sth,** s'extasier sur qch.

droop [dru:p] vi (a) (of head) (se) pencher; (of shoulders) tomber; (of eyelids) s'abaisser; (of flower) commencer à se faner; (of pers) s'affaisser. **'droopy** a tombant, pendant.

drop [drɔp] **I.** n (a) goutte f; **d. by d.**, goutte à goutte; Fig: **a d. in the ocean**, une goutte d'eau dans la mer (b) bonbon m, pastille f (c) chute f; baisse f (de prix); MilAv: parachutage m; (distance down) à-pic m; **d. in voltage**, chute de tension; tonneau m (de la hat, sans hésiter. **II.** v (**dropped**) **1.** vi (a) tomber goutte à goutte, dégoutter (**from**, de) (b) (of pers) tomber, se laisser tomber; **to d.** (**down**) **dead**, tomber (raide) mort; P: **d. dead!** va au diable! F: **I'm ready to d.**, je tombe de fatigue; **to d. into a chair**, s'affaler dans une chaise; **he let it d. that**, il a laissé échapper que; F: **let it d.!** n'en parlons plus! (c) (of prices) baisser; (of wind) tomber **2.** vtr (a) laisser tomber, lâcher; lancer (une bombe); jeter (l'ancre); Knit: sauter (une maille); **to d. s.o. a line**, envoyer, écrire, un mot à qn; **he dropped me a hint that**, il m'a fait comprendre que (b) perdre (de l'argent) (**over sth**, sur qch) (c) (in car) déposer (qn); (in boat) débarquer (qn) (d) omettre, supprimer (une lettre, une syllabe); ne pas prononcer (les h, etc) (e) baisser (les yeux, la voix); faire (une révérence) (f) abandonner (un travail, un projet); renoncer à (une idée); **let's d. the subject!** n'en parlons plus! F: **d. it!** en voilà assez! **'drop back, be'hind** vi rester en arrière. **'drop 'in** vi entrer en passant (**on s.o.**, chez qn). **'drop-kick** n Rugby Fb: coup (de pied) tombé; drop m. **'droplet** n gouttelette f. **'drop 'off 1.** vi tomber, se détacher (b) (of numbers) diminuer (c) F: **to d. o.** (**to sleep**), s'endormir, s'assoupir **2.** vtr (in car) déposer (qn). **'drop 'out** vi (a) tomber (dehors) (b) vivre en marge de la société; **to d. o. of a contest**, se retirer d'un concours; **to d. o. of college**, abandonner ses études. **'dropout** n (a) personne f qui a abandonné ses études (b) marginal, -ale. **'dropper** n Med: compte-gouttes m inv. **'droppings** npl fiente f; crottes fpl (de lapin).

dross [drɔs] n Metall: scories fpl; Fig: rebut m.

drought [draut] n sécheresse f.

drove [drouv] see **drive II.**

droves [drouvz] npl troupeaux mpl (de bêtes); foules fpl (de gens).

drown [draun] **1.** vtr (a) noyer; **to d. one's sorrows** (**in drink**), noyer son chagrin (dans la boisson); **drowned person**, noyé, -ée (b) inonder (du terrain) (c) étouffer, couvrir (un son) **2.** vpr & i **to d.** (**oneself**), se noyer. **'drowning 1.** a (homme) qui se noie **2.** n noyade f.

drowse [drauz] vi somnoler, s'assoupir. **'drowsily** adv d'un air somnolent. **'drowsiness** n somnolence f. **'drowsy** a (**-ier, -iest**) assoupi, somnolent; **to feel d.**, avoir sommeil, envie de dormir.

drudge [drʌdʒ] n homme m, femme f, de peine. **'drudgery** n travail pénible, ingrat; corvée(s) f(pl).

drug [drʌg] **1.** n (a) produit m pharmaceutique; drogue f (b) narcotique m, stupéfiant m; F: drogue; **to take, be on, drugs**, se droguer; **d. addict**, toxicomane mf; drogué, -ée; **d. addiction**, toxicomanie f; F: (of article) **to be a d. on the market**, être invendable **2.** vtr (**drugged**) donner un narcotique, un stupéfiant, à (qn); droguer (qn); ajouter un narcotique à (une boisson). **'druggist** n (a) pharmacien, -ienne (b) NAm: celui, celle, qui tient un drugstore. **'drugstore** n NAm: drugstore m.

druid ['druːid] n druide m.

drum [drʌm] **1.** n (a) Mus: tambour m; caisse f; pl batterie f; **d. brakes**, freins à tambour (b) **big** (**bass**) **d.**, grosse caisse; Anat: tympan m (de l'oreille) (c) bidon m, tambour (à huile); tonneau m (en fer) **2.** v (**drummed**) (a) vi battre du tambour; (of pers, fingers) tambouriner (b) vtr tambouriner (un air); **to d. sth into s.o.'s head**, enfoncer qch dans la tête de qn. **'drummer** n tambour m; (in popular music) batteur m. **'drum 'out** vtr expulser (qn). **'drumstick** n (a) baguette f de tambour (b) Cu: pilon m (d'une volaille). **'drum 'up** vtr racoler (des clients); faire le rappel de (ses amis).

drunk [drʌŋk] a also **'drunkard, 'drunken, 'drunkenly, 'drunkenness** see **drink.**

dry [drai] **1.** a (**drier, driest**) (a) sec, f sèche; (puits) tari, à sec; (pays) aride; (champagne) brut; Ski: (of slope) artificiel; **d. land**, terre ferme; **to run d.**, se dessécher; **to be kept d.**, craint l'humidité; (of pers) **to feel d.**, avoir la gorge sèche; **medium d.**, (vin) demi-sec; NAm: **d. goods** (Br = **drapery**), tissus mpl, nouveautés fpl; F: **d. run**, coup d'essai; **as d. as a bone, bone d.**, sec comme une allumette (b) (pays) sec (où les boissons alcooliques sont prohibées) (c) (sujet, discours) aride; sans intérêt; **d. humour**, esprit mordant; **a man of d. humour**, un pince-sans-rire **2.** v (**dried**) (a) vtr (faire) sécher; essuyer (la vaisselle); **to d. one's eyes**, s'essuyer les yeux (b) vi sécher; se dessécher. **'dry-'clean** vtr nettoyer à sec. **'dry-'cleaner's** n teinturerie f, pressing m. **'dry-'cleaning** n nettoyage m à sec. **'dryer, 'drier** n séchoir m; Hairdr: (fixed) casque m (sèche-cheveux); **spin d.**, essoreuse f. **'dry-'eyed** a les yeux secs. **'drying** a (vent) desséchant. **'drying 'up** n **to do the d. up**, essuyer la vaisselle. **'dryly** (also **'drily**) adv sèchement; d'un ton sec; (répondre) d'un air de pince-sans-rire. **'dryness** n (a) sécheresse f, aridité f (b) sévérité f (du ton); aridité (de l'esprit). **'dry off, 'out** vtr & i (faire) sécher; (of alcoholic) **to d. out**, (se faire) désintoxiquer. **'dry 'up** vi (a) (of well) se dessécher, tarir (b) F: se taire; sécher; P: **d. up!** la ferme! (c) essuyer la vaisselle.

d.t.'s [diː'tiːz] abbr Med: F: delirium tremens.

dual ['djuːəl] a double; **d. carriageway**, route à quatre voies; **d. control(s)**, double commande; **d.-purpose**, à double emploi.

dub [dʌb] vtr (**dubbed**) (a) surnommer (qn) (b) Cin: doubler (un film). **'dubbing** n Cin: doublage m.

dubious ['djuːbiəs] a (of thg) douteux; incertain; (air) de doute; (caractère) suspect, louche, équivoque; (of pers) qui doute; indécis, incertain; **to be d. about**, avoir des doutes sur. **'dubiously** adv d'un air de doute; en hésitant.

duchess ['dʌtʃis] n duchesse f. **'duchy** n (pl **-ies**) duché m.

duck [dʌk] **1.** n (a) Orn: canard m; (female of drake) cane f; **wild d.**, canard sauvage; Fig: **lame d.**, entreprise f qui marche mal; F: **dead d.**, (i) (pers) pauvre type m (ii) fiasco m; sitting **d.**, cible f facile; **to play at ducks and drakes**, faire des ricochets (sur l'eau); F: **to play ducks and drakes with one's money**, jeter son argent par les fenêtres; F: **to take to sth like a d. to water**, mordre à qch; F: **it's like water off a d.'s back**, c'est comme si on chantait (b) Cr: zéro m **2.** v

(a) vi plonger (dans l'eau); se baisser, baisser la tête (b) vtr plonger (qn) dans l'eau; faire faire le plongeon à (qn); baisser (subitement) la tête. 'ducking n to give s.o. a d., faire faire le plongeon, faire boire une tasse, à qn. 'duckling n caneton m. 'duckpond n mare f aux canards.

duct [dʌkt] n conduit m; Anat: canal m. 'ductless a Anat: (glande) endocrine.

dud [dʌd] a & n F: incapable (mf); he's a d., il est nul; c'est un raté; d. cheque, chèque sans provision; d. banknote, billet faux.

due [djuː] 1. a (a) dû, f due; (dette) exigible; bill d. on 1st May, effet payable le premier mai; you are d. £5, £5 is d. to you, on vous doit £5; (of bill) to fall d., venir à échéance (b) (merited) dû; juste, mérité; (soin) voulu; after d. consideration, après mûre réflexion; in d. course, en temps utile, voulu; d. to, causé par, attribuable à; par suite de; dû à; what is it d. to? à quoi cela tient-il? the train is d. (to arrive) at 2 o'clock, le train arrive à deux heures; he is d. (to arrive) this evening, il doit arriver ce soir; I'm d. for a rise, j'attends une augmentation de salaire 2. adv d. north, droit vers le nord 3. n (a) dû m; to give s.o. his d., rendre justice à, être juste envers, qn; F: give the devil his d., à chacun son dû (b) pl droits mpl, frais mpl; (of club) cotisation f.

duel ['djuːəl] 1. n duel m; to fight a d., se battre en duel 2. vi se battre en duel.

duet [djuː'et] n duo m; (for piano) morceau m à quatre mains.

duff [dʌf] a F: (renseignement) faux; (moteur) crevé.

duffel, duffle ['dʌfəl] n d. coat, duffle-coat m; d. bag, sac marin, de campeur.

dug [dʌg] see dig 2. 'dugout n (a) (canoe) pirogue f (b) Mil: tranchée-abri f.

duke [djuːk] n duc m. 'dukedom n duché m.

dull [dʌl] 1. a (a) (of pers) lent, lourd; (of mind) obtus; (of sight) faible; (of hearing) dur; (of ache, sound) sourd; (of sound) étouffé; Com: (of market) calme, inactif; (depressed) triste, morne; déprimé (b) (tedious) triste, ennuyeux; as d. as ditchwater, ennuyeux comme la pluie; deadly d., abrutissant, assommant (c) (of colour) triste, sombre, maussade; (blunt) (outil) émoussé 2. vtr engourdir (l'esprit); émousser (un outil, les sens); assourdir (un bruit); amortir (une douleur); ternir (une couleur). 'dullard n lourdaud, -aude. 'dullness n (a) lourdeur f d'esprit (b) ennui m; tristesse f (c) manque m d'éclat (d'une couleur). 'dully adv (a) lourdement (b) d'une manière ennuyeuse (c) (briller) faiblement.

duly ['djuːli] adv (a) dûment, justement (b) en temps voulu.

dumb [dʌm] a (a) muet, f muette; d. animals, les bêtes; Fig: we were struck d. by the news, la nouvelle nous a laissé abasourdis; d. show, pantomime f (b) F: bête, sot, f sotte; d. blonde, blonde évaporée; to act d., faire le niais. 'dumbbell n haltère m. dumb'found vtr abasourdir. 'dumbness n (a) mutisme m (b) F: bêtise f, sottise f.

dummy ['dʌmi] 1. n (a) Com: homme m de paille (b) Dressm: etc: mannequin m; marionnette f (de ventriloque) (c) chose f factice; maquette f (de livre) (d) (baby's) d. (NAm: = pacifier), tétine f, sucette f (e) Cards: mort m 2. a factice, faux, f fausse; d. run, coup d'essai.

dump [dʌmp] 1. n tas m (de déchets); dépôt m (de munitions); rubbish d., décharge publique; F: what a d.! quel trou! F: to be down in the dumps, avoir le cafard 2. vtr (a) décharger (un camion de matériau); déverser (du sable); jeter (des ordures); déposer (b) F: se débarrasser de; abandonner, plaquer (c) Com: écouler à perte (des marchandises); faire du dumping. 'dumper n d. (truck) (esp NAm: dump truck), camion m à benne; tombereau m. 'dumpy a (-ier, -iest) F: trapu, boulot, courtaud.

dumpling ['dʌmpliŋ] n Cu: boulette f (de pâte); apple d., pomme enrobée (de pâte).

dun [dʌn] vtr (dunned) harceler (un débiteur).

dunce [dʌns] n cancre m, âne m.

dune [djuːn] n (sand) d., dune f.

dung [dʌŋ] n bouse f (de vache); crottin m (de cheval); crotte f; (manure) fumier m. 'dunghill n (tas m de) fumier.

dungarees [dʌŋgə'riːz] npl Cl: combinaison f; bleu(s) m(pl) (de mécanicien); (child's, woman's) salopette f.

dungeon ['dʌndʒən] n cachot m.

dunk [dʌŋk] vtr F: tremper (du pain) (dans son café).

Dunkirk [dʌn'kəːk] Prn Geog: Dunkerque f.

duo ['djuːou] n duo m.

duodenal [djuːou'diːnl] a Anat: duodénal.

dupe [djuːp] 1. n dupe f 2. vtr duper, tromper (qn).

duplex ['djuːpleks] n esp NAm: duplex m.

duplicate 1. a & n ['djuːplikət] double (m); in d., en double (exemplaire) 2. vtr ['djuːplikeit] reproduire (un document) en double exemplaire; faire le double de (qch), (poly)copier (un document). dupli'cation n reproduction f; répétition f. 'duplicator n (also 'duplicating machine) duplicateur m.

duplicity [djuː'plisiti] n duplicité f; mauvaise foi.

durable ['djuərəbl] a durable; résistant. dura'bility n durabilité f; résistance f (de matériaux).

duration [djuə'reiʃn] n durée f; étendue f (de la vie).

duress [djuə'res] n under d., sous la contrainte.

during ['djuəriŋ] prep pendant, durant; d. the winter, au cours de l'hiver.

dusk [dʌsk] n crépuscule m; at d., à la nuit tombante. 'dusky a (-ier, -iest) (of complexion) brun foncé.

dust [dʌst] 1. n poussière f; d. cover, back, jacket, jaquette f (de livre) 2. vtr (a) saupoudrer (a cake with sugar, un gâteau de sucre); Toil: dusting powder, (poudre f de) talc m (b) épousseter (un meuble). 'dustbin n (NAm: = garbage, trash, can) poubelle f; boîte f à ordures. 'dustbowl n zone f semi-aride. 'dustcart n (NAm: garbage truck) camion m aux ordures, des éboueurs. 'duster n chiffon m; torchon m; feather d., plumeau m. 'dustman n (pl -men) éboueur m, Pej: boueur m; boueux m. 'dustpan n pelle f à poussière. 'dustsheet n housse f (pour meubles). 'duststorm n tempête f de poussière. 'dustup n F: querelle f; to have a d. with s.o., se quereller avec qn. 'dusty a (-ier, -iest) poussiéreux; recouvert de poussière; F: d. answer, réponse décevante; F: not so d., pas mal.

Dutch [dʌtʃ] 1. a hollandais; néerlandais; de Hollande; D. auction, vente à la baisse; D. barn, hangar à récoltes; D. courage, bravoure après boire; to go

D., payer chacun son écot (pour un repas) 2. (a) n Ling: hollandais m, néerlandais m; F: it's double D. to me, c'est de l'hébreu pour moi (b) npl the D., les Hollandais mpl, les Néerlandais mpl. 'Dutchman, -woman n (pl -men, -women) Hollandais, -aise; Néerlandais, -aise; F: then I'm a Dutchman, je veux bien être pendu.

duty ['dju:ti] n (a) devoir m (to, envers); to do one's d., faire son devoir; from a sense of d., par devoir; you are (in) d. bound to do it, votre devoir vous y oblige; d. call, visite de politesse (b) fonction(s) f(pl); to take up one's duties, entrer en fonctions (c) service m; to be on d., être de service, Nau: de garde; to be off d., ne pas être de service, Nau: de garde; Mil: avoir quartier libre; to do d. for, (of pers) remplacer (qn); (of thg) servir de; d. officer, officier de service, de jour (d) droit m; customs d., droit(s) de douane. 'dutiable a soumis aux droits de douane. 'dutiful a respectueux; (mari) plein d'égards. 'dutifully adv respectueusement. 'duty-'free a exempt de droits (de douane); (magasin) hors taxe.

duvet ['du:vei] n couette f.

dwarf [dwɔːf] 1. a & n nain, f naine 2. vtr rabougrir (une plante); rapetisser (qch) (par contraste); (of high building) écraser.

dwell [dwel] vi (dwelt) Lit: habiter, demeurer. 'dweller n habitant, -ante. 'dwelling n Lit: lieu m de séjour; Adm: domicile m; d. house, maison d'habitation. 'dwell (up)'on vtr insister, appuyer, s'étendre, sur (un sujet).

dwindle ['dwindl] vi to d. (away), diminuer; dépérir. 'dwindling a diminuant.

dye [dai] 1. n (a) teinture f, teint m; fast d., grand teint (b) matière colorante; colorant m; teinture (pour les cheveux) 2. vtr teindre; to d. sth black, teindre qch en noir; to d. one's hair, se teindre les cheveux. 'dyed-in-the-'wool a Fig: bon teint inv. 'dyeing n teinture. 'dyer n teinturier, -ière; d.'s and cleaner's (shop), teinturerie f, pressing m. 'dyestuff n matière colorante.

dying ['daiiŋ] 1. a mourant, agonisant; (son m) qui s'éteint 2. (a) n mort f; (death throes) agonie f; to my d. day, jusqu'à la mort (b) npl the d., les mourants mpl, les moribonds mpl, les agonisants mpl.

dyke [daik] n digue f, levée f.

dynamic [dai'næmik] a dynamique. dy'namics npl dynamique f. 'dynamism n dynamisme m.

dynamite ['dainəmait] 1. n dynamite f 2. vtr faire sauter (des roches) à la dynamite; dynamiter (un bâtiment).

dynamo ['dainəmou] n dynamo f.

dynasty ['dinəsti] n (pl dynasties) dynastie f. dy'nastic a dynastique.

dysentery ['disəntri] n Med: dysenterie f.

dyslexia [dis'leksiə] n dyslexie f. dys'lexic, dys'lectic a & n dyslexique (mf).

dyspepsia [dis'pepsiə] n dyspepsie f. dys'peptic a & n dyspepsique (mf), dyspeptique (mf).

dystrophy ['distrəfi] n dystrophie f; muscular d., dystrophie musculaire progressive.

E

E, e [i:] *n* (la lettre) E, e *m*; *Mus*: mi *m*; **key of E flat**, clef de mi bémol.

each [iːtʃ] **1.** *a* chaque; **e. day**, chaque jour; tous les jours; **e. one of us**, chacun, chacune, de nous, d'entre nous **2.** *pron* chacun, -une; **e. of us**, chacun d'entre nous; **we earn £10 e.**, we **e. earn £10**, nous gagnons dix livres chacun; **peaches at 20p e.**, pêches à 20p chacune, 20p pièce; **one of e.**, un de chaque; **e. other**, l'un(e) l'autre, les un(e)s les autres; **they adore e. other**, ils s'adorent; **to be afraid of e. other**, avoir peur l'un de l'autre; **separated from e. other**, séparés l'un de l'autre.

eager ['iːgər] *a* passionné; vif (désir); (regard) avide; **to be e. to do sth.**, être impatient de faire qch; *F:* **e. beaver**, zélé, -ée. **'eagerly** *adv* passionnément, avidement. **'eagerness** *n* impatience *f*; vif désir.

eagle [iːgl] *n* Orn: aigle *mf*; **golden e.**, aigle royal. **'eagle-'eyed** *a* aux yeux d'aigle. **'eaglet** *n* aiglon *m*.

ear¹ [iər] *n* oreille *f*; **e., nose and throat specialist**, oto-rhino-laryngologiste *mf*; **to have sharp ears**, avoir l'oreille, l'ouïe, fine; **to have an e. for music**, avoir de l'oreille; avoir l'oreille musicale; **to keep one's ears open, one's e. to the ground**, se tenir aux écoutes; **e. defenders**, protège-tympan *m inv*; *Sp:* **e. protector(s)**, protège-oreilles *m inv*; **your ears must have been burning**, les oreilles ont dû vous tinter; *F:* **I'm up to my ears in work**, je suis débordé de travail; *F:* **to play it by e.**, aller à vue de nez, au pifomètre; *F:* **I'm all ears**, je suis tout oreilles; j'écoute; *F: (of words)* **to go in one e. and out of the other**, entrer par une oreille et sortir par l'autre. **'earache** *n* mal *m* d'oreille(s); **to have e.**, avoir mal à l'oreille, aux oreilles. **'eardrum** *n* tympan *m* (de l'oreille). **'earmark** *vtr* affecter, assigner, réserver (**for**, à). **'earphone** *n* écouteur *m*; *pl* casque *m*. **'earplug** *n* (*for sleeping*) boule *f* Quiès (*Rtm*); *Av: etc:* protège-tympan. **'earring** *n* boucle *f* d'oreille. **'earshot** *n* within, out of, e., à, hors de, portée de voix. **'ear-splitting** *a* (bruit) qui vous fend les oreilles. **'earwig** *n* Ent: perce-oreille *m*.

ear² *n* épi *m* (de blé).

earl [əːl] *n* comte *m* (*f* **countess**, *qv*). **'earldom** *n* comté *m*; titre *m* de comte.

early ['əːli] (**-ier, -iest**) **1.** *a* (*a*) **in the e. morning**, de bon, de grand, matin; **in e. summer**, au début de l'été; **to be an e. riser**, être matinal; se lever de bon matin, tôt; **to keep e. hours**, se coucher (et se lever) tôt; **I'm going to have an e. night**, je vais me coucher de bonne heure; **it's e. days yet**, il est encore trop tôt (*b*) (*of man, church*) primitif; **the e. Christians**, les premiers chrétiens; **e. youth**, première jeunesse; **e. age**, âge tendre; **at an e. age**, dès l'enfance (*c*) (*of fruit, flowers*) précoce, hâtif; (*of death*) prématuré; **e. vegetables, fruit**, primeurs *fpl* (*d*) prochain, rapproché; **at an e. date**, prochainement; à une date prochaine; **next week at the earliest**, la semaine prochaine au plus tôt **2.** *adv* de bonne heure; tôt; **earlier (on)**, plus tôt; **too e.**, trop tôt; de trop bonne heure; **it's (still) e.**, il est (encore) tôt; **to arrive five minutes e.**, arriver avec cinq minutes d'avance; **to leave work ten minutes e.**, quitter le bureau dix minutes en avance; **e. in the morning**, le matin de bonne heure; très tôt le matin; **e. in the afternoon**, au début de l'après-midi; **as e. as the tenth century**, déjà au, dès le, dixième siècle; **as e. as possible**, le plus tôt possible; **to die e.**, mourir (i) jeune (ii) prématurément. **'early-'warning** *a* Mil: etc: **e.-w. system**, réseau de radars de pré-alerte.

earn [əːn] *vtr* gagner (de l'argent); mériter (des éloges); **to e. one's living**, gagner sa vie. **'earnings** *npl* (*a*) salaire *m* (*b*) profits *mpl*, bénéfices *mpl*.

earnest ['əːnist] **1.** *a* sérieux; (ouvrier) consciencieux; (*of request*) pressant; (*of prayer*) fervent **2.** *n* **in e.**, sérieusement; pour de bon; **to be in e.**, être sérieux; **ne pas plaisanter. 'earnestly** *adv* sérieusement; sincèrement; (travailler) avec zèle. **'earnestness** *n* gravité *f*, sérieux *m* (de ton); caractère sérieux (d'une discussion); ferveur *f* (d'une prière).

earth [əːθ] **1.** *n* (*a*) terre *f*; monde *m*; **on e.**, sur terre; **nothing on e.**, rien au monde; **where on e. have you been?** où diable étiez-vous? **to cost the e.**, coûter les yeux de la tête (*b*) (*ground*) terre, sol *m*; (*soil*) terre; **down to e.**, terre à terre; réaliste (*c*) terrier *m*, tanière *f* (d'un renard); **to run s.o. to e.**, se terrer; **to run s.o. to e.**, dénicher qn (*d*) El: masse *f*; **e. cable**, câble de terre **2.** *vtr* El: mettre (un appareil) à la masse, à la terre. **'earthen** *a* de, en, terre. **'earthenware** *n* poterie *f* (de terre); faïence *f*. **'earthly** *a* terrestre; *F:* **there's no e. reason for**, il n'y a pas la moindre raison (du monde) pour; **he hasn't an e. (chance)**, il n'a pas l'ombre d'une chance (de réussir). **'earthquake** *n* tremblement *m* de terre; séisme *m*. **'earthworks** *npl* travaux *m* en terre, de terrassement. **'earthworm** *n* ver *m* de terre. **'earthy** *a* (**-ier, -iest**) terreux; (*of pers*) terre à terre; (*of humour*) truculent.

ease [iːz] *n* (*a*) tranquillité *f*; repos *m*, bien-être *m*; **to be at e.**, être à l'aise; avoir l'esprit tranquille; *Mil:* **to stand at e.**, se mettre au repos; **ill at e.**, mal à l'aise; **to put s.o. at (his) e.**, mettre qn à son aise; **to take one's e.**, se mettre à l'aise; **life of e.**, vie de loisirs *mpl* (*b*) aisance *f* (de manières); simplicité *f* (de réglage); facilité *f* (de manœuvre); **with e.**, facilement; aisément **2.** *v* (*a*) *vtr* adoucir, calmer (la souffrance); soulager (un malade); tranquilliser (l'esprit); débarrasser, délivrer (qn de qch); détendre, relâcher (un cordage, un ressort); desserrer (une vis); *Dressm:* donner plus d'ampleur à (une robe) (*b*) *vi* **to e. (off, up)**, (*of pain*) s'atténuer; (*of tension*) se détendre; (*of pers*) se relâcher; (*slow down*) diminuer la vitesse; ralentir.

easel ['iːzl] *n* chevalet *m* (de peintre).

east [iːst] **1.** *n* (*a*) est *m*; **to the e.**, à l'est (**of, de**) (*b*) *Geog:* **the E.**, l'Orient *m*; **the Far E.**, l'Extrême-Orient *m*; **the Middle E.**, le Moyen-Orient; **the Near E.**, le Proche-Orient **2.** *adv* à l'est; **to travel e.**, voyager vers l'est; **e. of the Rhine**, à l'est du Rhin **3.** *a* (côté) est; (vent) d'est; (pays) de l'est; **E. End**, quartiers pauvres de la partie est de Londres. **'eastbound** *a* allant vers l'est, en direction de l'est. **'easterly** *a* (vent) d'est; (point) situé à l'est, vers l'est. **'eastern** *a* est, de l'est; oriental. **'eastward** *a* à l'est. **'eastward(s)** *adv* à l'est, vers l'est.

Easter ['iːstər] *n* Pâques *m*; **E. Day**, le jour de Pâques; **E. egg**, œuf de Pâques.

easy ['iːzi] (-ier, -iest) **1.** *a* (*a*) à l'aise; (esprit) tranquille; (vie) sans souci; (*of manners*) aisé, libre; (style) facile; **e. chair**, fauteuil *m* (*b*) (travail) facile; aisé; *F:* **as e. as anything**, simple comme bonjour; **that's e. to see**, cela se voit; **within e. reach of (sth)**, à distance commode de (qch) (*c*) (*of pers*) facile, accommodant, complaisant; **e. to live with**, facile à vivre; *F:* **I'm e.!** ça m'est égal! **by e. stages**, (voyager) par petites étapes; **to come in an e. first**, arriver bon premier; *Com:* **by e. payments, on e. terms**, avec facilités *fpl* de paiement **2.** *adv* **to take things e.**, prendre les choses en douceur; **take it e.!** ne vous en faites pas! **to go e. with, on, s.o., sth**, ménager qn, qch; aller doucement avec qn, qch; **easier said than done**, c'est plus facile à dire qu'à faire. **'easily** *adv* (*a*) facilement, sans difficulté; **he's e. 40**, il a bien 40 ans (*b*) (se fermer) sans effort, doucement (*c*) (répondre) tranquillement. **'easiness** *n* (*a*) facilité *f* (d'un travail) (*b*) (*of pers*) humeur *f* facile (*c*) grâce *f* (du style). **'easy-'going** *a* accommodant, complaisant; d'humeur facile; facile à vivre.

eat [iːt] *vtr & i* (ate [et]; eaten) manger; prendre (un repas); **to e. one's lunch, dinner, supper**, déjeuner, dîner, souper; **fit to e.**, mangeable; bon à manger; **to e. one's words**, se rétracter; **to e. like a horse**, manger comme un ogre; **to e. one's fill**, manger à sa faim; *Fig:* **to e. one's heart out**, se ronger le cœur; *F:* **I've got him eating out of my hand**, il fait tout ce que je veux; *F:* **he won't e. you!** il ne te mangera pas! *F:* **i'll e. my hat**, je veux bien être pendu; **to e. s.o. out of house and home**, ruiner qn en nourriture; *F:* **what's eating you?** quelle mouche te pique? **'eatable 1.** *a* mangeable; bon à manger **2.** *npl* comestibles *mpl*. **'eat a'way** *vtr* ronger, éroder; (*of acid*) attaquer (un métal). **'eater** *n* small, big, e., petit(e), gros(se), mangeur, -euse. **'eat 'into** *vtr* ronger (le bois). **'eat 'out** *vi* manger au restaurant. **eats** *npl F:* manger *m*; bouffe *f*. **'eat 'up** *vtr* finir (son pain); **to e. up the miles**, dévorer la route; **car that eats up petrol**, voiture qui consomme trop d'essence; **to be eaten up (with sth)**, être dévoré (d'orgueil).

eaves [iːvz] *npl* (*of house*) avant-toit *m*. **'eavesdrop** *vi* (eavesdropped) écouter aux portes. **'eavesdropper** *n* oreille indiscrète.

ebb [eb] **1.** *n* reflux *m*; baisse *f* (de la marée); déclin *m* (de la fortune); **the e. and flow**, le flux et le reflux; **e. tide**, marée descendante; (*of pers*) **to be at a low e.**, être très bas **2.** *vi* (*of tide*) baisser; (*of life*) décliner; **to e. and flow**, monter et baisser; **to e. away**, s'écouler.

ebony ['ebəni] *n* ébène *f*; bois *m* d'ébène.

ebullient [i'bʌljənt] *a* exubérant; enthousiaste. **e'bullience** *n* effervescence *f*.

eccentric [ik'sentrik] *a & n* excentrique (*mf*); original, -ale. **ec'centrically** *adv* excentriquement. **eccen'tricity** *n* excentricité *f*; originalité *f*.

ecclesiastic [ikliːzi'æstik] *n* ecclésiastique *m*. **ecclesi'astical** *a* ecclésiastique.

ECG *abbr* electrocardiogram.

echo ['ekou] **1.** *n* (*pl* echoes) écho *m*; **e. chamber**, chambre sonore; **e. sounder**, écho-sondeur *m* **2.** *v* (*a*) répéter (*b*) *vi* faire écho; retentir.

éclair [ei'kleər] *n Cu:* **(chocolate) é.**, éclair *m* (au chocolat).

eclectic [i'klektik] *a* éclectique.

eclipse [i'klips] **1.** *n* éclipse *f* **2.** *vtr* éclipser.

ecology [i'kɔlədʒi] *n* écologie *f*. **eco'logical** *a* écologique. **e'cologist** *n* écologiste *mf*.

economy [i'kɔnəmi] *n* (*pl* -ies) économie *f*; **to practise e.**, économiser; **political e.**, économie politique; **planned e.**, économie planifiée; *Av:* **e. class**, classe économique. **eco'nomic** *a* (*a*) économique (*b*) (loyer) rentable. **eco'nomical** *a* (*of pers*) économe; (*of methods*) économique. **eco'nomically** *adv* économiquement; **to use sth e.**, ménager qch. **eco'nomics** *npl* (*a*) économie politique (*b*) rentabilité *f* (d'un projet); aspects financiers (de l'urbanisme). **e'conomist** *n* économiste *mf* (politique). **e'conomize** *vtr & i* économiser (**on**, sur); ménager; faire des économies.

ecstasy ['ekstəsi] *n* transport *m* (de joie); ravissement *m*; extase *f*; **to be in e., go into ecstasies, over sth**, s'extasier sur qch.

Ecuador ['ekwədɔːr] *Prn Geog:* (République *f* de) l'Équateur *m*.

ecumenical [iːkjuˈmenikl] *a* œcuménique.

eczema ['eksimə] *n Med:* eczéma *m*.

eddy ['edi] **1.** *n* (*pl* eddies) (*of water, wind*) remous *m*; tourbillon *m* **2.** *vi* (eddied) (*of water*) faire des remous; (*of wind*) tourbillonner, tournoyer.

edge [edʒ] **1.** *n* (*a*) fil *m*, tranchant *m* (d'une lame); **to take the e. off sth**, émousser qch (*b*) arête *f* (d'une pierre); bord *m*, rebord *m*; tranche *f* (d'un livre); (*of pers*) **on e.**, énervé; **it sets my teeth on e.**, cela me fait mal aux dents; **to have the e. on s.o.**, être avantagé par rapport à qn; **on a knife e.**, (*of pers*) sur des charbons ardents; (*of result*) qui ne tient qu'à un fil (*c*) lisière *f*, bordure *f* (d'un bois); bord, rive *f* (d'une rivière); liséré *m*, bord (d'un tissu) **2.** *vtr & i* (*a*) aiguiser, affiler, affûter (un outil) (*b*) border (un mouchoir, la route) (*c*) **to e. (one's way) into a room**, se faufiler, se glisser, dans une pièce; **to e. one's chair nearer**, rapprocher, avancer, sa chaise; **to e. away**, s'éloigner (tout) doucement (**from**, de). **'edgeways, 'edgewise** *adv* de côté; de chant; *F:* **I can't get a word in e.**, impossible de placer un mot. **'edging** *n* (*in garden*) bordure; *Dressm:* liséré. **'edgy** *a F:* (*of pers*) nerveux; énervé.

edible ['edibl] *a* comestible; bon à manger; mangeable.

edict ['iːdikt] *n* édit *m*.

edifice ['edifis] *n* édifice *m*.

edify ['edifai] *vtr* (edified) édifier.

Edinburgh ['edinb(ə)rə] *Prn Geog:* Édimbourg.

edit ['edit] *vtr* annoter, éditer (un texte); rédiger, diriger (un journal); monter (un film); **edited by,** (série, journal) sous la direction de. **'editing** *n* annotation *f* (d'un texte); rédaction *f* (d'un journal); *Cin:* montage *m.* **edition** [i'diʃn] *n* édition *f*; **limited e.,** édition à tirage limité. **'editor** *n* éditeur, -trice (d'un texte); directeur, -trice (d'une série de textes); rédacteur, -trice (en chef) (d'un journal); *Cin:* monteur, -euse; *TV: WTel:* **programme e.,** éditorialiste *mf.* **edi'torial** 1. *a* (bureau) de rédaction; **the e. staff,** la rédaction 2. *n* Journ: article *m* de fond; éditorial *m.*

educate ['edjukeit] *vtr* (*a*) donner de l'instruction à, instruire (qn); **he was educated in France,** il a fait ses études en France (*b*) former (qn, le goût de qn); **educated man,** homme instruit, cultivé. **edu'cation** *n* (*a*) éducation *f* (*b*) enseignement *m*, instruction *f*; formation *f*; **he's had a good e.,** il a reçu une bonne éducation; **adult e.,** enseignement des adultes; **university e.,** éducation supérieure; études supérieures. **edu'cational** *a* (ouvrage) d'éducation, d'enseignement; (procédé) pédagogique; (film) éducatif; (ouvrage) éducateur; (programme) scolaire. **edu'cation(al)ist** *n* pédagogue *mf.* **edu'cationally** *adv* e. **subnormal,** (enfant) arriéré. **'educator** *n* éducateur, -trice.

Edward ['edwəd] *Prnm* Édouard. **Ed'wardian** [-'wɔːrd-] *a* qui a rapport à l'époque du roi Édouard VII; **the E. era,** la belle époque.

EEC *abbr European Economic Community.*

eel [iːl] *n* anguille *f.*

eerie ['iəri] *a* (-ier, -iest) surnaturel; qui donne le frisson.

efface [i'feis] *vtr* effacer; oblitérer (qch).

effect [i'fekt] 1. *n* (*a*) effet *m*; résultat *m*; conséquence *f*; action *f* (de la chaleur); **to have an e. on,** produire de l'effet sur; **to have no e.,** ne produire aucun effet; **to take e.,** (i) faire (son) effet (ii) (*of regulations*) entrer en vigueur (iii) (*of drugs*) agir, opérer; **to come into e.,** entrer en vigueur; **with e. from 10th October,** applicable à partir du 10 octobre; **to no e.,** en vain; sans résultat; **to put into e.,** mettre à exécution; **in e.,** en fait; en réalité; **for e.,** à effet (*b*) sens *m*, teneur *f* (d'un document); **words to that e.,** quelque chose d'approchant (*c*) **personal effects,** biens *mpl*, effets (personnels); *Th:* **stage effects,** effets scéniques; **sound effects,** bruitage *m*; **special effects,** trucage *m* 2. *vtr* effectuer, réaliser; opérer. **e'ffective** *a* (*a*) (remède) efficace; (rendement) effectif; (contrat) valide; *Adm:* (date) d'entrée en vigueur (*b*) (contraste) frappant; (tableau) qui fait de l'effet. **e'ffectively** *adv* (*a*) efficacement, utilement (*b*) effectivement; en réalité (*c*) d'une façon frappante. **e'ffectiveness** *n* (*a*) efficacité *f* (*b*) effet heureux. **e'ffectives** *npl esp NAm: Mil:* effectifs *mpl.* **e'ffectual** *a* efficace; (contrat) valide; (règlement) en vigueur. **e'ffectually** *adv* efficacement. **e'ffectuate** *vtr* effectuer.

effeminate [i'feminət] *a* efféminé. **e'ffeminacy** *n* caractère efféminé.

effervesce [efə'ves] *vi* être, entrer, en effervescence; (*of drinks*) mousser; (*of pers*) pétiller de joie. **effer'vescence** *n* effervescence *f.* **effer'vescent** *a* effervescent.

effete [i'fiːt] *a* mou, veule.

efficacious [efi'keiʃəs] *a* efficace. **'efficacy** *n* efficacité *f.*

efficiency [i'fiʃ(ə)nsi] *n* efficacité *f* (d'un remède); rendement *m* (d'une machine); bon fonctionnement (d'une administration); capacité *f*, compétence *f* (d'une personne). **e'fficient** *a* (*of method, work*) efficace; (machine) qui fonctionne bien; (*of pers*) capable, compétent. **e'fficiently** *adv* efficacement; avec compétence.

effluent ['efluənt] *n* effluent *m.*

effort ['efət] *n* (*a*) effort *m*; **to make an e. to do sth,** faire un effort pour, s'efforcer de, faire qch; **wasted e.,** peine perdue (*b*) (coup *m* d')essai *m*; **that's not a bad e.,** ce n'est pas mal réussi; **what do you think of his latest e.?** qu'est-ce que tu penses de ce qu'il vient de faire? **'effortless** *a* sans effort; facile. **'effortlessly** *adv* sans effort.

effrontery [i'frʌntəri] *n* effronterie *f.*

effusive [i'fjuːsiv] *a* démonstratif, expansif; (compliments) sans fin; **to be e. in one's thanks,** se confondre en remerciements. **e'ffusively** *adv* avec effusion. **e'ffusion** *n*, **e'ffusiveness** *n* effusion *f*; volubilité *f.*

egalitarian [igæli'teəriən] *a & n* égalitaire (*mf*).

egg [eg] *n* œuf *m*; **boiled e.,** œuf à la coque; **fried e.,** œuf sur le plat; **scrambled eggs,** œufs brouillés; *F:* **a bad e.,** un vaurien; *F:* **as sure as eggs is eggs,** aussi sûr que deux et deux font quatre; *F:* **to have e. on one's face,** être couvert de ridicule. **'eggcup** *n* coquetier *m.* **'egghead** *n F:* intellectuel, -elle. **egg'nog** (*also* e. **flip**) *Cu:* lait *m* de poule. **'egg 'on** *vtr* inciter, pousser (qn) (**to do sth,** à faire qch). **'eggplant** *n* aubergine *f.* **'egg-shaped** *a* ovoïde. **'eggshell** *n* coquille *f* d'œuf.

ego ['iːgou] *n* **the e.,** le moi, l'égo *m*; *F:* **e. trip,** glorification *f* de soi-même. **ego'centric** *a* égocentrique. **egoism** ['egouizm] *n* égoïsme *m.* **'egoist** *n* égoïste *mf.* **ego'istic(al)** *a* égoïste. **'egotism** *n* égotisme *m.* **'egotist** *n* égotiste *mf.* **ego'tistic(al)** *a* égotiste.

Egypt ['iːdʒipt] *Prn Geog:* Égypte *f.* **E'gyptian** *a & n* égyptien, -ienne.

eiderdown ['aidədaun] *n* édredon *m.*

eight [eit] *num a & n* huit (*m*); **to be e.** (years old), avoir huit ans; **page twenty-e.,** page vingt-huit; **it's e. o'clock,** il est huit heures; *F:* **to have had one over the e.,** avoir bu un coup de trop. **eigh'teen** *num a & n* dix-huit (*m*). **eigh'teenth** *num a & n* dix-huitième (*mf*); (**on**) **the e. (of May),** le dix-huit (mai); **Louis the E.,** Louis Dix-huit. **eighth** *num a & n* huitième (*mf*); (**on**) **the e. (of April),** le huit (avril); **Henry the E.,** Henri Huit. **'eightieth** *num a & n* quatre-vingtième (*mf*). **'eighty** *num a & n* (*pl* -ies) quatre-vingts (*m*); **e.-one,** quatre-vingt-un; **e.-first,** quatre-vingt-unième.

Eire ['eərə] *Prn Geog:* l'Eire *f.*

either ['aiðər, 'iːðər] 1. *a & pron* (*a*) l'un(e) et l'autre; **on e. side,** de chaque côté; des deux côtés (*b*) l'un(e) ou l'autre; **e. of them,** soit l'un(e), soit l'autre; n'importe lequel, laquelle; **I don't believe e. of you,** je ne vous crois ni l'un ni l'autre; **there is no evidence e. way,** les preuves manquent de part et d'autre 2. *conj & adv* **e. . . . or . . .,** ou . . ., ou . . .; soit . . ., soit

...; **e. come in** or **go out,** entrez ou sortez; **it's not him e.,** ce n'est pas lui non plus; **I don't e.,** ni moi non plus.

ejaculate [i'dʒækjuleit] *vtr & i* (*a*) *Physiol:* éjaculer (*b*) pousser (un cri); s'écrier. **ejacu'lation** *n* (*a*) *Physiol:* éjaculation *f* (*b*) cri *m*, exclamation *f*.

eject [i'dʒekt] **1.** *vtr* jeter, émettre (des flammes); expulser (un agitateur); *Av:* éjecter **2.** *vi Av:* s'éjecter. **e'jection** *n* expulsion *f*; *Av:* éjection *f*. **e'jector** *n Mec:* éjecteur *m*; *Av:* **e. seat,** siège éjectable.

eke [i:k] *vtr* to **e. out,** ménager, économiser, faire durer (ses revenus).

elaborate 1. *a* [i'læbərət] compliqué; (*of style*) travaillé; (*of inspection*) minutieux; (*of clothes*) recherché **2.** *vtr & i* [i'læbəreit] donner plus de détails (**on,** sur). **e'laborately** *adv* avec soin; minutieusement.

elapse [i'læps] *vi* (*of time*) s'écouler; (se) passer.

elastic [i'læstik] *a & n* élastique (*m*); **e. band,** élastique. **elas'ticity** *n* élasticité *f*; souplesse *f* (de corps).

elated [i'leitid] *a* transporté; plein de joie. **e'lation** *n* exaltation *f*; joie *f*, gaieté *f*.

elbow ['elbou] **1.** *n* coude *m*; **to lean one's e. on sth,** s'accouder sur qch; **at s.o.'s e.,** aux côtés de qn; *F:* **e. grease,** huile de coude **2.** *vtr* pousser (qn) du coude; **to e. s.o. aside,** écarter qn d'un coup de coude; **to e. one's way through the crowd,** se frayer un passage à travers la foule (en jouant des coudes). **'elbowroom** *n* **to have (enough) e.,** avoir ses coudées franches.

elder¹ ['eldər] **1.** *a* aîné, plus âgé; **my e. brother,** mon frère aîné; **e. statesman,** doyen *m* des hommes politiques **2.** *n* aîné, -ée; plus âgé, -ée; *Ecc:* ancien *m*. **'elderly 1.** *a* d'un certain âge; assez âgé **2.** *npl* **the e.,** les personnes âgées. **'eldest** *a* aîné; **my e. (son),** mon (fils) aîné.

elder² *n Bot:* **e. (tree),** sureau *m*. **'elderberry** (*pl* -ies), **-flower** *n* baie *f*, fleur *f*, de sureau.

elect [i'lekt] **1.** *vtr* (*a*) to **e. (to do sth),** choisir (de faire qch) (*b*) élire (qn) **2.** *a* élu; **the Mayor e.,** le futur maire. **e'lection** *n* élection *f*; **general, parliamentary, e.,** élections législatives; **e. committee,** comité électoral. **election'eering** *n* propagande, campagne, électorale. **e'lector** *n* électeur, -trice; votant, -ante. **e'lectoral** *a* électoral. **e'lectorate** *n* corps électoral; électeurs *mpl*.

electricity [ilek'trisiti] *n* électricité *f*. **e'lectric, e'lectrical** *a* électrique; **electrical engineering,** électrotechnique *f*. **elec'trician** *n* électricien *m*. **electrifi'cation** *n* (*a*) électrisation *f* (d'un corps) (*b*) électrification *f* (d'un chemin de fer, etc). **e'lectrify** *vtr* (*a*) électriser (un corps, son auditoire) (*b*) électrifier (un chemin de fer). **e'lectro'cardiogram** *n* électrocardiogramme *m*. **e'lectrocute** *vtr* électrocuter. **electro'cution** *n* électrocution *f*. **e'lectrode** *n* électrode *f*. **elec'trolysis** *n* électrolyse *f*. **e'lectron** *n* électron *m*; **e. microscope,** microscope électronique. **elec'tronic 1.** *a* électronique **2.** *npl* **electronics,** électronique *f*; **e. engineer,** ingénieur électronicien; électronicien, -ienne. **e'lectroplated** *a* (métal) plaqué, argenté.

elegance ['eligəns] *n* élégance *f*. **'elegant** *a* élégant. **'elegantly** *adv* élégamment; avec élégance.

elegy ['elədʒi] *n* (*pl* **elegies**) élégie *f*.

element ['elimənt] *n* élément *m*; *El:* résistance *f*; **to be in one's e.,** être dans son élément; **exposed to the elements,** exposé aux intempéries *fpl*; **the human e.,** le facteur humain. **ele'mentary** *a* élémentaire; *Sch:* **e. algebra,** rudiments *mpl* d'algèbre.

elephant ['elifənt] *n* (**bull**) **e.,** éléphant *m* (mâle); **cow e.,** éléphant femelle; *Fig:* **white e.,** objet inutile et encombrant. **ele'phantine** *a* (*a*) éléphantin; **e. wit,** esprit lourd (*b*) (*of size, proportions*) éléphantesque.

elevate ['eliveit] *vtr* élever; relever (son style). **'elevated** *a* (*a*) élevé; (*of thoughts*) haut; **e. position,** position élevée (*b*) (*overhead*) surélevé; (chemin de fer) aérien. **'elevating** *a* qui élève l'esprit; (principe) moralisateur. **ele'vation** *n* élévation *f*; **e. above sea level,** altitude *f*, hauteur *f*, au-dessus du niveau de la mer; **sectional e.,** coupe verticale; **front e.,** façade *f*. **'elevator** *n* (*a*) monte-charge *m inv*; **grain e.,** élévateur *m* à grains (*b*) *NAm:* (*Br* = **lift**) ascenseur *m* (*c*) *Av:* gouvernail *m* de profondeur.

eleven [i'levn] **1.** *num a & n* onze (*m*); **there are only e. of them,** ils ne sont que onze; **the e. o'clock train,** le train d'onze heures; **to be e. (years old),** avoir onze ans; **page e.,** page onze; **it's e. o'clock,** il est onze heures **2.** *n Sp:* équipe *f* de onze joueurs. **e'levenses** *n F:* casse-croûte *m inv* de onze heures (du matin). **e'leventh** *num a & n* onzième (*mf*); **at the e. hour,** au dernier moment; (**on) the e.,** le onze (du mois).

elf [elf] *n* (*pl* **elves**) elfe *m*.

elicit [i'lisit] *vtr* tirer (les faits) au clair; obtenir (une réponse) (**from** s.o., de qn); découvrir (la vérité).

eligible ['elidʒibl] *a* éligible (**to,** à); **to be e.,** avoir droit (**for,** à); **e. for a job,** admissible à un emploi; **e. young man,** bon parti. **eligi'bility** *n* éligibilité *f*.

eliminate [i'limineit] *vtr* éliminer; supprimer; écarter (une éventualité). **e'liminating** *a* (épreuve) éliminatoire. **elimi'nation** *n* élimination *f*; **by process of e.,** en procédant par élimination.

élite [ei'li:t] *n* élite *f*. **e'litist** *a & n* élitiste (*mf*).

Elizabethan [ilizə'bi:θən] *a* élisabéthain.

elk [elk] *n Z:* élan *m*; **Canadian e.,** orignal *m*.

elliptical [i'liptikl] *a* elliptique.

elm [elm] *n* orme *m*; **Dutch e. disease,** maladie des ormes.

elocution [elə'kju:ʃn] *n* élocution *f*, diction *f*.

elongate ['i:lɔŋgeit] *vtr* allonger, étendre.

elope [i'loup] *vi* s'enfuir (avec un amant, ensemble); (*of girl*) se laisser enlever.

eloquence ['eləkwəns] *n* éloquence *f*. **'eloquent** *a* éloquent; (regard) qui en dit long. **'eloquently** *adv* éloquemment.

else [els] **1.** *adv* autrement; ou bien; **come in, or e. go out,** entrez ou bien sortez; *F:* **or e.!** sinon! **2.** (*a*) *a* or *adv* **anyone e.,** toute autre personne; tout autre, n'importe qui d'autre; **did you see anybody e.?** avez-vous vu quelqu'un d'autre? **anything e.,** n'importe quoi d'autre; (*in shop*) **anything e., madam?** et avec cela, madame? **someone e.,** quelqu'un d'autre, un autre; **something e.,** autre chose; quelque chose d'autre; **no one e., nobody e.,** personne d'autre; **nothing e.,** rien d'autre; **nothing e., thank you,** plus rien, merci; **who e.?** qui d'autre? qui encore? **what**

e.? quoi encore? quoi de plus? **what e. can I do?** que puis-je faire d'autre, de mieux, de plus? **everything e.,** tout le reste (b) adv **everywhere e.,** partout ailleurs; **somewhere e.,** autre part; ailleurs; **nowhere e.,** nulle part ailleurs. **'else'where** adv ailleurs; autre part.

elucidate [i'lu:sideit] vtr élucider, éclaircir (un problème). **eluci'dation** n élucidation f.

elude [i'lu:d] vtr éluder, éviter (une question); échapper à (la poursuite); esquiver (un coup); se soustraire à (la justice).

elusive [i'lu:siv] a insaisissable, intangible; (of reply) évasif; (of personality) fuyant.

elves [elvz] see **elf**.

emaciated [i'meisieitid] a émacié; décharné. **emaci'ation** n amaigrissement m, émaciation f.

emanate ['eməneit] vi émaner (**from,** de).

emancipate [i'mænsipeit] vtr émanciper; affranchir (un esclave). **emanci'pation** n émancipation f; affranchissement m.

embalm [im'ba:m] vtr embaumer.

embankment [im'bæŋkmənt] n (a) digue f; levée f de terre (b) talus m; remblai m; (of river) berge f, quai m.

embargo [im'ba:gou] n (pl -oes) embargo m; **to put an e. on,** mettre un embargo sur; **under an e.,** séquestré.

embark [im'ba:k] 1. vtr embarquer (les passagers) 2. vi s'embarquer (**on,** à bord d'un navire, dans une affaire). **embar'kation** n embarquement m; **e. card,** carte d'accès à bord.

embarrass [im'bærəs] vtr embarrasser, gêner. **em-'barrassing** a embarrassant. **em'barrassment** n embarras m; gêne f.

embassy ['embəsi] n ambassade f.

embed [im'bed] vtr (**embedded**) enfoncer (un clou); noyer (dans le béton).

embellish [im'beliʃ] vtr embellir, orner (qch); enjoliver (un récit). **em'bellishment** n embellissement m, ornement m; enjolivure f.

embers ['embəz] npl braise f; cendres ardentes; charbons ardents.

embezzle [im'bezl] vtr détourner (des fonds). **em-'bezzlement** n détournement m de fonds. **em-'bezzler** n auteur m d'un détournement de fonds.

embitter [im'bitər] vtr aigrir (le caractère), envenimer (une querelle). **em'bittered** a aigri; envenimé (**by,** par).

emblem ['embləm] n emblème m; insigne (sportif). **emble'matic** a emblématique.

embody [im'bɔdi] vtr (**embodied**) (a) incarner (b) personnifier (une qualité) (c) Jur: incorporer (un article). **em'bodiment** n incarnation f; personnification f.

embolism ['embəlizm] n Med: embolie f.

emboss [im'bɔs] vtr travailler en relief; bosseler (du métal).

embrace [im'breis] 1. n étreinte f 2. v (a) vtr embrasser; étreindre (qn) (b) vi s'embrasser.

embroider [im'brɔidər] vtr broder (un tissu, sur les faits); enjoliver (un récit). **em'broidery** n broderie f.

embroiled [im'brɔild] a entraîné (**in,** dans).

embryo ['embriou] n Biol: embryon m; **in e.,** (i) Biol: (à l'état) embryonnaire (ii) (projet) embryonnaire, en germe. **embry'onic** a embryonnaire; Fig: en germe.

emend [i'mend] vtr corriger (un texte).

emerald ['emərəld] 1. n émeraude f 2. a & n e. (**green**), (vert) émeraude (m).

emerge [i'mɔ:dʒ] vi (a) émerger (**from,** de); surgir (de l'eau) (b) déboucher (**from,** de); sortir (d'un trou) (c) (of difficulty) se dresser; surgir; **from these facts it emerges that,** de ces faits il ressort que. **e'mergence** n émergence f (d'un fait); apparition f (d'un nouvel état). **e'mergent** a (pays) en voie de développement.

emergency [i'mɔ:dʒənsi] n situation f, circonstance f, critique; cas urgent, imprévu; Med: **an e. (case),** une urgence; **e. ward,** salle d'urgence; **to provide for emergencies,** parer aux éventualités; **in an e., in case of e.,** en cas d'urgence; **state of e.,** état d'urgence; **e. repairs,** réparations d'urgence; **e. exit,** sortie de secours; **e. rations,** vivres de réserve.

emery ['eməri] n émeri m; **e. paper,** papier d'émeri; Toil: **e. board,** lime émeri.

emigrate ['emigreit] vi émigrer. **'emigrant** a & n émigrant, -ante. **emi'gration** n émigration f.

eminence ['eminəns] n (a) éminence f, élévation f (de terrain) (b) grandeur f, distinction f; Ecc: **your E.,** votre Éminence. **'eminent** a éminent; distingué. **'eminently** adv éminemment; par excellence.

emirate ['emirət] n émirat m.

emit [i'mit] vtr (**emitted**) dégager, émettre (de la chaleur); exhaler (une odeur); lancer, jeter (des étincelles); rendre (un son). **e'mission** n émission f, dégagement m.

emotion [i'mouʃn] n émotion f; **to appeal to the emotions,** faire appel aux sentiments; **full of e.,** ému. **e'motional** a (choc) émotif; (état) émotionnel; **e. voice,** voix émue; **to be e.,** s'attendrir facilement. **e'motionally** adv avec émotion; **I am e. involved,** cela me concerne de trop près. **e'motive** a émotif.

emperor ['empərər] n empereur m.

emphasize ['emfəsaiz] vtr accentuer, appuyer sur, souligner (un fait); faire ressortir (une qualité). **'emphasis** n (a) force f; accentuation f (b) insistance f; **to put e. on a fact,** appuyer sur un fait (c) Ling: accent m d'insistance. **em'phatic** a (manière) énergique; (refus) net, positif. **em'phatically** adv énergiquement; (refuser) catégoriquement.

empire ['empaiər] n empire m; **e. builder,** constructeur d'empires.

empiric(al) [em'pirik(əl)] a empirique.

employ [im'plɔi] 1. n **to be in s.o.'s e.,** être employé par qn 2. vtr employer; user de (la force); **to be employed in doing sth,** s'occuper, être occupé, à faire qch. **employ'ee** n employé, -ée; pl personnel m. **em'ployer** n patron, -onne; employeur, -euse; (**body of**) **employers,** patronat m; **employers' association,** syndicat patronal. **em'ployment** n emploi m, travail m; place f, situation f; **e. agency,** bureau de placement; **to find e. for s.o.,** placer qn.

empower [im'pauər] vtr autoriser (qn) (**to do sth,** à faire qch).

empress ['empris] n impératrice f.

empty ['empti] 1. v (**emptied**) (a) vtr vider; décharger

(un wagon); verser (de l'eau); vidanger (un carter) *(b)*
vi (of river) se déverser (**into,** dans); *(of hall)*
se vider **2.** *a* (**-ier, -iest**) vide (**of,** de); (immeuble)
inoccupé; (estomac) creux; *(of words)* vain; **on an e.
stomach,** à jeun **3.** *npl* **empties,** caisses *fpl,* bouteilles
fpl, vides. **'emptiness** *n* vide *m.* **'empty-
'handed** *a* les mains vides. **'empty-'headed** *a*
sans cervelle.

emu [ˈiːmjuː] *n Orn:* émeu *m.*

emulate [ˈemjuleit] *vtr* imiter. **emu'lation** *n* émulation *f.*

emulsion [iˈmʌlʃn] *n* émulsion *f;* e. (**paint**), peinture
mate.

enable [iˈneibl, e-] *vtr* **to e. s.o. to do sth,** mettre qn
à même, permettre à qn, de faire qch.

enact [inˈækt] *vtr* décréter (une loi).

enamel [iˈnæməl] **1.** *n (a)* émail *m;* **e. bath,** baignoire
en fer émaillé *(b)* vernis *m;* **e. paint,** peinture au
vernis **2.** *vtr* (**enamelled**) *(a)* émailler (la porcelaine) *(b)* ripoliner (une porte); vernir (du fer);
enamelled kettle, bouilloire en fer émaillé.

enamoured, *NAm:* **-ored** [inˈæməd] *a* amoureux
(**of,** de); passionné (**of,** pour).

encampment [inˈkæmpmənt] *n* campement *m;*
camp *m.*

encapsulate [inˈkæpsjuleit] *vtr* capsuler, renfermer.

encase [inˈkeis] *vtr* enfermer; revêtir.

enchant [inˈtʃɑːnt] *vtr* enchanter; charmer, ravir
(qn). **en'chanter,** *f* **-tress** *n* enchanteur, en-
chanteresse. **en'chanting** *a* enchanteur; charmant, ravissant. **en'chantingly** *adv* à ravir. **en-
'chantment** *n* enchantement *m;* ravissement *m.*

encircle [inˈsɜːkl] *vtr* ceindre, encercler; entourer
(une armée). **en'circlement, en'circling** *n*
encerclement *m.*

enclave [ˈenkleiv] *n* enclave *f.*

enclose [inˈklouz] *vtr (a)* clôturer (un champ) (**with,**
de); entourer (une ville) *(b)* inclure, refermer, joindre
(**in,** dans); **please find enclosed,** veuillez trouver
ci-inclus, ci-joint. **en'closed** *a* (espace) clos; *Ecc:*
(ordre) cloîtré. **en'closure** *n (a) (act)* clôture *f (b)*
enclos *m,* clos *m;* enceinte *f; Turf:* pesage *m (c) Com:*
pièce jointe, annexée; document ci-joint.

encompass [inˈkʌmpəs] *vtr* entourer.

encore [ˈɒŋkɔːr] *n & int* bis *m.*

encounter [inˈkauntər] **1.** *n* rencontre *f* **2.** *vtr* rencontrer (un obstacle); éprouver (des difficultés); affronter (l'ennemi); essuyer (une tempête).

encourage [inˈkʌridʒ] *vtr* encourager (qn) (**to do sth,**
à faire qch); favoriser (la recherche). **en'couragement** *n* encouragement *m.* **en'couraging** *a* encourageant. **en'couragingly** *adv* d'une manière
encourageante.

encroach [inˈkroutʃ] *vi* **to e. on the land,** empiéter
sur le, gagner du, terrain.

encrusted [inˈkrʌstid] *a* **e. with,** incrusté, couvert
d'une croûte, de.

encumber [inˈkʌmbər] *vtr* encombrer (**with,** de);
gêner (qn, le mouvement). **en'cumbrance** *n*
embarras *m,* charge *f;* **to be an e. to s.o.,** être à
charge à qn; **without (family) encumbrances,** sans
charges de famille.

encyclop(a)edia [insaiklǝˈpiːdiǝ] *n* encyclopédie *f.*
encyclo'p(a)edic *a* encyclopédique.

end [end] **1.** *n (a)* bout *m,* extrémité *f;* fin *f;* mégot *m*
(de cigarette); *Games:* **to change ends,** changer de
camp; *(of swimming pool)* **deep, shallow, e.,** grand,
petit, fond; *F:* **to be thrown in at the deep e.,** être mis
en pleine eau; *F:* **to go off the deep e.,** se mettre
en colère; sortir de ses gonds; **the e. house,** la dernière maison (de la rue); **the third from the e.,** le
troisième avant la fin; *Fig:* **to get hold of the wrong
e. of the stick,** prendre qch à contresens; *F:* **to keep
one's e. up,** ne pas se laisser démonter; tenir bon; **e.
to e.,** bout à bout; **from e. to e.,** d'un bout à l'autre;
(of box) **on e.,** debout; *(of hair)* **to stand on e.,** se
dresser (sur la tête); se hérisser; **for two hours on e.,**
(pendant) deux heures de suite; **for days on e.,** pendant des jours et des jours *(b)* limite *f,* borne *f;* **to
the ends of the earth,** jusqu'au bout du monde *(c)*
bout, fin (du mois); terme *m* (d'un procès); **we shall
never hear the e. of it!** on n'entendra jamais la fin!
and there's an e. of it! et voilà tout! **there's no e. to
it!** cela n'en finit pas! **to put an e. to sth,** en finir
avec qch; achever qch; mettre fin à qch; **to come to
an e.,** prendre fin; **in the e.,** (i) à la longue (ii) à la fin;
enfin; **at the e. (of sth),** à la fin (du mois, de l'hiver);
au bout (de six mois); **at the e. of one's resources,** au
bout de ses ressources; **to be at an e.,** être terminé;
it's not the e. of the world! ce n'est pas la fin du
monde! **e. product,** (i) produit fabriqué (ii) *(also* **e.
result)** résultat *m; F:* **it'll do you no e. of good,** cela
vous fera énormément de bien; **to come to a sticky
e.,** mal finir *(d)* fin, but *m;* dessein *m;* **to this e., with
this e. in view,** dans cette intention; dans ce but;
Prov: **the e. justifies the means,** la fin justifie les
moyens **2.** *v (a) vtr* finir, achever, terminer (un
ouvrage); conclure (un discours); **to e. it all,** se suicider *(b) vi (also* **end up)** finir, se terminer, aboutir
(**at, in,** dans, en). **ending** *n* fin; conclusion *f* (d'un
livre); *(of word)* terminaison *f; (act)* achèvement *m;*
(of story) **happy e.,** dénouement heureux. **'endless**
a (voyage) sans fin, interminable; (espace) sans
bornes; infini; *(of pain)* continuel, incessant; **it's e.,**
cela n'en finit pas. **'endlessly** *adv* sans fin; sans
cesse; éternellement. **'endpaper** *n Bookb:* (page *f*
de) garde *f.* **'endways, -wise** *adv (a)* de chant,
debout *(b) (end to end)* bout à bout.

endanger [inˈdeindʒər] *vtr* mettre en danger; risquer
(sa vie); compromettre (ses intérêts).

endear [inˈdiər] *vtr* rendre cher (**to,** à); **he endeared
himself to everyone,** il s'est fait aimer de tout le
monde. **en'dearing** *a* qui inspire l'affection;
sympathique; (mot, geste) tendre, affectueux. **en-
'dearments** *npl* expressions *fpl* de tendresse; mots
mpl tendres.

endeavour, *NAm:* **-or** [inˈdevər] **1.** *n* effort *m,* tentative *f;* **to make every e. to do sth,** faire tout son
possible pour faire qch **2.** *vi* s'efforcer, essayer,
tenter, tâcher (de faire).

endemic [enˈdemik] *a* endémique.

endive [ˈendiv] *n Bot: (a) (curled)* chicorée (frisée)
(b) esp NAm: endive *f.*

endorse [inˈdɔːs] *vtr (a)* endosser (un chèque); viser (un
passeport); *Com:* avaliser (un effet); appuyer (l'opinion de qn); souscrire à (une décision); approuver
(une action); **to e. a driving licence,** inscrire les détails
d'un délit sur le permis de conduire. **en'dorse-**

ment *n* endossement *m*, endos *m* (d'un chèque); (*on passport*) mention spéciale; *Adm:* contravention inscrite sur le permis de conduire; approbation *f* (d'une action); adhésion *f* (à une opinion).

endow [in'dau] *vtr* doter (qn) (**with**, de); fonder (une œuvre charitable); **endowed with great talents**, doué de grands talents. **en'dowment** *n* dotation *f*; fondation *f*; e. **insurance** (**policy**), assurance en cas de vie, à capital différé.

endure [in'djuər] 1. *vtr* supporter, endurer; souffrir (avec patience) 2. *vi* durer, rester. **en'durable** *a* supportable. **en'durance** *n* endurance *f*, résistance *f* (à la fatigue); patience *f* (de qn); **beyond e.**, insupportable, intolérable; e. **test**, *MecE:* essai de durée; *Sp:* épreuve d'endurance. **en'during** *a* durable, permanent.

enema ['enimə] *n Med:* lavement *m*.

enemy ['enimi] 1. *n* ennemi, -ie; **the e.**, l'ennemi, l'adversaire *m* 2. *a* ennemi; e. **alien**, ressortissant d'un pays ennemi. **'enemy-'occupied** *a* occupé par l'ennemi.

energy ['enədʒi] *n* énergie *f*; force *f*; vigueur *f*; **atomic e.**, énergie atomique; **the e. crisis**, la crise de l'énergie. **ener'getic** *a* énergique. **ener'getically** *adv* avec énergie; énergiquement. **'energize** *vtr* donner de l'énergie à (qn); stimuler (qn); alimenter, amorcer (une dynamo). **'energy-pro'ducing** *a* (aliment) énergétique.

enervate ['enəveit] *vtr* affaiblir (le corps, la volonté). **'enervating** *a* (climat) débilitant.

enforce [in'fɔːs] *vtr* faire valoir (un argument, ses droits); appuyer (une demande); mettre en vigueur, appliquer (une loi); faire observer, imposer (un règlement); **to e. obedience**, se faire obéir.

engage [in'geidʒ] *vtr & i* (*a*) engager (sa parole); **to e. to do sth**, s'engager à faire qch (*b*) embaucher (des ouvriers); retenir (l'intérêt de qn); **to e. s.o. in a conversation**, **to e. in conversation with s.o.**, entrer en discussion, lier conversation, avec qn (*c*) mettre en prise (un engrenage); (*of cogwheel*) s'engrener, s'embrayer. **en'gaged** *a* (*a*) (*of pers*) fiancé; **to get e.**, se fiancer (*b*) (*of seat, pers*) occupé, pris; *Tp:* (*NAm:* = **busy**) occupé; (*of pers*) e. **in**, occupé (à faire qch). **en'gagement** *n* (*a*) engagement *m*; promesse *f* (*b*) rendez-vous *m*; **to have an e.**, être pris, occupé; e. **book**, agenda *m* (*c*) fiançailles *fpl*; e. **ring**, bague de fiançailles (*d*) *Mil:* combat *m*, engagement (*e*) *MecE:* embrayage *m*; mise *f* en prise. **en'gaging** *a* engageant; attirant; attrayant.

engine ['endʒin] *n* (*a*) machine *f*; appareil *m*; *Rail:* locomotive *f*; e. **driver** (*NAm:* = **engineer**), mécanicien *m*; *Nau:* e. **room**, salle des machines (*b*) moteur *m*. **engi'neer** 1. *n* (*a*) ingénieur *m*; **chemical e.**, ingénieur chimiste; **civil e.**, ingénieur constructeur (*b*) *Nau: & NAm: Rail:* (*Br* = **engine driver**) mécanicien (*c*) *Mil:* soldat *m* du génie; **the Engineers**, le génie 2. *vtr* (*a*) construire (en qualité d'ingénieur) (*b*) machiner (un coup); manigancer (une affaire). **engi'neering** *n* ingénierie *f*; (**mechanical**) e., mécanique *f*; **chemical e.**, génie *m* chimique; **civil e.**, génie civil; **industrial e.**, organisation industrielle; **production e.**, technique de la production; e. **works**, atelier de constructions *fpl* mécaniques.

England ['iŋglənd] *Prn Geog:* Angleterre *f*; **in E.**, en Angleterre; **the Church of E.**, l'église anglicane.

'English 1. *a & n* anglais, -aise; (histoire) d'Angleterre; **the E.**, les Anglais *mpl*; **the E. Channel**, la Manche 2. *n Ling:* anglais *m*; **the Queen's E.**, l'anglais correct. **'Englishman, -woman** (*pl* -**men**, -**women**) Anglais, -aise. **'English-speaking** *a* (*pays*) anglophone, de langue anglaise.

engrave [in'greiv] *vtr* graver. **en'graver** *n* graveur *m*. **en'graving** *n* gravure *f*; (*print*) estampe *f*.

engross [in'grous] *vtr* absorber, occuper (qn); **to become engrossed in sth**, s'absorber dans qch. **en'grossing** *a* absorbant.

engulf [in'gʌlf] *vtr* engloutir, engouffrer.

enhance [in'hɑːns] *vtr* rehausser (le mérite de qch); accroître (le plaisir); mettre en valeur (la beauté de qn).

enigma [i'nigmə] *n* énigme *f*. **enig'matic** *a* énigmatique. **enig'matically** *adv* d'une manière énigmatique.

enjoy [in'dʒɔi] *vtr* (*a*) aimer; prendre plaisir à (qch); goûter (la musique); **to e. one's dinner**, trouver le dîner bon; bien dîner; **I enjoyed this novel**, ce roman m'a plu; **I e. being in Paris**, je me plais à Paris; **to e. oneself**, s'amuser; **to e. doing sth**, prendre plaisir à faire qch (*b*) jouir de, posséder (la santé, la confiance de qn). **en'joyable** *a* agréable; (*of meal, evening*) excellent. **en'joyably** *adv* agréablement. **en'joyment** *n* (*a*) plaisir *m* (*b*) jouissance *f* (d'un droit).

enlarge [in'lɑːdʒ] 1. *vtr* agrandir; étendre; augmenter (sa fortune); élargir (un trou); développer (une idée) 2. *vi* s'agrandir, s'étendre, s'élargir; **to e. (up)on**, s'étendre sur (un sujet). **en'larged** *a* (*of edition*) augmenté; (*of tonsils*) hypertrophié. **en'largement** *n* agrandissement *m*. **en'larger** *n Phot:* agrandisseur *m*.

enlighten [in'laitn] *vtr* éclairer (qn sur un sujet). **en'lightened** *a* éclairé. **en'lightenment** *n* éclaircissements *mpl* (**on**, sur); *Hist:* **the** (**age of**) E., le siècle des lumières.

enlist [in'list] 1. *vtr* enrôler, engager (un soldat); recruter (des partisans); **to e. s.o.'s support for a cause**, rallier qn à une cause; **to e. the services of s.o.**, s'assurer le concours de qn 2. *vi* s'engager. **en'listed** *a esp US: Mil:* e. **man**, simple soldat *m*; homme de troupe. **en'listment** *n Mil:* engagement *m*.

enliven [in'laivən] *vtr* animer; stimuler (les affaires); égayer (une fête).

enmity ['enmiti] *n* inimitié *f*; hostilité *f*; haine *f*.

enormous [i'nɔːməs] *a* énorme; colossal; (*succès*) fou. **e'normously** *adv* énormément.

enough [i'nʌf] 1. *a & n* assez; e. **money**, assez d'argent; **I've had e. to drink**, j'ai assez bu; **I've had e. of it**, j'en ai assez; *F:* **I've had just about e.**, j'en ai par-dessus la tête; **that's e.**, (i) cela suffit (ii) en voilà assez! **that's e. for me**, cela me suffit; **more than e.**, plus qu'il n'en faut; **have you e. to pay the bill?** avez-vous de quoi payer? **he has e. to live on**, il a de quoi vivre; **it was e. to drive you crazy**, c'était à vous rendre fou 2. *adv* **good e.**, assez bon; **close e. to see**, assez près pour voir; **you know well e. what I mean**, vous savez très bien ce que je veux dire; **curiously e.**, **oddly e.**, chose curieuse; **she sings well e.**, elle ne chante pas mal.

enquire [in'kwaiər] *vtr & i* demander; s'informer (**about**, de); se renseigner (**about**, sur); faire des recherches (**into**, sur). **en'quiry** *n* (*a*) enquête *f*, recherche *f* (*b*) demande *f* de renseignements. *See also* **inquire**.

enrage [in'reidʒ] *vtr* rendre furieux; exaspérer.

enrapture [in'ræptʃər] *vtr* ravir, enchanter.

enrich [in'ritʃ] *vtr* enrichir; fertiliser (la terre). **en-'richment** *n* enrichissement *m*.

enrol [in'roul] *v* (**enrolled**) **1.** *vtr* enrôler, encadrer (des recrues); embaucher (des ouvriers); immatriculer (des étudiants) **2.** *vi* s'enrôler (dans l'armée); s'inscrire (à une société).

ensconce [in'skɔns] *vtr* **to e. oneself**, se nicher, se camper.

ensign ['ensən] *n Nau:* (*a*) drapeau *m*; pavillon national; **red e.** = pavillon marchand (*b*) *US: Navy:* enseigne *m* (de vaisseau de deuxième classe).

enslave [in'sleiv] *vtr* asservir. **en'slavement** *n* asservissement *m*.

ensue [in'sju:] *vi* s'ensuivre; **a long silence ensued**, il se fit un long silence. **en'suing** *a* (année) qui suit.

ensure [in'ʃuər] *vtr* assurer (**against**, **from**, contre).

entail [in'teil] *vtr* entraîner (des conséquences); occasionner (des dépenses); comporter (des difficultés).

entangle [in'tæŋgl] *vtr* empêtrer; emmêler (du fil); **to get entangled**, s'empêtrer; (*of thread*) s'emmêler. **en'tanglement** *n* embrouillement *m*, enchevêtrement *m*.

entente [ɔn'tɔnt] *n* entente *f*.

enter ['entər] **1.** *vi* (*a*) entrer (**into**, **through**, dans, par) (*b*) se faire inscrire (**for**, pour); se présenter (**for an exam**, à un examen) **2.** *vtr* (*a*) entrer, pénétrer, dans (une maison); monter dans (une voiture); s'engager dans, sur (une route); **to e. the Army**, se faire soldat; **it never entered my head that**, il ne m'est pas venu à l'esprit que (*b*) inscrire, porter (un nom) (**on a list**, sur une liste); engager (un cheval) (**for a race**, dans une course); **to e. a protest**, protester formellement. **'enter 'into** *vtr* entrer en (service, relations); entrer dans (les affaires); engager (une conversation, des négociations); conclure (un engagement); prendre part à (un complot); **that doesn't e. i. the matter**, c'est en dehors de l'affaire.

enterprise ['entəpraiz] *n* (*a*) entreprise *f* (*b*) esprit entreprenant. **'enterprising** *a* entreprenant.

entertain [entə'tein] *vtr* (*a*) amuser, divertir (qn); **to e. s.o. to dinner**, offrir un dîner à qn; **they e. a great deal**, ils reçoivent beaucoup (*b*) admettre, accueillir (une proposition); concevoir (une idée); éprouver (des craintes); nourrir (un espoir). **enter-'tainer** *n* artiste *mf* (de cabaret). **enter'taining 1.** *a* amusant, divertissant **2.** *n* **to do a lot of e.**, recevoir beaucoup (de monde). **enter'tainingly** *adv* d'une manière amusante. **enter-'tainment** *n* (*a*) divertissement *m*, amusement *m*; **much to the e. of the crowd**, au grand amusement de la foule; *Adm:* **e. allowance**, frais de représentation *f* (*b*) *Th: etc:* spectacle *m*.

enthral, *NAm:* **enthrall** [in'θrɔ:l] *vtr* (**enthralled**) captiver, passionner. **en'thralling** *a* passionnant.

enthusiasm [in'θju:ziæzm] *n* enthousiasme *m* (**for**, **about**, pour). **en'thuse** *vi* s'enthousiasmer, se passionner (**over**, **about**, de, pour). **en'thusiast** *n* en-

thousiaste *mf*; fervent(e), passionné(e) (de musique). **enthusi'astic** *a* enthousiaste; **to become e. about sth**, s'enthousiasmer pour qch. **enthusi'astically** *adv* avec enthousiasme.

entice [in'tais] *vtr* attirer, séduire (qn); entraîner (qn). **en'ticing** *a* (*of offer*) séduisant, attrayant; (*of dish*) alléchant.

entire [in'taiər] *a* (*a*) entier, tout; **the e. population**, la population (tout) entière (*b*) entier, complet; **an e. success**, un vrai succès. **en'tirely** *adv* entièrement, tout à fait; **you are e. mistaken**, vous vous trompez tout à fait. **en'tirety** *n* **in its e.**, en entier, intégralement.

entitle [in'taitl] *vtr* (*a*) intituler (un livre) (*b*) **to e. s.o. to do sth**, donner à qn le droit de faire qch; **to be entitled to sth**, avoir droit à qch; **to be entitled to do sth**, avoir le droit de faire qch. **en'titlement** *n* allocation à laquelle on a droit; **holiday e.**, congé annuel.

entity ['entiti] *n* entité *f*.

entomology [entə'mɔlədʒi] *n* entomologie *f*. **ento-mo'logical** *a* entomologique. **ento'mologist** *n* entomologiste *mf*.

entrails ['entreilz] *npl* entrailles *fpl*.

entrance¹ ['entrəns] *n* (*a*) entrée *f*; *PN:* **no e.**, défense d'entrer; **to make one's e.**, faire son entrée; **e. hall**, hall *m* (d'hôtel); **main e.**, entrée principale; **side e.**, porte *f* de service (*b*) admission *f*, accès *m*; (*to club*) **e. fee**, droit d'inscription *f*. **'entrant** *n* débutant, -ante (dans une profession); inscrit, -ite (pour une course); candidat, -ate (à un examen).

entrance² [in'trɑ:ns] *vtr* extasier, ravir, transporter (qn); **to be entranced by**, être en extase devant. **en-'trancing** *a* enchanteur, ravissant. **en'trancingly** *adv* à ravir.

entreat [in'tri:t] *vtr* **to e. s.o. to do sth**, prier, implorer, supplier, qn de faire qch. **en'treating** *a* (ton, regard) suppliant. **en'treaty** *n* prière *f*, supplication *f*; **at s.o.'s urgent e.**, sur les vives instances de qn; **look of e.**, regard suppliant.

entrée ['ɔntrei] *n Cu:* entrée *f*; *NAm:* (*Br* = **main course**) plat principal.

entrench [in'trentʃ] *vtr Mil:* retrancher; **firmly entrenched**, solidement retranché.

entrepreneur [ɔntrəprə'nə:r] *n* entrepreneur *m*. **entrepre'neurial** *a* (décision) d'entrepreneur.

entrust [in'trʌst] *vtr* **to e. s.o. with**, charger qn d'(une tâche); **to e. sth to s.o.**, confier qch à qn.

entry ['entri] *n* (*a*) entrée *f*; début *m* (dans la politique); *PN:* **no e.**, (i) (= **one way street**) sens interdit (ii) passage interdit (au public); **to make one's e.**, faire son entrée (*b*) enregistrement *m*; inscription *f* (d'un nom sur une liste, d'un concurrent); *Book-k:* **single, double, e.**, comptabilité *f* en partie simple, en partie double; **e. form**, feuille d'inscription (*c*) (item entered) article *m*; écriture *f*; (in competition) inscrit, -ite (pour une course); candidat, -ate (à un examen).

entwine [in'twain] **1.** *vtr* entrelacer; enlacer (**with**, de) **2.** *vi* s'entrelacer.

enumerate [i'nju:məreit] *vtr* énumérer, détailler. **enume'ration** *n* énumération *f*.

enunciate [i'nʌnsieit] **1.** *vtr* énoncer, déclarer (une opinion) **2.** *vtr & i* articuler (distinctement).

enunci'ation n (a) énonciation f (d'une opinion) (b) articulation f (d'un mot).

envelop [in'veləp] vtr (**enveloped**) envelopper (**in**, dans, de). **envelope** ['envəloup] n enveloppe f; **to put a letter in an e.**, mettre une lettre sous enveloppe; **in a sealed e.**, sous pli cacheté.

environment [in'vaiərənmənt] n milieu m, entourage m; ambiance f; environnement m; **Department of the E.**, Ministère de l'Environnement. **environ'mental** a (étude) de l'environnement. **environ'mentalist** n écologiste mf.

envisage [in'vizidʒ] vtr envisager.

envoy ['envoi] n envoyé, -ée (diplomatique).

envy ['envi] 1. n (a) envie f; **to be green with e.**, être dévoré d'envie (b) objet m d'envie 2. vtr (**envied**) envier; porter envie à (qn); **to e. s.o. sth**, envier qch à qn. '**envious** a envieux; **to be e. of s.o., sth**, envier qn, qch. '**enviously** adv avec envie.

enzyme ['enzaim] n Bio-Ch: enzyme f.

eon ['iːən] n éternité f.

ephemeral [i'femərəl] a éphémère.

epic ['epik] 1. a épique 2. n (a) poème m épique; épopée f (b) film m à grand spectacle.

epicentre, NAm: **-center** ['episentər] n épicentre m.

epicure ['epikjuər] n gourmet m, gastronome m. **epicu'rean** a épicurien.

epidemic [epi'demik] 1. a épidémique 2. n épidémie f.

epigram ['epigræm] n épigramme f.

epilepsy ['epilepsi] n épilepsie f. **epi'leptic** a & n épileptique (mf).

epilogue, NAm: **epilog** ['epilɔg] n épilogue m.

Epiphany [i'pifəni] n Ecc: Épiphanie f; fête f des Rois.

episcopal [i'piskəpəl] a épiscopal; **E. Church**, église épiscopale. **Episco'palian** 1. a épiscopalien 2. n membre m de l'Église épiscopale.

episode ['episoud] n épisode m.

epistle [i'pisl] n épître f.

epitaph ['epitɑːf] n épitaphe f.

epithet ['epiθet] n épithète f.

epitome [i'pitəmi] n **to be the e. of sth**, incarner qch; **the e. of elegance**, l'élégance même. **e'pitomize** vtr incarner (qch).

EPNS abbr electroplated nickel silver.

epoch ['iːpɔk] n époque f, âge m. '**epoch-making** a qui fait époque.

equable ['ekwəbl] a uniforme, régulier; (of temperament) égal. '**equably** adv d'humeur égale.

equal ['iːkwəl] 1. vtr (**equalled**) égaler (**in**, en); **four times five equals twenty**, quatre fois cinq font vingt 2. a (a) égal (**to**, **with**, à); **to be on e. terms, on an e. footing**, être sur un pied d'égalité (**with**, avec); **all things being e.**, toutes choses égales (d'ailleurs); **to be e. to the occasion**, être à la hauteur de la situation; **I don't feel e. to (doing) it**, je ne m'en sens pas le courage; Mth: **equal(s) sign**, signe d'égalité 3. n égal, -ale; pair m; **your equals**, vos pareils; **you won't find his e.**, vous ne trouverez pas son semblable; **to treat s.o. as an e.**, traiter qn d'égal à égal. **e'quality** n égalité f. '**equalize** 1. vtr égaliser; compenser, équilibrer (des forces) 2. vi s'équilibrer; Sp: égaliser. '**equalizer** n Sp: but égalisateur.

'**equally** adv également; pareillement; **e. tired**, tout aussi fatigué; **to contribute e.**, contribuer pour une part égale.

equanimity [ekwə'nimiti] n égalité f d'âme; sérénité f.

equate [i'kweit] vtr égaler; donner comme l'équivalent (**with**, de). **equation** [i'kweiʒn] n Mth: équation f.

equator [i'kweitər] n équateur m; **at the e.**, sous l'équateur. **equa'torial** a équatorial.

equestrian [i'kwestriən] 1. a (statue) équestre 2. n cavalier, -ière.

equidistant [iːkwi'distənt] a équidistant (**from**, de).

equilateral [iːkwi'lætərəl] a Mth: équilatéral.

equilibrium [iːkwi'libriəm] n équilibre m.

equine ['ekwain] a équin; **e. race**, race chevaline.

equinox ['iːkwinɔks] n équinoxe m. **equi'noctial** a équinoxial; (vent) d'équinoxe; **e. tides**, grandes marées.

equip [i'kwip] vtr (**equipped**) équiper; meubler, monter (une maison); outiller (une usine); **to e. s.o. with sth**, munir qn de qch; **well-equipped**, (laboratoire) bien installé; (ménage) bien monté. **e'quipment** n (a) équipement m; outillage m (d'une usine); installation f (d'un laboratoire) (b) équipement; appareils mpl; matériel m; **sports e.**, équipement sportif; **camping e.**, matériel de camping.

equity ['ekwiti] n (pl **equities**) équité f; justice f; pl Fin: actions fpl ordinaires. '**equitable** a équitable; juste. '**equitably** adv avec justice, équitablement.

equivalent [i'kwivələnt] a & n équivalent (m). **e'quivalence** n équivalence f.

equivocate [i'kwivəkeit] vi user d'équivoques, tergiverser. **e'quivocal** a équivoque. **e'quivocally** adv d'une manière équivoque. **equivo'cation** n tergiversation f.

ER abbr Elizabeth Regina.

era ['iərə] n ère f.

eradicate [i'rædikeit] vtr extirper (des préjugés); déraciner (des plantes).

erase [i'reiz] vtr effacer; raturer; gommer (un mot). **e'raser** n gomme f (à effacer). **e'rasure** n rature f.

erect [i'rekt] 1. a (of pers) droit, debout; **with head e.**, la tête haute 2. vtr dresser (un mât); ériger, construire (un édifice); installer (une machine). **e'rection** n (a) érection f; dressage m (d'un mât); construction f (d'un édifice); montage m, installation f (d'une machine) (b) bâtisse f, construction, édifice.

erode [i'roud] vtr éroder; ronger; corroder. **e'rosion** n érosion f; Fig: diminution f (des salaires).

erogenous [i'rɔdʒənəs] a érogène.

erotic [i'rɔtik] a érotique. **e'roticism** n érotisme m.

err [əːr] vi (a) pécher (b) se tromper.

errand ['erənd] n commission f, course f; **to run errands**, faire des courses; **e. boy**, garçon de courses.

erratic [i'rætik] a irrégulier; (of pers) capricieux; (of life) désordonné. **e'rratically** adv irrégulièrement; sans méthode, sans règle.

error ['erər] n erreur f, faute f; **typing e.**, faute de frappe; **compass e.**, déviation f du compas; **to see the e. of one's ways**, revenir de ses égarements; **in e.**,

par erreur. e'rroneous *a* erroné, faux. e'rro-
neously *adv* par erreur.

erudite ['erudait] *a* érudit, savant. eru'dition *n*
érudition *f*.

erupt [i'rʌpt] *vi* (*of volcano*) entrer en éruption; (*of
anger*) éclater; (*of pers*) exploser. e'ruption *n*
éruption *f* (de volcan, de boutons); accès *m* (de
colère).

escalate ['eskəleit] *vtr & i* (*of prices*) (faire) monter
(en flèche); (*of conflict*) (s')intensifier. esca'lation *n* escalade *f*. 'escalator *n* escalier roulant;
escalator *m*.

escape [i'skeip] 1. *n* (*a*) fuite *f*, évasion *f*; to make
one's e., s'échapper, se sauver; to have a narrow e.,
l'échapper belle; e. hatch, trappe de secours; *Jur:
Com:* e. clause, clause échappatoire (*b*) échappement
m, fuite (de gaz); e. velocity, vitesse de libération
de l'attraction terrestre 2. *v* (*a*) *vi* s'échapper, échapper
(from, out of, de); prendre la fuite; s'évader (de
prison); (*of gases*) se dégager, fuir; escaped prisoner,
évadé, -ée; to e. uninjured, s'en tirer indemne; he
escaped with a fright, il en a été quitte pour la peur
(*b*) *vtr* (*of pers*) échapper à (un danger); to e. notice,
passer inaperçu; he just escaped being killed, il a bien
failli être tué; his name escapes me, son nom
m'échappe. 'escapade *n* escapade *f*, frasque *f*.
esca'pee *n* évadé, -ée. e'scapism *n* évasion *f*
(de la réalité). e'scapist *a & n* personne *f* qui
cherche à fuir la réalité; e. literature, littérature
d'évasion. esca'pologist *n* prestidigitateur, -trice,
spécialiste de l'évasion.

escarpment [i'skɑːpmənt] *n* escarpement *m*.

escort 1. *n* ['eskɔːt] escorte *f*; (*male partner*) cavalier
m 2. *vtr* [i'skɔːt] escorter, faire escorte à (un convoi);
(*of man*) servir de cavalier à (une femme); to e.
s.o. home, reconduire qn.

Eskimo ['eskimou] *a & n* esquimau, -aude.

ESN *abbr educationally subnormal*.

esophagus [i'sɒfəgəs] *n NAm: see* oesophagus.

esoteric [esou'terik] *a* ésotérique.

ESP *abbr extrasensory perception*.

especial [i'speʃl] *a* spécial, particulier. e'specially
adv surtout, particulièrement.

espionage ['espiənɑːʒ] *n* espionnage *m*.

esplanade [esplə'neid] *n* esplanade *f*.

espresso [es'presou] *n* e. (coffee), (café *m*) express
m.

esquire [i'skwaiər] *n* (*abbr* Esq) J. Martin, Esq =
Monsieur J. Martin.

essay ['esei] *n* (*a*) essai *m*, tentative *f* (*b*) *Lit:* essai;
Sch: dissertation *f*; composition *f* (littéraire). 'es-
sayist *n* essayiste *mf*.

essence ['esəns] *n* (*a*) essence *f*; fond *m* (d'une affaire); in e., essentiellement (*b*) *Ch: Cu:* essence; extrait *m* (de viande). e'ssential 1. *a* essentiel,
indispensable 2. *n usu pl* l'essentiel *m*; qualités *fpl*
indispensables. e'ssentially *adv* essentiellement.

establish [is'tæbliʃ] *vtr* (*a*) établir (un gouvernement); fonder (une maison de commerce); créer (une
agence); constituer (une société); se faire (une réputation); affermir (sa foi); to e. oneself (in business),
s'établir dans les affaires; to e. oneself in a new house,
s'installer dans une maison neuve (*b*) établir, constater (un fait); prouver (un alibi); démontrer

(l'identité de qn). e'stablished *a* établi; (réputation) solide; (fait) avéré, acquis; (religion) d'état.
es'tablishment *n* (*a*) établissement *m*; business
e., maison *f* de commerce; the E., les institutions *fpl*
(d'un pays); le monde traditionnel; to be anti-E.,
être anticonformiste (*b*) personnel *m* (d'une maison);
Mil: effectif(s) *m* (*pl*).

estate [i'steit] *n* (*a*) domaine *m*; terre *f*, propriété *f*;
housing e., (i) lotissement *m* (ii) cité *f*; groupe *m* de
HLM; e. agent, agent immobilier; e. agency, e.
agents, agence immobilière; *Aut:* e. car (*NAm:* =
station wagon) break *m* (*b*) succession *f* (d'un
défunt).

esteem [i'stiːm] 1. *n* estime *f*, considération *f*; to hold
s.o. in high e., avoir qn en haute estime; to go up in
s.o.'s e., monter dans l'estime de qn 2. *vtr* (*a*) estimer
(qn); priser (qch) (*b*) estimer, considérer (as,
comme). 'estimable *a* estimable.

esthete ['iːsθiːt] *n NAm: see* aesthete. es'thetic *a
NAm: see* aesthetic.

estimate 1. *n* ['estimət] (*a*) appréciation *f*, évaluation *f*; at a rough e., à vue de nez; at the lowest e.,
au bas mot (*b*) *Com:* devis *m* (de construction); to
put in an e., soumissionner 2. *vtr* ['estimeit] estimer;
évaluer (les frais); estimated cost, coût estimatif;
estimated time of arrival, heure prévue d'arrivée.
esti'mation *n* (*a*) jugement *m*; in my e., à mon
avis (*b*) estime *f*.

estranged [i'streinʒd] *a* (époux) séparés.

estrogen ['iːstrədʒən] *n NAm: see* oestrogen.

estuary ['estjuəri] *n* estuaire *m*.

etc [et'setərə] *abbr et cetera*.

etch [etʃ] *vtr* graver à l'eau-forte. 'etcher *n* graveur
m à l'eau-forte. 'etching *n* (gravure *f* à l')eau-
forte *f*.

eternity [i'tɜːniti] *n* éternité *f*. e'ternal *a* éternel;
Fig: continuel; sans fin. e'ternally *adv* éternellement.

ether ['iːθər] *n* éther *m*. e'thereal *a* éthéré.

ethic(s) ['eθik(s)] *n* (*pl*) éthique *f*, morale *f*.
'ethic(al) *a* moral, éthique.

Ethiopia [iːθi'oupiə] *Prn Geog:* Éthiopie *f*.

ethnic ['eθnik] *a* ethnique.

ethnology [eθ'nɒlədʒi] *n* ethnologie *f*. eth-
no'logical *a* ethnologique. eth'nologist *n*
ethnologue *mf*.

ethos ['iːθɒs] *n* génie *m* (d'un peuple).

etiquette ['etiket] *n* étiquette *f*; convenances *fpl*;
cérémonial *m*; protocole *m* (diplomatique).

etymology [eti'mɒlədʒi] *n* étymologie *f*. etymo'logical *a* étymologique. etymo'logically
adv étymologiquement. ety'mologist *n* éty-
mologiste *mf*.

eucalyptus [juːkə'liptəs] *n Bot:* eucalyptus *m*.

Eucharist (the) [ðə'juːkərist] *n Ecc:* l'eucharistie *f*.

eulogy ['juːlədʒi] *n* panégyrique *m*. 'eulogize *vtr*
faire le panégyrique de.

eunuch ['juːnək] *n* eunuque *m*.

euphemism ['juːfəmizm] *n* euphémisme *m*.
euphe'mistic *a* euphémique. euphe'mistically *adv* par euphémisme.

euphonium [juː'founiəm] *n Mus:* saxhorn *m* basse.

euphoria [juː'fɔːriə] *n* euphorie *f*. eu'phoric *a*
euphorique.

Europe ['juərəp] *Prn Geog:* Europe *f.* **'eurocrat** *n* eurocrate *mf.* **'eurodollar** *n* eurodollar *m.* **Euro'pean** *a & n* européen, -enne; **E. Economic Community,** Communauté Économique Européenne. **'Eurovision** *n* Eurovision *f.*

euthanasia [juːθə'neiziə] *n* euthanasie *f.*

evacuate [i'vækjueit] *vtr* évacuer. **evacu'ation** *n* évacuation *f.* **evacu'ee** *n* évacué, -ée.

evade [i'veid] *vtr* éviter (un coup, un danger); esquiver (un coup); se soustraire à (la justice); éluder, tourner (une question); déjouer (la vigilance de qn); échapper à (ses poursuivants); **to e. tax,** frauder le fisc.

evaluate [i'væljueit] *vtr* évaluer. **evalu'ation** *n* évaluation *f.*

evangelical [iːvæn'dʒelikl] *a* évangélique. **e'vangelist** *n* évangéliste *m.*

evaporate [i'væpəreit] **1.** *vtr* faire évaporer (un liquide) **2.** *vi* s'évaporer, se vaporiser. **evapo'ration** *n* évaporation *f.*

evasion [i'veiʒn] *n* (*a*) évasion *f,* fuite *f;* dérobade *f;* **tax e.,** fraude fiscale (*b*) échappatoire *f;* faux-fuyant *m;* **without e.,** sans détours. **e'vasive** *a* évasif; **to take e. action,** faire une manœuvre d'évitement. **e'vasively** *adv* évasivement.

eve [iːv] *n* veille *f;* **Christmas E.,** la veille de Noël.

even ['iːvən] **1.** *a* (*a*) (*of surface*) uni; plat; égal; uniforme; (souffle) régulier; **to make e.,** aplanir (une surface); égaliser (l'espacement); **e. pace,** allure uniforme; **e. temper,** humeur égale; *Sp:* **to be e.,** être but à but; **to get e. with s.o.,** prendre sa revanche sur qn; **to break e.,** s'y retrouver; ne faire ni pertes ni profits; **e. chance,** une chance sur deux; **to lay e. money, evens,** parier à égalité (*b*) (nombre) pair; **odd or e.,** pair ou impair **2.** *adv* même (*with comparative*) encore; (*with negative*) seulement, même; **e. the cleverest,** même les plus habiles; **e. the children knew,** même les enfants le savaient; **that would be e. worse,** ce serait encore pire; **without e. speaking,** sans dire un mot; **even so, e. if,** même si; **e. though,** bien que + *sub;* **e. so,** mais cependant, quand même; **e. now,** à l'instant même; **e. then,** même alors. **'even-'handed** *a* équitable. **'evenly** *adv* (étendre) uniment; (respirer) régulièrement; (diviser) également; **e. matched,** de force égale. **'evenness** *n* égalité *f;* régularité *f* (de mouvement); calme *m* (d'esprit); égalité (d'humeur). **'even'out, 'up** *vtr & i* (s')égaliser; aplanir, niveler (une surface); **to e. things up,** rétablir l'équilibre. **'even-'tempered** *a* d'humeur égale.

evening ['iːvniŋ] *n* soir *m;* soirée *f;* **this e.,** ce soir; **tomorrow e.,** demain (au) soir; **in the e.,** le soir, au soir; **at nine o'clock in the e.,** à neuf heures du soir; **(on) the previous e., the e. before,** la veille au soir; **the next e.,** le lendemain (au) soir; **one fine summer e.,** (par) un beau soir d'été; **every e.,** tous les soirs; **all (the) e.,** toute la soirée; **e. paper,** journal du soir; *Th:* **e. performance,** (représentation de) soirée; **e. dress,** (*man's*) tenue, (*woman's*) robe, de soirée; **in e. dress,** en tenue de soirée.

evensong ['iːvnsɒŋ] *n Ecc:* vêpres *fpl.*

event [i'vent] *n* (*a*) cas *m;* **in the e. of his refusing,** au cas, dans le cas, où il refuserait; **in the e. of his death,** en cas de décès (*b*) événement *m;* **in the course of**

events, par la suite (*c*) issue *f,* résultat *m;* **in either e.,** dans l'un ou l'autre cas; **in any e.,** quoi qu'il arrive; **in the e.,** justement; **at all events,** en tout cas; **wise after the e.,** sage après coup (*d*) *Sp:* réunion sportive; *Equit:* concours *m* hippique; (*athletics*) **field events,** épreuves *fpl* sur terrain; **track events,** courses *fpl* sur piste. **e'ventful** *a* plein d'incidents; mouvementé; (jour) mémorable.

eventual [i'ventjuəl] *a* (*a*) (profit) éventuel (*b*) définitif; **his e. ruin,** sa ruine finale. **eventu'ality** *n* éventualité *f.* **e'ventually** *adv* finalement, en fin de compte, par la suite.

ever ['evər] *adv* **1.** (*a*) jamais; **seldom if e.,** rarement pour ne pas dire jamais; **the highest building that e. (there) was,** le bâtiment le plus haut qui ait jamais existé; **if e. I catch him,** si jamais je l'attrape; **nothing e. happens,** il n'arrive jamais rien; **he hardly e. smokes,** il ne fume presque jamais; **he's a liar if e. there was one,** c'est un menteur s'il en fut jamais; **do you e. miss the train?** vous arrive-t-il jamais de manquer le train? **it started to rain harder than e.,** il s'est mis à pleuvoir de plus belle; **it's as warm as e.,** il fait toujours aussi chaud; *P:* **did you e.!** par exemple! **e. since (then),** dès lors, depuis; **they lived happily e. after,** depuis lors ils vécurent toujours heureux (*b*) toujours; **e.-increasing,** toujours plus étendu; *Corr:* **yours e.,** bien (cordialement) à vous; **for e.,** pour toujours; à jamais; **gone for e.,** parti sans retour; **for e. and e.,** à tout jamais; **Scotland for e.!** vive l'Écosse! **he's for e. grumbling,** il ne cesse pas de se plaindre; il se plaint sans cesse (*c*) (*intensive*) **as quick as e. you can,** aussi vite que possible; **e. so pretty,** joli comme tout; **e. so difficult,** difficile au possible; **e. so long ago,** il y a bien longtemps; **I waited e. so long,** j'ai attendu un temps infini; **thank you e. so much,** merci mille fois; **e. so pleased,** très, tellement, content; **how e. did you manage?** comment diable avez-vous fait? **what e. shall we do?** qu'est-ce que nous allons bien faire? **what e.'s the matter with you?** mais qu'est-ce que vous avez donc? **why e. not?** mais pourquoi pas? **'evergreen** *a & n* (toujours) vert; (arbre *m,* plante *f*) à feuilles persistantes. **ever-'lasting** *a* (*a*) éternel (*b*) (*of object*) solide (*c*) perpétuel; (plaintes) sans fin. **ever'more** *adv* **for e.,** à (tout) jamais.

every ['evri] *a* (*a*) chaque; tout; tous les; **e. day,** chaque jour, tous les jours; **e. other day,** tous les deux jours; un jour sur deux; **e. few days,** tous les deux ou trois jours; **e. few minutes,** toutes les cinq minutes; **e. now and then, e. now and again, e. so often,** de temps en temps (*b*) (*intensive*) **I have e. reason to believe that,** j'ai tout lieu de croire que; **e. bit as good as,** tout aussi bon que; **with e. confidence,** avec une pleine confiance; **e. one,** chacun, chacune; **e. single one of them,** chacun d'entre eux; **e. man for himself,** (i) chacun pour soi (ii) (*in danger*) sauve qui peut! **e. one of them was there,** ils étaient tous là. **'everybody, 'everyone** *indef pron* chacun; tout le monde; tous; **e. else,** tous les autres; **e.'s here,** tout le monde est ici. **'everyday** *a* journalier, quotidien; **e. occurrence,** fait banal; **e. life,** la vie quotidienne; **e. clothes,** vêtements de tous les jours; **e. English,** l'anglais usuel; **in e. use,** d'usage courant. **'everything** *indef pron* tout; **they sell e.,** on y

vend de tout; **beauty isn't e.**, il n'y a pas que la beauté (qui compte). **'everywhere** *adv* partout.
evict [i'vikt] *vtr* évincer, expulser (qn) **(from, de)**. **e'viction** *n* éviction *f*, expulsion *f*.
evidence ['evidəns] *n* (*a*) évidence *f*; **in e.**, en évidence (*b*) signe *m*, marque *f*; preuve *f*; *Jur:* témoignage *m*; **to bear e. of**, faire preuve, témoigner, porter la marque, de; *Jur:* **to give e.**, témoigner; **to turn Queen's e.**, *US:* **State's e.**, témoigner contre ses complices (sous promesse de pardon). **'evident** *a* évident. **'evidently** *adv* évidemment, manifestement; **he was e. afraid**, il était évident qu'il avait peur.
evil ['i:vəl] **1.** *a* mauvais; (moment) funeste; (esprit) méchant, malfaisant; (influence) néfaste **2.** *n* mal *m*; **a social e.**, une plaie sociale. **'evildoer** *n* malfaiteur *m*. **'evilly** *adv* avec malveillance. **evil-'minded** *a* malintentionné, malveillant.
evince [i'vins] *vtr* montrer, témoigner.
evoke [i'vouk] *vtr* évoquer; susciter (un sourire). **evo'cation** *n* évocation *f*. **e'vocative** *a* évocateur.
evolve [i'vɔlv] **1.** *vtr* dérouler; développer; élaborer (une méthode); déduire (une théorie) **2.** *vi* (*of events*) se dérouler; (*of race, species*) se développer, évoluer. **evo'lution** [i:və-] *n* évolution *f*.
ewe [ju:] *n* brebis *f*.
ex- [eks] *pref* ex-; **ex-minister**, ex-ministre *m*; **ex-schoolmaster**, ancien professeur; **ex-wife**, ex-femme.
exacerbate [eg'zæsəbeit] *vtr* exacerber, aggraver (une douleur), exaspérer (qn).
exact [ig'zækt] **1.** *a* exact; **e. details**, détails précis; **e. copy**, copie textuelle (d'un document); **the e. word**, le mot juste **2.** *vtr* exiger **(from, de)**; extorquer (une rançon); réclamer (beaucoup de soins). **e'xacting** *a* (*of pers*) exigeant; (*of work*) astreignant. **e'x-actitude, e'xactness** *n* exactitude *f*, précision *f*; justesse *f*. **e'xactly** *adv* exactement, précisément; (*of time*) juste; **e.!** parfaitement!
exaggerate [ig'zædʒəreit] *vtr* exagérer. **exag-ge'ration** *n* exagération *f*.
exam [ig'zæm] *n* F: examen *m*.
examine [ig'zæmin] *vtr* examiner; inspecter (une machine); contrôler (un passeport); *Cust:* visiter (les bagages); vérifier (des comptes); *Sch:* faire passer un examen à (qn); *Jur:* interroger (qn). **exami'na-tion** *n* (*a*) examen *m*; visite *f*, inspection *f* (d'une machine); vérification *f* (des comptes); **on e.**, après examen (*b*) *Sch:* (*also F:* **ex'am**) examen; **oral e.**, épreuve orale. **exami'nee** *n Sch:* candidat, -ate. **e'xaminer** *n* (*a*) inspecteur, -trice (de machines) (*b*) *Sch:* examinateur, -trice; **the examiners**, le jury (d'examen).
example [ig'zɑ:mpl] *n* exemple *m*; précédent *m*; **to quote sth as an e.**, citer qch en exemple; **for e.**, par exemple; **to set an e.**, donner l'exemple; **to make an e. of s.o.**, punir qn pour l'exemple; **to take s.o. as an e.**, prendre exemple sur qn.
exasperate [ig'zɑ:spəreit] *vtr* exaspérer; irriter. **ex'asperating** *a* exaspérant. **e'xasperat-ingly** *adv* d'une manière exaspérante. **exaspe'ra-tion** *n* exaspération *f*; **to drive s.o. to e.**, pousser qn à bout.
excavate ['ekskəveit] **1.** *vtr* creuser (un tunnel);

fouiller (la terre); déterrer (des ruines) **2.** *vi* faire des fouilles. **exca'vation** *n* excavation *f*; *Archeol:* usu pl fouilles *fpl*. **'excavator** *n CivE:* excavateur, -trice.
exceed [ik'si:d] *vtr* (*a*) excéder, dépasser (les limites); **to e. one's powers**, sortir de sa compétence; *Aut:* **to e. the speed limit**, dépasser la limite de vitesse (*b*) surpasser **(in, en)**. **ex'ceedingly** *adv* extrême-ment, excessivement.
excel [ik'sel] *v* (**excelled**) **1.** *vi* exceller **(in, à)** **2.** *vtr* surpasser (qn); **to e. oneself**, se surpasser. **'excel-lence** *n* excellence *f*; perfection *f*; mérite *m*. **'ex-cellency** *n* **Your E.**, (votre) Excellence. **'excel-lent** *a* excellent, parfait. **'excellently** *adv* ad-mirablement; parfaitement.
except [ik'sept] **1.** *vtr* excepter, exclure **(from, de)**; **present company excepted**, les présents exceptés **2.** (*also* **ex'cepting**) *prep* excepté; à l'exception de; sauf; **he does nothing e. sleep**, il ne fait rien sinon dormir; **nobody heard it e. myself**, il n'y a que moi qui l'aie entendu; **e. by agreement**, sauf accord; **e. that**, excepté que, sauf que; **e. when, if**, sauf quand, si; **e. for**, à part. **ex'ception** *n* (*a*) exception *f*; **to make an e.**, faire une exception **(to, à)**; **the e. proves the rule**, l'exception confirme la règle; **without e.**, sans (aucune) exception; **with the e. of**, à l'exception de, exception faite de; **with certain exceptions**, sauf exceptions (*b*) objection *f*; **to take e. to sth**, (i) trou-ver à redire à qch (ii) s'offenser de qch. **ex'cep-tionable** *a* blâmable, critiquable. **ex'ceptional** *a* exceptionnel. **ex'ceptionally** *adv* excep-tionnellement.
excerpt ['eksə:pt] *n* extrait *m*, citation *f*.
excess [ik'ses, *esp attrib* 'ekses] *n* (*pl* **excesses**) excès *m*; excédent *m* (de poids); **to e.**, à l'excès; **in e. of**, au-dessus de; *Rail: etc:* **e. fare**, supplément *m*; **e. luggage**, excédent de bagages; bagages en surpoids *m*. **ex'cessive** *a* excessif; immodéré. **ex-'cessively** *adv* excessivement; (boire) à l'excès; extrêmement; **e. generous**, par trop généreux.
exchange [iks'tʃeindʒ] **1.** *n* (*a*) échange *m*; **in e. (for sth)**, en échange (de qch); **(car, etc, taken in)** part e., reprise *f* (*b*) *Fin:* (foreign) e., change *m*; **e. rate, rate of e.**, taux *m* du change; **foreign e. office**, bureau de change; **at the current rate of e.**, au cours (du jour); **e. control**, contrôle des changes (*c*) bourse *f* (des valeurs) (*d*) **telephone e.**, central *m* (téléphonique) **2.** *vtr* échanger, troquer (qch pour, contre, qch); faire un échange de. **ex'changeable** *a* échangeable.
exchequer [iks'tʃekər] *n* the E., (i) la Trésorerie, le fisc (ii) le Trésor public (iii) = le Ministère des Finances *fpl*; **Chancellor of the E.** = Ministre des Finances.
excise ['eksaiz] *n* (*a*) contributions indirectes (*b*) **Customs and E.**, la Régie.
excite [ik'sait] *vtr* provoquer, exciter (un sentiment); susciter (de l'intérêt); piquer (la curiosité de qn); agiter, énerver, surexciter (qn). **ex'citable** *a* (*of pers*) émotionnable, surexcitable. **ex'cited** *a* excité; (*of pers*) énervé, surexcité; **to get e.**, s'éner-ver. **ex'citedly** *adv* avec agitation. **ex'cite-ment** *n* agitation *f*; vive émotion; surexcitation *f*; **the thirst for e.**, la soif des sensations fortes; **the e. of departure**, l'émoi *m* du départ; **what's all the e.**

about? qu'est-ce qui se passe? **to cause great e.**, faire sensation. **ex'citing** *a* passionnant; sensationnel; (roman) plein de suspense, palpitant; **e. game,** partie mouvementée.

exclaim [iks'kleim] *vtr & i* s'écrier, s'exclamer. **excla'mation** *n* exclamation *f*; **e. mark,** point d'exclamation.

exclude [iks'klu:d] *vtr* exclure (**from**, de); écarter (le doute). **ex'cluding** *prep* à l'exclusion de. **ex'clusion** *n* (a) exclusion *f* (**from**, de) (b) refus *m* d'admission (**from**, à). **ex'clusive** *a* (a) exclusif; **to have e. rights in a production,** avoir l'exclusivité *f* d'une production; **e. interview,** interview accordée exclusivement à un seul journal (b) (*of club*) très fermé (c) **chapters one to twenty e.,** chapitres un à vingt exclusivement; **wrappings e., e. of wrappings,** sans compter, non compris, l'emballage. **ex'clusively** *adv* exclusivement.

excommunicate [ekskə'mju:nikeit] *vtr* excommunier. **excommuni'cation** *n* excommunication *f*.

excrement ['ekskrimənt] *n* excrément *m*.

excrescence [iks'kresns] *n* excroissance *f*.

excrete [iks'kri:t] *vtr* excréter. **ex'creta** *npl* excrétions *fpl*. **ex'cretion** *n* excrétion *f*.

excruciating [iks'kru:ʃieitiŋ] *a* (*of pain, F: of joke*) atroce. **ex'cruciatingly** *adv* atrocement; **it's e. funny,** c'est à se tordre (de rire).

excursion [iks'kə:ʃn] *n* excursion *f*; voyage *m* d'agrément; *Aut: etc:* randonnée *f*.

excuse 1. *n* [iks'kju:s] excuse *f*, prétexte *m*; **to make excuses,** s'excuser **2.** *vtr* [iks'kju:z] (a) excuser, pardonner (qn); **e. me!** (i) excusez-moi! (ii) pardon! **to e. oneself,** s'excuser (b) excuser, exempter, dispenser (qn de faire qch); **may I be excused?** est-ce que je peux sortir? **ex'cusable** *a* excusable, pardonnable.

ex-directory [eksdai'rektəri] *a* qui ne figure pas dans l'annuaire.

execrate ['eksikreit] *vtr* exécrer, détester. **'execrable** *a* exécrable. **'execrably** *adv* exécrablement. **exe'cration** *n* exécration *f*, détestation *f*.

execute ['eksikju:t] *vtr* (a) exécuter (un travail); accomplir (une opération); *Jur:* souscrire (un acte) (b) exécuter, jouer (un morceau de musique) (c) exécuter (un criminel). **exe'cution** *n* exécution *f* (d'un projet, d'un morceau de musique, d'un criminel); *Jur:* souscription *f* (d'un acte); **to put a plan into e.,** mettre un projet à exécution; **in the e. of one's duties,** dans l'exercice *m* de ses fonctions. **exe'cutioner** *n* bourreau *m*. **ex'ecutive 1.** *a* exécutif; (mobilier) du directeur **2.** *n* (a) (pouvoir) exécutif *m* (b) directeur, -trice; cadre *m*. **ex'ecutor** *f* -**trix** *n* exécuteur, -trice, testamentaire.

exemplary [ig'zempləri] *a* exemplaire; (élève) modèle. **ex'emplify** *vtr* (**exemplified**) exemplifier; servir d'exemple à (une règle).

exempt [ig'zempt] **1.** *vtr* exempter, dispenser (qn de qch) **2.** *a* exempt, dispensé; franc (d'impôts). **ex'emption** *n* exemption *f*, dispense *f* (**from** sth, de qch).

exercise ['eksəsaiz] **1.** *n* exercice *m*; **physical e.,** exercice physique; *Mil:* **tactical exercises,** évolutions *fpl* tactiques; **breathing exercises,** gymnastique *f* res-

piratoire; **to take e.,** prendre de l'exercice; *Sch:* **written e.,** exercice écrit; devoir *m*; **e. book,** cahier *m* **2.** *v* (a) *vtr* exercer; pratiquer (un métier); user d'(un droit); mettre à l'épreuve (la patience de qn) (b) *vi* prendre de l'exercice; s'entraîner.

exert [ig'zə:t] *vtr* employer (la force); déployer (son talent); exercer (une influence); **to e. oneself,** se remuer; se donner du mal, s'efforcer (pour faire qch). **ex'ertion** *n* effort(s) *m(pl)*.

exhaust [ig'zɔ:st] **1.** *vtr* épuiser; éreinter, exténuer (qn); **I'm exhausted,** je n'en peux plus **2.** *n* (a) échappement *m* (des gaz) (b) gaz *m* d'échappement (c) *Aut:* **e. (pipe),** tuyau *m* d'échappement. **ex'hausting** *a* épuisant. **ex'haustion** *n* épuisement *m*; **in a state of e.,** à bout de forces. **ex'haustive** *a* exhaustif; complet; **e. enquiry,** enquête approfondie. **ex'haustively** *adv* à fond; exhaustivement.

exhibit [ig'zibit] **1.** *n* (a) *Jur:* pièce *f* à conviction (b) objet exposé (à une exposition) **2.** *vtr* exhiber, montrer (un objet); faire preuve de (courage); présenter (qch à la vue); exposer (des tableaux); *Jur:* produire (une pièce à conviction). **exhi'bition** *n* exposition *f* (de tableaux); étalage *m* (de marchandises); démonstration *f* (d'un procédé); **to make an e. of oneself,** se donner en spectacle; **Ideal Home E.** = Salon *m* des Arts ménagers. **exhi'bitionist** *n* exhibitionniste *mf*. **exhi'bitor** *n* (*at exhibition*) exposant, -ante.

exhilarate [ig'ziləreit] *vtr* vivifier; revigorer; ragaillardir. **ex'hilarated** *a* ragaillardi. **ex'hilarating** *a* vivifiant. **exhila'ration** *n* gaieté *f* de cœur; joie *f* de vivre.

exhort [ig'zɔ:t] *vtr* exhorter (**s.o. to do sth.,** qn à faire qch).

exhume [eks'hju:m] *vtr* exhumer.

exile ['eksail] **1.** *n* (a) exil *m*, bannissement *m* (b) (*pers*) exilé, -ée; banni, -ie **2.** *vtr* exiler, bannir (**from**, de).

exist [ig'zist] *vi* exister; **to continue to e.,** subsister; **we e. on very little,** nous vivons de très peu. **ex'istence** *n* existence *f*; vie *f*; **to be in e.,** exister; **to come into e.,** naître. **ex'istent** *a* existant. **exis'tential** *a* existentiel. **exis'tentialism** *n* existentialisme *m*. **exis'tentialist** *a & n* existentialiste (*mf*). **ex'isting** *a* existant; actuel; présent; **in e. circumstances,** dans les circonstances actuelles.

exit ['eksit] **1.** *n* sortie *f*; **to make one's e.,** sortir; *Th:* quitter la scène; **e. permit,** permis de sortie **2.** *vi* sortir.

exodus ['eksədəs] *n* exode *m*; **there was a general e.,** il y a eu une sortie générale.

exonerate [ig'zɔnəreit] *vtr* disculper (qn) (**from**, de). **exone'ration** *n* disculpation *f*.

exorbitant [ig'zɔ:bitənt] *a* exorbitant; excessif. **ex'orbitantly** *adv* excessivement.

exorcize ['eksɔ:saiz] *vtr* exorciser. **'exorcism** *n* exorcisme *m*. **'exorcist** *n* exorciste *m*.

exotic [ig'zɔtik] *a* exotique.

expand [iks'pænd] **1.** *vtr* dilater (un gaz); étendre (les limites de qch); développer (une idée, la poitrine); élargir (l'esprit); déployer (les ailes) **2.** *vi* se dilater; (*of chest*) se développer; (*of empire*) s'étendre. **ex'panded** *a* étendu; (polystyrène) expansé. **ex'panding** a (univers) en expansion; (bracelet) extensible.

expanse [iks'pæns] n étendue f (de pays). **ex'pansion** n expansion f; dilatation f (d'un gaz, d'un métal); développement m (d'une idée, de la poitrine). **ex'pansive** a expansif; **in an e. mood**, en veine d'épanchement.

expatiate [iks'peiʃieit] vi discourir (longuement) (on, sur).

expatriate 1. vtr [eks'pætrieit] expatrier (qn) **2.** a & n [eks'pætriət] expatrié, -ée.

expect [iks'pekt] vtr attendre; s'attendre à (un événement); compter sur (l'arrivée de qn); **I knew what to e.**, je savais à quoi m'attendre; **I expected as much**, je m'y attendais; **as expected**, comme de raison; **to e. that s.o. will do sth, e. s.o. to do sth**, s'attendre à ce que qn fasse qch; **to e. to do sth**, compter, espérer, faire qch; **she's expecting a baby**, F: **she's expecting**, elle attend un bébé; **to e. sth from s.o.**, attendre, exiger, qch de qn; **to e. too much of s.o.**, trop attendre de qn; **what do you e. me to do?** qu'attendez-vous de moi? **I e. you to be punctual**, je vous demanderai d'arriver à l'heure; **how do you e. me to do it?** comment voulez-vous que je le fasse? **I e. so**, je pense, je crois bien, que oui. **ex'pectancy** n attente f; **eager e.**, vive impatience; **life e.**, espérance f de vie. **ex'pectant** a qui attend; **e. mother**, femme enceinte; future mère. **ex'pectantly** adv (regarder) avec l'air d'attendre qch. **expec'tation** n attente f, espérance f; **to come up to s.o.'s expectations**, répondre à l'attente de qn; **beyond one's expectations**, au-delà de ses espérances; **contrary to all expectations**, contre toute prévision; **in e. of**, dans l'attente de.

expedience, expediency [iks'pi:diəns(i)] n (a) convenance f, opportunité f (d'une mesure) (b) (of pers) opportunisme m. **ex'pedient 1.** a convenable, opportun **2.** n expédient m; moyen m.

expedite ['ekspidait] vtr activer, pousser (une mesure); accélérer, hâter (un processus); expédier, dépêcher (une affaire). **expe'dition** n (a) expédition f (b) (speed) promptitude f. **expe'ditionary** a expéditionnaire. **expe'ditious** a (procédé) expéditif; prompt. **expe'ditiously** adv promptement.

expel [iks'pel] vtr (expelled) expulser (qn); chasser (l'ennemi); renvoyer (un élève).

expend [iks'pend] vtr dépenser (de l'argent); consacrer (du soin); épuiser (ses ressources). **ex'pendable** a (matériel) non récupérable, non réutilisable; (of troops) sacrifiable. **ex'penditure** n dépense(s) f(pl) (d'argent); consommation f (de gaz).

expense [iks'pens] n dépense f, frais mpl; **regardless of e.**, sans regarder à la dépense; **at great e.**, à grands frais; **to go to great e.**, faire beaucoup de dépense; **to put s.o. to e.**, faire faire des dépenses à qn; Com: **e. account**, indemnité pour frais professionnels; **travelling expenses**, indemnité f de voyage; **a laugh at my e.**, un éclat de rire à mes dépens. **ex'pensive** a coûteux, cher; (passe-temps) onéreux; **to be e.**, coûter cher inv. **ex'pensively** adv (s'habiller) coûteusement; (vivre) à grands frais. **ex'pensiveness** n cherté f, prix élevé (d'un article).

experience [iks'piəriəns] **1.** n (a) expérience f;

practical e., pratique f; **he lacks e.**, il manque de pratique; **have you had any previous e.?** avez-vous déjà travaillé dans ce métier? **from e.**, par expérience (b) expérience f; aventure f; épreuve personnelle **2.** vtr éprouver; faire l'expérience de (qch). **ex'perienced** a qui a de l'expérience; expérimenté; (œil) exercé.

experiment 1. n [iks'perimənt] expérience f; essai m; **as an e.**, à titre d'essai **2.** vi [iks'periment] expérimenter, faire une expérience, des expériences (on, with, sur, avec). **experi'mental** a expérimental; fondé sur l'expérience; (sujet) d'expérience; **at the e. stage**, à l'essai. **experi'mentally** adv expérimentalement; à titre d'essai. **experimen'tation** n expérimentation f.

expert ['ekspə:t] **1.** a expert (in, at, en); habile **2.** n expert m; spécialiste mf. **exper'tise** n compétence f (in, en); adresse f (in, à); connaissances fpl techniques. **'expertly** adv en expert; habilement.

expire [iks'paiər] vi (a) expirer, mourir; (of hope) s'évanouir (b) (of law) expirer, cesser; (of passport) **to have expired**, être périmé. **expi'ration, ex'piry** n expiration f; cessation f; échéance f; terme m (d'une période).

explain [iks'plein] vtr expliquer, éclaircir (qch); **to e. oneself**, (i) s'expliquer (ii) se justifier. **ex'plain a'way** vtr donner une explication satisfaisante de. **expla'nation** [eksplə-] n explication f; éclaircissement m. **ex'planatory** a explicatif.

expletive [iks'pli:tiv] n juron m.

explicable [iks'plikəbl] a explicable.

explicit [iks'plisit] a explicite; formel, catégorique; **to be more e.**, préciser. **ex'plicitly** adv explicitement; catégoriquement.

explode [iks'ploud] **1.** vtr (a) démontrer la fausseté de (qch); discréditer (une théorie) (b) faire éclater (un obus); faire sauter (une mine); faire exploser (du gaz) **2.** vi faire explosion; éclater; sauter; (of dynamite) exploser; **to e. with laughter**, éclater de rire.

exploit 1. n ['eksploit] n exploit m **2.** vtr [iks'ploit] exploiter. **exploi'tation** n exploitation f.

explore [iks'plɔ:r] vtr explorer; Med: sonder. **explo'ration** n exploration f; **voyage of e.**, voyage de découverte. **ex'ploratory** a (puits) d'exploration; (voyage) de découverte; (conversation) préliminaire, exploratoire. **ex'plorer** n explorateur, -trice.

explosion [iks'plouʒn] n explosion f; (noise) détonation f. **ex'plosive 1.** a (matière) explosible; (mélange) explosif; détonant **2.** n explosif m.

exponent [iks'pounənt] n interprète mf (d'un système); protagoniste mf (d'un sport).

export 1. vtr [iks'pɔ:t] exporter **2.** n ['ekspɔ:t] exportation f; pl articles mpl d'exportation; **e. trade**, commerce d'exportation; **e. markets**, marchés pour les exportations; **e. duty**, droit de sortie. **expor'tation** n exportation f. **ex'porter** n exportateur, -trice.

expose [iks'pouz] vtr exposer; mettre (qch) à découvert, à nu, à jour; afficher (son ignorance); étaler (des marchandises); éventer (un secret); dévoiler (un crime); dénoncer (qn, un vice); **to e. oneself to danger**, s'exposer au danger; **to e. oneself, one's body**, faire de l'exhibitionnisme. **ex'posed** a exposé;

(engrenage) à déc:ouvert; (*laid bare*) à nu. **ex-'posure** *n* (*a*) exposition *f* (à l'air); **to die of e.**, mourir de froid; *Jur:* **indecent e.**, outrage public à la pudeur (*b*) *Phot:* (temps *m* de) pose *f*; **e. meter**, posemètre *m* (*c*) dévoilement *m* (d'un crime); dénonciation *f* (d'un escroc); **fear of e.**, crainte d'un scandale (*d*) exposition, orientation *f* (d'un lieu, d'une maison).

expostulate [iks'postjuleit] *vi* **to e. with s.o.**, faire des remontrances à qn. **expostu'lation** *n* (*often in pl*) remontrance(s) *f(pl)*.

expound [iks'paund] *vtr* exposer.

express¹ [iks'pres] 1. *a* (*a*) (*of order*) exprès, formel; explicite; **for this e. purpose**, dans ce but même (*b*) (train) express, rapide; (lettre) exprès *inv* 2. *n Rail:* express *m*, rapide *m* 3. *adv* sans arrêt. **ex'pressly** *adv* expressément, formellement; **I did it e. to please you**, je l'ai fait dans le seul but de vous plaire. **ex-'pressway** *n NAm:* (*Br* = **motorway**) autoroute *f*.

express² *vtr* exprimer; formuler (un souhait); énoncer (un principe); **to e. oneself**, s'exprimer. **ex'pression** *n* (*a*) expression *f* (d'une pensée); **beyond e.**, au delà de toute expression; inexprimable (*b*) expression, locution *f* (*c*) expression (du visage). **ex'pressive** *a* expressif; (geste) éloquent. **ex'pressively** *adv* avec expression.

expulsion [iks'pʌlʃn] *n* expulsion *f*; renvoi *m* (d'un élève).

expurgate ['ekspɔːgeit] *vtr* expurger. **expur'gation** *n* expurgation *f*.

exquisite ['ekskwizit, iks'kwizit] *a* exquis; (plaisir) vif; (supplice) raffiné; (sens) subtil. **ex'quisitely** *adv* (*a*) d'une manière exquise (*b*) extrêmement.

ex-serviceman [eks'sɔːvismən] *n* (*pl* **ex-servicemen**) ancien combattant; **disabled ex-s.**, mutilé *m* de guerre.

extant [iks'tænt] *a* existant; qui existe encore.

extempore [iks'tempɔri] 1. *adv* (parler) impromptu 2. *a* (discours) improvisé, impromptu *inv*. **ex-'temporize** *vtr & i* improviser.

extend [iks'tend] 1. *vtr* prolonger (une ligne, une période de temps); étendre, porter plus loin (les limites); accroître (ses connaissances); agrandir (son pouvoir); reculer (les frontières d'un état); tendre (la main); *Sp:* faire rendre son maximum à (un cheval, un coureur); **to e. a welcome to s.o.**, souhaiter la bienvenue à qn 2. *vi* s'étendre, s'allonger; se prolonger; continuer. **ex'tension** *n* (*a*) extension *f*; prolongement *m*; agrandissement *m* (d'une usine); prolongation *f* (de congé) (*b*) (r)allonge *f* (de table, de câble); annexe *f* (d'un bâtiment); *Tp:* poste *m* (supplémentaire); **e. ladder**, échelle à coulisse; *Sch:* **e. courses**, cours du soir organisés par une université. **ex'tensive** *a* étendu, vaste; ample; (travail) approfondi; **to make e. use of sth**, faire un usage considérable de qch. **ex'tensively** *adv* **to use sth e.**, se servir beaucoup de qch.

extent [iks'tent] *n* étendue *f* (d'un terrain); importance *f* (des dégâts); **to a certain e., to some e.**, jusqu'à un certain point; dans une certaine mesure; **to a great e.**, en grande partie; dans une large mesure; **to a slight e.**, quelque peu; **to such an e. that**, à un tel point que.

extenuating [iks'tenjueitiŋ] *a* **e. circumstance**, circonstance atténuante.

exterior [iks'tiəriər] 1. *a* extérieur (**to,** à); en dehors (**to, de**) 2. *n* extérieur *m*, dehors *mpl*; **on the e.**, à l'extérieur.

exterminate [iks'tɔːmineit] *vtr* exterminer. **extermi'nation** *n* extermination *f*.

external [iks'tɔːnl] 1. *a* externe; (mur) extérieur; (affaires) du dehors; *Med:* **for e. use only**, pour usage externe 2. *n* (*usu in pl*) extérieur *m*; **to judge by externals**, juger les choses selon les apparences *fpl*. **ex'ternally** *adv* extérieurement; à l'extérieur.

extinct [iks'tiŋkt] *a* (*of volcano*) éteint; (*of species*) disparu. **ex'tinction** *n* extinction *f*.

extinguish [iks'tiŋgwiʃ] *vtr* éteindre. **ex-'tinguisher** *n* (appareil) extincteur *m* (d'incendie).

extort [iks'tɔːt] *vtr* extorquer (**from s.o.**, à qn); arracher (une promesse) (**from s.o.**, à qn). **ex'tortion** *n* extorsion *f*; arrachement *m* (d'une promesse). **ex-'tortionate** *a* (prix) exorbitant.

extra ['ekstrə] 1. *a* (*a*) en sus, de plus; supplémentaire; (pile) de réserve; **e. charge**, supplément *m* (de prix); *Fb:* **e. time**, prolongation *f*; **as an e. precaution**, pour plus de précaution (*b*) de qualité supérieure; exceptionnel 2. *adv* (*a*) plus que d'ordinaire; **e. strong**, extra-solide; **e. special**, exceptionnel; **e. smart**, ultrachic (*b*) en plus; **the wine is e.**, le vin est en plus; **packing e.**, emballage non compris; **baths are e.**, il y a un supplément pour les bains 3. *n* (*a*) supplément (de menu); édition spéciale (d'un journal) (*b*) *Cin:* figurant, -ante (*c*) *pl* frais *m* supplémentaires; faux frais; **the little extras**, les petits à-côtés. **'extra-'fine** *a* extra-fin.

extract 1. *n* ['ekstrækt] extrait *m*; **meat e.**, concentré *m* de viande; *Sch:* **extracts**, morceaux choisis 2. *vtr* [iks'trækt] extraire, tirer; arracher. **ex'traction** *n* (*a*) extraction *f* (*b*) origine *f*; **to be of French e.**, être d'origine française. **ex'tractor** *n* **e. (fan)**, aérateur *m*.

extracurricular [ekstrəkə'rikjulər] *a Sch:* hors-programme *inv*; (activité) périscolaire.

extradite ['ekstrədait] *vtr* extrader. **extra'dition** *n* extradition *f*.

extramarital [ekstrə'mæritl] *a* extra-conjugal.

extramural [ekstrə'mjuərəl] *a Sch:* en dehors de la faculté; (cours) supplémentaire.

extraordinary [iks'trɔːdnri] *a* extraordinaire; (intelligence) rare, remarquable; (*of pers*) prodigieux; **e. meeting**, assemblée extraordinaire; **what an e. thing!** quelle affaire étrange! **extra'ordinarily** *adv* extraordinairement.

extrasensory [ekstrə'sensəri] *a* **e. perception**, perception extra-sensorielle.

extraterrestrial [ekstrətə'restriəl] *a* extra(-)terrestre.

extravagance [iks'trævəgəns] *n* (*a*) extravagance *f* (*b*) prodigalités *fpl*, dépenses folles; dépense inutile; folie *f*. **ex'travagant** *a* (*a*) extravagant; (*of claims*) exagéré; (*of praise*) outré (*b*) (*of pers*) dépensier; (goût) dispendieux; (prix) exorbitant. **ex-'travagantly** *adv* (*a*) d'une façon extravagante; **to talk e.**, dire des folies (*b*) excessivement; à l'excès. **extrava'ganza** *n Mus: Lit: etc:* œuvre *f* fantaisiste.

extreme [iks'tri:m] 1. *a* extrême; (opinion) extrémiste; **e. youth**, grande jeunesse; **an e. case**, un cas exceptionnel; **to be in e. danger**, être en (très) grand danger; *Pol:* **the e. left**, l'extrême gauche 2. *n* extrême *m*; **in the e.**, au dernier degré; **to go to extremes**, pousser les choses à l'extrême. **ex-'tremely** *adv* extrêmement; au dernier point; **to be e. witty**, avoir énormément d'esprit. **ex'tremist** *a* & *n* extrémiste (*mf*). **ex'tremity** [-'trem-] *n* (*a*) extrémité *f*; point *m* extrême; bout *m* (d'une corde) (*b*) (*usu pl*) extrémités (du corps).

extricate ['ekstrikeit] *vtr* dégager; **to e. oneself**, se tirer (d'un danger); **to e. oneself from difficulties**, se débrouiller, se tirer d'affaire.

extrovert ['ekstrəvɔ:t] *a* & *n* extroverti(e), extraverti(e).

exuberance [ig'zju:bərəns] *n* exubérance *f*. **ex-'uberant** *a* exubérant. **ex'uberantly** *adv* avec exubérance.

exude [ig'zju:d] *vtr* exuder; **she exudes kindness**, elle est la bonté même.

exult [ig'zʌlt] *vi* exulter, se réjouir (**at**, **in**, **de**); **to e. over s.o.**, triompher de qn. **ex'ultant** *a* (cri) de triomphe; **to be e.**, exulter. **ex'ultantly** *adv* d'un air de triomphe. **exul'tation** *n* exultation *f*.

eye [ai] 1. *n* œil *m*, *pl* yeux; **e. hospital**, hôpital ophtalmologique; **to have blue eyes**, avoir les yeux bleus; **to open one's eyes wide**, ouvrir les yeux tout grands; **to do sth with one's eyes open**, faire qch les yeux ouverts, *Fig:* en connaissance de cause; **to keep one's eyes open**, *F:* **skinned**, ouvrir l'œil (et le bon); **he couldn't keep his eyes open**, il dormait debout; **to open s.o.'s eyes (to sth)**, ouvrir les yeux à qn; **to shut one's eyes to s.o.'s faults**, fermer les yeux sur les défauts de qn; **to have the sun in one's eyes**, avoir le soleil dans les yeux; **with tears in one's eyes**, les larmes aux yeux; **I'm up to my eyes in work**, j'ai du travail par-dessus la tête; *F:* **that's one in the e. for him!** ça lui fait les pieds! **to catch s.o.'s e.**, attirer l'attention de qn; **to set,** *F:* **clap, eyes on sth**, apercevoir, voir, qch; **to have eyes in the back of one's head**, avoir des yeux d'Argus; **he only has eyes for her**, il n'a d'yeux que pour elle; **with one's own eyes**, de ses propres yeux; **before my very eyes**, sous mes yeux; **I could hardly believe my eyes**, j'en croyais à peine mes yeux; **in s.o.'s eyes**, aux yeux de qn; **in the eyes of the law**, devant la loi; **to make eyes at s.o.**, faire de l'œil à qn; **to see e. to e. with s.o.**, voir les choses du même œil que qn; **to keep an e. on s.o., sth**, surveiller qn, qch; **to keep one's e. on the ball**, suivre, fixer, la balle; **with an e. to**, en vue de; **to be all eyes**, être tout yeux; **to have an e. for a horse**, s'y connaître en chevaux; **to be very much in the public e.**, être très en vue; (*pers*) **private e.**, détective privé 2. *vtr* regarder, observer. **'eyeball** *n* globe *m* oculaire. **'eyebath** *n* œillère *f*. **'eyebrow** *n* sourcil *m*. **'eye-catching** *a* accrocheur. **'eyeful** *n F:* **to get an e.**, se rincer l'œil. **'eyelash** *n* cil *m*. **'eyelet** *n* œillet *m*; petit trou. **'eye-level** *a* à la hauteur des yeux; *DomEc:* (gril) surélevé. **'eyelid** *n* paupière *f*. **'eyeliner** *n Toil:* eye-liner *m*. **'eye-opener** *n* révélation *f*. **'eyepiece** *n* oculaire *m* (de télescope); viseur *m* (de théodolite). **'eyeshade** *n* visière *f*. **'eyeshadow** *n Toil:* ombre *f* à paupières. **'eyesight** *n* vue *f*; **my e. is failing**, ma vue baisse. **'eyesore** *n* qch qui blesse la vue; **that house is an e.**, cette maison est affreuse. **'eyestrain** *n* **to have e.**, avoir les yeux fatigués. **'eyetooth** *n* (*pl* -teeth) dent canine. **'eyewash** *n Med:* collyre *m* liquide; *F:* **that's all e.**, tout ça, c'est du boniment. **'eyewitness** *n* (*pl* -es) témoin *m* oculaire.

F

F, f [ef] *n* (la lettre) F, f *m* or *f*; *Mus:* fa *m*.

fable ['feibl] *n* fable *f*, conte *m*. **'fabled** *a* célèbre dans la fable; légendaire. **fabulous** ['fæbjuləs] *a* fabuleux; légendaire; *F:* merveilleux, prodigieux; (prix) fou. **'fabulously** *adv* fabuleusement; prodigieusement (riche).

fabric ['fæbrik] *n* (*a*) (*material*) tissu *m*; étoffe *f*; **silk and woollen fabrics,** soieries *fpl* et lainages *mpl* (*b*) structure *f*, fabrique *f* (d'un édifice); **the f. of society,** l'édifice social. **'fabricate** *vtr* fabriquer. **fabrication** *n* fabrication *f*.

façade [fə'sɑːd] *n* *Arch:* façade *f*.

face [feis] **I.** *n* (*a*) figure *f*, visage *m*; mine *f*; **to strike s.o. in the f.,** frapper qn au visage; **I'll never look him in the f. again,** je ne pourrai jamais plus le regarder dans les yeux; **he won't show his f. here again!** il ne se risquera pas de remettre les pieds ici! **I. to f.,** face à face; vis-à-vis (**with s.o.,** avec qn); **to set one's f. against,** s'opposer résolument à; **in the f. of danger,** devant le danger; **I told him so to his f.,** je le lui ai dit au nez; **to shut the door in s.o.'s f.,** fermer la porte au nez de qn; **f. cream,** crème de beauté; **f. pack,** masque (hydratant); *NAm: Cards:* **f. card** (*Br* = **court card**), figure; **to make, pull, faces,** faire des grimaces; **to keep a straight f.,** garder son sérieux; **to put a brave, good, f. on it,** faire contre mauvaise fortune bon cœur; **on the f. of it,** au premier aspect, à première vue; *Fin:* **f. value,** valeur nominale; **I took him at f. value,** je l'ai jugé sur les apparences; **to save, lose, f.,** sauver, perdre, la face; **they disappeared off the f. of the earth,** ils ont disparu de la surface du globe (*b*) face (d'une pièce de monnaie); recto *m* (d'un document); devant *m*, façade *f* (d'un immeuble); face (d'une falaise); cadran *m* (de montre); *Min:* front *m* de taille; **f. down, up,** face en dessous, en dessus. **II.** *v* **1.** *vtr* (*a*) affronter, faire face à, braver (un danger); **to f. facts,** regarder les choses en face; **let's face it!** voyons les choses comme elles sont! **the problem that faces us,** le problème qui se pose; **to be faced with a difficulty,** se heurter à une difficulté; **he didn't dare f. me,** il n'a pas osé me rencontrer face à face; *F:* **to f. the music,** tenir tête à l'orage (*b*) faire face à, se tenir devant; **facing each other,** l'un en face de l'autre; **facing the street,** qui donne sur la rue; **picture facing page 10,** gravure en regard de la page dix **2.** *vi* (*of house*) **to f., be facing north,** être exposé, orienté, au nord; **to f. both ways,** (i) faire face des deux côtés (ii) *Fig:* ménager la chèvre et le chou; **f. this way!** tournez-vous de ce côté! **'face-cloth** *n* = gant *m* de toilette. **'faceless** *a* sans visage; anonyme. **'facelift** *n Surg:* lifting *m*; **to have a f.,** se faire faire un lifting. **'face-saving** *a* qui sauve la face. **'face'up'to** *vtr* affronter, faire face à (un danger). **'facial** **1.** *a* facial **2.** *n* (*a*) massage facial (*b*) traitement *m* esthétique (pour le visage). **'facing** *n Const:* revêtement *m* (d'un mur); *Dressm:* revers *m* (d'un vêtement).

facet ['fæsit] *n* facette *f* (d'un diamant).

facetious [fə'siːʃəs] *a* facétieux, plaisant; (style) bouffon. **fa'cetiously** *adv* facétieusement.

facile ['fæsail] *a usu Pej:* facile.

facility [fə'siliti] *n* (*a*) facilité *f* (**in**, à, pour) (*b*) *usu pl* aménagements *mpl*; installations *fpl* (de cuisine); **we have no facilities for it,** nous ne sommes pas équipés pour cela. **fa'cilitate** *vtr* faciliter.

facsimile [fæk'simili] *n* fac-similé *m*.

fact [fækt] *n* fait *m*; **f. and fiction,** le réel et l'imaginaire; **it is a f. that,** il est de fait que; **apart from the f. that,** hormis que; **to know for a f. that,** savoir pertinemment que; **the f. is,** le fait est que, c'est que; **in (point of) f.,** en fait; **as a matter of f.,** (i) en réalité; à vrai dire (ii) en effet. **'fact-finding** *a* (commission) d'enquête. **'factual** *a* (connaissance) des faits. **'factually** *adv* en ce qui concerne les faits.

faction ['fækʃn] *n* faction *f*, cabale *f*.

factor ['fæktər] *n* (*a*) (*pers*) *Com:* agent *m* (dépositaire) (*b*) *Mth:* diviseur *m*, facteur *m*; **safety f.,** facteur, marge *f*, de sécurité; **the human f.,** l'élément humain.

factory ['fæktəri] *n* (*pl* **factories**) usine *f*, fabrique *f*; **f. inspector,** inspecteur du travail; **f. farming,** élevage industriel.

faculty ['fækəlti] *n* faculté *f*.

fad [fæd] *n* marotte *f*, manie *f*. **'faddy** *a* capricieux; difficile (sur la nourriture).

fade [feid] **1.** *vi* (*of flowers*) se faner, se flétrir; (*of colour*) passer; (*of cloth*) déteindre, se décolorer; **to f. (away),** (*of sound*) s'évanouir; (*of light*) s'affaiblir; (*of memory*) s'effacer; (*of pers*) dépérir; **to f. from sight,** se perdre de vue **2.** *vtr* faner (des fleurs); décolorer (un tissu); *Cin: TV:* **to f. (in, out),** faire arriver, faire partir (une scène) dans un fondu; *WTel: etc:* monter, diminuer, l'intensité de (la musique). **'fadeout** *n Cin: TV:* fading *m*.

faeces, *NAm:* **feces** ['fiːsiːz] *npl* fèces *fpl*.

fag [fæg] *n* (*a*) corvée *f* (*b*) *Sch:* jeune élève attaché au service d'un grand (*c*) *F:* cigarette *f*; sèche *f*; **f. end,** bout *m*; *F:* mégot *m* (de cigarette). **'fagged 'out** *a F:* épuisé, claqué.

faggot ['fægət] *n* (*a*) fagot *m* (de bois) (*b*) *Cu:* boulette *f* (de viande) (*c*) *P:* **old f.,** vieille chipie (*d*) *NAm: P:* homosexuel.

fail [feil] **I.** *adv phr* **without f.,** sans faute; à coup sûr. **II.** *v* **1.** *vi* (*a*) manquer, faillir, faire défaut; **to f. in one's duty,** manquer à son devoir; **to f. to do sth,** manquer, négliger, de faire qch (*b*) *Aut:* (*of brakes*) lâcher; (*of engine*) **to f. to start,** refuser de démarrer (*c*) (*of light, memory, health*) baisser; (*of eyesight*) faiblir (*d*) ne pas réussir; échouer; manquer son coup; *Sch:* être refusé (à un examen); **I f. to see why,** je ne vois pas pourquoi (*e*) *Com:* faire faillite **2.** *vtr* (*a*) *Sch:* refuser, recaler (un candidat) (*b*) **words f. me to express my thanks,** je ne sais comment vous exprimer mes remerciements; **I won't f. you,** vous pouvez compter sur moi. **failed** *a* (artiste) raté. **'failing 1.** *n* (*a*) défaillance *f* (de forces); baisse *f* (de la vue) (*b*) non-réussite *f*; échec *m* (*c*) défaut *m*; faiblesse *f* **2.** *prep* à défaut de; faute de (paiement); **f. advice to the contrary,** sauf avis contraire. **'fail-safe** *a* (dispositif) de sécurité positive. **'failure** *n* (*a*) manque *m*, manquement *m* (à une promesse); défaut (de paiement) (*b*) panne *f*; *El:* **power f.,** panne de courant; *Med:* **heart f.,** syncope (mortelle) (*c*) insuccès *m*, non-réussite; échec (à un examen); *Com:* faillite *f*; *Th:* four *m*, fiasco *m* (*d*) (*pers*) raté, -ée.

faint [feint] **1.** *a* (*of hope*) faible; (*of colour*) pâle; (*of sound*) léger; (*of idea*) vague; **not the faintest idea,** pas la moindre idée; (*of sound*) **to grow fainter,** s'affaiblir; (*of pers*) **to feel f.,** se sentir mal; être pris d'une défaillance **2.** *n* évanouissement *m*, défaillance **3.** *vi* s'évanouir; défaillir. **'faint-'hearted** *a* craintif; pusillanime. **'fainting** *n* évanouissement. **'faintly** *adv* faiblement; légèrement; **f. visible,** à peine visible. **'faintness** *n* faiblesse *f*, légèreté *f*.

fair¹ ['fɛər] *n* foire *f*; fête *f* foraine. **'fairground** *n* champ *m* de foire.

fair² **1.** *a* (*a*) (*of pers, hair*) blond; (*of skin*) blanc (*b*) juste, équitable; **f. play,** jeu loyal; fair-play *m inv*; **fair's f.!** il faut être juste; **it's not f.!** ce n'est pas juste! **as is only f.,** comme de juste; **f. enough!** ça va! d'accord! **it's all f. and square, f. and above board,** c'est de bonne guerre; **by f. means or foul,** d'une manière ou d'une autre (*c*) passable; assez bon; (nombre) respectable; **he has a f. chance of success,** il a des chances de réussir; **the room's a f. size,** la pièce est assez grande (*d*) beau; (vent) propice, favorable; **f. weather,** beau temps; (*of barometer*) **(at) set f.,** au beau fixe; **the f. sex,** le beau sexe; *Sch:* **f. copy,** corrigé *m* **2.** *adv* (agir) loyalement; **to play f.,** jouer beau jeu; **to hit s.o. f. (and square) on the chin,** frapper qn en plein menton. **'fair-'haired** *a* blond; aux cheveux blonds. **'fairly** *adv* (*a*) équitablement; (traiter qn) avec impartialité (*b*) (agir) honnêtement; **to come by sth f.,** obtenir qch par des moyens honnêtes (*c*) complètement, absolument (*d*) assez (riche); **f. good,** passablement bon; **f. certain,** à peu près certain. **'fairness** *n* (*a*) couleur blonde (des cheveux); blancheur (f de la peau) (*b*) équité *f*, honnêteté *f*; **in all f.,** en toute justice. **'fair-'sized** *a* assez grand. **'fair-'skinned** *a* à la peau blanche.

fairy ['fɛəri] **1.** *n* (*pl* fairies) (*a*) fée *f*; **f. godmother,** (i) marraine fée (ii) (*benefactress*) marraine gâteau; **f. queen,** reine des fées; **f. story, tale,** (i) conte de fées (ii) conte invraisemblable (iii) mensonge *m*; **f. lights,** lampions *mpl* (électriques) (*b*) *F:* (*male homosexual*) pédé *m*, tante *f* **2.** *a* féerique. **'fairyland** *n* (*a*) royaume *m* des fées (*b*) féerie *f*.

faith [feiθ] *n* foi *f*, confiance *f*; **to have f. in,** avoir confiance en; **the Christian f.,** la foi chrétienne; **to put one's f. in s.o.,** accorder toute sa confiance à qn; **f. healer, healing,** guérisseur, -euse, guérison, par la prière; **to keep f. with s.o.,** tenir ses engagements envers qn; **good f.,** bonne foi; **to do sth in all good f.,** faire qch en (toute) bonne foi; **bad f.,** mauvaise foi; perfidie *f*. **'faithful 1.** *a* (*a*) fidèle; (*of friend*) loyal (*b*) exact; (traduction) fidèle **2.** *npl* **the f.,** les fidèles

mpl; (*Islam*) les croyants *mpl*. **'faithfully** *adv* (*a*) fidèlement, loyalement; (promettre) formellement; *Corr:* **yours f.,** veuillez agréer l'expression de mes sentiments distingués (*b*) (copier) exactement. **'faithfulness** *n* fidélité *f*.

fake [feik] **1.** *a* & *n* (article) faux, truqué **2.** *vtr* truquer (des calculs); inventer (une histoire); **to f. illness,** faire semblant d'être malade.

falcon ['fɔːlkən] *n* *Orn:* faucon *m*.

fall [fɔːl] **1.** *n* (*a*) chute *f*; éboulement *m* (de terre); baisse *f* (des prix, de la température); dépréciation *f* (de la monnaie); perte *f*, ruine *f* (de qn); renversement *m* (d'un gouvernement); *Th:* baisser *m* (du rideau); **there has been a heavy f. of snow,** il est tombé beaucoup de neige (*b*) *usu pl* chute(s) *f(pl)* (d'eau) (*c*) *NAm:* (*Br* = **autumn**), automne *m* **2.** *vi* (fell; fallen) (*a*) tomber; (*of building*) s'écrouler; (*of tide, price, thermometer*) baisser; (*of ground*) aller en pente, descendre; **to f. into a trap,** donner dans un piège; **he fell (a hundred metres) to his death,** il a fait une chute mortelle (de cent mètres); **to f. into s.o.'s hands,** tomber entre les mains de qn; **to f. on one's feet,** retomber sur ses pieds; avoir de la chance; **to let sth f.,** laisser tomber qch; **night is falling,** la nuit tombe; **Christmas falls on a Thursday,** Noël tombe un jeudi; **to f. on, to, one's knees,** tomber à genoux; **to f. to pieces,** tomber en morceaux; **falling star,** étoile filante; **her eyes fell,** elle a baissé les yeux; **his face fell,** sa figure s'est allongée; **to f. from one's position,** déchoir de sa position; **the blame, the responsibility, falls on me,** le blâme, la responsabilité, retombe sur moi; **it fell to me to do it,** c'est moi qui ai dû le faire; **to f. into conversation,** entrer en conversation (**with,** avec); **to f. into a habit,** contracter une habitude; **to f. into a certain category,** entrer dans une certaine catégorie; **to f. on hard times,** connaître de mauvais jours; **to f. ill,** tomber malade; **to f. asleep,** s'endormir; **to f. vacant,** se trouver vacant; **to f. a victim to,** être victime de. **'fall a'bout** *vi* *F:* **to f. a. (laughing),** se tordre (de rire). **'fall a'way** *vi* (*of ground*) s'affaisser brusquement; aller en pente, descendre; (*of followers*) déserter. **'fall 'back** *vi* (*a*) tomber en arrière, à la renverse; (*of troops*) reculer (*b*) avoir recours (**on sth,** à qch); **some money to f. b. on,** de l'argent en réserve. **'fall be'hind** *vi* rester en arrière; **to f. b. with the rent,** être en retard pour payer son loyer. **'fall 'down** *vi* tomber (à terre, par terre); (*of building*) s'écrouler, s'effondrer; *F:* **to f. d. on the job,** tomber dans le travail; échouer dans une entreprise. **'fallen 1.** *a* tombé; perdu; **f. woman,** femme déchue **2.** *n* **the f.,** les morts *mpl* (sur le champ de bataille). **'fall 'for** *vtr* (*a*) **to f. f. a trick,** s'y laisser prendre (*b*) *F:* tomber amoureux de (qn). **'fallguy** *n* *esp NAm:* (*Br* = **scapegoat**), bouc *m* émissaire. **'fall 'in** *vi* (*of roof*) s'écrouler, s'effondrer; *Mil:* former les rangs; **f. in!** rassemblement! **to f. in with,** (i) rencontrer (ii) accepter (une proposition); accéder à (une demande). **'fall 'off** **1.** *vi* tomber; (*of profits*) diminuer **2.** *vtr* **to f. o. a ladder,** tomber (à bas) d'une échelle. **'fall 'out** *vi* (*a*) tomber (dehors); *Mil:* rompre les rangs; **f. o.!** rompez! **to f. o. of a window,** tomber d'une fenêtre (*b*) se brouiller, se fâcher (**with,** avec). **'fallout** *n* retombées (radioactives). **'fall 'over 1.** *vi* (*of pers*) tomber (par terre);

(*of thg*) se renverser, être renversé 2. *vtr* trébucher sur, tomber en se heurtant contre (un obstacle); *Fig:* **to f. o. oneself to do sth,** se mettre en quatre pour faire qch. **'fall 'through** *vi* ne pas aboutir; échouer. **'fall 'to** *vi(a)* entamer la lutte (*b*) s'attaquer au repas. **'fall (up)'on** *vtr* attaquer.

fallacy ['fæləsi] *n* (*a*) faux raisonnement (*b*) erreur *f*. **fa'llacious** *a* trompeur.

fallible ['fælibl] *a* faillible. **falli'bility** *n* faillibilité *f*.

fallopian [fə'loupiən] *a Anat:* (trompe) de Fallope.

fallow[1] ['fælou] *a* (*of land*) **to lie f.,** être en friche.

fallow[2] *a* f. **deer,** daim *m*.

false [fɔls] *a* faux; (*of hair*) artificiel, postiche; (*of coin*) contrefait; **f. report,** canard *m*; **f. alarm,** fausse alerte; **f. start,** faux départ. **'falsehood** *n* mensonge *m*; **to distinguish truth from f.,** distinguer le vrai du faux. **'falsely** *adv* faussement; à faux. **'falseness, 'falsity** *n* fausseté *f*. **'falsies** *npl F:* faux seins. **falsifi'cation** *n* falsification *f*. **'falsify** *vtr* (**falsified**) falsifier (un document); fausser (un bilan).

falsetto [fɔl'setou] *n* **f. (voice),** voix *f* de fausset.

falter ['fɔ:ltər] *vi* (*of voice, pers*) hésiter; (*of voice*) trembler; (*of pers*) vaciller; défaillir.

fame [feim] *n* renom *m*, renommée *f*; **to win f.,** se faire un grand nom, se rendre célèbre.

familiar [fə'miliər] *a* familier, intime; bien connu; **to be on f. terms with s.o.,** avoir des rapports d'intimité avec qn; **he is too f.,** il prend trop de privautés; **in f. surroundings,** en pays de connaissance; **to be on f. ground,** être sur son terrain; **to be f. with sth,** bien connaître qch; **his voice sounded f. (to me),** j'ai cru reconnaître sa voix. **famili'arity** *n* familiarité *f*, intimité *f*; connaissance *f* (**with,** de). **fa'miliarize** *vtr* **to f. s.o. with sth,** faire connaître qch à qn; **to f. oneself with sth,** se familiariser avec qch. **fa'miliarly** *adv* familièrement.

family ['fæmili] *n* (*pl* **families**) famille *f*; **to be one of, a friend of, the f.,** être de la maison, un ami de la maison; **it runs in the f.,** cela tient de famille; **f. dinner,** dîner en famille; **f. tree,** arbre généalogique; **f. hotel,** hôtel de famille; **f. likeness,** air de famille; **f. life,** vie familiale; **f. man,** (i) père de famille (ii) homme d'intérieur; *Com:* **in a f.-size(d) jar,** en pot familial; *Adm: O:* **f. allowance,** allocation familiale; **f. planning,** limitation des naissances; planning familial.

famine ['fæmin] *n* (*a*) famine *f* (*b*) disette *f*. **'famished** *a* affamé; *F:* **I'm f.,** je meurs de faim.

famous ['feiməs] *a* célèbre (**for,** par); renommé. **'famously** *adv F:* fameusement, à merveille.

fan[1] [fæn] **1.** *n* (*a*) éventail *m* (*b*) ventilateur (rotatif); *Aut:* **f. belt,** courroie de ventilateur; *DomEc:* **f. heater,** radiateur soufflant **2.** *vtr* (**fanned**) éventer (qn); souffler (le feu); attiser (une passion); envenimer (une querelle). **'fanlight** *n* imposte *f* (au-dessus d'une porte). **'fan 'out** *vi* se déployer (en éventail).

fan[2] *n* fanatique *mf*; passionné, -ée; fan *mf*; fana *mf*; admirateur, -trice; mordu, -ue; **film f.,** cinéphile *mf*; **f. club,** club de fans. **'fanmail** *n* courrier *m* des admirateurs (d'une vedette).

fanatic [fə'nætik] *n* fanatique *mf*. **fa'natical** *a* fanatique. **fa'natically** *adv* fanatiquement. **fa'naticism** *n* fanatisme *m*.

fancy ['fænsi] **1.** *n* (*pl* **fancies**) (*a*) imagination *f*, fantaisie *f* (*b*) idée *f* (*c*) fantaisie, caprice *m*; **as the f.**

takes me, comme l'idée me prend, *F:* comme ça me chante (*d*) fantaisie, goût *m*; **to take a f. to sth,** prendre goût à qch; **to take a f. to s.o.,** (i) prendre qn en affection (ii) s'éprendre de qn; **it caught my f.,** cela m'a séduit du premier coup **2.** *a* (de) fantaisie; (biscuits) assortis; *F:* (prix) trop élevé; **f. goods,** nouveautés *fpl*; **f. dress,** travesti *m*; déguisement *m*; **f. dress ball,** bal travesti; *F:* **f. man,** gigolo *m*; amant *m*; **f. woman,** maîtresse *f* **3.** *vtr* (**fancied**) (*a*) s'imaginer, se figurer (qch); **f. that!** figurez-vous ça! tiens! **f. meeting you!** je ne m'attendais guère à vous rencontrer! (*b*) croire, penser; **I f. I've seen him before,** j'ai l'impression de l'avoir déjà vu (*c*) se sentir attiré (vers qn, qch); **I don't f. his offer,** son offre ne me dit rien; **I f. a bit of chicken,** je mangerais volontiers un morceau de poulet; *Turf:* **strongly fancied horse,** cheval très coté; *F:* **to f. oneself,** se gober; **he fancies himself as a speaker,** il se croit orateur. **'fancier** *n* connaisseur, -euse (en chiens, en pigeons). **'fanciful** *a* (*of pers*) capricieux, fantasque; (projet) chimérique; (conte) imaginaire.

fanfare ['fænfɛər] *n* fanfare *m*.

fang [fæŋ] *n* croc *m* (de loup); crochet *m* (de vipère).

fantasy ['fæntəsi] *n* (*pl* **fantasies**) fantaisie *f*; idée *f* fantasque; fantasme *m*. **'fantasize** *vi* fantasmer. **fan'tastic** *a* fantastique; bizarre; invraisemblable; *F:* formidable; incroyable; *Com:* **f. reductions,** baisses phénoménales. **fan'tastically** *adv* incroyablement.

far [fɑ:r] (*comp* **farther, further;** *sup* **farthest, furthest**) **1.** *adv* (*a*) (*of place*) loin; **to go f.,** aller loin; **how f. is it from Paris to Bonn?** combien y a-t-il de Paris à Bonn? **as f. as the eye can see,** à perte de vue; **to live f. away, f. off,** demeurer au loin; **f. and wide,** de tous côtés; **f. and near,** partout; **f. from,** loin de; **to go so f. as to do sth,** aller jusqu'à faire qch; **that's going too f.,** cela dépasse les bornes; **how f. have you got?** où en êtes-vous (**with,** de)? **as f. as I know,** autant que je sache; **as f. as that goes,** pour ce qui est de cela; **as f. as I can,** dans la mesure de mes moyens; **so f. so good,** c'est fort bien jusque-là; **in so f. as,** dans la mesure où; en tant que; **f. from it,** loin de là; **f. be it from me to,** loin de moi l'idée de; **he's not f. off sixty,** il approche de la soixantaine; **by f.,** de loin; **by f. the best,** de beaucoup le meilleur (*b*) (*of time*) so f., jusqu'ici; **as f. as I can see,** autant que je puisse prévoir; **f. into the night,** bien avant dans la nuit; **as f. back as 1900,** déjà en 1900 (*c*) (*for emphasis*) beaucoup, bien, fort; **it's f. better,** c'est beaucoup mieux; **f. advanced,** fort avancé; **f. and away the best,** de beaucoup le meilleur, bien préférable **2.** *a* lointain, éloigné; **at the f. end of the street,** à l'autre bout de la rue. **faraway** *a* lointain, éloigné; (regard) perdu dans le vague. **'far-'fetched** *a* (*of argument, etc*) forcé, outré; tiré par les cheveux. **'far-'flung** *a* (*a*) très étendu (*b*) lointain, éloigné. **'far-'gone** *a F:* bien parti. **'far-'off** *a* lointain, éloigné. **'far-'out** *a F:* outré; avant-garde. **'far-'reaching** *a* de grande envergure, d'une grande portée. **'far-'seeing, 'far-'sighted** *a* prévoyant; clairvoyant; perspicace. **far'sightedness** *n* prévoyance *f*; perspicacité *f*.

farce [fɑ:s] *n* farce *f*; **the trial was a f.,** le procès a été grotesque. **'farcical** *a* grotesque; absurde.

fare ['fɛər] **1.** *n* (*a*) prix *m* du voyage; (*in taxi*) prix de la course; **single f.,** (prix du) billet simple; **return f.,**

aller et retour *m*, aller-retour *m*; **fares, please!** les places, s'il vous plaît! **to pay one's f.**, payer son billet (*b*) (*in taxi*) client, -ente; voyageur, -euse (*c*) chère *f*, manger *m*; **bill of f.**, menu *m* (du jour); **prison f.**, régime *m* de prison 2. *vi* **to f. well**, aller bien. **fare·'well** *int* & *n* adieu (*m*); **to bid s.o. f.**, dire adieu, faire ses adieux, à qn; **f. dinner**, dîner d'adieu.

farm [fɑːm] 1. *n* ferme *f*; élevage *m* (de truites); **f. labourer**, ouvrier agricole 2. *v* (*a*) *vtr* cultiver (des terres) (*b*) *vi* être cultivateur. **'farmer** *n* agriculteur *m*; cultivateur, -trice; **(tenant) f.**, fermier, -ière; **stock f.**, éleveur, -euse. **'farmhand** *n* ouvrier *m* agricole. **'farmhouse** *n* (maison *f* de) ferme. **'farming** *n* exploitation *f* agricole; agriculture *f*; **f. communities**, agglomérations rurales. **'farm 'out** *vtr* mettre (des enfants) en nourrice; sous-traiter (du travail). **'farmyard** *n* cour *f* de ferme; basse-cour *f*.

farrier ['færiər] *n* maréchal-ferrant *m*.

fart [fɑːt] *P:* 1. *n* pet *m* 2. *vi* péter.

farther ['fɑːðər] (*comp of* **far**) 1. *adv* plus loin (**than,** que); **f. off, away**, plus loin, plus éloigné; **f. on**, plus en avant; plus loin; plus en avance; **f. back**, plus en arrière 2. *a* plus lointain, plus éloigné; **at the f. end of the room**, à l'autre bout de la pièce. **'farthest** (*sup of* **far**) 1. *a* **f.** (*off*), le plus lointain, le plus éloigné; (*of way*) le plus long 2. *adv* le plus loin.

fascinate ['fæsineit] *vtr* fasciner, charmer, séduire; **to be fascinated by sth**, être fasciné par qch. **'fascinating** *a* fascinant; séduisant; (livre) passionnant. **fasci'nation** *n* fascination *f*; attrait *m*.

fascism ['fæʃizm] *n* fascisme *m*. **'fascist** *a* & *n* fasciste (*mf*).

fashion ['fæʃn] 1. *n* (*a*) manière *f* (de faire qch); **in a peculiar f.**, d'une façon étrange; **after a f.**, tant bien que mal (de mode *f*, vogue *f*; **in f.**, à la mode; en vogue; **out of f.**, passé de mode; démodé; **in the latest f.**, à la dernière mode; **to set the f.**, mener la mode; **to become the f.**, **come into f.**, devenir la mode; **it's (all) the f.**, c'est la grande vogue; **f. house**, maison de haute couture; **f. show**, présentation de collections; **f. magazine**, journal de modes 2. *vtr* façonner; confectionner. **'fashionable** *a* à la mode; en vogue; (endroit) mondain. **'fashionably** *adv* à la mode. **'fashioned** *a Cl:* **fully f.**, (entièrement) diminué, proportionné.

fast¹ [fɑːst] 1. *n* jeûne *m* 2. *vi* jeûner.

fast² 1. *a* (*a*) ferme, fixe, solide; (*of colour*) solide, résistant; (tissu) bon teint, grand teint; (*of grip*) tenace; *Nau:* **to make f.**, amarrer (un cordage) (*b*) rapide; **f. train**, rapide *m*; **you're a f. walker**, vous marchez vite; *F:* **he pulled a f. one on me**, il m'a joué un mauvais tour (*c*) (*of clock*) en avance; **my watch is five minutes f.**, ma montre avance de cinq minutes (*d*) *O:* (*of pers*) dissipé; de mœurs légères; (trop) émancipé 2. *adv* (*a*) ferme, solidement; **to hold f.**, tenir ferme; tenir bon; **to stand f.**, tenir bon; **to stick f.**, rester pris, collé; **to play f. and loose**, jouer double jeu (with, avec); **to be f. asleep**, dormir profondément (*b*) vite, rapidement; **not so f.!** pas si vite! doucement! **as f. as his legs could carry him**, à toutes jambes; **he'll do it f. enough if you pay him**, il ne se fera pas prier si vous le payez.

fasten ['fɑːsn] 1. *vtr* attacher (qch à qch); fixer, assurer; bien fermer (la porte); **to f. (up)**, agrafer, boutonner (sa robe) 2. *vi* s'attacher, se fixer; (*of garment*) s'agrafer, se boutonner; (*of door*) se fermer. **'fasten 'down** *vtr* fixer (à terre). **'fastener**, **'fastening** *n* attache *f*; (*of garment*) agrafe *f*; (*of window*) fermeture *f*; (*of purse*) fermoir *m*.

fastidious [fæs'tidiəs] *a* difficile (à contenter); délicat (**about** sth, sur qch). **fas'tidiously** *adv* avec une délicatesse exagérée.

fat [fæt] 1. *a* (**fatter; fattest**) gros; gras; **to get f.**, (s')engraisser; *F:* **a f. lot you know about it!** comme si vous en saviez quelque chose! 2. *n* (*a*) graisse *f*; *pl* matières grasses; **deep f.**, (grande) friture; *F:* **the f.'s in the fire!** le feu est aux poudres! (*b*) gras *m* (de viande); **to live off the f. of the land**, vivre comme un coq en pâte. **'fathead** *n F:* imbécile *mf*; andouille *f*. **'fatness** *n* embonpoint *m*; corpulence *f*. **'fatted** *a* **to kill the f. calf**, tuer le veau gras. **'fatten ('up)** *vtr* & *i* engraisser. **'fattening** *a* (aliment) qui fait grossir. **'fatty** *a* graisseux; (aliment) gras; (*of tissue*) adipeux.

fate [feit] *n* destin *m*, sort *m*; **to leave s.o. to his f.**, abandonner qn à son sort. **'fatal** *a* fatal; (*of blow, disease*) mortel; (décision) funeste; **f. mistake**, faute capitale. **fa'tality** *n* accident mortel; sinistre *m*; **there were no fatalities**, il n'y a pas eu de mort *f*. **'fatally** *adv* fatalement; mortellement (blessé). **'fated** *a* (*a*) (jour) fatal (*b*) destiné, condamné (**to do** sth, à faire qch) (*c*) voué à la destruction. **'fateful** *a* (parole) fatidique; (jour) décisif, fatal; (événement) inévitable.

father ['fɑːðər] *n* père *m*; **from f. to son**, de père en fils; **like f. like son**, tel père tel fils; **yes, F.**, oui, (mon) père; **God the F.**, Dieu le Père; **the Holy F.**, le Saint-Père; **F. Martin**, (i) (*belonging to religious order*) le Père Martin (ii) (*priest*) l'abbé Martin; **F. confessor**, père spirituel; **F. Christmas**, le père Noël; *F:* **the f. and mother of a row!** une de ces empoignades! **F.'s Day**, la Fête des Pères. **'fatherhood** *n* paternité *f*. **'father-in-law** *n* beau-père *m*. **'fatherland** *n* patrie *f*. **'fatherless** *a* orphelin de père. **'fatherly** *a* paternel.

fathom ['fæðəm] 1. *n Nau:* brasse *f* (= 6 ft = 1,83 m) 2. *vtr* sonder (un mystère); **I can't f. it (out)**, je n'y comprends rien; **I can't f. him**, je ne le comprends pas.

fatigue [fə'tiːg] 1. *n* (*a*) fatigue *f* (*b*) *Mil:* corvée *f* 2. *vtr* fatiguer. **fa'tiguing** *a* fatigant.

fatuous ['fætjuəs] *a* imbécile, idiot. **fa'tuity**, **'fatuousness** *n* imbécillité *f*. **'fatuously** *adv* d'un air imbécile.

faucet ['fɔːsət] *n NAm:* (*Br* = **tap**) robinet *m*.

fault [fɔːlt] 1. *n* (*a*) défaut *m* (de qn); imperfection *f*, vice *m* (de construction); **scrupulous to a f.**, scrupuleux à l'excès; **to find f. with s.o.**, trouver à redire contre qn (*b*) faute *f*; *Geol:* faille *f*; **to be at f.**, être en défaut, être fautif; **whose f. is it?** à qui la faute? **it wasn't my f.**, ce n'était pas de ma faute 2. *vtr* prendre (qn) en défaut; trouver un défaut dans (qch). **'faultfinder** *n* critiqueur, -euse; mécontent, -ente. **'faultfinding** *n* (*a*) (*of pers*) disposition *f* à critiquer (*b*) (*of device*) localisation *f* des défauts. **'faultiness** *n* défectuosité *f*, imperfection *f*. **'faultless** *a* sans défaut, sans faute; impeccable, irréprochable. **'faultlessly** *adv* parfaitement, d'une manière impeccable. **'faulty** *a* (**-ier, -iest**) défectueux, imparfait; (*of reasoning*) erroné; (*of style*) incorrect.

fauna ['fɔːnə] *n* faune *f*.

favour, *NAm:* -**or** ['feivər] 1. *n* (*a*) faveur *f*, approbation *f*; **to be in f. with s.o.**, être en faveur auprès de qn; **to be out of f.**, (i) être mal en cour (ii) ne plus être à la mode; **to find f. with s.o.**, trouver grâce aux yeux de qn (*b*) grâce *f*; bonté *f*; **to do s.o. a f.**, rendre (un) service, faire une faveur, à qn; obliger qn; **as a f.**, à titre gracieux; **to ask a f. of s.o.**, solliciter une grâce, une faveur, de qn (*c*) partialité *f*, préférence *f*; **to show f. to s.o.**, favoriser qn (*d*) **in f. of**, en faveur de; **to have everything in one's f.**, avoir tout pour soi; **to decide in s.o.'s f.**, donner gain de cause à qn; **to be in f. of sth**, être partisan de qch 2. *vtr* (*a*) favoriser, approuver, préférer; accorder une préférence à; être pour (un projet); **I don't f. the idea**, l'idée ne me plaît pas (*b*) avantager (qn); montrer de la partialité pour (qn) (*c*) faciliter (qch); **circumstances that f. our interests**, circonstances favorables à nos intérêts. '**favourable**, *NAm:* -**orable** *a* favorable; (*of weather*) propice; (*of terms, circumstances*) bon, avantageux. '**favourably**, *NAm:* -**orably** *adv* favorablement. '**favoured**, *NAm:* -**ored** *a* favorisé; **most f. nation**, nation la plus favorisée; **the f. few**, les élus *m*. '**favourite**, *NAm:* -**orite** *a & n* favori, -ite; préféré, -ée. '**favouritism**, *NAm:* -**oritism** *n* favoritisme *m*.

fawn¹ [fɔːn] 1. *n Z:* faon *m* 2. *a & n* (*colour*) fauve (*m*).

fawn² *vi* **to f. on s.o.**, (i) (*of dog*) caresser qn (ii) (*of pers*) faire le chien couchant auprès de qn; aduler qn. '**fawning** *a* servile.

FBI *abbr US: Federal Bureau of Investigation.*

fear ['fiər] 1. *n* crainte *f*, peur *f*; respect *m* (des lois); **deadly f.**, effroi *m*; **to be, go, stand, in f. of**, redouter, craindre, avoir peur de; **to go in f. of one's life**, craindre pour sa vie; **have no f.**, ne craignez rien! **for f. that**, de peur que + *sub*; **for f. of making a mistake**, de crainte d'erreur; **without f. or favour**, sans distinction de personnes; **to put the f. of God in(to) s.o.**, faire trembler qn; *F:* **no f.!** pas de danger! 2. *vtr* craindre, avoir peur de (qn, qch); appréhender (un événement); **to f. that**, craindre, avoir peur, que + *ne* + *sub*; **to f. for s.o.**, s'inquiéter au sujet de qn; **I f. it is too late**, je crains qu'il ne soit trop tard; **I f. I'm late**, je crois bien être en retard. '**fearful** *a* (*a*) (bruit) affreux, effrayant; **a f. mess**, un désordre effrayant (*b*) (*of pers*) peureux, craintif. '**fearfully** *adv* (*a*) affreusement, terriblement (*b*) peureusement. '**fearless** *a* intrépide, courageux. '**fearlessly** *adv* intrépidement, sans peur. '**fearlessness** *n* intrépidité *f*. '**fearsome** *a* redoutable, effrayant.

feasible ['fiːzəbl] *a* (*a*) faisable, possible, praticable; (*of story*) vraisemblable. **feasi'bility** *n* praticabilité *f*; faisabilité *f* (d'un projet).

feast [fiːst] 1. *n* (*a*) (jour *m* de) fête *f* (*b*) (*meal*) festin *m*, banquet *m* 2. *v* (*a*) *vi* faire festin; festoyer; **to f. on, se** régaler de (*b*) *vtr* régaler, fêter (qn); **to f. one's eyes on sth**, repaître ses yeux de qch.

feat [fiːt] *n* (*a*) exploit *m* (*b*) tour *m* de force; **f. of engineering**, triomphe *m* de l'ingénieur.

feather ['feðər] *n* plume *f*; *pl* plumage *m* (d'oiseau); **f. bed**, lit de plume(s); **f. duster**, plumeau *m*; **you could have knocked me down with a f.**, j'ai cru tomber de

mon haut; **birds of a f. flock together**, qui se ressemble s'assemble; **that's a f. in his cap**, il peut en être fier 2. *vtr Fig:* **to f. one's nest**, faire sa pelote. '**feather-brained** *a* écervelé, étourdi. '**featherweight** *n Box:* poids *m* plume.

feature ['fiːtʃər] 1. *n* (*a*) trait *m* (du visage) (*b*) trait, caractéristique *f* (d'un paysage); **main features**, grands traits; **special f.**, particularité *f*; spécialité *f* (*c*) *Journ:* article *m* vedette; *TV: WTel:* numéro *m* vedette; *Cin:* **f. (film)**, long métrage, *F:* grand film 2. *v* (*a*) *vtr* caractériser, distinguer; *Journ:* mettre (une nouvelle) en manchette; *Cin:* représenter (qn) (*b*) *vi* figurer. '**featureless** *a* sans traits bien marqués.

feces ['fiːsiːz] *npl NAm: see* **faeces**.

February ['februəri] *n* février *m*; **in F.**, en février, au mois de février.

feckless ['fekləs] *a* propre à rien.

fed [fed] *see* **feed** 2. '**fed 'up** *a F:* **to be f. up**, en avoir marre, plein le dos (**with, about, de**)

federate 1. *v* ['fedəreit] (*a*) *vtr* fédérer (*b*) *vi* se fédérer 2. *a* ['fedərət] fédéré. '**federal** *a* fédéral. **fede'ration** *n* fédération *f*.

fee [fiː] *n* honoraires *mpl* (d'un avocat); cachet *m* (d'un acteur); **school fees**, frais *mpl* de scolarité; **entrance f.**, droit *m* d'entrée; **registration f.**, (i) droit(s) d'inscription (ii) *Post:* taxe *f* de recommandation; **for a small f.**, moyennant une légère redevance. '**fee-paying** *a* **f.-p. school** = collège privé.

feeble ['fiːbl] *a* (*a*) faible, infirme, débile (*b*) (*of pers*) mou; (*of joke*) médiocre. '**feeble-'minded** *a* d'esprit faible. '**feebleness** *n* faiblesse *f*, débilité *f*. '**feebly** *adv* faiblement.

feed [fiːd] 1. *n* (*a*) alimentation *f*; pâturage *m* (d'animaux) (*b*) nourriture *f*, pâture *f*; fourrage *m* (pour les animaux); ration *f* (de nourriture); **to give a horse, a baby, his f.**, donner à manger à un cheval, un bébé; **to be off one's f.**, bouder sur la nourriture; *F:* **to have a good f.**, bien manger (*b*) *Tchn:* alimentation (d'une machine); **gravity f., pressure f.**, alimentation par gravité, sous pression 2. *v* (**fed**) (*a*) *vtr* nourrir; donner à manger à (qn); allaiter (un enfant); ravitailler (une armée); alimenter (une machine); **to f. on sth**, nourrir qn de qch (*b*) *vi* manger; (*of cattle*) paître, brouter; **to f. on sth**, se nourrir de qch. '**feed 'back** *vtr Cmptr:* réintroduire (de l'information). '**feedback** *n Elcs: etc:* réaction *f*; feed-back *m inv.* '**feeder** *n* (*a*) heavy f., gros mangeur (*b*) (*baby's bib*) bavoir *m* (*c*) route *f* de raccordement. '**feeding** *n* alimentation *f*; **f. bottle**, biberon *m* (de bébé). '**feed 'up** *vtr* engraisser; *F:* **I'm fed up**, j'en ai plein le dos, j'en ai marre (**with, about, de**).

feel [fiːl] *n* (*a*) toucher *m*; **to recognize sth by the f. of it**, reconnaître qch au toucher (*b*) sensation *f*; **to get the f. of sth**, s'habituer à qch; **he's got the f. of his car**, il a sa voiture bien en main 2. *v* (**felt**) (*a*) *vtr* toucher, palper; tâter (le pouls) (*b*) *vtr & i* **to f. about in the dark**, tâtonner dans l'obscurité; **to f. (about) for sth**, chercher qch à tâtons; **to f. one's way** (i) avancer à tâtons (ii) *Fig:* explorer le terrain; **to f. in one's pockets for sth**, chercher qch dans ses poches (*c*) *vtr* sentir; **to f. the floor trembling**, sentir trembler le plancher (*d*) *vtr & i* ressentir, éprouver; **to f. the cold**, être sensible au froid; être frileux; **to make one's authority felt**, affirmer son autorité; **I f. for him**, il a toute ma sympathie (e) vtr avoir conscience de (qch); **I felt it in my bones that**, qch m'a dit que; **I felt it necessary to intervene**, j'ai jugé nécessaire d'intervenir; **what I f. about it is**, mon sentiment là-dessus c'est que (f) vi to **f. cold**, avoir froid; **to f. ill**, se sentir malade; **my foot feels better**, mon pied va mieux; **he's not feeling himself**, il ne se sent pas très bien; **to f. all the better for it**, s'en trouver mieux; **to f. certain that**, être certain que; **I f. as if**, j'ai l'impression que; **I felt like crying**, j'avais envie de pleurer; **I don't f. like it**, ça ne me dit rien; **I f. like a cup of tea**, je prendrais bien une tasse de thé (g) vi (of thg) **to f. hard**, être dur au toucher; **this room feels damp (to me)**, cette pièce (me) paraît humide. **'feeler** n antenne f (d'insecte); tentacule m (de mollusque); Fig: **to put out feelers**, tâter le terrain. **'feeling** n (a) tâtage m (de qch) (b) **(sense of) f.**, toucher m; **to have no f. in one's arm**, avoir le bras mort (c) sensation (douloureuse) (d) sentiment m; **public f.**, le sentiment populaire; **feelings are running very high**, les esprits sont très montés; **no hard feelings!** sans rancune! **I had a f. of danger**, j'avais le sentiment d'être en danger; **there is a general f. that**, l'impression f règne que (e) sensibilité f, émotion f; **to have a f. for music**, être sensible à la musique; **have you no feelings!** vous n'avez donc pas de cœur! **with f.**, (parler) avec émotion; (chanter) avec âme; **bad f.**, rancune f.

feet [fi:t] npl see **foot 1**.

feign [fein] vtr feindre, simuler; affecter (la surprise). **feint 1.** n Mil: fausse attaque; Box: etc: feinte f **2.** vi feinter.

felicity [fə'lisiti] n félicité f, bonheur m.

feline ['fi:lain] a félin.

fell¹ [fel] vtr abattre (un arbre).

fell² see **fall 2**.

fellow ['felou] n (a) camarade m, compagnon m; **f. sufferer**, compagnon de misère; **f. feeling**, sympathie f; **f. creature**, semblable mf; **f. citizen**, concitoyen, -enne; **f. countryman, -woman**, compatriote mf; **f. traveller**, (i) compagnon de voyage (ii) Pol: communisant, -ante (b) (of pers) semblable m, pareil m (c) (at university) (professeur) chargé m de cours (d) membre m, associé, -ée (d'une société savante) (e) F: homme m; garçon m; **a good f.**, un brave garçon, un bon type; **a queer f.**, un drôle de type; **the poor little f.**, old f., le pauvre petit, vieux. **'fellowship** n (a) communion f, communauté f; (good) **f.**, camaraderie f (b) association f, corporation f; (con)fraternité f.

felon ['felən] n Jur: criminel, -elle. **fe'lonious** [-'louniəs] a criminel. **'felony** n crime m.

felt¹ [felt] n feutre m. **felt-'tip** n f.-t. (pen), (crayon m) feutre m.

felt² see **feel 2**.

female ['fi:meil] **1.** a féminin; (de) femme; (enfant) du sexe féminin; (of animal) femelle **2.** nf femme; (of animals, plants) femelle. **'feminine** a féminin; Gram: **this word is f.**, ce mot est (du) féminin. **femi'ninity** n féminité f. **'feminism** n féminisme m. **'feminist** a & n féministe (mf).

fen [fen] n marais m, marécage m.

fence [fens] **1.** n (a) clôture f, barrière f, palissade f; Equit: obstacle m; Fig: **to sit on the f.**, ménager la chèvre et le chou (b) F: receleur, -euse (d'objets volés) **2.** v (a) vi faire de l'escrime (b) vtr **to f. (in)**, clôturer (un terrain). **'fencer** n escrimeur, -euse. **'fencing** n (a) escrime f; **f. master**, maître d'escrime; **f. match**, assaut d'escrime (b) (matériaux mpl pour) clôture, barrière, palissade; **wire f.**, treillage m en fil de fer.

fend [fend] vi to **f. for oneself**, se débrouiller. **fender** n Furn: garde-feu m inv; (on boat) bourrelet m; NAm: Aut: (Br = **wing**) aile f. **'fend 'off** vtr parer, détourner.

fennel ['fenl] n Hort: fenouil m.

ferment 1. n ['fə:ment] (a) ferment m (b) fermentation f (des liquides) (c) agitation f populaire; **the town is in a (state of) f.**, la ville est en effervescence **2.** vtr & i [fə'ment] fermenter. **fermen'tation** n fermentation.

fern [fə:n] n Bot: fougère f.

ferocious [fə'rouʃəs] a féroce. **fe'rociously** adv férocement. **ferocity** [-'rɔsiti] n férocité f.

ferret ['ferit] **1.** n Z: furet m **2.** vi fureter; chasser au furet; **to f. (about) in one's pockets**, fureter, fouiner, dans ses poches. **'ferret 'out** vtr dénicher. **'ferreting** n chasse f au furet.

ferrous ['ferəs] a Ch: ferreux.

ferry ['feri] **1.** n (a) (endroit m de) passage m (d'un cours d'eau en bac); bac m (b) **f. (boat)**, bac; (passenger, car) **f.**, ferry(-boat) m **2.** vtr to **f. (across)**, passer (qn) en bac; transporter (en voiture). **'ferryman** n (pl **-men**) passeur m.

fertile ['fə:tail] a fertile, fécond; (œuf) fécondé. **fer'tility** [-'til-] n fertilité f, fécondité f. **fertili'zation** n fertilisation f; fécondation f. **'fertilize** vtr fertiliser; féconder. **'fertilizer** n engrais m.

fervour, NAm: **-or** ['fə:vər] n ferveur f; ardeur f. **'fervent** a ardent, fervent.

fester ['festər] vi suppurer; (of resentment) couver. **'festering** a (of wound) ulcéreux, suppurant.

festive ['festiv] n (air) de fête; **the f. season**, Noël m; **in a f. mood**, le cœur en fête. **'festival** n fête f; festival m (de musique, du film). **fes'tivity** n fête; réjouissance(s) f(pl); festivité f.

festoon [fes'tu:n] **1.** n feston m, guirlande f **2.** vtr festonner (**with**, de).

fetch [fetʃ] vtr (a) aller chercher; **come and f. me**, venez me chercher; **to f. water from the river**, aller puiser de l'eau dans la rivière (b) apporter (qch); amener (qn); (to dog) **f. (it)!** va chercher! **to f. and carry for s.o.**, aux ordres de qn (c) rapporter, atteindre (un certain prix); **it fetched a high price**, cela s'est vendu cher; F: to **f. s.o. a blow**, flanquer un coup à qn. **'fetch 'back** vtr ramener (qn); rapporter (qch). **'fetch 'in** vtr rentrer (le linge). **'fetching** a séduisant; ravissant. **'fetch 'up 1.** vtr monter (qch); faire monter (qn) **2.** vi aboutir; s'arrêter.

fête [feit] **1.** n fête **2.** vtr fêter; faire fête à (qn).

fetid ['fetid, 'fi:-] a fétide, puant.

fetish ['fetiʃ] n fétiche m.

fetter ['fetər] **1.** vtr enchaîner (qn); entraver (un cheval) **2.** n usu pl chaînes fpl, fers mpl; **in fetters**, enchaîné.

fettle ['fetl] n **in fine f.**, en pleine forme.

fetus, fetal ['fi:təs, 'fi:tl] NAm: see **foetus**.

feud ['fju:d] **1.** n inimitié f; (family, blood) **f.**, vendetta f **2.** vi se quereller (**over**, au sujet de).

feudal ['fjuːdl] *a* féodal. **'feudalism** *n* système féodal; féodalité *f*.

fever ['fiːvər] *n* fièvre *f*; **f. of excitement,** excitation fébrile, fiévreuse; **to be at f. pitch,** être fièvreux. **'fevered** *a* fiévreux. **'feverish** *a* fiévreux; fébrile. **'feverishly** *adv* fiévreusement, fébrilement. **'feverishness** *n* état fiévreux, fébrile.

few [fjuː] **1.** *a* (*a*) peu de; **he has f. friends,** il a peu d'amis; **with f. exceptions,** à de rares exceptions près; **trains every f. minutes,** trains à quelques minutes d'intervalle; **every f. days,** tous les deux ou trois jours; **a f. (books,** etc**),** quelques (livres, etc); **a f. more,** encore quelques-un(e)s; **he had a good f. enemies,** il avait beaucoup d'ennemis; **in a f. minutes,** dans quelques minutes (*b*) peu nombreux; **f. and far between,** très espacés; rares **2.** *n* (*a*) peu (de gens); **f. of them,** peu d'entre eux; **there are very f. of us,** nous sommes peu nombreux; **the happy f.,** une minorité de gens heureux (*b*) quelques-uns, -unes; **I know a f. of them,** j'en connais quelques-uns; **a f. of us,** quelques-uns d'entre nous; **there were a good f., quite a f.,** of them, il y en avait pas mal. **'fewer** *a & n* (*a*) moins (de); **20% f. visitors,** 20% de visiteurs en moins; **no f. than,** pas moins de (*b*) plus rares; moins nombreux; **the houses became f.,** les maisons devenaient plus rares. **'fewest** *a & n* (*a*) le moins (de) (*b*) les plus rares, les moins nombreux.

fiancé(e) [fi'ɔnsei] *n* fiancé, -ée.

fiasco [fi'æskou] *n* fiasco *m*.

fib [fib] *F:* **1.** *n* petit mensonge; blague *f* **2.** *vi* (**fibbed**) mentir; blaguer. **'fibber** *n* *F:* menteur, -euse; blagueur, -euse.

fibre, *NAm:* **fiber** ['faibər] *n* fibre *f*. **'fibreboard,** *NAm:* **'fiber-** *n* panneau *m* de fibres (agglomérées). **'fibreglass,** *NAm:* **'fiber-** *n* (*also* **glass fibre**) fibre de verre. **'fibroid** *Med:* **1.** *a* fibroïde **2.** *n* fibrome *m*. **fibro'sitis** *n* *Med:* rhumatisme *m*. **'fibrous** *a* fibreux.

fickle ['fikl] *a* inconstant, volage.

fiction ['fikʃn] *n* (*a*) fiction *f*; **legal f.,** fiction légale; **these stories are pure f.,** ces histoires sont de pure invention (*b*) (**works of**) **f.,** romans *mpl*; **light f.,** romans de lecture facile. **'fictional, fic'titious** *a* fictif.

fiddle ['fidl] **1.** *n F:* (*a*) violon *m*; *Fig:* **to play second f.,** jouer un rôle secondaire (**to** s.o., auprès de qn) (*b*) combine *f*; tripotage *m*; **to be on the f.,** faire du fricotage. **II.** *v* **1.** *vi* (*a*) jouer du violon (*b*) **to f. about, around,** bricoler; **to f. (about, around) with sth,** tripoter, trifouiller, jouer avec, qch; **don't f. with that drawer!** ne touche pas au tiroir! laisse le tiroir tranquille! **stop fiddling (about, around)!** tiens-toi tranquille! **2.** *vtr* truquer (les comptes); carotter (une permission). **'fiddler** *F:* *n* (*a*) joueur, -euse, de violon; violoniste *m* (*b*) combinard, -arde. **'fiddlesticks** *int F:* quelle blague! **'fiddling 1.** *a* futile, insignifiant **2.** *n* combines *fpl*. **'fiddly** *a* (**-ier, -iest**) *F:* (travail) délicat, minutieux.

fidelity [fi'deliti] *n* fidélité *f*, loyauté *f*; *Rec:* **high f.,** haute fidélité.

fidget ['fidʒit] **1.** *n F:* **he's a f.,** il ne tient pas en place; **what a f. you are!** tiens-toi donc tranquille! **2.** *vi* **to f. (about),** remuer continuellement; ne pas tenir en place; **don't f.!** tiens-toi tranquille! **'fidgets** *npl F:* **to**

have the f., ne pas tenir en place. **'fidgety** *a* (*a*) remuant, agité (*b*) nerveux, impatient.

field [fiːld] **1.** *n* (*a*) champ *m*; *Min:* gisement *m* (pétrolifère); **in the fields,** aux champs; **f. glasses,** jumelles *fpl*; **f. sports,** la chasse et la pêche; *Sp:* **f. events,** épreuves d'athlétisme; *Mil:* **f. hospital,** champ de bataille; **in the f.,** en campagne; **f. hospital,** ambulance divisionnaire; **f. gun,** canon de campagne; **f. artillery,** artillerie de campagne; **f. marshal,** maréchal *m*; **f. day,** (i) *Mil:* jour de grandes manœuvres (ii) *NAm: Sch:* réunion athlétique (iii) *Fig:* grande occasion (*b*) *Fb: etc:* terrain *m*; *Av:* **landing f.,** terrain d'atterrissage (*c*) théâtre *m*, champ; domaine *m* (d'une science); **in the political f.,** sur le plan politique; **f. study,** étude sur le terrain; **f. of vision,** champ visuel (*d*) *Turf:* **the f.,** le champ, les partants *m* **2.** *v* (*a*) *vi Games:* tenir le champ (*b*) *vtr* arrêter (une balle); réunir (une équipe); présenter (des candidats). **'fielder** *n Games:* chasseur *m*. **'fieldmouse** *n Z:* mulot *m*. **'fieldwork** *n* travaux *mpl* sur le terrain.

fiend [fiːnd] *n* (*a*) démon *m*, diable *m* (*b*) monstre *m* (de cruauté) (*c*) *F:* **fresh air f.,** maniaque *mf* du plein air. **'fiendish** *a* diabolique, satanique. **'fiendishly** *adv* diaboliquement.

fierce ['fiəs] *a* féroce; (*of battle*) acharné; (*of wind*) furieux, violent; (frein) brutal; (feu) ardent. **'fiercely** *adv* férocement; violemment; avec acharnement. **'fierceness** *n* violence *f*; férocité *f* (d'un animal); ardeur *f* (du feu); acharnement *m* (de la bataille).

fiery ['faiəri] *a* **1.** ardent, brûlant, enflammé **2.** (*of pers*) (i) fougueux, emporté, impétueux (ii) colérique.

fife [faif] *n Mus:* fifre *m*.

fifteen [fif'tiːn] *num a & n* quinze (*m*); **she is f.,** elle a quinze ans; *Rugby Fb:* **the French f.,** le quinze de France. **fif'teenth** *num a & n* quinzième (*mf*); **Louis the F.,** Louis Quinze; (**on) the f. (of August),** le quinze (août).

fifth [fifθ] *num a & n* cinquième (*mf*); **Henry the F.,** Henri Cinq; *Pol:* **f. column,** cinquième colonne.

fifty ['fifti] *num a & n* cinquante (*m*); **to go f.-f. with** s.o., se mettre de moitié avec qn; **about f.,** une cinquantaine (de livres, etc); **in the fifties,** dans les années cinquante. **'fiftieth** *num a & n* cinquantième (*mf*).

fig [fig] *n* figue *f*; **green figs,** figues fraîches; **f. (tree),** figuier *m*. **'figleaf** *n* feuille *f* (i) de figuier (ii) *Art:* de vigne.

fight [fait] **1.** *n* combat *m*, bataille *f*; lutte *f* (**against,** contre); (quarrel) rixe *f*, bagarre *f*; *Box:* match *m*; assaut *m*; **f. to the death,** combat à mort; **to show f.,** résister; **to put up a good f.,** bien se défendre; **there was no f. left in him,** il n'avait plus de cœur à se battre **2.** *v* (**fought**) (*a*) *vi* se battre; combattre; lutter; **dogs fighting over a bone,** chiens qui se disputent un os (*b*) *vtr* se battre avec, contre (qn); combattre (qn, un incendie); lutter contre (qn); **to f. a battle,** livrer (une) bataille; **to f. one's way (out),** se frayer un passage (pour sortir); *Jur:* **to f. a case,** se défendre dans un procès. **'fight 'back 1.** *vtr* lutter contre (une émotion); refouler (ses larmes) **2.** *vi* résister; se battre. **'fight 'down** *vtr* vaincre. **'fighter** *n* (*a*) combattant *m* (*b*) *Av:* chasseur *m*; avion *m* de chasse; **f.-bomber,** chasseur-bombardier *m*. **'fighting 1.** *n*

combat; *Sp:* boxe *f*; (*in crowd*) rixes *fpl*, bagarres *fpl*;
I've still got a f. chance, j'ai encore une chance (si je
résiste jusqu'au bout); *Mil:* f. strength, effectif *m* de
combat 2. *a* militant, de combat; f. forces, effectifs
sous les armes.

figment ['figmənt] *n* F. of the imagination, invention
f, imagination *f*.

figure ['figər, *NAm: also* 'figjər] 1. *n* (*a*) (*pers*) forme
humaine; silhouette *f*; *Art:* figure *f*; a fine f. of a man,
un bel homme; a f. of fun, un grotesque (*b*) (*of pers*)
taille *f*; to keep one's f., garder sa ligne (*c*) personnage
m, personnalité *f*; figure; (*in play*) the central f., le
pivot de l'action; father f., personne *f* qui joue le rôle
du père; to cut a fine f., faire belle figure (*d*) figure
(géométrique); illustration *f* (dans un livre); *Art:*
image *f*; f. of speech, (i) figure de rhétorique (ii) façon *f*
de parler (*e*) *Mth: etc:* chiffre *m*; in round figures, en
chiffres ronds; double figures, dix ou plus; a mistake in
the figures, une erreur de calcul; to be good at figures,
être bon en calcul; f. of eight, huit-de-chiffre(s) *m*; to
fetch a high f., se vendre cher; the figures for 1975, les
statistiques *f* pour 1975 2. *vi* (*a*) *esp NAm:* estimer
(that, que) (*b*) (*appear*) figurer, se trouver; *F:* that
figures! ça colle! **'figurative** *a* figuré; métaphorique; (art) figuratif. **'figuratively** *adv Ling:* au
figuré. **'figurehead** *n* (*a*) *Nau:* figure *f* de proue (*b*)
personnage purement décoratif; prête-nom *m*.
'figure 'on *vtr NAm:* compter sur. **'figure 'out**
vtr (*a*) calculer (une somme) (*b*) comprendre (les
paroles de qn).

filament ['filəmənt] *n* filament *m*.

filbert ['filbət] *n* noisette *f*.

filch [filtʃ] *vtr* voler, chiper, barboter, chaparder (sth
from s.o., qch à qn).

file¹ [fail] 1. *n* lime *f* 2. *vtr* limer. **'filing** *n* limage *m*.
'filings *npl* limaille *f*.

file² [fail] *n* (*a*) classeur *m*; card-index f., fichier *m*; *esp
NAm:* f. clerk, documentaliste *mf* (*b*) liasse *f* (de
papiers); dossier *m*; *Publ:* f. copy, exemplaire
d'archives 2. *vtr* classer (des fiches); *esp Adm:* déposer
(une plainte); *Jur:* to f. a petition, enregistrer une
requête. **'filing** *n* classement *m*; f. clerk, documentaliste; f. cabinet, classeur; fichier.

file³ 1. *n* file *f*; in single, Indian, f., en file indienne, à la
queue leu leu 2. *vi* marcher à la file, en file; to f. past
s.o., défiler devant qn; to f. in, out, entrer, sortir, à la
file, un à un.

filial ['filiəl] *a* filial.

filigree ['filigri:] *n* filigrane *m*; f. work, travail en
filigrane.

fill [fil] I. *n* (*a*) to eat one's f., manger à sa faim; *F:* I've
had my f. of it, j'en ai assez (*b*) (*quantity*) charge *f*,
plein *m*. II. *v* 1. *vtr* (*a*) remplir, emplir (with, de);
bourrer (sa pipe); charger (un wagon); to be filled with
admiration, être rempli d'admiration (*b*) combler
(une brèche); plomber (une dent) (*c*) pourvoir à (une
vacance); post to be filled, emploi à pourvoir (*d*)
occuper (un poste); the thoughts that filled his mind,
les pensées qui occupaient son esprit (*e*) (*fulfil*)
répondre à (un besoin) 2. *vi* (*a*) se remplir; the hall is
beginning to f., la salle commence à se garnir (*b*) (*of
sail*) se gonfler. **'filler** *n Paint:* mastic *m*. **'fill 'in**
vtr combler, remplir, boucher (un trou); condamner
(une porte); remblayer (un fossé); remplir (un for-

mulaire); insérer (la date); *F:* to f. s.o. in on sth,
éclaircir qn sur qch. **'filling** 1. *a* (*of food*) rassasiant
2. *n* (*a*) (r)emplissage *m*; chargement *m* (d'un wagon);
comblement *m* (d'un trou); *Dent:* plombage *m*; *Aut:* f.
station, poste d'essence, station-service *f* (*b*) *Cu:*
garniture *f* (d'un sandwich); cake with chocolate f.,
gâteau fourré au chocolat. **'fill 'out** *v* 1. *vtr* remplir
(un formulaire) 2. *vi* se gonfler; (*of pers*) engraisser.
'fill 'up 1. *vtr* remplir (un verre) jusqu'au bord;
combler (une mesure); boucher (un trou); remplir (un
formulaire) 2. *vi* se remplir, se combler; *Aut:* faire le
plein (with petrol, d'essence).

fillet ['filit] 1. *n.* filet *m* (de bœuf, de sole); f. steak,
tournedos *m* 2. *vtr Cu:* désosser (un poisson); détacher des filets de (poisson); filleted sole, filets *npl* de
sole.

fillip ['filip] *n* coup *m* de fouet; stimulant *m*.

filly ['fili] *n* (*pl* fillies) pouliche *f*.

film [film] 1. *n* couche *f* (d'huile); voile *m* (de brume);
Phot: pellicule *f*; *Cin:* film *m*; colour f., film (en)
couleurs; to make a f., tourner un film; the film
industry, l'industrie cinématographique; le cinéma; f.
library, cinémathèque *f*; f. club, ciné-club *m*; f. critic,
critique du cinéma; f. script, scénario *m*; f. test, bande
d'essai 2. *vtr Cin:* filmer; tourner (une scène).
'filmstar *n* vedette *f* (de cinéma). **'filmstrip** *n*
film fixe (d'enseignement). **'filmy** *a* (-ier, -iest) léger.

filter ['filtər] 1. *n* filtre *m*; épurateur *m* (d'essence); f.
paper, papier filtre; (*of cigarette*) f. tip, bout filtre;
Phot: colour f., filtre de couleur 2. *v* (*a*) *vtr* filtrer
(l'eau); épurer (l'air) (*b*) *vi* (*of water*) filtrer (through, à
travers, par); *Aut:* changer de file; to f. to the right, to
the left, glisser à droite, à gauche. **'filter-'tipped** *a*
(à) bout filtre.

filth [filθ] *n* ordures *fpl*; immondices *mpl*; saleté *f*; to
talk f., dire des obscénités *f*. **'filthy** *a* (-ier, -iest) (*a*)
sale; immonde; dégoûtant; f. hovel, taudis infect; f.
weather, temps de chien; in a f. temper, d'une humeur
massacrante; *F:* f. dirty, crasseux; f. rich, pourri de
fric (*b*) (*of book, talk*) ordurier, obscène; (crime)
crapuleux.

fin [fin] *n* (*of fish*) nageoire *f*; (*of shark*) aileron *m*; (*of
frogman*) palme *f*; *Av:* empennage *m*; *Aut:* ailette *f* (de
radiateur).

final ['fainl] 1. *a* (*a*) final, dernier; to put the f. touches
to sth, mettre la dernière main à qch; *Com:* f.
instalment, dernier versement; versement libératoire
(*b*) définitif; (décision, jugement) sans appel; am I to
take that as f.? c'est votre dernier mot? 2. *n Sp:*
(épreuve) finale *f*; *Sch:* to take one's finals = passer
son dernier examen de licence. **fi'nale** *n* finale *m*;
grand f., apothéose *f*. **'finalist** *n* finaliste *mf*.
fi'nality *n* irrévocabilité *f*. **'finalize** *vtr* mener
(qch) à bonne fin; mettre la dernière main à (qch).
'finally *adv* finalement .; enfin; définitivement.

finance [fai'næns, fi-] 1. *n* finance *f*; f. company,
société de crédits 2. *vtr* financer, commanditer (une
entreprise). **fi'nancial** *a* financier; f. statement,
bilan *m*; f. year, exercice *m* (comptable); année
budgétaire. **fi'nancier** *n* (*a*) financier *m* (*b*) bailleur
m de fonds. **fi'nancing** *n* financement *m*.

finch [fintʃ] *n Orn:* fringille *m*.

find [faind] 1. *n* découverte *f* (de pétrole); trouvaille
f 2. *vtr* (found) (*a*) trouver; découvrir; rencontrer

(le bonheur); **to f. some difficulty in doing sth,** éprouver quelque difficulté à faire qch; **we must leave everything as we f. it,** il faut tout laisser tel quel; **I often f. myself smiling,** je me surprends souvent à sourire (b) (by searching) **to f. a (lost) key,** retrouver une clef; **the key has been found,** la clef est retrouvée; **to try to f. sth,** chercher qch; **to f. s.o. a job,** trouver un emploi à qn; **he's nowhere to be found,** il est introuvable; **to f. a leak,** localiser une fuite; **I can't f. (the) time,** je n'ai pas le temps (de faire qch) (c) constater (**that,** que); **you'll f. that I'm right,** vous verrez que j'ai raison; **they will f. it easy,** cela leur sera facile; **to f. it impossible to do sth,** se trouver dans l'impossibilité de faire qch; **how do you f. this wine?** comment trouvez-vous ce vin? Jur: **to f. s.o. guilty,** déclarer qn coupable (d) fournir (l'argent), procurer (les capitaux) (pour une entreprise); obtenir (une sûreté); **wages £20 all found,** gages £20 tout fourni. **'finding** n (a) pl découvertes f; résultants m (de recherches) (b) Jur: conclusion f (d'un tribunal). **'find 'out** vtr & i (a) se rendre compte (des faits); découvrir (la vérité); **to f. out how to do sth,** découvrir le moyen de faire qch; **to f. out about sth,** se renseigner sur qch (b) découvrir le vrai caractère de (qn); trouver (qn) en défaut.

fine¹ [fain] Jur: 1. n amende f 2. vtr frapper (qn) d'une amende; condamner (qn) à une amende.

fine² 1. a (a) fin; (of metal) pur; (of distinction) subtil (b) beau; excellent; magnifique; **the f. arts,** les beaux-arts m; **to appeal to s.o.'s finer feelings,** faire appel aux sentiments élevés de qn; **of the finest quality,** de premier choix; **how's your wife?**—**f., thanks!** comment va votre femme?—très bien, merci! **that's f.!** voilà qui est parfait! Iron: **you're a f. one, you are!** tu es joli, toi! **you're a f. one to talk,** c'est bien à vous de parler; **the weather's f.,** il fait beau; **one f. day,** un de ces beaux jours (c) effilé; (tranchant) affilé; **f. nib,** plume pointue; Fig: **not to put too f. a point on it,** pour parler carrément 2. int bon! entendu! d'accord! 3. adv (a) (hacher) fin, menu; Fig: **to cut it f.,** arriver de justesse (b) très bien. **'finely** adv (a) finement (b) délicatement, subtilement (c) **f. chopped,** haché fin, menu (d) admirablement, magnifiquement. **'fineness** n (a) titre m, aloi m (de l'or); pureté f (d'un vin) (b) excellence f (c) finesse f (d'un tissu); délicatesse f, subtilité f (des sentiments). **'finery** n parure f; **decked out in all her f.,** parée de ses plus beaux atours. **'fine-'tooth** a (peigne) fin; Fig: **to go through sth with a f.-t. comb,** passer qch au peigne fin.

finger ['fiŋgər] 1. n (a) doigt m (de la main); **first f.,** index m; **middle f.,** médius m; **ring f.,** annulaire m; **little f.,** petit doigt; **to put one's f. on sth,** mettre le doigt sur qch; F: **don't you dare lay a f. on him,** je vous défends de le toucher; **he wouldn't lift a f. to help you,** il ne remuerait pas le petit doigt pour vous aider; **you could count them on the fingers of one hand,** on pourrait les compter sur les doigts de la main; **he has a f. in every pie,** il est mêlé à tout; **to keep one's fingers crossed** = toucher du bois; P: **pull your f. out!** grouille-toi! (b) DomEc: **f. bowl,** rince-doigts m inv 2. vtr toucher, tâter, palper; F: tripoter. **'fingerboard** n touche f (de violon). **'fingering** n (a) maniement m (b) Mus: doigté m. **'fingermark** n empreinte f de doigt (sale). **'fingernail** n ongle m (de la main). **'fingerprint** 1. n empreinte digitale 2.

vtr prendre les empreintes digitales de (qn). **'fingerstall** n doigtier m. **'fingertip** n bout m du doigt; **f. control,** commande au doigté; **French to his fingertips,** français jusqu'au bout des ongles; **to have sth at one's fingertips,** savoir qch sur le bout du doigt.

finicky ['finiki] a méticuleux, vétilleux.

finish ['finiʃ] 1. n (a) fin f; Sp: arrivée f (d'une course); **to fight to the f.,** aller jusqu'au bout; **that was the f. (of it),** c'était le coup de grâce; **to be in at the f.,** (i) assister à l'arrivée (ii) voir la fin de l'aventure (b) fini m, finesse f de l'exécution; apprêt m (d'un drap); Tchn: finition(s) f(pl); **paint with a gloss, matt, f.,** peinture vernis, mate 2. v (a) vtr finir, terminer, achever (b) vi finir, cesser, se terminer; s'achever; **I've finished with it,** je n'en ai plus besoin; F: **I've finished with you,** tout est fini entre nous; **wait till I've finished with him!** attendez que je lui aie réglé son compte! Rac: **to f. fourth,** arriver quatrième. **'finished** a (a) fini; (article) apprêté (b) (of pers, performance) soigné, parfait; (orateur) accompli. **'finishing** 1. a dernier; **f. touches,** finitions 2. n achèvement m; Tchn: finition; **f. school,** école d'arts d'agrément pour les jeunes filles; Sp: **f. line,** ligne d'arrivée. **'finish 'off** vtr & i finir, terminer; achever; donner le coup de grâce à (une bête blessée).

finite ['fainait] a fini, limité; Gram: fini.

Finland ['finlənd] Prn Geog: Finlande f. **Finn** n Finlandais, -aise; Finnois, -oise. **'Finnish** 1. a finlandais 2. n Ling: finnois m.

fir [fəːr] n (a) **f. (tree),** sapin m; **f. plantation,** sapinière f; **f. cone,** pomme de pin (b) (bois m de) sapin.

fire ['faiər] 1. n (a) feu m; **to light a f.,** faire du feu; **electric, gas, f.,** radiateur m électrique, à gaz; **log f.,** feu de bois; **a roaring f.,** une belle flambée; **f. irons,** garniture f de foyer; **f. screen,** (i) devant de cheminée (ii) écran ignifuge (b) incendie m; **bush f.,** feu de brousse; **f. broke out,** un incendie s'est déclaré; **to catch f.,** prendre feu; **to set f. to sth,** mettre (le) feu à qch; **on f.,** en feu, en flammes; **the house is on f.,** la maison brûle; F: **to get on like a house on f.,** (i) (with work) marcher rondement (ii) (with pers) s'entendre à merveille; **f. fighting,** lutte contre l'incendie; **f. alarm,** avertisseur d'incendie; **f. brigade,** corps m (de sapeurs)-pompiers mpl; **f. engine,** (i) (vehicle) voiture des pompiers (ii) pompe à incendie; **f. station,** caserne de pompiers; **f. escape,** (i) échelle à incendie (ii) escalier de secours; **f. extinguisher,** extincteur d'incendie; **f. insurance,** assurance-incendie f; **f. drill,** exercice de sauvetage (en cas d'incendie); **f. door,** porte coupe-feu (c) lumière f, éclat m; feux d'un diamant) (d) enthousiasme m (e) Mil: feu; tir m; coups mpl de feu; **to open f.,** ouvrir le feu; **to cease f.,** cesser le feu; **to come, be, under f.,** essuyer le feu (de l'ennemi); **we are under f.,** on tire sur nous 2. vtr & i (a) mettre le feu à (une maison); **to be fired with enthusiasm,** brûler d'enthousiasme (b) cuire (de la poterie) (c) **oil-fired (central) heating,** chauffage (central) à mazout (d) lancer (une fusée); **to f. at, on,** tirer sur; **to f. at s.o. with a revolver,** to f. **a revolver at s.o.,** tirer un coup de revolver sur qn; **to f. a question at s.o.,** poser une question à qn à brûle-pourpoint; **without firing a shot,** sans tirer un coup; **the revolver failed to f.,** le revolver a fait long feu; **the engine is firing badly,** le moteur tourne mal; **f. away!** allez-y! (e)

F: renvoyer, congédier (un employé). **'firearm** *n* arme *f* à feu. **'fireball** *n Meteor:* (*a*) bolide *m* (*b*) éclair *m* en boule. **'firebrand** *n* (*a*) tison *m*, brandon *m* (*b*) (*pers*) brandon de discorde. **'firebreak** *n* coupe-feu *m inv*. **'firebug** *n* incendiaire *mf*. **'firecracker** *n esp NAm:* pétard *m*. **'firedog** *n* chenet *m*. **'fire-eater** *n* (*a*) avaleur *m* de feu (*b*) batailleur, -euse. **'firefly** *n* (*pl* **-flies**) *Ent:* luciole *f*. **'fireguard** *n* pare-étincelles *m inv*; garde-feu *m inv*. **'firelight** *n* lumière *f* du feu. **'firelighter** *n* allume-feu *m inv*. **'fireman** *n* (*pl* **-men**) (*a*) (sapeur-) pompier *m* (*b*) chauffeur *m* (d'une machine à vapeur). **'fireplace** *n* cheminée *f*, foyer *m*. **'fireproof** 1. *a* incombustible, ignifuge; **f. door,** porte coupe-feu; **f. dish,** plat allant au feu, au four 2. *vtr* ignifuger. **'fire-raiser** *n* incendiaire *mf*. **'fireside** *n* foyer; coin *m* du feu. **'firetrap** *n* **this building's a real f.,** ce bâtiment est une véritable souricière (en cas d'incendie). **'firewater** *n F:* gnôle *f*. **'firewood** *n* bois *m* de chauffage; bois à brûler. **'firework(s)** *n*(*pl*) feu d'artifice. **'firing** *n* (*a*) *Cer:* cuisson *f* (*b*) chauffage *m*, chauffe *f* (d'un four) (*c*) *Aut:* allumage *m* (des cylindres) (*d*) (*of gun*) tir; feu; **f. squad,** peloton d'exécution; **f. line,** ligne de tir; **to be in the f. line,** (i) être exposé au feu (de l'ennemi) (ii) *Fig:* s'attirer des attaques.

firm[1] [fə:m] *n* maison *f* (de commerce); entreprise *f*; firme *f*; société *f*; compagnie *f*; **a big f.,** une grosse entreprise; **f. of solicitors** = étude *f* de notaire.

firm[2] 1. *a* (*a*) ferme; (*of post*) solide; (pas) assuré; **as f. as a rock,** inébranlable (*b*) (*of friendship*) constant; (*of intention*) résolu; (*of belief*) ferme; **to be f.,** tenir bon (**about,** sur) 2. *adv* **to stand f.,** tenir bon, tenir ferme. **'firmly** *adv* (*a*) fermement; **I f. believe that,** j'ai la ferme conviction que (*b*) d'un ton ferme. **'firmness** *n* fermeté *f*; solidité *f*.

first [fə:st] 1. *a* premier; **the f. of April,** le premier avril; **one hundred and f.,** cent unième; **at f. sight,** à première vue; **at f. place,** d'abord; en premier lieu; **at the f. opportunity,** dès que possible; **I'll do it f. thing tomorrow,** je le ferai dès demain matin; **at f. light,** au point du jour; **head f.,** (tomber) la tête la première; **on the f. floor,** (i) au premier étage (ii) *NAm:* au rez-de-chaussée; **Charles the F.,** Charles Premier; **f. cousin,** cousin germain; **f. name,** prénom *m*; **f. aid,** premiers secours; secourisme *m*; **f.-aid kit,** trousse de secours; **f.-aid post,** poste de secours; *Publ:* **f. edition,** édition originale; *Th:* **f. night, performance,** première *f*; *Sch:* **f. year, form** = (classe de) sixième *f*; *Post:* **f. day cover,** (enveloppe de) premier jour (d'émission); *Aut:* **f. gear,** première vitesse; **to put f. things f.,** mettre en avant les choses essentielles 2. *n* (*a*) (le) premier, (la) première; **we were the f. to arrive,** nous sommes arrivés les premiers; **to be the f. to do sth,** être le premier à faire qch; **to come in an easy f.,** arriver bon premier; **f. come, f. served,** les premiers vont devant; *Sch:* (*of degree*) **to get a f.** = avoir une mention (très) bien (*b*) commencement *m*; **from f. to last,** depuis le début jusqu'à la fin; **from the f.,** dès le commencement; **at f.,** d'abord (*c*) *Aut:* première (vitesse); **in f.,** en première 3. *adv* (*a*) premièrement; d'abord; **f. and foremost,** surtout et avant tout; **f. of all,** tout d'abord; en premier lieu; **f. and last,** en tout et pour tout; **to say f. one thing and then another,** dire tantôt blanc, tantôt

noir (*b*) **when I f. saw him,** quand je l'ai vu pour la première fois (*c*) plutôt; **I'd die f.,** plutôt mourir (*d*) **he arrived f.,** il est arrivé le premier; **you go f.!** passez devant! **ladies f.!** place aux dames! **'firstborn** *a & n* (enfant) premier-né, première-née. **'first-'class** 1. *a* de première classe; (marchandises) de première qualité; (hôtel) de premier ordre; (courrier) à tarif normal 2. *adv* (voyager) en première (classe); *Post:* (envoyer une lettre) à tarif normal. **'first'hand** *a* de première main. **'firstly** *adv* premièrement; en premier lieu. **'first-'rate** *a* excellent; de première classe; *F:* **that's f.-r.!** ça c'est extra!

fiscal ['fiskəl] *a* fiscal; (année) budgétaire.

fish [fiʃ] 1. *n* (*pl* **fishes,** *coll* **fish**) poisson *m*; **f. farm,** établissement piscicole; **f. tank,** vivier *m*; **f. shop,** poissonnerie *f*; **fried f.,** poisson frit; **f. and chips,** poisson frit, servi avec des frites; **f. and chip shop,** friterie *f*; **f. fingers,** *NAm:* **sticks,** filets de poisson panés; **f. knife,** couteau à poisson; *Fig:* **I've other f. to fry,** j'ai d'autres chats à fouetter; *F:* **he's a queer f.,** c'est un drôle de type; *F:* **he's like a f. out of water,** il n'est pas dans son élément; *F:* **to drink like a f.,** boire comme un trou 2. *vtr & i* pêcher; **to go fishing,** aller à la pêche; **to f. for trout,** pêcher la truite; **to f. for compliments,** chercher des compliments; **to f. up, out, a corpse,** (re)pêcher un cadavre; **he fished a pencil out of his pocket,** il a fouillé dans sa poche et a sorti un crayon. **'fishbone** *n* arête *f* (de poisson). **'fishcake** *n Cu:* croquette *f* de poisson. **'fisherman** *n* (*pl* **-men**) pêcheur *m*. **'fishery** *n* (*pl* **-ies**) (*a*) (*place*) pêcherie *f* (*b*) (*fishing*) pêche. **'fishhook** *n* hameçon *m*. **'fishing** *n* pêche; **f. boat,** bateau de pêche; **f. line,** ligne (de pêche); **f. net,** filet de pêche; **f. rod,** canne à pêche; **f. tackle,** articles de pêche; **f. ground,** pêcherie. **'fishmonger** *n* poisson-nier, -ière; **fishmonger's,** poissonnerie *f*. **'fishpond** *n* vivier; étang *m* (à poissons). **'fishy** *a* (-ier, -iest) (odeur) de poisson; *F:* louche; douteux; (histoire) qui ne tient pas debout.

fission ['fiʃn] *n Ph:* fission *f*.

fissure ['fiʃər] *n* fissure *f*, fente *f*; crevasse *f*.

fist [fist] *n* poing *m*; **to clench one's fists,** serrer les poings. **'fistful** *n* poignée *f*. **'fisticuffs** *npl* coups *mpl* de poing.

fit[1] [fit] *n* (*a*) accès *m*, attaque *f*; **f. of coughing,** quinte *f* de toux (*b*) crise *f* épileptique; **fainting f.,** évanouisse-ment *m*; **to have,** *F:* **throw, a f.,** piquer une crise; **he'll have a f. when he knows,** il en aura une congestion quand il le saura (*c*) accès, mouvement *m* (de mauvaise humeur); **f. of crying,** crise de larmes; **to be in fits (of laughter),** avoir le fou rire; **to work by fits and starts,** travailler par à-coups. **'fitful** *a* irrégulier; (sommeil) troublé. **'fitfully** *adv* irrégulièrement; par à-coups.

fit[2] 1. *a* (fitter; fittest) (*a*) bon, propre (for sth, à qch); **f. to eat,** bon à manger; mangeable; **f. to drink,** buvable, potable; **I've nothing f. to wear,** je n'ai rien à me mettre; **I'm not f. to be seen,** je ne suis pas pré-sentable; **to think, see, f. to do sth,** juger convenable de faire qch; **do as you think f.,** faites comme bon vous semble (*b*) capable; **f. for sth,** en état de faire qch; **f. for duty,** bon pour le service; *Mil:* valide; **f. to do sth,** capable de faire qch; **he's not f. for anything,** il n'est propre à rien; **that's all he's f. for,** il n'est bon qu'à cela; **I was f. to drop,** je tombais de fatigue (*c*) en bonne santé; **as f. as a fiddle, fighting f.,** en parfaite santé; **to keep f.,** rester, se maintenir, en forme. **II.** *n* ajustement *m*; **my dress is a tight f.,** ma robe est un peu serrée, un peu juste; **her dress is a perfect f.,** sa robe lui va parfaitement. **III.** *v* 1. *vtr* (*a*) (*of clothes*) aller à (qn); être à la taille de (qn); **these shoes don't f. me very well,** ces souliers ne me vont pas très bien (*b*) adapter, ajuster (**sth to sth,** qch à qch); **to be fitted for a new dress,** faire l'essayage *m* d'une nouvelle robe; **to make the punishment f. the crime,** proportionner les peines aux délits; **to f. parts together,** monter, assembler, des pièces (*c*) **to f. s.o. for doing sth,** préparer qn à faire qch (*d*) **to f. sth with sth,** munir, pourvoir, qch de qch 2. *vi* **to f. (together),** s'ajuster, s'adapter; **your dress fits well,** votre robe vous va bien. **'fit 'in** 1. *vtr* emboîter; faire cadrer (des projets) 2. *vi* s'emboîter; **to f. in with sth,** être en harmonie avec qch; **your plans don't f. in with mine,** vos projets ne s'accordent pas, ne cadrent pas, avec les miens; **he doesn't f. in,** il ne sait pas s'adapter. **'fitment** *n* installation *f*; accessoire *m*. **'fitness** *n* (*a*) (*of pers*) aptitude *f*; **f. to drive,** aptitude à conduire (*b*) (**physical**) **f.,** santé *f* (physique); bonne forme (*c*) à-propos *m* (d'une remarque). **'fit 'out** *vtr* équiper; armer (un navire); **to f. s.o. out,** équiper qn (de vêtements). **'fitted** *a* ajusté; **f. sheet,** drap housse; (*of pers*) **f. for sth, to do sth,** fait pour qch; apte à faire qch. **'fitter** *n* ajusteur *m*, monteur *m*; installateur *m* (d'appareils électriques, à gaz); poseur *m* (de tapis); *Dressm:* essayeur, -euse. **'fitting** 1. *a* convenable, approprié 2. *n* (*a*) ajustement *m*; **f. of sth on sth,** montage *m* de qch sur qch (*b*) essayage *m* (de vêtements); **f. room,** cabine d'essayage (*c*) *Com:* **made in three fittings,** fabriqué en trois tailles, (*of shoes*) en trois largeurs (*d*) **f. out,** équipement *m*; **f. up,** aménagement *m* (d'un magasin) (*e*) *pl* installations *fpl*; accessoires *mpl*; **brass fittings,** garnitures *fpl* en cuivre. **'fittingly** *adv* à propos. **'fit 'up** *vtr* aménager.

five [faiv] *num* *a* & *n* cinq (*m*). **'five-barred** *a* (barrière) à cinq barreaux. **'fivefold** 1. *a* quintuple 2. *adv* au quintuple. **'fivepenny** *a* valant cinq pence; **f. piece,** pièce de cinq pence. **'fiver** *n* *F:* billet *m* de cinq livres, *NAm:* de cinq dollars.

fix [fiks] 1. *n* *F:* (*a*) embarras *m*, difficulté *f*; **to be in a f.,** être dans le pétrin (*b*) piqûre *f* de drogue (*c*) truquage *m* (d'une élection); **it's a f.!** c'est truqué! 2. *vtr* (*a*) fixer; caler, monter, attacher; **to f. sth in one's memory,** se graver qch dans la mémoire; **to f. one's eyes on s.o.,** fixer qn du regard; **to f. one's attention on sth,** fixer son attention sur qch (*b*) fixer, établir (une limite); nommer (un jour); **there's nothing fixed yet,** il n'y a encore rien de décidé; *F:* **how are you fixed for money?** tu as de l'argent? (*c*) arranger (qch avec qn); **I've fixed it with him,** je me suis arrangé avec lui (*d*) réparer (qch); *F:* **I'll f. him!** je lui ferai son affaire! (*e*) *esp NAm:* préparer (un repas); *F:* **just wait while I f. my hair,** attends que je me coiffe (*f*) *F:* graisser la patte à (qn); truquer (un match). **fix'ation** *n* *Psy:* fixation *f*. **'fixative** *n* fixatif *m*. **fixed** *a* (*a*) fixe; (sourire) figé; **of f. length,** de longueur constante (*b*) *F:* (match) truqué. **fixedly** ['fiksədli] *adv* fixement. **'fixing** *n* fixation *f*. **'fix 'on** *vtr* se décider pour. **'fixture** *n* (*a*) appareil *m* fixe; *pl* aménagements *mpl* (d'une

maison); installations *fpl*; **£1000 for fixtures and fittings,** £1000 de reprise (*b*) *Sp:* match prévu; rencontre (prévue); **f. list,** calendrier *m* (de la saison). **'fix 'up** *vtr* arranger; **it's all fixed up,** c'est une affaire réglée; **to f. s.o. up with sth,** trouver qch pour qn; **I can f. you up for the night,** je puis vous héberger pour la nuit.

fizz, fizzle ['fiz(l)] *vi* (*of wine*) pétiller. **'fizzle 'out** *vi* (*of plan*) ne pas aboutir. **'fizzy** *a* (-ier, -iest) gazeux; (*of wine*) mousseux.

flabbergast ['flæbəgɑ:st] *vtr* *F:* abasourdir, ahurir (qn); **I was flabbergasted,** j'en étais sidéré.

flabby ['flæbi] *a* (-ier, -iest) flasque; mou; (*of cheeks*) pendant. **'flabbiness** *n* flaccidité *f*; mollesse *f* (de qn).

flag¹ [flæg] *n* **flag(stone),** carreau *m*; dalle *f*.

flag² 1. *n* drapeau *m*; *Nau:* pavillon *m*; **f. of convenience,** pavillon de complaisance; **f. officer,** officier général; **f. day,** jour de quête pour une œuvre de bienfaisance; *Fig:* **to keep the f. flying,** ne pas se laisser abattre 2. *vtr* (**flagged**) pavoiser (un édifice); **to f. (down) s.o., a car,** faire signe à qn, à une voiture, de s'arrêter. **'flagpole, -staff** *n* mât *m* de drapeau. **'flagship** *n* (navire *m*) amiral *m*.

flag³ *vi* (**flagged**) (*of plant*) languir; (*of pers*) s'alanguir; (*of conversation*) traîner, languir; (*of attention*) faiblir; (*of zeal*) se relâcher.

flagon ['flægən] *n* grosse bouteille ventrue.

flagrant ['fleigrənt] *a* (*of offence*) flagrant; (cas) notoire. **'flagrantly** *adv* d'une manière flagrante.

flair ['flɛər] *n* flair *m*; aptitude *f*; **to have a f. for,** avoir du flair pour, le don de.

flake [fleik] 1. *n* flocon *m* (de neige); écaille *f*, éclat *m*, paillette *f* (de métal); **soap flakes,** savon en paillettes 2. *vi* **to f. (off),** s'écailler. **'flake 'out** *vi* *F:* (*a*) s'évanouir (*b*) s'endormir; **flaked out,** crevé. **'flaky** *a* **f. pastry,** pâte feuilletée.

flamboyant [flæm'bɔiənt] *a* flamboyant.

flame [fleim] 1. *n* flamme *f*; (*colour*) rouge *m* feu; **in flames,** en flammes, en feu; **to burst into flame(s), go up in flames,** s'enflammer brusquement; *F:* **an old f.,** un ancien amour 2. *vi* flamber. **'flameproof, 'flame-resistant** *a* ignifuge; ininflammable. **'flamethrower** *n* lance-flammes *m inv*. **'flaming** *a* (*a*) (feu) flambant; (maison) en flammes; (soleil) ardent; **in a f. temper,** d'une humeur massacrante; *F:* **a f. row,** une querelle de tous les diables (*b*) *P:* **you f. idiot!** espèce d'imbécile!

flamingo [fləˈmiŋgou] *n* (*pl* **flamingoes**) *Orn:* flamant *m* (rose).

flammable ['flæməbl] *a esp NAm:* inflammable.

flan [flæn] *n* *Cu:* tarte *f* (aux fruits); quiche (lorraine).

Flanders ['flɑ:ndəz] *Prn Geog:* Flandre *f*.

flange [flændʒ] *n* bride *f*; collerette *f*, collet *m*; **cooling f.,** ailette *f* de refroidissement. **flanged** *a* *Aut:* (radiateur) à ailettes.

flank [flæŋk] 1. *n* flanc *m*; *Cu:* flanchet *m* 2. *vtr* flanquer (**by, de**).

flannel ['flænl] *n* *Tex:* flannelle *f*; **f. trousers,** *npl* **flannels,** pantalon *m* de flanelle; (**face**) **f. =** gant *m* de toilette. **flanne'lette** *n* *Tex:* pilou *m*.

flap [flæp] 1. *n* (*a*) battement *m*, coup *m* (d'aile); *F:* affolement *m*; **f. to get in(to) a f.,** s'agiter, s'affoler (*b*) patte *f* (de poche); rabat *m* (d'une enveloppe);

abattant *m* (de table); trappe *f* (de cave); *Av:* volet *m*
2. *v* (**flapped**) (*a*) *vtr* battre (des ailes); agiter (les bras)
(*b*) *vi* (*of sail, shutter*) battre, claquer; *F:* (*of pers*)
s'affoler. '**flapping** *n* battement *m*, claquement *m*.

flare ['flɛər] 1. *n* (*a*) flamboiement irrégulier (*b*) feu *m*
(de signal); fusée éclairante (*c*) évasement *m* (d'une jupe) 2. *vi* (*a*) flamboyer (*b*) (*of skirt*) s'évaser. **flared** *a* (*of skirt*) évasé. '**flare 'up**
vi s'enflammer brusquement; (*of anger*) éclater; (*of pers*) s'emporter; **he flares up at the least thing,** il monte comme une soupe au lait. '**flare-up** *n* (*a*) flambée soudaine; déclenchement *m* (d'une guerre); éruption *f* (de colère) (*b*) altercation *f*.

flash [flæʃ] 1. *n* (*a*) éclair *m*; éclat *m* (de flamme); lueur *f* (d'une arme à feu); **a f. of lightning,** un éclair; **f. of wit,** saillie *f* (d'esprit); **in a f.,** en un rien de temps; en un clin d'œil; *Fig:* **a f. in the pan,** un feu de paille; **f. flood,** crue subite; *AtomPh:* **f. burn,** brûlure par irradiation (*b*) *Phot:* flash *m*; **f. gun,** flash; **f. bulb,** ampoule (de) flash (*c*) (**news**) **f.,** flash (d'information)
2. *v* (*a*) *vi* jeter des éclairs; lancer des étincelles; (*of diamonds*) étinceler; **to f. past,** passer comme un éclair; **it flashed across my mind that,** l'idée m'est venue tout d'un coup que (*b*) *vtr* faire étinceler (ses bijoux); étaler (son argent); projeter, diriger (un rayon de lumière); lancer (un regard); *Aut:* **to f. one's headlights,** faire un appel de phares. '**flashback** *n* *Cin:* flash-back *m*. '**flasher** *n* (*a*) (*light*) clignotant *m* (*b*) *F:* (*pers*) exhibitionniste *m*. '**flashily** *adv* **f. dressed,** à toilette tapageuse. '**flashing** *a* éclatant; (yeux) étincelants; (feu, signal) clignotant. '**flashlight** *n* lampe *f* de poche. '**flashpoint** *n* *Ch:* point *m* d'inflammabilité; *Fig:* situation explosive. '**flashy** *a* (**-ier, -iest**) voyant, tapageur.

flask [flɑːsk] *n* flacon *m*; *Ch:* fiole *f*; **vacuum f.,** bouteille isolante.

flat [flæt] 1. *a* (**flatter; flattest**) (*a*) plat; horizontal; uni; (*of colour, paint*) mat; (pneu, accumulateur) à plat; **as f. as a pancake,** plat comme une galette; *Turf:* **f. racing,** le plat (*b*) (refus) net, catégorique; **that's f.!** voilà qui est net! (*c*) monotone, ennuyeux; (voix) terne; (son) sourd (*d*) (*of drink*) éventé, plat; **to go f.,** s'éventer (*e*) (taux, tarif) uniforme (*f*) *Mus:* **in D f.,** en ré bémol; **you're f.,** vous chantez en dessous du ton 2. *adv* (*a*) à plat; **to fall f. on one's face,** tomber à plat ventre; **stretched out f. on the ground,** étendu à plat sur le sol; **to fall f.,** manquer son effet; tomber à plat; **to work f. out,** travailler d'arrache-pied; **to go f. out,** filer à toute allure; **to be f. broke,** être à sec (*b*) nettement, positivement; **he told me f. that,** il m'a dit carrément que (*c*) *Mus:* (chanter) en dessous du ton 3. *n* (*a*) plat *m*; **with the f. of the hand,** avec la main plate (*b*) *NAm:* pneu *m* à plat (*c*) appartement *m*; **service f.,** appartement avec service; **block of flats,** immeuble *m* (*d*) *Mus:* bémol *m*. '**flat-'bottomed** *a* à fond plat.
'**flat-'chested** *a* qui a la poitrine plate.
'**flatfish** *n* poisson plat. '**flat-'footed** *a* aux pieds plats; *F:* (refus) absolu. '**flatiron** *n* fer *m* à repasser. '**flatlet** *n* petit appartement; studio *m*. '**flatly** *adv* nettement, carrément; (refuser) tout net. '**flatness** *n* égalité *f* (d'une surface); manque *m* de relief; monotonie *f* (de l'existence); (*of beer*) évent *m*. '**flatten** *vtr* & *i* (*a*) (s')aplatir; (s')aplanir; (*of rain*) coucher (le blé); **to f. oneself against a wall,** se plaquer

contre un mur (*b*) *F:* écraser (qn) (*c*) *Mus:* bémoliser (une note). '**flatten 'out** *vi* *Av:* se redresser (après un vol piqué).

flatter ['flætər] *vtr* flatter (qn). '**flatterer** *n* flatteur, -euse. '**flattering** *a* flatteur. '**flatteringly** *adv* flatteusement. '**flattery** *n* flatterie *f*.

flatulence ['flætjuləns] *n* flatulence *f*.

flaunt [flɔːnt] *vtr* étaler, afficher.

flautist ['flɔːtist] (*NAm:* = **flutist**) *n* *Mus:* flûtiste *mf*.

flavour, *NAm:* -**or** ['fleivər] 1. *n* saveur *f*; goût *m*; (*of ice cream*) parfum *m* 2. *vtr* assaisonner, parfumer; relever (une sauce); **vanilla flavoured,** (parfumé) à la vanille. '**flavouring,** *NAm:* -**oring** *n* assaisonnement *m*; parfum *m*. '**flavourless,** *NAm:* -**orless** *a* sans saveur; insipide.

flaw [flɔː] 1. *n* défaut *m*; défectuosité *f*, imperfection *f*; point *m* faible (d'un projet); (*in glass*) fêlure *f* 2. *vtr* endommager, défigurer. **flawed** *a* défectueux. '**flawless** *a* sans défaut; parfait; (technique) impeccable. '**flawlessly** *adv* parfaitement.

flax [flæks] *n* *Bot:* lin *m*. '**flaxen** *a* (*of hair*) blond (filasse); **f.-haired,** aux cheveux très blonds.

flay [flei] *vtr* écorcher (un animal); *Fig:* éreinter (qn).

flea [fliː] *n* *Ent:* puce *f*; *F:* **to send s.o. off with a f. in his ear,** envoyer promener qn; **f. market,** marché aux puces. '**fleabag** *n* *F:* sac *m* à puces. '**fleabite** *n* morsure *f* de puce; *Fig:* vétille *f*, bagatelle *f*. '**fleapit** *n* *P:* cinéma pouilleux.

fleck [flek] 1. *n* petite tache; moucheture *f* (de couleur); particule *f* (de poussière) 2. *vtr* tacheter, moucheter (**with,** de); **hair flecked with grey,** cheveux qui commencent à grisonner.

fled [fled] *see* **flee.**

fledged [fledʒd] *a see* **fully-fledged.**

fledgling ['fledʒliŋ] *n* *Orn:* oisillon *m*.

flee [fliː] *vi* (**fled** [fled]) fuir, s'enfuir, se sauver; se réfugier. '**fleeing** *a* en fuite.

fleece [fliːs] 1. *n* toison *f* 2. *vtr* *F:* tondre, écorcher, estamper (qn). '**fleece-lined** *a* doublé de molleton. '**fleecy** *a* (*of wool, clouds*) floconneux; (*of cloud*) moutonné; (*of material*) laineux.

fleet [fliːt] *n* (*a*) flotte *f*; **the F.** = la Marine nationale; **the F. Air Arm** = l'Aéronavale *f*; **a fishing f.,** une flottille de pêche (*b*) parc *m* (de voitures); **a f. of coaches,** une caravane de cars.

fleeting ['fliːtiŋ] *a* fugitif, fugace; (bonheur) éphémère; **f. visit,** courte visite.

Fleming ['flemiŋ] *n* *Geog:* Flamand, -ande. '**Flemish** 1. *a* flamand 2. (*a*) *n* *Ling:* flamand *m* (*b*) *npl* **the F.,** les Flamands *mpl.*

flesh [fleʃ] *n* chair *f*; **to make s.o.'s f. creep,** donner la chair de poule à qn; **f. wound,** blessure légère; **f. colour,** couleur (de) chair; **in the f.,** en chair et en os; **his own f. and blood,** les siens; **it's more than f. and blood can bear,** c'est plus que la nature humaine ne saurait endurer. '**fleshy** *a* charnu.

flew [fluː] *see* **fly².**

flex [fleks] 1. *vtr* fléchir (les genoux); faire jouer (ses muscles) 2. *n* *El:* cordon *m*, câble *m*; fil *m* (souple). **flexi'bility** *n* flexibilité *f*, souplesse *f*. '**flexible** *a* flexible; souple. '**flexitime** *n* horaire *m* souple.

flick [flik] 1. *n* petit coup (de fouet); (**with finger**) chiquenaude *f*; **f. of the wrist,** tour *m* de main; **at the f.**

of a switch, juste en appuyant sur un bouton 2. *vtr* (*with whip*) effleurer (un cheval); (*with finger*) donner une chiquenaude à (qch); to f. sth off with a duster, faire envoler, enlever, qch d'un coup de torchon; to f. through a book, feuilleter un livre. 'flick-knife *n* (*pl* -knives) couteau *m* à cran d'arrêt. flicks *npl F:* cinéma *m*; cinoche *m*.

flicker ['flikər] 1. *n* petit mouvement vacillant; (*of eyelid*) battement *m*; a f. of light, une petite lueur tremblotante 2. *vi* trembloter, vaciller; (*of eyelids*) cligner; (*of light*) clignoter; (*of needle*) osciller. 'flic-kering 1. *a* tremblotant 2. *n* tremblotement *m*, clignotement *m*.

flier ['flaiər] *n* aviateur, -trice.

flies [flaiz] *see* fly¹,².

flight¹ [flait] *n* (*a*) vol *m*; course *f*, trajectoire *f* (d'un projectile); (*distance*) volée *f*; f. of fancy, essor *m* de l'imagination; time of f., durée du trajet (d'un projectile); *Av:* it's an hour's f. from London, c'est à une heure de vol de Londres; f. 217 to Brussels, vol 217 à destination de, pour, Bruxelles; f. path, trajectoire de vol; f. deck, poste de pilotage; f. plan, plan de vol; f. recorder, enregistreur de vol (*b*) (*group*) vol, volée (d'oiseaux); escadrille *f* (d'avions); *MilAv:* f. lieutenant, capitaine aviateur: *Fig:* in the top f., parmi les tout premiers (*c*) f. of stairs, escalier *m*.

flight² *n* fuite *f*; to take (to) f., prendre la fuite; to put to f., mettre en fuite.

flighty ['flaiti] *a* (-ier, -iest) frivole, étourdi. 'flightiness *n* inconstance *f*.

flimsy ['flimzi] 1. *a* (-ier, -iest) sans solidité; (tissu) léger, peu solide; (*of excuse*) pauvre 2. *n* papier *m* pelure. 'flimsily *adv* d'une manière peu solide. 'flimsiness *n* manque *m* de consistance.

flinch [flintʃ] *vi* reculer, fléchir; tressaillir (de douleur); without flinching, sans broncher.

fling [fliŋ] 1. *n* jet *m*, coup *m*; *Fig:* to have a f. at sth, essayer (de faire) qch; to have one's f., faire la fête (tant qu'on est jeune) 2. *vtr* (flung [flʌŋ]) jeter; lancer; to f. one's arms round s.o.'s neck, se jeter au cou de qn; to f. money about, gaspiller son argent; to f. sth away, jeter qch de côté; se défaire de qch; to f. open the door, ouvrir la porte d'un mouvement brusque; ouvrir toute grande la porte; to f. s.o. out, flanquer qn à la porte; to f. out one's arm, étendre le bras d'un grand geste.

flint [flint] *n* silex *m*; (*for cigarette lighter*) pierre *f* (à briquet); *Prehist:* f. implements, outils en silex taillés.

flip [flip] 1. *n* chiquenaude *f*; f. side, revers *m* (d'un disque) 2. *vtr & i* (flipped) donner une chiquenaude à (qch); to f. sth over, retourner qch; *F:* to f. (one's lid), sortir de ses gonds. 'flip-flops *npl* claquettes *fpl* (en caoutchouc pour la plage). 'flipper *n* (*of animal*) nageoire *f*; (*of swimmer*) palme *f*. 'flipping *a F:* fichu.

flippant ['flipənt] *a* léger, désinvolte. 'flippancy *n* légèreté *f*, irrévérence *f*, désinvolture *f*. 'flippantly *adv* d'une manière désinvolte.

flirt [flə:t] 1. *n* (*of man*) flirteur *m*; (*of woman*) coquette *f* 2. *vi* flirter. flir'tation *n* flirt *m*. flir'tatious *a* (*of man*) flirteur *m*; (*of woman*) coquette.

flit [flit] 1. *vi* (flitted) (*a*) to f. (away), partir (*b*) to f. by, passer légèrement; to f. about, aller et venir sans bruit

2. *n F:* to do a moonlight f., déménager à la cloche de bois.

float [flout] 1. *n* (*a*) *Tchn:* flotteur *m*; (*cork*) bouchon *m* (*b*) (*vehicle*) char *m* de carnaval; milk f., voiture *f* de livraison du lait 2. *v* (*a*) *vi* flotter; surnager; (*in air*) planer; (*of boat*) être à flot; (*of swimmer*) faire la planche (*b*) *vtr* flotter (des bois); mettre (un navire) à flot; *Com:* lancer (une compagnie); *Fin:* émettre, lancer (un emprunt). 'floating *a* flottant; (navire) à flot; f. voter, voteur indécis. 'float 'off 1. *vtr* renflouer (une épave) 2. *vi* (*of ship*) se déséchouer.

flock [flɔk] 1. *n* bande *f* (d'animaux); troupeau *m* (de moutons); volée *f* (d'oiseaux); foule *f* (de visiteurs); *Ecc:* ouailles *fpl* (d'un pasteur) 2. *vi* to f. (together), s'attrouper, s'assembler; everyone is flocking to see the exhibition, tout le monde se précipite pour voir l'exposition; to f. to the sea, aller en foule au bord de la mer.

floe [flou] *n* masse *f* de glaces flottantes; banquise *f*.

flog [flɔg] *vtr* (flogged) (*a*) flageller; *F:* ne pas savoir se taire (sur un sujet); to f. oneself (to death), s'éreinter (à faire qch); *Fig:* to f. a dead horse, se dépenser en pure perte (*b*) *F:* vendre, bazarder (qch). 'flogging *n* flagellation *f*; châtiment *m* du fouet.

flood [flʌd] 1. *n* (*a*) f. (tide), flux *m* (de la marée); marée montante (*b*) inondation *f*; déluge *m*; crue *f* (d'une rivière); torrent *m* (de larmes) 2. *v* (*a*) *vtr* inonder; *Aut:* noyer (le carburateur) (*b*) *vi* (*of river*) déborder; être en crue; *Fig:* to f. in, entrer à flots. 'floodgate *n* vanne *f*. 'flooding *n* inondation *f*; submersion *f*; (*of river*) débordement *m*; *PN:* road liable to f., chemin sujet aux inondations. 'floodlight 1. *n* (*a*) projecteur *m* (*b*) lumière *f* de grande intensité 2. *vtr* (floodlit) illuminer par des projecteurs. 'flood-lighting *n* illumination *f* par des projecteurs.

floor [flɔ:r] 1. *n* (*a*) plancher *m*; parquet *m*; piste *f* (de danse); on the f., par terre; (*in meeting*) to have the f., prendre la parole; *F:* to wipe the f. with s.o., battre qn à plate(s) couture(s) (*b*) (*storey*) étage *m*; ground f., rez-de-chaussée *m*; first f., (i) premier étage (ii) *NAm:* rez-de-chaussée 2. *vtr* (*a*) parqueter (une pièce) (*b*) terrasser (un adversaire); *F:* clouer le bec à (qn). 'floorboard *n* planche *f* (du plancher). 'floorcloth *n* serpillière *f*. 'floorshow *n* spectacle *m* de cabaret. 'floorwalker *n* chef *m* de rayon.

flop [flɔp] 1. *n* (*a*) bruit sourd; floc *m* (*b*) *F:* fiasco *m*; (*of play*) four *m* 2. *vi* (flopped) (*a*) to f. (down), se laisser tomber, s'affaler (*b*) *F:* échouer; *Th:* faire four. 'floppy *a* (-ier, -iest) pendant, souple; (chapeau) mou; *Cmptr:* f. disc, disquette *f*.

flora ['flɔ:rə] *n* flore *f*. 'floral *a* floral.

florid ['flɔrid] *a* (*of style*) fleuri; orné à l'excès; to have a f. complexion, être haut en couleur.

florist ['flɔrist] *n* fleuriste *mf*.

floss [flɔs] *n* dental f., fil *m* de soie dentaire; *Comest:* candy f., barbe *f* à papa.

flotilla [flə'tilə] *n* flottille *f*.

flounce [flauns] 1. *n Dressm:* volant *m* 2. *vi* to f. in, out, entrer, sortir, avec un mouvement d'indignation, brusquement.

flounder ['flaundər] 1. *n Ich:* flet *m* 2. *vi* patauger; to f. about in the water, se débattre dans l'eau.

flour ['flauǝr] n farine f; **f. mill,** minoterie f; moulin à farine.

flourish ['flʌriʃ] **1.** n (a) grand geste; brandissement m (d'épée) (b) trait m de plume; (after signature) parafe m; fioriture f (de style) (c) Mus: fanfare f (de trompettes) **2.** v (a) vi (of plant) bien venir; (of pers) être florissant, prospérer; (of arts) fleurir (b) vtr brandir (un bâton). **'flourishing** a florissant; (commerce) prospère.

flout [flaut] vtr faire fi de (l'autorité de qn); se moquer d'(un ordre).

flow [flou] **1.** n (a) écoulement m (d'un liquide); El: passage m (d'un courant); flot m, flux m (de la marée); Cmptr: circulation f (de l'information); **f. diagram, chart,** organigramme m (b) volume m (de liquide débité); débit m (d'un lac); **f. of traffic,** débit de la circulation **2.** vi couler, s'écouler; (of river) se jeter (**into the sea,** dans la mer); (of tide) monter, remonter; (of blood, electric current) circuler; (of people) aller, venir, en masse; (of hair) flotter; (of blood, tears) se répandre; jaillir; (result) dériver, découler (**from,** de). **'flow 'back** vi refluer. **'flow 'in** vi (of money, people) affluer. **'flowing** a coulant; (of draperies) flottant; (of movement) gracieux.

flower ['flauǝr] **1.** n fleur f; **bunch of flowers,** bouquet m (de fleurs); **f. show,** exposition horticole; (bigger) floralies fpl; **f. bed,** parterre m; **f. garden,** jardin d'agrément; **at the f. shop,** chez le fleuriste; **in f.,** en fleur(s); **in full f.,** en plein épanouissement; **to burst into f.,** fleurir **2.** vi fleurir. **'flowered** a (tissu) à fleurs. **'flowering 1.** a (plante) à fleurs; (jardin) en fleurs **2.** n floraison f. **'flowerpot** n pot m à fleurs. **'flowery** a fleuri; (pré) couvert de fleurs.

flown [floun] see **fly²**.

flu [fluː] n F: grippe f.

fluctuate ['flʌktjueit] vi fluctuer; varier. **'fluctuating** a variable. **fluctu'ation** n fluctuation f; variation f.

flue [fluː] n tuyau m de cheminée; conduit m de fumée; **f. brush,** hérisson m (de ramoneur).

fluency ['fluːǝnsi] n facilité f (de parole). **'fluent** a coulant, facile; **to be a f. speaker,** avoir la parole facile; **he is a f. speaker of French, he is f. in French,** il parle le français couramment. **'fluently** adv couramment; (s'exprimer) avec facilité.

fluff [flʌf] **1.** n duvet m, peluches fpl; (under bed) moutons mpl; fourrure douce (d'un jeune animal) **2.** vtr (a) **to f. (out, up),** faire bouffer (les cheveux); hérisser (ses plumes) (b) Th: F: rater (son entrée). **'fluffy** a (-ier, -iest) (drap) pelucheux; (poussin) duveteux; **f. hair,** cheveux flous.

fluid ['fluːid] a & n fluide (m); liquide (m). **flu'idity** n fluidité f.

fluke [fluːk] n coup m de veine; chance f.

flummox ['flʌmǝks] vtr F: démonter, abasourdir (qn).

flung [flʌŋ] see **fling 2**.

fluorescence [fluǝ'resns] n fluorescence f. **fluo'rescent** a fluorescent.

fluorine ['fluǝriːn] n Ch: fluor m. **fluori'dation** n fluoration f. **'fluoride** n Ch: fluorure f.

flurry ['flʌri] **1.** n agitation f, bouleversement m; émoi m; rafale f (de neige) **2.** vtr **to get flurried,** perdre la tête.

flush¹ [flʌʃ] **1.** n (a) (in toilet) chasse f (d'eau) (b) accès m, élan m; **in the first f. of victory,** dans l'ivresse f de la victoire (c) éclat m (de lumière, de la jeunesse) (d) rougeur f, flot m de sang (au visage); **hot f.,** bouffée f de chaleur **2.** v (a) vtr **to f. (out),** donner une chasse à (un égout); **to f. the toilet,** tirer la chasse d'eau (b) vi rougir; **he, his face, flushed,** il a rougi; le sang lui est monté au visage. **flushed** a rouge; empourpré; **f. with success,** ivre de succès.

flush² a (a) F: **f. (with money),** en fonds (b) ras; de niveau; **to be f. with sth,** être à fleur, au ras, de qch.

fluster ['flʌstǝr] **1.** n agitation f, trouble m; **in a f.,** tout en émoi, bouleversé **2.** vtr faire perdre la tête à (qn); troubler (qn); **to be flustered,** se troubler.

flute [fluːt] n flûte f; **f. player,** joueur de flûte. **'fluted** a à cannelures fpl; (of column) cannelé. **'flutist** n NAm: (Br = **flautist**) flûtiste mf.

flutter ['flʌtǝr] **1.** n (a) voltigement m (d'un oiseau); battement m (des ailes); palpitation f (du cœur) (b) agitation f, trouble m; (**all) in a f.,** tout en émoi (c) F: (petite) spéculation; **to have a little f.,** faire un ou deux petits paris (**on,** sur) **2.** (a) vi voleter; battre des ailes; (of flag) flotter (au vent); (of heart) palpiter, battre (b) vtr battre (des ailes, des cils).

flux [flʌks] n **to be in a state of f.,** être sujet à des changements fréquents.

fly¹ [flai] n (pl **flies**) (a) Ent: mouche f; Fig: **a f. in the ointment,** un cheveu sur la soupe; **there are no flies on him,** il n'est pas bête; **he wouldn't hurt a f.,** il ne ferait pas de mal à une mouche (b) Fish: mouche; **f. fishing,** pêche à la mouche. **'fly-blown** a plein d'œufs de mouche. **'flypaper** n papier m tue-mouches. **'flyspray** n (bombe f d')insecticide m. **'flytrap** n Bot: (**Venus),** f, dionée f, attrape-mouche m. **'fly-weight** n Box: poids m mouche.

fly² **I.** n (also **flies**) braguette f (de pantalon); Th: **the flies,** les cintres m. **II.** v (**flies; flew** [fluː]; **flown** [floun]) **1.** vi (a) voler; (of flag) flotter; (of sparks) jaillir; **the bird has flown,** l'oiseau s'est envolé; **to f. high,** (i) voler haut (ii) Fig: (of pers) avoir de l'ambition; **as the crow flies,** à vol d'oiseau; **to f. to Paris,** se rendre à Paris en avion; **to f. over London,** survoler Londres (b) courir, aller à toute vitesse; (of time) fuir, filer; **it's late, I must f.,** il se fait tard, il faut que je me sauve; **time flies,** le temps s'envole; **to f. into a rage, off the handle,** s'emporter; **the door flew open,** la porte s'est ouverte en coup de vent; **to send s.o. flying,** envoyer rouler qn; **to let f. at s.o.,** (i) tirer sur qn (ii) flanquer un coup à qn (c) fuir, s'enfuir; **to f. to s.o. (for protection),** se réfugier auprès de qn **2.** vtr battre (un pavillon); faire voler (un cerf-volant); piloter (un avion); emmener (qn) en avion; transporter (qn, qch) par avion; survoler (la Manche). **'fly a'way** vi s'envoler. **'flyaway** a (of hair) fin. **'fly-by-night** a Fig: véreux. **'flyer,** **'flier** n aviateur, -trice. **'fly 'in 1.** vtr amener en avion **2.** vi arriver en avion. **'flying 1.** a (a) volant; **f. boat,** hydravion m; Mil: **f. column,** colonne mobile; **f. visit,** visite éclair; **to get off to a f. start,** se lancer sans anicroche; **to take a f. leap over a wall,** franchir un mur d'un saut **2.** n vol m, aviation f; **f. club,** aéro-club m; **f. hours,** heures de vol. **'flyleaf** n (pl -**leaves**) (page f de) garde f. **'fly 'off** vi s'envoler. **'flyover** n Aut: (NAm: = **overpass**) saut-de-mouton m; toboggan m. **'flypast** n défilé aérien. **'flysheet**

n double toit *m* (de tente). '**flywheel** *n Mec:* volant *m.*

foal [foul] *n* poulain *m.*

foam [foum] **1.** *n* écume *f;* (*on beer*) mousse *f;* **f. rubber,** caoutchouc mousse; **bath f., f. bath,** bain de mousse **2.** *vi* (*of sea*) écumer; (*of beer*) mousser; **to f. (at the mouth) (with rage),** écumer (de rage).

fob [fɔb] *vtr* (**fobbed**) **to f. s.o. off with sth, to f. sth off on s.o.,** refiler qch à qn.

fo'c'sle ['fouksl] *n* (*abbr* **forecastle**) *Nau:* gaillard *m;* (*in merchant vessel*) poste *m* de l'équipage.

focus ['foukəs] **1.** *n* (*pl* **focuses, foci** ['fousai]) foyer *m;* **in f.,** au point **2.** *v* (**focus(s)ed**) (*a*) *vtr* concentrer, faire converger (des rayons); mettre au point (un microscope); **all eyes were focused on him,** il était le point de mire de tous les yeux (*b*) *vi* (*of light*) converger (**on,** sur); *Phot:* **to f. on an object,** mettre au point sur un objet. '**focal** a focal; **f. point,** foyer. '**focusing** *n* mise *f* au point (d'un appareil).

fodder ['fɔdər] *n* fourrage *m.*

foe [fou] *n Lit:* ennemi *m.*

foetus, NAm: fetus ['fiːtəs] *n* (*pl* **f(o)etuses**) *Biol:* fœtus *m.* '**foetal, NAm: fetal** *a* fœtal.

fog [fɔg] **1.** *n* brouillard *m;* brume *f; F:* **I'm in a f.,** je ne sais plus où j'en suis; *Rail:* **f. signal,** pétard *m* **2.** *v* (**fogged**) (*a*) *vtr* brouiller (les idées); embrouiller (qn); *Phot:* voiler (un cliché) (*b*) *vi* **to f. (up),** (*of spectacles*) se couvrir de buée; *Phot:* (*of negative*) se voiler. '**fogbank** *n* banc *m* de brume. '**fogbound** *a* pris dans le brouillard. '**foggy** *a* (**-ier, -iest**) brumeux; (*esprit*) confus; *Phot:* (*cliché*) voilé; **f. day,** jour de brouillard; **it's f.,** il fait du brouillard; *F:* **I haven't the foggiest idea,** je n'en ai pas la moindre idée. '**foghorn** *n Nau:* sirène *f;* **voice like a f.,** voix de taureau. '**foglamp, -light** *n Aut:* (phare *m*) antibrouillard *m.*

fog(e)y ['fougi] *n* (*pl* **fogies**) *F:* **old f.,** vieille baderne.

foible ['fɔibl] *n* côté *m* faible, point *m* faible.

foil[1] [fɔil] *n Metalw:* feuille *f* (d'or, d'argent); **kitchen, aluminium, cooking, f.,** papier *m* d'aluminium; **to serve as a f. to (s.o., sth),** servir de repoussoir à (qn, qch).

foil[2] *n Fenc:* fleuret *m.*

foil[3] *vtr* faire échouer, faire manquer; déjouer (un complot).

foist [fɔist] *vtr* refiler (**sth on s.o.,** qch à qn); **to f. oneself on s.o.,** s'imposer à, chez, qn.

fold[1] [fould] *n* parc *m* à moutons; *Fig:* **to return to the f.,** rentrer au bercail.

fold[2] **1.** *n* pli *m*, repli *m; Geol:* plissement *m* **2.** *v* (*a*) *vtr* plier; **to f. sth (up) in sth,** envelopper qch dans, de, qch; **to f. one's arms,** (se) croiser les bras *vi* (*of shutters, screen*) se (re)plier; *F:* **to f. (up),** (*of business*) cesser les affaires; *Th:* (*of play*) être retiré. '**foldaway** *a* (siège) pliant; (lit) escamotable. '**fold back** *vtr* rabattre. '**folder** *n* chemise *f*, dossier *m;* (*leaflet*) prospectus *m.* '**fold 'in** *vtr Cu:* incorporer (des blancs d'œufs). '**folding** *a* pliant; **f. door,** porte brisée, à deux battants. '**fold 'up** *vtr & i* (se) replier.

foliage ['fouliidʒ] *n* feuillage *m.*

folio ['fouliou] *n* folio *m*, feuille *f* (de manuscrit); (**book in**) **f.,** (livre) in-folio *m.*

folk [fouk] *n* (*pl* **folk,** *occ* **folks**) gens *mfpl;* **country f.,** campagnards *mpl;* **my f.,** les miens; ma famille; *F: esp*

NAm: **hi, folks!** salut tout le monde! **f. dance,** danse folklorique; **f. song,** (i) chanson traditionnelle (ii) (*modern*) folk-song *m.* '**folklore** *n* folklore *m.* '**folksy** *a F:* (*a*) sociable (*b*) folklorique.

follow ['fɔlou] *v* **1.** *vtr* (*a*) suivre; poursuivre (l'ennemi, une carrière); **followed by his dog,** suivi de son chien; *F:* **to f. one's nose,** aller tout droit devant soi; **night follows day,** la nuit succède au jour; **to f. s.o.'s advice,** suivre le conseil de qn (*b*) suivre, comprendre (une explication); **I don't quite f. you,** je ne vous comprends pas très bien **2.** *vi* (*a*) **to f. (after),** suivre; **as follows,** ainsi qu'il suit; **our method is as follows,** notre méthode est la suivante; **to f. in s.o.'s footsteps,** marcher sur les traces de qn; **to f. close behind s.o.,** emboîter le pas à qn (*b*) s'ensuivre, résulter (**from,** de); **it doesn't f. that,** ce n'est pas à dire que + *sub* (*c*) suivre, comprendre. '**follow a'bout, a'round** *vtr* suivre partout. '**follower** *n* partisan, -ane; disciple *m.* '**following 1.** *a* suivant; **the f. day,** le jour suivant; **le lendemain; the f. resolution,** la résolution que voici **2.** *n* (*a*) (*in speech, document*) **the f.,** ce qui suit (*b*) *Pol:* parti *m;* **to have a big f.,** avoir un grand nombre de partisans; **programme that has a wide f.,** programme très suivi **3.** *prep* (*a*) par suite de (*b*) après. '**follow 'on** *vi* suivre; **to f. on (from) sth,** résulter de qch. '**follow 'through** *vtr* poursuivre (un projet) jusqu'au bout. '**follow 'up** *vtr* poursuivre (un avantage); exploiter (un succès). '**follow-up** *n* suite *f;* **f.-up letter,** lettre de rappel.

folly ['fɔli] *n* (*pl* **follies**) folie *f;* sottise *f.*

foment [fou'ment] *vtr* fomenter. **fomen'tation** *n* fomentation *f.*

fond [fɔnd] *a* affectueux, tendre; (souvenir) doux; **to be f. of s.o., sth,** aimer qn, qch; **they are f. of each other,** ils s'aiment; **to be f. of music,** être amateur *m* de musique; **f. of sweets,** friand de sucreries. '**fondly** *adv* (*a*) naïvement (*b*) tendrement, affectueusement. '**fondness** *n* affection *f*, tendresse *f* (**for s.o.,** pour, envers, qn); penchant *m*, prédilection *f*, goût *m* (**for sth,** pour qch).

fondle ['fɔndl] *vtr* caresser, câliner.

font [fɔnt] *n* fonts baptismaux.

food [fuːd] *n* nourriture *f;* aliments *mpl;* vivres *mpl; Husb:* pâture *f* (d'animaux); *Hort:* engrais *m;* **to be off one's f.,** ne pas avoir d'appétit; **hotel where the f. is good,** hôtel où la cuisine est bonne; **f. and drink,** le boire et le manger; **f. and clothing,** le vivre et le vêtement; (*in large store*) **f. hall,** rayon d'alimentation; **f. value,** valeur nutritive; **f. poisoning,** intoxication alimentaire; **f.(-processing) industry,** industrie alimentaire; **to give s.o. f. for thought,** donner à penser à qn. '**foodstuffs** *npl* produits *mpl* alimentaires.

fool [fuːl] **1.** *n* (*a*) imbécile *mf;* idiot, -ote; **to play, act, the f.,** faire l'idiot; **to make a f. of oneself,** se couvrir de ridicule; **to make a f. of s.o.,** se moquer de qn; **silly f.!** espèce d'idiot! **he's no f., nobody's f.,** il n'est pas bête; **any f. knows that,** le premier imbécile venu sait cela; **some f. of a politician,** quelque imbécile d'homme politique; **to go on a fool's errand,** y aller pour des prunes; **he lives in a fool's paradise,** il se fait des illusions; **more f. you!** ça t'apprendra à faire l'idiot! (*b*) *Cu:* purée *f* de fruits à la crème **2.** *v* (*a*) *vi* **to f. (about, around),** (i) faire l'idiot (ii) perdre son temps; **I was**

only **fooling**, je plaisantais (b) vtr duper (qn). **'foolery** n sottise f, bêtise f. **'foolhardiness** n témérité f. **'foolhardy** a téméraire, imprudent. **'foolish** a (a) (unwise) fou; **it's f. of him to**, c'est fou de sa part de (b) bête; absurde, ridicule; **to do sth f.**, faire une bêtise; **to look f.**, avoir l'air penaud; **to feel f.**, se sentir idiot. **'foolishly** adv (a) follement (b) sottement, bêtement. **'foolishness** n (a) folie f (b) bêtise f. **'foolproof** a (mécanisme) indéréglable, indétraquable. **'foolscap** n papier m ministre.

foot [fut] 1. n (pl **feet** [fi:t]) pied m; patte f (de chien, d'oiseau); (bas) bout m (d'une table); base f (d'une colonne); Meas: pied anglais (= 30,48cm); **to get to one's feet**, se lever; **to be on one's feet**, se tenir debout; **he leaped to his feet**, d'un bond il était debout; (after illness) **he's on his feet again**, il s'est remis; il est de nouveau sur pied; Fig: **he's beginning to find his feet**, il commence à s'acclimater; **to put one's feet up**, se reposer; F: **to put one's f. down**, (i) faire acte d'autorité (ii) Aut: accélérer; appuyer sur le champignon; **to put one's best f. forward**, (i) avancer vite (ii) faire de son mieux; **not to put a f. wrong**, ne faire aucune erreur; F: **to put one's f. in it**, mettre les pieds dans le plat; faire une gaffe; **to get one's f. in the door**, s'implanter chez qn; F: **to have cold feet**, avoir la frousse; F: **he gets under your feet**, il se met dans vos jambes; **to trample sth under f.**, fouler qch aux pieds; **on f.**, à pied; F: **my f.!** mon œil! **at the f. of the stairs, the page**, au, en bas de l'escalier, de la page; **f. passenger**, voyageur à pied; **f. soldier**, soldat de l'infanterie; fantassin m; **f. pump**, pompe à pied 2. vtr F: (a) **to f. it**, aller à pied (b) **to f. the bill**, payer la note. **'footage** n Cin: métrage m. **'foot-and-mouth (di'sease)** n Vet: fièvre aphteuse. **'football** n (a) ballon m (b) football m; **f. ground**, terrain de football. **'footballer** n footballeur m. **'footbath** n bain m de pieds. **'footbrake** n frein m à pédale, à pied. **'footbridge** n passerelle f. **'footfall** n (bruit m de) pas m. **'foothills** npl contreforts mpl. **'foothold** n prise f pour le pied; **to get a f.**, prendre pied. **'footing** n prise (pour le pied); Fig: position f (de qn); **to lose one's f.**, perdre pied; **to miss one's f.**, poser le pied à faux; Fig: **to gain a f.**, s'implanter; prendre pied; **to be on an equal f.**, être de pair, sur un pied d'égalité; **to be on a friendly f. with s.o.**, être en bons termes avec qn; **on a war f.**, sur le pied de guerre. **'footlights** npl Th: rampe f. **'footloose** a (of pers) qui ne s'établit nulle part. **'footman** n (pl -men) valet m de pied. **'footmark** n empreinte f de pied. **'footnote** n note f, renvoi m, en bas de la page. **'footpath** n sentier m; (in street) trottoir m. **'footplate** n Rail: plate-forme f (de locomotive). **'footprint** n empreinte de pied. **'footstep** n (bruit m de) pas m. **'footstool** n tabouret m. **'footwear** n chaussures fpl. **'footwork** n jeu m des pieds, des jambes.

footle ['fu:tl] vi F: **to f. about**, perdre son temps (à des futilités). **'footling** a F: insignificant.

for [fɔr] I. prep pour 1. (a) (representing) **A for Alpha**, A comme Alpha; **member f. Liverpool**, député pour Liverpool; **to act f. s.o.**, agir pour qn (b) **to have s.o. f. a teacher**, avoir qn comme professeur; **he wants her f. his wife**, il la veut pour femme (c) **to exchange one thing f. another**, échanger une chose contre une autre; **to sell sth f. £100**, vendre qch cent livres; F: **f. free**,

gratis, pour rien; **what's the French f. cat?** comment est-ce qu'on dit cat en français? (d) (in favour of) **he's (all) f. free trade**, il est pour le libre-échange; il est partisan du libre-échange (e) (purpose) **what f.?** pourquoi (faire)? **what's that thing f.?** à quoi sert ce truc-là? **clothes f. men**, vêtements pour hommes; **f. sale**, à vendre; **f. example**, par exemple; F: **he's (in) f. it!** qu'est-ce qu'il va prendre! (f) (because of) **to marry s.o. f. his money**, épouser qn pour son argent; **to choose s.o. f. his ability**, choisir qn en raison de sa compétence; **to jump f. joy**, sauter de joie (g) (direction) **ship (bound) f. America**, navire à destination de l'Amérique; **the train f. London**, le train allant à Londres, le train de Londres; **change here f. York**, direction de York, changez de train; **I'm leaving f. France**, je pars pour la France (h) **his feelings f. you**, ses sentiments envers vous; (i) (extent in space) **the road is lined with trees for 2km**, la route est bordée d'arbres pendant 2km; **we didn't see a house f. miles**, nous avons fait des kilomètres sans voir de maison; **bends f. 5km**, virages sur 5km (j) (extent in time) (future) **I'm going away f. a fortnight**, je pars pour quinze jours; **he'll be away f. a year**, il sera absent (pendant) un an; (past) **he was away f. a fortnight**, il a été absent (pendant) quinze jours; **I haven't seen him f. 3 years**, il y a trois ans que je ne l'ai pas vu; (past extending to present) **I've been here f. three days**, je suis ici depuis trois jours, il y a trois jours que je suis ici (k) (intention) **this book is f. you**, ce livre est pour vous; **I'll come f. you tomorrow**, je viendrai vous prendre demain; **to make a name f. oneself**, se faire un nom; **to write f. the papers**, écrire dans les journaux; **to act f. the best**, faire pour le mieux (l) **to care f. s.o., sth**, aimer qn, qch; **fit f. nothing**, bon à rien; **ready f. dinner**, prêt à dîner; **time f. dinner**, l'heure du dîner; **too stupid f. words**, d'une bêtise incroyable; **oh f. a bit of peace!** que ne donnerais-je pour avoir la paix! **now f. it!** allons-y! **cheque f. £50**, chèque de 50 (m) (with regard to) **he's big f. his age**, il est grand pour son âge; **as f. him**, quant à lui; **see f. yourself!** voyez vous-même! (n) (in spite of) **f. all that**, malgré tout (o) (owing to) **but f. her, if it wasn't f. her**, sans elle (p) (corresponding to) **word f. word**, mot pour mot; (traduire) mot à mot; **they sell 20 red bikes f. every black one**, pour chaque vélo noir vendu il y en a 20 rouges 2. (introducing inf clause) **it's easy (enough) f. him to come**, il lui est facile de venir; **I've brought it f. you to see**, je l'ai apporté pour que vous le voyiez; **it's not f. me to decide**, ce n'est pas à moi de décider; **he gave orders f. the trunks to be packed**, il a donné l'ordre de faire les malles; **it took an hour f. the taxi to get to the station**, le taxi a mis une heure pour aller à la gare; **to wait f. sth to be done**, attendre que qch se fasse; **it would be a disgrace f. you to back out now**, vous retirer maintenant serait honteux; **the best thing would be f. you to go away for a while**, le mieux serait que vous vous absentiez pendant quelque temps. II. conj car. **for'ever** adv (also **for ever**) (a) toujours, sans cesse (b) esp NAm: pour toujours. see **ever**.

forage ['fɔridʒ] 1. n fourrage(s) m(pl); Mil: **f. cap**, bonnet de police 2. vi fourrager; F: **to f. about in a drawer**, fouiller dans un tiroir.

forbade [fəˈbæd] see **forbid**.

forbearance [fɔ:'bɛərəns] *n* patience *f.* **for'bearing** *a* patient, indulgent.

forbid [fə'bid] *vtr* (**forbade** [fə'bæd]; **forbidden** [fə'bidn]) défendre, interdire (**s.o. to do sth**, à qn de faire qch); **smoking is forbidden**, il est défendu, interdit, de fumer; défense de fumer; **I'm forbidden to drink alcohol**, l'alcool m'est défendu; **God f.!** à Dieu ne plaise! **for'bidden** *a* défendu, interdit; (sujet) tabou. **for'bidding** *a* sinistre; (temps) sombre; (ciel) menaçant.

force [fɔ:s] 1. *n* (*a*) force *f*; violence *f*; **by sheer, brute, f.**, de vive force; **by sheer f. of will**, à force de volonté; **the f. of circumstances**, la contrainte, la force, des circonstances; **to resort to f.**, faire appel à la force; (*of law*) **to come into, to be in, f.**, entrer, être, en vigueur (*b*) influence *f*, autorité *f*; **f. of example**, influence de l'exemple (*c*) force, énergie *f* (d'un coup); intensité *f* (du vent); effort *m*; **f. of gravity**, (force de la) pesanteur; **nuclear f.**, force nucléaire (*d*) (*group of people*) force; **the (armed) forces**, les forces armées; **the police f.**, la police; **in (full) f.**, en force, en masse (*e*) vertu *f*, valeur *f* (d'un argument); signification *f* (d'un mot) 2. *vtr* (*a*) forcer; **to f. s.o.'s hand**, forcer la main à qn; **to f. the pace**, forcer l'allure; **she forced a smile**, elle s'est forcée à sourire (*b*) forcer (une porte, une serrure); **to f. one's way**, se frayer un chemin; **to f. one's way into a house**, entrer, pénétrer, de force dans une maison (*c*) pousser (qch); faire entrer (qn, qch) de force (**into**, dans) (*d*) **to f. s.o. to do sth**, forcer, contraindre, qn à faire qch; **to be forced to do sth**, être forcé de faire qch; **to f. sth on s.o.**, forcer qn à accepter qch; imposer qch à qn; **to f. sth from s.o.**, arracher qch à qn. **force 'back** *vtr* repousser, faire reculer (l'ennemi); refouler (ses larmes). **forced** *a* forcé. **force 'down** *vtr* faire descendre de force; forcer (un avion) à atterrir; avaler (qch) avec un grand effort. **'force-'feed** *vtr* (**-fed** [-fed]) nourrir (qn) de force; gaver (une oie). **'forceful** *a* plein de force; énergique; (langage) vigoureux. **'forcefully** *adv* avec force; vigoureusement. **'force 'out** *vtr* faire sortir de force. **'forcible** *a* (entrée) de, par, force; (*of pers, argument*) vigoureux, plein de force. **'forcibly** *adv* (*a*) (entrer) de force (*b*) vigoureusement.

forceps ['fɔ:seps] *n inv in pl Surg:* **(pair of) f.**, forceps *m.*

ford [fɔ:d] 1. *n* gué *m* 2. *vtr* traverser à gué.

fore [fɔ:r] 1. *a* antérieur; de devant 2. *n* avant *m*; **to the f.**, en vue, en évidence 3. *int Golf:* attention! gare devant! **'forearm** 1. *n* avant-bras *m inv* 2. *vtr* prémunir (qn). **fore'boding** *n* (mauvais) pressentiment. **'forecast** 1. *n* prévision *f*; *Turf:* pronostic *m* (des courses); **weather f.**, prévision météorologique 2. *vtr* prévoir. **forecastle** ['fouksl] *n* = **fo'c'sle**. **'forecourt** *n* avant-cour *f.* **'forefather** *n* aïeul *m*, *pl* aïeux. **'forefinger** *n* index *m.* **'forefront** *n* **to be in the f.**, être au premier rang, occuper le premier plan. **fore'go** *vtr* (**-went** [-'went]; **-gone** [-'gɔn]) renoncer à (qch). **'foregoing** *a* précédent, antérieur; **the ˉ**, ce qui précède. **'foregone** *a* décidé d'avance; **it was a f. conclusion**, c'était prévu (d'avance). **'foreground** *n* premier plan. **'forehand** *a & n Ten:* **f. (stroke)**, coup *m* d'avant-main. **forehead** ['fɔrhed, 'fɔrid] *n Anat:* front *m.*

'foreland *n* cap *m*, promontoire *m.* **'foreleg** *n* jambe *f*, patte *f*, de devant. **'forelock** *n* mèche *f* (de cheveux) sur le front. **'foreman** *n* (*pl* -**men**) (*a*) *Jur:* chef *m* du jury (*b*) *Ind:* contremaître *m*; chef *m* d'équipe. **'foremast** *n Nau:* mât *m* de misaine. **'foremost** 1. *a* premier; le plus avancé 2. *adv* **first and f.**, tout d'abord. **'forename** *n* prénom *m.* **'foreplay** *n* travaux *mpl* d'approche. **'forerunner** *n* avant-coureur *m*; précurseur *m.* **fore'see** *vtr* (**-saw** [-'sɔ:], **-seen** [-'si:n]) prévoir; entrevoir. **fore'seeable** *a* prévisible. **fore'shadow** *vtr* présager, annoncer. **'foreshore** *n* (*a*) plage *f* (*b*) laisse *f* de mer. **'foresight** *n* prévoyance *f.* **'foreskin** *n Anat:* prépuce *m.* **fore'stall** *vtr* anticiper, devancer. **'foretaste** *n* avant-goût *m.* **fore'tell** *vtr* (**-told** [-'tould]) prédire. **'forethought** *n* prévoyance. **fore'warn** *vtr* avertir (qn); *Prov:* **forewarned is forearmed**, un homme averti en vaut deux. **'forewoman** *n* (*pl* -**women**) (*a*) *Jur:* chef *m* du jury (*b*) *Ind:* contremaîtresse *f.* **'foreword** *n* préface *f*, avant-propos *m inv.*

foreign ['fɔrən] *a* étranger; **feelings f. to his nature**, sentiments qui lui sont étrangers; **f. travel**, voyages à l'étranger; **the F. Service**, le corps diplomatique; **the F. Legion**, la Légion étrangère; **f. trade**, commerce extérieur; **the F. Office** = le Ministère des Affaires étrangères; *Med:* **f. body**, corps étranger. **'foreigner** *n* étranger, -ère.

forensic [fə'rensik] *a* légal.

forest ['fɔrist] *n* forêt *f.* **'forester** *n* (garde) forestier *m.* **'forestry** *n* sylviculture *f*; **F. Commission** = (service *m* des) Eaux *fpl* et Forêts.

forfeit ['fɔ:fit] 1. *n* (*a*) amende *f* (*b*) (*in game*) gage *m* 2. *vtr* perdre (ses droits); **to f. one's life**, payer de sa vie. **'forfeiture** *n* perte *f* (de ses droits).

forgave [fə'geiv] *see* **forgive.**

forge [fɔ:dʒ] 1. *n* forge *f* 2. *vtr* (*a*) forger (le fer) (*b*) contrefaire (une signature); faire un faux de (qch). **'forge a'head** *vi* avancer à toute vitesse; pousser de l'avant. **forged** *a* (*a*) (fer) forgé (*b*) (document) faux, contrefait. **'forger** *n* faussaire *mf.* **'forgery** *n* (*a*) contrefaçon *f* (d'une signature); falsification *f* (de documents) (*b*) faux; **the signature was a f.**, la signature était contrefaite. **'forging** *n* 1. *Metalw:* (*a*) travail *m* de forge (*b*) pièce forgée 2. = **forgery**.

forget [fə'get] *vtr & i* (**forgot** [-'gɔt]; **forgotten** [-'gɔtən]) oublier; négliger (son devoir); **I forgot all about those books**, j'ai complètement oublié ces livres; **to f. how to do sth**, oublier comment faire qch; ne plus savoir faire qch; (*in reply to thanks, apology*) **f. it!** (i) de rien! (il n'y a) pas de quoi! (ii) ça ne fait rien! **f. about it!** n'y pensez plus! and **don't you f. it!** faites-y bien attention! **never to be forgotten**, inoubliable; **to f. to do sth**, oublier de faire qch; **don't f. to do it**, ne manquez pas de le faire; **to f. oneself**, s'oublier. **for'getful** *a* (*a*) oublieux (**of**, de); **he's very f.**, il a très mauvaise mémoire (*b*) négligent. **for'getfulness** *n* (*a*) manque *m* de mémoire; **a moment of f.**, un moment d'oubli *m* (*b*) négligence *f.* **for'get-me-not** *n Bot:* myosotis *m inv.*

forgive [fə'giv] *vtr* (**forgave** [-'geiv]; **forgiven** [-'givn]) pardonner (qch); **to f. s.o.**, pardonner à qn.

for'givable a pardonnable. **for'giveness** n (a) pardon m (b) indulgence f. **for'giving** a indulgent; peu rancunier.

forgo [fɔː'gou] vtr (**-went** [-'went]; **-gone** [-'gɔn]) renoncer à (qch).

forgot, forgotten see **forget**.

fork [fɔːk] **1.** n fourchette f (de table); Agr: fourche f; branche fourchue (d'un arbre); bifurcation f (de routes); **take the left f.,** prenez le chemin à gauche; Mus: **tuning f.,** diapason m **2.** vi (of road) bifurquer; f. **right for York,** prenez à droite pour York. **forked** a fourchu; (éclair) qui fait des zigzags. **'forklift** n f. **(truck),** chariot élévateur (à fourche). **'fork 'out** vtr & i F: **to f. o. (the money),** payer, les allonger. **'fork 'over** vtr fourcher (le sol).

forlorn [fɔ'lɔːn] a (a) désespéré (b) (endroit) abandonné, délaissé; f. **appearance,** mine triste.

form [fɔːm] **1.** n (a) forme f (d'un objet); sorte f, espèce f (d'une maladie); **different forms of worship,** différentes façons d'adorer Dieu; **in the f. of a cross,** en forme de croix; **in the f. of a dog,** sous la forme d'un chien; **statistics in tabular f.,** statistique sous forme de tableau; **to take f.,** prendre forme (b) forme, formalité f; **for form's sake,** pour la forme; **it's a mere matter of f.,** c'est une pure formalité; F: **you know the f.,** vous savez bien ce qu'il faut faire; **it's bad f.,** c'est de mauvais ton; cela ne se fait pas (c) formule f, forme (d'un acte); **it's only a f. of speech,** ce n'est qu'une façon de parler; **correct f. of words,** tournure correcte; **forms of address,** titres mpl de politesse (d) (document) formulaire m; formule (de télégramme); **printed f.,** imprimé m (e) Sp: forme; état m, condition f; **to be in (good) f.,** être en forme (f) Sch: classe f; f. **teacher,** professeur principal (g) banc m; banquette f **2.** v (a) vtr former, faire, façonner; organiser (une société); arrêter (un plan); contracter (une liaison); se faire (une idée); **to f. part of sth,** faire partie de qch; **they formed themselves into a committee,** ils se sont constitués en comité; **to be formed by,** se former par; **the ministers who f. the cabinet,** les ministres qui composent, constituent, le gouvernement (b) vi prendre forme; se former; **to f. into line,** se mettre en ligne. **'format** n format m. **for'mation** n formation f; f. **flying,** vol de groupe m. **'formative** a formateur; (année) de formation. **'formroom** n (salle f de) classe f.

formal ['fɔːm(ə)l] a (a) (of procedure) formel, en règle; (of order) positif; (contrat) en due forme; (of occasion) cérémonieux, solennel; f. **dress,** tenue (1) de cérémonie (ii) de soirée; f. **dinner,** grand dîner; dîner officiel (b) (of pers) compassé; formaliste; (art) conventionnel; (jardin) à la française. **for'mality** n (a) (formal act) formalité f (b) (attention to rules) raideur f; cérémonie f. **'formalize** vtr formaliser. **'formally** adv cérémonieusement.

former ['fɔːmər] **1.** a (a) antérieur, précédent, ancien; **my f. pupils,** mes anciens élèves; **in f. times,** autrefois; **he is a shadow of his f. self,** il n'est plus que l'ombre de ce qu'il était autrefois (b) (as opposed to the latter) **the f. alternative,** la première alternative **2.** pron **the f.,** celui-là, celle-là, ceux-là, celles-là. **'formerly** adv autrefois.

formidable ['fɔːmidəbl] a formidable, redoutable.

formula ['fɔːmjulə] n (pl **formulas,** Tchn: **formulae** [-mjuliː]) formule f. **'formulate** vtr formule

formu'lation n formulation f.

fornicate ['fɔːnikeit] vi forniquer. **forni'cation** n fornication f.

forsake [fə'seik] vtr (**forsook** [fə'suk; **forsake** [fə'seikn]) abandonner; délaisser (qn); renoncer (qch).

forsythia [fɔː'saiθiə] n Bot: forsythia m.

fort [fɔːt] n Mil: fort m.

forte ['fɔːtei, NAm: fɔːt] n fort m.

forth [fɔːθ] adv en avant; **to walk back and f.,** marche de long en large; aller et venir; **and so f.,** et ainsi d suite; Lit: **from this time f.,** désormais. **forth'coming** a (a) qui arrive; prochain, à venir (livre) en préparation; **the promised help was not f.,** le secours promis ont fait défaut (b) (of pers) sociable; expansif; ouvert; franc; **not (very) f.,** réservé. **'forthright** a franc. **forth'with** adv tout d suite.

fortify ['fɔːtifai] vtr (**fortified**) fortifier; alcooliser (u vin). **fortifi'cation** n fortification f.

fortitude ['fɔːtitjuːd] n force f d'âme.

fortnight ['fɔːtnait] n quinzaine f; quinze jours m **'fortnightly 1.** a bimensuel **2.** adv tous les quinz jours.

fortress ['fɔːtris] n forteresse f; place forte.

fortuitous [fə'tjuːitəs] a fortuit, imprévu **for'tuitously** adv fortuitement; par hasard.

fortune ['fɔːtʃən, -tjuːn] n (a) fortune f; hasard m chance f; often bonne chance; **by good f.,** par bonheur (b) destinée f, sort m; **to tell fortunes,** dire la bonn aventure; f. **teller,** diseur, -euse, de bonne aventure; **telling,** la bonne aventure (c) fortune; richesses fp biens mpl; **to make a f.,** faire fortune; **to come into a f** hériter une fortune; F: **to cost a small f.,** coûter u argent fou. **'fortunate** a heureux; (of occasion propice; **to be f.,** avoir de la chance; **to be f. enough to** avoir la chance de; **how f.!** quelle chance **'fortunately** adv (a) heureusement (b) par bon heur.

forty ['fɔːti] num a & n quarante (m); **about f. guests** une quarantaine d'invités; **f.-one, f.-two,** quarante e un, quarante-deux; **the forties,** les années quarante; **t be in one's forties,** avoir passé la quarantaine; F: **t have f. winks,** faire un petit somme. **'fortieth** num & n quarantième (mf).

forward ['fɔːwəd] **1.** a (a) (mouvement) progressif, e avant; (of plant, child) avancé; précoce (b) Pej: (c pers) effronté **2.** adv (also **forwards**) (a) **from that da f.,** à partir de ce jour-là; **to look f. to sth,** attendre qch avec plaisir, avec impatience (b) (direction) en avant **to move f.,** avancer; **to go straight f.,** aller tout droit; f. **en avant!** Fig: **to come f.,** se proposer, s'offrir; t **thrust, push, oneself f.,** se mettre en évidence; Com **carried f.,** à reporter (c) (position) à l'avant; **the seat i too far f.,** la banquette est trop avancée **3.** vtr (a avancer, favoriser (un projet) (b) expédier, envoyer faire suivre (une lettre); (on letter) **please f.,** prière d faire suivre **4.** n Sp: avant m. **'forwarding** n (a avancement m (d'un projet) (b) expédition f, envoi m (des marchandises); f. **address,** nouvelle adresse (pou faire suivre le courrier). **'forward-looking** progressiste. **'forwardness** n précocité f; Pe effronterie f.

forwent [fɔːˈwent] *see* forgo.

fossil [ˈfɔsl] *a* & *n* fossile (*m*); *F:* **an old f.**, un vieux fossile, une vieille croûte. **'fossilized** *a* fossilisé.

foster [ˈfɔstər] **1.** *vtr* élever (un enfant); entretenir, nourrir (une idée); favoriser (un projet) **2.** *a* **f. brother,** frère de lait; **f. child,** enfant placé dans une famille qui n'est pas la sienne; **f. mother,** (mère) nourricière; **f. sister,** sœur de lait; *Adm:* **placing of children in f. homes,** placement familial des enfants.

fought [fɔːt] *see* **fight 2.**

foul [faul] **1.** *a* (*a*) infect; fétide; (air) vicié; (*of water*) croupi; (linge) sale, souillé; (*of thoughts*) immonde; (*of language*) ordurier; (crime) atroce; *Sp: etc:* déloyal; *F:* horrible; *F:* **what f. weather!** quel sale temps! quel temps infect! **to fall f. of s.o.,** se brouiller avec qn; *Sp:* **f. play,** jeu déloyal; *Jur:* **f. play is not suspected,** on ne croit pas à un crime **2.** *n Sp:* faute *f*; coup illicite, déloyal; *Box:* coup bas **3.** *v* (*a*) *vtr* salir, souiller; obstruer (un tuyau); engager (un cordage); *Nau:* surjaler (l'ancre); (*of ship*) entrer en collision avec (un navire) (*b*) *vi* (*of rope*) s'engager. **'foul-'mouthed** *a* au langage ordurier. **'foul 'up** *vtr* embrouiller, gâcher (un projet).

found [faund] *vtr* fonder; créer (une institution); baser (son opinion) (**on,** sur); (*of novel*) **founded on fact,** reposant sur des faits véridiques. **foun'dation** *n* (*a*) fondation *f*; *Fig:* fondement *m*, assise *f*, base *f* (d'une doctrine); **to lay the f. stone,** poser la première pierre; **rumour without f.,** bruit dénué de tout fondement; *Cl:* **f. garment,** gaine *f* (*b*) *Toil:* **f. (cream),** fond *m* de teint. **'founder¹** *n* fondateur, -trice.

found² *see* **find 2. 'foundling** *n* enfant trouvé(e).

founder² [ˈfaundər] *vi* (*of hope, horse*) s'effondrer; (*of ship*) sombrer.

foundry [ˈfaundri] *n* (*pl* **foundries**) fonderie *f*.

fount [faunt] *n Lit:* source *f*; *Typ:* fonte *f*.

fountain [ˈfauntin] *n* fontaine *f*; **drinking f.,** poste *m*, jet *m*, d'eau potable; **f. pen,** stylo à encre.

four [fɔːr] *num a* & *n* quatre (*m*); **twenty-f.,** vingt-quatre; **the f. corners of the earth,** les quatre coins du monde; **to go on all fours,** courir à quatre pattes; **f. at a time,** quatre à quatre. **'four-'engined** *a* quadrimoteur. **'fourfold 1.** *a* quadruple **2.** *adv* quatre fois autant; au quadruple. **'four-'footed** *a* quadrupède; à quatre pattes. **'four-'leaf(ed), -'leaved** *a Bot:* (trèfle) à quatre feuilles. **'four-'letter 'word** *n F:* obscénité *f*; gros mot. **'four-'part** *a Mus:* à quatre voix. **'four-'poster (bed)** *n* lit *m* à colonnes. **'foursome** *n* groupe *m* de quatre personnes. **four'teen** *num a* & *n* quatorze (*m*). **four'teenth** *num a* & *n* quatorzième (*mf*); **Louis the F.,** Louis Quatorze. **fourth 1.** *num a* & *n* quatrième (*m*); **on the f. of June,** le quatre juin **2.** *n* (*a*) (*fraction*) quart *m* (*b*) *Mus:* quarte *f*. **'fourthly** *adv* quatrièmement; en quatrième lieu. **'four-wheel** *a* (voiture) à quatre roues; **car with f.-w. drive,** voiture à quatre roues motrices.

fowl [faul] *n* (*inv in pl or* **fowls**) volaille *f*; poule *f*, coq *m*; **wild f.,** gibier *m* d'eau; *Cu:* **boiling f.,** poule; *Vet:* **f. pest,** peste aviaire.

fox [fɔks] **1.** *n* (*pl* **foxes**) renard *m*; **f. cub,** renardeau *m*; *Cl:* **f. fur,** (fourrure *f* de) renard; *F:* (*of pers*) **a sly old f.,** un fin renard **2.** *vtr F:* mystifier, tromper (qn). **'foxglove** *n Bot:* digitale *f* (pourprée). **'foxhole** *n Mil:* trou *m* de tirailleur. **'foxhound** *n* chien courant. **'foxhunt(ing)** *n* chasse *f* au renard. **'foxtrot** *n Danc:* fox-trot *m inv.* **'foxy** *a* (-ier, -iest) *F:* (*a*) (visage) de renard (*b*) rusé, astucieux (*c*) *esp NAm:* (*of woman*) sexy.

foyer [ˈfɔiei] *n* foyer *m* (du public).

fraction [ˈfrækʃn] *n* fraction *f*; **to escape death by a f. of a second,** être à deux doigts de la mort. **'fractional** *a* fractionnaire. **'fractionally** *adv* (d')un tout petit peu.

fractious [ˈfrækʃəs] *a* (*a*) revêche (*b*) de mauvaise humeur; (enfant) pleurnicheur, -euse. **'fractiousness** *n* mauvaise humeur; (*of baby*) pleurnicherie *f*.

fracture [ˈfræktʃər] **1.** *n* fracture *f*; *Med:* **compound f.,** fracture compliquée **2.** *vtr* & *i* (se) casser, (se) briser; *Med:* (se) fracturer (un os).

fragile [ˈfrædʒail] *a* fragile; (*of pers*) faible; *F:* **to feel f.,** avoir mal aux cheveux. **fragility** [frəˈdʒiliti] *n* fragilité *f*.

fragment 1. *n* [ˈfrægmənt] fragment *m*; morceau *m* **2.** *vtr* & *i* [frægˈment] (se) fragmenter. **'fragmentary, frag'mented** *a* fragmentaire.

fragrance [ˈfreigrəns] *n* parfum *m*. **'fragrant** *a* parfumé; odorant.

frail [freil] *a* fragile; frêle; faible. **'frailty** *n* faiblesse *f*; fragilité *f*.

frame [freim] **1.** *n* construction *f*, structure *f*; (*of pers*) ossature *f*, charpente *f* (d'un bâtiment); cadre *m* (d'une bicyclette); monture *f* (d'un parapluie, d'une paire de lunettes); carcasse *f* (d'un navire); cadre, encadrement *m* (d'un tableau); chambranle *m*, châssis *m* (d'une fenêtre); *Cin: TV:* image *f*; *Hort:* châssis (de couches); **f. of mind,** état *m*, disposition *f*, d'esprit; **man with a gigantic f.,** homme d'une taille colossale; **f. of reference,** système *m* de référence; **f. house,** maison en bois **2.** *vtr* (*a*) former, régler (ses pensées); composer (un poème); imaginer (une idée); se faire (une opinion) (*b*) encadrer (un tableau) (*c*) *F:* monter un coup contre (qn); **I've been framed,** c'est un coup monté (contre moi). **'frame-up** *n F:* coup monté. **'framework** *n* charpente, ossature, carcasse; **within the f. of the United Nations,** dans le cadre des Nations Unies.

France [frɑːns] *Prn Geog:* France *f*; **in F.,** en France. **'Franco-'British** *a* franco-britannique.

franchise [ˈfræntʃaiz] *n* (*a*) droit *m* de vote (*b*) *Com:* contrat *m* de franchisage.

frank¹ [fræŋk] *a* franc, *f* franche; sincère. **'frankly** *adv* franchement; ouvertement. **'frankness** *n* franchise *f*, sincérité *f*.

frank² *vtr* affranchir (une lettre); **franking machine,** machine à affranchir.

frankfurter [ˈfræŋkfɜːtər] *n Cu:* saucisse *f* de Francfort.

frankincense [ˈfræŋkinsens] *n* encens *m*.

frantic [ˈfræntik] *a* frénétique; fou (de joie, de douleur); (effort) effréné, désespéré; *F:* **it drives him f.,** cela le met hors de lui. **'frantically** *adv* frénétiquement; (courir) comme un affolé.

fraternal [frəˈtɜːnl] *a* fraternel. **fra'ternity** *n* fraternité *f*; *NAm:* association *f* de camarades de classe.

fraterni'zation n fraternisation f. 'fraternize vi fraterniser.

fraud [frɔːd] n (a) Jur: fraude f (b) supercherie f, tromperie f (c) (pers) imposteur m; (place) attrape f. 'fraudulence n caractère frauduleux. 'fraudulent a frauduleux. 'fraudulently frauduleusement.

fraught [frɔːt] a (a) f. with danger, qui entraîne des conséquences funestes (b) F: (of thg) désolant, pénible; (of pers) désolé.

fray¹ [frei] n bagarre f; ready for the f., prêt à se battre.

fray² vtr & i (of material) (s')érailler, (s')effiler; (of collar) (s')effranger; (of rope) (s')user; my nerves are frayed, je suis à bout de nerfs; tempers were getting a little frayed, on commençait à se fâcher.

frazzle ['fræzl] n F: burnt to a f., carbonisé.

freak [friːk] 1. n caprice m, fantaisie f, lubie f; f. of fortune, jeu m de la fortune; f. (of nature), phénomène m; F: jazz f., fana mf du jazz; f. storm, orage complètement inattendu; f. weather, temps anormal; f. accident, accident incroyable, extraordinaire 2. vi F: to f. (out), se défouler; (of drug taker) se défoncer. 'freakish a bizarre.

freckle ['frekl] n tache f de rousseur. 'freckled a couvert de taches de rousseur.

free [friː] 1. a & adv (freer; freest) (a) libre; en liberté; f. house, débit de boissons libre de vendre les produits de n'importe quelle brasserie; f. will, libre arbitre m; of one's own f. will, de son propre gré; man is a f. agent, l'homme est libre; F: it's a f. country, vous avez (le droit d'agir selon) votre libre arbitre; to set f., libérer; to be allowed to go f., être mis en liberté; f. speech, parole libre; f. love, amour libre; f. trade, libre-échange m; f. fall, chute libre; f. verse, vers libres; f. church, église non-conformiste; to be f. to do sth, être libre de faire qch; f. from, of, s.o., sth, débarrassé de qn, qch; f. from care, sans souci; f. of tax, exempt d'impôt; you can bring in half a litre f., il y a une tolérance d'un demi-litre (b) (unoccupied) libre; is this table f.? est-ce que cette table est libre? I'm f. tomorrow, je suis libre demain; f. end, brin libre (d'un cordage); with his f. hand, avec sa main libre; to give s.o. a f. hand, donner carte blanche à qn (c) (of style) franc; (of bearing) souple, désinvolte; (of pers) libéral; (of pers, speech) ouvert; to be f. with one's money, être prodigue de son argent; f. and easy, désinvolte; to make f. with sth, se servir de qch sans se gêner; he made very f. with my whisky, il ne se gênait pas pour boire mon whisky; F: feel f.! faites comme chez vous! servez-vous! (d) (without charge) gratuit; admission f., entrée gratuite; post f., franco de port; catalogue sent f. on request, catalogue franco sur demande; Com: f. gift, sample, cadeau m, échantillon m 2. adv (for) f., gratuitement; gratis; pour rien 3. vtr affranchir (un peuple); libérer (qn); débarrasser (from, de); dégager (un sentier); to f. oneself from s.o.'s grasp, se dégager des mains de qn. 'freebie n F: prime (accordée à un journaliste). 'freedom n liberté f; indépendance f; franchise f (d'une conversation); exemption f (from, de); f. of speech, liberté d'expression; f. to do sth, liberté de faire qch; to receive the f. of the city, être nommé citoyen d'honneur de la ville; to give s.o. the f. of one's house, mettre sa maison à la disposition de qn. 'free-for-all n F: bagarre f, mêlée f.

'freehand a & adv à main levée. 'freehold a & n f. (property), propriété f sans réserve; pleine propriété. 'freelance 1. n journaliste indépendant, -ante 2. vi faire du travail indépendant. 'freely adv librement; (parler) franchement. 'freeman n (pl -men) citoyen, -enne, d'honneur (d'une ville). 'freemason n franc-maçon m. 'freemasonry n franc-maçonnerie f. 'free-'range a (œuf) de ferme. 'freestyle a & n f. (swimming), nage f libre. 'free'thinker n libre-penseur, -euse. 'freeway n esp NAm: Aut: autoroute f sans péage. 'free'wheel vi Cy: faire roue libre; Aut: rouler en roue libre.

freesia ['friːziə] n Bot: freesia m.

freeze [friːz] 1. n gel m, gelée f; blocage m (de prix) 2. vtr & i (froze [frouz]; frozen ['frouzn]) geler; esp Cu: congeler; (of weather) it's freezing, il gèle; the river is, has, frozen, la rivière est prise; F: I'm freezing, frozen, je (me) gèle; my hands are freezing, frozen, j'ai les mains gelées, glacées; the smile froze on his lips, le sourire s'est figé sur ses lèvres; to f., be frozen, to death, mourir de froid; to f. the blood (in one's veins), glacer le sang, le cœur; to f. wages, bloquer les salaires. 'freeze-'dry vtr (-'dried) lyophiliser. 'freeze 'over vi geler d'un bout à l'autre. 'freezer n congélateur m; (in refrigerator) freezer m. 'freeze 'up vi geler. 'freezing a & n (temps) glacial; (brouillard) givrant; f. point, point de congélation; the temperature dropped to f. point, la température a baissé jusqu'à zéro degré. 'frozen a gelé; glacé; (of food) congelé, surgelé.

freight [freit] n (a) fret m (b) transport m; f. train, train de marchandises; air f., transport par avion. 'freighter n (ship) cargo m; avion-cargo m.

French [frentʃ] 1. a français; F. Canadian, canadien français; F. Canada, le Canada français; F. lesson, leçon de français; F. master, mistress, professeur de français; F. Embassy, ambassade de France; esp NAm: F.-fried potatoes, F. fries (Br = (potato) chips), (pommes) frites fpl; F. bread, loaf, stick, baguette f; F. dressing, vinaigrette f; F. windows, esp NAm: doors, portes-fenêtres fpl; to take F. leave, filer à l'anglaise; F: F. letter, capote anglaise 2. (a) n Ling: français m; to speak F., parler français; Canadian F., français canadien, du Canada (b) npl the F., les Français m. 'Frenchman n (pl -men) Français m. 'French-'speaking a francophone. 'Frenchwoman n (pl -women) Française f.

frenzy ['frenzi] n frénésie f; transport m (de joie). 'frenzied a affolé, forcené; (of applause) frénétique.

frequent 1. a ['friːkwənt] (of custom) répandu; (of visits) fréquent; qui arrive souvent; (client) habituel 2. vtr [fri'kwent] fréquenter; hanter (un endroit). 'frequency n fréquence f; WTel: very high f., très haute fréquence; f. modulation, modulation de fréquence. 'frequently adv fréquemment; souvent.

fresh [freʃ] 1. a (a) frais; (of paragraph, attempt) nouveau; to put f. courage into s.o., ranimer le courage de qn; it is still f. in my mind, je l'ai encore frais à la mémoire; f. from London, nouvellement arrivé de Londres; bread f. from the oven, pain qui sort du four; in the f. air, en plein air; au grand air; f. water, (i) (newly drawn) eau fraîche (ii) (not salt) eau douce; as f. as a daisy, frais et dispos (b) (of pers) vigoureux, alerte; (*of horse*) fougueux (*c*) F: (*of pers*) effronté; **to get f. with s.o.,** prendre des libertés avec qn **2.** *adv* fraîchement, nouvellement. **'freshen** *vi* (*of wind*) fraîchir. **'freshener** *n* air f., désodorisant *m* (contre les odeurs domestiques). **'freshen 'up 1.** *vi* faire un bout de toilette **2.** *vtr* rafraîchir (l'air). **'fresher, 'freshman** *n* (*pl* **-men**) *Sch*: étudiant, -ante, de première année. **'freshly** *adv* fraîchement; nouvellement. **'freshness** *n* (*a*) fraîcheur *f* (*b*) vigueur *f*, vivacité *f* (*c*) F: effronterie *f*, toupet *m*. **'freshwater** *a* (poisson) d'eau douce.

fret [fret] *vi* (**fretted**) s'inquiéter; **child fretting for his mother,** enfant qui réclame sa mère en pleurnichant; **stop fretting,** ne te fais pas de mauvais sang. **'fretful** *a* agité; qui se fait du mauvais sang. **'fretfully** *adv* d'un air chagrin, inquiet. **'fretfulness** *n* irritabilité *f*.

fretwork ['fretwəːk] *n* travail ajouré (en bois). **'fret-saw** *n* scie *f* à découper.

Freudian ['frɔidiən] *a Psy*: freudien; **F. slip,** lapsus *m*.

friar ['fraiər] *n* frère *m*, religieux *m*.

friction ['frikʃn] *n* friction *f*.

Friday ['fraidi] *n* vendredi *m*; **he's coming (on) F.,** il viendra vendredi; **he comes on Fridays,** *esp NAm:* **he comes Fridays,** il vient le vendredi; **Good F.,** le vendredi saint; *F:* **man F.,** factotum *m*; **girl F.,** aide *f* de bureau.

fridge [fridʒ] *n F:* réfrigérateur *m*, frigo *m*.

fried, fries [fraid, fraiz] *see* **fry²**.

friend [frend] *n* ami, *f* amie; (*acquaintance*) connaissance *f*; **a f. of mine,** un(e) de mes ami(e)s; **to make friends with s.o.,** se lier d'amitié avec qn; **to make friends,** se faire des amis; **to be friends with s.o.,** être ami avec qn; **the Society of Friends,** les Quakers *m*; *Fig:* **to have friends at court,** avoir des amis bien placés. **'friendless** *a* sans amis. **'friendliness** *n* bienveillance *f*, bonté *f* (**to, towards,** envers); dispositions amicales. **'friendly** *a* (**-ier, -iest**) amical; sympathique; (*of pers*) bienveillant; **to be f. with s.o.,** être ami avec qn; **f. gathering,** réunion d'amis; **to be on f. terms with s.o.,** être en bons termes avec qn; **f. society,** association de bienfaisance. **'friendship** *n* amitié *f*.

frieze [friːz] *n Arch:* frise *f*; (*on wallpaper*) bordure *f*.

frigate ['frigət] *n Navy:* frégate *f*.

fright [frait] *n* (*a*) peur *f*; effroi *m*; **to take f.,** s'effrayer (**at,** de); **to give s.o. a f.,** faire peur à qn; **I got an awful f.,** j'ai eu une peur bleue (*b*) *F:* personne laide, grotesque. **'frighten** *vtr* effrayer; faire peur à (qn); **to be frightened,** avoir peur (**of,** de); **to be frightened to death,** mourir de peur; **to f. s.o. out of his wits,** faire une peur bleue à qn. **'frighten a'way, 'off** *vtr* effaroucher (des oiseaux); chasser (qn). **'frightened** *a* apeuré; **easily f.,** peureux. **'frightening** *a* effrayant. **'frighteningly** *adv* à faire peur. **'frightful** *a* effroyable, affreux, épouvantable. **'frightfully** *adv* terriblement, affreusement; **to be f. sorry,** regretter énormément. **'frightfulness** *n* horreur *f*, atrocité *f* (d'un crime).

frigid ['fridʒid] *a* glacial; (très) froid; (*of woman*) frigide. **'frigidly** *adv* très froidement. **fri'gidity** *n* frigidité *f*; grande froideur.

frill [fril] *n Cost:* volant *m*, ruche *f*; *Cu:* papillote *f*; **a plain meal without frills,** un repas simple sans pré-

sentation compliquée. **'frilly** *a* (**-ier, -iest**) (*of dress*) froncé, ruché; (*of style*) orné, fleuri.

fringe [frindʒ] *n* (*a*) frange *f* (*b*) (*edge*) bordure *f*, bord *m*; *pl* banlieue *f* (d'une ville); **to live on the f. of society,** vivre en marge de la société; **f. theatre,** petit théâtre expérimental; **f. area,** zone limitrophe; **f. benefits,** compléments de salaire; avantages accessoires.

frisk [frisk] **1.** *vi* **to f. (about),** s'ébattre, gambader **2.** *vtr* *F:* fouiller (qn). **'friskiness** *n* vivacité *f*. **'frisky** *a* (**-ier, -iest**) vif, folâtre; (cheval) fringant.

fritter ['fritər] **1.** *n Cu:* beignet *m* **2.** *vtr* **to f. (away),** gaspiller (son argent).

frivolous ['frivələs] *a* frivole; (*of question*) vain, futile. **fri'volity** [-'vɔliti] *n* frivolité *f*. **'frivolously** *adv* frivolement.

frizzle ['frizl] *vi* grésiller. **'frizzled** *a Cu:* bien frit, bien doré.

frizzy ['frizi] *a* frisotté; crêpelé, crépu.

fro [frou] *adv* **to go to and f.,** aller et venir.

frock [frɔk] *n Cost:* robe *f*; (*of monk*) froc *m*.

frog [frɔg] *n* grenouille *f*; *F:* **to have a f. in one's throat,** avoir un chat dans la gorge. **'frogman** *n* (*pl* **-men**) homme-grenouille *m*. **'frogmarch** *vtr* porter (qn) à quatre, le derrière en l'air. **'frogspawn** *n* œufs *mpl* de grenouille.

frolic ['frɔlik] **1.** *n* ébats *mpl*, gambades *fpl* **2.** *vi* (**frolicked**) **to f. (about),** s'ébattre, folâtrer.

from [frɔm, frəm] *prep* (*a*) (*place*) **de; to return f. London,** revenir de Londres; **f. Paris to London,** de Paris à Londres; **f. town to town,** de ville en ville; **f. above,** d'en haut; **f. a long way off,** de loin (*b*) **the bird lays f. four to six eggs,** l'oiseau pond de quatre à six œufs; **wine f. ten francs a bottle,** vins à partir de dix francs la bouteille (*c*) (*time*) **depuis, dès, à partir de; f. the beginning,** dès le commencement; **f. time to time,** de temps en temps; **f. his childhood,** depuis son enfance; **f. now on,** à partir d'aujourd'hui; **f. that day (on),** à partir de ce jour (*d*) (*distance*) **not far f.,** pas loin de; **10km f. Paris,** à 10km de Paris (*e*) **de, à; he stole a pound f. her,** il lui a volé une livre; **to dissuade s.o. f. doing sth,** dissuader qn de faire qch; **to shelter f. the rain,** s'abriter contre la pluie (*f*) (*change*) **f. bad to worse,** de mal en pis; **to increase the price f. five to ten pence,** augmenter le prix de cinq à dix pence (*g*) (*difference*) **d'avec, de; to distinguish good f. bad,** distinguer le bon d'avec le mauvais (*h*) **to pick s.o. out f. the crowd,** distinguer qn parmi la foule; **to drink f. the brook,** boire au ruisseau; **to drink f. the bottle,** boire à même la bouteille; **to take sth f. one's pocket,** prendre qch de, dans, sa poche; **he grabbed the gun f. the table,** il a saisi le revolver sur la table (*i*) (*origin*) **a train f. the north,** un train en provenance du nord; **he comes f. Manchester,** (i) il est natif, originaire, de Manchester (ii) il habite à Manchester; **a quotation f. Shakespeare,** une citation tirée de Shakespeare; **f. your point of view,** à votre point de vue; **I've brought you it f. a friend,** je te l'apporte de la part d'un ami; **tell him that f. me,** dites-lui cela de ma part; **I'm surprised at that (coming) f. him,** cela m'étonne de sa part; **painted f. nature,** peint d'après nature (*j*) **to act f. conviction,** agir par conviction; **f. what I heard,** d'après ce que j'ai entendu dire; **f. what I can see,** à ce que je vois; **f. the way he looks,** à le voir.

frond [frɔnd] n Bot: fronde f (de fougère).

front [frʌnt] **1.** n (a) devant m; façade f (d'un bâtiment); avant m (d'une voiture); premier rang (de la classe); début m (d'un livre); **in the f. of a car,** à l'avant d'une voiture; **in the f. of the train,** en tête de train; **in f.,** devant, en avant; **in f. of,** (i) en face de (ii) devant; (of pers) **to put on a bold f.,** faire bonne contenance (b) Mil: Pol: Meteor: front m; Fig: **on all fronts,** de tous côtés (c) (at seaside) promenade f; **on the f.,** face à la mer (d) F: (cover) façade; (of pers) prête-nom m **2.** a antérieur; de devant, d'avant; **f. seat,** siège (i) Th: au premier rang (ii) (in car) d'avant; Fig: **to have a f. seat,** être aux premières loges; **f. door,** porte d'entrée; **f. room,** pièce qui donne sur la rue, usu salon m; **f. wheel,** roue (d')avant; (of car) **f.-wheel drive,** traction avant; Journ: **f. page,** première page; F: la une; **f.-page news,** nouvelles sensationnelles; Mil: **f. line,** ligne de feu; **f.-line troops,** troupes du front; **f. rank,** premier rang; **f.-rank actress,** actrice de premier plan; **f. runner,** favori m; **f.-loading washing machine,** machine à laver à hublot; F: **f. man,** prête-nom m **3.** vtr & i (a) **to f. (on) sth,** faire face à qch; être tourné vers qch; donner sur (la rivière) (b) **house fronted with stone,** maison avec façade en pierre. **'frontage** n (longueur f de) façade (d'une maison). **'frontal** a Anat: frontal; (attaque, etc) de front; (nudité) (vue) de face. **'front'bencher** n Parl: membre m de la Chambre siégeant aux premières banquettes.

frontier ['frʌntiər, -'tiər] n frontière f; **f. town,** ville frontière.

frontispiece ['frʌntispi:s] n Typ: frontispice m.

frost [frɔst] **1.** n gelée f, gel m; (hoar) f., givre m; **ground f.,** gelée blanche; **ten degrees of f.,** dix degrés de froid, au-dessous de zéro **2.** vtr geler (un arbre fruitier); givrer (les vitres); glacer (un gâteau). **'frostbite** n gelure f. **'frostbitten** a gelé. **'frostbound** a gelé. **'frosted** a (of windows) givré; (of glass) dépoli; (gâteau) glacé. **'frostily** adv d'une manière glaciale. **'frosting** n givrage m (de vitres); dépolissage m (de verre); glaçage m (d'un gâteau). **'frosty** a (-ier, -iest) glacial; (jour) de gelée; (of windows) couvert de givre.

froth [frɔθ] **1.** n écume f; mousse f (de la bière) **2.** vi écumer; mousser; **to f. at the mouth,** avoir l'écume aux lèvres. **'frothy** a (-ier, -iest) écumeux, mousseux; (tissu) léger; (discours) vide.

frown [fraun] **1.** n froncement m (de sourcils); regard m sévère **2.** vi froncer les sourcils; **to f. at s.o.,** regarder qn en fronçant les sourcils; **to f. upon a suggestion,** désapprouver une suggestion.

frowsty ['frausti] a (pièce) qui sent le renfermé.

frowzy ['frauzi] a (a) (pièce) qui sent le renfermé (b) (of pers, clothes) mal tenu, peu soigné.

froze, frozen ['frouz, 'frouzn] see **freeze 2.**

frugal ['fru:gəl] a frugal; (of pers) économe. **fru'gality** [-'gæl-] n frugalité f. **'frugally** adv frugalement.

fruit [fru:t] n fruit m; **dried f.,** fruits secs; **stewed f.,** compote f de fruits; **f. cake,** cake m; **f. tree,** arbre fruitier; **f. salad,** salade de fruits; **f. machine,** machine à sous; **to bear f.,** porter fruit. **'fruiterer** n fruitier, -ière. **'fruitful** a (of tree) productif; (of soil) fertile, fécond; (of work) fructueux. **'fruitfully** adv fructueusement; à profit. **fru'ition** n réalisation f (d'un projet); **to come to f.,** réussir; **to bring to f.,** réaliser.

'fruitless a stérile, infructueux; (efforts) sans résultat(s). **fruity** a (-ier, -iest) (goût) de fruit; (vin) fruité; (of voice) étoffé; F: (scandale) corsé.

frump [frʌmp] n femme mal habillée. **'frumpish, 'frumpy** a (of woman) mal habillée; (chapeau) informe, démodé.

frustrate [frʌs'treit] vtr faire échouer (un projet); contrecarrer (qn); **to f. s.o.'s hopes,** frustrer qn dans son espérance. **frus'trated** a frustré. **frus'trating** a frustrant. **frus'tration** n frustration f.

fry¹ [frai] n coll Ich: frai m, fretin m, alevin m; F: **the small f.,** le menu fretin; les gens insignifiants.

fry² [frai] (fried) **1.** vtr (faire) frire (la viande); **fried egg,** œuf sur le plat **2.** vi (of food) frire. **fries** npl NAm: F: (Br = chips) (pommes) frites fpl. **'fryer** n DomEc: friteuse f. **'frying** n friture f; **f. pan,** poêle f; **to jump out of the f. pan into the fire,** tomber d'un mal dans un pire; tomber de Charybde en Scylla. **'fry-up** n F: (plat m de) restes réchauffés à la poêle.

ft abbr foot.

fuck [fʌk] V: **1.** n coït m; baise f; **I don't give a f.!** je m'en fous! **2.** vtr coïter avec, baiser (qn); **f. off!** va te faire foutre! **'fucking** a V: foutu.

fuddle ['fʌdl] vtr soûler, brouiller les idées de (qn). **'fuddled** a soûl; brouillé (dans ses idées).

fuddy-duddy ['fʌdidʌdi] n (pl fuddy-duddies) vieux croulant, vieille croulante.

fudge [fʌdʒ] **1.** n Cu: fondant (américain) **2.** vtr **to f. the issue,** éluder la question.

fuel ['fjuəl] **1.** n combustible m; (for engine) carburant m; **to add f. to the flames,** jeter de l'huile sur le feu; **f. tank,** réservoir à carburant; **f. oil,** mazout m **2.** v (fuelled) (a) vtr alimenter, charger (un fourneau); ravitailler (un navire) en carburant (b) vi **to f. (up),** se ravitailler en combustible, en carburant.

fug [fʌg] n atmosphère étouffante et chaude, qui sent le renfermé. **'fuggy** a F: qui sent le renfermé.

fugitive ['fju:dʒitiv] a & n fugitif, -ive.

fulfil [ful'fil] vtr (fulfilled) NAm: also **-fill** répondre à, remplir (l'attente de qn); satisfaire (un désir); exaucer (une prière); accomplir (une tâche); s'acquitter d(un devoir). **ful'filling** a (travail) satisfaisant. **ful'filment,** NAm: **-'fill-** n accomplissement m (d'une prophétie, d'un devoir); exaucement m (d'une prière); réalisation f (d'une condition).

full [ful] **1.** a (a) plein; rempli, comble; (jour) chargé; (of bus) complet; **f. to the brim,** rempli jusqu'au bord; **f. to overflowing,** plein à déborder; (of pers) **to be f. (up),** avoir (trop) bien mangé; Th: **f. house,** salle comble; **to be f. of one's own importance,** **f. of oneself,** être pénétré de sa propre importance, de soi-même (b) (of facts) ample, copieux; **f. particulars,** tous les détails; **in the fullest detail,** dans le plus grand détail (c) complet, entier; **f. pay,** paie entière; **in f. flower,** en pleine fleur; **f. meal,** repas complet; **to pay f. fare,** payer place entière; **f. weight,** poids juste; **f. price,** prix fort; **f. stop,** point (final); F: **to come to a f. stop,** s'arrêter net; roses in **f. bloom,** roses épanouies; in **f. uniform,** en grande tenue; **I waited two f. hours,** j'ai attendu deux bonnes heures; **f. member,** membre titulaire (d) (of face) plein; (of figure) rond; (of lips) gros; (of sleeve) large **2.** n plein m (de la lune); **in f.,** (publier) intégralement; (écrire) en toutes lettres;

name in f., nom et prénoms; to the f., complètement 3.
adv f. well, très bien; f. in the face, en pleine figure; to
turn a tap f. on, ouvrir un robinet en grand; to turn the
radio f. on, mettre la radio au plus fort. 'fullback n
Fb: arrière m. 'full-'blooded a (a) de race pure;
(cheval) pur-sang (b) vigoureux. 'full'blown a
épanoui; en pleine fleur; he's a f. doctor, il a tous ses
diplômes (de médecin). 'full-'bodied a (vin) corsé,
qui a du corps. 'full-'dress a (tenu) de cérémonie;
(débat) solennel. 'full-'grown a (of pers) adulte.
'full-'length a (portrait) en pied; (robe) longue; f.-
l. film, long métrage. 'ful(l)ness n plénitude f,
totalité f (de qch); ampleur f (d'un vêtement); abondance f (de détail); in the f. of time, quand les temps
seront révolus. 'full-'page a Journ: (réclame)
d'une page entière. 'full-'scale, 'full-'size(d) a
grandeur nature; (attaque) de grande envergure.
'full-'time a & adv à plein temps, à temps complet.
'fully adv pleinement; entièrement, complètement;
(armé) de toutes pièces; I'll write more f., j'écrirai plus
longuement; f. two hours, deux bonnes heures; au
moins deux heures. 'fully-'fashioned a entièrement diminué. 'fully-'fledged a (of doctor)
qualifié.

fulminate ['fʌlmineit] vi fulminer.

fulsome ['fulsəm] a excessif; f. flattery, flagornerie f,
adulation f.

fumble ['fʌmbl] vi to f. (about, around), fouiller;
tâtonner; to f. with sth, manier qch maladroitement.
'fumbling a maladroit, gauche.

fume [fjuːm] vi fumer, émettre de la fumée; F: (of pers)
rager, fumer (de rage). fumes npl fumée(s) f(pl),
vapeur(s) f(pl); exhalaison(s) f(pl); exhaust fumes,
gaz m d'échappement.

fumigate ['fjuːmigeit] vtr fumiger.

fun [fʌn] n amusement m, gaieté f; plaisanterie f; to
make f. of, poke f. at, s.o., se moquer de qn; for f., in
f., pour rire; par plaisanterie; for the f. of it, pour
le plaisir; he's, it's, great f., il est, c'est, très amusant;
to have f., s'amuser; se divertir. 'funfair n (a)
fête foraine (b) (amusement park) parc m d'attractions.

function ['fʌŋkʃn] 1. n (a) fonction f; charge f; in his f.
as a magistrate, en sa qualité de magistrat; to
discharge one's functions, s'acquitter de ses fonctions
(b) réception f, réunion f; cérémonie publique 2. vi
fonctionner; to f. as, faire fonction de; this gadget
won't f., ce truc ne marche pas. 'functional a
fonctionnel. 'functionary n fonctionnaire mf.

fund [fʌnd] 1. n fonds m; caisse f; to start a f., lancer
une souscription; funds, fonds mpl; ressources fpl
pécuniaires; to be in funds, être en fonds; Bank: no
funds, défaut de provision f 2. vtr pourvoir (un projet)
de fonds. 'fund-raising n moyens mpl de se
procurer des fonds (pour une œuvre de bienfaisance,
des réparations).

fundamental [fʌndə'mentl] 1. a fondamental; essentiel 2. n usu pl principe(s) m(pl); partie essentielle.
funda'mentally adv fondamentalement.

funeral ['fjuːnərəl] n funérailles fpl; obsèques fpl;
(burial) enterrement m; F: that's your f.! ça c'est
votre affaire! f. (procession), convoi m funèbre; f.
director, entrepreneur de pompes f funèbres; f. parlour, établissement de pompes funèbres.

funereal [fju:'niəriəl] a lugubre, funèbre; (of voice)
sépulcral.

fungus ['fʌŋgəs] n (pl fungi ['fʌŋgai, 'fʌndʒai]) champignon m; Med: fongus m. 'fungicide [-dʒi-] n
fongicide m.

funicular [fju'nikjulər] a & n funiculaire (m).

funk [fʌŋk] F: 1. n frousse f; to be in a blue f., avoir la
frousse, une peur bleue 2. vtr & i to f. (it), caner, se
dégonfler; to f. doing sth, avoir peur de faire qch.
'funky a F: amusant, chouette.

funnel ['fʌnl] n (a) (for pouring liquids) entonnoir m
(b) cheminée f (d'un bateau).

funny ['fʌni] a (-ier, -iest) (a) drôle; comique, amusant; he's trying to be f., il veut faire de l'esprit (b)
curieux, bizarre; a f. idea, une drôle d'idée; he's f.
that way, il est comme ça; there's sth f. about it, il y a
qch de louche dans cette affaire; this butter tastes f.,
ce beurre a un drôle de goût; F: I came over all f., je
me suis senti tout chose; (that's) f.! voilà qui est
curieux! F: no f. business! pas d'histoires! pas de
blagues! 'funnily adv drôlement; comiquement;
curieusement; f. enough, chose curieuse. 'funnybone n F: petit juif.

fur [fɜːr] 1. n (a) fourrure f; poil m (de lapin); pl peaux
fpl (d'animaux); f. coat, manteau de fourrure; Fig: to
make the f. fly, faire une scène violente (b) (in kettle)
tartre m; (in bottles) dépôt m 2. vtr (furred) entartrer,
incruster; furred tongue, langue chargée. 'fur-
'lined a (manteau) doublé de fourrure; (gant)
fourré. 'furrier n fourreur m. 'furry a (-ier, -iest)
(animal) à poil; (tissu) pelucheux.

furbish ['fɜːbiʃ] vtr to f. (up), (i) fourbir, polir (ii)
remettre à neuf.

furious ['fjuːriəs] a furieux; (of look) furibond; (of
battle) acharné; to be f. with s.o., être furieux contre
qn; to become f., entrer en fureur; at a f. pace, à une
allure folle; fast and f., frénétique. 'furiously adv
furieusement; avec acharnement; (conduire) à une
allure folle.

furl [fɜːl] vtr serrer, ferler (une voile); rouler (un
parapluie).

furlough ['fɜːlou] n Mil: congé m, permission f.

furnace ['fɜːnis] n fourneau m, four m; (hot place)
fournaise f; blast f., haut fourneau.

furnish ['fɜːniʃ] vtr (a) fournir, donner; pourvoir; to f.
s.o. with sth, fournir, pourvoir, munir, qn de qch (b)
meubler (une maison); furnished flat, appartement
meublé; to live in a furnished flat, loger en meublé.
'furnishings npl ameublement m; soft f., tapis mpl
et rideaux mpl; furnishing fabric, tissu
d'ameublement.

furniture ['fɜːnitʃər] n meubles mpl, mobilier m; piece
of f., meuble; f. polish, encaustique f; f. shop, magasin
d'ameublement; f. remover, déménageur m.

furore [fjuə'rɔːri], NAm: furor ['fjuərɔːr] n enthousiasme démesuré; to create a f., faire fureur.

furrow ['fʌrou] 1. n sillon m; (on forehead) ride
profonde 2. vtr labourer (la terre); sillonner (une
surface); rider profondément (le front).

further ['fɜːðər] 1. adv (a) = farther 1. (b) davantage, plus; until you hear f., jusqu'à nouvel avis; to go
no f. into sth, en rester là; f. back, à une période plus
reculée (c) d'ailleurs, de plus 2. a (a) = farther 2. (b)
additionnel, supplémentaire; without f. loss of time,

without f. ado, sans autre perte de temps; sans plus de cérémonie; sans plus; **on f. consideration,** après plus ample réflexion; **one or two f. details,** encore un ou deux détails; **f. education,** enseignement postscolaire **3.** *vtr* avancer, favoriser (un projet). **further-'more** *adv* en outre, de plus. **'furthermost** *a* (endroit) le plus lointain, le plus éloigné. **'furthest** *a & adv* = **farthest.**

furtive ['fə:tiv] *a (of glance)* furtif; *(of pers)* sournois. **'furtively** *adv* furtivement.

fury ['fjuəri] *n* furie *f*, fureur *f*; violence *f* (du vent); **to get into a f.,** entrer en fureur; *F:* **to work like f.,** travailler comme un fou.

furze [fə:z] *n Bot:* ajonc *m.*

fuse[1] [fju:z] *n* fusée *f* (d'obus); amorce *f*; *Min:* **(safety) f.,** cordeau *m.*

fuse[2] **I.** *n El:* fusible *m*; plomb *m*; **f. box,** boîte à fusibles; **f. wire,** (fil *m*) fusible; **the f. has gone, blown,** le plomb a sauté; **to blow a f.,** faire sauter un plomb. **II.** *v* **1.** *vtr (a)* fondre (un métal); fusionner, amalgamer (deux partis) *(b) El:* faire sauter les plombs d'un circuit) **2.** *vi (a) (of metals)* fondre; *(of parties)* fusionner, s'amalgamer *(b) El:* **the lights have fused,** les plombs ont sauté. **fused** *a* pourvu d'un fusible.

fuselage ['fju:zəla:ʒ] *n Av:* fuselage *m.*

fusilier [fju:zə'liər] *n Mil:* fusilier *m.*

fusillade [fju:zi'leid] *n* fusillade *f.*

fusion ['fju:ʒn] *n* fusion *f*; fonte *f* (d'un métal); fusionnement *m* (de deux entreprises); fusion (de deux partis).

fuss [fʌs] **1.** *n* bruit exagéré; *(of pers)* façons *fpl*; **a lot of f. (and bother) about nothing,** beaucoup de bruit pour

rien; **what's all the f. about!** qu'est-ce que c'est que toutes ces histoires? **to make a f.,** faire un tas d'histoires; faire des cérémonies; **to make a f. of s.o.,** être aux petits soins pour qn **2.** *v (a) vi* faire des histoires, des embarras; **to f. about, around,** faire l'affairé; **to f. over s.o.,** être aux petits soins pour qn *(b) vtr* tracasser, agiter (qn); *F:* **I'm not fussed,** ça ne me dit rien. **'fussily** *adv* d'une manière tatillonne; (habillé) avec trop de recherche. **'fussiness** *n* façons. **'fusspot** *n F:* tatillon, -onne. **'fussy** *a* **(-ier, -iest)** tatillon; tracassier; méticuleux; *(of style, dress)* trop pomponné; **don't be so f.!** ne soyez pas si difficile! **(about,** sur).

fusty ['fʌsti] *a* **(-ier, -iest)** (odeur) de renfermé; (pièce) qui sent le renfermé. **'fustiness** *n* odeur *f* de renfermé.

futile ['fju:tail] *a* futile, vain. **fu'tility** [-'til-] *n* futilité *f.*

future ['fju:tʃər] **1.** *a* futur; *(of events)* à venir; **my f. wife,** ma future; **at some f. date,** dans l'avenir; *Gram:* **f. tense,** temps futur **2.** *n (a)* avenir *m*; **in (the) f.,** à l'avenir; **in the near f.,** dans un proche avenir; **there's no f. in it,** cela n'a pas d'avenir *(b) Gram:* (temps) futur (*m*); **f. perfect,** futur antérieur; **in the f.,** au futur. **futu'ristic** *a* futuriste.

fuze [fju:z] *n & v NAm:* = **fuse.**

fuzz [fʌz] *n (a) (on fabric)* peluches *fpl*; *(on skin)* duvet *m (b)* cheveux crêpelés, crépus *(c) coll P:* **the f.,** la police, les flics *m.* **'fuzziness** *n* crêpelure *f* (des cheveux); *Art:* flou *m*; manque *m* de netteté. **'fuzzy** *a* **(-ier, -iest)** *(of hair)* crêpelé, crépu, frisotté; *(of ideas, view)* confus; *Phot:* flou.

G

G, g [dʒiː] n (a) (la lettre) G, g m (b) Mus: sol m;
G-string (i) Mus: corde de sol (ii) Cl: cache-sexe m inv.

g abbr gram(s).

gab [gæb] n F: **to have the gift of the g.**, avoir la langue
bien pendue.

gabardine, gaberdine [gæbə'diːn] n gabardine f.

gabble ['gæbl] **1.** n bredouillement m **2.** v (a) vi
bredouiller; **don't g.**, ne parlez pas si vite (b) vtr **to g.
(out)**, débiter (un discours) à toute vitesse.

gable ['geibl] n g. **(end)**, pignon m.

gad [gæd] vi **(gadded) to g. about**, courir la ville, le
monde.

gadget ['gædʒit] n gadget m; F: machin m, truc m.
'gadgetry n gadgets mpl; F: trucs mpl.

Gaelic ['geilik] a & n gaélique (m).

gaff¹ [gæf] Fish: **1.** n gaffe f **2.** vtr gaffer.

gaff² n F: **to blow the g.**, vendre la mèche.

gaffe [gæf] n gaffe f, bourde f.

gaffer ['gæfər] n (a) vieux m (b) P: contremaître m; (in
pub) patron m.

gag [gæg] **1.** n (a) bâillon m (b) F: plaisanterie f; Cin:
gag m **2.** v **(gagged)** (a) vtr bâillonner (b) vi (i) F:
plaisanter (ii) avoir des haut-le-cœur.

gaga ['gɑːgɑː] a F: gaga; gâteux.

gage [geidʒ] n & v NAm: = **gauge**.

gaiety ['geiəti] n gaieté f.

gaily ['geili] adv gaiement; allègrement; **g. coloured**,
aux couleurs vives.

gain [gein] **1.** n (a) gain m, profit m, avantage m,
bénéfice m (b) accroissement m, augmentation f;
hausse f (de valeur) **2.** vtr & i (a) gagner, acquérir; **you
will g. nothing by it**, vous n'y gagnerez rien; **to g.
weight**, prendre du poids; **to g. (in) popularity**, gagner
de la popularité; **to g. the upper hand**, prendre le
dessus; **to g. (ground) on s.o.**, gagner du terrain sur qn;
(in race) **to g. on s.o.**, prendre de l'avance sur qn (b) (of
clock) prendre de l'avance; **to g. five minutes a day**,
avancer de cinq minutes par jour. **'gainful** a
profitable; rémunérateur; (emploi) rémunéré.
gain'say vtr (-'said [-'sed]) contredire, démentir.

gait [geit] n démarche f; façon f de marcher.

gaiter ['geitər] n Cl: guêtre f.

gala ['gɑːlə] n fête f, gala m; Sp: grand concours (de
natation).

galaxy ['gæləksi] n (pl galaxies) galaxie f. **ga'lactic**
a galactique.

gale [geil] n coup m de vent; **it's blowing a g.**, le vent
souffle en tempête; **g. force winds**, vents forts; **g.
warning**, avis de tempête; **gales of laughter**, accès mpl
de rires.

gal(l) abbr gallon(s).

gall¹ [gɔːl] n (a) fiel m; bile f; **g. bladder**, vésicule f
biliaire (b) F: effronterie f, culot m. **'gallstone** n
calcul m biliaire.

gall² n Bot: **g. (nut)**, (noix f de) galle f.

gall³ vtr irriter; exaspérer; froisser (qn). **'galling** ‹
irritant, exaspérant; blessant, humiliant.

gallant ['gælənt] a (a) courageux, brave, vaillant (b
(of man) (occ [gə'lænt]) galant. **'gallantly** adv (a
bravement; courageusement (b) (occ [gə'læntli]
galamment. **'gallantry** n (a) bravoure f, vaillance
(b) galanterie f.

galleon ['gæliən] n ANau: galion m.

gallery ['gæləri] n (pl galleries) (a) galerie f; Th
(troisième) galerie; (in Parliament) tribune f (de la
presse, réservée au public); Fig: **to play to the g.**, joue
pour la galerie (b) (art) g., galerie; musée m (d'art)

galley ['gæli] n (a) yole f (d'amiral) (b) Hist: galère f (b
slave, galérien m; Nau: Av: cuisine f (c) Typ: galée f; g
(proof), (épreuve f en) placard m.

Gallic ['gælik] a (a) Hist: gaulois (b) français
'gallicism n Ling: gallicisme m.

gallivant ['gælivænt] vi courir la ville, le monde.

gallon ['gælən] n gallon m (=4,5 litres; US: = 3,78
litres).

gallop ['gæləp] **1.** n galop m; **to go for a g.**, faire une
galopade; **(at) full g.**, au grand galop **2.** v **(galloped**
(a) vi galoper; aller au galop; **to g. away, off**, partir au
galop (b) vtr faire aller (un cheval) au galop
'galloping a (cheval) au galop; **g. inflation**, in
flation galopante.

gallows ['gælouz] n potence f, gibet m.

galore [gə'lɔːr] adv en abondance, à profusion; ‹
gogo.

galvanize ['gælvənaiz] vtr galvaniser; **to g. s.o. int**
action, galvaniser qn. **galvani'zation** n galvani
sation f. **galva'nometer** n galvanomètre m.

Gambia (the) [ðə'gæmbiə] Prn Geog: la Gambie.

gambit ['gæmbit] n Chess: gambit m; Fig: manœuvr
f.

gamble ['gæmbl] **1.** n (a) jeu m de hasard (b
spéculation f; affaire f de chance **2.** vi jouer d
l'argent; **to g. on a throw of the dice**, miser sur u
coup de dé; **to g. on the Stock Exchange**, agioter; **to g
on a rise in prices**, jouer à la hausse; **she's gambling o**
getting home by 8 o'clock, elle compte rentrer avant :
heures. **'gamble a'way** vtr perdre (une fortune) au
jeu. **'gambler** n joueur, -euse; **g. on the Stock
Exchange**, spéculateur, -trice. **'gambling** n le jeu; g
debts, dettes du jeu; **g. den**, maison de jeu; tripot m

gambol ['gæmbəl] vi **(gambolled)** gambade
s'ébattre.

game¹ [geim] **1.** n (a) jeu m; amusement m, divertisse
ment m; **g. of skill, of chance**, jeu d'adresse, de hasard
card games, jeux de cartes; **Olympic games**, jeu
olympiques; Sch: **games**, sports mpl; **games teache**
professeur d'éducation sportive; **he's good at games**
c'est un sportif; **to play the g.**, jouer franc jeu; **to bea**
s.o. at his own g., battre qn avec ses propres armes
two can play at that g., à bon chat bon rat; Fig: **what'**

his g.? où veut-il en venir? **I can see your g.**, je vous vois venir; **to spoil s.o.'s g.**, déjouer les plans de qn; **the game's up**, l'affaire est dans l'eau (b) partie f (de cartes); manche f (d'une partie de cartes); match m (de football); *Ten:* **g., set and match**, jeu, set et partie (c) gibier m; **big g.**, (i) gros gibier (ii) (*esp in Africa*) les grands fauves; **g. birds**, gibier à plumes; **g. reserve**, parc à gibier; *Cu:* **g. pie**, pâté de gibier en croûte; *Fig:* **he's fair g.**, c'est une bonne proie **2.** a courageux, résolu; **to be g.**, avoir du cran; **I'm g.!** d'accord! **g. for anything**, prêt à tout, capable de tout. **'gamekeeper** n garde-chasse m. **'games-manship** n art m de gagner. **'gaming** n jeu m; **g. table**, table de jeu.

game² a **g. leg**, jambe boiteuse.

gamma ['gæmə] n gamma m; **g. rays**, rayons gamma.

gammon ['gæmən] n (quartier m de) jambon salé ou fumé.

gammy ['gæmi] a F: **g. leg**, jambe boiteuse.

gamut ['gæmət] n gamme f.

gander ['gændər] n *Orn:* jars m.

gang [gæŋ] n équipe f (d'ouvriers); convoi m (de prisonniers); bande f, gang m (de voleurs); **the whole g.**, toute la bande. **'gangland** n monde criminel; le milieu. **'gangplank** n passerelle f. **'gangster** n gangster m. **'gang 'up** vi s'allier (**with**, avec); se liguer (**on**, contre). **'gangway** n passage m; couloir (central) (d'autobus); allée f (de cinéma); *Nau:* passerelle f de service; **g. please!** dégagez, s'il vous plaît!

gangling ['gæŋgliŋ] a dégingandé.

ganglion ['gæŋgliən] n *Anat:* ganglion m.

gangrene ['gæŋgriːn] n *Med:* gangrène f. **'gangrenous** a gangreneux.

gannet ['gænit] n *Orn:* fou m (de Bassan).

gantry ['gæntri] n (pl **gantries**) pont (roulant) (à signaux); portique (roulant, *Space:* de lancement).

gaol [dʒeil] **1.** n prison f; **in g.**, en prison; **he's been in g. for five years**, il a fait cinq ans de prison **2.** vtr mettre (qn) en prison. **'gaolbird** n F: récidiviste mf. **'gaolbreak** n évasion f de prison. **'gaoler** n gardien, -ienne, de prison; *Hist:* geôlier, -ière.

gap [gæp] n trou m; trouée f, ouverture f; vide m (dans une haie); blanc m (sur une page); brèche f (dans un mur); jour m (entre des planches); interstice m (entre des rideaux); *El:* distance f, intervalle m (entre les électrodes); écartement m (des contacts); **his death leaves a g.**, sa mort laisse un vide; **the gaps in his education**, les lacunes f de son éducation; **trade g.**, déficit commercial; **credibility g.**, crise f de confiance; **age g.**, écart m d'âge; **g. of 20 years**, intervalle de vingt ans; **generation g.**, fossé m entre les générations; **to fill (in, up), to stop, a g.**, boucher un trou, combler un vide.

gape [geip] vi (a) bâiller; (*of thg*) **to g. (open)**, s'ouvrir (tout grand); (*of hole*) être béant; **boards that g.**, planches qui ne joignent pas (b) (*of pers*) rester bouche bée; **to g. at s.o.**, regarder qn bouche bée. **'gaping** a béant.

garage ['gærɑːʒ] **1.** n garage m; **g. proprietor**, garagiste m **2.** vtr garer; remiser (une voiture).

garb [gɑːb] n *Lit: & Hum:* costume m.

garbage ['gɑːbidʒ] n (a) immondices fpl; détritus mpl; déchets mpl (b) *esp NAm:* ordures ménagères; **g. can**

(*Br* = **dustbin**), poubelle f; **g. truck** (*Br* = **dustcart**), camion aux ordures, des éboueurs; **g. collector** (*Br* = **dustman**), éboueur m.

garble ['gɑːbl] vtr fausser (une citation); dénaturer (des faits); altérer (un texte); **garbled account**, compte rendu embrouillé, trompeur.

garden ['gɑːdn] **1.** n jardin m; **kitchen g., vegetable g.**, (jardin) potager (m); **g. of remembrance** = cimetière m d'un crématorium; **zoological gardens**, jardin zoologique; *F:* **to lead s.o. up the g. path**, faire marcher qn; **(public) garden(s)**, jardin public, parc m; **g. centre**, pépinière f; **g. party**, garden-party f; **g. produce**, produits maraîchers; **g. suburb, g. city**, cité-jardin f; **g. tools**, outils de jardinage **2.** vi jardiner; faire du jardinage. **'gardener** n jardinier, -ière; **landscape g.**, jardinier paysagiste; **market g., NAm: truck g.**, maraîcher, -ère. **'gardening** n jardinage; horticulture f; **market g., NAm: truck g.**, maraîchage m.

gargle ['gɑːgl] *Med:* **1.** n gargarisme m **2.** vi se gargariser.

gargoyle ['gɑːgɔil] n gargouille f.

garish ['gɛəriʃ] a voyant; (lumière) crue.

garland ['gɑːlənd] n guirlande f; couronne f (de fleurs).

garlic ['gɑːlik] n ail m; **g. sausage**, saucisson à l'ail. **'garlicky** a qui sent, qui a le goût de, l'ail.

garment ['gɑːmənt] n vêtement m.

garnet ['gɑːnit] n grenat m.

garnish ['gɑːniʃ] **1.** n garniture f **2.** vtr garnir (un plat). **'garnishing** n garniture f (d'un plat).

garret ['gærət] n mansarde f, soupente f.

garrison ['gærisən] **1.** n garnison f; **g. town**, ville de garnison **2.** vtr mettre (des troupes) en garnison; **to g. a town**, (i) mettre une garnison (ii) être en garnison, dans une ville.

garrulous ['gærələs, -rjul-] a loquace, bavard. **'garrulously** adv avec volubilité.

garter ['gɑːtər] n (a) jarretière f; fixe-chaussette m; *Knit:* **g. stitch**, point mousse (b) *NAm:* (*for woman's stocking*) (*Br* = **suspender**) jarretelle f.

gas [gæs] **1.** n (pl **gases**) (a) gaz m; **natural g.**, gaz naturel; **g. industry**, industrie du gaz; **cooking with g.**, cuisine au gaz; **g. cooker**, cuisinière à gaz; **g. fire**, radiateur à gaz; **g. lighter**, (i) allume-gaz m inv (ii) briquet m (à gaz); **g. meter**, compteur à gaz; **g. main, g. pipe**, tuyau à gaz; (*pers*) **g. fitter**, gazier m; poseur, ajusteur, d'appareils à gaz; *Dent: Med:* **to have g.**, se faire anesthésier; **tear g., CS g.**, gaz lacrymogène; **g. chamber**, chambre à gaz (b) *NAm:* essence f (c) **g. station**, station-service f; **to step on the g.**, marcher à pleins gaz **2.** v (**gassed**) (a) vtr asphyxier, *Mil:* gazer (qn); **to g. oneself**, s'asphyxier (b) vi F: bavarder. **'gasbag** n F: bavard, -arde. **'gaseous** a gazeux. **'gas-fired** a (chauffage central) au gaz. **'gaslight** n **by g.**, à lumière du gaz. **'gasman** n (pl -**men**) employé m du gaz. **'gasmask** n masque m à gaz. **'gasoline** n *NAm:* essence f. **gas'ometer** n gazomètre m. **'gassy** a (-ier, -iest) gazeux. **'gasworks** npl usine f à gaz.

gash [gæʃ] **1.** n coupure f, entaille f; (*on face*) balafre f **2.** vtr couper, entailler; balafrer (le visage).

gasket ['gæskit] n *MecE:* joint m d'étanchéité; garniture f (de joint); *ICE:* **cylinder head g.**, joint de culasse.

gasp [gɑːsp] 1. *n* hoquet *m* (de surprise); **to be at one's last g.,** (i) être à l'agonie (ii) être à bout de souffle 2. *vtr & i* **the news made me g.,** cette nouvelle m'a coupé le souffle; **to g. for breath,** haleter, suffoquer; **to g. out sth,** dire qch d'une voix entrecoupée.

gastric [ˈɡæstrik] *a* gastrique; **g. flu,** grippe gastro-intestinale; **g. ulcer,** ulcère de l'estomac. **gaˈstritis** *n* gastrite *f.* **gastroenteˈritis** *n* gastro-entérite *f.* **ˈgastronome** *n* gastronome *mf.* **gastroˈnomic** *a* gastronomique. **gaˈstronomy** *n* gastronomie *f.*

gate [ɡeit] *n* (*a*) porte *f*; portail *m*; (*in garden*) (*wooden*) barrière *f*; (*iron*) grille *f* d'entrée; (*at sportsground*) entrée *f*; *HydE:* (*of lock*) vanne *f* (*b*) (*number of spectators*) public *m* (à un match); **g. (money),** recette *f*; entrées *fpl.* **ˈgatecrash** *vtr & i* resquiller. **ˈgatecrasher** *n* resquilleur, -euse. **ˈgate-leg(ged)** *a* (table) à abattants. **ˈgatepost** *n* montant *m* de barrière; *F:* **between you, me and the g.,** soit dit entre nous. **ˈgateway** *n* porte (monumentale); portail *m.*

gâteau [ˈɡætou] *n* (*pl* gâteaux [-ouz]) gros gâteau à la crème.

gather [ˈɡæðər] 1. *vtr* (*a*) rassembler; assembler; recueillir (des choses); **to g. (in, up, together),** ramasser (des papiers); cueillir (des fleurs); récolter (des fruits); **to g. speed,** prendre de la vitesse; **to g. strength,** reprendre des forces; **to g. one's thoughts,** se recueillir; **he gathered her (up) in his arms,** il l'a serrée dans ses bras (*b*) *Needlew:* froncer (une jupe) (*c*) conclure; **I g. that,** je crois comprendre, je déduis, que 2. *vi* (*a*) **to g. (together),** se rassembler; se réunir, s'assembler; (*of thgs*) s'accumuler, s'amonceler, s'amasser; **a crowd gathered,** une foule s'est formée; **g. round!** approchez-vous! **a storm is gathering,** un orage se prépare. **ˈgathered** *a Needlew:* froncé; (jupe) à fronces. **ˈgathering** *n* (*a*) assemblée *f*; family *g.*, réunion *f* de famille; **we were a large g.,** nous étions nombreux (*b*) *Needlew:* (*also* gathers) fronces *fpl.*

gauche [ɡouʃ] *a* gauche, maladroit.

gaudy [ˈɡɔːdi] *a* (-ier, -iest) voyant, criard, éclatant; de mauvais goût. **ˈgaudily** *adv* de manière voyante; (peint) en couleurs criardes.

gauge, *NAm:* gage [ɡeidʒ] 1. *n* (*a*) calibre *m* (d'un écrou); *Rail:* écartement *m* (de la voie); **narrow g.,** voie étroite (*b*) (*instrument*) indicateur *m*; **fuel g.,** jauge *f* d'essence; **oil pressure g.,** manomètre *m* de pression d'huile; **tyre (pressure) g.,** indicateur de pression des pneus; manomètre pour pneus 2. *vtr* calibrer (un écrou); jauger, mesurer; prévoir (l'avenir); **to g. s.o.'s capacities,** estimer, jauger, les capacités de qn.

Gaul [ɡɔːl] *Hist:* 1. *Prn* Gaule *f* 2. *n* Gaulois, -oise.

gaunt [ɡɔːnt] *a* maigre, décharné; (*of place*) lugubre.

gauntlet [ˈɡɔːntlit] *n* gant *m* à crispin, à manchette; *Arm:* gantelet *m*; *Fig:* **to run the g.,** soutenir un feu roulant (**of criticism,** de critiques adverses).

gauze [ɡɔːz] *n* gaze *f.*

gave [ɡeiv] *see* **give.**

gavel [ˈɡævl] *n* marteau *m* de commissaire-priseur.

gawky [ˈɡɔːki] *a* dégingandé, gauche.

gay [ɡei] 1. *a* gai; (rire) enjoué; **to lead a g. life,** mener une vie de plaisir(s) 2. *a & n F:* homosexuel, -elle.

gaze [ɡeiz] 1. *n* regard *m* fixe 2. *vi* regarder fixement; **to g. at sth,** contempler qch.

gazelle [ɡəˈzel] *n Z:* gazelle *f.*

gazette [ɡəˈzet] *n* journal officiel; (*title*) gazette *f.* **gaˈzetteer** *n* répertoire *m* géographique.

GB *abbr* Great Britain.

GCE *abbr* General Certificate of Education.

gear [ɡiər] *n* (*a*) équipement *m*, appareil *m*; matériel *m* (de camping); attirail *m* (de pêche); *F:* **my g.,** (i) mes effets *m*, mes bagages *m* (ii) mes vêtements *m*, mes fringues *fpl* (*b*) *MecE:* mécanisme *m*; *Av:* **landing g.,** train *m* d'atterrissage (*c*) *MecE:* **(driving, transmission) g.,** transmission *f*, commande *f*; engrenages *mpl* (de transmission); **in g.,** en prise; embrayé; **out of g.,** hors de prise; débrayé; *Aut:* **first, bottom, g.,** première vitesse; **top g.,** prise (directe); **to change,** *NAm:* **shift, g.,** changer de vitesse 2. *vtr* **to g. up, down,** multiplier, démultiplier (un moteur); **wages geared to the cost of living,** salaires indexés au coût de la vie; **book geared to the needs of students,** livre adapté aux besoins des étudiants; *F:* **to be geared up for sth,** être préparé pour, prêt à, qch. **ˈgearbox** *n* (*pl* -boxes) *Aut:* boîte *f* de vitesses. **ˈgearstick,** *NAm:* **-shift** *n* (*also* gear lever) levier *m* de vitesse. **ˈgearwheel** *n* (roue *f* d')engrenage *m*; (*on bicycle*) pignon *m.*

gee [dʒiː] *int* (*a*) (*to horse*) **g. up!** hue! (*b*) *esp NAm:* **g. (whiz)!** ça alors!

geese [ɡiːs] *see* **goose.**

geezer [ˈɡiːzər] *n F:* **(old) g.,** vieux type.

gel [dʒel] 1. *n* gelée *f*; *Ch:* colloïde *m* 2. *vi* **(gelled)** (*of jelly*) prendre; (*of ideas*) se former, prendre. **ˈgelatin(e)** *n* gélatine *f.* **geˈlatinous** *a* gélatineux.

gelding [ˈɡeldiŋ] *n* (cheval *m*) hongre (*m*).

gelignite [ˈdʒelignait] *n* gélignite *f.*

gem [dʒem] *n* pierre précieuse; joyau *m*; *Fig:* (*of pers, mistake*) perle *f.* **ˈgemstone** *n* pierre gemme.

Gemini [ˈdʒeminai] *Prnpl Astr:* Gémeaux *mpl.*

gen [dʒen] *n F:* renseignements *mpl*, tuyaux *mpl.*

gender [ˈdʒendər] *n* genre *m.*

gene [dʒiːn] *n Biol:* gène *m.*

genealogy [dʒiːniˈælədʒi] *n* généalogie *f.* **geneaˈlogical** *a* généalogique. **geneˈalogist** *n* généalogiste *mf.*

general [ˈdʒenərəl] 1. *a* général; (effet) d'ensemble; **as a g. rule,** *adv phr* **in g.,** en règle générale; en général; **the rain has been pretty g.,** il a plu un peu partout; **g. election,** élections législatives; **in g. use,** (d'usage) courant; **the g. public,** le grand public; **g. knowledge,** connaissances générales; **g. store(s), shop,** magasin de village 2. *n* général *m.* **geneˈrality** *n* (*pl* -ies) généralité *f.* **generaliˈzation** *n* généralisation *f.* **ˈgeneralize** *vtr & i* généraliser. **ˈgenerally** *adv* généralement, en général; **g. speaking,** d'une façon générale. **ˈgeneral-ˈpurpose** *a* (à) toutes fins, (pour) tous usages; (d'usage) universel.

generate [ˈdʒenəreit] *vtr* générer; engendrer; produire (de la chaleur); *El:* **generating station,** centrale électrique. **geneˈration** *n* génération *f*; **first g., second g., Swiss,** suisse depuis une génération, depuis deux générations. **ˈgenerator** *n El: etc:* génératrice *f*; générateur *m.*

generic [dʒiˈnerik] *a* générique.

generous [ˈdʒenərəs] *a* généreux; **to take a g. helping,** se servir amplement. **geneˈrosity** [-ˈrɒsiti] *n* générosité f. **'generously** adv généreusement; (agir) magnanimement.

genesis ['dʒenəsis] n genèse f.

genetic [dʒi'netik] a génétique. **ge'neticist** n généticien, -ienne. **ge'netics** npl génétique f.

Geneva [dʒə'ni:və] Prn Geog: Genève f; **Lake G.,** le lac Léman.

genial ['dʒi:niəl] a cordial; (climat) doux; (feu) réconfortant. **geni'ality** n bonne humeur. **'genially** adv affablement.

genital ['dʒenitl] a génital. **'genitals** npl organes génitaux (externes).

genitive ['dʒenitiv] a & n Gram: génitif (m).

genius ['dʒi:niəs] n (pl **geniuses**) génie m; **to have a g. for business,** avoir le génie des affaires; **to have a g. for doing sth,** avoir le don de faire qch; **work of g.,** œuvre géniale.

Genoa ['dʒenouə] Prn Geog: Gênes f. **Geno'ese** a & n génois, -oise.

genocide ['dʒenousaid] n génocide m.

gent [dʒent] n F: monsieur m; Com: **gents'** footwear, chaussures pour hommes; PN: (public lavatory) **gents,** hommes; messieurs; **where's the gents** (NAm: **the men's room)?** où sont les WC?

genteel [dʒen'ti:l] a maniéré; affecté. **gen'tility** n manières affectées.

gentle ['dʒentl] a doux; (coup) léger; (exercice) modéré; (réprimande) peu sévère. **'gentleness** n douceur f. **'gently** adv doucement; **g. does it!** allez-y doucement!

gentleman ['dʒentlmən] n (pl **gentlemen**) (a) homme bien élevé; gentleman m; **g. farmer,** gentleman-farmer m (b) monsieur; (to audience) **ladies and gentlemen!** mesdames, mesdemoiselles, messieurs! PN: (public lavatory) **gentlemen,** hommes; messieurs; **gentlemen's hairdresser,** coiffeur pour hommes. **'gentlemanly** a bien élevé; (air) distingué.

gentry ['dʒentri] n petite noblesse; **landed g.,** aristocratie terrienne.

genuine ['dʒenjuin] a (a) authentique, véritable; Com: (article) garanti d'origine (b) (pers) sincère; franc; (acheteur) sérieux. **'genuinely** adv authentiquement; sincèrement.

genus ['dʒi:nəs] n (pl **genera** ['dʒenərə]) genre m.

geography [dʒi'ɔgrəfi] n géographie f. **ge'ographer** n géographe mf. **geographical** [dʒiə'græfikl] a géographique.

geology [dʒi'ɔlədʒi] n géologie f. **geo'logical** a géologique. **ge'ologist** n géologue mf.

geometry [dʒi'ɔmətri] n géométrie f. **geo'metrical** [dʒiə'metrikl] a géométrique.

geophysics [dʒiou'fiziks] npl géophysique f.

geranium [dʒə'reiniəm] n géranium m.

geriatric [dʒeri'ætrik] a (salle) des vieillards; **g. medicine,** gériatrie f. **geri'atrics** npl gériatrie.

germ [dʒə:m] n germe m; Med: microbe m; **g. warfare,** guerre bactériologique. **'germ-free** a (milieu) stérile. **'germicide** n germicide m. **'germinate** vtr & i (faire) germer. **germi'nation** n germination f.

Germany ['dʒə:məni] Prn Geog: Allemagne f; **West G.,** Allemagne de l'ouest; **East G.,** Allemagne de l'est. **'German 1.** a allemand; **West G., East G.,** ouest-allemand, est-allemand **2.** n (a) Allemand, -ande (b)

Ling: allemand m. **Ger'manic** a allemand; Hist: Ling: germanique.

gerund ['dʒerənd] n Gram: gérondif m.

gestation [dʒes'teiʃn] n gestation f.

gesticulate [dʒes'tikjuleit] vi gesticuler. **gesticu'lation** n gesticulation f.

gesture ['dʒestʃər] **1.** n geste m **2.** vi exprimer par, faire, des gestes.

get [get] v (pt & pp got [gɔt]; pp NAm: also **gotten**) **1.** vtr (a) (se) procurer; obtenir; **to g. sth for s.o.,** procurer qch à qn; **to g. sth to eat,** (i) trouver de quoi manger (ii) manger qch (au restaurant); **where did you g. that?** où avez-vous trouvé, acheté, cela? **I got this car cheap,** j'ai eu cette voiture bon marché (b) acquérir, gagner; **I'll see what I can g. for it,** je verrai ce qu'on m'en donnera; **to g. 10% interest,** recevoir 10% d'intérêt; **to g. nothing out of it,** n'y rien gagner; **if I g. the time,** si j'ai le temps; **to g. one's own way,** faire valoir sa volonté (c) recevoir (une lettre); attraper (un rhume); **he gets his shyness from his mother,** il tient sa timidité de sa mère; **he got a bullet in the shoulder,** il a reçu une balle dans l'épaule; (on radio) **we can't g. Moscow,** nous ne pouvons pas avoir Moscou; F: **to g. the sack,** être congédié; **to g. ten years,** attraper dix ans de prison (d) prendre, attraper (une bête); **we'll g. them yet!** on les aura! **you've got me this time!** cette fois-ci vous m'avez eu! (e) émouvoir (qn); **that really gets me, gets my goat,** ça m'énerve (f) F: comprendre; **I don't g. you,** je ne vous comprends pas; **g. me?** tu saisis? tu piges? **you've got it!** vous y êtes! (g) **to** (go and) **g. sth, s.o.,** aller chercher qch, qn; **how can I g. it to you?** comment vous le faire parvenir? **to g. the children to bed,** faire coucher les enfants; **that gets us nowhere, doesn't g. us anywhere,** cela ne nous mène à rien; **to g. lunch (ready),** préparer le déjeuner (h) **to g. s.o. to do sth,** faire faire qch à, par, qn; **to g. the house painted,** faire repeindre la maison; **to g. oneself noticed,** se faire remarquer; **g. him to read it,** faites-le-lui lire; **I can't g. the door to shut,** je n'arrive pas à fermer la porte; **to g. s.o. to agree,** décider qn à consentir; **to g. one's work finished,** venir à bout de son travail **2.** **to have got** (a) avoir; **what have you got there?** qu'avez-vous là? **I haven't got any,** je n'en ai pas (b) être obligé (de faire qch); **it's got to be done,** il faut que cela se fasse **3.** vi (a) devenir (riche); **to g. old,** devenir vieux; vieillir; **I'm getting used to it,** je commence à m'y habituer; **it's getting late,** il se fait tard; **to g. married,** se marier; **to g. dressed,** s'habiller; **to g. killed,** se faire tuer; **let's g. going!** allons-y! en route! **to g. talking to s.o.,** se mettre à parler à qn; entrer en conversation avec qn (b) arriver, se rendre (à un endroit); **how do you g. there?** comment fait-on pour y aller? **he'll g. here tomorrow,** il arrivera demain; **we're not getting anywhere, we're getting nowhere (fast),** nous n'aboutissons à rien; **to g. within s.o.'s reach,** se mettre à la portée de qn; **where have you got to?** où en êtes-vous (dans votre travail)? **where has he got to?** qu'est-ce qu'il est devenu? **he got as far as saying,** il a été jusqu'à dire; **to g. to know,** (i) faire la connaissance de (qn) (ii) apprendre (qch); **when you g. to know him,** quand on le connaît mieux; **you'll g. to like him,** tu finiras par l'aimer. **'get a'bout, a'round** vi circuler; (of pers) se déplacer; (after illness) sortir; (of news) se répandre. **'get a'cross 1.** vtr (a) traverser (une rue); passer (une rivière) (b) faire passer; faire traverser (qn) (c) faire comprendre (qch) (to s.o., à qn) 2. vi traverser, passer; Th: (of play) passer la rampe. 'get a'long vi (a) s'avancer (dans son chemin); **I'd better be getting a.**, il est temps que je parte; F: **g. a. with you!** (i) va-t'en! (ii) allons donc! tu plaisantes! (b) faire des progrès (dans son travail) (c) s'entendre (avec qn). 'get 'at vtr (a) atteindre (un endroit, qn); découvrir (la vérité); **that's what I'm trying to g. at,** c'est là que je veux en venir (b) F: acheter (qn); suborner (un témoin) (c) F: attaquer, dénigrer (qn); s'en prendre à (qn). get-'at-able a F: d'accès facile. 'get a'way 1. vi partir; (of car) démarrer; (of prisoner, etc) s'échapper; **to g. a. from,** quitter (un endroit, qn); F: **g. a. (with you)!** (i) va-t'en! (ii) allons donc! tu plaisantes! **there's no getting a. from it,** il faut bien l'admettre; (of burglar) **to g. a. with £100,** rafler £100; F: **to g. a. with it,** (i) faire accepter qch (ii) s'en tirer à bon compte 2. vtr éloigner, emmener (qn). 'getaway n F: fuite f, évasion f; (of car) démarrage m; **to make one's g.,** s'enfuir; **g. car,** voiture de fuite. 'get 'back 1. vi (a) reculer (b) revenir, retourner; **to g. b. home,** rentrer chez soi; **to g. b. (in)to bed,** se recoucher 2. vtr (a) se faire rendre (qch); retrouver, recouvrer (ses biens); reprendre (ses forces); **to g. one's money b.,** (i) rentrer dans ses fonds (ii) se faire rembourser; F: **to g. one's own b., g. b. at, s.o.,** prendre sa revanche sur qn (b) faire revenir, remettre (qch). 'get 'by vi (a) passer (b) se débrouiller; s'en tirer. 'get 'down vtr & i (a) descendre; **to g. d. to work, to business,** se mettre au travail; **to g. d. to the facts,** en venir aux faits (b) **to g. sth d. (in writing),** noter qch (par écrit) (c) avaler (qch) (d) déprimer, décourager (qn). 'get 'in 1. vtr & i entrer (dans une maison); monter (dans une voiture) 2. vi rentrer (chez soi); (of water) pénétrer; (of train) arriver; Pol: être élu (député) 3. vtr rentrer (la moisson); faire une provision (de charbon, bois); faire venir (qn); **I can't g. a word in (edgeways),** je n'arrive pas à placer un mot; Fig: **to g. one's hand in,** se faire la main; **to g. one's eye in,** ajuster son coup d'œil. 'get 'into vtr (a) entrer dans (une maison); monter dans (une voiture); pénétrer dans (un bois); **to g. i. parliament,** être élu député (b) mettre (des vêtements); **to g. i. a rage,** se mettre en colère; **to g. in the way of sth,** prendre l'habitude de (faire) qch; F: **what's got i. him?** qu'est-ce qu'il a? (b) (faire) (r)entrer (qch) dans (qch). 'get 'off 1. vtr & i descendre (de qch); F: **g. o.!** ôte-toi de là! **g. o. (me)!** lâche-moi! F: **I told him where to g. o.,** je lui ai dit ses quatre vérités 2. vi (a) partir; Av: décoller; **to g. o. (to sleep),** s'endormir (b) se tirer d'affaire; **to g. o. lightly,** s'en tirer à bon compte; **to g. o. with a fine,** en être quitte pour une amende (c) se faire exempter 3. vtr (a) enlever (des vêtements, une tache) (b) expédier (une lettre); faire partir (qn); Fig: **to g. sth o. one's hands,** se débarrasser de qch (c) faire acquitter (un prévenu); tirer (qn) d'affaire. 'get 'on 1. vtr & i· monter (sur une échelle, dans un train) 2. vi (a) **to g. on (with sth),** continuer (qch); **to g. on,** (of pers) se faire vieux; être sur le retour; **to be getting on,** comme ·er à vieillir; être sur le retour; **to be getting on for forty,** friser la quarantaine; **time's getting on,** l'heure avance; **it's getting on for midnight,** il est presque minuit (b) faire des progrès; réussir (dans la vie); **how are you getting on?** comment allez-vous?

how did you g. on in your exam? comment votre examen a-t-il marché? **I can't g. on without him,** je ne peux pas me passer de lui (c) s'entendre (with s.o., avec qn) 3. vtr mettre (des vêtements). 'get 'onto vtr (a) monter sur (une échelle); monter dans (un train); **we got o. (the subject of) divorce,** nous en sommes venus à parler du divorce; **to g. s.o. o. a subject,** amener qn à parler d'un sujet (b) F: contacter (qn) (c) F: découvrir le vrai caractère de (qn). 'get 'out 1. vtr sortir (qch); arracher (un clou); tirer (un bouchon); enlever (une tache); faire sortir (qn); emprunter (un livre) (**from the library,** à la bibliothèque); prendre (qch) (**from a drawer,** dans un tiroir); **to g. nothing o. of it,** n'y rien gagner 2. vi (a) sortir (**of sth,** de qch); descendre (**of a train,** d'un train); s'échapper (**of a cage,** d'une cage); **to g. o. of bed,** se lever; **to g. o. of s.o.'s way,** faire place à qn; **g. o. (of here)!** fiche-moi le camp! **to g. o. of a difficult position,** se tirer d'une position difficile; **to g. o. of (doing) sth,** se faire exempter de (faire) qch; **to g. o. of a habit,** perdre une habitude (b) (of secret) se faire jour. 'get 'over 1. vtr & i passer par-dessus, escalader (un mur) 2. vtr (a) se remettre d'(une maladie); venir à bout de, surmonter (des difficultés); revenir de (sa surprise); **he can't g. o. it,** il n'en revient pas (b) **to g. sth o. (and done with),** en finir avec qch. 'get 'round vtr & i tourner (un coin), contourner (une difficulté); persuader (qn); **to g. r. to doing sth,** trouver le temps de faire qch. 'get 'through vtr & i (a) passer (par un trou); se frayer un chemin (à travers la foule); **to g. t. (an exam),** être reçu (à un examen) (b) achever, arriver au bout de (son travail); venir à bout de (la nourriture); faire passer (la journée); **to g. t. a lot of work,** abattre du travail (c) parvenir (à franchir un obstacle); Tp: **to g. t. to s.o.,** obtenir la communication avec qn; **to g. (it) t. to s.o.,** faire comprendre (qch) à qn (d) faire adopter (un projet de loi); (faire) passer (qch) (à la douane). 'get to'gether 1. vi (of people) se rassembler, se réunir 2. vtr rassembler; réunir. 'get-to-gether n réunion f. 'get 'up 1. vtr & i monter (à une échelle) 2. vi se lever (**from a chair,** d'une chaise); se mettre debout; (of wind) se lever; **to g. up to chapter 5,** arriver au chapitre 5; **where have you got up to?** où en êtes-vous? **what are they getting up to?** qu'est-ce qu'ils font? 3. vtr (a) aider (qn) à monter (l'escalier); monter; **to g. up speed,** donner de la vitesse (b) réveiller (qn) (c) organiser (une fête); apprêter (un article); **to g. oneself up as a sailor,** se déguiser en marin. 'get(-)up n tenue f, toilette f; costume m.

geyser ['giːzər] n (a) Geol: geyser m (b) chauffe-bain m inv.

Ghana ['gɑːnə] Prn Geog: Ghana m.

ghastly ['gɑːstli] a (a) blême (b) horrible; (accident) affreux; F: (temps) abominable.

Ghent [gent] Prn Geog: Gand m.

gherkin ['gəːkin] n Cu: cornichon m.

ghetto ['getou] n ghetto m.

ghost [goust] 1. n fantôme m, revenant m; **g. story,** histoire de revenants; **not the g. of a chance,** pas la moindre chance; **g. of a smile,** sourire vague; Holy G., Saint-Esprit m; F: **g. (writer),** collaborateur, -trice, anonyme; nègre m 2. vi & tr **to g. for s.o.,** servir de nègre à qn; écrire (les discours de qn). **'ghostly** a (**-ier, -iest**) spectral.

ghoul [gu:l] n (a) Myth: goule f (b) (pers) amateur m du macabre. **'ghoulish** a macabre.

GI abbr US: (a) general, government, issue (b) soldat américain.

giant ['dʒaiənt] a & n géant (m); g. **strides**, pas de géant.

gibber ['dʒibər] vi baragouiner. **'gibberish** n baragouin m, charabia m.

gibe [dʒaib] **1.** n raillerie f **2.** vi to g. **at s.o.,** railler qn; se moquer de qn.

giblets ['dʒiblits] npl abattis m (de volaille).

giddy ['gidi] a (a) étourdi; **to feel g.,** être pris de, avoir le, vertige; **I feel g.,** la tête me tourne; **it makes me g.,** cela me donne le vertige (b) (of height) vertigineux. **'giddiness** n vertige, étourdissement m.

gift [gift] n (a) don m (b) cadeau m; **I wouldn't have it as a g.,** je n'en voudrais pas même comme cadeau (c) Com: (on presentation of coupons) prime f (d) talent m; don; **to have a g. for mathematics,** être doué pour les mathématiques. **'gifted** a doué.

gig [gig] n Th: etc: F: engagement m (d'un soir); gig f.

gigantic [dʒai'gæntik] a géant, gigantesque; colossal.

giggle ['gigl] **1.** n petit rire nerveux, bête; **to get the giggles,** avoir le fou rire **2.** vi rire nerveusement, bêtement.

gild [gild] vtr dorer; Fig: to g. **the lily,** orner la beauté même. **'gilding** n dorure f. **gilt 1.** a doré; Fin: g.-**edged securities,** fonds mpl d'État **2.** n dorure; doré m; Fin: **gilts,** fonds mpl d'État; F: **that takes the g. off the gingerbread,** voilà qui en enlève le charme.

gill [dʒil] n Meas: canon m (de vin) (= approx 0,142 l).

gills [gilz] npl ouïes fpl, branchies fpl (de poisson); lames fpl, lamelles fpl (d'un champignon); F: (of pers) **to be green about the gills,** avoir le teint vert.

gimlet ['gimlit] n vrille f; foret m.

gimmick ['gimik] n F: truc m; astuce f; **advertising g.,** truc publicitaire. **'gimmickry** n F: trucs mpl, astuces fpl. **'gimmicky** a plein de trucs, d'astuces.

gin [dʒin] n gin m.

ginger ['dʒindʒər] **1.** n gingembre m; g. **ale, beer,** boisson gazeuse au gingembre; Pol: g. **group,** groupe de pression **2.** a (of hair, pers) roux, F: rouquin; (biscuit) au gingembre. **'gingerbread** n pain m d'épice. **'gingerly** a & adv g., **in a g. fashion,** doucement, avec précaution. **'gingernut, -snap** n biscuit m au gingembre. **'ginger 'up** vtr stimuler, activer.

gingham ['giŋəm] n Tex: vichy m.

gipsy ['dʒipsi] n (pl **gipsies**) bohémien, -ienne; ro- manichel, -elle; (Spanish) gitan, -ane; g. **music,** mu- sique tsigane; Ent: g. **moth,** zigzag m.

giraffe [dʒi'ra:f] n Z: girafe f.

girder ['gə:dər] n poutre f.

girdle ['gə:dl] n (belt) ceinture f; (corset) gaine f; Anat: **pelvic g.,** ceinture pelvienne.

girl [gə:l] n jeune fille; **little g.,** petite fille, fillette; **girls' school,** école de filles; **old g.,** (i) ancienne élève (d'un lycée) (ii) F: (petite) vieille; **a French g.,** une jeune Française; **chorus g.,** girl f; **my oldest g.,** ma fille aînée; **when I was a g.,** quand j'étais jeune, petite. **'girlfriend** n (petite) amie. **'girlie** n F: jeune fille;

g. **magazine,** revue contenant des photos de femmes nues. **'girlish** a de petite fille, de jeune fille; (of boy) mou, efféminé.

giro ['dʒai(ə)rou] n Bank: **National G.,** (service m de) compte-chèques postaux; **bank g. (transfer, credit),** g. **(bank) system,** virement m bancaire; **(bank) g. credit slip,** bulletin de versement.

girth [gə:θ] n circonférence f (d'un arbre); tour m (de taille); (of pers) **of great g.,** d'une belle corpulence.

gist [dʒist] n fond m, essentiel m; essence f; **the g. of the matter,** le vif de la question.

give [giv] I. v (**gave** [geiv]; **given** ['givn]) **1.** vtr (a) to g. sth to s.o., to g. **s.o. sth,** donner qch à qn; **to g. s.o. a present,** faire un cadeau à qn; **to g. s.o. lunch,** offrir un déjeuner à qn; g. **me the good old days!** parlez-moi du bon vieux temps! (on telephone) g. **me Mr X,** passez- moi, donnez-moi, M. X; **to g. and take,** faire des concessions mutuelles; g. **or take a few minutes,** à quelques minutes près; **to g. s.o. sth to eat,** donner à manger à qn; **to g. s.o. ten years,** condamner qn à dix ans de prison; **to g. s.o. a note from s.o.,** remettre à qn un petit mot de qn; g. **him our congratulations,** félicitez-le de notre part; g. **her our love,** embrassez-la pour nous; **to g. s.o. one's support,** prêter son appui à qn; **to g. one's word,** donner sa parole; **to g. sth in exchange for sth,** donner qch pour, contre, qch; **what did you g. for it?** combien l'avez-vous payé? **I'll g. you £10 for it,** je vous en donnerai £10; **I'd g. a lot to know,** je donnerais beaucoup pour savoir; (of woman) **to g. oneself,** se donner (b) faire (un saut); laisser échapper (un rire); pousser (un cri); adresser (un sourire à qn); lancer (un regard); faire, donner (une réponse); **to g. sth a squeeze,** serrer qch; **to g. orders,** donner des ordres; (at shop) **to g. an order,** faire une commande; **to g. s.o. one's attention,** faire attention à qn; **to g. sth some thought,** considérer qch (c) donner, fournir (des détails); donner (un exemple); faire (une description); rendre (une moyenne, de l'intérêt); **given a triangle ABC,** soit un triangle ABC (d) donner (un concert); **to g. a toast,** proposer un toast (e) donner, passer (un rhume) (à qn); **to g. pleasure,** faire plaisir; **to g. oneself trouble,** se donner du mal; **to g. s.o. to believe, understand, that,** faire croire, donner à entendre, à qn que; **lamp that gives a poor light,** lampe qui éclaire mal; F: **to g. as good as one gets,** rendre coup pour coup; g. **it all you've got!** faites le maximum! P: **I gave him what for!** je l'ai arrangé de la belle façon! (f) **to g. way,** céder; (of ladder) (se) casser; (of ground) s'affaisser; (of legs) fléchir; **to g. way to s.o., a car,** céder la place à qn; le passage à une voiture; PN: Aut: g. **way** = céder la priorité **2.** vi (of cloth, elastic) prêter, donner; **the springs don't g. enough,** les res- sorts manquent de souplesse; **the door will g. if you push,** la porte cédera si vous la poussez. II. n élasticité f; g. **and take,** concessions mutuelles. **'give a'way** vtr (a) donner; faire cadeau de (qch); distribuer (des prix); conduire (la mariée) à l'autel (b) trahir, vendre (qn); **to g. oneself a.,** se révéler; **to g. the game a.,** vendre la mèche. **'giveaway** n F: révélation f involontaire; Com: **it's a g.!** c'est donné! **'give 'back** vtr rendre, restituer (qch) à qn); renvoyer (un écho). **'give 'in 1.** vtr donner (son nom); remettre (sa copie) **2.** vi céder. **'given 1.** a (a) at a g. **time,** à une heure convenue; NAm: g. **name,** prénom m (b) porté, enclin, à; adonné (à la boisson) 2. *prep* vu; g. **that**, étant donné que. **'give 'off** *vtr* dégager, émettre (un parfum). **'give 'onto** *vtr* (*of window*) donner sur. **'give 'out** 1. *vtr* distribuer (des livres); **to g. out a notice**, lire une communication; **it was given out that**, on a annoncé que 2. *vi* manquer; faire défaut; (*of supplies*) s'épuiser; (*of brakes*) lâcher; (*of engine*) tomber en panne; **my strength was giving o.**, j'étais à bout de forces. **'give 'over** *vtr* remettre qch (à qn); *P:* g. o.! arrête! assez! **'giver** *n* donneur, -euse; donateur, -trice. **'give 'up** *vtr* (*a*) abandonner (ses biens); céder (sa place) (à qn); renoncer à (un projet); résigner (son emploi); **to g. up smoking**, cesser de fumer; (*of riddle*) **I g. up**, je donne ma langue au chat; **to g. sth up as a bad job**, y renoncer; **to g. s.o. up (for lost)**, considérer qn comme perdu; **the doctors had given him up**, les médecins l'avaient condamné; **I'd given you up!** je ne vous attendais plus! (*b*) livrer (qn); consacrer (du temps à qch); **to g. oneself up**, se constituer prisonnier.

gizzard ['gizəd] *n* (*of bird*) gésier *m*.

glacier ['glæsiər] *n* glacier *m*. **glacial** ['gleisiəl] *a* (vent, accueil) glacial; (érosion) glaciaire.

glad [glæd] *a* (**gladder, gladdest**) heureux, content; joyeux; **he is only too g. to help you**, il ne demande pas mieux que de vous aider. **'gladly** *adv* avec plaisir, volontiers; avec joie. **'gladness** *n* joie *f*.

glade [gleid] *n* clairière *f*.

gladiolus [glædi'ouləs] *n* (*pl* **gladioli** [-lai]) *Bot:* glaïeul *m*.

glamour, *NAm:* -or ['glæmər] *n* fascination *f*; prestige *m* (d'un nom); **to lend g. to sth**, prêter de l'éclat à qch; **g. girl**, pin-up *f inv.* **'glamorous** *a* fascinateur; enchanteur; prestigieux.

glance [glɑːns] 1. *n* regard *m*, coup *m* d'œil; **at a g.**, d'un coup d'œil; **at first g.**, à première vue 2. *vi* **to g. at s.o.**, jeter, lancer, un coup d'œil à qn; jeter un regard sur qn; **to g. through, over**, parcourir, feuilleter (un livre). **'glance 'off** *vtr & i* dévier, ricocher (sur qch). **'glancing** *a* (*of blow*) oblique.

gland [glænd] *n Anat:* glande *f*. **'glandular** *a* glandulaire; **g. fever**, mononucléose infectieuse.

glare [gleər] 1. *n* (*a*) éclat *m*, éblouissement *m*, lumière éblouissante (du soleil); **in the full g. of publicity**, sous les feux *m* de la rampe (*b*) regard fixe et irrité 2. *vi* (*a*) briller d'un éclat éblouissant (*b*) **to g. at s.o.**, lancer un regard furieux à qn. **'glaring** *a* (*of light*) éblouissant; (soleil) aveuglant; (*of colour*) voyant; (*of fact*) manifeste; (*of injustice*) flagrant; **g. mistake**, faute grossière.

glass [glɑːs] *n* (*pl* **glasses**) (*a*) verre *m*; **g. industry**, industrie du verre; verrerie *f*; **stained g. window**, vitrail *m*; **safety g.**, verre de sûreté; **pane of g.**, vitre *f*; glace *f*, carreau *m*; **cut g.**, verre taillé; **g. wool, paper**, laine, papier, de verre; **g. fibre**, fibre de verre; **g. bowl**, bol de, en, verre; **g. door**, porte vitrée; **g. case**, vitrine *f*; **grown under g.**, cultivé sous verre, en serre *f* (*b*) vitre (de fenêtre); glace *f* (de voiture); verre (de montre) (*c*) verre (à boire); **g. of wine**, verre de vin; **liqueur g.**, verre à liqueur (*d*) lentille *f* (d'un instrument d'optique); **magnifying g.**, loupe *f*; **(field) g.**, longue-vue *f*; **field glasses**, jumelles *fpl*; **to wear glasses**, porter des lunettes *fpl*; **dark glasses**, lunettes de soleil (*e*) **(looking) g.**, glace, miroir *m* (*f*) baromètre *m*.

'glasscloth *n* (torchon *m*) essuie-verres *m inv.* **'glassful** *n* (plein) verre. **'glasshouse** *n* (*a*) *Hort:* serre (*b*) *F:* prison *f* militaire. **'glassware** *n* articles *mpl* de verre; verrerie *f*. **'glassy** *a* vitreux.

glaucoma [glɔː'koumə] *n Med:* glaucome *m*.

glaze [gleiz] 1. *n Cer:* glaçure *f*, vernis *m*; *Cu:* glace *f*, dorure *f* 2. *vtr & i* vitrer (une maison); vernisser (une poterie); *Cu:* glacer, dorer; (*of eyes*) **to g. (over)**, devenir vitreux. **glazed** *a* (*of door, window*) vitré; *Cer:* glacé, émaillé, vernissé; (papier) brillant; (regard) vitreux. **'glazier** *n* vitrier *m*. **'glazing** *n* vitrerie *f*; **double g.**, double vitrage *m*; doubles fenêtres *fpl*.

gleam [gliːm] 1. *n* (*a*) rayon *m*, lueur *f*; **g. of hope**, lueur d'espoir (*b*) reflet *m* (d'un couteau); miroitement *m* (d'un lac) 2. *vi* luire, reluire; (*of water*) miroiter.

glean [gliːn] *vtr* glaner. **'gleanings** *npl* glanure(s) *f*(*pl*).

glee [gliː] *n* joie *f*; *Mus:* **g. club** = chorale *f*. **'gleeful** *a* joyeux. **'gleefully** *adv* avec joie, joyeusement.

glen [glen] *n esp Scot:* vallée étroite.

glib [glib] *a* (*of answer*) spécieux; **g. tongue**, langue bien pendue. **'glibly** *adv* spécieusement; (parler) avec aisance; (répondre) sans hésiter.

glide [glaid] *vi* (*a*) (se) glisser, couler (*b*) (*of bird, aircraft*) planer; faire un vol plané; *Av:* **g. path**, trajectoire de descente. **'glider** *n* planeur *m*. **'gliding** *n Av:* vol plané.

glimmer ['glimər] 1. *n* faible lueur *f*; reflet *m* (de l'eau) 2. *vi* jeter une faible lueur; (*of water*) miroiter.

glimpse [glimps] 1. *n* vision momentanée; **to catch a g. of (s.o., wth)**, entrevoir (qn, qch) 2. *vtr* entrevoir.

glint [glint] 1. *n* trait *m*, éclair *m* (de lumière); reflet *m* 2. *vi* étinceler.

glisten ['glisn] *vi* reluire, scintiller; (*of water*) miroiter.

glitter ['glitər] 1. *n* scintillement *m*, éclat *m* 2. *vi* scintiller, briller. **'glittering** *a* brillant; resplendissant.

gloat [glout] *vi* **to g. over (sth)**, savourer (un spectacle); se réjouir méchamment de (la nouvelle); triompher de (l'infortune d'autrui).

globe [gloub] *n* globe *m*; sphère *f*; *Hort:* **g. artichoke**, artichaut *m*. **'global** *a* (*a*) (*of point of view*) global (*b*) mondial; **g. warfare**, guerre mondiale. **'globe-trotter** *n* globe-trotter *m*.

glofule ['glɔbjuːl] *n* globule *m*, gouttelette *f*.

gloom [gluːm] *n* (*a*) obscurité *f*, ténèbres *fpl* (*b*) mélancolie *f*; tristesse *f* pessimiste; **to cast a g. over, on**, jeter une ombre sur. **'gloomy** *a* (**-ier, -iest**) lugubre, sombre; morne; (*of thoughts*) noir; **to take a g. view of things**, voir tout en noir.

glory ['glɔri] 1. *n* (*pl* **glories**) gloire *f*; splendeur *f* (d'un spectacle); *F:* **g. hole**, capharnaüm *m*; débarras *m* 2. *vi* (**gloried**) **to g. in sth**, se glorifier de qch; se faire gloire de qch. **glorifi'cation** *n* glorification *f*. **'glorify** *vtr* (**glorified**) glorifier; rendre gloire à; exalter; **it was only a glorified shed**, ce n'était qu'une remise mais en plus grand, en mieux. **'glorious** *a* (*a*) glorieux; (*of victory*) éclatant (*b*) magnifique, splendide; (temps) superbe.

gloss [glɔs] *n* lustre *m*; vernis *m*; brillant *m*; **g. paint**, peinture (brillante) laquée. **'gloss 'over** *vtr* glisser sur (les défauts de qn); passer (un fait) sous silence.

'**glossy** a (-ier, -iest) lustré, glacé; brillant; g. **magazines**, n **glossies**, revues fpl de luxe.

glossary ['glɔsəri] n glossaire m; lexique m.

glove [glʌv] n gant m; (in large shop) g. **counter**, ganterie f; **rubber gloves**, gants de caoutchouc; **boxing gloves**, gants de boxe; **to handle s.o. with kid gloves**, ménager qn; Aut: g. **compartment**, boîte à gants.

glow [glou] 1. n (a) lueur f (rouge); incandescence f; feux mpl (du soleil couchant) (b) chaleur f; éclat m (du teint); **the exercise had given me a** g., l'exercice m'avait fouetté le sang 2. vi (of metal) rougeoyer; **to** g. **with pleasure, with enthusiasm**, rayonner de plaisir, brûler d'enthousiasme; **to be glowing with health**, éclater de santé; **his cheeks were glowing**, il avait les joues en feu. '**glowing** a rougeoyant; rayonnant; (of colours, words) chaleureux; (of pers) enthousiaste; **to paint sth in** g. **colours**, présenter qch sous un jour des plus favorables. '**glow-worm** n ver luisant.

glower ['glauər] vi to g. **at**, fixer les yeux sur (qch, qn) d'un air maussade, menaçant. '**glowering** a (air) maussade; (regard) farouche.

glucose ['glu:kous] n glucose m.

glue [glu:] 1. n colle (forte) 2. vtr (glued, gluing) coller; **he walked with his eyes glued to the road**, il marchait sans quitter la route des yeux.

glum [glʌm] a (glummer, glummest) renfrogné, maussade; (air) morne. '**glumly** adv d'un air maussade.

glut [glʌt] n surabondance f (d'une denrée); **there's a** g. **of pears**, le marché regorge de poires.

glutton ['glʌtn] n glouton, -onne; a g. **for work**, un bourreau de travail; g. **for punishment**, personne f qui sait encaisser; masochiste mf. '**gluttonous** a glouton. '**gluttony** n gloutonnerie f.

glycerine ['glisərin, -i:n] n glycérine f.

GMT abbr Greenwich Mean Time.

gnarled [nɑ:ld] a noueux.

gnash [næʃ] vtr to g. **one's teeth**, grincer des dents.

gnat [næt] n moucheron m, moustique m.

gnaw [nɔ:] vtr & i ronger. '**gnawing** a (of hunger) dévorant, tenaillant.

gnome [noum] n Myth: gnome m; F: **the gnomes of Zurich**, les banquiers suisses internationaux.

gnu [nu:] n Z: gnou m.

go [gou] I. v (goes [gouz]; pt went [went]; pp gone [gɔn]) 1. vi (a) aller; **to come and go**, aller et venir; **to go to Paris, to France**, aller à Paris, en France; **to go to a party**, aller à une soirée; **to go to the doctor's**, aller voir, aller chez, le médecin; **to go on a journey**, faire un voyage, partir en voyage; **to go to prison**, être mis en prison; **to go for a walk**, faire une promenade; aller se promener; **to go by the shortest way**, prendre par le plus court; **there he goes!** le voilà (qui passe)! **who goes there?** qui va là? **to go at 100km an hour**, faire 100 km, du cent, à l'heure; **you go first!** (i) partez le premier! (ii) à vous d'abord (b) (see also compound vbs) **to go up, down, across, a street**, monter, descendre, traverser, une rue; **to go into a room**, entrer dans une pièce; **to go behind s.o.'s back**, faire qch derrière le dos de qn (c) **which road goes to London?** quel est le chemin qui va à Londres? 2. **to go to school**, aller à l'école; **to go to sea, into the army**, se faire marin, soldat; **to go hungry, thirsty**, souffrir de la faim, de la soif; **wine that goes to the head**, vin qui monte à la tête; **to go one's**

own way, faire à sa guise; **promotion goes by seniority**, l'avancement se fait à l'ancienneté; F: **anything goes**, on fait ce qu'on veut; F: (of woman) **six months gone** (d) (of machinery) marcher; **to get sth going**, mettre qch en marche; F: **get going!** file! vas-y! F: **when he gets going he never stops**, une fois lancé il ne sait pas s'arrêter; **my watch won't go**, ma montre ne marche pas; **to keep industry going**, faire marcher l'industrie; **to keep the conversation going**, entretenir la conversation; **to go well, badly**, marcher bien, mal; **the way things are going**, au train où vont les choses; **how are things going?** comment ça va? **if all goes well**, si tout va bien; **what he says goes**, c'est lui qui commande (e) **the bell is going**, la cloche sonne; **it has just gone eight**, huit heures viennent de sonner; **it's gone four (o'clock)**, il est passé quatre heures; **to go crack, bang**, faire crac, pan; **go like this with your left foot**, faites comme ça du pied gauche; **I forget how the tune goes**, l'air de la chanson m'échappe; **how does the chorus go?** quelles sont les paroles du refrain? **vendre goes like descendre, vendre se conjugue comme descendre; these colours don't go (together)**, ces couleurs jurent (f) (of time) passer; **there were only 5 minutes to go**, il ne restait que 5 minutes; **the story goes that**, à ce qu'on raconte; **that's not dear as things go**, ce n'est pas cher au prix où sont les choses; **that goes without saying**, ça va sans dire; **it goes without saying that**, il va de soi que (g) partir; s'en aller; **after I've gone**, après mon départ; **we must go, be going**, il est temps de partir; **let me go!** laissez-moi partir, y aller! Sp: **go! partez! from the word go**, dès le commencement (h) disparaître; **it's all gone**, il n'y en a plus; **my strength is going**, mes forces s'affaiblissent; **her sight is going**, elle est en train de perdre la vue (i) se casser; (of cable) partir; (of fuse) sauter; (of dress) **to go at the seams**, se déchirer aux coutures (j) **to be going cheap**, se vendre bon marché; (at auction) **going! going! gone!** une fois! deux fois! adjugé! (k) mourir; **when I'm gone**, après ma mort (l) **to go and see s.o.**, aller voir qn; **to go and fetch s.o.**, to go for s.o., aller chercher qn; **he went (forward) to help her**, il a fait un mouvement pour l'aider; **I'm not going to be cheated**, je ne me laisserai pas avoir; **I was going to walk there**, j'avais l'intention d'y aller à pied; **I'm going to do it**, je vais le faire; **to go fishing**, aller à la pêche; **to go riding**, faire du cheval, se promener à cheval; **to go looking for sth**, partir à la recherche de qch; **there you go again!** vous voilà reparti! **to go to war**, entrer en guerre; **to go to a lot of trouble**, se donner beaucoup de peine (pour faire qch) (m) **it won't go into my case**, ça n'entre pas dans ma valise; **the key won't go into the lock**, la clef n'entre pas dans la serrure; **where does this book go?** où faut-il mettre ce livre? **six goes into twelve**, douze se divise par six; **four into three won't go**, trois n'est pas divisible par quatre; **the proceeds will go to charity**, les bénéfices seront distribués à des œuvres charitables (n) contribuer (à qch); **it only goes to show that**, cela montre que; **that just goes to show!** tu vois! (o) **the garden goes down to the river**, le jardin s'étend jusqu'à la rivière; **as far as the style goes**, quant au, pour ce qui est du, style (p) **to go mad**, devenir fou; **to go white, red, pale**, pâlir, rougir (q) **to let go**, lâcher prise; **let me go! let go of me!** lâchez-moi! **to let go of sth**, lâcher qch; **to let oneself go,** se laisser aller; **we'll let it go at that!** cela ira comme ça! **2.** *vtr* **to go it,** aller grand train; **to go it alone,** agir tout seul; **to go one better (than s.o.),** surenchérir (sur qn). **II.** *n* (*pl* **goes**) *F:* (*a*) **to be always on the go,** être toujours à courir, à trotter; **it's all go,** ça n'arrête pas (*b*) (*of pers*) énergie *f*; **to be full of go,** être plein d'entrain *m* (*c*) coup *m,* essai *m;* **to make a go of it,** réussir; **it's your go,** à vous de jouer; **to have a go at sth,** essayer de faire qch; **at one go,** d'un seul coup; **no go!** rien à faire! **III.** *a* Space: *F:* **all systems go,** tout paré et en ordre de marche (pour le départ). **'go a'bout 1.** *vtr & i* **to go a.** (**the streets**), circuler (dans les rues); (*of rumour*) **to go a.** (**town**), courir (les rues) **2.** *vtr* **to go a.** one's **work,** one's **business,** se mettre à son travail; s'occuper de, vaquer à, son travail; **how to go a. it,** comment s'y prendre. **'go after** *vtr* poursuivre. **'go a'gainst** *vtr* aller à l'encontre de (l'opinion de qn); (*of conditions*) être défavorable à. **'go a'head** *vi* **to go a.** (**with sth**), continuer (qch); **go a.!** allez-y! **'go-ahead** *F:* **1.** *a* actif, entreprenant; **go-a. signal,** feu vert **2.** *n* **to give s.o. the go-a.,** donner le feu vert à qn. **'go a'long** *vi* suivre son chemin; **I check the figures as I go a.,** je vérifie les chiffres à mesure; **to go a. with s.o.,** (i) accompagner qn (ii) être d'accord avec qn. **'go a'round** *vtr & i* = **go about 1. 'go 'at** *vtr* s'attaquer à. **'go a'way** *vi* s'en aller; partir; **to go a. for the weekend,** s'absenter pour le weekend. **'go 'back** *vi* (*a*) retourner; revenir; **to go b. home,** rentrer chez soi; **to go b. to a subject,** revenir sur un sujet; **to go b. to the beginning,** recommencer; **to go b. to sleep,** se rendormir; **to go b. on** one's **word,** revenir sur sa parole (*b*) (*step back*) reculer (*c*) (*in time*) remonter (to, à). **'go-between** *n* intermédiaire *mf.* **'go 'by 1.** *vi* passer; **as the years go by,** à mesure que les années passent; **to let an opportunity go by,** laisser passer une occasion **2.** *vtr* se régler sur; **to go by appearances,** juger d'après les apparences; **that's nothing to go by,** on ne peut pas se fonder là-dessus. **'go-by** *n F:* **to give s.o., sth, the go-by,** éviter qn, qch. **'go'down 1.** *vtr & i* descendre **2.** *vi* (*a*) (*to fall*) tomber; (*of sun*) se coucher; (*of ship*) couler (à fond); (*of wind, tem perature*) baisser; (*of swelling*) désenfler; (*of tyre*) se dégonfler; **to go d. well,** (*of food*) se laisser manger; (*of drink*) se laisser boire; (*of speech*) être bien reçu; *F:* **to go d. with flu,** attraper la grippe (*b*) continuer (jusqu'à la fin de la page) (*c*) (*to lose*) perdre le coup. **'goer** *n* (*a*) *F:* personne active; **he's a g.,** il est plein d'allant (*b*) **cinema g.,** habitué, -ée, du cinéma. **'go 'for** *vtr F:* (*a*) attaquer (qn); tomber sur (le dos de) (qn) (*b*) aller chercher, essayer d'obtenir (qch) (*c*) **I don't go f. him much,** je ne l'aime pas beaucoup. **'go-getter** *n F:* arriviste *mf.* **'go 'in** *vtr & i* entrer, rentrer; (*of sun*) se cacher; **to go in for,** faire (de la peinture); se présenter à (un examen); prendre part à (un concours). **'going 1.** *a* (prix) courant, actuel; **g. concern,** affaire qui marche **2.** *n Sp:* **good, heavy, g.,** terrain bon, lourd; *Fig:* **the g. is rough,** le chemin est rude; **to get out while the going's good,** partir pendant que la voie est libre; **that's good g.!** voilà qui n'est pas mal du tout! **it's heavy g. getting him to talk,** on a du mal à le faire parler; **comings and goings,** allées *fpl* et venues *fpl;* (*of bride*) **g. away outfit,**

tenue de voyage de noces. **going-'over** *n F:* **to give s.o. a g.-o.,** examiner, fouiller, qn. **goings-'on** *npl* événements *mpl,* activités *fpl;* **strange g.-on,** histoires *fpl* extraordinaires. **'go 'into** *vtr* (*a*) entrer dans; **to go i. fits of laughter,** éclater de rire (*b*) examiner, étudier (une question). **'go-kart** *n* kart *m.* **'goner** *n F:* **he's a g.,** il va bientôt mourir; il est fichu. **'go 'off 1.** *vi* (*a*) partir, s'en aller; *Th:* quitter la scène; **to go o. with sth,** emporter qch; **to go o. (to sleep),** s'endormir (*b*) (*of gun*) partir (*c*) (*of lights*) s'éteindre (*d*) (*of feeling*) passer (*e*) **everything went o. well,** tout s'est bien passé (*f*) (*of food*) se détériorer; (*of milk*) tourner; (*of meat*) se gâter **2.** *vtr* perdre le goût de (qch); **I've gone o. cheese,** je ne mange plus de fromage. **'go 'on 1.** *vi* (*a*) continuer; **time goes on,** le temps passe; **go on looking!** cherchez toujours! **I've got enough to be going on with,** j'en ai assez pour le moment; **he does go on,** impossible de l'arrêter; **he's going on for forty,** il frise la quarantaine; **it's going on for midnight,** il est presque minuit; **to go on to another question,** passer à une autre question; *F:* **go on (then)!** vas-y (alors)! *F:* **go on (with you)!** allons donc! tu plaisantes! **to go on at s.o.,** gronder qn (*b*) **what's going on here?** qu'est-ce qui se passe ici? **it's been going on for years,** cela dure depuis des années (*c*) se conduire (*d*) *Th:* entrer en scène (*e*) (*of lights*) s'allumer **2.** *vtr* se baser sur (qch). **'go 'out** *vi* (*a*) sortir; *WTel: TV:* (*of programme*) être diffusé; **to go o. for a walk,** aller se promener, faire une promenade; **to go o. to dinner,** (aller) dîner (i) au restaurant (ii) chez des amis; **he doesn't go o. much,** il sort peu; **to go o. (on strike),** se mettre en grève; **my heart went o. to him,** j'ai ressenti de la pitié pour lui (*b*) (*of fashion*) passer de mode; se démoder (*c*) (*of fire*) s'éteindre; (*of tide*) baisser, se retirer. **'go 'over.** *vtr* vérifier (un compte); examiner, revoir (un rapport); relire (un document); **to go o. sth in** one's **mind,** repasser qch dans son esprit **2.** *vi* passer (à l'ennemi); (*of speech*) **to go o. well,** être bien reçu. **'go 'found** *vi* (*a*) (*of wheel*) tourner; **my head's going r.,** la tête me tourne (*b*) faire un détour (*c*) (*of rumour, bottle*) circuler; **there isn't enough to go r.,** il n'y en a pas assez pour tout le monde. **go-'slow** *n* grève perlée. **'go 'through 1.** *vtr* (*a*) remplir (des formalités); passer par, subir (de rudes épreuves) (*b*) examiner (des documents); repasser (une leçon), qch dans son esprit); trier (des vêtements); *Cust:* visiter, fouiller (des valises); **to go t. s.o.'s pockets,** fouiller dans les poches de qn (*c*) dépenser (de l'argent) **2.** *vi* (*of law*) passer; (*of deal*) être conclu; **I mean to go t. with it,** j'irai jusqu'au bout. **'go 'under** *vi* couler; (*of business*) faire faillite. **'go 'up 1.** *vtr & i* monter **2.** *vi* (*a*) (*of prices*) augmenter; **to go up to bed,** monter se coucher; *Th:* **before the curtain goes up,** avant le lever du rideau; **a shout went up,** un cri s'est élevé (*b*) (*explode*) sauter; **to go up in flames,** s'enflammer brusquement. **'go 'with** *vtr* (*a*) marcher, aller, (de pair) avec (qch); accompagner (qn) (*b*) s'accorder avec; (*of colours*) s'assortir avec, être assorti à. **'go with'out** *vtr* se passer de; manquer de.

goad [goud] *vtr* **to g. s.o. (on),** aiguillonner qn; **to g. s.o. into doing sth,** talonner qn jusqu'à ce qu'il fasse qch.

goal [goul] *n* but *m.* **'goalkeeper,** *F:* **'goalie** *n Fb:* gardien *m* de but; *F:* **goal** *m.* **'goalmouth** *n Fb:*

entrée f du but. 'goalpost n montant m, poteau m, de but; the goalposts, le but.

goat [gout] n chèvre f; (he-g.) bouc m; F: it gets my g., ça me tape sur les nerfs.

gob [gɔb] n P: bouche f; gueule f; shut your g.! ferme-la!

gobble ['gɔbl] vtr avaler (qch) gloutonnement; (to child) don't g.! mange plus lentement! 'gobbledegook n F: charabia m.

goblet ['gɔblit] n verre m à pied; DomEc: bol m (de mixeur); Hist: coupe f.

goblin ['gɔblin] n Myth: lutin m.

god [gɔd] n dieu m; G., Dieu m; Th: F: the gods, le poulailler, le paradis; F: (my) G.! mon Dieu! thank G.! Dieu merci! 'godchild n (pl -children) filleul, f filleule. 'goddamn(ed) a P: sacré. 'god(-)daughter n filleule. 'goddess n (pl -es) déesse f. 'godfather n parrain m. 'godforsaken a misérable; (endroit) perdu. 'godmother nf marraine. 'godparents npl le parrain et la marraine. 'godsend n aubaine f. 'godson n filleul.

goes [gouz] see go I. & II.

goggle ['gɔgl] vi rouler de gros yeux; to g. at sth, regarder qch en roulant de gros yeux; F: the g. box, la télé. 'goggles npl lunettes (protectrices).

gold [gould] 1. n or m; Fin: g. standard, étalon-or m 2. a (collier) d'or, en or; g. leaf, feuille d'or, or en feuille; g. plate, vaisselle d'or. 'gold-digger n (a) chercheur m d'or (b) F: (woman) croqueuse de diamants. 'golden a d'or; g. wedding, noces d'or; g. eagle, aigle royal; g. opportunity, occasion magnifique; the g. mean, le juste milieu; Bot: g. rod, verge d'or; F: g. handshake, cadeau d'adieu, indemnité de départ. 'goldfinch n (pl -es) Orn: chardonneret m. 'goldfish n (inv in pl) poisson m rouge; g. bowl, bocal à poissons rouges. 'goldmine n mine f d'or; Fig: it's a g., c'est une affaire d'or. 'gold-'plated a plaqué or. 'goldrush n ruée f vers l'or. 'goldsmith n orfèvre m.

golf [gɔlf] 1. n golf m; g. club, (i) crosse, club, de golf (ii) (place) club de golf; g. course, terrain de golf 2. vi to go golfing, (aller) jouer au golf. 'golfer n golfeur, -euse.

golliwog ['gɔliwɔg] n poupée f en étoffe représentant un nègre.

gone [gɔn] see go I.

gong [gɔŋ] n (a) gong m (b) F: médaille f.

goo [gu:] n F: (a) substance collante (b) sentimentalité f à l'eau de rose. 'gooey a (gooier, gooiest) F: (a) gluant; (b) (sentimentalité) à l'eau de rose.

good [gud] 1. a (better, best) (a) bon; g. handwriting, belle écriture; g. story, bonne histoire; to look, smell, g., avoir l'air, sentir, bon; this is g. enough for me, cela fera mon affaire; cela me suffit; F: that's a g. one! en voilà une bonne! g. to eat, bon à manger; to have g. sight, avoir de bons yeux; to have a g. time, (bien) s'amuser; he's too g. for that job, il mérite une meilleure situation; g. doctor, médecin de premier ordre; g. reason, raison valable; this car ought to be g. for another 5 years, cette voiture devrait me faire encore 5 ans; F: he's g. for another 10 years, il a encore bien 10 ans à vivre (b) avantageux; g. opportunity, bonne occasion; I thought it a g. idea to do it, il m'a semblé bon de le faire; to earn g. money, gagner largement

sa vie (c) heureux; g. news, bonnes nouvelles; too g. to be true, trop beau pour y croire, pour être vrai; g. (for you, on you)! g. show! tant mieux (pour toi)! very g.! très bien! it's g. to be alive! il fait bon vivre! (d) g. morning! g. afternoon! bonjour! g. evening! bonsoir! (e) this medicine is very g. for coughs, ce remède est très bon pour la toux; yoghurt is g. for you, le yaourt vous fait du bien; to drink more than is g. for one, boire plus que de raison; g. for nothing, bon à rien (f) g. with one's hands, habile de ses mains; g. at French, fort, bon, en français; he's g. at games, c'est un sportif (g) g. man, homme (de) bien; g. conduct, bonne conduite; g. old Martin! ce bon vieux Martin! (h) (of child) sage; be g.! sois sage! as g. as gold, sage comme une image (i) aimable; that's very g. of you, c'est bien aimable, gentil, de votre part; would you be g. enough to, auriez-vous la gentillesse de? he's always been g. to me, il s'est toujours montré bon pour moi; he's a g. sort, c'est un bon garçon; F: g. Lord! g. heavens! grand Dieu! (j) a g. half, une bonne moitié; a g. time, a g. while, pas mal de temps; a g. hour, une bonne heure; a g. 10 kilometres, dix bons kilomètres; a g. 20 years ago, il y a bien 20 ans; a g. many, a g. deal, beaucoup; to come in a g. third, arriver bon troisième (k) it's as g. a way as any other, c'est une façon qui en vaut une autre; it's as g. as saying that, autant vaut dire que; my family is as g. as his, ma famille vaut bien la sienne; to give as g. as one gets, rendre coup pour coup; it's as g. as new, c'est comme neuf (l) to make g., se rattraper de (ses pertes); réparer (une injustice); combler (un déficit); remplir (sa promesse); effectuer (sa retraite); assurer (sa position); faire prévaloir (ses droits); (of pers) prospérer, faire son chemin; (after setback) se refaire une vie 2. n (a) bien m; to do g., faire du bien; he's up to no g., il prépare quelque mauvais coup (b) I did it for your g., je l'ai fait pour votre bien; for the g. of one's health, pour son bien; en vue de sa santé; for the common g., dans l'intérêt commun; it will do you g., cela vous fera du bien (to, de); what g. will that do you? à quoi cela vous avancera-t-il? that won't be much g., cela ne servira pas à grand-chose; what's the g. of that? à quoi bon (faire) cela? that's no g., cela ne sert à rien; cela ne vaut rien; he's no g., il est nul; much g. may it do you! grand bien vous fasse! it's no g. talking about it, inutile d'en parler; he'll come to no g., il tournera mal (c) to be £5 to the g., avoir £5 de gagné, de profit; it's all to the g., autant de gagné; tant mieux; he's gone for g., il est parti pour (tout) de bon. good'bye int & n au revoir (m inv); F: you can say g. to that, tu peux en faire ton deuil. 'good-for-nothing a & n propre à rien (m). 'good-'hearted a (of pers) qui a bon cœur. 'good-'humoured, NAm: -'humored a (of pers) d'un caractère facile; facile à vivre; (sourire) de bonne humeur. good-'humouredly, NAm: -'humoredly adv avec bonhomie. 'good-'looking a beau. 'good-'natured a (of pers) au bon naturel; bon enfant. 'good-'naturedly adv avec bonhomie. 'goodness n bonté f (de qn, de cœur); bonne qualité (d'un article); F: (my) g.! g. me! g. gracious! mon Dieu! thank g.! Dieu merci! for goodness' sake! pour l'amour de Dieu!

g. **(only) knows!** Dieu seul le sait! **'good-'night** *int & n* bonsoir (*m*); bonne nuit. **goods** *npl* (*a*) *Jur:* biens *mpl*, effets *mpl* (*b*) objets *mpl*, articles *mpl*; *Com:* marchandises *fpl*; **manufactured g.,** produits fabriqués; **consumer g.,** biens de consommation; g. **train, yard,** train, dépôt, de marchandises; *F:* to **deliver the g.,** tenir sa parole. **'good-'tempered** *a* de caractère facile, égal; facile à vivre. **good' will** *n* (*a*) bonne volonté; bienveillance *f* (*b*) *Com:* clientèle *f*; actif incorporel. **'goody** *F:* 1. *n* (*pl* **-ies**) (*a*) (*pers*) bon type (*b*) *pl* friandises *fpl* 2. *int* chouette! **'goody-goody** *n F:* (*pers*) sainte nitouche *f*.

goose [guːs] *n* (*pl* **geese** [giːs]) (*a*) oie *f*; **to cook s.o.'s g.,** faire son affaire à qn (*b*) *F:* (*pers*) niais, -aise. **'gooseberry** *n* (*pl* **gooseberries**) groseille *f* à maquereau; g. **(bush),** groseillier *m* (à maquereau). **'gooseflesh** *n* (*also* g. **pimples,** *NAm:* **bumps**) chair *f* de poule. **'goosestep** *n Mil:* pas *m* de l'oie.

gore [gɔːr] *vtr* (*of bull*) blesser (qn) avec les cornes; encorner (qn).

gorge [gɔːdʒ] *n* (*a*) *Geog:* gorge *f* (*b*) *Fig:* **it makes my g. rise,** cela me soulève le cœur.

gorge² *vi & pr* **to g. (oneself),** se gorger (**on,** de).

gorgeous [ˈgɔːdʒəs] *a* magnifique, splendide; *F:* épatant; superbe.

gorilla [gəˈrilə] *n Z:* gorille *m*.

gormless [ˈgɔːmlis] *a F:* idiot, bête.

gorse [gɔːs] *n Bot:* ajonc(s) *m*(*pl*).

gory [ˈgɔːri] *a* sanglant, ensanglanté.

gosh [gɔʃ] *int* mince (alors)!

gosling [ˈgɔzliŋ] *n Orn:* oison *m*.

gospel [ˈgɔspəl] *n* évangile *m*; **to take sth for g.,** *F:* **for the g. truth,** accepter qch comme parole d'évangile.

gossip [ˈgɔsip] 1. *n* (*a*) (*pers*) bavard, -arde; (*ill-natured*) commère *f* (*b*) bavardage *m*; (*ill-natured*) commérages *mpl*, potins *mpl*; *Journ:* g. **column,** échos *mpl*; g. **(column)** writer, échotier, -ière 2. *vi* bavarder; (*ill-naturedly*) potiner; faire des commérages (**about,** sur). **'gossiping** *n* bavardage; (*ill-natured*) commérage *m*. **'gossipy** *a F:* (*style*) anecdotique.

got, *NAm:* **gotten** [gɔt, ˈgɔtn] *see* **get.**

gothic [ˈgɔθik] *a* (architecture) gothique.

gouge [gaudʒ] 1. *n Tls:* gouge *f* 2. *vtr* gouger (le bois); creuser (une cannelure) à la gouge.

goulash [ˈguːlæʃ] *n Cu:* goulache *f*.

gourmand [ˈguəmənd] *n* gourmand, -ande.

gourmet [ˈguəmei] *n* gourmet *m*.

gout [gaut] *n Med:* goutte *f*.

govern [ˈgʌvən] *vtr & i* gouverner; administrer (une province); maîtriser (ses passions); **governing body,** conseil d'administration. **'governess** *n* gouvernante *f*. **'government** *n* gouvernement *m*; g. **loan,** emprunt public. **govern'mental** *a* gouvernemental. **'governor** *n* gouverneur *m*; directeur, -trice (d'une école).

gown [gaun] *n* robe *f*; toge *f* (d'universitaire, d'avocat); **dressing g.,** robe de chambre.

GP *abbr* General Practitioner.

grab [græb] 1. *n* **to make a g. for, at, sth,** faire un mouvement pour saisir qch 2. *vtr* (**grabbed**) **to g. (hold of) sth,** saisir qch.

grace [greis] *n* (*a*) grâce *f*; **with (a) good g.,** de bonne grâce; **to fall from g.,** tomber en disgrâce; **to be in s.o.'s good graces,** être dans les bonnes grâces de qn; **he had**

the g. to apologize, il a eu la bonne grâce de faire ses excuses; **it has the saving g. that,** cela a au moins ce mérite que; **to give s.o. seven days' g.,** accorder à qn sept jours de grâce (*b*) **to say g.,** (*before meal*) dire le bénédicité; (*after meal*) dire les grâces (*c*) (*also* **'gracefulness**) grâce, élégance *f*. **'graceful** *a* gracieux; élégant. **'gracefully** *adv* avec grâce, avec élégance. **gracious** [ˈgreiʃəs] *a* gracieux, bienveillant; (*of lifestyle*) élégant; *F:* **(good) g.! mon Dieu! good g. no!** jamais de la vie! **'graciously** *adv* gracieusement.

grade [greid] 1. *n* (*a*) grade *m*, rang *m*, degré *m*; qualité *f*; échelon *m* (d'une administration); **to make the g.,** atteindre le niveau requis; réussir; **high g.,** de qualité supérieure (*b*) *NAm: Sch:* classe *f*; g. **school** = école primaire (*c*) *NAm:* pente *f*, rampe *f*; *Rail:* g. **crossing,** passage à niveau 2. *vtr* classer (des marchandises); graduer (des exercices); régulariser (une pente); *NAm: Sch:* corriger et noter (des dissertations).

gradient [ˈgreidiənt] *n CivE:* rampe *f*; inclinaison *f*; pente *f*.

gradual [ˈgrædjuəl] *a* graduel; progressif; (*of slope*) doux. **'gradually** *adv* graduellement; peu à peu.

graduate 1. *n* [ˈgrædjuət] *Sch:* = licencié, -ée; diplômé, -ée 2. *v* [ˈgrædjueit] (*a*) *vi Sch:* = obtenir sa licence; *NAm:* = terminer ses études (au lycée) (*b*) *vtr* graduer; **graduated income tax,** impôt progressif. **gradu'ation** *n Sch:* remise *f* des diplômes.

graffiti [grəˈfiːti] *npl* graffiti *mpl*.

graft [grɑːft] 1. *n* (*a*) greffe *f*; greffon *m*; *F:* **hard g.,** travail *m*, boulot *m* (*b*) *esp NAm: F:* graissage *m* de patte; gratte *f* 2. *vtr* greffer. **'grafting** *n* greffe, greffage *m*; **skin g.,** greffe épidermique.

grain [grein] *n* (*a*) grain *m* (de blé, de sel) (*b*) céréale(s) *f*(*pl*) (*c*) grain (du cuir, du bois); fil *m* (de la viande); **against the g.,** à contre-fil; *F:* **it goes against the g.,** c'est à contrecœur que je le fais.

grammar [ˈgræmər] *n* grammaire *f*; **that's bad g.,** ce n'est pas grammatical; g. **school** = lycée *m*. **gra'mmatical** *a* grammatical. **gra'mmatically** *adv* grammaticalement.

gram(me) [græm] *n Meas:* gramme *m*.

gramophone [ˈgræməfoun] *n* gramophone *m*.

granary [ˈgrænəri] *n* grenier *m*; entrepôt *m* de grain.

grand [grænd] 1. *a* (*a*) grand; g. **piano,** piano à queue; g. **duke,** grand-duc *m*; g. **total,** total global (*b*) grandiose, magnifique; imposant; g. **old man,** vétéran *m* (*c*) *F:* excellent, splendide; épatant; **I'm not feeling too g.,** je ne suis pas dans mon assiette 2. *n F:* mille livres *fpl* (sterling); *NAm:* mille dollars *mpl*. **'grandchild** *n* (*pl* **-children**) petit-fils *m*, petite-fille *f*, petits-enfants *mpl*. **'grandad** *n F:* grand-papa *m*. **'grand-daughter** *n* petite-fille *f*. **grandeur** [ˈgrændjər] *n* grandeur *f*. **'grandfather** *n* grand-père *m*. **'grandiose** *a* grandiose. **'grandly** *adv* grandement; grandiosement. **'grandma** *n F:* grand-maman *f*. **'grandmother** *n* grand-mère *f*. **'grandpa** *n F:* grand-papa *m*. **'grandparents** *npl* grands-parents *mpl*. **'grandson** *n* petit-fils. **'grandstand** *n Sp:* tribune *f*.

granite [ˈgrænit] *n* granit *m*.

gran(ny) [ˈgræn(i)] *n* (*pl* **grannies**) *F:* grand-maman *f*.

grant [grɑːnt] 1. *n* aide *f* pécuniaire; subvention *f*; *Sch:*

bourse *f*, allocation *f*, d'études **2.** *vtr* accorder, concéder; exaucer (une prière); accéder à (une requête); admettre (un argument); **he was granted permission to do it,** il a reçu la permission de le faire; **to take sth for granted,** considérer qch comme convenu; **you take too much for granted,** vous présumez trop; **it must be granted that,** il faut reconnaître que; **granting, granted, that this story is true,** si l'on admet la vérité de cette histoire. **'grant-'aided** *a* subventionné.

granule ['grænju:l] *n* granule *m*. **'granular** *a* granulaire, granuleux. **'granulated** *a* granulé; (sucre) cristallisé.

grape [greip] *n* (grain *m* de) raisin *m*; **bunch of grapes,** grappe de raisin; **dessert grapes,** raisin(s) de table; **g. harvest,** vendange *f*; *F:* **sour grapes!** ils sont trop verts! *Bot:* **g. hyacinth,** muscari *m*. **'grapefruit** *n* (*no pl*) pamplemousse *m*. **'grapevine** *n* vigne *f*; *F:* téléphone *m* arabe.

graph [grɑ:f] *n* graphique *m*; **g. paper,** papier millimétré. **'graphic** *a* graphique; (*of description*) pittoresque, vivant. **'graphics** *npl* graphique *f*; art *m* graphique.

graphite ['græfait] *n* graphite *m*; mine *f* de plomb.

grapple ['græpl] *vi* **to g. with,** en venir aux prises avec.

grasp [grɑ:sp] **1.** *n* (*a*) poigne *f*; **to have a strong g.,** avoir de la poigne (*b*) prise *f*; **to lose one's g.,** lâcher prise; **within one's g.,** (avoir qch) à sa portée (*c*) compréhension *f*; **to have a good g. of modern history,** avoir une bonne connaissance de l'histoire moderne **2.** *vtr* (*a*) saisir; empoigner; serrer dans la main; **to g. s.o.'s hand,** serrer la main à qn (*b*) s'emparer de, se saisir de (qch); **to g. the opportunity,** saisir l'occasion (de faire qch) (*c*) comprendre; saisir. **'grasping** *a* âpre au gain; cupide.

grass [grɑ:s] **1.** *n* (*a*) herbe *f*; (*as food*) herbage *m*; (*lawn*) gazon *m*; **blade of g.,** brin d'herbe; *PN:* **keep off the g.,** défense de marcher sur le gazon; **to put out to g.,** mettre (un cheval) à l'herbe; *F:* mettre (qn) à la retraite; **g. snake,** couleuvre *f* (à collier); *F:* **he doesn't let the g. grow under his feet,** il ne perd pas son temps; *F:* **g. widow,** femme dont le mari est absent (*b*) *P:* dénonciateur, -trice; cafardeur, -euse (*c*) *P:* marijuana *f* **2.** *vi* cafarder; **to g. on s.o.,** dénoncer qn. **'grasshopper** *n* sauterelle *f*. **'grassland** *n* près *mpl*; prairies *fpl*. **'grassroots** *npl* **g. democracy,** le populisme; **to tackle a problem at g. level,** remonter à la source d'un problème. **'grassy** *a* herbeux.

grate[1] [greit] *n* (*a*) grille *f* (de foyer) (*b*) foyer *m*, âtre *m*; **a fire in the g.,** un feu dans la cheminée. **'grating**[1] *n* grille *f*, grillage *m*.

grate[2] **1.** *vtr* râper (du fromage); **to g. one's teeth,** grincer des dents **2.** *vi* grincer, crisser; **to g. on the ear,** écorcher l'oreille; **to g. on the nerves,** taper sur les nerfs. **'grater** *n* râpe *f*. **'grating**[2] *a* grinçant; (bruit) discordant; **g. sound,** grincement *m*.

grateful ['greitfl] *a* reconnaissant (**to s.o. for sth,** à, envers, qn de qch). **'gratefully** *adv* avec reconnaissance. **gratitude** ['græt-], **'gratefulness** *n* gratitude *f*, reconnaissance *f* (**to,** envers).

gratify ['grætifai] *vtr* (**gratified**) faire plaisir, être agréable, à (qn); satisfaire (le désir de qn). **'gratification** *n* satisfaction *f*. **'gratified** *a* satisfait, content; (sourire) de satisfaction. **'gratifying** *a* agréable; flatteur, satisfaisant.

gratis ['grætis] *a* & *adv* gratis.

gratuity [grə'tjuiti] *n* (*pl* **gratuities**) (*a*) prime *f* (de démobilisation) (*b*) (*tip*) gratification *f*, pourboire *m*. **gra'tuitous** *a* gratuit. **gra'tuitously** *adv* gratuitement.

grave[1] [greiv] **1.** *n* tombe *f*, tombeau *m*; **mass g.,** charnier *m*; *F:* **to have one's foot in the g.,** avoir un pied dans la tombe; **to make s.o. turn in his g.,** faire frémir qn dans sa tombe **2.** *a* grave; sérieux; **g. mistake,** lourde erreur. **'gravedigger** *n* fossoyeur *m*. **'gravely** *adv* gravement; sérieusement; grièvement (blessé). **'gravestone** *n* pierre tombale. **'graveyard** *n* cimetière *m*.

gravel ['grævl] *n* gravier *m*; **g. path,** allée sablée; **g. pit,** carrière de gravier.

gravity ['græviti] *n* (*a*) (*seriousness*) gravité *f*, sérieux *m* (*b*) *Ph:* pesanteur *f*; **specific g.,** poids *m* spécifique; **g. feed,** alimentation par gravité; **centre of g.,** centre de gravité. **'gravitate** *vi* graviter (**towards,** vers, **round,** autour de). **gravi'tation** *n* gravitation *f*.

gravy ['greivi] *n* *Cu:* (i) jus *m* (de la viande) (ii) sauce *f* (au jus); **g. boat,** saucière *f*.

gray [grei] *a* & *n* *see* **grey**.

graze[1] [greiz] **1.** *vi* paître, brouter **2.** *vtr* faire paître (un troupeau); paître (l'herbe); pâturer (un champ).

graze[2] **1.** *n* écorchure *f*, éraflure *f* **2.** *vtr* (*a*) écorcher, érafler (ses genoux) (*b*) effleurer, frôler (qn, qch).

grease [gri:s] **1.** *n* graisse *f*; **g. gun,** pistolet graisseur **2.** *vtr* graisser. **'greasepaint** *n* *Th:* fard *m*. **'greaseproof** *a* **g. paper,** papier parchemin, papier jambon; papier beurre. **'greasy** *a* (-**ier,** -**iest**) graisseux, huileux; taché de graisse; (chemin) gras, glissant.

great [greit] *a* grand; **Greater London,** le grand Londres; l'agglomération londonienne; **a g. deal of money,** beaucoup d'argent; **a g. many people,** beaucoup de gens; **the greater part of the day,** la plus grande partie de la journée; **the g. majority of women,** la plupart des femmes; **to a g. extent,** en grande partie; **to reach a g. age,** parvenir à un âge avancé; **g. difference,** grande, forte, différence; **to have no g. opinion of s.o.,** tenir qn en médiocre estime; **they are g. friends,** ils sont grands amis; *F:* **to be g. at tennis,** être fort au tennis; **to have a g. time,** s'amuser follement; *F:* (**that's**) **g.!** fameux! magnifique! **isn't he g.?** quel homme! *F:* **g. Scott!** grands dieux! **'great-'aunt** *n* grand-tante *f*. **'greatcoat** *n* pardessus *m*; *Mil:* capote *f*. **'great-'grandchild** *n* (*pl* -'**children**) arrière-petit-fils *m*; arrière-petite-fille *f*; arrière-petits-enfants *mpl*. **'great-'granddaughter** *n* arrière-petite-fille. **'great-'grandfather,** -'**grandmother** *n* arrière-grand-père *m*; arrière-grand-mère *f*. **'great-'grandson** *n* arrière-petit-fils. **'great-'great-'grandfather,** -**mother** *n* trisaïeul, -eule. **'greatly** *adv* grandement; **g. irritated,** très irrité; fort mécontent; **I would g. prefer,** je préférerais (de) beaucoup. **'greatness** *n* grandeur *f*. **'great-'uncle** *n* grand-oncle *m*.

Greece [gri:s] *Prn Geog:* Grèce *f*. **Greek 1.** *a* grec **2.** (*a*) Grec, *f* Grecque (*b*) *Ling:* grec *m*; *F:* **it's all G. to me,** c'est de l'hébreu pour moi.

greed [gri:d] *n* (*also* **'greediness**) avidité *f*, cupidité *f*; (*for food*) gourmandise *f*, gloutonnerie *f*. **'greedily** *adv* avidement; (manger) gloutonnement, goulûment. **'greedy** a (**-ier, -iest**) avide, cupide; âpre (au gain); (for food) gourmand, glouton.

green [gri:n] **1.** a (a) vert; (of bacon) non fumé; (of skin, face) blême; **to grow g.,** verdir; (of pers) **to go, turn, g.,** blêmir; **to keep s.o.'s memory g.,** entretenir la mémoire de qn; **she has g. fingers,** NAm: **a g. thumb,** en jardinage, elle a la main heureuse; **to make s.o. g. with envy,** faire pâlir qn d'envie (b) (of pers) jeune, inexpérimenté; naïf; **he's not as g. as he looks,** il n'est pas si niais qu'il en a l'air **2.** n (a) vert m; Cu: **greens,** légumes verts (b) pelouse f, gazon m; Golf: vert; **village g.,** pelouse communale, place f du village. **'greenback** n NAm: billet m de banque. **'greenery** n verdure f, feuillage m. **'greenfinch** n (pl **-finches**) verdier m. **'greenfly** n (pl **-flies**) puceron m, aphis m. **'greengage** n Bot: reine-claude f. **'greengrocer** n marchand, -ande, de légumes; fruitier, -ière. **'greenhouse** n serre f. **'greenish** a verdâtre. **'greenness** n verdeur f; verdure f (du paysage). **'greenroom** n Th: foyer m des artistes.

Greenland ['gri:nlənd] Prn Geog: Groenland m.

greet [gri:t] vtr saluer, aborder, accueillir (qn). **'greeting** n salutation f, salut m; **greetings card,** carte de vœux; **new year greetings,** compliments mpl du jour de l'an; **to send one's greetings,** envoyer le bonjour (à qn).

gregarious [gri'gɛəriəs] a grégaire; (of pers) sociable.

grenade [grə'neid] n grenade f; **hand g.,** grenade à main. **grenadier** [grenə'diər] n Mil: grenadier m.

grew [gru:] see **grow.**

grey [grei] **1.** a & n gris (m); (of skin, face) blême; (of outlook, day) sombre, morne; **g. matter,** matière grise (du cerveau); **to go, turn, g.,** (of hair) grisonner; (of face) blêmir **2.** vi (of hair) grisonner. **'grey-'haired** a aux cheveux gris. **'greyhound** n lévrier m; **g. racing,** courses de lévriers; **g. track,** cynodrome m. **'greyish** a grisâtre.

grid [grid] n grille f, grillage m; El: **the (national) g.,** le réseau (électrique national). **'gridiron** n (a) Cu: gril m (b) NAm: terrain m de football.

griddle ['gridl] n Cu: tôle f (pour galettes).

grief [gri:f] n chagrin m, douleur f; peine f; **to come to g.,** (i) faire de mauvaises affaires (ii) avoir un accident (iii) (of plan) échouer; mal tourner; F: **good g.!** mon Dieu! **'grievance** n (a) grief m; **to air one's grievances,** conter ses doléances spl (b) injustice f. **grieve 1.** vtr chagriner, affliger; peiner; **we are grieved to learn,** nous apprenons avec peine **2.** vi se chagriner, s'affliger (**over sth,** de qch); **to g. at sth,** pleurer qch. **'grievous** a douloureux; pénible; (of loss) cruel; (of injury) grave; Jur: **g. bodily harm,** graves blessures.

grill [gril] **1.** n (a) Cu: (food) grillade f; **g. (room),** grill (-room) m (b) Cu: (appliance) gril m (c) = **grille 2.** vtr Cu: (faire) griller; F: cuisiner (un détenu).

grille [gril] n grille f (de porte); Aut: **radiator g.,** calandre f.

grim [grim] a (**grimmer, grimmest**) sinistre; (humour) macabre; (paysage) lugubre; (sourire) sardonique; (visage) sévère; **it's a g. prospect,** ça s'annonce mal; **to hold on like g. death,** se cramponner en désespéré; **g. determination,** volonté inflexible; **how do you feel?— pretty g.,** comment ça va?—plutôt mal. **'grimly** adv

sinistrement; sévèrement; (se battre) avec acharnement.

grimace ['griməs] **1.** n grimace f **2.** vi. faire la grimace.

grime [graim] n saleté f; poussière f de charbon. **'grimy** a (**-ier, -iest**) sale, encrassé, noirci.

grin [grin] **1.** n large sourire m; sourire épanoui; **to give a broad g.,** avoir un grand sourire **2.** vi (**grinned**) (avoir un grand) sourire; **to g. and bear it,** (tâcher de) garder le sourire.

grind [graind] **1.** n labeur monotone et continu; **the daily g.,** le boulot journalier; **what a g.!** quelle corvée! **2.** v (**ground**) (a) vtr moudre (du café, du blé); dépolir (le verre); aiguiser (un outil); passer (un couteau) à la meule; jouer d'un orgue de Barbarie); **to g. sth (down) to dust,** pulvériser qch; **to g. out a tune,** tourner un air; **to g. sth under one's heel,** écraser qch sous ses pieds; **to g. the faces of the poor,** opprimer les pauvres; **to g. one's teeth,** grincer des dents (b) vi grincer; crisser. **'grinder** n broyeur m; DomEc: **coffee g.,** moulin m à café. **'grinding 1.** a **g. sound,** grincement m, crissement m; **g. poverty,** misère écrasante **2.** n (a) mouture f (du blé); broyage m; **g. mill,** broyeur (b) aiguisage m (c) grincement, crissement. **'grindstone** n meule f à aiguiser; **to keep s.o.'s nose to the g.,** faire travailler qn sans répit.

grip [grip] **1.** n (a) prise f; serrement m; étreinte f; adhérence f (de pneus); **to have a strong g.,** avoir une bonne poigne; **to get, come, to grips with,** en venir aux prises avec; **to get a g. on sth,** prendre prise à qch; **to lose one's g.,** lâcher prise; Fig: baisser (du point de vue mental); **to get, keep, a g. on oneself,** se contrôler, se maîtriser (b) poignée f (d'aviron, de pistolet) (c) (NAm: = **bobby pin**) pince f à cheveux (d) esp NAm: (Br = **holdall**) valise f, sac m **2.** v (**gripped**) (a) vtr saisir, empoigner; serrer (b) vi (of tyres) adhérer. **'gripping** a (of book) passionnant.

gripe [graip] F: **1.** n plainte f, ronchonnement m **2.** vi se plaindre, ronchonner. **'griping 1.** a **g. pain(s),** coliques fpl **2.** n F: ronchonnement.

grisly ['grizli] a affreux, sinistre.

gristle ['grisl] n cartilage m, croquant m. **'gristly** a cartilagineux.

grit [grit] **1.** n (a) grès m, sable m (b) F: courage m, cran m **2.** vtr (**gritted**) (a) **to g. one's teeth,** grincer des dents (b) sabler (une route). **grits** npl NAm: Cu: (**hominy**) **g.,** gruau m de maïs. **'gritty** a sablonneux, cendreux; (fruit) graveleux.

grizzle ['grizl] vi F: (a) ronchonner, grognonner (b) pleurnicher, geindre. **'grizzled** a (of hair) grisonnant. **'grizzly** a & n **g. (bear),** ours gris (d'Amérique); grizzli m.

groan [groun] **1.** n gémissement m **2.** vi gémir.

grocer ['grousər] n épicier, -ière; **the grocer's (shop),** l'épicerie f, l'alimentation f. **'grocery** n (pl **-ies**) n épicerie f; pl (articles mpl d')épicerie.

grog [grog] n grog m. **'groggy** a chancelant, titubant; (boxeur) groggy; **to feel (a bit) g.,** avoir les jambes en coton; ne pas être dans son assiette.

groin [groin] n Anat: aine f.

groom [gru:m] **1.** n valet m d'écurie; (before wedding) fiancé m; (at wedding) (nouveau) marié **2.** vtr panser (un cheval); **well groomed,** bien soigné.

groove [gru:v] n rainure f; cannelure f (de colonne);

sillon *m* (de disque); onglet *m* (de canif); *Fig:* **to get into a g.,** s'encroûter; devenir routinier.

grope [group] *vi* tâtonner; **to g. for sth,** chercher qch à tâtons, à l'aveuglette; **to g. one's way,** avancer à tâtons.

gross¹ [grous] *n* (*no pl*) (=144) grosse *f*; douze douzaines *fpl.*

gross² 1. *a* (*a*) (*fat*) gras; gros (*b*) grossier; (*ignorance*) crasse; (*abus*) choquant; **g. injustice,** injustice flagrante (*c*) *Com: etc:* (poids) brut 2. *vtr* (*of company, undertaking*) produire (tant de francs) brut. **'grossly** *adv* grossièrement; énormément (exagéré).

grotesque [grou'tesk] *a* grotesque.

grotto ['grɔtou] *n* (*pl* grotto(e)s) grotte *f.*

grotty ['grɔti] *a* (-ier, -iest) *F:* moche; dégueulasse.

grouch ['grautʃ] *vi* grogner. **'grouchy** *a* (-ier, -iest) maussade.

ground¹ [graund] *a* moulu; *see* **grind 2.**

ground² 1. *n* (*a*) sol *m,* terre *f;* **g. floor** (*NAm:* = **first floor**), rez-de-chaussée *m inv;* **sitting on the g.,** assis par terre; **to fall to the g.,** tomber à, par, terre; **to get off the g.,** (*of aircraft*) décoller; (*of scheme*) démarrer; **above g.,** sur terre; *Min:* à la surface; **at g. level,** au niveau du sol; **burnt to the g.,** brûlé de fond en comble; **that suits me down to the g.,** cela m'arrange le mieux du monde; **to be on firm g.,** connaître le terrain; être sûr de son fait; **to cut the g. from under s.o.'s feet,** couper l'herbe sous les pieds de qn; *Av:* **g. crew,** personnel au sol, non navigant, *F:* rampant (*b*) terrain *m;* **parade g.,** terrain de manœuvre; **football g.,** terrain de football; *Fig:* **to find (a) common g.,** trouver un terrain d'entente; **to cover a lot of g.,** faire beaucoup de chemin; **to shift one's g.,** changer d'arguments; **to gain g.,** gagner du terrain; (*of idea*) faire son chemin; **to lose g.,** perdre du terrain; **to stand one's g.,** tenir bon (*c*) *NAm: El:* (*Br* = **earth**) terre, masse *f* (*d*) *pl* parc *m,* jardin *m* (d'une maison), domaine *m* (*e*) *pl* raison *f,* cause *f,* motif(s) *m*(*pl*); **grounds for complaint,** grief *m;* **on what grounds?** à quel titre? **on health grounds,** pour des raisons de, pour raison de, santé; *Jur:* **grounds for divorce,** motifs de divorce (*f*) **coffee grounds,** marc *m* de café 2. *vtr* (*a*) *Av:* interdire (à qn) de voler; interdire de vol (un avion) (*b*) *NAm: El:* mettre à la terre. **'grounding** *n* connaissance *f* solide (d'un sujet); *Av:* interdiction *f* de vol. **'groundless** *a* (soupçon) mal fondé, sans fondement. **'groundnut** *n Bot:* arachide *f.* **'groundsheet** *n* tapis *m* de sol. **'groundsman** (*pl* **-men**) préposé *m* d'un terrain de jeux. **'groundswell** *n Nau:* lame *f,* houle *f,* de fond. **'groundwork** *n* base *f;* plan *m;* **to do the g.,** préparer le terrain.

group [gru:p] 1. *n* groupe *m;* **blood g.,** groupe sanguin; **in groups,** en, par, groupes; **g. action,** action collective; **to form a g.,** se grouper; **pop g.,** groupe pop; *Mil: Av:* **g. captain,** colonel *m* 2. *vtr & i* (se) grouper.

grouse¹ [graus] *n* (*no pl*) *Orn:* tétras *m;* grouse *m or f.*

grouse² *F:* 1. *n* (*a*) grogne *f* (*b*) (*cause for complaint*) grief *m* 2. *vi* ronchonner, grogner. **'grousing** *n F:* ronchonnement *m.*

grout [graut] *n Const:* mortier *m* liquide; coulis *m.*

grove [grouv] *n* futaie *f,* bosquet *m;* **orange g.,** orangeraie *f.*

grovel ['grɔvəl] *vi* (grovelled) ramper; se mettre à plat ventre (devant qn). **'grovelling** *a* rampant.

grow [grou] *v* (**grew** [gru:]; **grown** [groun]) 1. *vi* (*a*) (*of plant*) pousser; (*of seeds*) germer; **olives won't g. here,** l'olivier ne pousse pas ici (*b*) (*of pers*) grandir; **to g. into a man,** devenir homme; **to g. up,** grandir, atteindre l'âge adulte; **to g. out of one's clothes,** devenir trop grand pour ses vêtements; **he'll g. out of it,** cela lui passera avec l'âge (*c*) s'accroître, augmenter, grandir; **the crowd grew,** la foule augmentait; **habit that grows on one,** habitude qui vous gagne; **that picture's growing on me,** plus je regarde ce tableau plus il me plaît (*d*) devenir; **to g. old,** devenir vieux, vieillir; **to g. big(ger),** grandir; s'agrandir; grossir; augmenter; **to g. angry,** se fâcher; **it's growing dark,** il commence à faire nuit 2. *vtr* cultiver (des roses); laisser pousser (sa barbe). **'grower** *n* cultivateur, -trice. **'growing** *a* (*a*) croissant; qui pousse (*b*) grandissant; (enfant) en cours de croissance; (avis) de plus en plus répandu. **grown** *a* (**fully**) **g.,** grand; (*of pers*) adulte; (homme) fait; **when you are g. up,** quand tu seras grand. **'grown-'up** *n* grande personne; **grown-ups,** grands *mpl.* **growth** *n* (*a*) croissance *f;* accroissement *m,* augmentation *f;* développement *m* (économique); expansion *f* (de la population) (*b*) **yearly g.,** pousse annuelle (*c*) poussée *f* (des cheveux); **a week's g. on his chin,** le menton couvert d'une barbe de huit jours (*d*) *Med:* grosseur *f,* tumeur *f.*

growl [graul] 1. *n* grondement *m,* grognement *m* (d'un chien) 2. *vtr & i* grogner, gronder.

grown [groun] *see* **grow.**

grub [grʌb] 1. *n* (*a*) larve *f;* ver (blanc); asticot *m* (*b*) *P:* boustifaille *f;* **grub's up!** à la soupe! 2. *vi* (grubbed) fouiller (dans la terre); **to g. up a plant,** déraciner une plante. **'grubbiness** *n* saleté *f.* **'grubby** *a* (-ier, -iest) sale; malpropre.

grudge [grʌdʒ] 1. *n* rancune *f;* **to bear s.o. a g.,** have a g. against s.o., garder rancune à qn; en vouloir à qn 2. *vtr* **to g. s.o. his pleasures,** voir d'un mauvais œil les plaisirs de qn. **'grudging** *a* (consentement) donné à contrecœur. **'grudgingly** *adv* (faire qch) à contrecœur, de mauvaise grâce.

gruelling ['gruəliŋ] *a* éreintant, épuisant.

gruesome ['gru:səm] *a* horrible, macabre, affreux.

gruff [grʌf] *a* bourru, brusque; **g. voice,** grosse voix. **'gruffly** *adv* d'un ton bourru.

grumble ['grʌmbl] 1. *n* **without a g.,** (faire qch) sans murmurer; **to have a good g.,** rouspéter 2. *vi* grommeler, grogner; se plaindre (**about,** de); rouspéter; **to g. at s.o.,** rouspéter contre qn. **'grumbler** *n* grognon *mf;* mécontent, -ente; rouspéteur, -euse. **'grumbling** 1. *a* grognon, grondeur; *F:* **g. appendix,** appendice chronique 2. *n* rouspétance *f;* mécontentement *m.*

grumpy ['grʌmpi] *a* (-ier, -iest) maussade, renfrogné, grincheux. **'grumpily** *adv* maussadement.

grunt [grʌnt] 1. *n* grognement *m* 2. *vi* grogner; pousser un grognement. **'grunting** *n* grognement(s) *m*(*pl*).

guarantee [gærən'ti] 1. *n* (*a*) (*pers*) garant, -ante; caution *f* (*b*) garantie *f;* **two-year g.,** garantie de deux ans 2. *vtr* garantir; cautionner; se porter garant de, caution pour. **guaran'tor** *n* garant, -ante; caution.

guard [ga:d] 1. *n* (*a*) garde *f;* **to be on one's g.,** être sur ses gardes; **to put s.o. on his g.,** mettre qn en garde; **to be caught off one's g.,** être pris au dépourvu; (*of sentry*) **to be on g. (duty),** être de garde; **to go on, come off, g.,** monter la garde, descendre de garde; **to stand, keep, g.,** faire la garde; **to march s.o. off under g.,** emmener qn sous escorte *f* (*b*) *Mil:* garde *f*; (*one sentry*) garde *m*; **g. of honour,** garde d'honneur; **to form a g. of honour,** faire la haie; **to set a g. on a house,** faire surveiller une maison (*c*) chef *m* de train (*d*) *Mil:* **the Guards,** les Gardes *m* du corps (*e*) dispositif protecteur; garde-feu *m* **2.** *vtr & i* garder; protéger (qn, un mécanisme); surveiller (un prisonnier); **to g. against sth,** se garder de qch; parer à qch. **'guarded** *a* prudent; circonspect; (réponse) qui n'engage à rien. **'guardhouse, 'guardroom** *n Mil:* (*a*) corps de garde *m inv* (*b*) salle *f*, poste *m*, de police. **'guardian** *n* (*a*) gardien, -ienne (*b*) tuteur, -trice (d'un mineur); *g.* **angel,** ange gardien. **'guardrail** *n* garde-corps *m*. **'guardsman** *n* (*pl* **-men**) officier *m*, soldat *m*, de la Garde.

Guernsey ['gə:nzi] *Prn Geog:* Guernesey *m*.

guer(r)illa [gə'rilə] *n Mil:* guérillero *m*; **band of guer(r)illas,** guérilla *f*; *g.* **warfare,** guérilla.

guess [ges] **1.** *n* (*pl* **guesses**) conjecture *f*; estimation *f*; **to have, make, a g.,** hasarder une conjecture; essayer de deviner; **you've made a lucky g.,** tu es bien tombé; **your g. is as good as mine,** j'en sais autant que toi; **I give you three guesses,** tu devines? **it's anybody's g.,** qui sait? **at a g.,** au jugé **2.** *vtr & i* (*a*) **to g. at sth,** (essayer de) deviner qch; **to g. the length of sth,** estimer la longueur de qch; **to keep s.o. guessing,** mystifier qn; **g. who did it,** devinez qui l'a fait; **to g. right, wrong,** bien, mal, deviner; **you've guessed it!** vous y êtes! (*b*) *esp NAm:* croire, penser; **I g. you're right,** je suppose que vous avez raison; **I g. so!** sans doute! **'guesswork** *n* conjecture; **by g.,** au jugé; **by sheer g.,** à vue de nez.

guest [gest] *n* invité, -ée; (*at a meal*) convive *mf*; (*in a hotel*) client, -ente; **paying g.,** pensionnaire *mf*; **the landlord and his guests,** l'hôtelier et ses hôtes *mpl*; **g. artist,** artiste invité. **'guesthouse** *n* pension *f* de famille. **'guestroom** *n* chambre *f* d'ami(s).

guffaw [gə'fɔ:] **1.** *n* gros rire (bruyant) **2.** *vi* pouffer (de rire).

guide [gaid] **1.** *n* (*a*) guide *m*; **to take sth as a g.,** prendre qch pour règle; **g. dog,** chien d'aveugle (*b*) (*girl*) **g.,** éclaireuse *f*; guide *f* de France (*c*) (*book*) guide (**to a country,** d'un pays); manuel *m* (**to a sport,** d'un sport) (*d*) indication *f*, exemple *m*; **as a g.,** à titre indicatif **2.** *vtr* guider; conduire, diriger; **to be guided by,** se laisser guider par (qn); suivre (les conseils de qn). **'guidance** *n* (*a*) direction *f*; conduite *f*; **for your g.,** à titre d'indication; *Sch:* **vocational g.,** orientation professionnelle (*b*) guidage *m* (d'un missile). **'guidebook** *n* guide *m*. **'guided** *a* (excursion) sous la conduite d'un guide; (missile) (télé)guidé. **'guidelines** *npl* directives *fpl*. **'guiding** *a* qui sert de guide; (principe) directeur; *g.* **star,** guide *m*.

guild [gild] *n* association *f*; cercle *m*; *Hist:* guilde *f*.

guile [gail] *n* artifice *m*, ruse *f*, astuce *f*. **'guileless** *a* (*a*) franc, sincère (*b*) candide, naïf.

guillotine ['giləti:n] **1.** *n* guillotine *f*; (*for paper*) massicot *m* **2.** *vtr* guillotiner (qn); massicoter (du papier).

guilt [gilt] *n* culpabilité *f*. **'guiltily** *adv* d'un air coupable. **'guilty** *a* (**-ier, -iest**) coupable; **g. person, party,** coupable *mf*; **to plead g., not g.,** plaider coupable, non coupable; **verdict of g., not g.,** verdict de culpabilité, d'acquittement; **g. conscience,** mauvaise conscience; **g. look,** regard confus.

Guinea ['gini] **1.** *Prn Geog:* Guinée *f* **2.** *n g.* **fowl,** pintade *f*; *g.* **pig,** cobaye *m*, cochon d'Inde; (*of pers*) **to be a g. pig,** servir de cobaye.

guitar [gi'tɑ:r] *n Mus:* guitare *f*. **gui'tarist** *n* guitariste *mf*.

gulf [gʌlf] *n* (*a*) *Geog:* golfe *m*; **the G. Stream,** le Gulfstream (*b*) gouffre *m*, abîme *m*.

gull [gʌl] *n Orn:* mouette *f*; goéland *m*.

gullet ['gʌlit] *n Anat:* œsophage *m*; gosier *m*.

gullible ['gʌlibl] *a* facile à duper; crédule. **gulli'bility** *n* crédulité *f*; jobarderie *f*.

gully ['gʌli] *n* (*pl* **gullies**) *Geog:* (petit) ravin.

gulp [gʌlp] **1.** *n* (*a*) coup *m* (de gosier); **at one g.,** d'un (seul) coup (*b*) grosse bouchée **2.** *v* (*a*) *vtr* **to g. sth down,** avaler qch à grosses bouchées; n'en faire qu'une bouchée, qu'une gorgée; avaler à pleine gorge (*b*) *vi* essayer d'avaler; **he gulped,** sa gorge s'est serrée.

gum¹ [gʌm] **1.** *n* (*a*) (*adhesive*) gomme *f*, colle *f*; **g. arabic,** gomme arabique (*b*) (**chewing, bubble**) **g.,** chewing-gum *m* (*c*) (**fruit**) **g.,** boule *f* de gomme (*d*) *Bot:* **g. (tree),** gommier *m*; *F:* **to be up a g. tree,** être dans le pétrin **2.** *vtr* (**gummed**) gommer; coller. **'gumboot** *n* botte *f* de caoutchouc. **gummed** *a* (*of label*) gommé.

gum² *n Anat:* gencive *f*. **'gumboil** *n* abcès *m* à la gencive.

gumption ['gʌmpʃn] *n F:* jugeotte *f*, sens *m* pratique.

gun [gʌn] **1.** *n* (*a*) canon *m*; **the big guns,** l'artillerie *f*; les grosses pièces; *F:* (*of people*) les gros bonnets; **g. carriage,** affût *m* de (canon); (*at funeral*) prolonge *f* d'artillerie; **six-g. salute,** salve de six coups de canon; *F:* **to be going great guns,** être en pleine forme, en plein succès (*b*) (*rifle*) fusil *m* (de chasse); (*handgun*) revolver *m*; pistolet *m*; **spray g.,** pistolet (à peinture) **2.** *vtr* (**gunned**) *Aut:* (faire) emballer (le moteur). **'gunboat** *n* canonnière *f*; aviso-torpilleur *m*. **'gun down** *vtr* tuer (qn) d'un coup de revolver. **'gunfire** *n* canonnade *f*; feu *m*; tir *m* (rapide). **'gun for** *vtr F:* pourchasser; **he's gunning for us,** c'est à nous qu'il en veut. **'gunman** *n* (*pl* **-men**) voleur armé; terroriste *m*. **'gunner** *n* artilleur *m*; *Navy:* canonnier *m*. **'gunnery** *n* artillerie; tir au canon. **'gunpoint** *n* **at g.,** sous la menace d'un pistolet, d'un revolver; **to hold s.o. at g.,** menacer qn d'un pistolet, d'un fusil. **'gunpowder** *n* poudre *f* (à canon). **'gunrunner** *n* contrebandier *m* d'armes. **'gunship** *n Av:* (**helicopter**) **g.,** hélicoptère *m* de protection. **'gunshot** *n* coup *m* de fusil, de canon; coup de feu; **g. wound,** blessure de balle. **gunwale** ['gʌnl] *n Nau:* plat-bord *m*.

gurgle ['gə:gl] **1.** *n* glouglou *m* (d'un liquide); murmure *m* (d'un ruisseau); gloussement *m*, roucoulement *m* (de rire) **2.** *vi* glouglouter; faire glouglou; (*of stream*) murmurer; (*of pers*) glousser, roucouler.

guru ['gu:ru:] *n Rel:* gourou *m*.

gush [gʌʃ] **1.** *n* effusion *f* (de larmes); jet *m*, flot *m* (de sang) **2.** *vi* (*a*) **to g. (out),** jaillir, couler à flots; (*of torrent*) bouillonner (*b*) faire de longs discours flatteurs, sentimentaux. **'gushing** *a* jaillissant; (*torrent*) bouillonnant; (*pers*) exubérant, expansif.

gust [gʌst] *n* bouffée *f* (de fumée); **g. of rain,** ondée *f*. giboulée *f*; **g. of wind,** coup *m* de vent; rafale *f*, bourrasque *f*, *Nau:* grain *m*. **'gusty** *a* (vent) à rafales; (journée) de grand vent.

gusto ['gʌstou] *n* **to do sth with g.,** faire qch (i) avec plaisir (ii) avec élan, avec entrain.

gut [gʌt] **1.** *n* (*a*) *Anat:* boyau *m*, intestin *m*; *Mus:* corde *f* de boyau; **guts,** boyaux, intestins; *F:* **to have guts,** avoir du cran; *P:* **to sweat one's guts out,** se casser les reins; *Fig:* **g. reaction,** réaction dans son for intérieur **2.** *vtr* (**gutted**) vider (un poisson, une volaille); **the fire gutted the house,** le feu n'a laissé que les quatre murs de la maison. **'gutsy** *a F:* (*a*) goinfre (*b*) qui a du cran.

gutter ['gʌtər] *n* gouttière *f* (de toit); ruisseau *m* (de rue); caniveau *m*; *F:* **g. press,** bas-fonds *mpl* du journalisme. **'guttersnipe** *n* gamin, -ine, des rues.

guttural ['gʌtərəl] *a* guttural.

guy¹ [gai] **1.** *n* (*a*) effigie *f* burlesque de Guy Fawkes, chef de la Conspiration des Poudres (1605) (*b*) *F:* type

m, individu *m*; **a tough g.,** un dur **2.** *vtr* se moquer de (qn); ridiculiser.

guy² *n* (*also* **'guyrope**) corde *f* (de tente).

Guyana [gai'ɑːnə] *Prn Geog:* Guyane *f*.

guzzle ['gʌzl] *vtr & i* (*a*) bâfrer, bouffer (la nourriture); s'empiffrer (*b*) boire avidement, lamper (la boisson).

gym [dʒim] *n F:* (*a*) gymnase *m* (*b*) gymnastique *f*; **g. shoes,** chaussures de tennis, tennis *mpl*.

gymnasium [dʒim'neiziəm] *n* gymnase *m*. **'gymnast** [-næst] *n* gymnaste *mf*. **gym'nastic** *a* gymnastique. **gym'nastics** *npl* gymnastique *f*.

gynaecology, *NAm:* **gynecology** [gaini'kɔlədʒi] *n* gynécologie *f*. **gynae'cologist,** *NAm:* **gyne'cologist** *n* gynécologue *mf*.

gypsy ['dʒipsi] *n* (*pl* **gypsies**) *see* **gipsy.**

gyrate [dʒaiə'reit] *vi* tourner; tournoyer. **gy'ration** *n* giration *f*.

gyro ['dʒaiərou] *n Av:* **g. control,** commande gyroscopique. **gyro'compass** *n* (*pl* **-es**) gyrocompas *m*. **'gyroscope** *n* gyroscope *m*, gyro *m*. **gyro'scopic** *a* gyroscopique.

H

H, h [eiʃ] *n* (la lettre) H, h *m or f*; **to drop one's h's** [ˈeitʃiz] ne pas aspirer les h; **H-bomb,** bombe *f* H.

haberdasher [ˈhæbədæʃər] *n* mercier *m*; *NAm:* chemisier *m*. **haber'dashery** *n* mercerie *f*; *NAm:* chemiserie *f*.

habit [ˈhæbit] *n* (a) habitude *f*, coutume *f*; **to be in the h., to make a h., of doing sth,** avoir l'habitude de faire qch; **I don't make a h. of it,** ce n'est pas une habitude chez moi; **from, out of, by, (sheer) force of h.,** par (pure) habitude; **to get into bad habits,** prendre de mauvaises habitudes; **to get into, out of, the h. (of doing sth),** prendre, perdre, l'habitude (de faire qch) (b) *Cl:* habit *m* (de religieuse); **riding h.,** amazone *f*. **'habit-forming** *a* (drogue) qui cause une accoutumance. **ha'bitual** [-juəl] *a* habituel; (menteur) invétéré. **ha'bitually** *adv* habituellement; d'habitude. **ha'bituate** *vtr* **to h. s.o. to (doing) sth,** habituer, accoutumer, qn à (faire) qch.

habitat [ˈhæbitæt] *n Z: Bot:* habitat *m*.

habitation [hæbiˈteiʃn] *n* habitation *f*; **fit for h.,** habitable. **'habitable** *a* habitable.

hack¹ [hæk] *vtr* **to h. sth to pieces,** tailler qch en pièces. **'hacking** *a* h. cough, toux sèche et pénible. **'hacksaw** *n* scie *f* à métaux.

hack² 1. *n* (a) cheval de louage; cheval de selle (b) **h. (writer), (literary) h.,** écrivain *m* à la tâche; nègre *m* 2. *vi* **to go hacking,** (aller) se promener à cheval; **hacking jacket,** jaquette de cheval. **'hackwork** *n* travail *m* d'écrivain à la tâche.

hackney [ˈhækni] *n Adm:* **h. (cab, carriage),** voiture *f* de louage. **'hackneyed** *a* (sujet) rebattu, usé; **h. phrase,** expression devenue banale; cliché *m*.

had [hæd] *see* have.

haddock [ˈhædək] *n (no pl) Ich:* aiglefin *m*; **smoked h.,** haddock *m*.

haemoglobin, *NAm:* **hemo-** [hiːməˈgloubin] *n* hémoglobine *f*. **haemo'philia,** *NAm:* **hemo-** *n Med:* hémophilie *f*. **'haemorrhage,** *NAm:* **'hemo-** [ˈhemaridʒ] *n* hémorragie *f*. **'haemorrhoids,** *NAm:* **'hemorrhoids** *npl Med:* hémorroïdes *fpl*.

hag [hæg] *n* (vieille) sorcière; *F:* **old h.,** vieille taupe.

haggard [ˈhægəd] *a* hâve; décharné; (visage) égaré, hagard.

haggle [ˈhægl] *vi* marchander; **to h. about (the price of) sth,** chicaner sur (le prix de) qch.

Hague (the) [ðəˈheig] *Prn Geog:* la Haye.

hail¹ [heil] 1. *n* grêle *f* 2. *vi & tr* grêler; **it's hailing,** il grêle. **'hailstone** *n* grêlon *m*. **'hailstorm** *n* averse *f* de grêle.

hail² 1. *n esp Nau:* appel *m*; **within h.,** à portée de voix 2. *v* (a) *vtr* saluer (qn); héler (qn, un navire); appeler, héler (un taxi); **h.!** salut! *RCCh:* **the H. Mary,** l'Ave Marie *m* (b) *vi* *(of ship)* **to h. from,** être en provenance de; **where does he h. from?** d'où vient-il? **hail-**

'fellow-well-'met *a* **to be h.-f.-w.-m. with everyone,** être à tu et à toi avec tout le monde.

hair [ˈhɛər] *n* *(of head)* cheveu *m*; *(on body)* poil *m*; **coll** cheveux; *(on body)* poils; *(of animal)* pelage *m*, poil; *(of horse)* crin *m*; **head of h.,** chevelure *f*; **to do one's h.,** se coiffer; **to have one's h. done, cut,** se faire coiffer, se faire couper les cheveux; **to wash one's h.,** se laver les cheveux, la tête; **to have one's h. set,** se faire faire une mise en plis; *Fig:* **to split hairs,** couper les cheveux en quatre; **he escaped death by a h.'s breadth,** il a été à deux doigts de la mort; *F:* **to let one's h. down,** (i) se mettre à son aise (ii) s'amuser follement; **it was enough to make your h. stand on end,** c'était à faire dresser les cheveux (sur la tête); *F:* **h. of the dog that bit one,** boisson alcoolique prise pour faire passer une gueule de bois; *P:* **keep your h. on!** calme-toi! *F:* **to get in s.o.'s h.,** taper sur les nerfs à qn; **h. drier,** séchoir à cheveux; **h. spray,** laque *f*. **'hairbrush** *n* brosse *f* à cheveux. **'haircut** *n* coupe *f* de cheveux; **to have a h.,** se faire couper les cheveux. **'hairdo** *n* coiffure *f*. **'hairdresser** *n* coiffeur, -euse. **'hairdressing** *n* coiffure. **'hairgrip** *n (NAm: = bobby pin)* pince *f* à cheveux. **'hairless** *a* sans cheveux; *(of animal)* sans poils. **'hairline** *n* naissance *f* des cheveux; *Fig:* **h. distinction,** distinction subtile. **'hairnet** *n* filet *m* pour cheveux. **'hairpiece** *n* mèche *f* postiche. **'hairpin** *n* épingle *f* à cheveux; *(in road)* **h. bend,** virage en épingle à cheveux; lacet *m*. **'hairraising** *a* effrayant; à vous faire dresser les cheveux (sur la tête). **'hairslide** *n* barrette *f*. **'hairspring** *n* ressort spiral (de montre). **'hairstyle** *n* coiffure. **'hairy** *a* (-ier, -iest) velu, poilu; *(of scalp)* chevelu; *(of pers)* hirsute; *F: (of situation)* périlleux, épineux.

hake [heik] *n (no pl) Ich:* colin *m*.

hale [heil] *a* vigoureux; **h. and hearty,** frais et gaillard.

half [hɑːf] 1. *n (pl* halves [hɑːvz]*)* (a) moitié *f*; **h. the loaf,** la moitié du pain; **to cut sth in h.,** couper qch en deux; **to go halves with s.o.,** se mettre de moitié avec qn; **bigger by h.,** moitié plus grand; *F:* **he's too clever by h.,** il est beaucoup trop malin; **to do things by halves,** faire les choses à demi; *F:* **my better h.,** mon mari, ma femme; *(of wife)* ma chère moitié (b) demi *m*, demie *f*; **three and a h.,** trois et demi; **two hours and a h., two and a h. hours,** deux heures et demie (c) *Rail:* **return h.,** (billet *m* de) retour *m* (d) *(in train, bus)* demi-place *f*; *(in cinema)* demi-tarif *m* (e) *Sp:* **h.-time** *f* (f) *Sp: (pers)* demi 2. *a* demi; **h. an hour,** une demi-heure; **in h. a second,** en moins de rien; **at h. price,** à moitié prix 3. *adv* (a) à moitié; **he only h. understands,** il ne comprend qu'à moitié; **h. dressed,** à demi habillé; **h. naked,** à moitié nu; *(of work)* **h. done,** à moitié fait; **h. full, empty,** à moitié plein, vide; **h. closed, open,** entrouvert; **h. laughing, h. crying,** moitié riant, moitié pleurant; **I was h. afraid that,** j'avais quelque crainte que; *F:* **not h. bad**, pas mal du tout; *P:* **it isn't h. cold!** il fait rudement froid! *P:* **not h.!** tu parles! (*b*) **it's h. past two**, il est deux heures et demie (*c*) **h. as big**, moitié aussi grand; **h. as big again**, plus grand de moitié; **h. as much money as you**, moitié moins d'argent que vous. **'half-and-'half** *adv* moitié-moitié; moitié l'un, moitié l'autre; **how shall I mix them?**—h.-and-h., comment faut-il les mélanger?—à doses égales; je vous en mets combien de chaque (sorte)?—moitié-moitié. **'halfback** *n Sp:* demi(-arrière) *m.* **'half-baked** *a F:* (*of pers*) niais; (projet) qui ne tient pas debout. **'half-breed** *n* métis, -isse. **'half-brother** *n* demi-frère *m.* **'half-caste** *a & n* métis, -isse. **'half-'circle** *n* demi-cercle *m.* **half'cock(ed)** *a & n F:* **to go off at halfcock**, **to go off halfcock(ed)**, mal démarrer. **'half-'dozen** *n* demi-douzaine *f.* **'half-'fare** *n* (*in train, bus*) demi-place; (*in cinema*) demi-tarif. **'half-'hearted** *a* tiède; sans enthousiasme. **half-'heartedly** *adv* avec tiédeur; sans enthousiasme. **half-'holiday** *n* demi-journée *f* libre. **half-'hour** *n* demi-heure. **'half-'hourly** *a & adv* (qui a lieu) toutes les demi-heures. **half-'mast** *n* **at h.-m.**, en berne. **half-'moon** *n* demi-lune *f;* (*on finger-nails*) lunule *f.* **'half-'pay** *n* **on h.-p.**, en demi-solde *f.* **halfpenny** [ˈhɑːfpeni, *occ* ˈheipni] *n* (*pl* **-ies**) demi-penny *m.* **'half-shaft** *n Aut:* demi-arbre *m.* **'half-'sister** *n* demi-sœur *f.* **'half-'term** *n Sch:* **h.-t. (holiday)**, congé *m* de mi-trimestre. **'half-'timbered** *a* (maison) à colombage. **half-'time** *n Sp:* mi-temps. **'half-tone** *n Phot:* simili *f.* **'half-track** *n Veh:* (auto)chenille *f.* **'halfway** *adv* à moitié chemin; à mi-chemin; **h. up, down (the hill)**, à mi-côte, à mi-pente; *Fig:* **to meet s.o. h.**, faire la moitié des avances; couper la poire en deux. **'halfwit** *n* idiot, -ote. **'half-'yearly** **1.** *a* semestriel **2.** *adv* tous les six mois.

halibut [ˈhælibət] *n* (*no pl*) *Ich:* flétan *m.*

halitosis [hæliˈtousis] *n Med:* mauvaise haleine.

hall [hɔːl] *n* (*a*) grande salle; **dining h.**, salle à manger (d'un château); *Sch:* (*of college*) réfectoire *m;* **concert h.**, salle de concert; **music h.**, music-hall *m* (*b*) (**entrance**) **h.**, entrée *f;* hall *m; esp NAm:* couloir *m;* **h. porter**, concierge *mf* (*c*) (**large house**) manoir *m; Sch:* **h.** (**of residence**) = cité *f* universitaire. **'hallmark** *n* poinçon *m* (sur les objets d'orfèvrerie); *Fig:* empreinte *f.* **'hallstand** *n* portemanteau *m.* **'hallway** *n* vestibule *m,* entrée; *esp NAm:* couloir.

hallo [həˈlou] *int* (*greeting*) bonjour! salut! (*calling attention*) holà! ohé! (*indicating surprise*) tiens! *Tp:* allô!

hallow [ˈhælou] *vtr* sanctifier, consacrer; *Ecc:* **hallowed be thy name**, que ton nom soit sanctifié; **hallowed ground**, terre sainte. **Hallow'e'en** [-ˈiːn] *n* veille *f* de la Toussaint.

hallucination [həluːsiˈneiʃn] *n* hallucination *f.*

halo [ˈheilou] *n* (*pl* **haloes**) (*a*) *Astr:* halo *m* (*b*) auréole *f,* nimbe *m* (d'un saint).

halt [hɔːlt] *n* (*a*) halte *f,* arrêt *m;* *PN: Aut:* stop *m;* **to come to a h.**, faire halte; s'arrêter; **to call a h. to sth**, arrêter qch (*b*) *Rail:* (*small station*) halte **2.** *v* (*a*) *vi* s'arrêter; **h.!** halte! (*b*) *vtr* faire faire halte à. **'halting** *a* hésitant.

halter [ˈhɔ(ː)ltər] *n* licou *m.* **'halterneck** *n Cl:* encolure *f* bain-de-soleil.

halve [hɑːv] *vtr* (*a*) diviser, partager, en deux (*b*) réduire de moitié.

halves [hɑːvz] *see* **half 1.**

ham [hæm] **1.** *n* (*a*) *Cu:* jambon *m;* **h. and eggs**, œufs au jambon; **boiled h.**, jambon cuit (*b*) **h.** (**actor**), cabotin, -ine (*c*) (**radio**) **h.**, amateur *m* de radio **2.** *vtr & i* (**hammed**) *Th:* **to h.** (**it up**), jouer (un rôle) en charge. **'ham-'fisted** *a* maladroit. **'hamstring** **1.** *n* tendon *m* du jarret **2.** *vtr* (**hamstrung**) *Fig:* couper les moyens à (qn).

Hamburg [ˈhæmbəːg] *Prn Geog:* Hambourg. **'hamburger** *n Cu:* hamburger *m.*

hamlet [ˈhæmlit] *n* hameau *m.*

hammer [ˈhæmər] **I.** *n Tls:* marteau *m;* (*heavy*) masse *f;* (*at auction*) **to come under the h.**, être mis aux enchères; **to go at it h. and tongs**, se bagarrer. **II.** *v* **1.** *vtr* (*a*) marteler, battre au marteau; **to h. into shape**, façonner (un pot); **to h. sth into s.o.**, faire entrer qch dans la tête à qn (*b*) *F:* battre (qn) à plates coutures (*c*) *F:* critiquer (qn, un livre) **2.** *vi* travailler au marteau; **to h. at, on, the door**, frapper à la porte à coups redoublés. **'hammer 'in** *vtr* enfoncer (un clou) à coups de marteau. **'hammering** *n F:* **to give s.o. a good h.**, battre qn à plates coutures. **'hammer 'out** *vtr* perfectionner (un projet).

hammock [ˈhæmək] *n* hamac *m.*

hamper[1] [ˈhæmpər] *n* manne *f;* panier *m* (à provisions).

hamper[2] *vtr* embarrasser, gêner.

hamster [ˈhæmstər] *n Z:* hamster *m.*

hand [hænd] **1.** *n* (*a*) main *f;* **on one's hands and knees**, à quatre pattes; **to vote by show of hands**, voter à main levée; **to hold (sth) in one's h.**, tenir (un revolver) à la main, (des graines) dans la main, (le succès) entre les mains; **to take s.o. by the h.**, prendre qn par la main; **give me your h.!** donne-moi la main! **to take s.o.'s h.**, donner la main à qn; **to lay hands on sth**, mettre la main sur qch; s'emparer de qch; **hands off!** bas les mains, *F:* les pattes! **hands up!** haut les mains! **he can turn his h. to anything**, il sait tout faire; **to have a h. in sth**, se mêler de qch; y être pour qch; **I had no h. in it**, je n'y suis pour rien; **to give s.o. a (helping) h.**, donner un coup de main à qn; **to have one's hands full**, avoir fort à faire; **to have sth on one's hands**, avoir qch à sa charge, sur les bras; *Com:* **goods left on our hands**, marchandises invendues; **to change hands**, changer de main, de propriétaire; **to be in good hands**, être en bonnes mains; **to put oneself in s.o.'s (good) hands**, s'en remettre à qn (*b*) applaudissement(s) *m(pl)*; **to give s.o. a good h.**, applaudir vivement qn (*c*) *phrs* **to be (near) at h.**, être sous la main, à portée de la main; **Christmas was (close) at h.**, Noël était tout proche; **made by h.**, fait (à la) main; **hat in h.**, chapeau bas; **revolver in h.**, revolver au poing; **to have some money in h.**, avoir de l'argent disponible; **cash in h.**, espèces en caisse; **I've got 5 minutes in h.**, j'ai encore 5 minutes; **the matter in h.**, la chose en question; **to take sth in h.**, prendre qch en main; se charger de qch; **situation well in h.**, situation bien en main; **work in h.**, travail en cours; **on (the) one h.**, d'une part; **on the other h.**, d'autre part; par contre; **to do sth out of h.**, faire qch immédiatement, sur-le-champ; **to get out of h.**, perdre toute discipline; **your parcel has come to h.**, votre paquet m'est parvenu, est arrivé à destination; **the first excuse to h.**, le premier prétexte venu; **to be h. in glove with s.o.**, être d'intelligence, de mèche, avec qn; **to wait on s.o. h. and foot**, être aux petits soins avec qn; **h. in h.**, la main dans la main; **h. to h.**, (lutter) corps à corps; **to make money h. over fist**, faire des affaires d'or; **to live from h. to mouth**, vivre au jour le jour; **to win hands down**, gagner haut la main; **horse 15 hands high**, cheval de quinze paumes *fpl* (*d*) (*pers*) ouvrier, -ière; manœuvre *m*; *Nau*: matelot *m*; (*of ship*) **the hands**, l'équipage *m*; (*of ship*) **all hands on deck!** tout le monde sur le pont! **to be lost with all hands**, périr corps et biens; *Ind*: **to take on hands**, embaucher de la main-d'œuvre; **to be a good, dab, h. at doing sth**, être adroit à faire qch; **an old h.**, un expert (*e*) *Cards*: jeu *m*; (*cards*) main; (*game*) partie *f* (*f*) aiguille *f* (de montre) 2. *vtr* passer, remettre, donner (qch à qn); *Fig*: **to h. it to s.o.**, reconnaître la supériorité de qn. '**hand ' back** *vtr* rendre (qch à qn). '**handbag** *n* sac *m* à main. '**handball** *n esp NAm: Games*: hand-ball *m*. '**handbell** *n* sonnette *f*. '**handbill** *n* prospectus *m*. '**handbook** *n* manuel *m*; guide *m*; livret *m* (d'un musée). '**handbrake** *n* frein *m* à main. '**handclap** *n* **to give s.o. the slow h.**, battre lentement des mains pour manifester son ennui, son impatience, vis à vis de qn. '**handcuff** 1. *n* menotte *f* 2. *vtr* mettre des menottes à (qn). '**hand ' down** *vtr* descendre (qch) (et le remettre à qn); transmettre (une tradition). '**handful** *n* ouvrage *m*; **a h. of people**, une poignée de gens; **by the h.**, par poignées; **that child is quite a h.**, cet enfant me donne du fil à retordre. '**handicap** 1. *n* handicap *m*; désavantage *m*; **to have a physical h.**, être handicapé physiquement 2. *vtr* (**handicapped**) handicaper; **to be handicapped**, être handicapé, désavantagé. '**handicapped** 1. *a* handicapé 2. *npl* **the physically, mentally, h.**, les handicapés *m* physiques, mentaux. '**handicraft** *n* métier manuel; *pl* (i) artisanat *m* (ii) produits *mpl* de l'industrie artisanale. '**hand ' in** *vtr* remettre. '**handiwork** *n* ouvrage *m*; œuvre *f*; **is that your h.?** c'est toi qui as fait cela? '**handkerchief** [ˈhæŋkətʃi(:)f] *n* mouchoir *m*. '**hand-'knitted** *a* tricoté (à la) main. '**hand'made** *a* fait, fabriqué, (à la) main. '**hand ' on** *vtr* transmettre. '**hand ' out** *vtr* distribuer. '**handout** *n* (*a*) communiqué *m* (à la presse); prospectus *m* (publicitaire); *Sch*: notes (polycopiées) (données aux étudiants) (*b*) aumône *f*. '**hand'over** *vtr* remettre (qch à qn); livrer (qn à la justice); transmettre (ses pouvoirs) (**to**, à); céder (sa propriété). '**hand'picked** *a* trié sur le volet. '**handrail** *n* garde-fou *m*; rampe *f*, main courante (d'escalier). '**hand ' round** *vtr* faire passer, faire circuler (la bouteille, les gâteaux). '**handshake** *n* poignée *f* de main. '**handstand** *n Gym*: **to do a h.**, faire l'arbre droit. '**hand-to-'hand** *a* **h.-to-h. fighting**, corps à corps *m*. '**handwriting** *n* écriture *f*. '**handwritten** *a* manuscrit; écrit à la main. '**handy** *a* (-**ier**, -**iest**) (*a*) (*of pers*) adroit (de ses mains); **he's very h. about the house**, c'est un bon bricoleur (*b*) (*of tool*) maniable (*c*) commode; **that would come in very h.**, cela ferait bien l'affaire (*d*) à portée (de la main); **to keep sth h.**, tenir qch sous la main. '**handyman** *n* (*pl* -**men**) homme *m* à tout

faire; (*for pleasure*) bricoleur *m*.

handle [ˈhændl] 1. *n* manche *m* (de couteau); poignée *f* (de porte); anse *f* (de seau, de panier); bras *m* (de brouette); queue *f* (de poêle); *Aut*: **starting h.**, manivelle *f*; *F*: **to fly off the h.**, s'emporter, sortir de ses gonds 2. *vtr* manier, manipuler (qch); manœuvrer (un navire); conduire (une voiture); se servir d'(un fusil); prendre en main (une situation); s'occuper de (l'affaire); (*of pers*) **he's hard to h.**, il n'est pas commode. '**handlebar(s)** *n* (*pl*) guidon *m* (de vélo, de moto). '**handler** *n* (dog) h., dresseur, -euse (de chiens). '**handling** *n* maniement *m*; manœuvre *f* (d'une voiture, d'un bateau); manutention *f* (de marchandises); traitement *m* (de qn); **rough h.**, traitement brutal.

handsome [ˈhænsəm] *a* beau; (meuble) élégant; (*of action, conduct*) gracieux, généreux; **a h. man**, un bel homme; **to make a h. profit**, réaliser de beaux bénéfices. '**handsomely** *adv* (*a*) élégamment, avec élégance (*b*) généreusement.

hang [hæŋ] I. *v* (hung) 1. *vtr* (*a*) pendre, accrocher, suspendre (qch) (**on, from**, à); monter (une porte); **hall hung with flags**, salle ornée de drapeaux; **to h. one's head**, baisser la tête; (*of plan*) **to h. fire**, traîner (en longueur) (*b*) poser (un papier peint) (*c*) (hanged) pendre (un criminel) 2. *vi* (*a*) pendre, être suspendu (**on, from**, à); **picture hanging on the wall**, tableau suspendu, accroché, au mur; **to h. out of the window**, (*of pers*) se pencher à la fenêtre; (*of thg*) pendre à la fenêtre (*b*) (*of fog*) planer; (*of silence*) peser; (*of curtains, hair*) tomber (*c*) (*of criminal*) être pendu. II. *n F*: **to get the h. of sth**, (i) attraper le coup, saisir le truc, de, pour, qch (ii) comprendre, piger, qch. '**hang a'bout, a'round** *vtr & i* traîner, flâner (à la maison, dans les rues). '**hang ' back** *vi* rester en arrière; hésiter. '**hangdog** *a* **h. look**, air de chien battu. '**hang ' down** *vi* pendre; (*of hair*) tomber. '**hanger** *n* (clothes, coat) **h.**, cintre *m*. '**hanger-'on** *n* (*pl* **hangers-on**) (*pers*) parasite *m*. '**hang-glider** *n Sp*: libriste *mf*. '**hang-gliding** *n* (sport *m* de l')aile *f* libre. '**hanging** 1. (*a*) suspension *f* (de qch) (*b*) pendaison *f* (d'un criminel) (*c*) *usu pl* tenture(s) *f*(*pl*); tapisserie(s) *f*(*pl*) 2. *a* pendant; (pont) suspendu. '**hangman** *n* (*pl* -**men**) bourreau *m*. '**hang ' on** 1. *vi* se cramponner, s'accrocher (**to**, à qch); *Fig*: tenir; **h. on to your job**, ne lâchez pas votre situation; **h. on!** minute! *Tp*: ne quittez pas! **h. on (for) a minute!** attendez un instant! 2. *vtr* être suspendu à (qch); (*of result*) dépendre de (qch); **to h. on s.o.'s every word**, écouter avidement qn. '**hang ' out** 1. *vtr* prendre (qch) au dehors; étendre (le linge); arborer (un pavillon) 2. *vi* pendre (au dehors); *F*: habiter; **where do you h. out?** où nichez-vous? '**hang-over** *n* (*a*) gueule *f* de bois (*b*) reliquat *m* (d'une habitude). '**hang to'gether** *vi* (*of statements*) s'accorder, tenir debout. '**hang 'up** *vtr & i* accrocher, pendre (un tableau); *Tp*: **to h. up** (the receiver), raccrocher (l'appareil); **to h. up on s.o.**, couper la communication avec qn; *F*: **to be hung up**, être obsédé, frustré. '**hang-up** *n F*: trouble *m* psychique.

hangar [ˈhæŋər] *n Av*: hangar *m*.

hank [hæŋk] *n* écheveau *m* (de laine).

hanker [ˈhæŋkər] *vi* **to h. after sth**, avoir bien envie de qch. ' **hankering** n vif désir (pour qch); **to have a h. for sth**, avoir bien envie de qch.

hankie, -y ['hæŋki] n (pl **hankies**) F: mouchoir m.

hanky-panky ['hæŋki'pæŋki] n (no pl) F: supercherie f; finasseries fpl.

haphazard [hæp'hæzəd] a au hasard; fortuit.
hap'hazardly adv au hasard; au petit bonheur.

happen ['hæpən] vi (a) arriver; se passer, se produire; **don't let it h. again!** que cela n'arrive plus! **(just) as if nothing had happened**, comme si de rien n'était; **whatever happens**, quoi qu'il arrive; **as it happens**, justement; F: **worse things h. at sea**, il y a pire; **what's happened to him?** (i) qu'est-ce qui lui est arrivé? (ii) qu'est-ce qu'il est devenu? **if anything happened to you**, s'il vous arrivait quelque chose; **something has happened to him**, il lui est arrivé quelque chose (b) (chance) **he happened to pass that way**, il s'est trouvé passer par là; **if I h. to forget**, s'il m'arrive d'oublier; **the house happened to be empty**, la maison se trouvait vide; **do you h. to know whether**, sauriez-vous par hasard si? **to h. upon sth**, tomber sur qch. ' **happening** n événement m; Th: happening m.

happy ['hæpi] a (-ier, -iest) heureux; **to be h. to do sth, h. with sth**, être content de (faire) qch; h. **thought!** bonne inspiration! **h. Christmas!** joyeux Noël! ' **happily** adv heureusement; **to live h.**, vivre heureux. ' **happiness** n bonheur m; félicité f. ' **happy-go-'lucky** a (of pers) sans souci; insouciant; **in a h.-go-l. way**, au petit bonheur.

harangue [hə'ræŋ] 1. n harangue f 2. vtr haranguer (la foule).

harass ['hærəs, NAm: hə'ræs] vtr harceler; tracasser, tourmenter (qn). ' **harassment**, NAm: **ha'rassment** n harcèlement m; tracasserie f.

harbour, NAm: harbor ['ha:bər] 1. n port m; h. **master**, capitaine de port 2. vtr héberger (qn); receler (un criminel); retenir (la saleté); entretenir (des soupçons); **to h. a grudge against s.o.**, garder rancune à qn.

hard [ha:d] 1. a (a) dur; (of snow) durci; **to get h.**, durcir; (of pers) **to be as h. as nails**, (i) être musclé (ii) être dur; **h. currency**, devise forte; **h. cash**, espèces fpl; h. **frost**, forte gelée; h. **water**, eau calcaire; h. **liquor**, spiritueux mpl (b) difficile; (tâche) pénible; h. **work**, (i) travail difficile (ii) travail assidu (iii) travail ingrat; **it was h. work to**, j'avais du mal à; **to be h. to please**, être exigeant, difficile; **to be h. of hearing**, être dur d'oreille; Com: h. **sell**, vente agressive; **I find it h. to believe that**, j'ai de la peine à croire que; **it's h. to understand**, c'est difficile à comprendre (of pers, manner) dur, sévère (on, to, towards, envers); (fait) brutal; (hiver) rigoureux; **times are h.**, les temps sont rudes, durs; **to have a h. time of it**, en voir de dures; F: h. **luck!** h. **lines!** pas de chance! **to try one's hardest**, faire tout son possible 2. adv fort; **as h. as one can**, de toutes ses forces; **to hit h.**, cogner dur; **to look h. at s.o.**, regarder fixement qn; **to think h.**, réfléchir profondément; **to be h. at work**, F: **at it**, être en plein travail; **it's raining h.**, il pleut à verse; **to snow h.**, neiger dru; **to freeze h.**, geler dur; F: **to be h. up**, être à court d'argent), fauché; **to be h. pushed**, être dans la gêne; **to try h.**, faire un grand effort; **to try harder**, faire de plus grands efforts; **to work h.**, travailler dur. ' **hard-and-'fast** a (of rule) rigoureux, absolu.

' **hardback** n livre cartonné. ' **hardboard** n Isorel m (Rtm). ' **hard-'boiled** a (œuf) dur; (of pers) dur à cuire. ' **hardcore** n (a) Const: blocaille f (b) noyau m (de résistance); h. **pornography**, pornographie dure. ' **hard-'earned** a (salaire) péniblement gagné; (prix) bien mérité. ' **harden** vtr & i durcir; (of pers) **to become hardened**, s'endurcir; **hardened criminal**, criminel endurci. ' **hardening** n durcissement m. ' **hard-'fought** a (of election, battle) chaudement contesté; âprement disputé. ' **hard-'headed** a (of pers) positif, pratique; réaliste. ' **hard-'hearted** a impitoyable, au cœur dur. **hard-'liner** n Pol: faucon m. ' **hardly** adv (a) à peine; ne ... guère; **I h. know**, je n'en sais trop rien; **she can h. read**, c'est à peine si elle sait lire; **you'll h. believe it**, vous aurez de la peine à le croire; **I need h. say**, pas besoin de dire; h. **anyone**, presque personne (b) **he could h. have said that**, il n'aurait sûrement pas dit cela. ' **hardness** n dureté f; difficulté f (d'un travail); sévérité f, rigueur f (d'une règle). ' **hardship** n privation f; fatigue f; (dure) épreuve. ' **hardware** n (a) quincaillerie f; h. **dealer**, quincaillier m; h. **shop**, quincaillerie f (b) Tchn: éléments matériels (d'un système); F: armes fpl (c) Cmptr: matériel m, hardware m. ' **hard-'wearing** a (vêtement) de bon usage; durable. ' **hard-'working** a laborieux, travailleur, assidu. ' **hardy** a (-ier, -iest) robuste; endurci; (of plant) résistant; Bot: (plante) de pleine terre.

hare [hɛər] 1. n Z: lièvre m; **doe h.**, hase f; **young h.**, levraut m; Cu: **jugged h.**, civet m de lièvre 2. vi F: **to h. off**, se sauver, s'élancer, courir, à toutes jambes. ' **harebell** n Bot: campanule f. ' **harebrained** a écervelé, étourdi; (projet) insensé. ' **harelip** n bec-de-lièvre m.

haricot ['hærikou] n Bot: h. **(bean)** haricot blanc.

hark [ha:k] vi Lit: h.! écoutez! ' **hark 'back** vi F: **to h. b. to sth**, revenir à un sujet.

harm [ha:m] 1. n mal m, tort m; **to do s.o. h.**, faire du mal, du tort à qn; nuire à qn; **to see no h. in sth**, ne pas voir de mal à qch; **you'll come to no h.**, il ne vous arrivera aucun mal; **out of harm's way**, à l'abri du danger; en sûreté; **that won't do any h.**, cela ne gâtera rien; **there's no h. in trying**, on peut toujours essayer; **there's no h. in saying so**, il n'y a pas de mal à le dire 2. vtr faire du mal, du tort, à (qn); nuire à (qn). ' **harmful** a malfaisant, pernicieux; nuisible. ' **harmless** a (animal) inoffensif; (individu) sans malice; (passe-temps) innocent; (médicament) anodin.

harmony ['ha:məni] n harmonie f; (agreement) accord m; **to live in perfect h.**, vivre en parfaite intelligence; **in h. with**, conforme à, qui s'accorde avec. **har'monica** n Mus: harmonica m. **har'monious** a harmonieux. ' **harmonize** 1. vtr harmoniser 2. vi s'harmoniser; (of facts, pers) s'accorder.

harness ['ha:nis] 1. n (pl **harnesses**) (a) harnais m; Fig: **to get back into h.**, reprendre le collier; **to die in h.**, mourir à la peine (b) ceinture f (de parachutiste, de sécurité) 2. vtr harnacher (un cheval); atteler (un cheval à une voiture); aménager (une chute d'eau); exploiter (l'énergie atomique).

harp [ha:p] 1. n Mus: harpe f; **to play the h.**, jouer de la harpe 2. vi **to be always harping on about sth**, rabâcher toujours la même chose.

harpoon [hɑːˈpuːn] 1. *n* harpon *m* 2. *vtr* harponner.

harpsichord [ˈhɑːpsikɔːd] *n Mus:* clavecin *m*.

harrow [ˈhærou] *n Agr:* herse *f*. **ˈharrowing** *a* poignant; navrant; (cri) déchirant.

harsh [hɑːʃ] *a* (*a*) dur, rêche, rude (au toucher); âpre (au goût); strident (à l'oreille); (voix) rude (*b*) (caractère) dur, bourru; (maître) rude. **ˈharshly** *adv* durement; (traiter qn) sévèrement. **ˈharshness** *n* dureté *f*, rudesse *f* (au toucher); âpreté *f* (au goût); (*of pers, punishment*) sévérité *f*.

harum-scarum [ˈhɛərəmˈskɛərəm] *a F:* étourdi, écervelé.

harvest [ˈhɑːvist] 1. *n* (*a*) moisson *f*; récolte *f*; vendange *f* (du vin); **to get in the h.,** faire la moisson; **h. festival,** action de grâces (après la rentrée des récoltes); **h. home,** fête de la moisson (*b*) (époque *f* de) la moisson 2. (*a*) *vtr* moissonner (les blés); récolter (les fruits) (*b*) *vi* rentrer, faire, la moisson. **ˈharvester** *n* (*pers*) moissonneur, -euse; (*machine*) (**combine**) **h.,** moissonneuse(-batteuse) *f*.

has [hæz] *see* **have**. **ˈhas-been** *n* (*pl* **-beens**) *F:* homme fini, femme finie; vieille croûte.

hash [hæʃ] 1. *n* (*a*) *Cu:* hachis *m*; *F:* **to make a h. of sth,** gâcher, faire un beau gâchis de, qch; **he made a h. of it,** il a tout bousillé, saboté (*b*) *F:* **h.(-up),** réchauffé *m* (de vieilles idées) 2. *vtr* **to h. (up) meat,** hacher de la viande.

hashish [ˈhæʃiʃ] *n* hachisch *m*.

hassle [ˈhæsl] *F:* 1. *n* (*a*) dispute *f*, chamaille *f* (*b*) embêtement *m* 2. *vtr* embêter (qn).

haste [heist] *n* hâte *f*; **to make h.,** se hâter, se dépêcher (**to do,** de faire); **in h.,** à la hâte. **hasten** [ˈheisn] 1. *vtr* avancer (la mort de qn) 2. *vi* se hâter, se dépêcher (**to do,** de faire). **ˈhastily** *adv* à la hâte; précipitamment; (parler) sans réfléchir. **ˈhastiness** *n* précipitation *f*, hâte *f*; (*of temper*) emportement *m*. **ˈhasty** *a* (**-ier, -iest**) (départ) précipité; (repas) sommaire; (croquis) fait à la hâte; (aveu) irréfléchi; (*of temper*) emporté.

hat [hæt] *n* chapeau *m*; **to raise one's h. to s.o.,** saluer qn (d'un coup de chapeau); **to take off one's h.,** enlever son chapeau; *Fig:* **I take my h. off to him (for that)!** je lui tire mon chapeau! **to pass the h. round** (for s.o.), faire la quête (pour qn); *F:* **keep it under your h.,** gardez ça pour vous; *F:* **old h.,** vieux jeu; **to talk through one's h.,** débiter des sottises; *Sp:* **h. trick,** trois réussites de suite. **ˈhatshop** *n* (*for men*) chapellerie *f*; (*for women*) (boutique *f* de) modiste *f*; **at the h.,** chez la modiste.

hatch¹ [hætʃ] *n* (*pl* **hatches**) (*a*) *Nau:* écoutille *f*; **under hatches,** dans la cale; *F:* (*when drinking*) **down the h.!** cul sec! (*b*) passe-plats *m inv.* **ˈhatchback** *n Aut:* (voiture *f* à) hayon *m* arrière.

hatch² 1. *vtr* faire éclore (des poussins); (faire) couver (des œufs); ourdir, tramer (un complot) 2. *vi* **to h. (out),** éclore.

hatchet [ˈhætʃit] *n* hachette *f*, cognée *f*; hache *f* à main; *Fig:* **h. man,** tueur à gages; *Pol:* homme de main.

hate [heit] 1. *n* haine *f*; *F:* (**pet**) **h.,** objet *m* d'aversion; bête noire 2. *vtr* haïr, détester (qn); avoir horreur de (qch); **to h. to do sth,** détester faire qch; **I h. to trouble you,** je suis désolé de vous déranger; **she hates being kissed,** elle a horreur d'être embrassée; **she hates to be**

contradicted, elle n'admet pas qu'on la contredise; **to h. oneself for sth,** s'en vouloir de qch. **ˈhateful** *a* odieux; détestable. **ˈhatred** *n* haine *f* (*of*, de, contre).

haughty [ˈhɔːti] *a* (**-ier, -iest**) hautain, arrogant, altier. **ˈhaughtily** *adv* avec hauteur. **ˈhaughtiness** *n* hauteur *f*, arrogance *f*.

haul [hɔːl] 1. *vtr* tirer; traîner; remorquer (un bateau) 2. *n* (*a*) *Fish:* coup *m* de filet (*b*) *Fish:* prise *f*; pêche *f* (*c*) *F:* (*of burglar*) butin *m* (*d*) *Aut: etc:* parcours *m*, trajet *m*; **a long h.,** un long trajet; *Av:* **short, long, h.,** étape courte, longue. **ˈhaulage** *n* (*a*) transport routier; **h. contractor,** entrepreneur de transports (*b*) frais *mpl* de transport. **ˈhaul ˈdown** *vtr* descendre. **ˈhaulier** *n* entrepreneur de transports. **ˈhaul ˈin** *vtr* tirer (en dedans). **ˈhaul ˈup** *vtr* monter; hisser (un pavillon).

haunch [hɔːntʃ] *n Anat:* hanche *f*; *Cu:* cuissot *m* (de chevreuil); **haunches,** arrière-train *m* (d'un animal); **sitting on his haunches,** (*of pers*) accroupi; (chien) assis (sur son derrière).

haunt [hɔːnt] 1. *n* lieu fréquenté (par qn); repaire *m* (d'un animal); **it's a favourite h. of mine,** (i) c'est un de mes endroits favoris (ii) c'est un lieu où j'aime souvent aller 2. *vtr* fréquenter, hanter (un endroit); (*of ghost*) hanter; **this house is haunted,** il y a des revenants dans cette maison; **haunted by memories,** obsédé par des souvenirs; **haunted** *a* hanté; (air) égaré. **ˈhaunting** *a* qui vous hante; (souvenir) obsédant.

Havana [həˈvænə] 1. *Prn Geog:* Havane *f* 2. *n* **H.** (**cigar**), havane *m*.

have [hæv] (**had**; *pr he* **has**) *vtr* 1. (*a*) avoir, posséder; **he has no friends,** hasn't got any friends, il n'a pas d'amis; **all I h.,** tout ce que je possède; **he has a shop,** il tient un magasin; **I h. it!** j'y suis! **my bag has no name on it,** ma valise ne porte pas de nom; **I h. nothing to do,** je n'ai rien à faire; **I h. work to do,** j'ai à travailler (*b*) **we don't h. many visitors,** nous ne recevons pas beaucoup de visites; **we're having visitors tomorrow,** nous attendons des invités demain; **to h. s.o. to dinner,** avoir qn à dîner 2. **to h. a child,** avoir, donner naissance à, un enfant 3. (*a*) **there was no work to be had,** on ne pouvait pas obtenir de travail (*b*) **to h. news from s.o.,** recevoir des nouvelles de qn; **I h. it on good authority that,** je tiens de bonne source que (*c*) **I must h. them by tomorrow,** il me les faut pour demain; **let me h. your keys,** donnez-moi vos clefs; **I will let you h. it for £10,** je vous le céderai pour dix livres; **let me h. an early reply,** répondez-moi sans retard; *F:* **I let him h. it,** (i) je lui ai dit son fait (ii) je lui ai réglé son compte; *F:* **you've had it!** tu es foutu! 4. **to h. tea with s.o.,** prendre le thé avec qn; **to h. lunch,** déjeuner; **will you h. some wine?** voulez-vous prendre du vin? **I had some more,** j'en ai repris; **he is having his dinner,** il est en train de dîner; **to h. a cigar,** fumer un cigare; *F:* **I'm not having any!** on ne me la fait pas! ça ne prend pas! 5. (*a*) **to h. an idea,** avoir une idée; **to h. a right to sth,** avoir droit à qch (*b*) **to h. measles, avoir la rougeole;** (c) I h. a cold, je suis enrhumé; **he has (got) a sore throat, he has (got) earache,** il a mal à la gorge, aux oreilles; **to h. a dream,** faire un rêve; **to h. a game,** faire une partie (*c*) **to h. a lesson,** prendre une leçon; **to h. a bath, a shower,** prendre un bain, une douche; **to h. a wash,** se laver (*d*) **to h. a pleasant evening,** passer une soirée agréable; **I**

didn't h. any trouble at all, cela ne m'a donné aucune peine; **we had a rather strange adventure,** il nous est arrivé une aventure assez étrange 6. (a) prétendre, soutenir; **he will not h. it that she is delicate,** il n'admet pas qu'elle soit de santé délicate; **rumour has it that,** le bruit court que (b) **to h. s.o. by the throat,** tenir qn à la gorge; F: **you've been had!** on vous a eu! 7. **to h. sth done,** faire faire qch; **to h. a house built,** faire construire une maison; **to h. one's hair cut,** se faire couper les cheveux; **I had my watch stolen,** on m'a volé ma montre; **he had his leg broken,** il s'est cassé la jambe 8. (a) **which (one) will you h.?** lequel voulez-vous? **as luck would h. it,** le hasard a voulu que; **I'd h. you know that,** sachez que (b) **what would you h. me do?** que voulez-vous que je fasse? (c) **I will not h. such conduct,** je ne supporterai pas une pareille conduite; **I won't h. him teased,** je ne veux pas qu'on le taquine 9. **to h. to do sth,** devoir faire qch; être obligé de faire qch; être forcé de faire qch; **we shall h. to walk faster,** il nous faudra marcher plus vite; **I haven't got to work,** je n'ai pas besoin de travailler 10. (as auxiliary) (a) **to h. been,** avoir été; **to h. come,** **to h. hurt oneself,** être venu, s'être blessé; **I h. lived in London for three years,** voilà trois ans que j'habite Londres; j'habite Londres depuis trois ans; (emphatic) **well, you h. grown!** ce que tu as grandi! (b) **you h. forgotten your gloves—so I h.!** vous avez oublié vos gants—en effet! **you haven't swept the room—(yes,) I h.!** vous n'avez pas balayé la pièce—si! mais si! (no,) **I haven't!** c'est faux! 11. **I had, I'd, better say nothing,** je ferais mieux de ne rien dire; **I had, I'd, as soon stay here,** j'aimerais autant rester ici; **I'd much rather start at once,** j'aimerais bien mieux partir tout de suite. **have in** vtr **I had them in for a cup of tea,** je les ai fait entrer pour prendre une tasse de thé; **I had the doctor in,** j'ai fait venir le médecin; F: **to h. it in for s.o.,** garder à qn un chien de la chienne. **'have-'nots** npl the h.-n., les pauvres m. **'have 'on** vtr 1. (a) porter (un vêtement); **to h. nothing on,** être à poil, être nu (b) **I h. a lecture on this evening,** ce soir, je dois (i) faire (ii) assister à, une conférence; **I haven't got anything on,** je ne suis pas pris 2. **to h. s.o. on,** duper, faire marcher, qn 3. **to h. something on (a horse),** faire un pari. **'have 'out** vtr (se) faire arracher (une dent); F: **to h. it o. with s.o.,** s'expliquer avec qn. **'haves** npl the h., les riches m. **'have 'up** vtr citer (qn) en justice; **to be had up,** être cité devant le tribunal

haven ['heivn] n port m; Fig: abri m, asile m.

haversack ['hævəsæk] n sac m à dos, havresac m; Mil: musette f.

havoc ['hævək] n ravage m, dégâts mpl; **to play, wreak, h. (with sth),** faire de grands dégâts (dans qch); ravager (les récoltes); désorganiser (des projets).

haw [hɔː] n Bot: cenelle f.

Hawaii [hə'wai] Prn Geog: Hawaï m.

hawk [hɔːk] n Orn: faucon m; **to have eyes like a h.,** avoir des yeux d'aigle.

hawker ['hɔːkər] n colporteur m; démarcheur, -euse.

hawthorn ['hɔːθɔːn] n Bot: aubépine f.

hay [hei] n foin m; **to make h.,** faire les foins; faner; Prov: **to make h. while the sun shines,** battre le fer pendant qu'il est chaud; Med: **h. fever,** rhume des foins. **'haycock** n tas m, meulon m, de foin. **'hayfork** n fourche f à foin. **'hayloft** n fenil m;

grenier m à foin. **'haymaker** n (pers) faneur, -euse. **'haymaking** n fenaison f. **'hayrick, 'haystack** n meule f de foin. **'haywire** a F: **to go h.,** (of plans) mal tourner, tourner court; (of mechanism) se détraquer; (of pers) s'emballer; déménager, dérailler.

hazard ['hæzəd] 1. n (a) hasard m (b) risque m; danger m; péril m 2. vtr hasarder; risquer (sa vie). **'hazardous** a hasardeux, chanceux.

haze [heiz] n brume légère; Fig: vague f (d'oubli); incertitude f (de l'esprit). **'hazily** adv vaguement, indistinctement. **'hazy** a (-ier, -iest) brumeux, embrumé; (contour) flou; (of ideas) nébuleux, vague; **I'm a bit h. about it,** je n'en ai qu'une connaissance vague, qu'un souvenir vague.

hazel ['heizl] 1. n **h. (tree),** noisetier m, coudrier m 2. a noisette inv. **'hazelnut** n noisette f.

he [hiː] pers pron m 1. (unstressed) il; (a) **what did he say?** qu'a-t-il dit? qu'est-ce qu'il a dit? (b) **here he comes,** le voici qui vient; **he's an honest man,** c'est un honnête homme 2. (a) (stressed) lui; **he and I,** lui et moi; **I'm as tall as he is,** je suis aussi grand que lui; **he knows nothing about it,** il n'en sait rien, lui (b) esp Lit: celui; **who believes,** celui qui croit 3. n (of child) garçon m; (of animal) mâle m; **he-bear,** ours mâle; **he-goat,** bouc. **'he-man** n (pl -men) homme viril.

head [hed] I. n 1. tête f; **from h. to foot,** de la tête aux pieds; **he gives orders over my h.,** il donne des ordres sans me consulter; **h. down,** (la) tête baissée; **h. downwards,** la tête en bas; **h. first, h. foremost,** la tête la première; **to stand on one's h.,** faire le poirier; F: **I could do it standing on my h.,** c'est simple comme bonjour; **to turn h. over heels,** faire la culbute; **to fall h. over heels in love with s.o.,** tomber follement amoureux de qn; Rac: **to win by a h.,** gagner d'une tête; **to win by a short h.,** gagner de justesse; **to give s.o. his h.,** donner libre cours à qn; **to laugh one's h. off,** rire comme un fou; **to talk s.o.'s h. off,** bavarder comme une pie; F: **to bite s.o.'s h. off,** rembarrer qn 2. **to have a good h. for business,** avoir le sens des affaires; **to have a good h., no h., for heights,** ne pas avoir, avoir, le vertige; **what put that into your h.?** où avez-vous pris cette idée-là? **to take it into one's h. to do sth,** se mettre en tête de faire qch; **to put ideas into s.o.'s h.,** donner des idées à qn; **to get sth into one's h.,** se mettre qch dans la tête; **I can't get it into his h.,** je ne peux pas le lui enfoncer dans la tête; **his name has gone out of my h.,** j'ai complètement oublié son nom; **we put our heads together,** nous avons conféré ensemble; Prov: **two heads are better than one,** deux conseils valent mieux qu'un; **wine that goes to one's h.,** vin qui (vous) monte à la tête; **to be over the heads of the audience,** dépasser (l'entendement de) l'auditoire; **to lose one's h.,** perdre la tête; **to keep one's h.,** conserver son sang-froid; **to go off one's h.,** devenir fou; **not right, weak, in the h.,** faible d'esprit, un peu timbré; F: **to have a bad h.,** avoir mal à la tête 3. tête f (d'arbre, d'épingle, de piston); pointe f (d'asperge); pomme f (de chou, de canne); pied m (de céleri); haut m (de page, d'un escalier); chevet m (de lit); haut bout (de la table); source f (d'une rivière); mousse f (d'un verre de bière); **to bring matters to a h.,** forcer une décision; (of abscess) **to come to a h.,** mûrir; **things are coming to a h.,** une crise est proche 4. = **heading** 5. (a) **at the h. of,** en tête de (liste, d'un cortège); à la tête (d'un groupe) (*b*) (*pers*) chef *m* (de famille, d'une entreprise); directeur, -trice (d'une école); **h. of State,** chef d'État; **h. of a department,** chef de service, (*in large shop*) de rayon; **h. clerk,** chef de bureau; **h. gardener,** jardinier en chef; **h. office,** siège social, bureau principal 6. *inv* **thirty h. of cattle,** trente bœufs; **to pay so much per h., a h.,** payer tant par tête, par personne 7. (*of coin*) face *f*; **to toss, play, heads or tails,** jouer à pile ou face; *F:* **I can't make h. or tail of this,** je n'y comprends rien 8. *Mch:* **h. of steam, of water,** pression *f* de vapeur, d'eau. II. *v* 1. *vtr* (*a*) être à la tête (d'un parti); mener (un parti); venir en tête (d'un cortège, du scrutin); **to h. a letter,** mettre l'en-tête à une lettre; **the article is headed,** l'article est intitulé; **headed notepaper,** papier à en-tête (*b*) *Fb:* **to h. the ball,** faire une tête 2. *vi* s'avancer, se diriger (**for,** vers); (*of ship*) avoir le cap (sur); **we were heading for,** nous étions en route pour; **to be heading for ruin,** marcher tout droit vers la ruine. **'headache** *n* mal *m* de tête; *F:* (*of problem*) casse-tête *m inv*; **to have a h.,** avoir mal à la tête. **'headband** *n* bandeau *m*. **'headdress** *n* (*pl* **-es**) coiffure *f*; coiffe *f*. **'header** *n* (*a*) plongeon *m*; **to take a h.,** plonger (dans l'eau) la tête la première; piquer une tête (*b*) *Fb:* coup *m* de tête. **'headgear** *n* couvre-chef *m*. **'heading** *n* tête (de chapitre); rubrique *f* (d'article); en-tête *m* (de page); **under different headings,** sous des rubriques différentes. **'headlamp**, **'headlight** *n* *Aut:* phare *f*; **to dip the headlights,** se mettre en code; **dipped headlights,** phares code. **'headland** *n* cap *m*, promontoire *m*. **'headline** *n* *Journ:* titre *m* (de rubrique); **banner headlines,** gros titres; **to hit the headlines,** défrayer la chronique. **'headlong** 1. *adv* (tomber) la tête la première; (courir) à corps perdu 2. *a* (chute) la tête la première; **h. flight,** panique *f*. **head'master** *n* directeur *m* (d'une école); proviseur *m* (d'un lycée). **head'mistress** *n* (*pl* **-mistresses**) directrice *f*. **'head 'off** 1. *vi* se diriger (**towards,** vers) 2. *vtr* détourner (qn); faire rebrousser chemin à (qn); parer à (une question). **'head-on** *a* & *adv* de front; (collision) de plein fouet; (réunion) en face à face, en tête à tête. **'headphones** *npl* casque *m* (à écouteurs). **'headquarters** *npl* *Mil:* quartier général; siège social, bureau principal (d'une banque, d'une administration). **'headrest** *n* appui-tête *m*. **'headroom** *n* encombrement vertical; **there's not much h.,** le toit, le plafond, est plutôt bas. **'headscarf** *n* (*pl* **-scarves**) foulard *m*. **'headset** *n* casque *m* (à écouteurs). **'headship** *n* direction *f* (d'une école). **'headstone** *n* pierre tombale. **'headstrong** *a* volontaire; têtu. **'headway** *n* **to make h.,** faire des progrès; avancer; (*of ship*) faire de la route. **'headwind** *n* vent *m* contraire. **'heady** *a* (**-ier, -iest**) capiteux.

heal [hi:l] 1. *vtr* guérir; cicatriser (une blessure) 2. *vi* (*of wound*) **to h. (up),** guérir, se cicatriser, se refermer. **'healer** *n* guérisseur, -euse. **'healing** 1. *a* (onguent) cicatrisant 2. *n* guérison *f*; cicatrisation *f*.

health [helθ] *n* santé *f*; **good h., bonne santé; ill, poor, h.,** mauvaise santé; **to be in good h.,** être en bonne santé; **to be in poor h.,** se porter mal; **the National H. Service** =(le Service de la Santé de) la Sécurité sociale; **h. insurance,** assurance maladie; **to drink (to) s.o.'s h.,** boire à la santé de qn; **(your very) good h.!** (à votre) santé! **h. foods,** produits (i) diététiques (ii) alimentaires naturels; **h. food shop,** magasin diététique. **'health-giving** *a* (effet) salutaire; (air) tonifiant. **'healthily** *adv* sainement. **'healthy** *a* (**-ier, -iest**) sain; (*of pers*) en bonne santé; bien portant; (*of climate, food*) salubre; (appétit) robuste.

heap [hi:p] 1. *n* tas *m*, monceau *m*; **in a h.,** en tas; *F:* (*of pers*) **to be struck all of a h.,** en rester abasourdi; *F:* (*large number*) **heaps of times,** bien des fois, très souvent; **heaps of time,** largement le temps; **to have heaps of money,** avoir beaucoup, des tas, d'argent 2. *vtr* **to h. (up),** entasser, amonceler; amasser; **to h. insults on s.o.,** accabler qn d'injures; **to h. one's plate with strawberries,** remplir son assiette de fraises; *Cu:* **heaped measure,** mesure comble; **heaped spoonful,** cuillère bien pleine.

hear [ˈhiər] *vtr* & *i* (**heard** [həːd]) (*a*) entendre; **to h. s.o. speak,** entendre parler qn; **to make oneself heard,** se faire entendre; *F:* **I've heard that one before! connu! h.! h.!** très bien! très bien! (*b*) apprendre (une nouvelle); **to h. from s.o.,** recevoir des nouvelles, une lettre, de qn; *Corr:* **hoping to h. from you,** dans l'attente de vous lire; **to h. of, about, s.o.,** avoir des nouvelles de qn; entendre parler de qn; **he hasn't been heard of since,** depuis on n'en a plus entendu parler; **I never heard of such a thing!** a-t-on jamais entendu une chose pareille! **I've heard that he's leaving,** j'ai entendu dire qu'il allait partir; **this is the first I've heard of it,** c'est la première fois que j'en entends parler; **father won't h. of it,** mon père ne veut pas en entendre parler; mon père s'y oppose formellement (*c*) (*listen to*) écouter (qn, une prière); *Ecc:* assister à (la messe). **'hearing** *n* (*a*) audition *f*; audience *f*; **give me a h.!** veuillez m'entendre! (*b*) ouïe *f*; **within h.,** à portée de la voix; **it was said in my h.,** on l'a dit en ma présence; **h. aid,** audiophone *m*. **'hear 'out** *vtr* écouter jusqu'au bout. **'hearsay** *n* ouï-dire *m inv*.

hearse [həːs] *n* corbillard *m*.

heart [haːt] *n* (*a*) cœur *m*; *Med:* **to have h. trouble, a weak h.,** être cardiaque; **h. disease,** maladie de cœur, **h. attack,** crise cardiaque; **h. transplant,** greffe du cœur; **h.-lung machine,** cœur-poumon artificiel; **h. failure,** défaillance cardiaque; **to have one's h. in one's mouth,** avoir un serrement de cœur; **his heart's in the right place,** il a le cœur bien placé; **h. of gold, of stone,** cœur d'or, de pierre; **have a h.!** ayez un peu de cœur! **my h. sank,** j'ai eu un serrement de cœur; **to break s.o.'s h.,** briser le cœur à qn; **he died of a broken h.,** il est mort de chagrin; **with a heavy h.,** le cœur serré; **in my h. of hearts,** au plus profond de mon cœur; **from the bottom of my h.,** du fond de mon cœur; **he's a reactionary at h.,** au fond c'est un réactionnaire; **to learn sth (off) by h.,** apprendre qch par cœur; **to love s.o. with all one's h.,** aimer qn de tout son cœur; **to have s.o.'s welfare at h.,** avoir à cœur le bonheur de qn; **to take sth to h.,** prendre qch à cœur; **to have set one's h. on sth,** avoir qch à cœur; **he's a man after my own h.,** c'est un homme selon mon cœur; **to one's heart's content,** à cœur joie; **his h. isn't in it,** le cœur n'y est pas; **to lose h.,** perdre courage; **to take h.,** prendre courage; **not to have the h. to do sth,** ne pas avoir le cœur, le courage, de faire qch; **lonely h.,** personne célibataire, solitaire, (qui se sent bien) seule (*b*) cœur (de chou); fond *m* (d'artichaut); vif *m* (d'un arbre);

the h. of the matter, le fond du problème; in the h. of, au cœur (d'une ville); au beau milieu (d'une forêt) (c) *Cards:* queen of hearts, dame de cœur; have you any hearts? avez-vous du cœur? 'heartache n chagrin m. 'heartbeat n battement m de cœur. 'heartbreaking a navrant. 'heartbroken a to be h., avoir le cœur brisé. 'heartburn n *Med:* brûlures *fpl* d'estomac. 'hearten vtr encourager (qn). 'heartfelt a sincère; qui vient du cœur. 'heartily adv (saluer) cordialement; (accueillir) chaleureusement; (travailler, rire) de bon cœur; (manger) de bon appétit, avec appétit; to be h. sick of sth, être profondément dégoûté de qch. 'heartless a sans cœur; dur, cruel. 'heartrending a à fendre le cœur; navrant; (cri) déchirant. 'heart-searching n examen m de conscience. 'heart-throb n F: idole f. 'heart-to-'heart 1. a (conversation) intime 2. n to have a h.-to-h. with s.o., parler à qn à cœur ouvert. 'hearty a (-ier, -iest) (accueil) cordial, chaleureux; (rire) jovial; (of pers) vigoureux, robuste; (repas) copieux.

hearth [hɑ:θ] n foyer m, âtre m. 'hearthrug n devant m de foyer.

heat [hi:t] 1. n (a) chaleur f; ardeur f (du soleil, d'un foyer); feu m (d'une discussion); in the h. of the day, au plus chaud de la journée; h. haze, brume due à la chaleur; *Med:* prickly h., h. rash, spot, rougeur f (sur la peau due à la chaleur); (of animal) on h., en chaleur; to reply with some h., répondre avec une certaine vivacité; in the h. of the moment, dans la chaleur du moment (b) *Sp:* (épreuve f, manche f) éliminatoire f; dead h., course à égalité 2. vtr & i chauffer. 'heated a chauffé; (argument) animé. 'heatedly adv avec chaleur. 'heater n appareil m de chauffage; water h., chauffe-eau m inv; car h., chauffage m (de voiture); electric h., radiateur m (électrique). 'heating n chauffage m; central h., chauffage central. 'heatproof, 'heat-resistant, -resisting a calorifuge; thermorésistant; (plat) allant au feu. 'heatstroke n *Med:* coup m de chaleur. 'heatwave n *Meteor:* vague f de chaleur; canicule f.

heath [hi:θ] n bruyère f; lande f.

heathen ['hi:ðən] a & n païen, -ïenne.

heather ['heðər] n *Bot:* bruyère f, brande f.

heave [hi:v] v 1. vtr (a) lever, soulever (un fardeau); pousser (un soupir) (b) lancer, jeter (sth at s.o., qch contre qn) 2. vi (a) (se) gonfler, se soulever (b) (of pers) avoir des haut-le-cœur m (c) *Nau:* (pt & pp hove [houv]) to h. to, se mettre en panne, à la cape; to h. in(to) sight, paraître. II. n soulèvement m; effort m (pour soulever qch).

heaven ['hevən] n ciel m; in h., au ciel; to go to h., aller au ciel, en paradis m; it's h. on earth, c'est le paradis sur terre; the heavens opened, il a commencé à pleuvoir à torrents; (good) heavens! heavens above! juste ciel! thank h. (for that)! Dieu merci! for h.'s sake! pour l'amour du ciel! h. only knows! Dieu seul le sait! 'heavenly a céleste, F: what h. peaches! quelles pêches délicieuses! 'heaven-sent a providentiel.

heavy ['hevi] 1. a (-ier, -iest) (a) lourd; (coup) violent; (pas) pesant; h. goods vehicle, poids lourd; h. losses, grosses pertes; h. luggage, gros bagages; h. features, gros traits; h. beard, forte barbe; h. meal, repas lourd

à digérer; h. cold, gros rhume; h. eyes, yeux battus; h. shower, grosse averse; h. rain, pluie battante; *Mil:* h. fire, feu nourri; air h. with scent, air chargé de parfums (b) (travail) pénible, laborieux; h. day, journée chargée; h. work, gros travail; to find it h. going, avancer avec difficulté; h. weather, gros temps; he made h. weather of it, il s'est compliqué la tâche; h. sea, grosse mer; h. eater, gros mangeur; to be a h. sleeper, avoir le sommeil profond 2. adv food that lies h. on one's stomach, nourriture lourde, indigeste. 'heavily adv lourdement; time hangs h. on his hands, le temps lui pèse; h. underlined, fortement souligné; to lose h., perdre gros; to sleep h., dormir profondément; to drink h., boire beaucoup. 'heaviness n (a) lourdeur f, pesanteur f; poids m (d'un fardeau) (b) engourdissement m, lassitude f. 'heavy-'duty a (machine) à grand rendement; (pneu) tous-terrains; (vêtement) solide. 'heavy-'handed a à la main lourde; maladroit. 'heavyweight n *Box:* poids lourd.

Hebrew ['hi:bru:] 1. a hébreu (no f); hébraïque 2. (a) Hébreu m (b) *Ling:* hébreu m.

heck [hek] int F: zut! flûte! what the h. are you doing? que diable faites-vous? a h. of a lot, des masses de.

heckle ['hekl] vtr (at public meetings) interpeller, chahuter (l'orateur). 'heckler n interpellateur, -trice. 'heckling n interpellation f.

hectic ['hektik] a agité, fiévreux; (of lifestyle) bousculé; (c'a) mouvementé; to have a h. time, ne pas savoir où donner de la tête.

hector ['hektər] vtr intimider, rudoyer (qn). 'hectoring a (ton) autoritaire, impérieux.

hedge [hedʒ] 1. n haie f; quickset h., haie vive 2. v (a) vtr enfermer, enclore (un terrain); to be hedged in with difficulties, être entouré de difficultés; to h. one's bets, se couvrir (b) vi se réserver, chercher des échappatoires. 'hedgehog n hérisson m. 'hedgerow n haie.

heebie-jeebies [hi:bi'ji:biz] npl F: to have the h.-j., avoir la frousse, la trouille.

heed [hi:d] 1. vtr faire attention à, prendre garde à, tenir compte de 2. n to take h. of sth, tenir compte de qch. 'heedless a étourdi, insouciant, imprudent; h. of, peu soucieux de. 'heedlessly adv étourdiment.

heel [hi:l] 1. n (a) talon m; to wear high heels, porter des talons hauts; to tread on s.o.'s heels, marcher sur les talons de qn; to follow hard on s.o.'s heels, suivre qn de très près; to take to one's heels, prendre ses jambes à son cou; to come to h., (of dog) venir au pied; (of pers) se soumettre; (to dog) h.! au pied! to bring s.o. to h., rappeler qn à l'ordre; F: to cool, kick, one's heels, attendre, poireauter (b) talon (d'un soulier); (of pers) to be down at h., être dans la dèche (c) F: (pers) chameau m 2. v (a) vtr mettre un talon à (une chaussure) (b) vi (of ship) to h. (over), avoir de la bande, de la gîte. 'heeled a F: well h., riche.

hefty ['hefti] a (-ier, -iest) (homme) fort, solide; costaud; (of amount, price) gros, important.

heifer ['hefər] n *Husb:* génisse f.

height [hait] n (a) hauteur f; élévation f; wall six metres in h., mur haut de six mètres, qui a six mètres de haut (b) taille f, grandeur f (de qn); of average h., de taille moyenne (c) altitude f; **h. above sea level**, altitude au-dessus du niveau de la mer (d) (hill) hauteur; éminence f (de terrain) (e) apogée m (de la fortune); comble m (de la folie); sommet m (de l'éloquence); **at the h. of the storm**, au plus fort de l'orage; **in, at, the h. of summer**, en plein été; **the season is at its h.**, la saison bat son plein; **it's the h. of fashion**, c'est la (toute) dernière mode. **'heighten** vtr accroître, augmenter (un plaisir); accentuer, relever (un contraste).

heinous ['heinəs] a (crime) odieux.

heir [ɛər] n héritier m; Jur: **h. apparent**, héritier présomptif. **'heiress** n (pl -es) héritière f. **'heir- loom** n héritage m; meuble m, tableau m, bijou m, de famille.

held [held] see **hold** II.

helicopter ['helikɔptər] n Av: hélicoptère m. **'heliport** n héliport m, héligare f.

helium ['hi:liəm] n Ch: hélium m.

hell [hel] n (a) enfer m; F: **all h. was let loose**, c'était infernal (b) F: **(oh) h.!** mince, zut (alors)! **it's h. on earth!** c'est infernal! **to make a h. of a noise**, faire un bruit d'enfer, un vacarme infernal; **a h. of a price**, un prix élevé, salé; **a h. of a nerve**, un culot du diable; **a h. of a guy**, un type formidable; **go to h.!** va au diable! **to h. with him!** qu'il aille au diable! **come h. or high water**, advienne que pourra; **h. for leather**, à toute vitesse; **to give s.o. h.**, faire un enfer de la vie de qn; **to work like h.**, travailler comme un dératé; **what the h. do you want?** que diable désirez-vous? **hell'bent** a F: **to be h. on doing sth**, vouloir à tout prix faire qch. **'hellish** a infernal; diabolique. **'hellishly** adv F: diaboliquement; **h. expensive**, vachement cher.

hello [he'lou] int bonjour! salut! (calling attention) holà! ohé! (indicating surprise) tiens! Tp: allô!

helm [helm] n Nau: barre f (du gouvernail); gouvernail m, timon m. **'helmsman** n (pl -men) homme m de barre; timonier m.

helmet ['helmit] n casque m.

help [help] 1. n (a) aide f, assistance f, secours m; **with the h. of a friend**, avec l'aide d'un ami; **to call for h.**, crier au secours; **can I be (of) any h. to you?** puis-je vous aider? **to come to s.o.'s h.**, venir au secours de qn; **to be a h. to s.o.**, être d'un grand secours, rendre service, à qn (b) (pers) aide mf; (in shop) employé, -ée; **daily h.**, femme f de ménage; **home h.**, aide ménagère 2. vtr & i(a) aider, secourir, assister (qn); **to h. s.o. to do sth**, aider qn à faire qch; **to h. s.o. upstairs**, aider qn à monter l'escalier; **so h. me (God)!** que Dieu me juge si je ne dis pas la vérité! **that will not h. you**, cela ne vous servira à rien; **I got a friend to h. me**, je me suis fait aider par un ami; **h.!** au secours! (b) faciliter (le progrès) (c) (at table) servir (qn); **to h. s.o. to soup**, servir du potage à qn; **h. yourself**, servez-vous (d) (with negation, expressed or implied) **things we can't h.**, choses qu'on ne saurait empêcher; **I can't h. it**, je n'y peux rien; c'est plus fort que moi; **it can't be helped**, on n'y peut rien! tant pis! **I can't h. laughing**, je ne peux m'empêcher de rire; **don't be away longer than you can h.**, essayez d'être absent le moins de temps possible. **'helper** n aide; assistant, -ante. **'helpful** a (personne) serviable; (objet) utile. **'helpfully** adv utilement. **'helping** 1. a to lend a h. hand, prêter la main, son aide (à qn) 2. n portion f (de nourriture); **I had two helpings**, j'en ai repris. **'helpless** a (a) sans ressource, sans appui (b) faible, impuissant. **'helplessly** adv faiblement; (regarder) en spectateur impuissant. **'help 'out** vtr & i aider (qn); dépanner (qn).

helter-skelter ['heltə'skeltər] 1. adv (courir, fuir) pêle-mêle, à la débandade 2. a & n **h.-s. (flight)**, fuite désordonnée; débandade 3. n (at fair) toboggan m.

hem [hem] 1. n bord m (d'un vêtement); ourlet m (d'un mouchoir, d'une jupe) 2. vtr (hemmed) ourler. **'hem 'in** vtr cerner, entourer (l'ennemi); **hemmed in by mountains**, serré entre les montagnes, enserré par les montagnes.

hemisphere ['hemisfiər] n hémisphère m.

hemo- [hi:mou-] pref NAm: = **haemo-**.

hemp [hemp] n chanvre m.

hen [hen] n (chicken) poule f; (female bird) femelle f; F: **h. party**, réunion de femmes. **'hencoop, -house** n poulailler m. **'henpecked** a he's h., c'est elle qui porte la culotte; elle le mène par le bout du nez.

hence [hens] adv (a) (of time) dorénavant, désormais; **five years h.**, dans cinq ans (d'ici) (b) (consequence) **h. his anger**, de là, d'où sa fureur. **hence'forth** adv désormais, dorénavant, à l'avenir.

henchman ['hentʃmən] n (pl henchmen) partisan m, acolyte m.

henna ['henə] n Toil: henné m.

hepatitis [hepə'taitis] n Med: hépatite f.

her [hər, hɔːr] 1. pers pron (a) (unstressed) (direct) la, (before vowel sound) l'; (indirect) lui; **have you seen h.?** l'avez-vous vue? **look at h.**, regardez-la; **tell h.**, dites-lui; (refl) **she took her luggage with h.**, elle a pris ses bagages avec elle (b) (stressed) elle; **I'm thinking of h.**, je pense à elle; **I remember h.**, je me souviens d'elle; **I found him and h. at the station**, je les ai trouvés, lui et elle, à la gare; **it's h.**, c'est elle; **that's h.!** la voilà! 2. poss a son, f sa, pl ses; **h. husband**, son mari; **h. sister**, sa sœur; **h. handwriting**, son écriture; **h. friends**, ses ami(e)s; **she hurt h. hand**, elle s'est blessée (à) la main. **hers** poss pron le sien, la sienne, les siens, les siennes; **this book is h.**, ce livre est à elle; (written by her) ce livre est d'elle; **a friend of h.**, un de ses amis. **her'self** pers pron elle-même; (refl) se; **I saw Louise h.**, j'ai vu Louise elle-même; **she hurt h.**, elle s'est blessée, s'est fait mal; **by h.**, toute seule; (after illness) **she's looking h. again**, elle paraît complètement remise.

herald ['herəld] 1. n (a) héraut m (b) précurseur m 2. vtr annoncer, proclamer. **he'raldic** a héraldique. **'heraldry** n (art m, science f) héraldique f.

herb [hɔːb] n Bot: herbe f; Cu: **herbs**, fines herbes. **her'baceous** a Bot: herbacé; **h. border**, bordure de plantes herbacées. **'herbal** 1. n (book) herbier m 2. a (tisane) d'herbes. **'herbalist** n herboriste mf. **her'bivorous** a Z: herbivore.

herd [hɔːd] 1. n troupeau m (de bétail, de moutons, de gens); troupe f, bande f (d'animaux); foule f (de gens); **the h. instinct**, l'instinct grégaire 2. v (a) vi **to h. (together)**, (of animals) vivre, s'assembler, en troupeau (b) vtr garder (des animaux); diriger (des touristes); **to h. together**, rassembler en troupeau. **'herdsman** n (pl -men) gardien m de troupeau.

here ['hiər] 1. adv (a) ici; **in h.**, ici; **come in h., please**, venez par ici, s'il vous plaît; **near, round, h.**, près d'ici; **up to h., down to h.**, jusqu'ici; **from h. to London**, d'ici jusqu'à Londres; **between h. and London**, d'ici à Londres; entre ici et Londres; **h. and now**, tout de suite; **h. goes!** allons-y! (*on tombstone*) **h. lies**, ci-gît (*b*) (*at roll call*) présent! (*c*) (*on this earth*) **h. below**, ici-bas; **here's your hat**, voici votre chapeau; **h. are your books**, voici vos livres; **h. you are!** (i) vous voici! (ii) tenez! (ceci est pour vous); **h. she comes!** la voici (qui vient)! **h. I am!** me voici! me voilà! **here's to you!** à votre santé! **my friend h. will tell you**, mon ami que voici vous le dira (*d*) **h. and there**, par-ci par-là; ça et là; **h., there, and everywhere**, un peu partout; **that's neither h. nor there**, cela ne fait rien, cela n'a rien à voir (l'affaire) **2.** *int* (*calling attention*) holà! ohé! **'hereabout(s)** *adv* près d'ici, par ici. **here'with** *adv* ci-joint, ci-inclus; sous ce pli.

heredity [hi'rediti] *n* hérédité *f*. **he'reditary** *a* héréditaire.

heresy ['herəsi] *n* hérésie *f*. **'heretic** *n* hérétique *mf*. **he'retical** *a* hérétique.

heritage ['heritidʒ] *n* héritage *m*, patrimoine *m*.

hermetic [hə:'metik] *a* hermétique. **her'metically** *adv* (scellé) hermétiquement.

hermit ['hə:mit] *n* ermite *m*. **'hermitage** *n* ermitage *m*.

hernia ['hə:niə] *n Med:* hernie *f*.

hero ['hiərou] *n* (*pl* **heroes**) héros *m*; **h. worship**, culte *m* (des héros). **he'roic** *a* héroïque. **he'roically** *adv* héroïquement. **'heroine** *n* héroïne *f*. **'heroism** *n* héroïsme *m*.

heroin ['herouin] *n Ch:* héroïne *f*.

heron ['herən] *n Orn:* héron *m*.

herpes ['hə:pi:z] *n Med:* herpès *m*.

herring ['heriŋ] *n Ich:* hareng *m*; **red h.**, (i) hareng saur (ii) diversion *f*. **'herringbone** *n* arête *f* de hareng; **h.** (**pattern**), (dessin *m* à) chevrons *mpl*.

hesitate ['heziteit] *vi* hésiter; **to h. to do sth**, hésiter à faire qch. **'hesitant** *a* hésitant, irrésolu. **'hesitantly** *adv* avec hésitation. **'hesitating** *a* hésitant, incertain. **'hesitatingly** *adv* avec hésitation; en hésitant. **hesi'tation** *n* hésitation *f*; **he had no h. about it**, il n'a pas hésité une seconde.

hessian ['hesiən] *n Tex:* toile *f* de jute.

heterogeneous [hetərou'dʒi:niəs] *a* hétérogène. **hetero'sexual** *a & n* hétérosexuel, -elle.

het up [het'ʌp] *a F:* **to get h. up**, s'énerver; **don't get h. up about it**, ne t'en fais pas pour cela.

hew [hju:] *vtr* (**hewed**; **hewed**, **hewn**) couper, tailler.

hexagon ['heksəgən] *n* hexagone *m*. **hex'agonal** *a* hexagonal.

hey [hei] *int* (*calling attention*) ohé! holà! hé!

heyday ['heidei] *n* apogée *m*.

HGV *abbr* heavy goods vehicle.

hi [hai] *int* (*calling attention*) hé! là-bas! ohé! (*greeting*) salut!

hiatus [hai'eitəs] *n* (*pl* **hiatuses**) lacune *f*.

hibernate ['haibəneit] *vi* (*of animal*) hiberner. **hiber'nation** *n* hibernation *f*.

hiccup, hiccough ['hikʌp] **1.** *n* hoquet *m*; **to have (the) hiccups**, avoir le hoquet **2.** *vi* hoqueter.

hide¹ [haid] *v.tr* (**hid**; **hidden** ['hidn]) **1.** *v.tr* cacher (**from**, à); **to h. one's face**, se cacher la figure; **to h. one's light under a bushel**, cacher son talent; **to h. sth from sight**,

dérober, soustraire, qch aux regards; **clouds hid the sun**, des nuages voilaient le soleil **2.** *vi* se cacher. **hide-and-'seek** *n Games:* cache-cache *m*. **'hideaway, 'hideout** *n* cachette *f*. **'hiding¹** *n* **to go into h.**, se cacher; **to be in h.**, se tenir caché; **h. place**, cachette.

hide² *n* peau *f*; *Com:* cuir *m*; **to save one's h.**, sauver sa peau. **'hidebound** *a* (*of pers*) aux vues étroites. **'hiding²** *n F:* raclée *f*; **to give s.o. a good h.**, flanquer une raclée à qn.

hideous ['hidiəs] *a* hideux, affreux, effroyable; d'une laideur repoussante. **'hideously** *adv* hideusement, affreusement. **'hideousness** *n* hideur *f*, laideur *f*.

hierarchy ['haiəra:ki] *n* hiérarchie *f*.

hi-fi ['hai'fai] *a & n* (de) haute fidélité, hi-fi (*f*) *inv*.

higgledy-piggledy [higldi'pigldi] *adv F:* sans ordre, en pagaïe, pêle-mêle.

high [hai] **1.** *a* (*a*) haut; **wall two metres h.**, mur haut de deux mètres; **how h. is that tree?** quelle est la hauteur de cet arbre? **at h. tide**, à (la) marée haute (*b*) (*of neckline, collar*) haut, montant; **h. cheekbones**, pommettes saillantes; **to hold one's head h.**, porter la tête haute; **to be in a h. position, very h. up**, avoir un poste élevé; **higher education**, enseignement supérieur; **h. table**, table d'honneur; *Sch:* table des professeurs (au réfectoire); **h. and mighty**, haut et puissant (*c*) (prix, taux) élevé; (*of aims, thoughts*) noble; **it fetches a h. price**, cela se vend cher; cela atteint un prix élevé; **to play for h. stakes**, jouer gros (jeu); **h. speed**, grande vitesse; **to have a h. opinion of s.o.**, tenir qn en haute estime; **to have a h. opinion of oneself**, avoir une bonne opinion de soi; s'estimer; **to a h. degree**, à un haut degré; **to, in, the highest degree**, au plus haut degré; **h. fever**, forte fièvre; **h. wind**, vent fort, violent; **h. treason**, haute trahison; **h. colour**, vivacité *f* du teint; **to be in h. spirits**, être plein d'entrain; **h. spot**, point culminant (d'un match); **h. voice**, voix haute, élevée (*d*) (*principal*) **the h. street**, la grand-rue; *Ecc:* **h. mass**, la grand-messe; **h. altar**, maître autel (*e*) (*far advanced*) **h. noon**, plein midi; **it's h. time he went to school**, il est grand temps qu'il aille à l'école (*f*) *Cu:* (*of meat*) avancé, gâté; (*of game*) faisandé; *F:* (*of pers*) ivre, parti; dans un état d'euphorie dû aux drogues; **to get h.** (**on drugs**), se défoncer; (*of ship*) **h. and dry**, échoué; à sec; (*of pers*) **to leave s.o. h. and dry**, laisser qn en plan **2.** *adv* (*a*) haut; en haut; **higher** (**up**), plus haut; **higher and higher**, de plus en plus haut; **to aim h.**, viser haut; **to look h. and low for sth**, chercher qch partout; **to go as h. as £2000**, aller jusqu'à 2000 livres (*b*) fort, fortement; **to run h.**, (*of the sea*) être grosse, houleuse; (*of feelings*) s'échauffer **3.** *n* (*a*) *Meteor:* anticyclone *m*; zone *f* de haute pression (*b*) **on h.**, en haut (*c*) (*of prices*) maximum *m*; **all-time h.**, record le plus élevé. **'highball** *n NAm:* (i) whisky *m* à l'eau (ii) whisky-soda *m*. **'highbrow 1.** *n* pour les intellectuels **2.** *n* intellectuel, -elle. **'high-'class** *a* (marchandises) de premier ordre, de première qualité; (hôtel) de première classe. **'highflown** *a* (style, discours) ampoulé. **'high-flying** *a* (avion) qui vole très haut, à haute altitude. **'high-'grade** *a* (marchandises) de première qualité, de (premier) choix. **'high-'handed** *a* autoritaire; (autorité) tyrannique. **'highland 1.** *n* pays montagneux **2.** *a* (*a*) des montagnes; montagnard (b) des montagnes écossaises. **'highlander** n montagnard écossais. **'high-'level** a à un niveau supérieur. **'highlight** **1.** n rehaut m (d'une peinture); clou m (de la fête); point culminant (d'un match) **2.** vtr mettre en vedette. **'highly** adv fort, très (bien); fortement; **h. coloured,** haut en couleur; (of pers) **h. strung,** nerveux; **his services are h. paid,** on paie très cher ses services; to **think h. of s.o.,** avoir une haute opinion ddegree, à un haut degré; **to, in, the highest degree,** au plus haut degré; **h. fever,** forte fièvre; **h. wind,** vent fort, violent; **h. treason,** haute trahison; **h. colour,** vivacité f du teint; **to be in h. spirits,** être plein **'high-'powered** a (machine, avion) de grande puissance. **'high-pressure** a (machine) à haute pression; (vendeur) agressif; Meteor: (aire) anticyclonique. **'high-ranking** a haut (fonctionnaire). **'high-rise** a **h.-r. block,** immeuble-tour m. **'high-speed** a rapide, à grande vitesse; (moteur) grande vitesse; Phot: (objectif) à très grande ouverture. **'high-'spirited** a plein d'ardeur; (cheval) fougueux. **'highway** n grande route; Adm: voie publique; **the H. Code,** le code de la route; **the highways and byways,** les chemins et sentiers; NAm: **h. patrolman,** motard m. **'highwayman** n (pl **-men**) Hist: voleur m de grand chemin.

hijack ['haidʒæk] **1.** n vol armé (d'un véhicule); détournement m (d'un avion) **2.** vtr s'emparer de force d'un (véhicule), détourner (un avion). **'hijacker** n: pirate m de l'air, de la route. **'hijacking** n = **hijack 1.**

hike [haik] **1.** n (a) excursion f, (longue) promenade (à pied) (b) NAm: augmentation f (de prix, de salaire) **2.** vi faire une excursion, une (longue) promenade (à pied). **'hiker** n excursionniste mf. **'hiking** n excursions fpl, tourisme m, à pied.

hilarious [hi'lɛəriəs] a gai; hilare. **hi'lariously** adv avec hilarité. **hi'larity** n hilarité f, gaieté f.

hill [hil] n (a) colline f; coteau m; **up h. and down dale,** par monts et par vaux (b) éminence f; monticule m (c) (on road) côte f; PN: **h. 1 in 10,** pente 10%. **'hillbilly** n (pl **-ies**) US: montagnard, -arde; rustaud, -aude. **'hillock** n petite colline; butte f; tertre m. **'hillside** n coteau; flanc m de coteau. **'hilltop** n sommet m de la colline; haut m de la côte. **'hilly** a (terrain) accidenté; (route) à fortes pentes.

hilt [hilt] n poignée f, garde f (d'épée); Fig: **up to the h.,** (endetté) jusqu'à la gauche.

him [him] pers pron (a) (unstressed) (direct) le, (before vowel sound) l'; (indirect) lui; **do you love h.?** l'aimezvous? **call h.,** appelez-le; **I am speaking to h.,** je lui parle; (refl) **he took his luggage with h.,** il a pris ses bagages avec lui (b) (stressed) lui; **I'm thinking of h.,** je pense à lui; **I remember h.,** je me souviens de lui; **I found h. and her at the station,** je les ai trouvés, lui et elle, à la gare; **it's h.,** c'est lui; **that's h.!** le voilà! **him'self** pers pron lui-même; (refl) se; **I saw Louis h.,** j'ai vu Louis lui-même; **he hurt h.,** il s'est blessé, s'est fait mal; **by h.,** tout seul; (after illness) **he's looking h. again,** il paraît complètement remis.

hind [haind] a **h. legs,** (of dog) pattes f de derrière; (of horse) jambes f de derrière. **'hindquarters** npl arrière-train m. **'hindsight** n sagesse f d'après coup.

hinder ['hindər] vtr (a) gêner, embarrasser (qn); retarder, entraver (qch) (b) empêcher, retenir, arrêter (s.o. from doing sth, qn de faire qch). **'hindrance** n empêchement m, obstacle m; **to be a h. to s.o.,** gêner qn.

Hindu [hin'du:, 'hin-] a & n Ethn: hindou, -oue. **'Hindi** n Ling: hindi m. **'Hinduism** n hindouisme m.

hinge [hindʒ] **1.** n gond m (de porte); charnière f **2.** vi tourner, pivoter (on, autour de); **everything hinges on his reply,** tout dépend de sa réponse. **hinged** a (couvercle) à charnière(s); (of counter) **h. flap,** battant m.

hint [hint] **1.** n (a) insinuation f; **broad h.,** allusion peu voilée; **to give, drop, s.o. a h.,** toucher un mot à qn; donner à entendre à qn; **to know how to take a h.,** savoir entendre (qn) à demi-mot (b) signe m, indication f; **not a h. of surprise,** pas une ombre de surprise; **not the slightest h. of,** pas le moindre soupçon de; **hints for housewives,** conseils mpl aux ménagères **2.** vtr & i to **h. (at) (sth),** insinuer (qch); laisser entendre (qch); faire une allusion (voilée) à (qch).

hip [hip] n Anat: hanche f; **h. measurement,** tour de hanches; **h. pocket,** poche revolver. **'hipbone** n Anat: os m iliaque. **'hippie, -y** n (pl **-ies**) F: hippie mf, hippy mf. **'hipsters** npl pantalon m taille basse.

hippopotamus [hipə'pɒtəməs] n (pl **hippopotamuses**) Z: hippopotame m.

hire ['haiər] **1.** n location f (d'une voiture); embauchage m (de main-d'œuvre); **on h.,** à louer; (on taxi) **for h.,** libre; **h. purchase,** achat à crédit **2.** vtr (a) louer (une voiture); embaucher (un ouvrier); **hire(d) car,** voiture de location (b) **to h. (out),** louer, donner en location (une voiture).

his [hiz] **1.** poss a son, f sa, pl ses; **h. master,** son maître; **h. wife,** sa femme; **h. handwriting,** son écriture; **h. friends,** ses ami(e)s; **he fell on h. back,** il tomba sur le dos **2.** poss pron le sien, la sienne, les siens, les siennes; **he took my pen and h.,** il a pris mon stylo et le sien; **this book is h.,** ce livre est à lui; (written by him) ce livre est de lui; **a friend of h.,** un de ses amis.

hiss [his] **1.** n sifflement m (du gaz); Th: sifflet m **2.** vtr & i siffler.

history ['histəri] n (pl **histories**) histoire f; **h. book,** livre d'histoire; **natural h.,** histoire naturelle; Med: **(case) h.,** dossier médical (d'un malade). **historian** [hi'stɔːriən] n historien, -ienne. **historic(al)** [hi'stɔrik(l)] a (événement) historique; **place of h. interest,** monument historique. **hi'storically** adv historiquement.

histrionic [histri'ɔnik] a théâtral; (manière) peu sincère. **histri'onics** npl Pej: parade f d'émotion.

hit [hit] **1.** n (a) coup m (b) coup réussi; succès m; **to make a h.,** réussir; faire sensation (c) Th: TV: **h. (song, record, show, film),** chanson f, disque m, spectacle m, film m, à succès; **h. parade,** palmarès m; hit-parade m. **II.** v (hit; prp hitting) **1.** vtr (a) frapper; **h. or miss,** au hasard; **to h. one's foot against sth,** se heurter, se cogner, le pied contre qch; Fig: **to h. the headlines,** défrayer la chronique; **to h. the nail on the head,** tomber juste; F: **to h. the roof,** être furieux; **to h. the**

bottle, picoler; **to h. the sack, the hay**, se coucher, *F:* se pieuter; **to h. the road**, se mettre en route; **he didn't know what had h. him**, il se demandait ce qui lui était arrivé; **you've h. it!** vous y êtes! (*b*) atteindre; toucher; **to be h. by a bullet**, être atteint d'une balle; (*of allusion*) **to h. home**, porter (coup); piquer (qn) au vif; **to be hard h.**, être sérieusement touché (par qch) 2. *vi* se heurter, se cogner (**against**, contre). **hit-and-'run** *a & n* **h.-a.-r. (accident)**, accident *m* dont l'auteur est coupable du délit de fuite; **h.-a.-r. driver**, chauffard qui a pris la fuite (après un accident dont il est coupable). **'hit 'back** *vtr & i* se défendre; rendre coup pour coup (à qn). **'hit 'off** *vtr* **to h. it off with s.o.**, s'accorder avec qn. **'hit 'on** *vtr* découvrir, trouver (un moyen); découvrir, relever (un indice); **I h. on the idea of**, j'ai eu l'idée de. **'hit 'out** *vi* **to h. out at s.o.**, décocher un coup à qn.

hitch [hitʃ] **1.** *n* anicroche *f*; contretemps *m*; **there's a h. somewhere**, il y a quelque chose qui cloche; **it went off without a h.**, tout s'est passé sans accroc; *TV: etc:* **technical h.**, incident *m* technique **2.** *v* (*a*) *vtr* accrocher, attacher, fixer (qch); **to h. (up) one's trousers**, remonter son pantalon; *F:* **to get hitched**, se marier (*b*) *vtr & i F:* **to h. (a lift, a ride)**, faire du stop; **we hitched a ride to Paris**, on nous a pris en stop jusqu'à Paris. **'hitch-hike** *vi* faire du stop, de l'auto-stop. **'hitch-hiker** *n* auto-stoppeur, -euse. **'hitch-hiking** *n* auto-stop *m*.

hive [haiv] *n* ruche *f*; **a h. of industry**, une véritable ruche. **'hive 'off** *vtr F:* séparer (qch) (de la partie principale).

HM *abbr* Her, His, Majesty.

hoard [hɔːd] **1.** *n* amas *m*, accumulation (secrète); **h. of money**, trésor *m*, magot *m* **2.** *vtr* amasser, accumuler (de l'argent); mettre en réserve (des vivres). **'hoarder** *n* personne qui accumule des vivres (en temps de disette).

hoarding ['hɔːdiŋ] *n* palissade *f* (de chantier); (*for advertisement*) panneau *m* d'affichage.

hoarfrost ['hɔːfrɔst] *n* gelée blanche; givre *m*.

hoarse [hɔːs] *a* enroué, rauque. **'hoarsely** *adv* d'une voix enrouée, rauque. **'hoarseness** *n* enrouement *m*.

hoax [houks] **1.** *n* (*pl* **hoaxes**) canular *m*; farce *f* **2.** *vtr* (**hoaxes**) monter un canular à (qn).

hobble ['hɔbl] *vi* boitiller, clopiner; **to h. along**, avancer clopin-clopant.

hobby ['hɔbi] *n* (*pl* **hobbies**) passe-temps (favori); violon *m* d'Ingres. **'hobbyhorse** *n Fig:* dada *m*.

hobnailed ['hɔbneild] *a* (soulier) ferré, à gros clous.

hobnob ['hɔbnɔb] *vi* (**hobnobbed**) être à tu et à toi, frayer (**with s.o.**, avec qn).

hobo ['houbou] *n* (*pl* **hobo(e)s**) *NAm: F:* clochard *m*.

hock¹ [hɔk] *n* jarret *m* (de quadrupède).

hock² *n* vin *m* du Rhin.

hockey ['hɔki] *n* (jeu *m* de) hockey *m*.

hod [hɔd] *n* hotte *f* (de maçon).

hoe [hou] **1.** *n Tls:* houe *f*, binette *f* **2.** *vtr* (**hoed**) biner (le sol); sarcler (les mauvaises herbes).

hog [hɔg] **1.** *n* cochon *m*; porc *m*; *F:* (*pers*) goinfre *m*, glouton *m*; **to go the whole h.**, aller jusqu'au bout **2.** *vtr* (**hogged**) *F:* prendre plus que sa part de (qch); monopoliser (qch); **to h. the limelight**, accaparer la vedette; **to h. the road**, tenir toute la route.

'hogshead *n* tonneau *m*, barrique *f*.

Hogmanay ['hɔgmənei] *n Scot:* la Saint-Sylvestre.

hoi polloi [hɔipə'lɔi] *n* **the h. p.**, la foule, les masses *f*.

hoist [hɔist] **1.** *n* (*a*) **to give s.o. a h. (up)**, aider qn à monter (*b*) appareil *m* de levage; treuil *m*; (*for goods*) monte-charge *m inv* **2.** *vtr* **to h. (sth) (up)**, hisser (qch).

hold [hould] **I.** *v* (**held**) **1.** *vtr* (*a*) tenir (qch); **to h. sth in one's hand**, tenir qch à, dans, la main; **they held (each other's) hands**, ils se tenaient (par) la main; **to h. sth tight**, serrer qch; tenir qch serré; **to h. sth in position**, tenir qch en place; **to h. oneself in readiness**, se tenir prêt; **to h. s.o. to his promise**, contraindre qn à tenir sa promesse; *Fig:* **to h. sth against s.o.**, tenir rigueur à qn de qch (*b*) **to h. one's ground**, tenir bon, tenir ferme; **to h. one's own**, se maintenir; *Mil:* **to h. a fort**, défendre une forteresse; *F:* **I'll h. the fort while you're away**, je garderai la maison, je m'occuperai de tout, pendant votre absence; **to h. one's drink**, bien tenir le vin; **car that holds the road well**, voiture qui tient bien la route; *Tp:* **h. the line!** ne quittez pas! **to h. oneself upright**, se tenir droit; **to h. one's head high**, porter la tête haute; marcher le front haut (*c*) contenir, renfermer; **car that holds six people**, voiture à six places; **what the future holds**, ce que l'avenir nous réserve (*d*) tenir (une séance); célébrer (une fête); avoir (une consultation); **the motor show is held in October**, le salon de l'automobile a lieu au mois d'octobre (*e*) retenir, arrêter, empêcher; **to h. one's breath**, retenir son souffle; **there was no holding him**, il n'y avait pas moyen de l'arrêter; **h. it!** *F:* **h. your horses!** un moment! attendez! (*said by photographer*) **h. it!** ne bougez plus! **to h. water**, tenir l'eau; être étanche; *F:* (*of theory*) tenir debout (*f*) retenir (l'attention); avoir, posséder (un titre, un emploi); détenir (une charge, *Fin:* des actions); occuper (une position) (*g*) **to h. s.o. responsible**, tenir qn responsable; *F:* **to be left holding the baby**, devoir payer les pots cassés; **to h. s.o. in respect**, avoir du respect pour qn; **to h. an opinion**, avoir, professer, une opinion **2.** *vi* (*a*) (*of rope, board, nail*) tenir (bon); être solide; tenir ferme; (*on bus*) **h. tight!** = attention au départ! (*b*) durer; continuer; (*of weather*) se maintenir; (*of promise*) **to h. (good)**, être valable. **II.** *n* (*a*) prise *f*; **to have a h. over s.o.**, avoir prise sur qn; **to take h. of sth**, saisir qch; *F:* **where did you get h. of that?** où avez-vous trouvé, pêché, ça? *Wr: & Fig:* **no holds barred**, toutes prises autorisées (*b*) (*in ship*) cale *f*. **'holdall** *n* fourre-tout *m inv*. **hold 'back 1.** *vtr* retenir (qn, ses larmes); cacher, dissimuler (la vérité) **2.** *vi* rester en arrière; hésiter; se retenir (**from doing sth**, de faire qch). **'hold 'down** *vtr* baisser (la tête); maintenir à terre; occuper (un emploi); maintenir le niveau (des prix). **'holder** *n* (*a*) (*pers*) propriétaire *mf* (d'une terre); titulaire *mf* (d'un droit); détenteur, -trice (de titres) (*b*) (*device*) support *m*; monture *f*; **cigarette h.**, porte-cigarettes *m* (*c*) (*vessel*) récipient *m*. **'hold 'forth** *vi* disserter, pérorer. **'hold 'in** *vtr* contenir, maîtriser (une passion); rentrer (l'estomac). **'holding** *n* (*a*) *Fin:* avoir *m* (en actions); **h. company**, holding *m* (*b*) (petite) propriété; terrain *m*; ferme *f*. **'hold 'off 1.** *vtr* tenir (qn) à distance **2.** *vi* (*a*) **the rain is holding off**, jusqu'ici il ne pleut pas (*b*) s'abstenir; se réserver. **'hold 'on** *vtr* tenir; **h. on!** (i) tenez bon! (ii) *Tp:* ne quittez pas! (iii) (attendez) un instant! pas si vite! **to h. on to sth,** (i) s'accrocher à qch (ii) ne pas lâcher qch. **'hold 'out** l. *vtr* tendre, offrir 2. *vi* durer; **how long can you h. out?** combien de temps pouvez-vous tenir? **to h. out to the end,** tenir jusqu'au bout; **to h. o. against an attack,** soutenir une attaque; **to h. o. for sth,** exiger qch. **'hold 'over** *vtr* remettre (à plus tard). **'hold to'gether** 1. *vtr* maintenir ensemble 2. *vi* tenir ensemble. **'hold 'up** 1. *vtr* (*a*) (*support*) soutenir (*b*) lever (qch) (en l'air); **to h. s.o. up as an example,** citer qn comme exemple; **to h. s.o. up to ridicule,** tourner qn en ridicule (*c*) arrêter, entraver, bloquer, gêner (la circulation) (*d*) attaquer (qn, une banque) 2. *vi* se soutenir; (*of weather*) se maintenir. **'hold-up** *n* (*a*) arrêt *m*; embouteillage *m* (de voitures); panne *f* (du métro) (*b*) attaque *f*, vol *m*, à main armée; hold-up *m*. **'hold 'with** *vtr* I don't h. w. his opinions, his behaviour, je ne partage pas ses opinions; je n'approuve pas sa conduite.

hole [houl] 1. *n* trou *m*; creux *m*, cavité *f*; orifice *m*, ouverture *f*; œillet *m* (de ceinture); terrier *m* (de lapin); *F:* **to be in a h.,** être dans le pétrin; (*of place*) **what a rotten h.!** quel sale trou! (*of house*) quel taudis! (*of town*) quel bled! *Med: F:* **h. in the heart,** trou dans le cœur; *Mec: etc:* **inspection h.,** regard *m*; **to bore a h.,** percer un trou; **to make a h. (in sth),** faire un trou (à qch); trouer (un vêtement) 2. *vtr* trouer, percer. **'hole 'up** *vi esp NAm: F:* se cacher, se terrer.

holiday ['hɔlidei] 1. *n* (jour *m* de) fête *f*; jour férié; (jour de) congé *m*; **bank, public,** *NAm:* **legal, h.,** fête légale; **to take a h.,** prendre un congé; **the holidays,** les vacances *f*; **the summer holidays,** les grandes vacances; **a month's h.,** un mois de vacances; **where did you go on h., spend your h.?** où avez-vous passé vos vacances? **h. camp,** (i) camp (ii) (*for children*) colonie, de vacances; **h. season,** période des vacances 2. *vi* passer les vacances. **'holidaymaker** *n* vacancier, -ière; (*in summer*) estivant, -ante.

Holland ['hɔlənd] *Prn Geog:* Hollande *f*.

hollow ['hɔlou] 1. *a* creux, caverneux; (*of eyes*) cave; (son) sourd; (*of promise*) faux, trompeur; **in a h. voice,** d'une voix caverneuse 2. *adv* **to sound h.,** sonner creux; *F:* **to beat s.o. h.,** battre qn à plates coutures 3. *n* creux *m* (de la main); cavité *f* (d'une dent); excavation *f*; dépression *f* (du sol); bas-fond *m*; cuvette *f* 4. *vtr* **to h. (out),** creuser, évider. **'hollow-'cheeked, -'eyed** *a* aux joues creuses, aux yeux caves.

holly ['hɔli] *n Bot:* houx *m*.

hollyhock ['hɔlihɔk] *n Bot:* rose trémière.

holster ['houlstər] *n* étui *m* de revolver.

holy ['houli] *a* (-ier, -iest) saint, sacré; **the H. Ghost, Spirit,** le Saint-Esprit; **h. water,** eau bénite; **the H. Father,** le Saint-Père; *Geog:* **the H. Land,** la Terre Sainte. **'holiness** *n* sainteté *f*; *Ecc:* **His H.,** Sa Sainteté.

homage ['hɔmidʒ] *n* hommage *m*; **to pay h. to s.o.,** rendre hommage à qn.

home [houm] 1. *n* (*a*) chez-soi *m inv*; foyer (familial); (*house*) intérieur *m*; (*of animal*) habitat *m*; **to have a h. of one's own,** avoir un chez-soi; **Ideal H. Exhibition** = Salon des arts ménagers; **to make one's h. in France,** s'établir en France; **it's (a) h. from h.,** on y est comme chez soi; **there's no place like h.,** on n'est

nulle part si bien que chez soi; **to leave h.,** (i) quitter la maison (ii) partir (définitivement); quitter la famille, at **h.,** à la maison, chez soi; *Sp:* (jouer) sur le terrain du club; **to stay at h.,** rester à la maison; **is Mr X at h.?** M. X est-il chez lui? est-ce que je puis voir M. X? **to be not at h.** to anyone, consigner sa porte à tout le monde; **to feel at h. with s.o.,** se sentir à l'aise chez qn; **to make oneself at h.,** faire comme chez soi (*b*) patrie *f*; pays (natal); **at h. and abroad,** chez nous, dans notre pays, et à l'étranger; **to take an example nearer h.,** sans chercher plus loin (*c*) asile *m*, hospice *m*; **old people's h.,** maison de retraite; **children's h.,** home *m* d'enfants; **convalescent h.,** maison de repos; **nursing h.,** clinique *f* 2. *adv* à la maison; chez soi; **to go, come, h.,** (i) rentrer (à la maison) (ii) rentrer dans sa famille (iii) retourner au pays; **the train h.,** le train pour rentrer; **on the way h.,** en revenant, en rentrant, (chez soi); **to be h.,** être de retour; *NAm:* **to stay h.,** rester à la maison; **to send s.o. h. (from abroad),** rapatrier qn; *F:* **that's nothing to write h. about,** ce n'est pas bien extraordinaire; **the reproach went h.,** le reproche l'a touché au vif; **to strike h.,** frapper juste; **to drive, bring, sth h. to s.o.,** faire sentir, comprendre, qch à qn; **it will come h. to him one day,** il s'en rendra compte un jour; *Mec:* **to screw sth h.,** visser qch à fond, à bloc 3. *a* **h. life,** vie de famille; **h. address,** adresse personnelle; **h. town,** ville natale; **h. cooking,** cuisine familiale; **h. economics,** économie domestique; **the h. counties,** les comtés avoisinant Londres; *Sp:* **h. side,** équipe qui reçoit; **h. ground,** terrain du club; *Rac:* **h. straight,** dernière ligne droite; **the H. Office** = le Ministère de l'Intérieur; **the H. Secretary** = le Ministre de l'Intérieur; **h. trade,** commerce intérieur; *Pol:* **h. rule,** autonomie *f*; **to tell s.o. a few h. truths,** dire son fait à qn 4. *vi* (*of pigeon*) revenir au colombier; (*of pers, missile*) **to h. (in),** se diriger (on, vers, sur). **'home-baked** *a* fait à la maison; **h.-b. cake,** gâteau maison. **'home-'brewed** *a* (*of beer*) brassé à la maison. **'homecoming** *n* retour *m* au foyer, à la maison, au pays. **'home'grown** *a* (denrée) du pays; (fruits) du jardin. **'homeland** *n* patrie. **'homeless** 1. *a* sans foyer; sans abri 2. *npl* **the h.,** les sans-logis *m*. **'homely** *a* (*a*) (nourriture) simple, ordinaire; (goût) modeste; (atmosphère) accueillante (*b*) *NAm:* (*of pers*) (plutôt) laid. **'home-'made** *a* fait à la maison. **'homesick** *a* nostalgique; **she's h.,** elle a le mal du pays. **'homesickness** *n* nostalgie *f*; mal *m* du pays. **'homeward** 1. *a* (voyage) de retour 2. *adv* (*also* **homewards**) vers sa maison; *Nau:* **cargo h.,** cargaison de retour; **homeward bound,** sur le chemin du retour. **'homework** *n Sch:* devoirs *mpl.* **'homing** *a* **h. pigeon,** pigeon voyageur; **h. device,** (dispositif) auto-directeur *m*.

homeopathy [houmi'ɔpəθi] *n Med: esp NAm:* = **homoeopathy.**

homicide ['hɔmisaid] *n* (*crime*) homicide *m*; (*pers*) homicide *mf*. **homi'cidal** *a* homicide.

hominy ['hɔmini] *n US:* maïs *m*; *Cu:* **h. grits,** gruau de maïs.

homoeopathy, esp NAm: homeo- [houmi'ɔpəθi] *n Med:* homéopathie *f*. **'homoeopath, esp NAm: 'homeo-** *n* homéopathe *mf*. **homoeo'pathic, esp NAm: homeo-** *a* homéopathique.

homogeneous [hɔmou'dʒi:niəs] *a* homogène.

homogenize [hə'mɔdʒənaiz] *vtr* homogénéiser (le lait).

homosexual ['hɔmou'seksjuəl, hou-] *a & n* homosexuel, -elle.

honest ['ɔnist] *a* (*of pers*) honnête; loyal; (*of actions, words, appearance*) vrai, sincère; (*of method, means*) légitime, juste; **the h. truth,** la pure vérité. **'honestly** *adv* honnêtement; loyalement; (dire) sincèrement; **I can h. say that,** je peux dire franchement que. **'honesty** *n* (*a*) (*of pers*) honnêteté *f*; probité *f*; (*of statement*) véracité *f*, sincérité *f*; **in all h.,** en toute sincérité (*b*) *Bot:* lunaire *f*; monnaie-du-pape *f*.

honey ['hʌni] *n* miel *m*; *F:* (*term of endearment*) chéri, *f* chérie. **'honeybee** *n Ent:* abeille *f*. **'honeycomb 1.** *n* rayon *m* de miel; *Tex:* nid *m* d'abeille **2.** *vtr* cribler (de petits trous). **'honeydew** *n Hort:* **h. (melon),** melon *m* (à peau jaune) (d'hiver). **'honeyed** *a* (*of words*) mielleux. **'honeymoon** *n* lune *f* de miel; **h. (trip),** voyage *m* de noces; **couple on h., h. couple,** couple en voyage de noces. **'honeysuckle** *n Bot:* chèvrefeuille *m*.

honk [hɔŋk] *vtr & i* (*of goose, seal*) pousser un cri; (*of car horn*) klaxonner.

honor ['ɔnər] *n & vtr NAm:* = **honour. 'honorable** *a*, **'honorably** *adv NAm:* = **honourable, honourably.**

honorary ['ɔnərəri] *a* (emploi, membre) honoraire; (service) bénévole; (président) d'honneur; *Mil:* (rang) honorifique; *Sch:* **h. degree,** grade honorifique, honoris causa.

honour, *NAm:* **honor** ['ɔnər]. **1.** *n* (*a*) honneur *m*; **the seat of h.,** la place d'honneur; **in h. of s.o.,** (statue) à la gloire de qn; (dîner) en l'honneur de qn; **to make (it) a point of h. to do sth,** mettre son (point d')honneur, à faire qch; **in h. bound,** obligé par l'honneur, engagé d'honneur (**to do,** à faire); **word of h.,** parole d'honneur; **on my (word of) h.!** je vous donne ma parole! **to have the h. of doing, to do, sth,** avoir l'honneur de faire qch (*b*) distinction *f* honorifique; **honours list,** tableau d'honneur, palmarès *m*; *Sch:* **honours degree** = licence *f*; (*when introducing people, serving sth*) **to do the honours,** faire les honneurs (de sa maison) (*c*) **Your H., His H.,** Monsieur le juge, Monsieur le président **2.** *vtr* honorer (**with,** de); *Com:* honorer, faire honneur à (un effet). **'honourable,** *NAm:* **'honorable** *a* honorable; (*title*) **the H.** (*abbr* **the Hon.),** l'Honorable. **'honourably,** *NAm:* **'honorably** *adv* honorablement.

hooch [hu:tʃ] *n F:* boisson alcoolisée; gnôle *f*.

hood [hud] *n Cl:* capuchon *m*; cagoule *f* (de pénitent); capuche *f* (de femme, d'enfant); *Aut:* capote *f*; *NAm:* (*Br* = **bonnet**) capot *m*; (*of cooker*) hotte *f*; *Phot:* **lens h.,** parasoleil *m*. **'hooded** *a* (*of pers*) encapuchonné.

hoodlum ['hu:dləm] *n esp NAm: F:* voyou *m*. **'hoodwink** *vtr* tromper, donner le change à (qn).

hoof [hu:f] *n* (*pl* **hoofs** *or* **hooves** [hu:vz]) sabot *m* (d'animal).

hoo-ha ['hu:hɑ:] *n F:* **what's all this h.-ha about?** qu'est-ce qui se passe?

hook [huk] **1.** *n* crochet *m*; croc *m*; *Cl:* agrafe *f*; **h. and eye,** agrafe et œillet *m*; **(coat) h.,** patère *f*; **(fish) h.,** hameçon *m*; (**reaping**) **h.,** faucille *f*; **to take, leave, the phone off the h.,** décrocher le récepteur; *Fig:* **by h. or by crook,** d'une manière ou d'une autre; *Fig:* **to**

swallow sth h., line and sinker, gober tout ce qu'on vous dit; *P:* **to sling one's h.,** décamper; plier bagage; *F:* **to let s.o. off the h.,** faire grâce à qn **2.** *vtr* accrocher (qch à qch); prendre (un poisson) (à l'hameçon); gaffer (un poisson) (avec une gaffe); crocher (un bateau); *F:* attraper (un mari); **to h. (up) a garment,** agrafer un vêtement. **hooked** *a* (*a*) recourbé; (nez) crochu (*b*) muni de crochets, d'hameçons (*c*) *F:* **to be h. on sth,** être entiché de qch; **to get h. on morphine,** devenir morphinomane. **'hook-'nosed** *a* au nez crochu. **'hook-up** *n WTel: TV:* conjugaison *f* de postes. **'hook(e)y** *n F:* **to play h.,** faire l'école buissonnière.

hooligan ['hu:ligən] *n* voyou *m*. **'hooliganism** *n* vandalisme *m*.

hoop [hu:p] *n* cercle *m* (de tonneau); jante *f* (de roue); cerceau *m* (d'enfant); (*in croquet*) arceau *m*; (*of performing animal*) **to jump through hoops,** sauter à travers les cerceaux; *Fig:* **to put s.o. through the hoops,** rendre la vie dure à qn. **'hoop-la** *n* (*at fairs*) jeu *m* des anneaux.

hoot [hu:t] **1.** *vi* (*of owl*) (h)ululer, huer; (*of car*) klaxonner; (*of train*) siffler; (*of siren*) mugir; (*of pers*) huer; (*of pers*) **to h. with laughter,** rire aux éclats **2.** *n* (h)ululement *m* (de hibou); coup *m* de sirène, de klaxon, de sifflet; mugissement *m* (de sirène); (*of pers*) huée *f* (de dérision); *F:* **what a h.!** c'est à se tordre de rire! **I don't care a h., two hoots, about it,** je m'en fiche comme de l'an quarante. **'hooter** *n* sirène *f*; *Aut:* klaxon *m*; *P:* nez *m*, pif *m*.

hoover ['hu:vər] *Rtm:* **1.** *n* aspirateur *m* **2.** *vtr* passer (qch) à l'aspirateur.

hop¹ [hɔp] *n Bot:* houblon *m*. **'hopfield** *n* houblonnière *f*. **'hop-picker** *n* cueilleur, -euse, de houblon.

hop² **1.** *n* (petit) saut; sautillement *m*; (*on one foot*) saut à cloche-pied; *F:* (*dance*) sauterie *f*; *Av:* étape *f*; **to catch s.o. on the h.,** prendre qn au pied levé **2.** *vtr & i* (**hopped** [hɔpt]) sauter, sautiller; (*on one foot*) sauter à cloche-pied; *F:* **to h. it,** filer, ficher le camp; **h. it!** va-t'en! **'hopper** *n* trémie *f*. **'hopping** *a F:* **h. mad,** fou de colère. **'hopscotch** *n Games:* marelle *f*.

hope [houp] **1.** *vi* espérer; **to h. for sth,** espérer qch; **to h. against h.,** espérer contre toute espérance; **I h. to see you again,** j'espère vous revoir; *Corr:* **hoping to hear from you,** dans l'espoir de vous lire; **to h. for the best,** ne pas désespérer **2.** *n* espérance *f*; espoir *m*; **to be full of h., have high hopes,** avoir bon espoir; **in the h. of,** dans l'espoir, l'attente *f*, de; **to live in h. that,** caresser l'espoir que; **to have hopes of doing sth,** avoir l'espoir de faire qch; *NAm:* **h. chest** (*Br* = **bottom drawer**), trousseau *m* (de mariage); *Geog:* **the Cape of Good H.,** le cap de Bonne Espérance; *F:* **what a h.! some h.!** si vous comptez là-dessus! **'hopeful** *a* plein d'espoir; (avenir) qui promet; **the situation looks more h.,** la situation est plus encourageante; **to be h. that,** avoir bon espoir que. **'hopefully** *adv* (travailler) avec bon espoir, avec optimisme; *F:* **h. the snow will be gone by tomorrow,** espérons que la neige aura fondu demain. **'hopefulness** *n* (bon) espoir; confiance *f*. **'hopeless** *a* sans espoir; désespéré; (maladie) incurable; (enfant, menteur) incorrigible; **it's a h. job,** c'est désespérant; *F:* **you're h.!** tu es impossible! **'hopelessly** *adv* (vivre) sans espoir; (regarder) avec désespoir; (vaincu) irrémédiablement;

(amoureux) sans retour. **'hopelessness** n état désespéré.

horde [hɔːd] n horde f.

horizon [həˈraizn] n horizon m; **on the h.,** à l'horizon. **hori'zontal** a horizontal. **hori'zontally** adv horizontalement.

hormone [ˈhɔːmoun] n hormone f.

horn [hɔːn] n corne f; bois m (d'un cerf); (of insects) antenne f; (on vehicle) klaxon m; Mus: cor m; Fig: **to draw in one's horns,** (i) faire des économies (ii) en rabattre; Mus: **French h.,** cor d'harmonie; **hunting h.,** trompe f de chasse. **'horn-'rimmed** a (lunettes) à monture en corne. **'horny** a (-ier, -iest) corné, en corne; (of hands) calleux.

hornet [ˈhɔːnit] n Ent: frelon m.

horoscope [ˈhɔrəskoup] n horoscope m.

horrify [ˈhɔrifai] vtr (horrifies) horrifier; faire horreur à (qn); (shock) scandaliser (qn). **ho'rrendous** a F: terrible, affreux. **'horrible** a horrible, affreux; atroce. **'horribly** adv horriblement, affreusement. **'horrid** a horrible, affreux; (of pers) méchant; to be **h. to s.o.,** être méchant envers qn; **don't be h.!** (i) ne dites pas des horreurs pareilles! (ii) ne faites pas le, la, méchant(e)! **ho'rrific** a horrible; horrifique. **'horrifying** a horrifiant.

horror [ˈhɔrər] n horreur f; **to have a h. of (doing) sth,** avoir horreur de (faire) qch; **h. film,** film d'épouvante; **it gives me the horrors,** cela me donne le frisson; (of child) **a little h.,** un petit monstre. **'horror-stricken, -struck** a saisi d'horreur.

horse [hɔːs] n (a) cheval m; **draught h.,** cheval de trait; **the (Royal) H. Guards** = la Garde du corps (à cheval); **h. dealer,** maquignon m; Bot: **h. chestnut,** marron m d'Inde; **h. chestnut (tree),** marronnier d'Inde; Fig: **dark h.,** personne f dont on ne sait rien; Fig: **to get on one's high h.,** monter sur ses grands chevaux; **h. show,** concours hippique (b) Gym: (vaulting) **h.,** cheval d'arçons; **(clothes) h.,** séchoir m; (on sea) **white horses,** moutons mpl (d'écume). **'horseback** on **h.,** à cheval. **'horsebox** n (pl -boxes) (trailer on car) van m. **'horse-drawn** a tiré par des chevaux; (véhicule) attelé. **'horseflesh, -meat** n Cu: viande f de cheval. **'horsefly** n (pl -flies) Ent: taon m. **'horsehair** n crin m (de cheval). **'horseman, f -woman** n (pl -men, -women) cavalier, -ière; écuyer, -ère. **'horsemanship** n (art m de) l'équitation f. **'horseplay** n jeux brutaux. **'horsepower** n (abbr hp) Aut: Mec: puissance f (en chevaux); Meas: cheval-vapeur m. **'horseracing** n courses fpl de chevaux. **'horseradish** n Hort: Cu: raifort m. **'horseshoe** n fer m à cheval. **'hors(e)y** a (profil) chevalin; (of pers) qui ne parle que chevaux; qui s'intéresse aux chevaux.

horticulture [ˈhɔːtikʌltʃər] n horticulture f. **horti'cultural** a horticole.

hose [houz] **1.** n (a) Com: bas mpl (b) (also **'hose-pipe**) tuyau m; manche f (d'arrosage) **2.** vtr arroser (au jet d'eau); to **h. (down),** laver à grande eau, au jet d'eau. **'hosiery** n Com: bonneterie f.

hospitable [həˈspitəbl] a hospitalier; accueillant. **ho'spitably** adv avec hospitalité. **hospi'tality** n hospitalité f.

hospital [ˈhɔspitl] n hôpital m; **in h.,** à l'hôpital; **teaching h.,** centre hospitalier universitaire; **h. nurse,** infirmière f d'hôpital; **patients in h.,** hospitalisés mpl. **'hospitalize** vtr esp NAm: hospitaliser (qn).

host [houst] n (a) hôte m (b) Ecc: hostie f (c) (large number) armée f, foule f. **'hostess** n (pl -es) hôtesse f; **air h.,** hôtesse de l'air.

hostage [ˈhɔstidʒ] n otage m.

hostel [ˈhɔstəl] n foyer m (sous la direction d'une œuvre sociale); **youth h.,** auberge f de jeunesse. **'hosteller** n **youth h.,** ajiste mf.

hostile [ˈhɔstail, NAm: ˈhɔstəl] a hostile; opposé (to, à); ennemi (to, de). **ho'stility** n (pl -ies) hostilité f (to, contre); animosité f.

hot [hɔt] **1.** a (hotter; hottest) chaud; Cu: (spiced) piquant; épicé; (of feelings) violent; (of struggle) acharné; F: (of goods) recherché par la police; volé; **boiling h.,** bouillant; **burning h.,** brûlant; **to be (very) h.,** (of thg) être (très) chaud; (of pers) avoir (très) chaud; (of weather) faire (très) chaud; **h. flush,** rougeur brûlante; Cu: **h. dog,** hot-dog m; **h. water bottle,** bouillotte f; F: **to be in h. water,** être dans le pétrin; F: **to get into h. water,** se créer des ennuis; F: **h. air,** platitudes fpl; galimatias m; **h. air balloon,** ballon m; F: **to get all h. and bothered,** s'échauffer; F: **to get h. under the collar,** se mettre en colère; F: **how are you?** — **not so h.,** comment ça va? — pas terrible; F: **he's h. stuff at tennis,** au tennis c'est un as; **news h. off the press,** nouvelles de la dernière heure; **to be h. on the scent,** the trail, être sur la bonne piste; **to be h. on the trail of s.o.,** in **h. pursuit of s.o.,** poursuivre qn de près; Games: **you're getting h.,** tu brûles; Tp: F: **h. line,** ligne directe; F: **h. seat,** situation difficile; **h. spot,** (i) boîte de nuit (ii) point névralgique; **to have a h. temper,** s'emporter facilement; **h. contest,** chaude dispute; Rac: **h. favourite,** grand favori; **h. tip,** tuyau increvable; F: **to make things too h. for s.o.,** rendre la vie intolérable à qn **2.** adv **to blow h. and cold,** souffler le chaud et le froid; agir de façons contradictoires. **'hotbed** n foyer m (de corruption). **'hot-'blooded** a (of pers) emporté, passionné. **'hotfoot** adv à toute vitesse. **'hothead** n (pers) tête chaude, emballée. **'hot-headed** a impétueux; à la tête chaude. **'hothouse** n serre (chaude). **'hotly** adv (répondre) vivement, avec chaleur; (poursuivre) de près; (disputer) chaudement. **'hotplate** n plaque chauffante (de cuisinière). **'hotpot** n Cu: ragoût m. **'hotrod** n F: voiture gonflée. **hot-'tempered** a (of pers) vif; colérique. **'hot 'up** v (hotted) **1.** vtr chauffer, réchauffer (qch); F: gonfler (une voiture, un moteur) **2.** vi (of campaign, affair, argument) (s'é)chauffer.

hotchpotch [ˈhɔtʃpɔtʃ] n mélange confus.

hotel [houˈtel] n hôtel m; **private h., residential h.,** pension f de famille; **h. keeper,** hôtelier, -ière; **the h. trade,** l'industrie hôtelière; l'hôtellerie f. **ho'telier** n hôtelier, -ière.

hound [haund] **1.** n chien courant; **the (pack of) hounds,** la meute; **master of hounds,** maître d'équipage; **to ride to hounds,** chasser à courre **2.** vtr **to h. s.o. (down),** traquer qn, poursuivre qn avec acharnement, sans relâche; **to be hounded from place to place,** être pourchassé d'un endroit à l'autre; **to be hounded out of a country,** être chassé d'un pays.

hour [ˈauər] n heure f; **an h. and a half,** une heure et demie; **half an h.,** une demi-heure; **a quarter of an h.,** un quart d'heure; **h. by h.,** heure par heure; **to pay**

s.o. **by the h.**, payer qn à l'heure; **to be paid £5 an h.**, être payé £5 (de) l'heure; **to take hours over sth**, mettre des heures à faire qch; **five kilometres an h.**, cinq kilomètres à l'heure; **office hours**, heures de bureau; **after hours**, après l'heure de fermeture; **in the early, small, hours (of the morning)**, fort avant dans la nuit; au petit matin; **h. hand**, petite aiguille (de montre, de pendule). **'hourglass** n (pl **-es**) sablier m. **'hourly** 1. a (de) toutes les heures; (salaire) horaire, à l'heure; (rendement) horaire; (frequent) continuel 2. adv toutes les heures; d'heure en heure; (frequently) continuellement.

house 1. n [haus] (pl **houses** ['hauziz]) (a) maison f; **from h. to h.**, de porte en porte; **country h.**, (large) château m; (small) maison de campagne; **at, to, in, my h.**, chez moi; **to keep h. for s.o.**, tenir la maison de qn; **to move h.**, déménager; **to keep open h.**, tenir table ouverte; **h. of cards**, château de cartes; **h. agent**, agent immobilier; **h. arrest**, résidence surveillée; **under h. arrest**, aux arrêts; **h. surgeon**, interne en chirurgie (d'un hôpital); *Parl:* **the H.**, la Chambre (i) des Communes (ii) des Lords; **business h.**, maison de commerce; **publishing h.**, maison d'édition; **public h.**, café m, débit m de boissons; **drink on the h.**, consommation (offerte) aux frais de la maison, du patron (b) famille f, maison, dynastie f; **the H. of Valois**, les Valois mpl, la maison des Valois (c) *Th: Cin:* salle f; auditoire m; **full h.**, salle pleine; *PN:* **h. full**, complet; **first h.**, première séance 2. vtr [hauz] loger, héberger (qn); pourvoir au logement de (la population); (of object) **to be housed**, se trouver (**in**, dans, à). **'houseboat** n péniche (aménagée). **'housebound** a obligé de garder la maison. **'housebreaker** n cambrioleur m. **'housebreaking** n cambriolage m. **'housecoat** n *Cl:* peignoir m; robe f d'intérieur; (quilted) douillette f. **'housefly** n (pl **-flies**) mouche f domestique. **'houseful** n maisonnée f; pleine maison (d'invités). **'household** n (membres mpl de la) maison, famille; ménage m: **h. expenses**, frais de, du, ménage; **h. goods**, articles ménagers; **h. word**, mot d'usage courant. **'householder** n chef m de famille; propriétaire mf. **'housekeeper** n concierge mf (d'un immeuble); économe mf (d'un collège); femme f de charge, gouvernante f (d'une maison). **'housekeeping** n ménage; économie f domestique; soins mpl du ménage; **h. (money)**, argent m du ménage. **'housemaid** n bonne f; femme f de chambre. **'housemaster, -mistress** n (pl **-mistresses**) *Sch:* professeur chargé de la surveillance d'un internat. **'houseparty** n (pl **-ies**) partie f de campagne. **'house-proud** a she's very **h.-p.**, c'est une femme d'intérieur très méticuleuse. **'houseroom** n I wouldn't give it **h.**, je n'en voudrais pas même si on me le donnait. **'house-to-house** a (vente) à domicile; **h.-to-h. canvassing**, porte-à-porte m. **'housetop** n to proclaim sth from the housetops, crier qch sur les toits. **'housetrained** a (chien) propre. **'housewarming** n **h. (party)**, pendaison f de la crémaillère; **to have a h. party**, pendre la crémaillère. **'housewife** n (pl **-wives**) maîtresse f de maison; ménagère; femme f au foyer, d'intérieur. **'housework** n travaux mpl domestiques, de ménage; **to do the h.**, faire le ménage. **housing** ['hauziŋ] n (a) logement m; **the h. problem**, la crise du logement; **h. estate**, cité f, lotissement m; groupe m de HLM (D) *MecE:* logement; bâti m; cage f; carter m.

hove [houv] *see* **heave** I. 2. (c).

hovel ['hɔvl] n taudis m; masure f.

hover ['hɔvər] vi planer; (of pers) errer, rôder (autour de qn). **'hovercraft** n *Nau:* aéroglisseur m. **'hoverport** n hoverport m.

how [hau] adv (a) comment; **h. do you do?** bonjour; enchanté (de faire votre connaissance); **h. are you?** comment allez-vous? **h. is it that?** comment se fait-il que? **h.'s that?** *F:* **h. come?** comment ça? **to learn h. to do sth**, apprendre à faire qch; *F:* **and h.!** et comment! **h. do you like this wine?** comment trouvez-vous ce vin? (b) **h. much, h. many**, combien (de); **h. long ago?** il y a combien de temps? **h. long is this room?** quelle est la longueur de cette pièce? **h. old are you?** quel âge avez-vous? (c) **h. pretty she is!** comme elle est jolie! qu'elle est jolie! **h. I wish I could!** si seulement je pouvais! **h. she has changed!** ce qu'elle a changé! I told you **h.** there had been a storm, je lui ai raconté qu'il y avait eu un orage. **how'ever** 1. adv (a) **h. he may do it**, de quelque manière qu'il le fasse; **h. that may be**, quoi qu'il en soit; **h. good his work is**, quelque excellent que soit son travail; **h. intelligent she is**, si intelligente qu'elle soit; **h. little**, si peu que ce soit 2. conj toutefois, cependant, pourtant.

howl [haul] 1. vi & tr hurler; pousser des hurlements; (of wind) mugir, rugir 2. n (also **howling**) hurlement m; mugissement m (du vent). **'howler** n *F:* grosse gaffe; **schoolboy h.**, perle f. **'howling** a (of crowd) hurlant; **h. tempest**, tempête furieuse; *F:* **h. success**, succès fou.

hp abbr horsepower.

HP abbr hire purchase.

hub [hʌb] n moyeu m (de roue); *Fig:* pivot m (de l'univers); centre m (d'activité). **'hubcap** n *Aut:* enjoliveur m.

hubbub ['hʌbʌb] n remue-ménage m inv, vacarme m; **h. of voices**, brouhaha m de voix.

huddle ['hʌdl] 1. vtr & i entasser pêle-mêle, sans ordre; **to h. together**, se tasser; se serrer les uns contre les autres; **to h. up**, se pelotonner; **huddled (up) in a corner**, blotti dans un coin 2. n tas confus, fouillis m (d'objets); (petit) groupe (de personnes); **to go into a h.**, se réunir en petit comité.

hue¹ [hju:] n teinte f, nuance f.

hue² n **h. and cry**, clameur f de haro; *Jur:* clameur publique.

huff [hʌf] n **to be in a h.**, être froissé; **to go into a h.**, prendre la mouche. **'huffy** a vexé, fâché.

hug [hʌg] 1. n étreinte f; **to give s.o. a h.**, serrer qn dans ses bras; embrasser qn 2. vtr (**hugged**) étreindre, embrasser, serrer (qn); (of ship) serrer, longer (la côte); (of pers) longer, raser (un mur); (of car) **to h. the kerb**, serrer le trottoir.

huge [hju:dʒ] a énorme, vaste; (succès) immense, formidable. **'hugely** adv énormément; extrêmement. **'hugeness** n énormité f, immensité f.

hulk [hʌlk] n (a) carcasse f (de navire) (b) (pers) lourdaud, -aude. **'hulking** a gros, lourd; lourdaud.

hull [hʌl] n coque f (de navire).

hullabaloo [hʌləbə'lu:] n *F:* tintamarre m, vacarme m.

hullo [hʌ'lou] *int* = **hello.**

hum [hʌm] **1.** *v* (**hummed**) (*a*) *vi* (*of insect*) bourdonner; (*of machine*) ronfler; (*of aircraft*) vrombir; (*of pers*) fredonner; **to make things h.,** faire marcher rondement les choses (*b*) *vtr* fredonner (un air) **2.** *n* bourdonnement *m*; ronflement *m*; vrombissement *m* (d'avion). **'hummingbird** *n* colibri *m*; oiseau-mouche *m*.

human ['hju:mən] **1.** *a* humain; **h. being,** être humain; **h. nature,** nature humaine; **h. rights,** droits de l'homme **2.** *n* être humain. **humani'tarian** *a* humanitaire. **hu'manity** *n* (*pl* **-ies**) humanité *f*. **'humanize** *vtr* humaniser. **'humanly** *adv* everything **h. possible,** tout ce qui est humainement possible. **'humanoid** *a & n* humanoïde (*mf*).

humane [hju(:)'mein] *a* humain, compatissant; (*of pers*) clément; qui évite de faire souffrir. **hu'manely** *adv* humainement; avec humanité.

humble ['hʌmbl] **1.** *a* humble, modeste; *Fig:* **to eat h. pie** (*NAm:* = **to eat crow**), s'humilier **2.** *vtr* humilier, mortifier (qn); **to h. oneself,** s'humilier; **to h. s.o.'s pride,** (r)abattre l'orgueil de qn. **'humbleness** *n* humilité *f*. **'humbly** *adv* humblement.

humbug ['hʌmbʌg] *n* (*a*) charlatanisme *m*; blagues *fpl*; **h.!** tout ça c'est de la blague! (*b*) (*pers*) blagueur, -euse; fumiste *mf* (*c*) (*sweet*) berlingot *m*; = bêtise *f* de Cambrai.

humdinger [hʌm'diŋər] *n* *F:* quelque chose, quelqu'un, d'extraordinaire; **a real h. of a speech,** un discours formidable, sensationnel.

humdrum ['hʌmdrʌm] *a* monotone; **my h. daily life,** mon train-train quotidien.

humerus ['hju:mərəs] *n* (*pl* **humeri** ['hju:mərai]) *Anat:* humérus *m*.

humid ['hju:mid] *a* humide; (*of heat, skin*) moite. **hu'midifier** *n* humidificateur *m*. **hu'midify** *vtr* (**humidifies**) humidifier. **hu'midity** *n* humidité *f*.

humiliate [hju:'milieit] *vtr* humilier, mortifier (qn). **hu'miliating** *a* humiliant. **humili'ation** *n* humiliation *f*. **hu'mility** *n* humilité *f*.

humour, *NAm:* **humor** ['hju:mər] **1.** *n* (*a*) humeur *f*; disposition *f*; **to be in a good, bad, h.,** être de bonne, de mauvaise, humeur; **to be out of h.,** être (d'humeur) maussade (*b*) humour *m*; **to have a (good) sense of h.,** avoir (le sens) de l'humour; **to have no sense of h.,** ne pas avoir le sens de l'humour; **the h. of the situation,** le côté comique de la situation **2.** *vtr* ménager (qn); complaire à (qn); se prêter à tous les caprices de qn. **'humorist** *n* (*a*) farceur, -euse; *Th:* comique (*b*) écrivain humoristique; humoriste *mf*. **'humorous** *a* humoristique; (*of pers*) plein d'humour; drôle; comique; (*of writer*) humoriste. **'humorously,** *NAm:* **'humourlessly** *adv* drôlement, comiquement. **'humourless,** *NAm:* **'humorless** *a* dépourvu d'humour.

hump [hʌmp] **1.** *n* bosse *f* (de bossu, de chameau); *Fig:* **we're over the h. now,** le plus difficile est passé maintenant **2.** *vtr* (*a*) voûter (les épaules); arquer (le dos) (*b*) *F:* porter (un fardeau). **'humpbacked** *a* (*of pers*) bossu; (*of bridge*) bossu; (pont) en dos d'âne.

humus ['hju:məs] *n* *Hort:* humus *m*; terreau *m*.

hunch [hʌntʃ] **1.** *vtr* arrondir (le dos); voûter (les épaules); **hunched (up),** accroupi (le menton sur les genoux) **2.** *n* *F:* pressentiment *m*; **I have a h. that,** je soupçonne que; j'ai idée que. **'hunchback** *n* (*pers*)

bossu. -ue. **'hunchbacked** *a* bossu.

hundred ['hʌndrəd] *num a & n* cent (*m*); **a h. and one,** cent un; **about a h. houses,** une centaine de maisons; **two h. apples,** deux cents pommes; **two h. and one pounds,** deux cent une livres; **in 1900,** en dix-neuf cent; **to live to be a h.,** atteindre la centaine; **they were dying in hundreds,** ils mouraient par centaines; **a h. per cent,** cent pour cent. **'hundredth** *num a & n* centième (*mf*). **'hundredweight** *n* (*a*) poids *m* de 112 livres = 50,80 kg (*b*) *NAm:* poids *m* de 100 livres = 45,36 kg.

hung [hʌŋ] *see* **hang** I.

Hungary ['hʌŋgəri] *Prn Geog:* Hongrie *f*. **Hun'garian** *a & n* hongrois, -oise.

hunger ['hʌŋgər] **1.** *n* faim *f*; **h. strike,** grève de la faim **2.** *vi* **to h. after, for,** être affamé de. **'hungrily** *adv* avidement; voracement. **'hungry** *a* (**-ier, -iest**) **to be h.,** avoir faim; être affamé; **to be ravenously h.,** avoir une faim de loup; **a h. look,** l'œil avide.

hunk [hʌŋk] *n* gros morceau (de fromage); quignon *m* (de pain).

hunt [hʌnt] **1.** *n* (*a*) chasse *f* (*esp* à courre); recherche *f* (d'un objet, de qn); **tiger h.,** chasse au tigre (*b*) équipage *m* de chasse **2.** *v* (*a*) *vi* chasser à courre; **to h. for sth,** chercher qch (*b*) *vtr* chasser (un animal); poursuivre (un voleur); être à la recherche de. **'hunt 'down** *vtr* traquer; forcer (une bête); *F:* mettre (qn) aux abois. **'hunter** *n* (*a*) chasseur *m*; tueur *m* (de lions); dénicheur, -euse (d'antiquités) (*b*) cheval *m* de chasse. **'hunting** *n* chasse (à courre); **bargain h.,** chasse aux soldes; **to go house h.,** se mettre à la recherche d'une maison, d'un logement; **h. ground,** (i) terrain de chasse (ii) endroit propice (aux collectionneurs); **h. lodge,** pavillon de chasse. **'hunt 'out** *vtr* déterrer, dénicher (qch) (à force de recherches). **'huntsman** *n* (*pl* **-men**) chasseur *m*.

hurdle ['hə:dl] *n* claie *f*; *Sp: Turf:* haie *f*; *Fig:* obstacle *m*; **the hundred metre hurdles,** le cent mètres haies.

hurl [hə:l] *vtr* lancer (qch) avec violence (**at**, contre); **to h. oneself at s.o.,** se ruer, se jeter, sur qn; **to h. abuse at s.o.,** vociférer des injures à qn. **'hurl 'down** *vtr* jeter bas; précipiter.

hurrah [hu'rɑ:], **hurray** [hu'rei] *int & n* hourra (*m*); **h. for the holidays!** vivent les vacances!

hurricane ['hʌrikən] *n* ouragan *m*; **h. lamp,** lampe-tempête *f*.

hurry ['hʌri] **1.** *v* (**hurried**) (*a*) *vtr* presser; bousculer (qn); **work that cannot be hurried,** travail qui demande du temps (*b*) *vi* se hâter, se presser; se dépêcher; presser le pas; **to h. to a place,** se rendre à la hâte, en toute hâte, à un endroit: **she hurried home,** elle s'est dépêchée de rentrer; **to h. into, out of, a room,** entrer dans une, sortir d'une, pièce en toute hâte; **to h. after s.o.,** courir après qn **2.** *n* hâte *f*; précipitation *f*; **to be in a h.,** être pressé; **to go out in a h.,** sortir à la hâte; **he was in no h. to leave,** il n'était pas pressé de partir. **'hurried** *a* (pas) précipité, pressé; (travail) fait à la hâte; (mot) dit à la hâte. **'hurriedly** *adv* à la hâte, en toute hâte; précipitamment. **'hurry a'long 1.** *vi* marcher d'un pas pressé **2.** *vtr* entraîner (qn) précipitamment. **'hurry 'back 1.** *vtr* faire rentrer (qn) en toute hâte **2.** *vi* rentrer à la hâte. **'hurry 'on 1.** *vtr* faire hâter le pas à (qn); avancer (un travail); précipiter (une affaire) **2.** *vi* presser le pas. **'hurry**

'**up 1.** *vtr* presser; faire hâter le pas à (qn) **2.** *vi* se dépêcher, se hâter; **h. up!** dépêchez-vous!

hurt [hɔ:t] **1.** *vtr & i* (**hurt**) (*a*) faire (du) mal à, blesser (qn); **to h. one's foot,** se blesser au pied; **to be, get, h.,** être blessé; **to h. oneself,** se faire (du) mal, se blesser (*b*) faire de la peine à (qn); **to h. s.o.'s feelings,** blesser, peiner, qn (*c*) nuire à, abîmer, endommager (qch) **2.** *n* mal *m*; blessure *f*. '**hurtful** *a* nuisible, nocif; préjudiciable (à qn); blessant.

hurtle ['hɔ:tl] *vi* se précipiter, s'élancer (avec bruit, comme un bolide).

husband ['hʌzbənd] *n* mari *m*; époux *m*; **h. and wife,** les (deux) époux; **to live as h. and wife,** vivre maritalement. '**husbandry** *n* **animal h.,** élevage *m*.

hush [hʌʃ] **1.** *v* (*a*) *vtr* calmer, faire taire (un enfant); imposer silence à (qn) (*b*) *vi* se taire; faire silence **2.** *n* silence *m*; calme *m*; **h. money,** prime du silence; pot-de-vin *m* **3.** *int* chut! **hushed** *a* (*of conversation*) étouffé; **to talk in a h. voice,** chuchoter. '**hush-'hush** *a* F: archi-secret. '**hush 'up** *vtr* étouffer (un scandale).

husk [hʌsk] *n* cosse *f*, gousse *f* (de pois); écale *f* (de noix); balle *f* (de grain).

husky[1] ['hʌski] *a* (**-ier, -iest**) (*a*) (*of voice*) enroué, voilé (*b*) (*of pers*) costaud, fort. '**huskily** *adv* (parler) d'une voix enrouée. '**huskiness** *n* enrouement *m*, empâtement *m* (de la voix).

husky[2] *n* (*pl* **huskies**) chien *m* esquimau.

hustle ['hʌsl] **1.** *v* (*a*) *vtr* bousculer; pousser, presser (qn); **to h. things on,** pousser le travail; faire activer les choses (*b*) *vi* se dépêcher, se presser **2.** *n* bousculade *f*; activité *f* énergique; **h. and bustle,** tourbillon *m* d'activité.

hut [hʌt] *n* hutte *f*, cabane *f*; **mountain h.,** refuge *m*.

hutch [hʌtʃ] *n* (**rabbit**) **h.,** clapier *m*.

hyacinth ['haiəsinθ] *n Bot:* jacinthe *f*.

hybrid ['haibrid] *a & n Biol:* hybride (*m*).

hydrangea [hai'dreindʒə] *n Bot:* hortensia *m*.

hydrant ['haidrənt] *n* prise *f* d'eau; **fire h.,** bouche *f* d'eau.

hydraulic [hai'drɔ:lik] *a* hydraulique.

hydrochloric [haidrou'klɔrik] *a Ch:* (acide) chlorhydrique.

hydroelectric [haidroui'lektrik] *a* hydro-(-)électrique; **h. power,** énergie hydraulique.

hydrofoil ['haidroufɔil] *n* hydrofoil *m*.

hydrogen ['haidrədʒən] *n Ch:* hydrogène *m*; **h. peroxide,** eau oxygénée.

hydrophobia [haidrə'foubiə] *n Med:* hydrophobie *f*.

hydroplane ['haidrouplein] *n* hydroglisseur *m*.

hyena [hai'i:nə] *n Z:* hyène *f*.

hygiene ['haidʒi:n] *n* hygiène *f*. **hy'gienic** *a* hygiénique. **hy'gienically** *adv* hygiéniquement.

hymn [him] *n Ecc:* hymne *m & f*; cantique *m*; **h. book,** (*also* **hymnal** ['himnəl]) *n* livre *m* d'hymnes, recueil *m* de cantiques.

hypermarket ['haipəmɑ:kit] *n* hypermarché *m*.

hypersensitive [haipə'sensitiv] *a* hypersensible.

hyphen ['haifən] *n* trait *m* d'union. '**hyphenate** *vtr* mettre un trait d'union à (un mot); **hyphenated word,** mot à trait d'union.

hypnosis [hip'nousis] *n* hypnose *f*. **hypnotic** [hip'nɔtik] *a* hypnotique. '**hypnotism** *n* hypnotisme *m*. '**hypnotist** *n* hypnotiseur, -euse. '**hypnotize** *vtr* hypnotiser.

hypochondria [haipou'kɔndriə] *n* hypocondrie *f*. **hypo'chondriac** *a & n* hypocondriaque (*mf*); malade *mf* imaginaire.

hypocrisy [hi'pɔkrisi] *n* hypocrisie *f*. '**hypocrite** *n* hypocrite *mf*. **hypo'critical** *a* hypocrite. **hypo'critically** *adv* hypocritement.

hypodermic [haipə'dɔ:mik] **1.** *a* hypodermique **2.** *n* seringue *f* hypodermique.

hypotenuse [hai'pɔtənju:z] *n Mth:* hypoténuse *f*.

hypothermia [haipou'θɔ:miə] *n Med:* hypothermie *f*.

hypothesis [hai'pɔθəsis] *n* (*pl* **hypotheses** [hai'pɔθəsi:z]) hypothèse *f*. **hypothetical** [haipə'θetikl] *a* hypothétique; supposé. **hypo'thetically** *adv* par hypothèse.

hysterectomy [histə'rektəmi] *n* (*pl* **hysterectomies**) *Surg:* hystérectomie *f*.

hysteria [hi'stiəriə] *n Med:* hystérie *f*; crise *f* de nerfs. **hysterical** [hi'sterikl] *a Med:* hystérique; sujet à des crises de nerfs; (rire) nerveux, énervé; **h. sobs,** sanglots convulsifs; **she was h.,** elle avait une crise de nerfs. **hy'sterically** *adv* **to weep h.,** avoir une crise de larmes; **to laugh h.,** être pris d'un rire nerveux; avoir le fou rire. **hy'sterics** *npl* crise de nerfs; fou rire; **to have, go into, h.,** avoir une crise de nerfs, le fou rire.

I

I¹, i [ai] n (la lettre) I, i m; **to dot one's i's,** mettre les points sur les i.

I² pers pron (a) je, (before vowel sound) j'; **I sing,** je chante (b) moi; **it is I,** c'est moi; **I too,** moi aussi; **here I am,** me voici; (stressed) **'I'll do it,** c'est moi qui le ferai; **'he and 'I are great friends,** lui et moi, nous sommes de très bons amis.

ice [ais] **I.** n **1.** glace f; **my feet are like i.,** j'ai les pieds glacés; Fig: **to break the i.,** briser la glace; **to skate on, to be on, thin i.,** toucher à un sujet délicat; **to cut no i. with s.o.,** ne faire aucune impression sur qn; **to put a project on i.,** mettre un projet en veilleuse **2.** (a) Cu: **strawberry i.,** glace à la fraise (b) Ind: **dry i.,** neige f carbonique (c) (on roads) **black i.,** verglas m (d) Geol: **i. age,** période glaciaire; Geog: **i. floe,** banquise f; **i. bucket,** seau à glace; **i. cube,** glaçon m; Sp: **i. hockey,** hockey m sur glace, FrC: hockey; **i. skating,** patinage sur flace; **i. rink,** patinoire f; **i. pick,** (i) Mount: pioche à glace (ii) DomEc: poinçon à glace. **II.** v **1.** vtr geler, congeler **2.** vtr rafraîchir, frapper (une boisson) **3.** vtr glacer (un gâteau) **4.** vi **to i. up,** se givrer. **'iceberg** n iceberg m. **'icebox** n (a) glacière f (b) freezer m (c) NAm: réfrigérateur m. **'ice-breaker** n brise-glace(s) m. **ice-'cold** a glacial; (eau) glacée. **'ice-cream** n glace f. **'icehouse** n glacière f; **it's an i. in here,** on gèle ici. **'icicle** n glaçon m. **'icily** adv glacialement, d'un air glacial. **'iciness** n **1.** froid glacial **2.** froideur glaciale (d'un accueil). **'icing** n glace f (sur un gâteau); **i. sugar,** sucre m glace. **'icy** a **1.** couvert de glace; glacial; **i. road,** route verglacée **2.** (vent, accueil) glacé, glacées.

Iceland ['aisland] Prn Geog: l'Islande f. **'Icelander** n Islandais, -aise. **Ice'landic** (a) a islandais, d'Islande (b) n Ling: l'islandais m.

icon ['aikɔn] n Ecc: icône f.

idea [ai'diːə] n idée f; **what a funny i.!** en voilà une idée! quelle drôle d'idée! **to have some i. of chemistry,** avoir des notions de chimie; **the i. is to make him pay for it,** il s'agit de le lui faire payer; **I've got the general i.,** je vois à peu près ce dont il s'agit; **it was not my i.,** ce n'est pas moi qui en ai eu l'idée; **it's not my i. of pleasure,** ce n'est pas là ma conception du plaisir; **that's the i.!** c'est ça! **I have an i. that,** j'ai idée que; **I had no i., I hadn't the faintest, the foggiest, i.,** je l'ignorais absolument; je n'en avais pas la moindre idée; **I have an i. that I've already seen it,** j'ai l'impression de l'avoir déjà vu; **to get ideas into one's head,** se faire des idées; **who put that i. into your head?** qui t'a mis cette idée dans la tête? F: **what's the big i.?** qu'est-ce qui vous prend? **get the i.?** tu y es? tu piges?

ideal [ai'diːəl] a & n idéal (m). **i'dealism** n idéalisme m. **i'dealist** n idéaliste mf. **i'dealize** vtr idéaliser. **i'deally** adv idéalement; **i., everyone should go,** l'idéal serait que tous y aillent.

identify [ai'dentifai] vtr **1.** identifier (**sth with sth,** qch avec qch) **2. to i. s.o.,** établir l'identité de qn. **i'dentical** a identique (**with, to, à**). **i'dentically** adv identiquement. **identifi'cation** n identification f; **i. papers,** pièces fpl d'identité. **i'dentikit** n **i. picture,** portrait-robot m, pl portraits-robots. **i'dentity** n identité f; **i. card,** carte d'identité; **i. bracelet,** bracelet d'identité; **mistaken i.,** erreur f sur la personne.

ideology [aidi'ɔlədʒi] n idéologie f. **ideo'logical** a idéologique.

idiom ['idiəm] n **1.** langue f, idiome m (d'un pays, d'une région) **2.** idiotisme m, locution f; **a French i.,** un gallicisme; **an English i.,** un anglicisme. **idio'matic** a idiomatique. **i. phrase,** idiotisme m; expression f idiomatique. **idio'matically** adv (parler, s'exprimer) de façon idiomatique.

idiosyncrasy [idiou'siŋkrasi] n **1.** idiosyncrasie f **2.** petite manie; particularité f (de style). **idiosyn'cratic** a particulier, caractéristique.

idiot ['idiət] n (a) Med: idiot, -ote (b) imbécile mf; F: **you i.!** espèce d'imbécile! **'idiocy** n (a) idiotie (congénitale) (b) stupidité f. **idi'otic** a bête; **don't be i.!** ne fais pas l'imbécile! **that's i.,** (ça) c'est stupide. **idi'otically** adv bêtement, stupidement.

idle ['aidl] **1.** a (a) inoccupé, oisif; en chômage; (of machine) au repos; **to be, stand, i.,** rester à ne rien faire; **in my i. moments,** à mes heures perdues; **capital lying i.,** fonds dormants (b) paresseux, fainéant (c) inutile; futile; **i. threats,** menaces en l'air; **out of i. curiosity,** par simple curiosité **2.** vi (a) (of pers) fainéanter, paresser; flâner (b) (of engine) tourner au ralenti. **'idleness** n (a) oisiveté f, désœuvrement m (b) paresse f, fainéantise f. **'idler** n (a) oisif, -ive; désœuvré, -ée; flâneur, -euse (b) fainéant, -ante; paresseux, -euse. **'idly** adv (a) sans rien faire; sans travailler (b) paresseusement.

idol ['aidl] n idole f. **i'dolatrous** a idolâtre. **i'dolatry** n idolâtrie f. **'idolize** vtr idolâtrer, adorer (qn, qch).

idyll ['(a)idil] n idylle f. **i'dyllic** a idyllique.

if [if] conj **1.** (a) si; **if I'm late I apologize,** si je suis en retard, je m'en excuse; **if I wanted him I rang,** si j'avais besoin de lui, je sonnais (b) **if he does it, he will be punished,** s'il le fait, il sera puni; **if I am free, I shall go out,** si je suis libre, je sortirai; **if I were free, I would go out,** si j'étais libre, je sortirais; **if they are to be believed nobody was saved,** à les croire, personne n'aurait survécu; **you'll get five pence for it, if that,** on vous en donnera cinq pence et encore! **if not,** sinon; **if possible,** si possible; **if necessary,** s'il le faut; au besoin; **go and see him, if only to please me,** allez le voir, ne serait-ce que pour me faire plaisir (c) **if I were you,** si j'étais vous, à votre place; **if I am not**

mistaken, si je ne me trompe (*d*) (*exclamatory*) **if only I had known!** si seulement je l'avais su! **if only he comes in time!** pourvu qu'il vienne à temps! **if it isn't Simon!** ça, par exemple! mais c'est Simon! (*e*) **as if,** comme (si); **as if by chance,** comme par hasard; **as if to,** comme pour; **he leant forward as if to pick it up,** il s'est penché comme pour le ramasser 2. (*concessive*) **pleasant weather, if rather cold,** temps agréable, bien qu'un peu froid 3. (= *whether*) **do you know if he is at home?** savez-vous s'il est chez lui? **4.** *n* **your ifs and buts,** vos si (*inv*) et vos mais; **it's a very big if,** c'est une condition diffici'e à remplir.

igloo ['iglu:] *n* igloo *m*.

ignite [ig'nait] **1.** *vtr* mettre (le) feu à (qch) **2.** *vi* prendre feu; s'enflammer. **ig'nition** *n* (*a*) ignition *f* (*b*) *Aut:* allumage *m*; **i. key,** clef de contact; **i. switch,** contact *m*.

ignoble [ig'noubl] *a* ignoble; infâme, vil.

ignominious [ignə'miniəs] *a* ignominieux; honteux. **igno'miniously** *adv* ignominieusement; avec ignominie. **'ignominy** *n* ignominie *f*, honte *f*.

ignore [ig'nɔːr] *vtr* ne tenir aucun compte de (qch); fermer les yeux sur (une façon d'agir); ne pas relever (une injure); passer (qch) sous silence; **to i. s.o.,** feindre de ne pas voir qn, de ne pas reconnaître qn; **to i. the facts,** méconnaître les faits; **to i. an invitation,** ne pas répondre à une invitation. **'ignorance** *n* ignorance *f*; **to keep s.o. in i. of sth,** laisser ignorer qch à qn; **i. of the law is no excuse,** nul n'est censé ignorer la loi. **'ignorant** *a* ignorant; **to be i. of a fact,** ignorer un fait.

ILEA *abbr* *Inner London Education Authority.*

ill [il] (**worse, worst**) **1.** *a* (*a*) mauvais; **i. effects,** effets pernicieux; **of i. repute,** mal famé (*b*) méchant, mauvais; **i. deed,** mauvaise action (*c*) malade, souffrant; **to be i.,** être malade, souffrant; *F:* vomir; avoir mal au cœur; **to be taken i.,** tomber malade; **to be seriously i.,** être dans un état grave; avoir une maladie grave; **to look i.,** avoir mauvaise mine; **i. health,** mauvaise santé **2.** *n* (*a*) mal *m*; **to speak i. of s.o.,** dire du mal de qn (*b*) dommage *m*, tort *m* 3 *adv* mal; **i. informed,** (i) mal renseigné (ii) ignorant; **to be i. at ease,** (i) être mal à l'aise (ii) être inquiet. **ill-ad'vised** *a* **1.** malavisé **2.** (*of action*) peu judicieux. **'ill-'bred** *a* mal élevé; malappris. **'ill-dis'posed** *a* malintentionné, malveillant. **'ill-'fated** *a* (*of pers*) infortuné; (*jour*) néfaste. **'ill-'feeling** *n* ressentiment *m*, rancune *f*; **no i.-f.!** sans rancune! **'ill-'gotten** *a* (bien) mal acquis. **'ill-'humoured,** *NAm:* **-humored** *a* de mauvaise humeur; maussade, grincheux. **'ill-in'formed** *a* (*a*) mal renseigné (*b*) ignorant. **'ill-'mannered** *a* grossier; impoli. **'ill-'natured** *a* méchant; désagréable. **'ill-ness** *n* maladie *f*. **'ill-'tempered** *a* de mauvais caractère; maussade. **'ill-'timed** *a* mal à propos; **i.-t. arrival,** arrivée inopportune. **'ill-'treat** *vtr* maltraiter, brutaliser (qn, un animal). **'ill-treatment** *n* mauvais traitements. **'ill-'use** *vtr* maltraiter. **'ill-will** *n* malveillance *f*, rancune *f*.

illegal [i'li:gəl] *a* illégal. **i'llegally** *adv* illégalement.

illegible [i'ledʒibl] *a* illisible. **i'llegibly** *adv* illisiblement.

illegitimate [ili'dʒitimət] *a* illégitime. **ille'giti-**

macy *n* illégitimité *f*. **ille'gitimately** *adv* illégitimement.

illicit [i'lisit] *a* illicite; clandestin; **i. betting,** paris clandestins. **i'llicitly** *adv* illicitement.

illiteracy [i'litərəsi] *n* analphabétisme *m*. **i'lliterate** *a & n* analphabète (*mf*); illettré, -ée.

illogical [i'lɔdʒik(ə)l] *a* illogique; peu logique. **i'llogically** *adv* illogiquement.

illuminate [i'lu:mineit] *vtr* **1.** éclairer (une salle, l'esprit de qn) **2.** illuminer (un bâtiment pour une fête) **3.** enluminer (un manuscrit). **i'lluminated** *a* (enseigne) lumineuse. **i'lluminating** *a* **1.** éclairant **2.** **i. talk,** entretien qui apporte des éclaircissements. **illumi'nation** *n* **1.** (*a*) éclairage *m* (*b*) illumination *f* (d'un édifice) **2.** (*usu pl*) (*a*) illuminations (*b*) enluminures *fpl* (d'un manuscrit).

illusion [i'lu:ʒ(ə)n] *n* illusion *f*; tromperie *f*; **he had no illusions on that point,** il ne se faisait aucune illusion à cet égard. **i'llusionist** *n* prestidigitateur *m*; illusionniste *mf*. **i'llusory** *a* illusoire.

illustrate ['iləstreit] *vtr* **1.** expliquer, démontrer, par des exemples **2.** illustrer; orner (un livre) de gravures; **illustrated magazine,** (journal, magazine) illustré (*m*). **illus'tration** *n* **1.** explication *f*, exemple *m*; **by way of i.,** à titre d'exemple **2.** illustration *f*, gravure *f*, image *f*. **'illustrator** *n* illustrateur *m*.

illustrious [i'lʌstriəs] *a* illustre, célèbre.

ILO *abbr* *International Labour Organization*, Organisation internationale du travail, OIT.

image ['imidʒ] *n* **1.** image (sculptée); représentation *f* (d'un dieu); idole *f* **2.** **he's the living i. of his father,** c'est le portrait vivant de son père **3.** **(public) i.,** image de marque. **'imagery** *n* images *fpl*.

imagine [i'mædʒin] *vtr* **1.** (*a*) imaginer, concevoir; se figurer, se représenter (qch); **i. yourself in Paris,** supposez que vous êtes à Paris; **i. meeting you here!** qui aurait jamais pensé vous rencontrer ici! **just i my despair,** imaginez(-vous) (un peu) mon désespoir; **you can't i. it!** vous n'avez pas idée! **as may (well) be imagined,** comme on peut (se) l'imaginer (*b*) **I i. them to be fairly rich,** je les crois assez riches; **don't i. that I am satisfied,** n'allez pas croire que je sois satisfait **2. to be always imagining things,** se faire des idées; **I imagined I heard a knock at the door,** j'ai cru entendre frapper à la porte. **i'maginable** *a* imaginable; **the finest thing i.,** la plus belle chose qu'on puisse imaginer. **i'maginary** *a* imaginaire. **imagi'nation** *n* imagination *f*; **to have no i.,** manquer d'imagination; **in i.,** en imagination; **vivid i.,** imagination fertile; **it's your i.!** vous avez rêvé! **i'maginative** *a* imaginatif.

imbalance [im'bæləns] *n* déséquilibre *m*.

imbecile ['imbisil] *n* imbécile *mf*; *F:* **you i.!** espèce d'idiot! **imbe'cility** *n* imbécillité *f*; faiblesse *f* d'esprit.

imbibe [im'baib] *vtr* (*a*) absorber, s'assimiler (des connaissances) (*b*) boire, avaler (une boisson); aspirer (l'air frais) (*c*) (*of thg*) imbiber (qch); s'imprégner, se pénétrer, de (qch).

IMF *abbr* *International Monetary Fund,* Fonds Monétaire International, FMI.

imitate ['imiteit] *vtr* **1.** (*a*) imiter, copier (*b*) mimer, singer (qn); contrefaire (la voix de qn). **imi'tation** (*a*) *n* imitation *f*; **beware of imitations,** méfiez-vous des contrefaçons *f* (*b*) *a* factice; **i. leather**, similicuir *m*; **i. jewellery**, faux bijoux. **'imitative** [-tətiv] *a* imitatif. **'imitator** *n* imitateur, -trice.

immaculate [i'mækjulət] *a* 1. immaculé; sans tache; **the I. Conception**, l'Immaculée Conception 2. (*of dress*) irréprochable, impeccable. **i'mmaculately** *adv* 1. sans défaut 2. (vêtu) impeccablement.

immaterial [imə'tiəriəl] *a* 1. (esprit) immatériel 2. peu important; **that's quite i. to me**, cela m'est indifférent; peu importe; **it's i. whether he comes or not**, il importe peu qu'il vienne ou non; **the fact is (quite) i.**, cela n'a aucune importance.

immature [imə'tjuər] *a* pas mûr; (*of plan*) insuffisamment mûri; (*of pers*) très jeune (pour son âge); qui manque de maturité. **imma'turity** *n* manque *m* de maturité.

immediate [i'mi:djət] *a* 1. immédiat; sans intermédiaire; direct; **my i. object**, mon premier but; **in the i. future**, dans l'immédiat *m*; **in the i. vicinity**, dans le voisinage immédiat; **the i. family**, les proches parents 2. instantané; sans retard. **i'mmediately** 1. *adv* (*a*) immédiatement; **it does not affect me i.**, cela ne me touche pas directement (*b*) tout de suite; **i. on his return**, dès son retour; **i. after**, aussitôt après 2. *conj* **i. he received the money**, dès qu'il eut reçu l'argent; **i. I arrived**, dès mon arrivée.

immemorial [imi'mɔ:riəl] *a* **from time i.**, de temps immémorial, de toute antiquité.

immense [i'mens] *a* (étendue) immense, vaste; (quantité) énorme. **i'mmensely** *adv* immensément; *F:* **to enjoy oneself i.**, s'amuser énormément. **i'mmensity** *n* immensité *f*.

immerse [i'mə:s] *vtr* 1. immerger, submerger, plonger (qch) (dans un liquide) 2. **to be immersed in one's work**, être plongé, absorbé, dans son travail. **i'mmersion** *n* immersion *f*; **i. heater**, chauffe-eau *m inv* électrique.

immigrate ['imigreit] *vi* immigrer. **'immigrant** *a & n* immigrant, -ante; immigré, -ée. **immi'gration** *n* immigration *f*; **i. officer**, agent *m* du service de l'immigration.

imminent ['iminənt] *a* (danger) imminent. **'imminence** *n* imminence *f*.

immobile [i'moubail] *a* fixe; immobile. **immobility** [-'bili-] *n* immobilité *f*. **immobili'zation** [-bilai-] *n* immobilisation *f* (i) *Med:* d'un membre fracturé (ii) de la circulation (iii) *Fin:* de capitaux. **i'mmobilize** [-bil-] *vtr* immobiliser.

immoderate [i'mɔdərət] *a* immodéré, intempéré; extravagant. **i'mmoderately** *adv* immodérément.

immodest [i'mɔdist] *a* impudique; sans pudeur.

immoral [i'mɔrəl] *a* immoral; (*of pers*) dissolu. **immo'rality** *n* immoralité *f*.

immortal [i'mɔ:tl] *a & n* immortel (*m*). **immor'tality** *n* immortalité *f*. **i'mmortalize** *vtr* immortaliser (qn, le nom de qn); perpétuer (la mémoire de qn).

immovable [i'mu:vəbl] 1. *a* (*a*) fixe; à demeure (*b*) (volonté) inébranlable (*c*) (visage) impassible 2. *npl Jur:* **immovables**, biens immobiliers, immeubles.

immune [i'mju:n] *a Med:* à l'abri (de la contagion); immunisé. **i'mmunity** *n* immunité *f*. **immuni'zation** *n* immunisation *f*. **'immunize** *vtr* immuniser (qn) (**against**, contre) (une maladie).

immutable [i'mju:təbl] *a* immuable; inaltérable. **i'mmutably** *adv* immuablement.

imp [imp] *n* (*a*) diablotin *m*, lutin *m* (*b*) (*of child*) petit diable.

impact ['impækt] *n* (*a*) choc *m*, impact *m* (*b*) **to make a great i. on (sth)**, avoir une forte répercussion, une grande incidence, un effet retentissant, sur (qch).

impair [im'pɛər] *vtr* affaiblir; altérer, abîmer (la santé); diminuer (les forces).

impart [im'pa:t] *vtr* communiquer (des connaissances); annoncer (une nouvelle).

impartial [im'pa:ʃəl] *a* (*of pers, conduct*) impartial. **imparti'ality** *n* impartialité *f*. **im'partially** *adv* impartialement.

impassable [im'pa:səbl] *a* infranchissable; (chemin) impraticable.

impassioned [im'pæʃənd] *a* (discours) passionné, exalté.

impassive [im'pæsiv] *a* impassible; (visage) composé. **im'passively** *adv* sans s'émouvoir.

impatient [im'peiʃənt] *a* impatient; **to get, grow, i.**, s'impatienter. **im'patience** *n* (*a*) impatience *f* (*b*) intolérance *f*. **im'patiently** *adv* avec impatience; impatiemment.

impeach [im'pi:tʃ] *vtr* 1. *Jur:* accuser (qn) (de haute trahison) 2. mettre en doute; attaquer (la probité de qn).

impeccable [im'pekəbl] *a* impeccable. **im'peccably** *adv* de façon irréprochable; impeccablement.

impecunious [impi'kju:niəs] *a* impécunieux.

impede [im'pi:d] *vtr* mettre obstacle à, empêcher, entraver (qn, qch). **im'pediment** *n* empêchement *m*, obstacle *m* (to, à); **speech i.**, trouble *m* de la parole.

impel [im'pel] *vtr* (**impelled**) 1. pousser, forcer (s.o. **to do sth**, qn à faire qch) 2. pousser (en avant); **boat impelled by the wind**, bateau poussé par le vent.

impending [im'pendiŋ] *a* (danger) imminent, menaçant; **her i. arrival**, son arrivée prochaine; **the i. landing**, l'imminence du débarquement.

impenetrable [im'penitrəbl] *a* impénétrable (**to**, à); **i. mystery**, mystère insondable. **impenetra'bility** *n* impénétrabilité *f*.

imperative [im'perətiv] 1. *a & n Gram:* impératif (*m*); **in the i.**, à l'impératif 2. *a* urgent, impérieux; **discretion is i.**, la discrétion s'impose; **it is i. that he should come**, il faut absolument qu'il vienne. **im'peratively** *adv* impérativement.

imperceptible [impə'septibl] *a* imperceptible; (bruit) insaisissable; **an i. difference**, une différence insensible. **imper'ceptibly** *adv* imperceptiblement, insensiblement.

imperfect [im'pə:fikt] 1. *a* imparfait, incomplet; défectueux 2. *a & n Gram:* **i. (tense)**, (temps) imparfait (*m*); **verb in the i.**, verbe à l'imparfait. **imper'fection** *n* imperfection *f*, défectuosité *f*. **im'perfectly** *adv* imparfaitement.

imperial [im'piəriəl] *a* (*a*) impérial (*b*) (poids et mesures) qui ont cours légal dans le Royaume-Uni; **i. pint**, pinte légale. **im'perialism** *n* impérialisme *m*. **im'perialist** *a & n* impérialiste (*mf*). **im'perially** *adv* impérialement; majestueusement.

imperil [im'peril] *vtr* (**imperilled**) mettre en péril, en danger.

imperious [im'piəriəs] *a* impérieux, arrogant.
im'periously *adv* impérieusement.

impermeable [im'pə:miəbl] *a* imperméable, étanche.

impersonal [im'pə:sənəl] *a* (style) impersonnel; *Gram:* **i. verb**, verbe impersonnel. **im'personally** *adv* impersonnellement.

impersonate [im'pə:səneit] *vtr* se faire passer pour (qn); imiter (qn). **imperso'nation** *n* imitation *f* (de qn). **im'personator** *n* (a) imitateur, -trice (b) imposteur *m*.

impertinence [im'pə:tinəns] *n* impertinence *f*, insolence *f*; **a piece of i.**, une impertinence. **im'pertinent** *a* impertinent, insolent. **im'pertinently** *adv* avec impertinence; d'un ton insolent.

imperturbable [impə(:)'tə:bəbl] *a* imperturbable; calme; impassible.

impervious [im'pə:viəs] *a* (a) impénétrable; **i. to water**, imperméable, étanche à l'eau (b) (of pers) **i. to reason**, inaccessible, fermé, à la raison.

impetigo [impə'taigou] *n Med:* impétigo *m*; *F:* gourme *f*.

impetuous [im'petjuəs] *a* impétueux. **impetu'osity**, **im'petuousness** *n* impétuosité *f*. **im'petuously** *adv* impétueusement.

impetus ['impitəs] *n* vitesse acquise; élan *m*; **to give an i. to sth**, donner l'impulsion à qch.

impiety [im'paiəti] *n* impiété *f*.

impinge [im'pin(d)ʒ] *vi* empiéter sur (les droits d'autrui).

implacable [im'plækəbl] *a* implacable (**towards s.o.**, à, pour, qn). **im'placably** *adv* implacablement.

implant ['implɑ:nt] **1.** *vtr* inculquer (une idée); *Med:* faire une implantation **2.** *n* implant *m*.

implement[1] ['implimənt] *n* outil *m*, instrument *m*, ustensile *m*.

implement[2] ['impliment] *vtr* rendre effectif (un contrat); remplir (un engagement); accomplir (une promesse); donner suite à (une décision).

implicate ['implikeit] *vtr* impliquer. **impli'cation** *n* **1.** implication *f* (**in**, dans); **the i. of his words**, la portée de ses paroles; **by i.**, implicitement **2.** insinuation *f*.

implicit [im'plisit] *a* (condition) implicite; **i. faith**, confiance aveugle (**in**, dans); **i. obedience**, obéissance absolue. **im'plicitly** *adv* absolument; aveuglément.

implore [im'plɔ:r] *vtr* implorer; **to i. s.o. to do sth**, supplier qn de faire qch. **im'ploring** *a* (ton, regard) suppliant. **im'ploringly** *adv* d'un ton, d'un air, suppliant.

imply [im'plai] *vtr* **1.** impliquer; **what is implied**, ce qui en découle **2.** laisser supposer (que); **you seem to i. (that)**, vous laissez supposer (que). **im'plied** *a* (consentement) implicite, tacite.

impolite [impə'lait] *a* impoli (**to, towards**, envers). **impo'litely** *adv* impoliment. **impo'liteness** *n* impolitesse *f*.

imponderable [im'pondrəbl] *a & n* impondérable (*m*).

import I. *n* ['impɔ:t] **1.** sens *m*, signification *f* (d'un mot) **2.** (*usu pl*) *Com:* **imports**, articles *m* d'importation; importations *f*; **i. duty**, droit *m*

d'entrée. **II.** *vtr* [im'pɔ:t] *Com:* importer (des marchandises). **impor'tation** *n* importation *f*. **im'porter** *n* importateur, -trice.

importance [im'pɔ:təns] *n* (a) importance *f*; **to be of i.**, avoir de l'importance; **it is of the highest i.** (that), il est de la plus haute importance (que); **of vital i.**, d'une importance capitale; **to give i. to a word**, mettre un mot en valeur; **to attach the greatest i. to a fact**, attacher la plus haute importance à un fait (b) importance (d'une personne); **to be full of one's own i.**, être pénétré de son importance. **im'portant** *a* (a) important; **that's not i.**, ça n'a pas d'importance; **it's i. (that)**, il est important (de, que); il importe (de, que) (b) (of pers) **to look i.**, prendre des airs (d'importance).

importune [impɔ:'tju:n] *vtr* importuner (qn); harceler, presser (qn). **im'portunate** *a* importun; (visiteur) ennuyeux. **impor'tunity** *n* importunité *f*.

impose [im'pouz] **1.** *vtr* (a) **to i. conditions on s.o.**, imposer des conditions à qn (b) **to i. a tax on sugar**, imposer, taxer, le sucre; **to i. a penalty on s.o.**, infliger une peine à qn **2.** *vi* **to i. (up)on s.o.**, en imposer à qn; abuser de l'amabilité de qn. **im'posing** *a* (air) imposant; (spectacle) grandiose. **impo'sition** *n* **1.** imposition *f* (i) de conditions (ii) d'une tâche (iii) d'une taxe, d'un impôt **2.** abus *m* de la bonne volonté de qn.

impossible [im'pɔsəbl, -ibl] **1.** *a* (a) impossible; **it's i. for me to do it**, il m'est impossible de le faire; **to make it i. for s.o. to do sth**, mettre qn dans l'impossibilité de faire qch (b) (histoire) invraisemblable; **i. person**, personne difficile à vivre, impossible **2.** *n* **to attempt the i.**, tenter l'impossible *m*. **impossi'bility** *n* impossibilité *f*; chose *f* impossible. **im'possibly** *adv* **1. not i.**, peut être bien que **2.** *F:* (habillé) d'une façon impossible; **i. long**, insupportablement long.

impostor [im'pɔstər] *n* imposteur *m*. **im'posture** *n* imposture *f*.

impotence ['impətəns] *n* (a) *Med:* impuissance (sexuelle) (b) impotence *f*; faiblesse *f*. **'impotent** *a* (a) *Med:* impuissant (b) impotent.

impound [im'paund] *vtr* confisquer, saisir (des marchandises); mettre (un véhicule) en fourrière.

impoverish [im'pɔvəriʃ] *vtr* appauvrir (qn, un pays). **im'poverished** *a* appauvri, pauvre.

impracticable [im'præktikəbl] *a* infaisable, impraticable. **impractica'bility** *n* impraticabilité *f*.

impractical [im'præktikl] *a* (of pers) peu pratique; (projet) peu réaliste.

imprecise [impri'sais] *a* imprécis, vague.

impregnable [im'pregnəbl] *a* (forteresse) imprenable, inexpugnable.

impregnate ['impregneit] *vtr* (a) *Biol:* féconder (une femelle) (b) imprégner (**sth with sth**, qch de qch).

impresario [impre'sɑ:riou] *n* (pl **impresarios**) impresario *m*.

impress I. *n* ['impres] (a) impression *f*, empreinte *f* (b) marque distinctive; cachet *m*. **II.** *vtr* [im'pres] **1.** imprimer (un dessin sur du tissu); **to i. sth on the mind**, graver qch dans la mémoire **2. to i. sth upon s.o.**, faire bien comprendre qch à qn **3.** faire impression sur (qn); impressionner (qn); **he impressed me**, il m'a fait une impression favorable; **I'm not impressed,** cela me laisse froid; je ne suis pas emballé. **im'pression** n 1. (a) impression f; **to make a good i. on s.o.,** faire une bonne impression sur qn (b) **I'm under the i. (that),** j'ai l'impression (que); **to create the i. (that),** donner l'impression (que) 2. tirage m (d'un livre). **im'pressionable** a (of pers) impressionnable; sensible. **im'pressionism** n Art: impressionnisme m. **im'pressionist** a & n Art: impressionniste (mf). **impressio'nistic** a impressionniste. **im'pressive** a impressionnant. **im'pressively** adv d'une manière impressionnante.

imprint ['imprint] 1. n (a) empreinte f (b) firme f, rubrique f (d'un éditeur) 2. vtr imprimer; graver, fixer (dans la mémoire).

imprison [im'prizn] vtr emprisonner (qn). **im'prisonment** n emprisonnement m; **ten days' i.,** dix jours de prison.

improbable [im'prɔbəbl] a improbable; (histoire) invraisemblable. **improba'bility** n improbabilité f; invraisemblance f. **im'probably** adv peu probablement; invraisemblablement.

impromptu [im'prɔm(p)tju:] 1. adv (faire qch) sans préparation; impromptu 2. a (discours) impromptu inv, improvisé 3. n Lit: Mus: impromptu m.

improper [im'prɔpər] a 1. (expression) impropre; (terme) inexact 2. choquant; déplacé; malhonnête; indécent. **im'properly** adv 1. **word i. used,** mot employé abusivement 2. (se conduire) d'une façon inconvenante, indécente, malhonnête. **impropriety** [imprə'praiəti] n (a) impropriété f (de langage) (b) inconvenance f (de conduite).

improve [im'pru:v] 1. (a) vtr améliorer; perfectionner; **to i. the appearance of sth,** embellir qch (b) v ind tr **to i. (up)on sth,** améliorer qch; **to i. on s.o.,** faire mieux que qn 2. vi s'améliorer; **he has greatly improved,** il a fait de grands progrès; **business is improving,** les affaires reprennent. **im'provement** n amélioration f; perfectionnement m; embellissement m (d'une maison); **to be an i. on sth,** surpasser qch; **my new car is a great i. on the old one,** ma nouvelle voiture est bien supérieure à l'ancienne.

improvident [im'prɔvidənt] a (a) imprévoyant (b) prodigue. **im'providence** n imprévoyance f. **im'providently** adv sans prévoyance.

improvise ['imprəvaiz] vtr improviser (un discours). **improvi'sation** n improvisation f.

imprudent [im'pru:dənt] a imprudent. **im'prudence** n imprudence f. **im'prudently** adv imprudemment.

impudent ['impjudənt] a effronté, insolent. **'impudence** n impudence f, effronterie f, insolence f; **to have the i. to say,** avoir l'audace f, F: le culot, de dire. **'impudently** adv effrontément, insolemment.

impugn [im'pju:n] vtr attaquer, contester (une proposition); mettre en doute (la véracité de qch).

impulse ['impʌls] n 1. impulsion f; poussée motrice 2. impulsion; mouvement spontané; élan m; **to act on i.,** agir spontanément, par impulsion; **on the, a, first i.,** à première vue; **i. buying,** achat spontané; **sudden, rash, i.,** coup m de tête. **im'pulsive** a (of pers) impulsif; **i. action,** coup de tête. **im'pulsively** adv (agir) par impulsion.

impunity [im'pju:niti] n impunité f; **with i.,** impunément.

impure [im'pju:ər] a impur. **im'purity** n (pl -ies) 1. impureté f 2. pl saletés f; corps étrangers.

impute [im'pju:t] vtr imputer. **impu'tation** n imputation f.

in [in] I. prep 1. (of place) (a) en, à, dans; **in Europe,** en Europe; **in Japan,** au Japon; **in Paris,** à Paris; **in the United States,** aux États-Unis; **in the country,** à la campagne; (of book) **in the press,** sous presse; **in school,** à l'école; **in bed,** au lit; **in one's house,** chez soi; **in my hand,** dans ma main; **in the water,** dans l'eau; **in here,** ici; **in there,** là-dedans; **in the distance,** au loin; **in your place,** à votre place (b) (among) **in the crowd,** dans la foule; **he's in his sixties,** il a passé la soixantaine; **in the thirties,** dans les années trente 2. (in respect of) **blind in one eye,** aveugle d'un œil; **two metres in length,** long de deux mètres 3. (of ratio) **one in ten,** un sur dix; **once in ten years,** une fois en dix ans 4. (of time) (a) **in 1927,** en 1927; **in those days,** en ce temps-là; à cette époque-là; **at four o'clock in the afternoon,** à quatre heures de l'après-midi; **in the daytime,** pendant la journée; **in the evening,** le soir, pendant la soirée; **in summer, autumn, winter,** en été, en automne, en hiver; **in spring,** au printemps; **in August,** au mois d'août, en août; **in the future,** à l'avenir; **in the past,** par le passé; **never in my life,** jamais de ma vie; **in my time,** de mon temps (b) **to do sth in three hours,** faire qch en trois heures; **he'll be here in three hours,** il sera là dans trois heures; **in a little while,** sous peu; **I haven't seen you in years,** il y a des années que je ne vous ai vu 5. **in tears,** en larmes; **in good health,** en bonne santé; **in despair,** au désespoir 6. (clothed in) **in his shirt,** en chemise; **dressed in white,** habillé de blanc 7. **to go out in the rain,** sortir sous la pluie; **to work in the rain,** travailler sous la pluie; **in the sun,** au soleil 8. **in my opinion,** à mon avis 9. (a) **in a gentle voice,** d'une voix douce; **to be in (the) fashion,** être à la mode (b) **to write in French,** écrire en français; **to write in ink,** écrire à l'encre; **in writing,** par écrit (c) **in alphabetical order,** par ordre alphabétique (d) **in the form of,** sous forme de (e) **I've nothing in your size,** je n'ai rien à votre taille (f) (of degree, extent) **in part,** en partie; **in places,** par endroits; **in large quantities,** en grandes quantités (g) **in wood,** de, en, bois 10. **in that,** parce que, vu que, en ce sens que. II. adv 1. (a) à la maison, chez soi; **Mr Smith is in,** M. Smith y est, est ici, est à la maison (b) **the harvest is in,** la moisson est rentrée (c) **the train is in,** le train est en gare (d) **is the fire still in?** est-ce que le feu brûle encore? (e) **what is he in for?** pour quel crime est-il en prison? 2. (a) **strawberries are in,** c'est la saison des fraises; **stripes are in this year,** les rayures sont à la mode cette année (b) **I've got my hand in,** j'ai le tour de main (c) **to be (well) in with s.o.,** être en bons termes avec qn; **the Labour Party is in,** le parti travailliste est au pouvoir (d) **my luck is in,** je suis en veine 3. (a) **to be in for £100,** en avoir pour £100; **we're in for a storm,** nous aurons sûrement de l'orage; F: **he's in for it,** (i) le voilà dans de beaux draps! (ii) qu'est-ce qu'il va prendre! **you don't know what you're in for,** tu ne sais pas ce qui t'attend (b) **I wasn't in on it,** je n'étais pas dans le coup (c) **day in, day out,** jour après jour, sans trêve (d) **all in,** (i) (prix) tout compris (ii) F: **I'm all in,**

je suis éreinté. **III.** *n* the ins and outs of a matter, les coins *m* et recoins *m* d'une affaire. **'in-be'tween 1.** *n* celui qui est entre les deux **2.** *a* intermédiaire; **in-b. times,** dans les intervalles. **'in-depth** *a* (interview) en profondeur. **'in-flight** *a* en vol. **'in-'laws** *npl* belle-famille *f*, beaux-parents *mpl*. **'in-'patient** *n* malade hospitalisé.

inability [inə'biliti] *n* incapacité *f* (de faire qch); impuissance *f* (à faire qch).

inaccessible [inæk'sesəbl] *a* inaccessible (to, à); (*of pers*) inabordable. **inaccessi'bility** *n* inaccessibilité *f*.

inaccurate [in'ækjurət] *a* (calcul) inexact; (sens) incorrect. **in'accuracy** *n* inexactitude *f*; manque *m* de précision; imprécision *f*.

inactive [in'æktiv] *a* inactif. **in'action** *n* inaction *f*. **inac'tivity** *n* inactivité *f*; passivité *f*.

inadequate [in'ædikwət] *a* inadéquat, insuffisant. **in'adequacy** *n* insuffisance *f*. **in'adequately** *adv* insuffisamment.

inadmissible [inəd'misəbl] *a* inadmissible; (offre) inacceptable.

inadvertent [inəd'vəːtənt] *a* commis par inadvertance, par mégarde, par étourderie. **inad'vertence** *n* inadvertance *f*, étourderie *f*. **inad'vertently** *adv* par inadvertance, par mégarde.

inadvisable [inəd'vaizəbl] *a* peu sage; imprudent; à déconseiller.

inane [i'nein] *a* inepte, stupide; bête; niais; **i. remark,** ineptie *f*. **i'nanely** *adv* bêtement, stupidement. **inanity** [i'næniti] *n* inanité *f*, niaiserie *f*.

inanimate [in'ænimət] *a* inanimé.

inapplicable [inə'plikəbl] *a* inapplicable (to, à); (*on form*) delete where i., rayer les mentions inutiles.

inappropriate [inə'proupriət] *a* qui ne convient pas (to, à); (*of words*) impropre. **in'appropriately** *adv* d'une façon impropre.

inapt [in'æpt] *a* inapte **1.** (*of pers*) (*a*) incapable (*b*) inhabile, inexpert **2.** peu approprié (to, à). **in'aptitude** *n* inaptitude *f* (for, à).

inarticulate [inɑː'tikjulət] *a* (son) inarticulé; (*of pers*) muet, incapable de parler; **i. with rage,** bégayant de colère. **inar'ticulately** *adv* (parler, prononcer) indistinctement.

inartistic [inɑː'tistik] *a* sans valeur artistique; (*of pers*) dépourvu de sens artistique.

inattentive [inə'tentiv] *a* (*a*) inattentif, distrait; *Sch:* (élève) dissipé (*b*) peu attentionné, peu prévenant. **ina'ttention** *n* inattention *f*, distraction *f*. **ina'ttentively** *adv* distraitement.

inaudible [in'ɔːdibl] *a* (son) imperceptible; (voix) faible; **he is almost i.,** on l'entend à peine. **in'audibly** *adv* sans bruit; (parler, bouger) de manière à ne pas être entendu.

inaugurate [i'nɔːgjureit] *vtr* inaugurer. **in'augural** *a* & *n* i. **(address),** discours *m* d'inauguration. **inaugu'ration** *n* inauguration *f*.

inauspicious [inɔːs'piʃəs] *a* peu propice; (jour) néfaste; (retard) malencontreux. **inaus'piciously** *adv* d'une manière peu propice; malencontreusement.

inborn ['inbɔːn] *a* (*a*) inné; naturel (*b*) *Med:* congénital.

inbred ['inbred] *a* inné, naturel.

Inc. *abbr* Incorporated.

incalculable [in'kælkjuləbl] *a* incalculable. **in'calculably** *adv* incalculablement.

incandescent [inkæn'desnt] *a* incandescent. **incan'descence** *n* incandescence *f*.

incantation [inkæn'teiʃən] *n* incantation *f*.

incapable [in'keipəbl] *a* **1.** incapable (**of, de**); **i. of speech,** incapable de parler; **i. of pity,** inaccessible à la pitié **2.** (*a*) (*of pers*) incapable, incompétent (*b*) **drunk and i.,** ivre mort. **incapa'bility** *n* incapacité *f*.

incapacity [inkə'pæsiti] *n* incapacité *f*, incompétence *f*; **the i. of the staff,** la nullité du personnel. **inca'pacitate** *vtr* rendre (qn) incapable (de travailler). **inca'pacitated** *a* infirme.

incarcerate [in'kɑːsəreit] *vtr* incarcérer; emprisonner; mettre (qn) en prison. **incarce'ration** *n* emprisonnement *m*.

incarnation [inkɑː'neiʃ(ə)n] *n* **1.** incarnation *f* (du Christ) **2.** to be the i. of wisdom, être la sagesse incarnée. **in'carnate** *a* fait de chair; (*of Christ*) **to become i.,** s'incarner; **the devil i.,** le diable incarné.

incautious [in'kɔːʃəs] *a* imprudent. **in'cautiously** *adv* imprudemment.

incendiary [in'sendjəri] *a* & *n* incendiaire (*mf*); **i. bomb,** bombe incendiaire.

incense[1] ['insens] *n* encens *m*.

incense[2] [in'sens] *vtr* mettre en colère; exaspérer (qn). **in'censed** *a* exaspéré, en colère.

incentive [in'sentiv] **1.** *n* stimulant *m*, encouragement *m*; **it gave me an i.,** cela m'a encouragé **2.** *a* **i. pay,** prime *f* de rendement.

inception [in'sepʃən] *n* commencement *m*, début *m* (d'une entreprise).

incessant [in'sesnt] *a* incessant, continuel. **in'cessantly** *adv* sans cesse; incessamment.

incest ['insest] *n* inceste *m*. **in'cestuous** *a* incestueux.

inch [in(t)ʃ] **1.** *n* *Meas:* pouce *m* (=2,54cm); **he couldn't see an i. in front of him,** il ne, n'y, voyait pas à deux pas devant lui; **he's every i. a soldier,** il est soldat jusqu'au bout des ongles; **by inches, i. by i.,** peu à peu, petit à petit; **not to give way an i.,** ne pas reculer ni avancer d'une semelle; **within an i. of,** à deux doigts de **2.** (*a*) *vi* **to i. forward, along,** avancer peu à peu, petit à petit (*b*) *vtr* faire avancer (qch) petit à petit.

incident ['insidnt] *n* incident *m*; **journey full of incidents,** voyage mouvementé. **'incidence** *n* **the high i. of traffic accidents,** la fréquence, le taux élevé, des accidents de la route. **inci'dental 1.** *a* (événement) fortuit, accidentel; **i. expenses,** faux frais; **i. music,** musique d'accompagnement, de scène **2.** *n* éventualité *f*; *pl* **the incidentals,** les faux frais. **inci'dentally** *adv* **1.** incidemment **2.** soit dit en passant; à propos.

incinerator [in'sinəreitər] *n* incinérateur *m*; **domestic i., refuse i.,** incinérateur d'ordures.

incipient [in'sipiənt] *a* naissant; qui commence; **i. beard,** barbe naissante; **i. crack,** amorce de cassure.

incise [in'saiz] *vtr* **1.** faire une incision **2.** *Art:* graver. **in'cision** *n* incision *f*, entaille *f*. **in'cisive** *a* incisif, tranchant; (ton) mordant; (esprit) pénétrant. **in'cisively** *adv* incisivement; d'un ton mordant. **in'cisor** *n* (dent) incisive (*f*).

incite [in'sait] *vtr* inciter, stimuler, pousser (**s.o. to sth,**

qn à qch); **to i. s.o. to revolt,** pousser qn à la révolte.
in'citement *n* incitation *f* (to, à).

inclement [in'klemənt] *a* inclément.

incline [in'klain] **1.** *vi (a)* incliner, pencher (to, towards, à, vers); **inclined at an angle of 45°,** incliné à un angle de 45´ *(b)* avoir un penchant (to, pour qch, à faire qch); être enclin, porté (to, à); **to i. to pity,** incliner à la pitié **2.** *vtr* **I'm inclined to think that he's right,** je suis porté à croire qu'il a raison; **he's inclined to put on weight,** il a une tendance à l'embonpoint **3.** *n* ['inklain] pente *f*, déclivité *f*. **incli'nation** [-kli-] *n* **1.** inclination *f* (de la tête) **2.** inclinaison *f* (d'une pente) **3.** inclination, penchant *m* (to, for, à, pour); **to follow one's own i.,** en faire à sa tête; **to do sth from i.,** faire qch par goût. **in'clined** *a* **1.** (plan) incliné **2.** enclin, porté (to, à); **to be i. to do sth,** avoir de l'inclination, une tendance, à faire qch; **if you feel so i.,** si le cœur vous en dit.

include [in'klu:d] *vtr* comprendre, renfermer, embrasser, comporter; **we were six including our host,** nous étions six y compris notre hôte; **does that i. her?** est-ce que cela s'applique à elle aussi? **up to and including 31st December,** jusqu'au 31 décembre inclus. **in'cluded** *a* y compris; *(on bill)* **service i., not i.,** service compris, non compris; **the children i.,** y compris les enfants. **in'clusion** *n* inclusion *f*. **in'clusive** *a* qui comprend, qui renferme; **i. sum,** somme globale; *(at hotel)* **i. terms,** prix *m* tout compris; **five i. of the driver,** cinq y compris le chauffeur; **from the 4th to the 12th i.,** du 4 au 12 inclusivement. **in'clusively** *adv* inclusivement.

incognito [inkɔg'ni:tou] *n & adv* incognito *(m)*.

incoherent [inkou'hiərənt] *a* incohérent; (style) décousu. **inco'herence** *n* incohérence *f*. **inco'herently** *adv* sans cohérence, sans suite.

incombustible [inkəm'bʌstəbl] *a* incombustible.

income ['inkəm] *n* revenu(s) *m(pl)*; **earned i.,** revenus salariaux; **unearned, private, i.,** rente(s) *f (pl)*; **i. group,** tranche *f* de salaire, de revenu(s); **the lowest i. group,** les économiquement faibles; **i. tax,** impôt sur le revenu; **i.-tax return,** déclaration de revenu.

incoming ['inkʌmiŋ] **I.** *a* qui arrive; (locataire) entrant; **i. tide,** marée montante **II.** *n* **1.** entrée *f*, arrivée *f* **2.** *pl* recettes *f*, revenus *m*.

incommunicable [inkə'mju:nikəbl] *a* incommunicable.

incommunicado [inkəmju:ni'kɑ:dou] *a (of pers)* tenu au secret.

incomparable [in'kɔmprəbl] *a* incomparable (to, with, à); **i. artist,** artiste hors ligne. **in'comparably** *adv* incomparablement.

incompatible [inkəm'pætibl] *a* incompatible, inconciliable (with, avec). **incompati'bility** *n* incompatibilité *f*; inconciliabilité *f* (de deux théories, etc); **i. of temper,** incompatibilité d'humeur.

incompetent [in'kɔmpitənt] *a* inhabile; incompétent. **in'competence** *n* incompétence *f*, inhabilité *f* (d'une personne).

incomplete [inkəm'pli:t] *a* incomplet; inachevé. **incom'pletely** *adv* incomplètement.

incomprehensible [inkɔmpri'hensibl] *a* incompréhensible. **incompre'hensibly** *adv* incompréhensiblement. **incompre'hension** *n* manque *m* de compréhension, incompréhension *f*.

inconceivable [inkən'si:vəbl] *a* inconcevable. **incon'ceivably** *adv* inconcevablement; **i. poor,** d'une pauvreté inconcevable.

inconclusive [inkən'klu:siv] *a* peu concluant. **incon'clusively** *adv* d'une manière peu concluante.

incongruous [in'kɔŋgruəs] *a* **1.** sans rapport (to, with, avec) **2.** *(of remark)* incongru, déplacé; absurde. **inconsequent** [in'kɔnsikwənt] *a* inconséquent, illogique. **in'consequence** *n* inconséquence *f*. **inconse'quential** *a (a)* inconséquent *(b)* (affaire) sans importance.

inconsiderable [inkən'sidərəbl] *a* peu considérable; insignifiant.

inconsiderate [inkən'sidərət] *a (of pers)* sans égards pour les autres. **incon'siderately** *adv* **to behave i. to(wards) s.o.,** manquer d'égards envers qn.

inconsistent [inkən'sistənt] *a* **1.** incompatible (with, avec); contradictoire **2.** *(of pers)* inconsistant, inconséquent; illogique; incohérent; (histoire) qui ne tient pas debout. **incon'sistency** *n* **1.** inconsistance *f*; contradiction *f* **2.** inconséquence *f*, illogisme *m*.

inconsolable [inkən'soulabl] *a* inconsolable.

inconspicuous [inkən'spikjuəs] *a* peu apparent, peu frappant; effacé; **to remain i.,** passer inaperçu. **incon'spicuously** *adv* discrètement.

inconstant [in'kɔnstənt] *a* inconstant, volage. **in'constancy** *n* inconstance *f*.

incontestable [inkən'testəbl] *a* incontestable, indéniable. **incon'testably** *adv* incontestablement.

inconvenience [inkən'vi:njəns] **1.** *n* incommodité *f*, contretemps *m*; **I'm putting you to a lot of i.,** je vous dérange beaucoup; **he went to a great deal of i.,** il s'est donné beaucoup de mal; **without the slightest i.,** sans le moindre inconvénient **2.** *vtr* déranger, gêner (qn). **incon'venient** *a* malcommode; gênant; *(of time)* inopportun; **if it's not i. for you,** si cela ne vous dérange pas. **incon'veniently** *adv* incommodément; d'une façon gênante; (arriver) à un moment inopportun.

incorporate [in'kɔ:pəreit] *vtr* incorporer, unir (with, à); *Com:* constituer (une association) en société commerciale. **in'corporated** *a* **1.** faisant corps (with others, avec d'autres); incorporé **2.** *NAm: Com:* (société) anonyme.

incorrect [inkə'rekt] *a* **1.** inexact; **that's quite i.,** c'est tout à fait inexact **2.** *(of wording, behaviour)* incorrect; **it would be i. to say so,** ce serait déplacé de le dire. **inco'rrectly** *adv* **1.** inexactement **2.** incorrectement.

incorrigible [in'kɔridʒəbl] *a* incorrigible.

incorruptible [inkə'rʌptəbl] *a* incorruptible.

increase I. *n* ['inkri:s] *(a)* augmentation *f* (de prix, de salaire); accroissement *m* (de vitesse); redoublement *m* (d'efforts); hausse *f* (du coût de la vie); **i. in value,** plus-value *f* (d'une propriété); **I've had an i. in salary,** j'ai été augmenté, j'ai reçu une augmentation *(b) adv phr* **to be on the i.,** être en augmentation, augmenter **2.** *vi* [in'kri:s] augmenter, s'agrandir; s'accroître; se multiplier **3.** *vtr* [in'kri:s] augmenter (la production); grossir (le nombre); accroître (sa fortune); **to i. the cost of goods,** hausser le prix des marchandises; **to i. speed,** forcer la vitesse; **increased cost of goods,** hausse

de prix des marchandises. **in'creasing** *a* croissant.
in'creasingly *adv* de plus en plus (grand, difficile).
incredible [in'kredibl] *a* incroyable. **in'credibly**
adv incroyablement.
incredulous [in'kredjuləs] *a* incrédule; **i. smile,** sourire d'incrédulité *f*. **incre'dulity** *n* incrédulité *f*.
in'credulously *adv* avec incrédulité.
increment ['inkrimənt] *n* augmentation *f*.
incriminate [in'krimineit] *vtr* 1. incriminer (qn) 2.
impliquer (qn) (dans une accusation).
in'criminating *a* **i. documents,** pièces à conviction
f. **incrimi'nation** *n* incrimination *f*, accusation *f*
(de qn).
incubate ['inkjubeit] *vtr* couver (des œufs, une maladie). **incu'bation** *n* incubation *f*; *Med:* **i. period,**
période d'incubation (d'une maladie). **'incubator**
n incubateur *m*; couveuse (artificielle).
inculcate ['inkʌlkeit] *vtr* inculquer.
incumbent [in'kʌmbənt] 1. *n* titulaire *m* (d'une
fonction administrative) 2. *a* **to be i. on s.o. to do sth,**
incomber, appartenir, à qn de faire qch.
incur [in'kəːr] *vtr* (**incurred**) courir (un risque); encourir (un blâme, des frais); s'attirer (la colère de qn);
contracter (des dettes).
incurable [in'kjuərəbl] *a & n* incurable. **in'curably**
adv **to be i. lazy,** être d'une paresse incurable.
incurious [in'kjuːriəs] *a* sans curiosité.
incursion [in'kəːʃən] *n* incursion *f*.
indebted [in'detid] *a* 1. endetté 2. redevable (**to s.o.
for sth,** à qn de qch).
indecent [in'diːsənt] *a* peu décent, indécent; **i. assault,** attentat à la pudeur; **i. exposure,** outrage *m* à
la pudeur. **in'decently** *adv* indécemment; d'une
manière indécente.
indecipherable [indi'saifərəbl] *a* déchiffrable.
indecisive [indi'saisiv] *a* (*of argument, battle*) indécis, incertain; **an i. sort of person,** une personne plutôt
irrésolue. **inde'cision** *n* indécision *f*, irrésolution *f*.
indeed [in'diːd] *adv* 1. (*a*) en effet; vraiment (*b*)
(*intensive*) **I'm very glad i.,** je suis très très content;
thank you very much i., merci infiniment (*c*) (*concessive*) **I may i. be wrong,** il se peut toutefois que j'aie
tort 2. même; à vrai dire; **I think so, i. I am sure of it,** je
le pense et même j'en suis sûr 3. **yes i.!** (i) mais
certainement! (ii) (*contradicting*) mais si!
indefatigable [indi'fætigəbl] *a* infatigable, inlassable. **inde'fatigably** *adv* infatigablement, inlassablement.
indefensible [indi'fensəbl] *a* indéfendable; (argument) insoutenable.
indefinable [indi'fainəbl] *a* indéfinissable.
indefinite [in'definit] *a* indéfini, (idée) vague;
(nombre) indéterminé; *Gram:* (article, pronom) indéfini; **i. leave,** congé illimité. **in'definitely** *adv*
indéfiniment; vaguement; **to postpone sth i.,** remettre
qch indéfiniment.
indelible [in'delibl] *a* indélébile; ineffaçable; **i. ink,**
encre indélébile. **in'delibly** *adv* ineffaçablement; de
façon indélébile.
indemnify [in'demnifai] *vtr* 1. garantir (**from,
against,** contre) 2. indemniser, dédommager (**for a
loss,** d'une perte). **in'demnity** *n* (*a*) garantie *f*,
assurance *f* (contre une perte) (*b*) indemnité *f*,
dédommagement *f*,

indent [in'dent] 1. *vtr* denteler, découper (le bord de
qch); *Typ:* renfoncer, (faire) rentrer (une ligne) 2. *vi* **to
i. for sth,** (i) réquisitionner qch (à qn) (ii) passer
commande de qch (à qn). **inden'tation** *n* dentelure *f*, découpure *f*; empreinte creuse. **in'dented**
a (bord) dentelé; (littoral) échancré; (ligne) en alinéa,
en retrait. **in'dentures** *npl* contrat *m*
d'apprentissage.
independent [indi'pendənt] *a* indépendant; (état)
autonome; *Pol:* **i. candidate,** candidat non-inscrit;
to be i., être son propre maître; **to be (of) i. (means),**
vivre de ses rentes; **i. school** = école
libre. **inde'pendence** *n* indépendance *f*; **to show i.,**
faire preuve d'indépendance; *US:* **I. Day,** le quatre
juillet. **inde'pendently** *adv* (*a*) indépendamment
(**of, de**) (*b*) avec indépendance.
indescribable [indis'kraibəbl] *a* indescriptible;
(joie) indicible. **indes'cribably** *adv* indescriptible-
ment, indiciblement.
indestructible [indis'trʌktəbl] *a* indestructible.
index ['indeks] **I.** *n* 1. (*pl* **indexes**) **i.** (finger), index
m 2. (*pl* **indices**) indice *m*; **cost of living i.,** indice du
coût de la vie 3. (*pl* **indexes**) index; table *f* alphabétique, répertoire *m* (d'un livre); **card i.,** (i) fichier *m*,
classeur *m* (ii) catalogue *m* sur fiches; **i. card,** fiche *f*
4. *Ecc:* **to put a book on the I.,** mettre un livre à
l'Index. **II.** *vtr* faire l'index d'(un livre); classer (un
article).
India ['indjə] *Prn* l'Inde *f*. **'Indian** 1. (*a*) de l'Inde;
des Indes; indien; (encre) de Chine (*b*) *n* Indien, -ienne
2. *n* (*a*) Indien, -ienne, d'Amérique; **Red Indians,** (les)
Peaux-Rouges *m* (*b*) **West I.,** Antillais, -aise.
indiarubber [ˈindjəˈrʌbər] *n* gomme *f* (à effacer).
indicate ['indikeit] *vtr* indiquer. **indi'cation** *n*
indice *m*, signe *m*; **there is every i. (that),** tout porte à
croire (que); **there is no i. (that),** rien ne permet de
croire (que). **in'dicative** *a & n* indicatif (*m*); *Gram:*
(présent) de l'indicatif; **in the i.,** à l'indicatif.
'indicator *n* (tableau *m*) indicateur (*m*); *Aut:*
clignotant *m*.
indict [in'dait] *vtr* *Jur:* accuser, inculper (qn) (**for,** de);
traduire, poursuivre, (qn) en justice (**for,** pour).
in'dictable *a* **i. offence,** délit *m*. **in'dictment** *n*
accusation *f*; **i. for theft,** inculpation *f* de vol.
Indies (the) [ði'indiz] *Prnpl* les Indes *f*; **the East I.,** les
Indes (orientales); **the West I.,** les Antilles *f*.
indifferent [in'difərənt] *a* 1. indifférent (**to,** à); **he's i.
to everything,** tout lui est indifférent, égal 2. médiocre;
very i. quality, qualité très médiocre. **in-
'difference** *n* 1. indifférence *f*, manque *m* d'intérêt
(**to, towards, sth, s.o.,** pour qch, à l'égard de qn) 2.
médiocrité *f* (de talent). **in'differently** *adv* 1.
indifféremment; avec indifférence 2. médiocrement.
indigenous [in'didʒənəs] *a* indigène (**to,** de).
indigestion [indi'dʒestʃən] *n* dyspepsie *f*; mauvaise
digestion; **an attack of i.,** une indigestion.
indi'gestible *a* indigeste.
indignant [in'dignənt] *a* (air) indigné; (cri)
d'indignation; **to feel i. at sth,** s'indigner de qch; **to
make s.o. i.,** indigner qn. **in'dignantly** *adv* avec
indignation. **indig'nation** *n* indignation *f*.
indignity [in'digniti] *n* indignité *f*, affront *m*.
indigo ['indigou] *a & n* (*pl* **-o(e)s**) indigo *m*.
indirect [indi'rekt, -dai-] *a* 1. indirect; *Gram:* **i.**

speech, discours indirect **2.** (moyen, chemin) détourné. **indi′rectly** adv indirectement.

indiscreet [indis′kri:t] a **1.** indiscret; **would it be i. to ask you what you are going to do?** peut-on vous demander sans indiscrétion ce que vous comptez faire? **2.** peu judicieux; imprudent. **indis′creetly** adv (a) indiscrètement (b) imprudemment. **indis′cretion** n (a) manque m de discrétion (b) indiscrétion f (c) action inconsidérée; imprudence f (d) écart m de conduite.

indiscriminate [indis′kriminət] a **i. blows,** coups frappés au hasard, à tort et à travers. **indis′criminately** adv sans faire de distinction; au hasard; aveuglément.

indispensable [indis′pensəbl] a indispensable, de première nécessité; **it is not i.,** on peut s'en passer. **indis′pensably** adv indispensablement.

indisposed [indis′pouzd] a **1.** peu enclin, peu disposé **(to do sth,** à faire qch) **2. to be i.,** être souffrant; ne pas être dans son assiette. **indisposition** [-pə′ziʃən] n malaise m; indisposition f.

indisputable [indis′pju:təbl] a incontestable, indiscutable. **indis′putably** adv incontestablement, indiscutablement.

indissoluble [indi′sɔljubl] a indissoluble.

indistinct [indis′tiŋkt] a indistinct; (bruit) confus; (souvenir) vague. **indis′tinctly** adv indistinctement.

indistinguishable [indis′tiŋgwiʃəbl] a qu'on ne peut différencier **(from,** de); **i. to the naked eye,** imperceptible à l'œil nu.

individual [indi′vidjuəl] **1.** a (a) (of portion, attention) individuel (b) (of style, ideas) original, particulier **2.** n individu m; **a private i.,** un simple particulier. **indi′vidualist** n individualiste mf. **indi′vidualistic** a individualiste. **individu′ality** n individualité f. **indi′vidualize** vtr individualiser. **indi′vidually** adv individuellement.

indivisible [indi′vizibl] a indivisible.

Indochina [indou′tʃainə] Prn Geog: Indochine f.

indoctrinate [in′dɔktrineit] vtr endoctriner (qn). **indoctri′nation** n endoctrinement m.

Indo-European [′indoujuərə′pi:ən] **1.** a Ling: Ethn: indo-européen **2.** n (a) Indo-Européen, -éenne (b) Ling: indo-européen m.

indolence [′indələns] n indolence f, paresse f. **′indolent** a indolent, paresseux. **′indolently** adv indolemment.

Indonesia [ində′ni:zjə] Prn Geog: l'Indonésie f. **Indo′nesian** a & n Geog: Ethn: indonésien, -ienne.

indoor [′indɔ:r] a (travail) d'intérieur; (plante) d'appartement; **i. games,** sports pratiqués à l'intérieur; **i. swimming pool,** piscine couverte. **in′doors** adv à la maison; à l'intérieur; **to go i.,** entrer, rentrer (à la maison); **stay i.,** restez à la maison.

indubitable [in′dju:bitəbl] a indubitable. **in′dubitably** adv indubitablement.

induce [in′dju:s] vtr **1. to i. s.o. to do sth,** persuader à qn de faire qch; décider qn à faire qch **2.** amener, produire, causer, occasionner; **to i. sleep,** provoquer le sommeil. **in′ducement** n motif m, cause f (qui encourage qn à faire qch); **the i. of a good salary,** les attraits m d'un bon salaire.

induction [in′dʌkʃən] n **1. i. course,** stage m préparatoire **2.** El: induction f.

indulge [in′dʌldʒ] **1.** vtr (a) gâter (qn); **to i. oneself,** s'écouter; ne rien se refuser; **to i. s.o.'s fancies,** flatter les caprices de qn (b) se laisser aller à (un penchant) **2.** vi **to i. in a practice,** s'adonner à une habitude; **to i. in a cigar,** se permettre un cigare. **in′dulgence** n indulgence f, complaisance f **(to, towards, s.o.,** envers qn); RCCh: indulgence. **in′dulgent** a indulgent **(to s.o.,** envers, pour, qn). **in′dulgently** adv avec indulgence.

industry [′indəstri] n (pl **industries**) **1.** application f; assiduité f au travail; diligence f **2.** industrie f; **heavy i., light i.,** industrie lourde, légère; **the car i.,** l'industrie automobile. **in′dustrial** a industriel; (accidents) du travail; (maladie) professionnelle; **i. disputes, unrest,** conflits ouvriers, agitation ouvrière; **i. estate,** zone industrielle; **to take i. action,** se mettre en grève. **in′dustrialist** n industriel m. **industriali′zation** n industrialisation f. **in′dustrialize** vtr industrialiser. **in′dustrious** a travailleur, assidu, industrieux. **in′dustriously** adv industrieusement. **in′dustriousness** n assiduité f (au travail).

inedible [in′edibl] a **1.** immangeable **2.** non comestible.

ineffective [ini′fektiv] a inefficace, sans effet.

ineffectual [ini′fektjuəl] a inefficace; **i. person,** personne incompétente, incapable. **ine′ffectually** adv inefficacement; vainement.

inefficacious [inefi′keiʃəs] a inefficace. **in′efficacy** n inefficacité f.

inefficient [ini′fiʃənt] a (moyen, remède) inefficace; (of pers) incapable, incompétent. **ine′fficiency** n inefficacité f; incompétence f. **ine′fficiently** adv inefficacement; sans compétence.

inelegant [in′eligənt] a inélégant. **in′elegantly** adv sans élégance.

ineligible [in′elidʒibl] a inéligible; inapte (au service militaire); inacceptable; qui n'a pas droit (à qch, de faire qch).

inept [i′nept] a **1.** déplacé; mal à propos **2.** (of remark) inepte, absurde. **i′neptitude** n **1.** manque m d'à-propos (d'une observation) **2.** ineptie f, sottise f. **i′neptly** adv ineptement; stupidement.

inequality [ini:′kwɔliti] n inégalité f.

inequitable [in′ekwitəbl] a inéquitable. **in′equitably** adv inéquitablement, injustement.

ineradicable [ini′rædikəbl] a indéracinable; inextirpable.

inert [i′nə:t] a inerte. **i′nertia** [-ʃ(i)ə] n inertie f; Ph: Mec: force f d'inertie; (of pers) inertie, paresse f; Aut: **i. reel seat belt,** ceinture (de sécurité) à enrouleur m.

inescapable [inis′keipəbl] a inéluctable, inévitable.

inestimable [in′estiməbl] a inestimable, incalculable.

inevitable [in′evitəbl] a (a) inévitable (b) fatal; **it was i. that he should come back,** il devait inévitablement revenir. **in′evitably** adv inévitablement; fatalement.

inexact [inig′zækt] a inexact. **inex′actitude** n (a) inexactitude f (b) erreur f. **inex′actly** adv inexactement.

inexcusable [iniks'kju:zəbl] *a* inexcusable; impardonnable. **inex'cusably** *adv* inexcusablement.

inexhaustible [inig'zɔːstəbl] *a* inépuisable; (source) intarissable.

inexorable [in'eksərəbl] *a* inexorable. **in'exorably** *adv* inexorablement.

inexpensive [iniks'pensiv] *a* peu coûteux; bon marché; pas cher. **inex'pensively** *adv* (acheter) (à) bon marché; (vivre) économiquement; à peu de frais.

inexperience [iniks'piəriəns] *n* inexpérience *f*. **inex'perienced** *a* 1. inexpérimenté; he's still i., il est encore novice 2. inaverti; i. eye, œil inexercé.

inexpert [in'ekspəːt] *a* maladroit, peu habile. **in'expertly** *adv* mal, maladroitement.

inexplicable [iniks'plikəbl] *a* inexplicable. **inex'plicably** *adv* inexplicablement.

inexpressible [iniks'presəbl] *a* inexprimable; (charme) indicible. **inex'pressive** *a* (geste) inexpressif; sans expression; (visage) fermé.

inextricable [in'ekstrikəbl, iniks'trik-] *a* inextricable. **in'extricably** *adv* inextricablement.

infallible [in'fæləbl] *a* infaillible. **infalli'bility** *n* infaillibilité *f*. **in'fallibly** *adv* infailliblement.

infamous ['infəməs] *a* infâme; (personne, conduite) abominable. **'infamy** *n* infamie *f*.

infant ['infənt] *n* 1. enfant *mf* (en bas âge); nourrisson *m*; bébé *m*; **i. mortality**, mortalité *f* infantile; **i. school**, école pour les enfants de cinq à huit ans; **i. class**, classe enfantine; cours préparatoire 2. *Jur:* mineur, -eure. **'infancy** *n* 1. (*a*) première enfance; bas âge (*b*) débuts *mpl* 2. *Jur:* minorité *f*. **'infantile** *a* 1. (esprit) d'enfant; (raisonnement) enfantin; (remarque) puérile 2. (maladie) infantile.

infantry ['infəntri] *n* infanterie *f*.

infatuated [in'fætjueitid] *a* **to be, to become, i. with s.o.**, s'enticher, s'éprendre, de qn; avoir un béguin pour qn. **infatu'ation** *n* engouement *m*.

infect [in'fekt] *vtr* 1. infecter, corrompre, vicier (l'air, les mœurs) 2. (*a*) *Med:* contaminer (qn); infecter (une plaie) (*b*) communiquer (sa bonne humeur). **in'fection** *n* *esp* *Med:* infection *f*, contagion *f*; contamination *f*; **source of i.**, foyer *m* d'infection. **in'fectious** *a* (*a*) infectieux; **i. disease**, maladie contagieuse (*b*) **i. laughter, i. good humour**, rire communicatif; bonne humeur communicative. **in'fectiousness** *n* nature infectieuse (d'une maladie); contagion *f* (du rire).

infer [in'fəːr] *vtr* (**inferred**) 1. déduire, conclure (sth from sth, qch de qch; that, que). **inference** ['infərəns] *n* déduction *f*, conclusion *f*; **by i.**, par déduction.

inferior [in'fiəriər] 1. *a* inférieur; **i. piece of work**, ouvrage *m* de second ordre; **i. goods**, produits de qualité inférieure; **to feel i.**, avoir un sentiment d'infériorité; **to be in no way i. to s.o.**, ne le céder en rien à qn 2. *n* (*a*) inférieur, -eure (*b*) *Adm:* subordonné, -ée; subalterne *m*. **inferi'ority** *n* infériorité *f*; **i. complex**, complexe *m* d'infériorité.

infernal [in'fəːnəl] *a* 1. infernal; des enfers 2. *F:* (*a*) infernal, diabolique (*b*) **i. row**, bruit infernal. **in'fernally** *adv* *F:* diablement; **it's i. hot**, il fait une chaleur d'enfer.

inferno [in'fəːnou] (*pl* **infernos**) *n* enfer *m*.

infertile [in'fəːtail] *a* infertile. **infer'tility** *n* infertilité *f*.

infest [in'fest] *vtr* (*of vermin*) infester (**with**, de). **infes'tation** *n* invasion *f* (de parasites); infestation *f*.

infidelity [infi'deliti] *n* infidélité *f*.

infighting ['infaitin] *n* querelles *fpl* internes (entre les membres d'un groupe).

infiltrate ['infiltreit] 1. *vtr* pénétrer (dans qch); *Pol:* noyauter 2. *vi* s'infiltrer (dans qch). **infil'tration** *n* infiltration *f*; *Pol:* noyautage *m*.

infinite ['infinit] *a* (*a*) infini, illimité; sans bornes (*b*) **to have i. trouble (in) doing sth**, avoir une peine infinie à faire qch. **'infinitely** *adv* infiniment. **infini'tesimal** *a* infinitésimal. **in'finitive** *a* & *n* *Gram:* infinitif (*m*); **in the i.**, à l'infinitif. **in'finity** *n* 1. infinité *f*, infinitude *f* (de l'espace) 2. *Mth: etc:* infini *m*; **to i.**, à l'infini.

infirm [in'fəːm] *a* (*of pers*) infirme, débile. **in'firmary** *n* (*a*) infirmerie *f* (d'école, de caserne) (*b*) hôpital *m*. **in'firmity** *n* infirmité *f*.

inflame [in'fleim] 1. *vtr* enflammer (une plaie); allumer (les désirs); envenimer (une querelle) 2. *vi* s'enflammer; prendre feu; *Med:* (*of wound*) s'enflammer. **in'flamed** *a* enflammé. **inflamma'bility** *n* inflammabilité *f*. **in'flammable** *a* inflammable. **infla'mmation** *n* 1. inflammation *f* (d'un combustible) 2. *Med:* inflammation; **i. of the lungs**, fluxion *f* de poitrine. **in'flammatory** *a* (discours) incendiaire.

inflate [in'fleit] *vtr* 1. gonfler (un pneu) 2. hausser, faire monter (les prix). **in'flatable** *a* gonflable; (canot) pneumatique. **in'flated** *a* (*a*) gonflé; (talk) with pride, gonflé d'orgueil (*b*) **i. prices**, prix exagérés. **in'flation** *n* (*a*) gonflement *m* (*b*) *PolEc:* inflation *f*; **galloping i.**, inflation galopante. **in'flationary** *a* **i. policy**, politique inflationniste.

inflexible [in'fleksəbl] *a* inflexible, rigide. **inflexi'bility** *n* inflexibilité *f*; manque *m* de souplesse; rigidité *f*. **in'flexibly** *adv* inflexiblement. **in'flexion** *n* *Ling:* inflexion *f* (de la voix).

inflict [in'flikt] *vtr* infliger (**sth on s.o.**, qch à qn): occasionner (du chagrin à qn); *Jur:* infliger (une punition à qn); **to i. oneself on s.o.**, s'imposer; imposer sa compagnie à qn.

influence ['influəns] 1. *n* (*a*) influence *f* (**on s.o.**, sur qn); **to have great i. over s.o.**, avoir beaucoup d'influence sur qn; **to have an i. on sth**, influencer qch; influer sur qch; **under the i. of fear**, sous le coup de la peur; **under the i. of drink**, *F:* under the i., en état d'ivresse; *Jur:* **undue i.**, intimidation *f* (*b*) **to have i.**, avoir de l'influence, de l'autorité 2. *vtr* (*of pers*) influencer (qn); (*of thg*) influer sur (qch); **don't be influenced by what he says**, ne te laisse pas influencer par ce qu'il dit; **she's easily influenced**, elle est très influençable. **influ'ential** *a* influent; **to be i.**, avoir de l'influence; avoir le bras long; **to have i. friends**, avoir des amis en haut lieu, bien placés.

influenza [influ'enzə] *n* *Med:* grippe *f*.

influx ['inflʌks] *n* affluence *f*, afflux *m* (de gens); flot *m* (d'idées nouvelles).

inform [in'fɔːm] 1. *vtr* (*a*) **to i. s.o. of sth**, informer, avertir, qn de qch; faire part de qch à qn; **to keep s.o. informed**, tenir qn au courant; **to i. the police**, avertir la police (*b*) **to i. s.o. about sth**, renseigner qn sur qch; **I regret to have to i. you (that)**, j'ai le regret de vous annoncer (que) **2.** *vi* **to i. against s.o.**, dénoncer qn. **in′formant** *n* informateur, -trice. **infor′mation** *n* **1.** renseignements *mpl*; **a piece of i.**, un renseignement; **for your i.**, à titre d'information *f*; **to get i. about sth**, se renseigner sur qch; **i. bureau**, (bureau de) renseignements; **Ministry of I.**, le Ministère de l'Information; (*computers*) **i. processing**, informatique *f*; **i. retrieval (system)**, (système) de recherche *f* documentaire **2.** savoir *m*, connaissances *fpl*. **in′formative** *a* instructif. **in′formed** *a* bien renseigné; bien au courant. **in′former** *n* dénonciateur, -trice; *Pej:* délateur, -trice; *F:* mouchard *m*; **to turn i.**, dénoncer ses complices.

informal [in′fɔːml] *a* (dîner, etc) sans cérémonie, en famille; (style) familier; (*of meeting*) non officiel; **it will be quite i.**, ce sera sans cérémonie, à la bonne franquette; **i. dress**, tenue de ville. **infor′mality** *n* absence *f* de cérémonie; simplicité *f*. **in′formally** *adv* à titre non officiel; sans cérémonie; sans formalités.

infra dig [′infrə′dig] *adj phr F:* au-dessous de la dignité de (qn); au-dessous de soi.

infra-red [′infrə′red] *a* infrarouge.

infrasonic [′infrə′sɔnik] *a* infrasonore; **i. vibration**, infra-son *m*.

infrastructure [′infrəstrʌktʃər] *n* infrastructure *f*.

infrequent [in′friːkwənt] *a* rare; peu fréquent. **in′frequency** *n* rareté *f*. **in′frequently** *adv* rarement; **not i.**, assez souvent.

infringe [in′frindʒ] **1.** *vtr* enfreindre, violer (une loi); commettre (un délit de contrefaçon) **2.** *v ind tr* **to i. upon s.o.'s rights**, empiéter sur les droits de qn. **in′fringement** *n* infraction *f* (d'un règlement); violation *f* (d'une loi); **i. of patent, of copyright**, délit *m* de contrefaçon.

infuriate [in′fjuərieit] *vtr* rendre furieux. **in′furiated** *a* furieux; en fureur. **in′furiating** *a* exaspérant; **I find him i.**, il me met hors de moi. **in′furiatingly** *adv* à rendre furieux.

infuse [in′fjuːz] *vtr* **1. to i. courage into s.o.**, infuser du courage à qn **2.** infuser, faire infuser (le thé, une tisane). **in′fusion** *n* (*a*) infusion *f* (d'une tisane) (*b*) tisane.

ingenious [in′dʒiːniəs] *a* ingénieux. **in′geniously** *adv* ingénieusement. **ingenuity** [indʒi′njuːiti] *n* ingéniosité *f*.

ingenuous [in′dʒenjuəs] *a* ingénu, candide; naïf, *f* naïve. **in′genuously** *adv* ingénument, naïvement. **in′genuousness** *n* ingénuité *f*, naïveté *f*, candeur *f*.

ingot [′iŋgət] *n* lingot *m* (d'or).

ingrained [in′greind] *a* **i. dirt**, crasse *f*; **i. with dirt**, encrassé; **i. prejudices**, préjugés enracinés; **i. habits**, habitudes invétérées.

ingratiate [in′greiʃieit] *vpr* **to i. oneself with s.o.**, s'insinuer dans les bonnes grâces de qn. **in′gratiating** *a* insinuant.

ingratitude [in′grætitjuːd] *n* ingratitude *f*.

ingredient [in′griːdiənt] *n* ingrédient *m*; élément *m*.

ingrowing [′ingrouiŋ] *a* (*also* **ingrown**) (ongle) incarné.

inhabit [in′hæbit] *vtr* habiter, habiter dans (une

maison, un endroit). **in′habitable** *a* habitable. **in′habitant** *n* habitant, -ante (d'un village, d'une maison). **in′habited** *a* habité.

inhale [in′heil] *vtr* aspirer, humer, avaler (un parfum); avaler (la fumée d'une cigarette).

inherent [in′hiərənt, -′her-] *a* inhérent, naturel (**in**, à); **i. defect**, vice propre. **in′herently** *adv* essentiellement; intrinsèquement; **i. lazy**, né paresseux.

inherit [in′herit] *vtr* (*a*) hériter de (qch); succéder à (une fortune) (*b*) **to i. sth from s.o.**, hériter qch de qn. **in′heritance** *n* succession *f*, héritage *m*; patrimoine (national).

inhibit [in′hibit] *vtr* inhiber (un sentiment). **inhi′bition** *n* inhibition *f*.

inhospitable [inhɔs′pitəbl] *a* inhospitalier.

inhuman [in′hjuːmən] *a* inhumain; brutal. **inhu′manity** [-′mæniti] *n* inhumanité *f*, cruauté *f*. **in′humanly** *adv* inhumainement.

inimical [i′nimik(ə)l] *a* ennemi, hostile.

inimitable [i′nimitəbl] *a* inimitable. **i′nimitably** *adv* d'une manière inimitable.

iniquitous [i′nikwitəs] *a* inique. **i′niquitously** *adv* iniquement. **i′niquity** *n* iniquité *f*.

initial [i′niʃ(ə)l] **1.** *a* initial, premier; **the i. difficulties**, les difficultés du début; **i. cost**, coût initial **2.** *n* (*usu pl*) **initials**, initiales *f*; parafe *m*; sigle *m* (d'une organisation). **3.** *vtr* (**initialled**) parafer (une correction); viser (un acte). **i′nitially** *adv* au commencement; au début; initialement.

initiate [i′niʃieit] *vtr* **1.** commencer, ouvrir, amorcer (des négociations); lancer (une mode); **to i. a reform**, prendre l'initiative d'une réforme; **to i. proceedings against s.o.**, engager des poursuites, intenter une action, contre qn **2.** initier (qn à un secret). II [i′niʃiət] *a & n* initié, -ée. **initi′ation** *n* **1.** début(s) *m(pl)* (d'une entreprise) **2.** initiation *f* (**into**, à). **i′nitiative** *n* initiative *f*; **to do sth on one's own i.**, faire qch par soi-même; **to show, lack, i.**, faire preuve, manquer, d'initiative. **i′nitiator** *n* initiateur, -trice.

inject [in′dʒekt] *vtr* injecter; faire une piqûre à (qn). **in′jection** *n* piqûre *f*; injection *f*; **to have an i.**, se faire faire une piqûre; **intramuscular, intravenous, i.**, piqûre intramusculaire, intraveineuse.

injudicious [indʒu(ː)′diʃəs] *a* peu judicieux; malavisé.

injunction [in′dʒʌŋkʃən] *n* **1.** injonction *f*, ordre *m*; **to give s.o. strict injunctions to do sth**, enjoindre strictement à qn de faire qch **2.** *Jur:* ordre (donné par le juge), injonction.

injure [′indʒər] *vtr* **1.** nuire à, faire tort à (qn); **to i. s.o.'s interests**, compromettre, léser, les intérêts de qn **2.** (*a*) blesser; faire mal à (qn); **he injured his foot**, il s'est blessé au pied; **fatally injured**, blessé mortellement (*b*) endommager; avarier (des marchandises); **to i. one's eyes**, se gâter la vue. **′injured 1.** *a* (*a*) **the i. party**, l'offensé, -ée; **in an i. tone (of voice)**, d'une voix offensée (*b*) (bras) blessé, estropié **2.** *n* **the i.**, les blessés *m*; (*from accident*) les accidentés *m*. **in′jurious** *a* **1.** nuisible, pernicieux (**to s.o., sth**, à qn, qch) **2.** (langage) offensif. **′injury** *n* **1.** tort *m*, mal *m*; **to do s.o. an i.**, faire du tort à qn **2.** blessure *f*; **to do oneself an i.**, se blesser, se faire du mal; **industrial i.**, accident *m* du travail **3.** *Com: etc:* dommage *m*; avarie *f*.

injustice [in'dʒʌstis] *n* 1. injustice *f* 2. **you do him an i.,** vous êtes injuste envers lui.

ink [iŋk] 1. *n* encre *f*; **Indian i.,** encre de Chine; **invisible i.,** encre sympathique; **written in i.,** écrit à l'encre 2. *vtr* noircir d'encre, tacher d'encre. **ink 'in, ink 'over** *vtr* encrer (les lettres); **to i. in, over, a drawing,** repasser un dessin à l'encre. **ink 'out** *vtr* rayer (un mot) à l'encre. '**inkpad** *n* tampon encreur. '**inkpot,** '**inkstand,** '**inkwell** *n* encrier *m*. '**inky** *a* taché d'encre; barbouillé d'encre; **i.-black,** noir comme de l'encre.

inkling ['iŋkliŋ] *n* soupçon *m*; **he had an i. of the truth,** il entrevoyait la vérité; **he has no i. of the matter,** il ne se doute de rien.

inland ['inlænd] 1. *n* (l')intérieur *m* (d'un pays) 2. *a* intérieur; **i. trade,** commerce intérieur; **the I. Revenue,** le fisc 3. *adv* **to go i.,** pénétrer dans les terres.

inlay ['in'lei, in'lei] *vtr* (**inlaid**) incruster (**with,** de); marqueter (une table); *Metalw:* damasquiner. '**inlaid** *a* incrusté, marqueté; **i. work,** marqueterie *f*.

inlet ['inlet] *n* (*a*) (orifice *m* d')admission *f* (d'eau, d'essence); **i. pipe,** tuyau d'arrivée (*b*) *Geog:* petit bras de mer; crique *f*; anse *f*.

inmate ['inmeit] *n* (*a*) pensionnaire *mf* (d'une maison de retraite) (*b*) détenu, -ue (dans une prison).

inmost ['inmoust] *a* le plus profond; **i. thoughts,** pensées les plus secrètes.

inn [in] *n* auberge *f*; hôtellerie *f*. '**innkeeper** *n* aubergiste *mf*; hôtelier, -ière.

innards ['inədz] *npl* intestins *mpl*; entrailles *fpl*.

innate [i'neit] *a* inné; naturel; **i. common sense,** bon sens foncier.

inner ['inər] *a* intérieur; de dedans; **i. meaning,** sens intime; **i. circle,** cercle intime (d'amis); noyau *m*, groupe *m*, dirigeant (d'une société); **i. ear,** oreille interne; **i. city,** centre de la ville; centre-ville *m*; **i. harbour,** arrière-port *m*; *Aut:* **i. tube,** chambre à air; *F:* **the i. man,** l'estomac *m*.

innings ['iniŋz] *n inv* (*at cricket*) tour *m* de batte; **he had a good i.,** il a vécu longtemps.

innocent ['inəsənt] *a* 1. innocent; pas coupable 2. (*a*) pur; innocent (*b*) naïf, *f* naïve; **to put on an i. air,** faire l'innocent. '**innocence** *n* (*a*) innocence *f* (d'un accusé) (*b*) innocence; candeur *f*, naïveté *f*. '**innocently** *adv* innocemment.

innocuous [i'nɔkjuəs] *a* inoffensif. **i'nnocuously** *adv* inoffensivement.

innovate ['inəveit] *vi* innover. **inno'vation** *n* innovation *f*, changement *m*. '**innovator** *n* (in)novateur *m*.

innuendo [inju(:)'endou] *n* (*pl* **innuendo(e)s**) *n* allusion (malveillante), insinuation *f*.

innumerable [i'nju:mərəbl] *a* innombrable; sans nombre.

inoculate [i'nɔkjuleit] *vtr Med:* inoculer, vacciner (qn contre une maladie). **inocu'lation** *n Med:* inoculation (immunisante).

inoffensive [inə'fensiv] *a* inoffensif.

inoperable [in'ɔpərəbl] *a Med:* inopérable.

inopportune [in'ɔpətju:n] *a* inopportun; intempestif; hors de propos. **in'opportunely** *adv* inopportunément; mal à propos.

inordinate [i'nɔːdinət] *a* démesuré, excessif, immodéré. **i'nordinately** *adv* démesurément.

inorganic [inɔː'gænik] *a* inorganique; **i. chemistry,** chimie minérale.

input ['input] *n* 1. *El:* tension *f* d'entrée 2. **i. data,** (données d')entrée *f*.

inquest ['inkwest] *n* enquête *f*; **(coroner's) i.,** enquête judiciaire (en cas de mort suspecte).

inquire [in'kwaiər] *vtr & i* se renseigner (sur qch); **to i. the price of sth,** demander le prix de qch; **to i. (of s.o.) how to get somewhere,** demander son chemin (à qn); *PN:* **i. within,** s'adresser ici; **to i. after s.o.'s health,** s'informer de la santé de qn; **to i. about sth,** se renseigner sur qch; **to i. for s.o.** demander qn; **to i. into sth,** faire des recherches sur qch. **in'quiring** *a* curieux; **an i. glance,** un coup d'œil interrogateur. **in'quiringly** *adv* d'un air, d'un ton, interrogateur; **to glance i. at s.o.,** interroger qn du regard. **in'quiry** *n* 1. enquête; **committee of i.,** commission *f* d'enquête 2. demande *f* de renseignements; **to make inquiries about s.o.,** s'informer de, se renseigner sur, qn; **i. office, inquiries,** (bureau de) renseignements.

inquisitive [in'kwizitiv] *a* curieux. **in'quisitively** *adv* avec curiosité. **in'quisitiveness** *n* curiosité (indiscrète).

inroad ['inroud] *n* empiétement *m* (sur la liberté de qn); **to make inroads on one's capital,** entamer son capital.

inrush ['inrʌʃ] *n* irruption *f* (d'eau, de gens); entrée soudaine (d'air, de gaz).

insane [in'sein] *a* 1. fou; (esprit) dérangé; **to become i.,** perdre la raison; **to drive s.o. i.,** rendre qn fou 2. (désir) insensé, fou 3. *npl* **the i.,** les aliénés. **in'sanely** *adv* follement. **insanity** [in'sæniti] *n* folie *f*, démence *f*; *Med:* aliénation mentale.

insanitary [in'sænit(ə)ri] *a* insalubre; malsain.

insatiable [in'seiʃəbl] *a* insatiable. **in'satiably** *adv* insatiablement.

inscribe [in'skraib] *vtr* 1. inscrire; graver (un nom sur un tombeau) 2. dédicacer (un livre à qn). **in'scription** [-ipʃ(ə)n] *n* 1. inscription *f* (sur un monument); légende *f* (d'une pièce de monnaie) 2. dédicace *f* (d'un livre).

inscrutable [in'skru:təbl] *a* (dessein) impénétrable, incompréhensible; (visage) fermé.

insect ['insekt] *n* insecte *m*; **i. eater,** insectivore *m*; **i. repellent,** (crème) anti-moustique. **in'secticide** *n* insecticide *m*.

insecure [insi'kjuər] *a* 1. peu sûr; peu solide; mal affermi 2. exposé au danger; **to feel i.,** manquer de sécurité; être anxieux. **inse'curely** *adv* peu solidement; sans sécurité. **inse'curity** *n* insécurité *f*.

insemination [insemi'neiʃn] *n* **artificial i.,** insémination artificielle.

insensible [in'sensibl] *a* (*a*) insensible (*b*) sans connaissance. **insensi'bility** *n* insensibilité *f*. **in'sensibly** *adv* insensiblement.

insensitive [in'sensitiv] *a* insensible (**to,** à). **in'sensitiveness, insensi'tivity** *n* insensibilité *f*.

inseparable [in'sepərəbl] *a* inséparable (**from,** de). **in'separably** *adv* inséparablement.

insert 1. *vtr* [in'səːt] insérer, introduire (la clef dans la serrure) 2. *n* ['insəːt] (*a*) *Typ:* insertion *f* (*b*) encart *m* (*c*) *Dressm:* incrustation *f*. **in'sertion** *n* insertion *f*; *Typ:* **i. mark,** renvoi *m*.

inside ['in'said] **1.** n (a) dedans m, (côté) intérieur (m); **on the i.,** en dedans, au dedans; **to know the i. of an affair,** connaître les dessous d'une affaire; **his sweater is i. out,** son pull est à l'envers; **to turn a pocket i. out,** retourner une poche; **to turn everything i. out,** mettre tout sens dessus dessous; **to know sth i. out,** savoir qch à fond (b) intérieur (d'une maison) (c) F: l'estomac m, ventre m; **I've a pain in my i.,** j'ai mal à l'estomac, au ventre (d) Fb: **i. left,** intérieur gauche **2.** a intérieur, d'intérieur; **i. information,** renseignements privés; **it's an i. job,** c'est un coup monté par qn de la maison **3.** adv intérieurement; en dedans; **i. of three hours,** en moins de trois heures; **i. and outside,** au dedans et au dehors; **come i.!** entrez! **he's waiting i.,** il attend à l'intérieur; **to put s.o. i.,** mettre qn en taule **4.** prep à l'intérieur de; dans; **i. a week,** en moins d'une semaine.

insidious [in'sidiəs] a insidieux; (raisonnement) astucieux. **in'sidiously** adv insidieusement.

insight ['insait] n **1.** perspicacité f; pénétration f **2.** aperçu m; **to get an i. into sth,** avoir un aperçu de qch.

insignificant [insig'nifikənt] a insignifiant; de peu d'importance; (personne) sans importance. **insig'nificance** n insignifiance f.

insincere [insin'siər] a (a) peu sincère; de mauvaise foi (b) (of smile) faux, f fausse. **insin'cerity** n manque m de sincérité.

insinuate [in'sinjueit] **1.** vtr insinuer **2.** vpr **to i. oneself into s.o.'s favour,** s'insinuer (dans les bonnes grâces de qn) **3.** vtr donner adroitement à entendre (que), insinuer (que); laisser entendre, sous-entendre (que). **insinu'ation** n insinuation f; sous-entendu m.

insipid [in'sipid] a insipide, fade. **insi'pidity** n insipidité f; fadeur f.

insist [in'sist] vi insister; **he insisted that it was so,** il soutenait qu'il en était ainsi; **to i. on doing sth,** insister pour faire qch; **I i. (up)on it,** je le veux, j'y tiens, absolument; **if you i.,** si vous y tenez; **I won't i.,** je n'insiste pas. **in'sistence** n insistance f. **in'sistent** a qui insiste, insistant; (créancier) importun, pressant. **in'sistently** adv instamment; avec insistance.

insolent ['insolənt] a insolent (to, envers). **'insolence** n insolence f (to, envers). **'insolently** adv insolemment; avec insolence.

insoluble [in'soljubl] a **1.** Ch: (sel) insoluble **2.** (problème) insoluble. **insolu'bility** n insolubilité f (d'un produit chimique, d'un problème).

insolvent [in'solvənt] a (débiteur) insolvable; **to become i.,** faire faillite. **in'solvency** n (a) insolvabilité f (b) faillite f.

insomnia [in'somniə] n insomnie f. **in'somniac** a & n insomniaque (mf).

inspect [in'spekt] vtr examiner (qch) de près; inspecter; contrôler (les livres d'un négociant); vérifier (un moteur). **in'spection** n inspection f; vérification f; contrôle m (de billets); **i. chamber,** regard m; Aut: **i. pit,** fosse f (à réparations); Pub: **i. copy,** spécimen m. **in'spector** n inspecteur, -trice; contrôleur m (d'autobus, des contributions). **in'spectorate** n corps m d'inspecteurs.

inspire [in'spaiər] vtr **to i. s.o. with confidence, with admiration, with hatred,** inspirer confiance, de l'admiration, de la haine, à qn; **to be inspired (by),** être inspiré (par); **to be an i. to s.o.,** être une source d'inspiration pour qn. **inspi'ration** [-spi-] n inspiration f. **in'spiring** [-spai-] a inspirant.

instability [instə'biliti] n instabilité f.

install [in'stɔ:l] vtr installer (qn dans une fonction); installer, poser (une machine); **to i. oneself in a place,** s'installer dans un endroit; **to i. a workshop,** monter un atelier. **insta'llation** n installation f.

instalment, NAm: **installment** [in'stɔ:lmənt] n **1.** acompte m; versement partiel; **monthly i.,** mensualité f; **to pay by instalments,** échelonner les paiements; **to buy sth on the i. plan,** acheter qch à crédit, à tempérament **2.** fascicule m (d'un ouvrage); feuilleton m; épisode m (d'une histoire).

instance ['instəns] **1.** n exemple m, cas m; **for i.,** par exemple; **in the first i.,** en (tout) premier lieu; **in the present i., in this i.,** dans le cas actuel; dans cette circonstance **2.** vtr citer (qch, qn) en exemple; illustrer (par un exemple).

instant ['instənt] **I.** n instant m, moment m; **come this i.,** venez sur-le-champ. **II.** a **1.** Com: (abbr **inst**) de ce mois; **the 5th inst.,** le 5 courant **2.** immédiat **3. i. coffee,** café soluble, (café) instantané (m). **instan'taneous** a instantané. **'instantly** adv tout de suite.

instead [in'sted] **1.** prep phr **i. of sth,** au lieu de qch; **i. of s.o.,** à la place de qn **2.** adv au lieu de cela; **he did not go to Rome, he went to Venice i.,** au lieu d'aller à Rome, il est allé à Venise; **if he can't come, take me i.,** s'il ne peut pas venir, emmenez-moi à sa place.

instep ['instep] n cou-de-pied m; cambrure f (du pied, d'une chaussure).

instigate ['instigeit] vtr inciter, provoquer (qn) (**to do sth,** à faire qch). **insti'gation** n instigation f, incitation f; **at his i.,** à son instigation. **'instigator** n **1.** instigateur, -trice **2.** auteur m (de troubles).

instil [in'stil] vtr (**instilled**) instiller (un liquide) (**into,** dans); inculquer (des connaissances, des principes); **to i. an idea into s.o.,** faire pénétrer une idée dans l'esprit de qn.

instinct ['instiŋkt] n instinct m; **by i.,** d'instinct; **to have an i. for business,** avoir l'instinct des affaires. **in'stinctive** a instinctif. **in'stinctively** adv d'instinct; instinctivement.

institute ['institju:t] **1.** vtr (a) instituer, établir (b) Jur: ordonner, instituer (une enquête); **to i. (legal) proceedings against s.o.,** intenter un procès à qn **2.** n institut m. **insti'tution** n **1.** institution f; établissement m **2.** institution; chose établie **3. charitable i.,** établissement d'intérêt public. **insti'tutional** a institutionnel; **i. life,** vie dans un établissement. **insti'tutionalized** a **to be i.,** être marqué par sa vie dans un hôpital psychiatrique, etc.

instruct [in'strʌkt] vtr **1.** instruire (qn en, dans, qch); enseigner (qch à qn) **2. to i. s.o. to do sth,** charger qn de faire qch. **in'struction** n **1.** instruction f, enseignement m **2.** usu pl indications f, instructions, ordres m; (to sentry, etc) consigne f; **strict instructions,** ordre(s) formel(s); **instructions for use,** mode m d'emploi; **i. book,** manuel m d'entretien; Adm: **standing instructions,** règlement m; **to go beyond one's instructions,** aller au delà des ordres reçus. **in'structive** a instructif. **in'structor** *nm*, **in'structress** *nf*, maître (enseignant); instructeur *m*; *Sp:* moniteur, -trice; **swimming i.,** professeur *m* de natation, d'escrime; **driving i.,** moniteur, -trice, d'auto-école.

instrument ['instrumənt] *n* (*a*) instrument *m*, appareil *m* (*b*) **musical i.,** instrument de musique; **wind, stringed, i.,** instrument à vent, à cordes. **instru'mental** *a* **1. to be i. in doing sth,** contribuer à faire qch **2. i. music,** musique instrumentale. **instru'mentalist** *n Mus:* instrumentiste *mf*. **instrumen'tation** *n Mus:* instrumentation *f*.

insubordinate [insə'bɔːdinət] *a* insubordonné; insoumis. **'insubordi'nation** *n* insubordination *f*.

insufferable [in'sʌfərəbl] *a* insupportable, intolérable. **in'sufferably** *adv* insupportablement.

insufficient [insə'fiʃənt] *a* insuffisant. **insu'fficiency** *n* insuffisance *f*. **insu'fficiently** *adv* insuffisamment.

insular ['insjulər] *a* (*a*) (climat) insulaire (*b*) (esprit) étroit, borné. **insu'larity** *n* insularité *f*.

insulate ['insjuleit] *vtr* isoler; calorifuger (une chaudière); protéger (contre qch); *Const: Cin:* insonoriser (une salle). **'insulating** *a* **i. material,** isolant *m*; matériau isolant; **i. tape,** ruban isolant; chatterton *m*. **insu'lation** *n* isolation *f*; calorifugeage *m*; insonorisation *f*. **'insulator** *n* (*a*) (*material*) isolant *m* (*b*) (*device*) isolateur *m*.

insulin ['insjulin] *n* insuline *f*.

insult 1. *n* ['insʌlt] insulte *f*, affront *m* **2.** *vtr* [in'sʌlt] insulter (qn); dire des injures (à qn). **in'sulting** *a* offensant, injurieux.

insuperable [in'sjuːp(ə)rəbl] *a* insurmontable.

insure [in'ʃuər] *vtr* **1.** (i) assurer (ii) faire assurer (sa maison, sa voiture); **to i. one's life,** s'assurer, se faire assurer, sur la vie; prendre une assurance-vie **2.** garantir, assurer (le succès). **in'surance** *n* assurance *f*; **i. agent,** agent d'assurance; **i. company,** société, compagnie, d'assurance; **i. scheme,** régime d'assurance; **i. policy,** police d'assurance; **life i.,** assurance-vie *f*; *Aut:* **third party i.,** assurance aux tiers; **comprehensive i.,** assurance tous risques; *Adm:* **National i.,** assurance sociale.

insurgent [in'sɜːdʒənt] *a & n* insurgé, -ée.

insurmountable [insə(ː)'mauntəbl] *a* insurmontable.

insurrection [insə'rekʃən] *n* insurrection *f*, soulèvement *m*, émeute *f*.

intact [in'tækt] *a* intact.

intake ['inteik] *n* (*a*) appel *m* (d'air); prise *f*, adduction *f* (d'eau); admission *f* (de vapeur); **i. valve,** soupape *f* d'admission (*b*) consommation *f*; **food i.,** ration *f* alimentaire (*c*) *Mil:* le contingent (*d*) *Sch:* admission *f*.

intangible [in'tændʒəbl] *a* intangible, impalpable.

integral ['intigrəl] **1.** *a* (*a*) **to be an i. part of sth,** faire partie intégrante de qch (*b*) *Mth:* **i. calculus,** calcul intégral (*c*) (paiement) intégral **2.** *n Mth:* intégrale *f*.

integrate ['intigreit] **1.** *vtr* (*a*) intégrer (qch dans qch) (*b*) *NAm:* **to i. a school,** imposer la déségrégation raciale dans une école **2.** *vi* s'intégrer (dans un milieu social, racial). **inte'gration** *n* intégration *f*; *NAm:* **racial i.,** déségrégation raciale.

integrity [in'tegriti] *n* intégrité *f*, honnêteté *f*, probité *f*; **man of i.,** homme intègre.

intellect ['intəlekt] *n* intellect *m*; intelligence *f*, esprit *m*. **inte'llectual** *a & n* intellectuel, -elle. **inte'llectually** *adv* intellectuellement.

intelligence [in'telidʒəns] *n* **1.** intelligence *f*; entendement *m*, sagacité *f*; **i. test,** test *m* d'intelligence; **i. quotient, I.Q.,** quotient intellectuel **2.** renseignement(s) *m(pl)*; nouvelles *fpl*; informations *fpl*; *Mil:* **I. service,** service secret. **in'telligent** *a* intelligent; avisé. **in'telligently** *adv* intelligemment; avec intelligence. **intelli'gentsia** *n* intelligentsia *f*.

intelligible [in'telidʒəbl] *a* intelligible. **intelligi'bility** *n* intelligibilité *f*. **in'telligibly** *adv* intelligiblement.

intemperate [in'tempərət] *a* **1.** (*of pers*) intempérant, immodéré **2.** adonné à la boisson.

intend [in'tend] *vtr* **1. to i. to do sth,** avoir l'intention de faire qch; compter faire qch; **was it intended?** était-ce fait avec intention? **I i. to be obeyed,** je veux qu'on m'obéisse **2. to i. sth for s.o.,** destiner qch à qn; **he intends to be a schoolmaster,** il se destine au professorat; **I intended it as a compliment,** mon intention était de (vous) faire un compliment; **he intended no harm,** il l'a fait sans mauvaise intention. **in'tended** *a* **1.** (*a*) (voyage) projeté (*b*) **the i. effect,** l'effet voulu **2.** intentionnel; fait avec intention.

intense [in'tens] *a* (*a*) vif; fort, intense (*b*) **i. expression,** expression d'intérêt profond (*c*) trop sérieux. **in'tensely** *adv* excessivement; avec intensité; **to hate s.o. i.,** détester qn profondément, intensément. **in'tensify 1.** *vtr* intensifier, augmenter; (*of sound*) rendre plus fort, plus vif; (*of colour*) renforcer **2.** *vi* s'intensifier. **in'tensity** *n* intensité *f*; force *f*; violence *f* (d'une douleur). **in'tensive** *a* intensif; *Med:* **i. care unit,** service *m* de soins intensifs. **in'tensively** *adv* intensivement.

intent [in'tent] **1.** *a* (*a*) **to be i. on sth,** être absorbé par qch, être tout entier à qch; **to be i. on doing sth,** être résolu, déterminé, à faire qch (*b*) attentif; absorbé (par son travail); **i. gaze,** regard fixe, profond **2.** *n* intention *f*; dessein *m*; **with i. to defraud,** dans le but de frauder; **to all intents and purposes,** virtuellement, en fait. **in'tently** *adv* attentivement; (regarder) fixement.

intention [in'tenʃən] *n* (*a*) intention *f*; dessein *m*; **to do sth with the best (of) intentions,** faire qch avec les meilleures intentions du monde; **I had no i. of accepting,** je n'avais nullement l'intention d'accepter; **with the i. (of doing sth),** dans l'intention de faire qch (*b*) but *m*. **in'tentional** *a* intentionnel, voulu. **in'tentionally** *adv* à dessein; exprès; intentionnellement.

inter [in'tɜːr] *vtr* (**interred**) ensevelir, enterrer (qch, un mort). **in'terment** *n* enterrement *m*.

interact [intə'rækt] *vi* réagir réciproquement. **inte'raction** *n* action *f* réciproque.

interbreed [intə'briːd] (**interbred**) **1.** *vtr* croiser (des races) **2.** *vi* se croiser.

intercede [intə'siːd] *vi* **to i. (with s.o.) for s.o.,** intercéder (auprès de qn) en faveur de qn.

intercept [intə'sept] *vtr* intercepter; arrêter (qn) au passage. **inter'ception** *n* interception *f*.

intercession [intə'seʃən] n intercession f.
interchange 1. n ['intətʃeindʒ] (a) échange m, communication f (d'idées) (b) CivE: échangeur m (d'autoroute) 2. vtr [intə'tʃeindʒ] échanger (des lettres, des compliments, avec qn); échanger (des parties d'une machine); changer (deux choses de place). **inter'changeable** a interchangeable.
intercom ['intəkɔm] n interphone m.
intercontinental [intəkɔnti'nentl] a (vol, missile) intercontinental.
intercourse ['intəkɔːs] n (a) commerce m; relations fpl; rapports mpl (b) rapports (sexuels).
interest ['intərest] I. n 1. Com: (a) participation f; **to have an i. in the profits,** participer aux bénéfices; **to have a financial i. in sth,** avoir des capitaux, être intéressé, dans qch (b) **the shipping i.,** les armateurs m; le commerce maritime; **we look after British interests,** nous défendons les intérêts britanniques 2. avantage m, profit m; **to act in one's own i.,** agir dans son propre intérêt; **it's in my i. to do this,** j'ai intérêt à le faire 3. **to take an i. in s.o.,** s'intéresser à qn; **questions of public i.,** questions d'intérêt public; **to take no (further) i. in sth,** se désintéresser de qch 4. Fin: **simple, compound, i.,** intérêts simples, composés; **to bear i. at 10%,** porter intérêt à dix pour cent. II. vtr 1. intéresser (qn à, dans, une affaire) 2. éveiller l'intérêt de (qn); **to be interested in music,** s'intéresser à la musique; **I am not i.,** cela ne m'intéresse pas; **can I i. you (in)?** est-ce que cela vous intéresserait (de)? '**interested** a the i. party, l'intéressé m. '**interesting** a intéressant.
interfere [intə'fiːər] vi (a) intervenir (dans une affaire); s'interposer (dans une querelle); **don't i. in s.o. else's business,** ne vous mêlez pas des affaires des autres; **he's always interfering,** il a toujours le nez fourré partout (b) **don't i. with it!** n'y touchez pas! (c) **to i. with (sth),** gêner (la circulation); **it interferes with my plans,** cela dérange mes plans (d) Ph: interférer; WTel: brouiller. **inter'ference** n 1. intervention f, intrusion f (**in s.o. else's business,** dans les affaires de qn) 2. Ph: interférence f; WTel: parasites mpl. **inter'fering** a importun; qui se mêle de tout.
interim ['intərim] 1. n **in the i.,** pendant, dans, l'intérim 2. a (rapport, dividende) intérimaire.
interior [in'tiəriər] a & n intérieur (m).
interjection [intə'dʒekʃən] n interjection f.
interloper ['intələupər] n intrus, -use.
interlude ['intəluːd] n Th: Mus: intermède m; interlude m.
intermediary [intə'miːdjəri] a & n intermédiaire (m).
intermediate [intə'miːdiət] a intermédiaire; Sch: (de niveau) moyen.
interminable [in'təːminəbl] a interminable; sans fin. **in'terminably** adv interminablement; sans fin.
intermingle [intə'miŋgl] 1. vtr entremêler 2. vi s'entremêler.
intermission [intə'miʃən] n (a) Th: entracte m (b) interruption f; **without i.,** sans arrêt m.
intermittent [intə'mitənt] a intermittent. **inter'mittently** adv par intervalles, par intermittence.
intern 1. vtr [in'təːn] interner 2. n ['intəːn] NAm: (Br = **houseman**) interne m (d'un hôpital). **inter'nee** n interné, -ée. **in'ternist** n Med: spé-

cialiste mf des maladies organiques. **in'ternment** n internement m.
internal [in'təːnəl] a 1. intérieur; (maladie) organique; (conviction) intime; (angle, lésion) interne; **i. combustion engine,** moteur à combustion interne 2. **i. trade,** commerce m intérieur; NAm: **i. revenue,** le fisc. **in'ternally** adv intérieurement; Pharm: **not to be taken i.,** pour usage m externe; ne pas avaler.
international [intə'næʃənəl] a international.
interphone ['intəfoun] n interphone m, téléphone intérieur.
interplanetary [intə'plænit(ə)ri] a (exploration, vol) interplanétaire.
interplay ['intəplei] n effet m réciproque; réaction f; interaction f.
interpolate [in'təːpəleit] vtr interpoler, intercaler. **interpo'lation** n interpolation f.
interpose [intə'pouz] 1. vtr interposer 2. vi s'interposer, intervenir.
interpret [in'təːprit] vtr 1. interpréter, expliquer (un texte) 2. interpréter, traduire. **interpre'tation** n interprétation f. **in'terpreter** n interprète mf.
interrelated [intə(ː)ri'leitid] a (faits) étroitement liés entre eux.
interrogate [in'terəgeit] vtr interroger, questionner (qn); faire subir un interrogatoire (à qn). **interro'gation** n interrogation f; interrogatoire m (d'un prévenu); Gram: **i. mark,** NAm: **i. point,** point d'interrogation. **inte'rrogative** a interrogateur; (pronom) interrogatif. **inte'rrogatively** adv d'un air, d'un ton, interrogateur, -trice. **in'terrogator** n interrogateur.
interrupt [intə'rʌpt] vtr interrompre; couper la parole à (qn). **inte'rruption** n interruption f; dérangement m.
intersect [intə(ː)'sekt] 1. vtr entrecouper, entrecroiser (**with, by, de)** 2. vi (of lines) se couper, se croiser. **inter'section** n 1. intersection f (de lignes); (point) d'intersection 2. carrefour m; croisement m de routes.
intersperse [intə'spəːs] vtr entremêler, parsemer (**with, de).**
interval ['intəvəl] n (a) intervalle m; **at intervals,** par intervalles; **an hour's i. between two lectures,** une heure de battement entre deux conférences; **meetings held at short intervals,** séances très rapprochées (b) Meteor: **bright intervals,** belles éclaircies (c) Th: entracte m; Sp: mi-temps f inv (d) écart m, distance f (entre deux objets, points).
intervene [intə(ː)'viːn] vi 1. intervenir, s'interposer 2. (of event) survenir, arriver; (of time) **ten years intervened,** dix années se sont écoulées. **inter'vening** a **during the i. week,** pendant la semaine qui s'est écoulée entretemps. **inter'vention** n intervention f.
interview ['intəvjuː] 1. n (a) entrevue f; **to invite s.o. to an i.,** convoquer qn (b) Journ: interview f 2. vtr (a) avoir une entrevue avec (qn) (b) Journ: interviewer (qn). **'interviewer** n interviewer m; (for research) enquêteur, -euse.
intestine [in'testin] n Anat: intestin m.
intimate[1] ['intimət] 1. a (ami) intime; **to become i. with s.o.,** se lier d'amitié (avec qn); **to be on i. terms with s.o.,** être à tu et à toi avec qn; **to have an i.**

knowledge of sth, avoir une connaissance approfondie de qch; **i. connection,** rapport intime, étroit; **to be i. with s.o.,** (i) être intime avec qn (ii) (*sexually*) avoir des relations intimes avec qn **2.** *n* **his intimates,** ses intimes *mf,* ses familiers *m.* **'intimacy** *n* (*a*) intimité *f* (*b*) relations *fpl* intimes, rapports sexuels. **'intimately** *adv* intimement; à fond.

intimate² ['intimeit] *vtr* **to i. sth to s.o.,** signifier qch à qn.

intimidate [in'timideit] *vtr* intimider (qn); **easily intimidated,** timide, peureux. **in'timidating** *a* intimidant. **intimi'dation** *n* intimidation *f;* menaces *fpl.*

into ['intu, 'intə] *prep* **1.** dans, en; **to go i. a house,** entrer dans une maison; **to get i. a car,** monter dans une voiture; **to fall i. the hands of the enemy,** tomber entre les mains de l'ennemi; **to get i. difficulties,** s'attirer des ennuis; **late i. the night,** tard dans la nuit; *F:* **to be i. sth,** donner à fond dans qch **2. to change sth i. sth,** changer qch en qch; **to change dollars i. francs,** changer des dollars contre des francs; **to divide i. four,** diviser en quatre; **two i. four goes two,** quatre divisé par deux égale deux; **to grow i. a man,** devenir un homme; **to burst i. tears,** fondre en larmes.

intolerable [in'tɔlərəbl] *a* intolérable, insupportable. **in'tolerably** *adv* insupportablement.

intolerant [in'tɔlərənt] *a* intolérant (**of,** de). **in'tolerance** *n* intolérance *f.* **in'tolerantly** *adv* avec intolérance.

intonation [intə'neiʃ(ə)n] *n* intonation *f.*

intoxicate [in'tɔksikeit] *vtr* enivrer, griser (qn). **in'toxicated** *a* ivre; **i. with praise,** grisé d'éloges. **in'toxicating** *a* enivrant, grisant; **i. drink,** boisson alcoolisée. **intoxi'cation** *n* ivresse *f.*

intransigent [in'trænzidʒənt] *a* intransigeant. **in'transigence** *n* intransigeance *f.*

intransitive [in'trænsitiv] *a Gram:* intransitif.

intrepid [in'trepid] *a* intrépide.

intricate ['intrikət] *a* compliqué; complexe. **'intricacy** *n* complexité *f;* complication *f.* **'intricately** *adv* d'une manière complexe, compliquée.

intrigue 1. *vi* [in'tri:g] intriguer; mener des intrigues **2.** *vtr* intriguer; éveiller la curiosité de (qn) **3.** *n* ['intri:g] intrigue *f.*

intrinsic [in'trinsik] *a* intrinsèque. **in'trinsically** *adv* intrinsèquement.

introduce [intrə'dju:s] *vtr* **1.** (*a*) introduire; faire entrer; mettre (dans); **to i. s.o. (into s.o.'s presence),** faire entrer qn; introduire qn (auprès de qn); **to i. a subject,** amener un sujet (*b*) **to i. a Bill (before Parliament),** déposer un projet de loi (*c*) *Com:* lancer (un produit) (*d*) présenter (un programme de radio, TV) **2. to i. s.o. to s.o.,** présenter qn à qn. **intro'duction** *n* **1.** introduction *f* **2.** présentation *f* (de qn à qn) **3.** introduction, avant-propos *m inv* (d'un livre); *Mus:* introduction **4.** manuel *m* élémentaire; introduction (**to,** à). **intro'ductory** *a* (mots) d'introduction; *Com:* (prix) de lancement.

introspective [intrə'spektiv] *a* introspectif. **intro'spection** *n* introspection *f.*

introvert ['intrəvə:t] *n* introverti, -ie. **intro'version** *n* introversion *f.*

intrude [in'tru:d] *vi* faire intrusion (**on s.o.,** auprès de

qn); **I'm afraid of intruding,** je crains d'être importun, de vous déranger. **in'truder** *n* intrus, -use. **in'trusion** *n* intrusion *f.* **in'trusive** *a* importun, indiscret; *Ling:* (liaison) abusive.

intuition [intju(:)'iʃ(ə)n] *n* intuition *f.* **in'tuitive** *a* intuitif. **in'tuitively** *adv* intuitivement; par intuition.

inundate ['inʌndeit] *vtr* inonder (**with,** de); **to be inundated with requests,** être débordé de demandes. **inun'dation** *n* inondation *f.*

inure [i'njuər] *vtr* accoutumer, habituer, rompre, endurcir (qn à qch); **inured to hardship,** habitué aux privations.

invade [in'veid] *vtr* **1.** envahir **2.** empiéter sur (les droits de qn). **in'vader** *n* envahisseur *m.* **in'vading** *a* (armée) d'invasion.

invalid¹ [in'vælid] *a Jur:* (mariage) non valide; non-valable; (arrêt) nul et non avenu. **in'validate** *vtr Jur:* invalider, rendre nul (un testament); vicier (un contrat); casser (un jugement).

invalid² ['invalid] *a & n* malade (*mf*); infirme (*mf*); invalide (*mf*); **i. chair,** fauteuil roulant. **'invalid out** [-li:d] *vtr Mil:* réformer.

invaluable [in'vælju(ə)bl] *a* inestimable; d'un prix incalculable.

invariable [in'vɛəriəbl] *a* invariable. **in'variably** *adv* invariablement, immanquablement.

invasion [in'veiʒən] *n* invasion *f,* envahissement *m;* intrusion *f* (dans l'intimité de qn).

invective [in'vektiv] *n* invective *f;* **a torrent of i.,** un torrent d'injures *fpl.*

inveigh [in'vei] *vi* invectiver (**against,** contre).

inveigle [in'vi:gl, -'veigl] *vtr* entraîner (qn à faire qch).

invent [in'vent] *vtr* inventer; **newly invented process,** procédé d'invention récente. **in'vention** *n* invention *f;* **a story of his own i.,** une histoire de son cru. **in'ventive** *a* inventif. **in'ventiveness** *n* esprit inventif, d'invention; imagination *f.* **in'ventor** *n* inventeur, -trice.

inventory ['invəntri] *n* inventaire *m; NAm:* stock *m.*

inverse ['in'və:s] *a* **1.** *a* inverse; **in i. ratio, proportion,** en raison inverse (**to,** de) **2.** *n* inverse *m,* contraire *m* (**of,** de). **in'versely** *adv* inversement. **in'version** *n* renversement *m;* inversion *f; Med:* rétroversion *f* (de l'utérus).

invert [in'və:t] *vtr* **1.** renverser, retourner (un objet) (le haut en bas) **2.** invertir, renverser (l'ordre, les positions) **3.** retourner, mettre à l'envers. **in'verted** *a* (*a*) inverted commas, guillemets *mpl* (*b*) *Dressm:* (pli) creux (*c*) (*of pers*) inverti.

invertebrate [in'və:tibrət] *a & n Z:* invertébré (*m*).

invest [in'vest] *vtr* **1. to i. s.o. with an office,** investir qn d'une fonction **2.** *Fin:* placer, investir; **to i. money,** engager des capitaux, faire des placements; **to i. in property,** faire des placements en immeubles; **to i. in a new piece of furniture,** se payer un nouveau meuble. **in'vestiture** *n* (*a*) investiture *f* (d'un évêque) (*b*) remise *f* de décorations. **in'vestment** *n* placement *m,* investissement *m,* mise *f* de fonds; (société) de portefeuille *m,* de placement. **in'vestor** *n* actionnaire *mf;* **small investors,** petits épargnants.

investigate [in'vestigeit] *vtr* examiner, étudier (une

question); **to i. a crime,** faire une enquête sur un crime. **investi'gation** n investigation f; enquête f **(of, sur); question under i.,** question à l'étude f. **in'vestigator** n investigateur, -trice; enquêteur, -euse; **private i.,** détective privé.

inveterate [in'vetərət] a (of smoker, drunkard, criminal) invétéré; **i. hatred,** haine implacable.

invidious [in'vidiəs] a 1. haïssable, odieux; **i. task,** tâche ingrate 2. qui excite la jalousie; **i. comparison,** comparaison désobligeante.

invigilate [in'vidʒileit] vi Sch: surveiller (les candidats pendant un examen). **in'vigilator** n surveillant, -ante (à un examen).

invigorate [in'vigəreit] vtr (a) fortifier (qn) (b) (of the air, etc) vivifier, tonifier; revigorer.

invincible [in'vinsəbl] a invincible. **invinci'bility** n invincibilité f. **in'vincibly** adv invinciblement.

invisible [in'vizəbl] a invisible; **i. mending,** stoppage m. **invisi'bility** n invisibilité f. **in'visibly** adv invisiblement.

invite 1. vtr [in'vait] inviter; convier (qn à dîner); **to i. s.o. in,** prier qn d'entrer; **to i. s.o. out,** inviter qn à sortir; **to i. s.o. over for a meal,** inviter qn à venir dîner chez soi 2. n ['invait] F: invitation f. **invita-tion** [invi'teiʃ(ə)n] n invitation f. **in'viting** a invitant, attrayant; (plat) appétissant. **in'vitingly** adv d'une manière attrayante.

invoice ['invɔis] Com: 1. n facture f; **i. clerk,** facturier, -ière 2. vtr facturer (des marchandises). **'invoicing** n i. **of goods,** facturation f de marchandises.

invoke [in'vouk] vtr (a) invoquer (Dieu) (b) appeler (qn à son secours) (c) Jur: invoquer (les termes d'un contrat).

involuntary [in'vɔlənt(ə)ri] a involontaire. **in'voluntarily** adv involontairement.

involve [in'vɔlv] vtr 1. (often passive) **to be i. s.o. in a quarrel,** mêler qn à une querelle; **to be involved in a dispute, a plot,** être impliqué dans une dispute, un complot; **the car involved,** la voiture en cause (dans l'accident); **the forces involved,** les forces en jeu; **the person involved,** la personne en question; **I am emotionally involved,** cela me touche de trop, de très, près 2. comporter, entraîner; include; **to i. much expense,** nécessiter de grands frais. **in'volved** a (style) embrouillé, compliqué; (of pers) **to be i. (with s.o.),** avoir une liaison (amoureuse) (avec qn). **in'volvement** n engagement m; participation f; collaboration f.

invulnerable [in'vʌlnərəbl] a invulnérable.

inward ['inwəd] 1. a intérieur; interne; vers l'intérieur 2. adv = **inwards. 'inwardly** adv intérieurement; en dedans; **I was i. pleased,** dans mon for intérieur j'étais content. **'inwards** adv 1. vers l'intérieur; en dedans 2. dans l'âme; intérieurement.

iodine ['aiədi:n] n iode m; Pharm: teinture f d'iode.

ion ['aiən] n El: Ph: ion m.

iota [ai'outə] n iota m, rien m; **not an i. of truth,** pas un brin de vérité, pas un mot de vrai.

IRA abbr Irish Republican Army.

Iran [i'rɑːn] Prn Geog: l'Iran m. **Iranian** [i'reinjən] a n iranien, -ienne.

Iraq [i'rɑːk] Prn Geog: l'Irak m. **I'raqi** a & n irakien, -ienne.

irate [ai'reit] a furieux; en colère.

Ireland ['aiələnd] Prn Geog: l'Irlande f.

iridescent [iri'des(ə)nt] a irisé, iridescent; **i. colours,** couleurs chatoyantes.

iris ['aiəris] n 1. Anat: (pl irides) iris m (de l'œil) 2. Bot: (pl irises) iris m.

Irish ['aiəriʃ] 1. a irlandais; (République) d'Irlande 2. n (a) Ling: l'irlandais m (b) pl **the I.,** les Irlandais m **'Irishman,** pl -men n Irlandais m. **'Irishwoman,** pl -women n Irlandaise f.

irksome ['ə:ksəm] a (travail) ennuyeux, ingrat.

iron ['aiən] I. n 1. fer m; **made of i.,** de, en, fer; **cast i.,** fonte f; **corrugated i.,** tôle (ondulée); **old i.,** ferraille f; **i. ore,** minerai de fer; Med: **i. lung,** poumon d'acier m; **will of i.,** volonté de fer 2. fer à repasser 3. pl irons, fers, chaînes f. II. vtr repasser (le linge); **to i. out difficulties,** aplanir des difficultés. **'ironing** n repassage m (du linge); **i. board,** planche à repasser. **'ironmonger** [-mʌŋgər] n quincaillier m. **'ironmongery** n quincaillerie f. **'ironwork** n 1. serrurerie f; ferronnerie f (d'art) 2. pl ironworks, usine f sidérurgique; forges fpl. **'ironworker** n serrurier m; ferronnier m (d'art).

irony ['aiərəni] n ironie f. **i'ronical** a ironique. **i'ronically** adv ironiquement.

irradiate [i'reidieit] vtr (of light, heat) irradier, rayonner; (of light rays) illuminer. **irradi'ation** n irradiation f; illumination f.

irrational [i'ræʃənəl] a déraisonnable, absurde. **i'rrationally** adv déraisonnablement.

irreconcilable [irekən'sailəbl] a 1. (ennemi) irréconciliable; (haine) implacable 2. (croyance) incompatible, inconciliable (**with,** avec).

irrecoverable [iri'kʌv(ə)rəbl] a irrécouvrable.

irredeemable [iri'di:məbl] a (of pers) incorrigible; (perte) irrémédiable; (faute) irréparable; Fin: (obligation) non amortissable.

irrefutable [iri'fju:təbl] a irréfutable.

irregular [i'regjulər] a (a) irrégulier; contraire aux règles; **i. life,** vie déréglée (b) (of surface) inégal. **irregu'larity** n irrégularité f (de conduite); accident m (de terrain). **i'rregularly** adv irrégulièrement.

irrelevant [i'relivənt] a non pertinent; hors de propos; **that's i.,** cela n'a rien à voir avec la question. **i'rrelevance** n manque m d'à-propos. **i'rrelevantly** adv mal à propos; hors de propos.

irremediable [iri'mi:diəbl] a irrémédiable; sans remède. **irre'mediably** adv irrémédiablement.

irreparable [i'repərəbl] a irréparable; (perte) irrémédiable. **i'rreparably** adv irréparablement.

irreplaceable [iri'pleisəbl] a irremplaçable.

irrepressible [iri'presəbl] a irrésistible, irréprimable. **irre'pressibly** adv irrésistiblement.

irreproachable [iri'proutʃəbl] a irréprochable. **irre'proachably** adv irréprochablement.

irresistible [iri'zistəbl] a irrésistible. **irre'sistibly** adv irrésistiblement.

irresolute [i'rezəl(j)u:t] a 1. indécis 2. (caractère) irrésolu. **i'rresolutely** adv irrésolument.

irrespective [iri'spektiv] 1. a indépendant (**of,** de) 2. adv **i. of sth,** indépendamment de, sans tenir compte, de qch.

irresponsible [iri'spɔnsəbl] a (of pers) étourdi; (of

action) irréfléchi. **irresponsi'bility** n étourderie f; manque m de sérieux. **irre'sponsibly** adv étourdiment.

irretrievable [iri'triːvəbl] a irréparable, irrémédiable; introuvable. **irre'trievably** adv irréparablement, irrémédiablement; (perdu) à tout jamais.

irreverent [i'rev(ə)rənt] a irrévérent; irrévérencieux. **i'rreverence** n irrévérence f; manque m de respect (**towards s.o.**, envers, pour, qn). **i'rreverently** adv irrévérencieusement.

irrevocable [i'revəkəbl] a irrévocable. **i'rrevocably** adv irrévocablement.

irrigate ['irigeit] vtr irriguer (des champs); (*of river*) arroser (une région). **irri'gation** n irrigation f.

irritate ['iriteit] vtr 1. irriter, agacer 2. Med: irriter (une plaie). **'irritable** a irritable, irascible. **'irritably** adv d'un ton de mauvaise humeur. **'irritant** a & n irritant (m). **'irritating** a irritant; agaçant; Med: irritant. **irri'tation** n irritation f; agacement m; Med: irritation (de la gorge); **nervous i.**, énervement m.

irruption [i'rʌpʃ(ə)n] n irruption f.

is see **be.**

ISBN abbr International Standard Book Number(ing).

Islam ['izlɑːm] n Islam m (religion ou peuple). **Is-lamic** [iz'læmik] a islamique.

island ['ailənd] n île f; (**traffic**) **i.**, refuge m (pour piétons). **'islander** n insulaire mf; habitant, -ante, d'une île. **isle** n (*esp in Prn*) île f; **the British Isles**, les Îles Britanniques. **'islet** n îlot m.

ism [is(ə)m] n F: doctrine f, théorie f.

isolate ['aisəleit] vtr isoler (s.o., sth, from s.o., sth, qn, qch, de, d'avec, qn, qch). **'isolated** a isolé. **iso'lation** n isolement m; solitude f; **i. hospital**, hôpital d'isolement (des contagieux); **i. ward**, salle des contagieux. **iso'lationism** n Pol: isolationnisme m. **iso'lationist** a & n isolationniste (mf).

isotope ['aisoutoup] n Ch: Ph: isotope m.

Israel ['izreiəl] Prn Geog: Israël m. **Is'raeli** a & n israélien, -ienne.

issue ['isjuː] I. n 1. écoulement m 2. issue f, sortie f, débouché m (**out of**, de) 3. issue, résultat m, dénouement m; **to bring a matter to an i.**, faire aboutir une question; **to await the i.**, attendre le résultat; **the point at i.**, la question en discussion; **to force the i.**, forcer la main (à qn); **to confuse the i.**, brouiller les cartes; **I don't want to make an i. of it**, je ne veux pas trop insister 4. progéniture f. descendance f 5. (a) Fin: émission f (de billets de banque, d'actions, de timbres-poste) (b) publication f (d'un livre) (c) numéro m (d'une revue) (d) délivrance f (d'un passeport) (e) Mil: distribution f, versement m (de vivres); **i. shirt**, chemise réglementaire. **II.** v 1. vi (a) jaillir, s'écouler (**from**, de) (b) provenir, dériver (**from**, de) 2. vtr (a) émettre, mettre en circulation (des billets de banque, etc) (b) publier (un livre); lancer (un prospectus); Mil: **to i. an order**, publier, donner, un ordre (c) verser, distribuer (des provisions); délivrer (des billets, des passeports); **to i. s.o. with sth**, délivrer qch à qn.

isthmus ['is(θ)məs] (*pl isthmuses*) n Geog: isthme m.

it [it] pers pron 1. (a) (*subject*) il, f elle; **where is your hat?—it's in the cupboard**, où est ton chapeau?—il est dans l'armoire (b) (*object*) le, f la; **I don't believe it**, je

ne le crois pas; **give it to me, give me it**, donne-le, -la, moi; **he took her hand and pressed it**, il lui prit la main et la serra; **and my cake, have you tasted it?** et mon gâteau, y avez-vous goûté? (c) (*indirect object*) lui mf; **bring the cat and give it a drink**, amenez le chat et donnez-lui à boire (d) F: **this book is absolutely it!** c'est un livre épatant! **this is it!** nous y voilà! ça y est! **he thinks he's it** [hiːz'it], il se croit sorti de la cuisse de Jupiter **2.** (*impersonal use*) il maintenant allons-y! **there is nothing for it but to run**, il n'y a qu'une chose à faire, c'est de filer; **to have a bad time of it**, en voir de dures; **to face it**, faire front; **he hasn't got it in him (to)**, il n'est pas capable (de); il n'a pas ce qu'il faut (pour); **the worst of it is that**, le pire de l'histoire c'est que **3.** ce, cela, il; **who is it?** qui est-ce? **that's it**, (i) c'est ça (ii) ça y est! **it doesn't matter**, cela ne fait rien; **it's Monday**, c'est aujourd'hui lundi; **it's raining**, il pleut **4.** **it's nonsense talking like that**, c'est absurde de parler comme ça; **it makes you think**, cela (vous) fait réfléchir; **how is it that?** comment se fait-il que? **it's said that**, on dit que; **I thought it well to warn you**, j'ai jugé bon de vous avertir **5. at it**, **in it, to it**, y; **to consent to it**, y consentir; **to fall in it**, y tomber; **above it, over it**, au-dessus; dessus; **for it**, en; pour lui, pour elle, pour cela; **I feel (the) better for it**, je m'en trouve mieux; **from it**, en; **far from it**, tant s'en faut, il s'en faut; **of it**, en; **he's afraid of it**, il en a peur; **on it**, y, dessus; **don't tread on it**, ne marche pas dessus.

italic [i'tælik] a italique (m); **to print in italic(s)**, imprimer en italique(s). **i'talics** npl italique m; **the i. are mine**, c'est moi qui souligne.

Italy ['itəli] Prn Geog: l'Italie f. **Italian** [i'tæljən] **1.** a italien, d'Italie **2.** n (a) Italien, -ienne (b) Ling: l'italien m.

itch [itʃ] **1.** vi démanger; (*of pers*) avoir des démangeaisons; **my hand itches**, la main me démange; **to be itching to do sth**, brûler d'envie de faire qch **2.** n (*also itching*) démangeaison f. **'itching** a **i. powder**, poil à gratter. **'itchy** a qui démange; **to have i. feet**, brûler d'envie de partir; avoir la bougeotte.

item ['aitəm] n article m; détail m; **news items**, faits divers; **the last i. on the programme**, le dernier numéro du programme; **items on the agenda**, questions f à l'ordre du jour. **'itemize** vtr détailler.

itinerary [i'tinərəri] n itinéraire m. **i'tinerant** a (musicien) ambulant; (marchand) forain.

its [its] poss a son, f sa, (*before vowel sound*) son; pl ses; **I cut off its head**, je lui ai coupé la tête.

it's = **it is; it has.**

itself [it'self] pers pron lui-même, elle-même; (*refl*) se.

ITV abbr Independent Television.

IUD abbr (*birth control*) intra-uterine device, stérilet m.

IUS abbr International Union of Students.

I've = **I have.**

ivory ['aivəri] n **1.** ivoire m; (objet m d')ivoire **2.** attrib d'ivoire, en ivoire; (*of colour*) ivoire inv; **i. tower**, tour d'ivoire; Geog: **the I. Coast (Republic)**, la (République de la) Côte d'Ivoire.

ivy ['aivi] n **1.** (a) Bot: lierre m (b) Bot: **poison i.**, sumac vénéneux; FrC: herbe f à la puce **2.** NAm: **I. League**, qui fait partie du cercle des vieilles universités prestigieuses des états de l'est.

J

J, j [dʒei] *n* (la lettre) J, j *m*.

jab [dʒæb] I. *n* (*a*) coup *m* de pointe (*b*) F: piqûre *f*. II. *vtr & i* (**jabbed**) **to j.** (**at**) s.o., sth, with sth., piquer qn, qch, du bout de qch; **to j. sth into sth**, enfoncer qch dans qch.

jabber [ˈdʒæbər] 1. *vi* jacasser; jaser, baragouiner 2. *vtr* baragouiner (le français).

Jack¹ [dʒæk] 1. *Prnm* (*dim of* **John**) Jeannot; **before you could say J. Robinson**, sans qu'on ait le temps de dire ouf; F: **I'm all right, J.**, je m'en tire bien (et tant pis pour les autres) 2. *n* (*a*) (*pers*) **j. tar**, marin *m*; **every man j.**, tout le monde (*b*) *Cards:* valet *m* (*c*) *Aut:* cric *m* (*d*) *Games:* (*bowls*) cochonnet *m* (*e*) (*male of species*) **j. hare**, bouquin *m* 3. *vtr* (*a*) **to j. up**, soulever (une voiture) avec un cric; F: augmenter (les prix) (*b*) F: **to j. in**, abandonner (ses études, etc.) '**jackass** *n* âne *m*. '**jackboots** *npl* bottes *fpl* à genouillère. '**jackdaw** *n* choucas *m*. '**jack-in-the-box** *n* diable *m* (à ressort). '**jack-knife** 1. *n* (*pl* **-knives**) couteau *m* de poche 2. *vi* (*of articulated vehicle*) se mettre en travers (de la route). **jack-of-'all-trades** *n* homme *m* à tout faire. '**jackpot** *n* pot *m*; **to hit the j.**, gagner le gros lot.

jack² *n Nau:* **the Union J.**, le pavillon britannique.

jackal [ˈdʒækɔl] *n* chacal *m*, *pl* -als.

jacket [ˈdʒækit] *n* 1. *Cl:* veston *m* (d'homme); jaquette *f* (de femme); veste *f*; paletot *m*; **dinner j.**, smoking *m*; **bed j.**, liseuse *f*; *Cu:* **j. potatoes**, pommes de terre en robe de chambre 2. jaquette, couverture *f* (de livre).

jade [dʒeid] *n Miner:* jade *m*; **j. (green)**, vert jade *inv*.

jaded [ˈdʒeidid] *a* (*of pers, horse*) surmené, fatigué, éreinté; (goût) blasé.

jagged [ˈdʒægid] *a* déchiqueté, dentelé, ébréché; (pierre) aux arêtes vives.

jaguar [ˈdʒægjuər] *n Z:* jaguar *m*.

jail [dʒeil] 1. *n* prison *f*, F: taule *f*; **in j.**, en prison 2. *vtr* mettre (qn) en prison. '**jailbird** *n* F: récidiviste *mf*. '**jailbreaker** *n* évadé, -ée (de prison). '**jailer** *n* gardien, -ienne, de prison; *A:* geôlier, -ière.

jalopy [dʒəˈlɔpi] *n* (*pl* **jalopies**) F: vieux tacot; vieille guimbarde.

jam¹ [dʒæm] I. *n* foule *f* (de gens); **traffic j.**, embouteillage *m*; F: **to be in a j.**, être dans le pétrin. II. *v* 1. *vtr* (*a*) serrer, enfoncer (de force) (**sth in(to) sth**, qch dans qch); **to j. one's finger, get one's finger jammed, in the door**, se coincer le doigt dans la porte (*b*) coincer (une machine); enrayer (une roue) (*c*) bloquer, obstruer (un couloir) (*d*) *WTel:* brouiller (un message) (*e*) **to j. on the brakes**, serrer les freins à bloc 2. *vi* (*a*) (*of crowd*) se presser (*b*) (*of machine*) se coincer; (*of rifle*) s'enrayer; (*of brakes*) se bloquer. '**jamming** *n WTel:* brouillage *m*. **jam-'packed** *a* F: (autobus) bondé, comble.

jam² *n* confiture *f*; **strawberry j.**, confiture de fraises; F: **it's money for j.**, c'est donné. '**jamjar** *n* pot *m* à confitures.

Jamaica [dʒəˈmeikə] *Prn Geog:* Jamaïque *f*. **Ja-'maican** *a & n* jamaïquain, -aine.

jamb [dʒæm] *n* jambage *m*, montant *m*, chambranle *m* (de porte).

jamboree [dʒæmbəˈriː] *n* (*a*) réjouissances tapageuses (*b*) *Scout:* jamboree *m*.

jangle [ˈdʒæŋgl] 1. *vi* cliqueter; s'entrechoquer 2. *vtr* faire cliqueter, entrechoquer; **jangled nerves**, nerfs en pelote.

janitor [ˈdʒænitər] *n* portier *m*; concierge *m*.

January [ˈdʒænjuəri] *n* janvier *m*; **in J.**, en janvier; **(on) J. the first, (on) the first of J.**, le premier janvier.

Japan [dʒəˈpæn] *Prn Geog:* Japon *m*; **in J.**, au Japon. **Japa'nese** 1. *a & n* japonais, -aise 2. *n Ling:* japonais *m*.

japonica [dʒəˈpɔnikə] *n Bot:* cognassier *m* du Japon.

jar¹ [dʒɑːr] I. *n* choc *m*; secousse *f*; ébranlement *m*. II. *v* (**jarred**) 1. *vi* (*a*) rendre un son discordant (*b*) heurter, cogner; **to j. on s.o.'s feelings**, choquer les sentiments de qn; **to j. on s.o.'s nerves**, taper sur les nerfs de qn (*c*) (*of sound*) détonner; (*of action*) être en désaccord (**with**, avec) 2. *vtr* heurter, cogner, ébranler, secouer. '**jarring** *a* (*of sound*) discordant, dur.

jar² *n* récipient *m*; pot *m*; bocal *m*.

jargon [ˈdʒɑːgən] *n* jargon *m*.

jasmine [ˈdʒæzmin] *n Bot:* jasmin *m*.

jaundice [ˈdʒɔːndis] *n Med:* jaunisse *f*. '**jaundiced** *a* **to take a j. view of things**, voir tout en noir, d'un œil jaloux.

jaunt [dʒɔːnt] *n* (petite) excursion, promenade *f*.

jaunty [ˈdʒɔːnti] *a* 1. insouciant, désinvolte 2. enjoué, vif. '**jauntily** *adv* avec insouciance; de manière désinvolte.

javelin [ˈdʒævlin] *n* javelot *m*; *Sp:* **j. throwing**, lancer du javelot.

jaw [dʒɔː] *n* mâchoire *f*; **jaws of death**, griffes *fpl* de la mort. '**jawbone** *n* (os *m*) maxillaire *m*; mâchoire.

jay [dʒei] *n Orn:* geai *m*. '**jaywalker** *n* piéton *m* imprudent (en traversant la rue).

jazz [dʒæz] I. *n* 1. *Mus:* jazz *m* 2. F: baratin *m*; **and all that j.**, et tout le bataclan. II. *vtr* **to j. up** (i) tourner (une mélodie) en jazz (ii) rendre (qch) plus gai, plus voyant.

JC *abbr Jesus Christ*, Jésus-Christ.

jealous [ˈdʒeləs] *a* jaloux (**of**, de). '**jealously** *adv* jalousement. '**jealousy** *n* jalousie *f*.

jeans [dʒiːnz] *npl Cl:* jean *m*; blue-jean *m*.

jeep [dʒiːp] *n Aut:* jeep *f*.

jeer [ˈdʒiər] I. *n* raillerie *f*, moquerie *f*; huée *f*. II. *vtr & i* (**at**) s.o., sth, se moquer de, railler, qn, qch; (*of crowd*) huer qn, qch. '**jeering** I. *a* railleur, moqueur. II. *n* = JEER I.

jell [dʒel] *vi* (*a*) (*of jelly*) prendre (*b*) F: (*of ideas*) se former. **jelly** *n* (*pl* **-ies**) gelée *f.* '**jellyfish** *n* méduse *f.*

jemmy ['dʒemi] *n* (*pl* **jemmies**) pince-monseigneur *f.*

jeopardize ['dʒepədaiz] *vtr* exposer au danger; compromettre. '**jeopardy** *n* danger, péril *m*; **in j.,** en danger, en péril.

jerk [dʒəːk] I. *n* (*a*) saccade *f*, secousse *f*; à-coup *m* (*b*) *esp NAm:* F: idiot, -ote. II. *vtr* donner une secousse à (qch); tirer (qch) d'un coup sec; **he jerked himself free,** il s'est dégagé d'une secousse. '**jerkily** *adv* d'une manière saccadée; par à-coups. '**jerky** *a* saccadé; (style) décousu.

jerkin [dʒəːkin] *n* gilet *m.*

jerry ['dʒeri] *n* F: pot *m* de chambre. '**jerry-built** *a* (maison) de camelote, de carton. '**jerrycan** *n* jerrycan *m.*

Jersey ['dʒəːzi] 1. *Prn Geog:* (Île de) Jersey 2. *n Cl:* jersey *m*; tricot *m*; chandail *m*; **football j.,** maillot *m* 3. (*cloth*) jersey.

jest [dʒest] I. *n* plaisanterie *f*; **in j.,** pour rire. II. *vi* plaisanter. '**jester** *n* bouffon *m.*

Jesus ['dʒiːzəs] *Prnm* Jésus; **J. Christ,** Jésus-Christ. **Jesuit** ['dʒezjuit] *n* jésuite *m.*

jet¹ [dʒet] *n* jais *m*; **j. black,** noir comme (du) jais.

jet² *n* 1. jet *m* (d'eau) 2. (*a*) ajutage *m*, jet (de tuyau d'arrosage) (*b*) brûleur *m* (à gaz); *Aut:* gicleur *m* 3. *Av:* **j. (aircraft),** avion *m* à réaction; jet; **j. engine,** moteur *m* à réaction, réacteur *m*; **j. propulsion,** propulsion par réaction; **j. lag,** décalage horaire; **j. set,** monde des play-boys. **jet-pro'pelled** *a* (avion) à réaction.

jetsam ['dʒetsəm] *n* épaves rejetées sur la côte.

jettison ['dʒetisn] *vtr* jeter à la mer, se délester de (la cargaison); *Av:* larguer (des bombes); *Fig:* abandonner (un espoir).

jetty ['dʒeti] *n* (*pl* **jetties**) jetée *f*, digue *f*; **(landing) j.,** embarcadère *m.*

Jew [dʒuː] *n* juif *m.* '**Jewess** *nf* juive. '**Jewish** *a* juif.

jewel ['dʒuːəl] *n* 1. (*a*) bijou *m*, joyau *m*; **j. case,** coffret à bijoux (*b*) *pl* pierres précieuses 2. (*in watch*) rubis *m.* '**jewelled,** *NAm: also* '**jeweled** *a* 1. orné de bijoux 2. (*of watch*) monté sur rubis. '**jeweller,** *NAm: also* '**jeweler** *n* bijoutier *m*, joaillier *m*; **j.'s (shop),** bijouterie *f.* '**jewel(le)ry** *n* bijouterie, joaillerie *f*; **costume j.,** bijoux de fantaisie.

jib¹ [dʒib] *n Nau:* foc *m*; *MecE:* flèche *f* (de grue).

jib² *vi* (**jibbed**) (*of horse, pers*) regimber; **to j. at doing sth.,** rechigner à faire qch.

jiffy ['dʒifi] *n* F: **in a j.,** en un instant, en moins de rien; **I won't be a j.,** j'arrive.

jig [dʒig] *n* 1. *Danc:* gigue *f* 2. *MecE:* calibre *m*, gabarit *m.* '**jigsaw (puzzle)** *n* puzzle *m.*

jiggle ['dʒigl] *vtr & vi* secouer (qch) légèrement.

jilt [dʒilt] *vtr* F: laisser tomber (un amant).

jingle ['dʒiŋgl] I. *n* 1. tintement *m* (de clochettes); cliquetis *m* (de clefs) 2. (*advertising*) **j.,** ritournelle *f* publicitaire. II. *v* 1. *vi* (*of bells*) tinter; (*of keys*) cliqueter 2. *vtr* faire tinter, faire cliqueter. '**jingling** *n* = **jingle** I. 1.

jingoism ['dʒiŋgouizm] *n* chauvinisme *m.* **jingo'istic** *a* chauvin(iste).

jinx [dʒiŋks] *n* F: porte-malheur *m inv.*

jitters ['dʒitəz] *n* F: **to have the j.,** avoir la frousse. '**jittery** *a* F: **to be j.,** avoir la frousse.

jive [dʒaiv] I. *n* rock (and roll) *m.* II. *vi* danser le rock (and roll).

Jnr [dʒuːniər] *abbr Junior,* jeune.

job [dʒɔb] *n* 1. (*a*) tâche *f*, travail *m*, besogne *f*; **to do a j.,** exécuter un travail; **odd jobs,** petits travaux; **to do odd jobs,** bricoler; F: **odd j. man,** homme à tout faire; F: **to make a good j. of sth,** réussir qch, F: faire du bon boulot; **to make a bad j. of sth,** bousiller qch; **that's a good j.!** à la bonne heure! **it's a good j. that,** il est fort heureux que + *sub*; **to give sth up as a bad j.,** y renoncer; F: **that's a lovely j.,** c'est du beau travail; **that's just the j.,** cela fait juste l'affaire (*b*) tâche difficile; corvée *f*; **to have a j. to do sth, doing sth,** avoir du mal à faire qch 2. emploi *m*; poste *m*; **to look for a j.,** chercher du travail, un emploi; **he knows his j.,** il connaît son affaire; F: **jobs for the boys,** distribution des planques; **to be out of a j.,** être en chômage, chômer; **j. centre,** = Agence nationale pour l'emploi; **j. description,** description de la fonction; **j. lot,** (lot *m* d')articles dépareillés 3. intrigue *f*, *esp* cambriolage *m.* '**jobber** *n StExch:* marchand *m* de titres. '**jobbing** *a* (ouvrier) à la tâche; (jardinier) à la journée. '**jobless** 1. *a* sans travail 2. *npl* **the j.,** les chômeurs *mpl.*

jockey ['dʒɔki] I. *n* jockey *m.* II. *vtr & i* entraîner, amener (qn) (**into doing,** à faire); manœuvrer; **to j. for position,** intriguer pour se placer avantageusement.

jockstrap ['dʒɔkstræp] *n Cl:* suspensoir *m.*

jocular ['dʒɔkjulər] *a* jovial; enjoué.

jodhpurs ['dʒɔdpəz] *npl Cl:* culotte *f* de cheval.

jog [dʒɔg] I. *n* 1. (*a*) coup *m* (de coude) (*b*) secousse *f*, cahot *m* (d'une voiture) 2. (*a*) **j. (trot),** petit trot (*b*) *Sp:* **to go for a j.,** faire du jogging. II. *v* (**jogged**) 1. *vtr* (*a*) pousser (le coude à qn) (*b*) rafraîchir (la mémoire à qn) (*c*) (*of vehicle*) secouer (les passagers) 2. *vi* (*a*) **to j. along,** (i) aller au petit trot (ii) (*of vehicle*) avancer par saccades (iii) *Fig:* faire son petit bonhomme de chemin; aller cahin-caha; **we're jogging along,** les choses vont leur train (*b*) *Sp:* **to j., go jogging,** faire du jogging. '**jogger** *n Sp:* joggeur, -euse. '**jogging** *n Sp:* jogging *m.*

joggle ['dʒɔgl] *vtr & vi* F: ballotter.

join [dʒɔin] I. *n* joint *m*, jointure *f*; ligne *f* de jonction. II. *v* 1. *vtr* (*a*) **to j. (together, up),** joindre, unir, réunir; relier (une chose à une autre); raccorder (des tuyaux); **to j. forces with s.o.,** se joindre à qn; **to j. hands with s.o.,** prendre qn par la main (*b*) **to j. (on),** ajouter (*c*) se joindre, s'unir, à (qn); rejoindre (qn); **will you j. us?** voulez-vous vous joindre à nous? voulez-vous être des nôtres? **to go and j. s.o.,** aller retrouver qn; **to j. s.o. in a drink,** prendre un verre avec qn (*d*) *Mil:* rejoindre (son unité, son navire) (*e*) entrer dans (un club); adhérer, s'affilier, à (un parti); devenir membre d'(une société); s'engager dans (l'armée) (*f*) se joindre, s'unir, à (qch); **the path joins the road,** le sentier rejoint la route 2. *vi* **to j. (together),** se (re)joindre, s'unir (**with,** à); (*of lines*) se rencontrer. '**joiner** *n* menuisier *m.* '**joinery** *n* menuiserie *f.* '**join 'in** 1. *vtr & i* **to j. in (with),** prendre part à (une querelle); participer, s'associer, à (un projet); joindre sa voix à (une protestation) 2. *vi* se mettre à la partie. **joint I.** *n* 1. joint, jointure; *Carp:* assemblage *m* 2. *Anat:* articulation *f*; jointure; **out of j.,** (i) (bras) disloqué, déboîté (ii) *Fig:* (système) détraqué; **to put s.o.'s nose out of j.,** froisser, dépiter, qn 3. *Cu:* rôti *m* (de viande) 4. *P:* (a) endroit *m*; boîte *f* (louche); **gambling j.,** tripot *m* (b) (*drug*) joint. **II.** *vtr* 1. joindre, assembler (des pièces de bois) 2. découper (un poulet). **III.** *a* (travail) commun, combiné, collectif; (commission) mixte; *Bank:* (compte) conjoint; *Fin:* **j. stock,** capital social; **j. author,** coauteur *m*; **j. heir,** cohéritier, -ière; **j. owner,** copropriétaire *mf*; **j. ownership,** copropriété *f*; **j. tenant,** colocataire *mf*. **'jointed** *a* articulé. **'jointly** *adv* ensemble, conjointement; **to manage a business j.,** cogérer une affaire. **'join 'up** *vi* s'engager (dans l'armée).

joist [dʒɔist] *n Const:* solive *f*, poutre *f*.

joke [dʒouk] **I.** *n* plaisanterie *f*; *F:* blague *f*; **for a j.,** pour rire; **practical j.,** tour *m*; farce *f*; **to play a j. on s.o.,** jouer un tour à qn; **he can't take a j.,** il ne comprend pas la plaisanterie. **II.** *vi* plaisanter (**about,** sur); **you must be joking!** vous voulez rire! sans blague! **'joker** *n* 1. farceur, -euse; *F:* blagueur, -euse 2. *Cards:* joker *m*. **'joking** 1. *a* (ton) de plaisanterie 2. *n* plaisanterie(s) *f(pl)*. **'jokingly** *adv* en plaisantant; pour rire.

jolly [dʒɔli] **I.** 1. *a* (-ier, -iest) joyeux, gai; agréable 2. *adv F:* rudement, drôlement; **j. quickly,** bien vite. **II.** *vtr* **to j. s.o. along,** encourager qn par des plaisanteries. **jollifi'cation** *n F:* réunion joyeuse. **'jollity** *n* gaieté *f*.

jolt [dʒoult] **I.** *n* secousse *f*; (*of vehicle*) cahot *m* **II.** *vtr & i* cahoter; *vi* **j. along,** avancer en cahotant.

Jordan [dʒɔːdən] *Prn Geog:* 1. (*country*) Jordanie *f* 2. (*river*) Jourdain *m*.

joss stick [dʒɔsstik] *n* bâton *m* d'encens.

jostle [dʒɔsl] 1. *vi* jouer des coudes (dans une foule); **to j. against s.o.,** bousculer qn 2. *vtr* bousculer, coudoyer (qn).

jot [dʒɔt] **I.** *n* **not a j.,** pas un iota. **II.** *vtr* (**jotted**) **to j. sth down,** noter, prendre note de, qch. **'jotter** *n* bloc-notes *m*. **'jottings** *npl* notes *fpl*.

journal [dʒɔːnl] *n* journal *m*, -aux; revue (savante); *Book-k:* (livre) journal; *Nau:* journal de bord; *Pol:* compte rendu. **journa'lese** *n F:* style *m* journalistique. **'journalism** *n* journalisme *m*. **'journalist** *n* journaliste *mf*. **journa'listic** *a* journalistique.

journey [dʒɔːni] *n* voyage *m*; trajet *m*; **return j.,** (voyage de) retour *m*; **j. there and back,** voyage aller (et) retour; **train j.,** voyage en chemin de fer; **on a j.,** en voyage.

jovial [dʒouvjəl] *a* jovial. **jovi'ality** *n* jovialité *f*. **'jovially** *adv* jovialement.

jowl [dʒaul] *n* (a) mâchoire *f* (b) joue *f*.

joy [dʒɔi] *n* joie *f*, allégresse *f*. **'joyful** *a* joyeux. **'joyfully** *adv* joyeusement. **'joyride** *n* balade *f* en voiture (faite à l'insu du propriétaire). **'joystick** *n Av:* manche *m* à balai.

JP *abbr* Justice of the Peace.

Jr [dʒuːniər] *abbr* Junior, jeune.

jubilant [dʒuːbilənt] *a* joyeux; (visage) épanoui. **jubi'lation** *n* (a) joie *f*; jubilation *f* (b) réjouissance(s) *f(pl)*.

jubilee [dʒuːbiliː] *n* jubilé *m*; **golden j.,** fête *f* du cinquantième anniversaire (d'un couronnement).

judder [dʒʌdər] 1. *n* trépidation (des freins) 2. *vi* (*of brakes*) trépider.

judge [dʒʌdʒ] **I.** *n* 1. juge *m* 2. connaisseur, -euse; **to be a good j. of wine,** s'y connaître en vin. **II.** *vtr & i* juger; apprécier, estimer (une distance); **to j. it necessary to do sth,** juger nécessaire de faire qch; **j. for yourself,** jugez(-en) par vous-même; **judging by,** à en juger par. **'judg(e)ment** *n* 1. (a) jugement *m* (b) décision *f* judiciaire; arrêt *m*, sentence *f* 2. opinion *f*, avis *m* 3. bon sens; discernement *m*; **to have good j.,** avoir du jugement.

judicial [dʒuːdiʃl] *a* juridique; (enquête) judiciaire; (esprit) critique. **ju'diciary** *n* magistrature *f*. **ju'dicious** *a* judicieux. **ju'diciously** *adv* judicieusement.

judo [dʒuːdou] *n Sp:* judo *m*.

jug [dʒʌg] *n* 1. cruche *f*; (*for milk*) pot *m*; (*small*) cruchon *m*; (*big*) broc *m* 2. *P:* prison *f*, taule *f*. **jugged** *a Cu:* **j. hare,** civet *m* de lièvre.

juggernaut [dʒʌgənɔːt] *n Veh:* mastodonte *m*.

juggle [dʒʌgl] *vtr & i* jongler (**sth, with sth,** avec qch). **'juggler** *n* (a) jongleur, -euse (b) prestidigitateur, -trice. **'juggling** *n* jonglerie *f*.

jugular [dʒʌgjulər] *a Anat:* jugulaire.

juice [dʒuːs] *n* jus *m* (de viande, de fruit); suc *m* (gastrique); **to stew in one's own j.,** mijoter dans son (propre) jus. **'juicer** *n NAm: DomEc:* centrifugeuse *f*. **'juiciness** *n* nature juteuse. **'juicy** *a* (-ier, -iest) juteux; plein de jus; (récit) savoureux.

jukebox, -es [dʒuːkbɔks, -iz] *n* juke-box *m*.

July [dʒu(ː)lai] *n* juillet *m*; **in J.,** en juillet; (**on) the seventh of J., (on) J. the seventh,** le sept juillet.

jumble [dʒʌmbl] **I.** *n* 1. fouillis *m*; méli-mélo *m* 2. (objets *mpl* de) rebut *m*; **j. sale** (*NAm:* = **rummage sale**), vente de charité d'objets usagés. **II.** *vtr* **to j.** (**up**), brouiller; mettre pêle-mêle.

jumbo [dʒʌmbou] *n* 1. *F:* éléphant *m* 2. *Av:* **j.** (**jet**), (avion) gros porteur; jumbo-jet *m*.

jump [dʒʌmp] **I.** *n* 1. saut *m*, bond *m*; brusque hausse *f* (des prix); *Sp:* **high, long, j.,** saut en hauteur, en longueur; *F:* **he's for the high j.!** qu'est-ce qu'il va prendre! *Av: F:* **j. jet,** avion *m* à décollage et atterrissage verticaux; *Aut:* **j. lead(s)** (*NAm:* = **jumper**), câble *m* de démarrage 2. sursaut *m* 3. *Equit:* obstacle *m*. **II.** *v* 1. *vi* (a) sauter; bondir; (*of prices*) monter; **to j. off a wall,** sauter (à bas) d'un mur; **to j. up and down,** sautiller; **to j. at an offer,** sauter sur une offre; **to j. to a conclusion,** arriver prématurément à une conclusion; *F:* **j. to it!** grouillez-vous! (b) sursauter 2. *vtr* sauter; franchir (une haie); (*of train*) **to j. the rails,** dérailler; **to j. the queue,** passer avant son tour; resquiller; *Aut:* **to j. the lights,** brûler le feu (rouge); **to j. ship,** déserter le navire; **to j. the gun,** (i) *Sp:* voler le départ (ii) faire qch prématurément. **'jump a'bout** *vi* sautiller. **'jump a'cross** *vtr* franchir (qch) d'un bond. **'jump 'down** *vi* sauter à terre. **'jump 'up** *a* parvenu. **'jumper** *n* 1. *Cl:* pull(over) *m*, tricot *m* (b) *NAm:* (i) robe-chasuble *f* (ii) barboteuse *f* (pour enfant) 2. *NAm: Aut:* = **jump leads(s)**. **'jump 'in** *vi* 1. entrer d'un bond; (*into vehicle*) **j. in!** montez vite! 2. se jeter à l'eau. **jumping-'off place** *n* point *m* de départ. 'jump 'out *vi* sortir d'un bond; to j. out of bed, sauter (à bas) du lit; I nearly jumped out of my skin, cela m'a fait sursauter. 'jump 'up *vi* se (re)lever d'un saut. 'jumpy *a* agité, nerveux.

junction ['dʒʌŋkʃn] *n* (*a*) (point *m* de) jonction *f*; confluent *m* (de rivières); raccordement *m* (de tuyaux); embranchement *m*, bifurcation *f* (de routes, de voies de chemin de fer); (road) j., carrefour *m* (*b*) Rail: gare *f* de jonction.

juncture ['dʒʌŋktʃər] *n* conjoncture *f* (de circonstances); at this j., à ce moment; dans les circonstances actuelles.

June [dʒuːn] *n* juin *m*; in J., en juin; (on) the seventh of J., (on) J. the seventh, le sept juin.

jungle ['dʒʌŋgl] *n* jungle *f*.

junior ['dʒuːnjər] *a* & *n* 1. (*in age*) cadet, -ette; plus jeune; Martin J., Martin (i) le jeune, junior (ii) fils; Sch: the juniors, les petits (élèves); Sp: j. event, épreuve des cadets 2. (*in rank*) moins ancien; subalterne (*m*).

juniper ['dʒuːnipər] *n* Bot: (tree) genévrier *m*; (tree and berry) genièvre *m*.

junk¹ [dʒʌŋk] *n* Nau: jonque *f*.

junk² 1. *n* (chose(s) *f* (*pl*) de) rebut *m*; bric-à-brac *m* *inv*; camelote *f*; j. heap, dépotoir *m*; tas de ferraille; j. shop, magasin de brocanteur 2. *vtr* F: mettre au rebut, balancer. 'junkie *n* F: drogué, -ée, camé, -ée.

junket ['dʒʌŋkit] *n* 1. Cu: lait caillé 2. F: esp NAm: voyage officiel aux frais de la princesse. 'junketing *n* F: partie *f* de plaisir; bombe *f*.

junta ['dʒʌntə] *n* Pol: junte *f*.

jurisdiction [dʒuːris'dikʃn] *n* juridiction *f*; within our j., de notre compétence. juris'prudence *n* jurisprudence *f*.

jury ['dʒuːri] *n* jury *m*; jurés *mpl*; to be, serve, on the j., être du jury. 'juror, 'juryman, -men, -woman, -women *n* juré, -ée; membre *m* du jury.

just [dʒʌst] I. *a* juste; it's only j., ce n'est que justice; as was only j., comme de juste. II. *adv* 1. (*a*) juste, justement, au juste; j. here, juste ici; j. by the door, tout près de la porte; not j. yet, pas encore; j. how many are there? combien y en a-t-il au juste? j. over £50, un peu plus de £50; that's j. it, (i) c'est bien cela (ii) justement! j. so! c'est bien cela! parfaitement!

he did it j. for a joke, il l'a fait simplement histoire de rire (*b*) j. as well as him, tout aussi bien que lui; j. as you please! comme vous voudrez! leave my things j. as they are, laissez mes affaires telles quelles; j. as he was starting out, au moment où il partait; I'd j. as soon have this one, j'aimerais tout autant celui-ci; j. now, (i) actuellement; en ce moment (ii) pour l'instant; pour le moment (iii) tout à l'heure; j. you wait! tu verras! 2. he has j. written to you, il vient de vous écrire; he has j. come, il ne fait que d'arriver; (*of book*) j. out, vient de paraître 3. (I'm) j. coming! j'arrive! j. about, presque; he's j. going out, j. about to go out, il est sur le point de sortir 4. he (only) j. managed to do it, c'est tout juste s'il est arrivé à le faire; they j. missed the train, ils ont manqué le train de très peu; I (only) j. managed to avoid it, je l'ai évité de justesse; I was only j. saved from drowning, j'ai failli me noyer; I've only j. got enough, j'en ai tout juste assez; you're j. in time, vous arrivez juste à temps 5. (*a*) seulement; j. once, rien qu'une fois; j. one, un seul; j. a little bit, un tout petit peu (*b*) j. listen! écoutez donc! j. look at that! regarde-moi ça! 'justice *n* 1. justice *f*; to do s.o. j., faire justice à qn; the photo didn't do him j., la photo ne l'avantageait pas; to do oneself j., se faire valoir; to do j. to a meal, faire honneur à un repas; to bring s.o. to j., traduire qn en justice 2. magistrat *m*; juge *m*; j. of the peace = juge de paix. 'justly *adv* avec justice; avec juste raison; (célèbre) à juste titre. 'justness *n* 1. justice (d'une cause) 2. justesse *f* (d'une remarque).

justify ['dʒʌstifai] *vtr* (justified) justifier; légitimer (une action); prouver le bien-fondé de (ses mots). justi'fiable *a* justifiable. 'justifiably *adv* légitimement. justifi'cation *n* justification *f*. 'justified *a* justifié; fully j. decision, décision bien fondée; to be j. (in doing sth), avoir raison (de faire qch).

jut [dʒʌt] *vi* (jutted) to j. (out), être en saillie, faire saillie; to j. out over sth, surplomber qch.

jute [dʒuːt] *n* Bot: Tex: jute *m*.

juvenile ['dʒuːvənail] *a* juvénile; (livres) pour enfants; j. delinquency, délinquance *f* juvénile; j. delinquent, jeune délinquant, -ante.

juxtaposition [dʒʌkstəpə'ziʃn] *n* juxtaposition *f*; to be in j., se juxtaposer.

K

K, k [kei] *n* (la lettre) K, k *m*.
kaftan [ˈkæftæn] *n Cl:* kaftan *m*.
kale [keil] *n* (curly) k., chou frisé.
kaleidoscope [kəˈlaidəskoup] *n* kaléidoscope *m*.
kangaroo [kæŋgəˈruː] *n Z:* kangourou *m*.
kaolin [ˈkeiəlin] *n* kaolin *m*.
kapok [ˈkeipɔk] *n* kapok *m*.
kaput [kəˈput] *a F:* fichu, foutu.
karate [kəˈrɑːti] *n Sp:* karaté *m*.
kayak [ˈkaiæk] *n* kayak *m*.
kebab [kiˈbæb] *n Cu:* brochette *f*.
kedgeree [kedʒəˈriː] *n Cu:* plat *m* de riz accommodé avec du beurre, des œufs durs et du poisson.
keel [kiːl] *n Nau:* quille *f*; **on an even k.**, (i) (*of ship*) sans différence de tirant d'eau (ii) *Fig:* stable; calme. **'keel 'over** *vi* (*of ship*) chavirer; (*of pers*) tomber, *esp* s'évanouir.
keen [kiːn] *a* 1. (couteau) affilé, aiguisé; **k. edge**, fil tranchant 2. (vent, froid) vif, perçant, piquant; (son, chagrin) aigu; (appétit) rude 3. (*a*) ardent, zélé; **k. golfer**, enragé *m* de golf; *F:* **to be k. on sth**, être enthousiaste de, emballé pour, qch; **to be k. on s.o.**, avoir le béguin pour qn; **he isn't k. on it**, il n'y tient pas beaucoup; **he's k. on sport**, le sport le passionne (*b*) **k. competition**, concurrence acharnée 5. (œil) perçant, vif; **to have a k. ear**, avoir l'ouïe fine 6. (esprit) fin, pénétrant. **'keenly** *adv* âprement, vivement. **'keenness** *n* 1. finesse *f*, acuité *f* (d'un outil) 2. âpreté *f* (du froid) 3. ardeur *f*, zèle *m* 4. acuité (de la vision).
keep [kiːp] I. *n* 1. donjon *m* 2. (frais *mpl* de) subsistance *f*; nourriture *f*; **to earn one's k.**, gagner de quoi vivre; subvenir à ses (propres) besoins; **£20 a week and one's k.**, £20 par semaine logé et nourri 3. *F:* **for keeps**, pour de bon. II. *v* (**kept**) 1. *vtr* (*a*) observer, suivre (une règle); tenir, remplir (une promesse); rester fidèle à (un vœu); respecter (un traité); ne pas manquer à (un rendez-vous) (*b*) célébrer (une fête); fêter (un anniversaire); observer (le carême) (*c*) tenir (un journal, des comptes, un hôtel); avoir (un magasin); élever (des animaux); **badly kept road**, route mal entretenue; (*in shop*) **we don't k. cigars**, nous ne vendons pas de cigares (*d*) subvenir aux besoins de (qn); **he doesn't earn enough to k. himself**, il ne gagne pas de quoi vivre; **he has his parents to k.**, il a ses parents à sa charge (*e*) garder, conserver; réserver (une place) (**for s.o.**, à qn); maintenir (l'ordre); tenir (propre, chaud, en réserve); **to k. sth to oneself**, garder qch pour soi; **to k. sth from s.o.**, cacher qch à qn; **to k. s.o. waiting**, faire attendre qn; **to k. s.o. from doing sth**, empêcher qn de faire qch; **they k. themselves to themselves**, ils font bande à part; **to k. one's figure**, garder sa ligne; **where do you k. the glasses?** où mettez-vous les verres? (*f*) (*detain*) (re)tenir (qn) (en prison); garder (qn) (à la maison); **what's keeping you?** qu'est-ce qui vous retient? 2. *vi* (*a*) rester, se tenir; **to k. quiet**, rester tranquille; **to k.**

smiling, garder le sourire; **to k. left**, tenir la gauche; *Aut: etc:* serrer à gauche; **how are you keeping?** comment allez-vous? (*b*) continuer; **to k. (on) doing sth**, continuer à, de, ne pas cesser de, s'obstiner à, faire qch; **k. (on) looking!** cherchez toujours! **to k. straight on**, continuer tout droit; *F:* **to k. (on) at s.o.**, être toujours sur le dos de qn; **to k. (hard) at it**, (continuer à) travailler sans relâche (*c*) (*of food*) se garder, se conserver. **'keep a'way** 1. *vtr* éloigner 2. *vi* ne pas s'approcher (**from**, de). **'keep 'back** 1. *vtr* (*a*) arrêter (l'ennemi); retenir (l'argent) (*b*) ne pas dire, dissimuler (la vérité) 2. *vi* ne pas s'approcher; **k. back!** n'avancez pas! **'keep 'down** 1. *vtr* (*a*) empêcher de monter; **she kept her head down**, elle se tenait la tête baissée (*b*) opprimer (un peuple) (*c*) ne pas vomir (de la nourriture) 2. *vi* se tapir. **'keeper** *n* gardien, -ienne; surveillant, -ante; conservateur, -trice (de musée); (*gamekeeper*) garde-chasse *m*. **keep-'fit (class)** *n* (cours *m* de) gymnastique *f* d'entretien. **'keep 'in**. *vtr* (*a*) empêcher de sortir; *Sch:* mettre (un élève) en retenue (*b*) entretenir (un feu) (*c*) **to k. one's hand in**, se faire la main 2. *vi* **to k. in with s.o.**, rester en bons termes avec qn; cultiver qn. **'keeping** *n* 1. observation *f* (d'une règle); célébration *f* (d'une fête) 2. **to be in s.o.'s (safe) k.**, être sous la garde de qn 3. **in k. with**, en accord avec; **out of k. with**, en désaccord avec. **'keep 'off** 1. *vtr* empêcher de toucher; **k. your hands off!** n'y touchez pas! *PN:* **k. off the grass**, défense de marcher sur le gazon 2. *vi* se tenir éloigné; **if the rain keeps off**, s'il ne pleut pas. **'keep 'on** 1. *vtr* (*a*) garder (son chapeau); maintenir (le chauffage) (*b*) ne pas congédier (un employé) 2. *vi* (*a*) continuer (*b*) parler sans cesse (**about**, de). **'keep 'out** 1. *vtr* empêcher d'entrer 2. *vi* ne pas entrer; **to k. out of danger**, rester à l'abri du danger; **k. out of this!** mêlez-vous de ce qui vous regarde! *PN:* **k. out**, défense d'entrer. **'keepsake** *n* souvenir *m*. **'keep to** 1. *vtr* obliger (qn) (à tenir sa promesse) 2. *vi* s'en tenir à (une résolution); ne pas s'éloigner (du sujet); **to k. to the left**, tenir la gauche. **'keep 'together** 1. *vi* rester ensemble 2. *vtr* garder ensemble. **'keep 'up** 1. *vtr* (*a*) entretenir (une route); maintenir (une maison) (en bon état) (*b*) conserver (l'allure); **k. it up!** allez toujours! continuez! (*c*) soutenir (l'intérêt); sauver (les apparences) (*d*) empêcher (qn) de se coucher 2. *vi* marcher de front (**with**, avec); marcher aussi vite (**with**, que); **to k. up with the Joneses**, rivaliser avec ses voisins.
keg [keg] *n* barillet *m*, tonnelet *m* (de bière); caque *f* (de harengs).
kelp [kelp] *n* varech *m*.
ken [ken] *n* **to be beyond s.o.'s k.**, dépasser la compétence de qn.
kennel [ˈkenl] *n* (*a*) niche *f* (de chien de garde) (*b*) (*also pl*) chenil *m*.

Kenya ['kenjə, 'kiːnjə] *Prn Geog:* Kenya *m.*
kept [kept] *see* **keep II.**
kerb [kəːb] *n* (*NAm:* = **curb**) bord *m*, bordure *f*, trottoir; **to hit the k.,** heurter le trottoir.
kernel ['kəːnl] *n* amande *f* (de noyau).
kerosene ['kerəsiːn] *n* kérosène *m.*
kestrel ['kestrəl] *n Orn:* (faucon *m*) crécerelle (*f*).
ketchup ['ketʃəp] *n* ketchup *m.*
kettle ['ketl] *n* bouilloire *f.*
key [kiː] *n* 1. (*a*) clef *f*, clé *f*; remontoir *m* (de pendule); **k. man,** pilier *m* (d'un établissement); **k. position, industry,** poste·clef, industrie clef; **k. word,** mot-clé *m* (*b*) clef (d'une énigme); *Sch:* corrigé *m*; solutions *fpl* (de problèmes) 2. *Mus:* ton (majeur, mineur); **k. of C.,** ton d'ut; **in a high k.,** sur un ton haut; **k. signature,** armature *f* (de la clef) 3. touche *f* (de piano, de machine). **'keyboard** *n* clavier *m* (de piano, de machine). **keyed up** *a* tendu (**about,** dans l'attente de). **'keyhole** *n* trou *m* de (la) serrure. **'keynote** *n* (*a*) *Mus:* tonique *f* (*b*) note dominante (d'un discours). **'keyring** *n* porte-clefs *m inv.* **'keystone** *n* clef *f* de voûte.
kg *abbr* kilogram(me).
khaki ['kaːki] *a & n* kaki (*m*) *inv.*
kHz *abbr* kilohertz.
kibbutz [ki'buts] *n* (*pl* **kibbutzim**) kibboutz *m.*
kick [kik] I. *n* 1. coup *m* de pied; (*of horse*) ruade *f*; *F:* **drink with a k. in it,** boisson qui a du montant, qui tape; **to get a k. out of (doing) sth,** prendre plaisir à (faire) qch; **for kicks,** pour s'amuser 2. (*of gun*) recul *m.* II. *v* 1. *vi* (*a*) donner des coups de pied; (*of horse*) ruer (*b*) (*of gun*) reculer 2. *vtr* donner un coup de pied à; (*of horse*) décocher un coup de sabot à; **I could have kicked myself,** je me serais donné des gifles. **'kick a'bout, a'round** 1. *vtr* (*a*) donner des coups de pied à (un ballon) (*b*) *F:* maltraiter 2. *vi F:* traîner. **'kick a'gainst, 'at** *vtr* regimber contre. **'kick a'way** *vtr* repousser du pied. **'kick-back** *n F:* (*a*) réaction violente (*b*) ristourne *f*, dessous-de-table *m.* **'kick 'in** *vtr* enfoncer (une porte) à coups de pied. **'kick 'off** *vtr* enlever d'un coup de pied 2. *vi* (*a*) *Fb:* donner le coup d'envoi (*b*) *F:* démarrer. **'kick-off** *n* coup d'envoi. **'kick 'out** 1. *vtr* mettre (qn) à la porte 2. *vi* lancer (i) des coups de pied (ii) (*of horse*) des ruades (**at,** à). **'kick-start(er)** *n* démarreur *m* au pied; kick *m.* **'kick 'up** *vtr F:* **to k. up a row,** faire du tapage; **to k. up a fuss,** faire des histoires.
kid [kid] I. *n* 1. *Z:* chevreau *m*, *f* chevrette; **k. gloves,** gants (en peau) de chevreau; **to handle s.o. with k. gloves,** ménager qn 2. *F:* gosse *mf*; **my k. brother,** mon petit frère. II. *vtr & i* (**kidded**) *F:* **to k. (on),** faire marcher (qn); blaguer; **to k. s.o. (on) that,** faire croire à qn que; **I was kidding,** je l'ai dit par plaisanterie; **no kidding!** sans blague! **to k. oneself,** se faire des illusions. **'kiddie, -y** *n F:* gosse.
kidnap ['kidnæp] *vtr* (**kidnapped**) enlever (de vive force); kidnapper. **'kidnapper** *n* kidnappeur, -euse; ravisseur, -euse. **'kidnapping** *n* enlèvement *m*; kidnapping *m*; *Jur:* rapt *m.*
kidney ['kidni] *n* 1. *Anat:* rein *m*; **k. machine,** rein artificiel 2. *Cu:* rognon *m*; **k. bean,** haricot (i) nain (ii) rouge.
kill [kil] *n* (*a*) mise *f* à mort (d'un animal); *Fig:* **to**

be in at the k., participer au dénouement (*b*) gibier tué; (*of animal*) proie *f.* II. *vtr* 1. tuer; abattre (un animal); **to k. two birds with one stone,** faire d'une pierre deux coups; *F:* **dressed to k.,** pomponné; *F:* **to k. oneself (laughing),** crever de rire; *F:* **my feet are killing me,** j'ai atrocement mal aux pieds 2. tuer (le temps, une odeur, une couleur); détruire (des chances); arrêter (un moteur); amortir (le son). **'killer** *n* tueur, -euse; meurtrier, -ière; **k. disease,** maladie mortelle; **k. whale,** épaulard *m.* **'killing** I. *a* 1. (travail) tuant, assommant; (coup) meurtrier, fatal 2. *F:* tordant. II. *n* 1. tuerie *f*, massacre *m*; abattage *m* (d'animaux); *F:* **to make a k.,** faire un bénéfice énorme 2. meurtre *m.* **'killjoy** *n* rabat-joie *m inv.* **'kill 'off** *vtr* exterminer.
kiln [kiln] *n* four *m* (à céramique).
kilo ['kiːlou] *n* kilo *m.* **kilogram(me)** *n* kilogramme *m.* **'kilohertz** *n* kilohertz *m.* **kilometre,** *NAm:* **kilometer** ['kiləmiːtər, ki'lɔmitər] *n* kilomètre *m.* **'kilovolt** *n* kilovolt *m.* **'kilowatt** *n* kilowatt *m.*
kilt [kilt] *n* kilt *m.* **'kilted** *a* portant le kilt.
kilter ['kiltər] *n NAm: F:* **out of k.,** détraqué.
kin [kin] *n* parents *mpl*; **next of k.,** parent le plus proche; famille *f.*
kind¹ [kaind] *n* 1. genre *m*, espèce *f*; sorte *f*; **what k. is it?** de quelle sorte est-ce? **what k. of man is he?** quel genre d'homme est-ce? **nothing of the k.,** rien de la sorte; **sth of the k.,** qch de ce genre; **the only one of its k.,** unique en son genre; *F:* **I k. of expected it,** je m'en doutais presque; *F:* **he looks k. of stupid,** il a l'air plutôt bête 2. **payment in k.,** paiement en nature.
kind² *a* gentil, aimable (avec qn); bon (pour, envers); bienveillant; **it's very k. of you,** c'est bien aimable de votre part, à vous; **would you be so k. as to do it?** auriez-vous la gentillesse de le faire? **'kind-hearted** *a* bon; qui a bon cœur. **'kindliness** *n* bonté *f*, bienveillance *f.* **'kindly** 1. *a* bon, bienveillant 2. *adv* avec bonté; (**would you**) **k. put it back,** voulez-vous avoir la bonté de le remettre; *Com:* **k. remit by cheque,** prière de nous couvrir par chèque; **not to take k. to sth.,** ne pas aimer qch. **'kindness** *n* 1. gentillesse, bonté (pour); amabilité *f* 2. **to do s.o. a k.,** rendre service *m* à qn.
kindergarten ['kindəgaːtn] *n* jardin *m* d'enfants; école maternelle.
kindle ['kindl] 1. *vtr* allumer 2. *vi* s'allumer. **'kindling** *n* petit bois.
kindred ['kindrəd] 1. *n* parents *mpl* 2. *a* (sujet) connexe; **k. spirits,** âmes sœurs.
kinetic [ki'netik] *a Ph:* (énergie) cinétique.
king [kiŋ] *n* 1. (*a*) roi *m*; **K. John,** le roi Jean (*b*) magnat (industriel) 2. (*at draughts*) dame *f.* **'king-cup** *n Bot:* bouton *m* d'or. **'kingdom** *n* 1. royaume *m* 2. règne (animal); *F:* **k. come,** paradis *m*, éternité *f.* **'kingfisher** *n* martin-pêcheur *m.* **'king-pin** *n* cheville ouvrière. **'king-size(d)** *a Com:* (format) géant.
kink [kiŋk] *n* 1. (en)tortillement *m* (dans une corde) 2. aberration *f* (de l'esprit). **'kinky** *a* 1. (*of hair*) crépu 2. *F:* bizarre; (sexuellement) pervers.
kiosk ['kiːɔsk] *n* kiosque *m*; **telephone k.,** cabine *f* téléphonique.

kipper ['kipər] *n* hareng salé et fumé; kipper *m*.
kirk [kə:k] *n Scot:* église *f*.
kiss [kis] **I.** *n* (*pl* **kisses**) baiser *m; Med:* **k. of life**, bouche-à-bouche *m*. **II.** *vtr* embrasser (qn); donner un baiser à (qn); **to k. (one another)**, s'embrasser.
kit [kit] *n* **1.** effets *mpl*, bagages *mpl* (de voyageur); affaires *fpl* **2.** matériel *m*, équipement *m*; trousse *f* (d'outils); **repair k.**, nécessaire *m* de réparation; **model k.**, boîte *f* de construction; **first-aid k.**, trousse de premiers secours. **'kitbag** *n* sac *m* (de soldat). **'kit 'out, 'up** *vtr* (**kitted**) équiper.
kitchen ['kitʃin] *n* cuisine *f*; **k. table**, table de cuisine; **k. unit**, bloc-cuisine *m*; **k. garden**, (jardin) potager *m*. **kitche'nette** *n* cuisinette *f*. **'kitchenware** *n* (i) vaisselle *f* (ii) ustensiles *mpl*, batterie *f*, de cuisine.
kite [kait] *n* **1.** *Orn:* milan *m* **2.** cerf-volant *m*.
kitsch [kitʃ] *n* kitsch; art pompier.
kitten ['kitn] *n* chaton *m*; petit(e) chat(te); *F:* **to have kittens**, être dans tous ses états. **'kittenish** *a* espiègle. **'kitty** *n F:* **1.** chaton *m* **2.** cagnotte *f*, pot *m*, caisse *f*.
kiwi ['ki:wi:] *n Orn:* kiwi *m*; aptéryx *m*.
kleptomania [kleptə'meiniə] *n* kleptomanie *f*. **klepto'maniac** *a & n* kleptomane (*mf*).
km *abbr* kilomètre.
knack [næk] *n* tour *m* de main; *F:* truc *m*; **to have a k. for, the k. of, doing sth**, avoir le talent de faire qch.
knacker ['nækər] **1.** *n.* abatteur *m* de chevaux; équarrisseur *m*; **knacker's yard**, chantier d'équarrissage *2. vtr F:* éreinter; **I'm knackered**, je suis crevé.
knapsack ['næpsæk] *n* havresac *m*; sac à dos.
knave [neiv] *n* **1.** *Cards:* valet *m* **2.** *A:* fripon *m*.
knead [ni:d] *vtr* pétrir (la pâte); masser (les muscles).
knee [ni:] *n* genou *m*; **on one's knees**, à genoux; **to go down on one's knees**, s'agenouiller; se mettre à genoux. **'kneecap** *n Anat:* rotule *f*. **'knee-'deep** *a* jusqu'aux genoux.
kneel [ni:l] *vi* (**knelt** [nelt]) **to k. (down)**, s'agenouiller; se mettre à genoux.
knell [nel] *n* glas *m*.
knelt [nelt] *see* **kneel**.
knew [nju:] *see* **know**.
knickers ['nikəz] *npl* culotte *f*, slip *m* (de femme).
knick-knack ['niknæk] *n* babiole *f*, bibelot *m*.
knife [naif] **I.** *n* (*pl* **knives**) couteau *m* (de table); (*pocketknife*) canif *m*; **k. and fork**, couvert *m*; **flick k.**, couteau à cran d'arrêt; *F:* **to get one's k. into s.o.**, en vouloir à qn. **II.** *vtr* donner un coup de couteau à (qn); poignarder (qn).
knight [nait] **I.** *n* **1.** chevalier *m* **2.** *Chess:* cavalier *m* **II.** *vtr* faire, créer, (qn) chevalier. **'knighthood** *n* titre *m* de chevalier.
knit [nit] *v* (**knitted**) **1.** *vtr* (a) tricoter; **k. two**, deux à l'endroit (b) froncer (les sourcils) (c) *Fig:* joindre **2.** *vi* (a) tricoter (b) (*of bones*) se souder. **'knitting** *n* **1.** (*action*) tricotage *m*; **k. wool**, laine à tricoter; **k. machine**, tricoteuse *f* **2.** tricot *m*. **'knitwear** *n* tricots *mpl*.
knob [nɔb] *n* **1.** (a) bosse *f* (b) pommeau *m* (de canne); bouton *m* (de porte, de radio) **2.** noix *f* (de beurre); morceau *m* (de charbon). **'knobb(l)y** *a* noueux.

knock [nɔk] **I** *n* **1.** coup *m*; heurt *m*, choc *m*; **there was a k. (at the door)**, on a frappé à la porte **2.** *ICE:* cognement *m*. **III.** *v* **1.** *vtr* (a) frapper, heurter, cogner; **to k. s.o. on the head**, frapper qn sur la tête; assommer qn; **to k. one's head against sth**, se cogner la tête contre qch (b) *F:* critiquer, taper sur **2.** *vi* (a) frapper (**at, on**); cogner (b) *ICE:* cogner (**against, into,** contre). **'knock a'bout, a'round** *F:* **1.** *vtr* malmener (qn); maltraiter **2.** *vtr & i* **to k. about (the world)**, parcourir le monde; rouler sa bosse. **'knock 'back** *vtr F:* (a) s'envoyer (un verre) (b) **that knocked her back £100**, cela lui a coûté £100. **'knock 'down** *vtr* **1.** renverser; jeter par terre; démolir (un immeuble); abattre (un mur) **2.** (*at auction*) adjuger (qch) (**to s.o.,** à qn) **3.** (faire) baisser (le prix). **'knockdown** *a* (*prix*) de réclame. **'knocker** *n* marteau *m*, heurtoir *m* (de porte). **'knocking** *n* **1.** coups *mpl* (à la porte) **2.** *ICE:* cognement. **'knock 'in(to)** *vtr* **1.** enfoncer (un clou) **2.** se cogner, se heurter, contre. **'knock-'kneed** *a* **to be k.-k.**, être cagneux. **knock-knees** *npl* **to have k.-k.**, avoir les jambes cagneuses. **'knock 'off 1.** *vtr* (a) faire tomber (qch) (de la table) (b) rabattre (qch) (**a price,** sur un prix) (c) *F:* achever (un travail) (d) *F:* voler, chiper (qch) **2.** *vtr & i F:* **k. off (work)**, s'arrêter de travailler; débrayer. **'knock 'out** *vtr* **1.** faire sortir (un clou); repousser (un rivet) **2.** (a) assommer (qn); *Box:* mettre (qn) knock-out (b) (*of drug*) faire perdre connaissance à (qn) **3.** *Sp:* (*in tournament*) éliminer. **'knockout** *n* **1.** (a) *Box:* knock-out *m; F:* **k. drops**, soporifique *m* (b) *F:* phénomène *m* **2.** **k. (competition)**, concours *m* avec épreuves éliminatoires. **'knock 'over** *vtr* renverser; faire tomber (qch). **'knock to'gether** *vtr* assembler (qch) à la hâte. **'knock 'up 1.** *vtr* (a) réveiller (qn) (b) *F:* construire (qch) à la hâte; improviser (un repas) (c) *P:* mettre (une femme) enceinte **2.** *vi Ten:* (*also* **to have a knock-up**) faire des balles.
knoll [noul] *n* tertre *m*, monticule *m*, butte *f*.
knot [nɔt] **I.** *n* **1.** nœud *m*; **to tie a k.**, faire un nœud **2.** *Meas:* nœud *m; Nau:* **to make ten knots**, filer dix nœuds **3.** groupe *m* (de personnes). **II.** *vtr* (**knotted**) nouer; faire des nœuds, un nœud, à (une ficelle). **'knotty** *a* (bois, doigt) noueux; (problème) épineux.
know [nou] **I.** *n F:* **to be in the k.**, être au courant. **II.** *vtr & i* (**knew** [nju:]; **known**) **1.** savoir (qch, un fait, que, quand, pourquoi); **as far as I k., for all I k.**, autant que je sache; **as everyone knows**, comme tout le monde (le) sait; **I don't k.**, je ne sais pas; **not that I k. (of)**, pas que je sache; **I k. (that) only too well**, je ne le sais que trop; *F:* **(and) don't I k. it!** à qui le dites-vous! **to k. a thing or two**, être roublard; **to k. one's (own) mind**, savoir ce qu'on veut; **to k. how to do sth**, savoir faire qch; **to k. about sth**, être au courant de qch; **I don't k. about that**, je n'en suis pas bien sûr! **I k. nothing about it**, je n'en sais rien; **he knows (all) about electronics**, il s'y connaît en électronique; **to k. better than to**, bien se garder de; **he ought to k. better**, il devrait être plus raisonnable, prudent; **she doesn't k. any better**, elle ne peut (pas) faire mieux; **you k. best**, vous en êtes le meilleur juge; **he is known to be in France**, on sait qu'il est en

France; **he had never been known to laugh,** on ne l'avait jamais vu rire **2.** connaître (qn, un endroit, un sujet); **to k. of,** connaître; **do you k. his son?** avez-vous fait la connaissance de son fils? **3.** (*a*) reconnaître (**by his walk,** à sa démarche) (*b*) distinguer (**one from the other,** l'un de l'autre). **'know-all,** *NAm:* also **'know-it-all** *n F:* je-sais-tout *mf.* **'know-how** *n F:* savoir-faire *m*; technique *f*; connaissances *fpl* (techniques). **'knowing I.** *a* fin, malin, rusé; (sourire) entendu. **II.** *n* **there's no k. (how),** (il n'y a) pas moyen de savoir (comment). **'knowingly** *adv* **1.** sciemment **2.** (sourire) d'un air entendu. **knowledge** ['nɔlidʒ] *n* **1.** connaissance (d'un fait, de qn); **lack of k.,** ignorance *f*; **I had no k. of it,** je ne le savais pas; je l'ignorais; **to the best of my k.,** à ma connaissance; **it's common k. that,** il est notoire que; **without my k.,** à mon insu *m*; **not to my k.,** pas que je sache **2.** savoir *m*; connaissances *fpl*; **to have a k. of several languages,** connaître plusieurs langues; **to have a thorough k. of a subject,** connaître, posséder, un sujet à fond; **to**

have a working k. of sth, posséder des connaissances élementaires sur qch. **'knowledgeable** *a* bien informé. **known** *a* (re)connu; (fait) avéré.

knuckle ['nʌkl] *n* **1.** articulation *f* du doigt, jointure *f* **2.** *Cu:* manche *m* (d'un gigot); jarret *m* (de veau). **'knuckle 'down** *vi* se mettre (**to sth,** à qch). **'knuckleduster** *n* coup-de-poing (américain). **'knuckle 'under** *vi* se soumettre; céder.

koala [kou'ɑːlə] *n Z:* **k. (bear),** koala *m.*

kohlrabi [kɔl'rɑːbi] *n Bot:* chou-rave *m*, *pl* choux-raves.

Koran (the) [ðəkɔ'rɑːn] *n Rel:* le Coran, le Koran.

Korea [kə'riə] *Prn Geog:* Corée *f.* **Ko'rean** *a & n* coréen, -enne.

kosher ['kouʃər] *a* kascher *inv*, cascher *inv.*

kowtow [kau'tau] *vi* faire des courbettes (**to s.o.,** devant qn).

kudos ['kjuːdɔs] *n F:* prestige *m*; gloire *f.*

Kuwait [ku'weit] *Prn Geog:* Kuweit *m*, Koweït *m.*

kw *abbr* kilowatt.

L

L, l [el] *n* (la lettre) L, l *m; Aut:* **L plates,** plaques *fpl* d'apprenti conducteur.
l *abbr* litre.
la [lɑː] *n Mus:* la *m*.
lab [læb] *n F:* (= *laboratory*) labo *m*.
label ['leibl] **I.** *n* **1.** étiquette *f* **2.** *Com:* label *m.* **II.** *vtr* (**labelled,** *NAm:* **also labeled**) étiqueter.
labial ['leibjəl] **1.** *a* labial, -aux **2.** *n Ling:* labiale *f*.
labor ['leibər] *n & v NAm:* = **labour**.
laboratory [lə'bɔrətri, *NAm:* 'læbrətɔːri] *n* laboratoire *m;* **l. assistant,** laborantin, -ine; **language l.,** laboratoire de langues.
labour, *NAm:* **labor** ['leibər] **I.** *n* **1.** travail *m; Lit:* labeur *m,* peine *f;* **l. of love,** travail fait avec plaisir; *Jur:* **hard l.,** travaux forcés **2.** (*a*) main-d'œuvre *f;* ouvriers *mpl;* travailleurs *mpl;* **l. troubles,** agitation ouvrière (*b*) *Pol:* les travaillistes *m;* **the L. Party,** le parti travailliste **3.** *Med:* travail; **in l.,** en travail. **II.** *v* **1.** *vi* (*a*) travailler; peiner; **to l. up a hill,** gravir péniblement une côte (*b*) **to l. under a delusion,** se faire des illusions; être victime d'une illusion (*c*) (*of car engine*) peiner **2.** *vtr* insister (trop) sur (qch); **I won't l. the point,** je ne m'étendrai pas là-dessus. **la'borious** *a* laborieux. **la'boriously** *adv* laborieusement. **'laboured,** *NAm:* **'labored** *a* **1.** laborieux; (style) travaillé **2.** (respiration) pénible. **'labourer,** *NAm:* **'laborer** *n* ouvriers; **'labour-saving,** *NAm:* **'labor-** *a* (appareil) allégeant le travail.
Labrador ['læbrədɔːr] *n* L. (dog, retriever), labrador *m*.
laburnum [lə'bəːnəm] *n Bot:* cytise *m*.
labyrinth ['læbirinθ] *n* labyrinthe *m*.
lace [leis] **I.** *n* **1.** lacet *m* (de soulier); cordon *m* **2.** dentelle *f;* point *m* (d'Alençon). **II.** *vtr* **1. to l. (up),** lacer (des chaussures) **2.** additionner d'alcool (une boisson). **'lace-up (shoe)** *a & n* (chaussure *f*) à lacets. **'lacy** *a* de dentelles.
lacerate ['læsəreit] *vtr* lacérer; déchirer. **lace'ration** *n* lacération *f,* déchirure *f*.
lack [læk] **I.** *n* manque *m;* défaut *m;* **for l. of,** faute de. **II.** *vtr & i* **to l. (for), be lacking (in),** manquer (de qch). **'lacklustre,** *NAm:* **-luster** *a* terne.
lackadaisical [lækə'deizikl] *a* apathique.
laconic [lə'kɔnik] *a* laconique. **la'conically** *adv* laconiquement.
lacquer ['lækər] **I.** *n* **1.** (*liquid*) laque *f* **2.** (*surface*) laque *m.* **II.** *vtr* laquer.
lactation [læk'teiʃ(ə)n] *n Physiol:* lactation *f.* **'lactose** *n Ch:* lactose *f*.
lad [læd] *n* (*a*) jeune homme *m;* (jeune) garçon *m; F:* **come on, lads!** allez les gars *m*! (*b*) (**stable) l.,** lad *m,* garçon d'écurie.
ladder ['lædər] **I.** *n* **1.** échelle *f* **2.** (*in stocking*) maille filée, échelle. **II.** *vtr & i* filer.
laden ['leidn] *a* chargé; *Nau:* **fully l.,** (navire) en pleine charge.

ladle ['leidl] **I.** *n* louche *f.* **II.** *vtr* **to l. (out),** servir (du potage) à la louche; *Fig:* donner (des renseignements).
lady ['leidi] *n* (*pl* **ladies**) **1.** dame *f;* **young l.,** (i) (*girl*) jeune fille *f;* demoiselle *f* (ii) (*woman*) jeune femme *f;* **l. of the house,** maîtresse *f* de maison; **ladies and gentlemen!** mesdames, mesdemoiselles, messieurs! (*on WC*) **ladies,** *NAm:* **ladies' room,** dames; *F:* **where's the ladies?** où sont les toilettes? **ladies' tailor,** tailleur pour dames; **lady's watch,** montre de dame **2.** (*a*) **Our L.,** Notre-Dame; **L. Day,** fête de l'Annonciation (*b*) **my l.,** madame *f* (la comtesse). **'ladybird,** *NAm:* also **'ladybug** *n Ent:* coccinelle *f.* **lady-in-'waiting** *n* dame d'honneur. **'lady-like** *a* distingué; (femme) bien élevée. **'ladyship** *n* **her l.,** madame (la comtesse).
lag¹ [læg] **I.** *n* (time) l., retard *m;* décalage *m* (entre deux opérations). **II.** *vi* (**lagged) to l. (behind),** rester en arrière; traîner (derrière qn, qch).
lag² *vtr* (**lagged**) calorifuger (un chaudière). **'lagging** *n* (revêtement *m*) calorifuge *m*.
lag³ *n F:* **old l.,** récidiviste *mf*.
lager ['lɑːgər] *n* bière blonde.
lagoon [lə'guːn] *n* (*a*) (*sand, shingle*) lagune *f* (*b*) lagon *m* (d'atoll).
la(h) [lɑː] *n Mus:* **1.** (*fixed*) la *m* **2.** (*movable*) sus-dominante *f*.
laid [leid] *see* **lay²**.
lain [lein] *see* **lie²**.
lair [leər] *n* tanière *f,* repaire *m*.
laity ['leiiti] *n coll* **the l.,** les laïques *mpl*.
lake [leik] *n* lac *m*.
lama ['lɑːmə] *n Rel:* lama *m*.
lamb [læm] *n* agneau *m; F:* **poor l.!** pauvre petit(e)! **'lambwool** *n* laine *f* d'agneau.
lame [leim] **I.** *a* **1.** boiteux; (*through accident*) estropié; **to be l.,** boiter (**in one leg,** d'une jambe) **2.** (excuse) pauvre, faible, piètre. **II.** *vtr* estropier (qn).
lament [lə'ment] **I.** *n* lamentation *f.* **II.** *vtr & i* **to l. (for, over),** se lamenter (sur). **'lamentable** *a* lamentable, déplorable. **'lamentably** *adv* lamentablement. **lamen'tation** *n* lamentation *f.* **la-'mented** *a* the late l. X, le regretté X.
laminated ['læmineitid] *a* (métal) laminé; (verre) feuilleté; (papier) plastifié.
lamp [læmp] *n* (*a*) lampe *f* (à pétrole, de mineur); **standard l.,** lampadaire *m;* **street l.,** réverbère *m* (*b*) *occ* ampule *f* (électrique). **'lamplight** *n* lumière *f* de la lampe. **'lamppost** *n* réverbère. **'lampshade** *n* abat-jour *m inv.* **'lampstand** *n* pied *m* de lampe.
lance [lɑːns] **I.** *n* lance *f; Mil:* **l. corporal,** soldat de première classe. **II.** *vtr Med:* percer (un abcès). **'lancet** *n Med:* lancette *f*.
land [lænd] **I.** *n* **1.** terre *f;* **dry l.,** terre ferme; **by l. and sea,** sur terre et sur mer; **to see how the l. lies,**

tâter le terrain; **l. breeze,** brise de terre; **l. battle,** bataille terrestre; *Jur:* **l. act,** loi agraire **2.** (*country*) terre, pays *m* **3.** (*property*) terre(s); (*smaller*) terrain; **l. tax,** impôt foncier. **II.** *v* **1.** *vtr* (*a*) mettre à terre; débarquer; décharger (qch); poser (un avion) **2.** amener (un poisson) à terre; *F:* remporter (un prix); décrocher (une bonne situation) (*c*) amener; *F:* **that will l. you in prison,** cela vous vaudra de la prison; **to l. s.o. in trouble,** mettre qn dans de beaux draps; **to be landed with sth,** rester avec qch sur les bras **2.** *vi* (*a*) (*of pers*) descendre à terre; débarquer; (*of aircraft*) atterrir; (*on moon*) alunir (*b*) tomber (à terre); **to l. on one's feet,** retomber sur ses pieds. **'landed** *a* (*of property, owner*) foncier. **'landfall** *n* arrivée *f* en vue de terre. **'landing** *n* **1.** (*a*) débarquement *m;* mise *f* à terre; **l. stage,** débarcadère *m,* embarcadère *m* (flottant); **l. card,** carte de débarquement; *Nau:* **l. craft,** chaland de débarquement (*b*) *Av:* atterrissage *m;* **parachute l.,** parachutage *m;* **l. gear,** train d'atterrissage (*c*) *Fish:* **l. net,** épuisette *f* **2.** palier *m* (d'un escalier). **'landlord, -lady** *n* **1.** logeur, -euse (en garni) **2.** hôtelier, -ière **3.** propriétaire *mf* (d'un immeuble). **'landmark** *n* **1.** (point *m* de) repère *m* **2.** point décisif. **'landowner** *n* propriétaire (foncier, -ière). **landscape I.** *n* paysage *m;* **l. gardener,** jardinier paysagiste **2.** *vtr* aménager (un terrain). **'landslide** *n* **1.** éboulement *m,* glissement *m* (de terrain) **2.** *Pol:* (*b*) débâcle *f* (*b*) **l. (victory),** victoire écrasante.

lane [lein] *n* **1.** (*in country*) chemin *m;* (*in town*) ruelle *f* **2.** *Nau:* route *f* (de navigation); *Av:* couloir (aérien) **3.** *Aut:* (**traffic**) **l.,** voie *f;* **four-l. road,** route à quatre voies; **to change lanes,** changer de file *f;* *PN:* **get in l.** = serrez à gauche, à droite.

language [ˈlæŋgwidʒ] *n* **1.** langue *f;* **modern languages,** langues vivantes **2.** langage *m;* **bad l.,** gros mots, langage grossier.

languid [ˈlæŋgwid] *a* languissant. **'languidly** *adv* languissamment.

languish [ˈlæŋgwiʃ] *vi* languir (**for,** après). **'languishing** *a* languissant.

languor [ˈlæŋgər] *n* langueur *f.* **'languorous** *a* langoureux.

lank [læŋk] *a* **1.** (*of pers*) maigre; sec **2.** (*of hair*) plat (et gras). **'lanky** *a* (**-ier, -iest**) grand et maigre.

lanolin [ˈlænəlin] *n* lanoline *f.*

lantern [ˈlæntən] *n* lanterne *f;* (*bigger*) falot *m;* **Chinese l.,** lanterne vénitienne. **lantern-'jawed** *a* aux joues creuses.

lap¹ [læp] *n* **1.** genoux *mpl,* giron *m.* **'lapdog** *n* chien *m* d'appartement.

lap² *n Sp:* tour *m* (de piste); boucle *f;* circuit *m;* étape *f* (d'un voyage).

lap³ (**lapped**) **1.** *vtr* (*of animal*) **to l. (up),** laper; *F:* **he lapped it up,** il a tout gobé **2.** *vi* (*of waves*) clapoter.

lapel [ləˈpel] *n* revers *m* (de veston).

lapis lazuli [ˈlæpisˈlæzul(a)i] *n Miner:* lazulite *m;* lapis(-lazuli) *m inv.*

Lapland [ˈlæplænd] *Prn Geog:* Laponie *f.* **'Laplander** *n* Lapon, -one. **Lapp 1.** *a* lapon **2.** *n* Lapon, -one **3.** *n Ling:* lapon *m.*

lapse [læps] **I.** *n* **1.** (*a*) erreur *f,* faute *f;* manquement *m* (**from duty,** au devoir) **2.** marche *f* (du temps); laps *m* de temps; **l. of three months,** délai *m* de trois

mois. **II.** *vi* **1.** manquer (**from duty,** au devoir); **to l. into silence,** rentrer dans le silence **2.** (*of passport*) (se) périmer; (*of legacy*) devenir caduc; (*of law*) cesser d'être en vigueur. **lapsed** *a* **1.** (catholique) non pratiquant **2.** (passeport) périmé; (contrat) caduc.

lapwing [ˈlæpwiŋ] *n Orn:* vanneau (huppé).

larceny [ˈlɑːsəni] *n Jur:* vol *m* (simple).

larch [lɑːtʃ] *n* (*pl* **larches**) *Bot:* mélèze *m.*

lard [lɑːd] *n* saindoux *m;* graisse *f* de porc.

larder [ˈlɑːdər] *n* garde-manger *m inv.*

large [lɑːdʒ] **I.** *a* (**-er, -est**) (*a*) grand; gros; vaste; fort; **to grow large(r),** grossir, grandir (*b*) (repas) copieux; **a l. sum,** une grosse somme; **l. family,** famille nombreuse. **II.** *n* **at l.,** en liberté; **the public at l.,** le grand public. **'largely** *adv* en grande partie; pour une bonne part; **very l.,** pour la plupart. **'largeness** *n* grosseur *f* (du corps); grandeur *f;* importance *f* (des profits). **large-scale** *a* gros; (carte) à grande échelle; (entreprise) sur une grande échelle.

lark¹ [lɑːk] *n Orn:* alouette *f;* **to be up with the l.,** se lever au chant du coq. **'larkspur** *n Bot:* pied-d'alouette *m.*

lark² *n F:* blague *f,* rigolade *f;* **for a l.,** pour rire, histoire de rigoler. **lark a'bout, a'round** *vi F:* rigoler; s'amuser.

larva, -ae [ˈlɑːvə, -iː] *n Ent:* larve *f.*

larynx [ˈlæriŋks] *n* (*pl* **larynxes**) larynx *m.* **laryngitis** [lærinˈdʒaitis] *n Med:* laryngite *f.*

laser [ˈleizər] *n Ph:* laser *m.*

lash¹ [læʃ] **I.** *n* (*pl* **lashes**) **1.** (*a*) coup *m* de fouet (*b*) lanière *f* (de fouet) **2.** cil *m.* **II.** *vtr* & *i* (*a*) fouetter; (*of rain*) **to l. (against),** cingler (les vitres) (*b*) **to l. oneself into a fury,** entrer dans une violente colère (*c*) (*of animal*) **to l. its tail,** se battre les flancs avec la queue. **'lashings** *npl F:* des tas *mpl* (de qch).

'lash 'out *vi* (*a*) (*of horse*) ruer; (*of pers*) **to l. o. at s.o.,** (i) invectiver (contre) qn (ii) donner des coups de poing à qn (*b*) *F:* se livrer à de folles dépenses; **to l. out on sth,** se payer le luxe de qch.

lash² *vtr* attacher; *Nau:* amarrer; **to l. down,** lier, brider (un chargement).

lass [læs] *n* (*pl* **lasses**) *Dial:* jeune fille *f.*

lassitude [ˈlæsitjuːd] *n* lassitude *f.*

lasso [læˈsuː] **I.** *n* lasso *m.* **II.** *vtr* prendre (un cheval) au lasso.

last¹ [lɑːst] *n* forme *f* (à chaussure).

last² **I.** *a* **1.** dernier; **she was the l. (one) to arrive,** elle est arrivée la dernière; **the l. but one,** l'avant-dernier; **l. but not least,** le dernier, mais non le moindre; **l. thing (at night),** tard dans la soirée; **I'm down to my l. bottle,** il ne me reste plus qu'une bouteille **2. l. Monday,** lundi dernier; **l. week,** la semaine dernière; **l. year,** l'année dernière; **l. night** (i) la nuit dernière (ii) hier soir (iii) cette nuit; (**the**) **l. time I saw him,** la dernière fois que je l'ai vu; **the day before l.,** avanthier *m;* **the week before l.,** il y a deux semaines; **the year before l.,** il y a deux ans. **II.** *n* (*a*) **we shall never hear the l. of it,** on ne nous le laissera pas oublier; **that's the l. I saw of him,** je ne l'ai pas revu depuis; **the l. of the wine,** le reste du vin (*b*) **to the l.,** jusqu'au bout (*c*) **at (long) l.,** enfin; à la fin. **III.** *adv* (*a*) **when I saw him l., l. saw him,** la dernière fois que je l'ai vu (*b*) **he came l.,** il est arrivé le dernier (*c*) =

LASTLY. 'last-'ditch a (effort) suprême. 'lastly adv pour finir; en dernier lieu. 'last-minute a de dernière minute.

last³ vi & tr durer; se maintenir; (of weather) tenir; too good to l., trop beau pour durer; the supplies will not l. (out) two months, les vivres ne feront pas deux mois; my coat will l. the winter (out), mon pardessus fera encore l'hiver; it will l. me a lifetime, j'en ai pour la vie; he won't l. long in that job, il ne fera pas long feu dans ce poste. 'lasting a durable.

latch [lætʃ] n (pl latches) (a) loquet m; on the l., au loquet (b) serrure f de sûreté. 'latchkey n clef f de maison. 'latch 'on vi to l. on (to s.o., sth), (i) s'attacher (à qn) (ii) F: saisir (qch).

late [leit] I. a (-er, -est) 1. I am l., je suis en retard; the train is l., le train a du retard, a dix minutes de retard 2. tard; at a l. hour, à une heure avancée; it's (getting) l., il est, il se fait, tard; I was too l., je suis arrivé trop tard, je ne suis pas arrivé à temps; to be l. going to bed, se coucher tard; in the l. afternoon, en fin d'après-midi; in l. summer, vers la fin de l'été; in the l. sixties, dans les années approchant 1970; in later life, plus tard dans la vie; at a later meeting, à une réunion ultérieure; latest date, date limite 3. (of fruit, frost) tardif 4. (a) ancien, ex-; the l. minister, l'ancien ministre, l'ex-ministre (b) my l. father, feu mon père; the l. queen, feu la reine, la feue reine 5. récent, dernier; of l., dernièrement; depuis peu; his latest novel, son dernier roman; is there any later news? a-t-on des nouvelles plus récentes? F: have you heard the latest? sais-tu la dernière? II. adv (-er, -est) l. (arriver) en retard; too l., trop tard; better l. than never, mieux vaut tard que jamais. 2. tard; sooner or later, tôt ou tard; to stay up, go to bed, l., se coucher tard; very l. at night, très tard dans la nuit; l. in life, à un âge avancé; l. in the day, sur le tard; a moment later, un instant après; no later than yesterday, pas plus tard qu'hier; later (on), plus tard; at the latest, au plus tard; see you later! à tout à l'heure! 'latecomer n retardataire mf. 'lately adv dernièrement; depuis peu; till l., jusqu'à ces derniers temps. 'lateness n retard m.

latent ['leitənt] a latent; caché.

lateral ['lætərəl] a latéral. 'laterally adv latéralement.

latex ['leiteks] n Bot: latex m.

lath [lɑ:θ] n latte f.

lathe [leið] n Tls: tour m.

lather ['lɑːðər, 'læðər] I. n 1. mousse f (de savon) 2. (on horse) écume f. II. v 1. vtr savonner 2. vi (of soap) mousser.

Latin ['lætin] 1. a latin 2. n Ling: latin m. Latin-A'merican a latino-américain.

latitude ['lætitjuːd] n latitude f; at a l. of 30° north, à 30° de latitude nord.

latter ['lætər] a 1. dernier (des deux); the l., ce, le, dernier; celui-ci, ceux-ci 2. the l. half of June, la deuxième moitié de juin. 'latterly adv dernièrement.

lattice ['lætis] n treillis m, treillage m; l. window, fenêtre (i) treillagée (ii) à losanges.

laudable ['lɔːdəbl] a louable. 'laudably adv louablement. 'laudatory a élogieux.

laugh [lɑːf] I. n rire m; with a l., en riant; to raise a l., faire rire; to do sth. for a l., faire qch histoire de rire. II. v 1. vi (a) rire; to l. till one cries, rire aux larmes; to l. to oneself, rire tout bas; to l. up one's sleeve, rire sous cape; to l. in s.o.'s face, rire au nez de qn; to l. on the other side of one's face, perdre son envie de rire (b) to l. about, at, over, sth, rire de qch; there's nothing to l. at, il n'y a pas de quoi rire; to l. at s.o., se moquer, rire, de qn 2. vtr (a) avoir un rire (amer) (b) to l. s.o. out of court, se moquer des prétentions de qn. 'laughable a risible, ridicule, (offre) dérisoire. 'laughing 1. a riant; rieur 2. n rires mpl; it's no l. matter, il n'y a pas de quoi rire; l. gas, gaz hilarant. 'laughingly adv en riant. 'laughingstock n risée f; make a l. of oneself, se faire moquer de soi. 'laugh 'off vtr tourner (qch) en plaisanterie. 'laughter n rire(s).

launch [lɔːn(t)ʃ] I. n (pl launches) chaloupe f; motor l., vedette f; police l., vedette de la police. II. v 1. vtr (a) lancer (un projectile, qn, une affaire); déclencher (une offensive) (b) mettre à la mer 2. vi to l. (out), se lancer (into, dans). 'launching n lancement m; mise f à l'eau (d'un navire); l. pad, rampe de lancement.

laundry ['lɔːndri] n (pl laundries) 1. (place) blanchisserie f 2. lessive f; linge (i) blanchi (ii) à blanchir; l. list, liste de blanchissage. launde'rette, NAm: Rtm: 'laundromat n laverie f automatique.

laureate ['lɔːriət] a & n lauréat, -ate.

laurel ['lɔrəl] n Bot: laurier m; to rest on one's laurels, se reposer sur ses lauriers.

lava ['lɑːvə] n lave f.

lavatory ['lævətri] n cabinets mpl; toilettes fpl; W-C mpl.

lavender ['lævindər] 1. n lavande f; l. water, eau de lavande 2. a (colour) lavande inv.

lavish ['læviʃ] I. a 1. prodigue; to be l. with sth, prodiguer qch 2. somptueux; abondant; (repas) plantureux l. expenditure, dépenses folles. II. vtr prodiguer (sth on s.o., qch à qn). 'lavishly adv. 1. (dépenser) avec prodigalité 2. somptueusement. 'lavishness n prodigalité f.

law [lɔː] n 1. loi f; l. législation 2. his word is l., sa parole fait loi; to lay down the l. to s.o., faire la loi à qn; to be a l. unto oneself, n'en faire qu'à sa tête 3. droit m; to study, read, l., faire son droit; civil, criminal, l., droit civil, criminel; l. student, étudiant en droit 4. (a) court of l. = LAWCOURT; to go to l., avoir recours à la justice; to take the l. into one's own hands, faire soi-même la justice (b) F: the l., la police, les flics m. 'law-abiding a respectueux des lois. 'lawbreaker n transgresseur m de la loi. 'lawcourt n cour f de justice; tribunal m. 'lawful a légal. 'lawfully adv. légalement. 'lawless a sans loi; déréglé; désordonné. 'lawlessness n dérèglement m, désordre m; anarchie f. 'lawsuit n procès m. 'lawyer n (a) homme de loi, juriste m (b) (i) avocat m (ii) notaire m.

lawn [lɔːn] n pelouse f; gazon m. 'lawnmower n tondeuse f (à gazon).

lax [læks] a (of conduct) relâché; (of pers) négligent; (morale) facile. 'laxative a & n Med: laxatif (m). 'laxity, 'laxness n relâchement m (des mœurs); négligence f; mollesse f.

lay¹ [lei] *a* laïque; *Ecc:* (*of monk, nun*) convers; (frère) lai; **to the l. mind,** aux yeux du profane. **'layman, -men** *n* (*a*) *Ecc:* laïc *m*, laïque *m* (*b*) profane.

lay² *vtr* (**laid** [leid]) **1.** coucher; **to l. s.o. low,** terrasser, abattre, qn **2.** abattre (la poussière); exorciser (un fantôme) **3.** mettre, placer, poser (**sth on sth,** qch sur qch); reposer (la tête); **to l. a finger on s.o.,** toucher qn; **to l. one's hand(s) on sth,** mettre la main sur qch; **to l. s.o. to rest,** mettre qn au tombeau **4.** pondre (un œuf) **5.** faire (un pari); parier (une somme) **6.** soumettre (une demande); exposer, présenter (les faits) (**before s.o.,** à qn); imposer (une peine) (**upon s.o.,** à qn); **to l. a charge against s.o.,** porter plainte contre qn **7.** (*a*) poser (un tapis); asseoir (des fondements); ranger (des briques); préparer (un feu); **to l. the table,** mettre le couvert; **to l. for three,** mettre trois couverts (*b*) dresser, tendre (un piège) (*c*) former, faire (des projets). **'lay-about** *n F:* fainéant, -ante. **'lay a'side, 'lay 'by** *vtr* mettre (qch) de côté; **'lay-by** *n* (*on road*) aire *f*, terre-plein *m* (de stationnement). **'lay 'down** *vtr* **1.** (*a*) déposer, poser (qch); mettre bas (les armes); mettre (du vin) en cave; *Cards:* étaler (son jeu) (*b*) coucher, étendre (qn) (*c*) donner, sacrifier (sa vie) **3.** poser, établir (une règle); imposer, fixer (des conditions); **to l. d. that,** stipuler que. **'layer** *n* **1.** (*of hen*) good l., bonne pondeuse **2.** couche *f* (de peinture); assise *f*, lit *m* (de béton). **'lay 'in** *vtr* faire provision de, s'approvisionner de (qch). **'lay 'into** *vtr F:* (*a*) rouer (qn) de coups (*b*) engueuler (qn). **'lay 'off 1.** *vtr* licencier, renvoyer (des ouvriers) **2.** *vtr & i F:* laisser (qn) tranquille; **l. off (it)!** arrête! fiche-moi la paix! **'lay-off** *n* licenciement *m* (des ouvriers). **'lay 'on** *vtr* **1.** appliquer (un enduit); *F:* **to l. it on thick, with a trowel,** flatter qn grossièrement **2.** *vtr* installer (le gaz); **with water laid on,** avec l'eau courante **3.** arranger (qch) (**for s.o.,** pour qn). **'lay 'out** *vtr* **1.** arranger, disposer, étaler (des objets, des marchandises) **2.** étendre (qn) d'un coup **3.** dépenser (de l'argent) **4.** dessiner (un jardin); faire le tracé d'une route). **'layout** *n* tracé *m*; dessin *m*; disposition *f*. **'lay 'up** *vtr* **1.** accumuler (des provisions); **to l. up trouble for oneself,** se préparer bien des ennuis **2.** remiser (une voiture) **3.** **to be laid up,** être obligé de garder le lit.

lay³ *see* **lie².**

lazy ['leizi] *a* (**-ier, -iest**) paresseux, fainéant. **'laze (a'bout, a'round)** *vi* paresser, fainéanter. **'lazily** *adv* paresseusement. **'laziness** *n* paresse *f*; fainéantise *f*. **'lazybones** *n F:* paresseux, -euse.

lb *abbr* libra, pound.

lead¹ [led] *n* **1.** plomb *m*; white l., blanc *m* de plomb; **l. pipe,** tuyau de plomb **2.** mine *f* (de crayon, de plomb) **3.** *Nau:* (plomb de) sonde *f*. **'leaded** *a* (*a*) (*of window*) plombé (*b*) (*of petrol*) plombifère. **'leaden** *a* (teint, ciel) de plomb. **'lead-free** *a* (essence) sans plomb.

lead² [li:d] **I.** *n* **1.** **to be in the l.,** mener; **to take the l.,** prendre la tête; **to follow s.o.'s l.,** suivre l'exemple *m* de qn; **to give s.o. a l.,** mettre qn sur la voie; **a l. of ten metres,** une avance de dix mètres **2.** *Cards:* **to have the l.,** jouer le premier; **your l.!** à vous de jouer! **3.** *Th:* premier rôle **4.** (*for dog*) laisse *f*; **on a l.,** en laisse **5.** *El:* câble *m*, fil *m*. **II.** *v* (**led,** [led]) **1.** *vtr* (*a*)

mener, conduire; guider; **to l. the way,** (i) montrer le chemin (ii) aller devant, en tête; **he is easily led,** il va comme on le mène (*b*) mener (sa vie) (*c*) porter, amener (**s.o. to do sth,** qn à faire qch) (*d*) être à la tête de (la file); commander (une armée); diriger (un mouvement); **to l. the field,** être à la tête (*e*) *Cards:* jouer (trèfle); attaquer (de la dame) **2.** *vi* (*a*) mener, conduire (**to,** à); (*b*) **to l. to nothing,** n'aboutir, ne mener, n'amener, à rien (*b*) aller devant, en tête (*c*) *Cards:* jouer (le premier). **'lead a'way** *vtr* emmener. **'lead 'back** *vtr* ramener, reconduire. **'leader** *n* **1.** (*a*) conducteur, -trice; guide *m* (*b*) chef *m*; meneur, -euse (d'une émeute); *Mil:* commandant *m*; *Pol:* leader *m* **2.** *Sp:* coureur, -euse, cheval *m*, de tête **3.** *Journ:* (*a*) article *m* de fond, de tête; leader (*b*) éditorial *m*. **'leadership** *n* (*a*) conduite *f*; **under s.o.'s l.,** sous la conduite de qn (*b*) qualités *fpl* de chef (*c*) commandement *m*; direction *f* (d'un parti). **'leading** *a* **1.** **l. question,** question tendancieuse **2.** (*a*) premier, principal; **a l. man,** un homme important; *Journ:* **l. article = leader 3; l. part,** (i) *Th:* premier rôle (ii) rôle prépondérant; **l. man, lady,** vedette *f* (*b*) (voiture) de, en, tête. **'lead 'on 1.** *vi* **l. on!** en avant! **2.** (*a*) entraîner (qn) (*b*) tromper, en conter à (qn). **'lead 'up** *vi* **to l. up to a subject,** précéder, amener, un sujet.

leaf [li:f] *n* (*pl* **leaves**) **1.** feuille *f*; **in l.,** en feuilles **2.** feuillet *m* (de livre); **to turn over the leaves of a book,** feuilleter un livre; *Fig:* **to turn over a new l.,** changer de conduite; **to take a l. out of s.o.'s book,** prendre exemple sur qn **3.** battant *m* (de table). **'leaflet** *m* imprimé *m*; prospectus *m*; papillon *m* (publicitaire); *Pol:* tract *m*. **'leaf 'through** *vtr* feuilleter (un livre). **'leafy** *a* feuillu.

league [li:g] *n* **1.** ligue *f*; **he was in l. with them,** il était ligué, de connivence, avec eux **2.** *Fb:* championnat *m*.

leak [li:k] **I.** *n* fuite *f* (d'un liquide, d'informations); (*in boat*) voie *f* d'eau. **II.** *v* **1.** *vi* (*a*) (*of pipe*) fuir (*b*) (*of roof*) laisser entrer la pluie; (*of shoes*) prendre l'eau; (*of boat*) faire eau (*c*) **to l. (out),** (i) (*of liquid*) fuir, couler (ii) (*of information*) être divulgué; s'ébruiter **2.** *vtr* divulguer (des informations). **'leakage** *n* fuite, perte *f* (d'eau). **'leaky** *a* (tuyau) qui fuit, qui coule; (toit) qui laisse entrer la pluie; (chaussure) qui prend l'eau; (bateau) qui fait eau.

lean¹ [li:n] *a & n* (**-er, -est**) maigre (*m*). **'leanness** *n* maigreur *f*.

lean² *v* (**leant** [lent] *or* **leaned**) **1.** *vi* (*a*) s'appuyer (**against, on,** contre, sur); **to l. on one's elbow(s),** s'accouder; *F:* **to l. on s.o.,** exercer une pression sur qn (*b*) (*of pers*) se pencher (**over, sur; towards,** vers); (*of wall*) incliner, pencher **2.** *vtr* appuyer (une échelle) (**against,** contre). **'lean 'back** *vi* se pencher, se renverser, en arrière; s'adosser (**against,** à, contre). **'lean 'forward** *vi* se pencher en avant. **'leaning 1.** *a* appuyé (**against,** contre); (*not upright*) penché **2.** *n* **l. towards,** inclination *f* pour, à (qch); tendance *f* à (qch); penchant *m* pour, vers (qch). **'lean 'out** *vi* se pencher au dehors. **'lean 'over** *vi* (*of pers*) se pencher en avant; (*of tree*) pencher; *Fig:* **to l. over backwards to do sth,** se mettre en quatre pour faire qch. **'lean-to** *n* appentis *m*.

leap [li:p] *n* **1.** saut *m*, bond *m*; **a l. in the dark,** un saut dans l'inconnu; **by leaps and bounds,** à pas de géant 2. **l. year,** année bissextile. **II.** v (leapt [lept] or leaped) 1. vi (a) sauter, bondir; **to l. up, to one's feet,** se lever brusquement; **to l. at an offer,** sauter sur une offre (b) (of flame) **to l. (up),** jaillir 2. vtr **to l. (over),** sauter (un fossé); franchir (qch) d'un saut. **'leapfrog** n saute-mouton m. **'leap 'over** vi sauter par-dessus.

learn [lə:n] vtr & i (learnt [lə:nt] or learned) apprendre; **to l. how to do sth,** apprendre à faire qch; Fig: **he's learnt his lesson,** cela lui a donné une bonne leçon. **learned** ['lə:nid] a savant, instruit. **'learner** n 1. **to be a quick l.,** apprendre facilement 2. débutant, -ante 3. **l. (driver),** apprenti(e) conducteur, -trice. **'learning** n 1. étude f (de leçons) 2. érudition f, savoir m.

lease [li:s] **I.** n Jur: bail m; Fig: **new l. of,** NAm: **on, life,** regain m de vie. **II.** vtr louer (une maison) (à bail). **'leasehold** n 1. n (a) (tenure f à) bail (b) appartement, etc, loué à bail 2. a tenu à bail. **'leaseholder** n locataire mf (à bail).

leash [li:ʃ] n (pl leashes) laisse f; **on the l.,** en laisse.

least [li:st] 1. a (a) (the) **l.,** (le, la) moindre; (le, la) plus petit(e); **the l. meat,** le moins de viande; **not the l. chance,** pas la moindre chance (b) le moins important; **that's the l. of my worries,** c'est le dernier, le cadet, le moindre, de mes soucis 2. n (the) **l.,** (le) moins; **to say the l. (of it),** pour ne pas dire plus; **it's the l. I can do,** c'est la moindre des choses; **at (the) l.,** (tout) au moins; **at l. it didn't rain,** du moins il n'a pas plu; **I can at l. try,** je peux toujours essayer; **not in the l.,** pas le moins du monde; **it doesn't matter in the l.,** cela n'a pas la moindre importance 3. adv **(the) l.,** (le) moins; **he deserves it l. of all,** il le mérite moins que personne.

leather ['leðər] n cuir m; **l. articles,** articles de, en, cuir; maroquinerie f.

leave [li:v] **I.** n 1. permission f, autorisation f, permis m; **without so much as a by your l.,** sans même demander la permission 2. **l. (of absence),** congé m; Mil: permission; **on l.,** en congé 3. **to take (one's) l. (of s.o.),** prendre congé (de qn); **to take l. of one's senses,** perdre la raison. **II.** vtr (left [left]) 1. (a) laisser; oublier (qch); **take it or l. it,** c'est à prendre ou à laisser (b) laisser, léguer (de l'argent) (**to s.o.,** à qn) (c) **to l. the door open,** laisser la porte ouverte; **l. me alone!** laisse-moi tranquille! **left to oneself,** livré à soi-même; **let's l. it at that,** demeurons-en là (d) **to l. go of sth,** lâcher qch (e) **left luggage (office),** (bagages en) consigne f (f) **to l. s.o. to do sth,** laisser qn faire qch; **l. it to me,** remettez-vous-en à moi; laissez-moi faire; je m'en charge (g) **to be left (over),** rester; **I've none left,** il ne m'en reste plus 2. (a) quitter (un endroit, qn); sortir de (la salle); **to l. home,** (i) (forever) partir (ii) (to go out) sortir, partir de la maison; **to l. the table,** se lever de table; **we l. tomorrow for Rome,** nous partons demain pour Rome; **to l. harbour,** sortir du port (b) abandonner; quitter (sa femme) (c) (of train) **to l. the rails,** dérailler. **'leave a'bout** vtr laisser traîner (des objets). **'leave be'hind** vtr. laisser, oublier (qch); partir sans (qn). **'leave 'off** 1. vtr (a) cesser de porter (un vêtement) (b) renoncer (à qch); **to l. off work, working,** cesser le

travail, de travailler 2. vi cesser, (s')arrêter; **where did we l. off?** où en sommes-nous restés? **'leave 'out** vtr 1. (deliberately) exclure 2. (a) omettre (b) oublier; sauter (une ligne). **'leave 'over** vtr. 1. remettre (une affaire) à plus tard 2. **to be left over,** rester. **'leaving** n 1. départ m 2. **leavings,** restes mpl.

leaven ['levn] n levain m.

Lebanon ['lebənən] Prn Geog: Liban m. **Leba-'nese** a & n libanais, -aise.

lecherous ['letʃərəs] a lascif, lubrique.

lectern ['lektən] n lutrin m.

lecture ['lektʃər] **I.** n 1. conférence f, Sch: cours m **(on,** sur); **to give a l.,** faire une conférence; **l. theatre,** salle f de conférences 2. sermon m, semonce f. **II.** v faire une, des, conférence(s), faire un cours (on, sur) 2. vtr sermonner, semoncer (qn). **lecturer** n (a) conférencier, -ière (b) Sch: **(junior, assistant) l.,** maître assistant; **(senior) l.** = maître de conférences; chargé m de cours.

led [led] see lead² **II.**

ledge [ledʒ] n rebord m; saillie f; (on building) corniche f.

ledger ['ledʒər] n 1. Com: grand livre 2. Mus: **l. line,** ligne supplémentaire (à la portée).

lee [li:] n (a) Nau: côté m sous le vent; **l. shore,** terre sous le vent (b) abri m (contre le vent); **in the l. of a rock,** abrité par un rocher. **'leeward** Nau: **l.** a & adv sous le vent 2. n côté sous le vent. **'leeway** n (a) Nau: dérive f (b) retard m (à rattraper) (c) liberté f d'agir.

leech [li:tʃ] n (pl leeches) sangsue f.

leek [li:k] n poireau m.

leer ['liər] **I.** n regard m (i) malicieux, mauvais (ii) polisson. **II.** vi **to l.** (at s.o.,) lorgner (qn).

left¹ [left] 1. a gauche; **on my l. hand,** à ma gauche 2. adv à gauche; Mil: **eyes l.!** tête (à) gauche! 3. n (a) gauche f; **on my l.,** à ma gauche; **on, to, the l.,** à gauche (b) Box: gauche m (c) Pol: **the L.,** la gauche. **'lefthand** a (poche) de gauche; (virage) à gauche; **on the l. side,** à gauche. **'left'handed** a (a) (of pers) gaucher (b) (compliment) équivoque (c) (ciseaux) pour gaucher. **left'hander** n 1. (pers) gaucher, -ère 2. coup m du gaucher. **'leftist** a & n Pol: gauchiste (mf). **'left-'wing** a (of pers) gauchiste; (politique) de gauche.

left² see leave **II.** **leftovers** ['leftouvəz] npl restes mpl.

leg [leg] 1. n jambe f; patte f (d'animal, d'oiseau); **to be on one's last legs** (i) être épuisé (ii) être à bout de ressources (iii) tirer à sa fin; **to give s.o. a l. up,** (i) faire la courte échelle à qn (ii) Fig: donner à qn un coup d'épaule; **to stand on one l.,** se tenir sur un pied; F: **to pull s.o.'s l.,** se payer la tête de qn 2. Cu: cuisse f (de volaille); gigot m d'agneau 3. jambe (de pantalon); tige f (d'une bottine) 4. pied m (de table) 5. étape f (d'un voyage); Sp: manche f (d'un championnat) 2. vtr F: **to l. it,** faire la route à pied. **-legged** ['-legid,--legd] a **short-l.,** aux jambes courtes; **four-l.,** (animal) à quatre pattes. **'leggings** npl Cl: jambières fpl. **'leg-pull** n F: blague f. **'legroom** n place f pour les jambes. **'legwarmers** npl jambières.

legacy ['legəsi] *n* legs *m*; **to leave s.o. a l.**, faire un legs à qn. **lega'tee** *n* légataire *mf*.

legal ['li:gl] *a* 1. légal, licite; (propriétaire) légitime 2. légal; judiciaire, juridique; **l. document**, acte authentique; **the l. profession**, les hommes de loi; **to go into the l. profession**, faire une carrière juridique; **to take l. advice** = consulter un avocat; (*of company*) **l. department**, (service du) contentieux; **l. aid**, assistance judiciaire. **le'gality** *n* légalité *f*. **'legalize** *vtr* légaliser. **'legally** *adv* légalement; **l. responsible**, responsable en droit.

legend ['ledʒənd] *n* légende *f*. **'legendary** *a* légendaire.

legible ['ledʒibl] *a* lisible. **legi'bility** *n* lisibilité *f*. **'legibly** *adv* lisiblement.

legion ['li:dʒən] *n* légion *f*; **the Foreign L.**, la Légion étrangère.

legislate ['ledʒisleit] *vi* faire des lois; légiférer. **legis'lation** *n* législation *f*. **'legislative** *a* législatif. **'legislator** *n* législateur, -trice. **'legislature** *n* corps législatif.

legitimacy [li'dʒitiməsi] *n* légitimité *f*. **le'gitimate** *a* légitime; (théâtre) régulier. **le'gitimately** *adv* légitimement.

leisure ['leʒər, *NAm:* 'li:ʒər] *n* **l.** (**time**), loisir(s) *m(pl)*; temps *m* libre; **to have l. for reading**, avoir le loisir, le temps, de lire; **in my l. moments**, à mes moments perdus, de loisir; **at l.**, (i) pas occupé; libre (ii) sans se presser; **at one's l.**, à loisir. **'leisured** *a* qui a beaucoup de loisirs. **'leisurely** *a* (*of pers*) qui n'est jamais pressé; **l. pace**, allure mesurée; **in a l. fashion**, sans se presser.

lemon ['lemən] 1. *n* citron *m*; **l. (tree)**, citronnier *m*; **l. squash**, citronnade *f*; **l. squeezer**, presse-citron *m inv*; **l. juice**, jus de citron; (*drink*) citron pressé 2. *a* **l. (yellow)**, (jaune) citron *inv*; **lemon'ade** *n* limonade *f*; (*still*) citronnade.

lemur ['li:mər] *n Z:* maki *m*.

lend [lend] *vtr* (**lent**) prêter; **to l. s.o. a hand**, donner un coup de main à qn; **to l. an ear**, prêter l'oreille; **to l. oneself, itself, to sth**, se prêter à qch. **'lender** *n* prêteur, -euse. **'lending** *n* prêt *m*; **l. library**, bibliothèque de prêt.

length [leŋθ] *n* 1. longueur *f*; **to be two metres in l.**, avoir deux mètres de long, de longueur, être long de deux mètres; *Sp:* **by a l.**, (gagner) d'une longueur; **throughout the l. and breadth of the country**, dans toute l'étendue du pays; **to fall full l.**, tomber de tout son long 2. durée *f* (d'un séjour); **stay of some l.**, séjour assez prolongé; **l. of time**, temps *m*; **l. of service**, ancienneté *f*; **at l.**, (i) (parler) longuement; (expliquer qch) en détail (ii) (*at last*) enfin, à la fin 3. **to go to the l. of doing sth**, aller jusqu'à faire qch; **to go to great lengths**, faire tout son possible; **to go to any length(s)**, ne reculer devant rien 4. morceau *m*; bout *m* (de ficelle); coupon *m* (de tissu); **what l. of material do you need?** quel métrage vous faut-il? **'lengthen** 1. *vtr* rallonger (une jupe); allonger (une jupe, la vie); prolonger (la vie, une rue) 2. *vi* s'allonger; se prolonger; (*of days*) allonger. **'lengthily** *adv* longuement. **'lengthways**, **'lengthwise** *adv* dans le sens de la longueur; en long. **'lengthy** *a* (-ier, -iest) (discours) long, plein de longueurs.

leniency ['li:niənsi] *n* indulgence *f*, clémence *f* (**to, towards**, envers, pour). **'lenient** *a* indulgent, clément. **'leniently** *adv* avec indulgence; avec clémence.

lens [lenz] *n* (*pl* **lenses**) (*a*) lentille *f*; verre *m* (de lunettes); **contact l.**, verre, lentille, de contact (*b*) *Phot:* objectif *m* (*c*) *Anat:* cristallin *m*.

Lent¹ [lent] *n Ecc:* Carême *m*.

lent² *see* **lend**.

lentil ['lentl] *n Bot:* lentille *f*.

Leo ['li:ou] *Prn Astr:* le Lion.

leopard ['lepəd] *n* léopard *m*.

leotard ['li:əta:d] *n* maillot *m* (de danseur); collant *m*.

leper ['lepər] *n* lépreux, -euse. **'leprosy** *n* lèpre *f*. **'leprous** *a* lépreux.

leprechaun ['leprəkɔ:n] *n Myth:* farfadet *m*, lutin *m*.

lesbian ['lezbiən] 1. *a* lesbien 2. *n* lesbienne *f*.

lesion ['li:ʒ(ə)n] *n Jur: Med:* lésion *f*.

less [les] 1. *a* (*a*) moindre; **the distance is l. than I thought**, la distance est moindre que je ne le pensais; **a number l. than six**, un chiffre inférieur à, au-dessous de, six (*b*) **eat l. meat**, mangez moins de viande 2. *prep.* moins; **l. £5**, moins £5 3. *n* moins *m*; **in l. than an hour**, en moins d'une heure; **at l. than cost price**, à moins du prix de revient 4. *adv* moins; **l. known**, moins connu; **one man l.**, un homme de moins; **l. than six**, moins de six; **l. and l.**, de moins en moins; **even l.**, moins encore; **he's much l. intelligent than his sister**, il est beaucoup moins intelligent que sa sœur; **I'm l. afraid of it now**, je le crains moins maintenant; **no l.**, rien de moins; **no l. a person than**, rien moins que. **'lessen** 1. *vi* diminuer, s'amoindrir; (*of symptoms*) s'atténuer 2. *vtr* diminuer, amoindrir; atténuer (une douleur). **'lesser** *a* moindre; **to choose the l. of two evils**, de deux maux choisir le moindre.

lessee [le'si:] *n* locataire *mf* (à bail). **le'ssor** *n Jur:* bailleur, -eresse.

lesson ['lesn] *n* leçon *f*; cours *m*; **to take French lessons**, prendre des leçons de français; **driving lessons**, leçons de conduite; **let that be a l. to you!** que cela vous serve d'exemple.

let [let] *v* (**let**; **letting**) I. *vtr* 1. (*a*) permettre; laisser; **to l. s.o. do sth**, laisser qn de, faire qch; **to l. go of sth**, **to l. sth go**, lâcher qch; **when can you l. me have it?** quand pourrai-je l'avoir? (*b*) **to l. s.o. know about sth**, faire savoir qch à qn, faire part à qn de qch; **l. me hear the story**, racontez-moi l'histoire (*c*) **to l. s.o. pass**, laisser passer qn 2. louer (une maison). II. *v aux* (*1st & 3rd pers of imp*) **let's go!** allons! **let's hurry!** dépêchons-nous! **don't let's start yet**, ne partons pas encore; **just l. me catch you at it again!** que je vous y reprenne! **l. there be no mistake about it!** qu'on ne s'y trompe pas! **l. them all come!** qu'ils viennent tous! **l. me see!** voyons! attendez un peu! **'let 'down** *vtr* 1. (*a*) baisser (la glace) (*b*) (r)allonger (une robe) 2. décevoir (qn); I **won't l. you down**, vous pouvez compter sur moi. **'letdown** *n* désappointement *m*, déception *f*. **'let 'in** *vtr* 1. (*a*) laisser entrer, faire entrer; **to l. oneself in**, entrer (avec une clef); **my shoes l. in water**, mes chaussures prennent l'eau (*b*) **to l. s.o. in on a secret**, mettre qn dans le secret **2. I didn't know what I was letting myself in for,** je ne savais pas à quoi je m'engageais. **'let 'into** vtr to l. s.o. i. **the house,** laisser entrer qn dans la maison; **to l. s.o. i. a secret,** mettre qn dans le secret. **'let 'off** vtr **1.** (a) tirer, faire partir (un feu d'artifice) (b) lâcher (de la vapeur) **2.** (a) **to l. s.o. off (from) doing sth,** dispenser qn de faire qch (b) faire grâce, pardonner, à (qn); **to be l. off with a fine,** en être quitte pour une amende. **'let 'on** vi F: **don't l. on that I was there,** n'allez pas dire que j'y étais. **'let 'out** vtr **1.** laisser sortir, faire sortir; élargir (un prisonnier, une jupe); laisser échapper (un cri, un secret); vider (l'eau); **to l. one-self out,** sortir (en fermant la porte); **to l. the air out of sth,** dégonfler qch **2.** louer (des canots). **'let 'through** vtr laisser passer. **'letting** n location f; louage m. **'let 'up** vi (of rain) diminuer; (of frost) s'adoucir; (of pers) s'arrêter.

lethal ['li:θl] a mortel; **l. weapon,** arme meurtrière.

lethargy ['leθədʒi] n léthargie f; torpeur f. **le'thargic** a léthargique.

letter ['letər] I. n **1.** lettre f; **to the l.,** à la lettre, au pied de la lettre **2.** lettre; **are there any letters for her?** y a-t-il du courrier pour elle? **3. man of letters,** homme de lettres. II. vtr marquer (qch) avec des lettres, graver des lettres sur (qch). **'letterbox** n (pl -es) boîte f à lettres. **'lettercard** n carte-lettre f. **'letterhead** n en-tête m. **'lettering** n **1.** lettrage m **2.** lettres fpl; inscription f. **'letterpress** n **1.** impression f typographique **2.** texte m (d'un livre).

lettuce ['letis] n laitue f; salade f.

leuka(e)mia [lu:'ki:miə] n Med: leucémie f.

level ['levl] I. n **1.** niveau m (de la mer, de la société); **on a l. with,** au niveau, à la hauteur, de; **at eye l.,** à la hauteur des yeux; **room on a l. with the garden,** pièce de plain-pied avec le jardin; **at ministerial l.,** à l'échelon ministériel **2.** terrain m, surface f, de niveau; Aut: Rail: palier m; **on the l.,** (i) sur un terrain plat (ii) F: (of pers.) loyal; de bonne foi; **speed on the l.,** vitesse en palier **3.** Tls: (spirit) l., niveau (à bulle d'air). II. a **1.** (a) (not sloping) horizontal; (terrain) de niveau, à niveau (b) (flat) égal; uni (c) **l. with,** de niveau avec; au niveau de; à (la) hauteur de; **l. with the ground,** à ras de terre; **l. spoonful,** cuillerée rase; **to draw l. with,** arriver à la hauteur de; Rail: **l. crossing,** passage à niveau **2.** (ton) soutenu; F: **to do one's l. best,** faire tout son possible. III. v (levelled) **1.** vtr (a) niveler, aplanir (un terrain) (b) raser (une maison) (c) pointer, braquer (un fusil); diriger (une longue-vue) (at, sur); lancer (des accusations) (against s.o., contre qn); porter (un coup) (at s.o., à qn) **2.** vi esp NAm: F: **to l. with s.o.,** parler franchement à qn. **'level-'headed** a (of pers) (bien) équilibré. **'level 'off, 'out** vi (a) **1.** (of aircraft) voler en palier **2.** (of prices) se stabiliser.

lever ['li:vər] I. n levier m. II. vtr to **l. sth up,** soulever qch au moyen d'un levier. **'leverage** n force f, puissance f, de levier; Fig: prise f (**on s.o.,** sur qn).

leveret ['levərit] n Z: levraut m.

levity ['leviti] n légèreté f.

levy ['levi] I. n **1.** levée f (d'un impôt) **2.** impôt m, contribution f. II. vtr lever, percevoir (un impôt); imposer (une amende).

lewd [lju:d] a lubrique, lascif.

lexicon ['leksikən] n lexique m. **lexi'cographer** n lexicographe mf.

liable ['laiəbl] a **1.** Jur: responsable (**for,** de) **2.** sujet, exposé (**to,** à); **l. to a fine,** passible d'une amende; **l. for military service,** astreint au service militaire **3. difficulties are l. to occur,** des difficultés pourraient bien se présenter. **lia'bility** n (pl -ies) **1.** Jur: responsabilité **2.** (a) Com: **liabilities,** (ensemble m des) dettes f; **assets and liabilities,** actif et passif m (b) Fig: poids mort; (of thg) handicap m **3.** (a) **l. to a fine,** risque m d'amende (b) disposition f, tendance f (**to (do) sth,** à (faire) qch); **l. to explode,** danger m d'explosion.

liaison [li'eizɔn] n liaison f. **li'aise** vi F: faire, effectuer, la liaison (**with,** avec).

liar ['laiər] n menteur, -euse.

lib [lib] abbr F: liberation.

libel ['laibl] I. n diffamation f (par écrit); calomnie f; **l. action,** procès en diffamation. II. vtr (**libelled**) Jur: diffamer (qn) (par écrit); calomnier (qn). **'libellous,** NAm: **'libelous** a (écrit) diffamatoire; calomnieux.

liberal ['libərəl] **1.** a libéral; (of pers) d'esprit large; sans préjugés (b) libéral, généreux; **l. with one's money,** prodigue de son argent (c) abondant; **l. provision,** ample provision (de qch) **2.** a & n Pol: libéral, -ale. **'liberalism** n Pol: libéralisme m. **libe'rality** n (a) libéralité f; générosité f (b) largeur f d'esprit. **'liberally** adv libéralement.

liberate ['libəreit] vtr libérer; mettre en liberté. **libe'ration** n libération f; mise f en liberté. **'liberator** n libérateur, -trice.

liberty ['libəti] n (pl **liberties**) liberté f; **at l.,** en liberté; **at l. to do sth,** libre de faire qch; **to take the l. of doing sth,** se permettre de faire qch; **to take liberties,** se permettre, prendre, des libertés (**with,** avec).

Libra ['li:brə] Prn Astr: la Balance.

library ['laibrəri] n (pl **libraries**) bibliothèque f; **record l.,** discothèque f. **li'brarian** n bibliothécaire mf.

libretto [li'bretou] n (pl **libretti, -os**) libretto m; livret m; (d'opéra). **li'brettist** n librettiste mf.

Libya ['libiə] Prn Geog: Libye f. **'Libyan** a & n libyen, -enne.

lice [lais] npl see **louse**.

licence, NAm: **license** ['laisəns] n **1.** permis m, autorisation f; patente f; **l. to sell alcoholic drinks,** licence f de débit de boissons; **television l.,** impôt (annuel) sur un téléviseur; **marriage l.** = dispense f de bans; **driving,** NAm: **driver's, l.,** permis de conduire; **pilot's l.,** brevet de pilote **2.** licence; **poetic l.,** licence poétique.

license ['laisəns] n **1.** n NAm: = **licence 2.** vtr accorder un permis, une patente, à (qn); **licensed premises,** débit m de boissons; **licensed pilot,** pilote breveté. **licen'see** n (of public house) propriétaire mf; gérant, -ante.

licentious [lai'senʃəs] a licencieux.

lichen ['laikən, 'litʃən] n lichen m.

lick [lik] I. n **1.** coup m de langue; F: **a l. and a promise,** un brin de toilette **2. l. of paint,** petite couche de peinture **3.** F: **at a great l.,** à toute vitesse.

II. *vtr* **1.** lécher; **to l. one's lips,** se (pour)lécher les babines; **to l. s.o. into shape,** dégrossir qn; **to l. s.o.'s boots,** lécher les bottes de, à, qn **2.** *F:* battre (qn). **'licking** *n F:* (*a*) rossée *f,* raclée *f* (*b*) défaite *f,* raclée.

lid [lid] *n* **1.** couvercle *m*; *F:* **that puts the l. on it!** ça, c'est le comble! il ne manquait plus que ça! **2.** (*eyelid*) paupière *f*.

lie¹ [lai] **I.** *n* (*a*) mensonge *m*; **it's a pack of lies,** pure invention que tout cela; **to tell lies,** mentir; dire des mensonges (*b*) **to give the l. to sth,** donner un démenti formel à qch. **II.** *vi* (lying) mentir. **'lying¹ 1.** *a* (*of pers*) menteur **2.** *n* mensonge(s) *m*(*pl*).

lie² **I.** *vi* (lay [lei]; lain [lein]; lying) **1.** (*a*) être couché (à plat); (*of corpse*) reposer; **he was lying on the floor,** il était couché par terre; **to l. asleep,** être endormi; **to l. dead,** être (étendu) mort; (*on tombstone*) **here lies,** ci-gît (*b*) être, rester, se tenir; **to l. still,** rester tranquille, immobile; **to l. low** (i) rester tapi (ii) *Fig:* faire le mort (*c*) = **lie down 2.** (*of thg*) être, se trouver; **his clothes were lying on the ground,** ses vêtements étaient éparpillés par terre; **the snow lay thick, deep,** la neige était épaisse; **the snow did not l.,** la neige n'a pas tenu; **to l. heavy on,** peser sur; **the responsibility lies with the author,** la responsabilité incombe à l'auteur; **the difference lies in this,** la différence consiste en ceci; **a vast plain lay before us,** une vaste plaine s'étendait devant nous; **a brilliant future lies before him,** un brillant avenir s'ouvre devant lui. **II.** *n* (*a*) (*NAm:* **= lay**) disposition *f* (du terrain) **2.** *Golf:* assiette *f* (de la balle). **'lie a'bout** *vi* (*of thgs*) traîner; (*of pers*) paresser. **'lie 'back** *vi* se renverser (en arrière); **to l. back and take things easy,** se reposer. **'lie 'down** *vi* se coucher, s'étendre; s'allonger; (*to rest*) se reposer; *Fig:* **he won't take it lying down,** il ne se laissera pas faire. **'lie-'down** *n F:* **to have a l.-d.,** se coucher; faire une sieste. **'lie 'in** *vi* faire la grasse matinée. **'lie-'in** *n* **to have a l.-in,** faire la grasse matinée. **'lie 'up** *vi* (*a*) garder le lit (*b*) se cacher. **'lying²** *a* **l. (down),** couché, étendu; allongé.

lieu [lju:] *n* **in l. of,** au lieu de.

lieutenant [lef'tenənt, *NAm:* lu:-] *n* (*a*) lieutenant *m*; *Navy:* lieutenant de vaisseau; **second l.,** sous-lieutenant *m*; *Navy:* **l.-commander,** capitaine *m* de corvette; *Mil:* **l.-general,** général *m* de corps d'armée; **l.-colonel,** lieutenant-colonel *m*; *MilAv:* **flight l.,** capitaine d'aviation) (*b*) (*deputy*) adjoint, -ointe.

life [laif] *n* (*pl* lives) **1.** vie *f*; **it's a matter of l. and death,** c'est une question de vie ou de mort; **l.-and-death struggle,** lutte désespérée; **to come to l.,** s'animer; **to take s.o.'s l.,** tuer qn; **to take one's own l.,** se suicider; **to save s.o.'s l.,** sauver la vie de, à, qn; **to escape with one's l.,** s'en tirer la vie sauve; **run for your lives!** sauve qui peut! **I can't for the l. of me understand,** je ne comprends absolument pas; **not on your l.!** jamais de la vie! **full of l.,** plein de vie; **to put new l. into s.o., sth,** ranimer, galvaniser (qn, une entreprise); **he's the l. and soul of the party,** c'est le boute-en-train de la bande; **animal l.,** la vie animale; **bird l.,** les oiseaux *m* **2.** (*a*) vie, vivant *m* (de qn); **never in (all) my l.,** jamais de la vie; **at my time of life,** à mon âge; **early l.,** enfance *f*; **appointed for l.,** nommé à vie; **l. imprisonment,** emprisonnement à perpétuité; **l. insurance,** assurance-vie *f* (*b*) **l. (story),** biographie *f*; vie (*c*) durée *f* (d'une ampoule) **3. to depart this l.,** quitter ce monde; mourir; **the American way of l.,** la vie américaine; *F:* **what a l.!** quelle vie! **that's l.!** **such is l.!** c'est la vie! **he's seen l.,** il a beaucoup vécu. **'lifebelt** *n* ceinture *f* de sauvetage. **'lifeblood** *n* (*a*) sang *m* (*b*) *Fig:* âme *f* (d'une entreprise); pivot *m* (de l'économie). **'lifeboat** *n* (i) (*coastal*) canot *m* (ii) (*ship's*) embarcation *f,* de sauvetage. **'lifeguard** *n* (*at seaside*) gardien *m* de plage. **'lifejacket** *n* gilet *m* de sauvetage. **'lifeless** *a* sans vie; inanimé; sans vigueur. **'lifelike** *a* (portrait) vivant. **'lifeline** *n* (*a*) *Nau:* ligne *f* de sauvetage (*b*) corde *f* de communication (de plongeur) (*c*) *Fig:* moyen *m* unique de communication. **'lifelong** *a* (amitié) de toute la vie; (ami) de toujours. **'lifesaving** *n* sauvetage *m*. **'life-size(d)** *a* (portrait) de grandeur naturelle, (de) grandeur nature. **'lifetime** *n* vie; **in his l.,** de son vivant; **it's the work of a l.,** c'est le travail de toute une vie; **once in a l.,** une fois dans la vie.

lift [lift] **I.** *n* **1. to give s.o. a l.,** (i) (*in vehicle*) conduire, déposer, qn (ii) (*hitchhiker*) prendre qn en stop (iii) *F:* remonter le moral à qn **2.** (*NAm:* = ELEVATOR) ascenseur *m*; (goods) **l.,** monte-charge *m inv*; **l. attendant,** liftier *m*. **II.** *v* **1.** *vtr* (*a*) lever, soulever (un poids); lever (les yeux); **to l. up one's head,** redresser la tête; **to l. sth down,** descendre qch (*b*) arracher (des pommes de terre) (*c*) *F:* voler, chiper (*d*) lever (un embargo) **2.** *vi* se soulever; (*of fog*) se lever. **'lift-boy, -man** *n* liftier. **'lift 'off** *vi Space:* décoller. **'lift-off** *n Space:* décollage *m*.

ligament ['ligəmənt] *n Anat:* ligament.

ligature ['ligətjər] *n* ligature *f*; *Mus:* liaison *f*.

light¹ [lait] **I.** *n* **1.** (*a*) lumière *f*; **by the l. of,** à la lumière de; **l. year,** année-lumière *f*; *Phot:* **l. meter,** photomètre *m*; (*of crime*) **to come to l.,** se montrer; se dévoiler; **to bring to l.,** révéler; mettre en évidence; **to see the l.,** (i) voir le jour (ii) comprendre (iii) trouver son chemin de Damas (*b*) éclairage *m*; **against the l.,** à contre-jour; **to be, stand, in s.o.'s l.,** cacher le jour, la lumière, à qn; **to be in one's own l.,** tourner le dos à la lumière; *Fig:* **in a new l.,** sous un jour nouveau; **in the l. of,** dans le contexte de; **to throw l. on sth,** éclairer, éclaircir, qch **2.** (*a*) lumière, lampe *f* (de bureau); (*pers*) **leading l.,** personnalité *f* (*b*) feu *m*; **traffic lights,** feux de signalisation (routière); *F:* feu rouge; **the lights were (on) green,** le feu était au vert; *Fig:* **to see the red l.,** se rendre compte du danger; (*on vehicle*) **lights,** phares *mpl*; **tail, rear, lights,** feux arrière (*c*) (*on coast, at sea*) phare *m* **3. to set l. to sth,** mettre le feu à qch; (*for cigarette*) **have you got a l.?** avez-vous du feu? **4.** *Art: Phot:* clair *m* (d'une œuvre). **II.** *v* (lit *or* lighted) **1.** *vtr* (*a*) allumer; **to l. a fire,** faire du feu (*b*) éclairer (une maison) (by electricity), à l'électricité) **2.** *vi* s'allumer; (*of fire, wood*) prendre (feu). **III.** *a* (-er, -est) **1.** clair; (bien) éclairé; **it's l.,** il fait jour **2.** (*of hair*) blond; (*of colour*) clair; **l. blue,** bleu clair *inv*. **'lighten¹ 1.** *vtr* éclairer (les ténèbres; un visage); éclaircir (une couleur) **2.** *vi* s'éclairer. **'lighter¹** *n* briquet *m* (à gaz, à essence). **'lighthouse** *n Nau:* phare. **'lighting** *n* **1.** allumage *m* (d'une lampe) **2.**

éclairage; *Th:* éclairages *mpl;* **l. engineer,** éclairagiste *m;* **l.-up time,** heure d'éclairage (de véhicules). **'lightship** *n* bateau-feu *m.* **'light 'up 1.** *vtr* allumer, éclairer; illuminer (un chemin, un visage) **2.** *vi (a)* s'allumer; *(of face)* s'éclairer, s'illuminer *(b) F:* allumer une cigarette.

light² **I.** *a* (**-er, -est**) **1.** *(a)* léger; **to be l. on one's feet,** avoir le pas léger *(b) (deficient)* (poids) faible **2. to be a l. sleeper,** avoir le sommeil léger **3.** *(a) (of punishment)* léger *(b)* (travail) facile, peu fatigant **4. l. reading,** lecture(s) délassante(s), amusante(s); **to make l. of sth,** prendre qch à la légère. **II.** *adv* **to travel l.,** voyager avec peu de bagages. **'lighten²** *vtr* alléger. **'lighter²** *n Nau:* allège *f.* **'light-fingered** *a* voleur, chipeur. **'light-'headed** *a* **to feel l.-h.,** être pris de vertige; avoir la tête qui tourne. **'light-'hearted** *a* au cœur léger; allègre; gai. **'lightly** *adv* légèrement; à la légère; **to sleep l.,** avoir le sommeil léger; **to get off l.,** s'en tirer à bon compte. **'lightness** *n* légèreté *f.* **'light 'on** *vtr* trouver par hasard. **lights** *npl* mou *m* (de bœuf). **'lightweight 1.** *n Box:* poids léger **2.** *a* (pantalon) léger.

lightning ['laitniŋ] **I.** *n* éclairs *mpl,* foudre *f;* **a flash of l.,** un éclair; **struck by l.,** frappé par la foudre; **like l., as quick as l.,** rapide comme l'éclair; **l. conductor,** paratonnerre *m.* **II.** *a (of progress)* foudroyant; (visite) éclair *inv; Ind:* (grève) surprise *inv.*

like¹ [laik] **I.** *a* **1.** semblable, pareil, tel; **l. father, l. son,** tel père, tel fils; **they are as l. as two peas,** ils se ressemblent comme deux gouttes d'eau *k.* *(a)* **I want to find one l. it,** je veux trouver le pareil, la pareille; **a woman l. you,** une femme comme vous; **to be l. s.o., sth,** ressembler à qn, qch; **what's he l.?** comment est-il? **what's the weather l.?** quel temps fait-il? **she has been l. a mother to him,** elle lui a servi de mère; **I never saw anything l. it,** je n'ai jamais rien vu de pareil; **it costs something l. ten pounds,** cela coûte quelque dix livres; **that's something l.!** voilà qui est réussi, qui est bien! **there's nothing l. being frank,** rien de tel que de parler franchement; **she's nothing l. as pretty as you,** elle est (bien) loin d'être aussi jolie que vous *(b)* **that's just l. a woman!** voilà bien les femmes! **that's just l. me!** c'est bien de moi! **II.** *prep* comme; **just l. anybody else,** tout comme un autre; **he ran l. anything,** il courait comme un dératé; **don't talk l. that,** ne parlez pas comme ça. **III.** *adv F:* **l. enough, as l. as not,** probablement. **IV.** *n* semblable *mf,* pareil, -eille; **I never saw the l. of it,** je n'ai jamais vu chose pareille; **music, painting and the l.,** la musique, la peinture et autres choses du même genre; **his l.,** son pareil, ses pareils; *F:* **the likes of him,** des gens comme lui. **V.** *conj F:* (= AS) **l. I do,** comme moi. **'likelihood** *n* probabilité *f;* vraisemblance *f;* **in all l.,** selon toute probabilité; vraisemblablement. **'likely I.** *a* **1.** probable; vraisemblable; **that's a l. story!** la belle histoire! **it's l. to rain,** il est probable qu'il pleuvra; il y a des chances (pour) qu'il pleuve; **it's very l. (to happen),** c'est très probable; **it's not (very) l.,** c'est peu probable; il y a peu de chances; **he's not (very) l. to succeed,** il a peu de chances de réussir; **he's the most l., the likeliest, (one) to win,** c'est lui qui a le plus de chances de gagner **2.** bon

(endroit); (projet) qui promet; (livre) susceptible (**to interest s.o.,** d'intéresser qn); **the likeliest place to find him,** l'endroit où on a le plus de chances de le trouver. **II.** *adv* most, very, l., *NAm:* l., (très) probablement; vraisemblablement; **as l. as not,** probablement; *F:* **not l.!** pas de danger! **'liken** *vtr* assimiler. **'likeness** *n* ressemblance *f* (to, à); **family l.,** air *m* de famille; **portrait that is a good l.,** portrait bien ressemblant. **'likewise** *adv* **1.** *(moreover)* de plus; aussi **2.** *(similarly)* **to do l.,** faire de même, en faire autant.

like² *vtr* **1.** aimer; **I l. him,** je l'aime bien; il me plaît; je le trouve sympathique; **which do you l. best, better, most?** lequel préférez-vous? **how do you l. him?** comment le trouvez-vous? **he likes school,** il se plaît à l'école; **as much as you l.,** tant que vous voudrez; **your father won't l. it,** votre père ne sera pas content; **whether he likes it or not,** qu'il le veuille ou non; *F:* **I l. that!** par exemple! **2.** *(a)* **I l. to see them,** j'aime les voir; **he doesn't l. people to talk about it,** il n'aime pas qu'on en parle; **would you l. some more?** en voulez-vous, en voudriez-vous, encore un peu? **I should have liked to go there,** j'aurais bien voulu y aller *(b)* **as you l.,** comme vous voudrez; **as he likes,** comme il lui plaira; **to do (just) as one likes,** en faire à sa tête; **he thinks he can do anything he likes,** il se croit tout permis; **if you l.,** si vous voulez. **'likeable** *a* agréable, sympathique. **likes** *npl* goûts *mpl,* préférences *fpl;* **likes and dislikes,** sympathies *f* et antipathies. **'liking** *n* goût *m;* penchant *m;* **to one's l.,** à souhait; **is it to your l.?** cela est-il à votre goût? **to take a l. to sth,** prendre goût à qch; **I've taken a l. to him,** il m'est devenu sympathique; **to have a l. for,** aimer.

lilac ['lailək] **1.** *n Bot:* lilas *m* **2.** *a* lilas *inv.*

lilt [lilt] *n* rythme *m,* cadence *f.*

lily ['lili] *n (pl* **lilies)** *Bot:* lis *m;* **l. of the valley,** muguet *m.*

limb [lim] *n* **1.** membre *m;* **to tear l. from l.,** mettre en pièces **2.** (grosse) branche (d'un arbre); *Fig:* **out on a l.,** sur la corde raide.

limber ['limbər] *vtr* assouplir (le corps). **'limber 'up** *vi* se chauffer (les muscles).

limbo ['limbou] *n Theol:* les limbes *mpl;* **to be in l.,** être tombé dans l'oubli.

lime¹ [laim] *n* chaux *f;* **slaked l.,** chaux éteinte. **'limestone** *n* pierre *f* à chaux; calcaire *m.*

lime² *n Bot:* citron vert; lime *f.*

lime³ *n* **l.** (tree), tilleul *m.*

limelight ['laimlait] *n* **in the l.,** en bien en vue; en vedette.

limerick ['limərik] *n* poème *m* comique en cinq vers.

limit ['limit] **I.** *n* limite *f;* borne *f;* **within a l. of ten kilometres,** dans un rayon de dix kilomètres; **within limits,** dans une certaine limite; **age l.,** limite d'âge; **speed l.,** limitation *f* de vitesse; vitesse limite, maximale; *F:* **that's the l.!** ça, c'est le comble! **you're the l.!** vous êtes impossible! **II.** *vtr* limiter, borner, restreindre. **limi'tation** *n* limitation *f;* restriction *f;* **to know one's limitations,** connaître ses limites. **'limited** *a* limité; restreint; (esprit) borné; **l. company** = société anonyme; **l. (liability) company** = - société à responsabilité limitée; **l. edition,** (édition à) tirage limité. **'limitless** *a* sans bornes.

limp¹ [limp] **1.** n claudication f; **to have a l.,** boiter. **II.** vi boiter; clopiner. **'limping** a boiteux.

limp² a mou; flasque; (reliure) souple. **'limply** adv mollement. **'limpness** n mollesse f.

limpet ['limpit] n Moll: patelle f.

limpid ['limpid] a limpide; clair.

linctus ['liŋktəs] n Pharm: sirop m.

line¹ [lain] **I.** n **1.** ligne f; trait m; (on skin) ride f; **l. drawing,** dessin au trait; Fig: **one must draw the l. somewhere,** il y a limite à tout; (telephone) **on the l.,** au téléphone; au bout du fil **2.** (a) ligne; (side by side) rangée f, ligne (de personnes, d'objets); **to fall, get, into l.,** se mettre en ligne; former des rangs; s'aligner; Fig: **to come into l., be in l.,** se conformer (with, à); **to bring into l.,** mettre (qn) d'accord, (qch) en accord (with, avec) (b) (one behind the other) file f (de personnes, de voitures); esp NAm: queue f; **in l.,** à la file; en file; **to be lined, in (a) l.,** s'aligner, se ranger dans une file; NAm: **to stand in l.,** faire la queue; **he's in l. for promotion,** il y a toutes les chances qu'il sera promu (c) Mil: **l. of battle,** ligne de combat; **l. of attack,** ligne d'attaque; Fig: **all along the l.,** sur toute la ligne (d) (direction) **l. of argument,** raisonnement m; **what l. are you going to take?** quel parti allez-vous prendre? **along, on, these lines,** de cette façon, de ce genre; **on the right lines,** dans la bonne voie; **to take a tough l.,** prendre des mesures sévères; F: **to get a l. on,** (i) obtenir des tuyaux sur (qch) (ii) se renseigner sur (qn) (e) ligne (de mots écrits); vers m (de poésie); (of actor) **lines,** rôle m; (in dictating) **new l.,** à la ligne; F: **to drop s.o. a l.,** envoyer une (petit) mot à qn **3.** ligne (a) compagnie f (de navigation) (b) Rail: (track) voie **4.** ligne (de descendants); **in direct l.,** en ligne directe **5.** genre (d'affaires); métier m; **what's his l. (of business)?** qu'est-ce qu'il fait (comme travail)? **it's not (in) my l.,** ce n'est pas dans mes cordes **6.** Com: série f (d'articles); article m. **II.** vtr **1. lined paper,** papier réglé; **lined face,** visage ridé; (of face) **to become lined,** se rider **2. troops lined the streets,** des troupes faisaient la haie, s'alignaient, le long des trottoirs; **street lined with trees,** rue bordée d'arbres. **'linesman, -men** n Fb: juge m de touche. **'line 'up 1.** vtr (a) aligner (b) prévoir, avoir en vue; **to have sth lined up for s.o.,** préparer qch à qn **2.** vi s'aligner; se mettre en ligne. **'line-up** n (a) rangée (de personnes) (b) Sp: (formation f d'une) équipe.

line² vtr doubler (un vêtement); Tchn: garnir, revêtir; Fig: **to l. one's pocket(s),** faire sa pelote. **'lining** n doublure f (de robe); Aut: garniture f (de frein); Tchn: revêtement m.

linen ['linin] n **1.** (toile f de) lin m; fil m (de lin); **l. sheets,** draps fil **2.** linge m; lingerie f; **table l.,** linge de table; **l. basket,** panier à linge; **l. cupboard,** armoire à linge; F: **don't wash your dirty l. in public,** il faut laver son linge sale en famille.

liner ['lainər] n (a) Nau: paquebot m (b) **bin l.,** sac m à poubelle; **nappy l.,** couche f à jeter.

linger ['liŋər] vi s'attarder (over, sur); tarder, (of doubt) subsister; **to l. (on),** traîner; **to l. over a meal,** prolonger un repas. **'lingering** a (regard) prolongé; (doute) qui subsiste encore; (of death) lent.

lingerie ['lɛ̃:ʒəri(:)] n lingerie f (pour femmes).

lingo ['liŋgou] n F: **1.** langue f (d'un pays) **2.** argot m, jargon m.

linguist ['liŋgwist] n linguiste mf. **lin'guistic** a linguistique. **lin'guistics** npl linguistique f.

liniment ['linimənt] n liniment m.

link [liŋk] **I.** n **1.** chaînon m, maillon m, anneau m (d'une chaîne) **2.** lien m, trait m d'union; **missing l.,** vide m, lacune f (dans une théorie); anneau manquant; **air l.,** liaison aérienne. **II.** v **1.** vtr **to l. (together, up),** enchaîner, (re)lier, (re)joindre, (r)attacher (with, to, à); **closely linked facts,** faits étroitement unis; **to l. arms,** se donner le bras **2.** vi **to l. on to sth.,** se lier avec sth., se (re)joindre, s'attacher s'unir, à qch. **'link-up** n lien, liaison; WTel: TV: (émission f en) duplex m.

links [liŋks] npl terrain m de golf.

linoleum, F: lino [li'nouliəm, 'lainou] n linoléum m, lino m.

linseed ['linsi:d] n **l. oil,** huile f de lin.

lint [lint] n (a) Med: tissu, pansement, ouaté (b) peluche f (d'une étoffe).

lintel ['lintl] n linteau m.

lion ['laiən] n (a) lion m; **l. cub,** lionceau m; **the l.'s share,** la part du lion; **mountain l.,** puma m, couguar m (b) Fig: célébrité f. **'lioness** n lionne f. **'lion-hearted** a au cœur de lion.

lip [lip] n **1.** (a) lèvre f; babine f (d'un animal); Fig: **to keep a stiff upper l.,** serrer les dents; **to pay l. service to sth,** rendre à qch des hommages peu sincères (b) F: insolence f, toupet m; **none of your l.!** en voilà assez! **2.** bord m, rebord m (d'une tasse); bec m (d'un pot). **'lipread** vtr & i (lipread [-red]) lire sur les lèvres. **'lipreading** n lecture f sur les lèvres. **'lipstick** n rouge m à lèvres.

liquefy ['likwifai] vtr & i (se) liquéfier. **lique'faction** n liquéfaction f.

liqueur [li'kjuər] n liqueur f; **l. brandy,** fine f.

liquid ['likwid] **1.** a (a) liquide; Fin: **l. assets,** disponibilités f (b) (œil) limpide; (son) doux **2.** n liquide m; **l. measure,** mesure pour les liquides. **'liquidate** vtr liquider. **liqui'dation** n liquidation f; (of business) **to go into l.,** déposer son bilan. **'liquidize** vtr Cu: liquéfier; passer au mixeur. **'liquidizer** n DomEc: mixeur m.

liquor ['likər] n boisson f alcoolique; spiritueux m; NAm: **l. store** = marchand de vins.

liquorice ['likəris] n réglisse f.

lisp [lisp] **I.** n zézaiement m; **to have a l.,** zézayer. **II.** vi & tr zézayer.

lissom ['lisəm] a souple, agile, leste.

list¹ [list] **I.** n (a) liste f; wine l., carte f des vins; **to make a l.,** faire une liste (b) Com: catalogue m; **l. price,** prix (de) catalogue. **II.** vtr inscrire (des noms) (sur une liste); faire une liste de; cataloguer (des articles); classer (un monument).

list² vi (of ship) donner de la bande.

listen ['lisn] v ind tr **1. to l. to s.o., sth,** écouter qn, qch; **to l. to s.o. singing,** écouter chanter qn **2.** faire attention; écouter; **he wouldn't l. (to us),** il a refusé de nous entendre. **'listener** n auditeur, -trice; **to be a good l.,** savoir écouter. **'listen 'in** vi écouter la radio; être à l'écoute. **'listen ('out) 'for** vtr & i faire attention à.

listless ['listləs] a indifférent; sans énergie; apathique. **'listlessly** adv sans énergie. **'listlessness** n manque m d'énergie; indifférence f; apathie f.

lit [lit] *see* **light**[1].
litany ['litəni] *n* litanie *f*.
liter ['li:tər] *n NAm:* litre *m*.
literacy ['litərəsi] *n* fait *m* de savoir lire et écrire; degré *m* d'instruction, d'alphabétisation.
literal ['litərəl] *a* littéral, (sens) propre (d'un mot); (*of pers, mind*) prosaïque; **in a l. sense**, au pied de la lettre. **'literally** *adv* littéralement; (interpréter qch) au pied de la lettre.
literary ['lit(ə)rəri] *a* littéraire.
literate ['litərət] *a* qui sait lire et écrire.
literature ['litərətʃər] *n* (*a*) littérature *f* (*b*) *Com:* prospectus *mpl*; documentation *f*.
lithe [laið] *a* souple, agile.
lithograph ['liθəgra:f, -æf] I. *n* lithographie *f*. II. *vtr* lithographier. **li'thographer** *n* lithographe *mf*. **litho'graphic** *a* lithographique. **li'thography** *n* lithographie.
litigation [liti'geiʃn] *n* litige. **'litigant** *n* plaideur, -euse. **li'tigious** *a* litigeux.
litmus ['litməs] *n* tournesol *m*; **l. paper**, papier de tournesol.
litre, NAm: liter ['li:tər] *n* litre *m*.
litter ['litər] I. *n.* **1.** (*bed*) litière *f* **2.** *Agr:* litière (de paille) **3.** (*a*) détritus *m*; papiers jetés par terre (*b*) fouillis *m*, désordre *m* **4.** portée *f* (d'un animal). II. *vtr* mettre (une chambre) en désordre; joncher (le plancher) (with, de); (*of clothes*) **to l. the floor**, traîner sur le plancher; **table littered with papers**, table encombrée de papiers. **'litterbin** *n* boîte *f* à ordures. **'litterlout, NAm: -bug** *n* personne *f* qui jette des ordures n'importe où.
little ['litl] (*comp* **less**; *superl* **least**) I. *a* **1.** petit; **l. finger**, petit doigt; **wait a l. while!** attendez un petit moment! **poor l. girl!** pauvre petite! *F:* **tiny l.**, tout petit **2.** peu (de); **l. money**, peu d'argent; **a l. money**, un peu d'argent. II. *n.* **1.** (**a, the**) **l.**, (un, le) peu; **to eat l. or nothing**, manger peu ou point; **he knows, does, very l.**, il ne sait pas, ne fait pas, grand-chose; **I took very l. (of it)**, j'en ai pris très peu, moins que rien; **too l., so l., time**, trop peu, si peu, de temps; **I see very l. of him**, je le vois rarement; **you can get them for as l. as £10**, ils ne coûtent pas plus cher que £10; **l. by l.**, petit à petit; peu à peu; *Prov:* **every l. helps**, on fait feu de tout bois **2. a l. more (tea)**, encore un peu (de thé); **a l. longer**, (i) (objet) un peu plus long (ii) (rester) encore un peu. III. *adv* peu; **l. more than an hour ago**, il n'y a guère, il y a à peine, plus d'une heure; **l. did he know that**, il ne se doutait guère que; **l. known**, peu connu. **'littleness** *n* petitesse *f*.
liturgy ['litədʒi] *n* liturgie *f*. **li'turgical** *a* liturgique.
live I. *a* [laiv] **1.** (*a*) vivant; en vie; **a real l. burglar**, un cambrioleur en chair et en os (*b*) (question) d'actualité (*c*) (charbon) ardent (*d*) *TV: WTel:* (émission) en direct **2.** (*a*) (munitions) de guerre; (*of bomb*) amorcé (*b*) *El:* (fil) sous tension; *F:* **he's a real l. wire**, il est dynamique. II. *adv* [laiv] *TV: WTel:* (émettre) en direct. III. *v* [liv] **1.** *vi* (*a*) vivre; **long l. the king!** vive le roi! **as, so, long as I l.**, tant que je vivrai; *Prov:* **you l. and learn**, on apprend à tout âge; **l. and let l.**, il faut que tout le monde vive; **to l. by doing sth**, gagner sa vie à faire qch; **to l.**

well, faire bonne chère (*b*) **where do you l.?** où habitez-vous? **he lives at number 7 rue de Rivoli**, il habite au numéro 7, rue de Rivoli; **to l. in the country, in Bonn, in Spain, in a big house**, habiter (à) la campagne, (à) Bonn, en Espagne, (dans) une grande maison; **house not fit to l. in**, maison inhabitable; **to l. with s.o.**, habiter, vivre, avec, chez, qn; **to be easy to l. with**, être facile à vivre; **to l. together**, habiter, vivre, ensemble **2.** *vtr* vivre (sa vie); mener (une vie heureuse). **'live 'down** *vtr* faire oublier (un scandale). **'live 'for** *vtr* ne vivre que pour (qn, qch). **'live 'in** *vi* être logé et nourri; (*of student*) être interne. **livelihood** ['laiv-] *n* vie; moyens *mpl* d'existence. **liveliness** ['laiv-] *n* vivacité *f*, animation *f*, entrain *m*; vie. **lively** ['laiv-] *a* (**-ier, -iest**) (*a*) vif, animé, plein d'entrain; vivant; (argument) mouvementé; (air) entraînant; (*of pers*) gai; *F:* **things are getting l.**, ça chauffe! (*b*) **to take a l. interest in sth**, s'intéresser vivement à qch. **'liven 'up** ['laiv-] *vtr & i* (s')animer. **'live 'off** *vtr* (*a*) vivre de (légumes, de la terre) (*b*) vivre aux crochets de (qn). **'live 'on 1.** *vtr* vivre, se nourrir, de (légumes); **to have enough to l. on**, avoir de quoi vivre; **to l. on £100 a week**, vivre avec £100 par semaine **2.** *vi* survivre. **'live 'out** *vi* ne pas être logé; (*of student*) être externe. **livestock** ['laiv-] *n* bétail *m*, bestiaux *mpl*. **'live 'through** *vtr & i* passer (l'hiver); vivre (des événements). **'live 'up 1.** *vtr F:* **to l. it up**, faire la noce **2.** *vi* **to l. up to**, vivre selon (ses principes); faire honneur à (sa réputation); remplir (sa promesse). **living** ['liv-] I. *a* vivant; en vie; **l. or dead**, mort ou vif; **I didn't see a l. soul**, je n'ai pas vu âme qui vive. II. *n* **1.** vie; **l. standard, standard of l.**, niveau de vie; **l. space**, espace vital; **l. room**, salle de séjour **2. to earn, make, a l.**, gagner sa vie, de quoi vivre; **to work for one's l., for a l.**, travailler pour vivre **3.** *Ecc:* bénéfice *m*, cure *f* **4. the l.**, les vivants *mpl*; **he's still in the land of the l.**, il est encore de ce monde.
liver ['livər] *n Anat:* foie *m*. **'liverish** *a F:* **to feel l.**, avoir une crise de foie.
livery ['livəri] *n* livrée *f*.
livid ['livid] *a* (teint) livide; blême (**with anger**, de colère); (ciel) plombé; *F:* **to be absolutely l.**, être furieux, dans une colère folle.
lizard ['lizəd] *n* lézard *m*.
llama ['lɑ:mə] *n Z:* lama *m*.
load [loud] I. *n* (*a*) fardeau *m*; poids *m*; **that's a l. off my mind**, quel soulagement! (*b*) charge *f*, chargement *m* (d'un camion); cargaison *f* (d'un navire) (*c*) *F:* **loads of, a l. of**, des tas *m*, des quantités *f*, de; **we've got loads of time**, nous avons largement le temps. II. *v* **1.** *vtr* **to l. sth (up with) sth**, charger qch de qch; **to l. s.o. with favours**, combler qn de faveurs; **to be loaded (down) with**, être surchargé de; (*of pers*) être accablé de (soucis) **2.** *vi* **to l. (up)**, charger; prendre une charge. **'loaded** *a* (*a*) (camion) chargé (**with**, de) (*b*) (dé) pipé (*c*) (*of question*) insidieux (*d*) *F:* (*of pers*) **to be l.**, rouler sur l'or. **'loading** *n* chargement *m*.
loaf[1] [louf] *n* (*pl* **loaves**) pain *m*; **sugar l.**, pain de sucre.
loaf[2] *vi* **to l. (about)**, flâner, fainéanter. **'loafer** *n* flâneur, -euse; fainéant, -ante.

loam [loum] n terreau m; terre grasse.

loan [loun] I. n 1. prêt m; on l., prêté; à titre de prêt 2. emprunt m; **to have the l. of sth.,** emprunter qch; Fin: **to get, raise, a l.,** emprunter de l'argent (on, sur); **l. word,** mot d'emprunt. II. vtr prêter.

loathe [louð] vtr détester (qch); **doing sth,** (de) faire qch; **to do sth,** répugner à faire qch; **faire qch à contrecœur.**

loath [louθ] vtr détester (qch); **doing sth,** (de) faire qch). **'loathing** n dégoût m, répugnance f. **'loathsome** a dégoûtant, répugnant; repoussant, écœurant.

loaves [louvz] npl see **loaf.**

lobby ['lɔbi] n 1. (a) vestibule m (b) Parl: = salle f des pas perdus 2. Pol: etc: lobby m, groupe m de pression.

lobe [loub] n lobe m.

lobster ['lɔbstər] n homard m; **l. pot,** casier m à homards.

local ['loukəl] 1. a local, régional; (vin) du pays; (médecin) du quartier; Tp: (of call) urbain; **l. government** = administration départementale, communale 2. n (a) habitant, -ante, du pays; **the locals,** les gens m du pays (b) F: café m du coin. **lo'cality** n localité f; endroit m, lieu m; voisinage m; **in this l.,** dans cette région. **'localize** vtr localiser. **'locally** adv localement; dans la région; **staff recruited l.,** personnel engagé sur place. **lo'cate** vtr 1. localiser; découvrir; repérer 2. situer (un bâtiment). **lo'cation** n situation f, emplacement m; Cin: **on l.,** en extérieur.

loch [lɔχ] n Scot: lac m.

lock¹ [lɔk] n mèche f, boucle f (de cheveux).

lock² I. n 1. serrure f; fermeture f; **mortise l.,** serrure encastrée; **under l. and key,** sous clef; (of pers) **sous les verrous; l., stock and barrel,** tout sans exception 2. Aut: **(steering) l.,** angle m de braquage; **on full l.,** braqué au maximum 3. écluse f; **l. keeper, gardien d'écluse; éclusier m.** II. v 1. vtr (a) fermer à clef; **to l. s.o. in a room,** enfermer qn dans une pièce (b) bloquer, enrayer (les roues); **to be locked (together) in a struggle,** être engagés corps à corps dans une lutte; **to be locked in each other's arms,** se tenir étroitement embrassés 2. vi (a) (of door) fermer à clef (b) (of wheels) se bloquer, s'enrayer. **'locker** n armoire f; coffre m. **'lock 'in** vtr enfermer (à clef). **'lockjaw** n Med: tétanos m. **'lock 'on(to)** vtr & i esp Ball: accrocher (un objectif). **'lock 'out** vtr empêcher (qn) d'entrer en fermant la porte à clef; Ind: lock-outer (le personnel). **'lockout** n Ind: lock-out m inv. **'locksmith** n serrurier m. **'lock 'up 1.** vtr mettre sous clef; fermer (une maison) à clef; enfermer (qn) 2. vi fermer (boutique, la maison). **'lockup** n (a) cellule f, prison f (b) **l. (shop),** petit magasin (sans logement) (c) **l. (garage),** box m.

locket ['lɔkit] n Jewel: médaillon m.

locomotive [loukə'moutiv] 1. a locomotif 2. n locomotive f. **loco'motion** n locomotion f.

locum (tenens) ['loukəm('tenenz)] n remplaçant, -ante (d'un médecin).

locust ['loukəst] n Ent: criquet m pèlerin; (grande) sauterelle.

lodge [lɔdʒ] I. n 1. loge f (de concierge); pavillon m d'entrée (d'une propriété); **shooting l.,** pavillon de chasse 2. (in freemasonry) loge, atelier m. II. v 1. vtr (a) loger, héberger (qn) (b) to l. **a complaint,** porter plainte 2. vi (a) (se) loger, être en pension (**with s.o.,** chez qn) (b) (of thg) rester, se loger. **'lodger** n locataire mf; (meals provided) pensionnaire mf. **'lodging** n 1. logement m, hébergement m 2. **lodgings,** logement; appartement meublé; chambre meublée; **to live in lodgings,** vivre en meublé m.

loft [lɔft] n (a) grenier m (b) (in church) **organ l.,** tribune f (de l'orgue).

lofty ['lɔfti] a 1. haut, élevé 2. (of pers) hautain. **'loftily** adv (répondre) avec hauteur.

log¹ [lɔg] I. n 1. bûche f; tronçon m (de bois); rondin m; **to sleep like a l.,** dormir comme une souche; **l. cabin,** cabane en rondins 2. Nau: (device) loch m 3. carnet m de route; Nau: journal m, livre m de bord; Av: carnet de vol. II. vtr **(logged)** (a) porter (un fait) au journal, au carnet (b) noter (des résultats). **'logbook** n = **log¹** 3; Aut: F: = carte grise.

logarithm, F: **log²** ['lɔgəriðm] n logarithme m, log m; **log table,** table de logarithmes.

loggerheads ['lɔgəhedz] npl **to be at l. with s.o.,** être en conflit, en désaccord, avec qn.

logic ['lɔdʒik] n logique f. **'logical** a logique. **'logically** adv logiquement. **lo'gistics** npl logistique f.

logo ['lougou] n logo m.

loin [lɔin] n 1. loins, reins m; **l. cloth,** pagne m 2. Cu: filet m (d'agneau, de veau); longe f (de veau); aloyau m (et faux-filet m) (de bœuf); **l. chop,** côtelette de filet.

loiter ['lɔitər] vi flâner, traîner; Jur: rôder d'une manière suspecte. **'loiterer** n flâneur, -euse; rôdeur, -euse.

loll [lɔl] vi (of tongue) pendre; (of pers) être étendu; **to l. (back) in an armchair,** se prélasser dans un fauteuil. **'loll a'bout** vi fainéanter.

lollipop ['lɔlipɔp] n sucette f.

lolly ['lɔli] n F: 1. sucette f; **ice l.,** sucette glacée 2. argent m, pognon m.

London ['lʌndən] Prn Geog: Londres m. **'Londoner** n Londonien, -ienne.

lone [loun] a solitaire, seul.

lonely ['lounli] a solitaire, isolé; (endroit) désert; **to feel very l.,** se sentir bien seul. **'loneliness** n solitude f, isolement m. **'lonesome** a = **lonely.**

long¹ [lɔŋ] I. a (-er, -est) 1. long, longue; **to be ten metres l.,** avoir dix mètres de long, être long de dix mètres; **how l. is the room?** quelle est la longueur de la pièce? **the best by a l. way,** de beaucoup le meilleur; **the longest way round,** le chemin le plus long; **to make sth longer,** (r)allonger qch; **to pull a l. face,** faire une grimace 2. (in time) **how l. are the holidays?** combien de temps durent les vacances? **the days are getting longer,** les jours commencent à allonger; **it will take a l. time,** ce sera long; **they're a l. time (in) coming,** ils se font attendre; **a l. time ago,** il y a longtemps; **to wait for a l. time,** attendre longtemps; **he's been there for a l. time,** il est là depuis longtemps; **time ago at the longest,** trois jours (tout) au plus. II. n 1. **the l. and the short of it is that,** le fin mot de l'affaire c'est que 2. **before l.,** avant peu; sous peu; **for l.,** pendant longtemps; **he hasn't been there for l.,** il n'est pas là depuis longtemps; **it won't take l.,** cela ne sera pas long. III. adv

1. (a) longtemps; **so l. as, as l. as,** (i) tant que (ii) pourvu que + *sub;* **he wasn't l. in putting things straight,** il avait bientôt fait de réparer le désordre; **you weren't l. about it,** vous avez vite fait; **he won't be l.,** il ne tardera pas; il n'en a pas pour longtemps; **don't be l.!** dépêchez-vous! *F:* **so l.!** à bientôt! (b) **he hasn't been back l.,** il n'est pas de retour depuis longtemps; **I have l. been convinced of it,** j'en suis convaincu depuis longtemps (c) **how l.?** combien de temps? **how l. have you been here?** depuis combien de temps êtes-vous ici? **how l. do the holidays last?** combien de temps durent les vacances? **2. l. before, after,** longtemps avant, après; **not l. before,** peu de temps avant; **l. ago,** il y a longtemps; **he died l. ago,** il est mort depuis longtemps; **not l. ago,** depuis peu **3. all day l.,** à longueur de journée **4. I could no longer see him,** je ne le voyais plus; je ne pouvais plus le voir; **I couldn't wait any longer,** je ne pouvais pas attendre plus longtemps; **three months longer,** encore trois mois; pendant trois mois encore; **how much longer?** combien de temps encore? **'long-'distance** a (vol) sur long parcours; *Sp:* (coureur) de fond; *Tp:* (of call) interurbain; **l.-d. lorry driver,** routier *m.* **'long-drawn-'out** a prolongé; (histoire) interminable. **lon'gevity** n longévité *f.* **'longhaired** a (personne) aux cheveux longs; (animal) à poils longs. **'longhand** n écriture *f* ordinaire. **'long-'lived** a (race) qui vit longtemps; (amitié) de longue durée. **'long-'lost** a perdu depuis longtemps. **'long-'playing** a **l.-p. record,** (disque) 33 tours (*m inv*); microsillon *m.* **'long-'range** a (avion) long-courrier; (canon) à longue portée; (prévision météorologique) à longue échéance. **long-'sighted** a hypermétrope; presbyte. **'long-'standing** a ancien; de longue date. **'long-'suffering** a patient; indulgent. **'long-'term** a à longue échéance, à long terme. **'long-'winded** a (of pers) verbeux, intarissable; (of speech) interminable.

long² vi avoir bien envie **(to do sth,** de faire qch). **'long 'for** vi avoir grande envie de (qch); désirer (qch) ardemment. **'longing** n désir ardent, grande envie **(for,** de). **'longingly** adv avec (un œil d')envie.

longitude ['lɔndʒitjuːd,- 'lɔngi-] n longitude *f.*

loo [luː] n *F:* cabinets *mpl;* toilettes *fpl,* W-C *mpl.*

look [luk] **I.** n **1.** regard *m;* **to have a l. at sth,** jeter un coup d'œil sur, à, qch; regarder qch; **to have a l. round the town,** faire un tour dans la ville; **let me have a l.,** fais voir **2.** (a) aspect *m,* air *m;* allure *f,* apparence *f;* mine *f* (de qn); **I like the l. of him,** il me plaît, je le trouve sympathique; **by the look(s) of him,** à le voir; **by the look(s) of it,** autant qu'on puisse en juger (b) **(good) looks,** belle mine, beauté *f.* **II.** vi & vtr **1.** regarder; *Prov:* **l. before you leap,** il faut réfléchir avant d'agir; **to l. the other way,** (i) regarder de l'autre côté (ii) détourner les yeux; **l. (and see) what time it is,** regardez quelle heure il est; **l. where you're going,** regardez où vous allez **2. to l. s.o. (full) in the face,** regarder qn (bien) en face, dans les yeux; **I could never l. him in the face again,** je me sentirais toujours honteux devant lui; **to l. s.o. up and down,** regarder qn de haut en bas **3.** avoir l'air, paraître, sembler; **he looks young for his age,** il ne paraît pas son âge; **she looks her age,** elle paraît bien son âge; **he looks ill, well,** il a mauvaise, bonne, mine; **that looks good,** cela a l'air bon; cela fait bien; **things are looking bad,** les choses prennent une mauvaise tournure; **what does he l. like?** comment est-il? **he looks like his brother,** il ressemble à son frère; **he looks the part,** il a le physique de l'emploi; **it looks as if, it looks like, he's going to win,** on dirait qu'il va gagner; **you l. as if you've slept badly,** tu as l'air d'avoir mal dormi; **it looks like it,** cela en a l'air; on le dirait; **it looks like rain,** on dirait qu'il va pleuvoir **4.** *F:* **l. here!** voyons! dites donc! écoutez donc! **'look a'bout, a'round** vi to l. a. **(oneself),** regarder autour de soi; **to l. a. for sth, s.o.,** chercher qch, qn, du regard. **'look 'after** *v ind tr* soigner, s'occuper de; veiller à (ses intérêts); entretenir (une voiture); garder (un magasin); **he can l. a. himself,** il sait se débrouiller. **'look-alike** n sosie *m* (de qn). **'look at** *v ind tr* regarder, considérer; **to l. at him,** à le voir; **the hotel is not much to l. at,** l'hôtel ne paie pas de mine; **way of looking at things,** manière de voir les choses; **whichever way you l. at it,** de n'importe quel point de vue. **'look a'way** vi détourner les yeux, la vue. **'look 'back** vi (a) regarder en arrière; se retourner **(at sth,** pour regarder qch); *Fig:* **he never looked b.,** il est allé de mieux en mieux (b) **what a day to l. b. on!** quelle journée à se rappeler plus tard! **'look 'down 1.** vtr parcourir (une liste) **2.** vi regarder en bas; baisser les yeux; **to l. d. on,** (i) (also l. d. at) regarder de haut (ii) *Fig:* mépriser. **'look for** *v ind tr* chercher; **go and l. f. him,** va le chercher. **'look 'forward to** vtr attendre (qch) avec plaisir, avec impatience; **I'm looking f. to seeing him again,** je me réjouis, j'ai hâte, de le revoir. **'look 'in** vi (a) regarder à l'intérieur (b) **to l. in (again),** (re)passer; **to l. in on s.o.,** entrer chez qn en passant. **'look-in** n *F:* **he won't get a l.-in,** il n'a pas la moindre chance. **'looking glass** n miroir *m,* glace *f.* **'look 'into** *v ind tr* (a) **to l. i. s.o.'s eyes,** regarder qn dans les yeux (b) examiner, étudier (une question); s'informer de (qch). **'look 'on 1.** vtr considérer, regarder (**as,** comme); **I don't l. on it in that light,** je n'envisage pas la chose ainsi **2.** vi être spectateur; **suppose you helped me instead of looking on,** si vous m'aidiez au lieu de me regarder faire. **'look 'onto** vtr (of building) donner sur. **'look 'out 1.** vi (a) regarder (au) dehors; **to l. o. of the window,** regarder par la fenêtre (b) **room that looks out on the garden,** pièce qui donne sur le jardin (c) **to l. o. for s.o.,** guetter (l'arrivée de) qn (d) *F:* **l. o.!** (faites) attention! prenez garde! **2.** vtr chercher (qch). **'lookout** n **1.** (a) guet *m,* surveillance *f;* Nau: veille *f;* **to keep a, be on the, l. for s.o.,** guetter qn (b) poste *m* d'observation, de guet (c) (pers) guetteur *m;* Nau: homme de veille **2.** *F:* **that's a poor l. for him,** c'est de mauvais augure pour lui; **that's his l.,** ça c'est son affaire. **'look 'over** vtr jeter un coup d'œil sur, à; parcourir (qch) des yeux; examiner (qch); visiter (une maison). **'look 'round** vi (a) regarder (autour de soi); **to l. r. for s.o.,** chercher qn du regard (b) se retourner (pour voir); **don't l. r.!** ne regardez pas en arrière! **2.** vtr visiter (des jardins). **'look 'through** vtr parcourir, examiner (des papiers); repasser (un compte). 'look to vtr compter sur (qn) (to, for, pour). 'look 'up 1. vi (a) regarder en haut; lever les yeux (b) to l. up to s.o., respecter qn (c) (of business) reprendre; things are looking up for him, ses affaires vont mieux 2. vtr (a) chercher (un mot dans le dictionnaire, un train dans l'indicateur) (b) aller, venir, voir (qn). 'look upon v ind tr = look on[1].

loom[1] [lu:m] n métier m (à tisser).

loom[2] vi to l. (up), apparaître indistinctement; surgir, sortir (out of the fog, du brouillard); (of danger) menacer; (of event) to l. large, paraître imminent.

loony ['lu:ni] a & n F: fou, folle; toqué, -ée; l. bin, maison de fous.

loop [lu:p] I. n (a) boucle f (b) (contraceptive) stérilet m. II. vtr faire une boucle à (qch); Av: to l. the loop, boucler la boucle. 'loophole n 1. (in wall) meurtrière f 2. Fig: échappatoire f.

loose [lu:s] I. a (a) (not fixed) dégagé, mal assujetti; branlant; (dent) qui branle; (of page) détaché; (of knot) défait; lâche; (of screw) desserré; El: (of connection) mauvais; to come, get, work, l., se dégager, se détacher; branler; (of knot) se défaire; se relâcher; (of screw) se desserrer; (of machine parts) prendre du jeu; to let l., lâcher (un animal); to break l., s'échapper; l. sheets (of paper), feuilles volantes; l. end, bout pendant (d'une corde); Fig: to be at a l. end, ne rien avoir à faire; se tourner les pouces (b) (vêtement) ample, lâche, large; (peau) flasque (c) (marchandises) en vrac (d) (terre) meuble; (tissu) lâche; (of bowels) relâché; l. change, petite monnaie (e) (raisonnement) vague, peu exact; (style) lâche; (of translation) approximatif (f) (of pers, behaviour) dissolu; (of morals) relâché; (of woman) de mauvaise vie; l. living, mauvaise vie. II. vtr défaire (un nœud); délier; détacher. 'loosebox n box m (d'écurie). 'loose-fitting a (vêtement) ample, lâche, large. looseleaf a (album) à feuilles volantes, à feuillets mobiles. 'loosely adv 1. (tenir qch) sans serrer; (noué) lâchement 2. (parler) vaguement, inexactement. 'loosen v 1. vtr défaire, relâcher (un nœud); desserrer (un écrou); relâcher (son étreinte, les intestins); délier (la langue à qn) 2, vi (of knot) se défaire; (of screw) se desserrer; (of rope) se relâcher. 'looseness n 1. état branlant (d'une dent); (of machine parts) jeu 2. relâchement m (d'une corde); ampleur f (d'un vêtement) 3. (a) vague m, imprécision f (d'un raisonnement) (b) relâchement (de la discipline, des mœurs). 'loosen 'up vi se chauffer (les muscles).

loot [lu:t] I. n butin m. II. v 1. vtr piller, saccager (une ville) 2. vi se livrer au pillage. 'looter n pillard m. 'looting n pillage m.

lop [lɔp] vtr (lopped) élaguer, tailler (un arbre); to l. (off), couper. 'lop-eared a (lapin) aux oreilles pendantes. 'lop'sided a qui penche d'un côté; de travers, de guingois.

lope [loup] vi to l. (along), aller, courir, à petits bonds.

loquacious [lə'kweiʃəs] a loquace. lo'quacity [-'kwæs-] n loquacité f.

lord [lɔːd] n 1. seigneur m; maître m 2. the L., le Seigneur; Dieu m; F: (good) L.! mon Dieu! 3. (title) lord m; to live like a l., vivre en grand seigneur; my

l., (i) monsieur le baron, etc (ii) (to bishop) monseigneur (iii) monsieur le juge; monsieur le président; Parl: the House of Lords, la Chambre des Lords. to 'lord 'it vi prendre de grands airs; to l. it over s.o., vouloir en imposer à qn. 'lordliness n 1. dignité f 2. hauteur f. 'lordly a 1. de grand seigneur; noble 2. hautain, altier. 'lordship n your l., votre seigneurie; monsieur le comte, etc; (to bishop) monseigneur.

lore [lɔːr] n connaissances fpl (de la campagne).

lorry ['lɔri] n (pl lorries) camion m; l. driver, camionneur m; (long-distance) routier m. 'lorryload n chargement m (d'un camion).

lose [lu:z] v (lost [lɔst]) 1. vtr (a) perdre; to l. one's way, get lost, perdre son chemin; se perdre; s'égarer; F: get lost! fiche-moi le camp! F: you've lost me! je n'y suis plus! to l. one's life, perdre la vie; there were no lives lost, personne n'a été tué; to be lost at sea, périr en mer; to l. strength, s'affaiblir; to l. one's voice, avoir une extinction de voix; to l. weight, perdre du poids; I've lost 5 kilos, j'ai maigri de 5 kilos (b) faire perdre (qch à qn); the mistake lost him the match, cette faute lui a coûté le match (c) semer (un poursuivant) (d) ne pas entendre (les paroles de qn); I lost most of his last sentence, la plupart de sa dernière phrase m'a échappé (e) (of clock) retarder (5 minutes a day, de 5 minutes par jour) 2. vi (a) perdre (on a deal, on an article, au change, sur un article); you can't l. (by it), vous n'y perdez rien; to l. to s.o., se faire battre par qn (b) (of clock) retarder. 'lose 'out vi perdre (on the deal, au change). 'loser n 1. I'm the l. by it, j'y perds; he's a born l., il ne réussit jamais 2. perdant, -ante; to be a good, bad, l., être bon, mauvais, joueur. 'losing a (joueur) perdant; l. battle, bataille de vaincu. lost a perdu; (âme) en peine; l. in thought, perdu dans ses pensées; he looks l., il a l'air dépaysé; he's l. to the world, le monde n'existe plus pour lui; I'm l. for words, les mots me manquent; F: I'm l.! je n'y suis plus! l. property office, US: l. and found department, (service des) objets trouvés; the joke was l. on him, il n'a pas compris, saisi, la plaisanterie.

loss [lɔs] n (a) perte f; extinction f (de la voix); dead l., perte sèche; to sell at a l., vendre à perte; it's her l., c'est elle qui y perd; he's no great l.! la perte n'est pas grande; to be at a l., être dépaysé, désorienté; to be at a l. what to do, say, ne pas savoir que faire, que dire; I'm at a l. for words, les mots me manquent (b) Tchn: déperdition f (de chaleur); écoulement m (de sang).

lot [lɔt] n 1. to draw lots for sth, tirer au sort pour qch, tirer qch au sort; by l., par le tirage au sort; to throw in one's l. with s.o., partager le sort, la fortune, de qn 2. (a) sort, part f, partage m; it fell to my l. to decide, c'était à moi de décider (b) destin m, destinée f 3. (a) (at auction) lot m (b) esp NAm: (lot de) terrain m; parking l., parking m (c) F: (pers) a bad l., un mauvais sujet (d) the l., le tout; that's the l., c'est tout; the whole l. of you, vous tous 4. (a) a l. of, lots of, beaucoup de; lots of things to do, un tas de choses à faire; lots of people, énormément de gens; what a l. of people! que de monde! such a l. of, tant, tellement, de; quite a l., une quantité considérable, F: pas mal (de); I see quite a l. of him, je le vois assez souvent; *adv phr* **times have changed a l.,** les temps ont beaucoup, bien, changé.

loth [louθ] *a see* **loath**.

lotion ['louʃn] *n* lotion *f*.

lottery ['lɔtəri] *n* (*pl* **lotteries**) loterie *f*.

lotus ['loutəs] *n* lotus *m*; (*in yoga*) **l. position,** posture de méditation.

loud [laud] **1.** *a* (**-er, -est**) (*a*) bruyant, retentissant; grand (bruit); gros (rire); **l. voice,** voix forte; **in a l. voice,** à haute voix; **l. cheers,** vifs applaudissements (*b*) (*of colour*) criard, voyant; (*of clothes*) tapageur **2.** *adv* haut, fort, à haute voix; **loudest,** le plus fort; **out l.,** tout haut. **loud'hailer** *n* porte-voix *m inv.* **'loudly** *adv* (crier) haut, fort, à voix haute; (rire) bruyamment. **'loudmouth** *n F:* gueulard, -arde. **'loudmouthed** *a F:* fort en gueule, gueulard. **'loudness** *n* force *f* (d'un bruit); (grand) bruit. **loud'speaker** *n* haut-parleur *m.*

lounge [laundʒ] **I.** *n* **1.** salon *m*; **sun l.,** véranda *f*; **l. suit,** (i) complet-veston *m* (ii) (*on invitation*) tenue de ville **2.** *NAm: Furn;* canapé *m*; **l. chair,** fauteuil *m* **II.** *vi* se prélasser (dans un fauteuil). **'lounge a'bout** *vi* flâner; fainéanter. **'lounger** *n* lit *m* de plage; (fauteuil) relax(e) *m.*

louse [laus] *n* (*pl* **lice**) (*a*) pou *m*, *pl* poux (*b*) *P:* salaud *m.* **'lousy** [-zi] *a* **1.** pouilleux **2.** *F:* sale; moche; **l. trick,** sale tour; (*of pers*) **to feel l.,** se sentir patraque.

lout [laut] *n* rustre *m.* **'loutish** *a* rustre.

love [lʌv] **I.** *n* **1.** amour *m*; **there's no l. lost between them,** ils ne peuvent pas se sentir; **for the l. of God,** pour l'amour de Dieu; **to work for l.,** travailler pour rien; **give your parents my l.,** faites mes amitiés à vos parents; *Corr:* **l. to all,** affectueusement à tous; **not for l. or money,** à aucun prix; **to fall in l. with s.o.,** tomber amoureux de qn; **to be in l.,** être amoureux; **to make l.,** faire l'amour (**with,** to, avec); **to marry for l.,** faire un mariage d'amour; **l. match,** mariage d'amour; **l. letter,** billet doux; **l. story,** histoire, roman, d'amour **2.** (*pers*) (*a*) **my l.,** mon amour (*b*) *F:* mon petit, ma petite **3.** *Ten:* zéro *m*, rien *m*; **l. 15,** rien à quinze. **II.** *vtr* aimer; **to l. doing sth,** aimer, adorer, faire qch; **will you do it?—I'd l. to,** voulez-vous le faire?—avec le plus grand plaisir; **she'd l. to see you,** elle serait ravie de te voir. **'lovable** *a* sympathique. **'loveliness** *n* beauté *f*, charme *m.* **'lovely** *a* beau, charmant, ravissant; (repas) excellent; (soirée) très agréable; **l. and warm,** bien chaud; **it's been l. seeing you again,** j'ai été ravi de vous revoir. **'lovemaking** *n* (*a*) cour (amoureuse) (*b*) rapports sexuels. **'lover** *n* **1.** (*a*) amant, -ante; amoureux, -euse (*b*) (*outside marriage*) amant **2.** amateur *m*, ami(e) (de qch); **nature l.,** ami, amoureux, de la nature. **'loving** *a* affectueux, aimant; **nature-l.,** qui aime la nature; *Corr:* **your l. son,** votre fils affectueux. **'lovingly** *adv* affectueusement, tendrement.

low¹ [lou] **I.** *a* (**-er, -est**) (*a*) bas; (plafond) peu élevé; (rendement) faible; **l. down,** (bien) bas; **l. tide,** marée basse; *Geog:* **the L. Countries,** les Pays-Bas *m*; **cook over a l. heat,** faire cuire à feu doux; **the coal is getting l., we're (getting) l. on coal,** le charbon commence à manquer; **l. prices,** bas prix; **the lowest price,** le der nier prix; **£100 at the lowest,** £100 au bas mot; **l. speed,** petite vitesse; **in a l. voice,** à voix basse, à mi-voix; **lower jaw,** mâchoire inférieure; **lower classes, animals,** classes inférieures, animaux inférieurs; **lower school,** petites classes; *Ecc:* **l. mass,** messe basse (*b*) (malade) bien bas; **to feel, be, l., to be in l. spirits,** être déprimé, abattu (*c*) (*of behaviour*) mauvais; **l. trick,** sale tour; **lowest of the l.,** dernier des derniers. **II.** *adv* bas; **l. down,** (bien) bas; **l. paid,** mal payé; **the lowest paid workers,** les employés les moins payés; (*of stocks*) **to run l.,** s'épuiser. **III.** *n* (*a*) *Meteor:* dépression *f* (*b*) **all-time l.,** record le plus bas. **'lowbrow** *a* peu intellectuel; **'low-'budget** *a* bon marché; peu coûteux. **'low-cut** *a* (*of dress*) décolleté. **'lowdown I.** *n* bas; ignoble; sale (coup). **II.** *n F:* **to give s.o. the l.,** tuyauter qn (**on,** sur). **'lower** *vtr* baisser; descendre; mettre (une embarcation) à la mer; abaisser (une vitre); diminuer la hauteur de (qch); réduire (un prix); **to l. oneself** (**so far as**) **to,** s'abaisser à (faire qch). **'lowering**¹ *n* descente *f*; mise *f* à la mer (d'une embarcation); abaissement *m* (d'une vitre); diminution *f* de la hauteur (de qch); réduction *f*, diminution (de prix). **'low-fat** *a* (yaourt) maigre. **'low-flying** *a* (avion) volant à basse altitude. **'low-'grade** *a* de qualité inférieure. **'low-key** *a* calme; discret; mesuré; (décor) neutre, sobre. **'lowland** *n* plaine (basse); *Geog:* **the Lowlands,** la Basse-Écosse. **'low-'lying** *a* situé en bas; (terrain) bas. **'low-'pitched** *a* (son) grave.

low² *vi* (*of cattle*) meugler. **'lowing** *n* meuglement *m.*

lowering² ['lauəriŋ] *a* (ciel) sombre, menaçant.

loyal ['lɔiəl] *a* fidèle (**to,** à); loyal (**to,** envers). **'loyalist** *a & n* loyaliste (*mf*). **'loyally** *adv* loyalement. **'loyalty** *n* fidélité *f*; loyauté *f.*

lozenge ['lɔzindʒ] *n* (*sweet*) pastille *f*, tablette *f.*

LP *abbr* long-playing (record), (disque) 33 tours (*m inv*).

LPG *abbr* liquefied petroleum gas.

LSD *abbr* lysergic acid diethylamide.

Ltd *abbr* limited (company).

lubricate ['lu:brikeit] *vtr* lubrifier; graisser; **lubricating oil,** huile de graissage. **'lubricant** *n* lubrifiant *m.* **lubri'cation** *n* lubrification *f*, graissage *m.* **'lubricator** *n* graisseur *m.*

lucid ['lu:sid] *a* lucide. **lu'cidity** *n* lucidité *f.* **'lucidly** *adv* lucidement.

luck [lʌk] *n* **1.** hasard *m*, chance *f*, fortune *f*; **good l.,** bonne chance, bonheur *m*; **bad l.,** malchance *f*; **good l. (to you)!** bonne chance! **to be down on one's l.,** être dans la déveine; **to try one's l.,** tenter sa chance; **to bring s.o. (good) l., bad l.,** porter bonheur, malheur, à qn; **better l. next time!** ça ira mieux une autre fois; **worse l.!** tant pis! **bad, hard, tough, l.!** pas de chance, de veine *f*! **as l. would have it,** le hasard a fait que; par bonheur **2.** bonheur, bonne fortune, (bonne) chance; **to keep sth for l.,** garder qch comme porte-bonheur; **stroke, bit, of l.,** coup de chance, de hasard, de veine; **to be in l., out of l.,** avoir de la chance, ne pas avoir de chance. **'luckily** *adv* heureusement; par bonheur. **'lucky** *a* (*a*) (*of pers*) heureux, chanceux; **to be l.,** avoir de la chance; *F:* (**you**) **l. thing!** veinard, -arde! *Iron:* **you'll be l.!** tu peux toujours courir! (*b*) (coup) de bonheur; (jour) de veine; **how l.!** quelle chance! (of thg) **to be l.,** porter bonheur; **l. charm,** porte-bonheur m inv.

lucrative ['luːkrətiv] a lucratif.

ludicrous ['luːdikrəs] a ridicule; risible. **'ludicrously** adv ridiculement.

ludo ['luːdou] n jeu m des petits chevaux.

lug [lʌg] vtr **(lugged)** traîner, tirer.

luggage ['lʌgidʒ] n bagage(s) m(pl); **l. label,** étiquette à bagages; **l. rack,** Rail: filet m, porte-bagages m inv; Aut: galerie f; Rail: **l. van,** fourgon m (à bagages).

lugubrious [luːˈguːbriəs] a lugubre.

lukewarm ['luːkwɔːm] a tiède.

lull [lʌl] **I.** n moment m de calme; arrêt m (dans une conversation); Nau: accalmie f. **II.** vtr bercer, endormir (qn); calmer, apaiser, endormir (les soupçons). **lullaby** ['lʌləbai] n Mus: berceuse f.

lumber¹ ['lʌmbər] **I.** n **1.** vieux meubles; fatras m; **l. room,** débarras m **2.** esp NAm: bois m de charpente. **II.** vtr **1.** encombrer (une pièce); F: **to l. s.o. with sth,** charger qn de faire qch (qu'il ne veut pas faire); **to be lumbered with s.o., sth,** avoir qn, qch, sur les bras **2.** NAm: abattre (des arbres); débiter (du bois). **'lumberjack** n bûcheron m. **'lumberman,** pl -men n NAm: (a) exploitant forestier (b) bûcheron. **'lumberyard** n chantier m de bois.

lumber² vi **to l. along,** avancer à pas pesants, pesamment. **'lumbering** a lourd, pesant.

luminous ['luːminəs] a lumineux.

lump¹ [lʌmp] **I.** n **1.** (a) (gros) morceau, bloc m (de pierre); motte f (d'argile); morceau (de sucre); (in sauce) grumeau m; **l. sum,** (i) somme globale (ii) prix, paiement, forfaitaire; **to have a l. in one's throat,** avoir la gorge serrée (b) bosse f (au front); Med: grosseur f (au sein) **2.** F: (pers) empoté, -ée. **II.** vtr mettre en bloc, en tas. **'lump to'gether** vtr réunir; mettre ensemble. **'lumpy** a (of sauce) grumeleux.

lump² vtr F: **if he doesn't like it he can l. it,** si cela ne lui plaît pas, qu'il s'arrange.

lunacy ['luːnəsi] n aliénation mentale; folie f; **it's sheer l.,** c'est de la folie. **'lunatic** a & n fou, folle; aliéné, -ée; dément, -ente; **l. fringe,** cinglés mpl (d'un groupe).

lunar ['luːnər] a lunaire; (éclipse) de (la) lune.

lunch [lʌn(t)ʃ] **I.** n (pl lunches) déjeuner m; **to have l.,** déjeuner; **l. hour = lunchtime. II.** vi déjeuner. **luncheon** ['lʌn(t)ʃən] n déjeuner; **l. voucher,** chèque-repas m, ticket-repas m. **'lunchtime** n heure f du déjeuner.

lung [lʌŋ] n poumon m; **iron l.,** poumon d'acier; **l. cancer,** cancer du poumon.

lunge [lʌndʒ] **I.** n mouvement (précipité) en avant. **II.** vi se précipiter en avant.

lurch¹ [ləːtʃ] n **to leave s.o. in the l.,** planter là qn.

lurch² **I.** n (pl lurches) **1.** (of ship, car) embardée f; cahot m **2.** (of pers) pas titubant. **II.** vi **1.** (of ship, car) faire une embardée **2.** (of pers) tituber; **to l. along, in,** marcher, entrer, en titubant.

lure ['ljuər] **I.** n **1.** Fish: leurre m **2.** (a) piège m (b) attrait m (de la mer). **II.** vtr attirer, allécher; **lured into a trap,** attiré, entraîné, dans un piège.

lurid ['ljuərid] a **1.** (of colour) voyant, éclatant; (of light) vif; (of flames, sun) rougeoyant **2.** (of description) coloré, frappant; (film) corsé, à sensation; **l. description,** description saisissante; **he described it in l. detail,** il l'a décrit en ajoutant tous les horribles détails.

lurk [ləːk] vi (a) se cacher rester tapi (b) rôder. **'lurking** a caché; (soupçon) vague; **l. thought,** arrière-pensée f.

luscious ['lʌʃəs] a succulent, savoureux.

lush [lʌʃ] a (of vegetation) luxuriant; abondant; (of furnishings) luxueux, riche.

lust [lʌst] n luxure f; désir (charnel); **l. for power,** soif f du pouvoir.

lustre, NAm: **luster** ['lʌstər] n lustre m.

lusty ['lʌsti] a vigoureux, fort, robuste. **'lustily** adv vigoureusement.

lute [luːt] n Mus: luth m.

luxuriance [lʌgˈzjuəriəns] n luxuriance f, exubérance f. **lu'xuriant** a luxuriant, exubérant. **lu'xuriantly** adv avec exubérance. **lu'xuriate** vi prendre ses aises (dans un bain); s'abandonner (**in,** à).

luxury ['lʌkʃəri] n (pl luxuries) luxe m; **to live in (the lap of) l.,** vivre dans le (plus grand) luxe; **it's quite a l. for us,** c'est du luxe pour nous; **l. flat,** appartement de (grand) luxe. **luxurious** [lʌgˈzjuəriəs] a luxueux, somptueux; (vie) de luxe. **lu'xuriously** adv luxueusement; dans le luxe. **lu'xuriousness** n luxe.

lying¹, ² ['laiiŋ] a & n see **lie¹, ²**

lymph [limf] n Physiol: lymphe f; **l. gland,** ganglion lymphatique. **lym'phatic** a lymphatique.

lynch [lin(t)ʃ] vtr lyncher. **'lynching** n lynchage m.

lynx [liŋks] n (pl lynxes) Z: lynx m; loup-cervier m.

lyre ['laiər] n Mus: lyre f. **'lyrebird** n oiseau-lyre m, pl oiseaux-lyres.

lyric ['lirik] **1.** a lyrique **2.** n (a) poème m lyrique (b) usu pl paroles fpl (d'une chanson); **l. writer,** parolier, -ière. **'lyrical** a lyrique. **lyricism** ['lirisizm] n lyrisme m.

M

M, m [em] *n* (la lettre) M, m *m or f.*
M *abbr* motorway.
MA *abbr Sch:* Master of Arts.
ma'am [mɑːm] *n* madame; *F:* school m., maîtresse *f* d'école.
mac [mæk] *n F:* imper *m.*
macadam [mə'kædəm] *n* macadam *m.* **ma'cadamize** *vtr* macadamiser.
macaroni [mækə'rouni] *n Cu:* macaroni *m;* **m. cheese,** macaroni au gratin.
macaroon [mækə'ruːn] *n Cu:* macaron *m.*
macaw [mə'kɔː] *n Orn:* ara *m.*
mace¹ [meis] *n* masse *f.*
mace² *n Bot: Cu:* macis *m.*
macerate ['mæsəreit] *vtr & i* macérer.
Mach [mæk] *n* M. **(number),** (nombre de) Mach.
machete [mə'tʃeti] *n* machette *f.*
machination [mæki'neiʃn] *n* machination *f,* complot *m.*
machine [mə'ʃiːn] **1.** *n* (*a*) machine *f;* **m. tool,** machine-outil *m;* **sewing m., washing m.,** machine à coudre, à laver; **m. operator,** machiniste *m;* **m. shop,** atelier d'usinage; *Med:* **kidney m.,** rein artificiel; *Com:* **slot m.,** (i) distributeur *m* automatique (ii) *F:* machine à sous (*b*) (*pers*) automate *m,* robot *m* (*c*) *Pol:* **the party m.,** les rouages *mpl* du parti (*d*) **m. gun,** mitrailleuse *f;* **to m.-gun,** mitrailler; **m. gunner,** mitrailleur *m* **2.** *vtr Ind:* façonner (une pièce); usiner; *Dressm:* coudre, piquer, à la machine. **ma'chine-'made** *a* fait à la machine. **ma'chinery** *n* (*a*) mécanisme *m;* machines *fpl;* machinerie *f* (*b*) **the m. of government,** les rouages du gouvernement. **ma'chining** *n* usinage *m; Dressm:* couture *f* à la machine. **ma'chinist** *n* machiniste mécanicien *m; Dressm:* mécanicienne *f.*
machismo [mə'tʃizmou] *n F:* machisme *m.*
mackerel ['mækrəl] *n Ich:* maquereau *m.*
mackintosh ['mækintɔʃ] *n* imperméable *m.*
mad [mæd] **1.** *a* (**madder, maddest**) (*a*) fou, *f* folle; dément; **raving m., as m. as a hatter,** fou à lier; **to drive s.o. m.,** rendre qn fou; **nationalism gone m.,** nationalisme forcené; **m. with fear,** affolé (de peur); **m. plan,** projet insensé; *F:* **to run like m.,** courir comme un dératé; **m. for revenge,** assoiffé de revanche; **to be m. about, on, sth,** être fou, raffoler, de qch; **he's m. on sport,** c'est un sportif passionné (*b*) *F:* furieux, furibond; **to be m. with s.o.,** être furieux contre qn; **hopping m.,** fou furieux; **m. bull,** taureau furieux; **m. dog,** chien enragé **2.** *adv F:* **m. keen on sth,** fou de qch. **'madden** *vtr* rendre fou; exaspérer. **'maddening** *a* à rendre fou; exaspérant, enrageant. **'maddeningly** *adv* à rendre fou. **'madhouse** *n* maison *f* de fous. **'madly** *adv* **1.** follement; comme un fou **2.** (aimer) à la folie, éperdument. **'madman** *n* (*pl* **-men**) fou *m,* aliéné *m;* **like a m.,** (faire qch) comme

un forcené. **'madness** *n* folie *f.* **'madwoman** *nf* (*pl* **-women**) folle, aliénée.
madam ['mædəm] *nf* (*a*) madame, mademoiselle; **M. Chairman,** Madame la Présidente; *Corr:* **Dear M.,** Madame, Mademoiselle (*b*) *F:* (*pl* **madams**) **she's a little m.,** c'est une pimbêche.
madder ['mædər] *n Bot:* garance *f.*
made [meid] *see* **make.**
Madeira [mə'diərə] (*a*) *Prn Geog:* Madère *f;* **M. cake** = gâteau de Savoie (*b*) (*wine*) madère *m.*
madonna [mə'dɔnə] *n* madone *f.*
madrigal ['mædrigl] *n Mus:* madrigal *m.*
mag [mæg] *n F:* = magazine 3.
magazine [mægə'ziːn] *n* **1.** *Mil:* magasin *m;* dépôt (d'armes) **2.** *Sma:* chargeur *m,* magasin **3.** revue *f* (périodique), magazine *m.*
maggot ['mægət] *n* ver *m,* asticot *m.* **'maggoty** *a* véreux, plein de vers.
magic ['mædʒik] **1.** *n* magie *f,* enchantement *m;* **like m.,** comme par enchantement, comme par magie **2.** *a* magique, enchanté. **'magical** *a* magique. **'magically** *adv* magiquement; (comme) par enchantement. **ma'gician** *n* magicien, -ienne.
magisterial [mædʒi'stiəriəl] *a* magistral.
magistrate ['mædʒistreit] *n* magistrat *m,* juge *m.*
magnanimous [mæg'næniməs] *a* magnanime. **magna'nimity** *n* magnanimité *f.* **mag'nanimously** *adv* magnanimement.
magnate ['mægneit] *n* magnat *m.*
magnesia [mæg'niːʃə] *n Ch:* magnésie *f; Pharm:* **milk of m.,** magnésie hydratée.
magnesium [mæg'niːziəm] *n Ch:* magnésium *m.*
magnet ['mægnit] *n* (*a*) aimant *m* (*b*) électro-aimant *m.* **mag'netic** *a* (*a*) aimanté (*b*) magnétique; **m. pole,** pôle magnétique; **m. tape,** bande magnétique. **mag'netically** *adv* magnétiquement. **'magnetism** *n* magnétisme *m.* **'magnetize** *vtr* (*a*) aimanter (une aiguille) (*b*) magnétiser, attirer (qn). **mag'neto** *n* (*pl* **-tos**) *El:* magnéto *f.*
magnificence [mæg'nif is(ə)ns] *n* magnificence *f.* **mag'nificent** *a* magnifique; (repas) somptueux. **mag'nificently** *adv* magnifiquement.
magnify ['mægnifai] *vtr* (**magnified**) grossir, agrandir; amplifier (un son); exagérer (un incident); **magnifying glass,** loupe *f.* **magnifi'cation** *n* grossissement *m,* amplification *f.*
magnitude ['mægnitjuːd] *n* grandeur *f; Astr:* magnitude *f.*
magnolia [mæg'noulia] *n Bot:* magnolia *m.*
magnum ['mægnəm] *n* magnum *m* (de champagne).
magpie ['mægpai] *n Orn:* pie *f.*
mahogany [mə'hɔgəni] *n* acajou *m;* **m. table,** table en acajou.
maid [meid] *n* (*a*) *Lit:* jeune fille *f;* **the M. of Orleans,** la pucelle d'Orléans (*b*) **old m.,** vieille fille (*c*) bonne *f,* domestique *f;* **lady's m.,** femme *f* de chambre; **m. of**

honour, première demoiselle d'honneur. **'maiden** n (a) Lit: jeune fille (b) Lit: vierge f (c) **m. aunt,** tante non mariée; **m. name,** nom de jeune fille; **m. voyage, flight,** premier voyage, vol; Nau: voyage inaugural; **m. speech,** discours de début (d'un député). **'maidenhair** n Bot: **m. (fern),** capillaire m; cheveu m de Vénus.

mail¹ [meil] n Arm: (also **chainmail**) mailles fpl.

mail² 1. n (a) courrier m; lettres fpl; NAm: **m. drop** (Br = **letterbox**), boîte aux lettres (b) la poste; Com: **m. order,** achat m et vente f par correspondance 2. vtr envoyer, expédier (une lettre) par la poste; mettre (une lettre) à la poste. **'mailbag** n sac postal. **'mailbox** n (pl -es) NAm: (Br = **letterbox**) boîte f aux lettres. **'mailing** n **m. list,** liste de diffusion; liste d'adresses. **'mailman** n (pl -men) NAm: (Br = **postman**) facteur m.

maim [meim] vtr estropier, mutiler.

main [mein] 1. n CivE: canalisation maîtresse; El: conducteur principal; câble m de distribution; **water m., gas m.,** conduite f d'eau, de gaz; **m. drainage,** tout-à-l'égout m; **mains water,** eau de ville; El: **mains,** le secteur; **in the m.,** en général, en somme 2. a principal; premier, essentiel; **m. body,** gros m (de l'armée); Agr: **m. crop,** culture principale; **m. point, m. thing,** l'essentiel m, le principal; **m. course,** plat principal, de résistance; **m. road,** grande route; **m. street,** rue principale; Rail: **m. line,** voie principale, grande ligne. **'mainland** n continent m; terra f ferme. **'mainly** adv (a) principalement, surtout (b) en grande partie. **'mainmast** n Nau: grand mât. **'mainsail** n Nau: grand-voile f. **'mainspring** n 1. grand ressort, ressort moteur 2. mobile essentiel, cause principale. **'mainstay** n point m d'appui; soutien principal; pilier m.

maintain [mein'tein] vtr (a) maintenir (l'ordre); soutenir (la conversation); entretenir (des relations); conserver (la santé); garder, observer (une attitude, le silence); **to m. the speed,** conserver l'allure (b) entretenir, soutenir (une famille) (c) entretenir (une armée); soutenir, défendre (une cause); garder (un avantage) (d) soutenir (une opinion); **I m. that it's not true,** je soutiens que c'est faux. **'maintenance** n (a) maintien m (de l'ordre); entretien m (d'une famille) (b) Jur: pension f alimentaire (c) entretien (des routes, du matériel); **m. handbook,** manuel de maintenance.

maison(n)ette [meizə'net] n (appartement m) duplex (m).

maize [meiz] n maïs m.

majesty ['mædʒisti] n (pl **majesties**) majesté f; His M., Her M., Sa Majesté le Roi, Sa Majesté la Reine. **ma'jestic** a majestueux. **ma'jestically** adv majestueusement.

major¹ ['meidʒər] n Mil: (a) commandant m (b) **drum m.,** tambour-major m. **'major-'general** n général m de division.

major² 1. a **the m. portion,** la majeure partie, la plus grande partie; **m. decision,** décision capitale; Mus: **m. key,** ton majeur; Adm: **m. road,** route à priorité; **m. firms,** grandes entreprises 2. n (a) Jur: (pers) majeur, -eure (b) Sch: NAm: matière principale 3. vi Sch: NAm: **to m. in a subject,** se spécialiser dans un sujet. **majo'rette** n (drum) **m.,** majorette f. **ma'jority** n 1. (a) majorité f; **to be in a m.,** être en majorité; **elected**

by a m., élu à la pluralité des voix; **m. party,** parti majoritaire (b) la plus grande partie; le plus grande nombre; la plupart (des hommes) 2. Jur: **to attain one's m.,** atteindre sa majorité, devenir majeur.

Majorca [mə'jɔːkə] Prn Geog: Majorque f.

make [meik] n 1. (a) façon f, fabrication f, construction f (b) Com: Ind: marque f (d'un produit); **of French m.,** de fabrication française; F: **to be on the m.,** chercher à faire fortune, par tous les moyens. II v (**made** [meid]) 1. vtr (a) faire; construire (une machine); fabriquer (du papier); confectionner (des vêtements); ménager (une ouverture); **God made man,** Dieu a créé l'homme; Knit: **m. one,** faire un jeté simple; **you're made for this work,** vous êtes fait pour ce travail; **what's it made of?** c'est (fait) en quoi? **I don't know what to m. of it,** je n'y comprends rien; **what do you m. of it?** qu'en pensez-vous? **to show what one is made of,** montrer de quoi l'on est capable; **to m. a friend of s.o.,** faire de qn son ami (b) faire (son testament, le lit, le thé); **to m. trouble,** causer des ennuis (for s.o., à qn); **to m. a noise,** faire du bruit; **to m. peace,** faire, conclure, la paix (c) faire (une loi); établir (une règle); effectuer, faire (un versement); opérer (un changement); faire (un discours); **to m. a mistake,** faire une erreur, se tromper; **to m. one's escape,** s'échapper, se sauver (d) fermer, assurer (un raccordement); El: (of contact points) fermer (le circuit); **two and two m. four,** deux et deux font quatre; **they m. a handsome couple,** il font un beau couple; **he made an excellent captain,** il s'est montré excellent (i) chef d'équipe (ii) Sp: capitaine (e) **to m. £100 a week,** gagner, se faire, £100 par semaine; **to m. one's fortune,** faire fortune; F: **to m. a bit on the side,** se faire de la gratte; **to m. a name,** se faire un nom; **to m. friends,** (i) se faire des amis (ii) devenir amis; F: **to m. it,** réussir, y arriver; **we just made it,** nous sommes arrivés juste à temps; **he's got it made,** son avenir est assuré (f) faire la fortune de (qn); **the book that made his name,** le livre qui l'a rendu célèbre; **this will m. or break him,** cela fera ou son succès ou sa ruine; **that made my day,** ça m'a rendu heureux pour toute la journée; **it makes all the difference,** ça change tout; **to m. s.o. happy,** rendre qn heureux; **to m. s.o. angry,** fâcher qn; **to m. s.o. hungry,** donner faim à qn; **to m. s.o. one's heir,** constituer qn son héritier; **to m. sth known,** faire connaître qch; **to m. oneself comfortable,** se mettre à l'aise; **to m. oneself ill,** se rendre malade; **what time do you m. it?** quelle heure avez-vous? (g) **to m. s.o. speak,** faire parler qn; **you should m. him do it,** vous devriez le forcer à le faire; **what made you say that?** pourquoi avez-vous dit cela? 2. vi (a) **to m. for,** se diriger vers (un endroit), Nau: mettre le cap sur; **to m. for the open sea,** prendre le large (b) **to m. as if to do sth,** faire mine, faire semblant, de faire qch. **'make a'way** vi **to m. a. with sth,** partir avec qch; voler (de l'argent); **to m. away with s.o.,** tuer qn. **'make-believe** n semblant m; **that's all m.-b.,** tout cela c'est de la pure fantaisie; **the land of m.-b.,** le pays des chimères. **'make 'do** vi **to m. do with sth,** se contenter de qch; s'arranger, se débrouiller avec qch. **'make 'off** vi se sauver; décamper, filer; **to m. o. with the cash,** filer avec l'argent. **'make 'out** 1. vtr (a) faire, établir, dresser (une liste); rédiger (un mémoire); établir, relever (un compte); faire, établir (un chèque) (b) **how do you m. that out?** comment arrivez-vous à ce résultat, à cette conclusion? **he's made out to be richer than he is,** on le fait plus riche qu'il ne l'est; **he's not such a fool as people m. out,** il n'est pas si bête qu'on le croit (c) comprendre (une énigme); déchiffrer (une écriture); **I can't m. it out,** je n'y comprends rien; **I can't m. out his features,** je ne peux pas distinguer ses traits 2. vi F: réussir; faire des progrès; **he's making out very well,** il fait de bonnes affaires. **'make 'over** vtr céder, transférer (sth to s.o., qch à qn). **'maker** n 1. faiseur, -euse; Com: Ind: fabricant m; constructeur m (de machines) 2. **Our M.,** le Créateur. **'makeshift** n expédient m; moyen m de fortune; **a m. shelter,** un abri de fortune. **'make 'up** 1. vtr (a) compléter (une somme); combler (un déficit); **to m. up the difference,** parfaire la différence; **to m. up lost ground,** regagner le terrain perdu; **to m. it up to s.o. for sth,** dédommager qn de qch (b) faire (un paquet); Pharm: exécuter (une ordonnance); faire, confectionner (des vêtements); dresser (une liste); régler (un compte); inventer (une histoire, des excuses); **the whole thing is made up!** pure invention (que) tout cela! (c) **to m. up the fire,** arranger le feu (d) former, composer (un ensemble) (e) **to m. (oneself) up,** se maquiller (f) **to m. up one's mind,** se décider; prendre son parti (g) arranger, accommoder (un différend); **to m. it up (again),** se réconcilier 2. vi (a) **to m. up for lost time,** rattraper le temps perdu; **that makes up for it,** il y a là compensation; **to m. up for the lack of sth,** suppléer au manque de qch (b) **to m. up to s.o.,** faire des avances à qn; flatter qn. **'makeup** n 1. (a) composition f (de qch) (b) (of pers) caractère m 2. maquillage m; **m. bag,** trousse à maquillage; **m. remover,** démaquillant m; **m. artist,** maquilleur, -euse. **'making** n fabrication f; confection f (de vêtements); construction f (d'un pont); création f (d'un poste); **this incident was the m. of him,** c'est à cet incident qu'il doit sa fortune; **history in the m.,** l'histoire en train de se faire; **I haven't the makings of a hero,** je n'ai rien du héros; **he has the makings of a statesman,** il a l'étoffe d'un homme d'État.

maladjusted [mælə'dʒʌstid] a inadapté.

maladroit [mælə'drɔit] a maladroit.

malady ['mælədi] n (pl maladies) maladie f.

malaria [mə'lɛəriə] n Med: malaria f, paludisme m.

Malaya [mə'leiə] Prn Geog: Malaisie f. **Ma'lay** a & n malais, -aise. **Ma'layan** a malais.

Malaysia [mə'leiʒiə] Prn Geog Malaisie f.

male [meil] 1. a mâle; (sexe) masculin; **m. child,** enfant mâle 2. n mâle m.

malevolence [mə'levələns] n malveillance f (towards, envers). **ma'levolent** a malveillant. **ma'levolently** adv avec malveillance.

malformation [mælfɔː'meiʃn] n malformation f, difformité f.

malfunction [mæl'fʌŋkʃən] 1. n mauvais fonctionnement. 2. vi mal fonctionner.

malice ['mælis] n 1. malice f, méchanceté f; rancune f; **out of m.,** par malice; **to bear s.o. m.,** en vouloir à qn 2. Jur: intention criminelle; **with m. aforethought,** avec préméditation f. **ma'licious** a (a) méchant, malveillant; rancunier (b) Jur: fait avec intention crimi-

nelle. **ma'liciously** adv avec méchanceté, avec malveillance; par rancune.

malign [mə'lain] 1. a pernicieux, nuisible 2. vtr calomnier, diffamer. **malignancy** [mə'lignənsi] n (a) méchanceté f, malveillance f (b) Med: malignité f. **ma'lignant** a (a) malin, f maligne; méchant (b) Med: **m. tumour,** tumeur maligne. **ma'lignantly** adv avec malignité, méchamment.

malinger [mə'liŋgər] vi faire le malade. **ma'lingerer** n faux, fausse, malade.

mallard ['mæləːd] n Orn: col-vert m; canard m sauvage.

malleable ['mæliəbl] a malléable.

mallet ['mælit] n maillet m.

mallow ['mælou] n Bot: mauve f.

malnutrition [mælnju'triʃn] n malnutrition f, sous-alimentation f.

malt [mɔːlt] n malt m; **m. whisky,** whisky pur malt. **'malted** a **m. milk,** lait malté.

Malta ['mɔːltə] Prn Geog Malte f. **'Maltese** 1. a maltais; **M. cross,** croix f de Malte 2. n Maltais, -aise; Ling: maltais m.

maltreat [mæl'triːt] vtr maltraiter, malmener. **mal'treatment** n mauvais traitement.

mam(m)a [mə'maː] nf F: maman.

mammal ['mæməl] n Z: mammifère m.

mammary ['mæməri] a & n Anat: **the m. glands,** npl **the mammaries,** les glandes f mammaires.

mammoth ['mæməθ] 1. n mammouth m 2. a géant, monstre.

man [mæn] I. n (pl men [men]) 1. (a) homme m; chacun; **any m.,** n'importe qui; **no m.,** personne m; **no man's land,** (i) terrain m vague (ii) Mil: zone f neutre; **few men,** peu de gens (b) l'homme; **m. proposes, God disposes,** l'homme propose et Dieu dispose; **the m. in the street,** l'homme de la rue (c) Ind: etc: **m. hour,** heure de travail, de main-d'œuvre; heure-homme f; **m. year,** année-homme f. (a) PN: (on public convenience) **men,** hommes; Com: **men's department,** rayon hommes; **they replied as one m.,** ils ont répondu d'une seule voix; **to speak to s.o. as m. to m.,** parler à qn d'homme à homme; **to make a m. of s.o.,** faire un homme de qn; **he took it like a m.,** il a pris ça courageusement; **he's not the m. to refuse,** il n'est pas homme à refuser; **I'm your m.!** je suis votre homme! cela me va! F: **come here, young m.!** venez ici (i) jeune homme! (ii) mon petit! **good m.!** bravo (mon vieux)! **look at that, m.!** regarde un peu, mon vieux! (b) **an old m.,** un vieillard; **an ambitious m.,** un ambitieux; **a dead m.,** un mort (c) **an Oxford m.,** (i) un originaire, un habitant, d'Oxford (ii) un étudiant de l'Université d'Oxford (d) **odd-job m.,** homme à tout faire; F: **the weather m.,** Monsieur Météo 3. **m. and wife,** mari m et femme; **to live as m. and wife,** vivre maritalement; **her young m.,** (i) son amoureux (ii) son fiancé 4. (a) domestique m (b) employé m; Ind: **the employers and the men,** les patrons et les ouvriers (c) Mil: **officers and men,** officiers et hommes de troupe (d) Sp: joueur m 5. (chess) pièce f; (draughts) pion m. II. vtr (**manned**) (a) fournir du personnel à (une organisation); assurer le service (d'une machine); faire partie de l'équipage (d'un avion) (b) Mil: **to m. a gun,** servir une pièce (c) Nau: équiper (un canot) (d) **we need s.o. to m. this stall,** nous avons besoin de qn pour tenir ce stand; **the**

telephone is manned 24 hours a day, la permanence
téléphonique est assurée 24 heures sur 24.
'maneater *n (of animal)* mangeur *m* d'hommes.
'maneating *a* (tigre) mangeur d'hommes.
'manful *a* vaillant, courageux. **'manfully** *adv*
vaillamment, courageusement. **man'handle** *vtr*
maltraiter, malmener (qn); manutentionner (des
marchandises). **'manhole** *n* trou *m* de visite, regard
m (d'égout). **'manhood** *n* âge *m* d'homme; âge viril;
virilité *f*. **'manhunt** *n* chasse *f* à l'homme.
man'kind *n* le genre humain; l'homme, les
hommes. **'manlike** *a* (à l'aspect) humain; semblable
à un homme. **'manliness** *n* virilité *f*. **'manly** *a*
viril. **'man-made** *a* artificiel, synthétique; industriel. **manned** *a (of spacecraft)* habité. **'mannish** *a*
masculin; *Pej:* hommasse. **'manpower** *n coll Ind:*
main-d'œuvre *f; Mil:* effectif *m*. **'manservant** *n (pl
menservants)* domestique *m*, valet *m* de chambre.
'mansize(d) *a* de la grandeur, de la taille, d'un
homme; (travail) d'homme. **'manslaughter** *n Jur:*
homicide *m* (i) involontaire (ii) sans préméditation.
'mantrap *n* piège *m* à hommes.
manacle ['mænəkl] **1.** *n* menotte *f* **2.** *vtr* mettre,
passer, les menottes à (qn).
manage ['mænidʒ] *vtr* **1.** diriger, gérer (une entreprise, une affaire); diriger (une banque); régir (une
propriété); **to m. s.o.'s business,** gérer les affaires de qn
2. to know how to m. s.o., savoir prendre qn **3. to m. to
do sth,** s'arranger pour faire qch; **I'll m. it,** j'y
arriverai; **if you can m. to see him,** si vous pouvez vous
arranger pour le voir; **how do you m. not to dirty your
hands?** comment faites-vous pour ne pas vous salir les
mains? **£100 is the most that I can m.,** je ne peux offrir
plus de £100 **4.** *vi* **m. as best you can,** arrangez-vous
comme vous pourrez; **he'll m. all right,** il se dé-
brouillera. **'manageable** *a* **1.** (outil) maniable;
(canot) manœuvrable **2.** *(of pers)* traitable, docile **3.**
(of undertaking) réalisable, faisable.
'management *n* **1.** *(a)* maniement *m* (d'un outil)
(b) direction *f*, conduite *f* (d'une affaire); gérance *f*,
gestion *f* (d'une usine); **m. consultant,** conseil en
gestion; **bad m.,** mauvaise gestion; **under new m.,** (i)
changement *m* de propriétaire (ii) nouvelle direction
2. adresse *f*, savoir-faire *m* **3.** *coll* l'administration *f*, la
direction. **'manager** *n* directeur *m*, gérant *m*;
administrateur *m*; régisseur *m* (d'une propriété); *Cin:
Sp:* manager *m*; **general m.,** directeur général; **joint
m.,** cogérant *m*; **sales m.,** directeur commercial;
personnel m., chef *m* du personnel; **area m.,** directeur
régional. **'manageress** *nf* directrice, gérante.
mana'gerial [-'dʒiəriəl] *a* directorial; (poste) de
commande; **m. staff,** les cadres *mpl*. **'managing** *a*
directeur; gérant; **m. director,** directeur général.
mandarin ['mændərin] *n* **1.** *(pers)* mandarin *m* **2.** *Bot:*
(also **mandarine**) mandarine *f*.
mandate ['mændeit] *n* mandat *m*. **'mandatory** *a*
obligatoire.
mandolin(e) ['mændəlin] *n Mus:* mandoline *f*.
mane [mein] *n* crinière *f*.
maneuver [mə'nu:vər] *n & v NAm:* = **manoeuvre.**
manganese [ˌmæŋgə'ni:z] *n Ch:* manganèse *m*.
mange [meindʒ] *n* gale *f*. **'mangy** *a* (**-ier, -iest**) *(a)*
galeux *(b) F:* minable, miteux.

manger ['mein(d)ʒər] *n* mangeoire *f*; crèche *f*; **he's a
dog in the m.,** c'est un empêcheur de tourner en rond.
mangle ['mæŋgl] **1.** *n* essoreuse *f* (à rouleaux) **2.** *vtr (a)*
essorer (le linge) *(b)* déchirer, lacérer, mutiler (qn);
charcuter (un morceau de viande); mutiler (un texte);
déformer (un mot); estropier (une citation).
mango ['mæŋgou] *n (pl* **mangoes**) *Bot: (a)* mangue *f*
(b) **m. (tree),** manguier *m*.
mangrove ['mæŋgrouv] *n* palétuvier *m*; **m. swamp,**
mangrove *f*.
mania ['meiniə] *n* **1.** *Med:* (i) manie *f*; folie *f* (ii) folie
furieuse **2. to have a m. for (doing) sth,** avoir la passion
de (faire) qch. **'maniac** *a & n* fou, folle, à lier;
maniaque (*mf*); **sex m.,** obsédé sexuel.
manicure ['mænikjuər] **1.** *n* soin *m* des mains; **to give
oneself a m.,** se faire les ongles; **m. set,** trousse de
manucure. **2.** *vtr* soigner les mains de (qn); **to m. one's
nails,** se faire les ongles. **'manicurist** *n* manucure
mf.
manifest ['mænifest] **1.** *a* manifeste, évident **2.** *n
Nau:* manifeste *m; Av:* état *m* de chargement **3.** *vtr*
manifester, témoigner (qch); *(of symptom)* **to m. itself,**
se manifester, se révéler. **manifes'tation** *n* manifestation *f*. **'manifestly** *adv* manifestement.
mani'festo *n (pl -os) Pol:* manifeste *m*.
manifold ['mænifould] **1.** *a (a)* divers, varié; de
diverses sortes *(b)* multiple, nombreux **2.** *n ICE:*
tubulure *f;* collecteur *m*.
manipulate [mə'nipjuleit] *vtr* **1.** manipuler (un objet); actionner (un dispositif mécanique); agir sur (un
levier) **2.** *Pej:* tripoter, cuisiner (des comptes).
manipu'lation *n* **1.** manipulation *f*; manœuvre *f* **2.**
Pej: tripotage *m*.
manna ['mænə] *n* manne *f*.
mannequin ['mænikin] *n* mannequin *m*.
manner ['mænər] *n* **1.** manière *f*, façon *f* (de faire qch);
in a m. of speaking, en quelque sorte; pour ainsi dire;
it's a m. of speaking, c'est une façon de parler **2.**
maintien *m*, tenue *f*, air *m;* **I don't like his m.,** je n'aime
pas son attitude **3.** *pl (a)* manières; **bad manners,**
mauvaises manières; **it's very bad manners to do that,**
c'est très mal élevé de faire ça *(b)* **(good) manners,**
bonnes manières, savoir-vivre *m*, politesse *f;* **to teach
s.o. manners,** donner à qn une leçon de politesse; **to
forget one's manners,** oublier les convenances;
s'oublier; *(to child)* **where are your manners?** c'est
comme çà qu'on se tient? **4.** espèce *f*, sorte *f;* **all m. of
things,** toutes sortes de choses. **'mannered** *a* maniè-
ré. **'mannerism** *n* **1.** maniérisme *m* **2.** particularité
f (d'un écrivain). **'mannerly** *a* poli, bien élevé.
man(n)ikin ['mænikin] *n* **1.** nabot *m* **2.** *Art: Med:*
mannequin *m*.
manoeuvre, *NAm:* **maneuver** [mə'nu:vər] **1.** *n (a)*
manœuvre *f (b) Mil:* **troops on manoeuvres,** troupes en
manœuvre **2.** *vtr & i* manœuvrer; **to m. s.o. into a
corner,** (i) acculer qn dans un coin (ii) amener
adroitement qn dans une impasse. **ma'noeuv-
rable** *a* manœuvrable, maniable.
manor ['mænər] *n* **1.** **(house),** manoir *m*.
mansion ['mænʃən] *n (in country)* château *m*; *(in
town)* hôtel particulier; **m. (house),** manoir *m*.
mantel(piece) ['mæntl(pi:s)] *n (a)* manteau
m de cheminée *(b)* dessus *m*, tablette *f*, de cheminée.

mantle ['mæntl] n 1. Cl: A: mante f, pèlerine f 2. manteau m (de neige) 3. manchon m (de bec de gaz).

manual ['mænjuəl] 1. a manuel; **m. labour,** travail de manœuvre 2. n (a) manuel m (b) Mus: clavier m (d'un orgue). **'manually** adv manuellement, à la main.

manufacture [mænju'fæktʃər] 1. n (a) fabrication f, élaboration f (d'un produit industriel); confection f (de vêtements) (b) produit manufacturé 2. vtr fabriquer, construire; confectionner (des vêtements); **manufacturing industries,** industries de fabrication. **manu'facturer** n fabricant m, constructeur m.

manure [mə'njuər] 1. n engrais m; **farmyard m.,** fumier m (d'étable); **liquid m.,** purin m; **m. heap,** tas de fumier 2. vtr fumer, engraisser (la terre).

manuscript ['mænjuskript] a & n manuscrit (m).

Manx [mæŋks] 1. a Geog: de l'île de Man; **M. cat,** chat sans queue de l'île de Man 2. n Ling: mannois m.

many [meni] a & n (more, most qv) un grand nombre (de); beaucoup (de); bien des; plusieurs; **m. a time,** maintes fois; **m. times,** beaucoup de fois; **before m. days have passed,** avant longtemps; **for m. years,** pendant plusieurs années; **m. of us,** beaucoup d'entre nous; **there were so m. of them,** ils étaient si nombreux; **in so m. words,** en propres termes; **too m. people,** trop de monde; **a card too m.,** une carte de trop; **how m. horses?** combien de chevaux? **I have as m. books as you,** j'ai autant de livres que vous; **as m. again,** twice as m.,** deux fois plus, autant; **as m. as ten people saw it,** au moins dix personnes l'ont vu; **a good m. things,** pas mal de choses; **a great m. tourists,** un grand nombre de touristes. **'many-'coloured,** NAm: **-'colored** a multicolore. **'many-sided** (a) (figure) à plusieurs côtés (b) (problème) complexe (c) (of pers) aux talents variés; polyvalent.

map [mæp] 1. n (a) carte f; **ordnance survey m.** = carte d'état-major; **town m.,** plan m d'une ville; **m. of the world,** mappemonde f (b) **to put a town on the m.,** mettre une ville en vedette; **the village was wiped off the m.,** le village a été rayé de la carte; **it's off the m.,** c'est au bout du monde 2. vtr (mapped) (a) dresser une carte, un plan, de (la région) (b) **to m. out,** tracer (un itinéraire); dresser (un programme). **'mapmaker** n cartographe m. **'mapmaking, 'mapping** n cartographie f.

maple ['meipl] n érable m; **m. sugar, syrup,** sucre, sirop, d'érable.

maquis ['mæki:] n Geog: Pol: maquis m.

mar [mɑːr] vtr (marred) gâter, gâcher (le plaisir de qn); troubler (la joie de qn); **to make or m. s.o.,** faire la fortune ou la ruine de qn.

maraschino [mærə'ski:nou] n marasquin m.

marathon ['mærəθən] n Sp: marathon m; **m. runner,** marathonien m.

maraud [mə'rɔːd] vi marauder. **ma'rauder** n maraudeur, -euse. **ma'rauding** a maraudeur m.

marble ['mɑːbl] n 1. marbre m; **m. statue,** statue de marbre; **m. staircase,** escalier en marbre; **m. quarry,** marbrière f 2. Games: bille f; **to play marbles,** jouer aux billes.

March¹ [mɑːtʃ] n mars m; **in M.,** en mars, au mois de mars; **(on) the fifth of M.,** le cinq mars.

march² I. n (a) marche f; déroulement m (des événements); **on the m.,** en marche; **to do a day's m.,** faire une étape; **route m.,** marche d'entraînement (b) pas m, allure f; **slow m.,** pas de parade; **quick m.,** pas cadencé. **II.** v 1. vi marcher; **quick . . . m.!** en avant . . . marche! **to m. by, past** (s.o.), défiler (devant qn); **time marches on,** l'heure avance 2. vtr faire marcher (des troupes); **to m. s.o. off to prison,** emmener qn en prison. **'marching** n Mil: marche f; **m. orders,** ordre de marche; F: **to give s.o. his m. orders,** donner son congé à qn; mettre qn à la porte. **'march-'past** n défilé m.

marchioness ['mɑːʃənis] nf (pl marchionesses) marquise.

mare ['mɛər] n jument f.

margarine, F: **marge** [mɑːdʒə'riːn, mɑːdʒ] n margarine f.

margin ['mɑːdʒin] n 1. (a) marge f; lisière f; bord m (b) marge, écart m; **profit m.,** marge bénéficiaire; **safety m.,** marge de sécurité; **to give s.o. some m.,** accorder quelque liberté à qn; **m. of error,** marge d'erreur (c) Com: couverture f, provision f 2. marge, blanc m (d'une page); **to write sth in the m.,** écrire qch en marge, dans la marge. **'marginal** a marginal; en marge; Pol: **m. seat,** siège chaudement disputé. **'marginally** adv (très) légèrement.

marguerite [mɑːgə'riːt] n Bot: (grande) marguerite.

marigold ['mærigould] n Bot: souci m; **French m.,** œillet m d'Inde; **African m.,** rose f d'Inde.

marihuana, marijuana [mæri'(h)wɑːnə] n marihuana f, marijuana f.

marina [mə'riːnə] n marina f.

marinade [mæri'neid] Cu: 1. n marinade f 2. vtr (also **marinate**) (faire) mariner.

marine [mə'riːn] 1. a marin; **m. insurance,** assurance maritime; **m. engineering,** génie maritime 2. n (a) marine f; **merchant, mercantile, m.,** marine marchande (b) Mil: = fusilier marin; F: **tell that to the marines!** à d'autres! **'mariner** n marin m.

marionette [mæriə'net] n marionnette f.

marital ['mæritl] a marital; matrimonial; conjugal.

maritime ['mæritaim] a maritime.

marjoram ['mɑːdʒərəm] n Bot: marjolaine f.

mark¹ [mɑːk] 1. n (a) but m, cible f; **to hit the m.,** atteindre le but; frapper juste; **wide of the m.,** loin de la réalité (b) marque f, preuve f, signe m, témoignage m; **as a m. of respect,** en signe de respect (c) marque, tache f, signe, trace f, empreinte f; **to make one's m.,** se faire une réputation; arriver; **distinguishing m.,** marque distinctive; F: **he's not up to the m.,** il n'est pas à la hauteur; Ind: **m. II, III,** série f II, III; **punctuation m.,** signe de ponctuation; **question m.,** point m d'interrogation; **guide m., reference m.,** point de repère (d) Sch: point; note f (e) Nau: amer m; **highwater m.,** niveau m de la marée haute (f) Sp: ligne f de départ; **on your marks!** à vos marques! **to be quick off the m.,** prendre un départ 2. vtr (a) marquer; estampiller (des marchandises); piper (les cartes); **face marked by chickenpox,** visage marqué par la varicelle; **to m. an article,** mettre le prix à un article (b) Sch: corriger, noter (un devoir); **to m. s.o., sth, as,** désigner qch, qch, pour (c) marquer, repérer, indiquer; témoigner (son approbation); accentuer (le rythme); **to m. time,** Mil: marquer le pas; Fig: piétiner (sur place); **to m. an era,** faire époque; **m. my words!** croyez-moi! **'mark 'down** vtr baisser le prix de (qch); démarquer. **marked** a 1. marqué; **m. man,**

homme repéré 2. marqué, prononcé; (différence) marquée; **m. improvement,** amélioration sensible; **strongly m. features,** traits fortement accusés. **mar kedly** ['mɑːkidli] adv d'une façon marquée. **'marker** n 1. (pers) marqueur, -euse 2. (a) Tls: marquoir m (b) (stake) jalon m 3. **(book) m.,** signet m. **'marking** n 1. (a) marquage m; **m. ink,** encre à marquer (b) estampillage m 2. pl **markings,** marques f; (on animal) taches f, rayures f 3. Sch: correction f (d'un devoir). **'mark 'off** vtr (a) séparer, distinguer (b) cocher (des noms). **'mark 'out** vtr 1. délimiter (une frontière) 2. **to m. s.o., sth, out, for,** destiner qn, qch, à; désigner qn, qch, pour. **'marksman** n (pl **-men)** tireur m d'élite. **'marksmanship** adresse f au tir. **'mark 'up** vtr (a) marquer (le score) (b) augmenter, majorer, le prix (de qch). **'mark-up** n marge f (bénéficiaire); majoration f (d'un prix).

mark² n Num: mark m.

market ['mɑːkit] 1. n (a) marché m; **covered m.,** marché couvert, halle(s) f (pl); **m. gardening,** culture maraîchère; **m. garden,** jardin maraîcher; **m. gardener,** maraîcher, -ère; **m. day,** jour de marché; **cotton m.,** marché du coton (b) marché; débouchés mpl (d'un produit); **the Common M.,** le Marché Commun; **black m.,** marché noir; **m. research,** étude de marché; **he put his house on the m.,** il a mis sa maison en vente; (of pers) **to be in the m. for sth,** être acheteur de qch; **to find a m. for sth,** trouver un débouché pour qch; **m. price,** prix courant (c) **stock m.,** marché des titres; la Bourse 2. vtr **(marketed)** commercialiser; lancer (un article) sur le marché. **'marketable** a commercialisable. **marke'teer** n **black m.,** trafiquant, -ante, du marché noir. **'marketing** n (a) commercialisation f (b) marketing m.

marmalade ['mɑːməleid] n Cu: confiture f d'oranges.

marmoset [mɑːmə'zet] n Z: ouistiti m.

marmot ['mɑːmət] n Z: marmotte f.

maroon¹ [mə'ruːn] a & n (colour) marron pourpré (m) inv; (rouge) bordeaux inv.

maroon² vtr (a) abandonner (qn) sur une île déserte (b) **marooned,** isolé (par des inondations).

marquee [mɑː'kiː] n grande tente.

marquess, marquis ['mɑːkwis] n (pl **marquesses, marquises)** marquis m.

marriage ['mærɪdʒ] n mariage m; union (conjugale); **relation by m.,** parent par alliance; **m. settlement,** contrat de mariage; **m. certificate,** acte de mariage; **m. bureau,** agence matrimoniale. **'marriageable** a of **m. age,** d'âge à se marier. **'married** a m. **man,** homme marié; **m. couple,** ménage m; **m. life,** vie conjugale; **m. name,** nom de mariage. **'marry** v **(married)** 1. vtr (a) (of priest, parent) marier; to m. (off) **a daughter,** marier sa fille (b) se marier avec, à (qn); épouser (qn) 2. vtr & i **to m., to get married,** se marier; **to m. (for) money,** faire un mariage d'argent; **to m. again,** se remarier.

marrow ['mærou] n 1. **(bone) m.,** moelle f; **frozen to the m.,** transi de froid; glacé jusqu'à la moelle 2. Bot: **(vegetable) m.,** courge f. **'marrowbone** n os m à moelle.

marsh [mɑːʃ] n marais m, marécage m; **m. marigold,** souci m d'eau. **marsh'mallow** n (a) Bot: guimauve f (b) (pâte f de) guimauve. **'marshy** a marécageux.

marshal ['mɑːʃl] 1. n (a) Mil: **field m.** = maréchal m (de France); Av: **M. of the R.A.F.** = Commandant m en Chef des Forces aériennes; **Air Chief M.** = général m d'armée aérienne (b) maître m des cérémonies (c) US: fonctionnaire m ayant les attributions d'un shérif (d) **fire m.,** chef m du service d'incendie (dans une région, une usine) 2. vtr **(marshalled,** NAm: **marshaled)** placer (des personnes) en ordre, en rang; Mil: ranger (des troupes); Rail: trier (des wagons). **'marshalling** n disposition f en ordre (de personnes, de choses); Rail: triage m (des wagons); **m. yard,** gare de triage.

marsupial [mɑː'suːpiəl] a & n Z: marsupial (m).

marten ['mɑːtin] n Z: mart(r)e f.

martial ['mɑːʃl] a martial; **m. law,** loi martiale.

Martian ['mɑːʃən] a & n martien, -ienne.

martin ['mɑːtin] n Orn: **(house) m.,** martinet m; hirondelle f de fenêtre.

martinet [mɑːti'net] n personne f à cheval sur la discipline.

martyr ['mɑːtər] 1. n martyr, f martyre; **to be a m. to migraine,** être torturé par la migraine 2. vtr martyriser. **'martyrdom** n martyre m.

marvel ['mɑːvl] 1. n merveille f; prodige m; **it's a m. to me how,** cela me paraît un miracle que 2. vi **(marvelled,** NAm: **marveled)** s'émerveiller, s'étonner **(at,** de). **'marvellous,** NAm: **marvelous** a merveilleux, étonnant. **'marvel(l)ously** adv à merveille; merveilleusement.

Marxism ['mɑːksizm] n PolEc: marxisme m. **'Marxist** a & n marxiste (mf).

marzipan ['mɑːzipæn] n pâte f d'amandes; massepain m.

mascara [mæs'kɑːrə] n Toil: mascara m.

mascot ['mæskət] n mascotte f; porte-bonheur m inv.

masculine ['mæskjulin] a 1. masculin, mâle 2. (nom) masculin; n **in the m.,** au masculin. **mascu'linity** n masculinité f.

mash [mæʃ] 1. n purée f (de pommes de terre) 2. vtr broyer, écraser (qch); réduire (qch) en purée; Cu: **mashed potatoes,** purée de pommes de terre. **'masher** n broyeur m; **potato m.,** presse-purée m inv.

mask [mɑːsk] 1. n masque m; (silk or velvet) loup m; **to throw off the m.,** lever le masque; se démasquer 2. vtr masquer; **to m. one's face,** se masquer. **masked** a masqué; **m. ball,** bal masqué.

masochism ['mæsoukizm] n masochisme m. **'masochist** n masochiste mf. **maso'chistic** a masochiste.

mason ['meisn] n 1. maçon m 2. (freemason) franc-maçon m. **ma'sonic** a franc-maçonnique. **'masonry** n 1. maçonnerie f 2. (freemasonry) franc-maçonnerie f.

masquerade [mæskə'reid] 1. n mascarade f 2. vi **to m. as,** se déguiser en; se faire passer pour.

mass¹ [mæs] n (pl **masses)** Ecc: messe f; **high m.,** grand-messe f; **low m.,** messe basse; **requiem m.,** messe des morts; **to say m.,** dire la messe.

mass² n (a) masse f, amas m; **atomic m.,** masse atomique (b) foule f, multitude f (de gens); collection f, grande quantité f (de choses); F: **I've got masses of things to do,** j'ai un tas de choses à faire; **he was a m. of bruises,** il était tout couvert de bleus; **m. meeting,** réunion de masse; **m. grave,** fosse commune; charnier *m*; **m. production,** fabrication en série; **the great m. of the people,** la plus grande partie de la population; **the masses,** les masses; le grand public; **m. media,** les mass média *mpl*; **m. protest,** protestation en masse **2.** *vtr & i* (se) masser; (*of clouds*) s'amonceler. **'massive** *a* massif. **mass-'produce** *vtr* fabriquer en série.

massacre ['mæsəkər] **1.** *n* massacre *m*, tuerie *f* **2.** *vtr* massacrer.

massage ['mæsɑ:ʒ] **1.** *n* massage *m* **2.** *vtr* masser (le corps). **ma'sseur, ma'sseuse** *n* masseur, -euse.

mast [mɑ:st] *n* **1.** *Nau:* mât *m*; **to sail before the m.,** servir comme simple matelot **2.** pylône *m*. **'masthead** *n* tête *f* de mât.

master ['mɑ:stər] **1.** *n* (*a*) maître *m*; **to be m. in one's own house,** être maître chez soi; **to be one's own m.,** ne dépendre que de soi; **to be m. of the situation,** être maître de la situation; **to meet one's m.,** trouver son maître (*b*) (*employer*) maître, patron *m*, chef *m* (*c*) *Nau:* capitaine *m* (d'un navire marchand); patron (d'un bateau de pêche) (*d*) **m. of ceremonies,** maître des cérémonies (*e*) *Sch:* (*primary*) maître, instituteur *m*; (*secondary*) professeur *m*; **fencing m.,** maître d'armes; **m. class,** cours de grand maître; **M. of Arts** = licencié ès lettres; **to be m. of one's art,** posséder son art en maître; *Art:* **an old m.,** (i) un maître (ii) tableau *m* de maître (*f*) (*form of address to small boys*) **M. David Thomas,** Monsieur David Thomas (*g*) **m. mason,** maître maçon; **m. mariner,** capitaine au long cours; capitaine marchand; **it is the work of a m. hand,** c'est fait de main de maître; **m. stroke,** coup de maître; **m. switch,** commutateur principal; **m. plan,** plan d'ensemble détaillé; **m. key,** passe-partout *m inv*; **m. race,** race supérieure **2.** *vtr* maîtriser (un cheval); maîtriser, dompter (ses passions); surmonter (une difficulté); apprendre (un sujet) à fond; **to have mastered a subject,** posséder un sujet à fond. **'masterful** *a* impérieux, autoritaire. **'masterfully** *adv* impérieusement, avec autorité. **'masterly** *a* de maître; magistral; **in a m. way,** magistralement. **'mastermind 1.** *n* intelligence supérieure; cerveau *m* **2.** *vtr* diriger (un projet); tramer (un complot). **'masterpiece** *n* chef-d'œuvre *m*. **'mastery** *n* (*a*) maîtrise *f* (**of,** de); domination *f* (**over,** sur) (*b*) connaissance approfondie (d'un sujet).

masticate ['mæstikeit] *vtr* mâcher, mastiquer. **masti'cation** *n* mastication *f*.

mastiff ['mæstif] *n* mâtin *m*; mastiff *m*.

mastoid ['mæstɔid] *Anat:* **1.** *n* mastoïde **2.** *n* mastoïde *f*; *Med: F:* **mastoids,** mastoïdite *f*.

masturbate ['mæstəbeit] *vi & tr* (se) masturber. **mastur'bation** *n* masturbation *f*.

mat¹ [mæt] *n* (*a*) natte *f* (de paille) (*b*) (petit) tapis; carpette *f* (*c*) (*doormat*) paillasson *m*, essuie-pieds *m inv*; *F:* **to be on the m.,** être sur la sellette (*d*) **table m.,** (i) dessous *m* de plat (ii) (*also* **place m.**) rond *m* de table; napperon *m*. **'matted** *a* (*of cloth*) feutré; **m. hair,** cheveux emmêlés. **'matting** *n* natte(s) *f*(*pl*), paillassons *mpl*.

mat² *a* (*of colour, surface*) mat.

match¹ [mætʃ] **I.** *n* **1.** (*a*) égal; pareil; **to meet one's m.,** trouver à qui parler; **to be a m. for s.o.,** être de force à lutter avec qn; **he's more than a m. for me,** il est plus fort que moi (*b*) (*of thgs*) **to be a good m.,** aller bien

ensemble; **perfect m. of colours,** assortiment parfait de couleurs **2.** *Sp:* lutte *f*, partie *f*, match *m*; **football m.,** match de football; **tennis m.,** match de tennis **3.** mariage *m*, alliance *f*; **good m.,** beau mariage; **he's a good m.,** c'est un excellent parti. **II.** *v* **1.** *vtr* (*a*) égaler (qn); être l'égal de (qn); rivaliser avec (qn); **evenly matched,** de force égale; **there's nobody to m. him,** il n'a pas son pareil (*b*) **to m. s.o. against s.o.,** opposer qn à qn (*c*) apparier (des gants); rappareiller (un service à thé); assortir (des couleurs); **a well matched couple,** un couple bien assorti; **I need a hat to m. my dress,** j'ai besoin d'un chapeau qui aille avec ma robe **2.** *vi* s'assortir, s'harmoniser; **dress with hat to m.,** robe avec chapeau assorti. **'matching 1.** *a* assorti **2.** *n* assortiment *m*, appariement *m*. **'matchless** *a* incomparable, sans égal; sans pareil. **'matchmake** *vi* marier les gens. **'matchmaker** *n* marieur, -euse.

match² *n* allumette *f*; **safety m.,** allumette de sûreté; **to strike a m.,** frotter une allumette; **box of matches,** boîte d'allumettes. **'matchbox** *n* (*pl* **-es**) boîte *f* à allumettes. **'matchstick** *n* allumette *f*. **'matchwood** *n* bois d'allumettes; **smashed to m.,** réduit en miettes.

mate¹ [meit] *Chess:* **1.** *n* mat *m* **2.** *vtr* mettre (le roi) échec et mat; mater.

mate² **1.** *n* (*a*) camarade *mf*, compagnon *m*, *f* compagne; *F:* copain, copine; (**workman's**) **m.,** aide *mf*; *F:* **hi, m.!** dis donc, mon vieux! (*b*) (*one of a pair*) (*pers, animal*) compagnon, compagne; (*of animals*) mâle *m*, femelle *f* (*c*) *Sp:* **team m.,** coéquipier, -ière (*d*) *Nau:* (*on merchant vessel*) officier *m*; *Navy:* second *m*; **first m.,** second *m*; **second m.,** lieutenant *m* **2.** *vtr & i* (*of birds, animals*) (s')accoupler. **'mating** *n* accouplement *m*; **m. season,** saison des amours.

material [mə'tiəriəl] **1.** *a* (*a*) matériel; matérialiste; (*of comfort, interests*) matériel; **to have enough for one's m. needs,** avoir de quoi vivre matériellement (*b*) important, essentiel (**to,** pour); **m. witness,** témoin essentiel, témoin-clé *m* (*c*) (fait) pertinent **2.** *n* (*a*) matière *f*, matériau *m*; **raw material(s),** matière(s) première(s); **building materials,** matériaux de construction; **he was collecting m. for a book,** il se documentait pour écrire un livre; **war m.,** matériel de guerre; **materials,** fournitures *f*, accessoires *m*; **writing materials,** tout ce qu'il faut pour écrire (*b*) *Tex:* tissu *m*; étoffe *f*. **ma'terialism** *n* matérialisme *m*. **ma'terialist** *n* matérialiste *mf*. **materia'listic** *a* matérialiste. **ma'terialize** *vi* se matérialiser; se réaliser; (*of plan*) aboutir. **ma'terially** *adv* **1.** matériellement, essentiellement **2.** sensiblement.

maternal [mə'tə:nəl] *a* maternel. **ma'ternally** *adv* maternellement. **ma'ternity** *n* maternité *f*; **m. hospital,** maternité; clinique *f* d'accouchement; **m. dress,** robe de grossesse; **m. allowance,** allocation de maternité.

math [mæθ] *n NAm: F:* = **maths.**

mathematics [mæθə'mætiks] *npl* mathématiques *fpl*. **mathe'matical** *a* mathématique; **he's a m. genius,** c'est un mathématicien de génie. **mathe'matically** *adv* mathématiquement. **mathema'tician** *n* mathématicien, -ienne. **maths.** *NAm:* math *npl F:* math(s) *f*(*pl*).

matinée ['mætinei] *n* (*a*) *Th:* matinée *f* (*b*) **m. coat,** veste *f* (de bébé).

matins ['mætinz] *npl Ecc:* matines *fpl.*

matriarch ['meitriɑːk] *nf* femme qui exerce une autorité matriarcale. **'matri'archal** *a* matriarcal.

matricide ['mætrisaid] *n (crime)* matricide *m; (pers)* matricide *mf.*

matriculate [mə'trikjuleit] *vtr & i Sch:* (s')inscrire. **matricu'lation** *n* immatriculation *f,* inscription *f.*

matrimony ['mætriməni] *n* mariage *m.* **matri'monial** *a* matrimonial.

matrix ['meitriks] *n (pl* **matrixes, matrices** [-triksiz, -trisiːz]) matrice *f.*

matron ['meitrən] *nf* 1. matrone; femme d'un certain âge; **m. of honour,** dame d'honneur 2. intendante (d'une institution). **'matronly** *a* matronal; de matrone.

matt [mæt] *a (of colour, surface)* mat.

matter ['mætər] I. *n* 1. matière *f;* substance *f;* **vegetable m.,** matières végétales; *Anat:* grey m., matière grise; **to have plenty of grey m.,** être très intelligent 2. *Med:* matière (purulente); pus *m* 3. *(a)* matière, sujet *m* (d'un discours); **reading m.,** livres *mpl,* choses *fpl* à lire; **it's no laughing m.,** il n'y a pas de quoi rire *(b) Adm:* **printed m.,** imprimé *m* 4. **no m.!** n'importe! **no m. what he says,** quoi qu'il dise; **no m. how,** de n'importe quelle manière 5. affaire *f,* chose, cas *m;* **it's an easy m.,** c'est facile; **it's no great m.,** ce n'est pas grand-chose; **that's quite another m.,** c'est tout autre chose; **as matters stand,** au point où en sont les choses; **business matters,** affaires; **in matters of religion,** en ce qui concerne la religion; **a m. of taste, of opinion,** une question de goût, d'opinion; **within a m. of hours,** en quelques heures; **there's the m. of the £100,** il y a la question des £100; **for that m.,** quant à cela; **as a m. of fact,** (i) à vrai dire; en réalité (ii) aussi bien; **as a m. of course,** tout naturellement, comme de raison; **what's the m.?** qu'est-ce qu'il y a? qu'y a-t-il? **what's the m. with you?** qu'avez-vous? qu'est-ce que vous avez? **there's something the m.,** il y a quelque chose; **I don't know what's the m. with me,** je ne sais pas ce que j'ai; **there's nothing the m. with him,** il va tout à fait bien. II. *vi* importer (to s.o., à qn); avoir de l'importance; **it doesn't m.,** n'importe; cela ne fait rien; cela n'a pas d'importance; **nothing else matters,** tout le reste n'est rien; **what does it m. to you?** qu'est-ce que cela peut vous faire? **'matter-of-'fact** *a* pratique, terre-à-terre; prosaïque.

Matterhorn (the) [ðə'mætəhɔːn] *Prn Geog:* le (Mont) Cervin.

mattins ['mætinz] *npl* = **matins.**

mattress ['mætris] *n (pl* **mattresses)** matelas *m.*

mature [mə'tjuər] 1. *a* mûr 2. *vtr & i* mûrir. **ma'turity** *n* maturité *f.*

maudlin ['mɔːdlin] *a* larmoyant, pleurard.

maul [mɔːl] *vtr* meurtrir, malmener (qn); **to be mauled by a dog,** être lacéré, déchiqueté, par un chien.

Maundy Thursday ['mɔːndi'θəːzdi] *n* le jeudi saint.

Mauritania [mɔri'teiniə] *Prn Geog:* Mauritanie *f.*

Mauritius [mə'riʃəs] *Prn Geog:* l'île *f* Maurice.

mausoleum [mɔːsə'liːəm] *n* mausolée *m.*

mauve [mouv] *a & n* mauve *(m).*

maverick ['mævərik] *a & n* (politicien) non-conformiste *(mf).*

mawkish ['mɔːkiʃ] *a (a)* fade, insipide *(b)* d'une sensiblerie outrée.

maxi ['mæksi] *a & n Cl: F:* (jupe *f,* manteau *m)* maxi *(m* or *f).*

maxim ['mæksim] *n* maxime *f,* dicton *m.*

maximum ['mæksiməm] 1. *n (pl* **maxima)** maximum *m;* to reach one's m., plafonner 2. *a* maximum; **m. load,** charge limite; **m. speed,** vitesse maximale; vitesse limite, maximum; **m. temperatures,** températures maximales. **'maximize** *vtr* porter au maximum. maximiser (le profit).

may[1] [mei] *v aux* (*pt* **might** [mait]) 1. *(a)* **I m. do it with luck,** avec de la chance je peux le faire; **he m. not be hungry,** il n'a peut-être pas faim; **he m. miss the train,** il se peut qu'il rate le train *(b)* **how old might she be?** quel âge peut-elle bien avoir? **and who might you be?** qui êtes-vous, sans indiscrétion? **and what might you be doing here?** peut-on savoir ce que vous faites ici? **mightn't it be as well to warn him?** est-ce qu'on ne ferait pas bien de l'avertir? *(c)* **it m. be, might be, that he'll come tomorrow,** il se peut bien, il se pourrait bien, qu'il vienne demain; **be that as it m.,** quoi qu'il en soit; **that's as m. be,** c'est selon; **run as he might he couldn't overtake me,** il a eu beau courir, il n'a pas pu me rattraper *(d)* **we m., might, as well stay where we are,** autant (vaut) rester où nous sommes *(e)* **you might shut the door!** vous pourriez quand même fermer la porte! **he might have offered to help,** il aurait bien pu offrir son aide 2. **m. I?** vous permettez? **m. I come in?** puis-je entrer? **if I m. say so,** si j'ose dire 3. **I only hope it m. last,** pourvu que ça dure 4. **m. he rest in peace!** qu'il repose en paix! **much good m. it do you!** grand bien vous fasse! **'maybe** *adv* peut-être.

May[2] *n* 1. mai *m;* **in (the month of) M.,** en mai; au mois de mai; **(on) the seventh of M.,** le sept mai 2. *Bot:* aubépine *f;* fleurs *fpl* d'aubépine. **'Mayday** 1. *n (also* **May Day)** le premier mai 2. *int (distress signal)* mayday! **'mayfly** *n (pl* **-flies)** *Ent:* éphémère *m.* **'maypole** *n* mai *m.*

mayonnaise [meiə'neiz] *n Cu:* mayonnaise *f.*

mayor ['mɛər] *n* maire *m.* **'mayoress** *nf (pl* **-es)** femme du maire.

maze [meiz] *n* labyrinthe *m,* dédale *m.*

MB *abbr Bachelor of Medicine.*

MBE *abbr Member of the Order of the British Empire.*

MC *abbr* 1. *Master of Ceremonies* 2. *NAm: Member of Congress* 3. *Military Cross.*

MD *abbr Doctor of Medicine.*

me [mi, miː] *pers pron (a) (unstressed)* me; *(before a vowel sound)* m'; **he sees me,** il me voit; **he told me so,** il me l'a dit; **listen to me!** écoutez-moi! **he wrote me a letter,** il m'a écrit une lettre; **I'll take it with me,** je le prendrai avec moi *(b) (stressed)* moi; **he was thinking of me,** il pensait à moi; **that's for me,** ça c'est pour moi; *F:* **it's me,** c'est moi; **he's younger than me,** il est plus jeune que moi; **dear me!** mon Dieu! vraiment!

mead [miːd] *n* hydromel *m.*

meadow ['medou] *n* pré *m,* prairie *f; Bot:* **m. saffron,** safran *m* des prés. **'meadowsweet** *n Bot:* reine *f* des prés.

meagre, *NAm:* **meager** ['miːgər] *a* maigre; peu copieux. **'meagrely,** *NAm:* **'meagerly** *adv* maigrement.

meal[1] [miːl] *n* farine *f* (d'avoine, de seigle, de maïs). **'mealy** *a* farineux. **'mealy-'mouthed** *a* doucereux, mielleux.

meal[2] *n* repas *m*; **to have a huge m.**, manger comme quatre; *F:* **to make a m. of it**, en faire tout un plat. **'mealtime** *n* heure *f* du repas.

mean[1] [mi:n] **1.** *n* (*a*) milieu *m*, moyen terme; **golden m.**, juste milieu (*b*) *Mth:* moyenne *f* (*c*) (*often with sg const*) **means**, moyen(s) *m*(*pl*); **to find the means of doing sth**, trouver moyen de faire qch; **there's no means of doing it**, il n'y a pas moyen de le faire; **by all means!** mais certainement! mais oui! **may I come in?— by all means!** puis-je entrer?—je vous en prie; **by no means**, pas du tout, en aucune façon; nullement; **he's not stupid by any means**, il est loin d'être stupide; **by some means or other**, de toute manière; d'une manière ou de l'autre; **by means of sth**, au moyen, par le moyen, de qch; **a means to an end**, un moyen d'arriver au but (*d*) **means**, ressources *fpl*; **it's beyond my means**, c'est au-delà de mes moyens; **means test**=enquête sur la situation (de fortune) **2.** *a* moyen.

mean[2] *a* (*a*) misérable, pauvre; humble; minable; **he has no m. opinion of himself**, il ne se prend pas pour de la petite bière; **he's no m. scholar**, c'est un grand érudit; *esp NAm: F:* **he plays a m. guitar**, c'est un guitariste formidable (*b*) bas, méprisable; mesquin; **a m. trick**, un vilain tour; un sale coup; **how m. of him!** ce n'est pas chic de sa part! (*c*) *esp NAm:* (*Br=* **bad tempered**) difficile; méchant **3.** avare, radin; **he's m. about tipping**, il n'aime pas donner les pourboires. **'meanly** *adv* (*a*) misérablement, pauvrement (*b*) (se conduire) peu loyalement, indignement (*c*) en lésinant. **'meanness** *n* (*a*) médiocrité *f*, pauvreté *f*, petitesse *f*; bassesse *f* (d'esprit) (*b*) mesquinerie *f*, avarice *f*.

mean[3] *vtr* (**meant** [ment]) **1.** (*purpose*) (*a*) avoir l'intention (**to do sth**, de faire qch); se proposer (de faire qch); **what do you m. to do?** que comptez-vous faire? **he means no harm**, il le fait très innocemment; **I m. him no harm**, je ne lui veux pas de mal; **he didn't m. (to do) it**, il ne l'a pas fait exprès; **without meaning it**, sans le vouloir (*b*) **he means well**, il a de bonnes intentions (*c*) **I m. to be obeyed**, j'entends qu'on m'obéisse; **I m. to succeed**, je veux réussir; **to m. business**, avoir des intentions sérieuses; **I m. to have it**, je suis résolu à l'avoir **2.** (*a*) **I meant this book for you**, je vous destinais ce livre; **the remark was meant for you**, la remarque s'adressait à vous (*b*) **do you m. me?** est-ce de moi que vous parlez? est-ce de moi qu'il s'agit? **this portrait is meant to be the duke**, ce portrait est censé représenter le duc **3.** (*a*) (*of words*) vouloir dire; signifier; **the name means nothing to me**, ce nom ne me dit rien; **what is meant by this?** que veut dire ceci? (*b*) **what do you m.?** que voulez-vous dire? **what do you m. by that?** qu'entendez-vous par là? **you don't m. it!** vous voulez rire! vous plaisantez! **I m. it**, je parle sérieusement; **when I say no I m.** *no*, quand je dis non c'est non (*c*) **twenty pounds means a lot to him!** vingt livres, c'est une somme importante pour lui! **you don't know what it means to live alone**, vous ne savez pas ce que c'est que de vivre seul. **'meaning 1.** *a* (*a*) (*with adv prefixed*) **well m.**, bien intentionné (*b*) (regard) significatif; (sourire) d'intelligence **2.** *n* signification *f*, sens *m*, acception *f* (d'un mot); **if you take my m.**, si vous me comprenez; **look full of m.**, regard significatif; **what's the m. of that word?** que veut dire ce mot?

(*indignation*) **what's the m. of this?** qu'est-ce que cela signifie? **'meaningful** *a* (*a*) plein de sens (*b*) significatif. **'meaningless** *a* dénué de sens; qui ne signifie rien; **m. remark**, non-sens *m*.

meander [mi'ændər] **1.** *n* méandre *m*, repli *m*. **2.** *vi* (*a*) (*of river*) faire des méandres, serpenter (*b*) (*of pers*) errer çà et là.

meantime ['mi:ntaim], **meanwhile** ['mi:n(h)wail] *n & adv* **(in the) m.**, dans l'intervalle *m*; en attendant, entre-temps.

measles ['mi:zlz] *npl* (*usu with sg const*) *Med:* rougeole *f*, German *m.*, rubéole *f*.

measly ['mi:zli] *a F:* misérable, insignifiant, minable.

measure ['meʒər] **I.** *n* **1.** (*a*) mesure *f*; **cubic m.**, mesure de volume; **liquid m.**, mesure de capacité pour les liquides; **weights and measures**, poids et mesures (*b*) *Tail: etc:* **made to m.**, fait sur mesure(s) **2.** (*a*) mesure (à grain, à lait); **half m.**, demi-mesure *f* (*b*) **tape m.**, mètre *m* (à ruban) **3.** mesure, limite *f*; **beyond m.**, outre mesure; **in some m.**, dans une certaine mesure; **a m. of independence**, une certaine indépendance **4.** (*a*) mesure, démarche *f*; **safety measures**, mesures de sécurité; **to take extreme measures**, employer les grands moyens; **as a m. of**, par mesure de (*b*) projet *m* de loi. **II.** *v* **1.** *vtr* (*a*) mesurer; métrer; arpenter (un terrain); **to m. one's length (on the ground)**, s'étaler par terre (*b*) *Tail: etc:* mesurer (qn); prendre la mesure de (qn) (*c*) **to m. one's strength with s.o.**, mesurer ses forces avec qn (*d*) peser (ses paroles) **2.** *vi* **the column measures 10 metres**, la colonne mesure 10 mètres. **'measured** *a* **1.** mesuré, déterminé **2.** (à pas) cadencé; **m. tread**, marche scandée (*b*) **with m. steps**, à pas comptés **3.** (langage, ton) modéré. **'measurement** *n* **1.** mesurage *m* **2.** mesure *f*, dimension *f*; **to take s.o.'s measurements**, mesurer, prendre les mesures de, qn; **hip m.**, tour *m* de hanches. **'measure 'off** *vtr* mesurer (un tissu). **'measure 'out** *vtr* répartir (qch); verser (qch) dans une mesure. **'measure up** *vi* **to m. up to s.o., sth**, être à la mesure, à la hauteur, de qn, qch. **'measuring** *n* mesurage *m*; métrage *m*; mesure *f* (du temps); **m. glass**, verre gradué; **m. tape**, mètre *m* (à ruban).

meat [mi:t] *n* viande *f*; **m. extract**, concentré de viande; **minced**, *NAm:* **ground, m.**, hachis *m* (de viande); **m. diet**, régime carné; **m. broth**, bouillon gras; **m. hook**, croc de boucherie; **m. eater**, carnivore *m*, mangeur de viande; **m. and drink**, le boire et le manger; **it was m. and drink to them**, c'était leur plus grand plaisir; *Prov:* **one man's m. is another man's poison**, ce qui guérit l'un tue l'autre. **'meatball** *n* boulette *f* de viande. **'meaty** *a* **1.** (odeur, goût) de viande; (livre) étoffé.

Mecca ['mekə] *Prn Geog:* la Mecque.

mechanic [mi'kænik] *n* mécanicien *m*, *F:* mécano *m*; **motor m.**, **car m.**, mécanicien garagiste. **me'chanical** *a* **1.** mécanique **2.** **m. engineering**, mécanique *f*; **m. engineer**, ingénieur mécanicien **3.** (*of reply, smile*) machinal; automatique. **me'chanically** *adv* **1.** mécaniquement **2.** machinalement; automatiquement. **me'chanics** *npl* (*a*) la mécanique (*b*) mécanisme *m*. **'mechanism** *n* appareil *m*, dispositif *m*; mécanisme *m*. **mechani'zation** *n* mécanisation *f*. **'mechanize** *vtr* mécaniser.

medal ['medl] *n* médaille *f*. **me'dallion** *n* médaillon *m.* '**medallist,** *NAm:* '**medalist** *n* médaillé, -ée; **gold m.,** médaillé d'or.

meddle ['medl] *vi* **to m. with, in,** sth, se mêler de qch; **don't m. in my affairs,** ne vous mêlez pas de mes affaires. '**meddler** *n* touche-à-tout *m inv.* '**meddlesome** *a* qui touche à tout; qui se mêle de tout. '**meddling** **1.** *a* qui touche à tout **2.** *n* intervention *f* (**in, with,** dans).

media ['mi:diə] *npl see* **medium.**

mediaeval [medi'i:vl] *a* du moyen âge; médiéval; *Pej:* moyenâgeux.

mediate ['mi:dieit] **1.** *vi* s'entremettre, s'interposer; servir de médiateur (**between,** entre) **2.** *vtr* **to m. a peace,** intervenir en qualité de médiateur pour (r)amener la paix. **medi'ation** *n* médiation *f;* intervention (amicale). '**mediator** *n* médiateur, -trice.

medical ['medikl] **1.** *a* médical; (livre) de médecine; **the m. profession,** (i) le corps médical (ii) la profession de médecin; **m. student,** étudiant, -ante, en médecine; **m. practitioner,** médecin *m;* **m. officer of health** = médecin départemental; **m. examination,** examen médical **2.** *n F:* examen médical. '**medically** *adv* médicalement; **to be m. examined,** subir un examen médical. '**medicated** *a* médical, traitant. **medi'cation** *n* médication *f.*

medicine ['med(i)sin] *n* **1.** médecine *f;* **to study m.,** étudier la médecine **2.** (*a*) médicament *m;* remède *m;* **to give s.o. a dose of his own m.,** rendre la pareille à qn; **m. cabinet, chest, cupboard,** (armoire *f* à) pharmacie *f* (*b*) **m. man,** (sorcier *m*) guérisseur (*m*). **me'dicinal** *a* médicinal.

mediocre [mi:di'oukər] *a* médiocre. **medi'ocrity** *n* médiocrité *f.*

medieval [medi'i:vl] *n* = **mediaeval.**

meditate ['mediteit] **1.** *vtr* méditer (un projet) **2.** *vi* (*a*) **to m. on** sth, méditer sur qch (*b*) méditer; se recueillir. **medi'tation** *n* méditation *f;* recueillement *m.* '**meditative** *a* méditatif; recueilli. '**meditatively** *adv* d'un air méditatif.

Mediterranean [meditə'reiniən] *a Geog:* méditerranéen; **the M. (Sea),** la (mer) Méditerranée.

medium ['mi:diəm] **1.** *n* (*pl* **media, -iums**) **1.** milieu *m;* moyen terme (**between,** entre); **happy m.,** juste milieu **2.** (*a*) milieu, véhicule *m* (*b*) (**social**) **m.,** milieu, atmosphère *f,* ambiance *f* **3.** (*a*) intermédiaire *m,* entremise *f;* **through the m. of** the press, par voie de presse (*b*) moyen *m* (d'expression); agent *m;* **advertising m.,** organe *m* de publicité; **the (mass) media,** les (mass) média *mpl* (*c*) moyen *m* d'expression **4.** *Psychics:* médium *m.* **II.** *a* moyen; **m. sized,** de grandeur moyenne, de taille moyenne; **m. wave,** onde moyenne.

medley ['medli] *n* mélange *m;* méli-mélo *m; Mus:* potpourri *m.*

meek [mi:k] *a* doux, humble; **m. and mild,** doux comme un agneau. '**meekly** *adv* avec douceur; humblement. '**meekness** *n* douceur *f;* humilité *f.*

meet [mi:t] **1.** *v* (**met** [met]) **1.** *vtr* (*a*) rencontrer; se rencontrer avec; **to m. s.o. on the stairs,** croiser qn dans l'escalier; **to meet another car,** croiser une voiture (*b*) rencontrer (l'ennemi) (*c*) affronter (la mort, un danger); faire face à (une difficulté) (*c*) rejoindre, (re)trouver (qn); **to go to m. s.o.,** aller audevant de qn; aller à la rencontre de qn; **to arrange to**

m. s.o., prendre rendez-vous avec qn; **I'll m. you at the station,** je viendrai vous chercher à la gare (*d*) faire la connaissance de (qn); **I've already met him,** je l'ai déjà rencontré (*e*) **the scene that met my eyes,** le spectacle qui s'offrait à mes yeux; **there's more in it than meets the eye,** on ne voit pas le dessous des cartes (*f*) **the road meets the railway,** la route rejoint le chemin de fer (*g*) **to m. s.o.,** faire des concessions à qn (*h*) satisfaire, répondre, à (un besoin); faire face à (une demande); prévoir (une objection); **to m. s.o.'s wishes,** remplir les désirs de qn; (*i*) *Com:* honorer (un chèque) (*j*) **to m. expenses,** subvenir aux frais **2.** *vi* (*a*) se rencontrer, se voir; **they met in 1960,** ils se sont connus en 1960; **when shall we m. again?** quand nous reverrons-nous? (*b*) se réunir (en session); s'assembler (*c*) (*of thgs*) se réunir, se joindre; **our eyes met,** nos regards se sont croisés; **to make (both) ends m.,** joindre les deux bouts (*d*) **to m. with** sth, rencontrer, trouver, qch; **to m. with a loss,** subir une perte; **to m. with difficulties,** éprouver des difficultés; **to m. with a refusal,** essuyer un refus; **he met with an accident,** il lui est arrivé un accident; **we met up with him in Paris,** nous l'avons rencontré à Paris. **II.** *n* (*a*) rendez-vous de chasse (*b*) *esp NAm:* réunion *f.* '**meeting** *n* **1.** rencontre *f;* **m. place,** lieu de réunion; rendez-vous *m* **2.** (*a*) assemblée *f;* réunion *f; Pol: Sp:* meeting *m;* **to call a m. of** the shareholders, convoquer les actionnaires; **to address the m.,** prendre la parole; **she's in a m.,** elle est en conférence (*b*) *Rel:* (*Quakers*) **to go to m.,** aller au temple.

megacycle ['megəsaikl] *n El:* mégacycle *m.*

megalith ['megəliθ] *n* mégalithe *m.*

megalomania [megəlou'meiniə] *n* mégalomanie *f.* '**megalo'maniac** *a* & *n* mégalomane (*mf*).

megaphone ['megəfoun] *n* porte-voix *m inv; Sp:* mégaphone *m.*

megaton ['megətʌn] *n* mégatonne *f.*

melamine ['meləmi:n] *n* mélamine *f.*

melancholy ['melənkəli] **1.** *n* mélancolie *f* **2.** *a* (*of pers*) mélancolique; triste; (*of news*) triste, attristant. **melan'cholic** *a* mélancolique.

mellow ['melou] **I.** *a* **1.** (fruit) fondant, mûr; (vin) moelleux **2.** (*of voice*) moelleux, doux; (*of colour*) doux, velouté **3.** (*a*) (esprit) mûr; **to grow m.,** s'adoucir (*b*) *F:* un peu gris. **II.** *v* **1.** *vtr a* (*a*) (faire) mûrir (des fruits); donner du moelleux à (un vin, une couleur) (*b*) mûrir, adoucir (le caractère de qn) **2.** *vi* (*a*) mûrir; prendre du moelleux (*b*) (*of character*) s'adoucir. '**mellowness** *n* maturité *f* (des fruits); moelleux *m* (du vin); douceur *f* (du caractère).

melodrama ['melədra:mə] *n* mélodrame *m.* **melodra'matic** *a* mélodramatique. **melodra'matically** *adv* d'un air mélodramatique.

melody ['melədi] *n* (*pl* **melodies**) mélodie *f,* air *m.* **me'lodic** *a* mélodique. **me'lodious** [-'loud-] *a* mélodieux. **me'lodiously** *adv* mélodieusement.

melon ['melən] *n* melon *m;* **water m.,** pastèque *f.*

melt [melt] *v* (**melted,** *pp adj* **molten** ['moult(ə)n]) **1.** *vi* (*a*) (se) fondre (*b*) (*of pers*) s'attendrir; **to m. into tears,** fondre en larmes (*c*) (i) (*of solid in liquid*) fondre, se dissoudre (ii) (*of colour*) to m. into, fondre, se perdre, dans; **to m. into thin air,** disparaître **2.** *vtr a* (*a*) (faire) fondre (*b*) attendrir, émouvoir (qn) (*c*) (faire) dissoudre (le sucre, un sel). '**melt a'way** *vi* (*a*) (*of* *snow*) fondre complètement (*b*) (*of clouds*) se dissiper; (*of crowd*) se disperser; (*of anger*) s'évaporer. **'melt 'down** *vtr* fondre (de la ferraille, un métal). **'melting 1.** *a* (*a*) (*of snow*) fondant; (*of voice*) attendri (*b*) (*of words, scene*) attendrissant, émouvant **2.** *n* (*a*) fonte *f*; fusion *f*; **m. point,** point de fusion; **m. pot,** creuset *m*; *Fig:* **to put everything back in the m. pot,** remettre tout en question; **it's still in the m. pot,** c'est encore au stade des discussions (*b*) attendrissement *m* (des cœurs).

member ['membər] *n* **1.** *Anat: Z:* organe *m*; **male m.,** membre viril **2.** (*a*) membre (d'une famille, d'un club); adhérent, -ente (d'un parti); **he's a m. of the family,** il fait partie de la famille; **m. of the audience,** spectateur, -trice, auditeur, -trice, assistant, -ante; **m. of staff,** (i) employé, -ée (ii) *Sch:* professeur *m*; **the m. countries,** les pays membres (*b*) **M. of Parliament,** député *m*. **'membership** *n* **1.** qualité *f* de membre; adhésion *f*; **m. card,** carte de membre; **m. fee,** cotisation *f* **2.** nombre *m* des membres, effectif *m* (d'une société).

membrane ['membrein] *n* membrane *f*; **mucus m.,** muqueuse *f*.

memento [mi'mentou] *n* (*pl* memento(e)s) memento *m*, souvenir *m*.

memo ['memou] *n* (*pl* memos) *F:* note *f*; **m. pad,** bloc-notes *m*.

memoir ['memwɑːr] *n* (*a*) mémoire *m*, dissertation *f* (scientifique) (*b*) notice *f* biographique (*c*) **memoirs,** mémoires.

memorandum [memə'rændəm] *n* (*pl* memoranda, -dums) mémorandum *m*, note *f*; *Adm:* circulaire *f*.

memory ['meməri] *n* (*pl* memories) (*a*) mémoire *f*. **like a sieve,** mémoire de lièvre; **I've no m. for names,** je n'ai pas la mémoire des noms; **loss of m.,** perte de mémoire; amnésie *f*; **if my m. serves me right,** si j'ai bonne mémoire; **within living m.,** de mémoire d'homme; **to play sth from m.,** jouer qch de mémoire (*b*) mémoire, souvenir *m*; **childhood memories,** souvenirs d'enfance; **in m. of s.o.,** en, à la, mémoire de qn; **en souvenir de qn. 'memorable** *a* mémorable. **'memorably** *adv* mémorablement. **me'morial 1.** *a* commémoratif **2.** *n* monument *m*; **war m.,** monument aux morts. **'memorize** *vtr* apprendre (qch) par cœur; retenir (des chiffres).

men [men] *npl* *see* **man I. 'menfolk** *nmpl* les hommes. **'menswear** *n coll Com:* vêtements *mpl* d'hommes; habillement *m* pour hommes; **m. (department),** rayon *m* hommes.

menace [menəs] **1.** *n* menace *f*; (*of pers*) *F:* plaie *f* **2.** *vtr* menacer (qn). **'menacing** *a* menaçant. **'menacingly** *adv* d'un air, d'un ton, menaçant.

menagerie [mə'nædʒəri] *n* ménagerie *f*.

mend [mend] **I.** *n* (*in fabric*) reprise *f*, raccommodage *m*; **to be on the m.,** être en voie de guérison. **II.** *v* **1.** *vtr* (*a*) raccommoder (un vêtement); repriser (des chaussettes); réparer (une machine, une route) (*b*) rectifier, corriger; **to m. one's ways,** changer de conduite; se corriger (*c*) réparer (une faute) **2.** *vi* (*of invalid, health*) se remettre; (*of pers*) se corriger; (*of condition*) s'améliorer. **'mending** *n* (*a*) raccommodage *m*; reprisage *m*; réparation *f* (*b*) vêtements *mpl* à raccommoder.

mendacious [men'deiʃəs] *a* menteur; mensonger.

menial ['miːniəl] *a* (*of duties*) servile, bas.

meningitis [menin'dʒaitis] *n* *Med:* méningite *f*.

menopause ['menoupɔːz] *n* *Med:* ménopause *f*. **meno'pausal** *a* (femme) à la ménopause; (symptôme) dû à la ménopause.

menstruate ['menstrueit] *vi* (*of woman*) avoir ses règles. **menstru'ation** *n* menstruation *f*.

mental ['mentl] *a* mental; **m. reservation,** restriction mentale; arrière-pensée *f*; **m. arithmetic,** calcul mental, de tête; **m. deficiency,** débilité mentale: **m. defective,** débile (mental(e)); **m. hospital, home,** hôpital psychiatrique; **m. patient,** malade mental, -ale; **m. powers,** facultés intellectuelles; *F:* **he's m.!** il est fou! **men'tality** *n* mentalité *f*. **'mentally** *adv* mentalement; **m. defective, m. deficient,** débile (mental(e)); **m. handicapped,** handicapé mental.

menthol ['menθɔl] *n* menthol *m*.

mention ['menʃən] **1.** *n* mention *f*; **he made no m. of it,** il n'en a pas parlé **2.** *vtr* mentionner, citer, faire mention de (qch); parler de (qn, qch); **the sum mentioned,** la somme indiquée; **I forgot to m. that,** j'ai oublié de vous dire que; **I'll m. it to him,** je lui en toucherai un mot; **it must never be mentioned again,** il ne faut plus jamais en reparler; **it's not worth mentioning,** cela est sans importance; **nothing worth mentioning,** pour ainsi dire rien; **not to m.,** sans parler de, sans compter; **I heard my name mentioned,** j'ai entendu prononcer mon nom; **mentioning no names,** sans nommer personne; **don't m. it!** il n'y a pas de quoi!

mentor ['mentɔːr] *n* mentor *m*, guide *m*.

menu ['menjuː] *n* menu *m*; carte *f*.

mercenary ['məːsinəri] *a & n* mercenaire (*m*).

merchant ['məːtʃənt] **1.** *n* négociant, -ante; commerçant, -ante; marchand, -ande, en gros; **wine m.,** négociant en vins **2.** *a* marchand; de commerce; **m. bank,** banque d'affaires; **m. ship, vessel,** navire marchand; **m. seaman,** marin de la marine marchande; **m. navy,** marine marchande. **'merchandise** *n* marchandise(s) *f* (*pl*). **'merchandising** *n* marchandisage *m*.

Mercury ['məːkjuri] **1.** *Prnm Astr: Myth:* Mercure **2.** *n Ch:* mercure *m*. **mer'curial** *a* (*a*) vif, éveillé (*b*) (*of pers*) inconstant.

mercy ['məːsi] *n* (*a*) miséricorde *f*, grâce *f*, merci *f*; pitié *f*; **to have m. on s.o.,** avoir pitié de qn; **to beg for m.,** demander grâce; **to throw oneself on s.o.'s m.,** s'abandonner à la merci de qn; **m. killing,** euthanasie *f* (*b*) **at s.o.'s m.,** à la discrétion, à la merci, de qn; *Iron:* **I leave him to your tender mercies,** je le livre à vos soins (*c*) **thankful for small mercies,** reconnaissant des moindres bienfaits; **what a m.!** quel bonheur! quelle chance! **'merciful** *a* miséricordieux **(to,** pour); clément **(to,** envers). **'mercifully** *adv* (*a*) miséricordieusement (*b*) par bonheur. **'merciless** *a* impitoyable; sans pitié. **'mercilessly** *adv* impitoyablement; sans merci.

mere ['miər] *a* simple, pur, seul; **the m. sight of her,** sa seule vue; **by m. chance,** par pur hasard; **I shudder at the m. thought of it,** je frissonne rien que d'y penser; **he's a m. child,** ce n'est qu'un enfant. **'merely** *adv* simplement, seulement; **he m. smiled,** il s'est contenté de sourire.

merge [məːdʒ] **1.** *vtr* fondre, fusionner (deux systèmes, deux classes) **2.** *vi* se fondre, se perdre (**in, into,**

dans); se confondre (**in, into,** avec); (*of banks, companies*) s'amalgamer, fusionner; (*of roads*) se rejoindre (**avec,** with); (*of rivers*) confluer (**with,** avec). **'merger** *n* fusion *f*.
meridian [mə'ridiən] *a & n* méridien (*m*).
meringue [mə'ræŋ] *n Cu:* meringue *f*.
merino [mə'ri:nou] *n Agr: Tex:* mérinos *m*.
merit ['merit] **1.** *n* (*a*) mérite *m*; **according to one's merits,** (être récompensé) selon ses mérites; *Jur:* **the merits of a case,** le bien-fondé d'une cause; **to judge sth on its merits,** juger qch au fond; **to go into the merits of sth,** discuter le pour et le contre de qch (*b*) valeur *f*, mérite **2.** *vtr* mériter. **meri'tocracy** *n* méritocratie *f*. **meri'torious** *a* méritoire.
mermaid ['mə:meid] *nf* sirène. **'merman** *nm* (*pl* -**men**) triton.
merry ['meri] *a* (**merrier, merriest**) (*a*) joyeux, gai; **to make m.,** s'amuser; **Christmas!** joyeux Noël! *Prov:* **the more the merrier,** plus on est de fous plus on rit; *A: & Lit:* **m. England,** l'aimable Angleterre (*b*) *F:* un peu gris. **'merrily** *adv* gaiement, joyeusement. **'merriment** *n* gaieté *f*, réjouissance *f*; hilarité *f*. **'merry-go-round** *n* manège *m* (de chevaux *mpl* de bois). **'merrymaker** *n* fêtard, -arde. **merrymaking** *n* réjouissances *fpl*; partie *f* de plaisir.
mesh [meʃ] **1.** *n* (*a*) maille *f* (d'un filet); **wire m.,** grillage *m*; **m. tights,** (i) collant filet (ii) collant indémaillable; **m. bag,** filet (à provisions) (*b*) *MecE:* prise *f*, engrenage *m*; **in m.,** en prise; **to be caught in the meshes,** être pris dans l'engrenage. **2.** *vi* s'engrener.
mesmerize ['mezmə raiz] *vtr* hypnotiser (qn); **I was mesmerized,** j'étais fasciné (**par,** by).
mess [mes] **1.** *n* (*a*) saleté *f*; **to make a m. of the tablecloth,** salir la nappe; **dog's m.,** crotte *f* de chien (*b*) fouillis *m*, désordre *m*; gâchis *m*; **everything's in a m.,** tout est en désordre; **what a m.!** quel désordre! (*of pers*) **to get into a m.,** se mettre dans de beaux draps; **to make a m. of things,** tout gâcher; (*of pers*) **to be (in) a m.,** être très sale; **he looks a m.,** il n'est pas présentable (*c*) (i) (*for officers*) mess *m*; (*for men*) *Mil:* ordinaire *m*; *Navy:* plat *m* (ii) (*room*) mess *m*; *Navy:* réfectoire *m* (des hommes); *Navy:* carré *m*; **m. dress, kit,** tenue de mess, de soirée; **m. tin,** gamelle *f*; **m. jacket,** spencer *m* **2.** *v* (*a*) *vtr* salir, souiller (*b*) *vi Mil: etc:* manger (en commun), faire gamelle (**with,** avec). **'mess a'bout, 'mess a'round** *F:* **1.** *vtr* (*a*) embêter (qn); tripoter (qch) (*b*) déranger (qn); chambouler (les projets de qn) **2.** *vi* (*a*) patauger (dans la boue) (*b*) bricoler; perdre son temps; lambiner, traîner. **'mess 'up** *vtr* salir (qch); mettre en désordre; ébouriffer (les cheveux); gâcher, bousiller (un travail). **'mess-up** *n F:* gâchis *m*. **'messy** *a* (-**ier, -iest**) **1.** (*a*) sale, malpropre (*b*) en désordre; (*of work*) peu soigné **2.** qui salit; salissant.
message ['mesidʒ] *n* **1.** message *m*; **telephone m.,** message téléphonique; **to leave a m. for s.o.,** laisser un message, un mot, pour qn; *F:* **has he got the m.?** est-ce qu'il a compris, pigé? **2.** commission *f*, course *f*. **'messenger** *n* (*a*) messager, -ère; coursier, -ière; **motorcycle m.,** estafette *f* motocycliste (*b*) commissionnaire *m*; **m. boy,** garçon de courses (*c*) courrier *m* (diplomatique).
Messiah [mi'saiə] *Prn* Messie *m*.

Messrs ['mesəz] *nmpl Com: etc:* Messieurs, *abbr* MM.
met¹ [met] *see* **meet I.**
met² *a F:* (*abbr* **meteorological**) météo; **the m. office,** la météo.
metabolism [me'tæbəlizm] *n* métabolisme *m*. **meta'bolic** *a* métabolique.
metal ['metl] **1.** *n* (*a*) métal *m*; **m. polish,** produit *m* d'entretien (pour métaux) (*b*) métal, fonte *f*; **sheet m.,** métal en feuilles; **m. casing,** enveloppe métallique; *CivE:* **road m.,** cailloutis *m*, pierraille *f*; *Rail:* **the metals,** les rails *m* **2.** *vtr* (**metalled,** *NAm:* **metaled**) empierrer (une route). **me'tallic** *a* métallique. **me'tallurgist** *n* métallurgiste *m*. **me'tallurgy** *n* métallurgie *f*. **'metalwork** *n* (*a*) travail *m* des métaux; **art m.,** ferronnerie *f*, serrurerie *f*, d'art (*b*) métal ouvré. **'metalworker** *n* ouvrier *m* en métaux, métallurgiste.
metamorphosis [metə'mɔ:fəsis] *n* (*pl* **metamorphoses**) métamorphose *f*. **meta'morphose** *vtr & i* (se) métamorphoser (**to, into,** en).
metaphor ['metəfər] *n* métaphore *f*; **mixed m.,** métaphore disparate, incohérente. **meta'phorical** *a* métaphorique. **meta'phorically** *adv* métaphoriquement.
metaphysics [metə'fiziks] *npl* (*usu with sg const*) métaphysique *f*. **meta'physical** *a* métaphysique.
mete [mi:t] *vtr Lit:* **to m. out,** infliger (des punitions); décerner (des récompenses).
meteor ['mi:tiər] *n* météore *m*. **mete'oric** *a* météorique; **m. rise,** montée rapide. **'meteorite** *n* météorite *m or f*. **meteoro'logical** *a* météorologique. **meteo'rologist** *n* météorologue *mf*, météorologiste *mf*. **meteo'rology** *n* météorologie *f*.
meter¹ ['mi:tər] **1.** *n* compteur *m*; **electricity m.,** compteur électrique, d'électricité; **gas, water, m.,** compteur à gaz, à eau; **parking m.,** parcmètre *m*; *NAm:* **m. man, m. maid** (*Br* = **traffic warden**) contractuel(le); **m. reader,** releveur, -euse, de(s) compteur(s).
meter² *n NAm:* = **metre¹·²**
methane ['mi:θein] *n Ch:* méthane *m*.
method ['meθəd] *n* méthode *f*; **m. of doing sth,** façon *f*, méthode, manière *f*, de faire qch; procédé *m* pour faire qch; *Adm:* **m. of payment,** modalités *fpl* de paiement; **there's m. in his madness,** il n'est pas si fou qu'il en a l'air. **me'thodical** *a* méthodique; **to be m.,** avoir de l'ordre. **me'thodically** *adv* méthodiquement, avec méthode. **'Methodism** *n Rel:* méthodisme *m*. **'Methodist** *a & n Rel:* méthodiste (*mf*). **metho'dology** *n* méthodologie *f*.
meths [meθs] *n F:* alcool *m* à brûler.
methyl ['meθil] *n Ch:* méthyle *m*. **'methylated** *a* **m. spirit(s),** alcool *m* à brûler.
meticulous [mi'tikjuləs] *a* méticuleux. **me'ticulously** *adv* méticuleusement. **me'ticulousness** *n* méticulosité *f*.
metre¹, *NAm:* **meter** ['mi:tər] *n Pros:* mètre *m*, mesure *f*; **in m.,** en vers.
metre², *NAm:* **meter** *n* mètre *m*; **square m., cubic m.,** mètre carré, cube. **'metric** *a* (système) métrique; *F:* **to go m.,** adopter le système métrique. **metri'cation** *n* adoption *f* du système métrique.
metronome ['metrənoum] *n* métronome *m*.

metropolis [mi'trɔpəlis] *n* métropole *f*. **metro'politan** *a* métropolitain.

mettle [metl] *n* 1. (*of pers*) ardeur *f*, courage *m*, feu *m*; (*of horse*) fougue *f*; **to be on one's m.**, se piquer d'honneur 2. caractère *m*, tempérament *m*; **to show one's m.**, donner sa mesure.

mew [mju:] 1. *n* miaulement *m* 2. *vi* miauler. **'mewing** *n* miaulement *m*.

mews [mju:z] *n* (*a*) écuries *fpl* (*b*) ruelle *f* (sur laquelle donnaient les écuries); **m. flat**, appartement aménagé dans une ancienne écurie.

Mexico ['meksikou] *Prn Geog:* Mexique *m*; **M. (City),** Mexico. **'Mexican** *a & n* mexicain. -aine.

mezzanine ['mezəni:n] *n* **m. (floor),** mezzanine *f*, entresol *m*.

mezzo ['metsou] *adv Mus:* mezzo. **'mezzo- (-so'prano)** *n* (*a*) (*voice*) mezzo-soprano *m* (*b*) (*singer*) mezzo(-soprano) *f*.

MF *abbr WTel: Medium Frequency.*

mi [mi:] *n Mus:* (*fixed*) mi; (*movable*) médiante *f*.

MI *abbr Military Intelligence.*

miaow [mi(:)'au] 1. *n* miaulement *m*, miaou *m* 2. *vi* miauler.

mica ['maikə] *n* mica *m*.

mice [mais] *npl see* **mouse.**

Michaelmas ['miklməs] *n* **M. (Day)** la Saint-Michel; *Bot:* **M. daisy,** aster *m* d'automne.

mickey ['miki] *n F:* **to take the m. out of s.o.,** se payer la tête de qn.

micro- ['maikrou] *pref* micro-. **microbi'ology** *n* microbiologie *f*. **'microchip** *n Cmptr:* puce *f*. **'microdot** *n* micropoint *m*. **microelec'tronics** *n* (*used as sg const*) micro-électronique *f*. **'microfilm** *n* microfilm *m*. **'microgroove** *n* microsillon *m*. **'micromesh** *a* (bas) super-fin. **'micro'processor** *n* microprocesseur *m*. **'microwave** *n* micro-onde *f*.

microbe ['maikroub] *n* microbe *m*.

microcosm ['maikroukɔzm] *n* microcosme *m*.

microphone ['maikrəfoun] *n* microphone *m*.

microscope ['maikrəskoup] *n* microscope *m*; **electron m.,** microscope électronique; **visible under the m.,** visible au microscope. **micro'scopic** *a* microscopique. **mi'croscopy** *n* microscopie *f*.

mid [mid] *a* du milieu; mi-; **in m. afternoon,** au milieu de l'après-midi; **in m. air,** entre ciel et terre; **m. June,** la mi-juin; **in m. ocean,** en plein océan; **m. season,** demi-saison *f*. **'mid'day** *n* midi *m*; **m. sun,** soleil de midi. **'midland** 1. *a* du centre (d'un pays) 2. *npl* **the Midlands,** les comtés *m* du centre (de l'Angleterre). **'midnight** *n* minuit *m*; **m. mass,** messe de minuit; **to burn the m. oil,** travailler tard dans la nuit. **'midriff** *n* diaphragme *m*, estomac *m*; **bare m.,** ventre nu. **'midshipman** *n* (*pl* **-men**) aspirant *m* (de marine). **midst** *n* **in the m. of,** au milieu de; **in the m. of winter,** en plein hiver; **in the m. of all this,** sur ces entrefaites; **in our m.,** parmi nous. **'midstream** *n* **in m.,** au milieu du courant. **'midsummer** *n* (*a*) milieu *m* de l'été (*b*) solstice *m* d'été; **M. day,** la Saint-Jean. **'mid'way** *adv* à mi-chemin, à moitié chemin; **m. between Paris and London,** à mi-distance entre Paris et Londres. **mid'week** *n* milieu *m* de la semaine. **mid'winter** *n* (*a*) milieu *m* de l'hiver (*b*) solstice *m* d'hiver.

middle [midl] 1. *a* du milieu; central; moyen, intermédiaire; **to take a m. course,** adopter une solution intermédiaire; **m. class,** bourgeoisie *f*; **the upper, lower, m. class,** la haute, petite, bourgeoisie; **m. name,** second prénom; *Hist:* **the M. Ages,** le moyen âge; *Geog:* **(the) M. East,** le Moyen-Orient; **m. finger,** médius *m*, majeur *m* 2. *n* (*a*) milieu *m*, centre *m*; **in the m. of,** au milieu de; **in the m. of August,** à la mi-août; **right in the m. of sth,** au beau milieu de qch; **to be in the m. of doing sth,** être en train de faire qch; *F:* **in the m. of nowhere,** en plein bled (*b*) *F:* taille *f*, ceinture *f*; **the water came up to his m.,** l'eau lui arrivait à mi-corps. **middle-'aged** *a* d'un certain âge. **'middle-'class** *a* bourgeois. **'middleman** *nm* (*pl* **-men**) *Com:* intermédiaire. **'middle-of-the-'road** *a Fig:* modéré. **'middleweight** *a & n* (poids *m*) moyen (*m*). **'middling** 1. *a* médiocre; passable; moyen 2. *adv* assez bien; passablement.

midge [midʒ] *n Ent:* moucheron *m*.

midget ['midʒit] *n* 1. nain, *f* naine 2. *a* minuscule.

midwife ['midwaif] *n* (*pl* **midwives**) sage-femme *f*. **midwifery** ['midwifri] *n* obstétrique *f*.

might[1] [mait] *n* puissance *f*, force(s) *f*(*pl*); **to work with all one's m.,** travailler de toutes ses forces. **'mighty** 1. *a* (*a*) puissant, fort (*b*) grand, grandiose (*c*) *F:* grand; **you're in a m. hurry,** vous êtes drôlement pressé 2. *adv F:* fort, extrêmement, rudement. **'mightily** *adv* (*a*) puissamment, fortement (*b*) *F:* extrêmement.

might[2] *v aux see* **may**[1]. **'might-have-been** *n F:* (*pers*) raté(e).

mignonette [minjə'net] *n Bot:* réséda *m*.

migraine ['mi:grein] *n Med:* migraine *f*.

migrate [mai'greit] *vi* émigrer. **'migrant** 1. *a* (oiseau) migrateur; (ouvrier) migrant, saisonnier 2. *n* (*bird*) migrateur *m*; (*worker*) saisonnier *m*. **mi'gration** *n* migration *f*. **'migratory** *a* =**migrant** 1.

mike [maik] *n F:* micro *m*.

mild [maild] *a* (*a*) (*of pers*) doux; (*of reproach*) peu sévère; (*of regulation*) doux, peu sévère; (*of punishment*) léger; (climat) doux, tempéré; (ciel) clément; (hiver) doux; **it's milder here,** il fait meilleur ici (*b*) (plat) peu relevé; (tabac) doux; *Med:* **m. form of measles,** forme bénigne de la rougeole (*c*) (exercice) modéré; **the play was a m. success,** la pièce a obtenu un succès modéré. **' mildly** *adv* doucement, avec douceur; **to put it m.,** c'est un euphémisme; et encore, je suis gentil. **'mildness** *n* douceur *f*, clémence *f* (de qn, du temps); légèreté (d'une punition); bénignité *f* (d'une maladie).

mildew ['mildju:] 1. *n* moisissure *f*; (*on plants*) rouille *f*; (*on vine*) mildiou *m* 2. *vi* moisir, se rouiller. **' mildewed** *a* moisi; piqué de rouille; mildiousé.

mile [mail] *n Meas:* mille *m*; **five miles,** cinq milles = huit kilomètres; **you don't see anyone for miles (and miles),** on parcourt des kilomètres sans voir personne; **he lives miles away,** il habite loin d'ici; *F:* **to be miles away,** être dans la lune; *F:* **it sticks out a m.,** ça vous crève les yeux; *F:* **miles better,** beaucoup mieux. **' mileage** *n* distance en milles, = kilométrage *m*; **with low m.,** (voiture) qui a très peu roulé; **m. allowance,** indemnité de déplacement. **mil(e)'ometer** *n* = compteur *m* kilométrique.

'milestone n **1.** borne routière, = borne kilometrique **2.** Fig: jalon m.

milieu ['mi:ljə:] n milieu (social).

militant ['militənt] a & n militant, -ante; activiste (mf). **'militarism** n militarisme m. **'militarist** n militariste mf. **milita'ristic** a militariste. **'military 1.** a militaire; **m. service,** service militaire **2.** npl coll **the m.,** les militaires m, l'armée f. **'militate** vi militer (**against,** contre). **militia** [mi'liʃə] n milice f.

milk [milk] **1.** n (a) lait m; **m. diet,** régime lacté; **powdered m.,** lait en poudre; Cu: **m. pudding,** entremets au lait; **m. chocolate,** chocolat au lait; **m. shake,** milk-shake m; **m. bar,** milk-bar m; **m. jug,** pot à lait; Lit: **land of m. and honey,** pays de cocagne; Prov: **it's no use crying over spilt m.,** ce qui est fait est fait (b) **m. tooth,** dent de lait; Toil: **cleansing m.,** lait démaquillant (c) **coconut m.,** lait de coco **2.** vtr (a) traire (une vache) (b) F: dépouiller, exploiter (qn). **'milk-and-'water** a insipide. **'milking** n traite f; **m. machine,** trayeuse f (mécanique). **'milkman** nm (pl -men) laitier m. **'milksop** n F: poule mouillée. **'milky** a (-ier, -iest) laiteux; (boisson) au lait; **the M. Way,** la Voie lactée.

mill [mil] **I.** n **1.** n moulin m; (large) minoterie f; **m. wheel,** roue de moulin; F: **to go through the m.,** passer par de dures épreuves; F: **run of the m.,** ordinaire, quelconque (b) **coffee, pepper, m.,** moulin à café, à poivre **2.** Metalw: **(rolling) m.,** laminoir m **3.** (a) usine f, esp usine textile; **cotton m.,** filature f de coton; **m. hand,** ouvrier, -ière, de textile; **m. owner,** industriel du textile (b) **paper m.,** fabrique f de papier. **II.** v **1.** vtr moudre (le blé); broyer (du minerai); créneler (une pièce de monnaie); **milled edge,** crénelage m **2.** vi (of crowd) **to m. (about, around),** fourmiller; grouiller. **'millboard** n carton-pâte m inv. **'miller** n meunier m; Ind: minotier m. **'millpond** n réservoir m de moulin; **sea like a m.,** mer d'huile. **'millrace** n bief m de moulin. **'millstone** n meule f (de moulin); Fig: **a m. round his neck,** un boulet qu'il traînera avec lui. **'millstream** n courant m du bief.

millennium [mi'leniəm] n (a) RelH: millenium m (b) millénaire m; mille ans mpl.

millet ['milit] n Bot: millet m, mil m.

milligram(me) ['miligræm] n Meas: milligramme m. **'millibar** n Meas: millibar m. **'millilitre,** NAm: **'milliliter** n Meas: millilitre m. **'millimetre,** NAm: **millimeter** n Meas: millimètre m.

milliner ['milinər] n modiste f. **'millinery** n (articles mpl de) modes (fpl).

million ['miljən] n million m; **two m. men,** deux millions d'hommes; F: **he's one in a m.,** c'est la perle des hommes; **thanks a m.!** merci mille fois! NAm: **I feel like a m. dollars,** je me sens en pleine forme. **millio'naire** n millionnaire mf; = milliardaire mf. **'millionth** a & n millionième (mf).

millipede ['milipi:d] n mille-pattes m inv.

mime [maim] **1.** n mime m **2.** (a) vtr mimer (b) vi jouer par gestes.

mimic ['mimik] **1.** n imitateur, -trice **2.** vtr (**mimicked**) imiter, mimer, contrefaire; singer (qn). **'mimicry** n mimique f, imitation f.

mimosa [mi'mouzə] n Bot: mimosa m.

minaret [minə'ret] n minaret m.

mince [mins] **1.** n Cu: (a) (NAm: = ground meat) hachis m (de viande) (b) **m. pie,** tarte fourrée au mincemeat (mangée à Noël) **2.** (a) vtr hacher (menu); **minced meat** (NAm: = ground meat), hachis; viande hachée (b) vtr **not to m. matters,** parler carrément; **not to m. one's words,** ne pas mâcher ses mots (c) vi parler du bout des lèvres (d) vi marcher d'un air affecté. **'mincemeat** n (sorte de) compote f de raisins secs et de pommes; F: **to make m. of,** pulvériser (qch); réduire (qn) en bouillie. **'mincer** n hachoir m. **'mincing** a affecté, minaudier.

mind [maind] **I.** n **1.** to bear, keep, sth in m., (i) songer à qch; ne pas oublier qch (ii) tenir compte de qch; **to call sth to m.,** se rappeler, se souvenir de, qch; **he puts me in m. of his father,** il me rappelle son père; **it went (clean) out of my m.,** je l'ai (complètement) oublié (a) pensée f, avis m, idée f; **to give s.o. a piece of one's m.,** dire son fait à qn; **we're of one m., of the same m.,** nous sommes du même avis, nous sommes d'accord; **to my m.,** à mon avis (b) (purpose, desire) **to know one's own m.,** savoir ce qu'on veut; **to make up one's m.,** se décider; **to make up one's m. about sth,** prendre une décision au sujet de qch; **to be in two minds about sth,** être indécis sur qch; **to change one's m.,** changer d'avis; se raviser; **I've a good m. to do it,** je suis bien tenté, j'ai bien envie, de le faire (c) **to set one's m. on sth,** désirer qch ardemment; se mettre en tête de faire qch; **to give one's m. to sth,** s'adonner, s'appliquer, à qch; **to have sth in m.,** avoir qch en vue; **the person I have in m.,** la personne à qui je pense **3.** esprit m, âme f; **state of m.,** état d'esprit; **turn of m.,** mentalité f (de qn); **attitude of m.,** manière de penser; **peace of m.,** tranquillité d'esprit; **he has no strength of m.,** c'est un homme sans caractère **4.** (a) (opposed to body) âme; (opposed to matter) esprit; (opposed to emotions) intelligence f (b) esprit; **it never entered her m.,** cela ne lui est jamais venu à l'esprit; **she has something on her m.,** il y a quelque chose qui la préoccupe; **in the mind's eye,** dans l'imagination; **a walk will take my m. off it,** une promenade me changera les idées; **to be easy in one's m.,** avoir l'esprit tranquille; **that's a weight off my m.,** voilà qui me soulage l'esprit; **put it out of your m.,** n'y pensez plus (c) Prov: **great minds think alike,** les grands esprits se rencontrent (d) **m. reader,** liseur -euse, de pensées **5.** **to be out of one's m.,** avoir perdu la raison; **are you out of your m.? you must be out of your m.!** vous êtes fou! **to be in one's right m.,** avoir toute sa raison. **II.** vtr **1.** (a) faire attention à (qn, qch); **never m. that!** qu'à cela ne tienne! **never m. the money,** ne regardez pas à l'argent; F: **never you m.!** ça c'est mon affaire! **m. you, I've always thought that,** remarquez (que) j'ai toujours pensé (que) b) s'occuper de (qch); **m. your own business!** occupez-vous, mêlez-vous, de ce qui vous regarde! (c) **m. you're not late!** veillez à ne pas être en retard! **m. what you're doing!** faites attention à ce que vous faites! **m. you don't fall!** prenez garde de tomber! **m. the step!** attention à la marche! **m. your backs!** dégagez (s'il vous plaît)! **2.** (a) would **you m. shutting the door?** voudriez-vous bien fermer la porte? **do you m. if I smoke?** cela ne vous gêne pas que je fume? la fumée ne vous gêne pas? **you don't m. my mentioning it?** cela ne vous froisse pas que je vous le dise? **if you don't m.,** si vous n'y voyez p d'inconvénient; **I don't m.,** (i) cela m'est égal (ii) je veux bien; **I wouldn't m. a cup of tea,** je prendrais volontiers une tasse de thé; **I don't m. if I do,** ce n'est pas de refus (b) **never m.!** (i) ça ne fait rien! tant pis! (ii) ne vous inquiétez pas! **who minds what he says?** qui s'occupe de ce qu'il dit? **he doesn't m. the cost,** il ne regarde pas à la dépense; **don't m. them,** ne vous inquiétez pas d'eux **3.** soigner (qn); surveiller (des enfants); garder (des animaux); garder, veiller sur (la maison); s'occuper (du magasin). **'mind-'blowing** a P: hallucinant. **'mind-boggling** a P: ahurissant. **'minded** a disposé, enclin (**to do sth,** à faire qch); **commercially-m.,** commerçant. **'minder** n (a) (**child**) **m.,** surveillant, -ante, gardien, -ienne (d'enfants) (b) P: garde m du corps; ange gardien. **'mindful** a attentif (**of, à**). **'mindless** a sans intelligence; (destruction) irresponsable. **'mind 'out** vi faire attention; **m. o.!** attention!

mine[1] [main] **1.** n (a) mine f; **coal m.,** mine de houille, de charbon; **to work a m.,** exploiter une mine; **it's a m. of information,** c'est une mine de renseignements (b) Mil: etc: mine; **to lay a m.,** poser une mine; **m. detector,** détecteur de mines **2.** vtr & i (a) **to m. (for) coal,** exploiter le charbon (b) Mil: miner, saper (une muraille) (c) Mil: etc: miner (un port). **'minefield** n Mil: Navy: champ m de mines. **'minelayer** n Navy: mouilleur m de mines. **'minelaying** n Mil: Navy: pose f, mouillage m, de mines. **'miner** n Min: mineur m (de fond). **'mineshaft** n puits m de mine. **'minesweeper** n Navy: dragueur m de mines. **'mining** n **1.** Min: exploitation minière; **the m. industry,** l'industrie minière; **m. town,** ville minière; **m. engineer,** ingénieur des mines **2.** Mil: Navy: pose f, mouillage m, de mines.

mine[2] poss pron (a) le mien, la mienne, les miens, les miennes; **your country and m.,** votre patrie et la mienne; **these gloves are m.,** ces gants sont à moi, m'appartiennent; **this signature is not m.,** cette signature n'est pas de moi; **a friend of m.,** un(e) de mes ami(e)s; un(e) ami(e) à moi; **it's no business of m.,** ce n'est pas mon affaire (b) (my family) les miens (c) (my property) **m. and yours,** le mien et le tien, le vôtre; F: **what's yours is m.,** ce qui est à toi est à moi.

mineral ['minərəl] **1.** a minéral; **m. spring,** source (d'eau) minérale; **m. water,** (i) eau minérale (ii) boisson gazeuse **2.** n (a) minéral m; **m. deposits,** gisements miniers (b) **minerals,** boissons gazeuses. **mine'ralogist** n minéralogiste mf. **mine'ralogy** n minéralogie f.

mingle ['miŋgl] **1.** vtr mêler, mélanger **2.** vi (a) se mêler, se mélanger, se confondre (**with,** avec) (b) **to m. with the crowd,** se mêler à, dans, la foule.

mingy ['mindʒi] a F: **1.** (pers) radin **2.** (portion) misérable.

mini ['mini] **1.** n (a) Aut: Rtm: mini f (b) Cl: mini-jupe f **2.** a **a m. demonstration,** une mini manifestation. **'minibus** n (pl -es) minibus m. **'minicab** n radio-taxi m. **'miniskirt** n mini-jupe f.

miniature ['minitʃər] **1.** n miniature f; **in m.,** en miniature **2.** a en miniature; (jardin, bouteille) miniature; (livre) minuscule; (appareil-photo) de petit format; (caniche) nain.

minimum ['minimam] a & n (pl **minima**) minimum (m); **to reduce sth to a m.,** réduire qch au minimum.

'minimal a minimal. **'minimize** vtr réduire au minimum, minimiser.

minister ['ministər] **1.** n (a) Pol: ministre m (d'État) (b) Ecc: ministre, pasteur m **2.** vi **to m. to s.o.'s needs,** pourvoir aux besoins de qn. **minis'terial** a (a) Pol: ministériel; gouvernemental (b) Ecc: sacerdotal. **'ministering** a (ange) secourable. **minis'tration** n ministère m, soins mpl; Ecc: sacerdoce m; **to receive the ministrations of a priest,** être administré par un prêtre. **'ministry** n **1.** (a) Pol: ministère m, gouvernement m (b) Adm: ministère, département m **2.** Ecc: **the m.,** le sacerdoce; **he was intended for the m.,** on le destinait à l'Église **3.** entremise f (**of, de**).

mink [miŋk] n Z: vison m; **m. coat,** manteau de vison, vison.

minnow ['minou] n Ich: vairon m.

minor ['mainər] **1.** a (a) petit, mineur; **Asia M.,** l'Asie mineure (b) petit, menu, peu important; **of m. interest,** d'intérêt secondaire; **to play a m. part,** jouer un rôle subalterne; Med: **m. operation,** opération bénigne (c) Mus: **m. key,** ton mineur; F: **in a m. key,** plutôt triste **2.** n (a) Jur: mineur, -eure (b) NAm: Sch: matière f secondaire. **mi'nority** n (pl -ies) (a) minorité f; **in a, the, m.,** en minorité; **m. party,** parti minoritaire (b) Jur: minorité.

Minorca [mi'nɔːkə] Prn Geog: Minorque f.

minster ['minstər] n église abbatiale; grande église.

minstrel ['minstrəl] n ménestrel m.

mint[1] [mint] **1.** n **the M.** = (l'Hôtel m de) la Monnaie; **in m. condition,** à l'état (de) neuf; **to be worth a m. (of money),** (of pers) rouler sur l'or; (of thg) valoir une somme fabuleuse, une fortune **2.** vtr (a) **to m. money,** (i) frapper de la monnaie (ii) F: amasser de l'argent à la pelle (b) monnayer (de l'or).

mint[2] n (a) Bot: menthe f; Cu: **m. sauce,** vinaigrette à la menthe (b) bonbon m à la menthe.

minuet [minju'et] n Mus: Danc: menuet m.

minus ['mainəs] **1.** prep moins; **ten m. two equals eight,** dix moins deux égale huit; **it's m. 10 (C),** il fait moins 10 (degrés); **he escaped, but m. his luggage,** il s'est échappé, mais sans ses bagages **2.** a & n Mth: **m. (sign),** moins m; **m. quantity,** quantité négative.

minuscule ['minəskjuːl] a minuscule.

minute[1] ['minit] n **1.** (a) minute f; **ten minutes past, to, three,** NAm: **ten minutes after, of, three,** trois heures dix, trois heures moins dix; **m. hand,** grande aiguille (d'une montre) (b) **wait a m.!** (i) attendez un instant! F: (une) minute! (ii) mais dites donc …; **he came in this (very) m.,** il rentre à l'instant (même); **he'll be here any m.,** il va arriver d'une minute à l'autre; **I'll come in a m.,** j'arrive(rai) dans un instant; **I shan't be a m.,** j'en ai pour une seconde; **I've just popped in for a m.,** je ne fais qu'entrer et sortir **2.** Mth: minute (de degré) **3.** (a) note f (b) **minutes of a meeting,** compte-rendu m, procès-verbal m, d'une séance; **m. book,** registre des délibérations.

minute[2] [mai'njuːt] a (a) tout petit; menu, minuscule, minime; **the minutest details,** les moindres détails m (b) minutieux, détaillé. **mi'nutely** adv minutieusement; en détail, dans les moindres détails. **mi'nutiae** [mai'njuːʃiiː] npl minuties fpl, menus détails.

miracle ['mirəkl] n miracle m; **by a m.,** par miracle; F: **it's a m. he's still alive,** c'est (un) miracle qu'il soit encore en vie; **m. cure,** remède-miracle *m*; *Th:* **m. play,** miracle. **mi'raculous** *a* (*a*) miraculeux; **it's m.,** cela tient du miracle (*b*) extraordinaire, merveilleux. **mi'raculously** *adv* miraculeusement, par miracle.

mirage ['mirɑːʒ] *n* mirage *m*.

mire ['maiər] *n* (*a*) bourbier *m* (*b*) boue *f*, bourbe *f*.

mirror ['mirər] **1.** *n* miroir *m*, glace *f*; **hand m.,** glace à main; **shaving m.,** miroir à raser; *Aut:* **driving m., rear view m.,** rétroviseur *m* **2.** *vtr* **the trees are mirrored in the water,** les arbres se reflètent dans l'eau.

mirth [mɑːθ] *n* gaieté *f*; rires *mpl*.

misadventure [misəd'ventʃər] *n* mésaventure *f*; contretemps *m*; **death by m.,** mort accidentelle.

misanthrope ['misənθroup], **misanthropist** [mi'sænθrəpist] *n* misanthrope *mf*. **misan'thropic** *a* (personne) misanthrope; (humeur) misanthropique. **mi'santhropy** *n* misanthropie *f*.

misapply [misə'plai] *vtr* (**misapplied**) **1.** mal appliquer, mal employer (qch) **2.** détourner (des fonds).

misapprehension [misæpri'hen ʃ(ə)n] *n* malentendu *m*; méprise *f*; **to be (labouring) under a m.,** se tromper.

misappropriate [misə'prouprieit] *vtr* détourner (des fonds). **misappropri'ation** *n* détournement *m* (de fonds).

misbehave [misbi'heiv] *vi & pr* se conduire mal; (*of child*) se tenir mal. **misbe'haviour,** *NAm:* **-havior** *n* mauvaise conduite; inconduite *f*; écart *m* de conduite.

miscalculate [mis'kælkjuleit] **1.** *vtr* mal calculer (une somme) **2.** *vi* se tromper (sur qch). **miscalcu'lation** *n* faux calcul; erreur *f* de calcul; mécompte *m*.

miscarriage [mis'kæridʒ] *n* **1.** (*a*) échec *m*, insuccès *m* (d'un projet) (*b*) **m. of justice,** erreur *f* judiciaire **2.** *Med:* fausse couche; **to have a m.,** avorter; faire une fausse couche. **mis'carry** *vi* (**miscarried**) **1.** (*of scheme*) échouer; ne pas réussir **2.** *Med:* avorter; faire une fausse couche.

miscast [mis'kɑːst] *vtr* (**miscast**) *Th: Cin:* donner une mauvaise distribution à (une pièce, un film); **he was m. in the part,** il était mal choisi pour ce rôle.

miscellaneous [misə'leiniəs] *a* varié, divers. **miscellany** [mi'seləni] *n* mélange *m*; collection *f* d'objets variés; *Lit:* recueil *m*.

mischance [mis'tʃɑːns] *n* **by m.,** par malchance, par malheur.

mischief ['mistʃif] *n* (*a*) mal *m*; tort *m*; mauvais coup; **to make m.,** apporter le trouble; semer la discorde (*b*) malice *f*; **out of pure m.,** (i) par pure espièglerie (ii) par pure méchanceté; **he's full of m.,** il est très espiègle; **to get into m.,** faire des bêtises; **to keep s.o. out of m.,** empêcher qn de faire des sottises (*c*) (*pers*) *F:* polisson, -onne. **'mischiefmaker** *n* brandon *m* de discorde; mauvaise langue. **'mischievous** *a* (*a*) méchant, malfaisant; (*of thg*) mauvais, nuisible (*b*) (enfant) espiègle, malicieux; **m. trick,** espièglerie *f*. **'mischievously** *adv* (*a*) méchamment (*b*) nuisiblement (*c*) malicieusement, par espièglerie. **'mischievousness** *n* (*a*) méchanceté *f* (*b*) malice *f*, espièglerie *f*.

misconception [miskən'sepʃn] *n* (*a*) idée fausse (*b*) malentendu *m*.

misconduct [mis'kɔndʌkt] *n* inconduite *f*; *Jur:* adultère *f*.

misconstrue [miskən'struː] *vtr* mal interpréter (qch). **miscon'struction** *n* fausse interprétation.

miscount 1. *n* ['miskaunt] faux calcul; mécompte *m*; erreur *f* d'addition; *Pol:* erreur dans le dépouillement du scrutin **2.** *vtr & i* [mis'kaunt] mal compter.

misdeal [mis'diːl] *Cards:* **1.** *n* maldonne *f* **2.** *vtr & i* (**misdealt** [mis'delt]) faire maldonne.

misdeed [mis'diːd] *n* méfait *m*.

misdemeanour, *NAm:* **-demeanor** [misdi'miːnər] *n* **1.** *Jur:* délit contraventionnel **2.** écart *m* de conduite.

misdirect [misdai'rekt] *vtr* mal adresser (une lettre); mal diriger (une entreprise); mal renseigner (qn); *Jur:* (*of judge*) mal instruire (le jury).

miser ['maizər] *n* avare *mf*. **'miserliness** *n* avarice *f*. **'miserly** *a* avare.

miserable ['mizrəbl] *a* (*a*) (*of pers*) malheureux, triste; **I feel m.,** j'ai le cafard; **to make s.o.'s life m.,** rendre la vie dure à qn (*b*) (*of event, condition*) misérable, déplorable; (*of journey*) pénible, désagréable; **what m. weather!** quel temps abominable! (*c*) misérable, pauvre; (*of sum*) insignifiant; (*of salary*) dérisoire; **a m. £70,** soixante-dix misérables livres. **'miserably** *adv* (*a*) malheureusement, tristement (*b*) misérablement (*c*) pauvrement. **'misery** *n* (*pl* -ies) (*a*) souffrance(s) *f* (*pl*), supplice *m*; his **life was sheer m.,** sa vie fut un martyre; **to put s.o. out of his m.,** mettre fin aux souffrances de qn; **to put an animal out of its m.,** achever un animal (*b*) misère *f*, détresse *f*; **to make s.o.'s life a m.,** rendre qn malheureux; *F:* **what a m. you are!** comme tu es grincheux!

misfire [mis'faiər] **1.** *n* (*of gun, engine*) raté *m* **2.** *vi* (*a*) (*of gun*) rater (*b*) (*of engine*) avoir des ratés (*c*) (*of joke*) manquer son effet; foirer; (*of plan*) échouer.

misfit ['misfit] *n* (*of pers*) inadapté(e).

misfortune [mis'fɔːtʃən] *n* infortune *f*, malchance *f*, malheur *m*.

misgiving [mis'givin] *n* doute *m*, crainte *f*; **not without misgivings,** non sans appréhension.

misgovern [mis'gʌvən] *vtr* mal gouverner.

misguided [mis'gaidid] *a* (*of pers*) qui manque de jugement; (*of conduct*) peu judicieux; (*of attempt*) malencontreux. **mis'guidedly** *adv* sans jugement; malencontreusement.

mishandle [mis'hændl] *vtr* malmener, maltraiter (qn); mal manier (une machine); mal mener, mal gérer (un affaire).

mishap ['mishæp] *n* mésaventure *f*, contretemps *m*.

mishear [mis'hiər] *vtr* (**misheard** [mis'həːd]) mal entendre.

mishmash ['miʃmæʃ] *n* *F:* méli-mélo *m*.

misinform [misin'fɔːm] *vtr* mal renseigner (qn).

misinterpret [misin'təːprit] *vtr* mal interpréter. **misinterpre'tation** *n* (*a*) fausse interprétation (*b*) (*in translating*) contresens *m*.

misjudge [mis'dʒʌdʒ] *vtr* mal juger; mal évaluer; se tromper sur le compte de (qn).

mislay [mis'lei] *vtr* (**mislaid**) égarer, perdre (qch).

mislead [mis'liːd] *vtr* (**misled** [-'led]) (*a*) induire (qn) en erreur; tromper (qn) (*b*) égarer, fourvoyer (qn). **mis'leading** *a* trompeur; fallacieux.

mismanage [mis'mænidʒ] *vtr* mal administrer, ma

gérer (une affaire). **mis'management** n mauvaise administration, mauvaise gestion.

misname [mis'neim] vtr mal nommer.

misnomer [mis'noumər] n nom m impropre.

misogynist [mi'sɔdʒinist] n misogyne mf.

misplace [mis'pleis] vtr (a) mal placer (sa confiance) (b) égarer (un objet).

misprint ['misprint] n faute f d'impression, F: coquille f.

mispronounce [misprə'nauns] vtr mal prononcer. **mispronunci'ation** n faute f de prononciation.

misquote [mis'kwout] vtr citer (qch) à faux, inexactement, incorrectement. **misquo'tation** n citation inexacte.

misread [mis'ri:d] vtr (**misread** [mis'red]) mal lire, mal interpréter (qch).

misrepresent [misrepri'zent] vtr mal représenter; dénaturer, travestir (les faits). **misrepresen'tation** n faux rapport, présentation erronée (des faits).

miss[1] [mis] 1. n coup manqué, raté; **it was a near m.**, c'était moins une; **we had a near m. with that car**, cette voiture a failli nous percuter; F: **to give (s.o., sth) a m.**, passer le tour de (qn); ne pas aller voir (qn, qch). 2. vtr (a) manquer, rater (le but); vi **he never misses**, il ne manque jamais son coup; **to m. the point**, (i) répondre à côté (ii) ne pas comprendre; Th: **to m. one's cue**, manquer la réplique; vi **to m. one's way**, se tromper de route; s'égarer; **he missed his footing**, le pied lui a manqué (b) ne pas trouver, ne pas rencontrer, rater (qn); manquer, rater (un train); manquer, laisser échapper, rater (une occasion); **an opportunity not to be missed**, une occasion à saisir; F: **you haven't missed much**, vous n'avez pas manqué, raté, grand-chose; Fig: **to m. the boat, the bus**, manquer le coche; **I missed my holiday this year**, je n'ai pas eu de vacances cette année (c) manquer (un rendez-vous); F: sécher (un cours); **I never m. going there**, je ne manque jamais d'y aller; **he just missed being killed**, il a failli se faire tuer (d) ne pas saisir (une plaisanterie); **I missed that**, je n'ai pas (i) compris (ii) entendu; **you can't m. the house**, vous reconnaîtrez la maison sans hésiter (e) **to m. (out) a word**, passer, sauter, un mot; vi F: **to m. out on sth**, manquer, rater (qch) (f) remarquer l'absence de (qn, qch); remarquer qu'il manque (qch, qn); **we're sure to be missed**, on va sûrement remarquer notre absence (g) regretter (qn); regretter l'absence de (qn); **I m. you**, vous me manquez; **I don't m. it**, cela ne me manque pas (du tout). **'missing** a absent; égaré; perdu; disparu, manquant; **one man is m.**, il manque un homme à l'appel; npl **the m.**, les disparus m.

miss[2] nf (title) mademoiselle; pl **the Misses Martin**, F: **the Miss Martins**, les demoiselles Martin; (as address) Mesdemoiselles Martin; **thank you, Miss Martin**, merci mademoiselle.

missal ['misl] n Ecc: missel m.

misshapen [mis'ʃeipən] a difforme, contrefait; (of figure) déformé.

missile ['misail, NAm: 'misl] n (a) projectile m (b) Mil: missile m, engin m; **guided m.**, missile, engin, guidé; **anti-m. m.**, missile antimissile(s); **m. base**, base de lancement de missiles; **m. launcher**, lance-missiles m inv.

mission ['miʃən] n mission f; **her m. in life is to help**

lame dogs, elle s'est donné pour mission de secourir les malheureux; **trade m.**, mission commerciale. **'missionary** 1. n (pl -ies) missionnaire mf 2. a de missionnaire; **m. work**, œuvre missionnaire.

missive ['misiv] n lettre f, missive f.

misspell [mis'spel] vtr (**misspelt**) mal épeler, mal orthographier. **mis'spelling** n faute f d'orthographe.

mist [mist] 1. n (a) brume f; **Scotch m.**, bruine f, crachin m; **lost in the mists of time**, perdu dans la nuit des temps (b) buée f (sur une glace); voile m (devant les yeux); **to see things through a m.**, voir trouble 2. vi **to m. over**, (i) (of landscape) disparaître sous la brume (ii) (of windscreen, mirror) s'embuer (iii) (of eyes) se voiler. **'misty** a brumeux, embrumé; (of windscreen, mirror) embué; (of eyes) troublé; (of shape) estompé; **it's m.**, le temps est brumeux; **m. outlines**, contours vagues; **m. recollection**, souvenir vague, confus.

mistake [mi'steik] 1. n erreur f, méprise f, faute f; **grammatical mistake**, faute de grammaire; **to make a m.**, faire une faute, une erreur; se tromper (**about**, **over**, sur, au sujet de); **to do sth by m.**, faire qch par erreur; **there is, can be, no m. about that**, il n'y a pas à se tromper; **make no m.**, que l'on ne s'y trompe pas; F: **I'm unlucky and no m.!** décidément je n'ai pas de chance! 2. vtr (**mistook; mistaken**) (a) mal comprendre (les paroles de qn); se méprendre sur (les intentions de qn); **if I'm not mistaken**, si je ne me trompe (pas); **there's no mistaking it**, il n'y a pas à s'y tromper (b) **to m. s.o., sth, for s.o., sth**, confondre qn, qch, avec qn, qch; **to m. s.o. for s.o. else**, prendre une personne pour une autre. **mis'taken** a 1. (of opinion) erroné; (of idea) faux 2. **m. identity**, erreur sur la personne. **mis'takenly** adv par erreur, par méprise.

mister ['mistər] n (always abbreviated to Mr) **Mr Martin**, Monsieur Martin.

mistime [mis'taim] vtr faire (qch) mal à propos, à contretemps; mal calculer (un coup).

mistletoe ['misltou] n Bot: gui m.

mistranslate [mistræns'leit] vtr mal traduire. **mistrans'lation** n mauvaise traduction; erreur f de traduction.

mistress ['mistris] nf (pl **mistresses**) (a) maîtresse; **to be one's own m.**, être indépendante; **to be m. of oneself**, être maîtresse de soi(-même) (b) maîtresse (d'école); institutrice; professeur m (de lycée); **the French m.**, le professeur de français.

mistrust [mis'trʌst] 1. n méfiance f, défiance f (of, à l'égard de) 2. vtr se méfier de (qn, qch); ne pas avoir confiance en (qn). **mis'trustful** a méfiant. **mis'trustfully** adv avec méfiance.

misunderstand [misʌndə'stænd] vtr (**misunderstood**) 1. mal comprendre, se méprendre sur (qch); mal interpréter (une action); **if I have not misunderstood**, si j'ai bien compris; **we misunderstood each other**, il y a eu un malentendu 2. méconnaître (qn); se méprendre sur le compte de (qn). **misunder'standing** n 1. malentendu m, méprise f 2. mésentente f; brouille f. **misunder'stood** a mal compris; (of pers) incompris.

misuse 1. n [mis'ju:s] abus m; mauvais usage, emploi abusif (de qch) 2. vtr [mis'ju:z] faire (un) mauvais usage, (un) mauvais emploi, de (qch); abuser de (qch); **to m. a word,** employer un mot abusive-ment.

mite [mait] n **1.** A & Lit: **the widow's m.,** le denier de la veuve **2.** petit(e) gosse; mioche mf; **poor little m.!** pauvre petit! **3.** Arach: acarien m; mite f.

miter [¹'²] ['maitər] n NAm: = mitre [¹'²].

mitigate ['mitigeit] vtr **1.** adoucir, atténuer (la souf-france); apaiser (la douleur); mitiger (une peine) **2.** atténuer (une faute); **mitigating circumstances,** cir-constances atténuantes. **miti'gation** n adoucisse-ment m; mitigation f (d'une peine); atténuation f (d'une faute).

mitre¹, NAm: **miter**¹ ['maitər] n Ecc: mitre f.

mitre², NAm: **miter**² n Carp: onglet m.

mitt [mit] n (also **mitten**) **1.** mitaine f **2.** moufle f.

mix [miks] **1.** n mélange m; Cu: **cake m.,** préparation f pour gâteau(x) **2.** vtr (a) mêler, mélanger (b) préparer (un gâteau, une boisson) (c) gâcher (du mortier); Cu: retourner, mélanger (la salade); NAm: (Br = **shuffle**) battre, mélanger (les cartes) **3.** vi se mêler, se mélanger (**with,** avec, à); (of colours) to m. well, aller bien ensemble; s'accorder; **to m. with people,** fréquenter les gens; **to m. with the crowd,** se mêler à la foule. **mixed** a mêlé, mélangé, mixte; **person of m. blood,** sang-mêlé mf inv; **m. marriage,** mariage mixte; Cu: **m. grill,** mixed-grill m; **m. sweets,** bonbons assortis; **m. vegetables,** jardinière f, macédoine f, de légumes, m. **feelings,** sentiments mêlés; **m. motives,** motifs com-plexes; **m. company,** milieu hétéroclite; F: **they were a m. bag,** il y en avait de toutes sortes; il y avait un peu de tout; **m. blessing,** bonne chose qui a son mauvais côté; **m. school,** école mixte; Sp: **m. doubles,** double m mixte. **mixed-'up** a F: (of pers) complexe; déboussolé. **'mixer** n (a) (machine) Ind: mélangeuse f; agitateur m; **concrete m.,** bétonnière f (b) DomEc: **(electric) m.,** batteur m, mixe(u)r m (c) (of pers) **to be a good m.,** être très sociable. **'mixing** n **1.** mélange m (de qch avec qch) **2.** (a) préparation f (d'un gâteau); **m. bowl,** bol à mélanger (b) gâchage m (du mortier). **mixture** ['mikst∫ər] n mélange m; Pharm: mixtion f, mixture f; **cough m.,** sirop m contre la toux. **'mix'up** vtr (a) mêler, mélanger; embrouiller (ses papiers); **I always m. him up with his brother,** je le confonds toujours avec son frère; **to be mixed up in (sth),** être mêlé à (une affaire); être compromis dans (une affaire) (b) em-brouiller (qn); **I was getting all mixed up,** je ne savais plus où j'en étais; **everything had got mixed up,** tout était en pagaille. **'mix-up** n (pl **mix-ups**) confusion f; embrouillement m, pagaille f.

ml abbr millilitre.

mm abbr millimetre.

MO abbr Medical Officer.

moan [moun] **1.** n gémissement m, plainte f **2.** (a) vi gémir, se lamenter; pousser des gémissements (b) vtr dire (qch) en gémissant. **'moaning** n gémissement(s) m(pl).

moat [mout] n fossé(s) m(pl), douves fpl.

mob [mɔb] **1.** n (a) Pej: **the m.,** la populace; **m. rule,** voyoucratie f (b) foule f, cohue f; rassemblement m, attroupement m; émeutiers mpl (c) F: bande f **2.** vtr (**mobbed**) (a) (of angry crowd) houspiller, attaquer, malmener (qn) (b) (of admiring crowd) assiéger (qn); faire foule autour de (qn).

mobile ['moubail] **1.** a (a) mobile (b) itinérant, mobile; **m. library,** bibliobus m; NAm: **m. home,** maison préfabriquée; F: **are you m.?** êtes-vous motorisé? **2.** n Art: mobile m. **mo'bility** n mobilité f. **mobili'zation** n mobilisation f. **'mobilize** vtr & i mobiliser.

moccasin ['mɔkəsin] n Cl: mocassin m.

mocha ['mɔkə] n Comest: moka m.

mock [mɔk] **1.** a d'imitation; contrefait; faux; **m. leather,** imitation f cuir; **m. turtle soup,** consommé à la tête de veau; **m. trial,** simulacre m de procès; **m. exam,** examen blanc **2.** vtr & i **to m. (at) s.o.,** se moquer de qn qch; railler qn, qch. **'mocker** n moqueur, -euse. **'mockery** n (a) moquerie f, raillerie f (b) sujet m de moquerie; **to make a m. of sth,** tourner qch en dérision (c) semblant m, simulacre m (**of, de**); **the trial is a mere m.,** le procès n'est qu'un simulacre. **'mocking 1.** a moqueur, railleur **2.** n moquerie f, raillerie f. **'mockingbird** n Orn: moqueur m. **'mockingly** adv d'un ton, d'un air, moqueur, railleur; par dérision. **'mock-up** n maquette f.

mod [mɔd] F **1.** a moderne; **m. cons,** confort m moderne **2.** n mods and rockers = blousons noirs.

mode [moud] n **1.** mode m, méthode f, manière f; **m. of life,** train m de vie **2.** (fashion) mode f. **'modal** a modal.

model ['mɔdl] **I.** n modèle m; maquette f, modèle réduit; new m., nouveau modèle; **1975 m.,** modèle 1975; **to take s.o. as one's m.,** prendre modèle sur qn; **to be a m. of virtue,** être un exemple de vertu; (artist's) **m.,** modèle (b) (fashion) m., mannequin m; male m., mannequin masculin. **II.** a (a) **m. husband,** époux modèle (b) **m. aircraft,** modèle réduit d'avion. **III.** v (**modelled,** NAm: **modeled**) **1.** vtr (a) modeler; **to m. oneself on s.o.,** prendre exemple sur qn (b) (of mannequin) présenter (une robe) **2.** vi **she models,** elle est mannequin. **'modelling,** NAm: **'modeling** n **1.** modelage m; **m. clay,** pâte à modeler **2.** pré-sentation f (d'une robe) par un mannequin.

moderate I. a & n ['mɔd(ə)rət] **1.** a modéré; moyen; (buveur) tempéré; (langage) mesuré; (prix) modéré, modique; **of m. size,** de grandeur, de taille, moyenne; **m. opinions,** opinions modérées **2.** n Pol: modéré(e). **II.** v ['mɔdəreit] **1.** vtr modérer, tempérer; **moderating influence,** influence modératrice **2.** vi (of storm) se calmer, s'apaiser. **'moderately** adv modérément; avec modération; modiquement, moyennement. **mode'ration** n modération f, mesure f; sobriété f (de langage); **with m.,** avec modération; **in m.,** modérément.

modern ['mɔdən] a & n moderne (m); **m. times,** les temps modernes; **m. languages,** langues vivantes. **mo'dernity** n modernité f. **'modernize** vtr moderniser.

modest ['mɔdist] a (a) modeste; **to be m. about one's achievements,** ne pas se vanter de son succès (b) O: pudique (c) modéré; (fortune) modeste; **m. in one's requirements,** peu exigeant (d) (of style) sans pré-tentions. **'modestly** adv modestement, avec modestie (b) pudiquement (c) modérément (d) sans prétentions. **'modesty** n (a) modestie f; **with all m.,** soit dit sans vanité (b) O: pudeur f (c) modération f (d'une demande); modicité (d'un prix) (d) absence f de prétention.

modicum ['mɔdikəm] *n* **a m. of,** un minimum de; un petit peu de; **a m. of truth,** une petite part de vérité.

modify ['mɔdifai] *vtr* (**modified**) (*a*) modifier; apporter des modifications à (qch) (*b*) modérer; mitiger, atténuer (une peine); **to m. one's demands,** rabattre de ses prétentions. **modifi'cation** *n* modification *f*. **'modifier** *n* modificateur *m*; *Gram:* modificatif *m*.

modulate ['mɔdjuleit] *vtr & i* moduler. **modu-'lation** *n* modulation *f*.

module ['mɔdju:l] *n* module *m*; **command m.,** module de commande.

Mogul ['mougəl] *n Hist:* mogol *m* **2.** *F:* **m.,** gros bonnet.

mohair ['mouhɛər] *n* mohair *m*.

Mohammedan [mə'hæmidən] *a & n* musulman, -ane.

moist [mɔist] *a* (climat) humide; (peau) moite; **eyes m. with tears,** yeux mouillés de larmes. **moisten** ['mɔisən] **1.** *vtr* humecter, mouiller; arroser (la pâte;) **to m. a rag with water,** imbiber un chiffon d'eau **2.** *vi* s'humecter, se mouiller. **'moistness** *n* humidité *f*; moiteur *f* (de la peau). **'moisture** *n* humidité *f*; buée *f* (sur une glace). **'moisturize** humidifier; hydrater (la peau). **'moisturizer** *n* crème hydratante, hydratant *m*. **'moisturizing** *a* **m. cream,** crème hydratante.

molar ['moulər] *a & n* (dent *f*) molaire (*f*).

molasses [mə'læsiz] *npl* mélasse *f*.

mold [mould] *etc: NAm:* = **mould,** *etc*.

mole¹ [moul] *n* grain *m* de beauté.

mole² *n* (*animal and spy*) taupe *f*; **m. catcher,** taupier *m*. **'molehill** *n* taupinière *f*. **'moleskin** *n* (*a*) (peau *f* de) taupe (*f*) (*b*) *Tex:* velours *m* de coton.

mole³ *n* môle *m*; brise-lames *m inv*.

molecule ['mɔlikju:l] *n* molécule *f*. **mo'lecular** *a* moléculaire.

molest [mə'lest] *vtr* (*a*) molester, importuner (qn) (*b*) *Jur:* attenter à la pudeur de (qn).

mollify ['mɔlifai] *vtr* (**mollified**) apaiser, calmer (qn).

mollusc. *NAm:* **mollusk** ['mɔləsk] *n* mollusque *m*.

mollycoddle ['mɔlikɔdl] *vtr F:* dorloter, chouchouter.

molt [moult] *n & v NAm:* = **moult.**

molten [moultən] *a* fondu, en fusion.

moment ['moumənt] *n* **1.** moment *m*, instant *m*; I haven't a m. to spare, je n'ai pas un instant de libre; **wait a m.! just a m.! one m.!** un moment! une seconde! **to expect s.o. (at) any m.,** attendre qn d'un instant à l'autre; **to interrupt at every m.,** interrompre à tout bout de champ; **I have just this m., only this m.,** heard of it, je l'apprends à l'instant; **a m. ago,** il y a un instant; **the m. he arrives,** dès son arrivée; **at this m., at the (present) m.,** en ce moment; actuellement; **I'll come in a m.,** je viendrai dans un instant; **for the m.,** pour le moment; **not for a m.!** jamais de la vie! **the m. of truth,** la minute de vérité; *F:* **he has his moments,** de temps en temps il lui arrive de faire des étincelles **2.** *Mec:* **m. of inertia,** moment d'inertie **3.** (*of fact, event*) **of little m.,** de petite importance. **'momentarily** *adv* momentanément. **'momentary** *a* momentané. **mo'mentous** *a* important; (décision) capitale; **m. occasion,** occasion mémorable. **mo'mentum** *n* **1.** *Mec: Ph:* moment *m* **2.** (*impetus*) vitesse acquise; élan *m*; **to gather m.,** prendre de la vitesse; **to lose m.,** perdre son élan.

Monaco ['mɔnəkou] *Prn Geog:* (**Principality of**) **M.,** (Principauté *f* de) Monaco *m*.

monarch ['mɔnək] *n* monarque *m*. **mo'narchic** [-'nɑ:k-] *a* monarchique. **'monarchist** *a & n* monarchiste (*mf*). **'monarchy** *n* (*pl* **-ies**) monarchie *f*.

monastery ['mɔnəstri] *n* (*pl* **monasteries**) monastère *m*. **mo'nastic** *a* monastique; monacal. **mo'nasticism** *n* monachisme *m*.

Monday ['mʌndi] *n* lundi *m*.

monetary ['mʌnitəri] *a* monétaire. **'monetarism** *n* politique *f* monétaire.

money ['mʌni] *n* monnaie *f*; argent *m*; **paper m.,** billets *mpl* (de banque); papier-monnaie *m*; *F:* **he's (just) coining m.,** il gagne un argent fou; **m. market,** marché monétaire; *Com:* **ready m.,** argent comptant, liquide; **to pay in ready m.,** payer (au) comptant; *Post:* **m. order,** mandat-poste *m*; **to throw good m. after bad,** s'enfoncer davantage dans une mauvaise affaire; **spending m.,** argent pour dépenses courantes; **to be worth a lot of m.,** (i) (*thg*) avoir de la valeur (ii) (*pers*) être riche; **to have m. to burn,** avoir de l'argent à n'en savoir que faire; *F:* **I'm not made of m.,** je ne suis pas cousu d'or; **to be short of m.,** être à court d'argent; **to earn, to make, m.,** gagner de l'argent; faire fortune; **to be rolling in m.,** rouler sur l'or; **there's m. in it,** c'est une bonne affaire; **it will bring in big m.,** cela rapportera gros; **I want to get my m. back,** je voudrais être remboursé; **you've had your m.'s worth,** vous en avez eu pour votre argent; *F:* **for my m.,** à mon avis; **m. belt,** ceinture à porte-monnaie; *Arach:* **m. spider,** petite araignée rouge. **'moneybox** *n* (*pl* **-es**) tirelire *f*. **'moneyed** *a* riche; qui a de l'argent; **the m. classes,** les gens riches, fortunés. **'moneygrubber** *n* grippe-sou *m*. **'moneygrubbing** *n* rapacité *f* **2.** *a* rapace. **'moneylender** *n* prêteur *m* (d'argent). **'moneymaking 1.** *a* qui rapporte **2.** *n* acquisition *f* de l'argent.

Mongolia [mɔŋ'goulia] *Prn Geog:* Mongolie *f*. **'Mongol** *a & n* **1.** *Geog:* mongol, -ole **2.** *Med:* **m. (child),** mongolien, -ienne. **Mon'golian** *a Geog:* mongol. **'mongolism** *n Med:* mongolisme *m*.

mongoose ['mɔŋgu:s] *n* (*pl* **mongooses**) *Z:* mangouste *f*.

mongrel ['mʌŋgrəl] *n* (chien *m*) bâtard (*m*).

monitor ['mɔnitər] **1.** *n* (*a*) *Sch:* = chef *m* de classe (*b*) *Tp:* opérateur *m* d'interception (*b*) *WTel: etc:* appareil *m* de contrôle, surveillance; moniteur *m* **2.** *vtr* (*a*) *WTel: etc:* surveiller (des émissions) (*b*) contrôler (les performances d'une machine). **'monitoring** *n WTel:* interception *f* des émissions, monitoring *m*; **m. station,** centre d'écoute.

monk [mʌŋk] *nm* moine, religieux. **'monkish** *a* de moine. **'monkshood** *n Bot:* (aconit *m*) napel (*m*).

monkey ['mʌŋki] *n* (*a*) *Z:* singe *m*; **female m., she-m.,** guenon *f*; *F:* **you little m.!** petit monstre! **to make a m. out of s.o.,** se payer la tête de qn; **m. business,** (i) combine *f*, fricotage *m* (ii) conduite *f* malhonnête; **m. tricks,** espiègleries *fpl*; *P:* **I don't give a monkey's,** je m'en fous éperdument (*b*) **m. nut,** arachide *f*; *Com:* cacah(o)uète *m*; *Bot:* **m. puzzle (tree),** araucaria *m*; **m. wrench,** clef anglaise; clef à molette. **'monkey**

a'bout, a'round vi faire des sottises, faire l'imbécile; **to m. a. with sth,** tripoter qch.

mono ['mɔnou] a Rec: F: mono.

monochrome ['mɔnəkroum] n monochrome m; Art: camaïeu m.

monocle ['mɔnəkl] n monocle m.

monogamous [mə'nɔgəməs] a monogame. **mo'nogamy** n monogamie f.

monogram ['mɔnəgræm] n monogramme m.

monograph ['mɔnəgræf] n monographie f.

monolith ['mɔnəliθ] n monolithe m.

monologue ['mɔnəlɔg] n monologue m.

monomania [mɔnə'meiniə] n monomanie f. **mono'maniac** n monomane mf.

monoplane ['mɔnəplein] n monoplan.

monopolist [mə'nɔpəlist] n monopolisateur, -trice. **monopoli'zation** n monopolisation f. **mo'nopolize** vtr monopoliser. **mo'nopoly** n (pl -ies) monopole m.

monorail ['mɔnəreil] n monorail m.

monosyllable ['mɔnə'siləbl] n monosyllabe m. **monosy'llabic** a monosyllabe; monosyllabique.

monotonous [mə'nɔtənəs] a monotone. **'monotone** n in a m., sur un ton monocorde. **mo'notonously** adv avec monotonie. **mo'notony** n monotonie f.

monoxide [mə'nɔksaid] n Ch: carbon m., oxyde m de carbone.

monsoon [mɔn'su:n] n Meteor: mousson f.

monster ['mɔnstər] 1. n monstre m 2. a F: monstre; colossal; énorme. **monstrosity** [mɔn'strɔsiti] n (pl -ies) monstruosité f. **'monstrous** a monstrueux. **'monstrously** adv monstrueusement.

month [mʌnθ] n mois m; **calendar m.,** mois civil; **on the 19th of this m.,** le 19 courant; **what day of the m. is it?** quel jour du mois, le combien, sommes-nous? **a m. ago today,** il y a aujourd'hui un mois; **once a m.,** une fois par mois; F: **never in a m. of Sundays,** jamais de la vie; la semaine des quatre jeudis. **'monthly 1.** a mensuel; **m. instalment,** mensualité f; Med: **m. period,** règles fpl; Rail: **m. season ticket,** billet m d'abonnement, abonnement m, valable pour un mois 2. adv mensuellement; tous les mois 3. n revue, publication, mensuelle.

Montreal [mɔntri'ɔ:l] Prn Geog: Montréal m.

monument ['mɔnjumənt] n monument m; **ancient m.,** monument historique. **monu'mental** a monumental; **m. mason,** marbrier m.

moo [mu:] 1. n meuglement m, beuglement m; int meuh! 2. vi (mooed) meugler, beugler.

mooch [mu:tʃ] vi F: **to m. about,** flâner, traîner.

mood[1] [mu:d] n Gram: mode m.

mood[2] n humeur f, disposition f; **he's in one of his bad moods,** il est de (très) mauvaise humeur; **to be in the m. for reading,** avoir envie de lire; **he's in no m. for laughing,** il n'est pas d'humeur à rire; **I'm not in the mood,** ça ne me dit rien. **'moodily** adv d'un air maussade, morose. **'moodiness** n humeur f maussade. **'moody** a (-ier, -iest) d'humeur changeante; maussade.

moon[1] [mu:n] n lune f; **new, full, m.,** nouvelle lune, pleine lune; Fig: **to ask, cry, for the m.,** demander la lune; **once in a blue m.,** tous les trente-six du mois; F: **to be over the m.,** être enchanté, ravi. **'moonbeam** n

rayon m de lune. **'moonlight 1.** n clair m de lune; **in the m., by m.,** au clair de lune; à la clarté de la lune; F: **to do a m. flit,** déménager à la cloche de bois **2.** vi F: travailler au noir, faire du travail (au) noir. **'moonlighting** n F: travail m (au) noir. **'moonlighter** n F: travailleur, -euse, au noir. **'moonlit** a éclairé par la lune. **'moonrise** n lever m de la lune. **'moonshine** n (a) clair m de lune (b) F: balivernes fpl, fadaises fpl. **'moonstone** n pierre f de lune. **'moonstruck** a à l'esprit dérangé; dingue.

moon[2] vi **to m. about, around,** musarder, flâner; **to m. over s.o.,** languir pour qn.

moor[1] ['muər], **moorland** ['muələnd] n lande f, bruyère f. **'moorhen** n Orn: poule f d'eau.

moor[2] v Nau: 1. vtr amarrer (un navire); mouiller (une bouée) 2. vi s'amarrer. **'mooring** n amarrage m; **ship at her moorings,** navire sur ses amarres f.

moose [mu:s] n inv in pl Z: élan m du Canada, orignal m.

moot [mu:t] 1. a **m. point,** point discutable 2. vtr **the question was mooted,** la question fut soulevée.

mop [mɔp] 1. n (a) balai m à laver, balai-éponge m; lavette f à vaisselle (b) **m. of hair,** tignasse f 2. vtr (mopped) éponger, essuyer (le parquet); **to m. one's brow,** s'éponger le front. **'mopping 'up** n Mil: nettoyage m. **'mop 'up** vtr (a) éponger (de l'eau); essuyer (une surface) (b) Mil: nettoyer (une position).

mope [moup] vi être triste; se morfondre.

moped ['mouped] n cyclomoteur m, vélomoteur m.

moral ['mɔrəl] 1. a moral; **to raise m. standards,** relever les mœurs; **m. courage,** courage moral 2. n (a) morale f, moralité f (d'un conte) (b) **morals,** moralité, mœurs fpl. **mo'rale** n moral m. **'moralist** n moraliste mf. **mo'rality** n (a) moralité f; principes moraux; sens moral (b) bonnes mœurs. **'moralize** vi moraliser. **'moralizing 1.** a moralisant; moralisateur 2. n leçons fpl de morale. **'morally** adv moralement; **m. wrong,** immoral.

morass [mə'ræs] n marais m; fondrière f.

morbid ['mɔ:bid] a morbide; **m. curiosity,** curiosité malsaine, maladive. **'morbidly** adv morbidement. **'morbidness** n (a) morbidité f (b) tristesse maladive (des pensées).

mordant ['mɔ:dənt] a mordant, caustique.

more [mɔ:r] 1. a & indef pron plus (de); **m. than ten men,** plus de dix hommes; **he's m. than 30,** il a plus de 30 ans; **one m.,** un de plus, encore un; **one or m.,** un ou plusieurs; **there's only one m. thing to do,** il n'y a plus qu'une chose à faire; **(some) m. bread,** encore du pain; **to have some m. wine,** reprendre du vin; **do you want any, some, m.?** en voulez-vous encore? **what m. can I say?** que puis-je dire de plus? **nothing m.,** plus rien; **have you any m.?** en avez-vous d'autres? **I need m.,** il m'en faut davantage 2. n or indef pron **I needn't say m.,** pas besoin d'en dire davantage; **that's m. than enough,** c'est plus qu'il n'en faut; **what is m.,** de plus, (et) qui plus est 3. adv (a) plus, davantage; **m. and m.,** de plus en plus; **far m. serious,** beaucoup plus grave; **he was m. surprised than annoyed,** il était plutôt surpris que fâché; **m. than satisfied,** plus que satisfait; **m. like 30 than 20,** plutôt 30 que 20; **that's m. like it!** ça, c'est mieux! **m. or less,** plus ou moins (b) **once m.,** encore une fois, une fois de plus; **I don't want to go**

there any m., je ne veux plus jamais y aller 4. (a) a (the) more's the pity, c'est d'autant plus regrettable (b) n the m. one has the m. one wants, plus on a, plus on désire avoir (c) adv all the m. reason, à plus forte raison; raison de plus; **I'm all the m.** surprised as, je suis d'autant plus étonné que 5. (a) a **I have no m.** money, je n'ai plus d'argent; **no m.** soup, thank you, plus de potage, merci (b) n **I have no m.,** je n'en ai plus; **I can do no m.,** je ne peux pas faire plus; **let's say no m. about it,** n'en parlons plus; **is there any m.?** y en a-t-il encore? en reste-t-il? **many m.,** beaucoup d'autres; **as many m.,** encore autant (c) adv **the house doesn't exist any m.,** la maison n'existe plus; **I don't want to see him—no m. do I,** je ne veux pas le voir—ni moi non plus. **'moreish** a F: appétissant; **it's very m.,** ça a un goût de revenez-y. **more'over** adv de plus; en outre; d'ailleurs; du reste.
morgue [mɔːg] n morgue f.
moribund ['mɔribʌnd] a moribond.
morning ['mɔːniŋ] n (a) matin m; **tomorrow m.,** demain matin; **(the) next m.,** le lendemain matin; **the m. before,** la veille au matin; **every Monday m.,** tous les lundis matins; **at four in the m.,** à quatre heures du matin; **first thing in the m.,** dès le matin, dès demain matin; **in the early m., early in the m.,** de grand matin; **what do you do in the m.?** que faites-vous le matin? **good m.!** bonjour! **m. breeze,** brise matinale; **m. newspaper,** journal du matin; **m. sickness,** nausées du matin; **m. coat** (NAm: = cutaway) frac m, jaquette f, habit m; **m. dress,** tenue f de cérémonie, frac (b) matinée f; **in the course of the m.,** dans la matinée; **a morning's work,** une matinée de travail.
Morocco [mə'rɔkou] 1. Prn Geog: le Maroc 2. n (leather) maroquin m. **Mo'roccan** a & n marocain, -aine.
moron ['mɔːrɔn] n (homme, femme) faible (mf) d'esprit; F: idiot, -ote; crétin, -ine. **mo'ronic** a faible d'esprit; F: idiot, crétin.
morose [mə'rous] a chagrin, morose. **mo'rosely** adv d'un air chagrin, morose.
morphia ['mɔːfiə], **morphine** ['mɔːfiːn] n morphine f; **m. addict,** morphinomane mf.
morphology [mɔː'fɔlədʒi] n morphologie f.
Morse [mɔːs] Prn M. (code), (code m) Morse m.
morsel ['mɔːsl] n petit morceau; **choice m.,** morceau friand, de choix.
mortadella [mɔːtə'delə] n m. (sausage), mortadelle f.
mortal ['mɔːtl] 1. a (a) mortel; **m. remains,** dépouille mortelle (b) humain (c) mortel; funeste, fatal; **m. blow,** coup mortel; **m. sin,** péché mortel; **m. enemy,** ennemi mortel; **m. combat,** combat à mort; **to be in m. fear of sth,** avoir une peur mortelle de qch; F: **it's no m. use,** ça ne sert absolument à rien 2. n mortel, -elle; humain, -aine. **mor'tality** n mortalité f. **'mortally** adv mortellement; **m. wounded,** blessé à mort; **to be m. afraid,** avoir une peur mortelle.
mortar ['mɔːtər] n mortier m. **'mortarboard** n Sch: toque universitaire anglaise.
mortgage ['mɔːgidʒ] 1. n hypothèque f; emprunt-logement m; **to take out a m.,** prendre une hypothèque, obtenir un emprunt-logement; **to pay off a m.,** purger une hypothèque, rembourser un emprunt-logement 2. vtr hypothéquer. **mortga'gee** n créan-

cier m hypothécaire. **'mortgager, 'mortgagor** n débiteur m hypothécaire.
mortice ['mɔːtis] n = mortise.
mortician [mɔː'tiʃn] n NAm: (Br = undertaker) entrepreneur m de pompes funèbres, F: croque-mort m.
mortification [mɔːtifi'keiʃn] n 1. mortification 2. humiliation f. **'mortify** vtr (mortified) mortifier; humilier (qn). **'mortifying** a mortifiant, humiliant.
mortise ['mɔːtis] n Carp: mortaise f; **m. lock,** serrure encastrée.
mortuary ['mɔːtjuəri] 1. a mortuaire 2. n (pl mortuaries) morgue f.
mosaic [mou'zeiik] n mosaïque f; **m. flooring,** dallage en mosaïque.
Moscow ['mɔskou] Prn Geog: Moscou m.
Moslem ['muzləm, 'mɔ-] a & n musulman, -ane.
mosque [mɔsk] n mosquée f.
mosquito [mɔs'kiːtou] n (pl mosquitoes) Ent: moustique m; **m. net,** moustiquaire f.
moss [mɔs] n Bot: mousse f; **m. rose,** rose moussue; Knit: **m. stitch,** point m de riz. **'mossy** a (-ier, -iest) moussu.
most [moust] 1. a (a) le plus (de); **who made (the) m. mistakes?** qui a fait le plus de fautes? (b) **m. men,** la plupart des hommes; **in m. cases,** dans la majorité des cas; **for the m. part,** (i) pour la plupart (ii) le plus souvent 2. n & indef pron (a) le plus; **at m., at the (very) m.,** au maximum; (tout) au plus; **to make the m. (of sth),** tirer le meilleur parti (possible) de qch; faire valoir (son argent); bien employer (son temps); exploiter (qch) au maximum; profiter (de qch) au maximum (b) **m. of them,** la plupart d'entre eux; **m. of the work,** la plus grande partie du travail (c) **he's more reliable than m.,** on peut compter sur lui plus que sur la plupart des gens 3. adv (a) (as superlative of comparison) **what I want m.,** ce que je désire le plus; **the m. beautiful woman,** la plus belle femme; **those who have answered m. accurately,** ceux qui ont répondu le plus exactement (b) (intensive) très, fort, bien; **m. displeased,** fort mécontent; **m. likely, probably,** très probablement; **it's m. remarkable,** c'est tout ce qu'il y a de plus remarquable; **m. unhappy,** bien malheureux; **he has been m. rude,** il a été on ne peut plus grossier. **'mostly** adv (a) pour la plupart; principalement (b) le plus souvent, la plupart du temps.
motel [mou'tel] n motel m.
moth [mɔθ] n Ent: (a) (clothes) m., mite f (b) papillon m de nuit. **'mothball** npl boule f de naphtaline. **'motheaten** a mangé aux mites, mité. **'mothproof** 1. a traité à l'antimite; antimite(s) 2. vtr traiter à l'antimite.
mother ['mʌðər] 1. n mère f; **m. to be,** future maman; **unmarried m.,** mère célibataire; **Mother's Day,** la fête des mères; **m. country,** mère-patrie f; **m. tongue,** langue maternelle; Ecc: **M. Superior,** Mère supérieure 2. vtr (a) donner des soins maternels à (qn); servir de mère à (qn) (b) dorloter (qn). **'mothercraft** n puériculture f. **'motherhood** n maternité f. **'Mothering 'Sunday** n la fête des mères. **'mother-in-law** n (pl mothers-in-law) belle-mère f. **'motherland** n patrie f. **'motherless** a sans mère; orphelin (de mère).

'**motherly** a maternel. '**mother-of-pearl** n ' nacre f.

motion ['mouʃən] 1. n (a) mouvement m, déplacement m; **in m.,** en mouvement (b) (of vehicle, apparatus) marche f, mouvement; **car in m.,** voiture en marche; **to set in m.,** mettre en mouvement, en marche, en jeu; faire agir (une loi); esp NAm: **m. picture** (Br = **film**), film m; **m. picture industry,** cinéma m (c) mouvement (du bras); F: **to go through the motions,** faire semblant d'agir selon les règles (d) signe m, geste m (e) motion f, proposition f; **to propose a m.,** faire une proposition 2. vtr & i **to m. (to) s.o. to do sth,** faire signe à qn de faire qch. '**motionless** a immobile; sans mouvement.

motive ['moutiv] 1. a moteur; **m. power,** force motrice 2. n (a) motif m (**for doing sth,** pour faire qch); **from the best motives,** avec les meilleures intentions (b) mobile m (d'une action); **I wonder what his m. is,** je me demande quelle raison il fait cela. '**motivate** vtr motiver (une action); pousser (qn). **moti'vation** n motivation f.

motley ['mɔtli] a (a) Lit: (multicoloured) bariolé, bigarré (b) divers, hétéroclite.

motocross ['moutoukrɔs] n Sp: moto-cross m.

motor ['moutər] 1. (a) a moteur (b) n moteur m; **m. vehicle,** voiture, véhicule, automobile; **m. show,** salon de l'automobile; **m. mower,** tondeuse (à gazon) à moteur 2. vi circuler, voyager, en voiture. '**motorbike** n F: moto f. '**motorboat** n canot m automobile. '**motorcade** n défilé m de voitures. '**motorcar** n voiture f, automobile f. '**motorcycle** n motocyclette f, F: moto f. '**motorcycling** n motocyclisme m. '**motorcyclist** n motocycliste mf. '**motoring** n automobilisme m; **school of m.,** auto-école f. '**motorist** n automobiliste mf. **motori'zation** n motorisation. '**motorize** vtr motoriser. '**motorman** nm (pl -**men**) conducteur (de train, de métro). '**motorway** n (NAm: = **expressway**) autoroute f.

mottled ['mɔtld] a tacheté, moucheté; marbré.

motto ['mɔtou] n (pl **mottoes**) devise f.

mould', NAm: **mold¹** [mould] n terre végétale; terreau m.

mould², NAm: **mold²** 1. n moule m; **casting m.,** moule à fonte 2. vtr mouler; former (le caractère de qn). '**moulding,** NAm: '**molding** n 1. moulage m; formation f (du caractère) 2. moulure f.

mould³, NAm: **mold³** n moisi m, moisissure f. '**mouldy,** NAm: '**moldy** a (-ier, -iest) moisi; **to go m.,** moisir.

moulder, NAm: **molder** ['mouldər] vi **to m. (away),** tomber en poussière; s'effriter; Fig: (of pers) moisir.

moult, NAm: **molt** [moult] 1. n mue f 2. v (a) vi muer (b) vtr perdre (ses plumes). '**moulting,** NAm: '**molting** 1. a en mue 2. n mue f.

mound [maund] n (a) tertre m, monticule m, butte f; **burial m.,** tumulus m (b) monceau m, tas m (de pierres).

mount¹ [maunt] n mont m, montagne f; **M. Sinai,** le mont Sinaï

mount² I. n 1. (a) (montage m, support m (b) monture f (d'une lentille); **lens m.,** porte-objectif m inv (d'un microscope) (c) carton m de montage (d'un tableau)

2. monture (d'un cavalier). II. v 1. vi monter; Equit: se mettre en selle; monter à cheval 2. vtr (a) monter sur (la scène); (of car) **to m. the pavement,** monter sur le trottoir; **to m. a horse, a bicycle,** monter sur un cheval, une bicyclette; enfourcher une bicyclette (b) monter, gravir (un escalier, une colline); **to m. a ladder,** monter sur, à, une échelle; **to m. s.o. (on a horse),** hisser qn sur un cheval; **the mounted police,** la police montée; **to m. guard,** monter la garde (c) monter, sertir (un diamant); monter, entoiler (un tableau, une photographie); Th: monter (une pièce). '**mounting** n (a) entoilage m, montage m (d'un tableau, d'une photographie) (b) monture f, garniture f (de fusil). '**mount' up** vi (of costs) croître, monter, augmenter; **it all mounts up,** ça finit par chiffrer.

mountain ['mauntin] n montagne f; **to make a m. out of a molehill,** se faire une montagne de qch; **m. range,** chaîne de montagnes; **m. scenery,** paysage de montagne; **m. tribe,** tribu montagnarde; **m. rescue,** secours en montagne; Bot: **m. ash,** sorbier commun, sauvage; **a m. of work,** un travail monstre. **mountai'neer** 1. n alpiniste mf 2. vi faire de l'alpinisme. **mountai'neering** n alpinisme m. '**mountainous** a (pays) montagneux; Fig: gigantesque. '**mountainside** flanc m de la montagne.

mountebank ['mauntibæŋk] n charlatan m.

mourn [mɔːn] vtr & i pleurer, se lamenter, s'affliger; **to m. (for, over) sth,** pleurer, déplorer, qch; **to m. for s.o.,** pleurer (la mort de) qn. '**mourner** n affligé, -ée; **the mourners,** le cortège funèbre. '**mournful** a triste, lugubre, mélancolique. '**mournfully** adv tristement, lugubrement. '**mourning** n (a) affliction f, deuil m (b) deuil; **house of m.,** maison endeuillée (c) (habits mpl de) deuil; **to go into m.,** prendre le deuil.

mouse [maus] 1. n (pl **mice** [mais]) souris f 2. vi (of cat) chasser les souris. '**mousehole** n trou m de souris. '**mouser** n (cat) souricier m. '**mousetrap** n souricière f; tapette f; F: **m. (cheese),** fromage m ordinaire. '**mousy** a (a) timide (b) gris (de) souris; (of hair) queue-de-vache inv.

mousse [muːs] n Cu: mousse f.

moustache, NAm: **mustache** [məˈstɑːʃ, NAm: ˈmʌstæʃ] n moustache(s) f(pl).

mouth I. n [mauθ] (pl **mouths** [mauðz]) 1. bouche f; **to make s.o.'s m. water,** faire venir l'eau à la bouche de qn; F: **big m.,** gueulard m; grande gueule; **shut your m.!** ta gueule! **he kept his m. shut,** il n'a parlé à personne; **to put words into s.o.'s m.,** attribuer des paroles à qn; **by word of m.,** de bouche à oreille; F: **to be down in the m.,** avoir le cafard 2. bouche (de cheval); gueule f (de chien); Fig: **it's straight from the horse's m.,** (i) ça vient de source sûre (ii) c'est un tuyau increvable 3. (a) bouche (de puits); gueule (de four, de canon); ouverture f, entrée f (de tunnel) (b) embouchure f (de fleuve). II. vtr & i [mauð] (a) **to m. one's words,** déclamer ses phrases (b) former des mots avec les lèvres (sans faire entendre de sons). '**mouthful** n 1. bouchée f; gorgée f (d'eau) 2. F: nom m à coucher dehors. '**mouthorgan** n harmonica m. '**mouthpiece** n 1. bec m (de clarinette) 2. Pol: porte-parole m inv (d'un parti). '**mouth-to-'mouth** n **m.-to-m. (resuscitation),** bouche-à-bouche m inv. '**mouthwash** n eau f dentifrice; bain *m* de bouche. **'mouth-watering** *a* appétissant; qui fait venir l'eau à la bouche.

move [muːv] I. *n* (*a*) *Chess:* coup *m*; **to have first m.,** avoir le trait; **to make a m.,** jouer; **whose m. is it?** c'est à qui le tour, à qui de jouer? (*b*) coup, démarche *f*; **what's the next m.?** qu'est-ce qu'il faut faire maintenant? **he must make the first m.,** c'est à lui de faire le premier pas (*c*) mouvement *m*; **we must make a m.,** il faut partir; **to be always on the m.,** ne jamais rester en place; *F:* **to get a m. on,** se dépêcher; se grouiller (*d*) déménagement *m*. II. *v* I. *vtr* (*a*) déplacer (qch); **to m. one's position,** changer de place; **to m. one's chair nearer the fire,** approcher son fauteuil du feu; **he was moved to London,** on l'a envoyé (travailler) à Londres; *Chess:* **to m. a piece,** jouer une pièce (*b*) **to m. (house),** déménager; **to m. to the country,** aller s'installer à la campagne (*c*) remuer, bouger (la tête); (*of wind*) agiter (les branches); **he didn't m. a muscle,** il n'a pas sourcillé (*d*) mouvoir, animer (qch); mettre (qch) en mouvement (*e*) ébranler la résolution de (qn); **nothing will m. him,** il est inflexible (*f*) **to m. s.o. to do sth,** pousser, inciter, qn à faire qch; (*g*) émouvoir, toucher (qn); **to m. s.o. to anger,** provoquer la colère de qn; **to m. s.o. to tears,** émouvoir qn (jusqu')aux larmes; **to m. s.o. to pity,** exciter la pitié de qn (*h*) **to m. a resolution,** proposer une motion; **I m. that,** je propose que + *sub* 2. *vi* (*a*) se mouvoir, se déplacer; **keep moving! m. along!** circulez! **to m. to another seat,** changer de place; **moving train,** train en marche; **to m. in high society,** fréquenter la haute société (*b*) **to m. (about),** bouger, (se) remuer; **don't m.!** ne bougez pas! (*c*) marcher, aller, s'avancer; **the earth moves round the sun,** la terre tourne autour du soleil; **to m. towards the table,** s'avancer, se diriger, vers la table; **it's time we were moving, we must be moving,** il est temps de partir, il faut partir (*d*) agir; **he must m. first,** c'est à lui d'agir le premier. **'movable** 1. *a* mobile 2. *npl* **movables,** mobilier *m*. **'move a'bout, a'round** 1. *vtr* déplacer (qch) 2. *vi* aller et venir. **'move a'long** 1. *vi* avancer; (*on bench*) se pousser 2. *vtr* faire avancer. **'move a'way** 1. *vi* s'éloigner, s'en aller 2. *vtr* écarter, éloigner (qch). **'move 'back** 1. *vi* reculer; retourner, revenir 2. *vtr* (faire) reculer; remettre (un objet). **'move 'down** 1. *vi* descendre 2. *vtr* (faire) descendre. **'move 'forward** 1. *vtr* avancer, faire avancer (qn, qch) 2. *vi* (s')avancer. **'move 'in** 1. *vi* emménager 2. *vtr* (*a*) faire entrer (qn) (*b*) installer (son mobilier). **'movement** *n* mouvement *m*; geste *m* (du bras); **to watch s.o.'s movements,** surveiller les allées et venues de qn; *Physiol:* **(bowel) m.,** selle *f*. **'move 'off** *vi* s'éloigner, s'en aller; (*of train*) se mettre en marche; (*of car*) démarrer. **'move 'on** 1. *vi* (*a*) avancer; continuer son chemin; **m. on please!** circulez, avancez, s'il vous plaît! (*b*) (*of car*) se remettre en route 2. *vtr* faire circuler (la foule). **'move 'out** 1. *vi* déménager 2. *vtr* (*a*) sortir (qch); faire sortir (qn) (*b*) déménager (ses meubles). **'move 'over** 1. *vi* se pousser, se ranger 2. *vtr* pousser. **'mover** *n* 1. **prime m.,** premier moteur; inspirateur, -trice (d'un projet) 2. auteur *m* (d'une motion). **'move 'up** 1. *vi* monter; (*of employee*) avoir de l'avancement; *Sch:* passer dans la classe supérieure 2. *vtr* (faire) monter; donner de l'avancement à (un employé). **'movie** *n esp NAm:*

F: film *m*; **the movies,** le cinéma; **m. house,** (salle *f* de) cinéma; **m. camera,** caméra *f*. **'moving** 1. *a* (*a*) en mouvement; en marche (*b*) mobile; (*pavement, staircase*) roulant (*c*) moteur; **the m. spirit,** l'âme *f* (d'une entreprise) (*d*) émouvant, attendrissant, touchant 2. *n* **m. (out),** déménagement *m*; **m. in,** emménagement *m*. **'movingly** *adv* d'une manière émouvante.

mow [mou] *vtr* (**mowed; mown**) (*a*) faucher (le blé, un champ); **to mow s.o. down,** faucher qn (*b*) tondre (le gazon). **'mower** *n* (*pers*) faucheur *m*; (*machine*) faucheuse *f*; **(lawn) m.,** tondeuse *f* (à gazon); **motor m.,** tondeuse à moteur.

MP *abbr Member of Parliament.*

m.p.g. *abbr miles per gallon.*

m.p.h. *abbr miles per hour.*

Mr ['mistər] *abbr Mister,* Monsieur.

Mrs ['misiz] *abbr Mistress,* Madame.

Ms [miz] *abbr* (i) Mademoiselle (ii) Madame.

much [mʌtʃ] 1. *a* beaucoup (de); bien (du, de la, des); **with m. care,** avec beaucoup de soin; *Iron:* **m. good may it do you!** grand bien vous fasse! **how m. bread?** combien de pain? **how m. is it?** *F:* **how m.?** c'est combien? *F:* combien? 2. *adv* beaucoup, bien; **m. better,** beaucoup mieux; **m. worse,** bien pis; **it doesn't matter m.,** cela ne fait pas grand-chose; **m. the biggest,** de beaucoup le plus grand; **thank you very m.,** merci beaucoup; **it's (pretty, very) m. the same,** c'est à peu près la même chose; **m. to my surprise,** à ma grande surprise; *P:* **not m.!** et comment! 3. *n* (*a*) **m. remains to be done,** il reste encore beaucoup à faire; **do you see m. of one another?** vous voyez-vous souvent? **there isn't m. of it,** il n'y en a pas beaucoup; **it's not worth m.,** not up to m., cela ne vaut pas grand-chose (*b*) **this m.,** autant que ceci; **I'll say this m. for him,** je dirai ceci en sa faveur; **this m. is certain,** il y a ceci de certain; **there isn't all that m.,** il n'y en a pas tellement (*c*) **to make m. of sth,** attacher beaucoup d'importance à qch; faire grand cas de qch; **to make m. of s.o.,** (i) être aux petits soins pour (qn) (ii) flatter (qn); **I don't think m. of it,** je n'en pense pas beaucoup de bien 4. *adv phrs* (*a*) **m. as I like him,** quelle que soit mon affection pour lui (*b*) **as m.,** autant (de); **twice as m.,** deux fois plus; **I thought as m.,** je m'y attendais; je m'en doutais bien (*c*) **as m. as possible,** autant que possible; **it's as m. as he can do to read,** c'est tout juste s'il sait lire; **he looked at me as m. as to say,** il me regarda avec l'air de dire (*d*) **as m. (as), so m. (as),** tant (que), autant (que); **as m. as that?** tant que ça? à ce point-là? **he went away without so m. as saying goodbye,** il est parti sans même dire au revoir; **I haven't so m. as my fare,** je n'ai pas même le prix de mon voyage (*e*) **so m.,** tant (de); autant (de); **so m. money,** tant d'argent; **he has drunk so m.,** il a tellement bu; **so m. the better,** tant mieux; **so m. so that,** à ce point, à tel point, que; **so m. for his friendship!** voilà ce qu'il appelle l'amitié! **so m. for that!** voilà pour cela! **so m. per cent,** tant pour cent (*f*) **too m.,** trop (de); **m. too m.,** beaucoup trop (de); **£10 too m.,** £10 de trop; **it costs too m.,** ça coûte trop cher; **to make too m. of sth,** attacher trop d'importance à qch; **they were too m. for him,** il n'était pas de taille à leur résister; **this is (really) too m.!** *F:* **that's a bit m.!** (ça) c'est (vraiment) trop fort! **you can't have too m. of a good thing,** abondance de bien ne nuit pas. **'muchness** *n F:* **they're much of a m.,** ils se ressemblent beaucoup; **it's all much of a m.**, c'est toujours la même chose.

mucilage [´mjuːsilidʒ] *n* mucilage *m*.

muck [mʌk] *n* (*a*) fumier *m* (*b*) fange *f*; crotte *f*; ordures *fpl* (*c*) *F:* choses dégoûtantes; saletés *fpl* (*d*) *F:* **to make a m. of sth**, faire un gâchis de qch. **´muck a´bout, a´round** *F:* **1.** *vi* (*a*) traîner (*b*) faire l'imbécile (*c*) **to m. a. with sth**, tripoter qch **2.** *vtr* **to m. s.o. a.**, créer des ennuis, des complications, à qn. **´muck ´in** *vi F:* **to m. in with s.o.**, (i) crécher avec qn (ii) participer avec qn (à qch). **´muckiness** *n* saleté *f*. **´muck ´out** *vtr* nettoyer (une écurie). **´muckraking** *n F:* déterrement *m* de scandales. **´muck ´up** *vtr F:* (i) salir (qch) (ii) bousiller, gâcher (qch). **´muck-´up** *n* gâchis *m*. **´mucky** *a* (**-ier, -iest**) sale; boueux.

mucus [´mjuːkəs] *n* mucus *m*, mucosité *f*. **´mucous** *a* muqueux; **m. membrane**, muqueuse *f*.

mud [mʌd] *n* boue *f*, bourbe *f*; (**river**) *m*, vase *f*; **m. hut**, hutte de terre; **to throw m. at s.o.**, lancer des calomnies contre qn; *F:* **his name is m.**, il est très mal vu; *F:* **as clear as m.**, clair comme de l'eau de boudin; *F:* **m. pie**, pâté de sable. **´mudbank** *n* banc de vase. **´muddy** *a* (**-ier, -iest**) **1.** (*a*) boueux, fangeux, bourbeux; (cours d'eau) vaseux (*b*) (vêtement) crotté, couvert de boue **2.** (liquide) trouble; (couleur) sale; (teint) brouillé. **´mudflap** *n* pare-boue *m inv.* **´mudflat** *n Geog:* plage *f* de vase. **´mudguard** *n* garde-boue *m inv.* **´mudpack** *n Toil:* masque *m* de beauté.

muddle [´mʌdl] **1.** *n* confusion *f*, désordre *m*, embrouillement *m*; **to be in a m.**, (i) (*of thgs*) être en désordre, en pagaille (ii) (*of pers*) avoir les idées brouillées; **to get into a m. (about sth)**, s'embrouiller (au sujet de qch) **2.** *vtr* (*a*) embrouiller, brouiller (qch); **to m. things (up)**, embrouiller les choses; *F:* brouiller les fils (*b*) embrouiller (qn); brouiller l'esprit de (qn). **´muddle a´long** *vi* se débrouiller tant bien que mal. **´muddle-´headed** *a* à l'esprit confus, brouillon; (*of ideas*) embrouillé. **´muddler** *n* esprit brouillon. **´muddle ´through** *vi* se débrouiller, s'en tirer, tant bien que mal.

muff [mʌf] **1.** *n Cl:* manchon *m* **2.** *vtr F:* **to m. it**, rater, louper, son coup.

muffle [´mʌfl] *vtr* **1.** emmitoufler; **to m. oneself up**, s'emmitoufler **2.** assourdir (une cloche); étouffer (un son). **´muffled** *a* (*of sound*) sourd. **´muffler** *n* **1.** cache-nez *m inv* **2.** *NAm: Aut:* (*Br* = **silencer**) silencieux *m*.

mufti [´mʌfti] *n Mil:* tenue civile; **in m.**, en civil.

mug¹ [mʌg] *n* **1.** (*for beer*) chope *f*; (*for coffee*) (grosse) tasse; gobelet *m*; (*metal*) timbale *f* **2.** *F:* visage *m*; **ugly m.**, vilain museau **3.** *F:* (*pers*) dupe *f*, poire *f*; **it's a mug's game**, on se fait toujours avoir.

mug² *vtr* (**mugged**) **1.** *Sch: F:* **to m. up**, bûcher (un sujet) **2.** attaquer (qn) à main armée; agresser qn. **´mugger** *n* agresseur *m*. **´mugging** *n* (vol *m* avec) agression *f*.

muggy [´mʌgi] *a* (**-ier, -iest**) (temps) mou, lourd; (temps) chaud et humide.

mulatto [mjuˈlætou] *n* (*pl* **mulattoes**) mulâtre, -esse.

mulberry [´mʌlbəri] *n* (*pl* **mulberries**) *Bot:* mûre *f*; (*tree*) mûrier *m*.

mulch [mʌltʃ] *Hort:* **1.** *n* paillis *m* **2.** *vtr* pailler.

mule [mjuːl] *n Z:* (**he-**)**m.**, mulet *m*; (**she-**)**m.**, mule *f*; **m. driver**, muletier *m*; **m. track**, chemin muletier; **stub-**

born as a m., têtu comme une mule. **mule´teer** *n* muletier *m*. **´mulish** *a* entêté, têtu (comme une mule).

mull [mʌl] *vtr* **1.** *F:* **to m. over an idea**, ruminer une idée **2.** chauffer (du vin) avec des épices; **mulled wine**, vin chaud épicé.

mullet [´mʌlit] *n Ich:* **grey m.**, muge *m*; mulet *m*; **red m.**, rouget(-barbet) *m*.

mulligatawny [mʌligəˈtɔːni] *n* potage *m* au curry.

multi- [mʌlti] *pref* multi-. **multicoloured** *a* multicolore. **multimillio´naire** *n* milliardaire *mf.* **multi´national 1.** *a* multinational **2.** *n* multinationale *f*. **multi´purpose** *a* à usages multiples; polyvalent. **multi´racial** *a* multiracial. **multi´storey**, *NAm:* **multi´story** *a* (garage) à étages.

multiple [´mʌltipl] *a & n* multiple (*m*); **m. store**, magasin à succursales (multiples). **´multiple-´choice** *a* (questionnaire) à choix multiples, QCM. **multipli´cation** *n* multiplication *f*. **multi´plicity** *n* multiplicité *f*. **´multiply** *vtr & i* (**multiplied**) (se) multiplier.

multitude [´mʌltitjuːd] *n* multitude *f*; foule *f*.

mum¹ [mʌm] **1.** *int* **m.'s the word!** motus! **2.** *a* **to keep m.**, ne pas souffler mot (de qch).

mum² *n F:* maman *f*.

mumble [´mʌmbl] *vtr & i* marmotter, marmonner; manger ses mots.

mumbo-jumbo [´mʌmbouˈdʒʌmbou] *n* charabia *m*.

mummy¹ [mʌmi] *n* (*pl* **mummies**) momie *f*. **´mummify** *vtr* (**mummified**) momifier.

mummy² *n* (*pl* **mummies**) *F:* maman *f*.

mumps [mʌmps] *npl Med:* oreillons *mpl.*

munch [mʌntʃ] *vtr* mâcher, mâchonner.

mundane [mʌnˈdein] *a* banal; terre-à-terre; de ce monde.

municipal [mjuˈnisipəl] *a* municipal; **m. buildings** = hôtel *m* de ville. **munici´pality** *n* municipalité *f*.

munificence [mjuːˈnifisəns] *n* munificence *f*. **mu´nificent** *a* munificent, généreux.

munition [mjuːˈniʃən] *n* munitions, munitions *fpl* (de guerre); **m. factory**, usine de munitions.

mural [´mjuərəl] **1.** *a* mural **2.** *n* peinture murale.

murder [´məːdər] **1.** *n* meurtre *m*; *Jur:* homicide *m* volontaire; **premeditated m.**, assassinat *m*; **m.!** au meurtre! à l'assassin! **the m. weapon**, l'arme du crime; *F:* **it's (sheer) m.**, c'est infernal; *F:* **to shout blue m.**, crier comme un perdu; *F:* **he gets away with m.**, il peut faire n'importe quoi impunément; il peut tout se permettre **2.** *vtr* (*a*) assassiner (qn) (*b*) *F:* massacrer (une chanson). **´murderer** *nm* meurtrier, assassin. **´murderess** *nf* meurtrière. **´murderous** *a* meurtrier, assassin.

murky [´məːki] *a* obscur, ténébreux; **m. past**, passé trouble.

murmur [´məːmər] **1.** *n* murmure *m*; bourdonnement *m* (de voix); *Med:* **heart m.**, souffle *m* au cœur **2.** *vtr & i* (*a*) murmurer, susurrer (*b*) murmurer, dire (qch) à voix basse.

muscle [´mʌsl] *n* muscle *m*. **´muscle in** *vi F:* s'immiscer (**on sth**, dans qch); se pousser, jouer des coudes. **´muscular** *a* **1.** (force) musculaire **2.** (homme) musculeux, musclé.

muse¹ [mjuːz] *n* muse *f*.

muse² *vi* méditer, rêver; songer (**on**, à). **'musing** *a* pensif, rêveur.

museum [mjuːˈziəm] *n* musée *m*.

mush [mʌʃ] *n* **1.** bouillie *f* **2.** *F:* sentimentalité *f* (à l'eau de rose). **'mushy** *a* (-ier, -iest) **1.** en bouillie; (fruit) blet; **m. peas**, purée *f* de pois **2.** *F:* sentimental.

mushroom [ˈmʌʃrum] **1.** *n* champignon *m* (comestible); **m. soup**, potage aux champignons; **m. town**, ville champignon; **m. cloud**, champignon atomique **2.** *vi F:* pousser comme un champignon, des champignons. **'mushrooming** *n* **to go m.**, aller aux champignons.

music [ˈmjuːzik] *n* (*a*) musique *f*; **to set to m.**, mettre en musique; **background m.**, musique de fond; **m. lover**, mélomane *mf* (*b*) **m. case**, porte-musique *m inv*; **m. stand**, pupitre à musique (*c*) **m. hall**, music-hall *m*. **'musical 1.** *a* (*a*) musical; (instrument) de musique; **m. box**, boîte à musique (*b*) (*of pers*) **to be m.**, être (bon) musicien, (bonne) musicienne (*c*) (*of sound*) harmonieux, mélodieux **2.** *n* comédie musicale. **mu'sician** *n* musicien, -ienne. **mu'sicianship** *n* sens *m* de la musique. **musi'cologist** *n* musicologue *mf*. **musi'cology** *n* musicologie *f*.

musk [mʌsk] *n* (*a*) musc *m*; **m. cat**, civet *m* (*b*) **m. rose**, rose musquée. **'muskrat** *n* rat musqué. **'musky** *a* musqué; (odeur) de musc.

musket [ˈmʌskit] *n Sma: Hist:* mousquet *m*. **muske'teer** *n Hist:* mousquetaire *m*.

Muslim [ˈmuzləm] *a & n* musulman, -ane.

muslin [ˈmʌslin] *n* mousseline *f*.

musquash [ˈmʌskwɔʃ] *n* rat musqué.

mussel [ˈmʌsl] *n Moll:* moule *f*.

must [mʌst] **1.** *n F:* **it's a m.**, c'est une nécessité, c'est indispensable; **this film's a m.**, c'est un film qu'il faut absolument avoir vu; c'est un film à ne pas manquer **2.** *modal aux v inv* (**must not** *is often contracted into* **mustn't**) (*finite tenses of*) falloir, devoir (*a*) (*obligation*) **you m. be ready at four o'clock**, vous devrez être prêt à quatre heures; **you m. hurry up**, il faut vous dépêcher; **you mustn't tell anyone**, il ne faut le dire à personne; **do it if you m.**, faites-le s'il le faut; **he's stupid, I m. say**, il est stupide, il faut l'avouer (*b*) (*probability*) **it m. be the doctor**, ce doit être le médecin; **I m. have made a mistake**, j'ai dû me tromper; **if he says so it m. be true**, s'il le dit c'est que c'est vrai (*c*) **I saw that he m. have suspected something**, j'ai bien vu qu'il avait dû se douter de quelque chose.

mustache [ˈmʌstæʃ] *n NAm:* = **moustache.**

mustang [ˈmʌstæŋ] *n Z:* mustang *m*.

mustard [ˈmʌstəd] *n* moutarde *f*; **m. pot**, moutardier *m*.

muster [ˈmʌstər] **I.** *n* (*a*) rassemblement *m* (*b*) *Mil:* revue *f*; **to pass m.**, passer; être acceptable; être à la hauteur (*c*) appel *m*; **m. roll**, feuille d'appel (*d*) assemblée *f*, réunion *f*. **II.** *v* **1.** *vtr* (*a*) rassembler (ses partisans) (*b*) *Mil:* passer (des troupes) en revue (*c*) faire l'appel (*d*) **to m. (up) one's courage**, prendre son courage à deux mains; **he couldn't m. (up) enough energy**, il n'a pas eu suffisamment d'énergie (**to**, pour) **2.** *vi* se réunir, se rassembler.

musty [ˈmʌsti] *a* (-ier, -iest) **1.** (goût, odeur) de moisi; (of room) **to smell m.**, sentir le moisi, le renfermé **2.** (of ideas) vieux jeu. **'mustiness** *n* goût *m*, odeur *f*, de moisi; relent *m*.

mutate [mjuːˈteit] *vtr & i* (faire) subir une mutation. **'mutant** *a & n* mutant (*m*). **mu'tation** *n* mutation *f*.

mute [mjuːt] **1.** (*a*) *a* muet (*b*) *Ling:* (lettre) muette; **h m.**, h muet **2.** *n* (*of pers*) (*a*) muet, -ette (*b*) *Th:* personnage muet (*c*) *Mus:* sourdine *f*. **'muted** *a* (*of sound*) assourdi; (*of colour*) sourd; (*of protest*) voilé; (*of violin*) en sourdine.

mutilate [ˈmjuːtileit] *vtr* mutiler. **muti'lation** *n* mutilation *f*.

mutiny [ˈmjuːtini] **1.** *n* (*pl* **mutinies**) révolte *f*, mutinerie *f* **2.** *vi* se révolter, se mutiner. **muti'neer** *n* mutiné *m*, mutin *m*. **'mutinous** *a* rebelle, mutiné, mutin; (équipage) en révolte.

mutter [ˈmʌtər] **1.** *n* marmonnement *m* **2.** *vtr & i* marmonner, marmotter; grommeler. **'muttering** *n* marmonnement, marmottement *m*; grommellement *m*.

mutton [ˈmʌtn] *n Cu: O:* mouton *m*; **leg of m.**, gigot *m*; **m. chop**, côtelette de mouton.

mutual [ˈmjuːtjuəl] *a* (*of feelings*) mutuel, réciproque; **m. friend**, ami commun. **'mutually** *adv* mutuellement, réciproquement.

muzzle [ˈmʌzl] **1.** *n* (*a*) museau *m* (d'un animal) (*b*) bouche *f*, gueule *f* (d'une arme à feu) (*c*) muselière *f* (pour chien) **2.** *vtr* museler (un chien, *F:* la presse).

muzzy [ˈmʌzi] *a* (*a*) (*of pers*) brouillé, confus; **I feel m.**, je me sens un peu abruti (*b*) (*of outline*) flou.

my [mai] *poss a* mon, *f* ma, *pl* mes; **in my opinion**, à mon avis; **one of my friends**, un de mes amis; un ami à moi; **I've broken my arm**, je me suis cassé le bras; **my hair is grey**, j'ai les cheveux gris; **my idea would be to**, mon idée à moi serait de. **myself** *pers pron* (*a*) moi-(même); **I did it m.**, je l'ai fait moi-même; **I'm not m.**, je ne suis pas dans mon assiette; **I m. believe that**, pour ma part je crois que (*b*) **I've hurt m.**, je me suis fait mal; **I was enjoying m.**, je m'amusais (*c*) **I live by m.**, je vis tout seul; **I'll keep it for m.**, je le garderai pour moi.

myopia [maiˈoupiə] *n Med:* myopie *f*. **my'opic** *a* myope.

myriad [ˈmiriəd] *n* myriade *f*.

myrtle [ˈmɔːtl] *n Bot:* myrte *m*.

mystery [ˈmistəri] *n* (*pl* **mysteries**) mystère *m*; **to make a m. of sth**, faire mystère de qch; **it's a m. to me**, je n'y comprends rien; **there's no m. about it**, ça n'a rien de mystérieux. **mys'terious** *a* mystérieux. **mys'teriously** *adv* mystérieusement.

mystic [ˈmistik] *a & n* mystique (*mf*). **'mystical** *a* mystique. **'mysticism** *n* mysticisme *m*.

mystify [ˈmistifai] *vtr* (**mystified**) **1.** mystifier, intriguer (qn) **2.** désorienter, dérouter (qn). **mystifi'cation** *n* **1.** mystification *f* **2.** désorientation *f*, embrouillement *m*. **my'stique** *n* mystique *f*.

myth [miθ] *n* mythe *m*. **'mythical** *a* mythique. **mytho'logical** *a* mythologique. **my'thology** *n* mythologie *f*.

myxomatosis [miksəməˈtousis] *n* myxomatose *f*.

N

N n [en] *n* (la lettre) N, n *m*.

nab [næb] *vtr* (**nabbed**) *P*: arrêter, pincer (qn); **to get nabbed**, se faire pincer.

nadir ['neidiər] *n* nadir *m*.

nag[1] [næg] *n F*: bidet *m*, bourrin *m*.

nag[2] *vtr & i* (**nagged**) quereller (qn); gronder (qn) sans cesse; **to be always nagging (at) s.o.**, être toujours sur le dos de qn. **'nagging** *a* (*a*) (*of pers*) querelleur; grondeur; hargneux (*b*) (*of pain*) agaçant, énervant.

nail [neil] **I.** *n* **1.** ongle *m* (de doigt); **n. file**, lime à ongles; **n. scissors**, ciseaux à ongles; **n. varnish**, vernis à ongles **2.** clou *m*, *pl* clous; **to drive in a n.**, enfoncer un clou; *F*: **to hit the n. on the head**, tomber juste; mettre le doigt dessus **3.** *F*: **to pay on the n.**, payer argent comptant, payer rubis sur l'ongle. **II.** *vtr* **1. to n.** (**sth down**), clouer (qch); **he stood nailed to the spot**, il est resté cloué sur place **2.** clouter (des chaussures) **3.** *P*: saisir, coincer (qn). **'nailbiting** *n* habitude *f* de se ronger les ongles. **'nailbrush** *n* brosse *f* à ongles.

naive [nai'i:v] *a* naïf, ingénu. **na'ively** *adv* naïvement. **na'ivety** *n* naïveté *f*.

naked ['neikid] *a* **1.** (*a*) (*of pers*) nu; **stark n.**, tout nu (*b*) (*bras*) découvert, nu; (*pays, arbre*) dénudé **2. n. sword**, épée nue; **n. flame, n. light**, feu nu, flamme nue; **visible to the n. eye**, visible à l'œil nu; **the n. truth**, la pure vérité. **'nakedness** *n* nudité *f*.

namby-pamby ['næmbi'pæmbi] *a & n* gnan-gnan (*mf*).

name [neim] **I.** *n* **1.** (*a*) nom *m*; *Com*: raison sociale (d'une maison); **full n.**, nom et prénoms; **Christian n., first n.**, *NAm*: **given n.**, prénom *m*; **n. day**, fête *f* (de qn); **what's your n.?** comment vous appelez-vous? **my n. is**, je m'appelle; **to go by the n. of**, être connu sous le nom de; **to mention s.o. by n.**, nommer qn; (*to caller*) **what n. shall I say?** qui dois-je annoncer? **to put one's n. down** (*for sth*), (i) poser sa candidature (ii) s'inscrire (pour qch); **by n.**, de nom; **in the n. of**, au nom de; **to be master in n. only**, n'être maître que de nom (*b*) **to call s.o. names**, injurier qn **2.** réputation *f*, renommée *f*; **to get a bad n.**, se faire un mauvais renom; **he has several books to his n.**, il est l'auteur de plusieurs livres; **to have a n. for honesty**, avoir la réputation d'être honnête; **to make a n. for oneself, to make one's n.**, se faire une réputation; **to give sth a bad n.**, faire une mauvaise réputation à qch. **II.** *vtr* **1.** nommer; dénommer; **to n. s.o. after s.o.**, *NAm*: **for s.o.**, donner à qn le nom de qn **2.** désigner (qn, qch) par son nom **3.** (*a*) citer (un exemple) (*b*) fixer (le jour, un prix). **'name-dropping** *n* habitude *f* de se dire ami de gens connus. **'nameless** *a* **1.** sans nom; inconnu **2.** anonyme; **someone who shall be n.**, quelqu'un dont je tairai le nom **3.** (*of fear*) indicible, inexprimable; (*vice*) abominable. **'namely** *adv* (à) savoir; c'est-à-dire. **'nameplate** *n* plaque *f* (de porte); **manufacturer's n.**, plaque de constructeur. **'namesake** *n* homonyme *m*.

nanny ['næni] *nf* **1.** (*pl* **nannies**) bonne d'enfant, nurse **2. n. goat**, chèvre, *F*: bique.

nap[1] [næp] **I.** *n* petit somme; **afternoon n.**, sieste *f*. **II.** *vi* (**napped**) sommeiller; **to catch s.o. napping**, (i) prendre qn au dépourvu (ii) prendre qn en faute.

nap[2] *n* (*of velvet, cloth*) poil *m*; (*of cloth*) duvet *m*, lainer *m*; **against the n.**, à rebrousse-poil, à rebours.

nap[3] *n* **1.** *Cards*: napoléon *m*, nap *m* **2.** *Turf*: tuyau sûr.

napalm ['neipɑ:m] *n* napalm *m*.

nape [neip] *n* **n.** (**of the neck**), nuque *f*.

naphtha ['næfθə] *n* naphte *m*. **'naphthalene** *n* (*a*) *Ch*: naphtalène *m* (*b*) *DomEc*: naphtaline *f*.

napkin ['næpkin] *n* **1.** (**table**) **n.**, serviette *f* (de table); **n. ring**, rond de serviette **2.** (*see also* **nappy**) (*NAm*: = **diaper**) couche *f* (de bébé).

Napoleonic [næpouli'ɔnik] *a* napoléonien.

nappy ['næpi] *n* (*pl* **nappies**) (*NAm*: = **diaper**) couche *f* (de bébé).

narcissus [nɑː'sisəs] *n* (*pl* **narcissi**) *Bot*: narcisse *m*. **'narcissism** *n* narcissisme *m*. **narci'ssistic** *a* narcissique.

narcotic [nɑː'kɔtik] *a & n* narcotique (*m*); stupéfiant (*m*).

nark [nɑːk] **I.** *n F*: mouchard *m*. **II.** *vtr* embêter (qn), foutre (qn) en rogne.

narrate [nə'reit] *vtr* narrer, raconter (qch). **na'rration** *n* narration *f*. **narrative** **1.** *a* narratif **2.** *n* récit *m*, narration *f*. **na'rrator** *n* narrateur, -trice.

narrow ['nærou] **I.** *a* (-er, -est) (*a*) (chemin) étroit; (jupe) étriquée; **to grow n.**, se rétrécir (*b*) restreint, étroit, de faibles dimensions; (esprit) étroit, borné; **n. limits**, limites restreintes; **in the narrowest sense**, dans le sens le plus exact (*c*) **n. majority**, faible majorité; **he had a n. escape**, il l'a échappé belle. **II.** *v* **1.** *vtr* (*a*) resserrer, rétrécir (*b*) restreindre, limiter, borner; **to n.** (**down**) **an investigation**, limiter une enquête **2.** *vi* devenir plus étroit; se rétrécir. **'narrowboat** *n* bateau utilisé sur les canaux. **'narrowly** *adv* **1.** (*a*) (interpréter) étroitement, strictement (*b*) (examiner) minutieusement, de près **2.** tout juste; **he n. missed being run over**, il a failli être écrasé. **'narrow-'minded** *a* borné; à l'esprit étroit. **'narrow-'mindedness** *n* étroitesse *f*, petitesse *f*, d'esprit. **'narrowness** *n* **1.** (*a*) étroitesse *f* (*b*) petitesse *f*; limitation *f*; étroitesse (d'esprit) **2.** minutie *f* (d'un examen). **'narrows** *npl* passe étroite; goulet *m*.

NASA ['næsə] *abbr NAm*: National Aeronautics and Space Administration.

nasal ['neiz(ə)l] **1.** *a* nasal; **n. accent**, accent nasillard **2.** *n* *Ling*: nasale *f*. **'nasalize** *vtr* nasaliser.

nascent ['neisənt] *a* (*of plant, society*) naissant.

nasturtium [nə'stə:ʃəm] n Hort: capucine f.

nasty ['nɑ:sti] a (-ier, -iest) 1. (a) désagréable, dégoûtant; **to smell n.**, sentir mauvais (b) **n. weather**, sale, vilain, mauvais, temps; **n. job**, besogne difficile, dangereuse; **n. accident**, accident sérieux; **n. corner**, tournant dangereux 2. (of pers) méchant, désagréable; F: rosse; **to turn n.**, prendre un air méchant; **he's a n. piece of work**, c'est un sale type 3. (a) (of language, book) indécent, obscène (b) **to have a n. mind**, avoir l'esprit mal tourné. '**nastily** adv désagréablement; méchamment. '**nastiness** n aspect désagréable; méchanceté f.

nation ['neiʃ(ə)n] n 1. nation f; **people of all nations**, des gens de toutes les nationalités; Pol: **United Nations Organization**, Organisation des Nations Unies 2. **the whole n. rose in arms**, tout le pays s'est soulevé. **national** ['næʃənəl] a national, de l'État; (costume) national; (coutume) du pays; **n. park**, parc national; Mil: **n. service**, service militaire. '**nationalism** n nationalisme m. '**nationalist** a & n nationaliste (mf). **national'istic** a. **natio'nality** n nationalité f. **nationali'zation** n nationalisation f. '**nationalize** vtr nationaliser. '**nationally** adv nationalement; du point de vue national. '**nationwide** a répandu dans tout le pays.

native ['neitiv] 1. a (a) (of qualities) naturel, inné (b) (of place) natal, de naissance; **n. country**, terre natale; patrie f, pays m; **n. language**, langue maternelle; **n. speaker of English**, personne dont la langue maternelle est l'anglais 2. n (a) originaire mf (d'un pays, d'une ville); indigène mf (d'un pays) (b) (of plant, animal) indigène.

nativity [nə'tiviti] n nativité f; **n. play**, mystère de la Nativité.

NATO ['neitou] abbr North Atlantic Treaty Organization, Organisation du Traité de l'Atlantique Nord, OTAN.

natter ['nætər] F: I. n causerie f; **to have a n.**, bavarder, jacter II. vi bavarder, jacter.

natty ['næti] a (a) (of pers, dress) pimpant, coquet (b) (of gadget) bien imaginé.

natural ['nætʃərəl] a 1. (a) naturel; **n. history**, histoire naturelle; **n. law**, loi naturelle; **n. size**, grandeur nature (b) **in the n. state**, à l'état naturel, primitif; **n. gas**, gaz naturel 2. (a) natif, inné; **it is n. for a man to**, il est dans la nature de l'homme de (b) **it's n. he should go away**, il est (bien) naturel qu'il s'en aille; **as is n.**, comme de raison. '**naturalism** n naturalisme m. '**naturalist** n naturaliste nf. **natural'istic** a naturaliste. **naturali'zation** n naturalisation f (d'un étranger); acclimatation f (d'une plante). '**naturalize** vtr naturaliser (un étranger); acclimater (une plante, un animal). '**naturally** adv naturellement; **it comes n. to him**, c'est un don chez lui. '**naturalness** n 1. caractère naturel 2. naturel m; absence f d'affectation.

nature ['neitʃər] n 1. (a) (of thg) nature f, essence f, caractère m; **it is in the n. of things that**, il est dans l'ordre des choses que; **by, from, the n. of things**, vu la nature de l'affaire (b) (of pers) nature; naturel m, caractère; **it is not in his n.**, ce n'est pas dans sa nature; **by n.**, par tempérament; naturellement; **it's second n. to him**, il le fait presque par instinct 2.

espèce f, sorte f, genre m; **something of that n.**, quelque chose de la sorte 3. (a) (la) nature; **the laws of n.**, les lois fpl de la nature; **to draw from n.**, dessiner d'après nature; **n. study**, histoire naturelle (b) **human n.**, la nature humaine. -'**natured** suff de nature; **good-natured**, d'un bon naturel. '**naturism** n naturisme m. '**naturist** n naturiste mf.

naught [nɔ:t] n 1. rien m, néant m; Lit: **to bring sth to n.**, faire échouer qch 2. Mth: zéro m.

naughty ['nɔ:ti] a (-ier, -iest) (of child) vilain, méchant. '**naughtily** adv **to behave n.**, ne pas être sage. '**naughtiness** n mauvaise conduite (d'un enfant).

nausea ['nɔ:ziə] n 1. nausée f 2. F: dégoût m, nausée, écœurement m. '**nauseate** vtr écœurer, dégoûter (qn). '**nauseating** a écœurant, dégoûtant. '**nauseous** a (a) dégoûtant (b) NAm: (qn) qui a la nausée.

nautical ['nɔ:tik(ə)l] a nautique, marin.

naval ['neiv(ə)l] a naval; **n. war(fare)**, guerre navale; **n. base**, base navale; **n. officer**, officier de marine; **n. dockyard**, arsenal maritime.

nave [neiv] n nef f (d'église).

navel ['neiv(ə)l] n Anat: nombril m; **n. orange**, orange navel inv.

navigate ['nævigeit] vtr & i Nau: Av: naviguer. **naviga'bility** n navigabilité f. '**navigable** a (fleuve) navigable. **navi'gation** n navigation f; **radio n.**, navigation par radio; **n. officer**, officier de navigation. '**navigator** n navigateur m.

navvy ['nævi] n (pl navvies) terrassier m.

navy ['neivi] n 1. (pl navies) marine f de guerre; **the Royal N.** = la Marine nationale britannique; **merchant n.**, marine marchande 2. **n. (blue)**, bleu marine inv.

Nazi ['nɑ:tsi] a & n nazi, -ie. '**Nazism** n nazisme m.

NB abbr nota bene, notez bien, NB.

neap [ni:p] a (of n. (tide), marée f de morte-eau f, pl mortes-eaux.

Neapolitan [niə'politən] a & n napolitain, -aine; **N. ice cream**, tranche napolitaine.

near ['niər] (-er, -est) I. adv 1. (a) près, proche; **to come n., draw n., to s.o., sth**, s'approcher de qn, qch; **come nearer, approchez-vous; time is drawing n.**, l'heure approche; **n. at hand**, à proximité, tout près (b) **those n. and dear to him**, ceux qui le touchent de près 2. (a) **as n. as I can remember**, autant que je puisse m'en souvenir; **I came n. to crying**, j'étais sur le point de pleurer (b) **he's nowhere n. finished**, il est loin d'avoir fini. II. prep 1. près de, auprès de; **bring your chair near(er) the fire**, (r)approchez votre chaise du feu 2. **n. death**, sur le point de mourir; **to be n. the end**, toucher à sa, à la, fin; **he came n. to being run over**, il a failli être écrasé 3. **to come n. to s.o., sth**, se rapprocher de qn, qch (par la ressemblance); ressembler à qn, à qch; **nobody can come anywhere n. her**, il n'y a personne à son niveau; **you're nowhere n. it!** vous n'y êtes pas du tout! III. a 1. (ami) intime, cher; **our n. relations**, nos proches (parents) 2. **in the n. future**, dans un proche avenir; **the nearest hotel**, l'hôtel le plus proche; **the time is n. when**, l'heure est proche où; **to the nearest metre**, à un mètre près 3. **to go by the nearest road**, prendre par le plus court 4. **it was a n. thing**, nous l'avons échappé belle; F: il était moins cinq. **IV.** *vtr* (s')approcher de (qch); **the road is nearing completion**, la route est presque terminée; **to be nearing one's goal**, toucher au but. 'nearby *a* voisin, proche. 'near 'by *adv* tout près; tout proche. 'nearly *adv* **1.** (de) près **2.** (*a*) presque, à peu près, près de; **it's n. midnight**, il est bientôt minuit; **very n.**, peu s'en faut; **I n. fell**, j'ai failli tomber (*b*) **she's not n. so pretty as her sister**, elle est loin d'être aussi jolie que sa sœur. 'nearness *n* proximité *f*. 'nearside *n* *Aut*: côté *m* gauche (d'une voiture); gauche *f* (de la route). 'near-'sighted *a* myope. 'near-'sightedness *n* myopie *f*.

neat [ni:t] *a* (-er, -est) **1.** (*of spirits*) (*NAm:* = straight) pur; sans eau; **n. whisky**, whisky sec **2.** (*a*) simple et de bon goût; (*of room*) bien rangé, en ordre; **n. handwriting**, écriture soignée; **as n. as a new pin**, tiré à quatre épingles (*of style*) élégant; (*of phrase*) bien tourné **3.** (*of pers*) ordonné; qui a de l'ordre. 'neaten *vtr* ajuster (qch); ranger (qch). 'neatly *adv* **1.** avec ordre; **n. dressed**, habillé avec soin; **n. written**, écrit soigneusement **2.** adroitement; **n. turned**, (compliment) bien tourné. 'neatness *n* **1.** simplicité *f*, bon goût (dans la mise); apparence soignée (d'un jardin); netteté *f* (d'écriture); bon ordre (d'un tiroir) **2.** (*of pers*) (*a*) ordre *m*, propreté *f* (*b*) adresse *f*, habileté *f*.

nebula ['nebjulə] *n* (*pl* nebulæ [-li:]) *Astr*: nébuleuse *f*. 'nebulous *a* nébuleux.

necessary ['nesəsri] **1.** *a* (*a*) nécessaire, indispensable (to, for, à); **it is n. to do it**, il est nécessaire de le faire, il faut le faire; **to make all n. arrangements**, prendre toutes dispositions utiles; **if n.**, s'il le faut; le cas échéant; s'il y a lieu; au besoin; **to do no more than is strictly n.**, ne faire que le strict nécessaire, que l'essentiel (*b*) (résultat) inévitable **2.** *n* (*a*) *usu pl* = **necessity 2.** (*b*) *F:* **the n.**, (i) le nécessaire (ii) de l'argent *m*; **to do the n.**, (i) faire le nécessaire (ii) payer, casquer. nece'ssarily *adv* nécessairement; de (toute) nécessité; inévitablement; forcément. ne'cessitate, *vtr* nécessiter (qch); rendre (qch) nécessaire. ne'cessity *n* **1.** (*a*) nécessité *f*, obligation *f*, contrainte *f*; **of n.**, de (toute) nécessité, nécessairement; **case of absolute n.**, cas de force majeure (*b*) besoin *m*; **in case of n.**, au besoin **2.** *usu pl* le nécessaire; **bare necessities**, le strict nécessaire; **for me a car is a n.**, une voiture m'est indispensable.

neck [nek] **I.** *n* **1.** (*a*) cou *m*; **to have a stiff n.**, avoir un, le, torticolis; *F:* **to be up to one's n. in work**, avoir du travail par-dessus la tête; **to throw one's arms round s.o.'s n.**, se jeter au cou de qn; *F:* **to breathe down s.o.'s n.**, talonner qn; *Rac:* **to win by a n.**, gagner par une encolure; **to finish n. and n.**, arriver à égalité; **it's n. or nothing**, il faut jouer le tout pour le tout; *F:* **to save one's n.**, sauver sa peau; *F:* **to get it in the n.**, écoper; *F:* **to stick one's n. out**, prendre des risques; **he's a pain in the n.**, c'est un casse-pieds (*b*) *Cu:* collet *m* (d'agneau); collier *m* (de bœuf) *Cu:* encolure *f* (de robe); **V n.**, encolure en pointe, en V; **high n.**, col montant; **low n.**, décolleté *m* **2.** (*a*) goulot *m* (de bouteille); col (d'un vase); *Anat:* col (de l'utérus) (*b*) langue *f* (de terre). **II.** *vi* *F:* se bécoter; se faire des mamours. 'necking *n* pelotage *m*. 'necklace *n* collier *m* (de diamants,

de perles). 'necklet *n* collier (de fourrure). 'neckline *n* encolure *f*; décolletage *m* (d'une robe du soir). 'necktie *n* cravate *f*.

necromancy ['nekrəmænsi] *n* nécromancie *f*.

nectar ['nektər] *n* nectar *m*.

nectarine ['nektəri(:)n] *n* brugnon *m*; *Com:* nectarine *f*.

née [nei] *a* née; **Mrs Smith, n. Taylor**, Mme Smith, née Taylor.

need [ni:d] **I.** *n* **1.** (*a*) besoin *m*; **if n. be**, in case of n., en cas de besoin, au besoin; **si besoin est**; **there's no n. to go there**, il n'est pas nécessaire, il n'est pas besoin, d'y aller; **what n. is there to send for him?** à quoi bon le faire venir? (**there's**) **no n. to wait**, inutile d'attendre (*b*) **to have n.**, **be in n., of sth**, avoir besoin de qch; **I have no n. of your help**, je n'ai que faire de votre aide **2.** (*a*) adversité *f*; difficulté *f*; **in times of n.**, aux moments difficiles (*b*) besoin, indigence *f*; **to be in n.**, être dans le besoin **3. to supply s.o.'s needs**, pourvoir aux besoins de qn; **that will meet my needs**, cela fera mon affaire. **II.** *v* **1.** *vtr* (*a*) avoir besoin de (qn, qch); (*of thg*) réclamer, exiger, demander (qch); **this needs explaining**, ceci demande à être expliqué; **these facts n. no comment**, ces faits se passent de commentaires; **what he needs is a thrashing**, ce qu'il lui faudrait c'est une bonne raclée (*b*) **to n. to do sth**, être obligé, avoir besoin, de faire qch; **they n. to be told everything**, il faut qu'on leur dise tout; **you only needed to ask**, vous n'aviez qu'à demander **2.** *modal aux* **adults only n. apply**, seuls les adultes peuvent postuler; **you needn't wait**, inutile (pour vous) d'attendre; **I n. hardly tell you how grateful I am**, il n'est pas besoin de vous dire combien je vous suis reconnaissant **3.** *impers* **it needs a great deal of skill**, il faut beaucoup d'habileté. 'needful *a* nécessaire (to, for, à, pour). 'neediness *n* indigence *f*, nécessité *f*. 'needless *a* inutile, peu nécessaire, superflu; **she's very pleased, n. to say**, il va sans dire qu'elle est très contente; **n. to say we'll refund the money**, il va de soi que nous rembourserons l'argent. 'needlessly *adv* inutilement. 'needs *adv* **if n. must**, s'il le faut. 'needy *a* nécessiteux.

needle ['ni:dl] **I.** *n* (*a*) aiguille *f*; **knitting n.**, aiguille à tricoter; *Med:* **hypodermic n.**, aiguille hypodermique; **to look for a n. in a haystack**, chercher une aiguille dans une botte de foin (*b*) aiguille, saphir *m* (de tourne-disque). **II.** *vtr* agacer (qn). 'needlecord *n* velours *m* mille-raies. 'needlepoint *n* tapisserie *f* à l'aiguille. 'needlewoman *n* **she's a good n.**, elle travaille adroitement à l'aiguille. 'needlework *n* travaux *mpl* à l'aiguille; couture *f*.

ne'er-do-well ['nɛədu:wel] *a & n* propre à rien (*mf*).

nefarious [ni'fɛəriəs] *a* infâme.

negative ['negətiv] **I.** *a* négatif. **II.** *n* **1.** négative *f*; *Gram:* négation *f*; **to answer in the n.**, répondre négativement **2.** *Phot:* (cliché) négatif (*m*). **III.** *vtr* **1.** s'opposer à, rejeter (un projet) **2.** contredire, nier (un rapport). ne'gate *vtr* contredire, nier. ne'gation *n* négation *f*. 'negatively *adv* négativement.

neglect [ni'glekt] **I.** *n* **1.** (*a*) manque *m* d'égards (of, envers, pour) (*b*) manque de soin(s) (*c*) mauvais entretien (d'une machine) 2. négligence f, inattention f; **from n.**, par négligence. II. *vtr* 1. (*a*) manquer d'égards envers (qn) (*b*) manquer de soins pour (qn); négliger (ses enfants); **the garden looks neglected**, le jardin est mal tenu 2. négliger, oublier (ses devoirs); **to n. an opportunity**, laisser échapper une occasion; **to n. to do sth**, négliger, omettre, de faire qch. ne'**glected** *a* (*of appearance*) négligé; peu soigné; abandonné; **n. garden**, jardin mal tenu. ne'**glect-ful** *a* négligent; **to be n. of one's duty**, négliger ses devoirs.

négligé ['negliʒei] *n* négligé *m*, déshabillé *m*.

negligence ['neglidʒəns] *n* négligence f, incurie f; **through n.**, par négligence. '**negligent** *a* 1. négligent 2. (air, ton) nonchalant, insouciant. '**negligently** *adv* négligemment; avec négligence. '**negligible** *a* négligeable.

negotiate [ni'gouʃieit] 1. *vtr* (*a*) négocier, traiter (une affaire); négocier (un emprunt); **price to be negotiated**, prix à débattre (*b*) franchir (une haie); surmonter (une difficulté); *Aut:* **to n. a bend**, prendre un virage 2. *vi* **to n. for peace**, entreprendre des pourparlers de paix; **they refuse to n.**, ils refusent de négocier. ne'**gotiable** *a* 1. *Fin:* (effet) négociable 2. (barrière) franchissable; (chemin) praticable. **negoti'ation** *n* 1. négociation f (d'un emprunt); **to start negotiations**, engager des négociations (avec qn) 2. franchissement *m* (d'un obstacle); prise f (d'un virage). ne'**gotiator** *n* négociateur, -trice.

negro ['ni:grou] *a* & *n* (*pl* **negroes**) nègre (*m*), noir (*m*); **n. race**, race nègre, noire. '**negress** *nf* (*pl* **negresses**) négresse, noire. '**negroid** *a* négroïde.

neigh [nei] I. *n* hennissement *m*. II. *vi* hennir. '**neighing** *n* hennissement *m*.

neighbour, *NAm:* **neighbor** ['neibər] *n* voisin, -ine; *B:* prochain *m*. '**neighbourhood**, *NAm:* **-borhood** *n* 1. voisinage *m*; **to live in the n. of**, habiter à proximité de; *F:* **in the n. of £10**, environ £10 2. (*a*) alentours *mpl*, environs *mpl* (d'un lieu) (*b*) voisinage, quartier *m*. '**neighbouring**, *NAm:* **-boring** *a* avoisinant, voisin; proche. '**neighbourly**, *NAm:* **-borly** *a* (*of pers*) obligeant; **in a n. fashion**, en bon voisin, amicalement.

neither ['naiðər, 'ni:ðər] 1. *adv* & *conj* (*a*) **he will n. eat nor drink**, il ne veut ni manger ni boire; **n. here nor anywhere else**, ni ici ni ailleurs (*b*) non plus; **if you don't go n. shall I**, si vous n'y allez pas, je n'irai pas non plus (*c*) **n. does it seem that**, il ne semble pas non plus que; **I haven't read it, n. do I intend to**, je ne l'ai pas lu et d'ailleurs je n'en ai pas l'intention 2. *a* & *pron* ni l'un(e) ni l'autre; aucun(e); **n.** (**of them**) **knows**, ils ne le savent ni l'un ni l'autre; **on n. side**, ni d'un côté ni de l'autre.

nemesis ['nemesis] *n* châtiment mérité.

neo-classical [ni:ou'klasikəl] *a* néo-classique. **neo'fascist** *a* & *n* néo-fasciste (*mf*). **neo'nazi** *a* & *n* néo-nazi, -ie.

neolithic [ni:ou'liθik] *a* & *n* **the n.** (**age**), l'époque f néolithique, le néolithique.

neologism [ni'olədʒizm] *n* néologisme *m*.

neon ['ni:on] *n* néon *m*; **n. sign**, enseigne f au néon.

neophyte ['ni:oufait] *n* néophyte *mf*.

nephew ['nefju:] *n* neveu *m*.

nepotism ['nepətizm] *n* népotisme *m*.

nerve [nə:v] I. *n* 1. (*a*) *Anat:* nerf *m*; **n. centre**, centre nerveux; **n. gas**, gaz neurotoxique; **to be in a state of nerves**, être énervé; **to get on s.o.'s nerves**, taper sur les nerfs de qn; *Med:* **n. specialist**, neurologue *mf* (*b*) courage *m*; **to lose one's n.**, perdre son sang-froid; **he lost his n.**, le courage lui a manqué; il s'est dégonflé (*c*) *F:* audace f; toupet *m*; **what a n.!** quel culot! **you've got a n.!** tu es gonflé! 2. *Bot:* nervure f 3. *Lit:* tendon *m*, nerf; **to strain every n. to do sth**, déployer tous ses efforts pour faire qch. II. *vtr* **to n. oneself to do sth**, s'armer de courage pour faire qch. '**nerveless** *a* (*of pers, limb*) inerte, faible. '**nerve-racking** *a* énervant, exaspérant. '**nerviness** *n* *F:* nervosité f. '**nervous** *a* 1. *Anat:* **n. system**, système nerveux 2. (*of pers*) (*a*) excitable, irritable (*b*) intimidé; timide, peureux; **to feel n.**, avoir peur; (*of actor*) avoir le trac; **it makes me n.**, cela m'intimide. '**nervously** *adv* (*a*) timidement (*b*) craintivement. '**nervousness** *n* (*a*) nervosité f, état nerveux (*b*) timidité f. '**nervy** *a* *F:* énervé, irritable; nerveux; **to feel n.**, avoir les nerfs en pelote.

nest [nest] I. *n* 1. (*a*) nid *m*; **n. egg**, (i) nichet *m*; œuf en faïence (ii) *F:* argent mis de côté; pécule *m* (*b*) repaire *m*, nid (de brigands) 2. nichée f (d'oiseaux) 3. **n. of tables**, table f gigogne. II. *vi* (se) nicher; faire son nid.

nestle ['nesl] *vi* se nicher; se pelotonner; **to n. close** (**up**) **to s.o.**, se serrer contre qn; **to n. against s.o.**, se blottir contre qn. '**nestling** *n* oisillon *m*.

net[1] [net] I. *n* 1. (*a*) filet *m*; **butterfly n.**, filet à papillons (*b*) **hair n.**, filet, résille f (à cheveux) (*c*) *Ten:* filet (*d*) (*at circus*) **safety n.**, filet 2. *Tex:* tulle *m*; **n. curtains**, voilage *m*. II. *vtr* (**netted**) prendre (des poissons) au filet. '**netball** *n Sp:* netball *m*. '**netting** *n* (*a*) filet(s) (de protection) (*b*) grillage *m*; treillage *m*; **wire n.**, treillis *m* métallique (*c*) *Tex:* tulle. '**network** *n* réseau *m*, lacis *m* (de rues); *TV: WTel:* réseau, chaîne f; **spy n.**, réseau d'espionnage.

net[2] I. *a* (*of price, weight*) net, f nette; **n. proceeds of a sale**, (produit) net (*m*) d'une vente; **terms strictly n.**, sans déduction; payable au comptant. II. *vtr* (**netted**) produire (un bénéfice) net; toucher (une somme d'argent) net.

nether ['neðər] *a* inférieur, bas. '**Netherlands** (**the**) *Prn pl* les Pays-Bas *m*.

nettle ['netl] I. *n Bot:* ortie f; **stinging n.**, ortie brûlante. II. *vtr* piquer, irriter (qn). '**nettlerash** *n Med:* urticaire f.

neural ['njuərəl] *a* neural.

neuralgia [njuə'rældʒiə] *n Med:* névralgie f.

neuritis [njuə'raitis] *n Med:* névrite f.

neurology [njuə'rolədʒi] *n Med:* neurologie f. **neuro'logical** *a* neurologique. **neu'rologist** *n* neurologue *mf*.

neurosis [njuə'rousis] *n* (*pl* **neuroses**) *Med:* névrose f. **neurotic** [njuə'rɔtik] *a* & *n* névrosé, -ée; névrotique.

neurosurgery [njuərou'sə:dʒəri] *n* neurochirurgie f. **neuro'surgeon** *n* neurochirurgien, -ienne.

neuter ['nju:tər] I. *a* & *n* (*a*) *Gram:* neutre (*m*) (*b*) animal châtré. II. *vtr* châtrer (un animal). '**neutral** *a* & *n* neutre (*m*); **to remain n.**, rester neutre, garder la neutralité; *Aut:* **in n.**, au point mort. **neu-**

'**trality** n neutralité f. '**neutralize** vtr neutraliser.
neutron ['nju:trɔn] n neutron m; n. **bomb**, bombe f à neutrons.
never ['nevər] adv (a) (ne ...) jamais; I **n. go there**, je n'y vais jamais; n. **again**, jamais plus; he **n. came back**, il n'est plus revenu; I **shall n. forget it**, jamais je ne l'oublierai; n. **in (all) my life**, jamais de la vie (b) (emphatic) I **n. expected him to come**, je ne m'attendais pas du tout à ce qu'il vînt; he **n. said a word**, il n'a pas dit un mot; he's **eaten it all—n.!** il a tout mangé—pas possible! F: **well I n.!** ça par exemple! (c) n. **mind!** ne vous en faites pas! '**never-'ending** a perpétuel, éternel; sans fin; interminable. '**never-'never** n F: **to buy sth on the n.-n.**, acheter qch à crédit, à tempérament. **never-the'less** adv néanmoins, quand même, toutefois, pourtant. '**never-to-be-for'gotten** a inoubliable.
new [nju:] a (-er, -est) 1. (a) nouveau; (pays) neuf; (terre) vierge; **what's n.?** quoi de neuf? **that has made a n. man of him**, cela a fait de lui un autre homme; (for torch, radio) n. **battery**, pile f de rechange; Sch: **the n. boys**, les nouveaux (b) he's **n. to this work**, il est novice dans ce travail; I'm **n. to this town**, je suis nouveau venu dans cette ville 2. neuf, f neuve; **dressed in n. clothes**, habillé de neuf; Com: **as n.**, à l'état (de) neuf; **to make sth like n.**, remettre qch à neuf; **the subject is quite n.**, ce sujet n'a pas encore été traité 3. (pain) frais; (vin) nouveau, jeune; n. **moon**, nouvelle lune; n. **potatoes**, pommes de terre nouvelles. '**newborn** a nouveau-né; n. **babies**, (enfants) nouveau-nés (mpl). '**New 'Brunswick** Prn Geog: le Nouveau-Brunswick. '**newcomer** n nouveau venu, nouvelle venue. '**New 'England** Prn Geog: la Nouvelle-Angleterre. '**new'fangled** a d'une modernité outrée. **Newfoundland** ['nju:fəndlænd] 1. Prn Geog: Terre-Neuve f 2. n (dog) terre-neuve m inv. '**Newfoundlander** n Terre-neuvien, -ienne. '**New 'Guinea** Prn Geog: Nouvelle-Guinée. '**new-'laid** a (œuf) tout frais, du jour. '**newly** adv récemment, nouvellement, fraîchement; **the n.-elected members**, les députés nouveaux élus; **n.-painted wall**, mur fraîchement peint. '**newlyweds** npl nouveaux mariés. '**new-ness** n 1. nouveauté f (d'une mode) 2. état neuf (d'un objet). '**New Or'leans** Prn Geog: Nouvelle-Orléans. '**New 'World** n Nouveau Monde. '**New 'Year** n nouvel an; nouvelle année; N. Y.'s **Day**, le jour de l'an; N. Y.'s **Eve**, la Saint-Sylvestre; **to wish s.o. a happy N. Y.**, souhaiter la bonne année à qn. '**New 'York** Prn Geog: New York; attrib new-yorkais. '**New 'Yorker** n Newyorkais, -aise. '**New 'Zealand** Prn Geog: la Nouvelle-Zélande; attrib néo-zélandais. '**New 'Zealander** n Néo-Zélandais, -aise.
news [nju:z] n 1. nouvelle(s) f(pl); **what's the n.?** quelles nouvelles? quoi de nouveau, de neuf? I **have some n. for you**, j'ai une nouvelle à vous annoncer; **a sad piece of n.**, une triste nouvelle; **to break the n. to s.o.**, faire part d'une mauvaise nouvelle à qn; **no n. is good n.**, pas de nouvelles, bonnes nouvelles 2. (a) Journ: **official n.**, communiqué officiel; n. **in brief**, faits divers; **to be in the n.**, faire vedette; n.

stand, kiosque m (à journaux); bibliothèque f de gare (b) WTel: TV: informations fpl; téléjournal m; n. **bulletin**, bulletin d'informations (c) **to make n.**, faire sensation. '**newsagent** n marchand m de journaux. '**newscast** n TV: bulletin m d'informations. '**newscaster** n WTel: TV: présentateur, -trice; speaker m, speakerine f. '**news 'flash** n flash m. '**newsletter** n bulletin d'informations (d'une société); circulaire f. '**newsman** n journaliste m. '**newspaper** n journal m; n. **report**, reportage m; n. **man**, (i) marchand m de journaux (ii) journaliste m. '**newsprint** n papier m journal. '**newsreader** n présentateur, -trice. '**newsreel** n Cin: actualités fpl. '**newsroom** n salle f de rédaction. '**newsworthy** a (nouvelle) qui intéresserait le grand public. '**newsy** a plein de nouvelles.
newt [nju:t] n triton m.
newton ['nju:tn] n Ph: newton m.
next [nekst] I. a 1. (of place) prochain; le plus proche; **the n. room**, la chambre voisine; **her room is n. to mine**, sa chambre est à côté de la mienne; **sitting n. to me**, assis à côté de moi; n. **to the skin**, à même la peau; **the n. house**, la maison d'à côté; n. **door**, à côté; n. **door neighbour**, voisin immédiat, d'à côté 2. (a) (of time) prochain, suivant; **the n. day**, le lendemain; **the n. day but one**, le surlendemain; **the n. moment**, l'instant d'après; n. **year**, l'année prochaine; **this time n. year**, dans un an d'ici (b) **the n. chapter**, le chapitre suivant; **the n. time I see him**, la prochaine fois que je le reverrai; F: **what n.!** par exemple! et quoi encore! n. (**person**), **please!** au suivant! who's **n.?** c'est à qui? à qui le tour? (c) (in shoes) n. **the size**, la pointure au-dessus; **the n. best thing would be to**, à défaut de cela le mieux serait de; I **got it for n. to nothing**, je l'ai eu pour presque rien. II. adv 1. ensuite; après; **what shall we do n.?** qu'est-ce que nous allons faire maintenant, après cela? 2. **when you are n. that way**, la prochaine fois que vous passerez par là; **when I n. saw him**, quand je l'ai revu. III. n prochain(e), suivant(e); **the year after n.**, dans deux ans. IV. prep n. **to**, auprès de, à côté de (qn, qch). '**next 'door** adv & a **he lives n. d.**, il habite à côté; **the people n. d.**, the n. d. **neighbours**, les gens, les voisins, d'à côté. '**next-of-'kin** n (i) parent le plus proche (ii) pl la famille; **to inform the n.-of-k.**, prévenir la famille.
NHS abbr National Health Service.
nib [nib] n (bec m de) plume f.
nibble ['nibl] I. n (a) grignotement m (b) Fish: touche f. II. vtr & i grignoter; mordiller (qch); (of fish, F: of pers) **to n. (at the bait)**, mordre à l'hameçon; **to n. away, at**, réduire (qch) petit à petit.
nice [nais] a (-er, -est) 1. n. **distinction**, distinction délicate 2. (a) (of pers) gentil; sympathique; agréable; **he was as n. as could be**, il s'est montré aimable au possible; **to be n. to s.o.**, se montrer gentil, aimable, avec qn; **it's not n. of you to make fun of him**, ce n'est pas bien de vous moquer de lui; Iron: **that's a n. way to talk!** c'est du joli de parler comme ça! **she's a n.-looking woman**, c'est une jolie femme (b) (of thg) joli, bon; **a n. dress**, une jolie robe; **it's n. here**, il fait bon ici; **the garden is beginning to look n.**, le jardin s'embellit (c) (intensive) **it's n. and cool**,

le temps est d'une fraîcheur agréable; **n. and easy,** très facile (*d*) **n. people,** des gens bien; **not n.,** pas tout à fait convenable (*e*) **this is a n. mess we're in!** nous voilà dans de beaux draps! **that's a n. way to behave!** en voilà des manières! 'ni**cely** *adv* joliment, gentiment, bien; **that will do n.,** cela fera très bien l'affaire; **he's getting on n.,** (i) (*of invalid*) il fait des progrès (ii) ses affaires ne marchent pas mal. 'ni**ce-ness** *n* gentillesse *f*, amabilité *f* (de qn). 'ni**cety** *n* 1. **to a n.,** exactement, à la perfection 2. *pl* **niceties,** minuties *f*, finesses *f*.

niche [nitʃ, niːʃ] *n* niche *f*; **to find one's n.,** trouver sa voie; **to make a n. for oneself,** se caser.

Nick¹ [nik] *Prnm* Nicolas; *F:* **Old N.,** le diable.

nick² I. *n* 1. entaille *f*, encoche *f* 2. **in the n. of time,** juste à temps 3. *P:* **in good n.,** en bon état 4. *P:* prison *f*, taule *f*. II. *vtr* 1. entailler, encocher 2. *F:* (*a*) arrêter; **to get nicked,** se faire pincer (*b*) **to n. sth,** chiper, faucher, qch.

nickel ['nikl] I. *n* 1. nickel *m*; **n. plating,** nickelage *m* 2. *NAm:* pièce *f* de cinq cents. II. *vtr* (**nickelled**) nickeler (qch).

nickname ['nikneim] I. *n* surnom *m*; sobriquet *m*. II. *vtr* surnommer (qn).

nicotine ['nikətiːn] *n* nicotine *f*.

niece [niːs] *n* nièce *f*.

nifty ['nifti] *a F:* malin, astucieux; (travail) vite fait.

Niger *Prn Geog:* (*a*) (*river*) [*nai*'ʒeːr] Niger *m* (*b*) [niː'ʒeər] (République du) Niger. **Ni'gerian¹** (*a*) *a* nigérien (*b*) *n* Nigérien, -ienne.

Nigeria [nai'dʒiːriə] *Prn Geog:* Nigeria *m*. **Ni'gerian²** (*a*) *a* nigérian (*b*) *n* Nigérian, -ane.

niggardly ['nigədli] *a* (*of pers*) pingre; (*of sum*) mesquin.

nigger ['nigər] *a & n P: Pej:* nègre (*m*); (*colour*) **n. (brown),** (tête-de-)nègre *inv.*

niggle ['nigl] *vi* vétiller, tatillonner. 'ni**ggler** *n* (*of pers*) tatillon, -onne. 'ni**ggling** *a* (*of work*) fignolé; **n. details,** détails insignifiants.

nigh [nai] *adv Lit:* proche.

night [nait] *n* 1. (*a*) (i) nuit *f* (ii) soir *m*; **last n.,** (i) la nuit dernière; cette nuit (ii) hier (au) soir; **the n. before,** la veille (au soir); **tomorrow n.,** demain soir; **ten o'clock at n.,** dix heures du soir; **good n.!** bonsoir! bonne nuit! **at n.,** la nuit; **in the n.,** (pendant) la nuit; **by n.,** de nuit; **to have a n. out,** sortir le soir; **n. shift,** équipe de nuit; **to be on n. shift,** être de nuit; **n. nurse,** infirmière de nuit; **n. flight,** vol de nuit (*b*) *Th:* **first n.,** première *f* 2. obscurité *f*, ténèbres *fpl;* **n. is falling,** il commence à faire nuit, la nuit tombe. 'ni**ghtcap** *n* boisson (alcoolique) prise avant de se coucher. 'ni**ght-clothes** *npl* vêtements *m* de nuit. 'ni**ghtclub** *n* boîte *f* de nuit. 'ni**ghtdress** *n* chemise *f* de nuit. 'ni**ghtfall** *n* tombée *f* du jour, de la nuit; **at n.,** à la nuit tombante. 'ni**ghtgown,** *F:* 'ni**ghtie** *n* chemise de nuit. 'ni**ghtingale** *n Orn:* rossignol *m.* 'ni**ghtjar** *n Orn:* engoulevent *m.* 'ni**ghtlight** *n* veilleuse *f.* 'ni**ghtly** 1. *a* (de) tous les soirs 2. *adv* tous les soirs, toutes les nuits. 'ni**ghtmare** *n* cauchemar *m.* 'ni**ghtmarish** *a* cauchemardesque. 'ni**ghtshade** *n Bot:* woody *n.,* douce-amère *f;* **deadly n.,** belladone *f.* 'ni**ghtshirt** *n* chemise de nuit (d'homme). 'ni**ght-time** *n* la nuit. 'ni**ght-watchman** *n* (*pl* **-men**) gardien *m* de nuit.

nihilism ['niːilizm] *n* nihilisme *m.* 'ni**hilist** *n* nihiliste *mf.*

nil [nil] *n* rien *m*; néant *m*; zéro *m.*

Nile (the) [ðə'nail] *Prn Geog:* le Nil.

nimble ['nimbl] *a* (*of pers*) agile, leste; (*of mind*) délié, subtil. 'ni**mble-'footed** *a* aux pieds agiles. 'ni**mble-'witted** *a* à l'esprit délié. 'ni**mbly** *adv* agilement; lestement, légèrement.

nimbus ['nimbəs] *n* (*a*) *Meteor:* nimbus *m* (*b*) *Art:* nimbe *m.*

nincompoop ['niŋkəmpuːp] *n* nigaud *m,* niais *m.*

nine [nain] *num a & n* neuf (*m*); **n. times out of ten,** neuf fois sur dix; en général; **to be dressed up to the nines,** être sur son trente et un. 'ni**nepins** *npl* (jeu *m* de) quilles *fpl; F:* **to go down like n.,** tomber comme des mouches. **nine'teen** *num a & n* dix-neuf (*m*). **nine'teenth** *num a & n* dix-neuvième (*m*). 'ni**netieth** *num a & n* quatre-vingt-dixième (*m*). 'ni**nety** *num a & n* quatre-vingt-dix (*m*); **n.-one,** quatre-vingt-onze. **ninth** *num a & n* neuvième (*m*).

nip [nip] I. *n* 1. pincement *m*; **to give s.o. a n.,** pincer qn 2. morsure *f* (du froid); *Hort:* coup *m* de gelée; **there's a n. in the air,** l'air est piquant. II. *v* (**nipped**) 1. *vtr* (*a*) pincer (*b*) **to n. (sth) in the bud,** étouffer (qch) dans l'œuf (*c*) (*of cold*) pincer, piquer, mordre; brûler (les bourgeons) 2. *vi F:* **just n. round to the baker's,** cours vite chez le boulanger. 'ni**pper** *n F:* (*a*) gamin *m,* gosse *m* (*b*) *pl* pince(s) *f(pl),* pincette(s) *f(pl).* 'ni**ppy** *a F:* 1. alerte, vif; **tell him to look n.,** dis-lui de se grouiller 2. (vent) froid, piquant.

nipple ['nipl] *n* (*a*) *Anat:* mamelon *m,* bout *m* de sein (*b*) *MecE:* graisseur *m.*

nirvana [niə'vaːnə] *n* nirvāna *m.*

nisi ['naisai] *see* **decree** 1.

Nissen ['nisən] *n* **N. hut,** hutte préfabriquée (en tôle).

nit [nit] *n* 1. lente *f* 2. *F:* (*pers*) nigaud, -aude; andouille *f,* crétin, -ine. 'ni**t-pick** *vi F:* couper les cheveux en quatre. 'ni**tty-'gritty** *n F:* (fin) fond (d'une affaire). 'ni**t-wit** *n* = **nit** 2.

nitrogen ['naitrədʒən] *n* azote *m.* 'ni**trate** *n* nitrate *m.* 'ni**tric** *a* **n. acid,** acide nitrique. **nitro-'glycerin(e)** *n* nitroglycérine *f.* 'ni**trous** *a* nitreux, d'azote.

no [nou] I. *a* 1. nul, pas de, point de, aucun; **to have no heart,** n'avoir pas de cœur; **he made no reply,** il n'a pas répondu; **it's no distance,** ce n'est pas loin; **no two men are alike,** il n'y a pas deux hommes qui se ressemblent; **of no interest,** sans intérêt; **it's of no importance,** ça n'a aucune importance; **no-man's land,** (i) terrains *m* vagues (ii) *Mil:* no man's land *m; Mil:* **no-go area,** zone interdite; **no surrender!** on ne se rend pas! **no nonsense!** pas de bêtises! **no admittance,** entrée interdite; **no smoking,** défense de fumer 2. (*a*) peu; **it's no easy job,** ce n'est pas une tâche facile; **no such thing,** pas du tout; nullement (*b*) **he's no artist,** il n'est pas artiste; *NAm: F:* **no way!** jamais de la vie! (*c*) **there's no pleasing him,** il n'y a pas moyen de le satisfaire; **there's no getting out of it,** impossible de s'en tirer 3. *pron* **no-one** = **nobody** 1. II. *adv* **I'm no richer than he is,** je ne suis pas plus riche que lui; **he's no longer here,** il n'est plus ici 3. non; **have you seen him?**—**no,** l'avez-vous vu?—non; **no, no, you're mistaken!** mais non, vous vous trompez! **III.** *n* non *m inv*; **I won't take no for an answer,** je n'accepterai pas de refus; (*in voting*) **ayes and noes,** voix *f* pour et contre.

no. *abbr* number.

nob [nɔb] *n F:* (*a*) tête *f* (*b*) richard *m*, aristo *m*.

nobble ['nɔbl] *vtr F:* (*a*) acheter (un témoin) (*b*) doper (un cheval de course).

noble ['noubl] *a & n* noble (*m*). **no'bility** *n* noblesse *f.* **'nobleman** *n* (*pl* **-men**) noble *m*; gentilhomme *m.* **'nobleness** *n* noblesse *f* d'esprit. **'noble-woman** *n* (*pl* **-women**) aristocrate *f.* **'nobly** *adv* (*a*) noblement (*b*) magnifiquement; superbement.

nobody ['noubədi] **1.** *pron* personne *m*; nul *m*; aucun *m*; **who's there?**—**n.,** qui est là?—personne; **n. is perfect,** nul n'est parfait; **n. spoke to me,** personne ne m'a parlé; **there was n. else on board,** personne d'autre n'était à bord; **there was n. about,** il n'y avait personne **2.** *n* (*of pers*) nullité *f*, zéro *m*; **when he was still a n.,** quand il était encore inconnu.

nocturnal [nɔk'tə:n(ə)l] *a* nocturne. **'nocturne** *n Mus:* nocturne *m*; *Art:* effet *m* de nuit.

nod [nɔd] **I.** *n* (*a*) inclination *f* de la tête; signe *m* de tête affirmatif (*b*) **he gave me a n.,** il me fit un petit signe de la tête. **II.** *vtr & i* (**nodded**) **1. to n.** (**one's head**), (i) faire un signe de tête; incliner la tête (ii) faire un signe de tête affirmatif **2.** dodeliner de la tête **3. to n. off,** somnoler, sommeiller. **'nodding** *n* inclination *f* de tête; **to have a n. acquaintance with s.o.,** connaître qn vaguement.

node [noud] *n Bot: etc:* nœud *m*.

nog [nɔg] *n* **egg n.,** boisson faite d'alcool et d'un œuf battu; = lait *m* de poule. **'noggin** *n* verre *m*, petit pot.

noise [nɔiz] *n* **1.** bruit *m*, tapage *m*, vacarme *m*; **to make a n.,** faire du bruit, du tapage; **to make a n. in the world,** faire parler de soi; *F:* **the big n.,** le grand manitou (d'une entreprise) **2.** bruit; son *m*; **clicking n.,** cliquetis *m*; *WTel:* **background n.,** bruit de fond; **n. level,** niveau de bruit. **'noiseless** *a* sans bruit; silencieux. **'noiselessly** *adv* silencieusement; sans bruit. **'noisily** *adv* bruyamment, à grand bruit. **'noisy** *a* bruyant, tapageur; (enfant) turbulent; (*of street*) tumultueux; **to be n.,** faire du bruit, du tapage.

nomad ['noumæd] *a & n* nomade (*mf*). **no'madic** *a* nomade.

nom de plume ['nɔmdə'plu:m] *n* (*pl* **noms de plume**) pseudonyme *m*.

nomenclature [nə'meŋklətʃər] *n* nomenclature *f.*

nominal ['nɔmin(ə)l] *a* (*a*) nominal; **to be the n. head,** n'être chef que de nom; **n. rent,** loyer purement insignifiant (*b*) **n. value,** valeur nominale. **'nominally** *adv* nominalement; de nom.

nominate ['nɔmineit] *vtr* (*a*) nommer, choisir, désigner (qn à un emploi) (*b*) proposer, présenter (un candidat). **nomi'nation** *n* (*a*) nomination *f* (*b*) présentation *f*, investiture *f* (d'un candidat). **'nominative** *a & n Gram:* nominatif (*m*). **'nominator** *n* présentateur, -trice (d'un candidat). **nomi'nee** *n* candidat, -ate; désigné, -ée.

nonagenarian [nɔnədʒə'nɛəriən] *a & n* nonagénaire (*mf*).

non-aggression ['nɔnə'greʃən] *n* non-agression *f.*

non-alcoholic ['nɔnælkə'hɔlik] *a* non alcoolisé.

non-aligned ['nɔnə'laind] *a* non aligné. **'non-a'lignment** *n* non-alignement *m*.

nonchalant ['nɔnʃələnt] *a* nonchalant; indifférent. **'nonchalance** *n* nonchalance *f.* **'nonchalantly** *adv* nonchalamment; avec nonchalance.

non-combattant ['nɔn'kɔmbətənt] *a & n* non-combattant (*m*).

non-commissioned ['nɔnkə'miʃ(ə)nd] *a Mil:* **n.-c. officer,** sous-officier *m*; gradé *m*.

noncommittal ['nɔnkə'mit(ə)l] *a* qui n'engage à rien; (réponse) diplomatique.

non-committed ['nɔnkə'mitid] *a* non aligné.

non-conductor ['nɔnkən'dʌktər] *n* non-conducteur *m*; (*of heat*) calorifuge *m*; (*of electricity*) isolant *m*. **'non-con'ducting** *a* non conducteur.

nonconformist ['nɔnkən'fɔ:mist] *a & n* non-conformiste (*mf*). **'non-con'formism** *n* non-conformisme *m*.

non(-)contributory [nɔnkən'tribjutri] *a* sans versements, sans cotisations.

non-cooperation [nɔnkɔɔpə'reiʃn] *n* refus *m* de coopération.

nondescript ['nɔndiskript] *a* indéfinissable, inclassable; (style) quelconque.

none [nʌn] **1.** *pron* (*a*) aucun; **n. at all,** pas un(e) seul(e); **n. of this concerns me,** rien de ceci ne me regarde; **n. at all,** pas un(e) seul(e); **I know n. of them,** je n'en connais aucun; **strawberries! there are n.,** des fraises! il n'y en a pas; **n. of your cheek!** pas d'insolences de votre part! (*b*) **n. can tell,** personne ne le sait; **he knew, n. better, that,** il savait mieux que personne que (*c*) (*on forms*) néant *m* **2.** *adv* (*a*) **I like him n. the worse for it,** je ne l'en aime pas moins; **he was n. the worse for his accident,** il ne s'en portait pas plus mal après l'accident (*b*) **he was n. too soon,** il est arrivé juste à temps.

nonentity [nɔn'entiti] *n* (*pl* **nonentities**) personne insignifiante, de peu d'importance; non-valeur *f*; nullité *f*.

non-event [nɔni'vent] *n F:* événement manqué.

nonexistent ['nɔnig'zist(ə)nt] *a* non existant; inexistant.

non-fiction ['nɔn'fikʃən] *n* littérature générale.

non-inflammable ['nɔnin'flæməbl] *a* ininflammable.

non(-)intervention [nɔnintə'venʃn] *n Pol:* non-intervention *f.*

non-iron [nɔn'aiən] *a* (tissu) n'exigeant aucun repassage.

non(-)member [nɔn'membər] *n* (*at club*) personne étrangère, invité, -ée; **open to n.-members,** ouvert au public.

non-payment ['nɔn'peimənt] *n* non-paiement *m*; défaut *m* de paiement.

nonplus [nɔn'plʌs] *vtr* (**nonplussed**) confondre, interdire, interloquer (qn); **to be nonplussed,** être désemparé.

non-profitmaking ['nɔn'prɔfitmeikiŋ] *a* (societé) sans but lucratif.

non-resident ['nɔn'rezid(ə)nt] *a & n* non-résident (*m*); (*hotel*) **open to non-residents,** repas servis aux voyageurs de passage.

non-returnable [ˈnɔnriˈtɔːnəbl] *a* (emballage) perdu, non repris, non consigné.

nonsense [ˈnɔnsəns] *n* 1. non-sens *m* 2. absurdité *f*; **piece of n.,** bêtise *f*; **to talk n.,** dire des bêtises; **(what) n.!** quelle bêtise! bêtises que tout cela! **no n.!** pas de bêtises! **non'sensical** *a* absurde.

non sequitur [nɔnˈsekwitər] *n* phrase *f*, conclusion *f*, illogique.

non-skid [nɔnˈskid] *a* antidérapant.

non-smoker [ˈnɔnˈsmoukər] *n* (*a*) (*of pers*) non-fumeur *m* (*b*) *Rail: Av:* siège *m*, compartiment *m*, non-fumeurs.

non-starter [ˈnɔnˈstɑːtər] *n* (*a*) (cheval) non partant (*b*) projet voué d'avance à l'échec.

non-stick [ˈnɔnˈstik] *a* **n.-s. saucepan,** casserole qui n'attache pas.

nonstop [ˈnɔnˈstɔp] 1. *a* (train) direct; *Av:* (vol) sans escale 2. *adv* sans arrêt; (voler) sans escale; **to talk n.,** parler sans arrêt.

non-taxable [nɔnˈtæksəbl] *a* non imposable.

non-union [ˈnɔnˈjuːniən] *a* (ouvrier) non syndiqué.

non-violence [ˈnɔnˈvaiələns] *n* non-violence *f*.

noodles [ˈnuːdlz] *npl Cu:* nouilles *f*.

nook [nuk] *n* coin *m*; recoin *m*; **in every n. and cranny,** dans tous les coins et recoins.

noon [nuːn] *n* midi *m*. **'noonday** *n* **the n. sun,** le soleil de midi.

noose [nuːs] *n* nœud coulant; (*for trapping animals*) lacet *m*, collet *m*.

nor [nɔːr] *conj* 1. (ne, ni . . .) ni; **he has neither father n. mother,** il n'a ni père ni mère; **he hasn't any, n. have I,** il n'en a pas, ni moi non plus 2. **I don't know, n. can I guess,** je n'en sais rien, et je ne peux pas le deviner; **n. was this all,** et ce n'était pas tout.

norm [nɔːm] *n* norme *f*. **'normal** 1. *a* normal, régulier, ordinaire 2. *n* normale *f*; **temperature above n.,** température au-dessus de la normale. **nor'mality** *n* normalité *f*. **'normally** *adv* normalement.

Normandy [ˈnɔːməndi] *Prn Geog:* la Normandie. **'Norman** *a & n* normand, -ande; **N. architecture,** (i) l'architecture normande (ii) l'architecture romane (anglaise).

Norse [nɔːs] 1. *a* norvégien 2. *n* (*a*) *pl* Scandinaves *mfpl, esp* Norvégiens, -iennes (*b*) *Ling:* (i) norvégien *m* (ii) (*in Orkneys, Shetlands*) norse *m*. **'Norseman** *n* (*pl* -men) Scandinave.

north [nɔːθ] 1. *n* nord *m*; **on the n., to the n. (of),** au nord (de); **in the n. of England,** dans le nord de l'Angleterre 2. *adv* au nord; **to travel n.,** voyager vers le nord; **it's n. of here,** c'est au nord d'ici 3. *a* nord *inv*; **the n. coast,** la côte nord; **n. wall,** mur exposé au nord; **n. wind,** vent du nord; **the N. Sea,** la mer du Nord; **the N. Pole,** le Pôle nord. **North-'African** *a & n* nord-africain, -aine. **'North-A'merican** *a & n* nord-américain, -aine. **'north-bound** *a* (train) allant vers le nord, en direction du nord. **'north-'east** 1. *n* nord-est *m* 2. *a* (du) nord-est *inv* 3. *adv* vers le nord-est. **'north-'eastern** *a* (du) nord-est. **'northerly** [-ð-] *a* du nord; vers le nord; **n. wind,** vent du nord. **'northern** [-ð-] *a* (du) nord; septentrional; **N. Ireland,** l'Irlande *f* du Nord; **n. lights,** aurore boréale. **'northener** *n* habitant(e) du nord. **'northern-**

most *a* le plus au nord. **'northward** 1. *a* au, du, nord 2. *n* **to the n. (of),** au nord (de). **'northwards** *adv* vers le nord. **north'west** 1. *n* nord-ouest *m* 2. *a* (du) nord-ouest *inv* 3. vers le nord-ouest. **north'western** *a* (du) nord-ouest.

Norway [ˈnɔːwei] *Prn Geog:* la Norvège. **Norwegian** [nɔːˈwiːdʒən] 1. *a & n* norvégien, -ienne 2. *n Ling:* norvégien *m*.

nose [nouz] I. *n* 1. (*of pers, dog*) nez *m*; (*of many animals*) museau *m*; **to blow one's n.,** se moucher; **to hold one's n.,** se boucher le nez; **to speak through one's n.,** nasiller; parler du nez; **to pay through the n. for sth,** payer qch trop cher; **I did it under his very n.,** je l'ai fait sous son nez; **to poke one's n. into sth,** fourrer son nez dans qch; **to lead s.o. by the n.,** mener qn par le bout du nez; **to look down one's n. at s.o.,** regarder qn de haut en bas; **to cut off one's n. to spite one's face,** agir par colère contre son propre intérêt 2. odorat *m*; **to have a n. for sth,** avoir du flair pour qch 3. nez (d'un avion); *Aut:* **n. to tail,** pare-choc contre pare-choc. II. *v* 1. *vtr* (*of dog*) **to n. out the game,** flairer le gibier; *F:* **to n. sth out,** découvrir (qch); flairer (qch) 2. *vi* **to n. about, (a)round,** fureter, fouiner; **to n. one's way into sth,** entrer discrètement dans (une pièce, un club). **'nosebag** *n* musette *f* (de cheval). **'nosebleed** *n* **to have a n.,** saigner du nez. **'nosecone** *n* cône *m* avant (d'avion); ogive *f* (de fusée). **'nosedive** 1. *n* piqué *m*, descente *f* en piqué. 2. *vi* descendre en piqué; piquer de l'avant. **'nosegay** *n* bouquet *m*. **'nosey, 'nosy** *a* curieux, fouinard; fureteur; **a n. parker,** un indiscret, un fouinard.

nosh [nɔʃ] *n P:* bouffe *f*.

nostalgia [nɔsˈtældʒ(i)ə] *n* nostalgie *f*. **nos'talgic** *a* nostalgique.

nostril [ˈnɔstril] *n* (*of pers*) narine *f*; (*of horse*) naseau *m*.

nostrum [ˈnɔstrəm] *n* panacée *f*, remède *m* de charlatan.

not [nɔt] *adv* 1. (*a*) (ne) pas, (ne) point; **he will n., won't, come,** il ne viendra pas; **she is n., isn't, there,** elle n'est pas là; **you understand, do you n., don't you?** vous comprenez, n'est-ce pas? (*b*) **n. at all,** (i) pas du tout (ii) je vous en prie; **I think n.,** je crois que non; **why n.?** pourquoi pas? **n. negotiable,** non négociable 2. **n. including,** sans compter; **he asked me n. to move,** il m'a demandé de ne pas bouger; *F:* **n. to worry!** ne vous en faites pas! (*of party*) **we can't n. go,** impossible de s'en tirer 3. **n. that,** ce n'est pas que; **n. that I'm afraid of him,** non (pas) que je le craigne; **n. that I can remember,** pas autant qu'il m'en souvienne 4. **n. only, but also,** non seulement, mais encore; **respected but n. loved,** respecté mais non pas aimé 5. **I was n. sorry to leave,** j'étais bien content de partir; **n. without reason,** non sans raison 6. **n. a murmur was heard,** on n'entendit pas un murmure.

notable [ˈnoutəbl] *a* notable, insigne; (*of pers*) éminent. **'notably** *adv* 1. notablement, remarquablement 2. notamment, particulièrement.

notary [ˈnoutəri] *n* (*pl* **notaries**) *Jur:* **n. (public),** notaire *m*.

notation [nouˈteiʃ(ə)n] *n* notation *f*.

notch [nɔtʃ] I. *n* (*pl* **notches**) (*a*) entaille *f*, encoche *f*, cran *m* (*b*) brèche *f* (dans une lame). II. *vtr* (*a*) entailler, encocher (un bâton); **to n. up,** marquer (un point) (*b*) ébrécher (une lame).

note [nout] I. *n* 1. (*a*) note *f* (de musique) (*b*) touche *f* [d'un piano] (*c*) note, son *m*; **to sing a wrong n.,** chanter faux; **to strike the right n.,** être bien dans la note 2. marque *f*, signe *m*, indice *m* 3. (*a*) note, mémorandum *m*; **to make, keep, a n. of sth,** noter qch; prendre, tenir, note de qch; **I must make a n. of it,** il faut que je m'en souvienne (*b*) note, commentaire *m*, annotation *f*; **to make notes on a text,** annoter un texte (*c*) billet *m*; petite lettre; petit mot 4. (*a*) *Com:* billet, bordereau *m*; **n. of hand,** reconnaissance *f* (de dette); **advice n.,** note, lettre, d'avis (*b*) (*NAm:* = **bill**) (**bank**) **n.,** billet (de banque) 5. (*a*) distinction *f*, renom *m*; **a person of n.,** un homme de marque (*b*) attention *f*, remarque *f*; **to take a n. of sth,** remarquer qch. II. *vtr* 1. noter, constater, remarquer, prendre note de (qch); **it's worth noting that,** il convient de remarquer que 2. **to n. sth (down),** écrire, inscrire (qch). **'notebook** *n* carnet *m*, calepin *m*; bloc-notes *m*; **'notecase** *n* porte-billets *m inv*, portefeuille *m*. **'noted** *a* (*of pers*) distingué, éminent; (*of thg*) célèbre (**for sth,** par qch). **'notepaper** *n* papier *m* à lettres. **'noteworthy** *a* remarquable; digne d'attention, de remarque.

nothing ['nʌθiŋ] I. *n or pron* rien (*with* ne *expressed or understood*) (*a*) **n. could be simpler,** rien de plus simple; **to say n. of,** sans parler de; **it looks like n. on earth,** cela ne ressemble à rien; **as if n. had happened,** comme si de rien n'était; **there's n. in these rumours,** ces bruits sont sans fondement; *F:* **there's n. to it,** in it, c'est simple comme bonjour; **to be n. if not discreet,** être discret avant tout; **to create sth out of n.,** créer qch de toutes pièces (*b*) **n. new,** rien de nouveau; **n. much,** pas grand-chose; **there's n. more to be said,** il n'y a plus rien à dire (*c*) **I have n. to do with it,** je n'y suis pour rien; **that's n. to do with you,** cela ne vous regarde pas; **there's n. to cry about,** il n'y a pas de quoi pleurer; **n. doing!** rien à faire! (*d*) **he is n. of a scholar,** ce n'est pas du tout un savant; **n. of the kind,** rien de la sorte (*e*) **n. else,** rien d'autre; **n. but the truth,** rien que la vérité; **he does n. but complain,** il ne fait que se plaindre; **there was n. for it but to wait,** il ne nous restait plus qu'à attendre (*f*) **it's not for n. that,** ce n'est pas sans raison que; **all my efforts went for n.,** c'étaient des efforts perdus; **it counts for n.,** ça ne compte pour rien; **I got n. out of it,** j'en suis pour mes frais (*g*) **he is n. to me,** il m'est indifférent; **it's n. to me either way,** cela m'est égal (*h*) **to think n. of sth,** ne faire aucun cas de qch. II. *n* 1. *Mth:* zéro *m* 2. (*a*) néant *m*; rien *m*; **to come to n.,** ne pas aboutir; (*of hopes*) s'anéantir (*b*) vétille *f*, bagatelle *f*; **a hundred francs? a mere n.!** cent francs? une bêtise! III. *adv* aucunement, nullement; pas du tout; **n. like as big,** loin d'être aussi grand; **it's n. less than madness,** c'est de la folie ni plus ni moins; **n. daunted,** nullement intimidé. **'nothingness** *n* néant *m*.

notice ['noutis] I. *n* 1. (*a*) avis *m*, notification *f*; **n. of delivery,** accusé *m* de réception (*b*) préavis *m*, avertissement *m*; **to give s.o. n. of sth,** prévenir, avertir, qn de qch; **to do sth without n.,** faire qch sans avis préalable; **public n.,** avis au public; **until further n.,** jusqu'à nouvel ordre, nouvel avis (*c*) avis formel, instructions formelles; **to give s.o. n. to do sth,** aviser qn de faire qch (*d*) **ready to leave at short n.,** at a moment's n.,** prêt à partir à l'instant (*e*) **n. to quit,** congé *m*; **to give n. to an employee,** donner son congé à un employé; **to give in one's n.,** donner sa démission 2. (*a*) affiche *f*; indication *f*, avis (au public); **n. board,** écriteau *m*; tableau d'affichage; panneau d'affichage (*b*) (*in newspaper*) annonce *f* 3. **to take n. of sth,** tenir compte, prendre connaissance, de qch; **to take no n. of sth,** ne prêter aucune attention à qch; **to bring sth to s.o.'s n.,** faire observer qch à qn; **to attract n.,** se faire remarquer; *F:* **to sit up and take n.,** dresser l'oreille. II. *vtr* observer, remarquer, s'apercevoir de, tenir compte de (qn, qch); **I have never noticed it,** je ne l'ai jamais remarqué. **'noticeable** *a* perceptible, sensible; **it's not n.,** cela ne se voit pas. **'noticeably** *adv* perceptiblement, sensiblement.

notify ['noutifai] *vtr* annoncer, notifier (qch); déclarer (une naissance); **to n. s.o. of sth,** avertir, aviser, qn de qch; **to n. the police of sth,** signaler qch à la police. **noti'fiable** *a* (qch) qu'on est obligé de déclarer aux autorités. **notifi'cation** *n* avis *m*, notification *f*, annonce *f*; déclaration *f* (de naissance).

notion ['nouʃ(ə)n] *n* (*a*) notion *f*, idée *f*; **to have no n. of sth,** n'avoir aucune notion de qch (*b*) opinion *f*, pensée *f*; **I have a n. that,** j'ai dans l'idée que. **'notional** *a* *Gram:* notionnel, -elle.

notorious [nou'tɔːriəs] *a* d'une triste notoriété; (menteur) insigne; (malfaiteur) reconnu, notoire; (endroit) mal famé. **notoriety** [noutə'raiəti] *n* notoriété *f*. **no'toriously** *adv* notoirement; **n. cruel,** connu pour sa cruauté.

notwithstanding [notwiθ'stændiŋ, -wið-] *prep* malgré, en dépit de; **n. any clause to the contrary,** nonobstant toute clause contraire.

nougat ['nuːgɑː] *n* nougat *m*.

nought [nɔːt] *n Mth:* zéro *m*; **noughts and crosses** = morpion *m*.

noun [naun] *n Gram:* substantif *m*, nom *m*.

nourish ['nʌriʃ] *vtr* nourrir, alimenter (qn). **'nourishing** *a* nourrissant, nutritif. **'nourishment** *n* 1. alimentation *f*, nourriture *f* 2. aliments *mpl*, nourriture.

nous [naus] *n F:* savoir-faire *m*.

nova ['nouvə] *n* (*pl* novae [-viː]) *Astr:* nova *f*.

Nova Scotia ['nouvə'skouʃə] *Prn Geog:* Nouvelle-Écosse.

novel¹ ['nɔv(ə)l] *n* roman *m*; **detective n.,** roman policier. **'novelist** *n* romancier, -ière.

novel² *a* nouveau; original; **that's a n. idea!** voilà qui est original! **'novelty** *n* 1. chose nouvelle; innovation *f*; *Com:* (article *m* de) nouveauté *f* 2. nouveauté (de qch).

November [nou'vembər] *n* novembre *m*; **in N.,** au mois de novembre; **(on) the fifth of N.,** le cinq novembre.

novice ['nɔvis] *n* novice *mf*; apprenti, -ie; débutant, -ante. **no'viciate** *n* noviciat *m*.

now [nau] I. *adv* 1. (*a*) maintenant; actuellement, à l'heure actuelle; **n. or never!** c'est le moment où jamais! (*b*) **he won't be long n.,** il ne tardera plus guère (c) maintenant; tout de suite; **and n. I must go**, sur ce je vous quitte; **n. is the time to**, c'est le bon moment pour (d) (in narrative) alors; à ce moment-là; **all was n. ready**, dès lors tout était prêt (e) **just n.**, (i) (past) tout à l'heure, il y a un instant (ii) (present) en ce moment (f) (every) **n. and then**, de temps en temps; de temps à autre; **n. here n. there**, tantôt ici tantôt là; **up to n.**, jusqu'ici 2. (a) or; déjà; **n. it happened that**, or il advint que (b) **n. what's all this about?** qu'avez-vous donc? **come n.!** voyons, voyons! **well n.!** eh bien! **n. then!** (i) attention! (ii) voyons! **allons! II.** conj maintenant que, à présent que; **n. I'm older I think differently**, maintenant que je suis plus âgé je pense autrement. **III.** n in three days from n., d'ici trois jours; **between n. and then**, d'ici là; **by n.**, à l'heure qu'il est; **he ought to be here by n.**, il devrait déjà être arrivé; **until n.**, **up to n.**, jusqu'à présent, jusqu'ici; **from n. (on)**, désormais, à partir de maintenant. **'nowadays** adv aujourd'hui; de nos jours; à l'heure actuelle.

nowhere ['nouwεər] adv nulle part; **it's n. near big enough**, c'est loin d'être assez grand; **I'm getting n.**, je n'y arrive pas; **flattery will get you n.**, la flatterie ne vous mènera à rien.

noxious ['nɔkʃəs] a nuisible, nocif; malfaisant; (gaz) délétère.

nozzle ['nɔzl] n ajutage m; jet m, lance f (de tuyau); bec m, tuyau m (de soufflet); suceur m (d'aspirateur); Av: injecteur m; Aut: gicleur m.

NSPCC abbr National Society for the Prevention of Cruelty to Children.

nth [enθ] a F: **to the n. degree**, au suprême degré; **for the n. time**, pour la énième fois.

nuance ['njuːɑːns] n nuance f.

nub [nʌb] n essentiel m (d'une affaire).

nubile ['njuːbail] a nubile.

nucleus ['njuːkliəs] n (pl nuclei) noyau m (de cellule). **'nuclear** a nucléaire; **n. power**, énergie atomique; **n. power station**, centrale nucléaire; **n. weapon**, arme nucléaire.

nude [njuːd] a & n nu (m); **to draw from the n.**, dessiner d'après le nu; **in the n.**, tout nu. **'nudism** n nudisme m. **'nudist** n nudiste mf. **'nudity** n nudité f.

nudge [nʌdʒ] **I.** n coup m de coude. **II.** vtr pousser (qn) du coude.

nugget ['nʌgit] n pépite f (d'or).

nuisance ['njuːs(ə)ns] n (a) peste f, fléau m; **he's a perfect n.**, il est assommant; **go away, you're (being) a n.!** va-t'en, tu m'embêtes! **to make a n. of oneself**, embêter le monde (b) **that's a n.!** voilà qui est bien ennuyeux! **what a n.!** quel ennui! que c'est agaçant!

null [nʌl] a Jur: **n. and void**, nul et de nul effet, nul et non avenu; **to declare a contract n. and void**, déclarer un contrat nul et non avenu. **'nullify** vtr annuler, Jur: infirmer (un acte). **'nullity** n 1. nullité f 2. (of pers) non-valeur f; homme nul.

numb [nʌm] **I.** a engourdi. **II.** vtr engourdir; **numbed with horror**, glacé d'horreur. **'numbness** n engourdissement m; torpeur f (de l'esprit).

number ['nʌmbər] **I.** n 1. (a) Mth: nombre m (b) **they were six in n.**, ils étaient au nombre de six; **they are few in n.**, il sont peu nombreux; **without n.**, sans nombre (c) **a (large) n. of men came**, un grand nombre, beaucoup, d'hommes sont venus; **a great n. of people are of this opinion**, beaucoup de gens sont de cet avis; **a n. of people**, plusieurs personnes; **any n. of**, un grand nombre de; une quantité de (d) **in small numbers**, en petit nombre; **in ever increasing numbers**, de plus en plus nombreux (e) Lit: **one of their n.**, (l')un d'entre eux 2. chiffre m; **to write the n. on a page**, numéroter une page 3. numéro m (d'une maison); **I live at n. forty**, j'habite au numéro quarante; F: **to look after n. one**, penser à mézigue; Aut: **registration, licence, n.**, numéro minéralogique, d'immatriculation; **telephone n.**, numéro d'appel; F: **his number's up**, il a son compte; il est fichu 4. Gram: nombre 5. numéro (d'un journal); Th: numéro (du programme). **II.** vtr 1. compter, dénombrer; **his days are numbered**, ses jours sont comptés 2. numéroter (les maisons). **'numbering** n numérotage m; **n. machine, stamp**, numéroteur m. **'numberless** a innombrable; sans nombre. **'numberplate** n plaque f d'immatriculation.

numeral ['njuːmərəl] 1. a numéral 2. n chiffre m, nombre m. **'numeracy** n degré m d'aptitude en calcul. **'numerate** a qui a le sens de l'arithmétique. **'numerator** n Mth: numérateur m. **nu'merical** a numérique. **nu'merically** adv numériquement. **'numerous** a nombreux.

numismatics [njuːmiz'mætiks] npl (usu with sg const) la numismatique. **nu'mismatist** n numismate mf.

nun [nʌn] n Ecc: religieuse f; F: (bonne) sœur. **'nunnery** n couvent m (de religieuses).

nuncio ['nʌnsiou] n nonce m.

nuptial ['nʌpʃəl] a nuptial. **'nuptials** npl noces fpl.

nurse [nəːs] **I.** n 1. infirmier, -ière; garde-malade mf 2. (wet) n., nourrice f; (children's) n., nurse f; bonne f d'enfants. **II.** vtr 1. soigner (un malade); vi **she wants to n.**, elle voudrait être infirmière 2. (a) allaiter (un enfant) (b) nourrir, entretenir (un chagrin, un espoir); cultiver (une plante); Pol: **to n. a constituency**, chauffer ses électeurs 3. bercer (un enfant); tenir (qn, qch) dans ses bras. **'nursemaid** n bonne f d'enfants. **'nursery** n 1. (a) chambre f des enfants; nursery f; **n. rhyme**, comptine f (b) **day n.**, crèche f; garderie f; **n. school**, (école) maternelle (f); jardin m d'enfants 2. Hort: pépinière f; **n. gardener**, pépiniériste mf. **'nurseryman** n pépiniériste m. **'nursing I.** a 1. **n. mother**, mère qui allaite son enfant 2. (in hospital) **n. staff**, personnel infirmier. **II.** n (a) soins mpl (d'un(e) garde-malade) (b) profession f d'infirmière (c) **n. home**, (i) clinique (ii) maison f de santé (iii) maison de retraite.

nurture ['nəːtʃər] vtr nourrir, entretenir (les enfants, les sentiments).

nut [nʌt] n 1. (a) noix f; **hazel n.**, noisette f, aveline f; **cashew n.**, noix d'acajou; F: **tough, hard, n. to crack** (i) problème m difficile à résoudre (ii) personne f difficile, peu commode; F: **he can't sing for nuts**, il ne sait pas chanter du tout (b) P: tête f; **off one's n.**, timbré, toqué; **to go nuts**, perdre la boule; **he's nuts**, il est cinglé; **to be nuts about sth**, être fou de qch; raffoler de qch 2. écrou m; **wing n., butterfly n.**, écrou à oreilles, à ailettes; **nuts and bolts**, (i) écrous et boulons (ii) Fig: éléments essentiels (d'une affaire). **'nutcrackers** npl casse-noisettes m inv, casse-noix *m inv.* 'nutmeg *n* (noix *f*) muscade (*f*). 'nut-shell *n* coquille *f* de noix; **in a n.,** en un mot, en deux mots; bref. 'nutty *a* 1. au goût de noisette, de noix 2. *F:* **to be n. about s.o., sth,** raffoler de qn, de qch 3. *F:* fou, timbré.

nutrient ['nju:triənt] *n* nourriture *f*. nu'trition *n* nutrition *f*. nu'tritious, 'nutritive *a* nutritif, nourrissant.

nuzzle ['nʌzl] *vi* fourrer son nez (contre l'épaule de qn); se blottir contre qn.

nylon ['nailən] *n Tex:* nylon *m*; **n. stockings,** nylons, bas *mpl* (de) nylon.

nymph [nimf] *n* nymphe *f*. nympho'mania *n* nymphomanie *f*. nympho'maniac *n* nymphomane *f*.

O

O¹, o [ou] *n* **1.** (la lettre) O, o *m*; *Sch:* **O level (exam)** = premier examen du *General Certificate of Education* **2.** (*nought*) zéro *m*; 3103 ['θri:wanou'θri:] = 31.03 [trãteœzerotrwa].

O² *int* ô! oh!

oaf [ouf] *n* lourdaud *m*, ours mal léché. **'oafish** *a* lourdaud, stupide.

oak [ouk] *n* (*a*) **o. (tree)**, chêne *m*; **o. apple**, noix *f* de galle (*b*) (bois *m* de) chêne; **o. furniture**, meubles de, en, chêne.

oakum ['oukəm] *n* étoupe *f*, filasse *f*.

OAP *abbr* old-age pensioner, retraité(e).

oar [ɔːr] *n* (*a*) pagaie *f*, aviron *m*, rame *f*; *F:* **to stick one's o. in**, intervenir (mal à propos) (dans qch) (*b*) **good o.**, bon rameur. **'oarlock** *n NAm:* (*Br* = **rowlock**) tolet *m*. **'oarsman** *n* (*pl* -**men**) rameur *m*; *Nau:* nageur *m*.

oasis [ou'eisis] *n* (*pl* **oases**) oasis *f*.

oasthouse ['ousthaus] *n* sécherie *f* de houblon.

oath [ouθ] *n* (*pl* **oaths**) **1.** serment *m*; *Jur:* **to take an o.**, prêter serment; **I'll take my o. on it**, j'en jurerais; **on o.**, sous serment; (témoin) assermenté **2.** juron *m*; gros mot; **to swear an o.**, jurer.

oats [outs] *npl* avoine *f*; **field of o.**, champ d'avoine; **to sow one's wild o.**, faire des frasques. **'oatcake** *n* galette *f* d'avoine. **'oatmeal** *n* farine *f* d'avoine; *NAm:* (*Br* = **porridge**) flocons *mpl* d'avoine.

obdurate ['ɔbdjurət] *a* (*a*) endurci; têtu (*b*) inexorable, inflexible. **'obduracy** *n* (*a*) endurcissement *m* (de cœur); entêtement *m* (*b*) inflexibilité *f*.

OBE *abbr* Order of the British Empire.

obedience [ə'bi:djəns] *n* obéissance *f*; **to secure o.**, faire obéir. **o'bedient** *a* obéissant; soumis; docile. **o'bediently** *adv* avec obéissance, avec soumission; docilement.

obelisk ['ɔbilisk] *n* obélisque *m*.

obese [ou'bi:s] *a* obèse. **o'besity** *n* obésité *f*.

obey [ə'bei] *vtr* obéir à (qn, un ordre); (*of machine*) répondre (à); **to make oneself obeyed**, se faire obéir.

obituary [ə'bitjuri] *a & n* (*pl* **obituaries**) **o. notice**, notice *f* nécrologique; *Journ:* **the o. column**, the **obituaries**, nécrologie *f*.

object I. *n* ['ɔbdʒikt] **1.** (*a*) objet *m*, chose *f*; **o. lesson**, exemple *m* (*b*) **o. of pity**, objet, sujet *m*, de pitié **2.** (*a*) but *m*, objectif *m*, objet; **with this o.**, dans ce but, à cette fin; **what is the o. of all this?** à quoi vise tout cela? **to defeat one's o.**, manquer son but; **there's no o. in doing that**, il ne vise à rien de faire cela (*b*) **distance is no o.**, la longueur du trajet importe peu; **expense, money, is no o.**, il ne faut pas regarder à la dépense **3.** *Gram:* complément *m*, objet; **direct, indirect, o.**, complément direct, indirect. **II.** *vi* [əb'dʒekt] **to o. to sth**, faire une objection, trouver à redire, à qch; **to o. to s.o.**, soulever des objections contre qn; **to o. to doing sth**, se refuser à faire qch; **he objects to it**, il s'y oppose; **if you don't o.**, si vous n'y voyez pas d'inconvénient; **I o.!** je proteste! **ob'jection** *n* **1.**

objection *f*; **to raise an o.**, soulever une objection; **the o. has been raised that**, on a objecté que; **to take o. to s.o., to sth**, être mécontent de qn, se fâcher de qch; **I've no o. to that**, je ne m'oppose pas à cela; **if you have no o.**, si cela ne vous fait rien **2.** obstacle *m*; **I see no o.** (to it), je n'y vois pas d'inconvénient; **I have no o. to him**, je n'ai rien à dire contre lui. **ob'jectionable** *a* **1.** répréhensible, inacceptable, inadmissible **2.** désagréable; (langage) choquant; **idea that is most o. to me**, idée qui me répugne; **a most o. man**, un homme que personne ne peut souffrir. **ob'jective 1.** *a Gram:* **o. case**, accusatif *m* **2.** *n* (*a*) but *m*; objectif *m* (*b*) *Phot:* objectif. **objectively** *adv* objectivement. **objec'tivity** *n* objectivité *f*. **ob'jector** *n* protestataire *mf*; **conscientious o.**, objecteur *m* de conscience.

oblige [ə'blaidʒ] *vtr* **1.** obliger, astreindre (qn à faire qch); **to be obliged to do sth**, être obligé, tenu, de faire qch **2.** (*a*) **to o. a friend**, rendre service à un ami; **can you o. me with a light?** auriez-vous l'amabilité de me donner du feu? **(in order) to o. you**, pour vous être agréable; **he's always willing to o.**, il est très obligeant (*b*) **to be obliged to s.o.**, être obligé à qn; être reconnaissant à qn. **obligation** [ɔbli'geiʃ(ə)n] *n* (*a*) obligation *f*; **to be under an o. to do sth**, être dans l'obligation de faire qch; **I'm under no o.**, rien ne m'oblige (à faire qch); *Ecc:* **day of o.**, fête *f* d'obligation (*b*) dette *f* de reconnaissance; **to be under an o. to s.o.**, devoir de la reconnaissance à qn; **to put, lay, s.o. under an o. (to do sth)**, obliger qn (à faire qch) (*c*) *Com:* **without o.**, sans engagement; **to meet, fail to meet, one's obligations**, faire honneur, manquer, à ses engagements. **o'bligatory** [ə'bligətri] *a* obligatoire; de rigueur; **to make it o. to do sth**, imposer l'obligation de faire qch. **o'bliging** *a* obligeant, complaisant, serviable. **o'bligingly** *adv* obligeamment.

oblique [ə'bli:k] *a* oblique; de biais; **o. angle**, angle oblique. **o'bliquely** *adv* obliquement, de biais, en biais.

obliterate [ə'blitəreit] *vtr* (*a*) faire disparaître, effacer (*b*) oblitérer (un timbre). **oblite'ration** *n* **1.** (*a*) effacement *m* (*b*) rature *f* **2.** oblitération *f* (d'un timbre).

oblivion [ə'blivien] *n* (état *m* d')oubli *m*; **to sink into o.**, tomber dans l'oubli. **o'blivious** *a* oublieux (of, de); **o. of what is going on**, inconscient de ce qui se passe; **to be o. of the difficulties**, ignorer les difficultés.

oblong ['ɔblɔŋ] **1.** *a* oblong, -ongue; rectangulaire **2.** *n* rectangle *m*.

obnoxious [əb'nɔkʃəs] *a* (*a*) odieux; antipathique (to s.o., à qn) (*b*) repoussant, désagréable.

oboe ['oubou] *n Mus:* hautbois *m*. **'oboist** *n* hautboïste *mf*.

obscene [əb'si:n, ɔ-] *a* obscène. **ob'scenely** *adv* d'une manière obscène. **obscenity** [əb'seniti] *n* obscénité *f*.

obscure [əb'skjuər] I. *a* 1. obscur, ténébreux, sombre 2. (livre) obscur; (sentiment) vague; (argument) peu clair 3. (auteur) peu connu. II. *vtr* obscurcir; **clouds obscured the sun**, des nuages voilaient le soleil. **ob'scurely** *adv* obscurément. **ob'scurity** *n* obscurité *f*.

obsequies ['ɔbsikwiz] *npl* obsèques *f*, funérailles *f*.

obsequious [əb'si:kwiəs] *a* obséquieux. **ob'sequiously** *adv* obséquieusement. **ob'sequiousness** *n* servilité *f*.

observe [əb'zə:v] *vtr* 1. observer (la loi); garder (le silence); se conformer à (un ordre) 2. observer, regarder (les étoiles); surveiller (l'ennemi) 3. remarquer, noter (un fait); **at last I observed a dark stain**, enfin j'aperçus une tache foncée 4. dire, remarquer (que). **ob'servable** *a* visible; perceptible. **ob'servance** *n* 1. observation *f*, observance *f* 2. **religious observances**, pratiques religieuses. **ob'servant** *a* (*a*) observateur (*b*) **he's very o.**, rien ne lui échappe. **obser'vation** *n* 1. (*a*) observation *f*; **to keep, put, s.o. under o.**, mettre (un malade) en observation; surveiller qn; **to escape o.**, se dérober aux regards (*b*) *Nau:* **to take an o.**, faire le point (*c*) **o. car, coach**, voiture panoramique 2. **to make an o.**, faire une remarque. **ob'servatory** *n* observatoire *m*. **ob'server** *n* observateur, -trice.

obsess [əb'ses] *vtr* obséder; **to be obsessed with an idea**, être obsédé par une idée. **ob'session** *n* obsession *f*, hantise *f*. **ob'sessive** *a* obsédant. **ob'sessively** *adv* d'une façon obsédante.

obsolete ['ɔbsəli:t] *a* désuet; hors d'usage; tombé en désuétude. **obsolescence** [ɔbsə'lesəns] *n* désuétude *f*; obsolescence *f* (d'un outillage). **obso'lescent** *a* (mot) vieilli.

obstacle ['ɔbstəkl] *n* obstacle *m*, empêchement *m*; **to be an o. to sth**, faire obstacle à qch; **to put obstacles in s.o.'s way**, faire obstacle à qn; *Sp:* **o. race**, course d'obstacles.

obstetrics [ɔb'stetriks] *npl* obstétrique *f*. **obste'trician** *n* obstétricien, -ienne.

obstinate ['ɔbstinət] *a* obstiné (**in doing sth**, à faire qch); opiniâtre; **o. as a mule**, entêté, têtu, comme une mule. **'obstinacy** *n* obstination *f*, entêtement *m*, opiniâtreté *f*; **to show o.**, s'obstiner. **'obstinately** *adv* obstinément, opiniâtrement; **to refuse o.**, s'entêter à refuser.

obstreperous [əb'strep(ə)rəs] *a* bruyant, tapageur; turbulent.

obstruct [əb'strʌkt] *vtr* (*a*) obstruer, encombrer (la rue); boucher (un tuyau); **to o. the view**, gêner la vue (*b*) gêner, entraver (les mouvements de qn) (*c*) embarrasser, entraver (la circulation). **ob'struction** *n* 1. (*a*) engorgement *m* (d'un tuyau) (*b*) empêchement *m* (de qn) 2. encombrement *m*, embarras *m* (dans la rue); *Rail:* **o. on the line**, obstacle *m* sur la voie. **ob'structionist** *n Pol:* obstructionniste *mf*. **ob'structive** *a* obstructif; **o. tactics**, tactique d'obstruction.

obtain [əb'tein] *vtr* obtenir; se procurer (qch). **ob'tainable** *a* **where is that o.?** où peut-on se procurer cela?

obtrude [əb'tru:d] *vtr & i* mettre (qch) en avant; **to o. oneself on s.o.**, importuner qn. **ob'trusion** *n* intrusion *f*; importunité *f*. **ob'trusive** *a* importun,

indiscret; (*of smell*) pénétrant. **ob'trusiveness** *n* importunité *f*.

obtuse [əb'tju:s] *a* (angle, esprit) obtus. **ob'tuseness** *n* stupidité *f*.

obverse ['ɔbvə:s] *n* avers *m*, face *f* (d'une médaille).

obviate ['ɔbvieit] *vtr* éviter, parer à, obvier à (une difficulté).

obvious ['ɔbviəs] *a* évident, clair, manifeste; **o. fact**, fait patent; **it's quite o. that he is lying**, il ment, cela saute aux yeux; **it's the o. thing to do**, c'est tout indiqué, cela s'impose. **'obviously** *adv* évidemment, manifestement; **she's o. wrong**, il est clair qu'elle a tort.

occasion [ə'keiʒ(ə)n] I. *n* 1. cause *f*, occasion *f*; **I've no o. for complaint**, je n'ai pas à me plaindre; **if the o. arises, should the o. arise**, s'il y a lieu; le cas échéant 2. occasion, occurrence *f*; **on the o. of his marriage**, à l'occasion de son mariage; **on one o.**, une fois; **on several occasions**, à plusieurs reprises; **on great occasions**, dans les grandes occasions; **on rare occasions**, rarement; **on such an o.**, en pareille occasion. II. *vtr* occasionner, donner lieu à (qch). **o'ccasional** *a* **o. visitor**, visiteur qui vient de temps en temps; **o. showers**, ondées éparses. **o'ccasionally** *adv* de temps en temps.

occident ['ɔksidənt] *n* occident *m*. **occi'dental** *a* occidental.

occult [ɔ'kʌlt] *a* occulte. **'occultism** *n* occultisme *m*.

occupy ['ɔkjupai] *vtr* 1. (*a*) occuper, habiter (une maison) (*b*) *Mil:* occuper (un pays ennemi); s'emparer d'(une ville); **occupied territory**, territoire occupé 2. remplir (un espace); occuper (une place, le temps); **this seat is occupied**, cette place est prise 3. occuper (qn); donner du travail à (qn); **to o. one's mind**, s'occuper l'esprit. **'occupancy** *n* occupation *f*, habitation *f* (d'un immeuble). **'occupant** *n* occupant, -ante; locataire *mf* (d'une maison). **occu'pation** *n* 1. occupation *f*; **to be in o. of (a house)**, occuper (une maison); **army of o.**, armée d'occupation 2. (*a*) **to find s.o. (some) o.**, occuper qn (*b*) métier *m*, emploi *m*; **what's his o.?** quel est son métier, sa profession? **occu'pational** *a* **o. disease**, maladie professionnelle; **o. therapy**, ergothérapie *f*; **o. hazards**, risques *mpl* du métier; risques professionnels. **'occupier** *n* occupant, -ante; locataire *mf* (d'une maison).

occur [ə'kə:r] *vi* (**occurred**) 1. (*of event*) avoir lieu; arriver; se produire; **if another opportunity occurs**, si une autre occasion se présente; **don't let it o. again!** que cela ne se répète pas! 2. se rencontrer, se trouver 3. **it occurs to me that . . .**, il me vient à l'esprit que . . . . **o'ccurrence** *n* événement *m*, occurrence *f*; **an everyday o.**, un fait journalier.

ocean ['ouʃ(ə)n] *n* océan *m*; **o. floor**, fond sous-marin; **o. current**, courant océanique; **o.-going ship**, navire de haute mer. **oceanic** [ousi'ænik] *a* océanique. **ocea'nographer** *n* océanographe *mf*. **ocean'ography** *n* océanographie *f*.

Oceania [ouʃi'a:niə] *Prn Geog:* l'Océanie *f*.

ocelot ['ɔsilɔt] *n Z:* ocelot *m*.

ochre, *NAm:* **ocher** ['oukər] *n* ocre *f*; **yellow, red, o.**, ocre jaune, rouge.

o'clock [ə'klɔk] *adv phr* **six o'c.**, six heures; **twelve o'c.**, (i) midi *m* (ii) minuit *m*.

octagon ['ɔktəgən] *n* octogone *m*. **oc'tagonal** *a* octogonal.

octane ['ɔktein] *n* **o. rating**, indice d'octane *m*; **high o. petrol**, essence à haut indice d'octane.

octave ['ɔktiv, 'ɔteiv] *n* octave *f*.

octet [ɔk'tet] *n Mus:* octuor *m*.

October [ɔk'toubər] *n* octobre *m*; **in O.**, au mois d'octobre; **(on) the sixth of O.**, le six octobre.

octogenarian [ɔktoudʒi'nɛəriən] *a & n* octogénaire (*mf*).

octopus ['ɔktəpəs] *n* poulpe *m*; pieuvre *f*.

ocular ['ɔkjulər] *a* oculaire. **'oculist** *n* oculiste *mf*.

odd [ɔd] *a* (**odder**, **oddest**) **1.** (*a*) (nombre) impair (*b*) **£6 o.**, six livres et quelques; **fifty o.**, cinquante et quelques; **a hundred o. sheep**, une centaine de moutons; **a thousand o. soldiers**, un millier de soldats; **to be the o. man out**, rester en surnombre **2.** (*a*) dépareillé; **o. socks**, chaussettes dépareillées (*b*) **at o. times**, de temps en temps; **o. moments**, moments de loisir, moments perdus; **he writes the o. letter**, il écrit de temps en temps; **o.-job man**, homme à tout faire; **to do o. jobs**, bricoler; *Com:* **o. lot**, soldes *mpl* **3.** singulier, drôle; (*of pers*) excentrique, original; **that's o.!** c'est curieux, bizarre, singulier! **'oddball** *n NAm: F:* excentrique *mf*. **'oddity** *n* **1.** singularité *f*, bizarrerie *f* **2.** (*a*) personne *f* excentrique; original, -ale (*b*) chose *f* bizarre; curiosité *f*. **'oddly** *adv* bizarrement, singulièrement; **o. enough nobody arrived**, chose singulière, curieuse, personne n'est arrivé. **'oddments** *npl* **1.** *Com:* fonds *m* de boutique; fins *f* de série **2.** petits bouts; restes *m*. **'oddness** *n* singularité *f*, bizarrerie *f*. **odds** *npl* **1.** (*a*) avantage *m*; chances *f*; **the o. are against him**, les chances sont contre lui; **to fight against (great) o.**, lutter contre des forces supérieures (*b*) différence *f*; **what's the o.?** qu'est-ce que ça fait? **it makes no o.**, ça ne fait rien (*c*) *Rac:* cote *f* (d'un cheval); **long, short, o.**, forte, faible, cote; **the o. are that**, il y a gros à parier que **2. to be at o. with s.o.**, ne pas être d'accord avec qn **3. o. and ends**, petits bouts; bribes *f* et morceaux *m*; restes *m*.

ode [oud] *n* ode *f*.

odious ['oudjəs] *a* odieux (**to**, à); détestable. **'odiously** *adv* odieusement. **'odiousness** *n* caractère odieux, l'odieux *m* (d'une action). **'odium** *n* réprobation *f*.

odometer [ou'dɔmitər] *n* odomètre *m*.

odour, *NAm:* **odor** ['oudər] *n* **1.** (*a*) odeur *f* (*b*) parfum *m* **2. to be in good, bad, o. with s.o.**, être bien, mal, vu de qn. **'odourless** *a* inodore; sans odeur.

odyssey ['ɔdisi] *n* odyssée *f*.

oedema, *NAm:* **edema** [i'di:mə] *n* œdème *m*.

oesophagus, *NAm:* **esophagus** [i'sɔfəgəs] *n Anat:* œsophage *m*.

oestrogen ['i:strədʒən] *n BioCh:* œstrogène *m*.

of [*accented* ɔv, *unaccented* əv, v] *prep* de **1.** (*a*) (*separation*) **south of**, au sud de; **free of**, libre de; *NAm:* **five (minutes) of one**, une heure moins cinq (*b*) (i) (*origin*) **the works of Shakespeare**, les œuvres de Shakespeare (ii) (*cause*) **of necessity**, par nécessité; **to die (as the result) of a wound**, mourir (des suites) d'une blessure **2. it's very kind of you**, c'est bien aimable de votre part **3. made of wood**, fait de, en, bois **4.** (*a*) **to**

think of s.o., penser à qn (*b*) **guilty of**, coupable de (*c*) **doctor of medicine**, docteur en médecine; **bachelor of arts** = licencié(e) ès lettres (*d*) **well, what of it?** eh bien, et après? **5.** (*a*) (i) **the town of Rouen**, la ville de Rouen; **child of ten**, enfant (âgé) de dix ans (ii) **hard of hearing**, (un peu) sourd, dur d'oreille (*b*) **that fool of a sergeant**, cet imbécile de sergent (*c*) **all of a sudden**, tout d'un coup, tout à coup **6.** (*a*) **how much of it do you want?** combien en voulez-vous? **two of them**, deux d'entre eux; **there are several of us**, nous sommes plusieurs; **of the twenty only one was bad**, sur les vingt un seul était mauvais (*b*) **the best of men**, le meilleur des hommes; **the one he loved most of all**, celui qu'il aimait entre tous (*c*) **the one thing of all others that I want**, ce que je désire par-dessus tout, avant tout **7.** (*a*) **the widow of a doctor**, la veuve d'un médecin; **the first of June**, le premier juin (*b*) **a friend of mine**, un de mes amis; **it's no business of yours**, cela ne vous regarde pas **8. of late**, dernièrement.

off [ɔf] **I.** *adv* **1.** (*a*) **one kilometre o.**, à un kilomètre; **some way o.**, à quelques kilomètres d'ici; **to keep s.o. o.**, empêcher qn d'approcher (*b*) **I'm o. to London**, je pars pour Londres; **where are you o. to?** où allez-vous? **be o. with you!** allez-vous-en! filez! **they're o.!** les voilà partis! **I must be o.**, (il faut que) je me sauve; **o. we go!** (i) en route! (ii) nous voilà partis! **to go o. to sleep**, s'endormir **2.** (*a*) **to take o. one's shoes**, enlever ses chaussures; **with his coat o.**, sans manteau; **o. with your shoes!** enlève tes chaussures! **a button has come o.**, un bouton a sauté; **he gave me 10% o.**, il m'a fait une remise de 10%; **to take a day o.**, prendre un jour de congé; se libérer pour la journée (*b*) (*of gas, electricity, stove*) fermé; *Aut:* **the ignition is o.**, l'allumage est coupé; (*in restaurant*) *F:* **chicken is o.**, il n'y a plus de poulet; **the deal's o.**, l'affaire ne se fera pas (*c*) **meat that is slightly o.**, viande un peu avancée; **the beer's o.**, la bière est éventée; **the milk's o.**, le lait a tourné; *F:* **that's a bit o.**, ce n'est pas chic (*d*) **to finish o. a piece of work**, achever un travail **3. badly o.**, dans la gêne; **well o.**, riche, prospère; **he's better o. where he is**, il est bien mieux où il est; **he's worse o.**, sa situation a empiré **4. on and o.**, par intervalles; **right o., straight o.**, immédiatement, tout de suite. **II.** *prep* **1.** (*a*) de; **to fall o. a horse**, tomber de cheval; **to take sth o. a table**, prendre qch sur une table; **door o. its hinges**, porte qui est hors de ses gonds; **to take sth o. the price**, rabattre qch du prix; faire une remise (*b*) écarté de, éloigné de; **a few kilometres o. the coast**, à quelques kilomètres de la côte; **street o. the main road**, rue qui débouche sur la grande route; **house o. the road**, maison en retrait; maison éloignée de la route; *Sp:* **o. side**, hors jeu (*c*) *F:* **to be o. one's food**, ne pas avoir d'appétit **2.** *Nau:* **o. the Cape**, au large du Cap; **o. Calais**, devant Calais. **III.** *a* (*a*) *Aut:* **o. side**, côté droit; (*in Fr, NAm:*) côté gauche (*b*) **o. day**, (i) jour de liberté (ii) jour où l'on n'est pas en forme; **o. season**, morte-saison *f*. **'off-beat** *a F:* original, pas ordinaire. **off-'centre** *a* décentré. **'off-chance** *n* **on the o.-c.**, au hasard. **off-'colour** *a* **to be o.-c.**, ne pas être dans son assiette. **'offcut** *n* (*of wood, cloth*) chute *f*. **'off'hand 1.** *adv* (*a*) sans préparation; **to speak o.**, parler impromptu (*b*) sans façon; d'un air dégagé **2.** *a* (*a*) spontané (*b*) brusque, cavalier; désinvolte. **'off'handed** *a* **in an o. way**, sans façon, avec désinvolture. 'off-'handedly adv sans façon, avec désinvolture. 'off'handedness n brusquerie f, sans-façon m, désinvolture f. 'off-'key a & adv Mus: faux. 'off-licence n (a) licence f permettant exclusivement la vente de boissons alcoolisées à emporter (b) débit m où l'on vend des boissons alcoolisées à emporter. off-'limits a esp NAm: d'accès interdit. off'load vtr débarquer (un excédent de marchandises); se décharger de (son travail sur qn). 'off-'peak a o.-p. hours, heures creuses; o.-p. tariff, tarif de nuit. 'off-putting a F: déconcertant. 'off-season 1. n morte-saison f 2. a (prix) hors saison. 'offset 1. n (a) compensation f, dédommagement m; as an o. to my losses, en compensation de mes pertes (b) Typ: offset m; o. printing, impression f offset 2. vtr (a) compenser (des pertes) (b) Typ: imprimer (un livre) en offset. 'offshoot n rejeton m. 'offshore a o. wind, vent de terre; o. islands, îles au large de la côte. 'offside 1. n Aut: (in UK) côté droit; (in France, NAm:) côté gauche 2. off'side adv Sp: hors jeu. 'offspring n 1. progéniture f 2. rejeton m. off'stage a & adv (a) dans les coulisses (b) (of life) privé. 'off-white n blanc cassé.

offal ['ɔfl] n (NAm: = variety meats) abats mpl; abattis mpl.

offend [ə'fend] 1. vi to o. against, violer (la loi); pécher contre (la politesse) 2. vtr (a) offenser, froisser (qn); to be offended at, by, sth, s'offenser de qch; easily offended, très susceptible (b) (of thg) to o. the eye, choquer la vue; it offends our sense of justice, cela choque notre sentiment de la justice. o'ffence, NAm: offense n 1. to take o. at sth, se froisser de qch; to give o. to s.o., blesser, froisser, qn; I mean no o., je ne veux offenser personne 2. offense f, faute f; infraction f (à la loi); Jur: crime m, délit m; minor o., contravention f. o'ffender n 1. Jur: délinquant, -ante; the chief o., le grand coupable 2. offenseur m. o'ffending a offensant, fautif. o'ffensive 1. (a) Mil: offensif (b) offensant, choquant; (odeur) nauséabonde (c) to be o. to s.o., insulter qn 2. n to take the o., prendre l'offensive f. o'ffensively adv 1. Mil: offensivement 2. désagréablement; d'un ton injurieux. o'ffensiveness n nature offensante.

offer ['ɔfər] 1. n offre f; any offers? combien m'en offrez-vous? that's the best o. I can make, c'est le plus que je puis offrir; o. of marriage, demande f en mariage; Com: £10 or near(est) o., environ £10; on o., (en) réclame 2. vtr (a) to o. s.o. sth, offrir qch à qn; how much will you o. for it? combien m'en offrez-vous? house offered for sale, maison mise en vente; to o. to do sth, offrir de, s'offrir à, faire qch (b) to o. a remark, an opinion, faire une remarque, avancer une opinion (c) to o. resistance, offrir, opposer, une résistance. 'offering n offrande f; offre f. 'offertory n Ecc: 1. offertoire m 2. quête f.

office ['ɔfis] n 1. office m, service m; through the good offices of s.o., par les bons offices de qn 2. (a) fonctions fpl (b) charge f, emploi m; to be in o., (of government) être au pouvoir; (of pers) être en fonction; NAm: o. holder, fonctionnaire mf 3. (a) bureau m; (lawyer's) o., étude f; (of company) head o., registered offices, bureau central; siège social; o. hours, heures de bureau; o. worker, employé, -ée, de

bureau; o. block, immeuble de bureaux; o. work, travail de bureau; o. boy, coursier, garçon de courses (b) private o., cabinet particulier (c) the Foreign O. = le ministère des Affaires étrangères (d) (of house) the usual offices, cuisine f, salle f de bains, sanitaires mpl.

officer ['ɔfisər] n 1. (a) fonctionnaire m, officier m; police o., agent m de police, de la sûreté (b) membre du bureau (d'une société) 2. Mil: officier; staff o., officier d'état-major; Av: pilot o., sous-lieutenant m; flying o., lieutenant m.

official [ə'fiʃ(ə)l] 1. a (a) officiel; to do sth in one's o. capacity, faire qch dans l'exercice de ses fonctions (b) (style) administratif; o. news, nouvelles officielles 2. n fonctionnaire mf; railway o., employé(e) des chemins de fer. o'fficialdom n la bureaucratie. officia'lese n F: jargon administratif. o'fficially adv officiellement. o'fficiate vi 1. Ecc: officier (à un office) 2. to o. as host, remplir les fonctions d'hôte. o'fficious a empressé; trop zélé. o'fficiously adv to behave o., faire l'empressé. o'fficiousness n excès m de zèle.

offing ['ɔfiŋ] n Nau: in the o., au large; F: I've got a job in the o., j'ai un emploi en perspective, en vue.

often ['ɔfn, 'ɔftən] adv souvent, fréquemment; less o., moins souvent; not o., rarement; once too o., une fois de trop; how o.? combien de fois? tous les combien? as o. as not, more o. than not, le plus souvent; every so o., de temps en temps.

ogle ['ougl] 1. n œillade f 2. vtr & i lorgner; faire les yeux doux.

ogre ['ougər], f ogress ['ougris] n ogre m, f ogresse f.

oh [ou] int oh!

ohm [oum] n El: ohm m.

OHMS abbr On His, Her, Majesty's Service.

oil [ɔil] I. n 1. huile f; olive o., huile d'olive; fried in o., frit à l'huile; o.-painting, peinture à l'huile; o. colours, couleurs à l'huile 2. mineral o., pétrole m, huile minérale; fuel o., mazout m; the o. industry, l'industrie pétrolière; o.(-fired) heating, chauffage au mazout; o. well, puits de pétrole; o. rig, (i) plate-forme f de forage (ii) (on land) derrick m; o. slick, nappe de pétrole; marée noire 3. essential o., essence f. II. v 1. vtr huiler, graisser, lubrifier (une machine); to o. the wheels, graisser les roues; F: faciliter les choses 2. vi Nau: faire le plein de mazout. 'oil-bearing a pétrolifère. 'oilcan n (a) bidon m à huile (b) burette f à huile. oiled a graissé, huilé; F: he's well o., il est un peu parti, (un peu) éméché. 'oilfield n champ m, gisement m, pétrolifère. 'oiling n graissage m, huilage m, lubrification f. 'oilskin n Cl: ciré m. 'oilstone n Tls: pierre f à huile (pour affûter). 'oil-tanker n pétrolier m. 'oily a (oilier, oiliest) (a) huileux, gras, graisseux (b) (of manner) onctueux.

ointment ['ɔintmənt] n onguent m, pommade f.

O.K. (also okay) [ou'kei] F: 1. int très bien! ça va! d'accord! 2. a that's O.K., d'accord! I'm O.K., (moi) ça va; if it's O.K. with you, si ça ne vous ennuie pas; si vous êtes d'accord; everything's O.K., tout est en règle; tout va bien 3. n approbation f; to give the O.K., donner le feu vert 4. vtr (O.K.'d, okayed) approuver (un projet).

okey-doke, okey-dokey, okie-doke, okie-dokey ['ouki'douk(i)] int P: ça va! d'accord!

okra ['ɔkrə] n okra m.

old [ould] a (older, oldest) 1. (a) vieux; âgé; **to grow o.**, vieillir; **to be getting o.**, se faire vieux; **to make s.o. look o.**, vieillir qn; **an o. man**, un vieillard; **an o. woman**, une vieille; **o. people, o. folk(s)**, les vieux; **o. people's home**, maison de retraite; **an o. maid**, une vieille fille; **o. wives' tale**, conte de bonne femme; npl **o. and young**, grands et petits; **o. age**, vieillesse f; **in my o. age**, quand je serai vieux; **sur mes vieux jours; to die at a good o. age**, mourir à un âge avancé, à un bel âge (b) **o. clothes**, vieux habits; **o. wine**, vin vieux 2. **how o. are you?** quel âge avez-vous? **to be five years o.**, avoir cinq ans; **he's older than I am**, il est plus âgé que moi; il est mon aîné; **older brother**, frère aîné; **the oldest boy**, le plus âgé; **older** (des garçons); **to be o. enough to do sth**, être d'âge à faire qch 3. (a) vieux, ancien; (famille) de vieille souche; **an o. friend of mine**, un vieil ami à moi; **an o. dodge**, un coup classique (b) **o. hand**, ouvrier expérimenté; **he's an o. hand (at it)**, il a du métier 4. (a) Sch: **an o. boy**, un ancien élève; F: **the o. boy network** = la franc-maçonnerie des grandes écoles; **in the o. days**, autrefois (b) **the O. World**, l'ancien monde; **the O. Country**, la mère-patrie 5. F: (a) **any o. thing**, la première chose venue; n'importe quoi; **it's the same o. story**, c'est toujours la même histoire (b) **the o. man**, (i) papa (ii) le patron. **'old-'age** a o.-a. **pension**, pension f de retraite; allocation f de vieillesse; **o.-a. pensioner**, retraité, -ée. **'olden** a Lit: **in o. days**, au temps jadis. **'old-es'tablished** a ancien; établi depuis longtemps. **'old-'fashioned** a 1. (i) l'ancienne mode (ii) démodé 2. (of pers, ideas) vieux jeu; **she is, it is, a bit o.-f.**, elle est, c'est, un peu vieux jeu 3. F: **an o.-f. look**, un regard de travers. **'oldish** a vieillot. **'old-'time** a o.-t. **dances**, danses fpl du bon vieux temps. **'old-'timer** n vieux (de la vieille). **'old-'world** a (a) (village) vieux et pittoresque (b) du temps jadis.

oleaginous [ouli'ædʒinəs] a oléagineux.

oleander [ouli'ændər] n Bot: laurier-rose m.

olfactory [ɔl'fæktəri] a (nerf) olfactif.

oligarchy ['ɔligaːki] n oligarchie f.

olive ['ɔliv] n 1. **o.** (tree), olivier m; **o. grove**, oliv(er)aie f; **o. branch**, rameau d'olivier; **to hold out the o. branch**, faire les premiers pas (pour une réconciliation) 2. olive f; **o. oil**, huile d'olive 3. Cu: paupiette f 4. a (teint) olivâtre; **o.(-green) dress**, robe vert olive.

Olympic [ə'limpik] a **the O. Games**, n **the Olympics**, les jeux olympiques.

ombudsman ['ɔmbudzmən] n médiateur m.

omelet(te) ['ɔmlit] n Cu: omelette f.

omen ['oumen] n présage m; augure m; **to take sth as a good o.**, tirer un bon augure de qch; **bird of ill o.**, oiseau de malheur, de mauvais augure. **'ominous** ['ɔm-] a de mauvais augure; sinistre; inquiétant. **'ominously** adv sinistrement.

omit [ou'mit] vtr (omitted) 1. omettre (qch) 2. **to o. to do sth**, omettre, oublier, de faire qch. **omission** [ə'miʃn] n 1. omission f 2. négligence f.

omnibus ['ɔmnibəs] (pl omnibus(s)es) a & n Pub: **o.** (volume), gros recueil (de contes).

omnipotence [ɔm'nipətəns] n omnipotence f. **om'nipotent** a omnipotent.

omniscience [ɔm'nisiəns] n omniscience. **om'niscient** a omniscient.

omnivorous [ɔm'nivərəs] a omnivore.

on [ɔn] I. prep 1. (a) sur; **to tread on sth**, marcher sur qch; **don't tread on it**, ne marchez pas dessus; **to be on the telephone**, (i) être abonné au téléphone (ii) parler au téléphone; **on the piano**, au piano; **on the radio**, à la radio; **dinner on the train**, dîner dans le train; **on the high seas**, en haute mer; **on the third floor**, au, du, troisième (étage) (b) **on shore**, à terre; **on foot**, à pied; **on a, my, bicycle**, à bicyclette; **on horseback**, à cheval (c) **to be on the committee**, être membre du comité; **to be on the staff**, faire partie du personnel 2. (a) **hanging on the wall**, pendu au mur; **on the ceiling**, au plafond; **have you any money on you?** avez-vous de l'argent (sur vous)? **on page four**, à la page quatre (b) **just on a year ago**, il y a près d'un an; **just on £5**, (tout) près de £5 3. (a) **on the right, left**, à droite, à gauche; **on this side**, de ce côté (b) **to turn one's back on s.o.**, tourner le dos à qn (c) **to hit s.o. on the head**, frapper qn sur la tête (d) **house on the main road**, maison sur la grande route (e) **on (to)**, sur, à; **the cat jumped on to the table**, le chat a sauté sur la table; **room that looks on (to) the street**, pièce qui donne sur la rue 4. **to have sth on good authority**, savoir qch de source certaine; **on pain of death**, sous peine de mort; **it all depends on circumstances**, tout dépend des circonstances; **on condition that**, à condition que 5. (a) **on Sundays**, le(s) dimanche(s); **on the following day**, le lendemain; **on April 3rd**, le trois avril; **on the evening of June the first**, le premier juin au soir; **on the day of my arrival**, le jour de mon arrivée (b) **on a warm day like this**, par une chaleur comme celle-ci; **on and after Monday**, à partir de lundi; **on or about the twelfth**, vers le douze; **on that occasion**, à, en, cette occasion; **on my arrival**, à mon arrivée; **on application**, sur demande; **on examination**, après examen 6. **on the cheap**, à bon marché; **on the sly**, en cachette, en douce 7. **on sale**, en vente 8. **to congratulate s.o. on his success**, féliciter qn de son succès; **keen on sth**, amateur de qch 9. **I am here on business**, je suis ici pour mes affaires; **on holiday**, en vacances; **on the way**, en chemin 10. **to have pity on s.o.**, avoir pitié de qn; **attack on s.o.**, attaque contre qn; F: **the drinks are on me**, c'est moi qui paie cette tournée; **the police have nothing on him**, la police n'a rien contre lui 11. (a) **many live on less than that**, beaucoup vivent avec moins que ça (b) **he's on insulin**, il suit un traitement à l'insuline; **to be on drugs**, se droguer 12. **to put money on a horse**, parier sur un cheval. II. adv 1. (a) **to put the kettle on**, mettre la bouilloire à chauffer; (of actor) **to be on**, être en scène; F: **it's just not on**, il n'en est pas question; on ne peut pas tolérer ça (b) **to put one's clothes on**, s'habiller; **what did he have on?** qu'est-ce qu'il portait? **to have nothing on**, être tout(e) nu(e); **put the lid on**, mets le couvercle 2. **to fly on, work on**, continuer son vol, son travail; **to talk on**, continuer à parler; **go on!** (i) continuez! allez toujours! (ii) P: pas vrai! **move on!** circulez! **and so on**, et ainsi de suite 3. **to be sideways on to sth**, présenter le côté à qch 4. (a) **later on**, plus tard; **from that day on**, à dater de ce jour; **well on in April**, bien avant dans le mois d'avril; **well on in years**, d'un âge avancé (b) F: **to have s.o. on**, monter un bateau à qn 5. (of gas) ouvert; (of electric circuit) fermé; **to turn**

the tap on, ouvrir le robinet; to turn the light on, allumer (la lumière); the engine is on, le moteur est en marche; the brakes are on, les freins sont serrés; to leave the light on, laisser la lumière allumée; what's on (at the theatre)? qu'est-ce qu'on joue actuellement? this film was on last week, ce film a passé la semaine dernière; have you anything on this evening? êtes-vous occupé ce soir? on with your work! va vite faire ton travail! 6. F: (a) I'm on! ça me va! (b) I was on to him on the phone yesterday, je lui ai parlé au téléphone hier; the police are on to him, la police est sur sa piste (c) he's always on at me, il s'en prend toujours à moi 7. on and off, par intervalles; à différentes reprises; on and on, sans arrêt. 'oncoming a o. traffic, véhicules venant en sens inverse. 'onlooker n spectateur, -trice. 'onrush n ruée f, attaque f. 'onset n (a) assaut m, attaque f (b) at the o., de prime abord; the o. of winter, l'approche f de l'hiver. 'onslaught n assaut m, attaque f. 'on-the-'job a o.-the-j. training, formation sur le tas. 'onto prep = on (to), sur, à. 'onward 1. adv see 'onwards 2. a (of motion) en avant. 'onwards adv (a) en avant; plus loin (b) from tomorrow o., à partir de demain; from this time o., désormais, dorénavant.

once [wʌns] adv 1. (a) une fois; o. only, une seule fois; o. before, une fois déjà; o. a week, tous les huit jours; o. more, encore une fois; o. in a while, une fois en passant; o. and for all, une (bonne) fois pour toutes; o. again, o. more, encore une fois; more than o., plus d'une fois; o. or twice, une ou deux fois; just for this o., pour cette fois; for o. you are right, pour une fois tu as raison; o. in a while, de temps en temps (b) (if) o. you hesitate it's all up with you, pour peu que vous hésitiez vous êtes fichu 2. autrefois; o. (upon a time) there was, il était une fois; I knew him o., je l'ai connu autrefois; o. when I was young, un jour, quand j'étais petit(e). 3. (a) at o., (i) tout de suite; immédiatement (ii) à la fois, en même temps; don't all speak at o., ne parlez pas tous à la fois (b) all at o., soudainement, subitement. 'once-over n F: to give sth the o.-o., jeter un coup d'œil sur qch.

one [wʌn] I. num a 1. (a) un; twenty-o. apples, vingt et une pommes; seventy-o., soixante et onze; eighty-o., quatre-vingt-un; a hundred and o., cent un (b) that's o. way of doing it, c'est une manière comme une autre de le faire; that's o. comfort, c'est déjà une consolation; for o. thing I am tired, entre autres raisons, je suis fatigué 2. (a) seul, unique; my o. and only suit, mon seul et unique costume; the o. way of doing it, le seul moyen de le faire (b) as o. man, comme un seul homme (c) même; all in o. direction, tous dans la même direction; it's all o., cela revient au même; it's all o. to me, cela m'est égal. II. n 1. the typist has left out a o., la dactylo a oublié un un; number o., numéro un; F: soi-même; chapter o., premier chapitre; to look after number o., faire passer ses intérêts en premier 2. (a) there's only o. left, il n'en reste qu'un; the top step but o., l'avant-dernière marche; the last but o., l'avant-dernier, -ière; all in o., (vêtement) en une pièce; to be at o., être d'accord (avec qn) (b) o. (pound) fifty, une livre cinquante pence; o. (o'clock), une heure (c) F: to land s.o. o., balancer un coup de poing à qn (d) one too many, un de trop. III. dem pron (a) this o., celui-ci, f celle-ci; which o. do you like best?

lequel, laquelle, préférez-vous? the o. on the table, celui, celle qui est sur la table; she's the o. who helped him, c'est elle qui l'a aidé (b) our dear ones, ceux qui nous sont chers; to pick the ripe plums and leave the green ones, cueillir les prunes mûres et laisser les vertes; F: that's a good o.! en voilà une bonne! he's a sharp o., c'est un malin (c) F: to have a quick o., prendre un pot. IV. indef a o. day, un jour; o. stormy evening, (par) un soir de tempête. V. indef pron 1. (pl some, any) I haven't a pencil, have you got o.? je n'ai pas de crayon, en avez-vous un? o. of them, (i) l'un d'entre eux; l'un d'eux (ii) P: un homosexuel; he's o. of the family, il est de la famille; not o. (of them), pas un; o. and all, tous sans exception; o. after the other, l'un après l'autre; o. by o., un(e) à un(e); o. of these ladies will see to it, une de ces dames va s'en occuper; you can't have o. without the other, l'un ne va pas sans l'autre; he's a clever o., c'est un malin 2. I for o. shall come, quant à moi, je viendrai; I'm not o. to, je ne suis pas de ceux qui; F: I'm not much of a o. for sweets, je ne suis pas grand amateur de bonbons 3. (subject) on; (object) vous; o. never knows, on ne sait jamais; it's enough to kill o., il y a de quoi vous faire mourir 4. one's, son, f sa, pl ses; votre, pl vos; to give one's opinion, donner son avis; to cut one's finger, se couper le doigt 5. o. another, l'un l'autre; to look at o. another, se regarder. 'one-'armed a (of pers) manchot; F: o.-a. bandit, machine f à sous. 'one-'eyed a borgne. 'one-'horse a F: o.-h. town, trou m; bled m. 'one-'legged [-'legid] a unijambiste. 'one-man a o.-m. show, exposition individuelle; (spectacle) solo. 'one-off a (article, livre) spécial, hors-série. one'self pron (a) to flatter o., se flatter; to talk to o., se parler à soi-même; to speak of o., parler de soi (b) one must do it o., il faut le faire soi-même. 'one-'sided a (a) (of bargain) inégal (b) (of judgment) partial. 'one-'storey(ed) a (maison) de plein-pied. 'one-'time a o.-t. mayor, ancien maire. 'one-to-'one a univoque; o.-to-o. conversation, tête-à-tête m inv. 'one-'track a he's got a o.-t. mind, il est complètement polarisé; il a une idée fixe. one-'upmanship n l'art de se faire passer pour supérieur aux autres. 'one-'way a (a) (billet) simple (b) (rue) à sens m unique.

onerous ['ounərəs] a onéreux; (tâche) pénible.

onion ['ʌnjən] n oignon m; spring o., ciboule f; o. soup, soupe à l'oignon; o. skin, pelure d'oignon.

only ['ounli] I. a seul, unique; o. son, fils unique; his one and o. hope, son seul et unique espoir; his o. answer was to burst out laughing, pour toute réponse il éclata de rire; you're the o. one, il n'y a que vous; you are not the o. one, vous n'êtes pas le seul. II. adv seulement; ne . . . que; I've o. (got) three, je n'en ai que trois; staff o., réservé au personnel; o. he can say, lui seul pourrait le dire; I o. touched it, je n'ai fait que le toucher; you've o. to ask for it, vous n'avez qu'à le demander; I will o. say, je me bornerai à dire; o. to think of it, rien que d'y penser; if o. I knew! si seulement je le savais! o. yesterday, hier encore; pas plus tard qu'hier; if o., si seulement. III. conj mais; it's a beautiful dress o. it's rather expensive, c'est une belle robe, seulement elle coûte cher.

onomatopoeia [ɔnəmætə'pi:ə] n onomatopée f.

ono abbr or near(est) offer, environ.

Ontario [ɔn'tɛəriou] *Prn Geog:* l'Ontario *m.*
On'tarian *n* Ontarien, -ienne.
onus ['ounəs] *n* responsabilité *f*, charge *f.*
onyx ['ɔniks] *n* onyx *m.*
oodles ['uːdəlz] *npl F:* des tas (de qch).
ooze [uːz] **1.** *n* vase *f*, limon *m* **2.** *vi* suinter, dégoutter; **his courage oozed away**, son courage l'abandonnait; *F:* **he's oozing with money**, il roule sur l'or. **'oozing** *n* suintement *m.*
op [ɔp] *n F:* **1.** *Med:* opération *f* **2.** *Mil:* **combined op(s)**, opération (i) amphibie (ii) inter-armées.
opacity [ou'pæsiti] *n* opacité *f.*
opal ['oup(ə)l] *n* opale *f.*
opaque [ou'peik] *a* opaque.
OPEC ['oupek] *abbr Organization of Petroleum Exporting Countries*, Organisation des pays exportateurs de pétrole, OPEP.
open ['oup(ə)n] **I.** *a* **1.** ouvert (*a*) **half o.**, entrouvert, entrebâillé; **to cut o.**, ouvrir (avec un couteau, un ciseau); **to throw the door wide o.**, ouvrir brusquement la porte toute grande (*b*) (*of box*) ouvert; (*of bottle*) débouché; (*of letter*) décacheté; (*of parcel*) défait (*c*) **o. to the public**, ouvert, accessible, au public; (*of shop, office*) **o. from ten to five**, ouvert de dix heures à cinq heures (*d*) *Jur:* **in o. court**, en plein tribunal **2.** sans limites; sans bornes; **in the o. air**, *n* **in the o.**, au grand air, en plein air; (*dormir*) à la belle étoile; **o. country**, pays découvert; **in the o. country**, en pleine campagne; **the o. sea**, la haute mer; le large **3.** (*a*) **o. carriage**, voiture découverte (*b*) **o. ground**, (*in forest*) clairière; (*in town*) terrain *m* vague; **o. space**, espace *m* libre; **o. field**, champ sans enclos (*c*) **o. to every wind**, exposé à tous les vents (*d*) **to lay oneself o. to criticism**, s'exposer, donner prise, à la critique (*e*) **o. to conviction**, accessible à la conviction; **o. to improvement**, susceptible d'amélioration **4.** (*a*) manifeste; public; **o. secret**, secret de polichinelle; **o. letter**, lettre ouverte (dans la presse); **o. scandal**, scandale public (*b*) franc; **o. admiration**, franche admiration; **o. enemy**, ennemi déclaré; **to be o. with s.o.**, parler franchement à qn; ne rien cacher à qn **5. o. wound**, plaie (i) béante (ii) non cicatrisée; **o. at the neck**, (chemise) à col ouvert **6.** non serré **7.** (*a*) non obstrué; **o. road**, chemin libre; **o. view**, vue dégagée (*b*) **the job is still o.**, le poste est toujours vacant; **two courses are o. to us**, deux possibilités nous sont offertes; **it's o. to you to object**, vous avez le droit de faire des objections **8.** non résolu; **o. question**, question discutable; **to keep an o. mind**, rester sans parti pris **9.** *Com:* **o. account**, compte ouvert; compte courant; **o. cheque**, chèque ouvert, non barré. **II.** *v* **1.** *vtr* (*a*) ouvrir (une porte); baisser (une glace); déboucher, entamer (une bouteille); décacheter (une lettre); défaire, ouvrir (un paquet); inaugurer (une fête); *Med:* relâcher (les intestins); **to o. one's mail**, dépouiller son courrier; **to o. a new shop**, ouvrir un nouveau magasin (*b*) ouvrir (la main, les yeux); écarter (les jambes) (*c*) **to o. a way, path, through sth**, ouvrir, frayer, un chemin à travers qch (*d*) commencer; entamer, engager (des négociations, une conversation); ouvrir (le feu); *Com:* ouvrir (un compte) **2.** *vi* (*a*) s'ouvrir; (*of door*) ~~to an o., s entrouvrir, s'entrebâiller; door that opens into the garden~~, porte qui ouvre sur le jardin; ~~exit opening on to the street~~, sortie qui donne accès à la

rue; **the bank opens at ten**, la banque ouvre (ses portes) à dix heures; **as soon as the season opens**, dès l'ouverture de la saison (*b*) (*of flower*) s'ouvrir, s'épanouir; (*of view*) s'étendre (*c*) (*of play*) commencer. **'open-'air** *a* (assemblée) en plein air; (activités, jeux) de plein air. **'opencast** *a* (exploitation) à ciel ouvert. **'opener** *n* (*a*) (*of pers*) ouvreur, -euse (*b*) **can, tin, o.**, ouvre-boîtes *m inv*; **bottle o.**, décapsulateur *m*; **letter o.**, coupe-papier *m inv.* **'open-'handed** *a* libéral, généreux. **'open-'heart** *a* (chirurgie) à cœur ouvert. **'open-'hearted** *a* **1.** franc, expansif **2.** au cœur tendre, compatissant. **'opening** *n* **1.** (*a*) ouverture *f*; débouchage *m* (d'une bouteille); dépouillement *m* (du courrier); *Com:* **late o. Friday**, nocturne *f* le vendredi (*b*) **formal o.**, inauguration *f* (*c*) (*at cards*) attaque *f* **2.** trou *m*, ouverture, orifice *m*; clairière *f* (dans un bois) **3.** occasion *f* favorable, opportunité *f*; *Com:* débouché *m*, créneau *m* (pour une marchandise); **to give s.o. an o. against you**, prêter le flanc à un adversaire **4.** *attrib* d'ouverture; inaugural; **o. sentence**, phrase de début. **'openly** *adv* ouvertement, franchement, en toute franchise; au vu et au su de tout le monde. **'open'minded** *a* qui a l'esprit ouvert, large; impartial; **to be o.-m. about sth**, être sans préjugés, sans parti pris, sur qch. **'open-'mouthed** *a* **to stand o.-m.**, rester bouche bée. **'open-'necked** *a* à col ouvert. **'openness** *n* franchise *f.* **'open 'out** *v* **1.** *vtr* ouvrir, déplier (une feuille de papier) **2.** *vi* (*of view*) s'ouvrir, s'étendre. **'open 'up** *v* **1.** *vtr* ouvrir (une mine); exposer, révéler (une perspective); frayer (un chemin); ouvrir (un pays au commerce) **2.** *vi F:* **make s.o. o. up**, délier la langue à qn.
opera ['ɔp(ə)rə] *n* opéra *m*; *TV: F:* **soap o.**, feuilleton *m* (à l'eau de rose); **o. glasses**, jumelles *f* de théâtre; **o. house**, opéra; **o. singer**, chanteur, -euse, d'opéra. **ope'ratic** *a* d'opéra; **o. singer**, chanteur, -euse, d'opéra. **ope'retta** *n* opérette *f.*
operate ['ɔpəreit] **1.** *vi* (*a*) opérer; (*of machine*) fonctionner (*b*) *Med:* **to o. on s.o.**, opérer qn; **to be operated on**, subir une opération **2.** *vtr* faire manœuvrer (une machine); faire jouer (un mécanisme). **'operable** *a Med:* (tumeur) opérable. **'operating** *n Med:* **o. table, o. theatre**, table, salle, d'opération (*b*) *Com:* opérationnel. **ope'ration** *n* **1.** fonctionnement *m*, action *f*; **to be in o.**, fonctionner, jouer; (*of machine*) être en marche; (*of law*) **to come into o.**, entrer en vigueur **2.** *Mil: etc* opération *f* **3.** *Med:* opération, intervention chirurgicale; **to have, to undergo, an o.**, subir une opération, se faire opérer; **to perform an o. on s.o.**, opérer qn. **ope'rational** *a* opérationnel. **'operative 1.** *a* opératif, actif; (*of law*) **to become o.**, entrer en vigueur; **the o. word**, le mot qui compte **2.** *n* ouvrier, -ière. **'operator** *n* opérateur, -trice; **switchboard o.**, standardiste *mf*; **radio o.**, radio *m*; *StExch:* joueur, -euse; *F:* **a smart o.**, un commerçant habile.
ophthalmic [ɔf'θælmik] *a Med:* ophtalmique. **ophthal'mologist** *n* ophtalmologiste *mf*, ophtalmologue *mf.* **ophthal'mology** *n* ophtalmologie *f.*
opinion [ə'pinjən] *n* (*a*) opinion *f*; avis *m*; **in my o.**, à mon avis; **to be entirely of s.o.'s o.**, abonder dans le sens de qn, être tout à fait de l'avis de qn; **to be of the o. that**, être d'avis que; **matter of o.**, affaire d'opinion; **to**

express an o., to give one's o., donner, exprimer, son opinion; **to ask s.o.'s o.,** consulter qn, demander l'avis de qn; **to form an o.,** se faire une opinion; **to have a high, low, o. of s.o.,** avoir une bonne, une mauvaise, opinion de qn; **what's your o. of him?** que pensez-vous de lui? **public o.,** l'opinion (publique); **o. poll,** sondage *m* d'opinion publique *(b)* consultation *f* (de médecin). **o'pinionated** *a* opiniâtre.

opium ['oupjəm] *n* opium *m*; **o. addict,** opiomane *mf.*

Oporto [ə'pɔːtou] *Prn Geog:* Porto *m.*

opossum [ə'pɔsəm] *n Z:* opossum *m.*

opponent [ə'pounənt] *n* adversaire *mf*, antagoniste *mf.*

opportune ['ɔpətjuːn] *a* opportun, convenable, commode; à propos; **the o. moment,** le moment opportun. **'opportunely** *adv* opportunément, en temps opportun, à propos; (arriver) à point (nommé), juste à point. **oppor'tunist** *n* opportuniste *mf.* **oppor'tunity** *n* occasion *f* (favorable); **golden o.,** affaire *f* d'or; **when the o. occurs,** à l'occasion; **at the earliest, first, o.,** à la première occasion; **to miss an o.,** laisser passer une occasion; **if I get an o.,** si l'occasion se présente; *Com:* **fantastic sales opportunities,** soldes et occasions exceptionnels; **job opportunities,** débouchés *mpl.*

oppose [ə'pouz] *vtr* **1.** opposer **2.** s'opposer à (qn, qch); résister à (qn, qch); *Pol: etc:* **to o. the motion,** mettre opposition à la proposition. **o'pposed** *a* **1.** opposé, hostile; **papers o. to the government,** journaux hostiles au gouvernement **2. sth as o. to sth,** qch par opposition à, par contraste avec, qch. **o'pposing** *a* opposé; **the o. forces,** les forces qui s'opposent; *Sp:* **o. team,** équipe adverse.

opposite ['ɔpəzit] **1.** *a (a)* opposé (to, à); vis-à-vis, en face; **see the diagram on the o. page,** voir la figure ci-contre; **the house o.,** la maison (d')en face *(b)* contraire; **the o. sex,** l'autre sexe *m*; **o. poles,** pôles *m* contraires; **in the o. direction,** en sens opposé, inverse; *(of pers)* **o. number,** homologue *mf* **2.** *n* opposé *m*; le contre-pied; **the o. of what he said,** le contraire de ce qu'il a dit **3.** *adv* vis-à-vis; en face **4.** *prep* en face de, vis-à-vis de; **o. the church,** en face de l'église. **oppo'sition** *n (a)* opposition *f*; **in o. to public opinion,** contrairement à l'opinion publique *(b)* résistance *f*; **to meet with no o.,** ne rencontrer aucune résistance *(c)* (le) camp adverse; *Pol:* (le parti de) l'opposition; **o. spokesman,** porte-parole de l'opposition *(d)* **to set up (shop) in o. to s.o.,** ouvrir un magasin en concurrence avec qn.

oppress [ə'pres] *vtr (a)* opprimer *(b)* oppresser, accabler (l'esprit). **o'ppression** *n (a)* oppression *f*; abus *m* d'autorité *(b)* accablement *m* (de l'esprit). **o'ppressive** *a* **1.** oppressif, opprimant, tyrannique **2.** *(a) (of atmosphere)* lourd, étouffant *(b) (of grief)* accablant. **o'ppressively** *adv* **1.** oppressivement, tyranniquement **2.** d'une manière accablante. **o'ppressiveness** *n* **1.** caractère oppressif (d'un gouvernement) **2.** lourdeur (du temps). **o'ppressor** *n (a)* oppresseur *(b)* **the oppressors and the oppressed,** les opprimants *m* et les opprimés *m.*

opprobrium [ə'proubriəm] *n* opprobre *m.* **o'pprobrious** *a* injurieux.

opt [ɔpt] *vi* opter (for, pour). **'opt 'out** *vi* **to o. o. (of sth),** décider de ne pas participer (à qch).

optical ['ɔptik(ə)l] *a* **1.** optique **2.** (instrument) d'optique; **o. illusion,** illusion d'optique. **'optic** *a Anat:* **o. nerve,** nerf *m* optique. **op'tician** *n* (*NAm* = **optometrist**) opticien, -ienne. **'optics** *npl* l'optique *f.*

optimal ['ɔptiməl] *a* optimal.

optimist ['ɔptimist] *n* optimiste *mf.* **'optimism** *n* optimisme *m.* **opti'mistic** *a* optimiste. **opti'mistically** *adv* avec optimisme. **'optimum** *n (pl* **-a**) optimum; **o. conditions,** conditions optimum.

option ['ɔpʃ(ə)n] *n* option *f*, choix *m*; **I have no o.,** je n ai pas le choix; **to take an o. on,** prendre une option sur. **'optional** *a* facultatif.

optometrist [ɔp'tɔmətrist] *n NAm:* (*Br* = **optician**) opticien, -ienne.

opulence ['ɔpjuləns] *n* opulence *f*, richesse *f.* **'opulent** *a* opulent. **'opulently** *adv* avec opulence.

opus ['oupəs] *n* opus *m.*

or [ɔːr] *conj (a)* ou; *(with neg)* ni; **either one or the other,** soit l'un soit l'autre; l'un ou l'autre; **he can't read or write,** il ne sait ni lire ni écrire; **without money or luggage,** sans argent ni bagages; **in a day or two,** dans un jour ou deux; **ten kilometres or so,** une dizaine de kilomètres; **do it or else!** fais-le sinon (tu seras puni)! *(b)* **keep still or I'll shoot!** ne bougez pas, ou je tire!

oracle ['ɔrəkl] *n* oracle *m.* **o'racular** *a* (style) oraculaire, d'oracle.

oral ['ɔːr(ə)l] *a* **1.** oral; *Sch:* **o. examination** *n* o., (examen) oral *(m)* **2.** *Med:* **o. vaccine,** vaccin buccal; **o. administration,** administration par la bouche. **'orally** *adv* **1.** oralement; de vive voix **2.** *Med:* par la bouche; par voie buccale.

orange ['ɔrin(d)ʒ] *n* **1.** orange *f*; **blood o.,** sanguine *f* **2.** **o. (tree),** oranger *m*; **o. blossom,** fleurs *fpl* d'oranger; **o. grove,** orangeraie *f* **3.** *a & n (colour)* orangé *(m)*; orange *(m) inv.* **oran'geade** *n* orangeade *f.*

orang-outang, -utan [ə'ræŋuː'tæŋ, -'tæn] *n Z:* orang-outan(g) *m, pl* orangs-outan(g)s.

oration [ə'reiʃ(ə)n, ɔ-] *n* allocation *f*, discours *m*; **funeral o.,** oraison *f* funèbre. **'orator** *n* orateur *m.* **ora'torical** *a (a)* (style) oratoire *(b)* (discours) verbeux, ampoulé. **'oratory¹** *n* l'art *m* oratoire; l'éloquence *f.*

oratorio [ɔrə'tɔːriou, -ouz] *n (pl* **oratorios**) *Mus:* oratorio *m.*

oratory² ['ɔrət(ə)ri] *n Ecc:* oratoire *m*; chapelle privée.

orb [ɔːb] *n* orbe *m*; globe *m*, sphère *f.*

orbit ['ɔːbit] **I.** *n (a)* orbite *f*; **to put a satellite into o.,** mettre un satellite en orbite; **to go into o.,** être mis sur orbite *(b)* **the Russian o.,** la sphère d'influence soviétique. **II.** *vtr & i* décrire une orbite (autour de la lune).

orchard ['ɔːtʃəd] *n* verger *m*; **apple o.,** verger de pommiers.

orchestra ['ɔːkistrə] *n* orchestre *m.* **or'chestral** [-'kes-] *a* orchestral. **'orchestrate** *vtr Mus:* orchestrer. **orches'tration** *n* orchestration *f*, instrumentation *f.*

orchid ['ɔːkid] *n Hort:* orchidée *f.* **'orchis** *n Bot:* orchis *m.*

ordain [ɔː'dein] *vtr* **1.** *Ecc:* **to o. s.o. priest,** ordonner qn prêtre; **to be ordained,** recevoir les ordres; être reçu, ordonné, prêtre 2. (a) **so fate ordains**, ainsi le veut le sort (b) (*of pers*) décréter (une mesure); prescrire, ordonner.

ordeal [ɔː'diːl] *n* épreuve *f*; **it is an o. for me**, cela me met au supplice.

order ['ɔːdər] **I.** *n* **1.** ordre *m* (a) **workmanship of the highest o.**, travail de premier ordre, de qualité supérieure (b) *Ecc:* **holy orders**, ordres sacrés; **to be in holy orders**, être prêtre (c) **monastic o.**, ordre religieux; communauté *f*; **o. of knighthood**, ordre de chevalerie (d) **to wear all one's orders**, porter toutes ses décorations **2.** ordre, succession *f*, suite *f*; **in alphabetical o.**, en, par, ordre alphabétique; **out of (its) o.**, hors de son rang **3.** *Mil:* (a) **close o., open o.**, ordre serré, ouvert (b) **in review o.**, en grande tenue **4.** (a) **to set one's house in o.**, remettre de l'ordre dans ses affaires; **is your passport in o.?** votre passeport est-il en règle? (*of machine*) **in working o.**, en bon état de fonctionnement; **out of o.**, détraqué; en mauvais état; en panne; (téléphone) en dérangement; **to get out of o.**, se dérégler, se détraquer (b) *Parl: etc:* **in o.**, dans les règles; **to call s.o. to o.**, rappeler qn à l'ordre **5. law and o.**, l'ordre public **6. in o. to do sth**, afin de, pour, faire qch; **in o. to put you on your guard**, pour que vous soyez sur vos gardes; **in o. that they may see it**, afin qu'ils puissent le voir **7.** (a) commandement *m*, instruction *f*, *Mil: etc:* consigne *f*; **I have orders to do it**, j'ai ordre de le faire; **orders are orders**, les ordres sont les ordres; **until further orders**, jusqu'à nouvel ordre (b) *Com:* commande *f*; **o. book**, carnet de commandes; **made to o.**, fait sur commande; *F:* **that's a tall o.!** c'est demander un peu trop! **8.** (a) arrêt *m*; *Jur:* **o. of the court**, injonction *f* de la cour; **deportation o.**, arrêté *m* d'expulsion; *Mil:* **mention in orders**, citation *f* (à l'ordre du jour) (b) **money o.**, **postal o.**, mandat (postal), mandat-poste *m*; **banker's o.**, ordre de virement bancaire; **standing o.**, ordre de virement permanent. **II.** *vtr* (a) **to o. s.o. to do sth**, ordonner, commander, à qn de faire qch; **to o. s.o. about**, faire marcher, faire aller, qn; donner des ordres à qn (b) *Med:* prescrire, ordonner (un traitement) (c) *Com:* commander; **to o. a taxi**, appeler un taxi. **'orderliness** *n* **1.** bon ordre; méthode *f* **2.** habitudes *fpl* d'ordre **3.** discipline *f*; calme *m*. **'orderly I.** *a* (a) ordonné, méthodique; (*of life*) réglé, rangé, régulier; (*of pers*) **to be very o.**, avoir beaucoup de méthode (b) (*of crowd*) tranquille, discipliné. *n Mil:* planton *m*; **to be on o. duty**, être de planton; **o. officer**, officier de service; **medical o.**, infirmier *m*; **o. room**, salle des rapports.

ordinal ['ɔːdin(ə)l] *a & n* ordinal (*m*).

ordinance ['ɔːdinəns] *n* (*NAm:* = **bylaw**) ordonnance *f*, décret *m*, règlement *m*; **police o.**, arrêté *m*, ordonnance, de police.

ordinary ['ɔːdin(ə)ri] **I.** *a* **1.** ordinaire; coutumier; normal; **an o. tourist**, un touriste banal; **the o. Englishman**, l'Anglais moyen, typique; *Sch:* **o. level (exam)** = premier examen du *General Certificate of Education* **2.** *Pej:* **a very o. kind of man**, un homme très quelconque. **II.** *n* ordinaire *m*; **out of the o.**, exceptionnel; peu ordinaire. **'ordinarily, ordi'narily** *adv* ordinairement, normalement; à l'ordinaire, d'ordinaire; d'habitude.

ordination [ɔːdi'neɪʃ(ə)n] *n Ecc:* ordination *f*.

ordnance ['ɔːdnəns] *n* **1.** artillerie *f* **2.** *Mil:* **Royal Army O. Corps** = Service *m* du Matériel; **O. Survey**, service *m* topographique.

ore [ɔːr] *n* minerai *m*; **iron o.**, minerai de fer.

oregano [ɔri'gɑːnou] *n* origan *m*.

organ ['ɔːgən] *n* **1.** *Mus:* orgue *m*, orgues *fpl*; **street o.**, orgue de Barbarie **2.** (a) organe *m*; **the vocal organs**, l'appareil vocal (b) journal *m*, bulletin *m*, organe. **or'ganic** *a* **1.** (maladie) organique **2.** (a) **o. beings**, êtres organisés (b) **o. chemistry**, chimie *f* organique (c) **o. foods**, aliments produits à l'aide d'un engrais organique. **or'ganically** *adv* **1.** organiquement **2.** foncièrement; **the system is o. wrong**, le système est foncièrement mauvais **3. o. grown foods**, aliments produits à l'aide d'un engrais organique. **'organism** *n* organisme *m*. **'organist** *n Mus:* organiste *mf*. **organi'zation** *n* organisation *f*; organisme *m* (politique); entreprise *f*; **youth o.**, mouvement *m* de jeunesse. **'organize** *vtr* organiser (qch); arranger (un concert); **to get organized**, s'organiser. **'organizer** *n* organisateur, -trice.

orgasm ['ɔːgæzm] *n* orgasme *m*.

orgy ['ɔːdʒi] *n* orgie *f*; **o. of colour**, orgie de couleurs.

orient ['ɔːriənt] *n Geog:* **the O.**, l'Orient *m*. **ori'ental I.** *a* oriental; d'Orient **2.** *n* Oriental, -ale. **'orientate** *vtr* orienter. **orien'tation** *n* orientation *f*. **orien'teering** *n Sp:* exercice d'orientation.

orifice ['ɔrifis] *n* orifice *m*.

origin ['ɔridʒin] *n* origine *f*; **country of o.**, pays de provenance; **certificate of o.**, certificat d'origine. **o'riginal I.** *a* (a) originaire, primordial, primitif; **o. meaning of a word**, sens premier d'un mot (b) (ouvrage) original; **it's not an o. scheme**, le projet n'est pas inédit **2.** *n* original *m* (d'un tableau); **to read a French author in the o.**, lire un auteur français dans l'original. **origi'nality** *n* originalité *f*. **o'riginally** *adv* **1.** (a) originairement; à l'origine (b) originellement; dès l'origine **2.** originalement. **o'riginate I.** *vtr* faire naître, donner naissance à, être l'auteur de (qch) **2.** *vi* tirer son origine, dériver, provenir (**from, in,** de); avoir son origine (dans). **origi'nation** *n* création *f*, imitation *f* (d'une œuvre). **o'riginator** *n* créateur, -trice; auteur *m*; initiateur, -trice; promoteur *m* (d'une industrie).

oriole ['ɔːrioul] *n Orn:* (*European*) loriot *m*; (*American*) troupiale *m*, *FrC:* oriole *m*.

Orkneys (the) [ðiː'ɔːkniz] *Prn pl Geog:* les Orcades *f*.

ornament 1. *n* ['ɔːnəmənt] ornement *m* **2.** *vtr* ['ɔːnəment] orner, ornementer, décorer. **orna'mental** *a* ornemental; d'ornement. **ornamen'tation** *n* **1.** ornementation *f*, décoration *f* **2.** les ornements.

ornate [ɔː'neit] *a* orné; surchargé d'ornements.

ornery ['ɔːnəri] *a NAm: F:* grincheux.

ornithology [ɔːni'θɔlədʒi] *n* ornithologie *f*. **ornitho'logical** *a* ornithologique. **orni'thologist** *n* ornithologiste *mf*, ornithologiste *mf*.

orphan ['ɔːf(ə)n] **1.** *n & a* **an o.** (**child**), un(e) orphelin(e) **2.** *vtr* rendre orphelin(e). **'orphanage** *n* orphelinat *m*.

orthodontics [ɔːθou'dɔntiks] *npl Dent:* orthodontie *f*.

orthodox [´ɔ:θədɔks] *a* orthodoxe. **´orthodoxy** *n* orthodoxie *f.*

orthography [ɔ:´θɔgrəfi] *n* orthographe *f.* **ortho´graphical** *a* orthographique.

orthopaedic [ɔ:θə´pi:dik] *a* orthopédique. **ortho´paedics** *npl Med:* orthopédie *f.* **ortho´paedist** *n Med:* orthopédiste *mf.*

oscillate [´ɔsileit] *vi & tr* osciller; faire osciller. **osci´llation** *n* oscillation *f.* **o´scilloscope** *n* oscilloscope *m.*

osier [´ouziər] *n* osier *m*; **o. bed**, oseraie *f.*

osmosis [ɔz´mousis] *n Ph: Ch:* osmose *f.*

osprey [´ɔsprei] *n Orn:* balbuzard pêcheur.

osseous [´ɔsiəs] *a* osseux. **ossifi´cation** *n* ossification *f.* **´ossify** *vtr & i* (s')ossifier.

Ostend [ɔs´tend] *Prn Geog:* Ostende.

ostensible [ɔs´tensibl] *a* prétendu; qui sert de prétexte; soi-disant; feint. **os´tensibly** *adv* en apparence; censément; **he went out o. to**, il est sorti sous prétexte de, soi-disant pour.

ostentation [ɔsten´teiʃ(ə)n] *n* ostentation *f.* **osten´tatious** *a* plein d'ostentation; fastueux. **osten´tatiously** *adv* avec ostentation.

osteopath [´ɔstiəpæθ] *n* ostéopathe *m.*

ostracism [´ɔstrəsizm] *n* ostracisme *m.* **´ostracize** *vtr* ostraciser (qn).

ostrich [´ɔstritʃ] *n* (*pl* **ostriches**) autruche *f*; **o. feather**, plume *f* d'autruche.

other [´ʌðər] **1.** *a* autre (*a*) **the o. one**, l'autre; **the o. day**, l'autre jour; **every o. day**, tous les deux jours; **some o. day**, un autre jour (*b*) **the o. four**, les quatre autres; (*c*) **things being equal**, toutes choses égales (*c*) **people have seen it**, d'autres l'ont vu; **o. people's property**, le bien d'autrui; **any o. book**, tout autre livre **2.** *pron* autre (*a*) **one after the o.**, l'un après l'autre (*b*) **the others**, les autres, le reste (*c*) **some ... others ...**, les uns ... les autres ...; **I have no o.**, je n'en ai pas d'autre; **someone or o.**, quelqu'un; je ne sais qui; **one or o. of us**, l'un de nous; **this day of all others**, ce jour entre tous (*d*) (*of pers*) **the happiness of others**, le bonheur d'autrui **3.** *adv* autrement; **I could not do o. than**, je n'ai pu faire autrement que. **´otherwise** *adv* **1.** autrement (**than**, que); **he couldn't do o.**, il n'a pu faire autrement; **should it be o.**, dans le cas contraire; **if he's not o. engaged**, s'il n'est pas occupé à autre chose; **except where o. stated**, sauf indication contraire **2.** autrement; sans quoi, sans cela; dans le cas contraire **3.** sous d'autres rapports; par ailleurs; **o. he's quite sane**, à part ça il est complètement sain d'esprit. **other ´worldly** *a* détaché de ce monde.

otter [´ɔtər] *n Z:* loutre *f*; **o. (skin)**, loutre.

ouch [autʃ] *int* aïe!

ought [ɔ:t] *v aux* (*with present and past meaning, inv:* **o. not** *is frequently abbreviated to* **oughtn't**) (*parts of*) devoir, falloir **1.** (*obligation*) **one o. never to be unkind**, il ne faut, on ne doit, jamais être malveillant; **I thought I o. to tell you**, j'ai cru devoir vous en faire part; **to behave as one o.**, se conduire comme il faut **2.** (*vague desirability*) **you o. not to have waited**, vous n'auriez pas dû attendre; **you o. to see the exhibition**, vous devriez aller voir l'exposition; **you o. to have seen it!** il fallait voir ça! *F:* **I o. to be going**, il est temps que je parte **3.** (*probability*) **your horse o. to win**, votre

cheval a de grandes chances de gagner; **that o. to do**, je crois que cela suffira; *F:* **you o. to know**, vous êtes bien placé pour le savoir.

ounce [auns] *n Meas:* once *f* (= 28.35 g); **he hasn't an o. of courage**, il n'a pas pour deux sous de courage.

our [ɑ:r, ´auər] *poss a* notre, *pl* nos; **o. house and garden**, notre maison et notre jardin; **o. friends**, nos ami(e)s; **it's one of o. books**, c'est un livre (i) à nous (ii) que nous avons écrit (iii) publié par notre maison. **ours** *poss pron* le nôtre, la nôtre, les nôtres; **this is o.**, c'est le, la, nôtre; ceci est à nous; ceci nous appartient; **a friend of o.**, un(e) de nos ami(e)s. **our´selves** *pers pron pl* (*a*) **we did it o.**, nous l'avons fait nous-mêmes; **we o. are to blame**, c'est nous qui sommes à blâmer (*b*) (*at meal*) **we can help o.**, nous pouvons nous servir; **we enjoyed o.**, nous nous sommes amusés (*c*) (*after preposition*) **we say to o.**, nous nous disons; **amongst o.**, entre nous; **by o.**, tout seuls, toutes seules.

oust [aust] *vtr* **1. to o. s.o. from his post**, déloger qn de son poste **2.** prendre la place de (qn); évincer, supplanter (qn).

out [aut] **I.** *adv* **1.** dehors (*a*) **to go o.**, sortir; **o. you go!** sortez! **to throw sth o.**, jeter qch dehors; *Nau:* **the voyage out.**, l'aller *m* (*b*) **my father is o.**, mon père est sorti; **he's o. in the garden**, il est dans le jardin; **he's o. and about again**, il est de nouveau sur pied; *Ind:* **the men are o.**, les ouvriers sont en grève; **a long way o. (of the town)**, loin de la ville; **o. at sea**, en mer, au large; **o. there**, là-bas; **o. here**, ici; **the tide is o.**, la marée est basse **2. to lean o.**, se pencher au dehors; **to hang o. the washing**, étendre le linge **3.** (*a*) **to o. air**, découvert, exposé; **the sun is o.**, il fait du soleil; **the book is just o.**, le livre vient de paraître; **the secret is o.**, le secret est connu, éventé (*b*) **to pull o. a revolver**, tirer, sortir, un revolver; *F:* **o. with it!** achevez donc! allons, dites-le! expliquez-vous! (*c*) (*of flower*) épanoui; **the hawthorn is o.**, l'aubépine est en fleur (*d*) **all o.**, (aller) à toute vitesse (*e*) **o. loud**, tout haut, à haute voix; **to tell s.o. sth straight o.**, dire qch à qn carrément (*f*) *F:* **I'm not o. to do that**, je n'ai pas entrepris de faire cela **4.** **shoulder o. (of joint)**, épaule luxée; **I'm (quite) o. of practice**, je n'ai plus la main; **the Conservatives are o.**, les Conservateurs ne sont plus au pouvoir; *Games:* **o.** (déclaré) hors-jeu; *F:* **to be o. on one's feet**, tituber de fatigue **5. to be o. in one's calculations**, être loin de son compte; **I'm five pounds o.**, j'ai une erreur de cinq livres dans mes comptes; **I wasn't far o.**, je ne me trompais pas de beaucoup; **you've put me o.**, vous m'avez dérouté **6.** (*of fire*) éteint **7.** (*a*) à bout; achevé; **before the week is o.**, avant la fin de la semaine (*b*) **hear me o.**, écoutez-moi jusqu'au bout; **to fight it o.**, se battre jusqu'à une décision (*c*) **the plan is now definitely o.**, le plan a été définitivement abandonné **8.** **o. of** (*a*) hors de, au dehors de, en dehors de; **it is o. of my power to**, il n'est pas en mon pouvoir de; **to be o. of things**, être laissé à l'écart; **to feel o. of it**, se sentir dépaysé, de trop (*b*) **o. of season**, hors saison; **o. of date**, démodé; **times o. of number**, maintes et maintes fois; **to be o. of one's mind**, avoir perdu la raison (*c*) **to throw sth o. of the window**, jeter qch par la fenêtre; **to turn s.o. o. of the house**, mettre qn à la porte; **to get money o. of s.o.**, obtenir de l'argent de qn (*d*) dans, à, par; **to drink o. of a glass**, boire dans un verre; **to drink o. of the bottle**, boire à (même) la bouteille; **he took it**

o. of the drawer, il l'a pris dans le tiroir; to copy sth o. of a book, copier qch dans un livre; to look o. of the window, regarder par la fenêtre (e) parmi, d'entre; choose one o. of these ten, choisissez-en un parmi les dix; one o. of every three, un sur trois (f) hut made o. of a few old planks, cabane faite de quelques vieilles planches (g) o. of respect, par respect (pour qn); o. of curiosity, par curiosité; to act o. of fear, agir sous le coup de la peur (h) to be o. of, to have run o. of, tea, ne plus avoir de thé; Pub: o. of print, épuisé. II. n to know the ins and outs of sth, connaître qch dans tous ses détails. 'out and 'out 1. adv phr complètement, absolument 2. a an o. a. o. liar, un menteur fieffé, achevé. 'outback n Austr: l'intérieur m. out-'bid vtr (outbid; outbid) (at auction) renchérir sur (qn). 'outboard a Nau: o. motor, moteur m horsbord. 'outbreak n 1. éruption f; début m, ouverture f (des hostilités); Med: épidémie f (de grippe) 2. révolte f; émeute f. 'outbuilding n bâtiment extérieur; annexe f; pl outbuildings, dépendances f. 'outburst n éruption f, explosion f; éclat m (de rire); élan m (de générosité). 'outcast a & n expulsé, -ée; proscrit, -ite. 'outcaste a & n hors-caste (mf). out'class vtr Sp: surpasser. 'outcome n issue f, résultat m, dénouement m. 'outcrop n Geol: affleurement m. 'outcry n réclamations indignées. out'dated a démodé; vieux jeu. out'distance vtr distancer, dépasser (un concurrent). out'do vtr (outdid; outdone) surpasser (qn); l'emporter sur (qn). 'outdoor a extérieur; au dehors (jeux) de plein air; to put on one's o. clothes, s'habiller pour sortir. out'doors adv dehors; hors de la maison; en plein air; (coucher) à la belle étoile. 'outer a extérieur, externe; o. space, l'espace intersidéral; o. garments, vêtements m de dessus. 'outermost a le plus écarté; le plus à l'extérieur. 'outfit n 1. équipement m, équipage m; attirail m; tool o., jeu m d'outils; first aid o., trousse f de premiers secours 2. (of clothes) trousseau m; effets mpl; Mil: équipement 3. F: organisation f. 'outfitter n Com: marchand m de confections, confectionneur m. out'flank vtr (a) Mil: déborder (l'ennemi) (b) circonvenir (qn). 'outflow n écoulement m, dépense f (d'eau); décharge f (d'un égout). 'outgoing a (a) sortant; o. tide, marée descendante; o. mail, courrier à expédier (b) (of pers) sociable, qui se lie facilement. 'outgoings npl dépenses f; débours m; sorties f de fonds. out'grow vtr (outgrew; outgrown) devenir trop grand pour (ses vêtements); perdre (une habitude, le goût de qch). 'outhouse n (a) dépendance f (b) appentis m, hangar m. 'outing n (a) promenade f (b) excursion f, sortie f. out'landish a bizarre, étrange. out'last vtr durer plus longtemps que (qch); survivre à (qn). 'outlaw 1. n hors la loi m inv 2. vtr mettre (qn) hors-la-loi. 'outlay n débours mpl, dépenses fpl, frais mpl; capital o., dépenses d'établissement. 'outlet n 1. orifice m d'émission; issue f 2. Com: débouché m (pour marchandises). 'outline 1. n contour m, profil m; general o. of a plan, ébauche f d'un projet 2. vtr ébaucher (un projet); esquisser (qch). out'live vtr survivre à (qn). 'outlook n vue f; the o. is not very promising, les perspectives ne sont pas encourageantes; to share s.o.'s o., entrer dans les

idées, les vues, de qn. 'outlying a éloigné, écarté. outma'noeuvre, NAm: outma'neuver vtr déjouer (qn). out'moded a démodé. out'number vtr l'emporter en nombre sur, être plus nombreux que (l'ennemi). 'out-of-'date a (a) vieilli; démodé; vieux jeu (b) (passeport) périmé. 'out-of-'doors adv = outdoors. out-of-'pocket a o.-o.-p. expenses, menues dépenses; débours mpl. 'out-of-the-'way a 1. (of house) écarté 2. peu ordinaire; (of price) not o.-of-t.-w., pas exorbitant. out'pace vtr dépasser; distancer. 'out-patient n malade mf externe; out-patients' department, service m de consultations externes. 'outpost n Mil: poste avancé; poste colonial. 'output n rendement m (d'une machine); production f (d'une mine); débit m (d'un générateur).

outrage ['autreidʒ] 1. n (a) outrage m, atteinte f (b) (bomb) o., attentat m (à la bombe) (c) it's an o.! c'est un scandale! 2. vtr outrager, faire outrage à (la morale). out'rageous a (a) immodéré, indigne; (of price) excessif (b) outrageant, outrageux; (of conduct) scandaleux, atroce. out'rageously adv (a) immodérément; outre mesure; o. expensive, horriblement cher (b) d'une façon scandaleuse, indigne.

outright ['autrait] I. adv 1. (a) complètement; to buy sth o., acheter qch comptant, à forfait (b) to kill s.o. o., tuer qn net, sur le coup 2. franchement, carrément; to laugh o. (at s.o.), éclater de rire (au nez de qn); to refuse o., refuser net, carrément. II. a 1 o. sale, vente à forfait; o. purchase, marché m forfaitaire 2. (of manner) franc, carré.

outset ['autset] n commencement m; at the o., au début; tout d'abord; from the o., dès le début, dès l'origine, dès le principe.

outside [aut'said] 1. n (a) extérieur m, dehors m; on the o. of sth, à l'extérieur de qch; to open a door from the o., ouvrir une porte du dehors (b) at the o., tout au plus; au maximum (c) Fb: ailier m 2. a (a) du dehors, extérieur (b) an o. opinion, un avis du dehors, un avis étranger (c) it's an o. chance, il y a tout juste une chance (de réussite). 3. adv dehors, à l'extérieur, en dehors; I've left my dog o., j'ai laissé mon chien dehors, à la porte; he's playing o., il joue dehors; seen from o., vu de dehors 4. prep en dehors de, hors de, à l'extérieur de; o. the house, en dehors de la maison; o. the door, à la porte. out'sider n (a) étranger, -ère; profane mf; intrus, -use (b) Rac: outsider m.

outsize ['autsaiz] n Com: dimension f; pointure f, hors série; taille exceptionnelle; for outsizes, pour les grandes tailles; a o. packet, paquet géant.

outskirts ['autskɔ:ts] npl abords mpl; lisière f (d'une forêt); faubourgs mpl, banlieue f, approches fpl (d'une ville).

outspoken [aut'spoukən] a (of pers) franc; to be o., avoir son franc-parler. out'spokenly adv franchement; carrément. out'spokenness n franchise f; franc-parler m.

outstanding [aut'stændiŋ] a 1. (résultat) remarquable, exceptionnel; (trait) saillant; (incident) marquant; (artiste) éminent 2. (affaire) en suspens; (compte) impayé, dû; (paiement) en retard, arriéré. out'standingly adv éminemment; remarquablement, exceptionnellement; he's not o. talented, son talent n'est pas exceptionnel.

outstay [aut'stei] *vtr* 1. rester plus longtemps que (qn) 2. **to o. one's welcome,** abuser de, lasser, l'amabilité de ses hôtes.

outstretched [aut'stretʃt] *a* déployé; étendu; (bras) tendu; **with arms o.,** les bras étendus.

outvote [aut'vout] *vtr* obtenir une majorité sur (qn); **to be outvoted,** être mis en minorité.

outward ['autwəd] 1. *a (a)* en dehors; *Nau:* pour l'étranger; *Rail:* **o. half,** billet *m* d'aller; **the o. voyage,** l'aller *m (b)* extérieur; de dehors 2. *adv* au dehors; *Nau:* **o. bound,** (navire) (i) en partance, sortant (ii) faisant route pour l'étranger. **'outwardly** *adv* 1. à l'extérieur, au dehors 2. en apparence. **'outwards** *adv* au dehors; vers l'extérieur.

outwear [aut'wɛər] *vtr* (**outwore, outworn**) (*of clothes*) user (complètement); **outworn idea,** idée désuète, démodée

outweigh [aut'wei] *vtr* 1. peser plus que qch 2. l'emporter sur qch.

outwit [aut'wit] *vtr* (**outwitted**) 1. circonvenir (qn); déjouer les intentions de (qn); duper (qn) 2. dépister (la police).

oval ['ouv(ə)l] 1. *a* ovale; en ovale 2. *n* ovale *m*.

ovary ['ouvəri] *n* ovaire *m*.

ovation [ou'veiʃ(ə)n] *n* ovation *f*.

oven ['ʌv(ə)n] *n* four *m*; **in the o.,** au four; **to cook sth in a very slow o.,** faire cuire qch à four très doux; (*of poultry*) **o. ready,** prêt à cuire (au four); **this room's like an o.,** cette salle est une fournaise. **'ovenproof** *a* (plat) allant au four. **'ovenware** *n* vaisselle *f* allant au four.

over ['ouvər] I. *prep* 1. (*a*) sur, par-dessus; **to spread a cloth o. sth,** étendre une toile par-dessus, sur, qch; **I spilled water o. it,** j'ai renversé de l'eau dessus (*b*) **famous all o. the world,** célèbre dans le monde entier (*c*) **o. (the top of) sth,** par-dessus qch; **to throw sth o. the wall,** jeter qch par-dessus le mur; **to fall o. a cliff,** tomber du haut d'une falaise; **to stumble, trip, o. sth,** buter contre qch; **we're o. the worst,** le pire (moment) est passé 2. (*a*) **jutting out o. the street,** faisant saillie sur la rue; **his name is o. the door,** il a son nom au-dessus de la porte; **with water o. one's ankles,** avec de l'eau au-dessus des chevilles (*b*) **to have an advantage o. s.o.,** avoir un avantage sur qn (*c*) **bending o. his work,** courbé sur son travail; **to chat o. a glass of wine,** bavarder devant un verre de vin; **o. the phone,** au téléphone; **o. the radio,** à la radio; **sitting o. the fire,** assis tout près du feu 3. (*a*) **the house o. the way,** la maison d'en face; **o. the border,** au-delà de la frontière (*b*) **the bridge o. the river,** le pont qui traverse la rivière; **to jump o. a wall,** sauter (par-dessus) un mur 4. **o. fifty pounds,** plus de cinquante livres; **o. five (years old),** au-dessus, de plus, de cinq ans; **he's o. fifty,** il a dépassé la cinquantaine; **he spoke for o. an hour,** il a parlé pendant plus d'une heure; **o. and above,** en plus de, en sus de; **o. and above his wages,** en plus de son salaire 5. **o. the last three years,** au cours des trois dernières années. II. *adv* 1. (*a*) sur toute la surface; **all o.,** partout; d'un bout à l'autre; **to be dusty all o.,** être tout couvert de poussière; **to ache all o.,** avoir mal partout; **that's you all o.,** je vous reconnais bien là; **he's French all o.,** il est français jusqu'au bout des ongles (*b*) **to read a letter o.,** lire une lettre en entier; **to do sth all o. again,** refaire qch entièrement (*c*) **ten times o., dix fois de suite; twice o.,** à deux reprises; **o. and o. (again),** à plusieurs reprises; maintes et maintes fois 2. (*a*) par-dessus (qch); **to jump o.,** sauter par-dessus; **the milk boiled o.,** le lait s'est sauvé (*b*) **to lean o.,** (*of pers*) se pencher (à la fenêtre); (*of thg*) pencher 3. (*a*) **to fall o.,** (*of pers*) tomber (par terre); (*of thg*) se renverser; être renversé; **to knock sth o.,** renverser qch (*b*) **please turn o.,** voir au dos; tournez, s'il vous plaît; **to turn sth o. and o.,** tourner et retourner qch; **to bend sth o.,** replier qch 4. **to cross o.,** traverser (la rue); faire la traversée (de la Manche); **he's coming o. tomorrow,** il vient nous voir demain; **I've invited him o.,** je l'ai invité à venir (nous voir); **o. there,** là-bas; **o. here,** ici; de ce côté 5. en plus, en excès (*a*) **children of sixteen and o.,** les enfants qui ont seize ans et plus (*b*) **keep what's left o.,** gardez le surplus; **I have a card o.,** j'ai une carte de, en, trop; **o. and above,** en outre (*c*) **the question is held o.,** la question est différée (*d*) (*in compounds*) (i) trop; à l'excès; **o.-abundant,** surabondant; **o.-particular,** trop exigeant; **o.-scrupulous,** scrupuleux à l'excès (ii) **o.-confidence,** excès *m* de confiance (iii) **to overstretch a spring,** trop tendre, distendre, un ressort 6. fini, achevé; **the danger is o.,** le danger est passé; **the rain is o.,** la pluie s'est arrêtée; **o. and done with,** terminé; tout à fait fini; **the concert is just o.,** le concert vient de finir, de se terminer; **it's all o.,** c'est fini; tout est fini; **it's all o. with me,** c'en est fait de moi. **over'act** *vi* exagérer; *F:* en faire trop. **'overall** 1. *a* total, global, d'ensemble; **o. length,** longueur *f* hors tout 2. *n (a)* blouse *f (b) pl* **overalls,** salopette *f*; combinaison *f*; bleus *mpl* (de travail). **over'anxious** *a* trop inquiet, anxieux. **over'arm** *a Cr:* (service) par le haut. **over-'awe** *vtr* intimider (qn); en imposer à (qn). **over'balance** 1. *vtr* renverser (qch) 2. *vi (of pers)* perdre l'équilibre; (*of thg*) se renverser; tomber. **over'bearing** *a* arrogant, impérieux, autoritaire. **'overboard** *adv Nau:* par-dessus bord; **to fall o.,** tomber à la mer; **to throw sth o.,** (i) jeter qch à la mer (ii) abandonner (un projet); **man o.!** un homme à la mer! **to go o. for sth,** s'emballer pour qch. **over'burden** *vtr* surcharger, accabler (**with,** de); *F:* **ne's not overburdened with work,** ce n'est pas le travail qui l'écrase. **overcast** *a* (ciel) couvert, nuageux. **'over'charge** 1. *n* prix excessif; prix surfait 2. *vtr* & *i* **to o. s.o.,** faire payer trop cher un article à qn; majorer une facture. **'overcoat** *n* pardessus *m*; manteau *m*. **over'come** 1. *vtr* (**overcame**) triompher de, vaincre (ses ennemis); venir à bout de (ses difficultés); surmonter (un obstacle); maîtriser, dominer (son émotion) 2. *a* **to be o. with, by (sth),** être accablé de (douleur); être gagné par (le sommeil); succomber à (la chaleur, l'émotion); être paralysé (par la peur). **over'crowded** *a (a)* trop rempli (**with,** de); (train) bondé (**with people,** de monde) (*b*) (*of town, forest*) surpeuplé. **over'crowding** *n* encombrement *m*; surpeuplement *m*. **'overde'veloped** *a Phot:* (cliché) trop développé. **over'do** *vtr* (**overdid; overdone**) 1. **to o. things,** (i) se surmener (ii) exagérer 2. *Cu:* trop cuire (qch). **'overdose** *n* trop forte dose; surdose *f*. **'over-draft** *n Bank:* découvert *m*; solde débiteur. **over-'draw** *vtr* (**overdrew; overdrawn**) *Bank:* mettre (son compte) à découvert; **overdrawn account,** compte à découvert. **over'dress** *vtr & i* s'habiller avec une recherche excessive. **'overdrive** *n Aut:* vitesse surmultipliée. **over'due** *a* arriéré, en retard; **he's long o.,** il devrait être là depuis longtemps. **over-'eat** *vi* **(overate; overeaten)** trop manger. **over'eating** *n* excès *mpl* de table. **over'estimate** *vtr* surestimer; exagérer (le danger). **over'exert** *vtr* **to o. oneself,** se surmener. **'overex'ertion** *n* surmenage *m*. **'overex'pose** *vtr Phot:* surexposer. **'overex'posure** *n Phot:* surexposition *f*. **over'feed** *vtr* **(overfed)** suralimenter. **over'feeding** *n* suralimentation *f*. **over'filled** *a* (verre) plein à déborder. **overflow I.** [´ouvəflou] *n* **1.** (*a*) débordement *m* (d'un liquide) (*b*) inondation *f* **2.** trop-plein *m inv*; **o. pipe,** (tuyau *m* de) trop-plein; décharge *f*; déversoir *m* **3. o. meeting,** réunion *f* supplémentaire. **II.** [ouvə´flou] *v* **1.** *vtr* (*a*) déborder de (la coupe) (*b*) (*of river*) inonder (un champ); **to o. its banks,** sortir de son lit **2.** *vi* déborder. **over'flowing** *n* **full to o.,** plein à déborder; rempli à ras bord. **over'grown** *a* couvert (de qch); **o. with weeds,** (jardin) envahi par les mauvaises herbes. **'over'hang** *vtr* **(overhung)** surplomber. **'over'hanging** *a* surplombant, en surplomb. **overhaul 1.** *n* [´ouvəhɔːl] (*a*) révision *f* (d'une machine) (*b*) remise *f* en état (d'une machine) **2.** [ouvə´hɔːl] *vtr* (*a*) examiner en détail; réviser; remettre en état, réparer (*b*) *Nau:* rattraper, dépasser (un autre navire). **overhead 1.** *adv* [´ouvə´hed] au-dessus (de la tête); en haut, en l'air **2.** *a* [´ouvəhed] (*a*) **o. cable,** câble aérien (*b*) *Com:* **o. expenses,** *npl* **overheads,** frais généraux (*c*) *Aut:* (soupapes) en tête. **over'hear** *vtr* **(overheard)** surprendre (une conversation). **over'heat 1.** *vtr* surchauffer, trop chauffer **2.** *vi Aut:* **the engine is overheating,** le moteur chauffe. **overin'dulge 1.** *vtr* gâter (les enfants) **2.** *vi* **to o. in wine,** abuser du vin. **over'joyed** *a* transporté de joie; au comble de la joie; **to be o. to see s.o.,** être ravi de voir qn. **over'land 1.** *adv* par voie de terre **2.** *a* **o. route,** voie *f* de terre. **overlap 1.** [ouvə´læp] *vtr & i* **(overlapped)** (*a*) **to o. (one another),** (se) chevaucher (*b*) faire double emploi **2.** [´ouvə-] *n* chevauchement *m*. **over'lay** *vtr* **(overlaid)** recouvrir (de qch). **'over'leaf** *adv* au dos, au verso (de la page); **see o.,** voir au verso. **over'load** *vtr* **1.** surcharger **2.** surmener (une machine). **over'look** *vtr* **1.** avoir vue sur (qch); (*of building*) dominer, commander; (*of window*) donner sur (la rue) **2.** (*a*) oublier, négliger (qch); **I overlooked the fact,** ce fait m'a échappé (*b*) fermer les yeux sur (qch); **we'll o. it,** passons; **o. it this time,** fermez les yeux pour cette fois. **'over'much** *adv* (par) trop; à l'excès. **overnight 1.** *adv* [´ouvə´nait] (*a*) la veille (au soir) (*b*) (pendant) la nuit; *F:* (changer d'idée) soudainement; **to stay o.,** passer une nuit; rester jusqu'au lendemain; (*of food*) **to keep o.,** se conserver jusqu'au lendemain **2.** *a* [´ouvənait] de la veille; **o. stay,** séjour d'une seule nuit; **o. bag,** sac de voyage; **o. trip,** voyage de nuit, d'une nuit. **'over'pass** *n CivE: NAm:* (*Br* = **flyover**) saut-de-mouton. **over'pay** *vtr* **(overpaid)** surpayer; trop payer; payer (£10) de trop. **over'payment** *n* surpaye *f*; paiement *m* en trop. **over'play** *vtr* **to o. one's hand,** viser trop haut. **over'power** *vtr* maîtriser, dominer, vaincre. **over'powering** *a*

accablant; (désir) irrésistible; (odeur) très forte; *F:* (femme) imposante. **'overpro'duction** *n* surproduction *f*. **over'rate** *vtr* surestimer; faire trop de cas de (qch); **overrated restaurant,** restaurant surfait. **over'reach** *vpr* **to o. oneself,** (trop) présumer de ses forces. **overre'act** *vi* réagir avec excès. **over'ride** *vtr* **(overrode; overridden)** (*a*) outrepasser (un ordre) (*b*) avoir plus d'importance que (qch); **considerations that o. all others,** considérations qui l'emportent sur toutes les autres. **'overrider** *n Aut:* sabot *m* (de parechoc). **'over'ripe** *a* trop mûr. **over'rule** *vtr* (*a*) décider contre (l'avis de qn) (*b*) *Jur:* annuler, casser (un arrêt); rejeter (une réclamation) (*c*) passer outre à (une difficulté); passer à l'ordre du jour sur (une objection). **over'run 1.** *vtr* **(overran; overrun)** (*of invaders*) envahir (un pays); dévaster (un pays); (*of weeds*) envahir (un jardin); **house o. with mice,** maison infestée de souris **2.** *vi* dépasser (la limite); déborder. **over'seas 1.** *adv* outre-mer **2.** *a* d'outre-mer; (*of trade*) extérieur, étranger. **over'see** *vtr* **(oversaw; overseen)** surveiller (un atelier). **'overseer** *n* surveillant, -ante; *Ind:* contremaître, -tresse; chef *m* d'atelier. **over'shadow** *vtr* **1.** couvrir de son ombre **2.** éclipser (qn); surpasser en° éclat. **'over'shoot** *vtr* **(overshot)** dépasser, aller plus loin que (le point d'arrêt); *Av:* se présenter trop long (sur la piste); **to o. the mark,** dépasser le but. **'oversight** *n* oubli *m*, omission *f*; **through, by, an o.,** par mégarde, par inadvertance. **over'simplify** *vtr* trop simplifier. **'oversized** *a* au-dessus des dimensions normales. **over'sleep** *vi* **(overslept)** dormir trop tard, ne pas se réveiller à temps. **over'spend** *vi* **(overspent)** dépenser trop. **'overspill** *n* surplus de population; **o. town,** cité-satellite *f*. **over'state** *vtr* exagérer (les faits). **over'statement** *n* exagération *f*; récit exagéré. **over'stay** *vtr* dépasser (son congé); **to o. one's welcome,** lasser l'amabilité de ses hôtes. **over'step** *vtr* **(overstepped)** outrepasser, dépasser (les bornes); **don't o. the mark,** n'y allez pas trop fort. **'overstuffed** *a* rembourré, capitonné. **over'take** *vtr* **(overtook; overtaken) 1.** (*a*) rattraper, atteindre (qn) (*b*) doubler, dépasser (une voiture) **2.** (*of catastrophe*) frapper (qn). **over'taking** *n Aut:* dépassement *m*; **no o.,** défense de doubler. **'overtax** *vtr* (*a*) pressurer (le peuple); accabler (la nation) d'impôts (*b*) trop exiger de (qn); **to o. one's strength,** surmener; abuser de ses forces. **'over-the-'counter** *a* (vente) au comptant; (médicament) vendu sans ordonnance. **over'throw** *vtr* **(over-threw; overthrown)** défaire, vaincre (qn); renverser (un ministère); ruiner (les projets de qn). **'overtime 1.** *n Ind:* heures *f* supplémentaires (de travail) **2.** *adv* **to work o.,** faire des heures supplémentaires. **'overtones** *npl F:* nuance *f*, soupçon *m* (de tristesse, d'amertume).

overt [ou´vert] *a* évident, manifeste. **o'vertly** *adv* ouvertement.

overture [´ouvətjuər] *n* **1. to make overtures to s.o.,** faire des avances à qn **2.** *Mus:* ouverture *f*.

overturn [ouvə´təːn] **1.** *vtr* renverser; faire renverser (une voiture); (faire) chavirer (un canot) **2.** *vi* (*a*) se renverser; chavirer (*b*) *Aut:* capoter.

overweight [´ouvəweit] *a* (colis) qui excède, dépasse, le poids réglementaire; (*of pers*) **to become o.,**

prendre de l'embonpoint; engraisser; grossir; **I'm 10 pounds o.**, je pèse 5 kilos de trop.

overwhelm [ouvə'(h)welm] *vtr* 1. ensevelir (une ville dans la lave); submerger 2. (*a*) écraser, accabler (l'ennemi) (*b*) to be overwhelmed with work, être débordé, surchargé, de travail (*c*) combler (qn de bontés). **over'whelmed** *a* confus, honteux; o. with joy, au comble de la joie. **over'whelming** *a* irrésistible; accablant; o. majority, majorité écrasante; of o. importance, de toute première importance. **'over'whelmingly** *adv* to vote o. (for), voter en masse (pour); to win o., gagner par une victoire écrasante.

overwork ['ouvə'wə:k] 1. *n* surmenage *m* 2. *v* (*a*) *vtr* surmener; surcharger (qn) de travail (*b*) *vi* se surmener; travailler outre mesure.

owe [ou] *vtr* 1. to o. s.o. sth, to o. sth to s.o., devoir qch à qn; *vi* I still o. you for the petrol, je vous dois encore l'essence 2. I o. my life to you, je vous dois la vie; to what do I o. this honour? qu'est-ce qui me vaut cet honneur? I o. you an apology, je vous dois des excuses; you o. it to yourself to do your best, vous vous devez de faire de votre mieux. **'owing** 1. *a* dû; the money o. to me, l'argent qui m'est dû 2. *prep phr* o. to, à cause de, par suite de; o. to a recent bereavement, en raison d'un deuil récent.

owl [aul] *n Orn:* hibou *m*; the o., le hibou; barn o., (chouette) effraie; tawny o., chouette *f* des bois. **'owlet** *n* jeune hibou. **'owlish** *a* de hibou.

own [oun] **I.** *vtr* 1. posséder; who owns this land? qui est le propriétaire de cette terre? I don't o. a car, je n'ai pas de voiture 2. (*a*) reconnaître; dog that nobody will o., chien que personne ne réclame (*b*) avouer (qch); I o. I was wrong, j'admets que j'ai eu tort 3. *v ind tr* to o. up to a mistake, reconnaître, avouer, une erreur; to o. up to sth, faire l'aveu de qch; *vi F:* to o. up, faire des aveux; avouer. **II.** *a* (*a*) propre; her o. money, son propre argent; I saw him with my o. eyes, je l'ai vu de mes propres yeux; I do my o. cooking, je fais la cuisine moi-même (*b*) le mien, le

tien, etc; à moi, à toi, etc; the house is my o., la maison m'appartient. **III.** *n* my o., his o., etc, (*a*) le mien, le sien, etc; I have money of my o., j'ai de l'argent à moi; he has a copy of his o., il a son propre exemplaire; for reasons of his o., pour des raisons qui lui sont personnelles; to come into one's o., recevoir sa récompense; *F:* to get one's o. back, prendre sa revanche; he can hold his o., il sait se défendre (*b*) to do sth on one's o., faire qch (i) de sa propre initiative (ii) indépendamment, tout seul; I'm (all) on my o. today, je suis seul aujourd'hui; you're on your o. now! défends-toi comme tu peux! **'owner** *n* propriétaire *mf*, possesseur *m*; patron, -onne (d'une maison de commerce); who is the o. of this ball? à qui appartient ce ballon? joint owners, copropriétaires *mpl*; *Aut:* o.-driver, conducteur *m* propriétaire; o.-occupier, propriétaire-occupant. **'ownerless** *a* o. dog, chien sans maître. **'ownership** *n* (droit *m* de) propriété *f*; possession *f*.

ox [ɔks] *n* (*pl* oxen) bœuf *m*. **'oxcart** *n* char *m* à bœufs. **'oxeye** *n* o. daisy, marguerite *f* des champs. **'oxtail** *n Cu:* queue *f* de bœuf. **'ox-tongue** *n Cu:* langue *f* de bœuf.

OXFAM ['ɔksfæm] *abbr Oxford Committee for Famine Relief.*

oxide ['ɔksaid] *n Ch:* oxyde *m*. **oxidization** [ɔksidai'zei(ə)n] *n* oxydation *f*. **oxidize** ['ɔksidaiz] *vtr & i* (s')oxyder.

Oxon ['ɔksɔn] *abbr* 1. *Geog: Oxfordshire* 2. *Oxoniensis, of Oxford*, d'Oxford.

oxyacetylene [ɔksiə'setili:n] *a* o. torch, chalumeau *m* oxyacétylénique.

oxygen ['ɔksidʒən] *n Ch:* oxygène *m*; o. bottle, bouteille d'oxygène; *Med:* o. tent, tente à oxygène.

oyster ['ɔistər] *n* huître *f*; pearl o., huître perlière; o. bed, huîtrière *f*; o. breeding, ostréiculture *f*; o. farm, parc à huîtres; clayère *f*; o. shell, écaille d'huître; the world is his o., son ambition est sans limites.

oz *abbr Meas: ounce(s)*, once(s).

ozone ['ouzoun] *n Ch:* ozone *m*.

P

P, p [piː] *n (a)* (la lettre) P, p *m*; **to mind one's P's and Q's,** se surveiller *(b) F:* penny *m*; **a ten p (10p) stamp,** un timbre à dix pence.

p *abbr* page.

pa [pɑː] *n F:* papa *m*.

PA *abbr (a) personal assistant (b) public address (system).*

p.a. *abbr per annum.*

pace [peis] **1.** *n (a)* pas *m*; **ten paces off,** à dix pas de distance *(b)* vitesse *f*, train *m*, allure *f*; **at a walking p.,** au pas; **at a good, smart, p.,** à vive allure; **at a slow p.,** au petit pas; **to put s.o. through his paces,** mettre qn à l'épreuve; *Sp:* **to set the p.,** donner le pas; mener le train; **to keep p. with,** marcher du même pas que (qn); marcher de pair avec (qn, qch) **2.** *vi* **to p. up and down,** faire les cent pas **3.** *vtr (a)* arpenter (une pièce); **to p. off a distance,** mesurer une distance au pas *(b) Sp:* entraîner (qn). **'pacemaker** *n Med:* stimulateur *m* (cardiaque).

pacify ['pæsifai] *vtr* (**pacifies**) pacifier; apaiser, calmer.

pacific [pə'sifik] *a & n Geog:* **the P. (Ocean),** l'océan *m* Pacifique, le Pacifique. **'pacifier** *n NAm:* (*Br* = **dummy**) tétine *f*, sucette *f*. **'pacifism** *n* pacifisme *m*. **'pacifist** *a & n* pacifiste (*mf*).

pack [pæk] **1.** *v* **1.** *vtr (a)* emballer, empaqueter (qch); faire (sa valise) *(b)* tasser; entasser, serrer (des voyageurs dans une voiture) *(c)* remplir, bourrer (**sth with sth, qch de qch**) **2.** *vi (a)* faire sa valise; *F:* **to send s.o. packing,** envoyer promener qn *(b) (of earth)* se tasser *(c) (of people)* s'attrouper. **II.** *n (a)* paquet *m*; ballot *m* (de colporteur); sac *m* (de militaire); bât *m* (de bête de somme); **p. of lies,** tissu *m* de mensonges *(b)* bande *f* (de loups); **p. (of hounds),** meute *f*; *Rugby Fb:* **the p.,** le pack *(c)* jeu *m* (de cartes) *(d) Med:* enveloppement *m* (froid, humide). **'package 1.** *n* paquet, colis *m*; **p. deal,** contrat global; **p. tour,** voyage à prix forfaitaire **2.** *vtr* emballer, conditionner (des marchandises). **'packaging** *n* emballage *m*; conditionnement *m*. **'packed** *a* (train) bondé; (salle) comble; **p. lunch,** panier-repas *m*; **sandwiches** *mpl*. **'packer** *n* emballeur, -euse. **'packet** *n* paquet; colis; sachet *m* (d'aiguilles); *F:* **that'll cost a p.,** ça va coûter les yeux de la tête. **'packhorse** *n* cheval *m* de somme. **'pack 'in** *vtr F:* renoncer à (qch). **'packing** *n (a)* emballage *m*, empaquetage *m*; **to do one's p.,** faire sa valise; **p. case,** caisse d'emballage *(b)* (matière *f* pour) emballage. **'pack 'off** *vtr* envoyer (qn); **his father packed him off to America,** son père l'a expédié en l'Amérique. **'pack 'up** *vtr & i* emballer (ses effets); faire (ses valises); *F:* renoncer à (qch); *F:* cesser (le travail); *F: (of machine)* tomber en panne; **the telly has packed up,** la télé ne marche plus.

pact [pækt] *n* pacte *m*, convention *f*.

pad [pæd] **1.** *n (a)* bourrelet *m*, coussinet *m*;

Cr: jambière *f (b)* tampon *m*; **inking p.,** tampon encreur *(c)* bloc *m* (de papier); *(for notes)* bloc-notes *m (d)* patte *f* (de renard, de lièvre); pulpe *f* (du doigt); **launching p.,** aire *f* de lancement (d'une fusée) **2.** *vtr* (**padded**) rembourrer (un coussin); capitonner (un meuble); **to p. (out) a speech,** délayer un discours; **padded cell,** cabanon *m*. **'padding** *n (a)* remplissage *m*, rembourrage *m*; **p. (out),** délayage *m* (d'un discours) *(b)* rembourrage; ouate *f*, bourre *f*.

paddle ['pædl] **1.** *n* pagaie *f*; **p. steamer,** bateau à aubes **2.** *v (a) vtr & i* **to p. (a canoe),** pagayer *(b) vi* barboter, patauger (dans l'eau, la boue); **paddling pool,** bassin à patauger. **'paddle-boat** *n* bateau *m* à aubes.

paddock ['pædək] *n* enclos *m* (pour chevaux); *Turf:* pesage *m*, paddock *m*.

paddy ['pædi] *n* **p. field,** rizière *f*.

padlock ['pædlɔk] **1.** *n* cadenas *m* **2.** *vtr* cadenasser.

pagan ['peigən] *a & n* païen, -ïenne.

page¹ [peidʒ] **1.** *n* **p. (boy),** page *m*; *(in hotel)* groom *m*; (jeune) chasseur *m* **2.** *vtr* (faire) appeler (qn) (par haut-parleur).

page² *n* page *f*; **on p. 6,** à la page 6; **continued on p. 6,** suite page 6.

pageant ['pædʒənt] *n* grand spectacle pompeux, historique. **'pageantry** *n* apparat *m*.

paid [peid] *a see* **pay 1.**

pail [peil] *n* seau *m*.

pain [pein] **1.** *n* douleur *f*; souffrance *f*; *(mental)* peine *f*; **to be in (great) p.,** souffrir beaucoup; **to give, cause, s.o. p.,** faire mal à qn; **I've got a p. in my arm,** j'ai mal au bras; **shooting pains,** élancements *mpl*; *F:* **he's a p. in the neck,** il est, c'est un, casse-pieds; **to take pains, be at pains, to do sth,** se donner du mal pour faire qch; **on p. of death,** sous peine de mort **2.** *vtr* faire souffrir, faire mal à (qn); *(mentally)* faire de la peine à (qn). **pained** *a* (air) peiné. **'painful** *a* douloureux; *(of spectacle, effort)* pénible; **my hand is p.,** j'ai mal à la main, la main me fait mal. **'painfully** *adv* douloureusement; péniblement. **'painkiller** *n* calmant *m*. **'painless** *a* sans douleur; indolore. **'painlessly** *adv* sans douleur. **'painstaking** *a* soigneux, assidu; *(élève)* appliqué; *(travail)* soigné.

paint [peint] **1.** *n* peinture *f*; *PN:* **wet p.!** attention à la peinture; **box of paints,** boîte de couleurs *fpl* **2.** *v (a) vtr & i* peindre; *(in words)* dépeindre; *Th:* brosser (les décors); *F:* **to p. the town red,** faire la noce *(b) vi* faire de la peinture. **'paintbrush** *n (pl* **-brushes)** pinceau *m*. **'painter¹** *n (artist)* peintre *m*; *(house)* **p.,** peintre en bâtiment; peintre décorateur. **'painting** *n (a)* peinture *f* (de tableaux, de maisons) *(b) (picture)* tableau *m*. **'paintwork** *n* peintures *fpl*.

painter² *n Nau:* amarre *f*.

pair [pɛər] **1.** *n* paire *f*; **p. of scissors,** paire de ciseaux; **a p. of trousers,** un pantalon; **these two pictures are a p.,** ces deux tableaux se font pendant; **in**

pairs, (deux) par deux (b) (husband and wife) couple m
2. vtr appareiller, assortir (des gants); accoupler (des
oiseaux). **'pair 'off** vtr & i (s')arranger deux par
deux.

pajamas [pə'dʒæməz] npl NAm: (Br = **pyjamas**)
pyjama m.

Pakistan [pɑːki'stɑːn, pæk-] Prn Geog: Pakistan m.
Paki'stani a & n pakistanais, -aise.

pal [pæl] n F: camarade mf; copain m, copine f.

palace ['pæləs] n palais m.

palate ['pælət] n Anat: palais m. **'palatable** a
agréable au palais, au goût.

palatial [pə'leiʃl] a magnifique, grandiose.

palaver [pə'lɑːvər] n F: palabre(s) f(pl); **what a p.!**
quelle histoire!

pale [peil] 1. a (a) pâle, blême; **deadly p.,** pâle comme la
mort; **to turn p.,** pâlir (b) (of colour) clair; (of
moonlight) blafard 2. vi pâlir; blêmir. **'paleness** n
pâleur f.

Palestine ['pæləstain] Prn Geog: Palestine f.
Pales'tinian a & n palestinien, -ienne.

palette ['pælit] n Art: palette f.

paling ['peiliŋ] n (often pl) palissade f.

palisade [pæli'seid] n palissade f.

pall [pɔːl] 1. n (a) Ecc: drap m mortuaire (b) manteau m
(de neige); voile m (de fumée) 2. vi s'affadir; devenir
fade (on s.o., pour qn); **it never palls on you,** on ne s'en
dégoûte jamais.

palliate ['pælieit] vtr pallier (une faute); atténuer (un
vice). **'palliative** a & n palliatif (m).

pallid ['pælid] a pâle, décoloré; (of light) blafard; (of
face) blême. **'pallor** n pâleur f.

palm¹ [pɑːm] n (a) **p. (tree),** palmier m; **p. grove,**
palmeraie f; Ecc: **P. Sunday,** le dimanche des Rameaux (b) (branch) palme f.

palm² 1. n paume f (de la main); F: **to grease s.o.'s p.,**
graisser la patte à qn; F: **to have s.o. in the p. of one's
hand,** avoir qn sous sa coupe 2. vtr escamoter (une
carte). **'palmist** n chiromancien, -ienne. **'palmistry** n chiromancie f. **palm 'off** vtr refiler (sth
onto s.o., qch à qn).

palpable ['pælpəbl] a palpable; que l'on peut toucher;
(mensonge) manifeste. **'palpably** adv manifestement.

palpitate ['pælpiteit] vi palpiter. **palpi'tation** n palpitation f.

paltry ['pɔːltri] a (-ier, -iest) misérable, mesquin.

pamper ['pæmpər] vtr choyer, dorloter.

pamphlet ['pæmflit] n brochure f.

pan [pæn] 1. n (a) Cu: casserole f, poêlon m; **frying p.,**
poêle f; **baking p., roasting p.,** plat m à rôtir; **pots and
pans,** batterie f de cuisine (b) plateau m (d'une
balance); cuvette f (de WC) 2. v (**panned**) (a) vtr & i
Cin: panoramiquer (b) vtr décrier, éreinter (qn).
'pancake n crêpe f; **p. day,** mardi gras. **'pan 'out**
vi réussir; **things did not p. out as he intended,**
les choses ne se sont pas passées comme il l'aurait
voulu.

panacea [pænə'siːə] n panacée f.

pan-African ['pæn'æfrikən] a panafricain. **pan-
A'merican** a panaméricain.

panchromatic [pænkrou'mætik] a Phot: panchro-
matique.

pancreas ['pæŋkriəs] n Anat: pancréas m.

panda ['pændə] n Z: panda m; F: **p. car,** voiture pie (de
la police).

pandemonium [pændi'mouniəm] n pandémonium
m; bruit infernal.

pander ['pændər] vi **to p. to,** se prêter à (un vice);
flatter bassement (un goût).

pane [pein] n vitre f, carreau m.

panel ['pænl] 1. n (a) panneau m (de porte); caisson
m (de plafond); Aut: Av: **instrument p.,** tableau
m de bord; Elcs: Cmptr: **control p.,** pupitre m
de commande (b) tableau, liste f; Jur: TV: Sch: etc:
jury m; **p. game,** jeu télévisé, radiophonique, par équipes 2. vtr (**panelled**) recouvrir (une cloison) de panneaux; lambrisser. **'panelling,** NAm: **panel-
ing** n lambris m; boiserie f; **oak p.,** panneaux mpl
de chêne.

pang [pæŋ] n angoisse (subite); douleur f; serrement m
de cœur; **the pangs of death,** les affres f de la mort;
pangs of jealousy, tourments mpl de la jalousie; **pangs
of hunger,** tiraillements mpl d'estomac.

panic ['pænik] 1. n panique f; affolement m; **in a p.,** pris
de panique; **to throw s.o. into a p.,** affoler qn 2. vi
(**panicked**) être pris de panique; s'affoler. **'panicky**
a F: sujet à la panique; alarmiste. **'panic-stricken**
a pris de panique; affolé.

panorama [pænə'rɑːmə] n panorama m.
panoramic [-'ræm-] a panoramique.

pansy ['pænzi] n (pl **pansies**) (a) Bot: pensée f (b) F:
homosexuel m, tante f.

pant [pænt] vi haleter; **to p. for breath,** chercher à
reprendre haleine. **'panting** n essoufflement m.

panther ['pænθər] n Z: panthère f.

pantie ['pænti] n Cl: (**pair of**) **panties,** slip m (de
femme); **p. girdle,** gaine-culotte f; esp NAm: **p. hose**
(also **pantihose**) (Br = **tights**) collant m.

pantomime ['pæntəmaim] n (dumb show) pantomime f; Th: revue-féerie (représentée à Noël).

pantry ['pæntri] n (pl **pantries**) garde-manger m inv;
butler's p., office f.

pants [pænts] npl Cl: (**pair of**) **p.,** (underwear) caleçon
m; slip m (d'homme, de femme, d'enfant); esp NAm:
(Br = **trousers**) pantalon m; F: **a kick in the p.,** un
coup de pied au cul.

papacy ['peipəsi] n papauté f. **'papal** a papal.

paper ['peipər] 1. n (a) papier m; **brown p.,**
papier gris; **cigarette p.,** papier à cigarettes;
carbon p., papier carbone; **a sheet, a piece, of p.,**
une feuille, un morceau, de papier; **to put sth
down on p.,** mettre qch par écrit; **it's a good
scheme on p.,** c'est un bon projet en théorie;
the p. industry, l'industrie papetière; **p. mill,**
papeterie f; **p. clip,** trombone m; **p. knife,**
coupe-papier m inv (b) (morceau de) papier;
document m, pièce f; **old papers,** paperasse(s)
f(pl); **identity papers,** papiers d'identité; **voting
p.,** bulletin m de vote; Sch: **examination p.,** épreuve
écrite; copie f; **to correct papers,** corriger l'écrit (c)
journal m; **weekly p.,** hebdomadaire m (d) étude f,
mémoire m (sur un sujet scientifique, savant); communication f, exposé m (à une société savante) 2. a
(sac) en papier; (profit) fictif; **p. money,** papier-
monnaie m 3. vtr tapisser (une chambre); Fig: **to p.
over the cracks,** cacher les défauts. **'paperback** n
livre m de poche. **'paperboy** n livreur m de

journaux. 'paperweight *n* presse-papiers *m inv.* 'paperwork *n* paperasserie(s) *f (pl).*

paprika ['pæprikə] *n Cu:* paprika *m.*

par [pɑːr] *n* pair *m,* égalité *f;* **to be on a p. with,** être au niveau de, aller de pair avec; *F:* **to feel below p.,** ne pas être dans son assiette.

parable ['pærəbl] *n* parabole *f.*

parachute ['pærəʃuːt] 1. *n* parachute *m;* **to drop sth by p.,** parachuter qch; **p. jump,** saut en parachute; **p. drop,** parachutage *m;* **p. regiment,** régiment de parachutistes 2. *v (a) vtr* parachuter *(b) vi* **to p. (down),** descendre en parachute. 'parachutist *n* parachutiste *mf.*

parade [pə'reid] 1. *n (a)* procession *f,* défilé *m;* parade *f; Mil:* rassemblement *m;* exercice *m;* **on p.,** à l'exercice; **p. ground,** terrain de manœuvres; place d'armes; **mannequin p.,** défilé de mannequins; **fashion p.,** présentation *f* de collection *(b)* esplanade *f;* promenade *f* 2. *v (a) vtr* faire parade, étalage, de (ses richesses); *Mil:* faire l'inspection (des troupes) *(b) vi* défiler (dans les rues).

paradise ['pærədais] *n* paradis *m;* **bird of p.,** oiseau de paradis; **an earthly p.,** un paradis sur terre.

paradox ['pærədɔks] *n (pl* **paradoxes)** paradoxe *m.* para'doxical *a* paradoxal. para'doxically *adv* paradoxalement.

paraffin ['pærəfin] *n Ch:* paraffine *f; Pharm:* **liquid p.,** huile *f* de paraffine; *(fuel)* **p. (oil),** pétrole (lampant); kérosène *m;* **p. stove,** poêle à pétrole.

paragon ['pærəgən] *n* modèle *m* (de vertu).

paragraph ['pærəgrɑːf, -græf] *n (a)* paragraphe *m,* alinéa *m; (when dictating)* **new p.,** à la ligne *(b) Journ:* entrefilet *m.*

parakeet [pærə'kiːt] *n Orn:* perruche *f.*

parallel ['pærəlel] 1. *a* parallèle **(with, to,** à); *Fig:* semblable; (cas) analogue **(to, with,** à) 2. *n (a)* (ligne *f)* parallèle *f (b) Geog:* parallèle *m* (de latitude) *(c)* parallèle *m,* comparaison *f;* **to draw a p.,** établir un parallèle (entre deux choses). para'llelogram *n* parallélogramme *m.*

paralyse, *NAm:* paralyze ['pærəlaiz] *vtr* paralyser; **paralysed in one leg,** paralysé d'une jambe; **paralysed with fear,** paralysé par la peur. 'paralysing *a* paralysant. pa'ralysis *n Med:* paralysie *f.* para'lytic *a & n* paralytique *(mf); P:* ivre mort.

paramilitary [pærə'militri] *a* paramilitaire.

paramount ['pærəmaunt] *a* éminent, souverain; suprême.

paranoia [pærə'nɔiə] *n Med:* paranoïa *f.* para'noiac *a* paranoïaque. 'paranoid *a* paranoïde.

parapet ['pærəpit] *n* parapet *m;* garde-fou *m.*

paraphernalia [pærəfə'neiliə] *npl (a)* effets *mpl;* affaires *fpl (b)* attirail *m,* appareil *m* (de pêche, de sport).

paraphrase ['pærəfreiz] 1. *n* paraphrase *f* 2. *vtr* paraphraser.

paraplegic [pærə'pliːdʒik] *a & n Med:* paraplégique *(mf).*

parasite ['pærəsait] *n* parasite *m.* parasitic [pærə'sitik] *a* parasite **(on,** de).

parasol ['pærəsɔl] *n* ombrelle *f;* parasol *m.*

paratrooper ['pærətruːpər] *n* (soldat) parachutiste *(m).* 'paratroops *npl* (soldats) parachutistes.

parboil ['pɑːbɔil] *vtr Cu:* faire cuire à demi (dans l'eau.

parcel ['pɑːsl] 1. *n* paquet *m,* colis *m;* **parcels office,** bureau *m* de(s) messageries; **p. post,** service des colis postaux 2. *vtr* **(parcelled)** empaqueter; **to p. (up),** mettre en paquets; emballer (des livres). 'parcel 'out *vtr* partager; lotir (des terres).

parch [pɑːtʃ] *vtr* rôtir, griller (des céréales); **grass parched by the wind,** herbe desséchée par le vent; **to be parched (with thirst),** mourir de soif.

parchment ['pɑːtʃmənt] *n* parchemin *m.*

pardon ['pɑːdn] 1. *n* pardon *m; Ecc:* indulgence *f;* **I beg your p.!** (i) je vous demande pardon! (ii) *(asking s.o. to repeat sth)* *(also* **p.)** comment? que dites-vous? *Jur:* **free p.,** grâce *f;* **general p.,** amnistie *f* 2. *vtr* pardonner à (qn); *Jur:* gracier, amnistier (qn). 'pardonable *a* pardonnable, excusable.

pare [pɛər] *vtr* rogner (ses ongles); éplucher (un légume); **to p. (down),** réduire (les dépenses). 'parings *npl* rognures *fpl* (d'ongles); épluchures *fpl* (de fruits).

parent ['pɛərənt] *n* père *m,* mère *f; pl* parents *mpl;* **p. company,** société mère. 'parentage *n* origine *f,* naissance *f.* pa'rental *a* (autorité) des parents, des père et mère; (pouvoir) parental, paternel.

parenthesis [pə'renθəsis] *n (pl* **parentheses** [-'siːz]) parenthèse *f;* **in parentheses,** entre parenthèses.

Paris ['pæris] *Prn Geog:* Paris *m.* Parisian [pə'riziən] *a & n* parisien, -ienne.

parish ['pæriʃ] *n Ecc:* paroisse *f; Adm:* commune *f:* **p. church,** église paroissiale; **p. priest,** curé *m;* **p. council** = conseil municipal. pa'rishioner *n* paroissien, -ienne.

parish ['pæriʃ] *n Ecc:* paroisse *f; Adm:* commune *f:* **p. church,** église paroissiale; **p. priest,** curé *m;* **p. council** = conseil municipal. pa'rishioner *n* paroissien, -ienne.

parity ['pæriti] *n* égalité *f;* parité *f* (de rang, de valeur).

park [pɑːk] 1. *n* parc *m* (clôturé); **(public) p.,** jardin public; **national p.,** parc national; **p. keeper,** gardien de parc 2. *v (a) vtr* garer, parquer (sa voiture) *(b) vi* se garer, stationner. 'parking *n* stationnement *m* (d'une voiture); *PN:* **no p.,** défense de stationner; stationnement interdit; **p. place,** créneau de stationnement; **p. meter,** parcmètre *m; NAm:* **p. lot** *(Br =* carpark), parking *m.*

parliament ['pɑːləmənt] *n* parlement *m;* **Member of P.,** membre du Parlement; **the Houses of P.,** le palais du Parlement; **in p.,** au parlement. parliamen'tarian *a & n* parlementaire *(mf).* parlia'mentary *a* parlementaire; **p. election,** élection législative.

parlour, *NAm:* parlor ['pɑːlər] *n* salon *m;* **p. games,** jeux de société; **beauty p.,** salon de beauté.

parochial [pə'roukiəl] *a Ecc:* paroissial; *Pej:* (point de vue) provincial; (esprit) de clocher.

parody ['pærədi] 1. *n (pl* **parodies)** parodie *f,* pastiche *m* 2. *vtr* **(parodied)** parodier, pasticher.

parole [pə'roul] 1. *n* **prisoner on p.,** prisonnier (i) *Mil:* sur parole (ii) *Jur:* libéré conditionnellement 2. *vtr* libérer (un prisonnier) (i) sur parole (ii) conditionnellement.

paroxysm ['pærəksizm] *n* paroxysme *m;* crise *f* (de fou rire).

parquet ['pɑːkeı] n p. (floor), parquet m; p. flooring, parquetage m.

parrot ['pærət] n Orn: perroquet m; p. fashion, comme un perroquet.

parry ['pæri] vtr (parried) parer, détourner (un coup).

parsimony ['pɑːsımənı] n parcimonie f. **parsi'monious** a parcimonieux. **parsi'moniously** adv parcimonieusement.

parsley ['pɑːslı] n Bot: persil m; Cu: p. sauce, sauce persillée, au persil.

parsnip ['pɑːsnıp] n Cu: Hort: panais m.

parson ['pɑːsn] n Ecc: titulaire m d'un bénéfice (de l'église anglicane); ecclésiastique m; pasteur m. **'parsonage** n = presbytère m; cure f.

part [pɑːt] I. n (a) partie f; **good in parts**, bon en partie; **the funny p. is that,** le comique, c'est que; **to be, form, p. of sth,** faire partie de qch; **it's p. and parcel of,** c'est une partie intégrante de; **for the most p.,** pour la plupart; **ten parts (of) water to one of milk,** dix parties d'eau pour une partie de lait; **in that p. of the world, in those parts,** dans cette région; **what are you doing in these parts?** que fais-tu (par) ici? **in my p. of the world,** chez moi; **p. owner,** copropriétaire mf (b) pièce f (d'une machine, d'un moteur); **spare parts,** pièces de rechange, pièces détachées; **parts of speech,** parties du discours; **principal parts,** temps principaux (d'un verbe) (c) part f; **to take p.** in sth, prendre part, participer, à qch (d) Th: rôle m; personnage m; **to play one's p.,** remplir son rôle; **orchestral parts,** parties d'orchestre; **p. song,** chanson à plusieurs voix (e) parti m; **to take s.o.'s p.,** prendre parti pour qn; **an indiscretion on the p. of s.o.,** une indiscrétion de la part de qn; **for my p.,** quant à moi, pour ma part; **to take sth in good p.,** prendre qch en bonne part, du bon côté; **man of (many) parts,** homme à facettes. II. adv p. **eaten,** partiellement mangé; mangé en partie. III. v 1. vtr (a) séparer (**from,** de); **to p. one's hair,** se faire une raie; **to p. one's hair in the middle,** porter la raie au milieu (b) rompre (une amarre) 2. vi (a) se diviser; (of two people) se quitter, se séparer; (of roads) diverger; **to p. from s.o.,** quitter, se séparer de, qn; **to p. with sth,** céder, se défaire de, qch; **to p. with one's money,** débourser (c) (se) rompre; céder. **'parting** n séparation f; (of waters) partage m; (of hair) raie f; **the p. of the ways,** la croisée des chemins; **p. kiss,** baiser d'adieu; **p. shot,** riposte (lancée en partant). **'partly** adv partiellement; en partie. **'part-'time** a & adv à mi-temps, à temps partiel.

partial ['pɑːʃl] a (a) partial; injuste; **to be p. to sth,** avoir un faible pour qch; **I'm p. to a pipe,** je fume volontiers une pipe (b) partiel; en partie. **parti'ality** n partialité f (**for, to,** pour, envers); favoritisme m; penchant m (pour la boisson). **'partially** adv (a) avec partialité (b) partiellement; en partie.

participate [pɑː'tısıpeıt] vi **to p. in sth,** prendre part, participer, s'associer, à qch. **par'ticipant** n participant, -ante. **partici'pation** n participation f (**in,** à).

participle ['pɑːtısıpl] n Gram: participe m.

particle ['pɑːtıkl] n particule f; parcelle f (d'or); grain m (de sable, de bons sens).

particular [pə'tıkjulər] 1. a (a) particulier; spécial; (objet) déterminé; **that p. book,** ce livre-là; **my own p.**

feelings, mes propres sentiments, mes sentiments personnels; **to take p.** care over doing sth, faire qch avec un soin particulier; **for no p. reason,** sans raison précise; **in p.,** en particulier; notamment (b) (of pers) méticuleux, minutieux; pointilleux; **to be p. about one's food,** être difficile sur la nourriture; **to be p. about one's clothes,** soigner sa mise; **I'm not p. (about it),** je n'y tiens pas tellement 2. n détail m; particularité f; **alike in every p.,** semblables en tout point; **for further particulars apply to,** pour plus amples renseignements, s'adresser à. **particu'larity** n (pl -ies) particularité f. **par'ticularly** adv particulièrement; spécialement, en particulier.

partisan [pɑːtı'zæn] n partisan, -ane.

partition [pɑː'tıʃn] 1. n (a) partage m (d'un pays); morcellement m (d'une terre) (b) cloison f; glass p., vitrage m (c) compartiment m (de cale) 2. vtr partager (un pays); morceler (une terre); **to p. (off) a room,** cloisonner une pièce.

partner ['pɑːtnər] n associé, -ée; Sp: partenaire mf; dancing p., cavalier, -ière; **sleeping p.,** (associé) commanditaire m. **'partnership** n association f; Com: société f; **to go into p. with s.o.,** s'associer avec qn; **to take s.o. into p.,** prendre qn comme associé; **limited p.,** (société en) commandite f.

partridge ['pɑːtrıdʒ] n perdrix f; Cu: perdreau m.

party ['pɑːtı] n (pl parties) (a) parti m (politique); **to follow the p. line,** obéir aux directives du parti; **p. politics,** politique de parti (b) réception f; private p., réunion f intime; **evening p.,** soirée f; **dinner p.,** dîner m; **tea p.,** goûter m d'enfants; (of child) **p. dress,** belle robe; **to give a p.,** recevoir (du monde); **will you join our p.?** voulez-vous être des nôtres? (c) bande f, groupe m (de touristes); équipe f (de secours); Mil: détachement m (d) esp Jur: partie f; **a third p.,** un tiers, une tierce personne; **third p. insurance,** assurance au tiers; **to be (a) p. to a crime,** être complice d'un crime; **p. wall,** mur mitoyen; Tp: **p. line,** ligne partagée.

pass [pɑːs] I. v (passes) 1. vi passer; (move out of sight) disparaître; Aut: doubler; **they passed into the dining room,** ils sont passés dans la salle à manger; **words passed between them,** il y a eu un échange d'injures; **to p. along a street,** passer par une rue; **everyone smiles as he passes (by),** chacun sourit sur son passage; **the procession passed (by) slowly,** le cortège défilait lentement; **to let s.o. p.,** laisser passer qn; (of time) **to p. (by),** passer; s'écouler; **when five minutes had passed,** au bout de cinq minutes; **I don't know what passed between them,** j'ignore ce qui s'est passé entre eux 2. vtr (a) passer devant, près de (qn, qch); **to p. s.o. on the stairs,** croiser qn dans l'escalier (b) passer, franchir (la frontière); dépasser, doubler (une autre voiture) (c) dépasser (le but); outrepasser (les bornes de qch) (d) être reçu à, réussir (un examen) (e) Sch: recevoir (un candidat) (f) Parl: voter, adopter (un projet de loi) (g) transmettre, donner; refiler, écouler (un faux billet de banque); **p. me the salt,** passe-moi le sel; **to p. round the cakes,** faire passer, faire circuler, les gâteaux; Fb: Games: **to p. the ball,** passer le ballon; faire une passe; **to p. the time,** passer le temps; **it passes the time,** cela fait passer le temps (h) faire (des observations) **(on,** sur); **to p. sentence,** prononcer le jugement; **to p. water,** uriner. II. n (pl passes) (a) col *m*, défilé *m* (de montagne) (*b*) **things have come to a pretty p.!** voilà où en sont les choses! **things have come to such a p. that**, les choses en sont venues à (un) tel point que (*c*) *Sch:* **to get, obtain, a p.**, être reçu; **p. (mark)**, moyenne *f* (*d*) permis *m*, laissez-passer *m inv*; **(free) p.**, *Rail: Trans:* carte *f* de circulation; *Th:* billet gratuit, de faveur (*e*) *Fb: Games:* passe *f*; *F:* **to make a p. at s.o.**, faire des avances (amoureuses) à qn. **'passable** *a* (*a*) (rivière, bois) franchissable; (route) praticable (*b*) passable; assez bon. **'passably** *adv* passablement; assez. **passage** ['pæsidʒ] *n* (*a*) passage *m*; *esp Nau:* traversée *f* (*b*) adoption *f* (d'un projet de loi) (*c*) passage; corridor *m*, couloir *m* (*d*) passage (d'un texte). **'passageway** *n* passage. **'pass a'way** *vi* (*of memory*) disparaître; (*of pers*) mourir. **'passbook** *n* livret *m* (de banque). **passenger** *n* (*a*) voyageur, -euse; (*on ship, aircraft*) passager, -ère; **p. train**, train de voyageurs; *Aut:* **p. seat**, siège à côté du conducteur (*b*) *F:* non-valeur *f*; poids mort. **passer-'by** *n* (*pl* **passers-by**) passant, -ante. **'pass 'for** *vtr* passer pour. **'passing 1.** *a* (*a*) passant; qui passe; (remarque) en passant (*b*) passager; éphémère; (désir) fugitif **2.** *n* (*a*) passage (d'un train); écoulement *m* (du temps); (*overtaking*) dépassement *m* (d'une voiture); (*on road*) **p. place**, garage *m*; **in p.**, en passant; à propos (*b*) mort *f* (de qn). **'passkey** *n* (clef *f*) passe-partout *m inv*. **'pass 'off 1.** *vi* (*of pain*) disparaître; **everything passed o. well**, tout s'est bien passé **2.** *vtr* repasser (qch) (**on s.o.**, à qn); faire passer (qch) (**as sth**, pour qch); **to p. oneself o. as s.o.**, **sth**, se faire passer pour qn, qch. **'pass 'on 1.** *vi* (*a*) continuer son chemin; passer (**to another subject**, à un nouveau sujet) (*b*) mourir **2.** *vtr* remettre, faire circuler (qch); (faire) passer (qch); transmettre (une nouvelle). **'pass 'out** *vi* (*a*) *Sch:* sortir (après l'examen final) (*b*) (*to faint*) s'évanouir. **'pass 'over** *vtr* (*for promotion*) **to p. o. s.o.**, donner la préférence à qn d'autre. **'Passover** *n JewRel:* **the (Feast of the) P.**, la (Fête de la) Pâque. **'passport** *n* passeport *m*; *Fig:* passe-partout. **'pass 'through** *vtr* traverser (un pays, une crise); **I'm just passing through (Paris)**, je ne suis que de passage (à Paris). **'pass 'up** *vtr* laisser passer (une occasion). **'password** *n* mot *m* de passe. **past 1.** *a* passé; ancien; **p. president**, président sortant; ancien président; **he's a p. master at (doing) it**, il est expert en la matière; **the p. week**, la semaine dernière, passée; **for some time p.**, depuis quelque temps **2.** *n* passé *m*; **in the p.**, autrefois; dans le passé; *Gram:* au passé; **to be a thing of the p.**, ne plus exister; être périmé **3.** *prep* (*a*) au-delà de; **a little p. the bridge**, un peu plus loin que le pont; **just p. the corner**, juste après le coin; **to walk p. the house**, passer (devant) la maison (*b*) plus de; **it's p. four (o'clock)**, il est quatre heures passées; **half, quarter, p. four**, quatre heures et demie, et quart; **ten (minutes) p. four**, quatre heures dix; **it's half p.**, il est la demie; **he's p. eighty**, il a quatre-vingt ans passés; **she's p. thirty**, elle a passé la trentaine; **p. endurance**, insupportable; **p. (all) belief**, incroyable; **to be p. caring about sth**, être revenu de qch; **I'm p. work**, je ne suis plus d'âge à travailler; *F:* **he's p. it**, il est trop vieux (pour faire qch); *F:* **I wouldn't put it p. him**, il en est bien capable **4.** *adv* **to walk, go, p.**, passer.

passion ['pæʃn] *n* passion *f*; (*anger*) colère *f*, emporte-

ment *m*; **p. for work**, acharnement *m* au travail; **to have a p. for music**, avoir la passion de la musique; *Ecc:* **P. Sunday**, dimanche de la Passion; *Lit:* **p. play**, mystère de la Passion. **'passionate** *a* passionné; (*angry*) emporté; (discours) véhément. **'passionately** *adv* passionnément; (aimer qn) à la folie. **'passionflower** *n Bot:* passiflore *f*.

passive ['pæsiv] *a* & *n* passif (*m*); *Gram:* passif. **'passively** *adv* passivement.

pasta ['pæstə] *n* (*no pl*) *Cu:* pâtes *fpl* (alimentaires).

paste [peist] **1.** *n* (*a*) *Cu: Cer:* pâte *f*; pâté *m* (de viande); mousse *f* (de poisson); **anchovy p.**, beurre *m* d'anchois (*b*) (*glue*) colle *f* (*c*) (*of jewellery*) stras(s) *m*; **it's only p.**, c'est du toc **2.** *vtr* **to p. (up)**, coller (une affiche).

pastel ['pæstl] *n Art:* pastel *m*; **p. drawing**, (dessin au) pastel; **p. shades**, tons pastel.

pasteurize ['pæstjəraiz] *vtr* pasteuriser. **pasteuri'zation** *n* pasteurisation *f*.

pastille ['pæstil] *n* pastille *f*; (*soft*) pâte *f* (de fruits).

pastime ['pɑːstaim] *n* passe-temps *m inv*; divertissement *m*.

pastor ['pɑːstər] *n Ecc:* pasteur *m*.

pastry ['peistri] *n* (*a*) (*pl* **pastries**) pâtisserie *f* (*b*) pâte *f* (de pâtisserie). **'pastrycook** *n* pâtissier, -ière.

pasture ['pɑːstjər] *n* pâturage *m*.

pasty¹ ['peisti] *a* pâteux; (visage) terreux.

pasty² ['pæsti] *n* (*pl* **pasties**) *Cu:* = (petit) pâté (en croûte).

pat [pæt] **1.** *n* (*a*) coup léger; petite tape; caresse *f*; *Fig:* **to give s.o. a p. on the back**, féliciter qn (*b*) rondelle *f*, médaillon *m* (de beurre) **2.** *vtr* (**patted**) taper, tapoter; caresser; *Fig:* **to p. s.o. on the back**, féliciter qn; **to p. oneself on the back**, se féliciter **3.** *adv* **he had his answer off p.**, il a répondu sans hésiter.

patch [pætʃ] **1.** *n* (*a*) pièce *f* (pour raccommoder); (*over eye*) couvre-œil *m*; *Cy:* (*on inner tube*) pastille *f*; (*on tyre*) emplâtre *m*; *F:* **not to be a p. on s.o.**, ne pas arriver à la cheville de qn (*b*) tache *f* (de couleur); flaque *f* (d'huile); plaque *f* (de verglas); pan *m*, coin *m*, échappée *f* (de ciel bleu); morceau *m*, parcelle *f* (de terre); carré *m*, plant *m* (de légumes); **to go through a bad p.**, être dans la déveine **2.** *vtr* rapiécer (un vêtement); *Cy:* poser une pastille à (une chambre à air). **'patch 'up** *vtr* rafistoler (qch); arranger (une querelle). **'patchwork** *n* patchwork *m*. **'patchy** *a* (**-ier, -iest**) inégal.

pâté ['pɑːtei] *n Cu:* pâté *m*.

patent ['pætənt, 'pei-] **1.** *a* (*a*) **letters p.**, lettres patentes (*b*) (*of invention*) breveté; **p. medicine**, spécialité *f* pharmaceutique; **p. leather**, cuir verni (*c*) (fait) manifeste, clair; patent **2.** *n* (*a*) **p. of nobility**, lettres *fpl* de noblesse (*b*) brevet *m* d'invention; **to take out a p. for an invention**, faire breveter une invention; **infringement of a p.**, contrefaçon *f* (*c*) invention brevetée **3.** *vtr* faire breveter.

paternity [pə'tɜːniti] *n* paternité *f*. **pa'ternal** *a* paternel. **pa'ternally** *adv* paternellement.

path [pɑːθ] *n* (*pl* **paths** [pɑːðz]) (*a*) chemin *m*; sentier *m*; (*in garden*) allée *f* (*b*) cours *m*, trajet *m*, course *f* (d'un corps en mouvement); route *f* (du soleil); trajectoire *f* (de l'orage, d'une fusée). **'pathway** *n* sentier.

pathetic [pə'θetik] *a* pathétique, attendrissant; (*of*

pers) pitoyable. **pa'thetically** *adv* pathétique-
ment.

pathology [pə'θɔlədʒi] *n* pathologie *f.*
patho'logical *a* pathologique. **pa'thologist** *n* pathologiste *mf;* **(forensic) p.,** médecin *m*
légiste.

pathos ['peiθɔs] *n* pathétique *m.*

patience ['peiʃns] *n* (a) patience *f;* **to try s.o.'s p.,**
éprouver la patience de qn; **I've lost (my) p., my p.
is exhausted,** je suis à bout de patience; **I have no p.
with him,** il m'impatiente (b) *Cards:* réussite *f.* **'patient 1.** *a* patient; endurant; **to be p.,** patienter **2.**
n malade *mf;* patient, -ente. **'patiently** *adv* patiemment.

patio ['pætiou] *n* patio *m* (d'une maison).

patrimony ['pætriməni] *n* (*pl* **patrimonies)** patrimoine *m.*

patriot ['peitriot, 'pæ-] *n* patriote *mf.* **patri'otic** *a*
(of *pers)* patriote; (discours) patriotique.
patri'otically *adv* (agir) en patriote, patriotique-
ment. **'patriotism** *n* patriotisme *m.*

patrol [pə'troul] **1.** *n* patrouille *f;* **p. leader,** chef de
patrouille; **to be on p.,** être de patrouille; **to go on p.,**
faire la patrouille; **police p. car,** voiture de liaison
policière; *NAm:* **p. wagon** (*Br* = **Black Maria),**
voiture cellulaire; *F:* panier *m* à salade **2.** *vtr & i*
(patrolled) patrouiller, faire la patrouille (dans un
quartier). **pa'trolman** *n* (*pl* **-men)** (a) patrouilleur
m (b) *NAm:* agent *m* de police.

patron ['peitran] *n* (a) protecteur, -trice (des arts);
patron, -onne (d'une œuvre de charité); **p. saint,**
patron, -onne (b) *Com:* client, -ente (d'un magasin);
habitué, -ée (d'un théâtre). **patronage** ['pætrən-] *n*
(a) patronage *m;* protection *f* (b) *Pej:* air protecteur
(envers qn) (c) clientèle *f* (d'un hôtel). **patronize**
['pæ-] *vtr* (a) protéger (un artiste) (b) traiter (qn) avec
condescendance (c) être client (d'un magasin);
fréquenter (un cinéma). **patronizing** ['pæ-] *a* (ton)
de condescendance. **'patronizingly** *adv* d'un air
condescendant.

patter[1] ['pætər] *n* baratin *m,* boniment *m,* bagout *m.*

patter[2] **1.** *vi* (of *pers)* trottiner, marcher à petits pas
rapides et légers; (of *hail, rain)* grésiller, crépiter **2.**
n petit bruit (de pas rapides); crépitement *m,* grésillement *m* (de la pluie).

pattern ['pætən] **1.** *n* (a) modèle *m,* type *m* (b) *Dressm:*
patron *m* (en papier) (c) *Com:* échantillon *m;* **p. book,**
livre d'échantillons (d) dessin *m,* motif *m* (de papier
peint, de tissu) **2.** *vtr* modeler (**on,** sur). **'patterned**
a (tissu) imprimé, à dessins.

patty ['pæti] *n* (*pl* **patties)** *Cu:* = (petit) pâté (en
croûte).

paunch [pɔːntʃ] *n* panse *f,* ventre *m.*

pauper ['pɔːpər] *n* indigent, -ente.

pause [pɔːz] **1.** *n* pause *f,* arrêt *m; Mus:* repos *m;* **a p.
(in the conversation),** un silence **2.** *vi* faire une pause;
s'arrêter un instant; marquer un temps; hésiter.

pave [peiv] *vtr* paver (une rue); carreler (une cour); **to
p. the way,** préparer le terrain. **'pavement** *n*
trottoir *m; NAm:* chaussée *f.* **'paving** *n* (a) pavage
m, dallage *m,* carrelage *m* (b) pavé *m,* dalles *fpl,*
carreaux *mpl.* **'pavingstone** *n* pavé.

pavilion [pə'viliən] *n Sp: Arch:* pavillon *m.*

paw [pɔː] **1.** *n* patte *f* **2.** *vtr* donner des coups de patte à;

F: (of pers) tripoter; (of *horse)* **to p. (the ground),**
piaffer.

pawn[1] [pɔːn] **1.** *n* in **p.,** en gage; **to put one's watch in p.,**
mettre sa montre en gage **2.** *vtr* mettre (qch) en gage;
engager (qch). **'pawnbroker** *n* prêteur, -euse, sur
gages. **'pawnshop** *n* bureau *m* de prêt sur gages.

pawn[2] *n Chess:* pion *m;* **to be s.o.'s p.,** être le jouet de
qn.

pay [pei] **1.** *vtr & i* (paid) (a) payer; rembourser (un
créancier); **to p. s.o. £100,** payer £100 à qn; **to p. cash
(down),** payer (argent) comptant; *F:* **to p. through the
nose,** payer un prix excessif; *F:* **to make s.o. p. through
the nose,** écorcher qn; *Adm:* **p. as you earn, PAYE,**
retenue *f* de l'impôt à la source; (on *receipted bill)*
paid, pour acquit; **to p. a bill,** régler un compte; **to p. a
debt,** payer une dette; **to p. for sth,** payer qch; **how
much did you p. for it?** combien l'avez-vous payé? **to p.
in a cheque,** remettre un chèque à la banque; faire
porter un chèque au crédit de son compte; **to p. money
into s.o.'s account,** verser de l'argent au compte de qn;
to be paid by the hour, être payé à l'heure; **to p. s.o. to
do sth,** payer qn pour faire qch; **I wouldn't do it if you
paid me,** je ne le ferais pas même si on me payait (b)
faire (attention); rendre (hommage); **to p. s.o. a visit,**
rendre visite à qn; *F:* **to p. a visit,** aller faire pipi (c)
he'll p. for this! I'll make him p. for this! il me le payera!
it will p. you, vous y gagnerez; **business that doesn't p.,**
affaire qui ne rapporte pas, qui n'est pas rentable; **it
pays to advertise,** la publicité rapporte **2.** *n* paie *f,*
salaire *m* (d'un ouvrier, d'un employé); traitement *m*
(d'un fonctionnaire); *Mil:* solde *f;* **holidays with p.,**
congés payés; **to be in s.o.'s p.,** être à la solde, aux
gages, de qn; **p. day,** jour de paie; **p. slip,** bulletin,
feuille de paie; **p. cheque,** chèque de salaire; **p. packet,**
paie; **p. desk,** caisse *f;* **p. phone,** *NAm:* **p. station,**
cabine téléphonique. **paid** *a* payé; rétribué; ré-
muné; (employé) salarié; (tueur) à gages; **p. holidays,** congés payés; **to put p. to,** anéantir (des espoirs,
des projets); *Pol:* **(fully) p. up,** (membre) qui a payé,
qui est à jour de sa cotisation. **'payable** *a* payable;
acquittable; **rates p. by the tenant,** impôts à la charge
du locataire; **to make a cheque p. to s.o.,** faire un
chèque à l'ordre de qn. **'pay 'back** *vtr* rendre,
rembourser, restituer (de l'argent emprunté); rembourser (qn); **to p. s.o. back (in his own coin),** rendre
à qn la monnaie de sa pièce. **pay'ee** *n* bénéficiaire
mf. **'paying 1.** *a* rémunérateur; qui rapporte; rentable; payant; **p. guest,** pensionnaire *mf* **2.** *n* paiement *m,* versement *m* (d'argent); remboursement *m*
(d'un créancier); règlement *m* (d'une dette); *Bank:*
p. in book, slip, carnet, bulletin, de versement. **'paymaster** *n* trésorier *m.* **'payment** *n* paiement *m;*
versement *m;* remboursement *m;* règlement *m;* rémunération *f* (de services rendus); **on p. of £10,** moyennant
paiement de, contre paiement de, £10; **without p.,** à
titre gracieux. **'pay 'off 1.** *vtr* (a) régler (une dette);
rembourser (un créancier) (b) congédier (des ouvriers); licencier (des troupes); débarquer (des
marins) **2.** *vi* (of *deal, efforts)* être payant, rentable;
porter fruit. **'payoff** *n F:* paiement, règlement; *Pej:*
pot-de-vin *m.* **'pay 'out** *vtr* (a) payer, débourser
(b) *esp Nau:* (laisser) filer (un câble). **'payroll** *n*
livre *m* de paie; registre *m* des salaires; **to be on the p.,**
faire partie du personnel. **'pay 'up** *vtr & i* payer.

PAYE *abbr* pay as you earn.

PC *abbr* police constable.

PE *abbr* physical education.

pea [piː] *n Hort:* pois *m; Cu:* **green peas,** petits pois; *Cu:* **p. soup,** soupe aux pois; *Bot:* **sweet peas,** pois de senteur; **p. green,** vert feuille *m inv.* **'peashooter** *n* (petite) sarbacane.

peace [piːs] *n* (*a*) paix *f;* **at p.,** en paix (**with,** avec); **p. treaty,** traité de paix; **p. offering,** cadeau de réconciliation; **to make (one's) p. with s.o.,** faire la paix avec qn; **to keep the p.,** (i) ne pas troubler l'ordre public (ii) veiller à l'ordre public (*b*) traité *m* de paix (*c*) tranquillité *f;* **to live in p.,** vivre en paix; **to leave s.o. in p.,** laisser qn tranquille. **'peaceable** *a* pacifique; qui aime la paix. **'peaceably** *adv* pacifiquement. **'peaceful** *a* (*a*) paisible, calme, tranquille (*b*) pacifique. **'peacefully** *adv* (*a*) paisiblement; tranquillement (*b*) pacifiquement. **'peacefulness** *n* tranquillité, paix. **'peace-keeping** *n* **p.-k. force,** force de maintien de la paix. **'peace-loving** *a* qui aime la paix; pacifique. **'peacemaker** *n* pacificateur, -trice. **'peacetime** *n* temps de paix.

peach [piːtʃ] *n Hort:* pêche *f;* **p. (tree),** pêcher *m.*

peacock ['piːkɔk] *n Orn:* paon *m.* **'peahen** *n* paonne *f.*

peak [piːk] *n* (*a*) visière *f* (de casquette) (*b*) pic *m,* cime *f,* sommet *m* (de montagne); pointe *f* (d'un toit, d'une fièvre, d'une courbe); pointe *f* (d'une courbe, d'une charge); *El:* **p. load,** charge maximum (d'un générateur); *Ind:* **p. output,** record *m* (de production); prosperity was at its **p.,** la prospérité était à son apogée, son maximum; **p. hours,** heures de pointe, d'affluence. **peaked** *a* (casquette) à visière. **'peaky** *a F:* pâlot, malingre.

peal [piːl] 1. *n* (*a*) **p. of bells,** carillon *m;* **to ring a p.,** carillonner (*b*) grondement *m* (de tonnerre, de l'orgue); coup *m* (de tonnerre); **p. of laughter,** éclat *m* de rire 2. *v* **to p. (out)** (*a*) *vi* (*of bells*) carillonner; (*of thunder*) gronder; (*of the organ*) retentir; (*of laughter*) résonner (*b*) *vtr* sonner (les cloches) à toute volée.

peanut ['piːnʌt] *n Bot:* arachide *f; Com:* cacahuète *f; F: pl* trois fois rien; une bagatelle; **p. oil,** huile d'arachide; **p. butter,** beurre d'arachide.

pear [pɛər] *n* poire *f;* **p. (tree),** poirier *m.*

pearl [pɜːl] *n* perle *f;* **string of pearls, p. necklace,** collier de perles; **cultured pearls,** perles de culture; **p. oyster,** huître perlière; **mother of p.,** nacre *f;* **p. button,** bouton de nacre; **p. barley,** orge perlé; **p. diver,** pêcheur, -euse, de perles. **'pearly** *a* perlé, nacré.

peasant ['pezənt] *n* paysan, -anne; campagnard, -arde.

peat [piːt] *n* tourbe *f.*

pebble ['pebl] *n* caillou *m;* (*on shore*) galet *m; F:* **you're not the only p. on the beach,** il n'y a pas que toi (sur la terre). **'pebbledash** *n* crépi (moucheté). **'pebbly** *a* caillouteux; (plage) de galets.

peck [pek] 1. *n* coup *m* de bec; *F:* (*kiss*) bécot *m* 2. *v* (*a*) *vtr & i* **to p. (at),** picorer, picoter, becqueter; donner un coup de bec, des coups de bec, à; **to p. at one's food,** pignocher; *F:* **pecking order,** hiérarchie (sociale) (*b*) *vtr F:* (*kiss*) bécoter. **'peckish** *a F:* **to feel (a bit) p.,** se sentir le ventre creux.

peculiar [pi'kjuːliər] *a* (*a*) particulier; spécial; propre (**to s.o.,** à qn) (*b*) étrange; bizarre, singulier.

peculi'arity *n* (*a*) trait distinctif; particularité *f;* (*on passport*) **special peculiarities,** signes particuliers (*b*) bizarrerie *f,* singularité *f.* **pe'culiarly** *adv* (*a*) particulièrement (*b*) étrangement; singulièrement.

pecuniary [pi'kjuːniəri] *a* pécuniaire; **p. difficulties,** ennuis *m* d'argent.

pedagogical [pedə'gɔdʒikl] *a* pédagogique.

pedal ['pedl] 1. *n* pédale *f; Aut:* **clutch p.,** pédale d'embrayage; (*of piano*) **soft, loud, p.,** petite, grande, pédale 2. *vi* (**pedalled**) pédaler. **'pedalbin** *n DomEc:* poubelle *f* à pédale. **'pedalboat** *n* pédalo *m.* **'pedalcar** *n* voiture *f* à pédales.

pedant ['pedənt] *n* pédant, -ante. **pe'dantic** *a* pédant; pédantesque. **pe'dantically** *adv* en pédant.

peddle ['pedl] *vtr* faire le colportage de (qch); colporter (des marchandises); **to p. drugs,** faire le trafic des stupéfiants. **'peddler, 'pedlar** *n* colporteur *m;* (*drug*) *p.,* trafiquant *m* (de stupéfiants).

pedestal ['pedistl] *n* piédestal *m;* socle *m.*

pedestrian [pi'destriən] 1. *a* (*a*) pédestre (*b*) (style, livre) prosaïque, terre à terre 2. *n* piéton *m;* **p. crossing,** passage clouté, pour piétons; **p. precinct,** rue piétonnière, piétonne.

pedicure ['pedikjuər] *n* soins *mpl* du pédicure.

pedigree ['pedigriː] 1. *n* (*a*) arbre *m* généalogique (*b*) ascendance *f,* généalogie *f* (de qn) (*c*) *Breed:* certificat *m* d'origine, pedigree *m* (d'un animal) 2. *a* (chien) de (pure) race; (taureau) de bonne lignée.

pee [piː] *vi & n P:* **to p., have a p.,** faire pipi, pisser.

peek [piːk] *vi & n F:* **to p., have a p., at,** jeter un coup d'œil (furtif) à.

peel [piːl] 1. *n* pelure *f;* écorce *f,* peau *f; Cu:* zeste *m* (de citron, d'orange); **candied p.,** zeste confit 2. *v* (*a*) *vtr* peler (un fruit), éplucher (des pommes de terre); décortiquer (des amandes); écorcer (un bâton) (*b*) *vi* (*of paint*) s'écailler; (*of skin, nose*) peler. **'peeler** *n* éplucheur *m.* **'peelings** *npl* épluchures *fpl.* **'peel 'off** 1. *vtr* enlever (la peau d'un fruit, des vêtements) 2. *vi* (*a*) (*of paint*) s'écailler; (*of skin*) peler (*b*) (*of pers*) se déshabiller (*c*) (*of aircraft*) se détacher (de la formation).

peep [piːp] 1. *n* coup d'œil (furtif); **to get a p. at sth,** entrevoir qch 2. *vi* **to p. at sth,** regarder qch à la dérobée; jeter un coup d'œil (furtif) à qch; **to p. (out),** se laisser entrevoir, se montrer. **'peephole** *n* judas *m;* (trou *m* de) regard *m.* **peeping 'Tom** *n* voyeur *m.*

peer¹ [piər] *n* **p. of the Realm,** pair *m* du Royaume-Uni; **life p.,** pair à vie. **'peerage** *n* (*a*) pairie *f* (*b*) *coll* les pairs; la noblesse. **'peeress** *n* (*pl -es*) pairesse *f.*

peer² *vi* **to p. at s.o., sth,** scruter qn, qch, du regard; **to p. over the wall,** risquer un coup d'œil par-dessus le mur.

peevish ['piːviʃ] *a* irritable, maussade. **peeved** *a F:* fâché, embêté. **'peevishly** *adv* avec humeur, maussadement. **'peevishness** *n* maussaderie *f.*

peewit ['piːwit] *n Orn:* vanneau (huppé).

peg [peg] 1. *n* cheville *f* (en bois); fiche *f;* piquet *m* (de tente); (**hat, coat**) **p.,** patère *f;* **clothes p.** (*NAm:* = **clothespin**) pince *f* à linge; **clothes off the p.,** vêtements de confection; **he's a square p. in a round hole,** il n'est pas à sa place; *F:* **to take s.o. down a p. (or two),** rabattre le caquet à qn 2. *vtr* (**pegged**) cheviller (un assemblage); *Fin:* stabiliser (les prix); *Sp:* **it's still level pegging,** ils sont encore à égalité. **'peg a'way** *vi F:* travailler assidûment (at, à). **'peg 'down** *vtr* fixer (une tente) avec des piquets; *Fig:* entraver (qn). **'peg 'out 1.** *vtr* accrocher (du linge) avec des pinces **2.** *vi F:* mourir; casser sa pipe.

pejorative [pi'dʒɔrativ] *a* péjoratif.

Pekinese ['pi:ki'ni:z], *F:* **Peke** [pi:k] *n* (chien) pékinois *m*.

pelican ['pelikən] *n Orn:* pélican *m*; **p. crossing,** passage clouté (avec feux commandés par les piétons).

pellet ['pelit] *n* boulette *f* (de papier); pelote *f* (d'argile); pastille *f* (de plastique); *Sma:* grain *m* de plomb; *Pharm:* pilule *f*; *Husb:* granulé *m*.

pell-mell ['pel'mel] **1.** *adv* pêle-mêle **2.** *a* en désordre.

pelmet ['pelmit] *n* lambrequin *m*.

pelt [pelt] **1.** *vtr* **to p. s.o. with stones,** lancer des pierres à qn; **he pelted abuse at them,** il les a criblés d'injures **2.** *vi* (*a*) (*of rain*) **to p. (down),** tomber à verse; **pelting rain,** pluie battante (*b*) courir à toutes jambes.

pelvis ['pelvis] *n Anat:* bassin *m*.

pen¹ [pen] **1.** *n* parc *m*, enclos *m*; abri *m* (de sous marins) **2.** *vtr* (**penned**) **to p. (in, up),** parquer.

pen² *n* plume *f* (pour écrire); **fountain p.,** stylo *m*; **ballpoint p.,** stylo à bille; **to put p. to paper,** écrire; **p. name,** nom de plume; **p.-and-ink drawing,** dessin à la plume. **'penfriend** *n* correspondant, -ante. **'penknife** *n* (*pl* **-knives**) canif *m*.

penal ['pi:nl] *a* (*of laws*) pénal; **p. servitude,** travaux forcés. **'penalize** *vtr* sanctionner (un délit) d'une peine; infliger une peine à (qn); *Sp:* pénaliser (un joueur); handicaper (un coureur, un cheval). **penalty** ['pen-] *n* (*pl* **-ies**) (*a*) peine *f*, pénalité *f*; *Adm:* sanction (pénale); **the death p.,** la peine de mort; **to pay the p.,** subir les conséquences (*b*) *Sp:* pénalisation *f*, pénalité *f*; *Fb:* **p. (kick),** penalty *m*; **p. area,** surface de réparation.

penance ['penəns] *n* **to do p. for one's sins,** faire pénitence *f* de, pour, ses péchés.

pence [pens] *npl see* **penny**.

pencil ['pensl] **1.** *n* crayon *m*; **lead p.,** crayon à mine (de plomb); **coloured p.,** crayon de couleur; **written in p.,** écrit au crayon; **p. mark,** trait au crayon; **p. sharpener,** taille-crayon(s) *m* **2.** *vtr* **to p. (in),** marquer, écrire, au crayon.

pendant ['pendənt] *n* pendentif *m* (de collier).

pending ['pendiŋ] **1.** *a Jur:* (procès) pendant, en instance **2.** *prep* en attendant (qch).

pendulum ['pendjulɔm] *n* pendule *m*, balancier *m*.

penetrate ['penitreit] *vtr & i* pénétrer; **to p. through,** passer à travers. **'penetrating** *a* pénétrant; (son) mordant. **pene'tration** *n* pénétration *f*.

penguin ['peŋgwin] *n Orn:* manchot *m*; pingouin *m*.

penicillin [peni'silin] *n Med:* pénicilline *f*.

peninsula [pi'ninsjulə] *n* péninsule *f*; presqu'île *f*.

penis ['pi:nis] *n Anat:* pénis *m*.

penitence ['penitəns] *n* pénitence *f*; contrition *f*. **'penitent** *a & n* pénitent, -ente. **peni'tentiary** *n esp US:* prison *f*. **'penitently** *adv* d'un air contrit.

penny ['peni] *n* (*pl* **pennies, pence** ['peniz, pens]) penny *m*; **a ten pence piece,** une pièce de dix pence; **there were ten pennies on the table,** il y avait dix pennies sur la table; **they haven't got a p. to their name,**

ils sont sans le sou; *F:* **the p.'s dropped,** j'y suis! ça y est! *F:* **to spend a p.,** aller faire pipi; **they're two a p. nowadays,** c'est monnaie courante à l'heure actuelle; **a p. for your thoughts,** à quoi rêvez-vous? *Prov:* **in for a p., in for a pound,** quand le vin est tiré il faut le boire; **that will cost a pretty p.,** cela coûtera cher. **'penniless** *a* sans le sou, sans ressources.

pension ['penʃən] *n* pension *f*, retraite *f*; **Government p.,** pension sur l'État; **old age p.,** retraite (de) vieillesse; **retirement p.,** pension de retraite; **p. fund,** caisse de retraite. **'pensionable** *a* (*pers*) qui a droit à une pension, à une retraite; (*of job*) qui donne droit à une pension, à une retraite; (âge) de la (mise à la) retraite. **'pensioner** *n* retraité, -ée. **'pension 'off** *vtr* mettre (qn) à la retraite.

pensive ['pensiv] *a* pensif, songeur. **'pensively** *adv* pensivement; d'un air pensif.

pent [pent] *a* **p. up,** renfermé; (*of emotion*) refoulé; **to be p. up,** avoir les nerfs tendus.

pentagon ['pentəgən] *n* pentagone *m*.

pentathlon [pen'tæθlən] *n Sp:* pentathlon *m*.

Pentecost ['pentəkɔst] *n Ecc:* Pentecôte *f*.

penthouse ['penthaus] *n* appartement (de) terrasse construit sur le toit d'un immeuble.

penultimate [pen'ʌltimət] *a & n* pénultième (*mf*); avant-dernier, -ière.

penury ['penjuri] *n* indigence *f*; pauvreté *f*. **pe'nurious** *a* pauvre.

peony ['pi:əni] *n* (*pl* **peonies**) *Bot:* pivoine *f*.

people ['pi:pl] **1.** *n coll* (*with pl const except (a) where pl is* **peoples**) (*a*) peuple *m*; nation *f*; habitants *mpl* (d'une ville); **the French p.,** les Français *m*; **country p.,** les populations rurales; **the King and his p.,** le roi et ses sujets *mpl* (*b*) parents *mpl*; famille *f*; **my p. are abroad,** mes parents sont à l'étranger (*c*) citoyens *mpl*; **government by the p.,** gouvernement par le peuple; **people's democracy,** démocratie populaire; **the (common) p.,** la populace; le (bas) peuple (*d*) gens *mpl*; **young p.,** jeunes gens; **old p.,** les vieux *m*, les vieilles gens; **old people's home,** maison de retraite pour personnes âgées; **what do you p. think?** qu'en pensez-vous, vous autres? **why him, of all p.?** pourquoi lui? **there weren't many p.,** il n'y avait pas beaucoup de monde (*e*) personnes; **one thousand p.,** mille personnes (*f*) (*indefinite*) on; **p. say,** on dit **2.** *vtr* peupler (with, de).

pep [pep] *n F:* entrain *m*, fougue *f*; **full of p.,** plein d'allant *m*; **p. pill,** excitant *m*; **p. talk,** petit discours d'encouragement. **'pep 'up** *vtr* (**pepped**) *F:* ragaillardir (qn); remonter (une affaire); *Th:* corser (une pièce).

pepper ['pepər] **1.** *n* (*a*) (*spice*) poivre *m*; *Bot:* **p. plant,** poivrier *m*; *Cu:* **black, white, p.,** poivre noir, gris; **p. pot,** poivrière *f* (*b*) (*vegetable*) **red, green, p.,** poivron *m* rouge, vert **2.** *vtr* poivrer. **'peppercorn** *n* grain *m* de poivre. **'peppermill** *n* moulin *m* à poivre. **'peppermint** *n* (*a*) *Bot:* menthe (anglaise) (*b*) pastille *f* de menthe; **p. sweet, toothpaste,** bonbon, pâte dentifrice, à la menthe. **'peppery** *a* (trop) poivré; (*of pers*) irascible.

per [pə:r] *prep* par; **ten francs p. kilo,** dix francs le kilo; **as p. invoice,** suivant facture; **as p. sample,** conformément à l'échantillon; **sixty kilometres p. hour,** soixante kilomètres à l'heure; **p. day,** par jour; **p. annum,**

par an; **p. cent**, pour cent; *F:* **as p. usual,** comme d'habitude. **per'centage** *n* pourcentage *m.*

perambulator [pə'ræmbjuleitər] *n A: & Lit:* voiture *f* d'enfant; landau *m.*

perceive [pə'siːv] *vtr* percevoir (la vérité, une odeur); s'apercevoir de (qch, que); apercevoir (qn). **per'ceptible** *a* perceptible (à l'oreille, à l'œil); (différence) sensible. **per'ceptibly** *adv* sensiblement. **per'ception** *n* perception *f;* sensibilité *f.* **per'ceptive** *a (of pers)* perspicace; sensible.

perch[1] [pəːtʃ] 1. *n* perchoir *m* 2. *vtr & i* (se) percher; (se) jucher.

perch[2] *n (no pl) Ich:* perche *f.*

percolate ['pəːkəleit] *vi* s'infiltrer; *(of coffee)* filtrer, passer. **'percolator** *n* cafetière *f* automatique (à pression).

percussion [pə'kʌʃn] *n* percussion *f; Mus:* **p. instrument,** instrument de, à, percussion.

peremptory [pə'remptəri] *a* péremptoire; *(of refusal)* absolu; *(of tone)* dogmatique, tranchant. **pe'remptorily** *adv* péremptoirement; (parler) impérieusement.

perennial [pə'reniəl] 1. *a* éternel, perpétuel; (plante) vivace 2. *n* plante *f* vivace. **pe'rennially** *adv* à perpétuité.

perfect 1. ['pəːfikt] *(a) a* parfait; (ouvrage) achevé; **his English is p.,** son anglais est impeccable; *F:* **p. idiot,** parfait imbécile; **he's a p. stranger to me,** il m'est tout à fait inconnu *(b) a & n Gram:* **the p. (tense),** le parfait 2. *vtr* [pə'fekt] achever; rendre (qch) parfait; perfectionner, parfaire (qch); mettre (une invention) au point. **per'fecting** *n* perfectionnement *m.* **per'fection** *n* perfection *f.* **per'fectionist** *n* perfectionniste *mf.* **'perfectly** *adv* parfaitement.

perfidy ['pəːfidi] *n* perfidie *f.* **per'fidious** *a* perfide. **per'fidiously** *adv* perfidement.

perforate ['pəːfəreit] *vtr* perforer, percer, transpercer; perforer (du papier) en pointillé. **perfo'ration** *n* perforation *f; (on paper)* moletage *m,* pointillé *m.*

perform [pə'fɔːm] 1. *vtr (a)* célébrer (un rite); exécuter (un mouvement); accomplir (une tâche); remplir (son devoir); *Surg:* **to p. an operation on s.o.,** opérer qn *(b) Th:* jouer (une pièce); exécuter (une danse); **performing dogs,** chiens savants 2. *vi* **to p. in a play,** jouer dans une pièce; **to p. on the flute,** jouer de la flûte. **per'formance** *n (a)* fonctionnement *m* (d'une machine); rendement *m* (d'un moteur, d'un athlète) *(b) Th:* représentation *f* (d'une pièce); séance *f* (de cinéma); **evening p.,** soirée *f;* **afternoon p.,** matinée *f;* **no p. tonight,** ce soir relâche; *F:* **what a p.!** quelle histoire! **per'former** *n* artiste *mf; Mus:* exécutant, -ante; *Th:* acteur, -trice.

perfume 1. *n* ['pəːfjuːm] parfum *m;* odeur *f* agréable; **bottle of p.,** flacon de parfum 2. *vtr* [pə'fjuːm] parfumer. **per'fumery** *n* parfumerie *f.*

perfunctory [pə'fʌŋktəri] *a (a) (of inquiry)* fait pour la forme; (coup d'œil) superficiel; **p. inquiry,** enquête peu poussée *(b) (of pers)* négligent; peu zélé. **per'functorily** *adv* superficiellement; pour la forme.

perhaps [pə'hæps] *adv* peut-être; **p. so, p. not,** peut-être (bien) que oui, que non; **p. we'll come back tomorrow,** peut-être reviendrons-nous demain; **p. I have it,** il se peut que je l'aie.

peril ['peril] *n* péril *m,* danger *m;* **in p. of one's life,** en danger de mort; **at one's (own) p.,** à ses risques *m* et périls. **'perilous** *a* périlleux, dangereux. **'perilously** *adv* périlleusement, dangereusement.

perimeter [pə'rimitər] *n* périmètre *m; Sp: etc:* **p. track,** piste périphérique.

period ['piəriəd] *n (a)* période *f;* durée *f,* délai *m;* **within the agreed p.,** dans le délai convenu; **for a p. of three months,** pendant une période de trois mois; *Meteor:* **clear periods,** éclaircies *fpl (b)* époque *f,* âge *m;* **p. furniture,** meubles de style, d'époque *(c) Sch:* (heure *f* de) cours *m (d) Gram:* point *m* (de ponctuation); *F: esp NAm:* **he's no good, p.,** il est nul, un point, c'est tout! *(e)* règles *fpl* (d'une femme). **peri'odic** *a* périodique. **peri'odical** *a & n* périodique (*m*). **peri'odically** *adv* périodiquement.

peripheral [pə'rifərəl] *a* périphérique.

periscope ['periskoup] *n* périscope *m.*

perish ['periʃ] *vi* périr, mourir; *(of rubber)* se détériorer; *F:* **I'm perishing (cold), I'm perished,** je meurs de froid; **it's perishing (cold),** il fait un froid de loup, de canard. **'perishable** 1. *a* périssable 2. *npl* marchandises *fpl* périssables.

peritonitis [peritə'naitis] *n Med:* péritonite *f.*

periwinkle[1] ['periwiŋkl] *n Bot:* pervenche *f.*

periwinkle[2] *n Moll:* bigorneau *m.*

perjure ['pəːdʒər] *vpr* **to p. oneself,** se parjurer; commettre un parjure; *Jur:* porter faux témoignage. **'perjurer** *n* parjure *mf.* **'perjury** *n* parjure *m; Jur:* faux serment; faux témoignage; *Jur:* **to commit p.,** faire un faux serment.

perk[1] [pəːk] *v* **to p. up** *(a) vi* se raviver; se ranimer *(b) vtr* requinquer, ravigoter (qn). **'perkily** *adv* d'un air éveillé, dégagé. **'perky** *a* (-ier, -iest) éveillé; guilleret; (ton) désinvolte.

perk[2] *n F:* à-côté *m; pl* petits profits; avantages *m.*

perm [pəːm] *F:* 1. *n* permanente *f* 2. *vtr* **to p. s.o.'s hair,** faire une permanente à qn; **to have one's hair permed,** se faire faire une permanente.

permanent ['pəːmənənt] *a* permanent; **p. address,** adresse fixe; **p. wave,** permanente *f.* **'permanence** *n* permanence *f.* **'permanency** *n* emploi permanent. **'permanently** *adv* d'une façon permanente; en permanence.

permeate ['pəːmieit] *vtr & i* **to p. (through) sth,** filtrer à travers qch. **permea'bility** *n* perméabilité *f.* **'permeable** *a* perméable; pénétrable.

permissible [pə'misibl] *a* permis; acceptable. **per'mission** *n* permission *f;* autorisation *f.* **per'missive** *a* **p. society,** société permissive.

permit 1. *vtr* [pə'mit] **(permitted)** permettre; **to p. s.o. to do sth,** permettre à qn de faire qch; **p. me to tell you the truth,** laisser-moi vous dire la vérité; **I was permitted to visit the works,** on m'a autorisé à visiter l'usine 2. *n* ['pəːmit] permis *m;* autorisation *f; (to enter)* laissez-passer *m inv; Cust:* passavant *m.*

pernicious [pə'niʃəs] *a* pernicieux. **per'niciously** *adv* pernicieusement.

pernickety [pə'nikiti] *a F: (of pers)* vétilleux, pointilleux; *(of job)* délicat, minutieux; **p. old fool!** vieux tatillon! **p. about one's food,** difficile sur sa nourriture.

peroxide [pə'rɔksaid] *n Ch:* peroxyde *m;* **hydrogen p.,** eau oxygénée.

perpendicular [pəːpən'dikjulər] *a & n* perpendiculaire (*f*); (*of cliff*) à pic.

perpetrate ['pəːpitreit] *vtr* commettre, perpétrer (un crime). **'perpetrator** *n* auteur *m* (d'un crime, d'une farce).

perpetual [pə'petjuəl] *a* (*a*) perpétuel, éternel (*b*) sans fin; continuel. **per'petually** *adv* (*a*) perpétuellement (*b*) sans cesse. **per'petuate** *vtr* perpétuer, éterniser. **perpetu'ation** *n* préservation *f* (de qch) de l'oubli. **perpetuity** [pəːpi'tjuːiti] *n* perpétuité *f*; **in, for, p.,** à perpétuité.

perplex [pə'pleks] *vtr* embarrasser (qn); rendre (qn) perplexe. **per'plexed** *a* (*of pers*) perplexe, embarrassé. **per'plexedly** [-idli] *adv* d'un air perplexe. **per'plexing** *a* embarrassant, troublant; difficile (à comprendre). **per'plexity** *n* perplexité *f*, embarras *m*.

perquisite ['pəːkwizit] *n* à-côté *m*; *pl* petits profits.

persecute ['pəːsikjuːt] *vtr* persécuter (qn); tourmenter; harceler. **perse'cution** *n* persécution *f*; **p. mania,** délire, manie, de la persécution. **'persecutor** *n* persécuteur, -trice.

persevere [pəːsi'viər] *vi* persévérer (**with, in,** dans). **perse'verance** *n* persévérance *f*. **perse'vering** *a* persévérant, assidu (**in doing sth,** à faire qch).

Persia ['pəːʃə] *Prn Geog:* Perse *f*. **'Persian 1.** *a* persan; *AHist:* perse; **the P. Gulf,** le Golfe Persique; **P. carpet,** tapis de Perse **2.** *n* (*a*) Persan, -ane; *AHist:* Perse *mf* (*b*) *Ling:* persan *m*.

persist [pə'sist] *vi* persister; continuer; **to p. in doing sth,** persister, s'obstiner, à faire qch. **per'sistence** *n* persistance *f* (**in doing sth,** à faire qch). **per'sistent** *a* persistant; tenace; continu. **per'sistently** *adv* avec persistance; avec ténacité.

person ['pəːsn] *n* personne *f*; individu *m*; **in p.,** en personne; **on one's p.,** sur soi; *Tp:* **p. to p. call,** communication avec préavis; *Gram:* **in the first p. plural,** à la première personne du pluriel. **'personable** *a* bien (fait) de sa personne; qui présente bien. **'personage** *n* personnage *m*; personnalité *f*. **'personal** *a* personnel; **p. liberty,** liberté individuelle; **p. friend,** ami personnel; **p. matter,** affaire privée, personnelle; **p. appearance,** tenue *f*; **to give a p. touch to sth,** personnaliser qch; *Journ:* **p. column,** petites annonces; **don't make p. remarks, don't be p.,** ne faites pas d'allusions personnelles; **to make a p. application,** se présenter en personne; *Jur:* **p. property,** biens mobiliers; *Gram:* **p. pronoun,** pronom personnel. **perso'nality** *n* (*pl* **-ies**) personnalité; caractère *m* propre (de qn); **to have no, be lacking in, p.,** manquer de personnalité; **he's quite a p.,** c'est vraiment quelqu'un. **'personalized** *a* personnalisé. **'personally** *adv* personnellement; (intervenir) en personne; **p. I think,** pour ma part, je pense; **to deliver sth to s.o. p.,** remettre qch à qn en main propre. **personifi'cation** *n* personnification *f*. **per'sonify** *vtr* (**personified**) personnifier. **perso'nnel** *n coll* personnel *m*; **p. department, manager,** service, directeur, du personnel.

perspective [pə'spektiv] *n* perspective *f*; **to see sth in p.,** voir qch sous son vrai jour.

perspex ['pəːspeks] *n* (*no pl*) *Rtm:* plexiglas *m*.

perspicacious [pəːspi'keiʃəs] *a* perspicace; pénétrant. **perspicacity** [-'kæsiti] *n* perspicacité *f*.

perspire [pə'spaiər] *vi* transpirer; suer. **perspiration** [pəːspi'reiʃn] *n* transpiration *f*; sueur *f*; **bathed in p.,** trempé de sueur; en nage.

persuade [pə'sweid] *vtr* **to p. s.o. of sth,** persuader, convaincre, qn de qch; **to p. s.o. to do sth,** persuader qn de faire qch; **he persuaded me not to,** il m'en a dissuadé. **per'suasion** *n* persuasion *f*; *Ecc:* religion *f*, confession *f*. **per'suasive** *a* persuasif. **per'suasively** *adv* d'un ton persuasif.

pert [pəːt] *a* effronté, hardi. **'pertly** *adv* d'un air effronté. **'pertness** *n* effronterie *f*.

pertinacious [pəːti'neiʃəs] *a* obstiné, entêté, opiniâtre. **perti'naciously** *adv* obstinément, opiniâtrement. **pertinacity** [-'næsiti] *n* obstination *f*, opiniâtreté *f*, entêtement *m* (à faire qch).

pertinent ['pəːtinənt] *a* pertinent; à propos, juste; **to be p. to,** avoir rapport à. **'pertinently** *adv* d'une manière pertinente; à propos.

perturb [pə'təːb] *vtr* troubler, inquiéter. **pertur'bation** *n* perturbation *f*; agitation *f*, inquiétude *f*.

Peru [pə'ruː] *Prn Geog:* Pérou *m*. **Pe'ruvian** *a & n* péruvien, -ienne.

peruse [pə'ruːz] *vtr* lire (attentivement). **pe'rusal** *n* lecture (attentive).

pervade [pəː'veid] *vtr* s'infiltrer, se répandre, dans. **per'vading** *a* (*of smell*) pénétrant; (**all**) **p.,** qui se répand partout; (*of influence*) dominant. **per'vasive** *a* qui se répand partout; pénétrant.

perverse [pə'vəːs] *a* (*a*) pervers, méchant (*b*) contrariant. **per'versely** *adv* (*a*) avec perversité (*b*) d'une manière contrariante. **per'verseness,** **per'versity** *n* (*a*) perversité *f* (*b*) esprit contrariant, contraire. **per'version** *n* perversion *f*; travestissement *m* (de la vérité). **pervert 1.** *vtr* [pə'vəːt] pervertir; dépraver (le goût de qn) **2.** *n* ['pəːvəːt] perverti, -ie (sexuel(le)).

pessary ['pesəri] *n* (*pl* **pessaries**) *Med:* pessaire *m*.

pessimism ['pesimizm] *n* pessimisme *m*. **'pessimist** *n* pessimiste *mf*. **pessi'mistic** *a* pessimiste. **pessi'mistically** *adv* avec pessimisme.

pest [pest] *n* insecte *m*, animal *m*, plante *f*, nuisible; *F:* (*pers*) casse-pieds *mf inv*; **p. control,** (service de) dératisation *f*, désinsectisation *f*. **'pester** *vtr* tourmenter, importuner (qn); harceler (qn) (**with questions,** de questions). **'pesticide** *n* pesticide *m*. **pesti'lential** *a F:* assommant, empoisonnant.

pestle ['pesl] *n* pilon *m*.

pet [pet] **1.** *n* (*a*) animal familier; oiseau *m*, chien *m*, d'appartement; **p. shop,** boutique où l'on vend des animaux familiers; *PN:* **no pets,** les animaux sont interdits (*b*) enfant gâté; chouchou, -oute; **my p.!** mon chou! **2.** *a* favori; **p. subject,** marotte *f*, dada *m*; **p. name,** diminutif *m*; nom *m* d'amitié; **p. hate,** bête noire **3.** *v* (**petted**) *vtr* chouchouter; (*touch*) caresser, câliner (*b*) *vi F:* se peloter. **'petting** *n F:* pelotage *m*.

petal [petl] *n Bot:* pétale *m*.

peter ['piːtər] *vi* **to p. out,** (*of flame*) mourir; (*of stream*) s'épuiser; (*of path*) disparaître, se perdre; (*of plan*) tomber à l'eau; (*of conversation*) tarir.

petite [pə'tiːt] *a* (*of woman*) menue (et svelte).

petition [pə'tiʃn] *n* prière *f* (à Dieu); pétition *f*, requête *f*; *Jur*: **p. for a reprieve**, recours *m* en grâce; **p. for divorce**, demande *f* en divorce.

petrify ['petrifai] *vtr* **(petrified)** pétrifier (le bois); pétrifier (qn) de peur; **I was petrified**, j'étais paralysé de terreur.

petrol ['petrəl] *n* essence *f*; **high-grade, four-star, p.**, supercarburant *m*, *F*: super *m*; **p. tank**, réservoir à essence; (*at garage*) **p. pump**, pompe à essence. **pe'troleum** *n* pétrole *m*; **p. industry**, industrie pétrolière; **p. jelly**, vaseline *f*.

petticoat ['petikout] *n* (*full-length*) combinaison *f*, fond *m* de robe; (*waist slip*) jupon *m*.

pettifogging ['petifɔgin] *a* chicanier.

petty [peti] *a* (**-ier, -iest**) petit, insignifiant, sans importance; **p.(-minded)**, mesquin; **p. cash**, petite caisse; *Nau*: **p. officer**, officier marinier; gradé *m*. **'pettiness** *n* insignifiance *f*; petitesse *f* (d'esprit), mesquinerie *f*.

petulant ['petjulənt] *a* irritable; susceptible. **'petulance** *n* irritabilité *f*; **outburst of p.**, accès de mauvaise humeur. **'petulantly** *adv* avec humeur, avec irritation.

pew [pju:] *n* banc *m* d'église; *F*: **take a p.!** assieds-toi!

pewter ['pju:tər] *n* étain *m*. **'pewterware** *n* vaisselle *f* d'étain.

phallic ['fælik] *a* phallique.

phantom ['fæntəm] *n* fantôme *m*, spectre *m*.

pharmacy ['fɑ:məsi] *n* pharmacie *f*. **pharmaceutical** [fɑ:mə'sju:tikl] *a* pharmaceutique. **'pharmacist** *n* pharmacien, -ienne.

phase [feiz] **1.** *n* phase *f* **2.** *vtr* faire (qch) progressivement; échelonner (un programme); **phased** *a* par phases; progressif; par étapes; (programme) échelonné. **'phase 'in** *vtr* introduire, adopter, progressivement. **'phase 'out** *vtr* réduire, éliminer, progressivement.

PhD *abbr Doctor of Philosophy.*

pheasant ['feznt] *n Orn*: faisan *m*; (*hen*) faisane *f*.

phenobarbitone [fi:nou'bɑ:bitoun] *n Med*: phénobarbital *m*.

phenomenon [fi'nɔminən] *n* (*pl* **phenomena** [fi'nɔminə]) phénomène *m*. **phe'nomenal** *a* phénoménal; prodigieux. **phe'nomenally** *adv* phénoménalement.

philanthropy [fi'lænθrəpi] *n* philanthropie *f*. **philan'thropic** *a* philanthropique. **phi'lanthropist** *n* philanthrope *mf*.

philately [fi'lætəli] *n* philatélie *f*. **phi'latelist** *n* philatéliste *mf*.

Philippines (the) [ðə'filipi:nz] *Prn Geog*: les Philippines *f*.

philology [fi'lɔlədʒi] *n* philologie *f*. **philo'logical** *a* philologique. **phi'lologist** *n* philologue *mf*.

philosophy [fi'lɔsəfi] *n* philosophie *f*; **one's own p. about sth**, sa conception personnelle de qch. **phi'losopher** *n* philosophe *mf*. **philo'sophical** *a* (argument) philosophique; (*of pers*) philosophe, calme, modéré. **philo'sophically** *adv* philosophiquement. **phi'losophize** *vi* philosopher.

phlegm [flem] *n* flegme *m*. **phlegmatic** [fleg'mætik] *a* flegmatique. **phleg'matically** *adv* flegmatiquement.

phobia ['foubiə] *n* phobie *f*.

phone [foun] **1.** *n* téléphone *m*; **on the p.**, au téléphone;

p. call, coup de téléphone; **p. book**, annuaire *m*; **p. box**, cabine téléphonique **2.** *vtr & i* téléphoner (à qn). **'phone-in** *n WTel*: *TV*: programme *m* à ligne ouverte.

phonetic [fə'netik] *a* phonétique. **pho'netically** *adv* phonétiquement. **pho'netics** *npl* (*usu with sg const*) phonétique *f*.

phoney ['founi] *F*: **1.** *a* (**phonier, -iest**) faux; factice; (*of story, company*) bidon *inv*; (*of jewellery*) en toc; **that's a p. story**, c'est un canard, un bobard **2.** *n* (*pl* **phonies**) imposteur *m*; fumiste *mf*.

phosphate ['fɔsfeit] *n Ch*: phosphate *m*.

phosphorescent [fɔsfə'resnt] *a* phosphorescent. **phospho'rescence** *n* phosphorescence *f*. **'phosphorus** *n Ch*: phosphore *m*.

photo ['foutou] *n F*: photo *f*. **'photocopier** *n* photocopieur *m*. **'photocopy 1.** *n* (*pl* **-ies**) photocopie *f* **2.** *vtr* **(photocopied)** photocopier (un document). **photoe'lectric** *a* (cellule) photo-électrique. **'photo-'finish** *n Sp*: photo-finish *f inv*. **photogenic** [-'dʒenik] *a* photogénique. **'photograph 1.** *n* photographie *f*; **to take s.o.'s p.**, prendre une photographie de qn; **to have one's p. taken**, se faire photographier **2.** *vtr* photographier. **pho'tographer** *n* photographe *mf*; *Journ*: **press p.**, reporter *m* photographe. **photo'graphic** *a* photographique. **photo'graphically** *adv* photographiquement. **pho'tography** *n* photographie; **colour p.**, photographie en couleurs. **'photostat 1.** *n* photocopie **2.** *vtr* **(photostatted)** photocopier.

phrase [freiz] **1.** *n* locution *f*, expression *f*; tournure *f* de phrase; *Mus*: phrase *f* **2.** *vtr* exprimer (sa pensée); *Mus*: phraser; **a well phrased letter**, une lettre bien tournée. **'phrasebook** *n* recueil *m* de locutions. **phraseology** [-i'ɔlədʒi] phraséologie *f*.

physical ['fizikəl] *a* physique; (objet) matériel; **p. education, exercises, training**, *F*: **jerks**, exercices physiques; culture physique. **'physically** *adv* physiquement; **a p. handicapped person**, un(e) handicapé(e) physique. **physician** [fi'ziʃn] *n* médecin *m*.

physics ['fiziks] *npl* (*usu with sg const*) physique *f*. **'physicist** *n* physicien, -ienne.

physiognomy [fizi'ɔnəmi] *n* physionomie *f*.

physiology [fizi'ɔlədʒi] *n* physiologie *f*. **physio'logical** *a* physiologique. **physi'ologist** *n* physiologiste *mf*.

physiotherapy [fiziou'θerəpi] *n* kinésithérapie *f*. **physio'therapist** *n* kinésithérapeute *mf*, *F*: kiné(si) *mf*.

physique [fi'zi:k] *n* physique *m*; **to have a fine p.**, avoir un beau physique.

piano [pi'ænou] *n Mus*: piano *m*; **grand p.**, piano à queue; **p. key**, touche de piano. **pianist** ['piənist, 'pjæ-] *n* pianiste *mf*.

pick [pik] **1.** *vtr & i* (*a*) **to p. a hole in sth**, faire un trou dans, à, qch (avec ses ongles, un outil); **to p. holes in sth**, trouver à redire à qch; **to p. one's teeth**, se curer les dents; **to p. one's nose**, se curer le nez; **to p. a spot**, gratter un bouton; **to p. a bone**, ronger un os; *F*: **to have a bone to p. with s.o.**, avoir un compte à régler avec qn (*b*) (*of birds*) picoter, becqueter; **to p. at one's food**, manger du bout des dents (*c*) sélectionner; repérer (les gagnants); **to p. and choose**, se montrer difficile; *Games:* **to p. sides,** tirer les camps (*d*) cueillir (des fruits, des fleurs); **to p. s.o.'s pocket,** voler qch dans la poche de qn; **to p. pockets,** pratiquer le vol à la tire (*e*) crocheter (une serrure); **to p. s.o.'s brains,** exploiter l'intelligence de qn; **to p. a fight, a quarrel, with s.o.,** chercher bagarre à qn; chercher querelle avec qn 2. *n* (*a*) pic *m*, pioche *f* (*b*) choix *m*, élite *f*; **the p. of the bunch,** le dessus du panier; **take your p.!** choisissez! 'pickaxe, *NAm:* 'pickax *n* (*pl* -axes) pioche, pic. 'picker *n* cueilleur, -euse (de fruits, de fleurs). 'pickings *npl F:* bénéfices *mpl*; gratte *f.* 'pick-me-up *n F:* remontant *m.* 'pick 'off *vtr* enlever (des fleurs mortes); descendre, abattre (un à un) (des personnes). 'pick 'on *vtr* chercher querelle à (qn); **why p. on me?** pourquoi m'accuser, moi? 'pick 'out *vtr* (*a*) enlever (qch) (avec les doigts, avec un outil) (*b*) désigner, choisir; identifier (qn); distinguer (une mélodie). 'pick 'over *vtr* trier. 'pickpocket *n* pickpocket *m.* 'pick 'up 1. *vtr* (*a*) prendre; (*off the ground*) ramasser, relever (qch); décrocher (le téléphone); recueillir (des naufragés); **to p. up a child,** prendre un enfant dans ses bras; relever un enfant (qui est tombé); **to p. up a pound,** (i) ramasser un billet, une pièce, d'une livre (par terre) (ii) gagner une livre; **to p. s.o. up on the way,** prendre qn en passant; passer prendre qn; **I'll p. you up at the station,** je passerai vous chercher à la gare; *Knit:* **to p. up a stitch,** relever une maille (*b*) apprendre; s'initier (rapidement) à (une langue) (*c*) trouver, relever (une erreur); **to p. sth up cheap,** acheter qch bon marché (*d*) *F:* faire la connaissance de, ramasser (qn) (*e*) *WTel:* capter (un poste); (*of car, engine*) **to p. up (speed),** (re)prendre de la vitesse 2. *vi* (*after illness*) se rétablir; retrouver ses forces; **business is picking up,** les affaires reprennent. 'pick(-)up *n* (*a*) *Rec:* pick-up *m inv;* lecteur *m* (*b*) *Veh:* pick-up (*c*) *F:* partenaire *mf,* connaissance *f,* de rencontre.

picket ['pikit] 1. *n* (*a*) piquet *m* (*b*) *Ind:* piquet *m* (de grévistes); **p. line, strike p.,** piquet de grève 2. *vtr* **to p. a factory,** mettre un piquet de grève aux portes d'une usine.

pickle ['pikl] 1. *n Comest:* marinade *f*; saumure *f*; **pickles,** conserves *fpl* au vinaigre; pickles *mpl*; *F:* **to be in a p.,** être dans de beaux draps 2. *vtr Cu:* mariner; conserver (au vinaigre).

picnic ['piknik] 1. *n* pique-nique *m*; **the Vietnam war was no p.,** la guerre du Vietnam n'a pas été une partie de plaisir 2. *vi* (**picnicked**) pique-niquer; faire un pique-nique. 'picknicker *n* pique-niqueur, -euse.

picture ['piktʃər] 1. *n* (*a*) image *f*; tableau *m*; portrait *m* (de qn); (*painted*) peinture *f*; (*in book*) illustration *f*; **p. book,** livre d'images; **p. postcard,** carte postale illustrée; **he's the p. of health,** il respire la santé; **she's a perfect p.,** elle est à peindre; *F:* **to be in the p.,** être au courant; **put me in the p.,** mets-moi au courant; **to get a (mental) p. of sth,** se représenter qch (*b*) *Cin:* film *m*; **to go to the pictures,** aller au cinéma 2. *vtr* **to p. sth (to oneself),** se représenter, se figurer, s'imaginer, qch. pic'torial *a & n* (magazine) illustré (*m*). pictu'resque *a* pittoresque.

pie [pai] *n Cu:* **meat p.** = pâté *m* en croûte; **shepherd's, cottage, p.,** hachis *m* Parmentier; **apple p.,** (*with pastry lid*) tourte *f*, (*open*) tarte *f*, aux pommes. 'piecrust *n Cu:* pâte *f*, croûte *f* (d'une tourte, d'une tarte).

'piedish *n DomEc:* terrine *f.* 'pie-'eyed *a F:* ivre, soûl.

piebald ['paibɔːld] *a & n* (cheval) pie (*m*).

piece [piːs] 1. *n* (*a*) morceau *m* (de pain); bout *m* (de ruban); parcelle *f* (de terrain); fragment *m* (de verre); **p. by p.,** pièce *f* à pièce; **to come to pieces,** s'en aller en morceaux; **in pieces,** en morceaux; (*of pers, team*) **to go (all) to pieces,** s'effondrer; **to break sth to pieces,** mettre qch en morceaux; **to fall to pieces,** tomber en morceaux; **to pull s.o., sth, to pieces,** critiquer qn, qch, sévèrement (*b*) partie *f*, pièce (d'une machine); **to take a machine to pieces,** démonter une machine (*c*) *Com:* pièce (de drap); **to pay by the p.,** payer à la pièce; **all in one p.,** tout d'une pièce (*d*) **p. of work,** travail *m*; **a p. of my work,** un échantillon de mon travail; **p. out of a book,** passage *m* d'un livre; **p. of folly,** acte *m* de folie; **p. of (good) luck,** coup *m* de chance; **a p. of advice,** un conseil; **a p. of carelessness,** une étourderie; **a p. of news,** une nouvelle; **a p. of luggage,** une valise; **a p. of furniture,** un meuble (*e*) pièce (de monnaie); **five pence p.,** pièce de cinq pence (*f*) morceau (de musique, de poésie); *Journ:* article *m*; **to say one's p.,** prononcer son discours; *Mus:* **three p. ensemble,** trio *m* (*g*) *Chess:* pièce 2. *vtr* rapiécer, raccommoder (qch); **to p. together,** joindre, unir; (r)assembler (des fragments). 'piecemeal *adv* par morceaux; peu à peu. 'piecework *n* travail *m* à la pièce, à la tâche.

pier [piər] *n* (*a*) jetée *f*; digue *f*; **(landing) p.,** embarcadère *m* (*b*) *CivE:* pilier *m*.

pierce [piəs] *vtr* percer, transpercer, pénétrer; **to have one's ears pierced,** se faire percer les oreilles. 'piercing *a* (cri) aigu, perçant; (froid) pénétrant.

piety ['paiəti] *n* piété *f.*

pig [pig] *n* (*a*) porc *m*, cochon *m*; **sucking, suckling, p.,** cochon de lait; **p. farm,** porcherie *f*; **p. breeding,** élevage de porcs; **to buy a p. in a poke,** acheter chat en poche; *F:* **pigs might fly,** dans la semaine des quatre jeudis; **to eat like a p.,** manger comme un goinfre; **make a p. of oneself,** manger comme un goinfre (*b*) *F:* (*pers*) (*greedy*) goinfre; (*dirty*) sale type *m*; (*unkind*) vache *f*; *Metall:* **p. iron,** fer en gueuse. 'piggery *n* (*pl* -ies) porcherie. 'piggish *a* (*a*) sale, malpropre (*b*) goinfre (*c*) égoïste, désagréable. 'piggyback *n* **to give s.o. a p.,** porter qn sur son dos. 'piggybank *n* (cochon) tirelire *f, F:* = grenouille *f.* 'pigheaded *a* obstiné, entêté. 'piglet *n* porcelet *m*, cochonnet *m.* 'pigskin *n* peau *f* de porc. 'pigsty *n* (*pl* -ies) porcherie 'pigtail *n* natte *f* (de cheveux).

pigeon ['pidʒin] *n* pigeon *m*; **wood p.,** (pigeon) ramier *m*; **p. loft,** pigeonnier *m*; *Sp:* **clay p. shooting,** ball-trap *m.* 'pigeonhole 1. *n* casier *m*; case *f* (de bureau) 2 *vtr* classer.

pigment ['pigmənt] *n* pigment *m*; *Art:* colorant *m* pigmen'tation *n* pigmentation *f.*

pike [paik] *n* (*no pl*) *Ich:* brochet *m.*

pilchard ['piltʃəd] *n Ich:* pilchard *m.*

pile¹ [pail] *n CivE:* pieu *m*; **built on piles,** bâti sur piloti *m*; **p. driver,** sonnette *f.*

pile² 1. *n* (*a*) tas *m*, monceau *m*; pile *f* (d'assiettes, de linge); **atomic p.,** pile atomique; **to put in a p.,** mettre en tas; empiler; *F:* **to have piles of work,** avoir beaucoup, un tas, de travail (*b*) *F:* magot *m*; **to make one's p.,** faire fortune 2. *v* (*a*) *vtr* entasser (des objets) empiler (du bois); **to p. a table (high) with dishes** charger une table de plats (b) vi **they piled into the car,** ils se sont empilés dans la voiture; **fifteen of them piled out of the compartment,** ils sont descendus quinze du compartiment; (of cars) **to p. into one another,** se caramboler. **'pile 'on** vtr F: **to p. on the agony,** dramatiser (qch). **'pile 'up** l. vtr entasser, amonceler (de la terre); empiler (du bois); amasser (de l'argent) 2. vi s'amonceler, s'entasser. **'pile-up** n Aut: F: carambolage m.

pile³ n poil m (d'un tapis).

piles [pailz] npl Med: hémorroïdes fpl.

pilfer ['pilfər] vtr & i chaparder, chiper (sth from s.o., qch à qn). **'pilferer** n chapardeur, -euse. **'pilfering** n chapardage m.

pilgrim ['pilgrim] n pèlerin m. **'pilgrimage** n pèlerinage m; **to go on a p.,** faire un pèlerinage.

pill [pil] n pilule f; (of woman) **to be on the p.,** prendre la pilule; Fig: **to sugar the p.,** dorer la pilule.

pillage ['pilidʒ] l. n pillage m 2. vtr & i piller.

pillar ['pilər] n pilier m; colonne f; **he's a p. of the Church,** c'est un pilier de l'Église; **to drive s.o. from p. to post,** envoyer qn de droite à gauche; **p. box** (NAm: = mailbox), boîte f aux lettres; **p. box red,** rouge drapeau (m).

pillion ['piliən] n siège m arrière (de moto); **to ride p.,** monter derrière.

pillow ['pilou] n oreiller m. **'pillowcase, -slip** n taie f d'oreiller.

pilot ['pailət] l. n (a) Nau: Av: pilote m; **p. light,** veilleuse f (de cuisinière, de chauffe-eau); **p. film,** film d'essai; TV: **p. series,** présérie f; **p. scheme,** projet pilote (b) guide m 2. vtr piloter (un navire, un avion); mener, conduire, guider (qn à travers des obstacles).

pimento [pi'mentou] n Bot: Cu: piment m; poivron m.

pimp [pimp] n souteneur m.

pimple ['pimpl] n bouton m; **to come out in pimples,** avoir une poussée de boutons. **'pimply** a (-ier, -iest) boutonneux.

pin [pin] l. n épingle f; Tchn: goupille f; broche f (de serrure, Surg: dans un membre cassé); El: fiche f, broche (de prise de courant); Games: quille f; **safety p.,** épingle de nourrice; **drawing p.** (NAm: = thumbtack), punaise f; F: **p. money,** argent m de poche (d'une femme); **you could have heard a p. drop,** on aurait entendu voler une mouche; **for two pins I'd punch his face,** pour un rien je lui casserais la figure; **he doesn't care two pins,** il s'en moque, il s'en fiche; **to have pins and needles,** avoir des fourmillements m 2. vtr (pinned) épingler (qch); attacher (qch) avec une épingle; Tchn: goupiller; **to p. up one's hair,** épingler ses cheveux; **to p. up a hem,** rabattre un ourlet avec des épingles; **to p. sth (up) on the wall,** fixer qch au mur (avec des punaises); **to p. s.o. against a wall,** clouer qn à un mur; **to p. s.o.'s arms to his sides,** coller les bras de qn au corps. **'pinball** n Games: **p. (machine),** flipper m. **'pincushion** n pelote f à épingles. **'pin 'down** vtr clouer (l'ennemi); **pinned d. under a tree,** coincé sous un arbre; **to p. s.o. d. to do sth,** obliger qn à faire qch; **without pinning himself d. (to anything),** sans s'engager à rien. **'pin 'on** vtr **to p. sth on s.o.,** épingler qch sur qn; Fig: rendre qn responsable de qch; **to p. one's hopes on s.o., sth,** mettre tous ses espoirs en qn, dans qch. **'pinpoint**

vtr mettre le doigt sur (qch); localiser avec exactitude; indiquer exactement. **'pinprick** n piqûre f d'épingle; Fig: tracasserie f, coup m d'épingle. **'pinstripe** n Tex: rayure fine; **p. suit,** costume rayé. **'pin-up (girl)** n pin-up f inv.

pinafore ['pinəfɔːr] n tablier m; **p. dress** (NAm: = jumper), robe chasuble.

pincers ['pinsəz] npl (pair of) p., pince(s) f(pl), tenaille(s) f(pl).

pinch [pintʃ] l. vtr (a) pincer; serrer; **to p. off,** épincer (un bourgeon) (b) F: voler, chiper; **my purse has been pinched,** on m'a piqué mon porte-monnaie (c) arrêter, pincer (un criminel); **to get pinched,** se faire pincer 2. vi (of shoes) serrer; **to p. and scrape,** faire de petites économies 3. n (a) pincement m; **to give s.o. a p.,** pincer qn; Fig: **to feel the p.,** tirer le diable par la queue; **at a p.,** à la rigueur (b) pincée f (de sel); prise f (de tabac). **pinched** a (of face) tiré, hâve; **to be p. (for money),** être à court d'argent.

pine¹ [pain] n (a) **p. (tree),** pin m; Comest: **p. kernel, nut,** pigne f (b) (bois m de) pin. **'pinecone** n pomme f de pin. **'pinewood** n (a) (bois de) pin (b) (plantation) pinède f.

pine² vi **to p. (away),** languir; **to p. for s.o.,** se languir d'amour pour, languir après, qn.

pineapple ['painæpl] n ananas m.

ping-pong ['piŋpɔŋ] n Games: F: ping-pong m.

pinion ['pinjən] n (a) Orn: penne f (b) MecE: pignon m; **p. wheel,** roue à pignon.

pink [piŋk] l. n Bot: œillet m; **garden p.,** mignardise f; F: **in the p.,** en excellente santé 2. a & n rose (m). **'pinkish** a rosé, rosâtre.

pinnacle ['pinəkl] n pinacle m (d'un bâtiment); cime f, pic m (d'une montagne); apogée m (de la gloire).

pint [paint] n Meas: pinte f (= 0,568 litre; US: = 0,473 litre). **'pint-sized** a minuscule.

pioneer [paiə'niər] l. n pionnier m 2. vtr être le premier à faire, innover (qch); ouvrir la voie.

pious ['paiəs] a pieux. **'piously** adv pieusement.

pip [pip] l. n (a) point m (d'une carte, d'un dé) (b) pépin m (de fruit) (c) Mil: F: = galon m d'officier, ficelle f (d) WTel: top m; **the pips,** le signal horaire 2. vtr F: **to be pipped at the post,** se faire coiffer sur le poteau. **'pippin** n Hort: (pomme f) reinette f.

pipe [paip] l. n (a) tuyau m, tube m, conduit m, conduite f (b) Mus: pipeau m, chalumeau m; tuyau (d'orgue); pl (bagpipes) cornemuse f (c) pipe f (de fumeur); **peace p.,** calumet m de la paix; F: **put that in your p. and smoke it!** mettez ça dans votre poche et votre mouchoir par-dessus; **p. cleaner,** cure-pipe m; **p. dream,** rêve m (chimérique) 2. vtr (a) canaliser (l'eau, le gaz); amener (du pétrole) par pipeline; **piped music,** musique (de fond) enregistrée (b) dire, chanter, d'une voix flûtée; Navy: **to p. s.o. aboard,** rendre les honneurs du sifflet à qn (c) Needlew: passepoiler (une robe) (d) Cu: décorer (un gâteau) avec une douille. **'pipe 'down** vi F: se taire; cesser de parler; la boucler. **'pipeline** n conduite, canalisation f, (for oil) pipe-line m, oléoduc m; (for gas) gazoduc m; F: **it's in the p.,** c'est en route. **'piper** n joueur m de cornemuse; cornemuseur m. **'pipe 'up** vi (of voice) se faire entendre. **'piping** l. n (no pl) (a) coll tuyauterie f (b) Needlew: passepoil m 2. a (of voice) flûté 3. adv **p. hot,** tout chaud, tout bouillant.

piquant ['pi:kənt] *a* piquant. **'piquancy** *n* goût piquant (d'un plat); piquant *m* (d'un conte, d'une situation).

pique ['pi:k] **1.** *n* pique *f*, ressentiment *m*; **fit of p.**, accès de dépit *m* **2.** *vtr* (*a*) piquer, dépiter (qn) (*b*) piquer, exciter (la curiosité de qn).

pirate ['paiərət] **1.** *n* pirate *m*; contrefacteur *m* (d'un ouvrage littéraire); voleur, -euse (d'idées); **p. radio station**, poste, émetteur, pirate **2.** *vtr* s'approprier, voler (une invention); contrefaire (une marque de fabrique); démarquer (un livre). **'piracy** *n* piraterie *f*; contrefaçon *f* (d'un livre). **pi'ratical** *a* de pirate.

Pisces ['paisi:z] *Prn Astr:* les Poissons *m*.

piss [pis] *P:* **1.** *n* urine *f*; pisse *f* **2.** *vi* uriner, pisser.

pistachio [pis'ta:ʃiou] *n* (*pl* **pistachios**) *Bot:* pistache *f*.

pistil ['pistil] *n Bot:* pistil *m*.

pistol ['pistəl] *n* pistolet *m*; **p. shot**, coup de pistolet.

piston ['pistən] *n* piston *m*; **p. engine**, moteur à pistons; **p. ring**, segment de piston.

pit[1] [pit] **1.** *n* (*a*) fosse *f*, trou *m*; *Aut:* **inspection p.**, fosse de visite, à réparations; **p. of the stomach**, creux *m* de l'estomac (*b*) *Min:* puits *m* de mine; mine *f* (de charbon); **chalk p.**, carrière *f* à chaux; **to work in the pits**, être mineur (de fond) (*c*) *Th:* parterre *m*; **orchestra p.**, fosse d'orchestre (*d*) *Rac:* **the pits**, les stands *m* (de ravitaillement) **2.** *vtr* opposer (qn) (**against**, à); **to p. oneself, one's wits, against**, se mesurer avec, à. **'pitfall** *n* piège *m*. **'pithead** *n* bouche *f* de puits; carreau *m* de mine; **p. baths**, bains de la mine. **'pitted**[1] *a* (métal) piqué; (visage) grêlé.

pit[2] *n esp NAm:* noyau *m* (de fruit). **'pitted**[2] *a* (fruit) dénoyauté.

pit-a-pat ['pitəpæt] *adv* **to go p.-a-p.**, (*of rain*) crépiter; (*of feet*) trottiner; (*of heart*) battre, palpiter.

pitch[1] [pitʃ] *n* poix *f*; (*from coal tar*) brai *m*. **'pitch-'black**, -'dark** *a* it's **p.-d.**, il fait nuit noire, il fait noir comme dans un four. **'pitchpine** *n* faux sapin; pitchpin *m*.

pitch[2] **1.** *vtr* (*a*) dresser (une tente); établir (un camp) (*b*) *Mus:* **to p. one's voice higher, lower**, hausser, baisser, le ton de sa voix (*c*) lancer; jeter (une balle) **2.** *vi* (*a*) tomber; **to p. forward**, être projeté en avant (*b*) (*of aircraft, ship*) tanguer **3.** *n* (*a*) *Mus:* hauteur *f* (d'un son); diapason *m* (d'un instrument); **to have perfect p.**, avoir l'oreille absolue; **to rise in p.**, monter de ton (*b*) degré *m* (d'insolence); **to such a p. that**, à tel point que; **to the highest p.**, au plus haut degré (*c*) (*of aircraft, ship*) tangage *m* (*d*) *Sp:* terrain *m* (de football, de rugby) (*e*) emplacement *m*, place *f* (dans un marché) (*f*) (degré de) pente *f* (d'un toit). **'pitched** *a* **p. battle**, bataille rangée. **'pitchfork** *n* fourche *f* (à foin). **'pitch 'in** *vi F:* se mettre à la besogne. **'pitch 'into** *vtr* (*a*) tomber la tête la première dans (un étang) (*b*) s'attaquer à (un travail, un repas) (*c*) s'attaquer, dire son fait, à (qn).

pitcher ['pitʃər] *n* cruche *f*; broc *m*; *esp NAm:* pot *m* (à lait).

pith [piθ] *n* moelle *f* (d'une plante, d'un ouvrage); peau blanche (d'une orange); vigueur *f* (de l'esprit); essence *f* (d'un livre). **'pithiness** *n* (*of style*) concision *f*. **'pithy** *a* (-ier, -iest) (*of plant stem*) moelleux; (*of orange*) couvert de peau blanche; (*of style*) concis, vigoureux; (*of remark*) lapidaire.

pittance ['pitəns] *n* salaire *m* dérisoire; maigre salaire.

pity ['piti] **1.** *n* (*a*) pitié *f*; compassion *f*; **to take p. on s.o.**, prendre pitié de qn; **out of p. for s.o.**, par pitié pour qn; **for p.'s sake**, par pitié; de grâce (*b*) **what a p.!** quel dommage! **it's a (great) p. that**, il est (bien) dommage que **2.** *vtr* plaindre (qn); avoir pitié de, s'apitoyer sur (qn). **'piteous** *a* pitoyable. **'piteously** *adv* pitoyablement. **'pitiable** *a* pitoyable, piteux. **'pitiful** *a* (*a*) pitoyable; **it's p. to see him**, il fait pitié (*b*) *Pej:* piteux, lamentable; **he's a p. speaker**, c'est un orateur minable, lamentable. **'pitifully** *adv* (*a*) pitoyablement; **p. thin**, maigre à faire pitié; d'une maigreur pitoyable (*b*) *Pej:* lamentablement. **'pitiless** *a* impitoyable; (vent) cruel. **'pitilessly** *adv* sans pitié; impitoyablement. **'pitying** *a* compatissant; (regard) de pitié. **'pityingly** *adv* avec pitié.

pivot ['pivət] **1.** *n* pivot *m*; axe *m* (de rotation) **2.** *v* (*a*) *vi* pivoter, tourner (*b*) *vtr* monter (une pièce) sur pivot.

pizza ['pi:tsə] *n Cu:* pizza *f*.

placard ['plæka:d] **1.** *n* écriteau *m*; affiche *f* **2.** *vtr* placarder (un mur, une annonce); afficher (une annonce).

placate [plə'keit] *vtr* apaiser, calmer (qn).

place ['pleis] **1.** *n* (*a*) endroit *m*; lieu *m*; **this is the p.**, c'est ici; **nous y voilà; nous voilà arrivés; a native of the p.**, quelqu'un du pays; **to move from p. to p.**, se déplacer d'un endroit à un autre; **all over the p.**, partout; dans tous les coins; **in another p.**, autre part; ailleurs; **in places**, par endroits; **this is no p. for you**, vous n'avez que faire ici; *F:* **to be going places**, réussir (dans la vie); **p. of worship**, église *f*; **my p. of work**, mon lieu de travail; **meeting p.**, (lieu de) rendez-vous *m*; **p. of business**, maison *f* de commerce; établissement *m*; **at our p.**, chez nous; **market p.**, place *f* du marché; **p. name**, nom de lieu; **a little p. in the country**, une petite maison à la campagne (*b*) (*position*) place; **to hold sth in p.**, tenir qch en place; **he sat in my p.**, il s'est assis à ma place; **to change places with s.o.**, changer de place avec qn; **in your p.**, à votre place; **in (the) p. of**, au lieu de; **remark out of p.**, observation hors de propos, déplacée; **to look out of p.**, avoir l'air dépaysé; **to take p.**, avoir lieu; se dérouler; se passer; arriver; **his anger gave p. to pity**, sa colère a fait place à un sentiment de pitié (*c*) (*at table*) place; **p. (setting)**, couvert *m*; **p. mat**, napperon *m* (*d*) (*in street names*) rue *f*, ruelle *f* (*e*) place, rang *m*; **to put s.o. in his p.**, remettre qn à sa place; *Rac:* **to back a horse for a p.**, jouer un cheval placé; *Mth:* **answer to three decimal places**, résultat à trois décimales; **in the first p.**, en premier lieu; **in the second p.**, en second lieu; **who came in third p.?** qui a été (placé) troisième? (*in book*) **to lose, find, one's p.**, perdre, retrouver, la page (*f*) poste *m*, emploi *m*, situation *f*; **to take s.o.'s p.**, remplacer qn; **it's not my p. to do it**, ce n'est pas à moi de le faire **2.** *vtr* (*a*) placer, mettre; **to p. a book back on a shelf**, remettre un livre sur un rayon; (*of pers*) **to be awkwardly placed**, se trouver dans une situation délicate (*b*) *Com:* placer (des marchandises); passer (une commande); faire accepter (un livre) (**with a publisher**, par un éditeur); **to p. a matter in s.o.'s hands**, (re)mettre une affaire entre les mains de qn (*c*) placer; donner un rang à (qn); **to be well placed**, avoir bonne place; être bien placé (**to, pour**); **to be placed**

third, se placer, se classer, troisième; **I know his face but I can't p. him,** je le reconnais mais je ne peux pas le remettre.

placid ['plæsid] *a* placide, calme, tranquille. **pla'cidity** *n* placidité *f*, calme *m*, tranquillité *f*. **'placidly** *adv* avec calme; tranquillement.

plagiarism ['pleidʒərizm] *n* plagiat *m*. **'plagiarist** *n* plagiaire *mf*. **'plagiarize** *vtr* plagier.

plague [pleig] 1. *n* (*a*) fléau *m*, plaie *f* (*b*) *Med:* peste *f* 2. *vtr* tourmenter, harceler, embêter (qn); **to p. s.o. with questions,** harceler qn de questions.

plaice [pleis] *n* (*no pl*) *Ich:* carrelet *m*; plie *f*.

plain [plein] 1. *a* (*a*) clair, évident; **as p. as day,** clair comme le jour; **to make sth, oneself, p. to s.o.,** faire comprendre qch, se faire comprendre, à qn; **in p. English,** pour parler clairement; **marked in p. figures,** marqué en chiffres connus (*b*) simple; (*of fabric*) (*not patterned*) uni; (papier) non réglé; (*of cigarette*) sans filtre; **under p. cover,** sous pli discret; **in p. clothes,** en civil; *Knit:* **p.** (stitch), maille à l'endroit; **p. cooking,** cuisine simple; **p. chocolate,** chocolat à croquer; **p. truth,** vérité pure, simple; **I'll be quite p. with you,** je vais vous parler franchement; **p. answer,** réponse carrée; **p. speaking,** franchise *f*, franc-parler *m*; **a p. man,** un homme ordinaire (*c*) (*of woman*) sans beauté; plutôt laide; **to be p.,** manquer de beauté 2. *adv* clairement, franchement; distinctement; **I can't put it any plainer,** je ne peux pas m'exprimer plus clairement 3. *n* plaine *f*. **'plain-clothes** *a* (policier) en civil. **'plainly** *adv* (*a*) clairement; manifestement (*b*) (vivre) simplement; (parler) carrément; **to put it p.,** pour parler clair. **'plainness** *n* clarté *f* (de langage); netteté *f* (d'un objet lointain); simplicité *f* (de vie); franchise *f* (de langage); manque *m* de beauté. **'plainsong** *n* plain-chant *m*. **'plain-'spoken** *a* franc, carré.

plaintiff ['pleintif] *n* *Jur:* plaignant, -ante.

plaintive ['pleintiv] *a* plaintif. **'plaintively** *adv* plaintivement; d'un ton plaintif.

plait [plæt] 1. *n* natte *f*, tresse *f* (de cheveux) 2. *vtr* natter, tresser.

plan [plæn] I. *n* (*a*) plan *m* (d'une maison, d'un livre); *Surv:* levé *m* (d'un terrain); **to draw a p.,** tracer un plan (*b*) projet *m*, plan; **to draw up a p.,** dresser un plan; **to change one's plans,** prendre d'autres dispositions *fpl*; **according to p.,** comme prévu; **the best p. would be to,** le mieux serait de; **it would be a good p. to,** ce serait une bonne idée de. II. *v* (**planned**) 1. *vtr* (*a*) faire, dessiner, tracer, le plan de (qch); planifier (la production); **the school was planned for 500 pupils,** l'école était prévue pour 500 élèves (*b*) projeter (un voyage); combiner (une attaque); **to p. to do sth,** projeter, former le projet, se proposer, de faire qch; **they were planning to rob a bank,** ils étudiaient l'attaque d'une banque 2. *vi* faire des projets. **'planner** *n* planificateur, -trice; **town p.,** urbaniste *mf*. **'planning** *n* organisation *f* (d'un projet, d'un complot); *PolEc:* dirigisme *m*, planification *f*; *Ind: Com:* planning *m*; **town p.,** urbanisme *m*; **family p.,** contrôle *m* des naissances, planning familial.

plane¹ [plein] 1. *n* (*a*) *Mth: etc:* plan *m*; **horizontal p.,** plan horizontal; *Mec:* **inclined p.,** plan incliné (*b*) avion *m* 2. *a* plan, uni.

plane² 1. *n* *Tls:* rabot *m* 2. *vtr* raboter; aplanir.

plane³ *n* *Bot:* **p.** (tree), platane *m*.

planet ['plænit] *n* *Astr:* planète *f*. **plane'tarium** *n* planétarium *m*. **'planetary** *a* (système) planétaire.

plank [plæŋk] *n* planche *f*; madrier *m*. **'planking** *n* coll planches *fpl*.

plankton ['plæŋktən] *n* plancton *m*.

plant [plɑːnt] 1. *n* (*a*) plante *f*; **p. life,** (i) la vie végétale (ii) flore *f* (d'une région); **house p., pot p.,** plante d'appartement (*b*) installation industrielle; usine *f*; **automobile p.,** usine d'automobiles (*c*) appareil(s) *m* (*pl*); installation(s) *f* (*pl*); matériel *m*, équipement *m*; **heavy p.,** grosses machines 2. *vtr* planter; poser (une bombe); implanter (une idée); *F:* **to p. oneself in front of s.o.,** se planter, se camper, devant qn. **plan'tation** *n* plantation *f*. **'planter** *n* planteur *m*. **'plant 'out** *vtr* *Hort:* repiquer (des semis).

plaque [plɑːk, plæk] *n* plaque *f*.

plaster ['plɑːstər] 1. *n* (*a*) *Med:* emplâtre *m*; **sticking, adhesive, p.,** pansement adhésif; sparadrap *m* (*b*) *Const: Art: Med:* plâtre *m*; **p. of Paris,** plâtre de moulage; **p. cast,** *Med:* plâtre; (moulage *m* en) plâtre; **to put a leg in p.,** mettre une jambe dans le plâtre 2. *vtr* plâtrer (un mur); **to p. sth over,** enduire qch de plâtre; **plastered with mud,** tout couvert de boue. **'plastered** *a* *F:* ivre, soûl. **'plasterer** *n* plâtrier *m*.

plastic ['plæstik] 1. *a* (*a*) (art) plastique; **p. surgery,** chirurgie plastique, esthétique; **p. surgeon,** chirurgien esthétique 2. *a & n* (matière *f*) plastique (*m*); **a p. cup,** une tasse en (matière) plastique; **the plastics industry,** l'industrie des plastiques; **p. bomb, explosive,** plastic *m*. **'Plasticine** *n* *Rtm:* pâte *f* à modeler.

plate [pleit] 1. *n* (*a*) plaque *f*; lame *f* (de métal); *Dent:* appareil *n* dentaire; dentier *m*; *DomEc:* **hot p.,** (i) plaque chauffante (de cuisinière électrique) (ii) chauffe-assiettes *m inv*; **name p.,** plaque de porte; *Aut:* **number p.,** plaque d'immatriculation; **clutch p.,** disque *m* d'embrayage; **p. glass,** glace, verre, de vitrage (*b*) (*in book*) gravure *f*, estampe *f*; **full-page p.,** gravure hors texte (*c*) orfèvrerie *f*; vaisselle *f* d'or, d'argent; **it's only p.,** c'est du plaqué (*d*) *Sp:* coupe (donnée en prix) (*e*) assiette *f*; **dinner p.,** assiette plate; **soup p.,** assiette creuse; *F:* **to have a lot on one's p.,** avoir du pain sur la planche; *F:* **to hand s.o. sth on a p.,** servir qn sur un plateau; *Ecc:* **collection p.,** plateau de quête 2. *vtr* plaquer (un article) (en argent, en or). **'plateful** *n* assiettée *f*. **'platelayer** *n* *Rail:* poseur *n* de rails. **'platerack** *n* *DomEc:* égouttoir *m*.

plateau ['plætou] *n* (*pl* **plateaux, -eaus** ['plætouz]) *Geog:* plateau *m*.

platform ['plætfɔːm] *n* (*a*) plate-forme *f*; *Petr:* plate-forme de forage; **p. shoes,** chaussures à semelles compensées (*b*) *Rail:* quai *m*; **departure p.,** (quai de) départ *m*; **arrival p.,** (quai d')arrivée *f* (*c*) estrade *f*, tribune *f* (de réunion publique).

platinum ['plætinəm] *n* platine *m*; **p. blond(e),** platiné.

platitude ['plætitjuːd] *n* platitude *f*; lieu commun.

platonic [plə'tɔnik] *a* platonique.

platoon [plə'tuːn] *n* *Mil:* section *f*.

plausible ['plɔːzibl] *a* (argument) plausible; (prétexte) spécieux; (*of pers*) enjôleur; captieux. **plausi'bility** *n* plausibilité *f*. **'plausibly** *adv* plausiblement.

play [plei] I. *n* (*a*) jeu *m*; activité *f*; **in full p.,** en pleine activité; **to come into p.,** entrer en jeu; **to bring sth into p.,** mettre qch en jeu; **to make a p. for sth,** jouer le grand jeu pour obtenir qch; **to give full p. to sth,** donner libre cours à qch (*b*) *Tchn:* jeu (d'une pièce) (*c*) jeu; amusement *m*; **to be at p.,** être en train de jouer; **it's child's p.,** c'est un jeu d'enfant; **to say sth in p.,** dire qch pour plaisanter; **p. on words,** calembour *m*; jeu de mots (*d*) *Games:* jeu; **p. began at one o'clock,** la partie a commencé à une heure; **ball in p.,** out of **p.,** balle en jeu, hors jeu (*e*) pièce *f* (de théâtre); **Shakespeare's plays,** le théâtre de Shakespeare. II. *v* 1. *vi* (*of fountains, music, children*) jouer; (*of animals*) folâtrer; **to p. (at) soldiers,** jouer aux soldats; *F:* **what do you think you're playing at?** mais qu'est-ce que tu fais là? **to p. with a doll,** jouer avec une poupée; **to p. with one's glasses,** jouer (distraitement) avec ses lunettes; **to p. with fire,** jouer avec le feu; **to p. fair,** jouer franc jeu; **to p. for money,** jouer (pour) de l'argent; **to p. high, for high stakes,** jouer gros jeu; **to p. into s.o.'s hands,** fournir à qn des armes contre soi 2. *vtr* (*a*) **to p. football, chess,** jouer au football, aux échecs; **to p. ball,** jouer au ballon; *Fig:* coopérer; **to p. a match,** disputer un match; **to p. the piano, the flute,** jouer du piano, de la flûte; **to p. a piece of music,** jouer un morceau de musique (*b*) faire marcher (un tourne-disque); passer (un disque, une cassette) (*c*) *Th: Cin:* jouer (un rôle); **to p. Macbeth,** jouer Macbeth; tenir le rôle de Macbeth; **to p. the fool,** faire l'idiot; **to p. a joke, a trick, on s.o.,** jouer un tour à qn (*d*) *Cards:* jouer (une carte); **to p. clubs,** jouer trèfle; **to p. s.o. at chess,** faire une partie d'échecs avec qn (*e*) *Sp:* inclure (qn) dans l'équipe (*f*) diriger (une lance) (sur un feu). **'play-act** *vi Fig:* jouer la comédie. **'play-acting** *n Fig:* comédie. **'play 'back** *vtr* (faire) repasser (une bande). **'playbill** *n* affiche *f* (de théâtre). **'playboy** *n* playboy *m.* **'play 'down** *vtr* minimiser (l'importance de qch). **'played 'out** *a* très fatigué, éreinté; (*of idea, fashion*) démodé; vieux jeu. **'player** *n* (*a*) joueur, -euse (de football, de cartes; *Mus:* musicien, -ienne; *Th:* acteur, -trice (*b*) **record p.,** tourne-disque *m*; cassette **p.,** lecteur *m* de cassettes; magnétophone *m* à cassettes. **'playful** *a* espiègle, enjoué. **'playfully** *adv* gaiement; en badinant. **'playground** *n Sch:* cour *f* de récréation; covered **p.,** préau *m.* **'playgroup** *n* (école) maternelle *f.* **'playhouse** *n* théâtre *m.* **'playing** *n* jeu; **p. card,** carte à jouer; **p. field,** terrain de jeux. **'playmate** *n* camarade *mf* de jeu. **'play 'off** *vtr* (*a*) **to p. s.o. o. against s.o.,** opposer qn à qn (*b*) *Sp:* rejouer (un match nul). **'play-off** *n.Sp:* second match nécessité par un match nul. **'play 'on** *vtr* agir, faire pression sur (les sentiments de qn). **'playpen** *n* parc *m* (pour enfants). **'playroom** *n* salle *f* de jeux. **'play-school** *n* (école) maternelle. **'plaything** *n* jouet *m.* **'playtime** *n Sch:* récréation *f.* **'play 'up** *vtr & i* (*of pers, machine*) faire des siennes; (*of pers*) agacer, enquiquiner (qn); **my rheumatism is playing (me) up,** mon rhumatisme me fait mal; **to p. up to s.o.,** flatter qn. **'playwright** *n* auteur *m* dramatique; dramaturge *m.*

PLC, plc *abbr Public Limited Company.*

plea [pli:] *n* (*a*) *Jur:* défense *f*; **to put forward a p. of insanity,** plaider la folie (*b*) excuse *f*, prétexte *m*; **p. for mercy,** appel *m* à la clémence.

plead [pli:d] 1. *vi* (*a*) *Jur:* plaider (for, pour; against, contre); **to p. guilty, not guilty,** plaider coupable, non coupable (*b*) **to p. with s.o. to do sth,** supplier qn de faire qch 2. *vtr* (*a*) plaider; **to p. s.o.'s cause with s.o.,** plaider la cause de qn, intercéder pour qn, auprès de qn; **to p. insanity,** plaider la folie (*b*) prétexter (l'ignorance); invoquer, alléguer (une excuse). **'pleading** 1. *n* prières *fpl* (for, en faveur de); *Jur:* plaidoyer *m* 2. *a* suppliant. **'pleadingly** *adv* d'un ton, d'un regard, suppliant.

pleasant ['plezənt] *a* agréable, charmant, aimable; plaisant; (*of pers*) aimable; **p. it's very p. here,** il fait bon ici. **'pleasantly** *adv* agréablement.

please [pli:z] *vtr & i* plaire à (qn); faire plaisir à (qn); contenter (qn); **to be easily pleased,** être facile à contenter; **there is no pleasing him,** il n'y a pas moyen de lui plaire; **he's hard to p.,** il est difficile; **p. yourself! do as you p.!** faites comme il vous plaira, comme vous voudrez; **(if you) p.,** s'il vous plaît; s'il te plaît; **p. don't cry,** ne pleurez pas, je vous en prie; **p. tell me,** veuillez me dire; **may I?—p. do!** vous permettez?—je vous en prie; *PN:* **p. do not walk on the grass,** prière de ne pas marcher sur le gazon. **pleased** *a* satisfait, content; **to be p. with sth,** être satisfait de qch; **as p. as Punch,** heureux comme tout; **I'm very p. he's coming,** cela me fait grand plaisir, je suis très content, qu'il vienne; **I'll be p. to come,** je viendrai avec plaisir. **'pleasurable** *a* agréable; (expression) sympathique. **'pleasing** *a* agréable. **'pleasurably** *adv* agréablement. **'pleasure** ['pleʒər] *n* (*a*) plaisir; *m*; **with p.,** avec plaisir; volontiers; **to take p. in doing sth,** prendre (du) plaisir à faire qch; **it gave me great p.,** cela m'a fait grand plaisir; **p. trip,** partie de plaisir; **p. boat,** bateau de plaisance (*b*) volonté *f*, bon plaisir; **at p.,** à volonté; **at s.o.'s p.,** au gré de qn.

pleat [pli:t] *Dressm:* 1. *n* pli *m*; **flat pleats,** plis couchés; **box pleats,** doubles plis; **inverted pleats,** plis creux 2. *vtr* plisser (une jupe).

plebeian [pli'bi:ən] *a & n* plébien, -ienne.

plebiscite ['plebisit] *n* plébiscite *m.*

pledge [pledʒ] 1. *n* (*a*) gage *m*, nantissement *m*; **p. of good faith,** garantie *f* de bonne foi (*b*) promesse *f*, vœu *m*; **I'm under a p. of secrecy,** j'ai fait vœu de garder le secret 2. *vtr* (*a*) mettre (qch) en gage (*b*) engager (sa parole).

plenary ['pli:nəri] *a* complet; entier; **p. powers,** pouvoirs absolus; pleins pouvoirs; **p. assembly,** assemblée plénière.

plenipotentiary [plenipə'tenʃəri] *a & n* plénipotentiaire (*m*).

plenty ['plenti] *n* abondance *f*; **he has p. of everything,** il a tout ce qu'il faut; **p. of money,** beaucoup d'argent; **you have p. of time,** vous avez largement le temps; **to have p. to live on,** avoir largement de quoi vivre; **it's p. big enough,** c'est bien assez grand; **in p.,** en abondance; **to live in p.,** vivre dans l'abondance; **land of p.,** pays de cocagne. **'plentiful** *a* abondant, copieux. **'plentifully** *adv* abondamment; copieusement.

plethora ['pleθərə] *n* surabondance *f.*

pleurisy ['pluərisi] *n Med:* pleurésie *f.*

pliable ['plaiəbl] *a* flexible; souple; (caractère) docile.

plia'bility n flexibilité f; souplesse f; docilité f (de caractère).

pliers ['plaiəz] npl Tls: **(pair of) p.,** pince(s) f (pl), tenaille(s) f (pl).

plight [plait] n condition f; (triste) état m.

plimsolls ['plimsoulz] npl chaussures fpl de gymnastique, de tennis; tennis mpl.

plinth [plinθ] n Arch: plinthe f; socle m.

PLO abbr Palestinian Liberation Organization, Organisation de libération de la Palestine, OLP.

plod [plɔd] vi (plodded) marcher lourdement, péniblement; **to p. along,** marcher d'un pas pesant; **to p. on,** persévérer; **to p. (away),** travailler laborieusement (at sth, à qch). **'plodder** n travailleur, -euse, persévérant(e).

plonk [plɔŋk] F: 1. n (a) bruit sourd (b) vin m ordinaire 2. adv avec un bruit sourd 3. vtr **to p. sth down,** poser qch bruyamment et sans façons; **to p. oneself down,** s'asseoir lourdement; se laisser tomber.

plop [plɔp] F: 1. n flac m, plouf m 2. vi (plopped) faire flac; tomber en faisant plouf.

plot [plɔt] 1. n (a) (parcelle f, lot m, de) terrain m; **building p.,** terrain à bâtir, lotissement m; **vegetable p.,** coin m, carré m, des légumes (b) intrigue f, action f (d'un roman, d'une pièce de théâtre); **the p. thickens,** l'affaire se corse (c) complot m, conspiration f 2. v (plotted) (a) vtr relever, tracer (une route, un graphique); Nav: **to p. the position,** faire le point (b) vtr & i comploter, conspirer (against s.o., contre qn); tramer (une évasion). **'plotter** n conspirateur, -trice. **'plotting** n (a) levé m (d'un terrain) (b) tracé m, graphique m (c) complots mpl.

plough, NAm: plow [plau] 1. n charrue f 2. vtr & i labourer (la terre); tracer, creuser (un sillon); **to p. (one's way) through the snow,** avancer péniblement dans la neige; **to p. through a book,** lire laborieusement un livre jusqu'au bout; **to p. on,** continuer avec difficulté, laborieusement. **'plough 'back** vtr Com: réinvestir (les bénéfices) (dans une société). **'ploughing** n labour m; labourage m; Com: **p. back of profits,** autofinancement m. **'ploughman** n (pl -men) laboureur m; **ploughman's lunch,** déjeuner m de pain et de fromage. **'plough 'up** vtr faire passer la charrue sur (un champ); (of animals, explosions) défoncer (le terrain).

plover ['plʌvər] n Orn: pluvier m.

plow [plau] n & v NAm: see **plough.**

ploy [plɔi] n F: stratagème m.

pluck [plʌk] 1. vtr arracher (des plumes); plumer (une volaille); cueillir (des fleurs); pincer (de la guitare); **to p. one's eyebrows,** s'épiler les sourcils; **to p. (at) s.o.'s sleeve,** tirer qn par la manche 2. n courage m; F: cran m. **'pluck 'up** vtr **to p. up (one's) courage,** s'armer de courage; prendre son courage à deux mains (**to do sth,** pour faire qch). **'pluckily** adv avec courage. **'plucky** a (-ier, -iest) courageux; **to be p.,** avoir du cran.

plug [plʌg] 1. n (a) bonde f (de tonneau); bouchon m, tampon m (de baignoire, de lavabo); El: prise f (de courant); Elcs: Tp: fiche f; ICE: **(sparking) p.,** bougie f (b) F: réclame f; battage m 2. vtr (plugged) (a) **to p. (up),** boucher, obturer (une ouverture); obstruer (une cavité dentaire) (b) F: faire de la réclame, du battage, pour (un produit). **'plug a'way** vi F: persévérer (at,

dans). **'plughole** n bonde, trou m (d'écoulement) (de baignoire, de lavabo). **'plug 'in** vtr & i El: brancher (la télévision, une lampe).

plum [plʌm] n (a) prune f; **p. (tree),** prunier m; Cu: **p. pudding,** pudding m (de Noël) (b) morceau m de choix; **the plums,** les meilleurs (postes); **to have a p. job,** avoir une situation en or (c) **p. (colour),** prune.

plumage ['plu:midʒ] n plumage m.

plumb [plʌm] 1. n plomb m (de fil à plomb); **p. line,** fil à plomb; Nau: (ligne de) sonde f 2. a droit; vertical; d'aplomb 3. adv F: **p. in the middle,** en plein milieu 4. vtr sonder (la mer); vérifier l'aplomb de (qch); plomber (un mur). **'plumber** n plombier m. **'plumb 'in** vtr raccorder (une machine à laver). **'plumbing** n plomberie f.

plume [plu:m] n panache m; plumet m (de casque).

plummet ['plʌmit] vi plonger, tomber, verticalement; (of prices) s'effondrer.

plump¹ [plʌmp] a rebondi, grassouillet, dodu; (of chicken, pers) bien en chair; (of hands) potelé. **'plumpness** n embonpoint m. **'plump 'up** vtr secouer, brasser (un oreiller).

plump² vtr & i **to p. (down),** jeter, flanquer, déposer brusquement (qch); **to p. (oneself) down,** tomber lourdement; s'affaler (**in a chair,** dans un fauteuil). **'plump 'for** vtr F: choisir.

plunder ['plʌndər] 1. n (a) (act) pillage m (b) (goods) butin m 2. vtr piller.

plunge ['plʌndʒ] 1. n plongeon m; Fig: **to take the p.,** se jeter à l'eau 2. v (a) vtr plonger; immerger; **plunged in darkness,** plongé dans l'obscurité (b) vi plonger; se jeter (à corps perdu); (of ship) tanguer; **to p. forward,** s'élancer en avant; **she plunged to her death,** elle a fait une chute mortelle. **'plunger** n DomEc: ventouse f. **'plunging** a (décolleté) plongeant.

pluperfect [plu:'pə:fikt] a & n Gram: plus-que-parfait (m).

plural ['pluərəl] a & n Gram: pluriel (m); **in the p.,** au pluriel.

plus [plʌs] 1. prep plus 2. n (pl pluses ['plʌsiz]) **p. (sign),** plus m, signe m de l'addition; Fig: atout m, avantage m 3. a positif.

plush [plʌʃ] 1. n Tex: peluche f 2. a F: (also **'plushy**) luxueux, somptueux.

plutocrat ['plu:təkræt] n ploutocrate m. **plu'tocracy** n ploutocratie f.

plutonium [plu:'touniəm] n Ch: plutonium m.

ply¹ [plai] v (plied) 1. vtr manier (qch) (vigoureusement); exercer (son métier); **to p. s.o. with questions,** presser qn de questions; **to p. s.o. with drink,** verser de grandes rasades à qn 2. vi faire le service, la navette (**between, and,** entre, et); **to p. for hire,** faire un service de taxi.

ply² n épaisseur f (de contre-plaqué); fil m (de corde, de laine); **three-p. wool,** laine trois fils. **'plywood** n contre-plaqué m.

PM abbr Prime Minister.

p.m. [pi:'em] adv de l'après-midi, du soir; **at four p.m.,** à quatre heures de l'après-midi.

pneumatic [nju:'mætik] a pneumatique.

pneumonia [nju:'mouniə] n pneumonie f.

PO abbr Post Office.

poach¹ [poutʃ] vtr Cu: pocher (des œufs). **'poacher¹** n DomEc: pocheuse f (à œufs).

poach 294 **poke**

poach² vtr & i braconner (le gibier); to p. on s.o.'s
preserves, empiéter sur les prérogatives de qn; braconner sur les terres de qn. 'poacher² n braconnier
m. 'poaching n braconnage m.

pocket ['pɔkit] 1. n (a) poche f (de vêtement, de
minerai, de résistance); Bill: blouse f; air p., trou
d'air; (in pipe) poche d'air; trouser p., poche de
pantalon; hip p., poche revolver; breast p., poche de
poitrine; to put one's hands in one's pockets, mettre les
mains dans ses poches; he's always got his hand in his
p., il est toujours à débourser; to have s.o. in one's p.,
avoir qn dans sa manche; to go through s.o.'s pockets,
faire les poches à qn; p. handkerchief, mouchoir de
poche; p. dictionary, dictionnaire de poche; p. money,
argent de poche; to be in p., être bénéficiaire; to be out
of p., en être de sa poche 2. vtr (a) empocher; mettre
(qch) dans sa poche (b) Pej: soustraire (de l'argent);
F: chiper (qch) (c) Bill: blouser (la bille). 'pocket-
book n (a) carnet m (b) NAm: portefeuille m.
'pocketful n pleine poche. 'pocketknife n (pl
-knives) canif m.

pockmarked ['pɔkmɑːkt] a marqué de la petite
vérole; (visage) grêlé.

pod [pɔd] n cosse f, gousse f.

podgy ['pɔdʒi] a (-ier, -iest) boulot; rondelet.

poem ['pouim] n poème m; poésie f. 'poet n poète m.
poe'tess n (pl -es) femme f poète; poétesse f.
po'etic(al) a poétique. po'etically adv
poétiquement. 'poetry n poésie; to write p., écrire
des vers; a piece of p., une poésie.

poignant ['pɔinjənt] a poignant; vif. 'poignancy n
caractère poignant (d'une émotion). 'poignantly
adv d'une façon poignante.

poinsettia [pɔin'setiə] n Bot: poinsettia f.

point [pɔint] I. n (a) point m; decimal p., virgule f; three
p. five (3.5), trois virgule cinq (3,5); p. of departure,
point de départ; p. of view, point de vue; to consider
sth from all points of view, considérer qch sous tous
ses aspects (b) point, détail m (d'un argument); the
main p., l'essentiel m, l'important m; figures that give
p. to his argument, chiffres qui ajoutent du poids à sa
thèse; I see, take, your p., je vois ce que vous voulez
dire; p. taken! très juste! to make a p., faire ressortir un
argument; points to be remembered, considérations
fpl à se rappeler; to make a p. of doing sth, se faire un
devoir, ne pas manquer, de faire qch; p. of grammar,
of law, question f de grammaire, de droit; p. of
honour, point d'honneur; in p. of fact, en fait; à vrai
dire; case in p., cas d'espèce (c) the p., le point, le sujet,
la question; the p. is (that), c'est que; that's the p.,
justement; that's not the p., il ne s'agit pas de cela;
beside, off, the p., à côté de la question; hors de
propos; this is very much to the p., c'est bien dit; p. of
interest, détail intéressant; to have one's good points,
avoir ses qualités f; to be on the p. of doing sth, être sur
le point de faire qch; p. of no return, point de non-
retour; up to a (certain) p., jusqu'à un certain point; to
come to the p., arriver au fait; on this p., à cet égard;
your remark is not to the p., votre observation
manque d'à-propos; let's get back to the p., revenons
à nos moutons (d) what would be the p. (of doing sth)?
à quoi bon (faire qch)? there is no p. in (doing) it, cela
ne servirait à rien; I don't see the p. of the story, je ne
vois pas où l'histoire veut en venir; severe to the p. of

cruelty, sévère jusqu'à la cruauté (e) Games: point;
Box: to win on points, gagner aux points; Ten: match
p., set p., balle f de match, the set (f) Meas: degré m
(de thermomètre); freezing, boiling, p., point de congélation, d'ébullition (g) pointe f (d'une aiguille);
piquant m (d'une plaisanterie); to dance on point(s),
faire les pointes; Rail: points, aiguillage m; the points
of the compass, les aires f du vent; policeman on p.
duty, agent de circulation (h) Geog: pointe, promontoire m (i) El: (power) p., prise f (de courant)
(femelle). II. v 1. vtr (a) pointer, diriger (une longue-
vue); braquer (un fusil) (at, sur); to p. one's finger at
s.o., sth, montrer, indiquer, qn qch, du doigt; to p. the
way, montrer, indiquer, le chemin (à qn, vers un
endroit) (b) Const: jointoyer (un mur) 2. vi to p. at
s.o., sth, montrer qn, qch, du doigt; the needle of the
compass always points (to the) north, l'aiguille de la
boussole est toujours orientée vers le nord; everything
seems to p. to success, tout semble indiquer le succès;
this points to the fact that, ceci laisse supposer que.
'point-'blank 1. a (tir) à bout portant; (refus) net,
catégorique; (of question) fait de but en blanc 2. adv
(tirer) à bout portant; (refuser) catégoriquement;
(tirer, demander) de but en blanc. 'pointed a
pointu; (barbe) en pointe; (of comment) mordant;
(allusion) peu équivoque. 'pointedly adv d'un ton
mordant; d'une manière marquée. 'pointer n (a)
chien m d'arrêt; pointer m (b) aiguille (d'horloge);
baguette f (pour indiquer qch au tableau noir) (c)
conseil m, renseignement m; tuyau m. 'pointless a
(histoire) qui ne rime à rien; (plaisanterie) fade;
(démarche) inutile; it would be p. to, il ne servirait à
rien de. 'pointlessly adv inutilement. 'point-
lessness n inutilité f. 'point 'out vtr (a) montrer
(qch) du doigt (to s.o., à qn) (b) signaler, relever (une
erreur); to p. o. sth to s.o., attirer l'attention de qn sur
qch; faire remarquer qch à qn. 'point-to-'point a
& n Equit: p.-to-p. (race), course f au clocher.

poise [pɔiz] 1. n (a) équilibre m, aplomb m (b) port m
(du corps) 2. vtr équilibrer; tenir en équilibre; to be
poised, être en équilibre; to be poised ready to spring,
se tenir prêt à bondir.

poison ['pɔizn] 1. n poison m; to take p.,
s'empoisonner; p. gas, gaz toxique; to hate s.o. like p.,
ne pas pouvoir sentir qn; Bot: p. ivy, sumac vénéneux
2. vtr empoisonner; intoxiquer (qn); corrompre,
pervertir (l'esprit de qn). 'poisoner n empoison-
neur, -euse. 'poisoning n empoisonnement m;
intoxication f; food p., intoxication alimentaire; blood
p., empoisonnement du sang. 'poisonous a toxique; (of animal) venimeux; (of plant) vénéneux; p.
doctrine, doctrine pernicieuse, empoisonnée; she has
a p. tongue, elle a une langue de vipère; she's a p.
creature! c'est une vraie poison!

poke [pouk] I. n poussée f; (nudge) coup m de coude;
(with finger) coup du bout du doigt; to give s.o. a p. in
the ribs, cogner qn du coude. II. v 1. vtr (a) toucher
(qn, qch) du bout du doigt; pousser (qn) du coude (b)
tisonner (le feu) (c) mettre, fourrer (qch) (into, dans);
to p. one's head through the window, passer la tête par
la fenêtre; to p. one's nose into other people's business,
fourrer son nez dans les affaires d'autrui; to p. fun at
s.o., se moquer de qn 2. vi to p. (about), fouiller,
fureter (dans tous les coins); to p. into other people's

business, fourrer son nez dans les affaires d'autrui.
'**poker**¹ *n* tisonnier *m*.

poker² ['pouker] *n Cards:* poker *m*.

poky ['pouki] *a* (-ier, -iest) (*of room*) exigu et sombre.

Poland ['pouland] *Prn Geog:* Pologne *f*. **Pole**¹ *n* Polonais, -aise. '**Polish**¹ **1.** *a & n* polonais, -aise **2.** *n Ling:* polonais *m*.

pole² [poul] *n* perche *f*; mât *m* (de tente); **telegraph p.,** poteau *m* télégraphique; *F:* **to be up the p.,** être fou, toqué; *Sp:* **p. vaulting,** saut à la perche. '**poleax(e)** *vtr* assommer.

pole³ *n Geog:* pôle *m*; **South P.,** pôle sud; **the p. star,** l'étoile polaire; *Fig:* **to be poles apart,** être aux antipodes l'un de l'autre. '**polar** *a* polaire; **p. bear,** ours blanc. **polari'zation** *n* polarisation *f*. '**polarize** *vtr* polariser.

polemic [pɔ'lemik] *n* polémique *f*.

police [pɔ'liːs] **1.** *n inv* (*no pl*) **the p. (force),** la police; **p. superintendent** = commissaire de police; **p. inspector** = inspecteur de police; (*in CID*) commissaire de police; **p. constable, officer** = agent de police; **p. station** = commissariat *m* (de police); **p. car,** voiture de police; **p. dog,** chien policier; **p. state,** état policier; **river p.,** police fluviale; **Royal Canadian Mounted P.,** Gendarmerie royale du Canada; **the p. are after him,** la police est à ses trousses **2.** *vtr* assurer la police de (l'état); maintenir l'ordre dans (un pays). **po'liceman** *n* (*pl* -men) agent *m* de police. **po'licewoman** *nf* (*pl* -women) femme-agent (de police).

policy ['pɔlisi] *n* (*pl* policies) (*a*) politique *f*; ligne *f* de conduite; **foreign p.,** politique extérieure; **our p. is to satisfy our customers,** notre but *m* est de satisfaire nos clients (*b*) (**insurance**) **p.,** police *f* (d'assurance); **p. holder,** assuré, -ée.

poliomyelitis, *F:* **polio** [poulioumaiə'laitis, 'pouliou] *n Med:* poliomyélite *f*, polio *f*.

polish² ['pɔliʃ] **1.** *n* (*pl* polishes) (*a*) poli *m*, brillant *m*, lustre *m*; **high p.,** poli brillant; **to take the p. off sth,** dépolir qch (*b*) **household p.,** produit *m* d'entretien; (*for furniture, floors*) encaustique *f*, cire *f*, crème *f*; (**shoe**) **p.,** cirage *m*; **nail p.,** vernis *m* à ongles (*c*) politesse *f*; belles manières **2.** *vtr* polir; cirer (des chaussures, des meubles); astiquer (des meubles, le parquet). '**polish 'off** *vtr* terminer vite, expédier (un travail); vider (un verre); achever (un plat). '**polish 'up** *vtr* faire reluire (qch); astiquer (du métal); dérouiller (son français). '**polished** *a* poli; (*of furniture, shoes*) ciré; (*style*) raffiné. '**polisher** *n Tls:* polissoir *m*; (*for floors*) cireuse *f*.

polite [pɔ'lait] *a* poli, courtois (**to s.o.,** envers, avec, qn); **p. society,** le beau monde. **po'litely** *adv* poliment; avec politesse. **po'liteness** *n* politesse *f*.

politics ['pɔlitiks] *npl* (*usu with sg const*) la politique; **to talk p.,** parler politique; **to go into p.,** se lancer dans la politique. '**politic** *a* politique, avisé. **po'litical** *a* politique; **p. parties,** partis politiques; **p. science,** sciences politiques. **po'litically** *adv* politiquement. **poli'tician** *n* homme *m*, femme *f*, politique; *Pej:* politicien, -ienne.

poll [poul] **1.** *n* (*a*) vote *m* (par bulletins); scrutin *m*; **to go to the polls,** aller aux urnes *f*; **to declare the p.,** proclamer le résultat du scrutin; **heavy p.,** forte participation électorale (*b*) (**public opinion**) **p.,** son-

dage *m* (d'opinion publique); **Gallup p.,** (sondage) Gallup *m* **2.** *vtr* (*of candidate*) réunir (tant de voix); **to p. a vote,** donner sa voix. '**polling** *n* vote; élections *fpl*; **p. booth,** isoloir *m*; **p. station,** bureau de vote.

pollen ['pɔlən] *n Bot:* pollen *m*. '**pollinate** *vtr* transporter du pollen sur les stigmates (d'une fleur).

pollute [pə'luːt] *vtr* polluer; *Fig:* souiller, corrompre. **po'llution** *n* pollution *f*; *Fig:* souillure *f*.

polo ['poulou] *n Sp:* polo *m*; **water p.,** water-polo *m*; *Cl:* **p. neck,** col roulé. '**poloneck(ed)** *a* (chandail) à col roulé.

poltergeist ['pɔltəgaist] *n* esprit frappeur.

polyester [pɔli'estər] *n Tex:* polyester *m*.

polyethylene [pɔli'eθiliːn] *n Ch:* polyéthylène *m*.

polygamy [pə'ligəmi] *n* polygamie *f*. **po'lygamist** *n* polygame *mf*.

polyglot ['pɔliglɔt] *a & n* polyglotte (*mf*).

polygon ['pɔligən] *n* polygone *m*. **po'lygonal** *a* polygonal.

polymer ['pɔlimər] *n Ch:* polymère *m*.

Polynesia [pɔli'niːziə] *Prn Geog:* Polynésie *f*. **Poly'nesian** *a & n* polynésien, -ienne.

polyp ['pɔlip] *n* polype *m*.

polystyrene [pɔli'stairiːn] *n Ch:* polystyrène *m*.

polytechnic, *F:* **poly** [pɔli'teknik, 'pɔli] *n* (*pl* **polys**) = Institut universitaire de technologie.

polythene ['pɔliθiːn] *n* polyéthylène *m*, polythène *m*.

polyurethane [pɔli'juərəθein] *n Ch:* polyuréthane *m*.

pomegranate ['pɔmigrænit] *n Bot:* grenade *f*.

pom(my) ['pɔm(i)] *n* (*pl* pommies) *Austr: & NZ: F:* Anglais, -aise.

pomp [pɔmp] *n* pompe *f*, éclat *m*, faste *m*; **p. and circumstance,** (grand) apparat. **pom'posity** *n* suffisance *f*. '**pompous** *a* pompeux; (homme) suffisant. '**pompously** *adv* pompeusement, avec suffisance.

pond [pɔnd] *n* étang *m*; mare *f*; bassin *m* (de jardin).

ponder ['pɔndər] **1.** *vtr* réfléchir sur (une question); ruminer **2.** *vi* méditer; **to p. on, over, sth,** réfléchir à, méditer sur, qch. '**ponderous** *a* lourd, pesant.

pong [pɔŋ] *F:* **1.** *n* puanteur *f* **2.** *vi* puer.

pontiff ['pɔntif] *n Ecc:* pontife *m*; **the (sovereign) p.,** le (souverain) pontife, le pape. **pon'tifical** *a* pontifical. **pon'tificate** *vi* pontifier.

pontoon [pɔn'tuːn] *n* ponton *m*; **p. bridge,** pont de bateaux, pont flottant (*b*) *Cards:* vingt-et-un *m*.

pony ['pouni] *n* (*pl* ponies) poney *m*; **p. trekking,** randonnées *fpl* à dos de poney. '**ponytail** *n Hairdr:* queue *f* de cheval.

poodle ['puːdl] *n* caniche *mf*.

poof [puf] *n P:* homosexuel *m*, tante *f*.

pooh-pooh [puː'puː] *vtr F:* faire peu de cas, se moquer, de.

pool¹ [puːl] *n* (*a*) mare *f*; **swimming p.,** piscine *f*; **paddling p.,** bassin *m* à patauger (*b*) flaque *f* (d'eau, d'huile).

pool² **1.** *n* (*a*) *Games:* poule *f*, cagnotte *f*; **football pools,** concours *m* de pronostics de matchs de football (*b*) *Com:* fonds commun; groupe *m*, groupement *m* (de travailleurs, de marchandises); *PolEc:* pool *m*; **typing p.,** pool dactylographique, de dactylos (*c*) (jeu *m* de) billard *m* **2.** *vtr* mettre en commun (des capitaux).

poor [puǝr] 1. *a* (*a*) pauvre; **as p. as a church mouse,** pauvre comme Job (*b*) (*not good*) mauvais; (marchandises) (de qualité) médiocre; (terre) maigre; **p. excuse,** mauvaise excuse; **p. quality,** mauvaise qualité; **to have a p. opinion of s.o.,** avoir une pauvre opinion de qn; **he's p. at maths,** il est faible en maths; **p. thing!** le, la, pauvre! 2. *npl* **the p.,** les pauvres *m.* **'poorly** 1. *adv* pauvrement, médiocrement; **p. lit,** mal éclairé 2. *a* souffrant; **to look p.,** avoir mauvaise mine. **'poorness** *n* pauvreté *f*; infériorité *f*; mauvaise qualité.

pop¹ [pɔp] 1. *n* (*a*)·bruit sec; pan *m* (*b*) *F:* boisson gazeuse 2. *v* (**popped**) (*a*) *vi* éclater, péter; (*of cork*) sauter; (*of balloon*) crever; *F:* **to p. across, over, round, to the grocer's,** faire un saut (jusque) chez l'épicier (*b*) *vtr* crever (un ballon); faire sauter (un bouchon); *F:* **to p. sth into a drawer,** mettre, fourrer, qch dans un tiroir; **to p. one's head out of the window,** sortir (tout à coup) sa tête par la fenêtre; *F:* **he popped the question,** il lui a demandé de l'épouser. **'popcorn** *n Comest:* pop-corn *m.* **'popgun** *n* pistolet *m* d'enfant. **'pop 'in** *vi F:* entrer en passant; ne faire qu'entrer et sortir. **'pop 'off** *vi F:* (*a*) filer, déguerpir (*b*) mourir (subitement). **'pop 'out** *vi F:* sortir; **his eyes were popping out of his head,** les yeux lui sortaient de la tête. **'popper** *n F:* bouton-pression *m*, pression *m or f.* **'pop 'up** *vi F:* (*of question*) revenir sur le tapis.

pop² *n F: esp NAm:* papa *m.*

pop³ *F:* (= **popular**) *a & n* pop (*m inv*); **p. song,** chanson pop; **p. singer,** chanteur de pop; **p. music,** musique pop; **p. art,** pop'art *m.*

pope [poup] *n* pape *m.*

poplar ['pɔplǝr] *n Bot:* peuplier *m.*

poppy ['pɔpi] *n* (*pl* **poppies**) *Bot:* pavot *m*; **field p.,** coquelicot *m*; **p. day,** anniversaire de l'Armistice. **'poppycock** *n F:* bêtises *fpl.* **'poppyseed** *n* graine(s) *f*(*pl*) de pavot.

popular ['pɔpjulǝr] *a* (*a*) populaire; du peuple; **p. work, treatise,** ouvrage de vulgarisation; **p. error,** erreur courante (*b*) populaire; (livre) à la mode. **popu'larity** *n* popularité *f.* **populari'zation** *n* vulgarisation *f.* **'popularize** *vtr* populariser; vulgariser; rendre (qn) populaire. **'popularly** *adv* **it is p. believed that,** les gens croient que.

populate ['pɔpjuleit] *vtr* peupler; **thickly populated area,** région très peuplée. **popu'lation** *n* population *f*; **p. explosion,** explosion démographique.

porcelain ['pɔːslin] *n* porcelaine *f.*

porch [pɔːtʃ] *n* (*a*) porche *m*, portique *m* (*b*) *NAm:* véranda *f.*

porcupine ['pɔːkjupain] *n Z:* porc-épic *m.*

pore¹ [pɔːr] *n Anat:* pore *m.*

pore² *vi* **to p. over,** être plongé dans (un livre); méditer longuement (un problème).

pork [pɔːk] *n Cu:* (viande *f* de) porc *m*; **salt p.,** porc salé; **p. chop,** côtelette de porc; **p. pie,** pâté de porc (en croûte); **p. butcher,** charcutier, -ière.

pornography, *F:* **porn** [pɔːˈnɔɡrǝfi, pɔːn] *n* pornographie *f*; *F:* porno *f.* **porno'graphic,** *F:* **'porny** *a* (**-ier, -iest**) pornographique, *F:* porno.

porous ['pɔːrǝs] *a* poreux, perméable.

porpoise ['pɔːpǝs] *n Z:* marsouin *m.*

porridge ['pɔridʒ] *n* bouillie *f* d'avoine; porridge *m.*

port¹ [pɔːt] *n* port *m*; **free p.,** port franc; **naval p.,** fishing p., port militaire, de pêche; **p. of call,** port d'escale; (*of ship*) droits de port.

port² *n Nau:* bâbord *m.*

port³ *n* vin *m* de Porto; porto *m.*

portable ['pɔːtǝbl] *n* portatif; mobile.

portal [pɔːtl] *n* portail *m* (de cathédrale).

porter¹ ['pɔːtǝr] *n* (*a*) portier *m*, concierge *m*; **porter's lodge,** loge de concierge (*b*) *NAm: Rail:* garçon *m* (de wagon-lit).

porter² *n* porteur *m* (de bagages); chasseur *m* (d'hôtel). **'porterage** *n* frais *mpl* de transport. **'porterhouse** *n Cu:* **p. steak,** steak coupé entre le filet et le faux-filet.

portfolio [pɔːtˈfouliou] *n* (*a*) serviette *f* (pour documents) (*b*) chemise *f* (de carton) (*c*) portefeuille *m* (de ministre); **minister without p.,** ministre sans portefeuille (*d*) *Com:* portefeuille (d'assurances, de valeurs.

porthole ['pɔːthoul] *n Nau:* hublot *m.*

portion ['pɔːʃn] *n* (*a*) partie *f*; part *f*; côté *m* (d'un billet) (*b*) portion *f*, ration *f.* **'portion 'out** *vtr* partager (un bien); distribuer (les parts).

portly ['pɔːtli] *a* (**-ier, -iest**) corpulent, ventru.

portrait ['pɔːtrit] *n* portrait *m*; **p. painter,** portraitiste *mf.* **por'tray** *vtr* faire le portrait de (qn); dépeindre, décrire (des scènes, des personnages, des caractères). **por'trayal** *n* portrait; peinture *f*, représentation *f*; description *f* (d'une scène, d'un personnage).

Portugal ['pɔːtjugǝl] *Prn Geog:* Portugal *m.* **Portuguese** [-'giːz] 1. *a & n* portugais, -aise 2. *n Ling:* portugais *m.*

pose [pouz] 1. *n* pose *f*; attitude *f* (du corps) 2. *vtr & i* poser (un problème); (faire) poser (un modèle); faire prendre une pose à (qn); **to p. as a Frenchman,** se faire passer pour Français. **'poser** *n F:* question *f* difficile; colle *f.*

posh [pɔʃ] *a F:* chic.

position [pǝˈziʃǝn] 1. *n* position *f*; attitude *f*; place *f*; situation *f*; *Post: Bank:* guichet *m*; *Mil:* emplacement *m*; **in p.,** en place; **to put sth in p.,** mettre qch en place; *Nav:* **to work out one's p.,** faire le point; **to manoeuvre for p.,** manœuvrer pour s'assurer l'avantage; **to be in an awkward p.,** se trouver dans une situation difficile; **to be in a p. to do sth,** être à même, en mesure, de faire qch; **put yourself in my p.,** mettez-vous à ma place; **p. in society,** rang social; **in a high p.,** haut placé; *Sch:* **p. in class,** place dans la classe; (*at work*) **p. of trust,** poste *m* de confiance 2. *vtr* mettre en place, en position; mettre, placer, dans une position. **po'sitioning** *n* mise *f* en place, en position.

positive ['pɔzitiv] *a* (*a*) positif, affirmatif (*b*) (fait) authentique, indiscutable; **a p. miracle,** un véritable miracle (*c*) (*of pers, attitude*) convaincu, assuré, sûr, certain (**of, de**); (ton) absolu, tranchant. **'positively** *adv* (*a*) positivement, affirmativement (*b*) assurément, sûrement, certainement.

possess [pǝˈzes] *vtr* posséder; avoir (une qualité, des facultés); **all I p.,** tout mon avoir; **what possessed you (to do that)?** qu'est-ce qui vous a pris (de faire cela)? **to scream like one possessed,** crier comme un possédé. **po'ssession** *n* possession *f*; **to have sth·in one's p.,** avoir qch en sa possession; **to take p. of sth,** s'emparer de qch; **to take p. of a house,** entrer en possession d'une maison; **the information in my p.,** les renseignements dont je dispose; **in full p. of his faculties,** en pleine possession de ses facultés; **vacant p. (of a house),** libre possession, jouissance immédiate (d'une maison). **po'ssessive 1.** *a & n Gram:* possessif (*m*) **2.** *a* possessif; **a p. mother,** une mère abusive. **po'ssessiveness** *n* possessivité *f.* **po'ssessor** *n* possesseur *m;* propriétaire *mf.*

possible ['pɔsibl] **1.** *a* possible; **it's p.,** c'est possible; cela se peut bien; **it's p. (that) he'll come,** il se peut qu'il vienne; **it isn't p. to do it,** il n'est pas possible de le faire; **as many details as p.,** le plus de détails possible; **as far as p., if at all p.,** autant que possible; dans la mesure du possible; **as early as p.,** le plus tôt possible; **what p. interest can you have in it?** quel(le) (sorte d')intérêt cela peut-il présenter pour vous? **if p.,** si possible; **the p. nomination of this candidate,** la nomination éventuelle de ce candidat; **he is a p. candidate,** c'est un candidat possible, acceptable **2.** *n* (*a*) possible *m* (*b*) candidat, -ate, possible, acceptable. **possi'bility** *n* (*pl* -**ies**) possibilité *f;* **within the bounds of p.,** dans la limite du possible; **to prepare for all possibilities,** parer à toute éventualité; **this plan has possibilities,** ce projet offre des chances *f* de succès. **'possibly** *adv* (*a*) **I cannot p. do it,** il ne m'est pas possible de le faire; **it can't p. be!** ce n'est pas possible! **I'll do all I p. can,** je ferai tout mon possible (*b*) peut-être (bien); **p.!** c'est possible; cela se peut.

post¹ [poust] **1.** *n* poteau *m;* pieu *m;* montant *m* (de porte); **as deaf as a p.,** sourd comme un pot; *Rac:* **starting p., winning p.,** poteau de départ, d'arrivée **2.** *vtr* **to p. (up),** afficher (un avis); coller (des affiches); *PN:* **p. no bills,** défense d'afficher; **to be posted missing,** être porté (i) (*of ship*) disparu (ii) (*of pers*) manquant. **'poster** *n* affiche (murale); (*as decoration*) poster *m.*

post² **1.** *n* poste *m;* **trading p.,** comptoir *m; Mil:* **the last p.,** (i) la retraite au clairon (ii) la sonnerie aux morts **2.** *vtr* poster (qn à un endroit); *Mil:* affecter (qn) (à un commandement, à une unité). **'posting** *n esp Mil:* affectation *f* (à un poste).

post³ (*NAm:* = **mail**) **1.** *n* (*a*) courrier *m;* **by return of p.,** par retour du courrier; **the p. has come,** le facteur est passé; **to miss the p.,** manquer la levée; **what time's the next p.?** à quelle heure est la prochaine levée? (*b*) poste *f;* **to send sth by p.,** envoyer qch par la poste; **p. office,** bureau de poste; **the P. Office** = les Postes et Télécommunications; **p. office box,** boîte postale; **to take a letter to, put a letter in, the p.,** porter, mettre, une lettre à la poste **2.** *vtr* (*a*) mettre (une lettre) à la poste; poster (une lettre); **to p. sth to s.o.,** envoyer qch à qn par la poste (*b*) **to keep s.o. posted,** tenir qn au courant. **'postage** *n* affranchissement *m* (d'une lettre); **p. paid,** port payé; franco de port; **p. stamp,** timbre-poste *m;* **p. rates,** tarifs postaux; **additional p.,** surtaxe (postale). **'postal** *a* postal; **the p. service,** les Postes et Télécommunications; **p. rates,** tarifs postaux; **p. order,** mandat (postal). **'postbag** *n* sac postal. **'postbox** *n* (*pl* -**es**) boîte *f* aux lettres. **'postcard** *n* carte postale. **'postcode** *n* code postal. **post'haste** *adv* en toute hâte. **'postman** *n* (*pl* -**men**) facteur *m.* **'postmark 1.** *n* cachet *m* de la poste **2.** *vtr* timbrer (une lettre). **'postmaster, -mistress** *n* (*pl* -**mistresses**) receveur, -euse, des postes.

post- [poust-] *pref* post-. **post'date** *vtr* postdater (un chèque). **post'graduate** *a & n* **p.** (**student**), étudiant(e) licencié(e) qui continue ses études. **posthumous** ['pɔstjuməs] *a* posthume. **'posthumously** *adv* posthumement. **postim'pressionism** *n* post-impressionisme *m.* **post'mortem** *n* autopsie *f; Fig:* **to conduct a p. on sth,** examiner critiquement les résultats de qch. **post'natal** *a* post-natal. **post'pone** *vtr* remettre, ajourner, renvoyer (à plus tard) (une action, un départ); différer, arriérer (un paiement). **post'ponement** *n* remise *f,* renvoi *m* (à plus tard); ajournement *m.* **'postscript** *n* (*abbr* **PS**) postscriptum *m inv.* **'post'war** *a* d'après-guerre; **the p. period,** l'après-guerre *m inv.*

posterior [pɔs'tiəriər] *a & n* postérieur (*m*). **pos'terity** *n* postérité *f.*

posture ['pɔstʃər] **1.** *n* posture *f,* pose *f,* attitude *f* (du corps); position *f,* situation *f,* état *m* (des affaires) **2.** *vi* prendre une pose, une attitude.

posy ['pouzi] *n* (*pl* **posies**) petit bouquet (de fleurs).

pot [pɔt] **1.** *n* (*a*) pot *m; DomEc:* marmite *f;* (*for tea*) théière *f;* **pots and pans,** batterie *f* de cuisine; **flower p.,** pot à fleurs; **p. of jam,** pot de confiture; **coffee p.,** cafetière *f;* **chamber p.,** pot de chambre; *Cu:* **p. roast,** morceau de viande cuit à l'étouffée; *F:* **pots of money,** tas *mpl* d'argent; **to have pots of money,** rouler sur l'or; *F:* **to go to p.,** aller à la ruine; être fichu (*b*) *F:* marijuana *f;* herbe *f* **2.** *vtr* (**potted**) (*a*) mettre en pot (la viande, une plante) (*b*) *Bill:* blouser (une bille) (*c*) abattre (du gibier). **'pot'at** *vtr* lâcher un coup de fusil à (une bête). **'pot'bellied** *a F:* ventru, bedonnant. **'potbelly** *n* (*pl* -**ies**) *F:* gros ventre, bedon *m.* **'potbound** *a* (plante) dont le pot est trop petit. **'pothole** *n* (*in road*) trou *m;* nid *m* de poule; *Geol:* marmite *f* de géants. **'potholer** *n* spéléologue *mf.* **'potholing** *n* spéléologie *f.* **pot'luck** *n* **to take p.,** manger à la fortune du pot; choisir au hasard. **'potshot** *n F:* **to take a p. at sth,** lâcher au petit bonheur un coup de fusil à qch. **'potted** *a* (*a*) en pot; *Cu:* **p. meat,** terrine *f* de porc, etc (*b*) (*of book, version*) abrégé, condensé. **'potter¹** *n* potier *m;* **potter's wheel,** tour de potier. **'pottery** *n* (*pl* -**ies**) poterie *f;* **a piece of p.,** une poterie; **p. dish,** plat de, en, terre. **'potting** *n Hort:* **p. (up),** mise *f* en pot (de plantes); **p. shed,** serre de bouturages. **'potty** *F:* **1.** *a* toqué, timbré **2.** *n* (*pl* -**ies**) pot (de chambre) (d'enfant).

potash ['pɔtæʃ] *n Ch:* potasse *f.*

potassium [pə'tæsiəm] *n Ch:* potassium *m.*

potato [pə'teitou] *n* (*pl* **potatoes** [pə'teitouz]) pomme *f* de terre; **sweet p.,** patate *f* (douce); **boiled potatoes,** pommes (de terre) à l'eau; **baked potatoes,** pommes (de terre) au four; **mashed potatoes,** purée *f* de pommes (de terre); **chipped potatoes,** *NAm:* **French-fried potatoes,** pommes (de terre) frites; frites *fpl;* **p. crisps,** *NAm:* **chips,** (pommes) chips *mpl; F:* **to drop sth like a hot p.,** laisser tomber qch.

potency ['poutənsi] *n* force *f* (d'un argument, d'un alcool); puissance *f* (d'un argument); efficacité *f* (d'un médicament). **'potent** *a* (*of motive*) convaincant; (*of drug*) efficace, puissant; (poison) fort, violent.

potential [pə'tenʃl] **1.** *a* (ennemi, criminel) en puissance; (*of value*) virtuel; (danger) possible, latent; (client) éventuel; *Tchn:* potentiel **2.** *n* potentiel *m;*

potentialité *f*; **situation full of p.**, situation qui promet.
potenti'ality *n* (*pl* **-ies**) potentialité.
po'tentially *adv* potentiellement.

potpourri [poupu'ri:] *n* (*a*) fleurs séchées (*b*) *Lit: Mus:* pot-pourri *m*.

potter² ['pɔtər] *vi* s'occuper de bagatelles; traîner, flâner; **to p. about (at odd jobs)**, bricoler; **to p. about the house**, s'occuper à de petites tâches dans la maison; **he just potters (about)**, il s'occupe comme il peut; (*in car*) **to p. along**, y aller doucement.

pouch [pautʃ] *n* petit sac; bourse *f*; blague *f* (à tabac); *Dipl:* valise *f*; *Z:* poche ventrale (des marsupiaux).

pouf(fe) [pu:f] *n Furn:* pouf *m*.

poultice ['poultis] *n Med:* cataplasme *m*.

poultry ['poultri] *n coll* (*no pl*) volaille *f*; **p. farming**, élevage de volaille. **'poulterer** *n* marchand, -ande, de volaille.

pounce [pauns] *vi* (*of animal*) fondre, s'abattre (**on**, sur); (*of pers*) se précipiter, se jeter (**on**, sur).

pound¹ [paund] *n* (*a*) (*abbr* lb) (= 0,453 kg) livre *f*; **to sell sugar by the p.**, vendre le sucre à la livre; **40 pence a p.**, quarante pence la livre (*b*) (*symbol* £) livre; **p. sterling**, livre sterling; **p. note**, billet de (banque) d'une livre.

pound² *n* fourrière *f* (pour animaux errants, pour voitures).

pound³ 1. *vtr* broyer, piler, concasser (des pierres, des noix); pilonner (la terre); battre (qn); bourrer (qn) de coups de poing; *Mil:* marteler (une position); **to p. sth to pieces**, réduire qch en miettes 2. *vi* frapper, taper, dur; (*of heart*) battre à grands coups; **to p. away at sth**, cogner dur sur qch; **we heard their feet pounding on the stairs**, nous avons entendu résonner leurs pas sur l'escalier. **'pounding** *n* battement *m* frénétique (du cœur); grands coups *mpl* (à la porte); *F:* **to take a p.**, être pilonné, battu.

pour [pɔ:r] 1. *vtr* verser (du vin dans un verre) 2. *vi* (*of rain*) tomber à verse; **it's pouring (with rain)**, il's **pouring down**, il pleut à verse; **water poured into the cellar**, de l'eau entrait à flots dans la cave; **sweat was pouring off him**, il ruisselait de sueur; **tourists were pouring into the castle**, les touristes entraient dans le château en foule; **crowds poured in**, on entrait à flots, en foule; **invitations came pouring in**, c'était une avalanche d'invitations. **'pouring** *a* p. rain, pluie torrentielle. **'pour 'out** 1. *vtr* verser (une tasse de thé); donner libre cours à (ses sentiments); déverser (un torrent d'injures) 2. *vi* sortir à flots; (*of people*) sortir en foule.

pout [paut] 1. *n* moue *f* 2. *vi* faire la moue; (*sulk*) bouder.

poverty ['pɔvəti] *n* pauvreté *f*; manque *m* (de denrées, de ressources); dénuement *m* (d'idées); **to live in p.**, vivre dans la misère, dans la gêne. **'poverty-stricken** *a* réduit à la misère; (*of housing*) misérable.

PoW *abbr prisoner of war.*

powder ['paudər] 1. *n* poudre *f*; **face p.**, poudre de riz; **washing, soap, p.**, lessive *f* (en poudre); **to reduce sth to p.**, réduire qch en poudre; pulvériser qch; **p. room**, toilette pour dames 2. *vtr* (*a*) poudrer; saupoudrer (un gâteau) (**with**, de); se poudrer (le visage); **to p. one's nose**, se poudrer le nez; *Fig:* aller aux toilettes (*b*)

pulvériser (qch); **powdered milk**, lait en poudre.
'powdery *a* (*a*) poudreux (*b*) friable.

power ['pauər] 1. *n* (*a*) pouvoir *m*; **I'll do everything in my p.**, je ferai tout ce qui est dans mon pouvoir, tout mon possible; **it is beyond my p.**, cela ne m'est pas possible (*b*) faculté *f*, capacité *f*; **p. of speech**, la parole; **mental powers**, facultés intellectuelles (*c*) vigueur *f*, force *f*; énergie *f*; *F:* **more p. to your elbow!** allez-y! (*d*) puissance *f* (d'une machine); force (d'un aimant); **nuclear p.**, énergie nucléaire; **p. station**, centrale *f* (électrique); **p. cut, failure**, panne d'électricité; **p. point**, prise de courant *m*; **p. press**, presse mécanique (*e*) pouvoir, influence *f*, autorité *f*; **to come to p.**, arriver au pouvoir; **to be in p.**, être au pouvoir; **to fall into s.o.'s p.**, tomber au pouvoir de qn; **p. of life and death**, droit *m* de vie et de mort; **to have s.o. in one's p.**, avoir du pouvoir sur qn; *Jur:* **to act with full powers**, agir de pleine autorité (*f*) *Jur:* procuration *f*, mandat *m*, pouvoir (*g*) (*pers, country*) puissance; **world p.**, puissance mondiale; **the powers that be**, les autorités constituées; **the powers of darkness**, les puissances des ténèbres; *F:* **that'll do you a p. of good!** cela vous fera énormément de bien! (*h*) *Mth:* puissance; **three to the p. (of) ten** (3¹⁰), trois (à la) puissance dix 2. *vtr* fournir de l'énergie (à une machine); actionner; propulser; **nuclear powered**, à propulsion nucléaire. **'power-a'ssisted** *a Aut:* (*of steering*) assisté. **'power-boat** *n* vedette *f* automobile. **'powerful** *a* puissant; (*of physical strength*) fort, vigoureux; (remède) énergique. **'powerfully** *adv* puissamment, fortement; (*of man*) **p. built**, à forte carrure. **'powerhouse** *n* centrale *f* (électrique); *Fig:* personne vigoureuse et dynamique. **'powerless** *a* impuissant; **they are p. in the matter**, ils n'y peuvent rien.

p.p. *abbr per procurationem.*
PR *abbr public relations.*

practicable ['præktikəbl] *a* praticable. **practica'bility** *n* praticabilité *f*.

practical ['præktikəl] *a* pratique; **of no p. value**, inutilisable dans la pratique; **p. joke**, tour *m*; **he's very p.**, il a beaucoup de bon sens. **practi'cality** *n* (*pl* **-ies**) sens *m*, caractère *m*, pratique; *pl* processus *m*. **'practically** *adv* (*a*) pratiquement, en pratique (*b*) pour ainsi dire; **there's been p. no snow**, il n'y a presque pas de neige; **p. the whole of the audience**, la quasi-totalité de l'assistance.

practice, *NAm:* **practise** ['præktis] *n* (*a*) pratique *f*; exercice *m* (de la médecine); **to put one's ideas into p.**, mettre ses idées en pratique; **in p.**, dans la, en, pratique; (*of doctor*) **to be in p.**, exercer (*b*) (*of doctor*) clientèle *f*, cabinet *m*; (*of solicitor*) étude *f*; **group p.**, médecine de groupe (*c*) habitude *f*, coutume *f*, usage *m*; **to make a p. of doing sth**, faire une habitude de faire qch; **it's the usual p.**, c'est l'usage (*d*) *Sp: Mus:* entraînement *m*; exercice(s) *m*(*pl*); **to be in p.**, être en forme; **out of p.**, rouillé; **it takes years of p.**, cela demande des années de pratique; *Prov:* **p. makes perfect**, c'est en forgeant qu'on devient forgeron; **piano p.**, travail *m* au piano; **choir p.**, répétition (chorale); **p. match**, match d'entraînement; **target p.**, exercices de tir (*e*) *usu pl* pratiqués, menées *fpl*.

practise, *NAm:* **also practice** ['præktis] 1. *vtr* (*a*) pratiquer (une vertu); mettre en pratique, en action (un principe, une régle); **to p. what one preaches,** prêcher d'exemple (b) pratiquer, exercer (une profession) (c) étudier (le piano); s'exercer sur (la flûte); *Sp:* s'exercer à (un coup, un mouvement); essayer (son français) (**on s.o.,** sur qn) **2.** *vi* (a) (*of doctor*) exercer (b) *Sp: Mus:* s'exercer, faire des exercices. **'practised, 'practiced** a exercé, expérimenté; **p. in sth,** habile à qch. **'practising,** *NAm: also* **'practicing** a (avocat, médecin) exerçant; (chrétien, catholique) pratiquant. **prac'titioner** n practicien, -ienne; **medical p.,** médecin m; **general p.** (*abbr* **GP**), (médecin) généraliste (*mf*).

pragmatic [præg'mætik] a pragmatique.

prairie ['prɛəri] n usu pl **the prairies,** la prairie (de l'Amérique du Nord).

praise [preiz] **1.** n (*deserved*) éloge(s) m(pl); (*adulation or worship*) louange(s) f (pl); **I've nothing but p. for him,** je n'ai qu'à me louer de lui; **beyond all p.,** au-dessus de tout éloge; **in p. of,** à la louange de; **p. be to God!** Dieu soit loué! **2.** *vtr* louer (qn); faire l'éloge de. **'praiseworthy** a digne d'éloges; (travail) méritoire.

pram [præm] n (*NAm:* = **baby carriage**) voiture f d'enfant.

prance [prɑːns] vi (*of horse*) caracoler; piaffer; (*of pers*) se pavaner.

prank [præŋk] n (a) escapade f, frasque f, fredaine f (b) tour m, farce f; **to play pranks on s.o.,** jouer des tours à qn.

prattle ['prætl] n F: babiller; bavarder.

prawn [prɔːn] n crevette f rose; bouquet m; **Dublin Bay p.,** langoustine f; *Cu:* **p. cocktail,** crevettes à la mayonnaise.

pray [prei] *vtr & i* prier (**s.o. to do sth,** qn de faire qch); **to p. (to) God,** prier Dieu; **to p. for s.o., for sth,** prier pour qn, pour avoir qch; **he's past praying for,** il est perdu. **'prayer** n prière f (à Dieu); **the Lord's P.,** l'oraison dominicale; le Pater; **to say one's prayers,** dire ses prières; *Ecc:* **Morning, Evening, P.,** office m du matin, du soir; **p. book,** livre de prières; **the P. Book,** le rituel de l'Église anglicane; *Sch:* **prayers,** prière du matin en commun; **p. meeting,** réunion pour prières en commun; **p. wheel,** moulin à prières; **p. mat,** tapis à prières.

preach [priːtʃ] *vtr & i* prêcher; prononcer (un sermon); annoncer (l'Évangile); **to p. to the converted,** prêcher un converti. **'preacher** n prédicateur m; *NAm:* pasteur m.

prearrange [priə'reindʒ] *vtr* arranger d'avance.

precarious [pri'kɛəriəs] a précaire, incertain; **to make a p. living,** gagner précairement sa vie. **pre'cariously** adv précairement.

precast ['priːkɑːst] a (béton) prémoulé.

precaution [pri'kɔːʃn] n précaution f; **to take precautions against sth,** prendre ses précautions contre qch; **as a p.,** par mesure de précaution. **pre'cautionary** adv (mesures) de précaution.

precede [pri'siːd] *vtr* (a) précéder; **for a week preceding this match,** pendant une semaine avant ce match (b) avoir le pas, la préséance, sur (qn). **precedence** ['presidəns] n préséance; (droit m de) priorité f; **to take p. over,** avoir la préséance sur, prendre le pas sur

(qn); **ladies take p.,** les dames passent avant.

precedent ['presidənt] n précédent m; **to create a p.,** créer un précédent; **according to p.,** conformément à la tradition. **pre'ceding** a précédent; **the p. day,** la veille; **in the p. article,** dans l'article ci-dessus.

precept ['priːsept] n précepte m.

precinct ['priːsiŋkt] n (a) enceinte f, enclos m; **precincts,** pourtour m (d'une cathédrale); environs mpl (d'un endroit); **shopping p.,** centre commercial (fermé à la circulation automobile); **pedestrian p.,** zone piétonnière (b) limite f (du pourtour) (c) *US:* circonscription électorale.

precious ['preʃəs] **1.** a (a) précieux; **p. stones,** pierres précieuses (b) *F: Iron:* fameux, beau; sacré; **a p. lot he cares about it!** il s'en fout comme de l'an quarante! (c) *Lit:* (style) précieux **2.** n **my p.!** mon trésor! mon amour! **3.** adv *F:* **there are p. few of them,** il n'y en a guère; **p. little hope,** très peu d'espoir.

precipice ['presipis] n paroi f à pic; **to fall over a p.,** tomber dans un précipice. **pre'cipitous** a (a) escarpé, abrupt; à pic (b) (départ) précipité. **pre'cipitously** adv à pic.

precipitate [pri'sipiteit] *vtr* précipiter; *Meteor:* condenser; **to p. matters,** brusquer les choses. **precipi'tation** n précipitation f.

précis ['presi, pl -iːz] n précis m, résumé m.

precise [pri'sais] a (a) précis; exact; **at the p. moment when,** au moment précis où (b) (of pers) pointilleux; méticuleux. **pre'cisely** adv avec précision; **at six (o'clock) p.,** à six heures précises; **p. (so)!** précisément! **pre'ciseness** n précision f; méticulosité f; formalisme m. **precision** [pri'siʒn] n précision; exactitude f; **p. instruments,** instruments de précision.

preclude [pri'kluːd] *vtr* prévenir, exclure; écarter (qch); **to be precluded from doing sth,** être dans l'impossibilité de faire qch.

precocious [pri'kouʃəs] a précoce; (of plant) hâtif. **pre'cociously** adv précocement; avec précocité. **pre'cociousness** n précocité f.

preconceived [priːkən'siːvd] a préconçu. **precon'ception** n préconception f; idée, opinion, préconçue; préjugé m.

precondition [priːkən'diʃn] n condition préalable, requise; préalable m.

precursor [pri(ː)'kɔːsər] n précurseur m; avant-coureur m.

predate ['priː'deit] *vtr* antidater (un document); venir avant (un fait historique).

predatory ['predətəri] a prédateur; (of pers) rapace; (of soldiers) pillard; **p. animals,** bêtes de proie. **'predator** n prédateur m; bête de proie.

predecease ['priːdi'siːs] *vtr* prédécéder.

predecessor ['priːdisesər] n prédécesseur m; devancier, -ière.

predestine [pri'destin] *vtr* prédestiner.

predetermine [priːdi'təːmin] *vtr* déterminer d'avance; *Theol: Phil:* prédéterminer.

predicament [pri'dikəmənt] n situation difficile, fâcheuse; **we're in a fine p.!** nous voilà dans de beaux draps!

predict [pri'dikt] *vtr* prédire (un événement). **pre'dictable** a qui peut être prédit. **pre'dictably** adv comme on s'y attendait. **pre'diction** n prédiction f.

predilection [priːdiˈlekʃn] n prédilection f (for, pour).

predispose [priːdisˈpouz] vtr prédisposer; **to p. s.o. in favour of doing sth,** prédisposer qn à faire qch. **predispoˈsition** n prédisposition f (**to,** à).

predominate [priˈdɔmineit] vi prédominer, l'emporter par le nombre, par la quantité (**over,** sur). **preˈdominance** n prédominance f. **preˈdominant** a prédominant. **preˈdominantly** adv d'une manière prédominante. **preˈdominating** a prédominant.

pre-eminent [priːˈeminənt] a prééminent.

preen [priːn] vtr (of bird) lisser, nettoyer (ses plumes); **to p. oneself,** (i) se bichonner (ii) prendre un air avantageux.

prefabricate [priːˈfæbrikeit] vtr préfabriquer. **ˈprefab** n F: maison préfabriquée.

preface [ˈprefəs] **1.** n préface f; avant-propos m inv; préambule m (d'un discours) **2.** vtr écrire une préface pour (un ouvrage); faire précéder (des remarques) (**with,** de).

prefect [ˈpriːfekt] n Fr Adm: préfet m; Sch: élève des grandes classes chargé(e) de la discipline.

prefer [priˈfɔːr] vtr (**preferred**) (a) préférer, aimer mieux; **to p. sth to sth,** préférer qch à qch; aimer mieux qch que qch; **I would p. to go without,** j'aimerais mieux m'en passer (b) Jur: intenter (une action en justice); **to p. charges,** déposer, porter, plainte. **preferable** [ˈpref-] a préférable (**to,** à). **ˈpreferably** adv de préférence. **preference** [ˈpref-] n préférence f (**for,** pour); (droit m de) priorité f; **in p. to,** de préférence à; Fin: **p.,** NAm: **preferred, stock,** actions privilégiées, de priorité. **prefeˈrential** [pref-] a (traitement) préférentiel; (tarif) de faveur.

prefix [ˈpriːfiks] **1.** n (pl **prefixes**) préfixe m **2.** vtr préfixer.

pregnancy [ˈpregnənsi] n (pl **pregnancies**) grossesse f. **ˈpregnant** a (a) (femme) enceinte, grosse; (vache, jument) pleine; **three months p.,** enceinte de trois mois (b) (silence) chargé de sens; **p. with consequences,** lourd de conséquences.

preheat [priːˈhiːt] vtr préchauffer.

prehensile [priˈhensail] a préhensile.

prehistory [priːˈhistəri] n préhistoire f. **prehiˈstoric** a préhistorique.

prejudge [priːˈdʒʌdʒ] vtr préjuger de (la question); condamner (qn) d'avance.

prejudice [ˈpredʒudis] **1.** n (a) préjudice m, tort m, dommage m; **without p.,** sous toutes réserves (b) préjugé m; **to have a p. against sth,** avoir un préjugé contre qch **2.** vtr (a) nuire, porter préjudice, à (une réputation) (b) prévenir, prédisposer (**s.o. against s.o.,** qn contre qn). **ˈprejudiced** a prévenu (contre); **to be p.,** avoir des préjugés. **prejuˈdicial** a préjudiciable, nuisible (**to,** à).

prelate [ˈprelət] n prélat m.

preliminary [priˈliminəri] **1.** a préliminaire, préalable **2.** n prélude m (à une conversation); **preliminaries,** préliminaires mpl.

prelude [ˈpreljuːd] n prélude m (**to,** de).

premarital [priːˈmæritl] a prénuptial.

premature [ˈpremətjuər] a prématuré; F: **you're a bit p.!** tu vas trop vite! **ˈprematurely** adv prématurément; (né) avant terme.

premeditate [priːˈmediteit] vtr préméditer. **preˈmeditated** a prémédité; (crime) réfléchi; **p. insolence,** insolence calculée. **premediˈtation** n préméditation f.

premenstrual [priːˈmenstruəl] a prémenstruel.

premier [ˈpremiər] **1.** a premier (en rang, en importance) **2.** n premier ministre.

première [ˈpremiɛər] n Th: première f (d'une pièce, d'un film).

premise [ˈpremis] n (a) prémisse f (b) **premises,** le local, les locaux m; **business premises,** locaux commerciaux; **on the p.,** sur les lieux; **off the premises,** hors de l'établissement m.

premium [ˈpriːmiəm] n prime f; récompense f; prix (convenu); indemnité f; **insurance p.,** prime d'assurance; **to be at a p.,** faire prime; être très recherché; **p. bond,** bon m à lots.

premonition [preməˈniʃn] n prémonition f; pressentiment m (de malheur).

prenatal [ˈpriːˈneitl] a prénatal.

preoccupation [priːɔkjuˈpeiʃn] n préoccupation f (de l'esprit) (**with,** de); **my greatest p.,** mon plus grand souci. **preˈoccupied** a préoccupé; absorbé (par ses études, un souci).

prep [prep] Sch: F: **1.** n étude f, devoirs mpl (du soir); **p. room,** salle d'étude **2.** a **p. school,** école primaire privée; NAm: lycée privé.

prepack [priːˈpæk] vtr Com: préconditionner.

prepaid [priːˈpeid] a payé d'avance; **carriage p.,** port payé; franco de port.

prepare [priˈpɛər] **1.** vtr préparer; accommoder (un mets); **to p. a surprise for s.o.,** réserver une surprise à qn; **to p. the way for negotiations,** amorcer des négociations **2.** vi se préparer, se disposer (**for sth, to do sth,** à (faire) qch); **to p. for departure,** faire ses préparatifs de départ; **to p. for an examination,** préparer un examen. **prepaˈration** n (a) préparation f; pl préparatifs mpl (de voyage, de guerre); **in (course of) p.,** en (cours de) préparation; **to make one's preparations for sth,** faire ses préparatifs en vue de qch (b) Sch: = **prep 1. preˈparatory** a préparatoire, préalable (**to,** à); **p. school,** école primaire privée; NAm: lycée privé. **preˈpared** a préparé; **to be p. for anything,** être prêt, s'attendre, à toute éventualité; **be p. to be coolly received,** attendez-vous à être mal accueilli.

preponderance [priˈpondərəns] n prépondérance f (**over,** sur). **preˈponderant** a prépondérant.

preposition [prepəˈziʃn] n Gram: préposition f.

prepossessing [priːpəˈzesiŋ] a (visage) agréable; (air) prévenant; (aspect) attrayant, avenant; (of pers) sympathique.

preposterous [priˈpostərəs] a absurde; déraisonnable.

prerecord [priːriˈkɔːd] vtr préenregistrer; **prerecorded broadcast,** émission en différé.

prerequisite [priːˈrekwizit] n nécessité f, condition f, préalable; préalable m.

prerogative [priˈrɔgətiv] n prérogative f, privilège m.

preschool [priːˈskuːl] a préscolaire.

prescribe [priˈskraib] vtr prescrire, ordonner (qch à qn); **prescribed task,** tâche imposée; **in the prescribed time,** dans le délai prescrit. **prescription**

[-'skripʃn] n Med: ordonnance f; **on p.**, sur ordonnance.

presence ['prezəns] n présence f; **in the p. of**, en
présence de; **p. of mind**, présence d'esprit; **to keep
one's p. of mind**, garder son sang-froid. **'present**[1] 1.
a (a) présent; **to be p. at a ceremony**, être présent,
assister, à une cérémonie; **nobody else was p.**, personne d'autre n'était là; **some of you p. here**, quelques-
uns d'entre vous ici présents (b) actuel; **at the p. time**,
à présent; de nos jours; actuellement; aujourd'hui;
Gram: **the p. tense**, le temps présent (c) en question;
que voici; **the p. volume**, le présent volume, ce volume
2. n présent m; **the p.**, le (temps) présent; **up to the p.**,
jusqu'à présent; jusqu'ici; **at p.**, à présent; actuellement; **no more at p.**, rien de plus pour le moment; **as
things are at p.**, au point où en sont les choses; **for the
p.**, pour le moment; _Gram:_ **in the p.**, au présent.
'present-day a actuel; d'aujourd'hui. **'presently** adv (a) tout à l'heure; dans un instant;
bientôt (b) esp NAm: & Scot: actuellement; à présent.
present[2] 1. n ['prezənt] don m, cadeau m; **to make s.o.
a p. of sth**, faire cadeau de qch à qn; **it's for a p.**, c'est
pour offrir 2. vtr [pri'zent] présenter; donner (une
pièce, un film, une émission); **matter that presents
some difficulty**, affaire qui présente des difficultés; **to
p. oneself for an exam**, se présenter à un examen; **a
good opportunity presents itself**, une bonne occasion
se présente (de faire qch); **to p. sth to s.o.**, **to p. s.o. with
sth**, donner qch à qn; faire cadeau de qch à qn; **to p.
one's compliments (to s.o.)**, présenter ses compliments
(à qn); _Mil:_ **to p. arms**, présenter les armes.
pre'sentable a présentable; (of garment) portable, mettable. **presen'tation** n présentation f;
remise f (d'un cadeau). **pre'senter** n WTel: TV:
présentateur, -trice.
presentiment [pri'zentimənt] n pressentiment m.
preserve [pri'zə:v] 1. vtr (a) préserver, garantir (qn)
(**from**, de) (b) conserver (un bâtiment); maintenir (la
paix); garder (le silence) (c) Cu: conserver, mettre en
conserve (des aliments); **she's well preserved**, elle ne
paraît pas son âge (d) élever (du gibier) dans une
réserve; garder (une chasse) 2. n (a) Cu: preserve(s),
confiture f (de fruits) (b) **game p.**, réserve f; chasse
gardée; _Fig:_ **to trespass on s.o.'s preserves**, marcher
sur les plates-bandes de qn. **preser'vation**
[prezə-] n (a) conservation f; maintien m (de la paix)
(b) préservation f (de qn) (from, de). **preservative**
n Comest: agent m de conservation. **pre'served** a
conservé; (aliments) en conserve; **p. food**, conserves
fpl; **well p.**, (bâtiment) en bon état de conservation;
(of pers) bien conservé. **pre'serving** n Cu: conservation; _DomEc:_ **p. pan**, bassine f à confitures.
preshrunk [pri:'ʃrʌŋk] a irrétrécissable.
preside [pri'zaid] vi présider; **to p. at, over, a meeting**,
présider une réunion. **presidency** ['prez-] n présidence f. **'president** n président, -ente.
presi'dential a présidentiel.
press [pres] I. n (pl presses) (a) pressoir m (à cidre,
à huile); presse f (hydraulique, à raquette, pour pan-
talons); **printing p.**, presse d'imprimerie; **to pass (a
proof) for p.**, donner le bon à tirer; **ready for p.**, prêt à
mettre sous presse; **to go to p.**, être mis sous presse (b)
la presse, les journaux m; **p. agency**, agence de presse;
p. conference, conférence de presse; **p. cutting**, cou-

pure de journal; **p. photographer**, photographe de
presse; **to write for the p.**, faire du journalisme; **to have
a good, bad, p.**, avoir une bonne, mauvaise, presse. **II.**
v (presses) 1. vtr (a) appuyer sur (qch); presser (des
fruits, une fleur); serrer (la main de qn); **p. the button**,
appuyez sur le bouton; **his face was pressed against the
window**, il avait le visage collé à la vitre (b) repasser,
donner un coup de fer à (un vêtement) (c) harceler
(qn); **to p. s.o. to do sth**, presser qn de faire qch; **he
didn't need much pressing**, il ne s'est pas fait prier; **to p.
s.o. for an answer**, insister pour avoir une réponse
immédiate; **to p. a point**, insister sur un point; **to p.
one's advantage**, poursuivre son avantage; **to p. a gift
on s.o.**, forcer qn à accepter un cadeau 2. vi (a)
appuyer (on, sur); (of crowd) se presser; **time presses**,
le temps presse. **pressed** a p. **for time**, à court de
temps; **to be hard p. to find the money**, avoir beaucoup
de difficultés à trouver l'argent. **'pressgang** 1. n
Hist: presse (de matelots) 2. vtr F: **to p. s.o. into doing
sth**, forcer (la main à) qn pour qu'il fasse qch.
'pressing 1. a pressant; (travail) urgent; **since you
are so p.**, puisque vous insistez 2. n repassage m (d'un
vêtement); _Rec:_ matriçage m (d'un disque). **'press-
man** n (pl -men) journaliste m. **'press 'on** vi
presser le pas; continuer (son chemin); F: **p. on
regardless!** allons-y et tant pis! **'press-stud** n
bouton-pression m, pression m or f. **'press-up** n
Gym: traction f. **'pressure** ['preʃər] 1. n pression
f; _Ph:_ poussée f (d'un corps); **tyre p.**, pression des
pneus; **blood p.**, tension artérielle; **low blood p.**, **high
blood p.**, hypotension f, hypertension f; **to bring p. to
bear**, **put p. on**, exercer une pression sur; **p. of business**,
le poids des affaires; **under p.**, sous pression; sous la
pression des circonstances; **p. cabin**, cabine pres-
surisée; _DomEc:_ **p. cooker**, cocotte-minute f (Rtm),
autocuiseur m; _Pol:_ **p. group**, groupe de pression 2.
vtr=**pressurize** (b). **pressuri'zation** n pressurisation f. **'pressurize** vtr (a) pressuriser (une
cabine) (b) exercer une pression sur (qn).
prestige [pre'sti:ʒ] n prestige m; **p. apartments**, appartements de grand standing. **pre'stigious** a
prestigieux.
presume [pri'zju:m] 1. vtr présumer; supposer; **he was
presumed dead**, on le croyait mort; **to p. too much**,
trop présumer de soi 2. vi (a) se montrer présomptueux; prendre des libertés; **to p. to do sth**,
prendre la liberté de faire qch; **may I p. to advise you?**
puis-je me permettre de vous donner un conseil? **to p.
on s.o.'s friendship**, abuser de l'amitié de qn (b) **I p.
you've written to him**, je suppose que vous lui avez
écrit. **pre'sumably** adv p. **he'll come**, il est à croire
qu'il viendra; **p. you told him**, je suppose que tu le lui
as dit. **pre'suming** a présomptueux.
pre'sumption n (a) présomption f; **the p. is that
he's dead**, on présume qu'il est mort (b) présomption,
arrogance f. **pre'sumptuous** a présomptueux.
presuppose [pri:sə'pouz] vtr présupposer.
pretend [pri'tend] 1. vtr (a) feindre, simuler; **to p.
ignorance**, faire l'ignorant; **to p. to do sth**, faire
semblant de faire qch; **he pretended he was**, **to be, a
doctor**, il s'est fait passer pour un médecin; F: **it's only
p.**, c'est pour rire (b) prétendre; **he does not p. to be
artistic**, il ne prétend pas être artiste; **I can't p. to
advise you**, je n'ai pas la prétention de vous conseiller

2. *vi* faire semblant; jouer la comédie. **pre'tence,** *NAm:* **pre'tense** *n* (*a*) (faux) semblant; simulation *f*; prétexte *m*; **to make a p. of doing sth,** faire semblant de faire qch; **under the p. of friendship,** sous prétexte d'amitié; **to obtain sth by, under, false pretences,** obtenir qch par fraude, par des moyens frauduleux (*b*) prétention *f*, vanité *f*. **pre'tended** *a* (*of emotion*) feint, simulé; (*of pers*) prétendu. **pre'tender** *n* prétendant, -ante (**to the throne,** au trône); *Hist:* **the Young P.,** le jeune Prétendant. **pre'tension** *n* prétention (to, à); **to have pretensions to literary taste,** se piquer de littérature. **pre'tentious** *a* prétentieux. **pre'tentiously** *adv* prétentieusement.

preterite ['pretərit] *a & n Gram:* **p. (tense),** passé *m* (simple); prétérit *m*.

pretext ['pri:tekst] *n* prétexte *m*; **to find a p. for refusing,** trouver prétexte à un refus; **on, under, the p. of consulting me,** sous prétexte de me consulter.

pretty ['priti] 1. *a* (-ier, -iest) joli; beau; (*of manner*) gentil; **p. as a picture,** gentil, joli, à croquer; mignon comme tout; *Iron:* **this is a p. state of affairs!** c'est du joli! **that'll cost me a p. penny,** ça va me coûter cher 2. *adv* assez; passablement; **I'm p. well,** cela ne va pas trop mal; **p. much the same,** à peu près la même chose; *F:* **to be sitting p.,** être bien placé. **'prettily** *adv* joliment; gentiment. **'prettiness** *n* gentillesse *f*. **'pretty-'pretty** *a* trop joli; mignard.

prevail [pri'veil] *vi* (*a*) prévaloir (**over, against,** sur, contre); l'emporter (sur qn); **to p. on s.o. to do sth,** amener, décider, qn à faire qch; **he was prevailed on by his friends,** il s'est laissé persuader par ses amis (to, de) (*b*) prédominer, régner; **calm prevails,** le calme règne; **the conditions prevailing in France,** les conditions qui règnent en France. **pre'vailing** *a* (vent) dominant; **p. fashion,** mode actuelle; **p. opinion,** opinion courante. **prevalence** ['prevələns] *n* prédominance *f*; généralité *f* (de la corruption); fréquence *f* (d'une épidémie). **'prevalent** *a* répandu, général.

prevaricate [pri'værikeit] *vi* user d'équivoques; équivoquer; tergiverser. **prevari'cation** *n* équivoques *fpl*; tergiversation *f*.

prevent [pri'vent] *vtr* (*a*) empêcher, mettre obstacle à (qch); **to be unavoidably prevented from doing sth,** être dans l'impossibilité (matérielle) de faire qch (*b*) prévenir, détourner (un malheur); parer à (un accident); éviter (que qch se passe). **pre'ventable** *a* évitable; qui peut être évité. **pre'vention** *n* prévention *f*; **p. of accidents,** précautions *fpl* contre les accidents; **society for the p. of cruelty to children,** société protectrice des enfants. **pre'ventive** (*also* **pre'ventative**) 1. *a* (médicament) préventif; **p. medicine,** médecine préventive 2. *n* empêchement *m*; mesure préventive; **rust p.,** antirouille *m*.

preview ['pri:vju:] *n Art:* exhibition *f* préalable; *Cin:* avant-première *f*.

previous ['pri:viəs] 1. *a* précédent; préalable; antérieur, antécédent (to, à); **the p. day,** le jour précédent; la veille; **p. engagement,** engagement antérieur 2. *adv* **p. to my departure,** avant mon départ. **'previously** *adv* préalablement; auparavant; précédemment.

pre(-)war ['pri:'wɔːr] *a* d'avant-guerre.

prey [prei] 1. *n* proie *f*; **birds, beasts, of p.,** oiseaux, bêtes, de proie; **beasts (or birds) of p.,** les grands prédateurs; **to be (a) p. to,** être la proie (d'une bête);

être en proie à (la peur); **to fall (a) p. to,** tomber en proie à (la tentation) 2. *vi* **to p. (up)on sth,** faire sa proie de qch; **sth is preying on his mind,** il y a qch qui le travaille.

price [prais] 1. *n* prix *m*; *Turf:* cote *f*, *StExch:* cours *m*; **cost p.,** prix de revient, prix coûtant; **at a reduced p.,** à prix réduit; au rabais; **p. range,** écart des prix; **p. list,** tarif *m*; **p. tag,** étiquette *f*; **p. cut,** réduction de(s) prix; **p. freeze,** blocage des prix; **p. control,** contrôle des prix; **to rise in p.,** augmenter de prix; **what p. is that article?** quel est le prix de cet article? **his pictures fetch huge prices,** ses tableaux se vendent à prix d'or; **beyond p.,** sans prix; hors de prix; **you can buy it at a p.,** vous pouvez l'acheter en y mettant le prix; **this must be done at any p.,** il faut que cela se fasse à tout prix, coûte que coûte; **not at any p.,** pour rien au monde; à aucun prix; **to set a high p. on sth,** faire grand cas de qch; **to put a p. on s.o.'s head,** mettre à prix la tête de qn; **every man has his p.,** il n'y a pas d'homme qu'on ne puisse acheter; *F:* **what p. my chances of being appointed?** quelles sont mes chances d'être nommé? 2. *vtr* (*a*) mettre un prix à (qch); fixer le prix de (qch) (*b*) estimer, évaluer (qch) (*c*) s'informer du prix de (qch). **'priceless** *a* hors de prix; inestimable; *F:* (of joke, pers) impayable; marrant. **'price 'out** *vtr* **to p. oneself o. of the market,** perdre sa clientèle en pratiquant des prix excessifs. **'pricey** *a* (-ier, -iest) *F:* cher, coûteux.

prick [prik] 1. *n* piqûre *f* (d'aiguille); **pricks of conscience,** aiguillons *mpl* de la conscience 2. *v* (*a*) *vtr* piquer; crever (un ballon); **to p. one's finger,** se piquer le, au, doigt; **his conscience is pricking him,** sa conscience l'aiguillonne, le tourmente; **to p. a hole in sth,** faire un trou d'épingle dans qch (*b*) *vi* (*of skin*) picoter. **'pricking** *n* picotement *m* (de la peau); **prickings of conscience,** remords *mpl* (de conscience); *Hort:* **p. out,** repiquage *m* (de plants). **'prickle** 1. *n* piquant *m* (de plante, d'animal); épine *f* (de plante); picotement *m* (de la peau) 2. *v* (*a*) *vtr* piquer, picoter (*b*) *vi* avoir des picotements. **'prickly** *a* (-ier, -iest) (of plant, question) épineux; (of plant, animal) hérissé, armé de piquants; (sensation) de picotement; *F:* (of pers) irritable; *Bot:* **p. pear,** figue, (*tree*) figuier, de Barbarie; *Med:* **p. heat,** (fièvre) miliaire *f*. **'prick 'out** *vtr Hort:* repiquer (des plants). **'prick 'up** *vtr* **to p. up one's ears,** (*of animal*) dresser les oreilles; (*of pers*) dresser l'oreille.

pride [praid] 1. *n* (*a*) orgueil *m*; fierté *f*; (*self-respect*) amour-propre *m*; **puffed up with p.,** bouffi d'orgueil; **false p.,** vanité *f*; **proper p.,** orgueil légitime; **to take (a) p. in sth,** être fier de qch; **to have p. of place,** tenir la place d'honneur (*b*) bande *f* (de lions) 2. *vpr* **to p. oneself on (doing) sth,** être fier, s'enorgueillir, de (faire) qch.

priest [pri:st] *n* prêtre *m*; **parish p. =** curé *m*; **assistant p.,** vicaire *m*. **'priestess** *n* (*pl* -es) prêtresse *f*. **'priesthood** *n* (*a*) *coll* **the p.,** le clergé (*b*) prêtrise *f*; **to enter the p.,** se faire prêtre.

prig [prig] *n* poseur *m* (à la vertu); homme suffisant; **he's a real little p.,** il fait toujours le petit saint. **'priggish** *a* poseur, suffisant. **'priggishness** *n* suffisance *f*.

prim [prim] *a* (**primmer, primmest**) (*of pers*) collet monté *inv*; (*of manner*) guindé, compassé; (sourire) pincé. **'primly** adv d'un air collet monté. **'prim-ness** n air collet monté.

prima facie [praimɔ'feiʃiː] adv & a de prime abord, à première vue; Jur: **p. f. case**, affaire qui paraît bien fondée.

primary ['praimɔri] 1. a (a) premier, primitif; originel; **p. product**, produit de base; **p. colours**, couleurs fondamentales; Sch: **p. education**, enseignement primaire; Geol: **p. era**, ère primaire (b) premier, principal, essentiel; **p. cause**, cause première 2. n (pl -ies) US: Pol: (élection f) primaire f. **'primarily** adv (a) primitivement (b) principalement.

primate n (a) Ecc: ['praimit] primat m; archevêque m (b) Z: ['praimeit] primate m.

prime[1] [praim] 1. a (a) premier; principal; de premier ordre; **p. Minister**, premier ministre; **of p. importance**, de toute première importance (b) excellent; de première qualité; **p. quality meat**, viande de premier choix (c) premier, primitif; **p. cause**, cause première; Mth: **p. number**, nombre premier 2. n perfection f; **in the p. of life, in one's p.**, dans la fleur de l'âge; **to be past one's p.**, avoir passé le bel âge; être sur le retour.

prime[2] vtr (a) amorcer (une pompe) (b) faire la leçon à (qn); **to p. s.o. for a speech**, préparer qn à faire un discours; **to be well primed (with information)**, être bien au courant (c) Paint: apprêter (une surface). **'primer** n (a) premier livre (de lecture); premier cours (de géographie); initiation f (b) Paint: apprêt m.

primeval [prai'miːvəl] a primordial; (forêt) vierge.

primitive ['primitiv] a primitif; (of method) rude, grossier.

primordial [prai'mɔːdiəl] a primordial.

primrose ['primrouz] n Bot: primevère f.

primula ['primjulə] n Bot: primevère f.

prince [prins] n prince m; **p. charming**, prince charmant. **'princely** a princier; (cadeau) magnifique. **prin'cess** n (pl -es) princesse f. **princi'pality** n (pl -ies) principauté f.

principal ['prinsipəl] 1. a principal; **p. clerk**, premier commis 2. n (a) (pers) directeur, -trice (d'école); Th: rôle principal; Mus: soliste mf (b) Com: capital m, principal m (d'une dette). **'principally** adv principalement.

principle ['prinsipl] n principe m; **in p., as a p.**, en principe; **man of high principles**, homme qui a des principes; **to do sth on p.**, faire qch par principe; avoir pour principe de faire qch; **this works on the same p.**, ceci fonctionne sur, d'après, le même principe.

print [print] 1. n (a) empreinte (digitale, d'un pied); impression f; **thumb p.**, empreinte du pouce (b) Typ: matière imprimée; **he wants to see himself in p.**, il veut se faire imprimer; (of book) **out of p.**, épuisé; **in p.**, en vente (courante) (c) Typ: caractères mpl; **large, small, p.**, gros, petits caractères (d) édition f, impression; **to make a p. from a negative**, tirer une épreuve d'un cliché (e) estampe f, gravure f, image f; Phot: épreuve f (f) Tex: (tissu) imprimé (m); indienne f 2. v (a) vtr imprimer; tirer (un journal); **to have a book printed**, faire publier un livre; Post: **printed papers**, imprimés mpl; **please p.**, écrire en caractères d'imprimerie; Phot: **to p. a negative**, tirer une épreuve (d'un cliché); **incidents that p. themselves in the memory**, incidents qui se gravent dans la mémoire (b) vi **the book is now printing**, le livre est sous presse. **'printable** a

imprimable. **'printer** n imprimeur m; typographe m; **printer's error**, faute d'impression; coquille f. **'printing** n (a) impression; tirage m (d'un livre); (art of printing) imprimerie f; typographie f; **p. press**, presse d'imprimerie; **p. house, works**, imprimerie (b) écriture f en lettres moulées. **'print 'out** vtr Cmptr: imprimer. **'print-out** n Cmptr: listage m.

prior[1] ['praiər] 1. a préalable, précédent; antérieur (**to sth**, à qch); **to have a p. claim**, être le premier en date 2. adv p. **to my departure**, antérieurement à, avant, mon départ; **p. to sending the letter**, avant d'envoyer la lettre. **priority** [prai'ɔriti] n (pl -ies) priorité f; **to have p. over**, avoir la priorité sur.

prior[2] n Ecc: prieur m. **'prioress** n (pl -es) prieure f. **'priory** n (pl -ies) prieuré m.

prise [praiz] vtr **to p. sth up**, soulever qch à l'aide d'un levier; **to p. sth open**, forcer qch.

prism ['prizəm] n prisme m. **pris'matic** a prismatique.

prison ['prizən] n prison f; maison f d'arrêt; **to send s.o. to p.**, mettre qn en prison; **in p.**, en prison; **he's been in p.**, il a fait de la prison; **p. camp**, camp de prisonniers. **'prisoner** n prisonnier, -ière; **p. of war**, prisonnier de guerre; **to take s.o. p.**, faire qn prisonnier; Jur: **p. at the bar**, prévenu, -ue; accusé, -ée; (after sentence) détenu, -ue; coupable mf.

private ['praivit] 1. a (a) privé, particulier; **p. citizen**, simple particulier; **in p. life**, dans la vie privée; **to keep a matter p.**, tenir une affaire secrète; **p. entrance**, entrée particulière; **p. study**, études particulières; **in my p. opinion**, à mon avis personnel; **p. parts**, parties génitales; **p. and confidential**, secret et confidentiel; **to mark a letter p.**, marquer une lettre confidentiel, personnel; **p. conversation**, conversation intime; **p. interview**, entretien à huis clos; **p. arrangement**, accord à l'amiable; **p. house**, maison particulière; **p. room**, (in hotel) salon réservé; (in hospital) chambre particulière; **the funeral will be p.**, les obsèques auront lieu dans la plus stricte intimité; **p. education**, enseignement privé, libre; **p. detective**, F: eye, détective privé; (of doctor) **p. practice**, cabinet privé; **p. property**, propriété privée; PN: **p.**, défense d'entrer; entrée interdite au public; **p. income**, rentes fpl; fortune personnelle (b) (of pers) réservé; (of place) isolé 2. n (a) **in p.**, en privé; **to speak to s.o. in p.**, parler à qn en particulier (b) Mil: simple soldat m. **privacy** ['prai-, 'priv-] n intimité f; **to live in p.**, vivre retiré du monde; **in the p. of one's own home**, dans l'intimité du chez-soi; **there's no p. here**, on n'est jamais seul ici; **desire for p.**, désir de se cacher aux regards indiscrets; **lack of p.**, manque de secret. **'privately** adv en particulier; **p. owned**, qui appartient à un particulier; **to speak to s.o. p.**, parler à qn en particulier; (of medical treatment) **I've had it done p.**, je l'ai fait faire à mes frais.

privation [prai'veiʃn] n privation f.

privet ['privit] n Bot: troène m.

privilege ['privilidʒ] n privilège m; prérogative f; **parliamentary p.**, immunité parlementaire. **'privileged** a privilégié; **a p. few**, quelques privilégiés; **to be p. to do sth**, jouir du, avoir le, privilège de faire qch.

prize[1] [praiz] 1. n prix m; (in lottery) lot m; **to win the p.**, remporter le prix; (in lottery) gagner le gros lot; **the Nobel (peace) p.**, le prix Nobel (de la paix); **p. list,**

palmarès *m*; **p. money,** prix en espèces; *Box:* **p. ring,** ring des professionnels; **p. fighter,** boxeur professionnel; **p. fighting,** boxe professionnelle **2.** *a* (animal, poème) primé **3.** *vtr* estimer, priser, apprécier (qch); **to p. sth highly,** faire grand cas de qch; **his most (highly) prized possession,** l'objet qu'il prise au-dessus de tous. **'prizegiving** *n Sch:* distribution *f* des prix. **'prizewinner** *n* gagnant, -ante (d'un prix); lauréat, -ate. **'prizewinning** *a* (roman) primé.

prize² *vtr* = **prise.**

pro¹ [prou] *n* **the pros and cons,** le pour et le contre.

pro² *a & n Sp: F:* professionnel, -elle; pro *mf*.

probable ['prɔbəbl] *a* probable; (histoire) vraisemblable; **it's p. he'll come,** il est probable qu'il viendra. **proba'bility** *n* (*pl* **-ies)** probabilité *f*; vraisemblance *f*; **in all p.,** selon toute probabilité. **'probably** *adv* probablement; vraisemblablement.

probate ['proubeit] *n Jur:* validation *f*, homologation *f*(d'un testament). **pro'bation** *n* épreuve *f*, stage *m*; *Ecc:* probation *f* (d'un novice); *Jur:* mise *f* en liberté sous surveillance; probation; **to be on p.,** (*of employee*) faire son stage, être en stage; (*of offender*) être en liberté surveillée; **p. officer,** agent de probation; délégué à la liberté surveillée. **pro'bationary** *a* (période) stagiaire, de stage. **pro'bationer** *n* (*employee*) stagiaire *mf*; *Ecc:* novice *mf*; (*offender*) jeune délinquant, -ante, en liberté surveillée.

probe [proub] **1.** *vtr & i* sonder; explorer (une plaie); approfondir, fouiller (un mystère); **to p. into,** sonder, fouiller (le passé) **2.** *n* (*a*) sonde *f*; **space p.,** sonde spatiale (*b*) enquête *f*, sondage *m*. **'probing** *a* (*of question*) approfondi.

problem ['prɔbləm] *n* problème *m*; **the housing p.,** la crise du logement; **p. child,** enfant (d'un caractère) difficile; **it's a p. to know what to do,** il est bien difficile de savoir quoi faire. **proble'matic(al)** *a* problématique; douteux, incertain.

proceed [prə'si:d] *vi* (*a*) **to p. (on one's way),** continuer (son chemin); **before we p. any further,** avant d'aller plus loin; **to p. to a place,** aller, se rendre, à un endroit; **how shall we p.?** quelle est la marche à suivre? comment s'y prendre? **to p. cautiously,** agir avec prudence; **to p. to do sth,** se mettre à faire qch; **I'll turn p. to another matter,** je passe maintenant à une autre question (*b*) (*of action, game, play*) (se) continuer, se poursuivre; **things are proceeding as usual,** les choses se déroulent normalement; **to p. with,** poursuivre, continuer (ses études); **sounds proceeding from a room,** sons qui proviennent d'une pièce; *Jur:* **to p. against s.o.,** intenter un procès à qn. **pro'cedure** *n* (*a*) procédé *m*; **the correct p.,** la bonne méthode; la marche à suivre (*b*) procédure *f* (du Parlement, d'une réunion). **pro'ceeding** *n* façon *f* d'agir. **pro'ceedings** *npl* débats *mpl* (d'une assemblée); actes *mpl* (d'un congrès); réunion *f* (d'une société); **the whole p.,** toute l'affaire; **the evening's p.,** ce qui s'est passé pendant la soirée; *Jur:* **to take p. against s.o.,** intenter un procès à qn. **'proceeds** *npl* produit *m*, montant *m* (d'une vente).

process 1. *n* ['prouses] (*pl* **processes** ['prousesiz]) (*a*) processus *m*; **it's a slow p.,** c'est un long travail; **by a p. of elimination,** en procédant par élimination (*b*) cours *m*, déroulement *m* (des événements); **building in (the)**

p. of construction, immeuble en cours de construction; **to be in (the) p. of moving,** être en train de déménager (*c*) *Ind:* méthode *f*; procédé *m*; opération *f* (technique) (*d*) *Jur:* procès *m* **2.** *v* (**processes**) (*a*) *vtr* ['prouses] *Ind:* traiter (un produit, *Cmptr:* une information); transformer (qch); *Tex:* apprêter; *Adm:* faire l'analyse préalable de (documents); **processed cheese,** fromage industriel; crème *f* de fromage (*b*) *vi* ['prɔ'ses] défiler en cortège. **'processing** *n* traitement *m* (d'une matière première); transformation *f*; préparation industrielle (d'aliments); *Phot:* développement *m* (d'un film); **food p. industry,** industrie alimentaire; **data p.,** traitement *m* de l'information, des données. **pro'cession** *n* cortège *m*; défilé *m*; (*religious*) procession *f*. **'processor** *n* (*a*) *DomEc:* **food p.,** robot ménager (*b*) *Cmptr:* processeur *m*; **word p.,** machine de traitement de texte.

proclaim [prə'kleim] *vtr* proclamer (**s.o. king,** qn roi; **that,** que); déclarer (l'état d'urgence). **procla'mation** [prɔklə-] *n* proclamation *f*; déclaration (publique).

proclivity [prə'kliviti] *n* (*pl* **-ies)** penchant *m*, tendance *f*, inclination *f* (**to sth,** à qch).

procrastinate [prou'kræstineit] *vi* remettre (les affaires) au lendemain, à plus tard; temporiser. **procrasti'nation** *n* remise *f* des affaires à plus tard; procrastination *f*, temporisation *f*.

procreate ['proukrieit] *vtr* procréer. **procre'ation** *n* procréation *f*.

procure [prə'kjuər] *vtr* obtenir, procurer; **to p. sth for s.o.,** procurer qch à qn; **to p. sth (for oneself),** se procurer qch. **pro'curable** *a* procurable. **procu'ration** [prɔkju-] *n* acquisition *f* (de qch pour qn); *Jur:* procuration *f*. **pro'curement** *n* approvisionnement *m*. **pro'curer** *n* (*a*) personne *f* qui procure (qch à qn) (*b*) proxénète *m*. **pro'curing** *n* proxénétisme *m*.

prod [prɔd] **1.** *vtr* (**prodded**) pousser (du bout de qch); *Fig:* aiguillonner, stimuler, pousser (**s.o. into doing sth,** qn à faire qch) **2.** *n* coup (donné du bout de qch); *Fig:* **give him a p.,** aiguillonnez-le un peu.

prodigal ['prɔdigəl] *a & n* prodigue (*mf*); gaspilleur. **prodi'gality** *n* prodigalité *f*. **'prodigally** *adv* avec prodigalité.

prodigy ['prɔdidʒi] *n* prodige *m*; merveille *f*; **child, infant, p.,** enfant *mf* prodige. **pro'digious** *a* prodigieux; merveilleux. **pro'digiously** *adv* prodigieusement; merveilleusement, énormément.

produce 1. *vtr* [prə'dju:s] (*a*) présenter, produire (son passeport, des documents); fournir (des documents); donner (des raisons); faire sortir (un lapin) (**out of a hat,** d'un chapeau) (*b*) mettre (une pièce) *Th:* en scène, *WTel:* en ondes; *Cin:* produire (un film); *Publ:* éditer (un livre) (*c*) créer; *El:* faire jaillir (une étincelle) (*d*) *Ind:* fabriquer; produire (*e*) produire, causer, provoquer (un effet); **to p. a sensation,** faire sensation (*f*) rapporter, rendre (un bénéfice) **2.** *n* ['prɔdju:s] (*a*) rendement *m* (d'une mine, d'une exploitation) (*b*) *coll* produit(s) *m*(*pl*); denrées *fpl*; **dairy p.,** produits laitiers. **pro'ducer** *n* producteur, -trice; *Th: Cin:* metteur *m* en scène; *WTel:* TV: metteur *m* en ondes; réalisateur, -trice. **'product** ['prɔdʌkt] *n* produit(s). **pro'duction** *n* (*a*) présentation *f* (d'un billet) (*b*) *Th: Cin:* mise *f* en scène, *WTel:* en ondes (d'une pièce); réalisation *f* (d'un film); *Cin:* production *f* (*c*) production; fabrication *f* (de marchandises); **p. line**, chaîne de fabrication. **pro'ductive** *a* productif; (*of land*) fécond, fertile; (*of mine*) en rapport. **produc'tivity** *n* productivité *f*.

profane [prə'fein] **1.** *a* profane; (langage) impie **2.** *vtr* profaner. **profanity** [-'fæn-] *n* impiété *f* (d'une action); **to utter profanities**, proférer des jurons.

profess [prə'fes] *vtr* professer, faire profession de (sa foi); **to p. oneself satisfied**, se déclarer satisfait; **I do not p. to be a scholar**, je ne prétends pas être savant. **pro'fessed** *a* (*of monk, nun*) profès; (ennemi) déclaré; prétendu (savant). **pro'fession** *n* profession *f*; métier *m*; **he is a doctor by p.**, il exerce la profession de médecin; **the (learned) professions**, les professions libérales; **the p.**, (les membres *m* de) la profession; les gens du métier. **pro'fessional 1.** *a* professionnel; (usages) du métier; (diplomate) de carrière; **p. people, the p. classes**, les membres des professions libérales; **to take p. advice**, consulter un avocat, un médecin **2.** *n* professionnel, -elle; **to turn p.**, passer professionnel. **pro'fessionalism** *n* caractère professionnel (de qch); *esp Sp:* professionnalisme *m*. **pro'fessionally** *adv* professionnellement; **to consult s.o. p.**, consulter qn pour affaires. **pro'fessor** *n* professeur *m* (de faculté). **pro'fessorship** *n* professorat *m*.

proficient [prə'fiʃənt] *a* capable, compétent; **to be p. in maths**, être fort en maths; posséder à fond les mathématiques. **pro'ficiency** *n* capacité *f*, compétence *f* (**in a subject**, en une matière).

profile ['proufail] *n* profil *m*; silhouette *f*; *Journ:* portrait *m*; **to keep a low p.**, rester dans l'ombre; chercher à se faire oublier.

profit ['prɔfit] **1.** *n* profit *m*, bénéfice *m*; avantage *m*; **to turn sth to p.**, tirer profit de qch; *Com:* **net, clear, p.**, bénéfice net; **to sell at a p.**, vendre à profit; **to make huge profits**, réaliser de gros bénéfices; **p. and loss**, profits et pertes; **p. margin**, marge bénéficiaire **2.** *vi* to **p. by, from, sth**, profiter, bénéficier, de qch; tirer profit de (qch). **profita'bility** *n* rentabilité *f*. **'profitable** *a* profitable, avantageux, rentable. **'profitably** *adv* profitablement, avantageusement. **profi'teer 1.** *n* profiteur *m* **2.** *vi* faire des bénéfices excessifs. **profi'teering** *n* affairisme *m*. **'profitless** *a* sans profit. **'profit-sharing** *n Ind:* participation *f* aux bénéfices.

profligate ['prɔfligət] *a & n* (*a*) débauché, -ée (*b*) prodigue. **'profligacy** *n* (*a*) débauche *f* (*b*) prodigalité *f*.

profound [prə'faund] *a* profond; (secret) absolu. **pro'foundly** *adv* profondément. **profundity** [-'fʌnd-] *n* profondeur *f*.

profuse [prə'fju:s] *a* profus, abondant; **to be p. in one's apologies**, se confondre en excuses. **pro'fusely** *adv* profusément; (transpirer) abondamment; **to apologize p.**, se confondre en excuses. **profusion** [-'fju:ʒn] *n* profusion *f*, abondance *f*; **flowers in p.**, des fleurs à foison.

progeny ['prɔdʒəni] *n* progéniture *f*.

prognosticate [prɔg'nɔstikeit] *vtr* pronostiquer, présager, prédire (qch). **prog'nosis** *n* (*pl* **-es**) *Med:* pronostic *m*.

programme, esp NAm: -gram ['prougræm] **1.** *n*
programme *m*; *WTel: TV:* émission *f*; **what's (on) the p. today?** que faisons-nous aujourd'hui? *Th:* **p. seller**, vendeur, -euse, de programmes; *TV: etc:* **p. editor**, éditorialiste *mf*; *WTel:* **request p.**, émission des auditeurs **2.** *vtr* (**programmed**) programmer; **programmed teaching**, enseignement programmé. **'programmer** *n Cmptr:* (*pers*) programmeur, -euse; (*machine*) programmateur *m*. **'programming** *n* programmation *f*.

progress 1. *n* ['prougres] (*a*) marche *f* (du temps); évolution *f* (d'une maladie); avancement *m* (d'un travail); cours *m*, déroulement *m* (des événements); **the work now in p.**, le travail en cours (*b*) progrès *m*; **to make p. in one's studies**, faire des progrès dans ses études; **to make slow p.**, n'avancer que lentement; *Com: Ind:* **p. report**, état d'avancement (des travaux); rapport périodique **2.** *vi* [prə'gres] (**progresses**) (*a*) s'avancer; **as the year progresses**, au cours de l'année; **as the inquiry progresses**, à mesure que l'enquête avance (*b*) faire des progrès (**with**, dans); avancer; progresser. **pro'gression** *n* progression *f*. **pro'gressive** *a* progressif; (siècle) de progrès; (idée) progressiste; **by p. stages**, par degrés. **pro'gressively** *adv* progressivement; au fur et à mesure.

prohibit [prə'hibit] *vtr* (*a*) prohiber, défendre, interdire (qch); *PN:* **smoking prohibited**, défense de fumer; **to p. s.o. from doing sth**, défendre, interdire, à qn de faire qch (*b*) empêcher (qn) (**from doing**, de faire). **prohibition** [prou(h)i'biʃn] *n* prohibition *f*, interdiction *f*, défense *f* (de faire qch). **pro'hibitive** *a* prohibitif; (prix) inabordable; **the price of peaches is p.**, les pêches sont hors de prix.

project 1. *v* [prə'dʒekt] (*a*) *vtr* projeter; **projected buildings**, édifices en projet (*b*) *vi* faire saillie; (s')avancer; **to p. over sth**, surplomber qch **2.** *n* ['prɔdʒekt] (*a*) projet *m*; plan *m*; *Sch:* étude pratique (individuelle ou collective); **to form, carry out, a p.**, former, réaliser, un projet (*b*) *CivE:* ouvrage (réalisé); travaux (réalisés). **pro'jectile** *n* projectile *m*. **pro'jecting** *a* saillant, en saillie. **pro'jection** *n* (*a*) projection *f*; lancement *m* (d'un projectile); *Cin:* **p. room**, cabine de projection (*b*) conception *f* (d'un projet) (*c*) saillie *f*; porte-à-faux *m inv* (d'un balcon); avant-corps *m inv* (de façade). **pro'jectionist** *n Cin:* projectionniste *mf*. **pro'jector** *n* projecteur *m*.

proletariat [prouli'tɛəriət] *n* prolétariat *m*. **prole'tarian 1.** *a* prolétarien; prolétaire **2.** *n* prolétaire *mf*.

prolific [prə'lifik] *a* prolifique; fécond (**in, of**, en). **pro'liferate** *vi* proliférer. **prolife'ration** *n* prolifération *f*.

prologue ['proulɔg] *n* prologue *m* (**to**, de).

prolong [prə'lɔŋ] *vtr* prolonger. **prolon'gation** [proulɔŋ'geiʃn] *n* prolongation *f* (de la durée de qch); prolongement *m* (d'une ligne); (*in time*) délai accordé.

promenade, F: prom [prɔmə'nɑːd, prɔm] *n* (lieu *m* de) promenade *f*; (*at seaside*) front *m* de mer; esplanade *f*; *Th:* promenoir *m* (du parterre); **p. concert**, concert promenade; *Nau:* **p. deck**, pont promenade. **prome'nader** *n* auditeur, -trice, à un concert promenade.

prominence ['prɔminəns] *n* (*a*) proéminence *f*; relief *m* (*b*) saillie *f*, protubérance *f* (*c*) éminence *f*; **to give**

sth p., faire ressortir qch; **to come into p.**, (*of pers*) percer; (*of thg*) acquérir de l'importance. **'pro-minent** *a* (*a*) saillant; en saillie; proéminent (*b*) remarquable; **in a p. position**, très en vue; **to play a p. part**, jouer un rôle important (*c*) éminent; **a p. figure**, un personnage remarquable. **'prominently** *adv* éminemment; **goods p. displayed**, marchandises bien en vue.

promiscuous [prə'miskjuəs] *a* de mœurs douteuses; **she's completely p.**, elle couche avec n'importe qui. **promi'scuity** *n* promiscuité (sexuelle). **pro-'miscuously** *adv* immoralement; sans distinction.

promise ['prɔmis] **1.** *n* promesse *f*; **to make a p.**, faire une promesse; **to break one's p.**, manquer à sa promesse, de parole; **to keep one's p.**, tenir sa promesse; **child who shows p., child (full) of p.**, enfant qui promet; **to hold out a p. of sth to s.o.**, faire espérer qch à qn **2.** *vtr & i to* **p. s.o. sth**, promettre qch à qn; **to p. s.o. to do sth**, promettre à qn de faire qch; **he promised me he'd do it**, il m'a promis qu'il le ferait, de le faire; **to p. oneself sth**, se promettre qch; **it promises to be hot**, le temps s'annonce chaud; **the scheme promises well**, le projet s'annonce bien. **'promising** *a* plein de promesses; (jeune homme) qui promet; (début) prometteur; (avenir) qui s'annonce bien. **'promisingly** *adv* d'une façon prometteuse.

promontory ['prɔməntri] *n* (*pl* **promontories**) promontoire *m*.

promote [prə'mout] *vtr* (*a*) promouvoir (qn); donner de l'avancement à (qn); **to be promoted**, être promu; monter en grade (*b*) encourager (les arts); favoriser (le succès); avancer (les intérêts de qn); lancer (une société, un produit). **pro'moter** *n* promoteur *m* (d'une société, de vente); fondateur *m* (d'une société anonyme). **pro'motion** *n* promotion *f*; **to gain p.**, être promu; obtenir de l'avancement.

prompt [prɔmpt] **1.** *a* prompt; vif, rapide; immédiat; **p. delivery**, livraison immédiate **2.** *adv* **at three o'clock p.**, à trois heures précises **3.** *vtr* **to p. s.o. to do sth**, pousser, inciter, qn à faire qch; **to be prompted by a feeling of pity**, être animé par un sentiment de pitié (*b*) *Th:* souffler (un acteur). **'prompter** *n Th:* souffleur, -euse. **'prompting** *n* incitation *f* (**to do**, à faire) instigation *f* (de qn). **'promptly** *adv* promptement; avec empressement; sur-le-champ; immédiatement; (payer) ponctuellement. **'promptness** *n* promptitude *f*, empressement *m*.

prone [proun] *a* (*a*) couché (sur le ventre); étendu face à terre (*b*) **to be p. to (do) sth**, être enclin à (faire) qch; **to be accident p.**, être enclin aux accidents.

prong [prɔŋ] *n* fourchon *m* (de fourche); dent *f* (de fourchette). **pronged** *a* à fourchons; à dents; **three-p. attack**, attaque triple, sur trois fronts.

pronoun ['prounaun] *n Gram:* pronom *m*.

pronounce [prə'nauns] **1.** *vtr* (*a*) déclarer; *Jur:* prononcer (une sentence) (*b*) prononcer, articuler (un mot) **2.** *vi* (se) prononcer. **pro'nounced** *a* prononcé, marqué; (goût) très fort. **pro'nounce-ment** *n* déclaration *f*. **pronunci'ation** [-nʌn-] *n* prononciation *f*.

pronto ['prɔntou] *adv F:* illico; sur-le-champ.

proof [pru:f] **1.** *n* (*a*) preuve *f*; **positive p.**, preuve patente; **to give p. of sth**, faire preuve de, témoigner,

qch; **this is p. that he is lying**, cela prouve qu'il ment; **to produce p. to the contrary**, fournir la preuve contraire; **to put sth to the p.**, mettre qch à l'épreuve (*b*) teneur *f* en alcool (d'un spiritueux) (*c*) (**printer's**) **p.**, épreuve 2. *a p.* **against sth**, résistant à qch; à l'épreuve de qch; étanche à (l'humidité); immunisé contre (une maladie); insensible à (la flatterie) **3.** *vtr* imperméabiliser (un tissu). **'proofread** *vtr & i* (**proofread**) *Typ:* corriger les épreuves. **'proofreader** *n Typ:* correcteur, -trice, d'épreuves.

prop [prɔp] **1.** *n* appui *m*, support *m*; étai *m*; soutien *m* **2.** *vtr* (**propped**) **to p. (up)**, appuyer, soutenir, étayer (un mur).

propaganda [prɔpə'gændə] *n* propagande *f*.

propagate ['prɔpəgeit] *vtr & i* (se) propager; **to p. itself**, se propager. **propa'gation** *n* propagation *f*.

propel [prə'pel] *vtr* (**propelled**) propulser; pousser (en avant). **pro'pellant** *n* combustible *m*; *Space:* propergol *m*. **pro'peller** *n* propulseur *m*; *Nau: Av:* hélice *f*; **p. shaft**, *Aut:* arbre de transmission; *Av:* arbre de l'hélice; *Nau:* arbre de porte-hélice. **pro'pelling** *a* propulsif; **p. pencil**, porte-mine *m inv.*

propensity [prə'pensiti] *n* (*pl* **propensities**) propension *f*, penchant *m*, inclination *f*, tendance *f* (**to, towards, sth**, à, vers, qch; **for doing sth**, à faire qch).

proper ['prɔpər] **1.** *a* (*a*) **p. to sth**, propre, particulier, à qch; **to put sth to its p. use**, utiliser rationnellement qch; *Gram:* **p. noun**, nom propre (*b*) vrai, juste, approprié; **in a p. sense**, au sens propre; **architecture p.**, l'architecture proprement dite; *Mth:* **p. fraction**, fraction inférieure à l'unité (*c*) *F:* **to get a p. hiding**, recevoir une belle raclée; **we're in a p. mess**, nous voilà dans de beaux draps; **he's a p. fool**, c'est un parfait imbécile (*d*) convenable; **at the p. time**, en temps utile; **to think it p. to do** (**sth**), juger bon de (faire qch); **do as you think p.**, faites comme bon vous semblera; **to do the p. thing by s.o.**, agir loyalement avec qn; **the p. way to do it**, la meilleure manière de le faire; **the p. tool**, le bon outil; **to keep sth in p. condition**, tenir qch en bon état (*e*) comme il faut; correct **2.** *adv P:* (parler) correctement; **p. poorly**, vraiment malade. **'pro-perly** *adv* (*a*) **word p. used**, mot employé correctement; **p. speaking**, proprement dit (*b*) bien; de la bonne façon; **do it p. or not at all**, faites-le comme il faut ou pas du tout (*c*) *F:* (*intensive*) **he was p. drunk**, il était complètement, vraiment, soûl; **to tick s.o. off p.**, rembarrer vertement qn (*d*) convenablement; **to behave p.**, se conduire comme il faut.

property ['prɔpəti] *n* (*pl* **properties**) (*a*) propriété *f*, biens *mpl*, avoir(s) *m*(*pl*); **that's my p.**, cela m'appartient; **landed p.**, biens fonciers; **lost p.**, objets trouvés; **p. tax**, impôt foncier (*b*) immeuble(s) *m*(*pl*) (*c*) *Th: Cin:* accessoire *m*; **p. man**, accessoiriste *m* (*d*) propriété; qualité *f* (propre); **inherent p.**, attribut *m*.

prophecy ['prɔfisi] *n* (*pl* **prophecies**) prophétie *f*. **prophesy** ['prɔfisai] *v* (**prophesied**) **1.** *vi* parler en prophète; prophétiser **2.** *vtr* prophétiser, prédire (un événement). **'prophet, 'prophetess** *n* (*pl* **pro-phetesses**) prophète *m*, prophétesse *f*. **pro'phetic** *a* prophétique. **pro'phetically** *adv* prophétiquement.

propitiate [prə'piʃieit] *vtr* apaiser (qn); se faire

pardonner par (qn). **propiti'ation** n propitiation f; apaisement m (de qn); expiation f (d'une faute). **pro'pitious** a propice; favorable. **pro'pitiously** adv d'une manière propice.

proportion [prə'pɔːʃn] **1.** n (a) partie f; portion f; part f; **to divide expenses in equal proportions,** répartir équitablement les frais; **p. of an ingredient in a mixture,** dose f d'un ingrédient dans un mélange (b) rapport m, proportion f; **p. of the net load to the gross load,** rapport du poids utile au poids mort; **in due p.,** en proportions raisonnables; **in p. as,** à mesure que; **in p. to,** proportionnellement à; **out of p.,** mal proportionné; **out of all p. to,** sans mesure avec; **to have no sense of p.,** ne pas avoir le sens des proportions; **to lose all sense of p.,** ne garder aucune mesure (c) **proportions,** proportions (d'un édifice); dimensions fpl (d'une machine) **2.** vtr proportionner; **well proportioned,** bien proportionné. **pro'portional** a proportionnel; en proportion (**to,** de); proportionné (**to,** à); Pol: **p. representation,** représentation proportionnelle. **pro'portionally** adv en proportion (**to,** de); proportionnellement (**to,** à). **pro'portionate** a proportionné (**to,** à).

propose [prə'pouz] **1.** vtr proposer (une ligne de conduite, une motion); **to p. a toast,** porter un toast (à la santé de qn); **to p. to do sth,** se proposer de faire qch; **what do you p. to do now?** que comptez-vous faire maintenant? **2.** vi faire une demande en mariage (**to,** à); **he proposed to her,** il lui a demandé de l'épouser. **pro'posal** [-zəl] n (a) proposition f, offre f; **to make a p.,** faire, formuler, une proposition (b) demande en mariage (c) dessein m; projet m. **pro'poser** n auteur m d'une offre, d'une proposition. **propo'sition** [prɔpə'ziʃn] **1.** n proposition, offre; **paying p.,** affaire qui rapporte; affaire intéressante, rentable; **it's a tough p.,** c'est une question difficile à résoudre; F: **he's a tough p.,** il n'est guère commode **2.** vtr P: faire des propositions (indécentes) à (qn).

propound [prə'paund] vtr proposer (une énigme); émettre (une idée); poser (une question); exposer (un programme).

proprietor, proprietress [prə'praiətər, -tres] n propriétaire mf; patron, -onne (d'un hôtel); **garage p.,** garagiste m. **pro'prietary** a (a) (droit) de propriété, de propriétaire (b) Com: **p. article,** spécialité f; article, produit, breveté; **p. medicines,** spécialités pharmaceutiques.

propriety [prə'praiəti] n (pl **proprieties**) (a) propriété f, justesse f, à-propos m (d'une expression); rectitude f (de conduite) (b) bienséance f, décence f; **to observe the proprieties,** observer les convenances fpl.

props [prɔps] npl Th: F: accessoires mpl.

propulsion [prə'pʌlʃn] n propulsion f. **pro'pulsive** a propulsif; (effort) de propulsion.

pro rata [prou'rɑːtə] a & adv phr au prorata.

prosaic [prou'zeiik] a prosaïque; (esprit) banal. **pro'saically** adv prosaïquement.

proscribe [prou'skraib] vtr proscrire. **pro'scription** n proscription f.

prose [prouz] n (a) prose f; **in p.,** en prose; **p. writer,** prosateur m (b) Sch: **p. (translation),** thème m. **'prosy** a (of style) prosaïque.

prosecute ['prɔsikjuːt] vtr poursuivre (qn) (en jus-

tice); engager des poursuites contre (qn); poursuivre (une réclamation). **prose'cution** n Jur: poursuites fpl judiciaires; **the p.,** les plaignants; (in Crown case) = le Ministère public; **witness for the p.,** témoin à charge. **'prosecutor** n Jur: plaignant, -ante; **the Public P.** = le procureur de la République.

prospect 1. n ['prɔspekt] (a) vue f; perspective f; **wide p.,** horizon très étendu (b) perspective, expectative f; **to have sth in p.,** avoir qch en perspective, en vue; **there is very little p. of it,** on ne peut guère y compter; **no p. of agreement,** aucune perspective d'accord (c) **prospects,** avenir m, espérances fpl; **prospects of success,** chances fpl de succès; **the prospects for the harvest are excellent,** la récolte s'annonce excellente; **his prospects are brilliant,** un brillant avenir s'ouvre devant lui **2.** vtr & i [prəs'pekt] prospecter. **pro'specting** n prospection f. **pro'spective** a en perspective; **my p. son-in-law,** mon futur gendre; **p. visit,** visite prochaine; **a p. buyer,** un acheteur éventuel. **pro'spector** n prospecteur, -trice; chercheur m (d'or, de minerais). **pro'spectus** n (pl **-uses**) prospectus m.

prosper ['prɔspər] vi prospérer, réussir. **pro'sperity** n prospérité f. **'prosperous** a prospère, florissant. **'prosperously** adv avec prospérité.

prostate ['prɔsteit] n Anat: **p. (gland),** prostate f.

prosthesis [prɔs'θiːsis] n (pl **prostheses** [-siːz]) prothèse f.

prostitute ['prɔstitjuːt] **1.** n prostituée f; **male p.,** prostitué m **2.** vtr prostituer. **prosti'tution** n prostitution f.

prostrate 1. vtr [prɔ'streit] **to p. oneself before s.o.,** se prosterner devant qn; **prostrated by the heat,** accablé par la chaleur **2.** a ['prɔstreit] (a) prosterné; couché (à terre); étendu (b) abattu; accablé; Med: prostré. **pro'stration** n (a) prosternement m; prosternation f (b) abattement m; Med: prostration f.

protagonist [prou'tægənist] n protagoniste m.

protect [prə'tekt] vtr protéger (**from sth,** contre qch); sauvegarder (les intérêts de qn). **pro'tection** n (a) protection f, défense f (**against,** contre); sauvegarde f (des intérêts de qn); **under s.o.'s p.,** sous la protection de qn; **p. racket,** racket m (b) abri m. **pro'tective** a protecteur; (vêtement) de protection. **pro'tectively** adv d'un geste protecteur. **pro'tector** n protecteur, -trice. **pro'tectorate** n protectorat m.

protégé ['prɔtəʒei] n protégé, -ée.

protein ['proutiːn] n protéine f.

protest 1. n ['proutest] protestation f; **to make a p.,** protester; faire des représentations f; **a day of p.,** une journée revendicative; **p. meeting,** réunion de protestation; **under p.,** (signer) sous réserve; (faire qch) à son corps défendant, en protestant **2.** vtr & i [prə'test] protester; **to p. one's innocence,** protester de son innocence. **Protestant** ['prɔtistənt] a & n Ecc: protestant, -ante. **'Protestantism** n protestantisme m. **prote'station** n protestation f. **pro'tester** n protestataire mf.

protocol ['proutəkɔl] n protocole m.

prototype ['proutətaip] n prototype m.

protract [prə'trækt] vtr prolonger; faire traîner (une affaire) en longueur. **pro'tractor** n Mth: rapporteur m.

protrude [prə'tru:d] *vi* (s')avancer, faire saillie. **pro'truding** *a* en saillie; saillant; **p. teeth**, dents proéminentes. **pro'trusion** *n* saillie *f*; protubérance *f*.

protuberance [prə'tju:bərəns] *n* protubérance *f*; **pro'tuberant** *a* protubérant.

proud [praud] **1.** *a* (*a*) fier, orgueilleux; **to be p. of sth**, être fier de qch (*b*) (*of view, city*) noble, magnifique **2.** *adv F:* **to do s.o. p.**, se mettre en frais pour qn; **to do oneself p.**, ne se priver de rien. **'proudly** *adv* fièrement, orgueilleusement; avec fierté.

prove [pru:v] **1.** *vtr* (*a*) prouver, démontrer; **it remains to be proved**, cela n'est pas encore prouvé; **to p. oneself**, faire ses preuves (*b*) *Jur:* homologuer (un testament) **2.** *vi* se montrer; **to p. useful**, se révéler utile; **the news proved false**, la nouvelle s'est révélée fausse.

proverb ['prɔvə:b] *n* proverbe *m*. **pro'verbial** *a* proverbial. **pro'verbially** *adv* proverbialement.

provide [prə'vaid] **1.** *vtr* **to p. s.o. with sth**, fournir qch à qn; pourvoir qn de qch **2.** *vi* stipuler (que); **to p. against sth**, se prémunir contre (une attaque); **expenses provided for in the budget**, dépenses prévues au budget; **to p. for s.o.**, pourvoir aux besoins de qn; **to p. for oneself**, se suffire; **to be well provided for**, avoir largement de quoi vivre; **he provided for everything**, il a subvenu à tout; **this has been provided for**, on y a pourvu. **pro'vided, pro'viding (that)** *conj* pourvu que + *sub*; à condition que + *ind or sub*. **pro'vider** *n* pourvoyeur, -euse; fournisseur, -euse.

providence ['prɔvidəns] *n* providence (divine). **provi'dential** *a* providentiel. **provi'dentially** *adv* providentiellement.

province ['prɔvins] *n* province *f*; **in the provinces**, en province; *Fig:* **that is not (within) my p.**, ce n'est pas de mon ressort, de mon domaine. **provincial** [prə'vinʃl] *a & n* provincial, -ale.

provision [prə'viʒn] **1.** *n* (*a*) provision *f*; *pl* provisions *fpl* (de bouche); comestibles *mpl*; vivres *mpl*; **to make p. for sth**, pourvoir à qch; **the law makes no p. for a case of this kind**, la loi n'a pas prévu un cas semblable; **to make p. for one's family**, assurer l'avenir de sa famille; **to lay in (a store of) provisions**, faire des vivres (*b*) article *m* (d'un traité); clause *f*, stipulation *f* (d'un contrat); *pl* dispositions *fpl* (d'un décret); **p. must be made for**, il faudra prévoir; **there's no p. to the contrary**, il n'y a pas de clause contraire; **to come within the provisions of the law**, tomber sous le coup de la loi **2.** *vtr* approvisionner; ravitailler (une armée). **pro'visional** *a* provisoire; *Jur:* provisionnel. **pro'visionally** *adv* provisoirement; (nommer qn) à titre provisoire. **pro'visioning** *n* approvisionnement *m* (de troupes). **proviso** [prə'vaizou] *n* clause conditionnelle; condition *f*; **with the p. that**, à condition que. **pro'visory** *a* conditionnel.

provoke [prə'vouk] *vtr* (*a*) provoquer, pousser, inciter (**s.o. to do sth**, qn à faire qch); **to p. s.o. to anger**, mettre qn en colère (*b*) irriter, fâcher, agacer (*c*) exciter (la curiosité); faire naître (un sourire). **provocation** [prɔvə'keiʃn] *n* provocation *f*; **under p.**, sous le coup de la colère. **provocative** [-'vɔk-] *a* provocant; provocateur, -trice. **pro'vocatively** *adv* d'une manière provocante.

provost ['prɔvəst] *n Sch:* principal *m* (de collège); *Scot:* maire *m*.

prow [prau] *n Nau:* proue *f*, avant *m*.

prowess ['prauis] *n* prouesse *f*.

prowl [praul] **1.** *vi* rôder **2.** *n* **to be always on the p.**, être toujours à rôder. **'prowler** *n* rôdeur, -euse.

proximity [prɔk'simiti] *n* proximité *f*; **in p. to**, à proximité de.

proxy ['prɔksi] *n Jur:* (*a*) procuration *f*; pouvoir *m*; mandat *m*; **by p.**, par procuration (*b*) (*pers*) mandataire *mf*; fondé *m* de pouvoir(s).

prude [pru:d] *n* prude *mf*; bégueule *f*. **'prudery, 'prudishness** *n* pruderie *f*; pudibonderie *f*. **'prudish** *a* prude; pudibond. **'prudishly** *adv* avec pruderie; en prude.

prudence ['pru:dəns] *n* prudence *f*, sagesse *f*. **'prudent** *a* prudent, sage. **'prudently** *adv* prudemment.

prune¹ [pru:n] *n* pruneau *m*.

prune² *vtr* tailler (un rosier); élaguer (une branche); faire des coupures dans (un article). **'pruning** *n* taille *f*; **p. knife**, serpette *f*.

prurient ['pruəriənt] *a* lascif. **'prurience** *n* lascivité *f*.

Prussia ['prʌʃə] *Prn* Prusse *f*. **'Prussian** *a & n* prussien, -ienne; **P. blue**, bleu de Prusse.

pry¹ [prai] *vi* (**pried**) fureter; fouiller; chercher à voir (dans qch); *F:* fourrer le nez (**into sth**, dans qch). **'prying** *a* curieux, indiscret, fureteur.

pry² *vtr* (**pried**) soulever, mouvoir, à l'aide d'un levier; **to p. open**, forcer (une porte).

PS *abbr postscript.*

psalm [sɑ:m] *n* psaume *m*. **'psalmist** *n* psalmiste *m*.

pseud [sju:d] *n F:* faux intellectuel, fausse intellectuelle; bêcheur, -euse. **'pseudo, 'pseudy** *a F:* faux.

pseudonym ['sju:dənim] *n* pseudonyme *m*.

psychiatry [sai'kaiətri] *n* psychiatrie *f*. **psychi'atric** *a* psychiatrique. **psy'chiatrist** *n* psychiatre *mf*.

psychic ['saikik] *a* psychique; (phénomène) métapsychique.

psychoanalysis [saikouə'nælisis] *n* (*pl* **psychoanalyses**) psychanalyse *f*. **psycho'analyst** *n* psychanalyste *mf*. **psycho'analyze** *vtr* psychanalyser.

psychology [sai'kɔlədʒi] *n* psychologie *f*. **psycho'logical** *a* psychologique. **psycho'logically** *adv* psychologiquement. **psy'chologist** *n* psychologue *mf*.

psychopath ['saikoupæθ] *n* psychopathe *mf*. **psycho'pathic** *a* psychopathe; (état) psychopathique.

psychosomatic [saikousə'mætik] *a Med:* psychosomatique.

PT *abbr physical training.*

ptarmigan ['tɑ:migən] *n Orn:* lagopède muet.

PTO *abbr please turn over.*

pub [pʌb] *n F:* = bistro(t) *m*; pub *m*; **to go on a p. crawl**, faire la tournée des bistro(t)s.

puberty ['pju:bəti] *n* puberté *f*.

pubis ['pju:bis] *n Anat:* pubis *m*. **'pubic** *a* pubien; **p. hair**, poils du pubis.

public ['pʌblik] **1.** *a* public, *f* publique; **p. holiday**, fête légale; **p. service**, service public; **p. library**, bibliothèque municipale; **p. transport,** transports en commun; **p. conveniences,** toilettes publiques; **p. house** = café *m*, bistro(t) *m*; pub *m*; **to make a p. protest,** protester publiquement; **p. life,** vie publique; **p. spirit,** civisme *m*; **p. relations,** relations publiques; **p. address system,** sonorisation *f* pour diffusion en public 2. *n* public *m*; **the general p.,** le grand public; **in p.,** en public. **'publican** *n* = débitant, -ante, de boissons, patron, -onne, de café. **'publicly** *adv* publiquement; en public.

publicity [pʌ'blisiti] *n* publicité *f*; *Com:* réclame *f*; **p. campaign,** campagne de publicité. **'publicize** *vtr* faire connaître au public; faire de la réclame, de la publicité, pour (un article).

publish ['pʌbliʃ] *vtr* publier, faire paraître (un livre); (*of editor*) éditer (un livre); **just published,** vient de paraître. **publi'cation** *n* (*a*) publication *f*, parution *f* (d'un livre) (*b*) ouvrage publié; publication. **'publisher** *n* éditeur, -trice. **'publishing** *n* publication *f*; **p., the p. business,** l'édition *f*; **p. house,** maison d'édition.

pucker ['pʌkər] 1. *n* ride *f*, pli *m* (du visage); fronce *f*, faux pli (d'un tissu) 2. *v* (*a*) *vtr* rider, plisser; froncer; faire goder (un tissu) (*b*) *vi* **to p. (up),** se froncer; (*of material*) goder; (*of face*) se crisper.

pudding ['pudiŋ] *n* *Cu:* (*a*) pudding *m*, pouding *m*; **rice p.,** riz *m* au lait; **Christmas p.,** pudding de Noël; **black p.,** boudin *m*; **p. basin,** moule à puddings (*b*) entremets sucré; dessert *m*.

puddle ['pʌdl] *n* flaque *f* d'eau.

puerile ['pjuərail] *a* puéril.

puff [pʌf] 1. *n* (*a*) souffle *m* (d'air); bouffée *f* (de fumée); **to take a p. at one's pipe,** tirer une bouffée de sa pipe; **p. sleeves,** manches bouffantes; *F:* **out of p.,** à bout de souffle (*b*) **(powder) p.,** (*large*) houppe *f*; (*small*) houppette *f* (*c*) *Cu:* feuilleté *m* (à la crème et à la confiture); **p. pastry,** pâte feuilletée 2. *v* (*a*) *vi* souffler; haleter; **to p. (away) at one's pipe,** tirer des bouffées de sa pipe (*b*) *vtr* lancer (des bouffées de fumée); fumer (un cigare) par petites bouffées. **'puffball** *n* *Fung:* vesse-de-loup *f*. **puffed** *a* **p. sleeves,** manches bouffantes; *F:* (*of pers*) **p. (out),** à bout de souffle. **'puffiness** *n* bouffissure *f* (du visage). **'puff 'out** *vtr* gonfler (les joues); lancer (des bouffées de fumée). **'puff 'up** *vtr* gonfler (les joues). **'puffy** *a* (-ier, -iest) bouffi; boursouflé.

pug [pʌg] *n* **p. (dog),** carlin *m*. **'pug-'nosed** *a* au nez camus.

pugnacious [pʌg'neiʃəs] *a* querelleur, batailleur. **pugnacity** [-'næs-] *n* humeur querelleuse, batailleuse.

puke [pju:k] *vtr & i* vomir, dégueuler.

pull [pul] I. *n* (*a*) traction *f*, tirage *m*; force *f* d'attraction (d'un aimant); tirage *m* de traction; **uphill p.,** effort à la montée (*c*) *Row:* coup *m* (d'aviron) (*d*) avantage *m*; **to have a great deal of p.,** avoir du piston (**with s.o.,** chez qn) (*e*) gorgée *f* (de bière); **to take a p. at one's pipe,** tirer une bouffée de sa pipe (*f*) (*object*) **bell p.,** cordon *m* de sonnette. II. *v* 1. *vtr* (*a*) tirer, se déchirer (un muscle); appuyer sur (la gâchette d'un revolver); manier (un aviron); traîner (une charrette); attirer (la clientèle); **to p. a gun,** tirer, sortir, un revolver; **to p. the door to,** tirer,

fermer, la porte; **to p. sth apart, to pieces,** déchirer qch; mettre qch en morceaux; **to p. s.o. to pieces,** critiquer sévèrement qn; **p. your chair nearer to the fire,** approchez votre chaise du feu; **to p. a face,** faire une grimace; *F:* **to p. a fast one on s.o.,** avoir an (*b*) arracher (une plante); extraire, arracher (une dent) 2. *vi* tirer; *Row:* ramer; *Rac:* **to p. ahead,** se détacher du peloton; *Aut:* **the engine, the car, is not pulling very well,** le moteur peine. **'pull a'bout** *vtr* tirailler (qch); malmener (qn). **'pull 'at** *vtr* tirer; tirer sur (sà pipe, un cordage). **'pull a'way** 1. *vtr* arracher (qch) (**from s.o.,** à qn) 2. *vi* (*of car*) sortir; (*of pers*) s'arracher (des bras de qn); (*of runner*) se détacher (**from,** de). **'pull 'back** *vi* hésiter; se retirer. **'pull 'down** *vtr* baisser, (faire) descendre (un store); démolir (une maison); (*of illness*) abattre, affaiblir (qn). **'pull 'in** 1. *vtr* rentrer (un filet); retenir (un cheval); attirer (le public); *F:* (*of police*) arrêter (un suspect) 2. *vi* s'arrêter; (*of train*) **to p. in(to the station),** entrer en gare; *Aut:* **to p. in(to the kerb),** se ranger près du trottoir. **'pull-in** *n* parking *m*; café *m*, restaurant *m* (pour routiers). **'pull 'off** *vtr* (*a*) détacher (un couvercle); enlever (un vêtement) (*b*) *Sp: F:* gagner, remporter, décrocher (un prix) (*c*) *F:* réussir à (faire) (qch); venir à bout de (qch). **'pull 'on** *vtr* tirer (sur) (un cordage); mettre (son veston). **'pull 'out** 1. *vtr* tirer; extraire, arracher (une dent) 2. *vi* se retirer; partir; (*of car*) démarrer; sortir; (*of train*) **to p. out (of the station),** sortir de la gare; *Aut:* **to p. out from behind a vehicle,** déboîter (pour doubler). **'pull-out** *n* supplément *m* détachable (de magazine). **'pull 'over** 1. *vtr* faire tomber 2. *vi Aut:* se ranger. **'pullover** *n* *Cost:* pull-over *m*, *F:* pull *m*. **'pull 'round, 'through** 1. *vtr* remettre (qn) sur pied; ranimer (qn) 2. *vi* s'en tirer; (*after illness*) se remettre. **'pull to'gether** (*a*) *vi* tirer ensemble (*b*) *vtr* **to p. oneself t.,** se reprendre, se ressaisir. **'pull 'up** 1. *vtr* (*a*) (re)monter; hisser (un poids); hausser, lever (un store); retrousser (sa jupe); approcher (une chaise); **to p. one's socks up,** tirer ses chaussettes; *F:* se remuer, s'activer (*b*) arracher (une mauvaise herbe) (*c*) réprimander (qn); **to be pulled up (by the police),** se faire arrêter, siffler (par un agent) 2. *vi* s'arrêter.

pullet ['pulit] *n* jeune poule *f*; poulet *m*.

pulley ['puli] *n* poulie *f*.

Pullman ['pulmən] *Prn Rail:* **P. (car),** voiture *f* Pullman.

pulp [pʌlp] 1. *n* pulpe *f*; pâte *f* (à papier); **to reduce sth to (a) p.,** réduire qch en pulpe; **p. magazine, book,** magazine, livre, à sensation 2. *vtr* réduire en pulpe, en pâte; mettre au pilon. **'pulpy** *a* pulpeux, charnu.

pulpit ['pulpit] *n* chaire *f* (de prédicateur).

pulse [pʌls] *n* (*a*) pouls *m*; **to take, feel, s.o.'s p.,** prendre le pouls de qn (*b*) *Elcs:* pulsation *f*; *WTel:* impulsion *f*. **pul'sate** *vi* (*a*) (*of heart*) battre (*b*) palpiter, vibrer. **pul'sation** *n* pulsation *f*; battement *m*.

pulverize ['pʌlvəraiz] *vtr* pulvériser. **pulveri'zation** *n* pulvérisation *f*.

puma ['pju:mə] *n* *Z:* puma *m*.

pumice ['pʌmis] *n* **p. stone,** (pierre *f*) ponce *f*.

pummel ['pʌml] *vtr* **(pummelled)** bourrer (qn) de coups de poing. **'pummelling** *n* volée *f* de coups (de poing).

pump [pʌmp] 1. n pompe f; **hand p.**, pompe à bras; **foot p.**, pompe à pied; **bicycle p.**, pompe à bicyclette; **petrol p.**, pompe à essence; **p. attendant**, pompiste mf; (at spa) **p. room**, pavillon m (où l'on prend les eaux) 2. vtr & i pomper; **to p. up a tyre**, gonfler un pneu; **to p. a well dry**, assécher un puits; **to p. s.o.'s hand**, serrer vigoureusement la main à qn; **to p. s.o.**, sonder, pomper, qn.

pumpkin ['pʌmpkin] n Hort: potiron m, citrouille f.

pun [pʌn] n calembour m; jeu m de mots.

punch¹ [pʌntʃ] 1. n (a) Tls: chasse-clou(s) m; (for piercing) perçoir m; Rail: poinçon m (de contrôleur); (machine) poinçonneuse f; **paper p., hole p.**, perforateur m à papier; **hollow p.**, emporte-pièce m inv; **p. card**, carte perforée (b) coup m de poing (c) F: force f, énergie f 2. vtr (a) percer; découper; poinçonner; perforer (le cuir); **punched card**, carte perforée (b) donner un coup de poing à (qn); cogner sur (qn); **to p. s.o.'s face, to p. s.o. in the face**, donner un coup de poing sur le nez de qn. **'punchball** n Box: punching-ball m. **'punch-'drunk** a abruti (par les coups), groggy. **'punchline** n chute f (d'une histoire). **'punch-up** n F: bagarre f.

punch² n (beverage) punch m. **'punchbowl** n (a) bol m à punch (b) cuvette f (entre collines).

Punch³ Prn = Polichinelle m, Guignol m; **P. and Judy show**, (théâtre m de) Guignol.

punctilious [pʌŋk'tiliəs] a pointilleux, méticuleux. **punc'tiliously** adv méticuleusement.

punctual ['pʌŋktjuəl] a ponctuel; **always p.**, toujours à l'heure. **punctu'ality** n ponctualité f, exactitude f. **'punctually** adv ponctuellement; à l'heure.

punctuate ['pʌŋktjueit] vtr ponctuer. **punctu'ation** n ponctuation f; **p. mark**, signe de ponctuation.

puncture ['pʌŋktʃər] 1. n crevaison f; (hole) piqûre f; perforation f; Surg: ponction f 2. v (a) vtr crever; perforer (un abcès) (b) vi (of tyre) crever.

pundit ['pʌndit] n pontife m (de la politique).

pungent ['pʌndʒənt] a (of style, sarcasm) mordant, caustique; (of smell) âcre, piquant, irritant. **'pungency** n goût piquant; odeur forte; âcreté f, aigreur f (de paroles); mordant m (de sarcasme). **'pungently** adv d'une manière piquante.

punish ['pʌniʃ] vtr punir; corriger (un enfant); malmener (un adversaire); fatiguer (le moteur); **to p. s.o. for sth**, punir qn de qch. **'punishable** a punissable; **p. by a fine**, passible d'amende. **'punishing** 1. a F: dur; (coup) violent; (travail) éreintant 2. n punition f. **'punishment** n punition f; châtiment m; (for a child) correction f; **capital p.**, peine capitale; **as a p.**, en punition.

punk [pʌŋk] F: 1. n vaurien m; Mus: **p. (rock)**, le (rock) punk 2. a mauvais, moche; (of pers) qui ne vaut rien.

punt [pʌnt] 1. n bachot (conduit à la perche); **p. pole**, gaffe f, perche f 2. vtr conduire (un bateau) à la perche. **'punter** n (a) canotier m qui conduit à la perche (b) Turf: parieur m.

puny ['pju:ni] a (-ier, -iest) (of pers) chétif, faible, débile.

pup [pʌp] n jeune chien m; chiot m; F: (of pers) freluquet m; F: **to sell s.o. a p.**, tromper qn. **'puppy** n (pl -ies) jeune chien; chiot; (of pers) **p. fat**, adiposité d'enfance, d'adolescence; **p. love**, premier amour.

pupil¹ ['pju:pl] n Sch: élève mf; écolier, -ière.

pupil² n pupille f (de l'œil).

puppet ['pʌpit] n marionnette f; **glove, hand, p.**, marionnette à gaine; **p. government**, gouvernement fantoche; Th: **p. show**, spectacle, théâtre, de marionnettes. **puppe'teer** n marionnettiste mf.

purchase ['pə:tʃəs] 1. n (a) achat m; acquisition f; **p. price**, prix d'achat (b) prise f; (point m d')appui m; **to get a p. on sth**, prendre appui sur qch 2. vtr acheter, acquérir (qch); **purchasing power**, pouvoir d'achat. **'purchaser** n acheteur, -euse.

pure ['pjuər] a pur; (of pers) innocent; **p. gold**, or pur; **p. silk**, pure soie; **p. maths**, mathématiques pures; **p. chance**, pur hasard; **p. and simple**, pur et simple. **'purebred** a & n (chien, animal m) de race (pure). **'purely** adv purement. **'pureness** n pureté f.

purgatory ['pə:gətəri] n purgatoire m; **it was p. to me**, j'étais au supplice.

purge [pə:dʒ] 1. n purge f; (medicine) purgatif m 2. vtr purger; nettoyer (un égout); Pol: purger, éliminer (des adversaires); **to p. oneself of a crime**, se disculper d'un crime. **'purgative** [-gə-] a & n purgatif (m).

purify ['pjuərifai] vtr (purified) purifier; épurer (le gaz, l'huile). **purifi'cation** n purification f; épuration f. **'purifier** n épurateur m (de gaz, d'huile); purificateur m (d'atmosphère). **'purist** n puriste mf. **'purity** n pureté f.

Puritan ['pjuəritən] a & n puritain, -aine. **puri'tanical** a puritain.

purl [pə:l] Knit: 1. n **p. (stitch)**, (maille f) à l'envers 2 vtr tricoter (des mailles) à l'envers.

purple ['pə:pl] a & n violet (m); pourpre (m); **to get p. in the face**, devenir cramoisi; Lit: **p. passage**, morceau de bravoure. **'purplish** a violacé; (of the face) cramoisi.

purport [pə:'pɔ:t] vi **to p. to be**, (of pers) avoir la prétention d'être; (of thg) être censé être.

purpose ['pə:pəs] 1. n (a) dessein m, objet m; but m, fin f, intention f; **fixed p.**, dessein bien arrêté; **to do sth on p.**, faire qch exprès, à dessein, de propos délibéré; **for, with, the p. of doing sth**, dans le but de faire qch (b) résolution f; **steadfastness of p.**, ténacité f de caractère; détermination f; **man of p.**, homme résolu (c) **intended p.**, destination f; **for this p.**, à cet effet; **for all necessary purposes**, à tous usages; **for all practical purposes**, en réalité; dans la pratique; **to serve no p.**, ne servir à rien; **to speak to the p.**, parler à propos; **we're (talking) at cross purposes**, il y a malentendu (entre nous); **all that is to no p.**, tout cela ne sert à rien; **to work to good p., to some p.**, travailler utilement, efficacement. **'purpose-'built** a construit sur mesure; personnalisé, fonctionnalisé. **'purposeful** a (of action) prémédité; réfléchi; (of pers) avisé; tenace. **'purposefully** adv dans un but précis. **'purposely** adv à dessein; exprès.

purr [pə:r] 1. n ronron m, ronronnement m (de chat, de moteur); ronflement m, vrombissement m (d'un moteur) 2. vi (of cat, engine) ronronner; (of engine) ronfler, vrombir; **the cat's purring**, le chat fait ronron.

purse [pə:s] 1. n porte-monnaie m inv; bourse f; NAm: sac m à main; Sp: somme f d'argent; **that car is beyond my p.**, cette voiture est au-delà de mes moyens; Adm: **the public p.**, le Trésor 2. vtr **to p. (up) one's lips**, pincer les lèvres. **'purser** n Nau: Av: commissaire m.

'**pursestrings** npl Fig: **to hold the p.,** tenir les cordons m de la bourse.

pursue [pə'sju:] vtr (a) poursuivre (qn); rechercher (le plaisir); être à la poursuite (du bonheur) (b) continuer, suivre (son chemin); poursuivre (une enquête); **to p. a line of conduct,** suivre une ligne de conduite. **pur'suer** n poursuivant, -ante. **pur'suit** n (a) poursuite f; **to set out in p. of s.o.,** se mettre à la poursuite de qn; **in p. of happiness,** à la recherche du bonheur (b) carrière f, profession f; occupation f; **his literary pursuits,** ses travaux m littéraires.

purveyor [pə'veiər] n fournisseur, -euse (de provisions).

pus [pʌs] n Med: pus m.

push [puʃ] I. n (a) poussée f, impulsion f; **p. button,** bouton-poussoir m; **to give sth a p.,** pousser qch; F: **to give s.o. the p.,** flanquer qn à la porte (b) effort m; **to have plenty of p.,** avoir beaucoup d'initiative f, d'énergie f; être dynamique; F: **at a p.,** à la rigueur. II. v 1. vtr (a) pousser; appuyer sur (un bouton); **to p. one's finger into s.o.'s eye,** fourrer le doigt dans l'œil de qn; **don't p. (me)!** ne (me) poussez pas! ne (me) bousculez pas! **to p. oneself (forward),** se mettre en avant; **to p. one's luck,** aller un peu fort; **to p. s.o. into doing sth,** pousser qn à faire qch; **I'm terribly pushed (for time),** je suis très pressé; **to be pushed for money,** être à court d'argent; **to p. sth home,** pousser qch à fond; F: **he's pushing sixty,** il frise la soixantaine (b) faire la promotion (des produits); vendre (des drogues) 2. vi pousser; exercer une pression. '**push a'round** vtr F: mener (qn) par le bout du nez. '**push a'side** vtr écarter. '**push a'way** vtr repousser. '**push 'back** vtr repousser, faire reculer. '**pushbike** n F: bicyclette f, vélo m. '**push-button** a (fonctionnement) automatique; (guerre) presse-bouton inv. '**pushchair** n (NAm: = buggy) poussette f (d'enfant). '**pusher** n (a) F: arriviste mf (b) fournisseur, -euse, revendeur, -euse (de drogues). '**push 'forward** 1. vtr pousser en avant; (faire) avancer 2. vi avancer; se porter en avant. '**push 'in** 1. vtr enfoncer 2. vi entrer à toute force. '**pushing** a entreprenant, énergique; **a p. man,** un ambitieux. '**push 'off** vi Nau: pousser au large; F: **it's time to p. o.,** il est temps de se mettre en route, de partir; **p. o.!** fiche le camp! file! '**push 'on** 1. vtr pousser (en avant) 2. vi pousser (**to,** jusqu'à). '**push 'out** vtr pousser dehors; faire sortir; **to p. a boat o.,** mettre un bateau à l'eau; **to p. the boat o.,** Fig: faire la fête. '**push 'over** vtr faire tomber. '**pushover** n F: chose f facile à faire; **it's a p.,** c'est donné. '**push 'through** 1. vtr faire passer (qch) à travers (qch); mener à bien (un travail); faire accepter (un projet de loi) 2. vtr & i **to p. (one's way) t.,** se frayer un chemin (à travers). '**push 'to** vtr pousser, fermer (la porte). '**push 'up** vtr relever (qch) (en poussant). '**push-up** n Gym: traction f. '**pushy** a (-ier, -iest) F: arriviste.

pusillanimous [pju:si'læniməs] a pusillanime.

puss, pussy [pus, 'pusi] n (pl **pusses, pussies**) minet m, minette f; minou m.

put [put] v (**putting; put**) 1. vtr (a) mettre; **p. it on the table,** mettez-le, posez-le, placez-le, sur la table; **to p. milk in one's tea,** mettre du lait dans son thé; **to p. s.o. in his place,** remettre qn à sa place; **to p. one's**

signature **to sth,** apposer sa signature sur, à, qch; **to p. the matter right,** arranger l'affaire; **to p. the law into operation,** appliquer la loi; **to p. money into an undertaking,** placer de l'argent dans une affaire; **to p. s.o. against s.o.,** monter qn contre qn; **to p. money on a horse,** miser, parier, sur un cheval; **to p. a question to s.o.,** poser une question à qn; **I p. it to you that,** n'est-il pas vrai que? **to p. the case clearly,** exposer clairement la situation; **to p. it to him nicely,** présentez-lui la chose gentiment; **to p. it bluntly,** pour parler franc; **if one may p. it that way,** si l'on peut s'exprimer ainsi (b) **to p. the population at 10,000,** estimer, évaluer, la population à 10 000; **to p. a stop to sth,** mettre fin à qch; **to p. s.o. to bed,** mettre qn au lit; coucher (un enfant); **to p. s.o. through an ordeal,** faire subir une rude épreuve à qn; F: **to p. s.o. through it,** faire passer un mauvais quart d'heure à qn; **to p. s.o. to sleep,** endormir qn; **I'm putting you to a lot of trouble,** je vous donne beaucoup d'embarras; **to p. a bullet through s.o.'s head,** loger une balle dans la tête de qn; **to p. one's fist through the window,** enfoncer la fenêtre d'un coup de poing; Sp: **to p. the shot,** lancer le poids 2. vi Nau: **to p. (out) to sea,** prendre le large; **to p. into port,** faire escale, relâche. **put a'bout** 1. vtr faire circuler (un bruit) 2. vi Nau: virer de bord. '**put a'cross** vtr faire comprendre, faire accepter (qch à qn); communiquer (un message). '**put a'side** vtr mettre de côté. '**put a'way** vtr (a) ranger (des livres); remettre (qch) à sa place; garer (sa voiture); mettre de côté (de l'argent) (b) mettre (qn) en prison; F: coffrer (qn); (faire) enfermer (qn) (dans un asile) (c) F: bouffer (de la nourriture) (d) tuer (qn, un animal) (e) écarter, chasser (une pensée). '**put 'back** 1. vtr (a) remettre (qch) à sa place (b) retarder (une horloge, un départ, qn); **this decision has p. us b.,** cette décision nous a ramenés en arrière 2. vi Nau: rentrer au port. '**put 'by** vtr mettre de côté, en réserve. '**put 'down** vtr (a) déposer, poser; (of bus) débarquer (des voyageurs; **p. it down!** laissez cela! (b) supprimer, réprimer (une révolte) (c) noter (sur papier); mettre par écrit; **to p. down one's name,** s'inscrire; se faire inscrire (for, pour); **p. it down to my account,** mettez-le sur mon compte; **to p. sth down to s.o.,** attribuer qch à qn; **I'd p. her d. as 30,** je lui donnerais 30 ans (d) tuer, (faire) abattre (un animal); faire piquer (un chien) 2. vi (of aircraft) atterrir. '**put 'forward** vtr (a) émettre, avancer, proposer (un projet); **to p. oneself f.,** se mettre en avant; **to p. one's best foot f.,** presser le pas; Fig: s'efforcer de faire de son mieux (b) avancer (une horloge). '**put 'in** 1. vtr (a) mettre (qch) dedans; **to p. one's head in at the window,** passer sa tête par la fenêtre; **to p. in a (good) word for s.o.,** dire, placer, un mot en faveur de qn (b) présenter (une réclamation, des élèves à un examen) (c) passer (le temps); **to p. in an hour's work,** faire une heure de travail 2. vi **to p. in at a port,** faire escale, relâche; **to p. in for a post,** poser sa candidature à un poste; **to p. in for 2 days' leave,** demander 2 jours de congé. '**put 'off** 1. vtr (a) remettre (à plus tard); renvoyer; différer (de faire qch); **to p. off a case for a week,** ajourner une affaire à huitaine; **to p. s.o. off with an excuse,** se débarrasser de qn avec une excuse (b) déconcerter, déranger (qn); **you p. me off,** vous m'intimidez; **to p. s.o. off doing sth,** décourager qn de faire qch (c) dégoûter (qn) (d) éteindre (la lumière) **2.** *vi Nau:* pousser au large; démarrer. **'put 'on** *vtr (a)* mettre; **to p. the kettle on,** mettre de l'eau à chauffer *(b)* passer (un disque, une bande); monter (une pièce de théâtre); mettre (un train) en service; *Aut:* **to p. the brakes on,** freiner *(c)* mettre (ses vêtements); chausser (ses pantoufles); **to p. on one's shoes,** se chausser *(d)* affecter, prendre (un air innocent); *F:* **to put it on,** poser, afficher de grands airs *(e)* **to p. on weight,** grossir; prendre du poids *(f) (bet)* miser (de l'argent) *(g)* avancer (la pendule) *(h)* mettre, allumer (la lumière); mettre, ouvrir (la radio); faire marcher (la télévision); **to p. s.o. on to sth,** indiquer qch à qn; **who p. you on to it?** qui vous a donné le tuyau? *Tp:* **would you p. me on to Mr Martin, please?** voulez-vous me passer M. Martin, s'il vous plaît? **'put 'out** *vtr (a)* tendre, avancer (la main); étendre (le bras) *(b)* mettre (le chat) dehors; **to p. s.o. out (of the house),** mettre qn à la porte; **to p. the washing out to dry,** mettre du linge à sécher; **to p. one's head o. of the window,** passer sa tête par la fenêtre; sortir la tête à la fenêtre *(c)* tirer (la langue); **to p. o. o. (of joint),** se démettre, se déboîter (l'épaule, le genou) *(d)* éteindre (la lumière); fermer (le gaz) *(e)* déconcerter; ennuyer, contrarier (qn); incommoder, gêner (qn); **he never gets p. out,** il ne s'émeut jamais; **to p. oneself out for s.o.,** se déranger pour qn. **'put 'over** *vtr* = **put across 'put 'through** *vtr* mener à bien (un projet); faire accepter (un marché); *Tp:* passer (qn); **I'll p. you t. to him,** je vous le passe. **'put to'gether** *vtr (a)* mettre ensemble; monter, assembler (une robe, une machine) *(b)* mettre (deux choses) côte à côte; rapprocher, comparer (des faits). **'put 'up 1.** *vtr (a)* lever (une glace); ouvrir (un parapluie); dresser (une échelle); poser (un rideau); **p. up your hands!** haut les mains! *(b)* coller (une affiche) *(c)* augmenter (les prix) *(d)* proposer (un candidat) (aux élections); **to p. sth up for sale,** mettre qch en vente; **to p. sth up for auction,** mettre qch aux enchères *(e)* fournir (de l'argent) *(f)* offrir, opposer (une résistance); **to p. up a stout resistance,** se défendre vaillamment *(g)* loger, héberger (qn); **to p. a friend up**

for the night, héberger un ami pour une nuit *(h)* **to p. s.o. up to sth,** pousser qn à qch *(i)* construire (une maison); ériger (un monument) **2.** *vi (a)* loger, descendre (à un hôtel) *(b) (of candidate)* **to p. up for sth,** poser sa candidature à qch *(c)* **to p. up with,** supporter, *F:* encaisser; s'accommoder de (qch); se résigner à (qch); souffrir (des railleries); **to p. o. o. how,** chercher à comprendre comment. **'put-up** *a F:* **a p.-up job,** un coup monté. **'put upon** *vtr* en imposer à (qn); **I won't be p. u.,** je refuse qu'on se fiche de moi.

putrefy [ˈpjuːtrifai] *vtr & i (putrefied)* (se) putréfier. **putre'faction** *n* putréfaction *f.*

putrid [ˈpjuːtrid] *a* putride; en putréfaction; infect; *F:* moche.

putt [pʌt] *Golf:* **1.** *n* putt *m* **2.** *vtr & i* putter. **'putting** *n* putting *m;* **p. green,** green *m.*

putty [ˈpʌti] *n* mastic *m;* **p. knife,** couteau à mastic.

puzzle [ˈpʌzl] **1.** *n (a)* embarras *m;* perplexité *f (b)* énigme *f;* problème *m;* devinette *f; Games: (manual)* casse-tête *m inv;* *(jig-saw)* puzzle *m;* **crossword p.,** mots croisés **2.** *vtr* embarrasser, intriguer, déconcerter (qn). **'puzzle a'bout, 'over** *vtr* chercher à comprendre, à résoudre. **'puzzle 'out** *vtr* résoudre (un problème); trouver (une solution); **to p. o. o. how,** chercher à comprendre comment. **'puzzled** *a (air)* perdu; *(of pers)* perplexe. **'puzzler** *n F:* énigme; question *f* difficile. **'puzzling** *a* intrigant; curieux.

PVC *abbr polyvinyl chloride.*

pygmy [ˈpigmi] **1.** *n (pl* **pygmies)** pygmée *mf* **2.** *a* pygmée.

pyjamas [piˈdʒɑːməz] *npl (NAm: =* **pajamas)** pyjama *m.*

pylon [ˈpailən] *n* pylône *m.*

pyramid [ˈpirəmid] *n* pyramide *f.*

pyre [ˈpaiər] *n* bûcher *m* (funéraire).

Pyrenees (the) [ðəpirəˈniːz] *Prn Geog:* les Pyrénées *f.* **Pyre'nean** *a* pyrénéen; des Pyrénées.

pyrites [paiˈraitiːz] *n* pyrite *f.*

pyromaniac [pairouˈmeiniæk] *n* pyromane *mf.*

pyrotechnics [pairouˈtekniks] *npl* pyrotechnie *f.*

python [ˈpaiθən] *n Rept:* python *m.*

Q

Q, q [kju:] *n* (la lettre) Q, q *m*.

QC *abbr Jur:* Queen's Counsel.

QED *abbr quod erat demonstrandum,* ce qu'il fallait démontrer, CQFD.

quack[1] [kwæk] 1. *n & int* coin-coin (*m*) 2. *vi* (*of duck*) crier; faire coin-coin; (*of pers*) bavarder.

quack[2] *F:* (*a*) *a* q. **doctor,** charlatan *m*; q. **remedy,** remède de charlatan (*b*) *n* toubib *m,* charlatan.

quad [kwɔd] *n* 1. = **quadrangle** 2. = **quadruplet.**

Quadragesima [kwɔdrə'dʒesimə] *n Ecc:* la Quadragésime.

quadrangle ['kwɔdræŋgl] *n* quadrilatère *m; Sch:* cour (carrée).

quadrant ['kwɔdrənt] *n Mth:* quadrant *m;* quart *m* de cercle.

quadraphonic [kwɔdrə'fɔnik] *a* quadriphonique.

quadratic [kwɔ'drætik] *a Mth:* q. **equation,** équation *f* du second degré.

quadrilateral [kwɔdri'læt(ə)rəl] *a & n* quadrilatère (*m*).

quadruped ['kwɔdruped] *n* quadrupède *m.*

quadruple [kwɔ'drupl] 1. *a & n* quadruple (*m*) 2. *vtr & i* quadrupler. **'quadruplet** *n* quadruplé(e). **qua'druplicate** 1. *a* quadruple; **in q.,** en quatre exemplaires 2. *vtr* quadrupler; faire, tirer, quatre exemplaires (d'une lettre).

quagmire ['kwægmaiər, 'kwɔg-] *n* fondrière *f;* marécage *m.*

quail[1] [kweil] *n Orn:* caille *f.*

quail[2] *vi* fléchir, faiblir; **his heart, spirit, quailed,** il a perdu courage.

quaint [kweint] *a* pittoresque, vieillot; q. **ideas,** idées *f* (i) bizarres, un peu vieux jeu (ii) baroques; q. **style,** style (i) original (ii) désuet. **'quaintly** *adv* d'une façon originale, pittoresque.

quake [kweik] *vi* trembler (**with fear,** de peur); **to q. in one's shoes,** trembler dans sa peau.

Quaker ['kweikər] *n Ecc:* quaker *m,* quakeresse *f.*

qualify ['kwɔlifai] 1. *vtr* (*a*) *Gram:* qualifier (*b*) acquérir les connaissances *f,* qualités *f,* nécessaires (**for a job,** pour remplir un emploi); rendre qn apte (à faire qch); **does he q.?** est-ce qu'il remplit les conditions requises? (*c*) apporter des réserves à (un consentement); modifier, atténuer (une affirmation) 2. *vi* acquérir les connaissances requises, se qualifier (**for,** pour); **to q. as a doctor,** être reçu médecin; *Av:* **to q. as a pilot,** obtenir son brevet de pilote. **qualifi'cation** [-fi-] *n* (*a*) qualification *f;* **professional qualifications,** qualifications professionnelles; **qualifications for a job,** conditions *f,* qualités *f,* requises pour remplir une fonction; **what are your qualifications?** quels diplômes avez-vous? (*b*) **to accept without q.,** accepter (i) sans réserve (ii) sans condition. **'qualified** *a* 1. (*a*) (instituteur, -trice) diplômé(e); (pilote) breveté; (employé) compétent, qualifié; **to be q. to do sth,** être

qualifié pour faire qch (*b*) autorisé; **to be q. to.vote,** avoir qualité d'électeur 2. restreint, modéré; q. **acceptance,** acceptation conditionnelle. **'qualifying** *a* 1. *Gram:* (adjectif) qualificatif 2. (*a*) q. **examination,** (i) examen pour certificat d'aptitude (ii) examen d'entrée (*b*) *Sp:* q. **round,** série éliminatoire.

quality ['kwɔliti] *n* (*pl* **qualities**) (*a*) qualité *f;* **of good, poor, q.,** de bonne qualité; de qualité inférieure; *Com:* q. **goods,** marchandises de qualité; q. **(news)paper,** journal sérieux; **of the best q.,** de premier choix; q. **control,** contrôle de la qualité (*b*) **he has many good qualities, bad qualities,** il a beaucoup de qualités, de défauts *m* (*c*) **to act in the q. of,** agir en (sa) qualité de (*d*) qualité, timbre *m* (d'un son). **'qualitative** *a* qualitatif.

qualm [kwɑːm] *n* (*a*) scrupule *m,* remords *m;* **to have no qualms about doing sth,** ne pas se faire le moindre scrupule de faire qch (*b*) inquiétude *f.*

quandary ['kwɔndri] *n* (*pl* **quandaries**) **to be in a q.,** (i) se trouver dans une impasse; être dans l'embarras (ii) ne pas trop savoir que faire.

quango ['kwæŋgou] *n* (**Quasi autonomous nongovernmental organization**) = société nationale de service public.

quantify ['kwɔntifai] *vtr* 1. *Log:* quantifier 2. déterminer la quantité de (qch); évaluer avec précision.

quantity ['kwɔntiti] *n* (*a*) quantité *f;* **a q. of,** une quantité, des quantités de; **a small, a large, q. of,** une petite, une grande, quantité de; **in great quantities,** en grande quantité, en abondance (*b*) *Mth:* quantité; **unknown q.,** inconnue *f; F:* **he's an unknown q.,** on ne sait rien de lui; **negligible q.,** quantité négligeable, de peu d'importance (*c*) *CivE:* q. **surveying,** toisé *m;* métrage *m;* q. **surveyor,** métreur (vérificateur).

quantum ['kwɔntəm] *n* (*pl* **quanta**) quantum *m; Ph:* q. **theory,** théorie des quanta, théorie quantique; q. **mechanics,** mécanique quantique.

quarantine ['kwɔrəntiːn] 1. *n* quarantaine *f;* **to be in q.,** être en quarantaine 2. *vtr* mettre (qn, un chien) en quarantaine.

quarrel ['kwɔrəl] 1. *n* querelle *f,* dispute *f,* brouille *f;* **to try to pick a q. with s.o.,** chercher querelle à qn; **they've had a q.,** ils se sont disputés; ils (se) sont brouillés; **I have no q. with, against, him,** je n'ai rien à lui reprocher 2. *vi* (**quarrelled,** *NAm:* **quarreled**) (*a*) se quereller, se disputer (**with s.o. over, about, sth,** avec qn à propos de qch); se brouiller (avec qn) (*b*) **to q. with s.o. for having done sth,** reprocher à qn d'avoir fait qch; **to q. with sth,** trouver à redire à qch. **'quarrelling,** *NAm:* **quarreling** 1. *n* querelle(s) *f*(*pl*), dispute(s) *f*(*pl*) 2. *a* querelleur. **'quarrelsome** *a* querelleur; **he's a q. fellow,** il est mauvais coucheur.

quarry[1] ['kwɔri] *n* (*pl* **quarries**) *Ven:* proie *f;* gibier *m* (poursuivi à courre); (*pers*) gibier.

quarry² 1. *n* (*pl* **quarries**) (*a*) carrière *f* (de pierres) (*b*) **q. tile,** carreau *m* (de céramique) 2. *vtr* extraire, tirer, (la pierre) de la carrière; exploiter une carrière. '**quarrying** *n* exploitation *f* de carrières. '**quarry-man** *n* (*pl* -**men**) (ouvrier) carrier.

quart [kwɔːt] *n Meas:* un quart de gallon (**English q.** = 1 litre 136; **American liquid q.** = 0 litre 946; **American dry q.** = 1 litre 101).

quarter ['kwɔːtər] **I.** *n* 1. (*a*) quart *m*; **three quarters,** trois quarts; **two and a q.,** deux et un quart; **a q. (of a pound) of coffee,** un quart (de livre) de café; **to divide sth in(to) quarters,** diviser qch en quatre; **bottle one q. full,** bouteille au quart pleine (*b*) *Cu:* quartier *m* (de bœuf) 2. (*a*) trimestre *m*; terme *m* (de loyer (*b*) **moon at the first q.,** lune au premier quartier (*c*) **a q. of an hour,** un quart d'heure; **a q. to,** *NAm:* **of, six,** six heures moins le quart; **a q. past,** *NAm:* **after, six,** six heures un quart, et quart; **it's a q. to,** *NAm:* **of,** il est moins le quart (*d*) *NAm:* pièce *f* de vingt-cinq cents 3. (*a*) **what q. is the wind in?** de quel côté souffle le vent? (*b*) **the four quarters of the globe,** les quatre parties du globe; **from all quarters,** de partout; de tous côtés; **in high quarters,** en haut lieu; **to apply to the proper q.,** s'adresser à qui de droit 4. quartier *m* (d'une ville) 5. *pl Mil:* quartiers, logements *mpl.* **II.** *vtr* 1. diviser (une pomme) en quatre 2. *Mil:* cantonner, caserner (des troupes). '**quarter 'day** *n* (jour du) terme *m.* '**quarter-deck** *n* 1. *Nau:* gaillard *m* (d')arrière; *Navy:* plage *f* arrière 2. *Navy:* les officiers *mpl.* '**quarter-'final** *n Sp:* quart de finale. '**quarter-'hourly** *adv* tous les quarts d'heure. '**quarterly** 1. *a* trimestriel 2. *n* publication trimestrielle 3. *adv* par trimestre; tous les trois mois.

quartet(te) [kwɔː'tet] *n Mus:* quatuor *m.*

quarto ['kwɔːtou] *a* & *n* in-quarto (*m*) *inv.*

quartz [kwɔːts] *n Miner:* quartz *m*; **q. watch,** montre à quartz.

quash [kwɔʃ] *vtr* (*a*) *Jur:* casser, annuler (un jugement) (*b*) étouffer (un sentiment); apaiser, écraser (une révolte).

quasi ['kweisai] *pref* quasi, presque; **q.-contract,** quasi-contrat *m.*

quaver ['kweivər] 1. *n* (*a*) *Mus:* croche *f* (*b*) *Mus:* trille *m*, tremolo *m* (*c*) tremblement *m*, chevrotement *m* (de la voix) 2. *vi* chevroter, trembloter. '**quavering** 1. *a* voix, voix chevrotante, tremblotante 2. *n* tremblement, chevrotement.

quay [kiː] *n* quai *m.* '**quayside** *n* quai *m*; **at the q.,** à quai.

queasy ['kwiːzi] *a* (-**ier**, -**iest**) sujet à des nausées; **to feel q.,** avoir l'estomac barbouillé, avoir mal au cœur; **q. conscience,** conscience scrupuleuse à l'excès.

Quebec [kwi'bek] *Prn Geog:* (*a*) (*town*) Québec (*b*) (*province*) le Québec.

queen [kwiːn] **I.** *n* 1. reine *f*; **Q. Anne,** la reine Anne; **the Q. Mother,** la reine mère; **the kings and queens, les souverains *mpl* 2. (*a*) *Cards:* dame *f* (*b*) *Chess:* dame, reine 3. *Ent:* (*of bees, ants*) reine 4. **beauty q.,** reine de beauté 5. *P:* (*homosexual*) pédale *f*, tantouse *f.* **II.** *vtr* 1. **to q. it,** faire la grande dame, la reine 2. *Chess:* damer (un pion). '**queenly** *a* de reine; digne d'une reine.

queer [kwiər] **1.** *a* (*a*) bizarre, étrange, singulier; **q. ideas,** idées bizarres, biscornues; **q. in the head,** toqué, timbré; **a q.-looking chap,** une drôle de tête; *F:* **to be in Q. Street,** être dans une situation (financière) embarrassée (*b*) suspect (*c*) *P:* homosexuel; *n* **a q.,** un homosexuel (*d*) *F:* **I feel very q.,** je me sens patraque; je me sens tout drôle 2. *vtr F:* déranger, détraquer; **to q. s.o.'s pitch,** faire échouer les projets de qn. '**queerly** *adv* étrangement, bizarrement. '**queerness** *n* étrangeté *f*, bizarrerie *f.*

quell [kwel] *vtr* calmer, apaiser (une émotion); dompter, étouffer (une passion); réprimer (une révolte).

quench [kwen(t)ʃ] *vtr* **to q. one's thirst,** étancher sa soif; se désaltérer.

querulous ['kwerjuləs] *a* (ton) plaintif; grognon, maussade.

query ['kwiəri] 1. *n* (*pl* **queries**) (*a*) question *f* (*b*) point *m* d'interrogation 2. *vtr* (*a*) mettre (une affirmation) en question, en doute (*b*) marquer (qch) d'un point d'interrogation (*c*) chercher à savoir (**whether,** si).

quest [kwest] *n* recherche *f*; **to go in q. of s.o.,** se mettre à la recherche de qn.

question ['kwestʃən] 1. *n* (*a*) question *f*; **to ask s.o. a q., to put a q. to s.o.,** poser une question à qn; interroger qn; **to answer a q.,** répondre à une question; **list, set, of questions,** questionnaire *m*; *Gram:* **q. mark,** point d'interrogation (*b*) (*doubt*) **without q.,** sans aucun doute; **to obey without q.,** obéir aveuglément; **that's beyond q.,** c'est incontestable; **there is no q. about it,** il n'y a pas de doute (*c*) (*subject of discussion*) **that's the q.,** c'est toute la question; **that's not the q., that's another q.,** il ne s'agit pas de cela; **the matter, the person, in q.,** l'affaire, la personne, en question; **the q. is (whether),** il s'agit de savoir (si); **it's (quite) out of the q.,** c'est impossible; il ne saurait en être question (*d*) (*problem*) **the human rights q.,** la question des droits de l'homme; **the q. of unemployment,** le problème du chômage; **a q. of life or death,** une question de vie ou de mort; **a q. of time,** une question de temps 2. *vtr* (*a*) questionner, interroger (qn) (*b*) mettre (qch) en question, en doute; **I q. whether it would not be better,** je me demande s'il ne vaudrait pas mieux. '**questionable** *a* 1. contestable, discutable 2. équivoque; **in q. taste,** d'un goût douteux. '**questioner** *n* interrogateur, -trice. '**questioning** 1. *a* (regard) interrogateur 2. *n* interrogation *f.* '**question(-)master** *n* animateur, -trice (d'un jeu-concours). **questio'nnaire** *n* questionnaire *m.*

queue [kjuː] 1. *n* queue *f*, file *f* (de personnes, de voitures); **to form a q., to stand in a q.,** faire la queue; **to jump the q.,** passer avant son tour; **ticket q.,** la file d'attente devant le guichet 2. *vi* **to q. (up),** faire la queue; (*of cars*) prendre la file.

quibble ['kwibl] 1. *n* chicane *f* (de mots) 2. *vi* chicaner (sur les mots); vétiller; ergoter. '**quibbler** *n* ergoteur, -euse; chicaneur, -euse. '**quibbling** *n* chicane; ergoterie *f.*

quick [kwik] **1.** *a* (*a*) rapide; **the quickest way,** le chemin le plus court; **q. sale,** vente facile; **to have a q. lunch,** déjeuner sur le pouce; *F:* **to have a q. one,** prendre un verre (en vitesse); **as q. as lightning,**

prompt comme l'éclair; en un clin d'œil; **be q.!** faites vite! dépêchez-vous! (b) **q. child,** enfant vif, éveillé; **q. wit,** esprit prompt à la repartie; **q. ear,** oreille fine; **she has a q. temper,** elle s'emporte facilement; **q. to anger,** prompt à se fâcher (c) *Mus:* animé (d) **q. hedge,** haie vive 2. *n* vif *m*; chair vive; **to cut s.o. to the q.,** blesser qn au vif; **the q. and the dead,** les vivants et les morts 3. *adv* vite, rapidement; **as q. as possible,** aussi vite que possible; **to run quicker,** courir plus vite. '**quick-'acting** *a* (mécanisme) à action immédiate; (médicament) à action rapide. '**quicken** 1. *vtr* (a) exciter, stimuler (l'appétit); animer (la conversation) (b) hâter, presser, accélérer (le pas); (of pulse) accélérer 2. *vi* (of baby in womb) donner des signes de vie. '**quick-'freeze** *vtr* surgeler '**quickie** *n F:* (a) chose faite à la hâte (b) let's have **a q.,** viens prendre un verre (en vitesse). '**quicklime** *n* chaux vive. '**quickly** *adv* vite; rapidement; promptement; sans tarder. '**quickness** *n* 1. vitesse *f*, rapidité *f* 2. acuité *f* (de vision); finesse *f* (d'oreille); vivacité *f* (d'esprit). '**quicksand** *n* sable(s) mouvant(s); **to get caught in a q.,** s'enliser. '**quicksilver** *n* vif-argent *m*, mercure *m*. '**quickstep** *n Danc:* fox-trot *m* rapide. '**quick-'tempered** *a* emporté; prompt à la colère. '**quick-'witted** *a* d'esprit vif; éveillé.

quid [kwid] *n P:* livre *f* (sterling); **five q.,** cinq livres.

quiescent [kwai'esənt] *a* en repos; tranquille. **qui'escence** *n* repos *m*; tranquillité *f*.

quiet ['kwaiət] 1. *n* (a) tranquillité *f*, repos *m*, calme *m* (b) *F:* **to do sth on the q.,** faire qch en cachette; **I'm telling you that on the q.,** je vous dis ça entre nous (deux) 2. *a* (a) tranquille, calme, silencieux; **to keep q.,** rester tranquille; **be q.!** (i) taisez-vous! (ii) laissez-moi tranquille! **q. please!** silence s'il vous plaît! **try to be quieter,** essaye de faire moins de bruit (b) **q. disposition,** caractère doux, calme (c) simple; (of dress, colour) sobre; discret; **q. dinner,** dîner intime; **q. wedding,** mariage célébré dans l'intimité; (d) calme, tranquille, paisible; **to lead a q. life,** mener une vie calme; **he's had a q. sleep,** il a dormi paisiblement; **you may be q. on that score,** quant à cela vous pouvez être tranquille 3. (also **quieten**) (a) *vtr* apaiser, calmer (b) *vi* **to q., to quieten, down,** s'apaiser, se calmer. '**quietly** *adv* (a) tranquillement, doucement (b) silencieusement, sans bruit. **quietness** *n* 1. tranquillité *f*, repos *m*, calme *m* 2. sobriété *f* (de tenue).

quill [kwil] *n* 1. (a) *Orn:* **q. (feather),** penne *f* (b) **q. (pen),** plume *f* d'oie (pour écrire) 2. piquant *m* (de porc-épic).

quilt [kwilt] 1. *n* (NAm: = **comforter**) couverture piquée; édredon piqué; courtepointe *f*; **continental q.,** couette *f*; **q. cover,** housse pour couette 2. *vtr* piquer; capitonner (un fauteuil).

quince [kwins] *n* coing *m*; (tree) cognassier *m*.

quinine [kwi'ni:n, NAm: 'kwainain] *n Med:* quinine *f*.

quinsy ['kwinzi] *n Med:* amygdalite aiguë.

quintessence [kwin'tesəns] *n* quintessence *f*. **quinte'ssential** *a* quintessenciel.

quintet(te) [kwin'tet] *n Mus:* quintette *m*.

quintuple ['kwintjupl] *a & n* quintuple (*m*). **quin'tuplet** *n* 1. groupe *m* de cinq 2. quintuplé(e).

quip [kwip] 1. *n* sarcasme *m*, repartie *f*; raillerie *f*, mot piquant 2. *vi* railler; dire des mots piquants.

quire ['kwaiər] *n* = main *f* (de papier).

quirk [kwə:k] *n* bizarrerie *f*; **by a q. of fate,** par une ironie du sort. '**quirky** *a* (-ier, -iest) bizarre.

quit [kwit] 1. *a* quitte; **to be q. of s.o.,** être débarrassé de qn 2. *vtr & i* (pt & pp **quitted** or **quit**) (a) quitter (qn, un endroit); vider les lieux; s'en aller (b) **to q. one's job,** quitter son emploi; démissionner; NAm: **to q. doing sth,** cesser de faire qch; **q. fooling!** arrête de faire l'idiot! '**quitter** *n* personne *f* qui renonce facilement en face de difficultés imprévues.

quite [kwait] *adv* 1. tout à fait; entièrement; **q. new,** tout nouveau; **q. recovered,** complètement rétabli; **q. the best story of its kind,** sans exception la meilleure histoire de ce genre; **q. as much,** tout autant; **q. enough,** bien assez; **I q. understand,** j'ai bien compris; je me rends parfaitement compte; **q. right,** très bien; **q. so!** *F:* **q.!** parfaitement! d'accord! **not q.,** pas tout à fait; **I don't q. know what he will do,** je ne sais pas trop ce qu'il fera 2. **his story is q. a romance,** son histoire est tout un roman; **it's q. interesting,** cela ne manque pas d'intérêt; **q. a surprise,** une véritable surprise; **I q. believe that,** je veux bien croire que; *F:* **it's been q. a day!** quelle journée! **she's q. a girl,** elle est formidable; **I q. like him,** je l'aime assez.

quits [kwits] *a* quitte; **we are q.,** nous sommes quittes.

quiver ['kwivər] 1. *n* (a) tremblement *m*; frisson *m*; **with a q. in his voice,** d'une voix mal assurée; avec un frémissement dans la voix; **q. of the eyelid,** battement *m* de paupière (b) (for arrows) carquois *m* 2. *vi* trembler; tressaillir, frissonner; (of voice, light) trembloter; frémir (de crainte).

quixotic [kwik'sɔtik] *a* exalté, visionnaire; (projet) donquichottesque.

quiz [kwiz] 1. *n* (pl **quizzes**) WTel: TV: devinette *f*; jeu-concours *m*; Sch: NAm: examen oral 2. *vtr* (**quizzed**) poser des questions, des colles, à (qn). '**quiz master** *n* animateur, -trice d'un jeu-concours. '**quizzical** *a* railleur; **a q. smile,** un sourire moqueur.

quoit [kɔit] *n Games:* palet *m*; **to play quoits,** jouer au palet.

quorum ['kwɔ:rəm] *n* quorum *m*; nombre voulu; **not to have a q.,** ne pas atteindre le quorum.

quota ['kwoutə] *n* quote-part *f*; quotité *f*; quota *m*; Com: Adm: **to fix quotas for imports of butter,** fixer les quotas d'importation pour le beurre, contingenter les importations du beurre.

quote [kwout] 1. *vtr* (a) citer (un auteur, un passage, un exemple); **can I q. you?** est-ce que je peux vous citer? Com: **please q. this number,** prière de rappeler ce numéro; **q., unquote,** ouvrez les guillemets, fermez les guillemets (b) Com: établir, faire (un prix) 2. *n F:* (a) citation *f* (b) pl **guillemets** *mpl*. **quo'tation** *n* 1. citation *f*; **q. marks,** guillemets 2. StEx: cote *f*, cours *m*, prix *m*. '**quoted** *a StEx:* **q. shares,** valeurs cotées en Bourse.

quotient ['kwouʃ(ə)nt] *n Mth:* quotient *m*.

R

R, r [ɑːr] n (la lettre) R, r m; **the three Rs** (*Reading,* (w) *Riting and* (a) *Rithmetic*), l'enseignement m primaire.

RA *abbr Royal Academy.*

rabbi ['ræbai] n *JewRel:* rabbin m.

rabbit ['ræbit] n lapin m; **buck r.,** lapin mâle; **doe r.,** lapine f; **wild r.,** lapin de garenne; **r. hole,** terrier m (de lapin); **r. hutch,** clapier m; *Cu:* **Welsh r.,** fondue f au fromage sur canapé.

rabble ['ræbl] n *Pej:* cohue f; foule f (en désordre); **the r.,** la populace.

rabid ['ræbid] a (a) *Vet:* (chien) enragé (b) furieux; (haine) farouche; (partisan) fanatique.

rabies ['reibiːz] n *Med: Vet:* rage f.

RAC *abbr Royal Automobile Club.*

raccoon [rə'kuːn] n Z: raton laveur.

race¹ [reis] **1.** n *Sp:* course f; **to run a r.,** courir, disputer, une course; **long-distance r.,** course de fond; **to go to the races,** aller aux courses; **a r. against time,** une course contre la montre **2.** v (a) vi lutter de vitesse, faire une course (**with,** avec); courir à toute vitesse; (of engine) s'emballer; (of propeller) s'affoler; (of pulse) battre rapidement (b) vtr faire courir (un cheval); *Aut:* emballer (le moteur); **I'll r. you to school,** faisons une course jusqu'à l'école! au premier arrivé (de nous deux) à l'école! 'racecourse n champ m de courses; hippodrome m. 'racegoer n turfiste mf. 'racehorse n cheval m de course. 'racer n (a) (pers) coureur, -euse (b) cheval de course; bicyclette f, motocyclette f, voiture f, de course. 'racetrack n piste f (pour voitures); champ de courses (pour chevaux); hippodrome m. 'racing n courses fpl (de chevaux, d'automobiles); **r. car,** voiture de course; **r. stable,** écurie de courses. 'racy a (-ier, -iest) vif, piquant; (style) plein de verve.

race² n (a) race f; **the human r.,** la race humaine; **r. relations,** rapports entre les races (d'un même pays); **r. riot,** bagarre raciale (b) descendance f; lignée f. **racial** ['reiʃl] a racial, de (la) race; **r. discrimination,** discrimination raciale; **r. minorities,** les minorités raciales. 'racism n racisme m. 'racist a & n raciste (mf).

rack¹ [ræk] n **to go to r. and ruin,** aller à la ruine; (s'en) aller à vau-l'eau; (of house) se délabrer.

rack² n râtelier m (d'écurie, à bicyclettes); casier m (à bouteilles); (shelf) étagère f; **coat r.,** portemanteau m; *Av:* **bomb r.,** lance-bombes m inv; *Rail:* **luggage r.,** porte-bagages m inv; filet m (à bagages); *Aut:* **roof r.,** galerie f; **r. railway,** chemin de fer à crémaillère f.

rack³ 1. n *Hist:* chevalet m (de torture) **2.** vtr tourmenter, torturer (qn); **to r. one's brains,** se creuser la cervelle; **racked by remorse,** tenaillé par le remords.

racket¹, racquet ['rækit] n raquette f.

racket² n (a) tapage m; vacarme m; **to make a r.,** faire du boucan (b) racket m; **it's a r.,** c'est une escroquerie, c'est du vol (c) entreprise f de gangsters; **is he in on this**

r.? est-il dans le coup? **racke'teer** n gangster m; escroc m; trafiquant m; racketter m; racketteur m.

radar ['reidɑːr] n radar m; **navigation by r.,** navigation au radar; **r. operator,** radariste mf; **r. screen,** écran (de) radar.

radiate ['reidieit] **1.** vi rayonner; irradier; émettre des rayons; (of lines) partir d'un même centre **2.** vtr émettre, dégager (de la chaleur); répandre (le bonheur). 'radial a & n *Aut:* **r. (tyre),** pneu radial. 'radiance n rayonnement m; éclat m (de la beauté). 'radiant a radiant; (sourire) radieux; **r. heat,** chaleur rayonnante. 'radiantly adv d'un air radieux; **r. happy,** rayonnant de joie. radi'ation n irradiation f; rayonnement m; radiation f (nucléaire); **r. sickness,** mal des rayons. 'radiator n radiateur m; *Aut:* **r. cap,** bouchon de radiateur; **r. grill,** calandre f.

radical ['rædikal] a & n radical, -ale; **to make a r. change in sth,** changer qch radicalement. 'radically adv radicalement.

radii ['reidiai] npl see **radius.**

radio ['reidiou] **1.** n (a) radio(télégraphie) f; **r. communication** contact radio; **r. station,** poste radiotélégraphique, radiophonique; poste (émetteur) de radio; **r. operator,** (opérateur m de) radio m; **r. beacon,** radiobalise f; **r. control,** téléguidage m (b) **r. (set),** poste (récepteur) de radio; radio f; **on the r.,** à la radio **2.** vtr envoyer (un message) par radio. radio'active a radioactif. radioac'tivity n radioactivité f. 'radiocon'trolled a téléguidé, radioguidé. 'radiogram n (a) radiogramme m (b) combiné m (radiophone). 'radiograph n *Med:* radiographie f, F: radio f. radi'ographer n radiologue mf. radi'ography n *Med:* radiographie. radi'ologist n radiologue. radi'ology n radiologie f. radio'therapy n radiothérapie f.

radish ['rædiʃ] n radis m.

radium ['reidiəm] n radium m.

radius ['reidiəs] n (pl **radii** ['reidiai]) *Mth:* rayon m (de cercle); **within a r. of three kilometres,** dans un rayon de trois kilomètres.

RAF *abbr Royal Air Force.*

raffia ['ræfiə] n raphia m.

raffle ['ræfl] **1.** n tombola f; loterie f **2.** vtr mettre (qch) en loterie.

raft [rɑːft] n radeau m.

rafter ['rɑːftər] n *Const:* chevron m.

rag¹ [ræg] n (a) chiffon m; lambeau m; **rags (and tatters),** haillons mpl, guenilles fpl, loques fpl; **in rags,** en haillons; F: **the r. trade,** la confection; F: **to feel like a wet r.,** se sentir mou comme une chiffe (b) F: *Pej:* (newspaper) feuille f de chou, torchon m. **rag-and-'bone man** n chiffonnier m. 'ragbag n *Fig: Pej:* collection f hétéroclite (de choses, d'idées). 'ragged [-gid] a en lambeaux; en haillons.

rag² **1.** n *Sch:* F: brimade f; mauvais tour; farce f; chahut m **2.** v (**ragged**) (a) vtr brimer, taquiner (un camarade); chahuter (un professeur) (b) vi chahuter; faire du chahut.

rage [reidʒ] 1. n rage f, fureur f; emportement m; **to be in a r. with s.o.**, être furieux, en fureur, contre qn; **to fly into a r.**, s'emporter; (of thg) **to be all the r.**, faire fureur 2. vi être furieux; (of wind) faire rage; (of sea) être démonté; (of epidemic) sévir. **'raging** a furieux; en fureur; **r. sea**, mer déchaînée; **r. thirst**, soif ardente; **r. toothache**, rage de dents.

raid [reid] 1. n (by bandits) razzia f; (by police) descente f; Mil: raid m; **air r.**, raid aérien; **bank r.**, attaque f de banque 2. vtr faire une razzia, une descente, un raid, dans; razzier (une tribu); attaquer (une banque); F: dévaliser (le frigo). **'raider** n maraudeur m, pillard m.

rail [reil] n (a) barre f, barreau m; bâton m (de chaise) (b) barre d'appui; garde-fou m, parapet m (de pont); balustrade f (de balcon); rampe f (d'escalier); **curtain r.**, tringle m à rideau (c) pl (iron) grille f. (wood) palissade f; clôture f (d) Rail: rail m; **live r.**, rail de contact; **to go off the rails**, dérailler; **to travel by r.**, voyager par, en, chemin de fer; **r. traffic**, trafic ferroviaire. **'railcar** n automotrice f; autorail m. **'railhead** n tête f de ligne. **'railings** npl grille; parapet (de pont); balustrade (de balcon); rampe (d'escalier). **'railway**, NAm: **'railroad** n chemin m de fer; **r. line**, ligne de chemin de fer; voie ferrée; **r. station**, gare f; **r. cutting**, déblai m; **r. embankment**, remblai m; **r. network**, réseau ferroviaire; **r. timetable**, indicateur des chemins de fer. **'railwayman** n (pl -men) cheminot m.

rain [rein] 1. n pluie f; **driving r.**, pluie battante; **it looks like r.**, le temps est à la pluie; (in tropics) **the rains**, la saison des pluies; **r. cloud**, nuage de pluie 2. vtr & i pleuvoir; **it's raining**, il pleut, F: **it's raining cats and dogs**, il pleut à torrents, à seaux. **'rainbow** n arc-en-ciel m. **'raincheck** n NAm: **I'll take a r. (on that)**, ce sera partie remise. **'raincoat** n imperméable m, F: imper m. **'raindrop** n goutte f de pluie. **'rainfall** n précipitation f; **area of heavy r.**, région pluvieuse. **'rainproof** a imperméable. **'rainwater** n eau f de pluie. **'rainy** a (-ier, -iest) pluvieux; **a r. day**, un jour de pluie; **r. season**, saison des pluies; **to put sth by for a r. day**, garder une poire pour la soif.

raise [reiz] 1. vtr (a) dresser, mettre debout (une échelle); relever (qch qui est tombé); soulever (un malade, le peuple); **to r. s.o. from the dead**, ressusciter qn des morts (b) élever (un palais); ériger (une statue) (c) élever (une famille, du bétail); cultiver (des légumes) (d) produire (une ampoule); faire (une bosse); provoquer (un sourire); faire naître (une espérance); **to r. s.o.'s hopes**, exalter l'espoir de qn; **to r. s.o.'s spirits**, remonter le moral de qn; **he couldn't r. a smile**, il ne pouvait pas esquisser un sourire (e) soulever (une objection) (f) lever (le bras); soulever (un poids); porter (qn au pouvoir); relever (un store); **to r. one's voice**, élever, hausser, la voix (g) augmenter (le salaire de qn, les prix) (h) lever, mettre sur pied (une armée) (i) se procurer (de l'argent); (of the State) contracter (un emprunt) (j) évoquer (un esprit); F: **to r. hell**, faire un bruit de tous les diables (k) lever (un siège, un blocus) 2. n NAm: (Br = rise) augmentation f (de salaire).

raisin ['reizn] n raisin sec.

rake¹ [reik] 1. n Tls: râteau m 2. v (a) vtr râteler; ratisser (les feuilles) (b) vi **to r. (about) among some papers**, fouiller dans des documents. **'rake 'in** vtr amasser (de l'argent). **'rake 'off** vtr enlever au râteau. **'rake-off** n F: pourcentage m (illicite); gratte f. **'rake 'out** vtr enlever les cendres (du feu). **'rake 'up** vtr attiser (le feu); revenir sur (le passé); **to r. up s.o.'s past**, fouiller dans le passé de qn.

rake² n A: viveur m, roué m. **'rakish** a libertin, dissolu; (air) bravache, cavalier; **to wear one's hat at a r. angle**, porter son chapeau avec désinvolture sur l'oreille.

rally ['ræli] 1. n (a) ralliement m (de partisans); réunion f (de scouts) (b) Aut: (car) **r.**, rallye m automobile (c) reprise f (des forces); mieux momentané (d'un malade); Sp: dernier effort (pour gagner le match); Ten: échange m 2. v (rallied) (a) vtr rallier (ses partisans) (round, autour de) (b) vi se rallier; (of troops) se reformer; (of pers) reprendre ses forces (après une maladie); StExch: (of shares) se redresser, reprendre; **rallying point**, point de ralliement; **rallying cry**, cri de guerre.

ram [ræm] 1. n Z: bélier m; MecE: bélier hydraulique; mouton m (de marteau-pilon) 2. vtr (rammed) (a) battre, damer, tasser (le sol); enfoncer (un pieu) (b) tamponner (une voiture); éperonner (un navire); heurter (qch) (against, into, contre).

ramble ['ræmbl] 1. n promenade f (sans itinéraire bien arrêté); **to go for a r.**, faire une balade 2. vi (a) errer à l'aventure; (of plant) grimper (b) F: parler à bâtons rompus; **to r. on**, dire mille inconséquences. **'rambler** n (a) excursionniste mf (à pied) (b) Hort: rosier grimpant. **'rambling** a (a) errant, vagabond; (of plant) grimpant (b) (discours) décousu, sans suite; **r. house**, maison pleine de coins et de recoins.

ramify ['ræmifai] vi (ramified) se ramifier. **ramifi'cation** n ramification f.

ramp [ræmp] n rampe f; Aut: (repair) **r.**, pont élévateur; PN: Aut: (beware) **r.!** dénivellation f! **unloading r.**, rampe de débarquement.

rampage [ræm'peidʒ] 1. n **to be on the r.**, se comporter comme un fou; **to go on the r.**, se déchaîner 2. vi **to r. (about)**, se déchaîner; faire du tapage.

rampant ['ræmpənt] a **r. corruption**, la corruption omniprésente; **crime is r.**, la criminalité est en augmentation; **to be r.**, sévir.

rampart ['ræmpɑːt] n Fort: rempart m.

ramshackle ['ræmʃækl] a délabré.

ran [ræn] see run I.

ranch [rɑːntʃ] n ranch m.

rancid ['rænsid] a rance; **to smell r.**, sentir le rance.

rancour, NAm: **rancor** ['ræŋkər] n rancune f; rancœur f. **'rancorous** ['ræŋkərəs] a rancunier.

random ['rændəm] 1. n **at r.**, au hasard; **to hit out at r.**, lancer des coups à l'aveuglette 2. a **r. shot**, coup tiré au hasard.

randy ['rændi] a (-ier, -iest) F: lascif, paillard.

rang [ræŋ] see ring² II.

range [reindʒ] 1. n (a) rangée f (de bâtiments); chaîne f (de montagnes) (b) direction f, alignement m (c) champ m libre (d) NAm: grand pâturage (non clôturé) (e) étendue f, portée f; **r. of action**, champ d'activité; **within, beyond, my r.**, à, hors de, ma portée (f) gamme f (de couleurs); variation f (du ba-

rank 318 rate

classé (**as,** comme). **'rateable** *a Adm:* **r. value**=valeur locative imposable (d'un immeuble).
'ratepayer *n* contribuable *mf.* **'rating** *n* (a) estimation *f,* évaluation *f; Adm:* répartition *f* des impôts locaux (b) *Sp:* classe *f,* catégorie *f* (d'un athlète) (c) *Navy:* **the ratings,** les matelots *m* et gradés *m* (d) *WTel: TV:* indice *m* d'écoute.

rather ['rɑːðər] *adv* (a) plutôt (b) un peu; quelque peu; assez; **r. pretty,** assez joli; **r. plain,** plutôt laid; **r. a lot,** un peu trop; **I r. think you know him,** je crois bien que vous le connaissez; **r. nice,** pas mal (c) plutôt (**than,** que); **I would r. leave,** j'aimerais mieux partir; **I would r. that you came tomorrow,** je préférerais que vous veniez demain; **I'd r. be liked than feared,** plutôt être aimé que craint; **I'd r. not,** j'aime mieux pas; *F:* **do you know him?—r.!** le connaissez-vous?—bien sûr que oui! *F:* un peu!

ratify ['rætifai] *vtr* (**ratified**) ratifier; entériner (un décret); approuver (un contrat). **ratifi'cation** *n* ratification *f.*

ratio ['reiʃiou] *n* 1. raison *f,* rapport *m,* proportion *f;* **in the r. of,** dans le rapport, la proportion, de; **in direct r. to,** en raison directe de; **the student–staff r. is twenty to one,** le rapport élèves–maître est de vingt pour un 2. *MecE: etc:* taux *m* (de compression).

ration ['ræʃən] 1. *n* ration *f;* **to put s.o. on short rations,** rationner qn; **r. book,** carte d'alimentation 2. *vtr* rationner. **'rationing** *n* rationnement *m.*

rational ['ræʃənl] *a* (a) raisonnable; doué de raison; **to be quite r.,** avoir toute sa tête (b) (of explanation, argument) raisonné; conforme à la raison; **r. belief,** croyance rationnelle. **rationale** [ræʃə'nɑːl] *n* analyse raisonnée; raison *f* d'être. **rationali'zation** *n* rationalisation *f.* **'rationalize** *vtr & i* rationaliser; **to r. (one's behaviour),** essayer d'expliquer sa conduite. **'rationally** *adv* rationnellement; raisonnablement.

rattle ['rætl] **I.** *n* (a) hochet *m* (d'enfant); crécelle *f* (d'alarme); *Rept:* **rattles,** sonnettes *f* (d'un crotale) (b) bruit *m,* fracas *m* (d'une voiture); tapotis *m* (d'une machine à écrire); cliquetis *m* (d'une chaîne); grésillement *m* (de la grêle); *Med:* (death) **r.,** râle *m.* **II.** *v* 1. *vi* faire entendre des bruits secs; (of arms) cliqueter; (of window) branler; (of hail) grésiller; (of articles in box) ballotter; **to make the windows r.,** faire trembler les vitres; *Aut:* **to r. along,** rouler à toute vitesse, à grand bruit de ferraille 2. *vtr* (a) agiter (qch) avec bruit; faire cliqueter (des clefs) (b) consterner, bouleverser (qn); **he never gets rattled,** il ne se laisse pas épater. **'rattle 'off** *vtr* réciter, débiter, rapidement (un poème). **'rattle 'on** *vi* continuer à bavarder. **'rattlesnake** *vi Rept:* crotale *m,* serpent *m* à sonnettes.

raucous ['rɔːkəs] *a* (voix) rauque. **'raucously** *adv* d'une voix rauque.

ravage ['rævidʒ] 1. *n* ravage *m* 2. *vtr* ravager, dévaster (un pays, une ville).

rave [reiv] 1. *n* **r. review,** critique dithyrambique 2. *vi* délirer, divaguer; (in anger) tempêter; **to r. at, against,** **s.o.,** pester contre qn; *F:* **to r. about sth,** s'extasier sur qch. **'rave-up** *n F:* bringue *f.* **'raving** 1. *a* délirant, en délire; **r. (mad),** (fou) furieux; *F:* **you're r. mad!** t'es complètement fou! **r. lunatic,** fou furieux 2. *n* délire *m,* divagation *f;* **ravings,** délire; paroles incohérentes.

raven ['reivən] *n Orn:* (grand) corbeau.

ravenous ['rævənəs] *a* (animal, appétit) vorace; (of hunger) dévorant; (of pers) affamé; **to be r.,** avoir une faim de loup. **'ravenously** *adv* voracement; (manger) gloutonnement.

ravine [rə'viːn] *n* ravin *m.*

ravioli [rævi'ouli] *n Cu:* ravioli *mpl.*

ravish ['rævɪʃ] *vtr* ravir. **'ravishing** *a* ravissant; (spectacle) enchanteur. **'ravishingly** *adv* **r. beautiful,** ravissant.

raw [rɔː] 1. *a* (a) cru; **r. meat,** viande crue; **r. materials,** matières premières; **r. silk,** soie grège; **r. metal,** métal brut (b) sans expérience, inexpérimenté; **a r. hand,** un novice; **r. troops,** troupes non aguerries (c) (chair) à vif; **r. wound,** plaie vive; (of material) **r. edge,** bord coupé (d) (temps) âpre 2. *n* **to touch s.o. on the r.,** piquer qn au vif; **in the r.,** cru, brut; *F:* nu, à poil; **life in the r.,** la vie rude. **'raw-'boned** *a* décharné. **'rawhide** *n Leath:* cuir vert. **'rawness** *n* crudité *f* (des fruits); inexpérience *f* (d'une recrue); écorchure *f* (de la peau); âpreté *f* (du temps).

ray¹ [rei] *n* rayon *m;* **r. of light,** rayon lumineux; **a r. of hope,** une lueur d'espoir.

ray² *n Ich:* raie *f.*

rayon ['reiɔn] *n Tex:* rayonne *f.*

raze [reiz] *vtr* **to r. (to the ground),** raser (un édifice).

razor ['reizər] *n* rasoir *m;* **safety r.,** rasoir de sûreté; **electric r.,** rasoir électrique; **r. blade,** lame *f* de rasoir; *Fig:* **to be on a r. edge,** se trouver dans une situation critique.

RC *abbr Roman Catholic.*

Rd *abbr road.*

re¹ [rei] *n Mus:* ré *m.*

re² [riː] *prep* **re your letter of June 10th,** au sujet de votre lettre du 10 juin.

re³ *pref* re-; ré-; de nouveau; **to reread,** relire; **to reprint,** réimprimer; **to revisit,** revisiter, visiter de nouveau; **to reaccustom,** réhabituer.

reach [riːtʃ] **I.** *n* (pl **reaches**) (a) extension *f* (de la main); portée *f* (du bras); *Box:* allonge *f;* **within s.o.'s r.,** à la portée de qn; **out of r., beyond r.,** hors de portée; **within easy r.,** à portée de main; **hotel within easy r. of the station,** hôtel à proximité de la gare; **beyond the r. of human intellect,** au-dessus de l'entendement humain (b) partie droite (d'un fleuve) entre deux coudes; bief *m* (d'un canal). **II.** *v* (**reaches**) 1. *vtr* (a) atteindre; arriver à (un endroit); parvenir à (un but); **to r. perfection,** atteindre à la perfection; **your letter reached me today,** votre lettre m'est parvenue aujourd'hui; **r. me my gloves,** passez-moi mes gants (b) arriver à (une conclusion); **to r. an agreement,** arriver à un accord 2. *vtr & i to r. (to) sth,** arriver, s'élever, monter, descendre, jusqu'à qch; **to r. the bottom,** atteindre le fond; descendre jusqu'au fond 3. *vi* s'étendre; **as far as the eye could r.,** à perte de vue; **to r. (out) for sth,** tendre la main pour prendre qch; **he reached over to the table,** il a étendu la main vers la table. **'reach 'out** *vtr & i* **to r. o. (one's hand),** étendre, tendre, avancer, la main.

react [ri'ækt] *vi* réagir (**up)on,** sur; **against,** contre). **re'action** *n* réaction *f.* **re'actionary** *a & n* (pl **-ies**) réactionnaire (mf). **re'actor** *n* réacteur *m;* **atomic r.,** réacteur atomique; **breeder r.,** pile couveuse.

read [riːd] 1. *vtr & i* (**read** [red]) (a) lire; relever (un compteur); *Typ:* corriger (des épreuves); **to teach s.o. to r.,** apprendre à lire à qn; enseigner la lecture à qn; *Adm:* **read** [red] **and approved,** lu et approuvé; **I read it in a newspaper,** je l'ai lu dans un journal; *(at university)* **he's reading French,** il étudie le français; **to r. law,** faire son droit; **to r. sth aloud,** lire qch à haute voix; **to r. to s.o.,** faire la lecture à qn; **to take the minutes as read,** approuver le procès-verbal sans lecture; **the letter reads as follows,** la lettre est libellée comme suit; *(of pers)* **well read,** instruit, érudit; versé **(in,** dans); **to r. s.o.'s thoughts,** lire dans la pensée de qn; **to r. between the lines,** lire entre les lignes; **I can r. him like a book,** je le connais comme le fond de ma poche; *WTel:* **do you r. me?** vous (me) comprenez? *(b)* **the clause reads both ways,** l'article peut s'interpréter dans les deux sens; **the thermometer reads 30°,** le thermomètre indique trente degrés **2.** *n* action *f* de lire; **he was having a quiet r.,** il lisait tranquillement; **this book is a good r.,** ce livre est agréable à lire. **'readable** *a (of writing)* lisible; *(of book)* intéressant à lire. **'read 'back** *vtr* relire. **'reader** *n (a)* lecteur, -trice; *Typ:* correcteur -trice (d'épreuves); **he's not much of a r.,** il n'aime pas beaucoup la lecture; **publisher's r.,** lecteur, -trice, de manuscrits *(b) Sch:* = professeur *m* (de faculté) *(c) Sch:* livre *m* de lecture. **'readership** *n* nombre *m* de lecteurs, lectorat *m* (d'un journal). **'reading 1.** *a* **the r. public,** le public qui lit **2.** *n (a)* lecture(s) *f (pl)*; **to be fond of r.,** aimer la lecture; **book that makes good r.,** livre intéressant à lire; **r. lamp,** lampe de table; **r. room,** salle de lecture; **r. list,** liste de livres à lire *(b)* interprétation *f* (d'une énigme); lecture (d'un instrument de précision); relevé *m* (d'un compteur à gaz); **barometric r.,** hauteur *f* barométrique; **to take readings,** faire des relevés *m*; **what is your r. of the facts?** comment interprétez-vous les faits? **'read 'off** *vtr* lire (qch) d'un trait; relever (des cotes). **'read 'out** *vtr* lire (qch) à haute voix. **'read 'over, 'through** lire (d'un bout à l'autre); parcourir (rapidement). **'read 'up** *vtr & i* **to r. up (on) sth,** se documenter sur, étudier (un sujet).

readjust [ri:ə'dʒʌst] **1.** *vtr* rajuster **2.** *vi* se réadapter. **rea'djustment** *n* rajustement *m*.

ready ['redi] **1.** *a (-ier, -iest) (a)* prêt **(to do,** à faire); *Sp:* **r., steady, go!** à vos marques, prêts, partez! **to get sth r.,** préparer qch; **to get r.,** se préparer (**to,** à); **r. for use,** prêt à l'emploi; **r. for anything,** prêt à tout; **r. reckoner,** barème *m* (de calculs tout faits); **to be r. to face s.o.,** attendre qn de pied ferme; **r. to hand,** sous la main; **r. money,** argent comptant, liquide *(b)* prêt, disposé (à faire qch); **r. to die of hunger,** sur le point de mourir de faim *(c)* prompt; facile; **to be r. with an answer,** avoir la réplique prompte **2.** *adv* **r. dressed,** tout habillé; **table r. laid,** table toute préparée **3.** *n (of gun)* **at the r.,** paré à faire feu. **'readily** *adv* (faire qch) volontiers; (imaginer qch) facilement. **'readiness** *n* empressement *m* (à faire qch); bonne volonté; **r. of wit,** vivacité *f* d'esprit; **to be in r.,** être prêt. **'ready-'cooked** *a* (plat) tout cuit; (mets) à emporter. **'ready-'made** *a* (article) tout fait; (vêtement) de confection. **'ready-to-'wear** *a* **r.-to-w. clothes,** le prêt-à-porter.

real [ri(:)ol] **1.** *a (a)* vrai; **r. silk,** soie naturelle; **r. gold,** or véritable *(b)* véritable, réel; **a r. friend,** un vrai ami, un véritable ami; **it's the r. thing,** c'est authentique; c'est du vrai de vrai; **in r. life,** dans la réalité *(c)* r. **estate,** propriété immobilière **2.** *n F:* **for r.,** pour de vrai **3.** *adv NAm: F:* vraiment, très; **a r. fine day,** une très belle journée. **'realism** *n* réalisme *m*. **'realist** *a & n* réaliste *(mf)*. **rea'listic** *a* réaliste. **rea'listically** *adv* avec réalisme. **re'ality** [ri'æliti] *n (pl -ies)* la réalité; le réel; **in r.,** en réalité; **really** *adv* vraiment; réellement; **you r. must go,** il faut absolument que vous y alliez, que vous partiez; **is it r. true?** est-ce bien vrai? **not r.!** pas possible!

realize ['riəlaiz] *vtr (a)* réaliser (un projet, *Fin:* une propriété); *Com:* convertir (des biens) en espèces *(b)* bien comprendre (qch); se rendre compte de (qch). **reali'zation** *n (a)* réalisation *f* (d'un projet, *Fin:* d'une propriété); *Com:* conversion *f* en espèces (de biens) *(b)* conception nette, compréhension claire (d'un fait).

realm [relm] *n* royaume *m*; *Fig:* domaine *m* (de l'imagination).

realtor [ri'æltər] *n NAm: Rtm:* (*Br* = estate agent) agent immobilier.

ream [ri:m] *n* = rame *f* (de papier); *Fig:* **he's written reams,** il a écrit des pages et des pages.

reanimate [ri:'ænimeit] *vtr* ranimer, réanimer.

reap [ri:p] *vtr* moissonner (le blé, un champ); recueillir (le fruit de son travail); **to r. profit from sth,** tirer profit de qch. **'reaper** *n (pers)* moissonneur -euse; *(machine)* moissonneuse *f*; **r. binder,** moissonneuse-lieuse *f*.

reappear [ri:ə'piər] *vi* réapparaître, reparaître. **rea'ppearance** *n* réapparition *f*.

reappraisal [ri:ə'preizl] *n* réévaluation *f*.

rear¹ [riər] *n (a) Mil: (also* **rearguard***)* arrière-garde *f* (d'une armée); **to bring up the r.,** fermer la marche; **in, at, the r.,** en arrière, à l'arrière *(b)* arrière *m* (d'une maison); derrière *m*; dernier rang, queue *f* (d'un cortège) **2.** *a* (situé à l')arrière; d'arrière; postérieur; **r. admiral,** contre-amiral *m*; *Aut:* **r. view mirror,** rétroviseur *m*. **'rearguard** *n Mil:* arrière-garde; **r. action,** combat d'arrière-garde. **'rearmost** *a* dernier; de queue.

rear² **1.** *vtr* élever (une famille, des animaux); cultiver (des plantes) **2.** *vi (of horse)* **to r. (up),** se cabrer, se dresser.

rearm [ri:'ɑ:m] *vtr & i* réarmer. **re'armament** *n* réarmement *m*.

rearrange [ri:ə'reindʒ] *vtr* arranger de nouveau; remettre en ordre; réarranger. **rea'rrangement** *n* nouvel arrangement; remise *f* en ordre.

reason ['ri:zən] **1.** *n (a)* raison *f*, cause *f* (**for,** de); **for reasons best known to myself,** pour des raisons que je suis le seul à connaître; **for no r. at all,** sans motif; **the r. why,** la raison pour laquelle; le pourquoi; **you have r. to be glad,** vous avez des raisons de vous réjouir; **I have r. to believe that,** j'ai lieu de croire que; **everything within r.,** tout ce qui est raisonnable; **with (good) r.,** à bon droit; **all the more r. for going,** raison de plus pour y aller; **by r. of his infirmity,** à cause de, en raison de, son infirmité *(b)* raison; faculté *f* de raisonner; bon sens; **to lose one's r.,** perdre la raison; **to listen to r.,** entendre raison; **it stands to r.,** c'est évident; cela saute aux yeux **2.** *v (a) vi* **to r. with s.o.,** raisonner (avec) qn; **to r. that,** déduire que *(b) vtr* **to r.**

s.o. out of doing sth, faire entendre raison à qn. **'reasonable** a raisonnable; (offre) acceptable; (soupçon) bien fondé; (prix) modéré; **you must be r.,** il faut vous raisonner. **'reasonableness** n caractère m raisonnable; raison; modération f. **'reasonably** adv raisonnablement; **r. priced,** d'un prix abordable; **r. fit,** en assez bonne santé. **'reasoned** a (of analysis) raisonné; motivé; raisonnable. **'reasoning** n raisonnement m.

reassemble [ri:ə'sembl] 1. vtr rassembler; remonter, remettre (une machine) en état 2. vi se rassembler; **school reassembles tomorrow,** c'est demain la rentrée (des classes).

reassure [ri:ə'ʃuər] vtr rassurer, tranquilliser (qn) (**on, about,** sur); **to feel reassured,** se rassurer. **rea'ssurance** n réconfort m. **rea'ssuring** a rassurant.

reawaken [ri:ə'weikən] 1. vtr réveiller (qn) de nouveau 2. vi se réveiller de nouveau.

rebate ['ri:beit] n rabais m, escompte m.

rebel 1. a & n ['rebəl] rebelle (mf); insurgé, -ée 2. vi [ri'bel] (**rebelled**) se rebeller, se soulever (**against, contre**). **re'bellion** n rébellion f, révolte f (**against, contre**). **re'bellious** a rebelle. **re'belliousness** n esprit m de rébellion.

rebound 1. vi [ri'baund] rebondir 2. n ['ri:baund] rebond m, rebondissement m; retour m brusque; ricochet m (d'une balle).

rebuff [ri'bʌf] 1. n rebuffade f 2. vtr repousser.

rebuild [ri:'bild] vtr (**rebuilt**) rebâtir, reconstruire.

rebuke [ri'bju:k] 1. n réprimande f, reproche m 2. vtr réprimander (qn).

recalcitrant [ri'kælsitrənt] a récalcitrant.

recall [ri'kɔ:l] 1. n (a) rappel m (de qn, d'un souvenir); **total r.,** capacité f de se souvenir de tous les détails de qch (b) rétractation f, révocation f; **decision past r.,** décision irrévocable; **lost beyond r.,** perdu irrévocablement 2. vtr (a) rappeler (un ambassadeur, qch à qn); **I don't r. his name,** je ne me souviens pas de son nom; **to r. sth (to mind),** se rappeler qch (b) annuler (un jugement).

recapitulate [ri:kə'pitjuleit], F: **recap** ['ri:kæp] (**recapped**) vtr & i récapituler. **recapitu'lation,** F: **'recap** n récapitulation f; résumé m; **let's do a recap,** faisons le point.

recapture [ri:'kæptʃər] vtr reprendre; retrouver (sa joie); recréer.

recast [ri:'kɑ:st] vtr (**recast**) refondre (une cloche); refaire (une pièce, un roman); redistribuer les rôles (d'une pièce).

recede [ri'si:d] vi s'éloigner, reculer; (of forehead) fuir; **his hair is receding,** ses tempes se dégarnissent. **re'ceding** a qui s'éloigne; **r. tide,** marée descendante; **r. forehead,** front fuyant.

receipt [ri'si:t] 1. n (a) pl recettes fpl (b) réception f; **on r. of this letter,** au reçu, dès réception, de cette lettre; **to acknowledge r. of a letter,** accuser réception d'une lettre; **to pay on r.,** payer à la réception; Com: **I am in r. of your letter of 4th March,** j'ai bien reçu votre lettre du 4 mars (c) (document) reçu m, récépissé m, quittance f; **to give a r. for sth,** donner acquit de qch 2. vtr Com: acquitter (une facture).

receive [ri'si:v] vtr (a) recevoir; toucher (de l'argent); essuyer (un refus); WTel: capter (un poste); Jur:

receler (des objets volés); (on receipt) **received with thanks,** pour acquit; **to be well received,** trouver un accueil chaleureux; **to r. s.o. with open arms,** accueillir qn à bras ouverts; (of guilty pers) **to r. 30 days,** être condamné à un mois de prison. **re'ceived** a reçu; Ling: **r. pronunciation,** prononciation des gens cultivés. **re'ceiver** n (a) personne f qui reçoit (qch); destinataire mf (d'une lettre); réceptionnaire mf (d'un envoi); receleur, -euse (d'objets volés); (in bankruptcy) **the (official) r.,** l'administrateur m judiciaire; (in Fr) = syndic m de faillite (b) récepteur m (de téléphone); **to lift the r.,** décrocher (le combiné). **re'ceiving** n réception f; recel m (d'objets volés).

recent ['ri:sənt] a récent; nouveau; frais; **of r. date,** de fraîche date. **'recently** adv récemment; tout dernièrement; **as r. as yesterday,** pas plus tard qu'hier; **until quite r.,** jusqu'à ces derniers temps.

receptacle [ri'septəkl] n récipient m.

reception [ri'sepʃn] n (a) réception f; (in hotel) **r. (desk),** la réception; WTel: **the r. is poor in the evenings,** le soir, la réception est médiocre (b) (welcome) accueil m; **the play had a warm r.,** la pièce a été favorablement accueillie; **r. centre,** centre d'accueil (pour réfugiés). **re'ceptionist** n réceptionniste mf.

receptive [ri'septiv] a réceptif. **recep'tivity** n réceptivité f.

recess [ri'ses] 1. n (pl **recesses**) (a) vacances fpl parlementaires; NAm: Sch: (Br = **break**) récréation f; NAm: Jur: (Br = **adjournment**) suspension f (d'audience) (b) recoin m; enfoncement m (de muraille); embrasure f (de fenêtre); niche f (de statue); alcôve f 2. vi (**recesses**) NAm: (of assembly) suspendre la séance. **re'cession** n récession f.

recharge [ri:'tʃɑ:dʒ] vtr recharger (une batterie). **re'chargeable** a rechargeable, qui peut être rechargé.

recipe ['resipi] n Cu: recette f.

recipient [ri'sipiənt] n (pers) donataire mf; destinataire mf (d'une lettre); bénéficiaire mf (d'un chèque).

reciprocate [ri'siprəkeit] 1. vtr se rendre mutuellement (des services); payer de retour (un sentiment); **to r. s.o.'s kindness,** rendre l'amabilité de qn 2. vi retourner le compliment. **re'ciprocal** a réciproque, mutuel. **re'ciprocally** adv réciproquement, mutuellement. **reciprocity** [resi'prɔsiti] n réciprocité f.

recite [ri'sait] 1. vtr & i réciter 2. vtr énumérer (des dates, des détails). **re'cital** n récit m (d'un incident); énumération f (de détails); récitation f (d'une poésie); Mus: récital m. **reci'tation** n récitation f. **recitative** [resitə'ti:v] n Mus: récitatif m.

reckless ['reklis] a insouciant (**of,** de); imprudent; téméraire; Aut: **r. driving,** conduite imprudente. **'recklessly** adv témérairement; avec insouciance; imprudemment; **he spends r.,** il dépense sans compter. **'recklessness** n insouciance f (**of,** de); imprudence f, témérité f.

reckon ['rekən] vtr & i compter, calculer; estimer, juger; **to r. s.o. as,** considérer qn comme; **to r. on sth,** compter sur qch; **to have to r. with s.o.,** avoir affaire à qn; **a man to be reckoned with,** un homme avec qui il faut compter; **he had reckoned without his rivals,** il avait compté sans ses rivaux. **'reckoner** n **ready r.,**

barème *m* (de calculs tout faits). **'reckoning** *n* compte *m*, calcul *m*; **to be out in one's r.,** s'être trompé dans son calcul; **to the best of my r.,** autant que je puis en juger; **day of r.,** jour d'expiation.

reclaim [ri'kleim] *vtr* défricher (du terrain); assécher (un marais); récupérer (un sous-produit); réclamer (qch); **reclaimed land,** terrain reconquis. **recla'mation** [reklə-] *n* défrichement *m* (d'un terrain); assèchement *m* (des terres); récupération *f* (des sous-produits).

recline [ri'klain] 1. *vtr* reposer, appuyer (sa tête sur qch) 2. *vi* être couché, étendu; (*of head*) reposer, être appuyé (**on, sur**); **reclining on a couch,** étendu sur un canapé. **re'clining** *a* (siège) (à dossier) réglable.

recluse [ri'klu:s] *n* reclus, -use.

recognize ['rekəgnaiz] *vtr* reconnaître (qn, qch); **to r. one's mistake,** reconnaître, admettre, son erreur; **I don't r. you,** je ne vous remets pas; **to r. s.o. by his walk,** reconnaître qn à sa démarche. **recog'nition** *n* reconnaissance *f*; **he has changed beyond, out of, all r.,** il a tellement changé qu'il est méconnaissable; **in r. of,** en reconnaissance de. **recog'nizable** *a* reconnaissable. **'recognized** *a* reconnu, admis, reçu; **the r. term,** le terme consacré; *Com:* **r. agent,** agent accrédité.

recoil 1. *n* ['ri:kɔil] recul *m* (d'une arme à feu); mouvement *m* de recul, répugnance *f* (de qn) 2. *vi* [ri'kɔil] (*a*) (*of spring*) se détendre; (*of firearm*) reculer (*b*) (*of pers*) reculer (**from,** devant); se révolter (**from,** contre).

recollect [rekə'lekt] *vtr* se rappeler; se souvenir de (qch); **as far as I r.,** autant qu'il m'en souvienne. **reco'llection** *n* souvenir *m*; **to the best of my r.,** autant que je m'en souvienne.

recommend [rekə'mend] *vtr* recommander; conseiller (à qn de faire qch); **she has little to r. her,** elle n'a pas grand-chose pour elle; **not to be recommended,** à déconseiller. **recommen'dation** *n* recommandation *f*.

recompense ['rekəmpens] 1. *n* (*a*) récompense *f* (**for, de**) (*b*) dédommagement *m* (**for, de**) 2. *vtr* (*a*) récompenser (**s.o. for sth,** qn de qch) (*b*) dédommager (**s.o. for sth,** qn de qch).

reconcile ['rekənsail] *vtr* (*a*) réconcilier (deux personnes); **to become reconciled,** se réconcilier; **to r. oneself to sth,** se résigner à qch; **to r. s.o. to sth,** faire accepter qch à qn (*b*) concilier, faire accorder (des faits). **recon'cilable** *a* conciliable (**with,** avec). **reconcili'ation** [-sili-] *n* réconciliation *f* (entre deux personnes); conciliation *f* (d'opinions contraires).

recondite ['rekəndait] *a* (*of knowledge*) profond; (*of style*) obscur.

recondition [ri:kən'diʃn] *vtr* rénover; remettre à neuf, en état; *Com:* reconditionner; **reconditioned engine,** moteur révisé.

reconnaissance [ri'kɔnisəns] *n* *Mil:* reconnaissance *f*; **r. aircraft,** avion de reconnaissance.

reconnoitre, *NAm:* **reconnoiter** [rekə'nɔitər] 1. *vtr* reconnaître (le terrain) 2. *vi* faire une reconnaissance.

reconsider [ri:kən'sidər] *vtr* reconsidérer, considérer de nouveau, repenser (une question); revenir sur (une décision).

reconstruct [ri:kən'strʌkt] *vtr* reconstruire (un édifice); reconstituer (un crime). **recon'struction** *n* reconstruction *f*; reconstitution *f* (d'un crime).

record 1. *n* ['rekɔ:d] (*a*) *Jur:* enregistrement *m* (d'un fait); **to be on r.,** être enregistré; **to go on r. as a pacifist,** se déclarer pacifiste; (**to say sth**) **off the r.,** (dire qch) en confidence, hors antenne (*b*) minute *f* (d'un acte) (*c*) note *f*, mention *f*; **to make, keep, a r. of sth,** noter, faire une note de, qch; **for the r., to keep the r. straight,** pour mémoire (*d*) registre *m*; **r. of attendances,** registre de présence (*e*) *pl* archives *fpl*, annales *fpl* (*f*) monument *m*, document *m*, souvenir *m* (de qch) (*g*) dossier *m* (de qn); *Med:* fiche *f* (de patient); **service r.,** état *m* de service; **his past r.,** sa conduite passée; **police r.,** casier *m* judiciaire (*h*) *Sp:* record *m*; **world r.,** record mondial; **at r. speed,** à une vitesse record; **in r. time,** en un temps record; **to break the r.,** battre le record; **r. holder,** détenteur, -trice (d'un record) (*i*) disque *m*; **long-playing r.,** 33 tours *m inv*; **r. library,** discothèque *f*; **r. player,** tourne-disque *m* 2. *vtr* [ri'kɔ:d] (*a*) enregistrer (un fait); prendre acte de (qch); rapporter (des événements); *Adm:* recenser (des faits); (*of thermometer*) marquer (*b*) enregistrer (une chanson, une émission, sur bande). **'record-breaking** *a* (succès) qui bat tous les records. **re'corder** *n* (*a*) *Jur:* = juge *m* (*b*) **tape r.,** magnétophone *m*; **cassette r.,** enregistreur *m*, magnétophone *m*, à cassette(s) (*c*) *Mus:* flûte *f* à bec. **re'cording** 1. *a* enregistreur 2. *n* enregistrement *m*; **tape r.,** enregistrement sur bande.

recount¹ [ri'kaunt] *vtr* raconter.

recount² 1. *vtr* [ri:'kaunt] recompter 2. *n* ['ri:kaunt] *Pol:* nouveau dépouillement du scrutin.

recoup [ri'ku:p] *vtr* **to r. one's losses,** récupérer ses pertes.

recourse [ri'kɔ:s] *n* (*a*) recours *m*; **to have r. to sth,** avoir recours, recourir, à qch (*b*) expédient *m*.

recover¹ [ri'kʌvər] 1. *vtr* (*a*) recouvrer; retrouver (un objet perdu, son appétit); repêcher (un noyé); récupérer (des sous-produits, son argent); regagner (de l'argent perdu); rentrer en possession de (ses biens); rattraper (le temps perdu); **to r. one's breath,** reprendre haleine; **to r. lost ground,** regagner, refaire, le terrain perdu; se rattraper; **to r. one's health,** se rétablir; **to r. consciousness,** reprendre connaissance 2. *vi* (*a*) guérir, se rétablir, se remettre (**from an illness,** d'une maladie) (*b*) reprendre connaissance (*c*) **to r. from one's astonishment,** revenir, se remettre, de son étonnement (*d*) **to r. (oneself),** se remettre, se ressaisir (*e*) (*of market*) se ranimer, reprendre. **re'coverable** *a* récupérable. **re'covery** *n* (*a*) recouvrement *m* (d'un objet perdu); récupération *f* (de sous-produits); *Jur:* obtention *f* (de dommages-intérêts) (*b*) rétablissement *m*, guérison *f* (de qn); **to be past r.,** être dans un état désespéré; **he is making a good r.,** il est en bonne voie de guérison (*c*) redressement *m* (économique).

recover² [ri'kʌvər] *vtr* recouvrir (un canapé).

recreation [rekri'eiʃn] *n* récréation *f*; divertissement *m*; **r. ground,** terrain de jeux. **recre'ational** *a* (terrain) de jeux.

recrimination [rikrimi'neiʃn] *n* récrimination *f*.

recruit [ri'kru:t] 1. *n* recrue *f* 2. *vtr* recruter (une armée, des partisans). **re'cruiting, re'cruitment** *n* *Mil:* recrutement *m*.

rectangle [ˈrektæŋgl] n rectangle m. **recˈtangular** a rectangulaire.

rectify [ˈrektifai] vtr (**rectified**) rectifier, corriger (une erreur); réparer (un oubli). **rectifiˈcation** n rectification f.

rector [ˈrektər] n Ecc: = curé m; Sch: recteur m (d'une université); directeur m (d'un collège). **ˈrectory** n = presbytère m.

recumbent [riˈkʌmbənt] a couché, étendu; (on tomb) **r. figure**, gisant m.

recuperate [riˈk(j)uːpəreit] 1. vtr récupérer 2. vi se rétablir; se remettre (d'une maladie). **recupeˈration** n récupération f (de chaleur); rétablissement m (d'un malade).

recur [riˈkəːr] vi (**recurred**) se reproduire, se renouveler; (of occasion) se représenter. **recurrence** [-ˈkʌr-] n réapparition f, retour m; récidive f (d'une maladie). **recurrent** [-ˈkʌr-] a périodique; qui revient souvent; Mth: **r. series**, série récurrente. **reˈcurring** a périodique.

recycle [riːˈsaikl] vtr recycler (les vieux papiers).

red [red] a & n (**redder, reddest**) rouge (m); (of hair) roux; **to turn, go, r.**, rougir; **to see r.**, voir rouge, se mettre en colère; **it's like a r. rag to a bull**, c'est comme le rouge pour le taureau; **r. light**, feu rouge; Fig: **to see the r. light**, sentir le danger; Fig: **r. tape**, bureaucratie f; paperasserie f; **to be in the r.**, être déficitaire. **ˈredˈblooded** a vigoureux. **ˈredbreast** n Orn: (**robin**) r., rouge-gorge m. **ˈredbrick** a **r. university**, université provinciale moderne. **ˈredcurrant** n groseille f rouge. **ˈredden** 1. vtr rendre rouge; rougir 2. vi (of pers) rougir; (of sky) rougeoyer; (of leaves) roussir. **ˈreddish** a rougeâtre; (of hair) roussâtre. **ˈredˈeyed** a aux yeux rouges. **ˈredˈfaced** a rougeaud; rougissant (de gêne). **ˈredˈhaired, ˈredˈheaded** a roux. **ˈredˈhanded** a **to be caught r.-h.**, être pris en flagrant délit. **ˈredhead** n roux m, rousse f. **ˈredˈhot** a chauffé au rouge; (révolutionnaire) ardent. **ˈredˈletter** a **r.-l. day**, jour à marquer d'une pierre blanche. **ˈredˈlight** a **r.-l. district**, quartier réservé (des bordels). **ˈredness** n rougeur f; rousseur f (des cheveux). **ˈredskin** n Ethn: Peau-Rouge mf. **ˈredwood** n Bot: séquoia m.

redecorate [riːˈdekəreit] vtr repeindre et retapisser (une pièce).

redeem [riˈdiːm] vtr (a) racheter; rembourser (une obligation); dégager (une propriété hypothéquée); tenir (une promesse); amortir (une dette); purger (une hypothèque); **to r. one's watch (from pawn)**, retirer sa montre (b) libérer, racheter; **his good points r. his faults**, ses qualités compensent ses défauts; **to r. oneself**, se racheter. **reˈdeemer** n **the R.**, le Rédempteur. **reˈdeeming** a rédempteur; qui compense (un défaut). **reˈdemption** n Fin: remboursement m, amortissement m (d'une obligation); rédemption f (du genre humain); **crime past r.**, crime irréparable.

redirect [riːdaiˈrekt] vtr faire suivre (une lettre).

redouble [riːˈdʌbl] vtr redoubler (ses efforts).

redoubt [riˈdaut] n Fort: redoute f.

redoubtable [riˈdautəbl] a redoutable, formidable.

redress [riˈdres] 1. n redressement m, réparation f (d'un tort); réforme f (d'un abus); **legal r.**, réparation légale 2. vtr rétablir (l'équilibre); redresser, réparer (un tort); corriger, réformer (un abus).

reduce [riˈdjuːs] 1. vtr (a) réduire, rapetisser; (in length) raccourcir; Cu: (faire) réduire (une sauce) (b) réduire (la température); diminuer, baisser (le prix); **to r. speed**, réduire la vitesse; ralentir la marche; Ind: **to r. output**, ralentir la production; **to r. sth to ashes**, réduire qch en cendres; **to r. s.o. to silence**, faire taire qn; Med: **to r. a fracture, a dislocation**, réduire une fracture, une luxation; Mil: **to r. s.o. to the ranks**, casser qn 2. vi (to lose weight) maigrir. **reˈduced** a réduit; **at r. prices**, au rabais; en solde; **in r. circumstances**, dans la gêne. **reˈduction** n réduction f, diminution f (des prix); baisse f (de température); Com: rabais m; **to make a r. on an article**, faire un rabais sur un article.

redundant [riˈdʌndənt] a (a) (mot) redondant (b) surabondant; (personnel) superflu; (ouvriers) en surnombre; (of worker) **to be made r.**, être licencié. **reˈdundancy** n surplus m; excédent m; surnombre m; (of workers) licenciement m; **r. payment**, indemnité de licenciement.

re-echo [riːˈekou] v (**re-echoed**) 1. vtr répéter, renvoyer (un son) 2. vi retentir, résonner.

reed [riːd] n Bot: roseau m; jonc m (à balais); Mus: pipeau m; anche f (de hautbois); (in orchestra) **r. instruments, the reeds**, les instruments m à anche. **ˈreedy** a (**-ier, -iest**) (endroit) couvert de roseaux; **r. voice**, voix flûtée, ténue.

reef[1] [riːf] Nau: 1. n ris m; **r. knot**, nœud plat 2. vtr prendre un ris dans (une voile).

reef[2] n (a) récif m; Fig: écueil m; **coral r.**, récif de corail (b) Min: filon m.

reek [riːk] 1. n odeur forte, âcre; **r. of tobacco**, relent m de tabac 2. vi sentir mauvais; **to r. of garlic**, puer, empester, l'ail.

reel [riːl] 1. n (a) dévidoir m (pour tuyaux, câbles); bobine f (pour fil); moulinet m (de canne à pêche); Cin: bobine (de film) (b) danse écossaise 2. v (a) vtr dévider (le fil) (b) vi tournoyer; (stagger) chanceler, tituber; **my head's reeling**, la tête me tourne; **to make s.o.'s senses r.**, donner le vertige à qn. **reel ˈin** vtr remonter (un poisson). **ˈreel ˈoff** vtr débiter rapidement (des vers).

re-elect [riːiˈlekt] vtr réélire. **re-eˈlection** n réélection f.

re-embark [riːimˈbɑːk] vtr & i rembarquer. **re-embarˈkation** n rembarquement m.

re-enact [riːinˈækt] vtr reconstituer (une scène).

re-enter [riːˈentər] 1. vi rentrer; **to re-e. for an exam**, se représenter à un examen 2. vtr rentrer dans (un endroit). **re-ˈentry** n (pl **-ies**) rentrée f.

ref abbr (a) reference (b) F: referee.

refectory [riˈfektəri] n (pl **refectories**) réfectoire m.

refer [riˈfəːr] v (**referred**) 1. vtr rapporter, rattacher (un fait à une cause); **to r. a matter to s.o.**, en référer à qn; **to r. a matter to a tribunal**, soumettre une affaire à un tribunal; Bank: **to r. a cheque to drawer**, refuser d'honorer un chèque; **to r. s.o. to s.o.**, renvoyer qn à qn 2. vi (a) se référer, s'en rapporter (à une autorité); **to r. to a work**, consulter un ouvrage; **referring to your letter**, comme suite à votre lettre (b) faire allusion (à qn); **I'm not referring to you**, je ne parle pas de vous; (of statement) **to r. to sth**, se rapporter, avoir rapport, à qch; **this remark refers to you**, cette remarque vous concerne; **to r. to a fact,** faire mention d'un fait; **let's not r. to it again,** n'en reparlons plus. **referee** [refə'ri:] **1.** n (a) Sp: (F: **ref**) arbitre m (b) personne f à qui on peut s'en rapporter pour avoir des références sur qn; **to give s.o. as a r.,** se recommander de qn **2.** vtr & i Sp: remplir les fonctions d'arbitre; arbitrer (un match). **reference** ['refrəns] n (a) renvoi m, référence f (d'une question à une autorité); compétence f (d'un tribunal); **terms of r.,** mandat m (d'une commission); **r. library,** bibliothèque de référence; **r. book, work of r.,** livre, ouvrage, de référence; ouvrage à consulter; **with r. to my letter,** me référant à, comme suite à, ma lettre; **r. was made to this conversation,** on a fait allusion à cette conversation; **to make r. to a fact,** faire mention d'un fait; **to have r. to sth,** avoir rapport à qch; **in, with, r. to your letter,** en ce qui concerne votre lettre; **without r. to,** sans tenir compte de (b) renvoi m (dans un livre); (on map) **r. point,** point coté, point de référence; **coordonnée** f (c) usu pl renseignements mpl, références fpl (d'employé); **to give a r. about s.o.,** fournir des renseignements sur qn; **to have good references,** avoir de bonnes références; **to give s.o. as a r.,** se recommander de qn. **refe'rendum** n référendum m.

refill 1. vtr [ri:'fil] remplir (qch) (à nouveau) **2.** n ['ri:fil] recharge f, cartouche f (d'encre, de stylo); mine f de rechange (pour porte-mine); recharge (pour classeur). **re'fillable** a (briquet) rechargeable.

refine [ri'fain] v **1.** vtr raffiner (les métaux) **2.** vi se raffiner. **re'fined** a (or) fin, affiné; (sucre, goût) raffiné; (homme) cultivé, distingué. **re'finement** n raffinement m (d'une personne, des métaux); perfectionnement m (d'une machine). **re'finer** n raffineur, -euse. **re'finery** n (pl -ies) raffinerie f. **re'fining** n raffinage m (du pétrole, du sucre); affinage m (des métaux).

refit Nau: **1.** n ['ri:fit] radoub m **2.** vtr [ri:'fit] (**refitted**) remettre en état de service.

reflate [ri:'fleit] vtr relancer (l'économie). **re'flation** n relance f économique.

reflect [ri'flekt] **1.** vtr (of surface) réfléchir, refléter (la lumière, une image); renvoyer (la chaleur, la lumière); **to be reflected,** se réfléchir; (of behaviour) **to be reflected on s.o.,** rejaillir, se refléter, sur qn **2.** vi (think) **to r. (up)on,** méditer sur; réfléchir à, sur; **to r. that,** penser, se dire, que; (of action) faire du tort (**on s.o.,** à qn); nuire à (la réputation de) (qn). **re'flection** n (a) réflexion f (de la lumière, de la chaleur) (b) reflet m, image f (réfléchie) (c) (thought) réflexion f; pl réflexions, pensées fpl, considérations fpl; **this is a r. on your character,** c'est une atteinte à votre intégrité; **to cast reflections on s.o.,** faire des réflexions sur qn; **on r.,** (toute) réflexion faite; **to do sth without due r.,** faire qch sans avoir suffisamment réfléchi. **re'flector** n réflecteur m; Cy: catadioptre m, cataphote m.

reflex ['ri:fleks] **1.** n (pl reflexes) Med: réflexe m **2.** a (of movement) réflexe; Phot: **single lens r. (camera),** (appareil m) réflex m; Mth: **r. angle,** angle rentrant.

reflexive [ri'fleksiv] a & n Gram: **r. (verb),** verbe réfléchi; **r. pronoun,** pronom (personnel) réfléchi.

refloat [ri:'flout] vtr renflouer, (re)mettre à flot (un navire échoué).

reform [ri'fɔ:m] **1.** v (a) vtr réformer; corriger (qn) (b) vi se corriger **2.** n réforme f. **refor'mation** [refə-]

n réforme; Hist: **the R.,** la Réforme, la Réformation. **re'formatory** n Hist: maison f de correction. **re'former** n réformateur, -trice.

refractory [ri'fræktəri] a réfractaire.

refrain¹ [ri'frein] n Mus: refrain m.

refrain² vi se retenir, s'abstenir (**from,** de); **he could not r. from smiling,** il n'a pas pu s'empêcher de sourire.

refresh [ri'freʃ] vtr rafraîchir; (of rest) délasser (qn); **to awake refreshed,** s'éveiller bien reposé; **to r. oneself,** se rafraîchir; se restaurer. **re'fresher** n Sch: **r. course,** cours de recyclage m. **re'freshing** a rafraîchissant; réparateur; (sommeil) reposant. **re'freshment** n rafraîchissement m; Rail: **r. room,** buffet m.

refrigerator [ri'fridʒəreitər] n réfrigérateur m; frigidaire m (Rtm:) F: frigo m. **re'frigerate** vtr réfrigérer; frigorifier. **refrige'ration** n réfrigération f.

refuel [ri:'fjuəl] v (**refuelled**) **1.** vtr ravitailler (en combustible) (un avion, un navire) **2.** vi se ravitailler (en combustible). **re'fuelling** n ravitaillement m (en combustible).

refuge ['refju:dʒ] n refuge m, abri m (**from,** contre); **place of r.,** lieu d'asile m; **to take r.,** se réfugier. **refu'gee** n réfugié, -ée.

refund 1. vtr [ri:'fʌnd] rembourser (qn, de l'argent à qn); ristourner (un paiement en trop) **2.** n ['ri:fʌnd] remboursement m; Adm: ristourne f; **to get a r.,** se faire rembourser.

refurbish [ri:'fə:biʃ] vtr remettre à neuf, rénover.

refuse¹ ['refju:s] n déchets mpl (du marché, de fabrique); **household r.,** ordures ménagères; **town r.,** ordures; **garden r.,** détritus m de jardin; **r. bin,** poubelle f; boîte à ordures; **r. dump,** décharge publique; **r. collection,** service de voirie.

refuse² [ri'fju:z] vtr & i refuser (une offre, un don); rejeter, repousser (une requête); **to r. s.o. sth,** refuser qch à qn; **to r. to do sth,** refuser de faire qch; se refuser à faire qch. **re'fusal** n (a) refus m; **to give a flat r.,** refuser (tout) net (b) droit m de refuser; **to have the first r. of sth,** avoir la première offre de qch.

refute [ri'fju:t] vtr réfuter; **to r. a statement,** démontrer la fausseté d'une déclaration.

regain [ri'gein] vtr regagner; recouvrer (la liberté); **to r. possession of sth,** rentrer en possession de qch; **to r. consciousness,** reprendre connaissance, revenir à soi.

regal ['ri:gəl] a royal. **'regally** adv royalement.

regale [ri'geil] vtr régaler (**s.o. with a good meal,** qn d'un bon repas).

regard [ri'gɑ:d] **1.** n (a) égard m (**to, for,** à pour); attention f (**to, for,** à); **in, with, r. to,** quant à; **in this r.,** à cet égard; **to have no r. for human life,** faire peu de cas de la vie humaine; **having r. to,** si l'on tient compte de; **without r. for, to, race or colour,** sans distinction de race ni de couleur (b) égard, respect m, estime f; **to have (a) great r. for s.o.,** tenir qn en haute estime; **out of r. for s.o.,** par égard pour qn; **give my kind regards to your brother,** faites mes amitiés à votre frère **2.** vtr (a) considérer, regarder (**as,** comme); **to r. sth with suspicion,** avoir des soupçons au sujet de qch (b) regarder, concerner; **as regards,** en ce qui concerne. **re'garding** prep concernant; quant à; **r. your enquiry,** en ce qui concerne votre demande; **questions**

r. **France**, questions relatives à la France.
re'gardless 1. *a* peu soigneux (of, de); indifférent (of, à); r. **of expense**, sans regarder à la dépense **2.** *adv* sans se soucier (of, de); *F:* **press on r.**! allez-y quand même!

regatta [ri'gætə] *n* régates *fpl.*

regenerate [ri'dʒenəreit] **1.** *vtr* régénérer **2.** *vi* se régénérer. **regene'ration** *n* régénération *f.*

regent ['ri:dʒənt] *n* régent, -ente; **prince r.**, prince régent. **'regency** *n* (*pl* -**ies**) régence *f;* **R. armchair**, fauteuil régence.

reggae ['regei] *n Mus:* reggae *m.*

regime [rei'ʒi:m] *n* régime *m;* **the parliamentary r.**, le régime parlementaire.

regiment ['redʒimənt] *n* régiment *m.* **regi'mental** *a* du régiment, de régiment; régimentaire. **'regi-mented** *a* réglementé.

region ['ri:dʒən] *n* région *f;* **the car cost in the r. of £1000**, la voiture a coûté dans l'ordre de, dans les, mille livres sterling. **'regional** *a* régional.

register ['redʒistər] **I.** *n* (*a*) registre *m;* étendue *f* (de la voix) (*b*) compteur *m* (kilométrique, de vitesse); **cash r.**, caisse (enregistreuse); **r. office** = **registry office. II.** *v* **1.** *vtr* (*a*) enregistrer; inscrire (un nom); immatriculer (une voiture); faire enregistrer (une société); déclarer (une naissance); déposer (une marque de fabrique) (*b*) enregistrer (des bagages); recommander (une lettre) (*c*) (*of thermometer*) marquer (*d*) manifester, enregistrer (une émotion) **2.** *vi* s'inscrire sur le registre (d'un hôtel); se faire inscrire (**with the police**, à la police); *F:* **his name didn't r. with me**, son nom ne me disait rien; *F:* **it didn't r. (with her)**, elle n'a rien pigé. **'registered** *a* enregistré, inscrit, immatriculé; *Com:* (modèle) déposé; *Post:* **r. letter**, lettre recommandée; **r. parcel**, envoi en recommandé; **State r. nurse**, infirmière diplômée d'État. **regis'trar** *n Jur:* greffier *m; Adm:* officier *m* d'état civil; *Sch:* secrétaire *mf* et archiviste *mf* (d'une université); *Med:* interne *mf* (d'hôpital). **regi'stration** *n* enregistrement *m,* inscription *f;* immatriculation *f* (d'une voiture); recommandation *f* (d'une lettre); dépôt *m* (d'une marque de fabrique); **r. of luggage**, enregistrement des bagages; *Aut:* **r. number**, numéro d'immatriculation, minéralogique; **car with r. number SPF 342X**, voiture immatriculée SPF 342X; **r. fee**, *Post:* taxe de recommandation; *Adm:* droit d'inscription. **'registry** *n* **r. office**, bureau *m* de l'état civil; **to be married at a r. office** = se marier civilement, à la mairie.

regret [ri'gret] **1.** *n* regret *m;* **to have no regrets**, n'avoir aucun regret; ne rien regretter; **I say so with r.**, je le dis à regret; **much to my r.**, à mon grand regret **2.** *vtr* (**regretted**) regretter; **I r. to have to tell you**, je regrette d'avoir à vous dire; **I r. to have to inform you that**, j'ai le regret d'avoir à vous annoncer que; **we very much r. to hear**, nous sommes désolés d'apprendre; **it is to be regretted that**, il est regrettable, à regretter, que. **re'gretful** *a* (*of pers*) plein de regrets; (sentiment) de regret. **re'gretfully** *adv* avec regret, à regret. **re'grettable** *a* regrettable. **re'grettably** *adv* regrettablement.

regular ['regjulər] **1.** *a* (*a*) régulier; **as r. as clockwork**, réglé, exact, comme une horloge; **my r. time for going to bed**, l'heure habituelle à laquelle je me couche; **to do**

sth **as a r. thing**, faire qch régulièrement; **r. customer**, habitué, -ée; **r. staff**, employés permanents (*b*) réglé, rangé; **man of r. habits**, homme rangé dans ses habitudes (*c*) régulier, dans les règles; réglementaire; ordinaire; normal; **r. troops**, troupes régulières; **r. officer**, officier de carrière (*d*) *NAm:* **r. wine**, vin ordinaire (*e*) *F:* (*intensive*) vrai, véritable; **a r. hero**, un vrai héros; **a r. swindle**, une véritable escroquerie **2.** *n* (*a*) militaire de carrière (*b*) *F:* habitué, -ée (d'un restaurant). **regu'larity** *n* régularité *f.* **'regula-rize** *vtr* régulariser (un document, une situation). **'regularly** *adv* régulièrement. **'regulate** *vtr* régler. **regu'lation** *n* (*a*) réglage *m* (d'une machine) (*b*) règlement *m;* ordonnance *f;* **r. uniform**, uniforme réglementaire. **'regulator** *n* régulateur *m.*

rehabilitate [ri:(h)ə'biliteit] *vtr* réhabiliter; rééduquer (des handicapés); réadapter (des mutilés, des réfugiés). **rehabili'tation** *n* réhabilitation *f;* rééducation *f* (des mutilés); réadaptation *f;* **r. centre**, centre de rééducation professionnelle.

rehash 1. *n* ['ri:hæʃ] réchauffé *m* **2.** *vtr* [ri:'hæʃ] remanier (un vieux conte, une œuvre).

rehearse [ri'hə:s] *vtr & i* répéter (une pièce). **re'hearsal** *n Th:* répétition *f;* **dress r.**, (répétition) générale *f;* avant-première *f.*

rehouse [ri:'hauz] *vtr* reloger.

reign [rein] **1.** *n* règne *m;* **in the r. of George VI**, sous le règne de Georges VI **2.** *vi* régner (**over**, sur). **'reign-ing** *a* régnant.

reimburse [ri:im'bə:s] *vtr* rembourser. **reim'bursement** *n* remboursement *m.*

rein [rein] *f;* guide *f;* **to hold the reins of government**, tenir les rênes du gouvernement; **to give (free) r. to**, lâcher la bride à; **to give free r. to one's imagination**, donner libre cours *m* à son imagination; **to keep a tight r. on s.o.**, tenir la bride serrée à qn.

reincarnation [ri:inka:'neiʃn] *n* réincarnation *f.*

reindeer ['reindiər] *n inv in pl Z:* renne *m.*

reinforce [ri:in'fɔ:s] *vtr* renforcer; consolider (un bâtiment); arc-bouter (un mur); appuyer (une demande); **reinforced concrete**, béton armé. **rein'forcement** *n* renforcement *m;* renforçage *m* (d'un bâtiment); armature *f* (du béton); *Mil: usu pl* renforts *mpl.*

reinstate [ri:in'steit] *vtr* réintégrer (qn dans ses fonctions); rétablir (un fonctionnaire, qch); remettre (qch). **rein'statement** *n* réintégration *f* (de qn); rétablissement *m.*

reiterate [ri:'itəreit] *vtr* réitérer, répéter. **reite'ration** *n* réitération *f,* répétition *f.*

reject 1. *vtr* [ri'dʒekt] rejeter, repousser (qch); refuser (qch, un candidat); *Ind:* mettre (une pièce) au rebut **2.** *n* ['ri:dʒekt] article *m,* pièce *f,* de rebut; **export r.**, article de rebut non exportable. **re'jection** *n* rejet *m;* refus *m* (d'une offre); *Publ:* **r. slip**, note refusant un manuscrit.

rejoice [ri'dʒɔis] *vi* se réjouir (**at, over**, de); **to r. in sth**, jouir de qch; posséder qch. **re'joicing** *n* réjouissance *f,* allégresse *f.*

rejoin¹ [ri'dʒɔin] *vi* répliquer, répondre. **re'joinder** *n* réplique *f.*

rejoin² [ri:'dʒɔin] **1.** *vtr* rejoindre; **to r. one's ship**, rallier le bord **2.** *vi* (*of lines*) se réunir, se rejoindre.

rejuvenation [ridʒu:vi'neiʃn] *n* rajeunissement *m.*

rekindle [riːˈkindl] 1. *vtr* rallumer (le feu); ranimer (l'espoir) 2. *vi* se rallumer.

relapse [riˈlæps] 1. *n Med:* rechute *f* 2. *vi* retomber (**into**, dans); (*of patient*) rechuter, faire une rechute.

relate [riˈleit] 1. *vtr* (*a*) raconter, conter; faire le récit de (ses aventures); **strange to r.!** chose étonnante à dire (*b*) *Biol:* rapporter, rattacher (une espèce à une famille); établir un rapport entre (deux faits) 2. *vi* se rapporter, avoir rapport (**to**, à); **relating to**, relatif à. **reˈlated** *a* (*a*) ayant rapport (**to**, à); **r. ideas**, idées connexes (*b*) (*of pers*) apparenté (**to**, à); parent (**to**, de); (*by marriage*) allié (**to**, à); **he's r. to us**, il est notre parent; **they are closely r.**, ils sont proches parents. **reˈlation** *n* (*a*) relation *f*, récit *m* (d'évènements) (*b*) relation, rapport *m*; **in r. to**, relativement à; par rapport à; **sexual relations**, rapports sexuels; *Adm: Com:* **public relations**, service des relations avec le public, des relations publiques; **that bears no r. to the present situation**, cela n'a aucun rapport, rien à faire, avec la situation actuelle; **to enter into relations with s.o.**, entrer en rapport, en relations, avec qn (*c*) parent, -ente; **r. by marriage**, parent, -ente, par alliance; allié, -ée; **is he a r. of yours?** est-il de vos parents? **what r. is he to you?** quelle est sa parenté avec vous? **reˈlationship** *n* (*a*) rapport(s) *m*(*pl*) (entre deux personnes ou deux choses); relations *fpl* (*b*) parenté *f*; lien *m* de parenté; **blood r.**, consanguinité *f*.

relative [ˈrelətiv] 1. *a* relatif, qui se rapporte (**to**, à); *Gram:* **r. pronoun**, pronom relatif 2. *n* parent, -ente. **ˈrelatively** *adv* relativement (**to**, à); par rapport (à); **she's r. happy**, elle est assez heureuse. **relaˈtivity** *n* relativité *f*; **theory of r.**, théorie de la relativité.

relax [riˈlæks] *v* (**relaxes**) 1. *vtr* relâcher (la discipline, les muscles); décontracter (les muscles); détendre (l'esprit); mitiger (une loi, une peine) 2. *vi* (*of muscles*) se relâcher; (*of pers, muscles*) se détendre; **his face relaxed into a smile**, son visage s'est détendu et il a souri; **to r. for an hour**, se détendre pendant une heure. **relaxˈation** *n* (*a*) relâchement *m* (des muscles, de la discipline); mitigation *f* (d'une peine) (*b*) délassement, détente *f*, relaxation *f*; **for r.**, pour se détendre, se délasser. **reˈlaxed** *a* détendu, décontracté. **reˈlaxing** *a* qui détend; (séjour) relaxant, reposant; *Pej:* (climat) débilitant.

relay 1. *vtr* [riˈlei] relayer; retransmettre (une émission de radio, de télévision) 2. *n* [ˈriːlei] (*a*) relais *m*; relève *f* (d'ouvriers); **to work in relays**, se relayer; *Sp:* **r. race**, course de relais (*b*) *WTel:* radiodiffusion relayée; **r. station**, (station) relais.

release [riˈliːs] 1. *n* (*a*) délivrance *f* (**from**, de); décharge *f*, libération *f* (**from an obligation**, d'une obligation); mise *f* en liberté (d'un prisonnier); **order of r.**, (ordre de) levée *f* d'écrou (*b*) *Com:* sortie *f*, lancement *m*, mise en vente (d'un nouveau produit); *Cin:* mise en circulation (d'un film); *Journ:* autorisation *f* de publier (un article); *press:* **r.**, communiqué *m* de presse (*c*) *Av:* largage *m* (d'une bombe, d'un parachute) 2. *vtr* (*a*) décharger, libérer; *Adm:* mettre (du matériel) en disponibilité; **to r. s.o. from his promise**, relever qn de sa promesse (*b*) libérer (un prisonnier); **released on bail**, remis en liberté sous caution (*c*) mettre en vente, lancer, sortir (un nouveau produit); permettre la publication (d'un article); mettre (un film) en circulation (*d*) dégager (une pièce

coincée, du gaz); *Av:* larguer, lâcher (une bombe); lancer (un parachute); desserrer (le frein); **to r. one's hold**, lâcher prise; *Phot:* **to r. the shutter**, déclencher l'obturateur.

relegate [ˈreligeit] *vtr* reléguer. **releˈgation** *n* relégation *f*.

relent [riˈlent] *vi* se laisser attendrir; se laisser fléchir. **reˈlentless** *a* implacable. **reˈlentlessly** *adv* implacablement. **reˈlentlessness** *n* inflexibilité *f*.

relevant [ˈreləvənt] *a* qui a rapport (**to**, à); pertinent (**to**, à); **all r. information**, tous renseignements utiles. **ˈrelevance** *n* pertinence *f*, à-propos *m*.

reliable [riˈlaiəbl] *a* sûr; sur qui, sur lequel, on peut compter; (homme) sérieux; (machine) fiable, d'un fonctionnement sûr; **r. firm**, maison de confiance; **r. guarantee**, garantie solide; **from a r. source**, de bonne source. **reliaˈbility** *n* sûreté *f*; honnêteté *f*; fiabilité *f* (d'une machine). **reˈliably** *adv* sûrement; **to be r. informed that**, savoir de bonne source que.

reliant [riˈlaiənt] *a* **to be r. on s.o.**, avoir confiance en qn, dépendre de qn, compter sur qn. **reˈliance** *n* confiance *f*.

relic [ˈrelik] *n* (*a*) *Ecc:* relique *f* (*b*) *pl* reliques *fpl*, restes *mpl*; vestiges *mpl* (du passé).

relief¹ [riˈliːf] *n* (*a*) soulagement *m*; allégement *m*; **to heave a sigh of r.**, pousser un soupir de soulagement; **tax r.**, dégrèvement *m*; **r. valve**, soupape de sûreté (*b*) secours *m*; **to go to s.o.'s r.**, aller au secours de qn; **r. fund**, caisse de secours; **refugee r. work**, œuvre de secours aux réfugiés; **r. train**, train supplémentaire (*c*) *Mil:* délivrance *f* (d'une ville). **reˈlieve** *vtr* (*a*) soulager, alléger (les souffrances); tranquilliser (l'esprit de qn); **to r. one's feelings**, se décharger le cœur; **to r. oneself**, faire ses besoins; se soulager; **to r. boredom**, tromper, dissiper l'ennui (*b*) secourir, aider (qn); venir en aide à (qn) (*c*) **to r. s.o. of sth**, soulager, délester, qn d'(un fardeau); débarrasser qn d'(un manteau); dégager qn d'(une obligation); relever qn de (ses fonctions) (*d*) relayer (qn); *Mil:* relever (la garde); délivrer (une ville).

relief² *n Art:* relief *m*; modelé *m*; **to stand out in r.**, ressortir, se détacher (**against**, sur); **r. map**, carte en relief.

religion [riˈlidʒən] *n* religion *f*; culte *m*; *Adm:* confession *f*. **reˈligious** *a* religieux; pieux, dévot; (vie) de religion; (soin) scrupuleux. **reˈligiously** *adv* religieusement; pieusement; (faire qch) scrupuleusement.

relinquish [riˈliŋkwiʃ] *vtr* abandonner (une habitude, tout espoir); renoncer à (un projet); lâcher (un objet); *Jur:* délaisser (un droit, une succession). **reˈlinquishment** *n* abandon *m*; renonciation *f*.

reliquary [ˈrelikwəri] *n* (*pl* **reliquaries**) reliquaire *m*.

relish [ˈreliʃ] 1. *n* (*a*) goût *m*, saveur *f*; **to eat sth with r.**, manger qch de bon appétit; **he used to tell the story with great r.**, il se délectait à raconter cette histoire (*b*) *Comest:* sauce piquante (à base de légumes et de vinaigre); condiment *m* 2. *vtr* goûter, savourer (un mets); **to r. doing sth**, trouver du plaisir à faire qch; **we didn't r. the idea**, l'idée ne nous souriait pas.

reluctant [riˈlʌktənt] *a* (*a*) **to be r. to do sth**, être peu disposé à faire qch (*b*) (consentement) accordé à contrecœur. **reˈluctance** *n* répugnance *f* (à faire qch); **to do sth with r.**, faire qch à regret, à contrecœur.

re'luctantly *adv* à contrecœur; **I say it r.**, il m'en coûte de le dire.

rely [ri'lai] *vtr* **(relied) to r. (up)on s.o., sth,** compter sur qn, qch; se fier à qn.

remain [ri'mein] *vi* rester; **the fact remains that,** il n'en est pas moins vrai que; **it remains to be seen whether,** reste à savoir si; **that remains to be seen,** c'est ce que nous verrons; **to r. sitting,** rester, demeurer, assis; **to r. at home,** rester à la maison; **to r. behind,** rester, ne pas partir; **let it r. as it is,** laissez-le comme cela; **the weather remains fine,** le temps se maintient au beau; *Corr:* **I r., Sir, yours truly,** veuillez agréer, Monsieur, l'expression de mes sentiments distingués. **re'mainder** 1. *n* reste *m*; restant *m*; **the r. of his life,** le reste, restant, de sa vie; **coll the r.,** les autres *mf*; *Com:* **remainders,** fin(s) *f(pl)* de série; invendus soldés; *(books)* solde *m* d'édition 2. *vtr Publ:* solder (une édition). **re'maining** *a* **I have four r.,** il m'en reste quatre; **the r. travellers,** le reste des voyageurs; **our only r. hope,** le seul espoir qui nous reste. **re'mains** *npl* restes *mpl*; vestiges *mpl* (d'une civilisation).

remake ['ri:meik] *n Cin:* nouvelle version; remake *m*.

remand [ri'mɑ:nd] 1. *vtr Jur:* renvoyer (un prévenu) à une autre audience; **to r. s.o. for a week,** remettre le cas de qn à huitaine 2. *n Jur:* renvoi *m*; **to be on r.,** être renvoyé à une autre audience; **r. home** = maison d'éducation surveillée.

remark [ri'mɑ:k] 1. *n* remarque *f*; observation *f*, commentaire *m*; **to make a r.,** faire une observation, une réflexion; **to venture a r.,** se permettre un mot; *Pej:* **to pass remarks about s.o.,** faire des observations sur qn 2. *v* (*a*) *vtr* remarquer, observer; **it may be remarked that,** constatons que (*b*) *vi* faire une remarque, des remarques (on, sur); **I remarked (up)on it to my neighbour,** j'en ai fait l'observation à mon voisin. **re'markable** *a* remarquable; frappant. **re'markably** *adv* remarquablement.

remarry [ri:'mæri] *vtr & i* **(remarried)** se remarier (avec qn).

remedy ['remidi] 1. *n* remède *m* 2. *vtr* **(remedied)** remédier à (qch). **remedial** [ri'mi:diəl] *a* réparateur; (traitement) curatif; (cours) destiné à corriger les défauts de langage; **r. exercises,** gymnastique corrective.

remember [ri'membər] *vtr & i* se souvenir de; se rappeler (qch); **if I r. rightly,** si je m'en souviens bien; si j'ai bonne mémoire; **as far as I r.,** autant qu'il m'en souvient, qu'il m'en souvienne; **don't you r. me?** vous ne me remettez pas? **it will be something to r. you by,** ce sera un souvenir de vous; **that's worth remembering,** cela est à noter; **he remembered me in his will,** il ne m'a pas oublié dans son testament; **r. me (kindly) to them,** rappelez-moi à leur bon souvenir. **re'membrance** *n* souvenir; mémoire; **in r. of s.o.,** en souvenir de qn; **R. Day,** le dimanche le plus proche du 11 novembre (commémorant les victimes des deux guerres mondiales).

remind [ri'maind] *vtr* **to r. s.o. of sth,** rappeler qch à qn; **that reminds me!** à propos! **r. me to write to him,** faites-moi penser à lui écrire. **re'minder** *n* (*a*) mémento *m*; **as a r. that,** pour rappeler que (*b*) *Com:* **(letter of) r.,** lettre *f* de rappel *m* (*c*) *Com:* rappel de compte, d'échéance.

reminiscence [remi'nisəns] *n* réminiscence *f*; souvenir *m*; **to write one's reminiscences,** écrire ses souvenirs. **remi'nisce** *vi* raconter ses souvenirs. **remi'niscent** *a* **r. of s.o., sth,** qui rappelle, fait penser à, qn, qch. **remi'niscently** *adv* **he smiled r.,** il a souri à ce souvenir; **to talk r. of,** évoquer des souvenirs de.

remiss [ri'mis] *a* négligent, insouciant.

remission [ri'miʃn] *n Theol:* pardon *m*, rémission *f* (des péchés); *Med:* rémission *f*; *Jur:* remise *f* (d'une peine); **with r. of sentence,** avec sursis *m*.

remit [ri'mit] *vtr* **(remitted)** (*a*) remettre, pardonner (les péchés) (*b*) remettre (une peine, une dette); *Jur:* renvoyer (un procès) (*c*) *Com:* remettre, envoyer (de l'argent à qn). **re'mittal** *n* remise *f* (d'une dette, d'une peine); *Jur:* renvoi *m* (d'un procès à un autre tribunal). **re'mittance** *n Com:* remise *f* (d'argent); envoi *m* de fonds; versement *m*.

remnant ['remnənt] *n* reste *m*, restant *m*; *Com:* coupon *m* (de tissu); **remnants,** soldes *mpl*; fins *fpl* de série.

remonstrate ['remənstreit] *vi* **to r. with s.o. about sth,** faire des remontrances *f* à qn au sujet de qch; **to r. against sth,** protester contre qch. **re'monstrance** *n* protestation *f*; remontrance.

remorse [ri'mɔ:s] *n* remords *m*; **a feeling of r.,** un remords; **without r.,** sans pitié. **re'morseful** *a* plein de remords; repentant. **re'morsefully** *adv* avec remords. **re'morseless** *a* sans remords; sans pitié; impitoyable. **re'morselessly** *adv* sans remords; impitoyablement.

remote [ri'mout] *a* lointain; éloigné, écarté; (endroit) isolé; **in the remotest part of Asia,** au fin fond de l'Asie; **in the r. future,** dans un avenir lointain; **r. control,** télécommande *f*; **to operate sth by r. control,** télécommander qch; **a r. resemblance,** une vague ressemblance; **without the remotest chance of success,** sans la moindre chance de réussir; **I haven't the remotest idea,** je n'ai pas, je n'en ai pas, la moindre idée; **r. prospect,** éventualité peu probable. **remote-controlled** *a* télécommandé. **re'motely** *adv* (*a*) loin; au loin; **we're r. related,** nous sommes parents éloignés (*b*) vaguement. **re'moteness** *n* éloignement *m* (d'un village, d'un événement).

remould ['ri:mould] *n* pneu rechapé.

remove [ri'mu:v] 1. *vtr* (*a*) enlever; faire partir, enlever (une tache); écarter (un obstacle); supprimer (un abus); retirer (un élève, son chapeau); résoudre (une objection); révoquer (un fonctionnaire); **to r. (one's) make-up,** (se) démaquiller; **to r. s.o.'s name from a list,** rayer qn d'une liste (*b*) déplacer (qch); déménager (ses meubles); **a feeling not far removed from love,** un sentiment pas très éloigné de l'amour; **first cousin once removed,** cousin issu de germain 2. *n* **at a certain r. from,** à une certaine distance de; **only one r. from,** tout près de. **re'movable** *a* (*a*) détachable; amovible (*b*) transportable. **re'moval** *n* (*a*) enlèvement *m*; suppression *f* (d'un abus); *Surg:* ablation *f* (d'une tumeur) (*b*) déménagement *m*; **r. expenses,** frais de déplacement; **r. man,** déménageur *m*; **(furniture) r. van,** camion de déménagement. **re'mover** *n* (*a*) **(furniture) r.,** déménageur *m* (*b*) décapant *m* (pour vernis, pour peinture); **make-up r.,**

démaquillant m; **hair** r., crème épilatoire; **nail varnish** r., dissolvant m (pour vernis à ongles).

remunerate [ri'mju:nəreit] *vtr* rémunérer (qn de ses services). **remune'ration** n rémunération f (**for**, de). **re'munerative** a (travail) rémunérateur.

renaissance [rə'neisəns, -sɑ̃:s] n renaissance f; **R. style**, style (de la) Renaissance.

renal ['ri:nəl] a Anat: rénal; des reins.

render ['rendər] *vtr* (a) rendre; **to r. good for evil**, rendre le bien pour le mal; **to r. a service to s.o.**, rendre un service à qn; **to r. assistance to s.o.**, prêter secours à qn; **to r. oneself liable to (legal) proceedings**, s'exposer à des poursuites (judiciaires); **to r. an account of sth**, rendre compte de qch; Com: **as per account rendered, to account rendered**, suivant compte remis (b) interpréter (un morceau de musique); rendre; traduire (c) Cu: fondre (de la graisse) (d) Const: **to r. a wall (with cement)**, enduire un mur de ciment. **'rendering** n rendu m; interprétation f (d'un morceau de musique); traduction f (d'une phrase); enduit m (de ciment).

rendezvous ['rɒndivu:] **1.** n (inv in pl ['rɒndivu:z]) rendez-vous m inv **2.** vi (**rendezvoused**) [-vu:d]) se rencontrer.

renew [ri'nju:] *vtr* (a) renouveler; **to r. one's subscription**, se réabonner (**to a paper**, à un journal); **to r. one's acquaintance with s.o.**, renouer connaissance avec qn (b) remplacer (une pièce d'une machine, un vêtement). **re'newal** n renouvellement m; regain m (d'activité); **r. of subscription**, réabonnement m (**to**, à); **r. of acquaintance**, renouement m des relations; **r. of negotiations**, reprise f de négociations. **re'newed** a (of activity) redoublé.

renounce [ri'nauns] *vtr* renoncer à, abandonner (un droit, un projet); renier (son fils); dénoncer (un traité); abjurer (sa foi). **re'nouncement** n renoncement m; Jur: répudiation f (d'une succession).

renovate ['renəveit] *vtr* remettre à neuf; rénover; restaurer (une maison). **reno'vation** n rénovation f; remise f à neuf; restauration f.

renown [ri'naun] n renommée f, renom m. **re'nowned** a renommé (**for**, pour); célèbre (**for**, par).

rent[1] [rent] n déchirure f, accroc m (à un vêtement); fissure f (de terrain).

rent[2] **1.** n loyer m; **quarter's r.**, terme m; **r. collector**, receveur de loyers **2.** *vtr* (a) (of owner) louer (une maison) (b) (of tenant) louer, prendre en location (une maison). **'rental** n loyer; (prix m de) location f; **yearly r.**, redevance annuelle; **fixed r.**, (redevance d')abonnement m (au téléphone).

renunciation [rinʌnsi'eiʃn] n renoncement m, renonciation f (**of**, à, de); reniement m (de son fils).

reopen [ri:'oup(ə)n] **1.** *vtr* (a) rouvrir (un livre); Fig: **to r. an old wound**, raviver une plaie (b) reprendre (les hostilités) **2.** vi (of wound) se rouvrir; (of theatre) rouvrir; (of school) rentrer.

reorganize [ri:'ɔ:gənaiz] **1.** *vtr* réorganiser **2.** vi se réorganiser. **reorgani'zation** n réorganisation f.

rep [rep] n F: (a) représentant m (d'une maison de commerce) (b) Th: **to play in r.**, jouer dans un théâtre municipal (de province).

repair [ri'pɛər] **1.** n réparation f (d'une machine); réfection f (des routes); **emergency repairs**, répara-

tions d'urgence; dépannage m; **to be under r.**, être en réparation; **beyond r.**, irréparable; **r. shop**, atelier de réparations; **r. kit**, trousse de réparation; **to be in (good) r.**, être en bon état; **in bad, poor,** r., mal entretenu; **to keep sth in (good) r.**, entretenir qch **2.** *vtr* réparer; remettre en état; raccommoder (un vêtement). **re'pairer** n réparateur, -trice; **shoe r.**, cordonnier m. **reparable** ['repərəbl] a réparable. **repa'ration** n réparation f.

repartee [repɑ:'ti:] n repartie f.

repatriate [ri:'pætrieit] *vtr* rapatrier. **repatri'ation** n rapatriement m.

repay [ri:'pei] *vtr* (**repaid**) rendre; s'acquitter (d'une obligation); rembourser (de l'argent); récompenser (qn) (**for**, de); **to r. s.o. with ingratitude**, payer qn d'ingratitude; **how can I r. you?** comment pourrai-je m'acquitter envers vous? **to r. s.o. in full**, s'acquitter envers qn; **book that repays study**, livre qui vaut la peine d'être étudié. **re'payable** a remboursable. **re'payment** n remboursement m; récompense f (d'un service).

repeal [ri'pi:l] **1.** n abrogation f (d'une loi); révocation f (d'un décret); annulation f (d'une sentence) **2.** *vtr* abroger, annuler (une loi); révoquer (un décret).

repeat [ri'pi:t] **1.** v (a) *vtr* répéter; réitérer; renouveler (ses efforts, Com: une commande); Sch: redoubler (une classe); Pej: rapporter (un méfait); **to r. oneself**, se répéter (b) vi F: (of food) donner des renvois **2.** n répétition f; Mus: reprise f; TV: WTel: rediffusion f. **re'peated** a répété, réitéré, redoublé. **re'peatedly** adv à plusieurs reprises.

repel [ri'pel] *vtr* (**repelled**) repousser; dégoûter, répugner à (qn). **re'pellent** **1.** a répulsif; répugnant, repoussant; **to have a r. manner**, être d'un abord antipathique; **water r.**, (tissu) imperméable **2.** n **insect r.**, insectifuge m.

repent [ri'pent] *vtr* & i se repentir ((of) sth, de qch). **re'pentance** n repentir m. **re'pentant** a repentant, repenti.

repercussion [ri:pə'kʌʃn] n répercussion f.

repertoire ['repətwɑ:r] n Th: répertoire m.

repertory ['repətri] n r. theatre, théâtre municipal (de province); **r. company**, théâtre à demeure.

repetition [repi'tiʃn] n répétition f; réitération f (d'une action); renouvellement m (d'un effort). **re'petitive** a (livre) plein de répétitions; (of pers) rabâcheur.

replace [ri'pleis] *vtr* (a) replacer; remettre (qch) (à sa place, en place); Tp: **to r. the receiver**, raccrocher (le combiné) (b) remplacer (**by, with**, par); **I shall ask to be replaced**, je demanderai à me faire remplacer. **re'placeable** a remplaçable. **re'placement** n (a) remise f (à sa place) (d'un objet) (b) remplacement m, substitution f (c) **r. (part)**, pièce f de rechange (d) (pers) remplaçant, -ante.

replay ['ri:plei] n Sp: second match (après match nul); TV: (**action**) **r.**, répétition f (d'une séquence).

replenish [ri'pleniʃ] *vtr* remplir (de nouveau) (**with**, de); **to r. one's supplies**, se réapprovisionner (**with**, de). **re'plenishment** n (of fuel) remplissage m; (of food) réapprovisionnement m.

replete [ri'pli:t] a rempli.

replica ['replikə] n réplique f; double m (d'une œuvre d'art).

reply [ri'plai] 1. *n* (replies) réponse *f*; in r. to, en réponse à; what have you to say in r.? qu'avez-vous à répondre? r. paid, réponse payée 2. *vi & tr* (replied) répondre, répliquer (to, à).

report [ri'pɔːt] 1. *n* (*a*) rapport *m* (on, sur); compte rendu; exposé *m* (d'une affaire); procès-verbal *m* (d'une assemblée, d'un policier); *Sch*: bulletin (trimestriel); état *m* (d'ordinateur); expert's r., expertise *f*; weather r., bulletin *m* météorologique (*b*) bruit *m* qui court; rumeur *f*; newspaper, TV, r., reportage *m* (*c*) détonation *f* (d'une arme à feu); coup *m* (de fusil) 2. (*a*) *vtr* rapporter (un fait); rendre compte de (qch); (*of journalist*) faire le reportage de (qch); faire le compte rendu (d'une séance); signaler (un accident) (à la police); dénoncer (qn) (à la police); reported missing, porté absent (*b*) *vi* (i) se présenter (to s.o., devant qn) (ii) rendre compte de ses activités (to s.o., à qn); to r. (oneself) sick, se (faire) porter malade; to r. on sth, faire un rapport sur qch; *Mil*: to r. to one's unit, rallier son unité. **re'portedly** *adv* he r. said that, il aurait dit que. **re'porter** *n* journaliste *mf*; reporter *m*.

repose [ri'pouz] 1. *n* repos *m*; sommeil *m*; calme *m*, tranquillité *f* (d'esprit) 2. *vi* se reposer; (*of corpse*) reposer. **re'pository** *n* (*pl* -ies) (*a*) dépôt *m*, entrepôt *m*; furniture r., garde-meuble *m* (*b*) *Fig*: mine *f* (de renseignements).

reprehensible [repri'hensibl] *a* répréhensible. **repre'hensibly** *adv* de façon répréhensible.

represent [repri'zent] *vtr* représenter; he represents himself as a model of virtue, il se donne pour un modèle de vertu; exactly as represented, conforme à la description. **represen'tation** *n* (*a*) représentation *f*; *Pol*: proportional r., représentation proportionnelle (*b*) *Dipl*: démarche *f*; joint representations, démarche collective; to make representations to s.o., faire des démarches auprès de qn. **repre'sentative** 1. *a* représentatif; *Com*: r. sample, échantillon type 2. *n* (*a*) représentant, -ante, délégué, -ée (*b*) représentant (d'une maison de commerce) (*c*) *US*: *Pol*: = député *m*.

repress [ri'pres] *vtr* réprimer; retenir (ses désirs); refouler (ses sentiments). **re'pressed** *a* réprimé, contenu; a r. young man, un jeune homme renfermé. **re'pression** *n* répression *f*; *Psy*: unconscious r., refoulement *m*. **re'pressive** *a* répressif, réprimant; (mesures) de répression.

reprieve [ri'priːv] 1. *n* commutation *f* de la peine capitale; *Fig*: répit *m*, délai *m* 2. *vtr* *Jur*: accorder (à un condamné) une commutation de la peine capitale; *Fig*: accorder un délai à (qn).

reprimand ['reprimɑːnd] 1. *n* réprimande *f* 2. *vtr* réprimander (qn).

reprint 1. *vtr* [riː'print] réimprimer 2. *n* ['riːprint] réimpression *f*; nouveau tirage.

reprisal [ri'praizəl] *n* représailles *fpl*; as a r., en représailles.

reproach [ri'proutʃ] 1. *n* reproche *m*; to be a r. to (one's family), être la honte de (sa famille); beyond, above, r., irréprochable 2. *vtr* to r. s.o. with sth, reprocher qch à qn; to r. s.o. about sth, faire des reproches à qn au sujet de qch; I have nothing to r. myself with, je n'ai rien à me reprocher. **re'proachful** *a* réprobateur; (ton, air) de reproches. **re'proachfully** *adv* d'un air de reproche.

reprobate ['reprəbeit] *n* réprouvé, -ée; vaurien *m*.

reproduce [riːprə'djuːs] 1. *vtr* reproduire; copier (un texte) 2. *vi* se reproduire; se multiplier. **repro'duction** *n* reproduction *f*; *Cin*: *etc*: sound r., reproduction sonore; *Art*: correct r. of colour, rendu exact des couleurs. **repro'ductive** *a* *Anat*: (organe) reproducteur.

reproof [ri'pruːf] *n* reproche *m*, blâme *m*; réprimande *f*.

reproof [riː'pruːf] *vtr* réimperméabiliser.

reprove [ri'pruːv] *vtr* reprendre, réprimander (qn). **re'proving** *a* réprobateur. **re'provingly** *adv* d'un ton, d'un air, de reproche.

reptile ['reptail] *n* reptile *m*.

republic [ri'pʌblik] *n* république *f*. **re'publican** *a* & *n* républicain, -aine. **re'publicanism** *n* républicanisme *m*.

repudiate [ri'pjuːdieit] *vtr* répudier (ses dettes); désavouer (une opinion); *Com*: *Jur*: refuser d'honorer (un contrat). **repudi'ation** *n* répudiation *f*; désaveu *m* (d'une opinion); reniement *m* (d'une dette).

repugnant [ri'pʌgnənt] *a* répugnant (to s.o., à qn); to be r. to s.o., répugner à qn. **re'pugnance** *n* répugnance *f*; antipathie *f* (to, against, pour).

repulse [ri'pʌls] *vtr* repousser (un ennemi, une demande). **re'pulsion** *n* répulsion *f*; aversion *f*. **re'pulsive** *a* répulsif, repoussant. **re'pulsively** *adv* r. ugly, d'une laideur repoussante. **re'pulsiveness** *n* caractère repoussant.

repute [ri'pjuːt] *n* réputation *f*, renom *m*; to know s.o. by r., connaître qn de réputation; doctor of r., médecin réputé; place of ill r., endroit mal famé. **reputable** ['repjutəbl] *a* honorable, de bonne réputation. **repu'tation** [repju-] *n* réputation *f*, renom; to have the, a, r. of, for, being amusing, avoir la réputation d'être amusant; to ruin s.o.'s r., perdre qn de réputation. **re'puted** *a* réputé, censé, supposé; a. r. Hogarth, un tableau attribué à Hogarth; *Jur*: r. father, père putatif; he's r. wealthy, il a la réputation d'être riche. **re'putedly** *adv* censément; he's r. the best heart specialist, il passe pour le meilleur cardiologue.

request [ri'kwest] 1. *n* demande *f*, requête *f*; at s.o.'s r., à la demande de qn; samples sent on r., échantillons sur demande; r. (bus) stop, arrêt facultatif; *WTel*: r. programme, programme des auditeurs; to make a r., faire une demande (for, de); by (popular) r., à la demande générale; to grant a r., accéder à une demande 2. *vtr* demander (qch à qn, à qn de faire qch); *Com*: as requested, conformément à vos instructions.

requiem ['rekwiem] *n* requiem *m*; r. mass, messe *f* des morts.

require [ri'kwaiər] *vtr* (*a*) to r. sth of s.o., demander, réclamer, qch à qn; to r. s.o. to do sth, demander à qn de faire qch (*b*) exiger, demander; work that requires great precision, travail qui nécessite une grande précision; have you got all you r.? avez-vous tout ce qu'il vous faut? I'll do whatever is required, je ferai tout ce qu'il faudra. **re'quired** *a* exigé, demandé, voulu; in the r. time, dans le délai prescrit; the qualities r. for this post, les qualités requises pour ce poste; if r., s'il le faut; when r., au besoin.

re′quirement *n* (*a*) demande *f*, réclamation *f* (*b*) exigence *f*, besoin *m* (*c*) condition requise.

requisition [rekwi′zi∫n] *Mil:* **1.** *vtr* réquisitionner (des vivres, des locaux); avoir recours aux (services de qn) **2.** *n* demande *f*; *Mil:* réquisition *f*. **′requisite 1.** *a* (objet) requis (**to do sth,** pour faire qch); nécessaire (**to, à**); indispensable (**to,** pour) **2.** *n* (*a*) condition requise (**for,** pour) (*b*) chose *f* nécessaire; **toilet requisites,** accessoires *mpl* de toilette; **office requisites,** fournitures *fpl* de bureau; **travel requisites,** articles *mpl* de voyage.

reread [ri:′ri:d] *vtr* (**reread** [ri:′red]) relire.

reredos [′riədɔs] *n Ecc:* retable *m*.

reroute [ri:′ru:t, *NAm:* -′raut] *vtr* dérouter.

resat [ri:′sæt] *see* **resit.**

rescind [ri′sind] *vtr Jur: Adm:* rescinder (un acte); annuler (un vote); abroger (une loi).

rescue [′reskju:] **1.** *n* délivrance *f*; sauvetage *m*; **to come to s.o.'s r.,** venir au secours de qn; **r. party,** équipe *f* de sauvetage; **air-sea r.,** sauvetage aérien en mer **2.** *vtr* sauver, délivrer, secourir (qn); **to r. s.o. from drowning,** sauver qn qui se noie; **the rescued men,** les rescapés. **′rescuer** *n* (*from fire, drowning*) secouriste *mf*; sauveteur *m*; libérateur, -trice.

research [ri′sə:t∫] **1.** *n* recherche *f* (**for,** de); **scientific r.,** recherche scientifique; **r. work,** recherches *fpl*; **to do r.,** faire des recherches (**on,** sur); **r. worker,** chercheur, -euse; *Ind:* **r. department,** service de recherches **2.** *vtr & i* **to r. (into) sth,** faire des recherches sur qch; **well researched,** bien étudié, étudié à fond. **re′searcher** *n* chercheur.

resemble [ri′zembl] *vtr* ressembler à. **re′semblance** *n* ressemblance *f* (**to,** à, avec; **between,** entre); **to bear a r. to s.o.,** ressembler à qn.

resent [ri′zent] *vtr* (*a*) être offensé, irrité, de (qch); **you r. my being here,** ma présence vous déplaît (*b*) s'offenser de (qch). **re′sentful** *a* (*a*) plein de ressentiment; rancunier (*b*) froissé, irrité (**of,** de). **re′sentfully** *adv* avec ressentiment. **re′sentment** *n* ressentiment *m*.

reserve [ri′zə:v] **1.** *vtr* réserver (**sth for s.o.,** qch pour qn); mettre (qch) en réserve; **to r. a seat for s.o.,** retenir une place pour qn; **to r. the right to do sth,** se réserver le droit de faire qch **2.** *n* (*a*) réserve *f*; **to deep sth in r.,** tenir qch en réserve; **cash reserves,** réserve de caisse; **r. fund,** fonds de réserve; **r. (petrol) tank,** réservoir de réserve; (*at sale*) **r. price,** prix minimum; **without r.,** sans réserve; **nature r.,** réserve naturelle (*b*) *Sp:* remplaçant, -ante; *Mil:* **the Reserve(s),** la Réserve, les Réserves. **reser′vation** [rezə-] *n* (*a*) réservation *f*; **with reservations,** avec certaines réserves; **to accept sth without r.,** accepter qch sans réserve, sans arrière-pensée (*b*) *NAm:* parc national; réserve (zoologique, indienne) (*c*) (*on roads*) **central r.,** terre-plein central. **re′served** *a* réservé; (homme) renfermé, peu communicatif; **to be r. with s.o.,** se tenir sur la réserve avec qn. **re′servist** *n Mil:* réserviste *m*. **′reservoir** [-wɑːr] *n* réservoir *m*.

resettle [ri:′setl] *vtr* rétablir.

reshuffle [ri:′∫ʌfl] **1.** *n* remaniement *m* (ministériel, du personnel) **2.** *vtr* remanier (le personnel).

reside [ri′zaid] *vi* résider. **residence** [′rezidəns] *n* résidence *f*, demeure *f*; *Com:* **desirable r. for sale,** beile propriété à vendre; *Sch:* **(students') hall of r. =** cité *f* universitaire; **to take up r. in a country,** s'établir dans un pays; **r. permit,** permis de séjour; **in r.,** en résidence. **′resident 1.** *a* résidant; qui réside; (population) fixe; (professeur) à demeure; (*in hospital*) **r. physician,** interne *m*; **to be r. in a place,** résider dans un endroit **2.** *n* habitant, -ante; (*in hotel*) pensionnaire *mf*; (*of street*) riverain, -aine; *Adm:* (*living abroad*) résident, -ente. **resi′dential** *a* (quartier) résidentiel.

residue [′rezidju:] *n* reste(s) *m*(*pl*); *Ch:* résidu *m*; *Jur:* reliquat *m* (d'une succession). **re′sidual** *a* qui reste; restant; *Ch:* résiduel. **residuary** [ri′zidjuəri] *a Jur:* **r. legatee,** légataire (à titre) universel.

resign [ri′zain] *vtr & i* démissionner, donner sa démission (de son emploi); céder (qch à qn); **to r. oneself to doing sth,** se résigner à faire qch. **resignation** [rezig′nei∫n] *n* (*a*) démission *f* (d'un emploi); abandon *m* (d'un droit) (*b*) résignation *f*. **re′signed** *a* résigné (**to, à**); **to become r. to sth,** se résigner à qch. **re′signedly** [-idli] *adv* avec résignation; d'un air, d'un ton, résigné.

resilient [ri′ziliənt] *a* élastique; (*of pers*) **to be r.,** avoir du ressort. **re′silience** *n* résistance *f*, élasticité *f*; (*of pers*) ressort.

resin [′rezin] *n* résine *f*. **′resinous** *a* résineux.

resist [ri′zist] **1.** *vtr* résister à (la chaleur, la tentation, l'opinion); s'opposer à (un projet); refuser d'obéir à (un ordre); repousser (une suggestion); **I couldn't r. telling him,** je n'ai pas pu m'empêcher de lui dire **2.** *vi* résister. **re′sistance** *n* résistance *f*; **to offer no r.,** n'opposer aucune résistance; **she made no r.,** elle s'est laissé faire; **r. (movement),** résistance; **r. fighter,** résistant, -ante; **to take the line of least r.,** aller au plus facile. **re′sistant** *a* résistant. **re′sistor** *n El:* résistance.

resit [ri′sit] *vtr* (**resat; resitting**) se représenter à (un examen).

resolute [′rezəl(j)u:t] *a* résolu, déterminé. **′resolutely** *adv* résolument. **reso′lution** *n* (*a*) résolution *f*, délibération *f* (d'une assemblée); **to put a r. to the meeting,** soumettre une résolution (*b*) résolution, détermination *f*; **to make a r.,** prendre une résolution (*c*) résolution, fermeté *f*; **lack of r.,** manque de caractère.

resolve [ri′zɔlv] **1.** *n* résolution *f* **2.** *v* (*a*) *vtr* résoudre, dissiper (un doute) (*b*) résoudre, décider (de faire qch); se résoudre (**to do sth,** à faire qch).

resonant [′rezənənt] *a* réson(n)ant; (voix) sonore. **′resonance** *n* résonance *f*; *Mus:* vibration *f* (de la voix).

resort [ri′zɔ:t] **1.** *n* (*a*) ressource *f*, recours *m*; **the only r.,** la seule ressource; **without r. to compulsion,** sans avoir recours à la force; **as a, in the, last r.,** en dernier ressort (*b*) lieu *m* de séjour; **health r.,** station climatique, thermale; **holiday r.,** (centre *m* de) villégiature *f*; **seaside r.,** station balnéaire **2.** *vi* avoir recours, recourir (**to, à**); user (**to, de**); **to r. to blows,** en venir aux coups.

resound [ri′zaund] *vi* résonner; retentir (**with cries,** de cris); (*of event*) avoir du retentissement. **re′sounding** *a* réson(n)ant, retentissant; (rire) sonore; (succès) éclatant; **r. victory,** victoire fracassante.

resource [ri'zɔːs, -'sɔːs] n ressource f; **natural resources,** ressources naturelles; **to be at the end of one's resources,** être au bout de ses ressources; **he was left to his own resources,** il a dû se débrouiller tout seul. **re'sourceful** a (homme) de ressources, débrouillard; (projet) ingénieux. **re'sourcefully** adv habilement. **re'sourcefulness** n ressource.

respect [ri'spekt] 1. n (a) rapport m, égard m; **with r. to,** en ce qui concerne; quant à; **in some respects,** à certains égards; **in this r.,** à cet égard (b) respect m; **to have r. for s.o.,** avoir du respect pour qn; **to command r.,** savoir se faire respecter; **out of r. for,** par respect, par égard, pour; **worthy of r.,** respectable; digne d'estime f; **with (all) due r. (to you),** sans vouloir vous contredire; **to pay one's respects to s.o.,** présenter ses respects à qn 2. vtr respecter; honorer (qn); **to r. s.o.'s opinion,** respecter l'opinion de qn. **respecta'bility** n respectabilité f. **re'spectable** a respectable; digne de respect; convenable; (famille) honnête; **to put on some r. clothes,** mettre des vêtements convenables; **a r. sum (of money),** une somme respectable, rondelette. **re'spectably** a (vêtu) convenablement (b) pas mal; passablement. **re'spectful** a respectueux (to, envers, pour). **re'spectfully** adv respectueusement; avec respect. **re'spective** a respectif. **re'spectively** adv respectivement.

respiration [respi'reiʃn] n respiration f; **artificial r.,** respiration artificielle. **'respirator** n respirateur m. **respiratory** ['respirətri] a respiratoire.

respite ['respait] n répit m, relâche m; Jur: sursis m, délai m; **to work without r.,** travailler sans relâche.

resplendent [ri'splendənt] a resplendissant; éblouissant (de beauté, de santé).

respond [ri'spɔnd] vi répondre; être sensible (à la bonté, à l'affection); (of nerves) réagir; **to r. to music,** apprécier la musique; (of machine) **to r. to the controls,** obéir aux commandes. **re'sponse** n réponse f; réplique f; Ecc: répons m; (of nerves) réaction f. **responsi'bility** n (pl -ies) responsabilité f; **on one's own r.,** sous sa responsabilité, de son propre chef; **to take (the) r. for sth,** prendre la responsabilité de qch. **re'sponsible** a responsable; **to be r. for,** être chargé de; **to be r. to s.o.,** être responsable devant qn (**for sth,** de qch); **he's not r. for his actions,** il n'est pas maître de ses actes; **r. job,** poste à responsabilités; **job for a r. man,** emploi pour un homme sérieux; **she's a r. woman,** c'est une femme compétente. **re'sponsibly** adv avec sérieux. **re'sponsive** a impressionnable; sensible (to, à); (moteur) nerveux, souple; **to be r. to,** répondre à. **re'sponsiveness** n sensibilité f.

respray [riː'sprei] vtr repeindre (une voiture) au pistolet.

rest¹ [rest] **I.** n (a) repos m; **to have a good night's r.,** passer une bonne nuit; **at r.,** en repos; **to set s.o.'s mind at r.,** calmer, tranquilliser, l'esprit de qn; **to take a r.,** se reposer; **to be laid to r.,** être enterré; **to come to r.,** s'arrêter, s'immobiliser; **r. cure,** cure de repos; **r. centre,** centre d'accueil; **r. home,** maison de repos (pour convalescents, personnes âgées); **r. room,** toilettes fpl; (in factory) salle de repos; (b) Mus: pause f, silence m; **crotchet r.,** soupir m (c) support m; (of chair) **arm r.,** accoudoir m. **II.** v **1.** vi (a) se reposer;

may they r. in peace! qu'ils reposent en paix! (of actor) **to be resting,** se trouver sans engagement; **there the matter rests,** l'affaire en reste là, en est là (b) se poser, s'appuyer; **his hand resting on the table,** sa main posée, appuyée, sur la table; **a heavy responsibility rests on them,** une lourde responsabilité pèse sur eux; **resting place,** lieu de repos **2.** vtr appuyer (qch sur qch); poser (la main); déposer (un fardeau par terre); laisser reposer (qn); **to feel (quite) rested,** se sentir (bien) reposé; **God r. his soul!** Dieu donne le repos à son âme! **'restful** a paisible, tranquille; reposant. **'restless** a agité; (enfant) remuant; **r. audience,** assistance impatiente, énervée; **to get r.,** s'impatienter. **'restlessly** adv avec agitation; nerveusement. **'restlessness** n agitation f; turbulence f; nervosité f.

rest² n reste m, restant m; **to do the r.,** faire le reste; **for the r.,** quant au reste; **and all the r. of it,** et tout le reste; et tout ce qui s'ensuit; coll (with pl v) **the r.,** les autres mf; **the r. of us,** nous autres.

restaurant ['restərɔ̃nt] n restaurant m; Rail: **r. car,** wagon-restaurant m; **r. owner, manager,** restaurateur, -trice.

restitution [resti'tjuːʃn] n restitution f; **to make r. of sth,** restituer qch.

restive ['restiv] a (cheval) rétif; (of pers) indocile; nerveux, énervé, agité.

restore [ri'stɔːr] vtr (a) restituer, rendre (qch à qn) (b) restaurer (un monument); rénover (un meuble); **to r. sth to its former condition,** remettre qch en état (c) rétablir, réintégrer (qn dans ses fonctions); **to r. s.o. to health,** rétablir la santé de qn (d) rétablir (la liberté); ramener (la confiance); **to r. s.o.'s strength,** redonner des forces à qn. **resto'ration** [resta-] n restitution f (de qch à qn); restauration f (d'un régime, d'un monument); rétablissement m (de la santé). **re'storative** a & n Med: fortifiant (m); reconstituant (m). **re'storer** n restaurateur, -trice (d'un monument, d'un tableau, de meubles); Toil: **hair r.,** régénérateur m de cheveux.

restrain [ri'strein] vtr retenir, empêcher (**s.o. from doing sth,** qn de faire qch); retenir (sa curiosité); **to r. one's laughter,** se retenir de rire; **to r. oneself,** se contraindre; **to r. s.o.'s activities,** freiner les, mettre un frein aux, activités de qn. **re'strained** a (of anger) contenu; (style) sobre; **in r. terms,** en termes mesurés. **re'straint** n contrainte f; réserve f; sobriété f (de style); **wage r.,** limitation f des salaires; **to put a r. on oneself,** se contenir; **lack of r.,** abandon m; manque de réserve; **to speak without r.,** parler en toute liberté.

restrict [ri'strikt] vtr restreindre; limiter; réduire (les libertés). **re'stricted** a restreint, limité; (document) secret; **r. diet,** régime sévère; Adm: Aut: **r. area,** zone à vitesse limitée. **re'striction** n restriction f; limitation f (de vitesse, de dépenses). **re'strictive** a restrictif.

result [ri'zʌlt] **1.** n résultat m (of, de); aboutissement m (des efforts de qn); **the r. is that,** il en résulte que; **without r.,** sans résultat; **as a r. of,** par suite de **2.** vi résulter, provenir (from, de); aboutir (in, à); **little will r. from all this,** il ne sortira pas grand-chose de tout cela; **it resulted in nothing,** cela n'a mené à rien; **it will r. in unpleasant arguments,** cela entraînera des désagréments.

resume [ri'zjuːm] **1.** vtr (a) reprendre; **to r. one's seat,**

se rasseoir (b) renouer (des relations); **to r. work,** se remettre au travail **2.** *vi* reprendre; **the meeting will r. at 3 p.m.,** la séance est suspendue jusqu'à 15h. **resumption** [ri'zʌmpʃn] *n* reprise *f* (de négociations, des travaux).

résumé ['rezjuːmei] *n* résumé *m*; *esp NAm:* curriculum vitae *m inv.*

resurface [riː'səːfis] **1.** *vtr* refaire le revêtement (d'une route) **2.** *vi* (*of submarine*) revenir à la surface.

resurrect [rezə'rekt] *vtr* ressusciter; faire revivre. **resu'rrection** *n* résurrection *f.*

resuscitate [ri'sʌsiteit] *vtr* ressusciter; réanimer (un malade). **resusci'tation** *n* réanimation *f.*

retail ['riːteil] **1.** *n Com:* vente *f* au détail; détail; **wholesale and r.,** en gros et au détail **2.** *a* (prix) de détail; **r. dealer,** détaillant, -ante **3.** *v* (*a*) *vtr* détailler, vendre au détail (*b*) *vi* (*of goods*) se vendre au détail; **this retails at £20,** ceci se vend à un prix de détail de vingt livres **4.** *adv* au détail. **'retailer** *n* détaillant; marchand, -ande, au détail.

retain [ri'tein] *vtr* (*a*) retenir, maintenir (qch dans une position) (*b*) conserver, garder (un bien); **to r. control of the car,** rester maître de la voiture (*c*) garder (qch) en mémoire; **I can't r. anything,** j'oublie tout. **re'tainer** *n* provision *f*; avance *f.*

retaliate [ri'tælieit] *vi* rendre la pareille (à qn); user de représailles (envers qn). **retali'ation** *n* revanche *f*, représailles *fpl*; **in r.,** en revanche. **re'taliatory** *a* **r. measures,** représailles *fpl.*

retarded [ri'tɑːdid] *a* retardé; **mentally r.,** arriéré.

retch [riːtʃ, retʃ] **1.** *n* haut-le-cœur *m inv* **2.** *vi* avoir des haut-le-cœur.

retd *abbr* retired.

retention [ri'tenʃn] *n* conservation *f* (d'un usage); maintien *m* (d'une autorité); *Psy:* mémoire *f*; *Med:* rétention *f.* **re'tentive** (mémoire) fidèle.

reticent ['retisənt] *a* peu communicatif; réticent; réservé. **'reticence** *n* caractère peu communicatif; réticence *f*; réserve *f.* **'reticently** *adv* avec réticence.

retina ['retinə] *n Anat:* rétine *f* (de l'œil).

retinue ['retinjuː] *n* suite *f* (d'un prince).

retire [ri'taiər] *v* **1.** *vi* (*a*) se retirer (**to a place,** dans un endroit); *Mil:* reculer; *Sp:* abandonner; **to r. into oneself,** rentrer en soi-même (*b*) (aller) se coucher (*c*) **to r. from business,** se retirer des affaires; **to r. (on a pension),** prendre sa retraite **2.** *vtr* mettre (qn) à la retraite. **re'tired** *a* (*of place, life*) retiré; (*of pers*) à la retraite, retraité. **re'tirement** *n* retraite *f.* **re'tiring 1.** *a* (*of pers*) réservé; (*giving up work*) (président) sortant **2.** *n* **r. age,** âge de la retraite.

retort¹ [ri'tɔːt] **1.** *n* réplique *f* (**to,** à); riposte *f* **2.** *vtr & i* répliquer; riposter.

retort² *n Ch: Ind:* cornue *f.*

retrace [riː'treis] *vtr* remonter à l'origine de (qch); reconstituer, retracer (le passé); **to r. one's steps,** revenir sur ses pas.

retract [ri'trækt] **1.** *vtr* rétracter (qch); *Av:* escamoter, rentrer (le train d'atterrissage) **2.** *vi* se rétracter; se dédire. **re'tractable** *a* (*of undercarriage*) rentrant, escamotable.

retread ['riːtred] *n* pneu rechapé.

retreat [ri'triːt] **1.** *n* retraite *f*; recul *m* (des eaux); **to**

beat a r., battre en retraite **2.** *vi* se retirer; (*of glacier*) reculer; *Mil:* battre en retraite.

retrench [ri'trentʃ] **1.** *vtr* restreindre, réduire (ses dépenses) **2.** *vi* faire des économies. **re'trenchment** *n* réduction *f* (des dépenses); **policy of r.,** politique d'économies.

retrial ['riːtraiəl] *n Jur:* nouveau procès.

retribution [retri'bjuːʃn] *n* châtiment *m*; jugement *m.*

retrieve [ri'triːv] *vtr* (*a*) (*of dog*) rapporter (le gibier); *Cmptr:* extraire (une information) (*b*) recouvrer (des biens); retrouver (un objet perdu); rétablir (la fortune de qn); réparer (une erreur). **re'trievable** *a* (somme) recouvrable; (perte, erreur) réparable. **re'trieval** *n* recouvrement *m* (de biens); réparation *f* (d'une erreur); *Cmptr:* recherche *f* (d'informations); **beyond r.,** irréparable. **re'triever** *n* (*dog*) retriever *m.*

retrograde ['retrougreid] *a* rétrograde.

retrospect ['retrouspekt] *n* **when I consider these events in r.,** quand je jette un coup d'œil rétrospectif sur ces événements. **retro'spective 1.** *a* rétrospectif; (loi) avec effet rétroactif **2.** *n Art:* rétrospective *f.* **retro'spectively** *adv* rétrospectivement; rétroactivement.

return [ri'təːn] **I.** *n* (*a*) retour *m*; **the r. to school,** la rentrée (des classes); (immediately) **on my r.,** dès mon retour, à mon retour; **on my r. home,** de retour à la maison; **by r. (of post),** par retour (du courrier); **many happy returns (of the day)!** bon anniversaire! **r. (ticket),** (billet d')aller et retour *m*; **r. journey,** voyage de retour (*b*) *Com:* **returns,** recettes *fpl*; **quick returns,** un prompt débit (*c*) profit *m*; rendement *m*; **to bring in a fair r.,** rapporter un bénéfice raisonnable (*d*) renvoi *m*, retour (de marchandises avariées); **on sale or r.,** (marchandises) vendues avec faculté de retour, en dépôt (avec reprise des invendus), à condition (*e*) restitution *f* (d'un objet volé); ristourne *f* (d'une somme payée en trop); **in r. for sth,** en échange de qch; **in r. for which,** moyennant quoi; **in r.,** en retour (*f*) *Ten:* retour; *Sp:* **r. match,** match retour (*g*) récompense *f* (*h*) rapport (officiel); recensement *m* (de la population); **sales returns,** statistiques *fpl* de vente; **income tax r.,** déclaration *f* de revenu (*i*) élection *f* (d'un député); **to announce the election returns,** annoncer les résultats du scrutin. **II.** *v* **1.** *vi* (*come back*) revenir; (*go back*) retourner; **to r. home,** rentrer (chez soi); **they have returned,** ils sont de retour; **to r. to work,** reprendre le travail; **I shall r. to this subject later,** je reviendrai sur ce sujet plus tard **2.** *vtr* (*a*) rendre, restituer (un objet volé); renvoyer (un cadeau); rembourser (un emprunt); **to r. a book to its place,** remettre un livre à sa place (*b*) répondre, répliquer (*c*) déclarer, rapporter; *Jur:* **to r. a verdict of guilty,** déclarer l'accusé coupable (*d*) élire (un député); **returning officer,** directeur du scrutin. **re'turnable** *a* qui peut être rendu; (*of bottle*) consigné.

reunion [riː'juːniən] *n* réunion *f*; assemblée *f.* **reu'nite** *vtr* réunir.

Rev *abbr Ecc:* Reverend.

rev [rev] *F:* **1.** *n Aut:* (*abbr of* **revolution**) **4000 revs a minute,** 4 000 tours *mpl* (à la) minute; **r. counter,** compte-tours *m inv* **2.** *v* (**revved**) (*a*) *vtr* **to r. (up),**

(faire) emballer (le moteur) (b) vi to r. up, (of engine) s'emballer; (of driver) emballer le moteur.

reveal [ri'vi:l] vtr révéler, découvrir; laisser voir (une qualité); dévoiler (un mystère); to r. one's identity, se faire connaître. re'vealing a révélateur; (of dress) décolleté. revelation [revə'leiʃn] n révélation f; (the Book of) Revelation(s), l'Apocalypse f.

reveille [ri'væli] n Mil: réveil m.

revel ['revl] 1. n usu pl divertissement(s) m(pl), réjouissance(s) f (pl) 2. vi (revelled) (a) to r. in (doing) sth, se délecter à (faire) qch (b) se réjouir, se divertir; festoyer, faire la noce. 'reveller n joyeux convive; noceur, -euse. 'revelry n (pl -ies) = revel 1.

revenge [ri'vendʒ] 1. n vengeance f; (esp in games) revanche f; to take r. on s.o. for sth, se venger de qch sur qn; in r., par vengeance 2. vtr venger; to r. oneself, to be revenged, se venger (for sth, de qch; on s.o., de, sur, qn). re'vengeful a vindicatif.

revenue ['revənju:] n revenu m; rentes fpl; Adm: the Inland R., le fisc.

reverberate [ri've:bəreit] vi (of sound) retentir, résonner. reverbe'ration n renvoi m, répercussion f (d'un son).

revere [ri'viər] vtr révérer, vénérer. **reverence** ['revərəns] n respect religieux; vénération f. 're-verend a Ecc: (as title) le révérend père, abbé, pasteur; the R. Mother Superior, la révérende Mère supérieure. 'reverent a respectueux; plein de vénération. 'reverently adv avec respect; avec vénération.

reverie ['revəri] n rêverie f.

reversal [ri'və:səl] n renversement m; revirement m (d'opinion); Jur: réforme f, annulation f (d'un jugement). re'verse 1. a inverse, contraire, opposé (to, à); in the r. order, en ordre inverse; r. side, revers m, envers m (d'une médaille); dos m (d'un tableau) 2. n (a) inverse m, contraire m, opposé m; quite the r. of s.o., sth, tout le contraire de qn, qch; Aut: in r. (gear), en marche f arrière (b) revers (d'une médaille, de fortune); envers (d'une médaille); dos (d'un tableau); verso m (d'un feuillet); to suffer a r., essuyer une défaite 3. v (a) vtr renverser; retourner (un tableau); intervertir (l'ordre de qch); Jur: réformer (un jugement); révoquer (une sentence); to r. one's policy, faire volte-face; Tp: to r. the charges (NAm: = to call collect), appeler en PCV (b) vtr & i to r. (one's car), faire marche arrière; to r. (a car) out of a garage, sortir du garage en marche arrière. re'versible a (vêtement, tissu) réversible, à double face. re'versing n renversement; Aut: marche arrière; r. light, phare de recul.

revert [ri've:t] vi (of property) revenir, retourner (to, à); Biol: to r. to type, revenir au type primitif; to r. to our subject, pour en revenir à notre sujet. re'version n retour m; réversion f.

review [ri'vju:] 1. n (a) revue f (de troupes, du passé); examen m; to keep sth under r., suivre qch de très près (b) critique f (d'un livre, d'un film); r. copy, exemplaire fourni au critique (c) revue (périodique) 2. vtr passer (des faits, des troupes) en revue; examiner (des événements); faire la critique d'(un livre). re'viewer n critique m (littéraire, de cinéma).

revile [ri'vail] vtr injurier; insulter (qn).

revise [ri'vaiz] 1. vtr réviser (une leçon, un texte, des

lois); revoir, relire (un travail, une leçon); corriger (des épreuves) 2. vi Sch: réviser. **revision** [-'viʒn] n révision f.

revisit [ri:'vizit] vtr revisiter; visiter de nouveau.

revive [ri'vaiv] 1. vi ressusciter; reprendre connaissance, ses sens; (of courage) se ranimer; (of arts, of feelings) renaître; (of trade, customs) reprendre 2. vtr faire revivre, ressusciter (qn); ranimer, faire renaître (les espérances); renouveler (un usage); remonter (le courage de qn); remettre (une pièce au théâtre); remettre (une mode) en vogue; remettre (une loi) en vigueur; ressusciter (un journal, un parti politique). re'vival n renaissance f (des arts, des lettres); reprise f (d'une pièce au théâtre, Com: des affaires); (of pers) retour m à la vie; retour des forces; religious r., renouveau religieux.

revoke [ri'vouk] 1. vtr révoquer; annuler (un ordre); rétracter (une promesse); retirer (un permis de conduire) 2. vi Cards: faire une fausse renonce. revo'cation n révocation f; annulation f (d'un ordre); abrogation f (d'un décret).

revolt [ri'voult] 1. n révolte f 2. v (a) vi se révolter, se soulever (against, contre) (b) vtr révolter. re'volting a révoltant; dégoûtant, écœurant.

revolution [revə'l(j)u:ʃn] n (a) rotation f (autour d'un axe) (b) tour m, révolution f; Pol: révolution. revo'lutionary a & n (pl -ies) révolutionnaire (mf). revo'lutionize vtr révolutionner.

revolve [ri'vɔlv] 1. vtr retourner, repasser (un problème, une pensée); faire tourner (des roues) 2. vi tourner. re'volving a (planète) en rotation; (fauteuil) tournant, pivotant; r. door, tambour m.

revolver [ri'vɔlvər] n revolver m.

revue [ri'vju:] n Th: revue f.

revulsion [ri'vʌlʃn] n (a) revirement m (de sentiments); r. from s.o., réaction f contre qn (b) (disgust) révulsion f; écœurement m.

reward [ri'wɔ:d] 1. n récompense f; as a r. for, en récompense de 2. vtr récompenser, rémunérer (s.o. for sth, qn de qch). re'warding a (financially) rémunérateur; (travail) qui donne de la satisfaction.

rewire [ri:'waiər] vtr refaire l'installation électrique (d'une maison).

rhapsody ['ræpsədi] n rhapsodie f; Fig: transports mpl, dithyrambe m. 'rhapsodize vi to r. over sth, s'extasier sur qch.

rheostat ['ri:oustæt] n El: rhéostat m.

rhesus ['ri:səs] n Z: r. (monkey), (macaque) rhésus m; Med: r. factor, facteur rhésus (du sang); r. positive, negative, rhésus positif, négatif.

rhetoric ['retərik] n rhétorique f, éloquence f. rhe'torical a (terme) de rhétorique; (style) ampoulé; r. question, question pour la forme. rhe'torically adv (parler) avec emphase; (poser une question) pour la forme.

rheumatism ['ru:mətizm] n rhumatisme m. rheu'matic 1. a (of pain) rhumatismal; r. person, rhumatisant, -ante; r. fever, rhumatisme articulaire aigu 2. n rhumatisant. 'rheumatoid a r. arthritis, rhumatisme chronique articulaire.

Rhine (the) [ðə'rain] Prn Geog: le Rhin.

rhinoceros, F: rhino [rai'nɔsərəs, 'rainou] n (pl rhinoceroses, rhino(s)) Z: rhinocéros m.

rhododendron [rɔudǝ'dendrǝn] n Bot: rhododendron m.

rhubarb ['ru:bɑ:b] n Bot: rhubarbe f.

rhyme [raim] 1. n (a) rime f; **without r. or reason**, sans rime ni raison (b) poésie f; vers mpl 2. (a) vi rimer (avec); faire des vers (b) vtr faire rimer (un mot).

rhythm ['riðǝm] n rythme m; cadence f. **'rhythmic(al)** a rythmique, rythmé; cadencé; **r. tread**, marche scandée. **'rhythmically** adv avec rythme.

rib [rib] n côte f; nervure f (d'une feuille); baleine f (de parapluie).

ribald ['ribǝld] a licencieux, impudique; paillard; **r. song**, chanson grivoise. **'ribaldry** n paillardises fpl; grivoiserie f.

ribbon ['ribǝn] n ruban m; cordon m (d'un ordre); **to tear sth to ribbons**, mettre qch en lambeaux mpl; Adm: **r. development**, extension urbaine en bordure de route.

rice [rais] n riz m; **ground r.**, farine de riz; **brown r.**, riz complet; **polished r.**, riz glacé; Cu: **r. pudding** = riz au lait; **r. grower**, riziculteur m; **r. growing**, riziculture f; **r. plantation**, rizière f.

rich [ritʃ] 1. a riche; (of soil) fertile; (festin) somptueux; (voix) ample; **to grow r.**, s'enrichir; **r. food**, plats gras 2. npl **the r.**, les riches m. **'riches** npl richesse(s) f(pl). **'richly** adv richement; somptueusement; **r. deserved**, bien mérité. **'richness** n richesse, abondance f; fertilité f (du sol); somptuosité f; ampleur f (de la voix).

rick [rik] n meule f (de foin).

rickets ['rikits] n Med: rachitisme m; **to have r.**, être rachitique.

rickety ['rikiti] a (of furniture) branlant; délabré; (fauteuil) bancal.

ricochet ['rikǝʃei] 1. n ricochet m 2. vi (ricocheted [-ʃeid]) ricocher.

rid [rid] vtr (rid) débarrasser, délivrer (s.o. of sth, qn de qch); **to get r. of sth**, se débarrasser de qch; Com: **article hard to get r. of**, article d'écoulement difficile. **'riddance** n F: **good r.!** bon débarras!

ridden ['ridn] see ride II.

riddle¹ ['ridl] n énigme f, devinette f.

riddle² 1. n crible m 2. vtr passer (qch) au crible; **to r. s.o. with bullets**, cribler qn de balles.

ride [raid] I. n (a) promenade f (à cheval, à bicyclette, en voiture); **to go for a r.**, faire une promenade à cheval; **to go for a r. in the car**, faire un tour en voiture; **it's a short r. on the bus**, c'est un court trajet en autobus; F: **to give a child a r. on one's back**, porter un enfant sur son dos; **to take s.o. for a r.**, (i) emmener qn faire une promenade (à cheval, en voiture) (ii) F: faire marcher, duper, qn (b) (in forest) allée cavalière; piste f. II. v (rode; ridden) 1. vi (a) aller, se promener, monter, à cheval; **he rides well**, il est bon cavalier; il monte bien; **to r. on an elephant**, monter à dos d'éléphant (b) aller, se promener, en voiture; aller en autobus (c) (of boat) **to r. at anchor**, mouiller 2. vtr (a) courir (une course) (b) monter (un cheval); **to r. an elephant**, monter à dos d'éléphant; **to r. a bicycle**, aller, se promener, monter, à bicyclette; **to r. one's horse at a fence**, diriger son cheval sur une barrière; **ridden by fear**, hanté par la peur. **'ride 'out** vtr **to r. o. the storm**, Nau: étaler la tempête; Fig: surmonter la

crise. **'rider** n (a) cavalier, -ière; (horseracing) jockey m; (in circus) écuyer, -ère; **he's a good r.**, il monte bien (à cheval) (b) ajouté m, annexe f, clause additionnelle (d'un document); avenant m (d'un verdict). **'riderless** a (cheval) sans cavalier. **'ride 'up** vi (of garment) remonter. **'riding** n équitation f; **r. habit**, amazone f; **r. breeches**, culotte de cheval; **r. boots**, bottes (à l'écuyère); **r. school**, école d'équitation; (enclosed) manège m.

ridge [ridʒ] n arête f, crête f (de montagne); faîte m, crête f (d'un comble); chaîne f (de coteaux); Agr: billon m, butte f (de terre); ride f (sur le sable); strie f (sur une surface); Meteor: **r. of high pressure**, dorsale f barométrique.

ridicule ['ridikju:l] 1. n moquerie f, raillerie f, dérision f; **to hold s.o., sth, up to r.**, se moquer de qn, de qch; tourner qn, qch, en ridicule 2. vtr se moquer de, ridiculiser (qn, qch). **ri'diculous** a ridicule; **to make oneself r.**, se rendre ridicule. **ri'diculously** adv ridiculement; d'une façon ridicule. **ri'diculousness** n ridicule m.

rife [raif] a (of disease) **to be r.**, régner, sévir; (of rumour) courir (les rues).

riff-raff ['rifræf] n coll F: canaille f, racaille f.

rifle¹ ['raifl] vtr piller (une armoire); (fouiller et) vider (les poches de qn); violer, spolier (un tombeau).

rifle² n carabine f (de chasse); fusil (rayé).

rift [rift] n fente f; fissure f; **r. in the clouds**, éclaircie f.

rig [rig] 1. n derrick m; (offshore) plate-forme f de forage 2. vtr (rigged) truquer (les élections); **to r. the market**, provoquer une hausse, une baisse, factice. **'rigging** n gréement m (d'un navire). **'rig 'out** F: attifer (qn). **'rig-out** n F: tenue f. **'rig 'up** vtr monter, installer (un appareil); mâter (un mât de charge); F: **to r. sth up**, faire une installation de fortune.

right [rait] 1. a (a) Mth: **r. angle**, angle droit; **to meet at r. angles**, se croiser à angle droit (b) bon, juste; honnête, droit; **more than is r.**, plus que de raison; **it's only r.**, ce n'est que justice, c'est juste; **I thought it r. to**, j'ai cru, jugé, bon de (b) **to do the r. thing**, se conduire honorablement (c) correct, juste, exact; **to give the r. answer**, répondre juste; donner la bonne réponse; **the sum is r.**, l'addition est exacte; **to put an error r.**, redresser, corriger, rectifier, une erreur; **my watch is r.**, ma montre est à l'heure; **to be r.**, être juste; (of pers) avoir raison; **the r. word**, le mot juste; **the r. side of a material**, l'endroit m d'un tissu; **have you the r. amount?** avez-vous votre compte? **is that the r. house?** est-ce bien la maison? **the r. train**, le bon train; **the r. way**, **r. side**, **up**, à l'endroit; **to know the r. people**, avoir des relations utiles; **to be on the r. road**, être sur le bon chemin; **to put s.o. r.**, détromper qn; **in the r. place**, bien placé; à sa place; **the r. man (for the job)**, l'homme qu'il faut (pour la tâche); **you came at the r. moment**, vous êtes venu au bon moment; **the r. thing to do**, ce qu'il y a de mieux à faire; **that's r.!** c'est ça! c'est bien cela! **quite r.!** parfaitement! F: **r. (you are)!** bon! d'accord! **to get on the r. side of s.o.**, s'insinuer dans les bonnes grâces de qn; **he's on the r. side of forty**, il n'a pas encore quarante ans; **to be in one's r. mind**, avoir toute sa raison; **as r. as rain**, en parfaite santé; **to set things r.**, rétablir les choses; **things will come r. in the end**, les affaires s'arrangeront; **everything's all r.**, tout

est très bien; tout va bien; **all r.,** bien! entendu! O.K.!
d'accord! **it's all r.** with, by, me, je n'ai rien contre; **is it
(all) r.?** est-ce que ça va? **I'm all r. again now,** je suis
tout à fait remis maintenant; **he's all r.!** c'est un bon
type! (d) (côté) droit; **r. hand,** main droite; **on the r.
side,** du côté droit; à droite, sur la droite **2.** n (a) le
droit; la justice; le bien; **r. and wrong,** le bien et le mal;
to be in the r., avoir raison; être dans son droit (b)
droit, titre m; **to have a r., the r.,** to sth, avoir droit à
qch; **to have a r., the r.,** to do sth, avoir le droit de faire
qch; **by what r.?** de quel droit? **in one's own r.,** de son
chef; en propre; **r. of way,** Jur: (across property)
servitude f de passage; Aut: priorité f (de passage);
human rights, droits de l'homme; **by rights,** en toute
justice; **to be within one's rights,** être dans son droit; **to
set things to right,** arranger qch; mettre qch en ordre
(c) droite f; côté droit; **on the r.,** à droite; **on your r.,** à
votre droite; Aut: **to keep to the r.,** tenir la droite; Pol:
the R., la droite **3.** adv (a) **to go r. on,** continuer tout
droit; **to do sth r. away,** NAm: **r. off,** faire qch sur-le-
champ, immédiatement; **I'll be r. back,** je reviens tout
de suite; **to sink r. to the bottom,** couler droit au fond;
r. at the top, tout en haut; **r. in the middle,** au beau
milieu; **he threw it r. in my face,** il me l'a jeté en pleine
figure; **a wall r. round the house,** un mur tout autour
de la maison; **the wind was r. behind us,** nous avions le
vent juste dans le dos (b) **to do r.,** bien faire; bien agir;
it serves you r.! vous n'avez que ce que vous méritez!
(c) (répondre) correctement; (deviner) juste; **nothing
goes r. with me,** rien ne me réussit; **if I remember r.,** si
je me souviens bien; **to turn out (all) r.,** s'arranger; **I
got your letter all r.,** j'ai bien reçu votre lettre (d) à
droite; **to keep r.,** tenir la droite; **he owes money r. and
left,** il doit de l'argent de tous les côtés **4.** vtr redresser,
réparer (un tort); **to r. itself,** se redresser. **'right-
angled** a à angle droit; (triangle) rectangle. **'righteous** ['raitʃəs] a juste, vertueux; (of anger)
justifié. **'righteousness** n droiture f, vertu f.
'rightful a légitime; juste. **'rightfully** adv légitimement; à juste titre. **'right-hand** a (pouce,
gant) de la main droite; (tiroir) de droite; **on my r.-h.
side,** à ma droite; **on the r.-h. side,** du côté droit; Fig:
r.-h. man, homme de confiance; bras droit. **'right-
handed** a (of pers) droitier; (coup) du droit.
'rightly adv bien; correctement; à juste titre; **to act
r.,** bien agir; **I can't r. say,** je ne saurais dire au juste; **r.
or wrongly,** à tort ou à raison; **if I remember r.,** si je me
souviens bien. **'right-'minded** a bien pensant.
'rightness n justesse f (d'une décision); exactitude f
(d'une réponse). **'right-'wing** a Pol: (politique) de
droite.

rigid ['ridʒid] a rigide, raide; (of conduct) sévère, strict.
ri'gidity n rigidité f; (of conduct) sévérité f; intransigeance f. **'rigidly** adv rigidement; (agir)
sévèrement.

rigmarole ['rigmərəul] n galimatias m; litanie f.

rigour, NAm: **rigor** ['rigər] n rigueur f; sévérité f (de
la loi). **'rigorous** a rigoureux. **'rigorously** adv
rigoureusement.

rim [rim] n jante f (d'une roue); bord m (d'un vase);
monture f (de lunettes). **'rimless** a (lunettes) sans
monture.

rime [raim] n givre m; gelée blanche.

rind [raind] n peau f, pelure f (de fruit); couenne f (de

lard); croûte f (de fromage).

ring¹ [riŋ] **1.** n (a) (on finger) anneau m; (jewelled)
bague f; **wedding r.,** alliance f; **r. finger,** annulaire m
(b) rond m, anneau; MecE: segment m (de piston);
napkin r., rond de serviette; **r. binder,** classeur à
anneaux; **r. road,** route de ceinture (autour d'une
ville); périphérique m; **r. dove,** (pigeon) ramier m (c)
anneau (d'une planète); cerne m (autour des yeux); **to
have rings round one's eyes,** avoir les yeux cernés; Fig:
to run rings round s.o., surpasser qn (d) cercle m;
sitting in a r., assis en rond (e) groupe m, petite coterie
(de personnes); réseau m (d'espionnage); Com: syndicat m, cartel m; Pej: gang m (f) arène f, piste f (de
cirque); Box: ring m; Rac: **the R.,** l'enceinte f (du
pesage, des bookmakers) **2.** vtr entourer, encercler.
'ringleader n meneur m (de révolte); chef m (de
bande, d'émeute). **'ringlet** n boucle f (de cheveux);
anglaise f. **'ringmaster** n maître m de manège
(d'un cirque). **'ringworm** n Med: teigne f.

ring² **I.** n (a) son (clair); sonnerie f (de cloches);
tintement m; timbre m (de la voix); **r. of truth,** accent
m de la vérité; **it has a hollow r.,** cela sonne creux (b)
coup m de sonnette; **there's a r. at the door,** on sonne
(à la porte) (c) coup de téléphone, de fil; appel m
téléphonique; **I'll give you a r.,** je vous passerai,
donnerai, un coup de fil. **II.** v (rang; rung) **1.** vi (a)
sonner; (of bell) tinter; **his answer didn't r. true,** sa
réponse a sonné faux (b) résonner, retentir (with, de);
my ears are ringing, les oreilles me tintent; mes oreilles
bourdonnent; **to r. for the lift,** appeler l'ascenseur (c)
téléphoner **2.** vtr (a) (faire) sonner (une cloche); **to r.
the bell,** sonner à la porte; F: **does that r. a bell?** est-ce
que cela vous rappelle quelque chose? (b) donner,
passer, un coup de téléphone, de fil, à (qn). **'ringing
1.** a (son) sonore; retentissant; **in r. tones,** d'une voix
vibrante **2.** n sonnerie f; tintement m (de cloches);
bourdonnement m (dans les oreilles); Tp: **r.
tone,** tonalité d'appel. **'ring 'off** vi Tp: raccrocher.
'ring 'out vi sonner; retentir. **'ring 'up** vtr donner un coup de téléphone, passer un coup de fil,
à (qn).

rink [riŋk] n (ice skating) r., patinoire f; (roller skating)
r., skating m.

rinse [rins] **1.** vtr rincer; **to r. one's hands,** se rincer les
mains; **to r. one's mouth (out),** se rincer la bouche **2.** n
rinçage m; **to give the washing a r.,** rincer le linge.

riot ['raiət] **1.** n émeute f, orgie f (de couleurs, de
fleurs); **to run r.,** se déchaîner; F: **it's, he's, a r.,** c'est
rigolo; c'est un rigolo; **r. police,** compagnies de
sécurité; F: **to read s.o. the r. act,** semoncer, tancer, qn
2. vi se manifester de façon violente; s'ameuter.
'rioter n émeutier, -ière. **'rioting** n émeutes fpl,
troubles mpl. **'riotous** a tapageur, bruyant. **'riot-
ously** adv tapageusement.

rip [rip] **1.** n déchirure f; fente f **2.** v (ripped) (a) vtr
fendre; déchirer; **to r. open,** ouvrir en déchirant (b) vi
se déchirer; se fendre. **'ripcord** n corde f
d'ouverture (de parachute). **'rip 'off** vtr (a) arracher, détacher (qch); (b) F: voler,
rouler (qn). **'rip-off** n F: escroquerie f; **it's a r.-o.!**
c'est du vol (manifeste)! **rip 'out** vtr arracher (une
page d'un livre). **'rip-roaring** a F: tumultueux;
(succès) fulgurant.

ripe [raip] a (of fruit) mûr; (fromage) (bien) fait; **a r.

old age, un bel âge. **'ripen 1.** *vtr* (faire) mûrir **2.** *vi* mûrir. **'ripeness** *n* maturité *f*.

ripple ['ripl] **1.** *n* ride *f* (sur l'eau); ondulation *f*; (léger) clapotis (de l'eau); murmure(s) *m(pl)* (de conversation) **2.** *vi (of lake)* se rider; *(of corn, hair)* onduler.

rise [raiz] **1.** *vi* **(rose; risen)** *(a) (of pers, sun, wind)* se lever; *(of pers)* se mettre debout; *(after a fall)* se relever; **to r. from the dead,** ressusciter *(b) (of parliament)* lever la séance *(c)* **to r. (in revolt),** se soulever **(against,** contre) *(d) (of smoke, ground)* monter, s'élever; *(of dough)* lever; **to r. to the surface,** monter à la surface; **to r. to the bait,** mordre à l'hameçon; **the barometer is rising,** le baromètre est à la hausse, est en hausse; **prices have risen,** les prix ont augmenté *(e) (of hopes)* croître; *(of spirits)* remonter; **to r. to the occasion,** se montrer à la hauteur de la situation; **to r. to the rank of colonel,** monter au grade de colonel; **he rose from nothing,** il est parti de rien *(f) (of river)* prendre sa source **2.** *n (a)* montée *f*, côte *f* (sur une route); rampe *f*; éminence *f*, élévation *f* (de terrain); hausse *f*, augmentation *f* (des prix); **r. in value of a possession,** appréciation *f* d'un bien; **to ask for a r.** (*NAm:* **a raise),** demander une augmentation (de salaire); **to give r. to sth,** engendrer, donner lieu à, qch *(b)* avancement *m* (dans sa carrière); essor *m*; montée (au pouvoir); *F:* **to get, to take, a r. out of s.o.,** mettre qn en colère. **'riser** *n* **early r.,** personne matinale; un(e) matinal(e); **to be an early r.,** être matinal. **'rising 1.** *a* (soleil) levant; (route) qui monte; (prix, baromètre) en hausse; (vent) qui se lève; (sentiment) croissant; (homme) d'avenir; **r. damp,** humidité qui monte du sol; **r. tide,** marée montante; **the r. generation,** la nouvelle génération; *(of child)* **to be r. five,** aller sur ses cinq ans **2.** *n* ameutement *m*, soulèvement *m* (de la population); lever *m* (du soleil); hausse *f* (du baromètre); crue *f* (des eaux); **r. and falling,** mouvement *m* de hausse et de baisse.

risk [risk] **1.** *n* risque *m*; péril *m*; **to take, run, risks,** courir, prendre, des risques; **to run the r. of,** risquer de; **to be at r.,** être en danger, menacé; **at the r. of his life,** au risque, au péril, de sa vie; **at one's own r.,** à ses risques et périls; **it isn't worth the r.,** ça ne vaut pas le coup; **fire r.,** risque d'incendie **2.** *vtr* risquer; hasarder (qch); **I'll r. it,** je vais risquer, tenter, le coup; **I wouldn't r. a crossing in such weather,** je ne me risquerais pas à tenter la traversée par un temps pareil. **'riskiness** *n* nature hasardeuse (d'une entreprise). **'risky** *a* (-ier, -iest) risqué; hasardeux.

rissole ['risoul] *n Cu:* croquette *f*.

rite [rait] *n* rite *m*; **the last rites,** les derniers sacrements. **ritual** ['ritjuəl] **1.** *a* rituel **2.** *n* rituel *m*; rites *mpl*. **'ritually** *adv* selon les rites; rituellement.

rival ['raivəl] **1.** *a & n* rival, -ale; concurrent, -ente **2.** *vtr* **(rivalled)** rivaliser avec. **'rivalry** *n (pl* **-ies)** rivalité *f*; émulation *f*.

river ['rivər] *n (main)* fleuve *m*; *(tributary, smaller river)* rivière *f*; **r. port,** port fluvial; **r. bank,** rive *f* (d'un fleuve, d'une rivière). **'riverside** *n* bord *m* de l'eau; rive; **r. inn,** auberge située au bord d'une rivière.

rivet ['rivit] **1.** *n* rivet *m* **2.** *vtr* river; *Tchn:* riveter; **to r. s.o.'s attention,** fixer, capter, l'attention de qn. **'riveter** *n (pers)* riveur *m*. **'rivet(t)ing** *a* très intéressant; passionnant.

Riviera (the) [ðərivi'ɛərə] *Prn* **the (French) R.,** la Côte d'Azur.

RN *abbr Royal Navy.*

road [roud] *n (a)* route *f*, chemin *m*; voie *f*; *(in town)* rue *f*; **r. works,** travaux *mpl* (de voirie); **r. (traffic) accident,** accident de la circulation; **r. map,** carte routière; **r. transport,** transports routiers; **r. users,** usagers de la route; **to take the r.,** se mettre en route; **to be on the r.,** être en route; *(Th: of company, Com: of representative)* être en tournée; **r. sense,** sens pratique des dangers de la route; **he's on the right r.,** il est sur le bon chemin, *Fig:* dans la bonne voie; **the r. to London,** la route de Londres; **(on) the r. to success,** (sur) le chemin du succès; *(of car)* **to hold the r. well,** bien tenir la route; **r. test,** essai *m* (de voiture) sur route *(b) (also* **roadway)** chaussée *f*. **'roadblock** *n* barrage routier. **'roadhog** *n* chauffard *m*. **'roadhouse** *n* hôtellerie *f* en bord de route. **'roadside** *n* bord *m* de la route; **r. repairs,** dépannage *m*; **r. café,** café en bord de route, au bord de la route. **'roadway** *n* chaussée. **'roadworthy** *a (of car)* en état de marche.

roam [roum] **1.** *vi* errer, rôder **2.** *vtr* parcourir (les rues). **'roaming 1.** *a* errant, vagabond **2.** *n* course *f* à l'aventure.

roar [rɔːr] **1.** *n* hurlement *m*; rugissement *m* (de qn, de lion); grondement *m* (de canon); mugissement *m* (de taureau, de la mer); ronflement *m* (de fourneau); **roars of laughter,** grands éclats de rire **2.** *v (a) vi* hurler, rugir; *(of sea)* mugir; *(of thunder)* gronder; *(of fire)* ronfler; **to r. with laughter,** éclater de rire *(b) vtr* **to r. (out),** hurler, vociférer (un ordre). **'roaring 1.** *a* (homme) hurlant; (lion) rugissant; (taureau, vent) mugissant; (tonnerre) grondant; **r. fire,** belle flambée; **r. success,** succès fou; **to do a r. trade,** faire un gros commerce.

roast [roust] **1.** *v (a) vtr* (faire) rôtir (la viande); torréfier, griller (le café) *(b) vi (of meat)* rôtir; *(of pers)* se rôtir (au soleil) **2.** *n Cu:* rôti *m*; **a r. of veal, of pork,** un rôti de veau, de porc **3.** *a* **r. meat,** viande rôtie; **r. beef,** rôti de bœuf; rosbif *m*; **r. chicken,** poulet rôti. **'roaster** *n Cu:* volaille *f* à rôtir. **'roasting 1.** *n* rôtissage *m* (de la viande); torréfaction *f* (du café); **r. chicken,** poulet à rôtir **2.** *a* brûlant; *F:* **it's r. in here!** on crève de chaleur ici!

rob [rɔb] *vtr* **(robbed)** voler, dévaliser (qn); piller (un verger); **to r. s.o. of sth,** voler, dérober, qch à qn. **'robber** *n* voleur *m*. **'robbery** *n (pl* **-ies)** vol *m*; **armed r.,** vol à main armée; *F:* **it's daylight r.!** c'est de l'escroquerie! c'est du vol manifeste!

robe [roub] *n* robe *f* (d'office, de cérémonie, de magistrat); toge *f* (universitaire); **bath r.,** peignoir *m* de bain.

robin ['rɔbin] *n (a) Orn:* **r. (redbreast),** rouge-gorge *m (b) Bot:* **ragged r.,** lychnide *f* des prés.

robot ['roubɔt] *n* robot *m*; automate *m*.

robust [rou'bʌst] *a* robuste, vigoureux, solide. **ro'bustness** *n* robustesse *f*; vigueur *f*.

rock¹ [rɔk] *n (a)* rocher *m*, roc *m*; *Geol:* roche *f*; **a r.,** un rocher, une roche; *Geog:* **the R. (of Gibraltar),** le Rocher de Gibraltar; *Nau:* **to run on the rocks,** donner sur les écueils; *F:* **to be on the rocks,** *(of pers)* être sans le sou, fauché; *(of marriage)* crouler; **whisky on the rocks,** whisky aux glaçons *m*; **r. face,** paroi *f*; **r. climber,** varappeur *m*; **r. crystal,** cristal de roche; **r.**

salt, sel gemme; *Ich:* **r. salmon,** roussette *f; Cu:* **r. cake, bun,** rocher; **r. drawings,** dessins rupestres; **r. plant,** plante alpine; **r. garden,** (jardin de) rocaille *f;* **prices have reached r. bottom,** les prix sont au plus bas *(b) Comest:* **(stick of) r.,** bâton de sucrerie *f.* **'rockery** *n (pl* **-ies)** (jardin *m* de) rocaille. **'rocky[1]** *a* **(-ier, -iest)** rocailleux; rocheux; *Geog:* **the R. Mountains,** *npl* the Rockies, les (montagnes) Rocheuses.

rock[2] I. *v* 1. *vtr (a)* bercer, balancer; basculer (un levier); **to r. a child on one's knees,** balancer un enfant sur ses genoux; **the earthquake rocked the house,** le tremblement de terre a ébranlé la maison *(b) (shock)* secouer; *Fig:* **to r. the boat,** secouer la barque 2. *vi* se balancer. II. *n Mus:* rock *m;* **r. and roll,** rock (and roll) *m.* **'rocker** *n (a)* bascule *f* (de fauteuil); *F:* **to be off one's r.,** être fou, timbré *(b)* fauteuil *m* à bascule. **'rocking** I. *a* oscillant; *(unsteady)* branlant; **r. chair, horse,** fauteuil, cheval, à bascule 2. *n* balancement *m,* bercement *m;* oscillation *f.* **rocky[2]** *a* **(-ier, -iest)** *F:* branlant; chancelant.

rocket ['rɔkit] 1. *n* fusée *f;* **to fire, launch, a r.,** lancer une fusée; **r. launcher,** lance-fusées *m inv;* **r. base,** base de lancement de fusées; *F:* **he's just had a r. from his father,** son père vient de lui passer un savon 2. *vi (of prices)* monter en flèche.

rod [rɔd] *n* baguette *f;* verge *f; MecE:* tige *f;* **to make a r. for one's own back,** se préparer des ennuis; **to rule s.o. with a r. of iron,** gouverner qn avec une main de fer; mener qn à la baguette; **(fishing) r.,** canne *f* à pêche; **r. and line,** ligne *f* de pêche; **curtain, stair, r.,** tringle *f* de rideau, d'escalier.

rode [roud] *see* ride II.

rodent ['roudənt] *n Z:* rongeur *m.*

roe[1] [rou] *n (pl* **roe(s))** *Z:* **r. (deer),** chevreuil *m.* **'roebuck** *n* chevreuil (mâle).

roe[2] *n inv in pl* **(hard) r.,** œufs *mpl* (de poisson); **soft r.,** laite *f,* laitance *f.*

roger ['rɔdʒər] *int WTel:* (message) reçu et compris.

rogue [roug] *n* coquin, -ine; espiègle *mf; (child)* fripon, -onne; **rogues' gallery,** collection de portraits de criminels *mpl;* **r. elephant,** éléphant solitaire. **'roguish** *a* coquin, espiègle. **'roguishly** *adv* avec espièglerie. **'roguishness** *n* espièglerie *f.*

rôle [roul] *n* rôle *m.*

roll [roul] 1. *n (a)* rouleau *m* (de papier); bobine *f* (de film); *(of sweater)* **r. neck,** col roulé *(b)* **(bread) r.,** petit pain *(c) Adm:* rôle *m,* contrôle *m,* liste *f;* **to call the r.,** faire l'appel *m;* **r. call,** appel *m* (nominal); **r. of honour,** liste de ceux qui sont morts pour la patrie; *Sch:* tableau *m* d'honneur; *Jur: etc:* **to strike s.o. off the rolls,** rayer qn du tableau *(d) (of ship)* roulis *m; (of aircraft)* (vol *m* en) tonneau *m (e)* roulement *m* (de tambour, de tonnerre) 2. *v (a) vtr* rouler (une bille, ses yeux, une cigarette); enrouler (du papier); cylindrer (une route); laminer (des métaux); *Cu:* étendre (la pâte) au rouleau; **to r. one's r's,** rouler les r; grasseyer *(b) vi* rouler; *(of pers, animal)* se rouler; *(of thunder)* gronder; **the tears rolled down his cheeks,** les larmes coulaient sur ses joues; *F:* **to be rolling (in money, in it),** rouler sur l'or. **'roll a'bout** *vi* rouler ça et là. **'roll a'long** *vi* rouler. **'roll a'way** *vi* s'éloigner (en roulant). **'roll 'back** *vtr & i* rouler (en arrière). **'roll 'by** *vi* passer (en roulant). **rolled** *a* **r. gold,** doublé *m;* plaqué *m* (or). **'roller** *n (a)* rouleau *m* (à peinture, à

cheveux, transporteur); enrouleur *m* (de store); roulette *f* (de fauteuil); *Paperm:* calendre *f; Mec:* laminoir *m;* **road r.,** rouleau compresseur; **r. skating,** patin(age) à roulettes; **r. skates,** patins à roulettes; **r. towel,** serviette sans fin; **r. blind,** store sur rouleau; *(at fair)* **r. coaster,** montagnes *fpl* russes *(b) (of the sea)* lame *f* de houle. **'roller-skate** *vi* faire du patin à roulettes. **'roll 'in** *vi* entrer en roulant; *(of waves)* déferler; *F: (of orders, letters)* affluer; *F:* **he rolled in at midnight,** il a rappliqué à minuit. **'rolling** 1. *a* roulant; qui roule; (pays) ondulé, onduleux; *(of sea)* gros, houleux; **to have a r. gait,** se balancer, se dandiner, en marchant; *F:* **he's a r. stone,** il roule sa bosse 2. *n* roulement *m;* **r. pin,** rouleau (à pâtisserie); **r. mill,** usine de laminage *m; Rail:* **r. stock,** matériel roulant. **'roll-'neck(ed)** *a* (chandail) à col roulé. **'roll 'on** *vi (of time)* s'écouler; *F:* **r. on the holidays!** vivement les vacances! **'roll-on** *n* flacon *m* à bille. **'roll 'out** 1. *vtr* débiter (des vers); *Cu:* étendre (la pâte) au rouleau 2. *vi* sortir en roulant. **'roll 'over** 1. *vtr* retourner; culbuter (qn) 2. *vi* se retourner (en roulant); rouler (sur le sol); *(of animal, esp dog)* se rouler (sur le dos); **to r. o. and over,** rouler sur soi-même. **'rolltop** *n* **r. desk,** bûreau à cylindre *m.* **'roll 'up** 1. *vtr* rouler, enrouler (une carte); retrousser (ses manches); envelopper (qch) 2. *vi* se rouler (into, en); **to r. (oneself) up in a blanket,** s'enrouler dans une couverture; *F:* **he rolled up at midnight,** il est arrivé, il a rappliqué, à minuit.

Roman ['roumən] *a & n* romain, -aine; **R. numerals,** chiffres romains; **R. nose,** nez busqué, aquilin; **R. Catholic,** *a & n* catholique *(mf).* **Roma'nesque** *a Arch:* roman.

romance [rə'mæns, rou-] 1. *n (a)* the **R. languages,** les langues romanes *(b)* histoire *f* romanesque; roman *m;* **it's quite a r.,** c'est tout un roman; **love of r.,** amour du romanesque; **the r. of the sea,** la poésie de la mer *(c) (between two people)* idylle *f* 2. *vi* exagérer; inventer à plaisir. **ro'mantic** 1. *a* (histoire) romanesque; (paysage, *Art: Lit:* école, mouvement) romantique 2. *n* romantique *mf.* **ro'mantically** *adv* (décrire) de façon romanesque; (chanter) en romantique. **ro'manticism** *n* romantisme *m.* **ro'manticize** 1. *vtr* romancer (une idée, un incident); faire tout un roman d'(un incident) 2. *vi* donner dans le romantique.

Romania [rou'meiniə] *Prn Geog:* = Rumania.

Rome [roum] *Prn* Rome *f; Ecc:* **the Church of R.,** l'Église romaine; le catholicisme.

romp [rɔmp] 1. *n* gambades *fpl* 2. *vi* gambader; s'ébattre (bruyamment); *Rac:* **to r. home,** gagner haut la main; arriver dans un fauteuil; **to r. through an exam,** passer, réussir, un examen sans effort. **'romper(s)** *n(pl) Cl:* barboteuse *f* (d'enfant).

roof [ru:f] 1. *n* toit *m;* plafond *m* (de mine); voûte *f* (de tunnel); **the r. of the mouth,** la voûte du palais; **to be without a r. over one's head,** se trouver sans logement; **under the same r.,** sous le même toit; *F:* **to raise the r.,** faire beaucoup de bruit, du vacarme; *F: (of pers)* **to go through, to hit, the r.,** sortir de ses gonds 2. *Aut:* **sunshine r.,** toit ouvrant; **r. rack,** galerie *f* 2. *vtr Const:* couvrir (une maison); **to r. sth (over),** recouvrir qch d'un toit. **'roofing** *n* toiture *f;* couverture *f.* **'roof-**

top n toit; *Fig:* **to shout sth from the rooftops,** crier qch sur les toits.

rook¹ [ruk] n *Orn:* freux m. **'rookery** n (pl -ies) colonie f de freux.

rook² n *Chess:* tour f.

rook³ vtr *F:* refaire, rouler (qn).

room [ru(:)m] **1.** n (a) place f; espace m; **to take up a lot of r.,** occuper beaucoup de place; être très encombrant; **to be cramped for r.,** être à l'étroit; **to make r. for s.o.,** faire place à qn; **there's r. for improvement,** cela laisse à désirer (b) pièce f; salle f; (*bedroom*) chambre f (à coucher); **double r.,** chambre à deux personnes; **single r.,** chambre à une personne; **living r.,** salle de séjour; living m; **r. and board,** chambre et pension; (*in hotel*) **r. service,** repas servis dans les chambres; (*of wine*) **at r. temperature,** chambré; **furnished rooms to let,** chambres meublées à louer; **I have rooms in town,** j'ai un appartement en ville **2.** vi *NAm:* (*Br* = **lodge**) vivre en meublé; partager un logement (**with s.o.,** avec qn). **'roomful** n salle pleine. **'rooming house** n *NAm:* (*Br* = **lodging house**) maison f de rapport; immeuble m. **'room-mate** n compagnon m, compagne f, de chambre. **'roomy** a (-ier, -iest) (appartement) spacieux; (vêtement) ample.

roost [ru:st] **1.** n juchoir m; perchoir m; (*of crime*) **to come home to r.,** se retourner contre son auteur; **to rule the r.,** faire la loi (chez soi) **2.** vi (*of hens*) (se) percher, (se) jucher. **'rooster** n coq m.

root [ru:t] **I.** n racine f (d'une plante, d'un mot); source f (d'une idée); **to take r.,** prendre racine; **to pull up a plant by the roots,** déraciner une plante; **to put down roots,** s'enraciner; **r. crops,** racines alimentaires; *NAm:* **r. beer,** bière non alcoolisée (faite de racines); **r. cause,** cause première; *Mth:* **square r.,** racine carrée. **II.** v **1.** vtr enraciner; **to remain rooted to the spot,** rester cloué sur place **2.** vi (*of plant*) s'enraciner; prendre racine (b) **to r. (about, around),** fouiller (**among, in,** dans). **'root 'for** vtr *NAm:* encourager (son équipe) (de ses applaudissements). **'root 'out, 'up** vtr dénicher; extirper (un abus).

rope [roup] **1.** n corde f, cordage m; cordon m (de sonnette); grand collier (de perles); **to know the ropes,** connaître son affaire; **to show s.o. the ropes,** mettre qn au courant; **r. ladder,** échelle de corde **2.** vtr corder (un paquet); encorder (des alpinistes); **roped together,** en cordée. **'rope 'in** vtr entraîner (qn) dans un projet. **'rope 'off** vtr réserver (un espace) au moyen d'une corde tendue. **'rop(e)y** a (-ier, -iest) *F:* de mauvaise qualité.

rosary ['rouzəri] n (pl -ies) rosaire m; chapelet m.

rose¹ [rouz] see **rise 1.**

rose² **1.** n (a) rose f; (bush, tree), rosier m; **wild r.,** églantine f; **r. garden,** roseraie f; **life is not a bed of roses, not all roses,** tout n'est pas rose dans la vie (b) pomme f (d'arrosoir); rosace f (de plafond); **r. window,** rosace **2.** a & n (*colour*) rose (m). **rosé** ['rouzei] n (vin) rosé m. **'rosebud** n bouton m de rose. **'rose-coloured** a **to see things through r.-c. spectacles,** voir tout en rose. **'rosemary** n *Bot:* romarin m. **'rosewood** n bois m de rose. **'rosy** a (-ier, -iest) rose; rosé; **r. cheeks,** joues vermeilles; **a r. prospect,** une perspective souriante; **to paint everything in r. colours,** peindre tout en rose.

rosette [rou'zet] n cocarde f; rosette f (de ruban, d'une décoration).

rosin ['rɔzin] n colophane f.

rostrum ['rɔstrəm] n tribune f; (*at auction sale*) estrade f.

rot [rɔt] **1.** n (a) pourriture f; carie f; (*in timber*) **dry, wet, r.,** pourriture sèche, humide; **to stop the r.,** parer à la démoralisation; **the r. has set in,** le moral (de l'équipe) a flanché (b) *F:* bêtises fpl; **to talk r.,** dire des imbécillités **2.** v (**rotted**) (a) vi (se) pourrir; se décomposer; **to r. away,** tomber en pourriture (b) (faire) pourrir; putréfier. **'rotten** a pourri; (œuf) gâté; *Fig:* corrompu; *F:* (temps) de chien; **what r. luck!** quelle guigne! **r. job,** sale besogne; **I feel r.,** je me sens mal fichu, patraque. **'rotter** n *F:* **he's a r.!** quel sale type!

rota ['routə] n tableau m (de service).

rotate [rou'teit] **1.** vi tourner; (*of pers*) remplir ses fonctions à tour de rôle **2.** vtr faire tourner (qch); alterner (des cultures). **'rotary** a rotatif; **r. motion,** mouvement de rotation; **r. drier,** séchoir sur pied; **r. (printing) press,** rotative f. **ro'tating** a tournant. **ro'tation** n rotation f; **in, by, r.,** à tour de rôle; **r. of crops,** assolement m; *Mec:* **rotations per minute,** tours-minute mpl. **ro'tatory** a rotatoire; de rotation. **'rotor** n rotor m.

rotund [rou'tʌnd] a rond, arrondi. **ro'tundity** n rondeur f.

rouge [ru:ʒ] **1.** n *Toil:* rouge m (à joues) **2.** vtr **to r. one's cheeks,** se farder (les joues); se mettre du rouge aux joues.

rough [rʌf] **1.** a (a) (*of surface*) rêche, rugueux, rude; (*of road*) raboteux; (*of ground*) inégal, accidenté; **in the r. state,** à l'état brut; **to feel r.,** se sentir patraque, mal fichu (b) (*violent*) grossier; brutal; **r. sea,** mer grosse, agitée; *Nau:* **r. weather,** gros temps; **to have a r. crossing,** faire une mauvaise traversée; *F:* **he's had a r. time,** il a mangé de la vache enragée; *F:* **it was r. on him,** c'était dur pour lui; **r. handling;** *F:* **stuff,** brutalités fpl; **to be r. with s.o.,** brutaliser, rudoyer, qn; *F:* **a r. customer,** un sale type; **to give s.o. a r. handling,** malmener qn; **r. and ready,** exécuté grossièrement; (installation) de fortune; (*of pers*) cavalier; sans façons (c) (*of manners*) grossier; bourru, rude; **r. justice,** justice sommaire (d) approximatif; **r. sketch,** ébauche f, esquisse f; **r. translation,** essai de traduction, premier jet; **r. copy, draft,** brouillon m; **r. guess, estimate,** approximation f; **at a r. guess,** approximativement (e) (*of voice*) rude, rauque, âpre **2.** adv rudement; grossièrement; (jouer) brutalement; *F:* (coucher) sur la dure; *F:* **to cut up r.,** se mettre en colère **3.** n (a) **to take the r. with the smooth,** prendre le bien avec le mal; *Golf:* **in the r.,** dans l'herbe longue (b) *F:* (*pers*) vaurien m, voyou m **4.** vtr *F:* **to r. it,** vivre à la dure. **'roughage** n (*in diet*) ballast m. **'rough-and-'tumble** n mêlée f. **'roughen** vtr rendre rude, rugueux. **'rough-house** n *F:* chahut m, bousculade f. **'roughly** adv (a) rudement; brutalement; **to treat s.o. r.,** malmener qn (b) grossièrement; **r. made,** grossier; **to sketch sth r.,** faire un croquis sommaire de qch (c) approximativement; en gros; à peu près; **r. speaking,** en général. **'roughneck** n *F:* voyou m. **'roughness** n rudesse f; rugosité f; inégalité f (du sol); (*of pers*) grossièreté f, brusquerie f; agitation f (de la mer).

'**rough 'out** *vtr* ébaucher (un plan). '**roughshod**
a **to ride r. over s.o.**, traiter qn sans ménagement;
fouler qn aux pieds. '**rough 'up** *vtr F:* malmener,
rudoyer (qn).
roulette [ruːˈlet] *n* roulette *f*.
round [raund] **1.** *a* rond, circulaire; **r. table conference**,
table ronde; **r. shoulders**, épaules voûtées; **to make sth
r.**, arrondir qch; **r. dance**, ronde *f*; **r. trip**, voyage aller-
retour; **r. robin**, pétition (revêtue de signatures); **r.
dozen**, bonne douzaine; **in r. figures**, en chiffres ronds
2. *n* (*a*) cercle *m*, rond *m*; **theatre in the r.**, théâtre en
rond (*b*) tranche *f* (de pain); *Cu:* **r. of sandwiches**,
sandwich fait de deux tranches de pain de mie (et
coupé en quatre); **r. of toast**, rôtie *f*; **r. of beef**, gîte *f* à
la noix (*c*) **the daily r.**, la routine de tous les jours; le
train-train quotidien; **one continual r. of pleasures**,
une succession perpétuelle de plaisirs (*d*) tour *m*; **to
stand a r. (of drinks)**, payer une tournée (générale); **to
have a r. of golf**, faire une tournée de golf; **the story
went the round(s) (of the village)**, l'histoire a fait le
tour (du village) (*e*) tournée (du facteur, d'un médecin); *Mil:* ronde *f* (d'inspection); **to do one's round(s)**,
faire sa tournée; (*of doctor*) faire sa visite (à l'hôpital);
(*of soldier*) faire sa ronde (*f*) *Box:* round *m*, reprise *f*;
Ten: tour, série *f* (d'un tournoi); *Sp:* manche *f* (d'une
compétition); **r. of applause**, salve *f*
d'applaudissements; *Mil:* **a r. (of ammunition)**, une
cartouche (*g*) *Mus:* canon *m* **3.** *adv* **to go r.**,
tourner (en rond); décrire un cercle, des cercles; **the
wheels go r.**, les roues tournent; **to turn r.**, se
retourner; **all (the) year r.**, (pendant) toute l'année;
winter came r., l'hiver est revenu; **garden with a wall
right r., all r.**, jardin avec un mur tout autour; **to be six
feet r.**, avoir six pieds de tour; **all the country r. about**,
tout le pays à l'entour; **taking it all r.**, dans l'ensemble;
to hand r. the cakes, faire circuler les gâteaux; **there
isn't enough to go r.**, il n'y en a pas assez pour tout le
monde; **it's a long way r.**, cela fait un grand détour; **to
take the longest way r.**, prendre le chemin le plus long;
to ask s.o. r. for the evening, inviter qn à venir passer la
soirée (chez soi); **if you're r. this way**, si vous passez
par ici **4.** *prep* autour de; **r. the table**, autour de la
table; **r. (about) midday**, vers midi; **to travel r. the
world**, faire le tour du monde; **to show s.o. r. the
garden**, faire faire à qn le tour du jardin; **to look r. the
room**, jeter un coup d'œil autour de la pièce; **to go r.
the museum**, visiter le musée; **to go r. an obstacle**,
contourner un obstacle; **to go r. the corner**, (*of pers*)
tourner le coin; (*of car*) prendre le virage; *F:* **to go r.
the bend**, devenir fou, dingue **5.** *v* (*a*) *vtr* arrondir;
(*of pers*) tourner (un coin); (*of car*) prendre (un virage); *Nau:* doubler, franchir
(un cap) (*b*) *vi* s'arrondir; **to r. on s.o.**, s'en prendre à
qn. '**roundabout 1.** *n* (*at fair*) (manège *m* de)
chevaux *mpl* de bois; manège; *Aut:* rond-point *m* **2.** *a*
détourné; indirect; **to take a r. way**, faire un détour.
'**rounded** *a* arrondi. '**rounders** *n Games:* balle *f*
au camp. '**round-'eyed** *a* les, aux, yeux ronds.
'**roundish** *a* rondelet; arrondi. '**roundly** *adv*
(parler) rondement, carrément. '**round-necked** *a*
(pullover) au col ras le cou. '**roundness** *n* rondeur
f. '**round 'off** *vtr* achever (des négociations, un
discours). '**round 'on** *vtr* tomber sur (qn).
'**round-'shouldered** *a* voûté. '**round 'up** *vtr*

rassembler (le bétail); faire une rafle de (criminels);
arrondir (une somme).
rouse [rauz] *vtr* (*a*) **to r. s.o. (from sleep)**, (r)éveiller qn;
to r. oneself, se secouer; **to r. s.o. to action**, inciter qn à
agir (*b*) mettre (qn) en colère (*c*) éveiller (les passions);
soulever (l'indignation); susciter (l'admiration,
l'opposition). '**rousing** *a* (applaudissements) chaleureux; (discours) vibrant; **r. chorus**, refrain
entraînant.
rout[1] [raut] *Mil:* **1.** *n* déroute *f* **2.** *vtr* mettre (une
armée) en déroute. '**routed** *a* en déroute.
rout[2] *vtr & i* fouiller (dans des papiers). '**rout 'out**
vtr dénicher (qn); tirer (qn) (de son lit).
route [ruːt, *NAm:* raut] **1.** *n* (*a*) itinéraire *m*; route *f*;
sea r., route maritime; **bus r.**, ligne *f*, itinéraire,
parcours *m*, d'un autobus; *PN:* **all routes**, toutes
directions; *Mil:* **r. march**, marche d'entraînement **2.**
vtr (routeing) acheminer.
routine [ruːˈtiːn] *n* (*a*) routine *f*; **r. work**, travail de
routine; affaires courantes; **daily r.**, le train-train
journalier; **r. inquiries**, constatations d'usage; **to do
sth as a matter of r.**, faire qch d'office (*b*) *Th:* numéro
m (de danse).
roving [ˈrouviŋ] *a* vagabond; (ambassadeur) itinérant; **to have a r. eye**, avoir l'œil égrillard.
row[1] [rou] *n* rang *m* (de chaises, de gens); rangée *f* (de
maisons, d'arbres); ligne *f*; file *f* (de voitures); **in a r.**,
en rang, en ligne; **three times in a r.**, trois fois de suite;
in rows, par rangs; **in the front r.**, au premier rang.
row[2] [rou] **I.** *v* **1.** *vi* (*a*) ramer; *Nau:* nager; **to r. round
the island**, faire le tour de l'île à la rame (*b*) canoter;
faire du canotage; *Sp:* faire de l'aviron **2.** *vtr* conduire
(un bateau) à l'aviron; **to r. a race**, faire une course
d'aviron. **II.** *n* promenade *f* en canot; **to go for a r.**,
faire une promenade en canot. '**rower** *n* rameur,
-euse. '**rowing** *n* canotage; *Sp:* aviron *m*; **r. boat**,
canot à rames. **rowlocks** [ˈrɔləks] *npl* dames *fpl* de
nage; tolets *mpl*.
row[3] [rau] *n* (*a*) chahut *m*, tapage *m*, vacarme *m*; **to
make a r.**, faire du chahut, du tapage (*b*) querelle *f*,
dispute *f*; scène *f*; bagarre *f*; **to have a r. with s.o.**, se
disputer avec qn; **to get into a r.**, se faire attraper.
rowan [ˈrouən] *n Bot:* **r. (tree)**, sorbier *m*.
rowdy [ˈraudi] **1.** *a* (-ier, -iest) tapageur, chahuteur **2.**
n (*pl* **-ies**) voyou *m*. '**rowdiness** *n* tapage *m*.
'**rowdyism** *n* tapage, chahut *m*; violence *f*.
royal [ˈrɔiəl] *a* (*a*) royal; **the R. household**, la maison
du roi, de la reine; **r. blue**, bleu roi (*b*) royal, princier;
magnifique; **a r. feast**, un festin de roi **2.** *n P:* membre
m de la famille royale. '**royalist** *a & n* royaliste
(*mf*). '**royally** *adv* royalement. '**royalty** *n* (*pl* **-ies**)
(*a*) royauté *f* (*b*) (membre de) la famille royale (*c*) *pl*
droits *mpl* d'auteur; (*on patent, for use of oil pipeline*)
royalties *fpl*; redevances *fpl* (d'un inventeur).
rpm *abbr* revolutions per minute.
RSPCA *abbr Royal Society for the Prevention of
Cruelty to Animals*.
RSVP *abbr répondez s'il vous plaît; please answer*.
Rt *abbr Right*.
rub [rʌb] **1.** *v* (rubbed) (*a*) *vtr* frotter; prendre un frottis
(d'un cuivre); **to r. one's hands (together)**, se frotter les
mains; **to r. shoulders with other people**, frayer avec
d'autres gens; **to r. sth dry**, sécher qch en le frottant; **to
r. sth over a surface**, enduire une surface de qch; *Cu:*

to r. sth through a sieve, passer qch au tamis (b) vi frotter (against, contre); (of pers) se frotter (contre) 2. n frottement m; friction f; to give sth a r., donner un coup de torchon à (qch); frotter, astiquer (des cuivres); Fig: there's the r.! c'est là la difficulté! 'rub a'long vi F: se débrouiller; s'accorder (bien, mal). 'rub a'way vtr enlever (qch) par le frottement. 'rubbing n frottement, frottage m; frottis m (d'un cuivre). 'rub 'down vtr bouchonner (un cheval); frictionner (qn); poncer (de la peinture). 'rub-'down n to give a horse, s.o., a r.-d., bouchonner un cheval; frictionner qn; to give sth a r.-d., donner un coup de torchon à qch; poncer la peinture. 'rub 'in vtr faire pénétrer (un liniment) par des frictions; don't r. it in! n'insistez pas davantage (sur ma gaffe)! 'rub 'off 1. vtr enlever (qch) par le frottement 2. vi (of colour) s'enlever; Fig: it rubs o. on them, cela déteint sur eux. 'rub 'out vtr effacer, 'rub 'up vtr astiquer, frotter; F: to r. s.o. up the wrong way, prendre qn à rebrousse-poil.

rubber¹ ['rʌbər] n caoutchouc m; (eraser) (India) r., gomme f; foam r., caoutchouc mousse; r. dinghy, canot pneumatique; r. stamp, tampon m; r. ball, balle en, de, caoutchouc; r. band, élastique m; Bot: r. tree, arbre à gomme; Hort: r. plant, caoutchouc. 'rubberized a (tissu) caoutchouté. 'rubber-'stamp vtr entériner (automatiquement, sans délibérations). 'rubbery a caoutchouteux.

rubber² n (at bridge) robre m; the r. (game), la belle.

rubbish ['rʌbiʃ] n (a) immondices fpl, détritus mpl; household r., ordures ménagères; r. bin, poubelle f; boîte à ordures; r. dump, dépotoir m; décharge publique (c) to talk r., dire des bêtises f; (what) r.! quelle blague! 'rubbishy a sans valeur; (marchandises) de mauvaise qualité, de camelote.

rubble ['rʌbl] n (for building) blocaille f; (after demolition) décombres mpl.

rubicund ['ru:bikənd] a (of s.o.'s face) rougeaud.

ruby ['ru:bi] 1. n (pl rubies) Miner: rubis m 2. a & n rubis (m) inv; r. wedding, noces de vermeil.

rucksack ['rʌksæk] n (NAm:=backpack) sac m à dos.

ructions ['rʌkʃnz] npl F: disputes fpl; there'll be r., il va y avoir du grabuge; if you're late there'll be r., si tu es en retard, tu te feras engueuler.

rudder ['rʌdər] n gouvernail m. 'rudderless a (navire) sans gouvernail, à la dérive.

ruddy ['rʌdi] a (-ier, -iest) (a) (teint) coloré, haut en couleur; a large, r. man, un gros rougeaud (b) rougeâtre; the r. glow (of the fire), la lueur rouge (du feu) (c) P: (=bloody) all this r. work, tout ce sacré travail; he's a r. nuisance, c'est bien embêtant en-quiquinant.

rude [ru:d] a (a) primitif, rude (b) grossier; (vers) scabreux; (dessin) obscène (c) rude; violent, brusque; r. shock, choc violent (d) (santé) robuste (e) impoli; mal élevé; grossier; to be r. to s.o., dire des grossièretés à qn; être impoli avec qn. 'rudely adv (a) primitivement; grossièrement (b) violemment; brusquement (c) impoliment, grossièrement. 'rudeness n impolitesse f, grossièreté f.

rudiment ['ru:dimənt] n rudiment m; pl premières notions (d'une discipline). rudi'mentary a rudimentaire.

ruffian ['rʌfiən] n bandit m, brute f; voyou m.

ruffle ['rʌfl] vtr ébouriffer, agiter (les cheveux); (of bird) hérisser (ses plumes); troubler, rider (la surface de l'eau); to r. s.o., s.o.'s feelings, froisser, contrarier, qn; nothing ever ruffles him, rien ne le trouble jamais.

rug [rʌg] n (a) (blanket) couverture f; travelling r., plaid m (b) (for floor) (petit) tapis; carpette f; bedside r., descente f de lit.

rugby ['rʌgbi] n r. (football), F: rugger ['rʌgər], le rugby; R. Union, rugby à quinze; R. League, rugby à treize; r.-player, rugbyman m.

rugged ['rʌgid] a (a) (of ground) raboteux, accidenté, inégal; (of rock) déchiqueté; (of tree bark) rugueux; r. features, traits rudes, irréguliers (b) (of character) bourru, rude; (indépendance) farouche.

ruin ['ru:in] 1. n a ruine f; to fall in(to) ruin(s), to go to r., tomber en ruine; in ruin(s), en ruine; to be the r. of s.o., ruiner, perdre, qn; the building is a r., l'édifice est en ruine 2. vtr ruiner; abîmer (un vêtement); to r. one's prospects, gâcher son avenir; to r. one's health, se ruiner la santé; to r. s.o.'s reputation, perdre qn de réputation; her extravagance ruined him, ses folles dépenses l'ont ruiné. rui'nation n ruine, perte f; it'll be the r. of him, ce sera sa ruine. 'ruined a (bâtiment) en ruine; (château, homme) ruiné. 'ruinous a (a) (bâtiment) (tombé) en ruine (b) ruineux; r. expense, dépenses ruineuses. 'ruinously adv r. expensive, ruineux.

rule [ru:l] 1. n (a) règle f; as a (general) r., en règle générale; r. of thumb, méthode f empirique; to make it a r. to, se faire une règle de; r. of conduct, norme f de conduite; rules and regulations, statuts mpl et règlements mpl; Ind: work(ing) to r., grève f du zèle; the rules of the game, les règles du jeu; it's against the rules, c'est contre les règles; Aut: the r. of the road, le code de la route (b) empire m, autorité f; administration f; under British r., sous l'autorité britannique; majority r., règle majoritaire (c) Meas: règle (graduée); mètre m. II. v 1. vtr (a) gouverner (un état); régner sur (une nation); contenir (ses passions); to be ruled by s.o., être sous la coupe de qn; subir la loi de qn (b) régler, rayer (du papier); tracer (une ligne) à la règle 2. vi (a) régner (over, sur); the prices ruling in London, les prix qui se pratiquent à Londres (b) décider, déclarer (that, que). 'rule 'out vtr écarter, éliminer (une possibilité). 'ruler (a) souverain, -aine (b) règle, mètre. 'ruling 1. a souverain, dominant; (cours, prix) actuel, en vigueur, du jour; the r. classes, les classes dirigeantes 2. n décision f (d'un juge); to give a r. in favour of s.o., décider en faveur de qn.

rum [rʌm] n rhum m.

Rumania [ru:'meiniə] Prn: Geog: Roumanie f. Ru'manian 1. a roumain 2. n (a) Roumain, -aine (b) Ling: roumain m.

rumble ['rʌmbl] 1. n grondement m; roulement m (d'un train, d'un camion); F: tummy rumbles, borborygmes mpl 2. vi (of thunder) gronder (sourdement); rouler; (of stomach) gargouiller; (of cart) passer avec bruit. 'rumbling n grondement (de tonnerre); roulement m (de charrette); F: tummy rumblings, borborygmes.

ruminate ['ru:mineit] vi & tr ruminer; (of pers) méditer. **'ruminant** a & n Z: ruminant (m). **rumi'nation** n rumination f. **'ruminative** a méditatif.

rummage ['rʌmidʒ] **1.** vtr & i fouiller (dans) (une armoire); **to r. about among old papers,** fouiller, fourrager, dans de vieux documents **2.** n fouille f (dans de vieux objets); **r. sale,** vente de charité (d'objets usagés).

rumour, NAm: **rumor** ['ru:mər] n rumeur f, bruit m (qui court); on-dit m inv; **r. has it, there's a r. going round, that,** le bruit court que. **'rumoured** a it's r. **that,** le bruit court, on dit, que.

rump [rʌmp] n croupe f (d'un quadrupède); croupion m (de volaille); Cu: culotte f (de bœuf); F: (of pers) postérieur m, derrière m; Cu: **r. steak,** rumsteck m, romsteck m.

rumple ['rʌmpl] vtr chiffonner, froisser (une robe); ébouriffer (les cheveux).

rumpus ['rʌmpəs] n F: chahut m, vacarme m; **to kick up a r.,** faire du chahut.

run [rʌn] **I.** v (ran; run; prp running) **1.** vi (a) courir; **to r. upstairs,** monter l'escalier quatre à quatre; **to r. up, down, the street,** monter, descendre, la rue en courant; **to r. like the devil,** courir comme un dératé (b) fuir, s'enfuir, se sauver; filer; (of yacht) **to r. before the wind,** courir vent arrière; **to r. aground,** (s')échouer; **now we must r. for it!** maintenant sauvons-nous! Pol: **to r. for office,** se porter candidat (c) aller, marcher; circuler; **train running at fifty kilometres an hour,** train qui marche à cinquante kilomètres à l'heure; **train running to Paris,** train à destination de Paris; **trains running between London and the coast,** trains qui font le service entre Londres et la côte; **this train is not running today,** ce train est supprimé aujourd'hui; **the thought keeps running through my head,** cette idée me trotte continuellement par la tête; **it runs in the family,** cela tient de la famille; **the talk ran on this subject,** la conversation a roulé sur ce sujet; Th: **the play has been running for year,** la pièce tient l'affiche depuis un an; (of amount, number) **to r. to,** monter, s'élever, à; **I can't r. to that,** c'est au-dessus de mes moyens (d) (of engine, car) fonctionner, marcher; (of engine, wheel) tourner; **the engine's running,** le moteur est en marche; El: **to r. off the mains,** se brancher sur le secteur (e) (of colour) déteindre (au lavage); (of paint, nose) couler; (of eyes) pleurer; (of ice cream) fondre; **the floor was running with water,** le parquet ruisselait d'eau; **the river runs into a lake,** la rivière se jette, débouche, dans un lac; **a heavy sea was running,** la mer était grosse; (of mountain chain) **to r. north and south,** s'étendre du nord au sud; **the road runs quite close to the village,** la route passe tout près du village; **prices are running high,** les prix sont élevés; **money runs through his fingers,** l'argent lui fond dans les mains (f) (of stocking) filer, se démailler **2.** vtr (a) **to r. a race,** courir, disputer, une course; **to r. 6 km,** courir, faire, 6 km; **to r. an errand,** faire une course; **to r. the blockade,** forcer le blocus; **to r. a temperature,** avoir de la fièvre; **to r. s.o. close,** serrer qn de près; F: **to be r. off one's feet,** être éreinté; **to r. the car into the garage,** rentrer la voiture dans le garage; **to r. s.o. into town,** conduire qn en ville (en voiture); **to r. trains between London and the coast,** établir un service de

trains entre Londres et la côte (b) faire fonctionner (une machine); **I can't afford to r. a car,** je n'ai pas les moyens d'entretenir une voiture; **my car is cheap to r.,** ma voiture est économique (c) tenir (un hôtel, un commerce); éditer, gérer (un journal); diriger (une affaire, un théâtre); **to r. one's house,** tenir sa maison (d) faire la contrebande (des armes, de l'alcool) (e) faire courir (un cheval) (f) faire passer (des tuyaux) (à travers un mur); **to r. a thorn into one's finger,** s'enfoncer une épine dans le doigt; **to r. one's eye over sth,** jeter un coup d'œil sur qch, parcourir qch des yeux; **he ran his hand through his hair,** il s'est passé la main dans les cheveux (g) faire couler (de l'eau, un bain). **II.** n (a) **at r.,** au pas de course; **to break into a r.,** se mettre à courir; **we've got them on the r.,** nous les avons mis en déroute; **criminal on the r.,** criminel recherché par la police; **to make a r. for it,** se sauver (b) course f (à pied); Fig: **to have had a good r. for one's money,** en avoir pour son argent; Cr: **to make, score, six runs,** marquer six points (c) Aut: **to go for a r.,** faire une promenade; **trial r.,** course d'essai (d) trajet m; parcours m (en voiture, par le train); Av: **take-off r.,** parcours au décollage; **to have a r. of luck,** être en veine; **a r. of bad luck,** une suite de malheurs (e) ruée f (sur les valeurs); **there's a r. on that novel,** ce roman est très demandé, on demande beaucoup ce roman (f) Typ: **r. of ten thousand copies,** tirage m à dix mille (g) cours m, marche f (des événements); Cards: séquence f; Gaming: série f (à la rouge); **the ordinary r. of things,** la routine de tous les jours; Th: (of play) **to have a long r.,** tenir longtemps l'affiche; **in the long r.,** à la longue; **the ordinary r. of mankind,** le commun des mortels; **it's just r. of the mill,** c'est ce qu'il y a de plus ordinaire; **to have the r. of s.o.'s house,** avoir libre accès à la maison de qn; **to give s.o. the r. of one's library,** mettre sa bibliothèque à la disposition de qn (h) pâturage m (pour animaux); piste f (de toboggan, de ski) (i) (in stocking) maille filée. **'runabout** n petite voiture. **'run a'cross** vtr (a) traverser en courant (b) rencontrer (qn) par hasard. **'run a'long** vi **road that runs a. the river,** chemin qui longe la rivière; **r. a.!** allez-vous-en! va-t-en! filez! **'run a'way** vi s'enfuir, se sauver; filer; (of horse) s'emballer; **don't r. a. with the idea that,** n'allez pas vous mettre dans la tête, vous imaginer, que; **that runs a. with a lot of money,** cela mange beaucoup d'argent. **'runaway 1.** a & n fugitif, -ive **2.** a (cheval) emballé; (train, camion) fou. **'run 'down 1.** vi (a) (of clockwork, battery) se décharger; (of clock) s'arrêter (b) **the sweat ran down his forehead,** la sueur lui coulait sur le front **2.** vtr (a) dénigrer, déprécier (b) Aut: heurter, renverser (qn sur la route); **to get r. down,** se faire écraser (par une voiture) (c) laisser épuiser (les stocks); restreindre la production (d'une industrie); diminuer (les effectifs); (of pers) **to be, to feel, r. d.,** se sentir épuisé. **'run-down** a (of pers, look) épuisé; (of building) délabré. **'rundown** n restriction f (de la production); F: **to give s.o. a r. of sth,** mettre qn au courant de qch. **'run 'in** vtr (a) Aut: roder (un moteur, une voiture); **running in,** en rodage (b) F: (of police) arrêter (qn). **'run 'into** vi (a) **to r. into debt,** s'endetter (b) **to r. into sth,** entrer en collision avec, heurter, qch; **to r. i. s.o.,** se heurter contre qn; F: rencontrer qn par hasard. **'runner** n (a) coureur, -euse; (horse) partant *m* (*b*) *Hort:* coulant *m*, stolon *m* (d'une plante); r. **bean,** haricot *m* (à rames) (*c*) patin *m* (de traîneau); lame *f* (de patin); chariot *m* de roulement; trolley *m*; coulisseau *m* (de tiroir) (*d*) **carpet r.,** chemin *m* d'escalier, de couloir; **table r.,** chemin de table. **runner-'up** *n* (*pl* **runners-up**) second, -onde. ' **running** 1. *a* (*a*) r. **water,** eau courante; r. **cold,** rhume de cerveau; r. **commentary,** reportage en direct; *Needlew:* r. **stitch,** point devant; **three days r.,** trois jours de suite; **to keep up a r. battle,** lutter continuellement (with, avec) (*b*) (ruisseau) coulant; (plaie) qui suppure 2. *n* (*a*) *Sp:* course(s) *f*(*pl*) (à pied); **to be in the r.,** avoir des chances de réussir; **to be out of the r.,** ne plus avoir aucune chance; **to make the r.,** mener la course (*b*) marche *f*, fonctionnement *m* (d'une machine); roulement *m* (d'une voiture); **in r. order,** en (bon) état de marche; r. **costs,** frais d'entretien (*c*) direction *f* (d'un hôtel); exploitation *f* (d'une mine). ' **runny** *a* (-ier, -iest) (nez) qui coule; (sauce) trop liquide. ' **run 'off** 1. *vi* = **run away** 2. *vtr* (*a*) faire écouler (un liquide) (*b*) photocopier (qch) rapidement. ' **run 'on** 1. *vi* (*a*) continuer sa course; (*of time*) s'écouler; *Typ:* (*of text*) suivre sans alinéa; (*of words, letters*) être liés (*b*) continuer à parler 2. *vtr Typ:* faire suivre sans alinéa. ' **run 'out** 1. *vi* (*a*) sortir en courant; (*of liquid*) couler, fuir; (*of time*) se terminer; (*of lease*) expirer; (*of supplies*) venir à manquer; faire défaut; **we are running out of food,** les vivres s'épuisent; **I've r. o. of cigarettes,** je n'ai plus de cigarettes (*b*) (*of rope*) filer, se dérouler 2. *vtr* (laisser) filer (une corde). ' **run 'over** 1. *vtr* (*a*) parcourir (un document) (du regard) (*b*) *Aut:* passer sur le corps de (qn); **he's been r. o.,** il s'est fait écraser 2. *vi* (*of liquid*) déborder. ' **runproof,** ' **run-resist.** *a* (bas) indémaillable. **runs** *npl F:* **to have the r.,** avoir la diarrhée, la courante. ' **run 'through** *vtr* (*a*) traverser (la salle) en courant (*b*) parcourir (un document) (du regard); *Th:* répéter (son rôle) (*c*) gaspiller, dissiper (une fortune). ' **run 'up** 1. *vi* monter en courant; **to come running up,** arriver en courant; **to r. up to s.o.,** courir vers qn; **to r. up against s.o.,** (i) rencontrer qn par hasard (ii) se trouver en conflit avec qn; **to r. up against difficulties,** se heurter à des difficultés 2. *vtr* (*a*) laisser grossir (un compte); laisser accumuler (des dettes) (*b*) hisser (un pavillon) (*c*) *F:* confectionner (une robe) (à la hâte). ' **run-up** *n* période *f* préparatoire (avant une élection). ' **runway** *n Av:* piste *f* (d'envol).

rung[1] [rʌŋ] *see* **ring**[2] II.

rung[2] *n* échelon *m*, barreau *m* (d'une échelle); bâton *m* (d'une chaise).

rupture ['rʌptʃər] 1. *n* rupture *f*; brouille *f* (entre amis); *Med:* hernie *f* 2. *v* (*a*) *vtr* rompre (des relations); *Med:* se rompre (un tendon); **to r. oneself,** se faire une hernie (*b*) *vi* se rompre.

rural ['ruərəl] *a* rural; champêtre; de (la) campagne.

ruse [ru:z] *n* ruse *f*, stratagème *m*.

rush[1] [rʌʃ] *n* (*pl* **rushes**) jonc *m*.

rush[2] I. *n* (*pl* **rushes**) (*a*) course précipitée; **to make a r. at s.o.,** se précipiter sur qn; **a general r.,** une ruée générale; une bousculade; **the r. hour(s),** les heures d'affluence, de pointe (*b*) hâte *f*; r. **order,** commande urgente; **the r. of modern life,** la vie fiévreuse d'aujourd'hui; **to be in a r.,** être pressé (*c*) bouffée *f* (d'air); r. **of blood to the head,** coup *m* de sang (*d*) *Cin:* **rushes,** épreuves *fpl.* II. *v* 1. *vi* se précipiter; s'élancer; **to r. into the room,** entrer précipitamment, faire irruption, dans la pièce; **to r. back,** revenir à toute vitesse; **to r. at, on, s.o.,** se ruer, se jeter, sur qn; **to r. about,** courir çà et là; **the wind rushes up the chimney,** le vent s'engouffre dans la cheminée; **the blood rushed to his face,** le sang lui est monté au visage 2. *vtr* (*a*) pousser, entraîner, violemment; **they were rushed to hospital,** on les a transportés d'urgence à l'hôpital; **I don't want to r. you,** je ne voudrais pas vous bousculer; **don't r. me,** laissez-moi le temps de souffler; **to r. s.o. into sth,** entraîner qn dans qch sans lui donner le temps de réfléchir; **to r. a bill through (the House),** faire passer un projet de loi à la hâte, en toute hâte; **to be rushed,** être pressé; être débordé de travail (*b*) dépêcher, expédier (un travail); exécuter (une commande) d'urgence (*c*) (*of soldiers*) prendre d'assaut (une position); (*of crowd*) envahir (l'estrade).

rusk [rʌsk] *n Comest:* = biscotte *f* (*esp* pour bébés).

russet ['rʌsit] 1. *n Hort:* reinette grise 2. *a & n* (couleur *f*) roussâtre.

Russia ['rʌʃə] *Prn Geog:* Russie *f.* ' **Russian** 1. *n* (*a*) Russe *mf* (*b*) *Ling:* russe *m* 2. *a* russe.

rust [rʌst] 1. *n* rouille *f* 2. *vi* (se) rouiller. ' **rustproof** *a* antirouille *inv.* ' **rusty** *a* (-ier, -iest) rouillé; **to get r.,** se rouiller.

rustic ['rʌstik] 1. *a* rustique; paysan 2. *n* paysan, -anne; campagnard, -arde.

rustle ['rʌsl] I. *n* bruissement *m*; frou-frou *m* (de la soie); froissement *m* (de papiers). II. *v* 1. *vi* (*of wind, leaves, paper*) bruire; (*of silk*) faire frou-frou 2. *vtr* (*a*) faire bruire (des papiers) (*b*) *esp NAm:* voler (du bétail). ' **rustler** *n esp NAm:* voleur, -euse (de bétail). ' **rustle 'up** *vtr* **to r. up support,** rassembler des partisans; **to r. up a meal,** se débrouiller pour trouver à manger. ' **rustling** *n esp NAm:* vol *m* (de bétail).

rut [rʌt] *n* ornière *f*; (*of pers*) **to be in a r.,** s'encroûter; **to get out of the r.,** sortir de l'ornière. ' **rutted** *a* (chemin) coupé d'ornières.

ruthless ['ru:θlis] *a* impitoyable; sans pitié. ' **ruthlessly** *adv* impitoyablement; sans pitié. ' **ruthlessness** *n* nature *f* impitoyable (de qn).

rye [rai] *n* (*a*) seigle *m*; r. **bread,** pain de seigle (*b*) *NAm:* r. **(whiskey),** whisky *m*.

S

S, s [es] *n* (la lettre) S, s *m*.
Sabbath ['sæbəθ] *n* (a) *Jew:* sabbat *m* (b) *Ecc:* dimanche *m*. **sa'bbatical** *a & n* **s. (year),** année de congé (accordée à un professeur); année sabbatique.
sable[¹] ['seibl] *n* (martre *f*) zibeline *f*; (manteau de) zibeline, de martre; (pinceau) en poil de martre.
sabotage ['sæbətɑːʒ] **1.** *n* sabotage *m* **2.** *vtr* saboter (des appareils, une usine, un projet). **sabo'teur** *n* saboteur, -euse.
sabre, *NAm:* **saber** ['seibər] *n Mil:* sabre *m*; **s. cut,** (i) coup de sabre (ii) (*scar*) balafre *f*.
saccharin(e) ['sækərin, -iːn] *n* saccharine *f*.
sachet ['sæʃei] *n* sachet *m*.
sack[¹] **1.** *n* (grand) sac; **to put (sth) into sacks,** ensacher (qch); *F:* **to give s.o. the s.,** congédier (un employé); mettre (un employé) à la porte; sa(c)quer (qn); **to get the s.,** recevoir son congé; être mis à la porte; *F:* être sa(c)qué **2.** *vtr F:* mettre (un employé) à la porte; congédier, sa(c)quer (qn). **'sackcloth** *n* toile *f* à sac, d'emballage; **s. and ashes,** le sac et la cendre. **'sackful** *n* plein sac (de qch). **'sacking**[¹] *n* (a) *Tex:* toile *f* à sac (b) *F:* congédiement *m*.
sack[²] *vtr* saccager, mettre à sac (une ville). **'sacking**[²] *n* sac *m*.
sacrament ['sækrəmənt] *n Ecc:* sacrement *m*; **to receive the s.,** communier.
sacred ['seikrid] *a* (a) *Ecc:* sacré, saint; **the S. Heart,** le Sacré-Cœur (b) **s. music,** musique religieuse; **s. books,** livres sacrés (c) sacré, inviolable; **nothing was s. to him,** il ne respectait rien. **'sacredness** [-idnis] *n* (a) caractère sacré (**of a place,** d'un lieu) (b) inviolabilité *f* (d'une promesse).
sacrifice ['sækrifais] **1.** *n* (a) sacrifice *m*; **to offer sth as a s.,** offrir qch en sacrifice (**to,** à) (b) victime *f*; offrande *f* (c) sacrifice (de qch); renoncement *m* (à qch); **he succeeded at the s. of his health,** il a réussi en sacrifiant sa santé; **to make great sacrifices,** faire de grands sacrifices; *Com:* **to sell sth at a s.,** vendre qch à perte **2.** *vtr* sacrifier; renoncer à (qch); *Com:* vendre à perte.
sacri'ficial *a* sacrificiel.
sacrilege ['sækrilidʒ] *n* sacrilège *m*. **sacri'legious** *a* sacrilège.
sacristy ['sækristi] *n* (*pl* **sacristies**) *Ecc:* sacristie *f*. **'sacristan** *n Ecc:* sacristain *m*.
sacrosanct ['sækrousæŋkt] *a* sacro-saint.
sad [sæd] *a* (**sadder, saddest**) (a) triste; **to make s.o. s.,** attrister qn; **to look s.,** avoir l'air triste; **to be s. at heart,** avoir le cœur gros (b) (*of news*) triste, affligeant; (*of loss*) cruel; (*of mistake*) fâcheux; **to come to a s. end,** faire, avoir, une triste fin. **'sadden** *vtr* attrister. **'sadly** *adv* tristement. **'sadness** *n* tristesse *f*, mélancolie *f*.
saddle ['sædl] **1.** *n* (a) selle *f* (de cheval, de vélo, de moto); **in the s.,** en selle; **hunting s.,** selle anglaise (b)

col *m* (de montagne) (c) *Cu:* selle (de mouton) **2.** *vtr* (a) seller (un cheval) (b) **to s. s.o. with sth,** charger qn de qch; **she's saddled with five children,** elle a cinq enfants sur le dos. **'saddlebag** *n* sacoche *f* (de selle). **'saddler** *n* sellier *m*. **'saddlery** *n* sellerie *f*.
sadism ['seidizm] *n* sadisme *m*. **'sadist** *n* sadique *mf*. **sa'distic** *a* sadique.
sae *abbr* stamped addressed envelope.
safari [sə'fɑːri] *n* (*pl* **safaris**) safari *m*; **on s.,** en safari; **s. park,** réserve *f* d'animaux sauvages.
safe [seif] **1.** *a* (a) en sûreté; à l'abri; hors de danger; **s. and sound,** sain et sauf (b) sans danger; sûr; (*of bridge*) solide; **not s.,** dangereux; **to put sth in a s. place,** mettre qch en lieu sûr; **in s. hands,** en mains sûres (c) **is it s. to leave him alone?** n'est-ce pas imprudent de le laisser seul? **s. journey!** bon voyage! (d) (choix, investissement) prudent; judicieux; **to be on the s. side,** être du bon côté; **to play a s. game,** jouer serré; **it's s. to say (that),** on peut dire à coup sûr (que) **2.** *n* (a) coffre-fort *m* (b) **meat s.,** garde-manger *m*. **'safebreaker** *n* perceur *m* de coffre-fort. **'safe-'conduct** *n* sauf-conduit *m*. **'safeguard 1.** *n* sauvegarde *f*, garantie *f* (**against,** contre) **2.** *vtr* sauvegarder, protéger (les droits de qn); mettre (ses intérêts) à couvert. **'safekeeping** *n* **in s.,** en sécurité, en lieu sûr. **'safely** *adv* (a) **to arrive s.,** arriver sans accident, sain et sauf; arriver à bon port (b) sûrement; sans danger, sans risque (c) en lieu sûr (d) sans risque d'erreur. **'safety** *n* sûreté *f*, sécurité *f*; salut *m*; **in a place of s.,** en lieu sûr; **road s.,** prévention routière; *Ind: etc:* **s. measures,** mesures de sécurité; **s. factor,** coefficient *m* de sécurité; *Av: Aut:* **s. belt,** ceinture *f* de sécurité; (*on gun*) **s. catch,** cran *m* d'arrêt; **s. curtain,** rideau *m* de fer; **s. pin,** épingle de sûreté, de nourrice; **s. valve,** soupape *f* de sûreté.
saffron ['sæfrən] **1.** *n* safran *m* **2.** *a & n* (jaune *m*) safran *inv*.
sag [sæg] *vi* (**sagged**) (*of roof*) s'affaisser, fléchir (sous un poids); (*of cable*) se relâcher, se détendre; (*of cheek, hemline, curtain*) pendre.
saga ['sɑːgə] *n* saga *f*; roman-fleuve *m*; *F:* aventure *f*.
sagacious [sə'geiʃəs] *a* sagace, avisé; perspicace. **sa'gaciously** *adv* avec sagacité. **sa'gacity** *n* sagacité *f*; sagesse *f* (d'une remarque); intelligence *f* (d'un animal).
sage[¹] [seidʒ] **1.** *a* sage, prudent **2.** *n* philosophe *m*, sage *m*. **'sagely** *adv* sagement, avec sagesse.
sage[²] **1.** *n Bot:* sauge *f* **2.** *a & n* **s. green,** vert cendré *inv*.
Sagittarius [sædʒi'tɛəriəs] *Prn Astr:* Sagittaire *m*.
sago ['seigou] *n Cu:* sagou *m*; **s. pudding,** sagou au lait.
Sahara [sə'hɑːrə] *Prn* le Sahara.
said [sed] *see* **say** 1.
sail [seil] **1.** *n* (a) *Nau:* voile *f*; *coll* voile(s), voilure *f*, toile *f*; **to set s.,** prendre la mer (b) aile *f* (de moulin).

II. v **1.** vi (a) (of sailing ship) faire voile; (of steamer) naviguer, faire route; **to s. up the coast**, remonter la côte; **to s. around the world**, faire le tour du monde en bateau; **to s. around the cape**, doubler le cap (b) **to s. for New York**, partir, appareiller, pour New York; **the boat sailed into Southampton**, le bateau est arrivé à Southampton; **the boat sails at 10 o'clock**, le bateau part, prend la mer, à dix heures; **to be about to s.**, être en partance **2.** vtr **to s. the seas**, parcourir les mers **3.** vi planer (dans l'air); **to s. into a room**, entrer majestueusement dans une pièce; **to s. through an examination**, passer un examen sans le moindre effort, haut la main. **'sailboat** n NAm: (Br = **sailing boat**) voilier m. **'sailcloth** n toile f (à voile). **'sailing** **1.** a **s. ship, boat**, (NAm: = **sailboat**) voilier m **2.** n (a) navigation f; **it's all plain s.**, cela marche (i) tout seul (ii) comme sur des roulettes (b) allure f (d'un navire); **port of s.**, port de départ. **'sailor** n marin m (officier ou matelot); **s. hat**, béret de marin; **s. suit**, costume marin; **to be a good s.**, avoir le pied marin; **to be a bad s.**, être sujet au mal de mer. **'sailplane** n Av: planeur m.

saint [seint] n abbr **St, S.** saint, -e; **All Saints' (Day)**, la Toussaint; **saint's day**, fête (patronale); **St Peter's**, (l'église f) Saint-Pierre; **St Bernard** n (chien m) saint-bernard inv; **St George's day**, la Saint-Georges; Geog: **St Helena** Prn Sainte-Hélène f; **St Lawrence** Prn le (fleuve) Saint-Laurent. **'saintliness** n sainteté f. **'saintly** a (-ier, -iest) (de) saint.

sake [seik] n used only in the phr **for the s. of s.o., sth**, à cause de, pour l'amour de, qn, qch; **for the s. of regularity**, pour la bonne règle; **it's for your own s.**, c'est pour ton bien; **I forgive you for s.**, je vous pardonne par égard pour elle; **do it for my s.**, faites-le pour moi, pour me faire plaisir; **for goodness' s.**, pour l'amour de Dieu; **for old times' s.**, en souvenir du passé; **for economy's s.**, par (souci d')économie; **art for art's s.**, l'art pour l'art.

salad ['sæləd] n salade f; **green s.**, salade verte; **fruit s.**, macédoine f de fruits; **s. bowl**, saladier m; **s. dressing**, vinaigrette f; **s. cream**, sauce genre mayonnaise (en bouteille); **ham s.**, jambon servi avec de la salade; **s. oil**, huile de table; **s. shaker**, panier à salade; **s. days**, années f de jeunesse.

salami [sə'lɑ:mi] n Cu: salami m; saucisson m.

salary ['sæləri] n (pl **salaries**) traitement m, appointements mpl. **'salaried** a **s. staff**, employés qui touchent un traitement, des appointements.

sale [seil] n **1.** vente f; mise f en vente; **cash s.**, vente au comptant; **hire-purchase s.**, vente à crédit; **house for s.**, maison à vendre; **business for s.**, fonds à céder; **to put sth up for s.**, mettre qch en vente; **on s.**, en vente; **s. by auction**, vente aux enchères **2.** Com: (**clearance**) **s.**, soldes mpl; **s. price**, prix de solde **3.** **sales department**, service commercial, des ventes; **sales manager**, directeur commercial; **sales force**, équipe f de vente. **'saleable** a vendable; de vente facile. **'saleroom** n salle f de(s) vente(s). **'salesclerk** [-klɔ:k] n NAm: (Br = **sales, shop, assistant**) vendeur, -euse. **'salesgirl, -lady** (pl **-ladies**). **-woman** (pl **-women**) nf vendeuse. **'salesman** n (pl **-men**) **1.** vendeur m **2.** délégué commercial. **'salesmanship** n l'art m de la vente.

salient [seiliənt] a (a) (of angle) saillant; en saillie (b) (trait) saillant, frappant.

saliva [sə'laivə] n salive f.

sallow ['sælou] a (teint) jaunâtre, olivâtre. **'sallowness** n teint m jaunâtre.

sally ['sæli] n (pl **sallies**) boutade f, trait m d'esprit. **sally out, sally forth** vi (**sallied**) partir (en promenade); partir (d'un bon pas).

salmon ['sæmən] **1.** n inv in pl Ich: saumon m; **river full of s.**, rivière pleine de saumons; **s. trout**, truite saumonée; **s. steak**, darne de saumon **2.** a & n (colour) **s. (pink)**, saumon inv.

salmonella [sælmə'nelə] n Biol: Med: salmonelle f; F: (food poisoning) salmonellose f.

salon ['sælɔn] n salon m (de coiffure); **beauty s.**, institut m de beauté.

saloon [sə'lu:n] n (a) salle f, salon m; (in Eng) **s. bar** = bar m; **billiard s.**, salle de billard; **hairdressing s.**, salon de coiffure (pour hommes) (b) NAm: esp Hist: café m; débit m de boissons (c) Aut: **s. (car)**, conduite intérieure, berline f.

salsify ['sælsifai] n Bot: salsifis m.

salt [sɔlt] **I.** n **1.** (a) Cu: sel (commun); **cooking s.**, gros sel; **table s.**, sel fin; **to take a story with a pinch of s.**, prendre une histoire avec un grain de sel; **he isn't worth his s.**, il ne vaut pas le pain qu'il mange (b) F: **old s.**, loup m de mer **2.** Ch: **sel; spirit(s) of salts**, acide m chlorhydrique; **Epsom salts**, sulfate m de magnésie, Com: sels anglais. **II.** a salé; **s. water**, eau salée; eau de mer. **III.** vtr saler; saupoudrer (qch) de sel. **'saltcellar** n salière f. **'salt-free** a Med: **s.-f. diet**, régime m sans sel. **'salt(i)ness** n salinité f. **'saltpetre, NAm: -'peter** n salpêtre m. **'saltwater** n **s. fish**, poisson m de mer. **'salty** a (-ier, -iest) salé; saumâtre.

salubrious [sə'lu:briəs] a salubre, sain. **sa'lubrity** n salubrité f.

saluki [sə'lu:ki] n (dog) sloughi m.

salutary ['sæljutəri] a salutaire (**to**, à).

salute [sə'l(j)u:t] **I.** n (a) salut m, salutation f (b) Mil: **to give a s.**, faire un salut; **to take the s.**, passer les troupes en revue (c) **to fire a s.**, tirer une salve. **II.** v **1.** vtr saluer (qn) **2.** vi Mil: faire le salut militaire. **salu'tation** n salutation f.

salvage ['sælvidʒ] **1.** n (a) indemnité f, prime f, de sauvetage (b) sauvetage m (d'un navire); assistance f maritime; **s. company**, société f de sauvetage (c) objets sauvés (d'un navire, d'un incendie); récupération f (de matières pour l'industrie). **2.** vtr sauver, relever (un navire); sauver (des objets dans un incendie); récupérer (des matières usagées, des vieux journaux).

salvation [sæl'veiʃn] n salut m; **to find s.**, faire son salut; **the S. Army**, l'Armée du Salut. **sal'vationist** n salutiste mf.

salve [sælv] n baume m, onguent m.

salver ['sælvər] n plateau m (d'argent).

salvo ['sælvou] n (pl **salvoes**) n salve f; **s. of applause**, salve d'applaudissements.

Samaritan [sə'mæritən] n samaritain; (telephone service) **the Samaritans** = SOS Amitié.

same [seim] **1.** a & pron (le, la) même, (les) mêmes; **the s. person**, la même personne; **he's the s. age as myself**, il a le même âge que moi; **they're sold the s. day as they come in**, ils sont vendus le jour même de leur arrivée;

of the s. kind, similaire; in the s. way, de la même façon, de même; I'd do the s. again, je recommencerais; he got up and I did the s., il s'est levé et j'ai fait de même; the very s. thing, exactement la même chose; at the s. time, (i) en même temps (ii) à la fois; at the s. time that I heard it, au moment où je l'ai entendu; it all comes to the s. thing, tout cela revient au même; it's all the s., c'est tout un; it's all the s. to me, ça m'est égal; he's much, about, the s., son état reste inchangé; il ne va ni mieux, ni plus mal; the s. train as usual, le train habituel; always the s. old thing, toujours la même chose; F: the s. again? encore (un verre)? the s. again please! remets-moi ça, s'il te plaît! F: s. here! et moi aussi! et moi de même! d'accord! 2. adv to think the s., penser de même; just the s., all the s., malgré tout; quand même; all the s. it cost us a lot, n'empêche que cela nous a coûté cher; things go on just the s., tout marche comme d'habitude. 'sameness n 1. (a) identité f (with s.o., sth, avec qn, qch) (b) ressemblance f (with, à) 2. monotonie f, uniformité f (d'un paysage).

sample ['sɑːmpl] 1. n échantillon m (de tissu, de blé, Med: d'urine); prise f, prélèvement m (de minerai, de sang); fair s., échantillon représentatif; s. survey, (enquête f par) sondage m; up to s., conforme à l'échantillon 2. vtr (a) Com: prendre des échantillons de (qch) (b) déguster (un vin); goûter (un plat); essayer (un nouveau restaurant).

sanatorium [sænə'tɔːriəm] n (pl sanatoria, -iums) sanatorium m, F: sana m; Sch: infirmerie f.

sanctify ['sæŋktifai] vtr sanctifier; consacrer; custom sanctified by time, usage consacré par le temps. 'sanctified a (of pers) sanctifié, saint; (of thg) consacré. sanc'timonity n (pl -ies) 1. sainteté f 2. inviolabilité f; caractère sacré (de qch).

sanctimonious [sæŋkti'mouniəs] a (air) de petit saint; F: bondieusard.

sanction ['sæŋ(k)ʃən] I. n 1. Jur: sanction f 2. sanction, consentement m, approbation f. II. vtr 1. Jur: imposer des sanctions pénales à (qn) 2. (a) ratifier (une loi) (b) approuver, autoriser (qch); sanctioned by usage, consacré par l'usage.

sanctuary ['sæŋktjuəri] n (pl sanctuaries) 1. sanctuaire m 2. to take s., chercher asile 3. refuge m (de bêtes sauvages, d'oiseaux); wildlife s., réserve f zoologique; bird s., réserve d'oiseaux, ornithologique.

sand [sænd] 1. n sable m; choked (up) with s., ensablé; to build on s., bâtir sur le sable 2. pl sands, plage f, grève f 2. vtr & i to s. (down), poncer; frotter au papier de verre. 'sandbag 1. n sac m de sable. 2. vtr (sandbagged) protéger (un bâtiment) avec des sacs de sable. 'sand-bank n banc m de sable. 'sand-castle n château m de sable. 'sand-dune, -hill n dune f. 'sandman n (pl -men) marchand de sable. 'sandpaper 1. n papier m de verre 2. vtr frotter (qch) au papier de verre. 'sandpit n carrière f de sable; (for children) tas m de sable. 'sandstone n Geol: grès m. 'sandstorm n tempête f de sable. 'sandy a (-ier, -iest) 1. sableux, sablonneux; s. stretches of coast, longues grèves de sable 2. (of hair) roux pâle inv; blond roux inv.

sandal ['sændl] n sandale f; rope-soled sandals, espadrilles f.

sandwich ['sænwidʒ, -witʃ] 1. n sandwich m; two ham sandwiches, deux sandwiches au jambon; s. course, cours intercalaire 2. vtr serrer, intercaler (between, entre); to be sandwiched between two nuns, être (pris) en sandwich entre deux bonnes sœurs. 'sandwich-board n double panneau m publicitaire (porté par un homme-sandwich). 'sandwich-man n (pl -men) homme-sandwich m.

sane [sein] a (saner, sanest) sain d'esprit; raisonnable, sensé; to be s., avoir toute sa raison. 'sanely adv raisonnablement. sanity ['sæniti] n santé f d'esprit; bon sens.

sang [sæŋ] see sing.

sanguinary ['sæŋgwinəri] a (of battle) sanguinaire, sanglant.

sanguine ['sæŋgwin] a (a) (of complexion) d'un rouge sanguin; rubicond (b) (of temperament) sanguin (c) (of pers) confiant, optimiste; to feel s. about the future, avoir confiance en l'avenir.

sanitarium [sæni'tɛəriəm] n (pl sanitaria, -iums) NAm: = sanatorium.

sanitation [sæni'teiʃn] n système m sanitaire. 'sanitary a hygiénique; sanitaire; (ingénieur) sanitaire; (inspecteur) de la Santé publique; s. towel, NAm: napkin, serviette hygiénique.

sank [sæŋk] see sink².

Santa Claus ['sæntəklɔːz] Prn le Père Noël.

sap¹ [sæp] n sève f. 'sappy a plein de sève; (of timber) vert.

sap² vtr & i (sapped) saper, miner. 'sapper n Mil: sapeur m; F: the Sappers, le Génie.

sapling ['sæpliŋ] n jeune arbre m.

sapphire ['sæfaiər] 1. n saphir m 2. a & n (couleur de) saphir.

sarcasm ['sɑːkæzm] n 1. esprit m sarcastique 2. (piece of) s., sarcasme m. sar'castic a sarcastique, mordant; s. remark, sarcasme m. sar'castically adv d'une manière sarcastique.

sarcophagus [sɑːˈkɔfəgəs] (pl sarcophagi [-gai]) n sarcophage m.

sardine [sɑːˈdiːn] n Ich: sardine f; tinned sardines, sardines à l'huile.

Sardinia [sɑːˈdiniə] Prn Geog: Sardaigne f. Sar'dinian a & n sarde (mf).

sardonic [sɑːˈdɔnik] a (rire) sardonique. sar'donically adv sardoniquement; d'une manière sardonique.

sartorial [sɑːˈtɔriəl] a de tailleur; s. elegance, élégance de mise.

sash¹ [sæʃ] n Cl: écharpe f; ceinture f (en tissu); cordon m (de la Légion d'honneur).

sash² n Const: châssis m, cadre m (d'une fenêtre à guillotine); s. window, fenêtre à guillotine.

sat [sæt] see sit.

Satan ['seitən] Prn Satan m. satanic [sə'tænik] a satanique, diabolique.

satchel ['sætʃəl] n Sch: cartable m.

satellite ['sætəlait] n satellite m; s. state, pays, état, satellite; (town planning) s. town, agglomération f satellite.

satiate ['seiʃieit] vtr rassasier (qn) (jusqu'au dégoût) (with, de); blaser (qn) (with, de). 'satiated a rassasié. sati'ation n rassasiement m; satiété f. satiety [sə'taiəti] n satiété f; to s., (jusqu')à satiété.

satin ['sætin] n Tex: satin m; **s. finish,** (apprêt) satiné m.

satire ['sætaiər] n satire f. **satirical** [sə'tirikəl] a satirique. **sa'tirically** adv satiriquement. **'satirist** n auteur m, écrivain m, satirique; chansonnier m. **'satirize** vtr faire la satire (de qch).

satisfaction [sætis'fækʃən] n 1. (a) acquittement m, paiement m (d'une dette) (b) **s. for an offence,** réparation f, expiation f, d'une offense (c) assouvissement m (de la faim, d'un désir) 2. satisfaction f, contentement m (**at, with,** de); **to give s.o. s.,** satisfaire, contenter, qn; **it has not been done to my s.,** je ne, n'en, suis pas satisfait; **the work will be done to your s.,** le travail sera fait de manière à vous satisfaire 3. **that's a great s.,** c'est une grande source de bonheur, de satisfaction. **satis'factorily** adv de façon satisfaisante. **satis'factory** a satisfaisant; **to bring negotiations to a s. conclusion,** mener à bien des négociations; **to give a s. account of one's movements,** justifier ses déplacements.

satisfy ['sætisfai] vtr (**satisfied**) 1. (a) s'acquitter d'(une obligation); remplir (une condition) (b) satisfaire (qn); faire réparation à (qn); **to s. one's con-science,** par acquit de conscience 2. (a) satisfaire, contenter (qn); **to be satisfied with sth,** (i) être content, satisfait, de qch (ii) se contenter de qch (b) satisfaire, assouvir (un appétit, un désir); **food that satisfies,** nourriture rassasiante 3. convaincre, satisfaire; **I have satisfied myself (that),** je me suis assuré (que); **I am satisfied that he was telling the truth,** je suis convaincu qu'il disait la vérité. **'satisfied** a 1. (client) content, satisfait (de qch) 2. convaincu. **'satisfying** a satisfaisant; (of food) nourrissant; (of argument, reasons) convaincant.

saturate ['sætjureit] vtr (a) saturer, tremper, imbiber (**with,** de); **to become saturated (with),** s'imprégner (de) (b) Ch: Ph: saturer (une solution). **satu'ration** n imprégnation f; Ph: Ch: saturation f; **s. point,** point de saturation f; Com: **the market has reached s. point,** le marché est saturé.

Saturday ['sætədi] n samedi m; **she's coming on S.,** elle viendra samedi; **he comes on Saturdays,** il vient le samedi.

Saturn ['sætən] Prn Astr: Myth: Saturne m.

saturnine ['sætənain] a taciturne, sombre.

sauce [sɔːs] n 1. (a) sauce f (b) assaisonnement m; condiment m; **apple s.,** compote f de pommes; **white s.,** (sauce) béchamel (f); **tomato s.,** sauce tomate 3. F: (i) impertinence f, insolence f (ii) culot m, toupet m. **'sauceboat** n saucière f. **saucepan** ['sɔːspən] n casserole f; **double s.,** bain-marie m. **'saucer** n soucoupe f; **flying s.,** soucoupe volante. **'sauc-ily** adv avec impertinence, effronterie. **'sauciness** n F: impertinence f; toupet m. **'saucy** a (**-ier, -iest**) F: impertinent, effronté; coquin; (chapeau) coquet.

Saudi Arabia [saudiə'reibiə] Prn Geog: l'Arabie f Saoudite, Séoudite. **'Saudi (A'rabian)** a & n arabe (mf) (saoudit, séoudit, -ite).

sauerkraut ['sauəkraut] n Cu: choucroute f.

sauna ['sɔːnə] n sauna m.

saunter ['sɔːntər] 1. vi **to s. (along),** flâner; marcher nonchalamment 2. n flânerie f; promenade f.

sausage ['sɔsidʒ] n Cu: (a) (raw, to cook) saucisse f (b)

(precooked, smoked, ready to eat) saucisson m; **s. meat,** chair f à saucisse; **s. roll** = friand m.

savage ['sævidʒ] 1. a (a) sauvage, barbare; non civilisé (b) (animal) féroce; (coup) brutal 2. n sauvage mf 3. vtr (of animals) attaquer, mordre (qn, un autre animal); **the lion savaged his trainer,** le lion a attaqué son dompteur et l'a grièvement blessé. **'savagely** adv sauvagement, férocement. **'savagery** n 1. sauvagerie f, barbarie f (d'une nation) 2. férocité f; brutalité f (d'un coup).

save¹ [seiv] vtr 1. (a) sauver; **to s. s.o.'s life,** sauver la vie de, à, qn; **to s. s.o. from death,** arracher qn à la mort; **to s. s.o. from falling,** empêcher qn de tomber; Fb: (of goalkeeper) **to s. a goal,** arrêter le ballon; **to s. a game,** éviter la défaite (b) sauver, protéger; **to s. the situation,** se montrer, être, à la hauteur de la situation, des circonstances; **to s. appearances,** sauver, sauvegarder, les apparences 2. (a) mettre de côté; **s. a dance for me,** réservez-moi une danse; **s. some ice cream for me,** gardez-moi de la glace (b) économiser, épargner; **I have money saved,** j'ai de l'argent de côté; vi **to s. (up),** économiser (pour l'avenir) 3. ménager (ses vêtements); éviter (une dépense, de la peine); **to s. time,** gagner du temps; **I'm saving my strength,** je me ménage 4. **to s. s.o. sth,** éviter, épargner, qch à qn; **this has saved him a great deal of expense, of trouble,** cela lui a évité beaucoup de dépenses, d'ennuis. **'saving** 1. a Jur: Com: **s. clause,** clause de sauvegarde; réservation f 2. n (a) délivrance f, salut m (de qn); **this was the s. of him,** cela a été son salut (b) économie f, épargne f (c) pl **savings,** économies f; **to live on one's savings,** vivre de ses économies; **savings bank,** caisse f d'épargne.

save² prep sauf, excepté.

saveloy ['sævələi] n Cu: cervelas m.

saviour, NAm: **savior** ['seivjər] n sauveur m; Ecc: **Our S.,** Notre Sauveur.

savory ['seivəri] n Bot: Cu: sarriette f.

savour, NAm: **savor** ['seivər] 1. n saveur f, goût m. II. v 1. vtr savourer, déguster (un bon vin, des huîtres) 2. vi (of thg) **to s. of sth,** sentir qch, tenir de qch. **'savouriness,** NAm: **'savoriness** n saveur f, succulence f. **'savoury,** NAm: **'savory** 1. a savoureux, appétissant; succulent; **s. omelette,** omelette aux fines herbes 2. n (pl **-ies**) entremets non sucré.

saw¹ [sɔː] 1. n Tls: scie f; **chain s., power s.,** tronçonneuse f 2. vtr (**sawed; sawn**) scier; **to s. up wood,** débiter du bois. **'sawdust** n sciure f. **'sawmill** n scierie f. **sawn-off** a s.-o. shotgun, carabine f à canon scié. **'sawpit** n fosse f de scieur de long.

saw² [sɔː] see **see¹**.

saxophone, F: **sax** ['sæksəfoun, sæks] n Mus: saxophone m, F: saxo m. **saxophonist** [sæk'sofənist] n saxophoniste mf, F: saxo mf.

say [sei] I. vtr (**said** [sed]) 1. (a) dire; **to ask s.o. to s. a few words,** prier qn de prendre la parole; **who shall I s.?** qui dois-je annoncer? **to s. again,** répéter; **it isn't said,** cela ne se dit pas; **he says** [sez] **not,** il dit que non; **what did you s.?** qu'avez-vous dit? **to s. yes,** dire (que) oui; **to s. yes, no, to an invitation,** accepter, refuser, une invitation; **what do you s. to a drink?** si on prenait un verre? **so he says!** à l'en croire! (b) **all that can be said in a couple of words,** tout ça tient en deux mots;

you don't mean to s. he's 86! vous n'allez pas me dire qu'il a 86 ans! **as one might s.,** comme qui dirait; **one might as well as.,** autant dire; **I must s.,** j'avoue franchement; **that's to s.,** c'est-à-dire; à savoir; **have you said anything about it to him?** lui en avez-vous parlé? **the less said the better,** moins nous parlerons, mieux cela vaudra; **s. no more!** n'en dites pas davantage! **to s. nothing (of),** sans parler (de); **he has very little to s. for himself,** il est peu communicatif; **there's something to be said on both sides,** il y a du pour et du contre; **you don't s. (so)!** allons donc! pas possible! (*c*) **it is said that,** on dit que; **he's said to be rich,** on le dit riche; **he's said to have been there,** il y serait allé (*d*) **anyone would s. that he was asleep,** on dirait qu'il dort; **I should s. not,** je ne crois pas; je crois que non; **didn't I s. so!** quand je vous le disais! **let us, shall we, shall I, s.,** disons; **come soon, s. Sunday,** venez bientôt, disons dimanche (*e*) **well, s. it were true, what then?** eh bien, mettons que ce soit vrai, et alors? (*f*) **I s.!** (i) dites donc! (ii) pas possible! 2. dire, réciter; faire (ses prières); dire (la messe). **II.** *n* dire *m*, parole *f*, mot *m*; **to have one's s.,** dire son mot; **I've no s. in the matter,** je n'ai pas voix au chapitre. **'saying** *n* 1. (*a*) **it goes without s. (that),** il va de soi, cela va sans dire (que) (*b*) **there's no s.,** (il est) impossible de dire 2. (**common**) **s.,** dicton *m*; **as the s. goes,** comme dit le proverbe.

scab [skæb] *n* 1. (*on wound*) croûte *f* 2. *Ind: F:* (*of pers*) jaune *m*.

scaffold ['skæfəld] *n* échafaud *m* (pour exécutions). **'scaffolding** *n* *Const:* échafaudage *m*.

scald [skɔːld] *vtr* échauder, ébouillanter (qn, qch); **to s. one's foot,** s'échauder le pied. **'scalding** 1. *a* **s. (hot),** bouillant 2. *n* ébouillantage *m*.

scale [skeil] **I.** *n* 1. (*on fish, bud*) écaille *f*; *Med:* (*on skin*) squame *f* 2. incrustation *f*, dépôt *m*; tartre *m* (des dents); **boiler s.,** dépôt calcaire; tartre; **s. remover,** détartrant *m*. **II.** *v* 1. *vtr* (*a*) écailler (un poisson) (*b*) détartrer, nettoyer (ses dents, une chaudière) 2. *vi* (*a*) **to s. (off),** s'écailler; (*of skin*) se desquamer; (*of paint*) s'écailler (*b*) (*of boiler*) s'entartrer, s'incruster. **'scaly** *a* écailleux; squameux; tartreux.

scale² *n* 1. (*a*) échelle *f*, graduation(s) *f* (*pl*) (d'un thermomètre); série *f*, suite *f* (de nombres); **s. of salaries, salary s.,** échelle, barème *m*, des traitements (*b*) échelle (d'une carte); **to draw sth to s.,** dessiner qch à l'échelle; **on a large s.,** en grand; sur une grande échelle; **s. model,** modèle réduit (*c*) *Com:* **s. of prices,** éventail *m* des prix (*d*) envergure *f* (d'une entreprise); étendue *f* (d'une catastrophe); **on a national s.,** à l'échelle nationale; **to keep house on a small s.,** avoir un train de maison très simple 2. *Mus:* gamme *f*.

scale³ *vtr* 1. escalader; **to s. a mountain,** faire l'ascension d'une montagne 2. **to s. a map,** tracer une carte à l'échelle 3. **to s. down,** établir (un dessin) à une échelle réduite; **to s. wages up, down,** augmenter, réduire, les salaires selon le barème; **to s. down production,** ralentir la production.

scales [skeilz] *npl* (**pair of**) **s.,** balance *f*; **platform s.,** bascule *f*; **letter s.,** pèse-lettre *m*; **steelyard s.,** balance romaine; **bathroom s.,** pèse-personne *m*; **to turn the s. at 68 kilos,** peser 68 kilos; **to tip the s.,** faire pencher la balance (en faveur de qn).

scallop ['skɔləp] *n* (*a*) *Moll: Cu:* coquille *f* Saint-Jacques (*b*) *Needlew:* feston *m*, dentelure *f*.

scalp [skælp] 1. *n* (*a*) *Anat:* cuir chevelu (*b*) scalp *m* 2. *vtr* scalper (un ennemi).

scalpel ['skælpəl] *n* *Surg:* scalpel *m*.

scamp [skæmp] 1. *n* vaurien *m*; mauvais sujet; garnement *m*; **young s.,** petit galopin, petit polisson 2. *vtr* F: bâcler (un travail).

scamper ['skæmpər] 1. *n* (*a*) course *f* folâtre, allègre (*b*) course rapide; **to take the dog for a s.,** aller promener le chien 2. *vi* courir joyeusement, en gambadant; **to s. off,** se sauver à toutes jambes.

scampi ['skæmpi] *npl* *Cu:* langoustines *fpl*.

scan [skæn] **I.** *v* (**scanned**) 1. *vtr* (*a*) scander, mesurer (des vers) (*b*) examiner, scruter (l'horizon, la foule); **to s. the paper,** parcourir le journal (*c*) *TV:* balayer, explorer (l'image à transmettre) 2. *vi* (*of verse*) se scander. **II.** *n* *TV: Rad:* balayage *m*; **s. frequency,** fréquence *f* de balayage; *Med:* (**ultrasound**) **s.,** échographie *f*. **'scanner** *n* *radar* **s.,** balayeur *m* de radar; *Med:* (**ultrasound**) **s.,** scanner *m*. **'scanning** *n* 1. scansion *f* (de vers) 2. *TV: etc:* balayage *m*; **s. device,** appareil *m* explorateur; *Med:* (**ultrasound**) **s.,** échographie *f*.

scandal ['skændəl] *n* 1. scandale *m*; honte *f*; **it's a s.,** c'est scandaleux, c'est un scandale; **to create a s.,** faire un scandale 2. médisance *f*; cancans *mpl*; **to talk s.,** cancaner. **'scandalize** *vtr* scandaliser (qn); **to be scandalized,** être scandalisé. **'scandalous** *a* 1. scandaleux, infâme, honteux 2. *Jur:* (*of statement*) diffamatoire, calomnieux. **'scandalously** *adv* scandaleusement.

Scandinavia [skændi'neiviə] *Prn* Scandinavie *f*. **Scandi'navian** *a & n* scandinave (*mf*).

scant [skænt] *a* (**scantier, scantiest**) (*in certain phrases*) insuffisant, peu abondant, limité; **s. weight,** poids bien juste; **to have s. regard (for),** avoir peu d'égard, de considération (pour); **with s. courtesy,** peu poliment. **'scantily** *adv* insuffisamment, peu abondamment; **s. dressed,** à peine vêtu. **'scantiness** *n* insuffisance *f*, rareté *f*; pauvreté *f* (de la végétation); **the s. of my resources,** l'exiguïté *f* de mes ressources; **the s. of her dress,** l'étroitesse *f* de sa robe. **'scanty** *a* (**-ier, -iest**) insuffisant; à peine suffisant; peu abondant; (*of garment*) étroit, étriqué, **s. hair,** cheveux rares; **s. meal,** repas sommaire.

scapegoat ['skeipgout] *n* bouc *m* émissaire.

scar [skɑːr] **I.** *n* cicatrice *f*. **II.** *v* (**scarred**) 1. *vtr* laisser une cicatrice sur (la peau); marquer (qn) d'une cicatrice; balafrer 2. *vi* (*of wound*) se cicatriser.

scarce [skeəs] *a* rare; peu abondant; **good craftsmen are growing s.,** les bons artisans se font rares; **to make oneself s.,** décamper, filer. **'scarcely** *adv* 1. à peine; presque pas; **she could s. speak,** c'est à peine si elle pouvait parler; **you'll s. believe it,** vous aurez de la peine à le croire; **I s. know what to say,** je ne sais trop que dire 2. (*expressing incredulity*) sûrement pas; **s.!** j'en doute! **'scarcity** *n* (*pl* **-ies**), **'scarceness** *n* rareté *f*, manque *m*, pénurie *f*; **s. of rain,** rareté des pluies; **s. of labour,** manque de main-d'œuvre; **s. of water,** disette *f* d'eau.

scare [skeər] 1. *n* panique *f*, alarme *f*; rumeurs *fpl* (de guerre, d'épidémie); **you did give me a s.,** vous m'avez fait rudement peur 2. *v* (*a*) *vtr* effrayer, alarmer (qn); faire peur à (qn); **to s. away,** effaroucher (le gibier) (*b*) *vi* s'effrayer, s'alarmer; **I don't s. easily,** je ne m'effraie pas facilement. **'scarecrow** n épouvantail m. **'scared** a (air) effaré, épouvanté; affolé; **to be s. to death, out of one's wits,** F: **to be s.** stiff, avoir une peur bleue. **'scaremonger** n alarmiste mf. **'scary** a (-ier, -iest) effrayant; qui fait peur; (film, roman) d'épouvante.

scarf [skɑːf] n (pl **scarfs, scarves**) écharpe f, fichu m; cache-col m; (in silk) foulard m.

scarlet ['skɑːlət] a & n écarlate (f); **to blush s.,** devenir cramoisi; Med: **s. fever,** scarlatine f.

scarper ['skɑːpər] vi F: s'enfuir, déguerpir.

scathing ['skeiðiŋ] a acerbe, cinglant. **'scathingly** adv d'une manière acerbe; d'un ton cinglant.

scatter ['skætər] 1. vtr (a) disperser, mettre en fuite (b) éparpiller; jeter çà et là; semer à la volée; **to s. the floor with paper,** joncher le sol de papiers; **the region is scattered over with small towns,** la région est parsemée de petites villes 2. vi (of crowd) se disperser; (of shot) s'éparpiller; (of clouds) se dissiper. **'scatterbrain** n étourdi, -ie; écervelé, -ée. **'scatterbrained** a F: étourdi, écervelé; **to be s.,** avoir une tête de linotte. **'scattered** a dispersé, éparpillé; épars; **thinly s. population,** population clairsemée; **s. light,** lumière diffuse.

scavenge ['skævindʒ] vi fouiller dans les ordures. **'scavenger** n Z: insecte m, animal m, nécrophage; **s. beetle,** nécrophore m.

scenario [si'nɑːriou] n (pl **scenarios**) scénario m.

scene [siːn] n 1. Th: (a) scène f; **Act III, s. 2,** Acte III, scène 2 (b) **the s. is set in London,** l'action se passe à Londres; **to appear on the s.,** entrer en scène (c) **behind the scenes,** dans la coulisse 2. théâtre m, lieu m (d'un événement); **a change of s. will do him good,** un changement d'air lui fera du bien; **at the s. of the crime,** sur le(s) lieu(x) du crime; **the s. of operations,** le théâtre des opérations; F: **it's not my s.,** ce n'est pas mon genre 3. **the s. from my window,** la vue de ma fenêtre 4. scène; scandale m; dispute bruyante; **to make a s.,** faire une scène; **family scenes,** disputes de famille. **'scenery** n 1. Th: décors mpl; mise f en scène 2. paysage m; vue f. **'sceneshifter** n Th: machiniste m. **'scenic** a **s. road,** route touristique; **area of great s. beauty,** région qui offre de très beaux panoramas; (at fairground) **s. railway,** montagnes fpl russes.

scent [sent] 1. n (a) parfum m, senteur f; odeur f agréable (b) **bottle of s.,** flacon m de parfum (c) (of animal) fumet m, vent m; (of hounds) **to be on the right s.,** être sur la bonne piste; **to put (s.o.) off the s.,** dérouter, déjouer (qn) (d) odorat m, flair m (d'un chien). 2. vtr (a) (of hounds) flairer (le gibier); (of pers) **to s. trouble,** flairer des ennuis (b) (of flowers) parfumer, embaumer (l'air). **'scented** a parfumé (**with,** de); (of air) embaumé (**with,** de); **keen-s. dog,** chien qui a beaucoup de flair.

sceptic, NAm: **skeptic** ['skeptik] n sceptique mf. **'sceptical,** NAm: **skep-** a sceptique. **'sceptically,** NAm: **skep-** adv sceptiquement; avec scepticisme. **'scepticism,** NAm: **skep-** n scepticisme m.

sceptre, NAm: **scepter** ['septər] n sceptre m.

schedule ['ʃedjuːl, NAm: 'skedʒəl] I. n 1. (a) inventaire m; barème m (des prix); **s. of charges,** liste officielle des taux; tarif m (b) Adm: cédule f (d'impôts)

2. programme m; plan m (d'exécution d'un travail); calendrier m (de travaux); horaire m (d'un train); **everything went off according to s.,** tout a marché tel que, comme, prévu, selon les prévisions; **on s.,** (of train) à l'heure; (of work) à temps, à jour; **ahead of, behind, s.,** en avance, en retard; **I work to a very tight s.,** mon temps est très minuté. II. vtr 1. inscrire (qch) sur une liste, un inventaire; **scheduled as a place of historical interest,** classé comme monument historique 2. dresser le programme de (qch); **the mayor is scheduled to make a speech,** le maire doit prononcer un discours; **the train is scheduled to arrive at noon,** selon l'horaire m, l'indicateur m, le train arrive à midi; **scheduled flight,** vol régulier; Rail: etc: **scheduled services,** services réguliers.

scheme [skiːm] I. n 1. arrangement m; **colour s.,** combinaison f de couleurs 2. résumé m, exposé m (d'un sujet d'étude); plan m (d'un livre) 3. (a) plan, projet m; **s. for a canal,** étude f d'un canal (b) Adm: **pension s.,** plan, régime m, de retraite 4. machination f, intrigue f; complot m; **shady s.,** combinaison louche, F: combine f. II. v 1. vi intriguer, ruser, comploter (**to do sth,** pour faire qch) 2. vtr machiner, comploter, organiser (une prise d'otages); projeter (de faire qch). **sche'matic** a schématique. **'schemer** n Pej: intrigant, -ante. **'scheming** 1. a intrigant 2. n intrigues fpl, combinaisons fpl; F: combines fpl.

schism ['s(k)izm] n schisme m. **schis'matic** a & n schismatique (mf).

schist [ʃist] n Geol: schiste m.

schizophrenia [skitsou'friːniə] n schizophrénie f. **schizo'phrenic** a & n schizophrène (mf).

schnorkel ['ʃnɔːkl] a & n snorkel.

scholar ['skɔlər] n savant m, lettré, -ée, érudit, -ite; **he's no s.,** son éducation laisse à désirer. **'scholarly** a savant, érudit; **a very s. man,** un homme d'un grand savoir, d'une grande érudition. **'scholarship** n 1. savoir m; érudition f 2. Sch: bourse f (d'études). **scho'lastic** a (a) (philosophie) scolastique (b) (année) scolaire.

school[1] [skuːl] 1. n (a) école; **to go to s.,** aller à l'école; **s. leaving age,** âge m de fin de scolarité; **nursery s.,** (école) maternelle (f); **infant s.** = cours m préparatoire; **primary s.,** école primaire; **junior s.** = école primaire (de 8 à 11 ans); **grammar s.,** **secondary s.** = lycée m; **comprehensive s.** = collège m d'enseignement secondaire; **technical s.** = collège d'enseignement technique; **independent, private, s.,** école privée; **public s.,** (i) collège privé (avec internat) (ii) NAm: (Br: = **State school**) école d'État; **preparatory s.,** école privée pour élèves de 8 à 13 ans; NAm: **junior high s.** = collège d'enseignement secondaire (de 12 à 15 ans); NAm: **high s.,** (i) collège d'enseignement secondaire (de 15 à 18 ans) (ii) = lycée; **what s. were you at?** où avez-vous fait vos études? **s. equipment,** matériel scolaire; fournitures scolaires; **the s. year,** l'année scolaire; **s. bag,** cartable m; **s. bus,** car scolaire; **s. bus service,** service de ramassage scolaire; NAm: **to teach s.** (Br: = **to teach**), être dans l'enseignement (b) Art: etc: **s. of art,** école des beaux-arts; **the Italian s.,** l'école italienne; **s. of dancing,** cours m de danse; **s. of music,** académie f de musique; conservatoire m; **summer s.,** cours de vacances, cours d'été; **driving s.,** s.

of motoring, auto-école f 2. vtr former (un enfant, l'esprit de qn); discipliner (sa voix, ses gestes); dresser (un cheval, un chien). 'schoolbook n livre m de classe. 'schoolboy n écolier m, élève m; s. slang, argot scolaire. 'schoolgirl n écolière f, élève f. 'schooling n instruction f, éducation f. 'school-'leaver n jeune garçon, jeune fille (entre 16 et 18 ans) qui a terminé ses études secondaires. 'school-'leaving a s.-l. age, âge de fin de scolarité. 'schoolma'am, -marm n institutrice f; F: a real s., (i) une pédante (ii) une vraie prude. 'school-master n professeur m; instituteur m. 'school-mistress n (pl -es) professeur m; institutrice f. 'schoolroom n (salle f de) classe f. 'school-teacher n professeur m; instituteur, institutrice.

school² n banc m (de poissons); bande f (de mar-souins).

schooner¹ ['sku:nər] n Nau: schooner m; goélette f.

schooner² n (a) NAm: grande flûte (à bière) (b) grand verre (à porto, à vin de xérès).

science ['saiəns] n science f; s. faculty, faculté f des sciences; s. master, mistress, professeur de sciences; s. fiction, science-fiction f. scien'tific a scientifique; s. instruments, instruments de précision. scien'tifically adv scientifiquement. 'scientist n scientifique mf; savant m.

sci-fi ['saifai] n F: science-fiction f; la S.F.

Scilly ['sili] Prn Geog: the S. Isles, the Scillies, les Sorlingues f.

scintillate ['sintileit] vi scintiller, étinceler. 'scin-tillating a scintillant, étincelant, pétillant; brillant. scinti'llation n scintillation f; scintillement m.

scissors ['sizəz] npl (a pair of) s., (une paire de) ciseaux mpl; cutting-out s., ciseaux de couturière; nail s., ciseaux à ongles.

sclerosis [sklə'rousis] n Med: sclérose f; multiple s., sclérose en plaques.

scoff¹ [skɔf] vi se moquer; to s. at s.o., se moquer de qn; to s. at dangers, mépriser les dangers. 'scoffer n moqueur, -euse; railleur, -euse. 'scoffing 1. a moqueur 2. n moquerie f, raillerie f.

scoff² P: bouffer.

scold [skould] vtr gronder, réprimander (qn). 'scolding n semonce f, réprimande f.

scone [skɔn] n = (petit) pain au lait.

scoop [sku:p] I. vtr 1. to s. (out), excaver; évider (qch); to s. up, ramasser à la pelle 2. Journ: F: to s. (a rival paper), faire un scoop. II. n 1. (a) pelle f à main; (for ice cream) portionneur m à glace; (coal) s., pelle f à charbon 2. at one s., d'un seul coup 3. Journ: F: scoop m, reportage sensationnel.

scooter ['sku:tər] n (a) (child's) trottinette f, patinette f (b) (motorized) scooter m.

scope [skoup] n (a) portée f, étendue f; envergure f; that's outside my s., cela n'est pas de ma compétence; it's outside the s. of this book, cela sort du cadre de ce livre; to extend the s. of one's activities, élargir le champ de son activité (b) espace m, place f; to give full s. to s.o., donner (libre) cours, libre carrière, à qn.

scorch [skɔ:tʃ] I. v 1. vtr roussir, brûler légèrement (du linge); (of sun) dessécher (l'herbe) 2. vi roussir; brûler légèrement; F: to s. (along), brûler le pavé; aller un train d'enfer. II. n s. (mark), brûlure (légère). scorched a roussi, légèrement brûlé; (of grass)

desséché; (visage) brûlé; s. earth policy, politique de la terre brûlée. 'scorcher n F: (a) journée f torride (b) riposte cinglante. 'scorching 1. a brûlant, ardent; s. heat, chaleur f torride; s. hot, brûlant; it's s. (hot) here, on cuit ici. 2. n roussissement m; dessèchement m.

score [skɔ:r] I. n (a) éraflure f, entaille f; (on paint) rayure f (b) (nombre m de) points mpl; Fb: etc: what's the s.? où en est la marque? to keep the s., compter les points; F: to know the score, être au courant; connaître la musique; Fig: to pay off old scores, régler de vieux comptes (c) Mus: partition f (d) (inv in pl) vingt; vingtaine f (de gens) (e) pl F: scores, un grand nombre; scores of people, une masse de gens (f) point m, question f, sujet m; have no fear on that s., n'ayez aucune crainte sur ce point. II. v 1. vtr (a) érafler; strier; rayer; face scored with wrinkles, visage sillonné de rides (b) souligner (un passage) (c) Sp: compter, marquer (les points); gagner (une partie); Cr: to s. a century, faire une centaine; Fb: to s. a goal, marquer un but; to s. a success, remporter un succès (d) Mus: orchestrer (une composition) 2. vi Games: Sp: comp-ter, marquer, les points; Fb: marquer un but; Fig: that's where he scores, c'est là son point fort. 'scoreboard n Sp: tableau m (des points, des buts). 'scorecard n Golf: carte f du parcours; (shooting) carton m; Games: feuille f de marque. 'score 'off vi to s. off s.o., F: river son clou à qn. 'score 'out vtr rayer, biffer (un mot). 'sco-rer n Sp: marqueur m. 'scoring n 1. érafle-ment m; striation f; rayage m 2. Sp: marque f des points.

scorn [skɔ:n] 1. n dédain m, mépris m 2. vtr dédaigner, mépriser (qn, qch). 'scornful a dédaigneux, mé-prisant. 'scornfully adv dédaigneusement; avec mépris.

Scorpio ['skɔ:piou] Prn Astr: le Scorpion.

scorpion ['skɔ:piən] n Arach: scorpion m.

Scot [skɔt] n Écossais, -aise; she's a S., elle est Écossaise.

Scotch [skɔtʃ] 1. a (not used of pers in Scotland) écossais; S. terrier, scottish-terrier m; S. broth, potage m à base de mouton, de légumes et d'orge; S. mist, bruine f, crachin m; S. egg, œuf dur enrobé de chair à saucisse 2. n (a) dialecte écossais (b) whisky (écossais); a (glass of) S., un whisky, un scotch (c) Rtm: S. tape, ruban adhésif, Scotch m (Rtm) 3. vtr faire échouer (un projet).

scot-free [skɔt'fri:] a to get off s.-f., s'en tirer indemne, sans être puni.

Scotland ['skɔtlənd] Prn Geog: l'Écosse f; S. Yard, = la Sûreté.

Scots [skɔts] a & n (used in Scotland) écossais, -aise; Ling: écossais m; S. law, le droit écossais; Mil: the S. Guards, la Garde écossaise. 'Scotsman nm (pl -men) Écossais. 'Scotswoman nf (pl -women) Écossaise. 'Scottish a & n (used in Scotland) écossais, -aise.

scoundrel ['skaundrəl] n escroc m; (child) coquin, -ine.

scour¹ ['skauər] 1. vtr nettoyer, lessiver, frotter (le plancher); décaper (une surface métallique); to s. (out) a saucepan, récurer une casserole; scouring powder, poudre à récurer 2. n nettoyage m, récurage *m.* **'scourer** *n* (*pot*) s., cure-casseroles *m inv*; éponge *f* métallique, en nylon.

scour² *vtr* parcourir, battre (la campagne) (à la recherche de qn, qch).

scourge [skɔːdʒ] *n* fléau *m.*

scout [skaut] I. *n* 1. *Mil:* éclaireur *m*; s. **car, plane,** véhicule *m*, avion *m*, de reconnaissance 2. **boy s.,** (*Catholic*) scout *m*; (*non-Catholic*) éclaireur *m*; *NAm:* **girl s.,** guide *f*; éclaireuse 3. **talent s.,** dénicheur *m* de talents. II. *vi* 1. *Mil: etc:* aller en reconnaissance 2. **to s. (about, around) for sth,** aller à la recherche de qch; *Cin:* **to s. for talent,** rechercher de futures vedettes. **'scoutmaster** *n* chef *m* de troupe. **'scouting** *n* 1. *Mil:* reconnaissance *f* 2. scoutisme *m.*

scowl [skaul] I. *n* air menaçant, renfrogné; froncement *m* de(s) sourcils 2. *vi* se renfrogner; froncer les sourcils; **to s. at s.o.,** regarder qn de travers, d'un air menaçant. **'scowling** *a* renfrogné, menaçant.

scrabble ['skræbl] *vi* **to s. about,** gratter (ça et là) (**for sth,** pour trouver qch).

scraggy ['skrægi] *a* (-ier, -iest) (*of pers, animal*) décharné, maigre.

scram [skræm] *vi* (**scrammed**) *F:* décamper; ficher le camp.

scramble ['skræmbl] I. *v* 1. *vi* (*a*) monter, descendre, à quatre pattes; jouer des pieds et des mains; **to s. up a hill,** grimper une colline à quatre pattes (*b*) **to s. for sth,** se bousculer pour avoir qch (*c*) *Av: F:* décoller rapidement (en cas d'alerte) (*d*) *Sp:* faire du moto-cross 2. *vtr* (*a*) *Tp: Elcs: etc:* brouiller (une émission) (*b*) **scrambled eggs,** œufs brouillés. II. *n* 1. *Mount:* ascension *f* difficile; *Sp:* (**motorcycle**) s., moto-cross *m* 2. (*a*) mêlée *f*, lutte *f*, bousculade *f* (*b*) *Av: F:* décollage immédiat (en cas d'alerte). **'scrambler** *n* *Tp:* brouilleur *m.* **'scrambling** *n* 1. *Tp:* brouillage *m* 2. *Sp:* moto-cross *m.*

scrap¹ [skræp] I. *n* 1. petit morceau (de qch); bout *m*, chiffon *m*; **s. book,** album *m* (de découpures); **not a s. of evidence,** pas la moindre preuve; **to catch scraps of conversation,** saisir des bribes de conversation; **s. of comfort,** brin *m* de consolation 2. (*a*) *pl* **scraps,** restes *mpl* (d'un repas); déchets *m* (de papeterie, d'usine) (*b*) **s. paper,** papier brouillon; **s. heap,** tas de ferraille; **to put a plan on the s. heap,** mettre un projet au rancart; **s. metal,** ferraille *f*; **s. merchant,** marchand de ferraille; casseur *m*; **to sell sth for s.,** vendre qch à la casse. II. *vtr* (**scrapped**) 1. mettre (qch) au rebut; envoyer (une voiture) à la ferraille, à la casse 2. mettre (un projet) au rancart. **'scrapheap** *n* tas *m* de ferraille; **to throw sth on the s.,** mettre qch à la ferraille, au rebut. **'scrappy** *a* (-ier, -iest) **s. knowledge,** bribes *fpl* de connaissances; **s. dinner,** maigre repas (composé de restes).

scrap² *F:* 1. *vi* (**scrapped**) se bagarrer, se battre 2. *n* bagarre *f.*

scrape [skreip] I. *n* 1. (*a*) coup *m* de grattoir, de racloir (*b*) éraflure *f* 2. *F:* mauvaise affaire, mauvais pas; **to get out of a s.,** se tirer d'affaire, d'embarras. II. *v* 1. *vtr* (*a*) érafler, écorcher (la peau) (*b*) racler, gratter (qch); gratter (des carottes, des salsifis); **to s. one's boots,** s'essuyer les pieds; **to s. the (bottom of the) barrel,** racler les fonds de tiroirs (*c*) **to s. one's feet along the floor,** (se) frotter les pieds sur le plancher; **to s. the fiddle,** gratter du violon (*d*) **to s. together, up, a sum of**

money, amasser petit à petit une somme d'argent; **to s. a living,** trouver tout juste de quoi vivre; vivoter 2. *vi* (*a*) gratter; grincer (l'un contre l'autre) **b. to s. against the wall,** raser le mur (*c*) **to s. clear (of disaster),** échapper tout juste (à l'accident); friser (la catastrophe). **'scrape a'long** *vi* *F:* vivoter péniblement. **'scrape a'way, 'scrape 'off** *vtr* enlever, faire disparaître (qch) en grattant. **'scraper** *n* *Tls:* racloir *m.* **'scrape 'through** *vi* être reçu tout juste, de justesse (à un examen).

scratch [skrætʃ] I. *n* 1. (*a*) coup *m* d'ongle, de griffe (*b*) égratignure *f*, éraflure *f*; griffure; **to escape without a s.,** en sortir indemne, sans une égratignure 2. (*a*) grattement *m*; **to give one's head a s.,** se gratter la tête (*b*) grincement *m* (d'une plume) 3. *Sp:* scratch *m*; **to start from s.,** partir de zéro; **to come up to s.,** se montrer, être, à la hauteur (de l'occasion); **he's not up to s.,** il ne fait pas le poids. II. *v* 1. *vtr* égratigner, griffer; donner un coup de griffe à (qn); (*of thorn*) écorcher, érafler (la peau); (*of animal*) gratter (le sol); **to s. oneself,** s'égratigner; **to s. s.o.'s eyes out,** arracher les yeux à qn; **to s. one's head,** se gratter la tête; **you s. my back and I'll s. yours,** un service en vaut un autre; *Fig:* **to s. the surface,** effleurer le problème; **to s. together a few coins,** ramasser quelques pièces; **to s. out,** rayer, biffer (un mot); **to s. s.o. off a list,** rayer qn d'une liste 2. *vi* (*a*) **cat that scratches,** chat qui griffe (*b*) (*of pers, animal*) se gratter; (*of bird, animal*) gratter (dans la terre); **to s. about, around, for evidence,** dénicher des preuves; **to s. at the door,** gratter à la porte (*c*) (*of pen*) gratter (*d*) *Sp:* (*of competitor*) déclarer forfait. III. *a* (repas) improvisé, sommaire; *Sp:* **s. team,** équipe improvisée. **'scratchy** *a* (-ier, -iest) qui gratte; qui grince; (*of cloth*) rugueux, qui gratte la peau.

scrawl [skrɔːl] 1. *vtr* griffonner, gribouiller 2. *n* griffonnage *m*, gribouillage *m.*

scrawny ['skrɔːni] *a* (-ier, -iest) décharné, maigre.

scream [skriːm] I. *n* (*a*) cri perçant; **screams of laughter,** de grands éclats de rire (*b*) *F:* chose amusante, grotesque; **it was a perfect s.,** c'était tordant, *F:* marrant; **he's a s.,** il est marrant, impayable. II. *v* 1. *vi* pousser un cri perçant; crier (de peur, de douleur); *F:* **to s. with laughter,** rire aux éclats 2. *vtr* **to s. oneself hoarse,** s'enrouer à (force de) crier; **to s. abuse,** hurler des injures. **'screamingly** *adv* *F:* **s. funny,** tordant, crevant.

scree [skriː] *n* éboulis *m.*

screech [skriːtʃ] 1. *n* cri perçant; cri rauque; *Orn:* **s. owl,** effraie *f* 2. *vi* pousser des cris perçants, des cris rauques.

screen [skriːn] I. *n* 1. (*a*) *Furn:* écran *m*; (*against draught*) paravent *m* (*b*) cloison *f*, grille *f* (en fer forgé); **choir s.,** grille de chœur (*c*) rideau (protecteur); **s. of trees,** rideau d'arbres; **to act as a s. for a criminal,** couvrir un criminel; **smoke s.,** nuage artificiel; rideau de fumée (*d*) **safety s.,** écran de sécurité; **fire s.,** écran ignifuge 2. *Cin: TV:* écran (de projection); *coll* **the s.,** le cinéma; **s. star,** vedette de l'écran; **television s.,** écran de télévision; *F:* **the small s.,** le petit écran; **s. rights,** droits d'adaptation à l'écran; **s. test,** bande *f* d'essai 3. (*for camera*) filtre *m* 4. *CivE:* crible *m*, tamis *m.* II. *vtr* 1. (*a*) **to s. sth from view,** cacher, masquer, dérober, qch aux regards (*b*) abriter, protéger (qn, qch) 2. cribler (du gravier) 3. trier; sélectionner (du personnel); *Med:* soumettre (qn) à un test de dépistage; filtrer (des nouvelles) 4. *Cin:* mettre, porter (un roman) à l'écran; projeter (un film); *TV:* passer (une émission) à la télévision. **'screening** *n* 1. mise *f* à l'abri; dissimulation *f* aux regards 2. triage *m*; sélection *f* (du personnel); filtrage *m* (des nouvelles); *Med:* (test *m* de) dépistage *m* 3. criblage *m* (de gravier). **'screenplay** *n Cin:* scénario *m*. **'screenwriter** *n* scénariste *mf*.

screw [skru:] **I.** *n* 1. vis *f*; wing, butterfly, s., vis à oreilles, à ailettes; (écrou *m*) papillon *m*; s. **cap, top,** couvercle vissant (d'un bocal, d'une bouteille); *F:* **to have a s. loose,** être dingue, cinglé; **there's a s. loose somewhere,** il y a quelque chose qui cloche 2. *Av: Nau:* hélice *f* 3. *(a)* coup *m* de tournevis; tour *m* de vis; **give it another s.,** serrez-le encore un peu *(b) P:* gardien *m* de prison, gaffe *m* *(c) V:* coït *m.* **II.** *v* 1. *vtr (a)* visser; **to s. (sth) down,** visser (un couvercle); **to s. sth on,** visser, fixer, qch; **to s. sth tight,** visser qch à bloc; **to s. up a nut,** serrer un écrou; *F:* **his head's screwed on the right way,** il a la tête solide, la tête sur les épaules *(b)* **to s. money from s.o.,** extorquer de l'argent à qn 2. *vi (of tap)* tourner (à droite, à gauche); **the knob screws into the drawer,** le bouton se visse dans le tiroir. **'screwball** *a & n NAm: F:* loufoque *(mf)*, dingue *(mf)*. **'screwdriver** *n* tournevis *m.* **'screwed** *a F:* ivre, soûl. **'screw 'up** *vtr* **to s. up a piece of paper,** tortiller du papier; **to s. up one's eyes,** plisser les yeux; **to s. up one's courage,** prendre son courage à deux mains; *P:* **to s. sth up,** gâcher, bousiller, qch. **'screwy** *a (-ier, -iest) F:* dingue, cinglé.

scribble ['skribl] 1. *vtr* griffonner (quelques mots, une note dans un carnet) 2. *n (a)* griffonnage *m (b)* écriture *f* illisible; pattes *fpl* de mouche. **'scribbler** *n* écrivailleur, -euse; gratte-papier *m inv.* **'scribbling** *n* griffonnage *m*; **s. paper,** papier *m* brouillon.

scribe [skraib] *n* scribe *m.*

scrimmage ['skrimidʒ] *n* mêlée *f*; bousculade *f*; bagarre *f.*

script [skript] *n (a)* manuscrit *m; Sch:* copie *f* d'examen *(b) Cin:* scénario *m*; s. **girl,** script(-girl) *f.* **'scriptwriter** *n* scénariste *mf.*

scripture ['skriptʃər] *n* Holy S., l'Écriture sainte; *Sch:* S. (**lesson**), leçon *f* d'histoire sainte. **'scriptural** *a* biblique; des saintes Écritures.

scroll [skroul] *n (a)* rouleau *m* (de parchemin, de papier) *(b) Arch:* volute *f* (d'un chapiteau).

scrounge [skraundʒ] *vtr & i F:* écornifler; **to s. £5 off s.o.,** taper qn de £5; **to s. a meal,** se faire payer, offrir, un repas. **'scrounger** *n* pique-assiette *m*; tapeur *m.*

scrub[1] [skrʌb] *vtr* **(scrubbed)** récurer (une casserole); laver, frotter (le plancher) (avec une brosse dure). **'scrubber** *n* tampon *m* à récurer. **'scrubbing** *n* récurage *m*, nettoyage *m* (avec une brosse dure); s. **brush,** brosse de chiendent, brosse dure. **'scrub off** *vtr* faire disparaître (qch) en frottant. **'scrub up** *vi (of surgeon)* se brosser (les mains).

scrub[2] *n* broussailles *fpl*, brousse *f*. **'scrubby** *a* (-ier, -iest) *(of land)* couvert de broussailles. **'scrubland** *n* terrain broussailleux.

scruff [skrʌf] *n* (peau *f* de la) nuque; **to seize an animal by the s. of the neck,** saisir un animal par la peau du

cou. **'scruffy** *a* (-ier, -iest) mal soigné; *F:* mal fichu. **'scruffily** *adv* s. dressed, débraillé.

scrum [skrʌm] *n Rugby Fb:* mêlée *f*; s. **half,** demi *m* de mêlée; *F:* **what a s. in the Underground!** quelle bousculade dans le Métro!

scrumptious ['skrʌmpʃəs] *a F:* délicieux.

scruple ['skru:pl] 1. *n* scrupule *m*; **to have no scruples about doing sth,** n'avoir aucun scrupule à faire qch 2. *vi* **to s. to do sth,** avoir des scrupules à faire qch. **'scrupulous** *a* scrupuleux **(about, over, as to,** sur); méticuleux. **'scrupulously** *adv* scrupuleusement; méticuleusement; s. **clean,** d'une propreté irréprochable; impeccable. **'scrupulousness** *n* caractère scrupuleux; caractère méticuleux.

scrutinize ['skru:tinaiz] *vtr* scruter; examiner (qch) minutieusement. **'scrutinizing** *a* (regard) scrutateur, inquisiteur. **'scrutiny** *n* examen minutieux.

scuba ['sk(j)u:bə] *n* scaphandre *m* autonome; s. **diving,** plongée sous-marine autonome.

scuff [skʌf] *vtr* frotter, racler (qch) avec les pieds; érafler (ses chaussures); traîner (les pieds).

scuffle ['skʌfl] 1. *n* mêlée *f*, bousculade *f*; bagarre *f* 2. *vi (a)* se bousculer *(b)* se bagarrer *(c)* traîner les pieds.

scull [skʌl] 1. *n* aviron *m* de couple 2. *vi* ramer, nager, en couple. **'sculler** *n* rameur *m* de couple. **'sculling** *n* nage *f* à couple.

scullery ['skʌləri] *n (pl* **sculleries)** arrière-cuisine *f.*

sculp(t) [skʌlp(t)] 1. *vtr* sculpter (une statue) 2. *vi* faire de la sculpture. **'sculptor** *n* sculpteur *m.* **'sculptress** *n (pl -es)* femme sculpteur. **'sculpture** 1. *n* sculpture *f* 2. *vtr & i* sculpter.

scum [skʌm] *n* écume *f*; mousse *f* (sur un liquide); **to take the s. off,** écumer; **the s. of society,** le rebut de la société.

scurf [skɔ:f] *n* pellicules *fpl* (sur la tête).

scurrilous ['skʌriləs] *a (of language)* grossier, injurieux, ordurier; *(of pers)* ignoble. **scu'rrility** *n* grossièreté *f* (de langage); bassesse *f* (d'une personne, d'une action).

scurry ['skʌri] *vi* **(scurried)** courir à pas précipités; **to s. off, away,** détaler, décamper; **to s. through one's work,** expédier son travail.

scuttle[1] ['skʌtl] *n* **coal** s., seau *m* à charbon.

scuttle[2] *vtr Nau:* saborder (un navire).

scuttle[3] *vi* courir à pas précipités; **to s. off,** déguerpir, filer.

scythe [saið] 1. *n Tls:* faux *f* 2. *vtr* faucher.

sea [si:] *n* 1. *(a)* mer *f*; **by the s.,** au bord de la mer; s. **bathing,** bains de mer; **by s.,** par (voie de) mer; **beyond the sea(s),** outre-mer; s. **voyage,** voyage en mer; s. **breeze,** brise de mer; s. **battle,** bataille navale; s. **salt,** sel marin, de mer *(b)* **the open s., the high seas,** le large; **to put (out) to s.,** prendre le large; *Fig:* **to be all at s.,** être tout désorienté; **to get one's s. legs,** s'amariner; **to have one's s. legs,** avoir le pied marin *(c)* **inland s.,** mer intérieure; **the seven seas,** toutes les mers du monde *(d)* S. **Lord,** lord *m* de l'Amirauté *(e)* s. **fish,** poisson de mer; s. **fishing,** pêche maritime; s. **trout,** truite de mer; s. **elephant,** éléphant de mer; s. **anemone,** actinie *f* 2. *(a)* **heavy s.,** grosse mer; mer houleuse *(b)* lame *f*, houle *f*; **head s.,** mer debout *(c)* coup *m* de mer; paquet *m* de mer 3. océan *m*, multitude *f*; **a s. of faces,** un océan de visages. **'seabird** *n* oiseau *m* de mer. **'sea**

'coast n littoral m; côte f. 'seafarer n homme m de mer; marin m. 'seafood n fruits mpl de mer. 'seafront n bord m de mer, esplanade f; **a house on the s.**, une maison qui donne sur la mer. 'seagull n Orn: mouette f; goéland m. 'sealion n Z: otarie f. 'seaman n (pl -men) 1. marin m; matelot m 2. **a good s.**, un bon navigateur. 'seamanship n manœuvre f et matelotage m; la manœuvre. 'seaplane n hydravion m. 'seaport n port m de mer. 'seascape n Art: marine f. 'sea-shell n coquillage m. 'seashore n (a) bord m de mer (b) plage f. 'seasick a to be s., avoir le mal de mer. 'seasickness n mal m de mer. 'seaside n bord m de la mer; **s. resort**, station f balnéaire; plage f. 'seaway n 1. sillage m (d'un navire) 2. **the St Lawrence S.**, la voie maritime du Saint-Laurent. 'seaweed n algues marines. 'seaworthy a (of ship) en (bon) état de navigabilité.

seal¹ [si:l] n Z: phoque m. 'sealer n (a) navire armé pour la chasse au phoque (b) (pers) chasseur m de phoques. 'sealskin n peau f de phoque.

seal² 1. n (a) (on deed) sceau m; (on letter) cachet m; **to set one's s. to sth**, autoriser qch; donner son approbation à qch; **under the s. of secrecy**, sous le sceau du secret (b) cachet (de bouteille de vin); Ind: **s. of approval**, label m; Jur: (on property) official s., scellé m; Com: **lead s.**, plomb m (pour sceller une caisse) 2. vtr sceller (un acte); cacheter (une lettre, une bouteille); plomber (un colis); **my lips are sealed**, mes lèvres sont scellées; **his fate is sealed**, son sort est réglé; **sealing wax**, cire à cacheter. 'seal 'off vtr **the area was sealed off by the police**, le quartier a été bouclé par la police. **seal up** vtr fermer hermétiquement (un contenant).

seam [si:m] n (a) couture f; **French s.**, couture double; **flat s.**, couture rabattue; **saddle-stitched s.**, couture piquée; **room bursting at the seams**, salle pleine à craquer (b) (on face) fissure f, gerçure f (c) (in metal pipe) joint m; **welded s.**, joint soudé, soudure f (d) Min: veine f. 'seamless a sans couture; sans soudure. 'seamstress n (pl -es) couturière f. 'seamy a (-ier, -iest) **the s. side of life**, les dessous m de la vie.

séance ['seiɑ̃:ns] n séance f de spiritisme.

search [sə:tʃ] I. n 1. recherche(s) f (pl); **in s. (of)**, à la recherche (de); **s. party**, expédition de secours m 2. (a) Cust: visite f (b) Jur: perquisition f; **s. warrant**, mandat de perquisition 3. fouille f (dans un tiroir). II. v 1. vtr inspecter; chercher dans (un endroit); fouiller (un suspect); scruter (un visage); Cust: visiter (les valises de qn); fouiller (qn); Jur: perquisitionner dans (une maison); P: **s. me!** je n'ai pas la moindre idée! 2. vi **to s. for sth**, (re)chercher qch. 'searching a (examen) minutieux; (regard) pénétrant, scrutateur. 'searchlight n projecteur m.

season¹ ['si:zən] n 1. saison f; **holiday s.**, saison des vacances; **close s., open s.**, chasse, pêche, fermée, ouverte; (of fruit) **to be in s.**, être de saison; **strawberries are in s.**, c'est la saison des fraises; **when in s.**, pendant la saison; **out of s.**, hors saison; **low-s. price**, prix hors saison; **the high, busy, s.**, la haute saison 2. période f, temps m; **in s. and out of s.**, à tout propos; **s. ticket**, F: s., carte f d'abonnement; **s. ticket holder**, abonné, -ée. 'seasonable a 1. de (la) saison; **s.**

weather, temps de saison 2. (of advice) à propos, opportun. 'seasonably adv opportunément, à propos. 'seasonal a (commerce) saisonnier; **s. worker**, saisonnier, -ière.

season² 1. vtr (a) assaisonner, relever (un mets) (b) dessécher, étuver, conditionner (le bois); mûrir (le vin) (v) acclimater, endurcir (qn) (d) F: tempérer, modérer (une opinion) 2. vi (of wood) se sécher; (of wine) mûrir, se faire. 'seasoned a assaisonné; (of wine) mûr, fait; (of wood) sec; **highly s. dish**, plat relevé, épicé; (of pers) **to become s.**, s'acclimater; s'aguerrir. 'seasoning n Cu: assaisonnement m, condiment m; **to add s.**, assaisonner.

seat [si:t] I. n 1. (a) siège m; banquette f (de car); gradin m (d'amphithéâtre); fauteuil m (dans un théâtre); selle f (de vélo, de moto); lunette f (de WC); **folding s.**, pliant m; **flap s.**, strapontin m (b) **to take a s.**, s'asseoir; **to keep one's s.**, rester assis (c) Rail: Th: place (assise). **keep a s. for her**, gardez-lui une place (d) **he has a s. in the House**, il siège au Parlement 2. (a) siège, fond m (d'une chaise) (b) fond (de culotte); F: postérieur m; derrière m 3. siège, centre m (du gouvernement); foyer m (d'infection); **country s.**, château m 4. Equit: assiette f, assise f; **to have a good s.**, se tenir bien en selle; avoir de l'assiette. II. vtr 1. placer (qn); trouver place pour (qn); **please be seated**, veuillez vous asseoir; (of car) **to s. six**, à six places; **this table seats twelve**, on tient douze à cette table 2. (re)mettre, (re)faire, le siège (d'une chaise), (re)mettre un siège (à une chaise). 'seatbelt n ceinture f de sécurité. 'seater n a two-s. (car), une (voiture) à deux places. 'seating n (a) allocation f des places (b) **s. capacity**, nombre m de places (assises).

secateurs [sekə'tə:z] npl Hort: sécateur m.

secede [si'si:d] vi faire sécession (from, de); se séparer (d'un parti politique). se'ceding a sécessionniste. se'cession n sécession f.

seclude [si'klu:d] vtr tenir (qn, qch) retiré (from, de). se'cluded a (endroit) écarté, retiré; isolé; à l'abri des regards. se'clusion n solitude f, retraite f.

second¹ ['sekənd] n (a) seconde f (de temps); **I'll be back in a s.**, je reviens dans un instant; **in a split s.**, en un rien de temps; **wait a s.!** (attendez) une seconde! un instant! (on watch) **s. hand**, trotteuse f (b) Mth: seconde (de degré).

second² I. a second, deuxième; **the s. of January**, le deux janvier; **to live on the s. floor**, habiter au deuxième, NAm: au troisième (étage); **every s. day**, tous les deux jours; un jour sur deux; **the s. largest city in the world**, la deuxième ville du monde (en importance); **at tennis he is s. to none**, c'est le meilleur joueur de tennis; **s. to last**, avant-dernier; **in (the) s. place**, deuxièmement, en second lieu; **to marry for the s. time**, se marier en secondes noces; **it's only s. best**, c'est un pis-aller; **to travel s. class**, voyager en seconde; Aut: **s. (gear)**, deuxième (vitesse); **to be s. in command**, commander en second; **s. nature**, seconde nature; **s. sight**, clairvoyance f. II. n 1. (le) second, (la) seconde; (le, la) Deuxième; **Charles the S.**, Charles Deux 2. pl Com: **seconds**, articles m de deuxième qualité. III. vtr 1. seconder (qn); appuyer (qn), soutenir (ses amis); **to s. a motion**, appuyer une proposition 2. Mil: etc: [sə'kɔnd] mettre (un officier) en disponibilité; **to be seconded for service (with)**, être détaché (auprès de). **'secondary** *a* secondaire; *Sch:* **s. education,** enseignement du second degré; **s. causes,** causes secondes; **s. road** = route départementale. **'second'hand** *a* & *adv* d'occasion; **s. dealer,** brocanteur, -euse; **s. bookseller,** bouquiniste *mf.* **'secondly** *adv* deuxièmement; en second lieu. **se'condment** *n* détachement *m.* **'second-'rate** *a* médiocre, inférieur; de second ordre.

secret ['si:krit] **1.** *a* (a) secret; caché; **to keep sth s.,** tenir qch secret; garder le secret au sujet de qch; **s. agent,** agent secret **2.** *n* (*also* **'secrecy**) *n* discrétion *f;* **in s.,** en secret; **there's no s. about it,** il n'y a pas de mystère; **to let s.o. into the s.,** mettre qn dans le secret; **to be in the s.,** être au courant (de qch). **secrete¹** [si'kri:t] *vtr* cacher (qch); receler (des objets volés). **'secretive** *a* (*of pers*) réservé, dissimulé; *F:* cachottier. **'secretly** *adv* secrètement; en secret.

secretary ['sekrətri] *n* (*pl* **secretaries**) secrétaire *mf; Adm:* **executive s.,** secrétaire de direction; **company s.,** secrétaire général (d'une société); **private s.,** secrétaire particulier, -ière; *Pol:* **S. of State,** (i) Ministre *m* (ii) Secrétaire d'État; **S.-General to the United Nations,** Secrétaire général des Nations Unies. **secre'tarial** *a* (travail) de secrétaire; (cours) de secrétariat. **secre'tariat** *n* secrétariat *m.*

secrete² [si'kri:t] *vtr* (*of glands*) sécréter. **se'cretion** *n Physiol:* sécrétion *f.*

sect [sekt] *n* secte *f.* **sec'tarian** *a* sectaire.

section ['sekʃən] *n* (a) tranche *f* (b) *Mth:* **conic sections,** sections coniques (c) coupe *f,* profil *m;* **vertical s.,** coupe verticale (d) section; partie *f,* division *f;* **made in sections,** démontable; *Journ:* **sports s.,** les pages sportives; rubrique sportive. **'sectional** *a* (a) (dessin) en coupe, en profil (b) (intérêts) d'une classe, d'un parti (c) en sections; **s. bookcase,** bibliothèque démontable, par éléments.

sector ['sektər] *n* secteur *m.*

secular ['sekjulər] *a* séculier; laïque; **s. music,** musique profane.

secure [si'kjuər] **I.** *a* **1.** sûr; (avenir) assuré; **to feel s. of victory,** être certain de la victoire **2.** en sûreté; sauf; **s. against attack,** à l'abri de toute attaque **3.** (*of beam*) fixé, assujetti; solide; (*of foothold*) ferme, sûr. **II.** *vtr.* **1.** (a) mettre (qch) en sûreté, à l'abri (b) mettre en lieu sûr **2.** fixer, retenir (qch à sa place); verrouiller (la porte) **3.** obtenir, acquérir; se procurer (qch) (b) (*pers*) caution; garant *m;* **to secure s.o.'s services,** s'assurer de l'aide de qn. **se'curely** *adv* (a) sûrement; avec sécurité (b) solidement. **se'curity** *n* **1.** sécurité *f,* sûreté *f; Pol:* **S. Council (of UNO),** Conseil *m* de sécurité (de l'ONU); *Adm:* **social s.,** sécurité sociale; **job s.,** sécurité de l'emploi **2.** (moyen *m* de) sécurité; sauvegarde *f* **3.** *Com:* (a) caution *f;* **s. for a debt,** garantie *f* d'une créance; **to pay (in) a sum as a s.,** verser une provision; verser une somme en nantissement; **without s.,** à découvert (b) (*pers*) caution; garant *m;* **to stand s. for s.o.,** se porter garant pour qn, de qn (c) *Fin: usu pl* **securities,** titres *mpl,* valeurs *fpl.*

sedate [si'deit] **1.** *vtr Med:* donner un sédatif (à qn) **2.** *a* posé, calme; (maintien) composé. **se'dately** *adv* posément. **se'dation** *n Med:* sédation *f.* **'sedative** *a* & *n* sédatif (*m*); calmant (*m*).

sedentary ['sedəntri] *a* sédentaire.

sediment ['sedimənt] *n* sédiment *m,* dépôt *m;* lie *f*

(du vin). **sedi'mentary** *a* sédimentaire. **sedimen'tation** *n* sédimentation *f.*

sedition [si'diʃən] *n* sédition *f.* **se'ditious** *a* séditieux.

seduce [si'dju:s] *vtr* séduire, corrompre (qn). **se'ducer** *n* séducteur, -trice. **seduction** [-'dʌkʃən] *n* séduction *f,* corruption *f* (de qn). **se'ductive** *a* séduisant, attrayant; **s. offer,** offre alléchante. **se'ductively** *adv* d'une manière attrayante.

see¹ [si:] *vtr* (saw; seen) **1.** (a) voir; **to s. the sights of the town,** visiter les monuments de la ville; **I saw him leave,** je l'ai vu partir; **there's nothing to s.,** il n'y a rien à voir; **there was no one to be seen,** il n'y avait pas âme qui vive; **to s. s.o. in the distance,** apercevoir qn dans le lointain; **he's not fit to be seen,** il n'est pas présentable (b) **as far as the eye can s.,** à perte de vue; **it was too dark to s. clearly,** il faisait trop noir pour bien distinguer (c) **to s. s.o. coming,** voir venir qn; *Fig:* **you could s. it coming,** on voyait venir cela de loin (d) **I'll s. you to the door,** je vais vous accompagner jusqu'à la porte **2.** (a) comprendre, saisir; **I don't s. the point,** je ne saisis pas la nuance; **I s.!** je comprends! **as you can s.,** si ce que je vois (b) observer, remarquer (qch); s'apercevoir de (qch); **I can s. no fault in him,** je ne lui connais pas de défaut; **s. for yourself,** voyez par vous-même; **what can you s. in him, her?** que pouvez-vous lui trouver? (c) voir, juger, apprécier; **this is how I s. it,** voici comment j'envisage la chose; **if you s. fit to leave,** si vous trouvez bon de partir **3.** examiner; regarder avec attention; **we'll go and s.,** je vais aller voir; **let me s.,** (i) attendez un peu (ii) faites voir! **4. to s. (to it) that everything's in order,** s'assurer que tout est en ordre **5.** (a) fréquenter, avoir des rapports avec (qn); **he sees a great deal of the Smiths,** il fréquente beaucoup les Smith; **s. you on Thursday!** à jeudi! **s. you soon!** à bientôt! **s. you later,** à tout à l'heure; **s. you tomorrow!** à demain! (b) **to go and s. s.o.,** aller trouver qn; **to s. the doctor,** consulter le médecin; **to s. s.o. on business,** voir qn pour discuter affaires (c) recevoir (un visiteur). **'see about** *vtr* s'occuper de (qch); se charger de (qch); **I'll s. a. it,** (i) je m'en occuperai (ii) j'y réfléchirai. **'see 'in** *vtr* faire entrer (qn); **to s. the New Year in,** célébrer la Nouvelle Année (sur le coup de minuit). **'seeing** *n* vue *f;* vision *f;* **s. is believing,** voir c'est croire; **it's worth s.,** cela vaut la peine d'être vu; *conj phr* **s. that,** puisque, vu que. **'see 'off** *vtr* accompagner qn pour lui dire au revoir. **'see 'out** *vtr* accompagner (qn) jusqu'à la porte. **'see 'over** *vtr* visiter (une maison). **'see 'through 1.** *vi* (a) voir à travers (qch) (b) pénétrer les intentions de (qn); pénétrer (un mystère) **2.** *vtr* **to s. a business through,** mener une affaire à bonne fin; **to s. it through,** tenir jusqu'au bout. **'see-through** *a* (chemisier) transparent. **'see to** *vtr* s'occuper de (qn, qch); veiller à (qn, qch); **to s. to everything,** avoir l'œil à tout.

see² *n Ecc:* siège épiscopal.

seed [si:d] *n* (a) graine *f* (de tomate); pépin *m* (de pomme, de raisin) (b) *coll* semence *f;* graine(s); **to go to s.,** (i) monter en graine (ii) *F:* (*of pers*) se laisser aller; **s. potatoes,** pommes de terre de semence. **'seeded** *a Ten:* **s. players,** têtes *f* de série. **'seedling** *n Hort:* (jeune) plant *m.* **'seedsman** *n* (*pl -men*) grainetier *m.* **'seedy** *a* (**-ier, -iest**) (a) (fruit) plein de graines (*b*) F: (*of pers, hotel*) miteux; **s.-looking**, d'aspect *m* minable (*c*) (*of pers*) mal en train.

seek [si:k] *vtr* (**sought** [sɔ:t]) (*a*) chercher (un objet perdu); rechercher (de l'avancement, un emploi); **to s. shelter**, se réfugier (sous un arbre) (*b*) **to s. sth from s.o.**, demander qch à qn; **to s. advice**, demander conseil; **much sought after**, très recherché.

seem [si:m] *vi* (*a*) sembler, paraître; (*of pers*) avoir l'air (fatigué); **how does it s. to you?** que vous en semble? **how did he s. to you?** comment l'avez-vous trouvé? **it seems like a dream**, on croirait, on croit, rêver (*b*) **she seems to understand**, elle a l'air de comprendre; **I s. to have heard his name**, il me semble avoir entendu son nom **2.** *impers* **it seems to me that you are right**, il me semble que vous avez raison; **it seems best to leave her alone**, il vaut mieux la laisser seule (semble-t-il); **it seemed as though, as if**, il semblait que + *sub*; **on aurait dit que** + *ind*; **so it seems**, à ce qu'il paraît, paraît-il. **'seeming** *a* apparent; soi-disant *inv*. **'seemingly** *adv* apparemment; à ce qu'il paraît. **'seemly** *a* convenable.

seen [si:n] *see* **see**[1].

seep [si:p] *vi* (*of liquids*) suinter; s'infiltrer. **'seepage** *n* suintement *m*; infiltration *f*.

seersucker [ˈsiːəsʌkər] *n Tex*: crépon *m* de coton.

seesaw [ˈsiːsɔ:] **1.** *n* bascule *f* **2.** *vi* basculer; osciller; (*of pers*) **to s. between two opinions**, osciller entre deux opinions.

seethe [si:ð] *vi* bouillonner; (*of crowd*) s'agiter; **the street is seething with people**, la rue grouille de monde; **country seething with discontent**, pays en effervescence; **to be seething with anger**, bouillir de colère.

segment [ˈsegmənt] *n* segment *m*; quartier *m* (d'orange).

segregate [ˈsegrigeit] *vtr* isoler; mettre (qch) à part. **'segregated** *a* (*of school*) où on applique la ségrégation (raciale). **segre'gation** *n* ségrégation *f*; isolement *m*; *Pol*: **racial s.**, ségrégation raciale. **segre'gationist** *n* ségrégationniste *mf*; partisan, -ane, de la ségrégation raciale.

seismology [saizˈmɔlədʒi] *n* sismologie *f*. **'seismic** *a* sismique. **'seismograph** *n* sismographe *m*.

seize [si:z] **1.** *vtr* saisir; se saisir, s'emparer, de (qch); (to **s. s.o. by the throat**, prendre qn à la gorge; **to s. the opportunity**, saisir l'occasion; **to be seized with fright**, être saisi de peur **2.** *vi* **to s. (up)**, (*of engine*) gripper; coincer, (se) caler; (se) bloquer; *Med*: (*of joint*) s'ankyloser. **'seizure** *n* **1.** saisie *f* (de marchandises) **2.** *Med*: attaque *f*.

seldom [ˈseldəm] *adv* rarement; peu souvent; **I s. see him now**, je ne le vois plus guère.

select [siˈlekt] **1.** *vtr* choisir (**from**, parmi); sélectionner **2.** *a* choisi; de (premier) choix; d'élite; **s. club**, club très fermé; **s. audience**, public choisi. **se'lected** *a Lit*: **s. passages**, morceaux choisis. **se'lection** *n* choix *m*, sélection *f*; **a good s. of wines**, un bon choix de vins; **to make a s.**, faire un choix; **selections from Byron**, morceaux choisis de Byron. **se'lective** *a* sélectif; **to be s.**, choisir avec discernement.

self [self] **1.** *n* (*pl* **selves**) le moi; **one's better s.**, son meilleur côté; **he's quite his old s. again**, il est complètement rétabli **2.** *pron* (*on cheque*) (**pay**) **s.**, payez à moi-même. **'self-a'ddressed** *a* (enveloppe) adressée à soi-même. **'self-a'dhesive** *a*

autocollant. **'self-a'ssertive** *a* autoritaire. **'self-a'ssurance** *n*, **'self-'confidence** *n* confiance *f* en soi; assurance *f*; aplomb *m*. **'self-a'ssured**, **'self-'confident** *a* sûr de soi; plein d'assurance. **'self-'catering** *n* **s.-c. apartment**, appartement (loué pour les vacances) où l'on fait la cuisine soi-même. **'self-'centred** *a* égocentrique. **'self-'cleaning** *a* (four) autonettoyant. **'self-con'fessed** *a* (voleur) de son propre aveu. **'self-'conscious** *a* embarrassé, gêné; intimidé. **'self-'consciousness** *n* contrainte *f*, embarras *m*, gêne *f*; timidité *f*. **'self-con'tained** *a* **1.** (*of pers*) indépendant (d'esprit); peu communicatif **2.** (appareil, industrie) autonome **3. s.-c. flat**, appartement avec entrée particulière. **'self-con'trol** *n* sang-froid *m*; maîtrise *f* de soi. **'self-de'fence** *n* défense personnelle; *Jur*: légitime défense. **'self-de'nial** *n* abnégation *f* de soi; renoncement(s) *m(pl)*. **'self-determi'nation** *n Pol*: autodétermination *f*; **right of peoples to s.-d.**, droit des peuples à disposer d'eux-mêmes. **'self-'discipline** *n* auto-discipline *f*; discipline personnelle. **'self-'drive** *a* **s.-d. cars for hire**, location de voitures sans chauffeur. **'self-'educated** *a* autodidacte. **'self-em'ployed** *a* qui travaille à son (propre) compte. **'self-e'steem** *n* respect *m* de soi; amour-propre *m*. **'self-'evident** *a* (fait *m*) qui saute aux yeux. **'self-ex'planatory** *a* qui se passe d'explications. **'self-ex'pression** *n* libre expression *f*. **'self-'governing** *a* (territoire) autonome. **'self-'government** *n* autonomie *f*. **'self-'help** *n* efforts personnels. **'self-ig'nition** *n Aut*: auto-allumage *m*. **'self-im'portant** *a* suffisant, présomptueux. **'self-in'dulgent** *a* sybarite; qui se dorlote; qui ne se refuse rien. **'selfish** *a* égoïste, intéressé. **'selfishly** *adv* égoïstement, en égoïste. **'selfishness** *n* égoïsme *m*. **'selfless** *a* désintéressé. **'selflessness** *n* désintéressement *m*. **'self-made's. man**, homme qui est arrivé par lui-même. **'self-'pity** *n* attendrissement *m* sur soi-même; **full of s.-p.**, attendri sur soi-même. **'self-'portrait** *n* autoportrait *m*. **'self-po'ssessed** *a* maître de soi; qui a du sang-froid. **'self-po'ssession** *n* aplomb *m*, sang-froid *m*. **'self-preser'vation** *n* instinct de conservation (de soi-même). **'self-pro'pelled** *a* (*of vehicle*) autopropulsé. **'self-'raising**, *NAm*: **-rising** *n Cu*: **s.-r. flour**, farine préparée à la levure chimique. **'self-re'liance** *n* indépendance *f*. **'self-re'liant** *a* indépendant. **'self-re'spect** *n* respect *m* de soi; amour-propre *m*. **'self-'righteous** *a* pharisaïque, satisfait de soi. **'self-'sacrifice** *n* abnégation *f* (de soi). **'selfsame** *a* identique. **'self-'satisfied** *a* suffisant; content de soi. **'self-'service** *a* & *n Com*: libre-service (*m*); self-service; *n F*: self *m*. **'self-'starter** *n Aut*: démarreur *m*. **'self-'styled** *a* soi-disant *inv*; prétendu. **'self-su'fficient** *a* indépendant. **'self-su'pporting** *a* (financièrement) indépendant. **'self-'taught** *a* autodidacte. **'self-'willed** *a* opiniâtre, volontaire, obstiné. **'self-'winding** *a* (montre) à remontage automatique.

sell [sel] *vtr* (**sold**) **1.** (*a*) vendre (**to**, à); **he sold it for fifty pence**, il l'a vendu cinquante pence; *F*: **to s. an idea**, faire accepter une idée; **to be sold on sth**, être entiché de qch (b) **this book sells well,** ce livre se vend bien; **oranges are sold by the kilo,** les oranges se vendent au kilo; **land to s.,** terrain à vendre **2.** (a) vendre, trahir (un secret) (b) duper, tromper; F: **you've been sold a pup,** on vous a refait. **'sell-by** a F: **s.-by date,** date (de) limite de vente. **'seller** n vendeur, -euse; **seller's market,** marché à la hausse. **'selling** n vente f; écoulement m, placement m; **s. price,** prix m de vente. **'selling off** n liquidation f. **'sell 'off** vtr solder; liquider (son stock). **'sell 'out** vtr **1. we're sold out of this article,** nous sommes démunis de cet article; **the edition is sold out,** l'édition est épuisée **2.** Fin: réaliser (des actions). **'sellout** n **this play is a s.,** on a fait salle comble; on a joué à guichets fermés; **this article has been a s.,** cet article s'est vendu à merveille (et il ne nous en reste plus). **'sell 'up** vtr vendre, faire saisir (un failli).

Sellotape ['selouteip] n Rtm: ruban adhésif, Scotch m (Rtm).

selvedge ['selvidʒ] n Tex: lisière f.

semantic [si'mæntik] **1.** a sémantique **2.** n sémantique f.

semaphore ['semǝfɔːr] n sémaphore m.

semblance ['semblǝns] n apparence f; **to put on a s. of gaiety,** faire semblant d'être gai.

semen ['siːmen] n (no pl) sperme m, semence f.

semester [sǝ'mestǝr] n esp NAm: Sch: (Br = **term**) semestre m.

semi- ['semi] pref semi-; demi-; **s.-automatic gun,** arme (à feu) semi-automatique. **'semibreve** n Mus: ronde f. **'semicircle** n demi-cercle m. **'semi'circular** a semi-circulaire. **'semi'colon** n point-virgule m. **'semi'conscious** a à demi conscient. **'semide'tached** a **s.-d. house,** maisons jumelées; pavillon jumelé. **'semi'final** n Sp: demi-finale f. **'semi-o'fficial** a officieux. **'semi-'precious** a (of stone) semi-précieux. **'semi-quaver** n Mus: double croche f. **'semi-skilled** a (ouvrier) spécialisé.

seminar ['seminɑːr] n Sch: séminaire m.

seminary ['seminǝri] n (pl **seminaries**) séminaire m. **'seminarist** n séminariste m.

semolina [semǝ'liːnǝ] n Cu: semoule f.

senate ['senǝt] n (a) sénat m (b) Sch: conseil de l'université. **'senator** n sénateur m.

send [send] v (**sent**) **1.** vtr (a) envoyer; **to s. s.o. for sth,** envoyer qn chercher qch; **to s. s.o. home,** renvoyer qn chez lui; **to s. a child to bed,** envoyer un enfant se coucher; **to s. a child to school,** envoyer un enfant à l'école; **to s. s.o. on an errand,** envoyer qn faire une course (b) envoyer, expédier (un colis); **I'm sending you a present by post,** je vous fais parvenir un cadeau par la poste; **to s. clothes to the wash,** donner du linge à laver; **it sent a shiver down my spine,** cela m'a fait passer un frisson dans le dos; **the blow sent him sprawling,** le coup l'a envoyé rouler; F: **to s. s.o. packing,** envoyer promener qn; flanquer qn à la porte; Fig: **to s. s.o. to Coventry,** mettre qn en quarantaine **2.** vi **to s. for s.o.,** envoyer chercher qn; **I shall s. for it,** je vais le faire venir. **'send a'long** vtr **s. him along,** envoie-le moi! dis-lui de venir me voir! **'send a'way** vtr (a) renvoyer, congédier (qn) (b) expédier (un colis). **'send 'back** vtr renvoyer. **'send 'down** vtr faire descendre; renvoyer, expul-

ser (un étudiant); faire baisser (les prix). **'sender** n expéditeur, -trice (d'une lettre). **'send 'for** vtr envoyer chercher, faire venir (qn, qch). **'send 'in** vtr **1.** (a) faire (r)entrer (qn) (b) **to s. in one's name,** se faire annoncer **2.** (a) envoyer (un compte); remettre, faire parvenir (une demande) (b) **to s. in one's resignation,** donner sa démission. **'send 'off** vtr (a) envoyer (qn) (en mission) (b) expédier (une lettre) (c) Sp: exclure (un joueur) du terrain. **'sendoff** n réception n d'adieu. **'send 'on** vtr (a) faire suivre (une lettre) (b) transmettre (un message); expédier (des bagages) à l'avance. **'send 'out** vtr (a) faire sortir (qn); mettre (un élève) à la porte (b) lancer (des circulaires) (c) émettre (des signaux, de la chaleur). **'send 'round** vtr (a) faire circuler, faire passer (la bouteille) (b) envoyer (to s.o., to s.o.'s house, chez qn); **I'll s. s.o. round tomorrow,** j'enverrai qn demain. **send 'up** vtr **1.** faire monter (qn, un ballon); faire hausser, monter (les prix) **2.** F: parodier (qn, qch).

senile ['siːnail] a sénile. **senility** [si'niliti] n sénilité f.

senior ['siːniǝr] **1.** a (a) **William Jones s.,** William Jones père; **he's two years s. to me,** il est mon aîné de deux ans (b) s. **(in rank),** (de grade) supérieur; **s. partner,** associé principal; **the s. officer,** le doyen des officiers; **s. clerk,** premier commis; Jur: premier clerc; Sch: **s. boys, girls,** les grand(e)s; Adm: **s. citizens,** retraité(e)s; personnes âgées; le troisième âge **2.** n (a) aîné, -ée; doyen, -enne (d'âge) (b) (b) (le plus âgé), (la plus) ancienne; **to be s.o.'s s.,** être l'aîné de qn; avoir plus d'ancienneté que qn; Sch: **the seniors,** les grand(e)s. **seniority** [-'ɔriti] n **1.** priorité f d'âge; supériorité f d'âge **2.** ancienneté f (de grade); **to be promoted by s.,** avancer à l'ancienneté.

sensation [sen'seiʃǝn] n **1.** sensation f; sentiment m (de malaise); **I had a s. of falling,** j'avais l'impression de tomber **2.** sensation; effet sensationnel; **to create, make, cause, a s.,** faire sensation. **sen'sational** a sensationnel; (roman) à sensation; **s. happening,** sensation f; **s. writer,** auteur à sensation; F: **it's s.!** c'est fantastique, sensationnel!

sense [sens] **1.** n (a) sens m; **the five senses,** les cinq sens; **the s. of smell,** l'odorat m; **the s. of hearing,** l'ouïe f; **to have a keen s. of smell,** avoir l'odorat fin; **to be in one's senses,** être sain d'esprit; **any man in his senses,** tout homme jouissant de son bon sens; **to frighten s.o. out of his senses,** effrayer qn jusqu'à lui faire perdre la raison; **to bring s.o. to his senses,** ramener qn à la raison; **to come to one's senses,** (i) revenir à la raison (ii) (regain consciousness) revenir à soi; **to take leave of one's senses,** perdre la raison, la tête (b) sensation f (de plaisir, de chaleur); sens; **s. of injustice,** sentiment m d'injustice (c) sentiment, conscience f; **to have a s. of time,** avoir la notion de l'heure; **s. of humour,** sens de l'humour; **s. of direction,** sens de l'orientation (d) bon sens, intelligence f; **common s.,** bon sens; sens commun; **to see s.,** entendre raison; **to talk s.,** parler raison; **to have more s. than to do sth,** avoir trop de bons sens pour faire qch (e) sens, signification f; **this sentence doesn't make s.,** cette phrase ne veut rien dire; **I can't make s. of this passage,** je n'arrive pas à comprendre ce passage; **in the full s. of the word,** dans toute l'acception du terme; **in a s.,** d'une certaine façon; **in the s. (that),** en ce sens (que) **2.** vtr sentir (qch) intuitivement; pressentir (qch). **'senseless** a

1. stupide; déraisonnable; **a s. remark,** une bêtise **2. to knock s.o. s.,** assommer qn. **'senselessly** adv stupidement; bêtement. **'senselessness** n man-que m de bon sens; stupidité f.

sensibility [sensi'biliti] n (pl **sensibilities**) sensibilité f. **'sensible** a sensé, raisonnable; (choix) judicieux; (clothes) pratique; confortable. **'sensibly** adv raisonnablement; judicieusement.

sensitive ['sensitiv] a **1.** (of skin, tooth) sensible; (of skin, question) délicat; (of pers) **to be s. to cold,** être frileux (b) (of pers) susceptible; impressionnable (c) Ind: Fin: **s. market,** marché instable. **'sensitively** adv d'une manière sensible. **'sensitiveness, sensi'tivity** n (pl -**ies**) sensibilité f.

sensual ['sensjual] a sensuel; voluptueux. **sensu'ality** n sensualité f. **'sensually** adv avec sensualité, sensuellement.

sensuous ['sensjuas] a (of pleasure) voluptueux, sybaritique; (charme) voluptueux. **'sensuously** adv avec volupté.

sent [sent] see **send.**

sentence ['sentans] **1.** n (a) Jur: jugement m; sentence f, condamnation f; **death s.,** arrêt m de mort; **life s.,** condamnation à vie; **to pass a s.,** condamner qn (b) (term of imprisonment) peine f; **to serve a s.,** purger une, sa, peine (c) Gram: phrase f **2.** vtr Jur: con-damner (qn).

sententious [sen'tenʃas] a sentencieux, pompeux. **sen'tentiously** adv sentencieusement.

sentiment ['sentimant] n **1.** (a) sentiment m; **noble sentiments,** sentiments nobles (b) opinion f, avis m; **those are my sentiments,** voilà ce que je pense **2.** sentimentalité f. **senti'mental** a sentimental. **senti'mentalist** n sentimental, -ale. **sentimen'tality** n sentimentalité f. **senti'mentally** adv sentimentalement.

sentry ['sentri] n (pl **sentries**) sentinelle f; factionnaire m; **s. box,** guérite f; **to stand s., to be on, to do, s. duty,** être de faction; monter la garde.

sepal ['sepəl] n Bot: sépale m.

separate 1. a (a) séparé, détaché (**from,** de); **keep these bottles s.,** mettez ces bouteilles à part (b) distinct, indépendant; (entrée) particulière; (organi-sation) indépendante; **entered in a s. column,** inscrit dans une colonne spéciale. **II.** vtr & i ['separeit] (se) séparer; (se) détacher (de qn, qch); **he's separated (from his wife),** il est séparé (de sa femme). **'separ-able** a séparable. **'separately** adv séparément; à part; **sell them s.,** vends-les séparément. **'separates** npl Com: coordonnés mpl. **sepa'ration** n **1.** sépa-ration f (d'avec qn); **legal s. (of husband and wife),** séparation de corps (et de biens); séparation judi-ciaire **2.** écart m, distance f.

sepia ['si:pia] n Art: sépia f.

September [sep'tembər] n septembre m; **in S.,** au mois de septembre, en septembre.

septic ['septik] a Med: septique; **to become s.,** s'infecter; **s. tank,** fosse f septique. **septicae-mia,** NAm: -**cemia** [-'si:miə] n Med: septicémie f.

septuagenarian [septjuadʒi'nɛarian] n & a septua-génaire (mf).

sepulchre, NAm: **sepulcher** ['sepəlkər] n sépulcre m, tombeau m. **se'pulchral** a sépulcral; **s. vault,**

caveau m; **s. stone,** pierre tumulaire; **s. voice,** voix caverneuse.

sequel ['si:kwəl] n suite f (d'un roman).

sequence ['si:kwəns] n **1.** (a) succession f; ordre naturel; **in s.,** en série; **logical s.,** enchaînement m logique (b) suite f, série f (c) Gram: **s. of tenses,** concordance f des temps **2.** Cards: séquence f **3.** Cin: (film) s., scène f.

sequin ['si:kwin] n paillette f.

sequoia [si'kwɔia] n Bot: séquoia m.

serenade [sera'neid] **1.** n sérénade f **2.** vtr donner la sérénade à (qn).

serene [sə'ri:n] a serein, calme, tranquille; (ciel) clair. **se'renely** adv tranquillement; avec sérénité. **serenity** [-'reniti] n sérénité f, calme m, tranquillité f.

serge [sə:dʒ] n Tex: serge f.

sergeant ['sɑ:dʒant] n **1.** Mil: (infantry) sergent m; (artillery, armoured corps, cavalry) maréchal m des logis; (in all arms) sous-officier, m (b) **police s.,** brigadier m. **'sergeant-'major** n Mil: adjudant m; **regimental s.-m.,** adjudant-chef m.

serial ['siarial] **1.** a **s. number,** numéro de série **2.** n feuilleton m; TV: téléroman m. **'serialize** vtr publier, TV: diffuser (un roman) en feuilleton.

series ['siari:z] n inv **1.** série f, suite f; échelle f, gamme f (de couleurs); Ch: etc: **s. of reactions,** réactions en chaîne **2.** adv phr **in s.,** en série.

serious ['siarias] a **1.** sérieux; **s. injury,** blessure f grave; **s. mistake,** grosse faute; **his condition is s.,** il est dans un état grave, gravement malade **2.** (a) **s. promise,** promesse sérieuse, sincère (b) (of pers) réfléchi; **to give s. thought,** réfléchir; **I'm s.,** je ne plaisante pas. **'seriously** adv **1.** sérieusement; **s. ill,** gravement malade; **s. wounded,** grièvement blessé **2. to take sth s.,** prendre qch au sérieux. **'seriousness** n **1.** gravité f (d'une maladie, d'un événement) **2.** sérieux m (de maintien); **in all s.,** sérieusement.

sermon ['sə:mən] n sermon m; F: semonce f.

serpent ['sə:pənt] n serpent m.

serrated [sə'reitid] a denté en scie; **s. knife,** couteau à scie; **s. edge,** denture f.

serum ['siarəm] n (pl **serums, sera**) sérum m.

serve [sə:v] **1.** vtr (a) servir (un maître, un client, une cause); **to s. (at table),** servir (à table); (in shop) **are you being served?** est-ce qu'on s'occupe de vous? **he served ten years,** il a fait (i) dix ans de service (ii) dix ans de prison; Jur: **to s. on the jury,** être (membre), faire partie, du jury; **to s. in the army,** servir dans l'armée; **to s. one's apprenticeship,** faire son apprentissage; **to s. one's sentence,** F: one's **time,** purger sa peine (b) (of thg) être utile à (qn, qch); **it will s. the purpose,** cela fera l'affaire; **if my memory serves me right,** si j'ai bonne mémoire (c) (of bus route, railway) **to s. a place,** desservir (une localité) (d) (in shop) **to s. in a shop,** être vendeur, -euse; **to s. s.o. with a pound of butter,** servir une livre de beurre à qn; (at table) **to s. a dish,** servir un plat (e) F: **it serves you right!** c'est bien fait! vous ne l'avez pas volé! (f) (of bull) couvrir (une vache) (g) Ten: servir (la balle) (h) **to s. a writ on s.o.,** assigner qn **2.** vi (a) servir (**as, for, sth,** de qch); faire fonction (as **sth,** de qch); **to s. as an example,** servir d'exemple; **to s. as a pretext,** servir de prétexte. **'servant** n **1.** domestique mf; bonne f **2. civil s.,** fonctionnaire mf.

'**server** *n* 1. (a) serveur, -euse (b) *Ecc:* acolyte *m*, répondant *m* 2. **salad, fish, servers,** service *m*, couvert *m*, à salade, à poisson. '**service I.** *n* 1. service *m*; **public services,** services publics; **military s.,** service national, militaire; **to be in (domestic) s.,** être domestique 2. **the civil s.,** l'administration *f*; **to go into the civil s.,** devenir fonctionnaire; **the foreign s.,** le service diplomatique; **he's in the diplomatic s.,** il est de la carrière; **the (armed) services,** les forces armées; **the Senior S.,** la Marine nationale britannique; **s. families,** les familles de militaires 3. **s. flat,** appartement avec service; **s. lift,** monte-plats *m*; **s. hatch,** guichet *m*; **24-hour s.,** service permanent; (*in restaurant*) **s. charge,** service; **s. industry,** (i) secteur *m* tertiaire (ii) (*particular company*) société de service 4. **to do s.o. a s.,** rendre (un) service à qn; **I'm at your s.,** je suis à votre disposition *f*; **social services,** services sociaux; **to be of s. to s.o.,** être utile à qn 5. *Ecc:* office *m*; culte *m* 6. *Ten:* service 7. **tea s.,** service à thé; **dinner s.,** service de table 8. **bus s.,** service d'autobus 9. révision *f* (d'une voiture); **s. area,** *NAm:* **s. center,** aire *f* de service (au bord d'une autoroute); **s. station,** station-service *f*; **after-sales s.,** service après-vente. **II.** *vtr Aut: Mec: etc:* entretenir et réparer (un appareil); faire la révision (d'une voiture). '**serviceable** *a* (a) en état de fonctionner, utilisable (b) pratique, commode. '**serviceman** *n* (*pl* -**men**) militaire *m*; soldat *m*; (*esp in wartime*) mobilisé *m*; **disabled ex-s.,** mutilé *m* de guerre. '**servicing** *n* révision *f* (d'une voiture).

serviette [sɔːviˈet] *n* serviette *f* de table.

servile [ˈsɔːvail] *a* servile. **servility** [-ˈviliti] *n* servilité *f*.

servitude [ˈsɔːvitjuːd] *n* servitude *f*, esclavage *m*.

session [ˈseʃən] *n* session *f*; séance *f*; (*of Parliament*) **the House is now in s.,** la Chambre siège actuellement.

set [set] **I.** *n* 1. (a) ensemble *m*; jeu *m* (d'outils); série *f* (de casseroles); batterie *f* (d'ustensiles de cuisine); collection complète (des œuvres de qn); service *m* (de porcelaine); train *m* (de pneus); mobilier *m* (de salle à manger) (b) **wireless, television, s.,** poste *m* de radio, de télévision; téléviseur *m* (c) *Ten:* manche *f*, set *m* (d) groupe *m* (de personnes); bande *f* (de voleurs); **(literary) s.,** coterie *f* (littéraire) 2. (*of hair*) mise *f* en plis 3. direction *f* (du vent, du courant); assiette *f* (d'une poutre); voie *f*, chasse *f* (des dents d'une scie) 4. *Th: Cin:* décor *m*; mise en scène. **II.** *v* (**setting; set**) **I.** *vtr* (a) mettre, poser (un plat sur la table); **I haven't s. eyes on him,** je ne l'ai pas vu; **to s. one's heart on doing sth,** avoir, prendre, à cœur de faire qch; **to s. the table,** mettre le couvert, la table; **to s. the alarm for 6 o'clock,** mettre le réveil sur six heures; *Aut:* **to s. the milometer to zero,** ramener le compteur à zéro; **to have one's hair s.,** se faire faire une mise en plis; *Th:* **to s. a scene,** monter un décor; **the scene is s. (in),** l'action se passe (à) (b) sertir une pierre (précieuse); **ring s. with rubies,** bague ornée de rubis; **to s. words to music,** mettre des paroles en musique; **to s. a trap,** dresser, tendre, un piège; **to s. a chisel,** affûter un ciseau (k) *Typ:* **to s. type,** composer; **to s. the fashion,** fixer, mener, la mode; **to s. a bone,** réduire (une fracture); **to s. one's teeth,** serrer les dents; **to s. sth going,** mettre qch en train, en marche; **to s. s.o. to do sth,** mettre qn à faire qch; **to s. a man to work,** mettre un homme au travail; **to s. a good example,** donner un bon exemple; **to s. a**

problem, donner un problème à résoudre; *Sch:* **to s. an exam paper,** choisir les questions d'examen; **to s. an essay,** donner un sujet de dissertation (à une classe); **to s. a book,** mettre un livre au programme 2. *vi* (a) (*of sun*) se coucher (b) (*of broken bone*) se ressouder (c) (*of egg white*) se coaguler; (*of blood*) se figer; (*of milk*) (se) cailler; (*of jelly*) prendre; (*of cement*) prendre, durcir (d) **to s. to work,** se mettre au travail. **III.** *a* 1. **s. face, smile,** visage rigide; sourire figé; *F:* **to be all s.,** être prêt à commencer, à partir 2. **s. price,** prix fixe; **s. meal,** table *f* d'hôte; **s. phrase,** cliché *m*; **at s. hours,** à des heures réglées; **s. purpose,** ferme intention; **s. task,** tâche assignée; **s. book,** auteur au programme 3. **to be (dead) s. on sth,** être résolu, déterminé, à qch, à faire qch. '**set a'bout** *vi* **to s. about doing sth,** se mettre à faire qch; **I don't know how to s. about it,** je ne sais pas comment m'y prendre. '**set a'part, 'set a'side** *vtr* 1. mettre (qch) à part 2. (*esp set aside*) rejeter; mettre de côté (de l'argent); écarter (une proposition). '**set 'back** *vtr* (a) **house s. back from the road,** maison en retrait (de la route) (b) retarder (une horloge); **this will s. him back,** cela retardera sa guérison; *F:* **it s. me back £500,** ça m'a coûté £500. '**setback** *n* déconvenue *f*; revers *m* de fortune. '**set 'down** *vtr* 1. poser (qch); déposer (qn); (*of public transport*) **to s. down passengers,** déposer des passagers 2. **to s. sth down (in writing),** coucher qch par écrit; consigner (un fait). '**set 'in** *vi* commencer; **before winter s. in,** avant la venue de l'hiver; **it's setting in for rain,** le temps se met à la pluie; **if no complications s. in,** s'il ne survient pas de complications. '**set 'off 1.** *vtr* (a) déclencher; faire partir (une fusée) (b) **to s. off a gain against a loss,** compenser une perte par un gain 2. *vi* partir; se mettre en route. '**set 'out 1.** *vtr* arranger, disposer (des livres, une exposition); **his work is well s. out,** son travail est bien présenté 2. *vi* partir (en voyage); se mettre en route; s'embarquer; **to s. out in search of s.o.,** se mettre à la recherche de qn. '**set-square** *n* équerre *f*. '**setting** *n* cadre *m* (d'un récit); *Th:* mise *f* en scène; monture *f* (d'un diamant); aiguisage *m*, affûtage *m* (d'un outil); mise en plis (des cheveux); coucher *m* (du soleil); *Med:* réduction *f* (d'une fracture); *Typ:* composition *f*. '**set 'to** *vtr* **to s. to work,** se mettre au travail; s'y mettre. '**set-'to** *n F:* lutte *f*; combat *m*. '**set 'up** *vtr* monter (une machine); (*of printer*) composer (un manuscrit); établir (un record); fonder (une maison de commerce); ouvrir, créer (une agence, un magasin); ouvrir (une enquête); installer (un appareil); **to s. up house,** établir son domicile; **to s. (oneself) up (in business) as a grocer,** s'établir épicier. '**set-up** *n F:* organisation *f*. '**set u'pon** *vtr* attaquer (qn).

settee [seˈtiː] *n* canapé *m*; **bed s.,** canapé-lit *m*, divan-lit *m*.

setter [ˈsetər] *n* chien *m* d'arrêt; setter *m*.

settle [ˈsetl] **I.** *n* banc *m* à dossier. **II.** *v* 1. *vtr* (a) établir, installer (qn); s'installer (b) **to s. one's affairs,** mettre ses affaires en ordre (c) **to s. s.o.'s doubts,** dissiper les doutes de qn (d) calmer (les nerfs) (e) fixer, déterminer; **it's all settled,** c'est une affaire faite (f) résoudre, décider (une question); vider (une querelle); arranger, liquider (une affaire); **s. it among yourselves,** arrangez cela entre vous; **that settles it!** (i) voilà qui tranche la question! (ii) cela me décide! **nothing is settled,** rien n'est décidé (g) conclure (une affaire); régler, solder (un compte); payer (une dette) **2.** *vi* (a) se fixer; (*of bird*) se percher; **to s. (oneself) (down) in an armchair,** s'installer dans un fauteuil; **to s. (down) in a place,** s'établir dans un lieu; **to s. (down) to work,** se mettre sérieusement au travail; **I settled for £100,** j'ai accepté £100 (b) (*of snow*) ne pas fondre; (*of liquid*) se clarifier; déposer; (*of sediment*) se précipiter; **to let (sth) s.,** laisser déposer (un précipité); laisser reposer (une solution) (c) (*of ground, soil*) se tasser; (*of foundations*) s'affaisser. **'settled** a (a) invariable, sûr; (*of idea*) fixe, enraciné; **s. policy,** politique continue; **s. intention,** intention bien arrêtée; **s. weather,** temps stable (b) (*of pers*) rangé; *esp* marié (c) (*of question*) arrangé, décidé; (*of pers*) domicilié, établi. **'settle 'down** vi (*of pers*) se ranger; devenir sérieux; **he's settled down since he married,** le mariage l'a assagi; **he's beginning to s. down at school,** il commence à s'habituer à l'école. **'settlement** n (*also* **'settling**) **1.** (a) établissement m; installation f (b) peuplement m (d'un pays) **2.** règlement m (d'une affaire, d'un compte); *Com:* **in (full) s.,** pour solde de tout compte; **they have reached a s.,** ils sont parvenus à un accord. **'settler** n colon m. **'settle 'up** vi payer ses comptes; régler ses comptes (**with s.o.,** avec qn).

seven ['sevən] num a & n sept (m); **two sevens are fourteen,** deux fois sept font quatorze. **seven'teen** num a & n dix-sept (m). **seven'teenth** num a & n dix-septième (m); **Louis the S.,** Louis Dix-sept; **the s. of August, August the s.,** le dix-sept août. **'seventh** num a & n septième (m); **the s. of July, July the s.,** le sept juillet; **to be in the s. heaven,** être aux anges. **'seventieth** num a & n soixante-dixième (m). **'seventy** num a & n soixante-dix (m); *Belg: SwFr:* septante (m); **s.-one, s.-nine,** soixante et onze, soixante-dix-neuf; **she's in her seventies,** elle est septuagénaire; elle a plus de soixante-dix ans.

sever ['sevər] vtr couper (des liens); sectionner; rompre, cesser (les relations avec qn); interrompre (les communications); **to s. one's connection with s.o.,** cesser toutes relations avec qn; se dissocier de qn. **'severance** n séparation f (**from,** de); rupture f (de relations); interruption f (de communications); **s. pay,** indemnité de licenciement.

several ['sevərəl] **1.** a plusieurs, divers; quelques; **s. times,** plusieurs fois; **he and s. others,** lui et quelques autres **2.** pron **I have s.,** j'en ai plusieurs. **'severally** adv séparément, individuellement.

severe [si'viər] a **1.** sévère, strict, rigoureux (**with s.o.,** envers qn) **2.** (a) (temps) rigoureux, dur; **the cold was s.,** le froid sévissait (b) vif; rude; **s. pain,** vive douleur. **se'verely** adv **1.** sévèrement; avec sévérité **2.** grièvement; gravement (blessé). **severity** [-'veriti] n **1.** sévérité f, rigueur f **2.** (a) inclémence f (du temps) (b) gravité f (d'une maladie).

sew [sou] vtr (sewed; sewn) coudre; **to s. on a button,** coudre un bouton; **to s. (up) a seam,** faire une couture; *F:* **everything's sewn up,** tout est arrangé. **'sewing** n **1.** couture f; **s. needle,** aiguille à coudre; **s. cotton,** fil à coudre; **s. machine,** machine à coudre; **s. kit,** nécessaire à couture **2.** ouvrage m (à l'aiguille).

sewer ['s(j)u:ər] n *CivE:* égout m; **main s.,** égout

collecteur. **'sewage** n eau(x) f (pl) d'égout; **s. farm,** champs mpl d'épandage; **s. system,** système du tout-à-l'égout.

sex [seks] n sexe m; **to have s. with s.o.,** faire l'amour avec qn; **s. act,** l'acte sexuel; **s. organs,** organes sexuels; **s. shop,** sex shop m; **s. appeal,** charme m, *F:* sex-appeal m. **'sexless** a **1.** asexué **2.** *F:* froid, frigide. **'sexist** a sexiste. **'sexual** a sexuel; **s. intercourse,** rapports sexuels; **s. reproduction,** reproduction sexuée. **sexu'ality** n sexualité f. **'sexually** adv sexuellement. **'sexy** a (-ier, -iest) *F:* aguichant; sexy.

sextet [seks'tet] n *Mus:* sextuor m.

sexton ['sekstən] n *Ecc:* (a) sacristain m (b) sonneur m (des cloches, du carillon, d'une église) (c) fossoyeur m.

shabby ['ʃæbi] a (-ier, -iest) **1.** (vêtement) râpé, usé; (mobilier) pauvre, minable; **to look s.,** avoir l'air dépenaillé, miteux **2.** mesquin; **s. trick,** mesquinerie f. **'shabbily** adv **1.** pauvrement; **s. dressed,** dépenaillé **2.** (se conduire) mesquinement. **'shabbiness** n **1.** usure f, état usé (d'un vêtement); état défraîchi (d'un meuble); apparence pauvre, miteuse (de qn) **2.** mesquinerie f (de conduite).

shack [ʃæk] **1.** n cabane f, hutte f **2.** vi *P:* **to s. up with s.o.,** vivre, se coller, avec qn.

shade [ʃeid] **I.** n **1.** ombre f; **in the s. (of a tree),** à l'ombre (d'un arbre); **temperature in the s.,** température à l'ombre; **to put s.o. in(to) the s.,** éclipser qn; *Art:* **light and s.,** l'ombre et la lumière **2.** (a) nuance f; teinte f; **different shades of blue,** différentes nuances de bleu (b) **he's a s. better,** il va un tout petit peu mieux; **a s. longer,** un tantinet plus long **3.** (a) (*for eyes*) visière f; (*for lamp*) abat-jour m *inv* (b) *NAm:* (*Br* = **blind**) store m (de fenêtre); *esp NAm:* **shades** (*Br* = **sunglasses**) lunettes fpl de soleil. **II.** v **1.** vtr (a) ombrager; couvrir (qch) d'ombre; abriter (qch) (du soleil); voiler, masquer (une lumière); **a shaded spot,** un coin ombragé (b) ombrer (un dessin); nuancer (une couleur) **2.** vi (*of colour*) se fondre (into, en). **'shade 'off** **1.** vtr dégrader (une couleur) **2.** vi blue that shades off into green, bleu qui se fond en vert. **'shadiness** n **1.** ombre, ombrage m (d'un sentier, d'un arbre) **2.** *F:* aspect m louche (d'une affaire). **'shady** a (-ier, -iest) **1.** (a) qui donne de l'ombre, ombreux (b) ombragé, couvert d'ombre; **s. walk,** allée couverte **2.** *F:* (*of transaction*) louche; **s. pub,** bistrot louche; **the s. side of politics,** les dessous m de la politique.

shadow ['ʃædou] **1.** n (a) ombre f; obscurité f; **in the s.,** à, dans, l'ombre; dans l'obscurité; **to have shadows under one's eyes,** avoir les yeux cernés; *Toil:* **eye s.,** ombre à paupières; **to cast a s.,** projeter une ombre; faire ombre; **to be afraid of one's s.,** avoir peur de son ombre; **he's a s. of his past self,** il n'est plus que l'ombre de lui-même; **not the s. of a doubt,** pas l'ombre d'un doute; **to wear oneself to a s.,** s'épuiser; *Pol:* **s. cabinet,** cabinet fantôme; **s. minister,** ministre de l'opposition (b) compagnon, f compagne, inséparable **2.** vtr filer (qn). **'shadowing** n filature f (d'une personne suspecte). **'shadowy** a vague, indécis; **a s. form in the dusk,** une ombre dans la nuit tombante.

shaft¹ [ʃɑ:ft] n **1.** (a) hampe f (de lance) (b) manche m (de club de golf) **2.** flèche f, trait m (d'une satire) **3.**

rayon *m* (de lumière) **4.** tige *f* (de plume d'oiseau); fût *m* (d'une colonne) **5.** (*a*) *Mec:* arbre *m* (de transmission, à cames) (*b*) (*of horse-drawn vehicle*) brancard *m*.

shaft² *n Min:* puits *m*; cage *f* (d'un ascenseur).

shaggy ['ʃægi] *a* (**-ier, -iest**) poilu; à longs poils; (sourcils) en broussailles; (barbe) touffue; *F:* **s. dog story** = histoire farfelue.

shake [ʃeik] **I.** *n* **1.** (*a*) secousse *f*; **to give sth a good s.,** bien secouer, bien agiter, qch; **a s. of the head,** un hochement de tête; *F:* **in two shakes (of a lamb's tail),** en un rien de temps (*b*) **to be all of a s.,** trembler de tous ses membres; **to have the shakes,** avoir la tremblote **2. milk s.,** milk-shake *m* **3.** *F:* **to be no great shakes,** ne pas valoir grand-chose. **II.** *v* (**shook; shaken**) **1.** *vtr* (*a*) secouer; agiter (qch); **to s. one's head,** hocher la tête; faire non de la tête; **to s. one's fist at s.o.,** menacer qn du poing; **to s. hands with s.o.,** serrer la main à qn; s.! tope là! **to s. oneself free,** se dégager d'une secousse (*b*) ébranler; **to feel shaken after a fall,** se ressentir d'une chute; **he was shaken by the accident,** il a été bouleversé par l'accident **2.** *vi* trembler; (*of building*) chanceler, branler; (*of voice*) trembloter; chevroter; **to s. with fright,** trembler de peur; **to s. all over,** trembler de tout son corps. **'shake 'down 1.** *vtr* secouer (des fruits) **2.** *vi F:* s'habituer à une routine, un travail. **'shaken** *a* secoué; ébranlé; bouleversé. **'shake 'off** *vtr* **1.** se débarrasser, se défaire, de (qch); **to s. the dust off sth,** secouer la poussière de qch; **to s. off a bad habit,** se débarrasser d'une mauvaise habitude **2.** venir à bout d'(un rhume). **'shake 'out** *vtr* (*a*) secouer; vider (un sac) en le secouant (*b*) déferler (une voile, un drapeau). **'shake 'up** *vtr* **1.** secouer, brasser; agiter (une bouteille) **2.** éveiller, secouer, stimuler (qn). **'shake-up** *n* (*a*) **to get a good s.-up,** être pas mal secoué (*b*) *F:* changement *m*, remaniement *m* (de l'administration, du personnel). **'shakily** *adv* peu solidement; faiblement; (marcher) à pas chancelants; (écrire) d'une main tremblante; (parler) d'une voix chevrotante. **'shaking 1.** *a* tremblant; branlant; **s. voice,** voix tremblante, chevrotante **2.** *n* secousse *f*; ébranlement *m*; tremblement *m*; tremblotement *m*. **'shaky** *a* (**-ier, -iest**) peu solide; branlant; (santé) faible; (main) tremblante; (voix) mal assurée; (écriture) tremblée.

shale [ʃeil] *n* schiste (argileux, ardoisier).

shall [ʃæl, ʃ(ə)l] *modal aux v* (**should** [ʃud]; **shall not** and **should not** *are often contracted into* **shan't** [ʃɑːnt] *and* **shouldn't** [ʃudnt]) **I.** (*implying command, insistence*) **1.** (*a*) **thou shalt not kill,** tu ne tueras point; **ships s. carry three lights,** les navires sont tenus de porter trois feux; **all is as it should be,** tout est très bien (*b*) **he s. not, shan't, do it,** je lui interdis de le faire; **you s. do it!** vous le ferez, je le veux! (*c*) **you should do it at once,** vous devriez le faire tout de suite; **you should have seen him!** il fallait le voir! (*d*) **he should have arrived by this time,** il devrait être arrivé à l'heure qu'il est; **I should think so!** je crois bien! **2.** (*polite request*) **s. I open the window?** voulez-vous que j'ouvre la fenêtre? **3.** (*a*) (*exclamative & rhetorical questions*) **why should you suspect me?** pourquoi me soupçonner (,moi)? **whom should I meet but Jones!** voilà que je rencontre Jones! (*b*) **if he should come,** si par hasard il vient; **should I be free,** si je suis libre; **should the occasion**

arise, le cas échéant; **in case he shouldn't be there,** au cas où il n'y serait pas, s'il n'y était pas. **II.** *aux v* *forming the future tenses* **1. you shan't have any!** tu n'en auras pas! **you s. pay for this!** vous me le payerez! **2. tomorrow I s. go and he'll arrive,** demain, moi je partirai et lui arrivera; **will you be there?**—I s., y serez-vous?—oui (j'y serai); **no, I shan't,** non (je n'y serai pas) **3. if he comes I s. speak to him,** s'il vient je lui parlerai; **we should come if we were invited,** nous irions si nous étions invités **4. I should like a drink,** je prendrais quelque chose; **I shouldn't be surprised (if),** cela ne me surprendrait pas (que + *pr sub*).

shallot [ʃə'lɔt] *n* échalote *f*.

shallow ['ʃælou] **1.** *a* (*a*) (*of water, dish*) peu profond (*b*) (*of pers*) superficiel, frivole **2.** *n* (*usu pl*) bas-fond *m*, haut-fond *m*. **'shallowness** *n* (le) peu de profondeur; (*of pers, book*) caractère superficiel.

sham [ʃæm] **1.** *a* simulé, feint; (*of jewellery*) faux, *f* fausse, postiche, en toc **2.** *n* (*a*) feinte *f*, trompe-l'œil *m inv* (*b*) **he's a s.,** c'est un imposteur. **3.** *vtr* (**shammed**) feindre, simuler; **to s. sleep,** faire semblant de dormir; **he's only shamming,** tout ça c'est de la frime.

shamble ['ʃæmbl] *vi* **to s. along,** s'avancer d'un pas traînant, mal assuré.

shambles ['ʃæmblz] *npl* (*with sg const*) désordre *m*, gâchis *m*; **it's a s.!** tout est en désordre! **what a s.!** quelle pagaille!

shame [ʃeim] **1.** *n* honte *f*; **to put s.o. to s.,** faire honte à qn; **s. on you!** quelle honte! **to blush for, with, s.,** rougir (i) de honte (ii) de pudeur; **without s.,** (i) effronté (ii) effrontément; **it's a s.!** c'est honteux! **what a s.!** quel dommage! **it would be a s. (to),** il serait dommage (de) **2.** *vtr* faire honte à, humilier (qn); **to be shamed into doing sth,** faire qch par amour-propre. **'shame-faced** *a* honteux, penaud; embarrassé. **'shameful** *a* honteux, scandaleux. **'shamefully** *adv* honteusement, scandaleusement. **'shamefulness** *n* honte *f*, infamie *f*. **'shameless** *a* (*a*) éhonté, effronté; sans honte (*b*) honteux, scandaleux. **'shamelessly** *adv* effrontément; **to lie s.,** mentir impudemment. **'shamelessness** *n* effronterie *f*, impudence *f*. **'shaming** *a* mortifiant.

shampoo [ʃæm'puː] **1.** *n* shampooing *m*; **to give s.o. a s.,** faire un shampooing à qn; **s. and set,** shampooing et mise en plis; **carpet s.,** shampooing pour tapis **2.** *vtr* (*a*) **to s.o.'s hair,** laver la tête, faire un shampooing, à qn; **to s. one's hair,** se laver la tête; se faire un shampooing (*b*) nettoyer (une moquette).

shamrock ['ʃæmrɔk] *n* trèfle *m* d'Irlande.

shandy ['ʃændi] *n* (*pl* **shandies**) bière panachée; mélange *m* de bière et de limonade.

shan't [ʃɑːnt] *see* **shall.**

shanty¹ ['ʃænti] *n* (*pl* **shanties**) hutte *f*, cabane *f*, baraque *f*; **s. town,** bidonville *m*.

shanty² *n* (*pl* **shanties**) (**sea**) **s.,** chanson *f* de marins.

shape [ʃeip] **I.** *n* **1.** (*a*) forme *f*, configuration *f* (du terrain); façon *f*, coupe *f* (d'un habit); **square in s., of square s.,** carré, de forme carrée; **to get out of s.,** to lose (its) s., se déformer; **to put, knock an article into s.,** mettre un article au point; **to take s.,** prendre forme, prendre tournure; (*of pers*) **to be in good, poor, s.,** être, ne pas être, en forme; **no communication in any s. or form,** aucune communication de n'importe quelle sorte (*b*) *Cu:* moule *m*. **II.** *v* **1.** *vtr* façonner; tailler (la pierre); **to s. one's life,** régler sa vie; **to s. a coat,** ajuster une veste **2.** *vi* se développer; **the affair is shaping well,** (i) l'affaire prend bonne tournure (ii) l'affaire promet bien. **'shapeless** *a* informe; difforme. **'shape-lessness** *n* manque *m* de forme. **'shapely** *a* (-ier, -iest) bien fait, bien tourné.

share [ʃɛər] **I.** *n* 1. *(a)* part *f*, portion *f*; **the lion's s.,** la part du lion; **in equal shares,** par portions égales; **s. in profits,** participation *f* aux bénéfices; **to go shares, partager (with,** avec); **s. and s. alike,** en partageant également *(b)* **(fair) s.,** portion juste; lot *m*; **I had my fair s. of worries,** j'ai eu ma bonne part de soucis **2.** contribution *f*, cotisation *f*; **to pay one's s.,** payer sa (quote-)part; **to take a s. in the conversation,** prendre part, participer, à la conversation; **he doesn't do his s.,** il ne fait pas sa part (de travail); **to have a s. in an undertaking,** avoir un intérêt dans une entreprise **3.** *Fin:* action *f*, titre *m*; **s. index,** indice *m* de la Bourse. **II.** *v* **1.** *vtr* partager; **to s. sth with s.o.,** partager qch avec qn; **to s. and s. alike,** partager entre tous également **2.** *vtr & i* **to s. (in) sth,** prendre part à, participer à, qch; **to s. (in) s.o.'s grief,** partager la douleur de qn. **'sharecropper** *n Agr:* métayer, -ère. **'sharecropping** *n Agr:* métayage *m*. **'shareholder** *n Fin:* actionnaire *mf*. **'sharing** *n* 1. partage *m* 2. participation *f*. **'share-out** *n* partage *m*.

shark [ʃɑːk] *n* 1. *Ich:* requin *m* 2. *(pers)* escroc *m*; requin.

sharp [ʃɑːp] **I.** *a* 1. *(a)* tranchant, aiguisé, affilé; *(of point)* aigu, pointu *(b) (of features)* anguleux; *(of angle)* aigu; saillant; **s. turn,** tournant *m* brusque *(c) (of outline)* net *(d)* (descente) abrupte; **a s. rise in prices,** une forte augmentation de prix; **s. contrast,** contraste marqué **2.** *(of pers)* *(a)* fin, éveillé; *(of hearing)* fin, subtil; *(of sight)* perçant; *(of glance)* pénétrant; **a s. child,** un enfant à l'esprit vif, *Pej:* futé *(b)* rusé, malin; peu scrupuleux; **s. practice,** procédés *m* peu honnêtes; **to be too s. for s.o.,** être trop malin pour qn **3.** *(a)* (combat) vif, acharné *(b)* (orage) violent; **s. shower,** forte averse *(c)* (hiver) rigoureux; (vent) vif, perçant; (froid) pénétrant; **s. pain,** vive douleur *(d)* **s. pace,** allure vive, rapide *(e)* **s. tongue,** langue acérée; **in a s. tone,** d'un ton acerbe, cassant **4.** *(of sauce)* piquant; *(of apple)* aigre, acide; *(of wine)* vert **5.** *(of sound)* pénétrant, aigu. **II.** *n Mus:* dièse *m*. **III.** *adv* **1.** (tourner) brusquement; **turn s. right,** prenez tout de suite à droite, à angle droit **2.** ponctuellement, exactement; **at four o'clock s.,** à quatre heures précises; à quatre heures sonnantes, *F:* pile **3.** *F:* **look s.!** fais vite! dépêche-toi! *F:* grouille-toi! **4.** *Mus:* **to sing s.,** chanter faux (en haussant le ton). **'sharpen** *vtr* **1.** *(a)* affiler, affûter, aiguiser; *(of cat)* faire (ses griffes) *(b)* tailler en pointe; **to s. a pencil,** tailler un crayon **2. to s. s.o.'s wits,** dégourdir qn. **'sharpener** *n* aiguisoir *m*; *(for pencil)* taille-crayon(s) *m*. **'sharply** *adv* **1. s. divided,** nettement divisé **2. the road dips s.,** la route plonge brusquement **3.** *(a)* **he looked s. at her,** il la dirigea sur elle un regard pénétrant *(b)* (réprimander) sévèrement; **to answer s.,** répondre avec brusquerie. **'sharpness** *n* **1.** *(a)* acuité *f*, finesse *f*; tranchant *m* (d'un couteau) *(b)* netteté *f* (des contours) *(c)* caractère marqué (d'un contraste) **2.** *(a)* **s. of sight,** acuité de la vue *(b)* intelligence *f* **3.** sévérité

f, acerbité *f*. **'sharpshooter** *n Mil:* tireur *m* d'élite. **'sharp-'witted** *a* éveillé; intelligent; dégourdi.

shatter [ʃætər] **1.** *vtr* fracasser; briser (en éclats); détruire, ruiner, anéantir (les espérances, la confiance); briser (une carrière); *F:* **I was absolutely shattered!** j'étais complètement (i) bouleversé (ii) éreinté! **2.** *vi* se briser (en éclats); se fracasser. **'shattering** *a* (coup) écrasant; (nouvelle) renversante.

shave [ʃeiv] **I.** *n* rasage *m*; **to have a s.,** (i) se faire raser (ii) se raser; *F:* **to have a close, narrow, s.,** l'échapper belle. **II.** *v* **1.** *vtr* raser; faire la barbe à (qn); **to s. off one's moustache,** se raser la moustache **2.** *vi* **to s.** (oneself), se raser. **'shaven** *a* rasé; **clean-s.,** (visage) glabre; sans barbe ni moustache. **'shaver** *n* **electric s.,** rasoir *m* électrique. **'shaving** *n* **1.** action *f* de se raser; **s. brush,** blaireau *m*; **s. cream,** crème à raser; **s. soap,** savon à barbe; **s. stick,** bâton de savon à barbe **2.** *usu pl* **shavings,** copeaux *mpl* (de bois, de métal).

shawl [ʃɔːl] *n* châle *m*.

she [ʃi, ʃiː] *pers pron nom* **1.** *(a)* elle; **what's s. doing?** que fait-elle? **here s. comes,** la voici qui vient *(b)* (i) *(of female animals, motor cars)* elle (ii) *(of ships)* il; **s. sails tomorrow,** il appareille demain **2.** *(a) (stressed)* elle; **she and I,** elle et moi; **she knows nothing about it,** elle n'en sait rien, elle; **if I were s.,** si j'étais à sa place *(b) (antecedent to a rel pron)* (i) celle; **she who believes,** celle qui croit (ii) **it's** *she* **who did it,** c'est elle qui l'a fait **3.** *(used as a noun)* femelle *f*; **s.-ass,** ânesse *f*; **s.-bear,** ourse *f*; **s.-cat,** chatte *f*; **s.-monkey,** guenon *f*.

sheaf [ʃiːf] *(pl* **sheaves** [ʃiːvz]) *n* **1.** gerbe *f* (de blé, de fleurs) **2.** liasse *f* (de papiers).

shear [ʃiər] *vtr* (**sheared**; *pp* **shorn, sheared**) **1. to s. (off),** couper (une branche); **s. through sth,** trancher qch; *Metalw:* cisailler (une tôle) **2.** tondre (un mouton); **to be shorn of sth,** être dépouillé, privé, de qch. **'shearer** *n* tondeur *m* (de moutons). **'shearing** *n* taille *f* (d'une haie); cisaillement *m* (d'une tôle), tonte *f* (des moutons). **shears** *npl* **(pair of) s.,** cisaille(s) *f(pl)*; grands ciseaux *mpl*. **shorn** *a* (mouton) tondu; **s. of all his possessions,** dépouillé de tout ce qu'il possédait.

sheath [ʃiːθ] *n* fourreau *m*; gaine *f*; **(contraceptive) s.,** préservatif *m*; **s.-knife,** couteau *m* à gaine.

sheathe [ʃiːð] *vtr* (re)mettre au fourreau, rengainer.

shed¹ [ʃed] *n* hangar *m*; remise *f*; **lean-to s.,** appentis *m*; **building s.,** atelier *m* de construction; **vehicle s.,** remise *f* de véhicules; **garden s.,** resserre *f* dans un jardin; **bicycle s.,** remise, resserre, de vélos.

shed² *vtr* (**shedding; shed**) **1.** *(a)* perdre (ses feuilles) *(b)* décharger de (qn) *(c)* **to s. one's clothes,** se dévêtir *(d) (of animal, bird)* **to s. its skin, feathers,** changer de peau, de plumage, de poil; muer **2.** répandre, verser (des larmes, le sang); **to s. light on a matter,** éclairer une affaire; *El:* **to s. the load,** délester.

sheen [ʃiːn] *n* luisant *m*, lustre *m*; chatoiement *m*.

sheep [ʃiːp] *n inv* mouton *m*; *Fig:* **black s. (of the family),** brebis galeuse (de la famille); **to make sheep's eyes (at s.o.),** faire les yeux doux (à qn); **s. farmer,** éleveur, -euse, de moutons; **s. farming,** élevage de moutons; **s. pen,** parc, enclos, à moutons. **'sheep-dog** *n* chien *m* de berger. **'sheepfold** *n* parc *m* à moutons; bercail *m*. **'sheepish** *a* *(a) (ashamed)* penaud; interdit *(b) (afraid)* timide; gauche. **'sheep-**

ishly *adv* (a) d'un air penaud (b) d'un air timide. **'sheepishness** *n* (a) air penaud (b) timidité *f*. **'sheepskin** *n* peau *f* de mouton; s. **jacket**, canadienne *f*.

sheer¹ ['ʃiːər] *vi* (of ship, car) to s. **off**, faire une embardée; to s. **away**, changer de direction; to s. **away from sth**, éviter qch.

sheer² 1. *a* (a) pur, véritable, absolu; **it's s. madness**, c'est de la folie pure (et simple); c'est de la pure folie; **a s. impossibility**, une impossibilité absolue; **a s. waste of time**, une pure perte de temps; **by s. hard work**, à force de travail (b) (rocher) perpendiculaire; à pic; (of silk) léger, fin, diaphane; **s. nylon tights**, collant en nylon extra-fin 2. *adv* (a) tout à fait (b) à pic.

sheet [ʃiːt] *n* 1. drap *m* (de lit); **fitted s.**, drap housse 2. feuille *f*, morceau *m* (de papier); **loose s.**, feuille volante; Com: **order s.**, bulletin *m* de commande 3. feuille (de verre, de plastique); **s. metal**, tôle *f* 4. nappe *f* (d'eau); **s. lightning**, éclairs diffus; éclairs en nappe(s).

sheik(h) [ʃeik, ʃiːk] *nm* cheik(h), sheik *m*.

shelf [ʃelf] *n* (pl shelves [ʃelvz]) 1. tablette *f* (d'armoire); rayon *m* (de bibliothèque); **set of shelves**, étagère *f*; **s. space**, linéaire *m*; F: **to be on the s.**, être laissé pour compte 2. rebord *m*, corniche *f* (d'un rocher); Geog: **the continental s.**, le plateau continental 3. Com: (in supermarket) **s. filler**, réassortisseur, -euse; **s. life (of product)**, durée de vie (d'un produit); (of goods) **to stay on the shelves**, être difficile à vendre.

shell [ʃel] 1. *n* (a) coquille *f* (de mollusque, d'escargot); carapace *f* (de tortue); écaille *f* (d'huître); (empty) **shells**, coquillages *m*; **to retire into one's s.**, rentrer dans sa coquille (b) coquille (d'œuf, de noix); gousse *f*, cosse *f* (de pois) (c) forme *f* vide; simple apparence *f* (d) Cu: fond *m* de tarte (e) carcasse *f*, coque (de navire) (f) Mil: obus *m* 2. *vtr* (a) écosser (des petits pois); écaler (des noix) (b) Mil: bombarder. **'shellfish** *n coll* mollusques *mpl* et crustacés *mpl*; fruits *m* de mer. **'shell 'out** *vtr & i* F: payer (la note); casquer.

shelter ['ʃeltər] I. *n* lieu *m* de refuge; abri *m*; asile *m*; **bus s.**, abribus *m*; **bomb, air raid, s.**, abri; **under s.**, à l'abri, à couvert; **to take s.**, s'abriter, se mettre à l'abri. II. *v* 1. *vtr* abriter (qn); donner asile à, recueillir (un malheureux) 2. *vi & pr* s'abriter; se mettre à l'abri, à couvert (**from**, contre). **'sheltered** *a* abrité, protégé (against, from, contre).

shelve¹ [ʃelv] *vtr* ajourner (une question); mettre au rancart (un projet); **my request has been shelved**, ma demande est restée dans les cartons. **'shelving¹** *n* 1. ajournement *m* (d'une question) 2. (ensemble *m* de) rayons *mpl*; rayonnage *m*; **adjustable s.**, rayons mobiles.

shelve² *vi* aller en pente. **'shelving²** *a* en pente; (of shore) incliné.

shepherd ['ʃepəd] 1. *n* berger *m*; Ecc: **the Good S.**, le bon Pasteur; Cu: **shepherd's pie**, hachis *m* Parmentier 2. *vtr* accompagner (qn); conduire, piloter (des touristes). **shepher'dess** *n* (pl -es) bergère *f*.

sherbet ['ʃəːbət] *n* 1. s. (**powder**), poudre acidulée (pour préparer une boisson gazeuse) 2. NAm: (Br = **water ice**) sorbet *m*.

sheriff ['ʃerif] *n* shérif; US: chef *m* de la police (d'un comté); shérif.

sherry ['ʃeri] *n* (pl sherries) vin *m* de Xérès; xérès *m*.

Shetland ['ʃetlənd] *Prn* Geog: **the S. Islands**, les îles *f* Shetland; S. **wool**, shetland *m*; S. **pony**, poney shetlandais. **'Shetlander** *n* Shetlandais, -aise.

shield [ʃiːld] 1. *n* bouclier *m*; Tchn: tôle protectrice; écran protecteur 2. *vtr* protéger (**from, against**, contre); **to s. one's eyes**, se protéger les yeux.

shift [ʃift] I. *n* (a) changement *m* de position; renverse *f* (de la marée); **to make a s.**, changer de place; **s. of the wind**, saute *f* du vent; Typew: **s. key**, touche des majuscules (b) NAm: Aut: (Br = **gearstick, gear lever**) changement de vitesse (c) Ind: équipe *f*, brigade *f*; poste *m* (d'ouvriers); **to work in shifts**, se relayer; travailler par équipes; **day, night, s.**, équipe de jour, de nuit; **he's on day, night, s.**, il est de jour, de nuit; **s. work**, travail posté (d) expédient *m*; **to make s.**, s'arranger, se débrouiller. II. *v* 1. *vtr* changer (qch) de place; déplacer (les meubles); Th: **to s. the scenery**, changer le décor 2. *vi* (a) changer de place; se déplacer; NAm: Aut: (Br = **to change**) **to s. into third gear**, passer en troisième; **the wind has shifted**, le vent a tourné (b) **to s. for oneself**, se débrouiller. **'shiftiness** *n* sournoiserie *f*; manque *m* de franchise. **'shifting** 1. *a* (a) qui se déplace; **s. sands**, sables mouvants (b) (of scene) changeant; (of wind) inégal 2. *n* déplacement *m*; changement *m* (de position); NAm: Aut: (Br = **changing**) changement de vitesse. **'shiftless** *a* paresseux; peu débrouillard; (of pers, action) futile. **'shifty** *a* (-ier, -iest) roublard, retors; sournois; **s. eyes**, yeux fuyants.

shilly-shally ['ʃiliʃæli] *vi* hésiter; tergiverser. **'shilly-shallying** *n* hésitation *f*; tergiversation *f*; **stop this s.-s.**, décide-toi!

shimmer ['ʃimər] *vi* miroiter, luire, chatoyer. **'shimmering** *a* miroitant, luisant; chatoyant.

shin [ʃin] 1. *n* Anat: le (devant du) tibia; le devant de la jambe; Cu: jarret *m* (de bœuf) 2. *vi* (shinned) F: **to s. up a tree**, grimper à un arbre. **'shinbone** *n* Anat: tibia *m*.

shindig ['ʃindig] *n* NAm: (Br = **shindy**) tapage *m*, boucan *m*.

shindy ['ʃindi] *n* F: (NAm: = **shindig**) tapage *m*, boucan *m*; **to kick up a s.**, faire du boucan.

shine [ʃain] I. *v* (shone [ʃɔn]) 1. *vi* (a) briller; reluire; **the light is shining in my eyes**, j'ai la lumière dans les yeux; **the sun is shining**, il fait du soleil; **his face shone with happiness**, sa figure rayonnait de bonheur; **he doesn't s. in conversation**, il ne brille pas dans la conversation (b) **to s. on sth**, illuminer qch 2. *vtr* (a) **to s. a light on sth**, éclairer qch (avec une lampe); braquer une lampe sur qch (b) F: cirer (des chaussures). II. *n* 1. éclat *m*, lumière *f*; **come rain or s.**, par tous les temps 2. brillant *m*, luisant *m*; **to give a s. to the brasses**, faire reluire les cuivres; **to take the s. off sth**, défraîchir, délustrer, qch; faire ternir qch; **to give one's shoes a s.**, cirer ses chaussures. **'shining** *a* brillant, (re)luisant; **s. example**, exemple brillant (of, de). **'shiny** *a* (-ier, -iest) brillant; luisant; (vêtement) lustré par l'usage.

shingle ['ʃingl] *n* (a) coll galets *mpl*; (gros) cailloux *mpl* (b) Const: bardeau *m* (c) NAm: (Br = **plaque**)

plaque *f* (de cuivre) (de médecin, d'avocat).
'**shingly** *a* couvert de galets; caillouteux.

shingles ['ʃiŋglz] *npl Med:* zona *m*.

ship [ʃip] **I.** *n* (*usu referred to as* she, her) navire *m*;
bâtiment *m*; bateau *m*; **passenger s.**, paquebot *m*;
merchant s., navire marchand; **training s.**, navire-
école *m*; **His, Her, Majesty's ships,** les vaisseaux *m* de
la Marine Royale; **the ship's company,** l'équipage *m*;
on board s., à bord; **to take s., to go on board (a) s.**,
(s')embarquer. **II.** *v* (**shipped**) **1.** *vtr* (*a*) embarquer
(une cargaison) (*b*) expédier (des marchandises) (*c*)
Nau: **to s. a sea,** embarquer une lame **2.** *vi*
s'embarquer. '**shipbuilder** *n* constructeur *m* de
navires. '**shipbuilding** *n* construction navale.
'**shipment** *n* **1.** (*a*) embarquement *m* (*b*) expédition
f, envoi *m* (de marchandises) **2.** chargement *m*;
cargaison *f*. '**shipowner** *n* armateur *m*. '**shipper**
n **1.** chargeur *m*; expéditeur *m* **2.** affréteur *m*. '**shipping** *n* **1.** embarquement *m*; expédition *f*, envoi *m* (de
marchandises); **s. agent,** agent *m* maritime; **s. company,** compagnie *f* de navigation **2.** *coll* navires *mpl*
(d'un pays, dans un port) **3.** **s. routes,** routes *f* de
navigation. '**shipshape** *a* bien tenu; en bon ordre.
'**shipwreck 1.** *n* naufrage *m* **2.** *vtr* **to be shipwrecked,** faire naufrage. '**shipwright** *n* constructeur *m* de navires. '**shipyard** *n* chantier *m* de
constructions navales; chantier naval.

shire ['ʃaiər, *as suffix usu* ʃ(i)ər] *n* comté *m*; **s. horse,**
cheval de gros trait.

shirk [ʃəːk] *vtr* manquer à, se dérober à (une obligation); négliger son devoir; **to s. the question,** éluder
la question. '**shirker** *n* tire-au-flanc *m inv*.

shirt [ʃəːt] *n* chemise *f*; *sports.*, chemise sport; **lady's s.**,
chemisier *m*; *F:* **to put one's s. on a horse,** parier tout ce
qu'on possède sur un cheval; *F:* **keep your s. on!** ne
vous emballez pas! '**shirtsleeves** *npl* **to be in one's
s.**, être en bras de chemise. '**shirtwaister,** *NAm:*
'**shirtwaist** *n Cl:* robe *f* chemisier. **shirty** *a* (-ier,
-iest) *F:* irritable; en rogne; **to get s.**, se fâcher.

shiver[1] ['ʃivər] (*esp of glass*) **I.** (*a*) *vtr* fracasser; briser
(une vitre) en éclats (*b*) *vi* voler en éclats. **2.** *n* éclat *m*.

shiver[2] **I.** *vi* **to s. (with cold, with fear, with fever),**
frissonner, trembler (de froid, de peur, de fièvre);
grelotter (de froid). **II.** *n* frisson *m*, grelottement *m*,
tremblement *m*; **it gives me the shivers to think of it,** ça
me donne le frisson rien que d'y penser. '**shivery** *a*
to feel s., (i) avoir le frisson (ii) se sentir fiévreux.

shoal[1] ['ʃoul] *n* haut-fond *m*, banc *m*.

shoal[2] *n* banc *m* (de poissons).

shock[1] [ʃɔk] *n* **s. of hair,** tignasse *f*; toison *f*.

shock[2] **1.** *n* choc *m*; coup *m*; (*bump*) heurt *m*; **it gave
me a dreadful s.**, cela m'a porté un coup terrible; cela
m'a donné un choc; **the s. killed him,** il est mort de
saisissement; **electric s.**, décharge *f* électrique; *Med:*
electric s. treatment, traitement par électrochocs; **s.
wave,** onde de choc; *Aut:* **s. absorber,** amortisseur *m*;
Mil: **s. troops,** troupes d'assaut, de choc; *Med:* **in (a
state of) s.**, en état de choc **2.** *vtr* (*a*) choquer,
scandaliser (qn); **to be shocked at, by, sth,** être choqué
de, scandalisé par, qch; **easily shocked,** pudibond (*b*)
bouleverser (qn); **I was shocked to hear (that),** j'ai été
bouleversé d'apprendre (que). '**shocking** *a* choquant, révoltant, affreux; (*temps*) abominable; (douleur) atroce; **how s.!** quelle horreur! '**shockingly**

adv (*a*) abominablement; affreusement (*b*) extrêmement; **in s. bad taste,** du dernier mauvais goût.

shoddy ['ʃɔdi] *a* (-ier, -iest) (article) de mauvaise
qualité; de camelote. '**shoddily** *adv* mal. '**shoddi-
ness** *n* mauvaise qualité.

shoe [ʃuː] **I.** *n* **1.** chaussure *f*; **to put one's shoes on,** se
chausser; **I shouldn't like to be in his shoes,** je ne
voudrais pas être à sa place **2.** fer *m* (de cheval) **3.**
sabot *m* (d'un frein). **II.** *vtr* (**shod**) **1.** **to be well shod,**
être bien chaussé **2.** ferrer (un cheval). '**shoebrush**
n (*pl* -es) brosse *f* à cirer; brosse à chaussures.
'**shoehorn** *n* chausse-pied *m*. '**shoelace** *n* lacet
m (de chaussure). '**shoemaker** *n* **1.** bottier *m*;
fabricant *m* de chaussures **2.** cordonnier *m*. '**shoe-
string** *n* (*a*) *NAm:* (*Br* = **shoelace**) lacet *m* (de
chaussure) (*b*) *Fig:* **on a s.**, à peu de frais; **they're
doing it on a s.**, ils tirent sur la corde.

shone [ʃɔn] *see* **shine I.**

shoo [ʃuː] *vtr* (**shooed**) **to s. (away, off),** chasser.

shook [ʃuk] *see* **shake.**

shoot [ʃuːt] **I.** *v* (**shot** [ʃɔt]) **1.** *vi* (*a*) se précipiter, se
lancer; **to s. ahead of s.o.**, devancer qn rapidement; **he
shot into the room,** il est entré dans la pièce en trombe;
he shot past him, il est passé devant lui à toute vitesse
(*b*) (*of pain*) lanciner, élancer; (*of tree, bud*) pousser,
bourgeonner; (*of plant*) germer **2.** *vtr* (*a*) franchir (un
rapide); *Aut:* **to s. the lights,** brûler le feu rouge (*b*)
tirer (une balle); décharger (un fusil); **don't s.!** ne tirez
pas! **to s. at s.o.**, **at sth,** tirer, faire feu, sur qn, sur qch;
to s. wide of the mark, mal viser; *Sp:* **to s. a goal,**
marquer un but; *F:* **to s. a line,** exagérer (*c*) tuer (qn)
d'un coup de revolver; **he was shot dead,** il a été tué net
(d'un coup de revolver) (*d*) chasser (le gibier) (*e*)
Cin: tourner (un film). **II.** *n* **1.** pousse *f* (d'une plante);
(*of vine*) sarment *m* **2.** glissière *f*; déversoir *m*; **rubbish
s.**, vide-ordures *m inv* **3.** (*a*) partie *f* de chasse (*b*)
concours *m* de tir (*c*) (*area of land*) chasse gardée.
'**shoot 'down** *vtr* abattre, descendre (qn, un
avion). '**shooting 1.** *a* qui s'élance; jaillissant; **s.
star,** étoile filante; **s. pains,** douleurs lancinantes **2.** *n*
(*a*) tir *m* (au pistolet) (*b*) chasse *f*; **s. stick,** canne-siège
f (*c*) tournage *m* (d'un film) (*d*) meurtre *m*; fusillade *f*
(*e*) *F:* **the whole s. match,** tout le bataclan, tout le
tremblement. '**shoot 'up** *vi* (*of flames*) jaillir; (*of
prices*) augmenter rapidement; (*of plant*) pousser; (*of
child*) grandir (rapidement).

shop [ʃɔp] **1.** *n* (*a*) magasin *m*; (*small*) boutique *f*; **s.
assistant,** vendeur, -euse; employé(e) de magasin; **s.
window,** vitrine *f*; devanture *f* (de magasin); étalage *m*;
wine s., tobacconist's s., débit *m* de vins, de tabac;
grocer's s., épicerie *f*; (magasin d')alimentation *f*;
baker's s., boulangerie *f*; **butcher's s.**, boucherie *f*;
shoe s., magasin de chaussures; **mobile s.**,
camionnette-boutique *f*; **to set up s.**, ouvrir un
magasin; s'établir comme commerçant(e); **to shut up
s.**, fermer boutique; **to keep a s.**, tenir un commerce;
to go round the shops, courir les magasins; **to talk s.**,
parler métier; *F:* **you've come to the wrong s.**, vous
tombez mal; *F:* **everything was all over the s.**, tout était
en confusion, en désordre **2.** *Ind:* atelier *m*; **closed s.**,
atelier fermé aux (ouvriers) non-syndiqués; **s. floor,**
(i) l'atelier (ii) *coll* les ouvriers *mpl*; **s. steward,**
délégué(e) syndical(e) **2.** *vi* (**shopped**) **to s., to go
shopping,** faire des achats; faire ses courses. '**shop-**

girl *nf* vendeuse. **'shopkeeper** *n* commerçant, -ante. **shop-lifter** *n* voleur, -euse, à l'étalage. **'shoplifting** *n* vol *m* à l'étalage. **'shopper** *n* client, -ente (dans un magasin). **'shopping** *n* achats *mpl*; **to do one's s.,** faire ses courses *fpl*; **to go window s.,** faire du lèche-vitrines; s. **centre,** centre commercial; s. **basket,** panier à provisions; s. **bag,** cabas *m.* **'shop-soiled** *a* défraîchi, qui a fait l'étalage. **'shopwalker** *n* inspecteur, -trice, surveillant, -ante (de magasin).

shore¹ ['ʃɔːr] *n (a)* rivage *m*; littoral *m*; bord *m* (de la mer, d'un lac) *(b) Nau:* **on s.,** à terre; **off s.,** au large.

shore² 1. *n Const: etc:* étai *m*; étançon *m* 2. *vtr* **to s. (sth) up,** étayer, étançonner (un mur).

shorn [ʃɔːn] *see* **shear.**

short [ʃɔːt] I. *a* 1. court; **a s. way off,** à peu de distance; s. **steps,** petits pas; **a s. man,** un homme de petite taille; **to be s. in the arm,** avoir les bras courts; *(route)* a s. **cut,** raccourci *m; El:* s. **circuit,** court-circuit *m* 2. *(a)* court, bref; **of s. duration,** de peu de durée; **the days are getting shorter,** les jours raccourcissent; **for a s. time,** pour peu de temps; **in a s. time,** sous peu; bientôt; **a s. time ago,** il y a peu de temps; **a s. sleep,** un petit somme; **it was s. and sweet,** cela s'est fait vite; **to make s. work** of sth, expédier qch *(b)* **s. story,** nouvelle *f*; **in s.,** bref; **he's called Bob for s.,** on l'appelle familièrement Bob; **Bob is s. for Robert,** Bob est le diminutif de Robert *(c) (of reply)* brusque; sec; **to be s. with s.o.,** être sec, cassant, avec qn; **s. temper,** caractère emporté 3. *(a) (of weight)* insuffisant; **to give s. weight,** ne pas donner le poids; **I'm twenty francs s.,** il me manque vingt francs; **not far s. of it,** peu s'en faut; **it is little s. of folly,** ça frise la folie *(b)* **to be s. of sth,** être à court de qch; **to be s. of hands,** manquer de maind'œuvre; **to go s. of sth,** se priver de qch; **they never went s.,** ils n'ont jamais manqué du nécessaire. II. *n (a)* **the long and the s. of it,** le fin mot de l'affaire *(b) Cin:* court métrage *(c) El:* s. **(circuit),** court circuit. III. *adv* 1. **to stop s.,** s'arrêter net; **to cut s.o. s.,** couper la parole à qn; **to be taken s.,** (i) être pris au dépourvu (ii) être pris d'un besoin pressant 2. **to fall s. of sth,** être au-dessous de qch; **s. of burning it,** à moins de le brûler; **to stop s. of crime,** s'arrêter au seuil du crime. IV. *vtr El: F:* court-circuiter. **'shortage** *n* 1. insuffisance *f*, manque *m*; **the housing s.,** la crise du logement 2. pénurie *f*; **food s.,** disette *f.* **'short-bread, -cake** *n Cu:* = sablé *m.* **'shortcake** *n NAm: Cu:* gâteau fourré aux fruits et à la crème fraîche. **short-'change** *vtr* tricher (qn) sur la monnaie; ne pas donner son dû à (qn); *F:* rouler (qn). **short-'circuit** *El:* 1. *vtr* court-circuiter 2. *vi* se mettre en court-circuit. **'shortcoming** *n* défaut *m*, imperfection *f.* **'shortcrust** *n Cu:* s. **(pastry),** pâte brisée. **'shorten** *vi & tr* raccourcir. **'shortening** *n esp NAm: Cu: NAm:* graisse *f.* **'shortfall** *n* manque *m.* **'shorthand** *n* sténo(graphie) *f*; s. **typist,** sténo(dactylo) *mf.* **short-'handed** *a* à court de main-d'œuvre, de personnel. **'shortlist** 1. *n* liste des candidatures retenues 2. *vtr* sélectionner un candidat; retenir une candidature. **'short-'lived** *a* éphémère, de courte durée. **'shortly** *adv* 1. brièvement 2. (répondre) brusquement, sèchement 3. bientôt, prochainement; sous peu; s. **after(wards),** peu (de temps) après. **'shortness** *n* 1. *(a)* peu *m* de longueur *(b)* brièveté *f*, courte durée (de la vie); s. **of memory,** manque *m* de mémoire *(c)* brusquerie *f* (d'humeur) 2. manque, insuffisance *f* (de vivres). **shorts** *npl Cl:* **(pair of) s.,** short *m.* **'short-'sighted** *a* 1. myope 2. imprévoyant. **'short-'sightedness** *n* 1. myopie *f* 2. imprévoyance *f.* **'short-'sleeved** *a* à manches courtes. **'short-'staffed** *a* **to be s.-s.,** manquer de personnel. **'short-'tempered** *a* vif; d'un caractère emporté. **'short-term** *a Fin:* (placement) à court terme.

shot [ʃɔt] 1. *see* **shoot** 2. *a* chatoyant; s. **silk,** soie gorge-de-pigeon 3. *n (a)* plomb *m; F:* **like a s.,** (partir) comme une flèche; (accepter) sans hésitation; *Sp:* **putting the s.,** lancement *m* du poids *(b)* coup *m* (de feu); **to fire a s.,** tirer un coup de feu; *F:* **parting s.,** remarque qu'on lance en partant; *F:* **that was a s. in the dark,** il l'a dit, fait, à tout hasard *(c)* tireur, -euse; **he's a good s.,** il est bon chasseur *(d)* coup; **it's your s.,** à vous de jouer; **good s.!** bien joué! bien visé! *F:* **I'll have a s. at it,** je vais tenter le coup; *F:* **big s.,** gros bonnet. **'shotgun** *n* fusil *m* de chasse.

should [ʃud] *see* **shall.**

shoulder ['ʃəuldər] 1. *n (a)* épaule *f*; **breadth of shoulders,** carrure *f*; **slung across the s.,** en bandoulière; s. **blade,** omoplate *f*; s. **strap,** bretelle *f*; s. **bag,** sac à bandoulière; **to weep on s.o.'s s.,** pleurer sur l'épaule de qn; **put it round your s.,** mets-le sur les épaules; **to s.,** l'un à côté de l'autre; **to put one's s. to the wheel,** travailler d'arrache-pied *(b) Cu:* épaule (de mouton) *(c) (of road)* accotement *m*, bas-côté *m* 2. *vtr* pousser avec l'épaule; **to s. one's way through the crowd,** se frayer un chemin à travers la foule; **to s. s.o. out of the way,** écarter qn d'un coup d'épaule; **to s. the responsibility,** endosser la responsabilité.

shout [ʃaut] 1. *n (a)* cri *m* (de joie, de douleur); **shouts of laughter,** éclats *mpl* de rire *(b)* clameur *f*; **shouts of applause,** acclamations *fpl.* II. *v* 1. *vi* crier; pousser des cris; **to s. at s.o.,** crier après qn; **to s. for help,** appeler, crier, au secours; *vpr* **to s. oneself hoarse,** s'enrouer à force de crier 2. *vtr* crier (qch); vociférer (des injures); **to s. s.o. down,** huer qn. **'shouting** *n* cris *mpl*; acclamations *fpl*; **it's all over bar the s.,** c'est dans le sac, les applaudissements suivront.

shove [ʃʌv] *n F:* 1. coup *m* (d'épaule); poussée *f*; **to give s.o., sth, a s.,** pousser qn, qch 2. *vtr* pousser (qn, qch); enfoncer (ses doigts) (dans qch); **to s. sth, aside,** écarter qn, qch, d'une poussée; **to s. sth into a drawer,** fourrer qch dans un tiroir; *P:* **s. off!** fiche le camp!

shovel ['ʃʌvəl] 1. *n* pelle *f* 2. *vtr* **(shovelled)** pelleter; prendre, ramasser, enlever (le charbon, la neige) à la pelle; *F:* **to s. food into one's mouth,** enfourner sa nourriture. **'shovelful** *n* pelletée *f.*

show [ʃəu] 1. *n (a)* étalage *m*; **to vote by s. of hands,** voter *m* à main levée; s. **flat, house,** appartement *m*, maison *f*, témoin; s. **window,** vitrine *f*; **to be on s.,** être exposé; être en vitrine *(b)* exposition *f* (de tableaux, de marchandises); comices *m* agricoles; **motor s.,** salon *m* de l'automobile; **fashion s.,** présentation *f* de collection; s. **breeder,** s. **breeding,** éleveur *m*, élevage *m*, de bêtes à concours; *Equit:* s. **jumping,** jumping *m* *(c)* spectacle *m* (de théâtre); séance *f* (de cinéma); s. **business,** le monde du spectacle; **to go to a s.,** aller au spectacle; **the last s.,** la dernière représentation; **to steal the s.,** (r)emporter la vedette; **to**

make a s. of oneself, se donner en spectacle; *F:* to run the s., diriger l'affaire; *F:* good s.! compliments! bravo! **3.** (*a*) apparence *f*; semblant *m*; with some s. of reason, avec quelque apparence de raison; s. of resistance, simulacre *m* de résistance; to make a great s. of friendship, faire de grandes démonstrations d'amitié (*b*) parade *f*, ostentation *f*; to make a s. of learning, étaler son érudition; to do sth for s., faire qch pour la galerie. **II.** *v* (showed; shown) **1.** *vtr* (*a*) montrer; faire voir, exhiber (qch); to s. s.o. sth, montrer, faire voir, qch à qn; s. me it, s. it to me, montre-le moi; *F:* fais voir; we're going to s. some films this evening, on va passer des films ce soir; *TV:* this programme will be shown tomorrow, cette émission passera demain; to have sth to s. for one's money, en avoir pour son argent; he won't s. his face here again, il ne se montrera plus ici; colour that doesn't s. the dirt, couleur qui n'est pas salissante; (*of thg*) to s. itself, devenir visible; se révéler (*b*) représenter, figurer; machine shown in section, machine représentée en coupe (*c*) indiquer; (*of watch*) to s. the time, indiquer, marquer, l'heure; to s. a profit, se solder par un bénéfice; être bénéficiaire (*d*) to s. s.o. the way, indiquer le chemin à qn; to s. s.o. to his room, conduire qn à sa chambre; to s. s.o. in(to a room), faire entrer qn (dans une pièce); s. her in! faites-la entrer! to s. s.o. round, faire visiter (la maison) à qn; to s. s.o. out, faire sortir qn; to s. s.o. the door, mettre qn à la porte; to s. s.o. to the door, reconduire qn jusqu'à la porte (*e*) to s. an interest in s.o., témoigner de l'intérêt à qn; he shows his age, il accuse son âge; time will s., qui vivra verra; it only goes to s. (that), ce qui prouve que; *F:* I'll s. you! je vous apprendrai! **2.** *vi* se montrer, (ap)paraître; se laisser voir; your slip's showing, votre combinaison dépasse; it shows in your face, cela se voit, se lit, sur votre visage; to s. willing, faire preuve de bonne volonté; to s. to advantage, faire bonne figure. 'showcase *n* vitrine *f*. 'showdown *n* confrontation *f*; if it comes to a s., s'il faut en venir au fait. 'showiness *n* prétention *f*, clinquant *m*, faste *m*; ostentation *f*. 'showman *n* (*pl* -men) (*a*) forain, *m*; he's a great s., il a le sens de la mise en scène (*b*) montreur *m* de curiosités (à la foire). 'showmanship *n* art *m* de la mise en scène. 'show 'off **1.** *vtr* faire valoir (un bijou); mettre (un tableau) en valeur **2.** *vi Pej:* parader, poser; se pavaner; stop showing off! arrête de faire l'important, de te donner des airs! 'show-off *n* poseur, -euse. 'showpiece *n* article *m* d'exposition; monument *m* de grand intérêt. 'showroom *n Com:* salle *f* d'exposition. 'show 'up **1.** *vtr* démasquer (un imposteur); révéler (un défaut) **2.** *vi* (*a*) se détacher, ressortir (against, on, sur) (*b*) *F:* se présenter; faire acte de présence. 'showy *a* (-ier, -iest) prétentieux; voyant; s. hat, chapeau un peu tape-à-l'œil.

shower ['ʃauər] **1.** *n* (*a*) averse *f*; ondée *f* (*b*) avalanche *f* (d'injures); s. of stones, volée *f* de pierres (*c*) douche *f*; to take a s., prendre une douche (*d*) s. unit, bloc-douche *m*; s. cap, bonnet de douche (*e*) *NAm:* (*Br=approx* hen party) réception donnée en l'honneur d'une future mariée (où chacun apporte un cadeau) **2.** *vtr* (*a*) verser, faire pleuvoir (de l'eau) (*b*) to s. abuse on s.o., accabler qn d'injures; to s. blows (on s.o.), frapper dru (sur qn); to s. invitations on s.o.,

submerger qn d'invitations. 'showery *a* (temps) pluvieux.

shrank [ʃræŋk] *see* shrink.

shrapnel ['ʃræpnəl] *n* éclats *mpl* d'obus.

shred [ʃred] **1.** *n* brin *m*; lambeau *m*, fragment *m* (de tissu); to tear sth to shreds, mettre qch en lambeaux; there isn't a s. of evidence, il n'y a pas la moindre preuve, l'ombre d'une preuve **2.** *vtr* (shredded) râper (des légumes); couper (qch) en languettes; effilocher, déchiqueter (qch). 'shredder *n* effilocheuse *f*.

shrew¹ [ʃru:] *n Z:* musaraigne *f*.

shrew² [ʃru:] *n* mégère *f*. 'shrewish *af* (femme) acariâtre.

shrewd [ʃru:d] *a* sagace, perspicace; qui a du flair; s. businessman, homme d'affaires très habile, astucieux; s. reasoning, raisonnement judicieux; (*intensive*) I have a s. idea (that), je suis porté à croire (que). 'shrewdly *adv* avec perspicacité; avec finesse. 'shrewdness *n* sagacité *f*; perspicacité *f*, finesse *f*.

shriek [ʃri:k] **1.** *n* cri déchirant; cri perçant; shrieks of laughter, grands éclats de rire **2.** *v* (*a*) *vi* pousser des cris aigus; to s. with laughter, rire aux éclats; s'esclaffer de rire (*b*) *vtr* to s. (out) a warning, pousser un cri d'avertissement; hurler un avertissement.

shrill [ʃril] *a* aigu, strident. 'shrillness *n* stridence *f*. 'shrilly *adv* d'un ton aigu, criard.

shrimp [ʃrimp] *n Crust:* crevette (grise). 'shrimping *n* pêche *f* à la crevette; to go s., pêcher la crevette.

shrine [ʃrain] *n* **1.** tombeau *m* (de saint) **2.** chapelle *f*, autel *m* (consacré(e) à un saint).

shrink [ʃriŋk] (shrank [ʃræŋk]; shrunk [ʃrʌŋk]) **1.** *vi* (*a*) se contracter; (se) rétrécir; my shirt has shrunk in the wash, ma chemise a rétréci au lavage (*b*) faire un mouvement de recul; to s. (back) from (danger, etc), reculer devant (un danger, etc); to s. from doing sth, répugner à faire qch; to s. into oneself, rentrer dans sa coquille **2.** *vtr* (faire) rétrécir (un tissu). 'shrinkage *n* contraction *f* (du métal); rétrécissement *m* (d'un tissu). 'shrinking *a* **1.** qui se contracte **2.** (*of pers*) timide, craintif. 'shrunken *a* contracté; rétréci; (*of pers*) ratatiné; s. head, tête réduite.

shrivel ['ʃrivəl] (shrivelled) to s. (up) **1.** *vtr* rider, ratatiner (la peau); (*of sun, frost*) brûler (les plantes) **2.** *vi* se rider, se ratatiner.

shroud [ʃraud] *n* linceul *m*, suaire *m*. 'shrouded *a* enveloppé, voilé (in mist, de brume).

shrove [ʃrouv] *a* **S. Tuesday,** (le) mardi gras.

shrub [ʃrʌb] *n* arbrisseau *m*, arbuste *m*. 'shrubbery *n* (*pl* -ies) plantation *f*, massif *m*, d'arbustes.

shrug [ʃrʌg] **1.** *vtr* (shrugged) to s. (one's shoulders), hausser les épaules **2.** *n* haussement d'épaules; a resigned s., un geste de résignation; with a s., en haussant les épaules.

shrunk, shrunken ['ʃrʌŋk(ən)] *see* shrink.

shudder ['ʃʌdər] **1.** *n* frisson *m*, frémissement *m* (d'horreur); it gives me the shudders, j'en ai le frisson **2.** *vi* to s. with horror, frissonner, frémir, d'horreur; I s. at the thought of it, j'ai le frisson rien que d'y penser.

shuffle ['ʃʌfl] **1.** *vtr & i* to s. (one's feet), traîner les pieds; *Cards:* to s. (the cards), battre (les cartes); to s. off, s'en aller en traînant les pieds **2.** *vtr* (entre)mêler (des papiers).

shun [ʃʌn] *vtr* (shunned) fuir, éviter (qn, qch); to s. everybody, s'éloigner du monde.

shunt [ʃʌnt] *vtr Rail:* manœuvrer, garer (un train).

'shunting n Rail: garage m, manœuvre f; aiguillage m; s. yard, gare f de manœuvre et de triage.

shush [ʃʌʃ, ʃuʃ] 1. int chut! 2. vtr faire taire (qn).

shut [ʃʌt] v (shutting; shut) 1. vtr fermer (une porte, une boîte); to s. one's mouth, (i) fermer la bouche (ii) F: se taire 2. vi (se) fermer; the door won't s., la porte ne se ferme pas; the door s., la porte s'est (re)fermée. 'shut a'way vtr enfermer; mettre (qch) sous clef. 'shut 'down 1. vtr rabattre (un couvercle); fermer (une usine) 2. vi (of factory) fermer ses portes. 'shut-down n fermeture f (d'une usine). 'shut 'in vtr (a) enfermer (b) (of hills) entourer, encercler (un endroit). 'shut 'off vtr 1. couper (le courant, le moteur); fermer (l'eau) 2. séparer, isoler (from, de). 'shut 'out vtr (a) exclure (qn); the trees s. out the view, les arbres bouchent la vue (b) to s. s.o. out (of doors), fermer la porte à qn; s. the cat out! mets le chat dehors! 'shutter n 1. volet m; outside s., contrevent m; Venetian, metal, shutters, persiennes fpl 2. Phot: obturateur m; s. speed, vitesse f d'obturation. 'shuttering n Const: coffrage m (pour le béton armé). 'shutting n fermeture f. 'shut 'up 1. vtr (a) enfermer; to s. the dog up, enfermer le chien (b) fermer (une maison); to s. up shop, fermer boutique (c) F: faire taire (qn); réduire (qn) au silence 2. vi F: se taire; s. up! F: ta gueule! la ferme!

shuttle [ʃʌtl] 1. n navette f; to run a s. service, faire la navette; space s., navette spatiale 2. (a) vi faire la navette (between, entre) (b) vtr envoyer (qn) à droite et à gauche. 'shuttlecock n Games: volant m.

shy¹ [ʃai] vi (shying; shied) (of horse) faire un écart; broncher; to s. at sth, prendre ombrage de qch.

shy² a (shier, shiest) (of pers) timide; sauvage, farouche; to make s.o. s., intimider qn; to fight s. of sth, se défier, se méfier, de qch; don't pretend to be s., ne faites pas le, la, timide. 'shyly adv timidement. 'shyness n timidité f, réserve f; sauvagerie f; to lose one's s., s'enhardir.

shy³ 1. vtr (shying; shied) F: lancer (une pierre, une balle) (at, à) 2. n (pl shies) coconut s.=jeu m de massacre.

Siamese [saiə'mi:z] a & n siamois, -oise; S. twins, frères siamois, sœurs siamoises; S. cat, (chat) siamois (m).

Siberia [sai'biəriə] Prn la Sibérie. Si'berian a & n sibérien, -ienne.

sibling ['sibliŋ] n l'un(e) de deux, de plusieurs, enfants qui ont les mêmes parents; frère m, sœur f.

Sicily ['sisili] Prn la Sicile. Si'cilian a & n sicilien, -ienne.

sick [sik] a 1. malade; he's a s. man, il est malade; esp NAm: she's still s. (Br = ill), elle est encore malade; to go, report, s., se faire porter malade; to fall s., tomber malade; s. pay, indemnité f de maladie f; s. leave, congé de maladie; npl the s., les malades 2. to be s., vomir, rendre; a s. feeling, un malaise; to feel s., avoir mal au cœur; s. headache, migraine f 3. Fig: to be s. at heart, être abattu; F: he did look s.! il en faisait une tête. F: to be s. of sth, être dégoûté de qch; F: I'm s. of it! j'en ai plein le dos! F: I'm s. and tired of telling you, je me tue à vous le dire; P: you make me s.! tu me dégoûtes! tu m'écœures! 'sickbay n infirmerie f. 'sickbed n lit m de malade. 'sicken 1. vi (a) tomber malade (of, with, de); to be sickening for an illness, F: for sth, couver une maladie (b) to s. of sth, se lasser de qch 2. vtr dégoûter, écœurer (qn); his methods s. me, ses procédés me soulèvent le cœur. 'sickening a écœurant; dégoûtant; navrant. 'sickeningly adv d'une façon écœurante, dégoûtante; à vous écœurer, dégoûter; à vous soulever le cœur. 'sickliness n état maladif (de qn). 'sickly a (-ier, -iest) maladif, souffreteux; (couleur) délavée; (sourire) pâle; (soleil) blafard; (teint) terreux; (pâleur) maladive. 'sickness n 1. maladie f; air, car, s., mal m de l'air, de la route; s. benefit, assurance maladie 2. mal de cœur, nausées fpl. 'sickroom n chambre f de malade.

sickle ['sikl] n Agr: faucille f.

side [said] 1. n (a) côté m; flanc m; by s.o.'s s., à côté de qn; by, at, my s., à côté de moi, à mes côtés; s. by s., côte à côte; to split one's sides (with laughter), se tenir les côtes de rire; to be lying on one's s., être couché sur le côté; s. of bacon, flèche f de lard (b) côté d'un triangle); versant m, flanc (d'une montagne); paroi f (d'un fossé) (c) (surface) face f, côté (d'un disque, d'une médaille); the right s., le bon côté; l'endroit m (d'un tissu); le recto (d'une feuille de papier); the wrong s., l'envers m (d'un tissu, d'une robe); le verso (d'une feuille de papier); wrong s. out, à l'envers; (on box) this s. up = haut m; the bright s. of things, le bon côté des choses; the other s. of the picture, le revers de la médaille; to hear both sides, entendre le pour et le contre; his good sides, ses bons côtés; the weather's on the cool s., il fait plutôt froid; on his mother's s., du côté maternel; on this s., de ce côté-ci; on all sides, de tous côtés; with a dog on either s., flanqué de deux chiens; to be on the right s. of forty, avoir moins de quarante ans; to move to one s., se ranger; to put sth on one s., mettre qch de côté; to make sth on the s., se faire des petits à-côtés; s. entrance, entrée de côté; s. door, porte latérale; s. issue, question d'intérêt secondaire; s. effect, effet secondaire; s. street, rue latérale, transversale; s. view, vue de profil; s. plate, petite assiette; s. dish, plat d'accompagnement (d) parti m; he's on our s., il est de notre parti; you have the law on your s., vous avez la loi pour vous; to take sides with s.o., se ranger du côté, du parti, de qn; time's on our s., le temps travaille pour nous (b) section f, division f (c) Games: équipe f 2. vi to s. with s.o., se ranger du côté de qn; se mettre du parti de qn. 'sideboard n buffet m. 'sideboards npl, 'sideburns npl favoris mpl. 'sidecar n side-car m. 'sidelight n 1. Phot: etc: lumière f oblique; to throw a s. on a subject, donner un aperçu secondaire, indirect, sur un sujet 2. Aut: feu m de position, de stationnement. 'sideline n (a) Sp: ligne f de touche; to be on the sidelines, rester sur la touche (b) occupation f secondaire. 'sidelong a (regard) oblique. 'sidesaddle 1. n selle f de dame 2. adv to ride s., monter en amazone. 'sideshow n (at fair) spectacle forain. 'side-splitting a (of joke) tordant. 'sidestep v (sidestepped) (a) vtr éviter (une question) (b) vi faire un pas de côté. 'sidetrack vtr détourner l'attention de (qn). 'sidewalk n NAm: (Br = pavement) trottoir m. 'sideways 1. adv de côté, latéralement; to walk s., marcher en crabe 2. a (mouvement) latéral. 'siding n Rail: voie f de garage.

sidle ['saidl] vi to s. along, s'avancer de côté; to s. up to s.o., se glisser auprès de qn.

siege [si:dʒ] n Mil: siège m; to lay s. to a town, assiéger une ville; to declare a state of s., déclarer l'état de siège.

sienna [si'enə] n Art: terre f de Sienne; raw, burnt, s., terre de Sienne naturelle, brûlée.

siesta [si'estə] n sieste f.

sieve [siv] 1. n crible m; tamis m; passoire f; he's got a memory like a s., sa mémoire est une passoire 2. vtr passer au tamis; tamiser; passer.

sift [sift] vtr (a) passer au tamis; tamiser; passer au crible, au sas; to s. sugar over a cake, saupoudrer un gâteau de sucre (b) to s. through (sth), examiner minutieusement (les témoignages dans une affaire). 'sifter n saupoudreuse f (à sucre); saupoudroir m (à farine).

sigh [sai] 1. n soupir m; to breathe, heave, a s. of relief, pousser un soupir de soulagement 2. vi soupirer; pousser un soupir; to s. for sth., soupirer après qch. 'sighing n soupirs mpl.

sight [sait] I. n 1. (a) vue f; short s., myopie f; good, bad, s., bonne, mauvaise, vue; to lose one's s., perdre la vue; to become aveugle (b) to catch s. of s.o., apercevoir qn; to lose s. of s.o., perdre qn de vue; I can't bear the s. of him, je ne peux pas le sentir; to shoot s.o. at, on, s., tirer sur qn à vue; at the s. of, à la vue de, en voyant; at first s., au premier abord; love at first s., le coup de foudre; to know s.o. by s., connaître qn de vue 2. to come into s., (ap)paraître; to be within s., être à portée de la vue; être en vue; out of s., caché aux regards; to vanish out of s., disparaître; keep out of his s.! qu'il ne te voie pas! out of s. out of mind, loin des yeux, loin du cœur 3. (a) spectacle m; sad s., spectacle navrant; it's a s. well worth seeing, cela vaut la peine d'être vu (b) F: his face was a s.!, si vous aviez vu son visage! que do you look a s., what a s. you are! de quoi avez-vous l'air! it was a s. for sore eyes, c'était réjouissant à voir; it's not a pretty s., ce n'est pas beau, joli, à voir (c) pl the sights, les monuments m, les curiosités f (de la ville) 4. Opt: visée f; (on gun) mire f; to take s., viser 5. F: not by a long s., loin de là; he's a damn s. better, il va beaucoup mieux; a s. too much, vraiment trop. II. vtr 1. apercevoir 2. pointer (un fusil). 'sighted a qui voit; npl the s., les voyants; to be partially s., avoir un certain degré de vision; short-sighted, myope; long-s., far-sighted, prévoyant. 'sighting n several sightings of dolphin have been reported, on a vu des dauphins à plusieurs reprises. 'sightless a aveugle. 'sightread vtr & i (pp sightread) Mus: déchiffrer. 'sightreading n Mus: déchiffrage m. 'sightseeing n to go s., faire du tourisme; visiter les monuments de la ville. 'sightseer'n touriste mf.

sign [sain] I. n 1. signe m; to make an affirmative s., faire signe que oui; s. of the cross, signe m de la croix; to make the s. of the cross, se signer; (of deaf) s. language, langage par signes 2. (a) indice m, indication f; sure s., indice certain; s. of rain, signe de pluie; there's no s. of his coming, rien n'annonce sa venue; as a s. of friendship, en signe d'amitié (b) trace f; no s. (of), nulle, aucune, trace (de); to show no s. of life, ne donner aucun signe de vie; there was no s. of him, il restait invisible 3. (a) enseigne f (d'auberge, de magasin); neon s., réclame f néon (b) Aut: etc:

panneau indicateur; international road signs, signalisation routière internationale; s. of the Zodiac, signe du zodiaque. II. vtr & i signer (une lettre, son nom); to s. for the key, signer pour obtenir la clef. 'sign 'off vi (of worker) pointer au départ; WTel: TV: terminer l'émission. 'sign 'on 1. vtr embaucher (un ouvrier) 2. vi (of worker) pointer à l'arrivée; (of unemployed person) s'inscrire au chômage. 'signpost 1. n poteau indicateur. 2. vtr signaliser (une route); badly signposted road, route mal signalisée.

signal[1] ['signəl] 1. n signal m; time s., signal horaire; all clear s., signal de fin d'alerte; line engaged, NAm: busy, signal, signal d'occupation (de ligne); to give the s. (for departure), donner le signal (du départ); WTel: TV: station s., indicatif m (de l'émetteur); Aut: traffic signals, feux m de circulation; Rail: s. box, poste d'aiguillage 2. v (signalled, NAm: signaled) (a) vi faire des signaux; Aut: to s. before stopping, avertir avant de stopper (b) vtr signaler (un train); Aut: to s. a turn, annoncer, indiquer, un changement de direction; to s.o. to stop, faire signe à qn de s'arrêter. 'signalman n (pl -men) Rail: aiguilleur m.

signal[2] a insigne; (succès) éclatant, remarquable. 'signally adv remarquablement.

signature['signət∫ər] n signature f; to put one's s. to a letter, apposer sa signature à une lettre; s. tune, indicatif (musical). 'signatory a & n signataire (mf).

signet ['signit] n sceau m, cachet m; s. ring, (bague f) chevalière (f).

signify ['signifai] v (signified) 1. vtr signifier; vouloir dire; a broad forehead signifies intelligence, un front large est signe d'intelligence 2. vi importer; it doesn't s., cela ne fait rien; peu importe. significance [-'nifikəns] n 1. signification f; what is the s. of it? qu'est-ce que cela signifie? 2. importance f, conséquence f; of no s., sans importance, de peu d'importance. sig'nificant a 1. (mot) significatif 2. (événement) important, de grande portée. sig'nificantly adv (regarder qn) d'une manière significative. signifi'cation n signification f, sens m (d'un mot).

silence ['sailəns] 1. n (a) silence m; dead s., silence absolu; to keep s., garder le silence; se taire; to break (the) s., rompre le silence; to suffer in s., souffrir en silence (b) to pass over sth in s., passer qch sous silence 2. vtr (a) réduire (qn) au silence; faire taire (qn); étouffer (les plaintes); to s. criticism, faire taire la critique (b) étouffer, amortir (un bruit); Aut: to s. the exhaust, assourdir l'échappement m. 'silencer n silencieux m; Aut: (on exhaust system) pot m d'échappement. 'silent a silencieux; to keep, fall, s., se taire (about, sur); a s. man, un homme silencieux, taciturne; s. as the grave, muet comme la tombe; s. h, h muet. 'silently adv silencieusement; en silence.

silhouette [silu:'et] 1. n silhouette f 2. vtr silhouetter; to be silhouetted (against), se détacher (sur).

silicon ['silikən] n Ch: silicium m; s. chip, puce f, pastille f, de silicium.

silicone ['silikoun] n Ch: silicone f.

silicosis [sili'kousis] n Med: silicose f.

silk [silk] n (a) soie f; raw s., soie grège; sewing s., soie à coudre; a black s. dress, une robe de, en, soie noire; pl Com: silks, soierie f. 'silken a soyeux. 'silkiness n nature soyeuse (d'un tissu); moelleux *m* (d'une voix). **'silkscreen** *n* **s. printing,** sérigraphie *f*. **'silk-worm** *n* ver *m* à soie. **'silky** *a* (**-ier, -iest**) soyeux; **s. voice,** voix moelleuse, douceureuse.

sill [sil] *n* rebord *m* (de fenêtre); seuil *m* (de porte).

silly ['sili] *a* (**-ier, -iest**) sot, niais; **s. answer,** réponse stupide, ridicule; **you s. boy!** petit nigaud! **s. fool!** imbécile! **to do a s. thing,** faire une bêtise; **to knock s.o. s.,** étourdir, assommer, qn. **'silliness** *n* sottise *f*, niaiserie *f*, bêtise *f*.

silo ['sailou] *n* (*pl* **siloes**) 1. *Agr:* silo *m* 2. *Mil:* (*for guided missile*) **launching s.,** puits *m* de lancement.

silt [silt] 1. *n* dépôt (vaseux); vase *f*; limon *m* 2. *vtr & i* (*of harbour, river*) **to s. up,** (s')envaser; (s')ensabler.

silver ['silvər] *n* 1. (*metal*) argent *m* 2. (*a*) d'argent, en argent; **s. spoon,** cuiller d'argent; **he was born with a s. spoon in his mouth,** il est né coiffé; **s.-mounted,** monté en argent; **s.-plated,** argenté; plaqué argent; **s. paper,** papier d'étain; **s. grey,** gris argenté; **s. wedding,** noces d'argent 3. argent monnayé; **s. coin,** pièce d'argent; **one pound in s.,** une livre en monnaie, en pièces d'argent 4. *coll* argenterie *f* (de table). **'silverside** *n* *Cu:* gîte *m* à la noix. **'silversmith** *n* orfèvre *m*. **'silverware** *n* argenterie *f*. **'silvery** *a* (nuage) argenté; (écailles) d'argent; (son) argentin.

similar ['similər] *a* semblable, pareil (**to,** à). **simi'larity** *n* (*pl* **-ies**) ressemblance *f*, similarité *f*. **'similarly** *adv* pareillement, semblablement.

simile ['simili] *n* comparaison *f*, image *f*.

simmer ['simər] 1. *vi* (*a*) (*of liquid*) frémir; (*of soup, stews*) mijoter, cuire à feu doux (*b*) (*of revolt*) fermenter; (*of pers*) **to s. down,** s'apaiser peu à peu 2. *vtr* (faire) mijoter (un ragoût).

simper ['simpər] 1. *n* sourire affecté, minauder 2. *vi* minauder. **'simpering** 1. *n* minauderie(s) *f* (*pl*) 2. *a* minaudier.

simple ['simpl] *a* (*a*) simple; naturel (de caractère); sans affectation (*b*) naïf; crédule; niais (*c*) **s. problem,** problème simple, peu difficile; **as s. as ABC,** simple comme bonjour; *Com:* **s. interest,** intérêts *m* simples; **it's robbery, pure and s.!** c'est du vol pur et simple! **'simple-'minded** *a* simple d'esprit. **'simple-'mindedness** *n* simplicité *f* d'esprit. **'simpleton** *n* nigaud, -aude, niais, -aise. **sim'plicity** *n* simplicité *f*, candeur *f* (d'esprit); absence *f* de recherche, simplicité (dans la mise); **it's s. itself,** c'est simple comme bonjour. **'simplify** *vtr* (**simplified**) simplifier; **to become simplified,** se simplifier. **sim'plistic** *a* simpliste. **'simply** *adv* 1. (parler) simplement 2. (*a*) absolument; **you s. must,** il le faut absolument; **the weather's s. ghastly!** il fait un temps de chien (*b*) uniquement; tout simplement; **he did it s. to test you,** il l'a fait uniquement pour vous éprouver; **I s. said (that),** je me suis borné à dire (que).

simulate ['simjuleit] *vtr* simuler, feindre (une maladie). **simu'lation** *n* simulation *f*, feinte *f*. **'simulator** *n* simulateur *m*.

simultaneous [siməl'teiniəs] *a* simultané. **simulta'neity** *n* simultanéité *f*. **simul'taneously** *adv* (*a*) simultanément (*b*) en même temps (**with,** que).

sin [sin] 1. *n* péché *m*; **original s.,** péché originel; **the seven deadly sins,** les sept péchés capitaux; **the forgiveness of sins,** le pardon des offenses; (*of man and*

woman) **to live in s.,** vivre en concubinage 2. *vi* (**sinned**) pécher; commettre un péché, des péchés. **'sinful** *a* **s. person,** pécheur, *f* pécheresse; **s. pleasure,** plaisir coupable; **s. waste,** gaspillage scandaleux. **sinfully** *adv* d'une façon coupable. **'sinfulness** *n* 1. caractère *m* coupable (d'une action); culpabilité *f* 2. le péché. **'sinner** *n* pécheur, pécheresse.

since [sins] 1. *adv* (*a*) depuis; **I have not seen him s.,** je ne l'ai pas revu depuis; **ever s.,** depuis (lors) (*b*) **many years s.,** il y a bien des années; **long s.,** (i) depuis longtemps (ii) il y a longtemps; **not long s.,** il n'y a pas très longtemps; **how long s.?** depuis combien de temps? 2. *prep* depuis; **s. his death,** depuis sa mort; **he'd been up s. dawn,** il était levé dès l'aube; **s. when have you been here?** depuis quand êtes-vous ici? **s. that time, s. then,** depuis ce temps-là; depuis lors 3. *conj* (*a*) depuis que; que; **s. I've been here,** depuis que je suis ici; **it's a week s. he came,** il y a huit jours qu'il est arrivé; **it's a long time s. I saw her,** il y a longtemps que je ne l'ai vue; je ne l'ai pas vue depuis longtemps (*b*) puisque; étant donné que; **s. he's not of age,** puisqu'il est mineur; **I'll do it s. I must,** je le ferai puisqu'il le faut.

sincere [sin'siər] *a* sincère; franc. **sin'cerely** *adv* sincèrement; *Corr:* **yours s.,** veuillez agréer, (Monsieur, Madame,) l'expression de mes sentiments distingués. **sin'cerity** *n* sincérité *f*; bonne foi; **speaking in all s.,** en toute bonne foi.

sinecure ['sainikjuər] *n* sinécure *f*.

sinew ['sinju:] *n* 1. tendon *m* 2. *pl* **sinews,** nerf *m*, force *f*. **'sinewy** *a* (*of meat*) tendineux; **s. arm,** bras musclé, nerveux.

sing [siŋ] *v* (**sang** [sæŋ]; **sung** [sʌŋ]) 1. *vtr & i* chanter; **s. me a song!** chante-moi une chanson! **to s. in tune,** chanter juste; **to s. out of tune,** chanter faux; détonner 2. *vi* (*of the ears*) tinter, bourdonner; (*of kettle*) chanter. **'singer** *n* chanteur, -euse; (*operatic*) chanteur d'opéra; cantatrice *f*; *Ecc:* chantre *m*. **'singing** 1. *a* (oiseau) chanteur; qui chante. 2. *n* (*a*) chant *m* (*b*) bourdonnement *m*, tintement *m* (d'oreilles). **'singsong** 1. *a* (ton) traînant; **in a s. voice,** en psalmodiant 2. *n* (*a*) chant monotone (*b*) *F:* concert improvisé.

Singapore [siŋgə'pɔːr] *Prn Geog:* Singapour *m*.

singe [sindʒ] *vtr* brûler (qch) légèrement; roussir 2. flamber (une volaille).

single ['siŋgl] I. *a* 1. (*a*) seul, unique; **not a s. one,** pas un seul; pas un; **I haven't seen a s. soul,** je n'ai pas vu âme qui vive; (**one**) **s. case,** un cas unique 2. (*a*) **s. bed,** lit pour une personne; **s. bedroom,** chambre à un lit, pour une personne (*b*) célibataire; non marié(e); **a s. man, woman,** un, une, célibataire; **s. parent,** père, mère, célibataire; **she, he, is s.,** elle, il, n'est pas marié(e) (*c*) *Rail:* **s. ticket,** (billet *m* d')aller *m* (*d*) *Bot:* **s. flower,** fleur simple; *Cu:* **s. cream,** crème fraîche légère II. *n* (*a*) *Ten: Golf:* (partie *f*) simple (*m*); *Ten:* **men's singles,** simple messieurs (*b*) *Rail:* (billet d')aller (*c*) disque *m* 45 tours (*d*) *esp NAm:* **singles,** célibataires *mpl.* III. *vtr* **to s. (s.o., sth) out,** (i) choisir (qn, qch) (ii) remarquer, distinguer (qn, qch) (**for,** pour; **as,** comme). **'single-'barrelled** *a* (fusil) à un coup. **'single-'breasted** *a* (veston) droit. **'single-'engined** *a* **s.-e. aircraft,** (avion) monomoteur *m*. **'single-'handed** *a* seul, sans aide. **'single-'minded** *a* obstiné; résolu. **'single-**

ness n **with s. of purpose,** avec un seul but en vue.
'single-'track a Rail: (ligne) à voie unique.
'singly adv séparément; un à un.

singlet ['siŋglit] n **1.** maillot m de corps (pour homme)
2. Sp: maillot.

singular ['siŋgjulər] **1.** a & n Gram: singulier (m) **2.** a
singulier, bizarre. **singu'larity** n singularité f.
'singularly adv singulièrement (a) remarquablement (b) bizarrement.

sinister ['sinistər] a sinistre; **a s.-looking man,** un
homme à la mine patibulaire.

sink¹ [siŋk] n évier m (de cuisine); **to pour sth down the
s.,** jeter qch à l'égout.

sink² v (sank [sæŋk]; sunk [sʌŋk]) **1.** vi (a) aller au
fond; (of ship) couler; sombrer (b) s'enfoncer, pénétrer (into, dans); **his words begin to s.** in, ses paroles
commencent à faire impression (c) tomber (dans le
vice, dans l'oubli); **to s. deep(er) into crime,** s'enfoncer
dans le crime; **to s. into insignificance,** devenir insignifiant; **to s. into deep sleep,** s'endormir profonde-
ment (d) **to s. (down),** s'affaisser; **the fire is sinking,** le
feu baisse; (of pers) **to s. (down) into a chair,** se laisser
tomber, s'affaler, dans un fauteuil; **his heart sank,** le
cœur lui a manqué; son cœur s'est serré (e) descendre;
aller en descendant; **to s'abaisser; the sun is sinking,** le
soleil baisse (f) baisser (en valeur); diminuer;
s'affaiblir; (of pers) **the patient is sinking fast,** le
malade baisse rapidement; **he has sunk in my esteem,**
il a baissé dans mon estime **2.** vtr (a) couler, faire
sombrer (un navire) (b) enfoncer (un pieu); **to s. one's
teeth into sth,** mordre dans qch; **to s. money in an
undertaking,** placer de l'argent dans une entreprise (c)
creuser (un puits) (d) supprimer (une objection, des
différends). **'sinking 1.** a qui s'enfonce; **with a s.
heart,** avec un serrement de cœur **2.** n enfoncement m;
.that s. feeling, (i) sentiment de défaillance f (ii)
pressentiment fâcheux.

sinuous ['sinjuəs] a **1.** sinueux **2.** (of pers) souple,
agile. **sinu'osity** n (pl -ies) sinuosité f.

sinus ['sainəs] n (pl sinuses) Anat: sinus m; **she has bad
s. trouble,** elle a une mauvaise sinusite. **sinu'sitis** n
Med: sinusite f.

sip [sip] **1.** n petite gorgée **2.** vtr (sipped) boire (qch) à
petites gorgées; siroter.

siphon ['saifən] **1.** n siphon m **2.** vtr **to s. (off),**
siphonner (un liquide).

sir [sə:r, sər] n **1.** monsieur m; **yes, s.,** oui, monsieur;
Corr: **(Dear) Sir,** Monsieur **2.** (title) Sir (always used
with first name).

sire ['saiər] **1.** n (a) (in addressing a King) Sire (b) Breed:
père m; (of horses) étalon m; (of cattle) taureau m **2.**
vtr (of stallion) engendrer, procréer (un poulain).

siren ['saiərən] n sirène f.

sirloin ['sə:lɔin] n Cu: aloyau m; faux-filet m.

sissy ['sisi] n (pl sissies) F: (a) homme, garçon, un
peu efféminé (b) enfant peureux; poule mouillée.

sister ['sistər] n **1.** sœur f **2.** (a) Ecc: religieuse f; sœur
(b) Med: infirmière f en chef; **(ward) s.,** surveillante f
3. s. nations, nations sœurs; **s. company,** société sœur;
s. ship, sister(-)ship m. **'sisterhood** n fraternité f.
'sister-in-law n (pl sisters-in-law) belle-sœur f.
'sisterly a de sœur; comme une sœur; fraternel.

sit [sit] v (sitting; sat) **1.** vi (a) (of pers) s'asseoir; être
assis; rester assis; **to s. still,** rester tranquille; **to s.**

tight, ne pas céder; **to s. reading,** être assis à lire, en
train de lire; **to s. at (the) table,** s'asseoir, se mettre, à
table; s'attabler; **he sat through the whole play,** il est
resté jusqu'à la fin de la pièce; **s. straight!** tiens-toi
droit! **to s. for an exam(ination),** se présenter à un
examen, passer un examen; **to s. for one's portrait,**
poser pour son portrait (b) **to s. on a committee,** faire
partie d'un comité; **to s. in Parliament,** siéger au
parlement; (of assembly) siéger; être en séance; **to s. on
a project,** laisser dormir un projet; (of hen) **to s. (on
eggs),** couver (des œufs); (of food) **to s. heavy on the
stomach,** peser sur l'estomac **2.** vtr **to s. a horse,** se
tenir à cheval; **to s. a child on a chair,** asseoir un enfant
sur une chaise. **'sit 'down** vi s'asseoir; **please s. d.,**
veuillez vous asseoir; **to s. d. to table,** s'attabler, se
mettre à table. **'sit-down** a **s.-d. strike,** grève sur le
tas. **'sitter** n **1.** (for painter) modèle m **2. s. (in), baby
s.,** garde-bébé mf; baby-sitter mf. **'sitting** n séance
f, réunion f (d'une commission); **to paint a portrait in
three sittings,** faire, exécuter, un portrait en trois
séances; **to serve 200 people at one s.,** servir 200
personnes à la fois; (for a meal) **second s.,** deuxième
service m; **to write two chapters at one s.,** écrire deux
chapitres d'un seul jet; **s. room** salle f de séjour, F:
living m; salon m **2.** a assis; **s. tenant,** locataire en
possession des lieux; Parl: **our s. member,** le député
qui nous représente actuellement. **'sit 'out** vtr (a)
sauter (une danse) (b) rester (patiemment)
jusqu'à la fin (d'une conférence). **'sit 'up 1.** vi
(a) se redresser (sur sa chaise); **to make s.o. s. up,**
étonner qn; **s. up straight!** tiens-toi droit! (b) **to s. up
late,** veiller tard; **to s. up for s.o.,** veiller en attendant le
retour de qn; **to s. up with s.o.,** veiller qn, un malade **2.**
vtr **to s. s.o. up,** soulever qn pour l'asseoir.

sitcom ['sitkɔm] (abbr = situation comedy) n comédie f
de situation.

site [sait] **1.** n emplacement m (d'un édifice, d'une
ville); site m (archéologique); **caravan, camping, s.,** (i)
camping m (ii) emplacement; **building s.,** (i) terrain m
à bâtir (ii) chantier m de construction **2.** vtr placer,
situer, implanter, installer.

situate ['sitjueit] vtr situer (une maison). **'situated**
a well s. house, maison bien située. **situ'ation** n **1.**
situation f **2.** (job) emploi m, place f; **situations
wanted,** demandes d'emplois; **situations vacant,**
offres f d'emplois **3.** Th: **s. comedy,** comédie de
situation.

six [siks] num a & n six (m); **to be s. (years old),** avoir 6
ans; **s. o'clock,** six heures; **four sixes are twenty-four,**
quatre fois six font vingt-quatre; **there are s. of us,**
nous sommes six; Cards: **the s. of hearts,** le six de
cœur; **they arrived in sixes,** ils sont arrivés par groupes
de six; F: **everything's at sixes and sevens,** tout est en
désordre, est désorganisé; F: **it's s. of one and half a
dozen of the other,** c'est blanc bonnet et bonnet blanc.
'six-'sided a hexagonal. **six'teen** num a & n seize
(m); **she's s.,** elle a seize ans. **six'teenth** num a & n
seizième (m); **Louis the S.,** Louis Seize; **(on) the s. (of
August),** le seize (août). **sixth** num a & n sixième (m);
(on) the s. of June, le six juin; Sch: **s. form** = classe de
première; **s. former** = élève de première. **'sixtieth**
num a & n soixantième (m). **'sixty** num a & n
soixante (m); **he's in his sixties,** il a passé la soixantaine; **in the sixties,** dans les années soixante. **'sixty-**

'four num a & n soixante-quatre; F: the s.-f. thousand dollar question, la question cruciale.

size¹ [saiz] 1. n (a) grandeur f, dimension f, grosseur f; to take the s. of sth, mesurer qch; all of a s., tous de même taille; full s., grandeur naturelle; a town of that s., une ville de cette importance; F: that's about the s. of it, c'est à peu près cela; to cut a piece to s., couper un morceau à la dimension voulue; to cut s.o. down to s., remettre qn à sa place (b) (of pers) taille f (c) taille (de vêtements); encolure f (de chemise); pointure f (de chaussures); what s. do you take? what's your s.? what s. are you? (in dresses) quelle est votre taille? (in shoes) quelle est votre pointure? a s. larger, smaller, une taille, pointure, au-dessus, au-dessous; I take s. 7 in shoes = je chausse du 39 2. vtr classer (qn) par taille, par dimension. 'sizeable a assez grand; d'une belle taille. 'size 'up vtr to s. s.o. up, classer, juger, qn; to s. the situation up, mesurer l'importance, la gravité, de la situation.

size² n apprêt m; colle f.

sizzle ['sizl] 1. vi grésiller 2. n grésillement m.

skate¹ [skeit] n Ich: raie f.

skate² 1. n patin m; ice s., patin à glace; roller s., patin à roulettes; F: get your skates on! dépêche-toi! 2. vi patiner; to s. over sth, effleurer un sujet (difficile); Fig: to s. on thin ice, toucher à un sujet délicat. 'skate-board n planche f à roulettes. 'skater n patineur, -euse. 'skating n patinage m; s. rink, patinoire f.

skein [skein] n écheveau m (de laine).

skeleton ['skelitən] n 1. squelette m, ossature f (de l'homme, d'un animal); F: he's a real s., il n'a plus que la peau et les os; F: s. in the cupboard, NAm: in the closet, secret honteux de la famille; s. at the feast, rabat-joie m; trouble-fête m 2. charpente f, carcasse f (d'un navire); s. key, crochet m (de serrurier); clef f passe-partout; F: rossignol m 3. s. staff, personnel réduit; s. staff of three, permanence f de trois employés. 'skeletal a squelettique.

sketch [sketʃ] 1. n (a) croquis m, esquisse f; free-hand s., dessin m à main levée; s. map, croquis topographique (b) exposé m, ébauche f (d'un projet); aperçu m (c) Th: sketch m; saynète f 2. vtr to s. (out), esquisser (un objet, un projet); faire le croquis (d'un objet); ébaucher (un projet). 'sketchbook, -pad n cahier m, bloc m, de, à croquis. 'sketchily adv d'une manière incomplète, imprécise, vague. 'sketch in vtr ajouter des détails. 'sketching n (i) action f de dessiner un croquis (ii) dessin m à main levée. 'sketchy a (-ier, -iest) (ouvrage) qui manque de précision; s. knowledge, connaissances superficielles.

skewer ['skju:ər] 1. n Cu: brochette f 2. vtr embrocher (une volaille).

ski [ski:] 1. n ski m; s. binding, fixation f; s. boots, chaussures de ski; s. sticks, NAm: poles, bâtons de ski; s. run, piste de ski; s. jump, saut de ski; s. lift, remonte-pente m, téléski m 2. vi (skied) faire du ski; skier; to s. down the slope, descendre la piste à, en, skis. 'skier n skieur, -euse. 'skiing n le ski; to go s., faire du ski.

skid [skid] Aut: 1. n dérapage m 2. vi (skidded) déraper; glisser. 'skidding n dérapage m. 'skidlid n F: casque m (de moto). 'skidpan n Aut: piste savonnée.

skiff [skif] n 1. Nau: yole f 2. (rowing) skiff m.

skill [skil] n habileté f, adresse f, dextérité f; lack of s., maladresse f; manque m d'habileté. 'skilful, NAm: 'skillful a adroit, habile. 'skilfulness n habileté f, adresse f, dextérité f. 'skilled a habile; (ouvrier) qualifié; s. labour, main-d'œuvre spécialisée; to be s. in business, se connaître en affaires; it's a s. job, c'est un travail de spécialiste. 'skil(l)fully adv habilement, adroitement; avec adresse.

skillet ['skilit] n NAm: DomEc: (Br = frying pan) poêle f (à frire); poêlon m.

skim [skim] 1. n s. milk, lait écrémé 2. vtr & i (skimmed) (a) écumer (le bouillon); écrémer (le lait) (b) effleurer, raser (une surface); to s. through a book, parcourir rapidement un livre; to s. (NAm: = skip) stones, faire des ricochets. 'skimmed a s. milk, lait écrémé. 'skim off vtr prendre la meilleure part (de qch); sélectionner (des candidats, des élèves).

skimp [skimp] vtr 1. to s. (on), lésiner sur (la nourriture); être parcimonieux 2. to s. one's work, bâcler son travail. 'skimpy a (-ier, -iest) meal, maigre repas; s. garment, vêtement étriqué.

skin [skin] I. n 1. (a) peau f; rabbit s., peau de lapin; Fig: to have a thin s., être susceptible; to have a thick s., être insensible; next (to) one's s., à même, sur, la peau; Prov: beauty is only s. deep, la beauté n'est pas tout; (of snake) to cast, throw, its s., muer; to strip to the s., se mettre (tout) nu; wet to the s., mouillé jusqu'aux os; Toil: s. care, soins de la peau; s. cream, crème de beauté; Med: s. graft, greffe cutanée; s. test, cuti-réaction f; F: I nearly jumped out of my s., cela m'a fait sursauter; I escaped by the s. of my teeth, je l'ai échappé belle; to save one's s., sauver sa peau; F: I've got her under my s., je l'ai dans la peau; F: it's no s. off my nose, (i) ce n'est pas mon problème (ii) ça ne me coûte rien; pour ce que ça me coûte! (b) s. diving, plongée sous-marine (autonome); s. diver, plongeur, -euse, sous-marin(e) (autonome) 2. peau (d'orange, de banane); pelure f (d'oignon); Cu: potatoes baked in their skins, pommes de terre en robe de chambre, en robe des champs. II. vtr (skinned) écorcher, dépouiller (un lapin). 'skinflint n avare mf. 'skinhead n F: jeune homme à la tête rasée; jeune voyou. 'skinny a (-ier, -iest) maigre, décharné. 'skinny-'dip esp NAm: F: 1. n baignade f à poil 2. vi (skinny-dipped) se baigner, nager, tout nu, à poil. 'skin-tight a (vêtement) collant.

skip¹ [skip] v (skipped) 1. vi (a) sauter, sautiller, gambader (b) to s., NAm: to s. rope, sauter à la corde 2. vtr & i sauter, passer (un passage dans un livre); sauter (un repas); sécher (un cours); to s. over a word, sauter un mot; to s. from one subject to another, sauter d'un sujet à un autre; passer du coq à l'âne; NAm: to s. (Br = skim) stones, faire des ricochets; F: s. it! laisse courir! 'skipping n saut m à la corde; s. rope, corde à sauter.

skip² n Const: benne f.

skipper ['skipər] n 1. Nau: patron m 2. Sp: chef m d'équipe.

skirmish ['skə:miʃ] n Mil: escarmouche f, échauffourée f.

skirt [skə:t] 1. n Cl: jupe f 2. vtr contourner (un village); longer, serrer (le mur); the path skirts the wood, le sentier côtoie, contourne, le bois. 'skirting ('board) n (NAm: = baseboard) plinthe f.

skit [skit] *n* satire *f* (**on, de**).

skittle ['skitl] *n* quille *f*; *pl* (**game of**) **skittles**, jeu *m* de quilles.

skive [skaiv] *vi* F: **to s. (off)**, s'esquiver; tirer au flanc. **'skiver** *n* tire-au-flanc *m inv*.

skivvy ['skivi] *n* (*pl* **skivvies**) *Pej:* boniche *f*.

skulduggery [skʌl'dʌgəri] *n* F: maquignonnage *m*.

skulk [skʌlk] *vi* **1.** se cacher **2.** rôder furtivement.

skull [skʌl] *n* crâne *m*; **s. and crossbones**, tibias croisés et tête *f* de mort. **'skullcap** *n* calotte *f*.

skunk [skʌŋk] *n* **1.** Z: mouffette *f* **2.** (*fur*) skunks *m*, sconse *m* **3.** F: (*pers*) mufle *m*; salaud *m*.

sky [skai] *n* (*pl* **skies**) ciel *m*; **under the open s.**, (dormir) à la belle étoile; **to praise s.o. to the skies**, élever qn aux nues; F: **the s.'s the limit!** tout est possible! *Art:* **Turner's skies**, les ciels de Turner; **we live under other skies**, nous vivons sous un autre climat. **'sky-'blue** *a & n* bleu ciel. **'skydiving** *n* parachutisme *m* en chute libre. **'sky-'high** *adv* to blow sth **s.-h.**, faire sauter qch jusqu'aux cieux. **'skylark 1.** *n* Orn: alouette *f* des champs **2.** *vi* F: rigoler. **'skylarking** *n* rigolade *f*. **'skylight** *n* lucarne *f*. **'skyline** *n* ligne *f* d'horizon *m*. **'skyscraper** *n* gratte-ciel *m inv*. **'skyway** *n* **1.** route aérienne **2.** *NAm: Aut:* (*Br*=**flyover**) route surélevée. **'skywriting** *n* publicité aérienne (tracée par un avion).

slab [slæb] *n* plaque *f*, tranche *f* (de marbre); dalle *f* (de pierre); **s. of gingerbread**, pavé *m* de pain d'épice; **s. of cake**, grosse tranche de gâteau; **s. of chocolate**, tablette *f* de chocolat.

slack [slæk] *n* **I.** *n* **1.** (*a*) mou *m*, ballant *m* (d'un câble); **to take up the s. in a cable**, tendre un câble, rattraper le mou d'un câble (*b*) *Mec:* jeu *m*; **to take up the s.**, reprendre le jeu (*c*) période creuse; morte-saison *f*; ralentissement *m* (dans les affaires) **2.** *npl Cl:* **slacks**, pantalon *m*. **II.** *a* **1.** (*a*) mou, lâche, flasque; dégonflé (*b*) (main, prise) faible, sans force **2.** (*of pers*) négligent; **to be s. about one's work**, négliger son travail **3.** peu vif; faible; **business is s.**, les affaires ne marchent pas fort; **s. time**, accalmie *f*; **the s. season**, la morte-saison. **III.** *vi* **to s. (off)**, (*of rope*) prendre du lâche, du mou; (*of pers*) se relâcher; **to s. (up)**, ralentir. **'slacken 1.** *vtr* (*a*) ralentir (le pas); diminuer (de vitesse) (*b*) détendre (un cordage); desserrer (un écrou) **2.** *vi* **to s. off**, (*of pers*) se relâcher; devenir négligent; (*of rope*) prendre du mou. **'slackening** *n* ralentissement *m* (du zèle); diminution *f* (de force, de vitesse); relâchement *m* (d'un cordage, d'un effort); **s. of speed**, ralentissement. **'slacker** *n* paresseux, -euse. **'slackly** *adv* **1.** (lier qch) lâchement **2.** (agir) négligemment. **'slackness** *n* **1.** manque *m* d'énergie; négligence *f*; fainéantise *f* **2.** mou *m* (d'un cordage) **3.** *Com:* stagnation *f*, marasme *m* (des affaires).

slag [slæg] *n Metall:* scories *fpl*, crasses *fpl*; **s. heap**, crassier *m*; *Min:* terril *m*.

slain [slein] *see* **slay**.

slake [sleik] *vtr* **1. to s. one's thirst**, étancher sa soif; se désaltérer **2.** éteindre, amortir (la chaux).

slam[1] [slæm] **I.** *n* claquement *m* (d'une porte). **II.** *v* (**slammed**) **1.** *vtr* (faire) claquer (une porte); envoyer, lancer violemment, F: flanquer (**against**, contre; **into**, dans); **to s. the door in s.o.'s face**, claquer la porte au nez de qn; **she slammed the book (down) on the table,** elle a jeté le livre sur la table; **to s. on the brakes**, freiner brusquement **2.** *vi* (*of door*) claquer. **'slam- 'bang** *adv NAm:* (*Br*=**slap-bang**) en plein (**into**, dans).

slam[2] *n* (*at Bridge, Rugby*) chelem *m*.

slander ['slɑːndər] **1.** *n* calomnie *f*; diffamation *f* **2.** *vtr* calomnier, diffamer (qn). **'slanderer** *n* calomniateur, -trice; diffamateur, -trice. **'slanderous** *a* (propos) calomnieux, diffamatoire. **'slanderously** *adv* calomnieusement.

slang [slæŋ] **1.** *n* argot *m*; **s. phrase, expression**, expression argotique **2.** *vtr* injurier, F: engueuler (qn); **slanging match**, dispute *f*, F: engueulade *f*.

slant [slɑːnt] **I.** *n* **1.** pente *f*, inclinaison *f* **2.** biais *m*, biseau *m*; **on the s., at a s.**, obliquement; de biais **3.** point *m* de vue; **he has an interesting s. on the question**, il envisage la question d'une manière intéressante. **II.** *v* **1.** *vi* (*a*) être en pente; (s')incliner (*b*) être oblique, être en biais (*c*) (*of opinion*) pencher (vers), incliner (à) **2.** *vtr* incliner (qch); mettre (qch) en pente. **III.** *a* **s. eyes**, yeux bridés. **'slanted** *a* (nouvelle) faussée; (yeux) bridés. **'slant-'eyed** *a* aux yeux bridés. **'slanting** *a* (*a*) (toit) en pente, incliné (*b*) (direction) oblique. **'slantwise** *adv* obliquement; de biais.

slap [slæp] **1.** *n* claque *f*, tape *f*; **s. in the face**, (i) gifle *f* (ii) affront *m*; **s. on the back**, félicitations *fpl* **2.** *adv* **to run s. into sth**, se heurter en plein contre qch **3.** *vtr* (**slapped**) frapper (qn) avec la main (ouverte); donner une fessée à (un enfant); **to s. s.o.'s face**, gifler qn. **'slap-'bang** *adv* (*NAm:*=**slam-bang**) en plein (**into**, dans). **'slapdash** *a* sans soin; **s. work**, travail bâclé. **'slap-'happy** *a* F: (*a*) (*of pers*) insouciant; (travail) sans soin (*b*) plein d'entrain, fougueux. **'slapstick** *n* **s.** (**comedy**), farce bouffonne. **'slap- up** *a* F: fameux, chic, de premier ordre.

slash [slæʃ] **1.** *n* estafilade *f*, entaille *f*; balafre *f* **2.** *vtr* (*a*) taillader; balafrer (le visage); trancher net (un cordage) (*b*) **to s. a speech**, couper un discours; **to s. the price of sth**, vendre qch à prix sacrifié (*c*) critiquer, F: esquinter (un ouvrage littéraire) (*d*) cingler (un cheval) (d'un coup de fouet). **'slashing** *a* (*of criticism*) mordant, cinglant.

slat [slæt] *n* lame *f*, lamelle *f*.

slate [sleit] *n Const:* ardoise *f*; **s. industry**, ardoiserie *f*; **s. quarry**, ardoisière *f*; **s. (grey)**, gris ardoise; F: **put it on the s.**, mettez-le sur mon compte.

slaughter ['slɔːtər] **I.** *n* **1.** abattage *m* (de bétail) **2.** carnage *m*, massacre *m*. **II.** *vtr* **1.** abattre (des bêtes de boucherie) **2.** tuer, massacrer (des gens). **'slaughterhouse** *n* abattoir *m*.

Slav [slɑːv] *a & n Ethn:* slave (*mf*). **Sla'vonic I.** *a* slave **2.** *n Ling:* slave *m*.

slave [sleiv] **1.** *n* esclave *mf*; **s. trade**, traite des noirs; commerce des esclaves; F: **s. driver**, garde-chiourme *m* **2.** *vi* peiner; s'éreinter; bûcher (à un travail). **'slavery** *n* **1.** esclavage *m* **2.** travail tuant. **'slavish** *a* (imitation) servile. **'slavishly** *adv* (obéir) en esclave; (imiter) servilement.

slaver ['slævər] **1.** *n* bave *f*, salive *f* **2.** *vi* baver (**over**, sur).

slaw [slɔː] *n NAm:* (*Br*=**coleslaw**) salade *f* de chou cru.

slay [slei] *vtr* (**slew** [sluː]; **slain** [slein]) tuer; mettre à mort. **'slaying** *n* tuerie *f*; massacre *m*.

sleazy ['sli:zi] *a* (-ier, -iest) *F:* sordide, répugnant, *F:* dégueulasse.

sled, sledge [sled(ʒ)] 1. *n* traîneau *m*; luge *f* 2. *vi* aller en traîneau; faire de la luge.

sledgehammer ['sledʒhæmər] *n* marteau *m* de forgeron; marteau à deux mains; masse *f*.

sleek [sli:k] *a* lisse; luisant; (*of animal*) au poil soyeux. **'sleekness** *n* (*of hair, skin*) luisant *m*.

sleep [sli:p] I. *n* sommeil *m*; **sound s.,** sommeil profond; **short s.,** somme *m*; **to go to s.,** s'endormir; **to drop off to s.,** s'assoupir; **to send s.o. to s.,** endormir qn; **to have a good (night's) s.,** bien dormir; passer une bonne nuit; **to put a dog to s.** (= *kill*), piquer un chien; **to rouse s.o. from s.,** réveiller qn; **in my s.,** pendant que je dormais; **to walk in one's s.,** être somnambule; **s. tight!** dors bien! **my foot has gone to s.,** j'ai le pied engourdi. II. *vi & tr* (**slept**) 1. dormir; **to s. like a log,** dormir à poings fermés; dormir comme une marmotte; **I've not slept a wink all night,** je n'ai pas fermé l'œil de (toute) la nuit; j'ai passé une nuit blanche; **to s. on it,** repenser (à qch); **to s. the sleep of the just,** dormir du sommeil du juste 2. coucher; **to s. at a hotel,** coucher à un hôtel; **to s. away from home,** découcher; **to s. rough,** coucher sur la dure; **to s. with s.o.,** coucher avec qn. **'sleep a'round** *vi F:* coucher avec n'importe qui. **'sleeper** *n* 1. dormeur, -euse; **to be a light, a heavy, s.,** avoir le sommeil léger, profond 2. *Rail:* traverse *f* 3. *Rail:* wagon-lit *m*. **'sleepily** *adv* d'un air endormi, somnolent. **'sleep 'in** *vi* faire la grasse matinée; ne pas se réveiller à l'heure. **'sleepiness** *n* envie *f* de dormir; somnolence *f*. **'sleeping** 1. *a* dormant, endormi; *Prov:* **let's dogs lie,** ne réveillez pas le chat qui dort; *Com:* **s. partner,** commanditaire *m* 2. *n* sommeil *m*; **s. pill,** somnifère *m*; **s. bag,** sac de couchage; *Rail:* **s. car,** wagon-lit *m*; *Med:* **s. sickness,** maladie du sommeil. **'sleepless** *a* sans sommeil; **s. night,** nuit blanche. **'sleeplessness** *n* insomnie *f*. **'sleepwalk** *vi* être somnambule. **'sleepwalker** *n* somnambule *mf*. **'sleepwalking** *n* somnambulisme *m*. **'sleepy** *a* (-ier, -iest) somnolent; **to feel s.,** avoir envie de dormir; avoir sommeil; **s. look,** air endormi; **s. little town,** petite ville endormie. **'sleepyhead** *n F:* endormi, -ie.

sleet [sli:t] 1. *n* (*a*) grésil *m* (*b*) neige qui tourne à la pluie. 2. *v impers* grésiller; **it's sleeting,** il tombe de la neige fondue; la neige tourne à la pluie.

sleeve [sli:v] *n* manche *f*; pochette *f* (de disque); chemise *f* (de cylindre); **to have something up one's s.,** avoir une petite idée derrière la tête; **to have a few tricks up one's s.,** avoir plus d'un tour dans son sac. **'sleeveboard** *n* jeannette *f*. **'sleeveless** *a* (robe) sans manches.

sleigh [slei] *n* traîneau *m*.

sleight [slait] *n* **s. of hand,** prestidigitation *f*; tours *mpl* de passe-passe.

slender ['slendər] *a* 1. mince, ténu; (*of figure*) (*tall*) svelte, élancé; (*small*) menu; (*of finger*) fuselé 2. (*of hope*) faible; (*of income*) exigu, mince; **our s. means,** nos faibles ressources. **'slenderness** *n* 1. minceur *f*, ténuité *f*; sveltesse *f* 2. faiblesse *f* (des ressources).

slept [slept] *see* **sleep** 2.

sleuth ['slu:θ] *n F:* limier *m*, détective *m*.

slew [slu:] *see* **slay**.

slice [slais] I. *n* 1. tranche *f*; darne *f* (de gros poisson); rond *m*, rondelle *f* (de saucisson, de citron, de concombre); **s. of bread and butter,** tartine *f* de beurre; **s. of (good) luck,** coup *m* de veine 2. **fish s.,** truelle *f* à poisson. II. *vtr* 1. découper (qch) en tranches; **to s. thinly,** émincer (la viande) 2. *Sp:* (i) couper (ii) faire dévier, la balle. **'slice 'off** *vtr* trancher, couper (un morceau). **'slicer** *n* machine *f* à trancher (le pain); **bacon s.,** coupe-jambon *m inv.*

slick [slik] 1. *a F:* habile, adroit; **a s. customer,** un arnaqueur 2. *n* **oil s.,** traînée *f*, nappe *f*, de pétrole.

slide [slaid] I. *n* 1. glissade *f*, glissement *m*; éboulement *m*, glissement (de terrain); (*on ice*) glissoire *f*; (*in playground*) toboggan *m* 2. (*a*) (*for microscope*) porte-objet *m* (*b*) *Phot:* diapositive *f*, *F:* diapo *f* 3. (**hair**) **s.,** barrette *f*. II. *v* (**slid**) 1. *vi* glisser; (*of door*) coulisser; (*of land*) s'ébouler; **to s. (on ice),** faire des glissades; **he slid on the floor,** il a glissé sur le parquet; *Fig:* **to let things s.,** se désintéresser de tout 2. *vtr* (faire) glisser. **'sliding** *a* glissant; coulissant; **s. door,** porte à glissières, porte coulissante; **on a s. scale,** suivant une échelle mobile; **s. panel,** panneau mobile; **s. seat,** siège réglable; *Aut:* **s. roof,** toit ouvrant.

slight [slait] 1. *a* (*of pers*) mince, frêle; menu; (*of pain*) léger; (*of error*) petit; de peu d'importance; **not the slightest danger,** pas le moindre danger; **not in the slightest (degree),** pas le moins du monde; **to take offence at the slightest thing,** se piquer d'un rien; **I haven't the slightest idea,** je n'en ai pas la moindre idée 2. *n* manque *m* d'égards; affront *m* 3. *vtr* traiter (qn) sans considération; manquer d'égards envers (qn). **'slighting** *a* (air) de mépris. **'slightingly** *adv* avec mépris, dédaigneusement. **'slightly** *adv* 1. **s. built,** à la taille mince, svelte 2. légèrement, faiblement; **s. better,** un petit peu mieux; **I know him s.,** je le connais un peu.

slim [slim] 1. *a* (**slimmer, slimmest**) (*a*) mince; svelte, élancé; **s.-waisted,** à la taille svelte (*b*) (*of chance, hope*) mince, léger 2. *vi* (**slimmed**) (*a*) maigrir (*b*) suivre un régime amaigrissant. **'slimming** *a* amaigrissant. **'slimness** *n* minceur *f*; sveltesse *f*.

slime [slaim] *n* 1. limon *m*, vase *f* 2. bave *f* (de limace). **'sliminess** *n* (*a*) état vaseux (*b*) viscosité *f*. **'slimy** *a* (-ier, -iest) 1. (*a*) limoneux, vaseux (*b*) visqueux, gluant (*c*) couvert de vase 2. (*of pers*) servile, obséquieux.

sling [sliŋ] 1. *n* (*a*) fronde *f* (*b*) *Med:* écharpe *f*; **in a s.,** en écharpe (*c*) (*carrying strap*) bandoulière *f* (*d*) (*for hoisting*) élingue *f* 2. *vtr* (**slung**) (*a*) lancer, jeter; *F:* **to s. s.o. out,** flanquer qn à la porte (*b*) suspendre (un hamac); **to s. sth over one's shoulder,** jeter qch sur l'épaule 2. élinguer (un fardeau).

slink [sliŋk] *vi* (**slunk**) **to s. off,** partir furtivement. **'slinking** *a* furtif. **'slinky** *a* (-ier, -iest) (forme) svelte; (vêtement) collant.

slip [slip] I. *n* 1. (*a*) glissade *f*, glissement *m*; dérapage *m*; faux pas; *Aut:* **s. road,** bretelle *f* (*b*) **to give s.o. the s.,** fausser compagnie à qn (*c*) faute *f*, erreur *f*, d'inattention; **it was a s. of the tongue,** la langue lui a fourché (*d*) écart *m* (de conduite); peccadille *f* 2. (*a*) combinaison *f* (de femme) (*b*) (**pillow**) **s.,** taie *f* d'oreiller 3. *Nau:* cale *f*, chantier *m* de construction 4. bout *m* (de papier) 5. *Th:* **the slips,** les coulisses *fpl*. II. *v* (**slipped**) 1. *vi* (*a*) glisser; **to s. from s.o.'s hands,**

glisser des mains de qn; F: **you're slipping!** tu perds les pédales! (b) to s. **into the room,** se glisser dans la pièce; F: **I slipped round to the baker's,** j'ai fait un saut jusqu'à la boulangerie; **to let s.,** laisser tomber (qch); laisser échapper (une belle occasion) 2. vtr glisser (qch dans la main de qn); pousser (un verrou); Knit: glisser (une maille); to s. **one's arm around s.o.,** passer le bras autour de qn; **your name has slipped my memory,** votre nom m'échappe; **to s. a disc,** se faire une hernie discale; Aut: **to s. the clutch,** laisser patiner l'embrayage; to s. s.o.'s **notice,** échapper à l'attention de qn. **'slipcase** n esp Publ: étui m. **'slipcover** n Furn: housse f; Publ: étui. **'slipknot** n nœud coulant. **'slip-on** n (a) F: **s.-ons,** a **s.-on shoes,** mocassins mpl (b) NAm: Cl: (Br = **pullover**) pull-over m. **'slipover** n pull-over. **'slipper** n Cl: pantoufle f. **'slippery** a 1. glissant; **he's as s. as an eel,** il est souple comme une anguille 2. **to be on a s. slope,** être sur un terrain glissant 3. malin, rusé; **he's a s. customer,** on ne sait par où le prendre. **'slippy** a (-ier, -iest) F: glissant; **look s.!** P: grouille-toi! **'slip-road** n bretelle f (d'autoroute). **'slipshod** a (of pers) mal soigné; (of work) négligé, bâclé. **'slip-stream** n sillage m; Av: souffle m (de l'hélice). **'slip 'up** vi se tromper; faire une bourde; (of plan) échouer; tomber à l'eau. **'slip-up** n erreur f, bévue f. **'slipway** n Nau: cale f, chantier m de construction.

slit [slit] 1. n fente f; fissure f; déchirure f; **skirt with a s. on the side,** jupe fendue sur le côté 2. vtr (slitting; slit) fendre; **to s. s.o.'s throat,** couper la gorge à qn; égorger qn; to s. **open a sack,** éventrer un sac; **the blow s. his cheek (open),** le coup lui a déchiré la joue.

slither ['sliðər] vi glisser, manquer de tomber; (of snake) ramper.

sliver ['slivər] n lamelle f; éclat m (de bois); (mince) tranche f (de viande).

slob [slɔb] n F: rustaud, -aude.

slobber ['slɔbər] vi baver; **to s. over s.o.,** témoigner une tendresse exagérée envers qn.

sloe [slou] n Bot: 1. prunelle f; **s. gin,** (eau de vie de) prunelle 2. (tree) prunellier m.

slog [slɔg] vi (slogged) (a) to s. **away,** travailler avec acharnement (at sth, à qch); F: travailler dur, F: bosser (b) to s. **along,** marcher d'un pas lourd. **'slogger** n bûcheur, -euse, bosseur.

slogan ['slougən] n slogan m.

slop [slɔp] 1. npl **slops** (a) boissons renversées (b) aliments m liquides; bouillon m (pour un malade) (c) eaux ménagères (d) fond m de tasse 2. v (slopped) (a) vtr répandre (un liquide) (b) vi (of liquid) déborder. **'sloppily** adv s. **dressed,** débraillé. **'sloppy** a (-ier, -iest) (of pers) mou; flasque; peu soigné; (travail) bâclé, négligé; (vêtement) mal ajusté, trop grand; (roman, film) larmoyant; s. **sentimentality,** sensiblerie f; F: s. **joe,** gros pull très ample.

slope [sloup] 1. n pente f, inclinaison f; **steep, gentle, s.,** pente raide, douce; s. **down,** descente f; talus m; s. **up,** montée f; **mountain slopes,** flanc m, versants mpl de montagne; **ski s.,** piste f (de ski); **half-way down, up, the s.,** à mi-pente 2. vi être en pente; incliner, pencher; aller en pente; to s. **down,** descendre; to s. **up,** monter. **'sloping** a en pente, incliné; (jardin) en talus; s. **shoulders,** épaules tombantes.

slosh [slɔʃ] 1. vi (of liquid) to s. **(around),** clapoter; (of animal, child) to s. **(about),** patauger 2. vtr flanquer (de la peinture sur un mur). **sloshed** a ivre, soûl.

slot [slɔt] I. n entaille f, encoche f, rainure f; TV: (time) s., créneau m (horaire); s. **machine,** (i) distributeur m automatique (ii) machine à sous; s. **meter,** compteur à paiement préalable; **to put a coin in the s.,** introduire une pièce (de monnaie) dans la fente. II. v (slotted) 1. vtr insérer, mettre (sth **into** sth, qch dans qch) 2. vi s'introduire, se glisser (**into,** dans). **'slotted** a DomEc: s. **spoon,** cuillère à trous.

sloth [slouθ] n (a) paresse f (b) Z: paresseux m. **'slothful** a paresseux, fainéant; indolent. **'slothfully** adv paresseusement.

slouch [slautʃ] vi se laisser aller, traîner le pas (en marchant); manquer de tenue; être affalé (dans un fauteuil); **don't s.!** tenez-vous droit!

slovenly ['slʌvənli] a 1. (of pers) mal peigné, mal soigné; débraillé 2. (a) négligent; sans soin (b) (travail) négligé, F: bousillé; **done in a s. way,** fait sans soin. **'slovenliness** n négligence f; manque m de tenue, de soin; laisser-aller m inv; débraillé m (de la tenue).

slow [slou] I. a 1. (a) lent; s. **speed,** petite vitesse; ralenti m; Cin: (au) ralenti; **it's s. work,** ça ne va pas vite; Cu: **to cook in a s. oven,** cuire à feu doux; Rail: s. **train,** train m omnibus (b) **to be s. in starting sth, to start sth,** être lent à commencer qch (c) s. **(of intellect),** à l'esprit lourd; s. **child,** enfant retardé, arriéré (d) qui manque d'entrain; **business is s.,** les affaires stagnent 2. (of clock) en retard; **your watch is five minutes s.,** votre montre retarde de cinq minutes. II. adv lentement; **to go slower,** ralentir sa marche; **to go s.,** (i) aller lentement (ii) Ind: faire la grève perlée; **to go s. with one's provisions,** ménager ses vivres; PN: s.! ralentir! III. v 1. vi to s. **down, to s. up,** ralentir (son allure); diminuer de vitesse 2. vtr to s. **sth down,** ralentir qch; to s. s.o. **down,** retarder qn. **'slow-'burning** a à combustion lente. **'slowcoach,** NAm: **'slowpoke** n lambin, -ine. **'slowdown** n ralentissement m. **'slowly** adv lentement; s. **but surely,** lentement mais sûrement; **engine running s.,** moteur au ralenti. **'slow-'moving** a à marche lente. **'slowness** n lenteur f.

sludge [slʌdʒ] n vase f; fange f; Ind: tartres mpl boueux; (sewage) s., vidanges fpl. **'sludgy** a (-ier, -iest) vaseux, fangeux; boueux.

slug [slʌg] n (a) Moll: limace f (b) esp NAm: F: (Br = **bullet**) balle f.

sluggish ['slʌgiʃ] a paresseux, léthargique; (of market) stagnant; Aut: (moteur) peu nerveux. **'sluggishly** adv paresseusement; (of river) **to flow s.,** couler lentement. **'sluggishness** n paresse f (de qn, de l'intestin); lourdeur f (de l'esprit); lenteur f (d'une rivière).

sluice [slu:s] 1. n (a) écluse f; s. **gate,** vanne f (b) canal m de décharge (c) **to give sth a s. down,** laver (qch) à grande eau 2. vtr laver (qch) à grande eau; débourber (un égout).

slum [slʌm] n bas quartier (d'une ville); rue f sordide; taudis m; s. **clearance campaign,** lutte f contre les taudis. **'slummy** a (rue) sordide, misérable.

slumber ['slʌmbər] Lit: 1. n (a) sommeil m (paisible); assoupissement m; somme m 2. vi sommeiller; dormir (paisiblement). **'slumberwear** n Com: vêtements mpl de nuit.

slump [slʌmp] **1.** n Com: baisse soudaine; effondrement m (des cours); dégringolade f (de la livre sterling); **the s.,** la crise économique **2.** vi (a) Ind: (of prices) baisser tout à coup; s'effondrer, dégringoler (b) (of pers) tomber lourdement, s'affaler (**into a chair,** dans un fauteuil).

slung [slʌŋ] see **sling** 2.

slunk [slʌŋk] see **slink.**

slur[1] [sləːr] n affront m; **to cast a s. on s.o.,** ternir la réputation de qn.

slur[2] vtr & i (**slurred**) mal articuler; **to s. (over) a word,** bredouiller, escamoter, un mot; **to s. (over) a fact,** glisser sur un fait. **slurred** a brouillé, indistinct; (of outline) estompé.

slurp [sləːp] vtr & i F: boire (qch) avec bruit.

slush [slʌʃ] n neige à demi fondue; F: sensiblerie f; F: **s. fund,** caisse noire (pour payer des pots-de-vins). **'slushy** a (-ier, -iest) boueux; fangeux; F: (roman, film) à l'eau de rose.

slut [slʌt] n (dirty) souillon f; (immoral) salope f. **'sluttish** a (femme) malpropre, sale.

sly [slai] **1.** a (**slyer, slyest**) (a) rusé (b) sournois (c) malin, espiègle **2.** n **on the s.,** en cachette; **to do sth on the s.,** faire qch furtivement. **'slyly** adv (a) avec finesse (b) sournoisement. **'slyness** n (a) finesse f (b) sournoiserie f (c) malice f.

smack[1] [smæk] vi **to s. of sth,** avoir un léger goût de qch; **opinions that s. of heresy,** opinions qui sentent le fagot.

smack[2] **I.** n **1.** claquement m **2.** tape f; claque f; **s. in the face,** (gifle) affront m; **s. on the bottom,** fessée f; F: **to have a s. (at doing sth),** tenter, essayer (de faire qch). **II.** vtr frapper, taper (qn); **to s. s.o.'s face,** donner une gifle à qn; F: **to s. one's lips,** se lécher les babines. **III.** adv **s. in the middle,** en plein milieu.

smack[3] n (fishing) s., bateau m de pêche.

small [smɔːl] **1.** a (a) petit, menu; **s. man,** petit homme; homme de petite taille; **s. stature,** petite taille; **to make sth smaller,** rapetisser qch; **to make oneself s.,** se faire tout petit; **s. coffee,** une demi-tasse (de café); **he's a s. eater,** il n'est pas gros mangeur; **s. arms,** armes portatives, légères; **s. game,** menu gibier; Typ: **s. letters,** minuscules f; **s. print,** texte en petits caractères; **in s. numbers,** en petit nombre; **s. party,** réunion peu nombreuse; **s. voice,** voix fluette; **s. income,** revenu modeste; **s. harvest,** maigre récolte (b) peu important; peu considérable; **s. change,** menue monnaie; **in a s. way,** en petit; **a s. matter,** une bagatelle; **it's s. wonder (that),** il n'est guère étonnant (que); **it was no s. surprise to me,** à ma grande surprise; **the smallest detail,** le moindre détail; **s. hotel,** hôtel modeste; **s. shopkeeper,** petit commerçant; **in a small way,** en petit; **the smallest possible number of people,** le moins de gens possible (c) mesquin; **s. mind,** petit esprit; **to look s.,** avoir l'air penaud; **to make s.o. look s.,** humilier qn **2.** n (a) **s. of the back,** creux m des reins (b) F: **smalls,** sous-vêtements m **3.** adv (hacher) menu, en petits morceaux. **'smallholding** n petite exploitation agricole. **'smallish** a plutôt petit; assez petit. **'small-'minded** a (à l'esprit) mesquin. **'smallness** n petitesse f; modicité f (de revenus); le peu d'importance (d'une somme d'argent). **'smallpox**

n petite vérole; variole f. **'small-scale** a **1. s.-s. model,** modèle réduit f. **2. s.-s. business,** entreprise peu importante. **'small-time** a insignifiant, médiocre; **s.-t. crook,** petit escroc. **'small-town** a provincial.

smart [smɑːt] **I.** n douleur cuisante (d'une blessure). **II.** vi (of wound) (a) cuire, brûler; **my eyes are smarting,** les yeux me picotent (b) **to s. under an injustice,** souffrir sous le coup d'une injustice. **III.** a **1.** (coup) cinglant; (coup) sec **2. to walk at a s. pace,** marcher à vive allure; **look s. (about it)!** dépêchez-vous! **3.** habile; débrouillard, dégourdi; **s. answer,** réponse adroite; **to try to be s.,** faire le malin; F: **s. aleck,** je-sais-tout m inv **4.** élégant, distingué, chic; **to make oneself s.,** se faire beau. **'smarten** vtr & i **to s. up,** donner du chic à (qn); égayer (une pièce); **to s. (oneself) up,** se faire beau. **'smartly** adv (a) promptement; vivement (b) habilement, adroitement (c) (s'habiller) élégamment. **'smartness** n (a) vivacité f; esprit débrouillard (b) à-propos m (d'une réponse) (c) habileté peu scrupuleuse (d) élégance f; chic m.

smash [smæʃ] **I.** n (a) coup écrasant; Ten: smash m (b) désastre m; **car s.,** accident m (de la route) (c) Fin: débâcle f; faillite (commerciale) (d) F: **s. (hit),** succès fou. **II.** v **1.** vtr (a) casser, briser, fracasser; **to s. sth to pieces,** briser qch en morceaux; **to s. the door open,** enfoncer la porte; F: **to s. s.o.'s face in,** abîmer le portrait de qn (b) détruire (qch); écraser (une armée) **2.** vi (a) se heurter violemment (contre qch); **the car smashed into the wall,** la voiture s'est écrasée contre le mur (b) éclater en morceaux; se briser (c) Fin: faire faillite. **III.** adv (se heurter) de front (**into,** contre). **'smash-and-'grab** n F: **s.-and-g. (raid),** cambriolage m après bris de vitrine; F: **casse** m. **'smasher** n **she's a s.!** elle est drôlement belle! **it's a s.!** c'est formidable! **'smashing** a **1.** (coup) écrasant **2.** F: **that's s.!** c'est formidable! c'est super! **'smash 'up** vtr briser en morceaux; fracasser. **'smash-up** n destruction complète; Aut: Rail: collision f.

smattering ['smætəriŋ] n légère connaissance (d'une matière); **to have a s. of chemistry,** avoir des notions f de chimie.

smear ['smiər] **1.** n tache f, souillure f; Med: (cervical) **s. (test),** frottis vaginal; **s. campaign,** campagne de diffamation **2.** vtr (a) barbouiller, salir (**with,** de) (b) enduire (**with,** de) (c) maculer (une page écrite).

smell [smel] **I.** n **1.** (sense of) **s.,** odorat m; flair m (d'un chien); **to have a keen sense of s.,** avoir l'odorat fin **2.** (a) odeur f; parfum m (de fleurs); **musty s., stale s.,** relent m; **there's a nice, bad, s.,** ça sent bon, mauvais; **a s. of burning,** une odeur de brûlé (b) mauvaise odeur. **II.** v (smelt) **1.** vtr & i flairer (qch); sentir (une odeur, une fleur); sentir l'odeur de (qch); **I can s. sth burning,** ça sent le brûlé; **the dog smelt at my shoes,** le chien a flairé mes souliers **2.** vi (a) **to s. nice,** sentir bon (b) sentir (mauvais); avoir une forte odeur; **it smells!** ça sent mauvais! **'smell 'out** vtr (of dog) dépister (le gibier); (of pers) découvrir (un secret). **'smelly** a (-ier, -iest) malodorant; puant; **it's s.!** ça sent mauvais! ça pue!

smelt [smelt] vtr Metall: **1.** fondre; faire fondre (le minerai) **2.** extraire (le métal) par fusion. **'smelting** n (a) fonte f (b) extraction f (du métal); **s. works,** fonderie f.

smile [smail] **1.** n sourire m; **to be all smiles,** être tout souriant; **with a s.,** en souriant, avec un sourire; **with a s. on his lips,** le sourire aux lèvres; **to give s.o. a s.,** sourire, faire un sourire, à qn **2.** vi sourire; **to s. at s.o.,** sourire à qn; **to keep smiling,** garder le sourire. **'smiling** a souriant. **'smilingly** adv en souriant.

smirk [smɔːk] **1.** n sourire satisfait, affecté **2.** vi sourire d'un air satisfait, affecté.

smith [smiθ] n forgeron m; **shoeing s.,** maréchal ferrant. **'smithy** ['smiði] n (pl **-ies**) forge f.

smithereens [smiðə'riːnz] npl F: morceaux mpl; miettes fpl; **to blow, smash, sth to s.,** réduire qch en miettes; briser qch en mille morceaux.

smitten ['smitn] a frappé (de cécité); pris (de remords); **to be s. with the desire to do sth,** être pris du désir de faire qch; F: **to be s. (with a girl),** tomber amoureux, être amouraché, d'une jeune fille.

smock [smɔk] **1.** n blouse f, sarrau m **2.** vtr Needlw: orner (une robe) de smocks. **'smocking** n smocks mpl.

smog [smɔg] n brouillard enfumé; smog m.

smoke [smouk] **1.** n fumée f; **there's no s. without fire,** il n'y a pas de fumée sans feu; **to go up in s.,** brûler; (of project) s'en aller en fumée, n'aboutir à rien; **s. bomb,** bombe fumigène; **do you want to have a s.?** voulez-vous fumer? **2.** vtr & i fumer; **do you s.?** fumez-vous? I **s. a pipe,** je fume la pipe; **do you mind if I s.?** la fumée vous gêne-t-elle? **smoked** a (jambon, poisson, verre) fumé. **'smokeless** a (combustible) sans fumée; (zone) où la fumée est interdite. **'smoker** n (a) fumeur, -euse; **heavy s.,** grand fumeur (b) Rail: (also **smoking compartment**) compartiment m fumeurs. **'smoking** n **1.** fumage m (du jambon) **2.** action f, habitude f, de fumer (le tabac); PN: **no s.,** défense de fumer. **'smoky** a (**-ier, -iest**) (of atmosphere) fumeux, enfumé; (of room) plein, rempli, de fumée.

smooth [smuːð] **I.** a **1.** (a) (surface, pâte, papier) lisse; (chemin) uni, égal; (front) sans rides; **sea as s. as a millpond,** mer calme; mer d'huile; **s. skin,** peau douce, satinée; **to make s.,** lisser (ses cheveux); aplanir (une route) (b) (menton) glabre **2.** (a) doux, sans heurts; (voyage) (i) confortable (ii) sans anicroches (iii) (in boat) par mer calme; (of machine) **s. running,** fonctionnement doux, régulier (b) (vin) moelleux (c) (of pers, words) doucereux, mielleux; **he has a s. tongue,** c'est un beau parleur. **'smoothie** n F: beau parleur; personne mielleuse. **'smoothly** adv **1.** uniment; sans inégalités **2.** (marcher) doucement. **II.** vtr **to s. (down),** lisser (ses cheveux); égaliser (le terrain); aplanir (une planche); **to s. the way for s.o.,** aplanir la voie pour qn. **'smoothness** n **1.** (a) égalité f (d'une surface); satiné m (de la peau) (b) calme m (de la mer) **2.** douceur f (de la marche d'une machine). **'smooth 'off** vtr adoucir, arrondir (un angle). **'smooth 'out** vtr faire disparaître (un faux pli); aplanir (une difficulté). **'smooth 'over** vtr aplanir (une difficulté); arranger (les choses). **'smooth-'running** a qui marche bien; (of machine) à marche douce, régulière.

smother ['smʌðər] **1.** vtr (a) étouffer; suffoquer (qn) (b) recouvrir (un gâteau de crème Chantilly); **to be smothered in furs,** être emmitouflé de fourrures **2.** vi suffoquer.

smoulder, NAm: also smolder ['smouldər] vi (of coal) brûler lentement; (of fire, rebellion) couver (sous la cendre).

smudge [smʌdʒ] **1.** n tache f; noircissure f **2.** vtr salir (la page), barbouiller, maculer (son écriture). **'smudgy** a taché, barbouillé; (contour) estompé.

smug [smʌg] a (ton, air) suffisant; satisfait de soi-même. **'smugly** adv d'un air suffisant. **'smugness** n suffisance f.

smuggle ['smʌgl] **1.** vtr (faire) passer en contrebande, en fraude **2.** vi faire de la contrebande. **'smuggler** n contrebandier, -ière. **'smuggling** n contrebande f.

smut [smʌt] n **1.** parcelle f, tache f, de suie **2.** coll grivoiseries fpl, indécences fpl, ordures fpl; **to talk s.,** dire des saletés f, des cochonneries f. **'smuttiness** n **1.** noirceur f, saleté f **2.** obscénité f, grivoiserie f. **'smutty** a (**-ier, -iest**) **1.** noirci, sali (de suie) **2.** (of conversation) malpropre, ordurier, grivois.

snack [snæk] n léger repas; casse-croûte m inv; **to have a s.,** manger sur le pouce; manger un morceau; **s. bar,** snack(-bar) m.

snag [snæg] n (a) chicot m (d'arbre); souche f au ras de l'eau (b) obstacle caché; **to hit, strike, a s.,** se heurter à un obstacle; **that's the s.!** voilà la difficulté! **the s. is that he's left,** l'embêtant c'est qu'il est parti (c) accroc m (dans un vêtement).

snail [sneil] n escargot m; **edible s.,** escargot comestible; **at a snail's pace,** à une allure d'escargot.

snake [sneik] n serpent m; (common) grass s., couleuvre f à collier; F: **a s. in the grass,** un traître; **s. charmer,** charmeur de serpent; Games: snakes and ladders = le jeu de l'oie. **'snakebite** n morsure f de serpent. **'snakeskin** n peau f de serpent.

snap [snæp] **I.** n **1.** (a) coup m de dents (b) bruit sec, claquement m (de dents, de doigts); **with a s. of the fingers,** en faisant claquer ses doigts **2.** cassure f; rupture soudaine; **there was a s.,** qch a cassé, a pété **3.** **cold s.,** courte période de temps froid; coup de froid **4.** **s. (fastener),** (on clothes) bouton-pression m; pression m or f; (on bag) fermoir m **5.** Cu: ginger s., biscuit croquant au gingembre **6.** Phot: instantané m, photo f **7.** Cards: (jeu de) bataille f. **II.** a instantané, imprévu; **a s. decision,** décision prise sur le coup. **III.** v (snapped) **1.** vi (a) **to s. at sth, s.o.,** chercher à mordre qch, qn; (of trigger) faire du bruit, revenir brusquement (en place); **"that's enough!" he snapped,** "ça suffit!" dit-il d'un ton brusque; Fig: (of pers) **to s. out of it,** se secouer (b) (of teeth, whip) claquer; faire un bruit sec; **to s. shut,** se fermer avec un bruit sec (c) (break) (se) casser net; se rompre avec un bruit sec **2.** vtr (a) (of dog) happer (qch) (b) faire claquer (ses doigts); Fig: **to s. one's fingers at s.o.,** narguer qn, se moquer de qn (c) casser, rompre (net) (un bâton). **'snapdragon** n Bot: muflier m; gueule-de-loup f. **'snap 'off 1.** vtr enlever d'un coup de dents; casser net; F: **to s. s.o.'s head off,** rembarrer qn **2.** vi se casser. **'snappish** a hargneux, de mauvaise humeur. **'snappy** a (**-ier, -iest**) (a) irritable; hargneux (b) (of reply, style) vif; F: **look s.! make it s.!** grouille-toi! **'snapshot** n Phot: instantané m, photo f. **'snap 'up** vtr saisir, happer (qch); **to s. up a bargain,** sauter sur une occasion.

snare [snɛər] **1.** n (a) Ven: lacet m, collet m (b) piège m **2.** vtr prendre au piège.

snarl[1] [snɑːl] **1.** vi grogner, gronder; (of tiger) feuler **2.**

n grondement *m*, grognement *m*; (*of tiger*) feulement *m*. **'snarling** *a* (*of pers, animal*) hargneux.

snarl² *vtr* (*in traffic*) **to be snarled up**, être pris dans un embouteillage; (*of wool*) **to get snarled up**, s'emmêler. **'snarl-up** *n* embouteillage *m*, bouchon *m*.

snatch [snætʃ] **1.** *vtr & i* saisir, empoigner (qch); s'emparer brusquement (de qch); **to s. at sth**, essayer de saisir qch (*b*), ramasser vivement qch; **to s. an opportunity**, saisir une occasion; **to s. a meal**, avaler un repas en vitesse; **to s. some sleep**, réussir à faire un petit somme; **to s. sth out of s.o.'s hands**, arracher qch des mains de qn **2.** *n* (*a*) **to make a s. at sth**, chercher à saisir qch (*b*) courte période; **to work in, by, snatches**, travailler par à-coups; **snatches of song**, fragments *m* de chanson; **snatches of conversation**, bribes *f* de conversation.

snazzy ['snæzi] *a F:* élégant, chic.

sneak [sniːk] **I.** *v* **1.** (*a*) **to s. off**, partir furtivement; **to s. in, out**, se glisser furtivement, se faufiler, dans un endroit, hors d'un endroit (*b*) *Sch: P:* moucharder, cafarder **2.** *vtr* (*a*) *P:* chiper, chaparder (*b*) **to s. a look**, jeter un coup d'œil furtif (**at sth**, à qch). **II.** *n* *Sch: F:* mouchard *m*; rapporteur, -euse. **'sneakers** *npl* (chaussures *fpl* de) tennis *mpl*; baskets *mpl*. **'sneaking** *a* **1.** (*a*) furtif (*b*) **to have a s. liking for sth**, avoir un penchant inavoué pour qch **2.** rampant, servile. **'sneaky** *a* (*a*) furtif (*b*) sournois.

sneer [sniər] **I.** *n* **1.** sourire *m* de mépris; ricanement *m* **2.** sarcasme *m*. **II.** *vi* ricaner; **to s. at s.o.**, (i) parler de qn d'un ton méprisant (ii) lancer des sarcasmes à qn. **'sneering** *a* ricaneur; moqueur. **'sneeringly** *adv* d'un air méprisant; en ricanant.

sneeze [sniːz] **1.** *n* éternuement *m* **2.** *vi* éternuer; **that's not to be sneezed at**, cela n'est pas à dédaigner, *F:* il ne faut pas cracher dessus. **'sneezing** *a* **s. powder**, poudre à éternuer.

snide [snaid] *a* sarcastique; insidieux.

sniff [snif] **1.** *n* reniflement *m* **2.** *vtr & i* renifler; inhaler (de la cocaïne); *P:* sniffer; *F:* **it's not to be sniffed at**, il ne faut pas cracher dessus; **the dog sniffed (at) my hand**, le chien m'a flairé la main.

sniffle ['snifl] **1.** *n* *F:* petit rhume (de cerveau) **2.** *vi* renifler; être légèrement enrhumé. **'sniffling** *a* (*a*) enrhumé (*b*) pleurnicheur.

snigger ['snigər] *vi* rire sous cape; ricaner. **'sniggering** *n* rires *mpl* en dessous; ricanements *mpl*.

snip [snip] **1.** *vtr* (**snipped**) couper avec des ciseaux **2.** *n* (*a*) morceau coupé; petite entaille (*b*) coup *m* de ciseaux (*c*) *F:* affaire avantageuse.

snipe [snaip] *n* (*inv in pl*) *Orn:* bécassine *f*.

sniper ['snaipər] *n* *Mil:* tireur embusqué.

snippet ['snipit] *n* (*a*) bout *m*; morceau (coupé) (*b*) bribe *f* (de conversation).

snivel ['snivl] *vi* (**snivelled**) pleurnicher, larmoyer. **'snivelling 1.** *a* pleurnicheur; larmoyant **2.** *n* pleurnicherie *f*.

snob [snɔb] *n* prétentieux, -euse; snob *mf*; **intellectual s.**, poseur, -euse. **'snobbery** *n* snobisme *m*; **intellectual s.**, snobisme intellectuel; **inverted s.**, snobisme à rebours. **'snobbish** *a* poseur; snob. **'snobbishness** *n* snobisme *m*.

snog [snɔg] *vi* *P:* (*of couple*) s'embrasser; *P:* se peloter.

snooker ['snuːkər] *n* (sorte de) jeu *m* de billard.

snoop [snuːp] *vi* *F:* fureter, fouiner; fourrer le nez

partout; **to s. on s.o.**, espionner qn. **'snooper** *n* *F:* fureteur *m*, fouineur *m*.

snooze [snuːz] *F:* **1.** *n* petit somme, *F:* roupillon *m* **2.** *vi* sommeiller; faire un petit somme; *F:* piquer un roupillon. **'snoozing** *a* endormi, assoupi.

snore [snɔːr] **1.** *vi* ronfler **2.** *n* ronflement *m*. **'snoring** *n* ronflement.

snorkel ['snɔːkl] *n* schnorkel *m*; *Swim:* tuba *m*.

snort [snɔːt] **1.** (*a*) *vi* renifler fortement; (*of horse*) s'ébrouer (*b*) **to s. at sth**, dédaigner qch **2.** *n* reniflement *m*; ébrouement *m*. **'snorter** *F:* *n* (*a*) problème *m* difficile à résoudre; voilà qui va nous donner du fil à retordre! (*b*) petit verre (d'alcool). **'snorting** *n* reniflement.

snot [snɔt] *n* *P:* morve *f*; **s. rat**, mouchoir *m*. **'snotty** *a* morveux.

snout [snaut] *n* museau *m*; groin *m* (de porc).

snow [snou] **I.** *n* **1.** neige *f*; **there's been a fall of s.**, il est tombé de la neige; **s. shower**, chute de neige; **flurry of s.**, rafale de neige; *Ski:* **crusted s.**, (neige) tôlée (*f*); **powdered s.**, (neige) poudreuse (*f*) **2.** *P:* (*drug*) cocaïne *f*, *P:* coco *f*. **II.** *v impers* neiger; **it's snowing**, il neige; **to be snowed up**, être bloqué par la neige; **I'm snowed under with work**, je suis débordé, submergé, de travail. **'snowball 1.** *n* boule *f* de neige **2.** *vi* *F:* faire boule de neige. **'snow-blindness** *n* cécité *f* des neiges. **'snowbound** *a* bloqué par la neige. **'snowdrift** *n* congère *f*. **'snowdrop** *n* *Bot:* perce-neige *m inv.* **'snowfall** *n* (*a*) chute *f* de neige (*b*) (profondeur *f* d')enneigement *m*. **'snowflake** *n* flocon *m* de neige. **'snowline** *n* limite *f* des neiges éternelles. **'snowman** *n* (*pl* **-men**) bonhomme *m* de neige; **the abominable s.**, l'abominable homme des neiges; le yéti. **'snowmobile** *n* autoneige *f*; motoneige *f*. **'snowplough**, *NAm:* **snowplow** *n* chasse-neige *m inv.* **'snowshoes** *npl* raquettes *fpl*. **'snowstorm** *n* tempête *f* de neige. **'snow-'white 1.** *a* blanc comme neige **2.** *Prnf* Blanche-Neige. **'snowy** *a* (**-ier**, **-iest**) neigeux; de neige; enneigé.

snub¹ [snʌb] **1.** *n* mortification *f*, rebuffade *f* **2.** *vtr* (**snubbed**) infliger un affront à (qn).

snub² *a* (nez) camus, retroussé. **'snub-'nosed** *a* au nez retroussé.

snuff [snʌf] *n* tabac *m* à priser; **to take s.**, priser; **a pinch of s.**, une prise. **'snuffbox** *n* (*pl* **-es**) tabatière *f*.

snug [snʌg] *a* confortable; **to lie s. in bed**, être bien au chaud dans son lit; **it's very s. in here**, on est bien ici; il fait très bon ici. **'snuggle** *vi* **to s. up** (**to s.o.**), se pelotonner, se blottir (contre qn); **to s. down in bed**, se blottir dans son lit. **'snugly** *adv* confortablement; bien au chaud; **jacket that fits s.**, veste bien ajustée.

so [sou] **I.** *adv* **1.** si, tellement; tant, aussi; **it's so easy**, c'est tellement, si, facile; **he's so (very) kind**, il est si aimable; **the young and the not so young**, les jeunes et les moins jeunes; **I am not so sure of that**, je n'en suis pas bien sûr; **so serious a wound**, une blessure aussi grave; **he's not so feeble as he appears**, il n'est pas aussi faible qu'il en a l'air; **would you be so kind as to come?** voudriez-vous avoir la bonté de venir? **he's so rich (that) he doesn't know what he's worth**, il est riche au point d'ignorer sa fortune; **so much**, tellement, tant; **we enjoyed ourselves so much**, on s'est joliment bien

amusé; **I loved him so much,** je l'aimais tant **2.** (a)
ainsi; de cette manière; **stand just so,** tenez-vous ainsi,
comme ça; **why do you cry so?** pourquoi pleurez-vous
ainsi? **it so happened (that),** le hasard a voulu que
(+ sub); **and so on, and so forth,** et ainsi de suite; **so to
speak,** pour ainsi dire; **so saying,** à ces mots (b) **I think
so,** je le crois; **I'm afraid so,** j'en ai bien peur; **so I have
been told,** c'est ce qu'on m'a dit; **so it seems,** à ce qu'il
paraît; **I didn't say so!** je n'ai pas dit ça! **I told you so!**
didn't I say so! je vous l'avais bien dit! **I suppose so, I
expect so,** je le suppose; **I hope so,** je l'espère bien; **so
much so that,** à tel point que; tellement que; **is that so?**
vraiment? **it's not so,** il n'en est rien; **that's so,** c'est
bien vrai; **so be it!** soit! (c) **if so,** s'il en est ainsi; **how so?**
comment cela? **perhaps so,** cela se peut; **not so,** pas du
tout; **quite so!** parfaitement! **a week or so,** une semaine
environ; **a £100 or so,** une centaine de livres (d) **he's
right and so are you,** il a raison et vous aussi; **and so am
I,** et moi aussi (e) **you're late—so I am!** vous êtes en
retard—c'est vrai! **3.** conj phr **so that, so as to** (a) pour
que; **we hurried so as not to be late,** nous nous sommes
dépêchés pour ne pas être en retard (b) de sorte que
(+ ind or sub); **speak so as to be understood,** parlez de
sorte qu'on vous comprenne **4.** (used adverbially and
adjectivally) **so, so,** passablement; comme ci comme
ça. **II.** conj **1.** donc; c'est pourquoi; **he has a bad
temper so be careful,** il a mauvais caractère, alors
faites attention **2. so there you are!** vous voilà donc! **so
you're not coming?** ainsi vous ne venez pas? **so what?**
(i) et alors? (ii) et puis quoi encore? (iii) ça te regarde,
toi? **so that's what it is!** ah! c'est comme ça! **'so-and-
so** n F: (a) Pej: sale type m (b) Mr **So-and-So,**
Monsieur Untel. **'so-called** a soi-disant.

soak [souk] **I.** v **1.** vtr (a) tremper, détremper (b) **to s.
sth in sth,** tremper qch dans qch (c) F: écorcher (un
client); **to s. the rich,** faire payer les riches **2.** vi (a)
baigner, tremper (**in sth,** dans qch) (b) s'infiltrer,
s'imbiber (**into, dans**). **II.** n **1. to put in s.,** (faire)
tremper (le linge); faire macérer (des cornichons);
(faire) dessaler (la morue) **2.** P: ivrogne m, soûlard m.
soaked a trempé; **s. to the skin,** trempé jusqu'aux os.
'soak 'in 1. vi pénétrer **2.** vtr s'imprégner (d'eau),
absorber (l'eau). **'soaking 1.** n trempage m; **to get a
(good) s.,** se faire tremper **2.** a trempé, mouillé **3.** a &
adv **s. (wet),** trempé. **'soak 'up** vtr absorber.

soap [soup] **1.** n savon m; **bar of s.,** savonnette f; TV: F:
s. opera, feuilleton m à l'eau de rose **2.** vtr savonner.
'soapdish n porte-savon m inv. **'soapflakes** npl
savon m en paillettes. **'soapsuds** npl mousse f de
savon. **'soapy** a (-ier, -iest) **1.** savonneux, couvert de
savon **2.** Pej: (of pers) mielleux, doucereux.

soar [sɔːr] vi prendre son essor; monter, s'élever (dans
les airs); (of prices) monter (en flèche). **'soaring 1.** a
(a) qui monte dans les airs (b) **s. flight,** vol plané (c)
(ambition) sans bornes **2.** n (a) essor m (b) hausse f
(des prix) (c) vol plané (d'un oiseau).

sob [sɔb] **1.** n sanglot m; F: **s. story,** histoire à faire
pleurer; F: **s. stuff,** littérature sentimentale; F: mélo m
2. (a) vi (sobbed) sangloter (b) vtr dire (qch) en
sanglotant.

sober ['soubər] **1.** a (a) sobre, modéré, tempéré (b)
calme, posé; **in s. earnest,** bien sérieusement (c) **s.
truth,** simple vérité (d) (couleur) sobre, peu voyante;
(vêtement) discret, simple (e) (of pers) sobre; qui n'a

pas trop bu; **he's never s.,** il est toujours ivre; **to sleep
oneself s.,** cuver son vin. **II.** vi (a) **to s. up,** se dégriser,
se dessoûler (b) **to s. down,** s'assagir. **'sobering** a **s.
thought,** réflexion sérieuse. **'soberly** adv (a) sobrement, modérément (b) avec calme; tranquillement.
'sober-'minded a (of pers) sérieux; pondéré.
'soberness n (a) sobriété f, tempérance f (b) calme
m, tranquillité f, modération f. **sobriety** [-'braɪətɪ]
n sobriété f, tempérance f.

soccer ['sɔkər] n F: football m.

sociable ['souʃəbl] a sociable. **socia'bility** n sociabilité f. **'sociably** adv sociablement, amicalement.

social ['souʃəl] a (a) social; **s. problems,** problèmes
sociaux; **s. sciences,** sciences humaines; **s. security,**
sécurité sociale; **s. services,** services sociaux; **s. worker,** assistant(e) social(e); **s. system,** société f (b) **s.
ladder,** l'échelle sociale; **s. climber,** (i) arriviste mf (ii)
parvenu(e); **to have a busy s. life,** sortir beaucoup; **s.
events,** mondanités f; **s. gathering,** (i) soirée f (ii)
réception f; **s. evening,** n **s.,** réunion f; soirée intime.
'socialite n F: membre m de la haute société.
'socialize 1. vtr Pol: socialiser **2.** vi **he won't s.,** il ne
sort jamais; il n'accepte jamais une invitation. **'socially** adv socialement; **to know s.o. s.,** avoir
des rapports sociaux avec qn.

socialism ['souʃəlɪzm] n socialisme m. **'socialist** a
& n socialiste (mf). **socia'listic** a socialiste.

society [sə'saɪətɪ] n (pl **-societies**) société f; association f; **consumer s.,** société de consommation; **charitable s.,** œuvre f de bienfaisance; **learned s.,** société
savante.

sociology [sousɪ'ɔlədʒɪ] n sociologie f.
soci'ologist n sociologue mf.

sock[1] [sɔk] n **1.** chaussette f; **ankle socks,** socquettes f;
F: **pull your socks up!** tu peux faire mieux que ça! **2.**
semelle intérieure (d'une chaussure).

sock[2] n P: coup m; **to give s.o. a s. on the jaw,** casser la
gueule à qn.

socket ['sɔkɪt] n El: (for plug) prise f de courant; (for
lightbulb) douille f; alvéole m or f (de dent); orbite f
(de l'œil); cavité f articulaire (d'un os).

soda ['soudə] n (a) Ch: soude f; **caustic s.,** soude
caustique; **baking s.,** bicarbonate m de soude; **washing
s.,** cristaux mpl de soude (b) **s. (water),** eau f de seltz;
soda m; **s. fountain,** bar m pour glaces et
rafraîchissements.

sodden ['sɔdn] a (of field, lawn) (dé)trempé.

sodium ['soudɪəm] n Ch: sodium m.

sofa ['soufə] n sofa m; divan m; canapé m; **s. bed,**
divan-lit m.

soft [sɔft] a **1.** (a) (fromage, matelas) mou; (crayon,
roche) tendre; (cuir) souple; Com: **s. fruit,** fruits
rouges; **s. water,** eau douce, non calcaire; **s. drink,**
boisson sans alcool; **s. drugs,** drogues douces; **s.
furnishings,** tissus d'ameublement; Anat: **s. palate,**
voile m du palais; Fin: **s. currency,** devise faible; **s.
landing,** atterrissage en douceur (b) **s. to the touch,**
doux au toucher **2.** (a) doux; **s. voice,** voix douce; F: **s.
job, option,** petit boulot pépère; planque f (b) **s. heart,**
cœur tendre; **you mustn't be so s. with them,** il faut les
traiter plus sévèrement; **to become s.,** s'amollir; **to
have a s. spot (for s.o.),** avoir un faible pour qn **3.** a (of
pers) **s. (in the head),** faible d'esprit; niais. **'soft-
back, 'softcover** n NAm: (Br = **paperback**) livre

m de poche. **'softball** n NAm: Sp: genre m de baseball (joué avec une balle plus grande et plus molle). **'soft-'boiled** a Cu: (œuf) mollet, à la coque. **soften** ['sɔfn] 1. vtr (a) amollir, ramollir; assouplir (le cuir) (b) adoucir (la voix) (c) attendrir, émouvoir (qn) 2. vi (a) s'amollir, se ramollir (b) s'attendrir. **softener** ['sɔfnər] n water s., adoucisseur m d'eau; fabric s., adoucissant m. **softening** ['sɔfniŋ] n (a) amollissement m (du beurre) (b) attendrissement m (de qn) (c) assouplissement m (du cuir) (d) adoucissement m (du caractère). **'soft-'hearted** a au cœur tendre. **'softie, 'softy** n (pl -ies) F: sentimental(e); gros bébé. **'softly** adv (a) doucement; (marcher) sans bruit; s. spoken, à voix douce (b) tendrement (c) mollement. **'softness** n douceur f (de la peau, d'un climat); souplesse (du cuir, de caractère); flou m (des contours); mollesse f (d'une substance); manque de sévérité (d'une personne envers une autre). **'soft-'pedal** (soft-pedalled) 1. vi Mus: appuyer sur la pédale douce 2. vtr & i F: y aller doucement. **soft-'spoken** a (of pers) à voix douce. **'software** n Cmptr: logiciel m, software m. **'softwood** n bois m tendre.

soggy ['sɔgi] a (-ier, -iest) 1. (dé)trempé; saturé d'eau 2. (of bread) pâteux; lourd.

soil [sɔil] 1. n sol m, terrain m, terre f; rich s., terre grasse; light s., terre meuble 2. vtr souiller, salir. **soiled** a souillé, sali; s. linen, linge sale; shop s., (article) défraîchi, abîmé (en magasin); qui a fait l'étalage.

solar ['soulər] a (système) solaire; Anat: (plexus) solaire.

sold [sould] see sell.

solder ['souldər, NAm: sɔdər] 1. n soudure f; soft s., soudure tendre; hard s., brasure f 2. vtr souder, ressouder; soldering iron, fer m à souder.

soldier ['souldʒər] 1. n soldat m; three soldiers and two civilians, trois militaires et et deux civils; private s., simple soldat; old s., vétéran m 2. vi F: to s. on, persévérer. **'soldierly** a (allure) militaire, de militaire; martial.

sole[1] [soul] 1. n plante f (du pied); semelle f (de chaussure) 2. vtr ressemeler (des chaussures). **'soling** n ressemelage m.

sole[2] n Ich: sole f; lemon s., limande-sole f.

sole[3] a seul, unique; s. agent, agent exclusif. **'solely** adv uniquement; seulement; dans le seul but (de).

solemn ['sɔləm] a (a) solennel; s. fact, réalité sérieuse; s. duty, devoir sacré; s. ceremony, solennité f (b) (of pers) grave, sérieux; to keep a s. face, composer son visage. **solemnity** [-'lemniti] n (pl -ies) solennité f; gravité f (de maintien). **solemni'zation** [-nai-] n célébration f (d'un mariage, d'une fête religieuse). **'solemnize** vtr célébrer (un mariage, une fête religieuse). **'solemnly** adv (a) solennellement (b) gravement, sérieusement.

sol-fa ['sɔlfa:] n Mus: solfège m.

solicit [sə'lisit] 1. vtr solliciter (une faveur); to s. s.o. for sth, solliciter qch de qn 2. vtr & i (of prostitute) racoler. **solici'tation** n sollicitation f, demande f.

solicitor [sə'lisitər] n Jur: = avocat m; occ = notaire m.

solicitous [sə'lisitəs] a soucieux, désireux (of sth, de qch); s. about sth, préoccupé de qch; to be s. for s.o.'s comfort, se soucier du confort de qn. **so'licitously** adv avec sollicitude. **so'licitude** n sollicitude f, souci m, préoccupation f.

solid ['sɔlid] 1. a (a) solide; s. food, aliment solide; (of fluid) to become s., se solidifier; steps cut in the s. rock, escalier taillé dans la pierre vive (b) (or, argent) massif; (pneu) plein; s. mahogany table, table en acajou massif; s. measures, mesures de volume; to sleep for nine s. hours, dormir neuf heures d'affilée; three days' s. rain, trois jours de pluie continue; s. vote, vote unanime (c) en une seule pièce 2. adv pond frozen s., étang complètement gelé 3. n solide m. **soli'darity** n solidarité f. **so'lidify** v (solidified) 1. vtr solidifier 2. vi se solidifier; se figer. **so'lidity** n solidité f. **'solidly** adv solidement; fermement; (travailler) sans interruption, sans s'arrêter; (voter) à l'unanimité. **'solid-'state** a (appareil) transistorisé.

soliloquy [sə'liləkwi] n (pl soliloquies) monologue m; soliloque m.

solitary ['sɔlitri] a (a) solitaire; seul; isolé; not a s. one, pas un seul; s. confinement, régime m cellulaire (b) (lieu) solitaire, retiré. **'solitude** n solitude f, isolement m.

solo ['soulou] n Mus: solo m; to play s., jouer en solo; violin s., solo de violon; s. violin, violon solo; Cards: s. whist, whist m de Gand; Av: to make a s. flight, voler seul. **'soloist** n Mus: soliste mf.

solstice ['sɔlstis] n Astr: solstice m.

soluble ['sɔljubl] a 1. (sel) soluble 2. (problème) (ré)soluble. **solu'bility** n solubilité f (d'un sel); (ré)solution f (d'un problème).

solution [sə'lu:ʃn] n solution f.

solve [sɔlv] vtr résoudre (un problème); to s. a riddle, résoudre une énigme; to s. an equation, résoudre une équation. **'solvency** n Com: etc: solvabilité f (d'une entreprise). **'solvent** 1. a Com: solvable 2. a & n dissolvant (m); Ch: solvant m.

Somalia [sə'mɑ:liə] Prn Geog: la (République démocratique de) Somalie.

sombre, NAm: **somber** ['sɔmbər] a sombre, morne. **'sombrely,** NAm: **'somberly** adv sombrement.

some [sʌm] a 1. (a) quelque, quelconque; some books are expensive, il y a des livres qui sont chers; some people say, certains disent (que); he'll arrive s. day, il arrivera un de ces jours; I'll see you s. day this week, je vous verrai dans le courant de la semaine; s. other solution will have to be found, il faudra trouver quelque autre solution; s. way or another, d'une manière ou d'une autre; to make s. sort of reply, répondre d'une façon quelconque; s. book or other, un livre quelconque; give it to s. lawyer or other, remettez-le à n'importe quel notaire; ask s. experienced person, demandez l'avis d'une personne d'expérience (b) (partitive) de; to drink s. water, boire de l'eau; to eat s. fruit, manger des fruits (c) quelque; s. distance away, à quelque distance; after s. time, après un, au bout d'un, certain temps; s. days ago, il y a quelques jours; it takes s. time, cela prend pas mal de temps; at s. length, assez longuement; for s. time, (i) pendant quelque temps (ii) depuis quelque temps (b) there are s. others, il y en a d'autres (d) F: (intensive) (that was) s. storm! quelle tempête! it was s. dinner, c'était un dîner superbe; she's s. girl! c'est une fille formidable! **he's s. doctor,** (i) c'est un excellent médecin (ii) c'est un médecin (plutôt) quelconque 2. *pron* (a) (*pers*) certains *mpl*; **s. agree with us, and s. disagree,** les uns sont de notre avis, d'autres ne le sont pas; **s. of my friends,** certains de mes amis (b) **I have s.,** j'en ai; **take s.!** prenez-en! **if you have s.,** si vous en avez; **s. of them,** quelques-uns d'entre eux. 3. *adv* (a) environ, quelque *inv*; **s. twenty pounds,** une vingtaine de livres (b) **I waited s. few minutes,** j'ai attendu quelques minutes.

somebody, someone ['sʌmbədi, 'sʌmwʌn] *n* or *pron* (a) quelqu'un; **somebody's, someone's, knocking,** on frappe; **s. told me so,** quelqu'un, on, me l'a dit; **s. is missing,** il manque quelqu'un; **s. (or other) told him,** je ne sais qui lui a dit; **s. else,** quelqu'un d'autre; **Mr S.,** Monsieur Chose, Machin (b) **he's (a) somebody,** c'est un personnage; **he thinks he's somebody,** il se croit quelqu'un.

somehow ['sʌmhau] *adv* 1. de façon ou d'autre, d'une manière ou d'une autre; **we shall manage it s.,** nous y parviendrons tant bien que mal 2. **I never liked him s.,** je ne sais pourquoi, mais il ne m'a jamais été sympathique; **s. it's different,** il y a pourtant une différence.

someone ['sʌmwʌn] *see* **somebody.**

someplace ['sʌmpleis] *adv* NAm: (Br = **somewhere**) quelque part; **s. else,** ailleurs.

somersault ['sʌməsɔːlt] *n & vi* **to turn a s.,** to s., (*of pers*) faire la culbute; (*of car*) capoter; *Gym:* faire un saut périlleux.

something ['sʌmθiŋ] I. *n or pron* 1. quelque chose *m*; **s. has happened,** quelque chose est arrivé; il est arrivé quelque chose; **say s.!** dites quelque chose! **s. or other went wrong,** quelque chose a cloché; **s. to drink,** de quoi boire; **can I get you s.?** que puis-je vous offrir (à boire, à manger)? **let's have s. to eat,** mangeons quelque chose; **to ask for s. to drink,** demander à boire; **s. tells me he'll come,** quelque chose me dit qu'il viendra; **s. of the kind,** quelque chose du genre; **s. to live for,** une raison de vivre; **I have s. else to do,** j'ai autre chose à faire; *F:* **the four s. train,** le train de quatre heures et quelque 2. (a) **perhaps we shall see s. of you now,** peut-être nous verrons-nous plus (souvent) maintenant (b) **there's s. in what you say,** il y a un fond de vérité dans ce que vous dites; **there's s. in him,** il a du fond; **well, that's s.!** bon, c'est toujours quelque chose! **that was quite s.!** c'était vraiment quelque chose! II. *adv* quelque peu, tant soit peu; **that's s. like a cigar!** voilà un vrai cigare!

sometime ['sʌmtaim] 1. *adv* (*often written in two words*) **s. (or other),** tôt ou tard; **s. last year,** au cours de l'année dernière; **s. soon,** bientôt, un de ces jours; **I'll do it s.,** je le ferai un de ces jours; *F:* **see you s.!** à bientôt 2. *a* **s. chairman of the company,** ancien président de la société.

sometimes ['sʌmtaimz] *adv* quelquefois, parfois; **s. one, s. the other,** tantôt l'un, tantôt l'autre.

somewhat ['sʌm(h)wɔt] 1. *adv* quelque peu; un peu; tant soit peu; **to be s. surprised,** être passablement étonné. 2. *n* **he was s. of a coward,** il était quelque peu poltron; **it was s. of a relief,** c'était en quelque sorte un soulagement.

somewhere ['sʌm(h)weər] *adv* quelque part; **s. else,** ailleurs; autre part; **s. or other,** je ne sais où; **s. in the**

world, de par le monde; **he's s. about fifty,** il a la cinquantaine; **he lives s. near Oxford,** il habite dans les environs d'Oxford.

somnambulism [sɔm'næmbjulizm] *n* somnambulisme *m*. **som'nambulist** *n* somnambule *mf*.

somnolence ['sɔmnələns] *n* somnolence *f*. **'somnolent** *a* somnolent.

son [sʌn] *n* fils *m*. **'son-in-law** *n* (*pl* sons-in-law) gendre *m*, beau-fils *m*.

sonar ['souna:r] *n* sonar *m*.

sonata [sə'na:tə] *n Mus:* sonate *f*.

song [sɔŋ] *n* 1. chant *m*; **to burst into s.,** se mettre tout à coup à chanter; **s. thrush,** grive musicienne 2. chanson *f*; **marching s.,** chanson de route; *F:* **to buy sth for a s.,** acheter qch pour une bouchée de pain; **it went for a s.,** cela s'est vendu pour rien; *F:* **to make a s. (and dance) about sth,** faire des histoires *f* à propos de qch. **'songbird** *n* oiseau chanteur. **'songbook** *n* recueil *m* de chansons; chansonnier *m*. **'songwriter** *n* compositeur, -trice, de chansons.

sonic ['sɔnik] *a* sonique; *Nau:* **s. depth-finder,** sondeur acoustique; *Av:* **s. barrier,** mur du son; **s. boom,** bang *m*.

sonnet ['sɔnit] *n* sonnet *m*.

sonorous ['sɔnərəs] *a* sonore. **so'nority** *n* (*pl* -ies) sonorité *f*. **'sonorously** *adv* d'un ton sonore.

soon [su:n] *adv* 1. (a) bientôt, tôt; **s. after,** bientôt après; tôt après; **s. after four,** un peu après quatre heures; **he'll be here very s.,** il sera ici sous peu; **see you again s.!** à bientôt! **how s. can you be ready?** en combien de temps serez-vous prêt? **too s.,** trop tôt; avant l'heure; **all too s.,** trop vite; **he escaped none too s.,** il s'est échappé juste à temps (b) **as s. as,** aussitôt que, dès que; **as s. as I arrived in London,** dès mon arrivée à Londres; **as s. as he saw them,** dès qu'il les a vus; **as s. as possible,** le plus tôt possible (c) **I'd just as s. stay,** j'aime autant rester 2. (a) **the sooner the better,** le plus tôt sera le mieux; **sooner or later,** tôt ou tard; **no sooner said than done,** aussitôt dit, aussitôt fait; **no sooner had he finished than he was arrested,** à peine avait-il fini qu'il fut arrêté (b) **I'd sooner die,** j'aimerais mieux mourir; plutôt mourir! **I'd sooner come,** j'aimerais mieux venir.

soot [sut] *n* suie *f*. **'sooty** *a* (-ier, -iest) couvert de suie; noir de suie.

soothe [su:ð] *vtr* calmer, apaiser (la douleur); tranquilliser (l'esprit de qn). **'soothing** *a* calmant, apaisant. **'soothingly** *adv* avec douceur; (d'un ton) calmant.

sop [sɔp] *vtr* (sopped [sɔpt]) **to s. up a liquid,** éponger un liquide. **'sopping** *a* **to be s. (wet),** être (tout) trempé. **'soppy** *a* (-ier, -iest) *F:* (*of pers*) mou; avachi; (*of story*) sentimental; larmoyant.

sophistication [səfisti'keiʃn] *n* sophistication *f*; savoir-vivre *m inv*; raffinement *m*; recherche *f*; perfectionnement *m*. **so'phisticated** *a* (*of pers*) aux goûts raffinés; sophistiqué; (*of style*) recherché; (*of machinery*) perfectionné, sophistiqué.

sophomore ['sɔfəmɔ:r] *n NAm: Sch:* étudiant, -ante, de seconde année.

soporific [sɔpə'rifik] *a & n* soporifique (*m*); somnifère (*m*).

soprano [sə'pra:nou] *n* (*pl* sopranos) *Mus:* soprano *mf*; **s. voice,** voix *f* de soprano.

sorbet ['sɔːbei] n Cu: sorbet m.
sorcery ['sɔːsəri] n sorcellerie f. **'sorcerer, 'sor-ceress** n sorcier, -ière; magicien, -ienne.
sordid ['sɔːdid] a (a) sordide; sale, crasseux (b) vil, bas, ignoble. **'sordidness** n sordidité f; saleté f; crasse f.
sore [sɔːr] 1. a (a) douloureux; endolori; **s. to the touch,** douloureux au toucher; **that's s.!** ça me fait mal! **to be s. all over,** avoir mal partout (b) enflammé, irrité; **s. throat,** mal m de gorge; **he's got a s. throat,** il a mal à la gorge; **a s. point,** un point délicat; **that's his s. spot,** c'est son endroit sensible; Lit: **to be in s. need of sth,** avoir grandement besoin de qch (c) NAm: F: (Br = cross) fâché; **to get s.,** se fâcher 2. n plaie f; blessure f; écorchure f; ulcère m; **to (re)open an old s.,** raviver une douleur ancienne. **'sorely** adv grave-ment; **s. wounded,** grièvement blessé; **s. tried,** cruelle-ment éprouvé. **'soreness** n (a) endolorissement m (b) NAm: F: (Br = anger) (sentiment m de) rancune f.
sorrel[1] ['sɔrəl] n Bot: oseille f; **s. soup,** soupe f à l'oseille.
sorrel[2] a & n (cheval) alezan m.
sorrow ['sɔrou] n peine f, chagrin m, tristesse f; **to my s.,** à mon regret; **this was a great s. to me,** j'en ai eu beaucoup de peine. **'sorrowful** a affligé, chagriné, triste. **'sorrowfully** adv tristement.
sorry ['sɔri] a (-ier, -iest) fâché, désolé, peiné; **(I'm) s.!** pardon! **I'm so s. about it,** j'en suis désolé; **I'm extremely s.,** je regrette infiniment; **I'm so s. to hear that your father has died,** je suis désolé d'apprendre le décès de votre père; **he's s. he did it,** il regrette de l'avoir fait; **I'm s. to say (that),** je regrette d'avoir à vous dire (que); **I'm s. to keep you waiting,** je m'excuse de vous faire attendre; **I'm s. for him,** je le plains; **to be, feel, s. for oneself,** s'apitoyer sur son (propre) sort.
sort [sɔːt] 1. n sorte f, genre m, espèce f; **all sorts of people,** des gens de toutes sortes; **a strange s. of fellow,** un type bizarre; **they're not our s.,** ce ne sont pas des gens comme nous; **that's the s. of man he is,** il est comme ça; **he looks a good s.,** il a l'air bon garçon; **she's a (real) good s.,** c'est une brave fille; **something of that s.,** quelque chose de ce genre, dans ce genre-là; **nothing of the s.!** (i) rien de la sorte! (ii) pas du tout! **I shall do nothing of the s.,** je n'en ferai rien; **what s. of man is he?** comment est-il? **what s. of tree is it?** quelle sorte d'arbre est-ce? **what s. of day was it?** (i) quel temps faisait-il? (ii) avez-vous passé une journée agréable? **I have a s. of idea (that),** j'ai comme une idée, j'ai une sorte d'idée (que); **the trees formed a s. of arch,** les arbres formaient comme une arche; **it's a s. of table,** c'est une espèce de table; Pej: **we had coffee of a s.,** on nous a donné du soi-disant café (c) **to be out of sorts,** être indisposé 2. vtr trier, assortir; classer (des papiers); Post: **to s. the letters,** trier les lettres; **to s. out the bad ones,** trier les mauvais. **'sorter** n (a) (pers) trieur, -euse; classeur, -euse (b) (machine) trieuse f. **'sorting** n triage m, tri m; classement m; Post: **s. office, s. centre,** centre de tri. **sort out** vtr régler, arranger (une affaire); venir à bout (d'une difficulté); **things will s. themselves out,** les choses vont s'arranger d'elles-mêmes.
sortie ['sɔːtiː] n Mil: Av: sortie f, mission f.
soufflé ['suːflei] n Cu: soufflé m; **cheese s.,** soufflé au fromage; **s. dish,** moule à soufflé.
sought [sɔːt] see **seek**.

soul [soul] n âme f; **with all my s.,** de tout mon cœur, de toute mon âme; **he's the s. of honour,** il est l'honneur personnifié, la probité même; **he's the life and s. of the party,** c'est le boute-en-train de la soirée; **he's the s. of the enterprise,** c'est lui qui mène, fait marcher, l'affaire; **All Souls' Day,** la fête des Morts; **ship lost with all souls,** navire perdu corps et biens; **without meeting a living s.,** sans rencontrer âme qui vive; **s. (music),** soul m; **he's a good s.,** c'est une bonne personne; **poor s.!** le, la, pauvre! **'soul-destroying** a (emploi) abrutissant. **'soulful** a (a) plein d'âme; **s. eyes,** yeux expressifs (b) sentimental. **'soulfully** adv (chanter) (i) avec expression (ii) sentimentalement. **'soulless** a sans âme; terre à terre; (travail) abrutissant, dégradant. **'soul-searching** n examen m de conscience; **after a lot of s.-s.,** après mûre réflexion.
sound[1] [saund] I. n (a) son m, bruit m; **without a s.,** sans bruit; **there was not a s. to be heard,** on n'entendait pas le moindre bruit; **the s. of a dog barking,** le bruit d'un chien qui aboie; **to turn up, to turn down, the s.,** augmenter, diminuer, le volume (b) Av: **s. barrier,** mur du son; **s. wave,** onde sonore; **s. engineer,** ingénieur du son (c) **(the science of) s.,** l'acoustique f (d) **to catch the s. of sth,** entendre qch à demi; **I don't like the s. of it,** cela ne me dit rien qui vaille; **he's angry by the s. of it,** il est furieux à ce qu'il paraît. II. v 1. vi (a) sonner; résonner; retentir; **to s. hollow,** sonner creux (b) **that sounds well in a speech,** cela fait bon effet dans un discours; **it sounded a long way off,** on aurait dit que cela venait de loin; **it sounds like Mozart,** on dirait du Mozart 2. vtr (a) sonner (la cloche, le tocsin); **to s. the trumpet,** sonner de la trompette; Aut: **to s. the horn,** klaxonner (b) prononcer (une lettre) (c) Med: ausculter (un malade). **'sounding**[1] n résonnement m, retentissement m (du tambour); Med: auscultation f. **'soundless** a silencieux; muet. **'soundlessly** adv sans bruit; silencieusement. **'sound 'off** vi F: déblatérer (about sth, contre qch). **'soundproof** 1. a isolant; in-sonore; (of room) insonorisé 2. vtr insonoriser. **'soundproofing** n insonorisation f. **'sound-track** n bande f sonore.
sound[2] Nau: vtr sonder; vi prendre le fond. **'sound-ing**[2] n Nau: sondage m; **to take soundings,** sonder, prendre le fond; **s. balloon,** ballon-sonde m. **'sound out** vtr sonder.
sound[3] n détroit m; goulet m.
sound[4] 1. a (a) sain; **of s. mind,** sain d'esprit; (of pers) **to be s. in wind and limb** = avoir bon pied ton œil; **to be as s. as a bell,** être en parfaite santé (b) (of structure) solide; en bon état; pas endommagé; **s. timber,** bois sans tare; **s. fruit,** fruits sains (c) **s. financial position,** situation financière solide; **s. statesman,** homme d'état au jugement sain (d) (argument) valide; (raisonnement) juste; **a s. piece of advice,** un bon conseil; **it isn't s. finance,** ce n'est pas de la finance sérieuse (e) (sommeil) profond; **I'm a s. sleeper,** je dors bien; **to give s.o. a s. thrashing,** donner une bonne correction à qn 2. adv **s. asleep,** profondément endormi. **'soundly** adv 1. sainement; judicieuse-ment 2. **to sleep s.,** dormir profondément; dormir à poings fermés; **to thrash s.o. s.,** donner une bonne correction à qn. **'soundness** n (a) état sain

(d'esprit); bon état (des marchandises) (*b*) solvabilité *f*; solidité *f* (d'une maison de commerce) (*c*) solidité (d'un argument); justesse *f* (d'un jugement).

soup [su:p] *n* soupe *f*, potage *m*; **thick s.**, crème *f*, purée *f*; **cream s.**, velouté *m*; **clear s.**, consommé *m*; **onion s.**, soupe à l'oignon; *F:* **to be in the s.**, être dans le pétrin; **s. ladle**, louche *f*; **s. spoon**, cuillère à soupe; **s. plate**, assiette creuse; **s. tureen**, soupière *f*. **'soup 'up** *vtr F:* augmenter (la puissance de qch); *Aut:* **souped-up engine**, moteur gonflé; **souped-up publicity campaign**, publicité exagérée, mensongère.

sour [sauər] *a* (*a*) (fruit, crème) aigre; (pomme) acide; (vin) suret; **to turn s.**, tourner à l'aigre; **to turn sth s.**, (faire) aigrir qch; **to smell s.**, sentir l'aigre; **the plan went s.**, le projet a mal tourné (*b*) (*of pers*) revêche, aigre. **'sourly** *adv* avec aigreur. **'sourness** *n* (*a*) aigreur *f*, acidité *f* (d'un fruit) (*b*) (*of pers*) aigreur; humeur *f* revêche.

source [sɔ:s] *n* source *f*; **light s.**, source lumineuse; **the Rhone has its s. in the Alps**, le Rhône prend sa source dans les Alpes; **I have it from a good s.**, je le tiens de bonne source; **idleness is the s. of all evil**, l'oisiveté est (la) mère de tous les vices; **to trace a tradition back to its s.**, remonter aux sources, à l'origine, d'une tradition.

souse [saus] *vtr* (*a*) *Cu:* faire mariner (un aliment) (*b*) plonger, immerger (**in**, dans); tremper, noyer (qch, qn) (**with water**, d'eau).

south [sauθ] **1.** *n* sud *m*; **house facing the s.**, maison exposée au sud; **to the s. (of)**, au sud (de); **the S. of France**, le Midi (de la France) **2.** *adv* au sud; **to travel s.**, voyager vers le sud; (*of wind*) **to blow s.**, souffler du sud **3.** *a* sud *inv*; (vent) du sud; (pays) méridional; **the s. side**, le côté sud; **the s. coast**, la côté sud; **S. Africa**, Afrique du Sud; **S. American**, sud-américain. **'southbound** *a* (train) allant vers le sud. **south-'east 1.** *n* sud-est *m* **2.** *adv* vers le sud-est **3.** *a* du sud-est. **south-'easterly, south-'eastern** *a* (du) sud-est. **southerly** ['sʌð-] *a* (vent) du sud; (direction) vers le sud; **s. aspect**, exposition *f* au midi. **southern** ['sʌð-] *a* (du) sud; méridional; **s. lights**, aurore australe; **the S. Cross**, la Croix du Sud. **southerner** ['sʌð-] *n* habitant, -ante, du sud; méridional, -ale; *US: Hist:* sudiste *mf*. **'southernmost** *a* le plus au sud. **'southward(s)** *adv* vers le sud. **south-'west 1.** *n* sud-ouest *m* **2.** *aav* vers le sud-ouest **3.** *a* du sud-ouest. **south-'westerly, south-'western** *a* (du) sud-ouest.

souvenir [su:və'ni(:)ər] *n* souvenir *m*.

sou'wester [sau'westər] *n Cl:* chapeau *m* imperméable; suroît *m*.

sovereign ['sɔvrin] **1.** *n* (*a*) souverain, -aine (*b*) souverain *m* (ancienne pièce en or, valeur £1) **2.** *a* souverain, suprême; (droits) de souveraineté. **'sovereignty** *n* souveraineté *f*.

soviet ['souviet, 'sɔv-] **1.** *n* soviet *m* **2.** *a* soviétique; **S. Union**, Union *f* soviétique; **Union of S. Socialist Republics (USSR)**, Union des Républiques Socialistes Soviétiques (URSS).

sow¹ [sou] *vtr* (sowed; sown) semer; **to s. land with wheat**, ensemencer une terre en blé; **to s. discord**, semer la discorde. **'sower** *n* (*pers*) semeur, -euse; (*machine*) semoir *m*. **'sowing** *n* semailles *fpl*, semis *m*; **s. machine**, semoir.

sow² [sau] *n* truie *f*.

soy(a) ['sɔi(ə)] *n* soja *m*; **s. bean**, soja, soya *m*; **s. sauce**, sauce soja.

spa [spɑ:] *n* station thermale.

space [speis] **1.** *n* (*a*) espace *m*, intervalle *m* (de temps) (*b*) l'espace; **he sat staring into s.**, il était assis le regard perdu dans le vide; **s. flight**, voyage spatial; **s. station**, station spatiale; **s. suit**, scaphandre d'astronaute; **s. travel**, l'astronautique *f*; **s. race**, course interplanétaire (*c*) espace; place *f*; **in a confined s.**, dans un espace restreint; **to take up a lot of s.**, occuper beaucoup de place (*d*) espace libre; espacement *m*, intervalle; (*between lines of writing*) interligne *f*; (*on form*) (blank) **s.**, blanc *m*; **s. between two things**, écartement *m* de deux choses; **sign in the s. indicated**, signez dans la case indiquée **2.** *vtr* **to s. (out)**, espacer; échelonner (des paiements). **'spacecraft** *n* vaisseau spatial. **'spaceman** *n* (*pl* -men) (*a*) habitant *m* de l'espace (*b*) astronaute *m*, cosmonaute *m*. **'space-saving** *a* qui permet de gagner de la place; compact. **'spaceship** *n* vaisseau spatial. **'spacing** *n* espacement *m*; écartement; échelonnement *m*; *Typew:* **in single, double, s.**, à interligne simple, double. **'spacious** *a* vaste, spacieux; (*of garment*) ample. **'spaciousness** *n* vaste étendue *f*; proportions spacieuses (d'une salle).

spade¹ [speid] *n Tls:* bêche *f*; (*child's*) pelle *f*; *F:* **to call a s. a s.**, appeler les choses par leur nom; appeler un chat un chat. **'spadeful** *n* pleine bêche; pelletée *f*. **'spadework** *n* travaux *mpl* préliminaires (en vue d'une enquête).

spade² *n Cards:* pique *m*.

spaghetti [spə'geti] *n Cu:* spaghetti *mpl*.

Spain [spein] *Prn Geog:* Espagne *f*.

span [spæn] **1.** *n* (*a*) (*of bird, aircraft*) envergure *f* (*b*) portée *f* (entre deux appuis); largeur *f* (d'une voûte, d'une arche); écartement *m* (de deux piliers); travée *f* (d'un pont) (*c*) (court) espace de temps; **life s.**, durée *f*, espérance *f*, de vie **2.** *vtr* (spanned) (*of bridge*) franchir, enjamber (un ravin); (*in time*) embrasser (un siècle).

Spaniard ['spænjəd] *n* Espagnol, -ole.

spaniel ['spænjəl] *n* épagneul *m*.

Spanish ['spæniʃ] **1.** *a* espagnol; (oignon) d'Espagne **2.** *n* (*a*) *npl* the S., les Espagnols *m* (*b*) *n Ling:* espagnol *m*. **'Spanish-A'merican** *a* hispano-américain.

spank [spæŋk] *vtr* fesser (un enfant). **'spanking** *n* fessée *f*.

spanner ['spænər] *n* clef *f* (à écrous); **adjustable s.**, clef anglaise, clef à molette; **box s.**, clef en douille; *F:* **to throw a s. in the works**, mettre des bâtons dans les roues.

spar¹ [spɑ:r] *n Nau:* espar *m*.

spar² *vi* (sparred) **to s. with s.o.**, (*of boxer*) s'entraîner, *Fig:* (*of pers*) argumenter, avec qn; **sparring partner**, *Box:* sparring-partner *m*; *Fig:* adversaire *m*.

spare [speər] **1.** *a* de trop, de reste; disponible; **s. time**, moments perdus; loisirs *mpl*; **in my s. time**, quand j'ai du temps libre; **s. capital**, fonds disponibles; **s. room**, chambre d'ami(s); *Aut:* **s. parts**, *npl* spares, pièces de rechange, pièces détachées; **s. engine**, moteur de remplacement; **s. tyre**, *n* **s.**, pneu de rechange; **s. wheel**, roue de secours **2.** *vtr* (*a*) épargner, ménager; **to s. no expense**, ne pas regarder à la dépense; **to s. no pains**, ne pas ménager, marchander, sa peine (*b*) se passer de (qch); **can you s. it?** pouvez-vous vous en passer? **we can s. him,** nous n'avons pas besoin de lui; **to have nothing to s.,** n'avoir que le strict nécessaire; **to have enough and to s.,** avoir plus qu'il n'en faut (de qch); **I can't s. the time,** je n'ai pas le temps; **I have a minute to s.,** je peux disposer d'un instant; **no time to s.,** pas de temps libre; **can you s. me a few moments?** pouvez-vous m'accorder quelques moments? (c) faire grâce à (qn); **to s. s.o.'s life,** épargner la vie à qn; **to s. s.o.'s feelings,** ménager qn; **to s. s.o. the trouble of doing sth,** éviter à qn la peine de faire qch. **spare' rib** n Cu: côte découverte (de porc). **'sparing** a frugal; **to be s. with the butter,** ménager le beurre; **s. of praise,** avare de louanges. **'sparingly** adv frugalement; **to use sth s.,** ménager qch.

spark [spɑːk] 1. n étincelle f; (from fire) flammèche f; Fig: lueur f (d'esprit); ICE: **s. plug,** bougie f 2. vi émettre des étincelles. **'sparking** n El: émission f, (accidental) jaillissement m, d'étincelles; **s. plug,** bougie. **'spark 'off** vtr provoquer (une idée); déclencher (une révolution).

sparkle ['spɑːkl] 1. n (a) étincelle f; brève lueur (b) étincellement m; éclat m (des yeux); feux mpl (d'un diamant) 2. vi étinceler, scintiller; (of wine) pétiller; (of eyes) briller. **'sparkling** a étincelant, brillant; (vin) mousseux.

sparrow ['spærou] n Orn: moineau m; **hedge s.,** fauvette f d'hiver. **'sparrowhawk** n Orn: épervier m.

sparse [spɑːs] a clairsemé; épars. **'sparsely** adv peu abondamment; **s. populated,** peu peuplé.

spartan ['spɑːtən] a spartiate; (vie) austère.

spasm ['spæzəm] n accès m (de toux, de jalousie); Med: spasme m; **to work in spasms,** travailler par à-coups mpl. **spas'modic** a irrégulier, intermittent; (travail) fait par à-coups; Med: spasmodique. **spas'modically** adv (travailler) par à-coups.

spastic ['spæstik] Med: 1. a (paralysie) spasmodique 2. n paralysé, -ée, spasmodique; handicapé, -ée, moteur.

spat [spæt] see spit² I.

spate [speit] n crue f; avalanche f (de lettres); **river in s.,** rivière en crue; **to have a s. of work,** être débordé de travail.

spatial ['speiʃəl] a spatial.

spatter ['spætər] vtr **to s. s.o. with mud,** éclabousser qn de boue.

spatula ['spætjulə] n spatule f.

spawn [spɔːn] 1. n frai m, œufs mpl (de poisson); blanc m (de champignon) 2. v (a) vi (of fish) frayer (b) vtr Fig: engendrer, donner naissance à (qch).

spay [spei] vtr Vet: châtrer (une femelle).

speak [spiːk] v (spoke [spouk], spoken) 1. vi (a) parler; **without speaking,** sans rien dire; **to s. to s.o.,** parler à qn; s'adresser à qn, adresser la parole à qn; **I'll s. to him about it,** je lui en toucherai un mot; **I know him to s. to,** je le connais assez pour lui dire bonjour; **speaking for myself,** pour ma part; F: **s. for yourself!** parle pour toi-même! **roughly speaking,** approximativement; **so to s.,** pour ainsi dire; Tp: **who's speaking?** qui est à l'appareil? c'est de la part de qui? **Mr Thomas?—(yes,) speaking,** M. Thomas?—lui-même; **the facts s. for themselves,** ces faits parlent d'eux-mêmes, se passent de commentaires (b) faire un

discours; prendre la parole 2. vtr (a) dire (un mot, sa pensée); **to s. the truth,** dire la vérité; **to s. one's mind,** dire ce qu'on pense (b) parler; **do you s. French?** parlez-vous français? **English is spoken everywhere,** l'anglais se parle partout; PN: **French spoken,** ici on parle français. **'speaker** n (a) parleur, -euse; (in dialogue) interlocuteur, -trice; (in public) orateur m; **to be a fluent s.,** avoir la parole facile (b) Pol: **the S. = le Président** (des Communes) (c) (loudspeaker) haut-parleur m. **'speak 'for** vtr parler, plaider, pour (qn); **that speaks well for your courage,** cela en dit long sur votre courage; **to be spoken for,** être réservé. **'speaking** a & n 1. a (of doll) parlant; **English-s.,** de langue anglaise; anglophone 2. n parler m; parole f; **plain s.,** franchise f, franc-parler m; **not to be on s. terms (with s.o.),** être brouillé (avec qn); **public s.,** l'art m oratoire. **'speak 'of** vtr parler de; **speaking of,** à propos de; **she has no voice to s. of,** elle n'a pour ainsi dire pas de voix; **it's nothing to s. of,** cela ne vaut pas la peine d'en parler; **to s. well of s.o.,** dire du bien de qn; **to be well spoken of,** avoir une bonne réputation. **'speak 'out** vi parler franchement. **'speak 'up** vi parler plus haut; **to s. up for s.o.,** parler en faveur de qn.

spear [spiər] n lance f; (for throwing) javelot m; Fish: harpon m. **'spearhead** 1. n fer m de lance 2. vtr Mil: **to s. the crossing of a river,** forcer le premier le passage d'un fleuve. **'spearmint** n menthe verte.

spec [spek] n F: **on s.,** à tout hasard.

special ['speʃəl] 1. a spécial; particulier; **s. feature,** particularité f; Journ: **s. correspondent,** envoyé spécial; **to make a s. study of sth,** se spécialiser dans qch; Com: **s. price,** prix de faveur; **s. friend,** ami(e) intime; Post: **s. delivery** = envoi par exprès; **I've nothing s. to tell you,** je n'ai rien de particulier à vous dire; Cin: **s. effects,** trucage m 2. a & n s. **(constable),** personne f qui fait fonction d'agent de police 3. n train spécial; édition spéciale (d'un journal); (in restaurant) **today's s.,** plat m du jour. **'specialist** n spécialiste mf; **heart s.,** cardiologue mf. **speciality** [speʃi'æliti] n, NAm: **specialty** ['speʃəlti] n (pl -ies) spécialité f; **that's my s.,** c'est mon fort. **speciali'zation** n spécialisation f. **'specialize** vi se spécialiser (in, dans). **'specially** adv spécialement; particulièrement; surtout.

species ['spiːʃiːz] n (inv in pl) espèce f; **closely related s.,** espèces voisines.

specify ['spesifai] vtr (specified) spécifier, déterminer; préciser; **specified load,** charge prévue; **unless otherwise specified,** sauf indication contraire. **spe'cific** a (a) Tchn: spécifique; Ph: **s. gravity,** poids m spécifique (b) (of statement) précis; (of order) explicite; **s. aim,** but déterminé. **spe'cifically** adv (a) Tchn: spécifiquement (b) précisément. **specifi'cation** n spécification f (des détails); usu pl devis descriptif; caractéristiques fpl (d'une voiture).

specimen ['spesimin] n (a) spécimen m (d'une espèce) (b) exemple m; échantillon m (d'urine); prise f (de sang); F: (of pers) **queer s.,** drôle m de type; **s. page,** page spécimen; Publ: **s. copy,** livre à l'examen.

specious ['spiːʃəs] a spécieux; trompeur; captieux. **'speciousness** n apparence trompeuse.

speck [spek] n petite tache; point m; grain m, atome m (de poussière); **s. on the horizon,** point noir à l'horizon. **'speckled** a tacheté, moucheté; (of plumage) grivelé.

specs [speks] npl F: lunettes fpl.

spectacle ['spektəkl] n spectacle m; (glasses) **spectacles,** F: specs, lunettes fpl; s. **case,** étui à lunettes. **spectacular** [-'tæk] 1. a spectaculaire 2. n Th: superproduction f. **spectator** [-'teit-] n spectateur, -trice; assistant, -ante; **the spectators,** l'assistance f.

spectre, NAm: **specter** ['spektər] n spectre m, fantôme m.

spectrum ['spektrəm] n (pl spectra) Ph: spectre m; Fig: éventail m (de produits); **the colours of the s.,** les couleurs spectrales.

speculate ['spekjuleit] vi (a) to s. **about, on sth,** faire des conjectures sur qch (b) Fin: spéculer (**in,** sur). **specu'lation** n (a) spéculation f, méditation f (**on,** sur); conjecture f (b) Fin: spéculation; entreprise spéculative. **'speculative** a (a) spéculatif, contemplatif; conjectural (b) Fin: spéculatif. **'speculator** n Fin: spéculateur, -trice; StExch: agioteur m.

sped [sped] see **speed 2.**

speech [spiːtʃ] n (a) (faculty of) s., la parole; (**manner of**) s., élocution f; façon f de parler; **to lose the power of s.,** perdre la parole; s. **therapy,** orthophonie f; s. **therapist,** orthophoniste mf; Gram: **parts of s.,** parties du discours; **reported, indirect,** s., discours indirect (b) langue f (d'un peuple); parler m (d'une région) (c) discours; **to make a s.,** faire, prononcer, un discours; Sch: s. **day,** distribution f des prix. **'speechless** a muet; incapable de parler; (with surprise) interdit, interloqué.

speed [spiːd] 1. n (a) vitesse f; rapidité f; **at s.,** à grande vitesse; **at full s., at top s.,** à toute vitesse, à toute allure; **maximum s.,** vitesse maximum, limite; (of car) (vitesse) plafond (m); **to pick up s.,** prendre de la vitesse; s. **limit,** (of engine) vitesse maximale; (of car on a road) limitation de vitesse; F: s. **merchant,** chauffard m; F: s. **cop,** motard m (b) Phot: rapidité (d'une émulsion) (c) Aut: (gear) vitesse; **three-s. gearbox,** boîte à trois vitesses 2. vi (**speeded,** occ **sped**) (a) faire de la vitesse (b) Aut: (break speed limit) faire un excès de vitesse. **'speedboat** n canot m automobile; vedette f. **'speeding** n Aut: excès m de vitesse. **spee'dometer,** F: **'speedo** n indicateur m, compteur m, de vitesse. **'speed 'up 1.** vtr accélérer, activer (le travail) **2.** vi accélérer. **'speedway** n piste f (d'autodrome); s. **(racing),** courses fpl de moto. **'speedy** a (-ier, -iest) rapide; prompt.

speleology [spiːliˈɔlədʒi] n spéléologie f. **spele'ologist** n spéléologue mf.

spell¹ [spel] n (a) incantation f; formule f magique (b) charme m, maléfice m; **to cast a s. over s.o.,** jeter un sort sur qn; ensorceler qn. **'spellbound** a ensorcelé; magnétisé; envoûté; **to hold one's audience s.,** tenir ses auditeurs sous le charme.

spell² vtr & i (**spelled** or **spelt**) (a) épeler; (in writing) orthographier (un mot); **he can't s.,** il ne sait pas l'orthographe; **to s. out sth,** déchiffrer qch péniblement; Fig: **do I have to s. it out for you?** faut-il que je mette les points sur les i? **how is it spelt?** comment cela s'écrit-il? **what do these letters s.?** quel mot forment ces lettres? (b) signifier; **that would s. disaster!** ce serait

le désastre! **'spelling** n orthographe f; s. **mistake,** faute d'orthographe.

spell³ n (a) tour m (de travail); **to do a s. of duty,** faire un tour de service; **to take spells at the pumps,** se relayer aux pompes (b) (courte) période; temps m; **a s. of cold weather,** une période de froid; **during the cold s.,** pendant le coup de froid.

spend [spend] vtr (**spent**) (a) dépenser (**on,** en, pour); **to s. money on s.o.,** faire des dépenses pour qn; **without spending a penny,** sans rien débourser; F: **to s. a penny,** aller faire pipi (b) consacrer (du soin, du temps) (**on,** à) (c) passer, employer (son temps); **to s. Monday working,** passer lundi à travailler. **'spender** n **to be a big s.,** être très dépensier. **'spending** n dépense f; s. **power,** pouvoir d'achat; s. **money,** argent de poche. **'spendthrift** a & n dépensier, -ière. **spent** a épuisé; (of bullet) mort.

sperm [spɔːm] n sperme m; Z: s. **whale,** cachalot m.

sphere ['sfiər] n sphère f; milieu m, domaine m; **limited s.,** cadre restreint; **that doesn't come within my s.,** cela sort de ma compétence; s. **of influence,** sphère, zone f, d'influence; **in the political s.,** sur le plan politique. **'spherical** a sphérique.

sphinx [sfiŋks] n sphinx m.

spice [spais] 1. n épice f; aromate m; piquant m (de la vie); piment m (de l'aventure); **mixed spice(s),** épices mélangées; **to give s. to a story,** pimenter un récit 2. vtr épicer; pimenter (un récit). **'spiciness** n goût épicé; piquant, sel m (d'un récit). **'spicy** a (-ier, -iest) (of food) épicé; (goût) relevé; (of story) piquant; salé, épicé.

spick and span ['spikənˈspæn] adj phr reluisant de propreté; propre comme un sou neuf; (of pers) tiré à quatre épingles.

spider ['spaidər] n araignée f; **spider's web,** toile d'araignée. **'spidery** a s. **handwriting,** pattes fpl de mouche.

spiel [ʃpiːl] n F: boniment m, baratin m.

spigot ['spigət] n fausset m, broche f (de tonneau).

spike [spaik] 1. n pointe f; piquant m (de fil barbelé); Sp: **spikes,** chaussures fpl (de course) à pointes 2. vtr corser (une boisson); Fig: **to s. s.o.'s guns,** contrarier les projets de qn. **'spiky** a hérissé (de pointes).

spill [spil] 1. v (**spilt** or **spilled**) (a) vtr répandre, renverser (du vin, de l'eau); verser (du sang); F: **to s. the beans,** vendre la mèche (b) vi (of liquid) se répandre; s'écouler 2. n **to have a s.,** culbuter; (from bicycle) ramasser une pelle.

spin [spin] 1. v (**spun; spinning**) (a) vtr filer (la laine); lancer (une toupie); **to s. a coin,** jouer à pile ou face; **to s. s.o. round,** faire tourner qn (b) vi (of wheel) tourner; (of aircraft) descendre en vrille; (of compass) s'affoler; (of wheel) patiner (sur place); (of pers) **to s. round,** se retourner vivement; **to s. round and round,** tournoyer; **my head's spinning,** la tête me tourne; **blow that sent him spinning,** coup qui l'a envoyé rouler 2. n (a) tournoiement m; Av: vrille f; F: **to be in a flat s.,** ne pas savoir où donner de la tête; **to put s. on a ball,** donner de l'effet à une balle (b) DomEc: essorage m (du linge); s. **drier,** essoreuse f. **spin-'dry** vtr (**spindried**) DomEc: (faire) essorer (du linge). **'spinner** n (pers) fileur, -euse; DomEc: (machine) essoreuse. **'spinning** n filage m; Ind: filature f; s. **wheel,** rouet m; s. **top,** toupie. **'spin-off** n (a) avantage m, bénéfice *m*, supplémentaire (*b*) sous-produit *m*; retombées *fpl*. 'spin 'out *vtr* faire traîner (une affaire) en longueur; délayer (un discours); faire durer (une discussion).

spinach ['spinidʒ] *n Cu:* épinards *mpl*.

spindle ['spindl] *n Tex:* fuseau *m*; *MecE:* mandrin *m*; axe *m* (de pompe); arbre *m* (de tour). 'spindly *a* (*of pers*) maigrelet; (*of legs*) fuselé.

spindrift ['spindrift] *n* embrun *m*; poudrin *m*.

spine [spain] *n* (*a*) *Anat:* épine dorsale; colonne vertébrale (*b*) dos *m* (d'un livre); épine (de poisson); piquant *m* (de hérisson); arête *f* (de colline). 'spinal *a* spinal; s. column, colonne vertébrale; s. cord, moelle épinière. 'spinechilling *a* (film, histoire) à vous glacer le sang. 'spineless *a* (*of pers*) mou; qui manque de caractère. 'spiny *a* (-ier, -iest) épineux; couvert de piquants.

spinney ['spini] *n* petit bois; bosquet *m*.

spinster ['spinstər] *n Adm:* célibataire *f; often Pej:* vieille fille.

spiral ['spaiərəl] **1.** *n* spirale *f*; in a s., en spirale; *Av:* s. dive, descente spirale; **wage-price** s., montée *f* en flèche des prix et des salaires **2.** *a* spiral; en spirale; vrillé; s. staircase, escalier en colimaçon **3.** *vi* (spiralled) tourner, monter, en spirale; (*of rocket*) to s. up, monter en vrille.

spire ['spaiər] *n* aiguille *f*, flèche *f* (d'église).

spirit ['spirit] **1.** *n* (*a*) esprit *m*, âme *f*; I'll be with you in s., je serai avec vous de cœur; the Holy S., le Saint-Esprit; evil s., esprit malin; the leading s., l'âme, le chef (d'une entreprise) (*b*) esprit, disposition *f*; party s., l'esprit du parti; to enter into the s. of sth, entrer de bon cœur dans (la partie); to take sth in the wrong s., prendre qch en mauvaise part, de travers; that's the s.! à la bonne heure! (*c*) entrain *m*; to show s., montrer du caractère, du courage; to be in high spirits, être en train, en forme; to be in low spirits, être abattu, accablé; to be in good spirits, être de bonne humeur; to keep up one's spirits, ne pas perdre courage; their spirits rose, ils reprenaient courage; to raise s.o.'s spirits, remonter le moral de qn (*d*) *usu pl* spiritueux *mpl*; alcool *m*; surgical s. = alcool à 90°; s. lamp, lampe à alcool **2.** *vtr* to s. sth away, faire disparaître, subtiliser, escamoter, qch. 'spirited *a* (*of pers*) vif, animé; (*of horse*) fougueux; he gave a s. performance, il a joué avec brio, avec verve. 'spiritual **1.** *a* spirituel **2.** *n Mus:* negro s., (negro-)spiritual *m*. 'spiritualism *n* spiritisme *m*. 'spiritualist *a* & *n* spirite (*mf*). 'spiritually *adv* spirituellement.

spit¹ [spit] *n* (*a*) *Cu:* broche *f* (*b*) *Geog:* langue *f* de sable; flèche (littorale).

spit² [spit] **1.** *v* (spat; spitting) (*a*) *vi* cracher; (*of fire*) crépiter; it's spitting (with rain), il tombe quelques gouttes (*b*) *vtr* cracher (du sang); to s. sth out, cracher qch; *F:* s. it out! vide ton sac! **2.** *n* crachat *m*; salive *f; F:* he's the dead s. of his father, c'est son père tout craché; *F:* s. and polish, astiquage *m*. 'spitting **1.** *n* crachement *m; PN:* no s., défense de cracher **2.** *a F:* he's the s. image of his father, c'est son père tout craché. 'spittle *n* salive *f*, crachat *m*; bave *f*. spi'ttoon *n* crachoir *m*.

spite [spait] **1.** *n* (*a*) rancune *f*; malveillance *f*; dépit *m* (*b*) *prep phr* in s. of, en dépit de; malgré **2.** *vtr* to do sth to s. s.o., faire qch pour contrarier, vexer, qn.

'spiteful *a* rancunier, vindicatif, méchant, malveillant; s. tongue, langue venimeuse. 'spitefully *adv* par dépit; méchamment. 'spitefulness *n* méchanceté *f*; rancœur *f*; malveillance.

splash [splæʃ] **1.** *n* (*a*) éclaboussement *m*; clapotement *m*, clapotis *m* (des vagues); to make a s., (*in water*) faire floc; *F:* (*of pers, event*) faire sensation *f*; to fall into the water with a s., tomber dans l'eau en faisant floc; *Journ:* s. headline, grosse manchette (*b*) éclaboussure *f* (de boue); tache *f* (de couleur, de lumière) **2.** *v* (*a*) *vtr* éclabousser (with, de); to s. one's money about, prodiguer son argent, jeter son argent par la fenêtre; *Journ:* to s. a piece of news, faire la une des journaux; to s. oneself, one's face, with water, s'asperger (la figure) d'eau (*b*) *vi* (*of liquid*) rejaillir en éclaboussures; (*of waves*) clapoter; (*of tap*) cracher; to s. up, gicler; to s. (about) in the water, barboter, patauger, dans l'eau; I've splashed out on a new hat, je me suis payé un nouveau chapeau. 'splash 'down *vi* (*of spacecraft*) amerrir. 'splashdown *n* amerrissage *m* (d'un engin spatial).

spleen [splin] *n Anat:* rate *f; Fig:* mauvaise humeur; *Lit:* spleen *m*.

splendid ['splendid] *a* splendide; superbe; magnifique; that's s.! à la bonne heure! 'splendidly *adv* splendidement; magnifiquement. 'splendour, *NAm:* 'splendor *n* splendeur *f*, magnificence *f*; éclat *m*.

splice [splais] *vtr* **1.** épisser (un cordage) **2.** *Cin:* coller (un film); raccorder (une bande magnétique).

splint [splint] *n Surg:* éclisse *f*; attelle *f*; to put a limb in splints, éclisser un membre.

splinter ['splintər] **1.** *n* éclat *m* (de bois); écharde (logée sous la peau); esquille *f* (d'os fracturé); *Pol:* s. group, groupe séparatiste **2.** *vtr* & *i* (faire) voler en éclats; (faire) éclater. 'splintered *a* (bois) en éclats; (os) en esquilles.

split [split] **1.** *n* fente *f*; fissure *f*; déchirure *f* (dans une robe); crevasse *f* (dans une roche); division *f*, scission *f*, rupture *f* (dans un parti politique); *Cu:* banana s., banane fourrée à la crème; *Gym:* to do the splits, faire le grand écart **2.** *v* (split; splitting) (*a*) *vtr* fendre (du bois); cliver (la roche); déchirer (un vêtement); diviser, partager (une somme); to s. sth in two, couper qch en deux; *Ph:* to s. the atom, fissionner l'atome (*b*) *vi* se fendre; (*of cloth*) se déchirer; (*of party*) se diviser; to s. open, se fendre; to s. off, se séparer, se détacher; *F:* my head's splitting, j'ai un mal de tête fou; *F:* to s. on s.o., dénoncer qn; vendre (un complice) **3.** *a* fendu; s. peas, pois cassés; in a s. second, en un rien de temps; s. personality, dédoublement *m* de la personnalité. 'splitting **1.** *a* to have a s. headache, avoir un mal de tête fou **2.** *n* fendage *m; Ph:* fission *f* (de l'atome); s. (up), division, séparation *f* (de deux personnes). 'split 'up *vtr* & *i* (se) diviser; fragmenter (qch); (*of two people*) se séparer, rompre; the party s. up into three groups, le parti s'est divisé en trois groupes.

splodge, splotch [splɔdʒ, splɔtʃ] *n* tache *f* (de couleur).

splutter ['splʌtər] **1.** *v* (*a*) *vi* (*of pers*) crachoter, postillonner; (*stutter*) bredouiller, bafouiller; (*of engine*) bafouiller (*b*) *vtr* to s. (out), bredouiller (une excuse) **2.** *n* bredouillement *m* (de qn); bafouillage *m* (de qn, d'un moteur).

spoil [spɔil] v (**spoiled** or **spoilt**) **1.** vtr (a) gâter, abîmer, gâcher (qch); to s. **a piece of work**, gâcher un travail; **to get spoiled**, s'abîmer; **to s. s.o.'s appetite**, couper l'appétit à qn (b) gâter (un enfant) **2.** vi (of fruit) se gâter, s'abîmer; s'avarier; **to be spoiling for a fight**, brûler du désir de se battre. **spoils** npl butin m; **to claim one's share of the s.**, demander sa part du gâteau. **'spoilsport** n trouble-fête m inv. **spoilt** a gâté, abîmé, avarié; (bulletin de vote) nul; **s. child**, enfant gâté(e).

spoke¹, **spoken** ['spouk(ən)] see **speak**. **'spokesman** n (pl **-men**), **'spokesperson** n porte-parole m inv.

spoke² n rayon m (de roue); **to put a s. in s.o.'s wheel**, mettre des bâtons dans les roues de qn.

sponge [spʌndʒ]. **1.** n éponge f; Fig: **to throw in the s.**, s'avouer vaincu; **s. bag**, trousse de toilette; Cu: **s. (cake)**, gâteau m de Savoie; **s. finger**, langue-de-chat f **2.** v (a) vtr éponger (qch); **to s. down**, éponger (b) vi F: **to s. on s.o.**, vivre aux crochets de qn. **'sponger** n F: parasite m; écornifleur, -euse; pique-assiette mf inv. **'spongy** a (**-ier**, **-iest**) spongieux.

sponsor ['spɔnsər] **1.** n garant m, caution f, répondant m (**for s.o.**, de qn); (at baptism) parrain m, marraine f; WTel: Sp: personne f qui assure le patronage **2.** vtr être le garant de, répondre pour (qn); parrainer (qn); WTel: Sp: patronner; **sponsored walk**, marche pour aider une œuvre de charité. **'sponsorship** n caution; parrainage m.

spontaneous [spɔn'teiniəs] a spontané. **spontaneity** [spɔntə'ni:iti] n, **spon'taneousness** n spontanéité f. **spon'taneously** adv spontanément.

spooky ['spu:ki] a F: (histoires) de revenants; (endroit) hanté.

spool [spu:l] n bobine f (de coton); (of sewing machine, loom) can(n)ette f; Fish: tambour m (de moulinet); Typew: **ribbon spools**, bobines du ruban.

spoon [spu:n] **1.** n cuillère f, cuiller f; **dessert s.**, cuillère à dessert; **soup s.**, cuillère à soupe **2.** vtr **to s. sth out**, servir qch avec une cuillère. **'spoonfeed** vtr (**-fed**) nourrir (un enfant) à la cuillère; Fig: mâcher le travail à (un élève); subventionner (une industrie). **'spoonful** n cuillerée f.

spoor [spuər] n foulées fpl, piste f (d'un cerf).

sporadic [spə'rædik] a sporadique. **spo'radically** adv sporadiquement.

sport [spɔ:t] **1.** n (a) jeu m, divertissement m; (of hunting, fishing, shooting) **to have good s.**, faire bonne chasse, bonne pêche (b) sport m; **school sports (day)**, fête sportive; Aut: **sports car, model**, voiture de sport; **sports ground**, terrain de sport, de jeux; **sports jacket**, veston sport; **sports equipment**, accessoires, fournitures, articles, de sport (c) F: **he's a good s.**, (i) c'est un beau joueur (ii) c'est un chic type **2.** vtr porter, arborer (une fleur, un vêtement). **'sporting** a **s. man**, amateur m de sport; **in a s. spirit**, sportivement; F: **it's very s. of him**, c'est très chic de sa part; **you've a s. chance**, ça vaut la peine d'essayer. **'sportingly** adv sportivement. **'sportsman**, **-woman** n (pl **-men**, **-women**) (a) chasseur, -euse; pêcheur, -euse (b) amateur m de sport; sportif, -ive; **a real s.**, un beau joueur; un vrai sportif. **'sportsmanlike** a animé de l'esprit sportif. **'sportsmanship** n (a) qualités

fpl d'un vrai sportif; pratique f des sports sportivité f, esprit sportif. **'sportswear** n c vêtements mpl de sport. **'sporty** a F: sportif.

spot [spɔt] **1.** n (a) endroit m, lieu m; **the police are the s.**, la police est sur les lieux; **you should always on the s.**, vous devriez toujours être là; **the man on s.**, l'homme qui est sur place; **to do sth on the s.**, fai qch sur-le-champ, immédiatement; **to be killed on t s.**, être tué sur le coup; F: **to put s.o. on the s.**, mettre qn dans une situation difficile; F: **to be in a (tight)** être dans le pétrin; Com: **s. cash**, argent comptant; **put one's finger on a weak s.**, mettre le doigt sur un point faible; **s. check**, vérification sur place; contrô surprise m (b) tache f; pois m (de couleur); (on fac bouton m; **blue tie with red spots**, cravate bleue à po rouges; **a leopard's spots**, la moucheture d'un lé pard; f: **to knock spots off s.o.**, battre qn à plate couture(s) (c) goutte f (de pluie, de vin); F: **a s.** whisky, deux doigts m de whisky; **what about a s.** lunch? si nous allions déjeuner? **a s. of work**, un peu travail; **a s. of trouble**, un petit ennui (d) TV: WTe spot m publicitaire (e) (light) projecteur m; spot **2.** v (**spotted**) (a) tacher, souiller; **it's spotting with rain**, se met à pleuvoir (b) repérer; apercevoir; reconnaît Turf: prédire (le gagnant). **'spot-'check** co trôler à l'improviste. **'spotless** a sans tache; ir maculé. **'spotlessly** adv **s. clean**, d'une propre irréprochable. **'spotlight 1.** n projecteur; spot; to **the s. on sth**, mettre qch en vedette f. **'spot-'on** F: a exact, au point; **to be s.-on**, mettre dans le mille adv au point, exactement. **'spotted** a tacheté, moucheté; Tex: à pois. **'spotter** n (a) observateur m (b) **aircraft, train, s.**, personne f q regarde passer les avions, les trains (pour repérer l différents modèles). **'spotty** a (**-ier**, **-iest**) tache moucheté; (visage) couvert de boutons.

spouse [spauz] n époux m, épouse f; Jur: conjoir -jointe.

spout [spaut] **1.** n bec m (de théière); jet m (de pompe rainwater s.**, tuyau m (de décharge); F: **up the s** perdu, fichu **2.** v (a) vi (of liquid) jaillir; (of whal souffler (b) vtr faire jaillir, lancer (de l'eau); F: débit (des sottises) à jet continu.

sprain [sprein] **1.** n entorse f, foulure f **2.** vtr **to s. one wrist**, se fouler le poignet; **to s. one's ankle**, se faire un entorse (à la cheville).

sprang [spræŋ] see **spring II**.

sprat [spræt] n Ich: sprat m, harenguet m.

sprawl [sprɔ:l] vi s'étendre, s'étaler; (on a sofa) vautrer; **to go sprawling**, s'étaler par terre. **'spraw ing** a vautré; (ville) informe, tentaculaire.

spray¹ [sprei] n **s. of flowers**, branche f de fleu rameau fleuri.

spray² [sprei]. **1.** n (a) (on sea) embrun m (b) poussière f d'ea eau vaporisée; jet (pulvérisé) (de parfum) (c) (co tainer) atomiseur m (à parfum); vaporisateur n pulvérisateur m; (aerosol) bombe f, aérosol m **s. deodorant, paint**, déodoran peinture, en bombe **2.** vtr pulvériser, atomiser, v poriser (un liquide); asperger, arroser (des plantes peindre (qch) au pistolet. **'sprayer** n = **spray I.** (**'spraygun** n pistolet m (à peinture). **'spraying** pulvérisation f (des cultures).

spread [spred] **I.** n **1.** (a) étendue f (de pays) (b) (

bird's wings, *aircraft*) envergure *f*; différence *f* (entre deux prix); **middle-age s.,** l'embonpoint *m* de l'âge mûr (*c*) diffusion *f* (de l'éducation); propagation *f* (d'une doctrine); expansion *f* (*d*) festin *m*; repas (somptueux) (*e*) *Comest:* fromage *m*, pâté *m*, à tartiner (*f*) *Journ:* **double-page s.,** annonce *f*, article *m*, sur deux pages. **II.** *v* **(spread) 1.** *vtr* (*a*) étendre; tendre (un filet); déployer (des voiles); écarter (les doigts); **to s. out,** étaler (des marchandises) (*b*) répandre (du sable); épandre (du fumier); propager (une maladie); **instalments s. over several months,** versements échelonnés sur plusieurs mois (*c*) étaler (du beurre); **to s. butter on a slice of bread,** tartiner une tranche de pain **2.** *vi* s'étendre, s'étaler; (*of news*) se répandre; (*of disease*) se propager; (*of group*) **to s. (out),** se disperser; **to s. (oneself) out,** s'étendre (sur un divan); **the fire is spreading,** le feu gagne. **'spread-'eagle(d)** *a* vautré (sur le gazon, la plage).

spree [spriː] *n F:* partie *f* de plaisir; **to go on a s.,** faire la noce; **to go on a spending s.,** faire des achats extravagants.

sprig [sprig] *n* brin *m*, brindille *f*.

sprightly ['spraitli] *a* (**-ier, -iest**) éveillé, enjoué; vif.

spring [spriŋ] **I.** *n* (*a*) source *f* (d'eau) (*b*) printemps *m*; **in (the) s.,** au printemps; **s. flowers,** fleurs printanières; **s. day,** jour de printemps; **s. cleaning,** grand nettoyage (*c*) saut *m*, bond *m*; **to take a s.,** prendre son élan; faire un bond (*d*) élasticité *f* (*e*) ressort *m*; (*in seat*) *pl* suspension *f*; **s. (interior) mattress,** matelas à ressorts. **II.** *v* **(sprang** [spræŋ] **sprung** [sprʌŋ]) **1.** *vi* (*a*) bondir, sauter; **to s. up, to one's feet,** se lever d'un bond; **to s. forward,** se précipiter en avant; **to s. out of bed,** sauter du lit; **where did you s. from?** d'où sortez-vous? **the lid sprang open,** le couvercle s'est relevé brusquement; **hope springs eternal,** l'espérance reste toujours vivace; **to s. into existence,** naître, surgir (*b*) (*of water*) jaillir **2.** *vtr* (*a*) **to s. a leak,** (*se*) faire une voie d'eau (*b*) faire jouer (un piège); **to s. a surprise on s.o.,** faire une surprise à qn; **to s. a question on s.o.,** poser à qn une question imprévue (*c*) **sprung mattress,** matelas à ressorts; **sprung carriage,** voiture suspendue. **'springboard** *n* tremplin *m.* **'springbok** *n Z:* springbok *m.* **'spring-'clean** *vtr* (**spring-cleaned**) nettoyer à fond (une maison), *FrC:* faire le grand ménage. **'springiness** *n* élasticité *f.* **'springlike** *a* (*temps*) printanier; (*jour*) de printemps. **'spring-time** *n* printemps *m.* **'springy** *a* (**-ier, -iest**) élastique; flexible; (*pas*) léger; (*tapis*) moelleux.

sprinkle ['spriŋkl] *vtr* répandre, jeter (de l'eau, du sel, du sable); asperger (**with water,** d'eau); saupoudrer (**with salt,** de sel). **'sprinkler** *n* (*for gardens*) arroseur (automatique rotatif, à jet tournant); (*for sugar*) saupoudreuse *f*; *Ecc:* goupillon *m*; (**automatic**) **fire s.,** extincteur *m* (automatique) d'incendie. **'sprinkling** *n* arrosage *m* (d'eau); (léger) saupoudrage (de sucre); légère couche (de gravier); **a s. of knowledge,** quelques connaissances *fpl.*

sprint [sprint] *Sp:* **1.** *n* sprint *m* **2.** *vi* sprinter. **'sprinter** *n* sprinter *m.*

sprout [spraut] **1.** *v* (*a*) *vi* pousser; pointer; (*of seed*) germer (*b*) *vtr* pousser (des cornes); laisser pousser (une moustache) **2.** *n Bot:* jet *m*, rejeton *m*, pousse *f*; bourgeon *m*; (**Brussels**) **sprouts,** choux *mpl* de Bruxelles; **bean sprouts,** germes *mpl* de soja.

spruce¹ [spruːs] **1.** *a* pimpant; soigné; tiré à quatre épingles **2.** *vpr* **to s. oneself up,** se faire beau; se pomponner. **'spruceness** *n* mise pimpante.

spruce² *n Bot:* (sapin *m*) épicéa *m.*

sprung [sprʌŋ] *see* **spring II.**

spry [sprai] *a* (**spryer, spryest**) (*esp of elderly people*) vif, actif; plein d'entrain; plein d'allant.

spud [spʌd] *n F:* pomme *f* de terre, *F:* patate *f.*

spun [spʌn] *see* **spin I.**

spur [spəːr] **1.** *n* (*a*) éperon *m*; *Fig:* **to win one's spurs,** faire ses preuves (*b*) coup *m* d'éperon; stimulant *m*; aiguillon *m* (de la nécessité); **on the s. of the moment,** sous l'impulsion du moment (*c*) *Geog:* éperon, contrefort *m* (d'une chaîne de montagnes) **2.** *vtr* (**spurred**) éperonner (un cheval); **to s. s.o. on,** aiguillonner, stimuler, qn.

spurious ['spjuəriəs] *a* faux; contrefait. **'spuriousness** *n* fausseté *f.*

spurn [spəːn] *vtr* repousser, rejeter (une offre) avec mépris; traiter (qn) avec mépris.

spurt [spəːt] **1.** *n* (*a*) jaillissement *m*; jet *m*; giclée *f* (d'essence) (*b*) effort soudain; coup *m* de collier; *Sp:* **to put on a s.,** démarrer; **final s.,** pointe finale **2.** *vi* **to s. (up, out),** jaillir, gicler.

spy [spai] **1.** *n* (*pl* **spies**) espion, -onne; *F:* **police s.,** mouchard, -arde **2.** *v* (**spied**) (*a*) *vi* espionner; *F:* moucharder; **to s. on s.o.,** épier, espionner, qn (*b*) *vtr* apercevoir; **to s. out the land,** explorer le terrain. **'spyglass** *n* (*pl* **-es**) lunette *f* d'approche. **'spyhole** *n* trou *m.* **'spying** *n* espionnage *m.*

sq *abbr* square.

squabble ['skwɔbl] **1.** *n* querelle *f*, chamaillerie *f*; prise *f* de bec **2.** *vi* se quereller, se chamailler. **'squabbling** *n* querelles *fpl*; chamaillerie.

squad [skwɔd] *n* (*a*) *Mil:* escouade *f*; **firing s.,** peloton *m* d'exécution (*b*) brigade *f* (de cheminots); équipe *f* (de secours, de footballeurs); **s. car,** voiture de police.

squadron ['skwɔdrən] *n* (*a*) *Mil:* escadron *m* (*b*) *MilAv:* escadron, escadrille *f*; groupe *m*; **s. leader,** commandant *m* (de groupe) (*c*) *Navy:* escadre *f.*

squalid ['skwɔlid] *a* sale; misérable; sordide. **'squalor** *n* saleté *f*; misère *f*; aspect *m* sordide.

squall¹ [skwɔːl] *vi* (*of child*) crier, brailler, piailler. **'squalling** *a* criard, braillard.

squall² *n Nau:* grain *m*; coup *m* de vent; bourrasque *f*; rafale *f.* **'squally** *a* (temps) à grains, à rafales.

squander ['skwɔndər] *vtr* gaspiller (l'argent); dissiper, dilapider (sa fortune). **'squandering** *n* gaspillage *m.*

square ['skwɛər] **I.** *n* (*a*) carré *m*; carreau *m* (de carte quadrillée); case *f* (d'échiquier); **to divide a map into squares,** quadriller une carte; **to go back to s. one,** repartir à zéro (*b*) *Cl:* (*scarf*) carré, foulard *m* (*c*) (*of town*) place *f*; (*with garden*) square *m*; *Mil:* terrain *m* de manœuvre(s); *NAm:* bloc *m*, pâté *m* (de maisons) (*d*) *Draw:* **set s.,** équerre *f* (à dessin); **T s.,** équerre en T (*e*) *Mth:* carré (d'une expression) (*f*) *F:* **he's a s.,** il est un peu vieux jeu. **II.** *a* (*a*) carré; **s. dance,** danse à quatre; **s. measure,** mesure de surface; **s. metre,** mètre carré; **s. shoulders,** épaules carrées; *Mth:* **s. root,** racine carrée; **to get things s.,** mettre tout en ordre; **a s. deal,** une affaire honnête; **he always gives you a s. deal,** il est toujours loyal en affaires; **to be s. with s.o.,** être quitte envers qn; **to be (all) s.,** être à égalité; être quittes; **s. meal,** repas copieux; *F:* **to be s.,** être vieux jeu. **III.** *adv* à angles droits **(to, with, avec); set s. on its base,** d'aplomb sur sa base; **s. on the jaw,** en plein menton; **fair and s.,** loyalement, carrément. **IV.** *v* 1. *vtr (a)* carrer, équarrir (la pierre) *(b)* balancer, régler (un compte); arranger (qch); *F:* acheter (qn); graisser la patte à (qn) *(c) Mth:* élever (une expression) au carré; **four squared,** quatre au carré *(d)* **to s. (off),** quadriller (une feuille de papier) **2.** *vi* **his actions don't s. with his principles,** ses actions ne s'accordent pas, ne cadrent pas, avec ses principes. **'square-bashing** *n Mil: F:* = l'exercice *m.* **'squared** *a* (papier) quadrillé. **'squarely** *adv* carrément; (agir) honnêtement. **'square 'up** *vi* **to s. up with s.o.,** régler ses comptes avec qn; **to s. up to s.o.,** se mettre en posture de combat.

squash[1] [skwɔʃ] **1.** *v (a) vtr* écraser, aplatir; *F:* remettre (qn) à sa place *(b) vi* s'écraser; *(of people)* **to s. (up),** se serrer, se presser **2.** *n (a)* cohue *f;* bousculade *f (b)* **lemon, orange, s.,** citronnade *f,* orangeade *f; (to dilute)* sirop *m* de citron, d'orange *(c) Sp:* squash *m;* **s. court,** terrain *m* de squash. **'squashy** *a* mou (et humide); (terrain) détrempé.

squash[2] *n Bot:* gourde *f; esp NAm: (Br =* **vegetable marrow)** courge *f.*

squat [skwɔt] **1.** *vi* **(squatted)** *(a)* **to s. (down),** s'accroupir; *(of animals)* se tapir; **to be squatting,** être accroupi, tapi *(b)* s'établir comme squatter dans une maison inoccupée **2.** *a* ramassé, trapu. **'squatter** *n* squatter *m.*

squaw [skwɔ:] *n* femme *f* Peau-Rouge.

squawk [skwɔ:k] **1.** *n* cri *m* rauque; couic *m* **2.** *vi* pousser des cris rauques; faire couic.

squeak [skwi:k] **1.** *n* cri aigu (d'oiseau, de souris); crissement *m;* grincement *m;* craquement *m* (de chaussures); **to have a narrow s.,** l'échapper belle **2.** *vi* pousser des cris aigus; *(of shoes)* craquer; *(of machine)* grincer. **'squeaky** *a* (-ier, -iest) aigu; criard; (chaussures) qui craquent.

squeal [skwi:l] **1.** *n* cri aigu; cri perçant; grincement *m* (de freins); crissement *m* (de pneus) **2.** *vi* pousser des cris aigus; pousser des hauts cris; crier; *(of brakes)* grincer; *(of tyres)* crisser; *F:* **to s. on s.o.,** dénoncer qn.

squeamish ['skwi:miʃ] *a (a)* sujet aux nausées; **to feel s.,** avoir mal au cœur *(b)* difficile, délicat; dégoûté; **don't be so s.,** ne faites pas tant de façons. **'squeamishness** *n (a)* disposition *f* aux nausées *(b)* délicatesse exagérée.

squeegee ['skwi:dʒi:] *n* raclette *f* en caoutchouc.

squeeze [skwi:z] **I.** *n (a)* compression *f (b)* étreinte *f (c)* presse *f,* cohue *f;* **it was a tight s.,** on tenait tout juste; **a s. of lemon,** quelques gouttes *f* de citron; *Fin:* **the credit s.,** la restriction du crédit. **II.** *v* 1. *vtr (a)* presser; étreindre (qn); **to s. s.o.'s hand,** serrer la main à qn; **to s. a lemon,** exprimer le jus d'un citron; presser un citron; **to s. sth into a box,** faire entrer qch de force dans une boite *(b)* exercer une pression sur (qn); **to s. money out of s.o.,** extorquer de l'argent à qn **2.** *vi* se faufiler (par un trou); **to s. up,** se serrer; **to s. into a train,** entrer de force, se presser, dans un train. **'squeezer** *n DomEc:* presse *f;* **lemon s.,** presse-citrons *m inv.*

squelch [skweltʃ] *vi (of water)* gargouiller, gicler; *(of pers)* patauger (dans la boue).

squib [skwib] *n* pétard *m; F:* **damp s.,** affaire ratée.

squid [skwid] *n Moll:* calmar *m.*

squiggle ['skwigl] *n* écriture *f* illisible.

squint [skwint] **1.** *n* strabisme *m;* **he has a s.,** il louche; *F:* **let's have a s. (at it)!** fais voir! **2.** *vi* loucher; **to s. at sth,** regarder qch de côté.

squire ['skwaiər] *n* **the s.** = le châtelain (de l'endroit); *Hist:* écuyer *m* (d'un chevalier).

squirm [skwə:m] *vi (a)* se tordre, se tortiller *(b)* éprouver de l'embarras; ne pas savoir comment se tenir; être au supplice; **to make s.o. s.,** mettre qn au supplice.

squirrel ['skwirəl] *n Z:* écureuil *m.*

squirt [skwə:t] **1.** *v (a) vtr* faire jaillir (un liquide); **to s. in oil,** injecter de l'huile *(b) vi (of liquid)* jaillir, gicler **2.** *n* jet *m;* giclée *f* (de liquide).

SRN *abbr State Registered Nurse.*

St *abbr (a) Street (b) Saint.*

stab [stæb] **1.** *vtr* **(stabbed)** poignarder (qn); donner un coup de couteau à (qn); **to s. s.o. in the back,** poignarder qn dans le dos **2.** *n* coup de poignard, de couteau; *Fig:* **s. in the back,** attaque déloyale; **s. of pain,** élancement *m; F:* **to have a s. at sth,** tenter le coup. **'stabbing** **1.** *n* assassinat *m* à coups de couteau **2.** *a* **s. pain,** élancement, douleur lancinante.

stable[1] ['steibl] **1.** *n* écurie *f;* **racing s.,** écurie de courses **2.** *vtr* loger (un cheval). **'stableboy, -lad** *n* lad *m.* **'stabling** *n (a)* logement *m* (de chevaux) *(b) coll* écuries *fpl.*

stable[2] *a* stable; solide, fixe; *(of pers)* constant, ferme. **sta'bility** [stə-] *n* stabilité *f;* solidité *f* (d'une construction); fermeté *f* (d'une personne). **stabili'zation** *n* stabilisation *f.* **'stabilize** *vtr* stabiliser. **'stabilizer** *n* stabilisateur *m; Av:* empennage *m.*

stack [stæk] **1.** *n (a)* meule *f* (de foin); pile *f,* tas *m* (de bois); *F:* **I've got stacks of work,** j'ai beaucoup de travail, j'ai du pain sur la planche; **I've got stacks of them,** j'en ai des tas *(b)* souche *f* (de cheminée) **2.** *vtr* mettre (le foin) en meule; **to s. (up),** empiler, entasser.

stadium ['steidiəm] *n (pl* **stadia, -iums** ['steidiə, -iəmz]) stade *m.*

staff [stɑ:f] **1.** *n (a)* bâton *m;* mât *m* (de pavillon) *(b) coll* personnel *m; Mil:* état-major *m;* **(domestic) s.,** employés *mpl,* gens *mpl,* de maison; **teaching s.,** personnel enseignant; *Journ:* **editorial s.,** la rédaction **s. officer,** officier d'état-major; *Sch:* **s. room,** salle des professeurs *mpl; Mil:* **s. college** = école supérieure de guerre **2.** *vtr* pourvoir (un bureau) en personnel; **to be staffed with,** se composer de.

stag [stæg] *n Z:* cerf *m; Ent:* **s. beetle,** cerf-volant *m; F:* **s. party,** réunion entre hommes.

stage [steidʒ] **1.** *n (a) (platform)* estrade *f; Th:* scène *f; F:* les planches *f;* **the s.,** le théâtre; **s. play,** pièce de théâtre; **front of the s.,** avant-scène *f;* **to come on s.,** entrer en scène; **to go on the s.,** se faire acteur, actrice; **s. directions,** indications scéniques; **s. door,** entrée des artistes; **s. fright,** trac *m;* **s. name,** nom de théâtre; **s. manager,** régisseur *m;* **s. whisper,** aparté *m (b) Fig:* champ *m* (d'action); théâtre *(c)* phase *f,* période *f,* stade *m;* étape *f,* étape *m;* **the stages of an evolution,** les étapes d'une évolution; **to rise by successive stages,** monter par échelons *m;* **at this s.,** à ce point *(d) (of journey)* étape *f; (on bus route)* **fare s.,** section *f;* ▪

travel in, by, **easy stages,** voyager à petites étapes (e) (of space rocket) étage **2.** vtr monter (une pièce); organiser (une manifestation); monter (un coup). **'stagecraft** n Th: technique f de la scène. **'stagehand** n machiniste m. **'stagestruck** a passionné de théâtre; **he's s.-s.,** il brûle d'envie de faire du théâtre. **'staging** n Th: mise f en scène. **'stagy** a usu Pej: théâtral; histrionique.

stagger ['stægər] **1.** vi chanceler, tituber; **to s. along,** avancer en titubant; **to s. to one's feet,** se relever en chancelant **2.** vtr (a) confondre, consterner, renverser (qn); frapper (qn) de stupeur (b) disposer (des rivets) en quinconce; étaler, échelonner (les vacances). **'staggered** a **s. holidays,** congés échelonnés. **'staggering** a (of news) renversant, atterrant; **s. blow,** coup d'assommoir.

stagnant ['stægnənt] a (of water) stagnant; (of trade) en stagnation, dans le marasme. **stag'nate** vi être stagnant; stagner. **stag'nation** n stagnation f; marasme m (du commerce).

staid [steid] a posé, sérieux; sage. **'staidness** n caractère posé, sérieux.

stain [stein] **1.** n (a) tache f; souillure f; **s. remover,** détachant m; **he came out of the affair without a s. on his character,** il est sorti de l'affaire sans atteinte à sa réputation (b) couleur f, colorant m; **wood s.,** colorant pour bois **2.** vtr (a) tacher; souiller (with, de); ternir (une réputation) (b) teindre, teinter (le bois). **'stainless** a sans tache; immaculé; **s. steel,** (acier) inoxydable (m), inox m.

stair [steər] n marche f, degré m (d'un escalier); **stairs,** (also **'staircase)** escalier; **s. rod,** tringle d'escalier. **'stairwell** n cage f d'escalier.

stake [steik] **1.** n (a) pieu m, poteau m; Hort: tuteur m; **to be burnt at the s.,** mourir sur le bûcher (b) Gaming: mise f, enjeu m; **to play for high stakes,** jouer gros jeu; **the interests at s.,** les intérêts en jeu; **to have a s. in sth,** avoir des intérêts dans une affaire **2.** vtr (a) **to s.** (off, out), jalonner; **to s. a claim,** établir ses droits (b) Hort: ramer (des haricots); tuteurer (des tomates) (c) mettre (une somme) en jeu; jouer (une somme); miser (sur un cheval); **I'd s. my life on it,** j'en mettrais ma tête à couper.

stalactite ['stæləktait] n stalactite f.

stalagmite ['stæləgmait] n stalagmite f.

stale [steil] a (a) (pain) rassis; (œuf) qui n'est pas frais; (air) vicié; **s. smell,** odeur de renfermé (b) vieux, passé; **s. goods,** articles défraîchis; **s. joke,** vieille plaisanterie (c) fatigué, éreinté; (of athlete) **to go s.,** se surentraîner; **I'm s.,** je n'ai plus d'enthousiasme. **'stalemate** n Chess: pat m; Fig: **to reach s.,** arriver à une impasse. **'staleness** n état rassis (du pain); manque m de fraîcheur (d'un article, d'une nouvelle); odeur f de renfermé.

stalk¹ [stɔːk] **1.** vi **to s.** (along), marcher d'un pas majestueux; marcher à grands pas **2.** vtr traquer (une bête) à l'approche; filer (qn). **'stalker** n chasseur m à l'approche. **'stalking** n (deer) **s.,** chasse f à l'approche.

stalk² n tige f (de plante); queue f (de fruit); trognon m (de chou).

stall [stɔːl] **1.** n (a) stalle f (d'écurie, d'étable); (in church) **choir s.,** stalle (b) étalage m (en plein vent); éventaire m; (at exhibition) stand m; **newspaper s.,**

kiosque m; Th: **(orchestra) stalls,** fauteuils mpl d'orchestre **2.** v (a) vtr Aut: caler (le moteur); Av: mettre (l'appareil) en perte de vitesse; F: repousser; faire attendre (qn) (b) vi (of engine) caler; (of aircraft) se mettre en perte de vitesse; (of pers) **to s. (for time),** chercher à gagner du temps. **'stallholder** n marchand, -ande, en plein vent; (at exhibition) vendeur, -euse.

stallion ['stæljən] n étalon m.

stalwart ['stɔːlwət] a (a) robuste, vigoureux (b) vaillant, résolu.

stamen ['steimen] n Bot: étamine f.

stamina ['stæminə] n vigueur f, résistance f.

stammer ['stæmər] **1.** n (stutter) bégaiement m; (mumble) balbutiement m **2.** vtr & i bégayer; balbutier. **'stammerer** n bègue mf. **'stammering 1.** a (personne) bègue **2.** n bégaiement; balbutiement. **'stammeringly** adv en bégayant.

stamp [stæmp] **I.** n (a) battement m de pied; **with a s.** (of the foot), en frappant du pied (b) timbre m, empreinte f; **date s.,** timbre dateur; **rubber s.,** tampon m (c) étampe f, poinçon m (d) timbre; marque (apposée); **to bear the s. of genius,** porter la marque du génie (e) (postage) **s.,** timbre(-poste) m; **used s.,** timbre oblitéré; **National Insurance s.** = cotisation f de la sécurité sociale; Com: **trading s.,** timbre-prime m; **s. collector,** philatéliste mf; **s. album,** album de timbres; **s. machine,** distributeur automatique de timbres-poste; Adm: **s. duty,** droit de timbre. **II.** v **1.** vtr (a) **to s. one's foot,** frapper du pied; trépigner; **to s. one's feet,** trépigner, piétiner; (for warmth) battre la semelle (b) frapper, imprimer, une marque sur (qch); frapper, estamper (la monnaie, le cuir); contrôler, poinçonner (l'or, l'argent) (c) timbrer (un document); viser (un passeport); estampiller (des marchandises); timbrer, affranchir (une lettre); **the letter is insufficiently stamped,** l'affranchissement est insuffisant (d) Metalw: étamper (des objets en métal) **2.** vi **to s. about,** trépigner, piétiner; **to s. upstairs,** monter l'escalier à pas bruyants; **to s. on sth,** piétiner qch; fouler qch aux pieds. **'stamped** a (document) timbré; **s. addressed envelope,** enveloppe timbrée. **'stamping** n (a) timbrage m (de documents) (b) piétinement m; F: **s. ground,** endroit favori. **'stamp out** vtr éteindre (un feu) en piétinant dessus; écraser (une rébellion); supprimer (un abus).

stampede [stæm'piːd] **1.** n fuite précipitée; panique f; débandade f (de troupes); ruée f **2.** v (a) vi fuir en désordre, à la débandade; se ruer, se précipiter (for, towards, vers, sur) (b) vtr jeter la panique parmi (des animaux).

stance [stæns, stɑːns] n position f (des pieds); posture f; **to take up one's s.,** se mettre en posture (pour jouer).

stanch [stɔːntʃ] vtr see staunch².

stand [stænd] **I.** n (a) **to take a firm s.,** se planter, se camper solidement, sur ses jambes; Fig: se montrer résolu (b) résistance f; **to make a s. against s.o., sth,** résister, s'opposer, à qn, qch (c) situation f, position f; **to take (up) one's s. near the door,** se placer, prendre position, près de la porte; **to take one's s. on a principle,** se fonder sur un principe (d) station f (de taxis) (e) support m, pied m (de lampe); dessous m (de carafe) (f) étalage m; (at exhibition) stand m; (in sports ground) tribune f; NAm: Jur: (witness) **s.**

(*Br* = witness box) = barre *f* des témoins. **II.** *v* (**stood** [stud]) **1.** *vi* (*a*) être debout; se tenir debout; rester debout; **I could hardly s.,** je pouvais à peine me tenir; **to s. on one's own feet,** ne dépendre que de soi; **I didn't leave him a leg to s. on,** j'ai détruit ses arguments de fond en comble; **to s. six feet high,** avoir six pieds de haut; **to s.** (**up**), se lever; (**go and**) **s. by the window,** mettez-vous à la fenêtre; **to let a liquid s.,** laisser reposer un liquide; **to let the tea s.,** laisser infuser le thé (*b*) se trouver, être; **the chapel stands on a hill,** la chapelle se dresse sur une hauteur; **the tears stood in his eyes,** il avait les larmes aux yeux; **to let sth. in the sun,** laisser qch exposé au soleil; **to buy the house as it stands,** acheter la maison en l'état; **nothing stands between you and success,** rien ne s'oppose à votre succès; **he stood in the doorway,** il se tenait dans l'embrasure de la porte; **to s. talking,** rester à parler; **don't leave her standing there,** ne la laissez pas plantée là; (*in competition*) **to be left standing,** être laissé sur place (*c*) rester, durer; **to s. fast,** tenir (pied); tenir bon; **the contract stands,** le contrat tient; **the objection stands,** cette objection subsiste (*d*) **to s. convicted of a crime,** être déclaré coupable d'un crime; **to s. in need of sth,** avoir besoin de qch; **you s. in danger of being killed,** vous risquez de vous faire tuer; **I don't s. to lose anything,** je n'ai rien à perdre; **to s. as candidate, as surety,** se porter candidat, caution; **he stands first on the list,** il vient en tête de la liste; **the thermometer stands at 30°,** le thermomètre marque 30°; **the amount standing to your credit,** votre solde créditeur; **how do we s.?** où en sont nos comptes? **as things s., as it stands,** au point où en sont les choses; **I don't know where I s.,** j'ignore quelle est ma position **2.** *vtr* (*a*) mettre, poser; **to s. sth against the wall,** dresser qch contre le mur; **to s. sth upright,** mettre qch debout (*b*) **to s. one's ground,** tenir bon, ferme (*c*) supporter, subir; **to s. the cold,** supporter le froid; **to s. rough handling,** résister à des manipulations brutales; **we had to s. the loss,** nous avons supporté la perte; **I can't s. him,** je ne peux pas le sentir; **I can't s. it any longer,** je n'y tiens plus; j'en ai assez; **I won't s. (for) any more of that,** je ne supporterai plus ce genre de chose; j'en ai assez (*d*) payer, offrir; **to s. s.o. a drink,** payer à boire à qn; **I'm standing this one,** c'est ma tournée. **'stand a'side** *vi* s'écarter, se ranger; **to s. a. in favour of s.o.,** se désister en faveur de qn. **'stand 'back** *vi* se tenir en arrière; reculer; **house standing back from the road,** maison en retrait (de la route). **'stand 'by 1.** *vi* (*a*) se tenir prêt; *Mil:* être en état d'alerte; *Nau: Av:* se tenir paré (*b*) se tenir là (sans intervenir) **2.** *vtr* (*a*) se tenir près de (qn) (*b*) soutenir, défendre (qn); rester fidèle à (a promesse); **I s. by what I said,** je m'en tiens à ce que j'ai dit. **'standby** *n* ressource *f*; **s. engine,** locomotive de réserve; *Mil:* **to be on s. (duty),** être en état d'alerte; *Av:* (*of passenger*) **to be on s.,** être sur la, sur une, liste d'attente; **s. ticket,** billet standby, sans garantie. **'stand 'down** *vi* se désister (**in favour of s.o.,** en faveur de qn); *Mil:* quitter son service; (*of guard*) descendre de garde. **'stand 'for** *vtr* (*a*) signifier, vouloir dire (qch) (*b*) supporter, tolérer (qch). **'stand 'in** *vi* **to s. in for s.o.,** remplacer qn. **'stand-in** *n* remplaçant, -ante (temporaire); *Th:* doublure *f*; **to be s.o.'s s.-in,** doubler qn. **'standing 1.** *a* (*a*) (qui se tient) debout; (récoltes) sur pied; (*of water*) stag-

nant, dormant; **s. stone,** menhir *m* (*b*) (prix) fixe; *Com:* **s. expenses,** frais généraux; **s. rule,** règle fixe; *Bank:* **s. order,** ordre de virement permanent; **s. joke,** plaisanterie courante, traditionnelle **2.** *n* (*a*) station *f* debout; **s. room, place(s)** debout; **there wasn't even s. room,** il n'y avait pas où mettre le pied (*b*) durée *f*; **friend of long s., of 20 years' s.,** ami de longue date, de vingt ans (*c*) rang *m*, position *f*; standing *m*; **s. of a firm,** importance *f* d'une maison. **'stand 'off** *vtr Ind:* congédier (des ouvriers). **stand-'offish** *a F:* (*of pers*) peu accessible, distant, réservé. **'stand 'out** *vi* (*a*) **to s. o. against sth,** résister à qch, tenir bon contre qch; **to s. o. for sth,** s'obstiner à demander qch (*b*) (*jut out*) avancer; faire saillie; **to s. o. against sth,** se détacher sur qch; **to s. o. in relief,** ressortir; **to make a figure s. o.,** détacher une figure; **the qualities that s. o. in his work,** les qualités marquantes de son œuvre; *Nau:* **to s. o. to sea,** gagner le large. **'stand 'over 1.** *vi* rester en suspens; **to let a question s. o.,** remettre une question à plus tard **2.** *vtr* surveiller (qn) (de près); **if I don't s. o. him he does nothing,** si je ne suis pas toujours sur son dos il ne fait rien. **'standpoint** *n* point *m* de vue. **'standstill** *n* arrêt *m*; immobilisation *f*; **to come to a s.,** s'arrêter; **to bring sth to a s.,** arrêter qch; **business is at a s.,** les affaires ne marchent pas. **'stand 'to** *vi Mil:* être en état d'alerte. **'stand 'up 1.** *vi* (*a*) se lever, se mettre debout; **to s. up straight,** se tenir droit; **to s. up for s.o., sth,** défendre qn, soutenir (une cause); **to s. up to s.o.,** résister à qn; affronter courageusement qn; tenir tête à qn **2.** *vtr* mettre (qch) debout; *F:* **to s. s.o. up,** poser un lapin à qn; faire faux bond à qn. **'stand-up** *a* (col) droit, montant; (combat) en règle; (repas) pris debout.

standard ['stændəd] *n* (*a*) bannière *f*; *Mil:* étendard *m*; *Nau:* pavillon *m*; *Mil:* **s. bearer,** porte-étendard *m inv* (*b*) étalon *m* (de poids); *Fin:* **the gold s.,** l'étalon (d')or; **s. weight,** poids étalon; poids normal; **s. thickness,** épaisseur type, courante; (*of car*) **s. model,** voiture de série; *British:* **s. time,** heure légale anglaise; **s. authors,** auteurs classiques; **s. English,** anglais des gens cultivés; **s. joke,** plaisanterie habituelle (*c*) modèle *m*, type *m*; norme *f*; **s. of living,** niveau *m* de vie; **judged by that s.,** selon ce critère; **to aim at a high s.,** rechercher l'excellence; **up to s.,** à la hauteur (*d*) (*stand*) pied *m*; (*in street*) (lamp) **s.,** réverbère *m*; torchère *f*; pylône *m* d'éclairage; *Furn:* **s. lamp,** lampadaire *m*. **standardi'zation** *n* étalonnage *m*, étalonnement *m* (des poids); standardisation *f* (d'une machine). **'standardize** *vtr* étalonner; normaliser (une condition); *Ind:* standardiser (des produits).

stank [stæŋk] *see* stink 2.

stanza ['stænzə] *n* stance *f*, strophe *f*.

staple¹ ['steipl] **1.** *n* crampon *m* (à deux pointes); agrafe *f* **2.** *vtr* agrafer, cramponner (qch); brocher (un livre). **'stapler** *n* agrafeuse *f*. **'stapling** *n* agrafage *m*; fixage *m* à l'aide de crampons; brochage *m* (d'un livre).

staple² **1.** *n* (*a*) produit principal (d'un pays) (*b*) matière première, matière brute **2.** *a* **s. diet,** nourriture de base; **s. industry,** industrie principale.

star [sta:r] **1.** *n* (*a*) étoile *f*; astre *m*; *Typ:* astérisque *m*; **I thank my lucky stars that,** je bénis mon étoile de ce que (+ *ind*); **born under a lucky s.,** né sous une bonne étoile; *F:* **to see stars,** voir trente-six chandelles; **the stars and stripes, the s.-spangled banner,** la bannière étoilée (des États-Unis); **four s. hotel,** hôtel quatre étoiles, de grand luxe (*b*) *Cin: Th:* étoile, vedette *f,* star *f;* **s. part,** rôle de vedette **2.** *v* **(starred)** (*a*) *vtr* marquer (un mot) d'un astérisque; *Cin: Th:* présenter (qn) dans un rôle de vedette (*b*) *vi Th: Cin:* être en vedette; **starring role,** rôle de vedette, de star. **'star-dom** *n Cin: Th:* célébrité *f;* **to rise to s.,** devenir une vedette. **'starfish** *n* astérie *f;* étoile *f* de mer. **'stargazing** *n* rêvasserie(s) *f(pl).* **'starless** *a* (nuit) sans étoiles. **'starlet** *n Cin:* starlette *f.* **'starlight** *n* lumière *f* des étoiles; **by s.,** à la lumière des étoiles. **'starlit** *a* (ciel) étoilé. **'starry** *a* (-ier, -iest) étoilé; (par)semé d'étoiles. **'starry-'eyed** *a* qui voit tout en rose; (amoureux) extasié.

starboard ['stɑːbəd] *n Nau:* tribord *m.*

starch [stɑːtʃ] **1.** *n* amidon *m;* fécule *f* (de pommes de terre); matières féculentes **2.** *vtr* empeser, amidonner. **'starch-reduced** *a* (produit) débarrassé de matières féculentes. **'starchy** *a* (-ier, -iest) **s. foods,** féculents *mpl.*

stare ['stɛər] **1.** *n* regard *m* fixe; **stony s.,** regard dur; **vacant s.,** regard vague **2.** *v* (*a*) *vi* regarder fixement; **to s. into the distance,** regarder au loin; **to s. in s.o.'s face,** dévisager qn; **to s. at s.o.,** regarder qn fixement; dévisager qn (*b*) *vtr* **to s. s.o. in the face,** dévisager qn; fixer qn du regard; **ruin is staring us in the face,** notre ruine est imminente; *F:* **it's staring you in the face,** ça vous saute aux yeux. **'staring 1.** *a* **s. eyes,** yeux fixes; yeux grands ouverts; regard ébahi **2.** *adv* **stark s. mad,** complètement fou.

stark [stɑːk] **1.** *a* (*of town*) morne; (*of desolation*) absolu; (*of light*) cru **2.** *adv* **s. naked,** tout nu; nu comme un ver; **s. staring mad,** complètement fou.

starling ['stɑːliŋ] *n Orn:* étourneau *m.*

start [stɑːt] **I.** *n* (*a*) tressaillement *m,* sursaut *m;* **to wake with a s.,** se réveiller en sursaut; **he gave a s.,** il a tressailli, a sursauté; **to give s.o. a s.,** faire tressaillir qn (*b*) saut *m;* mouvement *m* brusque; **to work by fits and starts,** travailler par à-coups (*c*) commencement *m,* début *m;* (*for journey*) départ *m;* **for a s.,** pour commencer; **to make a good s.,** bien commencer; **to make an early s.,** commencer, partir, de bonne heure; **at the s.,** au début; **from s. to finish,** du commencement jusqu'à, à la fin; **to give s.o. a s.,** lancer qn (dans les affaires); **he had a good s. in life,** il a bien débuté dans la vie; **to make a fresh s. (in life),** recommencer (sa vie); *Sp:* **false s., faux** départ; **to give s.o. a two second s.,** donner à qn deux secondes d'avance, une avance de deux secondes. **II.** *v* **1.** *vi* (*a*) tressaillir, tressauter, sursauter; **to s. with surprise,** avoir un mouvement de surprise; **tears started from his eyes,** les larmes ont jailli de ses yeux (*b*) (*of rivets*) se détacher (*c*) commencer, débuter; **starting Monday,** à partir de lundi; **to s. again,** recommencer; **he started (out) as a doctor,** il a commencé par être médecin; **to s. in life,** débuter dans la vie; **to s. in business,** se lancer, se mettre, dans les affaires; **to s. with,** d'abord; en premier lieu; au début; **to s. by doing sth,** commencer par faire qch; **to s. on a job,** entamer un travail; **to s. off, out,** partir, se mettre en route; **to s. back,** reprendre le chemin (de la maison); (*of car*) **to s. (off, up),** démarrer; **I can't get it to s.,** je ne peux pas la faire

marcher **2.** *vtr* (*a*) commencer (un travail); entamer (un nouveau pain); **to s. life afresh,** recommencer sa vie; **to s. doing sth,** commencer à, de, faire qch; se mettre à faire qch (*b*) *Sp:* donner le signal de départ à (des coureurs) (*c*) lancer (une entreprise); fonder (un commerce); ouvrir (une école); *F:* **now you've started sth!** en voilà une affaire! **to s. a fire,** provoquer un incendie (*d*) **to s. (up),** mettre (une machine) en marche; démarrer (une voiture); **to s. s.o. on a career,** lancer qn dans une carrière; **if you s. him on this subject he'll never stop,** si vous le lancez sur ce sujet il ne tarira pas. **'starter** *n* (*a*) *Sp:* partant *m* (*b*) *Sp:* starter *m* (qui donne le signal de départ) (*c*) *Aut:* démarreur *m* (*d*) *Cu:* hors-d'œuvre *m;* **to have sth as a s.,** prendre qch pour commencer (le repas). **'starting** *n* **s. point,** point de départ; *Sp:* **s. pistol,** pistolet de starter; **s. price,** *Com:* prix initial; *Turf:* dernière cote (d'un cheval) avant le départ.

startle ['stɑːtl] *vtr* effrayer, alarmer (qn); faire tressaillir, faire sursauter (qn); **to s. s.o. out of his sleep,** éveiller qn en sursaut. **'startled** *a* effrayé; (cri) d'alarme. **'startling** *a* effrayant, saisissant; (événement) sensationnel.

starve [stɑːv] **1.** *vi* (*a*) **to s. to death,** mourir de faim (*b*) manquer de nourriture; **I'm starving,** je meurs de faim **2.** *vtr* (*a*) faire mourir (qn) de faim (*b*) priver (qn) de nourriture. **star'vation** *n* privation *f,* manque *m,* de nourriture; **to die of s.,** mourir de faim; **s. wages,** salaire de famine. **starved** *a* affamé; **s. of affection,** privé d'affection. **'starving** *a* affamé; mourant de faim.

stash [stæʃ] *vtr F:* **to s. (sth) away,** cacher (un trésor); mettre (son argent) de côté.

state [steit] **1.** *n* (*a*) état *m,* condition *f;* **in a good s.,** en bon état; **this is a fine s. of things to be in!** nous voilà bien! c'est du joli! **I am not in a fit s. to travel,** je ne suis pas en état de voyager; **s. of health,** état de santé; **s. of mind,** disposition *f* d'esprit; *F:* **to be in a terrible s.,** être dans tous ses états (*b*) rang *m,* dignité *f* (*c*) pompe *f,* parade *f;* apparat *m;* **to live in s.,** mener grand train; **to dine in s.,** dîner en grand gala; (*of body*) **to lie in s.,** être exposé (sur un lit de parade); **lying in s.,** exposition *f* (d'un corps); **robes of s.,** costume d'apparat; **s. coach,** voiture d'apparat; **s. ball,** grand bal officiel; **s. reception,** réception solennelle (d'un prince); **s. apartments,** salons d'apparat (*d*) **the S.,** l'État; **Secretary of S.,** (i) Secrétaire d'État (ii) *US:* = Ministre des Affaires étrangères; **head of s.,** chef d'état; **affairs of s.,** affaires d'État; **s.-aided,** subventionné par l'État; **s. control,** étatisme *m;* **s.-controlled,** étatisé; **the United States of America,** *F:* **the States,** les États-Unis (d'Amérique) **2.** *vtr* énoncer, déclarer; fixer (une heure); arrêter (une date); **condition stated in the contract,** condition énoncée dans le contrat; **as stated above,** ainsi qu'il a été mentionné ci-dessus; **I have seen it stated that,** j'ai lu quelque part que; **he is stated to have been in Paris,** on affirme l'avoir vu à Paris; **to s. a claim,** exposer une réclamation; *Jur:* **to s. the case,** exposer les faits. **'stated** *a* **at s. intervals,** à intervalles définis; **on s. days,** à jours fixes. **'stateless** *a Adm:* **s. person,** apatride *mf.* **'stateliness** *n* majesté *f;* aspect imposant; dignité *f.* **'stately** *a* (-ier, -iest) majestueux, imposant; plein de dignité; noble, élevé; **s. home**=château historique de l'Angleterre. **'statement** a (a) exposition f, exposé m (des faits); rapport m, compte rendu; déposition f (d'un témoin); **official s. (to the press),** communiqué m; **according to his own s.,** suivant sa propre déclaration; **to contradict a s.,** nier une affirmation (b) Com: état m, Bank: relevé m, de compte. **'stateroom** n grand appartement; Nau: cabine f de luxe. **'statesman** n (pl **-men**) homme m d'état. **'statesmanlike** a diplomatique; **to act in a s. way,** se conduire en homme d'état. **'statesmanship** n art m de gouverner.

static ['stætik] 1. a statique 2. n WTel: parasites mpl.

station ['steiʃn] 1. n (a) position f, place f; poste m; station f; Mil: Av: base (aérienne); Austr: **sheep s.,** élevage m de moutons; **lifeboat s.,** station de sauvetage; El: **power s.,** centrale f électrique; Aut: **petrol, service, s.,** station-service f; **police s.,** commissariat m, poste, de police; **fire s.,** caserne f de pompiers; **radio, TV, s.,** poste émetteur; station radio, de télévision; Ecc: **the Stations of the Cross,** le chemin de (la) Croix (b) position, condition f; rang m; **s. in life,** situation sociale (c) **(railway) s.,** gare f; **passenger s., goods s.,** gare de voyageurs, de marchandises; **coach, bus, s.,** gare routière; **underground, tube, s.,** station de métro; **s. hotel,** hôtel de la gare; NAm: Aut: **s. wagon** (Br = **estate car**), break m 2. vtr placer, mettre (qn dans un endroit); poster (des troupes); **to s. oneself,** se poster; **to be stationed at,** Mil: être en garnison à; Navy: être en station à. **'stationary** a stationnaire; immobile; (voiture) en stationnement. **'stationmaster** n chef m de gare.

stationer ['steiʃənər] n papetier m; **stationer's shop,** papeterie f. **'stationery** n papeterie; **office s.,** fournitures fpl de bureau.

statistics [stə'tistiks] npl statistique(s) f (pl); F: **vital s.,** mensurations fpl (d'une femme). **sta'tistical** a statistique; **s. tables,** statistiques. **sta'tistically** adv statistiquement. **statis'tician** n statisticien, -ienne.

statue ['stætju:] n statue f. **statu'esque** a sculptural. **statu'ette** n statuette f.

stature ['stætʃər] n stature f; taille f.

status ['steitəs] n (a) statut légal (de qn); Adm: **civil s.,** état civil (b) condition f, position f, rang m; **social s.,** rang social; **s. symbol,** signe extérieur de prestige m, de standing m; **without any offficial s.,** sans titre officiel; **s. quo,** statu quo m inv.

statute ['stætju:t] n (a) acte m du Parlement; loi f; **s. book,** code m (des lois); **s. law,** droit écrit; jurisprudence f (b) pl statuts mpl, règlements mpl (d'une société). **'statutory** a (a) établi, imposé, par la loi; réglementaire; **s. holiday,** fête légale (b) statutaire; conforme aux statuts.

staunch[1] ['stɔ:ntʃ] a sûr, dévoué; **s. friend,** ami à toute épreuve. **'staunchly** adv avec fermeté; avec résolution. **'staunchness** n fermeté f; dévouement m.

staunch[2] vtr étancher (le sang); étancher le sang de (la blessure).

stave [steiv] 1. n (a) douve f (d'un tonneau) (b) stance f, strophe f (d'un poème); Mus: portée f 2. vtr (**staved** or **stove**) **to s. in,** défoncer, enfoncer (un bateau, une barrique); **to s. off,** prévenir, parer à (un danger); conjurer (un désastre); tromper (la faim).

stay[1] [stei] **I.** n séjour m; visite f (chez un ami); **fortnight's s.,** séjour de quinze jours; Jur: **s. of proceedings,** suspension f d'instance; **s. of execution,** sursis m. **II.** v 1. vi (a) rester; demeurer sur les lieux; F: **to s. put,** rester sur place; ne pas bouger; **to s. at home,** rester à la maison; **to s. in bed,** garder le lit; **to s. to dinner, for dinner,** rester à dîner; **this word is here to s.,** ce mot est entré dans la langue (b) séjourner (dans un endroit); **he's staying with us for a few days,** il est venu passer quelques jours chez nous; **to s. at a hotel,** descendre, s'installer, dans un hôtel 2. vtr arrêter (le progrès de qn); enrayer (une épidémie); Jur: remettre (une décision); surseoir à, suspendre (son jugement); **horse that can s. three km,** cheval qui peut courir, tenir, pendant trois km; **to s. the course,** avoir du fond. **'stay-at-home** a & n casanier, -ière. **'stay a'way** vi ne pas venir; s'absenter. **'stayer** n Sp: coureur m de fond; cheval m qui a du fond; stayer m. **'stay 'in** vi ne pas sortir; rester à la maison. **'staying** n **s. power,** résistance f; endurance f; **horse with good s. power,** cheval qui a du fond. **'stay 'out** vi rester dehors; ne pas rentrer; **to s. o. all night,** découcher; Ind: **the men are staying out,** la grève continue toujours. **'stay 'up** vi ne pas se coucher; **to s. up late,** veiller tard; (of child) se coucher plus tard que d'habitude.

stay[2] n support m; soutien m; appui m, étai m.

STD abbr Tp: subscriber trunk dialling = téléphone automatique, l'automatique.

stead [sted] n **to stand s.o. in good s.,** être fort utile à qn; in s.o.'s s., à la place de qn.

steadfast ['stedfɑ:st] a ferme; constant. **'steadfastly** adv fermement; avec constance. **'steadfastness** n fermeté f (d'esprit); constance f; ténacité f.

steady ['stedi] 1. a (**-ier, -iest**) (a) ferme, solide; fixe, rigide; **to keep s.,** ne pas bouger; **to have a s. hand,** avoir la main sûre; **with a s. hand,** d'une main assurée (b) continu, soutenu; persistant; régulier; **s. progress,** progrès réguliers; **s. pace,** allure modérée, réglée; **s. downpour,** pluie persistante; Com: **s. demand for sth,** demande soutenue pour qch (c) (of pers) ferme, constant; assidu; rangé, posé; sérieux; (cheval) calme 2. adv & int **s.!** ne bougez pas! **s. (on)!** doucement! du calme! attention (de ne pas tomber)! F: (of boy or girl) **to go s.,** se fréquenter, sortir ensemble 3. v (**steadied**) (a) vtr (r)affermir; **to s. oneself against sth,** s'appuyer contre qch; **to s. the nerves,** calmer les nerfs; **to s. a young man (down),** assagir un jeune homme (b) vi **the market has steadied (down),** le marché s'est redressé; **young man who has steadied down,** jeune homme qui s'est rangé; **prices are steadying,** les prix se raffermissent. **'steadily** adv (a) fermement; **to walk s.,** marcher d'un pas ferme (b) régulièrement; sans arrêt; **his health gets s. worse,** sa santé va (en) empirant (c) (travailler) fermement, avec fermeté; assidûment (d) (se conduire) d'une manière rangée; avec sagesse. **'steadiness** n (a) fermeté f; sûreté f (de main) (b) assiduité f, persévérance f, application f; régularité f (de mouvement) (c) stabilité f (des prix) (d) (of pers) conduite rangée; sagesse f.

steak [steik] n Cu: (a) tranche f (de viande, de poisson) (b) bifteck m, steak m; (cut from the ribs) entrecôte f; **fillet s.,** tournedos m.

steal [sti:l] *v* (**stole** [stoul]; **stolen** ['stoulən]) **1.** *vtr* voler, dérober, soustraire (sth from s.o., qch à qn); **to s. a glance at s.o.**, jeter un coup d'œil furtif à qn; regarder qn à la dérobée; **to s. a march on s.o.**, devancer qn **2.** *vi* **to s. away**, s'en aller à la dérobée, furtivement; **to s. into the room**, se glisser dans la pièce; **to s. off**, s'esquiver. **'stealer** *n* voleur, -euse (de moutons). **'stealing** *n* vol *m*.

stealth [stelθ] *n* **by s.**, à la dérobée; furtivement. **'stealthily** *adv* à la dérobée, furtivement; (entrer) à pas de loup. **'stealthiness** *n* caractère furtif (d'une action). **'stealthy** *a* (-ier, -iest) furtif; (regard) dérobé.

steam [sti:m] **I.** *n* vapeur *f* (d'eau); buée *f*; **room full of s.**, salle remplie de buée; **heated by s.**, chauffé à la vapeur; **to get up s.**, mettre (la chaudière) sous pression; **to run out of s.**, *Mch:* ne plus être sous pression; *Fig:* être épuisé; **to let off s.**, *Mch:* lâcher la vapeur; *F:* dépenser son trop-plein d'énergie; donner libre cours à ses sentiments; **under one's own s.**, tout seul, sans aide; **at full s.**, à toute vapeur; *Nau:* **full s. ahead**, en avant toute! **s. engine**, machine à vapeur; *Rail: F:* locomotive *f*. **II.** *v* **1.** *vtr* (faire) cuire à la vapeur; **to s. open a letter**, décacheter une lettre à la vapeur **2.** *vi* (*a*) jeter, exhaler, de la vapeur; fumer (*b*) marcher (à la vapeur); (*of windscreen, spectacles*) **to s. up**, s'embuer; *F:* **to get all steamed up**, se laisser emporter (par la colère). **'steamboat** *n* vapeur *m*. **'steamer** *n* *Nau:* vapeur *m*; *Cu:* marmite *f* à vapeur. **'steaming** *a* fumant; **s. hot**, tout chaud. **'steam-roller** *n* rouleau compresseur; *F:* force *f* irrésistible. **'steamship** *n* vapeur *m*. **'steamy** *a* (-ier, -iest) plein de vapeur, de buée; (*of atmosphere*) humide.

steel [sti:l] **1.** *n* (*a*) acier *m*; **the iron and s. industry**, l'industrie sidérurgique; **stainless s.**, acier inoxydable; **sheet s.**, tôle *f* d'acier; **heart of s.**, cœur de fer, d'acier; **muscles of s.**, muscles d'acier (*b*) (*for sharpening knives*) affiloir *m* **2.** *vtr* **to s. oneself to do sth**, s'endurcir à faire qch; s'armer de courage pour faire qch; **to s. oneself against sth**, se cuirasser contre qch. **'steelworks** *npl* aciérie *f*. **'steely** *a* (-ier, -iest) d'acier; (regard) dur; (bleu) acier; (*of pers*) inflexible.

steep¹ [sti:p] *a* escarpé; à pic; raide; **s. climb**, montée raide; *F:* **that's a bit s.!** c'est un peu fort! **s. price**, prix exorbitant. **'steeply** *adv* en pente rapide; à pic; (*of prices*) **to rise s.**, monter en flèche. **'steepness** *n* raideur *f*, escarpement *m* (d'une pente).

steep² *vtr* baigner, tremper; mettre (qch) à tremper; **to s. sth in sth**, saturer, imbiber, qch de qch; **steeped in prejudice**, imbu de préjugés.

steeple ['sti:pl] *n* (*a*) clocher *m* (*b*) flèche *f* (de clocher). **'steeplechase** *n* steeple-chase *m*, steeple *m*. **'steeplejack** *n* réparateur *m* de clochers, de cheminées d'usines.

steer¹ ['stiər] *vtr & i* gouverner; diriger; conduire (une voiture); barrer (un yacht); **to s. a northerly course**, faire route au nord; **to s. clear of sth**, éviter qch. **'steering** *n* conduite *f* (d'un bateau, d'une voiture); direction *f*; **power(-assisted) s.**, direction assistée; **s. wheel**, volant *m*; **s. column**, colonne de direction; *Adm:* **s. committee**, comité d'organisation *f*.

steer² *n* (jeune) bœuf *m*; bouvillon *m*.

stem¹ [stem] **1.** *n* (*a*) *Bot:* tige *f* (de plante, de fleur); queue *f* (de fruit, de feuille); tronc *m*, souche *f*

(d'arbre); pied *m* (de verre à boire) (*b*) souche (de famille); *Ling:* thème *m*, radical *m* (d'un mot) (*c*) *Nau:* étrave *f*, avant *m*; **from s. to stern**, de l'avant à l'arrière **2.** *vi* (**stemmed**) **to s. from**, être issu de, provenir de, être le résultat de (qch).

stem² *vtr* (**stemmed**) contenir, endiguer (un cours d'eau); lutter contre (la marée); remonter (le courant); résister à (une attaque).

stench [stentʃ] *n* odeur *f* infecte; puanteur *f*.

stencil ['stensl] **1.** *n* (*a*) patron (ajouré); poncif *m*, pochoir *m* (*b*) peinture *f* au pochoir (*c*) *Typewr:* stencil *m* **2.** *vtr* (**stencilled**) peindre, marquer (qch) au pochoir; polycopier (un document).

stenographer [stə'nɔgrəfər] *n* sténographe *mf*, sténo *mf*.

stentorian [sten'tɔ:riən] *a* (voix) de stentor.

step [step] **I.** *n* (*a*) pas *m*; **to take a s.**, faire un pas; **to turn one's steps towards**, se diriger, diriger ses pas, vers; **at every s.**, à chaque pas; **s. by s.**, pas à pas; petit à petit; **to retrace one's steps**, revenir sur ses pas; **that's a great s. forward**, c'est déjà un grand pas de fait; **with a quick s.**, d'un pas rapide (*b*) pas, cadence *f*; **to keep s.**, **to be in s.**, marcher au pas; être au pas; **to fall into s.**, se mettre au pas; **to be out of s.**, marcher à contre-pas (**with**, de); **waltz s.**, pas de valse (*c*) démarche *f*; mesure *f*; **to take the necessary steps**, faire les démarches nécessaires; prendre toutes dispositions utiles; **to take steps to do sth**, se préparer à faire qch; **a s. in the right direction**, un pas dans la bonne voie; **the first s. will be to**, la première chose à faire sera de; (*in hierarchy*) **to go up a s.**, avancer en grade (*d*) marche *f*, degré *m* (d'un escalier); marchepied *m* (d'un véhicule); **top s.** (of a stair), marche palière; (**flight of**) **steps**, escalier; (*stone*) perron *m*; (**pair of**) **stairs**, escabeau *m*; échelle *f* double; **folding steps**, échelle pliante **2.** *vi* (**stepped**) faire un pas, des pas; marcher; aller; **s. this way**, venez par ici; **to s. aside to let s.o. pass**, s'écarter pour laisser passer qn; **to s. back, forward**, faire un pas en arrière, en avant; **the car drew up and he stepped in, out**, la voiture s'est arrêtée et il y est monté, en est descendu; **s. inside for a moment**, entrez un instant; **s. over to my place**, venez chez moi; **somebody stepped on my foot**, on m'a marché sur le pied; **to s. on the gas, to s. on it**, *Aut:* appuyer sur le champignon; *F:* se dépêcher; **to s. on the brakes**, donner un coup de frein; **to s. up to s.o.**, s'approcher de qn. **'stepbrother** *n* demi-frère *m*. **'stepchild** *n* (*pl* -**children**) beau-fils *m*, belle-fille *f*. **'stepdaughter** *n* belle-fille. **'step 'down** *vi* démissionner. **'stepfather** *n* beau-père *m*. **'step 'in** *vi* entrer; *Fig:* intervenir. **'stepladder** *n* escabeau *m*. **'stepmother** *n* belle-mère *f*. **'step 'out** *vi* sortir; **to s. o. briskly**, marcher rapidement; allonger le pas. **'stepsister** *n* demi-sœur *f*. **'stepson** *n* beau-fils. **'step 'up** *vtr* augmenter (la production); intensifier (une campagne); *El:* survolter (le courant).

steppe [step] *n* *Geog:* steppe *f*.

stereo ['steriou] **1.** *a* stéréo *inv* **2.** *n* (appareil *m*) stéréo *f*. **stereo'phonic** *a* stéréophonique. **'stereoscope** *n* stéréoscope *m*. **stereo'scopic** *a* stéréoscopique. **'stereotype 1.** *n* stéréotype *m*; *Typ:* cliché *m* **2.** *vtr* (**stereotyped**) *Typ:* clicher. **'stereotyped** *a* stéréotypé; **s. phrase**, cliché *m*.

sterile ['sterail] *a* stérile. **sterility** [stə'riliti] *n* stérilité f. **sterili'zation** [sterilai-] n stérilisation f. **'sterilize** vtr stériliser. **'sterilizer** n stérilisateur m.

sterling ['stə:liŋ] 1. a (a) (monnaie) de bon aloi, d'aloi; **pound s.**, livre sterling; **s. area**, zone sterling (b) (of quality) de bon aloi, vrai, solide; **man of s. worth**, homme de valeur f 2. n (livre f) sterling m.

stern¹ [stə:n] a sévère, dur. **'sternly** adv sévèrement, durement. **'sternness** n sévérité f; austérité f; dureté f.

stern² n Nau: arrière m; poupe f; **s. light**, feu d'arrière, de poupe.

sternum ['stə:nəm] n Anat: sternum m.

steroid ['steroid] n Bio-Ch: stéroïde m.

stet [stet] Typ: 1. imp bon; à maintenir 2. vtr (stetted) maintenir (un mot) (sur l'épreuve).

stethoscope ['steθəskoup] n Med: stéthoscope m.

stevedore ['sti:vdɔ:r] n docker m; arrimeur m.

stew [stju:] 1. n Cu: ragoût m; civet m (de chevreuil); F: **to be in a s.**, être dans tous ses états 2. v (a) vtr Cu: (faire) cuire (la viande) en ragoût; (faire) cuire (des fruits) en compote (b) vi Cu: mijoter; F: **to let s.o. s. in his own juice**, laisser qn mijoter (dans son jus). **stewed** a (a) **s. beef**, ragoût de bœuf; bœuf (à la) mode; bœuf en daube; **s. fruit**, compote f de fruits (b) (thé) trop infusé.

steward ['stju:əd] n (a) intendant m (d'une propriété); maître m d'hôtel (d'un cercle); Nau: commis m aux vivres (b) (waiter) Nau: Av: garçon m (de cabine); steward m (c) commissaire m (d'une réunion sportive); Ind: **shop s.**, délégué, -ée, d'atelier, d'usine, du personnel; délégué syndical. **stewar'dess** n (pl -es) Nau: femme f de chambre; Av: hôtesse f (de l'air).

stick¹ [stik] n bâton m (de bois, de sucrerie, d'orge, de cire à cacheter); Hort: rame f; Comest: branche f (de céleri); tige f (de rhubarbe); Av: chapelet m (de bombes); (walking) s., canne f; hockey s., crosse f de hockey; Av: **the s.**, le manche à balai; (for firewood) **to gather sticks**, ramasser du bois sec, du petit bois; **without a s. of furniture**, sans un meuble; F: (of pers) **queer s.**, drôle de type m; F: **to take a lot of s.**, être beaucoup critiqué; **the big s.**, la manière forte; la force; F: **he lives out in the sticks**, il vit dans la brousse; Ent: **s. insect**, phasme m.

stick² v (stuck [stʌk]) 1. vtr (a) piquer, enfoncer (into, dans); **to s. a pin through sth**, passer une épingle à travers qch; **he stuck the spade into the ground**, il a planté la bêche dans le sol; F: **to get stuck in**, se cramponner, se maintenir (b) F: **to s. a rose in one's buttonhole**, mettre une rose à sa boutonnière; **to s. one's hat on one's head**, planter son chapeau sur sa tête; **s. it in your pocket**, fourrez-le dans votre poche (c) coller; **to s. a stamp on a letter**, timbrer une lettre; **to s. down an envelope**, fermer, coller, une enveloppe (d) F: supporter, souffrir; **to s. it**, tenir (le coup); **I can't s. him**, je ne peux pas le sentir 2. vi (a) s'enfoncer, se planter; **with a needle sticking in it**, avec une aiguille piquée dedans (b) coller, s'attacher, tenir (to, à); **the envelope won't s.**, l'enveloppe ne colle pas; **the vegetables have stuck to the pan**, les légumes ont attaché; **his shirt stuck to his back**, il avait la chemise collée au dos; **the name stuck to him**, ce nom lui (en) est resté; **to s. by, to, a friend**, ne pas abandonner un

ami; **to s. together**, se serrer les coudes; faire preuve de solidarité; **to s. (to s.o.) like glue**, se cramponner (à qn); **to s. to one's post**, rester à son poste; **s. to it!** persévérez! **to s. to one's promise**, tenir sa promesse; **to s. to an opinion**, maintenir une opinion; **to s. to one's guns**, ne pas en démordre; **to s. to the facts**, s'en tenir aux faits; **to s. to the point**, ne pas s'écarter de la question; F: **to s. to sth**, garder qch pour soi; F: **I'm stuck with it, him**, je ne peux pas m'en débarrasser; **to s., to be stuck**, être pris, engagé; (in mud) s'embourber, être embourbé; (of machine parts) coincer; (of boat) s'enliser; **I'm stuck**, je n'avance plus; je suis en panne; **it sticks in my throat**, je ne peux pas avaler ça; **the lift has stuck**, l'ascenseur est en panne; **the switch was stuck**, le contact était collé; F: **to be stuck for a title**, ne pas trouver de titre. **'stick a'round** vi F: attendre; rester. **'stick at** vi **to s. at nothing**, ne reculer devant rien; **to s. at a job for six hours**, travailler à qch pendant six heures d'arrache-pied; **s. at it!** persévérez! **'sticker** n étiquette gommée. **'stickiness** n nature collante. **'sticking** 1. a adhésif; **s. plaster**, sparadrap m 2. n (a) adhérence f (b) arrêt m, coincement m. **'stick-in-the-mud** n F: **an old s.-in-t.-m.**, un vieux routinier. **'stick-on** a s.-**on label**, étiquette adhésive, autocollante. **'stick 'out** 1. vtr sortir (qch); bomber (la poitrine); tirer (sa langue); F: **to s. one's neck o.**, prendre des risques; F: **it sticks out a mile!** c'est clair comme le jour! **to s. it out**, tenir jusqu'au bout 2. vi faire saillie; **to s. o. beyond sth**, dépasser qch; **his ears s. o.**, il a les oreilles décollées; F: **to s. o. for sth**, s'obstiner à demander qch. **'stick 'up** 1. vtr (a) F: lever (la main); **s. 'em up!** haut les mains! (b) afficher (un avis) (c) F: attaquer (une banque) à main armée; braquer 2. vi se dresser; F: **to s. up for s.o.**, prendre la défense de qn. **'stick-up** n F: vol m à main armée; braquage m. **'sticky** a (-ier, -iest) collant, gluant; adhésif; (of substance, hands) poisseux; **s. tape**, ruban adhésif; **s. weather**, temps lourd; **to get one's hands s.**, s'engluer les mains; F: **to be on a s. wicket**, être dans une situation difficile; F: **he's s. about these things**, il est peu accommodant sur ces choses; **to come to a s. end**, finir mal. **'stuck-'up** a F: prétentieux.

stickleback ['stiklbæk] n Ich: épinoche f.

stickler ['stiklər] n **s. for sth**, rigoriste mf à l'égard de qch; **to be a s. for etiquette**, être à cheval sur l'étiquette.

stiff [stif] 1. a (a) raide, rigide, dur, inflexible; **s. shirt**, chemise empesée (de soirée); **s. brush**, brosse dure; **s. joint**, articulation ankylosée; **s. neck**, torticolis m; (of pers) **to be s.**, avoir des courbatures; (with cold) être engourdi; **s. as a post**, droit comme un piquet; **the body was already s.**, le cadavre était déjà raide (b) (of pers) raide, guindé; **s. bow**, salut contraint, froid (c) inflexible, obstiné; **to offer s. resistance**, résister opiniâtrement (d) (of handle, mechanism) qui fonctionne mal; **s. control lever**, commande dure (e) (of paste, consistency) ferme; **s. breeze**, forte brise f (montée) raide, pénible; (examen) difficile; (prix) élevé; **a s. whisky**, un whisky bien tassé, fort 2. n P: cadavre m; macchabée m. **'stiffen** 1. vtr (a) raidir, renforcer; **age has stiffened his joints**, l'âge lui a noué les membres (b) raidir (qn), rendre (qn) obstiné 2. vi se raidir; devenir raide; (of pers) se guinder; (of paste) devenir ferme; prendre de la consistance; (*of wind*) fraîchir. **'stiffly** *adv* avec raideur; d'un air guindé. **'stiff-'necked** *a* obstiné, entêté. **'stiffness** *n* (*a*) raideur *f*, rigidité *f*; dureté *f* (d'un ressort); courbatures *fpl*, engourdissement *m* (dans les jambes); **s. of manner**, raideur, contrainte *f*; air guindé (*b*) fermeté *f*, consistance *f* (d'une pâte); raideur (d'une pente); difficulté *f* (d'un examen).

stifle ['staifl] 1. *vtr* étouffer, suffoquer; réprimer (une émotion); **stifled by the smoke**, asphyxié par la fumée 2. *vi* suffoquer, étouffer. **'stifling** *a* étouffant, suffocant; **it's s. in here**, on étouffe ici.

stigma ['stigmə] *n* (*pl* **stigmas, stigmata** ['stigməz, 'stigmətə]) stigmate *m*. **'stigmatize** *vtr* stigmatiser (qn).

stile [stail] *n* échalier *m*.

stiletto [sti'letou] *n* stylet *m*; **s. heel**, talon aiguille.

still¹ [stil] 1. *a* tranquille, immobile; **to keep s.**, ne pas bouger; se tenir tranquille; **his heart stood s.**, son cœur a cessé de battre; **s. night**, nuit calme, silencieuse; **s. wine**, vin non mousseux; *Art:* **s. life**, nature morte 2. *n* (*a*) **in the s. of the night**, dans le calme de la nuit (*b*) *Cin:* photo. **'stillborn** *a* mort-né. **'stillness** *n* tranquillité *f*, calme *m*, silence *m*.

still² 1. *adv* encore; **he's s. here**, il est toujours ici; **I s. have 500 francs**, il me reste encore 500 francs; **they are s. playing**, ils jouent encore; **s. more, s. less**, encore plus, encore moins 2. *conj* cependant, pourtant, néanmoins, toutefois; **s. I did see her**, toujours est-il que je l'ai vue.

still³ *n* alambic *m*.

stilt [stilt] *n* (**pair of**) **stilts**, échasses *fpl*. **'stilted** *a* (style) guindé.

stimulate ['stimjuleit] *vtr* stimuler; aiguillonner, activer (**to**, à); aiguiser (l'appétit); encourager (la production). **'stimulant** *a & n* stimulant (*m*). **'stimulating** *a* stimulant. **stimu'lation** *n* stimulation *f*. **'stimulus** *n* (*pl* **-i**) stimulant, aiguillon *m*; *Med:* stimulus *m*; **to give trade a s.**, donner de l'impulsion *f* au commerce.

sting [stiŋ] 1. *n* dard *m*, aiguillon *m* (d'abeille); piqûre *f* (de guêpe); douleur cuisante (d'une blessure); mordant *m* (d'une observation) 2. *v* (**stung** [staŋ]) (*a*) *vtr* (*of bee, nettle*) piquer; (*of blow*) cingler (qn); (*of smoke*) **to s. the eyes**, picoter les yeux; **that reply stung him (to the quick)**, cette réponse l'a piqué (au vif); *F:* **to be stung**, attraper le coup de fusil (*b*) **vi my eyes were stinging**, les yeux me cuisaient. **'stinging** *a* cuisant; (coup) cinglant; **s. nettle**, ortie brûlante.

stingy ['stindʒi] *a* (**-ier, -iest**) mesquin, chiche, ladre. **'stingily** *adv* chichement, mesquinement. **'stinginess** *n* mesquinerie *f*, ladrerie *f*; pingrerie *f*.

stink [stiŋk] 1. *n* puanteur *f*; odeur infecte; *F:* **to raise a s. (about sth)**, faire de l'esclandre *m*; rouspéter (à propos de qch) 2. *v* (**stank** [staŋk], **stunk** [staŋk]) (*a*) *vi* puer; sentir mauvais; empester; **to s. of garlic**, puer l'ail; *P:* **he stinks**, c'est un type infect! *P:* (*of thg, plan*) **it stinks!** c'est moche! (*b*) *vtr* **to s. s.o. out**, chasser qn par la mauvaise odeur; **to s. the room out**, empester la pièce. **'stinker** *n P:* (*of pers*) sale type *m*; **to write s.o. a s.**, écrire une lettre carabinée à qn. **'stinking** 1. *a* puant, empesté, infect; *F:* **a s. cold**, un sale rhume 2. *adv F:* **to be s. rich**, avoir un argent fou.

stint [stint] 1. *n* tâche assignée; temps *m*, période *f*;

daily s., tâche quotidienne; **he had a two-year s. in the army**, il a fait ses deux ans dans l'armée 2. *vtr* lésiner sur (qch); **to s. oneself**, se refuser le nécessaire; **to s. oneself for one's children**, se priver pour ses enfants; **to s. s.o. of sth**, refuser qch à qn; priver qn de qch.

stipend ['staipend] *n* traitement *m*, appointements *mpl* (d'un ecclésiastique, d'un magistrat).

stipple ['stipl] *vtr* pointiller; **stippled design**, dessin au pointillé.

stipulate ['stipjuleit] *vtr & i* stipuler; prescrire (un délai). **stipu'lation** *n* stipulation *f*; **with the s. that**, à condition que.

stir [stəːr] I. *n* (*a*) remuement *m*; **to give one's coffee a s.**, remuer son café (*b*) mouvement *m* d'agitation (d'une grande ville); **a great s.**, un grand remue-ménage (*c*) agitation *f*, émoi *m*; **to make a s.**, faire du bruit; faire sensation. II. *v* (**stirred**) 1. *vtr* (*a*) remuer; mouvoir; activer, agiter; tisonner (le feu); tourner (une crème); **to s. one's tea**, remuer son thé; **to s. up trouble**, *F:* **to s. it**, fomenter la discorde; **to s. up the peoples**, ameuter le peuple; **he needs stirring up!** il a besoin d'être secoué! (*b*) émouvoir, troubler (qn); **to s. s.o. to pity**, émouvoir la compassion de qn 2. *vi* bouger, remuer; **he didn't s. out of the house**, il n'est pas sorti de la maison; **there's not a breath of air stirring**, on ne sent pas un souffle d'air; **he hasn't stirred yet**, il n'est pas encore levé. **'stirring** *a* (*a*) actif, remuant; **s. times**, époque troublée (*b*) émouvant; (discours) entraînant.

stirrup ['stirəp] *n* étrier *m*; **s. cup**, coup de l'étrier.

stitch [stitʃ] I. *n* (*pl* **stitches**) (*a*) *Needlew:* point *m*; piqûre *f* (à la machine); *Knit:* maille *f*; *Med:* point de suture; **to put a few stitches in a garment**, faire un point à un vêtement; *F:* **he hasn't a dry s. on him**, il est complètement trempé; **without a s. on**, complètement nu; *Knit:* **to drop a s.**, sauter une maille; **to put stitches in a wound**, suturer, faire une suture à, une plaie (*b*) **s. (in the side)**, point de côté; *F:* **to be in stitches (with laughter)**, se tordre de rire 2. *vtr* coudre (un vêtement); (*on machine*) piquer; *Bookb:* brocher (un livre); **to s. up a tear**, recoudre une déchirure; *Med:* **to s. (up) a wound**, suturer une plaie.

stoat [stout] *n Z:* hermine *f* (d'été).

stock [stɔk] I. *n* (*a*) *Hort:* sujet *m*; porte-greffe *m* (*b*) race *f*, famille *f*, lignée *f*; (*of pers*) **of good s.**, de bonne souche (*b*) fût *m*, bois *m* (de fusil) (*c*) *Nau:* **stocks**, chantier *m*; cale *f* de construction; **ship on the stocks**, navire en construction, sur cale(s) (*d*) *Hist:* *pl* (*punishment*) ceps *mpl* (*e*) provision *f*, approvisionnement *m*; **to lay in a s. of wood**, faire (une) provision de, s'approvisionner en, bois (*f*) *Com:* **s. (in trade)**, marchandises *fpl*; stock *m*; **surplus s.**, soldes *mpl*; **in s.**, en magasin, en stock; **out of s.**, épuisé; **to take s.**, faire l'inventaire; *Fig:* **to take s. (of the situation)**, faire le point (*g*) (*livestock*) bétail *m*; **fat s.**, bétail de boucherie; **s. farming**, élevage *m* (de bétail) (*h*) *Cu:* bouillon *m*; **s. cube**, bouillon-cube *m* (*i*) *Fin:* fonds *mpl*, valeurs *fpl*; actions *fpl*; **Government s.**, fonds d'état; **stocks and shares**, valeurs mobilières; titres *mpl*; **s. market**, marché des titres; **the S. Exchange**, Bourse (de Londres) (*j*) *Bot:* matthiole *f*; giroflée *f* des jardins. II. *a* normal; **s. size**, taille courante; **s. argument**, argument habituel, bien connu; **s. phrase**, phrase toute faite; *Sp:* **s. car**, stock-car *m*. III. *v* 1. *vtr* (*a*) monter (une ferme) en bétail; approvisionner (un magasin) (**with**, de); empoissonner (un étang); peupler (une forêt); **well stocked**, (magasin) bien approvisionné (*b*) tenir, garder, avoir (qch) en magasin; stocker (des marchandises) **2.** *vi* to s. **up with sth**, s'approvisionner en qch. '**stockbroker** *n* agent *m* de change. '**stockist** *n Com:* stockiste *mf*. '**stockman** *n* (*pl* **-men**) *Austr:* bouvier *m*. '**stockpile 1.** *n* stocks *mpl* de réserve **2.** *vtr & i* stocker. '**stockpiling** *n* stockage *m;* constitution *f* de réserves. '**stockpot** *n Cu:* pot *m* à bouillon; pot-au-feu *m inv.* '**stockroom** *n* magasin *m*, réserve *f*. '**stockstill** *adv* to stand **s.-s.**, rester complètement immobile. '**stocktaking** *n Com:* inventaire *m*. '**stocky** *a* (**-ier, -iest**) trapu; ragot.

stockade [stɔ'keid] *n* palissade *f*, palanque *f*.

stocking ['stɔkiŋ] *n Cl:* bas *m;* **fully fashioned s.**, bas diminué; *Med:* **elastic stockings**, bas pour varices; *Knit:* **s. stitch**, point (de) jersey; **to stand six feet in one's s.** (*also* **stockinged**) **feet** = mesurer 1,82m sans chaussures.

stodge [stɔdʒ] *n F:* aliment bourratif. '**stodgy** *a* (**-ier, -iest**) (repas) lourd; (aliment) bourratif; (livre) indigeste; *F:* (*of pers*) lourd, lourdaud.

stoic(al) ['stouik(əl)] *a* stoïque. '**stoically** *adv* stoïquement. '**stoicism** [-sizm] *n* stoïcisme *m*.

stoke [stouk] *vtr* charger (un foyer); chauffer (un four); entretenir le feu (d'un four). '**stoker** *n* chauffeur *m*.

stole[1], **stolen** ['stoul(ən)] *see* **steal**.

stole[2] [stoul] *n Cl:* étole *f*.

stolid ['stɔlid] *a* lourd, lent, impassible. **sto'lidity** *n* flegme *m*. '**stolidly** *adv* flegmatiquement.

stomach ['stʌmək] **1.** *n* ventre *m;* (*organ*) estomac *m;* **to crawl on one's s.**, ramper à plat ventre; **s. pump**, pompe stomacale; **s. trouble, upset s.**, troubles de digestion; crise de foie **2.** *vtr* endurer, supporter, tolérer (qch); digérer (une insulte); **I can't s. it any longer**, j'en ai plein le dos. '**stomachache** *n* mal *m* de ventre; douleurs *fpl* d'estomac; **to have (a) s.**, avoir mal au ventre.

stone [stoun] **1.** *n* (*a*) pierre *f;* caillou *m;* **to leave no s. unturned (in order to do sth)**, remuer ciel et terre (pour faire qch); **to throw stones at s.o.**, lancer des pierres à qn; (**within**) **a s.'s throw (from here)**, à quelques cm, à deux pas (d'ici) (*b*) *Const:* moellon *m;* pierre de taille; **not to leave a s. standing**, ne pas laisser pierre sur pierre (*c*) (*gravestone*) pierre tombale; (*grindstone*) meule *f* (de moulin); (*oilstone*) pierre à huile; **precious stones**, pierres précieuses; pierreries *fpl* (*d*) (*material*) pierre (à bâtir); **s. quarry**, carrière *f* (de pierre); broken **s.**, pierraille *f*, cailloutis *m* (*e*) *Med:* calcul *m* (du rein) (*f*) noyau *m* (de fruit); **s. fruit**, fruit à noyau (*g*) (*inv in pl*) *Meas:* = 6,348 kg; **to weigh 12 s.** = peser 76 kilos **2.** *a* (mur) de, en, pierre; (pot de) grès; **s. cold**, froid comme (le) marbre, complètement froid; **s. dead**, raide mort; **s. deaf**, complètement sourd; **s. blind**, complètement aveugle **3.** *vtr* (*a*) **to s. s.o. (to death)**, lapider qn (*b*) dénoyauter (des fruits); épépiner (des raisins secs). '**stoned** *a P:* ivre, soûl; (*on drugs*) drogué. '**stonemason** *n* maçon *m*. '**stonewall** *vi* (*in debate*) faire de l'obstruction. '**stoneware** *n* poterie *f* de grès. '**stonework** *n* maçonnerie *f*. '**stonily** *adv* froidement; (regarder) d'un air glacial. '**stoniness** *n* nature pierreuse (du sol); dureté *f* (de

cœur). '**stony** *a* (**-ier, -iest**) pierreux; dur comme la pierre; (accueil) froid; **s. heart**, cœur de roche, de marbre; **s. look**, regard glacial; *F:* **s. broke**, fauché, à sec; **I'm s. broke**, je suis complètement fauché.

stood [stud] *see* **stand II.**

stooge [stu:dʒ] **1.** *n* (*a*) *Th:* faire-valoir *m inv* (*b*) souffre-douleur *m inv* **2.** *vi Th:* servir de faire-valoir (à un acteur).

stool [stu:l] *n* (*a*) tabouret *m;* **folding s.**, pliant *m;* **wooden s.**, escabeau *m;* **to fall between two stools**, s'asseoir entre deux chaises; *F:* **s. pigeon**, mouchard *m;* indicateur, -trice (de police) (*b*) *pl Med:* selles *fpl*.

stoop [stu:p] **1.** *n* inclination *f* en avant; **to walk with a s.**, marcher le dos voûté **2.** *vi* (*a*) se pencher, se baisser; **to s. to go through the door**, se baisser pour passer par la porte (*b*) s'abaisser, descendre (à (faire) qch); **a man who would s. to anything**, un homme prêt à toutes les bassesses (*c*) avoir le dos rond; être voûté. '**stooping** *a* penché, courbé; voûté.

stop [stɔp] **I.** *n* (*a*) arrêt *m;* interruption *f;* **to put a s. to sth**, arrêter, faire cesser, qch; mettre fin à qch (*b*) arrêt, halte *f;* pause *f;* **ten minutes' s.**, dix minutes d'arrêt; **to come to a s.**, s'arrêter, faire halte; **to bring sth to a s.**, arrêter qch; **bus s.**, arrêt d'autobus; **request s.**, arrêt facultatif; *Av:* **scheduled s.**, escale prévue; **s. signal**, signal d'arrêt; *Aut:* **stop** *m* (*c*) *Gram:* **full s.**, point *m;* (*in telegram*) **stop** (*d*) *Mus:* jeu *m*, registre *m* (d'orgue); *Fig:* **to pull out all the stops**, donner le maximum (*e*) dispositif *m* de blocage; arrêt, taquet *m*, butée *f;* **door s.**, heurtoir *m*. **II.** *v* (**stopped**) **1.** *vtr* (*a*) boucher (une voie d'eau); plomber, obturer (une dent); **to s. (up)**, boucher, fermer (un trou); obstruer (un tuyau); (*of pipe*) **to get stopped (up)**, se boucher, s'obstruer; **to s. one's ears**, se boucher les oreilles; **to s. a gap**, boucher un trou; combler une lacune (*b*) arrêter; interrompre (la circulation); couper (l'électricité, la respiration à qn); parer (un coup); **to s. s.o. short**, arrêter qn (tout) court; **s. thief!** au voleur! **to s. s.o. from doing sth**, empêcher qn de faire qch; **I can't s. it happening**, je ne peux pas l'empêcher; **to s. (payment of) a cheque**, faire opposition à un chèque, au paiement d'un chèque; **to s. a clock, a machine**, arrêter une pendule, une machine; (*of abuse*) **it ought to be stopped**, il faudrait y mettre fin (*c*) cesser (ses efforts); arrêter (de parler); **s. it!** assez! ça suffit! **it's stopped raining**, il ne pleut plus; la pluie a cessé (*d*) retenir (le salaire de qn); supprimer (la pension de qn); **to s. s.o.'s allowance**, couper les vivres à qn; *Mil:* **all leave is stopped**, toutes les permissions sont suspendues **2.** *vi* s'arrêter; cesser (de faire qch); (*of car*) stopper; (*of pers*) **to s. short**, s'arrêter tout court; **to s. dead**, s'arrêter net, pile; *PN:* **all buses s. here** = arrêt fixe; *PN: Aut:* **s., stop; s. light**, le (feu) stop; feu rouge; *Rail:* **how long do we s. at Aix?** combien d'arrêt à Aix? **to pass a station without stopping**, brûler une gare; *Nau:* **to s. at a port**, faire escale dans un port; **my watch has stopped**, ma montre (s')est arrêtée; **without stopping**, (parler) sans s'arrêter, sans arrêt, sans cesse; (travailler) d'arrache-pied; **he didn't s. at that**, il ne s'en est pas tenu là; **the matter won't s. there**, l'affaire n'en demeurera pas là; **the rain's stopped**, la pluie a cessé; **to s. at home**, rester à la maison; **he's stopping with us a few days**, il est venu passer quelques jours chez nous; **to s. at a hotel**, descendre dans, séjourner à, un hôtel. **'stop 'by** vi esp NAm: faire une petite visite chez qn. **'stopcock** n robinet m d'arrêt. **'stopgap** n bouche-trou m; **it'll do as a s.,** cela servira à boucher un trou. **'stop 'off** vi s'arrêter, faire étape. **'stopover** n Av: escale. **'stoppage** n (a) arrêt; suspension f (du travail); retenue f (sur un salaire) (b) obstruction f, engorgement m (d'un tuyau); Med: occlusion f(c) arrêt, halte; interruption f (du travail); Ind: (strike) débrayage m. **'stopper** n bouchon m; F: **to put a s. on s.o.'s activities,** enrayer les activités de qn. **'stopping** I. n arrêt; plombage m (d'une dent); **s. place,** (point d')arrêt 2. a **s. train,** train omnibus. **'stop-'press** n Journ: **s.-p. (news),** informations fpl de dernière heure. **'stopwatch** n (pl -es) chronomètre m (à déclic).

store [stɔːr] I. n (a) provision f, approvisionnement m; **to lay in a s. of sth,** faire (une) provision de, s'approvisionner en, qch; **to keep sth in s.,** garder qch en réserve; **what the future holds in s.,** ce que l'avenir nous réserve; **that's a treat in s.,** c'est un plaisir à venir; **to set great s. by sth,** faire grand cas de qch (b) **stores,** provisions, approvisionnements, vivres mpl (c) entrepôt m, magasin m; (for furniture) gardemeuble m (d) (shop) magasin; boutique f; **village s.,** alimentation f, épicerie f, du village; **(department) s.,** grand magasin. II. v 1. vtr (a) **to s. (up),** amasser, accumuler (qch); mettre (qch) en réserve; emmagasiner (l'électricité, la chaleur); Comptr: stocker, mémoriser (des données) (b) mettre (des meubles) en dépôt; mettre (le foin) en grange; **stored furniture,** mobilier au garde-meuble 2. vi (of food) se conserver. **'storage** n (a) emmagasinage m; accumulation f (de pouvoir); **plenty of s. space,** grand volume de rangement; Furn: **s. unit,** meuble de rangement; **s. tank,** réservoir de stockage; **(night) s. heating,** chauffage par accumulation (pendant la nuit); **to take goods out of s.,** sortir des marchandises (b) caves fpl, greniers mpl (d'une maison); (for goods) entrepôts mpl, magasins mpl (d'une maison de commerce) (c) frais mpl d'entrepôt. **'storehouse** n magasin, entrepôt; Fig: mine f (de renseignements). **'storekeeper** n magasinier m; NAm: (Br = shopkeeper) marchand, -ande; boutiquier, -ière. **'storeroom** n office f, réserve f.

storey ['stɔːri] n étage m (d'une maison); **on the third s.,** NAm: **on the fourth s.,** au troisième (étage).

stork [stɔːk] n Orn: cigogne f.

storm [stɔːm] 1. n orage m; (wind) tempête f; **s. cloud,** nuée (d'orage); Fig: nuage à l'horizon, nuage menaçant; **s. centre,** centre de la tempête, Fig: d'agitation; **a s. in a teacup,** une tempête dans un verre d'eau; **to raise a s.,** soulever une tempête; **s. of abuse, of applause,** tempête d'injures, d'applaudissements; **to take by s.,** prendre d'assaut (un fort); emporter (un auditoire); **s. troops,** troupes d'assaut 2. v (a) vi (of wind, rain) faire rage; (of pers) tempêter (b) vtr prendre d'assaut, livrer l'assaut à (une place forte). **'stormy** a (-ier, -iest) (temps, ciel) orageux, d'orage; **s. sea,** mer démontée; **s. discussion,** discussion orageuse; **s. meeting,** réunion houleuse.

story[1] ['stɔːri] n (pl stories) histoire f, récit m, conte m; intrigue f (d'un roman); Journ: F: article m; **according to his own s.,** d'après lui; F: **that's quite another s.,** ça

c'est une autre histoire; **it's the (same) old s.,** c'est toujours la même histoire; **it's a long s.,** c'est toute une histoire; **these bruises tell their own s.,** ces meurtrissures en disent long; **short s.,** nouvelle f; **detective s.,** (roman m) policier m; **cock-and-bull s.,** histoire à dormir debout; F: **to tell stories,** dire des mensonges. **'storybook** n livre m de contes. **'storyteller** n conteur, -euse.

story[2] n (pl stories) NAm: = **storey.**

stout[1] [staut] a (a) fort, vigoureux; brave, vaillant; ferme, résolu; **to put up a s. resistance,** se défendre vaillamment; **s. heart,** cœur vaillant; **s. fellow,** gaillard solide (b) (of thg) fort, solide; (of cloth) résistant (c) gros, corpulent; **to grow s.,** prendre de l'embonpoint. **'stout-'hearted** a vaillant, intrépide. **'stoutly** adv fortement, vigoureusement; vaillamment; **to maintain sth s.,** affirmer qch énergiquement; **to deny sth s.,** nier qch fort et ferme; **s. built,** solidement bâti. **'stoutness** n (of pers) embonpoint m.

stout[2] n stout m; bière brune forte.

stove[stouv] n (a) poêle m, fourneau m; DomEc: **oil s.,** poêle à mazout (b) DomEc: (cooker) cuisinière f (à gaz, électrique); (smaller) réchaud m (c) Ind: four m. **'stovepipe** n tuyau m de poêle.

stow [stou] 1. vtr (a) **to s. (away),** mettre en place, ranger (des objets) (b) Nau: arrimer (des marchandises) 2. vi **to s. away,** s'embarquer clandestinement (à bord d'un navire). **'stowage** n Nau: arrimage m. **'stowaway** n passager, -ère, clandestin(e).

straddle ['strædl] vtr enfourcher (un cheval); se mettre à califourchon sur (une chaise).

straggle ['strægl] vi **to s. (along),** marcher sans ordre, à la débandade. **'straggler** n traînard, -arde. **'straggling, 'straggly** a disséminé; (cheveux) épars; **s. village,** village aux maisons éparses.

straight [streit] 1. a (a) droit; rectiligne; **s. line,** ligne droite; droite f; **s. hair,** cheveux raides, plats (b) (mouvement) en ligne droite (c) honnête; loyal; **s. answer,** réponse franche, sans équivoque; **to be s. with s.o.,** agir loyalement avec qn (d) F: (of pers) normal; hétérosexuel (e) net; tout simple; Pol: **s. fight,** campagne électorale à deux candidats; **s. whisky,** whisky sec, sans eau; Th: **s. part,** rôle sérieux; (of comedian) **s. man,** faire-valoir m (f) droit; d'aplomb; **to put sth s.,** redresser, ajuster, qch; **your tie isn't s.,** votre cravate est de travers; **s. face,** visage impassible (g) en ordre; **to put the room s.,** remettre de l'ordre dans la pièce; **to put things s.,** arranger les choses; débrouiller l'affaire; F: **get this s.!** comprends-moi bien! 2. n aplomb m; (of pers) **to be on the s.,** agir loyalement; **material cut on the s.,** tissu coupé de droit fil; Rac: **the s.,** la ligne droite 3. adv (a) droit; **to shoot s.,** tirer juste; **keep s. on,** continuez tout droit; **to go s.,** aller droit; Fig: vivre honnêtement; **to read a book s. through,** lire un livre d'un bout à l'autre (b) directement; **I'll come s. back,** je ne fais que l'aller et retour; **to go s. to the point,** aller droit au fait; **to drink s. from the bottle,** boire à même la bouteille; **to walk s. in,** entrer sans frapper; **s. away,** tout de suite; immédiatement, aussitôt; (deviner qch) du premier coup; **s. off,** sur-le-champ; tout de suite (c) tout droit, directement; **s. across the road,** c'est juste en face; **s. above sth,** juste au-dessus de qch; **to look s.o. s. in the face, in the eye(s),** regarder qn bien en face, droit dans les yeux; **I tell you s.,** je vous le dis tout net; **s. out,** franchement; **to play s.,** jouer beau jeu. **'straighten** v 1. vtr (a) rendre (qch) droit; (re)dresser (qch); défausser (une barre de fer); **to s. one's back,** se redresser (b) **to s. (up),** ranger (qch); mettre (qch) en ordre; **to s. (out) one's affairs,** mettre ses affaires en ordre; **I'll try to s. things out,** je vais essayer d'arranger les choses; **to s. one's tie,** arranger sa cravate 2. vi se redresser; devenir droit; (of pers) **to s. up,** se redresser. **'straight'forward** a loyal; franc; **to give a s. answer,** répondre sans détours. **straight'forwardly** adv (agir) avec droiture, loyalement; (parler) carrément, franchement, sans détours. **straight'forwardness** n droiture f, honnêteté f, franchise f. **'straightness** n rectitude f; droiture f (de conduite).

strain¹ [strein] I. n (a) tension f; **s. on the rope,** tension de la corde; **breaking s.,** effort m de rupture; **the s. of modern life,** la tension de la vie moderne; **mental s.,** surmenage (intellectuel); **eye s.,** fatigue f occulaire (b) Med: entorse f, foulure f; MecE: déformation f (d'une pièce); **s. in the back,** tour m de reins (c) Mus: Poet: usu pl accents mpl; **he went on in the same s.,** il s'est étendu dans ce sens. II. v 1. vtr (a) tendre, surtendre (un câble); **to s. one's voice,** forcer sa voix; **to s. one's ears,** tendre l'oreille; **to s. one's eyes doing sth,** se fatiguer, s'abîmer, les yeux à faire qch; **to s. one's eyes to see sth,** s'efforcer pour voir qch; **to s. one's resources,** grever ses ressources; **to s. s.o.'s friendship,** exiger trop de l'amitié de qn (b) fouler, forcer (un membre); **to s. one's back,** se donner un tour de reins; **to s. one's heart,** se forcer le cœur; **to s. a muscle,** se froisser un muscle; **to s. one's shoulder,** se fouler l'épaule; **to s. oneself doing sth,** se surmener, s'éreinter, à faire qch; F: **he doesn't exactly s. himself,** il ne se foule pas; il ne se fatigue pas trop (c) forcer (une poutre); MecE: déformer (une pièce) (d) filtrer, passer (un liquide); faire égoutter (les légumes) 2. vi faire un grand effort; peiner; **to s. to do sth,** faire tous ses efforts pour faire qch; **to s. at sth,** tirer sur qch. **strained** a (a) tendu; **s. ankle,** cheville foulée; **s. heart,** cœur forcé (b) (rire) forcé, contraint (c) (liquide) filtré. **'strainer** n filtre m, tamis m; Cu: passoire f.

strain² n (a) qualité héritée, inhérente; tendance f; **a s. of weakness,** un fond de faiblesse (b) race f, lignée f; (of virus) souche f.

strait [streit] n usu pl détroit m; **the Straits of Dover,** le Pas de Calais; **to be in dire straits,** être dans une situation désespérée. **'straitened** a **to be in s. circumstances,** être dans la gêne. **'straitjacket** n camisole f de force. **'straitlaced** a prude; collet monté inv.

strand¹ [strænd] n brin m (de cordage, de fil à coudre); fil m (de perles, d'une histoire); tresse f (de cheveux).

strand² vtr & i échouer. **'stranded** a (of ship) échoué; (of pers) abandonné; en panne; **to leave s.o. s.,** laisser qn en plan.

strange [streindʒ] a (a) (unknown) inconnu; **I can't work with s. tools,** je ne peux pas travailler avec des outils qui ne sont pas les miens; **this writing is s. to me,** je ne connais pas cette écriture; **I felt s. in those surroundings,** je me sentais dépaysé dans ce milieu (b) singulier, bizarre, étrange; **s. to say,** chose étrange (à dire); **it's s. that you haven't heard of it,** il est étonnant que vous ne l'ayez pas appris. **'strangely** adv étrangement, singulièrement; **s. enough,** chose étrange. **'strangeness** n étrangeté f, singularité f; bizarrerie f; **the s. of the work,** la nouveauté du travail. **'stranger** n étranger, -ère; inconnu -ue; **I'm a s. here,** je ne suis pas d'ici; **he's a complete s. to me,** il m'est tout à fait inconnu; **he's no s. to fear,** il sait ce que c'est d'avoir peur; **you're quite a s.!** on ne vous voit plus! vous vous faites rare!

strangle ['stræŋgl] vtr étrangler; **strangled voice,** voix étranglée. **'stranglehold** n **to have a s. on s.o.,** tenir qn à la gorge. **'strangler** n étrangleur, -euse. **strangu'lation** n strangulation f.

strap [stræp] 1. n courroie f; bracelet m (pour montre); bande f, sangle f (de cuir, de toile); barrette f (de chaussure); bretelle f (de robe); Tchn: lien m (en métal); bride f (de bielle); (in the underground) **(standing passenger's) s.,** poignée f d'appui 2. vtr **(strapped) to s. sth (up),** attacher, lier, qch avec une courroie; Med: mettre un pansement adhésif à (une blessure). **'straphanger** n voyageur, -euse, debout (dans le métro). **'strapless** a (robe) sans bretelles. **'strapping** a robuste; **s. fellow,** grand gaillard.

stratagem ['strætədʒəm] n ruse f (de guerre); stratagème m. **strategic(al)** [-'tiːdʒik-] a stratégique. **stra'tegically** adv stratégiquement. **'strategist** n stratège m. **'strategy** n (pl -ies) stratégie f.

stratify ['strætifai] vtr (stratified) stratifier. **stratifi'cation** n stratification f. **'stratosphere** n stratosphère f. **stratum** ['strɑːtəm] n (pl strata ['strɑːtə]) couche f; **social strata,** couches sociales.

straw [strɔː] n paille f; **s. hat,** chapeau de paille; **s. mat,** paillasson m; **s. mattress,** paillasse f; **to drink through a s.,** boire (qch) avec une paille; Fig: **to clutch at straws,** se raccrocher à n'importe quoi; **s. in the wind,** indication f de l'opinion publique; **s. poll, vote,** sondage d'opinion publique; **it's the last s. (that breaks the camel's back)!** c'est la goutte d'eau qui fait déborder le vase; c'est le comble! il ne manquait plus que ça! **s.(-coloured),** paille inv.

strawberry ['strɔːbəri] n (pl strawberries) fraise f; (plant) fraisier m; **wild s.,** fraise des bois; **s. jam,** confiture de fraises; **s. ice,** glace à la fraise; (on skin) **s. mark,** fraise.

stray [strei] 1. a (animal) égaré, perdu; (enfant) abandonné; (exemple) isolé; **s. bullets,** balles perdues; **s. thoughts,** pensées détachées; **a few s. houses,** quelques maisons isolées 2. n animal égaré; bête perdue 3. vi s'égarer, errer; s'écarter (de qch); **to let one's thoughts s.,** donner libre cours à ses pensées.

streak [striːk] 1. n raie f; bande f, strie f; trait m, filet m (de lumière); **the first s. of dawn,** la première lueur du jour; **like a s. of lightning,** comme un éclair; F: **s. of luck, lucky s.,** coup m de veine; **he had a s. of cowardice,** il était un peu lâche de nature 2. vi (a) strier; zébrer; **to s. past,** passer comme un éclair (b) F: courir tout nu (en public). **streaked** a rayé, strié (with, de). **'streaker** n F: coureur, -euse, nu(e) (en public). **'streaky** a (a) en raies (b) rayé, strié; (of bacon) entrelardé; **s. bacon** = petit salé.

stream [stri:m] I. n (a) cours m d'eau; ruisseau m; flot m d'eau; Sch: niveau m; in a thin s., en mince filet m (b) coulée f (de lave); flot(s) m(pl) (de gens); s. of abuse, torrent m d'injures; people entered in streams, les gens entraient à flots; s. of cars, défilé ininterrompu de voitures; in one continuous s., à jet continu (c) courant m; with the s., au fil de l'eau; against the s., contre le courant, à contre-courant. II. v 1. vi (of liquid) couler (à flots); (of liquid, surface) ruisseler; (of hair, banner) flotter au vent; people were streaming over the bridge, les gens traversaient le pont à flot continu; they streamed in, out, ils entraient, sortaient, à flots; her eyes were streaming (with tears), ses larmes coulaient à flots 2. vtr Sch: répartir (des élèves) en sections de force homogène. 'streamer n banderole f; paper streamers, serpentins mpl. 'streaming 1. a ruisselant; face s. with tears, visage baigné de larmes; to be s. with perspiration, être en nage; I've got a s. cold, j'ai attrapé un gros rhume (de cerveau) 2. n Sch: répartition f (des élèves) en sections de force homogène. 'streamline vtr caréner (une voiture); rationaliser (des méthodes). 'streamlined a caréné, fuselé, profilé; (fuselage) aérodynamique; (système) rationalisé. 'streamlining n carénage m, profilage m (d'une voiture); rationalisation f (des méthodes).

street [stri:t] n rue f; to turn s.o. (out) onto the s., mettre qn sur le pavé; the man in the s., l'homme de la rue; he's streets ahead of his competitors, il dépasse nettement tous ses concurrents; they're not in the same s. as him, ils n'arrivent pas à sa hauteur; Fig: that's right up my s., c'est parfaitement dans mes cordes; s. guide, indicateur des rues; s. level, rez-de-chaussée m inv; s. door, porte sur la rue; porte d'entrée; s. light, lamp, réverbère m; s. lighting, éclairage des rues; s. market, marché en plein air; s. sweeper, (pers) balayeur des rues; (machine) balayeuse f (de rues); s. musician, musicien des rues, de carrefour. 'streetcar n NAm: (Br = tram) tramway m. 'streetwalker n putain f; prostituée f.

strength [streŋθ] n (a) force(s) f(pl); intensité f (d'un courant); solidité f (d'un matériel); with all one's s., de toutes ses forces; s. of mind, force de caractère; fermeté f d'esprit; s. of will, résolution f; by sheer s., de vive force; to regain one's s., reprendre des forces; to do sth on the s. of what one has been told, faire qch en se fiant à ce qu'on vous a dit; to get the job on the s. of one's qualifications, obtenir un poste grâce à ses diplômes; to be present in great s., être présents en grand nombre (b) Mil: effectif(s) m(pl) (d'une unité); at full s., à effectif complet; to be on the s., faire partie de l'effectif. 'strengthen 1. vtr consolider (un mur); renforcer (une poutre); fortifier (qn); (r)affermir (l'autorité de qn) 2. vi se fortifier. 'strengthening 1. a fortifiant; (of drink) remontant 2. n renforcement m; consolidation f; armement m (d'une poutre).

strenuous ['strenjuəs] a (of pers) actif, énergique; (travail) acharné, ardu; (effort) tendu; s. life, vie toute d'effort; to offer s. opposition to sth, faire une opposition vigoureuse à qch. 'strenuously adv vigoureusement; avec acharnement; énergiquement. 'strenuousness n ardeur f, vigueur f; acharnement m.

stress [stres] 1. n (pl stresses) (a) force f, contrainte f; Mec: tension f, travail m; Med: tension nerveuse; stress m; period of storm and s., période de trouble et d'agitation (b) insistance f; to lay s. on a fact, insister sur un fait (c) Ling: accent m; s. mark, accent écrit 2. vtr (stresses) insister, appuyer, sur (qch); souligner (un mot); accentuer (une syllabe, un mot). 'stressful a stressant.

stretch [stretʃ] I. n (a) allongement m, extension f; Rac: at full s., à toute allure; by a s. of the imagination, par un effort d'imagination (b) élasticité f (d'un tissu) (c) étendue f (de pays); level s. (of road), palier m; for a long s. of time, longtemps; at a s., tout d'un trait; d'affilée; F: to do a five-year s., faire cinq ans de prison. II. a (tissu) extensible, élastique. III. v (stretches) 1. vtr (a) tendre (de l'élastique); élargir (ses chaussures); to s. (out), allonger (le bras); tendre (la main); to s. (oneself) (out), s'étirer; to s. one's legs, allonger les jambes; (for exercise) se dégourdir les jambes; stretched (out) on the ground, étendu (de tout son long) par terre; (of bird) to s. its wings, déployer ses ailes; Fig: to be fully stretched, (of pers) donner son maximum; (of resources) être poussé à bout (b) forcer (le sens d'un mot); to s. the truth, outrepasser les bornes de la vérité; to s. a point, faire une concession 2. vi (a) s'étirer; s'élargir; s'allonger; (of elastic) s'étendre; material that stretches, tissu qui prête; (of meal) it will s. to four, on en fera quand même quatre portions; my resources won't s. to that, mes moyens ne vont pas jusque-là (b) (of landscape) s'étendre. 'stretcher n brancard m; civière f; s. bearer, brancardier m. 'stretchy a (-ier, -iest) élastique; extensible.

strew [stru:] vtr (pp strewed or strewn) to s. the ground with sand, to s. sand over the ground, jeter, répandre, du sable sur le sol; toys were strewn all over the floor, des jouets étaient éparpillés sur le plancher; to s. the pavement with flowers, parsemer, joncher, le pavé de fleurs.

stricken ['strikən] a blessé; (of pers) affligé; accablé (with grief, de douleur); the s. city, la ville sinistrée; s. vessel, navire en détresse.

strict [strikt] a (a) exact; strict; (étiquette) rigide; in the strict(est) sense of the word, au sens précis du mot; s. neutrality, neutralité rigoureuse; s. orders, ordres formels; s. discipline, discipline sévère (b) (of pers) sévère; to be s. with s.o., traiter qn avec beaucoup de rigueur. 'strictly adv (a) exactement, rigoureusement; s. speaking, à proprement parler; s. in confidence, à titre tout à fait confidentiel (b) étroitement; strictement; smoking (is) s. prohibited, défense formelle, défense expresse, de fumer; it is s. forbidden, c'est absolument défendu (c) sévèrement; (élevé) avec rigueur. 'strictness n exactitude rigoureuse, précision f (d'une traduction); rigueur f, (des règles); sévérité f (de la discipline). 'stricture n to pass strictures on s.o., sth, adresser des critiques f à qn; trouver à redire à qch.

stride [straid] 1. n (a) (grand) pas m; enjambée f; Sp: foulée f; Fig: to make great strides, faire de grands progrès; to take sth in one's s., faire qch sans le moindre effort; to get into one's s., prendre son allure normale; adopter, prendre, la cadence (d'un travail) 2. vi (strode [stroud]; stridden ['stridn]) to s. along, avancer à grands pas; **to s. away,** s'éloigner à grands pas; **to s. over,** enjamber (un obstacle).

strident ['straidənt] *a* strident.

strife [straif] *n* lutte *f*; conflits *mpl*.

strike [straik] I. *n* (*a*) *Ind:* grève *f*; **to come out on s.,** se mettre en grève; **token s.,** grève symbolique; **sympathy s.,** grève de solidarité; **lightning s.,** grève surprise; **sitdown s.,** grève sur le tas; **s. pay,** allocation de grève (*b*) découverte *f* (de pétrole); **lucky s.,** coup *m* de veine (*c*) *Fish:* touche *f*; *Games:* (*baseball*) balle manquée (par le batteur); (*tenpin bowling*) honneur *m* double (*d*) *Mil:* attaque *f*; *MilAv:* raid (aérien); **s. aircraft,** avion d'assaut. II. *v* (**struck** [strʌk]) 1. *vtr & i* (*a*) frapper; **ready to s. a blow for freedom,** prêt à se battre pour défendre la liberté; **to s. at s.o.,** porter un coup à qn; **to s. home,** frapper juste; **to s. a medal,** frapper une médaille; **to s. a chord,** plaquer un accord; **that strikes a familiar note,** cela rappelle quelque chose; **to s. a bargain,** faire, conclure, un marché (*b*) frotter (une allumette); faire jaillir (des étincelles); (*of snake*) **to s. (s.o.),** foncer (sur qn); **to s. terror into s.o.,** frapper qn de terreur; (*of plant*) **to s. (root),** prendre (racine); **struck by lightning,** frappé par la foudre; **struck with terror,** saisi d'effroi; **to s. (against) sth,** heurter (contre) qch; **his head struck the pavement,** sa tête a porté sur le trottoir; (*of ship*) **to s. (on) the rocks,** donner, toucher, sur les écueils; **a sound struck my ear,** un bruit m'a frappé l'oreille; **the thought strikes me that,** l'idée me vient que; **how did she s. you?** quelle impression vous a-t-elle faite? **he strikes me as (being) sincere,** il me paraît sincère; **that's how it struck me,** voilà l'effet que cela m'a fait; **it strikes me that,** il me semble que; **what struck me was,** ce qui m'a frappé, c'est; **I was greatly struck,** j'ai été très impressionné (*c*) tomber sur, découvrir (une piste); trouver (le pétrole); **I've struck on an idea,** j'ai eu une idée; *F:* **he's struck it rich,** il tient le filon; **to s. tents,** plier les tentes; **to s. camp,** lever le camp; **to s. an attitude,** poser; **to s. an average,** établir, prendre, une moyenne 2. *vi* (*a*) (*of clock*) sonner; **it's just struck ten,** dix heures viennent de sonner; **the clock struck six,** six heures ont sonné (*b*) **to s. across country,** prendre à travers champs; **to s. into the jungle,** s'enfoncer, pénétrer, dans la jungle; **the road strikes off to the right,** la route tourne à droite (*c*) *Ind:* se mettre en grève. **'strikebound** *a* paralysé par une grève. **'strikebreaker** *n Ind:* briseur, -euse, de grève. **'strike 'down** *vtr* renverser (d'un coup de poing); **struck d. by disease,** terrassé par la maladie. **'strike 'off** *vtr* (*a*) trancher (la tête de qn) (*b*) rayer (un nom d'une liste); radier (un médecin). **'strike 'out** 1. *vtr* rayer (un mot) 2. *vi* **to s. o. at s.o.,** porter un coup à qn; **to s. o. for the shore,** se mettre à nager dans la direction du rivage; **to s. o. for oneself,** voler de ses propres ailes. **'striker** *n Ind:* gréviste *mf*. **'strike 'up** 1. *vtr & i* entonner (une chanson); commencer à jouer (un morceau) 2. *vtr* **to s. up a friendship with s.o.,** se lier d'amitié avec qn; **to s. up (a) conversation,** entrer en conversation (with s.o., avec qn). **'striking** 1. *a* (*a*) **s. clock,** pendule à sonnerie (*b*) (spectacle) remarquable, frappant, saisissant 2. *n* **within s. distance,** à portée (de la main). **'strikingly** *adv* d'une manière frappante; **s. beautiful,** d'une beauté frappante.

string [striŋ] 1. *n* (*a*) ficelle *f*; corde *f*, cordon *m*; **ball of** **s.,** pelote de ficelle; **to pull the strings,** tirer les fils, les ficelles; **s. bag,** filet à provisions; **s. bean,** haricot vert; *Fig:* **with no strings attached,** sans conditions; *Mus:* **the strings,** les instruments *m* à cordes; **s. orchestra,** orchestre à cordes; **to have more than one s. to one's bow,** avoir plus d'une corde à son arc (*b*) chapelet *m*, rang *m* (d'oignons); file *f* (de voitures); *Turf:* écurie *f*; **long s. of tourists,** longue procession de touristes 2. *vtr* (**strung** [strʌŋ]) (*a*) garnir (qch) de cordes; corder (une raquette de tennis); bander (un arc); **highly strung,** nerveux; impressionnable (*b*) enfiler (des perles); accrocher (des guirlandes) (*c*) *Cu:* enlever les fils (des haricots). **'string a'long** *F:* 1. *vtr* tenir (qn) en suspens; tromper (qn); faire marcher (qn) 2. *vi* **to s. a. with s.o.,** suivre qn, être copain avec qn. **stringed** *a* (instrument) à cordes. **'string 'out** *vtr* faire traîner (une conversation) en longueur. **'string 'up** *vtr* pendre (qn) haut et court; *F:* **to be strung up,** s'énerver (about, à propos de). **'stringy** *a* (**-ier, -iest**) filandreux; fibreux.

stringent ['strindʒənt] *a* rigoureux, strict. **'stringency** *n* rigueur *f*, sévérité *f* (des règles).

strip [strip] I. *n* (*a*) bande *f*; **s. of land,** bande, langue *f*, de terre; *Av:* (**landing**) **s.,** piste *f* d'atterrissage; **s. cartoon, comic s.,** bande dessinée; **s. lighting,** éclairage au néon, fluorescent; *F:* **to tear s.o. off a s.,** laver la tête à qn (*b*) *Sp:* tenue *f* (d'une équipe). II. *v* (**stripped**) 1. *vtr* (*a*) mettre (qn) tout nu; déshabiller (qn); **stripped to the waist,** nu jusqu'à la ceinture; **to s. s.o. of sth,** dépouiller qn de qch; **trees stripped of their leaves,** arbres dépouillés de leurs feuilles (*b*) défaire (un lit); (*of thieves*) vider (une maison); **to s. (down),** démonter (un moteur, un fusil); **to s. off, from, sth,** enlever qch de qch 2. *vi* (*of pers*) **to s. (off),** se déshabiller; **to s. to the skin,** se mettre tout nu; **to s. to the waist,** se mettre nu jusqu'à la ceinture; (*of paint, bark*) **to s. (off),** s'enlever, se détacher. **'stripper** *n* (*a*) décapant *m* (pour peinture) (*b*) *F:* (*pers*) strip-teaseuse *f*. **'striptease** *n* striptease *m*; **s. artist,** stripteaseuse.

stripe [straip] *n* raie *f*, barre *f* (d'un tissu); raie, rayure *f*, zébrure *f* (sur le pelage); bande *f* (de pantalon); *Mil:* galon *m*; **to lose one's stripes,** être dégradé. **striped** *a* (chaussettes) à raies; (pelage) rayé, zébré.

stripling ['striplin] *n* tout jeune homme; adolescent *m*.

strive [straiv] *vi* (**strove** [strouv]; **striven** ['strivn]) s'efforcer (de faire qch); **to s. for sth,** essayer d'obtenir qch; **to s. after effect,** rechercher l'effet; **to s. against,** lutter contre (qn, qch).

strobe [stroub] *n F:* stroboscope *m*.

strode [stroud] *see* **stride 2.**

stroke [strouk] 1. *n* (*a*) coup *m*; **with one s., at a s.,** d'un seul coup (*b*) coup (d'aviron); *Swim:* brassée *f*; (*style of swimming*) nage *f* (*c*) *MecE:* mouvement *m*, course *f* (du piston); **two-s.,** (moteur à) deux temps *m*; *F:* **he hasn't done a s. of work,** il n'a rien fait; **s. of (good) luck,** coup de chance, de veine; **s. of genius,** trait *m* de génie (*d*) coup (d'horloge); **on the s. of nine,** sur le coup de neuf heures; **à neuf heures sonnant(es);** *Med:* **to have a s.,** avoir une attaque (*e*) coup de crayon; trait; *Typ:* barre *f*; **with a s. of the pen,** d'un trait de plume (*f*) *Row:* (*pers*) chef *m* de nage; **to row s.,**

donner la nage (g) caresse f de la main 2. vtr passer la main sur, caresser (de la main).

stroll [stroul] 1. n petit tour; **to go for a s.,** aller faire un tour 2. vi errer à l'aventure; flâner; se balader. **'stroller** n (a) flâneur, -euse; promeneur, -euse (b) NAm: (Br = **pushchair**) poussette f (d'enfant).

strong [strɔŋ] I. a fort; solide; (candidat) sérieux; (argument) puissant; El: (courant) intense; **s. conviction,** ferme conviction; **s. character,** caractère fort, ferme; (in health) **he's not very s.,** il est peu robuste; **to grow stronger,** reprendre des forces; **s. voice,** voix forte, puissante; **he's as s. as an ox,** il est fort comme un bœuf; **to be s. in the arm,** avoir le bras fort; **a s. man,** un homme à poigne; **s. measures,** mesures énergiques; **manners aren't his s. point,** la politesse n'est pas son fort; **s. in numbers,** en grand nombre; **company two hundred s.,** compagnie forte de deux cents personnes; **s. reasons,** fortes raisons; Cards: **s. suit,** (couleur) longue f; **s. evidence,** preuves convaincantes; **s. wind,** grand vent; **s. drink,** boissons fortes; **s. light,** vive lumière; (liquid) **s. solution,** solution concentrée; **to have a s. smell,** sentir fort; **s. cheese,** fromage qui pique 2. adv F: **it's still going s.,** ça marche toujours à merveille; **he's still going s.,** il est toujours solide. **'strong-arm** a **to use s.-a. tactics,** appliquer, avoir recours à la manière forte. **'strongbox** n (pl -es) coffre-fort m. **'stronghold** n forteresse f; place forte; Fig: citadelle f (du syndicalisme). **'strongly** adv (a) fortement; solidement, fermement (b) fortement; vigoureusement, énergiquement; **to be s. in favour of sth,** être chaud partisan de qch; **s. worded letter,** lettre en termes énergiques; **I don't feel very s. about it,** cela ne m'enthousiasme guère. **'strong-'minded** a à l'esprit décidé. **'strongroom** n chambre forte. **'strong-willed** a à l'esprit décidé.

strove [strouv] see **strive**.

struck [strʌk] see **strike** II.

structure ['strʌktʃər] n (a) structure f (b) édifice m, bâtiment m; CivE: ouvrage m d'art; **the social s.,** l'édifice social. **'structural** a (a) de construction; **s. steel, iron,** acier, fer, de construction, charpentes métalliques; **s. engineer,** ingénieur constructeur m (b) structural.

struggle ['strʌgl] 1. n lutte f; **desperate s.,** lutte désespérée; combat acharné; **he gave in without a s.,** il n'a opposé aucune résistance 2. vi lutter (with, against, avec, contre); se débattre; se démener; **to s. hard to succeed,** faire tous ses efforts pour réussir; **they struggled for the prize,** ils se disputaient le prix; **we struggled through,** nous avons surmonté tous les obstacles; **he struggled to his feet,** il s'est levé avec difficulté; **to s. along,** marcher péniblement. **'struggling** a (artiste) qui vit péniblement.

strum [strʌm] vtr & i (strummed) **to s. (on) the piano, the guitar,** tapoter (un air) au piano; jouer (un air) à la guitare; gratter de la guitare.

strung [strʌŋ] see **string** 2.

strut¹ [strʌt] 1. n démarche affectée 2. vi (strutted) **to s. (about),** se pavaner, se rengorger; **to s. in, out,** entrer, sortir, d'un air important.

strut² n entretoise f; support m, étai m.

strychnine ['strikni:n] n strychnine f.

stub [stʌb] 1. n (a) souche f (d'arbre); bout m (de crayon, de cigare); F: mégot m (de cigarette) (b) souche, talon m (de chèque) 2. vtr (stubbed) **to s. one's toe against sth,** se cogner, se heurter, le pied contre qch; **to s. out a cigarette,** éteindre une cigarette (en l'écrasant par le bout). **'stubby** a (of plant) tronqué; (of pers) trapu; (of fingers) boudiné.

stubble ['stʌbl] n (a) chaume m (b) barbe (piquante) de plusieurs jours. **'stubbly** a **s. beard,** barbe (piquante) de plusieurs jours.

stubborn ['stʌbən] a obstiné, opiniâtre, entêté, têtu; (cheval) rétif; (fièvre) rebelle. **'stubbornly** adv obstinément. **'stubbornness** n entêtement m; obstination f, opiniâtreté f; ténacité f (de volonté).

stucco ['stʌkou] n stuc m; **s. work,** stucage m.

stuck [stʌk] see **stick²**.

stud¹ [stʌd] 1. n clou m à grosse tête; clou (de passage clouté); pl (on football boots) crampons mpl; bouton m (de chemise) 2. vtr (studded) garnir de clous; clouter. **'studded** a (a) garni de clous; clouté (b) parsemé (with, de); **sky s. with stars,** ciel piqué d'étoiles.

stud² n écurie f (de chasse); (for breeding) **s. (farm),** haras m; **s. (horse),** étalon m; **s. mare,** (jument) poulinière f; **s. book,** registre m (des chevaux); stud-book m; (of horse) **to be at s.,** être en haras.

student ['stju:dənt] n étudiant, -ante; **medical s.,** étudiant en médecine; **s. organization,** organisation étudiante; **s. life,** vie d'étudiant; **the s. body,** les étudiants; **he is a good s.,** il est très studieux.

studio ['stju:diou] n (of artist) atelier m; Cin: TV: WTel: studio m; **s. couch,** lit m canapé.

studious ['stju:diəs] a studieux; **with s. politeness,** avec une politesse étudiée. **'studiously** adv (a) studieusement (b) avec empressement; **he s. avoided me,** il s'ingéniait à m'éviter; **s. polite,** d'une politesse étudiée. **'studiousness** n attachement m à l'étude.

study ['stʌdi] 1. n (pl studies) (a) étude f; **to make a s. of sth,** étudier qch; **to finish one's studies,** achever ses études; **home s. course,** programme d'études chez soi; **s. group,** groupe de travail; F: **his face was a s.,** il fallait voir son visage! **brown s.,** rêverie f (b) (room) bureau m; cabinet m de travail; Sch: salle f d'étude; **s. bedroom,** chambre d'étudiant(e) 2. vtr & i (studied) étudier; observer (les astres); **to s. under Professor Martin,** suivre les cours du professeur Martin; **to s. economics,** faire des études de sciences économiques; étudier l'économie; **he's studying to be a doctor,** il fait des études de médecine; **he's studying,** il fait ses études; (at the moment) il travaille; **to s. for an examination,** préparer un examen; **to s. hard,** travailler ferme. **'studied** a étudié, recherché; prémédité, calculé; **s. carelessness,** négligence voulue.

stuff [stʌf] 1. n (a) matière f, substance f, étoffe f; **he's the s. heroes are made of,** il est du bois dont on fait les héros; F: **he writes good s.,** il écrit bien; **this wine is good s.,** ce vin est bon; **I don't like that s. you gave me,** je n'aime pas ce que vous m'avez donné là; **that's the s.!** c'est du bon! voilà ce qu'il faut! **come on, do your s.!** allons! montre-nous ce que tu sais faire! **he knows his s.,** il s'y connaît; **silly s., sottises** fpl; **s. and nonsense!** quelle bêtise! allons donc! (b) Tex: étoffe, tissu m (de laine) 2. vtr bourrer (with, de); rembourrer (un meuble); empailler (un animal); Cu: farcir (un poulet); **to s. oneself (with food),** se bourrer; bâfrer; F: (pers) **stuffed shirt,** individu suffisant; crâneur, -euse; P: **get stuffed!** va te faire foutre! **to s. up a hole,**

boucher un trou; **my nose is all stuffed up,** je suis enchifrené; **to s. sth into sth,** fourrer qch dans qch; **to s. one's fingers in one's ears,** se boucher les oreilles avec les doigts. **'stuffing** n bourrage m, rembourrage m; empaillage m (d'un animal); Cu: farce f; **to knock the s. out of s.o.,** (i) battre qn à plates coutures (ii) dégonfler qn (iii) épuiser qn.

stuffy ['stʌfi] a (-ier, -iest) (a) mal ventilé; mal aéré; **room that smells s.,** pièce qui sent le renfermé; **it's a bit s. in here,** cela manque d'air ici (b) F: (of pers) collet monté inv; crâneur. **'stuffiness** n manque m d'air; odeur f de renfermé.

stumble ['stʌmbl] **1.** n trébuchement m; faux pas; bronchement m (de cheval) **2.** vi trébucher; faire un faux pas; (of horse) broncher; **to s. over sth,** buter contre qch; **to s. in one's speech, in speaking,** hésiter en parlant; **to s. across, on, s.o., sth,** rencontrer qn, qch, par hasard; tomber sur qn, qch. **'stumbling 1.** a qui trébuche; (cheval) qui bronche; (of speech) hésitant **2.** n (a) trébuchement; faux pas; **s. block,** pierre f d'achoppement (b) hésitation f.

stump [stʌmp] **I.** n (a) souche f (d'arbre); chicot m (de dent); moignon m (de bras, de jambe); bout m (de cigare, de crayon); F: mégot m (de cigare, de cigarette) (b) Cr: piquet m (du guichet). **II.** v **1.** vi **to s. along,** clopiner; **to s. in, out,** entrer, sortir, clopin-clopant **2.** vtr (a) F: coller (un candidat); faire sécher (qn); **to be stumped,** ne savoir plus que faire, que dire; sécher; **this stumped me,** sur le coup je n'ai su que répondre (b) Cr: mettre (un batteur) hors jeu. **'stump** 'up vtr & i F: **to s. up (the money),** payer, F: casquer. **'stumpy** a (-ier, -iest) (of pers) trapu, ramassé.

stun [stʌn] vtr (stunned) (a) étourdir, assommer (b) renverser, abasourdir; **the news stunned me,** c'était un coup de massue; **stunned with surprise,** stupéfait. **'stunning** a (a) (coup) étourdissant; (malheur) accablant (b) F: épatant; **she's really s.,** elle est ravissante.

stung [stʌŋ] see sting 2.

stunk [stʌŋk] see stink 2.

stunt¹ [stʌnt] vtr rabougrir. **'stunted** a rabougri.

stunt² n (a) coup m, affaire f, de publicité (b) tour m de force; Av: acrobatie f (en vol). **'stuntman** n (pl -men) Cin: cascadeur m.

stupefy ['stju:pifai] vtr (stupefied) stupéfier; (surprise) abasourdir; **stupefied with grief,** hébété, abruti, par la douleur; **I'm absolutely stupefied,** je n'en reviens pas. **stupe'faction** n stupéfaction f. **'stupefying** a stupéfiant.

stupendous [stju:'pendəs] a prodigieux; F: formidable. **stu'pendously** adv prodigieusement.

stupid ['stju:pid] a stupide; sot; F: bête; **how s. of me!** que je suis bête; **don't be s.!** ne faites pas l'idiot! **I did a s. thing,** j'ai fait une bêtise. **stu'pidity** n stupidité f; bêtise. **'stupidly** adv stupidement; bêtement.

stupor ['stju:pər] n stupeur f.

sturdy ['stə:di] a (-ier, -iest) vigoureux, robuste; (of opposition, resistance) hardi, résolu, ferme. **'sturdily** adv (a) fortement; **s. built,** robuste (b) hardiment, vigoureusement. **'sturdiness** n vigueur f, robustesse f.

sturgeon ['stə:dʒən] n Ich: esturgeon m.

stutter ['stʌtər] **1.** n bégaiement m **2.** vtr & i bégayer.

'stutterer n bègue mf. **'stuttering 1.** a bègue **2.** n bégaiement m.

sty [stai] n (pl sties) étable f à porcs; porcherie f.

stye [stai] n Med: orgelet m.

style [stail] **1.** n (a) style m, manière f; **s. of living,** manière de vivre; **to live in s.,** mener grand train; **to win in fine s.,** gagner haut la main; **furniture in Empire s., meubles style Empire; Com: made in three styles,** fabriqué en trois genres, sur trois modèles; **something in that s.,** quelque chose de ce genre; **the latest s.,** la dernière mode; **that's not my s.,** ce n'est pas mon genre (b) style, manière d'écrire; **in a humorous s.,** sur un ton de plaisanterie (c) ton, chic m, cachet m; **there's no s. about her,** elle manque de chic **2.** vtr Com: créer (une robe); **to s. s.o.'s hair,** coiffer qn. **'stylish** a élégant, chic. **'stylishly** adv élégamment; avec chic. **'stylishness** n élégance f, chic. **'stylist** n styliste mf; (hair) s., coiffeur, -euse (d'art). **styli'zation** n stylisation f. **'stylize** vtr styliser.

stylus ['stailəs] n (pl styluses) Engr: style m; Elcs: (on record player) pointe f de lecture.

suave [swɑ:v] a doucereux, mielleux. **'suavely** adv doucereusement. **'suaveness, 'suavity** n manières mielleuses.

sub [sʌb] F: **1.** n (a) cotisation f (à un club) (b) Journ: secrétaire mf de la rédaction; Publ: rédacteur, -trice (c) Sp: remplaçant, -ante (d) sous-marin m **2.** v **(subbed)** F: (a) vtr Journ: mettre au point (un article) (b) vi **to s. for s.o.,** remplacer qn.

subaltern ['sʌbltən] **1.** a subalterne **2.** n Mil: lieutenant m; sous-lieutenant m.

subaqua [sʌb'ækwə] a (sport) subaquatique.

subcommittee [sʌbkə'miti] n sous-comité m.

subconscious [sʌb'kɔnʃəs] a & n subconscient (m); inconscient (m). **sub'consciously** adv inconsciemment.

subcontinent [sʌb'kɔntinənt] n **the Indian s.,** le sous-continent indien.

subcontract 1. n [sʌb'kɔntrækt] sous-traité m **2.** vi [sʌbkən'trækt] **to s. for (sth),** sous traiter (une affaire). **subcon'tractor** n sous-entrepreneur m, sous-traitant m.

subdivide [sʌbdi'vaid] vtr & i (se) subdiviser. **subdi'vision** n subdivision f; sous-division f.

subdue [səb'dju:] vtr subjuguer, assujettir (un tribu); maîtriser (un incendie); dompter (un mouvement de colère); adoucir (la lumière, la voix). **sub'dued** a (of pers) préoccupé; déprimé; (of light) adouci, tamisé, atténué; (conversation) à voix basse; **s. colours,** couleurs sobres.

sub-edit [sʌb'edit] vtr mettre au point (un article). **sub'editor** n Journ: secrétaire mf de rédaction; Publ: rédacteur, -trice.

subheading [sʌb'hediŋ] n sous-titre m.

subject 1. ['sʌbdʒikt] n (a) (pers) sujet, -ette; **British s.,** sujet britannique (b) sujet (du verbe, de conversation); **s. (matter),** sujet (d'un livre); contenu m (d'une lettre); **this will be the s. of my next lecture,** cela fera l'objet de ma prochaine conférence; **to hark back to a s.,** revenir sur un sujet; **while we are on this s.,** pendant que nous sommes sur ce sujet; **on the s. of,** au sujet de; **to change the s.,** parler d'autre chose; changer de sujet; Sch: **what subjects do you teach?** quelles matières enseignez-vous? **2.** ['sʌbdʒikt] a (a) (pays) assujetti, soumis (**to**, à) (*b*) sujet (au rhumatismes); **prices s. to** 5%, **discount**, prix bénéficiant d'une remise de 5%; **s. to stamp duty**, soumis au timbre; **plan s. to modifications**, projet qui pourra subir des modifications; (*conditional*) **s. to ratification**, sous réserve de ratification; **s. to correction**, sauf correction 3. [sʌbˈdʒekt] *vtr* assujettir, subjuguer (un peuple); soumettre (qn, qch, à qch); **to be subjected to much criticism**, être en butte à de nombreuses critiques. **sub'jection** *n* soumission *f*, assujettissement *m* (**to**, à); **to be in (a state of) s.**, être soumis (à qn); être dans la sujétion. **sub'jective** *a* subjectif. **sub'jectively** *adv* subjectivement.

sub judice [sʌbˈdʒuːdisi] *Jur*: **the case is s. j.**, l'affaire n'est pas encore jugée.

subjunctive [səbˈdʒʌŋktiv] *a & n* subjonctif (*m*); **in the s.**, au subjonctif.

sublet [sʌbˈlet] *vtr* (*pt & pp* **sublet**; *prp* **subletting**) sous-louer.

sublieutenant [sʌblefˈtenənt] *n Navy*: enseigne *m* (de vaisseau) première classe.

sublime [səˈblaim] *a & n* sublime (*m*); **s. indifference**, suprême indifférence *f*. **su'blimely** *adv* sublimement; **s. unconscious of sth**, dans une ignorance absolue de qch.

subliminal [sʌbˈliminəl] *a* subliminal; (publicité) subliminaire.

submachine gun [sʌbməˈʃiːngʌn] *n* mitraillette *f*.

submarine [sʌbməˈriːn] *a* sous-marin (*m*).

submerge [səbˈmɜːdʒ] 1. *vtr* submerger, immerger; inonder, noyer (un champ) 2. *vi* (*of submarine*) plonger; effectuer sa plongée. **sub'merged** *a* submergé; (champ) noyé; **s. speed**, vitesse en plongée (d'un sous-marin); **s. reef**, écueil sous-marin. **sub'mergence, sub'mersion** *n* submersion *f*.

submission [səbˈmiʃn] *n* (*a*) soumission *f*; résignation *f* (à une défaite); **to starve s.o. into s.**, réduire qn par la famine (*b*) docilité *f*, humilité *f*. **sub'missive** *a* soumis, humble. **sub'missively** *adv* d'un ton soumis; avec docilité; humblement; avec résignation. **sub'missiveness** *n* soumission, docilité. **sub'mit** *v* (**submitted**) 1. *vi & pr* se soumettre (**to**, à); se plier (à une nécessité); se résigner (à un malheur); **to s. that**, représenter, alléguer, que 2. *vtr* soumettre; **to s. sth to s.o.'s inspection**, soumettre, présenter, qch à l'inspection de qn; **to s. proofs of identity**, présenter des pièces d'identité.

subnormal [sʌbˈnɔːməl] *a* au-dessous de la normale; (*of pers*) faible d'esprit; **educationally s.**, arriéré.

subordinate I. [səˈbɔːdinət] *a & n* 1. *a* (rang) inférieur, subalterne; (rôle) secondaire, accessoire; *Gram*: subordonné (**to**, à) 2. *n* subordonné, -ée. II. [səˈbɔːdineit] *vtr* subordonner (**to**, à). **subordi'nation** *n* subordination *f* (**to**, à); soumission *f* (**to**, à).

subpoena [sʌbˈpiːnə] *Jur*: 1. *n* citation *f*, assignation *f* (de témoins, sous peine d'amende) 2. *vtr* citer (qn) à comparaître; signifier une assignation à (qn).

subscribe [səbˈskraib] *vtr & i* souscrire; **to s. to an opinion**, souscrire à une opinion; **I cannot s. to that**, je ne peux pas consentir à cela; **to s. ten pounds**, souscrire pour (la somme de) dix livres; **to s. to a charity**, verser sa contribution à une œuvre de charité; *Fin*: **subscribed capital**, capital souscrit; **to s. to a loan**,

souscrire à un emprunt; **to s. to a newspaper**, s'abonner à un journal, être abonné, à un journal. **sub'scriber** *n* **s. to a charity, for shares**, souscripteur *m* à une œuvre de charité, à des actions; abonné, -ée (à un journal, du téléphone); *Tp*: **s. trunk dialling**, (téléphone) automatique *m*. **subscription** [-ˈskripʃn] *n* souscription *f* (à une œuvre de charité, *Fin*: à un emprunt); abonnement *m* (à un journal); adhésion *f* (**to an opinion**, à une opinion); **to pay a s.**, verser une cotisation; **to get up a s.**, se cotiser; **s. list**, liste des souscripteurs; **to take out a s. to a newspaper**, s'abonner à un journal; **s. to a club**, cotisation (annuelle) à un club.

subsequent [ˈsʌbsikwənt] *a* (chapitre) qui suit, suivant; **at a s. meeting**, lors d'une séance ultérieure; **at our s. meeting**, quand je l'ai rencontré plus tard. **'subsequently** *adv* plus tard; dans la suite; postérieurement (**to**, à).

subservient [səbˈsɜːviənt] *a* obséquieux, servile. **sub'servience** *n* soumission *f*, servilité *f*.

subside [səbˈsaid] *vi* (*of ground*) s'affaisser, se tasser; (*of water*) baisser; (*of storm, anger*) s'apaiser, se calmer; (*of pers*) se taire; **to s. into an armchair**, s'affaler dans un fauteuil; **the flood is subsiding**, la crue diminue. **sub'sidence** *n* affaissement *m*; subsidence *f*.

subsidiary [səbˈsidiəri] *a & n* (*pl* **subsidiaries**) subsidiaire, auxiliaire; **s. (company)**, filiale *f*.

subsidy [ˈsʌbsidi] *n* (*pl* **subsidies**) subvention *f*; *Ind*: prime *f*. **'subsidize** *vtr* subventionner; primer (une industrie); **to be subsidized by the State**, recevoir une subvention de l'État.

subsistence [səbˈsistəns] *n* existence *f*; **means of s.**, moyens de subsistance *f*, de subsister; **a bare s. wage**, un salaire à peine suffisant pour vivre.

subsoil [ˈsʌbsɔil] *n Geol*: sous-sol *m*.

subsonic [sʌbˈsɔnik] *a Av*: subsonique.

substance [ˈsʌbstəns] *n* substance *f*; matière *f*; fond *m*, essentiel *m* (d'un argument); solidité *f*; **argument that has little s.**, argument qui n'a rien de solide; **he's a man of s.**, il a du bien. **sub'stantial** (*a*) substantiel; réel; (point) important; **s. reasons**, raisons sérieuses; **a s. difference**, une différence appréciable, sensible; **s. meal**, repas copieux (*b*) (construction, livre) solide; (drap) résistant; **of s. build**, (homme) bien taillé; **s. firm**, maison de commerce bien assise. **sub'stantially** *adv* (*a*) substantiellement; réellement; en substance (*b*) solidement; **s. built**, (homme) bien taillé, (ameublement) solide (*c*) fortement; considérablement; **this contributed s. to our success**, cela a contribué pour une grande part à notre succès. **sub'stantiate** *vtr* établir, justifier (une affirmation); établir le bien-fondé d'une réclamation).

substandard [sʌbˈstændəd] *a* de qualité inférieure.

substantive [ˈsʌbstəntiv] *a & n* substantif (*m*).

substitute [ˈsʌbstitjuːt] 1. *n* (*a*) (*pers*) suppléant, -ante; remplaçant, -ante; **to act as a s. for s.o.**, remplacer qn, se substituer à qn; **to find a s. (for oneself)**, se faire suppléer (*b*) (*of foodstuffs*) succédané *m* (for, de); **coffee s.**, ersatz *m* de café; **beware of substitutes**, se méfier des contrefaçons *f* 2. *v* (*a*) *vtr* substituer; **to s. steel for stone**, substituer l'acier à la pierre; remplacer la pierre par l'acier (*b*) *vi* **to s. for**

s.o., remplacer, suppléer, qn. **substi'tution** *n* substitution *f*, remplacement *m*.

substratum [sʌb'strɑːtəm] *n* (*pl* **substrata** [-'strɑːtə]) couche inférieure.

subtenancy [sʌb'tenənsi] *n* sous-location *f*. **sub'tenant** *n* sous-locataire *mf*.

subterfuge ['sʌbtəfjuːdʒ] *n* subterfuge *m*.

subterranean [sʌbtə'reiniən] *a* souterrain.

subtitle ['sʌbtaitl] **1.** *n* sous-titre *m* **2.** *vtr Cin:* sous-titrer.

subtle ['sʌtl] *a* (parfum, esprit) subtil; (parfum) délicat; (esprit) fin, raffiné; (*of pers*, *method*) rusé, astucieux. **'subtlety** *n* (*pl* **-ies**) subtilité *f* (de l'esprit, d'une distinction); raffinement *m*, finesse *f* (d'une politique); distinction subtile (dans un argument). **'subtly** *adv* subtilement; avec finesse.

subtract [səb'trækt] *vtr Mth:* soustraire, retrancher (**from**, de). **sub'traction** *n Mth:* soustraction *f*.

suburb ['sʌbəːb] *n* banlieue *f*; **the suburbs**, la banlieue; **garden s.**, cité-jardin *f*. **su'burban** [sə-] *a* suburbain; de banlieue. **su'burbia** *n F:* la banlieue.

subvention [sʌb'venʃn] *n* subvention *f*.

subversion [səb'vəːʃn] *n* subversion *f*. **sub'versive** *a* subversif. **sub'vert** *vtr* subvertir.

subway ['sʌbwei] *n* (*a*) passage souterrain (*b*) *NAm:* (*Br* = **underground**) métro *m*.

succeed [sək'siːd] *v* **1.** *vtr & i* succéder à (qn, qch); **to s. to the throne**, succéder à la couronne; **day succeeds day**, les jours se suivent **2.** *vi* réussir; mener à bien; **how to s.**, le moyen de parvenir; **to s. in doing sth**, réussir à faire qch. **suc'ceeding** *a* (*a*) suivant (*b*) à venir; futur (*c*) successif. **suc'cess** *n* (*pl* **-es**) succès *m*, réussite *f*; **without s.**, sans succès; sans y parvenir; **to be a s.**, (*of venture*) réussir; (*of play*) avoir du succès; **the evening was a great s.**, la soirée a été très réussie; **to make a s. of sth**, réussir qch. **suc'cessful** *a* (projet) couronné de succès; (résultat) heureux; (portrait) réussi; **s. play**, pièce qui a du succès; **to be s. in doing sth**, réussir à faire qch; **he's s. in everything**, tout lui réussit; **s. candidates**, candidats élus; *Sch:* candidats reçus. **suc'cessfully** *adv* avec succès. **suc'cession** *n* (*a*) succession *f*; suite *f*; série *f*; **in s.**, successivement; **for two years in s.**, pendant deux années successives, consécutives, de suite; **in rapid s.**, coup sur coup; **after a s. of losses**, après des pertes successives (*b*) succession (à la couronne); **in s. to s.o.**, en remplacement de qn. **suc'cessive** *a* successif, consécutif. **suc'cessively** *adv* successivement. **suc'cessor** *n* successeur *m* (**to**, **of**, **de**); **to appoint a s. to s.o.**, remplacer qn.

succinct [sʌk'siŋkt] *a* succinct. **suc'cinctly** *adv* succinctement.

succulence ['sʌkjuləns] *n* succulence *f*. **'succulent 1.** *a* succulent **2.** *n Bot:* plante grasse.

succumb [sə'kʌm] *vi* succomber; céder; **to s. to one's injuries**, succomber à, mourir de, ses blessures.

such [sʌtʃ] **1.** *a* (*a*) tel, pareil, semblable; **beasts of prey s. as the lion or the tiger**, des bêtes fauves telles que le lion ou le tigre; **men s. as you, s. men as you**, des gens comme vous; **s. a man**, un tel homme; **s. things**, de telles choses; **did you ever see s. a thing!** a-t-on jamais vu (une) chose pareille! **in s. cases**, en pareils cas; **some s. plan**, un projet de ce genre; **on s. an occasion**, en semblable occasion; **there is no s. thing**, cela n'existe pas; **no s. body exists**, il n'existe aucun corps de cette nature; **I said no s. thing**, je n'ai rien dit de la sorte; **here it is, s. as it is**, le voici mais il ne vaut pas grand-chose; **in s. (and s.) a place**, en tel endroit; **on s. and s. a date**, à une certaine date; **s. a one**, un tel, une telle; **in s. a way that**, de telle sorte que; de manière, de façon, que; **to take s. steps as (shall) appear necessary**, prendre toutes mesures qui paraîtront nécessaires; **until s. time as**, jusqu'à ce que + *sub* (*b*) (*intensive*) **s. big houses**, de si grandes maisons; **s. a clever man**, un homme si habile; **s. courage**, un tel courage; **I had s. a fright!** j'ai eu une de ces peurs! **I had never heard s. good music**, je n'avais jamais entendu d'aussi bonne musique; **he is s. a liar**, il est si, tellement, menteur **2.** *pron* **I'll send you s. as I have**, je vous enverrai ce que j'ai; **history as s.**, l'histoire en tant que telle; **he was a very brave man and well known as s.**, il était très courageux et connu pour tel. **'suchlike** *F:* **1.** *a* semblable, pareil; de ce genre **2.** *pron usu pl* **tramps and s.**, clochards et autres.

suck [sʌk] **1.** *n* action *f* de sucer; succion *f*; **to take a s. at a sweet**, sucer un bonbon **2.** *vtr & i* sucer; (*of baby*) téter (le lait); **to s. (at) sth**, sucer qch; **to s. one's thumb**, sucer son pouce; **to s. s.o. dry**, sucer qn jusqu'au dernier sou, jusqu'à la moelle. **'suck 'down** *vtr* engloutir; entraîner au fond. **'sucker** *n* ventouse *f* (de sangsue, sur une machine); *Bot:* rejeton *m*, drageon *m*, surgeon *m* (d'arbre); *F:* (*of pers*) poire *f*; **to be a s. for sth**, raffoler de qch. **'suck 'in** *vtr* sucer, absorber; aspirer; engloutir (dans un tourbillon). **'sucking** *a* (*also* **suckling**) **s. pig**, cochon *m* de lait. **'suckle 1.** *vtr* allaiter (un enfant) **2.** *vi* (*of baby*) téter. **'suck 'up 1.** *vtr* sucer, aspirer, pomper (un liquide, de l'air); (*of sponge*) absorber, boire (l'eau) **2.** *vi F:* **to s. up to s.o.**, faire de la lèche à qn; lécher les bottes à qn. **'suction** *n* succion *f*; aspiration *f*; appel *m* (d'air); **s. pump**, pompe aspirante.

Sudan (the) [ðəsuː'dæn] *Prn Geog:* le Soudan. **Suda'nese** [suːdə'niːz] *a & n* soudanais, -aise.

sudden ['sʌdn] *a* soudain; subit; (mouvement, tournant) brusque; **all of a s.**, soudain, tout à coup. **'suddenly** *adv* (*a*) soudain; subitement; tout à coup (*b*) brusquement; soudainement. **'suddenness** *n* (*a*) soudaineté *f*; **with startling s.**, en coup de théâtre (*b*) brusquerie *f* (d'un départ).

suds [sʌdz] *npl* (**bubbles**) mousse *f* (de savon); (**water**) eau savonnée.

sue [suː] *vtr & i* poursuivre (qn) en justice; intenter un procès à qn); **to s. s.o. for damages**, poursuivre qn en dommages-intérêts; **to s. for libel**, attaquer en diffamation.

suede [sweid] *n* (*for shoes*) daim *m*; (*for gloves*) (peau *f* de) suède *m*.

suet ['suit] *n Cu:* graisse *f* de rognon.

Suez ['suiz] *Prn Geog:* Suez; **the S. Canal**, le canal de Suez.

suffer ['sʌfər] **1.** *vtr* (*a*) éprouver, souffrir (une perte); subir (une peine); endurer, ressentir (une douleur); **to s. defeat**, essuyer, subir, une défaite (*b*) tolérer; **he doesn't s. fools gladly**, il ne supporte pas les imbéciles **2.** *vi* (*a*) souffrir (**from**, de); **to s. for one's misdeeds**, supporter la conséquence de ses méfaits; **to s. from neglect**, souffrir, pâtir, d'un manque de soins; **country suffering from labour troubles**, pays en proie à l'agitation ouvrière (b) subir une perte, un dommage; **the vines have suffered from the frost,** les vignes ont souffert de la gelée. **'sufferance** n on s., (faire qch) par tolérance. **'sufferer** n (*from calamity*) victime f, sinistré, -ée; (*from accident*) accidenté, -ée; (*from illness*) malade mf; **fellow s.,** compagnon m d'infortune. **'suffering 1.** a souffrant, qui souffre **2.** n souffrances fpl; douleurs fpl.

suffice [sə'fais] vtr & i suffire (à qn); **that will s. for him,** cela lui suffira; **s. it to say that I got nothing,** il ne me reste à dire que je n'ai rien obtenu. **sufficiency** [-'fiʃənsi] n quantité, fortune, suffisante; **to have a bare s.,** avoir tout juste de quoi vivre. **su'fficient** a assez; suffisant; **one lamp is s.,** il suffit d'une lampe; **a hundred francs will be s.,** j'aurai assez de cent francs; **this is s. to feed them,** cela suffit pour les nourrir. **su'fficiently** adv suffisamment; assez.

suffix ['sʌfiks] n (pl **suffixes**) Gram: suffixe m.

suffocate ['sʌfəkeit] vtr & i étouffer; suffoquer. **'suffocating** a suffocant; étouffant; **it's s. in this room,** on suffoque dans cette pièce. **suffo'cation** n suffocation f; étouffement m, asphyxie f.

suffrage ['sʌfridʒ] n suffrage m; **universal s.,** suffrage universel.

sugar ['ʃugər] **1.** n sucre m; **the s. industry,** l'industrie sucrière; **granulated s.,** sucre cristallisé; **caster s.,** sucre en poudre; sucre semoule; **lump s.,** sucre en morceaux; **brown s.,** cassonade f; **s. beet,** betterave f à sucre; **s. cane,** canne f à sucre; **s. refinery,** raffinerie f (de sucre); **s. almond,** dragée f; **s. basin, bowl,** sucrier m; **s. tongs,** pince f à sucre; Bot: **s. maple,** érable m à sucre; F: **s. daddy,** protecteur âgé; papa-gâteau m **2.** vtr sucrer; **sugared almond,** dragée f; Fig: **to s. the pill,** dorer la pilule. **'sugarloaf** n pain m de sucre. **'sugary** a (trop) sucré; (sourire) mielleux; (ton) doucereux.

suggest [sə'dʒest] vtr (a) suggérer, proposer (qch à qn); **a solution suggested itself to me,** une solution m'est venue à l'esprit (b) inspirer, faire naître (une idée); **prudence suggests a retreat,** la prudence conseille la retraite (c) insinuer; **are you suggesting that I'm lying?** est-ce que vous insinuez que je mens? (d) évoquer; **his nose suggests a rabbit,** son nez donne l'idée d'un lapin. **su'ggestible** a (of pers) influençable (par la suggestion); suggestible. **su'ggestion** n suggestion f; **to make a s.,** faire une suggestion, une proposition; **a s. of a foreign accent, of regret,** une pointe d'accent étranger, une nuance de regret. **su'ggestive** a suggestif; évocateur.

suicide ['suisaid] n (a) (pers) suicidé, -ée (b) (act) suicide m; **to commit s.,** se suicider; **attempted s.,** tentative f de suicide. **sui'cidal** a suicidaire; **s. tendencies,** tendances suicidaires; Fig: **this would be s.,** ce serait un véritable suicide que d'agir de la sorte.

suit [su:t] **1.** n (a) Jur: procès m; **to bring a s. against s.o.,** intenter un procès à qn (b) Cl: ensemble m; costume m, complet m (pour homme); tailleur m (pour femme); **lounge s.,** complet veston; **flying s.,** combinaison f de vol (c) Cards: couleur f; **politeness is not his long s.,** la politesse n'est pas son fort; **to follow s.,** Cards: fournir (la couleur demandée); Fig: en faire autant; emboîter le pas **2.** vtr (a) **to be suited to sth,** être adapté à qch; être fait pour qch; **they are suited to each other,** ils sont faits l'un pour l'autre; Th: **he is not**

suited to the part, le rôle ne lui convient pas (b) convenir à, aller à, accommoder (qn); **that suits me best,** c'est ce qui m'arrange le mieux; **that suits me,** ça me va à merveille; **I shall do it when it suits me,** je le ferai quand cela me conviendra; **s. yourself,** faites comme vous voudrez; **this hat suits you,** ce chapeau vous va (bien). **suita'bility** n convenance f; à-propos m (d'une remarque); adéquation f; **s. of s.o. for a job,** aptitude f de qn à un poste. **'suitable** a convenable, qui convient; (exemple) approprié; **I've found nothing s.,** je n'ai rien trouvé qui me convienne; **the most s. date,** la date qui conviendrait le mieux; **s. to, for, sth,** bon à qch; propre, approprié, adapté, à qch; **s. to the occasion,** qui convient à la circonstance; **is it a book s. for children?** est-ce un livre pour les enfants? **'suitably** adv convenablement; (répondre) à propos; (agir) comme il convient. **'suitcase** n valise f. **'suitor** n soupirant m.

suite [swi:t] n suite f (d'un prince, d'orchestre). **s. (of rooms),** appartement m; **s. (of furniture),** salon m (en trois pièces); canapé avec deux fauteuils assortis; **dining (room) s.,** salle f à manger; **bathroom s.,** salle de bains.

sulfur, NAm: n NAm: see **sulphur**.

sulk [sʌlk] **1.** npl **to have (a fit of) the sulks,** bouder; faire la tête **2.** vi bouder; faire la tête; être maussade. **'sulkily** adv en boudant; d'un air bouder, maussade. **'sulkiness** n bouderie f, maussaderie f. **'sulky** a (-ier, -iest) boudeur, maussade; **to be s.,** bouder; **to look s.,** faire la tête.

sullen ['sʌlən] a maussade, renfrogné, morose; sombre; (silence) obstiné. **'sullenly** adv d'un air maussade, renfrogné; (obéir) de mauvaise grâce. **'sullenness** n maussaderie f; air renfrogné.

sulphur, NAm: **sulfur** ['sʌlfər] n soufre m; **s. mine,** soufrière f. **'sulphate,** NAm: **'sulfate** n sulfate m; **copper s.,** sulfate de cuivre. **'sulphide,** NAm: **'sulfide** n sulfure m. **sul'phonamide,** NAm: **sul'fonamide** n Ch: sulfamide m. **sulphuric,** NAm: **sulfuric** [sʌl'fjuərik] a sulfurique. **'sulphurous,** NAm: **'sulfurous** a sulfureux.

sultan ['sʌltən] n sultan m. **sul'tana** n (a) (woman) sultane f (b) raisin sec (de Smyrne).

sultry ['sʌltri] a (-ier, -iest) (of heat) étouffant, suffocant; (of weather) très lourd; (of voice) chaud; (of pers) sensuel. **'sultriness** n chaleur étouffante; lourdeur f (de l'atmosphère).

sum [sʌm] **1.** n (a) somme f, total m; montant m; **s. total,** somme totale, globale; montant total; **s. (of money),** somme (d'argent); **to spend vast sums,** dépenser des sommes folles (b) problème m, exercice m (d'arithmétique); **to do a s. in one's head,** faire un calcul de tête; **to do sums,** faire du calcul **2.** vtr & i (summed) **to s. up,** résumer, faire un résumé de (qch); récapituler; **to s. up the situation at a glance,** évaluer, se rendre compte de, la situation d'un coup d'œil; **to s. s.o. up,** juger, classer, qn. **'summarily** adv sommairement. **'summarize** vtr résumer sommairement; récapituler (les débats). **'summary 1.** a sommaire **2.** n (pl **-ies**) sommaire m, résumé m; **a. s. of the news, a news s.,** résumé des nouvelles. **summing-'up** n évaluation f (de la situation); Jur: résumé (des débats).

summer ['sʌmər] n été m; **in s.,** en été; **in high s.,** en plein été; **last s.,** l'été dernier; **a summer('s) day,** un jour d'été; **s. clothes,** vêtements d'été; **s. visitor,** estivant, -ante; **s. resort,** station estivale; **the s. holidays,** les grandes vacances. **'summerhouse** n pavillon m. **'summertime** n été; Adm: (NAm: = **daylight saving time**) heure f d'été. **'summery** a d'été.

summit ['sʌmit] n sommet m; cime f, faîte m (d'une montagne); Fig: summum m (de la félicité); Pol: **s. (meeting),** (conférence f au) sommet.

summon ['sʌmən] vtr appeler, faire venir (qn); convoquer (une assemblée); Jur: sommer (qn) de comparaître; **to s. a witness to appear,** citer, assigner, un témoin. **'summons 1.** n (pl -es) appel (fait d'autorité); convocation urgente; Jur: citation f (à comparaître); assignation f; sommation f; **to take out a s. against s.o.,** faire assigner qn **2.** vtr Jur: citer (qn) à comparaître; assigner (qn); appeler (qn) en justice. **'summon'' up** vtr faire appel à (son courage); rassembler (ses forces).

sump [sʌmp] n Aut: carter m (à huile); fond m de carter; Min: puisard m.

sumptuous ['sʌmptjuəs] a somptueux. **'sumptuously** adv somptueusement. **'sumptuousness** n somptuosité f.

sun [sʌn] **1.** n soleil m; **the sun's shining,** il fait du soleil; **(full) in the s.,** au (grand) soleil; Fig: **to have a place in the s.,** avoir une place au soleil; **to get a touch of the s.,** prendre un coup de soleil; **s. lounge,** solarium m; **s. oil, lotion,** huile, lotion, solaire; **s. lamp,** lampe ultraviolette (pour le bronzage); Aug: **s. visor,** pare-soleil m inv **2.** vtr (**sunned**) exposer (qch) au soleil; **to s. oneself,** prendre le soleil; se chauffer au soleil. **'sunbathe** vi prendre un bain de soleil. **'sunbather** n personne f qui prend un bain de soleil. **'sunbathing** n bains mpl de soleil. **'sunbeam** n rayon m de soleil. **'sunbed** n lit m de plage. **'sunblind** n store m. **'sunburn** n (suntan) bronzage; (painful) coup de soleil. **'sunburnt, sunburned** a (suntanned) bronzé; hâlé; (painfully) brûlé par le soleil. **'Sunday** n dimanche m; **in one's S. best,** dans ses habits du dimanche. **'sundial** n cadran m solaire. **'sundown** n coucher m du soleil. **'sundress** n (pl -es) robe f bain de soleil. **'sunflower** n tournesol m; **s. seed oil,** huile de tournesol. **'sunglasses** npl lunettes fpl de soleil. **'sunless** a sans soleil. **'sunlight** n (lumière f du) soleil; **in the s.,** au (grand) soleil. **'sunlit** a ensoleillé. **'sunlounger** n lit m de plage. **'sunny** a (-ier, -iest) (journée) de soleil; (endroit) ensoleillé; (côté) exposé au soleil; (visage) radieux, rayonnant; (caractère) heureux; **it's s.,** il fait du soleil. **'sunrise** n (NAm: = **sun-up**) lever m du soleil. **'sunroof** n Aut: toit ouvrant. **'sunset** n coucher du soleil; **at s.,** au soleil couchant. **'sunshade** n ombrelle f; (for table) parasol m. **'sunshine** n (lumière f du) soleil; Aut: **s. roof,** toit ouvrant. **'sunspot** n Astr: tache f solaire. **'sunstroke** n Med: insolation f; coup de soleil. **'suntan** n bronzage; **s. oil,** huile solaire. **'suntanned** a bronzé; hâlé. **'suntrap** n endroit très ensoleillé. **'sun-up** n NAm: (Br = **sunrise**) lever du soleil.

Sun abbr Sunday.

sundae ['sʌndei] n Cu: glace aux fruits recouverte de noix et de crème Chantilly.

sundry ['sʌndri] **1.** a pl divers; **s. expenses,** frais divers; **on s. occasions,** à différentes occasions **2.** n all and s., tous sans exception; tout le monde (et son père); **he told all and s. about it,** il le racontait à tout venant; **sundries,** (i) articles divers (ii) frais divers.

sung [sʌŋ] see sing.

sunk [sʌŋk] see sink². **'sunken** a (rocher) submergé; (navire) sous-marin; (of cheeks, eyes, road) creux; (of eyes) enfoncé; (jardin) en contrebas.

super ['su:pər] F: **1.** a superbe, formidable **2.** n (= police superintendent) commissaire m (de police).

superabundance [su:pərə'bʌndəns] n surabondance f (of, de). **supera'bundant** a surabondant.

superannuate [su:pər'ænjueit] vtr mettre (qn) à la retraite. **super'annuated** a (a) suranné, démodé (b) retraité; (mis) à la retraite. **superannu'ation** n retraite par limite d'âge; **s. fund,** caisse des retraites; **s. contribution,** retenue pour la retraite.

superb [su:'pə:b] a superbe. **su'perbly** adv superbement.

supercharged ['su:pətʃɑ:dʒd] a Aut: (moteur) suralimenté, surcomprimé, à compresseur. **'supercharger** n Aut: compresseur m.

supercilious [su:pə'siliəs] a hautain; (air) dédaigneux. **super'ciliously** adv avec hauteur. **super'ciliousness** n hauteur f.

superficial [su:pə'fiʃəl] a superficiel; **to have a s. knowledge of sth,** avoir des connaissances superficielles de qch; **she has a s. mind,** elle manque de profondeur. **super'ficially** adv superficiellement.

superfine ['su:pəfain] a superfin; surfin.

superfluous [su:'pə:fluəs] a superflu. **su'perfluously** adv d'une manière superflue; inutilement.

superhuman [su:pə'hju:mən] a surhumain.

superimpose [su:pərim'pouz] vtr superposer; Phot: **superimposed,** en surimpression.

superintend [su:pərin'tend] vtr diriger, surveiller; présider à (un scrutin). **superin'tendent** n directeur, -trice; surveillant, -ante; chef m (des travaux); **police s.** = commissaire m de police.

superior [su:'piəriər] **1.** a (a) supérieur; (article) de qualité supérieure; **to be s. in numbers,** être supérieur en nombre, avoir la supériorité du nombre (b) (of pers) orgueilleux; (air) de supériorité; (sourire) suffisant, condescendant **2.** n supérieur, -eure; Ecc: Mother S., mère supérieure. **superiority** [-'ɔriti] n supériorité f.

superlative [su:'pə:lətiv] **1.** a suprême; excellent **2.** a & n Gram: superlatif (m). **su'perlatively** adv au suprême degré; **s. ugly,** d'une laideur sans pareille.

superman ['su:pəmæn] n (pl supermen [-men]) surhomme m.

supermarket ['su:pəmɑ:kit] n supermarché m.

supernatural [su:pə'nætʃərəl] a & n surnaturel (m).

supernumerary [su:pə'nju:mərəri] a & n (pl supernumeraries) surnuméraire (mf).

superpower ['su:pəpauər] n superpuissance f.

supersede [su:pə'si:d] vtr remplacer; supplanter (qn); **method now superseded,** méthode périmée.

supersonic [su:pə'sɔnik] a Av: supersonique.

superstition [su:pə'stiʃn] n superstition f.

super'stitious *a* superstitieux. **super-'stitiously** *adv* superstitieusement.

superstructure ['su:pəstrʌktʃər] *n* superstructure *f*; tablier *m* (d'un pont).

supertanker ['su:pətæŋkər] *n Nau:* pétrolier géant.

supervise ['su:pəvaiz] *vtr* surveiller; diriger (une entreprise). **supervision** [-'viʒn] *n* surveillance *f*; direction *f* (d'une entreprise); **under police s.,** sous la surveillance de la police. **'supervisor** *n* surveillant, -ante; directeur, -trice. **'supervisory** *a* (comité) de surveillance.

supine ['su:pain] *a* (a) (*of pers*) couché, étendu, sur le dos (b) mou; indolent, inerte.

supper ['sʌpər] *n* souper *m*; dîner *m*; **to have s.,** souper; dîner; **the Last S.,** la (Sainte) Cène. **'suppertime** *n* heure *f* du souper, du dîner.

supplant [sə'plɑ:nt] *vtr* supplanter; prendre la place de (qn); remplacer, évincer (qn).

supple ['sʌpl] *a* souple; flexible; **to become s.,** s'assouplir. **'suppleness** *n* souplesse *f*; flexibilité *f*. **supply**[1] ['sʌpli] *adv* avec souplesse.

supplement I. ['sʌplimənt] *n* supplément *m*; *Journ:* **literary s.,** supplément littéraire; **colour s.,** supplément illustré 2. ['sʌpliment] *vtr* ajouter un supplément à (un livre); **to s. one's income by sth,** augmenter ses revenus en faisant qch. **supple'mentary** *a* supplémentaire.

supplication [sʌpli'keiʃn] *n* supplication *f*; supplique *f*.

supply[2] [sə'plai] 1. *n* (*pl* **supplies**) (a) approvisionnement *m*, fourniture *f*; *Mil:* ravitaillement *m*; **food s.,** ravitaillement en vivres (b) provision *f*; **to get, lay, in a s. of sth,** se faire une provision de, s'approvisionner de, en, qch; *PolEc:* **s. and demand,** l'offre *f* et la demande; **in short s.,** (marchandises) en manque; **supplies,** fournitures (de bureau, de photographie); réserves *f*; stocks *m*; **food supplies,** vivres *m*; **s. ship,** (transport) ravitailleur *m*; **s. teacher,** remplaçant, -ante (d'un professeur) 2. *vtr* (**supplied**) (a) **to s. s.o. with sth,** fournir, pourvoir, approvisionner, qn de qch; **to s. s.o. with food,** alimenter qn; **to s. sth,** fournir, apporter, qch; amener (l'eau, le gaz) (b) réparer (une omission); répondre à (un besoin); **to s. s.o.'s needs,** fournir, subvenir, aux besoins de qn. **su'pplier** *n* fournisseur, -euse.

support [sə'pɔ:t] 1. *n* appui *m*, soutien *m*; support *m* (athlétique, d'une voûte); *Hort:* tuteur *m*; **moral s.,** appui moral; **collection in s. of a charity,** quête au profit d'une œuvre; **to be without means of s.,** sans ressources; *Jur:* **without visible means of s.,** sans moyens d'existence connus; **the sole s. of his old age,** son seul soutien dans sa vieillesse; **to give s. to a proposal,** venir à l'appui d'une, appuyer la, proposition; **documents in s. of an allegation,** documents à l'appui d'une allégation; **in s. of this theory,** pour corroborer cette théorie; *Mil:* **air s.,** soutien aérien; **s. unit,** unité de soutien 2. *vtr* (a) supporter, soutenir, appuyer, maintenir (une voûte); tuteurer (un arbuste) (b) appuyer (qn); soutenir, corroborer (une théorie); faire une donation à (une œuvre de charité); **thanks to the team that supported me,** grâce à l'équipe qui me secondait (c) entretenir (la vie); subvenir à l'entretien de (qn); faire vivre, faire subsister (une famille); **to s. oneself,** gagner sa vie (d) supporter, tolérer (une

injure). **su'pporter** *n* défenseur *m*; adhérent, -ente (d'un parti); partisan, -ane (de qn); *Sp:* supporter *m*. **su'pporting** *a* (mur) d'appui, de soutènement; *Cin:* (film) supplémentaire; *Th:* **s. cast,** la troupe qui seconde les premiers rôles.

suppose [sə'pouz] *vtr* (a) supposer; **s. you are right, supposing (that) you are right,** supposez, supposons, que vous ayez raison; **supposing he came back,** si par supposition il revenait; **s. we change the subject,** si nous changions de sujet (b) s'imaginer; croire, penser; **you'll do it, I s.,** je suppose que vous le ferez; **you mustn't s. that,** n'allez pas imaginer que; **he's supposed to have a chance,** on lui croit des chances; **so I supposed,** c'est ce que je pensais; **I s. so,** probablement; sans doute; **I s. not,** probablement pas; **I don't s. he'll do it,** je ne pense pas qu'il le fasse; **he's supposed to be rich,** il est censé être riche; **I'm not supposed to know,** je suis censé ne pas le savoir. **su'pposed** *a* supposé, prétendu; soi-disant; **the s. culprit,** le présumé coupable. **su'pposedly** [sə'pouzidli] *adv* censément; soi-disant; **he went away, s. with the intention of coming back,** il est parti soi-disant pour revenir. **suppo'sition** *n* supposition *f*, hypothèse *f*; **on the s. that,** supposé que + *sub*.

suppository [sə'pɔzitəri] *n* (*pl* **suppositories**) *Pharm:* suppositoire *m*.

suppress [sə'pres] *vtr* (a) réprimer (une révolte); supprimer (un journal); interdire (une publication); faire disparaître (un abus); étouffer (un scandale, un bâillonnement); refouler (ses sentiments); **to s. one's feelings,** se contenir (b) cacher, dissimuler (qch); supprimer (un fait); *TV: WTel:* antiparasiter. **su'ppressed** *a* étouffé; **s. anger,** colère réprimée, refoulée; **s. excitement,** agitation contenue. **su'ppression** *n* répression *f* (d'une émeute); suppression *f* (d'un livre); étouffement *m* (d'un scandale); refoulement *m* (des émotions); dissimulation *f* (de la vérité); *TV: WTel:* antiparasitage *m*. **su'ppressor** *n TV: WTel:* (dispositif) antiparasite (*m*).

supranational [s(j)u:prə'næʃənl] *a* supranational.

supreme [su(:)'pri:m] *a* suprême; **s. contempt,** mépris souverain; **s. court,** cour souveraine. **supremacy** [-'preməsi] *n* suprématie *f* (over, sur). **su'premely** *adv* suprêmement.

surcharge ['sə:tʃɑ:dʒ] 1. *n* droit *m* supplémentaire; surtaxe *f* (d'une lettre); surcharge *f* (sur un timbre-poste) 2. *vtr* (sur)taxer (une lettre); surcharger (un timbre-poste).

sure [ʃuər] 1. *a* sûr, certain; **to be s. of, about, sth,** être sûr, certain, de qch; **I'm s. of it,** j'en suis sûr, certain; j'en ai la certitude; **I'm not so s. of that,** je n'en suis pas bien sûr; **I'm s. (that) you're wrong,** je suis sûr que vous vous trompez; **to be s. of oneself,** être sûr de soi (-même); **I don't know, I'm s.,** ma foi, je ne sais pas; **to make s. of sth,** s'assurer de qch; **with a s. hand,** d'une main assurée; **in s. hands,** en mains sûres; **a s. thing,** une affaire sûre; une chose certaine; *Rac:* certitude *f*; *NAm: F:* **s. thing!** bien sûr! **I don't know for s.,** je n'en suis pas bien sûr; **tomorrow for s.,** demain sans faute; **he'll be killed for s.,** nul doute qu'il va se faire tuer; **it's s. to be fine,** il fera sûrement beau; **he's s. to come,** il viendra à coup sûr; il viendra sûrement; **be s. to come early,** ne manquez pas d'arriver de bonne heure; **be s. not to lose it,** veillez à ne pas le perdre 2. *adv* **as s. as**

eggs are eggs, aussi sûr que deux et deux font quatre; **s. enough he was there,** il était bien là; **he'll come s. enough,** il viendra à coup sûr; *esp NAm:* **s.!** bien sûr! **it s. is cold,** il fait vraiment froid. **'sure-'footed** *a* au pied sûr; **to be s.-f.,** avoir le pied sûr. **'surely** *adv* sûrement; **slowly but s.,** lentement mais sûrement: **s. you don't believe that!** vous ne croyez pas cela, voyons! **s. you're not going to leave us?** vous n'allez tout de même pas nous quitter! **'sureness** *n* sûreté *f;* certitude *f.* **'surety** *n* (*pers*) caution *f;* garant, -ante; **to stand s. for s.o.,** se porter caution pour qn.

surf [sə:f] **1.** *n* barre *f* (de plage); ressac *m;* brisants *mpl* sur la plage **2.** *vi* faire du surfing. **'surfboard** *n* planche *f* de surfing. **'surfboat** *n* surf-boat *m.* **'surfer, 'surfboarder** *n* surfeur, -euse. **'surfing, 'surfriding** *n* surf *m,* surfing *m.*

surface ['sə:fis] **1.** *n* (*a*) surface *f;* **to rise to the surface** (**of the water**), remonter sur l'eau; (*of submarine*) revenir en surface; **to send a letter by s. mail,** envoyer une lettre par voie *f* de terre, de mer; **s. water,** eau superficielle (*b*) extérieur *m,* dehors *m;* **on the s. everything was well,** tout allait bien en apparence; **he doesn't probe beneath the s.** (**of things**), il ne s'arrête à la surface; **his politeness is only on the s.,** sa politesse est toute en surface; (*on record*) **s. noise,** bruit de surface (*c*) aire *f,* étendue *f;* **the earth's s.,** la superficie de la terre **2.** *v* (*a*) *vtr* apprêter la surface de (qch); *CivE:* revêtir (une route) (**with,** de) (*b*) *vi* (*of submarine*) faire surface, revenir en surface; *F:* (*of pers*) réapparaître.

surfeit ['sə:fit] *n* surabondance *f;* réplétion *f* (d'aliments); **to have a s. of sth,** être rassasié de qch.

surge [sə:dʒ] **1.** *n Nau:* levée *f* de la lame; houle *f; El:* à-coup *m* (de courant); **s. of anger, of enthusiasm,** vague *f* de colère, d'enthousiasme **2.** *vi* (*of sea*) être houleux; (*of crowd*) se répandre en flots (dans la rue); **the blood surged to her cheeks,** le sang lui a reflué au visage; **anger surged (up) within her,** un flot de colère est monté en elle. **'surging** *a* (*of sea*) houleux.

surgeon ['sə:dʒən] *n* chirurgien, -ienne; **house s.,** interne *mf* en chirurgie; **dental s.,** chirurgien dentiste; **veterinary s.,** vétérinaire *mf.* **'surgery** *n* (*pl* -ies) (*a*) chirurgie *f;* **plastic s.,** chirurgie esthétique (*b*) cabinet *m* de consultation (d'un médecin); cabinet (d'un dentiste); **s. (hours),** heures *f* de consultation. **'surgical** *a* chirurgical; **s. instruments,** instruments de chirurgie; **s. appliances,** appareils chirurgicaux; appareils orthopédiques; **s. spirit** = alcool à 90°.

surly ['sə:li] *a* (-**ier,** -**iest**) bourru; hargneux, maussade, revêche. **'surliness** *n* air bourru.

surmise [sə:'maiz] **1.** *n* conjecture *f,* supposition *f* **2.** *vtr & i* conjecturer, deviner; **as I surmised,** comme je m'en doutais (bien).

surmount [sə:'maunt] *vtr* surmonter.

surname ['sə:neim] *n* nom *m* de famille.

surpass [sə:'pɑ:s] *vtr* surpasser; **you've surpassed yourself,** vous vous êtes surpassé; **the result surpasses our hopes,** le résultat a excédé, dépassé, nos espérances.

surplice ['sə:plis] *n* surplis *m.*

surplus ['sə:pləs] *n* surplus *m,* excédent *m;* **to have a s. of sth,** avoir qch en excès; **s. provisions,** vivres de surplus, en surplus; **s. population,** surplus de la population; *Com:* **sale of s. stock,** vente de soldes *mpl;* **government s.** (**stock**), les surplus du gouvernement.

surprise [sə:'praiz] **1.** *n* surprise *f;* étonnement *m;* **to**

take s.o. by s., prendre qn à l'improviste, au dépourvu; *Mil:* **to take a town by s.,** enlever une ville par surprise; **s. visit,** visite à l'improviste; visite surprise; **to give s.o. a s.,** faire une surprise à qn; **it was a great s. to me,** j'en ai été grandement surpris; **to my great s., much to my s.,** à ma grande surprise; **to recover from one's s.,** revenir de son étonnement; **to pause in s.,** s'arrêter surpris **2.** *vtr* surprendre; étonner; **to s. s.o. in the act,** prendre qn sur le fait, en flagrant délit; **to be surprised at sth,** être surpris de qch; **I'm surprised to see you,** je m'étonne de vous voir; **I shouldn't be surprised if,** cela ne m'étonnerait pas que; **I'm surprised at you!** vous m'étonnez! **sur'prised** *a* (air, regard) étonné, surpris. **sur'prising** *a* surprenant, étonnant; **that's s.,** cela m'étonne. **sur'prisingly** *adv* étonnamment; **I found him looking s. young,** j'ai été surpris de lui trouver l'air si jeune.

surrealism [sə'riəlizm] *n* surréalisme *m.* **su'rrealist** *a & n* surréaliste (*mf*). **surrea'listic** *a* surréaliste.

surrender [sə'rendər] **1.** *n* (*a*) reddition *f* (d'une forteresse); **no s.!** on ne se rend pas! (*b*) abandon *m,* cession *f* (de biens); remise *f* (des armes à feu); *Ins:* rachat *m* (d'une police) **2.** *v* (*a*) *vtr* rendre, livrer (une forteresse); abandonner, céder (un droit, ses biens); *Ins:* racheter (une police) (*b*) *vi* se rendre; se livrer (à la justice).

surreptitious [sʌrəp'tiʃəs] *a* subreptice, clandestin. **surrep'titiously** *adv* subrepticement, clandestinement, furtivement.

surround [sə'raund] **1.** *n* encadrement *m,* bordure *f* **2.** *vtr* entourer; **the walls that s. the town,** les murailles qui entourent la ville; **to be surrounded with, by, dangers,** être entouré de dangers. **su'rrounding** *a* entourant, environnant; **the s. countryside,** le pays d'alentour. **su'rroundings** *npl* entourage *m,* milieu *m,* ambiance *f;* cadre *m;* (*countryside*) environs *mpl,* alentours *mpl* (d'une ville).

surtax ['sə:tæks] *n* surtaxe (progressive sur le revenu).

surveillance [sə'veiləns] *n* surveillance *f,* contrôle *m;* **under s.,** sous surveillance.

survey 1. ['sə:vei] *n* (*a*) aperçu *m;* vue générale (d'un sujet); examen attentif; étude *f* (de la situation); enquête *f; Surv:* levé *m* des plans; relevé *m;* (*document*) plan *m,* levé (du terrain); **aerial s.,** levé aérien; **to make a s. of a property,** relever une propriété (*b*) inspection *f,* visite *f;* expertise *f* **2.** [sə'vei] *vtr* (*a*) regarder, contempler, promener son regard sur (un paysage); mettre (une question) à l'étude; passer (la situation) en revue; *Surv:* relever; faire le levé de, lever le(s) plan(s) de (la ville); arpenter (un champ); faire l'hydrographie (d'une côte) (*b*) inspecter, visiter; faire l'expertise de l'état de, expertiser (un navire). **sur'veying** *n* levé de plans; (**land**) **s.,** géodésie *f;* topographie *f.* **sur'veyor** *n* (architecte) expert (*m*); (**land**) **s.,** géomètre expert; arpenteur *m* (géomètre); **quantity s.,** métreur (vérificateur).

survive [sə'vaiv] **1.** *vi* survivre; (*of custom*) subsister **2.** *vtr* survivre à (qn, à une blessure); **to s. an illness, a shipwreck,** réchapper d'une maladie, d'un naufrage. **sur'vival** *n* survie *f* (d'un accidenté); survivance *f;* **s. of the fittest,** survivance du plus apte; **s. kit,** équipement de survie. **sur'vivor** *n* survivant, -ante; rescapé(e) (d'une catastrophe).

susceptible [sə'septibl] *a* sensible (**to**, à); susceptible; **s. to a disease**, prédisposé à une maladie; **s. of proof**, susceptible d'être prouvé. **suscepti'bility** *n* (*pl* -**ies**) sensibilité *f*; susceptibilité *f*; prédisposition *f* (à une maladie); **s. to impressions**, suggestibilité *f*; **to avoid wounding anyone's susceptibilities**, éviter tout froissement.

suspect 1. ['sʌspekt] *a* & *n* suspect, -e; **to regard s.o. as s.**, tenir qn pour suspect 2. [sə'spekt] *vtr* (*a*) soupçonner (qn de qch); suspecter (qn); **to be suspected**, être suspect; **I s. him of running into debt**, je le soupçonne de faire des dettes (*b*) s'imaginer, se douter de (qch); flairer (le danger); **I suspected as much**, je m'en doutais; **he suspects nothing**, il ne se doute de rien; **I s. you're right**, je crois bien que vous avez raison.

suspend [sə'spend] *vtr* (*a*) **to s. sth from the ceiling**, suspendre, pendre, qch au plafond (*b*) suspendre (son jugement, les paiements, le travail, un service d'autobus, un fonctionnaire); renvoyer (un élève) provisoirement; *Jur:* **to s. judgement**, surseoir au jugement. **su'spended** *a* suspendu; (*of services*) interrompu; *Jur:* (*of proceedings*) en suspens; *Ch:* (particules) en suspension; *Jur:* **he was given a s. sentence of six months**, il a été condamné à six mois de prison avec sursis; **the scheme is in a state of s. animation**, le projet est en suspens. **su'spenders** *npl Cl:* (*women's, for stockings*) jarretelles *fpl*; (*men's, for socks*) fixe-chaussettes *mpl*; *NAm:* (**br**=**braces**) (*for trousers*) bretelles *fpl*; (*women's undergarment*) **suspender belt**, porte-jarretelles *m inv.* **su'spense** *n* suspens *m*; (*in film, novel*) suspense *m*; **to keep s.o. in s.**, tenir qn en suspens, en haleine; **s. novel**, roman à suspense. **su'spension** *n* suspension *f*; retrait *m* temporaire (d'un permis de conduire); **s. bridge**, pont suspendu; *Ch:* **in s.**, en suspension.

suspicion [sə'spiʃən] *n* soupçon *m*; **to look at s.o. with s.**, regarder qn avec défiance; **to have suspicions about s.o.**, avoir des doutes sur qn; soupçonner qn; **to arouse s.**, éveiller les soupçons; **to arouse s.o.'s suspicions**, éveiller la défiance de qn; **above s.**, au-dessus de tout soupçon; **evidence not above s.**, témoignages sujets à caution; *Jur:* **to arrest s.o. on s.**, arrêter qn préventivement; **I had my suspicions about it**, je m'en doutais. **su'spicious** *a* (*a*) suspect; (*of conduct*) louche, équivoque; **it looks s. to me**, cela me paraît louche (*b*) méfiant, soupçonneux; **to be s. about s.o.**, avoir des soupçons à l'égard de qn. **su'spicious-looking** *a* suspect, louche. **su'spiciously** *adv* (*a*) d'une manière suspecte, équivoque, louche; **it looks to me s. like measles**, ça m'a tout l'air d'être la rougeole (*b*) d'un air méfiant; (regarder qn) avec méfiance. **su'spiciousness** *n* (*a*) caractère suspect, louche, équivoque (de qn, qch) (*b*) caractère soupçonneux; méfiance *f*.

suss [sʌs] *vtr P:* **to s. s.o. (out)**, cataloguer qn.

sustain [sə'stein] *vtr* (*a*) soutenir, supporter; **enough to s. life**, de quoi entretenir la vie; de quoi vivre; *Mus:* **to s. a note**, soutenir, prolonger, une note; *Jur:* **objection sustained**, réclamation admise (*b*) éprouver, subir (une perte); recevoir (une blessure). **su'stained** *a* soutenu; **s. applause**, applaudissements prolongés. **su'staining** *a* soutenant; **s. food**, nourriture fortifiante, qui soutient.

sustenance ['sʌstinəns] *n* aliments *mpl*, nourriture *f*; means of s., moyens de subsistance; moyens de vivre.

swab [swɔb] 1. *n* torchon *m*; serpillière *f*; *Med:* tampon *m* (d'ouate); *Nau:* vadrouille *f*; *Med:* **to take a s. of s.o.'s throat**, faire un prélèvement dans la gorge de qn 2. *vtr* (**swabbed**) nettoyer, essuyer (avec un torchon, *Med:* avec un tampon).

swag [swæg] *n F:* rafle *f*, butin *m* (d'un cambrioleur); *Austr:* baluchon *m*, paquet *m* (de clochard). 'swag-man *n* (*pl* -men) *Austr:* clochard *m*.

swagger ['swægər] 1. *n* (*a*) air important; **to walk with a s.**, marcher avec un air avantageux (*b*) rodomontades *fpl*; fanfaronnades *fpl* 2. *vi* (*a*) crâner, se pavaner; **to s. in, out**, entrer, sortir, d'un air important (*b*) faire de l'esbroufe. 'swaggering *a* (air) important, crâneur.

swallow¹ ['swɔlou] 1. *n* gorgée *f* (d'eau); **at one s.**, d'un seul coup 2. *vtr* & *i* avaler; ravaler (ses larmes); **to s. sth down**, avaler qch; gober (un œuf); **to s. sth up**, avaler, dévorer, qch; (*of the sea*) engloutir qch; **to s. one's pride**, mettre son orgueil dans sa poche; **you'll have a job to make them s. that story**, tu auras du mal à leur faire avaler ça; *Fig:* **to s. the bait**, se laisser prendre à l'appât; **story that is hard to s.**, histoire invraisemblable. 'swallowhole *n Geol:* aven *m*, gouffre *m*.

swallow² *n Orn:* hirondelle *f*; *Swim:* **s. dive** (*NAm:* = **swan dive**), saut de l'ange. 'swallowtail *n Ent:* **s. (butterfly)**, machaon *m*.

swam [swæm] *see* **swim** 2.

swamp [swɔmp] 1. *n* marais *m*, marécage *m* 2. *vtr* inonder, submerger; remplir (un bateau) d'eau; **to be swamped with work**, être débordé de travail. 'swampy *a* marécageux.

swan [swɔn] 1. *n* cygne *m*; *NAm: Swim:* **s. dive** (*Br* = **swallow dive**), saut de l'ange 2. *vi* (**swanned**) **to s. around**, se pavaner; flâner. 'swansdown *n* duvet *m* de cygne. 'swansong *n* chant *m* du cygne.

swank [swæŋk] *F:* 1. *n* (*a*) épate *f* (*b*) (*pers*) crâneur, -euse 2. *vi* se donner des airs; crâner; faire de l'épate. 'swanky *a F:* (*of pers*) prétentieux; (*of place, thg*) élégant, chic.

swap [swɔp] *F:* 1. *n* troc *m*, échange *m*; **to get sth as a s. for sth**, recevoir qch en échange de qch; **to do a s.**, faire un troc; (*in stamp collecting*) **swaps**, doubles *mpl* 2. *vtr* & *i* (**swapped**) **to s. sth for sth**, échanger, troquer, qch contre, pour, qch; **shall we s.?** si nous faisions un échange? **to s. places with s.o.**, changer de place avec qn. 'swapping *n F:* échange, troc.

swarm [swɔːm] 1. *n* essaim *m* (d'abeilles); vol *m* (de sauterelles); nuée *f* (de moucherons); fourmillement *m* (d'insectes); **s. of children**, essaim, troupe *f*, d'enfants 2. *vi* (*of bees*) essaimer; faire l'essaim; (*of pers*) accourir en foule, se presser (autour de, dans, qch); (*of insects, animals, people*) pulluler, grouiller; **to s. with**, fourmiller, grouiller, de; **street swarming with people**, rue qui grouille, regorge, de monde.

swarthy ['swɔːði] *a* (-**ier**, -**iest**) basané, bistré.

swastika ['swɔstikə] *n* svastika *m*; croix gammée.

swat [swɔt] 1. *n* (**fly**) **s.**, tapette *f* (à mouches) 2. *vtr* (**swatted**) écraser (une mouche). 'swatter *n* (**fly**) **s.**, tapette *f* (à mouches).

swathe [sweið] *vtr* emmailloter; envelopper; **head swathed in bandages**, tête enveloppée de bandages.

sway [swei] **I.** *n* (*a*) balancement *m*, oscillation *f* (*b*) empire *m*, domination *f*; **under his s.,** sous son influence *f*. **II.** *v* **1.** *vi* se balancer; osciller; **tree that sways in the wind,** arbre qui se balance au vent **2.** *vtr* (*a*) faire osciller; balancer, agiter (les arbres) (*b*) gouverner, diriger; **papers that s. public opinion,** journaux qui influencent l'opinion. **'swaying 1.** *a* oscillant; **s. crowd,** foule ondoyante **2.** *n* balancement, oscillation; *Rail:* mouvement *m* de lacet (des voitures).

swear [swɛər] *v* (**swore** [swɔːr]; **sworn** [swɔːn]) **1.** *vtr* jurer; **to s. an oath,** faire un serment; **to s. to do sth,** jurer de faire qch; **I could have sworn I heard footsteps,** j'aurais juré entendre des pas; **to s. s.o. to secrecy,** faire jurer le secret à qn; **to s. sth on one's honour,** jurer qch sur l'honneur **2.** *vi* jurer; proférer un juron; **to s. like a trooper,** jurer comme un charretier; **to s. at s.o.,** injurier qn; **to s. to sth,** attester qch sous serment; **I'd s. to it,** j'en jurerais; **I s. by aspirin for headaches,** pour les maux de tête, je ne jure que par l'aspirine. **'swear 'in** *vtr* faire prêter serment à (un témoin, un jury); **to be sworn in,** prêter serment. **'swearing** *n* (*a*) attestation *f* sous serment; prestation *f* de serment; **s. in of the jury,** assermentation *f* du jury (*b*) jurons *mpl*; gros mots. **'swearword** *n* gros mot; juron *m*.

sweat [swɛt] **1.** *n* sueur *f*; transpiration *f*; **by the s. of one's brow,** à la sueur de son front; *F:* **to be in a s. about sth,** s'inquiéter de qch; **to be in a cold s.,** avoir des sueurs froides; *F:* **it's an awful s.!** quelle corvée! *F:* **no s.!** pas de problème! **2.** *vtr & i* (*a*) suer; transpirer; (*of walls*) suinter; **to s. profusely,** suer à grosses gouttes; **to s. blood,** suer du sang (*b*) (*of worker*) peiner; **to s. workers,** exploiter la main-d'œuvre. **'sweatband** *n* *Sp:* bandeau *m*. **'sweater** *n* *Cl:* pullover *m*; sweater *m*. **'sweating** *n* transpiration *f*; suintement *m* (d'un mur); exploitation *f* (de la main-d'œuvre). **'sweat 'out** *vtr* *F:* **to s. it o.,** endurer jusqu'à la fin. **'sweatshirt** *n* *Cl:* sweat-shirt *m*. **'sweatshop** *n* atelier *m* où les ouvriers sont exploités. **'sweaty** *a* (**-ier, -iest**) en sueur; (vêtement) imprégné de sueur; (odeur) de sueur; **s. hands,** mains moites.

Sweden ['swiːdən] *Prn Geog:* la Suède. **Swede** *n* (*a*) (*pers*) Suédois, -oise (*b*) (*vegetable*) rutabaga *m*. **'Swedish 1.** *a* suédois **2.** *n* *Ling:* suédois *m*.

sweep [swiːp] **I.** *n* (*a*) coup *m* de balai, de faux; **at one s.,** d'un seul coup; **to give the room a s.,** balayer la pièce; **to make a clean s.,** faire table rase; **to make a clean s. of the staff,** liquider tout le personnel (*b*) mouvement *m* circulaire (du bras); portée *f* (d'un phare); *Mil:* balayage *m* (d'une région); **with a wide s. of the arm,** d'un geste large (*c*) boucle *f* (d'une rivière); **fine s. of grass,** belle étendue de gazon (*d*) (*chimney*) **s.,** ramoneur *m* (*e*) *F:* sweepstake *m*. **II.** *v* (**swept** [swɛpt]) **1.** *vtr* (*a*) balayer (une pièce, la poussière); ramoner (une cheminée); **to s. the horizon with a telescope,** parcourir l'horizon avec une lunette; *Fig:* **to s. the board,** remporter un succès complet; **the latest craze to s. the country,** la dernière chose qui fait fureur dans tout le pays; *Fig:* **to s. sth under the carpet,** enterrer une question (*b*) emporter, entraîner; **a wave swept him overboard,** une lame l'a jeté à la mer; *F:* **to be swept off one's feet by s.o.,** s'emballer pour qn **2.** *vi* (*a*) **to s. (along),** avancer rapidement, d'un mouvement rapide et uni; **to s. into a room,** entrer dans une pièce d'un air majestueux; **the enemy swept down on us,** l'ennemi s'est abattu sur nous; **hills sweeping down to the sea,** collines qui descendent, dévalent, vers la mer; **to s. on,** continuer d'avancer (irrésistiblement); *Nau:* **to s. for mines,** draguer des mines. **'sweep a'long** *vtr* entraîner, emporter. **'sweep a'side** *vtr* écarter (d'un geste large). **'sweep a'way** *vtr* balayer (la neige, les nuages); **bridge swept away by the torrent,** pont emporté, entraîné, par le torrent. **'sweeper** *n* (*pers*) balayeur, -euse; (*machine*) balayeuse *f*; balai *m* (mécanique). **'sweeping 1.** *a* (geste) large; **s. bow,** révérence profonde; **s. statement,** déclaration par trop générale; **s. reform,** réforme complète, radicale; **s. changes,** changement de fond en comble **2.** *n* balayage *m*; **(chimney) s.,** ramonage *m*; **sweepings,** balayures *fpl*, ordures *fpl*. **'sweep 'off** *vtr* enlever, emporter, avec violence. **'sweep 'out 1.** *vtr* balayer (une pièce) **2.** *vi* sortir d'un air majestueux. **'sweepstake** *n* sweepstake. **'sweep 'up** *vtr* balayer, ramasser (la poussière).

sweet [swiːt] **1.** *a* (*a*) doux, sucré; **as s. as honey,** doux comme le miel; **to have a s. tooth,** aimer les douceurs; être friand de sucreries; **my tea is too s.,** mon thé est trop sucré; *Cu:* **s. and sour sauce,** sauce aigre-douce (*b*) **s.(-scented, -smelling),** qui sent bon; odorant; au parfum délicieux; **s. pea,** pois de senteur; **s. william,** œillet *m* de(s) poète(s) (*c*) (*of breath*) sain, pur; (*of food*) frais; (son) doux, mélodieux; **s. temper,** caractère doux, aimable; **revenge is s.,** la vengeance est douce (*d*) agréable; (*of pers*) charmant, gentil; (sourire) doux; **a s. little kitten,** un petit chat adorable; **to keep s.o. s.,** cultiver la bienveillance de qn; *F:* **to be s. on s.o.,** être amoureux de qn **2.** *n* (*a*) (*NAm:* = **candy**) bonbon *m*; **boiled s.,** bonbon à sucer; **sweets,** sucreries *fpl*, confiseries *fpl* (*b*) (*at meal*) entremets sucré. **'sweetbread** *n* *Cu:* ris *m* de veau, d'agneau. **'sweetcorn** *n* *Cu:* maïs doux. **'sweeten** *vtr* sucrer (un plat); purifier (l'air); adoucir (la vie); *F:* graisser la patte à (qn). **'sweetener** *n* *Cu:* édulcorant *m*, *esp* saccharine *f*. **'sweetening** *n* substance *f* pour sucrer. **'sweetheart** *n* **they are childhood sweethearts,** ils s'aiment depuis leur enfance; **(my) s.!** mon amour! **'sweetie** *n* *F:* bonbon; (*to pers*) **s. (pie)!** chéri, -ie! **'sweetish** *a* douceâtre. **'sweetly** *adv* doucement; avec douceur; (chanter) mélodieusement; (agir) agréablement, gentiment; (*of machine*) **to run s.,** fonctionner sans à-coups. **'sweetness** *n* douceur *f*; (*of pers*) gentillesse *f*, charme *m*. **'sweetshop** *n* (*NAm:* = **candy store**) confiserie *f*. **'sweet-'tempered** *a* au caractère doux.

swell [swɛl] **I.** *n* *Nau:* houle *f*; levée *f* (de la lame); *Mus:* (*of organ*) soufflet *m*. **II.** *a* *NAm:* *F:* (*Br* = **great**) épatant; **he's a s. guy,** c'est un chic type. **III.** *v* (**swelled** [swɛld]; **swollen** ['swəʊlən]) **1.** *vtr* (r)enfler, gonfler; **river swollen by the rain,** rivière grossie par la pluie; **eyes swollen with tears,** yeux gonflés de larmes; **to s. the crowd,** se joindre à la foule **2.** *vi* **to s. (up), (s')en-fler, (se) gonfler; (*of number, crowd*) augmenter, grossir; (*of sea*) se soulever; **to s. (out),** être bombé; bomber; **his heart swelled with pride,** son cœur se gonflait d'orgueil. **'swelling** *n* enflement *m*, gonflement *m*; (*lump*) bosse *f*, enflure *f* (au front); tumeur *f*; grosseur *f*.

swelter ['sweltər] *vi* étouffer de chaleur. **'swelter-ing** *a* s. **heat,** chaleur étouffante, accablante.

swept [swept] *see* **sweep II.**

swerve [swə:v] **1.** *n* écart *m*, déviation *f*; *Aut:* embardée *f* **2.** *vi* faire un écart, un crochet; *(of car)* **to s. (across the road),** faire une embardée.

swift [swift] **1.** *a* rapide; vif; *(of reply)* prompt; **s. to act,** prompt à agir **2.** *n Orn:* martinet *m.* **'swiftly** *adv* rapidement, vite; promptement. **'swiftness** *n* rapidité *f*, vitesse *f*; promptitude *f*.

swig [swig] *F:* **1.** *n* grand trait, grand coup, lampée *f* (de bière) **2.** *vtr* **(swigged)** boire (un verre) à grands traits; lamper (qch).

swill [swil] **1.** *n* (*a*) lavage *m* à grande eau; **to give a glass a s. (out),** rincer un verre (*b*) pâtée *f* (pour les porcs); eaux grasses **2.** *vtr* laver (le plancher) à grande eau; rincer (un verre); *P:* boire avidement (qch).

swim [swim] **1.** *n* **to have a s.,** nager un peu; se baigner; **to go for a s.,** aller nager; aller se baigner; *F:* **to be in the s.,** être dans le mouvement **2.** *vtr & i* (**swam** [swæm]; **swum** [swʌm]; **swimming**) nager; **to s. (across) the river,** traverser la rivière à la nage; **to s. with the tide,** suivre le courant; **to s. (the) breast stroke,** nager la brasse; **to s. a race,** faire une course de natation (**with s.o.,** contre qn); **meat swimming in gravy,** viande nageant dans la sauce; **eyes swimming with tears,** yeux noyés de larmes; **my head's swimming,** la tête me tourne; **everything swam before my eyes,** tout tournait autour de moi. **'swimmer** *n* nageur, -euse. **'swimming 1.** *a* **s. eyes,** yeux noyés de larmes; **s. head,** tête qui tourne **2.** *n* nage, natation *f*; **s. bath(s),** pool, piscine *f.* **'swimmingly** *adv F:* comme sur des roulettes; à merveille. **'swimsuit** *n* maillot *m* (de bain).

swindle ['swindl] **1.** *n* escroquerie *f* **2.** *vtr* escroquer (qn); *F:* rouler (qn); **to s. s.o. out of sth,** escroquer qch à qn. **'swindler** *n* escroc *m*.

swine [swain] *n inv in pl* cochon *m*, porc *m*; *Lit:* pourceau *m*; *F: (of pers)* salaud *m*; sale cochon.

swing [swiŋ] **I.** *n* (*a*) balancement *m*; tour *m* (de manivelle); oscillation *f* (d'un pendule); *Box: Golf:* swing *m*; *F:* **to take a s. at s.o.,** donner un coup de poing à qn; *Pol:* **the s. of the pendulum,** le jeu de bascule (entre les partis); **to be in full s.,** *(of dance, party)* battre son plein; *(of factory, organization)* être en plein travail, en pleine activité; **s. of public opinion,** revirement *m* de l'opinion publique; **to give a child a s.,** balancer un enfant (*b*) amplitude *f* (d'une oscillation); *Nau:* évitage *m* (d'un navire à l'ancre); **to walk with a s.,** marcher d'un pas rhythmé; **song that goes with a s.,** chanson entraînante; *F:* **everything went with a s.,** tout a très bien marché; **to get into the s. of things,** se mettre dans le bain, au courant (*c*) balançoire *f.* **II.** *v* (**swung** [swʌŋ]) **1.** *vi* (*a*) **to s. (to and fro),** se balancer; *(of bell)* branler; *(of pendulum)* osciller; **to s. (round an axis),** tourner, pivoter; basculer; *(of door)* **to s. open,** s'ouvrir; **to s. to, to shut,** se refermer; **to s. on its hinges,** tourner sur ses gonds; *(of ship)* **to s. at anchor,** éviter sur l'ancre (*b*) se balancer (sur une balançoire); *(of pers)* **to s. round,** se retourner vivement; faire volte-face; **the car swung right round,** la voiture a fait un tête-à-queue; **to s. along,** marcher d'un pas rhythmé; **to s. (oneself) into the saddle,** sauter en selle; **to s. from**

branch **to branch,** sauter d'une branche à l'autre; **to s. into action,** passer (vivement) à l'action **2.** *vtr* (*a*) (faire) balancer (qch); faire osciller (un pendule); **to s. one's arms,** balancer les bras (en marchant); **to s. the hips (in walking),** se dandiner (*b*) faire tourner (qch); *Av:* lancer (l'hélice); *Nau:* **boat swung out,** embarcation parée au dehors; *Aut:* **to s. a car round,** faire faire un brusque virage à une voiture; **to s. it right round,** lui faire faire un tête-à-queue; **to s. the voting in favour of s.o.,** faire voter en faveur de qn; *F:* **to s. a deal,** mener à bien une affaire; **to s. a hammock,** pendre, suspendre, accrocher, un hamac. **'swing-bridge** *n* pont tournant. **'swingdoor** *n* porte battante. **'swinging I.** *a* (*a*) balançant, oscillant; **s. arms,** bras ballants; **s. stride,** allure rhythmée; **s. tune,** air entraînant (*b*) *F:* dans le vent, avant-garde *inv* **2.** *n* balancement, oscillation; mouvement *m* de bascule, de rotation; *Nau:* évitage *m.* **'swing-'wing** *a* (avion) à géométrie variable.

swingeing ['swindʒiŋ] *a* énorme; *(of tax)* excessif; **s. majority,** majorité écrasante.

swipe [swaip] **1.** *n F: (at ball)* coup *m* à toute volée; **to take a s. at s.o.,** donner un coup de poing, *Fig:* de patte, à qn **2.** *vtr* (*a*) frapper (la balle) à toute volée; donner un coup de poing à (qn) (*b*) chiper, chaparder (qch) (**from s.o.,** à qn).

swirl [swə:l] **1.** *n* remous *m* (de l'eau); tourbillon *m* (de poussière) **2.** *vi* tournoyer, tourbillonner; *(of dust)* **to s. up,** monter en tourbillons.

swish [swiʃ] **1.** *n* bruissement *m* (de l'eau); froufrou *m* (d'une robe); sifflement *m* (d'un fouet); crissement *m* (d'une faux) **2.** *v* (*a*) *vi (of water)* bruire; *(of silk)* froufrouter; *(of whip)* siffler (*b*) *vtr* faire siffler (sa canne); *(of animal)* **to s. its tail,** battre l'air de sa queue **3.** *a F:* chic, rupin.

Swiss [swis] **1.** *a* suisse; **the S. government,** le gouvernement helvétique **2.** *n* Suisse *m*, Suissesse *f*; **the S.,** les Suisses.

switch [switʃ] **1.** *n Rail:* aiguille *f*; changement *m* de voie; *El:* interrupteur *m*; commutateur *m*; *Aut:* **ignition s.,** contact *m* **2.** *vtr & i* aiguiller (un train) (sur un embranchement); **to s. the conversation to another subject,** détourner la conversation; **to s. on the light,** allumer (l'électricité); *Aut:* **to s. on the ignition,** mettre le contact; *TV: WTel:* **to s. on,** mettre la télévision, la radio; **to s. off the engine,** couper l'allumage; **s. the light off, please,** éteignez (l'électricité, la lumière), s'il vous plaît; *TV: WTel:* **to s. off,** arrêter la télévision, la radio; **to s. over to another television channel,** changer de chaîne. **'switchback** *n* montagnes *fpl* russes; **s. road,** route qui monte et descend. **'switchboard** *n El: Tp:* tableau *m* de distribution; *Tp: (in office)* standard *m.* **s. operator,** standardiste *mf.*

Switzerland ['switsələnd] *Prn Geog:* la Suisse; **French-speaking, German-speaking, Italian-speaking, S.,** la Suisse romande, alémanique, italienne.

swivel ['swivl] **1.** *n* émerillon *m*; maillon tournant; pivot *m*; **s. chair,** siège tournant **2.** *v* (**swivelled**) (*a*) *vi* pivoter, tourner (*b*) *vtr* faire pivoter (un siège).

swollen ['swoulən] **1.** *see* **swell III. 2.** *a* enflé, gonflé; (rivière) en crue; *F:* **to have a s. head,** être bouffi d'orgueil.

swoop [swu:p] **1.** *n* descente *f* (d'un faucon sur sa proie, de police); attaque brusquée; **at one fell s.,** d'un seul coup **2.** *vi (of police)* faire une descente; **to s. (down) on sth,** s'abattre, foncer, sur qch.

swop [swɔp] *n & v* (**swopped**)=**swap.**

sword [sɔ:d] *n* épée *f*; *Mil:* sabre *m*; **to cross swords with s.o.,** croiser le fer avec qn; *Fig:* mesurer ses forces avec qn; **s. arm,** bras droit; **s. thrust,** coup d'épée; **with drawn s.,** sabre au clair; **s. cut,** coup de sabre; *(on face)* balafre *f*; **s. dance,** danse au sabre. **'swordbelt** *n* ceinturon *m*. **'swordfish** *n Ich:* espadon *m*. **'swordplay** *n* maniement *m* de l'épée; escrime *f*. **'swordsman** *n (pl -men)* épéiste *m*; **fine s.,** fine lame. **'swordsmanship** *n* habileté *f* au maniement de l'épée. **'swordstick** *n* canne *f* à épée.

swore [swɔ:r] *see* **swear.**

sworn [swɔ:n] **1.** *see* **swear 2.** *a* assermenté; **s. enemies,** ennemis jurés, acharnés; **s. statement,** déclaration sous serment.

swot [swɔt] *Sch: F:* **1.** *n (pers)* bûcheur, -euse **2.** *vtr & i* (**swotted**) bûcher, potasser; **to s. for an exam,** potasser un examen; **to s. up (on) sth,** bûcher qch.

swum [swʌm] *see* **swim 2.**

swung [swʌŋ] *see* **swing II.**

sycamore ['sikəmɔ:r] *n Bot:* sycomore *m*.

sycophant ['sikəfənt] *n* flagorneur, -euse.

syllable ['siləbl] *n* syllabe *f*. **syllabic** [-'læbik] *a* syllabique.

syllabus ['siləbəs] *n (pl* **syllabuses**) programme *m*, sommaire *m* (d'un cours).

sylph [silf] *n* sylphe *m*, sylphide *f*. **'sylphlike** *a* de sylphide.

symbiosis [simbai'ousis] *n Biol:* symbiose *f*.

symbol ['simbəl] *n* symbole *m*; emblème *m*. **symbolic** [-'bɔlik] *a* symbolique. **sym'bolically** *adv* symboliquement. **'symbolism** *n* symbolisme *m*. **'symbolist** *n* symboliste *mf*. **symboli'zation** *n* symbolisation *f*. **'symbolize** *vtr* symboliser.

symmetry ['simitri] *n* symétrie *f*. **sy'mmetrical** *a* symétrique. **sy'mmetrically** *adv* symétriquement.

sympathize ['simpəθaiz] *vi* **to s. with s.o.,** avoir de la compassion pour qn; *(agree)* s'associer aux sentiments de qn; **they called to s.,** ils sont venus exprimer leurs condoléances; **I s. with his point of view,** je comprends son point de vue. **sympa'thetic** *a* compatissant; **he's always very s.,** il est toujours prêt à vous écouter; **s. audience,** auditoire bien disposé. **sympa'thetically** *adv* d'une manière compatissante. **'sympathizer** *n* sympathisant, -ante (d'une cause); **to be a s. with s.o. (in his grief),** compatir au chagrin de qn. **'sympathy** *n (pl -ies)* *(a)* compassion; **accept my deep s.,** agréez mes condoléances *fpl*; **to feel s. for s.o.,** avoir de la compassion pour qn *(b)* sympathie *f*, solidarité *f* **(for s.o.,** à l'égard de qn); **popular s. is on his side,** il a

l'opinion pour lui; **in s. with s.o.,** en sympathie avec qn; **I know you're in s. with them,** je sais que vous êtes de leur côté; **to strike in s.,** commencer, faire, une grève de solidarité; **prices went up in s.,** les prix sont montés par contrecoup.

symphony ['simfəni] *n (pl* **symphonies**) symphonie *f*; **s. concert,** concert symphonique. **sym'phonic** *a* symphonique.

symposium [sim'pouziəm] *n (pl* **symposia** [-iə]) symposium *m*; conférence *f* (académique).

symptom ['simptəm] *n* symptôme *m*; **to show symptoms of sth,** présenter des indices *m* de qch. **sympto'matic** *a* symptomatique.

synagogue ['sinəgɔg] *n* synagogue *f*.

synchronize ['siŋkrənaiz] **1.** *vtr* synchroniser **2.** *vi (of events)* arriver, avoir lieu, simultanément. **synchroni'zation** *n* synchronisation *f*.

syncopate ['siŋkəpeit] *vtr Mus:* syncoper. **synco'pation** *n* syncope *f*.

syndicalism ['sindikəlizm] *n* syndicalisme *m*. **'syndicalist** *n* syndicaliste *mf*.

syndicate 1. ['sindikət] *n* syndicat *m* **2.** ['sindikeit] *vtr* syndiquer (des ouvriers, une industrie); *Journ:* publier (un article) simultanément dans plusieurs journaux.

syndrome ['sindroum] *n Med:* syndrome *m*.

synod ['sinəd] *n Ecc:* synode *m*, concile *m*.

synonym ['sinənim] *n* synonyme *m*. **sy'nonymous** *a* synonyme (**with,** de).

synopsis [si'nɔpsis] *n (pl* **synopses** [-i:z]) résumé *m*, sommaire *m*.

syntax ['sintæks] *n* syntaxe *f*.

synthesis ['sinθisis] *n (pl* **syntheses** [-i:z]) synthèse *f*. **'synthesize** *vtr* synthétiser. **'synthesizer** *n* synthétiseur *m*.

synthetic [sin'θetik] *a* synthétique. **syn'thetically** *adv* synthétiquement.

syphilis ['sifilis] *n Med:* syphilis *f*. **syphi'litic** *a & n* syphilitique *(mf)*.

Syria ['siriə] *Prn Geog:* la Syrie. **'Syrian** *a & n* syrien, -ienne.

syringe [si'rindʒ] **1.** *n* seringue *f* **2.** *vtr* seringuer.

syrup ['sirəp] *n* sirop *m*; *Cu:* **(golden) s.,** mélasse raffinée; sirop de sucre. **'syrupy** *a* sirupeux.

system ['sistəm] *n (a)* système *m*; *(body)* organisme *m*; réseau (routier, télégraphique); *F:* **the s.,** l'ordre établi; **digestive s.,** appareil digestif; *F:* **to get sth out of one's s.,** se purger de qch; *Cmptr:* **systems analyst,** analyste-programmeur, -euse *(b)* méthode *f*; **to lack s.,** manquer de méthode, d'organisation *f*. **syste'matic** *a* systématique, méthodique; **he's s.,** il a de l'ordre. **syste'matically** *adv* systématiquement; *(travailler)* avec méthode. **systemati'zation** *n* systématisation *f*. **'systematize** *vtr* systématiser.

T

T, t [ti:] *n* **1.** (la lettre) T, t *m*; *Fig: to cross one's t's*, mettre les points sur les i; **to a T**, exactement; **it suits me to a T**, cela me va à merveille **2. T square**, té *m*, équerre en T; **T junction**, tête de carrefour; *Cl:* **T shirt**, tee-shirt *m*.

ta [tɑ:] *int P:* merci.

TA *abbr Mil: Territorial Army.*

tab [tæb] *n* **1.** (*a*) patte *f* (de vêtement); écusson *m* (d'officier d'état-major) (*b*) ferret *m* (de lacet) (*c*) attache *f*; tirant *m* (de botte) (*d*) onglet *m* (de fichier) **2.** étiquette *f* (pour bagages); *F:* **to keep tabs on s.o.**, surveiller qn, tenir qn à l'œil **3.** *NAm:* facture *f*, note *f*.

tabby ['tæbi] *n* **t. (cat)**, chat tigré.

tabernacle ['tæbənækl] *n* tabernacle *m*.

table ['teibl]. I. *n* **1.** (*a*) table *f*; guéridon *m*; *nest of* **tables**, table gigogne; **card t.**, table de jeu; **picnic t.**, table pliante, de camping (*b*) **to lay the t.**, mettre la table, le couvert; **to clear the t.**, desservir; **to sit down to t.**, se mettre à table; **to drink s.o. under the table**, faire rouler qn sous la table; **he has awful t. manners**, il se tient très mal à table; **t. knife**, couteau de table; **t. linen**, linge de table; **t. mat**, (i) dessous d'assiette (ii) napperon individuel; **t. wine**, vin de table (*c*) *Ecc:* **the communion t.**, la Sainte Table **2.** *Fig: to turn the tables on s.o.*, retourner un argument contre qn; retourner la situation; **the tables are turned**, les rôles sont renversés **3.** |table, tableau| *m*; **t. of** |contents, |table |des matières; **multiplication t.**, table de multiplication; **tide t.**, annuaire *m* des marées; *Rail:* **t. of fares**, barème *m* des prix. II. *vtr Parl:* **to t. a bill**, (i) déposer un projet de loi (ii) *NAm:* ajourner (indéfiniment) un projet de loi. **'tablecloth** *n* nappe *f*. **'tableland** *n Geog:* plateau *m*. **'tablespoon** *n* cuiller *f* à servir. **'tableware** *n* articles *mpl*, vaisselle *f*, de table.

tableau ['tæblou] *n* (*pl* **tableaux** [-ouz]) *Th:* tableau (vivant).

tablet ['tæblit] *n* **1.** plaque commémorative **2.** (*a*) *Pharm:* comprimé *m*, cachet *m* (*b*) tablette *f* (de chocolat); **t. of soap**, savonnette *f*.

tabloid ['tæblɔid] *n* tabloïd *m*.

taboo [tə'bu:] **1.** *n* (*pl* **taboos**) tabou *m* **2.** *a* tabou, proscrit.

tabular ['tæbjulər] *a* tabulaire; **appendix in t. form**, annexe en forme de tableau.

tabulate ['tæbjuleit] *vtr* classifier (des résultats); présenter sous forme de table, de tableau. **'tabulator** *n Typwr:* tabulateur *m*.

tachograph ['tækougræf] *n Aut:* tachygraphe *m*.

tacit ['tæsit] *a* (aveu) tacite. **'tacitly** *adv* tacitement.

taciturn ['tæsitən] *a* taciturne. **taci'turnity** *n* taciturnité *f*.

tack[1] [tæk]. I. *n* **1.** petit clou; pointe *f*; broquette *f*; semence *f*; *F:* **to get down to brass tacks**, en venir au fait **2.** *Needlw:* point *m* de bâti **3.** *Nau:* bord *m*, bordée *f*; **to be on the right t.**, être sur la bonne voie; **let's try another t.**, essayons une autre tactique. II. *v* **1.** *vtr* (*a*)

to t. sth (down), clouer qch (avec des broquettes); **to t. sth on to sth**, attacher qch à qch (*b*) *Needlw:* faufiler, bâtir **2.** *vi Nau:* (i) virer (de bord) (ii) tirer des bordées; louvoyer **3.** *vi F:* **to t. on to s.o.**, se coller à qn. **'tacking** *n* (*a*) clouage *m* (*b*) *Needlw:* bâti *m* (*c*) *Nau:* virement *m* de bord.

tack[2] *n Equit:* sellerie *f*; **t. room**, sellerie.

tackle ['tækl]. I. *n* **1.** attirail *m*, appareil *m*; **fishing t.**, articles *mpl* de pêche **2.** *Nau: etc:* palan *m* **3.** *Fb:* tackle *m*, arrêt *m*; *Rugby Fb:* plaquage *m*; (hockey) interception *f*. II. *vtr* (*a*) empoigner; saisir (qn) à bras-le-corps; *Fig:* **I'll tackle him about it**, je lui en parlerai (*b*) s'attaquer à, attaquer (la nourriture); aborder (un problème); **I don't know how to t. it**, je ne sais pas comment m'y prendre.

tacky ['tæki] *a* (-ier, -iest) collant; (vernis) presque sec; (*of surface*) poisseux.

tact [tækt] *n* tact *m*, savoir-faire *m*. **'tactful** *a* (homme) de tact; délicat; **to be t.**, avoir du tact. **'tactfully** *adv* avec tact; **to deal t. with s.o.**, ménager qn. **'tactless** *a* (*a*) dépourvu de tact (*b*) **t. question**, question indiscrète. **'tactlessly** *adv* sans tact.

tactics ['tæktiks] *npl* tactique *f*. **'tactical** *a* tactique; **t. error**, erreur de tactique. **'tactically** *adv* du point de vue tactique. **tac'tician** *n* tacticien, -ienne.

tadpole ['tædpoul] *n* têtard *m*.

taffeta ['tæfitə] *n* taffetas *m*.

tag [tæg]. I. *n* **1.** (*a*) morceau *m* (de ruban) qui pend (*b*) tirant *m* (de botte) (*c*) étiquette *f* (d') ferret *m* (de lacet) **2.** cliché *m* **3.** **t. end**, queue *f* (d'une affaire); bribes *fpl* (d'une conversation) **4.** (jeu *m* de) chat *m*. II. *v* (tagged) **1.** *vtr* étiqueter (des marchandises) **2.** *vi* **to t. along**, traîner (behind s.o., derrière qn); **to t. on to s.o.**, s'attacher à qn.

tail [teil]. I. *n* **1.** (*a*) queue *f* (d'animal); (*of peacock*) **to spread his t.**, faire la roue; **with his t. between his legs**, (i) (*of dogs*) la queue entre les jambes (ii) *F:* (*of pers*) l'oreille basse; **to turn t.**, montrer les talons (*b*) pan *m* (de chemise); **coat tails**, queue d'un habit; **to wear tails**, porter l'habit à queue (*c*) *Av:* queue (d'un avion); **t. spin**, (descente *f* en) vrille *f* (*d*) arrière *m* (d'une voiture); **to be on s.o.'s t.**, suivre qn de près; (*of detective*) filer qn; **t. end**, bout *m*; queue (d'un défilé); fin *f* (d'un orage); *Aut:* **t. light**, feu *m* arrière **2.** *F:* fileur *m* **3.** (*of coin*) pile *f*, revers *m*. II. *vtr* (*a*) équeuter, enlever les queues (des cerises) (*b*) (*of detective*) filer (qn). **'tail a'way** *vi* (*a*) (*of competitors in race*) s'espacer, s'égrener (*b*) diminuer, décroître (*c*) finir en queue de poisson. **'tailback** *n Aut:* bouchon *m*. **'tailboard**, **'tailgate** *n* hayon *m* (arrière). **'tailless** *a* sans queue. **'tail 'off** *vi* (*a*) (*of sound*) s'éteindre (*b*) (*of novel*) finir en queue de poisson. **'tailwind** *n* vent *m* arrière.

tailor ['teilər]. I. *n* tailleur *m* (d'habits); **tailor's chalk**, craie de tailleur; **tailor's dummy,** mannequin *m.* II. *vtr* faire, façonner (un complet); **(woman's) tailored suit,** (costume *m*) tailleur *m*; **tailored shirt,** chemise cintrée.

'**tailoring** *n* 1. métier *m* de tailleur 2. ouvrage *m* de tailleur. '**tailor-made** *a* (*a*) (*of suit*) fait sur mesure (*b*) adapté aux besoins particuliers de l'utilisateur; personnalisé; (outil) spécial; **it's t. for me,** c'est fait pour moi.

taint [teint] 1. *n* (*a*) corruption *f,* infection *f* (*b*) tare *f* héréditaire |(*c*)| trace *f* |(d'infection)| 2.| *vtr* |infecter (l'air); corrompre (les mœurs); gâter (la nourriture). '**tainted** *a* infecté, corrompu; **t. meat,** viande gâtée.

take [teik] I. *n Cin:* prise *f* de vues; *Rec:* enregistrement *m.* II. (**took** [tuk]; **taken** ['teik(ə)n]) *vtr* I. (*a*) prendre; **to t. sth on one's back,** charger qch sur son dos (*b*) **to t. sth from s.o.,** enlever, prendre, qch à qn; **to t. sth from the table, out of a drawer,** prendre qch sur la table, dans un tiroir; **t. the saucepan off the heat,** retirez la casserole du feu (*c*) **to t. (hold of) s.o., sth,** saisir, empoigner, s'emparer de, s'emparer de qn, qch; **she took my arm,** elle m'a pris le bras; **to t. the opportunity,** profiter de l'occasion; **to t. a chance,** risquer le coup (*d*) **prendre** (une ville); **to t. s.o. prisoner,** faire qn prisonnier; **to t. s.o. by surprise,** surprendre qn; **to be taken ill,** tomber malade; **he was very much taken with the idea,** l'idée l'enchantait; **I wasn't taken with him,** il ne m'a pas fait bonne impression (*e*) **to t. a passage from a book,** emprunter un passage à un livre 2. (*a*) louer, prendre (une maison, une voiture) (*b*) prendre (un billet); **all the seats are taken,** toutes les places sont prises; (*of seat, table*) **taken,** occupé; **to t. a paper,** s'abonner à un journal (*c*) **to t. a seat,** s'asseoir; **t. your seats!** prenez vos places! (*d*) **t. the turning on the left,** prenez à gauche; **to t. the wrong road,** se tromper de chemin; **he took the corner at full speed,** il a pris le virage à toute vitesse (*e*) **to t. legal advice,** consulter un avocat (*f*) *Ecc:* **to t. (holy) orders,** recevoir les ordres 3. (*a*) gagner, remporter (un prix); *Cards:* **to t. a trick,** faire une levée (*b*) passer, se présenter à (un examen); **she's taking a degree in law,** elle fait son droit (*c*) *Com:* **to t. so much per week,** faire (une recette de) tant par semaine 4. prendre (de la nourriture, un médicament) 5. (*a*) faire (une promenade); prendre (un bain); **to t. a nap,** faire un petit somme; **to t. a few steps,** faire quelques pas; *Phot:* **to t. a print,** tirer une épreuve; **to t. notes,** prendre des notes (*b*) prendre (une photo); **to have one's photograph taken,** se faire photographier (*c*) **to t. sth apart, to pieces,** démonter qch 6. *Ecc:* célébrer (un office); *Sch:* **she takes them in English,** elle fait la classe d'anglais 7. (*a*) prendre, accepter, recevoir; **t. it or leave it!** c'est à prendre ou à laisser; **t. that!** attrape (ça)! **what will you t. for it?** combien en voulez-vous? **to t. a bet,** tenir un pari; **to t. all responsibility,** assumer toute la responsabilité; **to t. things as one finds them,** prendre les choses comme elles sont; **t. it from me!** croyez-moi! **to t. s.o. seriously,** prendre qn au sérieux; **to t. sth the wrong way,** mal comprendre qch; **I wonder how he'll t. it,** je me demande comment il va prendre la chose; **he can't t. a joke,** il ne comprend pas la plaisanterie; **I can't take any more,** je n'en peux plus; **I can't t. any more of him,** je ne peux plus le supporter (*b*) **car that takes six people,** voiture qui tient six personnes; **the petrol tank takes 40 litres,** le réservoir à essence a une capacité de 40 litres; **to t. heavy loads,** supporter de lourdes charges 8. **to t. a dislike to s.o.,** prendre qn en grippe; **to t. a decision about sth,** prendre une décision à propos de qch 9. (*a*) **t. the pensioners,** prenez le cas des retraités; **to t. the news to be true,** tenir la nouvelle pour vraie; **how old do you t. him to be?** quel âge lui donnez-vous? **I t. it that,** je suppose que (*b*) **I took him for someone else,** je l'ai pris pour qn d'autre; **I took him for an Englishman,** je le croyais anglais; *F:* **what do you t. me for?** pour qui me prenez-vous? 10. (*a*) **that will t. some explaining,** voilà qui va demander des explications; **the work took some doing,** le travail a été difficile; **the journey takes five days,** le voyage prend cinq jours; **it will t. him two hours,** il en aura pour deux heures; **it won't t. long,** ce ne sera pas long; **it took four men to hold him,** il a fallu le tenir à quatre; *F:* **he hasn't got what it takes,** il lui manque ce qui lui faut (**to be a leader,** pour être chef) (*b*) **verb that takes a preposition,** verbe qui veut la préposition (*c*) **I t. size six,** j'ai 39 de pointure; je chausse du 39 11. (*a*) (*lead*) conduire, mener, emmener; prendre (qn avec soi); **to t. oneself to bed,** aller se coucher; **to t. the dog for a walk,** promener le chien; **I'll t. you with me,** je t'emmène avec moi; **he took him across the road,** il l'a fait traverser la rue (*b*) (*carry*) **to t. sth to s.o.,** porter qch à qn; **to t. some food,** emporter des provisions; **to t. s.o. to hospital,** transporter qn à l'hôpital (*c*) **his father took a stick to him,** son père lui a donné des coups de bâton. III. *vi* (*a*) avoir du succès; **the play has taken,** la pièce marche, a du succès; **the fire has taken,** le feu a pris (*b*) *Med:* (*of vaccine*) prendre. '**take after** *vi* tenir de (qn), ressembler à (qn); **she doesn't t. a. her father,** elle n'a rien de son père. '**take away** *vtr* (*a*) enlever, emporter (qch); emmener (qn); **sandwiches to t. a.,** sandwiches à emporter (*b*) **to t. a knife a. from a child,** retirer un couteau à un enfant (*c*) **to t. a. sth from sth,** ôter qch de qch; soustraire (un nombre d'un autre); **to t. a child a. from school,** retirer un enfant de l'école. '**takeaway** 1. *a* (plat, sandwich) à emporter 2. *n* magasin qui vend des plats à emporter. '**take back** *vtr* (*a*) reconduire (qn); reporter (qch à qn); **it takes me back to my childhood,** cela me rappelle mon enfance (*b*) reprendre (un employé) (*c*) **I t. back what I said,** je retire ce que j'ai dit. '**take down** *vtr* (*a*) descendre, décrocher (qch) (*b*) démolir (un mur); démonter (une machine) (*c*) *F:* **to t. s.o. a peg (or two),** remettre qn à sa place (*d*) noter, inscrire (un nom); **to t. d. a few notes,** prendre quelques notes; **to t. sth d. in shorthand,** prendre qch en sténo. '**take 'in** *vtr* 1. (*a*) faire entrer (qn) (*b*) rentrer (le linge); *Nau:* (*of boat*) **to t. in water,** faire eau; prendre l'eau (*c*) recueillir (qn); loger (qn); **to t. in lodgers,** prendre des locataires; **to t. in washing,** faire des lessives (*d*) reprendre (une couture); serrer (une manche) (*e*) *Nau:* **to t. in sail,** diminuer de voile(s) (*f*) comprendre, inclure; **the tour takes in three cities,** l'excursion passe par trois grandes villes (*g*) comprendre; se rendre compte de (qch); **to t. in the situation,** juger de la situation; **to t. in everything at a glance,** tout embrasser d'un coup d'œil (*h*) **he takes it all in,** il croit tout ce qu'on lui dit (*i*) *F:* **to be taken in,** se laisser avoir; **I've been taken in,** on m'a eu. '**take off** 1. *vtr* **to t. s.o.'s attention o. sth,** distraire l'attention de qn; **not to t. one's eyes o. sth,** ne pas quitter qch des yeux;

to t. s.o. o. a list, rayer qn d'une liste 2. *vtr* (a) enlever, ôter, retirer; to t. o. one's clothes, se déshabiller; *Tp:* to t. o. the receiver, décrocher le récepteur; *Aut:* to t. o. the brake, desserrer le frein (b) emmener (qn); to t. oneself o., s'en aller; *F:* décamper (c) to t. so much o. (the price of sth), rabattre tant (sur le prix de qch) (d) imiter, singer (qn) (e) to t. three days o., prendre trois jours de congé 3. *vi* (a) *Av:* décoller (b) *F:* (of pers) décamper. 'takeoff n (a) *Av:* décollage m (b) caricature *f*, imitation *f*. 'take'on v 1. *vtr* (a) se charger de, entreprendre (un travail); assumer (une responsabilité) (b) accepter le défi de (qn) (c) engager, embaucher (un ouvrier) (d) prendre, revêtir (une couleur, l'apparence de qch); the word takes on another meaning, le mot prend une autre signification (e) (of train) to t. on passengers, prendre des voyageurs (f) mener (qn) plus loin 2. *vi F:* don't t. on so! ne vous désolez pas comme ça! 'take'out *vtr* (a) sortir (qch de sa poche); arracher (une dent); enlever (une tache) (b) *F:* the heat takes it out of me, la chaleur m'épuise; don't t. it o. on me, ne vous en prenez pas à moi (c) faire sortir (qn); promener, sortir (le chien); he's taking me out to dinner, il m'emmène dîner (d) prendre (un brevet); souscrire (une police d'assurance). 'take'over *vtr* (a) to t. o. a business, prendre la suite des affaires; acheter une entreprise commerciale; to t. o. the liabilities, prendre les dettes à sa charge; *vi* to t. o. from s.o., remplacer qn (dans ses fonctions) (prendre (qn, qch). 'takeover n (a) prise *f* de possession (du pouvoir) (b) prise de contrôle; t. bid, offre *f* publique d'achat (OPA). 'taker n preneur, -euse (d'un bail); at that price there were no takers, à ce prix on n'a pas pu trouver d'acheteurs; any takers? est-ce qu'il y a des amateurs? 'take to *vi* (a) to t. to flight, to t. to one's heels, prendre la fuite; to t. to the woods, se réfugier dans les bois; to t. to the road again, reprendre la route (b) to t. to drink, se mettre à boire; to t. to writing, se mettre à écrire (c) to t. to s.o., éprouver de la sympathie pour qn; I didn't t. to him, il ne m'était pas sympathique; I shall never t. to it, je ne m'y ferai jamais. 'take'up 1. *vtr* (a) relever, ramasser (qch) (b) enlever (un tapis); dépaver (une rue) (c) faire monter (qn) (dans une chambre); there's a lift to t. you up, vous pouvez monter en ascenseur (d) *Rail:* to stop to t. up passengers, s'arrêter pour prendre des voyageurs (e) raccourcir (une jupe) (f) to t. up the slack in a rope, retendre une corde (g) absorber (de l'eau) 2. *vtr* (a) *Com:* honorer (un effet); souscrire à (des actions) (b) relever (un défi) (c) adopter (une idée); suivre (un conseil); aborder la discussion (d'une question) (d) embrasser (une carrière); s'adonner à (une occupation); adopter (une méthode); épouser (une querelle); he's taken up photography, il fait de la photo; to t. up one's duties again, reprendre ses fonctions (f) prendre (qn) sous sa protection (g) to t. s.o. up on sth, prendre qn au mot; I'll t. you up on that, (i) je vous prendrai au mot sur cela (ii) je vous défie de le prouver; to t. s.o. up short, couper la parole à qn (h) to t. up too much room, occuper trop de place; être encombrant; to t. up all s.o.'s attention, absorber l'attention de qn; he's entirely taken up with his business, il est entièrement occupé par son activité 3. *vi* to t. up with s.o., (i) se lier d'amitié avec qn (ii) se

mettre à fréquenter (qn). 'taking 1. *a* (style) attrayant; (visage) séduisant; (of manners) engageant 2. *n* (a) prise *f* (d'une ville) (b) *Com:* takings, recette *f*, produit *m*.

talc [tælk] n (poudre *f* de) talc m. 'talcum n (no pl) t. powder, (poudre de) talc.

tale [teil] n 1. conte m; récit *m*, histoire *f*; old wives' t., conte de bonne femme; he lived to tell the t., il a survécu 2. (a) racontar m, potin m (b) to tell tales, rapporter, cafarder. 'talebearer n rapporteur, -euse. 'talebearing, 'taletelling n rapportage m, cafardage m.

talent ['tælənt] n 1. talent m; aptitude *f*; don m (de faire qch); he has no t. for business, il n'est pas doué pour les affaires 2. (a) personne bien douée (b) *coll* gens *mpl* de talent; exhibition of local t., exposition d'œuvres d'artistes régionaux; *Cin: etc:* t. scout, spotter, dénicheur de talent(s), de vedettes. 'talented a doué; plein de talent.

talisman ['tælizmən] n talisman m.

talk [tɔːk] I. n 1. (a) paroles *fpl*; he's all t., ce n'est qu'un bavard (b) bruit m, dires *mpl*, racontages *mpl*; there's some t. of his returning, il est question qu'il revienne; there has been t. of it, on en a parlé; it's all t., tout ça c'est des racontars (c) propos *mpl*; bavardage *m*; idle t., paroles en l'air; small t., banalités *fpl*; to indulge in small t., causer de choses et d'autres; double t., propos (i) ambigus (ii) insincères (c) baby t., babil enfantin 2. (a) entretien m; conversation *f*; causerie *f*; to have a t. with s.o., s'entretenir avec qn (b) *Pol: etc:* talks, dialogue m, pourparlers *mpl* (c) causerie; to give a t. on, about, sth, faire une causerie sur qch; *TV:* t. show, entretien télévisé 3. it's the t. of the town, c'est la fable de la ville; she's the t. of the town, elle défraie la chronique. II. *v* 1. *vi* (a) parler; to learn to t., apprendre à parler (b) parler, discourir; *F:* that's no way to t.! (i) en voilà un langage! (ii) il ne faut pas dire des choses pareilles! to t. through one's hat, débiter des sottises; now you're talking! à la bonne heure! *you can* t.! c'est bien à vous de parler! to t. about sth, parler de qch; to t. of one thing and another, parler de choses et d'autres; what are you talking about? (i) de quoi parlez-vous? (ii) qu'est-ce que vous racontez? he knows what he's talking about, il sait ce qu'il dit; il s'y connaît; t. about luck! tu parles d'une chance! (c) to t. of doing sth, parler de faire qch (d) to t. on the radio, parler à la radio (e) to make s.o. t., faire avouer qn; they're afraid he'll t., ils craignent qu'il ne vende la mèche (f) to t. to s.o., s'entretenir avec qn; parler à, avec, qn; to t. to oneself, parler tout seul; *F:* who do you think you're talking to? à qui croyez-vous (donc) parler? *F:* I'll t. to him! je vais lui dire son fait! (g) jaser, bavarder (h) cancaner; people will t., (i) cela fera scandale (ii) le monde est cancanier; to get oneself talked about, faire parler de soi 2. *vtr* (a) to t. French, parler français; to t. politics, parler politique; to t. (common) sense, parler raison (b) to t. oneself hoarse, s'enrouer à force de parler (c) to t. s.o. into, out of, doing sth, persuader, dissuader, qn de faire qch; to t. s.o. round, amener qn à changer d'avis. 'talkative a causeur; jaseur; bavard, loquace. 'talkativeness n loquacité *f*. 'talk'down *vi* to t. d. to s.o., parler à qn avec condescendance. 'talker n 1. parleur, -euse 2. he's a great t., il est très bavard. 'talkie n *Cin:* film parlant. **'talking 1.** *a* parlant; **t. film,** film parlant **2.** *n* (*a*) discours *mpl,* propos *mpl;* **that's enough t.,** (c'est) assez parlé; **t. point,** sujet de conversation (*b*) (i) conversation *f* (ii) bavardage *m;* **to do all the t.,** faire (tous) les frais de la conversation; **no t. please!** silence s'il vous plaît! (*c*) **to give s.o. a good t.-to,** passer un savon à qn. **'talk 'over** *vtr* discuter (une question); **let's t. it o.,** discutons la chose.

tall [tɔːl] *a* (**taller, tallest**) **1.** (*of pers*) (*a*) grand; de haute taille (*b*) **how t. are you?** combien mesurez-vous? **he was taller by a head,** il dépassait de la tête; **she is getting t.,** elle se fait grande; **he has grown t.,** il a grandi **2.** (*of thg*) haut, élevé; **how t. is that mast?** quelle est la hauteur de ce mât? **tree ten metres t.,** arbre haut de dix mètres **3.** *F:* (histoire) incroyable; **that's a t. story!** celle-là est raide! vous m'en contez de belles! **that's a t. order!** voilà qui va être difficile. **'tallboy** *n Furn:* commode haute. **'tallness** *n* (*a*) (*of pers*) grande taille (*b*) hauteur *f.*

tallow ['tælou] *n* suif *m;* **t. candle,** chandelle *f.*

tally ['tæli] **1.** *n* (*a*) pointage *m;* **to keep t. of goods,** pointer les marchandises (sur une liste); **t. clerk,** pointeur *m* (*b*) compte *m* **2.** *v* (*a*) *vtr* pointer (des marchandises) (*b*) *vi* **to t. with sth,** correspondre à, s'accorder avec, qch; **they don't t.,** ils ne s'accordent pas.

tally-ho ['tæli'hou] *int & n Ven:* taïaut (*m*).

talon ['tælən] *n* serre *f* (d'aigle); griffe *f* (de tigre).

tamarisk ['tæmərisk] *n Bot:* tamaris *m.*

tambourine [tæmbə'riːn] *n Mus:* tambourin *m.*

tame [teim] **1.** *a* (*a*) (animal) apprivoisé, domestiqué (*b*) domestique (*c*) *F:* (*of pers*) soumis, docile; anodin, insipide; **the story has a t. ending,** l'histoire se termine sur une note banale **2.** *vtr* (*a*) apprivoiser (*b*) domestiquer (une bête) (*c*) mater (qn, une passion); dompter (un lion). **'tamely** *adv* (*a*) docilement; **to submit t.,** n'offrir aucune résistance (*b*) fadement. **'tameness** *n* **1.** (*a*) nature douce (d'un animal) (*b*) docilité *f* (de qn) **2.** insipidité *f,* banalité *f* (d'un conte). **'tamer** *n* apprivoiseur, -euse (d'oiseaux); dompteur, -euse (de fauves); **'taming** *n* (*a*) apprivoisement *m* (*b*) domestication *f* (c) domptage *m* (de fauves).

tamper ['tæmpər] *vi* (*a*) **to t. with,** toucher à (un mécanisme); altérer (un document); falsifier (un registre); fausser (une serrure); tripatouiller (des comptes) (*b*) **to t. with a witness,** suborner un témoin.

tampon ['tæmpən] *n* tampon *m* (périodique).

tan [tæn] **1.** *n* (*a*) tan *m* (*b*) couleur du tan (i) tanne *m* (ii) hâle *m,* teint hâlé (de la peau) **2.** *a* tanné; tan *inv;* (chaussures) en cuir jaune; (gants) en tanné; **black and t. dog,** chien noir et feu *inv* **3.** *v* (**tanned**) *vtr* (*a*) tanner (les peaux); *F:* **to t. s.o.'s hide,** tanner le cuir à qn (*b*) (*of sun*) hâler, bronzer (la peau) (*c*) *vi* se hâler, se bronzer; **I t. easily,** je bronze facilement. **'tanned** *a* (*a*) (cuir) tanné (*b*) (teint) basané, hâlé, bronzé. **'tanner** *n* tanneur *m.* **'tannery** *n* tannerie *f.* **'tanning** *n* **1.** (*a*) tannage *m* (*b*) bronzage *m* **2.** *F:* raclée *f.*

tandem ['tændəm] *n* **t. (bicycle),** tandem *m* de tourisme.

tang [tæŋ] *n* saveur piquante; montant *m;* **the t. of the sea,** le piquant de l'air marin.

tangent ['tæn(d)ʒənt] *n* tangente *f;* **to fly off at a t.,** changer de sujet.

tangerine [tæn(d)ʒə'riːn] *n* mandarine *f.*

tangible ['tæn(d)ʒibl] *a* **1.** tangible; **t. assets,** valeurs matérielles **2.** réel; **t. difference,** différence sensible. **'tangibly** *adv* **1.** tangiblement **2.** sensiblement.

Tangier(s) [tæn'dʒiər, -'dʒiəz] *Prn Geog:* Tanger *m.*

tangle ['tæŋgl] **1.** *n* embrouillement *m;* emmêlement *m* (de cheveux); fouillis (de broussailles); enchevêtrement *m* (de branches); **to be (all) in a t.,** (*of string*) être (tout) embrouillé; (*of wool, hair*) être (tout) enchevêtré; *Fig:* (*of pers*) ne plus savoir où on en est; **to get into a t.,** s'embrouiller; s'enchevêtrer **2.** *vtr* **to t. sth (up),** embrouiller, (em)mêler (des fils); embrouiller (une affaire); **to get tangled (up),** (*of thgs*) s'emmêler; (*of thgs, pers*) s'embrouiller.

tango ['tæŋgou] *n Danc:* tango.

tank [tæŋk] *n* **1.** (*a*) réservoir *m;* **water t.,** réservoir à eau, d'eau; **fish t.,** vivier *m;* **storage t.,** réservoir de stockage; *Aut:* **petrol t.,** réservoir à essence (*b*) **t. lorry,** *NAm:* **truck,** camion-citerne *m* **2.** (*a*) *Ind:* cuve *f,* bac *m* (*b*) *Pol:* **think t.,** comité *m* d'experts **3.** (*a*) *Mil:* char *m* (de combat); **the tanks,** les blindés (*b*) *Cl:* **t. top,** débardeur *m.* **'tanker** *n Nau:* navire-citerne *m;* **oil t.,** (navire) pétrolier (*m*); *Aut:* **t. (lorry),** *NAm:* **t. (truck),** camion-citerne *m.* **'tank 'up** *vi* **1.** *Aut:* faire le plein (d'essence) **2.** *P:* **to get tanked up,** se soûler.

tankard ['tæŋkəd] *n* pot *m,* chope *f* (en étain).

tannoy ['tænɔi] *n* (*Rtm*) système *m* de haut-parleurs.

tantalize ['tæntəlaiz] *vtr* tourmenter, taquiner (qn). **'tantalizing** *a* tentant; **t. slowness,** lenteur désespérante. **'tantalizingly** *adv* (*a*) cruellement (*b*) d'un air provocant.

tantamount ['tæntəmaunt] *a* **t. to,** équivalent à; **that is t. to saying I'm a liar,** cela revient à dire que je mens.

tantrum ['tæntrəm] *n* accès *m* de colère; **to get into a t.,** piquer une colère.

Tanzania [tænzə'niːə] *Prn Geog:* Tanzanie *f.*

tap¹ [tæp] **1.** *n* (*a*) robinet *m;* (*of cask*) cannelle *f,* cannette *f;* **to turn on, turn off, the t.,** ouvrir, fermer, le robinet; **t. water,** eau du robinet (*b*) (*of beer*) **on t.,** (i) en perce (ii) au tonneau **2.** *vtr* (**tapped**) (*a*) percer (un fût) (*b*) inciser (un arbre); gemmer (un pin); tirer (du vin); exploiter (les ressources naturelles); faire un branchement (sur une conduite d'eau, de gaz); **to t. a telephone conversation,** écouter une communication téléphonique; *F:* **to t. s.o. for fifty francs,** taper qn de cinquante francs. **'tapping¹** *n* (*a*) perçage *m* (d'un tonneau); incision *f,* gemmage *m* (d'un arbre) (*b*) tirage *m* (du vin) (*c*) branchement *m* (sur une conduite d'eau) (*d*) *Tp:* **telephone t.,** écoute(s) *f(pl)* téléphonique(s) (*e*) exploitation *f* (des ressources naturelles). **'taproom** *n* bar *m.* **'taproot** *n Bot:* racine pivotante; pivot *m.*

tap² **1.** *n* (*a*) tape *f;* petit coup; **there was a t. at the door,** on frappa doucement à la porte (*b*) **t. dance,** dancing, (danse à) claquettes *fpl;* **t. dancer,** danseur, -euse, de claquettes; **to t. dance,** faire des claquettes **2.** *v* (**tapped**) (*a*) *vtr* frapper légèrement; taper, tapoter (*b*) *vi* **to t. at, on, the door,** frapper à la porte; **to t. out a message,** émettre un message (en morse). **'tapping²** *n* petits coups; tapotement *m.*

tape [teip] **1.** *n* (*a*) ruban *m;* bande *f* (de toile); **masking t.,** ruban-cache *m;* **adhesive t.,** ruban adhésif; *Pharm:* sparadrap *m;* *El:* **insulating t.,** chatterton *m* (*b*) *Sp:* fil *m* d'arrivée (*c*) **t. measure,** mètre *m*; centimètre *m* (de couturière) (*d*) **ticker t.,** bande de téléimprimeur; **magnetic t.,** bande magnétique; **t. recorder,** magnétophone *m*; **t. recording,** enregistrement *m* (sur bande) **2.** *vtr* (*a*) attacher (un paquet) avec du ruban adhésif (*b*) mesurer (un terrain) au cordeau; (*of pers*) **I've got him taped,** j'ai pris sa mesure (*c*) **to t.(-record),** enregistrer (qch) sur bande. **'tapeworm** *n* ténia *m*; ver *m* solitaire. **'taping** *n* enregistrement *m* (sur bande).

taper ['teipər] **1.** *n Ecc:* cierge *m* **2.** (*a*) *vtr* effiler; tailler en pointe (*b*) *vi* **to t. (off),** s'effiler; aller en diminuant; se terminer en pointe. **'tapered** *a* effilé. **'tapering** *a* en pointe; effilé, fuselé.

tapestry ['tæpistri] *n* (*pl* **tapestries**) tapisserie *f.*

tapioca [tæpi'oukə] *n* (*no pl*) tapioca *m.*

tar [tɑːr] **1.** *n* goudron *m*; **to spoil the ship for a ha'p'orth of t.,** faire des économies de bouts de chandelle **2.** *vtr* **(tarred)** goudronner. **'tarring** *n* goudronnage *m.* **'tarry** *a* goudronneux; couvert de goudron.

tarantula [tə'ræntjulə] *n* (*pl* **tarantulas, -lae**) *Arach:* tarentule *f.*

tardy ['tɑːdi] *a* tardif.

target ['tɑːgit] *n* cible *f*; but *m*, objectif *m*; **to hit the t.,** atteindre le but; **t. practice,** exercices de tir; **sitting t.,** cible facile; *Com:* **t. date,** date limite; **to be on t.,** (i) (*of missile*) suivre la trajectoire prévue (ii) ne pas avoir de retard; **I've set myself a t. of £500,** je me suis fixé comme objectif de réunir £500.

tariff ['tærif] *n* **1.** tarif *m*; **t. wall,** barrière douanière **2.** tableau *m*, liste *f*, des prix.

tarmac ['tɑːmæk] *n* **1.** *CivE: Rtm:* macadam goudronné **2.** *Av:* (*a*) aire *f* de stationnement (*b*) piste *f* (d'envol).

tarnish ['tɑːniʃ] **1.** *n* ternissure *f* **2.** *vtr & i* (se) ternir.

tarot ['tærou] *n Cards:* tarot *m*; **t. card,** tarot.

tarpaulin [tɑː'pɔːlin] *n* (*a*) toile goudronnée (*b*) bâche *f.*

tarragon ['tærəgən] *n Bot: Cu:* estragon *m.*

tart¹ [tɑːt] **1.** *n* (*a*) *Cu:* tarte *f*; (*small*) tartelette *f* (*b*) *P:* prostituée *f*, poule *f* **2.** *vtr F:* **to t. oneself up,** s'attifer.

tart² *a* (*a*) au goût âpre, aigrelet (*b*) (*tone*) acerbe, aigre. **'tartly** *adv* avec aigreur; d'un ton acerbe. **'tartness** *n* acerbité *f*, goût *m* âpre (d'un fruit); verdeur *f* (d'un vin); aigreur *f* (du ton).

tartan ['tɑːt(ə)n] *n Tex: Cl:* tartan *m*, chemise écossaise.

Tartar¹ ['tɑːtər] **1.** *a & n Geog:* tartare **2.** *n* homme *m* intraitable; (*of woman*) mégère *f.*

tartar² *n Ch:* tartre *m.* **tar'taric** *a* tartrique.

task [tɑːsk] *n* **1.** tâche *f*; travail *m*; ouvrage *m*; *Sch:* devoir *m*; **a hard t.,** une tâche difficile; **to carry out one's t.,** remplir sa tâche **2.** **to take s.o. to t. for sth,** prendre qn à partie, réprimander qn, pour avoir fait qch **3.** *Mil:* **t. force,** corps *m* expéditionnaire. **'taskmaster** *n* chef *m* de corvée; surveillant *m*; **hard t.,** véritable tyran *m.*

Tasmania [tæz'meiniə] *Prn Geog:* Tasmanie *f.* **Tas'manian** *a & n* tasmanien, -ienne.

tassel ['tæsəl] *n* **1.** *Furn: Cl:* gland *m* **2.** *Bot:* épi *m* mâle (du maïs).

taste [teist] **I.** *n* **1.** (*a*) **(sense of) t.,** goût *m*; **t. bud,** papille gustative (*b*) saveur *f*, goût; **it has no t.,** cela n'a pas de goût, est insipide; **it has a burnt t.,** cela a un goût de brûlé (*c*) **a t. of sth,** un petit peu (de fromage); une petite gorgée (de vin); **have a t. of this claret,** goûtez donc à ce bordeaux (*d*) **he's already had a t. of prison,** il a déjà tâté de la prison **2.** goût, penchant (particulier), prédilection *f* **(for,** pour); **to have a t. for sth,** avoir du goût pour qch; avoir le goût de (qch); **to develop a t. for sth,** prendre goût à qch; **to find sth to one's t.,** trouver qch à son goût; *Cu:* **add sugar to t.,** ajoutez du sucre à volonté; **it's a matter of t.,** c'est une affaire de goût; **everyone to his t.,** (à) chacun son goût **3.** **to have (good) t.,** avoir du goût; **it's (in) bad t.,** c'est de mauvais goût. **II.** *v* **1.** *vtr* (*a*) percevoir la saveur de (qch); sentir (qch) (*b*) déguster (des vins) (*c*) goûter à (qch); manger un petit morceau d'(un mets); tâter de (qch); **he hadn't tasted food for three days,** il n'avait pas mangé depuis trois jours (*d*) **to t. happiness,** connaître le bonheur **2.** *vi* **to t. of sth,** avoir un goût de qch. **'tasteful** *a* de bon goût. **'tastefully** *adv* avec goût. **'tastefulness** *n* bon goût *m.* **'tasteless** *a* **1.** sans goût, sans saveur; fade, insipide **2.** (vêtement, ameublement) qui manque de goût, de mauvais goût. **'tastelessly** *adv* sans goût. **'tastelessness** *n* **1.** insipidité *f*, fadeur *f* **2.** manque *m* de goût. **'taster** *n* dégustateur, -trice (de vins). **'tastiness** *n* saveur *f*, goût *m* agréable. **'tasting** *n* dégustation *f* (de vins). **'tasty** *a* **(tastier, tastiest)** (mets) savoureux; (morceau) succulent.

ta-ta [tæ'tɑː] *int P:* au revoir! salut!

tatters ['tætəz] *npl* **in t.,** (vêtement) en lambeaux *m*, en loques *f.* **'tattered** *a* (vêtement) en lambeaux; (*of pers*) déguenillé.

tattle ['tætl] **1.** *n* (*a*) bavardage *m*, commérage *m* (*b*) cancans *mpl*; potins *mpl* **2.** *vi* (*a*) bavarder (*b*) cancaner; faire des cancans. **'tattler** *n* (*a*) bavard, -arde (*b*) cancanier, -ière.

tattoo¹ [tə'tuː] *n Mil:* **1.** retraite *f* (du soir) **2.** torchlight t., retraite aux flambeaux.

tattoo² **1.** *n* (*pl* **tattoos**) tatouage *m* **2.** *vtr* tatouer. **ta'ttooing** *n* tatouage *m.* **ta'ttooist** *n* tatoueur *m.*

tatty ['tæti] *a* **(-ier, -iest)** *F:* défraîchi; miteux.

taught [tɔːt] *see* **teach.**

taunt [tɔːnt] **1.** *n* raillerie *f*; sarcasme *m* **2.** *vtr* (*a*) railler; accabler (qn) de sarcasmes (*b*) **to t. s.o. with sth,** reprocher qch à qn (avec mépris). **'taunting 1.** *a* railleur **2.** *n* railleries *fpl.*

Taurus ['tɔːrəs] *Prn Astr:* le Taureau.

taut [tɔːt] *a* tendu, raide, raidi. **'tauten** *vtr* raidir (un câble). **'tautness** *n* raideur *f.*

tautology [tɔː'tɔlədʒi] *n* tautologie *f.* **tauto'logical** *a* tautologique.

tavern ['tævən] *n A:* taverne.

tawdry ['tɔːdri] *a* **(-ier, -iest)** d'un mauvais goût criard; (bijoux) de camelote; **t. existence,** misère dorée. **'tawdriness** *n* clinquant *m*; faux brillant.

tawny ['tɔːni] *a* **(-ier, -iest)** fauve; tirant sur le roux; *Orn:* **t. owl,** chouette *f* hulotte.

tax [tæks] **I.** *n* (*pl* **taxes**) **1.** impôt *m*, contribution *f*, taxe *f*; **income t.,** impôt sur le revenu; **t. collector,** percepteur *m*; **t. year,** année fiscale; **value added t.,** taxe à la valeur ajoutée; **t. avoidance,** évasion fiscale; **t. evasion,** fraude fiscale; **t. free,** exempt d'impôts; **I paid £500 in t.,** j'ai payé £500 d'impôts, de contributions **2.** charge *f*; fardeau *m*; **to be a t. on s.o.,** être une charge pour qn. **II.** *vtr* **1.** (*a*) taxer, imposer (les objets de luxe); frapper (qch) d'un impôt (*b*) imposer (qn) (*c*) mettre à l'épreuve; **to t. s.o.'s patience to the limit,** mettre à bout la patience de qn **2. to t. s.o. with doing sth,** accuser qn d'avoir fait qch. **'taxable** *a* imposable. **tax'ation** *n* (*a*) imposition *f* (de la propriété); taxation *f*; **the t. authorities,** l'administration fiscale; *F:* le fisc (*b*) charges fiscales (*c*) revenu réalisé par les impôts; les impôts *m*. **'tax-de'ductible** *a* sujet à dégrèvements (d'impôts). **'taxing** *a* éprouvant. **'taxman** *nm* (*pl* **-men**) *F:* percepteur. **'taxpayer** *n* contribuable *mf*.

taxi ['tæksi] **1.** *n* (*pl* **taxis**) taxi *m*; **t. driver,** chauffeur *m* de taxi; **t. rank,** station de taxis **2.** *vi* (**taxied, taxying**) (*of aircraft*) rouler au sol. **'taxicab** *n* taxi *m*. **'taximeter** *n* taximètre *m*.

taxidermy ['tæksidə:mi] *n* taxidermie *f*. **'taxidermist** *n* taxidermiste *m*; empailleur *m* (d'animaux).

TB *abbr tuberculosis,* tuberculose.

tea [ti:] *n* (*pl* **teas**) **1.** thé *m*; **t. plant,** arbre à thé; **t. rose,** rose thé *f* **2.** (*a*) thé; **China t.,** thé de Chine; **t. caddy,** boîte à thé; **t. chest,** caisse à thé (*b*) (**afternoon**) **t.,** thé; = goûter *m*; **high t.,** repas *m* du soir (arrosé de thé); **t. break,** pause-thé *f*; **to give a t. party,** (i) donner un thé (ii) organiser un goûter d'enfants; **t. service, set,** *F:* **t. things,** service à thé; **t. towel,** torchon *m* (à vaisselle) **3.** infusion *f*, tisane *f*; **mint t.,** thé à la menthe. **'teabag** *n* sachet *m* de thé. **'teacake** *n Cu:* (genre de) brioche plate. **'teacloth** *n* **1.** nappe *f*; napperon *m* **2.** torchon *m*. **'teacup** *n* tasse *f* à thé. **'tealeaf** *n* (*pl* **-leaves**) feuille *f* de thé. **'teapot** *n* théière *f*. **'tearoom, 'teashop** *n* salon *m* de thé. **'teaspoon** *n* cuiller *f* à thé. **'teaspoonful** *n* cuiller(ée) *f* à thé. **'teatime** *n* l'heure *f* du thé.

teach [ti:tʃ] *vtr* (**taught** [tɔ:t]) enseigner, instruire (qn); enseigner (qch); **to t. s.o. sth,** enseigner, apprendre, qch à qn; **she teaches the young pupils,** elle fait la classe aux petits; **he teaches French,** il enseigne le français; il est professeur de français; *vi* **she teaches,** *NAm:* **she teaches school,** elle est dans l'enseignement; **to t. s.o. (how) to do sth,** apprendre à qn à faire qch; **to t. oneself sth,** apprendre qch tout seul; **that will t. him!** ça lui apprendra! **to t. s.o. a thing or two,** dégourdir qn. **'teachable** *a* (sujet) enseignable. **'teacher** *n* (i) instituteur, -trice; maître, maîtresse, d'école (ii) professeur *m* (iii) enseignant, -ante; **to become a t.,** entrer dans l'enseignement; **history t.,** professeur d'histoire. **'teach-in** *n* colloque *m*; séance *f* d'études. **'teaching** *n* **1.** enseignement *m*, instruction *f*; **the t. profession,** (i) le corps enseignant (ii) l'enseignement **2.** enseignement; leçons *fpl* **3.** (*a*) doctrine *f* (*b*) **teachings,** préceptes *mpl*.

teak [ti:k] *n* teck *m*.

team [ti:m] **1.** *n* (*a*) attelage *m* (de chevaux) (*b*) équipe *f*; **football t.,** équipe de football; **t. member,** équipier *m*; **t. mate,** coéquipier *m*; **t. games,** jeux d'équipe; **t. spirit,** esprit d'équipe **2.** *vi* s'associer; entrer en collaboration; **t. up with s.o.,** se joindre à qn (pour faire qch). **'teamster** *n NAm:* camionneur *m*, routier *m*. **'teamwork** *n* travail *m* d'équipe.

tear¹ [tiər] *n* larme *f*; **to burst into tears,** fondre en larmes; **to shed tears of joy,** verser des larmes de joie; **to bring tears to s.o.'s eyes,** faire venir les larmes aux

yeux de qn; **t. gas,** gaz lacrymogène. **'teardrop** *n* larme *f*. **'tearful** *a* tout en pleurs; **in a t. voice,** (i) avec des larmes dans la voix (ii) *Pej:* en pleurnichant. **'tearfully** *adv* en pleurant; les larmes aux yeux. **'tearjerker** *n F:* film larmoyant. **'tearstained** *a* (visage) ruisselant de larmes.

tear² [tɛər] **1.** *n* déchirure *f*, accroc *m* **2.** *v* (tore; torn) (*a*) *vtr* déchirer; **to t. sth to pieces,** déchirer qch en morceaux; **to t. sth in half,** déchirer qch en deux; **to t. a hole in sth,** faire un trou dans, un accroc à, qch; **this material tears easily,** ce tissu se déchire facilement; **to t. a muscle,** se déchirer un muscle; *F:* **that's torn it,** il ne manquait plus que ça; **torn between two choices,** tiraillé entre deux choix; **to t. sth down, away, off, out,** arracher qch (de qch); **to t. one's hair,** s'arracher les cheveux (*b*) *vi* **to t. at sth,** déchirer, arracher, qch avec des doigts impatients; **to t. along,** aller à toute vitesse, à fond de train; **he was tearing along (the road),** il dévorait la route. **'tear a'way** *vtr* arracher (qch); **to t. s.o. a. from his work,** arracher qn à son travail; **I could not t. myself a.,** je ne pouvais me décider à partir. **'tearing** *n* déchirement *m*; **t. away, off, out,** arrachement *m*; *F:* **to be in a t. hurry,** être terriblement pressé. **'tear 'off** *vtr* arracher (qch); *F:* **to t. s.o. off a strip,** passer un savon à qn. **'tear 'up** *vtr* **1.** déchirer (une lettre) **2. to t. up a tree by the roots,** déraciner un arbre.

tease [ti:z] **1.** *n* taquin, -ine **2.** *vtr* taquiner, tourmenter (qn). **'teaser** *n F:* problème *m* difficile; colle *f*. **'teasing 1.** *a* taquin, railleur **2.** *n* taquinerie *f*.

teasel ['ti:zl] *n Bot:* cardère *f*.

teat [ti:t] *n* (*a*) mamelon *m*; bout *m* de sein (*b*) tétine *f* (de biberon).

technique [tek'ni:k] *n* technique *f*. **'technical** *a* technique; **t. hitch,** incident technique; **t. offence,** quasi-délit *m*. **techni'cality** *n* détail *m* technique. **'technically** *adv* techniquement. **tech'nician** *n* technicien, -ienne. **tech'nologist** *n* technologue *mf*, technologiste *mf*. **techno'logical** *a* technologique. **tech'nology** *n* technologie *f*.

teddy ['tedi] *n* **t. (bear),** ours *m* en peluche, nounours *m*.

tedious ['ti:diəs] *a* fatigant; ennuyeux; pénible. **'tediously** *adv* d'une manière ennuyeuse. **'tediousness, 'tedium** *n* ennui *m*.

tee [ti:] *n Golf:* tee *m*.

teem [ti:m] *vi* **to t. with,** foisonner (de gibier), fourmiller d'(insectes); abonder en (poisson); grouiller (de monde); **the rain was teeming down,** il pleuvait à verse. **'teeming** *a* grouillant; **teeming rain,** pluie torrentielle.

teens [ti:nz] *npl* l'âge *m* de 13 à 19 ans; **to be in one's t.,** être adolescent(e). **'teenage** *a* adolescent; de jeune. **'teenager** *n* adolescent, -ente.

teeny(-weeny) ['ti:ni('wi:ni)] *a F:* minuscule.

teeshirt ['ti:ʃə:t] *n* tee-shirt *m*.

teeter ['ti:tər] *vi* chanceler; **to t. on the brink of,** être à deux doigts de.

teeth [ti:θ] *see* **tooth. teethe** [ti:ð] *vi* faire ses (premières) dents. **'teething** *n* dentition *f*; **t. ring,** anneau de dentition; *Fig:* **t. troubles,** difficultés initiales.

teetotal [ti:'toutl] *a* antialcoolique; qui ne boit pas d'alcool. **tee'totalism** *n* abstention *f* de boissons

alcoolisées. **tee'totaller**, *NAm:* **tee'totaler** *n*
abstinent, -ente; personne qui ne boit pas d'alcool.
telecommunication [telikəmju:ni'keiʃ(ə)n] *n* télécommunications *fpl.*
telegram ['teligræm] *n* télégramme *m*, dépêche *f*;
radio t., radiotélégramme *m.*
telegraph ['teligrɑːf] **1.** *n* télégraphe *m*; **t. pole,**
poteau télégraphique **2.** *vtr & i* télégraphier
tele'graphic *a* télégraphique. **te'legraphist** *n*
télégraphiste *mf.* **te'legraphy** *n* télégraphie *f.*
telepathy [te'lepəθi] *n* (*no pl*) télépathie *f.*
tele'pathic *a* télépathique; (personne) télépathe.
telephone ['telifoun] **1.** *n* téléphone *m*; **t. subscriber,**
abonné du téléphone; **public t.** = taxiphone *m*; **t. box,**
cabine téléphonique; **are you on the t.?** avez-vous le
téléphone? **you're wanted on the t.,** on vous demande
au téléphone; **t. number,** numéro de téléphone; **t.
directory, book,** annuaire *m* (du téléphone); **t. operator,** téléphoniste *mf*; standardiste *mf*; **t. call,** appel
téléphonique **2.** (*a*) *vi* téléphoner; **to t. for a taxi,**
appeler un taxi (par téléphone) (*b*) *vtr* téléphoner (un
message); téléphoner à (qn). **tele'phonic** *a* téléphonique. **te'lephonist** *n* téléphoniste *mf.*
te'lephony *n* téléphonie *f.*
telephoto [teli'foutou] *n* **t. lens,** téléobjectif *m.*
teleprinter ['teliprintər] *n* téléimprimeur *m*, téléscripteur *m*; **t. operator,** télétypiste *mf.*
telescope ['teliskoup] **1.** *n* (*a*) (**refracting**) **t.,** lunette *f*
(d'approche), longue-vue *f* (*b*) (**reflecting**) **t.,** télescope *m* (à miroir, à réflexion) **2.** *vtr & i* (se) télescoper;
parts made to t., pièces qui s'emboîtent.
tele'scopic *a* (*a*) télescopique; **t. lens,** téléobjectif
m (*b*) (parapluie) pliant.
teletype ['telitaip] *n* télétype *m*, téléscripteur *m.*
televiewer ['telivjuər] *n* téléspectateur, -trice.
television ['teliviʒ(ə)n] *n* télévision *f*; **colour t.,** télévision (en) couleur; **on (the) t.,** à la télévision; **t. (set),**
téléviseur *m*, (poste *m* de) télévision; **t. programme,**
émission de télévision; **t. news,** journal télévisé.
'televise *vtr* téléviser.
telex ['teleks] **1.** *n Rtm:* télex *m* **2.** *vtr* télexer (un
message).
tell [tel] *v* (**told** [tould]) **I.** *vtr* **1.** (*a*) dire; **to t. the truth,**
(i) dire la vérité (ii) à vrai dire (*b*) **to t. s.o. sth,** dire,
apprendre, qch à qn; faire savoir qch à qn; **can you t.
me the way to the station?** pouvez-vous m'indiquer le
chemin de la gare? **I can't t. you how pleased I am,**
je ne saurais vous dire combien je suis content; **I
have been told that,** on m'a dit que; **I don't want to
have to t. you that again,** tenez-vous cela pour dit;
I told you so! je vous l'avais bien dit! (*c*) **you're telling
me!** à qui le dites-vous? **t. me another!** à d'autres! (*c*)
raconter (une histoire); **I'll t. you what happened,** je
vais vous raconter ce qui est arrivé; **t. me something
about yourself,** parlez-moi un peu de vous(-même) (*d*)
F: **to hear t. that,** entendre dire que (*e*) annoncer,
proclamer (un fait); révéler (un secret); *F:* **that would
be telling!** ça c'est mon secret! (*f*) (*of clock*) **to t. the
time,** marquer l'heure **2.** (*a*) **to t. s.o. about s.o., sth,**
parler de qn, de qch, à qn; **t. me what you know
about it,** dites-moi ce que vous en savez (*b*) **it's not so
easy, let me t. you,** ce n'est pas si facile, je vous assure;
he'll be furious, I (can) t. you! il va être furieux, je peux
vous l'assurer! (*c*) **to t. s.o. to do sth,** ordonner, dire, à

qn de faire qch; **do as you're told,** faites ce qu'on
vous dit; **he'll do as he's told,** il marchera; **I told him
not to,** je lui ai défendu de (*d*) **to t. right from
wrong,** discerner le bien du mal; **you can't t. her
from her sister,** on ne peut pas la distinguer de sa
sœur; elle ressemble à sa sœur à s'y tromper; **one can
t. him by his voice,** on le reconnaît à sa voix; **he can't
t. the time,** il ne sait pas lire l'heure (*e*) **one can t.
she's intelligent,** on sent qu'elle est intelligente; **I
can t. it from the look in your eyes,** je le lis dans
vos yeux **3. all told,** tout compris; somme toute;
toutes dépenses confondues; **I made £100 out of it all
told,** tout compte fait j'en ai retiré £100. **II.** *vi* (*a*)
produire son effet; porter (coup); **these drugs t. on one,**
l'effet de ces drogues se fait sentir (*b*) **time will t.,** qui
vivra verra; **who can t.?** qui sait? **you never can t.,** on ne
sait jamais; **more than words can t.,** plus qu'on ne
saurait dire (*c*) **it will t. against you,** cela vous nuira (*d*)
to t. of sth, annoncer, accuser, révéler, qch (*e*) *P:* **to t.
on s.o.,** rapporter sur le compte de qn. **'teller** *n* (*a*)
caissier, -ière (*b*) *Pol:* scrutateur *m*; recenseur *m.*
'telling 1. *a* efficace; **t. blow,** coup qui porte **2.** *n* (*a*)
récit *m*; narration *f* (d'une histoire) (*b*) divulgation
f, révélation *f* (d'un secret) (*c*) *F:* **t. off,** engueulade *f*. **'tell 'off** *vtr F:* engueuler (qn). **'telltale**
n (*a*) (*of pers*) rapporteur, -euse (*b*) **t. sign,** signe
révélateur.
telly ['teli] *n* (*pl* **tellies**) *F:* télé *f.*
temerity [ti'meriti] *n* témérité *f*, audace *f.*
temp [temp] *n F:* (secrétaire *mf*, dactylo *mf*) intérimaire (*mf*); *F:* intérim *mf.*
temper ['tempər] **I.** *n* **1.** (*of steel*) trempe *f* **2.** (*of pers*)
sangfroid *m*, calme *m*; **to lose one's t.,** se mettre en
colère; s'emporter; **to keep one's t.,** rester calme **3.** (*a*)
humeur *f*, caractère *m*, tempérament *m*; **to have a bad
t.,** avoir mauvais caractère; **fiery, even, t.,** caractère
fougueux, égal (*b*) état *m* d'esprit; **in a vile t.,** d'une
humeur massacrante; **to be in a good, a bad, t.,** être de
bonne, de mauvaise, humeur (*c*) colère *f*; mauvaise
humeur; **fit of t.,** accès de colère; **to be in a t.,** être en
colère; **to get into a t.,** se fâcher; **to put s.o. in a t.,**
mettre qn en colère. **II.** *vtr* **1.** (*a*) donner la trempe à
(l'acier) (ii) adoucir (un métal) **2.** tempérer; modérer
(son ardeur); maîtriser (son chagrin).
'temperament *n* tempérament *m*, humeur *f.*
tempera'mental *a* (*a*) capricieux, fantasque (*b*)
qui s'emballe ou se déprime facilement.
temperance ['temp(ə)rəns] *n* (*a*) tempérance *f*; modération *f* (*b*) tempérance, sobriété *f* (*c*) abstention *f*
des boissons alcoolisées. **'temperate** *a* **1.** (*of pers*)
tempérant, sobre; (*of language*) modéré, mesuré **2.** (*of
climate*) tempéré.
temperature ['tempritʃər] *n* température *f*; **room t.,**
température ambiante; *Med:* **to take s.o.'s t.,** prendre
la température de qn; **to have a t.,** avoir de la fièvre.
tempest ['tempist] *n* tempête *f*. **tem'pestuous** *a*
(*a*) tempétueux (*b*) (*of meeting*) orageux; (*of pers*)
agité, violent.
template ['templit] *n Metalw: Carp:* gabarit *m*,
patron *m.*
temple¹ ['templ] *n* temple *m.*
temple² *n Anat:* tempe *f*. **'temporal¹** *a* (os) temporal.
tempo ['tempou] *n* (*pl* **tempi**) (*a*) *Mus:* tempo *m* (*b*) to

upset the t. of production, perturber la cadence de production.

temporal² ['tempərəl] a temporel.

temporary ['temp(ə)rəri] a (a) provisoire; **on a t. basis**, par intérim; provisoirement; **t. appointment**, emploi temporaire; **t. secretary**, secrétaire intérimaire (b) momentané; **the improvement is only t.**, l'amélioration n'est que passagère. **'temporarily** adv (a) temporairement, provisoirement; par intérim (b) momentanément; pour le moment. **'temporize** vi temporiser; chercher à gagner du temps.

tempt [tem(p)t] vtr 1. tenter; **to t. s.o. to do sth**, induire qn à faire qch; **to let oneself be tempted**, se laisser tenter; céder à la tentation; **I was greatly tempted**, l'occasion était bien tentante; **I am tempted to accept**, j'ai bien envie d'accepter 2. **to t. providence, fate**, tenter la providence, le sort. **temp'tation** n tentation f; **to yield to t.**, céder à la tentation; se laisser tenter. **'tempter** n tentateur. **'tempting** a tentant, alléchant; (of offer) séduisant, attrayant; (of food) appétissant. **'temptingly** adv d'une manière tentante. **'temptress** nf tentatrice.

ten [ten] num a & n dix (m); **about t. years ago**, il y a une dizaine d'années; **t. to one he finds out**, je vous parie qu'il le découvrira; Com: **the top t.** = palmarès m (de la chanson). **tenth 1.** num a & n dixième (mf) **2.** n (fractional) dixième m. **'tenthly** adv dixièmement.

tenable ['tenəbl] a soutenable.

tenacious [tə'neiʃəs] a tenace. **te'naciously** adv obstinément; avec ténacité. **te'nacity** n ténacité f.

tenant ['tenənt] n locataire mf; **sitting t.**, occupant(e). **'tenancy** n location f; **during my t.**, pendant que j'étais locataire.

tench [tenʃ] n Ich: tanche f.

tend¹ [tend] vtr soigner (un malade); surveiller (des enfants, une machine); garder (des moutons); entretenir (un jardin); soigner (le feu). **'tender¹** n 1. Nau: ravitailleur m; Rail: tender m 2. **bar t.**, barman m.

tend² vi 1. tendre, se diriger, aller (**towards**, vers); **that tends to annoy him**, cela tend à le fâcher; **blue tending to green**, bleu tirant sur le vert 2. **to t. to do sth**, être porté, enclin, à faire qch; être susceptible de faire qch; **he tends to forget**, il est porté à oublier; **to t. to shrink**, avoir tendance à rétrécir. **'tendency** n tendance f; inclination f; disposition f (**to**, à); penchant m (à qch); **to have a t. to do sth**, avoir tendance à faire qch.

tender² ['tendər] a 1. (viande) tendre 2. (cœur) tendre, sensible; (of conscience) délicat; **t. to the touch**, sensible, douloureux, au toucher 3. (a) (of plant) délicat, fragile; peu résistant (au froid) (b) jeune, tendre; **t. youth**, la tendre, verte, jeunesse; **of t. years**, (enfant) en bas âge 4. (of pers) tendre, affectueux. **tender'hearted** a compatissant; au cœur tendre, sensible. **'tenderloin** n Cu: filet m de bœuf. **'tenderly** adv 1. (toucher qch) doucement, délicatement 2. tendrement; avec tendresse. **'tenderness** n 1. sensibilité f (de la peau) 2. délicatesse f, fragilité f (d'une plante) 3. tendresse f (des sentiments); affection f (**for**, pour) 4. tendreté f (de la viande). **'tenderize** vtr attendrir (la viande).

tender³ 1. n (a) Com: soumission f, offre f; **to invite tenders**, faire, lancer, un appel d'offres (b) **legal t.**, cours légal; (of money) **to be legal t.**, avoir cours 2. v

(a) vtr offrir (ses services); **to t. one's resignation**, offrir de démissionner; **to t. one's apologies**, présenter ses excuses (b) vi Com: **to t. for**, faire une soumission pour (qch); soumissionner (qch).

tendon ['tendən] n Anat: tendon m.

tendril ['tendril] n Bot: vrille f.

tenement ['tenimənt] n t. (**house**), immeuble m.

tenet ['tenət] n (a) dogme m (b) croyance f; opinion f.

tenner ['tenər] n F: billet m de dix livres.

tennis ['tenis] n (no pl) (a) tennis m; **to play t.**, jouer au tennis; **t. ball**, balle de tennis; **t. court**, court (de tennis); **t. shoes**, tennis mpl; **t. player**, joueur, -euse, de tennis; Med: **t. elbow**, synovite f du coude (b) **table t.**, tennis de table; ping-pong m.

tenor ['tenər] n 1. contenu m, sens général (d'un document); cours m, marche f; progrès m (des affaires, de la vie) 2. Mus: ténor m; **t. voice**, voix de ténor; **t. sax(ophone)**, saxo(phone) m ténor.

tense¹ [tens] n Gram: temps m; **in the future t.**, au temps futur.

tense² a 1. (cord) tendu, raide 2. (of nerves, situation) tendu; **t. moment**, moment angoissant; **t. silence**, silence impressionnant; **t. voice**, voix étranglée (par l'émotion); **he's t.**, il est contracté. **'tensely** adv 1. raidement 2. les nerfs tendus; d'une voix tendue; avec anxiété. **'tenseness** n rigidité f; tension f (des muscles, des relations). **tension** ['tenʃ(ə)n] n (a) tension f; **muscular t.**, tension musculaire (b) tension (nerveuse) (c) pression f (d'un gaz) (d) El: tension, voltage m (e) tension (d'un ressort).

tent [tent] n tente f; **t. peg**, piquet de tente; **to pitch a t.**, monter une tente; Med: **oxygen t.**, tente à oxygène.

tentacle ['tentəkl] n Z: tentacule m.

tentative ['tentətiv] a (a) expérimental, d'essai; **t. offer**, offre préliminaire (b) hésitant, indécis. **'tentatively** adv à titre d'essai; provisoirement; avec hésitation.

tenterhooks ['tentəhuks] npl **to be on t.**, être au supplice, sur des charbons ardents; **to keep s.o. on t.**, faire languir qn.

tenuous ['tenjuəs] a ténu.

tenure ['tenjər] n Jur: (période de) jouissance f; (période d')occupation f.

tepee ['ti:pi(:)] n tente f (des Amérindiens).

tepid ['tepid] a tiède. **'tepidly** adv tièdement; sans enthousiasme.

term [tə:m] I. n 1. A: & Lit: terme m, fin f, limite f 2. (a) terme, période f, durée f; **t. of imprisonment**, peine f de prison; **during his t. of office**, lorsqu'il exerçait ses fonctions; **long-t., short-t., transaction**, opération à long, à court, terme; **in the long t.**, à la longue; **in the short t.**, dans l'immédiat (b) Sch: trimestre m (c) Jur: session f 3. pl (a) Com: etc: **terms**, conditions f; clauses f, termes (d'un contrat); **name your own terms**, précisez vos conditions; **under the terms of the clause**, sous le bénéfice de la clause; **to dictate terms**, imposer des conditions; **to come to terms**, arriver à un accord, parvenir à une entente; **to come to terms with death**, accepter la mort; **terms of reference**, attributions fpl (d'une commission) (b) **terms of payment**, conditions de paiement; **terms strictly cash**, payable au comptant; **on easy terms**, avec facilités de paiement; **not on any terms**, à aucun prix 4. pl relations f, rapports m; **to be on friendly, on**

good, terms with s.o., vivre en bons termes avec qn; **to be on bad terms with s.o.**, être en mauvais termes avec qn; **we are on the best of terms**, nous sommes au mieux ensemble 5. (a) *Mth:* terme; **to express one quantity in terms of another**, expliquer une quantité en fonction d'une autre; **in terms of financial risk**, en ce qui concerne les risques financiers (b) **terms of a problem**, énoncé *m* d'un problème 6. (a) terme, expression *f*; **legal, medical, t.**, terme de droit, de médecine (b) **to speak in disparaging terms of s.o.**, tenir des propos désobligeants envers qn; **I told him in no uncertain terms**, je le lui ai dit sans mâcher mes mots. II. *vtr* appeler, désigner. **terminal** ['tə:minl] **1.** *a* terminal; *Med:* (maladie) en phase terminale; **t. case**, malade condamné **2.** *n* (a) *Rail:* terminus *m*; *Av:* **air t.**, aérogare *f* (b) *El:* borne *f* (de prise de courant). **'terminally** *adv* **to be t. ill**, être en phase terminale; **the t. ill**, les malades incurables. **'terminate** *v* **1.** *vtr* terminer; mettre fin à (un engagement); résoudre, résilier (un contrat); être à la fin de (qch) **2.** *vi* se terminer, finir (in, en, par); aboutir (in, at, à). **termi'nation** *n* (a) terminaison *f*, fin *f* (d'un procès); cessation *f* (de relations) (b) **t. of pregnancy**, interruption *f* de grossesse. **'terminus** *n* (*pl* -mini) terminus *m*.

terminology [tə:mi'nɔlədʒi] *n* terminologie *f*. **termino'logical** *a* terminologique.

termite ['tə:mait] *n Ent:* termite *m*; fourmi blanche.

tern [tə:n] *n Orn:* sterne *m*; hirondelle *f* de mer.

terrace ['terəs] **1.** *n* (a) terrasse *f* (b) *Fb:* **the terraces**, les gradins *mpl* (c) **t. (of houses)**, rangée *f* de maisons (attenantes) **2.** *vtr* disposer (un jardin) en terrasses. **'terraced** *a* **1.** (jardin) en terrasse **2. t. houses**, rangée de maisons (attenantes).

terracotta [terə'kɔtə] *n* terre cuite.

terrain [tə'rein] *n* terrain *m*.

terrapin ['terəpin] *n* tortue *f* d'eau douce.

terrestrial [te'restriəl] *a* terrestre.

terrible ['teribl] *a* terrible, affreux, épouvantable; atroce; **I'm t. at maths**, je suis nul en math. **'terribly** *adv* terriblement, affreusement, atrocement; **t. rich**, extrêmement riche; **t. expensive**, hors de prix; **that's t. kind of you**, vous êtes vraiment trop aimable.

terrier ['teriər] *n* (chien *m*) terrier (*m*).

terrific [tə'rifik] *a* (a) terrifiant, épouvantable (b) *F:* terrible; énorme; **t. speed**, allure vertigineuse; **t.!** formidable! **te'rrifically** *adv* (a) d'une manière terrifiante (b) *F:* terriblement; formidablement (bien). **'terrify** *vtr* terrifier, effrayer, terroriser, épouvanter; **to t. s.o. out of his wits**, rendre qn fou de terreur; **to be terrified of s.o.**, avoir une peur bleue de qn. **'terrifying** *a* terrifiant, terrible, épouvantable. **'terrifyingly** *adv* épouvantablement; d'une manière terrifiante.

territory ['terit(ə)ri] *n* (*pl* **territories**) territoire *m*. **terri'torial** *a* territorial; **the T. Army**, *n* the Territorials, l'armée territoriale.

terror ['terər] *n* **1.** terreur *f*, effroi *m*, épouvante *f*; **to be in (a state of) t.**, être dans la terreur; **to go in t. of s.o.**, avoir une peur bleue de qn; **to be in t. of one's life**, craindre pour sa vie **2. to be the t. of the village**, être la terreur du village; *F:* **he's a little t.**, c'est un enfant terrible. **'terrorism** *n* terrorisme *m*. **'terrorist** *n* terroriste *mf*. **'terrorize** *vtr* terroriser.

'terrorstricken, 'terrorstruck *a* saisi de terreur; épouvanté.

terry ['teri] *n* **t. (towelling)**, tissu *m* éponge; **t. towel**, serviette éponge.

terse [tə:s] *a* **1.** (style) concis, net **2.** (réponse) brusque. **'tersely** *adv* **1.** avec concision **2.** brusquement. **'terseness** *n* **1.** concision *f*; netteté *f* (de style) **2.** brusquerie *f* (d'une réponse).

terylene ['terili:n] *n Rtm:* térylène *m*.

test [test] I. *n* **1.** (a) épreuve *f*; **to put s.o., sth, to the t.**, mettre qn, qch, à l'épreuve, à l'essai; **to be equal to, to stand, the t.**, supporter l'épreuve; **to undergo a t.**, subir une épreuve; **the acid t.**, l'épreuve concluante (b) essai *m*, épreuve; **endurance t.**, épreuve d'endurance; **t. bench**, banc d'essai; **field t.**, essai sur le terrain; *Aut:* **t. drive**, course d'essai; *Av:* **t. pilot**, pilote d'essai (c) *Ch: Ph:* test *m*; **t. paper**, papier réactif; **t. tube**, éprouvette *f*; **t.-tube baby**, bébé-éprouvette *m* (d) *Med:* **blood t.**, analyse *f* de sang; *F:* prise *f* de sang; **Wassermann t.**, réaction *f* de Wassermann (e) *Jur:* **t. case**, précédent *m* (*f*) *TV:* **t. card**, mire *f* **2.** (a) examen *m*; *Aut:* **driving t.**, (examen du) permis de conduire (b) *Sch:* **t. (paper)** = composition *f*; **oral t.**, épreuve orale; oral *m*; *Cin:* **screen t.**, bout *m* d'essai (c) *Cr:* **t. (match)**, match international. II. *vtr & i* (a) éprouver; mettre (qn, qch) à l'épreuve, à l'essai (b) essayer (une machine); contrôler, vérifier (des poids et mesures); examiner (la vue de qn); expérimenter (un procédé) (c) *Sch:* **to t. s.o. in algebra**, examiner qn en algèbre (d) faire des analyses (de sang); *Ch:* analyser (l'eau); *Psy:* tester (un animal, qn); *Ch:* **to t. for alcaloids**, faire la réaction des alkaloïdes; **to t. for sugar**, faire une recherche de sucre; **to t. for gas**, faire des essais pour découvrir une fuite de gaz (e) (*into microphone*) **testing, testing**, un, deux, trois. **'testing** *a* **t. time**, période éprouvante; **t. ground**, terrain d'essai.

testament ['testəmənt] *n* **1.** testament *m*; dernières volontés **2.** *Rel:* **Old T., New T.**, Ancien, Nouveau, Testament. **testa'mentary** *a* testamentaire. **tes'tator, *f* tes'tatrix** *n* (*pl* -trices, -trixes) testateur, -trice.

testicle ['testikl] *n Anat:* testicule *m*.

testify ['testifai] *v Jur:* (a) *vtr* **to t. sth (on oath)**, déclarer, affirmer, qch (sous serment) (b) *vi* **to t. in s.o.'s favour, against s.o.**, témoigner en faveur de qn; déposer contre qn (c) *v ind tr* **to t. to sth**, témoigner de qch, attester, affirmer, qch. **testi'monial** *n* **1.** certificat *m*; (lettre *f* de) recommandation *f*; attestation *f* **2.** témoignage *m* d'estime (offert en reconnaissance de services). **'testimony** *n* témoignage *m*; *Jur:* attestation *f*; déposition *f* (d'un témoin); **to bear t. to sth**, rendre témoignage de qch.

testy ['testi] *a* (-ier, -iest) irritable. **'testily** *adv* d'un air irrité.

tetanus ['tetənəs] *n Med:* tétanos *m*; **t. injection**, injection antitétanique.

tetchy ['tetʃi] *a* (-ier, -iest) irritable. **'tetchily** *adv* d'un air irrité.

tête-à-tête ['teita:'teit] *n* (*pl* tête-à-têtes) tête-à-tête *m inv*.

tether ['teðər] **1.** *n* longe *f*, attache *f* (d'un cheval); **to be at the end of one's t.**, être à bout de forces, de nerfs **2.** *vtr* attacher (un animal).

text [tekst] *n* **1.** texte *m* (d'un manuscrit) **2.** citation tirée de l'Écriture sainte. '**textbook** n Sch: manuel m; t. **example**, exemple classique. '**textual** a t. **error**, erreur dans le texte.

textile ['tekstail] 1. a textile 2. n (i) tissu m (ii) textile m; **the t. industries**, l'industrie textile; le textile.

texture ['tekstʃər] n texture f; grain m (du bois); contexture f (d'un tissu, des muscles).

TGWU abbr Transport and General Workers Union.

Thailand ['tailænd] Prn Geog: Thaïlande f.

thalidomide [θə'lidəmaid] n Pharm: Rtm: thalidomide f; **t. baby**, victime de la thalidomide.

Thames [temz] Prn Geog: **the T.**, la Tamise; **he'll never set the T. on fire**, il n'a pas inventé le fil à couper le beurre, il n'a pas inventé la poudre.

than [ðæn, unstressed ðən] conj (a) que; (with numbers) de; **I have more, less, t. you**, j'en ai plus, moins, que vous; **more t. twenty**, plus de vingt; **more t. once**, plus d'une fois; **better t. anyone**, mieux que personne; **I'd rather phone him t. write**, j'aimerais mieux lui téléphoner que lui écrire; **she would do anything rather t. let him suffer**, elle ferait n'importe quoi plutôt que de le laisser souffrir; **no sooner had we arrived t. the music began**, à peine étions-nous arrivés que la musique a commencé (b) **any person other t. himself**, tout autre que lui.

thank [θæŋk] 1. npl thanks, remerciement(s) m; **give him my thanks**, remerciez-le de ma part; **many thanks!** F: thanks very much, thanks awfully! merci beaucoup! **thanks!** merci! F: **thanks for coming**, merci d'être venu; **to give thanks to s.o.**, remercier qn; **to give thanks to God**, rendre grâce à Dieu; **to propose a vote of thanks to s.o.**, voter des remerciements à qn; **thanks to you**, grâce à vous; F: **that's all the thanks I get!** voilà comme, comment, on me remercie! 2. vtr (a) remercier (qn); dire merci à (qn); **to t. s.o. for sth**, remercier qn de qch; **t. God!** t. **goodness!** Dieu merci! **t. you**, je vous remercie; merci; **no t. you**, (non) merci! **t. you very much**, merci beaucoup, bien; **t. you for coming**, merci d'être venu; **t. you note**, mot de remerciement (b) O: **I'll t. you to mind your own business!** occupez-vous donc de ce qui vous regarde! (c) **to have s.o. to t. for sth**, devoir qch à qn; **you've only yourself to t.**, c'est à vous seul qu'il faut vous en prendre. '**thankful** a reconnaissant; **to be t. that**, s'estimer heureux que, être bien content que; **that's something to be t. for**, il y a de quoi nous féliciter. '**thankfully** adv avec reconnaissance, avec gratitude. '**thankfulness** n reconnaissance f, gratitude f. '**thankless** a ingrat. **thanks'giving** n action f de grâce(s); **T. Day**, fête célébrée (i) US: le 4e jeudi de novembre (ii) Can: le 2e lundi d'octobre.

that [ðæt] I. dem pron, pl those [ðouz] 1. cela; F: ça (a) **give me t.**, donnez-moi cela, ça; **what's t.?** qu'est-ce que c'est que ça? **who's t.?** qui est-ce? **that's Mr Martin**, c'est M. Martin; **is t. you, Anne?** c'est toi, Anne? **that's my opinion**, voilà mon avis; **those are my things**, ce sont mes affaires; **is t. all?** c'est tout? **that's where he lives**, c'est là qu'il habite; **after t.**, après cela; **t. was two years ago**, il y a deux ans de cela; **with t. she took out her handkerchief**, là-dessus elle a sorti son mouchoir; **what do you mean by t.?** qu'entendez-vous par là? **they all think t.**, c'est ce qu'ils pensent tous; **t. is** (**to say**), c'est-à-dire (b) (stressed) **so that's settled**, alors, c'est décidé; **it needs a good actor and an expert**

one at t., cela demande un bon acteur et de plus, un acteur expérimenté; **that's right! that's it!** c'est cela! ça y est! **that's all**, voilà tout; **that's odd!** voilà qui est curieux! **and that's t.!** et voilà! **and t. was t.**, plus rien à dire; **that's enough of t.!** en voilà assez! 2. (opposed to this, these) celui-là, f celle-là; pl ceux-là, f celles-là; **this is new and t. is old**, celui-ci est neuf et celui-là est vieux 3. celui, f celle; pl ceux, f celles; **what's t. you're holding?** qu'est-ce que vous avez dans la main? **all those I saw**, tous ceux que j'ai vus; **I'm not one of those who**, je ne suis pas de ceux qui; **there are those who maintain it**, certains l'affirment. II. dem a, pl those (a) ce, (before vowel or h mute) cet; f cette; pl ces; (for emphasis and in opposition to this, these) ce … -là; **t. book, those books**, ce livre(-là), ces livres(-là); **t. one**, celui-là, celle-là; **at t. time, in those days**, en ce temps-là; à cette époque; **everyone is agreed on t. point**, tout le monde est d'accord là-dessus; **t. fool of a gardener**, cet imbécile de jardinier (b) F: **well, how's t. leg of yours?** eh bien, et cette jambe? (c) **all those flowers that you have there**, toutes ces fleurs que vous avez là (d) **I don't have t. much confidence in him**, je n'ai pas assez confiance en lui (e) (that with pl noun; those with noun sg coll) **what about t., those, five pounds you owe me?** et ces cinq livres que vous me devez? III. dem adv 1. **t. high**, aussi haut que ça; **t. far**, aussi loin que ça; **cut off t. much**, coupez-en grand comme ça 2. tellement; si; **is he t. tall?** est-il si grand (que ça)? IV. rel pron sg & pl 1. (for subject) qui; (for object) que; **the house t. stands at the corner**, la maison qui se trouve au coin; **the letter t. I sent you**, la lettre que je vous ai envoyée; **miser t. he was, he wouldn't pay**, avare comme il était, il n'a pas voulu payer; **idiot t. I am!** idiot que je suis! 2. (governed by prep) lequel, f laquelle; pl lesquels, f lesquelles; **the envelope t. I put it in**, l'enveloppe dans laquelle je l'ai mis; **the man t. we're talking about**, l'homme dont nous parlons; **nobody has come t. I know of**, personne n'est venu que je ne sache 3. (after expression of time) où; que; **the night t. we went to the theatre**, le soir où nous sommes allés au théâtre; **during the years t. he had been in prison**, pendant les années qu'il avait été en prison. V. conj 1. (introducing subordinate clause; often omitted in rapid speech) que (a) **it was for her t. they fought**, c'est pour elle qu'ils se sont battus; **I'll see to it t. everything is ready**, je veillerai à ce que tout soit prêt; **he's so ill t. he can't work**, il est si malade qu'il est incapable de travailler (b) **I wish t. it had never happened**, j'aurai voulu que cela ne soit jamais arrivé; **I hope t. you'll come**, j'espère que vous viendrez (c) **so t.**, afin que, pour que + sub; **come nearer so t. I can see you**, approchez, que je vous voie; **I'm telling you so t. you'll know**, je vous préviens pour que vous soyez au courant 2. **t. he should behave like this!** dire qu'il se conduit comme cela!

thatch [θætʃ] 1. n chaume m (de toiture) 2. vtr couvrir (un toit) de, en, chaume; **thatched roof**, toit de chaume; **thatched cottage**, chaumière f. '**thatcher** n couvreur m en chaume.

thaw [θɔː] 1. n dégel m; fonte f des neiges 2. v (a) vtr dégeler; **to t.** (**out**), décongeler (la viande) (b) vi (of snow) fondre; (of frozen food) **to t.** (**out**), se décongeler; dégeler; impers **it's thawing**, il dègèle; (of pers) **to**

t. (out), se dégeler; se réchauffer. 'thawing n 1. dégel m (d'un cours d'eau); fonte f (des neiges) 2. décongélation f (d'aliments congelés).

the [ðiː; unstressed before consonant ðə; unstressed before vowel ði] I. def art 1. le, f la; (before vowel or h mute) l'; pl les (a) t. father and (t.) mother, le père et la mère; on t. other side, de l'autre côté; t. Alps, les Alpes; I spoke to t. postman, j'ai parlé au facteur; give it to t. woman, donnez-le à la femme; he has gone to t. fields, il est allé aux champs; t. voice of t. people, la voix du peuple; t. roof of t. house, le toit de la maison; t. arrival of t. guests, l'arrivée des invités; t. Martins, les Martin; George t. Sixth, Georges Six; she's t. most beautiful woman I know, c'est la plus belle femme que je connaisse; F: well, how's t. throat then? eh bien, et cette gorge? P: t. wife, ma femme (b) (with noun in apposition: omitted in Fr) Mr Long, t. manager of the firm, M. Long, directeur de la maison (c) he's not t. person to do that, ce n'est pas une personne à faire cela; t. impudence of it! quelle audace! he hasn't t. patience to wait, il n'a pas la patience d'attendre (d) t. beautiful, le beau; translated from t. Russian, traduit du russe; t. poor, les pauvres (e) F: to have t. measles, avoir la rougeole (f) (generalizing) who invented t. wheel? qui a inventé la roue? (g) to be paid by t. hour, être payé à l'heure; eight apples to t. kilo, huit pommes au kilo 2. (demonstrative force) ce, cet, f cette; pl ces; I was away at t. time, j'étais absent à cette époque; I shall see him in t. summer, je le verrai cet été; do leave t. child alone! mais laissez-la donc cette enfant! (in café) and what will t. ladies have? et ces dames, que prendront-elles? 3. (stressed) [ðiː] he's the surgeon here, c'est lui le grand chirurgien ici; Long's is the shop for furniture, la maison Long est la meilleure pour les meubles. II. adv (a) all t. more, all t. less, d'autant plus, d'autant moins; it will be all t. easier for you, cela vous sera d'autant plus facile (b) t. sooner t. better, le plus tôt sera le mieux; t. less said t. better, moins on en parlera mieux cela vaudra; t. more t. merrier, plus on est de fous plus on rit.

theatre, NAm: theater ['θiːətər] n 1. (a) théâtre m; salle f de spectacle(s); to go to the t., aller au théâtre; t. company, troupe de théâtre (b) the t., l'art m dramatique; le théâtre 2. (lecture) t., amphithéâtre m; Med: (operating) t., salle d'opération 3. t. of war, théâtre de la guerre. 'theatregoer, NAm: 'theater- n amateur m de théâtre; habitué(e) du théâtre. the'atrical a 1. théâtral; t. company, troupe d'acteurs 2. (of behaviour) théâtral, histrionique. the'atrically adv 1. théâtralement 2. de façon théâtrale. the'atricals npl amateur t., théâtre d'amateurs.

thee [ðiː] pers pron, objective case; A: & Poet: te; (before vowel sound) t'; (stressed) toi.

theft [θeft] n vol m; Jur: petty t., larcin m.

their [ðɛər] poss a 1. (a) leur, pl leurs; t. father and mother, leur père et leur mère; leurs père et mère; t. eyes are blue, ils ont les yeux bleus; they have t. own car, a car of t. own, ils ont leur propre voiture (b) T. Majesties, leurs Majestés 2. (after indef pron) F: nobody in t. right mind, personne jouissant de bon sens. theirs poss pron le leur, la leur, les leurs; this house is t., cette maison est la leur, est à eux, est à elles,

leur appartient; he's a friend of t., c'est un de leurs amis.

them [ðem] pers pron pl, objective case 1. (unstressed) (a) (direct) les mf; (indirect) leur mf; I like t., je les aime; I shall tell t. so, je le leur dirai; call t., appelez-les; speak to t., parlez-leur (b) they took the keys away with t., ils ont emporté les clefs avec eux 2. (stressed) eux, f elles; I'm thinking of t., c'est à eux, elles, que je pense 3. many of t., nombre, beaucoup, d'entre eux; both of t., the two of t., tous les deux; all of t., every one of t., tous; every one of t. was killed, ils ont tous été tués; give me half of t., donnez-m'en la moitié; neither of t., ni l'un ni l'autre; none of t., aucun d'eux; most of t., la plupart d'entre eux; lay the tables and put some flowers on t., préparez les tables et mettez-y des fleurs 4. it's t.! ce sont eux! c'est eux! them'selves pers pron (a) (emphatic) eux-mêmes, elles-mêmes; they t. are resigned to it, eux pour leur part, s'y sont résignés (b) (refl) they've hurt t., ils se sont fait mal (c) (after prep) all by t., tous seuls, toutes seules; they whispered among t., ils chuchotaient entre eux.

theme [θiːm] n 1. sujet m, thème m 2. Mus: thème, motif m; t. and variations, air m avec variations; t. song, chanson principale; chanson leitmotiv; (signature tune) indicatif m.

then [ðen] 1. adv (a) alors; en ce temps-là; à cette époque; t. and there, séance tenante; sur-le-champ; now and t., de temps en temps (b) puis, ensuite, alors; they travelled in France and t. in Spain, ils voyagèrent en France et ensuite en Espagne; what t.? et puis? et (puis) après? (c) d'ailleurs, aussi (bien); et puis; you weren't there, but t. neither was I, tu n'y étais pas, moi non plus d'ailleurs; it's beautiful, but t. it is expensive, c'est beau, mais aussi ça coûte cher 2. conj en ce cas, donc, alors; well, t. go! eh bien (alors) partez! well t., are you coming? alors, vous venez, vous viendrez? t. you should have told me, en ce cas vous auriez dû me le dire; you knew all the time t.? vous le saviez donc d'avance? 3. n ce temps-là; cette époque-là; before t., avant cela; by t. they had gone, ils étaient déjà partis; till t., (i) jusqu'alors (ii) jusque-là; (ever) since t., dès lors; depuis ce temps-là; between now and t., d'ici là; every now and t., de temps à autre 4. a the t. president, le président de l'époque, d'alors.

thence [ðens] adv A: & Lit: de là.

theodolite [θiˈɔdəlait] n théodolite m.

theology [θiˈɔlədʒi] n théologie f. theologian [θiəˈloudʒiən] n théologien, -ienne. theo'logical a théologique; t. college, séminaire m.

theorem ['θiərəm] n théorème m.

theory ['θiəri] n (pl theories) théorie f; in t., en théorie. theo'retical a théorique. theo'retically adv théoriquement. theore'tician, 'theorist n théoricien, -ienne. 'theorize vi faire de la théorie; se lancer dans des théories.

therapy ['θerəpi] n (pl therapies) Med: thérapie f; occupational t., thérapie rééducative; speech t., orthophonie f. thera'peutic a thérapeutique. thera'peutics n (with sg const) thérapeutique f. 'therapist n thérapeute mf; occupational t., spécialiste mf de thérapie rééducative.

there [ðɛər, unstressed ðər] I. adv 1. (stressed) (a) là, y; put it t., mettez-le là; he's still t., il est encore là; il y est toujours; we're t., nous voilà arrivés; who's t.? qui est là? *F:* **he's not all t.,** il n'a pas toute sa tête; il a un petit grain; **he's all t.,** c'est un malin; **here and t.,** çà et là; **here, t. and everywhere,** un peu partout (*b*) **I'm going t.,** j'y vais; **a hundred kilometres t. and back,** cent kilomètres aller et retour (*c*) (*emphatic*) **that man t.,** cet homme-là; **hurry up t.!** dépêchez-vous là-bas! (*d*) **t. is, t. are,** voilà; **t.'s the bell ringing,** voilà la cloche qui sonne; **t. they are!** les voilà! **there's a dear!** tu seras bien gentil! **t. you are!** (et) voilà! ça y est! **2.** (*unstressed*) (*a*) **t. is, t. are,** il y a; il existe; **t. was once a king,** il était une fois un roi; **there's a page missing,** il manque une page; **there's one slice left,** il reste une tranche; **there's someone at the door,** il y a quelqu'un à la porte (*b*) **t. comes a time when,** il arrive un moment où **3.** (*stressed*) quant à cela; en cela; **there's the difficulty,** c'est là qu'est, voilà, la difficulté; *F:* **t. you have me!** ça, ça me dépasse. **II.** *int* (*stressed*) voilà; **t. now!** (i) voilà (ii) allons bon! **t., I told you so!** je vous l'avais pourtant bien dit! **t., take this book,** tenez! prenez ce livre; **t.! t t.! don't worry!** là, là, ne vous inquiétez pas! **I shall do as I like, so t.!** je ferai comme il me plaira, na! **III.** *n* **he left t. last night,** il est parti (de là) hier soir; **in t.,** là-dedans; là; **somewhere round t., near t.,** quelque part par là; **over t.,** là-bas; **under t.,** là-dessous; **up t.,** là-haut. **there'abouts** *adv* **1.** près de là; dans le voisinage; **somewhere t.,** quelque part par là **2.** à peu près; environ; **it's four o'clock or t.,** il est à peu près quatre heures, il est quatre heures environ. **there'after** *adv A: & Lit:* par la suite. **there'by** *adv* par ce moyen; de ce fait; de cette façon; ainsi. **'therefore** *adv* donc; par conséquent; **it's probable, t., that he will consent,** par conséquent, il est probable qu'il consentira. **thereu'pon** *adv* **t. he left us,** sur ce il nous a quittés.

therm [θɔːm] *n Ph: etc:* 100,000 Btu (unités britanniques de chaleur). **thermal** *a* **1.** thermal **2.** *Ph:* thermal, thermique.

thermodynamic [θɔːmoudai'næmik] *a* thermodynamique.

thermometer [θɔ'mɔmitər] *n* thermomètre *m.*

thermonuclear [θɔːmou'njuːkliər] *a* thermonucléaire.

Thermos ['θɔːmɔs] *a & n Rtm:* (marque déposée désignant les articles fabriqués par Thermos (1925) Limited) **T. (flask),** (bouteille *f*) Thermos *m or f inv.*

thermostat ['θɔːmɔstæt] *n* thermostat *m.* **thermo'static** *a* thermostatique.

these *see* **this.**

thesis ['θiːsis] *n* (*pl* **theses** ['θiːsiːz]) thèse *f.*

they [ðei] **1.** *pers pron nom pl* (*a*) (*unstressed*) ils, *f* elles; **t. are dancing,** ils, elles, dansent; **here t. come,** les voici (qui arrivent) (*b*) (*stressed*) eux, *f* elles; **t. alone,** eux seuls; **t. know nothing about it,** quant à eux, ils n'en savent rien; **we are as rich as t. are,** nous sommes aussi riches qu'eux (*c*) ceux, *f* celles (qui font qch) **2.** *indef pron* on; **t. say that,** on dit que; **that's what t. say,** voilà ce qu'on raconte; *F:* **nobody ever admits they're wrong,** on ne veut jamais reconnaître ses torts.

thick [θik] **I.** *a* (**thicker, thickest**) **1.** épais; (*of book, thread*) gros; **wall two metres t.,** mur qui a deux mètres d'épaisseur; **t. skinned,** (i) à la peau épaisse (ii) (*of pers*) peu sensible, peu susceptible; **t. lipped,** lippu; à grosses lèvres **2.** (*of wheat, forest*) serré, touffu, dru; (*of hair*) abondant, épais; (*of crowd*)

compact, serré; **t. beard,** barbe fournie **3.** (*a*) (*of liquid*) épais, visqueux; (*of mist*) dense, épais; (*of darkness*) profond; (*of air*) épais (*b*) (*of voice*) étouffé (*c*) *F:* (*of pers*) t., obtus, borné **4.** *F:* **to be very t. with s.o.,** être très lié avec qn; **they're as t. as thieves,** ils s'entendent comme larrons en foire **5.** *F:* **that's a bit t.!** ça c'est un peu raide, un peu fort! **II.** *n* **1.** (*a*) partie charnue, gras *m* (de la jambe) (*b*) **in the t. of the forest,** au beau milieu de la forêt; **in the t. of it,** en plein dedans; **in the t. of the fight,** au (plus) fort de la mêlée **2. to go through t. and thin for s.o.,** courir tous les risques pour qn; **to stick to s.o. through t. and thin,** rester fidèle à qn à travers toutes les épreuves. **III.** *adv* **1.** en couche épaisse; **snow lay t. on the ground,** une neige épaisse couvrait le sol; **to cut the bread t.,** couper le pain en tranches épaisses; *F:* **to lay it on a bit t.,** exagérer **2. the blows fell t. and fast,** les coups pleuvaient dru. **'thicken** *v* **1.** *vtr* épaissir; épaissir, lier (une sauce) **2.** *vi* (*a*) (s')épaissir (*b*) (*of sauce*) épaissir (*c*) (*of plot*) se compliquer, se corser. **'thicket** *n* hallier *m,* fourré *m.* **'thickheaded** *a F:* bête; borné. **'thickly** *adv* **1.** en couche(s) épaisse(s); en tranches épaisses **2.** épais; **the snow fell t.,** la neige tombait dru **3.** (parler) d'une voix étouffée; (*when drunk*) d'une voix pâteuse. **'thickness** *n* **1.** (*a*) épaisseur *f* (d'un mur); grosseur *f* (des lèvres) (*b*) épaisseur (d'une forêt); abondance *f* (de la chevelure) (*c*) consistance *f* (d'un liquide); épaisseur (du brouillard) (*d*) étouffement *m* (de la voix) **2.** couche *f* (de papier). **'thick'set** *a* **1.** (*of hedge*) épais; dru; (*of beard*) fourni **2.** (*of pers*) trapu.

thief [θiːf] *n* (*pl* **thieves**) voleur, -euse; **stop t.!** au voleur! **set a t. to catch a t.,** à voleur, voleur et demi. **thieve** *v* (*a*) *vtr* voler (qch) (*b*) *vi* être voleur, -euse. **'thieving 1.** *a* voleur **2.** *n* vol *m;* **petty t.,** larcin *m.*

thigh [θai] *n* cuisse *f;* **t. boots,** cuissardes *fpl.* **'thighbone** *n* fémur *m.*

thimble ['θimbl] *n* dé *m* (à coudre). **'thimbleful** *n* doigt *m* (de cognac).

thin [θin] **I.** *a* (**thinner, thinnest**) **1.** (*a*) (*of paper*) mince, fin; (*of thread*) ténu, fin; (*of fabric*) fin, léger; **to cut the bread in t. slices,** couper le pain en tranches minces (*b*) (*of pers*) maigre, mince; **long t. fingers,** doigts effilés; **to grow thinner,** maigrir, s'amaigrir; **t. lipped,** aux lèvres minces; **as t. as a rake,** maigre comme un clou **2.** (*of hair*) clairsemé, rare; (*of audience*) clairsemé; **his hair was getting t.,** ses cheveux s'éclaircissaient; **t. on the ground,** peu nombreux **3.** (*of liquid*) clair; peu consistant; (*of blood*) appauvri; (*of voice*) fluet, grêle; **t. soup,** potage clair **4.** *F:* **t. excuse,** pauvre excuse; **my patience is wearing t.,** je suis presque à bout de patience; **to have a t. time (of it),** (i) s'ennuyer (ii) manger de la vache enragée. **II.** *n* **through thick and t.,** à travers toutes les épreuves. **III.** *adv* **to cut t.,** couper en tranches minces; (*of wheat*) **t. sown,** clairsemé **IV.** *vi* (**thinned**) **1.** *vtr* (*a*) **to t. (down),** amincir (qch) (*b*) **to t. (down),** diluer, délayer (la peinture); allonger (une sauce) (*c*) **to t. (out),** éclaircir (les arbres); **to t. out seedlings,** éclaircir des jeunes plants **2.** *vi* s'amincir, s'effiler; (*of hair, trees, crowd*) s'éclaircir; **his hair is thinning,** il perd ses cheveux. **'thinly** *adv* **1.** (*a*) en couche(s) mince(s); en tranches minces (*b*) clair; **t. sown,** clairsemé; **t. populated,** à faible densité de population 2. à peine; **t. dressed,** vêtu (i) légèrement (ii) insuffisamment; **t. veiled allusion,** allusion à peine voilée. **'thinner** n (occ thinners) diluant m, dissolvant m. **'thinness** n 1. (a) minceur f; légèreté f (d'un tissu) (b) maigreur f, minceur (d'une personne) 2. rareté f (des cheveux) 3. fluidité f (d'un liquide); raréfaction f (de l'air); caractère grêle, fluet (d'une voix). **'thinning** n (a) **t. (down),** (i) amincissement m (ii) délayage m; dilution f; **t. agent,** diluant, dissolvant (b) **t. (out),** éclaircissement m.

thine [ðain] A: & Poet: 1. poss pron le tien, la tienne; pl les tiens, les tiennes; **what is mine is t.,** ce qui est à moi est à toi 2. poss a ton, ta, tes.

thing [θiŋ] n 1. (a) chose f; objet m, article m; **to go the way of all things,** mourir; **things to be washed,** du linge à laver (b) F: **what's that t.?** qu'est-ce que c'est que ce machin-là? (c) **tea things,** service m à thé; **to wash up the tea things, the dinner things,** faire la vaisselle (d) pl vêtements m, effets m; **bring along your swimming things,** apportez votre maillot de bain (e) pl affaires f, effets; **to pack up one's things,** faire ses valises; **to put one's things away,** ranger ses affaires (f) Jur: **things personal,** biens meubles 2. être m, créature f; **poor t.,** le, la, pauvre! **poor little things!** pauvres petits! **she's a dear old t.,** c'est une bonne vieille très sympathique 3. (a) **that was a silly t. to do,** quelle bêtise! **how could you do such a t.?** comment avez-vous pu faire une chose pareille? **you take things too seriously,** vous prenez les choses trop au sérieux; **he gets things done,** il est efficace; **to think things over,** réfléchir; **it's just one of those things,** ce sont des choses qui arrivent; **to talk of one t. and another,** parler de choses et d'autres; **that's the very t.,** c'est juste ce qu'il faut; **that's the t. for me!** voilà mon affaire! **the t. is this,** voici ce dont il s'agit; **the t. is, I haven't got any money,** le problème c'est que je n'ai pas d'argent; **the important t. is that,** l'important c'est que; **neither one t. nor the other,** ni l'un ni l'autre; **what with one t. and another,** tant et si bien que; **entre une chose et l'autre; for one t.,** en premier lieu; **and another t.,** en plus; **that's quite another t.,** c'est tout autre chose; F: **he's onto a good t.,** il est sur un bon filon; **I don't know a t. about chemistry,** je ne comprends rien à la chimie; **it doesn't mean a t. to me,** (i) je n'y comprends rien (ii) je ne m'en souviens pas; **to know a t. or two,** (i) avoir plus d'un tour dans son sac (ii) être bien renseigné; **I could tell you a t. or two,** je pourrais en conter; **first t. in the morning,** (i) très tôt dans la matinée (ii) dès demain matin; **last t. at night,** (très) tard dans la soirée; F: **he's got a t. about that,** c'est son idée fixe; **do your own t.,** fais comme il te plaira (b) **things are going badly,** les affaires vont mal; **as things are,** dans l'état actuel de choses; **since that is how things are,** puisqu'il en est ainsi; F: **how are things? how's things?** (i) comment vont les affaires? (ii) comment ça va? 4. **the latest t. in shoes,** chaussure(s) dernier cri; **it's the (very) latest t.,** c'est tout ce qu'il y a de plus moderne 5. F: **it's not the done t.,** cela ne se fait pas. **'thingumabob, 'thingumajig, 'thingummy** n F: chose m, machin m, truc m.

think [θiŋk] I. n to have a (quiet) t., réfléchir; F: **you've got another t. coming!** tu peux toujours courir! II. v (thought [θɔːt]) vtr & i 1. penser, réfléchir; **to t. aloud,** penser tout haut; **to t. hard,** se creuser la tête; F: **to t.**

big, être ambitieux; **what are you thinking?** à quoi pensez-vous? **I know what you're thinking,** je connais vos pensées; **to act without thinking,** agir sans réfléchir; **t. before you speak,** pesez vos paroles; **give me time to t.,** laissez-moi réfléchir; **his name was—let me t.,** il s'appelait—voyons; **to t. again,** se raviser; **to t. twice before doing sth,** y regarder à deux fois avant de faire qch 2. songer, s'imaginer, se figurer; **I (really) can't t. why,** je me demande bien pourquoi; **what will people t.?** qu'en dira-t-on? **one would have thought that,** c'était à croire que; **anyone would t. he was asleep,** on dirait qu'il dort; **who'd have thought it?** qui l'aurait dit! **just t.!** songez donc! **to t. he's only ten!** et dire qu'il n'a que dix ans! 3. (a) **I've been thinking that,** l'idée m'est venue que (b) **did you t. to bring any money?** avez-vous pensé à apporter l'argent? 4. (a) **do you t. you could do it?** vous sentez-vous capable de le faire? **it's better, don't you t., to get it over?** il vaut mieux en finir n'est-ce pas? **I thought it was all over,** je croyais que tout était fini; **I thought I heard him,** j'ai cru l'entendre; **I t. she's pretty,** je la trouve jolie; **everyone thought he was mad,** on le tenait pour fou; **I rather t. it's going to rain,** j'ai dans l'idée qu'il va pleuvoir; **it is thought that,** on suppose que + ind; **I t. so,** je pense que oui; c'est ce qui me semble; **I t. not, I don't t. so,** je pense que non; **I should hardly t. so,** c'est peu probable; **I should t. so!** je crois bien! **I shouldn't t. so,** je ne crois pas; F: **that's what you t.!** tu penses! (b) juger, considérer, croire, trouver, penser; **I hardly t. it likely that,** il n'est guère probable que + sub; **I thought her a fool,** je l'avais prise pour une sotte; **they are thought to be rich,** ils passent pour (être) riches; **do as you t. best,** faites comme bon vous semble(ra) 5. **I little thought I would see him again,** je ne m'attendais guère à le revoir; **I thought as much, I thought so,** je m'y attendais; je m'en doutais (bien). **'thinkable** a concevable, imaginable. **'think'about, 'of** v ind tr (a) penser à (qn, qch); songer à (qn, qch); **I've thought about your proposal,** j'ai réfléchi à votre proposition; **one can't t. of everything,** on ne saurait penser à tout; **I can't t. of his name,** son nom ne me revient pas; **I can't t. of the right word,** le mot juste m'échappe; **come to t. of it,** à la réflexion; **he can't sleep for thinking about it,** il perd le sommeil à force d'y penser; F: il n'en dort pas; **the best thing I can t. of,** ce que je vois de mieux; **that's worth thinking about,** cela mérite réflexion; **what am I thinking of, about?** où ai-je la tête? (b) s'imaginer, se figurer; **t. of a number,** pensez à un chiffre; **I thought of him as being tall,** je le voyais grand; F: **t. of that! t. of it!** qui l'aurait cru? **t. of it, I'm in love with him,** je l'aime, figure-toi; **when I t. of what might have happened!** quand je pense à ce qui aurait pu arriver! (c) **it's not to be thought of,** ce n'est pas à considérer; **to t. of the expense,** regarder à la dépense; **to t. of s.o.'s feelings,** avoir égard aux sentiments de qn (d) **to t. of, about, doing sth,** méditer, projeter, de faire qch; penser à faire qch; **I couldn't t. of it!** c'est impossible! il n'en est pas question! (e) vtr **what do you t. of it, about it?** qu'en pensez-vous? **to t. a great deal of oneself,** avoir une haute idée de sa personne; **to t. too much of sth,** attacher trop d'importance à qch; **I told him what I thought of him,** je lui ai dit son fait (f) **to t. well of s.o.,** estimer qn; **people t. well of him, he is well thought of,** il est bien vu; **to t. better of it,** changer d'opinion; **I don't t. much of it,** ça ne me dit pas grand-chose. **'think 'back** *vi* essayer de se souvenir (de qch). **'thinker** *n* penseur, -euse. **'thinking** 1. *a* pensant; qui pense 2. *n* (*a*) pensée(s) *f(pl)*, réflexion(s) *f(pl)*; **he did some hard t.,** il a réfléchi profondément (*b*) **to my (way of) t.,** à mon avis; **I hope to bring you round to my way of t.,** j'espère vous amener à mon point de vue. **'think 'of** *v ind tr see* **think about. 'think 'out** *vtr* (*a*) imaginer, méditer (qch); **to t. o. a plan,** élaborer un plan; **carefully thought out answer,** réponse bien étudiée; **that wants thinking out,** cela demande mûre réflexion (*b*) **he thinks things out for himself,** il juge des choses par lui-même. **'think 'over** *vtr* réfléchir sur, aviser à (une question); **t. it o. (carefully),** réfléchissez-y bien; **on thinking it over,** après réflexion. **'think 'up** *vtr* imaginer (une méthode, un projet).

third [θəːd] 1. *num a* troisième; **t. person,** (i) *Jur:* tierce personne, tiers *m* (ii) *Gram:* troisième personne; **t. party insurance,** assurance au tiers; **George the T.,** Georges Trois; **(on) the t. (of March),** le trois (mars); **t. rate pianist,** pianiste de troisième ordre 2. *n* (*a*) *Mus:* tierce *f* (*b*) *Sch:* **to get a t. (class degree)**=obtenir une licence avec mention *passable* (*c*) *Aut:* troisième vitesse *f*, troisième *f* 3. *n* (*fraction*) tiers *m*; **a t. of the inhabitants were killed,** un tiers des habitants a été tué, ont été tués. **'thirdly** *adv* troisièmement; en troisième lieu *m*.

thirst [θəːst] 1. *n* soif *f*; **to quench one's t.,** se désaltérer; **t. for knowledge,** soif de connaissances; **to satisfy one's t. for adventure,** apaiser sa soif d'aventures 2. *vi* avoir soif (**for,** de); **to t. for blood,** être altéré de sang. **'thirstily** *adv* avidement. **'thirsting** *a* altéré, assoiffé; **t. for blood,** assoiffé, avide, de sang. **'thirsty** *a* altéré; assoiffé; **to be t.,** avoir soif; *F:* **this is t. work,** cela donne soif.

thirteen [θəːˈtiːn] *num a & n* treize (*m*); **she's t. (years old),** elle a treize ans. **thir'teenth** 1. *num a & n* treizième (*m*); **(on) the t. (of May),** le treize (mai) 2. *n* (*fraction*) treizième *m*.

thirty [ˈθəːti] *num a & n* trente (*m*); **t.-three,** trente-trois; **t.-first,** trente et unième; **about t. people,** une trentaine de personnes; **the thirties,** les années trente. **'thirtieth** *num a & n* trentième (*m*); **(on) the t. (of June),** le trente (juin).

this [ðis] I. *dem pron, pl* **these** [ðiːz] 1. ceci; ce; **what's t.? what are these?** qu'est-ce que c'est (que ça)? **who's t.?** qui est-ce? **you'll be sorry for t.,** vous le regretterez; **what good is t.?** à quoi cela sert-il? **after t.,** après cela, ensuite, désormais; **it ought to have come before t.,** cela devrait être déjà arrivé; **t. is odd,** voilà qui est curieux; **t. is what he told me,** voici ce qu'il m'a dit; **t. is a free country,** nous sommes dans un pays libre; **t. is Mr Martin,** je vous présente M. Martin; **these are my children,** ce sont mes enfants; **t. is where he lives,** c'est ici qu'il habite; **listen to t.,** écoutez bien ceci; **what's t. (I hear?),** qu'est-ce que j'apprends? **it was like t.,** voici comment les choses se sont passées; **what's all t.?** qu'est-ce qu'il y a? qu'est-ce qui se passe? **t. will you have t. or that?** voulez-vous ceci ou cela? **to talk of t. and that,** parler de choses et d'autres 3. celui-ci, *f* celle-ci, *pl* ceux-ci, *f* celles-ci; **I prefer these to those,** je préfère ceux-ci à ceux-là. II. *dem a, pl* **these** (*a*) ce, (*before vowel or h mute*) cet, *f* cette, *pl* ces; (*for*

emphasis) ce . . . -ci; **t. book, these books,** ce livre(-ci), ces livres(-ci); **one of these days,** un de ces jours; **in t. day and age,** de nos jours; **by t. time,** à l'heure qu'il est; **to run t. way and that,** courir de-ci de-là; **for t. reason,** voilà pourquoi; **pour cette raison** (*b*) *Pej:* **he's one of these artist chaps,** c'est un de ces artistes (*c*) **I've known him t. three years,** je le connais depuis trois ans. III. *dem adv* **t. high, as high as t.,** haut comme ça; **t. far,** jusqu'ici, jusque là.

thistle [ˈθisl] *n Bot:* chardon *m*. **'thistledown** *n* duvet *m* de chardon.

thither [ˈðiðər] *adv A: & Lit:* là; y; **to run hither and t.,** courir çà et là.

tho' [ðou] *conj & adv F:*=**though.**

thong [θɔŋ] *n* lanière *f* de cuir.

thorax [ˈθɔːræks] *n* (*pl* **thoraces**) *Anat:* thorax *m*. **tho'racic** *a* thoracique.

thorn [θɔːn] *n* (*a*) épine *f*; **a t. in the flesh,** une épine au pied (*b*) *Bot:* épine. **'thorny** *a* épineux.

thorough [ˈθʌrə] *a* (*a*) (*of search*) minutieux; (*of knowledge*) profond; (*of work*) consciencieux; **to give a room a t. cleaning,** nettoyer une chambre à fond; **to be t. in one's work,** travailler consciencieusement (*b*) **a t. musician,** un musicien consommé; **a t. republican,** un républicain convaincu; **a t. scoundrel,** un fieffé coquin. **'thoroughbred** 1. *a* (cheval) pur sang *inv*; (chien) de race 2. *n* (*of horse*) pur-sang *m inv*; animal *m* de race. **'thoroughfare** *n* voie *f* de communication; **public t.,** voie publique; **a main t.,** une des principales artères (d'une ville); *PN:* **no t.,** rue barrée; passage interdit. **'thoroughgoing** *a* (*a*) (*of search, inspection*) minutieux, complet (*b*) (travailleur) consciencieux; (coquin) fieffé. **'thoroughly** *adv* tout à fait; (savoir une langue) parfaitement; (renouveler) entièrement; (nettoyer) à fond. **'thoroughness** *f* perfection *f*, minutie *f* (du travail).

those *see* **that.**

thou [ðau] *pers pron A: & B:* tu; (*stressed*) toi.

though [ðou] 1. *conj* (*a*) quoique, bien que+*sub or occ ind*; **I am sorry for him t. he is nothing to me,** je le plains même s'il ne m'est rien; **t. not beautiful, she was attractive,** sans être belle elle était séduisante (*b*) **strange t. it may seem,** si étrange que cela paraisse; **even t. you'll laugh at me,** même que vous allez vous moquer de moi (*c*) **as t.,** comme si; **it looks as t. he's gone,** il semble qu'il soit parti; **as t. nothing had happened,** comme si de rien n'était 2. *adv* (*a*) cependant, pourtant (*b*) **did he t.!** vraiment! il a dit, fait, cela?

thought[1] [θɔːt] *n* 1. pensée *f*; **capable of t.,** capable de penser 2. (*a*) pensée, idée *f*; **happy t.,** heureuse idée; **gloomy thoughts,** pensées sombres; *F:* **a penny for your thoughts,** à quoi pensez-vous? **to read s.o.'s thoughts,** lire dans la pensée de qn; **t. reading,** lecture de la pensée; **t. reader,** liseur, -euse, de pensées; **I can't read your thoughts,** je ne suis pas devin (*b*) **the mere t. of it,** rien que d'y penser; **he never gave it a single t.,** il n'y a jamais pensé; **I didn't give it another t.,** je n'y ai pas repensé (*c*) *pl* esprit *m*, pensée; **to collect one's thoughts,** rassembler ses idées, ses esprits; **her thoughts were elsewhere,** son esprit était ·ailleurs 3. (*a*) réflexion *f*, considération *f*; **lack of t.,** irréflexion *f*; **after much t.,** après mûre réflexion; **he has no t. for others,** il est peu soucieux des autres, il n'a pas de considération pour les autres; **on second thoughts**, (toute) réflexion faite (b) pensées, rêverie f, méditation f; **lost in t.**, perdu dans ses pensées **4.** (a) intention f, dessein m; **to have thoughts, some t., of doing sth**, songer à faire qch; **you must give up all thought(s) of seeing him**, il faut renoncer à le voir; **it's the t. that counts**, c'est l'intention qui compte (b) O: **I had no t. of meeting you here**, je ne m'attendais pas à vous rencontrer ici. **'thoughtful** a **1.** (a) pensif, méditatif, rêveur (b) réfléchi, prudent **2.** prévenant; plein d'égards (**of**, pour); **he was t. enough to warn me**, il a eu la prévenance de m'avertir. **'thoughtfully** adv **1.** (a) pensivement; d'un air rêveur (b) d'une manière réfléchie, prudente **2.** avec prévenance. **'thoughtfulness** n **1.** (a) méditation f, recueillement m (b) réflexion f, prudence f **2.** prévenance f, égards mpl (**of**, pour, envers). **'thoughtless** a **1.** irréfléchi; étourdi; **t. action**, étourderie f **2. t. of others**, qui manque d'égards, de prévenance, pour les autres. **'thoughtlessly** adv **1.** étourdiment; (agir) sans réflexion, à la légère **2. to treat s.o.**, manquer d'égards envers qn. **'thoughtlessness** n **1.** irréflexion f; étourderie f **2.** manque m d'égards, de prévenance (**of**, pour, envers).

thought² see **think II.**

thousand ['θauz(ə)nd] num a & n mille (m) inv; n millier m; **about a t. men**, un millier d'hommes; quelque mille hommes; **I paid five t. for it**, je l'ai payé cinq mille (livres, dollars); **the year 4000 B.C.**, l'an quatre mille avant J.-C.; **a t. years**, mille ans; un millénaire; **thousands of people**, des milliers de gens; **in thousands**, par milliers; **he's one in a t.**, c'est un homme entre mille; **a. t. apologies!** mille pardons! **no, no, a t. times no!** non, non, et cent fois non! **'thousandth** num a & n millième (mf).

thrash [θræʃ] **1.** vtr (a) battre (qn); rosser (qn); **to t. s.o. soundly**, donner une bonne raclée à qn (b) Sp: etc: battre (qn) à plates coutures (c) **to t. out**, (i) débattre (une question); discuter (une question) à fond (ii) démêler (un problème) (d) **to t. one's arms and legs about**, se démener **2.** vi **to t. about**, se débattre, se démener. **'thrashing** n (a) rossée f, correction f; **to give s.o. a t.**, flanquer une raclée à qn (b) Sp: etc: défaite f.

thread [θred] n **1.** filament m, fil m (de soie); **to hang by a t.**, ne tenir qu'à un fil **2.** (a) Needlw: fil (de coton, de nylon); **sewing t.**, fil à coudre; **gold t.**, fil d'or (b) Tex: fil (de trame, de chaîne); **the t. of life**, la trame de la vie; **to lose the t. of the conversation**, perdre le fil de la conversation (c) (**length of**) **t.**, brin m, bout m (de coton) **3.** Tchn: filet m (de vis). **II.** vtr **1.** (a) enfiler (une aiguille, des perles) (b) **to t. one's way**, se faufiler **2.** fileter (une vis). **'threadbare** a (of clothes) râpé, usé; (of argument) usé (jusqu'à la corde), rebattu.

threat [θret] n menace f; **to be under the t. of sth**, être menacé de qch; **idle t.**, menace en l'air; **there is a t. of rain**, la pluie menace. **'threaten 1.** vtr (a) menacer; **to t. s.o. with sth**, menacer qn de qch; **race threatened with extinction**, race en voie d'extinction (b) **to t. to do sth**, menacer de faire qch **2.** vi **a storm is threatening**, l'orage menace; un orage s'annonce. **'threatening** a (ton, air) menaçant; (lettre) de menaces; **t. language**, menaces verbales; Jur: intimidation f; **the weather**

looks t., le temps menace. **'threateningly** adv d'un air menaçant, d'une manière menaçante.

three [θri:] num a & n trois (m); **to be t. (years old)**, avoir trois ans; **to come in in threes, t. by t., t. at a time**, entrer par trois; Cards: **t. of diamonds**, trois de carreau; **t. star hotel**, hôtel trois-étoiles; **t. act play**, pièce en trois actes; **t. sided, t. party, conversations**, conversations tripartites. **'three-'cornered** a triangulaire; **t.-c. hat**, tricorne m. **three-di'mensional** a tridimensionnel; à trois dimensions; (film) en relief; Mus: **t.-four time**, trois-quatre m. **'threefold 1.** a triple **2.** adv trois fois plus, autant; **to increase t.**, tripler. **three-'legged** a (tabouret) à trois pieds. **'three-'piece** a en trois pièces; **t.-p. suite**, (salon m comprenant un) canapé et deux fauteuils assortis. **'three-ply** a (of wool) à trois fils. **'three-point** a Aut: **t.-p. turn**, demi-tour m en trois manœuvres. **three-'quarter 1.** n Rugby: Fb: trois-quarts m inv **2.** adv **t.-quarters full**, plein aux trois quarts, aux trois quarts pleins. **'threesome** n groupe m de trois (personnes); **in a t.**, à trois. **'three-way** a (division) en trois; (discussion) à trois. **three-'wheeler** n (a) voiture f à trois roues (b) tricycle m.

thresh [θreʃ] vtr battre (le blé). **'thresher** n batteuse f. **'threshing** n battage m (du blé); **t. machine**, batteuse.

threshold ['θreʃ(h)ould] n seuil m, pas m; **to cross the t.**, franchir le seuil; **on the t. of**, au seuil de; sur le seuil de.

threw see **throw II.**

thrice [θrais] adv A: & Lit: trois fois.

thrift [θrift] n économie f, épargne f. **'thriftiness** n économie. **'thriftless** a dépensier; imprévoyant. **'thriftlessness** n gaspillage m; imprévoyance f. **'thrifty** a économe.

thrill [θril] **I.** n (a) frisson m, tressaillement m (b) (vive) émotion; **it gave me quite a t.**, ça m'a vraiment fait quelque chose; **to get a t. out of doing sth**, avoir des sensations en faisant qch. **II.** v **1.** vtr (a) faire frissonner, faire frémir (qn); F: **she's thrilled with her new car**, elle est ravie de sa nouvelle voiture (b) émouvoir, émotionner (qn); électriser (un auditoire); **to be thrilled**, ressentir une vive émotion à la vue de qch) **2.** vi tressaillir, frissonner (de joie). **'thriller** n roman m, film m, à suspense. **'thrilling** a (spectacle) émouvant, saisissant, émotionnant; (voyage) palpitant; (roman) sensationnel.

thrive [θraiv] vi (pt & pp thrived) (a) (of child, plant) bien se développer; F: profiter; (of adult) bien se porter; (of business) bien marcher; (of plant) **thrives in all soils**, s'accommode de tous les sols; **he thrives on it**, il s'en trouve bien (b) (of pers) prospérer; **to t. on other people's misfortunes**, exploiter la misère humaine. **'thriving** a vigoureux; bien portant; (of pers, business) prospère, florissant.

throat [θrout] n (a) gorge f; **to take s.o. by the t.**, empoigner qn à la gorge; **to cut s.o.'s t.**, couper la gorge à qn; F: **to cut one's own t.**, travailler à sa propre ruine; **they were cutting each other's throats**, ils se faisaient une concurrence désastreuse (b) gorge, gosier m; **to have a sore t.**, avoir mal à la gorge; **to clear one's t.**, s'éclaircir, se racler, la gorge; F: **he's always ramming it down my t.**, il m'en rebat toujours les oreilles; **to jump down s.o.'s t.,** rembarrer qn; **it sticks in my t.,** je ne peux pas avaler ça. **'throaty** a (of voice) d'arrière-gorge; guttural.

throb [θrɔb] **1.** n palpitation f, pulsation f (du cœur); vrombissement m (d'une machine) **2.** vi (**throbbed**) (a) (of heart) battre fort; palpiter; (of engine) vrombir (b) **my finger is throbbing,** mon doigt lancine. **'throbbing 1.** a (of heart) palpitant; (of engine) vrombissant; (of pain) lancinant **2.** n (a) battement fort, pulsation f, palpitation f (du cœur); vrombissement m (d'une machine) (b) élancement m.

throes [θrouz] npl douleurs fpl, angoisse f, agonie f; **the t. of death,** les affres f de la mort; l'agonie; **we're in the t. of moving house,** nous sommes en plein déménagement.

thrombosis [θrɔm'bousis] n Med: thrombose f; **coronary t.,** infarctus m du myocarde.

throne [θroun] n trône m; **to come to the t.,** monter sur le trône; **heir to the t.,** héritier du trône.

throng [θrɔŋ] **1.** n (a) foule f (b) (disorderly) cohue f **2.** v (a) vi s'assembler en foule; affluer (à, dans, un endroit); **to t. round s.o.,** se presser autour de qn (b) vtr encombrer, emplir; **the room was thronged with people,** la pièce était bondée.

throttle ['θrɔtl] **1.** n (a) Mch: régulateur m (b) ICE: papillon m des gaz; **to open the t.,** mettre les gaz **2.** (a) vtr étrangler (qn); serrer (qn) à la gorge; étrangler (le moteur) (b) vi **to t. down,** mettre le moteur au ralenti; fermer les gaz; Av: **to t. back,** couper les gaz. **'throttling** n étranglement m.

through [θru:] **I.** prep **1.** (a) à travers; par; **t. a hedge,** au travers d'une haie; **to go t. sth,** traverser qch; passer par qch; **I'm on my way t. Paris,** je suis de passage à Paris; **to look t. the window,** regarder par la fenêtre; **to look t. a telescope,** regarder dans un télescope; **to go t. s.o.'s pockets,** fouiller qn; Aut: **to go t. a red light,** brûler un feu rouge; **he's been t. it,** il en a vu de dures; **to talk t. one's nose,** parler du nez; **he got t. his exam,** il a été reçu à son examen; F: **to put s.o. t. it,** faire subir un interrogatoire serré à qn; **I'm halfway t. this book,** j'ai lu la moitié de ce livre (b) pendant, durant; **all t. his life,** sa vie durant; durant toute sa vie; **t. the ages,** à travers les âges; esp NAm: **Monday t. Friday** (Br = Monday to Friday), du lundi à vendredi; du lundi au vendredi **2.** t. s.o., par qn; par l'entremise, l'intermédiaire, de qn; **t. sth,** par le moyen de qch; **to send sth t. the post,** envoyer qch par la poste **3.** (a) en conséquence de, par suite de, à cause de (qch); **t. ignorance,** par ignorance; **absent t. illness,** absent par suite, pour cause, de maladie; **to act t. fear,** agir sous le coup de la peur (b) par l'action de (qn, qch); **it's t. me that he missed the train,** c'est à cause de moi qu'il a raté son train; **it all happened t. him,** il est cause de tout. **II.** adv **1.** (a) à travers; **the water poured t.,** l'eau coulait à travers; **to let s.o. t.,** laisser passer qn; F: **England are t. to the semi-final,** l'Angleterre jouera la demi-finale (b) **t. and t.,** de bout en bout; de part en part; (connaître qch) comme le fond de sa poche; **to run s.o. t. (with a sword),** transpercer qn; **wet t.,** trempé jusqu'aux os (b) d'un bout à l'autre; jusqu'au bout; jusqu'à la fin; **to see sth t.,** mener qch à bonne fin; **we must go t. with it,** il faut aller jusqu'au bout; **to be t. with sth,** (i) avoir fini qch (ii) en avoir assez; **are you t. with it?** l'as-tu fini? **I'm t. with him,** j'en ai fini

avec lui **2.** (a) directement; **to book t. to Paris,** prendre un billet direct pour Paris (b) **to get t. to s.o.,** (i) Tp: obtenir la communication avec qn (ii) F: faire comprendre qch à qn; Tp: **I'll put you t. to the secretary,** je vous passe la secrétaire; **you're t.,** vous avez la communication. **III.** a Rail: **t. carriage for Geneva,** voiture directe pour Genève; **t. passenger to Paris,** voyageur, -euse, direct(e) pour Paris; **t. traffic,** transit m; PN: **no t. road,** voie sans issue. **through'out 1.** prep (a) **t. the country,** dans tout le pays; **t. the world,** à travers le monde; dans le monde entier (b) **t. the year,** pendant toute l'année **2.** adv (a) partout (b) tout le temps. **'throughway** n NAm: autoroute f.

throw [θrou] **I.** n (a) jet m, lancement m; lancer m (du javelot); coup m (de dés); **within a stone's t.,** à quelques pas (b) Wr: mise f à terre (de l'adversaire). **II.** vtr (threw [θru:]; thrown [θroun]) **1.** (a) jeter, lancer; vi **he can t. a hundred metres,** il est capable de lancer à cent mètres; **to t. s.o. a kiss,** envoyer un baiser à qn; **to t. the dice,** jeter les dés; **to t. sth in s.o.'s face,** jeter qch à la figure de qn; **to t. a glance at s.o.,** jeter un coup d'œil à, sur, qn; **to t. oneself forwards, backwards,** se jeter en avant; se rejeter en arrière; **to t. oneself into sth,** (i) se jeter dans (la rivière) (ii) se lancer à corps perdu dans (une entreprise); **to t. oneself on s.o.'s mercy,** se remettre à la merci de qn; F: **she threw herself at him,** elle s'est jetée à sa tête; **to t. temptation in s.o.'s way,** exposer qn à la tentation; **to t. the blame on s.o.,** rejeter la faute sur qn (b) **to t. a sheet over sth,** couvrir qch d'un drap; **to t. s.o. into prison,** jeter, mettre, qn en prison; **to t. a switch,** basculer un interrupteur; **to t. s.o. into confusion,** jeter qn dans l'embarras; **to t. open the door,** ouvrir la porte toute grande **2.** projeter; **to t. a picture on the screen,** projeter une image sur l'écran; **to t. some light on the matter,** jeter de la lumière sur la question; éclairer la question **3.** **to t. a fit,** (i) tomber en convulsions (ii) F: piquer une crise de nerfs; F: **to t. a party,** organiser une soirée **4.** Wr: renverser (son adversaire); (of horse) désarçonner (son cavalier); (of rider) **to be thrown,** être désarçonné **5.** (of reptile) **to t. its skin,** muer **6.** tourner, façonner (un pot) **7.** F: **his question threw me for a moment,** pendant un moment je ne savais que répondre à sa question. **'throw a'bout** vtr (a) jeter (des objets) çà et là; gaspiller (son argent) (b) **to t. one's arms a.,** faire de grands gestes; **to t. oneself a.,** se démener; **to be thrown about,** être ballotté. **'throw a'way** vtr (a) jeter (sa cigarette); rejeter (qch); mettre (qch) au rebut (b) gaspiller (son argent); **to t. a. a chance,** laisser passer une occasion; **to t. a. one's life,** se sacrifier inutilement (c) (of actor) **to t. a. a line,** énoncer une phrase avec une indifférence calculée. **'throwaway** a **1.** à jeter, jetable **2.** **t. line,** aparté m. **'throw 'back** vtr (a) rejeter; renvoyer, relancer (une balle) (b) **to t. one's head back,** rejeter la tête en arrière (c) **to be thrown back upon s.o., sth,** être obligé de se rabattre sur qn, qch. **'throwback** n retour m (en arrière); **it's a t. to,** ça remonte à. **'throw 'down** vtr jeter (qch) (de haut en bas); jeter (qch) à terre; **to t. oneself d.,** se jeter à terre; **to t. d. one's arms,** (i) abandonner ses armes (ii) se rendre. **'thrower** n lanceur, -euse. **'throw 'in** vtr (a) jeter (qch) dedans; Fb: **to t. in the ball,**

thru · 427 · ticket

thru [θru:] *NAm:* = **through**. **'thruway** *n* auto-route *f*.

remettre le ballon en jeu (*b*) ajouter (qch); donner (qch) en plus (*c*) intercaler, insérer (une observation); placer (un mot) (*d*) **to t. in one's lot with s.o.**, partager le sort de qn (*e*) **to t. in one's hand, one's cards**, abandonner, quitter, la partie; **to t. in the towel**, (i) *Box:* jeter l'éponge (ii) *Fig:* s'avouer vaincu. **'throw-in** *n Fb:* remise *f* en jeu (du ballon). **'throw 'off** *vtr* 1. (*adv use*) (*a*) jeter (de la vapeur) (*b*) enlever, ôter (ses vêtements); se débarrasser, se défaire, de (qn, qch); abandonner (un déguisement); lever (le masque); guérir (d'un rhume) 2. (*prep use*) (*a*) **to t. s.o. o. his bicycle**, faire tomber qn de sa bicyclette (*b*) **to t. the dogs o. the scent**, dépister les chiens. **'throw 'on** *vtr* enfiler ses vêtements à la hâte. **'throw 'out** *vtr* (*a*) jeter (qn, qch) dehors; se débarrasser de (qch); mettre (qn) à la porte (*b*) répandre, émettre (de la chaleur) (*c*) rejeter, repousser (un projet de loi) (*d*) **to t. o. one's chest**, bomber le torse (*e*) lancer (un défi); émettre (une proposition) (*f*) troubler (un orateur); **to t. s.o. o. in his calculations**, tromper les calculs de qn. **'throwouts** *npl Com:* rebuts *m*. **'throw 'over** *vtr* laisser tomber (un ami); lâcher, plaquer (qn). **'throw to'gether** *vtr* (*a*) assembler, rassembler (qch) à la hâte; *F:* torcher (un article) (*b*) **chance had thrown them together**, le hasard les avait réunis. **'throw 'up** *vtr & i* (*a*) jeter (qch) en l'air (*b*) *F:* vomir, rendre (*c*) lever haut, mettre haut (les mains) (*d*) construire (une maison) à la hâte (*e*) renoncer à, abandonner (un projet); **to t. everything up**, tout plaquer; **to t. up one's job**, donner sa démission.

thrush¹ [θrʌʃ] *n Orn:* grive *f*.

thrush² *n Med:* muguet *m*.

thrust [θrʌst] 1. *n* (*a*) poussée *f*; *Mil:* poussée (*b*) coup *m* de pointe; *Fenc:* coup d'estoc; **that was a t. at you**, c'était une attaque à votre adresse (*b*) *MecE: etc:* poussée 2. *v* (*pt & pp* **thrust**) (*a*) *vtr* pousser (avec force); **to t. one's hands into one's pockets**, fourrer les mains dans ses poches; **to t. a knife into s.o.'s back**, planter un couteau dans le dos de qn; **to t. sth on s.o.**, forcer qn à accepter qch; **to t. oneself upon s.o.**, s'imposer à qn, chez qn; **to t. (one's way) through the crowd**, se frayer un chemin à travers la foule (*b*) *vi* **to t. at s.o.**, porter un coup de pointe à qn. **'thrust a'side** *vtr* repousser, écarter (qch) brusquement. **'thrust 'forward** *vtr* pousser (qn, qch) en avant; avancer, tendre, brusquement (la main).

thud [θʌd] 1. *n* bruit sourd 2. *vi* (**thudded**) tomber avec un bruit sourd; résonner sourdement.

thug [θʌg] *n* brute *f*; voyou *m*.

thumb [θʌm] 1. *n* pouce *m*; **he's all thumbs**, il est maladroit de ses mains; **to be under s.o.'s t.**, être sous la domination de qn; **she's got him right under her t.**, elle le fait marcher comme elle veut; **to stick out like a sore t.**, choquer la vue; *F:* **he gave her the thumbs up sign**, il lui a fait signe que tout allait bien; **t. index**, répertoire à onglets 2. *vtr* (*a*) **to t. through a book**, feuilleter un livre (*b*) **to t. one's nose at s.o.**, faire un pied de nez à qn (*c*) *F:* **to t. a lift**, faire de l'auto-stop, du stop. **'thumbnail** *n* ongle *m* du pouce; **t. sketch**, croquis *m* sur le vif. **'thumbprint** *n* empreinte *f* de pouce. **'thumbscrew** *n* vis *f* à oreilles, à papillon.

'thumbtack *n NAm:* (*Br* = **drawing pin**) punaise *f*.

thump [θʌmp] 1. *n* (*a*) coup sourd; cognement *m*; **to fall with a t.**, tomber lourdement (*b*) coup de poing; bourrade *f* 2. *vtr & i* bourrer (qn) de coups; taper (sur la table); cogner (à la porte); **my heart was thumping**, mon cœur battait fort. **'thumping** *a F:* **a t. great lie**, un mensonge énorme.

thunder [ˈθʌndər] 1. *n* (*a*) tonnerre *m*; **there's t. in the air**, (i) le temps est à l'orage (ii) *Fig:* l'atmosphère est orageuse (*b*) **t. of applause**, tonnerre d'applaudissements 2. *vtr & i* (*a*) tonner; **it's thundering**, il tonne; **the train thundered past**, le train est passé avec un bruit de tonnerre (*b*) **to t. (out) threats**, proférer des menaces d'une voix tonnante. **'thunderbolt** *n* 1. (coup *m* de) foudre *f* 2. nouvelle foudroyante. **'thunderclap** *n* coup *m* de tonnerre. **'thundercloud** *n* nuage orageux. **'thundering** *a* 1. tonnant; fulminant 2. *F:* **in a t. rage**, dans une colère épouvantable; **t. great lie**, mensonge énorme. **'thunderous** *a* (*of voice*) tonnant; **t. applause**, tonnerre *m* d'applaudissements. **'thunderstorm** *n* orage *m*. **'thunderstruck** *a* abasourdi, foudroyé. **'thundery** *a* orageux.

Thursday [ˈθəːzdi] *n* jeudi *m*; **Maundy T.**, jeudi saint.

thus [ðʌs] *adv* 1. ainsi; de cette façon 2. ainsi, donc 3. **t. far**, jusqu'ici; jusque-là.

thwack [θwæk] *n* coup *m*; claque *f*.

thwart¹ [θwɔːt] *n* banc *m* de nage (d'une embarcation).

thwart² *vtr* contrecarrer (qn); déjouer (une intrigue, les projets de qn); **to be thwarted**, essuyer un échec.

thy [ðai] *poss a* (**thine** *before a vowel*) *A: & Lit:* ton, *f* ta, *pl* tes.

thyme [taim] *n Bot:* thym *m*.

thyroid [ˈθairɔid] *a & n* thyroïde (*f*).

ti [tiː] *n Mus:* si *m*.

tiara [tiˈɑːrə] *n* diadème *m*.

Tibet [tiˈbet] *Prn Geog:* Tibet *m*. **Ti'betan** *a & n* tibétain, -aine.

tibia [ˈtibiə] *n* (*pl* **tibiae**) *Anat:* tibia *m*.

tic [tik] *n Med:* tic *m*.

tichy [ˈtitʃi] *a* (-ier, -iest) *F:* minuscule.

tick¹ [tik] 1. *n* (*a*) tic(-)tac *m* (d'une pendule) (*b*) *F:* moment *m*, instant *m*; **half a t.!** un instant! une seconde! **he'll do it in two ticks**, il fera ça en moins de rien (*c*) marque *f*, pointage *m*, coche *f*; **to put a t. against a name**, cocher un nom 2. *v* (*a*) *vi* faire tic(-)tac; **the minutes are ticking by**, le temps passe; *F:* **I'd like to know what makes him t.**, je voudrais bien savoir ce qui le pousse (*b*) *vtr* cocher (un nom); marquer (une réponse) juste. **'ticker** *n* 1. *F:* (*a*) montre *f* (*b*) cœur *m* 2. **t. tape**, (i) bande *f* (de téléimprimeur) (ii) *US:* (*at parades*) = serpentin *m*. **'ticking¹** *n* 1. tic(-)tac *m* (d'une pendule) 2. *F:* **t. off**, réprimande *f*; **to give s.o. a t. o.**, passer un savon à qn. **'tick 'off** *vtr* 1. cocher (un nom) 2. *F:* attraper (qn); passer un savon à qn. **'tick 'over** *vi Aut:* (*of engine*) tourner au ralenti; **my business is just ticking over**, mes affaires vont doucement. **'tick-'tock** *n* tic(-)tac *m*.

tick² *n Arach:* tique *f*.

tick³ *n F:* crédit *m*; **to buy sth on t.**, acheter qch à crédit.

ticket [ˈtikit] 1. *n* (*a*) (*NAm:* = **transportation**) billet *m* (de chemin de fer, de théâtre); ticket *m* (de métro, d'autobus); titre *m* de transport; **left-luggage t.**,

cloakroom t., bulletin *m* de consigne; **platform t.**, ticket de quai; **t. collector**, contrôleur, -euse (de billets); **season t.**, carte *f* d'abonnement; **season t. holder**, abonné(e); **single t.**, (billet d')aller *m*; **return t.**, (billet d')aller et retour (*b*) *Aut:* **(parking) t.**, papillon *m*, P.V. *m*; **to get a t.**, attraper un P.V. (*b*) *Com:* **(price) t.**, étiquette *f* (*c*) *Pol: US:* liste *f* des candidats; *F:* **the democratic t.**, le programme du parti démocrate (*d*) *P:* **that's the t.!** voilà qui fera l'affaire! à la bonne heure! **2.** *vtr* (**ticketed**) étiqueter (des marchandises).

ticking² ['tikiŋ] *n* toile *f* à matelas.

tickle ['tikl] **1.** *n* chatouillement *m* **2.** *v* (*a*) *vtr* chatouiller; (*of food*) **to t. the palate**, chatouiller le palais; **to t. s.o.'s fancy**, amuser qn; **to be tickled to death, tickled pink**, **at**, **by**, **sth**, (i) s'amuser beaucoup de qch (ii) être ravi de qch (*b*) *vi* **my hand tickles**, la main me démange. **'tickling** **1.** *a* qui chatouille **2.** *n* chatouillement *m.* **'ticklish, 'tickly** *a* (**-ier**, **-iest**) **1.** chatouilleux; (toux) d'irritation; (couverture) qui chatouille **2.** (*of pers*) susceptible; (*of task, subject*)' délicat; **he's in a t. situation**, il est dans une situation délicate.

tiddler ['tidlər] *n* *F:* (*a*) petit poisson; *esp* épinoche *f* (*b*) petit enfant; mioche *mf.* **'tiddl(e)y¹** *a* (**-ier**, **-iest**) minuscule.

tiddl(e)y² ['tidli] *a* (**-ier**, **-iest**) *F:* ivre, pompette.

tiddlywinks ['tidliwiŋks] *n* jeu *m* de puce.

tide [taid] **1.** *n* marée *f*; **high, low**, **t.**, marée haute, basse; **against the t.**, à contre-marée; *Fig:* à contre-courant; **to go with the t.**, suivre le courant; **the t. has turned**, la chance a tourné **2.** *vtr* **to t. (s.o.) over**, aider (qn) à surmonter une difficulté; **that will t. us over**, cela nous dépannera. **'tidal** *a* **1.** **t. wave**, (i) raz *m* de marée (ii) vague *f* (d'enthousiasme) **2.** **t. river**, fleuve à marée. **'tidemark** *n* **1.** (*a*) ligne *f* de marée haute (*b*) laisse *f* de haute mer **2.** *F:* ligne de crasse (dans une baignoire). **'tideway** *n* lit *m* de la marée.

tidy ['taidi] **I.** *a* (**-ier**, **-iest**) **1.** (*a*) (*of room*) bien rangé, en (bon) ordre; **clean and t. room**, chambre propre et nette (*b*) (*of pers*) ordonné; qui a de l'ordre **2.** *F:* assez bon; passable; **a t. sum**, une somme rondelette. **II.** *n* vide-poches *m* *inv*; **sink t.**, coin *m* d'évier. **III.** *vtr* ranger; mettre de l'ordre dans (une chambre); **to t. oneself (up)**, faire un brin de toilette; **to t. one's hair**, s'arranger les cheveux; **to t. away**, ranger (qch); **to t. (things) up**, ranger; tout remettre en place. **'tidily** *adv* proprement; soigneusement; avec soin. **'tidiness** *n* bon ordre, propreté *f*; (*of pers*) sens de l'ordre.

tie [tai] **I.** *n* **1.** lien *m*; attache *f*; **family ties**, liens de famille; **ties of friendship**, liens d'amitié **2.** lacet *m* (de chaussure) **3.** *Cl:* cravate *f*; **bow t.**, nœud *m* papillon; (*on invitation*) **black t.** = smoking *m* **4.** *Mus:* liaison *f* **5.** (*a*) *Sp:* match *m*, course *f*, à égalité; **t. breaker**, match de barrage (*b*) *Fb:* **cup t.** = match de championnat (*c*) **the election has ended in a t.**, les candidats ont obtenu un nombre égal de suffrages. **II.** *v* (**tied**; **tying**) **1.** *vtr* (*a*) attacher; lier (qn à qch); *Fig:* **to t. s.o.'s hands**, lier les mains à qn; *Fig:* **to be tied hand and foot**, avoir les mains liées; **to be tied to one's bed**, être cloué au lit (*b*) lier, nouer (un lacet, une ficelle); faire (un nœud, sa cravate) (*c*) *Mus:* lier (deux notes) **2.** *vi* *Sp: etc:* être, arriver, à égalité (**with**, avec); (*of candidates*) obtenir un nombre égal de suffrages; *Sch:* **to t. for first**

place, être premier ex æquo (**with**, avec). **'tie 'back** *vtr* retenir (les cheveux) en arrière. **'tie 'down** *vtr* (*a*) immobiliser (qn); assujettir (qch) (*b*) assujettir (qn) à certaines conditions; **tied down to one's job**, assujetti à ses fonctions. **'tie 'in** *vi* (*a*) se rattacher (à qch) (*b*) avoir un rapport (avec qch). **'tie-in** *n* rapport *m*; association *f.* **'tie 'on** *vtr* attacher (avec une ficelle). **'tie-on a t.-on label**, étiquette *f* à œillet(s). **'tiepin** *n* épingle *f* de cravate. **'tie 'up** *vtr* **1.** (*a*) ficeler (un paquet); se nouer (les cheveux); bander, panser (un bras blessé) (*b*) attacher (un chien); ligoter (qn) (*c*) *vtr* & *i* amarrer (un bateau); immobiliser (ses capitaux) (*d*) *F:* **just now I'm tied up**, pour l'instant je suis très occupé **2.** *vi* avoir des rapports (avec qch); **we are tied up with another firm**, nous avons des accords avec une autre maison; **that ties up with what I was saying**, cela rejoint ce que je disais. **'tie-up** *n* association *f*, rapport *m*, lien *m* (entre deux choses).

tier [tiər] *n* rangée *f* (de sièges); étage *m*; **in tiers**, par étages; en gradins; **to rise in tiers**, s'étager; **four-t. cake**, pièce montée à quatre étages.

tiff [tif] *n* petite querelle; *F:* prise *f* de bec.

tiger ['taigər] *n* tigre *m*; *Bot:* **t. lily**, lis tigré; *Ent:* **t. moth**, écaille *f* **'tigress** *n* tigresse *f.*

tight [tait] **I.** *a* **1.** (*of partition*) imperméable (à l'eau, à l'air); (*of ship, container*) étanche; (*of joint*) hermétique **2.** (*a*) (*of cord*) raide, tendu; **to draw a cord t.**, serrer un cordon; **to keep a t. hold over s.o.**, tenir qn serré (*b*) (*of clothes*) **(skin) t.**, collant; **too t.**, étriqué; trop juste; **t. shoes**, chaussures trop étroites; *F:* **to be in a t. corner**, être dans une mauvaise passe (*c*) (*of furniture, mortise*) bien ajusté; (*of knot, screw*) serré (*d*) **t. schedule**, horaire minuté; **I work to a very t. schedule**, mon temps est très minuté **3.** (*of money, credit*) resserré, rare; *F:* **money's a bit t. with me**, je suis à court d'argent **4.** *F:* ivre, soûl; **to get t.**, prendre une cuite. **II.** *adv* **1.** **shut t.**, hermétiquement clos; (yeux) bien fermés **2.** (*a*) fortement, fermement; **to hold sth t.**, tenir qch serré; **hold t.!** tenez bon! **to screw a nut t.**, serrer un écrou à bloc (*b*) étroitement; **to squeeze sth t.**, serrer qch étroitement. **'tighten** *v* **1.** *vtr* (*a*) serrer, resserrer (une vis, un nœud); tendre, raidir (un cordage); *Fig:* **to t. one's belt**, se serrer la ceinture (*b*) **to t. (up) restrictions**, renforcer des restrictions **2.** *vi* (*a*) se (res)serrer (*b*) (*of cable*) devenir tendu; se tendre; raidir. **tight'fisted** *a* *F:* avare, radin. **tight-'fitting** *a* (*a*) (vêtement) collant (*b*) (*of lid*) qui ferme bien; (*of door*) qui ferme hermétiquement. **'tightly** *adv* = **tight II.** **'tightness** *n* (*a*) raideur *f* (*b*) étroitesse *f* (d'un vêtement) (*c*) *Med:* oppression *f* (de la poitrine). **'tightrope** *n* corde raide; **t. walker**, funambule *mf.* **'tights** *npl* *Cl:* collant *m.*

tile [tail] **1.** *n* (*a*) tuile *f* (de toiture); *F:* **to spend a night on the tiles**, traîner dehors toute la nuit (*b*) carreau *m* **2.** *vtr* (*a*) couvrir de tuiles, en tuiles (*b*) carreler (un plancher). **tiled** *a* **1.** (toit) de, en, tuiles **2.** (pavage) carrelé, en carreaux; (paroi) à carreaux vernissés. **'tiling** *n* **1.** (*a*) pose *f* des tuiles (*b*) carrelage *m* **2.** *coll* (*a*) couverture *f* en tuiles (*b*) carreaux *mpl*, carrelage.

till¹ [til] *vtr* labourer, cultiver (un champ). **'tilling** *n* labour *m*, culture *f.*

till² *n* caisse *f*; tiroir-caisse *m*; **t. money**, encaisse *f*; *F:* **to be caught with one's hand in the t.**, être surpris la main dans le sac.

till[3] 1. *prep* (a) jusqu'à; **t. now, t. then,** jusqu'ici, jusque-là; **from morning t. night,** du matin au soir (b) **not t. Monday,** pas avant lundi; **he won't come t. after dinner,** il ne viendra qu'après le dîner 2. *conj* (a) jusqu'à ce que + *sub:* **t. the doors are shut,** jusqu'à ce que les portes soient fermées; **to laugh t. one cries,** rire aux larmes (b) **he won't come t. he's invited,** il ne viendra que lorsqu'il qu'il aura été invité.

tiller ['tilər] *n Nau:* barre franche (de direction).

tilt [tilt] 1. *n* (a) inclinaison *f,* pente *f* (b) **(at) full t.,** à fond de train; **to run full t. into sth,** donner en plein contre qch 2. *v* (a) *vi* **to t. (up),** s'incliner; pencher; **to t. backwards, forwards,** incliner vers l'arrière, vers l'avant; **to t. over,** (i) se pencher, s'incliner (ii) *(of table)* se renverser (b) *vtr* pencher, incliner; rabattre (son chapeau) **(over one's eyes,** sur les yeux); **to t. one's chair back,** se balancer sur sa chaise.

timber ['timbər] *n* 1. (a) bois *m* d'œuvre; **t. merchant,** marchand de bois (b) **standing t.,** bois sur pied; arbre *m* de haute futaie 2. *(piece of)* **t.,** poutre *f,* madrier *m.* '**timbered** *a* (maison) en bois; *(of land)* boisé; **half t.,** à colombage. '**timberyard** *n* chantier *m* de bois.

time [taim] I. *n* 1. temps *m;* **t. will tell,** qui vivra verra; **in (the course of) t., as t. goes on, by,** avec le temps; à la longue; **race against t.,** course contre la montre 2. (a) **in a short t.,** en peu de temps; sous peu; **in three weeks' t.,** dans trois semaines; **in no t. (at all),** en un rien de temps, en moins de rien; **within the required t.,** dans le délai prescrit; **to take a long t. over sth,** mettre longtemps à faire qch; **for some t. (to come),** pendant quelque temps; **for some t. (past),** depuis quelque temps; **I haven't seen him for a long t.,** voilà longtemps que je ne l'ai vu; **a short t. after,** peu (de temps) après; **after a t.,** au bout d'un certain temps; **after a long t.,** longtemps après; **he's taking a long t.!** il prend son temps! **all the t.,** tout le temps; **all this t.,** pendant tout ce temps; *Sp:* **to keep the t.,** chronométrer; *Cin:* **running t.,** durée *f* de projection (b) *El:* **t. switch,** minuterie *f;* **t. bomb,** bombe à retardement; *Phot:* **t. exposure,** pose *f* 3. (a) **my t. is my own,** je suis libre de mon temps; **when I have the t.,** quand j'aurais le temps; **to have t. on one's hands,** avoir du temps à perdre; *F:* **I've no t. for him,** il m'embête; **to play for t.,** chercher à gagner du temps; **you've plenty,** *F:* **heaps, of t.,** vous avez tout le temps qu'il vous faut; **there's no t. to lose,** il n'y a pas de temps à perdre; **to waste t.,** perdre du temps; **to make up for lost t.,** rattraper le temps perdu; **to lose no t. in doing sth,** s'empresser de faire qch; **to make t.,** trouver le temps **(to do sth,** pour faire qch); **it takes t.,** cela prend du temps; **to take one's t. over sth,** mettre le temps (qu'il faut) à faire qch; **take your t.,** prenez votre temps; **time's up!** c'est l'heure! *(in pub)* **gentlemen, please!** on ferme! *Fb: etc:* **to play extra t.,** jouer les prolongations *fpl* (b) *F:* **to do t.,** faire de la prison; **if I had my t. over again,** si j'avais à recommencer ma vie 4. (a) époque *f;* **sign of the times,** un signe des temps; **in former times,** autrefois; dans le temps; **in times to come,** à l'avenir; **in our times,** de nos jours (b) **to be ahead of one's t.,** être en avance sur son temps; **to move with the times,** être à la page; **to be behind the times,** être en retard sur son siècle 5. (a) moment *m;* **I was away at the t.,** j'étais absent à ce moment-là, à cette époque; **at that t.,** en ce temps-là;

at the present t., à l'heure qu'il est; actuellement; à présent; **at a given t.,** à un moment donné; **at the t. fixed,** à l'heure convenue; **at one t. it was different,** autrefois il n'en était pas ainsi; **at no t.,** jamais; à aucun moment; **at times,** parfois; quelquefois; **at all times,** (i) toujours (ii) à n'importe quel moment; **between times,** entre temps; **at various times,** à diverses reprises; **(at) any t. (you like),** n'importe quand; quand vous voudrez; **if at any t.,** si à l'occasion; **he may turn up at any t.,** il peut arriver d'un moment à l'autre; **some t. or other,** un jour ou l'autre; **some t. next month,** dans le courant du mois prochain; **this t. tomorrow,** demain à la même heure; **by the t. I got there,** le temps que j'arrive; **from t. to t.,** de temps en temps; **from that t. (onwards),** dès lors; à partir de ce moment-là; **at the right t.,** en temps utile; **we shall see when the t. comes,** nous verrons (cela) le moment venu; **now's the t. to,** c'est le (bon) moment de; **to choose one's t.,** choisir son heure; **this is no t., this is not the t. to,** ce n'est pas le moment de (b) **all in good t.,** chaque chose en son temps; **in his own good t.,** à son heure 6. (a) heure *f;* **summer t.,** l'heure d'été; **Greenwich Mean T.,** l'heure de Greenwich; **(standard) t. belt, t. zone,** fuseau *m* horaire (b) **what's the t.?** quelle heure est-il? **what t. do you make it?** quelle heure avez-vous? **to look at the t.,** regarder sa montre; **watch that keeps (good) t., that loses t.,** montre qui est toujours à l'heure, qui retarde; *Tp:* **t. signal,** signal horaire; *F:* **to pass the t. of day with s.o.,** échanger quelques mots avec qn; **at this t. of day,** à cette heure de la journée (c) **dinner t.,** l'heure du dîner; **on t.,** à l'heure; **to be ahead of, behind, t.,** être en avance, en retard; **I was just in t.,** je suis arrivé juste à temps; **in good t.,** (i) à temps (ii) de bonne heure; **it's t. we left,** il est temps de partir; *F:* **it's high t.! and about t. too!** c'est pas trop tôt! (d) **t. of the year,** époque de l'année; saison *f;* **at my t. of life,** à mon âge (e) **to die before one's t.,** mourir avant l'âge, prématurément; **his t. had not yet come,** son heure n'était pas encore venue 7. *Ind:* (a) **t. clock,** pendule de pointage; **t. sheet,** feuille de présence (b) **t. and motion study,** étude des temps et mouvements 8. *F:* **we had a good t.,** on s'est bien amusé; **to have a bad t., a rough t. (of it),** (i) en voir de dures (ii) passer un mauvais quart d'heure; **to give s.o. a rough t.,** en faire voir de dures à qn 9. fois *f;* **next t.,** la prochaine fois; **several times over,** (faire qch) à plusieurs reprises; plusieurs fois; **four times running,** quatre fois de suite; **t. and t. again, t. after t.,** à maintes reprises; maintes et maintes fois; **he gets it every t.,** il réussit à chaque coup; **two things at a t.,** deux choses à la fois; **to run upstairs four at a t.,** monter l'escalier quatre à quatre; **for weeks at a t.,** des semaines durant; **£6 a t.,** £6 chaque fois; **four times as big,** quatre fois plus grand 10. *adv phr* (a) **at the same t.,** en même temps; (faire deux choses) à la fois (b) **at the same t. you mustn't forget that,** d'autre part il ne faut pas oublier que 11. (a) *Mus:* **t. value,** valeur *f* (d'une note) (b) *Mus:* mesure *f;* **triple t.,** mesure à trois temps; **t. signature,** fraction *f* indiquant la mesure; **to beat t.,** battre la mesure; **in strict t.,** en mesure; **to keep t.,** jouer, chanter, en mesure (c) *Mus:* tempo *m; Gym:* **in quick t.,** au pas accéléré 12. *F:* **the big t.,** le haut de l'échelle; **big-t. operator,** gros trafiquant; **small-t. crook,** petit escroc. II. *vtr* 1. (a) fixer l'heure de (qch)

(b) **to t. a blow, a remark,** choisir le moment de porter un coup, de placer un mot; (of remark) **well timed,** opportun, à propos; **ill timed,** inopportun, mal à propos (c) régler (une horloge) (d) Aut: etc: régler (l'allumage); mettre (le moteur) au point **2.** calculer la durée de (qch) **3.** (a) **to t. how long it takes s.o. to do sth,** mesurer le temps que quelqu'un met à faire qch (b) Sp: chronométrer (une course); prendre le temps (d'un coureur); **timed race,** course contre la montre (c) Mil: minuter (une opération). **'time-con-'suming** a qui prend beaucoup de temps; long. **'time-'honoured** a consacré (par l'usage). **'timekeeper** n **1.** Sp: chronométreur m **2. to be a good t.,** être toujours à l'heure. **'time-lag** n décalage m. **'timeless** a éternel. **'timely** a opportun, à propos. **'timepiece** n pendule f; montre f. **'timer** n (a) Aut: distributeur m d'allumage (b) compte-minutes m inv; sablier m. **'time(-)'saving 1.** a qui permet de gagner du temps **2.** n gain m de temps. **'timeserver** n opportuniste mf. **'timetable** n **1.** horaire m; indicateur m (des chemins de fer) **2.** Sch: emploi m du temps. **'timework** n Ind: travail m à l'heure. **'timing** n **1.** Aut: etc: (a) réglage m (de l'allumage) (b) distribution f **2.** (a) Sp: chronométrage m (b) minutage m (d'une opération) **3.** (a) **error of t.,** mauvais calcul; erreur de jugement (b) rythme m (d'un mouvement) **4. t. mechanism,** mouvement d'horlogerie (d'une bombe); El: minuteur m.

timid ['timid] a timide, peureux, craintif. **ti'midity** n timidité f. **'timidly** adv timidement, craintivement.

timorous ['timərəs] a timoré, timide.

timpani ['timpəni] npl Mus: timbales fpl.

tin [tin] **1.** n (a) étain m (b) **t. (plate),** fer-blanc m; **t. mug,** timbale f; Mil: etc: **t. hat,** casque m; **t. whistle,** flageolet m (c) tôle f (d) **cake t.,** moule m à gâteaux; tourtière f (e) boîte f (de conserves); **t. of sardines,** boîte de sardines; **t. opener,** ouvre-boîtes m inv **2.** vtr **(tinned)** (a) étamer (b) mettre (des sardines) en conserve. **'tinfoil** n papier m d'aluminium. **'tinned** a en conserve, en boîte; **t. foods,** conserves fpl. **'tinny** a (goût) métallique; (son) grêle, fêlé. **'tinplate** n fer-blanc m. **'tinpot** a F: qui ne vaut pas grand-chose. **'tintack** n semence f; clou m de tapissier.

tinder ['tindər] n mèche f de briquet; amadou m.

ting-a-ling ['tiŋəliŋ] n & adv drelin drelin (m).

tinge [tin(d)ʒ] **1.** n teinte f, nuance f **2.** vtr teinter, nuancer.

tingle ['tiŋgl] **1.** n (a) **I have a t. in my ears,** j'ai les oreilles qui tintent (b) picotement m, fourmillement m **2.** vi (a) (of ears) tinter (b) picoter; **my hand tingles,** j'ai des picotements dans la main; **her cheeks tingled with the cold,** le froid lui piquait les joues. **'tingling 1.** a (a) (oreilles) qui tintent (b) **t. sensation,** picotement **2.** n = **tingle 1.**

tinker ['tiŋkər] **1.** n (a) rétameur, étameur, ambulant (b) romanichel **2.** vi **to t. (about),** bricoler; **to t. with (sth),** retaper, rafistoler (une machine). **'tinkering** n bricolage m, rafistolage m.

tinkle ['tiŋkl] **1.** n tintement m; F: **I'll give you a t.,** je vous passerai un coup de fil **2.** (a) vi tinter (b) vtr faire tinter. **'tinkling** n tintement m.

tinsel ['tins(ə)l] n (a) (decoration) cheveux mpl d'ange;

guirlande f d'arbre de Noël (b) Fig: clinquant m.

tint [tint] **1.** n teinte f, nuance f **2.** vtr teinter, colorer; **to get one's hair tinted,** se faire faire un shampooing colorant.

tiny ['taini] a minuscule; **a t. bit,** un tout petit peu.

tip¹ [tip] **1.** n (a) bout m, extrémité f, pointe f; **to have sth on the t. of one's tongue,** avoir qch sur le bout de la langue; **asparagus tips,** pointes d'asperge (b) (of walking stick) bout ferré, embout m; (of billiard cue) procédé m **2.** vtr **(tipped)** mettre un bout à (qch); emboutir (une canne). **'tipped** a gold-t., à bout doré; **(filter) t. cigarettes,** cigarettes à bout filtre. **'tiptoe 1.** n & adv (on) t., sur la pointe des pieds **2.** vi marcher sur la pointe des pieds; **to t. in, out,** entrer, sortir, sur la pointe des pieds. **'tiptop** a de premier ordre; excellent.

tip² I. n **1.** pente f, inclinaison f **2.** pourboire m; **the t. is included,** le service est compris **3.** Turf: etc: tuyau m; **if you take my t.,** si vous voulez me croire; **to give s.o. a t.,** tuyauter, renseigner, qn **4. rubbish t.,** décharge f publique; dépotoir m. **II.** v **(tipped)** **1.** vtr (a) **to t. over,** renverser (qch); chavirer (un canot); **to t. up,** relever (un strapontin); faire basculer (une charrette); **to t. out,** déverser, décharger; **to t. sth into sth,** verser qch dans qch; **to t. rubbish,** déposer des ordures (b) faire pencher, faire incliner (c) donner un pourboire à (qn) (d) Turf: tuyauter (qn); donner un tuyau à (qn); **to t. a horse to win,** pronostiquer qu'un cheval sera le gagnant; F: **he's widely tipped for the job,** on lui donne toutes les chances pour le poste; **to t. s.o. off,** (i) donner un tuyau à qn (ii) avertir qn **2.** vi **to t. over,** se renverser, basculer; (of boat) chavirer; (of plank) **to t. up,** se soulever, basculer. **'tipper** n **t.** (truck, lorry), camion m à benne (basculante). **'tipping** n **1.** (a) inclinaison f (b) **t. over,** renversement m; chavirement m (d'un canot) (c) basculage m (d) versage m, déversement m; PN: no t., défense de déposer des ordures **2.** pourboires mpl; distribution f de pourboires **3.** Rac: tuyautage m. **'tip-off** n tuyau m; **to give s.o. a t.-o.,** prévenir, renseigner, qn. **'tipster** n Turf: pronostiqueur m. **'tip-up** a (charrette) à bascule; **t.-up seat,** strapontin m.

tipple ['tipl] F: **1.** n boisson f alcoolisée; **what's your t.?** qu'est-ce que vous voulez boire? **2.** vi picoler. **'tippler** n picoleur, -euse.

tipsy ['tipsi] a (-ier, -iest) gris, ivre; F: pompette; **to get t.,** se griser. **'tipsiness** n (légère) ivresse.

tirade [tai'reid] n tirade f; diatribe f (against, contre).

tire¹ ['taiər] **1.** vtr fatiguer, lasser; **to t. s.o. out,** (i) épuiser, briser, qn de fatigue (ii) excéder qn **2.** vi se fatiguer, se lasser (of s.o., sth, de qn, qch); **he never tires of telling me,** il ne se lasse pas de me le dire. **'tired** a (a) fatigué; las; **to get t.,** se fatiguer; **she was t. out,** elle n'en pouvait plus de fatigue; F: **you make me t.,** tu m'embêtes (b) **to be t. of sth,** être las de qch; en avoir assez de qch; **t. of arguing, he agreed,** de guerre lasse, il a donné son consentement. **'tiredness** n lassitude f, fatigue f. **'tireless** a inlassable, infatigable. **'tirelessly** adv inlassablement, infatigablement. **'tiresome** a **1.** fatigant; (discours) ennuyeux **2.** exaspérant; (of child) assommant; **how t.!** que c'est assommant! **'tiring** a fatigant.

tire² n NAm: = **tyre.**

tissue ['tisju:] n **1.** (a) tissu m; Fig: **t. of lies,** tissu de mensonges (b) mouchoir m en papier; **t. paper,** papier de soie 2. *Biol:* tissu (nerveux, musculaire).

tit[1] [tit] n *Orn: (also* **titmouse)** mésange f.

tit[2] n **t. for tat,** donnant donnant; œil pour œil, dent pour dent; **to give s.o. t. for tat,** rendre à qn la pareille.

tit[3] n P: (a) bout m de sein (b) sein m, nichon.

titanic [tai'tænik] a titanesque.

titbit ['titbit] n friandise f.

titillate ['titileit] vtr titiller, chatouiller. **titi'llation** n titillation f, chatouillement m.

title ['taitl] n 1. (a) titre m (b) **t. (of nobility),** titre de noblesse; **to have a t.,** être titré (c) *Sp:* **to hold the t.,** détenir le titre (de champion); **t. holder,** détenteur, -trice, du titre 2. titre (d'un livre); **t. page,** (page de) titre; *Th:* **t. rôle,** rôle qui donne le titre à la pièce; *Cin:* **credit titles,** générique m 3. (a) **t. to property,** titre de propriété (b) **t. (deed),** titre (constitutif) de propriété; acte m. **'titled** a titré.

titter ['titər] 1. n (a) rire étouffé (b) petit rire nerveux, bête 2 vi (a) avoir un petit rire étouffé (b) rire nerveusement, bêtement.

tittle-tattle ['titltætl] n potins mpl, cancans mpl, commérages mpl.

titular ['titjulər] a titulaire; (of function) nominal.

tizzy ['tizi] n (pl tizzies) **to be in a t.,** être dans tous ses états; ne pas savoir où donner de la tête.

TNT abbr *Exp:* trinitrotoluene.

to [tu:; unstressed before consonant tə; unstressed before vowel tu] I. prep a 1. (a) **what school do you go to?** à quelle école allez-vous? **I'm off to Paris,** je pars pour Paris; **he went to France, to Japan, to the U.S.A.,** il est allé en France, au Japon, aux États-Unis; **she came home to her family,** elle est rentrée auprès de sa famille; **I'm going to the grocer's,** je vais chez l'épicier; **from town to town,** de ville en ville; **flights to America,** vols à destination de l'Amérique (b) **the road to London,** la route de Londres; **journey to Paris,** voyage à Paris; **the shortest way to the station,** le plus court chemin pour aller à la gare; **to bed!** (i) je vais me coucher (ii) allez vous coucher! 2. vers, à; **to the east,** vers l'est; **to the right,** à droite; *PN:* **to the trains,** accès m aux quais 3. elbow to elbow, coude à coude; **I told him so to his face,** je le lui ai dit en face; **to clasp s.o. to one's heart,** serrer qn sur son cœur; **to fall to the ground,** tomber à, par, terre 4. (a) **from morning to night,** du matin au soir; **from day to day,** de jour en jour; **d'un jour à l'autre** (b) **ten (minutes) to six,** six heures moins dix 5. (a) **soaked to the skin,** trempé jusqu'aux os; **to this day,** jusqu'à ce jour; **moved to tears,** ému jusqu'aux larmes; **fight to the death,** bataille à mort (b) **generous to a fault,** généreux à l'excès; **accurate to a millimetre,** exact à un millimètre près; **a year to the day,** un an jour pour jour 6. (a) **to this end,** à cet effet, dans ce but; **to sit down to dinner,** se mettre à table pour dîner; **to come to s.o.'s help,** venir à l'aide de qn (b) **to my despair,** à mon grand désespoir; **to everyone's surprise,** à la surprise de tous 7. en; **to run to seed,** monter en graine; **to put to flight,** mettre en fuite; **to pull to pieces,** mettre en pièces 8. **to sing sth to the tune of,** chanter qch sur l'air de 9. **heir to an estate,** héritier d'une propriété; **secretary to the manager,** secrétaire du directeur; **ambassador to the king,** ambassadeur auprès du roi; **apprentice to a joiner,** apprenti chez un menuisier; **the key to the door,**

la clef de la porte 10. (a) **compared to this one,** comparé à celui-ci; **that's nothing to what I've seen,** cela n'est rien à côté de ce que j'ai vu (b) **six votes to four,** six voix contre quatre; **three (goals) to two,** trois (buts) à deux; **to bet ten to one,** parier dix contre un 11. **to all appearances,** selon les apparences; **to write to s.o.'s dictation,** écrire sous la dictée de qn; **not to my taste,** pas à mon goût; **to the best of my recollection,** autant que je m'en souvienne 12. **to drink to s.o.,** boire à la santé de qn 13. **what did he say to my suggestion?** qu'est-ce qu'il a dit de ma proposition? **that's all there is to it,** c'est tout ce qu'il y a à dire; c'est tout; **there's nothing to it,** c'est simple comme bonjour; ce n'est rien 14. (a) **to give sth to s.o.,** donner qch à qn; **what's that to you?** qu'est-ce que cela vous fait? **to keep sth to oneself,** garder qch pour soi (b) envers, pour; **he has been a father to me,** il a été comme un père pour moi (c) **known to the ancients,** connu des anciens; **used to doing sth,** accoutumé à faire qch. II. (with the inf) 1. (a) pour; **he came to help me,** il est venu (pour) m'aider; **so to speak,** pour ainsi dire (b) **happy to do it,** heureux de le faire; **ready to listen,** prêt à écouter; **old enough to go to school,** d'âge à aller à l'école; **good to eat,** bon à manger; **too hot to drink,** trop chaud pour qu'on puisse le boire (c) **to look at her you wouldn't imagine that,** à la voir on ne s'imaginerait pas que; **he woke to find the lamp still burning,** en s'éveillant il trouva la lampe encore allumée; **he left the house never to return,** il quitta la maison pour n'y plus revenir 2. (a) **to have a great deal to do,** avoir beaucoup à faire; **there was not a sound to be heard,** on n'entendait pas le moindre bruit; **nothing to speak of,** rien qui vaille la peine d'en parler; **the first to complain,** le premier à se plaindre (b) **tendency to do sth,** tendance à faire qch; **this is the time to do it,** c'est le moment de le faire 3. (inf used as noun) **to lie is shameful,** il est honteux de mentir; **it's better to do nothing,** il vaut mieux ne rien faire; **to learn to do sth,** apprendre à faire qch 4. (inf in finite clause) **I want him to do it,** je veux qu'il le fasse; **you'd like it to be true,** vous voudriez bien que cela soit vrai 5. **fifty employees are to go,** cinquante employés vont être licenciés 6. **I didn't want to go but I had to,** je ne voulais pas y aller mais il a bien fallu; **you ought to,** vous devriez le faire; **I want to,** je voudrais bien; j'ai envie de le faire. III. adv (stressed) 1. (a) **to come to,** reprendre connaissance (b) **to pull the door to,** fermer la porte 2. **to go to and fro,** aller et venir; faire la navette; **movement to and fro,** (mouvement de) va-et-vient m inv. **to-'do** n remue-ménage m; **what a to-do!** quelle affaire! quelle histoire! **'toing and 'froing** n va-et-vient m inv.

toad [toud] n 1. (a) crapaud m (b) F: sale type m 2. *Cu:* **t. in the hole,** saucisses cuites au four dans de la pâte à crêpes. **'toadstool** n champignon m, esp champignon vénéneux. **'toady** 1. n flagorneur, -euse 2. vi **t. to s.o.,** flagorner qn. **'toadying** n flagornerie f.

toast [toust] 1. n (a) pain grillé, toast m; **piece of toast,** toast, rôtie f; **t. rack,** porte-toast m inv; **anchovies on t.,** anchois sur canapé (b) toast; to give, propose, a t., porter un toast à qn; boire à la santé de qn 2. v (a) vtr & i rôtir, griller (b) vtr porter un toast à (qn); boire à la santé de (qn). **'toaster** n grille-pain m inv.

tobacco [tə'bækou] n (pl tobaccos) tabac m; **t. pouch,** blague à tabac. **to'bacconist** n marchand m de tabac; **tobacconist's (shop)**, bureau *m* de tabac.

toboggan [tə'bɔgən] **1.** *n* toboggan *m*, luge *f*; **t. run**, piste de toboggan **2.** *vi* faire du toboggan, de la luge.

tocsin ['tɔksin] *n* tocsin *m*.

today [tə'dei] *adv & n* aujourd'hui (*m*); **t. week**, d'aujourd'hui en huit; **today's paper**, le journal d'aujourd'hui; *Fig:* **here t. and gone tomorrow**, ça va, ça vient; **the young people of t.**, les jeunes d'aujourd'hui.

toddle ['tɔdl] **1.** *n* pas chancelant (d'un enfant) **2.** *vi* marcher à petits pas (chancelants); trottiner; **to t. along**, suivre son petit bonhomme de chemin. '**toddler** *n* enfant *mf* qui commence à marcher; **the toddlers**, les tout petits.

toddy ['tɔdi] *n* (*pl* **toddies**) grog chaud.

toe [tou] **1.** *n* (*a*) orteil *m*; doigt *m* de pied; **big t.**, gros orteil; **from top to t.**, de la tête aux pieds; **to be on one's toes**, être alerte; **to tread on s.o.'s toes**, marcher sur les pieds de qn (*b*) bout *m*, pointe *f* (de chaussure) **2.** *vtr Fig:* **to t. the line**, obéir; s'exécuter. '**toecap** *n* bout renforcé (de chaussure). '**toeclip** *n Cy:* cale-pied *m*. '**toenail** *n* ongle *m* d'orteil.

toffee ['tɔfi] *n* caramel *m* (au beurre); **t. apple**, pomme caramélisée; *F:* **he can't sing for t.**, il ne sait pas chanter du tout.

tog [tɔg] *vtr & i* (**togged**) *F:* **to t. (oneself) up**, s'attifer; **all togged up**, en grand tralala. **togs** *npl F:* fringues *fpl*.

together [tə'geðər] *adv* (*a*) ensemble; **to go t., to belong t.**, aller ensemble; **t. with**, avec; en même temps que (*b*) **to assemble, rassembler, réunir** (*c*) **to act t.**, agir de concert; **all t.**, tout le monde ensemble; tous à la fois; **all t. now!** tous en chœur! (*d*) **for hours t.**, des heures durant; **for months t.**, pendant des mois entiers. **to'getherness** *n* solidarité *f*.

toggle ['tɔgl] *n Cl:* olive *f*, bouton *m* (de duffel-coat).

toil [tɔil] **1.** *n* travail dur, pénible; labeur *m*, peine *f* **2.** *vi* travailler, peiner; se donner du mal; **to t. up a hill**, gravir péniblement une colline.

toilet ['tɔilit] *n* **1.** toilette *f*; **t. case**, trousse, nécessaire, de toilette; **t. soap**, savon de toilette **2.** (*lavatory*) toilettes *fpl*, cabinets *mpl*; **t. paper**, papier hygiénique; **t. roll**, rouleau de papier hygiénique. '**toiletries** *npl* articles *mpl* de toilette.

token ['touk(ə)n] *n* **1.** indication *f*, marque *f*, témoignage *m*; **as a t. of respect**, en signe, comme marque, de respect; **by this t., by the same t.**, (i) donc; d'ailleurs (ii) de même; **t. strike**, grève symbolique **2.** (*a*) jeton *m* (*b*) **gift t.**, bon *m* d'achat; **book t.**, chèque-livre *m*; **record t.**, chèque-disque *m*.

told *see* **tell.**

Toledo [tə'leidou] *Prn Geog:* Tolède.

tolerate ['tɔləreit] *vtr* tolérer, supporter (la douleur); **I can't t. noise**, je ne supporte pas le bruit. '**tolerable** *a* (*a*) tolérable, supportable (*b*) passable; assez bon. '**tolerably** *adv* passablement; **I'm t. well**, je me porte assez bien. '**tolerance** *n* tolérance *f*. '**tolerant** *a* tolérant (**of**, à l'égard de). '**tolerantly** *adv* avec tolérance. **tole'ration** *n* tolérance *f*.

toll¹ [toul] *n* **1.** péage *m*; **t. bridge, t. motorway**, pont, autoroute, à péage **2.** (*of disease*) **to take its t.**, (i) faire beaucoup de victimes (ii) laisser ses traces (**of s.o.**, sur qn); **the t. of the roads**, les accidents de la route; le nombre des victimes de la route.

toll² **1.** *vtr* (*a*) tinter, sonner (une cloche) (*b*) (*of bell*) sonner (l'heure); **t. s.o.'s death**, sonner le glas pour la mort de qn **2.** *vi* (*of bell*) sonner. '**tolling** *n* (*a*) tintement *m* (de cloche) (*b*) glas *m*.

Tom [tɔm] **1.** *Prnm F:* **any T, Dick or Harry**, le premier venu; n'importe qui **2.** *n* **t. (cat)**, matou *m*.

tomahawk ['tɔməhɔːk] *n* hache *f* de guerre (des Amérindiens); tomahawk *m*.

tomato [tə'mɑːtou, *NAm:* -'mei-] *n* (*pl* **tomatoes**) tomate *f*; **t. sauce**, sauce tomate.

tomb [tuːm] *n* tombe *f*; tombeau *m*. '**tombstone** *n* pierre tombale.

tombola [tɔm'boulə] *n* (*pl* **tombolas**), tombola *f*.

tomboy ['tɔmbɔi] *nf* garçon manqué.

tome [toum] *n* tome *m*; gros volume.

tomfool ['tɔm'fuːl] *a F:* idiot, absurde; **t. scheme**, projet insensé. **tom'foolery** *n F:* bêtise(s) *f*(*pl*); niaiserie(s) *f*(*pl*).

tommygun ['tɔmigʌn] *n* mitraillette *f*.

tommyrot ['tɔmirɔt] *n F:* bêtises *fpl*.

tomorrow [tə'mɔrou] *adv & n* demain (*m*); **t. night**, demain soir; **t. week**, (de) demain en huit; **the day after t.**, après-demain.

tomtom ['tɔmtɔm] *n* tam-tam *m*.

ton [tʌn] *n* **1.** tonne *f*; **metric t.**, tonne (métrique); *F:* **there's tons of it**, il y en a des tas; **this suitcase weighs a t.**, cette valise est rudement lourde **2.** *Nau:* **register t.**, tonneau *m*; **t. of displacement**, tonne de déplacement. '**tonnage** *n Nau:* (*of ship*) jauge *f*, tonnage *m*; (*of port*) tonnage.

tonality [tou'næliti] *n* tonalité *f*. '**tonal** *a* tonal.

tone [toun] **I.** *n* **1.** son *m*, sonorité *f*; timbre *m* (de la voix, d'un instrument de musique); *Rec:* **t. control**, bouton de tonalité *f*; *Tp:* **ringing t.**, tonalité d'appel **2.** (*a*) ton *m*, voix *f*; intonation *f*; **t. of voice**, accent *m*; **don't speak to me in that t. of voice!** ne me parlez pas sur ce ton! **in low tones**, à voix basse; **in an impatient t.**, d'un ton d'impatience (*b*) *Fin:* **the t. of the market**, l'allure *f* du marché (*c*) *Med:* tonus *m* (des muscles) **3.** ton, nuance *f* (d'une couleur); *Mus:* ton. **II.** *vi* **to t. with sth**, s'harmoniser avec qch. '**tone-'deaf** *a* atteint d'amusie; **he's t. d.**, il n'a pas d'oreille. '**tone down** *vtr* adoucir, atténuer (une expression). '**toneless** *a* **t. voice**, voix blanche. '**tonelessly** *adv* d'une voix blanche.

tongs [tɔŋz] *npl* (**pair of**) **t.**, pinces *fpl*; (**fire**) **t.**, pincettes *fpl*; **sugar t.**, pince à sucre; **curling t.**, fer *m* à friser.

tongue [tʌŋ] *n* **1.** (*a*) langue *f*; **to put one's t. out at s.o.**, tirer la langue à qn; **to have one's t. hanging out**, tirer la langue; avoir soif (*b*) **to have a glib t.**, avoir la langue bien pendue; **to find one's t.**, retrouver la parole; **to keep a civil t. in one's head**, rester courtois; **t. in cheek**, ironiquement; **t. twister**, phrase difficile à prononcer **2.** langue, idiome *m* (d'un peuple) **3.** langue (de terre, de feu); patte *f*, languette *f* (de chaussure); battant *m* (de cloche). '**tongue-tied** *a* muet; interdit.

tonic ['tɔnik] **1.** *a* tonique; **t. water**, *n* **t.**, eau tonique; **gin and t.**, gin-tonic *m* **2.** *n* (*a*) *Med:* tonique *m*, fortifiant *m* (*b*) *Mus:* tonique *f*.

tonight [tə'nait] *adv & n* ce soir; cette nuit.

tonsil ['tɔns(il)] *n* **1.** amygdale *f*. **tonsi'llectomy** *n* amygdalectomie *f*. **tonsi'llitis** *n Med:* angine *f*; amygdalite *f*.

tonsure ['tɔnʃər] 1. *n* tonsure *f* 2. *vtr* tonsurer.

too [tu:] *adv* 1. trop, par trop; **t. many people,** trop de gens; **to work t. hard,** trop travailler; **t. much money,** trop d'argent; **ten pounds t. much,** dix livres de trop; **this job's t. much for me,** ce travail est au-dessus de mes forces; **I've listened to him for t. long,** je l'ai trop écouté; **I know him all t. well,** je ne le connais que trop; **you're t. kind,** vous êtes trop gentil; **he's not t. well,** il ne va pas très bien 2. aussi; également; **I want some t.,** il m'en faut également; moi aussi il m'en faut 3. d'ailleurs; de plus; en outre; 30° **in the shade, and in September t.,** 30° à l'ombre et en septembre en plus.

took *see* **take.**

tool [tu:l] 1. *n* (*a*) outil *m*; instrument *m*, ustensile *m*; **garden(ing) tools,** outils de jardinage (*b*) instrument; **to make a t. of s.o.,** se servir de qn; **he was a mere t. in their hands,** il était devenu leur créature (*c*) **you have to learn the tools of your trade,** on ne peut pratiquer un métier sans apprentissage 2. *vtr* ciseler (le cuir); **tooled leather,** cuir repoussé. **'toolbag** *n* sac *m* à outils. **'toolbox** *n* boîte *f* à outils. **'tooling** *n* ciselage *m.* **'toolkit** *n* outillage *m*; jeu *m* d'outils. **'toolmaker** *n* outilleur *m.* **'toolshed** *n* remise *f*; cabane *f* à outils.

tooth [tu:θ] *n* (*pl* **teeth** [ti:θ]) 1. dent *f*; **milk, first, t.,** dent de lait; **set of teeth, denture** *f*, dentition *f*; (**set of**) **false teeth,** dentier *m*; **t. powder,** poudre dentifrice; **to cut one's teeth,** faire, percer, ses dents; **to have a t. out,** se faire arracher une dent; **in the teeth of all opposition,** en dépit de toute opposition; **to show one's teeth,** montrer les dents; **to fight t. and nail,** se battre avec acharnement; **to get one's teeth into sth,** s'acharner à faire qch; se mettre à fond à faire qch; **to set one's teeth,** serrer les dents; *F:* **to be long in the t.,** n'être plus dans sa première jeunesse; **I'm fed up to the (back) teeth with it,** j'en ai ras le bol 2. dent (de scie); **teeth of a wheel,** denture. **'toothache** *n* mal *m*, rage *f*, de dents; **to have t.,** avoir mal aux dents. **'toothbrush** *n* brosse *f* à dents. **'toothcomb** *n* peigne fin; **to go through sth with a fine t.,** passer qch au peigne fin, au crible. **toothed** *a* **t. wheel,** roue dentée. **'toothless** *n* sans dent(s); édenté. **'toothpaste** *n* (pâte *f*) dentifrice (*m*). **'toothpick** *n* cure-dent(s) *m.* **'toothy** *a* (-ier, -iest) à dents saillantes.

tootle ['tu:tl] *vi* **to t. along,** suivre son petit bonhomme de chemin.

top¹ [tɔp] 1. *n* 1. haut *m*, sommet *m*, cime *f*, faîte *m* (d'une montagne, d'un arbre); **at the t. of the tree,** (i) en haut de l'arbre (ii) *Fig:* au premier rang de sa profession; **from t. to bottom,** de haut en bas; de fond en comble; **from t. to toe,** de la tête aux pieds; **put it on t. of the other one,** mettez-le par-dessus l'autre; **to come out on t.,** avoir le dessus; **things are getting on t. of him,** il est dépassé; il ne s'en sort pas; **on t. of the one he's already got,** en plus de celui qu'il a déjà; **on t. of it all,** et pour comble, et en plus de tout cela; **to feel on t. of the world,** se sentir en pleine forme 2. surface *f*; dessus *m* (d'une table); impériale *f* (d'un autobus); **t. of the milk,** crème (séparée du lait) 3. (*a*) dessus *m* (d'une chaussure); couvercle *m* (d'une boîte); bouchon *m* (d'une bouteille); capuchon *m* (de stylo); *F:* **to blow one's t.,** s'emporter (*b*) *Cl:* haut *m* 4. tête *f* (de page); haut (d'une page) 5. haut bout (de la table);

at the t. of the street, au bout de la rue; *Sch:* **he's t. of the form,** c'est le premier de la classe; *F:* **he's the tops!** il est champion! *F:* **to say sth off the t. of one's head,** dire qch sans en être certain 6. **to shout at the t. of one's voice,** crier à tue-tête; **to be on t. of one's form,** être en pleine forme 7. **turnip tops,** fanes *f* de navets 8. *Nau:* hune *f.* **II.** *a* 1. supérieur; du dessus, du haut, d'en haut; **t. floor, t. storey,** dernier étage; **t. hat,** (chapeau *m*) haut-de-forme *m*; **t. speed,** vitesse maximale; **at t. speed,** à toute vitesse; *F:* **to be t. dog,** avoir le dessus; *Mus:* **the t. notes,** les notes hautes; *Aut:* **t. gear,** prise (directe); quatrième (vitesse); *Adm:* **t. secret,** ultra-secret; **to feel on t. form,** se sentir en pleine forme 2. premier, principal; **t. people,** personnalités *fpl*; l'élite *f*; *Sch:* **t. pupil,** premier, -ière, de la classe; **he got the t. mark,** he came t., **in history,** il a obtenu la meilleure note en histoire; **the world's t. ten players,** les dix meilleurs joueurs du monde; *Com:* **the t. ten = palmarès** *m* (de la chanson). **III.** *vtr* (**topped**) 1. écimer, étêter (un arbre); **to t. and tail gooseberries,** éplucher des groseilles à maquereau 2. surmonter, couronner, coiffer (**with,** de); *Cu:* garnir (un dessert) (**with,** de); **and to t. it all,** et pour comble 3. dépasser, surpasser (qch); **to t. s.o. by a head,** dépasser qn de la tête 4. **to t. a list,** être à la tête d'une liste 5. *Golf:* calotter (la balle). **'topcoat** *n* 1. *Cl:* pardessus *m* 2. *Paint:* couche *f* de finition. **'top'heavy** *a* trop lourd du haut; peu stable. **'topknot** *n* petit chignon. **'topless** *a* (danseuse) aux seins nus; (costume) sans haut; **t. swimsuit,** monokini *m.* **'top-'level** *a* (réunion, discussion) au sommet. **'topmost** *a* le plus haut; le plus élevé. **'top'off** *vtr* terminer (**with,** par). **'topping** *n* 1. écimage *m* (d'un arbre) 2. *Cu:* garniture *f* (pour un dessert); **vanilla t.,** crème à la vanille. **'top-'ranking** *a* haut placé. **'topside** *n* *Cu:* tende *f* de tranche (de bœuf). **'topsoil** *n* *Agr:* couche *f* arable. **'top'up** *vtr* **to t. up a drink, a glass,** remplir un verre; *F:* **let me t. you up,** encore un peu? *Aut:* **to t. up the battery, the oil,** rajouter de l'eau, de l'huile. **'top-up** *n* (remplissage *m* d')appoint *m.*

top² *n* toupie *f.*

topaz ['toupæz] *n* topaze *f.*

topic ['tɔpik] *n* matière *f* (d'une discussion); sujet *m*, thème *m* (d'une conversation). **'topical** *a* d'actualité. **topi'cality** *n* actualité *f.*

topography [tɔ'pɔgrəfi] *n* (*pl* **topographies**) topographie *f.* **topo'graphic(al)** *a* topographique.

topple ['tɔpl] 1. *vi* **to t. (down, over),** tomber, s'écrouler, culbuter, dégringoler 2. *vtr* **to t. sth over,** faire tomber, faire dégringoler, qch; renverser (un gouvernement).

topsy-turvy ['tɔpsi'tə:vi] *a & adv* sens dessus dessous; **the whole world's (turned) t.-t.,** c'est le monde à l'envers; **everything's t.-t.,** tout est en désarroi.

torch [tɔ:tʃ] *n* 1. torche *f*, flambeau *m* 2. (**electric**) **t.,** lampe *f* de poche. **'torchlight** *n* lueur *f* de(s) flambeaux; **t. procession,** retraite *f* aux flambeaux.

tore *see* **tear²** **II.**

torment 1. ['tɔ:ment] *n* tourment *m*, torture *f*, supplice *m*; **he suffered torments,** il souffrait le martyre; **to be in t.,** être au supplice 2. [tɔ:'ment] *vtr* (*a*) tourmenter, torturer (qn); **tormented by remorse,** en proie aux remords (*b*) taquiner, harceler (qn, un animal).

torn *see* **tear²** II.

tornado [tɔː'neidou] *n* (*pl* **tornadoes**) tornade *f*.

torpedo [tɔː'piːdou] **1.** *n* (*pl* **torpedoes**) torpille *f*; **to carry out a t. attack,** attaquer à la torpille; **t. tube,** (tube *m*) lance-torpille(s) (*m*); **t. boat,** vedette lance-torpilles **2.** *vtr* torpiller.

torpid ['tɔːpid] *a* engourdi, torpide. **'torpor** *n* engourdissement *m*, torpeur *f*.

torque [tɔːk] *n Mec: Ph:* moment *m* de torsion.

torrent ['tɔrənt] *n* torrent *m*; (*of rain*) **to fall in torrents,** tomber à torrents, à verse; **t. of abuse,** torrent d'injures. **to'rrential** *a* torrentiel; **t. rain,** pluie diluvienne.

torrid ['tɔrid] *a* torride.

torsion ['tɔːʃn] *n Mec: etc:* torsion *f*.

torso ['tɔːsou] *n* (*pl* **torsos**) torse *m*.

tortoise ['tɔːtəs] *n* tortue *f*. **'tortoiseshell** *n* écaille *f* (de tortue).

tortuous ['tɔːtjuəs] *a* tortueux.

torture ['tɔːtʃər] **1.** *n* torture *f*, tourment *m*, supplice *m* **2.** *vtr* torturer (qn); mettre (qn) à la torture, au supplice; **tortured by remorse,** tenaillé par le remords. **'torturer** *n* (*a*) tortionnaire *m* (*b*) *Hist:* bourreau *m*.

toss [tɔs] **I.** *n* **1.** (*a*) lancée *f*, lancement *m* (d'une balle) (*b*) **t.** (**of a coin**), coup *m* de pile ou face; *Sp:* tirage *m* au sort; **to win, lose, the t.,** gagner, perdre, à pile ou face; *Sp:* gagner, perdre, le tirage au sort **2. t. of the head,** brusque mouvement *m* de tête **3. to take a t.,** faire une chute (de cheval). **II.** *v* (**tossed**) **1.** *vtr* (*a*) lancer, jeter, (une balle) en l'air; (*of bull*) lancer (qn) en l'air; (*of horse*) désarçonner (son cavalier); **to t. sth to s.o.,** jeter qch à qn; **to t. s.o. in a blanket,** faire sauter qn dans une couverture; **to t. the salad,** mélanger la salade (*b*) **to t. a coin,** jouer à pile ou face; *vi* **to t. for sth,** jouer qch à pile ou face; **let's t. for it,** on le joue à pile ou face; **who's paying? — I'll t. you for it,** qui est-ce qui paye? jouons à pile ou face et le perdant payera (*c*) **to t. one's head,** relever brusquement la tête (*d*) agiter, secouer, ballotter; **to be tossed about,** être ballotté **2.** *vi* (*a*) **to t. and turn, to t.** (**about**) **in bed,** se tourner et se retourner dans son lit (*b*) (*of ship*) **to pitch and t.,** tanguer (*c*) (*of waves*) s'agiter. **'tossing** *n* **1.** lancement *m* en l'air **2.** agitation *f*, ballottement *m*. **'toss 'off** *vtr* avaler d'un trait (un verre de vin); expédier (un travail); écrire (un article) au pied levé. **'toss-up** *n* **1.** coup *m* de pile ou face **2.** affaire *f* à issue douteuse; **it's a t.-up,** les chances sont égales.

tot¹ [tɔt] *n* **1.** (**tiny**) **t.,** tout(e) petit(e) enfant **2.** goutte *f*, petit verre (de whisky).

tot² *v* (**totted**) **1.** *vtr* **to t. up,** additionner; faire le total; **to t. up expenses,** faire le compte des dépenses **2.** *vi* (*a*) faire le total (*b*) (*of expenses*) **to t. up,** s'élever (**to, à**).

total ['tout(ə)l] **1.** *a & n* (*a*) total, global; **t. amount,** somme totale, globale; **they were in t. ignorance of it,** ils l'ignoraient complètement; **t. failure,** échec complet (*b*) *n* total *m*; montant *m*; tout *m*; **grand t.,** total général; **sum t.,** somme totale; **the t. amounts to £100,** la somme s'élève à £100 **2.** *vtr & i* (**totalled,** *NAm:* **totaled**) (*a*) additionner (les dépenses); faire le total de (*b*) **to t.** (**up to**) **£100,** s'élever à £100. **totali'tarian** *a & n* totalitaire (*mf*). **totali'tarianism** *n* totalitarisme *m*. **to'tality** *n* totalité *f*. **'totally** *adv* totalement, entièrement, complètement.

totalizator [toutəlai'zeitər] *n* (*F:* **tote¹** [tout]) totalisateur *m* (des paris); = pari mutuel.

tote² ['tout] *vtr esp NAm:* transporter, trimballer; porter (un revolver).

totem ['toutəm] *n* totem *m*; **t. pole,** mât totémique.

totter ['tɔtər] *vi* **1.** (*of pers*) chanceler; **to t. in,** entrer d'un pas chancelant **2.** (*of building*) menacer ruine; chanceler, branler. **'tottering** *a* chancelant; **t. steps,** pas chancelants, pas mal assurés.

toucan ['tuːkæn] *n Orn:* toucan *m*.

touch [tʌtʃ] **I.** *n* **1. to touch** *n*, contact *m*; **I felt a t. on my arm,** je sentis qu'on me touchait le bras **2.** (le sens du) toucher; tact *m*; **soft, hard, to the t.,** mou, dur, au toucher; **to know sth by the t.,** reconnaître qch au toucher; **the cold t. of marble,** le contact froid du marbre **3.** (*a*) léger coup (*b*) touche *f* (de pinceau); coup (de crayon); **to add a few touches to a picture,** faire quelques retouches à un tableau; **to put the finishing touch(es), to add the final t., to sth,** mettre la dernière main à qch; mettre qch au point **4.** (*a*) **he's lost his t.,** il a perdu la main; **this room needs a woman's t.,** il manque une touche féminine dans cette pièce (*b*) *Mus:* toucher; **to have a light t. on the piano,** avoir un toucher délicat **5. t. of garlic,** pointe *f* d'ail; **t. of rouge,** soupçon *m* de rouge; **a t. of bitterness,** une nuance d'amertume; **there's a t. of colour in her cheeks,** ses joues ont pris un peu de couleur; **t. of originality,** note *f* d'originalité; **t. of flu,** petite grippe **6.** contact; **to be in t. with s.o.,** être en contact avec qn; **to get in t. with s.o.,** joindre, contacter, qn; se mettre en, prendre, contact avec, qn; **to get in t. with the police,** se mettre en communication avec la police; **I'll be in t.,** je vous ferai signe; **to put s.o. in t. with s.o.,** mettre qn en rapport avec qn; **to be out of t. with s.o.,** ne plus être au courant de qch; **I've lost t. with him,** je l'ai perdu de vue **7.** *Fb:* touche; **kick into t.,** envoi *m* en touche. **II.** *v* **1.** *vtr* (*a*) toucher; effleurer; **to t. sth with one's finger,** toucher qch du doigt; **to t. s.o. on the shoulder,** toucher qn à l'épaule; **to t. one's hat,** porter, mettre, la main à son chapeau; *F:* **t. wood!** touchons du bois! **don't t.!** ne, n'y, touchez pas! **I wouldn't t. it with a barge pole,** je n'y toucherais pas avec des pincettes; (*of ship*) **to t. the bottom,** *vi* **to t.,** toucher le fond; toucher (*b*) **his garden touches mine,** son jardin touche au mien, le mien (*c*) faire jouer (un ressort); **he touched the bell,** il a appuyé sur le bouton de la sonnette (*d*) *v ind tr* **to t. on a subject,** aborder, effleurer, un sujet (*e*) toucher, atteindre; **the law can't t. him,** la loi ne peut rien contre lui; **the curtains t. the floor,** les rideaux descendent jusqu'au plancher; **nobody can t. him in comedy,** personne ne joue la comédie aussi bien, comme lui (*f*) **I never t. wine,** je ne bois jamais de vin (*g*) toucher, émouvoir, attendrir (qn); **to be touched by s.o.'s kindness,** être touché de la bonté de qn; **to t. s.o. to the quick,** toucher qn au vif (*h*) toucher, regarder (qn); **the question touches you closely,** la question vous touche de près; **flowers touched by the frost,** fleurs atteintes par la gelée **2.** *vi* (*of pers, thgs*) **se toucher;** être, venir, en contact. **'touch and 'go** *n* **it was t. and go whether we would catch the train,** nous avons failli manquer le train; **it was t. and go with him,** il revient de loin; **a t.-and-go affair,** une affaire très risquée. **'touch 'down 1.** *vtr & i Rugby Fb:* toucher dans les buts 2. *vi Av:* faire escale. **'touchdown** *n Av:* atterrissage *m.* **touched** *a F:* toqué, timbré. **'touchiness** *n* susceptibilité *f,* irascibilité *f.* **'touching 1.** *a* touchant, émouvant, attendrissant **2.** *prep* concernant. **'touchingly** *adv* d'une manière touchante. **'touchline** *n Fb: etc:* ligne *f* de touche. **'touch 'off** *vtr* décharger (un canon); faire partir, faire exploser (une mine). **'touch-'type** *vi* taper au toucher. **'touch 'up** *vtr* faire des retouches à (un tableau); faire des raccords (de peinture); rafraîchir (les couleurs de qch). **'touchy** *a* susceptible, ombrageux, irascible; **he's very t.,** il se froisse, s'offusque, pour un rien.

tough [tʌf] **I.** *a* **1.** dur, résistant; **t. meat,** (viande) coriace **2.** *(of pers)* fort, solide; *F:* **a t. guy,** un dur **3.** *(of pers)* raide, inflexible; *F:* **he's a t. customer,** il n'est pas commode; c'est un dur à cuire; **to get t. with s.o.,** se montrer dur envers qn **4.** *F:* *(a)* **t. job,** tâche rude, difficile *(b)* **t. luck,** pas de veine! **that's t.!** c'est vache! **to have a t. time,** en voir de dures. **II.** *n F:* dur *m;* brute *f.* **'toughen 1.** *vtr (a)* durcir *(b)* endurcir (qn) **2.** *vi (a)* durcir *(b)* *(of pers)* s'endurcir. **'toughly** *adv* **1.** durement **2.** avec acharnement; vigoureusement. **'toughness** *n* **1.** dureté *f;* résistance *f* **2.** *(a)* force *f,* solidité *f (b)* résistance à la fatigue **3.** inflexibilité *f* **4.** difficulté *f* (d'un travail).

toupee, toupet ['tu:pei] *n* (mèche) postiche (*m*).

tour ['tuər] **1.** *n (a)* voyage *m* (circulaire); **conducted, guided, t.,** (i) voyage organisé (ii) *(in museum)* visite guidée; **package t.,** voyage à prix forfaitaire; **walking t.,** excursion *f,* randonnée *f,* à pied; **to go on a world t.,** faire le tour du monde *(b)* **t. of inspection,** tournée *f* d'inspection; **t. of duty,** (i) tour *m* de service (ii) journée *f* (de travail) *(c) Th:* tournée **2.** *vtr & i (a)* **to t. a country,** faire le tour d'un pays; voyager dans un pays; **to go touring,** faire du tourisme *(b) Th:* **to t. the provinces,** être en, faire une, tournée en province. **'tourer** *n* voiture *f* de tourisme. **'touring 1.** *a* **t. car,** voiture de tourisme; **touring company,** troupe en tournée **2.** *n* tourisme *m.* **'tourism** *n* tourisme. **'tourist** *n* touriste *mf;* **t. agency,** agence, bureau, de tourisme; **t. centre,** centre, ville, touristique; **the t. trade,** le tourisme; **t. class,** classe touriste. **'touristy** *a Pej:* (trop) touristique.

tournament ['tuənəmənt] *n* tournoi *m* (de tennis, de bridge).

tourniquet ['tuənikei] *n Med:* tourniquet *m,* garrot *m.*

tousle ['tauzl] *vtr* ébouriffer (les cheveux); **tousled hair,** cheveux ébouriffés.

tout [taut] **1.** *n (a)* *(for hotels)* rabatteur *m;* *(for insurance companies)* démarcheur, -euse; *(for shops)* racoleur *m;* **ticket t.,** revendeur, -euse, de billets au marché noir *(b)* **(racing) t.,** pronostiqueur *m;* donneur *m* de tuyaux **2.** *vi & tr* revendre (des billets); **to t. for custom,** racoler des clients; **to t. a product,** faire l'article d'un produit.

tow¹ [tou] **1.** *n (a)* **to take a car in t.,** prendre une voiture en remorque; **to be taken in t.,** se mettre à la remorque; *F:* **he always has his family in t.,** il trimbale toujours sa famille avec lui; *Aut:* **on t.,** en remorque; **t. bar,** timon de remorque *(b) Aut:* **we can give you a t.,** nous pouvons vous remorquer; *NAm:* **t. truck,** dépanneuse *f* **2.** *vtr* remorquer (un navire, une voiture);

touer (un chaland); *(from towpath)* haler (un chaland); **my car's been towed away by the police,** la police a mis ma voiture en fourrière. **'towboat** *n* remorqueur *m.* **'towing** *n* remorque *f,* remorquage *m;* touage *m;* *(from towpath)* halage *m.* **'towline, 'towrope** *n* (câble *m* de) remorque *f.* **'towpath** *n* chemin *m* de halage.

tow² *n* étoupe (blanche); filasse *f.* **'tow-'headed** *a* aux cheveux (blond) filasse.

towards [tə'wɔ:dz] *prep* *(occ* **toward)** **1.** vers; du côté de; **he came t. me,** il est venu vers moi **2.** envers, à l'égard de (qn); **his feelings t. me,** ses sentiments envers, pour, moi; **his sentiments t. me** à mon égard **3.** pour; **to save t. sth,** économiser pour qch; **I'd like to give something t. it,** je voudrais apporter ma contribution **4.** vers, sur; **t. noon,** vers midi; **t. the end of the week,** en fin de semaine; **t. the end of his life,** sur la fin de sa vie.

towel ['tauəl] **1.** *n (a)* serviette *f* (de toilette); essuie-mains *m inv;* **roller t.,** serviette sans fin (pour rouleau); **t. rail,** porte-serviettes *m inv (b)* **sanitary t.,** serviette hygiénique, périodique **2.** *vtr* **(towelled,** *NAm:* **toweled) to t. (s.o.) (dry),** essuyer, frotter, (qn) avec une serviette. **'towelling,** *NAm:* **'toweling** *n* **1.** friction *f* avec une serviette **2.** tissu-éponge *m.*

tower ['tauər] **1.** *n* tour *f;* **church t.,** clocher *m;* **water t.,** château *m* d'eau; *Av:* **control t.,** tour de contrôle; **t. block,** tour (d'habitation); **he's a t. of strength,** c'est un puissant secours **2.** *vi (of building)* s'élever très haut; **to t. over, above (sth),** dominer (qch). **'towering 1.** *(a)* très haut, très élevé *(b)* imposant **2. in a t. rage,** au paroxysme de la colère.

town [taun] *n* **1.** ville *f;* **county t.** =chef-lieu *m* (de département); *F:* **to go out on the t.,** faire la bombe; **t. clerk** =secrétaire *mf* de mairie; **t. council,** conseil municipal; **t. hall,** hôtel de ville; =mairie *f* **2. to go into t.,** aller, se rendre, en ville; **he's out of t.,** il est en voyage; *F:* **to go to t.,** (i) bien s'amuser (ii) dépenser sans compter **3. t. planning,** urbanisme *m;* **t. planner,** urbaniste *m.* **'townsfolk** *npl* citadins *m.* **'township** *n* commune *f;* bourg *m,* bourgade *f.* **'townsman,** *f* **-woman** *n (pl* **-men, -women)** habitant, -ante, de la ville; citadin, -ine. **'townspeople** *npl* habitants *m* de la ville; citadins *m.*

toxic ['tɔksik] *a Med:* toxique. **to'xaemia,** *NAm:* **to'xemia** *n* toxémie *f.* **toxi'cologist** *n* toxicologue *mf.* **toxi'cology** *n* toxicologie *f.* **'toxin** *n* toxine *f.*

toy [tɔi] **1.** *n* jouet *m, F:* joujou *m;* **t. trumpet,** trompette d'enfant; **t. poodle,** caniche nain **2.** *vi* **to t. with sth,** s'amuser, jouer, avec qch; **to t. with one's food,** manger du bout des dents; **to t. with an idea,** caresser une idée. **'toyshop** *n* magasin *m* de jouets.

trace¹ [treis] **I.** *n* **1.** *(usu pl)* trace(s) *f (pl)* (de qn, d'un animal); empreinte *f* (d'un animal) **2.** *(a)* trace, vestige *m;* **they could find no t. of him,** on n'a pas pu retrouver sa trace; **there's no t. of it,** il n'en reste pas trace *(b)* quantité *f* minime; soupçon *m;* **without a t. of jealousy,** sans la moindre jalousie. **II.** *vtr* **1.** tracer (un plan) **2.** *(a)* faire le tracé d'(un plan) *(b)* calquer (un dessin) **3.** suivre la trace, la piste (de qn, d'une bête); **he has been traced to Paris,** on a suivi sa piste jusqu'à Paris; **to t. lost goods,** recouvrer des objets perdus **4.**

retrouver les vestiges (d'un ancien édifice); retrouver (une influence); **he traces his family back to the Crusades**, il fait remonter sa famille aux croisades; to **t. an event back to its source**, remonter à l'origine d'un événement. **'tracer** n 1. traceur m (radioactif) 2. *Mil:* t. bullet, (balle) traçante f. **'tracery** n réseau m (de rosace). **'tracing** n 1. calquage m; **t. paper**, papier calque 2. calque m.

trace² n *Harn:* trait m; *(of pers)* **to kick over the traces**, (i) s'insurger (ii) s'émanciper.

trachea [trə'kiːə] n *(pl* tracheae [-'kiːiː]) *Anat:* trachée f.

track [træk] 1. n *(a)* trace(s) f *(pl)*, piste f (de qn, d'une bête); sillon m (d'une roue); **to follow in s.o.'s tracks**, suivre, marcher sur, les traces de qn; **to be on s.o.'s t.**, être sur la piste de qn; **to be on the right t.**, être sur la bonne voie; **to be on the wrong t.**, faire fausse route; **to keep t. of s.o.**, suivre les progrès de qn; **I've lost t. of him**, je l'ai perdu de vue; **to throw s.o. off the t.**, dépister qn; *F:* **to make tracks**, filer, s'éclipser; **to stop in one's tracks**, s'arrêter net *(b)* piste, chemin m, sentier m; **mule t.**, sentier muletier; **cycle t.**, piste cyclable; **(racing) t.**, piste; **t. racing**, courses sur piste; **motor-racing t.**, autodrome m; *(of car, Fig: pers)* **t. record**, carrière f, dossier m *(c)* *Rail:* voie (ferrée); **the train left the t.**, le train a déraillé *(d)* *Rec:* plage f, piste (de disque); **sound t.**, piste sonore *(e)* *Veh:* chenille f 2. *vtr* suivre (une bête) à la piste; traquer (un malfaiteur); suivre la trajectoire d'(une comète). **'track 'down** *vtr* dépister (le gibier, un criminel); découvrir (qch). **tracked** a (véhicule) chenillé. **'tracker** n traqueur m (de gibier); **t. dog**, chien policier. **'tracking** n 1. poursuite f (d'un animal, de qn) à la piste; **t. (down)**, dépistage m (du gibier, d'un criminel) 2. **t. station**, station de dépistage. **'tracksuit** n survêtement m.

tract¹ [trækt] n 1. étendue f (de pays) 2. *Anat:* appareil m (respiratoire), conduit vocal.

tract² n brochure f; tract m.

tractable ['træktəbl] a *(of pers, character)* docile; traitable.

traction ['trækʃ(ə)n] n traction f; **t. engine**, tracteur m; locomobile f; *Rail:* **t. wheels**, roues motrices.

tractor ['træktər] n tracteur m.

trade [treid] I. n 1. *(a)* métier m; commerce m; **to carry on a t.**, exercer un métier; **he's a carpenter by t.**, il est charpentier de son métier; **everyone to his t.**, chacun son métier *(b)* (corps de) métier; **the building t.**, le bâtiment; **the printing t.**, l'imprimerie f; **to be in the t.**, être du métier; **t. name**, (i) *(product)* appellation commerciale (ii) *(firm)* raison commerciale; **t. secret**, secret de fabrication; **t. discount**, remise f *(c)* **trade(s) union**, syndicat (ouvrier); **to form a t. union**, se syndiquer; **trade(s) unionism**, syndicalisme m; **trade(s) unionist**, syndicaliste mf 2. *(a)* commerce, négoce m, affaires fpl; **to be in the t.**, être dans le commerce; **he's doing a roaring t.**, il fait des affaires d'or *(b)* **t. winds**, (vents) alizés *(mpl)* *(c)* **illicit t.**, trafic m. II. v 1. vi *(a)* faire le commerce, le négoce (in, de); faire des affaires **(with s.o.**, avec qn) *(b)* **to t. on s.o.'s ignorance**, exploiter, tirer profit de, l'ignorance de qn 2. *vtr* **to t. sth for sth**, échanger, troquer, qch contre qch. **'trade 'in** *vtr* donner (qch) en reprise; faire une reprise; **I'm trading in my old car for a new one**, j'échange ma

vieille voiture contre une neuve. **'trade-in** n objet donné en reprise. **'trademark** n marque f de fabrique; **registered t.**, marque déposée. **'trade-off** n *esp NAm:* compromis m. **'trader** n négociant, -ante; commerçant, -ante; marchand, -ande. **'tradesman** nm *(pl* -men) marchand, commerçant, fournisseur. **'trading** n commerce m, négoce m; **t. stamp**, timbre-prime m; **t. estate**, zone industrielle.

tradition [trə'diʃ(ə)n] n tradition f; **according to t.**, selon la tradition. **tra'ditional** a traditionnel. **tra'ditionally** adv traditionnellement.

traffic ['træfik] I. n 1. trafic m; *Pej:* **drug t.**, trafic des stupéfiants 2. *(a)* mouvement m, circulation f; **road t.**, circulation routière; **heavy t.**, circulation intense; **t. jam**, embouteillage m; bouchon m; **t. island**, refuge m; **t. lights, signals**, feux mpl de circulation, de signalisation routière; **t. warden**, contractuel(le) *(b)* **ocean t.**, navigation f au long cours *(c)* **rail t.**, trafic ferroviaire; **goods, passenger, t.**, trafic marchandises, voyageurs II. vi *Pej:* **to t. in sth**, trafiquer en, faire le trafic de, qch. **'trafficker** n *Pej:* trafiquant, -ante (in, de, en).

tragedy ['trædʒidi] n *(pl* tragedies) tragédie f; **the t. of his death**, sa mort tragique. **'tragic** a tragique; **t. actor, actress**, tragédien, -ienne; *F:* **to put on a t. act**, jouer la comédie. **'tragically** adv tragiquement; **to take things t.**, prendre les choses au tragique.

trail [treil] I. n 1. traînée f (de fumée, de sang, d'une comète) 2. *(a)* piste f, trace f (d'une bête, de qn); **to pick up the t.**, retrouver la trace; **false t.**, fausse piste; **to be on s.o.'s t.**, être sur la piste de qn *(b)* sentier (battu); piste (dans une forêt). II. v 1. vtr *(a)* **to t. sth (along)**, traîner qch après soi; *(of car)* remorquer (une caravane); **to t. one's dress in the dust**, traîner sa robe dans la poussière *(b)* traquer (une bête, un criminel) 2. vi *(a)* traîner; **your dress is trailing on the ground**, votre robe traîne (par terre) *(b)* *(of pers)* **to t. along**, se traîner; **to t. behind**, traîner derrière (les autres); *Fig:* être en retard sur les autres; **her voice trailed away, off**, sa voix s'estompa *(c)* *(of plant)* ramper; grimper. **'trailblazer** n pionnier, -ière. **'trailer** n 1. *Aut:* remorque f; *NAm:* caravane f (de camping) 2. *Cin:* film m annonce. **'trailing** a traînant; *(of plant)* rampant, grimpant.

train [trein] I. n 1. traîne f (d'une robe) 2. train m, convoi m (de wagons); succession f, série f (d'événements); **t. of thought**, enchaînement m d'idées; fil m des pensées 3. *Rail:* *(a)* train; **main line t.**, train de grande ligne; **through t.**, train direct; **slow t.**, train omnibus; **fast t.**, (train) rapide *(m)*; **express t.**, train express; **relief t.**, train supplémentaire; **to travel by t.**, voyager en train, par le train; *PN:* **to the trains**, accès m aux quais; **t. spotter**, personne qui observe les trains (pour repérer les différents modèles) *(b)* rame f (de métro) *(c)* **t. ferry**, ferry(-boat) m *(d)* *F:* **to ride the gravy t.**, se la couler douce. II. v 1. vtr *(a)* former, instruire (qn); dresser (un animal); exercer (l'oreille, les yeux); *Sp:* entraîner (qn); *Hort:* palisser (un arbre fruitier); **to t. s.o. for sth, to do sth**, exercer qn à qch, à faire qch *(b)* pointer (un canon); braquer (une lunette) **(on**, sur) 2. vi *(a)* s'exercer *(b)* *Sp:* s'entraîner *(c)* **to t. as a typist**, suivre un cours de dactylographie. **trained** a (soldat) instruit; (chien) dressé; (œil) exercé; *Sp:* (coureur) entraîné; **t. nurse**, infirmière diplômée; **she's not t.**, elle n'a reçu aucune formation professionnelle. **trai'nee** n élève mf; stagiaire mf. **'trainer** n 1. dresseur m (d'animaux) 2. Sp: entraîneur m 3. chaussure f de sport. **'training** n 1. (a) éducation f, instruction f; formation f; **physical t.**, éducation physique; **he has received a good t.**, il a fait un bon apprentissage; **t. centre**, centre de formation; **to acquire a business t.**, se former aux affaires (b) **military t.**, dressage m; **t. ship**, navire-école m militaire (c) Sp: entraînement m; **to go into t.**, s'entraîner; **to be in t.**, (i) être à l'entraînement (ii) être bien entraîné; être en forme (d) dressage (d'un animal) 2. palissage m (d'un arbre fruitier).

traipse [treips] vi to t. **around**, traîner çà et là; se balader.

trait [treit] n trait m (de caractère).

traitor ['treitər] n traître m; **to turn t.**, passer à l'ennemi; se vendre; **to be a t. to (one's country)**, trahir (sa patrie). **'traitress** nf traîtresse.

trajectory [trə'dʒektəri] n trajectoire f.

tram(car) ['træmkɑːr] n tram(way) m. **'tramline** n 1. ligne de tram(way) 2. **tramlines**, (i) voie f de tram(way) (ii) Ten: couloir m.

tramp [træmp] I. n 1. bruit m de pas lourds 2. marche f; promenade f à pied 3. (pers) (a) clochard, -arde; chemineau m, vagabond, -onde (b) NAm: prostituée f 4. Nau: t. **(steamer)**, tramp m. II. v 1. vi marcher d'un pas lourd 2. vi to t. **on sth**, piétiner, écraser, qch 3. vi & tr (a) marcher, voyager à pied; **to t. the country**, parcourir le pays à pied (b) vagabonder; **to t. the streets**, battre le pavé.

trample ['træmpl] 1. vi to t. **on s.o.**, sth, piétiner, écraser, qn, qch; **to t. on s.o.'s feelings**, bafouer les sentiments de qn 2. vtr (a) **to t. sth underfoot**, fouler qch aux pieds; **to t. down the grass**, fouler l'herbe; **he was trampled to death**, il a été écrasé par la foule (b) piétiner (le sol). **'trampling** n piétinement m; bruit m de pas.

trampoline [træmpə'liːn] n Gym: tremplin m.

trance [trɑːns] n 1. Med: extase f 2. **(hypnotic) t.**, transe f; **to fall into a t.**, entrer en transe.

tranquil ['træŋkwil] a tranquille; serein; calme. **tran'quillity**, NAm: **tran'quility** n tranquillité f, calme m, sérénité f. **'tranquillize**, NAm: **'tranquilize** vtr tranquilliser, calmer, apaiser. **'tranquillizer**, NAm: **'tranquilizer** n Med: tranquillisant m, calmant m.

trans- [træns, trænz] pref trans-. **trans'alpine** a transalpin. **transat'lantic** a transatlantique. **transconti'nental** a transcontinental. **trans'sexual** a trans-sexuel.

transact [trænz'ækt] vtr **to t. business with s.o.**, faire des affaires avec qn; traiter, régler, une affaire. **trans'action** n transaction f; opération (commerciale); **cash t.**, opération au comptant.

transcend [træns'end] vtr 1. transcender 2. surpasser (qn). **trans'cendent** a transcendant. **transcen'dental** a transcendantal.

transcribe [træns'kraib] vtr transcrire. **'transcript**, **trans'cription** n transcription f.

transect [træn'sekt] vtr couper transversalement.

transept ['trænsept] n Arch: transept m.

transfer I. n ['trænsfər] 1. (a) transfert m; déplacement m, mutation f (d'un fonctionnaire) (b) Bank: virement m, transfert m; **t. of funds**, virement de fonds 2. (a) décalcomanie f (b) auto-collant m. II. v [træns'fər] **(transferred)** 1. (a) transférer; déplacer (un fonctionnaire); muter (un militaire); **transfer(red) charge call**, communication en PCV (b) Bank: virer (une somme) 2. décalquer (un dessin); Phot: reporter. **trans'ferable** a transmissible; (on ticket) **not t.**, non cessible; strictement personnel.

transfigure [træns'figər] vtr transfigurer. **transfigu'ration** n transfiguration f.

transfix [træns'fiks] vtr transpercer (qn, qch); **transfixed with fear**, cloué au sol par la peur.

transform [træns'fɔːm] vtr transformer; **to be transformed into**, se transformer en. **transfor'mation** n transformation f. **trans'former** n El: transformateur m.

transfuse [træns'fjuːz] vtr Med: transfuser, faire une transfusion. **trans'fusion** n transfusion f; **blood t.**, transfusion de sang, sanguine.

transgress [træns'gres] vtr & i transgresser; pécher. **trans'gressor** n transgresseur m; pécheur, f pécheresse.

tranship [træn'ʃip] vtr transborder (des voyageurs).

transient ['trænziənt] a transitoire; (bonheur) passager; (beauté) éphémère.

transistor [træn'zistər] n Elcs: transistor m. **tran'sistorize** vtr transistoriser.

transit ['trænzit] n 1. transport m (de marchandises); **goods lost in t.**, marchandises perdues en cours de route 2. transit m; **in t.**, en transit; **t. duty**, droit de transit. **tran'sition** n transition f; passage m (du jour à la nuit). **tran'sitional** a transitionnel; de transition.

transitive ['trænzitiv] a & n transitif (m).

transitory ['trænzitəri] a transitoire, passager, éphémère.

translate [træns'leit] 1. vtr traduire; **the word is translated by**, le mot se traduit par 2. vi (pers) traduire; **it won't t.**, c'est intraduisible. **tran'slatable** a traduisible. **tran'slation** n traduction f; Sch: version f. **tran'slator** n traducteur, -trice.

transliteration [trænzlitə'reiʃən] n translit(t)ération f.

translucence [trænz'luːsəns] n translucidité f. **trans'lucent** a translucide.

transmit [trænz'mit] vtr **(transmitted)** (a) transmettre (b) WTel: TV: transmettre, émettre. **trans'missible** a transmissible. **trans'mission** n 1. transmission f, émission f 2. Aut: **t. shaft**, arbre de transmission 3. programme radiodiffusé, télévisé. **trans'mitter** n (a) transmetteur m, émetteur m (b) WTel: TV: (poste) émetteur; poste d'émission.

transmute [trænz'mjuːt] vtr transformer, changer **(into**, en); transmuer.

transom ['trænsəm] n traverse f, linteau m (de fenêtre).

transparent [træns'pærənt, -'peər-] a 1. transparent; (eau) limpide 2. clair, qui saute aux yeux. **trans'parency** n 1. transparence f 2. Phot: diapositive f.

transpire [træns'paiər] vi (a) transpirer (b) **it transpired that**, on a appris que (c) se passer. **transpi'ration** n transpiration f.

transplant 1. n ['trænsplɑːnt] Surg: transplantation

f; **heart t.**, greffe *f* du cœur **2.** *vtr* [træns'plɑːnt] (*a*) *Hort:* repiquer (des plants) (*b*) *Surg:* transplanter, greffer (un organe).

transport 1. *n* ['trænspɔːt] (*a*) transport *m* (de marchandises, de voyageurs); **public t.**, les transports en commun; **road, rail, t.**, transport routier, ferroviaire; **t. café**, restaurant *m* de routiers (*b*) moyen *m* de transport; *Navy:* transport; **t. aircraft**, avion de transport; *F:* **have you got t.?** est-ce que vous avez votre, une, voiture? (*c*) transport (de joie) **2.** *vtr* [træns'pɔːt] *vtr* (*a*) transporter (des marchandises, des voyageurs) (*b*) **to be transported with joy**, être transporté de joie. **transpor'tation** *n* (*a*) *esp NAm:* (i) transport *m* (ii) moyen *m* de transport (*b*) *NAm: Rail:* (*Br* = **ticket**) billet *m*, titre *m* de transport. **trans'porter** *n* transporteur *m*; **car t.**, camion *m*, wagon *m*, transporteur de voitures; **t. bridge**, (pont) transbordeur *m*.

transpose [træns'pouz] *vtr* transposer. **transpo'sition** *n* transposition *f*.

trans-ship [træn(z)'ʃip] = **tranship**.

transubstantiation [trænsəbstænʃi'eiʃn] *n* transubstantiation *f*.

transverse ['trænzvɜːs] *a* transversal. **trans'versely** *adv* transversalement.

transvestite [trænz'vestait] *n* travesti, -ie.

trap [træp] I. *n* **1.** (*a*) piège *m*; **to set a t.**, dresser, tendre, un piège; **to catch (an animal) in a t.**, prendre (une bête) au piège; **caught like a rat in a t.**, fait comme un rat (*b*) piège, ruse *f*; **police t.**, (i) souricière *f* (ii) *Aut:* zone *f* de contrôle de vitesse; **he fell into a t.**, il s'y laissa prendre **2.** (*a*) **t. (door)**, trappe *f* (*b*) *P:* **shut your t.!** (ferme) ta gueule! II. *vtr* (**trapped**) (*a*) prendre (une bête) au piège; piéger; **to t. one's finger in the door**, se coincer le doigt dans la porte; **trapped by the flames**, cerné par les flammes (*b*) tendre des pièges (*c*) *vi Can:* trapper. **'trapper** *n* trappeur *m*. **'trapshooting** *n Sp:* ball-trap *m*.

trapeze [trə'piːz] *n* trapèze *m*; **t. artist**, trapéziste *mf*.

trappings ['træpiŋz] *npl* atours *mpl*; apparat *m*.

Trappist ['træpist] *a & n Ecc:* trappiste (*m*).

trash [træʃ] *n* (*a*) chose(s) *f* (*pl*) sans valeur; camelote *f*, *NAm:* ordures *fpl*, déchets *mpl*; **t. can**, poubelle *f* (*b*) mauvaise littérature (*c*) **to talk a lot of t.**, dire des sottises (*d*) (*people*) vauriens *mpl*, propres à rien *mpl*. **'trashy** *a* sans valeur, de pacotille.

trauma ['trɔːmə] *n* (*pl* **traumas, traumata**) *Med:* trauma *m*. **trau'matic** *a* traumatique; traumatisant. **'traumatism** *n* traumatisme *m*.

travel ['træv(ə)l] I. *n* (*a*) voyages *mpl*; **t. agency, agent**, agence, agent, de voyages (*b*) **is he still on his travels?** est-il toujours en voyage? II. *vi* (**travelled**, *NAm:* **traveled**) **1.** (*a*) voyager; faire des voyages; **he is travelling**, il est en voyage; **to t. round the world**, faire le tour du monde; **to t. through a region**, parcourir une région; **distance travelled**, distance parcourue (*b*) (*of news*) circuler, se répandre; **the train was travelling at 150km an hour**, le train marchait à 150km à l'heure **2. to t. (for a firm)**, voyager (pour une maison); représenter une maison. **'travelator** *n* tapis roulant. **'traveller**, *NAm:* **'traveler** *n* **1.** voyageur, -euse; **fellow t.**, compagnon de voyage, de route; **traveller's cheque**, *NAm:* **traveler's check**, chèque de voyage **2. (commercial) t.**,

représentant *m* (de commerce). **'travelling**, *NAm:* **'traveling 1.** *a* (*a*) (cirque) ambulant; **t. salesman**, représentant *m* (de commerce) (*b*) (grue) mobile **2.** *n* voyages *mpl*; **t. bag**, sac de voyage; **t. expenses**, frais de voyage, de route, de déplacement; **t. scholarship**, bourse de voyage. **'travel-sick** *a* **to be t.-s.**, avoir le mal de la route, de l'air, de mer. **'travel-'sickness** *n* mal *m* de la route, de l'air, de mer.

traverse ['trævəs, trə'vɜːs] **1.** *n Mount:* (i) traverse *f* (ii) traversée *f* **2.** *v* (*a*) *vtr* traverser, passer à travers (une région); passer (la mer) (*b*) *vi Mount:* prendre une traverse.

travesty ['trævisti] *n* (*pl* **travesties**) travestissement *m*; *Pej:* simulacre *m*.

trawl [trɔːl] **1.** *n* **t. (net)**, chalut *m*, traille *f* **2.** *v* (*a*) *vi* pêcher au chalut; chaluter (*b*) *vtr* prendre (le poisson) au chalut. **'trawler** *n* chalutier *m*. **'trawling** *n* pêche *f* au chalut, chalutage *m*.

tray [trei] *n* (*a*) plateau *m* (*b*) casier *m* (d'une malle) (*c*) corbeille *f* (à correspondance). **'traycloth** *n* napperon *m*.

treachery ['tretʃəri] *n* (*pl* **treacheries**) trahison *f*, perfidie *f*. **'treacherous** *a* (*of pers*) traître, déloyal; (*of action*) déloyal, perfide; **road conditions are t.**, l'état des routes est dangereux. **'treacherously** *adv* (agir) traîtreusement, perfidement.

treacle ['triːkl] *n* (*no pl*) mélasse *f*.

tread [tred] I. *n* **1.** (*a*) pas *m*; **to walk with measured t.**, marcher à pas mesurés (*b*) bruit *m* de pas **2.** (*a*) giron *m* (de marche d'escalier) (*b*) *Aut:* bande *f* de roulement, chape *f* (d'un pneu); **non-skid t.**, roulement antidérapant. II. *v* (**trod** [trɔd]; **trodden** ['trɔdn]) **1.** *vi* marcher; poser les pieds; **to t. softly**, marcher doucement, à pas feutrés; **to t. on sth**, (i) marcher sur qch (ii) écraser qch; **to t. carefully, warily**, avancer avec précaution **2.** *vtr* (*a*) **to t. down**, piétiner (le sol); **to t. sth under foot**, écraser qch du pied; fouler qch aux pieds (*b*) **to t. grapes**, fouler la vendange, le raisin; **to t. water**, nager debout. **'treadle** *n* pédale *f*; **t. sewing machine**, machine *f* (à coudre) à pédale. **'treadmill** *n Fig:* besogne ingrate; routine ennuyeuse.

treason ['triːz(ə)n] *n Jur:* trahison *f*; **high t.**, haute trahison; lèse-majesté *f*. **'treasonable** *a* séditieux; traître; (acte) de trahison.

treasure ['treʒər] **1.** *n* trésor *m*; **t. hunt**, chasse *f* au(x) trésor(s); **t. trove**, trésor (découvert par par hasard); *F:* **my help's a real t.**, ma femme de ménage est une perle **2.** *vtr* (*a*) priser, estimer, tenir beaucoup à (qch) (*b*) garder (qch) soigneusement; **to t. sth in one's memory**, garder précieusement le souvenir de qch. **'treasurer** *n* trésorier, -ière. **'treasury** *n* trésor (public); trésorerie *f*; (*in Eng*) **the T.** = le Ministère des Finances; **t. bill**, bon *m* du Trésor.

treat [triːt] I. *n* **1.** (*a*) régal *m*; festin *m* (*b*) *F:* **to stand t.**, payer la tournée; **it's my t.**, c'est ma tournée **2.** plaisir *m*; fête *f*; **to give oneself a t.**, faire un petit extra; **to give s.o. a t.**, faire plaisir à qn; **a t. in store**, un plaisir à venir. II. *v* **1.** *vi* (*a*) **to t. with s.o.**, traiter, négocier, avec qn (*b*) **to t. of a subject**, traiter d'un sujet. **2.** *vtr* (*a*) traiter; **to t. s.o. well**, bien traiter qn; **to t. s.o., an animal, roughly**, maltraiter qn, un animal; **to t. s.o. with respect**, montrer du respect envers qn; **to t. sth as a joke**, considérer qch comme une plaisanterie (*b*) régaler (qn); payer à boire à (qn); **to t. oneself to sth**, s'offrir, se payer, qch; **to t. s.o. to the theatre,** inviter qn au théâtre (c) *Med:* traiter, soigner (un malade); **to t. s.o. for rheumatism,** soigner qn pour les rhumatismes; **to be treated in hospital,** recevoir des soins à l'hôpital (d) traiter (un métal, un thème). **treatise** ['tri:tiz] *n* traité *m* (on, de). **'treatment** *n* **1.** (a) traitement *m* (de qn); **his t. of his friends,** la façon dont il traite ses amis; sa manière d'agir envers ses amis (b) traitement (d'un sujet) **2.** *Med:* traitement; soins médicaux; **patient undergoing t.,** malade en traitement. **'treaty** *n* **1.** traité *m* (de paix); convention *f* **2.** accord *m*, contrat *m*; **to sell by private t.,** vendre (qch) à l'amiable.

treble ['trebl] **1.** *a* (a) triple (b) *Mus:* **t. voice,** (voix de) soprano *m*; **t. clef,** clef de sol **2.** *adv* trois fois plus **3.** *n* (a) triple *m* (b) *Mus:* (pers, voice) soprano *m*; **to sing the t.,** chanter le dessus (c) *Elcs:* **t. control,** touche de tonalité aiguë **4.** *vtr & i* (se) tripler. **'trebly** *adv* trois fois autant.

tree [tri:] *n* arbre *m*; **fruit t.,** arbre fruitier; **t. trunk,** tronc d'arbre; **t. house,** cabane construite dans un arbre; **to climb a t.,** grimper sur un arbre; **to be at the top of the t.,** être au haut, au sommet, de l'échelle; **family t.,** arbre généalogique. **'treeless** *a* sans arbres. **'treetop** *n* cime *f* (d'un arbre).

trefoil ['trefɔil] *n* trèfle *m*.

trek [trek] **1.** *n* voyage (long et difficile); **it's quite a t.,** c'est loin loin; **day's t.,** étape *f* **2.** *vi* (**trekked**) faire un voyage long et difficile, faire un trajet dur et pénible.

trellis ['trelis] *n* (*also* **trelliswork**) treillis *m*, treillage *m*.

tremble ['trembl] **1.** *n* tremblement *m*; (*in voice*) tremblotement *m*; *F:* **to be all of a t.,** être tout tremblant; trembloter **2.** *vi* (a) trembler, vibrer (b) trembler, frissonner; frémir. **'trembling 1.** *a* tremblant, tremblotant **2.** *n* tremblement *m*; tremblotement *m*; **in fear and t.,** tout tremblant. **'tremolo** *n* (*pl* -os) *Mus:* trémolo *m*. **'tremor** *n* tremblement *m*. **'tremulous** *a* tremblotant, frémissant; timide; **t. voice,** voix chevrotante. **'tremulously** *adv* en tremblant; timidement.

tremendous [tri'mendəs] *a* **1.** terrible **2.** *F:* immense, énorme; formidable; **a t. lot of,** une quantité énorme de; **a t. crowd,** un monde fou; **t. success,** succès fou. **tre'mendously** *adv* terriblement, extrêmement, énormément.

trench [tren(t)ʃ] **1.** *n* (*pl* **trenches**) tranchée *f*, fossé *m* **2.** *vtr* creuser un fossé, une tranchée, dans (le sol). **'trenchcoat** *n* trench-coat *m*.

trenchant ['tren(t)ʃənt] *a* (ton) incisif, (*of reply*) mordant.

trend [trend] *n* direction *f*; tendance *f* (de l'opinion, de la mode). **'trendsetter** *n* lanceur, -euse, de modes; personne *f* qui donne le ton. **'trendy** *a* *F:* à la page; dans le vent; (*of clothes*) dernier cri.

trepidation [trepi'dei∫(ə)n] *n* agitation violente; émoi *m*.

trespass ['trespəs] *vi* s'introduire sans autorisation sur la propriété de qn; *PN:* **no trespassing,** entrée interdite; propriété privée. **'trespasser** *n* intrus, -use; *PN:* **trespassers will be prosecuted,** défense d'entrer sous peine d'amende, de poursuites.

trestle ['tresl] *n* tréteau *m*, chevalet *m*; **t. table,** table à tréteaux.

trial ['traiəl] *n* **1.** *Jur:* (a) jugement *m*; **to bring s.o. to t.,** faire passer qn en jugement; **t. by jury,** jugement par jury (b) procès *m*; **famous trials,** causes *f* célèbres **2.** (a) essai *m*; épreuve *f*; *Sp:* **t. (game),** match de sélection (b) **to give sth a t.,** faire l'essai de qch; **on t.,** à l'essai; *Com:* **t. order,** commande d'essai; **t. run,** (i) *Aut:* essai sur route (ii) période d'essai (c) (*usu pl*) concours *m* (de chiens de berger) **3.** épreuve douloureuse; peine *f*; **he's a great t. to his parents,** il fait le martyre de ses parents.

triangle ['traiæŋgl] *n* triangle *m*. **tri'angular** *a* triangulaire.

tribe [traib] *n* tribu *f*. **'tribal** *a* de tribu; (système) tribal; **t. warfare,** guerre tribale. **'tribesman** *n* (*pl* -men) membre *m* de la tribu.

tribunal [trai'bju:n(ə)l] *n* tribunal *m*.

tribute ['tribju:t] *n* **1.** tribut *m*; **to pay t.,** payer tribut (**to,** à) **2.** tribut, hommage *m*; **to pay (a) t. to s.o.,** rendre hommage à qn; **floral tributes,** gerbes *f* et couronnes *f* (de fleurs). **'tributary 1.** *a* tributaire **2.** *n* affluent *m* (d'un fleuve).

trice [trais] *n* **in a t.,** en un clin d'œil, en moins de rien.

triceps ['traiseps] *n* *Anat:* triceps *m*.

trick [trik] **I.** *n* **1.** (a) tour *m*, ruse *f*; supercherie *f* (b) farce *f*, tour; **to play a t. on s.o.,** jouer un tour à qn; **my eyes have been playing tricks on me,** j'ai dû avoir la berlue; **you've been up to your tricks again,** vous avez encore fait des vôtres (c) truc *m*; **the tricks of the trade,** les ficelles, les astuces, du métier; **t. of the light,** illusion *f* d'optique; **he knows a t. or two, all the tricks,** il est roublard; **to know the t. of it,** avoir le truc, le chic; **that should do the t.,** ça fera l'affaire; *Phot: Cin:* **t. photography,** truquage *m*, trucage *m* (d) tour d'adresse; **card t.,** tour de cartes; **conjuring t.,** tour de prestidigitation, de passe-passe; *F:* **the whole bag of tricks,** tout le bataclan; **he doesn't miss a t.,** rien ne lui échappe; *F:* **how's tricks?** (i) comment vas-tu? (ii) quoi de neuf? **2.** manie *f*, tic *m*, habitude *f*; **he has a t. of arriving just when we're about to eat,** il a le don d'arriver juste au moment où nous nous mettons à table **3.** *Cards:* levée *f*; **to take a t.,** faire une levée, un pli. **II.** *vtr* attraper, duper (qn); mystifier (qn); **I've been tricked,** je me suis fait avoir; **to t. s.o. into doing sth,** amener qn par (la) ruse à faire qch; **to t. s.o. out of sth,** escroquer qch à qn. **'trickery** *n* tricherie *f*; fraude *f*, supercherie *f*; ruse *f*. **'trickiness** *n* **1.** fourberie *f* **2.** complication *f*, délicatesse *f* (d'un mécanisme, d'une situation). **'trickster** *n* escroc *m*; filou *m*. **'tricky** *a* **1.** rusé, astucieux; *F:* **he's a t. customer,** c'est un rusé **2.** délicat; compliqué; **a t. situation,** une situation délicate.

trickle ['trikl] **1.** *n* (a) filet *m* (d'eau); **there was a steady t. of people,** les gens arrivaient en petit nombre mais régulièrement; **sales were down to a t.,** il n'y avait presque plus de ventes (b) *El:* **t. charger,** chargeur à régime lent **2.** *vi* (a) couler (goutte à goutte); **water was trickling down the wall,** l'eau dégoulinait le long du mur; **tears trickled down her cheeks,** les larmes coulaient le long de ses joues; **the news is trickling through,** on commence à recevoir peu à peu des nouvelles (b) **the ball trickled into the hole,** la balle a roulé tout doucement dans le trou. **'trickling** *n* dégouttement *m*; écoulement *m* goutte à goutte.

tricolour ['trikələr] *n* drapeau tricolore (français).

tricycle ['traisikl] *n* tricycle *m*.

trident ['traidənt] n trident m.

tried see try II.

trier ['traiər] n F: he's a t., il ne se décourage jamais; il est persévérant.

trifle ['traifl] 1. n (a) bagatelle f, vétille f; **to quarrel over a t.**, se quereller pour un oui, pour un non (b) petite somme d'argent; **it was sold for a mere t.**, on l'a vendu pour une somme dérisoire (c) **a t.**, un tout petit peu; un soupçon; **a t. too wide**, un peu trop large (d) Cu: = diplomate m 2. vi (a) jouer, badiner (**with**, avec); **he's not a man to be trifled with**, on ne plaisante pas avec lui (b) **to t. with sth**, manier (qch); jouer avec (qch) (c) s'amuser; s'occuper à des riens. **'trifling 1.** a insignifiant; peu important; **t. incidents**, menus incidents 2. n (a) badinage m (b) gaspillage m du temps (en futilités).

trigger ['trigər] 1. n (a) poussoir m à ressort; **t. action**, déclenchement m (b) (of firearm) détente f; gâchette f; F: **to be t. happy**, avoir la gâchette facile 2. vtr **to t. (off)**, déclencher, provoquer (une explosion, une révolution).

trigonometry [trigə'nɔmitri] n trigonométrie f.

trill [tril] 1. n (a) Mus: trille m (b) consonne roulée 2. v (a) vi Mus: faire des trilles (b) vtr Mus: triller (une note); **trilled consonant**, consonne roulée.

trillion ['triljən] n (i) trillion m (10^{18}) (ii) NAm: billion m (10^{12}).

trilogy ['trilədʒi] n trilogie f.

trim [trim] I. n 1. **in good t.**, (i) en bon ordre (ii) (of pers) en bonne santé; en forme; **everything was in perfect t.**, tout était en parfait état 2. (a) Nau: assiette f; Av: équilibrage m; **in t., out of t.**, équilibré, non équilibré (b) Nau: orientation f (des voiles) 3. coupe f (de cheveux); **to have a t.**, se faire rafraîchir les cheveux 4. (on garment) garniture f; Aut: finitions fpl extérieures; **the car has a red interior t.**, la voiture a un intérieur rouge. II. a soigné; **a t. figure**, une taille fine; **a t. little garden**, un petit jardin coquet, net. III. vtr (trimmed) 1. tailler (une haie); rafraîchir (la barbe); couper, rafraîchir (les cheveux); rogner (les tranches d'un livre); **to t. a lamp**, moucher, tailler, une lampe; Cu: **to t. meat**, parer la viande; **to t. off the fat**, enlever le gras 2. Nau: orienter (les voiles) 3. Cl: orner, garnir (**with**, de); décorer (un arbre de Noël); **trimmed with lace**, garni de dentelles. **'trimming 1.** n 1. taille f (d'une haie); ébarbage m (des tranches d'un livre) 2. Cl: (a) garnissage m (b) garniture f, ornement m (de vêtements, de rideaux); Cu: F: **the (usual) trimmings**, accompagnements mpl, garniture (d'un plat).

trimaran ['traiməræn] n Nau: trimaran m.

Trinidad ['trinidæd] Prn Geog: (île f de) Trinidad, (île de) la Trinité.

Trinity ['triniti] n la (sainte) Trinité; **T. Sunday**, (fête f de) la Trinité.

trinket ['triŋkit] n (a) colifichet m; breloque f (b) bibelot m.

trio ['tri:ou] n (pl trios) trio m.

trip [trip] I. n 1. excursion f; voyage m d'agrément; **the t. takes two hours**, on fait le trajet en deux heures; **round t.**, (i) voyage circulaire (ii) voyage d'aller et retour; **he does three trips to Ireland a month**, il va en Irlande trois fois par mois; **we'll have to have another t. to the doctor**, il faudra retourner chez le médecin 2. (drugs) voyage, trip m. II. v (tripped) 1. vi (a) **to t.**

(along), aller d'un pas léger (b) trébucher; faire un faux pas; **to t. over sth**, buter contre qch (c) **to t. up**, se tromper (d) P: (drugs) faire un trip 2. vtr **to t. s.o. (up)**, (i) faire une croche-pied à qn; (of obstacle) faire trébucher qn (ii) prendre qn en défaut, en erreur. **'tripper** n touriste mf; excursionniste mf; **they're day trippers**, ils sont venus passer la journée. **'tripwire** n fil m de détente.

tripe [traip] n (a) Cu: tripe(s) f(pl) (b) bêtises fpl; **this is a lot of t.**, tout ça c'est des sottises.

triple ['tripl] 1. a triple; trois fois plus; Mus: **t. time**, mesure ternaire, à trois temps 2. n triple m 3. vtr & i (se) tripler. **'triplets** npl triplés, -ées. **'triplicate** n triple m; triplicata m; **in t.**, en trois exemplaires. **'triply** adv triplement.

tripod ['traipɔd] n trépied m.

tripos ['traipɔs] n Sch: = licence f ès lettres, ès sciences (à Cambridge).

triptych ['triptik] n Art: triptyque m.

trite [trait] a banal; (sujet) rebattu; **t. remarks**, lieux communs. **'tritely** adv banalement. **'triteness** n banalité f.

triumph ['traiəmf] 1. n (a) triomphe m, succès m (b) air m, sentiment m, de triomphe; jubilation f; **he came home in t.**, il est rentré chez lui en triomphe 2. vi triompher; **to t. over s.o.**, triompher de qn; l'emporter sur qn. **triumphal** [-'ʌmf(ə)l] a triomphal. **tri'umphant** a triomphant; triomphal. **tri'umphantly** adv triomphalement.

trivia ['triviə] npl vétilles fpl, futilités fpl. **'trivial** a (a) insignifiant; sans importance; **t. offence**, peccadille f (b) banal. **trivi'ality** n (a) insignifiance f (b) banalité f (d'une observation) (c) **to talk trivialities**, dire des futilités.

trod, trodden see tread II.

trolley ['trɔli] n (a) chariot m; (two-wheeled) diable m; Rail: **luggage t.**, chariot à bagages (b) **shopping t.**, chariot, F: caddie m; **tea, dinner, t.**, table roulante. **'trolleybus** n trolleybus m.

trollop ['trɔləp] nf putain f.

trombone [trɔm'boun] n Mus: trombone m.

troop [tru:p] I. n 1. troupe f, bande f (de personnes) 2. Mil: (a) pl **troops**, troupes; **t. train**, train militaire; **t. carrier**, (i) véhicule blindé de transport m de personnel (ii) avion de transport de troupes (b) (unit) peloton m (de cavalerie) 3. Scout: troupe. II. v 1. vi **to t. up**, s'assembler, s'attrouper; **to t. in, out, off**, entrer, sortir, partir, en troupe, en bande 2. vtr Mil: **to t. the colour**, présenter le drapeau. **'trooper** n Mil: soldat m de la cavalerie; F: **to swear like a t.**, jurer comme un charretier. **'trooping** n Mil: **t. the colour**, présentation f du drapeau. **'troopship** n transport m de troupes.

trophy ['troufi] n trophée m.

tropic ['trɔpik] n Geog: tropique m; **the T. of Cancer, of Capricorn**, le tropique du cancer, du capricorne (b) **the tropics**, les tropiques; **in the tropics**, sous les tropiques. **'tropical** a (climat) tropical; (maladie) des tropiques.

trot [trɔt] 1. n trot m; **to set off at a t.**, partir au trot; **to break into a t.**, prendre le trot; **they've had 5 wins on the t.**, ils ont gagné 5 fois de suite; F: **to keep s.o. on the t.**, ne laisser aucun repos à qn 2. vi (trotted) (of horse) trotter, aller au trot; (of pers) trotter, courir; **she**

trotted round to the butcher, elle a fait un saut chez le boucher; **to t. in,** entrer au trot. **'trot 'out** *vtr* faire étalage de (ses connaissances); débiter (des excuses). **'trotter** *n* 1. (*horse*) trotteur, -euse 2. *Cu:* **sheep's, pigs', trotters,** pieds *m* de mouton, de porc. **'trotting** *n* t. race, course de trot.

trouble ['trʌbl] I. *n* 1. (*a*) peine *f*, chagrin *m*; malheur *m*; **his troubles are over,** il est au bout de ses malheurs (*b*) ennui *m*, difficulté *f*; **money troubles,** soucis *mpl* d'argent; **what's the t.?** qu'est-ce qu'il y a? **the t. is that,** l'ennui, la difficulté, c'est que; **you'll have t. with him,** il va vous causer des ennuis, il vous donnera du fil à retordre (*c*) **to get into t.,** s'attirer des ennuis; **to get into t. with the police,** avoir des ennuis avec la police; **to get s.o. into t.,** créer des ennuis à qn; **to get s.o. out of t.,** tirer qn d'affaire; **he's asking for t.,** il se prépare des ennuis (*d*) **to make t.,** semer la discorde; **there's going to be t.,** il y aura du grabuge, du vilain (*e*) **there was t. in the streets,** il y a eu des désordres dans la rue; **t. spot,** point chaud, névralgique; **labour troubles,** conflits ouvriers (*f*) *Med:* **trouble(s)** *m(pl)*; **stomach t., troubles** digestifs; **to have heart t.,** être malade du cœur; **I have back t.,** je souffre du dos (*g*) panne *f*; *Aut:* **engine t.,** panne de moteur; **t.-free journey,** voyage sans incidents 2. dérangement *m*; peine; **to take the t. to do sth, to go to the t. of doing sth,** prendre, se donner, la peine de faire qch; **it's not worth the t.,** ce n'est pas la peine; **to give oneself a lot of t.,** se donner beaucoup de peine; **nothing is too much t. for him,** rien ne lui coûte; **it's no t.!** ce n'est rien! II. *v* 1. *vtr* (*a*) affliger, tourmenter, chagriner (qn); inquiéter, préoccuper (qn); **to be troubled about s.o.,** s'inquiéter au sujet de qn; **that doesn't t. him much,** cela ne le préoccupe guère; ça lui donne fort peu de soucis (*b*) affliger; **my arm troubles me,** mon bras me fait souffrir (*c*) déranger, incommoder, gêner (qn); **I'm sorry to t. you,** excusez-moi de vous déranger; **I won't t. you with the details,** je vous fais grâce des détails; **may I t. you to shut the door?** cela vous dérangerait(-il) de fermer la porte? 2. *vi* (*a*) s'inquiéter (**about, de,** au sujet de); **without troubling about the consequences,** sans s'inquiéter des conséquences (*b*) se déranger, se mettre en peine; **don't t. to write,** ne vous donnez pas la peine d'écrire; **don't t.!** **you needn't t.!** ne vous dérangez pas! **'troubled** *a* 1. (*of liquid*) trouble; **to fish in t. waters,** pêcher en eau trouble 2. (*a*) inquiet, agité; **t. sleep,** sommeil agité (*b*) *Pol: Hist:* **t. period,** époque de troubles. **'troublemaker** *n* fomentateur, -trice, de troubles; provocateur, -trice. **'troubleshooter** *n* dépanneur *m*; *Pol: Ind:* conciliateur, -trice. **'troublesome** *a* ennuyeux, gênant; (enfant) énervant; (rival) gênant; (toux) pénible.

trough [trɔf] *n* 1. (**feeding**) **t.,** auge *f*, mangeoire *f*; **drinking t.,** abreuvoir *m* 2. **t. of the sea,** creux *m* de la lame 3. *Meteor:* **t. of low pressure,** zone dépressionnaire.

trounce [trauns] *vtr* *Sp:* battre (qn) à plate(s) couture(s).

troupe [tru:p] *n* *Th:* troupe *f*.

trousers ['trauzɔz] *npl* (**pair of**) **t.,** pantalon *m*; **short t.,** culottes *fpl* courtes; **t. suit,** tailleur-pantalon *m*; *F:* **she wears the t.,** c'est elle qui porte la culotte.

trousseau ['tru:sou] *n* (*pl* **trousseaus, -eaux**) trousseau *m*.

trout [traut] *n* (*inv in pl*) *Ich:* truite *f*; **salmon t.,** truite saumonée; **t. fishing,** pêche à la truite; **t. stream,** ruisseau à truites.

trowel ['trau(ə)l] *n* 1. truelle *f*; *F:* **to lay it on with a t.,** exagérer; y aller un peu fort 2. *Hort:* déplantoir *m*.

truant ['tru:ənt] *n* élève absent (de l'école) sans permission; **to play t.,** faire l'école buissonnière; sécher les cours. **'truancy** *n* absentéisme *m* scolaire.

truce [tru:s] *n* trêve *f*; **to call a t.,** faire trêve; faire la paix.

truck¹ [trʌk] *n* 1. **I have no t. with him,** (i) je n'ai pas affaire à lui (ii) je n'ai rien à faire avec lui 2. *NAm:* produits *mpl* maraîchers; **t. gardener, farmer,** maraîcher *m*.

truck² I. *n* 1. (*a*) (*two-wheeled*) diable *m*; (*four-wheeled*) chariot *m*; **fork-lift t.,** chariot élévateur à fourche (*b*) *NAm:* *Aut:* camion *m*; **delivery t.,** camionnette *f* 2. *Rail:* wagon *m* (à marchandises); **cattle t.,** fourgon *m* à bestiaux II. *vtr* *esp NAm:* camionner (des marchandises). **'truckdriver, 'trucker** *n* *NAm:* camionneur *m*. **'trucking** *n* *NAm:* camionnage *m*. **'truckload** *n* **a t. of fruit,** un camion de fruits.

truculence ['trʌkjulɔns] *n* brutalité *f*, férocité *f*. **'truculent** *a* brutal, féroce. **'truculently** *adv* brutalement, férocement.

trudge [trʌdʒ] 1. *n* marche *f* pénible 2. *vi* marcher lourdement, péniblement; **to t. along,** avancer péniblement.

true [tru:] I. *a* 1. vrai; exact; **t. adventures,** aventures vécues; **that's t.!** c'est juste! c'est bien vrai! **to come t.,** se réaliser; **this also holds t. for,** il en est de même pour 2. véritable; vrai; réel; **t. repentance,** repentir sincère; **to get a t. idea of the situation,** se faire une idée juste de la situation 3. *MecE: etc:* juste, droit; **to make a piece t.,** ajuster une pièce; **the table isn't t.,** la table n'est pas d'aplomb 4. fidèle, loyal (**to, à**); **to be t. to oneself,** ne pas se démentir; **to be t. to one's promise,** rester fidèle à une promesse 5. (*of voice, instrument*) juste. II. *adv* (chanter, viser) juste; (*of wheel*) **to run t.,** tourner rond; **the wheel is not running t.,** la roue est désaxée. III. *n* **out of t.,** hors d'aplomb; (*of beam*) tordu, dénivelé; (*of wheel*) voilé, décentré, désaxé; **to run out of t.,** (i) se décentrer (ii) être décentré; tourner à faux; ne pas tourner rond. **'truism** *n* truisme *m*. **'truly** *adv* 1. (*a*) vraiment, véritablement; **I am t. grateful,** je vous suis sincèrement reconnaissant (*b*) *Corr:* **yours t. =** veuillez agréer l'expression de mes sentiments distingués 2. en vérité; à vrai dire; *F:* (**really and) t.?** vrai de vrai? 3. (servir qn) fidèlement, loyalement 4. vraiment, justement; **well and t.,** bel et bien.

truffle ['trʌfl] *n* truffe *f*.

trump [trʌmp] 1. *n* *Cards:* **t. (card),** atout *m*; **to play trumps,** jouer atout; **spades are trumps,** c'est pique atout; **no trumps,** sans atout; *Fig:* **to play one's t. card,** jouer son atout; *F:* **he always turns up trumps,** (i) la chance le favorise (ii) on peut toujours compter sur lui 2. *vtr* (*a*) *Cards:* couper (une carte); *vi* jouer atout (*b*) **to t. up an excuse,** inventer une excuse; **to t. up a charge,** forger une accusation (contre qn).

trumpet ['trʌmpit] 1. *n* trompette *f*; *Mil:* **t. major,** trompette-major *m*; **t. player,** trompettiste *m* 2. *vi*

(trumpeted) (a) sonner de la trompette (b) (of elephant) barrir. **'trumpeter** n (a) Mil: trompette m (b) (by profession) trompettiste m. **'trumpeting** n (a) sonnerie f de trompette (b) (of elephant) barrit m, barrissement m.

truncate [trʌŋ'keit] vtr tronquer (un texte).

truncheon ['trʌn(t)ʃən] n bâton m (d'agent de police); matraque f.

trundle ['trʌndl] 1. vtr pousser (qch) bruyamment 2. vi to t. along, rouler bruyamment.

trunk [trʌŋk] n 1. (a) tronc m (d'arbre) (b) tronc (du corps) (c) **t. road**, grande route; route nationale; Rail: **t. line**, grande ligne (d) Tp: **t. call**, communication interurbaine 2. (a) malle f (b) NAm: Aut: coffre m 3. trompe f (d'éléphant) (c) Cl: **trunks**, slip m (d'homme); **(bathing) trunks**, slip de bain.

truss [trʌs] I. n 1. (a) botte f (de foin) (b) touffe f, grappe f (de fleurs) 2. ferme f (de comble, de pont); armature f (de poutre); **t. girder**, poutre armée 3. Med: bandage m herniaire. II. vtr Cu: trousser, brider (une volaille); to **t. s.o. (up)**, ligoter qn.

trust [trʌst] I. n 1. confiance f (in, en); **to put one's t. in s.o., sth**, faire confiance à qn, qch; to **have t. in**, avoir confiance en; **to take sth on t.**, croire (qn) sur parole; accepter qch de confiance 2. espérance f, espoir m 3. (a) responsabilité f; **position of t.**, poste de confiance; **breach of t.**, abus de confiance (b) **he committed it to my t.**, il l'a confié à ma garde 4. Jur: fidéicommis m, fiducie f; **to hold sth in t.**, tenir qch par fidéicommis 5. Fin: trust m, syndicat m. II. v 1. vtr (a) se fier, se confier, à (qn, qch); mettre sa confiance en (qn); **he's not to be trusted**, on ne peut pas se fier à lui; **to t. s.o. with sth**, confier qch à qn; **to t. s.o. to do sth**, compter sur qn pour faire qch; F: **t. him (to say that)!** c'est bien de lui! **I couldn't t. myself to speak**, j'étais trop ému pour me risquer à rien dire; F: **she won't t. him out of her sight**, elle le surveille tout le temps (b) to **t. sth to s.o.**, confier qch à qn, aux soins, à la garde, de qn (c) Com: F: faire crédit à (un client) (d) espérer (que + ind); **I t. he will come**, j'espère (bien) qu'il viendra 2. vi (a) se confier (in, en); se fier (in, à); avoir confiance (in, en) (b) **to t. to sth**, mettre ses espérances, son espoir, en qch; **to t. to luck**, se confier au hasard. **'trusted** a (personne) de confiance; **tried and t.**, (ami, remède) éprouvé. **trus'tee** n Jur: 1, fidéicommissaire m; mandataire mf 2. administrateur, -trice (d'une institution); **board of trustees**, conseil m d'administration. **'trustful, 'trusting** a plein de confiance; confiant. **'trustfully, 'trustingly** adv avec confiance. **'trustworthiness** n 1. (of pers) loyauté f, honnêteté f 2. crédibilité f, véracité f (d'un témoignage). **'trustworthy** a 1. (of pers) (digne) de confiance, digne de foi; loyal; honnête; irrécusable; **a t. person**, une personne de confiance 2. (renseignement) digne de foi; (témoignage) irrécusable.

truth [tru:θ] n (pl **truths** [tru:ðz]) (a) vérité f; **the t. is, to tell the t., I forgot**, pour dire la vérité, à vrai dire, j'ai oublié; F: **the honest t.**, la vérité vraie; **there's some t. in what you say**, il y a du vrai dans ce que vous dites; Jur: **the t., the whole t., and nothing but the t.**, la vérité, toute la vérité, rien que la vérité (b) chose vraie; **to tell s.o. a few home truths**, dire ses quatre vérités à qn. **'truthful** a 1. (of pers) véridique 2. (témoignage) vrai; (portrait) fidèle. **'truthfully** adv 1. véridique-

ment; sans mentir 2. fidèlement. **'truthfulness** n véracité f; fidélité f (d'un portrait).

try [trai] I. n (a) essai m, tentative f; **to have a t. at (doing) sth**, essayer de faire qch; **let's have a t.!** essayons toujours! **at the first t.**, du premier coup (b) Rugby Fb: essai; **to score, to convert, a t.**, marquer, transformer, un essai (en but). II. v (pt & pp **tried**) 1. vtr (a) éprouver (qn); mettre (qn, qch) à l'épreuve (b) Lit: affliger (qn); **sorely tried**, durement éprouvé (c) **to t. one's eyes**, se fatiguer les yeux (d) essayer; faire l'essai de (qch); **to t. a dish**, goûter d'un plat (e) Jur: juger (une cause, un accusé) (f) essayer, tenter; **to t. one's hand at sth**, essayer de faire qch; **to t. one's strength against s.o.**, se mesurer avec qn; **to t. the door**, essayer d'ouvrir la porte (g) **to t. to do, t. and do, sth**, tâcher, essayer, de faire qch; **he tried his hardest to save them**, il a fait tout son possible pour les sauver; **she tried hard to keep back her tears**, elle a fait de grands efforts pour retenir ses larmes; **it's worth trying**, cela vaut la peine d'essayer 2. vi (a) faire un effort, des efforts, une tentative; **to t. again**, faire une nouvelle tentative; **t. again!** essaye encore une fois! (b) **to t. for (sth)**, tâcher d'obtenir (qch); poser sa candidature à (un emploi). **tried** a **well t.**, éprouvé; qui a fait ses preuves. **'trying** a 1. difficile, dur, pénible 2. vexant; contrariant; agaçant; **he's very t.**, il est insupportable. **'try on** vtr 1. essayer (un vêtement) 2. **to t. it on with s.o.**, bluffer qn; essayer de voir jusqu'où on peut aller avec qn; **he's just trying it on**, il fait le malin. **'try-on** n F: bluff m. **'try out** vtr essayer, faire l'essai de (qch); mettre (qch) à l'essai. **'tryout** n essai m.

tsar [tsɑːr] n tsar m. **tsa'rina** nf tsarine f.

tsetse ['tsetsi] n Ent: **t. (fly)**, (mouche f) tsétsé f.

TT abbr 1. teetotal(ler) 2. tuberculin tested.

tub [tʌb] n 1. (a) baquet m, cuve f; bac m (à fleurs) (b) baquet (à lessive); (in washing machine) cuve (c) petit pot (à glaces) 2. (a) baignoire f (b) tub m 3. Nau: F: old t., vieux rafiot. **'tubby** a F: (of pers) dodu, boulot.

tuba ['tjuːbə] n Mus: tuba m.

tube [tjuːb] n 1. (a) tube m, tuyau m (b) tube (de couleur, de pâte dentifrice) (c) **inner t.**, chambre f d'air (d'un pneu) (d) Ch: **test t.**, éprouvette f (e) Rail: F: (in London) **the t.** = le métro; **t. station** = station de métro 2. Anat: tube; canal; trompe f (de Fallope) 3. NAm: F: **the t.**, la télé. **'tubing** n coll tubes mpl; tuyauterie f; **rubber t.**, tube, tuyau, en caoutchouc. **'tubular** a tubulaire.

tuber ['tjuːbər] n Bot: tubercule m. **'tubercle** n Med: tubercule m. **tu'bercular** a tuberculeux. **tu'berculin** n Med: tuberculine f; **t. tested milk** = lait cru certifié. **tubercu'losis** n Med: tuberculose f. **tu'berculous** a Med: tuberculeux.

TUC abbr Trades Union Congress.

tuck [tʌk] 1. n (a) (petit) pli; rempli m (b) Sch: friandises fpl 2. vtr (a) faire des plis à (une jupe) (b) replier; serrer, mettre; **to t. one's legs under one**, replier les jambes sous soi; **she tucked her arm in mine**, elle a passé son bras sous le mien; **to t. a blanket round s.o.**, envelopper qn d'une couverture; **to t. one's shirt into one's trousers**, rentrer sa chemise dans son pantalon; **to t. sth away**, cacher qch. **'tuckbox** n (pl -boxes) Sch: boîte f à provisions. **'tuck 'in** vtr (a) serrer, rentrer; **to t. in the bedclothes**, border le lit (b) **to t. s.o.**

in, border qn (dans son lit) 2. *vi F:* bien bouffer; **t. in!** allez-y! mangez! **'tuck-in** *n F:* to have a good t.-in, s'envoyer un bon repas; bien bouffer. **'tuck 'into** *vtr F:* to t. i. a meal, attaquer un repas. **'tuckshop** *n Sch:* boutique *f* à provisions. **'tuck 'up** *vtr (a)* relever, retrousser (sa jupe) *(b)* border (qn) (dans son lit).

Tuesday ['tju:zdi] *n* mardi *m;* Shrove T., mardi gras.

tuft [tʌft] *n* touffe *f* (d'herbe, de plumes, de cheveux); huppe *f* (d'un oiseau). **'tufted** *a Orn:* huppé.

tug [tʌg] I. *n* 1. traction (subite); saccade *f;* to give a good t., tirer fort; he gave a t. at the bell, il a tiré (sur) la sonnette; I felt a t. at my sleeve, j'ai senti qu'on me tirait par la manche; t. of war, (i) *Sp:* lutte *f* de traction à la corde (ii) *Fig:* lutte acharnée et prolongée 2. *Nau:* remorqueur *m.* II. *v* 1. *vtr & i* (**tugged**) tirer fort; to t. at sth, tirer sur qch 2. *vtr Nau:* remorquer. **'tugboat** *n Nau:* remorqueur *m.*

tuition [tju(:)'iʃən] *n* instruction *f;* private t., leçons particulières; cours particuliers; t. fees, frais d'inscription.

tulip ['tju:lip] *n Bot:* tulipe *f.*

tulle [tju:l] *n Tex:* tulle *m.*

tumble ['tʌmbl] I. *n* 1. *(a)* culbute *f,* chute *f;* to take a t., faire une chute *(b)* t. drier, séchoir à linge rotatif (à air chaud) 2. culbute (d'acrobate). II. *v* 1. *vi (a)* to t. (down, over), tomber (par terre); faire une chute; culbuter, faire la culbute; building that is tumbling down, édifice qui s'écroule, qui tombe en ruine *(b)* to t. about, s'agiter *(c)* to t. into bed, to t. out of bed, se jeter dans son lit; bondir hors du lit; to t. out, tomber (de la voiture, par la fenêtre); they were tumbling over one another, ils se bousculaient *(d) (of acrobat)* faire des culbutes *(e) F:* to t. to an idea, comprendre, saisir, une idée 2. *vtr* to t. sth down, over, culbuter, renverser, faire tomber, qch. **'tumbledown** *a* croulant, délabré; (maison) qui tombe en ruine. **'tumbler** *n* 1. verre *m* à (boire) sans pied; gobelet *m* 2. t. (drier), séchoir à linge rotatif (à air chaud).

tummy ['tʌmi] *n (pl* tummies) *F:* ventre *m;* t. ache, mal de ventre.

tumour, *NAm:* tumor ['tju:mər] *n Med:* tumeur *f.*

tumult ['tju:mʌlt] *n* tumulte *m;* agitation *f,* émoi *m.* **tu'multuous** *a* tumultueux. **tu'multuously** *adv* tumultueusement.

tumulus ['tju:mjuləs] *n (pl* tumuli [-lai]) tumulus *m.*

tun [tʌn] *n* tonneau *m,* fût *m.*

tuna ['tju:nə] *n (no pl) Ich:* thon *m.*

tundra ['tʌndrə] *n Geog:* toundra *f.*

tune [tju:n] I. *n* 1. air *m* (de musique); *F:* give us a t.! jouez-nous un air! faites-nous un peu de musique! *Fig:* to call the t., donner le note; to change one's t., changer de ton; to be fined to the t. of £50, avoir une amende de £50 2. *Mus:* accord *m;* the piano is in t., out of t., le piano est accordé, désaccordé; to be out of t., détonner; to sing in t., out of t., chanter juste, faux 3. accord, harmonie *f;* to be in t. with one's surroundings, être en harmonie avec son milieu. II. *vtr & i* 1. accorder, mettre d'accord (un instrument); *(of orchestra)* to t. up, s'accorder 2. *WTel:* to t. in to a station, capter un poste; to be tuned (in) to, être à l'écoute de 3. *Aut:* to t. (up), caler, régler, mettre au point (un moteur); *(of engine)* to be tuned up, être au point. **'tuneful** *a* mélodieux, harmonieux.

'tunefully *adv* mélodieusement, harmonieusement. **'tuneless** *a* discordant; sans mélodie. **'tuner** *n* 1. (piano) t., accordeur *m* (de pianos) 2. *WTel:* tuner *m.* **'tuning** *n* 1. *Mus:* accord *m;* t. fork, diapason *m* 2. *Aut:* t. (up), réglage *m,* mise *f* au point (du moteur) 3. *WTel:* t. (in), réglage; t. knob, bouton de réglage.

tungsten ['tʌŋstən] *n* tungstène *m.*

tunic ['tju:nik] *n* tunique *f.*

Tunisia [tju:'nizjə] *Prn Geog:* Tunisie *f.*

tunnel ['tʌn(ə)l] I. *n* tunnel *m;* galerie (creusée par une taupe); to drive a t. through a mountain, percer un tunnel sous une montagne 2. *vtr & i* (**tunnelled,** *NAm:* **tunneled**) to t. (through) a mountain, percer un tunnel dans, sous, une montagne; to t. in, out, entrer, sortir en creusant un tunnel. **'tunnelling** *n* percement *m* d'un tunnel.

tunny ['tʌni] *n (no pl) Ich:* t. (fish), thon *m.*

turban ['tə:bən] *n Cl:* turban *m.*

turbid ['tə:bid] *a* (liquide) trouble.

turbine ['tə:bain] *n* turbine *f.*

turbo- ['tə:bou] *pref* turbo-. **'turbojet** *n* turboréacteur *m;* avion *m* à turboréacteur. **'turboprop** *n* turbopropulseur *m;* avion *m* à turbopropulseur.

turbot ['tə:bət] *n Ich:* turbot *m.*

turbulent ['tə:bjulənt] *a* turbulent. **'turbulence** *n* turbulence *f.*

tureen [tə'ri:n] *n* soupière *f.*

turf [tə:f] I. *n (pl* turves, turfs) 1. *(a)* (i) gazon *m* (ii) motte *f* de gazon *(b) (in Ireland)* tourbe *f* 2. *Rac:* the t., le turf; t. accountant, bookmaker *m.* II. *vtr* 1. to t. (over), gazonner (un terrain) 2. *F:* to t. s.o. out, flanquer qn dehors, à la porte.

Turkey[1] ['tə:ki] *Prn Geog:* Turquie *f.* Turk *n* Turc, *f* Turque. **'Turkish** 1. *a* turc; de Turquie; T. bath, bain turc; T. towel, serviette éponge; T. delight, rahat-lo(u)koum *m* 2. *n Ling:* turc *m.*

turkey[2] *n* 1. *Orn:* t. (cock), dindon *m; (hen)* dinde *f* 2. *Cu:* dinde, dindonneau *m.*

turmeric ['tə:mərik] *n Bot: Cu:* curcuma *m;* safran *m* des Indes.

turmoil ['tə:moil] *n* trouble *m,* tumulte *m,* agitation *f;* émoi *m;* everything is in a t., c'est le bouleversement complet.

turn [tə:n] I. *n* 1. tour *m,* révolution *f* (d'une roue); to give sth a t., tourner qch (une fois); meat done to a t., viande cuite à point 2. *(a)* tournant *m;* virage *m;* no right, left, t., défense de tourner à droite, à gauche; U t., demi-tour *m;* three-point t., demi-tour en trois manœuvres; at every t., à tout bout de champ *(b)* tournure *f* (des affaires); to take a tragic t., tourner au tragique; to take a t. for the better, s'améliorer; prendre meilleure tournure; the patient has taken a t. for the worse, le malade a empiré *(c)* t. of the tide, étale *m;* renversement *m* de la marée *(d) F:* it gave me quite a t., ça m'a donné un (vrai) coup *(e) F:* she had one of her turns, elle a eu une de ses crises, une de ses attaques 3. to take a t. in the garden, faire un tour dans le jardin 4. *(a)* tour (de rôle); it's your t., c'est votre tour; c'est à vous (de jouer); in t., tour à tour; à tour de rôle; t. and t. about, chacun son tour; to speak out of t., parler mal à propos; to take turns with s.o., relayer qn; they take it in turns, ils se relaient *(b) Th:* numéro *m* (de music-hall) 5. *(a)* to do s.o. a good t., rendre (un) service à qn; **to do s.o. a-bad t.,** jouer un mauvais tour à qn; *Prov:* **one good t. deserves another,** un service en vaut un autre (b) intention f; **it will serve my t.,** cela fera mon affaire (pour le moment) 6. (a) **humorous t. of mind,** esprit humoristique (b) **t. of phrase,** tournure f de phrase (c) **car with a good t. of speed,** voiture rapide 7. (a) tournant, coude m (d'un chemin); **(sharp) t.,** virage; **twists and turns,** tours et détours mpl (b) tour (d'une corde). **II.** v 1. vtr (a) (faire) tourner (une roue); **to t. the key in the lock,** donner un tour de clef dans la serrure; **to t. the gas low,** mettre le gaz en veilleuse (b) **to t. (over) a page,** tourner une page; **to t. a garment inside out,** retourner un vête-ment; **to t. everything upside down,** mettre tout sens dessus dessous; **without turning a hair,** sans sourciller, sans broncher; **onions t. my stomach,** les oignons m'écœurent (c) **to t. aside a blow,** détourner un coup; ~~to t. the conversation, détourner la conversation; to t.~~ **one's thoughts to,** tourner ses pensées vers (d) (re)tourner (la tête); diriger (les yeux) **(towards,** vers); **t. your face this way,** tournez-vous, regardez, de ce côté (e) **he turns everyone against him,** il se met tout le monde à dos; **they turned his argument against him,** ils ont retourné son argument contre lui (f) **to t. the corner,** tourner le coin; **he has turned forty,** il a passé la quarantaine; **it's turned seven,** il est sept heures passées (g) changer, convertir, transformer **(into,** en); **his love turned to hate,** son amour s'est transformé en haine; **to t. a theatre into a cinema,** convertir un théâtre en cinéma; **the heat has turned the milk sour,** la chaleur a fait tourner le lait; **autumn turns the leaves yellow,** l'automne fait jaunir les feuilles; **success has turned his head,** le succès lui a tourné la tête (h) tourner, façonner au tour (un pied de table); **well turned sentence,** phrase bien tournée 2. vi (a) tourner; **the wheel turns,** la roue tourne; **my head's turning,** la tête me tourne (b) **to toss and t.,** se tourner et se retourner (dans son lit); **to t. upside down,** se retourner (c) se tourner; se retourner; **he turned to look at the view,** il s'est retourné pour regarder la vue; *Mil:* **right t.!** à droite…droite! (d) tourner, se diriger; **to t. to the left,** tourner, prendre, à gauche; **the wind is turning,** le vent change; **to t. to another subject,** passer à une autre question; **to t. to the dictionary,** consulter le dictionnaire; **I don't know which way to t.,** je ne sais où donner de la tête; **I didn't know who to t. to,** je ne savais pas à qui m'adresser (e) **the tide is turning,** la marée change; **his luck has turned,** sa chance a tourné (f) **to t. against s.o.,** se retourner contre qn (g) se changer, se convertir, se transformer **(into,** en); **it's turning to rain,** le temps se met à la pluie; **everything he touches turns to gold,** tout ce qu'il touche se change en or; **the milk has turned (sour),** le lait a tourné; **the leaves are beginning to t.,** les feuilles commencent à jaunir; **he turned red,** il a rougi; **to t. socialist,** devenir socialiste. **'turn a'round** vtr & i esp NAm: = **turn round. 'turn a'way** 1. vtr (a) détourner (les yeux) (b) détourner, écarter (c) renvoyer (qn) 2. vi se détourner; **to t. a. from s.o.,** (i) tourner le dos à qn (ii) abandonner qn. **'turn 'back** 1. vtr (a) faire faire demi-tour à (qn); faire revenir (qn) sur ses pas (b) rabattre son col 2. vi rebrousser chemin; se retourner; faire demi-tour. **'turncoat** n renégat, -ate. **'turn 'down** vtr (a) rabattre; corner (la page d'un livre); **to**

t. d. the bed(clothes), ouvrir le lit (b) baisser (le gaz, la radio) (c) **to t. d. a candidate,** refuser un candidat; **to t. d. an offer,** repousser une offre; F: **she turned me down flat,** elle m'a refusé catégoriquement. **'turn 'in** 1. vtr (a) **to t. one's toes in,** tourner les pieds en dedans (b) F: rendre, rapporter (qch) (c) F: quitter (son emploi) (d) F: vendre (qn) à la police 2. vi (a) **his toes t. in,** il a les pieds tournés en dedans (b) F: (aller) se coucher. **'turning** n 1. (a) mouvement giratoire; rotation f (b) changement m de direction; virage m; **t. point,** moment décisif; **at the t. point of his career,** au tournant de sa carrière 2. tournant m (d'une route); coude m; virage; **take the first t. to the right,** prenez la première (rue, route) à droite. **'turn 'off** 1. vtr (a) fermer, couper (l'eau, le gaz); éteindre (l'électricité, le gaz); fermer (un robinet) (b) F: **he turns me off,** il me dégoûte 2. vi (a) changer de route; tourner (à droite, à gauche) (b) **to t. o. the main road,** quitter la grande route. **'turnoff** n 1. embranchement m 2. F: **it's a right t.!** c'est vraiment dégoûtant! **'turn 'on** 1. vtr (a) ouvrir (l'eau, le gaz, un robinet); allumer (l'électricité, le gaz); **shall I t. on the light?** voulez-vous que j'allume? (b) F: **to t. s.o. on,** éveiller l'intérêt de qn; **that really turns me on,** ça me fait quelque chose 2. vi **to t. on s.o.,** attaquer qn; se retourner contre qn. **'turn 'out** 1. vtr (a) mettre (qn) dehors, à la porte; évincer, chasser (un locataire) (b) mettre (le bétail) au vert (c) vider (ses poches); **to t. o. a drawer,** (i) vider (ii) mettre de l'ordre, dans un tiroir; **to t. o. a room,** nettoyer une pièce à fond (d) Cu: démouler (une crème) (e) produire, fabriquer (des marchandises); **turned out by the dozen,** confectionnés à la douzaine (f) (of pers) **well turned out,** élégant, soigné (g) **to t. o. the light,** éteindre (h) **to t. one's toes o.,** tourner les pieds en dehors 2. vi (a) sortir; **they turned out to see him,** ils sont venus pour le voir (b) **things have turned out well,** les choses ont bien tourné, ont réussi; **it will t. o. all right,** cela s'arrangera; **as it turned out,** en l'occurrence; **the weather has turned out fine,** le temps s'est mis au beau; **it turns out that,** il se trouve que. **'turnout** n 1. assemblée f (de gens); **there was a large t.,** il y avait beaucoup de monde, il y avait foule 2. nettoyage m à fond (d'une pièce). **'turn 'over** 1. vtr (a) retourner (qch); tourner (une page); **to t. o. the pages of a book,** feuilleter un livre; **please t. o.,** tournez s'il vous plaît; **to t. (sth) o. in one's mind,** ruminer (une idée); retourner (un projet) dans sa tête (b) **to t. sth o. to s.o.,** remettre qch entre les mains de qn 2. vi se tourner, se retourner; (of car) **to t. right o.,** capoter. **'turnover** n (a) Com: chiffre m d'affaires; **quick t. of goods,** écoulement m rapide de marchandises; **t. of staff,** rotation f du personnel (b) Cu: **apple t.,** chausson m aux pommes. **'turnpike** n NAm: autoroute f (à péage). **'turn 'round** 1. vtr retourner; faire faire demi-tour à (un navire) 2. vi (a) tourner; (of crane) virer, pivoter; **to t. r. and round,** tournoyer (b) se retourner; faire volte-face; **t. r. and let me see your face,** tournez-vous que je voie votre visage. **'turnstile** n tourniquet(-compteur) m (pour entrées). **'turntable** n 1. Rail: plaque tournante 2. Rec: platine f. **'turn 'up** 1. vtr (a) relever (son col); retrousser (ses manches); **turned-up nose,** nez retroussé; **to t. up one's nose at sth,** renifler sur qch (b) retourner (le sol, une carte); déterrer (un trésor);

dénicher (qch) (c) trouver, se reporter à (une citation) (d) P: **t. it up!** la ferme! (e) monter (le gaz); **to t. up the radio,** mettre la radio plus fort 2. vi (a) se replier; **her nose turns up,** elle a le nez retroussé (b) **the ace of clubs turned up,** l'as de trèfle est sorti (c) arriver (à l'improviste); **he'll t. up one of these days,** il reparaîtra un de ces jours; **something is sure to t. up,** il se présentera sûrement une occasion; **till something better turns up,** en attendant mieux. 'turn-up n (a) revers m (d'un pantalon) (b) Cards: retourne f; F: **that's a t. (for the book)!** ça c'est une sacrée surprise!

turnip ['tə:nip] n navet m.

turpentine ['tə:p(ə)ntain] n (abbr **turps**) térébenthine f.

turquoise ['tə:kwɔiz] 1. n turquoise f 2. a & n t. (blue), turquoise (m) inv.

turret ['tʌrit] n tourelle f.

turtle ['tə:tl] n tortue f de mer; **t. soup,** consommé m à la tortue; (of boat) **to turn t.,** chavirer. 'turtledove n Orn: tourterelle f. 'turtleneck n col montant; NAm: col roulé.

Tuscany ['tʌskəni] Prn Geog: Toscane f.

tusk [tʌsk] n défense f (d'éléphant, de sanglier).

tussle ['tʌsl] 1. n lutte f, bagarre f, mêlée f, corps-à-corps m inv; **to have a t.,** en venir aux mains (avec qn) 2. vi lutter (avec qn); **to t. over sth,** se disputer qch.

tussock ['tʌsək] n touffe f d'herbe.

tut [tʌt] int t. (t.)! allons donc!

tutor ['tju:tər] 1. n (a) Sch: directeur, -trice, d'études (d'un groupe d'étudiants) 2. private t., précepteur m 2. vtr instruire (qn); **to t. s.o. in Latin,** donner à qn des leçons particulières de latin. **tu'torial** n Sch: cours (individuel) fait par le directeur d'études.

tuxedo [tʌk'si:dou] n (pl **tuxedos**) Cl: NAm: (Br = dinner jacket) smoking m.

TV abbr television.

twaddle ['twɔdl] n F: fadaises fpl; **to talk t.,** dire des balivernes, des sottises.

twang [twæŋ] 1. n (a) son (de corde pincée) (b) nasal t., ton nasillard; nasillement m; **to speak with a t.,** parler du nez; nasiller 2. v (a) vtr pincer les cordes d'(un instrument); **to t. a guitar,** pincer de la guitare (b) vi Mus: (of string) vibrer.

tweak [twi:k] vtr pincer; tirer, tordre; **to t. a boy's ears,** tirer les oreilles à un gamin.

twee [twi:] a F: Pej: it's a bit t., c'est un peu maniéré.

tweed [twi:d] n 1. tweed m, cheviotte f écossaise 2. pl Cl: **tweeds,** complet m, costume m, de tweed.

tweet [twi:t] 1. n pépiement m; gazouillement m 2. vi (of bird) pépier; gazouiller.

tweezers ['twi:zəz] npl pince f à épiler.

twelve [twelv] num a & n douze (m); **t. o'clock,** (i) midi m (ii) minuit m. **twelfth** num a & n douzième (m); Louis the T., Louis Douze; T. Night, le jour, la fête, des Rois.

twenty ['twenti] num a & n vingt (m); t.-one, vingt et un; t.-two, vingt-deux; t.-first, vingt et unième; (on) the t.-first of May, le vingt et un mai; about t. people, une vingtaine de gens; the twenties, les années vingt. 'twentieth num a & n vingtième (m); (on) the t. of June, le vingt juin.

twerp [twə:p] n P: andouille f, nouille f, idiot, -ote.

twice [twais] adv deux fois; t. as big, deux fois plus grand (que qch); he's t. as old as I am, il a

deux fois mon âge; t. over, à deux reprises; to think t. about doing sth, y regarder à deux fois, hésiter, avant de faire qch; he didn't have to be asked t., il ne se fit pas prier.

twiddle ['twidl] vtr & i to t. (with) sth, jouer avec, tripoter, qch; to t. one's thumbs, se tourner les pouces.

twig¹ [twig] n brindille f (de branche).

twig² [twig] vtr (twigged) F: comprendre, saisir, piger.

twilight ['twailait] (a) n crépuscule m; demi-jour m; aube naissante; in the (evening) t., au crépuscule; entre chien et loup (b) a crépusculaire.

twill [twil] n Tex: (tissu) sergé (m).

twin [twin] 1. a & n (a) jumeau, jumelle; t. brother, t. sister, frère jumeau, sœur jumelle (b) n t. beds, lits jumeaux; t.-engined aircraft, bimoteur m 2. vtr (twinned) jumeler; twinned towns, villes jumelées. 'twinning n jumelage m (de deux villes).

twine [twain] 1. n ficelle f 2. v (a) vtr tordre, tortiller (des fils); entrelacer (une guirlande); to t. sth round sth, (en)rouler qch autour de qch; entourer qch de qch (b) vi se tordre, se tortiller; to t. round sth, s'enrouler, s'enlacer, autour de qch.

twinge [twin(d)ʒ] n (a) t. (of pain), élancement m (b) t. of conscience, remords m (de conscience); to feel a t. of sadness, avoir un pincement au cœur.

twinkle ['twiŋkl] 1. n (a) scintillement m, clignotement m (des étoiles) (b) pétillement m (du regard); in a t., en un clin d'œil 2. vi (a) scintiller, étinceler (b) (of eyes) to t. with mischief, pétiller de malice. 'twinkling 1. a scintillant; pétillant 2. n scintillement m, clignotement m; in the t. of an eye, en un clin d'œil.

twirl [twə:l] 1. n (a) tournoiement m; (of dancer) pirouette f (b) volute f (de fumée); (in writing) fioriture f 2. v (a) vtr to t. (round), (i) faire tournoyer; faire des moulinets avec (sa canne) (ii) tortiller (sa moustache) (b) vi to t. (round) tournoyer; (of dancer) pirouetter.

twirp [twə:p] n = twerp.

twist [twist] I. n 1. (a) fil m retors; cordon m; cordonnet m (b) torsade f, tortillon m (de cheveux); tortillon, cornet m (de papier) (c) t. of tobacco, rouleau m de tabac; add a t. of lemon, ajoutez un zeste de citron 2. (a) (effort m de) torsion f; to give one's ankle a t., se fouler la cheville (b) with a t. of the wrist, d'un tour de poignet (c) Danc: twist m 3. (a) twists and turns, tours et détours; zigzags (b) F: to go round the t., devenir dingue, cinglé 4. perversion f (d'esprit). II. v 1. vtr (a) tordre, tortiller; to t. together, torsader, câbler (des fils); to t. sth round sth, rouler, entortiller, qch autour de qch; F: she can t. him round her little finger, elle le mène par le bout du nez (b) to t. one's ankle, se fouler la cheville; to t. s.o.'s arm, (i) tordre le bras à qn (ii) Fig: exercer une pression sur qn (c) dénaturer (les paroles de qn); déformer (le sens de qch, la vérité) 2. vi (a) (of worm) se tordre, se tortiller (b) former une spirale; (of smoke) former des volutes (c) to get all twisted (up), s'entortiller (d) (of road) tourner; faire des zigzags, des lacets; to t. and turn, serpenter (e) Danc: twister. 'twisted a (a) tordu, tors; (fil) retors (b) (distorted) tordu; (of tree) tortueux (c) (of meaning, truth) perverti, déformé; t. mind, esprit tordu. 'twister n F: escroc m. 'twisting a (sentier) tortueux. 'twist 'off vtr

enlever en dévissant, en tordant. **'twist 'round** *vi*
(*of pers*) se retourner.

twit¹ [twit] *n* F: andouille *f*, imbécile *m*.

twit² *vtr* (**twitted**) taquiner (qn) (**about,** à propos de).

twitch [twitʃ] I. *n* (*pl* **twitches**) 1. secousse *f*; petit
coup sec 2. crispation nerveuse (des mains); mouve-
ment convulsif; (*facial*) tic *m*. II. *v* 1. *vtr* (*a*) tirer
vivement; donner une secousse à (qch) (*b*) contracter
(ses traits); crisper (les mains); (*of cat*) **to t. its tail,**
faire de petits mouvements de la queue 2. *vi* (*of face*)
se contracter nerveusement; (*of eyelids*) clignoter; (*of
hands*) se crisper nerveusement; **his face twitches,** il a
un tic.

twitter ['twitər] 1. *n* (*a*) gazouillement *m*, gazouillis *m*
(*b*) F: **to be in a t.,** être dans tous ses états 2. *vi*
gazouiller. **'twittering** *n* gazouillement.

two [tu:] *num a & n* deux (*m*); **to break sth in t.,** casser
qch en deux; **the t. of us,** we **t.,** nous deux; **to come in t.
by t., t. and t., in twos,** entrer deux par deux; *Fig:* **to
put t. and t. together,** tirer ses conclusions (après avoir
rapproché les faits); **that makes t. of us,** c'est aussi
mon cas; et moi aussi; **to have t. of everything,** avoir
tout en double; **to be in t. minds about sth,** être indécis
sur qch; **mother of t.,** mère de deux enfants. **'two-
edged** *a* (épée, argument) à deux tranchants, à
double tranchant. **'two-faced** *a* hypocrite.
'twofold 1. *a* double 2. *adv* doublement; au double.
'two-'legged [-'legid] *a* bipède. **'two-piece** *a &
n Cl:* **t.-p.** (**suit**), (*men's*) costume *m* deux-pièces;
(*woman's*) tailleur *m*. **'two-ply** *a* (laine) deux fils.
'two-'seater *n* avion *m*, voiture *f*, à deux places.
'twosome *n* partie *f* à deux joueurs; couple *m*
(d'amis); **in a t.,** à deux. **'two-stroke** *a* (moteur) à
deux temps; **t.-s. mixture,** (mélange) deux-temps *m*.
'two-'time *vtr esp NAm:* tromper (qn). **'two-
way** *a* (rue) à double sens; (trafic) dans les deux sens;
El: (commutateur) à deux directions; **t.-w. radio,**
poste émetteur-récepteur. **two-'wheeler** *n* deux-
roues *m inv.*

tycoon [tai'ku:n] *n Com: Ind:* magnat *m*.

tyke [taik] *n* F: vilain chien; cabot *m*.

type [taip] I. *n* 1. (*a*) type *m*; marque *f*, modèle *m*;
people of every t., des gens de toutes sortes; *F:* **she's
not my t.,** ce n'est pas mon genre (*b*) *F:* **he's an odd t.,** il
est bizarre 2. *Typ:* (i) caractère *m*, type (ii) *coll*
caractères; **to set t.,** composer; **in large, small, t.,** en
gros, en petits, caractères. II. *vtr* 1. *Med:* déterminer
le groupe (sanguin) 2. taper, écrire, à la machine;
dactylographier; **to t. out, up** (**a letter**), taper (une
lettre) (à la machine). **'typecast** *vtr Th: Cin:*
donner toujours les mêmes rôles à (un acteur).
'typeface *n* œil *m* (de caractère). **'typescript** *n*
manuscrit dactylographié. **'typeset** *vtr* composer.
'typesetter *n* compositeur, -trice. **'typesetting**
n composition *f*. **'typewriter** *n* machine *f* à écrire.
'typewriting *n* dactylographie *f*. **'typewritten**
n (document) dactylographié, tapé à la machine.
'typing *n* dactylographie *f*, F: dactylo *f*; **t. error,**
faute de frappe; **t. paper,** papier *m* machine; **t. pool,**
pool *m* de dactylos. **'typist** *n* dactylo *mf*; **audio t.,**
audiotypiste *mf*. **ty'pography** *n* typographie *f*.

typhoid ['taifɔid] *n Med:* typhoïde *f*.

typhoon [tai'fu:n] *n* typhon *m*.

typhus ['taifəs] *n Med:* typhus *m*.

typical ['tipik(ə)l] *a* typique; **the t.** Frenchman, le
Français type; **with t. charm he said,** avec son charme
habituel il a dit; **that's t. of him,** c'est bien de lui.
'typically *adv* d'une manière typique; typiquement. **'typify** *vtr* (*a*) symboliser (qch) (*b*) être
caractéristique de (qch); être le type (même) de
(qch).

tyranny ['tirəni] *n* (*pl* **tyrannies**) tyrannie *f*.
ty'rannical *a* tyrannique. **ty'rannically** *adv*
tyranniquement. **'tyrannize** *vi & tr* faire le tyran; **to
t.** (**over**) s.o., tyranniser qn. **'tyrant** *n* tyran *m*.

tyre ['taiər] *n* (*NAm:* = **tire**) *Aut:* pneu *m*; **radial t.,**
pneu à carcasse radiale; **t. pressure,** pression de
gonflage *m*; **t. lever,** démonte-pneu *m*.

tyro ['taiərou] *n* (*pl* **tyros**) novice *mf*; débutant, -ante.

Tyrol (the) [ðəti'roul] *Prn Geog:* le Tyrol. **Tyro-
lean** [tirə'li:ən] *a* tyrolien, -ienne.

tzar, tzarina [tsɑr, tsɑ:'ri:nə] *see* **tsar, tsarina.**

U

U, u [juː] *n* (la lettre) U, u *m*; **U and non-U**, ce qui est bien, comme il faut, et ce qui ne l'est pas; *Aut:* **U-turn**, demi-tour *m*; **no U-turns**, demi-tour interdit; *Cin:* U **(film)**, (film) pour tout le monde.

ubiquitous [juːˈbikwitəs] *a* qui se trouve partout; que l'on rencontre partout. **u'biquity** *n* ubiquité *f*.

udder [ˈʌdər] *n* mamelle *f*, pis *m* (de vache).

UFO (*occ* [ˈjuːfou]) *abbr unidentified flying object.*

Uganda [juːˈgændə] *Prn Geog:* Ouganda *m*.

ugh [uː] *int* pouah! beurk!

ugly [ˈʌgli] *a* (**uglier, ugliest**) (*a*) laid; **u. as sin**, laid comme un pou; **to grow u.**, (s')enlaidir; **u. duckling**, vilain petit canard; *F:* **u. customer**, sale type (*b*) (*of thg*) vilain; (incident) regrettable; **u. rumour**, bruit sinistre. **'ugliness** *n* laideur *f*.

UHF *abbr ultra-high frequency.*

UHT *abbr ultra-heat treated.*

UK *abbr United Kingdom.*

ulcer [ˈʌlsər] *n* ulcère *m*. **'ulcerate** *vtr & i* (s')ulcérer. **ulce'ration** *n* ulcération *f*. **'ulcerous** *a* ulcéreux.

ullage [ˈʌlidʒ] *n Winem:* creux *m* du tonneau.

ulna [ˈʌlnə] *n Anat:* cubitus *m*.

Ulster [ˈʌlstər] *Prn Geog:* (i) Ulster *m* (ii) Irlande *f* du Nord.

ulterior [ʌlˈtiəriər] *a* **1.** ultérieur **2. u. motive**, motif secret, caché; **without u. motive**, sans arrière-pensée.

ultimate [ˈʌltimət] **1.** *a* final; **u. purpose**, but final; **u. decision**, décision définitive **2.** *n* (*a*) **the u.**, l'absolu *m* (*b*) **the u. in luxury**, le summum de luxe; **the u. in vulgarity**, le comble de la vulgarité. **'ultimately** *adv* à la fin; en fin de compte; finalement. **ulti'matum** *n* ultimatum *m*. **'ultimo** *adv Com:* du mois dernier.

ultra [ˈʌltrə] **1.** *a* extrême; **u.-short waves**, ondes ultra-courtes **2.** *n Pol:* ultra *m*. **ultra'fashionable** *a* du tout dernier cri, ultra-chic. **ultra'high** *a* **u. frequency**, très haute fréquence. **ultrama'rine** *a & n* (bleu *m* d')outremer *m inv*. **ultra'modern** *a* ultramoderne. **ultra'sensitive** *a* ultrasensible. **ultra'short** *a* ultracourt. **ultra'sonic** *a* ultrasonique. **ultra'violet** *a* ultraviolet.

umber [ˈʌmbər] *n* (terre *f* d')ombre *f*.

umbilical [ʌmˈbilikl] *a* ombilical.

umbrage [ˈʌmbridʒ] *n A:* ombrage *m*, ressentiment *m*; **to take u.**, s'offenser, se froisser (**at sth**, de qch).

umbrella [ʌmˈbrelə] *n* parapluie *m*; (*of jellyfish*) ombrelle *f*; **beach u.**, parasol *m*; **u. stand**, porteparapluies *m inv*; *Bot:* **u. pine**, pin parasol; *Av:* **air u.**, ombrelle de protection aérienne, parapluie aérien.

umlaut [ˈumlaut] *n Ling:* tréma *m*.

umpire [ˈʌmpaiər] **I.** *n* arbitre *m*, juge *m*. **II. 1.** *vtr* arbitrer (un match) **2.** *vi* être l'arbitre. **'umpiring** *n* arbitrage *m*.

umpteen [ʌmpˈtiːn] *a & n F:* je ne sais combien; des tas (de livres). **ump'teenth** *a* énième.

UN *abbr United Nations.*

unabashed [ʌnəˈbæʃt] *a* **1.** sans perdre contenance **2.** aucunement ébranlé.

unabated [ʌnəˈbeitid] *a* non diminué.

unable [ʌnˈeibl] *a* incapable; **to be u. to do sth**, être dans l'impossibilité de faire qch; **u. to speak**, incapable de parler; **we are u. to help you**, nous ne sommes pas en mesure de vous aider; nous ne pouvons pas vous aider.

unabridged [ʌnəˈbridʒd] *a* non abrégé; intégral; **u. edition**, édition intégrale.

unacceptable [ʌnəkˈseptəbl] *a* inacceptable; (théorie) irrecevable; (conduite) inadmissible.

unaccommodating [ʌnəˈkɔmədeitiŋ] *a* peu accommodant; désobligeant.

unaccompanied [ʌnəˈkʌmpənid] *a* **1.** non accompagné, seul **2.** *Mus:* sans accompagnement; **sonata for u. violin**, sonate pour violon seul.

unaccountable [ʌnəˈkauntəbl] *a* (*a*) (phénomène) inexplicable (*b*) (conduite) bizarre. **una'ccountably** *adv* inexplicablement. **una'ccounted a five passengers are still u. for**, on reste sans nouvelles de cinq passagers; **two books are still u. for**, il manque toujours deux livres.

unaccustomed [ʌnəˈkʌstəmd] *a* inaccoutumé, inhabituel; (*of pers*) **u. to sth**, peu habitué à qch.

unacknowledged [ʌnəkˈnɔlidʒd] *a* (lettre) restée sans réponse.

unacquainted [ʌnəˈkweintid] *a* **to be u. with (s.o., sth)**, ne pas connaître (qn); ignorer (un fait).

unadorned [ʌnəˈdɔːnd] *a* sans ornement; (*of truth*) tout nu.

unadulterated [ʌnəˈdʌltəreitid] *a* pur; sans mélange; (vin) non frelaté; *F:* **pure u. laziness**, paresse pure et simple.

unaffected [ʌnəˈfektid] *a* **1.** (*a*) sans affectation; (joie, douleur) sincère (*b*) naturel, simple; (style) sans recherche (*c*) (*of pers*) sans affectation, sans pose **2.** (*of pers*) impassible, insensible (**by sth**, à qch) **3.** inaltérable (**by air, by water**, à l'air, à l'eau). **una'ffectedly** *adv* sans affectation; sincèrement; naturellement; simplement.

unafraid [ʌnəˈfreid] *a* sans peur, qui n'a pas peur.

unaided [ʌnˈeidid] *a* sans aide; **he can walk u. now**, il peut marcher tout seul maintenant.

unalloyed [ʌnəˈlɔid] *a* (métal) pur, sans alliage; (bonheur) parfait.

unalterable [ʌnˈɔːltərəbl] *a* immuable, invariable. **un'altered** *a* toujours le même; inchangé; sans changement.

unambiguous [ʌnæmˈbigjuəs] *a* non équivoque; (réponse) sans ambiguïté. **unam'biguously** *adv* sans ambiguïté.

unambitious [ʌnæmˈbiʃəs] *a* **1.** sans ambition; peu ambitieux **2.** (projet) modeste.

un-American [ʌnəˈmerikən] *a* antiaméricain.

unanimity [juːnəˈnimiti] *n* unanimité *f.* **u'nanimous** *a* unanime; (vote) à l'unanimité. **u'nanimously** *adv* à l'unanimité.

unannounced [ʌnəˈnaunst] *a* **he came in u.**, il est entré sans se faire annoncer.

unanswerable [ʌnˈɑːnsərəbl] *a* (argument) irréfutable; **u. question**, question à laquelle on ne peut pas répondre. **un'answered** *a* **1.** (*of letter*) (i) sans réponse (ii) à répondre **2.** (argument) irréfuté.

unappealing [ʌnəˈpiːliŋ] *a* peu attrayant.

unappetizing [ʌnˈæpitaizin] *a* peu appétissant.

unappreciated [ʌnəˈpriːʃieitid] *a* peu apprécié; peu estimé.

unapproachable [ʌnəˈproutʃəbl] *a* **1.** inabordable, inaccessible; (*of pers*) d'un abord difficile **2.** incomparable, sans pareil.

unarmed [ʌnˈɑːmd] *a* (*of pers*) non armé; (combat) sans armes.

unashamed [ʌnəˈʃeimd] *a* sans honte; sans pudeur. **una'shamedly** *adv* sans honte.

unasked [ʌnˈɑːskt] *a* (faire qch) spontanément, sans y être invité.

unassisted [ʌnəˈsistid] *a* sans aide.

unassuming [ʌnəˈsjuːmin] *a* sans prétention(s); modeste.

unattached [ʌnəˈtætʃt] *a* **1.** qui n'est pas attaché (**to**, à); indépendant (**to**, de) **2.** libre; (*of pers*) **to be u.**, être sans attaches.

unattainable [ʌnəˈteinəbl] *a* inaccessible (**by**, à); hors de (la) portée (**by**, de).

unattended [ʌnəˈtendid] *a* (*a*) seul; sans escorte (*b*) (*car, shop*) sans surveillance; (*luggage*) abandonné; **u. to**, négligé.

unattractive [ʌnəˈtræktiv] *a* peu attrayant; (*of pers*) peu sympathique.

unauthorized [ʌnˈɔːθəraizd] *a* non autorisé, sans autorisation.

unavailable [ʌnəˈveiləbl] *a* (article) épuisé; (personne) qui n'est pas disponible.

unavailing [ʌnəˈveiliŋ] *a* inutile; vain.

unavoidable [ʌnəˈvɔidəbl] *a* inévitable; (événement) qu'on ne peut prévenir. **una'voidably** *adv* inévitablement; **u. detained**, retenu pour raison majeure.

unaware [ʌnəˈwɛər] *a* ignorant, pas au courant (**of sth**, de qch); **to be u. of sth**, ignorer qch. **una'wares** *adv* (faire qch) inconsciemment; **to take s.o. u.**, prendre qn au dépourvu.

unbalanced [ʌnˈbælənst] *a* déséquilibré.

unbaptized [ʌnbæpˈtaizd] *a* non baptisé.

unbearable [ʌnˈbɛərəbl] *a* insupportable, intolérable; **u. pain**, douleur atroce. **un'bearably** *adv* insupportablement.

unbeatable [ʌnˈbiːtəbl] *a* imbattable. **un'beaten** *a* invaincu; non battu; (record) qui n'a pas été battu.

unbecoming [ʌnbiˈkʌmin] *a* **1.** peu convenable **2.** (*of garment*) peu seyant.

unbeknown(st) [ʌnbiˈnoun(st)] *adv* **u. to anyone**, (faire qch) à l'insu de tous.

unbelievable [ʌnbiˈliːvəbl] *a* incroyable.

unbe'lievably *adv* incroyablement. **unbe-'liever** *n* incrédule *mf.* **unbe'lieving** *a* incrédule.

unbend [ʌnˈbend] *v* (**unbent**) **1.** *vtr* redresser (un tuyau); déplier (la jambe) **2.** *vi* se détendre. **un'bending** *a* inflexible, ferme, raide; intransigeant.

unbias(s)ed [ʌnˈbaiəst] *a* impartial; neutre; sans parti pris.

unbidden [ʌnˈbidn] *a* sans y avoir été invité.

unbleached [ʌnˈbliːtʃt] *a* écru.

unblemished [ʌnˈblemiʃt] *a* sans défaut; (réputation) sans tache.

unblock [ʌnˈblɔk] *vtr* dégager (un passage); déboucher (un tuyau).

unblushing [ʌnˈblʌʃiŋ] *a* sans vergogne; éhonté. **un'blushingly** *adv* (*a*) sans rougir (*b*) sans vergogne.

unbolt [ʌnˈboult] *vtr* déverrouiller (une porte).

unborn [ʌnˈbɔːn] *a* qui n'est pas (encore) né; (enfant) à naître; (générations) à venir, futures.

unbounded [ʌnˈbaundid] *a* sans bornes; illimité; **u. ambition**, ambition démesurée.

unbreakable [ʌnˈbreikəbl] *a* incassable.

unbridled [ʌnˈbraidld] *a* (*of passion*) débridé, effréné.

unbroken [ʌnˈbrouk(ə)n] *a* **1.** (*a*) non brisé, non cassé (*b*) intact (*c*) (*of rule*) toujours observé; (*of promise*) inviolé; *Sp:* **u. record**, record qui n'a pas été battu (*d*) (*of silence*) ininterrompu, continu; **u. sheet of ice**, nappe de glace continue **2.** (*a*) (cheval) non rompu, non dressé (*b*) **u. spirit**, esprit insoumis.

unburden [ʌnˈbɜːd(ə)n] *vtr* **to u. the mind**, soulager l'esprit; **to u. oneself**, s'épancher.

unbusinesslike [ʌnˈbiznislaik] *a* (*a*) (*of pers*) peu commerçant; qui n'a pas le sens des affaires (*b*) (procédé) irrégulier; **to u.**, manquer de méthode.

unbutton [ʌnˈbʌt(ə)n] *vtr* déboutonner.

uncalled-for [ʌnˈkɔːldfɔːr] *a* (*of remark*) déplacé; (*of rebuke*) injustifié.

uncanny [ʌnˈkæni] *a* mystérieux; troublant; (bruit) inquiétant.

uncared-for [ʌnˈkɛədfɔːr] *a* peu soigné; négligé; (enfant) délaissé; (jardin) à l'abandon.

uncarpeted [ʌnˈkɑːpitid] *a* sans tapis, sans moquette.

unceasing [ʌnˈsiːsiŋ] *a* (*a*) incessant, continu (*b*) (travail) assidu; (effort) soutenu. **un'ceasingly** *adv* sans cesse.

unceremonious [ˈʌnseriˈmouniəs] *a* (*of pers*) sans façon, sans gêne. **uncere'moniously** *adv* sans façons; brusquement.

uncertain [ʌnˈsɜːt(ə)n] *a* **1.** (*a*) incertain; (*of time, amount*) indéterminé (*b*) (résultat) douteux; **it's u. who will win**, on ne sait pas au juste qui gagnera **2.** (*a*) mal assuré; (avenir) incertain; **u. temper**, humeur inégale; **in no u. terms**, sans mâcher les mots (*b*) **to be u. of, about, sth**, être incertain de qch; **to be u. what to do**, hésiter sur le parti à prendre. **un'certainly** *adv* d'une façon incertaine. **un'certainty** *n* **1.** incertitude *f*; **to remove any u.**, pour dissiper toute équivoque **2. to prefer a certainty to an u.**, préférer le certain à l'incertain.

unchallengeable [ʌnˈtʃælindʒəbl] *a* incontestable. **un'challenged** *a* (droit) incontesté; **to let (sth)**

pass u., ne pas relever (une affirmation); ne pas récuser (un témoignage).

unchangeable [ʌnˈtʃein(d)ʒəbl] a immuable, inchangeable. **un'changed** a inchangé. **un'changing** a invariable, immuable.

uncharitable [ʌnˈtʃæritəbl] a peu charitable.

uncharted [ʌnˈtʃɑːtid] a inexploré.

unchecked [ʌnˈtʃekt] a 1. (passion) sans frein; (colère) non contenue; **to advance u.,** avancer sans rencontrer d'opposition 2. non vérifié; non relu.

unchristian [ʌnˈkristjən] a peu chrétien.

uncivilized [ʌnˈsivilaizd] a peu civilisé, barbare; **u. hour,** heure indue.

unclaimed [ʌnˈkleimd] a non réclamé; **u. right,** droit non revendiqué.

unclassified [ʌnˈklæsifaid] a non (classé) secret.

uncle [ˈʌŋkl] n oncle m; **yes u.!** oui, mon oncle!

unclean [ʌnˈkliːn] a 1. impur 2. malpropre.

unclear [ʌnˈkliər] a peu clair; obscur.

unclouded [ʌnˈklaudid] a (of sky) sans nuage; (of vision) clair; (of liquid) limpide.

uncoil [ʌnˈkɔil] 1. vtr dérouler 2. vi & pr (of snake, rope) **to u. (itself),** se dérouler.

uncollected [ʌnkəˈlektid] a (of luggage) non réclamé; (of tax) non perçu.

uncoloured [ʌnˈkʌləd] a (a) non coloré; **u. account,** rapport impartial (de qch) (b) incolore.

uncombed [ʌnˈkoumd] a (of hair) non peigné, mal peigné, ébouriffé.

uncomfortable [ʌnˈkʌmftəbl] a 1. inconfortable, peu confortable; incommode; (vêtement) gênant; **this is a very u. armchair,** on est très mal (assis) dans ce fauteuil 2. **to make things u. for s.o.,** créer des ennuis à qn 3. **to feel u.,** (i) être mal à l'aise (ii) se sentir gêné; **to be, feel, u. about sth,** se sentir inquiet au sujet de qch. **un'comfortably** adv 1. peu confortablement 2. **the enemy were u. near,** la proximité de l'ennemi était inquiétante.

uncommitted [ʌnkəˈmitid] a (of pers) non engagé; libre; indépendant; Pol: neutraliste, non aligné.

uncommon [ʌnˈkɔmən] a (a) peu commun; (mot) peu usité; **not u.,** assez fréquent (b) peu ordinaire. **un'commonly** adv singulièrement; **u. good,** excellent.

uncommunicative [ʌnkəˈmjuːnikətiv] a peu communicatif; renfermé; taciturne.

uncomplaining [ʌnkəmˈpleiniŋ] a patient, résigné. **uncom'plainingly** adv sans se plaindre.

uncomplicated [ʌnˈkɔmplikeitid] a peu compliqué, simple.

uncomplimentary [ˈʌnkɔmpliˈment(ə)ri] a peu flatteur.

uncompromising [ʌnˈkɔmprəmaiziŋ] a intransigeant; **u. honesty,** honnêteté absolue.

unconcealed [ʌnkənˈsiːld] a non dissimulé.

unconcern [ʌnkənˈsəːn] n insouciance f; indifférence f. **uncon'cerned** a (a) insouciant, indifférent (b) **to be u. about sth,** être sans inquiétude au sujet de qch. **uncon'cernedly** [-idli] adv d'un air indifférent; sans se (laisser) troubler.

unconditional [ʌnkənˈdiʃənəl] a inconditionnel; (soumission) sans condition. **uncon'ditionally** adv inconditionnellement; sans condition.

unconfirmed [ʌnkənˈfəːmd] a non confirmé.

uncongenial [ʌnkənˈdʒiːniəl] a (of pers) peu sympathique; (travail) peu agréable.

unconnected [ʌnkəˈnektid] a sans rapport (**with,** avec); **the two events are quite u.,** les deux événements n'ont aucun rapport entre eux.

unconscionable [ʌnˈkɔnʃənəbl] a déraisonnable, excessif.

unconscious [ʌnˈkɔnʃəs] 1. a inconscient; **to be u. of sth,** ne pas avoir conscience, ne pas s'apercevoir, de qch 2. a sans connaissance; évanoui; **to become u.,** perdre connaissance; **to knock s.o. u.,** assommer qn 3. n **the u.,** l'inconscient m. **un'consciously** adv inconsciemment. **un'consciousness** n 1. inconscience f (**of,** de) 2. évanouissement m.

unconsidered [ʌnkənˈsidəd] a (of remark) inconsidéré.

unconstitutional [ʌnkɔnstiˈtjuːʃənəl] a anticonstitutionnel.

uncontested [ʌnkənˈtestid] a (droit) incontesté; Pol: **u. seat,** siège qui n'est pas disputé.

uncontrollable [ʌnkənˈtrouləbl] a (enfant) ingouvernable; (mouvement) irréprimable; (désir) irrésistible; **u. laughter,** fou rire; **fits of u. temper,** violents accès de colère. **uncon'trollably** adv irrésistiblement; **she sobbed u.,** elle ne pouvait s'arrêter de sangloter. **uncon'trolled** a sans frein; (of passion) effréné; (of inflation) rampant.

unconventional [ʌnkənˈvenʃən(ə)l] a peu conventionnel; non-conformiste. **uncon'ventionally** adv de manière peu conventionnelle.

unconvinced [ʌnkənˈvinst] a sceptique (**of sth,** à l'égard de qch); **I am still u.,** je ne suis toujours pas convaincu. **uncon'vincing** a peu convaincant; (excuse) peu vraisemblable. **uncon'vincingly** adv d'une manière peu convaincante.

uncooked [ʌnˈkukt] a (aliment) non cuit, cru.

uncooperative [ʌnkəˈɔprətiv] a peu coopératif.

uncork [ʌnˈkɔːk] vtr déboucher (une bouteille).

uncorrected [ʌnkəˈrektid] a (a) (of proof) non corrigé (b) (of error) non rectifié; Ph: **u. result,** résultat brut.

uncouple [ʌnˈkʌpl] vtr dételer, découpler (des wagons).

uncouth [ʌnˈkuːθ] a grossier; fruste.

uncover [ʌnˈkʌvər] vtr découvrir (qch). **un'covered** a mis à découvert; découvert.

uncritical [ʌnˈkritik(ə)l] a dépourvu de sens critique; sans discernement; (auditoire) peu exigeant.

uncrossed [ʌnˈkrɔst] a (chèque) non barré.

uncrowned [ʌnˈkraund] a non couronné.

uncrushable [ʌnˈkrʌʃəbl] a (tissu) infroissable.

unction [ˈʌŋkʃ(ə)n] n Ecc: **extreme u.,** extrême-onction f.

uncultivated [ʌnˈkʌltiveitid] a inculte.

uncurl [ʌnˈkəːl] vtr défriser (les cheveux); déplier (les jambes).

uncut [ʌnˈkʌt] a non coupé; (of hedge) non taillé; (diamant) brut; (of edition) intégral.

undamaged [ʌnˈdæmidʒd] a non endommagé; indemne; (of reputation) intact.

undated [ʌnˈdeitid] a non daté; sans date.

undaunted [ʌnˈdɔːntid] a aucunement intimidé.

undeceive [ʌndiˈsiːv] vtr Lit: désabuser (**of,** de); détromper (qn).

undecided [ˌʌndiˈsaidid] *a* indécis, non résolu; (*of pers*) indécis, irrésolu; **to be u. how to act**, ne pas savoir quel parti prendre.

undefeated [ˌʌndiˈfiːtid] *a* invaincu.

undefended [ˌʌndiˈfendid] *a* (*a*) sans défense (*b*) *Jur:* **u. case**, débats non contentieux.

undefinable [ˌʌndiˈfainəbl] *a* indéfinissable. **unde'fined** *a* (*a*) non défini (*b*) indéterminé; vague.

undelivered [ˌʌndiˈlivəd] *a* non livré; **if u. return to sender**, en cas de non-livraison prière de retourner à l'expéditeur.

undemocratic [ˌʌndeməˈkrætik] *a* antidémocratique.

undemonstrative [ˌʌndiˈmɔnstrətiv] *a* peu expansif, peu démonstratif; réservé.

undeniable [ˌʌndiˈnaiəbl] *a* indéniable, incontestable. **unde'niably** *adv* incontestablement; indiscutablement.

under [ˈʌndər] **I.** *prep* **1.** (*a*) sous; au-dessous de; **to swim u. water**, nager sous l'eau; **put it u. that**, mettez-le là-dessous; **he pulled a stool out from u. the table**, il a tiré un tabouret de sous la table; **to file sth u.** *miscellaneous*, classer qch sous la rubrique *divers* (*b*) moins de; **salaries u. £5000**, salaires inférieurs à £5000; **he's u. thirty**, il a moins de trente ans; **the u.-thirties**, les moins de trente ans; **children u. ten**, les enfants au-dessous de dix ans; **u. one's breath**, à mi-voix **2.** (*a*) **u. lock and key**, sous clef; **visible u. the microscope**, visible au microscope; **to be u. sentence of death**, être condamné à mort; **to be u. attack**, être attaqué; **u. these circumstances**, dans ces conditions; **u. his father's will**, d'après le testament de son père; **u. this law**, selon cette loi; **I'm u. no obligation to do it**, rien ne m'oblige à le faire (*b*) **he had a hundred men u. him**, il avait cent hommes sous ses ordres; **to be u. the authority of**, relever de; **u. government control**, soumis au contrôle de l'État; **u. the influence of alcohol**, *F:* **u. the influence**, sous l'empire de la boisson; **u. Louis XIV**, sous Louis XIV; *F:* **to be u. the doctor**, être sous les ordres du médecin **3. u. repair**, en réparation; **u. observation**, (malade) en observation; **question u. examination**, question prise en considération. **II.** *adv* **1.** (au-)dessous; **to stay u. for 2 minutes**, rester 2 minutes sous l'eau; **as u.**, comme ci-dessous; *F:* **down u.**, aux antipodes **2. to keep a rebellion u.**, mater une rébellion. **under-'age** *a* mineur. **'underarm** *adv* par en-dessous. **'underbelly** *n* **1.** bas-ventre *m* (d'un animal) **2.** point *m* vulnérable. **'underblanket** *n* protège-matelas *m*. **under'capitalized** *a* sous-financé. **'undercarriage** *n Av:* train *m* d'atterrissage. **under'charge 1.** *vtr* ne pas faire payer assez à (qn) **2.** *vi* demander trop peu (**for sth**, pour qch). **'underclothes** *npl*, **'underclothing** *n* sous-vêtements *mpl*; lingerie (féminine). **'undercoat** *n* première couche (de peinture), couche de fond. **under'cook** *vtr* ne pas assez cuire. **under'cover** *a* secret. **'undercurrent** *n* (*a*) courant *m* de fond; (*in sea*) courant sous-marin (*b*) **u. of discontent**, vague *f* de fond de mécontentement. **'undercut** *n Cu:* filet *m* (de bœuf). **under'cut** *vtr* (**under'cut; under'cutting**) vendre moins cher que (qn). **'underde'veloped** *a Phot:* (cliché) insuffisamment développé; **u. countries**, pays sous-développés. **'underdog** *n* opprimé, -ée, défavorisé, -ée. **under'done** *a* (*a*) pas assez cuit (*b*) pas trop cuit; (bifteck) saignant. **underem'ployed** *a* sous-employé. **underestimate 1.** *n* [ˌʌndərˈestimət] sous-évaluation *f* **2.** *vtr* [ˌʌndərˈestimeit] sous-estimer. **underex'pose** *vtr* sous-exposer (un film). **underex'posure** *n* sous-exposition *f* (d'un film). **under'fed** *a* mal nourri, sous-alimenté. **'underfelt** *n* thibaude *f* (pour moquette). **'underfloor** *a* **u. heating**, chauffage par le sol. **under'foot** *adv* **the snow crunched u.**, la neige craquait sous les pieds; **to trample sth u.**, fouler qch aux pieds. **'undergardener** *n* aide-jardinier *m*. **'undergarment** *n* sous-vêtement *m*. **under'go** *vtr* (**under'went; under'gone**) subir (un changement, une épreuve); suivre (un traitement); éprouver (une déception). **under'graduate** *n* étudiant, -ante (qui prépare la licence); **u. life**, vie d'étudiant. **underground 1.** *adv* [ˌʌndəˈgraund] (*a*) sous (la) terre (*b*) clandestinement, secrètement; **to go u.**, passer dans la clandestinité **2.** *a* [ˈʌndəgraund] (*a*) sous (la) terre; (tuyau) sous le sol; (câble) souterrain (*b*) clandestin **3.** *n* [ˈʌndə-] (*a*) **the u.** = le métro (*b*) **the u.**, la résistance. **'undergrowth** *n* broussailles *fpl*; sous-bois *m*. **under'hand** *a* secret; clandestin; (*of pers*) sournois. **'underlay** *n* thibaude *f* (pour moquette). **under'lie** *vtr* (**under'lain; under'lying**) être à la base, à l'origine, de (qch). **under'line** *vtr* souligner. **'underling** *n* subalterne *m*; subordonné, -ée. **under'lining** *n* soulignement *m*. **under'lying** *a* **1.** au-dessous; (*of rock*) sous-jacent **2.** (principe) fondamental; **u. causes**, raisons profondes (d'un événement). **under'manned** *a* à court de personnel, de main-d'œuvre. **under'mentioned** *a* (mentionné) ci-dessous. **under'mine** *vtr* miner, saper (une muraille); miner (la santé de qn); ébranler (la confiance de qn). **'undermost** *a* le plus bas, la plus basse. **under'neath 1.** *prep* au-dessous de; sous; **from u. sth**, de dessous qch **2.** *adv* au-dessous; dessous **3.** *n* dessous *m* **4.** *a* d'en dessous. **under'nourished** *a* sous-alimenté. **under'paid** *a* sous-payé. **'underpants** *npl* (*for men*) slip *m*, caleçon *m*. **'underpass** *n* passage souterrain. **under'pin** *vtr* (**under'pinned**) étayer (un mur, une société). **under'populated** *a* sous-peuplé. **under'priced** *a* dont le prix est trop bas. **under'privileged** *a* déshérité; défavorisé; économiquement faible; *npl* **the u.**, les économiquement faibles. **unde'rrate** *vtr* sous-estimer. **'underseal** *vtr Aut:* traiter contre la rouille. **under'secretary** *n* sous-secrétaire *mf*; **permanent u.**, directeur général (d'un ministère). **under'sell** *vtr* (**under'sold**) vendre à meilleur marché, moins cher, que (qn). **under'sexed** *a* de faible libido. **'undershirt** *n esp NAm:* maillot *m*, tricot *m*, de corps. **'underside** *n* dessous *m*. **'undersigned** *a & n* soussigné, -ée. **under'sized** *a* trop petit. **'underskirt** *n* jupon *m*. **under'slung** *a Aut:* (châssis) surbaissé. **under'staffed** *a* à court de personnel; **to be u.**, manquer de personnel. **'understate** *vtr* minimiser. **'understatement** *n* **1.** amoindrissement *m* (des faits) **2.** affirmation *f* qui reste au-dessous de la vérité, de la réalité; *F:* **that's the u. of the year!** si tu crois que c'est assez dire! **'understudy 1.** *n Th:* doublure *f* **2.** *vtr* doubler (un rôle). **under'take** *vtr* (**under'took; under'taken**) **1.** entreprendre (un voyage) **2.** (*a*) se charger de, entreprendre (une tâche); **to u. to do sth,** se charger de faire qch (*b*) **to u. that,** garantir, assurer, que. **'undertaker** *n* entrepreneur *m* des pompes funèbres; *F:* croque-mort *m;* **the undertaker's,** les pompes funèbres. **undertaking** [ʌndə'teikiŋ] *n* **1.** (*a*) entreprise *f* (de qch) (*b*) ['ʌndəteikiŋ] métier *m* d'entrepreneur des pompes funèbres **2.** entreprise (commerciale); **it's quite an u.,** c'est toute une affaire **3.** engagement *m,* promesse *f.* **'undertone** *n* **in an u.,** à mi-voix. **under'value** *vtr* **1.** sous-estimer, sous-évaluer **2.** mésestimer (qn, qch). **'undervest** *n esp NAm:* maillot *m,* tricot *m,* de corps. **underwater 1.** *a* ['ʌndəwɔ:tər] sous-marin; **u. fishing,** pêche sous-marine **2.** *adv* [ʌndə'wɔ:tər] sous l'eau; sous la mer. **'underwear** *n* sous-vêtements *mpl;* lingerie (féminine). **'underworld 1.** *n* enfers *mpl* **2.** (*a*) *n* pègre *f,* milieu *m* (*b*) *a* du milieu. **'underwrite** *vtr* (**under'wrote; under'written**) *Fin:* garantir (une émission); *Ins:* souscrire (un risque). **'underwriter** *n Fin:* syndicataire *m; Ins:* assureur *m.*

understand [ʌndə'stænd] *v* (**under'stood**) **1.** *vtr* (*a*) comprendre; entendre; **I don't u. French,** je ne comprends pas le français; **he understands business matters,** il s'y connaît en affaires; **this sentence can be understood in several ways,** cette phrase peut s'interpréter de plusieurs façons; **to u. each other,** se comprendre; **I can't u. it,** je n'y comprends rien; (**is that) understood?** (c'est bien) compris? **that's easily understood,** cela se comprend facilement (*b*) **to give s.o. to u. sth,** donner à entendre qch à qn; **I u. you're coming to work here,** si j'ai bien compris, vous venez travailler ici; **am I to u. that?** ai-je bien compris que? **I u. he'll consent,** je crois savoir qu'il consentira (*c*) *Gram:* sous-entendre (un mot), supposer (une condition); **that's understood,** cela va sans dire **2.** *vi* comprendre; **now I u.!** je comprends! j'y suis maintenant! **you don't u.,** vous n'y êtes pas; **to u. about sth,** comprendre qch. **under'standable** *a* compréhensible; **that's u.,** cela se comprend; c'est (bien) normal. **under'standably** *adv* naturellement; à juste titre. **under'standing 1.** *a* compréhensif, bienveillant **2.** *n* (*a*) entendement *m,* compréhension *f;* intelligence *f;* **lacking in u.,** incompréhensif; **according to my u. of it,** si j'ai bien compris (*b*) accord *m,* entente *f* (*c*) arrangement *m;* **to have an u.,** avoir un arrangement (avec qn); **there's an u. between them,** ils sont d'intelligence; **to come to an u.,** s'accorder, s'entendre (avec qn) (*d*) **on the u. that,** à condition que + *ind* or *sub.* **under'standingly** *adv* avec compréhension.

undeserved [ʌndi'zɔ:vd] *a* immérité. **unde'servedly** [-idli] *adv* (*a*) à tort; injustement (*b*) sans le mériter. **unde'serving** *a* sans mérite; peu méritoire; **u. of attention,** qui ne mérite pas l'attention.

undesirable [ʌndi'zaiərəbl] *a & n* indésirable (*mf*); (personnage) peu désirable.

undetected [ʌndi'tektid] *a* **to go u.,** passer inaperçu.

undetermined [ʌndi'tɔ:mind] *a* indéterminé, incertain.

undeterred [ʌndi'tɔ:d] *a* sans se laisser décourager (by, par).

undeveloped [ʌndi'veləpt] *a* non développé; **u. land,** terrains inexploités.

undies ['ʌndiz] *npl F:* (*esp for women*) lingerie *f,* dessous *mpl.*

undigested [ʌnd(a)i'dʒestid] *a* mal digéré; **u. knowledge,** connaissances mal assimilées.

undignified [ʌn'dignifaid] *a* peu digne; **to be u.,** manquer de dignité.

undiluted [ʌndai'l(j)u:tid] *a* non dilué; non délayé; (vin) pur; (joie) sans mélange.

undiplomatic ['ʌndiplə'mætik] *a* peu diplomatique; (*of pers*) peu diplomate.

undipped [ʌn'dipt] *a Aut:* **to drive with u. headlights,** être en phares; conduire avec les phares allumés.

undischarged [ʌndis'tʃɑ:dʒd] *a Jur:* **u. bankrupt,** failli non réhabilité; **u. debt,** dette non acquittée.

undisciplined [ʌn'disiplind] *a* indiscipliné.

undiscovered [ʌndis'kʌvəd] *a* non découvert; (*of country*) inconnu.

undiscriminating [ʌndis'kri_mineitiŋ] *a* sans discernement, qui manque de discernement.

undisguised [ʌndis'gaizd] *a* non déguisé.

undisputed [ʌndis'pju:tid] *a* incontesté.

undistinguished [ʌndis'tingwiʃt] *a* médiocre; banal; quelconque; (*of appearance*) peu distingué.

undisturbed [ʌndis'tɔ:bd] *a* **1.** (*of pers*) tranquille; (*of sleep*) paisible **2.** (*of peace*) que rien ne vient troubler; **we found everything u.,** rien n'avait été dérangé.

undivided [ʌndi'vaidid] *a* **1.** entier **2.** non partagé; **to give one's u. attention,** donner toute son attention.

undo [ʌn'du:] *vtr* (**undid** [-'did]; **undone** [-'dʌn]) **1.** détruire (une œuvre); réparer (une faute); **you can't u. the past,** ce qui est fait est fait **2.** défaire (un nœud, un paquet); dégrafer, déboutonner (sa robe). **un'doing** *n Lit:* ruine *f,* perte *f;* **gambling will be his u.,** le jeu sera sa ruine. **un'done** *a* **1.** défait; **to come u.,** se défaire, se dénouer, se délacer, se découdre, se dégrafer **2.** inaccompli; **to leave some work u.,** laisser du travail inachevé.

undoubted [ʌn'dautid] *a* (fait) indubitable, incontestable. **un'doubtedly** *adv* indubitablement, incontestablement.

undreamed, undreamt [ʌn'dri:md, ʌn'dremt] *a* **u. of,** (i) insoupçonné (ii) inimaginable.

undress [ʌn'dres] *v* **1.** *vi & pr* se déshabiller **2.** *vtr* déshabiller. **un'dressed** *a* déshabillé.

undrinkable [ʌn'driŋkəbl] *a* (*unpleasant*) imbuvable; (*dangerous*) non potable.

undue [ʌn'dju:] *a* (*a*) injuste, injustifiable; **to exert u. influence over s.o.,** faire pression sur qn (*b*) (*of haste*) exagéré, indu; **u. optimism,** optimisme excessif, peu justifié. **un'duly** *adv* **1.** (réclamer) indûment **2.** (*a*) injustement (*b*) à l'excès, trop; **u. high price,** prix excessif; **he worries u. about his health,** sa santé le préoccupe trop.

undulate ['ʌndjuleit] *vtr & i* onduler, **'undulating** *a* ondulé, onduleux; (terrain) vallonné. **undu'lation** *n* ondulation *f;* accident *m* de terrain.

undying [ʌn'daiiŋ] *a* immortel; éternel.

unearned ['ʌn'ɔ:nd] *a* **1.** immérité **2. u. income,** rentes *fpl.*

unearth [ʌnˈɔːθ] *vtr* déterrer.

unearthly [ʌnˈɔːθli] *a* (a) surnaturel (b) **u. pallor,** pâleur mortelle; **u. light,** lueur sinistre (c) *F:* **at an u. hour,** à une heure indue; **u. reason,** raison absurde.

uneasy [ʌnˈiːzi] *a* (a) mal à l'aise; gêné (b) inquiet; (sommeil) agité; (b) inquiet; **to be u. in one's mind,** ne pas avoir l'esprit tranquille. **un'easily** *adv* (a) d'un air gêné (b) avec inquiétude; (dormir) d'un sommeil agité. **un'easiness** *n* inquiétude *f.*

uneatable [ʌnˈiːtəbl] *a* immangeable. **un'eaten** *a* non mangé; **u. food,** restes *mpl.*

uneconomic [ʌniːkəˈnɔmik, ˌʌnek-] *a* **1.** non économique **2.** (travail) pas rentable. **uneco'nomical** *a* (méthode) peu économique.

uneducated [ʌnˈedjukeitid] *a* (a) sans éducation (b) (*speech, accent*) populaire.

unemotional [ʌniːˈmouʃənəl] *a* impassible. **une'motionally** *adv* avec impassibilité.

unemployed [ʌnimˈplɔid] *a* (a) désœuvré (b) en chômage, sans travail; *npl* **the u.,** les chômeurs *m.* **unem'ployable** *a* incapable de travailler. **unem'ployment** *n* chômage *m;* **u. benefit,** allocation de chômage.

unending [ʌnˈendiŋ] *a* **1.** interminable; sans fin **2.** éternel.

unendurable [ʌninˈdjuərəbl] *a* insupportable.

unenterprising [ʌnˈentəpraiziŋ] *a* peu entreprenant; qui manque d'initiative; (*of plan*) qui manque d'audace.

unenthusiastic [ʌnenθjuːziˈæstik] *a* peu enthousiaste. **unenthusi'astically** *adv* sans enthousiasme.

unenviable [ʌnˈenviəbl] *a* peu enviable.

unequal [ʌnˈiːkwəl] *a* (a) inégal (b) **to be u. to the task,** ne pas être à la hauteur de la tâche; **to be u. to doing sth,** ne pas être de force à faire qch. **un'equalled** *a* inégalé; sans égal. **un'equally** *adv* inégalement.

unequivocal [ʌniːˈkwivəkl] *a* clair, net; sans équivoque. **une'quivocally** *adv* sans équivoque.

unerring [ʌnˈɜːriŋ] *a* infaillible, sûr.

UNESCO [juːˈneskou] *abbr United Nations Educational, Scientific and Cultural Organisation.*

unethical [ʌnˈeθikl] *a* qui manque de probité; immoral.

uneven [ʌnˈiːv(ə)n] *a* **1.** inégal; rugueux; (terrain) accidenté; **u. temper,** humeur inégale; **u. breathing,** respiration irrégulière **2.** (nombre) impair. **un'evenly** *adv* **1.** inégalement **2.** irrégulièrement. **un'evenness** *n* inégalité *f;* irrégularité *f.*

uneventful [ʌniˈventfəl] *a* sans incident; **u. life,** vie calme, peu mouvementée.

unexceptionable [ʌnikˈsepʃ(ə)nəbl] *a* (conduite) irréprochable; (personne) tout à fait convenable.

unexceptional [ʌnikˈsepʃənəl] *a* qui n'a rien d'exceptionnel.

unexciting [ʌnikˈsaitiŋ] *a* insipide; peu passionnant; (vie) monotone.

unexpected [ʌnikˈspektid] **1.** *a* (visiteur, résultat) inattendu; (événement) imprévu; (secours) inespéré; **u. meeting,** rencontre inopinée; **it was completely u.,** on ne s'y attendait pas du tout **2.** *n* **the u.,** l'imprévu *m.* **unex'pectedly** *adv* de manière inattendue; inopinément.

unexplained [ʌnikˈspleind] *a* inexpliqué.

unexplored [ʌnikˈsplɔːd] *a* (pays) inexploré.

unexposed [ʌnikˈspouzd] *a* (film) vierge.

unexpurgated [ʌnˈekspəgeitid] *a* (livre) non expurgé; **u. edition,** édition intégrale.

unfailing [ʌnˈfeiliŋ] *a* **1.** (moyen) infaillible, sûr; (courage) inlassable; (bonté) inaltérable; (espoir) inébranlable **2.** (source) intarissable, inépuisable (**of,** de). **un'failingly** *adv* infailliblement.

unfair [ʌnˈfeər] *a* **1.** (*of pers*) injuste; peu équitable; **to be u. to s.o.,** défavoriser qn; **it's u.!** ce n'est pas juste! **to be put at an u. disadvantage,** être défavorisé, désavantagé **2.** inéquitable; **u. competition,** concurrence déloyale. **un'fairly** *adv* **1.** injustement; peu équitablement; **he has been u. treated,** il est (la) victime d'une injustice **2. to act u.,** agir avec mauvaise foi. **un'fairness** *n* **1.** injustice *f* (envers qn); partialité *f* **2.** déloyauté *f;* mauvaise foi.

unfaithful [ʌnˈfeiθfəl] *a* infidèle.

unfamiliar [ʌnfəˈmiljər] *a* **1.** peu familier; (visage) étranger, inconnu **2.** (*of pers*) **to be u. with sth,** ne pas connaître, mal connaître, qch.

unfashionable [ʌnˈfæʃ(ə)nəbl] *a* démodé, passé de mode; qui n'est pas à la mode.

unfasten [ʌnˈfɑːsn] *vtr* détacher (qch de qch); défaire (un vêtement, un nœud); ouvrir, déverrouiller (une porte).

unfavourable, *NAm:* **unfavorable** [ʌnˈfeiv(ə)rəbl] *a* défavorable, peu favorable; (vent) contraire; (critique) adverse; **to show oneself in an u. light,** se montrer sous un jour désavantageux. **un'favourably,** *NAm:* -'**favorably** *adv* défavorablement; **u. disposed towards s.o.,** hostile à qn.

unfeeling [ʌnˈfiːliŋ] *a* insensible, impitoyable; (cœur) froid, indifférent. **un'feelingly** *adv* sans pitié; froidement.

unfeigned [ʌnˈfeind] *a* sincère.

unfeminine [ʌnˈfeminin] *a* peu féminin.

unfertilized [ʌnˈfɜːtilaizd] *a* non fécondé.

unfinished [ʌnˈfiniʃt] *a* (a) inachevé; **to have some u. business,** avoir une affaire à régler (b) non façonné; mal fini.

unfit [ʌnˈfit] *a* **1.** (a) impropre, peu propre, à la consommation; non comestible; **u. for publication,** impubliable; **u. for habitation,** inhabitable; **u. for vehicles,** (chemin) impraticable pour les voitures (b) (*of pers*) **u. for military service,** inapte au service (militaire) **2. to be u.,** en mauvaise santé; ne pas être en forme; **he's u. to travel,** il n'est pas en état de voyager.

unflattering [ʌnˈflæt(ə)riŋ] *a* peu flatteur.

unflinching [ʌnˈflin(t)ʃiŋ] *a* stoïque, impassible. **un'flinchingly** *adv* sans broncher.

unfold [ʌnˈfould] *v* **1.** *vtr* (a) déplier, ouvrir (un journal); déployer (une carte); décroiser (les bras) (b) exposer (un projet); dévoiler (un secret) **2.** *vi & pr* se déployer, se dérouler.

unforeseeable [ʌnfɔːˈsiːəbl] *a* imprévisible. **unfore'seen** *a* imprévu, inattendu; **unless something u. happens,** sauf imprévu.

unforgettable [ʌnfəˈgetəbl] *a* inoubliable. **unfor'gotten** *a* inoublié.

unforgivable [ʌnfəˈgivəbl] *a* impardonnable. **unfor'givably** *adv* **he was u. rude,** son impolitesse est impardonnable. **unfor'giving** *a* implacable, rancunier.

unformed [ʌn'fɔ:md] *a* informe.

unforthcoming [ʌnfɔ:θ'kʌmiŋ] *a* réservé; réticent.

unfortunate [ʌn'fɔ:tʃənət] **1.** *a* (*a*) malheureux; **to be u.,** avoir de la malchance (*b*) (événement) malencontreux; (erreur) regrettable; **in u. circumstances,** dans de tristes circonstances; **it is u. that,** il est fâcheux, malheureux, que + *sub*; **how u.!** quel dommage! **un'fortunately** *adv* malheureusement; par malheur.

unfounded [ʌn'faundid] *a* sans fondement.

unframed [ʌn'freimd] *a* sans cadre.

unfreeze [ʌn'fri:z] *v* (**unfroze; unfrozen**) **1.** *vtr* (*a*) (faire) dégeler (*b*) débloquer (des crédits) **2.** *vi* (se) dégeler.

unfrequented [ʌnfri'kwentid] *a* peu fréquenté; (endroit) écarté.

unfriendly [ʌn'frendli] *a* peu amical; inamical; (action) hostile; (accueil) froid; **u. towards s.o.,** mal disposé pour, envers, qn. **un'friendliness** *n* manque *m* d'amitié; froideur *f* (**towards,** envers); hostilité *f* (**towards,** envers, contre).

unfulfilled [ʌnful'fild] *a* (*prophesy*) inaccompli; (*desire*) non satisfait; (*prayer*) inexaucé; (*promise*) non tenu; **to feel u.,** éprouver un sentiment d'insatisfaction.

unfurl [ʌn'fɜ:l] *vtr* déployer.

unfurnished [ʌn'fɜ:niʃt] *a* non meublé.

ungainly [ʌn'geinli] *a* gauche, disgracieux.

ungenerous [ʌn'dʒenərəs] *a* peu généreux.

ungetatable [ʌnget'ætəbl] *a F:* inaccessible.

ungodly [ʌn'gɔdli] *a* impie; *F:* **at an u. hour,** à une heure indue.

ungovernable [ʌn'gʌv(ə)nəbl] *a* ingouvernable; (désir, passion) irrépressible.

ungracious [ʌn'greiʃəs] *a* peu gracieux; peu aimable; **it would be u. to refuse,** j'aurais mauvaise grâce de refuser. **un'graciously** *adv* de mauvaise grâce. **un'graciousness** *n* mauvaise grâce.

ungrammatical [ʌngrə'mætik(ə)l] *a* non grammatical; incorrect. **ungra'mmatically** *adv* incorrectement.

ungrateful [ʌn'greitful] *a* ingrat; peu reconnaissant. **un'gratefully** *adv* avec ingratitude.

ungrudging [ʌn'grʌdʒiŋ] *a* donné de bon cœur; (*praise*) très sincère. **un'grudgingly** *adv* de bon cœur; généreusement.

unguarded [ʌn'gɑːdid] *a* **1.** sans surveillance **2.** (*of remark*) inconsidéré, irréfléchi; **in an u. moment,** dans un moment d'inattention. **un'guardedly** *adv* inconsidérément.

unhampered [ʌn'hæmpəd] *a* libre (de ses mouvements); **u. by rules,** sans être gêné par des règlements.

unhappy [ʌn'hæpi] *a* **1.** (*a*) malheureux, triste; infortuné; **to make s.o. u.,** causer du chagrin à qn (*b*) inquiet; **I'm u. about leaving the house empty,** je n'aime pas laisser la maison vide **2.** malheureux; **u. state of affairs,** situation regrettable. **un'happily** *adv* (*a*) malheureusement; par malheur (*b*) tristement (*c*) **they're u. married,** c'est un ménage malheureux. **un'happiness** *n* chagrin *m*; tristesse *f*.

unharmed [ʌn'hɑːmd] *a* sain et sauf; indemne; intact.

unhealthy [ʌn'helθi] *a* **1.** malsain, insalubre **2.** (*a*) (*of pers*) maladif; **u. complexion,** visage terreux (*b*) **u. influence,** influence malsaine; **u. curiosity,** curiosité morbide. **un'healthiness** *n* **1.** insalubrité (du climat) **2.** mauvaise santé.

unheard [ʌn'hɜːd] *a* **u. of,** inouï, incroyable.

unheated [ʌn'hiːtid] *a* non chauffé.

unheeded [ʌn'hiːdid] *a* négligé; **his warning went u.,** on n'a pas tenu compte de son avertissement.

unhelpful [ʌn'helpfəl] *a* (critique) peu utile; (conseil) vain, futile; (*of pers*) peu secourable, peu obligeant; **don't be so u.!** tâche donc un peu de nous aider!

unhesitating [ʌn'heziteitiŋ] *a* qui n'hésite pas; ferme, résolu; (réponse) prompte. **un'hesitatingly** *adv* sans hésiter; sans hésitation.

unhindered [ʌn'hindəd] *a* sans obstacle; **to go u.,** passer librement.

unhinged [ʌn'hindʒd] *a* (cerveau) détraqué.

unhitch [ʌn'hitʃ] *vtr* décrocher (qch).

unholy [ʌn'houli] *a F:* **u. muddle,** désordre affreux, invraisemblable.

unhook [ʌn'huk] *vtr* décrocher.

unhoped [ʌn'houpt] *a* **u. for,** inespéré.

unhurried [ʌn'hʌrid] *a* lent; **in an u. way,** sans se presser.

unhurt [ʌn'hɜːt] *a* sans mal; indemne; sain et sauf; sans mal.

unhygienic [ʌnhai'dʒiːnik] *a* non hygiénique.

UNICEF ['juːnisef] *abbr United Nations (International) Children's (Emergency) Fund.*

unicorn ['juːnikɔːn] *n* licorne *f*.

unidentified [ʌnai'dentifaid] *a* non identifié; **u. flying object,** objet volant non identifié.

unification [juːnifi'keiʃ(ə)n] *n* unification *f*.

uniform ['juːnifɔːm] **1.** *a* (*of temperature*) constant **2.** *n* uniforme *m*; **out of u.,** en civil. **'uniformed** *a* en uniforme. **uni'formity** *n* uniformité *f*. **'uniformly** *adv* uniformément.

unify ['juːnifai] *vtr & i* (s')unifier.

unilateral [juːni'læt(ə)rəl] *a* unilatéral. **uni'laterally** *adv* unilatéralement.

unimaginable [ʌni'mædʒinəbl] *a* inimaginable. **uni'maginative** *a* dénué d'imagination; peu maginatif. **uni'maginatively** *adv* sans imagination.

unimpaired [ʌnim'pɛəd] *a* (*of health*) non altéré; (*of force*) non diminué.

unimportant [ʌnim'pɔːt(ə)nt] *a* sans importance; **it's quite u.,** cela n'a pas d'importance.

unimpressed [ʌnim'prest] *a* peu impressionné (**by,** par).

uninflammable [ʌnin'flæməbl] *a* ininflammable.

uninhabitable [ʌnin'hæbitəbl] *a* inhabitable. **unin'habited** *a* inhabité, désert.

uninhibited [ʌnin'hibitid] *a* sans inhibitions; (*of emotion*) non refréné.

uninitiated [ʌni'niʃieitid] *n* **the u.,** les non-initiés *m*.

uninjured [ʌn'indʒəd] *a* sans blessure; sain et sauf; indemne.

uninspired [ʌnin'spaiəd] *a* qui manque d'inspiration; (style) banal. **unin'spiring** *a* qui n'est pas inspirant.

uninsured [ʌnin'ʃuəd] *a* non assuré (**against,** contre).

unintelligent [ʌnin'telidʒənt] *a* inintelligent.

unintelligible [ʌnin'telidʒibl] *a* inintelligible. **unin'telligibly** *adv* inintelligiblement.

unintentional [ʌnin'tenʃ(ə)nəl] *a* involontaire; **it was quite u.,** ce n'était pas fait exprès. **unin'tentionally** *adv* involontairement; sans le faire exprès.

uninterested [ʌn'intristid] *a* non intéressé; indifférent **(in, à). un'interesting** *a* non intéressant; sans intérêt; inintéressant.

uninterrupted [ʌnintə'rʌptid] *a* **1.** ininterrompu **2.** continu; **u. correspondence,** correspondance suivie. **uninte'rruptedly** *adv* sans interruption.

uninvited [ʌnin'vaitid] *a* **to come u.,** venir sans invitation; **u. guest,** visiteur inattendu; **to do sth u.,** faire qch sans y avoir été invité. **unin'viting** *a* (*of appearance*) peu attirant, peu attrayant; (*of food*) peu appétissant.

union ['ju:njən] *n* **1.** (*a*) union *f* (*b*) mariage *m* (*c*) concorde *f*; **in perfect u.,** en parfaite harmonie **2.** (*a*) **the (American) U.,** les États-Unis; **customs u.,** union douanière (*b*) **trade(s), NAm: labor, u.,** syndicat (ouvrier) *m*; **to join a u.,** se syndiquer; **u. member,** syndiqué(e); **non-u. workers,** ouvriers non syndiqués **3. U. Jack,** pavillon du Royaume-Uni. **'unionism** *n* syndicalisme *m*. **'unionist** *n* (*a*) **trade(s) u.,** syndicaliste *mf*; syndiqué, -ée (*b*) *Pol:* unioniste *mf*. **'unionize** *vtr* syndiquer.

unique [ju:'ni:k] *a* unique. **u'niquely** *adv* exceptionnellement. **u'niqueness** *n* caractère unique.

unisex ['ju:niseks] *a* unisexe.

unison ['ju:nisən] *n* **1.** *Mus:* unisson *m*; **in u.,** à l'unisson **(with,** de) **2. to be in u. with s.o.,** être en accord avec qn.

unit ['ju:nit] *n* **1.** unité *f*; *Com:* **u. price,** prix unitaire **2.** (*a*) unité (de longueur, de poids); **standard u.,** module *m*; *Tp:* **u. charge,** taxe unitaire; *Fin:* **monetary u.,** unité monétaire; **u. trust,** société d'investissement à capital variable **3.** (*a*) *Med:* **intensive care u.,** centre *m* de soins intensifs; **X-ray u.,** service de radiologie (*b*) *Mil:* **fighting u.,** unité combattante (*c*) *MecE:* unité, élément *m*; *Aut:* **motor u.,** bloc-moteur *m*; *Cmptr:* **(visual) display u.,** console *f* de visualisation (*d*) **u. furniture,** mobilier par éléments; **kitchen u.,** élément de cuisine; **hob u.,** table *f* de cuisson.

unite [ju:'nait] **1.** *vtr* (*a*) unir; réunir (qch à qch); allier (qch à qch) (*b*) mettre (les gens) d'accord; unifier (un parti) **2.** *vi* (*a*) s'unir, s'unifier **(with,** à) (*b*) (*of two or more pers or thgs*) s'unir; se réunir; (*of party*) s'unifier; (*of states*) se confédérer; **to u. against s.o.,** s'unir contre qn; **to u. in doing sth,** se mettre d'accord pour faire qch. **u'nited** *a* uni, unifié; **u. efforts,** efforts conjugués; **to present a u. front,** présenter un front uni; **the U. Kingdom,** le Royaume-Uni; **the U. States (of America),** les États-Unis (d'Amérique). **'unity** *n* unité *f*; accord *m*; **u. is strength,** l'union fait la force; **in u.,** en harmonie **(with,** avec).

universe ['ju:nivə:s] *n* univers *m*. **uni'versal** *a* universel; **he's a u. favourite,** tout le monde l'aime; *MecE:* **u. joint,** joint universel. **uni'versally** *adv* universellement.

university [ju:ni'və:siti] *n* université *f*; **he's been to u., he's had a u. education,** il a fait des études supérieures; **u. professor,** professeur de faculté; **u. town,** ville universitaire.

unjust [ʌn'dʒʌst] *a* injuste **(to,** envers, avec, pour); **u. suspicions,** soupçons mal fondés. **unjusti'fiable** *a* injustifiable. **unjusti'fiably** *adv* sans justification. **un'justified** *a* injustifié. **un'justly** *adv* injustement.

unkempt [ʌn'kem(p)t] *a* **1.** (*of hair*) mal peigné; (*of appearance*) débraillé **2.** (*of garden*) peu soigné; mal tenu.

unkind [ʌn'kaind] *a* (i) dur; méchant (ii) peu aimable; pas gentil; **that's u. of him,** ce n'est pas gentil de sa part; **he was u. enough to,** il a eu la méchanceté de. **un'kindly** *adv* (i) méchamment, durement (ii) peu aimablement; **don't take it u. if,** ne le prenez pas en mauvaise part si. **un'kindness** *n* manque *m* de gentillesse; méchanceté *f*.

unknown [ʌn'noun] **1.** *a* (*a*) inconnu **(to,** à, de); ignoré **(to,** de); (écrivain) obscur, inconnu; **u. person,** inconnu, -ue; **the U. Soldier,** le Soldat inconnu; *adv* **u. to anyone,** à l'insu de tout le monde (*b*) *Mth:* **u. quantity,** (quantité) inconnue (*f*) **2.** *n* (*a*) (*pers*) inconnu, -ue (*b*) *Mth:* inconnue (*c*) **the u.,** l'inconnu. **un'knowing** *a* ignorant; inconscient **(of,** de). **un'knowingly** *adv* inconsciemment; sans le savoir.

unladen [ʌn'leidn] *a* *Nau:* sans charge; **u. weight,** poids à vide.

unladylike [ʌn'leidilaik] *af* mal élevée; (*of manners*) peu distingué.

unlawful [ʌn'lɔ:ful] *a* illégal; illicite. **un'lawfully** *adv* illégalement; illicitement.

unleavened [ʌn'lev(ə)nd] *a* (pain) azyme, sans levain.

unless [ʌn'les] *conj* à moins que + *sub*; **you'll be late u. you leave at once,** vous arriverez trop tard à moins de partir immédiatement; **u. I am mistaken,** si je ne me trompe; **u. I hear to the contrary,** sauf avis contraire.

unlicensed [ʌn'laisənst] *a* non autorisé; illicite; (*of car*) sans vignette; **u. premises,** établissement où la vente des boissons alcooliques n'est pas autorisée.

unlike [ʌn'laik] *a* différent, dissemblable; **u. sth,** différent de qch; **he's not u. his sister,** il ressemble assez à sa sœur; **he, u. his father,** lui, contrairement à son père; **that was very u. him!** cela ne lui ressemble pas! je ne le reconnais pas là!

unlik(e)able [ʌn'laikəbl] *a* peu sympathique; (*of thg*) peu agréable.

unlikely [ʌn'laikli] *a* **1.** (*a*) improbable, peu probable; (*of explanation*) invraisemblable; **most u.,** fort improbable; **it's not (at all) u.,** cela se pourrait bien; **it's u. to happen,** cela ne risque pas d'arriver (*b*) **he's u. to come,** il est peu probable qu'il vienne **2. he's an u. man for the job,** il ne semble pas être destiné à ce travail. **un'likelihood** *n* improbabilité *f*.

unlimited [ʌn'limitid] *a* illimité; sans borne(s).

unlined [ʌn'laind] *a* **1.** sans doublure **2.** (visage) sans rides; (papier) non réglé.

unlit [ʌn'lit] *a* non éclairé.

unload [ʌn'loud] *vtr & i* décharger (un bateau, des marchandises, un fusil); *Fig:* se débarrasser, se défaire, de (qch). **un'loaded** *a* **1.** déchargé **2.** non chargé; (fusil) non armé. **un'loading** *n* déchargement *m*.

unlock [ʌn'lɔk] *vtr* **1.** ouvrir (une porte); **it's unlocked,** ce n'est pas fermé à clef **2.** débloquer (une roue).

unlooked-for [ʌn'luktfɔːr] a inattendu.

unloved [ʌn'lʌvd] a qui n'est pas aimé.

unlucky [ʌn'lʌki] a 1. (a) malheureux, infortuné; **to be u.**, ne pas avoir de chance; F: n'avoir pas de veine (b) (of thg) malheureux, malencontreux; **that's u.**, ce n'est pas de chance 2. qui porte malheur; **u. star**, étoile maléfique; **it's u.**, ça porte malheur. **un'luckily** adv malheureusement, par malheur. **un'luckiness** n manque m de chance; F: déveine f.

unmade [ʌn'meid] a (lit) défait.

unmanageable [ʌn'mænidʒəbl] a 1. intraitable; (of child) indocile; (of ship) difficile à manœuvrer 2. difficile à manier; (of hair) rebelle.

unmanned [ʌn'mænd] a (of vehicle) non habité, sans équipage; Space: **u. flight**, vol inhabité.

unmarked [ʌn'mɑːkt] a (a) sans marque(s); (of police car) banalisé (b) (of essay) non corrigé.

unmarketable [ʌn'mɑːkitəbl] a invendable.

unmarried [ʌn'mærid] a célibataire; qui n'est pas marié; **u. mother**, mère célibataire.

unmask [ʌn'mɑːsk] vtr démasquer.

unmentionable [ʌn'menʃ(ə)nəbl] a (chose) dont il ne faut pas parler.

unmerciful [ʌn'mɔːsiful] a impitoyable; sans pitié. **un'mercifully** adv impitoyablement.

unmethodical [ʌnmi'θɔdik(ə)l] a peu méthodique; (of pers) qui manque de methode.

unmistakable [ʌnmis'teikəbl] a (a) (preuve) indubitable; (sentiment) clair; (différence) marquée (b) facilement reconnaissable. **unmis'takably** adv sans aucun doute; clairement, nettement.

unmitigated [ʌn'mitigeitid] a (a) (mal) non mitigé (b) véritable; **u. lie**, pur mensonge; **u. disaster**, échec total.

unmixed [ʌn'mikst] a sans mélange; pur.

unmounted [ʌn'mauntid] a (of gem) non serti; (of photo) non encadré.

unmoved [ʌn'muːvd] a impassible; **u. by sth**, aucunement ému de, par, qch; **u. by their entreaties**, insensible à leurs prières.

unmusical [ʌn'mjuːzik(ə)l] a 1. peu mélodieux 2. peu musicien, -ienne.

unnamed [ʌn'neimd] a au nom inconnu; anonyme.

unnatural [ʌn'nætʃrəl] a (a) qui n'est pas naturel; anormal; contre nature (b) (of style) peu naturel, artificiel. **un'naturally** adv anormalement; de manière peu naturelle; **not u.**, naturellement.

unnecessary [ʌn'nesis(ə)ri] a peu, pas, nécessaire; inutile, superflu; **it is u. to say that**, (il est) inutile de dire que. **unnece'ssarily** adv inutilement; pour rien.

unnerve [ʌn'nɔːv] vtr faire perdre son courage, son sang-froid, à (qn); déconcerter (qn). **un'nerving** a déconcertant.

unnoticed [ʌn'noutist] a inaperçu, inobservé; **to pass u.**, passer inaperçu.

unnumbered [ʌn'nʌmbəd] a non numéroté.

UNO abbr United Nations Organization.

unobjectionable [ʌnəb'dʒekʃnəbl] a (personne) à qui on ne peut rien reprocher; (chose) à laquelle on ne peut trouver à redire.

unobservant [ʌnəb'zɔːvənt] a peu observateur. **unob'served** a inobservé, inaperçu; **to go out u.**, sortir sans être vu.

unobstructed [ʌnəb'strʌktid] a 1. non bouché, non obstrué; (of street) non encombré; (of view) libre 2. sans rencontrer d'obstacles.

unobtainable [ʌnəb'teinəbl] a impossible à obtenir, à se procurer.

unobtrusive [ʌnəb'truːsiv] a discret. **unob'trusively** adv discrètement.

unoccupied [ʌn'ɔkjupaid] a (a) désœuvré, sans occupation (b) inoccupé, inhabité (c) (of seat) libre, disponible.

unofficial [ʌnə'fiʃ(ə)l] a non officiel; (renseignement) officieux; **u. strike**, grève sauvage; **in an u. capacity**, à titre privé, non officiel. **uno'fficially** adv à titre officieux.

unopened [ʌn'oupənd] a qui n'a pas été ouvert; **u. letter**, lettre non décachetée.

unopposed [ʌnə'pouzd] a sans opposition.

unorganized [ʌn'ɔːgənaizd] a mal organisé; (of labour) inorganisé.

unoriginal [ʌnə'ridʒinəl] a qui manque d'originalité; peu original.

unorthodox [ʌn'ɔːθədɔks] a peu orthodoxe.

unostentatious [ʌnɔsten'teiʃəs] a peu fastueux; simple; sans ostentation. **unosten'tatiously** adv sans ostentation.

unpack [ʌn'pæk] 1. vtr déballer, dépaqueter (des objets); défaire (une valise) 2. vi défaire sa valise. **un'packing** n déballage m; **my u. won't take long**, il me faudra peu de temps pour défaire mes valises.

unpaid [ʌn'peid] a 1. non payé; (of pers) non salarié; (of post) non rétribué 2. (of bill) impayé; **u. debt**, dette non acquittée.

unpalatable [ʌn'pælətəbl] a (a) d'un goût désagréable (b) (of truth) désagréable.

unparalleled [ʌn'pærəleld] a incomparable, sans égal.

unpardonable [ʌn'pɑːdnəbl] a impardonnable.

unpatriotic [ʌnpætri'ɔtik] a (of pers) peu patriote; (of action) peu patriotique.

unperturbed [ʌnpə'tɔːbd] a (a) impassible (b) non déconcerté.

unpick [ʌn'pik] vtr défaire (une couture).

unpin [ʌn'pin] vtr (unpinned) détacher (qch) (**from**, de).

unplaced [ʌn'pleist] a (cheval) non placé; (candidat) non classé.

unplanned [ʌn'plænd] a (événement) imprévu; (enfant) non prévu.

unpleasant [ʌn'plez(ə)nt] a désagréable, déplaisant; **u. weather**, mauvais temps; **to make u. remarks**, dire des choses désobligeantes. **un'pleasantly** adv désagréablement; de façon déplaisante. **un'pleasantness** n 1. caractère m désagréable, déplaisant (de qch) 2. ennui m; **there'll be some u.**, il y aura de la dispute.

unplug [ʌn'plʌg] vtr (unplugged) El: débrancher.

unpolished [ʌn'pɔliʃt] a 1. non poli; mat; (of stone) brut; (of floor) non ciré, non astiqué; (of shoes) non ciré 2. (of pers) rude, fruste.

unpolluted [ʌnpə'l(j)uːtid] a non pollué.

unpopular [ʌn'pɔpjulər] a impopulaire; **to be generally u.**, être mal vu de tous. **unpopularity** [-'læriti] n impopularité f.

unpractical [ʌn'præktikl] *a (of pers)* peu pratique; qui manque de sens pratique.

unprecedented [ʌn'presidentid] *a* sans précédent.

unpredictable [ʌnpri'diktəbl] *a* imprévisible; *(of weather)* incertain.

unprejudiced [ʌn'predʒudist] *a* sans préjugés; impartial.

unprepared [ʌnpri'pɛəd] *a* 1. non préparé; (discours) improvisé 2. **to be u. for sth**, ne pas s'attendre à qch 3. sans préparation; **to go into sth u.**, se lancer à tête perdue dans qch.

unprepossessing [ʌnpri:pə'zesiŋ] *a* peu engageant; qui fait mauvaise impression.

unpretentious [ʌnpri'tenʃəs] *a* sans prétention(s); modeste.

unprincipled [ʌn'prinsipld] *a* sans principes; sans scrupules.

unprintable [ʌn'printəbl] *a* impubliable; que l'on n'oserait pas répéter.

unproductive [ʌnprə'dʌktiv] *a* improductif.

unprofessional [ʌnprə'feʃ(ə)n(ə)l] *a (a)* **u. conduct**, conduite contraire au code professionnel *(b)* **for an architect he's very u.**, comme architecte il est plutôt amateur.

unprofitable [ʌn'prɔfitəbl] *a* peu lucratif; peu rentable. **un'profitably** *adv* sans profit.

unpromising [ʌn'prɔmisiŋ] *a* peu prometteur.

unpronounceable [ʌnprə'naunsəbl] *a* imprononçable.

unprotected [ʌnprə'tektid] *a* sans protection, sans défense.

unproved, unproven [ʌn'pru:vd, -'prouvən] *a* non prouvé.

unprovided-for [ʌnprə'vaididfɔ:r] *a (pers)* sans ressources.

unprovoked [ʌnprə'voukt] *a* non provoqué; fait sans provocation.

unpublished [ʌn'pʌbliʃt] *a* inédit; non publié. **un'publishable** *a* impubliable.

unpunctual [ʌn'pʌŋ(k)tjuəl] *a* inexact; peu ponctuel.

unpunished [ʌn'pʌniʃt] *a* impuni; **to go u.**, rester impuni.

unqualified [ʌn'kwɔlifaid] *a* 1. *(a)* non qualifié; incompétent *(b)* sans diplôme(s), non diplômé; **I'm quite u. to talk about it**, je ne suis nullement qualifié pour en parler 2. **u. praise**, éloges sans réserve; **u. success**, succès formidable.

unquestionable [ʌn'kwestʃənəbl] *a* indiscutable; incontestable. **un'questionably** *adv* incontestablement, sans aucun doute. **un'questioned** *a* 1. (droit) indisputé, incontesté 2. **to let a statement pass u.**, laisser passer une affirmation sans la relever. **un'questioning** *a* (obéissance) aveugle; inconditionnel.

unquote ['ʌnkwout] *vi (used only in imp) (in dictation)* fermez les guillemets; *(in report)* fin *f* de citation.

unravel [ʌn'rævəl] **(unravelled)** 1. *vtr* effiler, effilocher (un tissu); débrouiller, démêler (des fils); éclaircir (un mystère) 2. *vi* s'effiler, s'effilocher.

unreadable [ʌn'ri:dəbl] *a* illisible.

unready [ʌn'redi] *a* mal préparé (pour qch). **un'readiness** *n* impréparation *f*.

unreal [ʌn'riəl] *a* irréel. **unrea'listic** *a* peu réaliste. **unre'ality** *n* irréalité *f*.

unreasonable [ʌn'ri:znəbl] *a* 1. déraisonnable; **don't be u.**, soyez raisonnable 2. *(a)* (demande) immodérée; (prix) excessif *(b)* **at an u. hour**, à une heure indue. **un'reasonably** *adv* d'une manière peu raisonnable. **un'reasoning** *a* irraisonné.

unrecognizable [ʌn'rekəgnaizəbl] *a* méconnaissable; difficile à reconnaître. **un'recognized** *a (of talent)* méconnu; *(of government)* non reconnu; **to do sth u.**, faire qch sans être reconnu.

unrecorded [ʌnri'kɔ:did] *a* non enregistré; non mentionné.

unrefined [ʌnri'faind] *a* 1. brut; non raffiné 2. (homme) peu raffiné, fruste.

unreformed [ʌnri'fɔ:md] *a* non amendé.

unrehearsed [ʌnri'hɜ:st] *a (of speech)* improvisé; *(of play)* (joué) sans répétition(s).

unrelated [ʌnri'leitid] *a (of events)* qui n'a aucun rapport (**to**, avec); *(of pers)* **they are u.**, il n'y a aucun lien de parenté entre eux.

unrelenting [ʌnri'lentiŋ] *a (of pers)* implacable (**towards**, à, pour, à l'égard de); *(of persecution)* acharné.

unreliable [ʌnri'laiəbl] *a* (personne) sur qui on ne peut pas compter; (caractère) instable; (renseignement) sujet à caution; (résultat) incertain; *(source of information)* douteux; (machine) peu fiable. **unrelia'bility** *n* manque *m* de sérieux (de qn); inexactitude *f* (d'un résultat); manque de fiabilité (d'une machine).

unrelieved [ʌnri'li:vd] *a (of pain)* non soulagé, constant; *(of boredom)* mortel.

unremarkable [ʌnri'mɑ:kəbl] *a* médiocre.

unremitting [ʌnri'mitiŋ] *a* sans relâche; infatigable, inlassable.

unremunerative [ʌnri'mju:nərətiv] *a* peu rémunérateur; mal payé.

unrepeatable [ʌnri'pi:təbl] *a (a)* (remarque) qu'on ne peut pas répéter *(b)* (prix) exceptionnel; (offre) unique.

unrepentant [ʌnri'pentənt] *a* impénitent.

unrepresentative [ʌnrepri'zentətiv] *a* peu représentatif.

unrequited [ʌnri'kwaitid] *a* (amour) non partagé.

unreserved [ʌnri'zɜ:vd] *a* 1. sans réserve; franc; *(of approval)* entier 2. **u. seats**, places non réservées. **unre'servedly** [-idli] *adv* sans réserve; franchement.

unresponsive [ʌnri'spɔnsiv] *a* qui ne réagit pas; insensible (**to**, à).

unrest [ʌn'rest] *n* troubles *mpl*; **social u.**, malaise social; **industrial u.**, agitation ouvrière.

unrestricted [ʌnri'striktid] *a* illimité; (accès) libre.

unrewarded [ʌnri'wɔ:did] *a* sans récompense. **unre'warding** *a (a)* peu rémunérateur *(b)* ingrat.

unripe [ʌn'raip] *a* qui n'est pas mûr.

unrivalled, NAm: also unrivaled [ʌn'raivəld] *a* sans rival; incomparable.

unroll [ʌn'roul] *vtr, pr & i* (se) dérouler.

unromantic [ʌnrə'mæntik] *a* peu romantique.

unruffled [ʌn'rʌfld] *a (of pers)* calme; *(of hair)* lisse.

unruled [ʌn'ru:ld] *a (of paper)* uni, non réglé.

unruly [ʌn'ru:li] *a* indiscipliné.

unsaddle [ʌn'sædl] *vtr* desseller (un cheval).

unsafe [ʌn'seif] *a* 1. dangereux; peu sûr; *(of undertak-*

ing) hasardeux; (*of chair*) peu solide 2. exposé au danger.

unsaid [ʌn'sed] *a* **to leave sth u.,** passer qch sous silence.

unsaleable [ʌn'seiləbl] *a* invendable.

unsalted [ʌn'sɔltəd] *a* non salé; (beurre) frais.

unsatisfactory [ʌnsætis'fækt(ə)ri] *a* peu satisfaisant; qui laisse à désirer; (*of explanation*) peu convaincant. **un'satisfied** *a* 1. peu satisfait (with, de) 2. **I'm still u. about it,** je n'en suis pas encore convaincu 3. (*of appetite*) non rassasié. **un'satisfying** *a* 1. peu satisfaisant 2. peu convaincant 3. (*of meal*) insuffisant.

unsaturated [ʌn'sætʃəreitid] *a Ch:* non saturé.

unsavoury, *NAm:* **unsavory** [ʌn'seivəri] *a* 1. (goût) désagréable; d'un goût désagréable; **u. smell,** mauvaise odeur 2. (scandale) répugnant; (réputation) équivoque.

unscathed [ʌn'skeiθd] *a* indemne.

unscientific [ʌnsaiən'tifik] *a* non scientifique; peu scientifique.

unscramble [ʌn'skræmbl] *vtr* déchiffrer.

unscrew [ʌn'skru:] *vtr & i* (se) dévisser.

unscripted [ʌn'skriptid] *a* sans préparation; improvisé.

unscrupulous [ʌn'skru:pjuləs] *a* peu scrupuleux; sans scrupules. **un'scrupulously** *adv* peu scrupuleusement; sans scrupules. **un'scrupulousness** *n* manque *m* de scrupules.

unseasonable [ʌn'si:z(ə)nəbl] *a* (*of fruit*) hors de saison; **u. weather,** temps qui n'est pas de saison. **un'seasonably** *adv* **u. warm,** chaud pour la saison.

unseasoned [ʌn'si:zənd] *a* 1. (*of food*) non assaisonné 2. (*of timber*) vert.

unseat [ʌn'si:t] *vtr* (*of horse*) désarçonner (son cavalier).

unseeded [ʌn'si:did] *a Ten:* (*of player*) non classé.

unseeing [ʌn'si:iŋ] *a* qui ne voit pas; aveugle.

unseen *a* inaperçu; **to do sth u.,** faire qch sans être vu; **u. translation,** *n* u., version *f*.

unseemly [ʌn'si:mli] *a* inconvenant.

unselfconscious [ʌnself'kɔnʃəs] *a* naturel. **unself'consciously** *adv* sans contrainte, sans la moindre gêne.

unselfish [ʌn'selfiʃ] *a* (*of pers*) généreux; sans égoïsme; (motif) désintéressé. **un'selfishly** *adv* généreusement. **un'selfishness** *n* générosité *f*; désintéressement *m*.

unserviceable [ʌn'sə:visəbl] *a* inutilisable; (*of machine*) hors d'usage.

unsettle [ʌn'setl] *vtr* perturber; ébranler (les idées de qn); troubler le repos de (qn). **un'settled** *a* 1. perturbé; (pays) troublé; (temps) variable; (esprit) troublé, inquiet; **the u. state of the weather,** l'incertitude *f* du temps 2. (*a*) (*of question*) indécis (*b*) (*of bill*) impayé, non réglé. **un'settling** *a* perturbateur; inquiétant.

unshakeable [ʌn'ʃeikəbl] *a* inébranlable. **un'shaken** *a* inébranlé, ferme.

unshaved, unshaven [ʌn'ʃeivd, -'ʃeivn] *a* non rasé.

unshrinkable [ʌn'ʃriŋkəbl] *a* irrétrécissable.

unsightly [ʌn'saitli] *a* laid, disgracieux.

unsigned [ʌn'saind] *a* non signé.

unsinkable [ʌn'siŋkəbl] *a* insubmersible.

unskilled [ʌn'skild] *a* inexpert, inexpérimenté; *Ind:* **u. labour,** main-d'œuvre non spécialisée; **u. worker,** ouvrier non qualifié; manœuvre *m*. **un'skilful,** *NAm:* **un'skillful** *a* maladroit; malhabile (à qch).

unsociable [ʌn'souʃəbl] *a* insociable. **un'social** *a* insocial; **to work u. hours,** travailler à des heures indues.

unsold [ʌn'sould] *a* invendu.

unsolicited [ʌnsə'lisitid] *a* non sollicité; volontaire; (faire qch) spontanément.

unsolved [ʌn'sɔlvd] *a* (problème) non résolu.

unsophisticated [ʌnsə'fistikeitid] *a* naturel; (*of pers*) ingénu, simple.

unsound [ʌn'saund] *a* (*a*) **of u. mind,** qui n'est pas sain d'esprit (*b*) (*of timber*) avarié; (*of foundations, bridge*) peu solide; en mauvais état; (*of theory*) mal fondé; (*of decision*) peu judicieux; (*of investment*) peu sûr; (*of politician*) incompétent.

unsparing [ʌn'spɛəriŋ] *a* prodigue (**of,** de); **u. in one's efforts,** infatigable; **to be u. of one's strength,** ne pas ménager ses forces. **un'sparingly** *adv* sans ménager ses efforts; généreusement.

unspeakable [ʌn'spi:kəbl] *a* 1. (douleur) inexprimable; **u. muddle,** désordre sans nom 2. *F:* détestable, inqualifiable; **it's u.!** ça n'a pas de nom! **un'speakably** *adv F:* **u. bad,** exécrable.

unspecified [ʌn'spesifaid] *a* non spécifié.

unspoiled, unspoilt [ʌn'spɔild, -'spɔilt] *a* (*a*) intact (*b*) (enfant) qui n'a pas été gâté (*c*) (paysage) qui n'est pas défiguré.

unspoken [ʌn'spoukən] *a* inexprimé; tacite.

unsporting [ʌn'spɔ:tiŋ] *a* peu loyal; déloyal.

unstable [ʌn'steibl] *a* instable.

unstamped [ʌn'stæmpt] *a* (*of letter*) non affranchi.

unsteady [ʌn'stedi] *a* (*of table*) instable, peu stable, peu solide; branlant; (*of footsteps*) chancelant; (*of voice*) mal assuré; (*of rhythm*) irrégulier; **to be u. on one's feet,** marcher d'un pas chancelant; tituber. **un'steadily** *adv* (marcher) d'un pas chancelant; (tenir qch) d'une main tremblante. **un'steadiness** *n* instabilité *f*; manque *m* d'aplomb (d'une table); irrégularité *f*.

unstick [ʌn'stik] *vtr* (**unstuck** [-'stʌk]) décoller (qch); **to come unstuck,** (i) se décoller (ii) *F:* (*of plan*) s'effondrer; tomber à l'eau.

unstinting [ʌn'stintiŋ] *a* sans réserve; sans bornes; **u. efforts,** efforts illimités.

unstitch [ʌn'stitʃ] *vtr* dépiquer, découdre (un vêtement); **to come unstitched,** se découdre.

unstressed [ʌn'strest] *a* inaccentué.

unsubstantiated [ʌnsəb'stænʃieitid] *a* non prouvé; non corroboré.

unsuccessful [ʌnsək'sesful] *a* 1. (*of effort*) vain, infructueux; (*of application*) refusé; **u. attempt,** tentative sans succès; coup manqué; **it was completely u.,** cela a été un échec total 2. (*of pers*) qui n'a pas réussi; qui a échoué; **u. candidate,** candidat refusé; (*at election*) candidat non élu. **unsu'ccessfully** *adv* sans succès; en vain.

unsuitable [ʌn's(j)u:təbl] *a* 1. (*of pers*) peu fait (**to, for,** pour); **he's quite u. for the job,** ce n'est pas l'homme qu'il faut pour ce poste 2. (*of thg*) impropre, mal adapté (à); (*of remark*) inconvenant; déplacé; (*of time*) inopportun; (*of marriage*) mal assorti; **u. for the occasion**, qui ne convient pas à la circonstance; **to choose an u. time to**, mal choisir le moment de; **film u. for children**, film à déconseiller aux enfants. **unsuita'bility** n 1. inaptitude *f* (de qn à qch) 2. caractère *m* impropre. **un'suited** *a* inapte (à qch); **they are u. to each other**, ils s'accordent mal.

unsupported [ʌnsə'pɔːtid] *a* (*of statement*) sans preuves; (*of pers*) non soutenu; sans soutien financier.

unsure [ʌn'ʃuər] *a* peu sûr, précaire; (*of pers*) incertain (**about**, de); **to be u. of oneself**, manquer de confiance en soi-même.

unsuspected [ʌnsəs'pektid] *a* insoupçonné. **unsus'pecting** *a* qui ne se doute de rien; **naturally u.**, peu soupçonneux.

unsuspicious [ʌnsəs'piʃəs] *a* peu soupçonneux.

unsweetened [ʌn'swiːtnd] *a* non sucré.

unswerving [ʌn'swəːviŋ] *a* inébranlable; constant.

unsympathetic [ʌnsimpə'θetik] *a* peu compatissant; froid; indifférent; antipathique. **unsympa'thetically** *adv* froidement; avec indifférence.

unsystematic [ʌnsistə'mætik] *a* non systématique; sans méthode. **unsyste'matically** *adv* sans méthode.

untangle [ʌn'tæŋgl] *vtr* démêler (de la laine).

untapped [ʌn'tæpt] *a* (*of resources*) inexploité.

untaxed [ʌn'tækst] *a* exempt d'impôts; non imposé.

unteachable [ʌn'tiːtʃəbl] *a* à qui l'on ne peut rien apprendre.

untenable [ʌn'tenəbl] *a* (*of theory*) insoutenable; (*of position*) intenable.

untested [ʌn'testid] *a* inéprouvé; qui n'a pas encore été mis à l'épreuve; (*of drug*) non essayé; (*of water*) non analysé.

unthinkable [ʌn'θiŋkəbl] *a* impensable; **it's u. that he should be acquitted**, il est inconcevable qu'il soit acquitté. **un'thinking** *a* étourdi; irréfléchi. **un'thinkingly** *adv* sans réfléchir.

untidy [ʌn'taidi] *a* (*a*) (*of room*) en désordre; mal rangé; (*of hair*) ébouriffé, mal peigné; (*of writing*) brouillon; **u. appearance**, tenue débraillée (*b*) (*of pers*) désordonné. **un'tidily** *adv* sans ordre; sans soin. **un'tidiness** *n* désordre *m*; manque *m* d'ordre, de soin.

untie [ʌn'tai] *v* (**un'tied; un'tying**) 1. *vtr* dénouer (sa ceinture); défaire, délier (un nœud, un paquet); détacher (un chien); déficeler (un paquet) 2. *vi* **to come untied**, se défaire, se dénouer.

until [ʌn'til] 1. *prep* (*a*) jusqu'à; **u. evening**, jusqu'au soir; **u. now**, jusqu'ici, jusque-là; **she didn't arrive u. yesterday**, elle n'est arrivée qu'hier (*b*) **not u.**, pas avant; **he won't come u. after dinner**, il ne viendra qu'après le dîner; **I've never seen it u. now**, c'est la première fois que je le vois 2. *conj* (*a*) jusqu'à ce que + *sub*; **I'll wait u. he comes**, j'attendrai jusqu'à ce qu'il vienne (*b*) **he won't come u. you invite him**, il ne viendra pas avant d'être invité; **I won't leave him u. he's recovered**, je ne le quitterai pas tant qu'il n'est pas guéri.

untimely [ʌn'taimli] *a* (*a*) (*of death*) prématuré; **to come to an u. end**, mourir avant l'âge (*b*) (*of question, action*) inopportun.

untiring [ʌn'taiəriŋ] *a* infatigable. **un'tiringly** *adv* infatigablement.

untold ['ʌn'tould] *a* (richesse) immense, incalculable; **u. suffering**, souffrances inouïes.

untouchable [ʌn'tʌtʃəbl] *a & n* intouchable (*mf*). **un'touched** *a* 1. (*a*) non touché; (*of food*) **u. by hand**, non manié (*b*) **he had left the food u.**, il n'avait pas touché à la nourriture 2. (*pers*) indemne; (*thg*) intact 3. (*pers*) indifférent, insensible (**by**, à).

untoward [ʌntə'wɔːd; *NAm:* ʌn'tɔːd] *a* fâcheux.

untrained [ʌn'treind] *a* qui n'a pas reçu de formation professionnelle; (*of animal*) non dressé; (*of ear*) inexercé.

untranslatable [ʌntræns'leitəbl] *a* intraduisible.

untried [ʌn'traid] *a* qui n'a pas été essayé; qui n'a pas été mis à l'épreuve.

untroubled [ʌn'trʌbəld] *a* calme, tranquille.

untrue [ʌn'truː] *a* (*of statement*) faux; erroné; (*of pers*) infidèle.

untrustworthy [ʌn'trʌstwəːði] *a* 1. (*of pers*) indigne de confiance 2. (renseignement) douteux, sujet à caution; (témoin) récusable.

untruth [ʌn'truːθ] *n* mensonge *m*. **un'truthful** *a* 1. (*of pers*) menteur 2. (*of news*) mensonger, faux. **un'truthfully** *adv* mensongèrement. **un'truthfulness** *n* 1. (*of pers*) caractère menteur 2. fausseté *f* (d'une histoire).

untuned [ʌn'tjuːnd] *a Mus:* mal accordé.

untwist [ʌn'twist] *vtr* détordre.

unusable [ʌn'juːzəbl] *a* inutilisable. **unused** *a* 1. [ʌn'juːzd] (*a*) inutilisé; non employé; (bâtiment) désaffecté (*b*) qui n'a pas encore servi; neuf 2. [ʌn'juːst] peu habitué (**to**, à); **to be u. to sth**, ne pas avoir l'habitude de qch.

unusual [ʌn'juːʒju(ə)l] *a* peu commun; peu ordinaire; exceptionnel; insolite; **that's u.**, (i) cela se fait peu (ii) cela se voit rarement; **nothing u.**, rien d'anormal. **un'usually** *adv* exceptionnellement; rarement; **u. tall**, d'une taille exceptionnelle; **he was u. attentive**, il s'est montré plus attentif que d'habitude.

unutterable [ʌn'ʌtrəbl] *a* inexprimable; *F:* **u. fool**, parfait imbécile.

unvarnished [ʌn'vaːniʃt] *a* (*of surface*) non verni; (*of truth*) pur et simple.

unvarying [ʌn'vɛəriiŋ] *a* invariable, constant.

unveil [ʌn'veil] *vtr* dévoiler (a, une statue). **un'veiling** *n* inauguration *f* (d'une statue).

unventilated [ʌn'ventileitid] *a* non aéré; sans ventilation.

unvoiced [ʌn'vɔist] *a* (*of vowel, consonant*) sourd; (*of opinion*) inexprimé.

unwanted [ʌn'wɔntid] *a* 1. non voulu; (enfant) non désiré 2. superflu.

unwarranted [ʌn'wɔrəntid] *a* injustifié; **u. remark**, observation déplacée.

unwary [ʌn'wɛəri] *a* imprudent.

unwashed [ʌn'wɔʃt] *a* non lavé.

unwearying [ʌn'wiəriiŋ] *a* inlassable.

unwelcome [ʌn'welkəm] *a* (*a*) (visiteur) importun (*b*) (*of news*) fâcheux.

unwell [ʌn'wel] *a* indisposé; souffrant.

unwholesome [ʌn'houlsəm] *a* malsain.

unwieldy [ʌn'wiːldi] *a* 1. (*of pers*) lourd, gauche 2. difficile à manier; peu maniable.

unwilling [ʌnˈwiliŋ] *a* de mauvaise volonté; (consentement) donné à contrecœur; (complice) malgré lui; **u. to do sth**, peu disposé à faire qch; **I was u. for my wife to know**, je ne voulais pas que ma femme le sache. **un'willingly** *adv* à contrecœur; de mauvaise grâce. **un'willingness** *n* **1.** mauvaise volonté; mauvaise grâce **2.** manque *m* d'enthousiasme.

unwind [ʌnˈwaind] *v* (**unwound** [-ˈwaund]) **1.** *vtr* dérouler **2.** *vi* se dérouler; *F:* (*of pers*) se détendre.

unwise [ʌnˈwaiz] *a* imprudent; peu prudent, peu sage; (*of action*) peu judicieux. **un'wisely** *adv* imprudemment.

unwitting [ʌnˈwitiŋ] *a* involontaire. **un'wittingly** *adv* involontairement.

unworkable [ʌnˈwɔːkəbl] *a* (projet) inexécutable, impraticable.

unworldly [ʌnˈwɔːldli] *a* détaché de ce monde.

unworthy [ʌnˈwɔːði] *a* **u. of sth**, indigne de qch.

unwrap [ʌnˈræp] *vtr* (**unwrapped**) défaire, ouvrir (un paquet).

unwritten [ʌnˈrit(ə)n] *a* qui n'est pas écrit; (*of tradition*) oral; (*of agreement*) verbal; **u. law**, convention toujours respectée.

unyielding [ʌnˈjiːldiŋ] *a* qui ne cède pas; raide, ferme; (*of pers*) inébranlable, inflexible.

unzip [ʌnˈzip] *v* (**unzipped**) **1.** *vtr* ouvrir la fermeture éclair (*Rtm*) **2.** *vi F:* **it unzips at the side**, ça s'ouvre sur le côté.

up [ʌp] **I.** *adv* **1.** (*a*) en montant; vers le haut; **to go up**, monter; **my room is three flights up**, ma chambre est au troisième, *NAm:* au quatrième, (étage); **to throw sth up (in the air)**, jeter qch en l'air; **all the way up**, **right up (to the top)**, jusqu'au haut (de la colline), jusqu'en haut (de l'escalier); **halfway up**, (jusqu')à mi-hauteur; **to put one's hand up**, lever la main; **hands up!** haut les mains! **to put up the results**, afficher les résultats (*b*) **to walk up and down**, se promener de long en large; **to go up north**, aller dans le nord; **to go up to London**, aller à Londres; **he's going up to Oxford**, il va faire ses études à l'université d'Oxford (*c*) **from £10 up**, à partir de £10 **2.** (*a*) haut, en haut; **what are you doing up there?** que faites-vous là-haut? **up above**, en haut; **up above sth**, au-dessus de qch; **the moon is up**, la lune est levée; **the blinds are up**, on a relevé les stores; **the shops had their shutters up**, les magasins avaient leurs volets mis; **the new building is up**, le nouveau bâtiment est terminé; **the river's up**, la rivière est en crue; **the road's always up**, la route est toujours en réparation (*b*) en dessus; **face up**, face en dessus; (*on packing case*) **this side up**, haut; dessus (*c*) **up in London**, à Londres; **up in Yorkshire**, au nord, dans le Yorkshire; **relations up from the country**, parents de province en visite à la ville (*d*) *Sp:* **to be one goal up**, mener par un but; **to be one up on s.o.**, avoir l'avantage sur qn **3.** (*a*) **to go up**, (i) (*of prices*) augmenter (ii) (*of commodity*) subir une hausse; **the thermometer has gone up**, le thermomètre a monté; **business is looking up**, les affaires sont à la hausse; **he's something quite high up in the Civil Service**, il est haut placé dans l'administration (*b*) **to screw up**, visser, serrer (un écrou); **to get up steam**, mettre (la chaudière) sous pression, faire monter la pression; **his blood was up**, il était monté; le sang lui bouillait (*c*) **to be well up in a subject**, connaître un sujet à fond (*d*) **to**

speak up, parler plus fort **4.** (*a*) **put it up against the other one**, mettez-le tout près de l'autre; **lean it up against the wall**, appuyez-le contre le mur (*b*) **to be up against difficulties**, rencontrer, se heurter à, des difficultés; **to be up against it**, être dans le pétrin **5.** (*a*) debout, levé; **to be up late**, (i) veiller tard (ii) se lever tard; **to get up**, se lever; **to be up and about**, être sur pied; **to be up all night**, ne pas se coucher de la nuit; **to stay up**, veiller; **to be up and coming**, être plein d'avenir; promettre bien (*b*) **up with X!** vive X! **6.** (*a*) **to be up in arms**, se révolter; être en révolte (*b*) *F:* **what's up?** qu'est-ce qui se passe? **something's up**, il y a quelque chose (i) qui ne va pas (ii) qui se mijote; **what's up with him?** qu'est-ce qui lui prend? **7.** **time's up**, il est l'heure (de finir, de fermer); c'est l'heure; **his leave's up**, sa permission est expirée; *F:* **the game's up**, tout est perdu; **it's all up with him**, il est fichu; **I thought it was all up with me**, j'ai cru que ma dernière heure était venue **8.** (*a*) **to go up to s.o.**, s'approcher de, s'avancer vers, qn; **up to the ears in mud**, couvert de boue jusqu'aux oreilles; **where are you up to?** où en êtes-vous (du livre que vous lisez)? (*b*) **up to now, to here**, jusqu'ici; **up until then**, jusqu'alors; **to be up to date**, être à la mode, *F:* à la page; **up to £100 a week**, jusqu'à £100 par semaine (*c*) **to be up to one's job**, être à la hauteur de sa tâche; **he's not up to it**, il n'est pas capable de le faire; **I don't feel up to it**, je ne m'en sens pas le courage, la force; **it's not up to much**, cela ne vaut pas grand-chose (*d*) **what are you up to?** qu'est-ce que vous faites? **he's up to something**, il a quelque chose en tête (*e*) **it's up to him to decide**, c'est à lui de décider. **II.** *prep* **1.** **to go up the stairs, a hill**, monter l'escalier, une côte; **the cat is up the tree**, le chat est en haut de l'arbre **2.** **up the river**, en amont; **it's up river from here**, c'est en amont d'ici; **further up the street**, plus loin dans la rue; **to walk up and down the platform**, arpenter le quai. **III.** *a* ascendant, montant; *Rail:* **up line**, voie en direction de Londres, d'un terminus important; **up train**, train montant. **IV.** *n* (*a*) **ups and downs**, (i) ondulations *f* (du terrain) (ii) les hauts et les bas (de la vie) (iii) avatars *mpl* (de la politique); *attrib* **up-and-down movement**, (i) mouvement de montée et de descente (ii) jeu vertical d'une pièce (*b*) *F:* **to be on the up and up**, être en train de faire son chemin. **V.** *v* **1.** *vtr F:* hausser (les prix) **2.** *vi P:* se lever d'un bond; **they upped and went**, sans plus attendre ils sont partis. **'up-and-'coming** *a* (jeune homme) plein d'avenir; prometteur. **'upbringing** *n* éducation *f*; **what sort of (an) u. did he have?** comment a-t-il été élevé? **up'country** *adv esp NAm: Austr:* vers l'intérieur. **up'date** *vtr* mettre à jour. **up'end** *vtr* mettre (qch) debout. **upgrade 1.** [ˈʌpgreid] *n* pente ascendante; montée *f* (d'une route); **to be on the u.**, (i) (*of prices*) monter (ii) (*of business*) reprendre **2.** [ʌpˈgreid] *vtr* (*a*) améliorer (un produit) (*b*) nommer (qn) à un niveau supérieur; promouvoir (qn). **up'heaval** *n* **1.** soulèvement *m*; bouleversement *m* **2.** agitation *f* (politique). **uphill 1.** *a* [ˈʌphil] (*of road*) montant; (*of struggle*) pénible, difficile **2.** *adv* [ʌpˈhil] **to go u.**, monter. **up'hold** *vtr* (**upheld**) soutenir (une opinion); prêter son appui à (qn); confirmer (une décision); **to u. the law**, faire observer la loi. **up'holder** *n* défenseur *m* (d'une cause). **up'holster** *vtr* (i) rembourrer (ii) tapisser, garnir (un canapé). **up'holsterer** *n* tapissier *m*. **up'holstery** *n* (i) tapisserie *f* d'ameublement (ii) garniture intérieure (d'une voiture). **'upkeep** *n* (frais *mpl* d')entretien *m*. **'uplands** *npl* hautes terres. uplift **1.** *n* ['ʌplift] moral u., inspiration morale **2.** *vtr* [ʌp'lift] élever (l'âme). **up'lifted** *a* exalté, inspiré. **u'pon** *prep* (= on) sur; **I came u. it by accident**, je l'ai trouvé par hasard; **you brought it u. yourself**, ne t'en prends qu'à toi-même! **'upper I.** *a* **1.** (*a*) supérieur; (plus) haut; (plus) élevé; de dessus; d'au-dessus; **u. jaw**, mâchoire supérieure; **u. storey**, étage supérieur; *Th:* **u. circle**, deuxième balcon; **temperature in the u. twenties**, température qui dépasse 25˚ (*b*) **u. reaches**, amont *m* (d'une rivière) **2.** supérieur; **the u. classes**, la haute société; **to get the u. hand**, prendre le dessus; **to let s.o. get the u. hand**, se laisser tyranniser, mener, par qn; *Sch:* **the u. forms**, les grandes classes, les classes supérieures. **ii.** *n* empeigne *f* (d'une chaussure); *F:* **to be down on one's uppers**, être dans la gêne. **'uppermost I.** *a* (*a*) le plus haut, le plus élevé (*b*) de la plus grande importance; **to be u.**, tenir le premier rang; prédominer; **the problem u. in my mind**, le problème qui me préoccupe le plus **2.** *adv* (le plus) en dessus; **face u.**, face en dessus. **'uppish, 'uppity** *a* *F:* présomptueux, arrogant. **'upright I.** *a* **1.** vertical; perpendiculaire; droit; **u. piano**, piano droit; **u. freezer**, congélateur armoire **2.** (*of pers*) droit, juste, honnête. **II.** *adv* debout; (*of pers*) **to stand u.**, se tenir droit; **to set sth u.**, mettre qch debout. **III.** *n* **1.** montant *m* (d'une échelle); *Fb:* **the uprights**, les montants de but **2.** piano droit. **'uprising** *n* soulèvement *m*; insurrection *f*. **'uproar** *n* tumulte *m*, vacarme *m*, tapage *m*; **the town is in an u.**, la ville est en effervescence. **up'roarious** *a* tumultueux, tapageur; **u. laughter**, grands éclats de rire. **up'roariously** *adv* tumultueusement; (rire) à gorge déployée; **u. funny**, désopilant. **up'root** *vtr* déraciner (une plante, un mal); arracher (qn de son foyer). **upset I.** ['ʌpset] *n* **1.** renversement *m* (d'une voiture, d'un bateau) **2.** (*a*) désorganisation *f*, bouleversement *m*, désordre *m* (*b*) ennui *m*; difficultés *fpl* (*c*) bouleversement (d'esprit) (*d*) indisposition *f*; dérangement *m*; **I have a stomach u.**, j'ai l'estomac dérangé. **II.** [ʌp'set] *v* (upset; upset; *prp* upsetting) **1.** *vtr* (*a*) renverser; (faire) chavirer (un bateau) (*b*) désorganiser, bouleverser, déranger (les plans de qn) (*c*) troubler, bouleverser, émouvoir (qn); **the least thing upsets him**, il s'impressionne pour un rien; **don't u. yourself**, ne vous en faites pas (*d*) indisposer (qn); déranger (l'estomac); troubler (la digestion) **2.** vi (*of cup*) se renverser; (*of boat*) chavirer. **III.** [ʌp'set] *a* (*a*) bouleversé, ému; **don't get, be, u.**, ne vous en faites pas (*b*) (estomac) dérangé. **up'setting** *a* bouleversant, inquiétant. **'upshot** *n* résultat *m*. **'upside 'down** *adv phr* (*a*) sens dessus dessous; la tête en bas; **to hold sth u. down**, tenir qch à l'envers (*b*) en désordre, bouleversé; **to turn everything u. down**, tout bouleverser; tout mettre sens dessus dessous. **up'stage I.** (*a*) *n Th:* arrière-scène *f* (*b*) *adv* à l'arrière-scène **2.** *vtr* reléguer (qn) au second plan; souffler la vedette à (qn). **upstairs 1.** *adv* [ʌp'stɛəz] en haut (de l'escalier); **to go up.**, monter (l'escalier) **2.** (*a*) *a* ['ʌpstɛəz] (*of room*) d'en haut, du haut; à l'étage supérieur (*b*) *n* [ʌp'stɛəz] l'étage. **up'standing** *a* (*a*)

droit; bien bâti (*b*) honnête. **'upstart** *n* parvenu, -ue. **upstream 1.** *adv* [ʌp'stri:m] (*a*) en amont (*b*) en remontant le courant **2.** *a* ['ʌpstri:m] d'amont. **'upsurge** *n* poussée *f*, vague *f* (d'enthousiasme); regain *m* (d'activité). **'upswept** *a Aut: Av:* profilé. **'uptake** *n* **to be slow on the u.**, avoir la compréhension lente; **quick on the u.**, à l'esprit vif, éveillé. **up'tight** *a F:* tendu; agité; crispé; **to get u.**, s'énerver. **up-to-'date** *a* très récent; moderne. **up-to-the-'minute** *a* de dernière heure. **'upturned** *a* (*of nose*) retroussé. **'upward I.** *a* montant, ascendant; **u. movement**, mouvement ascensionnel; **u. tendency**, tendance à la hausse **2.** *adv* = **'upwards**. **'upwards** *adv* **1.** de bas en haut; vers le haut; en montant **2.** en dessus; **to put sth face u.**, mettre qch à l'endroit (sur qch); (*of pers*) **lying face u.**, couché sur le dos **3.** au-dessus; **£100 and u.**, £100 et au-dessus; **u. of fifty cows**, plus de cinquante vaches; **children from ten (years) u.**, des enfants à partir de dix ans. **Ural** ['juərəl] *Prn Geog:* **the U. (river)**, l'Oural *m*; **the U. mountains, the Urals**, les monts Oural, l'Oural. **uranium** [ju'reiniəm] *n* uranium *m*. **urban** ['ɜ:bən] *a* urbain; **u. sprawl**, urbanisation incontrôlée. **urbani'zation** *n* urbanisation *f*. **'urbanize** *vtr* urbaniser. **urbane** [ɜ:'bein] *a* courtois, poli, civil. **ur'banely** *adv* courtoisement; avec urbanité. **ur'banity** *n* urbanité *f*; courtoisie *f*. **urchin** ['ɜ:tʃin] *n* **1.** (*a*) galopin *m*, gamin *m* (*b*) gosse *mf*; marmot *m* **2. sea u.**, oursin *m*. **Urdu** ['ɜ:du:] *n Ling:* ourdou *m*. **ureter** [ju'ri:tər] *n Anat:* uretère *m*. **urge** [ɜ:dʒ] **I.** *n* impulsion *f*; poussée *f*; **to feel an u. to do sth**, se sentir le besoin de faire qch. **II.** *vtr* **1. to u. s.o. (on)**, encourager, exciter, qn; **to u. a horse forward, on**, pousser, presser, un cheval; **to u. s.o. to do sth**, pousser qn à faire qch; **to u. on a piece of work**, hâter un travail **2.** insister sur (un point); faire valoir (une excuse) **3.** conseiller fortement, recommander; **to u. that sth should be done**, insister pour que qch soit fait. **urgent** ['ɜ:dʒ(ə)nt] *a* urgent, pressant; **it's u.**, c'est urgent; **u. need**, besoin pressant; **the matter is u.**, l'affaire presse; c'est urgent; **the doctor had an u. call**, on a appelé le médecin d'urgence; **at their u. request**, à leurs instances pressantes. **'urgency** *n* **1.** urgence *f*; **it's a matter of u.**, il y a urgence **2.** nécessité urgente. **'urgently** *adv* d'urgence; avec insistance; **a doctor is u. required**, on demande d'urgence un médecin. **urine** ['juərin] *n* urine *f*. **urinal** [-'rainəl] *n* urinoir *m*. **'urinary** *a* urinaire. **'urinate** *vi* uriner. **urn** [ɜ:n] *n* urne *f*; **tea u.**, fontaine *f* à thé. **Uruguay** ['ju:rəgwai] *Prn Geog:* Uruguay *m*. **Uru'guayan** *a & n* uruguayen, -enne. **us** *pers pron, objective case* **1.** (*unstressed*) [əs] nous; **he sees us**, il nous voit; **give us some**, donnez-nous-en; **there are three of us**, nous sommes trois; **we'll take him with us**, nous l'amènerons avec nous **2.** (*stressed*) [ʌs] (*a*) nous; **between them and us**, entre eux et nous; **they can't deceive us women**, on ne peut pas nous tromper, nous autres femmes (*b*) (*after verb to be*) **it's us!** c'est nous! **he wouldn't believe it was us**, il ne voulait pas croire que c'était nous 3. (= me) *F:* **let us, let's, have a look,** laissez-moi regarder.

US(A) *abbr United States (of America).*

use I. [ju:s] *n* 1. *(a)* emploi *m*, usage *m*; utilisation *f*; **I'll find a u. for it,** je trouverai un moyen de m'en servir; **to make u. of sth,** se servir de qch; utiliser, employer, qch; **to make good u. of sth, to put sth to good u.,** faire bon usage de qch; tirer profit de qch; **word in everyday u.,** mot d'usage courant; **not in u.,** hors d'usage; (mot) désuet; hors de service; **for u. in case of fire,** à employer en cas d'incendie; **directions for u.,** mode *m* d'emploi *(b)* **to improve with u.,** s'améliorer à l'usage 2. *(a)* jouissance *f*, usage; **he has lost the u. of his left leg,** il a perdu l'usage de la jambe gauche *(b)* **to have the u. of the bathroom,** avoir le droit de se servir de la salle de bain; **I'd like to have the u. of it,** je voudrais pouvoir m'en servir *(c) Jur:* usufruit *m* 3. utilité *f*; **can I be of any u. (to you)?** puis-je vous être utile à quelque chose? **it's of no u. to me,** je n'en ai pas besoin; **it's not much u.,** cela ne sert pas à grand-chose; *F:* **a fat lot of u. that'll be to you!** si tu crois que ça va t'avancer! *F: Iron:* **you're a lot of u.!** je te retiens! **he's no u.,** il est incapable; **to have no u. for sth,** n'avoir que faire de qch; *F:* **I've no u. for him,** je ne peux pas le voir; **it was no u.,** c'était inutile; **it's no u. discussing the matter,** (c'est) inutile de discuter la question; **it's no u. crying,** ce n'est pas la peine de pleurer; **it's no u.!** impossible! **what's the u. of making plans?** à quoi bon faire des projets? II. [ju:z] *vtr* 1. *(a)* employer, se servir de; **are you using this knife?** est-ce que vous servez de ce couteau? **u. your head!** ne sois pas si bête! **u. your eyes!** ouvrez les yeux! *(of thg)* **to be used for sth,** servir à qch; **I used the money to rebuild my house,** j'ai utilisé l'argent à reconstruire ma maison; **word no longer used,** mot désuet; **to reserve the right to u. sth,** se réserver l'usage de qch; **I u. that as a hammer,** cela me sert de marteau; **you may u. my name (as a reference),** vous pouvez vous réclamer de moi *(b)* **to u. force,** employer, avoir recours à, la force; **to u. every means (at one's disposal),** employer tous les moyens (à sa disposition); **to u. one's influence,** user de son influence; **to u. discretion,** agir avec discrétion *(c) esp NAm: F:* **I could u. some coffee,** je prendrais volontiers du café 2. *(a)* (bien, mal) agir envers qn; **to u. sth carefully,** traiter qch avec soin; **roughly used,** maltraité *(b)* **I feel I've been used,** j'ai l'impression qu'on s'est tout bonnement servi de moi 3. **to u. sth (up),** épuiser, consommer, qch; **it's all used up,** il n'en reste plus; **to u. up the scraps, leftovers,** utiliser, *Cu:* accommoder, les restes 4. *(as aux past tense)* [ju:st] **as children we used to play together,** quand nous étions enfants nous jouions ensemble; **I used to do it,** j'avais l'habitude de le faire; **things aren't what they used to be,** ce n'est plus comme autrefois; **she used not, usen't, to like him,** autrefois elle ne l'aimait pas. **usable** ['ju:z] *a* utilisable. **usage** ['ju:z-, 'ju:s-] *n* 1. traitement *m* 2. usage *m*, coutume *f* 3. *(a)* emploi *m*, usage (d'un mot) *(b)* utilisation *f*. **used** *a* 1. [ju:zd] usé, usagé; (timbre-poste) oblitéré; (nappe) sale; **u. car,** voiture d'occasion; **hardly u.,** presque neuf 2. [ju:st] **to be u. to sth, to doing sth,** être habitué, accoutumé, à

qch, à faire qch; **to get u. to sth,** s'habituer à qch; **I'm not used to it,** je n'en ai pas l'habitude; **you'll get u. to it in time,** vous vous y ferez à la longue. **useful** *a* utile; pratique; **the book was very u. to me,** ce livre m'a été très utile; **it will come in very u.,** cela rendra bien service; **to make oneself u.,** se rendre utile. **usefully** *adv* utilement. **usefulness** *n* utilité *f*. **useless** *a* inutile; bon à rien; (effort) vain; **to be u.,** ne servir à rien; *a* person, incompétent(e); *F:* **it's worse than u.,** c'est au-dessous de tout. **uselessly** *adv* inutilement; en vain. **uselessness** *n* inutilité *f*. **user** *n* usager, -ère (de la route); utilisateur, -trice (d'un appareil). **usual** ['ju:ʒʊəl] 1. *a* usuel, habituel, ordinaire; **at the u. time,** à l'heure habituelle; **the u. terms,** les conditions d'usage; **it's u. to pay in advance,** il est d'usage de payer d'avance; **it's the u. practice,** c'est la pratique courante; **earlier than u.,** plut tôt que d'habitude; **as u.,** comme d'ordinaire, comme d'habitude; **business as u.,** les affaires continuent, la vente continue 2. *n (in bar)* **the u.!** comme d'habitude! **usually** *adv* ordinairement, habituellement; d'ordinaire, d'habitude; **he was more than u. polite,** il s'est montré encore plus poli que d'habitude.

usher ['ʌʃər] I. *n (a) Jur:* (huissier) audiencier *m (b) Cin: Th:* placeur *m;* (at wedding) garçon *m* d'honneur. II. *(a) vtr* **to u. (s.o.) in,** introduire (qn), faire entrer (qn) *(b) vi F:* (at wedding) servir de garçon d'honneur. **usherette** *nf Cin: Th:* ouvreuse.

USSR *abbr Union of Soviet Socialist Republics.*

usurer ['ju:ʒərər] *n* usurier, -ière. **usurious** *a* (intérêt) usuraire. **usury** *n* usure *f.*

usurp [ju:'zɔ:p] *vtr* usurper. **usurper** *n* usurpateur, -trice. **usurping** *a* usurpateur.

utensil [ju:(')'tens(i)l] *n* ustensile *m;* **household, cooking, utensils,** ustensiles de ménage; **set of kitchen utensils,** batterie *f* de cuisine.

uterus ['ju:tərəs] *n Anat:* utérus *m.*

utility [ju:'tiliti] *n (a)* utilité *f;* **u. vehicle,** véhicule utilitaire; **u. room,** pièce réservée à la lessive, au repassage *(b)* **public u. services,** *NAm:* **utilities,** services publics. **utilitarian** *a* utilisable. **utilizable** *a* utilisable. **utilization** *n* utilisation *f;* mise *f* en valeur. **utilize** *vtr* utiliser, se servir de (qch); tirer profit de, mettre en valeur (qch).

utmost ['ʌtmoust] 1. *a* extrême, dernier; **the u. ends of the earth,** les (derniers) confins de la terre; **it is of the u. importance that,** il est extrêmement important que 2. *n* **to the u.,** le plus possible; **to do one's u.,** faire tout son possible.

Utopia [ju:'toupiə] *n* utopie *f.* **utopian** *a* utopique.

utter¹ ['ʌtər] *a* complet; absolu; **he's an u. stranger to me,** il m'est complètement étranger; **it's u. rubbish, nonsense,** c'est complètement absurde; **u. fool,** parfait imbécile; **u. poverty,** misère la plus profonde. **utterly** *adv* complètement, absolument, tout à fait. **uttermost = utmost.**

utter² *vtr* 1. jeter, pousser (un cri); prononcer, proférer (un mot); lancer (un juron); **he didn't u. a word,** il n'a pas soufflé mot 2. émettre (de la fausse monnaie).

V

V, v [viː] n (la lettre) V, v m; Cl: **V neck**, décolleté en V, en pointe.

V & A abbr Victoria and Albert Museum.

vac [væk] n Sch: F: vacances fpl.

vacant ['veikənt] a 1. vacant, vide, libre; disponible; **v. site**, NAm: lot, terrain vague; **v. space**, place vide; **v. room, seat**, chambre, place, libre, inoccupée; Jur: (of house) **with v. possession**, avec jouissance immédiate; (of job) à pourvoir; **situations v.**, offres fpl d'emploi(s) 2. (esprit) inoccupé; (regard) distrait, vague, sans expression; **v. stare**, air hébété. **'vacancy** n 1. vide m, vacuité f; **to stare into v.**, regarder dans le vide, dans le vague 2. vacance f; poste vacant, à pourvoir; (at hotel) chambre f libre; **to fill a v.**, pourvoir à un poste; (at hotel) **no vacancies!** complet! **v. exists for a secretary**, on recherche secrétaire. **'vacantly** adv (regarder) en fixant le vide, d'un air distrait. **vacate** [və'keit] vtr (a) quitter (un emploi); **to v. office**, donner sa démission (b) quitter (une chambre d'hôtel, une maison); Jur: **to v. the premises**, vider les lieux. **va'cation** 1. n (a) vacances fpl; **the long v.**, les grandes vacances; **to be on v.**, être en vacances; **to take a v.**, prendre des vacances (b) (also **va'cating**) évacuation f (d'une maison) 2. vi NAm: prendre ses vacances.

vaccinate ['væksineit] vtr vacciner; **to get vaccinated**, se faire vacciner. **vacci'nation** n vaccination f. **'vaccine** n vaccin m (antivariolique, contre la polio).

vacillate ['væsileit] vi vaciller; hésiter (entre deux opinions). **'vacillating** a vacillant; irrésolu. **vaci'llation** n vacillation f; hésitation f.

vacuum ['vækjuəm] 1. n Ph: vide m; **v. pack**, emballage sous!vide; **v. cleaner**, aspirateur m; **v. flask**, NAm: **bottle**, bouteille isolante 2. vtr F: passer (une pièce) à l'aspirateur. **va'cuity** n vacuité f; vide m. **'vacuous** a vide d'expression; (observation, rire) bête; (air) hébété; (regard) vide d'expression. **'vacuum-'packed** a emballé sous vide.

vagabond ['vægəbɔnd] a & n vagabond, -onde.

vagary ['veigəri] n caprice m, fantaisie f.

vagina [və'dʒainə] n Anat: vagin m. **va'ginal** a Anat: vaginal; Med: **v. douche**, douche vaginale.

vagrant ['veigrənt] n Jur: vagabond, -onde. **'vagrancy** n vagabondage m.

vague [veig] a (of pers, look) vague; (of memory) imprécis; (of outline) estompé, flou; (of colour) indéterminé; (of answer) vague; **I haven't the vaguest idea**, je n'en ai pas la moindre idée; **I have a v. idea (that)**, il me semble (que); **he was rather v. about it**, il ne l'a pas précisé; il n'en était pas certain. **'vaguely** adv vaguement. **'vagueness** n vague m, imprécision f.

vain [vein] a 1. (of promise, pleasure, hope) vain; faux (espoir) 2. (effort) inutile, vain 3. vaniteux 4. **in v.**, en vain; vainement; **we protested in v.**, nous avons eu beau protester; **to labour in v.**, travailler inutilement;

it was all in v., c'était peine perdue. **'vainly** adv 1. vainement, en vain; inutilement 2. avec vanité.

valance ['væləns] n frange f, bordure f, de lit; lambrequin m (d'une fenêtre).

valentine ['væləntain] n carte (envoyée à son ami(e) le jour de la Saint-Valentin.

valet ['vælei] n valet m de chambre; (in hotel) **v. service**, buanderie f et nettoyage m.

valiant ['væljənt] a vaillant, courageux. **'valiantly** adv vaillamment.

valid ['vælid] a (contrat) valide, valable; (passeport) valide, en règle; (argument) solide; (excuse) valable; **v. for three months**, bon pour trois mois; **no longer v.**, périmé. **'validate** vtr valider. **va'lidity** n validité f (d'un document); force f (d'un argument).

valley ['væli] n vallée f; (small) vallon m; **the Rhone V.**, la vallée du Rhône.

valour, NAm: **valor** ['vælər] n courage m.

value ['væljuː] 1. n (a) valeur f; **of little, of great, v.**, de peu de, de grande, valeur; **to be of v.**, avoir de la valeur; **of no v.**, sans valeur; **to set a v. (up)on sth**, évaluer qch; **to set a high v. on sth**, faire grand cas de qch; Com: **market v.**, valeur marchande; **increase in v.**, plus-value f; **decrease in v.**, moins-value f; **v. added tax**, taxe à la valeur ajoutée (b) Com: **for v. received**, valeur reçue; **to get good v. for one's money**, en avoir pour son argent; **this article is very good v.**, cet article est à un prix très avantageux; **it's v. for money**, cela vaut son prix 2. vtr (a) Com: évaluer, estimer, priser (des marchandises); **to get sth valued**, faire expertiser qch (b) estimer, faire grand cas de (qn, qch); tenir à (la vie). **'valuable 1.** a (of object, help, time) précieux; (objet) de valeur, de prix; Jur: **for a v. consideration**, à titre onéreux 2. npl **valuables**, objets m de valeur, de prix. **valu'ation** n 1. évaluation f, estimation f; Jur: expertise f; **to make a v.**, faire une expertise; **to get a v. of sth**, faire expertiser qch 2. valeur estimée; **to take s.o. at his own v.**, estimer qn selon l'opinion qu'il a de lui-même. **'valued** a estimé, précieux. **'valueless** a sans valeur. **'valuer** n commissaire-priseur m, expert m.

valve [vælv] n 1. soupape f; clapet m; valve f (de pneu); **safety v.**, soupape de sûreté 2. Anat: valvule f (du cœur) 3. WTel: lampe f; valve 4. Mus: piston m (d'un instrument) 5. Moll: valve. **'valvular** a valvulaire.

vampire ['væmpaiər] n 1. Myth: vampire m 2. Z: **v. (bat)**, vampire.

van¹ [væn] n F: **in the v.**, (gens) d'avant-garde.

van² n 1. Aut: camionnette f; fourgon m; camion m (de déménagement) 2. Rail: wagon m; **luggage v.**, fourgon (à bagages); **guard's v.**, fourgon de queue. **'vanman** n (pl **-men**) livreur m.

vandal ['vænd(ə)l] n vandale mf. **'vandalism** n vandalisme m. **'vandalize** vtr saccager (un bâtiment); **several pictures have been vandalized**, plusieurs tableaux ont été mutilés par des vandales.

vane [vein] *n* (*a*) aile *f* (d'un moulin à vent) (*b*) (**weather**) **v.**, girouette *f*.

vanilla [və'nilə] *n* vanille *f*; **v. ice cream**, glace à la vanille; **v. sugar**, sucre vanillé.

vanish ['væniʃ] *vi* disparaître; (*of suspicions*) se dissiper, s'évanouir; (*of difficulties*) s'aplanir; (*of hope*) s'évanouir; *F:* (*of pers*) disparaître; s'éclipser; **to v. into thin air**, se volatiliser. **'vanishing** *n* disparition *f*; **v. point**, point de fuite; **profits have dwindled to v. point**, les bénéfices se sont réduits à néant; **v. trick**, tour de passe-passe; *Toil:* **v. cream**, crème de jour.

vanity ['væniti] *n* **1.** vanité *f* **2.** vanité; orgueil *m*; **to do sth out of v.**, faire qch par vanité **3.** *Furn:* coiffeuse *f*; **v. case**, trousse de toilette.

vanquish ['væŋkwiʃ] *vtr* vaincre.

vantage ['vɑːntidʒ] *n* **v. point**, position avantageuse.

vapid ['væpid] *a* plat, insipide; (*style*) fade.

vapour, *NAm:* **vapor** ['veipər] *n* vapeur *f*; buée *f* (sur les vitres); *Av:* **v. trail**, traînée *f* de condensation. **vapori'zation** *n* (*a*) vaporisation *f* (*b*) pulvérisation *f* (d'un liquide). **'vaporize** *vtr & i* (*a*) (se) vaporiser (*b*) (*of liquid*) (se) pulvériser. **'vaporizer** *n* (*a*) (*evaporator*) vaporisateur *m* (*b*) atomiseur *m*.

varicose ['værikous] *a Med:* **v. vein**, varice *f*.

varnish ['vɑːniʃ] **1.** *n* vernis *m*; *Toil:* **nail v.**, vernis à ongles; **v. remover**, (i) *Ind:* décapant *m* (ii) *Toil:* dissolvant *m* **2.** *vtr* vernir; vernisser (la poterie). **'varnishing** *n* vernissage *m*; **v. day**, vernissage (au Salon de peinture).

vary ['veəri] **1.** *vtr* varier, diversifier; faire varier; **to v. one's diet, one's reading**, diversifier son régime, ses lectures **2.** *vi* (*a*) varier, changer; être variable (*b*) **to v. from sth**, différer de qch (*c*) différer (d'avis); **on this point historians v.**, sur ce point les historiens ne sont pas d'accord. **varia'bility** *n* variabilité *f*. **'variable 1.** *a* variable; changeant **2.** *n Mth:* variable *f*. **'variance** *n* **to be at v. with s.o.**, être en désaccord avec qn; **authors are at v. about the date**, les auteurs ne sont pas d'accord sur la date (de qch); **theory at v. with the facts**, théorie incompatible avec les faits. **'variant** *n* variante *f*. **vari'ation** *n* **1.** variation *f*, changement *m* **2.** différence *f*, écart *m* (entre deux rapports) **3.** *pl Mus:* variations (on, sur). **'varied** *a* varié; divers. **'variegated** *a NatHist:* panaché; **to become v.**, (se) panacher. **varie'gation** *n Bot:* panachure *f*. **va'riety** *n* **1.** variété *f*, diversité *f*; **in a v. of ways**, de diverses manières; **for a v. of reasons**, pour toutes sortes de raisons; **a large, wide, v. of materials**, un grand choix de tissus **2.** *Bot:* variété (de fleurs) **3.** *Th:* **v. show**, spectacle de variétés; **v. turns**, numéros de music-hall **4.** *NAm:* **meats** (*Br* = **offal**), abats *mpl*. **'various** *a* **1.** varié, divers; **of v. kinds**, de diverses sortes; **in v. ways**, diversement; **to talk about v. things**, parler de chose(s) et d'autre(s) **2.** différent; plusieurs; **for v. reasons**, pour plusieurs raisons; **at v. times**, à différentes reprises; **on v. occasions**, en diverses occasions. **'varying** *a* variable, changeant; varié, divers; **with v. results**, avec des résultats divers.

vase [vɑːz] *n* vase *m*; **flower v.**, vase à fleurs.

vasectomy [və'sektəmi] *n Surg:* vasectomie *f*.

Vaseline ['væsəliːn] *n Rtm:* Vaseline *f*.

vast [vɑːst] *a* vaste, immense; **his v. knowledge**, l'étendue *f* de ses connaissances; **to spend v. sums**, dépenser énormément d'argent. **'vastness** *n* immensité *f* (de l'océan); amplitude *f* (d'une catastrophe).

vat [væt] *n* cuve *f*; bac *m*. **'vatful** *n* cuvée *f*.

VAT [væt, viːei'tiː] *abbr value added tax*, taxe à la valeur ajoutée, TVA.

Vatican ['vætikən] *Prn* **the V.**, le Vatican; **V. Council**, Concile du Vatican.

vault¹ [vɔːlt] **1.** *n* (*a*) *Arch:* voûte *f* (*b*) (*of bank*) chambre forte; **wine v.**, cave *f* (*c*) **family v.**, caveau *m* de famille **2.** *vtr* voûter (une cave). **'vaulted** *a* voûté; en voûte. **'vaulting** *n Arch:* voûte(s).

vault² **1.** *n* saut *m*; **pole v.**, saut à la perche **2.** *vi & tr* **to v. (over) sth**, sauter (un obstacle). **'vaulting** *n Gym:* exercice *m* du saut; **'voltige** *f*; **v. horse**, cheval d'arçon; **pole v.**, saut à la perche.

vaunt [vɔːnt] *vtr* vanter (qch); **our much vaunted justice**, notre justice tant vantée, si célèbre.

VC *abbr* Victoria Cross.

VD *abbr* venereal disease.

VDU *abbr Cmptr:* visual display unit.

veaʻ [viːl] *n Cu:* veau *m*; **v. cutlet**, côtelette de veau.

veer [viər] *vi* (*a*) (*of wind*) tourner, sauter (*b*) (*of ship*) virer (vent arrière); changer de bord (*c*) (*of pers*) **to v. round**, changer d'opinion.

vegan ['viːgən] *n* végétalien, -ienne.

vegetable ['vedʒtəbl] **1.** *a & n Bot:* végétal (*m*) **2.** *n* légume *m*; **early vegetables**, primeurs *f*; **v. dish**, légumier *m*; **v. salad**, macédoine de légumes; **v. garden**, potager *m*. **vege'tarian** *a & n* végétarien, -ienne. **vege'tarianism** *n* végétarisme *m*. **'vegetate** *vi* végéter. **vege'tation** *n* végétation *f*.

vehemence ['viːəməns] *n* véhémence *f*; violence *f*. **'vehement** *a* véhément; violent. **'vehemently** *adv* avec véhémence; avec violence.

vehicle ['viːikl] *n* véhicule *m*, voiture *f*; *Aut:* **commercial v.**, véhicule utilitaire; **heavy goods v.**, poids lourd; **speech is the v. of thought**, le langage est le véhicule de la pensée. **vehicular** [vi'hikjulər] *a Adm:* **v. traffic**, circulation des voitures.

veil [veil] **1.** *n* voile *m* (de religieuse, de mariée); (*on hat*) voilette *f*; *Ecc:* **to take the v.**, prendre le voile; *F:* **to draw a v. over sth**, jeter un voile sur qch **2.** *vtr* voiler; cacher, dissimuler (ses sentiments). **'veiled** *a* voilé; caché, dissimulé; **in thinly v. terms**, en termes à peine voilés.

vein [vein] *n* **1.** *Anat:* veine *f* **2.** *Bot: Ent:* nervure *f* (de feuille, d'aile) **3.** *Min:* veine, filon *m* **4.** (*in wood, marble*) veine **5.** disposition *f*; **in melancholy v.**, d'humeur mélancolique; **the poetic v.**, la veine poétique. **'veined** *a* **1.** veiné, à veines **2.** *Bot: Ent:* nervuré. **venous** ['viːnəs] *a* (sang, système) veineux.

veldt [velt] *n* veld(t) *m*.

vellum ['veləm] *n* vélin *m*.

velocity [vi'lɔsiti] *n* vitesse *f*.

velour(s) [və'luər] *n Tex:* velours *m* de laine.

velvet ['velvit] *n* velours *m*; **v. coat**, habit de velours; *Fig:* **to be on v.**, jouer sur le, du, velours. **velve'teen** *n* velours de coton. **'velvety** *a* velouté.

venal ['viːn(ə)l] *a* vénal; mercenaire. **ve'nality** *n* vénalité *f*.

vend [vend] *vtr* (*a*) *Jur:* vendre (*b*) vendre (des journaux, des choses de peu de valeur). **'vending** *n* vente *f*; **v. machine**, distributeur *m* automatique.

'**vendor** *n* vendeur, -euse; **street v.,** marchand, -ande, des quatre saisons; marchand ambulant.

vendetta [ven'deta] *n* vendetta *f.*

veneer [və'ni(:)ər] *n.* **1.** *n (a)* placage *m*, revêtement *m* (de bois mince) *(b)* bois *m* de placage *(c) Fig:* masque *m*; apparence extérieure; vernis *m* (de connaissances, de politesse) **2.** *vtr* plaquer (le bois).

venerate ['venəreit] *vtr* vénérer. '**venerable** *a* vénérable (vieillard). **vene'ration** *n* vénération *f* (**for,** pour); **to hold s.o. in v.,** avoir de la vénération pour qn.

venereal [vi'niəriəl] *a Med:* **v. disease,** maladie véné- rienne.

Venetian [vi'ni:ʃ(ə)n] *a & n Geog:* vénitien, -ienne; **V. blind,** store vénitien; **V. glass,** verre de Venise.

Venezuela [vene'zweilə] *Prn Geog:* le Vénézuéla. **Vene'zuelan** *a & n* vénézuélien, -ienne.

vengeance ['vendʒəns] *n* vengeance *f*; **to take v. on s.o.,** se venger sur, de, qn; **to take v. for sth,** tirer vengeance, se venger, de qch; *F:* **with a v.,** furieuse- ment; pour de bon; (travailler) d'arrache-pied.

venial ['vi:niəl] *a* (péché) véniel; *(of fault)* léger, pardonnable.

Venice ['venis] *Prn* Venise *f.*

venison ['venizn] *n* venaison *f*; **haunch of v.,** quartier de chevreuil.

venom ['venəm] *n* venin *m.* '**venomous** *a* **1.** *(of animal)* venimeux; *(of plant, mushroom)* vénéneux **2.** *(of criticism)* venimeux; **v. tongue,** langue de vipère; mauvaise langue. '**venomously** *adv* d'une manière venimeuse; méchamment.

vent[1] [vent] **1.** *n (a)* **v. (hole),** trou *m*, orifice *m*; évent *m*; cheminée *f* (volcanique); trou (de flûte) *(b)* **to give v. to one's anger,** donner libre cours à sa colère **2.** *vtr* **to v. one's anger on s.o.,** passer, décharger, sa colère sur qn.

vent[2] *n Cl:* fente *f* (dans la basque d'un veston).

ventilate ['ventileit] *vtr* **1.** aérer (une chambre); ventiler (un tunnel) **2.** *(of question)* discuter ouverte- ment; mettre au grand jour. **venti'lation** *n* **1.** aération *f*, aérage *m*, ventilation *f*; *Min:* **v. shaft,** puits d'aérage **2.** mise *f* en discussion publique (d'une question). '**ventilator** *n* ventilateur *m*; soupirail *m* (d'une cave); *(over door)* vasistas *m*; *Aut:* volet *m* d'aération; *(window)* déflecteur *m.*

ventricle ['ventrikl] *n* ventricule *m* (du cœur).

ventriloquist [ven'triləkwist] *n* ventriloque *mf.* **ven'triloquism** *n* ventriloquie *f.*

venture ['ventʃər] **I.** *n* **1.** entreprise (risquée, hasar- deuse) **2.** *Com:* entreprise (commerciale); **joint v.,** affaire *f* en participation **3.** **at a v.,** à l'aventure, au hasard. **II.** *v* **1.** *vtr (a)* oser (faire qch); se risquer à (faire qch) *(b)* hasarder (une conjecture) *(c)* hasarder, aventurer, risquer (sa vie, son argent) **2.** *vi (a)* **to v. on (doing) sth,** se risquer à faire qch *(b)* **to v. into an unknown country,** s'aventurer en pays inconnu; **to v. out of doors,** se hasarder à, oser, sortir; **to v. too far,** aller trop loin. '**venturesome** *a* **1.** *(of pers)* aventureux, entreprenant **2.** *(of action)* risqué, hasar- deux.

venue ['venju:] *n* lieu *m* de réunion.

Venus ['vi:nəs] *Prnf* Vénus.

veracious [və'reiʃəs] *a* véridique. **ve'raciously** *adv* véridiquement; avec véracité. **ve'racity** *n* vé- racité *f.*

veranda(h) [və'rændə] *n* véranda *f.*

verb [və:b] *n* verbe *m.* '**verbal** *a (a)* verbal; oral; (entente, offre) verbale; (mémoire) auditive *(b)* (tra- duction) littérale. '**verbalize** *vtr* rendre (une idée) par des mots; s'exprimer verbalement. '**verbally** *adv* verbalement; de vive voix. **ver'batim** *a & adv* mot à mot; (rapport) textuel.

verbena [və(:)'bi:nə] *n Bot:* verveine *f.*

verbiage ['və:biidʒ] *n* verbiage *m.* **verbose** [-'bous] *a* verbeux; diffus, prolixe. **ver'bosely** *adv* avec verbosité. **ver'bosity** *n* verbosité *f*, prolixité *f.*

verdict ['və:dikt] *n* **1.** *Jur:* verdict *m*; **to bring in a v. of guilty, not guilty,** prononcer, rendre, un verdict de culpabilité, de non-culpabilité **2.** jugement *m*, dé- cision *f*; **to give one's v. (on, about),** se prononcer (sur).

verdigris ['və:digris] *n* vert-de-gris *m inv.*

verge [və:dʒ] **1.** *n (a)* bord *m* (d'un fleuve); orée *f* (d'une forêt); bordure *f* (de gazon); accotement *m* (d'une route); *Aut: PN:* **soft v.,** accotement non stabilisé *(b)* **on the v. of ruin,** à deux doigts de la ruine; **on the v. of tears,** au bord des larmes **2.** *vi (a)* **to v. on,** toucher à, être contigu à (qch) *(b)* frôler; **courage verging on foolhardiness,** courage qui confine à, frise, la témérité; **he's verging on forty,** il frise la quaran- taine.

verger ['və:dʒər] *n Ecc:* bedeau *m.*

verify ['verifai] *vtr* (**verified**) **1.** confirmer (un fait, des soupçons) **2.** vérifier, contrôler (des renseignements, des comptes). **veri'fiable** *a* vérifiable. **verifi- cation** [-fi'keiʃ(ə)n] *n* vérification *f*, contrôle *m.*

verisimilitude [verisi'militju:d] *n* vraisemblance *f.*

veritable ['veritəbl] *a* véritable.

vermicelli [və:mi'tʃeli] *n* vermicelle *m.*

vermilion [və:'miljən] **1.** *n* vermillon *m* **2.** *a* (de) vermillon; vermeil.

vermin ['və:min] *n* **1.** *(body parasites; Pej: of people)* vermine *f* **2.** *(rats, etc)* animaux *mpl* nuisibles. '**vermifuge** *a & n* vermifuge (*m*). '**verminous** *a* couvert, grouillant, de vermine.

vermouth ['və:məθ] *n* vermout(h) *m.*

vernacular [və'nækjulər] *a & n Ling:* vernaculaire (*m*); (langue) du pays.

verruca [ve'ru:kə] *n (pl* **verrucae**) verrue *f* plantaire.

versatile ['və:sətail] *a (a)* aux talents variés; (objet, outil) adaptable *(b)* (esprit) souple. **versa'tility** *n* souplesse *f*, universalité *f* (d'esprit); adaptabilité *f.*

verse [və:s] *n (a)* vers *m* (de poésie) *(b)* couplet *m* (d'une chanson); strophe *f* (d'un poème) *(c)* verset *m* (de la Bible) *(d) coll* vers *mpl*; **in v.,** en vers; **free v.,** vers libres. **versifi'cation** *n* versification *f.* '**versify** *vtr & i* versifier; écrire des vers; mettre (qch) en vers.

versed [və:st] *a* versé (**in,** en, dans).

version ['və:ʃ(ə)n] *n* **1.** version *f*, traduction *f* **2.** version (des faits); interprétation *f* (d'un fait); **accord- ing to his v.,** selon son dire; d'après lui **3.** modèle *m*; **military v. of an aircraft,** version militaire d'un avion.

versus ['və:səs] *prep Jur: Sp:* contre; **Martin v. Thomas,** Martin contre Thomas.

vertebra ['və:tibrə] *n (pl* **vertebrae**) vertèbre *f.* '**vertebral** *a* vertébral. '**vertebrate** *a & n* ver- tébré (*m*).

vertex ['və:teks] *n (pl* **vertices**) *Anat:* vertex *m*; *Mth:* sommet *m* (d'une courbe).

vertical ['vɜːtik(ə)l] **1.** *a* vertical; (falaise) à pic **2.** *n* verticale *f*. **'vertically** *adv* verticalement.

vertigo ['vɜːtigou] *n Med:* vertige *m*.

verve [vɜːv] *n* verve *f*, brio *m*.

very ['veri] **I.** *a* **1.** *Lit:* vrai, véritable **2.** (a) même; **you're the v. man I wanted to see,** vous êtes justement l'homme que je voulais voir; **come here this v. minute!** venez ici à l'instant! **at that v. moment,** à cet instant même; **this v. day,** aujourd'hui même; **a year ago to the v. day,** il y a un an jour pour jour; **these are his v. words,** ce sont là ses propres paroles (b) **at the v. beginning,** tout au commencement (c) **I shudder at the v. thought of it,** je frémis rien que d'y penser. **II.** *adv* **1.** très, fort, bien; **v. well,** très bien; **v. good,** (i) très bon (ii) très bien, fort bien; **you're not v. polite,** vous êtes peu poli; **it's v. kind of you,** c'est gentil de votre part; **it's not so v. difficult,** ce n'est pas tellement difficile; **so v. little,** si peu; **there's v. little of it,** il y en a très peu; **v. (v.) few,** très (très) peu; **v. much,** beaucoup; **I was v. (much) surprised,** j'en ai été très surpris **2.** (*emphatic*) **the v. first, last,** le tout premier, dernier; **the v. best,** tout ce qu'il y a de meilleur, de mieux; **the v. best of friends,** le meilleur ami du monde; **the v. next day,** dès le lendemain; **at the v. most, least,** tout au plus, au moins; **at the v. latest,** au plus tard; **the v. same,** absolument, exactement, le même; **for your v. own,** pour vous seul.

vespers ['vespəz] *npl Ecc:* vêpres *fpl*.

vessel ['vesl] *n* **1.** récipient *m* **2.** navire *m*, bâtiment *m* **3.** *Anat:* blood **v.,** vaisseau sanguin.

vest[1] [vest] *n* **1.** *NAm:* (*waistcoat*) gilet *m* **2.** (*for man*) maillot *m* de corps; (*for woman*) chemise américaine; *FrC:* camisole *f*; *Sp:* maillot.

vest[2] *vtr* **to v. s.o.** with authority, investir qn de l'autorité nécessaire; **authority vested in the people,** l'autorité dont jouit le peuple; **right vested in the Crown,** droit dévolu à la Couronne **'vested v. interests,** droits acquis; **to have a v. interest in a firm,** avoir des capitaux investis dans une entreprise.

vestibule ['vestibjuːl] *n* vestibule *m*.

vestige ['vestidʒ] *n* vestige *m*, trace *f*; **not a v. of common sense,** pas la moindre trace, pas un grain, de bon sens.

vestment ['vestmənt] *n* vêtement *m*; (church) vestments, vêtements sacerdotaux. **'vestry** *n* sacristie *f*.

Vesuvius [vi's(j)uːviəs] *Prn Geog:* Vésuve *m*.

vet [vet] **1.** *n* vétérinaire *mf* **2.** *vtr* (vetted) (a) examiner (qn, une bête) (b) revoir, corriger (l'œuvre de qn) (c) *Adm:* effectuer un contrôle de sécurité sur (un candidat). **'vetting** *n* examen (médical); contrôle *m* de sécurité (sur un candidat).

vetch [vetʃ] *n Bot:* vesce *f*.

veteran ['vetərən] **1.** *n* vétéran *m*; (war) **v.,** ancien combattant **2.** *a* de vétéran; ancien; de toujours; **he's a v. golfer,** il joue au golf depuis toujours; **v. car,** (i) (*in Eng*) ancêtre *m* (vieille voiture d'avant 1905) (ii) (*international categories*) vétéran *m* (1905-1918).

veterinary ['vetrənri] *a* vétérinaire; **v. surgeon,** vétérinaire *mf*.

veto ['viːtou] **1.** *n* (*pl* vetoes) veto *m*; **to have a v., the right of v.,** avoir le droit de veto **2.** *vtr* interdire (qch); mettre, opposer, son veto à (qch).

vex [veks] *vtr* vexer, fâcher. **vex'ation** *n* (a) contrariété *f*, ennui *m* (b) dépit *m*. **vex'atious,**

'vexing *a* fâcheux, ennuyeux, contrariant; vexant.

vexed *a* **1.** vexé, contrarié; **v. at sth,** vexé, fâché, de qch; **v. with s.o.,** fâché contre qn; **to be v. with oneself,** s'en vouloir; **to get v.,** se fâcher **2. v. question,** question souvent débattue, non résolue.

VHF *abbr very high frequency,** très haute fréquence, THF.

via ['vaiə] *prep* via; par la voie de; **to travel v. Calais,** passer par Calais.

viable ['vaiəbl] *a* viable. **via'bility** *n* viabilité *f* (d'une entreprise).

viaduct ['vaiədʌkt] *n* viaduc *m*.

vibrate [vai'breit] **1.** *vi* vibrer; trépider **2.** *vtr* faire vibrer. **vibes** *npl* vibrations *fpl*; **the v. are good,** ça marche; ça gaze. **'vibrant** *a* vibrant. **vi'brating** *a* vibrant; (mouvement) vibratoire. **vi'bration** *n* vibration *f*; oscillation *f*. **vi'brator** *n* (*for massage*) vibromasseur *m*.

viburnum [vai'bɜːnəm] *n Bot:* viorne *f*.

vicar ['vikər] *n Ch of Eng:* pasteur *m*; *RCCh:* = curé *m*. **'vicarage** *n Ch of Eng:* presbytère *m*; cure *f*.

vicarious [vi'keəriəs] *a* **v. punishment,** châtiment souffert (i) par un autre (ii) pour un autre; **v. pleasure,** plaisir donné par le plaisir d'un autre. **vi'cariously** *adv* à la place d'un autre; indirectement.

vice[1] [vais] *n* **1.** vice *m*; *Adm:* **v. squad,** brigade des mœurs **2.** défaut *m* **3.** vice (d'un cheval).

vice[2], *NAm:* **vise** [vais] *n Tls:* étau *m*; **bench v.,** étau d'établi.

vice[3] ['vaisi] *prep* à la place de (qn); **Mr Martin v. Mr Thomas,** M. Martin qui succède à M. Thomas, démissionnaire.

vice- [vais] *pref* vice-. **'vice-'admiral** *n* vice-amiral *m*. **'vice-'chairman** *n* vice-président *m*. **'vice-'chairmanship** *n* vice-présidence *f*. **'vice-'chancellor** *n* **1.** vice-chancelier *m* **2.** recteur *m* (d'une université). **'vice-'consul** *n* vice-consul *m*. **'vice-'marshal** *n* **air v.-m.,** général *m* de division aérienne. **'vice-'presidency** *n* vice-présidence *f*. **'vice-'president** *n* vice-président *m*. **'viceroy** *n* vice-roi *m*.

vice versa ['vais'vɜːsə] *adv phr* vice versa.

vicinity [vi'siniti] *n* voisinage *m*, proximité *f*; abords *mpl*, alentours *mpl* (d'un lieu); **in the v.,** dans le voisinage; **to live in the v. of Dover,** demeurer à proximité de, dans les environs de, Douvres.

vicious ['viʃəs] *a* **1.** vicieux **2.** (a) méchant, haineux; **v. criticism,** critique méchante (b) violent, brutal; rageur (c) **it's a v. circle,** c'est un cercle vicieux (d) (*of animal*) vicieux. **'viciously** *adv* **1.** vicieusement **2.** méchamment; violemment; rageusement. **'viciousness** *n* **1.** nature vicieuse; vice *m* **2.** méchanceté *f*; violence *f*.

vicissitude [vi'sisitjuːd] *n* vicissitude *f*.

victim ['viktim] *n* victime *f*; **to be the v. of,** être (la) victime de; **to fall a v. to s.o.'s charm,** succomber au charme de qn; **v. of an accident,** accidenté, -ée. **victimi'zation** *n* oppression *f*; (*after strike*) **no v.!** point de représailles! **'victimize** *vtr* (a) prendre (qn) comme victime; exercer des représailles contre (les meneurs d'une grève) (b) tromper, escroquer (qn).

Victoria [vik'tɔːriə] *Prnf* **Queen V.,** la reine Victoria. **Vic'torian** *a & n* victorien, -ienne; du règne de la reine Victoria. **Victori'ana** *npl* antiquités *fpl* de l'ère victorienne.

victory ['viktəri] *n* victoire *f*. **'victor** *n* vainqueur *m*. **vic'torious** *a* victorieux; **to be v.**, être victorieux **(in, à)**; vaincre qn. **vic'toriously** *adv* victorieusement; en vainqueur.

victuals ['vitlz] *npl* vivres *mpl*; victuailles *fpl*.

video ['vidiou] *n* TV: vidéo *m*. **'videoca'ssette** *n* vidéocassette *f*. **'videodisc** *n* vidéodisque *m*. **'video'frequency** *n* vidéofréquence *f*. **'videophone** *n* vidéophone *m*. **'video-recorder** *n* magnétoscope *m*. **'videotape 1.** *n* bande-vidéo *f* 2. *vtr* enregistrer sur magnétoscope.

vie [vai] *vi* (**vied, vying**) **to v. with s.o.**, le disputer à qn; rivaliser avec qn.

Vienna [vi'enə] *Prn Geog:* Vienne *f*. **Vie'nnese** *a & n* viennois, -oise.

Vietnam [vjet'næm, -'nɑːm] *Prn Geog:* Vietnam *m*, Viêt-nam. **Vietna'mese** *a & n* vietnamien, -ienne.

view [vjuː] **I.** *n* **1.** vue *f*; regard *m*; coup *m* d'œil; **I should like a closer v. of it**, je voudrais l'examiner de plus près; **the collection is on v.**, la collection est ouverte au public; **private v.**, vernissage *m* (d'une exposition de peinture) **2. in v.**, en vue; **in full v. of the crowd**, sous les regards de la foule; **we were in v. of land**, nous étions en vue de la terre; (*of telescope*) **field of v.**, champ de vision; **angle of v.**, angle de champ *m* **3.** (*prospect*) vue, perspective *f*; **front v. of the hotel**, l'hôtel vu de face; **you'll get a better v. from here**, vous verrez mieux d'ici; **views of Paris**, vues de Paris; **it's worth while climbing up for the v.**, le panorama vaut le déplacement; **point of v.**, point de vue; **to keep sth in v.**, ne pas perdre qch de vue **4.** manière *f* de voir; opinion *f*; **to express a v.**, exprimer une opinion; **to take the right v. of sth**, voir juste; **to hold extreme views**, avoir des idées extrémistes; **in my v.**, à mon avis *m*; **to share s.o.'s views**, partager les sentiments de qn **5. in v. of**, étant donné (que), vu (que); **in v. of his being late**, étant donné qu'il était en retard; **in v. of the distance**, vu l'éloignement; **in v. of what happened**, en raison de ce qui est arrivé **6.** vue, intention *f*; **to fall in with s.o.'s views**, entrer dans les vues de qn; **will this meet your views?** cela vous conviendra-t-il? **to have sth in v.**, avoir qch en vue; méditer (un voyage); **whom have you in v.?** à qui pensez-vous? vous avez un candidat (à proposer)? **with this in v.**, à cette fin; **with a v. to doing sth**, en vue de, dans le but de, faire qch. **II.** *v* **1.** *vtr* (*a*) regarder (qn, qch); examiner (qn, qch); visiter (une maison à vendre); visionner (un film) (*b*) envisager; **I don't v. the thing in that light**, je n'envisage pas la chose ainsi **2.** *vi* TV: regarder la télévision. **'viewer** *n* **1.** spectateur, -trice; TV: téléspectateur, -trice **2.** Phot: visionneuse *f*. **'viewfinder** *n* Phot: viseur *m*. **'viewpoint** *n* point *m* de vue.

vigilance ['vidʒiləns] *n* vigilance *f*. **'vigilant** *a* vigilant, éveillé, alerte. **'vigilantly** *adv* avec vigilance.

vigour, *NAm:* **vigor** ['vigər] *n* vigueur *f*, énergie *f*. **'vigorous** *a* vigoureux, robuste. **'vigorously** *adv* vigoureusement, avec énergie.

vile [vail] *a* **1.** vil, bas, infâme **2.** abominable, exécrable; **v. weather**, sale temps; **v. temper**, humeur massacrante, exécrable. **'vilely** *adv* **1.** vilement; bassement **2.** abominablement. **'vileness** *n* **1.** bas-

sesse *f*, caractère *m* ignoble (de qn, d'un sentiment) **2. the v. of the weather**, le temps abominable.

vilify ['vilifai] *vtr* dénigrer (qn). **vilifi'cation** [-fikeiʃ(ə)n] *n* dénigrement *m*.

villa ['vilə] *n* (*a*) villa *f* (*b*) pavillon *m* de banlieue.

village ['vilidʒ] *n* village *m*; **at the v.** grocer's, chez l'épicier du village; **v. green**, pré communal; **v. inn**, auberge de campagne. **'villager** *n* villageois, -oise.

villain ['vilən] *n* scélérat *m*; gredin *m*; bandit *m*; *F:* **you little v.!** oh, le vilain! la vilaine! petit garnement! *Th:* **the v.**, le traître. **'villainous** *a* **1.** vil, infâme **2.** *F:* **v. weather**, sale temps. **'villainously** *adv* **1.** d'une manière infâme **2.** *F:* exécrablement, abominablement. **'villainy** *n* (*pl* -ainies) infamie *f*.

vim [vim] *n F:* vigueur *f*, énergie *f*, entrain *m*.

vindicate ['vindikeit] *vtr* défendre, soutenir (qn); justifier (qn, sa conduite); prouver, maintenir (son dire); **to v. one's rights**, revendiquer ses droits; faire valoir son bon droit. **vindi'cation** *n* défense *f*, justification *f*; **in v. of sth**, pour justifier qch.

vindictive [vin'diktiv] *a* vindicatif; rancunier. **vin'dictively** *adv* par rancune; par esprit de vengeance. **vin'dictiveness** *n* esprit *m* de vengeance; esprit rancunier.

vine [vain] *n* (*a*) vigne *f*; **v. grower**, viticulteur *m*; vigneron *m*; **v. growing**, viticulture *f*; **v.-growing district, industry**, pays, industrie, vinicole, viticole (*b*) *NAm:* plante grimpante. **'vineleaf** *n* feuille *f* de vigne. **'vinestock** *n* cep *m* de vigne.

vinegar ['vinigər] *n* vinaigre *m*; **cider, wine v.**, vinaigre de cidre, de vin.

vineyard ['vinjəd] *n* clos *m* de vigne; vignoble *m*; **the best vineyards**, les meilleurs crus.

vino ['viːnou] *n F:* vin *m* ordinaire.

vintage ['vintidʒ] *n* **1.** vendanges *fpl*; récolte *f* du raisin **2.** année *f* (de belle récolte); **of the 1973 v.**, de l'année 1973; **v. wine**, un millésimé; vin d'appellation, de grand cru; grand vin; **guaranteed v.**, appellation contrôlée; **v. year**, année de bon vin **3. v. car**, voiture construite entre 1916 et 1930. **'vintner** *n* négociant *m* en vins.

vinyl ['vainil] *n Ch:* vinyle *m*.

viola¹ [vi'oulə] *n Mus:* **1.** alto *m*; **v.** (**player**), altiste *mf* **2. v. da gamba**, viole *f* de gambe.

viola² ['vaiələ] *n Bot:* pensée *f*.

violate ['vaiəleit] *vtr* violer; manquer à (une règle); enfreindre (la loi). **vio'lation** *n* violation *f*; infraction *f* (à un ordre); **v. of s.o.'s privacy**, intrusion *f* auprès de, chez, qn.

violence ['vaiələns] *n* **1.** (*a*) violence *f*, intensité *f* (du vent) (*b*) **to use v.**, user de violence; **to do v. to one's feelings**, se faire violence **2.** *Jur:* robbery with v., vol avec agression; **acts of v.**, voies *f* de fait. **'violent** *a* **1.** violent; *Aut:* **v. braking**, freinage brutal; **to become v.**, s'emporter; **to die a v. death**, mourir de mort violente **2.** (*a*) violent, aigu, fort; **v. dislike**, vive aversion; **in a v. hurry**, extrêmement pressé; **v. cold**, gros rhume (*b*) **v. colour**, couleur criarde, éclatante. **'violently** *adv* **1.** violemment; avec violence **2.** vivement; extrêmement; **to be v. ill**, être terriblement malade; **to fall v. in love with s.o.**, tomber follement amoureux, -euse, de qn.

violet ['vaiələt] **1.** *n Bot:* violette *f* **2.** *a & n* (*colour*) violet (*m*).

violin [vaiə'lin] *n* violon *m*. **vio'linist** *n* violoniste *mf*.

V P *abbr very important person*, personnage de marque.

viper ['vaipər] *n* vipère *f*.

virgin ['vəːdʒin] **1.** *n* vierge *f*; **the Blessed V.**, la Sainte Vierge **2.** *a* de vierge; virginal; **v. oil**, huile vierge; **v. snow**, neige virginale; **v. forest**, forêt vierge. **'virginal** *a* virginal. **vir'ginity** *n* virginité *f*.

Virginia [vəː'dʒiniə] *Prn Geog:* Virginie *f*; *Bot:* **V. creeper**, vigne *f* vierge; **V. (tobacco)**, tabac de Virginie; virginie *f*.

Virgo ['vəːgou] *Prn Astr:* la Vierge.

virile ['virail] *a* viril, mâle. **vi'rility** *n* virilité *f*.

virtual ['vəːtjuəl] *a* de fait; en fait; **he's the v. head of the business**, c'est lui le vrai chef de la maison; **this was a v. confession**, de fait, c'était un aveu. **'virtually** *adv* virtuellement; de fait; **I'm v. certain of it**, j'en ai la quasi-certitude; j'en suis pratiquement certain.

virtue ['vəːtjuː] *n* **1.** vertu *f*; **to make a v. of necessity**, faire de nécessité vertu **2.** qualité *f*; avantage *m*; **he has many virtues**, il a beaucoup de qualités; **the great v. of the scheme**, le grand avantage du projet; *(of plants)* **healing virtues**, propriétés curatives **3.** *prep phr* **by v. of**, en vertu de; en raison de. **'virtuous** *a* vertueux. **'virtuously** *adv* vertueusement.

virtuoso [vəːtju'ouzou] *n* (*pl* **virtuosi**) *Mus:* virtuose *mf*. **virtu'osity** *n* virtuosité *f*.

virulence ['virjuləns] *n* virulence *f*. **'virulent** *a* virulent. **'virulently** *adv* avec virulence.

virus ['vaiərəs] *n* (*pl* **viruses**) *Med:* virus *m*; **v. disease**, maladie virale.

visa ['viːzə] **1.** *n* (*on passport, document*) visa *m* **2.** *vtr* (**visaed** ['viːzəd]) viser; apposer un visa à (un passeport).

vis-à-vis ['viːzaːviː] **1.** *n* vis-à-vis *m* **2.** *prep* (*a*) vis-à-vis (*b*) par rapport à.

viscera ['visərə] *npl* viscères *m*. **'visceral** *a* viscéral.

viscosity [vis'kɔsiti] *n* viscosité *f*. **'viscous** *a* visqueux.

viscount ['vaikaunt] *n* vicomte *m*. **'viscountess** *n* vicomtesse *f*.

visible ['vizibl] *a* visible; **to become v.**, apparaître; **with v. satisfaction**, avec une satisfaction évidente; **v. to the naked eye**, visible à l'œil nu. **visi'bility** *n* visibilité *f*; **good, bad, v.**, bonne, mauvaise, visibilité. **'visibly** *adv* visiblement, manifestement; (grandir) à vue d'œil.

vision ['viʒ(ə)n] *n* **1.** (*a*) vision *f*, vue *f*; **field of v.**, champ visuel (*b*) **man of v.**, homme d'une grande perspicacité, qui voit loin dans l'avenir **2.** (*a*) imagination *f*, vision; **visions of wealth**, visions de richesses (*b*) apparition *f*, fantôme *m*; **to see visions**, avoir des visions. **'visionary** *a & n* visionnaire *mf*.

visit ['vizit] **1.** *n* (*a*) (**social**) *v.*, visite *f*; **to pay s.o. a v.**, faire une visite à qn; *F:* **to pay a v.**, aller faire pipi (*b*) visite, séjour *m*; **to be on a v. to**, *NAm:* **with, friends**, être en visite chez des amis (*c*) **inspection v.**, tournée *f*, visite d'inspection; *Ecc:* **pastoral v.**, visite pastorale; **private, official, v.**, visite privée, officielle **2.** *vtr* (*a*) rendre visite à (qn); aller voir (qn, qch); visiter (un malade, un endroit) (*b*) (*of official*) visiter, inspecter. **visi'tation** *n* (*official*) visite d'inspection; (*by bishop*) visite pastorale. **'visiting 1.** *a* en visite; *Sp:*

v. team, les visiteurs *m*; **v. professor**, professeur invité; *NAm:* **v. nurse** (*Br* = **district nurse**) infirmière visiteuse **2.** *n* visites *fpl*; **they are not on v. terms**, ils ne se voient pas; (*at hospital*) **v. hours**, heures de visite; **v. card**, carte de visite. **'visitor** *n* (*a*) visiteur, -euse; invité, -ée; (*in hotel*) client, -ente; **visitors' book**, registre des voyageurs; livre *m* d'or; **she's got visitors**, elle a du monde (*b*) **health v.**, infirmière visiteuse.

visor ['vaizər] *n* (*a*) visière *f* (de casque, de casquette) (*b*) **sun v.**, pare-soleil *m inv*.

vista ['vistə] *n* **1.** échappée *f* (de vue) **2.** **to open up new vistas**, ouvrir de nouvelles perspectives.

visual ['vizju(ə)l] *a* visuel; perceptible à l'œil; (enseignement) par l'image; **v. memory**, mémoire visuelle. **'visualize** *vtr* se représenter (qch); évoquer l'image de (qch); **I can't v. it**, je n'arrive pas à me le représenter. **'visually** *adv* visuellement.

vital ['vait(ə)l] *a* **1.** vital; essentiel à la vie **2.** essentiel; capital; **question of v. importance**, question d'importance capitale; **it is v. that**, il est indispensable, essentiel, que **3. v. error**, erreur fatale **4.** (*of pers*) plein d'entrain **5. v. statistics**, (i) statistiques *f* démographiques (ii) *F:* mensurations *f* (d'une femme). **vi'tality** *n* vitalité *f*; vigueur *f*; **she's bubbling over with v.**, elle déborde de vie. **'vitally** *adv* d'une manière vitale.

vitamin ['vitəmin, 'vait-] *n* vitamine *f*; **v. deficiency**, carence vitaminique; avitaminose *f*; **with added vitamins**, vitaminé.

vitiate ['viʃieit] *vtr* vicier.

vitreous ['vitriəs] *a* (*a*) vitreux (*b*) *Anat:* (corps) vitré (de l'œil). **'vitrify** *vtr & i* (se) vitrifier.

vitriol ['vitriəl] *n* vitriol *m*. **vitri'olic** *a* (acide) vitriolique; (critique) mordante.

vituperation [vitjuːpə'reiʃ(ə)n] *n* injures *fpl*, insultes *fpl*, invectives *fpl*. **vi'tuperate 1.** *vtr* injurier **2.** *vi* vitupérer, déblatérer (contre qn, qch).

viva ['vaivə] *n Sch: F: abbr viva voce*, examen oral, oral *m*.

vivacious [vi'veiʃəs] *a* vif, animé, enjoué. **vi'vaciously** *adv* avec enjouement; avec entrain; avec verve. **vi'vacity** *n* vivacité *f*; verve *f*, entrain *m*.

vivid ['vivid] *a* **1.** vif, éclatant; **v. flash of lightning**, éclair aveuglant **2. v. imagination**, imagination vive; **v. description**, description vivante; **v. recollection**, souvenir très net. **'vividly** *adv* **1.** vivement; avec éclat **2.** (décrire qch) d'une manière vivante. **'vividness** *n* **1.** vivacité *f*, éclat *m* (des couleurs) **2.** vigueur *f*, pittoresque *m* (du style).

viviparous [vi'vipərəs] *a Z:* vivipare.

vivisection [vivi'sekʃ(ə)n] *n* vivisection *f*.

vixen ['viksn] *n* **1.** *Z:* renarde *f* **2.** mégère *f*.

viz [viz] *adv* à savoir; c'est-à-dire.

vizier [vi'ziər] *n Hist:* vizir *m*.

vocabulary [və'kæbjuləri] *n* (*a*) vocabulaire *m* (*b*) lexique *m*.

vocal ['vouk(ə)l] *a* (*a*) vocal; **v. score**, partition *f* de chant; *Anat:* **v. cords**, cordes vocales (*b*) verbal; oral. **'vocalist** *n* chanteur, -euse; cantatrice *f*. **'vocalize 1.** *vtr Ling:* vocaliser **2.** *vi Mus:* faire des vocalises. **'vocally** *adv* vocalement; oralement.

vocation [və'keiʃ(ə)n] *n* vocation *f*. **vo'cational** *a* **v. training**, enseignement professionnel; **v. guidance**, orientation professionnelle.

vocative [ˈvɔkətiv] *a* & *n* vocatif (*m*).

vociferate [vəˈsifəreit] *vi* & *tr* vociférer, crier (**against**, contre). **vocife'ration** *n* vociférations *fpl*, cris *mpl*. **vo'ciferous** *a* vociférant, bruyant, criard. **vo'ciferously** *adv* bruyamment; en vociférant.

vodka [ˈvɔdkə] *n* vodka *f*.

vogue [voug] *n* vogue *f*, mode *f*; **in v.**, en vogue, à la mode; **the v. for miniskirts**, la mode, la vogue, des minijupes.

voice [vɔis] **1.** *n* (*a*) voix *f*; **to raise one's v.**, hausser la voix; **to lose one's v.**, avoir une extinction de voix; **in a low v.**, à voix basse; à demi-voix; **in a loud v.**, à voix haute; **at the top of his v.**, à tue-tête; **v. test**, audition *f*; (*of singer*) **to be in (good) v.**, en voix; **he likes the sound of his own v.**, il aime à s'entendre parler (*b*) voix, suffrage *m*; **we have no v. in the matter**, nous n'avons pas voix au chapitre 2. *vtr* exprimer, énoncer (une opinion); *Ling:* voiser (une consonne). **'voiceless** *a* sans voix; muet.

void [vɔid] **1.** *a* (*a*) vide (*b*) (*of office*) vacant, inoccupé (*c*) *Jur:* nul; **null and v.**, nul et de nul effet, nul et non avenu (*d*) dépourvu, dénué (**of**, de); **v. of sense**, (projet) dénué de sens **2.** *n* vide *m*; **to fill the v.**, combler le vide.

volatile [ˈvɔlətail] *a* **1.** *Ch:* volatil **2.** volage, inconstant. **vo'latilize 1.** *vtr* *Ch:* volatiliser **2.** *vi* se volatiliser.

volcano [vɔlˈkeinou] *n* (*pl* **volcanoes**) volcan *m*; **active, dormant, extinct, v.**, volcan actif, dormant, éteint. **vol'canic** *n* volcanique.

vole [voul] *n* *Z:* (**field**) **v.**, campagnol *m* (des champs); **water v.**, rat *m* d'eau.

volition [vəˈliʃ(ə)n] *n* volonté *f*; **of one's own v.**, (faire qch) de son propre gré.

volley [ˈvɔli] **1.** *n* (*a*) volée *f*, salve *f* (d'armes à feu); grêle *f* (de pierres) (*b*) volée, bordée *f* (d'injures) (*c*) *Ten:* (balle prise de) volée **2.** (*a*) *vtr* & *i* *Ten:* **to v.** (**a return**), reprendre une balle de volée; **to half v. a ball**, prendre une balle à la demi-volée (*b*) *vi* (*of guns*) partir ensemble. **'volleyball** *n* *Sp:* volley-ball *m*; **v. player**, volleyeur, -euse.

volt [voult] *n* *El:* volt *m*. **'voltage** *n* tension *f* (en volts); **high, low, v.**, haute, basse, tension.

voluble [ˈvɔljubl] *a* (*of speech*) facile, aisé; (*of pers*) **to be v.**, avoir la langue bien pendue; parler avec volubilité. **volu'bility** *n* volubilité *f*. **'volubly** *adv* avec volubilité.

volume [ˈvɔljuːm] *n* **1.** volume *m*, livre *m*; **v. one**, tome premier; **in two volumes**, (ouvrage) en deux volumes; *F:* **it speaks volumes for him**, cela en dit long en sa faveur **2. volumes of smoke, of water**, nuages *m* de fumée, torrents *m* d'eau **3.** *Ph:* volume; **v. of a reservoir**, cubage *m*, capacité *f*, d'un réservoir **4.** volume (d'un son); ampleur *f* (de la voix); **v. control**, bouton de réglage de volume. **vo'luminous** *a* volumineux.

volunteer [vɔlənˈtiːər] **1.** *n* (*a*) *Mil:* volontaire *m*; **v. army**, armée de volontaires (*b*) volontaire; personne bénévole **2.** (*a*) *vtr* offrir volontairement, spontanément, ses services; **to v. information**, donner spontanément des renseignements (*b*) *vi* s'offrir (pour une tâche); se proposer volontairement (pour qch); *Mil:* s'engager comme volontaire. **'voluntarily** *adv*

volontairement, spontanément; bénévolement; de (son) plein gré. **'voluntary** *a* (*a*) volontaire, spontané (*b*) **v. work**, travail *m* bénévole; **v. organization**, organisation bénévole.

voluptuous [vəˈlʌptjuəs] *a* voluptueux. **vo'luptuously** *adv* voluptueusement. **vo'luptuousness** *n* volupté *f*.

vomit [ˈvɔmit] **1.** *n* vomissure *f*; vomi *m* **2.** *vtr* & *i* vomir, rendre. **'vomiting** *n* vomissement *m*.

voracious [vəˈreiʃəs] *a* vorace, dévorant; **v. appetite**, appétit de loup; **v. reader**, lecteur vorace. **vo'raciously** *adv* avec voracité. **vo'racity** *n* voracité *f*.

vortex [ˈvɔːteks] *n* (*pl* **vortices**) (*a*) tourbillonnement *m* (d'air); tourbillon *m* (de fumée) (*b*) (*whirlpool*) tourbillon.

votary [ˈvoutəri] *n* fervent, -ente (**of**, de); dévot, -ote.

vote [vout] **I.** *n* **1.** (*a*) vote *m*, scrutin *m*; **to put a question to the v.**, mettre une question aux voix; **to take the v.**, procéder au scrutin; **to count the votes**, dépouiller le scrutin (*b*) (**individual**) **v.**, voix *f*, suffrage *m*; **to have a v.**, avoir le droit de vote; **to give one's v. to s.o.**, donner son vote à qn; **to record one's v.**, voter **2. v. of censure**, motion *f* de censure; **v. of confidence**, vote de confiance; **to carry a v.**, adopter une résolution; **postal v.**, vote par correspondance; **to pass a v. of thanks**, voter des remerciements (à qn). **II.** *vi* & *tr* voter; **to v. for a candidate**, voter pour un candidat; **to v. communist**, voter communiste; **to v. s.o. in**, élire qn; **v. for Martin!** votez Martin! **to v. a sum**, voter une somme; **to v. by (a) show of hands**, voter à main levée; **to v. down**, repousser (une motion); *F:* **I v. we go**, je propose que nous y allions. **'voter** *n* électeur, -trice. **'voting** *n* (participation *f* au) vote; scrutin *m*; **v. paper**, bulletin de vote.

votive [ˈvoutiv] *a* votif; **v. offering**, ex-voto *m inv*.

vouch [vautʃ] *vi* **to v. for the truth of sth**, témoigner de, répondre de, la vérité de qch; **to v. for a fact**, garantir un fait; **to v. for s.o.**, répondre de qn; se porter garant de qn. **'voucher** *n* *Com:* fiche *f*; reçu *m*, bon *m*; **gift v.**, bon d'achat; **luncheon v.**, chèque-repas *m*.

vow [vau] **1.** *n* vœu *m*, serment *m*; **monastic vows**, vœux monastiques; **to take one's vows**, prononcer ses vœux; **to make a v.**, faire un vœu; **to break a v.**, manquer à un vœu **2.** *vtr* vouer, jurer; **to v. obedience**, jurer obéissance.

vowel [ˈvauəl] *n* voyelle *f*; **v. sound**, son vocalique.

voyage [ˈvɔiidʒ] **1.** *n* voyage *m* sur mer; **on the v. out, home**, à l'aller, au retour **2.** *vi* voyager par, sur, mer; naviguer. **'voyager** *n* voyageur, -euse, par mer; passager, -ère.

VP *abbr Vice-President*, vice-président, -ente.

VR *abbr Victoria Regina*.

VSOP *abbr* (*of brandy*) *Very Special Old Pale*.

vulcanize [ˈvʌlkənaiz] *vtr* vulcaniser (le caoutchouc). **vulcani'zation** *n* vulcanisation *f*.

vulgar [ˈvʌlgər] *a* **1.** vulgaire, commun; **v. display of wealth**, gros luxe de mauvais goût; **v. expressions**, expressions vulgaires; **to make v. remarks**, dire des vulgarités *f* **2.** (*a*) vulgaire; commun; **v. error**, erreur très répandue (*b*) **the v. tongue**, la langue commune, la langue vulgaire (*c*) *Mth:* **v. fraction**, fraction ordinaire. **'vulgarism** *n* expression *f* vulgaire, vulgarisme *m*. **vul'garity** *n* vulgarité *f*. grossièreté *f*, trivialité *f*. **vulgari'zation** *n* vulgarisation *f*. **'vulgarize** *vtr* vulgariser. **'vulgarly** *adv* vulgairement, grossièrement; communément. **'Vulgate** *n* la Vulgate.

vulnerable ['vʌln(ə)rəbl] *a* vulnérable. **vulnera'bility** *n* vulnérabilité *f*.
vulture ['vʌltʃər] *n* vautour *m*.
vulva ['vʌlvə] *n* Anat: vulve *f*.
vying *see* **vie.**

W

W, w [ˈdʌbljuː] *n* (la lettre) W, w *m*.

wad [wɔd] **1.** *n* (*a*) tampon *m* (d'ouate); bouchon *m* (de paille) (*b*) liasse *f* (de billets de banque) (*c*) *F:* sandwich épais **2.** *vtr* (**wadded**) ouater (un vêtement); capitonner (un fauteuil). **'wadding** *n* bourre *f*; ouate *m*; rembourrage *m*.

waddle [ˈwɔdl] **1.** *n* dandinement *m*; démarche *f* de canard **2.** *vi* se dandiner; marcher en canard; **to w. along,** marcher, avancer, en se dandinant.

wade [weid] *vi* marcher dans l'eau; **to w. across a stream,** passer un ruisseau à gué; **to w. in,** (i) entrer dans l'eau (ii) *F:* intervenir, s'interposer; *F:* **to w. through a book,** venir péniblement à bout d'un livre; **to w. into a pile of work,** se mettre (furieusement) au travail. **'wader** *n* **1.** *Orn:* échassier *m* **2.** personne *f* qui marche dans l'eau **3.** *pl* **waders,** bottes *fpl* d'égoutier, de pêcheur; (bottes) cuissardes (*fpl*).

wafer [ˈweifər] *n Cu:* gaufrette *f*; *Ecc:* hostie *f*; **to cut sth w. thin,** couper qch en tranches très minces.

waffle¹ [ˈwɔfl] *n Cu:* gaufre *f*; **w. iron,** gaufrier *m*.

waffle² *F:* **1.** *n* verbosité *f*; verbiage *m* **2.** *vi* parler pour ne rien dire; faire du remplissage; **he just waffles on,** il parle sans arrêt et pour ne rien dire.

wag [wæg] **1.** *n* agitation *f*, frétillement *m* (de la queue); hochement *m* (de la tête); (*of dog*) **with a w. of his tail,** en remuant la queue. **II.** *v* (**wagged**) **1.** *vtr* (*of dog*) agiter, remuer (la queue); **to w. one's finger at s.o.,** menacer qn du doigt **2.** *vi* s'agiter, se remuer; **his tongue was beginning to wag,** sa langue se déliait; **that'll set people's tongues wagging,** cela va faire parler les gens. **'wagtail** *n Orn:* bergeronnette *f*, hochequeue *m*.

wage [weidʒ] **1.** *n* salaire *m*, paie *f*; **w. packet,** (enveloppe de) paie; **living w.,** minimum vital; **to earn good wages,** être bien payé; toucher un bon salaire; **w. earner,** *NAm:* **w. worker,** (i) salarié, -iée (ii) soutien de famille; **minimum w.** = salaire minimum interprofessionnel de croissance (SMIC) **2.** *vtr* **to w. war,** faire la guerre.

wager [ˈweidʒər] **1.** *n* pari *m*; gageure *f* **2.** *vtr* parier; gager.

waggle [ˈwægl] *vtr & i* (*of dog*) agiter, remuer (la queue); (*of tooth*) (faire) branler; (*of loose screw*) (faire) jouer.

wag(g)on [ˈwægən] *n* **1.** charrette *f*; chariot *m* **2.** *Rail:* wagon découvert (à marchandises); **covered goods w.,** fourgon *m* **3.** *F:* **to be on the (water) w.,** s'abstenir de boissons alcoolisées; **to come off the w.,** se remettre à boire. **'wag(g)oner** *n* charretier *m*, roulier *m*. **'wag(g)onload** *n* (charge *f* de) wagon *m*; charretée *f* (de foin).

waif [weif] *n* (*a*) *Jur:* épave *f* (*b*) **waifs and strays,** (enfants) abandonnés (*mpl*).

wail [weil] **1.** *n* (*a*) cri plaintif; plainte *f*, gémissement *m* (*b*) vagissement *m* (de nouveau-né) (*c*) hurlement *m* (de sirène, du vent) **2.** *vi* (*a*) gémir; se plaindre; (*of newborn child*) vagir; (*of siren, wind*) hurler (*b*) **to w. about sth,** se lamenter sur qch. **'wailing 1.** *a* (cri) plaintif; (enfant) qui gémit **2.** *n* plaintes *fpl*; gémissements *mpl*.

wainscot [ˈweinskət] **1.** *n* lambris *m*; boiseries *fpl* (d'une pièce) **2.** *vtr* (**wainscot(t)ed**) lambrisser. **'wainscot(t)ing** *n* **1.** lambrissage *m* **2.** boiseries *fpl*.

waist [weist] *n* (*of pers*) taille *f*; **w. measurement,** tour de taille; **down, up, to the w.,** jusqu'à la ceinture; **stripped to the w.,** (le) torse nu; **to put one's arm round s.o.'s w.,** prendre qn par la taille; **dress with a short w.,** robe à taille courte. **'waistband** *n* ceinture *f* (de jupe). **'waistcoat** *n* gilet *m*. **'waistline** *n* taille *f*; **to watch one's w.,** surveiller sa ligne.

wait [weit] **I.** *v* **1.** *vi* (*a*) attendre; **w. a moment!** attendez un moment! **to w. for s.o., sth,** attendre qn, qch; **what are you waiting for?** qu'attendez-vous? **w. until tomorrow,** attends jusqu'à demain; **I'll w. until he's ready,** j'attendrai qu'il soit prêt; **to keep s.o. waiting,** faire attendre qn; **he didn't w. to be told twice,** on n'a pas dû le lui dire deux fois; **Com: repairs while you w.,** réparations à la minute; **w. and see!** attendez voir! (**we must**) **w. and see,** il n'y a plus qu'à attendre; **everything comes to him who waits,** tout vient à point à qui sait attendre (*b*) **to w. (at,** *NAm:* **on, table),** servir (à table) **2.** *vtr* *F:* **don't w. dinner for me,** ne m'attendez pas pour vous mettre à table. **II.** *n* (*a*) attente *f*; **it was a long w.,** nous avons dû attendre longtemps; **twenty minutes' w. between the two trains,** battement *m* de vingt minutes entre les deux trains (*b*) **to lie in w.,** être à l'affût; **to lie in w. for s.o.,** guetter qn. **'waiter** *n* garçon *m* (de restaurant); serveur *m* (dans un restaurant); **head w.,** maître *m* d'hôtel; **dumb w.,** monteplats *m inv*. **'waiting** *n* **1.** attente *f*; *Aut:* **no w.,** stationnement interdit; **w. room,** salle, salon, d'attente; **w. list,** liste d'attente **2.** (*in restaurant*) service *m*. **'wait 'on** *vi* **to w. on s.o.,** servir qn; **to w. on s.o. hand and foot,** être aux petits soins auprès de qn. **'waitress** *n* (*pl* **-es**) serveuse *f*. **'wait 'up** *vi* veiller pour attendre qn; **don't w. up for me,** couchez-vous sans m'attendre; ne m'attendez pas pour vous coucher.

waive [weiv] *vtr* renoncer à, abandonner (ses prétentions); déroger à (un principe); ne pas insister sur (une condition). **'waiver** *n* abandon *m* (d'un droit); dérogation *f*.

wake¹ [weik] *n* (*a*) *Nau:* sillage *m*; **to be in the w. of a ship,** être dans les eaux d'un navire (*b*) **in the w. of the storm,** à la suite de la tempête; **to follow in s.o.'s w.,** marcher sur les traces de qn.

wake² *n* **1.** (*Ireland*) veillée *f* mortuaire **2.** (*N. of Eng.*) **wakes week,** la semaine de congé annuel.

wake³ *v* (*pt* **woke** [wouk], **waked** [weikt]; *pp* **woke, waked, woken** [ˈwoukən]) **1.** *vi* (*a*) veiller; être éveillé; rester éveillé (*b*) **to w. (up),** se réveiller; **w. up!** (i) réveillez-vous! (ii) F: secoue-toi! he's **waking up to the truth**, la vérité commence à se faire jour (dans son esprit); to **w. up to find oneself famous**, se réveiller célèbre **2.** *vtr* éveiller (un souvenir); to **w. s.o. (up)**, réveiller qn; F: **he needs something to w. him up**, il lui faut quelque chose pour le secouer; F: **it's enough to w. the dead**, c'est (un bruit) à réveiller les morts. **'wakeful** *a* (a) éveillé; peu disposé à dormir (b) sans sommeil; **w. night**, nuit blanche (c) vigilant. **'wakefulness** *n* (a) insomnie *f* (b) vigilance *f*. **'waken 1.** *vtr* (a) réveiller (qn) (b) éveiller (une émotion) **2.** *vi* se réveiller. **'wakening** *n* réveil *m*. **'wakey** *int* F: **w. (w.)! debout!** réveillez-vous! **'waking 1.** *a* **w. hours**, heures de veille **2.** *n* **between sleeping and w.**, entre la veille et le sommeil.

Wales [weilz] *Prn* pays *m* de Galles; **North W., South W.**, la Galles du Nord, du Sud; **New South W.**, la Nouvelle-Galles du Sud; **the Prince of W.**, le Prince de Galles.

walk [wɔːk] **I.** *v* **1.** *vi* (a) marcher; to **w. on all fours**, marcher à quatre pattes; to **w. with a limp**, boiter (en marchant); to **w. in one's sleep**, être somnambule; **I'll w. with you**, je vais vous accompagner (b) *(as opposed to drive)* aller à pied; to **w. home**, rentrer à pied; to **w. round the town**, faire le tour de la ville (à pied) (c) *(for pleasure)* se promener, faire des promenades (à pied); **I like walking**, j'aime bien me promener (à pied) **2.** *vtr* to **w. the streets**, courir les rues; *(of prostitute)* faire le trottoir; to **w. s.o. off his legs, feet**, épuiser qn à force de le faire marcher; **I'll w. you home**, je vous raccompagne à la maison; to **w. a horse, a dog**, conduire, promener un cheval; promener un chien; to **w. the plank**, subir le supplice de la planche; **you can w. it in ten minutes**, vous en avez pour dix minutes à pied. **II.** *n* (a) marche *f*; **it's an hour's w. from here**, c'est à une heure de marche d'ici; **it's only a short walk from here**, on peut facilement s'y rendre à pied (b) promenade *f* (à pied); to **go for a w.**, aller se promener, faire une promenade; to **take the dog for a w.**, promener le chien; **sponsored w.**, marche entreprise au profit d'une œuvre de bienfaisance (c) démarche *f*; **I know him by his w.**, je le reconnais à sa démarche (d) allée *f* (de jardin); avenue *f*; **covered w.**, allée couverte (e) **w. of life**, (i) couche, classe, condition, sociale (ii) métier *m*, carrière *f*. **'walkabout** *n* bain *m* de foule. **'walk a'cross** *vi* to **w. across to speak to s.o.**, traverser (la rue) pour parler à qn. **'walk a'way** *vi* s'en aller; partir; *Sp:* to **w. a. from a competitor**, distancer un concurrent; F: to **w. away with sth**, emporter qch (en partant); voler qch. **'walker** *n* marcheur, -euse; promeneur, -euse; piéton *m*; **he's a good w.**, il est bon marcheur; **he's a fast w.**, il marche vite. **'walkie-'talkie** *n* talkie-walkie *m*. **'walk 'in** *vi* entrer; **(please) w. in**, entrez sans frapper. **'walking 1.** *n* la marche; promenades *fpl* (à pied); to **like w.**, aimer la marche; **w. shoes**, chaussures de marche; **w. stick**, canne *f*; **it's within w. distance**, on peut s'y rendre à pied **2.** *a* F: **he's a w. dictionary**, c'est un dictionnaire ambulant. **'walk 'into** *vtr* entrer dans (une pièce); to **w. i. a wall**, se heurter à, contre, un mur; **I walked into him in the street**, je l'ai rencontré par hasard dans la rue. **'walk 'off 1.** *vi* (a) s'en aller, partir (b) F: to **w. o. with the silver**,

décamper avec l'argenterie (volée); **he walked off with the first prize**, il a gagné facilement le premier prix **2.** *vtr* to **w. o. one's lunch**, faire une promenade de digestion. **'walk 'on** *vi Th:* remplir un rôle de figurant(e). **'walk 'out** *vi* (a) sortir; F: to **w. o. on s.o.**, (i) abandonner qn (ii) quitter qn en colère (b) *Ind:* F: se mettre en grève. **'walkout** *n Ind:* F: grève *f*; to **cause a w.**, provoquer le départ d'un groupe (en signe de protestation). **'walk 'over** *vi* to **w. o. to s.o.**, s'avancer vers qn. **'walkover** *n* F: victoire *f* facile. **'walk 'up** *vi* to **w. up to s.o.**, s'avancer vers qn; s'approcher de qn; to **w. up to the fifth floor**, monter (à pied) jusqu'au cinquième (étage), *NAm:* jusqu'au quatrième; to **w. up and down**, (i) monter et descendre (un escalier, une colline) à pied (ii) faire les cent pas. **'walk-up** *a & n NAm:* (immeuble *m*) sans ascenseur. **'walkway** *n esp NAm:* passage *m* (pour piétons).

wall [wɔːl] **1.** *n* (a) mur *m*; **main walls**, gros murs; **cavity w.**, mur double; **surrounding w.**, mur d'enceinte; **blank w.**, mur plein; to **come up against a blank w.**, se heurter à un mur; **you might just as well talk to a brick w.**, autant vaut parler à un sourd; **walls have ears**, les murs ont des oreilles; to **bang one's head against a brick wall**, se cogner, se taper, la tête contre les murs; **you're driving me up the wall**, vous allez me rendre fou; to **have one's back to the w.**, être acculé au mur; **the weakest always go to the w.**, le plus faible est toujours battu; to **go to the w.**, (i) succomber, perdre la partie (ii) faire faillite; to **leave only the bare walls standing**, ne laisser que les quatre murs; **w. painting**, peinture murale; **w. map**, carte murale; **w. clock**, pendule murale (b) muraille *f*; le mur (de Berlin, d'Adrien); **the Great W. of China**, la muraille de Chine; **tariff walls**, barrières douanières (c) paroi *f* (de la poitrine, d'une cellule, *Min:* d'une galerie); flanc *m* (d'un pneu) **2.** *vtr* to **w. (in)**, murer, entourer de murs; to **w. up**, murer (une porte); **walled garden**, jardin entouré de murs. **'wallflower** *n Bot:* giroflée *f*; F: *(of pers at dance)* to **be a w.**, faire tapisserie. **'wallpaper** *n* papier peint. **'wall-to-'wall** *a* **w.-to-w. carpet(ing)**, moquette *f*.

wallaby ['wɔləbi] *n (pl wallabies)* Z: wallaby *m*.

wallet ['wɔlit] *n* portefeuille *m*.

Walloon [wɔ'luːn] **1.** *a* wallon **2.** *n* (a) *(pers)* Wallon, -onne (b) *Ling:* wallon *m*.

wallop ['wɔləp] F: **1.** *n* (a) gros coup, fessée *f* (b) **down he went with a w.**, et patatras, le voilà par terre! **2.** *vtr* rosser (qn), flanquer une tournée à (qn). **'walloping** F: **1.** *a* énorme; **a w. (great) lie**, un mensonge phénoménal **2.** *n* volée *f* (de coups); rossée *f*, raclée *f*.

wallow ['wɔləu] *vi (of animal)* se vautrer, se rouler dans la boue; *(of ship)* être ballotté (par les flots); *(of pers)* to **w. in blood**, se rouler dans le sang; F: to **be wallowing in money**, rouler sur l'or; to **w. in self-pity**, s'attendrir sur soi-même.

walnut ['wɔːlnʌt] *n* (a) noix *f* (b) **w. (tree)**, noyer *m*; **w. oil**, huile de noix; **w. cake**, gâteau aux noix (c) *(bois m de)* noyer; (meuble) de, en, noyer.

walrus ['wɔːlrəs] *n (pl walruses)* Z: morse *m*; F: **w. moustache**, moustache à la gauloise.

waltz [wɔːls] **1.** *n* valse *f* **2.** *vi* valser; to **w. in, out, off**, entrer, sortir, partir, d'un pas joyeux.

wan [wɔn] *a* pâlot; blême; (*of light*) blafard; **a w. smile,** un pâle sourire.

wand [wɔnd] *n* **1.** baguette *f* magique, de fée **2.** bâton *m* (de commandement); verge *f* (d'huissier).

wander ['wɔndər] *vi* (*a*) errer (sans but); se promener au hasard; (*of river, road*) serpenter; **to w.** à l'aventure; **to let one's thoughts w.,** laisser vaguer ses pensées; **to w. away from the subject,** s'écarter du sujet, faire une digression; **his mind wanders at times,** il a des absences; **to w. off a path,** s'éloigner du chemin (*b*) (*of pers*) divaguer; radoter. '**wanderer** *n* vagabond, -onde; **the w. has returned,** notre voyageur nous est revenu. '**wandering 1.** *a* (*a*) errant, vagabond; **the w. Jew,** le Juif errant (*b*) (esprit) distrait (*c*) (discours) incohérent **2.** *n* (*a*) vagabondage *m*; pérégrinations *fpl* (*b*) rêverie *f* (*c*) *Med:* égarement *m* (de l'esprit); divagation *f*. '**wanderlust** *n* la passion des voyages; l'esprit *m* d'aventure.

wane [wein] **1.** *vi* (*of moon, power*) décroître, décliner; (beauté) qui se perd; (*of enthusiasm*) s'attiédir **2.** *n* déclin *m*; moon on the w., lune à son décours, qui décroît. '**waning** *n* décours *m* (de la lune); déclin.

wangle ['wæŋgl] *F:* **1.** *vtr* obtenir (qch) par subterfuge; resquiller; **to w. a week's leave,** carotter huit jours de congé **2.** *n* moyen détourné; truc *m*; **the whole thing's a w.,** tout ça, c'est de la resquille, c'est fricoté. '**wangler** *n F:* resquilleur, -euse. '**wangling** *n F:* fricotage *m*; resquille; le système D.

want [wɔnt] **I.** *v* **1.** *vi* manquer (de qch); être dépourvu (de qch); **to w. for nothing,** ne manquer de rien **2.** *vtr & i* (*a*) manquer de, ne pas avoir (qch) (*b*) (*of pers*) avoir besoin de (qch); (*of thg*) exiger, réclamer (qch); **he wants rest,** il a besoin de repos; **this work wants a lot of patience,** ce travail exige beaucoup de patience; **you w. to see it!** tu devrais le voir! il faut voir ça! **have you everything you w.?** avez-vous tout ce qu'il vous faut? **I've (got) all I w.,** j'en ai assez; **that's just what I w.,** voilà juste ce qu'il me faut, juste mon affaire; **do you w. a job?** (i) est-ce que tu cherches un emploi? (ii) ça ne te gênerait pas de m'aider? **wanted, a good cook,** on demande une bonne cuisinière; **your hair wants cutting,** vous avez besoin de vous faire couper les cheveux; **it only wants a coat of paint,** il ne manque plus qu'une couche de peinture; *F:* **that wants a bit of doing,** ce n'est pas si facile que ça (*c*) désirer, vouloir; **he knows what he wants,** il sait ce qu'il veut; **how much do you w. for it?** c'est combien? *Iron:* **you don't w. much!** tu n'es pas difficile! **you're wanted (on the phone),** on vous demande (au téléphone); **we're not wanted here,** nous sommes de trop ici; **to be wanted by the police,** être recherché par la police; **I don't w. him,** je n'ai pas besoin de lui; **to w. s.o. (sexually),** désirer qn; **what does he w. with me?** que me veut-il? **I w. to tell you about it,** je voudrais vous en parler; **I w. to see him,** j'ai envie de le voir; **I don't w. to, je n'en ai pas envie; I don't w. him to see me,** je ne veux pas qu'il me voie; **I don't w. it known,** je ne veux pas que cela se sache. **II.** *n* **1.** manque *m*, défaut *m*; **for w. of something better,** faute de mieux; **for w. of something (better) to do,** par désœuvrement **2.** indigence *f*, misère *f* **3.** besoin *m*; **a long-felt w.,** une lacune à combler; *Journ:* **w. ad,** offre *f* d'emploi. '**wanted** *a* (*a*) désiré, voulu (*b*) recherché par la police. '**wanting 1.** *a* **to be w.,** faire défaut;

w. in intelligence, dépourvu d'intelligence **2.** *prep* sans; **he arrived w. money,** il est arrivé sans argent.

wanton ['wɔntən] *a* **w. cruelty,** cruauté gratuite; **w. destruction,** destruction voulue, pour le simple plaisir de détruire. '**wantonly** *adv* (blesser, insulter) sans motif.

war [wɔːr] **1.** *n* guerre *f*; **total w.,** guerre totale; **civil w.,** guerre civile; **cold w.,** guerre froide; **world w.,** guerre mondiale; **to make, wage, w. on s.o.,** faire la guerre à, contre, qn; **to go to w.,** entrer en guerre; **to go off to w.,** partir pour la guerre; **to be at w.,** être en guerre; **w. of words,** dispute *f*; *F:* **you look as if you've been in the wars,** vous avez l'air de vous être battu; **w. clouds were gathering,** il y avait des menaces de guerre; **w. game,** kriegspiel *m*; jeu de stratégie militaire; **w. correspondent,** correspondant de guerre; **w. cry,** cri de guerre; **w. dance,** danse guerrière; *Fin:* **w. loan,** emprunt de guerre; **w. grave,** sépulture militaire; **w. widow,** veuve de guerre; **w. cemetery,** cimetière militaire; **w. memorial,** monument aux morts **2.** *vi* (**warred**) faire la guerre (**against sth,** à qch). '**warfare** *n* la guerre; **class w.,** la lutte des classes. '**warhead** *n* (*a*) cône *m* de charge (d'une torpille) (*b*) tête *f*, ogive *f* (de fusée); **nuclear w.,** tête nucléaire. '**warhorse** *n* cheval de bataille; *F:* **an old w.,** (i) un vieux militaire (ii) un vétéran de la politique. '**warlike** *a* (exploit) guerrier. '**warmonger** *n* belliciste *mf*. '**warpaint** *n* **1.** peinture *f* de guerre (des Peaux-Rouges) **2.** *F:* (*of woman*) **to put on the w.,** se maquiller. '**warpath** *n F:* **to be on the w.,** chercher noise; être d'une humeur massacrante. '**warring** *a* **w. nations,** nations en guerre. '**warship** *n* navire *m* de guerre. '**wartime** *n* temps *m* de guerre; **on a w. footing, under w. conditions,** sur le pied de guerre.

warble ['wɔːbl] **1.** *vi* (*of bird*) gazouiller **2.** *n* gazouillement *m*; gazouillis *m*. '**warbler** *n Orn:* (*a*) bec-fin *m* (*b*) fauvette *f*. '**warbling** *n* gazouillement; gazouillis.

ward [wɔːd] **I.** *n* **1.** pupille *mf*; *Jur:* **w. in Chancery,** pupille sous tutelle judiciaire **2.** (*a*) salle *f* (d'hôpital); **emergency w.,** salle d'urgence (*b*) quartier *m* (d'une prison) **3.** circonscription électorale. *vtr* **to w. off a blow,** parer un coup; **to w. off an illness,** prévenir une maladie. '**warden** *n* (*a*) directeur *m* (d'une institution) (*b*) gardien *m* (d'un parc) (*c*) **traffic w.,** contractuel, -elle (qui surveille le stationnement des voitures). '**warder** *n*, '**wardress** *n* gardien, -ienne (de prison, de musée). '**wardrobe** *n* (*a*) (*NAm:* = closet) (*furniture*) armoire *f*, penderie *f* (*b*) (= clothes) garde-robe *f*; *Th:* **w. keeper, w. mistress,** costumier, -ière. '**wardroom** *n Navy:* carré *m* des officiers.

ware [wɛər] *n* (*a*) *coll* articles fabriqués; ustensiles *mpl* (en aluminium) (*b*) *pl* marchandises *fpl*; **to boost one's wares,** vanter ses marchandises. '**warehouse** *n* entrepôt *m*; magasin *m*; **bonded w.,** entrepôt en douane. '**warehouseman** *n* (*pl* -men) (*a*) magasinier *m* (*b*) garde-magasin *m*.

warm [wɔːm] **I.** *a* (*a*) chaud; **to be w.,** (i) (*of water*) être chaud (ii) (*of pers*) avoir chaud; **to get w.,** (*of water*) chauffer; (*of pers*) se réchauffer; **I can't get w.,** je ne peux pas me réchauffer; (*in game*) **you're getting w.,** vous brûlez; **to keep oneself w.,** se tenir au chaud;

porter des vêtements chauds; **w. oven,** four moyen; **w. coat,** manteau chaud; (*of weather*) **it's w.,** il fait chaud; *Meteor:* **w. front,** front chaud; **the water is just w.,** l'eau est à peine chaude (*b*) chaleureux; **w. welcome,** accueil chaleureux; **w. heart,** cœur généreux, chaud; **it's w. work,** c'est une rude besogne (*c*) (*of colour*) chaud; (*of interior*) accueillant. **II.** *n* **in the w.,** au chaud; **come and have a w.,** venez vous réchauffer. **III.** *v* 1. *vtr* chauffer; **to w. oneself by the fire,** s'asseoir auprès du feu pour se réchauffer; **it warms the heart,** ça réchauffe le cœur 2. *vi* (se) chauffer; se réchauffer; **to w. to s.o.,** trouver qn de plus en plus sympathique. **'warm-'blooded** *a Z:* à sang chaud. **'warmer** *n* **bottle w.,** chauffe-biberon *m*. **'warm-'hearted** *a* au cœur chaud, généreux. **'warming** *n* chauffage *m*; **w. pan,** bassinoire *f*. **'warmly** *adv* (*a*) (vêtu) chaudement (*b*) (applaudir) chaudement; (remercier qn) chaleureusement; (répondre) vivement, avec chaleur. **'warmth** *n* (*a*) chaleur *f* (*b*) cordialité *f*, chaleur (d'un accueil) (*c*) emportement *m*, vivacité *f*. **'warm 'up** *v* 1. *vtr* chauffer; réchauffer; faire réchauffer (un plat) 2. *vi* s'échauffer; s'animer; (*of pers*) devenir plus cordial; **the lecturer was warming up to his subject,** le conférencier s'animait peu à peu.

warn [wɔ:n] *vtr* avertir; prévenir; **to w. s.o. of a danger,** avertir qn d'un danger; **to w. s.o. against sth,** mettre qn en garde contre qch; **he warned her not to go,** il lui a conseillé fortement de ne pas y aller; **you have been warned!** vous voilà prévenu! **I shan't w. you again,** tenez-vous-le pour dit; **to w. the police,** alerter la police. **'warning** 1. *a* (geste) avertisseur, d'avertissement 2. *n* avertissement *m*; **air-raid w.,** alerte *f*; **w. device,** avertisseur *m* (*b*) avertissement, avis *m*, préavis *m*; **without w.,** sans préavis; à l'improviste; sans prévenir; **to give s.o. fair w.,** donner à qn un avertissement formel; **let this be a w. to you,** que cela vous serve de leçon, d'exemple.

warp [wɔ:p] **I.** *v* 1. *vtr* (*a*) gauchir, voiler (le bois, une tôle); fausser, pervertir (l'esprit) (*b*) *Tex:* ourdir (*c*) *Nau:* touer (un navire) 2. *vi* se déformer; gondoler; (*of timber*) gauchir; (*of wheel*) se voiler; **wood that warps,** bois qui travaille. **II.** *n* 1. *Tex:* chaîne *f* 2. *Nau:* amarre *f*, touée *f* 3. voilure *f*, courbure *f*, gauchissement *m* (d'une planche). **'warped** *a* (*a*) (bois) gondolé, gauchi; (*of wheel*) voilé (*b*) (esprit) perverti, faussé. **'warping** *n* 1. (*a*) gauchissement *m* (du bois); gondolage *m* (de la tôle) (*b*) perversion *f* (de l'esprit) 2. *Tex:* ourdissage *m*.

warrant ['wɔrənt] 1. *n* (*a*) garantie *f*; justification *f* (*b*) mandat *m* (d'arrêt, de perquisition); **w. for payment,** ordonnance *f* de paiement; **travel w.,** feuille *f* de route; *Mil* **w. officer** = adjudant *m* 2. *vtr* (*a*) garantir (qch); **it won't happen again, I w. you!** cela n'arrivera pas deux fois, je vous en réponds! (*b*) justifier; **nothing can w. such behaviour,** rien ne justifie une pareille conduite. **'warranted** *a Com:* garanti. **'warranty** *n* (*pl* **-ies**) (*a*) autorisation *f*; justification *f* (*b*) garantie *f*.

warren ['wɔrən] *n* (rabbit) **w.,** (i) garenne *f* (ii) dédale *m*, labyrinthe *m* (de ruelles).

warrior ['wɔriər] *n* guerrier *m*, soldat *m*; **the Unknown W.,** le Soldat inconnu.

Warsaw ['wɔ:sɔ:] *Prn* Varsovie *f*; **W. Pact,** pacte de Varsovie.

wart [wɔ:t] *n* verrue *f*; **to paint s.o. warts and all,** peindre qn sans le flatter. **'warthog** *n Z:* phacochère *m*.

wary ['wɛəri] *a* (**-ier, -iest**) (*a*) prudent, circonspect (*b*) **to be w. of sth, s.o.,** se méfier de qch, qn. **'warily** *adv* prudemment, avec circonspection. **'wariness** *n* prudence *f*, circonspection *f*.

was [wɔz, wəz] *see* **be.**

wash [wɔʃ] **I.** *v* 1. *vtr* (*a*) laver; **to w. (oneself),** se laver, faire sa toilette; **to w. one's hands, one's hair,** se laver les mains, la tête; **to w. one's hands of sth,** se laver les mains de qch; **to w. sth in cold water,** laver qch à l'eau froide (*b*) blanchir, lessiver, laver (le linge); **hand w. only,** laver à la main seulement; **to w. sth clean,** bien nettoyer qch (en le lavant); (*of sea*) **to w. sth ashore,** rejeter qch sur le rivage; **washed away by the tide,** emporté par la mer; **he was washed overboard,** il a été enlevé par une vague 2. *vi* (*of pers*) se laver; **material that won't w.,** tissu qui ne se lave pas; *F:* **that (story) won't w.!** ça ne prend pas! **the waves were washing over the deck,** les vagues balayaient le pont. **II.** *n* 1. (*a*) lavage *m*; **to give sth a w.,** laver qch; (*of pers*) **to have a w.,** se laver; faire un brin de toilette (*b*) **I send the sheets to the w.,** j'envoie les draps à la blanchisserie; *F:* **it'll all come out in the w.,** (i) la vérité se saura un jour ou l'autre (ii) ça se tassera 2. **colour w.,** badigeon *m* 3. *Nau:* sillage *m*, remous *m* (d'un navire). **'washable** *a* lavable. **'wash-and-'wear** *a* (chemise) qui ne nécessite aucun repassage. **'washbasin** *n* lavabo *m*. **'washbowl** *n* cuvette *f*; bassine *f*. **'washcloth** *n NAm:* (*Br* = **facecloth**) = gant *m* de toilette. **'washday** *n* jour *m* de lessive. **'wash 'down** *vtr* (*a*) laver à grande eau (*b*) *F:* **to w. d. one's dinner with a glass of beer,** faire descendre son dîner avec un verre de bière. **'wash'down** *n* toilette *f* rapide; **I'll give the car a w.,** je vais rapidement laver la voiture. **'washer** *n* (*a*) (*pers*) laveur, -euse; **w. up, w. upper,** laveur, -euse, de vaisselle; (*in restaurant*) plongeur *m* (*b*) machine *f* à laver (*c*) *Aut:* **windscreen,** *NAm:* **windshield, w.,** lave-glace *m* (*d*) (*for tap*) rondelle *f* (de caoutchouc). **'washerwoman** *n* blanchisseuse *f*. **'wash-house** *n* (*a*) buanderie *f* (*b*) laverie *f* (*c*) lavoir *m*. **'washing** *n* (*a*) lavage *m*; ablutions *fpl* (*b*) lessive *f* (du linge); **w. day,** jour de lessive; **w. machine,** machine à laver; **w. powder,** lessive (en poudre); détergent *m* (pour le linge); *Aut:* **w. bay,** installation de lavage (*c*) linge *m* (à blanchir) 3. **w. up,** la vaisselle; (*in restaurant*) la plonge; **to do the w. up,** faire la vaisselle; **w.-up liquid,** lave-vaisselle *m*; détergent *m* pour la vaisselle; **w.-up machine,** lave-vaisselle; **w.-up bowl** (*NAm:* = **dishpan**), bassine *f* (à vaisselle). **'washleather** *n* (peau *f* de) chamois *m*. **'wash 'off** *vtr* enlever, effacer, (qch) par le lavage, à l'eau. **'wash 'out** 1. *vtr* enlever (une tache) (par le lavage); **to w. o. a few handkerchiefs,** laver (rapidement) quelques mouchoirs; *F:* **I'm completely washed out,** je suis complètement vanné, à plat; *Sp:* (*of match*) **to be washed out,** être décommandé à cause de la pluie 2. *vi* (*of stain*) partir à l'eau, au lavage. **'washout** *n F:* (*a*) fiasco *m*; four *m* (*b*) **he's a w.,** c'est un raté. **'washrag** *n NAm:* = **washcloth. 'washroom** *n* (*a*) cabinet *m* de toilette (*b*) les toilettes; **(where is) the w. please?** où sont les toilettes s'il vous plaît? **'washstand** *n* (*a*) table *f* de toilette (*b*) *NAm:*

lavabo *m.* '**wash 'up** *vtr & i* (*a*) to w. up (the dishes) (*NAm:* = **to do the dishes**), faire la vaisselle (*b*) *NAm:* (*Br* = **to have a wash**) (*of pers*) se laver (*c*) (*of sea*) rejeter (qn, qch) sur le rivage; *F:* **to be washed up**, être ruiné, fichu.

wasn't = was not *see* be.

wasp [wɔsp] *n* guêpe *f*; **wasps' nest**, guêpier *m.* '**waspish** *a F:* irritable; méchant; **w. tone**, ton aigre, irrité.

waste [weist] **1.** *vtr* (*a*) consumer, user; **wasted by disease**, miné, amaigri, par la maladie (*b*) gaspiller (son argent); laisser passer (une occasion); **to w. one's time**, perdre son temps; **it's just wasting one's words!** c'est parler en pure perte! **you're wasting your energy**, vous vous dépensez inutilement; **the joke was wasted on him**, il n'a pas compris la plaisanterie; **wasted life**, vie manquée; **w. not, want not**, qui épargne gagne **2.** *a* **w. land, w. ground,** (i) terre *f* inculte (ii) (*in town*) terrain *m* vague; (*of ground*) **to lie w.**, rester en friche; **to lay w.**, dévaster, ravager (un pays) **3.** *n* (*a*) région *f* inculte; désert *m* (*b*) gaspillage *m* (d'argent); **w. of time**, perte *f* de temps (*c*) déchets *mpl*, rebut *m*; **household w.**, ordures *fpl*; **radioactive w.**, déchets radioactifs; **w. disposal unit**, broyeur à ordures. '**wastage** *n* (*a*) perte *f* (de chaleur) (*b*) gaspillage *m.* '**waste a'way** *vi* dépérir. '**wastebin**, *NAm:* '**wastebasket** *n* corbeille *f* à papier. '**wasted** *a* (argent) gaspillé; (temps) perdu; **w. effort**, peine perdue. '**wasteful** *a* gaspilleur; prodigue; **w. habits**, habitudes de gaspillage. '**wastefully** *adv* avec prodigalité; en pure perte. '**wastefulness** *n* prodigalité *f*; gaspillage *m.* '**wasteland** *n* (i) terrain vague (ii) désert (culturel). **waste'paper** *n* papier *m* de rebut; **w. basket, bin**, corbeille à papier. '**waster** *n* **1.** gaspilleur, -euse; **time w.**, personne qui perd son temps; (travail) qui vous fait perdre votre temps **2.** vaurien *m*, propre *m* à rien. '**wasting** *n* gaspillage; **w. (away)**, dépérissement *m.*

watch [wɔtʃ] **I.** *n* **1.** garde *f*; surveillance *f*; **to be on the w.,** (i) être en observation; se tenir aux aguets (ii) être sur ses gardes; **to be on the w. for s.o.**, guetter qn; **to keep a w. on s.o.**, surveiller qn; **w. committee**, comité qui veille à l'ordre public (de la commune); **w. tower**, tour d'observation, du guet **2.** *Hist:* **the w.**, la ronde de nuit **3.** *Nau:* (*a*) quart *m*; **to be on w.**, être de quart; **officer of the w.**, officier de quart (*b*) (*men*) bordée *f* **4.** montre *f*; **it's six o'clock by my w.**, il est six heures à ma montre. **II.** *v* **1.** *vtr* (*a*) observer; regarder attentivement; surveiller (qn); **we are being watched**, on nous observe, nous regarde; **to w. the expenses**, regarder à la dépense; **to w. one's step**, (i) prendre garde de ne pas tomber (ii) éviter de faire un faux pas; **w. it!** attention! **w. your head**, attention de ne pas vous frapper la tête; **w. your language**, surveiller votre langage; **w. you don't fall**, prenez garde de ne pas tomber (*b*) regarder; voir; **I watched her working**, je la regardais travailler; **to w. television**, regarder la télévision; **to w. a football match**, assister à un match de football; regarder un match de football à la télévision (*c*) **to w. s.o.'s interests**, veiller aux intérêts de qn **2.** *vi* **to w. (out) for s.o.**, attendre qn; guetter qn; **w. out!** prenez garde! attention! **w. out for X!** gare à X! '**watchdog** *n* chien *m* de garde. '**watcher** *n* **bird w.**, observateur, -trice (des mœurs) des oiseaux.

'**watchful** *a* vigilant; alerte; attentif. '**watchfully** *adv* avec vigilance. '**watchfulness** *n* vigilance *f.* '**watching** *n* (*a*) surveillance *f* (*b*) **bird w.**, observation *f* (des mœurs) des oiseaux. '**watchmaker** *n* horloger *m.* '**watchmaking** *n* horlogerie *f.* '**watchman** *n* (*pl* -**men**) gardien *m*; *Nau:* homme *m* de garde; *Ind:* **night w.**, veilleur *m* de nuit. '**watchword** *n* mot *m* d'ordre.

water ['wɔːtər] **I.** *n* (*a*) eau *f*; **salt w.**, eau salée; eau de mer; **fresh w.**, eau douce; (*for drinking*) eau fraîche; **a drink of w.**, un verre d'eau; **drinking w.**, eau potable; **hot, cold, w.**, eau chaude, froide; **hot w. bottle**, bouillotte *f*; **to throw cold w. on a scheme**, décourager un projet; *F:* **to be in hot w.**, être dans le pétrin; **to have w. laid on**, (i) faire installer (ii) avoir, l'eau courante; **running w.**, eau courante; (*in hotel*) **hot and cold w. in all rooms**, eau courante (chaude et froide) dans toutes les chambres; **to turn on the w.**, ouvrir l'eau; ouvrir le robinet; (*at spa*) **to take the waters**, prendre les eaux; faire une cure; **the waters of a river, of a lake**, les eaux d'une rivière, d'un lac; **on land and w.**, sur terre et sur eau; by w., par mer; par bateau; **to be under w.**, être inondé, submergé; **to swim under w.**, nager sous l'eau; **above w.**, à flot; surnageant; **to keep one's head above w.**, (i) se maintenir à la surface (ii) *Fig:* faire face à ses engagements (*c*) **high, low, w.**, marée haute, basse; *F:* **to be in deep water(s)**, être dans de mauvais draps; *Prov:* **still waters run deep**, il n'y a pire eau que l'eau qui dort; *Med:* **w. on the brain**, hydrocéphalie *f*; **w. on the knee**, épanchement de synovie; **to make, pass, w.**, uriner (*b*) transparence *f*, eau (d'un diamant); orient *m* (d'une perle); **of the first w.**, de la plus belle eau (*c*) **w. bed**, matelas à eau; **w. biscuit** (*NAm:* = **cracker**), craquelin *m*; **w. heater**, chauffe-eau *m inv*; **w. ice**, sorbet *m*; **w. lily**, nénuphar *m*; **w. main**, conduite principale d'eau; **w. melon**, pastèque *f*; **w. polo**, water-polo *m*; **w. power**, force *f* hydraulique; **w. rat**, rat *m* d'eau; **w. rate**, taxe d'abonnement à l'eau; **w. skiing**, ski nautique; **w. softener**, adoucisseur d'eau; **w. supply**, service des eaux (d'une ville); *Geol:* **w. table**, nappe aquifère; **w. tower**, château d'eau. **II.** *v* **1.** *vtr* (*a*) arroser (son jardin; (*of river*) une région (*b*) couper (son vin) (*c*) faire boire, abreuver (des bêtes) (*d*) *Tex:* moirer (la soie) **2.** *vi* (*of eyes*) pleurer, larmoyer; **it made his mouth w.**, il en avait l'eau à la bouche. '**watercolour**, *NAm:* -**color** *n* aquarelle *f*; **watercolours**, couleurs *fpl* à l'eau (pour aquarelle); **to paint in watercolours**, faire de l'aquarelle. '**watercourse** *n* cours d'eau. '**watercress** *n* cresson *m* de fontaine. '**water 'down** *vtr* diluer, délayer (un liquide); atténuer (une expression); édulcorer (une histoire). '**watered** *a Tex:* (soie) moirée. '**waterfall** *n* chute *f* d'eau; cascade *f.* '**waterfowl** *n* (*no pl*) oiseau *m* aquatique; *coll* gibier *m* d'eau; sauvagine *f.* '**waterfront** *n* bord *m* de l'eau, de mer; les quais *m*; *NAm:* **on the w.**, chez les dockers. '**watering** *n* (*a*) arrosage *m* (du jardin); **w. can**, arrosoir *m* (*b*) dilution *f* (d'une boisson) (*c*) abreuvage *m* (des bêtes) (*d*) larmoiement *m* (des yeux). '**waterless** *a* sans eau. '**waterline** *n* ligne *f* de flottaison. '**waterlogged** *a* (terrain) imbibé d'eau, détrempé. '**watermark** *n* (*a*) filigrane *m* (*b*) *Nau:* laisse *f* de mer. '**waterproof 1.** *a & n Cl:* imperméable (*m*) **2.** *vtr* imperméabiliser.

'**watershed** n Geog: ligne f de partage des eaux; Fig: point décisif; tournant m. '**waterside** n bord m de l'eau; **along the w.**, le long de la rive. '**waterspout** n Meteor: trombe f. '**watertight** a étanche (à l'eau); **w. regulations**, règlement qui a prévu tous les cas. '**waterway** n voie f navigable. '**waterworks** npl 1. usine f de distribution d'eau 2. F: (a) **to turn on the w.**, se mettre à pleurer (b) **there's something wrong with my w.**, j'ai des ennuis avec mes voies urinaires. '**watery** a aqueux; qui contient de l'eau; noyé d'eau; (yeux) larmoyants; (potage) clair, peu consistant.

Waterloo [wɔːtə'luː] Prn **the Battle of W.**, la bataille de Waterloo; **to meet one's W.**, arriver à un échec total.

watt [wɔt] n El: watt m. '**wattage** n El: puissance f, consommation f, en watts.

wave [weiv] I. n 1. (in sea) vague f; Art: **new w.**, nouvelle vague; **to come in waves**, arriver par vagues; **w. of enthusiasm**, vague d'enthousiasme 2. Ph: onde f; **long waves**, grandes ondes; **medium, short, waves**, ondes moyennes, ondes courtes 3. ondulation f (des cheveux); **to have a natural w. (in one's hair)**, avoir des cheveux qui ondulent naturellement; **permanent w.**, permanente f 4. balancement m, ondoiement m; **with a w. of his hand**, d'un geste, d'un signe, de la main. II. v 1. vi (a) s'agiter; flotter (au vent) (b) **to w. to s.o.**, saluer qn de la main; faire signe à qn (de la main); **I waved to him to stop**, je lui ai fait signe d'arrêter (c) **my hair waves naturally**, mes cheveux ondulent naturellement 2. vtr (a) agiter (le bras, un mouchoir); brandir (une canne, un parapluie); **to w. one's hand**, faire signe de la main; **to w. goodbye to s.o.**, dire au revoir de la main; agiter la main, son mouchoir, en signe d'adieu (b) **to w. s.o. on**, faire signe à qn de continuer, d'avancer (c) **to have one's hair waved**, se faire faire une permanente. '**wave a'bout, a'round** vtr agiter (dans tous les sens). '**wave a'side, 'wave a'way** vtr écarter (qn) d'un geste; faire signe à qn de s'éloigner; **to w. aside an objection**, écarter une objection. '**waveband** n Ph: bande f de fréquences. **waved** a ondulé. '**wavelength** n Ph: longueur f d'onde; F: **we're not on the same w.**, on n'est pas sur la même longueur d'onde. '**wavy** a (-ier, -iest) onduleux; ondulé; (ligne) tremblée, onduleuse; (chevelure, surface) ondulée.

waver ['weivər] vi (a) (of flame) vaciller, trembloter (b) (of pers) vaciller, hésiter; (of courage) défaillir. **waverer** n indécis, -ise; irrésolu, -ue. '**wavering** 1. a (a) (of flame) vacillant, tremblotant (b) (of pers) irrésolu, hésitant; (of voice) tremblotant; défaillant 2. n (a) tremblement m, vacillement m (d'une flamme) (b) vacillation f, hésitation f, irrésolution f.

wax¹ [wæks] 1. n cire f; (in ear) cérumen m; fart m (pour skis); **w. paper**, papier paraffiné; Ecc: **w. taper**, cierge m; **w. museum**, musée de cire 2. vtr cirer, encaustiquer (un meuble); farter (des skis). '**waxbill** n Orn: bec-de-cire m. '**waxen** a cireux; de cire. '**waxing** n encaustiquage m; fartage m (des skis). '**waxwing** n Orn: jaseur m. '**waxwork** n personnage m en cire; **waxworks**, musée de cire. '**waxy** a cireux.

wax² vi (a) (of moon) croître; **to w. and wane**, croître et

décroître (b) Lit: **to w. eloquent**, déployer toute son éloquence (en faveur de qch).

way¹ [wei] n 1. (a) chemin m, route f; voie f; Rail: **the permanent w.**, la voie ferrée; NAm: **w. train** (Br = **stopping train**), (train m) omnibus (m); **over, across, the w.**, de l'autre côté de la rue, de la rue; en face; PN: Aut: **give w.** = priorité à droite; **to make w. for s.o.**, se ranger, céder le pas à qn (b) **by the w.**, (i) incidemment, en passant (ii) au fait; pendant que j'y pense; dites donc; **by w. of warning**, en guise d'avertissement; **he's by w. of being a socialist**, il est vaguement socialiste 2. (a) **to show s.o. the w.**, montrer la route à qn; **which is the w. to the station?** pouvez-vous m'indiquer le chemin de la gare? **to ask one's w.**, demander son chemin; **to lose one's w.**, se perdre; se tromper de chemin; s'égarer; **to go the wrong w.**, faire fausse route; **to go the shortest w.**, prendre par le plus court; **to know one's w. about**, savoir se débrouiller; **she went by w. of Germany**, elle est passée par l'Allemagne; **on the w.**, en cours de route; chemin faisant; **on the w. home**, en rentrant; en revenant chez moi; **it's on the w. to London**, c'est sur la route de Londres; **there's a baby on the w.**, elle attend un bébé; **I must be on my w.**, il faut que je parte; **to go one's own w.**, (i) faire à sa guise (ii) faire bande à part; **to go out of one's w.**, se donner du mal pour faire qch; **to go out of one's w. to look for difficulties**, rechercher la difficulté; **the village is completely out of the w.**, le village est complètement écarté, isolé, au bout du monde; F: **that's nothing out of the w.!** ça n'a rien d'extraordinaire! Ecc: **the W. of the Cross**, le chemin de la Croix; **w. in**, entrée f; **w. out**, sortie f; **to find a w. out of a difficulty**, trouver la solution d'une difficulté, trouver une solution; **to find one's w. to a place**, parvenir à un endroit; **to make one's w. through a crowd**, se frayer un chemin à travers la foule; **to make one's w. (in the world)**, réussir; arriver; **to work one's w. up**, s'élever à force de travailler; **to pay one's w.**, se suffire; **I can't see my w. to doing it now**, je ne vois pas, pour le moment, comment le faire; **to stand, be, in s.o.'s w.**, (i) barrer le passage à qn (ii) faire obstacle à qn; gêner, embarrasser, qn; **this table is in the w.**, cette table nous gêne, est encombrante; **he's always getting in my w.**, il est toujours à me gêner; **get out of the, my, w.!** rangez-vous! ôtez-vous du chemin! **to put sth out of the w.**, ranger qch; **I'm trying to keep out of his w.**, j'essaie de l'éviter; **to make w. for s.o.**, faire place à qn; **I'll go part of the w. with you**, je ferai un bout de chemin, une partie du trajet, avec vous; **all the w.**, jusqu'au bout; tout le long du chemin; **it's a long w. from here**, c'est (bien) loin d'ici; **I've a long w. to go**, j'ai beaucoup de chemin à faire; **he'll go a long w.**, il ira loin; il fera son chemin; il réussira; **to know how to make a little go a long w.**, savoir ménager ses sous (b) côté m, direction f; **which w. is the wind blowing?** d'où vient le vent? **this w. out**, (vers la) sortie; **this w. and that**, de-ci, de-là; de tous côtés; **he looked the other w.**, il a détourné la tête, les yeux; **I don't know which w. to turn**, je ne sais pas de quel côté me tourner, me mettre; **if the opportunity comes your w.**, si vous en avez l'occasion; F: **down our w.**, chez nous (c) sens m; **both ways**, dans les deux sens; F: **you can't have it both ways**, il faut choisir; **the other w. round**, dans l'autre sens; F: **it's the other w. round**, c'est le contraire; **the**

wrong w., à contre-sens; à rebrousse-poil; **the wrong w. up**, à l'envers; sens dessus dessous; **the right w. up**, dans le bon sens; **one w. street**, rue à sens unique (d) moyen m; **to find a w. to do sth**, trouver le moyen de faire qch; Pol: **Committee of Ways and Means** = la Commission du Budget (e) façon f, manière f; **in this w.**, de cette façon; **in no w.**, en aucune façon; **no w.!** jamais de la vie! **he's in no w. to blame**, on ne peut absolument pas l'en blâmer; **in a friendly w.**, en ami; amicalement; **in a big w.**, en grand; **without wishing to criticize it in any w.**, sans vouloir aucunement le critiquer; **to go the right w. to work**, s'y prendre bien; **in one w. or another**, d'une façon ou d'une autre; **there are no two ways about it**, il n'y a pas à discuter; **the w. things are going**, du train où vont les choses; **that's his w.**, il est comme ça; **to my w. of thinking**, selon moi, à moi sens; **our w. of living**, notre façon de vivre; notre genre m de vie; **the American w. of life**, la vie (à l')américaine; la façon de vivre des Américains; **that's always the w. with him**, il est toujours comme ça; **to do things (in) one's own w.**, faire les choses à sa guise; **to get into the w. of doing sth**, (i) prendre l'habitude de faire qch (ii) apprendre à faire qch; **he's got a w. with him**, il est insinuant; on le suit (en dépit de tout); **he has a w. with children**, il sait prendre les enfants; **I know his little ways**, je connais ses petites manies; **to get one's (own) w.**, arriver à ses fins; **he wants it all his own w.**, il veut n'en faire qu'à sa tête; **he had it all his own w.**, il n'a pas rencontré de résistance; **in many ways**, à bien des égards, à bien des points de vue; **in some ways**, à certains points de vue; **in every w.**, sous tous les rapports, en tous points; à tous les points de vue; **in one w.**, d'un certain point de vue (f) cours m; **in the ordinary w.**, d'habitude; **in the ordinary w. of business**, au cours des affaires; **things are in a bad w.**, les choses vont mal; **he's in a bad w.**, (i) ses affaires vont mal; il est dans le pétrin (ii) il est bien malade; **the flood is making w.**, l'inondation fait des progrès (g) erre f (d'un navire); **ship under w.**, navire en marche, faisant route; **to get under w.**, (of ships) appareiller; (of pers) se mettre en route; (of meeting) commencer; **we must get the work under w.**, il faut faire démarrer le travail. **'wayfarer** n voyageur, -euse (à pied). **'wayfaring** n voyages mpl (à pied). **way'lay** vtr (**way'laid**) attirer (qn) dans une embuscade; arrêter (qn) au passage. **'wayside** n bord m de la route; **to fall by the w.**, rester en chemin; **w. inn**, auberge au bord de la route; **w. flowers**, fleurs qui poussent en bordure de route. **'wayward** a (a) volontaire, rebelle (b) capricieux, fantasque.

way² adv F: (= away) **it was w. back in 1900**, cela remonte à 1900; **w. up the mountain**, tout en haut de la montagne; **w. down in the valley**, en bas dans la vallée; **to be w. out in one's calculations**, faire une grosse erreur; être loin du compte.

WC [dʌblju:'si:] n (abbr for **water closet**) WC mpl, waters mpl.

we [wi:] pers pron, nom pl (a) nous; **we were playing**, nous jouions; **here we are!** nous voilà! **we had a wonderful time**, nous nous sommes, on s'est, bien amûsé(s) (b) (stressed) **we are English, they are French**, nous, nous sommes anglais, eux, ils sont français; **you don't think that we did it?** vous ne pensez pas que c'est nous qui l'avons fait? **we English, nous**

autres Anglais (c) (indefinite) on; nous; **as we say in England**, comme on dit en Angleterre; **we are living in difficult times**, nous vivons dans une période difficile; **we all make mistakes sometimes**, tout le monde peut se tromper.

weak [wi:k] a (a) faible; (of health) débile; **to grow w.**, weaker, s'affaiblir; **to have a w. stomach**, avoir l'estomac fragile, peu solide; **to have a w. heart**, avoir le cœur malade, être cardiaque; **to have w. eyes**, eyesight, avoir la vue faible, une mauvaise vue; F: **I feel w. at the knees**, j'ai les jambes comme du coton; **the weaker sex**, le sexe faible; **w. in the head**, faible d'esprit; **w. character**, caractère m faible; **that's his w. side**, c'est son côté faible; **in a w. moment**, dans un moment de faiblesse (b) (of solution) dilué; (of petrol) **w. mixture**, mélange m pauvre; **w. tea**, thé léger, faible; **to be w. in French**, être faible en français. **'weaken** 1. vtr affaiblir; amollir (l'esprit) 2. vi s'affaiblir; faiblir; **his courage weakened**, son courage a fléchi, faibli; **the dollar has weakened**, le dollar a baissé. **'weakening** 1. a (a) affaiblissant (b) faiblissant; qui faiblit 2. n affaiblissement m. **'weak-'kneed** a F: sans caractère; mou. **'weakling** n (a) être m faible, débile (b) homme faible de caractère. **'weakly** 1. adv (a) faiblement, sans force (b) sans énergie 2. a débile, faible (de santé). **'weak-'minded** a (a) faible d'esprit (b) indécis, irrésolu. **'weakness** n faiblesse f; **to have a w. for sth, for s.o.**, avoir un faible pour qch, pour qn; **it's one of her weaknesses**, c'est un de ses points faibles.

weal [wi:l] n marque f, trace f (d'un coup de fouet).

wealth [welθ] n 1. richesse(s) f(pl); **a man of great w.**, un homme très riche 2. abondance f, profusion f (de détails). **'wealthy** a (-ier, -iest) riche; **w. heiress**, riche héritière; n **the w.**, les riches m.

wean [wi:n] vtr (a) sevrer (un nourrisson) (b) faire passer une mauvaise habitude (à qn). **'weaning** n sevrage m.

weapon ['wepən] n arme f.

wear [wɛər] I. v (wore [wɔːr], worn [wɔːn]) 1. vtr (a) porter (un vêtement); **he was wearing a hat**, il portait un chapeau; **to w. black**, porter du noir; être en noir; **what shall I w.?** qu'est-ce que je vais mettre? **I've nothing fit to w.**, je n'ai rien à me mettre, rien de mettable; **he was wearing his slippers**, il était en pantoufles; **to w. one's hair long**, porter les cheveux longs (b) user; **to w. sth into holes, to w. holes in sth**, trouer qch (par usure); **to w. oneself to death**, se tuer à force de travail 2. vi (of garment) **to w. into holes**, se trouer; **it will w. for ever**, c'est inusable; **to w. well**, (of material) faire bon usage; (of pers) être bien conservé; **worn at the knees**, usé aux genoux; **to w. thin**, (of clothes) être usé, râpé; (of patience) être à bout (de patience). II. n (a) usage m; **men's w.**, vêtements mpl pour hommes; **dresses for evening w.**, robes de soirée; **material that will stand hard w.**, tissu d'un bon usage; **shoes that still have some w. in them**, chaussures qui sont toujours portables; **to be the worse for w.**, (of garment) être usé, défraîchi; F: (of pers) (i) être éreinté (ii) avoir trop bu, avoir la gueule de bois; **to show signs of w.**, montrer des signes de fatigue (b) usure f; fatigue f (d'une machine); **w. and tear**, (i) usure (ii) frais mpl d'entretien; Jur: **fair w. and tear**, usure normale. **'wearable** a (vêtement) mettable, portable. **'wear a'way 1.** vtr (a) user, ronger; **he's worn away to a shadow,** il n'est plus que l'ombre de lui-même (b) effacer (une inscription) **2.** vi (a) s'user (b) s'effacer. **'wear 'down 1.** vtr user; **to w. one's heels d.,** user ses talons; **to w. d. s.o.'s resistance,** user à la longue, épuiser peu à peu, la résistance de qn **2.** vi s'user. **'wearer** n personne f qui porte un vêtement; **this new style does not suit many wearers,** ce nouveau style est difficile à porter. **'wearing** a fatigant, épuisant; **w. day,** journée fatigante, épuisante. **'wear 'off** vi s'effacer, disparaître; (of pain) se calmer; **when the novelty has worn off,** quand l'attrait de la nouveauté aura passé. **'wear 'on** vi **as the evening wore on,** à mesure que la soirée s'avançait; **as the years wore on,** avec le temps. **'wear 'out 1.** vtr (a) user (un vêtement); **to w. oneself o.,** s'user, s'épuiser; **to be worn out,** (of garment) être usé; (of pers) être épuisé; éreinté (b) épuiser, lasser (la patience de qn) **2.** vi s'user.

weary ['wiəri] **(-ier, -iest) I.** a **1.** fatigué; las **2.** las, dégoûté (of, de); **to grow w. of sth,** se lasser de qch; **to be w. of life,** être dégoûté de la vie. **II.** v (**wearied**) **1.** vi (a) se lasser, se fatiguer (b) trouver le temps long **2.** vtr lasser, fatiguer (qn). **'wearily** adv d'un air, d'un ton, las, fatigué; avec lassitude; (marcher) péniblement. **'weariness** n lassitude f, fatigue f. **'wearisome** a, **'wearying** a ennuyeux; fastidieux; F: assommant.

weasel ['wi:zəl] n Z: belette f.

weather ['weðər] **I.** n temps m (qu'il fait); **fine, bad, w.,** beau, mauvais, temps; **in all weathers,** par tous les temps; **in this, such, w.,** par le temps qu'il fait, par un temps pareil; **do you like this very hot w.?** aimez-vous ces grandes chaleurs? **w. permitting,** si le temps le permet; **what's the w. like?** quel temps fait-il? F: **to make heavy w. of a job,** compliquer les choses; F: (of pers) **to be under the w.,** être indisposé; ne pas être dans son assiette; **w. bureau, centre,** bureau météorologique; **w. forecast, report,** bulletin météorologique, F: météo f; F: **w. man,** météo m; **w. ship,** navire-météo m; **w. map, chart,** carte météorologique. **II.** v **1.** vtr (a) Geog: désagréger, altérer (b) Nau: **to w. a headland,** doubler un cap (à la voile); **to w. a storm,** (i) survivre à une tempête (ii) fig: se tirer d'affaire **2.** vi (a) (of rock) se désagréger, s'altérer (b) (of building) prendre de la patine; se patiner. **'weatherbeaten** a battu des vents, par la tempête; (of pers) bronzé, hâlé, basané. **'weatherboarding** n planche f de recouvrement. **'weathercock** n (a) girouette f (b) girouette, personne inconstante. **'weathered** a patiné. **'weathering** n (a) altération f, désagrégation f (des roches) (b) patine f. **'weatherman** n (pl -men) météorologue m, météorologiste m. **'weatherproof** a imperméable; étanche. **'weatherstrip** n (for door, window) calfeutrage m.

weave [wi:v] **I.** v (**wove** [wouv]; **woven** ['wouvən]) **1.** vtr (a) Tex: tisser (b) tresser (une guirlande, un panier); **to w. one's way through the crowd,** se frayer un chemin à travers la foule **2.** vi F: **to get weaving,** s'y mettre; **get weaving!** vas-y! grouille-toi! **II.** n Tex: (a) armure f (b) tissage m. **'weaver** n **1.** Tex: tisserand, -ande **2. w. (bird),** tisserin m. **'weaving** n tissage m.

web [web] n (a) Tex: tissu m; **w. of lies,** tissu de mensonges; **spider's w.,** toile f d'araignée (b) palmure f, membrane f (d'un palmipède). **webbed** a palmé, membrané; **w. feet,** pieds palmés. **'web-'footed** a palmipède, aux pieds palmés.

wed [wed] v (pt & pp **wed(ded)**) **1.** vtr épouser (qn); marier avec (qn); (of priest) marier (un couple); **to be wedded to an idea,** être obstinément attaché à une idée **2.** vi se marier. **'wedding** n mariage m, noce(s) f (pl); **church w.,** mariage religieux, à l'église; **silver, golden, diamond, w.,** noces d'argent, d'or, de diamant; **w. day,** jour du mariage, des noces; **w. breakfast,** repas de noce; **w. cake,** gâteau de mariage; **w. dress,** robe de mariée; **w. guest,** invité, -ée (à un mariage); **w. march,** marche nuptiale; **w. present,** cadeau de noces, de mariage; **w. ring,** alliance f; **w. night,** nuit de noces; **w. list,** liste de mariage; **w. anniversary,** anniversaire de mariage; **w. ceremony,** bénédiction, cérémonie, messe, nuptiale.

we'd = we would see will III.

wedge [wedʒ] **1.** n (a) coin m (de serrage); cale f (de fixation); **to drive in a w.,** enfoncer un coin; **it's the thin end of the w.,** c'est un premier empiétement (b) **w. of cake,** morceau m (triangulaire) de gâteau (c) **w. heel,** semelle compensée **2.** vtr (a) coincer, assujettir (b) caler (un meuble); **to w. a door open,** maintenir une porte ouverte avec une cale (c) enclaver, enfoncer, serrer (qch dans qch); **wedged in between two fat women,** coincé, serré, entre deux grosses femmes; **to w. sth in sth,** enfoncer qch dans qch; **to be wedged in,** être coincé.

Wednesday ['wenzdi] n mercredi m; **Ash W.,** le mercredi des Cendres.

wee [wi:] a tout petit; minuscule; **a w. bit,** un tout petit peu.

weed [wi:d] **1.** n (a) mauvaise herbe (b) F: personne malingre, chétive (c) F: (cigarette f de) marijuana f **2.** vtr sarcler; désherber. **'weeder** n (pers) sarcleur, -euse; (tool) sarcloir m. **'weediness** n F: maigreur f; apparence f malingre. **'weeding** n sarclage m; désherbage m. **'weedkiller** n herbicide m, désherbant m. **'weed 'out** vtr éliminer; rejeter. **'weedy** a (a) couvert de mauvaises herbes (b) F: (of pers) malingre.

week [wi:k] n (a) semaine f; **this w.,** cette semaine; **next w.,** la semaine prochaine; **last w.,** la semaine dernière; **in the middle of the w.,** dans le courant de la semaine; **three weeks ago,** il y a trois semaines; **w. in w. out,** toutes les semaines; semaine après semaine; **what day of the w. is it?** quel jour de la semaine sommes-nous? **twice a w.,** deux fois par semaine; P: **to knock s.o. into the middle of next w.,** donner à qn un fameux coup; **I haven't seen him for, in, weeks,** je ne l'ai pas vu depuis des semaines (b) huit jours; **once a w.,** une fois par semaine; tous les huit jours; **he stayed a w. with us,** il a passé huit jours chez nous; **a w. from now, today w.,** d'aujourd'hui en huit; **yesterday w.,** il y a eu hier huit jours; **tomorrow w.,** demain en huit; **within the w.,** dans la huitaine; **in a w. or so,** dans une huitaine; **in two weeks' time,** dans quinze jours; Ind: **forty-hour w.,** semaine de quarante heures; **what I can't do in the w. I do on Sundays,** ce que je n'arrive pas à faire en semaine je le fais le dimanche. **'weekday** n jour m ouvrable; jour de semaine; **on**

weep 478 well

week-end m; at the w., pendant le week-end, la fin de
semaine. 'weekly 1. a (salaire) de la semaine; (visite,
publication) hebdomadaire 2. n (journal m, revue f)
hebdomadaire m 3. adv tous les huit jours; twice w.,
deux fois par semaine.
weep [wiːp] 1. vi (wept [wept]) pleurer; to w. bitterly,
pleurer à chaudes larmes; to w. for joy, pleurer de joie;
it's enough to make you w., c'est à faire pleurer 2. n
crise f de larmes. 'weeping 1. a (enfant) qui pleure;
w. willow, saule pleureur 2. n pleurs mpl; larmes fpl.
'weepy a F: larmoyant; to feel w., avoir envie de
pleurer.
weevil ['wiːvil] n Ent: charançon m.
wee-wee ['wiːwiː] F: 1. n pipi m 2. vi faire pipi.
weft [weft] n Tex: trame f.
weigh [wei] 1. vtr (a) peser (qch); to w. sth in one's
hand, soupeser qch; to w. oneself, se peser; to w. the
consequences, calculer les conséquences; it's weighing
on my mind, ça me tracasse; to w. the pros and cons,
peser le pour et le contre (b) Nau: to w. anchor, lever
l'ancre; appareiller 2. vi peser, avoir du poids; to
w. heavy, light, peser lourd, peu; it weighs 2 kilos, ça
pèse 2 kilos; F: it weighs a ton, c'est rudement
lourd. 'weighbridge n pont-bascule m. 'weigh
'down vtr surcharger; branch weighed down with
fruit, branche surchargée de fruits; weighed down with
sorrow, accablé de chagrin, de tristesse. 'weigh 'in
vi (of jockey, boxer) se faire peser avant la course, le
match. 'weighing n 1. pesée f (de qch); Turf:
pesage m; w.-in room, le pesage; w. enclosure, (enceinte f du) pesage 2. Nau: levage m (de l'ancre);
appareillage m. weight n (a) poids m; to sell by w.,
vendre au poids; it's worth its w. in gold, cela vaut son
pesant d'or; (of pers) to lose, gain, w., perdre, prendre,
du poids; maigrir, grossir; to pull one's w., y mettre du
sien (b) poids, pesanteur f, lourdeur f; to try the w. of
sth, soupeser qch; specific w., poids spécifique, vo-
lumique; atomic w., poids atomique; what a w.!
comme c'est lourd! (c) set of weights, série de poids;
weights and measures, poids et mesures (d) (for
papers) presse-papiers m inv (e) charge f; that's a w.
off my mind, voilà qui me soulage (f) force f (d'un
coup) (g) importance f; his word carries w., sa parole a
du poids, de l'autorité; to throw one's w. around, faire
l'important. 'weightiness n 1. pesanteur f, lourdeur f (de qch) 2. importance f, force f (d'une
opinion). 'weighting n indemnité f (de résidence).
'weightless a w. conditions, état m d'apesanteur.
'weightlessness n apesanteur f. 'weight-
lifter n haltérophile m. 'weightlifting n
haltérophilie f. 'weighty a (-ier, -iest) 1. pesant,
lourd 2. (motif) grave, important; (argument)
puissant.
weir [wiǝr] n 1. barrage m (dans un cours d'eau) 2.
déversoir m (d'un étang).
weird [wiː)ǝd] a (a) surnaturel; mystérieux (b)
étrange, singulier. 'weirdie n F: excentrique mf,
drôle m de type. 'weirdly adv étrangement.
'weirdness n (a) étrangeté inquiétante (b) caractère singulier. 'weirdo, 'weirdy n F: excentrique
mf; drôle d'oiseau.
welcome ['welkǝm] 1. vtr souhaiter la bienvenue à
(qn); faire bon accueil à (qn); to w. a piece of news, se

réjouir d'une nouvelle 2. n (a) bienvenue f; to overstay
one's w., lasser l'amabilité de ses hôtes (b) accueil m;
hearty w., bon accueil; to have a cold w., être reçu
froidement 3. a (a) to make s.o. w., faire bon accueil à
qn; int w.! soyez le bienvenu, la bienvenue! to be w.,
être le, la, bienvenu(e); w. to England! bienvenue en
Angleterre! (b) this is w. news, nous nous réjouissons
de cette nouvelle; a w. change, un changement
bienvenu; this cheque is most w., ce chèque tombe à
merveille (c) you're w. to try, libre à vous d'essayer;
you're w. to it, c'est à votre disposition; esp NAm:
(thanking s.o.) you're w.! je vous en prie.
weld [weld] 1. vtr souder (au blanc); unir (à chaud) 2. n
soudure f. 'welder n (a) (pers) soudeur m (b)
machine f à souder. 'welding n soudage m, soudure
f; oxyacetylene w., soudure autogène; w. torch, chalumeau m.
welfare ['welfɛǝr] n bien-être m; prospérité f;
social w., sécurité sociale; child w., protection f de
l'enfance; the W. State, l'État providence; w.
work = assistance sociale; w. worker = assistant(e)
social(e).
well¹ [wel] 1. n (a) puits m; oil w., puits de pétrole (b)
puits, cage f (d'un ascenseur) 2. vi to w. up, jaillir; (of
spring) sourdre.
well² (better; best) I. adv 1. (a) bien; to work w., bien
travailler; he'll do w., il fera son chemin, il ira loin;
very w., très bien; to do well, bien réussir (à un
examen); (of sick person) aller mieux; you did w. to
leave, vous avez bien fait de partir; to do as w. as one
can, faire de son mieux; w. done! bravo! F: we did
ourselves w.! on s'est bien soigné(s), bien nourri(s)! he
accepted, as w. he might, il a accepté et rien de
d'étonnant; you might just as w. say (that), autant dire
(que); you could just as w. have stayed, vous auriez
tout aussi bien pu rester; very w.! très bien! entendu!
(b) we were very w. received, on nous a fait un bon
accueil; it speaks w. for him, cela lui fait honneur; she
deserves w. of you, elle mérite bien votre reconnaissance; it was w. intended, c'était fait avec une
bonne intention (c) you're w. out of it! soyez heureux
d'en être quitte! it went off w., cela s'est bien passé;
you've come off w., vous avez eu de la chance 2.
(intensive) it's w. worth trying, cela vaut vraiment la
peine d'essayer, cela vaut le coup; w. after six
(o'clock), six heures bien sonnées; we went on w. into
the small hours, nous avons continué tard dans la
nuit; he's w. over fifty, il a bien dépassé la cinquantaine; to be w. up in history, in French, être calé en
histoire, en français 3. pretty w. all of them, presque
tous; F: it serves him jolly w., damn w., right, il l'a bien
mérité 4. (a) as w., aussi; take me as w., emmenez-moi
aussi, également (b) as w. as, de même que; comme;
non moins que 5. (a) w., as I was telling you, donc, eh
bien, comme je vous disais; w., and what of it? eh bien,
et après? (b) (expressing astonishment, etc) w.! ça
alors! pas possible! w., it can't be helped! tant pis! on
n'y peut rien; w., w.! que voulez-vous! (c) w. then, why
worry? eh bien alors, pourquoi vous faire de la bile? 6.
(used with participles to form adjectives) w. advised,
sage, prudent, judicieux; w. behaved, (enfant) sage;
(animal) bien dressé; w. built, solide; w. educated,
instruit; cultivé; w. fed, bien nourri; w. heeled, à l'aise,
riche; w. informed, bien renseigné; (milieu) bien

informé; **w. kept,** (jardin) bien entretenu; (mains) soignées; (secret) bien gardé; **w. known,** célèbre, réputé, bien connu; **w. made,** bien fait, bien fini; **w. mannered,** poli, bien élevé; **w. meaning,** bien intentionné; **w. meant,** fait avec une bonne intention; **w. off,** riche; **you don't know when you're w. off,** vous ne connaissez pas votre bonheur; **w. read,** instruit, cultivé; **w. spent,** (temps) bien employé; (argent) dépensé avantageusement; **w. spoken,** qui parle bien; **w. timed,** opportun; bien calculé; **w. worn,** (vêtement) usé; (livre) beaucoup servi; (argument) rebattu; usé jusqu'à la corde. **II.** *a* 1. **to be w.,** être bien portant, en bonne santé; **to look w.,** avoir bonne mine; **I'm not w.,** je ne vais pas bien, ne me sens pas bien; **to get w.,** guérir, se rétablir; **I don't feel w.,** je ne me sens pas bien 2. *(a)* **it would be just as w. to do it,** il serait bon de le faire; **it would be just as w. if you came,** il y aurait avantage à ce que vous veniez; **it was just as w. that you were there,** il est bien heureux que vous vous soyez trouvé là; heureusement que vous vous trouviez là *(b)* **all's w. that ends w.,** tout est bien qui finit bien; **all's w.,** tout va bien *(c)* **that's all very w. (but),** tout cela est bien joli (mais); **it's all very w. for you to say that,** libre à vous de le dire; vous avez beau le dire (mais); **he's all very w. in his way (but),** il n'y a rien à dire contre lui (mais); **w. and good!** soit! bon! **III.** *n* 1. *pl* **the w. and the sick,** les bien portants et les malades 2. **to wish s.o. w.,** vouloir du bien à qn; **I wish him w.,** je lui souhaite bonne chance. **'wellbeing** *n* bien-être *m*. **'well-to-'do** *a* riche, aisé. **'well-wisher** *n* ami(e), partisan(e) (de qn, d'une cause); admirateur, -trice.

we'll [wi:l] = **we shall** *see* **shall**; = **we will** *see* **will III.**

Wellington ['weliŋtən] *Prn* **W. boots,** *n* **wellingtons,** *F:* **wellies** ['weliz] bottes *f* en caoutchouc.

Welsh [welʃ] 1. *a* gallois, du Pays de Galles; **W. dresser,** vaisselier *m* 2. *n (a) pl* **the W.,** les Gallois *(b)* *Ling:* gallois *m* 3. *vi* décamper; filer; lever le pied; partir sans payer; **to w. on s.o.,** partir sans payer ses dettes à qn, sans remplir ses obligations. **'Welshman** *n (pl* **-men)** Gallois *m*. **'Welshwoman** *n (pl* **-women)** Galloise *f*.

wend [wend] *vtr* **to w. one's way home,** s'acheminer vers la maison.

went [went] *see* **go I.**

wept [wept] *see* **weep.**

were [wɜːr] *see* **be.**

we're [wiər] = **we are** *see* **be.**

weren't [wɜːnt] = **were not** *see* **be.**

werewolf ['wiəwulf] *n (pl* **werewolves** [-wulvz]) loup-garou *m*.

west [west] 1. *n (a)* ouest *m*; occident *m*; couchant *m*; **the sun sets in the w.,** le soleil se couche à l'ouest; **to the w. (of),** à l'ouest (de); **house facing the w.,** maison exposée à l'ouest *(b)* *Pol:* **the W.,** l'Occident, l'Ouest; **the Far W.,** les États de l'ouest (des États-Unis) 2. *a* ouest *inv*; occidental, -aux; **w. wind,** vent *m* d'ouest; **w. wall,** mur qui fait face à l'ouest, exposé à l'ouest; **W. Berlin,** Berlin Ouest; **the W. Country,** les comtés de l'ouest (de l'Angleterre); **the W. End (of London),** le quartier (chic) du centre-ouest (de Londres); **W. Germany,** Allemagne de l'Ouest; **W. Africa,** l'Afrique occidentale; **the W. Indies,** les Antilles *f*; **W.**

Indian, antillais; des Antilles 3. *adv* à l'ouest; **to travel w.,** voyager vers l'ouest; *F:* **that's another plate gone w.!** encore une assiette de cassée! **'westbound** *a (of traffic, train)* allant vers l'ouest, en direction de l'ouest. **'westerly** 1. *a* (vent) d'ouest; (courant) qui se dirige vers l'ouest. 2. *a* à l'ouest 2. *n Cin:* western *m*. **'western** 1. *a* ouest *inv*; de l'ouest; occidental; **W. Europe,** l'Europe occidentale; **the w. world,** le monde occidental 2. *n Cin:* western *m*. **'westerner** *n* occidental, -ale, *pl* -aux; *NAm:* habitant(e) des États de l'Ouest (des États-Unis). **'westernize** *vtr* occidentaliser. **'westward** 1. *n* to w., vers l'ouest 2. *a* à l'ouest; de l'ouest. **'westwards** *adv* vers l'ouest, à l'ouest.

wet [wet] **I.** *a (wetter; wettest) (a)* mouillé; humide; imbibé d'eau; **to get one's feet w.,** se mouiller les pieds; *(of pers)* **to be w. through, soaking w., dripping w.,** être trempé (jusqu'aux os); *(of garment)* **wringing w., soaking w.,** mouillé à tordre; *F: (pers)* **w. blanket,** rabat-joie *m inv*; **the ink is still w.,** l'encre n'est pas encore sèche; *PN:* **w. paint!** = attention, peinture fraîche! **cheeks w. with tears,** joues baignées de larmes *(b)* **w. weather,** temps humide, pluvieux; **it's going to be w.,** il va pleuvoir; **three w. days,** trois jours de pluie; **the w. season,** la saison de pluies 3. *F:* **he's a bit w.,** c'est une nouille, une andouille. **II.** *n* 1. humidité *f* 2. pluie *f*; **to go out in the w.,** sortir sous la pluie 3. *F:* **he's a w.,** c'est une nouille, une andouille. **III.** *vtr (wetted)* mouiller; **to w. oneself, one's pants,** mouiller sa culotte. **'wetness** *n* humidité *f*. **'wetsuit** *n* combinaison *f* de plongée. **'wetting** *n* **to get a w.,** se faire tremper.

we've [wi:v] = **we have** *see* **have.**

whack [(h)wæk] *F:* 1. *vtr (a)* battre, rosser (qn); fesser (un enfant); battre (ses adversaires) à plates coutures *(b)* **I'm completely whacked,** je suis complètement épuisé, éreinté, à plat 2. *n (a)* coup (de bâton) bien appliqué *(b)* **let's have a w. at it,** essayons le coup *(c)* part *f*, portion *f*, (gros) morceau; **he did, paid, more than his w.,** il a fait, payé, plus que sa part. **'whacking** *F:* 1. *a* énorme, colossal; **a w. great cabbage,** un chou immense, énorme 2. *n* rossée *f*; raclée *f*; fessée *f*.

whale [(h)weil] 1. *n Z:* baleine *f*; **w. calf,** baleineau *m* 2. *F:* **we had a w. of a time,** on s'est drôlement bien amusés 2. *vi* faire la pêche à la baleine. **'whaleboat** *n* baleinier *m*. **'whalebone** *n* fanon *m* de baleine; baleine (d'un corset). **'whaler** *n (a) (pers)* baleinier *m*, pêcheur *m* de baleines *(b) (ship)* baleinier; baleinière *f*. **'whaling** *n* pêche à la baleine.

wharf [(h)wɔːf] *n* appontement *m*; débarcadère *m*, embarcadère *m*; quai *m*. **'wharfage** *n* droit *m* de quai.

what [(h)wɔt] **I.** *a* 1. *(rel)* (ce) que, (ce) qui; **he took away from me w. little I had,** il m'a pris le peu qui me restait; **with w. capital he had,** avec ce qu'il possédait de capital 2. *(interr)* quel, *f* quelle; **w. time is it?** quelle heure est-il? **w. right has he to do that?** quel droit a-t-il de faire ça? de quel droit fait-il cela? **w. good is this?** à quoi cela sert-il? **w. day of the month is it?** quelle est la date? nous sommes le combien? 3. *(excl)* **w. an idea!** quelle idée! **w. a pity!** quel dommage! **w. an idiot he is!** qu'il est bête! **w. a lot of people!** que de gens! **II.** *pron* 1. *(rel)* **what's done cannot be undone,** ce qui est fait est fait; **w. I need,** ce dont j'ai besoin; **w. I want,** ce que je veux; **w. I like most,** ce que j'aime le plus; **and w. is more,** et qui plus est; **this is w. it's all about,** voilà ce dont il s'agit; **come w. may,** advienne que pourra; **w. he will,** quoi qu'il dise; il a beau dire; **w. with golf and tennis I haven't much free time,** entre le golf et le tennis il me reste peu de temps libre; *P:* **to give s.o. w. for,** donner une bonne raclée à qn; laver la tête à qn **2.** (*interr*) (*a*) (*direct*) qu'est-ce qui? qu'est-ce? qu'est-ce que c'est? quoi? **w. are you doing here?** qu'est-ce que vous faites ici? **w. is it?** (i) qu'est-ce que c'est? (ii) qu'est-ce qu'il y a? **what's the matter?** qu'y a-t-il? de quoi s'agit-il? qu'est-ce que vous avez? **what's his name?** comment s'appelle-t-il? **what's that to you?** qu'est-ce que cela peux vous faire? **what's the good, the use?** à quoi bon? **w. can we do?** que faire? **what's the French for** *dog*? comment dit-on *dog* en français? **what's he made of?** comment est-il? **what's it made of?** en quoi est-ce? **w. about a game of bridge?** si on faisait une partie de bridge? **w. do you take me for?** pour qui me prenez-vous? **w. about you?** et vous donc? **well, w. about it?** (i) eh bien, quoi? et puis après? (ii) eh bien, qu'en dites-vous? **what's that?** qu'est-ce que c'est que ça? **what's that for?** à quoi cela sert-il? *F:* à quoi ça sert? **w. on earth for?** mais pourquoi donc? *F:* **so w.?** et puis après? alors? **w. did you say?** pardon? **w. of it?** et puis après? qu'est-ce que ça fait? **w. then? so w.?** et après? **and w. have you, and w. not,** et je ne sais quoi encore (*b*) (*indirect*) ce qui, ce que; **tell me what's happening,** dites-moi ce qui se passe; **I don't know w. to do,** je ne sais que faire; **I wonder w. he's doing,** je me demande ce qu'il fait; **I'll tell you w., I know w.,** écoute (j'ai une idée); *F:* **he knows what's w.,** il s'y connaît; c'est un malin, un rusé **3.** (*excl*) **w. next!** par exemple! **w. he must have suffered!** ce qu'il a dû souffrir! **w.! can't you come?** comment! vous ne pouvez pas venir? **what**'**ever 1.** *pron* **w. you like,** tout ce que vous voudrez; n'importe quoi; **w. it may, might, be,** quoi que ce soit; **w. happens,** quoi qu'il arrive **2.** *a* (*a*) **w. price they are asking,** quel que soit le prix qu'on demande; **at w. time,** quelle que soit l'heure; à n'importe quelle heure; **under any pretext w.,** sous quelque prétexte que ce soit (*b*) **no hope w.,** pas le moindre espoir; **is there any hope w.?** y a-t-il un espoir quelconque? y a-t-il quelque espoir? **nothing w.,** absolument rien; **none w.,** pas un seul. **'whatnot** *n* **1.** *Furn:* étagère *f* **2.** *F:* machin *m*, truc *m*. **'what's-it, 'what's-its (-his, -her) -name** *n*, **'what-d'you-call-it (-him, -her)** *n F:* machin *m*, truc *m*; old Mr W., le père Machin. **whatso'ever** *a* nothing **w.,** absolument rien.

wheat [(h)wiːt] *n* blé *m*; froment *m*; **w. germ,** germe *m* de blé. **'wheatmeal** *n* farine *f* de froment. **'wheatsheaf** *n* gerbe *f* de blé.

wheedle [('h)wiːdl] *vtr* enjôler, cajoler (qn); **to w. s.o. into doing sth,** amener qn à faire qch à force de cajoleries; **to w. money out of s.o.,** soutirer de l'argent à qn. **'wheedling 1.** *a* enjôleur; câlin **2.** *n* cajoleries *fpl*.

wheel [(h)wiːl] **I.** *n* (*a*) roue *f*; **there are wheels within wheels,** c'est une affaire compliquée; il y a toutes sortes de forces en jeu; **the wheels of government,** les rouages *m* de l'administration (*b*) *Aut:* **steering w.,** volant *m*; **to take the w.,** *Aut:* prendre le volant; *Nau:* prendre la barre (*c*) **potter's w.,** tour *m* de potier; *Pyr:* **catherine w.,** soleil *m*, roue à feu. **II.** *v* **1.** *vtr* (*a*) tourner; faire pivoter (*b*) rouler (une brouette); pousser (une bicyclette) à la main **2.** *vi* (*a*) tourner en rond; tournoyer (*b*) *Mil:* **left w.!** à gauche, marche! **to w. round,** faire demi-tour; se retourner (brusquement). **'wheelbarrow** *n* brouette *f*. **'wheelbase** *n* (*of vehicle*) empattement *m*. **'wheelchair** *n* fauteuil roulant. **'wheeled** *a* (*with adj prefixed*) **two-w.,** à deux roues. **'wheeler** *n* (*with number prefixed*) **two-w., four-w.,** voiture *f* à deux, à quatre, roues. **'wheelwright** *n* charron *m*.

wheeze [(h)wiːz] **1.** *vi* respirer péniblement **2.** *n* respiration *f* asthmatique. **'wheezy** *a* asthmatique.

whelk [welk] *n Moll:* buccin *m*.

whelp [(h)welp] **1.** *n* petit *m* (d'un animal); lion's w., lionceau *m* **2.** *vi & tr* (*of lion, dog*) mettre bas.

when [(h)wen] **1.** *interr adv* (*a*) **w. will you go?** quand partirez-vous? **w. is your birthday?** quelle est la date de votre anniversaire? **w. is the meeting?** quand la réunion aura-t-elle lieu? à quand la réunion? **w. on earth is he going to arrive?** quand donc, quand diable, va-t-il arriver? **since w.?** depuis quand? *F:* (*when pouring drink*) **say w.!** comme ça? **the day w. I first met her,** le jour où je l'ai rencontrée pour la première fois; **at the very time w.,** au moment même où; alors même que; **one day w. I was on duty,** un jour que j'étais de service **2.** *conj* quand, lorsque; **w. I was young,** quand j'étais jeune; **w. he was born,** lors de sa naissance; **w. it's finished,** une fois terminé; **I'll come w. I've finished this work,** je viendrai quand j'aurai terminé ce travail; **when I think of what he said,** quand je pense à ce qu'il a dit; **he walked w. he could have taken the car,** il est allé à pied alors qu'il aurait pu prendre la voiture **3.** *pron* (*interr*) **until w. can you stay?** jusqu'à quand pouvez-vous rester? **since w. have you been living in Paris?** depuis quand habitez-vous Paris? **when**'**ever** *conj & adv* toutes les fois que; chaque fois que; **I go w. I can,** j'y vais aussi souvent que possible; **come w. you like,** venez quand vous voudrez; venez n'importe quand; **next Monday or w.,** lundi prochain ou n'importe quel jour de la semaine, ou quand vous voulez.

where [(h)weər] **1.** *adv* (*interr*) où? **w. am I?** où suis-je? **tell me w. he is,** dites-moi où il est; **w. have we got to? w. are we up to?** où en sommes-nous? **where's the way out?** où est la sortie? par où sort-on? **w. do you come from?** (i) d'où venez-vous? (ii) de quel pays êtes-vous? **2.** *rel adv & conj* **I shall stay w. I am,** je resterai (là) où je suis; **go w. you like,** allez où vous voulez, voudrez; **that's w. you are mistaken,** voilà où vous vous trompez; **the house w. he was born,** la maison où, dans laquelle, il est né; **sa maison natale; I can see it from w. we are,** je le vois d'où nous sommes. **'whereabouts 1.** *adv & conj* où; de quel côté; **do you know w. the town hall is?** savez-vous de quel côté se trouve l'hôtel de ville? **2.** *n* lieu *m* où se trouve qn, qch; **nobody knows his w.,** personne ne sait où il est. **'whereas** *conj* (*a*) (*introducing formal statement*) attendu que, vu que, puisque (*b*) alors que, tandis que. **'wherefore** *n* the whys and wherefores, les pourquoi et les comment. **wher'ever** *conj & adv* **w. I go,** partout où je vais; n'importe où je vais; **I'll go w.**

you want me to, j'irai où vous voudrez; w. you are, où que vous soyez; w. they come from, d'où qu'ils viennent; at home, in the office or w., à la maison, au bureau ou n'importe où, ou Dieu sait où.

'wherewithal [-wiðɔːl] n F: the w., l'argent m, le nécessaire; les moyens m; I haven't the w. to buy it, je n'ai pas de quoi l'acheter.

whet [(h)wet] vtr (whetted) 1. aiguiser, affûter, affiler, repasser (un outil) 2. stimuler, aiguiser (l'appétit); F: to w. one's whistle, boire un coup; se rincer la dalle.

'whetstone n pierre f à aiguiser.

whether ['(h)weðər] conj si; I don't know w. it is true, je ne sais pas si c'est vrai; it depends on w. you're in a hurry or not, cela dépend de si vous êtes pressé ou non; w. he comes or not we'll leave, qu'il vienne ou non nous allons partir.

whey [(h)wei] n petit lait.

which [(h)witʃ] I. a (a) (interr) quel, f quelle, pl quels, quelles; w. colour do you like best? quelle couleur aimez-vous le mieux? w. way shall we go? par où irons-nous? quelle route est-ce que nous allons prendre? w. one? lequel? laquelle? w. one of you? lequel d'entre vous? I'm going with friends—w. friends? j'y vais avec des amis—lesquels? (b) they are coming on June 4th, by w. date we shall be in London, ils viendront le 4 juin, date à laquelle nous serons à Londres. II. pron 1. lequel, f laquelle, pl lesquels, lesquelles; w. have you chosen? lequel avez-vous choisi? w. of the dresses did you buy? laquelle des robes avez-vous achetée? w. of you can answer? lequel d'entre vous peut répondre? of w. is he speaking? duquel parle-t-il? tell me w. is w., dites-moi comment les distinguer; I don't mind w., cela m'est égal 2. (a) (rel) que; qui; the house w. is to be sold, la maison qui est à vendre; the pen w. is on the table, le stylo qui est sur la table; books w. I have read, des livres que j'ai lus; things w. I need, des choses dont j'ai besoin (b) ce qui; ce que; he looked like a retired colonel, w. indeed he was, il avait l'air d'un colonel en retraite, ce qu'il était en effet; he told me of many things that happened, all of w. were true, il m'a raconté beaucoup d'incidents qui étaient tous exacts 3. (with prep) the house of w. I was speaking, la maison dont, de laquelle, je parlais; the box in w. I put it, la boîte dans laquelle je l'ai mis(e); the countries to w. we are going, les pays où nous irons, que nous allons visiter; the hotels at w. we stayed, les hôtels où nous sommes descendus; I have nothing with w. to write, je n'ai pas de quoi écrire; after w. he went out, après quoi il est sorti. which'ever rel pron & a 1. pron celui qui, celui que, n'importe lequel; w. is best for him, celui qui, celle qui, ce qui, lui convient le mieux; take w. you like, prenez celui, celle, que vous voudrez, n'importe lequel, laquelle 2. a n'importe quel; take w. book you like, prenez le livre que vous voudrez; prenez n'importe quel livre; w. way I turn, de quelque côté que je me tourne.

whiff [(h)wif] 1. n (a) bouffée f (de fumée, d'air) (b) F: mauvaise odeur 2. vi (a) souffler par bouffées (b) F: puer.

while [(h)wail] 1. n (espace m de) temps m; after a w., après quelque temps; in a little w., sous peu; avant peu; a little w. ago, il y a peu de temps; a long w., longtemps; a long w. ago, il y a longtemps; for a (short) w., pendant quelque temps; pendant un moment; stay a little w. longer, restez encore un peu; a good w., quite a w., pas mal de temps; it will take me quite a long w. to do that, cela me prendra pas mal de temps, assez longtemps; all the w., tout le temps; once in a w., de temps en temps; de temps à autre; to be worth one's w., valoir la peine; I'll make it worth your w., vous serez bien payé de votre peine; it's not worth our w. waiting, cela ne vaut pas la peine, ce n'est pas la peine, d'attendre; it is perhaps worth w. saying (that), il vaut peut-être la peine de dire (que) 2. vtr to w. away the time, faire passer le temps 3. conj (a) pendant que, tandis que; w. he was here, pendant qu'il était ici; w. (he was) reading he fell asleep, tout en lisant, il s'est endormi; w. this was going on, sur ces entrefaites (b) tant que; w. I live you will not go without anything, tant que je vivrai vous ne manquerez de rien (c) quoique, bien que; w. I admit that it is difficult, quoique j'admette, tout en admettant, que c'est difficile (d) tandis que; I was dressed in white, w. my sister wore grey, j'étais habillée de blanc, tandis que ma sœur portait du gris. whilst conj=while 3.

whim [(h)wim] n caprice m, fantaisie f. 'whimsical a (a) capricieux; fantasque (b) bizarre.

whimper ['(h)wimpər] 1. vi pleurnicher, geindre; (of dog) pousser des petits cris plaintifs 2. n (a) pleurnicherie f, pleurnichement m (b) geignement m, plainte f; (of dog) petit cri plaintif. 'whimpering 1. a pleurnicheur 2. n (a) pleurnichement; pleurnicheries fpl (b) plaintes fpl; (of dog) petits cris plaintifs.

whine [(h)wain] 1. vi se plaindre; (of child) pleurnicher; (of dog) geindre 2. n plainte f; geignement m. 'whining 1. a geignant; pleurnicheur; (ton) plaintif 2. n plaintes fpl; geignement m.

whinny ['(h)wini] 1. vi (whinnied) (of horse) hennir 2. n (pl whinnies) hennissement m (de cheval).

whip [(h)wip] I. v (whipped) 1. vtr (a) fouetter; donner le fouet à (un cheval); whipped cream, crème fouettée, Chantilly (b) he whipped the revolver out of his pocket, il a sorti vivement le revolver de sa poche (c) Needlw: surjeter (une couture) 2. vi (a) the rain was whipping against the window panes, la pluie fouettait, cinglait, les vitres (b) he whipped behind the door, il s'est jeté derrière la porte; to w. round the corner, tourner vivement le coin. II. n 1. fouet m; riding w., cravache f 2. Parl: (a) chef m de file, whip m (b) appel m (aux membres d'un parti) 3. Cu: (lemon) w.=mousse f (au citron). 'whip a'way vtr he whipped it away, out of sight, il l'a caché d'un mouvement rapide. 'whip'hand n to have the w., avoir l'avantage. 'whiplash n mèche f de fouet; tongue like a w., langue cinglante. 'whip 'off vtr enlever (qch) vivement, d'un geste rapide. 'whipping n to give a child a w., donner le fouet à un enfant; Cu: w. cream, crème fraîche à fouetter; Fig: w boy, bouc m émissaire. 'whip 'round vi se retourner vivement. 'whipround n F: to have a w. for s.o., organiser une souscription en faveur de qn. 'whip 'up vtr fouetter, battre (des œufs, de la crème); stimuler (l'intérêt de qn); F: I'll w. you up sth to eat, je vais te préparer rapidement qch à manger.

whippet ['(h)wipit] n (dog) whippet m.

whirl [(h)wəːl] I. v 1. vi (a) to w. (round), tourbillonner, tournoyer; (*of dancer*) pirouetter; **my head's whirling,** la tête me tourne (*b*) **to w. along,** rouler, filer, à toute vitesse 2. *vtr* (*a*) (*of wind*) faire tournoyer (les feuilles mortes (*b*) **the train whirled us along,** le train nous emportait à toute vitesse. II. *n* (*a*) mouvement *m* giratoire, giration *f* (*b*) tourbillon *m,* tourbillonnement *m,* tournoiement *m;* **my head's in a w.,** la tête me tourne. 'whirlpool *n* tourbillon (d'eau); remous *m;* gouffre *m.* 'whirlwind *n* tourbillon *m* (de vent); trombe *f;* **to come in like a w.,** entrer en trombe, en coup de vent.

whirr [(h)wəːr] 1. *n* bruissement *m* (d'ailes); ronflement *m,* ronronnement *m* (de machines); vrombissement *m* (d'une hélice d'avion) 2. *vi* (*of machinery*) tourner à toute vitesse; ronfler, ronronner; (*of propeller*) vrombir.

whisk [(h)wisk] 1. *vtr* (*a*) (*of cow*) agiter (sa queue) (*b*) **to w. sth away, off,** enlever qch d'un geste rapide (*c*) *Cu:* battre (des œufs); fouetter (de la crème) 2. *n* (*a*) coup *m* (de queue) (*b*) (*for dusting*) époussette *f* (*c*) *Cu:* batteur *m,* fouet *m* (à œufs).

whiskers ['(h)wiskəz] *npl* moustache(s) *fpl* (de chat); (*side whiskers*) favoris *mpl;* (*beard*) barbe *f;* (*moustache*) moustache(s).

whisk(e)y ['(h)wiski] *n* whisky *m.*

whisper ['(h)wispər] I. *n* chuchotement *m;* **to speak in a w.,** parler tout bas; *Th:* **stage w.,** aparté *m.* II. *v* 1. *vi* chuchoter; parler bas; **to w. to s.o.,** chuchoter à l'oreille de qn 2. *vtr* **to w. a word to s.o.,** dire, glisser, un mot à l'oreille de qn; **whispered conversation,** conversation *f* à voix basse; **it is whispered (that),** le bruit court (que). 'whisperer *n* chuchoteur, -euse. 'whispering *n* chuchotement *m;* **w. gallery,** galerie *f* à écho; voûte *f* acoustique; **w. campaign,** campagne sournoise.

whist [(h)wist] *n Cards:* whist *m;* **w. drive,** tournoi *m* de whist.

whistle ['(h)wisl] I. *n* 1. sifflement *m;* coup *m* de sifflet 2. sifflet *m;* **to blow a w.,** donner un coup de sifflet. II. *v* 1. *vi* (*a*) siffler; **to w. for one's dog,** siffler son chien; *F:* **he can w. for his money!** il peut courir après son argent! (*b*) donner un coup de sifflet; **the bullet whistled past his ear,** il a entendu le sifflement de la balle près de son oreille 2. *vtr* siffler, siffloter (un air). 'whistler *n* siffleur, -euse. 'whistle-stop *n* (*a*) *NAm:* Rail: halte *f* (à arrêt facultatif) (*b*) **w.-s. tour,** tournée (électorale) rapide. 'whistling *n* sifflement *m;* sifflotement *m.*

whit¹ [(h)wit] *n* brin *m,* iota *m;* **he's not a w. the better for it,** il ne s'en porte aucunement mieux.

Whit² *a* W. Sunday, (le dimanche de) la Pentecôte; W. Monday, le lundi de la Pentecôte.

white ['(h)wait] 1. *a* blanc, *f* blanche; (cheveux) blancs; (Noël) sous la neige; (gelée) blanche; (sauce) béchamel (*f*); (pain, vin) blanc; **the w. races,** les races blanches; **a w. man,** un blanc; **he's going w.,** il commence à blanchir; **as w. as a sheet, as a ghost,** pâle comme un linge, comme la mort; **as w. as snow,** blanc comme (la) neige; **w. with fear,** blanc, blême, de peur; **w. spirit,** white-spirit *m;* **w. coffee,** café au lait; (café) crème *m; NAm:* **the W. House,** la Maison Blanche 2. *n* (*a*) blanc *m,* couleur blanche; **dressed in w.,** habillé en, de, blanc (*b*) (*pers*) blanc, blanche; homme, femme, de la race blanche (*c*) **w. of egg,** blanc d'œuf; **w. of the**

eye, blanc de l'œil. 'whitebait *n* (*inv in pl*) blanchaille *f;* **a dish of w.,** une friture. 'white-'collar *a* **w.-c. worker,** employé de bureau. 'white-'haired *a* aux cheveux blancs. 'whiten *vtr* blanchir. 'whiteness *n* (*a*) pâleur *f.* 'whitethorn *n* aubépine *f.* 'whitewash 1. *n* blanc *m* de chaux; badigeon blanc 2. *vtr* (*a*) blanchir à la chaux; badigeonner en blanc (*b*) blanchir, disculper (qn). 'whitewashing *n* (*a*) peinture *f* à la chaux; badigeonnage *m* en blanc (*b*) réhabilitation *f* (de qn). 'whitewood *n* bois blanc.

whiting ['(h)waitiŋ] *n* (*inv in pl*) *Ich:* merlan *m.*

whitlow ['(h)witlou] *n Med:* panaris *m.*

Whitsun(tide) ['(h)witsən(taid)] *n* la Pentecôte.

whittle ['(h)witl] *vtr* **to w. down,** amenuiser (qch); rogner (la pension de qn).

whiz(z) [(h)wiz] 1. *vi* (**whizzed**) (*of bullet*) siffler; **to w. past,** passer en sifflant; passer à toute vitesse 2. *n* sifflement *m* (d'une balle). 'whiz(z)-kid *n* jeune prodige *m.*

who [huː] *pron* nom 1. (*interr*) qui? qui est-ce qui? **w. is that man?** qui, quel, est cet homme? **w. is it? w. is that?** qui est-ce? **w. on earth is it?** qui cela peut-il bien être? **w. found it?** qui l'a trouvé? *F:* **w. does he think he is?** pour qui se prend-il? **who's speaking?** (qui est-ce) qui parle? **w. did you say?** qui ça? **tell me who's w.,** ditesmoi qui sont tous ces gens-là; *F:* **w. are you looking for?** qui cherchez-vous? 2. (*rel*) (*a*) qui; **my friend w. came yesterday,** mon ami qui est venu hier; **those w. don't work,** ceux qui ne travaillent pas (*b*) lequel, *f* laquelle, *pl* lesquel(le)s; **this girl's father, w. is very rich,** le père de cette fille, lequel est très riche. whodunit [huːˈdʌnit] *n F:* roman policier. who'ever *pron* (*a*) celui qui; quiconque; **w. finds it may keep it,** celui qui le trouvera, quiconque le trouvera, peut le garder (*b*) qui que + *sub;* **w. you are, speak!** qui que vous soyez, parlez! (*c*) **w. she marries will be lucky,** celui qu'elle épousera sera heureux; **w. you like,** qui vous voudrez.

WHO *abbr* World Health Organization, Organisation mondiale de la santé, OMS.

whoa [wou] *int* (*to horse*) ho! holà! *F:* (*to pers*) doucement! attendez!

whole [houl] 1. *a* intégral, entier; complet; **roasted w.,** rôti entier; **he swallowed it w.,** (i) il l'a avalé tout rond (ii) *F:* il a pris ça pour de l'argent comptant; **w. number,** nombre entier; **w. length,** longueur totale; **to tell the w. truth,** dire toute la vérité; **to last a w. week,** durer toute une semaine; **w. families were killed,** des familles entières se sont fait tuer; **the w. world,** le monde entier; **the w. lot of you,** vous tous 2. *n* tout *m,* totalité *f,* ensemble *m;* **the w. of the school,** l'école entière; toute l'école; **the w. of our resources,** la totalité de nos ressources; **as a w.,** dans son ensemble; en totalité; **on the w.,** à tout prendre; en somme; dans l'ensemble. 'wholemeal (pain) complet; (farine) de son. 'wholesale 1. *n* (vente *f* en) gros *m;* **w. and retail,** gros et détail 2. *a* (*a*) **w. trade, firm,** commerce *m,* maison *f,* de gros; **w. price,** prix *m* de gros (*b*) **w. slaughter,** tuerie *f* en masse; massacre *m* 3. *adv* (vendre, acheter) en gros. 'wholesaler *n* grossiste *mf.* 'wholewheat *a* (pain) complet; (farine) de son. 'wholly *adv* (*a*) tout à fait; complètement, entièrement (b) intégralement; en totalité; **w. or partly**, en tout ou en partie.

wholesome ['houlsəm] a sain; (air, climat) salubre. '**wholesomeness** n nature saine; salubrité f (du climat, de l'air).

whom [hu:m] pron (object) **1.** (interr) qui? **w. did you see?** qui avez-vous vu? **of w. are you speaking?** de qui parlez-vous? **2.** (rel) (a) (direct) que; **the man w. you saw**, l'homme que vous avez vu (b) (ind after prep) **the friend to w. I lent the book**, l'ami à qui j'ai prêté le livre; **the man of w. I was speaking**, l'homme dont je parlais; **the two officers between w. she was sitting**, les deux officiers entre lesquels elle était assise.

whoop [hu:p] **1.** n cri m (de joie); Med: quinte f (de la coqueluche) **2.** vi pousser des cris (de joie); Med: faire la quinte convulsive de la coqueluche; **whooping cough**, coqueluche. **whoopee** ['wupi] **1.** int hourra! **2.** n F: **to make w.**, faire la noce, la bombe; s'amuser, se régaler. **whoops** int houp-là!

whopper ['(h)wɔpər] n F: quelque chose de colossal, d'énorme; mensonge m énorme. '**whopping** a énorme; colossal.

whore [hɔ:r] n prostituée f, putain f.

whose [hu:z] poss pron **1.** (interr) de qui? (ownership) à qui? **w. are these gloves?** **w. gloves are these?** à qui sont ces gants? **w. daughter are you?** de qui êtes-vous la fille? **2.** (rel) dont; **the pupil w. work I showed you**, l'élève dont je vous ai montré le travail.

why [(h)wai] **1.** adv (a) (interr) pourquoi? pour quelle raison? **w. didn't you say so?** pourquoi ne l'avez-vous pas dit? il fallait le dire! **w. not?** pourquoi pas? **w. not tell her?** pourquoi ne pas lui dire? (b) that's (the reason) **w.**, voilà pourquoi; **I'll tell you w.**, je vais vous dire pourquoi **2.** n pourquoi m **3.** int **w., it's David!** tiens, c'est David! **w. of course!** mais bien sûr! **w., you're not afraid, are you?** voyons, vous n'avez pas peur? **w., what's the matter?** mais qu'avez-vous donc?

WI abbr Women's Institute.

wick [wik] n mèche f (d'une lampe, d'une bougie).

wicked ['wikid] a **1.** mauvais, méchant **2.** malicieux. '**wickedly** adv **1.** méchamment **2.** malicieusement. '**wickedness** n méchanceté f, perversité f.

wicker ['wikər] n osier m; **w. chair**, fauteuil en osier. '**wickerwork** n vannerie f; osier.

wicket ['wikit] n **1.** guichet m (d'une porte) **2.** (a) (in large door) porte à piétons (b) **w. (gate)**, petite porte à claire-voie; portillon m (de passage à niveau) **3.** NAm: (in post office, bank) guichet **4.** Cr: guichet; **w. keeper**, gardien de guichet.

wide [waid] **1.** a (a) large; **to be 10 metres w.**, avoir 10 mètres de large; **how w. is the room?** quelle est la largeur de la pièce? (b) étendu, vaste, ample; **the w. world**, le vaste monde (c) (vêtement) ample, large (d) éloigné, loin; **to be w. of the mark**, être loin du compte (e) F: malin, retors; **a w. boy**, un malin, un débrouillard **2.** adv (a) loin; **far and w.**, de tous côtés; **w. apart**, espacé; (jambes) écartées (b) (ouvrir) largement; **to fling the door w. open**, ouvrir la porte toute grande; **to be w. awake**, être complètement, tout à fait, éveillé. '**wide-angle** a Phot: (objectif) grand angulaire. '**wide-eyed** a les yeux grand ouverts, écarquillés. '**widely** adv largement; **w. read paper**, journal à grande circulation; **to be w. read**, (of author)

avoir un public très étendu; **w. known**, très connu; **he has travelled w.**, il a beaucoup voyagé. '**widen 1.** vtr élargir; accroître (ses connaissances); évaser (un trou); étendre (les limites de qch) **2.** vi s'élargir; s'agrandir (en large); **the breach is widening**, la rupture s'accentue. '**widespread** a (a) (of wings) étendu (b) répandu; universel; **w. opinion**, opinion largement répandue. **width** [widθ] n largeur f; **to be 10 metres w.**, avoir 10 mètres de largeur.

widow ['widou] n veuve f. '**widowed** a (homme) veuf; (femme) veuve; **he lives with his w. mother**, il habite avec sa mère qui est veuve. '**widower** n veuf m. '**widowhood** n veuvage m.

width [widθ] see **wide**.

wield [wi:ld] vtr manier (une épée); exercer (le pouvoir).

wife [waif] n (pl wives [waivz]) femme f, épouse f; **she was his second w.**, il l'avait épousée en secondes noces; **the farmer's w.**, la fermière; P: **the w.**, la ménagère, la bourgeoise; **old wives' tale**, conte de bonne femme. '**wifely** a (qualités) d'épouse, de femme mariée; **w. duties**, devoirs conjugaux.

wig [wig] n perruque f; postiche m.

wiggle ['wigl] vi & tr F: (se) tortiller; (se) remuer; **to w. one's toes**, remuer, agiter, les orteils. '**wiggly** a (trait) ondulé; (dent) qui branle.

wigwam ['wigwæm] n wigwam m.

wild [waild] **1.** a (a) sauvage; (fleur) des champs; (lapin) de garenne; (bête) farouche; (pays) inculte; (vent) furieux, violent; **a w. night**, une nuit de tempête; **w. beast**, bête f sauvage; **w. horses wouldn't drag it out of me**, rien au monde ne me le ferait dire (b) (pers) dissipé, dissolu; **w. life**, vie déréglée, de bâton de chaise (c) (pers) affolé; (regard) farouche; **w. eyes**, yeux égarés; **w. with joy**, fou, éperdu, de joie; F: **to be w. with s.o.**, être furieux contre qn; **it makes me w.**, ça me met en rage, me rend furieux (d) (of idea) fantasque, insensé; (enthousiasme) délirant; (applaudissements) frénétiques; **w. talk**, propos en l'air **2.** n (of animal) **in the w.**, à l'état sauvage; **the call of the w.**, l'appel de la jungle; **the wilds**, région sauvage; régions inexplorées; la brousse. '**wildcat** n chat m sauvage. **w. scheme**, projet insensé; **w. strike**, grève sauvage. '**wilderness** ['wildənis] n désert m; lieu m sauvage; pays m inculte. '**wildfire** n **to spread like w.**, se répandre comme une traînée de poudre. '**wildfowl** n coll gibier m à plume; gibier d'eau. '**wildlife** n coll faune f et flore f; la nature; **w. sanctuary**, réserve naturelle. '**wildly** adv (a) d'une manière extravagante; **to talk w.**, dire des folies; **w. inaccurate**, complètement inexact (b) (répondre) au hasard, au petit bonheur. '**wildness** n (a) état m sauvage (d'un pays, d'un animal); fureur f (du vent) (b) dérèglement m (des mœurs) (c) extravagance f (d'idées, de paroles).

wildebeest ['wildibi:st] n Z: gnou m.

wile [wail] vtr séduire, charmer (qn). **wiles** npl ruses fpl, artifices mpl.

wilful, NAm: **willful** ['wilful] a (a) (of pers) obstiné, entêté; volontaire (b) (of action) fait exprès, de propos délibéré; (meurtre) prémédité. '**wilfully**, NAm: '**willfully** a (a) obstinément (b) exprès; à dessein.

will [wil] n (a) volonté f; **to have a w. of one's own**, être volontaire; savoir ce qu'on veut; **to lack strength**

of w., manquer de caractère; **where there's a w. there's a way,** vouloir c'est pouvoir; **to work with a w.,** travailler de bon cœur, avec courage (b) décision f; volonté; Ecc: **Thy w. be done,** que ta volonté soit faite (c) bon plaisir; gré m; **at w.,** à volonté; à discrétion; **free w.,** libre arbitre m; **of one's own free w.,** de son plein gré; **I did it against my w.,** je l'ai fait malgré moi, à contrecœur, contre mon gré; **with the best w. in the world,** avec la meilleure volonté du monde (d) Jur: testament m; **the last w. and testament of X,** les dernières volontés de X; **to make one's w.,** faire son testament; **to leave s.o. sth in one's w.,** léguer qch à qn. **II.** vtr **1.** (a) **as fate willed,** comme le sort l'a voulu (b) **to w. s.o. into doing sth,** faire faire qch à qn (par un acte de volonté); (in hypnotism) suggestionner qn **2.** léguer (qch à qn); disposer de (qch) par testament. **III.** modal aux v def (pres **will;** pt & condit **would; w. not** often contracted to **won't**) **1.** (a) vouloir; **what would you expect me to do?** que voulez-vous que je fasse? **say what you w.,** quoi que vous disiez; **would to heaven I were free!** si seulement j'étais libre! **he could if he would,** il le pourrait s'il le voulait; **the engine won't start,** le moteur ne veut pas démarrer; **just wait a moment, w. you?** voulez-vous attendre un instant? **he won't have any of it,** il refuse d'en entendre parler; **I** won't **have it!** je ne le veux pas! **won't you sit down,** asseyez-vous, je vous en prie; **won't you have a cup of tea?** vous prendrez bien une tasse de thé? (b) (emphatic) **accidents w. happen,** on ne peut pas éviter les accidents; **he w. have his little joke,** il aime à plaisanter; **I quite forgot—you** would! je l'ai complètement oublié!—c'est bien de vous! **he will talk non stop,** il ne peut s'empêcher de parler; **he will go out in spite of his cold,** il persiste à sortir malgré son rhume (c) (habit) **this hen w. lay up to six eggs a week,** cette poule pond jusqu'à six œufs par semaine; **she would often come home tired out,** elle rentrait souvent très fatiguée (d) (conjecture) **would this be your cousin?** c'est là sans doute votre cousin? **2.** (auxiliary forming future tenses) **I will, I will not, you will, often I'll, I won't, you'll in** conversational style) (a) (emphatic) **I won't be caught again,** on ne m'y reprendra plus (b) **they'll go,** ils iront; **w. he be there?—he w.,** y sera-t-il?—oui (, bien sûr); **I'll starve!—no, you won't,** je mourrai de faim!—mais non! **you won't forget, will you?** vous ne l'oublierez pas, n'est-ce pas? vous m'écrirez, n'est-ce pas? **I think he'll come,** je crois qu'il viendra; **I'll dictate and you'll write,** moi je vais dicter et vous, vous allez écrire (c) (command) **you w. be here at three o'clock,** soyez ici à trois heures (d) (conditional) **he would come if you invited him,** il viendrait si vous l'invitiez. **'willing** a de bonne volonté; bien disposé; serviable; **a few w. men,** quelques hommes de bonne volonté; **w. hands,** mains empressées; **to be w.,** consentir, être consentant; **w. to do sth,** prêt à faire qch; **w. to help,** prêt à rendre service; F: **to show w.,** faire preuve de bonne volonté; **w. or not,** bon gré, mal gré. **'willingly** adv (a) de plein gré (b) (gladly) de bon cœur; volontiers. **'willingness** n (a) bonne volonté; **with the utmost w.,** de très bon cœur (b) consentement m. **'willpower** n volonté f; **to have no w.,** manquer de volonté.

will-o'-the-wisp ['wiləðəwisp] n feu follet.

willow ['wilou] n w. (tree), saule m; **weeping w.,** saule pleureur; **w. pattern,** décoration chinoise, motif chinois (en bleu). **'willowy** a souple, svelte, élancé.

willy-nilly ['wili'nili] adv bon gré, mal gré; de gré ou de force.

wilt [wilt] vi (a) (of plant) se flétrir, faner (b) (of pers) dépérir, languir.

wily ['waili] a (-ier, -iest) rusé; astucieux; malin.

win [win] **1.** n Sp: victoire f; **to have three wins in succession,** gagner trois fois de suite; **to back a horse for a w.,** jouer un cheval gagnant **2.** vtr & i (pt & pp **won** [wʌn]; **winning**) (a) gagner; remporter (une victoire, le prix); **to w. by a short head,** gagner de justesse (b) acquérir (de la popularité); captiver (l'attention); gagner (la confiance de qn); s'attirer (la sympathie de qn); **to w. a reputation,** se faire une réputation; **this action won him a decoration,** cette action lui a valu une décoration; **to w. s.o.'s love,** se faire aimer de qn; **to w. the day,** l'emporter. **'win 'back** vtr reconquérir; regagner (son argent). **'winner** n gagnant, ante; vainqueur m; F: **it's a w.,** c'est formidable; c'est un succès. **'winning 1.** a (a) **w. number,** numéro gagnant; (in lottery) numéro sortant; **w. stroke,** coup décisif (b) **w. ways,** manières avenantes; **w. smile,** sourire engageant, attrayant, séduisant **2.** n (a) victoire f; **w. post,** poteau d'arrivée; **the w. of the war,** le fait d'avoir gagné la guerre; **the w. of the war is the prime objective,** gagner la guerre est notre objectif principal (b) **winnings,** gains mpl (au jeu). **'win 'over** vtr gagner (qn); **to w. o. one's audience,** se concilier ses auditeurs. **'win 'through** vi parvenir à bout de ses difficultés.

wince [wins] vi faire une grimace de douleur; tressaillir de douleur; **without wincing,** sans sourciller, sans broncher.

winch [wintʃ] **1.** n treuil m (de hissage) **2.** vtr **to w. sth up,** hisser qch à l'aide d'un treuil.

wind¹ [wind] **1.** n (a) vent m; **the north w., the west w.,** le vent du nord, de l'ouest; **high w.,** vent fort, violent; **to see which way the w. blows,** regarder de quel côté vient le vent; **to go like the w.,** aller comme le vent; F: **to have, get, the w. up,** avoir le trac, la frousse; F: **to put the w. up s.o.,** faire une peur bleue, donner la frousse, à qn; **to sail, run, before the w.,** courir vent arrière; **in the teeth of the w.,** contre le vent; Fig: **to sail close to the w.,** friser (i) la malhonnêteté (ii) l'insolence (iii) l'indécence; **to take the w. out of s.o.'s sails,** déjouer les plans de qn; couper l'herbe sous le pied de qn; **w. gauge,** anémomètre m; **w. tunnel,** tunnel m aérodynamique; soufflerie f; F: **to get w. of sth,** avoir vent de qch (b) Med: flatuosité f; **to have w.,** avoir des gaz; **to break w.,** lâcher un pet; péter (c) souffle m, respiration f, haleine f; **to get one's second w.,** reprendre haleine (d) Mus: **w. instrument,** instrument m à vent; **the w.,** les instruments à vent **2.** vtr couper la respiration, le souffle, à (qn); **it completely winded me,** ça m'a complètement essoufflé, m'a mis à bout de souffle. **'windbag** n F: orateur verbeux; **he's just a w.,** il parle pour ne rien dire. **'windbreak** n brise-vent m. **'windcheater** n blouson m. **'windfall** n fruit tombé, abattu par le vent; Fig: aubaine f; profit, héritage, inattendu. **'windmill** n moulin m à vent. **'windpipe** n Anat: gosier m.

'**windproof** *a* à l'épreuve du vent. '**windscreen**, *NAm:* '**windshield** *n Aut:* pare-brise *m inv;* **w. wiper,** essuie-glace *m;* **w. washer,** lave-glace *m.* '**windsock** *n Av:* manche *f* à vent. '**windsurfer** *n* (*a*) planche *f* à voile (*b*) (*pers*) véliplanchiste *mf.* '**windsurfing** *n* to go **w.,** faire de la planche à voile. '**windswept** *a* balayé par le vent; venteux. '**windward** 1. *a & adv* au vent 2. *n* côté *m* du vent. '**windy** *a* (**-ier, -iest**) (*a*) venteux; **w. day,** journée de grand vent; **it's w.,** il fait du vent (*b*) balayé par le vent; exposé aux quatre vents; *F:* (*of pers*) **to be w.,** avoir le trac, la frousse.

wind² [waind] *v* (*pt & pp* **wound** [waund]) 1. *vi* tourner; faire des détours; (*of path, river*) serpenter; **road that winds up, down, the hill,** route qui monte, descend, en serpentant; **the river winds across the plain,** la rivière traverse la plaine en serpentant 2. *vtr* (*a*) enrouler; *Tex:* dévider (le fil); **to w. wool into a ball,** enrouler la laine en pelote (*b*) remonter (sa montre). '**wind** '**down** *vi* relaxer, se détendre. '**winding** 1. *a* (chemin) sinueux, qui serpente; (route) en lacets; (rue) tortueuse 2. *n* (*a*) mouvement sinueux; cours sinueux, replis *mpl* (*b*) *Tex:* bobinage *m;* **w. machine,** bobineuse *f* (*c*) remontage *m* (d'une horloge). '**wind** '**up** 1. *vtr* (*a*) enrouler (un cordage); remonter (une horloge); hisser (qch avec un treuil); *F:* (*of pers*) **to be all wound up,** avoir les nerfs en pelote (*b*) terminer (qch); *Com:* liquider (une société); régler, clôturer (un compte) 2. *vi* finir, terminer; **the company wound up,** la société s'est mise en liquidation; *F:* **he'll w. up in prison,** il finira en prison.

windlass ['windləs] *n* (*pl* **windlasses**) treuil *m.*

window ['windou] *n* (*a*) fenêtre *f;* **to look out of the w.,** regarder par la fenêtre; **I've broken a w.,** j'ai cassé une vitre, un carreau; **w. seat,** banquette *f* (dans l'embrasure d'une fenêtre); **w. cleaner,** laveur de vitres; **w. box,** caisse, bac, à fleurs (sur le rebord d'une fenêtre); **stained-glass w.,** vitrail *m* (d'église) (*b*) *Veh:* glace *f; Aut:* **rear w.,** lunette *f* arrière; *Rail:* **it is dangerous to lean out of the w.,** il est dangereux de se pencher dehors (*c*) (*of ticket office*) guichet *m* (*d*) *Com:* vitrine *f,* devanture *f;* **in the w.,** en vitrine; *F:* **w. shopping,** lèche-vitrines *m;* **to go w. shopping,** lécher les vitrines, faire du lèche-vitrines; **w. dressing,** (i) art *m* de l'étalage (ii) *Fig:* façade *f;* camouflage *m.* '**windowledge**, '**windowsill** *n* (*outside*) rebord *m,* (*inside*) appui *m,* de fenêtre. '**windowpane** *n* vitre *f,* carreau *m.*

wine [wain] 1. *n* vin *m;* **white, red, rosé, w.,** vin blanc, rouge, rosé; **dry, sweet, w.,** vin sec, doux; **sparkling w.,** vin mousseux; **w. production, producing,** viticulture *f;* **w.-producing region,** région viticole; **glass of w.,** verre de vin; **w. merchant,** négociant en vins; **w. grower,** viticulteur, -trice; **w. vinegar,** vinaigre de vin; (*in restaurant*) **w. list,** carte *f* des vins; **w. cellar,** cave *f* à vins; **w. waiter,** sommelier *m* 2. *vtr* **to w. and dine s.o.,** offrir à qn un repas soigné; fêter qn. '**wine-coloured**, *NAm:* **-colored** *a* lie-de-vin *inv.* '**wineglass** *n* (*pl* **-es**) verre *m* à vin. '**winegrowing** 1. *n* viticulture *f* 2. *a* (industrie) viticole. '**winerack** *n* casier *m* à bouteilles.

wing [wiŋ] *n* (*a*) aile *f* (d'oiseau, d'avion); **to take s.o. under one's wing,** prendre qn sous son aile, sous sa

protection (*b*) aile (d'un bâtiment); oreillette *f* (d'un fauteuil); *Mil:* escadre (aérienne); **w. commander,** lieutenant-colonel *m;* **the wings,** (i) *Th:* les coulisses *f* (ii) *Sp:* (*pers*) les ailiers *m* (iii) *Av:* la voilure (d'un avion). **winged** *a* ailé. '**wingless** *a* sans ailes. '**wingspan** *n* envergure *f.*

wink [wiŋk] 1. *n* clignement *m* d'œil; clin *m* d'œil; **in a w.,** en un clin d'œil; **with a w.,** en clignant de l'œil; *F:* **to tip s.o. the w.,** avertir qn (en faisant un clin d'œil); *F:* **to have forty winks,** faire un petit somme, une petite sieste; **I didn't sleep a w.,** je n'ai pas fermé l'œil de la nuit 2. *vi* (*a*) cligner des yeux; **to w. at s.o.,** cligner de l'œil, faire un clin d'œil, à qn (*b*) (*of light*) vaciller, clignoter. '**winking** *n* clignement *m* de l'œil; **as easy as w.,** simple comme bonjour.

winkle ['wiŋkl] *n Moll:* bigorneau *m.*

winner ['winər] *see* **win.**

winter ['wintər] 1. *n* hiver *m;* **in w.,** en hiver; **in the w. of 1984,** pendant l'hiver de 1984; **w. clothes,** vêtements *m* d'hiver; **w. sports,** sports *m* d'hiver; **w. resort,** station *f* d'hiver 2. *vi* hiverner; passer l'hiver (**at, à**). '**wintertime** *n* l'hiver. '**wintry** *a* d'hiver; hivernal; **w. weather,** temps d'hiver; **w. smile,** sourire glacial; sourire décourageant.

wipe [waip] 1. *vtr* essuyer (qch); effacer (le tableau); **to w. one's eyes,** s'essuyer les yeux; **to w. one's nose,** se moucher; **to w. (up),** essuyer la vaisselle; **to w. sth dry, clean,** bien essuyer qch 2. *n* coup *m* de torchon, de mouchoir, d'éponge; **give it a w.!** essuyez-le un peu! '**wipe a**'**way** *vtr* essuyer (ses larmes). '**wipe** '**off** *vtr* effacer (un tableau); essuyer (une éclaboussure). '**wiper** *n* **windscreen**, *NAm:* **windshield w.,** essuie-glace *m.* '**wipe** '**out** *vtr* (*a*) liquider, amortir (une dette) (*b*) exterminer (une armée, une famille) (*c*) *F:* tuer, assassiner (qn). '**wipe up** *vtr & i* (*a*) enlever (une saleté) (*b*) essuyer la vaisselle.

wire ['waiər] 1. *n* (*a*) fil *m* métallique; fil de fer; **copper w.,** fil de laiton; **w. netting, chicken w.,** grillage *m,* treillage *m,* en fil de fer; **w. brush,** brosse métallique; **barbed w.,** (fil de fer) barbelé (*m*); **w. mattress,** sommier métallique; **telegraph wires,** fils télégraphiques; **w. tapping,** écoute téléphonique; *F:* **to get one's wires crossed,** se tromper; *F:* (*pers*) **a live w.,** une personne dégourdie (*b*) télégramme *m* 2. *vtr* (*a*) faire l'installation électrique, poser l'électricité, dans (une maison) (*b*) télégraphier (qch à qn). '**wired** *a* monté sur fil de fer; (*of enclosure*) grillagé. '**wireless** 1. *a* sans fil 2. *a & n* **w. (set),** (poste *m* de) radio *f.* '**wirepulling** *n F:* intrigues *fpl.* '**wiring** *n* pose *f* de fils électriques; installation *f* électrique. '**wiry** *a* (**-ier, -iest**) (*of hair*) raide, rude; (*of pers*) sec et nerveux.

wise [waiz] *a* sage; prudent; **the W. Men,** les Rois Mages; **to look w.,** prendre un (petit) air entendu; **he's none the wiser for it,** il n'en est pas plus avancé; **to do sth without anyone being any the wiser,** faire qch à l'insu de tout le monde; **say nothing and nobody will be any the wiser,** si tu te tais personne n'en saura rien; **the wisest thing to do is to go,** le plus sage est de partir. **wisdom** ['wizdəm] *n* sagesse *f;* **w. tooth,** dent de sagesse. '**wisecrack** *n* mot *m* d'esprit désobligeant; vanne *f.* '**wisely** *adv* sagement; prudemment.

wish [wiʃ] I. • 1. *vi* **to w. for sth,** désirer, souhaiter, qch; **to have everything one could w. for,** avoir tout à souhait; **what more could you w. for?** que voudriez-vous de plus? **2.** *vtr* vouloir: **to w. to do sth,** désirer, vouloir, faire qch; **I don't w. you to do it,** je ne veux pas que vous le fassiez; **I w. I were in your place,** je voudrais être à votre place; **I w. I had seen it, him,** j'aurais bien voulu le voir; **I w. he would come!** pourvu qu'il vienne! **I w. I hadn't done it,** je regrette de l'avoir fait; **I w. I could (do it),** si seulement je pouvais (le faire); *F:* **it's been wished on me,** c'est une chose que je n'ai pas pu refuser: **to w. s.o. well,** (i) être bien disposé envers qn (ii) souhaiter bonne chance à qn; **to w. s.o. goodnight,** dire bonsoir à qn; souhaiter une bonne nuit à qn; **I w. you a happy New Year,** je vous souhaite une bonne et heureuse année. **II.** *n* (*pl* wishes) (*a*) désir *m*; vœu *m*; **I haven't the slightest w. to go,** je n'ai aucune envie d'y aller: **everything seems to go according to his wishes,** tout semble lui réussir à souhait; **you shall have your w.,** votre désir sera exaucé; **against my wishes,** contre mon gré (*b*) souhait *m*, vœu; **my best wishes to your mother,** présentez mon meilleur souvenir à votre mère; *Corr:* **with best wishes,** (bien) amicalement. **'wishbone** *n* fourchette *f* (d'un poulet). **'wishful** *a F:* **that's w. thinking,** c'est prendre ses désirs pour des réalités.

wishy-washy ['wiʃiwɔʃi] *a F:* fade, insipide.

wisp [wisp] *n* brin *m* (de paille); traînée *f* (de fumée); mèche folle (de cheveux); **she's only a w. of a girl,** elle est toute menue. **'wispy** *a* (*of grass, hair*) très fin.

wisteria [wi'stiəriə] *n Bot:* glycine *f.*

wistful ['wistful] *a* (regard) plein d'un vague désir, d'un vague regret; **w. smile,** sourire (i) désenchanté (ii) pensif. **'wistfully** *adv* d'un air songeur et triste; d'un air de regret.

wit [wit] *n* (*a*) (*usu pl*) esprit *m*, entendement *m*; intelligence *f*; **to have lost one's wits,** avoir perdu la raison; **to collect one's wits,** se ressaisir; **to have one's wits about one,** avoir toute sa présence d'esprit; **that will sharpen your wits,** cela va vous aiguiser l'intelligence; **to be at one's wits' end,** ne plus savoir de quel côté se tourner; **to live by one's wits,** vivre d'expédients; **to have a battle of wits,** jouer au plus fin; **he hasn't the wits to see it,** il n'est pas assez intelligent pour s'en apercevoir; **use your wits!** réfléchis un peu! (*b*) vivacité *f* d'esprit; **flash of w.,** trait d'esprit (*c*) (*pers*) homme, femme, d'esprit. **'witticism** *n* mot *m* d'esprit. **'wittily** *a* spirituellement; avec esprit. **'wittiness** *n* esprit *m.* **'witty** *a* (-ier, -iest) spirituel; plein d'esprit.

witch [witʃ] *n* sorcière *f*; **w. hunt,** chasse aux sorcières; **w. doctor,** sorcier (guérisseur); *F:* **old w.,** vieille sorcière; *F:* **you little w.!** petite ensorceleuse! **'witchcraft** *n* sorcellerie *f*; magie noire.

with [wið] *prep* (*a*) avec; **to work w. s.o.,** travailler avec qn; **he's staying w. friends,** il est chez des amis; **is there someone w. you?** êtes-vous accompagné? **I'll be w. you in a moment,** je serai à vous dans un moment (*b*) **girl w. blue eyes,** jeune fille aux yeux bleus; **child w. a cold,** enfant enrhumé; **w. his hat on,** le chapeau sur la tête; **he came w. his overcoat on,** il est venu en pardessus; **have you a pencil w. you?** avez-vous un crayon sur vous? **w. your intelligence,** intelligent comme vous l'êtes; **to leave a child w. s.o.,** laisser un enfant à la garde de qn; **this decision rests w. you,** c'est à vous de décider (*c*) **w. all his faults,** malgré tous ses défauts (*d*) **to trade w. France,** faire du commerce avec la France; **I have nothing to do w. him,** je n'ai rien à faire avec lui; **I can do nothing w. him,** je ne peux rien en faire; **all's well with him,** il va bien; **to be sincere w. oneself,** être sincère avec soi-même; **it's a habit w. me,** c'est une habitude chez moi; **I sympathize w. you,** je vous plains sincèrement; **I don't agree w. you,** je ne suis pas de votre avis; **I'm w. you there!** (i) je comprends (ii) j'en conviens! d'accord! **I am not w. you,** je ne (vous) comprends pas; *F:* **to be w. it,** être dans le vent, à la page (*e*) **w. a cry,** en poussant un cri; **w. these words he left me,** là-dessus, alors, sur ce, il m'a quitté; **to wrestle w. s.o.,** lutter avec qn; **to fight w. s.o.,** se battre contre qn; **to part w. sth,** se défaire de qch (*f*) **to cut sth w. a knife,** couper qch avec un couteau, au couteau; **to walk w. a stick,** marcher avec une canne; **to take sth w. both hands,** prendre qch à deux mains; **to strike w. all one's might,** frapper de toutes ses forces; **w. pleasure,** avec plaisir; **he's in bed w. flu,** il est retenu au lit avec la grippe; **to tremble w. rage,** trembler de rage; **to be stiff w. cold,** être engourdi par le froid; **to be ill w. measles,** avoir la rougeole; **red w. blood,** rouge de sang; **to fill a vase w. water,** remplir un vase d'eau; **it's pouring w. rain,** il pleut à verse (*g*) **to work w. courage,** travailler avec courage; **to receive s.o. w. open arms,** recevoir qn à bras ouverts; **w. all due respect,** avec tout le respect que je vous dois; **w. the object (of),** dans l'intention (de); **I say it w. regret,** je le dis à regret; **w. a few exceptions,** à part quelques exceptions; **down w. the President!** à bas le Président! **to hell w. him!** qu'il aille au diable!

withdraw [wið'drɔ:] (**withdrew** [-dru:], **withdrawn**) **1.** *vtr* (*a*) retirer (sa main); ramener (des troupes) en arrière; **to w. coins from circulation,** retirer des pièces de la circulation; **to w. money from the bank,** retirer une somme d'argent de la banque (*b*) retirer (une offre, une plainte, une promesse); revenir sur une promesse; *Com:* **to w. an order,** annuler une commande; *Jur:* **to w. an action,** abandonner un procès **2.** *vi* se retirer; s'éloigner; se replier (sur soi-même); *Mil:* se replier; (*of candidate*) **to w. in favour of s.o.,** se désister en faveur de qn. **with'drawal** *n* retrait *m* (de troupes, d'une somme d'argent, d'une plainte); rétractation *f* (d'une offre); retraite *f*; *Mil:* repli *m* (des troupes); désistement *m* (d'un candidat); **w. symptoms,** (état de) manque *m.* **with'drawn** *a* (*of pers*) réservé.

wither ['wiðər] **1.** *vi* (*of plant*) se dessécher, se faner **2.** *vtr* (*a*) dessécher, flétrir, faner (une plante); ternir (la beauté) (*b*) **to w. s.o. with a look,** foudroyer qn du regard. **'withered** *a* (*a*) (*of plant*) desséché, fané (*b*) **w. arm,** bras atrophié. **'withering 1.** *n* dessèchement *m* **2.** *a* (regard) foudroyant. **'witheringly** *adv* d'un regard foudroyant; d'un ton de mépris.

withhold [wið'hould] *vtr* (*pt & pp* **withheld**) (*a*) refuser (son consentement) (*b*) cacher (la vérité) (*c*) retenir (un montant d'argent sur un paiement).

within [wið'in] **1.** *adv* **from w.,** de l'intérieur **2.** *prep* (*a*) à l'intérieur de; **w. four walls,** entre quatre murs; **w. these four walls,** (soit dit) entre nous; **to keep w. the law,** rester dans les limites de la légalité; **w. the meaning of the act,** selon les prévisions de la loi; **to live w. one's income,** vivre dans les limites de ses moyens;

w. **reason,** dans les limites du possible; **weight w. a kilo,** poids à un kilo près (b) **w. sight,** en vue; **w. call,** à (la) portée de la voix; **situated w. five kilometres of the town,** situé à moins de cinq kilomètres de la ville; **w. a radius of ten kilometres,** dans un rayon de dix kilomètres; **w. an inch of death,** à deux doigts de la mort; **w. an hour,** dans, avant, une heure; **w. ten days,** dans un délai de dix jours; **w. the week,** avant la fin de la semaine; **w. the next five years,** d'ici cinq ans; **w. a short time,** (i) à court délai (ii) peu de temps après; **w. living memory,** de mémoire d'homme.

without [wið'aut] prep sans; **w. friends,** sans amis; **to be w. food,** manquer de nourriture; **he arrived w. money or luggage,** il est arrivé sans argent ni bagages; **w. anybody knowing,** sans que personne le s!che, à l'insu de tous; **w. looking,** sans regarder; **not w. difficulty,** non sans difficulté; **w. seeing me,** sans me voir; **that goes w. saying,** cela va sans dire; **to go w. sth,** se passer de qch.

withstand [wið'stænd] vtr (pt & pp **withstood**) résister à (la douleur); supporter (la chaleur); Mil: soutenir (une attaque).

witness ['witnis] I. n (a) témoignage m; **to bear w. to sth,** témoigner de qch (b) (pers) témoin m (**of an incident,** d'un incident); **to call s.o. as a w.,** citer qn comme témoin; **w. box** = barre f des témoins; **w. for the defence, the prosecution,** témoin à décharge, à charge. II. v 1. vtr (a) être témoin d'(un incident) (b) attester (un acte); certifier (une signature) 2. vi **to w. to sth,** témoigner de qch; **to w. against s.o.,** témoigner contre qn.

wizard ['wizəd] n sorcier m; magicien m; **a financial w.,** un génie de la finance.

wizened ['wizənd] a desséché, ratatiné; (visage) parcheminé.

wobble ['wɔbl] 1. vi vaciller; (of table) branler; (of pers) chanceler; (of wheel) tourner à faux 2. n branlement m, oscillation f; tremblement m; Aut: **front wheel w.,** shimmy m. '**wobbly** a branlant, vacillant; hors d'aplomb; (chaise) bancale; **my legs feel w.,** j'ai les jambes en coton.

woe [wou] n malheur m, chagrin m, peine f; **to tell a tale of w.,** faire le récit de ses malheurs. '**woebegone** a triste, désolé, abattu. '**woeful** a malheureux, (histoire) attristante. '**woefully** adv tristement.

woke, woken [wouk, 'woukən] see **wake**[3].

wolf [wulf] 1. n (pl **wolves** [wulvz]) (a) loup m; **she-w.,** louve f; **w. cub,** louveteau m; **prairie w.,** coyote m; **to cry w.,** crier au loup; **that will keep the w. from the door,** cela vous mettra à l'abri du besoin (b) F: tombeur m (de femmes); **w. whistle,** sifflement admiratif (au passage d'une jolie femme) 2. vtr **to w. one's food,** avaler sa nourriture à grosses bouchées; engloutir sa nourriture. '**wolfhound** n lévrier m d'Irlande. '**wolfish** a vorace.

woman ['wumən] n (pl **women** ['wimin]) femme f; **a young w.,** une jeune femme; **an old w.,** une vieille (femme); P: **the old w.,** ma femme, la bourgeoise; **w. doctor,** femme médecin; **w. friend,** amie f; **w. hater,** misogyne m; **Women's Liberation Movement,** F: **women's lib,** Mouvement pour la libération de la femme (MLF); **women's magazine,** revue féminine;

women's team, équipe féminine. '**womanhood** n to grow to w., devenir femme. '**womanizer** n coureur m de jupons. '**womankind** n coll les femmes. '**womanly** a féminin; **she's so w.,** elle est tellement femme. '**womenfolk** npl **my w.,** les femmes de la famille.

womb [wu:m] n Anat: matrice f, utérus m.

won [wʌn] see **win** 2.

wonder ['wʌndər] I. n 1. merveille f, prodige m; **to promise wonders,** promettre monts et merveilles; **to work wonders,** faire des merveilles; **the seven wonders of the world,** les sept merveilles du monde; **a nine days' w.,** la merveille d'un jour; **it's a w. he hasn't lost it,** il est étonnant qu'il ne l'ait pas perdu; **no w.,** rien d'étonnant 2. (a) étonnement m, surprise f (b) émerveillement m; **to fill s.o. with w.,** émerveiller qn. II. v 1. vi s'étonner, s'émerveiller (**at,** de); **I shouldn't w.,** cela ne m'étonnerait pas; **it's not to be wondered at,** cela n'est pas étonnant; **it makes me w.,** cela m'intrigue 2. vtr (a) s'étonner 2. vtr (a) s'étonner; **I w. he didn't buy it,** je m'étonne qu'il ne l'ait pas acheté (b) se demander; **I w. whether he will come,** je me demande s'il viendra; **I w. why,** je voudrais bien savoir pourquoi; **I w. who invented that,** je suis curieux de savoir qui a inventé cela; **I w. what I should do,** je ne sais pas que faire, ce qu'il faudrait que je fasse. '**wonderful** a merveilleux, prodigieux; **w. to relate,** chose étonnante, remarquable; **we had a w. time,** nous nous sommes très bien amusés; **it was w.!** c'était magnifique! '**wonderfully** adv merveilleusement; **w. well,** à merveille. '**wondering** a songeur; étonné. '**wonderland** n pays m des merveilles. '**wonderment** n étonnement m.

wonky ['wɔŋki] a F: branlant; patraque; détraqué.

won't [wount] = will not see **will** III.

wood [wud] n (a) (small forest) bois m; **you can't see the w. for the trees,** les arbres empêchent de voir la forêt; on se perd dans les détails; **we're not out of the woods yet,** nous ne sommes pas encore tirés d'affaire; **w. anemone,** anémone des bois; **w. pigeon,** (pigeon) ramier m (b) (material) bois; **made of w.,** fait de, en, bois; **w. shavings,** copeaux m; **touch w.!** NAm: knock on w.! touchons du bois! **w. carving, engraving,** sculpture, gravure, sur bois; **w. pulp,** pâte à papier (c) Golf: bois. '**woodchuck** n Z: marmotte f d'Amérique. '**woodcock** n Orn: bécasse f. '**woodcraft** n connaissance f de la forêt. '**woodcut** n gravure f sur bois. '**woodcutter** n bûcheron m. '**wooded** a boisé. '**wooden** a (a) de bois, en bois (b) (of movement, manner) raide, gauche. '**woodland** n pays boisé; bois m. '**woodlouse** n (pl -lice) cloporte m. '**woodpecker** n Orn: pic m; **green w.,** pivert m. '**woodshed** n bûcher m; hangar m à bois. '**woodsman** n (pl -men) chasseur m (en forêt); forestier m, occ bûcheron m. '**woodwind** n Mus: les bois m. '**woodwork** n (a) travail m du bois; charpenterie f; menuiserie f (b) bois travaillé; boiseries fpl; charpente f; menuiserie. '**woodworm** n ver m du bois; **this table's got w.,** cette table est vermoulue.

woof [wuf] (of dog) 1. n aboiement m 2. vi aboyer.

wool [wul] n 1. laine f; **w. cloth,** tissu de laine; **w. dress,** robe en laine; **ball of w.,** pelote de laine; **the w. trade,** commerce des laines; **knitting w.,** laine à tricoter; F: **to**

pull the w. over s.o.'s eyes, jeter de la poudre aux yeux de qn **2.** pelage *m* (d'animal) **3. steel, wire, w.,** paille *f* de fer. **'woolgathering** *n* F: rêvasserie *f*; **to be w.,** être dans la lune. **'woollen** *a* de laine; **w. goods,** *npl* **woollens,** lainages *mpl.* **'woolliness** *n* manque *m* de netteté; imprécision *f* (de raisonnement). **'woolly,** *NAm: also* **wooly 1.** *a* (-ier, -iest) (*a*) laineux, de laine (*b*) (*of ideas, plans*) flou, peu net **2.** *n* (vêtement *m* en) tricot *m*; **put on your w.!** mets ton tricot! *pl* **woollies** lainages; vêtements chauds (d'hiver).

word [wəːd] **1.** *n* (*a*) mot *m*; **w. for w.,** (répéter qch) mot pour mot; (traduire qch) mot à mot; **in a w.,** en un mot; bref; **in other words,** en d'autres termes; autrement dit; **I told him in so many words (that),** je lui ai dit expressément (que); **bad isn't the w. for it,** mauvais n'est pas assez dire; **words of a song,** paroles *fpl* d'une chanson; **spoken words,** paroles; **w. blindness,** dislexie *f*; **in the words of the poet,** selon le poète; **a man of few words,** un homme qui parle peu; **to call on s.o. to say a few words,** prier qn de prendre la parole; **he didn't say a w.,** il n'a pas soufflé mot; **I can't get a w. out of him,** je ne peux pas le faire parler; **to put sth into words,** exprimer qch; **in so many words,** explicitement; **to put one's w. in,** intervenir; placer son mot; **without a w.,** sans mot dire; **you've taken the words out of my mouth,** c'est justement ce que j'allais dire; **to have the last w.,** avoir le dernier mot; F: **the last w. in colours,** les couleurs les plus nouvelles; **he's too stupid for words,** il est d'une bêtise indicible; **words fail me!** j'en perds la parole! **I'd like a w. with you,** j'ai un mot à vous dire; **I'll have a w. with him about it,** je lui en parlerai; **to say a good w. for s.o.,** dire un mot en faveur de qn; F: **to have words with s.o.,** se disputer avec qn; **w. of command,** ordre *m*; commandement *m*; *Cmptr:* **w. processing,** traitement *m* de textes; **w. processor,** machine de traitement de textes; **by w. of mouth,** de vive voix; verbalement (*b*) (*message*) avis *m*; nouvelle *f*; **to send s.o. w. of sth,** faire dire, faire savoir, qch à qn; prévenir qn de qch; **there's still no w. from her,** nous sommes toujours sans nouvelles d'elle; **w. came (that),** on nous a rapporté (que) (*c*) **to keep one's w.,** tenir (sa) parole; **to break one's w.,** manquer à sa parole; **to take s.o. at his w.,** croire qn sur parole; **you can take my w. for it,** croyez-m'en; je vous en réponds; **I'll take your w. for it,** je vous crois sur parole; **my w.!** tiens! qui l'aurait cru? **2.** *vtr* formuler (qch) par écrit; rédiger (un document, un télégramme); **it might have been differently worded,** on aurait pu l'exprimer en d'autres termes; **well worded,** bien exprimé. **'wordbook** *n* lexique *m*, vocabulaire *m*. **'wordiness** *n* verbosité *f*. **'wording** *n* mots *mpl*; termes *mpl* (d'un document); langage *m*; choix *m* des termes (d'un article); **your w. is not clear,** vous ne vous exprimez pas clairement. **'wordy** *a* verbeux; prolixe. **'word-'perfect** *a* (*of actor*) **to be w.-p.,** savoir son rôle sur le bout du doigt.

wore [wɔːr] *see* **wear I.**

work [wəːk] **I.** *n* (*a*) travail *m*; **to be at w.,** travailler; **he was hard at w.,** il était en plein travail; **to start w.,** to set **to w.,** se mettre au travail; **the forces at w.,** les forces en jeu; **to go the right way to w.,** s'y prendre bien (*b*) travail, ouvrage *m*, besogne *f*, tâche *f*; **a piece of w.,** un travail, un ouvrage, une œuvre; F: (*pers*) **a nasty piece of w.,** un sale type; **I've so much w. to do,** j'ai tellement

(de travail) à faire; **the brandy had done its w.,** l'eau-de-vie avait fait son effet; **to do s.o.'s dirty w.,** faire les sales besognes de qn; **a day's w.,** (le travail d')une journée; **that's a good day's w.,** j'ai bien travaillé aujourd'hui; **it's all in a day's w.,** ça fait partie de ma routine; c'est comme ça tous les jours; **it was thirsty w.,** c'était un travail qui donnait soif (*c*) ouvrage, œuvre (d'un auteur); tableau *m* (d'un peintre); **the works of Shakespeare,** l'œuvre, les œuvres, de Shakespeare; **a w. of art,** une œuvre d'art; (*charitable acts*) **good works,** bonnes œuvres (*d*) travail, emploi *m*; **office w.,** travail de bureau; **to be off w.,** ne pas travailler (parce qu'on est malade); **to go to w.,** se rendre au bureau, à l'usine, au travail; F: aller au boulot; **to be at w.,** être au bureau, à l'usine; **to be out of w.,** être sans travail, chômer; *Mil:* **defensive works,** ouvrages défensifs; **public works,** travaux publics; *PN:* **road works ahead!** travaux! chantier! F: **the whole works,** tout le bataclan, tout le tralala! **to give s.o. the works,** passer qn à tabac (*e*) rouages *mpl*, mécanisme *m*, mouvement *m* (d'une horloge) (*f*) *pl* (*often with sg const*) usine *f*; atelier *m*; **steel works,** aciérie *f*; **works committee,** comité d'entreprise; **price ex works,** prix départ usine. **II.** *v* **1.** *vi* (*a*) travailler; **to w. hard,** travailler dur, ferme; **he is working on a history of the war,** il travaille à, il prépare, une histoire de la guerre; **to w. to rule,** faire la grève du zèle; **to w. with an end in view,** travailler pour atteindre un but (*b*) (*of machine*) fonctionner, aller, marcher; **system that works well,** système qui fonctionne bien; **the pump isn't working,** la pompe ne marche pas; **medicine that works,** médicament qui produit son effet, qui agit; **his plan didn't w.,** son projet n'a pas réussi; F: **that won't w. with me!** ça ne prend pas avec moi! **2.** *vtr* (*a*) faire travailler (qn); **he works his men too hard,** il surmène ses hommes; **to w. oneself to death,** se tuer au, de, travail, à travailler (*b*) faire fonctionner, faire marcher (une machine); faire jouer (un ressort); **can you w. it?** sais-tu comment t'en servir? **to be worked by electricity,** marcher à l'électricité (*c*) faire (un miracle); **I'll w. it, things, so that,** je ferai en sorte que + *subj*; **his keys worked a hole in his pocket,** ses clefs ont fini par faire un trou dans sa poche; **to w. one's hands free,** parvenir à se dégager les mains; **to w. one's way through the crowd,** se frayer un chemin à travers la foule; **he was working his way through college,** il travaillait pour payer ses études; *Nau:* **to w. one's passage,** payer son passage en travaillant; **to w. oneself into a rage,** laisser monter sa colère; **to w. s.o. into a frenzy,** rendre qn fou d'inquiétude); affoler qn (*d*) exploiter (une mine); broder (un dessin); *Com:* (*of representative*) **to w. the south-eastern area,** faire le sud-est. **'workable** *a* (matériau) maniable; (mine) exploitable; (projet) réalisable. **'workaday** *a* de tous les jours; banal. **'workbag** *n* sac *m* à ouvrage. **'workbasket** *n* *Needlw:* corbeille *f* à ouvrage. **'workbench** *n* établi *m*. **'workbook** *n* cahier *m* de devoirs. **'workbox** *n* (*pl* **-es**) *Needlw:* boîte *f* à ouvrage. **'workday** *n* jour *m* ouvrable. **'worker** *n* travailleur, -euse; *esp Ind:* ouvrier, -ière; **heavy w.,** travailleur de force; **to be a hard w.,** travailleur dur; **white-collar, office, w.,** employé(e) (de bureau); **w. priest,** prêtre-ouvrier *m*; **w. bee,** ouvrière; **w. of miracles,** faiseur *m* de miracles. **'work 'in** *vtr* incorporer (qch à, dans, qch); introduire (qch dans qch). 'working 1. *a* (*a*) qui travaille; ouvrier; **the w. class,** la classe ouvrière; **w.-class district,** quartier populaire; **w. day,** jour ouvrable; journée de travail; **w. hours,** heures de travail; **w. lunch,** déjeuner d'affaires; **w. wife,** femme mariée qui travaille; **w. population,** population active; **in w. order,** en état de marche; **w. party,** équipe *f* (*b*) qui fonctionne; **w. parts (of a machine),** mécanisme *m* (d'une machine) 2. *npl* **workings** (*a*) chantier *m* d'exploitation (d'une mine) (*b*) rouages *mpl*; marche *f*, fonctionnement *m* (d'un mécanisme); **the workings of the mind,** le travail de l'esprit. 'workless 1. *a* sans travail 2. *npl* **the w.,** les chômeurs *m*; les sans-travail *m*. 'workman *n* (*pl* **-men**) ouvrier *m*. 'workmanlike *a* bien fait, bien travaillé; **in a w. manner,** avec compétence. 'workmanship *n* exécution *f*; façon *f*; **sound w.,** construction soignée; **a fine piece of w.,** un beau travail. 'workmate *n* camarade *mf* de travail; collègue *mf*. 'work 'off 1. *vtr* se débarrasser (de qch); perdre (du poids); dépenser (de l'énergie); cuver (sa colère); **to w. o. one's bad temper on s.o.,** passer sa mauvaise humeur sur qn 2. *vi* (of *nut*) se détacher. 'work 'on *vi* 1. continuer à travailler 2. (*a*) **we have no data to w. on,** nous n'avons pas de données sur lesquelles nous baser (*b*) **to w. on s.o.,** agir sur qn. 'work 'out 1. *vtr* (*a*) mener à bien (*b*) développer (une idée); résoudre (un problème); **the plan is being worked out,** le projet est à l'étude 2. *vi* (*a*) réussir; marcher; **my plan didn't w. out,** mon projet est tombé à l'eau; **how will things w. o.?** à quoi tout cela aboutira-t-il? **it worked out very well for me,** ça a bien marché pour moi (*b*) **how much does it w. o. at?** le total s'élève à combien? **I have to w. it out,** je dois d'abord le calculer; **he tried to w. it o. (in his mind),** il essaya d'y réfléchir; **it works out at £100,** le total s'élève à £100. 'workroom *n* atelier *m*. 'workshop *n* atelier *m*; **mobile w.,** camion-atelier. 'workshy *a* F: qui boude à la besogne; flemmard. 'work-to-rule *n* Ind: grève *f* du zèle. 'work 'up 1. *vtr* (*a*) développer (une situation); **to w. up an appetite,** s'ouvrir l'appétit; **to w. one's way up to the top,** arriver au sommet par ses propres moyens (*b*) préparer (un sujet) (*c*) exciter, émouvoir (qn); **to be worked up,** être énervé 2. *vi* **what are you working up to?** à quoi voulez-vous en venir?

world [wɔːld] *n* monde *m*; **in this w.,** en ce bas ici-bas; **he's not long for this w.,** il n'a pas longtemps à vivre; **to bring a child into the w.,** mettre un enfant au monde; **to be alone in the w.,** être seul au monde; **the happiest man in the w.,** l'homme le plus heureux du monde; **what in the w. is the matter with you?** mais qu'avez-vous donc? **I wouldn't do it for the w.,** je ne le ferais pour rien au monde; **to go round the w.,** faire le tour du monde; **the Old W.,** le vieux monde, le vieux continent; **the New W.,** le nouveau monde; **the ancient w.,** l'antiquité *f*; **all the w. over,** dans le monde entier; **it's a small w.!** que le monde est petit! **w. politics,** politique mondiale; **w. power,** puissance mondiale; **w. war,** guerre mondiale; **it's the way of the w.,** ainsi va le monde; **man of the w.,** homme qui connaît la vie; **he wants the best of both worlds,** il veut tout avoir; **to come down, up, in the w.,** descendre, monter, dans l'échelle sociale; **he has gone down in the w.,** il a connu

des jours meilleurs; F: **it's something out of this w.,** c'est quelque chose d'extraordinaire; **the theatrical w.,** le monde, le milieu, du théâtre; **the sporting w.,** le monde du sport; **that will do you a w. of good,** cela vous fera énormément de bien; **to think the w. of s.o.,** avoir une très haute opinion de qn. 'world-'famous *a* de renommée mondiale. 'worldli-ness *n* mondanité *f*. 'worldly *a* (*a*) du monde, de ce monde; **all his w. goods,** toute sa fortune (*b*) mondain. 'worldwide *a* universel; répandu partout; mondial.

worm [wɔːm] 1. *n* (*a*) ver *m* (de terre); *Ent:* asticot *m*; *Fig:* **the w. has turned,** il en a assez de se laisser mener par le bout du nez (*b*) *Med: Vet:* **to have worms,** avoir des vers 2. *vtr* (*a*) **to w. one's way,** se glisser, se faufiler; **to w. oneself into s.o.'s favour,** s'insinuer dans les bonnes grâces de qn (*b*) **to w. a secret out of s.o.,** tirer les vers du nez à qn. 'wormeaten *a* vermoulu; piqué des vers; (fruit) véreux, plein de vers. 'wormwood *n* armoise amère; absinthe *f*.

worn [wɔːn] *see* **wear** I.

worry ['wʌri] I. *v* (worried) 1. *vtr* (*a*) (of *dog*) harceler (des moutons) (*b*) tourmenter, tracasser (qn); **it worries me,** cela m'inquiète; **to w. oneself,** se tourmenter; se faire du mauvais sang; **sth is worrying him,** il est soucieux 2. *vi* se tourmenter, se tracasser, s'inquiéter; **I am worried about this,** cela m'inquiète; **don't w. about him,** ne vous en faites pas pour lui; **don't w.! not to w.!** soyez tranquille! ne vous en faites pas! II. *n* (*pl* **worries**) ennui *m*, souci *m*; **financial worries,** soucis d'argent; **he's always been a w. to me,** il a été le tourment de ma vie; *F:* **what's your w.?** qu'est-ce qu'il y a qui cloche? **that's the least of my worries,** c'est le moindre, le dernier, de mes soucis. 'worried *a* soucieux, inquiet.

worse [wɔːs] 1. *a & n* (*comp of* **bad** & **ill**) pire; plus mauvais; **she's w. than him,** elle est pire que lui; **in w. condition,** en plus mauvais état; **it gets w. and w.,** cela va de mal en pis; **to make matters w.,** pour comble de malheur; **that only made matters worse,** cela n'a pas arrangé les choses; **(and) what's w.,** (et) le pire, ce qui est pire, (c'est que); **it might have been w.,** ce n'est qu'un demi-mal; **I'm none the w. for it,** je ne m'en porte pas plus mal; **he escaped with nothing w. than a fright,** il en a été quitte pour la peur; **he escaped none the w.,** il s'en est tiré sans aucun mal; **so much the w. for him,** tant pis pour lui 2. *n* **there was w. to come,** le pire était à venir; **I have been through w. than that,** j'en ai vu d'autres; **to change for the w.,** s'altérer; **he has taken a turn for the w.,** son état s'est aggravé 3. *adv* pis; plus mal; **he behaves w. than ever,** il se conduit plus mal que jamais; **you might do w.,** vous pourriez faire pis; **he's w. off than before,** sa situation s'est détériorée; il a moins d'argent qu'avant; **the noise went on w. than ever,** le vacarme a recommencé de plus belle. 'worsen 1. *vtr* empirer; aggraver 2. *vi* empirer; s'aggraver; se détériorer; se gâter.

worship ['wɔːʃip] 1. *vtr* (worshipped) adorer (Dieu, qn); avoir un culte pour (qn); **to w. money,** faire de l'argent son idole; **he worships the ground she treads on,** il vénère la trace de ses pas 2. *n* (*a*) culte *m*; **place of w.,** lieu consacré au culte; église *f*; temple *m*; **times of w.,** heures des offices; **to be an object of w.,** être un objet d'adoration; **his W. the Mayor,** Monsieur le maire; **yes, your W.,** oui, (i) Monsieur le maire (ii) Monsieur le juge. **'worshipful** *a* honorable; (*freemasonry*) vénérable. **'worshipper** *n* adorateur, -trice; (*in church*) **the worshippers,** les fidèles *m.*

worst [wɔːst] (*sup of* **bad(ly)** & **ill**) **1.** *a* (le) pire, (le) plus mauvais; **his w. mistake,** sa plus grave erreur; **his w. enemy,** son pire ennemi; **at the w. possible time,** au pire, au plus mauvais, moment **2.** *n* **the w. of the storm is over,** le plus fort de la tempête est passé; **that's the w. of cheap shoes,** c'est là l'inconvénient des chaussures bon marché; **when things are at their w.,** quand les choses vont au plus mal; (*in a fight*) **to get the w. of it,** avoir le dessous; **at (the) w.,** au pis aller; **if the w. comes to the w.,** en mettant les choses au pire; **the w. has happened,** c'est la catastrophe **3.** *adv* (le) pis, (le) plus mal; **that frightened me w. of all,** c'est cela qui m'a effrayé le plus.

worsted ['wustid] *n* laine peignée.

worth [wɔːθ] **1.** *a* (*a*) **to be w. so much,** valoir tant; **that's w. something,** cela a de la valeur; **two cars w. £3000 each,** deux voitures valant £3000 chacune; **whatever it may be w.,** vaille que vaille; **it's not w. the money,** cela ne vaut pas le prix, n'est pas avantageux; **I'm telling you this for what it's w.,** je vous dis cela sans y attribuer grande valeur (*b*) **it's not w. the trouble, w. it,** cela ne, n'en, vaut pas la peine; **is it w. my while going?** est-ce que ça vaut la peine, le coup, que j'y aille? **book w. reading,** livre qui mérite d'être lu; **a thing w. having,** une chose précieuse, utile; **it's w. thinking about,** cela mérite réflexion; **it's w. knowing,** c'est bon à savoir (*c*) **he's w. millions,** il est riche à millions; c'est un millionnaire; **to die w. a million,** mourir en laissant un million; **that's all I'm w.,** voilà tout mon avoir; **to run for all one is w.,** courir de toutes ses forces, à toute vitesse **2.** *n* valeur *f*; **of great, little, no w.,** de grande, de peu de, d'aucune, valeur; **he showed his true w.,** il a montré sa vraie valeur; **give me a pound's w.,** donnez-m'en pour une livre; **to want one's money's w.,** en vouloir pour son argent. **'worthless** *a* sans valeur; qui ne vaut rien; mauvais. **'worthlessness** *n* peu *m* de valeur; nature *f* méprisable. **'worthwhile** *a* qui en vaut l'effort, la peine, *F:* le coup.

worthy ['wɔːði] *a* (-ier, -iest) digne; estimable; **to be w. of sth,** être digne de qch; **the town has no museum w. of the name,** la ville n'a aucun musée digne de ce nom. **'worthily** *adv* (*a*) dignement (*b*) à juste titre. **'worthiness** *n* mérite *m*.

would [wud] *see* **will III. 'would-be** *a* prétendu.

wound¹ [wuːnd] **1.** *n* (*a*) blessure *f* (*b*) plaie *f* **2.** *vtr* blesser; faire une blessure à (qn); **to w. s.o.'s feelings,** froisser qn. **'wounded 1.** *a* blessé; **the w. man,** le blessé **2.** *npl* **the w.,** les blessés. **'wounding** *a* blessant.

wound² [waund] *see* **wind².**

woven ['wouv(ə)n] *see* **weave I.**

WPC *abbr* woman police constable.

WRAF *abbr* Women's Royal Air Force.

wrap [ræp] **1.** *vtr* (**wrapped**) envelopper; **to w. sth (up) in paper,** envelopper qch dans du papier; **to w. (oneself) up,** se couvrir (de vêtements chauds); s'emmitoufler; **to be wrapped up in one's work,** être

entièrement absorbé par son travail; **to be wrapped in mystery,** être entouré, enveloppé, de mystère; **wrapped up in one's thoughts,** plongé dans ses pensées; **to w. sth round sth,** enrouler qch autour de qch; *F:* **he wrapped his car round a tree,** il a encadré un arbre **2.** *n* (*shawl*) châle *m*; (*rug*) couverture *f*; *F:* **to keep sth under wraps,** garder qch secret. **'wrapover,** *esp NAm:* **'wraparound** *a & n Cl:* **w. (skirt),** jupe *f* portefeuille. **'wrapper** *n* papier *m* d'emballage; couverture *f* (d'un livre); bande *f* (de journal). **'wrapping** *n* (*a*) (*action*) emballage *m*; mise *f* en paquet(s); **w. paper,** papier d'emballage; (*b*) (papier, toile *f*, d')emballage; **gift w.,** emballage-cadeau *m.*

wrath [rɔːθ] *n Lit:* courroux *m*, colère *f.*

wreath [riːθ] *n* **1.** couronne *f*, guirlande *f* (de fleurs); (*for funeral*) couronne mortuaire **2.** volute *f*, panache *m* (de fumée).

wreathe [riːð] *vtr* enguirlander; couronner de fleurs; **face wreathed in smiles,** visage rayonnant; **mountain wreathed in mist,** montagne couronnée de brouillard.

wreck [rek] **1.** *n* (*a*) épave *f*; navire naufragé; **the building is a total w.,** le bâtiment n'est qu'une ruine; **my car's a complete w.,** ma voiture est bonne pour la casse; **human w.,** épave, loque, humaine; **to be a nervous w.,** avoir les nerfs détraqués (*b*) naufrage *m* (d'un navire); **to be saved from the w.,** échapper au naufrage **2.** *vtr* (*a*) causer le naufrage d'(un navire); **to be wrecked,** faire naufrage (*b*) faire dérailler (un train); démolir, détruire (un bâtiment); faire échouer, saboter (une entreprise); détruire, ruiner (les espérances de qn); briser (un mariage); anéantir (des chances). **'wreckage** *n* épaves *fpl*; débris *mpl*. **wrecked** *a* naufragé; **w. life,** existence brisée. **'wrecker** *n* (*a*) (*of ships*) naufrageur *m*; pilleur *m* d'épaves; (*authorized*) exploiteur *m* d'épaves (*b*) destructeur *m*, démolisseur *m* (de villes, d'une civilisation) (*c*) *NAm: Aut:* (*Br*=**breakdown van**) camion *m* de dépannage; dépanneuse *f*. **'wrecking** *n* destruction *f*; démolition *f*

wren¹ [ren] *n Orn: F:* roitelet *m*; **golden-crested w.,** roitelet huppé.

Wren² *nf F:* membre *m* du *Women's Royal Naval Service* (WRNS).

wrench [rentʃ] **1.** *n* (*a*) mouvement violent de torsion; **to give sth a w.,** tirer (sur) qch violemment; **to pull sth off with a w.,** arracher qch d'un effort violent; **he gave his ankle a w.,** il s'est donné une entorse (*b*) déchirement *m*; **it will be a w. to leave,** il m'en coûtera de partir (*c*) *Tls:* clef *f* (à écrous); tourne-à-gauche *m inv*; **adjustable w., monkey w.,** clef anglaise, clef à molette **2.** *vtr* tordre; tourner violemment; **to w. a lid off,** arracher un couvercle (avec un effort violent); **to w. oneself free,** se dégager d'une forte secousse; **to w. one's ankle,** se fouler la cheville; **to w. one's shoulder,** se démettre l'épaule.

wrestle ['resl] *vi* **to w. with s.o.,** lutter avec, contre, qn; **to w. with (sth),** lutter contre (les difficultés); résister à (la tentation); s'attaquer à (un problème). (corps à corps); **all-in w.,** catch *m*. **'wrestler** *n* lutteur, -euse. **'wrestling** *n* lutte *f*

wretch [retʃ] *n* (*pl* **wretches**) malheureux, -euse; infortuné, -ée; misérable *mf*; **poor w.,** pauvre diable *m*;

you little w.! petit fripon! petite friponne! 'wretched a (a) (of pers) misérable; malheureux; infortuné; **to feel w.**, être mal en train; ne pas être dans son assiette; (depressed) avoir le cafard; **to look w.**, avoir l'air malheureux (b) pitoyable; lamentable; maigre (repas); **what w. weather!** quel temps de chien! **where's that w. umbrella?** où est ce diable de parapluie? **what's that w. boy doing?** qu'est-ce qu'il fait, ce sacré garçon? 'wretchedly adv misérablement; (s'acquitter) de façon pitoyable, lamentable; **to be w. poor**, être dans la misère; **w. ill**, malade comme un chien. 'wretchedness n misère f; tristesse f.

wrick [rik] **1.** n **to have a w. in the neck**, avoir le torticolis **2.** vtr to w. one's neck, se donner un torticolis; **to w. one's ankle**, se fouler la cheville, se donner une entorse.

wriggle ['rigl] v **1.** vi se tortiller; (of fish) frétiller; (of pers) s'agiter; **stop wriggling**, arrête de gigoter; **to w. out of a difficulty**, se tirer d'une position difficile; **to try to w. out of it**, chercher à s'esquiver; **to w. through sth**, se faufiler à travers qch (avec difficulté) **2.** vtr **to w. one's toes**, remuer, agiter, les orteils; **to w. one's way into sth**, se faufiler, s'insinuer, dans qch. 'wriggling **1.** n tortillement m **2.** a (enfant) remuant.

wring [rin] vtr (wrung [rʌn]) (a) tordre; **to w. (out) the washing**, tordre, essorer, le linge; **to w. the neck of a chicken**, tordre le cou à un poulet; F: **I'd like to w. your neck!** tu m'exaspères, à la fin! **to w. one's hands**, se tordre les mains; **to w. s.o.'s hand**, étreindre, serrer fortement, la main de qn (b) arracher (un secret à qn); extorquer (de l'argent à qn); exprimer, faire sortir, l'eau (d'un vêtement mouillé). 'wringer n DomEc: essoreuse f (à rouleaux). 'wringing a w. (wet), (of clothes) mouillé à tordre; (of pers) trempé jusqu'aux os.

wrinkle ['rinkl] **1.** n (on face) ride f; (on water) ondulation f, ride; (in garment) faux pli. **II.** v **1.** vtr (a) rider, plisser; **to w. one's forehead**, froncer les sourcils (b) plisser, froisser, chiffonner (une robe); **her stockings were wrinkled**, ses bas tirebouchonnaient **2.** vi se rider; faire des plis.

wrist [rist] n poignet m. 'wristband n poignet, manchette f (de chemise). 'wristbone n os m du poignet. 'wristwatch n (pl -es) montre-bracelet f.

writ [rit] n Jur: acte m judiciaire; mandat m; **to serve a w. on s.o.**, assigner qn en justice.

write [rait] vtr (wrote [rout]; written ['ritn]) (a) écrire; **to w. one's name**, écrire son nom; **how is it written?** comment cela s'écrit-il? **to w. sth down**, inscrire, noter, qch; **paper written all over**, papier couvert d'écriture; **his guilt was written in his eyes**, on lisait dans ses yeux qu'il était coupable (b) écrire (une lettre, un roman); rédiger (un article); **he writes for the papers**, il fait du journalisme; **he writes**, il est écrivain; **he writes on, about, gardening**, il écrit des articles sur l'horticulture; **he wrote to me yesterday**, il m'a écrit hier; F: **that's nothing to w. home about**, (i) ça n'a rien d'extraordinaire (ii) ça c'est plutôt moche! **I have written to ask him to come**, je lui ai écrit de venir; **w. for our catalogue**, demandez notre catalogue. 'write 'back vi répondre (à une lettre). 'write 'down vtr mettre par écrit; inscrire, noter (qch). 'write 'in vtr (a) écrire pour faire venir (qch); demander (un catalogue) (b) insérer (une correction, un mot). 'write 'off vtr (a) Fin: **to w. o. capital**, réduire le

capital; amortir du capital (b) Com: défalquer (une mauvaise créance); **to w. o. so much for wear and tear**, déduire tant pour l'usure; **three machines were written off**, il y a eu trois appareils de détruits. 'write-off n perte totale; **the car's a w.-o.**, la voiture est bonne pour la casse. 'writer n (a) **to be a good, bad, w.**, avoir une belle, une mauvaise, écriture (b) écrivain m, auteur m; **woman w.**, (femme) auteur; **writer's cramp**, crampe des écrivains. 'write 'up vtr 1. Journ: écrire, rédiger (un fait divers) **2.** mettre (son agenda) à jour; Sch: **w. up your notes**, recopiez vos notes. 'write-up n Journ: article m; **a good w.-up**, un article élogieux, une bonne critique. 'writing n (a) écriture f; **good, bad, w.**, bonne, mauvaise, écriture; **to answer in w.**, répondre par écrit; **in his own w.**, écrit de sa main: **w. desk**, secrétaire m; bureau m; **w. paper**, papier à lettres; **the w. on the wall**, un avertissement (d'une catastrophe imminente) (b) (profession) métier m d'écrivain; **the art of w.**, l'art d'écrire; **writings**, ouvrages mpl littéraires; œuvre m (d'un auteur). 'written a écrit; **w. consent**, consentement par écrit; **w. exam**, écrit m.

WRNS abbr Women's Royal Naval Service.

wrong [rɔn] I. a 1. mauvais; mal inv; **stealing is w., it is w. to steal**, c'est mal de voler **2.** (a) faux, f fausse; (réponse) inexacte; (affirmation) erronée; (terme) impropre, incorrect; **my watch is w.**, ma montre n'est pas à l'heure; (of pers) **to be w.**, avoir tort; se tromper; **you were w. to leave**, tu as eu tort de partir (b) **to be in the w. place**, ne pas être à sa place; **to drive on the w. side of the road**, conduire du mauvais côté de la route; F: **to get out of bed on the w. side**, se lever du pied gauche; **the w. side of the material**, l'envers m du tissu; **your shirt's the w. side out**, votre chemise est à l'envers; **to stroke a cat the w. way**, caresser un chat à rebrousse-poil; **you're doing it the w. way**, vous vous y prenez mal; (of food) **it went down the w. way**, je l'ai avalé de travers; F: **to be on the w. side of forty**, avoir (dé)passé la quarantaine (c) **I went to the w. house**, je me suis trompé de maison; **that's the w. book**, ce n'est pas là le livre qu'il faut; **to be on the w. track**, suivre une mauvaise piste; **to do, say, the w. thing**, commettre un impair; Tp: **w. number**, erreur f de numéro; faux numéro; Mus: **w. note**, fausse note **3. what's w. (with you?)** qu'avez-vous? qu'est-ce qui ne va pas? **what's w. with that?** qu'avez-vous à redire à cela? **what do you find w. with this book?** qu'est-ce que vous reprochez à ce livre? **something's w. (somewhere)**, il y a quelque chose qui ne va pas, qui cloche; **I hope nothing's w.**, j'espère qu'il n'est rien arrivé (de malheureux); **there's nothing w.**, tout va bien; rien ne cloche; **there's nothing w. with him**, il va bien; **there's nothing w. with it**, ça marche bien. II n 1. mal m; **to know right from w.**, distinguer le bien et le mal; **two wrongs do not make a right**, deux noirs ne font pas un blanc **2.** tort m, injustice f; Jur: dommage m, préjudice m; **to be in the w.**, avoir tort; être dans son tort. III. adv 1. (a) mal; inexactement, incorrectement; **to guess w.**, mal deviner; **you've spelt my name w.**, vous avez mal écrit, orthographié, mon nom (b) à tort, à faux; F: **you've got me w.**, vous m'avez mal compris **2. to go w.**, (of pers) se tromper de chemin; faire fausse route; (be mistaken) se tromper; (of events) mal tourner; (of machinery) se détraquer; être en panne;

you can't go w.! c'est très simple! **everything's going w.,** tout va mal; **our plans went w.,** nos projets sont tombés à l'eau. **IV.** *vtr* (*a*) faire (du) tort à (qn); faire injure à (qn) (*b*) être injuste pour, envers (qn). **'wrongdoer** *n* malfaiteur *m*. **'wrongdoing** *n* mal *m*; *pl* méfaits *mpl*. **'wrongful** *a* injuste; w. **dismissal,** renvoi injustifié (d'un employé). **'wrongfully** *adv* injustement; à tort. **'wrongly**

adv (*a*) à tort; **I've been w. accused,** on m'a accusé injustement; **rightly or w.,** à tort ou à raison (*b*) mal; **to choose w.,** mal choisir.

wrote [rout] *see* **write.**

wrought [rɔːt] *a* w. **iron,** fer forgé.

wrung [rʌŋ] *see* **wring.**

wry [rai] *a* tordu; de travers; **a w. smile,** un petit sourire forcé.

X

X, x [eks] *n* (la lettre) X, x *m*; **for x number of years,**
pendant x années; *Cin:* **X certificate** = interdit aux
moins de 18 ans. **'X-ray 1.** *n* rayon *m* X; **X-r.**
examination, examen radiographique; *F:* radio *f*; **X-r.**
treatment, radiothérapie *f* **2.** *vtr* radiographier (qn);
to be X-rayed, se faire radiographier, *F:* se faire faire
une radio, passer à la radio.

Xerox ['ziərɔks] **1.** *n Rtm:* (*a*) machine *f* Xerox;
photocopieuse *f* (*b*) photocopie *f* **2.** *vtr* photocopier.

Xmas ['eksməs] *n F:* Noël *m*.

xylophone ['zailəfoun] *n Mus:* xylophone *m.* **xy-**
'lophonist *n* joueur, -euse, de xylophone.

Y

Y, y [wai] *n* (la lettre) Y, y *m*; i grec; **Y-shaped**, en (forme d')Y; *Cl: Rtm:* **Y-fronts**, slip *m* d'homme.

yacht [jɔt] **1.** *n* yacht *m*; **y. club**, yacht-club *m* **2.** *vi* faire du yachting. **'yachting** *n* yachting *m*; navigation *f* de plaisance. **'yachtsman** *n* (*pl* **-men**) yachtman *m*; plaisancier *m*.

yack(ety-yack) ['jæk(əti'jæk)] **1.** *n P:* jacasserie *f* **2.** *vi* jacasser.

yak¹ [jæk] *n Z:* ya(c)k *m*.

yak² *vi P:* jacasser.

yam [jæm] *n Bot:* igname *f*.

yank¹ [jæŋk] *F:* **1.** *n* secousse *f*, saccade *f*; **give it a y.!** tirez bien fort! **2.** *vtr* tirer (d'un coup sec); **to y. out a tooth**, arracher une dent d'un seul coup.

Yank², Yankee ['jæŋki] *n F:* (a) *NAm:* habitant, -ante, des États du Nord (b) Américain, -aine (des États-Unis); Yankee *mf*; *P:* Amerloque *mf*.

yap [jæp] **1.** *n* jappement *m* (d'un chien) **2.** *vi* (**yapped**) (*of dog*) japper; (*of pers*) jacasser. **'yapping 1.** *n* jappement *m* (d'un chien); (*of pers*) jacasserie *f* **2.** *a* jappeur, -euse.

yard¹ [jɑːd] *n* **1.** *Meas:* yard *m* (0,914m); (*in Canada*) verge *f*; **square y.**, yard carré (0,765m²); **by the y.** = au mètre **2.** *Nau:* vergue *f*. **'yardage** *n* = métrage *m*. **'yardarm** *n Nau:* bout *m* de vergue. **'yardstick** *n* mesure *f*.

yard² *n* (a) cour *f* (d'une maison); *NAm:* jardin *m* (derrière une maison) (b) New Scotland Y., *F:* **the Y.** = la Sûreté (c) chantier *m*; dépôt *m*; **builder's y.**, chantier de construction; *Rail:* **goods y.**, dépôt de marchandises.

yarn [jɑːn] *n* **1.** *Tex:* fil *m*; filé *m* (de coton) **2.** histoire *f*, conte *m*; **to spin a y.**, en conter; raconter une histoire.

yawn [jɔːn] **1.** *n* bâillement *m*; **to give a y.**, bâiller; **to stifle a y.**, étouffer un bâillement **2.** (a) *vi* bâiller (b) *vtr* **to y. one's head off**, bâiller à se décrocher la mâchoire. **'yawning** *n* bâillement *m*.

yeah [jɛə] *adv P:* oui; ouais; *Iron:* **oh y.?** vraiment?

year [jiər] *n* (a) an *m*; année *f*; **in the y. 1850**, en l'an 1850; **in the y. of our Lord**, en l'an de grâce; **next y.**, l'an prochain; l'année prochaine; **twice a y.**, deux fois par an; **last y.**, l'an dernier; l'année dernière; **a y. ago last March**, il y a eu, il y aura, un an au mois de mars; **to have ten thousand a y.**, avoir dix mille livres de revenu; **to be ten years old**, avoir dix ans (b) **the New Y.**, le nouvel an; **New Year's Day**, le jour de l'an; **New Year's Eve**, la Saint-Sylvestre; **to see the New Y. in**, faire la veillée, le réveillon, de la Saint-Sylvestre; **to wish s.o. a happy New Y.**, souhaiter la bonne année à qn (c) **calendar y.**, année civile; **leap y.**, année bissextile; **school y.**, année scolaire; **he's in my y.**, il est de ma promotion, c'est un camarade de classe; *Com:* **financial y.**, exercice *m*; **half y.**, semestre *m*; **to rent sth by the y.**, louer qch à l'année; **from one year's end to the next**, d'un bout de l'année à l'autre; **all the y.**

round, tout au long de l'année; **y. in y. out**, **y. after y.**, une année après l'autre; **years ago**, il y a bien des années (d) **from his earliest years**, dès son plus jeune âge; **old for his years**, (i) plus vieux que son âge (ii) (*of child*) précoce; **he's getting on in years**, il prend de l'âge; il n'est plus jeune; *F:* **I haven't seen you for (donkey's) years**, voilà une éternité que je ne vous ai vu; **it's enough to put years on one**, c'est à vous donner des cheveux blancs; **it takes years off her**, cela la rajeunit. **'yearbook** *n* annuaire *m*. **'yearling** *n* animal *m* d'un an; **y. colt**, poulain d'un an. **year-'long** *a* qui dure un an. **'yearly 1.** *a* annuel; (location) à l'année **2.** *adv* annuellement.

yearn [jəːn] *vi* **to y. for sth**, languir après qch; mourir d'envie de qch. **'yearning** *n* désir ardent, envie *f* (for, de).

yeast [jiːst] *n* levure *f*; **brewer's y.**, levure de bière.

yell [jel] **1.** *n* (a) hurlement *m*; cri aigu; **to give a y.**, pousser un cri, un hurlement (b) *F:* **it was a y.**, c'était tordant, à se tordre de rire **2.** *vi* hurler; crier à tue-tête; **to y. with pain**, hurler de douleur.

yellow ['jelou] **1.** *a* (a) jaune; **the y. races**, les races jaunes; **y. fever**, fièvre jaune; *Tp:* **y. pages** = annuaire *m* des professions; les pages jaunes (b) *F:* (*of pers*) poltron, lâche **2.** *n* jaune *m*; **chrome y.**, jaune de chrome **3.** *vtr & i* jaunir; **papers yellowed with age**, papiers jaunis par le temps. **'yellowhammer** *n Orn:* bruant *m* jaune. **'yellowish** *a* jaunâtre. **'yellowness** *n* teinte *f* jaune (de qch); teint *m* jaune (de qn).

yelp [jelp] **1.** *n* jappement *m*; glapissement *m* **2.** *vi* japper; (*of fox*) glapir. **'yelping 1.** *a* jappant, glapissant **2.** *n* jappement; glapissement.

Yemen (the) [ðə'jemən] *Prn* le Yémen.

yen [yen] *n F:* **to have a y. for sth**, avoir une envie folle de qch.

yep [jep] *adv NAm: P:* oui, ouais.

yes [jes] *adv* (a) oui; (*contradicting*) si; **to say y.**, dire (que) oui; **to answer y. or no**, répondre par oui ou non; **y., of course**, mais oui, bien sûr (b) (*interrogatively*) (i) vraiment? (ii) et puis après? (c) *F:* **y. man**, béni-oui-oui *m inv*.

yesterday ['jestədei] *adv & n* hier (*m*); **the day before y.**, avant-hier (*m*); **y. week**, il y a eu hier huit jours; **a week y.**, d'hier en huit; **yesterday's paper**, le journal d'hier; **y. morning, evening**, hier matin, soir; **y. was the tenth**, hier c'était le dix.

yet [jet] **1.** *adv* (a) déjà; jusqu'ici; **not y.**, pas encore; **not y. started**, pas même, pas encore, commencé; **it won't happen just y.**, nous n'en sommes pas encore là; **you needn't go just y.**, tu n'as pas besoin de partir tout de suite; **nothing has been done (as) y.**, jusqu'ici, jusqu'à présent, on n'a rien fait (b) malgré tout; **he'll win y.**, malgré tout il gagnera (c) *esp Lit:* encore; **we have ten minutes y.**, nous avons encore dix minutes; **y. again**, encore une fois; **y. more**, encore plus; **y. one more**, encore un autre 2. *conj* néanmoins, cependant, tout de même; **y. I like him,** malgré tout il me plaît.

yew [ju:] *n* y. **(tree),** if *m*.

YHA *abbr Youth Hostels Association.*

Yid [jid] *n P: Pej:* youpin, -ine. **'Yiddish** *a & n Ling:* yiddish (*m*).

yield [ji:ld] 1. *n* production *f*; rapport *m*; rendement *m*; **these shares give a poor y.,** ces actions rapportent mal; **net y.,** revenu net 2. *vtr (a)* rendre, donner (*b*) rapporter, produire; **money that yields interest,** argent qui rapporte (*c*) céder (du terrain, un droit) 3. *vi (a)* se rendre; céder **(to, à); to y. to reason,** entendre raison; **to y. to temptation,** succomber à la tentation (*b*) s'affaisser, fléchir, plier; **the plank yielded under our weight,** la planche a cédé sous notre poids. **'yield-ing** *n (a)* rendement *m* (*b*) soumission *f* (*c*) affaissement *m*, fléchissement *m*.

yippee [ji'pi] *int F:* hourra! bravo!

YMCA *abbr Young Men's Christian Association.*

yob [jɔb], **yobbo** ['jɔbou] *nm P:* voyou, loubar(d).

yodel ['joudl] *vi* **(yodel(l)ed),** iodler, jodler.

yoga ['jougə] *n* yoga *m*.

yog(h)urt ['jɔgət] *n* yaourt *m*, yog(h)ourt *m*.

yoke [jouk] I. *n* 1. joug *m*; **y. oxen,** bœufs d'attelage 2. empiècement *m* (d'une robe). II. *vtr* accoupler (des bœufs).

yolk [jouk] *n* jaune *m* d'œuf.

you [ju:] *pers pron* (i) *sg & pl* vous (ii) *sg (to relative, child, animal*) tu, te, toi (*a*) (*subject*) vous; tu; **y. are very kind,** vous êtes bien aimable(s); tu es bien aimable; **there y. are,** vous voilà; te voilà; **y. all,** vous tous (*b*) (*object*) vous; te; **I'll see y. tomorrow,** je vous, te, reverrai demain (*c*) (*after prep*) **between y. and me,** (i) entre vous et moi; entre toi et moi (ii) entre nous soit dit; **there's a fine apple for y.!** regardez-moi ça, si ce n'est pas une belle pomme! **all of y.,** vous tous; *F:* **go on with y.!** à d'autres! pour qui me prends-tu? **away with y.!** allez-vous-en! va-t-en! (*d*) **y. and I will go by train,** vous et moi, toi et moi, nous prendrons le train; **I am older than y.,** je suis plus âgé que vous, que toi; **if I were y.,** (si j'étais) à votre, ta, place; **is it y.?** est-ce (bien) vous, toi? *F:* **hi! y. there!** eh! dites donc, là-bas! (*e*) **y. Frenchmen,** vous autres Français; **y. idiot (y.)!** espèce d'imbécile! **don't y. be afraid,** n'ayez, n'aie, pas peur (*f*) (*indefinite*) on; **y. never can tell,** on ne sait jamais. **your** *poss a* 1. (i) *sg & pl* votre, *pl* vos (ii) *sg (of relative, child, animal*) ton, ta, *pl* tes; **y. house,** votre maison; ta maison; **y. friends,** vos ami(e)s; tes ami(e)s; **have you hurt y. hand?** vous vous êtes fait mal à la main? **y. turn!** à vous, à toi (de jouer)! **turn your head(s),** tournez la tête; tourne la tête 2. (*indefinite*) son, sa, *pl* ses; **y. cannot alter y. nature,** on ne peut pas changer son caractère. **yours** *poss pron* (i) *sg & pl* le vôtre, la vôtre, les vôtres (ii) *sg (of relative, child, animal*) le tien, la tienne, les tiens, les tiennes; **this book is y.,** ce livre est à vous, à toi; **is it really y.?** c'est

bien le vôtre, le tien? **he's a friend of y.,** c'est un de vos, de tes, amis; *F:* **what's y.?** qu'est-ce que tu prends? **the bathroom's all y.,** la salle de bains est libre; *Corr:* **y. (sincerely),** (i) bien amicalement (ii) *Com:* veuillez agréer l'expression de mes sentiments distingués, respectueux. **your'self** (*pl* **yourselves**) *pers pron* vous-même; toi-même (*a*) **do you do the cooking y.?** est-ce que vous faites la cuisine vous-même? *F:* **he's a do it y. enthusiast,** c'est un bricoleur passionné (*b*) **have you hurt y.?** est-ce que vous vous êtes fait mal? est-ce que tu t'es fait mal? **are you enjoying y.?** vous amusez-vous? tu t'amuses bien? (*c*) **all by y.,** tout seul; **are you living by y.?** est-ce que vous vivez seul? tu vis seul? **see for yourselves,** voyez vous-mêmes.

young [jʌŋ] 1. *a (a)* jeune; **younger,** plus jeune; **my younger sister,** ma jeune sœur; **younger son, daughter,** fils cadet, fille cadette; **the youngest,** le, la, plus jeune; le cadet, la cadette; **he is younger than I,** il est plus jeune que moi; **when I was twenty years younger,** quand j'avais vingt ans de moins; **you're looking years younger!** comme vous avez rajeuni! **the younger generation,** les jeunes; **in his young(er) days,** dans son jeune âge; **I'm not as y. as I was,** je n'ai plus mes jambes de vingt ans; **we are only y. once,** la jeunesse n'a qu'un temps; **y. man,** jeune homme; **y. lady, woman,** jeune fille; jeune femme; **y. people,** jeunes gens; **y. Mr Thomas,** (i) M. Thomas fils (ii) le jeune M. Thomas (*b*) **the night is still y.,** la nuit n'est que peu avancée 2. *npl inv (a)* **the y.,** les jeunes; la jeunesse; **the y. and the not so y.,** les jeunes et les moins jeunes; **books for the y.,** livres pour la jeunesse (*b*) **animal and its y.,** animal et ses petits. **'youngster** *n* un, une, jeune; **the youngsters,** (i) les jeunes (ii) les enfants, les gosses.

youth [ju:θ] *n (pl* **youths**) 1. (*a*) jeunesse *f*; adolescence *f*; **from y. upwards,** dès sa jeunesse; **in his early y.,** dans sa première jeunesse, quand il était tout jeune (*b*) **y. club,** foyer des jeunes; **y. hostel,** auberge de jeunesse; **y. hosteller,** ajiste *mf*; **y. hostelling,** ajisme *m* 2. jeune homme; adolescent *m* 3. *coll* les jeunes. **'youthful** *a (a)* jeune; juvénile; **to look y.,** avoir l'air jeune (*b*) **y. indiscretions,** erreurs de jeunesse. **'youthfulness** *n* jeunesse *f*; air *m* de jeunesse.

yowl [jaul] *vi (of dog)* hurler; *(of cat)* miauler.

yucky ['jʌki] *a F:* dégoûtant, infect, *P:* dégueulasse.

Yugoslavia, [ju:gou'slɑ:viə] *Prn* Yougoslavie *f. Prn* la Yougoslavie. **'Yugoslav(ian)** *a & n* yougoslave (*mf*).

yuk [jʌk] *int F:* pouah!

yukky *see* **yucky.**

Yule [ju:l] *n* **Y. log,** bûche de Noël. **'Yuletide** *n A:* l'époque *f*, les fêtes *fpl*, de Noël.

yum-yum ['jʌmjʌm] *int* miam-miam! **'yummy** *a F:* délicieux.

Z

Z, z [zed, *NAm:* ziː] *n* (la lettre) Z, z *m.*
Zaire [zɑːˈiər] *Prn* Zaïre *m.*
Zambezi [zæmˈbiːzi] *Prn* the (river) Z., le Zambèze.
Zambia [ˈzæmbiə] *Prn* Zambie *f.*
zany [ˈzeini] *a F:* loufoque; fou.
zeal [ziːl] *n* zèle *m*; empressement *m.* **zealot** [ˈzelət] *n* fanatique *mf.* **'zealous** *a* zélé; empressé. **'zeal-ously** *adv* avec zèle.
zebra [ˈzebrə, ˈziːbrə] *n Z:* zèbre *m*; z. **crossing** = passage pour piétons, passage clouté.
zed [zed], *NAm:* **zee** [ziː] *n* (la lettre) Z, z *m.*
zenith [ˈzeniθ] *n Astr:* zénith *m.*
zephyr [ˈzefər] *n* zéphyr *m.*
zero [ˈziərou] **1.** *n* (*pl* **zeros**) zéro *m*; *Mil: etc:* z. **hour**, l'heure H; **10° below z.**, 10° au-dessous de zéro; moins 10°; **down to z.**, tombé à zéro **2.** *vi* to z. **in on sth**, se diriger vers qch.
zest [zest] *n* (*a*) enthousiasme *m*, entrain *m*; **to eat with z.**, manger avec appétit (*b*) saveur *f*, goût *m*; **this added a bit of z. to the adventure**, cela a donné du piquant à l'aventure (*c*) zeste *m* (d'orange, de citron).
zigzag [ˈzigzæg] **1.** *n* zigzag *m*; **in zigzags**, en zigzag **2.** *vi* zigzaguer; faire des zigzags; (marcher) en zigzag.
zinc [ziŋk] *n* zinc *m*; *Paint:* z. **white**, oxyde *m*, blanc *m*, de zinc.
zing [ziŋ] *n NAm: F:* vitalité *f.*
zinnia [ˈziniə] *n Bot:* zinnia *m.*
Zion [ˈzaiən] *Prn* Sion *m.* **'Zionism** *n Pol:* sionisme *m.* **'Zionist** *a & n Pol:* sioniste (*mf*).
zip [zip] **I.** *n* **1.** sifflement *m* (d'une balle) **2.** *F:* énergie *f*; **put a bit of z. into it**, mettez-y du nerf **3.** z. **fastener**, fermeture *f* éclair (*Rtm*); z. **pocket**, poche avec

fermeture éclair **4.** *NAm:* z. **code**, code postal. **II.** *v* (**zipped**) **1.** *vi* siffler (comme une balle); **to z. past**, passer comme un éclair **2.** *vtr F:* **can you z. me up?** peux-tu m'aider avec ma fermeture éclair? **'zipper** *n* fermeture éclair *inv* (*Rtm*); z. **bag**, (sac) fourre-tout *m* à fermeture éclair. **'zippy** *a F:* plein d'entrain; **look z.!** grouille-toi!
zircon [ˈzɔːkən] *n* zircon *m.*
zither [ˈziðər] *n Mus:* cithare *f.*
zodiac [ˈzoudiæk] *n* zodiaque *m.*
zombie [ˈzɔmbi] *n* zombi *m*; **she looks like a z.**, elle a l'air à demi morte.
zone [zoun] **1.** *n* zone *f*; **time z.**, fuseau *m* horaire; *Geog:* **torrid z.**, zone torride; **the Canal Z.**, la Zone du Canal (de Panama); **frontier z.**, zone frontière; **danger z.**, zone dangereuse; **free z.**, zone franche **2.** *vtr* répartir (une ville) en zones. **'zonal** *a* zonal. **'zoning** *n* zonage *m*, répartition *f* en zones.
zoo [zuː] *n* zoo *m*; z. **keeper**, gardien, -ienne, de zoo.
zoology [zuːˈɔlədʒi] *n* zoologie *f.* **zoo'logical** *a* zoologique; z. **gardens**, jardin zoologique. **zo-'ologist** *n* zoologiste *mf.*
zoom [zuːm] **I.** *n* **1.** bourdonnement *m*, vrombissement *m* **2.** *Av:* montée *f* en chandelle. **3.** *Cin:* zoom *m*; changement *m* rapide de plan; z. **lens**, zoom. **II.** *vi* **1.** bourdonner; vrombir **2.** *Av:* monter en chandelle; *F:* **he suddenly zoomed up**, il est arrivé en trombe; **he zoomed past**, il est passé comme une flèche **3.** *Cin:* **to z. in (on sth)**, faire un zoom (sur qch).
zucchini [zuˈkiːni] *n* courgette *f.*
Zulu [ˈzuːluː] *a & n* zoulou, -oue; du Zoulouland. **'Zululand** *Prn* Zoulouland *m.*

PART TWO

FRENCH−ENGLISH

Tableau des signes phonétiques

Consonnes et semi-consonnes

[p]   pain [pɛ̃]; tape [tap]

[b]   beau [bo]; abbé [abe]; robe [rɔb]

[m]   mon [mɔ̃]; flamme [flam]

[f]   feu [fø]; bref [brɛf]; phrase [fraz]

[v]   voir [vwar]; vie [vi]; wagon [vagɔ̃]

[t]   table [tabl̩]; nette [nɛt]; théâtre [teatr̩]

[d]   donner [dɔne]; sud [syd]

[n]   né [ne]; canne [kan]; automne [otɔn]

[s]   sou [su]; rébus [rebys]; cire [sir]; scène [sɛn]; six [sis]

[z]   cousin [kuzɛ̃]; zéro [zero]; deuxième [døzjɛm]

[l]   lait [lɛ]; aile [ɛl]; facile [fasil]

[l]   table [tabl̩]; sensible [sɑ̃sibl̩]; noble [nɔbl̩]

[ʃ]   chose [ʃoz]; chercher [ʃɛrʃe]

[ʒ]   gilet [ʒilɛ]; manger [mɑ̃ʒe]; âge [ɑʒ]

[k]   camp [kɑ̃]; képi [kepi]; quatre [katr̩]; écho [eko]

[g]   garde [gard]; guerre [gɛr]; second [sǝgɔ̃]

[ɲ]   campagne [kɑ̃paɲ]; gnaule [ɲol]

[ŋ]   (in words of foreign origin) parking [parkiŋ]; smoking [smɔkiŋ]

[r]   rare [rar]; arbre [arbr̩]; rhume [rym]

[r̩]   être [ɛtr̩]; marbre [marbr̩]; neutre [nøtr̩]

[ks]   accident [aksidɑ̃]; action [aksjɔ̃]; xylophone [ksilɔfɔn]

[gz]   exister [egziste]; examen [egzamɛ̃]

[j]   yacht [jɔt, jat]; piano [pjano]; ration [rasjɔ̃]; voyage [vwajaʒ]; travailler [travaje]; cahier [kaje]

[w]   ouate [wat]; ouest [wɛst]; noir [nwar]; (also in words of foreign origin) tramway [tramwɛ]; watt [wat]

[ɥ]   muet [mɥɛ]; huit [ɥit]; luire [lɥir]; aiguille [egɥij]

Voyelles

[i]   vite [vit]; signe [siɲ]; sortie [sɔrti]

[e]   été [ete]; donner, donné [dɔne]; légal [legal]

[ɛ]   elle [ɛl; très [trɛ]; terre [tɛr]; rêve [rɛv]; père [pɛr]

[a]   chat [ʃa]; tache [taʃ]; toit [twa]; phare [far]

[ɑ]   âge [ɑʒ]; âgé [ɑʒe]; tâche [tɑʃ]

[ɔ]   donner [dɔne]; album [albɔm]; fort [fɔr]

[o]   dos [do]; impôt [ɛ̃po]; chaud [ʃo]

[u]   tout [tu]; goût [gu]; août [u]; cour [kur]

[y]   cru [kry]; ciguë [sigy]; mur [myr]

[ø]   feu [fø]; nœud [nø]; heureuse [ørøz]

[œ]   seul [sœl]; œuf [œf]; sœur [sœr]; cueillir [kœjir]

[ǝ]*   le [lǝ]; ce [sǝ]; entremets [ɑ̃trǝmǝ]

[ɛ̃]   vin [vɛ̃]; plein [plɛ̃]; thym [tɛ̃]; prince [prɛ̃s]; plainte [plɛ̃t]

[ɑ̃]   enfant [ɑ̃fɑ̃]; temps [tɑ̃]; paon [pɑ̃]; centre [sɑ̃tr̩]; branche [brɑ̃ʃ]

[ɔ̃]   mon [mɔ̃]; plomb [plɔ̃]; longe [lɔ̃ʒ]; comte [kɔ̃t]

[œ̃]   un [œ̃]; lundi [lœ̃di]; humble [œ̃bl̩]

* The symbol (ǝ) (in brackets) indicates that the mute *e* is pronounced in careful speech but not in rapid speech.

A

A, a [ɑ] *nm* (the letter) A, a.

à [a] *prep* (*contracts with* le *into* au, *with* les *into* aux) **1.** (*a*) (*direction*) aller à l'église, au cinéma, to go to church, to the cinema; son voyage à Paris, his journey to Paris; au feu! fire! au voleur! stop thief! (*b*) (de) 20 à 30 personnes, between 20 and thirty people **2.** (*position*) (*a*) à l'horizon, on the horizon; à l'ombre, in the shade; à la maison, at home; à deux kilomètres d'ici, two kilometres from here (*b*) au fond, basically **3.** (*direction in time*) du matin au soir, from morning to night; à jamais, for ever; à jeudi! see you (on) Thursday! **4.** à deux heures, at two o'clock; à mon arrivée, on my arrival; au vingtième siècle, in the twentieth century; à l'avenir, in (the) future **5.** se battre homme à homme, to fight man to man; *Ten:* quinze à, fifteen all **6.** (*introducing indirect object of many verbs*) attacher un cheval à un arbre, to tie a horse to a tree; donner qch à qn, to give sth to s.o.; penser à qn, to think of s.o. **7.** (*possession*) ce livre est à Paul, this is Paul's book; un ami à moi, a friend of mine; c'est à vous de décider, it's up to you to decide **8.** tasse à thé, teacup; moulin à vent, windmill; chambre à deux lits, twin-bedded room; homme aux cheveux noirs, dark haired man **9.** (*a*) (*manner*) à pied, on foot; à la main, by hand **10.** vendre des huîtres à la douzaine, to sell oysters by the dozen; à la française, in the French manner; manger à sa faim, to eat one's fill; recevoir qn à bras ouverts, to receive s.o. with open arms (*b*) à mon avis, in my opinion; à ce qu'il dit, according to him; à cette condition, on this condition (*c*) un timbre à deux francs, a two-franc stamp **11.** parallèle à, parallel to; c'est gentil à lui, it's kind of him **12.** (*introducing verb in infinitive*) (*a*) penser à faire qch, to think of doing sth (*b*) il ne me reste qu'à vous remercier, it only remains for me to thank you (*c*) apprendre à lire, to learn to read (*d*) il est à plaindre, he is to be pitied; j'ai une lettre à écrire, I've got a letter to write; maison à vendre, house for sale; machine à coudre, sewing machine (*e*) laid à faire peur, frightfully ugly; un bruit à tout casser, an ear-splitting noise (*f*) je suis prêt à vous écouter, I'm ready to listen to you; facile à comprendre, easy to understand (*g*) il est le seul à le faire, he's the only one to do it (*h*) à les en croire, if they are to be believed; à en juger par les résultats, judging by the results.

A2 *abbr TV:* Antenne 2 = BBC 2.

abaissement [abɛsmɑ̃] *nm* **1.** lowering (of blind); to reduce (prices) **2.** fall; subsidence, sinking; fall (in temperature) **3.** *Lit:* abasement, humiliation.

abaisser [abɛse] **1.** *vtr* (*a*) to lower; to pull down (blind) (*b*) to lower (one's voice); to reduce (prices) (*c*) to humiliate (s.o.) **2.** s'a. (*a*) to fall away, to dip, to slope down; (*of temperature*) to fall (*b*) to humble oneself; s'a. à faire qch, to stoop to doing sth. **abaissant** *a* degrading; lowering.

abandon [abɑ̃dɔ̃] *nm* **1.** (*a*) surrender, renunciation (*b*) *Sp:* retirement, withdrawal **2.** desertion (of children, duty) **3.** neglect; à l'a., neglected; (*of garden, children*) running wild **4.** lack of restraint; parler avec a., to speak freely.

abandonner [abɑ̃dɔne] *vtr* **1.** (*a*) to desert, abandon; to leave; mes forces m'abandonnent, my strength is failing me; abandonné par les médecins, given up by the doctors; a. la partie, to throw in one's hand (*b*) *vi Sp:* to retire (*c*) to surrender, renounce, give up **2.** s'a. (*a*) to neglect oneself (*b*) to give way to despair (*c*) to be unconstrained; to let oneself go (*d*) s'a. à (qch), to give oneself up to (sth); to become addicted to (vice); s'a. au sommeil, to give way to sleep. **abandonné** *a* abandoned, deserted.

abasourdir [abazurdir] *vtr* to astound, stun. **abasourdissant** *a* astounding, stunning, staggering.

abat-jour [abaʒur] *nm inv* lampshade.

abats [aba] *nmpl* (i) offal (ii) giblets.

abattage [abataʒ] *nm* **1.** (*a*) felling (of trees) (*b*) *Min:* cutting **2.** slaughtering.

abattant [abatɑ̃] *nm* flap (of table, counter).

abattement [abatmɑ̃] *nm* **1.** (*a*) exhaustion (*b*) despondency, depression **2.** *Fin:* abatement; allowance (against tax).

abattis [abati] *nmpl* (*a*) *Cu:* giblets (*b*) *P:* limbs.

abattoir [abatwar] *nm* slaughterhouse.

abattre [abatṛ] *vtr* (*conj like* BATTRE) **1.** (*a*) to knock down, pull down; a. de la besogne, to get through a lot of work (*b*) to fell, cut down (trees) (*c*) to cut off (*d*) to slaughter, kill, destroy (*e*) to bring down; to shoot down (aircraft) (*f*) (*of wind*) to blow down, beat down (*g*) to dishearten, depress (s.o.); ne vous laissez pas a.! don't let it get you down! (*h*) a. ses cartes, to lay one's cards on the table **2.** s'a. (*a*) to fall, to crash down, to collapse (*b*) s'a. sur qch, to pounce, swoop down on sth; to beat down on sth. **abattu** *a* dejected, depressed, demoralized.

abbatiale [abasjal] *nf* abbey church.

abbaye [abei] *nf* abbey.

abbé [abe] *nm* **1.** abbot **2.** *RCCh:* priest.

abbesse [abɛs] *nf* abbess.

abc [abese] *nm inv* **1.** alphabet **2.** rudiments (of a science).

abcès [apsɛ] *nm* abscess; a. à la gencive, gumboil.

abdication [abdikasjɔ̃] *nf* (*a*) abdication (*b*) renunciation, surrender (of authority).

abdiquer [abdike] *vtr & i* to abdicate (throne); to renounce, surrender (rights).

abdomen [abdɔmɛn] *nm* abdomen. **abdominal, -aux** *a* abdominal; *nmpl* abdominaux, stomach muscles.

abeille [abɛj] *nf* bee; a. mâle, drone.

aberration [abɛrasjɔ̃] *nf* aberration. **aberrant** *a* aberrant; absurd.

abêtir (s') [sabetir] *vi & pr* to become stupid.

abhorrer [abɔre] *vtr* to abhor, to loathe.

abîme [abim] *nm* abyss, chasm, gulf, depth(s).

abîmer [abime] **1.** *vtr* to spoil, damage, injure **2. s'a.** (*a*) **s'a. dans ses pensées,** to be lost in thought (*b*) to get spoiled.

abjection [abʒɛksjɔ̃] *nf* abjectness. **abject** *a* abject (poverty); mean, contemptible, despicable (person, conduct).

abjuration [abʒyrasjɔ̃] *nf* abjuration, renunciation.

abjurer [abʒyre] *vtr* to abjure; to renounce.

ablation [ablasjɔ̃] *nf Med:* removal.

ablution [ablysjɔ̃] *nf* ablution, washing.

abnégation [abnegasjɔ̃] *nf* abnegation, self-sacrifice.

aboi [abwa] *nm* **aux abois,** at bay.

aboiement [abwamɑ̃] *nm* bark, barking.

abolir [abɔlir] *vtr* to abolish, suppress.

abolition [abɔlisjɔ̃] *nf* abolition, suppression.

abolitionnisme [abɔlisjɔnism] *nm* abolitionism. **abolitionniste** *a & n* abolitionist.

abominable [abɔminabl] *a* abominable, foul; frightful. **abominablement** *adv* abominably; frightfully.

abomination [abɔminasjɔ̃] *nf* abomination; **avoir qch en a.,** to loathe sth; **ce café est une a.,** this coffee is abominable.

abominer [abɔmine] *vtr* to abominate, loathe.

abondamment [abɔ̃damɑ̃] *adv* abundantly.

abondance [abɔ̃dɑ̃s] *nf* **1.** abundance, plenty **2.** wealth (of details, ideas); **parler avec a.,** to have a great flow of words. **abondant** *a* abundant, plentiful; rich (style); lush (foliage); copious (meal, tears).

abonder [abɔ̃de] *vi* **1.** to abound (**en,** in); to be plentiful **2. a. dans le sens de qn,** to be entirely of s.o.'s opinion.

abonné, -ée [abɔne] **1.** *a* **être a. à,** to subscribe to (paper); to have (gas, electricity) **2.** *n* (*a*) subscriber (to paper) (*b*) season-ticket holder (*c*) **abonnés du gaz,** gas consumers.

abonnement [abɔnmɑ̃] *nm* **1.** subscription (to paper) **2.** (**carte d')a.,** season ticket **3.** *Adm:* (water) rate; (telephone) rental.

abonner [abɔne] **1.** *vtr* to take out a subscription for (s.o.) **2.** (*a*) **s'a. à un journal,** to take out a subscription to a paper (*b*) to take a season ticket (*c*) **s'a. au téléphone,** to have the telephone installed.

abord [abɔr] *nm* **1.** access, approach (to land); **île d'un a. difficile,** island difficult of access **2.** *pl* approaches (**d'un endroit,** to a place); surroundings, outskirts **3.** (*of pers*) **d'un a. facile, difficile,** approachable, unapproachable **4.** *adv phr* **d'a., tout d'a.,** first, at first, to begin with, in the first place; **dès l'a.,** from the outset; **à l'a.,** at first sight, to begin with. **abordable** *a* **1.** accessible; (*of prices*) reasonable **2.** (*of pers*) approachable.

abordage [abɔrdaʒ] *nm Nau:* **1.** boarding (as act of war) **2.** collision.

aborder [abɔrde] **1.** *vi* to land; **a. à port,** to reach a port **2.** *vtr* (*a*) to accost, approach (s.o.) (*b*) to approach, tackle (a question) (*c*) to board (ship in a fight) (*d*) to collide with (ship).

aborigène [abɔriʒɛn] **1.** *a* aboriginal **2.** *n* aboriginal, aborigine, native.

aboutir [abutir] *vi* **1. a. à, dans, en, qch,** to end at, in, sth; to lead to sth; to result in sth; **n'a. à rien,** to come to nothing **2.** (*of plan*) to succeed; **faire a. qch,** to bring sth to a successful conclusion.

aboutissement [abutismɑ̃] *nm* outcome; success.

aboyer [abwaje] *vi* (**j'aboie**) (*of dog*) to bark; (*of pers*) to shout.

abracadabrant [abrakadabrɑ̃] *a* amazing; preposterous.

abrasif, -ive [abrazif, -iv] *a & nm* abrasive.

abrégé [abreʒe] *nm* précis, summary; **en a.,** in abridged, abbreviated, form; in a few words, in brief.

abréger [abreʒe] *vtr* (**j'abrège; n. abrégeons**) **1.** to shorten, to cut short; **pour a.,** to be brief **2.** to abridge, cut down (article); to abbreviate (word) **3.** (*of days*) **s'a.,** to grow shorter.

abreuver [abrœve] *vtr* **1.** to water (horses, cattle) **2.** to flood, irrigate; **l'Égypte est abreuvée par le Nil,** Egypt is watered by the Nile **3. s'a.,** to drink.

abreuvoir [abrœvwar] *nm* (*a*) watering place (in river) (*b*) drinking trough.

abréviation [abrevjasjɔ̃] *nf* abbreviation.

abri [abri] *nm* shelter, cover; **a. public,** public shelter; **prendre a.,** to take cover; **personne sans a.,** homeless person; **à l'a.,** sheltered, under cover; **se mettre à l'a. (de la pluie),** to take shelter (from the rain); **à l'a. de qch,** sheltered from sth; **a. contre le vent,** windscreen.

abribus [abribys] *nm* bus shelter.

abricot [abriko] *nm* apricot.

abricotier [abrikɔtje] *nm* apricot tree.

abriter [abrite] *vtr* **1.** to shelter, screen, shield **2.** to house, to accommodate **3. s'a.,** to take shelter (**contre,** from).

abrogation [abrɔgasjɔ̃] *nf* abrogation, repeal (of law).

abroger [abrɔʒe] *vtr* (**n. abrogeons**) to abrogate, to rescind, repeal (law).

abrupt [abrypt] *a* **1.** abrupt, steep (descent) **2.** (*pers*) abrupt, blunt. **abruptement** *adv* steeply; abruptly.

abruti [abryti] *nm F:* fool, idiot, moron.

abrutir [abrytir] *vtr* (*a*) to stupefy (*b*) to exhaust; **ce travail m'abrutit,** this work is wearing me out. **abrutissant** *a* exhausting; mind-destroying.

abrutissement [abrytismɑ̃] *nm* exhaustion; mindless state.

absence [apsɑ̃s] *nf* **1.** absence; **en l'a. de ma secrétaire,** while my secretary is away; **remarquer l'a. de qn,** to miss s.o. **2.** (*a*) **a. d'imagination,** lack of imagination (*b*) **avoir des absences,** to be absentminded. **absent 1.** *a* (*a*) absent; away; (*b*) missing, absent; (*c*) **son esprit est a.,** his mind is far away **2.** *n* absentee.

absentéisme [apsɑ̃teism] *nm* absenteeism.

absenter (s') [sapsɑ̃te] *vpr* to go away (from home); to stay away (from school).

abside [apsid] *nf Arch:* apse.

absinthe [apsɛ̃t] *nf* absinth(e).

absolu [apsɔly] **1.** *a* (*a*) absolute; **règle absolue,** hard and fast rule; **refus a.,** flat refusal; (*b*) **pouvoir a.,** absolute power; **caractère a.,** autocratic nature; (*c*) peremptory (tone) **2.** *nm* **l'a.,** the absolute. **absolu-**

ment *adv* absolutely; entirely (unnecessary); utterly (impossible); strictly (forbidden); **vous devez a. y aller!** you simply *must* go there!

absolution [apsɔlysjɔ̃] *nf Theol:* absolution.

absorber [apsɔrbe] *vtr* 1. to absorb, soak up 2. to take (food, medicine); to drink (sth) 3. to absorb, engross; **son travail l'absorbe,** he's completely wrapped up in his work 4. **s'a.,** to become absorbed, engrossed (**dans,** in); **être absorbé dans ses pensées,** to be lost in thought. **absorbant** *a & nm* absorbent.

absorption [apsɔrpsjɔ̃] *nf* absorption.

absoudre [apsudr̥] *vtr* (*prp* **absolvant**; *pp* **absous, absoute;** *pr ind* **j'absous**) (*a*) to forgive (s.o. sth) (*b*) to absolve (s.o. from a sin).

abstenir (s') [sapstənir] *vpr* (*conj like* TENIR) to abstain from voting; **s'a. de qch,** to abstain from sth; to forgo sth; **s'a. de faire qch,** to refrain from doing sth.

abstention [apstãsjɔ̃] *nf* abstention.

abstentionnisme [apstãsjɔnism] *nm Pol:* abstention. **abstentionniste** *a & n* abstentionist.

abstinence [apstinãs] *nf* 1. abstinence; abstemiousness 2. abstention (**de,** from). **abstinent, -ente** *a* abstinent, abstemious.

abstraction [apstraksjɔ̃] *nf* (*a*) abstraction; **faire a. de qch,** to disregard sth (*b*) **moment d'a.,** absent-minded moment.

abstraire [apstrɛr] (*conj like* TRAIRE) 1. *vtr* to abstract; to separate 2. **s'a.,** to cut oneself off. **abstrait** *a* 1. abstracted 2. abstract (idea); abstruse (question). **abstraitement** *adv* abstractedly.

absurdité [apsyrdite] *nf* 1. absurdity 2. **dire des absurdités,** to talk nonsense. **absurde** *a* absurd.

abus [aby] *nm* 1. (*a*) abuse, misuse (**de,** of); **a. de pouvoir,** misuse of power (*b*) over-indulgence (**de,** in); excess (*c*) **a. de confiance,** breach of trust 2. abuse; corrupt practice 3. error, mistake 4. *F:* **il y a de l'a.!** that's going too far!

abuser [abyze] 1. *vi* **a. de qch** (i) to misuse sth (ii) to take (an unfair) advantage of sth; **vous abusez de vos forces,** you are overtaxing yourself; **j'abuse de votre temps,** I am wasting your time; **a. de l'alcool,** to drink too much; **vous abusez!** that's a bit much! 2. *vtr* to deceive 3. **s'a.,** to delude oneself; **si je ne m'abuse,** if I'm not mistaken.

abusif, -ive [abyzif, -iv] *a* 1. incorrect, improper; **emploi a.,** misuse 2. excessive; **mère abusive,** possessive mother. **abusivement** *adv* incorrectly, improperly; excessively.

acabit [akabi] *nm Pej:* **du même a.,** of the same type, sort.

acacia [akasja] *nm Bot:* acacia.

académicien [akademisjɛ̃] *nm* academician; member of the *Académie française.*

académie [akademi] *nf* 1. (*a*) academy (*b*) educational district (of France) 2. society (of letters, science, art); **l'A. française,** the French Academy (of letters) 3. (*a*) riding school (*b*) school (of music); (art) school. **académique** *a* academic; **occuper un fauteuil a.,** to be a member of the French Academy.

acajou [akaʒu] *nm* 1. mahogany 2. **noix d'a.,** cashew nut.

acariâtre [akarjɑtr̥] *a* (*esp of women*) bad-tempered, cantankerous.

accablement [akɑbləmã] *nm* dejection, despondency; exhaustion.

accabler [akɑble] *vtr* 1. to overpower, overwhelm, crush; **a. qn d'injures,** to heap abuse on s.o. 2. to overburden (with taxes, work). **accablant** *a* overwhelming; overpowering (heat).

accalmie [akalmi] *nf* lull.

accaparer [akapare] *vtr* to corner, hoard (goods); **le travail l'accapare,** the work takes up all his time; **a. la conversation,** to monopolize the conversation. **accaparant** *a* engrossing, absorbing. **accapareur, -euse** 1. *a* possessive (pers) 2. *n* monopolizer.

accéder [aksede] *vi* (**j'accède; j'accéderai**) 1. to have access (**à,** to) 2. **a. à une condition,** to agree to a condition 3. **a. au trône,** to accede to the throne.

accélérateur [akseleratœr] *nm* accelerator.

accélération [akselerasjɔ̃] *nf* (*a*) acceleration; *Aut:* **pédale d'a.,** accelerator (pedal) (*b*) speeding up (of work).

accélérer [akselere] *vtr* (**j'accélère; j'accélérerai**) 1. to accelerate; to speed up 2. **s'a.,** to quicken.

accent [aksã] *nm* 1. accent; stress; **sans a.,** unstressed 2. **a. aigu, grave,** acute, grave, accent 3. pronunciation, accent 4. tone of voice 5. *pl* (*a*) **accents du désespoir,** accents of despair (*b*) **accents de la Marseillaise,** strains of the Marseillaise.

accentuation [aksãtɥasjɔ̃] *nf* 1. stressing (of syllable) 2. accentuation.

accentuer [aksãtɥe] *vtr* 1. to stress (syllable) 2. to mark (vowel) with an accent; to accentuate 3. to emphasize; **traits fortement accentués,** pronounced features; **a. le chômage,** to increase unemployment 4. **s'a.,** to become accentuated, more pronounced.

acceptation [aksɛptasjɔ̃] *nf* acceptance.

accepter [aksɛpte] *vtr* to accept; to agree to (condition); **a. de faire qch,** to agree to do sth; **il accepte tout d'elle,** he puts up with anything from her. **acceptable** *a* (*a*) acceptable (**à,** to); reasonable (offer) (*b*) in fair condition.

acception [aksɛpsjɔ̃] *nf* meaning, sense (of word).

accès [aksɛ] *nm* 1. access, approach; **avoir, donner, a. à qch,** to have, to give, access to sth; **d'a. facile,** easily accessible; *PN:* **a. interdit,** no entry, no admittance; **a. aux quais,** to the trains 2. fit, attack; outburst; **a. de fièvre,** bout of fever; **a. d'enthousiasme,** burst of enthusiasm.

accessible [aksɛsibl] *a* 1. accessible; attainable 2. (*pers*) approachable.

accession [aksɛsjɔ̃] *nf* 1. accession (to power, to the throne) 2. attainment (of independence).

accessoire [aksɛswar] 1. *a* accessory; secondary 2. *nm* accessory; *pl Th:* props; **accessoires de toilette,** toilet requisites.

accessoiriste [aksɛswarist] *n Th: etc:* property man, girl.

accident [aksidã] *nm* 1 (*a*) accident, **par a.,** accidentally, by accident (*b*) mishap; accident; **a. mortel,** fatality; **a. d'avion,** air crash; **nous sommes arrivés sans a.,** we arrived safely 2. *Mus:* accidental 3. unevenness (of the ground). **accidenté, -ée** 1. *a* (*a*) eventful (life) (*b*) uneven (ground) (*c*) damaged (car)

2. n victim of an accident; **les accidentés,** the injured, the casualties. **accidentel, -elle** a accidental.

accidentellement adv accidentally; by accident, by chance; (to die) in an accident.

accidenter [aksidɑ̃te] vtr to injure (pers); to damage (car).

acclamation [aklamasjɔ̃] nf acclamation, cheering, cheers.

acclamer [aklame] vtr (a) to acclaim, applaud, cheer (b) **a. qn empereur,** to hail s.o. as emperor.

acclimatation [aklimatasjɔ̃] nf acclimatization; **jardin d'a.,** zoological gardens.

acclimater [aklimate] vtr **1.** to acclimatize (à, to) **2. s'a.,** to become acclimatized.

accointances [akwɛ̃tɑ̃s] nf pl Pej: dealings, relations (avec, with).

accolade [akɔlad] nf **1.** embrace **2.** accolade; **recevoir l'a.,** to be knighted **3.** Typ: brace, bracket.

accoler [akɔle] vtr to join side by side; Typ: to brace, to bracket.

accommodation [akɔmɔdasjɔ̃] nf **1.** adapting, adaptation **2.** accommodation (of the eye).

accommodement [akɔmɔdmɑ̃] nm compromise, arrangement.

accommoder [akɔmɔde] **1.** vtr (a) to suit (s.o.); **difficile à a.,** difficult to please (b) to cook, prepare (food) (c) **a. qch à qch,** to fit, adapt, sth to sth **2.** vi **a. sur, à, qch,** to focus on sth **3. s'a.** (a) **il s'accommode partout,** he is very adaptable (b) **s'a. de qch,** to make the best of sth (c) **s'a. à qch,** to adapt oneself to sth (d) **s'a. avec qn,** to come to an agreement with s.o. **accommodant** a accommodating, good-natured, easy-going.

accompagnateur, -trice [akɔ̃paɲatœr, -tris] n **1.** Mus: accompanist **2.** (tour) guide; courier.

accompagnement [akɔ̃paɲmɑ̃] nm **1.** Mus: accompaniment; **sans a.,** unaccompanied **2.** Cu: garnish; vegetables (served with meat).

accompagner [akɔ̃paɲe] vtr (a) to go, come, with (s.o.); **a. qn à la gare,** to see s.o. off at the station (b) to escort (s.o.); **accompagné de sa femme,** accompanied by his wife (c) **a. qn au piano,** to accompany s.o. on the piano; **elle s'accompagne elle-même,** she plays her own accompaniment.

accomplir [akɔ̃plir] vtr **1.** to accomplish, achieve (purpose); to carry out, fulfil (order, promise) **2.** to complete, finish; **il a quarante ans accomplis,** he's turned forty. **accompli** a accomplished.

accomplissement [akɔ̃plismɑ̃] nm **1.** accomplishment, carrying out (of duty); fulfilment (of wish) **2.** completion.

accord [akɔr] nm **1.** agreement, understanding; bargain; settlement **2.** agreement (sur, on); harmony; **d'a.,** in agreement, in accordance (avec, with); **se mettre d'a. avec qn,** to come to an agreement with s.o.; **être d'a. avec qn,** to agree with s.o.; **ils ne sont pas d'a.,** they disagree; **d'a.!** agreed! **d'un commun a.,** by mutual consent **3.** Gram: agreement, concordance; **les règles d'a.,** the concords **4.** Mus: chord; **a. parfait,** perfect chord.

accordéon [akɔrdeɔ̃] nm accordion; **en a.,** (i) pleated (skirt) (ii) F: wrinkled (trousers); **voiture en a.,** crumpled car.

accorder [akɔrde] **1.** vtr (a) to reconcile (b) Gram: **a.**

le verbe avec le sujet, to make the verb agree with the subject (c) Mus: to tune (d) to grant (favour); to award (damages); to allow (discount); **pouvez-vous m'a. quelques minutes?** can you spare me a few minutes? **2. s'a.** (a) to agree, come to an agreement; (b) **s'a. (bien, mal) avec qn,** to get on (well, badly) with s.o. (c) to correspond, harmonize, fit in (avec, with); to be in keeping (d) Gram: to agree (e) (of dress) to go (avec, with) (f) Mus: to tune (up).

accordeur [akɔrdœr] nm tuner.

accoster [akɔste] vtr **1.** to accost (s.o.); to go, come, up to (s.o.) **2.** to berth (a boat); vi to berth.

accotement [akɔtmɑ̃] nm shoulder, verge (of road); Rail: shoulder.

accoter [akɔte] vtr to lean (sth against sth); **s'a. à, contre, un mur,** to lean against a wall.

accouchée [akuʃe] nf mother (of newborn child).

accouchement [akuʃmɑ̃] nm delivery, childbirth; **a. prématuré,** premature delivery.

accoucher [akuʃe] **1.** vi (a) to give birth; **a. d'un garçon,** to give birth to a boy (b) F: **alors, accouche!** come on, out with it, spit it out! **2.** vtr **a. qn,** to deliver s.o.'s baby.

accoucheur, -euse [akuʃœr, -øz] n (a) **(médecin) a.,** obstetrician (b) nf midwife.

accouder (s') [sakude] vpr to lean on one's elbows.

accoudoir [akudwar] nm armrest.

accouplement [akupləmɑ̃] nm **1.** coupling, linking; yoking (of oxen); El: connecting **2.** pairing, mating.

accoupler [akuple] vtr **1.** (a) to couple; to yoke (oxen) (b) to mate (animals) (c) to couple (up) (parts) (d) El: to connect (batteries) **2. s'a.,** to mate.

accourir [akurir] vi (conj like COURIR; aux avoir or être) to run (up); to rush up; **ils ont accouru, sont accourus, à mon secours,** they came running to help me.

accoutrement [akutrəmɑ̃] nm usu Pej: garb; F: get-up.

accoutrer [akutre] vtr usu Pej: to rig (s.o.) out, get (s.o.) up (de, in).

accoutumance [akutymɑ̃s] nf **1.** (a) familiarization (à, with) (b) Med: **a. (à une drogue),** tolerance (for a drug) **2.** habit.

accoutumer [akutyme] vtr **1. a. qn à qch,** to accustom s.o. to sth; **être accoutumé à qch,** to be used to sth **2. s'a. à qch,** to get accustomed, used, to sth. **accoutumé** a usual; **comme à l'accoutumée,** as usual.

accréditer [akredite] vtr **1.** to accredit (an ambassador) **2.** to credit, believe (sth) **3.** (of rumour) **s'a.,** to gain ground.

accroc [akro] nm **1.** tear, rent (in clothes) **2.** hitch, difficulty, snag.

accrochage [akrɔʃaʒ] nm **1.** (a) Aut: scraping, knocking (of vehicle against another); (small) collision; Box: clinch (b) Rail: coupling **2.** altercation; Mil: brush, skirmish.

accrocher [akrɔʃe] **1.** vtr (a) to hook, catch (sth); **a. sa robe à un clou,** to catch one's dress on a nail; **a. une voiture,** to hit a car (b) to attract (s.o.'s attention, a client) (c) to couple (carriage) (d) to hang (sth) up **2.** vi **les négociations ont accroché,** there's been a hitch in the negociations 3. s'a. (a) s'a. à qch, qn, to fasten on to, cling to, sth, s.o. (b) to get caught (à, on); (of cars) to bump into each other (c) Box: to clinch (d) F: to have a row. **accrocheur, -euse** a (a) tenacious (b) eye-catching (poster); catchy (slogan).

accroire [akrwar] vtr (used only in) **faire a. à qn que** to make s.o., believe that.

accroissement [akrwasmã] nm (a) growth (b) increase.

accroître [akrwatr̩] vtr (prp **accroissant**; pp **accru**; pr ind **j'accrois, il accroît**) to increase; **s'a.**, to increase, grow.

accroupir (s') [sakrupir] vpr to squat, to crouch (down); **accroupi**, squatting, crouching.

accu [aky] nm Aut: etc: F: battery.

accueil [akœj] nm reception, welcome; **faire bon a. à qn**, to welcome s.o.

accueillir [akœjir] vtr (conj like CUEILLIR) to receive, greet (s.o.); **bien, mal, a. qn**, to give s.o. a good, a bad, reception. **accueillant** a hospitable, welcoming.

acculer [akyle] vtr to drive s.o. back (**contre**, against); to drive (s.o.) to the wall; **s'a. à, contre, qch**, to set one's back against sth.

accumulateur [akymylatœr] nm El: accumulator; battery.

accumulation [akymylasjɔ̃] n 1. accumulating; storage (of energy) 2. accumulation.

accumuler [akymyle] vtr to accumulate, amass; to store.

accusateur, -trice [akyzatœr, -tris] 1. a accusatory, incriminating 2. n accuser.

accusatif [akyzatif] a & nm Gram: accusative.

accusation [akyzasjɔ̃] nf 1. accusation, charge 2. Jur: **mettre qn en a.**, to commit s.o. for trial.

accuser [akyze] vtr 1. **a. qn de qch**, to accuse s.o. of sth 2. **a. qch**, to own to sth; **elle accuse 30 ans**, she looks at least 30 3. to define, show up, accentuate 4. **a. réception de qch**, to acknowledge (receipt of) sth. **accusé, -ée** 1. a prominent, pronounced; marked 2. n accused; (in court) defendant 3. nm **a. de réception**, acknowledgement (of receipt).

acerbe [asɛrb] a sharp, harsh.

acéré [asere] a (a) sharp(-pointed) (b) sharp, stinging (tongue).

acétate [asetat] nm Ch: acetate.

acétique [asetik] a Ch: acetic.

acétone [asetɔn] nf Ch: acetone.

acétylène [asetilɛn] nm acetylene.

achalandé [aʃalɑ̃de] a magasin bien a., (i) well patronized shop (ii) well stocked shop.

acharné [aʃarne] a fierce (opponent), relentless (efforts); **hommes acharnés les uns contre les autres**, men fighting desperately against each other; **joueur a.**, inveterate gambler; **lutte acharnée**, desperate struggle.

acharnement [aʃarnəmã] nm relentlessness; **a. au travail, pour le travail**, passion for work; **se battre avec a.**, to fight tooth and nail.

acharner (s') [saʃarne] vpr **s'a. contre, sur, qn**, to dog s.o.; to pursue s.o. relentlessly; **s'a. à, sur, qch**, to work desperately hard at sth; **s'a. inutilement**, to waste one's efforts.

achat [aʃa] nm purchase; buying; **faire l'a. de qch**, to buy sth; **faire des achats**, to shop, to go shopping; **prix d'a.**, purchase price.

acheminement [aʃminmã] nm forwarding, despatch (of goods).

acheminer [aʃmine] vtr 1. to forward, to despatch (goods) 2. **s'a. vers sa maison**, to set out for, to make one's way, home.

acheter [aʃte] vtr (j'achète, n. achetons) (a) a. qch, to buy, purchase, sth (b) a. qch à qn, to buy sth from s.o. (c) je vais lui a. un livre, I am going to buy him a book (d) F: to bribe (s.o.), to buy (s.o.) off.

acheteur, -euse [aʃtœr, -øz] n buyer, purchaser.

achèvement [aʃɛvmã] nm completion (of work).

achever [aʃve] v (j'achève) 1. vtr (a) to end, conclude, finish (off), complete; **a. de faire qch**, to finish doing sth; **achève de boire ton café**, drink up your coffee (b) to destroy (animal); F: **cette perte l'a achevé**, this loss was the end of him 2. **s'a.** (a) to draw to a close; to end (b) (of work) to reach completion. **achevé** a (a) accomplished (artist); perfect (piece of work) (b) downright (liar); utter (fool).

acide [asid] 1. a acid, tart, sour 2. nm acid.

acidité [asidite] nf acidity, sourness, tartness.

acidulé [asidyle] a slightly sour.

acier [asje] nm steel; **lame d'a., en a.**, steel blade; **regard d'a.**, steely look.

aciérie [asjeri] nf steelworks.

acné [akne] nf acne.

acolyte [akɔlit] nm Pej: confederate, associate.

acompte [akɔ̃t] nm instalment, down payment; deposit; advance (on salary).

aconit [akɔnit] nm Bot: aconite.

Açores (les) [lezasɔr] Prnfpl Geog: the Azores.

à-côté [akote] nm 1. aside (remark) 2. (a) usu pl side issues of a question) (b) F: extras; **avoir des à-côtés**, to make a bit on the side.

à-coup [aku] nm jerk; jolt; **par à-coups**, in fits and starts; **sans à-coups**, smoothly.

acoustique [akustik] 1. a acoustic 2. nf acoustics.

acquéreur [akerœr] nm buyer, purchaser.

acquérir [akerir] vtr (prp **acquérant**; pp **acquis**; pr ind **j'acquiers, n. acquérons, ils acquièrent**; pr sub **j'acquière, n. acquérions**; impf **j'acquérais**; ph **j'acquis**; fu **j'acquerrai**) 1. to acquire, obtain, get, win, gain 2. to purchase, to buy.

acquiescement [akjɛsmã] nm acquiescence, assent.

acquiescer [akjese] v ind tr (n. **acquiesçons**) a. à qch, to acquiesce in sth, to agree, to assent, to sth.

acquis [aki] 1. a (a) acquired (knowledge) (b) established, accepted (fact); **tenir pour a.**, to take for granted 2. nm acquired knowledge; experience.

acquisition [akizisjɔ̃] nf acquisition; purchase.

acquit [aki] nm 1. Com: receipt, acquittance; **pour a.**, received (with thanks) 2. **par a. de conscience**, for conscience sake.

acquittement [akitmã] nm 1. discharge, payment (of debt) 2. Jur: acquittal.

acquitter [akite] 1. vtr (a) a. qn (d'une obligation), to release s.o. (from an obligation) (b) a. un accusé, to acquit an accused person (c) to fulfil (an obligation); a. une dette, to discharge a debt (d) a. une facture, to receipt a bill 2. s'a. (a) s'a. d'une obligation, to fulfil (an obligation); **s'a. de son devoir**, to do one's duty (b) **se bien a.**, to acquit oneself well.

âcreté [akrəte] *nf* acridity, bitterness, pungency. **âcre** *a* acrid, bitter, pungent.

acrimonie [akrimɔni] *nf* acrimony. **acrimonieux, -euse** *a* acrimonious.

acrobate [akrɔbat] *n* acrobat.

acrobatie [akrɔbasi] *nf* (a) acrobatics (b) acrobatic feat (c) *Av:* **a. aérienne**, aerobatics. **acrobatique** *a* acrobatic.

acte [akt] *nm* 1. (a) action, act, deed; **a. de courage**, brave action; **faire a. de bonne volonté**, to give proof of good will (b) **a. de foi**, act of faith 2. *Jur:* (a) deed, title; **a. de vente**, bill of sale (b) **a. judiciaire**, writ; **a. d'accusation**, bill of indictment (c) record; **a. de naissance, de décès**, birth, death, certificate; **prendre a. de qch**, to record, to take note of, sth; **donner a. de qch**, to admit sth (d) *pl* records (of proceedings) 3. *Th:* act.

acteur, -trice [aktœr, -tris] *nm* actor, actress.

actif, -ive [aktif, -iv] 1. *a* (a) active; regular (army); *PolEc:* **population active**, working population (b) active, brisk, alert 2. *nm* (a) *Com:* assets (b) *Gram:* **verbe à l'a.**, verb in the active voice. **activement** *adv* actively, briskly.

action [aksjɔ̃] *nf* 1. (a) action, act; **homme d'a.**, man of action (b) action, deed, exploit; **bonne a.**, good deed 2. (a) (i) **a. sur qch**, effect on sth (ii) **a. sur qn**, influence over s.o.; **sans a.**, ineffectual, ineffective (b) **a. de l'eau**, agency of water 3. (a) *Th:* action (b) plot (of play, novel) 4. *Fin:* share; **a. ordinaire**, ordinary share; **société par actions**, joint stock company 5. *Jur:* action, lawsuit 6. *Mil:* action, engagement.

actionnaire [aksjɔnɛr] *n* shareholder.

actionnement [aksjɔnmɑ̃] *nm* activation.

actionner [aksjɔne] *vtr* 1. *Jur:* to sue 2. *MecE:* to activate; **actionné à la main**, hand operated.

activer [aktive] *vtr* 1. (a) to stimulate; to speed up (work) (b) *Ch:* to activate 2. **s'a.**, to be busy, to bustle about; to get a move on.

activiste [aktivist] *a & n* activist.

activité [aktivite] *nf* 1. activity; potency (of drug) 2. (a) activity, occupation (b) *pl* activities; *Sch:* **activités dirigées**, projects 3. **en a.**, in action, in operation, in progress, at work; (of volcano) active.

actrice *see* **acteur**.

actuaire [aktɥɛr] *nm* *Ins:* actuary.

actualité [aktɥalite] *nf* 1. actuality, reality 2. topic of the day; **d'a.**, topical; **les actualités**, current events; *TV:* the news. **actuel, -elle** *a* of the present day; existing, current; topical; **à l'heure actuelle**, at the present time. **actuellement** *adv* (just) now, at present.

acuité [akɥite] *nf* acuteness, sharpness (of point); shrillness of a sound.

acuponcteur, acupuncteur [akypɔ̃ktœr] *nm* acupuncturist.

acuponcture, acupuncture [akypɔ̃ktyr] *nf* acupuncture.

adage [adaʒ] *nm* adage.

adaptation [adaptasjɔ̃] *nf* adaptation.

adapter [adapte] 1. *vtr* to fit, adjust (sth to sth); to adapt (sth to sth) 2. **s'a.** (a) **s'a. à qch**, to fit, suit, sth (b) to adapt (oneself). **adaptable** *a* adaptable.

addition [adisjɔ̃] *nf* 1. addition, adding (to); adding up 2. (a) *Mth:* addition (b) (in restaurant) bill, *NAm:* check. **additionnel, -elle** *a* additional.

additionner [adisjɔne] *vtr & i* to add up (sum); **lait additionné d'eau**, watered down milk.

adepte [adɛpt] *n* follower.

adéquat [adekwa] *a* adequate, appropriate.

adhérence [aderɑ̃s] *nf* adhesion; adherence; grip (of tyre on road). **adhérent, -ente** 1. *a* adherent (à, to); adhesive, sticking 2. *n* member (of a party).

adhérer [adere] *vi* (**j'adhère, j'adhérerai**) 1. to adhere, stick; (of wheels) **a. à la route**, to grip the road 2. to adhere (to opinion) 3. **a. à un parti**, to join (a party).

adhésion [adezjɔ̃] *nf* 1. adhesion, sticking 2. adhesion, adherence (à, to); membership (of a party). **adhésif, -ive** *a & nm* adhesive.

adieu, pl -eux [adjø] 1. *int* good-bye! farewell! 2. *nm* farewell; **faire ses adieux à qn**, to say goodbye to s.o.

adipeux, -euse [adipø, -øz] *a* adipose, fatty (tissue).

adjacent [adʒasɑ̃] *a* adjacent (à, to); adjoining.

adjectif, -ive [adʒɛktif, -iv] 1. *a* adjectival 2. *nm* adjective.

adjoindre [adʒwɛ̃dr] *vtr* (conj like JOINDRE) 1. to add; to attach 2. **a. un collaborateur**, to appoint an assistant (à qn, for s.o.); **s'a. un collaborateur**, to take on an assistant. **adjoint, -ointe** *a & n* assistant; **a. au maire**, deputy mayor.

adjonction [adʒɔ̃ksjɔ̃] *nf* 1. adding; attaching 2. appointment.

adjudant [adʒydɑ̃] *nm* *Mil:* warrant officer class II.

adjudication [adʒydikasjɔ̃] *nf* (a) adjudication, award; allocation (of contract) (b) (i) sale by auction (ii) invitation to tender; **par voie d'a.**, (i) by tender (ii) by auction.

adjuger [adʒyʒe] *vtr* (n. adjugeons) **a. qch à qn**, (i) to award, allocate, sth to s.o. (ii) (at auction) to knock down sth to s.o.; **une fois! deux fois! adjugé!** going! going! gone! **s'a. qch**, to appropriate sth.

adjurer [adʒyre] *vtr* **a. qn de faire qch**, to implore, entreat, s.o. to do sth.

admettre [admɛtr] *vtr* (conj like METTRE) 1. to admit; to let (s.o.) in; **il fut admis dans le salon**, he was shown into the drawing room; **se faire a. dans un club**, to gain admittance to a club 2. (a) to allow, permit (sth); to accept (excuses); **l'usage admis**, the accepted custom (b) to admit, to acknowledge (sth); **admettons que j'ai tort**, assuming, supposing, (that) I'm wrong 3. *Sch:* **être admis à un examen**, to pass, to get through, an exam.

administrateur, -trice [administratœr, -tris] *n* 1. administrator 2. director (of bank, company) 3. trustee.

administration [administrasjɔ̃] *nf* 1. administering (of justice) 2. (a) administration, management (of business); **mauvaise a.**, mismanagement; **conseil d'a.**, board of directors (b) governing (of country) 3. government service; **l'A.** = the Civil Service. **administratif, -ive** *a* administrative. **administrativement** *adv* administratively.

administrer [administre] *vtr* 1. to administer, manage, run (business); to govern (country) 2. to dispense (justice); to administer (medicine) **3.** *Jur:* to produce (proof).

admirateur, -trice [admiratœr, -tris] *n* admirer.

admiration [admirasjɔ̃] *nf* admiration; **faire l'a. de qn,** to fill s.o. with admiration. **admiratif, -ive** *a* admiring. **admirativement** *adv* admiringly.

admirer [admire] *vtr* to admire. **admirable** *a* admirable, wonderful. **admirablement** *a* admirably, wonderfully.

admissibilité [admisibilite] *nf* admissibility; eligibility. **admissible** *a* admissible; eligible; *n* eligible candidate.

admission [admisjɔ̃] *nf* **1.** admission, entry; **(à, dans, to)**; *Sch:* entrance **(à, to) 2.** *Mch: ICE:* intake; **période d'a.,** induction stroke.

admonester [admɔneste] *vtr* to admonish.

ADN *abbr acide désoxyribonucléique.*

adolescence [adɔlesɑ̃s] *nf* adolescence. **adolescent, -ente 1.** *a* adolescent **2.** *n* adolescent; teenager.

adonner (s') [sadɔne] *vpr (a)* **s'a. à qch,** to devote oneself to sth *(b)* **s'a. à la boisson,** to take to drink.

adopter [adɔpte] *vtr* **1. a. un enfant,** to adopt a child **2. a. un projet de loi,** to pass a bill. **adoptif, -ive** *a* adopted (child); adoptive (parents).

adoption [adɔpsjɔ̃] *nf* adoption (of child); *Parl:* passage, carrying (of bill).

adorateur, -trice [adɔratœr, -tris] *n* adorer, worshipper.

adoration [adɔrasjɔ̃] *nf* adoration; worship.

adorer [adɔre] *vtr* to adore, worship (s.o., sth). **adorable** *a* adorable; delightful. **adorablement** *adv* adorably; delightfully.

adosser [adose] *vtr* **1.** to place (two things) back to back **2. a. qch à, contre, qch,** to lean, to rest, sth against sth **3. s'a. à, contre, qch,** to lean against sth. **adossé** *a (a)* back to back *(b)* **a. à qch,** with one's back against sth.

adoucir [adusir] *vtr* **1.** *(a)* to soften (voice, water); to tone down (colour); to subdue (light); to sweeten (drink) *(b)* to alleviate, relieve (pain, sorrow) *(c)* to pacify, mollify **2. s'a.** *(a) (of voice)* to grow softer; to soften *(b) (of weather)* to grow milder *(c) (of pain)* to decrease *(d) (of character)* to mellow.

adoucissement [adusismɑ̃] *nm* **1.** softening (of voice) **2.** alleviation (of pain) **3.** sweetening; softening.

adoucisseur [adusisœr] *nm* (water) softener.

adrénaline [adrenalin] *nf* adrenalin.

adresse [adrɛs] *nf* **1.** *(a)* address; **carnet d'adresses,** address book *(b)* **une observation à votre a.,** a remark meant for you *(c) Cmptr:* address *(d)* headword (in dictionary) **2.** *(a)* skill, dexterity; **tour d'a.,** sleight of hand *(b)* tact, diplomacy.

adresser [adrɛse] *vtr* **1.** *(a)* to address (letter) *(b)* **on m'a adressé à vous,** I have been referred to you *(c)* to aim, address (remarks); **cette remarque lui est adressée,** this remark is meant for him; **a. la parole à qn,** to speak to s.o. **2. s'a.** *(a)* **s'a. à qn,** to apply to s.o.; **s'a. ici,** enquire here *(b)* **s'a. à qn,** to speak to s.o. *(c)* **s'a. à l'imagination,** to appeal to the imagination; **le livre s'adresse aux enfants,** the book is written for children.

adroit [adrwa] *a* **1.** dexterous, skilful; **a. de ses mains,**

clever with one's hands **2.** shrewd, adroit (answer). **adroitement** *adv* skilfully; cleverly; shrewdly, adroitly.

adulateur, -trice [adylatœr, -tris] *n* adulator, flatterer.

adulation [adylasjɔ̃] *nf* adulation.

adulte [adylt] *a & n* adult, grown-up.

adultère [adylter] **1.** *a* adulterous **2.** *n* adulterer, *f* adulteress **3.** *nm* adultery.

advenir [advənir] *v (conj like* VENIR; *used only in the 3rd pers)* **1.** *vi* to occur, happen; to come (about); **je ne sais ce qui en adviendra,** I don't know what will come of it **2.** *v impers* **quoi qu'il advienne, advienne que pourra,** come what may.

adverbe [advɛrb] *nm* adverb. **adverbial, -aux** *a* adverbial; **locution adverbiale,** adverbial phrase.

adversaire [advɛrsɛr] *nm* adversary, opponent.

adverse [advɛrs] *a* opposing (party); adverse (fortune).

adversité [advɛrsite] *nf* adversity.

aération [aerasjɔ̃] *nf* **1.** ventilation, airing (of room) **2.** aeration (of water).

aérateur [aeratœr] *nm* ventilator.

aérer [aere] *vtr* **(j'aère, j'aérerai) 1.** to ventilate; to air (room, clothes) **2.** to aerate (water).

aérien, -ienne [aerjɛ̃, -jɛn] *a* **1.** aerial, atmospheric (phenomenon); aerial (plant); **défence aérienne,** air defence; **ligne aérienne,** airline **2.** (light and) airy (footstep) **3.** overhead (cable); elevated (railway).

aéro-club [aerɔklyb, -klœb] *nm* flying club; *pl aéroclubs.*

aérodrome [aerɔdrom] *nm* aerodrome, airfield.

aérodynamique [aerɔdinamik] **1.** *a* aerodynamic; streamlined **2.** *nf* aerodynamics.

aérofrein [aerɔfrɛ̃] *nm* air brake.

aérogare [aerɔgar] *nf* air terminal.

aéroglisseur [aerɔglisœr] *nm* hovercraft.

aérogramme [aerɔgram] *nm* air letter.

aéronautique [aerɔnotik] **1.** *a* aeronautical **2.** *nf* aeronautics.

aéronaval, -ale, -als [aerɔnaval] **1.** *a* air and sea (forces) **2.** *nf* **l'Aéronavale** = the Fleet Air Arm.

aéroport [aerɔpɔr] *nm* airport. **aéroporté** *a* airborne (troops); air-lifted (equipment).

aérosol [aerɔsɔl] *nm* aerosol.

aérospatial, -aux [aerɔspasjal, -o] *a* aerospace.

AF *abbr allocations familiales.*

affabilité [afabilite] *nf* affability. **affable** *a* affable. **affablement** *adv* affably.

affaiblir [afɛblir] *vtr* **1.** to weaken **2. s'a.,** to become weak(er); to lose one's strength; *(of sound)* to become fainter; *(of storm)* to abate, to die down.

affaiblissement [afɛblismɑ̃] *nm* weakening.

affaire [afɛr] *nf* **1.** *(a)* business, concern; **ce n'est pas votre a.,** it's none of your business; **occupez-vous de vos affaires,** mind your own business; **ça c'est mon a.,** (i) that's my business (ii) (you can) leave it to me *(b)* **a. d'argent,** money matter; **a. de cœur,** love affair; **c'est une a. de goût,** it's a question of taste; **ce n'est que l'a. d'un instant,** it won't take a minute *(c) (things, pers, required)*; **ça fait mon a.,** that's just what I need; **cela ne fera pas l'a.,** that won't do *(d)* (difficult) business; **c'est une sale a.,** it's a nasty business, a nasty piece of work; **ce n'est pas une a.,**

it's nothing serious; **la belle a.!** is that all? so what? **en voilà une a.!** what a lot of fuss about nothing! **se tirer d'a.,** to manage **2.** (*a*) (business) transaction, deal; **une bonne a.,** a good deal; **faire des affaires,** to do business; **chiffre d'affaires,** turnover; **homme d'affaires,** businessman; **voyage d'affaires,** business trip (*b*) **parler affaires,** to talk business (*c*) **avoir a. à qn,** to have to deal with s.o.; to be dealing with s.o.; **vous aurez a. à moi!** you'll be hearing from me! (*d*) business, firm **3.** *pl* (*a*) things, belongings; **ranger ses affaires,** to put one's things away; to tidy up (*b*) **les affaires de l'État,** affairs of State; **le Ministère des affaires étrangères** = the Foreign (and Commonwealth) Office; *NAm:* the State Department **4.** *Jur:* case, lawsuit.

affairer (s') [safere] *vpr* to bustle about; **s'a. autour de qn,** to fuss around s.o. **affairé** *a* busy.

affaissement [afɛsmã] *nm* subsidence; sinking; sagging (of floor).

affaiser (s') [safese] *vpr* (*a*) (*of ground*) to subside; (*of beam*) to sag; (*of floor*) to cave in (*b*) (*of pers*) to collapse.

affaler (s') [safale] *vpr* to collapse; **s'a. dans un fauteuil,** to sink, *F:* to flop, into an armchair.

affamer [afame] *vtr* to starve (s.o.). **affamé** *a* starving, famished.

affectation [afɛktasjõ] *nf* **1.** (*a*) affectation; affectedness; **sans a.,** unaffectedly (*b*) pretence; show (of generosity) **2.** (*a*) assignment (of sth); appropriation (of funds) (*b*) appointment; posting.

affecter [afɛkte] *vtr* **1.** to assign, allocate (**à,** to, for); to appropriate (funds) **2.** to pretend (to do sth) **3.** to have a partiality for (sth) **4.** to assume, take on (shape) **5.** (*a*) to affect, move, touch (s.o.) (*b*) to affect (career, health). **affecté** *a* affected (manners).

affectif, -ive [afɛktif, -iv] *a* affective, emotional.

affection [afɛksjõ] *nf* **1.** affection; fondness (**pour,** for); **avoir de l'a. pour qn,** to be fond of s.o. **2.** *Med:* ailment; affection.

affectionner [afɛksjone] *vtr* to be fond of (s.o., sth). **affectionné** *a* affectionate, loving.

affectueux, -euse [afɛktɥø, -øz] *a* affectionate, loving. **affectueusement** *adv* affectionately.

affermir [afɛrmir] *vtr* **1.** to strengthen, make firm **2.** to strengthen, consolidate (power, belief) **3.** **s'a.,** to become stronger, firmer.

affermissement [afɛrmismã] *nm* strengthening.

affichage [afiʃaʒ] *nm* billsticking, billposting.

affiche [afiʃ] *nf* poster, bill; placard; advertisement; **a. de théâtre,** playbill; (*of play*) **tenir l'a., rester à l'a.,** to run.

afficher [afiʃe] *vtr* **1.** to stick, post (up) (bills, notices); **a. une vente,** to advertise a sale; *PN:* **défense d'a.,** stick no bills **2.** (*a*) to display, to show off (sth) (*b*) **s'a.,** to show off; **il s'affiche avec sa maîtresse,** he is seen everywhere with his mistress.

affilée (d') [dafile] *adv phr* in a row; **cinq heures d'a.,** five hours at a stretch.

affiler [afile] *vtr* to sharpen (blade).

affiliation [afiljasjõ] *nf* affiliation.

affilier [afilje] *vtr* **1.** to affiliate (**à,** to, with) **2.** **s'a. à un parti,** to join a party. **affilié, -ée** *a & n* affiliated (member).

affinage [afinaʒ] *nm* refining; maturing.

affinement [afinmã] *nm* refinement.

affiner [afine] *vtr* **1.** (*a*) to refine; to ripen (cheese) (*b*) to sharpen (the senses) **2.** **s'a.,** (*of pers*) to become more refined; (*of features*) to become finer.

affinité [afinite] *nf* affinity.

affirmatif, -ive [afirmatif, -iv] **1.** *a* (*a*) affirmative; **signe a.,** nod (*b*) positive (person) **2.** *nf* **répondre par l'a.,** to answer in the affirmative, to answer yes; **dans l'a.,** if so. **affirmativement** *adv* in the affirmative.

affirmation [afirmasjõ] *nf* affirmation; assertion.

affirmer [afirme] *vtr* **1.** (*a*) to affirm; to insist, to maintain; **pouvez-vous l'a.?** can you swear to it? (*b*) to assert (one's authority) **2.** **s'a.,** to assert oneself.

affleurer [aflœre] **1.** *vtr Carp:* to make flush **2.** *vi* (*a*) to be level, flush (*b*) *Geol:* (*of lode*) to outcrop.

affliction [afliksjõ] *nf* affliction, sorrow.

affliger [afliʒe] *vtr* (**n. affligeons**) **1.** to afflict (**de,** with); to pain, distress, grieve **2.** **s'a.,** to be grieved, distressed (about sth). **affligé** *a* afflicted; **a. de rhumatisme,** suffering from rheumatism. **affligeant** *a* distressing, sad.

affluence [aflyãs] *nf* crowd; **heures d'a.,** rush hour.

affluent [aflyã] *nm* tributary (of river).

affluer [aflye] *vi* (*of liquid*) to flow; (*of blood*) to rush; **a. à, dans, un endroit,** to crowd, to flock, to a place.

afflux [afly] *nm* rush, flow; influx (of people).

affolement [afɔlmã] *nm* panic; **pas d'a.!** don't panic!

affoler [afɔle] *vtr* **1.** to drive (s.o.) crazy, to throw (s.o.) into a panic **2.** **s'a.,** to panic, to get into a panic. **affolant** *a* alarming. **affolé** *a* panic-stricken.

affranchir [afrãʃir] *vtr* **1.** to free; to set free; to emancipate (slave) **2.** to pay the postage on (letter); to frank; to stamp (letter); **colis affranchi,** pre-paid parcel.

affranchissement [afrãʃismã] *nm* **1.** emancipation, freeing (of slave) **2.** (*a*) stamping, franking (*b*) postage (of letter).

affres [afr] *nfpl* anguish, spasm; **les a. de la mort,** the pangs, the throes, of death.

affrètement [afrɛtmã] *nm* chartering.

affréter [afrete] *vtr* (**j'affrète; j'affréterai**) to charter (ship, plane).

affreux, -euse [afrø, -øz] *a* **1.** frightful, hideous, ghastly **2.** frightful, horrible, dreadful, shocking (news, crime). **affreusement** *adv* frightfully; hideously; horribly, dreadfully.

afriolant [afrijɔlã] *a* tempting, enticing.

affront [afrõ] *nm* affront, insult, snub.

affrontement [afrõtmã] *nm* confronting, confrontation.

affronter [afrõte] *vtr* **1.** to face, confront (s.o.); to encounter (enemy); to brave (the cold) **2.** **s'a.,** (*of enemies*) to confront each other; (*of theories*) to conflict.

affubler [afyble] *vtr Pej:* **a. qn de qch,** to rig s.o. out, dress s.o. up, in sth; **a. qn d'un nom,** to give s.o. a name.

affût [afy] *nm* **1.** hide; **chasser un animal à l'a.,** to stalk an animal; **être, se mettre, à l'a. de qn,** to lie in wait for s.o.; **à l'a. de nouvelles**, on the look-out for news **2.** gun carriage.

affûtage [afytaʒ] *nm* sharpening (of tool).

affûter [afyte] *vtr* to sharpen (tool).

afin [afɛ̃] *adv* **1. a. de (faire qch)**, to, in order to, so as to (do sth) **2. a. que** + *sub*, so that, in order that.

AFP *abbr Agence France Presse.*

Afrique [afrik] *Prnf* Africa. **africain, -aine** *a & n* African.

AG *abbr assemblée générale.*

agacement [agasmɑ̃] *nm* irritation, annoyance.

agacer [agase] *vtr* (**n. agaçons**) to annoy, to irritate (s.o.); **tu m'agaces!** you're getting on my nerves! **a. un chien**, to tease a dog. **agaçant** *a* annoying, irritating.

agate [agat] *nf Miner:* agate.

âge [ɑʒ] *nm* **1.** (*a*) age; **quel â. avez-vous?** how old are you? **d'un â. avancé**, elderly; **être d'â. légal**, to be of age; **être d'â. à faire qch**, to be old enough to do sth (*b*) **enfant en bas â.**, infant; **d'un certain â.**, middle-aged; **l'â. de raison**, the age of discretion (*c*) old age; **le troisième â.**, the over sixties (*d*) **â. mental**, mental age **2.** age, period, epoch; **l'â. de bronze**, the bronze age; *Hist:* **le moyen â.**, the middle ages; **l'â. d'or**, the golden age. **âgé** *a* old, aged; **â. de dix ans**, ten years old; **dame âgée**, elderly lady.

agence [aʒɑ̃s] *nf* (*a*) agency; **a. de placement**, employment bureau; **a. de presse**, press agency; **a. de voyages**, travel agency (*b*) branch office.

agencement [aʒɑ̃smɑ̃] *nm* **1.** arrangement **2.** *pl* fixtures, fittings.

agencer [aʒɑ̃se] *vtr* (**n. agençons**) to arrange (house); **local bien agencé**, well designed, well equipped, premises.

agenda [aʒɛ̃da] *nm* diary.

agenouiller (s') [saʒnuje] *vpr* to kneel (down).

agent [aʒɑ̃] *nm* **1.** agent, agency **2.** (*a*) agent; **a. d'assurances**, insurance agent; **a. immobilier**, estate agent; **a. du gouvernement**, government official; **a. (de police)**, policeman (*b*) **a. de change**, stockbroker **3.** *Mil:* **a. de liaison**, liaison officer; **a. secret**, secret agent.

agglomération [aglɔmerasjɔ̃] *nf* agglomeration; built-up area; **l'a. londonienne**, Greater London.

aggloméré [aglɔmere] *nm* (*a*) *Const:* conglomerate (*b*) briquette (*c*) fibreboard.

agglomérer [aglɔmere] *vtr* (**j'agglomère, n. agglomérons**) **1.** to agglomerate **2. s'a.**, to agglomerate; to cohere.

agglutination [aglytinasjɔ̃] *nf* agglutination.

agglutiner [aglytine] *vtr & pr* to bind; to agglutinate.

aggravation [agravasjɔ̃] *nf* aggravation; worsening; increase (of taxation).

aggraver [agrave] *vtr* **1.** (*a*) to aggravate (disease); to worsen (*b*) **s'a.**, to worsen; **son état s'est aggravé**, he has taken a turn for the worse **2.** to increase (taxation).

agilité [aʒilite] *nf* agility, nimbleness. **agile** *a* agile, nimble; active; quick (mind). **agilement** *adv* nimbly.

agir [aʒir] *vi* **1.** to act; **c'est le moment d'a.**, it's time to act, to take action; **faire a. qn**, to get s.o. to act; **bien, mal, a. envers qn**, to behave well, badly, to-

wards s.o.; **est-ce ainsi que vous agissez envers moi?** is that how you treat me? **2.** to act, operate; **le remède agit vite**, the medicine quickly takes effect; **a. sur qn**, to exercise an influence on s.o. **3.** *Jur:* to take proceedings. **s'agir (de)** *v impers* (*a*) to concern; to be the matter; **de quoi s'agit-il?** what's the matter? what is it all about? **il ne s'agit pas d'argent**, it's not a question of money; **il s'agit de lui**, it concerns him; **il ne s'agit pas de cela**, that is not the point (*b*) **il s'agirait de savoir si elle vient**, the question is whether she's coming; **il s'agit de se dépêcher**, we've got to hurry. **agissant** *a* **1.** active **2.** effective.

agissements [aʒismɑ̃] *nmpl Pej:* dealings; machinations.

agitateur, -trice [aʒitatœr, -tris] *n* (political) agitator.

agitation [aʒitasjɔ̃] *nf* (*a*) agitation; restlessness, fidgetiness (*b*) commotion, agitation; (labour) unrest (*c*) excitement; disturbance.

agiter [aʒite] *vtr* **1.** (*a*) to wave (handkerchief); **le chien agite sa queue**, the dog is wagging his tail (*b*) to shake (tree, bottle); to flutter (wings); to sway (branches) (*c*) to stir (mixture) **2.** (*a*) to agitate; to excite patient; **agité par la fièvre**, restless with fever (*b*) to trouble; to stir up (the masses) **3.** to debate (question) **4. s'a.** (*a*) to be agitated; to bustle around; to fidget; **s'a. dans l'eau**, to splash about in the water; **s'a. dans son sommeil**, to toss (about) in one's sleep (*b*) to become agitated, excited; (*of sea*) to get rough. **agité** *a* **1.** choppy, rough (sea) **2.** restless (night, patient); fitful (sleep) **3.** (*a*) excited; fidgety (*b*) troubled (mind) (*c*) **vie agitée**, hectic life.

agneau, -eaux [aɲo] *nm* (*a*) lamb (*b*) lambskin.

agonie [agɔni] *nf* death agony; throes of death; **être à l'a.**, to be at one's last gasp.

agoniser [agɔnize] *vi* to be dying. **agonisant, -ante** *a* dying.

agrafe [agraf] *nf* hook, fastener; clasp; buckle (of strap); staple (for paper).

agrafer [agrafe] *vtr* to fasten, to clip, together; to hook (up); to staple.

agrafeuse [agraføz] *nf* stapler.

agraire [agrɛr] *a* agrarian; land (reform).

agrandir [agrɑ̃dir] *vtr* **1.** (*a*) to make (sth) larger; to enlarge; to extend (house); **a. en long, en large**, to lengthen, to widen (*b*) to magnify **2. s'a.**, to grow larger; to become greater; to get bigger, wider; to expand.

agrandissement [agrɑ̃dismɑ̃] *nm* (*a*) enlarging, extending (*b*) extension (of house); *Phot:* enlargement (*c*) expansion.

agréable [agreabl] *a* agreeable, pleasant, nice; **si cela peut vous être a.**, if you like; **a. au goût**, pleasant to the taste; **peu a.**, disagreeable; **pour vous être a.**, to oblige you. **agréablement** *adv* agreeably, pleasantly.

agréer [agree] **1.** *vtr* (*a*) to accept, recognize, agree to (sth); **a. un contrat**, to approve an agreement; *Corr:* **veuillez a. l'assurance de mes salutations distinguées**, yours faithfully, yours sincerely (*b*) **fournisseur agréé**, registered dealer **2.** *v ind tr* to please; **si cela lui agrée**, if that suits him.

agrégat [agrega] *nm* aggregate.

agrégation [agregasjɔ̃] *nf* highest competitive examination for teaching posts in the *lycées* and universities.

agrégé, -ée [agreʒe] *a & n Sch:* (graduate) who has passed the *agrégation* examination.

agréger [agreʒe] *vtr* (a) to aggregate (b) to incorporate (s.o. into group).

agrément [agremã] *nm* 1. (a) pleasure, amusement; **voyage d'a.**, pleasure trip (b) attractiveness, charm 2. *usu pl* amenities (of place); charm (of person) 3. approval; consent.

agrémenter [agremãte] *vtr* to embellish.

agrès [agrɛ] *nmpl Gym:* apparatus.

agresser [agrese] *vtr* to attack.

agresseur [agresœr] *nm* agressor.

agression [agresjɔ̃] *nf* aggression; attack. **agressif, -ive** *a* aggressive. **agressivement** *adv* aggressively.

agricole [agrikɔl] *a* agricultural, farm (produce); farming (population).

agriculteur [agrikyltœr] *nm* farmer.

agriculture [agrikyltyr] *nf* agriculture, farming.

agripper [agripe] *vtr* to clutch (at), grip; **s'a. à qch**, to cling to sth.

agronome [agronɔm] *nm* agronomist.

agronomie [agronɔmi] *nf Agr:* agronomy. **agronomique** *a* agronomical.

agrumes [agrym] *nmpl* citrus fruits.

aguerrir [agerir] *vtr* 1. to harden (s.o) (to war) 2. **s'a.**, to become hardened.

aguets [agɛ] *nmpl* **aux a.**, watchful, on the lookout.

aguichant [agiʃã] *a* seductive, provocative.

ah [ɑ] *int* ah! oh! **ah bon?** (i) really? (ii) oh, well.

ahurir [ayrir] *vtr* to bewilder; to dumbfound; to stun; to confuse, stupefy. **ahuri, -ie** *a* stunned, dumbfounded; stupefied. **ahurissant** *a* bewildering, staggering.

ahurissement [ayrismã] *nm* stupefaction.

aide¹ [ɛd] *nf* help, assistance, aid; **venir en a. à qn**, to help s.o.; **appeler à l'a.**, to call for help; **à l'a.! help!** **à l'a. de qch**, with the help of sth; **sans a.**, unaided, without help.

aide² *nm & f* assistant, helper; **a. de camp**, aide-de-camp; **a. familiale**, home help, mother's help.

aide-mémoire [ɛdmemwar] *nm inv* manual; memorandum.

aider [ɛde] 1. *vtr* to help, assist, aid (s.o.); **je me suis fait a. par un ami**, I got a friend to help me, to give me a hand; **a. qn à monter, à descendre**, to help s.o. up, down; **Dieu aidant**, with God's help 2. *vi* **a. à qch**, to contribute towards sth 3. **s'a.** (a) **s'a. de qch**, to use, to make use of, sth (b) **s'a. les uns les autres**, to help one another

aïe [aj] *int* (*indicating twinge of pain*) ow! ouch! **a. a. a.!** oh dear!

aïeul [ajœl] *nm* 1. (*pl* aïeuls) grandfather 2. (*pl* aïeux [ajø]) ancestor.

aïeule [ajœl] *nf* 1. grandmother 2. ancestress.

aigle [ɛgl] (a) *nm & f Orn:* eagle; **a. royal**, golden eagle; **regard d'a.**, penetrating glance; **aux yeux d'a.**, eagle-eyed (b) *nm* **ce n'est pas un a.**, he's no genius.

aiglefin [ɛgləfɛ̃] *nm Ich:* haddock.

aigre [ɛgr] *a* (a) sour, acid, tart; *nm* **tourner à l'a.**, (i) to turn sour (ii) (*of quarrel*) to turn nasty (b) bitter, keen (wind). **aigrement** *adv* bitterly. **aigredoux, -douce** *a* sweet and sour (sauce); bittersweet (fruit); catty (remark).

aigrefin [ɛgrəfɛ̃] *nm* swindler, crook.

aigrelet, -ette [ɛgrəlɛ, -ɛt] *a* sourish, tart.

aigrette [ɛgrɛt] *nf* 1. aigrette, plume 2. *Orn:* egret.

aigreur [ɛgrœr] *nf* (a) sourness, tartness (b) harshness (of tone) (c) *Med:* **aigreurs**, acidity.

aigrir [egrir] 1. *vtr* (a) to turn (sth) sour (b) to embitter (pers) 2. *vi* to turn sour 3. **s'a.** (a) to turn sour (b) (*of pers*) to become embittered.

aigu, -uë [egy] *a* 1. sharp, pointed (instrument); **angle a.**, acute angle 2. acute, sharp (pain); keen (intelligence) 3. shrill, high-pitched 4. **accent a.**, acute accent.

aiguillage [eguijaʒ] *nm Rail:* points, *NAm:* switches.

aiguille [eguij] *nf* 1. needle; **travail à l'a.**, needlework 2. (a) **a. de glace**, icicle; **a. de pin**, pine needle (b) *Rail:* **a. de raccordement**, points 3. needle, point (of peak); (church) spire 4. needle (of compass); pointer (of balance); hand (of clock); **petite a.**, hour hand; **grande a.**, minute hand; **a. trotteuse**, second hand.

aiguiller [eguije] *vtr Rail:* to shunt, *NAm:* to switch.

aiguilleur [eguijœr] *nm Rail:* pointsman, *NAm:* switchman; *Av:* **a. du ciel**, air traffic controller.

aiguillon [eguijɔ̃] *nm* 1. (a) goad (b) spur, incentive 2. (a) *Bot:* prickle, thorn (b) sting (of wasp).

aiguillonner [eguijɔne] *vtr* 1. to goad 2. to spur on.

aiguiser [egize] *vtr* 1. to sharpen 2. to stimulate (wits); to whet (appetite).

ail, *pl* **ails, aux** [aj,o] *nm* garlic.

aile [ɛl] *nf* 1. wing; **battre de l'a.**, to flutter; **la peur lui donnait des ailes**, fear lent him wings 2. (a) wing (of aeroplane); sail (of windmill); blade (of propeller); wing (of nose) (b) *Aut:* wing, *NAm:* fender (c) *Fb:* wing.

aileron [ɛlrɔ̃] *nm* 1. (a) pinion (of bird) (b) fin (of shark) 2. *Av:* aileron, wing tip.

ailette [ɛlɛt] *nf* fin; blade.

ailier [ɛlje] *nm Fb:* winger.

ailleurs [ajœr] *adv* 1. elsewhere, somewhere else; **partout a.**, everywhere else; **nulle part a.**, nowhere else 2. (a) **d'a.** (i) besides, moreover (ii) however (iii) for that matter (b) **par a.** (i) in other respects (ii) moreover (iii) incidentally.

aimable [ɛmabl] *a* amiable; kind; nice; **vous êtes bien a.**, **c'est très a. de votre part**, it's very kind of you; **peu a.**, disagreeable. **aimablement** *adv* kindly, nicely.

aimant [ɛmã] *nm* magnet.

aimanter [ɛmãte] *vtr* to magnetize; **champ aimanté**, magnetic field.

aimer [ɛme] *vtr* 1. (a) to like, care for, to be fond of (s.o., sth); **se faire a. de qn**, to win s.o.'s affection; **j'aurais aimé le voir**, I would have liked to have seen him; **il aime faire du ski**, he likes skiing (b) **j'aime(rais) autant rester ici**, I would just as soon stay here (c) **a. mieux**, to prefer; **j'aime mieux rester ici**, I'd rather stay here 2. **a. qn (d'amour)**, to love s.o.; **ils s'aiment**, they are in love (with each other).

aine [ɛn] *nf Anat:* groin.

aîné [ɛne] *a* elder, older (of two); eldest, older (of

more than two); *n* **il est mon a. de 3 ans,** he is 3 years older than me, he is 3 years my senior.

aînesse [ɛnɛs] *nf* primogeniture; **droit d'a.,** (i) law of primogeniture (ii) birthright.

ainsi [ɛ̃si] **1.** *adv* (a) like this, like that; in this, in that, way; **s'il en est a.,** if that is the case, if (it is) so; **puisqu'il en est a.,** under the circumstances; **et a. de suite,** and so on; **pour a. dire,** so to speak, as it were (b) **a. soit-il,** (i) so be it (ii) *Ecc:* amen (c) for example, for instance **2.** *conj* (a) so; **a. vous ne venez pas?** so you're not coming? (b) as also; **cette règle a. que la suivante me paraît, me paraissent, inutile(s),** this rule, as well as the next one, seems to me to be unnecessary.

air[1] [ɛr] *nm* **1.** (a) air, atmosphere; **sans a.,** airless; **cela manque d'a.,** it's close, stuffy, in here; **donner de l'a. à,** to ventilate, to air; **prendre l'a.,** to enjoy the fresh air; **à a. conditionné,** air conditioned; **vivre de l'a. du temps,** to live on (next to) nothing, on air; **au grand a., en plein a.,** in the open air; **vie de plein a.,** outdoor life; **concert en plein a.,** open-air concert (b) (*of aircraft*) **prendre l'a.,** to take off; **Armée de l'A.** = Royal Air Force (c) **en l'a.,** in the air; **être en l'a.,** to be in a state of confusion; **paroles en l'a.,** idle talk; *F:* **tout flanquer en l'a.,** (i) to abandon, to chuck up, everything (ii) to mess everything up **2.** wind; **courant d'a.,** draught; **il fait de l'a.,** it's breezy.

air[2] *nm* **1.** (a) appearance, look; **avoir bon a.,** (i) to look distinguished (ii) (*of dress*) to be smart; **a. de famille,** family likeness; **avoir un a. de fête,** to look festive (b) **avoir l'a.,** to look, to seem; **l'a. fatigué,** to look tired; **elle a l'a. intelligent(e),** she looks intelligent; **cela en a tout l'a.,** it looks like it; **n'avoir l'a. de rien,** (i) to appear insignificant (ii) (*of house*) to look like nothing much (iii) (*of job*) to look (deceptively) easy; **le temps a l'a. d'être à la pluie,** it looks like rain **2.** manner, way; **se donner des airs,** to give oneself airs, to look important.

air[3] *nm* tune, air, melody; (*in opera*) aria.

airain [ɛrɛ̃] *nm Lit:* bronze.

aire [ɛr] *nf* **1.** (a) surface; floor; **a. (d'une grange),** threshing floor (b) (*on motorway*) parking area; *Av:* **a. de stationnement,** tarmac; *Space:* **a. de lancement,** launching site **2.** area (of field, triangle) **3.** eyrie (of eagle).

airelle [ɛrɛl] *nf Bot:* bilberry; *NAm:* blueberry.

aisance [ɛzɑ̃s] *nf* (a) ease; freedom (of movement) (b) **être dans l'a.,** to be well off.

aise [ɛz] **1.** *nf* ease, comfort; **être à l'a.,** à **son a.,** (i) to be comfortable (ii) to be well off; **ne pas être à son a., se sentir mal à l'a.,** (i) to feel uncomfortable (ii) to feel off colour; **mettez-vous à votre a.,** make yourself comfortable; **aimer ses aises,** to like one's comforts; **à votre a.!** please yourself! **2.** *a Lit:* **bien a.,** very pleased. **aisé** *a* **1.** (a) easy, free (manner) (b) well-to-do, well off **2.** easy (task). **aisément** *adv* easily.

aisselle [ɛsɛl] *nf* armpit.

ajonc [aʒɔ̃] *nm Bot:* furze, gorse.

ajouré [aʒure] *a* perforated; openwork (design); **travail a.,** (i) *Carp:* fretwork (ii) *Needlew:* hemstitched work.

ajournement [aʒurnəmɑ̃] *nm* postponement, adjournment; *Sch:* referring; *Mil:* deferment.

ajourner [aʒurne] *vtr* (a) to postpone, put off,

adjourn, defer (meeting, decision) (b) *Sch:* to refer (candidate); *Mil:* to grant deferment to (conscript).

ajouter [aʒute] *vtr* **1.** to add; **a. des chiffres,** to add up figures; **sans a. que,** without adding that; let alone the fact that; **a. à qch,** to add to sth **2.** **"venez aussi," ajouta-t-il,** "you come too," he added **3.** **a. foi à qch,** to believe sth.

ajustage [aʒystaʒ] *nm* **1.** fitting (of dress) **2.** assembly (of machine).

ajustement [aʒystəmɑ̃] *nm* adjustment.

ajuster [aʒyste] *vtr* **1.** (a) to adjust, set (tool) (b) to true up (sth) (c) to fit (dress); **robe ajustée,** tight fitting dress (d) **a. son fusil,** to aim one's gun (e) **a. qch à qch,** to fit, adapt, sth to sth **2.** **s'a.,** to fit (together).

ajusteur [aʒystœr] *nm* (metal) fitter.

alambic [alɑ̃bik] *nm Ch:* still.

alanguir [alɑ̃gir] **1.** *vtr* to make languid **2.** **s'a.,** to grow languid.

alanguissement [alɑ̃gismɑ̃] *nm* languor.

alarme [alarm] *nf* alarm; **donner, sonner, l'a.,** to give, sound, the alarm; *Rail:* **tirer la sonnette d'a.,** to pull the communication cord.

alarmer [alarme] *vtr* **1.** to alarm, frighten, startle (s.o.) **2.** **s'a.,** to take fright (**de,** at). **alarmant** *a* alarming, frightening.

alarmiste [alarmist] *a & n* alarmist.

Albanie [albani] *Prnf* Albania. **albanais, -aise** *a & n* Albanian.

albâtre [albɑtr] *nm* alabaster.

albatros [albatrɔs] *nm Orn:* albatross.

albinos [albinos] *n & a inv* albino.

album [albɔm] *nm* album.

albumine [albymin] *nf Ch:* albumin.

alcali [alkali] *nm Ch:* alkali. **alcalin** *a* alkaline.

alchimie [alʃimi] *nf* alchemy.

alchimiste [alʃimist] *nm* alchemist.

alcool [alkɔl] *nm* (a) alcohol; **a. à brûler,** methylated spirit; **a. à 90°** = surgical spirit (b) alcohol, spirits; **je ne bois pas d'a.,** (i) I don't drink spirits (ii) I don't drink (alcohol); **a. de poire** = pear brandy. **alcoolique** *a & n* alcoholic. **alcoolisé** *a* alcoholic.

alcoolisme [alkɔlism] *nm* alcoholism.

alcootest [alkotest] *nm* breathalyser (test).

alcôve [alkov] *nf* alcove.

aléa [alea] *nm* risk, hazard. **aléatoire** *a* risky; random.

alène [alɛn] *nf Tls:* awl; **a. plate,** bradawl.

alentour [alɑ̃tur] **1.** *adv* around, round about; **le pays d'a.,** the neighbouring country **2.** *nmpl* **aux alentours de la ville,** in the vicinity of the town; **aux alentours de 3 heures,** round about 3 o'clock.

alerte [alɛrt] **1.** *int* look out! **2.** *nf* alarm, warning; **a. aérienne,** air-raid warning; **fin d'a.,** all clear; **fausse a.,** false alarm **3.** *a* alert, brisk, quick.

alerter [alɛrte] *vtr* to alert, warn.

alexandrin [alɛksɑ̃drɛ̃] *nm* alexandrine.

alezan, -ane [alzɑ̃, -an] *a & n* chestnut (horse).

algèbre [alʒɛbr] *nf* algebra; **par l'a.,** algebraically; **c'est de l'a. pour moi,** it's all Greek to me. **algébrique** *a* algebraic.

Alger [alʒe] *Prn* Algiers.

Algérie [alʒeri] *Prnf* Algeria. **algérien, -ienne** *a & n* Algerian.

algue [alg] *nf Bot:* seaweed.

alias [aljɑs] *adv* alias.

alibi [alibi] *nm* alibi.

aliénation [aljenasjɔ̃] *nf* 1. alienation; estrangement 2. **a. mentale**, insanity.

aliéné, -ée [aljene] *n* mental patient.

aliéner [aljene] *vtr* (**j'aliène; j'aliénerai**) 1. (*a*) *Jur:* to alienate (property) (*b*) to give up (one's freedom) 2. to alienate, estrange (affections); **s'a. un ami**, to alienate a friend.

alignement [aliɲmɑ̃] *nm* 1. alignment; aligning 2. alignment, line (of wall).

aligner [aliɲe] *vtr* 1. to align, draw up, line up; to put (thgs) in a line 2. **s'a.**, to be in line with; to fall into line; **s'a. sur**, to conform to.

aliment [alimɑ̃] *nm* food. **alimentaire** *a* 1. **régime a.**, diet; *Jur:* **pension a.**, alimony 2. nutritious (food); **produits alimentaires**, food (products).

alimentation [alimɑ̃tasjɔ̃] *nf* 1. (*a*) feeding; supply (of market) (*b*) groceries; **magasin d'a.**, grocer's shop (*c*) food, nourishment 2. *Tchn:* feed(ing).

alimenter [alimɑ̃te] *vtr* 1. to feed, nourish (s.o.); to supply (market) with food 2. **s'a.**, to feed on (sth).

alinéa [alinea] *nm Typ:* 1. first line of paragraph; **en a.**, indented 2. paragraph.

aliter [alite] *vtr* to keep (s.o.) in bed; **s'a.**, to take to one's bed. **alité** *a* confined to bed.

alizé [alize] *a & nm* **les (vents) alizés**, the trade winds.

allaitement [alɛtmɑ̃] *nm* suckling, breastfeeding; **a. au biberon, a. naturel**, bottle feeding, breastfeeding.

allaiter [alɛte] *vtr* to suckle, to (breast)feed (child).

allant [alɑ̃] 1. *a* active, lively 2. *nm* drive, energy.

allécher [aleʃe] *vtr* (**j'allèche; j'allécherai**) to allure, attract, entice, tempt. **alléchant** *a* alluring, attractive, enticing, tempting.

allée [ale] *nf* 1. **allées et venues**, comings and goings 2. (*a*) walk (*esp* lined with trees); avenue; drive (*b*) path (in garden).

allégation [alegasjɔ̃] *nf* allegation.

allégeance [aleʒɑ̃s] *nf* allegiance.

allégement [aleʒmɑ̃] *nm* lightening, alleviation; reduction.

alléger [aleʒe] *vtr* (**j'allège, n. allégeons; j'allégerai**) (*a*) to lighten; to reduce (taxes) (*b*) to alleviate, relieve (pain).

allégorie [alegɔri] *nf* allegory. **allégorique** *a* allegorical.

allègre [alɛgr] *a* lively, cheerful, jolly, lighthearted. **allégrement** *adv* cheerfully, lightheartedly.

allégresse [alegrɛs] *nf* joy, cheerfulness, liveliness.

alléguer [alege] *vtr* (**j'allègue; j'alléguerai**) 1. to allege; **a. l'ignorance**, to plead ignorance 2. to quote (author).

Allemagne [almaɲ] *Prnf* Germany. **allemand, -ande** 1. *a & n* German 2. *nm* **l'a.**, (the) German (language).

aller¹ [ale] *vi* (*pr ind* **je vais, tu vas, il va, n. allons, ils vont**; *pr sub* **j'aille**; *imp* **va (vas-y), allons**; *impf* **j'allais**; *fu* **j'irai**; *aux* **être**) 1. (*a*) to go; **a. chez qn**, to call on s.o., to go and see s.o.; **ne faire qu'a. et revenir**, to be always on the go; **je ne ferai qu'a. et revenir**, I shall come straight back; **il va sur ses quarante ans**, he is getting on for forty; **il ira loin**, he will go far; **vous n'irez pas loin avec 50 francs**, 50 francs won't

get you very far; **nous irons jusqu'au bout**, we shall carry on to the end (*b*) **a. à pied, en vélo, en voiture**, to go on foot, by bike, by car; to walk, to cycle, to drive (*c*) *with adv acc* **a. bon train**, to go at a good pace; *with cogn acc* **a. son (petit bonhomme de) chemin**, to go one's way (*d*) **allez, je vous écoute**, go on, I'm listening (*e*) **chemin qui va à la gare**, road leading to the station (*f*) **plat allant au four**, ovenproof dish 2. (*a*) to go, be going (well, badly); **les affaires vont**, business is good; **ça ira!** we'll manage! **il y a qch qui ne va pas**, there's sth wrong; **je vous en offre 100 francs—va pour 100 francs**! I'll give you 100 francs for it—all right, 100 francs! **cela va sans dire, cela va de soi**, that goes without saying (*b*) (*of machine*) to go, work, run; **la pendule va bien**, (*i*) (*of clock's right*) (*ii*) the clock keeps good time (*c*) (*of clothes*) to fit (*d*) **ça n'ira pas dans le panier**, it won't go into the basket (*e*) **comment allez-vous?** how are you? **je vais bien**, *F:* **ça va**, I'm well, I'm all right; **écoute, je vais mieux**, I'm better; **ça va mal**, things aren't going too well; **ça va mal a.!** there's going to be trouble! 3. **a. à qn**, (i) (*of colours*) to suit s.o. (ii) (*of clothes*) to fit s.o. (iii) (*of climate, food*) to agree with s.o. (iv) (*of plan*) to suit s.o.; **ça me va!** agreed! *F:* **ça va!** all right! O.K.! 4. (*of colours*) **a. avec qch**, to go well with sth, to match sth 5. (*a*) **a. voir qn**, to go and see s.o.; to call on s.o.; **a. trouver qn**, to go and find s.o.; **a. se promener**, to go for a walk; **n'allez pas vous imaginer que**, don't imagine that; **allez donc savoir!** how is one to know? (*b*) to be going, to be about (to do sth); **il va s'en occuper**, he is going to see about it; **elle allait tout avouer**, she was about to confess everything; **a. en augmentant**, to increase 6. (*a*) **j'y vais! on y va!** coming! (*b*) **allez-y doucement!** easy does it! **y a. de tout son cœur**, to put one's heart and soul into it; **allons-y!** well, here goes! **vas-y! allez-y!** go! (*c*) *F:* **y a. de sa personne**, (i) to take a hand in it oneself (ii) to do one's bit 7. *v impers* **il va de soi**, it stands to reason, it goes without saying; **il en va de même pour lui**, it's the same with him; **il y va de sa vie**, it's a matter of life and death to him 8. *int* **allons, dépêchez-vous!** come on, hurry up! **allons donc!** (i) come along! (ii) nonsense! **allons bon!** there now! bother! **mais va donc!** get on with it! **j'ai bien souffert, allez!** I've been through a lot, believe me! **s'en aller** *vpr* (*pr ind* **je m'en vais**; *imp* **va-t'en, allons nous-en**) 1. to go away; to leave; **les voisins s'en vont**, the neighbours are moving; **les taches ne s'en vont pas**, the stains won't come off; **allez-vous-en!** go away! **s'en a. en fumée**, to end in smoke 2. **je m'en vais vous raconter ça**, I'll tell you all about it.

aller² *nm* 1. going; outward journey; **à l'a.**, on the way there; **a.-retour**, journey there and back; **billet a.-retour, d'a. et retour**, return ticket; *NAm:* round trip ticket; *F:* **un a.**, a single (ticket); *Sp:* **match a.**, away match 2. **pis a.**, last resort; **au pis a.**, if the worst comes to the worst.

allergie [alɛrʒi] *nf Med:* allergy. **allergique** *a* allergic.

alliage [aljaʒ] *nm* alloy.

alliance [aljɑ̃s] *nf* 1. (*a*) alliance; marriage, union; **parent par a.**, relation by marriage (*b*) **traité d'a.**, treaty of alliance 2. wedding ring.

allier [alje] *v* (*impf & pr sub* **n. alliions**) 1. *vtr* (*a*) to ally, unite (b) to alloy, mix (metals); to match (colours) (à, with) (c) to combine (qualities) (à, with) 2. s'a. (a) to form an alliance; to ally (b) s'a. à une famille, to marry into a family. **allié, -ée** 1. a (a) allied (nation) (b) related (by marriage) 2. n (a) ally (b) relation by marriage.

alligator [aligatɔr] nm Rept: alligator.

allô, allo [alo] int Tp: hullo! hallo! hello!

allocation [alɔkasjɔ̃] nf 1. allocation, granting (of money, supplies); Fin: allotment (of shares) 2. allowance, grant; **allocations familiales**, family allowances; **a. (de) chômage**, unemployment benefit.

allocution [alɔkysjɔ̃] nf short speech.

allongement [alɔ̃ʒmɑ̃] nm lengthening, extension; elongation.

allonger [alɔ̃ʒe] vtr (n. allongeons) 1. (a) to lengthen; to let down (garment) (b) to stretch out (one's arm); to crane (one's neck) (c) F: a. qn, to fork out the money 2. s'a. (a) (of days) to grow longer; **son visage s'allongea**, his face fell (b) to lie down at full length; F: **s'a. (par terre)**, to fall flat on the ground (c) to stretch out, to extend.

allouer [alwe] vtr (a) to allocate (salary) (b) grant (indemnity) (c) to allocate (shares, rations) (d) to allot, allocate (time).

allumage [alymaʒ] nm (a) lighting; switching on (b) Aut: ignition.

allume-cigare [alymsigar] nm cigar lighter; pl allume-cigares.

allume-gaz [alymgaz] nm inv gas lighter (for cooker).

allumer [alyme] vtr 1. to light; abs to switch on the light(s); to light up 2. to inflame, excite (passion); to fire (the imagination) 3. s'a., to take fire, to catch fire; (of eyes) to light up; **ça ne s'allume pas**, the light's not working.

allumette [alymet] nf 1. match; **a. de sûreté**, safety match 2. Cu: **a. au fromage**, cheese straw.

allumeur, -euse [alymœr, -øz] n 1. (pers) lighter 2. nm (a) igniting device (b) Aut: distributor 3. nf P: **allumeuse**, sexpot.

allure [alyr] nf 1. (a) walk, bearing; (of pers) **avoir de l'a.**, to have style (b) pace; **marcher à vive a.**, to walk at a brisk pace (c) speed; **à toute a.**, at full speed (d) working (of engine) 2. (a) behaviour (b) aspect, look; **l'a. des affaires**, the way things are going.

allusion [alyzjɔ̃] nf allusion; innuendo; **faire a. à qch**, to refer to, to hint at, sth. **allusif, -ive** a allusive.

alluvions [alyvjɔ̃] nmpl Geol: alluvium. **alluvial, -iaux** a alluvial.

almanach [almana] nm almanac.

aloi [alwa] nm standard, quality; **de bon a.**, genuine.

alors [alɔr] adv 1. then; at that, at the time 2. (a) then; in that case; **a. vous viendrez?** well then, you're coming? **et (puis) a.?** (i) and what then? (ii) so what? (b) therefore, so; **il n'était pas là, a. je suis revenu**, he wasn't there, so I came back 3. conj phr **a. (même) que**, (at the very time) when, even when; even though 4. then, next.

alouette [alwet] nf Orn: lark.

alourdir [alurdir] vtr 1. (a) to make (sth) heavy (b)

to weight (sth) down (c) to dull (the senses) 2. s'a., to grow (i) heavy (ii) stupid.

alourdissement [alurdismɑ̃] nm increased heaviness; dulling (of the senses).

aloyau [alwajo] nm sirloin (of beef).

alpaga [alpaga] nm Z: Tex: alpaca.

alpage [alpaʒ] nm mountain pasture.

alpe [alp] nf 1. alp, mountain 2. Geog: **les Alpes**, the Alps. **alpestre** a alpine. **alpin** a alpine.

alphabet [alfabe] nm 1. alphabet 2. Sch: spelling book. **alphabétique** a alphabetical; **par ordre a.**, alphabetically, in alphabetical order.

alphabétiser [alfabetize] vtr to teach (s.o.) to read and write.

alpinisme [alpinism] nm mountaineering.

alpiniste [alpinist] n mountaineer, climber.

alsacien, -ienne [alzasjɛ̃, -jɛn] a & n Alsatian.

altérant [alterɑ̃] a thirst producing.

altération [alterasjɔ̃] nf 1. change; impairing (of health); deterioration (of food); breaking (of the voice) 2. adulteration (of food); falsification (of document) 3. great thirst.

altercation [alterkasjɔ̃] nf altercation, dispute.

altérer [altere] vtr (j'altère; j'altérerai) 1. (a) to change (for the worse); to impair (health); to spoil (food); **voix altérée**, broken voice (b) s'a., to deteriorate 2. to tamper with (sth); to adulterate (food); to falsify (document); to twist (the truth) 3. to make (s.o.) thirsty.

alternance [alternɑ̃s] nf alternance; alternation; **en a.**, alternately.

alternateur [alternatœr] nm El: alternator.

alternatif, -ive [alternatif, -iv] 1. a (a) alternate (b) El: alternating (current) 2. a alternative (plan) 3. nf **alternative**, alternative. **alternativement** adv alternately, in turn.

alterner [alterne] vi (a) to alternate (b) to take turns (pour, in + ger); to take it in turn (pour, to + inf); **ils alternent pour veiller**, they take it in turns to sit up.

altesse [altes] nf (title) highness.

altier, -ière [altje, -jɛr] a haughty.

altitude [altityd] nf altitude, height; **à 100 mètres d'a.**, at an altitude of 100 metres; **en a.**, at a high altitude; **prendre de l'a.**, to gain altitude; Av: to climb.

alto [alto] nm Mus: 1. alto (voice) 2. viola.

altruisme [altrɥism] nm altruism. **altruiste** 1. a altruistic 2. n altruist.

aluminium [alyminjɔm] nm aluminium.

alun [alœ̃] nm alum.

alunir [alynir] vi to land on the moon.

alunissage [alynisaʒ] nm moon landing.

alvéole [alveɔl] nm or f 1. (a) alveole; cell (of honeycomb) (b) pigeonhole (of desk) 2. socket (of tooth) 3. cavity (in stone).

amabilité [amabilite] nf kindness; **ayez l'a. de**, would you be kind enough to; **faire des amabilités à qn**, to be polite to s.o.

amadouer [amadwe] vtr (a) to coax, wheedle, persuade (b) to soften.

amaigrir [amegrir] vtr to make thin; to emaciate; s'a., to grow thin. **amaigrissant** a slimming.

amaigrissement [amegrismɑ̃] nm (a) growing thin; emaciation (b) slimming.

amalgame [amalgam] *nm* (*a*) amalgam (*b*) mixture, medley.

amalgamer [amalgame] *vtr* to amalgamate; to combine.

amande [amɑ̃d] *nf* almond.

amandier [amɑ̃dje] *nm* almond tree.

amant, -ante [amɑ̃, -ɑ̃t] *n* lover, *f* mistress.

amarrage [amaraʒ] *nm* mooring.

amarre [amar] *nf* (mooring) rope; *pl* moorings.

amarrer [amare] *vtr* to moor; to make fast.

amas [amɑ] *nm* (*a*) heap, pile, accumulation (*b*) store (of provisions) (*c*) mass (of papers, of ideas) (*d*) *Astr:* cluster (*e*) *Min:* lode.

amasser [amase] *vtr* 1. to heap up, pile up 2. to hoard up, to store up; to amass (a fortune) 3. to gather (troops) together 4. **s'a.**, to pile up, accumulate; (*of crowd*) to gather.

amateur [amatœr] *nm* 1. (*a*) lover (of sth); **a. d'art**, art lover; **être a. de qch**, to be fond of sth (*b*) bidder (at sale); **est-ce qu'il y a des amateurs?** any takers? 2. amateur; *Pej:* dilettante; **championnat d'a.**, amateur championship; **travail d'a.**, amateurish work.

amateurisme [amatœrism] *nm* amateurism.

amazone [amazon] *nf* (*a*) *Myth:* Amazon; *Geog:* **l'A.**, the (river) Amazon (*b*) horsewoman; **monter en a.**, to ride sidesaddle.

ambages [ɑ̃baʒ] *nfpl* **parler sans a.**, to speak in plain language, without beating about the bush.

ambassade [ɑ̃basad] *nf* 1. embassy 2. mission.

ambassadeur [ɑ̃basadœr] *nm* ambassador.

ambassadrice [ɑ̃basadris] *nf* ambassadress (*a*) woman ambassador (*b*) ambassador's wife.

ambiance [ɑ̃bjɑ̃s] *nf* surroundings, environment; atmosphere. **ambiant** *a* surrounding; **température ambiante**, room temperature.

ambidextre [ɑ̃bidekstr] *a* ambidextrous.

ambiguïté [ɑ̃biɡɥite] *nf* ambiguity. **ambigu, -uë** *a* ambiguous.

ambition [ɑ̃bisjɔ̃] *nf* ambition (**de**, of, for); **sans a.**, unambitious(ly). **ambitieux, -euse** 1. *a* ambitious 2. *n* ambitious person; careerist. **ambitieusement** *adv* ambitiously.

ambitionner [ɑ̃bisjone] *vtr* to be ambitious of; **il ambitionne de**, his ambition is to.

ambivalence [ɑ̃bivalɑ̃s] *nf* ambivalence. **ambivalent** *a* ambivalent.

amble [ɑ̃bl] *nm Equit:* amble.

ambre [ɑ̃br] *nm* 1. **a. gris**, ambergris 2. **a. jaune**, (yellow) amber. **ambré** *a* amber-coloured; warm (complexion).

ambulance [ɑ̃bylɑ̃s] *nf* ambulance.

ambulancier, -ière [ɑ̃bylɑ̃sje, -jɛr] *n* ambulance man, ambulance woman.

ambulant [ɑ̃bylɑ̃] *a* strolling, travelling; **marchand a.**, hawker; *F:* **c'est un cadavre a.**, he's a walking corpse.

âme [ɑm] *nf* 1. (*a*) soul; **rendre l'â.**, to give up the ghost; **bonne â.**, kind soul (*b*) (departed) soul, spirit; **errer comme une â. en peine**, to wander about like a lost soul (*c*) heart, feeling; **â. sœur**, kindred spirit; **en mon â. et conscience**, in all conscience (*d*) moving spirit (of an undertaking) (*e*) **ne pas rencontrer â. qui vive**, not to meet a (living) soul 2. (*a*) bore (of gun) (*b*) soundpost (of violin).

amélioration [ameljɔrasjɔ̃] *nf* improvement.

améliorer [ameljɔre] *vtr* to improve; **s'a.**, to get better; to improve.

amen [amɛn] *int & nm inv* amen.

aménagement [amenaʒmɑ̃] *nm* (*a*) fitting out (of house) (*b*) *pl* fittings; fixtures, installations.

aménager [amenaʒe] *vtr* (**n. aménageons**) to fit out (house); to fit up (bedroom); **étable aménagée**, converted cowshed; **route aménagée**, made-up road.

amende [amɑ̃d] *nf* 1. fine; **être condamné à une a.**, to be fined; **mettre à l'a.**, to penalize 2. **faire a. honorable**, to make amends.

amendement [amɑ̃dmɑ̃] *nm* 1. improvement (of the soil) 2. *Pol:* amendment (to a bill).

amender [amɑ̃de] *vtr* (*a*) to improve (soil) (*b*) *Pol:* to amend (bill) (*c*) (*of pers*) **s'a.**, to turn over a new leaf.

amener [amne] *vtr* (**j'amène, n. amenons**) 1. to bring; to lay on (water, gas); **amenez votre ami**, bring your friend along; **a. qn à faire qch**, to get, induce, s.o. to do sth; **a. qn à son opinion**, to bring s.o. round to one's point of view; **a. la conversation sur un sujet**, to lead the conversation on to a subject 2. *Nau:* to strike (colours); to lower (sail) 3. *P:* **s'a.**, to turn up.

aménité [amenite] *nf* 1. charm (of manners); grace (of style) 2. *pl Iron:* uncomplimentary remarks.

amenuiser (s') [samənɥize] *vpr* to dwindle, to lessen; to run low.

amer, -ère [amɛr] *a* bitter. **amèrement** *adv* bitterly.

américain, -aine [amerikɛ̃, -kɛn] 1. *a & n* American 2. *nm* **l'a.**, American (English).

américaniser [amerikanize] *vtr* to Americanize.

américanisme [amerikanism] *nm* Americanism.

Amérique [amerik] *Prnf* America.

amerrir [amerir] *vi Av:* to make a sea landing; (*of space capsule*) to splash down.

amerrissage [amerisaʒ] *nm Av:* (sea) landing; splashdown (of space capsule).

amertume [amɛrtym] *nf* bitterness.

améthyste [ametist] *nf* amethyst.

ameublement [amœbləmɑ̃] *nm* 1. furnishing (of house) 2. furniture; **tissu d'a.**, furnishing fabric.

ameublir [amœblir] *vtr* to loosen (soil).

ameuter [amœte] *vtr* to stir up, to rouse (a mob); **s'a.**, to form a mob.

ami [ami] 1. *n* (*a*) friend; **a. intime**, close friend; **a. d'enfance**, childhood friend; **mon a.**, (i) (*between friends*) my dear fellow (ii) (*from wife to husband*) my dear; **mon amie**, my dear, my love; **sans amis**, friendless (*b*) **son a.**, her boyfriend; **son amie**, his girlfriend (*c*) (*of words*) **faux amis**, deceptive cognates 2. *a* friendly (**de**, to).

amiable [amjabl] *a Jur:* amicable; **à l'a.**, amicably; **arranger une affaire à l'a.**, to settle a difference out of court; **vente à l'a.**, private sale.

amiante [amjɑ̃t] *nm* asbestos.

amibe [amib] *nf* amoeba.

amical, -aux [amikal, -o] *a* friendly; **peu a.**, unfriendly; *nf* **amicale**, (professional) association. **amicalement** *adv* in a friendly way; *Corr:* **bien a.**, best wishes; yours.

amidon [amidɔ̃] *nm* starch.

amidonner [amidɔne] *vtr* to starch.

amincir [amɛ̃sir] vtr 1. to make (sth) thinner; to thin down 2. s'a., to get thinner.

amincissement [amɛ̃sismɑ̃] nm thinning (down); (of pèrs) growing thinner; slimming.

amiral, -aux [amiral, -o] 1. nm admiral. 2. a (vaisseau) a., flagship.

amirale [amiral] nf admiral's wife.

amirauté [amirote] nf Admiralty.

amitié [amitje] nf 1. friendship; prendre qn en a., to take (a liking) to s.o.; se lier d'a. avec qn, to make friends with s.o.; par a., out of friendship 2. (a) kindness, favour (b) Corr: mes amitiés à, my best regards to; sincères amitiés de, with best wishes from.

ammoniac, ammoniaque [amɔnjak] nf Ch: ammonia.

amnésie [amnezi] nf Med: amnesia. amnésique 1. a amnesic 2. n amnesiac.

amnistie [amnisti] nf amnesty.

amnistier [amnistje] vtr (pr sub & impf n. amnistiions) to amnesty.

amocher [amɔʃe] vtr F: to damage (sth); P: to beat (s.o.) up; se faire a., to get beaten up.

amoindrir [amwɛ̃drir] 1. vtr to reduce, decrease, lessen, diminish; to belittle (s.o.) 2. vi & pr to diminish, to grow less.

amoindrissement [amwɛ̃drismɑ̃] nm reduction, decrease, diminution.

amollir [amɔlir] vtr 1. to soften; to weaken 2. s'a., to soften, to become soft; (of courage) to weaken.

amollissement [amɔlismɑ̃] nm softening; weakening.

amonceler [amɔ̃sle] vtr (j'amoncelle) 1. to pile up, heap up; to accumulate 2. s'a., to pile up; (of snow) to drift.

amoncellement [amɔ̃sɛlmɑ̃] nm 1. heaping (up), piling (up), accumulation 2. heap, pile; a. de neige, snowdrift.

amont [amɔ̃] nm (a) upper waters (of river); en a., upstream; up river (b) uphill slope.

amoral, -aux [amɔral, -o] a amoral.

amorçage [amɔrsaʒ] nm 1. beginning; priming (of pump) 2. baiting.

amorce [amɔrs] nf 1. beginning, start (of negotiations, reform) 2. (a) Exp: detonator (b) Sma: percussion cap (c) priming (of pump) 3. bait.

amorcer [amɔrse] vtr (n. amorçons) 1. (a) to begin (building, negotiations) (b) to prime (pump); to cap (shell) 2. to bait (trap); to decoy, entice (pers, animal) 3. s'a., to begin; une baisse des cours s'amorce, shares are showing a downward trend.

amorphe [amɔrf] a (a) amorphous (b) flabby.

amortir [amɔrtir] vtr 1. to deaden, muffle (sound); to dull (pain); to break (fall); to absorb (shock) 2. to slake (lime) 3. (a) to redeem, pay off (debt); cela s'amortira tout seul, it will pay for itself (b) to write off (equipment). amortissable a Fin: redeemable.

amortissement [amɔrtismɑ̃] nm 1. breaking (of fall); absorption (of shock) 2. (a) redemption, paying off (of debt) (b) depreciation.

amortisseur [amɔrtisœr] nm Aut: shock absorber.

amour [amur] nm (occ f in poetry, often f in pl in 1, 2) 1. (a) love, affection, passion; avec a., lovingly; marriage d'a., love match; faire l'a., to make love (b) pl love affairs; les premières amours, first love, calf love 2. mon a., my love, my darling; l'a. de la famille, the idol of the family 3. quel a. d'enfant! what a darling child! quel a. de bijou! what a lovely jewel! tu es un a.! you're an angel! amoureux, -euse 1. a (a) loving (look); être a. de qn, to be in love with s.o. (b) amorous (gesture) 2. n lover, suitor. amoureusement adv lovingly; amorously.

amour-propre [amurprɔpr] nm (a) self-respect; pride (b) self-esteem, vanity, conceit.

amovible [amɔvibl] a 1. (of official) removable 2. (of parts of machine) detachable; interchangeable.

ampère [ɑ̃pɛr] nm El: ampere, amp.

ampèremètre [ɑ̃pɛrmɛtr] nm El: ammeter.

amphibie [ɑ̃fibi] 1. a amphibious 2. nm amphibian.

amphithéâtre [ɑ̃fiteatr] nm 1. amphitheatre 2. lecture theatre 3. Th: upper gallery.

amphore [ɑ̃fɔr] nf 1. amphora 2. jar.

ampleur [ɑ̃plœr] nf width, fullness (of garment); copiousness (of meal); volume (of voice); extent (of disaster). ample a 1. ample, full (dress) 2. roomy, spacious 3. full (account); plentiful, ample (supply). amplement adv amply, fully; nous avons a. le temps, we have plenty of time.

amplificateur [ɑ̃plifikatœr] nm amplifier.

amplification [ɑ̃plifikasjɔ̃] nf 1. (a) amplification, development (b) exaggeration 2. magnification; WTel: amplification.

amplifier [ɑ̃plifje] vtr (impf & pr sub n. amplifiions) 1. (a) to amplify, to develop (subject) (b) to exaggerate 2. to magnify; to amplify (sound).

amplitude [ɑ̃plityd] nf 1. amplitude 2. range (of temperature).

ampoule [ɑ̃pul] nf 1. phial 2. (light) bulb 3. blister.

amputation [ɑ̃pytasjɔ̃] nf (a) amputation (b) F: cut (in article).

amputer [ɑ̃pyte] vtr (a) to amputate (limb) (b) to cut (article).

amulette [amylɛt] nf amulet, charm.

amuse-gueule [amyzgœl] nm cocktail snack; pl amuse-gueules.

amuser [amyze] vtr 1. to amuse, entertain; si tu penses que ça m'amuse! if you think I enjoy (doing) that! 2. s'a (a) to enjoy oneself; to have a good time; ils s'amusent dans le jardin, they're playing in the garden; amusez-vous bien! enjoy yourselves! (b) s'a. avec qch, to play, to fiddle, with sth; s'a. à faire qch, to amuse oneself doing sth; F: ne t'amuse pas à recommencer, don't you dare do that again (c) s'a. de qn, to make a fool of s.o. amusant a amusing, funny.

amuseur, -euse [amyzœr, -øz] n entertainer.

amygdale [amidal] nf tonsil.

an [ɑ̃] nm year; tous les ans, every year; dans quatre ans, in four years' time; avoir dix ans, to be ten (years old); le jour de l'an, le nouvel an, New Year's day; en l'an 2000, in the year 2000.

anachronisme [anakrɔnism] nm anachronism. anachronique a anachronistic.

anagramme [anagram] nf anagram.

analogie [analɔʒi] nf analogy. analogique a analogical. analogue 1. n analogous, similar (à, to) 2. nm analogue.

analphabétisme [analfabetism] *nm* illiteracy. **analphabète** *a* & *n* illiterate.

analyse [analiz] *nf* (*a*) analysis; **a. grammaticale**, parsing; **a. logique**, analysis (*b*) (blood, urine) test; **il s'est fait faire des analyses**, he had some tests done. **analytique** *a* analytical.

analyser [analize] *vtr* to analyse; **a. une phrase**, (i) to parse, (ii) to analyse, a sentence.

analyste [analist] *n* analyst.

ananas [anana(s)] *nm* pineapple.

anarchie [anarʃi] *nf* anarchy. **anarchique** *a* anarchic.

anarchisme [anarʃism] *nm* anarchism. **anarchiste** *a* & *n* anarchist.

anathème [anatɛm] *nm* anathema.

anatife [anatif] *nm Crust:* barnacle.

anatomie [anatɔmi] *nf* anatomy. **anatomique** *a* anatomical.

ancestral, -aux [ɑ̃sɛstral, -o] *a* ancestral.

ancêtre [ɑ̃sɛtr̩] *n* (*a*) ancestor; forerunner (*b*) *F:* old man.

anchois [ɑ̃ʃwa] *nm* anchovy.

ancien, -ienne [ɑ̃sjɛ̃, -jɛn] *a* **1.** ancient, old; antique (furniture) **2.** ancient, old(en), early; past; **les peuples anciens**, people of antiquity; **l'A. Testament**, the Old Testament **3.** former, old; ex-; **a. élève**, old pupil (of a school); **anciens combattants**, ex-servicemen, *NAm:* veterans **4.** senior (officer); **les (élèves) anciens**, the senior pupils; **il est votre a.**, he is senior to you **5.** *nm* (*a*) **les anciens**, the ancients (*b*) *F:* **l'a.**, the old man (*c*) **l'a.**, antiques. **anciennement** *adv* formerly.

ancienneté [ɑ̃sjɛnte] *nf* **1.** age, antiquity (of monument) **2.** seniority; length of service.

ancrage [ɑ̃kraʒ] *nm* anchorage.

ancre [ɑ̃kr̩] *nf* anchor; **lever l'a.**, to weigh anchor.

ancrer [ɑ̃kre] *vtr* (*a*) to anchor (ship); **idée bien ancrée**, firmly rooted idea **2. s'a.**, to get a firm footing.

Andorre [ɑ̃dɔr] *Prn* Andorra.

andouille [ɑ̃duj] *nf* (*a*) *Cu:* chitterlings (made into a sausage) (*b*) *F:* clot; **faire l'a.**, to play the fool.

âne [ɑn] *nm* **1.** (*a*) ass; donkey; **promenade à dos d'â.**, donkey ride (*b*) **en dos d'â.**, ridged; **pont en dos d'â.**, humpbacked bridge **2.** fool, ass; **bonnet d'â.**, dunce's cap.

anéantir [aneɑ̃tir] *vtr* to annihilate, to destroy; to dash (s.o.'s hopes); **je suis anéanti**, I'm exhausted, dead beat.

anéantissement [aneɑ̃tismɑ̃] *nm* annihilation, destruction; (state of) prostration, exhaustion.

anecdote [anɛkdɔt] *nf* anecdote. **anecdotique** *a* anecdotal.

anémie [anemi] *nf Med:* anaemia. **anémique** *a* anaemic.

anémier [anemje] *vtr* to make (s.o.) anaemic; **s'a.**, to become anaemic.

anémone [anemɔn] *nf* **1.** anemone **2. a. de mer**, sea anemone.

ânerie [ɑnri] *nf F:* (*a*) stupidity (*b*) foolish remark; **dire des âneries**, to talk tripe.

ânesse [ɑnɛs] *nf* she ass.

anesthésie [anɛstezi] *nf Med:* anaesthesia; **a. générale**, general anaesthetic. **anesthésique** *a* & *nm* anaesthetic.

anesthésier [anɛstezje] *vtr Med:* to anaesthetize.

anesthésiste [anɛstezist] *n Med:* anaesthetist.

ange [ɑ̃ʒ] *nm* **1.** angel; **a. gardien**, guardian angel; **a. déchu**, fallen angel; **être aux anges**, to be in (the) seventh heaven; **sois un a.!** be an angel, be a darling! **un a. passa**, there was a silence **2. a. (de mer)**, angel fish.

angélique [ɑ̃ʒelik] **1.** *a* angelic **2.** *nf Cu:* angelica. **angéliquement** *adv* angelically.

angelet, angelot [ɑ̃ʒlɛ, ɑ̃ʒlo] *nm* cherub.

angélus [ɑ̃ʒelys] *nm* angelus (bell).

angine [ɑ̃ʒin] *nf Med:* **1.** quinsy; tonsillitis **2. a. de poitrine**, angina (pectoris).

anglais, -aise [ɑ̃glɛ, -ɛz] **1.** *a* English; *F:* **filer à l'anglaise**, to take French leave **2.** *n* Englishman, Englishwoman **3.** *nm* English (language).

angle [ɑ̃gl̩] *nm* **1.** angle; **a. droit**, right angle; **à angles droits**, rectangular **2.** corner, angle (of wall); **a. de la rue**, street corner **3.** angle, point of view.

Angleterre [ɑ̃glətɛr] *Prnf* England.

anglican, -ane [ɑ̃glikɑ̃, -an] *a* & *n Rel:* Anglican; **l'église anglicane**, the Church of England.

angliciser [ɑ̃glisize] *vtr* to anglicize (word).

anglicisme [ɑ̃glisism] *nm* anglicism.

angliciste [ɑ̃glisist] *n* (*a*) Anglicist (*b*) student of English.

anglo-américain [ɑ̃glɔamerikɛ̃] *a* Anglo-American.

anglo-normand, -ande [ɑ̃glɔnɔrmɑ̃, -ɑ̃d] *a* & *n* Anglo-Norman; **les îles Anglo-Normandes**, the Channel Islands.

anglophilie [ɑ̃glɔfili] *nf* anglophilia. **anglophile** *a* & *n* anglophil(e).

anglophobie [ɑ̃glɔfɔbi] *nf* anglophobia. **anglophobe 1.** *a* anglophobic **2.** *n* anglophobe.

anglophone [ɑ̃glɔfɔn] **1.** *a* English-speaking **2.** *n* English speaker.

anglo-saxon, -onne [ɑ̃glɔsaksɔ̃, -ɔn] *a* & *n* Anglo-Saxon; English-speaking (country).

angoisse [ɑ̃gwas] *nf* anguish; distress; **vivre dans l'a. d'un accident**, to live in fear and dread of an accident.

angoisser [ɑ̃gwase] *vtr* to distress, to cause anguish. **angoissant** *a* distressing; agonizing; tense, anxious (moment). **angoissé** *a* anguished, distressed.

anguille [ɑ̃gij] *nf Ich:* (*a*) eel; **il y a a. sous roche**, there's something in the wind (*b*) **a. de mer**, conger eel.

angulaire [ɑ̃gylɛr] **1.** *a* angular **2.** *nm Phot:* **grand a.**, wide-angle lens.

anguleux, -euse [ɑ̃gylø, -øz] *a* angular, bony.

anicroche [anikrɔʃ] *nf* difficulty, hitch, snag; **sans a.**, smoothly, without a hitch.

aniline [anilin] *nf Dy:* aniline.

animal, -aux [animal, -o] **1.** *a* animal (kingdom, instinct) **2.** *nm* animal; *F:* **quel a.!** what a brute!

animateur, -trice [animatœr, -tris] *n* (*a*) life and soul (of an enterprise) (*b*) *TV: etc:* compère (*c*) *Cin:* animator (*d*) leader, organizer.

animation [animasjɔ̃] *nf* **1.** animation, liveliness; **plein d'a.**, full of life **2.** *Cin:* animation.

animer [anime] *vtr* **1.** to animate; to give life to (s.o., sth); **animé par un nouvel espoir**, buoyed up with new hope; **son visage s'anima**, his face lit up **2.** to move, propel; **animé par un sentiment de jalousie**, prompted by a feeling of jealousy 3. to enliven (conversation); to stir up (feelings); **la conversation s'anime**, the conversation is getting more lively; **la rue s'anime**, the street is coming to life. **animé** *a* 1. lively; busy; **marché a.**, brisk market 2. *Cin:* **dessin a.**, cartoon.

animosité [animɔzite] *nf* animosity, spite (**contre**, against).

anis [ani(s)] *nm* (*a*) *Bot:* anise (*b*) (**graine d'**)**a.**, aniseed.

ankyloser [ākiloze] *vtr* (*a*) to ankylose; **être ankylosé**, to be stiff (*b*) **s'a.**, to become, get, stiff.

annales [anal] *nfpl* annals; (public) records.

anneau, -eaux [ano] *nm* 1. ring; *Gym:* **anneaux**, rings 2. (*a*) link (of chain) (*b*) coil (of snake).

année [ane] *nf* year; **a. civile**, calendar year; **pendant toute une a.**, for a whole year; **à l'a.**, annually; **étudiant de première a.**, first year student; **les années trente**, the thirties; **d'a. en a.**, from year to year.

année-lumière [anelymjɛr] *nf* light year; *pl* **années-lumière**.

annexe [anɛks] *nf* 1. annex(e) (to building) 2. (*a*) rider; schedule; appendix (*b*) enclosure (with letter) 3. *a* **établissement a.**, annex(e); **lettre a.**, covering letter; **industries annexes**, subsidiary industries.

annexer [anɛkse] *vtr* 1. to annex (territory) 2. to append, attach (document); **pièces annexées**, enclosures.

annexion [anɛksjɔ̃] *nf* annexation.

annihilation [aniilasjɔ̃] *nf* annihilation.

annihiler [aniile] *vtr* to annihilate, to destroy.

anniversaire [aniversɛr] *nm* (*a*) anniversary (*b*) birthday.

annonce [anɔ̃s] *nf* 1. (*a*) announcement, notice (*b*) (*at cards*) declaration; bid (*c*) sign, indication 2. advertisement; **petites annonces**, classified advertisements, small ads.

annoncer [anɔ̃se] *vtr* (**n. annonçons**) 1. to announce, give notice of, give out; **a. une mauvaise nouvelle à qn**, to break bad news to s.o. 2. to advertise 3. (*a*) to promise, foretell; to point to (success); **cela n'annonce rien de bon**, it doesn't look promising (*b*) to give proof of (sth); to show (sth) 4. to announce (s.o.) 5. **s'a.** (*a*) to announce oneself (*b*) **le temps s'annonce beau**, the weather promises to be fine.

annonceur, -euse [anɔ̃sœr, -øz] *n* 1. advertiser 2. *WTel: TV:* announcer.

annonciateur, -trice [anɔ̃sjatœr, -tris] 1. *nm Tp:* indicator board 2. *a* **signes annonciateurs du printemps**, signs that spring is on its way.

annonciation [anɔ̃sjasjɔ̃] *nf* (**fête de**) **l'A.**, (Feast of the) Annunciation; Lady day.

annotation [anɔtasjɔ̃] *nf* annotation, note.

annoter [anɔte] *vtr* to annotate (text); to write notes.

annuaire [anɥɛr] *nm* 1. annual, yearbook 2. calendar 3. (yearly) list; **a. (du téléphone)**, (telephone) directory.

annuel, -elle [anɥɛl] *a* annual, yearly. **annuellement** *adv* annually, yearly.

annuité [anɥite] *nf* 1. annual instalment (in repayment of debt) 2. (terminable) annuity.

annulaire [anylɛr] *nm* ring finger, third finger.

annulation [anylasjɔ̃] *nf* annulment; cancellation.

annuler [anyle] *vtr* 1. (*a*) to annul; to render void, to repeal (law, judgment) (*b*) to cancel (contract) 2. **s'a.**, to cancel each other out.

anoblir [anɔblir] *vtr* to raise (s.o.) to the peerage.

anoblissement [anɔblismɑ̃] *nm* ennoblement.

anode [anɔd] *nf El:* anode.

anodin [anɔdɛ̃] *a* harmless; innocuous; insignificant.

anomalie [anɔmali] *nf* anomaly; *Biol:* abnormality.

ânon [anɔ̃] *nm* ass's foal.

ânonner [anɔne] *vtr* to stumble through (speech); to hum and haw; to mumble.

anonymat [anɔnima] *nm* anonymity; **sous l'a.**, anonymously; **garder l'a.**, to remain anonymous. **anonyme** *a* (*a*) anonymous (letter) (*b*) *Com:* **société a.**, limited(-liability) company. **anonymement** *adv* anonymously.

anorak [anɔrak] *nm* anorak.

anorexie [anɔrɛksi] *nf* anorexia.

anormal, -aux [anɔrmal, -o] *a* abnormal; **enfant a.**, educationally subnormal child. **anormalement** *adv* abnormally.

ANPE *abbr* *Agence nationale pour l'emploi* = Job Centre.

anse [ɑ̃s] *nf* 1. handle (of jug, basket) 2. *Geog:* bight, cove.

antagonisme [ātagɔnism] *nm* antagonism. **antagoniste** 1. *a* antagonistic, opposed 2. *n* antagonist, opponent.

antan [ātā] *adv Lit:* **d'a.**, of yesteryear.

antarctique [ātarktik] 1. *a* Antarctic 2. *Prnm Geog:* **l'A.**, Antarctica, the Antarctic.

antécédent [ātesedā] 1. *a* antecedent, previous 2. *nm Gram:* antecedent (*b*) *pl* previous history; antecedents.

antédiluvien, -ienne [ātedilyvjɛ̃, -jɛn] *a* antediluvian.

antenne [ātɛn] *nf* 1. *Rad: TV: etc:* aerial, antenna; **a. de télévision**, television aerial; **à l'a.**, on the air; **garder l'a.**, to stay tuned in; **passer sur les antennes**, to be broadcast, to be televised 2. (*a*) antenna, feeler (of insect) (*b*) *Mil:* outpost; (surgical) unit.

antérieur [āterjœr] *a* 1. anterior (**à**, to); former (period); earlier (date); previous (year); prior (engagement) 2. fore (limb); front (wall). **antérieurement** *adv* previously, earlier; before.

antériorité [āterjorite] *nf* precedence.

anthologie [ātɔlɔʒi] *nf* anthology.

anthracite [ātrasit] 1. *nm* anthracite 2. *a inv* charcoal grey.

anthropoïde [ātrɔpɔid] *a* & *nm* anthropoid.

anthropologie [ātrɔpɔlɔʒi] *nf* anthropology. **anthropologique** *a* anthropological.

anthropologiste, anthropologue [ātrɔpɔlɔ-ʒist, -lɔg] *nm* anthropologist.

antiaérien, -ienne [ātiaerjɛ̃, -jɛn] *a* anti-aircraft (gun).

antialcoolique [ātialkɔlik] *a* anti-alcohol; **campagne a.**, campaign against alcohol.

antiatomique [ātiatɔmik] *a* antinuclear; **abri a.**, (nuclear) fall-out shelter.

antibiotique [ātibjɔtik] *a* & *nm* antibiotic.

antibrouillard [ātibrujar] *a* & *nm Aut:* (**phare**) **a.**, foglamp.

antibuée [ãtibчe] *a & nm* (**dispositif**) **a.**, demister.

anticancéreux, -euse [ãtikãserø, -øz] *a* **centre a.**, cancer hospital.

antichambre [ãtiʃãmbɾ] *nf* antechamber, anteroom.

antichoc [ãtiʃɔk] *a inv* shockproof.

anticipation [ãtisipasjɔ̃] *nf* anticipation; **payer par a.**, to pay in advance; **roman d'a.** = science fiction novel.

anticiper [ãtisipe] **1.** *vtr* to anticipate (sth); to forestall (s.o.'s action); **paiement anticipé**, payment in advance; **avec mes remerciements anticipés**, thanking you in anticipation **2.** *vi* **a. sur les événements**, to anticipate events.

anticlérical, -aux [ãtiklerikal, -o] *a* anticlerical.

anticonformisme [ãtikɔ̃fɔrmism] *nm* nonconformism.

anticorps [ãtikɔr] *nm* antibody.

anticyclone [ãtisiklon] *nm* anticyclone.

antidater [ãtidate] *vtr* to backdate.

antidérapant [ãtiderapã] *a Aut: etc:* non-skid (tyre).

antidiphtérique [ãtidifterik] *a* **vaccin a.**, diphtheria vaccine.

antidote [ãtidɔt] *nm* antidote.

antigel [ãtiʒɛl] *a & nm inv* antifreeze.

Antilles [ãtij] *Prnfpl* **les A.**, the West Indies; **la mer des A.**, the Caribbean. **antillais, -aise** *a & n* West Indian.

antilope [ãtilɔp] *nf Z:* antelope.

antimilitariste [ãtimilitarist] *n* antimilitarist.

antimite(s) [ãtimit] (*a*) *a* mothproof (*b*) *a* moth destroying; *nm* mothkiller; mothballs.

antimoine [ãtimwan] *nm Ch:* antimony.

antiparasite [ãtiparazit] *a & nm WTel: Aut:* (**dispositif**) **a.**, suppressor.

antipathie [ãtipati] *nf* antipathy. **antipathique** *a* unpleasant.

antipodes [ãtipɔd] *nmpl* **les a.**, the antipodes; **aux antipodes**, (i) on the other side of the world (ii) poles apart.

antiquaire [ãtikɛr] *nm* antique dealer.

antique [ãtik] *a* (*a*) ancient (*b*) antique (furniture) (*c*) antiquated.

antiquité [ãtikite] *nf* **1.** antiquity **2.** ancient times, antiquity **3.** **l'a. grecque**, ancient Greek civilization **4.** (*a*) *pl* antiquities (*b*) antiques; **magasin d'antiquités**, antique shop.

antirouille [ãtiruj] *nm* rust preventive.

antisémitisme [ãtisemitism] *nm* antisemitism.

antisepsie [ãtisɛpsi] *nf Med:* antisepsis. **antiseptique** *a* antiseptic.

antitétanique [ãtitetanik] *a* antitetanus (serum).

antithèse [ãtitɛz] *nf* antithesis.

antitoxine [ãtitɔksin] *nf Med:* antitoxin. **antitoxique** *a & nm* antitoxic.

antivenimeux, -euse [ãtivənimø, -øz] *a* **sérum a.**, antivenom.

antivol [ãtivɔl] *a inv & nm* (**dispositif**) **a.**, anti-theft device.

antonyme [ãtɔnim] *nm* antonym.

antre [ãtr] *nm* (*a*) cave (*b*) den, lair.

anus [anys] *nm* anus.

Anvers [ãvɛr(s)] *Prnm Geog:* Antwerp.

anxiété [ãksjete] *nf* anxiety. **anxieux, -euse** *a* anxious, worried. **anxieusement** *adv* anxiously.

aorte [aɔrt] *nf Anat:* aorta.

août [u, ut] *nm* August; **au mois d'a., en a.**, in (the month of) August; **le premier, le sept, a.**, (on) the first, the seventh, of August.

apaisement [apɛzmã] *nm* appeasement; calming (down); relief.

apaiser [apɛze] *vtr* **1.** to appease, pacify, calm (s.o.); **la foule s'est apaisée**, the crowd calmed down **2.** to soothe (pain); to satisfy (hunger); to quench (thirst); to calm (fears); **le vent s'est apaisé**, the wind dropped. **apaisant** *a* appeasing, soothing.

apanage [apanaʒ] *nm* privilege, right.

aparté [aparte] *nm* **1.** *Th:* aside; **en a.**, (in an) aside **2.** private conversation.

apathie [apati] *nf* apathy. **apathique** *a* apathetic.

apatride [apatrid] *n Jur:* stateless person.

apercevoir [apɛrsəvwar] *vtr* (*conj like* RECEVOIR) **1.** to perceive, see; to catch sight of, to catch a glimpse of (s.o., sth); **cela ne s'aperçoit pas**, it isn't visible; it doesn't show; **enfin nous avons aperçu un hotel**, at last we saw a hotel **2.** **s'a. de qch**, to realize, notice, sth; to become aware of sth; **sans s'en a.**, without noticing it.

aperçu [apɛrsy] *nm* **1.** glimpse **2.** general idea; outline, summary; **par a.**, at a rough estimate.

apéritif [aperitif] *nm* aperitif, drink.

apesanteur [apəzɑ̃tœr] *nf* weightlessness.

à-peu-près [apøprɛ] *nm inv* approximation.

apeuré [apœre] *a* scared, frightened.

aphone [afɔn] *a* voiceless.

aphorisme [afɔrism] *nm* aphorism.

aphrodisiaque [afrɔdizjak] *a & nm* aphrodisiac.

aphte [aft] *nm* (mouth) ulcer.

à-pic [apik] *nm* cliff, bluff; *pl* **à-pics**.

apiculteur [apikyltœr] *nm* bee keeper.

apiculture [apikyltyr] *nf* bee keeping.

apitoiement [apitwamã] *nm* pity, compassion.

apitoyer [apitwaje] *vtr* (**j'apitoie**) to move to pity; **il essaie de m'a.**, he's trying to make me feel sorry for him; **s'a. sur qn**, to feel pity for s.o.

aplanir [aplanir] *vtr* to flatten (surface); to plane (wood); to level (road); to smooth away, to iron out (difficulties).

aplatir [aplatir] *vtr* **1.** to make (sth) flat; to flatten (surface); **a. qch à coups de marteau**, to beat sth flat **2.** **s'a.** (*a*) to become flat, to flatten out (*b*) **s'a.** (**par terre**), (i) to lie flat on the ground (ii) *F:* to fall down flat; **s'a. devant qn**, to grovel before s.o. **aplati** *a* flat.

aplatissement [aplatismã] *nm* **1.** flattening **2.** *Fig:* humiliation.

aplomb [aplɔ̃] *nm* **1.** perpendicularity; balance; **d'a.**, upright; vertical(ly); plumb; *F:* **je ne suis pas d'a. aujourd'hui**, I'm out of sorts today; **voilà qui vous remettra d'a.**, that will get you back on your feet **2.** (self-)assurance; **perdre son a.**, to lose one's nerve.

apocalypse [apokalips] *nf* apocalypse; *B:* **l'A.**, the Book of Revelation, the Apocalypse. **apocalyptique** *a* apocalyptic.

apogée [apoʒe] *nm Astr:* apogee; *Fig:* height, zenith.

apolitique [apolitik] *a* apolitical.

apologie [apoloʒi] *nf* apology (**de**, for); defence, vindication (**de**, of). (NOTE: *never* = EXCUSE, *qv*).

apoplexie [apɔplɛksi] *nf Med:* apoplexy.
apostat, -ate [apɔsta, -at] *a & n* apostate.
apostolique [apɔstɔlik] *a* apostolic.
apostrophe [apɔstrɔf] *nf (a)* apostrophe *(b)* reproach.
apostropher [apɔstrɔfe] *vtr* to shout at (s.o.).
apothéose [apoteoz] *nf* **1.** apotheosis **2.** *Th:* grand finale.
apôtre [apotr] *nm* apostle.
apparaître [aparɛtr] *vi (conj like* PARAÎTRE; *aux usu* être, *occ* avoir) **1.** to appear; to become visible; to come into sight; **a. à travers le brouillard,** to loom out of the fog **2.** to become evident.
apparat [apara] *nm* state, pomp, display; **dîner d'a.,** banquet.
appareil [aparɛj] *nm* **1. l'a. de la justice,** the machinery of the law **2.** *(a)* apparatus, equipment; **l'a. digestif,** the digestive system *(b)* device, appliance; mechanism *(c)* machine (i) *Tp:* telephone; **qui est à l'a.?** who's speaking? (ii) *Av:* aircraft (iii) *Phot:* **a. (photographique),** camera (iv) *Dent:* brace (v) **a. à sous,** slot machine; fruit machine **3.** *Med:* splint.
appareillage [aparɛjaʒ] *nm Nau:* casting off.
appareiller¹ [aparɛje] *vtr* **1.** to install, fit up (workshop) **2.** *Nau:* *(a)* **a. une voile,** to trim a sail *(b) vi* to cast off.
appareiller² *vtr* to match (gloves, colours).
apparence [aparɑ̃s] *nf* **1.** *(a)* appearance; look; **une a. de vérité,** a semblance of truth; **selon toute a.,** to all appearances *(b)* **sous de fausses apparences,** under false pretences; **en a.,** outwardly; on the surface **2. pour sauver les apparences,** for the sake of appearances. **apparent** *a* **1.** *(a)* visible, apparent; **peu a.,** hardly noticeable *(b)* obvious, evident **2.** apparent, not real. **apparemment** *adv* apparently.
apparenter (s') [saparɑ̃te] *vpr* **1.** to marry (into a family) **2.** to have sth in common (à, with). **apparenté** *a* related (by marriage); closely connected.
apparier [aparje] *vtr (impf & pr sub* n. **appariions)** to match (socks); to pair off (opponents).
apparition [aparisjɔ̃] *nf* **1.** appearance; coming out; publication (of book) **2.** apparition, ghost.
appartement [apartəmɑ̃] *nm* flat, *NAm:* apartment; (hotel) suite.
appartenance [apartənɑ̃s] *nf* **1.** membership (à, of) **2.** property.
appartenir [apartənir] *vi (conj like* TENIR) **1.** *(a)* to belong (à, to); to be owned (à, by); **cela n'appartient pas à mes fonctions,** this does not come within the scope of my duties *(b)* **s'a.,** to be one's own master **2.** *v impers* **il ne m'appartient pas de le critiquer,** it's not for me to criticize him.
appât [apɑ] *nm (a)* bait; **mordre à l'a.,** to rise to the bait *(b)* lure (of success).
appâter [apɑte] *vtr* to lure, to entice; to bait (hook).
appauvrir [apovrir] **1.** *vtr* to impoverish; to weaken **2. s'a.,** to grow poorer.
appauvrissement [apovrismɑ̃] *nm* impoverishment; degeneration.
appel [apɛl] *nm* **1.** *(a)* appeal; **faire a. à qn,** to appeal to s.o., to send for s.o.; **faire a. à son courage,** to summon up one's courage *(b)* *Jur:* appeal at law; **faire a. d'une décision,** to appeal against a decision; **jugement sans a.,** final judgment **2.** call; **cri d'a.,**
call for help; **a. d'incendie,** fire alarm; *Fin:* **faire un a. de fonds,** to call up capital; *Com:* **a. d'offres,** invitation to tender; *Aut:* **faire un a. de phares,** to flash one's headlights; *Tp:* **a. téléphonique,** phone call; **a. avec préavis,** personal call **3.** roll call, call-over; *Sch:* **faire l'a.,** to call the register.
appelant, -ante [aplɑ̃, -ɑ̃t] *Jur:* *(a) a* appealing (party) *(b) n* appellant (against a judgment).
appeler [aple] *vtr* **(j'appelle, n. appelons) 1.** *(a)* to call, to call to (s.o.); **a. au secours,** to call for help *(b)* to call, hail (a taxi); **a. qn de la main,** to beckon (to) s.o. *(c)* *Tp:* **a. qn,** to phone s.o., to ring s.o. up; **a. Paris à l'automatique,** to dial Paris; **a. un médecin,** to phone for a doctor **2.** *(a)* to call in, send for, summon; **faire a. un médecin,** to send for a doctor; *Mil:* **a. une classe,** to call up a class; *Jur:* **a. qn en justice,** to summon(s) s.o., to sue s.o. *(b)* **être appelé à qch,** to be destined for sth **3.** to call (by name); to name; **a. les choses par leur nom,** to call a spade a spade; **vous appelez ça danser?** do you call that dancing? **4.** *(a)* to appeal to, call on (s.o., sth) *(b)* to call for; to invite (criticism); **ce problème appelle une solution immédiate,** the problem calls for an immediate solution **5.** to provoke, arouse **6.** *vi (a) Jur:* **a. d'un jugement,** to appeal against a sentence *(b)* **en a. à qn,** to appeal to s.o. **5. s'a.,** to be called, named; **comment vous appelez-vous?** what is your name? *F:* **voilà qui s'appelle pleuvoir!** it's raining with a vengeance!
appellation [apelasjɔ̃] *nf* *(a)* appellation; name; term *(b)* designation; trade name *(c)* *Vit:* **a. contrôlée,** guaranteed vintage.
appendice [apɛ̃dis] *nm* **1.** appendix (of book) **2.** *Anat:* appendix.
appendicite [apɛ̃disit] *nf Med:* appendicitis.
appentis [apɑ̃ti] *nm (a)* lean-to (building, roof) *(b)* outhouse.
appesantir [apəzɑ̃tir] *vtr* **1.** to weigh (sth) down; **yeux appesantis par le sommeil,** eyes heavy with sleep **2. s'a. sur un sujet,** to dwell on a subject.
appétit [apeti] *nm* **1.** appetite; **manger avec a.,** to eat heartily; **avoir un a. d'oiseau,** to eat like a bird; **avoir de l'a.,** to have a hearty appetite; *Prov:* **l'a. vient en mangeant,** (i) eating whets the appetite (ii) the more you have the more you want **2.** desire, craving. **appétissant** *a* tempting, appetizing.
applaudir [aplodir] **1.** *vtr* to applaud (s.o., sth); *F:* **se faire a. à tout casser,** to bring the house down **2.** *vi* to clap, to applaud **3. s'a. (de qch),** to congratulate oneself, to pat oneself on the back (for having done sth).
applaudissement [aplodismɑ̃] *nm usu pl* applause, clapping.
applicable [aplikabl] *a* applicable; suitable (word).
applicateur [aplikatœr] *nm* applicator.
application [aplikasjɔ̃] *nf* **1.** application; applying; **a. de peinture,** coat of paint **2.** application (of a rule); enforcement (of a law); **mettre une théorie en a.,** to put a theory into practice **3.** application (to one's work); **avec a.,** industriously.
applique [aplik] *nf (a)* (wall) bracket (for lamps) *(b)* bracket lamp, wall lamp.
appliquer [aplike] *vtr* **1.** to apply (sth to sth) **2.** to enforce (a law); **a. une loi à un cas particulier,** to

apply a law to a special case **3. a. son esprit à qch,** to apply one's mind to sth **4. s'a.** (*a*) **s'a. à qch,** to apply oneself to sth; to take pains over sth (*b*) **à qui s'applique cette remarque?** to whom does this remark apply? **appliqué** *a* **1.** studious, hard-working (pers) **2. sciences appliquées,** applied sciences.

appoint [apwɛ̃] *nm* **1.** *Com:* balance, odd money; **faire l'a.,** to give the right change, money **2.** contribution.

appointements [apwɛ̃tmɑ̃] *nmpl* salary.

appontement [apɔ̃tmɑ̃] *nm* (wooden) wharf; landing stage.

apponter [apɔ̃te] *vi Av:* to land (on deck of aircraft carrier).

apport [apɔr] *nm* **1.** contribution (of capital) **2.** *Fin:* (*a*) initial share (in undertaking) (*b*) supply, input (of heat) (*c*) **l'a. des fruits en vitamines,** the vitamins provided by fruit.

apporter [apɔrte] *vtr* **1.** to bring; **a. des nouvelles,** to bring news (à, to) **2. a. du soin à faire qch,** to do sth carefully; **a. des difficultés,** to raise problems **3.** to bring in (capital) **4.** to cause, to bring about (changes); **ce que l'avenir apportera,** what the future has in store.

apposer [apoze] *vtr* to affix, put; to append (signature).

apposition [apozisjɔ̃] *nf* apposition.

appréciation [apresjasjɔ̃] *nf* **1.** valuation, estimate; **faire l'a. des marchandises,** to value goods **2.** judgement; opinion; appreciation (of work of art) **3.** rise in value, appreciation.

apprécier [apresje] *vtr* (*pr sub & impf* **n. appréciions**) **1.** (*a*) to appraise; to estimate the value of (sth); to value (sth) (*b*) to determine, estimate (distance); to judge (differences) **2.** to appreciate (good thing). **appréciable** *a* appreciable. **appréciateur, -trice** *a* appreciative. **appréciatif, -ive** *a* **devis a.,** estimate.

appréhender [apreɑ̃de] *vtr* **1. a. qn,** to arrest, to apprehend, s.o. **2.** to dread, fear (sth).

appréhension [apreɑ̃sjɔ̃] *nf* apprehension (de, of). **appréhensif, -ive** *a* apprehensive (de, of).

apprendre [aprɑ̃dr̩] *vtr* (*conj like* PRENDRE) **1.** (*a*) to learn (lesson); **a. à faire qch,** to learn (how) to do sth (*b*) to learn, hear of, get to know of (sth); **je l'ai appris de bonne part,** I have it on good authority **2. a. qch à qn** (*a*) to teach s.o. sth; **ça t'apprendra!** serves you right! (*b*) to inform, to tell, s.o. of sth.

apprenti, -ie [aprɑ̃ti] *n* (*a*) apprentice (*b*) novice, beginner.

apprentissage [aprɑ̃tisaʒ] *nm* apprenticeship; **être en a.,** to be apprenticed (to s.o.); **faire l'a. de qch,** to serve one's apprenticeship in sth.

apprêt [aprɛ] *nm* **1.** dressing, finishing (of fabrics) **2.** (*a*) finish (of fabrics) (*b*) *Paint:* size.

apprêter [aprɛte] *vtr* **1.** to prepare; to make ready **2.** to dress, finish (fabrics) **3.** *Paint:* to size (surface) **4. s'a.** (*a*) to get ready (to go out); to get dressed (*b*) (*of storm, trouble*) to be brewing. **apprêté** *a* affected (manner).

apprivoisement [aprivwazmɑ̃] *nm* taming, domestication.

apprivoiser [aprivwaze] *vtr* **1.** to tame (animal) **2.**

s'a., to become tame. **apprivoisable** *a* tameable. **apprivoisé** *a* tame.

approbation [aprɔbasjɔ̃] *nf* approval, approbation. **approbateur, -trice** *a* approving.

approche [aprɔʃ] *nf* **1.** (*a*) approach; advance; **à l'a. de l'hiver,** as winter draws near; **à son a.,** as he came up; **d'une a. difficile,** difficult of access; **d'a. facile,** (i) easily accessible (ii) easy to understand (*b*) **chasser à l'a.,** to stalk (game). **2.** *pl* **approches,** approaches, surrounding area (of a town).

approcher [aprɔʃe] *vtr* **1.** (*a*) **a. qch de qn, de qch,** to bring, draw, sth near (to) s.o., sth; **approchez votre chaise,** pull up your chair (*b*) to approach, come near; to come close to (s.o., sth); **on ne peut pas l'a.,** (i) you can never see him (ii) he's unapproachable **2.** *vi* (*a*) to approach, draw near; **la nuit approchait,** night was falling; **approche!** come here! (*b*) **a. de qn,** to approach s.o.; **nous approchons de Paris,** we are getting near Paris (*c*) **a. de qch,** to resemble sth; **cela approche de la folie,** that borders on insanity **3. s'a. de qn, de qch,** to come up to s.o., to sth; **approche-toi!** come here! **approchable** *a* approachable, accessible. **approchant** *a* approximating, similar (de, to); **offre approchante,** near offer; **quelque chose d'a.,** something like it.

approfondir [aprɔfɔ̃dir] *vtr* **1.** (*a*) to deepen, excavate (river bed) (*b*) to increase (one's sadness) **2.** to go deeply, thoroughly, into (sth); to study (sth) thoroughly **3. s'a.,** to grow deeper; to deepen. **approfondi** *a* elaborate, careful, extensive (research); thorough (knowledge).

approfondissement [aprɔfɔ̃dismɑ̃] *nm* deepening.

appropriation [aprɔprijasjɔ̃] *nf* appropriation; embezzlement (of funds).

approprier [aprɔprie] *vtr* (*pr sub & impf* **n. approprions**) **1.** to adapt (sth) to (sth) **2. s'a. qch,** to appropriate sth. **approprié** *a* appropriate, adapted (à, to); proper, suitable.

approuver [apruve] *vtr* **1.** (*a*) **a. qch,** to approve of, be pleased with, sth; **a. de la tête,** to nod approval (*b*) **a. qn,** to commend s.o. (**d'avoir fait qch,** for doing sth) **2.** to consent to, to agree to (sth); **a. un contrat,** to ratify a contract; **a. une nomination,** to confirm an appointment; **lu et approuvé,** read and approved.

approvisionnement [aprɔvizjɔnmɑ̃] *nm* **1.** supplying **2.** supplies, stock, provisions.

approvisionner [aprɔvizjɔne] **1.** *vtr* to supply (de, with); to cater for (s.o.); to stock (shop) **2. s'a.,** to get a stock, a supply (en, de, of); to stock up (en, with); **s'a. au marché,** to shop at the market.

approximation [aprɔksimasjɔ̃] *nf* approximation, rough estimate. **approximatif, -ive** *a* approximate; rough (estimate). **approximativement** *adv* approximately; roughly.

appui [apɥi] *nm* **1.** (*a*) support, prop, stay (*b*) rest; *Arch:* balustrade; **a. de fenêtre,** window ledge, window sill **2.** (*a*) support; **mur d'a.,** supporting wall; **barre d'a.,** handrail (*b*) **a. moral,** moral support; **être sans a.,** to be friendless.

appui(e)-bras [apɥibra] *nm* armrest; *pl* **appuis-bras, appuie-bras.**

appui(e)-tête [apɥitɛt] *nm* head-rest; *pl* **appuis-tête, appuie-tête.**

appuyer [apɥije] v (j'**appuie**, n. **appuyons**) 1. vtr (a) to support; to prop (up) (b) to support (a petition); to second (a proposal) 2. vtr (a) **a. qch contre qch**, to lean, to rest, sth against sth; **a. son opinion sur qch**, to base one's opinion on sth; **théorie appuyée sur des faits**, theory supported by facts (b) to press (sth on sth); Mus: **a. (sur) une note**, to dwell on, sustain, a note 3. vi (a) to bear (sur, on) (b) **a. sur le bouton**, to press the button; **a. sur une syllabe**, to stress a syllable 4. **s'a.** (a) **s'a. sur, contre, à, qch**, to lean, rest, on, against, sth; **s'a. sur qn**, to depend on s.o., to rely on s.o. (b) F: to put up with (sth).

âpre [apr] a 1. rough, harsh; tart (taste) 2. biting, sharp (rebuke); **temps â.**, raw weather 3. keen (competition); **à. au gain**, grasping (person). **âprement** adv bitterly, harshly, roughly.

après [aprɛ] a 1. prep (order in time, space) (a) after; **a. tout**, after all; **jour a. jour**, day after day; **a. quoi**, after which (b) **je viens à. lui**, I come next to him (c) **courir a. qn**, to run after s.o.; **il est toujours a. moi**, he is always nagging at me (d) prep phr **d'a.**, according to; after; from; **d'a. ce qu'il dit**, according to what he said; **peint d'a. nature**, painted from nature; **paysage d'a.** Turner, landscape after Turner; **d'a. l'article 12**, under article 12; **d'a. vos instructions**, in accordance with your instructions (e) **a. avoir dîné**, after dinner 2. adv (a) afterwards, later; **le jour (d')a.**, the next day; the day after; F: **et puis a.?** what of it? **et a.?** (i) what then? (ii) so what? (b) conj phr **a. que**, after, when (c) F: **tout le monde leur court a.**, everybody runs after them.

après-demain [apredmɛ̃] adv & nm inv the day after tomorrow.

après-guerre [apregɛr] nm post-war period, years; pl **après-guerres**.

après-midi [apremidi] nm or f inv afternoon.

après-rasage [aprerazaʒ] a inv (lotion) **a.-r.**, aftershave (lotion).

après-ski [apreski] nm inv **des a.-s.**, snowboots; **tenue d'a.-s.**, après-ski outfit.

âpreté [aprǝte] nf roughness, harshness; tartness; sharpness, bitterness.

à-propos [apropo] nm 1. aptness, appropriateness (of an expression); **manquer d'à-p.**, to be irrelevant 2. opportuneness; **manque d'à-p.**, untimeliness.

apte [apt] a 1. **a. à qch**, fitted, qualified, for sth; **a. au service**, fit for military service 2. apt, suitable (example).

aptitude [aptityd] nf aptitude, fitness (à, pour, for); **avoir une a. à (faire qch)**, to have a gift (for sth), to have the ability (to do sth).

aquaplane [akwaplan] nm Sp: aquaplane; surfboard.

aquarelle [akwarɛl] nf watercolour; **peindre à l'a.**, to paint in water colours.

aquarium [akwarjɔm] nm aquarium.

aquatique [akwatik] a aquatic (bird, sport).

aqueduc [ak(ǝ)dyk] nm aqueduct.

aquilin [akilɛ̃] a aquiline; **nez a.**, Roman nose.

ara [ara] nm Orn: macaw.

arabe [arab] 1. (a) a & n Arab (person, horse) (b) a Arabian (customs) 2. a & nm Ling: etc: Arabic (language, numerals).

arabesque [arabɛsk] nf arabesque.

Arabie [arabi] Prnf Geog: Arabia; **A. séoudite, saoudite**, Saudi Arabia.

arable [arabl] a arable (land).

arachide [araʃid] nf peanut, groundnut.

araignée [arɛɲe] nf (a) spider; **toile d'a.**, cobweb, spider's web (b) **a. de mer**, spider crab.

aratoire [aratwar] a agricultural.

arbalète [arbalɛt] nf crossbow.

arbitrage [arbitraʒ] nm arbitration; Sp: refereeing, umpiring.

arbitraire [arbitrɛr] 1. a arbitrary; discretionary 2. nm arbitrariness; arbitrary nature (of sth). **arbitrairement** adv arbitrarily.

arbitre [arbitr] nm (a) Jur: arbitrator, referee (b) Games: referee, umpire (c) arbiter (of fashion).

arbitrer [arbitre] vtr (a) Jur: to arbitrate (b) Games: to referee, umpire (match).

arborer [arbore] vtr to raise; to set up; to hoist (flag); **a. une cravate rouge**, to wear, to sport a red tie.

arboriculture [arborikyltyr] nf arboriculture.

arbre [arbr] nm 1. (a) tree; **a. fruitier**, fruit tree; **a. vert**, evergreen (tree); **les arbres cachent la forêt**, you can't see the wood for the trees (b) **a. généalogique**, family tree (c) **a. de Noël**, Christmas tree 2. MecE: shaft, axle; **a. à cames**, camshaft.

arbrisseau, -eaux [arbriso] nm shrub.

arbuste [arbyst] nm bush; shrub.

arc [ark] nm 1. bow; **tir à l'a.**, archery 2. Arch: Anat: arch 3. Mth: El: arc.

arcade [arkad] nf 1. (a) archway (b) **arcades**, arcade 2. Anat: arch.

arc-boutant [arkbutɑ̃] nm Arch: flying buttress; pl **arcs-boutants**.

arc-bouter [arkbute] vtr 1. to buttress 2. **s'a.-b. contre un mur**, to brace oneself against a wall.

arceau [arso] nm 1. arch (of vault) 2. ring bow (of padlock); (croquet) hoop.

arc-en-ciel [arkɑ̃sjɛl] nm rainbow; pl **arcs-en-ciel**.

archaïsme [arkaism] nm archaism. **archaïque** a archaic.

archange [arkɑ̃ʒ] nm archangel.

arche[1] [arʃ] nf **l'a. de Noé**, Noah's ark.

arche[2] nf arch (of bridge).

archéologie [arkeɔlɔʒi] nf archaeology. **archéologique** a archaeological.

archéologue [arkeɔlɔg] n archaeologist.

archer [arʃe] nm archer.

archet [arʃɛ] nm Mus: etc: bow.

archétype [arʃetip] nm archetype.

archevêché [arʃǝveʃe] nm 1. archbishopric 2. archbishop's palace.

archevêque [arʃǝvɛk] nm archbishop.

archi- [arʃi] pref (a) enormously, tremendously; **archiplein**, chock-a-block (b) (title) arch-; **archidiacre**, archdeacon.

archiduc [arʃidyk] nm archduke.

archipel [arʃipɛl] nm Geog: archipelago.

architecte [arʃitɛkt] nm architect; **a. urbaniste**, townplanner.

architecture [arʃitɛktyr] nf architecture. **architectural, -aux** a architectural.

archives [arʃiv] nfpl archives; records.

archiviste [arʃivist] n 1. archivist; keeper of public records 2. (filing) clerk.

arçon [arsɔ̃] *nm Harn:* saddle bow.

arctique [arktik] (*a*) *a* arctic (*b*) *Prnm Geog:* **l'A.,** the Arctic.

ardent [ardɑ̃] *a* burning hot, scorching; blazing (fire) **2.** ardent, passionate, eager, fervent. **ardemment** *adv* ardently, fervently.

ardeur [ardœr] *nf* **1.** heat **2.** ardour, fervour; enthusiasm.

ardoise [ardwaz] *nf* slate; **(couleur) gris a.,** grey (colour).

ardu [ardy] *a* **1.** steep, difficult (path) **2.** arduous, difficult (task).

are [ar] *nm* 100 square metres.

arène [arɛn] *nf* arena; bullring; **les arènes d'Arles,** the amphitheatre of Arles.

arête [arɛt] *nf* **1.** (fish)bone; **grande a.,** backbone (of fish) **2.** (*a*) line; edge (*b*) *Geog:* arête, (serrated) ridge **3.** bridge (of the nose).

argent [arʒɑ̃] *nm* **1.** silver; **vaisselle d'a.,** (silver) plate **2.** money; **a. liquide,** ready money, cash (in hand); **gagner de l'a.,** to make money; **en avoir pour son a.,** to have good value for money. **argenté** *a* **1.** silver(y); **gris a.,** silver-grey **2.** silver-plated **3.** *F:* rich, well-off. **argentin¹, -ine** *a* silvery (waves); silvertoned (voice).

argenter [arʒɑ̃te] *vtr* to silver.

argenterie [arʒɑ̃tri] *nf* (silver) plate; silverware.

Argentine [arʒɑ̃tin] *Prnf Geog:* Argentina, the Argentine (Republic). **argentin², -ine** *a & n* Argentinian.

argile [arʒil] *nf* (*a*) clay (*b*) **a. cuite,** terracotta, earthenware. **argileux, -euse** *a* clayey.

argot [argo] *nm* slang. **argotique** *a* slangy.

arguer [argɥe] *v* (**j'arguë**) **1.** *vtr* to infer, assert, deduce **2.** *vi* to argue.

argument [argymɑ̃] *nm* **1.** argument; **tirer a. de qch,** to argue from sth **2.** outline, summary (of book).

argumentation [argymɑ̃tasjɔ̃] *nf* argumentation.

argumenter [argymɑ̃te] *vi* (*a*) to argue (**contre,** against) (*b*) *F:* to be argumentative.

argus [argys] *nm* guide to secondhand cars; = Glass's Guide.

aridité [aridite] *nf* aridity, dryness. **aride** *a* arid, dry, barren.

aristocrate [aristɔkrat] *n* aristocrat. **aristocratique** *a* aristocratic.

aristocratie [aristɔkrasi] *nf* aristocracy.

arithméticien, -ienne [aritmetisjɛ̃, -jen] *n* arithmetician.

arithmétique [aritmetik] **1.** *a* arithmetical **2.** *nf* arithmetic.

arlequin [arlǝkɛ̃] *nm* Harlequin.

armateur [armatœr] *nm Nau:* (ship)owner.

armature [armatyr] *nf* **1.** frame (of window); reinforcement (of concrete work); truss (of girder) **2.** *El:* armature **3.** *Mus:* key signature.

arme [arm] *nf* **1.** arm, weapon; **armes à feu,** firearms; **armes portatives,** small arms; **a. nucléaire,** nuclear weapon; **en armes,** in arms; **faire des armes,** to fence; **prendre les armes,** to take up arms (**contre,** against); **aux armes!** shoulder arms; **place d'armes,** parade-ground; **passer qn par les armes,** to have s.o. (court-martialled and) shot; **à armes égales,** on equal terms; **avec armes et baggages,** (with) bag and bag-

gage **2.** arm (as a branch of the army) **3.** *pl Her:* (coat of) arms.

armée [arme] *nf* **1.** army; **a. active,** regular army; **l'a. de terre,** the army, the land forces; **l'a. de l'air,** the air force; **l'a. de mer,** the navy **2.** (*a*) **l'A. du salut,** the Salvation Army (*b*) **une a. de fonctionnaires,** an army of officials.

armement [armǝmɑ̃] *nm* **1.** (*a*) arming, equipping (of army) (*b*) armament, equipment (*c*) *pl* armaments; weaponry; **course aux armements,** arms race **2.** strengthening **3.** *Nau:* commissioning, fitting out; **port d'a.,** port of registry **4.** (*a*) loading (of gun) (*b*) setting (of camera shutter) **5.** mounting gear (of machine).

Arménie [armeni] *Prnf Geog:* Armenia. **arménien, -ienne** *a & n* Armenian.

armer [arme] **1.** *vtr* (*a*) to arm (**de,** with) (*b*) to fortify; to strengthen (*c*) *Nau:* to equip, commission (ship) (*d*) to arm (a fuse); to set (camera); to cock (firearm) **2.** *vi* to arm, to prepare for war **3.** **s'a.** (*a*) to arm oneself; to take up arms (*b*) **s'a. de courage,** to summon up (one's) courage. **armé** *a* (*a*) armed (*b*) fortified, strengthened (*c*) cocked; **pistolet à l'a.,** pistol at full cock.

armistice [armistis] *nm* armistice.

armoire [armwar] *nf* (*a*) cupboard (*b*) wardrobe.

armoiries [armwari] *nfpl Her:* (coat of) arms.

armure [armyr] *nf* (*a*) armour (*b*) defence.

armurier [armyrje] *nm* **1.** arms manufacturer; gunsmith **2.** armourer.

arnaquer [arnake] *vtr P:* to swindle.

arnaqueur, -euse [arnakœr, -øz] *n P:* swindler, hustler.

arnica [arnika] *nf Bot: Pharm:* arnica.

aromate [arɔmat] *nm* aromatic; spice. **aromatique** *a* aromatic.

aromatiser [arɔmatize] *vtr* to flavour.

arôme [arom] *nm* aroma; flavour.

arpège [arpɛʒ] *nm Mus:* arpeggio.

arpentage [arpɑ̃taʒ] *nm* surveying.

arpenter [arpɑ̃te] *vtr* **1.** to survey, measure (land) **2. a. le terrain,** to stride over the ground; **a. le quai,** to pace up and down the platform.

arpenteur [arpɑ̃tœr] *nm* (land) surveyor.

arquer [arke] **1.** *vtr* to bend, curve (wood); **a. le dos,** to hump the back; (*of cat*) to arch its back **2.** *vi* to bend **3. s'a.,** to bend, to curve. **arqué** *a* arched, curved; **avoir les jambes arquées,** to be bow-legged.

arrachage [araʃaʒ] *nm* pulling up, rooting up (of plants); pulling out, drawing, extraction (of tooth).

arraché [araʃe] *nm Sp:* (*weightlifting*) snatch; **gagner à l'a.,** to snatch a win.

arrachement [araʃmɑ̃] *nm* (*a*) parting (*b*) wrench.

arrache-pied (d') [daraʃpje] *adv phr* without interruption; relentlessly.

arracher [araʃe] *vtr* to tear (out, up, away); to pull (up, out, away); to draw (nail); to uproot (tree); to lift (potatoes); to pull out (tooth); to tear down (poster); to extract (promise); **a. qch à qn,** to snatch sth from s.o.; **se faire a. une dent,** to have a tooth out; **a. les yeux à qn,** to scratch s.o.'s eyes out; **s'a. les cheveux,** to tear one's hair; **cela m'arrache le cœur,** it breaks my heart.

arraisonnement [arɛzɔnmɑ̃] *nm Nau:* boarding, examination (of ship).

arraisonner [arεzɔne] *vtr Nau:* **a. un navire,** to stop and examine a ship.

arrangement [arɑ̃ʒmɑ̃] *nm* 1. (a) arranging (b) arrangement; layout (c) *Mus:* arrangement 2. agreement, settlement, understanding.

arranger [arɑ̃ʒe] *vtr* (**n. arrangeons**) 1. (a) to arrange; to put in order; to tidy (up) (room); to straighten (one's tie) (b) *F:* **a. qn.** to tell s.o. off, to sort s.o. out (c) to arrange (a piece of music) 2. to repair, to mend 3. to organize (concert); to plan (sth) 4. to settle (quarrel); **a. les choses,** to put things right; **cela n'arrange rien,** that's not much help 5. **faire qch pour a. qn,** to do sth to help s.o. (out). **s'arranger** *vpr* 1. (a) to manage; **arrangez-vous pour être là,** you must make sure to be there; **il s'arrange de tout,** he is very adaptable (b) to tidy oneself up; to get dressed 2. (a) **s'a. avec qn,** to come to an agreement with s.o.; **arrangez-vous,** sort it out among yourselves (b) **ça s'arrangera,** things will turn out all right. **arrangeant** *a* obliging.

arrérages [areraʒ] *nmpl* arrears.

arrestation [arεstasjɔ̃] *nf* arrest; **en état d'a.,** under arrest.

arrêt [arε] *nm* 1. (a) stop, stoppage; stopping; **point d'a.,** stopping place; **a. en cours de route,** break of journey; **sans a.,** non-stop, continuously; **dix minutes d'a.,** ten minutes' stop, break; **temps d'a.,** pause; **a. de travail,** stoppage of work; *Med:* **a. de cœur,** cardiac arrest; heart failure; *Rail:* **signal d'a.,** stop signal (b) (bus) stop; **a. facultatif,** request stop (c) catch (of door); **cran d'a.,** safety catch 2. (a) decree (b) *Jur:* judgment; **a. de mort,** death sentence 3. seizure; detention (of ship) 4. arrest; **mandat d'a.,** warrant (for arrest) 5. **chien d'a.,** setter, pointer.

arrêté [arεte] 1. *a* fixed, decided (ideas); **dessein a.,** settled plan 2. *nm* (a) order, decree; **a. municipal,** by(e)-law (b) *Com:* **a. de compte,** settlement of an account.

arrêter [arεte] 1. *vtr* (a) to stop (s.o., sth); to check; to hold up; to bring (vehicle) to a standstill; to detain; to arrest (growth); *Aut:* **a. le moteur,** to switch off the engine; *Fb:* **a. un but,** to save a goal (b) to fix, fasten (shutter); **a. l'attention,** to arrest attention (c) to arrest, seize; **faire a. qn,** to have s.o. arrested (d) to decide; **a. un jour,** to fix a day (e) *Com:* to close, to settle (account) 2. *vi* to stop, halt; **elle n'arrête pas de parler,** she never stops talking; **arrête! arrêtez!** stop (it)! **s'arrêter** *vpr* 1. to stop; to come to a stop, to a standstill; **s'a. en route,** to break one's journey; **s'a. de fumer,** to give up smoking 2. to fix one's attention (on sth); to dwell (on sth); **s'a. aux apparences,** to pay too much attention to appearances.

arrhes [ar] *nfpl* (money) deposit.

arrière [arjεr] 1. *adv* (a) **(en) a.,** behind; **rester en a.,** to lag behind; **en a. de son temps,** behind the times (b) **en a.,** in arrears (c) **en a.,** backwards; **a.,** back! **faire marche a.,** to back; *Aut:* to reverse 2. *a inv* back; *Aut:* **feu a.,** rear light; **siège a.,** (i) *Aut:* back seat (ii) (*motorbike*) pillion seat 3. *nm* (a) back (part), rear (of house) (b) stern (of ship) 4. *nm Fb:* (full) back.

arriéré [arjere] 1. *a* (a) late, behind(hand), in arrears; overdue (payment) (b) backward (child); (*of pers*)

être a., to be behind the times; **pays arriérés,** underdeveloped countries 2. *nm* arrears (of account); backlog; **a. du loyer,** arrears of rent.

NOTE. *In all the following compounds* **arrière** *is inv, the noun takes the plural.*

arrière-bouche [arjεrbuʃ] *nf* back of the mouth.

arrière-boutique [arjεrbutik] *nf* back shop.

arrière-cour [arjεrkur] *nf* backyard.

arrière-cuisine [arjεrkɥizin] *nf* scullery.

arrière-garde [arjεrgard] *nf* 1. *Mil:* rearguard 2. *Navy:* rear squadron.

arrière-gorge [arjεrgɔrʒ] *nf* back of the throat.

arrière-goût [arjεrgu] *nm* aftertaste.

arrière-grand-mère, -grand-père [arjεrgrɑ̃mεr, -grɑ̃pεr] *n* great-grandmother, -grandfather.

arrière-grands-parents [arjεrgrɑ̃parɑ̃] *nmpl* great-grandparents.

arrière-pays [arjεrpei] *nm inv* hinterland.

arrière-pensée [arjεrpɑ̃se] *nf* (a) mental reservation (b) ulterior motive.

arrière-petit-fils, -petite-fille [arjεrpətifis, -pətitfij] *n* great-grandson, -granddaughter.

arrière-plan [arjεrplɑ̃] *nm* background; **à l'a.-p.,** at the back, *Th:* upstage.

arrière-saison [arjεrsεzɔ̃] *nf* late season, late autumn.

arrière-train [arjεrtrɛ̃] *nm* hindquarters (of animal).

arrimage [arimaʒ] *nm Nau:* (a) stowing (b) stowage.

arrimer [arime] *vtr Nau:* (a) to stow (cargo) (b) to trim (ship).

arrivage [arivaʒ] *nm* arrival; consignment (of goods).

arrivant [arivɑ̃] *nm* (*pers*) arrival, newcomer.

arrivée [arive] *nf* 1. arrival, coming; **à mon a.,** when I arrived 2. *Mch:* inlet; intake 3. *Sp:* (winning) post, finish.

arriver [arive] *vi* (*aux être*) 1. (a) to arrive, come; **il est arrivé en courant,** he came running up; **il arrive de voyage,** he's just back from a trip; **a. à temps,** to be on time; **a. en retard,** to be late; **l'avion devait a. à midi,** the plane was due (to arrive) at midday; **arrive!** come on! (b) **a. à un endroit,** to reach, to get to, a place; **a. à bon port,** to arrive safely; **l'eau m'arrivait aux genoux,** the water came up to my knees (c) **il faudra bien en a. là,** it must come to that 2. (a) to succeed; **il n'arrivera jamais à rien,** he will never achieve anything (b) **a. à faire qch,** to succeed in doing sth; **je n'arrive pas à y croire,** I just can't believe it 3. to happen; **cela arrive tous les jours,** it happens every day; *impers* **il lui est arrivé un accident,** he had an accident; **faire a. un accident,** to cause an accident; **quoi qu'il arrive,** whatever happens; **il m'arrive d'oublier,** I sometimes forget.

arrivisme [arivism] *nm* unscrupulous ambition.

arriviste [arivist] *n* climber, go-getter.

arrogance [arɔgɑ̃s] *nf* arrogance. **arrogant** *a* arrogant.

arroger (s') [sarɔʒe] *vpr* (**n. n. arrogeons**) **s'a. un droit,** to assume a right.

arrondir [arɔ̃dir] 1. *vtr* (a) to round (sth) (off); to make (sth) round; **a. sa fortune,** to get together a considerable capital; **les yeux arrondis par l'étonne-**

ment, in wide-eyed astonishment (*b*) **a. les angles**, to smooth things over; *Ling:* **a. une voyelle**, to round a vowel (*c*) to round off (number) (**à**, **to**) **2. s'a.**, to become rounded; to round out, fill out. **arrondi 1.** *a* rounded, round **2.** *nm* (*a*) round; rounded form (*b*) hemline (of skirt).

arrondissement [arɔ̃dismɑ̃] *nm Adm:* = district (of Paris, large city); = borough.

arrosage [arozaʒ] *nm* watering; irrigation.

arroser [aroze] *vtr* (*a*) to water (plants); *Cu:* to baste (a joint); **j'ai été bien arrosé**, I got absolutely soaked; *F:* **a. un repas**, to wash down a meal (with wine); **ça s'arrose!** we must drink to that! (*b*) to irrigate (meadow).

arroseur *nm*, **arroseuse** *nf* [arozœr, -øz] **1.** *nm* sprinkler **2.** *nf* water cart.

arrosoir [arozwar] *nm* watering can.

arsenal, -aux [arsənal, -o] *nm* (*a*) arsenal (*b*) gear; collection.

arsenic [arsənik] *nm* arsenic.

art [ar] *nm* **1.** (*a*) art; craft; **l'a. culinaire**, the art of (good) cooking (*b*) art; **beaux-arts**, fine arts; **œuvre d'a.**, work of art **2.** skill; artistry.

artère [arter] *nf* **1.** *Anat:* artery **2.** main road; thoroughfare. **artériel, -elle** *a* arterial; **tension artérielle**, blood pressure.

arthrite [artrit] *nf Med:* arthritis. **arthritique** *a & n* arthritic (patient).

arthrose [artroz] *nf Med:* osteoarthritis.

artichaut [artiʃo] *nm* (globe) artichoke.

article [artikl] *nm* **1.** critical point; **à l'a. de la mort**, at the point of death **2.** (*a*) article, clause (of treaty); **a. de foi**, article of faith (*b*) items (of bill); **articles divers** (*c*) article (in newspaper) **3.** *Com:* article, commodity; **a. (en) réclame**, special offer; **articles de voyage**, travel goods; **articles de bureau**, office accessories **4.** *Gram:* article.

articulation [artikylasjɔ̃] *nf* **1.** (*a*) *Anat:* articulation, joint; **a. du doigt**, knuckle (*b*) connection, joint **2.** speech, articulation.

articuler [artikyle] *vtr* **1.** to articulate, to joint **2.** to articulate; to pronounce distinctly; **articulez!** speak clearly! **articulé** *a* (*a*) articulated; jointed (*b*) articulate (speech).

artifice [artifis] *nm* **1.** artifice; contrivance, trick **2.** **feu d'a.**, fireworks (display). **artificiel, -elle** *a* **1.** (*a*) artificial (*b*) forced (laugh) **2.** imitation (pearl). **artificiellement** *adv* artificially. **artificieux, -euse** *a* crafty, cunning.

artillerie [artijri] *nf* **1.** artillery; **a. navale**, naval guns **2.** gunnery.

artilleur [artijœr] *nm* artilleryman, gunner.

artimon [artimɔ̃] *nm Nau:* mizzenmast.

artisan [artizɑ̃] *nm* **1.** artisan, craftsman **2.** architect, author. **artisanal, -aux** artisanal; **métier a.**, craft; **fabrication artisanale**, small-scale production by craftsmen.

artisanat [artizana] *nm* **1.** craftsmen **2.** cottage industry.

artiste [artist] **1.** *n* (*a*) artist; **a. peintre**, painter (*b*) *Th: Mus:* performer (*c*) *Th:* actor, actress; singer; entertainer; artiste **2.** *a* artistic. **artistique** *a* artistic. **artistiquement** *adv* artistically.

aryen, -yenne [arjɛ̃, -jɛn] *a & n* Aryan.

as [ɑs] *nm* **1.** ace; **as de pique**, ace of spades; *P:* **être (plein) aux as**, to be rolling (in it) **2.** *Av:* ace; *Games:* crack player, star; *Aut:* **as du volant**, crack (racing) driver.

ascendance [asɑ̃dɑ̃s] *nf* ancestry, lineage.

ascendant [asɑ̃dɑ̃] **1.** *a* ascending; upward; *Av:* **vol a.**, climbing flight **2.** *nm* (*a*) *Astr:* ascendant (*b*) ascendancy, influence (*c*) *pl* **ascendants**, ancestry.

ascenseur [asɑ̃sœr] *nm* lift; *NAm:* elevator.

ascension [asɑ̃sjɔ̃] *nf* (*a*) ascent, ascension; **faire l'a. d'une montagne**, to climb a mountain; *Ecc:* **Fête de l'A.**, Ascension Day (*b*) progress; rise. **ascensionnel, -elle** *a* ascensional; upward (motion); *Av:* **force ascensionnelle**, lift; **vitesse ascensionelle**, climbing speed.

ascète [aset] *n* ascetic. **ascétique** [asetik] *a & n* ascetic.

ascétisme [asetism] *nm* asceticism.

ascorbique [askɔrbik] *a* ascorbic (acid).

asepsie [asepsi] *nf Med:* asepsis. **aseptique** *a* aseptic.

aseptiser [aseptize] *vi* to sterilize; to disinfect.

Asie [azi] *Prnf Geog:* Asia. **asiatique** *a & n* Asiatic, asian.

asile [azil] *nm* **1.** (*a*) sanctuary (*b*) **a. politique**, political asylum **2.** shelter, refuge, retreat; **sans a.**, homeless; **a. de vieillards**, old people's home; **a. d'aliénés, de fous**, lunatic asylum; *Lit:* **a. de paix**, haven of peace.

asocial, -aux [asosjal, -o] *a* asocial.

aspect [aspɛ] *nm* **1.** sight, aspect **2.** aspect, appearance, look; **avoir un a. imposant**, to look imposing; **considérer une affaire sous tous ses aspects**, to look at a thing from all points of view.

asperge [aspɛrʒ] *nf* **1.** asparagus **2.** *F:* (*pers*) beanpole.

asperger [aspɛrʒe] *vtr* (*n. aspergeons*) to sprinkle, to spray, to splash (with water).

aspérité [asperite] *nf* **1.** unevenness, ruggedness, roughness (of surface) **2.** asperity, harshness (of character).

asphalte [asfalt] *nm* asphalt.

asphalter [asfalte] *vtr* to asphalt.

asphyxie [asfiksi] *nf* asphyxiation, suffocation.

asphyxier [asfiksje] *vtr* (*pr sub & impf* n. asphyxiions) **1.** to asphyxiate, suffocate; *Min:* to gas **2.** to stifle.

aspic [aspik] *nm* **1.** *Rept:* asp **2.** *Cu:* meat, fish, in aspic.

aspirant, -ante [aspirɑ̃, -ɑ̃t] **1.** *a* sucking; **pompe aspirante**, suction pump **2.** *n* (*a*) candidate (*b*) *Navy:* midshipman (*c*) *Mil:* officer cadet.

aspirateur [aspiratœr] *nm* vacuum cleaner.

aspiration [aspirasjɔ̃] *nf* **1.** aspiration, yearning (**à**, **vers**, for, after) **2.** *Ling:* aspiration **3.** (*a*) inhaling (of air) (*b*) suction, sucking up.

aspirer [aspire] **1.** *v ind tr* to aspire (**à**, to, after); to yearn for **2.** *vtr* (*a*) to inhale, breathe in (*b*) to suck up (water) (*c*) *Ling:* to aspirate (a sound).

aspirine [aspirin] *nf Pharm:* aspirin.

assagir [asaʒir] *vtr* to make (s.o.) wiser; to sober (s.o.) (down); **s'a.**, to become wiser.

assaillant [asajɑ̃] *nm* assailant.

assaillir [asajir] *vtr* (*prp* **assaillant**; *pr ind* **j'assaille**) to assail, assault, attack.

assainir [asɛnir] *vtr* to make (sth) healthier; to cleanse, purify (atmosphere); to stabilize (currency).

assainissement [asɛnismã] *nm* cleansing, purifying; stabilization.

assaisonnement [asɛzɔnmã] *nm* dressing; seasoning.

assaisonner [asɛzɔne] *vtr* to season (food) (**de**, with); to dress (salad).

assassin, -ine [asasɛ̃, -in] 1. *n* assassin; murderer; murderess; **à l'a.!** murder! 2. *a* provocative (smile).

assassinat [asasina] *nm* assassination, murder.

assassiner [asasine] *vtr* 1. to assassinate, murder 2. *F:* to pester (s.o.) to death (**de**, with).

assaut [aso] *nm* 1. assault, attack, onslaught; **donner l'a.**, to attack; **prendre d'a.**, to (take by) storm; **troupes d'a.**, storm troops 2. match, bout.

assèchement [asɛʃmã] *nm* drying, drainage.

assécher [aseʃe] *v* (**j'assèche; j'assécherai**) 1. *vtr* to dry, drain (marsh) 2. *vi & pr* to dry up.

assemblage [asãblaʒ] *nm* 1. gathering, collection 2. assembling, assembly, putting together (of parts) 3. joint; coupling.

assemblée [asãble] *nf* (*a*) assembly; meeting; (family) gathering (*b*) *Pol:* **A. nationale** = House of Commons.

assembler [asãble] *vtr* 1. (*a*) to assemble; to convene (committee); to collect, gather (*b*) to assemble, fit together (machine); to collate (documents); *MecE: etc:* to joint, to couple 2. **s'a.**, to assemble, meet, gather.

assener, asséner [asene] *vtr* (**j'assène, n. assenons, n. assénons**) to strike (blow).

assentiment [asãtimã] *nm* assent, consent.

asseoir [aswar] *v* (*prp* asseyant; *pp* assis; *pr ind* j'assieds, ils asseyent, *or* j'assois, ils assoient; *pr sub* j'asseye, *or* j'assoie; *impf* j'asseyais *or* j'assoyais; *ph* j'assis; *fu* j'assoirai) 1. *vtr* (*a*) to set, seat; **asseyez-le sur le gazon**, sit him down on the lawn; **faire a. qn**, to ask s.o. to sit down (*b*) to lay (foundations); **a. une théorie sur des faits**, to base a theory on facts; **a. son autorité**, to establish one's authority 2. **s'a.**, to sit down; **s'a. (sur son séant)**, to sit up; *F:* **les ordres du patron, je m'assois dessus!** I don't care a damn about the boss's orders!

assermenter [asɛrmãte] *vtr* to swear (s.o.) in. **assermenté** *a* sworn (in).

assertion [asɛrsjɔ̃] *nf* assertion.

asservir [asɛrvir] *vtr* to enslave, to subjugate.

asservissement [asɛrvismã] *nm* enslavement; subservience, slavery.

assesseur [asesœr] *nm* assessor.

assez [ase] *adv* 1. (*a*) enough; **elle parle a. bien l'anglais**, she speaks English quite well (*b*) **avez-vous a. d'argent?** have you enough money? **j'en ai a.!** I've had enough of it! I'm sick of it! **en voilà a.!** that's enough of that! (*c*) **c'est a. parler**, enough said (*d*) **être a. près pour voir**, to be near enough to see (*e*) *int* **a.!** that's enough! stop (it)! 2. rather, fairly; **elle est a. jolie**, she is quite pretty; **je suis a. de votre avis**, I'm rather inclined to agree with you; **avoir a. de bon sens**, to have plenty of common sense; **il parle a. peu**, he doesn't talk much.

assidu [asidy] *a* (*a*) assiduous; industrious, hardworking, persevering; untiring (efforts); **travailleur**

a., hard worker (*b*) unremitting, unceasing (care, etc) (*c*) regular (visitor). **assidûment** *adv* assiduously.

assiduité [asidɥite] *nf* 1. (*a*) assiduity; steadiness; perseverance; devotion (to work) (*b*) *Sch:* regular attendance 2. constant attention(s), care.

assiégeant, -ante [asjeʒã, -ãt] *n* besieger.

assiéger [asjeʒe] *vtr* (**j'assiége, n. assiégeons; j'assiégerai**) 1. (*a*) to besiege, lay siege to (a town) (*b*) **a. qn de demandes**, to pester s.o. with requests 2. to surround, to beset.

assiette [asjɛt] *nf* 1. (*a*) seat (on horse); trim (of boat); *F:* **ne pas être dans son a.**, to be out of sorts (*b*) position; site (of building) 2. foundation (of road); basis (of a tax) 3. (*a*) plate; **a. plate**, dinner plate; **a. creuse**, soup plate; *F:* **a. au beurre**, cushy job, *NAm:* the gravy train (*b*) **a. anglaise**, assorted cold meats.

assiettée [asjete] *nf* plateful.

assignation [asiɲasjɔ̃] *nf* 1. allocation (of shares, funds) 2. *Jur:* (*a*) serving of writ, summons (*b*) subpoena.

assigner [asiɲe] *vtr* 1. (*a*) to fix, appoint (time) (*b*) to allocate (a sum for payment) 2. *Jur:* (*a*) to summon, subpoena (witness) (*b*) to serve a writ against (s.o.).

assimilation [asimilasjɔ̃] *nf* assimilation; comparison; classification.

assimiler [asimile] *vtr* 1. to assimilate 2. to assimilate, compare (**à**, to, with); **a. à**, to class as, to put in the same category as.

assis [asi] *a* (*a*) seated; **il était a. près du feu**, he was sitting by the fire (*b*) *Rail: Th:* **places assises**, seats.

assise [asiz] *nf* 1. (*a*) seating, foundation (*b*) *Geol:* bed, stratum 2. *Constr:* course (of masonry) 3. (*a*) *Jur:* **les assises**, the assizes; **cour d'assises**, Assize Court (*b*) **assises d'un congrès**, sittings of a congress.

assistance [asistãs] *nf* 1. presence, attendance (of magistrate) 2. (*a*) audience; *Ecc:* congregation (*b*) spectators, onlookers 3. assistance, help; **a. sociale**, welfare work.

assistant, -ante [asistã, -ãt] *n* 1. *usu pl* (*a*) bystander, onlooker, spectator (*b*) member of the audience 2. (*a*) assistant (*b*) foreign assistant (in school) (*c*) laboratory assistant (*d*) **assistante sociale**, welfare officer, social worker.

assister [asiste] 1. *vi* **a. à qch**, to attend sth; to be (present) at sth; to witness sth 2. *vtr* to help, assist; **a. qn de ses conseils**, to give s.o. advice.

association [asɔsjasjɔ̃] *nf* 1. association (of words, ideas) 2. (*a*) society, company; association (*b*) *Com:* partnership.

associé, -ée [asɔsje] *n* (*a*) *Com:* partner (*b*) associate.

associer [asɔsje] *v* (*pr sub & impf* n. associions) 1. *vtr* to associate, unite, join; **a. des idées**, to associate ideas 2. **s'a.** (*a*) **s'a. à qch**, to share in, participate in, join in, sth; **s'a. à un crime**, to be a party to a crime (*b*) **s'a. à, avec, qn**, (*a*) to enter into partnership with s.o. (*b*) to join forces with s.o.

assoiffé [aswafe] *a* thirsty; thirsting for.

assolement [asɔlmã] *nm* rotation (of crops).

assoler [asɔle] *vtr* to rotate (crops).

assombrir [asɔ̃brir] *vtr* **1.** (*a*) to darken, obscure; **ciel assombri**, overcast sky (*b*) to cast a gloom over (s.o., sth); **visage assombri**, gloomy face **2.** (*a*) to darken; to cloud over (*b*) to become gloomy.

assommer [asɔme] *vtr* **1.** (*a*) to fell (an ox); to brain (s.o.), to club (s.o.) to death (*b*) to knock (s.o.) out, to stun (s.o.) **2.** F: to bore (s.o.) (to death). **assommant** *a* F: boring, tedious, deadly dull.

Assomption [asɔ̃psjɔ̃] *nf Ecc:* (**fête de**) **l'A.**, (feast of) the Assumption.

assonance [asɔnɑ̃s] *nf* assonance.

assortiment [asɔrtimɑ̃] *nm* **1.** match(ing) (of colours) **2.** (*a*) assortment, collection; range (*b*) set (of tools).

assortir [asɔrtir] *v* (**j'assortis, n. assortissons**) **1.** *vtr.* to match (colours); **a. son style à la matière**, to suit one's style to the subject **2.** **s'a.**, to match; to harmonize; to go well together. **assorti** *a* **1.** matched, paired; **pull avec jupe assortie**, jumper with matching skirt **2.** assorted, mixed (sweets); **fromages assortis**, assortment of cheeses **3.** **bien, mal, a.**, well, badly, stocked (shop).

assoupi [asupi] *a* **1.** dozing **2.** dormant.

assoupir [asupir] *vtr* **1.** (*a*) to make (s.o.) drowsy, to send (s.o.) to sleep (*b*) to calm (pain), to lull (the senses) **2.** **s'a.**, to drop off to sleep; to doze off; to grow sleepy; (*of pain*) to die down. **assoupissant** *a* soporific.

assoupissement [asupismɑ̃] *nm* **1.** calming, lulling **2.** drowsiness.

assouplir [asuplir] **1.** *vtr* (*a*) to make supple (*b*) to ease (regulations) **2.** **s'a.**, to become supple; **s'a. les muscles**, to limber up.

assouplissement [asuplismɑ̃] *nm* suppling; easing (of regulations); **exercises d'a.**, limbering up exercises.

assourdir [asurdir] *vtr* **1.** to make (s.o.) deaf; to deafen **2.** (*a*) to deaden, muffle (sound) (*b*) to soften, tone down (colour). **assourdissant** *a* deafening.

assouvir [asuvir] *vtr* to appease, to satisfy (hunger).

assouvissement [asuvismɑ̃] *nm* satisfaction, appeasement.

assujetti, -ie [asyʒeti] *a* subject (à, to).

assujettir [asyʒetir] *vtr* **1.** to subdue, subjugate (province); to subject (s.o. to a rule) **2.** **s'a.**, to submit to (sth). **assujettissant** *a* exacting, demanding.

assujettissement [asyʒetismɑ̃] *nm* (*a*) subjection, subjugation; subservience (*b*) obligation.

assumer [asyme] *vtr* to assume; to take upon oneself; to take up (one's duties); to hold (post); to fulfill (role).

assurance [asyrɑ̃s] *nf* **1.** (*a*) assurance; (self) confidence; self assurance (*b*) *Corr:* **veuillez agréer l'a. de mes sentiments distingués** = yours faithfully **2.** security, pledge, assurance **3.** (*a*) making sure, safe (*b*) *Com:* insurance, assurance; **police d'a.**, insurance policy; **a. sur la vie, a.-vie**, life insurance; **a. aux tiers, tous risques**, third-party, comprehensive, insurance (*c*) **assurances sociales**, national insurance.

assuré [asyre] **1.** *a* firm, sure (step); assured, confident (air); certain (cure); safe (retreat); **voix mal assurée**, unsteady voice **2.** *n Ins:* policy holder. **assurément** *adv* assuredly, certainly.

assurer [asyre] *vtr* **1.** (*a*) to make (sth) firm; to fix, secure (sth) (*b*) to ensure (result); to consolidate (one's fortune); **un service régulier est assuré entre Paris et Londres**, there is a regular service between Paris and London **2. a. qn de son affection**, to assure s.o. of one's affection **3.** *Ins:* to insure; **se faire a. sur la vie**, to take out a life insurance (policy). **s'assurer** *vpr* **1. s'a. sur ses pieds**, to steady oneself on one's feet **2. s'a. qch, de qch**, to make sure, certain, of sth; **s'a. que**, to make sure that; **je vais m'en a.**, I'll go and check **3.** to take out an insurance (**contre**, against).

assureur [asyrœr] *nm Ins:* (*a*) insurer (*b*) underwriter.

astérisque [asterisk] *nm* asterisk.

asthme [asm] *nm* asthma. **asthmatique** *a & n* asthmatic.

asticot [astiko] *nm* maggot; *Fish:* gentle.

asticoter [astikɔte] *vtr F:* to tease, to needle.

astiquer [astike] *vtr* to polish.

astre [astr] *nm* star. **astral, -aux** *a* astral (body).

astreindre [astrɛ̃dr] *vtr* (*conj like* PEINDRE) to compel, oblige; to tie down (**à un devoir**, to a duty); **s'a. à un régime sévère**, to keep to a strict diet. **astreignant** *a* exacting, demanding.

astreinte [astrɛ̃t] *nf* obligation.

astringent [astrɛ̃ʒɑ̃] *a & nm* astringent.

astrologie [astrɔlɔʒi] *nf* astrology. **astrologique** *a* astrological.

astrologue [astrɔlɔg] *nm* astrologer.

astronaute [astronot] *n* astronaut.

astronautique [astronotik] *nf* astronautics.

astronome [astronɔm] *nm* astronomer.

astronomie [astronɔmi] *nf* astronomy. **astronomique** *a* astronomical.

astuce [astys] *nf* **1.** astuteness; cleverness **2.** shrewdness **3.** witticism, pun. **astucieux, -euse** *a* astute, shrewd, clever. **astucieusement** *adv* astutely, shrewdly, cleverly.

asymétrique [asimetrik] *a* asymmetrical.

atavisme [atavism] *nm* atavism. **atavique** *a* atavistic.

atelier [atəlje] *nm* **1.** (*a*) (work)shop, workroom (*b*) studio (of artist) **2.** staff (of shop, workroom).

atermoiements [atɛrmwamɑ̃] *nmpl* procrastination.

atermoyer [atɛrmwaje] *vi* to procrastinate.

athée [ate] **1.** *a* atheistic **2.** *n* atheist.

athéisme [ateism] *nm* atheism.

Athènes [atɛn] *Prnf Geog:* Athens.

athlète [atlɛt] *n* athlete. **athlétique** *a* athletic.

athlétisme [atletism] *nm* athletics.

atlantique [atlɑ̃tik] *a* **l'océan A.**, *nm* **l'A.**, the Atlantic (Ocean).

atlas [atlɑs] *nm* atlas.

atmosphère [atmɔsfɛr] *nf* atmosphere. **atmosphérique** *a* atmospheric.

atoll [atɔl] *nm Geog:* atoll.

atome [atom] *nm Ph:* atom. **atomique** *a* atomic; atom(ic) bomb.

atomiseur [atɔmizœr] *nm* atomizer, spray.

atomiste [atɔmist] *nm* atomic physicist.

atone [atɔn] *a* **1.** dull, vacant (look) **2.** *Ling:* unstressed.

atout [atu] *nm Cards:* trump.

âtre [ɑtɽ] *nm* hearth.

atrocité [atrɔsite] *nf* 1. atrociousness 2. atrocity; **dire des atrocités**, to say dreadful things. **atroce** *a* atrocious, heinous, abominable (crime); excruciating, agonizing (pain); awful, ghastly. **atrocement** *adv* atrociously; horribly, terribly.

atrophie [atrɔfi] *nf* atrophy.

atrophier [atrɔfje] *vtr* to atrophy; **s'a.**, to atrophy; to waste (away).

attabler (s') [satable] *vpr* to sit down to table.

attachant [ataʃɑ̃] *a* engaging (personality).

attache [ataʃ] *nf* 1. fastening; tying up; *Nau:* port d'a., home port 2. (*a*) tie, fastener, fastening; head rope (of horse); leash (of dog); **mettre un cheval à l'a.**, to tether a horse (*b*) **attaches**, close ties, links, connections (*c*) *Anat:* **a. de la main, du pied**, wrist joint, ankle joint.

attachement [ataʃmɑ̃] *nm* attachment, affection.

attacher [ataʃe] 1. *vtr* (*a*) to attach; to fasten, bind; to tie (up); to do up; to tether (horse); **a. avec une corde**, to rope (together); **a. avec des épingles**, to pin (on, together) (*b*) **a. de l'importance à qch**, to attach importance to sth 2. *vi* (*of food*) to catch, stick. **s'attacher** *vpr* 1. to attach oneself, to cling, to stick (à, to); to be fastened, tied (à, on, to); to fasten (à, on) 2. **s'a. à qn**, to become attached to, fond of, s.o. **attaché** 1. *a* (*a*) fastened, tied up (*b*) **être a. à qn**, to be attached to s.o. 2. *nm Dipl: etc:* attaché.

attaque [atak] *nf* (*a*) attack, assault, onslaught; **passer à l'a.**, to take the offensive; **a. aérienne**, air raid (*b*) **être d'a.**, to be on top form; **il est toujours d'a.**, he is still going strong (*c*) *Med:* attack (of gout); bout (of fever); **a. d'épilepsie**, epileptic fit; **a. d'apoplexie**, stroke.

attaquer [atake] *vtr* 1. (*a*) to attack, to assault (*b*) to attack, criticize; *Jur:* **a. qn en justice**, to bring an action against s.o. 2. (*a*) to tackle (subject); to tuck into (a meal) (*b*) *Mus:* to strike up 3. **s'a. à qn**, to attack s.o.; **s'a. à un problème**, to grapple with a problem.

attarder [atarde] *vtr* 1. to keep, make (s.o.) late; to delay (s.o.) 2. **s'a.**, to be delayed (*b*) to stay (too) late (*c*) to linger; to lag behind; to dawdle. **attardé** *a* (*a*) late (*b*) behind the times (*c*) backward (child).

atteindre [atɛ̃dɽ] *v* (*conj like* PEINDRE) 1. *vtr* (*a*) to reach; to overtake; to attain; **a. qn**, to catch s.o. up, to catch up with s.o.; **comment puis-je vous a.?** how can I get in touch with you? **a. son but**, to achieve one's end (*b*) **a. le but**, to hit the target; **atteint d'une maladie**, suffering from an illness; **le poumon est atteint**, the lung is affected 2. *v ind tr* **a. à qch**, to reach, attain, achieve, sth.

atteinte [atɛ̃t] *nf* 1. reach; **hors d'a.**, out of reach 2. blow; **porter a. à**, to undermine; **porter a. aux intérêts de qn**, to interfere with s.o.'s interests.

attelage [atlaʒ] *nm* 1. harnessing 2. (*a*) team; yoke (of oxen) (*b*) carriage (and horses) 3. *Rail:* coupling.

atteler [atle] *vtr* (**j'attelle, n. attelons**) 1. to harness (horses); to yoke (oxen) 2. **a. une voiture**, to put horses to a carriage 3. *Rail:* **a. des wagons**, to couple (up) wagons 4. **s'a. à une tâche**, to settle down to a job.

attelle [atɛl] *nf Med:* splint.

attenant [atnɑ̃] *a* **a. à**, adjoining.

attendre [atɑ̃dɽ] *vtr* 1. (*a*) to wait for, to await (s.o., sth); **le déjeuner nous attend**, lunch is ready; **l'avenir nous attend**, the future lies before us; **faire a. qn**, to keep s.o. waiting; **se faire a.**, to be late; **attendez voir**, (i) wait and see (ii) let me see (*b*) *vi* **a. jusqu'à demain**, to wait until tomorrow; **attendez!** wait a bit! just a minute! **sans plus a.**, without waiting any longer; **il ne perdra rien pour a.**, he's got it coming to him (*c*) **en attendant**, meanwhile, in the meantime; **en attendant de vous voir**, until I see you (*d*) *F:* **a. après qn, qch**, to wait for, to want, s.o., sth 2. to expect; **elle attend un bébé**, she's expecting a baby. 3. **s'a. à qch**, to expect sth; **il faut s'a. à tout**, one must be ready for anything; **je m'y attendais**, I expected as much.

attendrir [atɑ̃driʀ] *vtr* 1. to tenderize (meat) 2. to soften (s.o.'s heart); to move, to touch (s.o.) 3. **s'a. sur qch**, to be moved by sth; **il s'attendrit facilement**, he is very emotional. **attendri** *a* fond, compassionate. **attendrissant** *a* touching, moving.

attendrissement [atɑ̃drismɑ̃] *nm* pity, emotion.

attendu [atɑ̃dy] 1. *a* expected; long-awaited 2. *prep* given, considering (the circumstances); *conj phr* **a. que + *ind***, considering that; seeing that.

attentat [atɑ̃ta] *nm* murder, assassination, attempt; **a. à la bombe**, bomb attack; **a. aux droits**, violation of rights; **a. aux mœurs**, indecent behaviour.

attente [atɑ̃t] *nf* 1. wait(ing); **salle d'a.**, waiting room 2. expectation(s), anticipation; **être dans l'a. de qch**, to be waiting for sth; **dans l'a. de vos nouvelles**, looking forward to hearing from you.

attenter [atɑ̃te] *v ind tr* to make an attempt (**à la vie de qn**, on s.o.'s life); to violate (s.o.'s rights).

attention [atɑ̃sjɔ̃] *nf* (*a*) attention, care; **attirer l'a.**, to catch the eye; to be conspicuous; **ne faire aucune a. à qch**, to take no notice of sth; **(faites) a.!** take care! look out! watch it! **a. à la peinture**, wet paint; **a. à la marche**, mind the step; **faites a. de ne pas vous perdre**, be careful not to get lost; **faire a. à ce que**, to make sure that (*b*) **être plein d'attention(s) pour qn**, to be full of attention for s.o. (*c*) **il a eu l'a. de m'avertir**, he was considerate enough to warn me. **attentif, -ive** *a* attentive (à, to); careful; **être a.**, to pay attention. **attentionné** *a* thoughtful, considerate. **attentivement** *adv* attentively, carefully.

atténuation [atenuasjɔ̃] *nf* attenuation, lessening, reducing; toning down; mitigation (of punishment); extenuation (of crime).

atténuer [atenue] *vtr* 1. (*a*) to attenuate, lessen, reduce; to tone down; to subdue (light): to mitigate (punishment); **a. une chute**, to break a fall (*b*) *Phot:* to reduce (negative) 2. to extenuate (offence) 3. **s'a.**, to lessen; to diminish; to fade. **atténuant** *a Jur:* extenuating (circumstances).

atterrer [atere] *vtr* to overwhelm, astound; to shatter. **atterré** *a* stunned; **d'un air a.**, with a look of consternation.

atterrir [aterir] *vi Av:* to land, to touch down; *F:* **a. en prison**, to land up in prison.

atterrissage [aterisaʒ] *nm Av:* landing, touchdown.

attestation [atɛstasjɔ̃] *nf* attestation; certificate.

attester [atɛste] *vtr* 1. **a. qch**, to attest, to certify, sth; to testify to sth 2. **a. qn (de qch)**, to call s.o. to witness (to sth).

attiédir [atjedir] *vtr* 1. to make tepid, lukewarm (to cool (s.o.'s passions) 2. **s'a.**, to grow lukewarm, to cool (off, down).

attifer [atife] F: *vtr* 1. to dress (s.o.) up, to deck (s.o.) out 2. **s'a.**, to get oneself up (**de**, in).

attirail [atiraj] *nm* (*a*) gear (*b*) F: paraphernalia.

attirance [atirɑ̃s] *nf* attraction (**pour**, for).

attirer [atire] *vtr* 1. (*a*) (*of magnet*) to attract, draw; **a. qn dans un coin**, to draw s.o. into a corner (*b*) **a. qch à, sur, qn**, to bring sth on s.o.; **a. l'attention**, to attract attention; **s'a. des reproches**, to come in for criticism; **s'a. des ennuis**, to cause trouble for oneself 2. **a. qn dans un piège**, to lure s.o. into a trap. **attirant** *a* attractive.

attiser [atize] *vtr* to poke (up) (fire); *Fig:* to stir up (trouble).

attitré [atitre] *a* regular, appointed, recognized.

attitude [atityd] *nf* 1. attitude, posture; bearing 2. behaviour.

attraction [atraksjɔ̃] *nf* 1. (*a*) attraction (of magnet) (*b*) attractiveness (of person) 2. **attractions**, attractions; sideshows.

attrait [atrɛ] *nm* (*a*) attraction, lure; appeal; **dépourvu d'a.**, unattractive (*b*) **attraits**, charms (of woman).

attrapade [atrapad] *nf* F: ticking off.

attrape [atrap] *nf* F: trick, hoax.

attrape-nigaud [atrapnigo] *nm* F: trick; con; *pl* attrape-nigaud(s).

attraper [atrape] *vtr* 1. (*a*) to catch; to trap, (en)snare (*b*) **a. qn**, to trick, cheat, s.o. 2. (*a*) to catch (ball, thief, bus) (*b*) **une pierre l'a attrapé au front**, a stone hit him on the forehead (*c*) **a. froid**, to catch cold, to catch a chill (*d*) F: **a. qn**, to tell s.o. off; **tu vas te faire a.**, you'll get it in the neck.

attrayant [atrɛjɑ̃] *a* attractive, engaging, alluring; **peu a.**, unattractive.

attribuer [atribɥe] *vtr* 1. to assign, to allocate (**à**, to); to confer (**à**, on); to award; *Th:* **a. un rôle à qn**, to cast s.o. for a part 2. to attribute, ascribe (fact); to impute (crime); to attach (importance) (**à**, to); **tableau attribué à X**, painting believed to be by X 3. **s'a. qch**, to lay claim to sth. **attribuable** *a* attributable (**à**, to).

attribut [atriby] *nm* attribute.

attribution [atribysjɔ̃] *nf* assigning, attribution; allocation; awarding; *Th:* casting.

attrister [atriste] *vtr* 1. to sadden, grieve 2. **s'a. de qch**, to be saddened by sth.

attroupement [atrupmɑ̃] *nm* crowd; mob.

attrouper (s') [satrupe] *vpr* to gather together, to form a crowd.

au [o] *see* **à** *and* **le**.

aubade [obad] *nf* dawn serenade.

aubaine [obɛn] *nf* windfall, godsend.

aube¹ [ob] *nf* 1. dawn, daybreak; *Fig:* dawn 2. *Ecc:* alb.

aube² *nf* (*a*) paddle, blade (of wheel); **roue à aubes**, paddle wheel (*b*) vane (of turbine).

aubépine [obepin] *nf* hawthorn, may (tree).

auberge [obɛrʒ] *nf* inn; **a. de jeunesse**, youth hostel.

aubergine [obɛrʒin] 1. *nf Bot:* aubergine, eggplant 2. *a inv* aubergine-coloured.

aubergiste [obɛrʒist] *n* innkeeper.

aucun, -une [okœ̃, -yn] 1. *pron* (*a*) anyone, any (*b*) (*with negation expressed or understood, with* **ne** *or* **sans**) (i) no one, nobody (ii) none, not any; **je n'ai a. soupçon**, I haven't the slightest suspicion; **a. des deux ne viendra**, neither of them will come (iii) not one (*c*) *pl Lit:* **d'aucuns**, some, some people 2. *a* (*a*) any (*b*) (*with implied negation*) **avez-vous aucune intention de le faire?** do you have any intention of doing it? (*c*) **sans a. bénéfice**, without any profit; **le fait n'a aucune importance**, the fact is of no importance.

aucunement *adv* (*with negation expressed or understood*) in no way, not at all; by no means; not in the slightest; not in the least; **je ne le connais a.**, I don't know him at all.

audace [odas] *nf* 1. audacity; boldness, daring 2. impudence; audacity; **vous avez l'a. de me dire cela!** you have the nerve to tell me that! **audacieux, -euse** *a* 1. audacious; bold, daring 2. impudent; brazen (lie). **audacieusement** *adv* audaciously, boldly, daringly; impudently.

au-dedans, au-dehors, au-delà *see* **dedans, dehors, delà.**

au-dessous [odsu] *adv* 1. (*a*) below, under (it); underneath; **les locataires a.-d.**, the tenants below (*b*) **les enfants âgés de sept ans et a.-d.**, children of seven years and under 2. *prep phr* **a.-d. de** (*a*) below, under; **a.-d. du genou**, below the knee; **15 degrés a.-d. de zéro**, 15 degrees below zero; **il est a.-d. de lui de se plaindre**, it is beneath him to complain (*b*) **épouser qn a.-d. de soi**, to marry beneath one (*c*) **a.-d. de cinq ans**, under five (years of age); **a.-d. de 30 kilos**, less than 30 kilos (*d*) **son travail est a.-d. de mon attente**, his work falls short of what I expected; **c'est a.-d. de tout**, it's worse than useless.

au-dessus [odsy] *adv* 1. (*a*) above (it) (*b*) **le salon est a.-d.**, the drawing room is upstairs (*c*) **mille francs et a.-d.**, a thousand francs and upwards 2. *prep phr* **a.-d. de** (*a*) above; **a.-d. de la porte**, above, over, the door; **les avions volent a.-d. de nos têtes**, the planes are flying overhead; **2 degrés a.-d. de zéro**, 2 degrees above zero; **a.-d. de 50 francs**, more than 50 francs (*b*) **a.-d. de cinq ans**, over five (years of age) (*c*) **vivre a.-d. de ses moyens**, to live beyond one's means.

au-devant [odvɑ̃] *used only in such phrases as* **aller, courir, a.-d.** 1. *adv* **quand il y a un problème, je vais a.-d.**, when there's a problem, I anticipate it 2. *prep phr* (*a*) **aller a.-d. de qn**, to go to meet s.o.; **aller a.-d. des désirs de qn**, to anticipate s.o.'s wishes (*b*) **aller a.-d. du danger**, to court danger.

audibilité [odibilite] *nf* audibility. **audible** *a* audible.

audience [odjɑ̃s] *nf* (*a*) hearing; (*of king*) **tenir une a.**, to hold an audience (*b*) *Jur:* hearing (by the court); sitting, session, court; **l'a. est reprise**, the case is resumed.

audio-visuel, -elle [odjovizɥɛl] 1. *a* audio-visual 2. *nm* audio-visual methods.

audit [odi] *see* **ledit.**

auditeur, -trice [oditœr, -tris] *n* listener; **les auditeurs**, the audience. **auditif, -ive** *a* auditory.

audition [odisjɔ̃] *nf* **1.** hearing (of sounds) **2.** (*a*) (piano) recital (*b*) audition (of singer); *Jur:* **a. des témoins,** hearing, examination, of the witnesses.

auditionner [odisjɔne] *vtr & i* to audition.

auditoire [oditwar] *nm* **1.** auditorium **2.** audience.

auditorium [oditɔrjɔm] *nm* (broadcasting) studio.

auge [oʒ] *nf* trough.

augmentation [ɔgmɑ̃tasjɔ̃] *nf* increase; rise, *NAm:* raise (in wages).

augmenter [ɔgmɑ̃te] **1.** *vtr* to increase, augment; **édition augmentée,** enlarged edition; **a. qn,** to raise s.o.'s (i) salary (ii) rent; **a. les prix,** to raise prices **2.** *vi* to increase; **le crime augmente,** crime is on the increase; **la valeur a augmenté de 10%,** the value has gone up 10%.

augure [ogyr] *nm* augury, omen; **de bon a.,** auspicious; **oiseau de mauvais a.,** a bird of ill omen.

augurer [ogyre] *vtr* to augur, forecast, foresee.

auguste [ogyst] *a* august, majestic.

aujourd'hui [oʒurdɥi] *adv* today; **cela ne se pratique plus a.,** this is not done nowadays; **d'a. en huit,** today week; **il y a a. huit jours,** a week ago today.

au(l)ne [on] *nm Bot:* alder.

aumône [omon] *nf* alms; **vivre d'a.,** to live on charity.

aumônier [omonje] *nm* chaplain.

auparavant [oparavɑ̃] *adv* before(hand), previously; first; **comme a.,** as before.

auprès [oprɛ] *adv* **1.** close to, near to **2.** *prep phr* **a. de** (*a*) close to; by, close by, beside, near; **il a toujours qn a. de lui,** he always has s.o. with him; **ambassadeur a. de,** ambassador to (*b*) **agir a. de qn,** to use one's influence with s.o.; **être bien a. de qn,** to be in favour with s.o. (*c*) compared with.

auquel [okɛl] *see* **lequel.**

auréole [oreɔl] *nf* (*a*) halo (of saint) (*b*) halo (of moon) (*c*) (stain) ring.

auréoler [oreɔle] *vtr* to exalt, to glorify.

auriculaire [orikylɛr] **1.** *a* auricular (confession) **2.** *nm* the little finger.

Aurigny [oriɲi] *Prnm Geog:* Alderney.

aurore [orɔr] *nf* (*a*) dawn, daybreak; break of day (*b*) **a. boréale,** northern lights.

auscultation [oskyltasjɔ̃] *nf Med:* auscultation.

ausculter [oskylte] *vtr Med:* to sound (patient).

auspices [ɔspis] *nmpl* auspices; **sous de mauvais a.,** inauspiciously.

aussi [osi] **1.** *adv* (*a*) (in comparisons) as; **il est a. grand que son frère,** he is as tall as his brother; **c'est tout a. bon,** it's just as good (*b*) so; **après avoir attendu a. longtemps,** after waiting for such a long time; **il est a. travailleur que vous,** he is as hardworking as you (*c*) (i) also, too; **gardez a. celui-là,** keep this one as well (ii) so; **j'ai froid—moi a.,** I'm cold—so am I (*d*) *conj phr* **a. bien que,** as well as; **lui a. bien qu'elle,** both him and her (*e*) **a. bizarre qu'il soit,** strange as it may be **2.** *conj* (*a*) therefore, consequently, so (*b*) *F:* **a., c'est ta faute,** after all, it's your fault (*c*) **a. bien,** moreover, for that matter, besides.

aussitôt [osito] (*a*) *adv* immediately, directly, at once; **a. dit, a. fait,** no sooner said than done; **a. après son retour,** as soon as he left (*b*) *conj phr* **a. que** + *ind,* as soon as (*c*) **a.** + *pp* **a. l'argent reçu je**

vous paierai, as soon as I get the money I'll pay you.

austérité [osterite] *nf* austerity. **austère** *a* austere (life); severe (style). **austèrement** *adv* austerely.

austral, -als, -aux [ɔstral, -o] *a* southern.

Australie [ɔstrali] *Prnf* Australia. **australien, -ienne** *a & n* Australian.

autant [otɑ̃] *adv* **1.** (*a*) as much, so much; as many, so many; **a. vous l'aimez, a. il vous hait,** he hates you as much as you love him; **tout a.,** quite as much, quite as many; **encore a., une fois a.,** twice as much; as much again; **j'aimerais a. aller au cinéma,** I would just as soon go to the cinema; **il se leva, j'en fis a.,** he got up and I did the same (*b*) (i) **le travail est fini ou a. vaut,** the work is as good as finished; **a. vaut rester ici,** we may as well stay here (ii) **a. dire mille francs,** we might as well say a thousand francs; **la bataille était a. dire perdue,** the battle was as good as lost; **a. le faire tout de suite,** better do it right away **2. a. que** (*a*) as much as, as many as; **j'en sais a. que toi,** your guess is as good as mine; *F:* **a. ça qu'autre chose,** it's all the same to me (*b*) as far as, as near as; (pour) **a. que je sache,** as far as I know **3. a. de,** as much, as many, so much, so many; **ils ont a. d'amis que vous,** they have as many friends as you; **c'est a. de gagné,** that's so much gained; so much to the good **4. d'a.,** accordingly; **d'a. plus,** especially, particularly; **d'a. moins (que),** all the less (because); **c'est d'a. plus facile que,** it's all the easier as **5. pour a.,** for all that.

autel [otɛl] *nm* altar; **conduire qn à l'a.,** (i) to give s.o. away (in marriage) (ii) to marry s.o.

auteur [otœr] *nm* **1.** author, originator; perpetrator (of crime); promoter (of scheme); **a. d'un accident,** party at fault in an accident; person who caused an accident **2.** author, writer; composer (of music); painter; **droit d'a.,** copyright; **droits d'a.,** royalties.

authenticité [otɑ̃tisite] *nf* authenticity. **authentique** *a* authentic. **authentiquement** *adv* authentically.

authentification [otɑ̃tifikasjɔ̃] *nf* authentification.

authentifier [otɑ̃tifje] *vtr* to authenticate.

auto [oto] *nf F: O:* (motor) car.

auto- [oto] *pref* **1.** auto- **2.** self- **3.** motor.

auto-allumage [otoalymaʒ] *nm Aut:* pre-ignition.

autobiographie [otobjografi] *nf* autobiography. **autobiographique** *a* autobiographic(al).

autobus [otobys] *nm* bus.

autocar [otokar] *nm* coach; *NAm:* bus.

autoclave [otoklav] *nm* autoclave, digester.

autocollant [otokɔlɑ̃] **1.** *a* self-adhesive **2.** *nm* sticker.

autocratie [otokrasi] *nf* autocracy. **autocrate 1.** *nm* autocrat **2.** *a* autocratic. **autocratique** *a* autocratic.

autocritique [otokritik] *nf* self criticism.

autocuiseur [otokɥizœr] *nm Cu:* pressure cooker.

autodafé [otodafe] *nm Hist:* auto-da-fé.

autodéfence [otodefɑ̃s] *nf* self-defence.

autodidacte [otodidakt] *a* self-taught.

autodrome [otodrom] *nm* motor-racing track.

auto-école [otoekɔl] *nf* school of motoring, driving school; *pl* **auto-écoles.**

autographe [otograf] *a & n* autograph.

automate [otomat] *nm* automaton.

automation [otomasjɔ̃] *nf* automation.

automatique [otomatik] **1.** *a* automatic **2.** *nm* (*a*) *Tp:* = subscriber trunk dialling, STD (*b*) automatic (pistol). **automatiquement** *adv* automatically.

automatisation [otomatizasjɔ̃] *nf* automation.

automitrailleuse [otomitrajøz] *nf* armoured car.

automne [otɔn] *nm* autumn; *NAm:* fall. **automnal, -aux** *a* autumnal.

automobile [otomɔbil] **1.** *a* (*a*) self-propelling; **voiture a.**, a motor vehicle; **canot a.**, motor boat (*b*) automobile (club); car, motor (insurance) **2.** *nf* (motor) car, *NAm:* automobile.

automobilisme [otomɔbilism] *nm* motoring.

automobiliste [otomɔbilist] *n* motorist.

autonomie [otonɔmi] *nf* autonomy; self-government. **autonome** *a* autonomous, self-governing.

autonomiste [otonɔmist] *n* autonomist.

autopsie [otopsi] *nf* autopsy; post-mortem (examination).

autopsier [otopsje] *vtr* to perform an autopsy on.

autorail [otoraj] *nm* railcar.

autorisation [otorizasjɔ̃] *nf* authorization; permission; permit.

autoriser [otorize] *vtr* **1. a. qn à faire qch**, to authorize s.o. to do sth **2.** to sanction (an action) **3.** to allow, permit, give permission (to do sth) **4. s'a. de qch**, to use sth as an excuse for doing sth. **autorisé** *a* authorized; authoritative (source); permitted, allowed.

autoritarism [otoritarism] *nm* authoritarianism.

autorité [otorite] *nf* **1.** (*a*) authority; **il n'a pas d'a. sur ses élèves**, he can't keep order; **faire qch d'a.**, to take it upon oneself to do sth (*b*) **avoir de l'a. sur qn**, to have influence over s.o.; **faire a. en qch**, to be an authority on sth; **sa parole a de l'a.**, his word carries weight **2. les autorités**, the authorities. **autoritaire 1.** *a* authoritative **2.** *n* authoritarian. **autoritairement** *adv* authoritatively.

autoroute [otorut] *nf* motorway, *NAm:* superhighway. **autoroutier, -ière** *a* motorway (network).

auto-stop [otostɔp] *nm* hitch-hiking; **faire de l'a.-s.**, to hitch-hike; to hitch a lift.

auto-stoppeur, -euse [otostɔpœr, -øz] *n* hitch-hiker.

autour [otur] **1.** *adv* round, around (it, them) **2.** *prep phr* **a. de**, round, about; **assis a. de la table**, sitting round the table; **tourner a. du pot**, to beat about the bush.

autre [otr] *a & pron* **1.** (*a*) other, further; **un a. jour**, another day; **une a. fois**, later; another time; **un jour ou l'a.**, one day; **d'autres vous diront que**, others will tell you that; **l'a. monde**, the next world; **sans faire d'a. observation**, without making any further remark (*b*) **nous autres Anglais**, we English; **vous autres**, all of you (*c*) **cela peut arriver d'un jour à l'a.**, it may happen any day; **je le vois de temps à a.**, I see him now and then (*d*) **l'un et l'a.**, both; **les uns et les autres**, (i) all (and sundry) (ii) both parties (*e*) **l'un ou l'a.**, either; **ni l'un ni l'a.**, neither (*f*) **l'un dit ceci, l'a. dit cela**, one says this and the other says that; **les uns par ci les autres par là**, some one way, some

another (*g*) **l'un l'a.**, each other, one another; **elles se moquent les unes des autres**, they make fun of each other (*h*) **l'un dans l'a.**, **on se fait mille francs**, one thing with another, on an average, we earn a thousand francs **2.** (*a*) other, different; **c'est un a. homme**, he's a new man; **une tout a. femme**, quite a different woman; **j'ai d'autres idées**, I have different ideas; *F:* **j'en ai vu bien d'autres**, that's nothing, I've been through worse than that (*b*) someone, something, else; **adressez-vous à quelqu'un d'a.**, ask someone else; **personne d'a. ne l'a vu**, no one else, nobody else, saw him; **que pouvait-il faire d'a.!** what else could he do? **(dites cela) à d'autres!** nonsense! tell that to the marines! (*c*) *indef pron m* (i) **a. chose**, something else; something different; **as-tu a. chose à faire?** have you anything else to do? (ii) **a. chose, and another thing; not only that, but; c'est tout a. chose!** that's quite a different matter!

autrefois [otrəfwa] *adv* formerly; in the past; once; **c'était l'usage a.**, it was the custom in former times; **sa vie d'a.**, his past life.

autrement [otrəmɑ̃] *adv* **1.** (*a*) otherwise; differently; in another way; **nous ne pouvons faire a.**, we have no alternative; **a. dit**, in other words (*b*) **c'est bien a. sérieux**, that is far more serious **2.** or (else); **venez demain, a. il sera trop tard**, come tomorrow, otherwise it will be too late.

Autriche [otriʃ] *Prnf Geog:* Austria. **autrichien, -ienne** *a & n* Austrian.

autruche [otryʃ] *nf Orn:* ostrich; **faire l'a.**, to bury one's head in the sand.

autrui [otrɥi] *pron indef* others; other people.

auvent [ovɑ̃] *nm* (*a*) open shed (*b*) porch roof (*c*) canopy.

aux [o] *see* **à** and **le**.

auxiliaire [ɔksiljɛr] **1.** *a* auxiliary (verb, troops); **bureau a.**, sub-office **2.** *n* (*a*) auxiliary (*b*) helper, assistant (*c*) *nmpl* auxiliaries.

auxquels, -elles [okɛl] *see* **lequel**.

avachir (s') [savaʃir] *vpr* (i) to become flabby, sloppy (ii) to let oneself go. **avachi** *a* flabby, sloppy; (*of pers*) slack; **a. sur la table**, slumped over the table.

aval¹ [aval] *nm Fin:* endorsement (on bill); **donneur d'a.**, guarantor (of bill).

aval² *nm* **1.** downstream side; **en a.**, downstream **2.** down slope.

avalanche [avalɑ̃ʃ] *nf* avalanche; flood (of compliments).

avaler [avale] *vtr* to swallow (down); **ça s'avale facilement**, it goes down easily; **a. son repas**, to bolt one's meal; **a. la fumée**, to inhale; **a. un roman**, to race through a novel; **celle-là est dure à a.**, that's a tall story; **j'ai avalé de travers**, it went down the wrong way; **a. ses mots**, to mumble; *F:* **tu as avalé ta langue?** have you lost your tongue?

avaliser [avalize] *vtr Com:* to endorse, to guarantee (bill).

avance [avɑ̃s] *nf* **1.** advance, lead; **avoir de l'a. sur qn**, to be ahead of s.o.; to have a lead over s.o.; **ma montre prend de l'a.**, my watch gains; **arriver avec cinq minutes d'a.**, to arrive with five minutes to spare; **le train a 10 minutes d'a.**, the train is 10 minutes early; *ICE:* **mettre de l'a. à l'allumage**, to advance the ignition **2.** projection; **balcon qui forme a.,** balcony that juts out **3.** (a) **a.** (**de fonds**), advance, loan (b) pl **faire des avances à qn,** to make advances to s.o. **4.** adv phr (a) **d'a., à l'a.,** in advance; beforehand; **jouir d'a. de qch,** to look forward to sth; **payé d'a.,** prepaid; **c'est décidé à l'a.,** it's a foregone conclusion (b) **l'horloge est en a.,** the clock is fast; **nous sommes en a.,** we are early; Sch: **il est en a. sur sa classe,** he is ahead of his class.

avancé [avɑ̃se] a (a) **position avancée,** advanced position (b) **opinions avancées,** progressive ideas (c) **élève a.,** pupil ahead of his class (d) **à une heure avancée de la nuit,** late in the night; **à une heure peu avancée,** quite early on; **l'été est bien a.,** summer is nearly over (e) **a. en âge,** getting on (in years); **à un âge a.,** late in life (f) F: **vous voilà bien a.!** a lot of good that's done you!

avancée [avɑ̃se] nf prominence, projection.

avancement [avɑ̃smɑ̃] nm **1.** promotion **2.** advance(ment), progress.

avancer [avɑ̃se] v (n. **avançons**) **1.** vtr (a) to advance, put forward; to hold out, stretch out (one's hand); to pull forward (a chair) (b) **a. une proposition,** to put forward a proposal (c) to make (sth) earlier; to hasten (sth) on; to bring forward (meeting); **a. une montre,** to wind on a watch (d) **a. de l'argent à qn,** to advance money to s.o. (e) to promote, to further (science, s.o.'s interests); **à quoi cela vous avancera-t-il?** what good will that do you? **2.** vi (a) to advance; to move, to step, to go, forward; **a. d'un pas,** to take one step forward; **faire a. qn,** to make s.o. move on; **a. en âge,** to be getting on in years; **ma montre avance d'une minute par jour,** my watch gains a minute a day (b) to progress; to make headway (c) to be ahead of time; **l'horloge avance,** the clock is fast; **j'avance de 5 minutes,** I'm, my watch is, 5 minutes fast (d) to jut out, to project **3.** **s'a.** (a) to move forward, to advance; **s'a. vers qch,** to head towards sth (b) to progress (c) to jut out.

avant [avɑ̃] **1.** prep before; **a. J.-C., B.C.; a. une heure,** (i) by one o'clock (ii) within an hour; **pas a. de nombreuses années,** not for many years to come; (surtout et) **a. tout,** first of all; above all; **a. toute chose,** in the first place **2.** (a) prep phr **a. de** + inf; **je vous reverrai a. de partir,** I shall see you before I leave (b) conj phr **a. que** + sub; **je vous reverrai a. que vous (ne) partiez,** I shall see you again before you leave; **a. que vous ayez fini,** by the time you have finished (c) **pas a. de, que,** not before, not until **3.** (= **auparavant**) adv (a) **il était arrivé quelques mois a.,** he had arrived some months before (b) **réfléchis a.,** think first (c) **il l'a mentionné a.,** he mentioned it earlier **4.** adv (a) far, deep; **pénétrer très a. dans les terres,** to penetrate far inland (b) far, late; **bien a. dans la nuit,** far into the night **5.** adv phr **en a. de** partir, far into the night **5.** adv phr **en a.,** in front; before; forward; Mil: **en a., marche!** quick march! **envoyer qn en a.,** to send s.o. ahead; **regarder en a.,** to look ahead; **faire deux pas en a.,** to move forward two steps; Nau: **en a. à toute vitesse,** full steam ahead; prep phr **il est en a. de son siècle,** he's ahead of his time; **en a. de nous,** ahead of us **6.** (in adj relation to n) (a) fore, forward, front; Aut: **traction a.,** front-wheel drive (b) **d'a.,** previous; **la nuit d'a.,** the night before **7.** nm (a) Nau: bow; **le**

logement de l'équipage est à l'a., the crew's quarters are forward; **aller de l'a.,** to go ahead (b) front; nose (of aircraft) (c) Fb: forward.

avantage [avɑ̃taʒ] nm **1.** advantage; **a. pécuniaire,** monetary gain; **a. en nature,** perquisite; **c'est un a. précieux,** it's a great asset; **tirer a. de qch.,** to turn sth to advantage **2.** (a) Sp: **donner l'a. à qn,** to give s.o. odds (b) Ten: (advantage) (c) **avoir l'a. sur qn,** to have the advantage of s.o.; **il y a a. à** + inf, it is best to + inf.

avantager [avɑ̃taʒe] vtr (n. **avantageons**) (a) to favour; to give an advantage (b) **l'uniforme l'avantage,** he looks well in uniform. **avantageux, -euse** a **1.** advantageous, favourable; **cet article est très a.,** this article is very good value; **prix a.,** reasonable price **2.** conceited. **avantageusement** adv advantageously.

NOTE. In all the following compounds AVANT is inv, the noun or adj takes the plural.

avant-bras [avɑ̃bra] nm inv forearm.

avant-coureur [avɑ̃kurœr] **1.** nm forerunner **2.** am premonitory (symptom).

avant-dernier, -ière [avɑ̃dɛrnje, -jɛr] a & n last but one.

avant-garde [avɑ̃gard] nf (a) advance(d) guard (b) avant-garde; **théâtre d'a.-g.,** avant-garde theatre.

avant-goût [avɑ̃gu] nm foretaste.

avant-guerre [avɑ̃gɛr] nm or f pre-war period; **d'a.-g.,** pre-war.

avant-hier [avɑ̃tjɛr] adv the day before yesterday.

avant-plan [avɑ̃plɑ̃] nm foreground.

avant-port [avɑ̃pɔr] nm Nau: outer harbour.

avant-poste [avɑ̃pɔst] nm Mil: outpost.

avant-première [avɑ̃prəmjɛr] nf Cin: etc: preview.

avant-propos [avɑ̃prɔpo] nm inv preface, foreword.

avant-scène [avɑ̃sɛn] nf Th: (a) apron (b) stage box.

avant-train [avɑ̃trɛ̃] nm forequarters (of animal).

avant-veille [avɑ̃vɛj] nf two days before.

avare [avar] **1.** a miserly, avaricious; **être a. de son argent,** to be mean with one's money **2.** n miser.

avarice [avaris] nf avarice. **avaricieux, -ieuse** a avaricious, miserly.

avarie [avari] nf damage.

avarier (s') [savarje] vpr to deteriorate, to go bad.

avatar [avatar] nm (a) Hindu Rel: avatar (b) transformation (c) misadventure.

avec [avɛk] **1.** prep (a) with; **déjeuner a. qn,** to have lunch with s.o.; **le public est a. nous,** the public is behind us (b) Com: **et a. cela, madame?** anything else, madam? (c) **se lever a. le soleil,** to get up at sunrise **2.** (a) (suggesting cause) **on n'y arrive plus a. cette vie chère,** it is becoming impossible to manage with the cost of living as high as it is (b) **je l'aime a. tous ses défauts,** I love him in spite of all his faults **3.** **a. courage,** with courage; courageously **4.** **cela viendra a. le temps,** that will come in time; **a. l'aide de qn,** with s.o.'s help **5.** **se marier a. qn,** to marry s.o.; **lier conversation a. qn,** to get into conversation with s.o. **6.** **être d'accord a. qn,** to agree with s.o. **7.** **en comparaison a. qch,** in comparison with sth **8.** **se battre a. qn,** to fight s.o. **9.** **être sévère a. qn,** to be hard on s.o. **10.** **a. elle on ne sait jamais,** you never can tell with her 11. *F*: **elle est grande et a. ça mince,** she's tall and slim as well; **a. ça qu'il n'a pas triché!** don't say he didn't cheat! 12. *prep phr* **d'a.,** from; **séparer le bon d'a. le mauvais,** to separate the good from the bad 13. *adv* with it, with them.

aven [avɛn] *nm Geol*: swallowhole.

avenant [avnɑ̃] 1. *a* (*a*) pleasing, prepossessing (*b*) **à l'a.,** in keeping (**de,** with) 2. *nm Ins*: additional clause.

avènement [avɛnmɑ̃] *nm* (*a*) advent, coming (of Christ) (*b*) accession (to the throne).

avenir [avnir] *nm* future; **jeune homme d'un grand a.,** youth of great promise; **homme d'a.,** man with a future; **dans l'a.,** at some future date; **à l'a.,** in future.

Avent [avɑ̃] *nm Ecc*: Advent.

aventure [avɑ̃tyr] *nf* 1. (*a*) adventure; **a. effrayante,** terrifying experience; **a.** (love) affair 2. chance, luck, venture; **tenter l'a.,** to try one's luck; **errer à l'a.,** to wander about aimlessly; **par a., d'a.,** by chance.

aventurer [avɑ̃tyre] *vtr* 1. to venture (a remark); to risk (one's life) 2. **s'a.,** to venture (**dans,** into); to take risks. **aventuré** *a* risky. **aventureux, -euse** *a* adventurous; risky. **aventureusement** *adv* adventurously; riskily.

aventurier, -ière [avɑ̃tyrje, -jɛr] *n* adventurer, adventuress.

avenue [avny] *nf* avenue; drive.

avérer (s') [savere] *vpr* to be proved correct; to be confirmed; **il s'avère que,** it turns out that; **s'a. faux,** to be proved false.

averse [avers] *nf* (sudden) shower; downpour.

aversion [avɛrsjɔ̃] *nf* aversion (**pour,** to, for); dislike (**pour,** to, for, of); **avoir qch en a.,** to loathe sth.

avertir [avɛrtir] *vtr* **a. qn de qch,** to warn, notify, inform, s.o. of sth; **je vous en avertis!** I give you fair warning! **averti** *a* informed, aware; well-informed; experienced.

avertissement [avɛrtismɑ̃] *nm* (*a*) warning (*b*) reprimand; *Sp*: warning (*c*) **a. (au lecteur),** foreword.

avertisseur, -euse [avɛrtisœr, -øz] 1. *a* warning 2. *nm* warning signal; *Aut*: horn; **a. d'incendie,** fire alarm.

aveu, -eux [avø] *nm* avowal, confession; **de l'a. de tout le monde,** by common consent.

aveugle [avœgl] 1. *a* (*a*) blind, sightless; **devenir a.,** to go blind; **a. d'un œil,** blind in one eye (*b*) *n* **un, une, a.,** a blind man, woman; **les aveugles,** the blind 2. blind, unreasoning (hatred); implicit (trust); **être a. aux défauts de qn,** to be blind to s.o.'s faults. **aveuglément** *adv* blindly.

aveuglement [avœgləmɑ̃] *nm* blinding; blindness.

aveugle-né, -née [avœgləne] *a & n* (man, woman) blind from birth.

aveugler [avœgle] *vtr* (*a*) to blind (s.o.) (*b*) to dazzle, blind (*c*) **s'a. sur les défauts de qn,** to turn a blind eye to s.o.'s faults. **aveuglant** *a* blinding, dazzling.

aveuglette (à l') [alavœglɛt] *adv phr* blindly; **avancer à l'a.,** to grope one's way along.

aviateur, -trice [avjatœr, -tris] *n* aviator; airman, -woman.

aviation [avjasjɔ̃] *nf* aviation; flying; air travel; **compagnie d'a.,** airline; **terrain d'a.,** airfield; **usine d'a.,** aircraft factory.

avicole [avikɔl] *a* poultry (farm, farming).

aviculteur, -trice [avikyltœr, -tris] *n* poultry farmer.

aviculture [avikyltyr] *nf* poultry farming.

avidité [avidite] *nf* avidity; eagerness; greed(iness); **avec a.,** (i) greedily (ii) eagerly. **avide** *a* avid, eager, greedy; **a. de qch,** (i) greedy for sth (ii) eager for sth. **avidement** *adv* avidly, eagerly, greedily.

avilir [avilir] *vtr* 1. to degrade 2. **s'a.,** to demean oneself. **avilissant** *a* degrading.

avilissement [avilismɑ̃] *nm* degradation.

avion [avjɔ̃] *nm* aircraft, aeroplane, *F*: plane; *NAm*: airplane; **aller à Paris en a.,** to fly to Paris; **par a.,** (by) air mail; **a. de chasse,** fighter; **a. de ligne,** airliner.

avion-taxi [avjɔ̃taksi] *nm* charter plane; air taxi; *pl* **avions-taxis.**

aviron [avirɔ̃] *nm* 1. oar 2. rowing; **faire de l'a.,** to row.

avis [avi] *nm* 1. (*a*) opinion, judgment; **ils ne sont pas du même a.,** they disagree; **à, selon, mon a.,** in my opinion; **de l'a. de tous,** in the opinion of all; **je suis de votre a.,** I agree with you; **j'ai changé d'a.,** I've changed my mind; **je suis d'a. qu'il vienne,** in my opinion he ought to come (*b*) advice, counsel; **demander l'a. de qn,** to ask s.o.'s advice 2. notice, notification, announcement; **a. (au public),** notice (to the public); **a. au lecteur,** foreword (to book); **jusqu'à nouvel a.,** until further notice; **sauf a. contraire,** unless otherwise informed; *Com*: **a. de crédit,** credit advice.

aviser [avize] 1. *vtr* (*a*) to perceive, to catch sight of (s.o.) (*b*) **a. qn de qch,** to inform, to advise, s.o. of sth 2. *vi* **a. à qch,** to decide what to do about (a situation); **il est temps d'a.,** it is time to make a decision 3. **s'a. de qch,** to think of sth; **s'a. de faire qch,** to take it into one's head to do sth. **avisé** *a* prudent, sensible; **bien a.,** well advised.

avitaminose [avitaminoz] *nf* vitamin deficiency.

aviver [avive] *vtr* 1. to revive, brighten (colours); to irritate (wound); to stir up, excite (passion); to revive, stir up (fire); to sharpen (appetite) 2. **s'a.,** to brighten up, to revive; to be stirred up.

avocat¹, -ate [avoka, -at] *n* 1. barrister; counsel; *NAm*: attorney; **consulter son a.,** to consult one's lawyer; **a. général,** assistant public prosecutor (in court of appeal); **être reçu a.,** to be called to the bar 2. advocate; **a. du diable,** devil's advocate.

avocat² *nm Bot*: avocado (pear).

avoine [avwan] *nf* oat(s); **farine d'a.,** oatmeal.

avoir¹ [avwar] *vtr* (*prp* **ayant**; *pp* **eu**; *pr ind* **j'ai, tu as, il a, n. avons, v. avez, ils ont**; *pr sub* **j'aie, il ait**; *impf* **j'avais**; *fu* **j'aurai**; *avoir is the aux of all transitive and many intransitive vbs*) 1. (*a*) to have, possess; to run (a car); to keep (chickens); to hold (opinion); **il a encore son père,** his father is still alive (*b*) **qu'est-ce que vous avez là?** what have you got there? **elle avait une robe bleue,** she was wearing a blue dress (*c*) **a. les yeux bleus,** to have blue eyes; **a. qch en horreur,** to have a horror of sth (*d*) **a. dix ans,** to be ten (years old) 2. (*a*) to get, obtain (sth); **j'ai eu mon train,** I caught my train (*b*) **a. un enfant,** to have a child 3. *F*: to get the better of (s.o.); **on vous a eu!** you've been had! 4. *Lit:* = **faire,** *etc, chiefly in ph*;

il eut un mouvement brusque, he made a sudden movement 5. to feel ill; qu'avez-vous? qu'est-ce que vous avez? what's the matter with you? a. la grippe, to have flu 6. en a. (a) nous en avons pour deux heures, it will take us two hours; j'en ai assez, I've had enough; I'm sick of it (b) en a. à, contre, qn, to have a grudge against s.o. 7. (a) a. qch à faire, to have sth to do; vous n'avez pas à vous inquiéter, you have no need to worry (b) je n'ai que faire de cela, I don't need that 8. impers y a. (a) combien y a-t-il de blessés? how many wounded are there? il n'y en a qu'un, there's only one; il y en a un qui va être surpris, someone is in for a surprise; il n'y a pas de quoi, please! don't mention it (b) qu'est-ce qu'il y a? what's the matter? (c) il y a deux ans, two years ago; il y avait six mois que j'attendais, I had been waiting for the last six months (d) combien y a-t-il d'ici à Londres? how far is it (from here) to London? 9. aux use j'ai fini, I've finished; je l'ai vue hier, I saw her yesterday; quand il eut fini de parler, when he had finished speaking; j'aurai bientôt fini; I shall soon have finished.

avoir² nm property; tout mon a., all I possess; Com: doit et a., debit and credit.

avoisiner [avwazine] vtr a. qch, to be near sth, close, adjacent, to sth; to border on sth. avoisinant a neighbouring; nearby.

avortement [avɔrtəmɑ̃] nm 1. (a) a. (spontané), miscarriage (b) a. (provoqué), abortion 2. failure.

avorter [avɔrte] vi 1. to miscarry, to abort; se faire a., to have an abortion 2. le projet a avorté, the plan proved abortive.

avorteur, -euse [avɔrtœr, -øz] n abortionist.

avorton [avɔrtɔ̃] nm puny man; runt; stunted plant.

avoué [avwe] nm Jur: = solicitor, NAm: attorney.

avouer [avwe] vtr 1. to acknowledge; s'a. coupable, to admit one's guilt; s'a. vaincu, to acknowledge defeat 2. to confess, to own up to (a fault); ceci me surprend, je l'avoue, I must say this surprises me.

avril [avril] nm April; en a., in April; au mois d'a., in the month of April; le sept a., (on) April the seventh; le premier a. (i) the first of April (ii) April Fool's day; poisson d'a.! April fool!

axe [aks] nm 1. axis (of ellipse); a. d'une route, centre line of a road; a. de circulation, major route 2. axle, spindle. axial, -aux a axial (line).

axer [akse] vtr to centre; être axé sur, autour de, to centre on.

axiome [aksjom] nm axiom. axiomatique a axiomatic.

ayant [ɛjɑ̃] 1. see avoir. 2. nm Jur: a. droit, rightful claimant or owner; interested party; beneficiary; pl ayants droit.

azalée [azale] nf Bot: azalea.

azimut [azimyt] nm azimuth; F: dans tous les azimuts, all over the place.

azotate [azɔtat] nm Ch: nitrate.

azote [azɔt] nm Ch: nitrogen. azoté a nitrogenous.

aztèque [aztɛk] a & n Ethn: Aztec.

azur [azyr] nm azure, blue; Geog: la Côte d'A., the (French) Riviera.

azurer [azyre] vtr to tinge with blue. azuré a azure, (sky-)blue.

azyme [azim] a unleavened (bread).

B

B, b [be] *nm* (the letter) B, b.

baba [baba] 1. *nm Cu:* baba 2. *a inv F:* dumbfounded.

babillage [babijaʒ] *nm* babble, prattle, twitter(ing), chatter(ing).

babiller [babije] *vi* to prattle; to chatter; to babble; to twitter.

babines [babin] *nfpl Z: Fig:* chops.

babiole [babjɔl] *nf* knick-knack, trinket.

bâbord [babɔr] *nm Nau:* port (side).

babouche [babuʃ] *nf* Turkish slipper.

babouin [babwɛ̃] *nm* baboon.

bac[1] [bak] *nm* 1. ferry(boat); pontoon; **b. à voitures,** car ferry; **passer le b.,** to cross the ferry 2. tank, vat; container (for food); **b. à glace,** ice tray.

bac[2] *nm F:* = **baccalauréat.**

baccalauréat [bakalɔrea] *nm* = General Certificate of Education, GCE A levels.

bâche [baʃ] *nf* canvas cover; **b. goudronnée,** tarpaulin.

bachelier, -ière [baʃəlje, -jɛr] *n Sch:* one who has passed the baccalauréat.

bâcher [baʃe] *vtr* to cover with a tarpaulin.

bachot [baʃo] *nm F:* = **baccalauréat; boîte à b.,** crammer.

bachotage [baʃɔtaʒ] *nm Sch: F:* cramming.

bachoter [baʃɔte] *vi Sch: F:* to cram.

bacille [basil] *nm Biol:* bacillus, germ.

bâcler [bakle] *vtr F:* to scamp, to botch (work); **travail bâclé,** slapdash work.

bactérie [bakteri] *nf* bacterium, *pl* -ia. **bactérien, -ienne** *a* bacterial.

bactériologie [bakterjɔlɔʒi] *nf* bacteriology. **bactériologique** *a* bacteriological.

bactériologiste [bakterjɔlɔʒist] *n* bacteriologist.

badaud, -aude [bado, -od] *n* stroller, idler.

baderne [badɛrn] *nf Pej:* **vieille b.,** old fogey.

badigeon [badiʒɔ̃] *nm* distemper; **b. à la chaux,** whitewash.

badigeonner [badiʒɔne] *vtr* to distemper, to whitewash (a wall).

badinage [badinaʒ] *nm* joking, banter.

badine [badin] *nf* cane, switch.

badiner [badine] *vi* to jest, to joke.

baffe [baf] *nf P:* slap, clout.

bafouer [bafwe] *vtr* to ridicule, jeer at (s.o.).

bafouiller [bafuje] *vtr & i F:* (*a*) to splutter, stammer (*b*) to talk nonsense.

bafouilleur, -euse [bafujœr, -øz] *n* stammerer, splutterer.

bâfrer [bafre] *F:* 1. *vi* to guzzle 2. *vtr* to wolf one's food.

bagage [bagaʒ] *nm* 1. **plier b.,** (i) to pack up one's bags, *Mil:* one's kit (ii) *F:* to clear out 2 *esp pl* luggage; **bagages à main,** hand luggage; **voyager avec peu de b.,** to travel light.

bagagiste [bagaʒist] *nm* luggage handler.

bagarre [bagar] *nf* fight, brawl; quarrel.

bagarrer [bagare] *vi F:* 1. to fight (**pour,** for) 2. **se b.,** to fight, to brawl; to quarrel. **bagarreur, -euse** *a & n* quarrelsome, violent (person); *n* brawler.

bagatelle [bagatɛl] *nf* trifle; **acheter qch pour une b.,** to buy sth for a song.

bagnard [baɲar] *nm* convict.

bagne [baɲ] *nm* (*a*) *A:* convict prison (*b*) **condamné à 5 ans de b.,** sentenced to 5 years' penal servitude; *F:* **quel b.!** what a grind!

bagnole [baɲɔl] *nf F:* car; **vieille b.,** old banger.

bagou(t) [bagu] *nm F:* glibness (of tongue); **avoir du b.,** to have the gift of the gab.

bague [bag] *nf* (*a*) (jewelled) ring (*b*) band (*c*) *MecE:* **b. d'assemblage,** collar.

baguenauder [bagnode] *vi & pr F:* to mooch about, to loaf around.

baguette [bagɛt] *nf* rod, wand, stick; (conductor's) baton; long thin loaf of French bread; **baguettes,** chopsticks; **b. magique,** magic wand; **baguettes de tambour,** drumsticks.

bah [ba] *int* bah! pooh!

bahut [bay] *nm* (*a*) chest (*b*) sideboard (*c*) *P:* school.

bai [bɛ] *a* bay (horse); **b. châtain,** chestnut bay.

baie[1] [bɛ] *nf Geog:* bay.

baie[2] *nf Arch:* bay, opening; **fenêtre en b.,** bay window.

baie[3] *nf Bot:* berry.

baignade [bɛɲad] *nf* 1. bathe 2. bathing place.

baigner [bɛɲe] 1. *vtr* (*a*) to bathe; to steep; **baigné de sueur,** dripping with sweat (*b*) (*of sea*) to wash (coast); (*of river*) to water (a district) (*c*) to bath (baby) 2. *vi* to soak, steep (in sth) 3. **se b.** (*a*) to take a bath (*b*) to bathe; to have a bathe, a swim.

baigneur, -euse [bɛɲœr, -øz] (*a*) *n* bather (*b*) *nm* (*toy*) baby doll.

baignoire [bɛɲwar] *nf* 1. bath; (bath)tub 2. *Th:* ground-floor box.

bail, *pl* **baux** [baj, bo] *nm* lease (to tenant); **prendre à b.,** to take a lease on (a house); **donner à b.,** to lease (out).

bâillement [bajmɑ̃] *nm* yawn(ing).

bâiller [baje] *vi* 1. to yawn; **b. à se décrocher la mâchoire,** to yawn one's head off 2. (*of seams*) to gape; (*of door*) to be ajar.

bailleur, -eresse [bajœr, bajrɛs] *n* 1. lessor 2. **b. de fonds,** financial backer.

bâillon [bajɔ̃] *nm* gag.

bâillonner [bajɔne] *vtr* to gag.

bain [bɛ̃] *nm* 1. (*a*) bath; **b. de mousse,** bubble bath; **prendre un b. de soleil,** to sunbathe; **salle de bain(s),** bathroom; *F:* **être dans le b.,** to be in the know; **ils sont dans le même b.,** they're in the same boat (*b*) bath(tub) (*c*) **bains publics,** public baths (*d*) *pl* watering place; spa (*e*) swim; bathing; **bains de mer** (i) sea bathing (ii) seaside resort 2. *Ch: Phot:* bath.

bain-marie [bɛmari] *nm Cu:* double saucepan; double boiler; *pl bains-marie.*

baïonnette [bajɔnɛt] *nf* bayonet.

baisemain [bɛzmɛ̃] *nm* hand kissing.

baiser¹ [beze] *vtr* (*a*) to kiss (s.o.) (*b*) *P:* **se faire b.,** to be had.

baiser² *nm* kiss.

baisse [bɛs] *nf* 1. subsidence (of water); ebb (of tide) 2. fall, drop (in prices).

baisser [bese] 1. *vtr* to lower (curtain, blind); to open, let down (car window); **b. la tête,** to hang one's head; **donner tête baissée dans un piège,** to fall headlong into a trap; **b. les yeux,** to look down; **b. la voix,** to lower one's voice; **b. la radio,** to turn down the radio; **b. les prix,** to lower, reduce, prices 2. *vi* (*a*) to be on the decline; (*of tide*) to ebb; **la température baisse,** it's getting colder; **le jour baisse,** it's getting dark; **sa vue baisse,** his sight is failing; **le malade baisse,** the patient is sinking; **il a baissé dans mon estime,** he has gone down in my estimation (*b*) (*of prices*) to fall, to come down 3. **se b.,** to stoop; to bend down.

bajoues [baʒu] *nfpl Z:* chops; (*of pers*) flabby cheeks.

bal, *pl* **bals** [bal] *nm* 1. ball, dance; **b. masqué,** fancy dress, masked, ball 2. ballroom, dance hall.

balade [balad] *nf F:* walk, stroll; **b. en voiture,** run in the car.

balader [balade] *F:* 1. *vtr* to take (s.o., dog) for a walk; to drag (sth) 2. **se b.,** to go for a walk; *vi & pr* to stroll, saunter; **se b. en voiture,** to go for a drive.

baladeuse [baladøz] *nf* (*a*) trailer (of car) (*b*) inspection lamp, portable lamp.

balafre [balafr] *nf* 1. slash, gash (*esp* in face) 2. scar.

balafrer [balafre] *vtr* 1. to gash, slash (*esp* the face) 2. to scar.

balai [balɛ] *nm* 1. broom; (long-handled) brush; **b. mécanique,** carpet sweeper; **manche à b.,** broom stick; **passer le b.,** to give the floor a sweep 2. *Aut:* blade (of windscreen wiper).

balance [balɑ̃s] *nf* 1. (*a*) balance; (pair of) scales; weighing machine; **faire pencher la b.,** to tip the scales (*b*) *Astr:* **la B.,** Libra 2. **b. d'un compte,** balancing of an account; **faire la b.,** to make up the balance (sheet) 3. *Fish:* shrimp net.

balancement [balɑ̃smɑ̃] *nm* 1. swing(ing), sway-(ing), rocking 2. balance.

balancer [balɑ̃se] *v* (**n. balançons**) 1. *vtr* (*a*) to balance; **b. un compte,** to balance an account; **b. le pour et le contre,** to weigh up the pros and cons (*b*) to swing (one's arms); to rock (baby); to sway (one's hips) (*c*) *F:* to fling, to chuck (stones); to throw (sth) out; to fire (employee); to give (sth) up 2. *vi* (*a*) *Lit:* to waver (*b*) to swing 3. **se b.** (*a*) to swing; to sway, rock; **se b. sur sa chaise,** to rock backwards and forwards on one's chair (*b*) to see-saw, to swing (*c*) *P:* **je m'en balance,** I couldn't care less!

balancier [balɑ̃sje] *nm* 1. balancing pole (of tight-rope walker) 2. pendulum.

balançoire [balɑ̃swar] *nf* (*a*) see-saw (*b*) (child's) swing.

balayage [balɛjaʒ] *nm* 1. sweeping 2. *Rad: Elcs:* scanning.

balayer [balɛje] *vtr* (**je balaie, je balaye**) 1. to sweep (out) (room); to sweep up (dirt); **le vent a balayé les nuages,** the wind has chased away the clouds 2. *Rad: Elcs:* to scan.

balayette [balɛjɛt] *nf* (hand) brush.

balayeur, -euse [balɛjœr, -øz] *n* (road) sweeper.

balbutiement [balbysimɑ̃] *nm* stuttering, stammering; mumbling.

balbutier [balbysje] (*pr sub & impf* **n. balbutiions**) *vtr & i* to stutter, to stammer; to mumble (sth).

balcon [balkɔ̃] *nm* 1. balcony 2. *Th:* **premier, deuxième, b.,** dress circle, upper circle.

baldaquin [baldakɛ̃] *nm* canopy (of bed).

Bâle [bɑl] *Prnf Geog:* Basel, Basle.

baléare [balear] *a & n Geog:* **les (îles) Baléares,** the Balearic Islands.

baleine [balɛn] *nf* 1. whale; **blanc de b.,** spermaceti 2. (whale)bone (of corset); *pl* ribs (of umbrella).

baleinier, -ière 1. *a* whaling (industry) 2. *nm* whaler 3. *nf* whaleboat.

balisage [balizaʒ] *nm* (*a*) *Nau:* buoys; *Av: etc:* beacons (*b*) beaconing; marking out.

balise [baliz] *nf* (*a*) *Nau:* beacon; **b. flottante,** buoy (*b*) *Av:* (approach) light; beacon.

baliser [balize] *vtr* to mark out (with beacons).

balistique [balistik] 1. *a* ballistic 2. *nf* ballistics.

baliverne [balivern] *nf* nonsense; **dire des balivernes,** to talk nonsense.

ballade [balad] *nf* ballad(e).

ballant [balɑ̃] 1. *a* swinging, dangling (arms) 2. *nm* (*a*) swing, roll, sway (*b*) slack (in rope).

ballast [balast] *nm* 1. *CivE: etc:* ballast (of road, railway track) 2. *Nau:* ballast tank (of submarine).

balle¹ [bal] *nf* 1. ball; **b. de tennis,** tennis ball; **jouer à la b.,** to play ball; *Ten:* **faire des balles,** to have a knock-up; **b. de match,** match point 2. bullet; shot; **b. perdue,** stray bullet 3. *Com:* bale (of cotton).

balle² *nf* husk, chaff (of wheat).

baller [bale] *vi* to hang (down); to be slack; **laisser b. ses bras,** to let one's arms dangle.

ballerine [balrin] *nf* 1. *Th:* ballerina, ballet-dancer 2. ballet shoe.

ballet [balɛ] *nm Th:* ballet.

ballon [balɔ̃] *nm* 1. (*a*) balloon; **b. dirigeable,** airship; **b. d'enfant,** toy balloon (*b*) *Med:* (oxygen) bottle 2. ball; **b. de football, de rugby,** football, rugby ball 3. (*a*) *Ch:* balloon flask (*b*) (**verre**) **b.,** brandy glass, balloon glass.

ballonnement [balɔnmɑ̃] *nm* distending (of stomach).

ballonner [balɔne] *vtr* to distend (stomach).

ballot [balo] *nm* 1. bundle 2. *F:* nit(wit), clot; **a c'est b.,** it's crazy.

ballottage [balɔtaʒ] *nm Pol:* failure to gain absolute majority; **scrutin de b.,** second ballot.

ballotter [balɔte] 1. *vtr* to toss, to shake (about); **b. qn (de l'un à l'autre),** to drive s.o. from pillar to post 2. *vi* to roll around; to swing to and fro; (*of ship*) to toss.

bal(l)uchon [balyʃɔ̃] *nm* bundle (of clothes); **faire son b.,** to pack up.

balnéaire [balneɛr] *a* **station b.,** (i) seaside resort (ii) spa.

balourdise [balurdiz] *nf* (*a*) clumsiness (*b*) stupid blunder. **balourd, -ourde** *a* & *n* awkward, clumsy (person).

baltique [baltik] *a* & *Prnf Geog:* **la (mer) B.**, the Baltic (Sea). **balte** *a* Baltic.

balustrade [balystrad] *nf* 1. balustrade 2. (hand)-rail; railing.

balustre [balystr̩] *nm* (*a*) baluster (*b*) *pl* banister.

bambin, -ine [bãbɛ̃, -in] *n F:* little child.

bambocher [bãbɔʃe] *vi F:* to live it up.

bambou [bãbu] *nm Bot:* bamboo (cane).

ban [bã] *nm* 1. (*a*) *A:* proclamation (*b*) (round of) applause; **un b. pour M. le maire!** = three cheers for the mayor! (*c*) *pl* banns (of marriage) 2. **être au b. de la société**, to be outlawed by society 3. **le b. et l'arrière-b.**, the whole lot.

banal, -als [banal] *a* commonplace, ordinary, trite; **pas b.**, unusual, out of the ordinary.

banaliser [banalize] *vtr* to make (sth) commonplace; **voiture banalisée**, unmarked police car.

banalité [banalite] *nf* 1. banality, triteness 2. *pl* small talk; clichés, platitudes.

banane [banan] *nf* banana.

bananier [bananje] *nm* 1. banana tree 2. banana boat.

banc [bã] *nm* 1. bench, seat; **b. d'église**, pew; **b. des ministres** = government front bench; *Jur:* **b. des accusés**, dock; **b. des témoins**, witness box 2. (work)-bench; **b. d'essai**, test bed; testing ground 3. (*a*) layer (of rock) (*b*) **b. de sable**, sandbank; **b. de roches**, reef; **b. d'huîtres**, oyster bed 4. shoal (of fish).

bancaire [bãkɛr] *a* banking; **chèque b.**, bank cheque.

bancal, -als [bãkal] *a* (*a*) (*of pers*) limping (*b*) wobbly, rickety (furniture).

bandage [bãdaʒ] *nm* (*a*) bandaging (*b*) bandage; **b. herniaire**, truss.

bande[1] [bãd] *nf* 1. (*a*) band, strip (of cloth, paper, metal); stretch (of land); stripe (on material); wrapper (round newspaper); **b. dessinée**, strip cartoon, comic strip (*b*) (surgical) bandage; (adhesive) tape (*c*) (reel of) (cine)film; **b. sonore**, sound track; **b. magnétique**, magnetic tape (*d*) *Bill:* cushion; **par la b.**, in a roundabout way (*e*) *WTel:* **b. de fréquences**, frequency band (*f*) (ammunition) belt (of machine gun) 2. *Nau:* keel, list(ing); **donner de la b.**, to list.

bande[2] *nf* 1. band, party, troop; **faire b. à part**, to keep oneself to oneself; **toute la b.**, the whole crowd; **b. d'imbéciles!** bunch of idiots! 2. flock (of birds); pack (of wolves); pride (of lions).

bandeau, -eaux [bãdo] *nm* 1. headband 2. bandage (on head); **mettre un b. à qn**, to blindfold s.o.

bandelettes [bãdlɛt] *nfpl* bandages, wrappings (of mummies).

bander [bãde] *vtr* (*a*) to bandage, bind (up) (wound); **b. les yeux à qn**, to blindfold s.o. (*b*) to stretch, to tighten; **b. un arc**, (i) to bend (ii) to string, a bow.

banderole [bãdrɔl] *nf* banderole, streamer.

bandit [bãdi] *nm* (*a*) bandit; brigand, highwayman (*b*) crook, swindler.

bandoulière [bãduljɛr] *nf* shoulderstrap; **porter qch en b.**, to carry sth across one's shoulder.

banjo [bãʒo] *nm* banjo.

banlieue [bãljø] *nf* suburbs; commuter belt; **de b.**, suburban; commuter.

banlieusard, -arde [bãljøzar, -ard] *n* suburbanite, commuter.

banni, -e [bani] *n* exile, outlaw.

bannière [banjɛr] *nf* banner.

bannir [banir] *vtr* to banish; to exile; to outlaw.

banissement [banismã] *nm* banishment.

banque [bãk] *nf* 1. (*a*) bank (*b*) banking (*c*) *Med:* **b. du sang**, blood bank 2. *Cards:* bank; **faire sauter la b.**, to break the bank.

banqueroute [bãkrut] *nf* bankruptcy; **faire b.**, to go bankrupt.

banquet [bãkɛ] *nm* banquet, feast.

banquette [bãkɛt] *nf* bench, seat; *Th:* **jouer devant les banquettes**, to play to empty benches.

banquier [bãkje] *nm Fin: Cards:* banker.

banquise [bãkiz] *nf* ice floe, ice pack.

baptême [batɛm] *nm* 1. baptism, christening; **recevoir le b.**, to be baptised; **nom de b.**, Christian name 2. blessing (of bell); naming (of ship); **b. de l'air**, first flight.

baptiser [batize] *vtr* (*a*) to baptize; to christen (s.o., ship); to bless (bell) (*b*) to name, to nickname; to dub. **baptismal, -aux** *a* baptismal.

baptiste [batist] *a* & *n Ecc:* Baptist.

baquet [bakɛ] *nm* tub, bucket.

bar [bar] *nm* 1. bar 2. *Ich:* bass.

baragouin [baragwɛ̃] *nm* gibberish.

baragouiner [baragwine] *vtr* & *i F:* (*a*) to speak a language badly; **b. l'anglais**, to speak broken English (*b*) to talk gibberish.

baraque [barak] *nf* (*a*) hut, shack, shed (*b*) *F:* hole, dump (*c*) stall (at fair).

baraquement [barakmã] *nm usu pl* shacks; *Mil:* hutted camp.

baratin [baratɛ̃] *nm F:* (*a*) chatter; (sales) patter (*b*) smooth talk.

baratiner [baratine] *vtr* & *i F:* (*a*) to chatter (*b*) to shoot a line; to make sales talk.

baratineur, -euse [baratinœr, -øz] *n F:* (*a*) gasbag (*b*) smooth talker.

baratte [barat] *nf* churn.

Barbade [barbad] *Prnf Geog:* Barbados.

barbant [barbã] *a F:* boring.

barbare [barbar] 1. *a* (*a*) barbaric (*b*) barbarous 2. *n* barbarian.

barbarie [barbari] *nf* 1. barbarism 2. barbarity, cruelty.

barbarisme [barbarism] *nm Gram:* barbarism.

barbe [barb] *nf* (*a*) beard; **sans b.**, cleanshaven; **b. de 8 jours**, a week's growth; **rire dans sa b.**, to laugh up one's sleeve; **b. à papa**, candy floss (*b*) *F:* **quelle b.!** what a drag! **la b.!** shut up! (*c*) beard (of goat); wattle (of bird); barb (of feather).

barbeau, -eaux [barbo] *nm* cornflower.

Barbe-Bleue [barbəblø] *Prnm* Bluebeard.

barbecue [barbəky] *nm* barbecue.

barbelé [barbəle] *a* barbed; **fil de fer b.**, *nm* **b.**, barbed wire.

barber [barbe] *F:* 1. *vtr* to bore (s.o.) (stiff) 2. **se b.**, to be bored (stiff).

barbiche [barbiʃ] *nf* goatee (beard).

barbier [barbje] *nm A:* & *FrC:* barber.

barbiturique [barbityrik] (*a*) *a* barbituric (*b*) *nm* barbiturate.

barboter [barbɔte] *vi* to paddle, splash (about).

barbouillage [barbujaʒ] *nm* 1. daubing; scrawling, scribbling 2. daub; scrawl, scribble.

barbouiller [barbuje] *vtr* 1. (*a*) to daub; to smear (**de**, with) (*b*) to smear (one's face) 2. to scrawl, to scribble 3. *F:* **avoir le cœur barbouillé**, to feel sick, queasy.

barbouilleur, -euse [barbujer, -øz] *n* dauber; scribbler.

barbu [barby] 1. *a* bearded 2. *nf Ich:* **barbue**, brill.

barda [barda] *nm P:* kit, gear.

barde¹ [bard] *nf Cu:* bard, bacon (put over roast).

barde² *nm* bard, poet.

barder¹ [barde] *vtr* 1. *Hist:* to bard; **bardé de fer**, armour-clad, steel-clad; **bardé de**, stuck all over with 2. *Cu:* to bard (roast).

barder² *v impers F:* **ça va b.!** things are really going to hot up!

barème [barɛm] *nm* (*a*) scale (of salaries) (*b*) (printed) table, schedule (of fares); (price) list.

baril [bari(l)] *nm* barrel, cask, keg.

barillet [barijɛ] *nm* cylinder (of revolver).

barioler [barjɔle] *vtr* to variegate; to paint (sth) in gaudy colours. **bariolé** *a* gaudy; splashed with colour.

bariolure [barjɔlyr] *nf* splashes (of colour).

baromètre [barɔmɛtr] *nm* barometer. **barométrique** *a* barometric.

baron, -onne [barɔ̃, -ɔn] *n* baron, baroness.

baroque [barɔk] *a* odd, strange, weird; baroque (style).

baroud [baru] *nm* **b. d'honneur**, last stand.

barque [bark] *nf* (small) boat.

barrage [baraʒ] *nm* (*a*) barrier, obstruction; **b. routier**, roadblock (*b*) dam, weir (*c*) *Mil:* barrage.

barre [bar] *nf* 1. (*a*) bar, rod (of metal); bar (of chocolate) (*b*) bar, barrier; *Danc:* barre; **b. d'appui**, handrail; *Gym:* **b. fixe**, horizontal bar (*c*) *Nau:* tiller; helm; **homme de b.**, helmsman (*d*) *Jur:* bar (of a lawcourt); **b. des témoins** = witness box; **paraître à la b.**, to appear before the court; **at the bar** 2. (sand)bar (of river); (harbour) boom; **b. d'eau**, (tidal) bore 3. (*a*) line, dash, stroke; **b. d'un t**, cross of a t (*b*) *Mus:* **b. de mesure**, bar (line).

barreau, -eaux [baro] *nm* 1. small bar; rail; rung (of ladder) 2. *Jur:* bar; **être reçu au b.**, to be called to the bar.

barrer [bare] *vtr* 1. (*a*) to bar (door) (*b*) to bar, obstruct; to dam; to block, to close (road) 2. to cross (a t, an A); **b. un chèque**, to cross a cheque; **chèque barré**, crossed cheque 3. to cross out, strike out (word) 4. *Nau:* to steer; to cox 5. *P:* **se b.**, to clear off.

barrette [barɛt] *nf* 1. *Ecc:* biretta 2. (hair) slide.

barreur [barœr] *nm* helmsman; cox; **sans b.**, coxless.

barricade [barikad] *nf* barricade.

barricader [barikade] *vtr* to barricade; **se b.**, (i) to barricade oneself (**dans**, in) (ii) to lock oneself up (**dans sa chambre**, in one's room).

barrière [barjɛr] *nf* barrier; fence; (ticket collector's) gate; gate (of level crossing).

barrique [barik] *nf* large barrel; cask.

barrir [barir] *vi* (*of elephant*) to trumpet.

barrissement [barismɑ̃] *nm* trumpeting (of elephant).

baryton [baritɔ̃] *a & nm* baritone (voice).

baryum [barjɔm] *nm Ch:* barium.

bas, basse [bɑ, bɑs] 1. *a* (*a*) low; **maison basse de toit**, house with a low roof; **b. sur pattes**, short-legged; **en b. âge**, young; **voix basse**, deep voice; **acheter qch à b. prix**, to buy sth cheap; **mer basse**, low tide; **la tête basse**, with one's head down (*b*) mean, base, low (*c*) low(er); *Cu:* **b. morceaux**, cheap cuts (of meat); **les b. quartiers**, the poor quarters (of a town); **ce b. monde**, here below; **au b. mot**, at the lowest estimate 2. *adv* (*a*) low (down); **plus b.**, further down, lower down; **voler b.**, to fly low; **voir plus b.**, see below; **traiter qn plus b. que terre**, to humiliate s.o. (*b*) *F:* **b. les pattes!** hands off! (*c*) (*of animals*) **mettre b.**, to give birth to, to drop (young); **mettre b. les armes**, to lay down one's arms (*d*) **parler (tout) b.**, to (speak in a) whisper 3. *nm* (*a*) lower part (of sth); bottom, foot (of ladder, of page); **b. du dos**, small of the back; **de haut en b.**, from top to bottom (*b*) *adv phr* **en b.**, (down) below; **aller en b.**, to go down(stairs); **les gens d'en b.**, the people below, downstairs; **tomber la tête en b.**, to fall head first; *prep phr* **en b. de**, at the foot of, at the bottom of; **en b. de l'escalier**, downstairs; *adv phr* **à b.**, down; **à b. les dictateurs!** down with dictators! **sauter à b. du lit**, to jump out of bed (*c*) **les hauts et les b.**, the ups and downs (*d*) stocking 4. *nf Mus:* **basse**, bass (part). **bassement** *adv* basely, meanly.

basalte [bazalt] *nm* basalt.

basané [bazane] *a* sunburnt, (sun)tanned; swarthy.

bas-bleu [bablø] *nm* bluestocking; *pl* bas-bleus.

bas-côté [bakote] *nm* 1. (side) aisle (of church) 2. shoulder, side (of road).

bascule [baskyl] *nf* rocker; **(jeu de) b.**, seesaw(ing); **chaise à b.**, rocking chair; **wagon à b.**, tipwagon.

basculer [baskyle] *vtr & i* 1. (*a*) to rock, swing; to seesaw (*b*) to tip (up); **(faire) b. une charrette**, to tip a cart 2. to fall over, to overbalance; topple over.

base [bɑz] *nf* 1. foot, bottom (of mountain); foundation (of building); *Toil:* **b. de maquillage**, foundation cream, makeup base 2. *Mil: etc:* base (of operations); **b. aérienne**, air base; **b. de lancement**, launching site 3. basis, foundation; grounds (for suspicion); **sans b.**, without foundation; **l'anglais de b.**, basic English; **produits à b. d'amidon**, starch products; **boisson à b. de gin**, gin-based drink, gin cocktail 4. radix, root, basis (of logarithm) 5. *Ch:* base.

base-ball [bɛzbol] *nm Sp:* baseball.

baser [bɑze] 1. *vtr* to base, ground, found (opinion) (**sur**, on) 2. **se b. sur qch**, to base one's argument on sth.

bas-fond [bafɔ̃] *nm* 1. low ground, hollow; **les b.-fonds de la société**, the dregs of society 2. shallow, shoal; *pl* bas-fonds.

basilic [bazilik] *nm Bot:* basil.

basilique [bazilik] *nf Arch:* basilica.

basket(-ball) [baskɛt(bol)] *nm Sp:* basketball; **baskets**, basketball shoes.

basketteur, -euse [baskɛtœr, -øz] *n* basketball player.

basque¹ [bask] *a & n Ethn:* Basque. **basquais, -aise** *a* Basque.

basque² *nf* skirt, tail (of jacket).

bas-relief [barəljɛf] *nm* bas relief, low relief; *pl bas-reliefs.*

basse *see* **bas.**

basse-cour [baskur] *nf* (*a*) farmyard (*b*) poultry; *pl basses-cours.*

basse-fosse [basfos] *nf* dungeon; *pl basses-fosses.*

bassesse [basɛs] *nf* 1. baseness, lowness 2. low, mean, contemptible, action.

basset [basɛ] *nm* basset (hound).

bassin [basɛ̃] *nm* 1. basin, bowl, pan 2. (*a*) ornamental lake; pond, pool (*b*) reservoir, tank 3. dock, basin 4. (*a*) *Geol:* basin (*b*) (river) basin (*c*) **b. houiller,** coal basin 5. *Anat:* pelvis.

bassine [basin] *nf* pan; basin; bowl.

bassiner [basine] *vtr* to bathe (wound).

bassiste [basist] *n* (double) bass player.

basson [basɔ̃] *nm Mus:* 1. bassoon 2. bassoonist.

bastingage [bastɛ̃gaʒ] *nm Nau:* (*a*) bulwark, topside (*b*) (hand)rail; **accoudé aux bastingages,** leaning over the rails.

bastion [bastjɔ̃] *nm* bastion.

bas-ventre [bavɑ̃tr̩] *nm* lower abdomen; *pl bas-ventres.*

bât [ba] *nm* pack(saddle); **cheval de b.,** packhorse; *F:* **c'est là que le b. (le) blesse,** that's his weak point.

bataclan [bataklɑ̃] *nm F:* belongings, paraphernalia; **vendez tout le b.!** sell the whole caboodle!

bataille [bataj] *nf* 1. battle, fight; **champ de b.,** battlefield 2. (*a*) **porter son chapeau en b.,** to wear one's hat askew (*b*) **cheveux en b.,** dishevelled hair 3. *Cards:* beggar-my-neighbour.

batailler [bataje] *vi* to fight, battle. **batailleur, -euse** *a* aggressive.

bataillon [batajɔ̃] *nm Mil:* battalion.

bâtard, -arde [batar, -ard] 1. *a & n* (*a*) (enfant) b., bastard (child), illegitimate (child) (*b*) (**chien**) **b.,** mongrel 2. (type of) French loaf.

bâtardise [batardiz] *nf* illegitimacy; bastardy.

bateau, -eaux [bato] *nm* (*a*) boat; vessel; craft; **b. à vapeur,** steamer, steamboat; **b. à voiles,** sailing boat; **b. de sauvetage,** lifeboat; **faire du b. à voiles, à rames,** to go sailing, boating (*b*) entrance to drive (where pavement curves).

bateau-citerne [batositɛrn] *nm* tanker; *pl bateaux-citernes.*

bateau-mouche [batomuʃ] *nm* river boat (in Paris); water bus; *pl bateaux-mouches.*

bateleur, -euse [batlœr, -øz] *n A:* juggler, tumbler.

batelier, -ière [batəlje, -jɛr] *n* boatman, -woman; ferryman, -woman.

bâti [bati] *nm* 1. frame(work), structure, support 2. *Needlew:* tacking, basting.

batifoler [batifɔle] *vi F:* to romp; to lark, to play about.

bâtiment [batimɑ̃] *nm* 1. **le b.,** the building trade 2. building 3. ship, vessel; **b. de guerre,** warship.

bâtir [batir] *vtr* 1. (*a*) to build, to construct; (**se**) **faire b. une maison,** to have a house built; **terrain à b.,** building site (*b*) to build up (a fortune); to develop (theory) (*c*) **homme bien bâti,** well built man 2. *Needlew:* to tack, to baste.

bâtisse [batis] *nf* (large) building.

bâtisseur, -euse [batisœr, -øz] *n* builder.

batiste [batist] *nf Tex:* batiste, cambric.

bâton [batɔ̃] *nm* 1. (*a*) stick, staff, rod; (policeman's) truncheon; rung (of chair); **b. de vieillesse,** support, prop, of old age; **mettre des bâtons dans les roues,** to put a spoke in s.o.'s wheel; to throw a spanner in the works (*b*) **conversation à bâtons rompus,** rambling conversation (*c*) staff, pole; **b. de pavillon,** flagstaff (*d*) (*wand of office*) **b.** pastoral, pastoral staff, crozier 2. stick, roll; **b. de rouge (à lèvres),** lipstick 3. vertical stroke (of the pen).

batracien [batrasjɛ̃] *nm Z:* batrachian.

battage [bataʒ] *nm* 1. beating; threshing 2. *F:* publicity campaign; hard sell.

battant [batɑ̃] 1. *a* beating; **pluie battante,** driving rain; downpour; **mener les choses tambour b.,** to hustle things on; *F:* (**tout**) **b. neuf,** brand new 2. *nm* (*a*) clapper, tongue (of bell) (*b*) leaf, flap (of table); **porte à deux battants,** folding doors (*c*) door (of cupboard) (*d*) (*pers*) fighter.

batte [bat] *nf* (cricket) bat.

battement [batmɑ̃] *nm* 1. (*a*) beat(ing); tap(ping); flap(ping); bang(ing); blinking (of eyelids) (*b*) throb(bing); **b. de cœur,** heartbeat; **avoir des battements de cœur,** to have palpitations 2. interval; **20 minutes de b.,** 20 minutes' break; 20 minutes' wait; 20 minutes to spare.

batterie [batri] *nf* 1. *Mus:* (*a*) beat (of drum) (*b*) drums 2. *Artil:* battery; **pièces en b.,** guns in action 3. (*a*) set, collection; **b. de cuisine,** (set of) kitchen utensils; pots and pans (*b*) *Aut: Elcs:* battery.

batteur, -euse [batœr, -øz] *n* 1. *nm* (*pers*) (*a*) **b. en grange,** thresher (*b*) *Ven:* beater (*c*) *F:* **b. de pavé,** loafer, idler (*d*) *Cr:* batsman (*e*) *Mus:* drummer 2. *nm* (egg) whisk 3. *nf* **batteuse,** threshing machine.

battoir [batwar] *nm* (*a*) (carpet) beater (*b*) (washerwoman's) beetle (*c*) *F:* (large) hand; paw.

battre [batr̩] *v* (*pr ind* **je bats, il bat**) 1. *vtr* (*a*) to beat, thrash, flog (s.o.); to beat (a carpet); **b. le tambour,** to beat the drum; **b. du blé,** to thresh wheat; **b. des œufs,** to beat (up), to whisk, eggs (*b*) to hammer (iron); *Prov:* **b. le fer pendant qu'il est chaud,** to strike while the iron is hot (*c*) to beat, defeat; **b. qn à plate(s) couture(s),** to beat s.o. hollow (*d*) **b. la campagne,** (i) to scour the country (ii) *F:* to be delirious; *Ven:* **b. un bois,** to beat a wood (*e*) *Nau:* **b. un pavillon,** to fly a flag (*f*) **b. les cartes,** to shuffle the cards 2. *vtr & i* (*a*) **b. la mesure,** to beat time; **la montre bat,** the watch ticks (*b*) **b. le réveil,** to sound the reveille; **le cœur lui battait,** his heart was beating (*c*) **la pluie bat (contre) la fenêtre,** the rain lashes the window; **battu par les vagues,** buffeted by the waves; **porte qui bat,** banging door; **le vent fait b. les volets,** the shutters are banging in the wind (*d*) **b. des mains,** to clap one's hands; **b. du pied,** (i) to stamp one's foot (ii) to tap one's foot; **b. des paupières,** to blink 3. **se b.,** to fight (**avec, contre,** with, against).

battue [baty] *nf Ven:* beat.

baudet [bodɛ] *nm* donkey, ass.

baudrier [bodrije] *nm* crossbelt, shoulder belt.

baume [bom] *nm* balm, balsam.

baux *see* **bail.**

bauxite [boksit] *nf Miner:* bauxite.

bavardage [bavardaʒ] *nm* (*a*) chattering; gossiping

(b) chatter; gossip. **bavard, -arde 1.** a talkative **2.** n chatterbox; gossip.

bavarder [bavarde] vi (a) to chatter (b) to gossip (c) to talk, to blab.

bavarois, -oise [bavarwa, -waz] a & n Bavarian.

bave [bav] nf slaver; dribble; slime (of snail); foam (of horse); spittle (of toad).

baver [bave] vi (a) to slaver; to dribble; to foam at the mouth (b) P: **en b.,** (i) to be taken aback (ii) to have a rough time of it (c) (of pen) to run. **baveux, -euse** a dribbling (mouth); runny (omelette).

bavette [bavɛt] nf **1.** bib **2.** Cu: undercut of the sirloin.

Bavière [bavjer] Prnf Geog: Bavaria.

bavoir [bavwar] nm bib.

bavure [bavyr] nf (a) smudge; **sans b.,** faultless(ly) (b) mistake.

bayer [baje] vi (**je baye, baie, n. bayons**) **b. aux corneilles,** to stand stargazing.

bazar [bazar] nm **1.** (oriental) bazaar **2.** (a) general store (b) F: clutter, shambles (c) F: gear; **tout le b.,** the whole caboodle.

bazarder [bazarde] vtr F: to chuck (sth) out; to flog (sth).

bazooka [bazuka] nm bazooka.

BCG abbr (vaccin) bilié (de) Calmette et Guérin.

béant [beã] a gaping.

béat, -ate [bea, -at] a (a) Ecc: blessed (b) self-satisfied, smug; **sourire b.,** beatific smile. **béatement** adv smugly.

béatification [beatifikasjɔ̃] nf beatification. **béatifique** a beatific.

béatifier [beatifje] vtr (pr sub & impf n. **béatifiions**) Ecc: to beatify.

béatitude [beatityd] nf (a) beatitude (b) bliss.

beau [bo], **bel, belle** [bɛl] pl **beaux, belles** (the form **bel** is used before m sg ns beginning with a vowel or a mute h) **1.** a (a) beautiful, handsome; lovely; **un bel homme,** a good-looking man; **le b. sexe,** the fair sex; **de beaux arbres,** beautiful, fine, trees (b) fine; **de beaux sentiments,** fine, noble, feelings; **une belle mort,** a glorious death (c) **b. danseur,** excellent dancer; **belle santé,** good health; **bel âge,** ripe old age; **belle occasion,** fine opportunity; **belle situation,** excellent job; **c'est trop b. pour être vrai,** it's too good to be true; Cards: **avoir (un) b. jeu,** to have a good hand; **b. joueur,** good loser; **voir tout du b. côté,** to see the bright side of everything (d) smart, spruce; **le b. monde,** society; the fashionable set; **se faire b.,** to smarten oneself up (e) **b. temps,** fine weather; **un b. jour,** one (fine) day (f) Iron: **tout cela est fort b. mais,** that's all very well, but; **vous avez fait du b. travail!** well done! **il en a fait de belles,** the things he's been up to! **vous en avez fait une belle!** you have put your foot in it! (g) **j'ai eu une belle peur!** I got an awful fright! **au b. milieu de la rue,** right in the middle of the street; **un b. gâchis,** a fine mess; P: **un b. salaud,** an absolute bastard **2.** adv phrs **bel et bien,** entirely, well and truly; **il est bel et bien venu,** he really, actually, came; **de plus belle,** all the more; (even) more, worse, than ever **3.** v phrs (a) **l'échapper belle,** to have a narrow escape (b) **il ferait b. voir cela,** that would be a fine thing to see (c) **il fait b. (temps),** it is fine (weather) (d) **avoir b.**

faire qch, to do sth in vain; **j'avais b. chercher, je ne trouvais rien,** however hard I looked, I found nothing **4.** n (a) **une belle,** a beautiful woman, a beauty; **la Belle au bois dormant,** the Sleeping Beauty (b) (of dog) **faire le b.,** to sit up and beg **5.** nm (a) **le b.,** the beautiful; beauty (b) **le plus b. de l'histoire c'est que,** the best part of the story is that (c) fine weather; **le temps est au b. (fixe),** the weather is set fair **6.** nf (a) **jouer la belle,** to play the deciding game (b) **se faire la belle,** to escape; to break out (of prison).

beaucoup [boku] **1.** nm inv (a) much, a great deal; a lot; **c'est déjà b. s'il veut bien vous parler,** it's something that he condescended to speak to you (b) (a great) many; a lot; **b. de,** much; (a great) many; a great deal of; **avec b. de soin,** very carefully; **il y est pour b.,** he's had a great deal to do with it; **b. d'entre nous,** many of us (c) adv phr **de b.,** much, by far, by a great deal; **c'est de b. le meilleur,** it is far and away the best **2.** adv much; **elle parle b.,** she talks a lot; **il est b. plus âgé,** he is much older; **il a b. voyagé,** he's travelled a great deal.

beau-fils [bofis] nm **1.** stepson **2.** occ son-in-law; pl beaux-fils.

beau-frère [bofrɛr] nm brother-in-law; pl beaux-frères.

beau-père [bopɛr] nm **1.** father-in-law **2.** stepfather; pl beaux-pères.

beaupré [bopre] nm Nau: bowsprit.

beauté [bote] nf **1.** beauty; **être en b.,** to be looking one's best; **finir en b.,** to end with a flourish; **grain de b.,** beauty spot; **de toute b.,** extremely beautiful; F: **se (re)faire une b.,** to put one's makeup on **2.** beauty; beautiful woman; **les beautés touristiques,** the sights.

beaux-arts [bozar] nmpl fine arts; **école des b.-a.,** **les B.-A.,** art school.

beaux-parents [boparã] nmpl parents-in-law, F: in-laws.

bébé [bebe] nm (a) baby (b) (baby) doll.

bébête [bebɛt] a F: silly.

bec [bɛk] nm **1.** beak; bill (of bird); **coup de b.,** peck **2.** F: mouth; gourmet; **être, rester, le b. dans l'eau,** to be left in the lurch; **prise de b.,** quarrel, slanging match **3.** (a) nose (of tool); lip (of jug); spout (of coffee pot); **b. de plume,** pen nib (b) **b. de gaz,** gaslamp; **b. Bunsen,** Bunsen burner; P: **tomber sur un b. (de gaz),** to come a cropper.

bécane [bekan] nf F: bicycle; bike.

bécarre [bekar] a & nm Mus: natural (sign).

bécasse [bekas] nf Orn: woodcock.

bec-de-lièvre [bɛkdəljɛvr] nm harelip; pl becs-de-lièvre.

bêche [bɛʃ] nf spade.

bêcher [bɛʃe] vtr to dig.

bécot [beko] nm F: kiss.

bécoter [bekɔte] vtr F: to give (s.o.) a kiss.

becquée [beke] nf beakful; **donner la b. à,** to feed.

becqueter [bɛkte] vtr (**je becquète**) (of bird) (a) to peck at (sth) (b) P: (of pers) to eat.

bedaine [bədɛn] nf F: potbelly, paunch.

bedeau, -eaux [bədo] nm Ecc: verger.

bedonnant [bədɔnã] a F: pot-bellied.

bédouin, -ine [bedwɛ, -win] a & n bedouin.

bée [be] *af* **bouche b.**, agape; **rester bouche b.**, to stand open-mouthed.

beffroi [bɛfrwa] *nm* belfry.

bégaiement [begɛmɑ̃] *nm* stammering, stuttering.

bégayer [begeje] *v* (**je bégaye, bégaie**) **1.** *vi* to stutter, stammer **2.** *vtr* to stammer out (an excuse).

bégonia [begɔnja] *nm* begonia.

bègue [bɛg] *n* stammerer, stutterer.

béguin [begɛ̃] *nm F:* **avoir le b. pour qn**, to fancy s.o.

beige [bɛʒ] *a* beige.

beignet [bɛɲɛ] *nm Cu:* (*a*) fritter (*b*) doughnut.

bel [bɛl] *see* **beau.**

bêlement [bɛlmɑ̃] *nm* bleating.

bêler [bɛle] *vi* to bleat.

belette [bəlɛt] *nf* weasel.

Belgique [bɛlʒik] *Prnf Geog:* Belgium. **belge** *a & n* Belgian.

bélier [belje] *nm* **1.** *Z:* ram **2.** *Astr:* **le B.**, Aries.

belladone [beladɔn] *nf Bot:* belladonna, deadly nightshade.

belle [bɛl] *see* **beau.**

belle-famille [bɛlfamij] *nf F:* wife's, husband's, family; in-laws; *pl* **belles-familles.**

belle-fille [bɛlfij] *nf* **1.** daughter-in-law **2.** step-daughter; *pl* **belles-filles.**

belle-mère [bɛlmɛr] *nf* **1.** mother-in-law **2.** step-mother; *pl* **belles-mères.**

belle-sœur [bɛlsœr] *nf* sister-in-law; *pl* **belles-sœurs.**

belligérance [beliʒerɑ̃s] *nf* belligerence. **belligérant, -ante** *a & nm* belligerent.

belliqueux, -euse [belikø, -øz] *a* warlike, belli-cose; quarrelsome.

belvédère [belvedɛr] *nm* **1.** belvedere **2.** viewpoint.

bémol [bemɔl] *nm Mus:* flat.

bénédicité [benedisite] *nm* grace (before meal).

bénédictin, -ine [benediktɛ̃, -in] *a & n* Benedictine (monk, nun).

bénédiction [benediksjɔ̃] *nf* blessing, benediction; **quelle b.!** what a godsend!

bénéfice [benefis] *nm* **1.** profit, gain; **vendre à b.**, to sell at a profit **2.** benefit; **concert donné au b. de**, concert given in aid of; **b. du doute**, benefit of the doubt **3.** *Ecc:* living, benefice.

bénéficiaire [benefisjɛr] *n* recipient; beneficiary.

bénéficier [benefisje] *v ind tr (pr sub & impf n. bénéficiions)* to profit (**de**, by); to have the advantage (**de**, of); to gain (**de**, by, from); **faire b. qn d'une remise**, to give, allow, s.o. a discount. **bénéfique** *a* beneficial.

Bénélux [benelyks] *Prnm* Benelux.

bénévole [benevɔl] *a* **1.** benevolent; kindly; indulgent **2.** unpaid (service); voluntary. **bénévolement** *adv* benevolently; voluntarily.

bénin, -igne [benɛ̃, -iɲ] *a* (*a*) benign, kindly (*b*) slight (accident); mild (disease); benign (tumour).

bénir [benir] *vtr* **1.** (*a*) to bless; **(que) Dieu vous bénisse!** God bless you! (*b*) to bless, to ask God's blessing on (s.o.) (*c*) to glorify (God); **le ciel en soit béni!** thank heaven! **2.** to consecrate (church, bread). **bénit** *a* consecrated, blessed; **eau bénite**, holy water.

bénitier [benitje] *nm Ecc:* stoop, stoup; font.

benjamin, -ine [bɛ̃ʒamɛ̃, -in] *n* youngest child.

benne [bɛn] *nf* (*a*) *Min:* skip, truck, tub (*b*) scoop (of crane); bucket (of dredger) (*c*) dumper (lorry); tipper wagon (*d*) (cable)car.

benzène [bɛ̃zɛn] *nf* benzene.

BEPC *abbr Sch:* brevet d'études du premier cycle.

béquille [bekij] *nf* **1.** crutch **2.** (motorcycle) stand.

berbère [bɛrbɛr] *a & n* Berber.

berceau, -eaux [bɛrso] *nm* **1.** (*a*) cradle, cot; *NAm:* crib (*b*) birthplace **2.** *Hort:* arbour, bower.

bercement [bɛrsəmɑ̃] *nm* rocking; swaying.

bercer [bɛrse] *vtr* (**n. berçons**) **1.** (*a*) to rock **2.** (*a*) to soothe (*b*) **b. qn de promesses**, to delude s.o. with promises **3. se b. d'une illusion**, to cherish an illusion; to delude oneself.

berceuse [bɛrsøz] *nf* lullaby, cradle song.

béret [berɛ] *nm* beret.

berge¹ [bɛrʒ] *nf* (steep) bank (of river).

berge² *nf P:* year; **il a 40 berges**, he's 40 (years old).

berger, -ère [bɛrʒe, -ɛr] *n* **1.** shepherd, shepherdess; **chien de b.**, sheepdog; **b. allemand**, German shepherd (dog) **2.** *nf* **bergère**, easy-chair.

bergerie [bɛrʒəri] *nf* sheepfold.

bergeronnette [bɛrʒərɔnɛt] *nf Orn:* wagtail.

berline [bɛrlin] *nf* (*a*) *A:* berlin(e) (*b*) *Aut:* saloon, *NAm:* sedan (*c*) *Min:* truck.

berlingot [bɛrlɛ̃go] *nm* **1.** (boiled) sweet **2.** (pyramid-shaped) carton.

berlinois, -oise [bɛrlinwa, -waz] **1.** *a* of Berlin **2.** *n* Berliner.

berlue [bɛrly] *nf* **avoir la b.**, to be seeing things.

bermuda(s) [bɛrmyda] *nm Cl:* Bermuda shorts.

Bermudes [bɛrmyd] *Prnfpl Geog:* **les (îles) B.**, Bermuda.

bernard-l'(h)ermite [bɛrnarlɛrmit] *nm inv* hermit crab.

berne [bɛrn] *nf Nau:* **pavillon en b.**, flag at half mast.

berner [bɛrne] *vtr* to fool (s.o.); to hoax (s.o.).

bernique [bɛrnik] **1.** *nf* limpet **2.** *int F:* no go! nothing doing!

besace [bəzas] *nf A:* beggar's bag.

besicles [bəzik[l]] *nfpl A:* spectacles; *F:* specs.

besogne [b(ə)zɔɲ] *nf* work; task, job.

besoin [bəzwɛ̃] *nm* **1.** (*a*) necessity, want, need; requirement; **pourvoir aux besoins de qn**, to provide for s.o.'s needs; *F:* **faire ses besoins**, to relieve oneself; **au b.**, if necessary; if need(s) be; **en cas de b.**, in case of necessity (*b*) **avoir b. de qch**, to need, want, sth; **il n'a pas b. de venir**, he needn't come; **pas b. de dire que**, needless to say, it goes without saying that; *Iron:* **vous aviez bien b. d'y aller!** of course, you *had* to go there! (*c*) *impers* **il n'est pas b.**, there is no need; **si b. est**, if need(s) be **2.** poverty, indigence; **être dans le b.**, to be in need.

bestialité [bɛstjalite] *nf* bestiality; brutishness.

bestial, -aux¹ *a* bestial, beastly, brutish. **bestialement** *adv* bestially, brutishly.

bestiaux² [bɛstjo] *nmpl* livestock, cattle.

bestiole [bɛstjɔl] *nf* tiny creature.

bêta, -asse [bɛta, -as] *F:* (*a*) *a* silly, stupid (*b*) *n* idiot.

bétail [betaj] *nm coll:* (*no pl*) livestock; cattle.

bête [bɛt] *nf* **1.** *n* (*a*) beast, animal; **b. à cornes**, horned beast (*b*) creature; bug; **petites bêtes**, (i) insects (ii) vermin; **b. à bon Dieu**, ladybird; **chercher la petite**

b., to be over-critical 2. *F:* (a) n idiot, fool (b) a silly, stupid, foolish; **pas si b.!** I'm not such a fool! **il est b. comme ses pieds,** he's a real idiot (c) **c'est b. comme chou, c'est tout b.,** it's dead simple. **bêtement** *adv* stupidly, foolishly; **tout b.,** purely and simply.

Bethléem [bɛtleɛm] *Prnm BHist:* Bethlehem.

bêtise [betiz] *nf* 1. stupidity, silliness 2. nonsense, absurdity; **dire des bêtises,** to talk nonsense; **faire des bêtises,** to play the fool 3. blunder; stupid mistake 4. trifle 5. **bêtises de Cambrai** = mint humbugs.

béton [betɔ̃] *nm* concrete; **b. armé,** reinforced concrete.

bétonneuse [betɔnøz] *nf* concrete mixer.

bette [bɛt] *nf Bot:* (spinach) beet; Swiss chard.

betterave [bɛtrav] *nf* beet(root); **b. sucrière,** sugar beet; **b. fourragère,** mangel-wurzel, fodder beet.

beuglement [bøgləmɑ̃] *nm* lowing; bellowing.

beugler [bøgle] *vi* to low; to bellow.

beurre [bœr] *nm* 1. butter; *Cu:* **au b.,** cooked in butter; **b. d'anchois,** anchovy paste; **b. noir,** brown butter; *F:* **avoir un œil au b. noir,** to have a black eye; **entrer comme dans du b.,** to get in with the greatest of ease; **faire son b.,** to make a packet; **ça mettra du b. dans les épinards,** that will ease the situation 2. **b. de cacahuètes,** peanut butter.

beurrer [bœre] *vtr* to butter.

beurrier [bœrje] *nm* butter dish.

beuverie [bøvri] *nf* drinking session; booze-up.

bévue [bevy] *nf* blunder, mistake.

biais [bjɛ] 1. *a* oblique, slanting, bevelled 2. *nm* (a) slant (of wall); **en b.,** on the slant; aslant; askew; **tailler un tissu dans le b.,** to cut material on the bias; **regarder qn de b.,** to look sideways at s.o. (b) indirect manner, means; expedient; **aborder une question de b.,** to approach a question in a roundabout way; **considérer qch par deux b.,** to look at sth from two angles.

biaiser [bjɛze] *vi* 1. to be on the slant; to turn away (towards sth) 2. to prevaricate; to dodge the issue.

bibelot [biblo] *nm* 1. curio; trinket 2. *pl* odds and ends.

biberon [bibrɔ̃] *nm* (baby's feeding) bottle; **nourrir au b.,** to bottle-feed.

bibine [bibin] *nf P:* weak beer.

Bible [bibl] *nf* Bible.

bibliobus [biblɔbys] *nm* mobile library.

bibliographe [bibliɔgraf] *n* bibliographer.

bibliographie [bibliɔgrafi] *nf* bibliography. **bibliographique** *a* bibliographical.

bibliophile [bibliɔfil] *n* bibliophile, book lover.

bibliothécaire [bibliɔtekɛr] *n* librarian.

bibliothèque [bibliɔtɛk] *nf* 1. (a) (building, room) library (b) *Rail:* bookstall 2. bookcase 3. library; collection of books.

biblique [biblik] *a* biblical.

bicarbonate [bikarbɔnat] *nm Ch:* bicarbonate.

bicéphale [bisefal] *a* two-headed.

biceps [bisɛps] *nm Anat:* biceps; *F:* **avoir des b.,** to be muscular.

biche [biʃ] *nf* 1. *Z:* doe 2. *F:* **ma b.,** my darling.

bichonner [biʃɔne] *vtr* 1. (a) to make (s.o.) spruce (b) to mollycoddle (s.o.) 2. **se b.,** to spruce oneself up.

bicolore [bikɔlɔr] *a* bicolour(ed).

bicoque [bikɔk] *nf F:* shack.

bicorne [bikɔrn] *nm* cocked hat.

bicyclette [bisiklɛt] *nf* bicycle, cycle, bike; **faire de la b.,** to go cycling.

bide [bid] *nm* 1. *P:* belly 2. *F: Th:* flop.

bidet [bidɛ] *nm* 1. nag; pony 2. *Hyg:* bidet.

bidon [bidɔ̃] *nm* 1. (a) can, drum (for oil); (milk) churn (b) *Mil:* water bottle (c) *P:* belly (d) *P:* rubbish 2. *a P:* fake, phoney.

bidonville [bidɔ̃vil] *nm* shantytown.

bidule [bidyl] *nm P:* thingummy, whatsit.

bief [bjɛf] *nm* 1. (canal) reach, level 2. millrace.

bielle [bjɛl] *nf* (a) (tie) rod; push rod; crank arm (b) **tête de b.,** crank head; *ICE:* big end.

bien [bjɛ̃] 1. *adv* (a) well; **il parle b.,** he is a good speaker; **écoutez b.,** listen carefully; **il faut b. les soigner,** they must be well looked after; **vous avez b. fait,** you did the right thing; **c'est b. fait (pour lui),** it serves him right; **tout va b.,** everything's fine, O.K.; **aller, se porter, b.,** to be well, in good health; *Iron:* **ça commence b.!** that's a good start! **b.!** (i) good! (ii) that's enough! (iii) all right! **très b.!** very good! well done! (b) right, proper; **ce n'est pas b. de vous moquer de lui,** it's not kind of you to make fun of him (c) comfortable; **vous ne savez pas quand vous êtes b.,** you don't know when you're well off (d) **je ne me sens pas b.,** I don't feel well (e) **être b. avec qn,** to be on good terms with s.o. (f) of good appearance, position, quality; **il est très b.,** he is very gentlemanly; **ce sont des gens b.,** they are people of good position; **tu es très b. dans cette robe,** that dress suits you perfectly (g) indeed, really, quite; **c'est b. cela,** that's right; **je l'ai regardé b. en face,** I looked him full in the face; **je veux b. le croire,** I can well believe it, him; **qu'est-ce ça peut b. être?** what on earth can it be? **c'est b. lui,** it really *is* him; *F:* **c'est b. à moi ça?** you're sure that's mine? **je l'avais b. dit!** didn't I say so! **b. entendu,** of course; **il est b. venu, mais j'étais occupé,** he did come, but I was busy (h) very; **b. malheureux,** very unhappy; **c'est b. simple,** it's quite simple (i) much, many, a great deal, a great many; **je l'ai vu b. des fois,** I have seen him many times; **b. d'autres,** many others (j) **je suis b. obligé,** I have to; **je voudrais b. mais,** I'd like to, but 2. *adv phr* (a) **aussi b.,** in any case, anyway; just as well (b) **tant b. que mal,** somehow (or other) 3. *conj phr* (a) **b. que + sub,** though, although (b) **si b. que + ind,** so that, and so; with the result that (c) **ou b.,** or else, otherwise 4. *int* **eh b.!** (oh) well! **eh b. ça alors!** well, I'm damned! 5. *nm* (a) good; **le b. et le mal,** good and evil; right and wrong; **homme de b.,** good, upright, man (b) **c'est pour votre b.,** it is for your own good; **grand b. vous fasse!** much good may it do you! **vouloir du b. à qn,** to wish s.o. well; **tout le monde dit du b. de lui,** everyone speaks well of him (c) possession, property, wealth; **avoir du b. (au soleil),** to be a man of property (d) *Jur:* **biens mobiliers,** personal estate; **biens immobiliers,** real estate (e) **biens de consommation,** consumer goods; **biens de production,** capital goods (f) *adv phr* **il a changé en b.,** he has changed for the better; **mener une affaire à b.,** to bring a matter to a satisfactory conclusion.

bien-aimé [bjɛ̃nɛme] *a & n* beloved; *pl* bien-aimés.

bien-être [bjɛ̃nɛtr] *nm no pl* (*a*) well-being (*b*) comfort; welfare.

bienfaisance [bjɛ̃fəzɑ̃s] *nf* charity; **œuvre de b.**, charitable organisation. **bienfaisant** *a* 1. beneficent, charitable 2. beneficial, salutary.

bienfait [bjɛ̃fɛ] *nm* 1. benefit, kindness, service 2. gift, blessing, boon.

bienfaiteur, -trice [bjɛ̃fɛtœr, -tris] *n* benefactor, benefactress.

bien-fondé [bjɛ̃fɔ̃de] *nm no pl* validity, merits; *Jur:* cogency.

bienheureux, -euse [bjɛ̃nœrø, -øz] *a* 1. blissful, happy 2. *Ecc:* blessed; **les b.**, the blest.

biennale [bienal] *nf* biennial event.

bien-pensant, -ante [bjɛ̃pɑ̃sɑ̃(t)] *a & n* right-minded (person).

bienséance [bjɛ̃seɑ̃s] *nf* propriety. **bienséant** *a* proper.

bientôt [bjɛ̃to] *adv* (very) soon; before long; *F:* **à b.!** good-bye, see you (again) soon! **il est b. 10 heures**, it's nearly 10 o'clock.

bienveillance [bjɛ̃vejɑ̃s] *nf* benevolence, kindness (**envers**, to). **bienveillant** *a* kind, kindly, benevolent.

bienvenu, -e [bjɛ̃vəny] 1. *a* well-timed, apposite (remark) 2. *n* **soyez le b.**, **la bienvenue! welcome!** 3. *nf* welcome; **souhaiter la bienvenue à qn**, to welcome s.o.

bière¹ [bjɛr] *nf* beer; **b. blonde**, lager, light ale; **b. brune**, brown ale.

bière² *nf* coffin.

biffer [bife] *vtr* to cross out (word).

bifteck [biftɛk] *nm* (beef)steak.

bifurcation [bifyrkasjɔ̃] *nf* fork (of road).

bifurquer [bifyrke] *vtr & i* to fork; to branch off, to turn off.

bigamie [bigami] *nf* bigamy. **bigame** 1. *a* bigamous 2. *n* bigamist.

bigarré [bigare] *a* (*a*) variegated, multicoloured (*b*) motley, mixed (crowd).

bigarreau, -eaux [bigaro] *nm* whiteheart (cherry).

bigarrure [bigaryr] *nf* medley, mixture (of colours).

bigorneau, -eaux [bigɔrno] *nm Moll:* winkle.

bigoterie [bigɔtri] *nf* bigotry. **bigot, -ote** 1. *a* (over-)devout 2. *n* bigot.

bigoudi [bigudi] *nm* (hair) curler, roller.

bigre [bigr] *int F:* gosh! **bigrement** *adv F:* **b. froid**, awfully cold; **vous avez b. raison!** you're dead right!

bijou, -oux [biʒu] *nm* jewel, gem; *pl* jewellery; *F:* **mon b.!** my pet!

bijouterie [biʒutri] *nf* (*a*) jeweller's trade (*b*) jeweller's (shop).

bijoutier, -ière [biʒutje, -jɛr] *n* jeweller.

bikini [bikini] *nm* bikini.

bilan [bilɑ̃] *nm* 1. *Fin:* (*a*) balance sheet (*b*) **déposer son b.**, to file one's petition (in bankruptcy) 2. (*a*) results (of a situation); assessment (of facts); **faire le b. de**, to take stock of (*b*) **b. de santé**, (medical) check-up.

bilatéral, -aux [bilateral, -o] *a* bilateral, two-sided (contract).

bilboquet [bilbɔkɛ] *nm* cup-and-ball.

bile [bil] *nf* 1. bile 2. (*a*) bad temper (*b*) *F:* **se faire de la b.**, to worry, to fret. **bileux, -euse** *a F:* easily

upset. **bilieux, -euse** *a* 1. bilious 2. irritable, irascible.

bilingue [bilɛ̃g] *a* bilingual.

billard [bijar] *nm* 1. (game of) billiards; **faire un b.**, to play a game of billiards; **b. électrique**, pinball machine 2. billiard table; *F:* **passer sur le b.**, to have an operation.

bille [bij] *nf* 1. (*a*) billiard ball (*b*) *P:* face, mug 2. marble 3. *MecE: etc:* ball; **roulement à billes**, ball bearing(s); **stylo (à) b.**, ballpoint pen 4. (saw)log.

billet [bijɛ] *nm* 1. *esp Lit:* note, short letter; **b. doux**, love letter 2. notice, invitation; **b. de faire-part**, card announcing a family event (birth, marriage, death) 3. ticket; **b. simple, b. d'aller**, single ticket; **b. d'aller (et) retour**, return ticket; *NAm:* round trip ticket; **b. circulaire**, round trip ticket; **b. de faveur**, complimentary ticket 4. *Com:* (*a*) promissory note, bill (*b*) **b. (de banque)**, (bank)note, *NAm:* bill 5. **b. de santé**, health certificate 6. permit, permission; *Sch:* **b. de sortie**, exeat 7. *Mil:* **b. de logement**, billet.

billion [biljɔ̃] *nm* billion; *NAm:* trillion.

billot [bijo] *nm* block (of wood).

bimensuel, -elle [bimɑ̃sɥɛl] *a* fortnightly, bimonthly.

bimoteur [bimɔtœr] *a & nm* twin-engine(d) (aircraft).

binaire [binɛr] *a Mth:* binary.

biner [bine] *vtr Agr:* to hoe; to harrow.

binette [binɛt] *nf* 1. hoe 2. *P:* face, mug.

biniou [binju] *nm* Breton bagpipes.

binôme [binom] *nm* binomial.

biochimie [bjɔʃimi] *nf* biochemistry.

biographe [bjɔgraf] *n* biographer.

biographie [bjɔgrafi] *nf* biography. **biographique** *a* biographical.

biologie [bjɔlɔʒi] *nf* biology. **biologique** *a* biological.

biologiste [bjɔlɔʒist] *n* biologist.

bioxyde [biɔksid] *nm Ch:* dioxide.

bipartite [bipartit] *a* bipartite.

bipède [biped] *a & nm* biped.

biphasé [bifaze] *a El:* two-phase (current).

biplace [biplas] *a & nm Aut: Av:* two-seater.

biplan [biplɑ̃] *nm* biplane.

bique [bik] *nf F:* 1. nanny goat 2. (*woman*) old hag.

biquet, -ette [bikɛ, -ɛt] *n Z:* kid.

Birmanie [birmani] *Prnf Geog:* Burma. **birman, -ane** *a & n* Burmese.

bis¹, bise² [bi, biz] *a* greyish-brown.

bis² [bis] *adv* twice 1. *adv & nm* (*a*) *Th:* encore (*b*) *Mus:* repeat 2. *adv* (*in address*) **10 b.**, (i) 10A (ii) 10B.

bisaïeul, -eule [bizajœl] *n* great-grandfather, great-grandmother.

bisannuel, -elle [bizanɥɛl] *a* biennial.

biscornu [biskɔrny] *a F:* 1. mis-shapen; crooked 2. bizarre, queer (ideas); illogical (argument).

biscotte [biskɔt] *nf* rusk.

biscuit [biskɥi] *nm* biscuit, *NAm:* cookie; **b. de savoie**, sponge cake; **b. à la cuiller**, sponge finger.

biscuiterie [biskɥitri] *nf* biscuit factory.

bise² [biz] *nf* north wind.

bise³ *nf P:* kiss.

biseau, -eaux [bizo] *nm* 1. chamfer, bevel; **taillé en b.,** bevelled, chamfered 2. *Tls:* bevel.

bismuth [bismyt] *nm Ch:* bismuth.

bison [bizɔ̃] *nm Z:* bison; *esp NAm:* buffalo.

bisou [bizu] *nm F:* kiss.

bissecteur, -trice [bisɛktœr, -tris] 1. *a* bisecting 2. *nf* **bissectrice,** bisector.

bisser [bise] *vtr* to encore (performer).

bissextile [bisɛkstil] *af* **année b.,** leap year.

bistouri [bisturi] *nm Surg:* lancet.

bistre [bistr̩] *a & nm* bistre; **teint b.,** swarthy complexion.

bistro(t) [bistro] *nm F:* café, bar, pub.

bitume [bitym] *nm Miner:* 1. bitumen, asphalt 2. pitch, tar.

bitum(in)er [bitum(in)e] *vtr* to asphalt (road). **bitumineux, -euse** *a* bituminous.

bivouac [bivwak] *nm Mil:* bivouac.

bivouaquer [bivwake] *vi* to bivouac.

bizarrerie [bizarri] *nf* 1. peculiarity, oddness 2. whimsicalness; eccentricity, oddity. **bizarre** *a* peculiar, eccentric, odd, strange, bizarre; **le b. de l'affaire, c'est que,** the funny thing is that. **bizarrement** *adv* peculiarly, strangely.

bizuter [bizyte] *vtr Sch: F:* to rag.

bizut(h) [bizy] *nm Sch: F:* freshman, fresher.

blabla(bla) [blabla(bla)] *nm F:* claptrap.

blackbouler [blakbule] *vtr* to blackball; *F:* to fail (candidate).

black-out [blakaut] *nm* blackout; **faire le b.-o. sur qch,** to hush sth up.

blafard, -arde [blafar, -ard] *a* pale, wan.

blague [blag] *nf* 1. **b. (à tabac),** (tobacco) pouch 2. *F:* (*a*) tall story; bunkum; **b. à part,** joking apart; seriously; **sans b.?** really? (*b*) joke; hoax; **quelle b.!** what a joke! **une sale b.,** a dirty trick 3. mistake, blunder.

blaguer [blage] *F:* 1. *vi* to joke, to kid 2. *vtr* to tease, to make fun of. **blagueur, -euse** 1. *a* teasing 2. *n* joker.

blaireau, -eaux [blɛro] *nm* 1. *Z:* badger 2. badger brush, shaving brush.

blairer [blere] *vtr P:* **je ne peux pas le b.,** I can't stand him.

blâme [blɑm] *nm* 1. blame, disapproval 2. *Adm:* reprimand; **donner un b.,** to reprimand.

blâmer [blɑme] *vtr* 1. to blame 2. *Adm:* to reprimand. **blâmable** *a* blameworthy.

blanc, blanche [blɑ̃, blɑ̃ʃ] 1. *a* (*a*) white; **vieillard à cheveux blancs,** white-haired old man (*b*) lightcoloured; pale; **b. comme un linge,** as white as a sheet; **verre b.,** colourless glass (*c*) innocent, pure (*d*) blank (page); plain (paper); **nuit blanche,** sleepless night; **examen b.,** mock exam; **voix blanche,** toneless voice; **vers blancs,** blank verse 2. *nm* (*a*) white; **robe d'un b. sale,** dingy white dress; **b. cassé,** off white; **mariage en b.,** white wedding (*b*) **le b. des yeux,** the white of the eyes; **regarder qn dans le b. des yeux,** to look s.o. straight in the eye (*c*) **b. d'une cible,** bull's eye of a target (*d*) blank, gap, space; **chèque en b.,** blank cheque (*e*) white (man) (*f*) **saigner qn à b.,** to bleed s.o. white; **chauffé à b.,** white hot (*g*) **cartouche à b.,** blank cartridge; **tirer à b.,** to fire a blank, blanks (*h*) **b. de poulet,** breast of chicken; **b. d'œuf,** white of egg, egg white (*i*) **b. de chaux,** whitewash (*j*) **(articles de) b.,** linen; **vente de b.,** white sale (*k*) white wine 3. *nf* **blanche** (*a*) white (woman) (*b*) *Mus:* minim. **blanchâtre** *a* whitish.

blanc-bec [blɑ̃bɛk] *nm* greenhorn; *pl* **blancs-becs.**

blanchaille [blɑ̃ʃɑj] *nf* 1. *Fish:* small fry 2. *Cu:* whitebait.

Blanche-Neige [blɑ̃ʃnɛʒ] *Prnf* Snow White.

blancheur [blɑ̃ʃœr] *nf* whiteness.

blanchir [blɑ̃ʃir] 1. *vtr* (*a*) to whiten; to make white (*b*) *Tex:* to bleach (*c*) to wash, launder; **donner du linge à b.,** to send clothes to the wash (*d*) to exonerate (s.o.) (*e*) **b. (à la chaux),** to whitewash (*f*) *Cu:* to blanch 2. *vi* to whiten; to turn white; **il commence à b.,** he is going white 3. **se b.,** to clear one's name.

blanchissage [blɑ̃ʃisaʒ] *nm* laundering.

blanchissement [blɑ̃ʃismɑ̃] *nm* whitening.

blanchisserie [blɑ̃ʃisri] *nf* laundry.

blanchisseur, -euse [blɑ̃ʃisœr, -øz] *n* launderer, laundress.

blanquette [blɑ̃kɛt] *nf Cu:* blanquette (of veal).

blaser [blaze] *vtr* to make (s.o.) blasé, indifferent. **blasé, -ée** *a* blasé, indifferent.

blason [blazɔ̃] *nm* coat of arms.

blasphémateur, -trice [blasfematœr, -tris] *n* blasphemer.

blasphème [blasfɛm] *nm* blasphemy. **blasphématoire** *a* blasphemous.

blasphémer [blasfeme] *vtr & i* (**je blasphème; je blasphémerai**) to blaspheme.

blatte [blat] *nf Ent:* cockroach.

blé [ble] *nm* wheat; **b. dur,** hard wheat, durum wheat; **b. noir,** buckwheat.

bled [blɛd] *nm F:* village, place; **b. perdu,** god-forsaken place; dump.

blême [blɛm] *a* 1. livid, ghastly 2. pale, wan.

blêmir [blemir] *vi* to turn pale.

blessé, -ée [blese] *n* wounded, injured, person; casualty.

blesser [blese] 1. *vtr* (*a*) to wound, injure, hurt (*b*) to offend, hurt (s.o.); **b. la vue,** to offend the eye; **cette suspicion me blesse,** I resent this suspiciousness 2. **se b.** (*a*) to injure, hurt, oneself (**avec,** with) (*b*) **il se blesse pour un rien,** he's very quick to take offence. **blessant** *a* cutting.

blessure [blesyr̩] *nf* wound, injury.

blet, blette[1] [blɛ, blɛt] *a* overripe (fruit).

blette[2] *nf see* **bette.**

bleu, *pl* **bleus** [blø] 1. *a* blue; **aux yeux bleus,** blueeyed; **colère bleue,** towering rage; **biftek b.,** very rare steak 2. *nm* (*a*) blue (colour); **b. ciel,** sky blue; **b. marine, b. roi,** navy blue, royal blue; **b.-noir,** blueblack (*b*) bruise; **mon bras est couvert de bleus,** my arm is all black and blue (*c*) greenhorn, novice; *Mil:* raw recruit (*d*) blue cheese (*e*) *Cu:* **poisson au b.,** fish *au bleu* (*f*) *pl* **bleu(s) (de chauffe),** overalls, dungarees, boiler suit (*g*) *Tchn:* blueprint. **bleuâtre** *a* bluish.

bleuet [bløɛ] *nm Bot:* cornflower.

bleuir [bløir] *vtr & i* to make (sth) blue; to become blue. **bleuté** *a* bluish; blue-tinted (glass).

blindage [blɛ̃daʒ] *nm* (armour) plating.

blinder [blɛ̃de] *vtr* 1. to armour (plate); to plate (ship, tank, car) 2. to harden (s.o.), to make (s.o.)

immune (**contre qch,** to sth). **blindé 1.** *a* armoured, armour-plated **2.** (*a*) *nf* **blindée,** armoured car (*b*) *nmpl* **les blindés,** the armour.

bloc [blɔk] *nm* **1.** block, lump (of wood); **tout d'un b.,** in one go; **coulé en b.,** cast in one piece; **acheter qch en b.,** to buy sth en bloc; **visser qch à b.,** to screw sth up tight **2.** *Pol: etc:* group; coalition; **faire b.,** to unite **3.** pad (of paper); **b. à dessin,** sketch pad **4.** unit; *Cin:* **b. sonore,** sound unit **5.** *F:* prison, clink.

blocage [blɔkaʒ] *nm* (*a*) sticking, jamming; locking on (of brakes) (*b*) *PolEc:* pegging; freezing (of prices, wages).

bloc-cuisine [blɔkɥizin] *nm* kitchen unit; *pl blocs-cuisines.*

bloc-évier [blɔkevje] *nm* sink unit; *pl blocs-éviers.*

bloc-moteur [blɔkmɔtœr] *nm* engine block; *pl blocs-moteurs.*

bloc-notes [blɔknɔt] *nm* writing pad; *pl blocs-notes.*

blocus [blɔkys] *nm* blockade.

blond, -onde [blɔ̃, -ɔ̃d] **1.** *a* fair, blond (hair, pers); fair-haired (person); **bière blonde,** lager; pale ale; (**cigarette**) **blonde,** Virginia cigarette **2.** *n* fair-(-haired) man, woman; blond(e) **3.** *nm* **cheveux (d'un) b. doré,** golden hair; **b. cendré,** ash blond.

blondinet, -ette [blɔ̃dinɛ, -ɛt] *n* fair haired child.

blondir [blɔ̃dir] *vi* (of hair) to get fairer.

bloquer [blɔke] **1.** *vtr* (*a*) to combine; to group together (*b*) to jam (piece of machinery); to lock (wheels); **b. les freins,** to jam on the brakes; **bloqué par la neige,** snowbound (*c*) to stop (cheque); to freeze (prices) (*d*) to block, obstruct (road) **2.** **se b.,** to jam; to get jammed.

blottir (se) [səblɔtir] *vpr* to curl up, to crouch; **blotti dans un coin,** huddled in a corner.

blouse [bluz] *nf* overall, smock; (surgeon's) gown.

blouson [bluzɔ̃] *nm* (lumber)jacket, windcheater; *F: O:* **b. noir,** teddy boy.

blue-jean(s) [blud͡ʒin(z)] *nm Cl:* jeans; *pl blue-jeans.*

blues [bluz] *nm Mus:* blues.

bluff [blœf] *nm F:* bluff; **c'est du b.,** he's bluffing.

bluffer [blœfe] *vtr & i* (*a*) *Cards:* to bluff (s.o.) (*b*) *F:* trick (s.o.); to bluff.

bluffeur, -euse [blœfœr, -øz] *n* bluffer.

BN *abbr Bibliothèque Nationale.*

BNP *abbr Banque Nationale de Paris.*

boa [bɔa] *nm Rept: Cl:* boa.

bobard [bɔbar] *nm F:* tall story; fib.

bobine [bɔbin] *nf* **1.** (*a*) bobbin, spool, reel; roll (of film) (*b*) *El:* coil **2.** *P:* face, mug.

bobo [bɔbo] *nm F:* (child's language) pain, sore, cut; **ça fait b.?** does it hurt?

bocage [bɔkaʒ] *nm* **1.** copse **2.** *Geog:* bocage.

bocal, -aux [bɔkal, -o] *nm* (*a*) (wide-mouthed) bottle, jar; **mettre des fruits en bocaux,** to bottle (*b*) goldfish bowl.

bock [bɔk] *nm* (*a*) beer glass (*b*) glass of beer.

bœuf, *pl* **bœufs** [bœf, bø] *nm* **1.** ox, bullock; **jeune b.,** steer; **bœufs de boucherie,** beef cattle **2.** beef; **b. (à la) mode,** stewed beef **3.** *a inv F:* amazing; **c'est b.,** it's fantastic.

bohème [bɔɛm] *a & n* Bohemian; **mener une vie de b.,** to lead a free and easy life. **bohémien, -ienne** *a & n* **1.** *Geog:* Bohemian **2.** gipsy.

boire[1] [bwar] *vtr* (*prp* **buvant;** *pp* **bu;** *pr ind* **je bois, ils boivent;** *pr sub* **je boive;** *impf* **je buvais;** *fu* **je boirai**) **1.** to drink; **b. qch à petits coups,** to sip sth; **b. qch d'un trait,** to drink sth at one gulp; **b. à sa soif,** to drink one's fill; *F:* **b. un coup,** to have a drink; **ce vin se laisse b.,** this wine is very drinkable; **b. les paroles de qn,** to drink in s.o.'s every word; *F:* **b. la tasse,** to get a mouthful (when swimming); **il y a à b. et à manger,** it's got its pros and cons **2.** to drink (alcohol); **il a (trop) bu,** he's had one too many; **il boit comme un trou,** he drinks like a fish **3.** (of plants) to soak up, to absorb (moisture).

boire[2] *nm* drink, drinking; **le b. et le manger,** food and drink.

bois [bwa] *nm* **1.** wood, forest; **petit b.,** thicket **2.** timber (trees); **abattre le b.,** to fell timber **3.** wood, timber, lumber; **b. de chauffage,** firewood; **petit b.,** kindling; **chantier de b.,** timber yard; **en b.,** wooden; **b. dur,** hardwood; **b. de sapin, b. blanc,** deal, whitewood; **je leur ferai voir de quel b. je me chauffe,** I'll show them (what I'm made of); *F:* **touchez du bois!** touch wood! **4.** (*a*) woodcut (*b*) **b. de lit,** bedstead (*c*) *Mus:* **les b.,** the woodwind **5.** *pl* antlers. **boisé** *a* wooded.

boiserie [bwazri] *nf* woodwork, panelling.

boisson [bwasɔ̃] *nf* drink, beverage; **pris de b.,** under the influence of drink.

boîte [bwat] *nf* **1.** box; **b. en fer,** tin, can; canister; **conserves en b.,** tinned, canned food; **mettre en b.,** to can (food); **b. aux lettres,** letterbox, pillarbox, postbox, *NAm:* mailbox; **b. postale 260,** Post Office box 260; **b. d'allumettes,** box of matches; **b. à outils,** toolbox; **b. à musique,** musical box; *Anat:* **b. crânienne,** brainpan **2.** *Aut:* **b. de vitesses,** gearbox; *El:* **b. à fusible,** fusebox **3.** *P:* (*a*) one's office, shop, school; **sale b.,** rotten hole (*b*) **b. (de nuit),** nightclub.

boitement [bwatmã] *nm* limping.

boiter [bwate] *vi* to limp; to walk with a limp; **b. d'un pied,** to be lame in one foot. **boiteux, -euse 1.** *a* (*a*) lame, limping (*b*) wobbly, rickety, shaky (furniture, argument); clumsy (lines) **2.** *n* lame man, woman.

boîtier [bwatje] *nm* case; **b. de montre,** watch case.

boitiller [bwatije] *vi* to limp slightly.

bol [bɔl] *nm* (*a*) bowl, basin (*b*) *P:* luck; **avoir du b.,** to be lucky.

boléro [bolero] *nm* bolero.

bolide [bolid] *nm* (*a*) meteor; (*b*) racing car; **lancé comme un b. sur la route,** hurtling along the road.

Bolivie [bolivi] *Prnf Geog:* Bolivia. **bolivien, -ienne** *a & n* Bolivian.

bombance [bɔ̃bãs] *nf F:* feast(ing); carousing; **faire b.,** to go on a binge.

bombardement [bɔ̃bardəmã] *nm* **1.** bombardment; shelling; pelting **2.** *Av:* bombing; **b. aérien,** air raid.

bombarder [bɔ̃barde] *vtr* **1.** to bombard, bomb, shell; **b. de pierres,** to pelt with stones; **b. qn de questions,** to fire questions at s.o. **2.** *F:* **on l'a bombardé ministre,** he's been made a minister out of the blue.

bombardier [bɔ̃bardje] *nm* (aircraft) bomber.

bombe [bɔ̃b] *nf* **1.** bomb; **b. à retardement,** time bomb; **cela fait l'effet d'une b.,** it was a real bombshell **2.** (*a*) *Cu:* **b. glacée,** ice pudding (*b*) *Com:*

aerosol, spray **3.** riding hat **4. faire la b.,** to go on a binge.

bomber [bɔ̃be] *vtr* (*a*) to cause (sth) to bulge; **b. la poitrine,** to throw out one's chest; **b. le torse,** to swagger (*b*) to bend, arch (one's back). **bombé** *a* convex, curved, rounded, bulging; cambered (road).

bon¹, bonne¹ [bɔ̃, bɔn] **1.** *a* (*a*) good, upright, honest (person) (*b*) good (book, smell); pleasant (evening); comfortable (armchair); **la bonne société,** polite society; *F:* **cela est b. à dire,** it's easier said than done (*c*) (*of pers*) clever, capable; **b. en anglais,** good at English (*d*) good, right, correct, proper; **si j'ai bonne mémoire,** if my memory is reliable; **en b. état,** in working order (*e*) good, kind (**pour, envers,** to); **vous êtes bien b. de m'inviter,** it is very kind of you to invite me (*f*) good, profitable, advantageous; **c'est b. à savoir,** it's worth knowing; **acheter qch à b. marché,** to buy sth cheap(ly); **à quoi b.?** what's the good of it? what's the point, the use? (*g*) good; fit, suitable; **b. à manger,** (i) good to eat (ii) safe to eat; *Mil:* **b. pour le service,** fit for duty; **il n'est b. à rien,** he's useless; **si b. vous semble,** if you think it advisable (*h*) good, favourable; **souhaiter la bonne année à qn,** to wish s.o. a happy New Year; **b. week-end!** have a good weekend! (*i*) good, sound, safe; **billet b. pour trois mois,** ticket valid for three months; *F:* **son compte est b.!** he's in for it! (*j*) good, full; **un b. rhume,** a bad cold; **j'ai attendu deux bonnes heures,** I waited two solid hours; **arriver b. premier,** to come in an easy first (*k*) **pour de b.,** seriously, really, in earnest; **est-ce pour de b.?** are you serious? **c'est b.!** good! enough said! (*l*) *int* **b.!** good! fine! right! **b.,** all right, I'm coming **2.** *adv* **tenir b.,** to stand fast, to hold one's own; **tenez b.!** hold tight! **sentir b.,** to smell nice; **il fait b. vivre,** it's good to be alive **3.** *n* (*a*) **les bons,** the good; *F:* the goodies (*b*) **cela a du b.,** it has its good points (*c*) **en voilà une bonne!** that's a good one!

bon² *nm* **1.** order, voucher, ticket; coupon; **b. de caisse,** cash voucher; **b. de livraison,** delivery note **2.** *Fin:* bond, bill, draft; **b. du Trésor,** treasury bond.

bonbon [bɔ̃bɔ̃] *nm* sweet, *NAm:* candy; **b. acidulé,** acid drop.

bonbonne [bɔ̃bɔn] *nf* (*a*) *Ind:* carboy (*b*) demijohn.

bonbonnière [bɔ̃bɔnjɛr] *nf* **1.** sweetbox **2.** bijou flat.

bond [bɔ̃] *nm* **1.** bound, leap, jump; spring; **faire un b.,** to leap; **les prix ont fait un b.,** prices have shot up; **franchir qch d'un b.,** to clear sth at one jump; **se lever d'un b.,** to spring, to leap, to one's feet **2.** (*of ball*) bounce; **faire faux b. à qn,** to stand s.o. up.

bonde [bɔ̃d] *nf* **1.** bung (of cask) (*b*) plug (of sink) (*c*) *HydE:* sluice gate **2.** bunghole; plughole.

bondé [bɔ̃de] *a* chock-full, packed.

bondir [bɔ̃dir] *vi* (*a*) to leap, to bound; to spring up, jump up; **b. sur qch,** to spring at, pounce on, sth; **b. de joie,** to jump for joy; *F:* **cela me fait b.,** it makes me hopping mad (*b*) to gambol, skip.

bondissement [bɔ̃dismã] *nm* bound, leap.

bonheur [bɔnœr] *nm* **1.** good fortune, good luck, success; **porter b.,** to bring (good) luck; **par b.,** luckily, fortunately; **au petit b. (la chance),** haphazardly **2.** happiness; **faire le b. de qn,** to make s.o. happy; **quel b.!** what bliss! what a delight!

bonhomie [bɔnɔmi] *nf* simple good-heartedness; good nature.

bonhomme [bɔnɔm] *nm* *F:* fellow, chap, bloke, *NAm:* guy; **un vilain b.,** nasty piece of work; **pourquoi pleures-tu, mon b.?** why are you crying sonny? **il va son petit b. de chemin,** he's jogging quietly along; (*in car*) he's bumbling along; **dessiner des bonshommes,** to draw funny people; **b. en pain d'épice,** gingerbread man; **b. de neige,** snowman; *pl* **bonshommes** [bɔ̃zɔm].

bonification [bɔnifikasjɔ̃] *nf* **1.** improvement (of land) **2.** (*a*) *Com:* bonus (*b*) *Sp:* advantage.

bonifier (se) [səbɔnifje] *vpr* to improve.

boniment [bɔnimã] *nm* (*a*) sales talk; patter (*b*) *F:* tall story, fib.

bonjour [bɔ̃ʒur] *nm* good day, good morning, good afternoon; hello; how d'you do? **donnez-lui le b. de ma part,** give him my regards.

bonne² [bɔn] *nf* maid; **b. à tout faire,** general help; maid of all work; **b. d'enfants,** nanny.

Bonne-Espérance [bɔnɛsperãs] *Prnf Geog:* **le Cap de B.-E.,** the Cape of Good Hope.

bonne-maman [bɔnmamã] *nf* *F:* grandma(ma); gran(ny); *pl* **bonnes-mamans.**

bonnement [bɔnmã] *adv* **tout b.,** quite simply.

bonnet [bɔnɛ] *nm* (*a*) brimless cap, hat; (woman's, child's) bonnet; **c'est b. blanc et blanc b.,** it's six of one and half a dozen of the other; **b. de nuit,** nightcap; **b. de bain,** bathing cap; **b. à poil,** bearskin; *F:* **gros b.,** bigwig, big shot (*b*) cup (of brassière).

bonneterie [bɔntri] *nf* **1.** hosiery **2.** hosiery trade; hosier's shop.

bonnetier, -ière [bɔntje, -jɛr] *n* hosier.

bon-papa [bɔ̃papa] *nm* *F:* grandpa(pa), grandad; *pl* **bons-papas.**

bonsoir [bɔ̃swar] *nm* good evening, good night; *F:* **b.!** nothing doing!

bonté [bɔ̃te] *nf* (*a*) goodness, kindness; **b. divine!** good heavens! **ayez la b. de,** please be so kind as to (*b*) *pl* kindnesses, kind actions.

bonze [bɔ̃z] *nm* **1.** bonze, Buddhist monk **2.** *F:* big shot **3.** *F:* **vieux b.,** old fogey.

boomerang [bumrãg] *nm* boomerang.

borax [bɔraks] *nm* *Ch:* borax.

bord [bɔr] *nm* **1.** *Nau:* (*a*) side (of ship); **par-dessus b.,** overboard; **moteur hors b.,** outboard (motor); **b. du vent, sous le vent,** weather side; lee side; **faux b.,** list; **le long du b.,** alongside (*b*) tack, leg; **courir un b.,** to make a tack (*c*) **les hommes du b.,** the ship's company, the crew; **journal de b.,** ship's log; logbook; **à b. d'un navire,** on board a ship; **à b.,** on board (ship); aboard. **2.** (*a*) edge; border, hem; brink, verge; rim, brim; lip (of cup); **b. du trottoir,** kerb, *NAm:* curb; **au b. des larmes,** on the verge of tears; **remplir un verre jusqu'au b., à ras b.,** to fill a glass to the brim; **b. de la rivière,** river bank; **b. de la route,** roadside; **aller au b. de la mer,** to go to the seaside (*b*) brim (of hat); **chapeau à larges bords,** wide-brimmed hat.

bordeaux [bɔrdo] **1.** *nm* Bordeaux (wine); **b. rouge,** claret. **2.** *a inv* maroon, burgundy.

bordée [bɔrde] *nf* *Nau:* **1.** broadside; **b. de jurons,** torrent of abuse **2.** tack; **tirer des bordées,** to tack; to beat up to windward **3.** watch; **b. de tribord, de bâbord,** starboard watch, port watch.

bordel [bɔrdɛl] *nm* brothel; *P:* **quel b.!** what a shambles!

bordelais, -aise [bɔrdəlɛ, -ɛz] *a & n* (native, inhabitant) of Bordeaux.

border [bɔrde] *vtr* to border; to edge, fringe, sth with sth; (*of trees*) to line (road); **b. un lit,** to tuck in the bedclothes; **b. qn,** to tuck s.o. in.

bordereau, -eaux [bɔrdəro] *nm* statement; invoice; note; **b. de paie,** wage(s) slip; salary advice (note); **b. de crédit,** credit note.

bordure [bɔrdyr] *nf* 1. border, rim; edge; fringe; **en b. de,** alongside, along the side of 2. frame.

boréal, -aux [bɔreal, -o] *a* boreal, north(ern).

borgne [bɔrɲ] *a* 1. one-eyed; blind in one eye 2. disreputable, shady (house).

borique [bɔrik] *a* boric, boracic (acid).

borne [bɔrn] *nf* 1. (*a*) boundary mark, stone, post (*b*) **b. kilométrique** = milestone (*c*) *F:* kilometre (*d*) *pl* boundaries, limits; **cela dépasse les bornes,** that's going too far; **sans bornes,** limitless 2. *El:* terminal.

borner [bɔrne] *vtr* 1. (*a*) to mark (out) the boundary of (field); to stake (claim) (*b*) to form the boundary of (country); **le chemin qui borne la forêt,** the path bordering the forest (*c*) to limit, restrict (view, power); to set limits, bounds, to (ambition) 2. **se b.** (*a*) to restrict oneself, to exercise self-restraint; **je me borne au strict nécessaire,** I confine myself to the absolute essentials (*b*) to be limited, restricted (**à. qch,** to sth); **leur science se borne à cela,** this is the extent of their knowledge. **borné** *a* limited; (*pers*) narrow-minded.

bosquet [bɔskɛ] *nm* grove, thicket, copse.

bosse [bɔs] *nf* 1. hump (of camel) 2. (*a*) bump, swelling, lump (*b*) unevenness, bump; **avoir la b. du commerce,** to have a good head for business.

bosseler [bɔsle] *vtr* (**je bosselle**) 1. to emboss (plate) 2. to dent; **casserole toute bosselée,** battered saucepan.

bosser [bɔse] *vi P:* to work hard, to slog.

bosseur, -euse [bɔsœr, -øz] *n P:* hard worker, slogger.

bossu, -ue [bɔsy] 1. *a* hunchbacked (person); humped (animal) 2. *n* hunchback.

bot [bo] *a* **pied b.,** club foot.

botanique [bɔtanik] 1. *a* botanical 2. *nf* botany.

botaniste [bɔtanist] *n* botanist.

botte¹ [bɔt] *nf* bunch (of carrots); sheaf, bale (of hay).

botte² *nf* (high) boot; **bottes à l'écuyère,** riding boots; **bottes cuissardes,** waders; **bottes en caoutchouc,** wellingtons, gumboots; **sous la b. de l'envahisseur,** under the invader's heel.

botte³ *nf Fenc:* thrust.

botter [bɔte] *vtr* 1. (*a*) to put boots, shoes, on (s.o.); **bien botté,** well shod (*b*) to kick (ball); *F:* **il lui a botté les fesses,** he gave him a kick up the backside (*c*) *F:* **ça me botte,** I dig that 2. **se b.,** to put one's boots on.

bottier [bɔtje] *nm* bootmaker.

bottillon [bɔtijɔ̃] *nm* ankle boot.

Bottin [bɔtɛ̃] *nm Rtm:* French telephone and street directory.

bottine [bɔtin] *nf* ankle boot.

bouc [buk] *nm* (billy) goat; **(barbe de) b.,** goatee (beard); **b. émissaire,** scapegoat.

boucan [bukɑ̃] *nm P:* row, din, racket.

bouche [buʃ] *nf* 1. mouth; **parler la b. pleine,** to talk with one's mouth full; **garder qch pour la bonne b.,** to keep something as a titbit; **faire la petite b.,** to turn one's nose up; **c'est une fine b.,** he's a gourmet; **b. cousue!** mum's the word! *F:* **il en avait plein la b.,** he was full of it, he could talk of nothing else; **de b. à oreille,** by word of mouth 2. mouth (of horse, fish) 3. mouth (of river); opening, aperture (of well); muzzle (of gun); **b. de métro,** underground entrance; **b. d'accès,** manhole; **b. d'incendie,** fire hydrant; **b. d'aération,** air vent.

bouche-à-bouche [buʃabuʃ] *nm inv* mouth-to-mouth resuscitation; kiss of life.

bouchée [buʃe] *nf* 1. mouthful; **mettre les bouchées doubles,** to do a job in double quick time; **ne faire qu'une b. de qch,** to make short work of sth 2. *Cu:* **b. à la reine,** chicken vol-au-vent.

boucher¹ [buʃe] *vtr* 1. to fill up (gap); to block (up), choke (up), clog; to block (view); **b. un trou,** to plug a hole; **cela servira à b. un trou,** it will serve as a stopgap; **b. une bouteille,** to cork a bottle; **b. le passage à qn,** to stand in s.o.'s way 2. **se b.,** to get blocked (up), clogged; **se b. le nez,** to hold one's nose; **se b. les oreilles,** to put one's fingers in one's ears. **bouché** *a* blocked; (*of weather*) overcast; **avoir l'esprit b.,** to be thick.

boucher² *nm* butcher.

bouchère [buʃɛr] *nf* (*a*) butcher's wife (*b*) (woman) butcher.

boucherie [buʃri] *nf* 1. (*a*) butcher's (shop) (*b*) butchery 2. *Fig:* slaughter, butchery.

bouche-trou [buʃtru] *nm* stopgap; *pl* bouche-trous.

bouchon [buʃɔ̃] *nm* 1. wisp, handful (of straw) 2. (*a*) stopper, plug, bung; cap, top (of bottle); cork; (radiator) cap (*b*) traffic jam; holdup.

bouclage [buklaʒ] *nm* (*a*) *F:* locking up (*b*) sealing off.

boucle [bukl] *nf* 1. buckle 2. (*a*) loop, bow (of ribbon) (*b*) loop (of river); bend (of road) (*c*) *Av: Cmptr:* loop 3. ring; **boucles d'oreilles,** earrings 4. curl, ringlet (of hair) 5. *Sp:* lap.

boucler [bukle] 1. *vtr* (*a*) to buckle (belt); to fasten (strap); *P:* **boucle-la! tu vas la b.!** (will you) belt up! *F:* **b. une affaire,** to clinch a matter; **b. sa valise,** to pack one's bags (*b*) to loop, tie up, knot (ribbon); *Av:* **b. la boucle,** to loop the loop (*c*) *F:* to lock up, imprison (*d*) to seal off (area) (*e*) *Sp:* to lap (competitor) 2. *vi* (*of hair*) to curl, to be curly. **bouclé** *a* curly.

bouclier [buklij(ə)e] *nm* shield.

Bouddha [buda] *Prnm* Buddha.

bouddhisme [budism] *nm* Buddhism. **bouddhique** *a* Buddhist(ic). **buddhiste** *a & n* Buddhist.

bouder [bude] 1. *vi* to sulk 2. *vtr* **b. qn,** to refuse to have anything to do with s.o.; **ils se boudent,** they're not on speaking terms.

bouderie [budri] *nf* sulkiness; sulk. **boudeur, -euse** *a* sulky.

boudin [budɛ̃] *nm* 1. (*a*) *Cu:* **b. (noir),** black pudding; **b. blanc,** white pudding (*b*) *F:* **boudins,** fat, podgy fingers 2. corkscrew curl; roll, twist (of tobacco). **boudiné** *a* (*a*) **b. dans,** squeezed into, bulging out of (*b*) podgy (fingers).

boudoir [budwar] nm (a) boudoir (b) Comest: (trifle) sponge, sponge finger.

boue [bu] nf 1. mud, slush 2. sediment, mud, sludge. **boueux, -euse** 1. a muddy 2. nm = **boueur.**

bouée [bue] nf Nau: 1. buoy, rubber ring (for non-swimmer); **b. à cloche,** bell buoy 2. **b. de sauvetage,** lifebuoy.

boueur [bucer] nm dustman, NAm: garbage collector.

bouffe [buf] nf F: food, grub.

bouffée [bufe] nf 1. puff (of smoke); whiff (of scent); **b. de chaleur,** blast of hot air; Med: hot flush 2. outburst (of anger); fit (of pride).

bouffer [bufe] 1. vi (of dress) to puff (out), swell out 2. F: (a) vi to gobble, to scoff (b) vtr & i to eat (sth); **on n'a rien à b.,** there's no grub. **bouffant** a puffed (sleeve); full (skirt); baggy (trousers).

bouffir [bufir] 1. vtr to swell, puff up, out 2. vi to become swollen, bloated; to puff up. **bouffi** a puffy, swollen (eyes); bloated (face).

bouffissure [bufisyr] nf swelling, puffiness.

bouffon, -onne [bufɔ̃, -ɔn] 1. a farcical, comical 2. nm buffoon, clown, jester.

bouffonnerie [bufɔnri] nf buffoonery, clowning.

bougeoir [buʒwar] nm (flat) candlestick; candle holder.

bougeotte [buʒɔt] nf F: **avoir la b.,** to be fidgety; to have itchy feet.

bouger [buʒe] v (n. bougeons) 1. vi (a) to move, budge, stir; **rester sans b.,** to stand still; **ne bougez pas,** don't move (b) **les prix ne bougent pas,** prices are steady (c) Pol: to stir 2. vtr F: **il ne faut rien b.,** you must not move anything 3. F: **se b.,** to move; to shift (oneself).

bougie [buʒi] nf 1. candle; **à la b.,** by candlelight 2. El: watt 3. ICE: **b. (d'allumage),** spark(ing) plug 4. P: face, mug.

bougonnement [bugɔnmɑ̃] nm grumbling, grousing. **bougon, -onne** 1. n grumbler, grouser 2. a grumpy.

bougonner [bugɔne] vi to grumble.

bougre [bugr] nm F: 1. chap, bloke; **pauvre b.,** poor devil 2. (a) **b. d'imbécile,** bloody idiot (b) int blast! **bougrement** adv F: damned.

bouillabaisse [bujabɛs] nf Cu: Provençal fishsoup; bouillabaisse.

bouillie [buji] nf gruel; **réduire en b.,** to crush to a pulp.

bouillir [bujir] vi (prp bouillant; pr ind je bous, n. bouillons; impf je bouillais) to boil; **faire b. qch,** to boil sth; **b. de colère,** to seethe with anger; **ça me fait b.,** it makes my blood boil. **bouillant** a 1. boiling 2. fiery (temper).

bouilloire [bujwar] nf kettle.

bouillon [bujɔ̃] nm 1. bubble; **le sang coulait à gros bouillons,** the blood was gushing out 2. (a) Cu: (meat, vegetable) stock; **b. gras,** clear (meat) soup; beef tea; **b. cube,** stock cube; **boire un b.,** (i) to get a mouthful (when swimming) (ii) to suffer a heavy loss (in business) (b) Biol: **b. de culture,** culture medium.

bouillonnement [bujɔnmɑ̃] nm bubbling, foaming, frothing.

bouillonner [bujɔne] vi to bubble, seethe, foam, froth up.

bouillotte [bujɔt] nf hot water bottle.

boulanger [bulɑ̃ʒe] nm baker.

boulangère [bulɑ̃ʒɛr] nf (a) baker's wife (b) (woman) baker.

boulangerie [bulɑ̃ʒri] nf 1. bakery trade 2. (a) bakery (b) baker's (shop).

boule [bul] nf 1. (a) ball, sphere, globe; F: **se mettre en b.,** to get angry; **b. dans la gorge,** lump in one's throat (b) F: **perdre la b.,** to go off one's head, to go nuts (c) **b. de scrutin,** ballot (ball) 2. Games: (croquet, hockey) ball; bowl; **jouer aux boules,** to play bowls; **jeu de boules,** (game of) bowls.

bouleau, -eaux [bulo] nm (silver) birch (tree).

bouledogue [buldɔg] nm bulldog.

boulet [bulɛ] nm 1. (a) **b. (de canon),** cannonball (b) ball and chain; Fig: **traîner un b.,** to have a millstone round one's neck 2. (coal) nut.

boulette [bulɛt] nf 1. pellet (of paper) 2. Cu: meatball 3. F: **faire une b.,** to drop a brick.

boulevard [bulvar] nm boulevard; **théâtre de b.** = variety show.

bouleversant [bulvɛrsɑ̃] a upsetting, bewildering.

bouleversement [bulvɛrsəmɑ̃] nm (a) upheaval, disruption (b) distress, anxiety.

bouleverser [bulvɛrse] vtr (a) to upset, overthrow; to disrupt (b) to upset, to distress (s.o.). **bouleversant** a distressing; staggering.

boulier [bulje] nm **b. (compteur),** abacus.

boulon [bulɔ̃] nm bolt.

boulonner [bulɔne] 1. vtr to bolt (down) 2. vi F: to work hard, to slog.

boulot, -otte [bulo, -ɔt] 1. a & n plump, tubby (person) 2. nm F: work, job.

boum [bum] 1. int & nm bang! boom! 2. nm Com: boom; **en plein b.,** in full swing 3. nf (young people's) party.

bouquet [bukɛ] nm 1. (a) bunch of flowers, posy, bouquet (b) cluster, clump (of trees) 2. bouquet (of wine) 3. Pyr: crowning piece; F: **ça, c'est le b.,!** that takes the biscuit! 4. prawn.

bouquin [bukɛ̃] nm F: book.

bouquiner [bukine] vi F: to read.

bouquiniste [bukinist] nm second-hand bookseller.

bourbier [burbje] nm slough, (quag)mire; mess.

bourde [burd] nf F: blunder, bloomer.

bourdon [burdɔ̃] nm 1. Mus: drone (of bagpipes) 2. great bell 3. (a) Ent: bumble-bee (b) P: **avoir le b.,** to be down in the dumps.

bourdonnement [burdɔnmɑ̃] nm buzz(ing); drone, droning; Med: buzzing in the ears.

bourdonner [burdɔne] vi to buzz, to drone.

bourg [bur] nm small market town.

bourgade [burgad] nf large village, township.

bourgeois, -oise [burʒwa, -waz] a & n 1. n (a) burgess; citizen (b) commoner 2. a & n (a) middle-class (person); **cuisine bourgeoise,** home cooking (b) Pej: philistine; a bourgeois (c) P: **la bourgeoise,** the wife, the missus. **bourgeoisement** adv conventionally; comfortably.

bourgeoisie [burʒwazi] nf the middle class(es); **la petite b.,** the lower middle class.

bourgeon [burʒɔ̃] nm Bot: bud.

bourgeonner [burʒɔne] *vi Bot:* to (come into) bud; to b(o)urgeon.

bourgmestre [burgmɛstr] *nm* burgomaster.

Bourgogne [burgɔɲ] 1. *Prnf Geog:* Burgundy 2. *nm* (vin de) B., Burgundy (wine).

bourguignon, -onne [burgiɲɔ̃, -ɔn] *a & n* Burgundian.

bourlinguer [burlɛ̃ge] *vi (a)* to sail *(b) F:* b. de par le monde, to knock about the world.

bourrade [burad] *nf* blow; thump; poke (in the ribs).

bourrage [buraʒ] *nm Sch:* cramming; *F:* b. de crâne, eyewash; brainwashing.

bourrasque [burask] *nf* squall; gust of wind; (snow) flurry.

bourratif [buratif] *a* stodgy, filling (food).

bourre [bur] *nf* 1. padding, wadding 2. wad (of firearm).

bourreau [buro] *nm* 1. executioner; hangman 2. torturer, tormentor; b. de travail, glutton for work; b. des cœurs, ladykiller.

bourrelet [burlɛ] *nm* 1. *(a)* pad, wad, cushion *(b)* draught excluder 2. b. de graisse, roll of fat; *F:* spare tyre.

bourrer [bure] *vtr* 1. to stuff, pad (cushion); to cram (cupboard); to fill (pipe with tobacco); *F:* b. un élève, to cram a pupil; *F:* b. le crâne à qn, to stuff s.o.'s head with nonsense; to brainwash s.o.; aliment qui bourre, filling food; b. qn (de coups), to beat s.o. up 2. se b., to stuff oneself (with food). **bourré** *a (a)* stuffed, crammed (de, with) *(b) P:* drunk, plastered.

bourrique [burik] *nf (a)* she ass; donkey *(b) F:* dunce, ass; têtu comme une b., as stubborn as a mule; faire tourner qn en b., to drive s.o. mad.

bourru [bury] *a* surly.

bourse [burs] *nf* 1. purse, pouch; la b. ou la vie! your money or your life! sans b. délier, without spending a penny; faire b. commune, to pool resources 2. *Sch:* b. (d'études), grant; scholarship 3. stock exchange; jouer à la B., to speculate; b. de commerce, commodities exchange; b. de l'emploi, job centre. **boursier, -ière** 1. *a* Stock Exchange (transactions) 2. *n* grant, scholarship, holder.

boursouflé [bursufle] *a* swollen, bloated; style b., inflated, turgid, style.

boursoufler [bursufle] *vtr* 1. to puff up, swell (face); to blister (paint) 2. *(of paint)* se b., to blister. **boursouflure** [bursuflyr] *nf* swelling, puffiness (of face); blister (of paint).

bousculade [buskylad] *nf* scuffle; hustle; jostle; crush; rush.

bousculer [buskyle] *vtr* 1. b. qn, to jostle, hustle, s.o.; to knock into s.o. 2. b. qn, to rush s.o.; il est toujours bousculé, he's always in a rush. se b., to jostle one another.

bouse [buz] *nf* b. de vache, cow dung; cowpat.

bousiller [buzije] *vtr F:* to bungle, botch (up) a piece of work; to wreck, to smash up (a car); b. qn, to bump s.o. off.

boussole [busɔl] *nf* compass; *F:* perdre la b., to go off one's head.

bout [bu] *nm* 1. end; extremity; au b. de la rue, at the end, at the bottom, of the street; le haut b. de la table, the head of the table; b. à b., end to end, end on; joindre les deux bouts, to make ends meet; au b.

du compte, after all; in the end; *adv phr* de b. en b., from beginning to end, from end to end; d'un b. à l'autre, from one end to the other, from end to end; c'est le b. du monde, (i) it's a dump (ii) it's the outside limit; au b. d'une heure, after an hour; aller jusqu'au b., to go on to the bitter end; to see it through; être à b., to be exhausted; pousser qn à b., to exasperate s.o.; à b. de patience, at the end of one's tether; être au b. de son rouleau, (i) to have run out of resources (ii) to be at the end of one's tether; venir à b. de (faire) qch, to succeed in doing sth 2. end, tip, end-piece; b. du doigt, de la langue, fingertip; tip of the tongue; b. de pied, toecap; à b. portant, (at) point blank (range); b. filtre, filter tip (of cigarette); on ne sait jamais par quel b. le prendre, one never knows how to approach him 3. bit, fragment; scrap (of paper); piece (of string); un b. de jardin, a bit of garden; un b. de temps, a (little) while; un bon b. de temps, quite a while; cela fait un b. de chemin, it's quite a long way.

boutade [butad] *nf* 1. whim, caprice 2. sally; flash of wit.

boute-en-train [butɑ̃trɛ̃] *nm inv* live wire; the life and soul of a party.

bouteille [butɛj] *nf (a)* bottle; b. isolante, vacuum flask; mettre en bouteilles, to bottle; *F:* prendre de la b., to get long in the tooth *(b)* (gas) cylinder.

boutique [butik] *nf* shop; (small) store; fermer b., to shut up shop; to close down; *F:* parler b., to talk shop; *F:* c'est une sale b.! it's a rotten dump!

boutiquier, -ière [butikje, -jɛr] *n* shopkeeper.

bouton [butɔ̃] *nm* 1. bud; b. de rose, rosebud; en b., budding, in bud 2. button; b. de plastron, stud; b. de col, collar stud; boutons de manchettes, cuff links 3. knob (of door, radio); handle (of door); (push) button; *El:* switch; b. de sonnerie, bellpush 4. spot, pimple (on face). **boutonneux, -euse** *a* spotty, pimply.

bouton-d'or [butɔ̃dɔr] *nm* buttercup.

boutonner [butɔne] 1. *vtr* to button (up) (coat, dress) 2. se b., to button (up); to button oneself up.

boutonnière [butɔnjɛr] *nf* buttonhole.

bouture [butyr] *nf Hort:* cutting.

bouturer [butyre] *vtr* to propagate by cuttings.

bouvier [buvje] *nm* herdsman.

bouvreuil [buvrœj] *nm Orn:* bullfinch.

bovin [bɔvɛ̃] 1. *a* bovine 2. *nmpl* cattle.

bowling [boliŋ] *nm* 1. (tenpin) bowling 2. bowling alley.

box [bɔks] *nm* 1. horse-box, loose box 2. *(a)* cubicle (in dormitory) *(b) Jur:* b. des accusés, dock 3. lock-up (garage); *pl* boxes.

boxe [bɔks] *nf* boxing.

boxer¹ [bɔkse] *vtr & i* to box.

boxer² [bɔkser] *nm* boxer (dog).

boxeur [bɔksœr] *nm* boxer.

boyau, -aux [bwajo] *nm* 1. bowel, gut; (corde de) b., (cat)gut 2. *(a)* hosepipe *(b) Cy:* tubular tyre 3. narrow passage.

boycott(age) [bɔjkɔt(aʒ)] *nm* boycott, boycotting.

boycotter [bɔjkɔte] *vtr* to boycott.

BP *abbr Boîte postale.*

brabançon, -onne [brabɑ̃sɔ̃, -ɔn] *a & n* Brabantine; la Brabançonne, the Belgian national anthem.

bracelet [braslɛ] nm **1.** bracelet, bangle; strap (of wristwatch) **2.** metal band, ring.
bracelet-montre [braslɛmɔ̃tr̩] nm wristwatch; pl *bracelets-montres.*
braconnage [brakɔnaʒ] nm poaching.
braconner [brakɔne] vi to poach.
braconnier [brakɔnje] nm poacher.
braderie [bradri] nf jumble sale; clearance sale.
braguette [bragɛt] nf flies, fly (of trousers).
braillement [brajmã] nm bawling.
brailler [braje] **1.** vi to bawl **2.** vtr to bawl out (a song). **braillard, -arde 1.** a bawling **2.** n bawler.
braire [brɛr] vi to bray.
braise [brɛz] nf (glowing) embers; **yeux de b.,** glowing eyes.
braiser [breze] vtr Cu: to braise.
bramer [brame] vi (a) (of stag) to bell (b) to howl.
brancard [brãkar] nm (a) shaft (of stretcher) (b) stretcher.
brancardier [brãkardje] nm stretcher bearer.
branchage [brãʃaʒ] nm (a) coll branches, boughs (of trees) (b) pl cut, fallen, branches.
branche [brãʃ] nf **1.** (a) branch, bough; **céleri en branches,** sticks of celery (b) branch (of family); **la b. maternelle,** the mother's side (c) branch (of river, nerve, industry) **2.** leg (of compasses); side (of spectacle frame); blade (of propeller).
branchement [brãʃmã] nm plugging in, connecting (up); branch; connection.
brancher [brãʃe] vtr El: to plug in; to connect up; Tp: to put (s.o.) through.
branchies [brãʃi] nfpl gills (of fish).
brandir [brãdir] vtr to brandish, flourish.
branle [brãl] nm (a) oscillation, swing (motion) (b) impulse, impetus; **mettre qch en b.,** to set sth going; **se mettre en b.,** to get going.
branle-bas [brãlba] nm inv **1.** Navy: **b.-b. de combat!** action stations! **2.** commotion, confusion.
branler [brãle] **1.** vtr to shake, nod (one's head) **2.** vi to shake, to move; to be loose; **dent qui branle,** loose tooth.
braquer [brake] vtr **1.** (a) **b. un fusil sur qch,** to aim, to point, a gun at sth (b) **b. les yeux sur qn,** to fix one's eye(s) on s.o. (c) Aut: to manoeuvre, to turn (car) (d) to antagonize (s.o.); **b. qn contre qn,** to turn s.o. against s.o. **2.** vi Aut: to turn the wheel; **la voiture braque bien, mal,** the car has a good, a poor, lock.
braquet [brakɛ] nm Cy: gear ratio.
bras [bra] nm **1.** (a) arm; Fig: **avoir le b. long,** to have a lot of influence; **offrir le b. à qn,** to offer s.o. one's arm; **b. dessus b. dessous,** arm in arm; **les b. m'en tombent,** I'm astounded; **rester les b. croisés,** to twiddle one's thumbs; **ouvrir les b. à qn,** to receive s.o. with open arms; **avoir qn sur les b.,** to have s.o. on one's hands; **voiture à b.,** handcart; **à bout de b.,** at arm's length; **saisir qn à b.-le-corps,** to grapple with s.o.; **en b. de chemise,** in one's shirtsleeves (b) pl hands, workmen; **manquer de b.,** to be shorthanded **2.** arm(rest) (of chair); arm (of lever); jib (of crane); limb (of cross); handle (of pump); (pickup) arm; **b. d'un fleuve,** arm of a river.
brasier [brazje] nm glowing fire; Fig: inferno.

brassage [brasaʒ] nm **1.** brewing (of beer) **2.** mixing, stirring.
brassard [brasar] nm armband.
brasse [bras] nf **1.** Swim: breast stroke; **b. papillon,** butterfly stroke **2.** Nau: fathom.
brassée [brase] nf armful.
brasser [brase] vtr **1.** to brew (beer) **2.** to mix, stir (up); **b. des affaires,** to be doing good business.
brasserie [brasri] nf **1.** brewery **2.** brewing **3.** restaurant (with bar); brasserie.
brasseur, -euse [brasœr, -øz] n **1.** brewer **2.** big businessman; **b. d'affaires,** tycoon.
brassière [brasjɛr] nf (baby's) (sleeved) vest.
bravade [bravad] nf bravado.
brave [brav] a **1.** brave, courageous **2.** good, honest, worthy; **c'est un b. homme,** F: **un b. type,** he's a good sort. **bravement** adv bravely.
braver [brave] vtr **1.** to brave; to face (sth) bravely **2.** to defy, dare (s.o.).
bravo [bravo] **1.** int bravo! well done! hear, hear! **2.** nmpl **des bravos,** applause, cheers.
bravoure [bravur] nf bravery.
break [brɛk] nm Aut: estate (car), station wagon.
brebis [brəbi] nf **1.** ewe **2.** sheep; **b. égarée, b. galeuse,** lost sheep, black sheep.
brèche [brɛʃ] nf breach, opening, gap, break (in hedge, wall); **être toujours sur la b.,** to be always on the go.
bredouille [brəduj] a inv **rentrer, revenir, b.,** to come back empty handed.
bredouillement [brədujmã] nm mumbling.
bredouiller [brəduje] **1.** vi to mumble **2.** vtr **b. une excuse,** to mumble an excuse.
bref, brève [brɛf, brɛv] **1.** a brief, short; **soyez b.,** be brief; **raconter qch en b.,** to relate sth in a few words **2.** adv briefly, in short.
brelan [brəlã] nm Cards: three of a kind; **b. d'as,** three aces.
breloque [brəlɔk] nf charm (on bracelet).
brème [brɛm] nf Ich: bream.
Brême [brɛm] Prnf Geog: Bremen.
Brésil [brezil] Prnm Geog: Brazil. **brésilien, -ienne** a & n Brazilian.
Bretagne [brətaɲ] Prnf Geog: Brittany.
bretelle [brətɛl] nf **1.** strap; (rifle) sling **2.** Cl: (a) shoulder strap (b) **(paire de) bretelles,** (pair of) braces, NAm: suspenders **3.** (a) Rail: crossover (b) access road; (motorway) sliproad.
breton, -onne [brətɔ̃, -ɔn] a & n Breton.
breuvage [brœvaʒ] nm beverage, drink.
brève [brɛv] a see bref.
brevet [brəvɛ] nm **1.** **b. (d'invention),** (letters) patent **2.** (a) diploma, certificate; Sch: = (GCE) O-level; Nau: **b. de capitaine,** master's certificate, F: master's ticket; Av: **b. de pilote,** pilot's licence (b) guarantee.
breveter [brəvte] vtr **(je brevète)** to patent (invention). **brevetable** a patentable. **breveté** a (a) patented (b) qualified.
bréviaire [brevjɛr] nm Ecc: breviary.
bribe [brib] nf usu pl **des bribes,** scraps, fragments; **bribes de conversation,** snatches of conversation; **par bribes,** piecemeal; bit by bit.
bric [brik] nm used in: **de b. et de broc,** haphazardly; F: any old how.

bric-à-brac [brikabrak] *nm inv* (a) odds and ends, bric-a-brac (b) junk shop.

brick [brik] *nm Nau:* brig.

bricolage [brikolaʒ] *nm* pottering about, tinkering about; odd jobs; **mordu du b.,** do-it-yourself enthusiast.

bricole [brikɔl] *nf usu pl* odd jobs; trifles, odds and ends; **s'occuper à des bricoles,** to potter about.

bricoler [brikole] **1.** *vtr* to knock together (a table); to tinker with (sth) **2.** *vi* to potter about, to do odd jobs.

bricoleur, -euse [brikɔlœr, -øz] *n* handyman; do-it-yourself enthusiast.

bride [brid] *nf* (a) bridle (b) rein(s); **aller à b. abattue,** to ride at full speed, *F:* to ride hell for leather; **laisser la b. sur le cou à un cheval, à qn,** to give a horse his head; to give s.o. a free hand; **tenir un cheval en b.,** to curb a horse; **tenir qn en b.,** to keep a tight rein on s.o.

brider [bride] *vtr* **1.** (a) to bridle (horse) (b) **b. ses passions,** to curb one's passions **2.** to tie up, fasten (up); *Cu:* to truss (fowl). **bridé** a tied up, constricted; **yeux bridés,** slanting eyes.

bridge [bridʒ] *nm Cards: Dent:* bridge.

bridger [bridʒe] *vi* (**je bridgeais**) to play bridge.

bridgeur, -euse [bridʒœr, -øz] *n* bridge player.

brièveté [brivte] *nf* shortness, brevity. **brièvement** *adv* briefly.

brigade [brigad] *nf* **1.** *Mil:* brigade; *Av:* **b. aérienne,** group, *NAm:* wing **2.** squad, detachment (of policemen); team (of workmen).

brigadier [brigadje] *nm* (a) *Mil:* corporal (b) **b. (de police),** (police) sergeant.

brigand [brigɑ̃] *nm* brigand; crook; ruffian.

brigandage [brigɑ̃daʒ] *nm* brigandage, robbery.

briguer [brige] *vtr* to solicit, to canvass for (sth); **b. des voix,** to canvass (for votes).

brillant [brijɑ̃] **1.** *a* (a) brilliant; sparkling, glittering (gem); shiny, glossy (b) splendid, striking; brilliant (pupil, speaker) (c) **je ne suis pas b.,** I'm not feeling too well **2.** *nm* (a) brilliancy, brilliance, brightness; sparkle, glitter; glossiness (b) polish, shine (on shoes) **3.** *nm* brilliant (diamond). **brillamment** *adv* brilliantly.

briller [brije] *vi* **1.** to shine; to glisten, gleam, glint; (of stars) to twinkle, sparkle; (of headlights) to glare **2.** (of pers) to shine, to be successful; **b. dans la conversation,** to be a brilliant conversationalist; **b. par son absence,** to be conspicuous by one's absence.

brimade [brimad] *nf* **1.** rough joke **2.** *pl* ragging.

brimer [brime] *vtr* (a) to rag (b) to bully; **je suis brimé,** I'm being got at.

brin [brɛ̃] *nm* **1.** blade (of grass); sprig, twig (of myrtle); wisp (of straw); **un beau b. de fille,** a handsome girl **2.** *F:* bit, fragment; **un b. d'air,** a breath of air; **un b. d'envie,** a touch of envy; **un b. de toilette,** a quick wash (and brush-up) **3.** strand (of rope); ply (of wool) **4.** *adv* **il est un b. ennuyeux,** he's a bit of a bore.

brindille [brɛ̃dij] *nf* twig, sprig.

bringue [brɛ̃g] *nf P:* **1. grande b.,** gangling girl **2.** binge; **faire la b.,** to go on a binge.

bringuebaler [brɛ̃gbale] *F:* **1.** *vi* to swing, to joggle, to shake about **2.** *vtr* to cart about.

brio [brijo] *nm* (a) *Mus:* brio (b) **avec b.,** brilliantly.

brioche [brijɔʃ] *nf Cu:* brioche; *F:* paunch.

brique [brik] *nf* **1.** brick **2.** *a inv* brick-red.

briquet [brike] *nm* (cigarette) lighter.

bris [bri] *nm* **1.** breaking (of glass) **2.** *Jur:* **b. de clôture,** breach of close.

brisant [brizɑ̃] *nm* (a) reef (b) breaker.

brise [briz] *nf* breeze.

brisé [brize] *a* **b. de fatigue,** tired out.

brise-fer [brizfɛr] *nm or f inv* destructive child.

brise-glace [brizglas] *nm inv* (ship) icebreaker.

brise-lames [brizlam] *nm inv* breakwater.

briser [brize] *vtr* **1.** (a) to break, smash; **b. une porte,** to break open a door; **b. qch en éclats,** to smash sth to smithereens (b) to crush (ore) (c) to break (treaty); to break down (opposition); to wear (s.o.) out; to break (s.o.'s heart); **brisé par la douleur,** crushed by grief (d) to break off (conversation) **2.** *vi & pr* (a) to break (with s.o.) (b) (of waves) (se) **b.,** to break (c) (of glass) se **b.,** to break; to be smashed; (of hopes) to be shattered, dashed.

briseur, -euse [brizœr, -øz] *n* breaker; **b. de grève,** strike breaker; blackleg.

brise-vent [brizvɑ̃] *nm inv* windbreak.

brisure [brizyr] *nf* break.

britannique [britanik] **1.** *a* British **2.** *n* Briton, British subject; *pl* the British.

broc [bro] *nm* pitcher; (large) jug.

brocante [brɔkɑ̃t] *nf* antiques, secondhand goods (trade).

brocanter [brɔkɑ̃te] *vi* to deal in, to sell, antiques; to deal in, to sell, secondhand goods.

brocanteur, -euse [brɔkɑ̃tœr, -øz] *n* dealer in antiques, in secondhand goods.

brocart [brɔkar] *nm Tex:* brocade.

broche [brɔʃ] *nf* **1.** *Cu:* (a) spit (b) meat skewer **2.** peg, pin **3.** *Tex:* spindle **4.** brooch.

brocher [brɔʃe] *vtr Bookb:* to stitch, sew (book); **livre broché,** paperback (book).

brochet [brɔʃe] *nm Ich:* pike.

brochette [brɔʃɛt] *nf* **1.** (a) skewer (b) *Cu:* kebab **2.** **b. de décorations,** row of medals.

brochure [brɔʃyr] *nf* **1.** stitching (of books) **2.** brochure, pamphlet.

broder [brɔde] *vtr* to embroider; **b. une histoire,** to elaborate (on) a story.

broderie [brɔdri] *nf* embroidery.

brome [brom] *nm Ch:* bromine.

bromure [brɔmyr] *nm Ch:* bromide.

bronche [brɔ̃ʃ] *nf Anat:* bronchus, *pl* bronchi; bronchial tube.

broncher [brɔ̃ʃe] *vi* **1.** (of horse) (a) to stumble (b) to shy **2.** *F:* (a) to flinch; **sans b.,** without turning a hair (b) *F:* to budge, to move.

bronchite [brɔ̃ʃit] *nf Med:* bronchitis.

bronzage [brɔ̃zaʒ] *nm* suntan.

bronze [brɔ̃z] *nm* (metal, object) bronze.

bronzer [brɔ̃ze] **1.** *vtr* to tan (skin); **teint bronzé,** suntanned complexion **2.** *vi & pr* (se) **b.,** to (get a) tan, to go brown; to sunbathe.

brossage [brɔsaʒ] *nm* brushing.

brosse [brɔs] *nf* (a) brush; **b. à cheveux, à habits,** hairbrush, clothes brush; **b. à dents,** toothbrush; **b. métallique,** wire brush; **donner un coup de b. à qch,**

to give sth a brush; *Hairdr:* **cheveux en b.**, crew cut (*b*) (paint) brush; **passer la b. sur qch**, to paint sth out.

brosser [brɔse] *vtr* **1.** to brush; to scrub (floor); **se b.**, to brush oneself down; **se b. les dents**, to brush one's teeth; *F:* **tu peux te b.!** you can whistle for it! **2.** to paint (boldly).

brouette [bruɛt] *nf* wheelbarrow.

brouhaha [bruaa] *nm F:* hubbub; uproar; hum (of conversation).

brouillage [brujaʒ] *nm WTel: Elcs:* jamming; interference.

brouillard [brujar] *nm* fog; mist; haze; **il fait du b.**, it's foggy; **je suis dans le b.**, I can't make head or tail of it.

brouille [bruj] *nf* quarrel; tiff.

brouiller [bruje] *vtr* **1.** to mix up, jumble; to muddle (s.o.); **b. des œufs**, to scramble eggs; **b. les cartes**, (i) to shuffle the cards (ii) to spread confusion **2.** to cause a misunderstanding between (people) **3.** *WTel: Elcs:* to jam (transmission) **4. se b.** (*a*) to become mixed, confused; **le temps se brouille**, the weather is breaking up (*b*) **yeux brouillés de larmes**, eyes blurred with tears (*c*) to quarrel, to fall out.

brouillon, -onne [brujɔ̃, -ɔn] **1.** *a* disorganized; muddleheaded **2.** *n* muddler **3.** *nm* (rough) draft; *Sch:* rough work; (**papier**) **b.**, scrap paper.

broussaille [brusɑj] *nf usu pl* brushwood; undergrowth, scrub; **cheveux en b.**, unkempt hair. **broussailleux, -euse** *a* bushy; scrubby.

brousse [brus] *nf Geog:* (i) the bush (ii) *Austr:* the outback; *F:* the back of beyond.

brouter [brute] **1.** *vtr & i* **b. (l'herbe)**, to browse, to graze (on the grass) **2.** *vi* (*of brake*) to judder.

broyage [brwajaʒ] *nm* crushing, grinding.

broyer [brwaje] *vtr* (**je broie, n. broyons**) to pound, crush, grind, pulverize; *F:* **b. du noir**, to be down in the dumps. **broyeur, -euse 1.** *a* grinding **2.** *nm* grinder.

bru [bry] *nf* daughter-in-law.

brugnon [brynɔ̃] *nm* nectarine.

bruine [brɥin] *nf* fine rain; drizzle.

bruiner [brɥine] *v impers* to drizzle.

bruire [brɥir] *vi def* (*prp* **bruissant**; *pr ind* **il bruit, ils bruissent**; *impf* **il bruissait**) to rustle; to rumble; (*of machinery*) to hum; (*of brook*) to murmur; (*of bees*) to buzz.

bruissement [brɥismɑ̃] *nm* rumbling; hum(ming) (of machinery); murmuring (of brook); buzzing (of bees).

bruit [brɥi] *nm* **1.** (*a*) noise; sound; clatter (of dishes); **b. métallique**, clang; **b. de pas**, (sound of) footsteps; **b. sourd**, thud, thump; **faire du b.**, to make a noise, to be noisy; **quel b.!** what a row, a racket! **b. de fond**, background noise (*b*) noise, fuss; **beaucoup de b. pour rien**, much ado about nothing; **faire grand b. de qch**, to make a great to-do about sth; **sans b.**, silently, quietly **2.** rumour, report; **le bruit court que**, rumour has it that.

bruitage [brɥitaʒ] *nm Th: Cin: TV:* sound effects.

bruiteur [brɥitœr] *nm Th: Cin: TV:* sound effects man.

brûlé [bryle] **1.** *a* burnt; *Cu:* **crème brûlée**, caramel custard; **crème brûlée**; **cerveau b.**, daredevil **2.** *nm*

odeur de b., smell of burning; **ça sent le b.**, there's trouble brewing.

brûle-parfum(s) [brylparfœ̃] *nm inv* perfume burner.

brûle-pourpoint (à) [abrylpurpwɛ̃] *adv phr* point-blank.

brûler [bryle] **1.** *vtr* (*a*) to burn; to burn (down) (house); to burn (up) (rubbish) (*b*) to use, consume, burn (fuel, electricity) (*c*) (*of acid*) to corrode (*d*) to scorch; to burn (toast); to roast (coffee); **le lait est brûlé**, the milk has caught; **terre brûlée par le soleil**, sun-scorched earth; **b. le pavé, la route**, to tear along the road (*e*) *Aut:* **b. les feux, un feu rouge**, to jump the lights, to go through a red light; **b. un concurrent**, to race past a competitor (*f*) (*of frost*) to nip (buds); **la fumée me brûlait les yeux**, the smoke made my eyes smart (*g*) *F:* **b. un espion**, to uncover a spy **2.** *vi* (*a*) to burn; to be on fire; *Med:* to be feverish; **b. lentement**, to smoulder; *F:* **on brûle ici**, it's baking here; *Games:* **tu brûles**, you're getting hot (*b*) **b. de curiosité**, to be consumed with curiosity; **b. d'indignation**, to seethe with indignation; **b. (du désir) de faire qch**, to be burning, dying, to do sth; **les mains lui brûlent**, he's itching to get on with the job (*c*) (*of meat*) to burn; (*of milk*) to catch **3. se b.**, to burn oneself; **se b. les doigts, la langue**, to burn one's fingers, one's tongue. **brûlant** *a* (*a*) burning; boiling (hot); scalding (hot); scorching (sun); **question brûlante**, burning question (*b*) fiery, passionate (words).

brûleur [brylœr] *nm* burner.

brûlure [brylyr] *nf* **1.** burn, scald; **(sensation de) b.**, burning sensation; **b. d'estomac**, heartburn **2.** frost nip.

brume [brym] *nf* haze, mist, fog. **brumeux, -euse** *a* misty, hazy, foggy; hazy (ideas).

brumisateur [brymizatœr] *nm Toil:* atomizer, spray.

brun, *f* brune [brœ̃, bryn] **1.** *a* brown; dark (complexion); (sun)tanned (complexion); **elle est brune**, she's dark-haired **2.** *nf* brown (colour) **3.** *nf* **brune**, brown ale. **brunâtre** *a* brownish.

brunette [brynɛt] *nf* brunette.

brunir [brynir] **1.** *vi* (*of hair*) to darken; to become dark, (sun)tanned; to go brown **2.** *vtr* to darken (hair); to tan (skin).

brushing [brœʃiŋ] *nm Hairdr:* blow-dry.

brusquer [bryske] *vtr* **1.** to be brusque, curt with (s.o.); to treat s.o. harshly **2. b. les choses**, to rush things; **attaque brusquée**, surprise attack. **brusque** *a* abrupt, off-hand, curt, brusque; sudden (stop); sharp (bend). **brusquement** *adv* abruptly, curtly; suddenly; sharply.

brusquerie [bryskəri] *nf* abruptness.

brut [bryt] *a* **1.** unpolished (marble); unrefined (sugar), crude (oil); rough, uncut (diamond); extra-dry (champagne); **produit b.**, primary product; **matières brutes**, raw materials **2.** *Com:* gross (weight) **3.** *nm* crude oil; crude.

brutaliser [brytalize] *vtr* to ill-treat, to maltreat; to bully. **brutal, -aux** *a* (*a*) brutal, savage (*b*) coarse, rough; **force brutale**, brute force; **vérité brutale**, plain truth; **arrêt b.**, sudden stop, abrupt stop. **brutalement** *adv* brutally, savagely; roughly; plainly; suddenly, abruptly.

brutalité [brytalite] *nf* **1.** (*a*) brutality, brutishness (*b*) brutality, savage cruelty (*c*) roughness, coarseness **2.** brutal act.

brute [bryt] *nf* brute; boor; bully; **sale b.!** filthy beast! **frapper comme une b.,** to hit out violently.

Bruxelles [brysɛl] *Prnf* Brussels.

bruyant [brɥijɑ̃] *a* **1.** noisy; resounding (success) **2.** loud; boisterous (laughter). **bruyamment** *adv* noisily, loudly.

bruyère [brɥijɛr] *nf* **1.** (*a*) heather, heath (*b*) heath(land) **2.** briar; **pipe en b.,** briar pipe.

BT(S) *abbr Brevet de technicien* (*supérieur*).

bu, -e [by] *see* **boire.**

buanderie [bɥɑ̃dri] *nf* wash house, laundry.

bûche [byʃ] *nf* (*a*) log; **b. de Noël,** yule log; *F:* **ramasser une b.,** to come a cropper (*b*) *F:* blockhead.

bûcher¹ [byʃe] *nm* **1.** woodshed **2.** (*a*) stake (*b*) (funeral) pyre.

bûcher² *vtr & i F:* to work hard; to swot (up).

bûcheron [byʃrɔ̃] *nm* (*a*) woodcutter (*b*) lumberjack.

bûcheur, -euse [byʃœr, -øz] *n F:* hard worker, swot.

bucolique [bykɔlik] *a & nf* bucolic.

budget [bydʒɛ] *nm* budget. **budgétaire** *a* budgetary; fiscal, financial (year).

buée [bɥe] *nf* steam, vapour, condensation; mist, moisture (on mirror).

buffet [byfɛ] *nm* **1.** sideboard; **b. de cuisine,** (kitchen) dresser **2.** buffet (meal); **b. de gare,** station buffet.

buffle [byfl] *nm Z:* buffalo.

buis [bɥi] *nm* **1.** *Bot:* box(tree) **2.** box(wood).

buisson [bɥisɔ̃] *nm* bush.

bulbe [bylb] *nm* **1.** *Bot:* bulb **2.** *Anat:* bulb **3.** *Arch:* onion-shaped dome. **bulbeux, -euse** *a* bulbous.

Bulgarie [bylgari] *Prnf* Bulgaria. **bulgare** *a & n* Bulgarian.

bulldozer [buldozɛr] *nm* bulldozer.

bulle [byl] *nf* **1.** *EccHist:* (papal) bull **2.** (*a*) bubble (of air); **faire des bulles,** to blow bubbles (*b*) balloon (in comic strip).

bulletin [byltɛ̃] *nm* **1.** (news) bulletin; **b. météorologique,** weather report; *Sch:* **b. trimestriel,** end-of-term report **2.** ticket, receipt; certificate; form; **b. de paie,** pay slip; **b. de vote,** ballot paper; **b. de commande,** order form.

buraliste [byralist] *n* (*a*) clerk (in post office) (*b*) receiver of taxes (*c*) tobacconist.

bureau, -eaux [byro] *nm* **1.** desk; bureau **2.** (*a*) office; study; **b. d'études,** planning department; **b. de poste,** post office; **b. de location,** box office; **b. de placement,** employment agency; **b. de tabac,**

tobacconist's (shop) (*b*) (office) staff **3.** board, committee **4.** department, division.

bureaucrate [byrɔkrat] *n* bureaucrat. **bureaucratique** *a* bureaucratic.

bureaucratie [byrɔkrasi] *nf* bureaucracy; *F:* red tape.

burette [byrɛt] *nf* **1.** cruet **2.** oilcan.

burin [byrɛ̃] *nm* **1.** burin, etcher's needle **2.** (cold) chisel.

burlesque [byrlɛsk] *a* **1.** burlesque **2.** comical, ludicrous.

bus [bys] *nm F:* bus.

buse [byz] *nf* **1.** *Orn:* buzzard **2.** *F:* fool.

busqué [byske] *a* aquiline, hooked (nose).

buste [byst] *nm* (*a*) chest (of pers) (*b*) bust.

bustier [bystje] *nm* long-line (strapless) bra(ssiere).

but [by(t)] *nm* **1.** mark (to aim at); target; objective; **coup au b.,** direct hit **2.** *Fb: etc:* goal; **marquer un b.,** to score a goal **3.** object, aim, purpose; **dans le b. de faire qch,** with the intention of doing sth; **dans ce b.,** with this end in view; **aller droit au b.,** to go straight to the point; **errer sans b.,** to wander about aimlessly **4.** *adv phr* (*a*) **b. à b.,** even; without any advantage to either party (*b*) **tirer de b. en blanc,** to fire point-blank; **faire qch de b. en blanc,** to do sth on the spur of the moment.

butane [bytan] *nm Ch:* butane; calor gas.

butée [byte] *nf MecE:* **b. (d'arrêt),** stop.

buter [byte] **1.** *vi* (*a*) **b. contre qch,** to strike, knock against sth; to bump into sth; to stumble over sth; **b. contre un problème,** to come up against a problem (*b*) (of beams) to abut, rest (**contre,** against) **2.** *vtr* (*a*) to antagonize (s.o.) (*b*) *P:* to bump (s.o.) off **3.** (*a*) **se b. à un obstacle,** to come up against an obstacle (*b*) **se b. à faire qch,** to be set on doing sth. **buté** *a* stubborn, obstinate.

buteur [bytœr] *nm Sp:* (goal) scorer.

butin [bytɛ̃] *nm* booty, spoils; loot.

butiner [bytine] *vi* (of bees) to gather pollen.

butoir [bytwar] *nm Tchn:* stop; **b. de porte,** door stop(per).

butor [bytɔr] *nm* lout, oaf.

butte [byt] *nf* **1.** hillock, mound **2.** **b. (de tir),** butts; **être en b. à,** to be exposed to.

buvable [byvabl] *a* drinkable; *Med:* to be taken orally.

buvard [byvar] **1.** *a & nm* (**papier**) **b.,** blotting paper **2.** *nm* blotter; blotting pad.

buvette [byvɛt] *nf* refreshment bar.

buveur, -euse [byvœr, -øz] *n* drinker.

Bx-A. *abbr Beaux-Arts.*

byzantin, -ine [bizɑ̃tɛ̃, -in] *a & n* Byzantine.

C

C, c [se] nm (the letter) C, c.

C abbr Celsius, centigrade.

c. abbr centime.

c' see ce¹.

ça see cela.

çà [sa] adv çà et là, here and there.

cabale [kabal] nf cabal. **cabalistique** a cabalistic.

caban [kabɑ̃] nm Nau: peajacket, reefer (jacket).

cabane [kaban] nf (a) hut, shanty; Pej: shack; (log) cabin; (rabbit) hutch (b) P: jail, nick, clink.

cabanon [kabanɔ̃] nm (a) hut, shed (b) (country) cottage.

cabaret [kabarɛ] nm (a) A: tavern, inn (b) night club; cabaret.

cabaretier, -ière [kabartje, -jɛr] n A: innkeeper.

cabas [kaba] nm shopping bag.

cabestan [kabɛstɑ̃] nm capstan.

cabillau(d) [kabijo] nm (fresh) cod.

cabine [kabin] nf (a) cabin; Av: c. de pilotage, cockpit (b) hut; c. de bain, bathing hut; c. téléphonique, phone box; Rail: c. d'aiguillage, signal box; Cin: c. de projection, projection room (c) cage (of lift); cab (of locomotive, crane).

cabinet [kabinɛ] nm 1. closet; small room; c. de toilette = dressing room; F: les cabinets, the lavatory, the loo, NAm: the john; c. de travail, study 2. (a) office; (doctor's) consulting room, surgery (b) practice (of doctor, lawyer) 3. (in museum) c. d'estampes, print room 4. (a) Pol: cabinet (b) c. (d'un ministre), (minister's) departmental staff; chef de c. = principal private secretary 5. Furn: cabinet.

câblage [kablaʒ] nm cabling; El: wiring.

câble [kabl] nm (a) cable, rope; c. d'amarrage, mooring line (b) El: cable, lead, flex.

câbler [kable] vtr to cable.

caboche [kabɔʃ] nf F: head, nut. **cabochard, -arde** a pigheaded.

cabosser [kabose] vtr F: to dent (metal).

cabot [kabo] nm dog; Pej: tyke.

cabotage [kabotaʒ] nm coastal trade.

caboteur [kabotœr] nm coaster.

cabotin, -ine [kabotɛ̃, -in] a & n F: third-rate actor, actress; ham (actor); show-off.

cabotinage [kabotinaʒ] nm ham acting; showing off.

cabotiner [kabotine] vi F: to show off.

cabrer [kabre] 1. vtr (a) to rear up (horse); c. qn contre qn, to turn s.o. against s.o. (b) c. un avion, to nose up 2. se c., (of horse) to rear; Av: to nose up; F: (of pers) to jib (at sth).

cabri [kabri] nm Z: kid.

cabriole [kabrijɔl] nf (a) caper (b) somersault.

cabrioler [kabrijole] vi to caper (about).

cabriolet [kabrijolɛ] nm (a) A: cabriolet (b) Aut: convertible.

caca [kaka] nm F: excrement; (to child) as-tu fait c.? have you done your job? c. d'oie, yellowish green.

cacah(o)uète [kakawɛt] nf peanut.

cacao [kakao] nm cocoa.

cacatoès [kakatoɛs] nm Orn: cockatoo.

cachalot [kaʃalo] nm Z: sperm whale.

cache [kaʃ] 1. nf A: hiding place; cache 2. nm (a) Phot: mask (b) cover, guard.

cache-cache [kaʃkaʃ] nm inv hide-and-seek.

cache-col [kaʃkɔl] nm inv Cl: scarf, muffler.

Cachemire [kaʃmir] 1. Prnm Geog: Kashmir 2. nm Tex: (a) cashmere (b) Paisley pattern.

cache-nez [kaʃne] nm inv scarf, muffler.

cache-pot [kaʃpo] nm inv flowerpot holder.

cacher [kaʃe] 1. vtr (a) to hide, conceal, secrete (b) to hide (one's face) from view; to cover up (picture); to mask (one's feelings); c. qch à qn, to hide sth from s.o.; il ne cache pas que, he makes no secret of the fact that; il me cache la lumière, he's in my light 2. se c., to hide, to be hidden, to lie in hiding; se c. de qn, to keep out of s.o.'s sight; je ne m'en cache pas, I make no secret of it; sans se c., openly.

cache-radiateur [kaʃradjatœr] nm inv radiator cover.

cachet [kaʃɛ] nm 1. (a) seal (b) mark, stamp; c. de la poste, postmark; il a beaucoup de c., he has style; manteau qui a du c., stylish coat 2. tablet, pill 3. fee (of consultant, artiste).

cache-tampon [kaʃtɑ̃pɔ̃] nm inv hunt-the-thimble.

cacheter [kaʃte] vtr (je cachette) to seal (up).

cachette [kaʃɛt] nf hiding place; hideout; en c., secretly.

cachot [kaʃo] nm (a) dungeon (b) solitary confinement.

cachotterie [kaʃɔtri] nf mystery; faire des cachotteries, to keep things secret. **cachottier, -ière** a secretive.

cacophonie [kakɔfɔni] nf cacophony.

cactus [kaktys] nm Bot: cactus.

c.-à-d. abbr c'est-à-dire.

cadastre [kadastr] nm cadastral survey; cadastre. **cadastral, -aux** a cadastral.

cadavre [kadavr] nm (a) corpse; (dead) body (b) P: empty (bottle); dead soldier. **cadavérique** a deathly; deadly pale.

cadeau, -eaux [kado] nm present; gift; faire un c. à qn, to give s.o. a present; F: il ne lui a pas fait de c., he didn't spare him.

cadenas [kadna] nm padlock.

cadenasser [kadnase] vtr to padlock.

cadence [kadɑ̃s] nf cadence, rhythm (of verse); en c., rhythmically, in time; à la c. de, at the rate of; forcer la c., to force the pace.

cadencer [kadɑ̃se] vtr (je cadençai(s)) to give rhythm to (one's style). **cadencé** a rhythmic(al).

cadet, -ette [kadɛ, -ɛt] 1. a & n (a) la (sœur) cadette, the younger, the youngest, sister; **il est mon c. de deux ans**, he's two years younger than me, he's two years my junior; **c'est le c. de mes soucis**, that's the least of my worries (*b*) junior (in rank); *Sp:* minor **2.** *nm Hist:* cadet.

cadrage [kadraʒ] *nm Phot:* centring (of image).

cadran [kadrã] *nm* dial; face; **c. solaire**, sundial.

cadre [kadr̩] *nm* **1.** (*a*) frame (of picture, door) (*b*) (*on form*) space, box (*c*) border (of map) (*d*) setting (of scene) (*e*) compass, limits, framework; **sortir du c. de ses fonctions**, to go beyond one's duties; **dans le c. de ce programme**, as part of this programme (*f*) crate, case, container (*g*) *WTel:* frame aerial **2.** frame (of bicycle) **3.** (*a*) *Mil:* **les cadres**, officers (*b*) executive; manager; **c. supérieur**, senior executive (*c*) books (of company); **être mis hors c.**, to be seconded; **rayé des cadres**, dismissed.

cadrer [kadre] **1.** *vi* to tally, to conform (**avec**, with) **2.** *vtr* to centre (photograph).

caduc, -uque [kadyk] *a* **1.** out of date; oldfashioned **2.** *Bot:* deciduous **3.** null and void (legacy).

CAF *abbr Caisse d'allocations familiales.*

cafard [kafar] **1.** *nm* (*a*) cockroach (*b*) *F:* **avoir le cafard**, to be depressed, to have the blues **2.** sneak. **cafardeux, -euse** *a* depressed; feeling blue.

cafarder [kafarde] *vi* to sneak.

café [kafe] *nm* **1.** (*a*) coffee; **grain de c.**, coffee bean (*b*) **c. au lait**, **c. crème**, white coffee; **c. soluble**, instant coffee; **glace au c.**, coffee ice cream; **c. complet**, continental breakfast (*c*) *a inv* coffee-coloured **2.** café.

caféier [kafeje] *nm* coffee tree.

caféine [kafein] *nf Ch:* caffein(e).

cafetier, -ière [kaftje, -jɛr] **1.** *n* café owner **2.** *nf* (*a*) coffee pot (*b*) coffee maker.

cafouillage [kafujaʒ] *nm F:* mess, muddle; misfiring (of engine).

cafouiller [kafuje] *vi F:* to get into a muddle; (*of engine*) to misfire; (*of TV set*) to be on the blink. **cafouilleur, -euse** *a & n* muddle-headed (*pers*); *n* muddler.

cage [kaʒ] *nf* **1.** (*a*) cage; (rabbit) hutch (*b*) cage (of mine shaft) **2.** (protective) cover; casing **3.** (stair) well; (lift) shaft **4.** *esp Fb:* goal.

cageot [kaʒo] *nm* crate.

cagibi [kaʒibi] *nm* box room.

cagneux, -euse [kaɲø, -øz] *a* knock-kneed; **genoux c.**, knock knees.

cagnotte [kaɲɔt] *nf* (*a*) kitty (*b*) *F:* nest egg.

cagoule [kagul] *nf* (*a*) (monk's) cowl (*b*) hood (of penitent, robber) (*c*) balaclava (helmet).

cahier [kaje] *nm* (*a*) notebook, exercise book (*b*) journal.

cahin-caha [kaɛ̃kaa] *adv F:* **aller c.-c.**, to jog along; (*of health*) to be so-so.

cahot [kao] *nm* jolt; bump.

cahoter [kaɔte] *vtr & i* to bump along (in cart). **cahotant** *a* rough, bump*y* (road); jolting (car).

cahute [kayt] *nf* shack.

caïd [kaid] *nm P:* gang leader; big boss.

caillasse [kajas] *nf* loose stones.

caille [kaj] *nf Orn:* quail.

cailler [kaje] *vtr, i & pr* **1.** (*of milk, blood*) to clot, curdle **2.** *P:* **ça caille, on se caille**, it's bloody cold, it's freezing.

caillot [kajo] *nm* (blood) clot.

caillou, pl -oux [kaju] *nm* **1.** (*a*) pebble; stone (*b*) boulder (*c*) (*diamond*) rock, stone **2.** *P:* head, nut. **caillouteux, -euse** *a* stony, pebbly.

cailloutis [kajuti] *nm* gravel; road metal.

caïman [kaimã] *nm Rept:* cayman, caiman.

Caire (le) [lɛkɛr] *Prnm* Cairo.

caisse [kɛs] *nf* **1.** (*a*) (packing) case; crate (*b*) box; chest **2.** case (of clock); body(work) (of vehicle) **3.** *Com:* (*a*) cash box; till; **c. (enregistreuse)**, cash register; **les caisses de l'État**, the coffers of the State (*b*) cashdesk; check-out; **tenir la c.**, to be cashier; **faire la c.**, to do the till; **livre de c.**, cashbook (*d*) fund; **c. noire**, slush fund (*e*) bank; **c. d'épargne**, savings bank **4.** *Mus:* drum.

caissette [kɛsɛt] *nf* small box.

caissier, -ière [kɛsje, -jɛr] *n* cashier.

caisson [kɛsɔ̃] *nm Mil: CivE:* caisson; *Med:* **mal, maladie, des caissons**, caisson disease; *F:* the bends.

cajoler [kaʒɔle] *vtr* to cuddle, pet (child).

cajolerie [kaʒɔlri] *nf* cuddle.

cajou [kaʒu] *nm* cashew (nut).

cake [kɛk] *nm* fruit cake.

calage [kalaʒ] *nm* wedging (of chair); chocking (of wheel).

calamité [kalamite] *nf* calamity, disaster. **calamiteux, -euse** *a* calamitous.

calandre [kalãdr̩] *nf* (*a*) calender (*b*) *Aut:* radiator grille.

calcaire [kalkɛr] **1.** *a* chalky (soil); **eau c.**, hard water **2.** *nm* (*a*) limestone (*b*) fur (in kettle).

calciner [kalsine] *vtr* to char; **rôti calciné**, joint burnt to a cinder; **calciné par le soleil**, scorched by the sun.

calcium [kalsjɔm] *nm Ch:* calcium.

calcul [kalkyl] *nm* **1.** (*a*) calculation, reckoning; **erreur de c.**, miscalculation; **tout c. fait**, taking everything into account (*b*) arithmetic; **c. différentiel**, differential calculus; **c. des probabilités**, probability theory **2.** *Med:* stone, calculus.

calculateur, -trice [kalkylatœr, -tris] **1.** *a* calculating **2.** *n* (*pers*) calculator **3.** *nm* computer **4.** *nf* calculator.

calculer [kalkyle] *vtr* (*a*) to calculate, compute, reckon; to work out (a price); **tout bien calculé**, taking everything into account (*b*) to plan (one's move); to weigh (up) (consequences).

cale [kal] *nf* **1.** (*a*) hold (of ship) (*b*) **c. de lancement**, slip(way) (*c*) **c. sèche**, dry dock; **c. de radoub**, graving dock **2.** (*a*) wedge, chock (*b*) prop, strut.

calé [kale] *a F:* (*a*) bright (person) (*b*) difficult (problem); **ça c'est c.!** that's clever!

calebasse [kalbɑs] *nf* calabash.

calèche [kalɛʃ] *A Veh:* barouche.

caleçon [kalsɔ̃] *nm* underpants; **c. de bain**, swimming trunks.

calembour [kalãbur] *nm* pun.

calendrier [kalãdri(j)e] *nm* (*a*) calendar (*b*) timetable.

cale-pied [kalpje] *nm inv Cy:* toe clip.

calepin [kalpɛ̃] *nm* notebook.

caler [kale] **1.** *vtr* (*a*) to wedge (furniture); to chock (up) (wheel) (*b*) to prop up (books, patient) (*c*) *F:* **ça cale l'estomac**, it fills you up (*d*) *Aut:* to stall (engine); *vi* (*of engine*) to stall (*e*) *vi* F: to give up; **je cale,** I can't go on **2. se c.,** to settle (oneself) comfortably (in armchair).

calfeutrage [kalføtraʒ] *nm* draughtproofing.

calfeutrer [kalføtre] **1.** *vtr* to block up (gaps); to make (room) draughtproof **2. se c.,** to make oneself snug.

calibre [kalibṛ] *nm* **1.** (*a*) calibre, bore (of firearm) (*b*) size, diameter (of bullet); grade (of eggs) (*c*) *Fig:* calibre **2.** *Tls:* gauge.

calibrer [kalibre] *vtr* to gauge; to grade (eggs).

calice [kalis] *nm* **1.** chalice **2.** *Bot:* calyx.

calicot [kaliko] *nm* (*a*) *Tex:* calico (*b*) banner.

califourchon (à) [akalifurʃɔ̃] *adv phr* astride.

câlin, -ine [kalɛ̃, -in] **1.** *a* caressing, winning (ways); tender, loving **2.** *n* (*pers*) cuddler.

câliner [kaline] *vtr* to caress, cuddle.

câlinerie [kalinri] *nf* (*a*) tenderness (*b*) cuddle.

calleux, -euse [kalø, -øz] *a* horny, callous.

calligraphie [kaligrafi] *nf* calligraphy.

calligraphier [kaligrafje] *vtr* (*pr sub & impf n.* **calligraphiions**) to write (letter) ornamentally.

callosité [kalozite] *nf* callosity.

calmant [kalmɑ̃] **1.** *a* calming; soothing; *Med:* tranquillizing; painkilling **2.** *nm Med:* tranquillizer; painkiller; sedative.

calmar [kalmar] *nm* calamary, squid.

calme [kalm] **1.** *nm* calm(ness); stillness (of night); peace (of mind); quietness, peacefulness; **du c.!** (i) keep cool! (ii) quieten down! *Nau:* **c. plat,** dead calm **2.** *a* calm; still, quiet; cool, composed (pers); smooth (sea). **calmement** *adv* calmly, quietly, coolly.

calmer [kalme] **1.** *vtr* to calm (down); to quieten (down); to allay (fears); to soothe (pain); to quench (thirst); to cool (ardour); to pacify (child, mob); to appease (hunger) **2. se c.,** to become calm; to calm (down), to quieten (down); (*of storm*) to abate; (*of wind*) to drop.

calomniateur, -trice [kalɔmnjatœr, -tris] *n* slanderer, libeller.

calomnie [kalɔmni] *nf* calumny, slander, libel.

calomnier [kalɔmnje] *vtr* to slander, libel. **calomnieux, -euse** *a* slanderous, libellous.

calorie [kalɔri] *nf PhMeas:* calorie. **calorifique** *a* calorific.

calorifugeage [kalɔrifyʒaʒ] *nm* (heat) insulation, lagging. **calorifuge** *a* (heat-)insulating.

calorifuger [kalɔrifyʒe] *vtr* (**n. calorifugeons**) to insulate, lag (pipe).

calot [kalo] *nm Mil:* forage cap.

calotte [kalɔt] *nf* (*a*) skullcap; crown (of hat) (*b*) **c. glaciaire,** icecap.

calque [kalk] *nm* (*a*) tracing; **(papier) c.,** tracing paper (*b*) exact copy (*c*) *Ling:* calque.

calquer [kalke] *vtr* (*a*) to trace; to make a tracing of (drawing) (*b*) to copy exactly.

calumet [kalyme] *nm* calumet; **le c. de la paix,** the pipe of peace.

calvaire [kalver] *nm* calvary; agony, suffering.

calvinisme [kalvinism] *nm Ecc:* Calvinism. **calviniste** *a & n* Calvinist.

calvitie [kalvisi] *nf* baldness.

camaïeu, -eux [kamajø] *nm* monochrome (painting).

camarade [kamarad] *n* friend; mate; *Pol:* comrade; **c. d'école,** schoolfriend.

camaraderie [kamaradri] *nf* companionship, goodfellowship.

Cambodge [kãbɔdʒ] *Prnm Hist: Geog:* Cambodia. **cambodgien, -ienne** *a & n* Cambodian.

cambouis [kãbwi] *nm* dirty oil, dirty grease.

cambrer [kãbre] **1.** *vtr* to bend; to arch (foot, back); to curve (wood) **2. se c.,** to arch one's back. **cambré** *a* arched (back); **pied c.,** foot with a high instep.

cambriolage [kãbrijɔlaʒ] *nm* burglary.

cambrioler [kãbriole] *vtr* to break into (house); to burgle; *NAm:* to burglarize.

cambrioleur, -euse [kãbrijɔlœr, -øz] *n* burglar.

cambrousse [kãbrus] *nf* F: country; **en pleine c.,** (out) in the sticks.

cambrure [kãbryr] *nf* (*a*) camber (of wood, of road); arch (of foot); curve (of back) (*b*) **c. du pied,** instep; **c. des reins,** small of the back.

came [kam] *nf* **1.** *MecE:* cam, lifter **2.** *P:* dope, junk, snow.

camé, -ée[1] [kame] *n P:* drug addict, junkie.

camée[2] *nm* cameo.

caméléon [kameleɔ̃] *nm Rept:* chameleon.

camélia [kamelja] *nm Bot:* camellia.

camelot [kamlo] *nm F:* street hawker.

camelote [kamlɔt] *nf* (*a*) *F:* cheap goods; junk; trash (*b*) *P:* goods; stuff.

caméra [kamera] *nf* film camera; cinecamera; *TV:* camera.

Cameroun [kamrun] *Prnm Geog:* Cameroon. **camerounais, -aise** *a & n* Cameroonian.

camion [kamjɔ̃] *nm* lorry, *NAm:* truck; **c. de déménagement,** removal van.

camion-citerne [kamjɔ̃sitɛrn] *nm* tanker (lorry); *NAm:* tank truck; *pl* **camions-citernes.**

camionnage [kamjɔnaʒ] *nm* haulage.

camionnette [kamjɔnɛt] *nf* (delivery) van.

camionneur [kamjɔnœr] *nm* (*a*) lorry driver, *NAm:* truck driver (*b*) haulage contractor.

camisole [kamizɔl] *nf* **c. de force,** strait jacket.

camomille [kamɔmij] *nf* camomile.

camouflage [kamuflaʒ] *nm* camouflaging; camouflage.

camoufler [kamufle] *vtr* to camouflage; to conceal; to disguise (truth).

camp [kɑ̃] *nm* **1.** camp; **lever le c.,** to strike camp; **c. de vacances,** holiday camp; *F:* **ficher le c.,** to clear off **2.** (*a*) party, faction (*b*) *Games:* side.

campagne [kãpaɲ] *nf* **1.** (*a*) plain; open country; **en pleine c.,** in the open country (*b*) country(side) **2.** *Mil:* (the) field; **en c.,** in the field **3.** *Mil: Pol:* campaign; **faire c.,** to fight a campaign; **mener une c. contre qch,** to campaign against sth. **campagnard, -arde 1.** *a* country **2.** *n* countryman, countrywoman.

campanule [kãpanyl] *nf Bot:* campanula.

campement [kãpmã] *nm* camp, encampment.

camper [kãpe] **1.** *vi* to camp **2.** *vtr* (*a*) to encamp (troops) (*b*) to place, fix, put (*c*) to construct (story); to portray (character) **3. se c.,** to stand firmly; **se c. devant qn,** to plant oneself in front of s.o.

campeur, -euse [kãpœr, -øz] *n* camper.

camphre [kɑ̃fr̩] *nm* camphor.
camping [kɑ̃piŋ] *nm* **1.** camping **2.** camp site.
campus [kɑ̃pys] *nm* campus.
camus [kamy] *a* flat-, snub-nosed (person).
Canada [kanada] *Prnm* Canada. **canadien, -ienne** *a & n* **1.** Canadian **2.** *nf* fur-lined lumber jacket.
canadianisme [kanadjanizm] *nm* Canadianism.
canaille [kanɑj] *nf* (*a*) *coll* rabble (*b*) scoundrel, rogue; rascal.
canaillerie [kanɑjri] *nf* **1.** low(-down) trick **2.** crookedness (of action).
canal, -aux [kanal, -o] *nm* **1.** channel; **par le c. de la poste,** through the post **2.** canal **3.** (*a*) conduit, tube, duct (*b*) *Anat:* canal, duct (*c*) *TV:* channel.
canalisation [kanalizasjɔ̃] *nf* piping, pipes; mains ducting; (electric) cable.
canaliser [kanalize] *vtr* **1.** to canalize (river) **2.** to channel (resources); to direct (crowd).
canapé [kanape] *nm* **1.** sofa, couch, settee **2.** *Cu:* (cocktail) canapé.
canard [kanar] *nm* **1.** duck; (*male bird*) drake; **c. de Barbarie,** Muscovy duck; drake; **c. sauvage,** wild duck; *F:* **mon petit c.,** ducky, pet **2.** *F:* (*a*) false report, hoax (*b*) newspaper, rag **3.** *Mus:* false note.
canarder [kanarde] *vtr* to snipe at (s.o.).
canari [kanari] *nm Orn:* canary.
Canaries [kanari] *Prnf pl Geog:* **les (îles) C.,** the Canary Islands, the Canaries.
cancan [kɑ̃kɑ̃] *nm* **1.** *F: pl* gossip **2.** cancan (dance). **cancanier, -ière** *a* gossipy.
cancaner [kɑ̃kane] *vi* to gossip, to tittle-tattle.
cancer [kɑ̃sɛr] *nm* **1.** *Med:* cancer **2.** *Astr:* **le C.,** Cancer. **cancéreux, -euse** *a* cancerous; cancer (patient). **cancérigène** *a* carcinogenic.
cancérologue [kɑ̃serɔlɔg] *n* cancerologist.
cancre [kɑ̃kr̩] *nm F:* dunce.
cancrelat [kɑ̃krəla] *nm* cockroach.
candélabre [kɑ̃delabr̩] *nm* candelabrum, *pl* -abra.
candeur [kɑ̃dœr] *nf* ingenuousness.
candidat, -ate [kɑ̃dida, -at] *n* candidate; applicant (à une place, for a place); examinee.
candidature [kɑ̃didatyr] *nf* candidature; **poser sa c. à un poste,** to apply for a post.
candide [kɑ̃did] *a* ingenuous, artless. **candidement** *adv* ingenuously.
cane [kan] *nf* (female) duck.
caneton [kantɔ̃] *nm* (male) duckling.
canette¹ [kanɛt] *nf* (female) duckling.
canette² *nf* beer bottle.
canevas [kanvɑ] *nm* (*a*) canvas (*b*) outline, framework (of novel).
caniche [kaniʃ] *nm* poodle.
canicule [kanikyl] *nf* heatwave; **la c.,** the dog days. **caniculaire** *a* scorching (heat).
canif [kanif] *nm* penknife.
canin, -ine [kanɛ̃, -in] **1.** *a* canine; **exposition canine,** dog show **2.** *nf* **canine,** canine (tooth).
caniveau, -eaux [kanivo] *nm* gutter (in street).
cannage [kanaʒ] *nm* (*a*) caning (of chairs) (*b*) canework.
canne [kan] *nf* **1.** cane, reed; **c. à sucre,** sugar cane **2.** walking stick; cane **3. c. à pêche,** fishing rod.
canneler [kanle] *vtr* (**je cannelle, n. cannelons**) to

flute, to groove.
cannelle [kanɛl] *nf* cinnamon.
cannelure [kanlyr] *nf* groove; *Arch:* fluting.
canner [kane] *vtr* to cane (chair).
cannibale [kanibal] *a & n* cannibal.
cannibalisme [kanibalism] *nm* cannibalism.
canoë [kanɔe] *nm* canoe; **faire du c.,** to canoe.
canoéiste [kanɔeist] *n* canoeist.
canon¹ [kanɔ̃] *nm* **1.** gun, cannon **2.** barrel (of rifle).
canon² *nm* **1.** *Ecc:* canon, rule (of an order) **2.** *Mus:* canon, round, catch.
cañon [kapɔ̃] *nm Geog:* canyon.
canonnade [kanɔnad] *nf* cannonade, gunfire.
canonnier [kanɔnje] *nm* g̲unner.
canonnière [kanɔnjɛr] *nf* gunboat.
canot [kano] *nm* (open) boat; dinghy; **c. automobile,** motorboat.
canotage [kanɔtaʒ] *nm* boating.
canotier [kanɔtje] *nm* (*hat*) boater.
cantate [kɑ̃tat] *nf Mus:* cantata.
cantatrice [kɑ̃tatris] *nf* (opera) singer.
cantine [kɑ̃tin] *nf* canteen; *Sch:* dining hall; *Sch:* **déjeuner à la c.,** to have school meals.
cantique [kɑ̃tik] *nm* hymn.
canton [kɑ̃tɔ̃] *nm* canton, district. **cantonal, -aux** *a* cantonal; district.
cantonade [kɑ̃tɔnad] *nf* **parler à la c.,** to speak to the company at large.
cantonnement [kɑ̃tɔnmɑ̃] *nm Mil:* (*a*) quartering, billeting (of troops) (*b*) quarters, billet, cantonment.
cantonner [kɑ̃tɔne] *vtr* **1.** to quarter, billet (troops); to confine (**dans qch,** in sth) **2. se c.,** to confine oneself (to sth).
cantonnier [kɑ̃tɔnje] *nm* roadman.
canular [kanylar] *nm F:* hoax.
caoutchouc [kautʃu] *nm* **1.** rubber; *Rtm:* **c. mousse,** foam rubber **2.** elastic band, rubber band. **caoutchouteux, -euse** *a* rubbery.
caoutchouter [kautʃute] *vtr* to rubberize (sth).
cap [kap] *nm* **1.** cape, headland; **le c. Horn,** Cape Horn; **le C.,** Capetown; **doubler un c.,** to round a cape; **franchir le c. de la quarantaine,** to turn forty **2.** *Nau: Av:* course, heading; **changement de c.,** change of course; **mettre le c. sur,** to head for.
CAP *abbr Certificat d'aptitude professionnelle.*
capable [kapabl̩] *a* capable; **c. de qch, de faire qch,** capable of sth, of doing sth; **il est c. de tout,** he's liable to do anything; **cette maladie est c. de le tuer,** this illness might well kill him.
capacité [kapasite] *nf* **1.** capacity (of vessel) **2.** (*a*) capacity, ability, capability (*b*) *Jur:* capacity; **avoir c. pour faire qch,** to be (legally) entitled to do sth.
caparaçonner [kaparasɔne] *vtr* to caparison (horse).
cape [kap] *nf* (hooded) cape, cloak; **rire sous c.,** to laugh up one's sleeve.
CAPES [kapes] *abbr Certificat d'aptitude pédagogique à l'enseignement secondaire.*
capharnaüm [kafarnaɔm] *nm* junk room.
capillaire [kapilɛr] **1.** *a* capillary; **lotion c.,** hair lotion **2.** *nm Anat:* capillary.
capitaine [kapitɛn] *nm* (*a*) *Mil: Nau:* captain; *Nau: MilAv:* **c. (d'aviation)** = flight lieutenant; *NAm:* (air) captain; **c. de port,** harbour master; **c. au long**

cours, master mariner (*b*) chief, leader; **un grand c.,** a great (military) leader; **c. d'industrie,** captain of industry.

capital, -aux [kapital, -o] 1. *a* (*a*) capital (punishment) (*b*) fundamental, essential, principal; **décision capitale,** major decision; **d'une importance capitale,** of paramount importance (*c*) **lettre capitale,** *nf* **capitale,** capital (letter); **en capitales d'imprimerie,** in block capitals 2. *nm* capital, assets; **c. et intérêt,** principal and interest; **c. social,** registered capital 3. *nf* **capitale,** capital (city).

capitalisation [kapitalizasjɔ̃] *nf* capitalization (of interest).

capitaliser [kapitalize] 1. *vtr* to capitalize (interest) 2. *vi* to save.

capitalisme [kapitalism] *nm* capitalism. **capitaliste** *a & n* capitalist.

capiteux, -euse [kapitø, -øz] *a* heady (wine); sensuous (charm).

capitonnage [kapitɔnaʒ] *nm* padding.

capitonner [kapitɔne] *vtr* to pad.

capitulation [kapitylasjɔ̃] *nf* capitulation, surrender.

capituler [kapityle] *vi* to capitulate; to surrender.

caporal, -aux [kapɔral, -o] *nm Mil: etc:* corporal.

capot [kapo] *nm* cover, hood, casing; *Aut:* bonnet (of car), *NAm:* hood.

capote [kapɔt] *nf* 1. *Mil:* greatcoat 2. *Aut:* adjustable hood, *NAm:* top.

capoter [kapɔte] *vi* 1. *Nau:* to capsize; to turn turtle 2. *Aut:* to overturn.

câpre [kɑpr] *nf Bot: Cu:* caper.

caprice [kapris] *nm* caprice, whim, freak; **faire des caprices,** to be temperamental, moody; (*of child*) **faire un c.,** to throw a tantrum; **caprices de la mode,** vagaries of fashion. **capricieux, -ieuse** *a* capricious, whimsical; temperamental. **capricieusement** *adv* capriciously, whimsically.

Capricorne [kaprikɔrn] *Prnm Astr:* Capricorn.

capsule [kapsyl] *nf Pharm:* capsule; cap, capsule (of bottle); (space) capsule.

capsuler [kapsyle] *vtr* to cap, to put a capsule on (a bottle).

capter [kapte] *vtr* 1. to win (s.o.) over, to win (s.o.'s confidence) 2. *WTel: Tp:* to pick up (transmission); to intercept (messages); to tap (a line).

captif, -ive [kaptif, -iv] *a & n* captive.

captiver [kaptive] *vtr* to captivate, charm. **captivant** *a* captivating, charming.

captivité [kaptivite] *nf* captivity.

capture [kaptyr] *nf* 1. capture, seizure (of ship) 2. capture, prize, catch.

capturer [kaptyre] *vtr* to capture, to seize, to catch.

capuche [kapyʃ] *nf* hood.

capuchon [kapyʃɔ̃] *nm* 1. (*a*) hood; (monk's) cowl (*b*) hooded cloak 2. cap, top (of pen).

capucine [kapysin] *nf Bot:* nasturtium.

caquet [kakɛ] *nm* 1. cackle, cackling (of hens) 2. (noisy) chatter; **elle lui a rabattu le c.,** she shut him up.

caqueter [kakte] *vi* (**je caquète, je caquette**) 1. (*of hen*) to cackle 2. *F:* to chatter.

car¹ [kar] *conj* for, because.

car² *nm* (*a*) coach; bus (*b*) **c. de police,** police van.

carabine [karabin] *nf* rifle.

carabiné [karabine] *a F:* heavy (cold); violent, raging (fever).

carabinier [karabinje] *nm* (*in Italy*) police officer; carabiniere; (*in Spain*) frontier guard; carabinero.

caracoler [karakɔle] *vi Equit:* to caracole.

caractère [karaktɛr] *nm* 1. character, letter; graphic sign; *Typ:* (metal) type; **caractères d'imprimerie,** block capitals; **en gros, en petits, caractères,** in large, in small, type 2. characteristic, feature; **l'affaire a pris un c. grave,** the matter has taken a serious turn; **de c. officiel,** of an official nature 3. (*a*) character, nature, disposition; **avoir (un) mauvais c., (un) bon c.,** to be bad-tempered, good-tempered (*b*) personality, character; **manquer de c.,** to lack strength of character. **caractériel, -ielle** *a* of character; emotional (disorder); **enfant c.,** emotionally disturbed child.

caractériser [karakterize] 1. *vtr* to characterize, to be characteristic of 2. **se c.,** to be characterized, to be distinguished (**par,** by). **caractérisé** *a* typical, unquestionable, indisputable. **caractéristique** *a & nf* characteristic.

carafe [karaf] *nf* decanter; carafe.

caraïbe [karaib] *a & n Geog:* Caribbean; **les Caraïbes,** the Caribbean.

carambolage [karɑ̃bɔlaʒ] *nm F:* pile-up (of cars).

caramboler [karɑ̃bɔle] *vtr* 1. **c. une voiture,** to run into a car 2. **se c.,** to collide.

caramel [karamɛl] *nm* caramel; **c. au beurre,** butterscotch, toffee.

caraméliser [karamelize] *vtr* to caramelize (sugar); to mix caramel with (sth); to coat (sth) with caramel.

carapace [karapas] *nf* shell (of lobster).

carat [kara] *nm* carat.

caravane [karavan] *nf* 1. (*a*) caravan (*b*) procession, stream (of tourists) 2. caravan, *NAm:* (house) trailer. **caravaning** 1. *a* caravan (route) 2. *nm Aut:* caravan(n)er.

caravan(n)ing [karavaniŋ] *nm* caravan(n)ing.

caravansérail [karavɑ̃seraj] *nm* caravanserai.

carbonate [karbɔnat] *nm Ch:* carbonate; **c. de soude,** sodium carbonate, *Com:* washing soda.

carbone [karbɔn] *nm* carbon; **(papier) c.,** carbon (paper). **carbonique** *a* carbonic.

carboniser [karbɔnize] *vtr* to carbonize; to char (wood); to burn (meat) to a cinder; **mort carbonisé,** burnt to death.

carburant [karbyrɑ̃] *nm* fuel.

carburateur [karbyratœr] *nm* carburettor.

carburation [karbyrasjɔ̃] *nf* carburation.

carbure [karbyr] *nm Ch:* carbide.

carburer [karbyre] *vi* (*a*) to vaporize (fuel); **le moteur carbure mal,** the engine is badly tuned; the mixture is wrong (*b*) *F:* to work, to go well.

carcan [karkɑ̃] *nm* (*a*) *Hist:* iron collar (*b*) yoke, restraint.

carcasse [karkas] *nf* 1. carcass 2. frame(work); shell, skeleton (of house, ship).

cardan [kardɑ̃] *nm MecE:* universal joint.

carder [karde] *vtr* to card (wool).

cardiaque [kardjak] 1. *a* cardiac (murmur); **crise c.,** heart attack; **être c.,** to have heart trouble 2. *n* heart patient.

cardinal, -aux [kardinal, -o] **1.** *a* cardinal (number) **2.** *nm Ecc:* cardinal.

cardiologie [kardjɔlɔʒi] *nf Med:* cardiology.

cardiologue [kardjɔlɔg] *n* cardiologist.

carême [karɛm] *nf (a)* Lent *(b)* (Lenten) fast(ing).

carence [karɑ̃s] *nf* **1.** default(ing), reneging; inefficiency **2.** *Med:* deficiency.

carène [karɛn] *nf* hull (of ship).

caréner [karene] *vtr* **(je carène, je carénerai) 1.** to careen (ship) **2.** *Av:* to streamline.

caresse [karɛs] *nf* caress.

caresser [karese] *vtr* **1.** to caress, stroke; **c. qn du regard,** to look affectionately at s.o. **2.** to cherish (hope); to toy with (idea). **caressant** *a* affectionate; tender; soft, gentle (wind).

cargaison [kargɛzɔ̃] *nf* cargo, freight; load.

cargo [kargo] *nm* cargo boat; freighter.

caricature [karikatyr] *nf (a)* caricature; cartoon *(b) F:* (pers) fright.

caricaturer [karikatyre] *vtr* to caricature.

caricaturiste [karikatyrist] *n* caricaturist; cartoonist.

carie [kari] *nf* **c. dentaire,** tooth decay, (dental) caries.

carier (se) [səkarje] *vpr* to decay. **carié** *a* decayed, bad (tooth).

carillon [karijɔ̃] *nm (a)* chime(s); **(horloge à) c.,** chiming clock *(b)* peal of bells *(c)* (door) chime.

carillonner [karijɔne] **1.** *vi (a)* to ring a peal *(b)* to chime *(c)* **c. à la porte,** to ring the (door)bell very loudly **2.** *vtr* to chime (air); to broadcast (news).

carlingue [karlɛ̃g] *nf Av:* cabin.

carmin [karmɛ̃] *nm* carmine (colour).

carnage [karnaʒ] *nm* carnage, slaughter.

carnassier, -ière [karnasje, -jɛr] **1.** *a* carnivorous **2.** *nm* carnivore.

carnaval, *pl* **-als** [karnaval] *nm* carnival. **carnavalesque** *a* carnivalesque.

carne [karn] *nf F:* tough meat.

carnet [karnɛ] *nm* notebook; book (of stamps); **c. de chèques,** cheque book; *Sch:* **c. (de notes),** school report.

carnivore [karnivɔr] **1.** *a* carnivorous **2.** *nm* carnivore.

carotide [karɔtid] *a & nf Anat:* carotid (artery).

carotte [karɔt] *nf* **1.** *Bot:* carrot; *a inv F:* **cheveux (rouge) c.,** carroty, ginger, hair; *F:* **ses carottes sont cuites,** he's done for **2.** *(a)* plug (of tobacco) *(b) Min:* core (sample).

carotter [karɔte] *vtr F: (a)* to steal, to pinch *(b)* to do (s.o.); to diddle (s.o.).

carpe [karp] **1.** *nf Ich:* carp **2.** *nm Anat:* carpus.

carpette [karpɛt] *nf* rug; *Fig: Pej:* doormat.

carquois [karkwa] *nm* quiver.

carre [kɑr] *nf* edge (of ski).

carré, -ée [kare] **1.** *a (a)* square; *Mth:* **nombre c.,** square number; **partie carrée,** foursome; *F:* **tête carrée,** (i) level-headed man (ii) stubborn man *(b)* plain, straight(forward), blunt (answer, pers) **2.** *nm (a) Mth:* square; **mettre au c.,** to square; **6 au c.,** 6 squared *(b)* slip (of paper); (silk) square; **c. de choux,** cabbage patch; *Navy:* **c. (des officiers),** wardroom **3.** *nf F:* **carrée,** room, digs. **carrément** *adv (a)* square(ly) *(b)* bluntly, straight out; **y aller c.,** to go right ahead; **il est c. impossible,** he's just impossible (to deal with).

carreau, -eaux [karo] *nm* **1.** small square; **tissu à carreaux,** check(ed) material **2.** *(a)* (floor) tile; (wall) tile *(b)* window (pane) *(c) F:* **carreaux,** glasses, specs **3.** *(a)* (tiled) floor (of room); **rester sur le c.,** (i) to be killed on the spot (ii) to be out of the running *(b)* **c. de mine,** pit head **4.** *Cards:* diamond; **se garder, se tenir à c.,** to take every precaution.

carrefour [karfur] *nm* crossroads.

carrelage [karlaʒ] *nm* **1.** tiling **2.** tiled floor.

carreler [karle] *vtr* **(je carrelle)** to tile (floor, wall).

carrelet [karlɛ] *nm* **1.** *Ich:* plaice **2.** square fishing net.

carreleur [karlœr] *nm* tiler.

carrer (se) [səkare] *vpr* to settle oneself (firmly) (in an armchair).

carrière¹ [karjɛr] *nf* **1.** course (of life); **la c. du succès,** the road to success **2.** **donner libre c. à son imagination,** to give free rein to one's imagination **3.** career; **il est de la c.,** he's in the diplomatic service.

carrière² *nf* (stone) quarry.

carriériste [karjerist] *n* careerist.

carriole [karjɔl] *nf* light cart.

carrossable [karɔsabl] *a* **route c.,** road suitable for motor vehicles.

carrosse [karɔs] *nm* (horse drawn) coach.

carrosserie [karɔsri] *nf Aut:* **1.** coachbuilding **2.** body, coachwork (of car).

carrossier [karɔsje] *nm Aut:* coach builder.

carrousel [karuzɛl] *nm* **1.** *Equit:* carousel **2.** merry-go-round (of cars).

carrure [karyr] *nf* breadth across the shoulders; **homme d'une belle c.,** well-built man.

cartable [kartabl] *nm* school satchel.

carte [kart] *nf* **1.** map; chart; **c. d'état-major =** Ordnance Survey map; **c. routière,** road map **2.** *(a)* (piece of) card(board); **c. (à jouer),** (playing) card; **jouer cartes sur table,** to put one's cards on the table *(b)* **c. de visite,** visiting card; **c. postale,** postcard; **c. de vœux,** greetings card *(c)* **c. d'identité,** identity card; **c. d'abonnement,** season ticket; **c. de lecteur,** library ticket; *Aut:* **c. grise =** (vehicle) registration document *(d)* **donner c. blanche à qn,** to give s.o. carte blanche, a free hand *(e)* **c. (de restaurant),** menu; **c. des vins,** winelist; **manger à la c.,** to eat à la carte.

cartel [kartɛl] *nm* **1.** wall clock **2.** *Pol:* coalition, cartel.

carter [kartɛr] *nm Mch:* casing, housing (of gear); (bicycle) chain guard; *Aut:* crankcase.

cartilage [kartilaʒ] *nm Anat:* cartilage; *(in meat)* gristle.

cartographe [kartɔgraf] *n* cartographer.

cartographie [kartɔgrafi] *nf* cartography.

cartomancie [kartɔmɑ̃si] *nf* fortune telling (by cards).

cartomancien, -ienne [kartɔmɑ̃sjɛ̃, -jɛn] *n* fortune teller (by cards).

carton [kartɔ̃] *nm* **1.** cardboard; pasteboard **2.** *(a)* (cardboard) box; **carton** *(b)* (cardboard) file **3.** *Art:* sketch **4.** *(at shooting range)* **faire un c.,** to fill a target; **faire un bon c.,** to make a good score.

cartonnage [kartɔnaʒ] *nm* **1.** (cardboard) packing **2.** *Bookb:* boarding, casing.

carton-pâte [kartɔpɑt] *nm* papier mâché; pasteboard; *pl* cartons-pâtes.

cartouche [kartuʃ] **1.** *nm Arch:* cartouche **2.** *nf* (*a*) cartridge (*b*) carton (of cigarettes).

cartouchière [kartuʃjer] *nf* (*a*) cartridge pouch (*b*) cartridge belt.

carvi [karvi] *nm Bot:* **(graines de) c.,** caraway (seeds).

cas [kɑ] *nm* **1.** case, instance; **c. limite,** borderline case; **c. imprévu,** unforeseen event; emergency; **c'est bien le c. de le dire,** there's no mistake about it; *F:* you can say that again **2.** case, matter, affair; **ce n'est pas le c.,** that is not the case; **c. de conscience,** matter of conscience **3. faire (grand) c. de qch,** to value sth (highly) **4.** *Gram:* case **5. en ce c.,** in that case; **en aucun c.,** under no circumstances, on no account; **en tout c.,** in any case, at any rate; anyhow, anyway; **le c. échéant,** should the occasion arise; **selon le c.,** as the case may be; **au c. où il viendrait,** if he comes.

casanier, -ière [kazanje, -jɛr] *a & n* stay-at-home.

casaque [kazak] *nf* (jockey's) blouse.

cascade [kaskad] *nf* (*a*) cascade, waterfall (*b*) peal(s) (of laughter); stream; torrent (of words).

cascader [kaskade] *vi* to cascade.

cascadeur, -euse [kaskadœr, -øz] *n Cin:* stuntman, stuntgirl.

case [kɑz] *nf* **1.** hut, cabin **2.** (*a*) compartment; pigeonhole (*b*) division, space (on printed form) (*c*) square (on chessboard); *F:* **il a une c. vide,** he's got a screw loose.

casemate [kazmat] *nf* blockhouse.

caser [kɑze] **1.** *vtr* (*a*) to put away; to file (papers); *F:* **c. qn,** to find a job for s.o.; **être bien casé,** to have (i) a good job (ii) a good home; **elle a 3 filles à c.,** she has 3 daughters to marry off **2. se c.,** to (get married and) settle down; to find a job; to find somewhere to live.

caserne [kazɛrn] *nf* (*a*) barracks (*b*) **c. de pompiers,** fire station.

casernement [kazɛrnəmɑ̃] *nm* **1.** barracking, quartering (of troops) **2.** barrack block.

caserner [kazɛrne] *vtr* to barrack (troops).

cash [kaʃ] *adv F:* **payer c.,** to pay cash down.

casier [kazje] *nm* **1.** (*a*) pigeonhole, locker (*b*) **c. judiciaire,** police record **2.** (*a*) (wine)bin, rack; **c. à bouteilles,** bottle rack (*b*) **c. (à homards),** lobsterpot.

casino [kazino] *nm* casino.

caspien, -ienne [kaspjɛ̃, -jɛn] *a* **la mer Caspienne,** the Caspian (Sea).

casque [kask] *nm* (*a*) helmet; crash helmet (of motorcyclist); **Casques bleus,** United Nations peacekeeping troops; (*b*) *WTel:* **c. (téléphonique),** headphones, headset (*c*) (hair) drier. **casqué** *a* wearing a helmet.

casquer [kaske] *vi P:* to pay (up), to fork out.

casquette [kaskɛt] *nf* (peaked) cap.

cassable [kasabl] *a* breakable.

cassant [kasɑ̃] *a* **1.** brittle **2.** curt, abrupt (tone of voice) **3.** *P:* **c'est pas c.,** it won't break your back.

cassation [kasasjɔ̃] *nf* **1.** *Jur:* cassation; **Cour de c.,** supreme court of appeal **2.** *Mil:* reduction (of NCO) to the ranks.

casse [kas] **1.** *nf* (*a*) breakage, damage; *F:* **il y aura de la c.,** there will be trouble (*b*) breakages (*c*) **vendre à la c.,** to sell for scrap **2.** *nm P:* break-in.

cassé [kɑse] *a* broken; worn out (person); cracked (voice).

casse-cou [kasku] *nm inv* daredevil.

casse-croûte [kaskrut] *nm inv* snack.

casse-noisettes [kasnwazɛt], **casse-noix** [kasnwa] *nm inv* (pair of) nutcrackers.

casse-pieds [kaspje] *a & nm inv F:* **ce qu'il est c.-p., quel c.-p.,** what a bore, what a pain in the neck.

casse-pipes [kaspip] *nm inv P:* war; front (line).

casser [kɑse] **1.** *vtr* (*a*) to break; to snap; to crack (nuts); to crack (voice); *F:* **c. les oreilles à qn,** to deafen s.o.; *F:* **c. les pieds à (qn),** to bore s.o. stiff; to get on s.o.'s nerves; *F:* **c. la figure à qn,** to smash s.o.'s face in; **c. sa pipe,** to kick the bucket; *F:* **ça ne casse rien,** it's nothing special, it's no great shakes; **un spectacle à tout c.,** a fantastic show (*b*) to cashier, to break (officer); to demote (employee) (*c*) *Jur:* to annul, to quash (verdict) **2.** *vi* to break, to snap, to give way **3. se c.,** to break, snap, give way; **se c. la jambe,** to break one's leg; *F:* **se c. la figure,** (i) to fall flat on one's face (ii) to kill oneself (iii) to fail, to come a cropper; **se c. la tête,** to rack one's brains; *P:* **te casse pas la tête!** don't overdo it! **se c. le nez,** to find nobody in.

casserole [kasrɔl] *nf* **1.** (*a*) (sauce)pan (*b*) *P:* **passer à la c.,** to get bumped off **2.** tinny piano.

casse-tête [kastɛt] *nm inv* **1.** club **2.** puzzle; *F:* headache.

cassette [kasɛt] *nf* (*a*) casket (*b*) moneybox (*c*) *Rec:* cassette.

casseur [kasœr] *nm* (*a*) aggressive person; troublemaker (*b*) scrap (metal) dealer (*c*) *P:* burglar.

cassis [kasis] *nm* **1.** (*a*) blackcurrant (fruit, bush) (*b*) blackcurrant liqueur **2.** *P:* head, nut **3.** *CivE:* crossdrain (across road).

cassoulet [kasulɛ] *nm Cu:* stew of beans, pork, goose (made in Languedoc).

cassure [kasyr] *nf* (*a*) break, fracture, crack (*b*) *Geol:* fault (*c*) fold mark, crease.

castagnettes [kastaɲɛt] *nfpl* castanets.

caste [kast] *nf* caste; **esprit de c.,** class consciousness; **hors c.,** outcaste.

castor [kastɔr] *nm Z: Com:* beaver.

castration [kastrasjɔ̃] *nf* castration; gelding; neutering.

castrer [kastre] *vtr* to castrate; to geld; to neuter.

cataclysme [kataklism] *nm* cataclysm, disaster.

catacombes [katakɔb] *nfpl* catacombs.

catadioptre [katadiɔptr] *nm* reflector; (on road) cat's eye.

catafalque [katafalk] *nm* catafalque.

catalan, -ane [katalɑ̃, -an] **1.** *a & n* Catalan, Catalonian **2.** *nm Ling:* Catalan.

catalepsie [katalɛpsi] *nf Med:* catalepsy. **cataleptique** *a* cataleptic.

Catalogne [katalɔɲ] *Prnf Geog:* Catalonia.

catalogue [katalɔg] *nm* catalogue, list.

cataloguer [katalɔge] *vtr* (*a*) to catalogue; to list (*b*) *F:* to label (s.o.).

catalyse [kataliz] *nf Ch:* catalysis. **catalytique** *a* catalytic.

catalyseur [katalizœr] *nm* catalyst.
cataphote [katafɔt] *nm Rtm:* cat's eye.
cataplasme [kataplasm] *nm* poultice.
catapulte [katapylt] *nf* catapult.
catapulter [katapylte] *vtr* to catapult.
cataracte [katarakt] *nf* 1. cataract, falls 2. *Med:* cataract.
catarrhe [katar] *nm Med:* catarrh.
catastrophe [katastrɔf] *nf* catastrophe, disaster; **atterrir en c.**, to make a crash landing; **partir en c.**, to go off in a mad rush. **catastrophé** *a* dumbfounded, shattered, stunned. **catastrophique** *a* catastrophic, disastrous.
catch [katʃ] *nm* (all-in) wrestling.
catcheur, -euse [katʃœr, -øz] *n* (all-in) wrestler.
catéchiser [kateʃize] *vtr* (*a*) *Ecc:* to catechize (*b*) *F:* to tell (s.o.) what to say; to lecture (s.o.).
catéchisme [kateʃism] *nm* catechism.
catéchiste [kateʃist] *n* catechist.
catégorie [kategɔri] *nf* category; type, grade; class. **catégorique** *a* categorical; **refus c.**, flat refusal. **catégoriquement** *adv* categorically; flatly.
catégorisation [kategɔrizasjɔ̃] *nf* categorization, classification.
catégoriser [kategɔrize] *vtr* to categorize.
caténaire [katenɛr] *a & nf* (**suspension**) **c.**, catenary (suspension).
cathédrale [katedral] *nf* cathedral.
cathode [katɔd] *nf El:* cathode. **cathodique** *a* cathodic.
catholicisme [katɔlisism] *nm* (Roman) Catholicism.
catholique [katɔlik] 1. *a* catholic, universal; *F:* **ce n'est pas très c.**, I don't like the sound of it 2. *a & n* (Roman) Catholic.
catimini [katimini] *adv* **en c.**, on the sly; **sortir en c.**, to sneak out.
cation [katjɔ̃] *nm El:* cation.
Caucase [kokaz] *Prnm Geog:* the Caucasus.
cauchemar [koʃmar, ko-] *nm* nightmare. **cauchemardesque** *a* nightmarish.
causalité [kozalite] *nf* causality.
cause [koz] *nf* 1. cause; **être la c. de qch**, to be the cause of sth; **c'est elle qui est en c.**, it's her fault; **et pour c.**, and for a very good reason; **absent pour c. de santé**, absent on medical grounds; **à c. de**, because of, on account of; owing to; **c'est à c. de toi!** it's all your fault! 2. (*a*) *Jur:* cause, (law) suit; action; **avocat sans c.**, briefless barrister; **affaire en c.**, case before the court; **la c. est entendue**, there's nothing more to add; **être en c.**, (i) to be a party to a suit (ii) *F:* to be concerned in sth; **mettre en c. la probité de qn**, to question s.o.'s honesty; **cela est hors de c.**, that's irrelevant; **mettre qn hors de c.**, to exonerate s.o.; **en connaissance de c.**, with full knowledge of the facts (*b*) **faire c. commune avec qn**, to make common cause with s.o.; to side with s.o.
causer¹ [koze] *vtr* to cause; to bring about; **c. des ennuis à qn**, to get s.o. into trouble.
causer² *vi* to talk, to chat; **cause toujours**, you can talk as much as you like (I'm not listening). **causant** *a* chatty, talkative (pers).
causerie [kozri] *nf* talk, chat.
causette [kozɛt] *nf F:* **faire la c.**, to have a chat, a natter.

causeur, -euse [kozœr, -øz] *n* talker.
causticité [kostisite] *nf* causticity. **caustique** *a* caustic.
cautère [kotɛr] *nm Med:* cautery.
cautérisation [koterizasjɔ̃] *nf* cauterization.
cautériser [koterize] *vtr* to cauterize (wound).
caution [kosjɔ̃] *nf* 1. security, guarantee; bail (bond); **se porter c. pour qn**, to bail s.o. out; **mettre qn en liberté sous c.**, to release s.o. on bail; *Com:* **verser une c.**, to pay a deposit; **sujet à c.**, unreliable, unconfirmed (news) 2. surety, guaranty; *Com:* **se porter c. pour qn**, to stand surety for s.o.
cautionnement [kosjɔnmɑ̃] *nm Com:* (*a*) surety bond, guarantee (*b*) security, guaranty.
cautionner [kosjɔne] *vtr* to stand as guarantor for (s.o.); to guarantee (sth).
cavalcade [kavalkad] *nf* cavalcade; pageant.
cavaler [kavale] *P:* 1. *vi & pr* (**se**) **c.**, to run (at full speed); to scarper 2. *vtr* **c. qn**, to get on s.o.'s nerves.
cavalerie [kavalri] *nf* (*a*) cavalry (*b*) stable (of horses).
cavalier, -ière [kavalje, -jɛr] 1. *n* rider; horseman, horsewoman; *a* **piste, allée, cavalière**, riding track, bridle path 2. (*a*) *Mil:* trooper; cavalryman (*b*) *arm Chess:* knight (*c*) *nm* escort (to a lady) (*d*) *n* partner (at dance); **faire c. seul**, to go it alone 3. *a* cavalier, offhand (manner). **cavalièrement** *adv* in a cavalier manner, offhandedly.
cave [kav] 1. *nf* cellar 2. *a* hollow, sunken (cheeks).
caveau, -eaux [kavo] *nm* (*a*) (burial) vault (*b*) small (wine) cellar.
caverne [kavɛrn] *nf* cave, cavern. **caverneux, -euse** *a* cavernous, hollow (voice).
caviar [kavjar] *nm* caviar; **c. rouge**, salmon roe.
caviste [kavist] *nm* cellarman.
cavité [kavite] *nf* cavity, hollow.
CC *abbr Corps consulaire.*
CCP *abbr Compte chèque postal.*
CD *abbr Corps diplomatique.*
CDN *abbr Comité de désarmement nucléaire,* Campaign for Nuclear Disarmament, CND.
ce¹ [s(ə)] *dem pron neut* (**c'** before parts of *être* beginning with a vowel) 1. (*as neuter subject of* **être, devoir être, pouvoir être**) (*a*) (*with adj or adv complement*) **c'est faux!** it's not true! **ce n'est pas trop tôt!** and about time too! **est-ce** [ɛs] **assez?** is that enough? (*b*) (*with n or pron as complement; with a 3rd pers pl complement, colloquial usage allows the sing*) **c'est moi, c'est nous, ce sont eux,** *F:* **c'est eux**, it is I, we, they, *F:* it's me, us, them; **c'est un bon soldat**, he's a good soldier; **ce ne sont pas mes chaussures**, these are not my shoes; *inv phr* **si ce n'est**, except, unless (*c*) **ce ... ici** = **ceci**; **ce n'est pas un hôtel ici!** this is not a hotel! (*d*) **ce ... là** = **cela**; **est-ce que ce sont là vos enfants?** are those your children? (*e*) (*subject isolated for the sake of stress*) **Paris, c'est bien loin!** it's a long way to Paris! (*f*) (*anticipating the subject*) **c'est demain dimanche**, tomorrow's Sunday (*g*) (i) *F:* (*as temporary subject when an adj is followed by a noun clause or an inf subject*) **c'était inutile de sonner,** you need not have rung (ii) **c'est à vous de vous en occuper**, it's up to you to see to it (*h*) **c'est ... qui, c'est ... que** (*used to bring a word into prominence*) **c'est**

un bon petit garçon que Jean! what a fine little chap John is! **c'est moi qui lui ai écrit**, it was I, *F:* me, who wrote to him (*i*) **c'est que** (*introducing a statement*) **c'est que maman est malade**, the point is, mummy's ill; **c'est qu'il fait froid!** it's cold and no mistake! **ce n'est pas qu'il n'y tienne pas**, it's not that he's not keen on it (*j*) **est-ce que** [ɛskə] (*introducing a question*) **est-ce que je peux entrer?** may I come in? 2. (*used as object to* **dire, faire,** *etc*) **ce disant**, in so doing; **pour ce faire**, in order to do this; **ce disant**, so saying 3. (*used as neuter antecedent to a rel pron*) (*a*) **ce qui, ce que,** *etc* = what; **je sais ce qui est arrivé**, I know what's happened; **voilà ce que c'est que mentir**, that's what comes of telling lies; **voici ce dont il s'agit**, this is what it's all about; **à ce qu'on dit**, according to what they say (*b*) **ce qui, ce que,** *etc* = which; **il est parti, ce que je ne savais pas**, he has gone, (a fact) which I didn't know (*c*) **tout ce qui, que**, everything, all (that); **faites tout ce que vous voudrez**, do whatever you like (*d*) *F:* **ce que** = how; **(qu'est-)ce qu'elle a changé!** how she has changed! 4. (= **cela**) **on l'a attaqué et ce en plein jour**, he was attacked and in broad daylight; **sur ce**, thereupon 5. *conj phr* **tenez-vous beaucoup à ce qu'il vienne?** are you very anxious for him to come? 6. *prep phr* **pour ce qui est de la qualité**, as regards quality.

ce² (**cet**), **cette, ces** [sə, (sɛt), sɛt, se] *dem a* (*the form* **cet** *is used before a noun or adj beginning with a vowel or* h *mute*) 1. this, that, *pl* these, those; **un de ces jours**, one of these days; **j'ai mal dormi cette nuit**, I slept badly last night 2. (*a*) that, these; **c'est une de ces personnes**, he's, she's, one of these people (*b*) the; **rien de ce genre**, nothing of the kind 3. (*a*) **ce dernier**, the latter (*b*) *F:* **mais laissez-la donc, cette enfant!** oh do leave the child alone! 4. *pl* **ces dames sont au salon**, the ladies are in the drawing-room 5. **ce . . . -ci**, this; **ce . . . -là**, that; **prenez cette tasse-ci**, take this cup; **je le verrai ces jours-ci**, I'll see him in a day or two 6. *F:* (*a*) **cette question!** what an absurd question! (*b*) **j'ai une de ces faims!** I'm ravenous!

ceci [səsi] *dem pron neut inv* this (thing, fact); **écoutez bien c.**, (now) listen to this; **le cas offre c. de particulier, que**, the case is peculiar in this, that.

cécité [sesite] *nf* blindness.

céder [sede] *v* (**je cède; je céderai**) 1. *vtr* (*a*) to give up, yield (**à**, to); to surrender (right); **c. le pas à qn**, to give way to s.o. (*b*) *Jur:* to transfer, make over, assign (**à**, to); to sell (lease); **maison à c.**, business for sale (*c*) **le c. à qn en qch**, to be inferior to s.o. in sth; **pour l'intelligence elle ne (lui) cède à personne**, in intelligence she's second to none 2. *vi* (*a*) to yield, give way (under pressure); **le câble a cédé sous l'effort**, the rope parted under the strain; **c. au sommeil**, to succumb to sleep (*b*) to give in (**à**, to).

CEDEX [sedɛks] *abbr Post: Courrier d'entreprise à distribution exceptionnelle.*

cédille [sedij] *nf Gram:* cedilla.

cèdre [sɛdr] *nm* cedar (tree, wood).

CEE *abbr Communauté économique européenne.*

ceindre [sɛ̃dr] *vtr* (*conj like* PEINDRE) 1. (*a*) to gird; to buckle on (sword); to put on (sash); **tête ceinte d'une couronne**, wearing a crown (*b*) **c. qn de qch**, to gird, encircle, s.o. with sth 2. to encircle (a town with walls).

ceinture [sɛ̃tyr] *nf* 1. (*a*) belt; girdle; sash; waistband; **c. de sauvetage**, lifebelt; *Aut: Av:* **c. de sécurité**, seat belt, safety belt; (*judo*) **c. noire**, black belt; *F:* **se serrer la c.**, to tighten one's belt (*b*) waist, middle (of the body); **au-dessous de la c.**, below the belt 2. enclosure; circle (of walls); belt (of hills) 3. *Rail:* circle line.

ceinturer [sɛ̃tyre] *vtr* 1. to girdle, surround 2. to seize (s.o.) round the waist.

ceinturon [sɛ̃tyrɔ̃] *nm Mil:* belt.

cela [səla, sla] *F:* **ça** [sa] *dem pron neut* (*a*) that (thing, fact); **qu'est-ce que c'est que c.**, *F:* **que ça?** what is that? **il y a deux ans de c.**, that was two years ago; **sans c. je ne serais pas venu**, otherwise I wouldn't have come; **à part c.**, with that one exception, except on that point; **s'il n'y a que ça de nouveau**, if that's all that's new (*b*) that, it (**cela** *is the pron used as neuter subject to all vbs other than* **être**, *and may be used with* **être** *as more emphatic than* **ce**) **c. ne vous regarde pas**, it's no business of yours; **ça y est!** that's that! that's it! (*c*) *F:* (*disparagingly of people and things*) **c'est ça les hommes!** that's men for you! (*d*) *F:* **ceci . . . cela**; **il m'a dit ceci et c.**, he told me this, that and the other; **comment allez-vous?—comme** (**ci comme**) **ça**, how are you?—so-so; (*e*) *F:* **ça alors!** you don't say! well I'll be damned! **c'est ça**, that's it, that's right; **ce n'est plus ça**, it's not the same anymore; **il n'y a que ça**, there's nothing like it; **et avec c., madame?** anything else, madam? **je suis comme ça**, I'm like that; *F:* **comme ça, vous partez?** so you're going are you? **allons, pas de ça!** hey! none of that! **où ça?** where? **comment ça?** how?

célébration [selebrasjɔ̃] *nf* celebration.

célébrer [selebre] *vtr* (**je célèbre; je célébrerai**) 1. to celebrate (mass, Christmas) (i) to solemnize (rite) (ii) to observe, keep (feast) 2. to praise (s.o.); **c. les louanges de qn**, to sing s.o.'s praises. **célébrant** *a & nm Ecc:* celebrant. **célèbre** *a* celebrated, famous (**par**, for).

célébrité [selebrite] *nf* (*a*) celebrity, fame (*b*) (*pers*) celebrity.

céleri [selri] *nm* **c. (en branche(s))**, celery.

céleri-rave [selrirav] *nm* celeriac; *pl* **céleris-raves.**

célérité [selerite] *nf* speed, rapidity.

céleste [selɛst] *a* celestial, heavenly.

célibat [seliba] *nm* celibacy, single life.

célibataire [selibatɛr] *a & n* unmarried, single, celibate (man, woman); *nm* bachelor; *nf* spinster.

celle, celle-ci, celle-là *see* **celui.**

cellier [selje] *nm* storeroom (for wine, food).

cellule [selyl] *nf* 1. cell 2. *Rec:* cartridge. **cellulaire** *a* cellular; **fourgon c.**, prison van, *F:* Black Maria.

cellulite [selylit] *nf Med:* cellulitis.

celluloïd [selylɔid] *nm* celluloid.

cellulose [selyloz] *nf Ch: Com:* cellulose.

celte [sɛlt] 1. *a* Celtic 2. *n* Celt. **celtique** *a* Celtic.

celui, celle, *pl* **ceux, celles** [səlɥi, sɛl, sø, sɛl] *dem pron* 1. (*a*) (*completed by an adj clause*) the one, *pl* those; **c. qui était parti le dernier**, the one who started last (*b*) he, she, *pl* those; **c. qui mange peu dort bien**, he who eats little sleeps well; **celle à qui j'ai écrit**, the woman I wrote to 2. (*followed by de*) **mes livres et ceux de Jean**, my books and John's 3. **tous ceux ayant la même idée**, all those with the same idea 4. **celui-ci, ceux-ci,** this (one), these; the latter; **celui-là, ceux-là,** that (one), those; the former; **ah celui-là, quel idiot!** oh him! what an idiot!

cénacle [senakl] *nm* 1. cenacle 2. (literary) club, coterie.

cendre [sɑ̃dr̩] *nf* (*a*) ash(es), cinders; **mercredi des Cendres,** Ash Wednesday; **visage couleur de c.,** ashen face (*b*) *pl* (mortal) remains, ashes (*c*) **cendres,** volcaniques, volcanic ash. **cendré, cendreux, -euse** *a* ash-grey, ashen, ashy.

cendrée [sɑ̃dre] *nf Sp:* cinder track; dirt track.

cendrier [sɑ̃drije] *nm* (*a*) ashpan (*b*) ashtray.

Cendrillon [sɑ̃drijɔ̃] 1. *Prnf* Cinderella 2. *nf* drudge.

Cène [sɛn] *nf* **la C.,** the Last Supper.

cénotaphe [senɔtaf] *nm* cenotaph.

cens [sɑ̃s] *nm Adm:* **c. électoral,** property qualification (for the franchise).

censé [sɑ̃se] *a* **être c. faire qch,** to be supposed to do sth; **je ne suis pas c. le savoir,** I am not required to know that. **censément** *adv* supposedly; practically.

censeur [sɑ̃sœr] *nm* 1. critic 2. *Adm:* censor 3. *Sch:* vice-principal, deputy headmaster, -mistress (of *lycée*).

censure [sɑ̃syr] *nf* 1. (*a*) censorship (*b*) *Cin: etc:* (board of) censors (*c*) *Psy:* (the) censor 2. censure.

censurer [sɑ̃syre] *vtr* 1. to censure, to find fault with (sth) 2. to censor (film).

cent¹ [sɑ̃] 1. (*a*) *num a* (*takes a pl s when multiplied by a preceding numeral but not when followed by another numeral; tirm when used as an ordinal*) (a, one) hundred; **c. élèves,** a hundred pupils; **deux cents hommes,** two hundred men; **deux c. cinquante hommes,** two hundred and fifty men; **page deux c.,** page two hundred; **vous avez c. fois raison,** you're absolutely right; **c. fois mieux,** a hundred times better; *F:* **je ne vais pas t'attendre (pendant) c. sept ans,** I'm not going to wait for you for ever; **faire les c. pas,** to pace up and down; *F:* **faire les quatre cents coups,** (i) to kick up a hell of a racket (ii) to be up to all sorts of tricks; *F:* **être aux c. coups,** to be desperate; *F:* **je vous le donne en c.,** you'll never guess (*b*) *nm inv* a hundred; **sept pour c.,** seven per cent; **il y a c. à parier contre un que,** it's a hundred to one that; **c. pour c.,** a hundred per cent 2. *nm var Sp:* **c. mètres,** the hundred metres.

cent² [sɛnt] *nm esp FrC:* (*coin*) cent.

centaine [sɑ̃tɛn] *nf* (approximate) hundred; **une c. de francs,** a hundred francs or so; **des centaines de livres,** hundreds of books; **atteindre la c.,** to live to be a hundred.

centaure [sɑ̃tɔr] *nm Myth:* centaur.

centenaire [sɑ̃tnɛr] 1. *a* age-old; **chêne c.,** ancient oak 2. *n* centenarian 3. *nm* centenary (anniversary).

centième [sɑ̃tjɛm] 1. *num a & n* hundredth 2. *nm* hundredth (part) 3. *nf Th:* hundredth performance.

centigrade [sɑ̃tigrad] *a* centigrade.

centigramme [sɑ̃tigram] *nm* centigramme.

centilitre [sɑ̃tilitr̩] *nm* centilitre.

centime [sɑ̃tim] *nm* centime; **je n'ai pas un c.,** I haven't got a penny.

centimètre [sɑ̃timɛtr̩] *nm* 1. centimetre 2. tape measure.

centrage [sɑ̃traʒ] *nm* centring, centering.

central, -aux [sɑ̃tral, -o] 1. *a* (*a*) central; middle (point); **quartier c. d'une ville,** town centre (*b*) principal, main, head (office) 2. *nm* **c. téléphonique,** telephone exchange 3. *nf* (*a*) **centrale (électrique),** power station (*b*) **centrale (syndicale),** group of affiliated trade unions (*c*) (central) prison.

centralisation [sɑ̃tralizasjɔ̃] *nf* centralization. **centralisateur, -trice** *a* centralizing (force).

centraliser [sɑ̃tralize] *vtr* to centralize.

centre [sɑ̃tr̩] *nm* (*a*) centre; middle central point; **c. ville,** town centre, city centre; **c. commercial,** shopping centre, shopping precinct; **c. hospitalier,** hospital complex; **il se croit le c. de l'univers,** he thinks the world revolves around him (*b*) *Pol:* centre (*c*) *Fb: etc:* centre (player).

centrer [sɑ̃tre] *vtr* (*a*) to centre (**sur,** on); **c. l'attention de qn sur qch,** to focus s.o.'s attention on sth (*b*) to centre the ball.

centrifuger [sɑ̃trifyʒe] *vtr* to centrifuge. **centrifuge** *a* centrifugal (force).

centrifugeuse [sɑ̃trifyʒøz] *nf* centrifuge.

centripète [sɑ̃tripɛt] *a* centripetal.

centuple [sɑ̃typl̩] *a & nm* centuple; hundredfold; **le c. de 10,** a hundred times 10.

centupler [sɑ̃typle] *vtr & i* to increase a hundred times, a hundredfold.

cep [sɛp] *nm* **c. de vigne,** vinestock.

CEP *abbr Caisse d'Épargne de Paris.*

cépage [sepaʒ] *nm* (variety of) vine.

cèpe [sɛp] *nm Bot:* boletus, cepe.

cependant [s(ə)pɑ̃dɑ̃] 1. *adv* meanwhile; in the meantime; **c. que,** while 2. *conj* yet, still, nevertheless, however.

céramique [seramik] *nf* ceramic; pottery; **la c.,** ceramics; **dalles en c.,** ceramic tiles.

cerceau, -eaux [sɛrso] *nm* hoop.

cercle [sɛrkl̩] *nm* 1. (*a*) circle; **faire c.,** to make a circle, a ring (**autour de qch,** around sth); **c. vicieux,** vicious circle; **c. d'activités,** sphere of activities (*b*) circle, set (of friends); **c. littéraire,** literary circle, society (*c*) club 2. (binding) hoop, ring; metal rim (of wheel) 3. (*a*) dial (*b*) **quart de c.,** quadrant.

cercler [sɛrkle] *vtr* 1. to encircle, to ring; **lunettes cerclées d'or,** gold-rimmed spectacles 2. to hoop (barrel); to rim (**de,** with).

cercueil [sɛrkœj] *nm* coffin, *NAm:* casket.

céréale [sereal] *nf* cereal.

cérébral, -ale, -aux [serebral, -o] *a* cerebral; intellectual, mental (work).

cérémonial, -als [seremɔnjal] *nm* ceremonial.

cérémonie [seremɔni] *nf* ceremony; **habit de c.,** formal dress; **sans c.,** informal(ly); **faire des cérémonies,** to stand on ceremony. **cérémonieux, -ieuse** *a* ceremonious, formal. **cérémonieusement** *adv* ceremoniously, formally.

cerf [sɛr, sɛrf, *pl* sɛr] *nm* stag.

cerfeuil [sɛrfœj] *nm Bot:* chervil.

cerf-volant [sɛrvɔlɑ̃] *nm* (paper) kite; *pl* **cerfs-volants.**

cerise [s(ə)riz] 1. *nf* cherry 2. *nm & a inv* cherry-red, cerise.

cerisier [s(ə)rizje] *nm* cherry tree.

cerne [sɛrn] *nm* ring (round moon, round eyes).

cerner [sɛrne] vtr (a) to encircle, surround; **avoir les yeux cernés,** to have rings round the eyes (b) to grasp, determine (argument).

certain, -aine [sɛrtɛ̃, -ɛn] 1. a (a) certain, sure; **il est c. qu'il viendra,** he will definitely come (b) **il est c. de réussir,** he is sure to succeed; **je n'en suis pas bien c.,** I'm not entirely convinced (c) fixed, stated (date, price) 2. indef a & pron (a) some, certain; **certains affirment que,** some people maintain that; **après un c. temps,** after a certain time; **jusqu'à un c. point,** up to a point; **d'un c. âge,** middle-aged; elderly; **dans un c. sens,** in a sense, in a way (b) Pej: **un c. M. Martin,** a certain Mr Martin. **certainement** adv certainly, undoubtedly; **vous l'avez c. lu,** I'm sure you've read it; **c.!** of course!

certes [sɛrt] adv (oui) **c.!** yes indeed!

certificat [sɛrtifika] nm certificate; testimonial; attestation; diploma.

certification [sɛrtifikasjɔ̃] nf certification, attestation; witnessing.

certifier [sɛrtifje] vtr to certify, attest; to witness (signature); **c. qch à qn,** to assure s.o. of sth.

certitude [sɛrtityd] nf certainty; **j'en ai la c.,** I am sure of it.

cerveau, -eaux [sɛrvo] nm (a) brain; **rhume de c.,** cold in the head (b) mind, intellect, brains; F: **avoir le c. dérangé,** to be cracked (c) brain(s), mastermind (of plan).

cervelas [sɛrvəla] nm Cu: saveloy.

cervelet [sɛrvəlɛ] nm Anat: cerebellum.

cervelle [sɛrvɛl] nf (a) Anat: brain(s); **brûler la c. à qn,** to blow s.o.'s brains out; Cu: **c. de veau,** calves' brains (b) mind, brains; **se creuser la c.,** to rack one's brains (pour, to); **elle a une c. de moineau,** she's feather-brained.

cervical, -aux [sɛrvikal, -o] a Anat: cervical.

ces [se] see **ce²** 1.

CES abbr Collège d'enseignement secondaire.

césarienne [sezarjɛn] af & nf Med: caesarean (section).

cessation [sɛsasjɔ̃] nf cessation, ceasing; suspension (of payments).

cesse [sɛs] nf **sans c.,** unceasingly; constantly, incessantly, continuously; **il n'aura de c. que,** he won't stop until.

cesser [sese] 1. vi to cease, leave off, stop; **faire c. (qch),** to put a stop to (sth); **c. de fumer,** to give up smoking 2. vtr to stop, leave off (work); to give up (business); to discontinue (payments); **c. toutes relations avec qn,** to break off all relations with s.o.

cessez-le-feu [seselfø] nm inv ceasefire.

cession [sɛsjɔ̃] nf Jur: transfer, assignment; **faire c. de,** to transfer.

c'est-à-dire [sɛtadir] conj phr 1. that is (to say) 2. **c'est-à-dire que** + ind, the fact is that; the thing is that.

cet, cette [sɛt] see **ce²**.

CET abbr Collège d'enseignement technique.

ceux [sø] see **celui**.

Ceylan [selɑ̃] Prnm Geog: Hist: Ceylon.

CFDT abbr Confédération française démocratique du travail.

CFTC abbr Confédération française des travailleurs chrétiens.

CGC abbr Confédération générale des cadres.

CGT abbr Confédération générale du travail.

chacal, -als [ʃakal] nm Z: jackal.

chacun, -une [ʃakœ̃, -yn] indef pron 1. each (one), every one; **trois francs c.,** three francs each; **ils sont partis c. de son côté, de leur côté,** they went their separate ways 2. everybody, everyone; **c. (a) son goût,** every man to his taste; **c. son tour,** each in turn.

chagrin [ʃagrɛ̃] 1. a A: sad, troubled; morose 2. nm grief, sorrow, trouble; **avoir du c.,** to be upset; **faire du c. à qn,** to grieve, to distress, s.o.

chagriner [ʃagrine] vtr to grieve, distress, upset.

chah [ʃa] nm shah.

chahut [ʃay] nm F: noise, din; **faire du c.,** to make a din, a racket.

chahuter [ʃayte] 1. vi F: to kick up a racket, to make a din 2. vtr (a) to knock (things) about (b) to rag (s.o.).

chahuteur, -euse [ʃaytœr, -øz] F: (a) a rowdy, unruly (b) n rowdy.

chai [ʃɛ] nm wine and spirits storehouse.

chaîne [ʃɛn] nf 1. (a) chain (b) shackles, fetters, bonds (c) Surv: **c. d'arpenteur,** chain measure (d) Nau: cable (e) **c. de montage, de fabrication,** assembly line, production line 2. (a) **c. de montagnes,** mountain range; **c. d'idées,** train of thought (b) chain (of hotels) 3. (hi-fi) system; WTel: TV: network; TV: channel 4. Tex: warp.

chaînette [ʃɛnɛt] nf small chain.

chaînon [ʃɛnɔ̃] nm (a) link (of chain) (b) secondary chain (of mountains).

chair [ʃɛr] nf flesh; **en c. et en os,** in the flesh; **être (bien) en c.,** to be plump, F: tubby 2. (a) **c. (à saucisse),** sausagemeat (b) flesh, pulp (of fruit) 3. **c. de poule,** gooseflesh; **ça vous donne la c. de poule,** it makes your flesh creep; a inv **(couleur) c.,** flesh-coloured 4. **sa propre c.,** his own flesh and blood.

chaire [ʃɛr] nf 1. (bishop's) throne 2. pulpit 3. (a) chair, desk, rostrum (of lecturer) (b) professorship, chair.

chaise [ʃɛz] nf 1. chair, seat; **c. d'enfant,** highchair; **c. longue,** deckchair; Jur: US: **c. électrique,** (electric) chair 2. Hist: **c. à porteurs,** sedan chair.

chaisier, -ière [ʃɛzje, -jɛr] n chair attendant (in park).

chaland [ʃalɑ̃] nm barge, lighter.

châle [ʃal] nm shawl.

chalet [ʃalɛ] nm chalet.

chaleur [ʃalœr] nf 1. (a) heat, warmth; **vague de c.,** heatwave; (on label) **craint la c.,** store in a cool place; Med: **avoir des chaleurs,** to have hot flushes (b) **les (grandes) chaleurs,** the hot weather, the hot season (c) ardour, zeal; **parler avec c.,** to speak warmly 2. heat, rut (of animals); **en c.,** on heat. **chaleureux, -euse** a warm (thanks); cordial (welcome). **chaleureusement** adv warmly, cordially.

challenge [ʃalɑ̃ʒ] nm Sp: (a) contest, tournament (b) trophy.

chaloupe [ʃalup] nf launch; **c. de sauvetage,** lifeboat.

chalumeau, -eaux [ʃalymo] nm 1. Mus: pipe 2. blowlamp; blowtorch.

chalut [ʃaly] nm Fish: trawl; **pêcher au c.,** to trawl.

chalutier [ʃalytje] nm (a) (boat) trawler (b) trawler-man.

chamailler (se) [səʃamaje] vpr F: to squabble, to bicker. **chamailleur, -euse** a & n quarrelsome (pers); n squabbler.

chamaillerie [ʃamajəri] nf F: squabble.

chamarrer [ʃamare] vtr Lit: to bedeck, adorn.

chambard [ʃãbar] nm F: (a) shambles, mess; upheaval (b) din, racket.

chambardement [ʃãbardəmã] nm F: upheaval.

chambarder [ʃãbarde] vtr F: (a) to upset, to ransack (room) (b) to rearrange, reorganize.

chambellan [ʃãbelã] nm chamberlain.

chambouler [ʃãbule] vtr F: to ruin, mess up (plans); **tout c.**, to turn everything upside down.

chambranle [ʃãbrãl] nm frame (of door); mantelpiece.

chambre [ʃãbr̥] nf 1. (a) c. (à coucher), bedroom; c. à grand lit, double room; c. à deux lits, twin-bedded room; c. d'ami, spare (bed)room; c. d'enfants, nursery; faire sa c. à part, to sleep in separate rooms; faire sa c., to clean (out), tidy, one's room; c. forte, strongroom; c. froide, cold store; travailler en c., to work at home (b) c. à gaz, gas chamber 2. Adm: chamber, house; division of a court of justice; c. de commerce, chamber of commerce; c. de députés, Chamber of Deputies 3. Tchn: chamber; cavity, space; c. à air, inner tube (of tyre); Phot: c. noire, (i) camera (body) (ii) darkroom.

chambrée [ʃãbre] nf Mil: barrack-room.

chambrer [ʃãbre] vtr to bring (wine) to room temperature.

chameau, -eaux [ʃamo] nm (a) Z: camel (b) F: (of man) brute; (of woman) cow.

chamelier [ʃaməlje] nm camel driver.

chamelle [ʃamɛl] nf she-camel.

chamois [ʃamwa] nm Z: chamois; (peau de) c., washleather, chamois leather, shammy.

champ [ʃã] nm 1. (a) field; fleur des champs, wild flower; prendre, couper, à travers champs, to go, cut, across country; prendre la clef des champs, to decamp, run off; à tout bout de c., repeatedly; at any moment (b) c. de foire, fairground; c. d'aviation, airfield; c. de courses, racecourse, NAm: racetrack (c) c. de bataille, battlefield; mort au c. d'honneur, killed in action; c. de tir, (i) shooting range, rifle range (ii) field of fire 2. (a) field of action; range, scope; avoir du c., to have (elbow) room; laisser le c. libre à qn, to leave s.o. a clear field; le c. est libre, the coast is clear (b) Cin: etc: shot, picture; field (of telescope); Phot: profondeur de c., depth of focus; hors c., off camera; out of shot (c) c. magnétique, magnetic field.

Champagne [ʃãpaɲ] 1. Prnf Geog: Champagne 2. nm (also vin de C.) champagne 3. nf fine c., liqueur brandy.

champêtre [ʃãpɛtr̥] a rustic, rural; garde c., country policeman.

champignon [ʃãpiɲɔ̃] nm 1. c. (comestible), mushroom; edible fungus; c. vénéneux, poisonous fungus; toadstool 2. Aut: F: accelerator (pedal).

champion, -ionne [ʃãpjɔ̃, -jɔn] 1. n champion 2. a F: first-rate.

championnat [ʃãpjɔna] nm championship.

chance [ʃãs] nf 1. chance, likelihood; il a peu de chances de réussir, he has little chance of succeeding; il y a une c., it's just possible; il y a une c. sur cent qu'elle le voie, it's a hundred to one against her seeing him 2. (good) luck, fortune; tenter sa c., to try one's luck; souhaiter bonne c. à qn, to wish s.o. (good) luck; pas de c.! hard luck! avoir de la c., to be lucky; c'est bien ma c.! just my luck! par c., luckily, fortunately. **chanceux, -euse** a lucky, fortunate.

chanceler [ʃãsle] vi (je chancelle) to stagger, to totter, to wobble; to waver, to falter (in one's resolution). **chancelant** a staggering, tottering; wavering; delicate (health).

chancelier [ʃãsəlje] nm chancellor; (in Britain) Grand C., Lord Chancellor; C. de l'Échiquier, Chancellor of the Exchequer.

chancellerie [ʃãsɛlri] nf chancellery; chancery (of embassy).

chandail [ʃãdaj] nm Cl: sweater, pullover.

Chandeleur [ʃãdlœr] nf la C., Candlemas.

chandelier [ʃãdəlje] nm candlestick; candelabra.

chandelle [ʃãdɛl] nf 1. (a) (tallow) candle; économies de bouts de c., cheeseparing economy; en voir trente-six chandelles, to see stars (b) (church) candle, taper; je vous dois une fière c., I owe you more than I can repay 2. P: dewdrop, snot (on the end of the nose) 3. (a) c. romaine, Roman candle (b) Av: chandelle (c) Ten: lob; Fb: high kick (d) Gym: shoulder stand.

change [ʃãʒ] nm 1. Fin: exchange; gagner, perdre, au c., to gain, to lose, on the deal; lettre de c., bill of exchange; bureau de c., foreign exchange office; cours du c., exchange rate; contrôle des changes, exchange control 2. donner le c. à qn, to sidetrack s.o.

changeant [ʃãʒã] a changing; altering; changeable, variable; fickle; unsettled (weather).

changement [ʃãʒmã] nm change; changing; alteration; Adm: transfer; il vous faut un c. d'air, you need a change; sans c., unchanged, unaltered; PN: c. de propriétaire, under new management; c. en mieux, change for the better; c. de vitesse, (i) gears, gear lever (ii) gear change.

changer [ʃãʒe] v (n. changeons) 1. vtr to change, to exchange; c. les draps, to change the sheets 2. vtr (a) to change, alter; cette robe vous change, that dress makes you look different (b) la campagne me changera, the country will be a (good) change for me; ça me changera les idées, it will take my mind off things 3. vi (a) to (undergo a) change; le temps va c., the weather is going to change; c. de visage, to alter one's expression; Iron: pour c., for a change (b) c. de train, to change (trains); c. de place avec qn, to change places with s.o., to change seats with s.o.; c. de domicile, to move (house); c. de vêtements, se c., to change (one's clothes); to get changed; c. d'avis, to change one's mind; c. de route, to take another road; Nau: to alter course; c. de vitesse, to change gear; c. de ton, to change one's tune.

changeur, -euse [ʃãʒœr, -øz] 1. n (pers) money changer 2. nm (a) c. (de disques), record changer (b) c. de monnaie, change machine.

Changhaï [ʃãgaj] Prnm Geog: Shanghai.

chanoine [ʃanwan] *nm Ecc:* canon.

chanson [ʃãsɔ̃] *nf* song; **c. folklorique**, folk song; *F:* **c'est toujours la même c.!** it's the same old story.

chansonnette [ʃãsɔnɛt] *nf* ditty.

chant [ʃã] *nm* 1. singing; song; **leçon de c.**, singing lesson; **c. du cygne**, swan song; **au c. du coq**, at cockcrow 2. (*a*) song; **c. de Noël**, Christmas carol (*b*) melody, air; **c. funèbre**, dirge; **c. grégorien**, Gregorian chant 3. canto (of long poem).

chantage [ʃãtaʒ] *nm* blackmail; **faire du c.**, to blackmail.

chanter [ʃãte] 1. *vtr* to sing; **c. victoire**, to crow; **c. toujours la même chanson**, to be always harping on the same string; **qu'est-ce que vous me chantez là?** what are you telling me? 2. *vi* (*of birds*) to sing; (*of cock*) to crow; (*of cricket*) to chirp; *F:* **c'est comme si je chantais**, I'm wasting my breath; **faire c. qn**, to blackmail s.o.; **si ça me chante**, if it appeals to me. **chantant** *a* sing-song, lilting (voice); tuneful (air).

chanteur, -euse [ʃãtœr, -øz] *n* singer.

chantier [ʃãtje] *nm* 1. (*a*) yard, site; depot; **c. (de construction)**, (i) building site (ii) builder's yard (iii) road works; **avoir une œuvre en c.**, to have a piece of work in hand; **quel c.!** what a mess! what a shambles! *PN:* **c. interdit au public**, no admittance except on business 2. **c. naval**, shipyard.

chantonner [ʃãtɔne] *vtr & i* to hum; to sing softly; to croon.

chantre [ʃãtr] *nm* 1. *Ecc:* cantor; chorister; **grand c.**, precentor 2. poet.

chanvre [ʃãvr] *nm* hemp.

chaos [kao] *nm* chaos. **chaotique** *a* chaotic.

chapardage [ʃapardaʒ] *nm F:* (petty) thieving, pilfering.

chaparder [ʃaparde] *vtr F:* to steal, to pinch, to pilfer. **chapardeur, -euse** 1. *a* thieving, pilfering 2. *n* thief, pilferer.

chapeau, -eaux [ʃapo] *nm* 1. (*a*) hat; **c. mou**, (soft) felt hat; **saluer qn d'un coup de c.**, to raise one's hat to s.o.; **tirer son c. à qn**, to take off one's hat to s.o.; **c.!** well done! bravo! (*b*) *Bot:* cap 2. cover, lid; *Cu:* piecrust; cap (of pen); *Aut:* **c. de roue**, hub cap.

chapeauter [ʃapote] *vtr* to be in charge, to oversee.

chapelet [ʃaplɛ] *nm* rosary; *F:* **défiler son c.**, to speak one's mind; **c. d'oignons**, string of onions; **c. de bombes**, stick of bombs; **c. d'injures**, stream of insults.

chapelier, -ière [ʃapəlje, -jɛr] *n* hatter.

chapelle [ʃapɛl] *nf* (*a*) chapel; **c. de la Vierge**, Lady chapel; **c. ardente**, mortuary chapel (*b*) *Ecc:* **maître de c.**, choir master (*c*) *Lit:* clique, coterie.

chapelure [ʃaplyr] *nf Cu:* breadcrumbs.

chaperon [ʃaprɔ̃] *nm* 1. hood; *Lit:* **le Petit C. rouge**, Little Red Riding Hood 2. chaperon.

chaperonner [ʃaprɔne] *vtr* to chaperon.

chapiteau, -eaux [ʃapito] *nm* 1. *Arch:* capital (of column) 2. big top (of circus).

chapitre [ʃapitr] *nm* 1. *Ecc:* chapter (of canons) 2. (*a*) chapter (of book) (*b*) head(ing); item (of expenditure); **sur ce c.**, on that subject, on that score.

chapitrer [ʃapitre] *vtr* to admonish, to reprimand (s.o.); to tell (s.o.) off.

chapon [ʃapɔ̃] *nm Cu:* capon.

chaque [ʃak] 1. *a* each, every; **c. chose à sa place**, everything in its place; **c. fois qu'il vient**, whenever he comes 2. *pron F:* (= **chacun**) **100 francs c.**, 100 francs each.

char [ʃar] *nm* 1. (*a*) chariot (*b*) waggon; **c. à bœufs**, bullock cart; **c. funèbre**, hearse (*c*) **c. (de carnaval)**, float 2. *Mil:* **c. (de combat)**, tank.

charabia [ʃarabja] *nm F:* gibberish, gobbledygook.

charade [ʃarad] *nf* (*a*) riddle (*b*) charade.

charbon [ʃarbɔ̃] *nm* 1. (*a*) coal (*b*) **c. (de bois)**, charcoal; **être sur des charbons ardents**, to be on tenterhooks (*c*) *Ch:* carbon 2. *Med: Vet:* anthrax.

charbonnage [ʃarbɔnaʒ] *nm* 1. coal mining 2. *pl* collieries; **les charbonnages de France**, the French Coal Board.

charbonnier [ʃarbɔnje] 1. *nm Nau:* collier 2. *n* coalman.

charcuter [ʃarkyte] *vtr F:* to hack up (meat); to butcher (s.o.).

charcuterie [ʃarkytri] *nf* 1. pork butchery; delicatessen trade 2. pork butcher's shop; = delicatessen (shop) 3. pork meat(s); delicatessen.

charcutier, -ière [ʃarkytje, -jɛr] *n* 1. pork butcher 2. *F:* butcher.

chardon [ʃardɔ̃] *nm* thistle.

chardonneret [ʃardɔnrɛ] *nm Orn:* goldfinch.

charge [ʃarʒ] *nf* 1. load, burden; (on ship) cargo; **c. utile**, carrying capacity; (*of taxi*) **prise en c.**, minimum fare; **être à c. à qn**, to be a burden to s.o. 2. *Tchn:* (*a*) load; stress; **c. admissible**, safe load (*b*) (*of furnace, gun*) **c. d'explosif**, explosive charge (*c*) *El:* charge; **mettre une batterie en c.**, to put a battery on charge 3. (*a*) charge, responsibility, trust; **prendre en c.**, to take charge (of s.o., sth); **enfants confiés à ma c.**, children in my care; **femme de c.**, housekeeper (*b*) office; **charges publiques**, public offices 4. charge, expense; **les réparations sont à votre c.**, you are responsible for repairs; **charges sociales**, national insurance contributions; **être à la c. de qn**, to be dependent on s.o.; **charges de famille**, dependents; **enfants à c.**, dependent children; **loyer plus les charges**, rent plus service charge (and maintenance costs); **à c. de revanche**, on condition that I may do as much for you 5. *Art:* caricature 6. *Mil:* charge 7. *Jur:* charge, indictment; **témoin à c.**, witness for the prosecution.

chargé [ʃarʒe] 1. *a* loaded, laden; crowded (train); **conscience chargée**, guilty conscience; **jour c.**, busy day; **temps c.**, heavy, overcast, weather 2. (*a*) *nm* **c. d'affaires**, chargé d'affaires (*b*) *n Sch:* **chargé(e) de cours** = (university) lecturer.

chargement [ʃarʒəmã] *nm* (*a*) loading, lading (*b*) load, freight, cargo.

charger [ʃarʒe] *vtr* (**n. chargeons**) 1. (*a*) to load; **c. des marchandises**, to load goods; *F:* (*of taxi driver*) **c. un client**, to pick up a fare (*b*) to weigh (down); **chargé de paquets**, weighed down with parcels; **nourriture qui charge l'estomac**, food that lies heavy on the stomach (*c*) **c. qn de reproches**, to heap reproaches on s.o. (*d*) to load (gun, camera); to fill (pipe); to refill (pen); to charge (battery) 2. (*a*) to entrust (s.o. with sth); to instruct (s.o. to do sth); **être chargé de qch**, to be in charge of sth (*b*) **se c. de**

faire qch, to undertake to do sth; **je m'en chargerai,** I'll see to it, I'll take care of it 3. to caricature (s.o.); to turn (portrait) into a caricature 4. (*of troops, bull*) to charge 5. *Jur:* to indict, to charge (s.o.).

chargeur [ʃarʒœr] *nm* 1. (*pers*) loader; *Nau:* shipper 2. (*a*) *Sma:* magazine; (cartridge) clip (*b*) *Phot:* cartridge (*c*) (battery) charger.

chariot [ʃarjo] *nm* 1. (*a*) waggon; cart (*b*) truck, trolley (*c*) *Cin:* dolly 2. (*a*) carriage (of typewriter) (*b*) *Av:* **c. d'atterrissage,** undercarriage; landing gear.

charité [ʃarite] *nf* 1. charity, love; *Prov:* **la c. bien ordonnée commence par soi-même,** charity begins at home 2. act of charity; **faire la c. à qn,** to give money to s.o. **charitable** *a* charitable, kindly (**envers,** to, towards). **charitablement** *adv* charitably, kindly.

charivari [ʃarivari] *nm* row, racket; hullabaloo.

charlatan [ʃarlatã] *nm* charlatan, quack; mountebank. **charlatanesque** *a* quack (remedy). **charlatanisme** [ʃarlatanism] *nm* charlatanism.

charme¹ [ʃarm] *nm* 1. charm, spell; **tenir qn sous le c.,** to hold the audience spellbound; **se porter comme un c.,** to be as fit as a fiddle 2. charm, attraction; **elle a beaucoup de c.,** she's absolutely charming; **c'est ce qui en fait le c.,** that's what makes it so attractive; **faire du c.,** to turn on the charm.

charme² *nm Bot:* hornbeam.

charmer [ʃarme] *vtr* 1. to charm, bewitch 2. to charm, delight; **être charmé de faire qch,** to be delighted to do sth. **charmant** *a* charming; delightful. **charmeur, -euse** 1. *a* charming 2. *n* (*a*) (snake) charmer (*b*) charming person.

charnel, -elle [ʃarnɛl] *a* (*a*) carnal (*b*) worldly. **charnellement** *adv* carnally.

charnier [ʃarnje] *nm* mass grave.

charnière [ʃarnjɛr] *nf* (*a*) hinge; *F:* **nom à c.,** double-barrelled name (*b*) turning point.

charnu [ʃarny] *a* fleshy.

charognard [ʃarɔɲar] *nm Orn: Fig:* vulture.

charogne [ʃarɔɲ] *nf* 1. carrion 2. *P:* (*pers*) swine.

charpente [ʃarpãt] *nf* frame(work), framing; **bois de c.,** timber; (*of pers*) **avoir la c. solide,** to be solidly built. **charpenté** *a* built, constructed; **homme solidement c.,** well built man.

charpenterie [ʃarpãtri] *nf* carpentry.

charpentier [ʃarpãtje] *nm* carpenter.

charpie [ʃarpi] *nf* shredded linen; **mettre qch en c.,** to tear sth to shreds.

charretée [ʃarte] *nf* cartload, cartful.

charretier [ʃartje] *nm* carter; **language de c.,** coarse language.

charrette [ʃarɛt] *nf* cart; **c. à bras,** handcart; barrow.

charrier [ʃarje] (*impf & pr sub* n. charriions) 1. *vtr* (*a*) to cart, carry, transport (*b*) to carry along, wash down, drift; **rivière qui charrie du sable,** river that carries sand (*c*) *P:* to poke fun at (s.o.) 2. *vi P:* to exaggerate; to pile it on.

charron [ʃarɔ̃] *nm* cartwright; wheelwright.

charrue [ʃary] *nf* plough; *F:* **mettre la c. devant les bœufs,** to put the cart before the horse.

charte [ʃart] *nf* 1. charter 2. (ancient) deed; title.

charter [ʃartɛr] 1. *nm* charter(ed) aircraft; charter flight 2. *a* charter (ticket); chartered (aircraft).

chartreux, -euse [ʃartrø, -øz] 1. *n* Carthusian (monk, nun) 2. *nf* **chartreuse,** Carthusian monastery; charterhouse.

chas [ʃa] *nm* eye (of needle).

chasse [ʃas] *nf* 1. (*a*) hunting; **c. à courre,** (stag)-hunting, (fox)hunting; **c. au daim** (**à l'affût**), deer-stalking; **c. à l'homme,** manhunt; **c. sous-marine,** underwater fishing; **c. aux appartements,** flat hunting; **aller à la c.,** to go hunting, shooting; **la c. est ouverte,** the shooting season has begun; **la c. vient de passer,** the hunt has just gone by; **faire bonne c.,** to make a good bag (*b*) **c. gardée,** private game preserve; *Fig:* **ah non, c. gardée!** hands off! **louer une c.,** to rent a shoot (*c*) chase; **donner c. à qch,** to chase, to pursue, sth; **faire la c. à qch,** to hunt sth down, out (*d*) *MilAv:* **la c.,** the fighters 2. **c. d'eau,** flushing system, flush; **tirer la c. (d'eau),** to flush the toilet.

châsse [ʃas] *nf* 1. reliquary, shrine 2. mounting; frame (of spectacles).

chasse-clou(s) [ʃasklu] *nm* nail punch; *pl chasse-clous.*

chassé-croisé [ʃasekrwaze] *nm* (*a*) *Danc:* set to partners (*b*) rearrangement, reshuffle; *pl chassés-croisés.*

chasse-neige [ʃasnɛʒ] *nm inv* snowplough.

chasser [ʃase] 1. *vtr* (*a*) to chase, hunt; **c. la perdrix,** to go partridge shooting; **c. à courre,** to ride to hounds; to hunt; **c. au fusil,** to shoot (*b*) to drive, to chase, (s.o.) out, away; to expel; to dismiss (employee); to dispel (fog); to drive in (nail); **c. une mouche (du revers de la main),** to brush away a fly; **c. une odeur,** to get rid of a smell 2. *vi* (*a*) to hunt, to go hunting; to go shooting; **c. au lion,** to hunt lions (*b*) to drive; **nuages qui chassent du nord,** clouds driving from the north (*c*) *Aut:* to skid; *Nau:* (*of anchor*) to drag.

chasseur [ʃasœr] *nm* 1. hunter; huntsman; **c. de têtes,** headhunter; **c. d'images,** keen photographer 2. (*in hotel*) messenger; porter; pageboy, *NAm:* bellboy, bellhop 3. *AMil:* chasseur 4. *Mil: Av:* fighter; *Navy:* **c. de sous-marins,** submarine chaser.

chasseur-bombardier [ʃasœrbɔ̃bardje] *nm* fighter-bomber; *pl chasseurs-bombardiers.*

châssis [ʃasi] *nm* (*a*) frame; **c. de porte, de fenêtre,** door frame, window frame (*b*) *Hort:* (cold) frame (*c*) *Aut:* chassis; **faux c.,** subframe.

chasteté [ʃastəte] *nf* chastity. **chaste** *a* chaste, pure. **chastement** *adv* chastely, purely.

chasuble [ʃazybl] *nf Cl:* (*a*) chasuble (*b*) **robe c.,** pinafore dress.

chat, chatte [ʃa, ʃat] *n* 1. cat; *m* tom(cat), *f* queen; **le C. botté,** Puss in Boots; *F:* **mon petit c., ma petite chatte,** my darling; **il n'y a pas un c.,** there isn't a soul (here); **avoir un c. dans la gorge,** to have a frog in one's throat; *Prov:* **c. échaudé craint l'eau froide,** once bitten twice shy 2. *Games:* (*a*) **jouer au c.,** to play tig, tag (*b*) (*pers*) it, he.

châtaigne [ʃatɛɲ] *nf* (*a*) *Bot:* (sweet) chestnut (*b*) *P:* blow, clout.

châtaignier [ʃatɛɲje] *nm* chestnut (tree).

châtain [ʃatɛ̃] *a usu inv in f* (chestnut-)brown; brown-haired (pers); **cheveux c. clair,** light brown hair.

château, -eaux [ʃato] *nm* 1. **c. (fort),** (fortified) castle; **bâtir des châteaux en Espagne,** to build castles in the air; **c. de cartes,** house of cards 2. (*a*) country seat; mansion; manor; chateau (*b*) (royal) palace 3. **c. d'eau,** water tower; *Rail:* tank.

châteaubriand, -briant [ʃɑtobriɑ̃] *nm Cu:* thick piece of filet steak.

châtelain [ʃɑtlɛ̃] *n* 1. *Hist:* lord (of the manor) 2. owner, tenant, of a château.

châtelaine [ʃɑtlɛn] *nf* 1. *Hist:* lady (of the manor) 2. (woman) owner, tenant, of a château.

chat-huant [ʃaɥɑ̃] *nm* tawny owl, brown owl; *pl* chats-huants.

châtier [ʃɑtje] *vtr* to punish; to polish (style).

châtiment [ʃɑtimɑ̃] *nm* punishment.

chatoiement [ʃatwamɑ̃] *nm* shimmer(ing); sheen; glistening.

chaton [ʃatɔ̃] *n* 1. kitten 2. *nm Bot:* catkin 3. *Jewel:* (*a*) setting (of stone) (*b*) stone.

chatouille [ʃatuj] *nf F:* tickle; **craindre la c., les chatouilles,** to be ticklish.

chatouillement [ʃatujmɑ̃] *nm* tickling; tickle (in one's throat, nose).

chatouiller [ʃatuje] *vtr* to tickle; **c. la curiosité,** to arouse curiosity. **chatouilleux, -euse** *a* (*a*) ticklish (*b*) sensitive, touchy.

chatoyer [ʃatwaje] *vi* (**il chatoie**) (*a*) to shimmer (*b*) to glisten, sparkle.

châtrer [ʃɑtre] *vtr* to castrate; to geld (stallion); to neuter (cat).

chatterie [ʃatri] *nf* 1. *pl* wheedling ways, coaxing 2. titbit, dainty.

chatterton [ʃatɛrtɔn] *nm* (adhesive) insulating tape.

chaud, chaude [ʃo, -od] 1. *a* warm; hot; **tout c.,** piping hot; **guerre chaude,** shooting war; **chaude dispute,** heated discussion; **à sang c.,** warm-blooded; **pleurer à chaudes larmes,** to weep bitterly; **il n'est pas c. pour le projet,** he's not keen on the project; **voix chaude,** sultry voice; *Art:* **tons chauds,** warm tints; *v phr* **il fait c.,** it's warm (weather) 2. *nm* heat, warmth; (*on label*) **tenir au c.,** to be kept in a warm place; **cela ne me fait ni c. ni froid,** it's all the same to me; **attraper un c. et froid,** to catch a chill; **avoir c.,** (*of pers*) to be warm; *F:* **il a eu c.,** he got a real fright. **chaudement** *adv* warmly; (to protest) hotly.

chaudière [ʃodjɛr] *nf* boiler.

chaudron [ʃodrɔ̃] *nm* cauldron.

chaudronnerie [ʃodrɔnri] *nf* 1. boiler-making 2. boiler works; coppersmith's works.

chaudronnier [ʃodrɔnje] *nm* boiler maker; coppersmith.

chauffage [ʃofaʒ] *nm* (*a*) warming, heating (of room) (*b*) heating system; *Aut:* (car) heater; **c. central,** central heating; **c. au mazout,** oil(-fired) heating.

chauffard [ʃofar] *nm F:* (*a*) roadhog (*b*) hit-and-run driver.

chauffe-eau [ʃofo] *nm inv* water heater; immersion heater.

chauffe-plats [ʃofpla] *nm inv* plate warmer, hot plate.

chauffer [ʃofe] 1. *vtr* (*a*) to heat (up), to warm (up); **c. une maison au gaz,** to heat a house with gas (*b*) **chauffé au rouge, à blanc,** red-hot, white-hot; **c. une chaudière,** to stoke up a boiler (*c*) *F:* to cram (s.o.) for an exam; **c. qn à blanc,** to incite s.o. 2. *vi* (*a*) to get, become, warm, hot (*b*) *F:* **ça va c.,** things are getting hot (*c*) to overheat 3. **se c.,** to warm oneself; **se c. au mazout,** to have oil-fired (central) heating.

chaufferie [ʃofri] *nf* boiler room; *Nau:* stokehold.

chauffeur [ʃofœr] *nm* 1. stoker, fireman 2. *Aut:* driver; chauffeur; **elle est c. de taxi,** she's a taxi-driver; **voiture sans c.,** self-drive car.

chaume [ʃom] *nm* (*a*) straw (*b*) thatch; **toit de c.,** thatched roof (*c*) stubble.

chaumière [ʃomjɛr] *nf* thatched cottage.

chaussée [ʃose] *nf* 1. causeway (across marsh) 2. roadway; carriageway, *NAm:* pavement; **c. bombée,** cambered road; **c. déformée,** uneven road surface.

chausse-pied [ʃospje] *nm* shoehorn; *pl* chausse-pieds.

chausser [ʃose] *vtr* 1. to put on one's (shoes); to put on one's (spectacles); **chaussé de pantoufles,** wearing slippers 2. (*a*) to put shoes on (s.o.); **se c.,** to put one's shoes on (*b*) to supply, fit, (s.o.) with footwear; **ces chaussures chaussent étroit,** these are narrow-fitting shoes; **combien chaussez-vous?** what size do you take?

chaussette [ʃosɛt] *nf* sock.

chausseur [ʃosœr] *nm* shoemaker.

chausson [ʃosɔ̃] *nm* 1. slipper (*b*) ballet shoe (*c*) (baby's) bootee 2. *Cu:* **c. aux pommes,** apple turn-over.

chaussure [ʃosyr] *nf* 1. (*a*) footwear (*b*) (boot and) shoe industry, trade 2. shoe.

chauve [ʃov] *a* (*a*) bald; bald-headed; **c. comme un œuf,** as bald as a coot (*b*) bare, denuded (mountain).

chauve-souris [ʃovsuri] *nf Z:* bat; *pl* chauves-souris.

chauvin, -ine [ʃovɛ̃, -in] 1. *n* chauvinist 2. *a* chauvinist(ic).

chauvinisme [ʃovinism] *nm* chauvinism.

chaux [ʃo] *nf* lime; **c. vive,** quicklime; **c. éteinte,** slaked lime; **blanchir à la c.,** to whitewash.

chavirer [ʃavire] 1. *vi* (*a*) (*of boat*) to capsize, turn turtle, overturn (*b*) to sway, to reel, to spin (round) 2. *vtr* (*a*) to upset, capsize (boat) (*b*) to overturn (sth) (*c*) *F:* **j'en suis tout chaviré,** it's completely upset me.

chef [ʃɛf] *nm* 1. *Lit:* **faire qch de son propre c.,** to do sth on one's own initiative 2. head (of family); chief (of tribe); leader (of political party); principal, head (of business); **c. de famille,** head of the family; **c. d'État,** head of state; **c. (cuisinier),** chef; **c. d'orchestre,** conductor; *Sp:* **c. d'équipe,** captain; **c. de bureau,** chief clerk; **c. de service,** head of department, section head; **c. d'atelier,** (shop) foreman; **ingénieur en c.,** chief engineer; *Rail:* **c. de gare,** stationmaster; **c. de train,** guard; *Mil:* **c. de bataillon,** major 3. *Jur:* **c. d'accusation,** charge.

chef-d'œuvre [ʃɛdœvr] *nm* masterpiece; *pl* chefs-d'œuvre.

chef-lieu [ʃɛfljø] *nm* chief town (of department); *pl* chefs-lieux.

cheftaine [ʃɛftɛn] *nf Scout:* captain; Brown Owl; (woman) cubmaster.

cheik(h) [ʃɛk] *nm* sheik(h).

chelem [ʃlɛm] *nm* Cards: **grand, petit, c.**, grand, little, slam.

chemin [ʃ(ə)mɛ̃] *nm* 1. (a) way, road; F: **c. des écoliers**, long way round; **il y a dix minutes de c.**, it is ten minutes away; **faire son c.**, to make one's way; **c. faisant**, on the way; **faire un bout de c. avec qn**, to accompany s.o. a little way; **montrer le c.**, to lead the way; **être sur le bon c.**, to be on the right track; **à moitié c.**, half way; **se mettre en c.**, to set out; **il est dans mon c.**, he's in my way; **ne pas y aller par quatre chemins**, to go straight to the point; **s'arrêter en c.**, to stop on the way (b) road, path, track; **c. vicinal**, by-road; **c. piéton**, footpath; **c. creux**, sunken lane; **c. de halage**, tow path 2. **c. de fer**, railway, NAm: railroad; **en, par, c. de fer**, by rail.

chemineau, -eaux [ʃ(ə)mino] *nm* tramp, vagrant.

cheminée [ʃ(ə)mine] *nf* 1. (a) fireplace; **pierre de c.**, hearthstone (b) **(manteau de) c.**, mantelpiece, chimney-piece 2. (a) chimney (stack) (b) funnel (of locomotive) 3. **c. d'aération**, ventilation shaft.

cheminement [ʃ(ə)minmɑ̃] *nm* (a) progress, advance (b) development (of thought).

cheminer [ʃ(ə)mine] *vi* to walk; to proceed, to advance.

cheminot [ʃ(ə)mino] *nm* railwayman, NAm: railroader.

chemise [ʃ(ə)miz] *nf* 1. shirt; **en bras, en manches, de c.**, in one's shirtsleeves; **c. de nuit**, nightshirt; (woman's) nightdress; **c. américaine**, (woman's) vest; **je m'en moque comme de ma première c.**, I don't give a damn 2. folder; portfolio.

chemiserie [ʃ(ə)mizri] *nf* (a) shirt (making) trade (b) shirt (and underwear) shop.

chemisette [ʃ(ə)mizɛt] *nf* short-sleeved shirt.

chemisier [ʃ(ə)mizje] *nm* 1. shirt-maker 2. blouse.

chenal, -aux [ʃ(ə)nal, -o] *nm* 1. channel, fairway (of river) 2. millrace.

chenapan [ʃ(ə)napɑ̃] *nm* A: scoundrel.

chêne [ʃɛn] *nm* oak; **c. vert**, holm oak.

chêne-liège [ʃɛnljɛʒ] *nm* cork-oak; *pl chênes-lièges*.

chenet [ʃ(ə)nɛ] *nm* firedog; andiron.

chènevis [ʃɛnvi] *nm* hempseed.

chenil [ʃ(ə)ni(l)] *nm* kennels.

chenille [ʃ(ə)nij] *nf* (a) caterpillar (b) band (of caterpillar tractor).

cheptel [ʃɛptɛl] *nm* livestock.

chèque [ʃɛk] *nm* cheque, NAm: check; **c. de £60**, cheque for £60; **c. barré**, crossed cheque; **c. en blanc**, blank cheque; **c. sans provision**, dud cheque; **c. postal** = Girocheque; **c. de voyage**, traveller's cheque.

chèque-cadeau [ʃɛkkado] *nm* gift token; *pl chèques-cadeau*.

chèque-repas [ʃɛkrəpa], **chèque-restaurant** [ʃɛkrɛstɔrɑ̃] *nm* luncheon voucher; *pl chèques-repas, chèques-restaurant.*

chéquier [ʃekje] *nm* cheque book.

cher, chère¹ [ʃɛr] *a & adv* 1. dear, beloved; **tout ce qui m'est c.**, all that I hold dear; **mon vœu le plus c.**, my dearest wish; Corr: **C. Monsieur**, Dear Mr X; Dear Sir; *n* **mon c.**, my dear (fellow); **ma chère**, my dear (girl) 2. (a) dear, expensive, costly; **c'est trop c. pour moi**, I can't afford it (b) *adv* **payer qch c.**, to pay a high price for sth; **cela ne vaut pas c.**, it's not worth much; **vendre c.**, to charge high prices; **il me le payera c.**, I will make him pay dearly for it; F: **je l'ai eu pour pas c.**, I got it cheap.

chercher [ʃɛrʃe] *vtr* (a) to search for, look for; to seek; **je l'ai cherché partout**, I hunted for it everywhere; **c. une solution**, to try to find a solution; **c. aventure**, to seek adventure; F: **tu l'as cherché**, you've asked for it (b) **aller c. qn, qch**, to (go and) fetch s.o., sth; **envoyer c. qn**, to send for s.o.; **je suis allé le c. à la gare**, I went to meet him at the station; F: **ça va c. dans les 10,000 francs**, it will fetch about 10,000 francs (c) **c. à faire qch**, to try to do sth.

chercheur, -euse [ʃɛrʃœr, -øz] 1. *a* **esprit c.**, enquiring mind 2. *n* seeker; researcher; research worker; **c. d'or**, gold digger.

chère² [ʃɛr] *nf* fare, food; **faire bonne c.**, to have a good meal.

chèrement [ʃɛrmɑ̃] *adv* 1. dearly, lovingly 2. dearly; at a high price.

chérir [ʃerir] *vtr* to cherish; to love (s.o.) dearly. **chéri, -ie** 1. *a* cherished, dear 2. *n* darling.

cherté [ʃɛrte] *nf* dearness; **c. de la vie**, high cost of living.

chérubin [ʃerybɛ̃] *nm* cherub.

chétif, -ive [ʃetif, -iv] *a* 1. weak, puny, sickly (person) 2. poor, miserable, wretched; paltry. **chétivement** *adv* weakly, punily; poorly, miserably.

cheval, -aux [ʃ(ə)val, -o] *nm* 1. (a) horse; **c. de trait**, draught horse; **c. de labour**, plough horse; **c. de selle**, saddle horse; **c. de chasse**, hunter; **c. de course**, racehorse; **à c.**, on horseback; **monter à c.**, to ride; **être à c. sur qch**, to sit astride sth; F: **c'est un c. à l'ouvrage**, he works like a Trojan; **remède de c.**, drastic remedy; **fièvre de c.**, raging fever; **c. de retour**, old lag (b) Ich: **c. marin**, seahorse 2. **c. d'arçons**, **c.-arçons**, vaulting horse; **c. à bascule**, rocking horse; **chevaux de bois**, roundabout, merry-go-round 3. Mch: (= **cheval-vapeur**) horsepower.

chevalerie [ʃ(ə)valri] *nf* 1. knighthood 2. chivalry. **chevaleresque** *a* chivalrous, knightly.

chevalet [ʃ(ə)valɛ] *nm* (a) support, stand; trestle, frame; **c. de peintre**, easel (b) bridge (of violin).

chevalier [ʃ(ə)valje] *nm* (a) knight; **c. errant**, knight errant; **c. d'industrie**, adventurer; **c. servant**, faithful admirer; **faire qn c.**, to dub s.o. knight (b) Chevalier (of the Legion of Honour).

chevalière [ʃ(ə)valjɛr] *nf* signet ring.

chevalin [ʃ(ə)valɛ̃] *a* equine; horsy (face); **boucherie chevaline**, horse-butcher's (shop).

cheval-vapeur [ʃ(ə)valvapœr] *nm* Mec: (French) horsepower; *pl chevaux-vapeur.*

chevauchée [ʃ(ə)voʃe] *nf* 1. ride 2. cavalcade.

chevauchement [ʃ(ə)voʃmɑ̃] *nm* overlapping.

chevaucher [ʃ(ə)voʃe] 1. *vi* (a) to ride (on horseback) (b) to overlap 2. *vtr* (a) to ride (on horse); to straddle, to be astride (a horse) (b) to span (gap) 3. **se c.**, to overlap.

chevelure [ʃ(ə)vlyr] *nf* (a) (head of) hair (b) tail (of comet). **chevelu** *a* long-haired; hairy.

chevet [ʃ(ə)vɛ] *nm* bedhead; **lampe de c.**, bedside lamp; **au c. de qn**, at s.o.'s bedside.

cheveu, -eux [ʃ(ə)vø] *nm* 1. (a single) hair; **être à un c. de la ruine**, to be within a hair's breadth of ruin; **arriver comme un c. sur la soupe**, to arrive at an awkward moment; **il y a un c.**, there's a snag **2.** *pl* hair; **couper les cheveux en quatre**, to split hairs; **tiré par les cheveux**, far-fetched; *F:* **avoir mal aux cheveux**, to have a hangover; **cheveux d'ange**, (i) *(Christmas decoration)* angel hair (ii) (type of) vermicelli.

cheville [ʃ(ə)vij] *nf* **1.** peg, pin; **c. en fer**, bolt; **c. ouvrière**, king pin (of vehicle, of enterprise); **être en c. avec qn**, to be in cahoots with s.o. **2.** peg, plug **3.** *Anat:* ankle; **il ne vous arrive pas à la c.**, he can't hold a candle to you.

cheviller [ʃəvije] *vtr* to pin, bolt, peg, together.

chèvre [ʃɛvr̩] **1.** *nf* goat, *esp* she goat, *F:* nanny goat; **barbe de c.**, goatee; **ménager la c. et le chou**, to sit on the fence **2.** *nm* goat('s) cheese.

chevreau, -eaux [ʃəvro] *nm* kid.

chèvrefeuille [ʃɛvrəfœj] *nm Bot:* honeysuckle.

chevreuil [ʃəvrœj] *nm* roe deer; *m* roe buck; *Cu:* venison.

chevron [ʃəvrɔ̃] *nm* **1.** rafter (of roof) **2.** *Her:* chevron; *Tex:* **tissu à c.**, herringbone pattern material **3.** *Mil:* chevron, (service) stripe.

chevronné [ʃəvrɔne] *a* senior, experienced.

chevrotement [ʃəvrɔtmɑ̃] *nm* quaver(ing).

chevroter [ʃəvrɔte] *vtr & i* to sing, speak, in a quavering voice; to quaver.

chevrotine [ʃəvrɔtin] *nf* buckshot.

chez [ʃe] *prep* **1.** *(a)* **c. qn**, at s.o.'s house, home; **il n'est pas c. lui**, he's not at home, not in; **je vais c. moi**, I'm going home; **il habite c. nous**, he lives with us; **acheter qch c. l'épicier**, to buy sth at the grocer's; *(on letters)* **c. . . .**, care of, c/o . . .; **faites comme c. vous**, make yourself at home *(b)* **son c-soi**, one's home, one's house; **derrière c. moi**, behind my house **2.** with; **c'est une habitude c. moi**, it's a habit with me; **c. les jeunes**, among young people; **c. les animaux**, in the animal kingdom.

chiader [ʃjade] *P:* **1.** *vi* to swot **2.** *vtr* to swot (up) for (an exam).

chialer [ʃjale] *vi P:* to snivel, to blubber.

chiasse [ʃjas] *nf P:* **avoir la c.**, (i) to have diarrhoea, the runs (ii) to have the wind up.

chic [ʃik] **1.** *nm (a)* skill, knack; **il a le c. pour (faire) cela**, he has the knack of doing that *(b)* smartness, stylishness; **il a du c.**, he has style; **femme qui a du c.**, smart woman **2.** *a inv (a)* smart, stylish; **les gens c.**, the smart set *(b) F:* **on a passé une c. soirée**, we had a great evening; **un c. type**, a good bloke, *NAm:* a swell guy; **c'est c. de ta part**, that's really good of you **3.** *int F:* **c. (alors)!** great!

chicane [ʃikan] *nf* **1.** *(a)* chicanery, pettifogging *(b)* quibbling, wrangling **2.** zigzag (in road).

chicaner [ʃikane] **1.** *vi* to chicane; to quibble; to haggle **2.** *vtr* **c. qn**, to wrangle with s.o. **(sur**, about). **chicanier, -ière 1.** *a* quibbling **2.** *n* quibbler.

chiche¹ [ʃiʃ] *a* **1.** *(a) (of thg)* scanty, poor *(b) (of pers)* stingy, niggardly **2.** *F:* **être c. de faire qch**, to dare to do sth; **c. (que je le fais)!** bet you I will! **c.!** I dare you! **chichement** *adv* stingily, meanly.

chiche² *a Bot:* **pois c.**, chick pea.

chichis [ʃiʃi] *nmpl F:* **faire des c.**, to make a fuss.

chicorée [ʃikɔre] *nf* **1.** chicory (for coffee) **2.** endive.

chicot [ʃiko] *nm* stump (of tree, tooth).

chien, f chienne [ʃjɛ̃, ʃjɛn] *n* **1.** dog; *f* bitch; **jeune c.**, puppy; **c. de berger**, sheepdog; **c. de garde**, guard dog, watchdog; **c. de chasse**, gundog; retriever; **c. courant**, hound; **c. d'arrêt**, pointer; **c. couchant**, setter; **faire le c. couchant**, to fawn on, to toady; **c. d'aveugle**, guide dog; **c. policier**, police dog; **vivre comme c. et chat**, to lead a cat and dog life; **se regarder en chiens de faïence**, to glare at one another; **entre c. et loup**, in the twilight; *F:* **vie de c.**, dog's life; **quel temps de c.!** what beastly weather! **2.** *F: (a)* **avoir du c.**, to have charm *(b) a* **être c.**, to be mean, stingy **3.** hammer (of gun).

chiendent [ʃjɛ̃dɑ̃] *nm Bot:* couch grass.

chien-loup [ʃjɛ̃lu] *nm* wolfhound, Alsatian; *pl* **chiens-loups.**

chier [ʃje] *vi V:* to shit, to crap; **tu me fais c.**, you're a pain in the arse.

chiffe [ʃif] *nf F:* spineless individual; drip, weed; **mou comme une c.**, like a wet rag.

chiffon [ʃifɔ̃] *nm* **1.** rag; **c. à poussière**, duster; *F:* **parler chiffons**, to talk (about) clothes **2.** **mettre ses vêtements en c.**, to leave one's clothes in a heap; **c. de papier**, scrap of paper.

chiffonner [ʃifɔne] **1.** *vtr (a)* to rumple, to crease (dress); to crumple (piece of paper) *(b)* to annoy, bother (s.o.) **2.** **se c.**, to crease, to crumple.

chiffonnier [ʃifɔnje] *nm* **1.** ragman **2.** *Furn:* chiffonier.

chiffrage [ʃifraʒ] *nm (a)* numbering (of pages) *(b)* calculating *(c)* ciphering, coding *(d)* marking *(e) Mus:* figuring.

chiffre [ʃifr̩] *nm* **1.** *(a)* figure, number, numeral, digit; **c. arabe**, Arabic numeral; **nombre de 3 chiffres**, 3-figure number *(b)* amount, total; *Com:* **c. d'affaires**, turnover **2.** *(a)* cipher, code *(b)* combination (of safe) **3.** *(a)* monogram *(b) Typ:* colophon.

chiffrer [ʃifre] **1.** *vtr (a)* to number (pages of book) *(b)* to calculate (amount); **détails chiffrés**, figures (of scheme) *(c)* to cipher; to code; to write (dispatch) in code; **message chiffré**, code message *(d)* to mark (linen) *(e) Mus:* to figure (bass) **2.** *vi & pr* **ça doit c.**, it must add up; **à combien cela se chiffre-t-il?** how much does it work out at?

chignole [ʃiɲɔl] *nf* drill.

chignon [ʃiɲɔ̃] *nm* chignon, bun.

Chili [ʃili] *Prnm Geog:* Chile. **chilien, -ienne** *a & n* Chilean.

chimère [ʃimɛr] *nf* chim(a)era; dream, (idle) fancy. **chimérique** *a (a)* visionary, fanciful; **rêve c.**, pipe dream *(b)* chimerical.

chimie [ʃimi] *nf* chemistry. **chimique** *a* chemical; **produit c.**, chemical. **chimiquement** *adv* chemically.

chimiste [ʃimist] *n* (research) chemist.

chimpanzé [ʃɛ̃pɑ̃ze] *nm Z:* chimpanzee.

Chine [ʃin] **1.** *Prnf Geog:* China; **encre de C.**, Indian ink **2.** *nm* rice paper.

chiné [ʃine] *a Tex:* chiné (fabric).

chiner [ʃine] *vtr F:* to tease (s.o.); to pull (s.o.'s) leg.

chinois, -oise [ʃinwa, -waz] **1.** *a (a)* Chinese *(b) F:* complicated, fussy **2.** *n* Chinese **3.** *nm Ling:* Chinese; **c'est du c.**, it's all Greek to me.

chinoiserie [ʃinwazri] *nf* **1.** Chinese curio **2.** *F:* un-

chiot [ʃjo] *nm* puppy.

chiottes [ʃjɔt] *nfpl P:* lavatory, bog, *NAm:* john.

chiper [ʃipe] *vtr F:* (a) to pinch, to swipe (sth) (b) to catch (cold).

chipie [ʃipi] *nf (woman)* minx.

chipoter [ʃipɔte] *vi* (a) to pick at one's food (b) to waste time (c) to haggle, to quibble. **chipoteur, -euse 1.** *a* haggling, quibbling **2.** *n* haggler, quibbler.

chips [ʃips] *nmpl Cu:* (potato) crisps.

chique [ʃik] *nf* (a) quid (of tobacco) (b) F: swelling (on cheek).

chiqué [ʃike] *nm F:* sham, pretence; **c'est du c.,** it's all bluff; **faire du c.,** to put on an act.

chiquement [ʃikmã] *adv F:* **1.** smartly, stylishly **2.** splendidly, (damn) well.

chiquenaude [ʃiknod] *nf* flick (of the finger).

chiquer [ʃike] *vtr & i* to chew (tobacco).

chiromancie [kirɔmɑ̃si] *nf* palmistry.

chiromancien, -ienne [kirɔmɑ̃sjɛ̃, -jɛn] *n* palmist.

chiropracteur [kirɔpraktœr] *nm* chiropractor.

chiropraxie [kirɔpraksi] *nf* chiropractic.

chirurgie [ʃiryrʒi] *nf* surgery. **chirurgical, -aux** *a* surgical.

chirurgien, -ienne [ʃiryrʒjɛ̃, -jɛn] *n* surgeon; **c. dentiste,** dental surgeon.

chiure [ʃjyr] *nf* fly speck.

chlore [klɔr] *nm Ch:* chlorine.

chlorer [klɔre] *vtr* to chlorinate.

chlorhydrique [klɔridrik] *a Ch:* hydrochloric (acid).

chloroforme [klɔrɔfɔrm] *nm* chloroform.

chloroformer [klɔrɔfɔrme] *vtr* to chloroform.

chlorophylle [klɔrɔfil] *nf* chlorophyll.

chlorure [klɔryr] *nm Ch:* chloride.

choc [ʃɔk] *nm* **1.** shock, impact, bump; **résistant aux chocs,** shock-proof; **c. sourd,** thud; **c. des verres,** clink of glasses; **c. des opinions,** clash of opinions; *Com:* **prix c.,** drastic reductions **2.** shock (to nervous system); *Med:* **c. opératoire,** post-operative shock.

chocolat [ʃɔkɔla] *nm* chocolate; **c. à croquer,** plain (eating) chocolate; **c. chaud,** drinking chocolate. **chocolaté** *a* chocolate-flavoured. **chocolatier, -ière 1.** *a* chocolate (industry) **2.** *n* chocolate maker.

chocolaterie [ʃɔkɔlatri] *nf* chocolate factory.

chocottes [ʃɔkɔt] *nfpl P:* **avoir les c.,** to have the jitters.

chœur [kœr] *nm* **1.** chorus; **chanter en c.,** to sing in chorus; **tous en c.!** all together! **2.** (a) choir (b) *Arch:* choir, chancel.

choir [ʃwar] *vi (pp* chu; *pr ind* je chois; *fu* je choirai, je cherrai; *the aux is* être) (a) *A:* to fall (b) **se laisser c.** (dans un fauteuil), to sink, to flop (into an armchair); **laisser c. qn, qch,** to drop s.o., to give s.o. up.

choisir [ʃwazir] *vtr* to choose, select, pick; **c. de partir,** to choose to leave. **choisi** *a* (a) selected (b) select, choice.

choix [ʃwa] *nm* choice, selection; **l'embarras du c.,** the difficulty of choosing; **faites votre c.,** take your pick; **je vous laisse le c.,** choose for yourself; **nous n'avons pas le c.,** we have no option; **viande ou poisson au c.,** choice of meat or fish; **de premier c.,** first-class, best quality; **grade one; de c.,** choice, selected.

choléra [kɔlera] *nm Med:* cholera. **cholérique 1.** *a* choleraic **2.** *n* cholera patient.

cholestérol [kɔlesterɔl] *nm Med:* cholesterol.

chômage [ʃomaʒ] *nm* unemployment; **être en c., au c.,** to be unemployed, out of work, *F:* jobless; **s'inscrire au c.,** to sign on (the dole); **c. partiel,** short-time working; **c. technique,** lay-offs.

chômer [ʃome] *vi* **1.** to have a holiday; **jour chômé,** public holiday **2.** to be idle; to be unemployed; **les usines chôment,** the works are at a standstill.

chomeur, -euse [ʃomœr, -øz] *n* unemployed person; **les chômeurs,** the unemployed, *F:* the jobless.

chope [ʃɔp] *nf* (a) tankard (b) mugful; pint.

choper [ʃɔpe] *vtr P:* **1.** to steal, to pinch **2.** to arrest, to nab **3.** to catch (cold).

chopine [ʃɔpin] *nf* half-litre bottle.

choquer [ʃɔke] **1.** *vtr* (a) to stroke, knock (sth against sth); **c. les verres,** to clink glasses (b) to shock; to displease, offend; **être choqué de qch,** to be scandalized by sth; **mot qui choque,** offensive word (c) to distress **2. se c.,** to be shocked, scandalized; to take offence (**de,** at). **choquant** *a* shocking, offensive.

choral, pl -als [kɔral] **1.** *a* choral **2.** *nm* choral(e) **3.** *nf* **chorale,** choral society, choir.

chorégraphe [kɔregraf] *n* choreographer.

chorégraphie [kɔregrafi] *nf* choreography. **chorégraphique** *a* choreographic.

choriste [kɔrist] *nm* chorus singer (in opera); choir member; (church) chorister.

chorus [kɔrys] *nm* **faire c.,** to voice one's agreement (**avec qn,** with s.o.).

chose [ʃoz] **1.** *nf* thing; **j'ai un tas de choses à faire,** I have masses of things to do; **de deux choses l'une,** it's a choice of two things; **dites bien des choses de ma part à Marie,** give my regards to Mary; **j'ai bien des choses à te dire,** I have lots to tell you; **la c. en question,** the case in point; **il a très bien pris la c.,** he took it very well; **c'est tout autre c.,** this is quite a different matter; **avant toute c.,** first of all, above all; **dans l'état actuel des choses,** as things stand; **il fait bien les choses,** he does things in style **2.** *n* (a) **Monsieur C., Madame C.,** Mr What's-his-name, Mrs What's-her-name (b) whatsit; thingummy **3.** *a inv F:* **être, se sentir, tout c.,** to feel peculiar; to be out of sorts; to feel funny.

choucas [ʃuka] *nm* jackdaw.

chouchou, -oute [ʃuʃu, -ut] *n F:* pet, darling.

chouchouter [ʃuʃute] *vtr F:* to pet, coddle (child).

choucroute [ʃukrut] *nf Cu:* sauerkraut.

chouette¹ [ʃwɛt] *nf* owl; **c. effraie,** barn owl; **c. hulotte,** tawny owl.

chouette² *a & int F:* terrific, great; **c. (alors)!** great! fantastic!

chou-fleur [ʃuflœr] *nm* cauliflower; *pl* **choux-fleurs**.

chow-chow [ʃuʃu] *nm* chow (dog); *pl* **chows-chows**.

choyer [ʃwaje] *vtr* (**je choie**) to pet, to coddle; to cherish (hope).

chrétienté [kretjɛ̃te] *nf* Christendom. **chrétien, -ienne** *a* & *n* Christian. **chrétiennement** *adv* as a, like a, Christian.

Christ [krist] *nm* **1.** **le Christ**, Christ; **Jésus-C.** [ʒezykri] Jesus Christ **2.** crucifix.

christianisation [kristjanizasjɔ̃] *nf* christianization.

christianiser [kristjanize] *vtr* to christianize.

christianisme [kristjanism] *nm* Christianity.

chromatique [krɔmatik] *a* (*a*) *Mus: Opt:* chromatic (*b*) *Biol:* chromosomal.

chrome [krom] *nm* *Ch:* chromium; *F:* **faire les chromes**, to polish the chrome (of a car).

chromer [krome] *vtr* to chromium-plate (metal).

chromo [krɔmo] *nm* *F:* chromo(lithograph).

chronique [krɔnik] **1.** *a* chronic (disease) **2.** *nf* (*a*) chronicle; *Journ:* news, report, column. **chroniquement** *adv* chronically.

chroniqueur, -euse [krɔnikœr, -øz] *n* **1.** chronicler **2.** *Journ:* columnist; (sports) editor.

chrono [krɔno] *nm* *F:* stopwatch; **du 220 (km/h) (au) c.**, recorded speed of 220 (km/h).

chronologie [krɔnɔlɔʒi] *nf* chronology. **chronologique** *a* chronological; time. **chronologiquement** *adv* chronologically.

chronométrage [krɔnɔmetraʒ] *nm* timing.

chronomètre [krɔnɔmɛtr] *nm* (*a*) chronometer (*b*) stopwatch. **chronométrique** *a* chronometric.

chronométrer [krɔnɔmetre] *vtr* (**je chronomètre, je chronométrerai**) *Sp:* to time (race).

chronométreur [krɔnɔmetrœr] *nm* timekeeper.

chrysalide [krizalid] *nf* *Ent:* chrysalis, pupa.

chrysanthème [krizɑ̃tɛm] *nm* *Bot:* chrysanthemum.

chuchotement [ʃyʃɔtmɑ̃] *nm* whisper(ing).

chuchoter [ʃyʃɔte] *vtr* & *i* to whisper.

chuintement [ʃɥɛ̃tmɑ̃] *nm* hiss(ing).

chuinter [ʃɥɛ̃te] *vi* to hiss.

chut [ʃyt, ʃt] *int* hush! sh!

chute [ʃyt] *nf* **1.** (*a*) fall; **faire une c. (de cheval)**, to have a fall; to fall off one's horse; **c. libre**, free fall; *PN:* **attention, c. de pierres**, danger! falling stones; **c. de pluie, de neige**, rainfall, snowfall; **c. du jour**, nightfall; **c. d'eau**, waterfall; **c. des cheveux**, hair loss; **c. des prix**, fall, drop, in prices (*b*) (down)fall, collapse (of ministry); **il m'a entraîné dans sa c.**, he dragged me down with him; *Th:* **c. d'une pièce**, failure of a play **2. c. des reins**, small of the back **3.** (*a*) off-cut (of wood) (*b*) snippet, clipping (of material).

chuter [ʃyte] *vi* (*a*) *F:* to fall; to come a cropper (*b*) *Th:* to flop.

Chypre [ʃipr] *Prnf* Cyprus. **chypriote** *a* & *n* Cypriot.

ci¹ [si] *adv* **de ci, de là**, here and there; **ci-gît**, here lies; *see also* **ce² 5.**

ci² *dem pron neut inv* *F:* **faire ci et ça**, to do this, that and the other; **comme ci, comme ça**, so so.

ci-après [siaprɛ] *adv* here(in)after; below.

cible [sibl] *nf* target.

ciboire [sibwar] *nm* *Ecc:* ciborium.

ciboule [sibul] *nf* *Bot: Cu:* spring onion.

ciboulette [sibulɛt] *nf* *Bot: Cu:* chives.

cicatrice [sikatris] *nf* scar.

cicatrisation [sikatrizasjɔ̃] *nf* healing.

cicatriser [sikatrize] **1.** *vtr* to heal (wound) **2.** *vi* & *pr* (of wound) to heal (up).

ci-contre [sikɔ̃tr] *adv* opposite; in the margin; *Book-k:* **porté ci-c.**, as per contra.

ci-dessous [sidsu] *adv* hereunder; undermentioned; below.

ci-dessus [sidsy] *adv* above(-mentioned).

cidre [sidr] *nm* cider.

Cie *abbr* Compagnie.

ciel, *pl* **ciels, cieux** [sjɛl, sjø] *nm* **1.** (*a*) sky, heaven; **à c. ouvert**, open, open-air; out of doors; **(couleur) bleu c.**, sky-blue; **entre c. et terre**, in mid-air (*b*) (*pl often* **ciels**) climate; **les ciels de l'Italie**, the skies of Italy **2.** heaven; *F:* **tomber du c.**, to come out of the blue; **(juste) c.!** (good) heavens! **3.** *Furn:* (bed) tester.

cierge [sjɛrʒ] *nm* candle.

cieux [sjø] *see* **ciel**.

cigale [sigal] *nf* *Ent:* cicada.

cigare [sigar] *nm* (*a*) cigar (*b*) *P:* head, nut.

cigarette [sigarɛt] *nf* cigarette.

cigogne [sigɔɲ] *nf* *Orn:* stork.

ciguë [sigy] *nf* *Bot:* hemlock.

ci-inclus [siɛ̃kly] *a* & *adv* (*inv when it precedes the noun*) **la copie ci-incluse**, the enclosed copy; **ci-i. copie de votre lettre**, herewith, enclosed, a copy of your letter.

ci-joint [siʒwɛ̃] *a* & *adv* (*inv when it precedes the noun*) attached, herewith; **les pièces ci-jointes**, the enclosed documents.

cil [sil] *nm* (eye)lash.

ciller [sije] *vi* to blink.

cime [sim] *nf* summit (of hill); top (of tree); peak (of mountain).

ciment [simɑ̃] *nm* cement; **c. armé**, reinforced concrete.

cimenter [simɑ̃te] *vtr* to cement.

cimenterie [simɑ̃tri] *nf* cement works.

cimetière [simtjɛr] *nm* cemetery, graveyard; **c. de voitures**, scrapyard.

ciné [sine] *nm* *F:* flicks, *NAm:* movies.

cinéaste [sineast] *nm* film director; film maker.

ciné-club [sineklœb] *nm* film club; *pl* **ciné-clubs**.

cinéma [sinema] *nm* (*a*) cinema, *NAm:* movies; **faire du c.**, to be a film actor; **acteur de c.**, film actor; **c. muet**, silent films; **il est dans le c.**, he's in the film business; *F:* **quel c.!** what a performance! what a fuss! (*b*) cinema, film theatre.

cinémascope [sinemaskɔp] *nm* *Rtm:* Cinemascope.

cinémathèque [sinematɛk] *nf* film library.

cinématographique [sinematɔgrafik] *a* cinematographic; film (production).

cinéphile [sinefil] *n* film enthusiast, *F:* film buff.

cinérama [sinerama] *nm* *Rtm:* Cinerama.

cingler [sɛ̃gle] **1.** *vi* *Nau:* to steer a given course **2.** *vtr* to lash, cut (horse) with a whip; to lash out at (s.o.); **la grêle lui cinglait le visage**, the hail stung his face. **cinglant** *a* lashing (rain); biting, cutting (wind); bitter (cold); scathing, cutting (remark).

cinglé, -ée *F:* 1. *a* nuts, cracked 2. *n* crackpot.

cinq [sɛ̃k] *num a inv & nm inv (as card a before a noun or adj beginning with a consonnant sound)* [sɛ̃]) five; **c. garçons** [sɛ̃garsɔ̃] five boys; **c. hommes** [sɛ̃kɔm] five men; **le c. mars** [ləsɛ̃(k)mars] the fifth of March; *F:* **il était moins c.,** it was a near thing; **en c. sec,** in two ticks. **cinquième** *num a & n* fifth. **cinquièmement** *adv* fifthly, in the fifth place.

cinquantaine [sɛ̃kɑ̃tɛn] *nf (about)* fifty; **avoir passé la c.,** to be in one's fifties.

cinquante [sɛ̃kɑ̃t] *num a inv & nm inv* fifty. **cinquantième** *num a & n* fiftieth.

cinquantenaire [sɛ̃kɑ̃tnɛr] *nm* fiftieth anniversary; golden jubilee.

cintre [sɛ̃tr] *nm* 1. curve, bend 2. arch (of tunnel) 3. coathanger 4. *Th:* **les cintres,** the flies. **cintré** *a (a)* arched (window) *(b)* bent, curved *(c)* waisted; **taille cintrée,** nipped-in waist.

cirage [siraʒ] *nm (a)* polishing *(b)* (wax, shoe) polish; *F:* **être dans le c.,** to be all at sea.

circoncire [sirkɔ̃sir] *vtr (prp* **circoncisant;** *pp* **circoncis;** *ph* **je circoncis;** *pr sub* **je circoncise)** to circumcise. **circoncision** [sirkɔ̃sizjɔ̃] *nf* circumcision.

circonférence [sirkɔ̃ferɑ̃s] *nf* circumference.

circonflexe [sirkɔ̃flɛks] *a* circumflex (accent).

circonlocution [sirkɔ̃lɔkysjɔ̃] *nf* circumlocution.

circonscription [sirkɔ̃skripsjɔ̃] *nf* division, district, area; **c. électorale,** constituency.

circonscrire [sirkɔ̃skrir] *(conj like* ÉCRIRE) 1. *vtr (a)* to circumscribe; to surround, encircle (**par,** with, by) *(b)* to limit, bound; **c. son sujet,** to define the scope of one's subject; **c. un incendie,** to bring a fire under control 2. **se c.,** to be limited.

circonspection [sirkɔ̃spɛksjɔ̃] *nf* circumspection, caution, wariness. **circonspect** *a* circumspect, cautious, wary.

circonstance [sirkɔ̃stɑ̃s] *nf* 1. circumstance, event, occasion; **en pareille c.,** in such a case; **étant donné les circonstances,** in the circumstances; **vers de c.,** occasional verse; **paroles de c.,** appropriate words 2. *Jur:* **circonstances atténuantes,** extenuating circumstances. **circonstancié** *a* detailed (account). **circonstanciel, -ielle** *(a)* circumstantial *(b) Gram:* adverbial (complement).

circonvenir [sirkɔ̃vnir] *vtr (conj like* VENIR) to circumvent, thwart; to outwit (s.o.).

circonvolution [sirkɔ̃vɔlysjɔ̃] *nf Anat:* convolution.

circuit [sirkɥi] *nm* 1. *(a)* circumference (of a town) *(b) Sp:* lap; circuit *(c)* **c. (touristique),** organized tour *(d)* **circuits commerciaux,** commercial channels 2. deviation; circuitous route; detour 3. *El:* circuit; **mettre en c.,** to connect, to switch on; **couper le c.,** to switch off; **c. fermé,** closed circuit; *Elcs:* **c. imprimé, intégré,** printed, integrated, circuit.

circulation [sirkylasjɔ̃] *nf* 1. circulation (of blood, air); **mettre en c.,** to put into circulation; to put (book) on the market 2. traffic; **accident de la c.,** road accident; *Rail:* **c. des trains,** running of trains 3. movement (of workers, goods). **circulaire** *a & nf* circular. **circulatoire** *adv* circulatory.

circuler [sirkyle] *vi* 1. *(of blood, air)* to circulate, flow; **faire c. l'air,** to circulate the air; **faire c. la**

bouteille, to pass the bottle round 2. to circulate, move about; **circulez!** move along! **les autobus circulent jour et nuit,** the buses run day and night; **faire c. une nouvelle,** to spread a piece of news.

cire [sir] *nf (a)* wax; (ear)wax; **c. d'abeilles,** beeswax; **c. à cacheter,** sealing wax *(b)* (wax) polish.

ciré [sire] *nm* oilskin.

cirer [sire] *vtr* to wax; to polish (floors, shoes). **cireux, -euse** *a* waxy; waxen.

cireur, -euse [sirœr, -øz] 1. *n* shoeblack 2. *nf (machine)* (electric) (floor) polisher.

cirque [sirk] *nm* 1. *(a)* (floor) circus *(b)* amphitheatre 2. *Geol:* cirque.

cirrhose [siroz] *nf Med:* cirrhosis.

cisaille(s) [sizaj] *nf sg or pl* shears; wirecutters.

cisailler [sizaje] *vtr* to cut, to shear (metal); to prune (branches).

ciseau, -eaux [sizo] *nm* 1. chisel; **c. à froid,** cold chisel 2. *pl (a)* **(paire de) ciseaux,** (pair of) scissors *(b)* shears *(c) Wr:* scissors (hold).

ciseler [sizle] *vtr* **(je cisèle, je ciselle)** to chase (gold); to chisel, carve (wood).

ciselure [sizlyr] *nf* chasing, engraving; chiselling, carving.

citadelle [sitadɛl] *nf* citadel.

citadin, -ine [sitadɛ̃, -in] 1. *n* city dweller 2. *a* urban.

citation [sitasjɔ̃] *nf* 1. quotation, citation 2. *Jur:* citation, summons; **c. des témoins,** subpoena of witnesses 3. *Mil:* **c. à l'ordre du jour** = mention in dispatches.

cité [site] *nf (a)* city; large town *(b)* **c. (ouvrière),** housing estate; **c. universitaire** = students' hall(s) of residence.

cité-dortoir [sitedɔrtwar] *nf* dormitory town; *pl* **cités-dortoirs.**

cité-jardin [siteʒardɛ̃] *nf* garden city; *pl* **cités-jardins.**

citer [site] *vtr* 1. to quote, cite; **c. qn en exemple,** to hold s.o. up as an example 2. *Jur:* to summon; to subpoena (witness) 3. *Mil:* **c. qn (à l'ordre du jour)** = to mention s.o. in dispatches.

citerne [sitɛrn] *nf* cistern, tank.

citoyen, -enne [sitwajɛ̃, -ɛn] *n* citizen.

citoyenneté [sitwajɛnte] *nf* citizenship.

citrique [sitrik] *a Ch:* citric (acid).

citron [sitrɔ̃] *nm (a)* lemon; *F:* **c. vert,** lime *(b) a inv* lemon-yellow, lemon(-coloured) *(c) P:* head, nut.

citronnade [sitrɔnad] *nf* lemon squash.

citronnier [sitrɔnje] *nm* lemon tree.

citrouille [sitruj] *nf (a)* pumpkin *(b) P:* head, nut.

civet [sivɛ] *nm Cu:* stew; **c. de lièvre** = jugged hare.

civière [sivjɛr] *nf* stretcher.

civil [sivil] *a* 1. *(a)* civil (rights); **guerre civile,** civil war *(b) Jur:* **droit c.,** civil law *(c)* lay, secular; civilian; civil (marriage); *nm* **un c.,** a civilian; **en c.,** (i) in plain clothes (ii) *Mil:* in civilian clothes; **dans le c.,** in civilian life 2. *A:* polite, courteous. **civilement** *adv* 1. **se marier c.,** to contract a civil marriage; *Jur:* **c. responsable,** liable for damages 2. politely, courteously.

civilisation [sivilizasjɔ̃] *nf* civilization.

civiliser [sivilize] 1. *vtr* to civilize 2. **se c.,** to become civilized.

civilité [sivilite] nf **1.** civility, courtesy **2.** pl **civilités,** compliments.

civisme [sivism] nm good citizenship. **civique** a civic (duties); civil (rights).

clair [klɛr] **1.** a (a) clear; unclouded, limpid (b) obvious, plain (meaning); **explication claire,** lucid explanation; **il est c. qu'elle a tort,** she's obviously wrong; **c. comme le jour,** crystal clear (c) bright, light (room); **il fait c.,** it's (day)light; **il ne fait pas c.,** there isn't much light (d) light, pale (colour); **robe bleu c.,** pale blue dress (e) thin (soup); light (fabric) **2.** adv plainly, clearly; **je commence à y voir c.,** I'm beginning to understand **3.** nm (a) light; **au c. de (la) lune,** in the moonlight (b) **en c.,** in plain language; **message en c.,** message in clear (ie not in code) (c) **tirer qch au c.,** to clear sth up (d) **passer le plus c. de son temps à dormir,** to spend most of one's time sleeping. **clairement** adv clearly, plainly.

claire-voie [klɛrvwa] nf open-work, lattice(-work); **clôture à c.-v.,** fence, paling; pl **claires-voies.**

clairière [klɛrjɛr] nf clearing, glade.

clairon [klɛrɔ̃] nm (a) bugle (b) bugler.

claironner [klɛrɔne] vtr to trumpet (piece of news). **claironnant** a loud, brassy (sound); resonant (voice).

clairsemé [klɛrsəme] a scattered, sparse (vegetation); thin (hair).

clairvoyance [klɛrvwajɑ̃s] nf perspicacity, clear-sightedness. **clairvoyant, -ante** a perceptive, clear-sighted.

clamecer [klamse] vi P: to die, to snuff it.

clamer [klame] vtr **c. son innocence,** to protest one's innocence.

clameur [klamœr] nf clamour; outcry.

clandestinité [klɑ̃destinite] nf clandestineness; **dans la c.,** in secret; **passer dans la c.,** to go underground. **clandestin, -ine** a clandestine; secret; underground; illicit; **passager c.,** stowaway. **clandestinement** adv clandestinely; secretly, illicitly.

clapet [klapɛ] nm (a) valve (b) P: **elle a un de ces clapets!** she never stops (talking)!

clapier [klapje] nm rabbit hutch; **(lapin de) c.,** tame rabbit.

clapotement [klapɔtmɑ̃] nm lapping (of waves).

clapoter [klapɔte] vi (of waves) to lap.

clapotis [klapɔti] nm lap(ping) (of waves).

clapper [klape] vi **c. de la langue,** to click one's tongue.

claquage [klakaʒ] nm straining (of ligament); strained ligaments.

claque [klak] nf **1.** smack, slap **2.** Th: hired clappers; claque **3.** a & nm **(chapeau) c.,** opera hat.

claqué [klake] a F: worn out, dog-tired.

claquement [klakmɑ̃] nm slam(ming), bang(ing); crack(ing); snap(ping); click(ing).

claquer [klake] **1.** vi (a) (of door) to slam, to bang; (of flag) to flap; (of tongue) to click; **il claque des dents,** his teeth are chattering (b) P: to die; to snuff it; (of business) to go bust; (of machinery) to go phut; (of light bulb) to go **2.** vtr & i **(faire) c.,** to slam, to bang (the door); to crack (a whip); to snap (one's fingers); to click (one's heels) **3.** vtr (a) to slap (child) (b) F: to wear (s.o.) out (c) F: to squander, to blow (one's money) **4.** **se c. un muscle,** to pull a muscle.

claquette [klakɛt] nf **(danse à) claquettes,** tap dance, tap dancing.

clarification [klarifikasjɔ̃] nf clarification.

clarifier [klarifje] vtr to clarify; **se c.,** to become clear.

clarinette [klarinɛt] nf clarinet.

clarinettiste [klarinɛtist] n clarinettist.

clarté [klarte] nf **1.** (a) clearness, clarity; limpidity (of water); transparency (of glass) (b) lucidity (of style); **c. d'esprit,** clear thinking (c) **avoir des clartés sur un sujet,** to have some knowledge of a subject **2.** light, brightness (of sun, moon).

classe [klas] nf **1.** class, division, category; Adm: rank, grade; **c. d'âge,** age group; **la c. moyenne,** the middle class; **de première c.,** first-rate; top quality (product); **c. touriste,** tourist class; **billet de première c.,** first-class ticket; F: **avoir de la c.,** to have class, to have style **2.** Sch: (a) class, form; **classes supérieures,** upper forms (b) **aller en c.,** to go to school; **être en c.,** to be at school; **livre de c.,** schoolbook; **(salle de) c.,** classroom; **M. Martin leur fait la c.,** Mr Martin is their teacher **3.** Mil: (a) annual contingent (of recruits); **la c. 1965,** the class of 1965; **faire ses classes,** to undergo basic training (b) (rank) **(soldat de) deuxième c.,** private; **(soldat de) première c.,** lance-corporal.

classement [klasmɑ̃] nm **1.** classification; position, place (in class, in race); Sch: **c. trimestriel,** end of term list; **donner le c.,** to give the results (of a competition) **2.** (a) sorting out (of articles) (b) filing (of documents).

classer [klase] vtr **1.** to class(ify); **monument classé,** listed monument **2.** (a) to sort out (articles) (b) to file (documents); **c. une affaire,** to consider a matter closed **3.** **se c. troisième,** to come in third; **il se classe parmi les meilleurs,** he ranks among the best.

classeur [klasœr] nm (a) filing cabinet (b) (looseleaf) file, binder.

classification [klasifikasjɔ̃] nf classification.

classifier [klasifje] vtr (impf & pr sub n. **classifiions**) to classify (plant).

classique [klasik] **1.** a (a) classical (music); classic (beauty) (b) standard (work); classic (joke); F: **c'est le coup c.,** it's an old trick, it's an old one **2.** nm (a) classical author (b) (Greek, Latin) classic (c) classical music.

clause [kloz] nf clause.

claustrophobie [klostrɔfɔbi] nf claustrophobia.

clavecin [klavsɛ̃] nm Mus: harpsichord.

clavicule [klavikyl] nf collarbone.

clavier [klavje] nm **1.** keyboard (of piano, typewriter); manual (of organ) **2.** range.

clé, clef [kle] nf **1.** (a) key; **fermer une porte à c.,** to lock a door; **tenir qch sous c.,** to keep sth under lock and key; **louer une maison clés en main,** to rent a house with vacant possession; **mettre la c. sous la porte,** to do a moonlight flit (b) **position c.,** key position; **industrie c.,** key industry (c) key (to a code); clue (to a puzzle) **2.** Mus: (a) clef (b) key signature **3.** Arch: **c. de voûte,** keystone **4.** Tls: wrench, spanner; **c. anglaise,** adjustable spanner; monkey wrench **5.** peg (of stringed instrument).

clématite [klematit] nf Bot: clematis.

clémence [klemɑ̃s] nf **1.** clemency, leniency **(pour,**

envers, to(wards)) 2. mildness (of the weather). **clément** *a* 1. clement, lenient (**pour, envers,** to(wards)) 2. mild (weather).

clémentine [klemɑ̃tin] *nf* clementine.

clenche [klɑ̃ʃ] *nf* latch (of door lock).

cleptomane [klɛptɔman] *n* kleptomaniac.

cleptomanie [klɛptɔmani] *nf* kleptomania.

clerc [klɛr] *nm* 1. (a) *Ecc:* cleric (b) *Hist:* scholar (c) **être grand c. en la matière,** to be an expert on the subject 2. clerk (in office).

clergé [klɛrʒe] *nm* clergy.

clérical, *pl* **-aux** [klerikal, -o] *a & n* clerical.

clic [klik] *nm* click(ing); **c.-clack,** click-clack, clickety-clack.

cliché [kliʃe] *nm* 1. *Typ:* plate 2. *Phot:* negative 3. cliché.

client, -ente [kliɑ̃, -ɑ̃t] *n* client, customer; (doctor's) patient; (taxi driver's) fare; (hotel) guest, patron; *F:* **un drôle de c.,** a queer customer.

clientèle [kliɑ̃tɛl] *nf* (a) (doctor's, lawyer's) practice; customers, clientele (of shop) (b) custom; **accorder sa c. à un magasin,** to patronize a shop.

clignement [kliɲmɑ̃] *nm* blinking, winking; **faire un c. d'œil,** to wink.

cligner [kliɲe] *vtr & i* **c. les yeux, des yeux,** to screw up one's eyes; to blink; **c. de l'œil à qn,** to wink at s.o.

clignotant [kliɲɔtɑ̃] *nm Aut:* indicator.

clignotement [kliɲɔtmɑ̃] *nm* blinking; flickering, flashing, winking, twinkling.

clignoter [kliɲɔte] *vi* (a) **c. des yeux,** to blink (b) (*of light*) to flicker; (*of star*) to twinkle; to flash.

climat [klima] *nm* 1. climate 2. *Fig:* atmosphere. **climatique** *a* climatic (conditions).

climatisation [klimatizasjɔ̃] *nf* air conditioning.

climatiser [klimatize] *vtr* to air-condition.

climatiseur [klimatizœr] *nm* air conditioner.

clin d'œil [klɛ̃dœj] *nm* wink; **faire un c. d'œil,** to wink; **en un c. d'œil,** in the twinkling of an eye.

clinique [klinik] 1. *a* clinical 2. *nf* clinic; nursing home.

clinquant [klɛ̃kɑ̃] 1. *nm* tinsel; **(bijoux de) c.,** imitation jewelry 2. *a* flashy, tawdry.

clique [klik] *nf* 1. clique, gang, set 2. *Mil:* band 3. *pl F:* **prendre ses cliques et ses claques,** to pack up and go.

cliquet [klikɛ] *nm Mec:* catch, pawl.

cliqueter [klikte] *vi* (**il cliquette**) (*of chains*) to rattle; (*of swords*) to clash; (*of glasses*) to clink, to chink; (*of keys*) to jingle.

cliquetis [klikti] *nm* rattling, clashing, clinking, clanking, jingling.

clivage [klivaʒ] *nm* 1. cleaving (of diamonds) 2. cleavage (of rocks) 3. gulf, rift.

cloaque [klɔak] *nm* cesspool, cesspit.

clochard [klɔʃar] *nm F:* tramp, *NAm:* hobo.

cloche [klɔʃ] *nf* 1. bell 2. *Ch:* belljar; *Hort:* cloche; *DomEc:* dish cover; *c.* **à plongeur,** diving bell; **(chapeau) c.,** cloche (hat) 3. *P:* imbecile, idiot; **avoir l'air c.,** to look stupid.

cloche-pied (à) [aklɔʃpje] *adv phr* **sauter à c.-p.,** to hop on one foot.

clocher¹ [klɔʃe] *nm* belfry, bell tower; steeple; church tower; **esprit de c.,** parochialism.

clocher² *vi F:* **il y a quelque chose qui cloche,** there's something wrong (somewhere).

clochette [klɔʃɛt] *nf* small bell; handbell.

cloison [klwazɔ̃] *nf* 1. partition, division; **mur de c.,** dividing wall 2. *Nau:* bulkhead.

cloisonnement [klwazɔnmɑ̃] *nm* partitioning (off) (of room).

cloisonner [klwazɔne] *vtr* to partition (off) (room).

cloître [klwatr] *nm* cloister(s).

cloîtrer [klwatre] *vtr* 1. to cloister (s.o.); to shut (s.o.) away; **religieuse cloîtrée,** enclosed nun 2. **se c.,** (i) to enter a convent (ii) to shut oneself up.

clopin-clopant [klɔpɛ̃klɔpɑ̃] *adv F:* **aller c.-c.,** to limp along, hobble along.

clopiner [klɔpine] *vi* to hobble, limp (along).

cloque [klɔk] *nf* blister.

cloquer [klɔke] *vi* to blister.

clore [klɔr] *vtr def* (*pp* **clos;** *pr ind* **je clos, ils closent**) (a) *A: & Lit:* to close, to shut (up) (b) to end (discussion); to close (meeting) (c) *A:* to enclose (park).

clos [klo] 1. *a* (a) closed, shut; **à la nuit close,** after dark (b) concluded 2. *nm* enclosure; **c. de vigne,** vineyard.

clôture [klotyr] *nf* 1. enclosure, fence, fencing; **mur de c.,** enclosing wall 2. (a) closing, closure (of offices) (b) conclusion (of sitting); *StExch:* **cours en c.,** closing price 3. *Com:* winding up (of account).

clôturer [klotyre] *vtr* 1. to enclose (field) 2. to close, conclude, end (session) 3. *Com:* to wind up, close (accounts).

clou [klu] *nm* 1. (a) nail; **chaussures à clous,** hobnailed boots; *F:* **des clous!** nothing doing! (b) stud (of pedestrian crossing); **traverser dans les clous,** to cross at a pedestrian crossing (c) **c. cavalier,** staple (d) star turn, chief attraction (of show) 2. *Med:* boil 3. **c. de girofle,** clove 4. *P:* (**vieux**) **c.,** ancient car, old banger.

clouer [klue] *vtr* 1. to nail (sth); *F:* **c. le bec à qn,** to shut s.o. up 2. to pin (s.o., sth) down; **rester cloué sur place,** to stand rooted to the spot; **être cloué au lit,** to be bedridden, confined to bed.

clouté [klute] *a* studded (shoes); **passage clouté,** pedestrian crossing.

clown [klun] *nm* clown; buffoon.

club [klœb] *nm* club.

cm *abbr* centimètre.

CNPF *abbr* Conseil national du patronat français.

CNRS *abbr* Centre national de la recherche scientifique.

coaccusé, -ée [kɔakyze] *n Jur:* co-defendant.

coacquéreur [kɔakerœr] *nm* joint purchaser.

coagulation [kɔagylasjɔ̃] *nf* coagulation.

coaguler (se) [sɔkagyle] *vpr* to coagulate, to clot; to curdle. **coagulant** *a & nm* coagulant.

coaliser (se) [sɔkɔalize] *vpr* to form a coalition; to unite.

coalition [kɔalisjɔ̃] *nf* coalition.

coassement [kɔasmɑ̃] *nm* croak(ing) (of frog).

coasser [kɔase] *vi* (*of frog*) to croak.

cobalt [kɔbalt] *nm* cobalt.

cobaye [kɔbaj] *nm Z:* guinea pig; **servir de c.,** to act as a guinea pig.

Coblence [kɔblɑ̃s] *Prnm Geog:* Koblentz, Coblentz.

cobra [kɔbra] *nm Rept:* cobra.

cocaïne [kɔkain] *nf Pharm:* cocaine.

cocarde [kɔkard] *nf* cockade, rosette; *Av:* roundel, *Aut:* sticker.

cocasse [kɔkas] *a F:* comical, laughable.

coccinelle [kɔksinel] *nf Ent:* ladybird.

coccyx [kɔksis] *nm Anat:* coccyx.

cocher¹ [kɔʃe] *nm* coachman; **c. de fiacre,** cabman.

cocher² *vtr* (*a*) to notch; to mark off (*b*) to tick (off) (names).

cochère [kɔʃɛr] *af* **porte c.,** carriage gateway.

cochon [kɔʃɔ̃] **1.** *nm* (*a*) pig, hog; **c. de lait,** suck(l)ing pig; *F:* **un c. n'y retrouverait pas ses petits,** what a pigsty! (*b*) **c. d'Inde,** guinea pig **2.** *a & n P:* (*a*) a indecent, dirty (story); swinish (pers, trick) (*b*) *n* dirty pig; swine.

cochonnaille [kɔʃɔnaj] *nf F:* (i) pork (ii) cooked meats; delicatessen.

cochonnerie [kɔʃɔnri] *nf P:* **1.** dire des cochonneries, to tell dirty jokes, dirty stories **2.** (*a*) filth, rubbish (*b*) revolting food **3.** dirty trick.

cochonnet [kɔʃɔne] *nm* (*a*) piglet (*b*) (bowls) jack.

cocktail [kɔktɛl] *nm* (*a*) cocktail (*b*) cocktail party.

coco [koko, kɔ-] *nm* **1.** noix de c., coconut **2.** liquorice water **3.** *F:* egg **4.** *F:* (*a*) fellow, bloke; **drôle de c.,** queer stick (*b*) **mon petit c.,** my darling.

cocon [kɔkɔ̃] *nm* cocoon; *Fig:* shell.

cocorico [kɔkɔriko] *onomat & nm* cock-a-doodle-doo!

cocotier [kɔkɔtje] *nm* coconut palm.

cocotte [kɔkɔt] *nf* **1.** *F:* hen, chicken **2.** *F:* (*a*) **ma c.,** (my) darling (*b*) prostitute, tart **3.** *Cu:* casserole (dish) **4.** **hue c.!** gee up!

cocotte-minute [kɔkɔtminyt] *nf Rtm:* pressure-cooker; *pl* cocottes-minute.

cocu, -e [kɔky] *a & n* cuckold.

codage [kɔdaʒ] *nm* coding.

code [kɔd] *nm* **1.** statute book; **c. civil** = Common Law; **c. pénal,** penal code; *Aut:* **C. de la route,** Highway Code; **se mettre en c.,** to dip one's headlights; (phares) c., dipped headlights **2.** code, cipher; **c. télégraphique,** telegraphic code.

coder [kɔde] *vtr* to code (message).

codétenu, -ue [kɔdetny] *n* fellow prisoner.

codification [kɔdifikasjɔ̃] *nf* codification.

codifier [kɔdifje] *vtr* to codify (laws).

codirecteur, -trice [kɔdirektœr, -tris] *n* codirector; joint manager, joint manageress.

coefficient [kɔefisjã] *nm* coefficient; *Ind:* **c. de sécurité,** safety factor.

coéquipier [kɔekipje] *nm Sp:* team mate.

coercition [kɔersisjɔ̃] *nf* coercion.

cœur [kœr] *nm* **1.** (*a*) heart; **maladie de c.,** heart disease; **opération à c. ouvert,** open-heart surgery; **en (forme de) c.,** heart-shaped (*b*) **avoir mal au c.,** to feel sick; **cela soulève le c.,** it's sickening, nauseating; *F:* **avoir le c. bien accroché,** to have a strong stomach **2.** (*a*) soul, feelings, mind; **avoir qch sur le c.,** to have sth on one's mind; **en avoir le c. net,** to be clear in one's mind (about it); **avoir la rage au c.,** to be seething with anger; **parler à c. ouvert,** to have a heart to heart talk; **remercier qn du fond du c.,** to thank s.o. wholeheartedly, from the bottom of one's heart; **avoir le c. gros,** to be sad at heart; **avoir le c.**

sur la main, to be generous; **homme de c.,** good-hearted man; **si le c. vous en dit,** if you feel like it; **je n'ai pas le c. à faire cela,** I am not in the mood to do that; **prendre qch à c.,** to take sth to heart; **avoir à c. de faire qch,** to set one's heart on doing sth (*b*) **apprendre qch par c.,** to learn sth by heart **3.** courage, spirit, pluck; **donner du c. à qn,** to give s.o. courage; *F:* **avoir du c. au ventre,** to have plenty of guts; **faire contre mauvaise fortune bon c.,** to make the best of a bad job **4.** (*a*) **avoir le c. à l'ouvrage,** to have one's heart in one's work; **faire qch de bon c.,** to do sth willingly; **y aller de bon c.,** to get down to it; **le c. n'y est pas,** my heart isn't in it (*b*) **aimer qn de tout son c.,** to love s.o. with all one's heart (*c*) **il a bon c.,** he's kind-hearted; **il n'a pas de c.,** he's heartless **5.** middle, midst; centre (of town); heart (of palm, of artichoke); **au c. de l'hiver,** in the depth of winter **6.** *Cards:* heart(s).

coexistence [kɔegzistãs] *nf* coexistence (avec, with).

coexister [kɔegziste] *vi* to coexist (avec, with).

coffrage [kɔfraʒ] *nm* framing, formwork, casing.

coffre [kɔfr̩] *nm* **1.** (*a*) chest, bin (*b*) *Anat: F:* chest (*c*) safe (deposit box); coffer (*d*) boot, *NAm:* trunk (of car) **2.** case (of piano, lock).

coffre-fort [kɔfrəfɔr] *nm* safe; *pl* coffres-forts.

coffrer [kɔfre] *vtr F:* to put (s.o.) in prison, inside.

coffret [kɔfre] *nm* small box; casket; **c. à bijoux,** jewel case.

cogérant, -ante [kɔʒerã, -ãt] *n* joint manager, joint manageress.

cognac [kɔɲak] *nm* cognac; brandy.

cognée [kɔɲe] *nf* axe.

cognement [kɔɲmã] *nm* knocking; thump(ing), banging.

cogner [kɔɲe] **1.** *vtr* (*a*) to drive in, hammer in (nail) (*b*) to knock, beat, thump (s.o., sth); to hit (s.o.); **c. qn en passant,** to bump into s.o. (in passing) (*c*) *P:* to beat (s.o.) up **2.** *vi* to knock, thump (sur, on); to bump (contre, against); (of engine) to knock **3.** se c. contre, à, qch, to knock against sth; **c'est à se c. la tête contre les murs,** it's enough to drive you up the wall.

cogneur [kɔɲœr] *nm F:* (pers) bruiser.

cohabitation [kɔabitasjɔ̃] *nf* cohabitation, living together.

cohabiter [kɔabite] *vi* to cohabit (avec, with).

cohérence [kɔerãs] *nf* coherence. **cohérent** *a* coherent.

cohésion [kɔezjɔ̃] *nf* cohesion, cohesiveness.

cohorte [kɔɔrt] *nf* **1.** *Hist:* cohort **2.** *F:* mob, band (of people).

cohue [kɔy] *nf* (*a*) crowd, throng (*b*) crush.

coi, coite [kwa, kwat] *a* silent; **se tenir c.,** to keep quiet.

coiffe [kwaf] *nf* headdress.

coiffer [kwafe] **1.** *vtr* (*a*) to cover (the head); **ce chapeau vous coiffe bien,** that hat suits you; **montagne coiffée de neige,** snow-capped mountain (*b*) **c. un chapeau,** to put on a hat (*c*) **c. qn,** to do s.o.'s hair; **se faire c.,** to have one's hair done (*d*) *Sp: F:* to overtake; **se faire c. (au poteau),** to be beaten at the post (*e*) *F:* to control (an organization) **2.** (*a*) **se c. d'une casquette,** to wear a cap (*b*) **se c.,** to do one's hair. **coiffé** *a* **elle est bien coiffée,** her hair looks lovely; **je ne suis pas encore coiffé(e),** I haven't done my hair yet.

coiffeur, -euse [kwafœr, -øz] *n* 1. hairdresser 2. *nf* dressing table.

coiffure [kwafyr] *nf* 1. headdress 2. hairstyle 3. hairdressing.

coin [kwɛ̃] *nm* 1. (*a*) corner; **maison du c.,** corner house; **l'épicier du c.,** the l cal grocer; **c. repas,** dining area; **regard en c.,** side glance; **du c. de l'œil,** out of the corner of one's eye (*b*) (retired) spot, nook; **un petit c. pas cher,** a cheap little place; *F:* **le petit c.,** the loo; **coins et recoins,** nooks and crannies; **chercher qch dans tous les coins,** to look high and low for sth (*c*) **c. du feu,** inglenook; **au c. du feu,** by the fireside (*d*) patch (of land); **c. de ciel,** patch of blue sky 2. wedge 3. stamp, die; hallmark.

coincer [kwɛ̃se] *v* (**n. coinçons**) 1. *vtr* (*a*) to wedge (up), chock (up) (rails) (*b*) to jam (drawer); **voiture coincée entre deux camions,** car stuck between two lorries (*c*) *F:* to corner (s.o.); **vous êtes coincé,** you're stymied (*d*) *F:* to arrest s.o., to nab s.o. 2. **se c.,** to jam, to stick; to bind.

coïncidence [kɔɛ̃sidɑ̃s] *nf* coincidence. **coïncident** *a* coincident.

coïncider [kɔɛ̃side] *vi* to coincide (**avec,** with).

coing [kwɛ̃] *nm Bot:* quince.

coke [kɔk] *nm* coke.

col [kɔl] *nm* 1. (*a*) *A: & Lit:* neck (of pers) (*b*) neck (of bottle) 2. collar; **faux c.,** detachable collar; **c. raide, mou,** stiff, soft, collar 3. **c. bleu, blanc,** blue-collar worker; white-collar worker 4. *Geog:* pass, col.

colchique [kɔlʃik] *nf Bot:* autumn crocus.

coléoptère [kɔleɔptɛr] *nm* beetle.

colère [kɔlɛr] 1. *nf* anger; **c. bleue,** towering rage; **être, se mettre, en c.,** to be angry, to get angry (**contre qn,** with s.o.); to lose one's temper; **avoir des colères,** to have fits of anger 2. *a* angry (voice); irascible (pers). **coléreux, -euse, colérique** *a* quick-tempered (pers).

colibacille [kɔlibasil] *nm* colon bacillus.

colibri [kɔlibri] *nm Orn:* humming bird.

colifichet [kɔlifiʃɛ] *nm* trinket.

colimaçon [kɔlimasɔ̃] *nm* snail; **escalier en c.,** spiral staircase.

colin [kɔlɛ̃] *nm Ich:* hake.

colin-maillard [kɔlɛ̃majar] *nm Games:* blind man's buff.

colique [kɔlik] *nf* colic; severe stomach pains; **avoir la c.,** (i) to have stomach ache (ii) to have diarrhoea.

colis [kɔli] *nm* parcel, package; **par c. postal,** by parcel post.

collaborateur, -trice [kɔlabɔratœr, -tris] *n* (*a*) collaborator; fellow worker, associate; contributor (to magazine) (*b*) *Pol:* collaborationist.

collaboration [kɔlabɔrasjɔ̃] *nf* collaboration (**avec,** with).

collaborer [kɔlabɔre] *vi* to collaborate (**avec,** with); to contribute (to newspaper).

collage [kɔlaʒ] *nm* gluing, sticking; pasting; *Art:* collage; **c. du papier peint,** paper hanging.

collant [kɔlɑ̃] 1. *a* (*a*) sticky (*b*) close-fitting, skin-tight (garment) 2. *nm* (*a*) (pair of) tights (*b*) leotard.

collatéral, pl -aux [kɔlateral, -o] *a* collateral.

collation [kɔlasjɔ̃] *nf* snack.

colle [kɔl] *nf* 1. adhesive; paste; glue; size 2. *Sch: F:* (*a*) poser (*b*) oral exam (*c*) detention.

collecte [kɔlɛkt] *nf* collection (for the poor).

collecter [kɔlɛkte] *vtr* to collect.

collecteur, -trice [kɔlɛktœr, -tris] 1. *n* collector 2. *a & nm* (**égout**) **c.,** main sewer.

collectif, -ive [kɔlɛktif, -iv] 1. *a* collective, joint (action) 2. *nm* (*a*) *Gram:* collective noun (*b*) *Fin:* **c. budgétaire,** bill of supply. **collectivement** *adv* collectively.

collection [kɔlɛksjɔ̃] *nf* collection (of stamps); line (of samples); **présentation de collections,** fashion show.

collectionner [kɔlɛksjɔne] *vtr* to collect (stamps).

collectionneur, -euse [kɔlɛksjɔnœr, -øz] *n* collector.

collectiviser [kɔlɛktivize] *vtr* to collectivize.

collectivité [kɔlɛktivite] *nf* 1. collectivity; community; organization; **vivre en c.,** to lead a communal life 2. collective ownership.

collège [kɔlɛʒ] *nm* 1. college; **c. électoral,** electoral body 2. school; **c. d'enseignement secondaire** = secondary school; **c. technique,** technical college; **c. libre,** private school. **collégial, -iale, -iaux** *a* collegiate.

collégien, -ienne [kɔleʒjɛ̃, -jɛn] *n* schoolboy, schoolgirl.

collègue [kɔlɛg] *n* colleague.

coller [kɔle] 1. *vtr* (*a*) to paste, stick, glue (**à, sur,** to; on); **c. du papier peint sur un mur,** to paper a wall; **c. son oreille à la porte,** to press one's ear to the door; *F:* **c. une gifle à qn,** to slap s.o.'s face (*b*) *F:* to put; **colle ça dans un coin,** stick it in a corner; **c. un élève,** (i) to keep a pupil in (ii) to catch out a pupil (with a difficult question); **c. un candidat,** to fail a candidate; **il me colle!** he sticks to me like glue! 2. *vi* to stick, adhere, cling (**à,** to); **robe qui colle au corps,** clinging dress; *F:* **ça ne colle pas entre eux,** they don't hit it off; *F:* **ça colle?** how's things? O.K.? *F:* **ça ne colle pas,** there's something wrong, it doesn't work 3. **se c.,** to stick, adhere closely; **se c. contre un mur,** to stand close to a wall; **elle s'est collée contre lui,** she clung to him; *F:* **se c. devant la télé,** to be glued to the telly.

collet [kɔlɛ] *nm* 1. collar (of coat); **saisir qn au c.,** to seize s.o. by the collar; *a inv* **elle est très c. monté,** she is very prim (and proper), very formal 2. neck (of tooth) 3. flange, collar (of pipe) 4. snare, noose.

colleter [kɔlte] *vtr* (**je collette, n. colletons**) (*a*) to collar (s.o.) (*b*) **se c. avec qn,** to grapple with s.o.

colleur, -euse [kɔlœr, -øz] *n* gluer, paster; **c. d'affiches,** billsticker.

collier [kɔlje] *nm* 1. necklace 2. (*a*) chain (of mayor) (*b*) **c. de chien,** dog collar; **donner un coup de c.,** to put one's back into it (*c*) **c. de barbe,** narrow beard (following line of jaw) 3. *MecE:* collar, ring.

collimateur [kɔlimatœr] *nm Astr: Surv:* collimator, laying prism; **avoir qn dans le c.,** to have s.o. in one's sights.

colline [kɔlin] *nf* hill.

collision [kɔlizjɔ̃] *nf* collision; **entrer en c. avec qch,** to collide with sth; to run into (car); **c. des intérêts,** clash of interests.

colloque [kɔlɔk] *nm* conference; symposium.

collusion [kɔlyzjɔ̃] *nf Jur:* collusion.

collyre [kɔlir] *nm* eye lotion.

colmater [kɔlmate] *vtr* to fill in, to plug up (hole); to seal off (leak).

colombe [kɔlɔ̃b] *nf Orn:* dove.

Colombie [kɔlɔ̃bi] *Prnf Geog:* **1.** Colombia **2.** **C. britannique,** British Columbia. **colombien, -ienne** *a & n* Colombian.

colombier [kɔlɔ̃bje] *nm* dovecot.

colon [kɔlɔ̃] *nm* **1.** colonist, settler **2.** child at holiday camp **3.** *Mil: P:* colonel.

côlon [kolɔ̃] *nm Anat:* colon.

colonel [kɔlɔnɛl] *nm* colonel; *Mil: Av:* group captain.

colonialisme [kɔlɔnjalism] *nm Pol:* colonialism. **colonialiste** *a & n* colonialist.

colonie [kɔlɔni] *nf* colony, settlement; **c. de vacances,** children's holiday camp. **colonial, -iaux** *a & nm* colonial.

colonisation [kɔlɔnizasjɔ̃] *nf* colonization.

coloniser [kɔlɔnize] *vtr* to colonize. **colonisateur, -trice 1.** *a* colonizing **2.** *n* colonizer.

colonnade [kɔlɔnad] *nf Arch:* colonnade.

colonne [kɔlɔn] *nf* **1.** (*a*) column, pillar (*b*) *Anat:* **c. vertébrale,** spine, spinal column **2.** **c. montante,** rising main **3.** (*a*) *Mil:* column; **c. de secours,** relief (column) (*b*) *Pol:* **cinquième c.,** fifth column.

coloration [kɔlɔrasjɔ̃] *nf* **1.** colouring, colouration **2.** colour, colouring (of skin).

colorer [kɔlɔre] *vtr* to colour, tinge, tint; to stain (wood); **c. qch en vert,** to colour sth green **2.** **se c.,** (*of fruit*) to colour; (*of face*) to become flushed. **colorant** *a & nm* colouring. **coloré** *a* coloured; ruddy (complexion); colourful (style).

coloriage [kɔlɔrjaʒ] *nm* (*a*) colouring (*b*) coloured drawing.

colorier [kɔlɔrje] *vtr* (*impf & pr sub* **n. coloriions**) to colour (drawing).

coloris [kɔlɔri] *nm* colour(ing) (of painting); shade; *Com:* **carte de c.,** shade card.

colosse [kɔlɔs] *nm* colossus; giant. **colossal, -aux** *a* colossal, gigantic, huge.

colportage [kɔlpɔrtaʒ] *nm* hawking, peddling.

colporter [kɔlpɔrte] *vtr* to hawk, to peddle.

colporteur, -euse [kɔlpɔrtœr, -øz] *n* (*a*) hawker, pedlar (*b*) **c. de fausses nouvelles,** newsmonger.

coltiner [kɔltine] **1.** *vtr* to carry (load) on one's back **2.** *F:* **je ne vais pas me c. ça tout seul,** I'm not doing it on my own.

colza [kɔlza] *nm Bot:* rape (seed), coleseed.

coma [kɔma] *nm* coma. **comateux, -euse** *a* comatose.

combat [kɔ̃ba] *nm* **1.** (*a*) combat, fight, battle, action; **c. terrestre,** land operation; **c. de rue,** street fight(ing); **engager le c.,** to go into action; **hors de c.,** (i) (*pers*) disabled (ii) (*machinery*) out of action; (*b*) **c. de boxe,** boxing match **2.** conflict; struggle; battle (of wits).

combattant [kɔ̃batã] **1.** *a* combatant, fighting (unit) **2.** *nm* combatant; fighter; **anciens combattants,** ex-servicemen.

combattre [kɔ̃batr] *v* (*conj like* BATTRE) **1.** *vtr* to combat, to fight (against) (enemy, temptation) **2.** *vi*

to fight, strive, struggle. **combatif, -ive** *a* combative, pugnacious; **esprit c.,** fighting spirit.

combien [kɔ̃bjɛ̃] *adv* (& *conj when introducing a clause*) **1.** (*exclamative*) (*a*) how (much)! **si vous saviez c. je l'aime!** if you knew how much I love him! (*b*) how (many)! **c. de gens!** what a lot of people! **2.** (*interrogative*) (*a*) how much? **c. vous dois-je?** how much do I owe you? (**c'est**) **c.?** *F:* **ça fait c.?** how much is it? **depuis c. de temps est-il ici?** how long has he been here? **à c. sommes-nous de Paris?** how far are we from Paris? (*b*) **c. de fois?** how many times? how often? (*c*) *nm inv F:* **le c. sommes-nous?** what's the date? **il y a un car tous les c.?** how often does the bus run?

combinaison [kɔ̃binɛzɔ̃] *nf* **1.** (*a*) combination, arrangement; grouping (of letters); (colour) scheme (*b*) plan, scheme (*c*) *Ch: Mth:* combination **2.** *Cl:* (*a*) overalls, boiler suit; flying suit (*b*) (woman's) slip.

combinard, -arde [kɔ̃binar, -ard] *a & n P:* schemer.

combine [kɔ̃bin] *nf* scheme, trick; fiddle; **il a une c. pour entrer sans payer,** he knows a way of getting in without paying.

combiné [kɔ̃bine] *nm* (*a*) *Ch:* combination (*b*) (telephone) receiver (*c*) *Sp:* combination.

combiner [kɔ̃bine] **1.** *vtr* (*a*) to combine, unite (forces); to arrange (ideas) (*b*) *Ch:* to combine (*c*) to contrive, devise (plan) **2.** **se c.,** to combine, to unite (**à, avec,** with).

comble [kɔ̃bl] **1.** *nm* **pour c. de malheur,** to cap it all; **ça, c'est le c.!** that's the limit, the last straw! **2.** *nm* (*a*) roof (timbers); **loger sous les combles,** to live in an attic; **de fond en c.,** from top to bottom (*b*) highest point; height (of happiness); **être au c. de la joie,** to be overjoyed **3.** *a* (*of hall*) packed; **salle c.,** house filled to capacity.

combler [kɔ̃ble] *vtr* **1.** to fill in (ditch); to make good (a loss); to fill (gap) **2.** to overwhelm (s.o., sth); to fulfil (s.o.'s desires); **vous me comblez,** you are too kind; **il est comblé,** he has everything he could wish for.

combustible [kɔ̃bystibl] **1.** *a* combustible **2.** *nm* fuel; (*rockets*) propellant.

combustion [kɔ̃bystjɔ̃] *nf* combustion.

comédie [kɔmedi] *nf* (*a*) comedy; **c. musicale,** musical (comedy) (*b*) **jouer la c.,** (i) to act in a play (ii) to put on an act; (*to child*) **pas de c.,** behave yourself. **comédien, -ienne** [kɔmedjɛ̃, -jɛn] *n* (*a*) actor, actress (*b*) sham (*c*) show-off.

comestible [kɔmɛstibl] **1.** *a* edible, eatable **2.** *nmpl* food(s).

comète [kɔmɛt] *nf* comet.

comice [kɔmis] *nm* **c. agricole,** agricultural association; **comices agricoles,** agricultural show.

comique [kɔmik] **1.** *Th:* (*a*) a comic (actor, part); **le genre c.,** comedy (*b*) *nm* (i) comedy (ii) comic; comedian **2.** (*a*) *a* comica(l), funny (*b*) *nm* **le c. de l'histoire c'est que,** the funny part, the joke, is that. **comiquement** *adv* comically.

comité [kɔmite] *nm* committee, board; **c. d'entreprise,** joint production committee; **être en petit c.,** to be an informal gathering.

commandant [kɔmãdã] **1.** *a* commanding, in command of **2**. *nm* (*a*) commander, commanding officer; *Nau:* captain (of ship); *Navy:* executive officer; *Av:* **c. de bord**, captain (*b*) (*rank*) *Mil:* Major; *MilAv:* squadron leader.

commande [kɔmãd] *nf* **1**. (*a*) *Com:* order; **passer une c.**, to place an order; **fait sur c.**, made to order; **ouvrage écrit sur c.**, commissioned work (*b*) **sourire de c.**, forced smile **2**. *MecE:* (*a*) control, operation; **levier de c.**, (i) operating lever (ii) *Av:* control column; **prendre les commandes**, to take the controls (*b*) drive, driving (gear).

commandement [kɔmãdmã] *nm* **1**. command, order; *Rel:* commandment **2**. command; authority; **prendre le c.**, to take command.

commander [kɔmãde] **1**. *vtr* (*a*) to command; to order (sth); **c. un dîner**, to order a dinner; **c. à qn de faire qch**, to order s.o. to do sth; **apprendre à se c.**, to learn to control oneself; **ces choses-là ne se commandent pas**, these things are beyond our control (*b*) to command (respect) (*c*) *Mil:* to command, to order; to be in command (of) (*d*) (*of fort*) to command, dominate (town) (*e*) *MecE:* to control, operate (valve); to drive (machine) **2**. *vi* (*a*) **je lui ai commandé de se taire**, I told him to be quiet; **c. à son impatience**, to control one's impatience (*b*) **qui est-ce qui commande ici?** who's in charge here?

commandeur [kɔmãdœr] *nm* commander (of the *Légion d'Honneur*).

commanditaire [kɔmãditɛr] *nm Com:* sleeping partner.

commanditer [kɔmãdite] *vtr* to finance (enterprise).

commando [kɔmãdo] *nm Mil:* commando (unit).

comme¹ [kɔm] *adv* **1**. (*a*) as, like; **faites c. moi**, do as I do; **se conduire c. un fou**, to behave like a madman; **tout c. un autre**, (just) like anyone else; *F:* **j'ai c. une idée que**, I have a sort of idea that; **(alors) c. ça vous venez de Paris?** and so you come from Paris? (*b*) **doux c. un agneau**, (as) gentle as a lamb; **blanc c. neige**, snow-white; *F:* **drôle c. tout**, terribly funny (*c*) **c. (si)**, as if, as though; **il faisait c. si rien ne s'était passé**, he pretended that nothing had happened; **il leva la main c. pour me frapper**, he lifted his hand as if to strike me; *F:* **c'est tout c.**, it amounts to the same thing; **c. quoi il ne fallait pas le faire**, which goes to show you shouldn't have done it (*d*) **les bois durs c. le chêne**, hard woods such as oak **2**. (*before finite verbs*) (*a*) as; **faites c. il vous plaira**, do as you please (*b*) *adj & adv phr* **c. il faut**, proper(ly); *F:* **il est très c. il faut**, he's well-bred; **tiens-toi c. il faut**, don't slouch; sit up properly **3**. as; in the way of; **qu'est-ce que vous avez c. légumes?** what have you got in the way of vegetables? **4**. (*exclamative*) how! **c. il est maigre!** how thin he is!

comme² *conj* **1**. as; seeing that; **c. vous êtes là**, since you are here **2**. (just) as; **c. il allait frapper, il fut arrêté**, (just) as he was about to strike he was arrested.

commémoration [kɔmemɔrasjɔ̃] *nf* commemoration. **commémoratif, -ive** *a* commemorative (**de**, of).

commémorer [kɔmemɔre] *vtr* to commemorate.

commencement [kɔmãsmã] *nm* (*a*) beginning,

start; **au c.**, at the beginning, at the outset; **du c. jusqu'à la fin**, from start to finish (*b*) *pl* beginnings.

commencer [kɔmãse] (*n.* **commençons**) **1**. (*a*) *vtr* to begin, start (*b*) *vi* **il commence à pleuvoir**, it's beginning to rain; **c. par faire qch**, to begin by doing sth; *F:* **ça commence bien!** that's a good start! *F:* **je commence à en avoir assez!** I've had just about enough! **2**. *vi* **ça vient de c.**, it's just started. **commençant -ante** **1**. *a* beginning **2**. *n* beginner.

comment [kɔmã] *adv* **1**. *interr* how; **c. allez-vous?** how are you? **c. (dites-vous)?** what (did you say?) **c. faire?** what's to be done? **c. est-il?** what's he like? **2**. *excl* what! why! **c.! vous n'êtes pas encore parti!** what, haven't you gone yet! **mais c. donc!** why, of course! *F:* **ça t'a plu?—et c.!** did you like it?—and how! **3**. *nm inv* **les pourquoi et les c.**, the whys and wherefores.

commentaire [kɔmãtɛr] *nm* **1**. commentary (**sur**, on) **2**. comment remark; *F:* **ça se passe de c.**, it speaks for itself; *F:* **pas de commentaires!** that's final!

commentateur, -trice [kɔmãtatœr, -tris] *n* commentator.

commenter [kɔmãte] *vtr* **1**. to comment on, annotate (text) **2**. to comment on, criticize (s.o., sth).

commérage [kɔmeraʒ] *nm* **commérage(s)**, gossip.

commerçant, -ante [kɔmersã, -ãt] **1**. *a* commercial; business (district); **rue commerçante**, shopping street; **peu c.**, bad at business **2**. *n* dealer; tradesman; shopkeeper; **c. en gros, en détail**, wholesaler, retailer.

commerce [kɔmɛrs] *nm* **1**. commerce; trade; **c. en gros, en détail**, wholesale, retail, trade; **le petit c.**, (i) small traders (ii) shopkeeping; **hors c.**, not on sale to the general public **2**. *A: & Lit:* intercourse, dealings; **être en c. avec qn**, to be in touch with s.o. **commercial, pl -iaux 1**. *a* commercial **2**. *nf Aut:* small van.

commercer [kɔmɛrse] *vi* (**je commerçai(s)**) to trade (**avec**, with).

commercialisation [kɔmɛrsjalizasjɔ̃] *nf* marketing.

commercialiser [kɔmɛrsjalize] *vtr* to market (product).

commère [kɔmɛr] *nf* (*pers*) gossip.

commettre [kɔmɛtr] *vtr* (*conj like* METTRE) **1**. **c. qn à qch**, to put s.o. in charge of sth **2**. to commit (crime); to make (a mistake) **3**. **se c. avec qn**, to associate with s.o.

commis [kɔmi] *nm O:* **1**. clerk **2**. (*a*) shop assistant (*b*) **c. voyageur**, commercial traveller.

commisération [kɔmizerasjɔ̃] *nf* commiseration.

commissaire [kɔmisɛr] *nm* (*a*) commissioner; (government) representative (*b*) **c. (de police)** = (police) superintendent (*c*) *Nau:* **c. du bord**, purser (*d*) *Sp:* steward.

commissaire-priseur [kɔmisɛrprizœr] *nm* auctioneer; *pl* **commissaires-priseurs**.

commissariat [kɔmisarja] *nm* (*a*) **c. (de police)**, police station (*b*) department (of ministry).

commission [kɔmisjɔ̃] *nf* **1**. commission; **vente à c.**, sale on commission; **c. de deux pour cent**, commission of two per cent **2**. message, errand; **faire les commissions**, to do the shopping **3**. committee, board; **c. d'enquête**, board of inquiry.

commissionnaire [kɔmisjɔnɛr] *nm* **1**. *Com:* commission agent; broker **2**. messenger.

commissionner [kɔmisjɔne] *vtr* to commission.
commissure [kɔmisyr] *nf* corner (of mouth).
commode [kɔmɔd] **1.** *a* (*a*) convenient, suitable (moment); handy (tool); convenient, comfortable (house) (*b*) **ce n'est pas c.**, it isn't easy (*c*) **c. à vivre**, easy to live with; *F:* **il n'est pas c.**, he's an awkward customer **2.** *nf* chest of drawers. **commodément** *adv* comfortably.
commodité [kɔmɔdite] *nf* convenience.
commotion [kɔmosjɔ̃] *nf* **1.** commotion; upheaval; *Med:* **c. cérébrale**, concussion **2.** shock.
commotionner [kɔmosjɔne] *vtr* (*a*) *Med:* **être fortement commotionné**, to have severe concussion (*b*) to give (s.o.) a shock.
commuer [kɔmɥe] *vtr Jur:* to commute (sentence).
commun [kɔmœ̃] **1.** *a* (*a*) common (à, to); **jardin c.**, shared garden; **amis communs**, mutual friends; **vie commune**, common life; **d'un c. accord**, with one accord; **en c.**, in common; **vivre en c.**, to live communally (*b*) common; universal, general (custom); usual, everyday (occurrence); **le sens c.**, common sense; *Gram:* **nom c.**, noun (*c*) vulgar, common **2.** *nm* (*a*) common run (of persons); **hors du c.**, out of the ordinary (*b*) *pl* **les communs**, outbuildings. **communément** *adv* commonly.
communauté [kɔmynote] *nf* **1.** (*a*) community (of interests) (*b*) *Jur:* joint estate (of married couple) **2.** (*a*) community, society (*b*) (religious) community, order (*c*) *Pol:* community. **communautaire** *a* community (centre).
commune [kɔmyn] *nf* **1.** (*in Eng*) **la Chambre des Communes, les Communes**, the (House of) Commons **2.** *FrAdm:* (*smallest territorial division*) commune, approx = (i) parish (ii) municipality. **communal, -aux** *a* common (land); communal; council (property).
communiant, -ante [kɔmynjɑ̃, -ɑ̃t] *n Ecc:* communicant; **premier c., première communiante**, child taking his, her, first communion.
communication [kɔmynikasjɔ̃] *nf* **1.** (*a*) communication; communicating; **entrer, se mettre, en c. avec qn**, to get into contact with s.o.; **portes de c.**, communicating doors (*b*) *Tp:* **c. téléphonique**, (telephone) call; **c. en PCV**, reverse, transferred, charge call, *NAm:* collect call; **vous avez la c.**, you're through; **la c. est mauvaise**, the line is bad **2.** (*a*) communication, message (*b*) (scientific) paper. **communicatif, -ive** *a* communicative, talkative; infectious (laughter).
communier [kɔmynje] *vi Ecc:* (*impf & pr sub* **n. communiions**) to receive Holy Communion.
communion [kɔmynjɔ̃] *nf* communion; **faire sa première c.**, to take one's first communion; **être en c. avec qn**, to be in communion with s.o.
communiqué [kɔmynike] *nm* communiqué; **c. de presse**, press release.
communiquer [kɔmynike] **1.** *vtr* to communicate; to impart, convey (information); **c. qch par écrit**, to report in writing; **c. une maladie à qn**, to pass on an illness to s.o. **2.** *vi* to be in communication, to communicate; **porte qui communique au, avec le, jardin**, door that leads into the garden **3.** (*of fire*) **se c.**, to spread (à, to). **communicant** *a* communicating (rooms).

communisme [kɔmynism] *nm* communism. **communisant, -ante 1.** *a* communistic **2.** *n* communist sympathizer.
communiste [kɔmynist] *n* communist.
commutateur [kɔmytatœr] *nm El:* switch.
commutation [kɔmytasjɔ̃] *nf* commutation.
commuter [kɔmyte] *vtr Jur:* to commute.
compact [kɔ̃pakt] *a* compact, dense; solid (majority).
compagne [kɔ̃paɲ] *nf* (female) companion; partner (in life); (*of animals*) mate; **c. de classe**, classmate.
compagnie [kɔ̃paɲi] *nf* **1.** company; **tenir c. à qn**, to keep s.o. company; **fausser c. à qn**, to give s.o. the slip **2.** company; party; **toute la c.**, everybody; all of them, of us; **fréquenter la mauvaise c.**, to keep bad company **3.** *Com: Th:* company; **c. aérienne**, airline; **la maison Thomas et C.** (*usu et Cie*), the firm of Thomas and Company (*usu & Co*) **4.** *Mil:* company **5.** covey (of partridges).
compagnon [kɔ̃paɲɔ̃] *nm* companion; comrade; **c. d'études**, fellow student; **c. de voyage**, travelling companion; **c. d'infortune**, fellow sufferer.
comparaison [kɔ̃parezɔ̃] *nf* **1.** comparison; **en c. de qch**, in comparison with sth; **sans c. le plus grand**, by far the tallest **2.** simile.
comparaître [kɔ̃parɛtr] *vi* (*conj like* PARAÎTRE) *Jur:* **c. (en justice)**, to appear (before a court of justice).
comparer [kɔ̃pare] *vtr* to compare (à, avec, to, with). **comparable** *a* comparable. **comparatif, -ive** *a* comparative. **comparativement** *adv* comparatively. **comparé** *a* comparative.
comparse [kɔ̃pars] *n* (*a*) *Th:* supernumerary; **rôle de c.**, walk-on part (*b*) stooge.
compartiment [kɔ̃partimɑ̃] *nm* compartment.
compartimentage [kɔ̃partimɑ̃taʒ] *nm* compartmentalization.
compartimenter [kɔ̃partimɑ̃te] *vtr* (*a*) to divide into compartments (*b*) to compartmentalize.
comparution [kɔ̃parysjɔ̃] *nf Jur:* appearance.
compas [kɔ̃pa] *nm* **1.** (pair of) compasses; **c. à pointes sèches**, dividers; **avoir le c. dans l'œil**, to have an accurate eye **2.** **c. (de mer)**, (mariner's) compass.
compassion [kɔ̃pasjɔ̃] *nf* compassion.
compatibilité [kɔ̃patibilite] *nf* compatibility. **compatible** *a* compatible.
compatir [kɔ̃patir] *vi* (*a*) to compensate; to offset **c. au chagrin de qn**, to sympathize with, to feel for, s.o. in his grief. **compatissant** *a* compassionate, sympathetic (**pour**, to, towards).
compatriote [kɔ̃patriɔt] *n* compatriot.
compensation [kɔ̃pɑ̃sasjɔ̃] *nf* (*a*) compensation; set-off; offset (of losses); **il y a c.**, that makes up for it (*b*) equalization, balancing (of forces). **compensatoire** *a* compensatory.
compenser [kɔ̃pɑ̃se] *vtr* (*a*) to compensate; to offset (a fault); to make up for (sth.); **c. une perte**, to make good a loss (*b*) to compensate, set off (debts). **compensé** *a* compensated; **semelle compensée**, wedge heel.
compère [kɔ̃pɛr] *nm* **1.** accomplice **2.** *O:* comrade; **un bon c.**, a pleasant companion.
compétence [kɔ̃petɑ̃s] *nf* **1.** competence, jurisdiction (of court); **cela ne rentre pas dans sa c.**, that

does not come within his province; **sortir de sa c.,** to exceed one's powers **2.** competence, ability; proficiency, skill. **compétent** *a* competent; **l'autorité compétente,** the authority concerned.

compétition [kɔ̃petisjɔ̃] *nf* (*a*) competition, rivalry (*b*) *Sp:* contest, match; **c. sportive,** sporting event. **compétitif, -ive** competitive.

compilateur, -trice [kɔ̃pilatœr, -tris] *n* compiler.

compilation [kɔ̃pilasjɔ̃] *nf* compilation.

compiler [kɔ̃pile] *vtr* to compile.

complainte [kɔ̃plɛ̃t] *nf Mus: Lit:* lay, lament.

complaire [kɔ̃plɛr] *v ind tr* (*conj like* PLAIRE) **1.** *Lit:* **c. à qn,** to please, humour, s.o. **2. se c. à faire qch,** to take pleasure in doing sth.

complaisance [kɔ̃plezɑ̃s] *nf* **1.** obligingness; **auriez-vous la c. de** + *inf,* would you be so kind as to + *inf* **2.** complacency, (self-)satisfaction. **complaisant** *a* (*a*) obliging (*b*) indulgent (*c*) complacent, self-satisfied. **complaisamment** *adv* obligingly; complacently, with satisfaction.

complément [kɔ̃plemɑ̃] *nm* (*a*) complement; rest, remainder (*b*) *Gram:* complement; **c. (d'objet),** object (of verb). **complémentaire** *a* complementary; further (information).

complet, -ète [kɔ̃plɛ, -ɛt] **1.** *a* (*a*) complete, entire, whole; full (report); thorough (examination); **athlète c.,** all-round athlete; **échec c.,** total, utter, failure; *F:* **c'est c.!** that's the limit! (*b*) full (bus, *Th:* house); *PN:* **c.,** full (up); (*outside hotel*) no vacancies **2.** *nm* (*a*) **c.(-veston),** suit (*b*) **au c.,** full, complete; **nous étions au grand c.,** we turned up in full force. **complètement** *adv* completely, wholly, totally, fully; utterly (ruined).

compléter [kɔ̃plete] *vtr* (**je complète; je compléterai**) (*a*) to complete; to make up (a sum of money) (*b*) **ils se complètent,** they complement each other.

complexe [kɔ̃plɛks] **1.** *a* complex; complicated; intricate; **nombre c.,** compound number **2.** *nm* (*a*) *Psy:* complex; **avoir des complexes,** to be inhibited (*b*) (industrial) complex.

complexer [kɔ̃plɛkse] *vtr* to give (s.o.) a complex.

complexité [kɔ̃plɛksite] *nf* complexity.

complication [kɔ̃plikasjɔ̃] *nf* **1.** complication **2.** complexity **3.** *Med:* complication(s).

complice [kɔ̃plis] *a & n* accessory (**de,** to); accomplice, abettor (**de,** of); **c. en adultère,** co-respondent.

complicité [kɔ̃plisite] *nf* complicity.

compliment [kɔ̃plimɑ̃] *nm* **1.** compliment **2.** *pl* compliments, greetings; **faites-lui mes compliments,** give him my regards **3.** congratulation; **je te fais mes compliments,** I congratulate you.

complimenter [kɔ̃plimɑ̃te] *vtr* to compliment; to congratulate (**de, sur,** on).

compliquer [kɔ̃plike] **1.** *vtr* to complicate **2. se c.,** to become complicated; (*of plot*) to thicken; **se c. l'existence,** to make life difficult for oneself. **compliqué** *a* complicated, elaborate; intricate (mechanism); *Med:* compound (fracture); **ce n'est pas c.,** it's simple.

complot [kɔ̃plo] *nm* plot, conspiracy.

comploter [kɔ̃plɔte] *vi* to plot (**contre,** against).

comploteur [kɔ̃plɔtœr] *nm* plotter.

componction [kɔ̃pɔ̃ksjɔ̃] *nf* compunction.

comportement [kɔ̃pɔrtəmɑ̃] *nm* behaviour.

comporter [kɔ̃pɔrte] *vtr* **1.** to allow (of), to admit of (sth) **2.** to call for, require (sth) **3.** to comprise, include (sth); **les inconvénients que cela comporte,** the difficulties which this involves, entails **4. se c.,** to behave (**envers,** towards); **se c. mal,** to misbehave.

composer [kɔ̃poze] **1.** *vtr* (*a*) to compose (symphony); *vi Mus:* to compose; *vi Sch:* to sit an exam (*b*) to set (type); *Tp:* **c. un numéro,** to dial a number (*c*) **les personnes qui composent notre famille,** the people who make up our family (*d*) **c. son visage,** to compose one's features **2.** *vi* to compromise, come to terms (**avec,** with) **3. se c. (de),** to consist (of). **composant** *a & nm* component, constituent (part). **composé 1.** *a* compound; composed (attitude) **2.** *nm* compound.

compositeur, -trice [kɔ̃pozitœr, -tris] *n* **1.** *Mus:* composer **2.** *Typ:* compositor, typesetter.

composition [kɔ̃pozisjɔ̃] *nf* **1.** (*a*) composing, composition (of sonata); construction (of novel); composition (of water) (*b*) *Typ:* typesetting **2.** (*a*) composition, compound (*b*) *Lit: Mus:* composition; *Sch:* (i) essay (ii) test, paper **3.** arrangement, compromise; **entrer en c. avec qn,** to come to terms with s.o.

compost [kɔ̃pɔst] *nm* compost.

composter [kɔ̃pɔste] *vtr* to (date) stamp, to punch (ticket).

compote [kɔ̃pɔt] *nf* stewed fruit, compote; *F:* **j'ai les jambes en c.,** my legs feel like jelly.

compotier [kɔ̃pɔtje] *nm* fruit dish.

compréhension [kɔ̃preɑ̃sjɔ̃] *nf* comprehension, understanding. **compréhensible** *a* comprehensible, understandable. **compréhensif, -ive** *a* comprehensive; understanding.

comprendre [kɔ̃prɑ̃dr] *vtr* (*conj like* PRENDRE) **1.** to comprise, include; **y compris,** including **2.** to understand; **je n'arrive pas à c. cette phrase,** I can't make sense of this sentence; **ai-je bien compris que tu pars?** do you mean to say that you're going? **je n'y comprends rien,** I can't make it out; **je lui ai fait c. que** + *ind,* I made it clear to him that; **se faire c.,** to make oneself understood; **cela se comprend,** of course, that's understandable; **je comprends bien!** I can well imagine it!

compresse [kɔ̃prɛs] *nf* compress.

compresseur [kɔ̃prɛsœr] *nm* compressor.

compression [kɔ̃presjɔ̃] *nf* **1.** compression **2.** restriction, cutback; reduction (of staff). **compressible** *a* compressible; reducible.

comprimer [kɔ̃prime] *vtr* **1.** to compress **2.** to repress, restrain (one's feelings); to hold back (tears). **comprimé 1.** *a* compressed (air); **outil à air c.,** pneumatic tool **2.** *nm Pharm:* tablet.

compromettre [kɔ̃prɔmɛtr] *v* (*conj like* METTRE) **1.** *vtr* (*a*) to compromise (s.o.); **être compromis,** to be implicated (*b*) to endanger (life) **2.** *vi* to compromise **3. se c.,** to compromise oneself; to commit oneself. **compromettant** *a* compromising.

compromis [kɔ̃prɔmi] *nm* compromise.

compromission [kɔ̃prɔmisjɔ̃] *nf Pej:* compromising; surrender (of principle).

comptabiliser [kɔ̃tabilize] *vtr* to enter (sth) in the accounts.

comptabilité [kɔ̃tabilite] *nf* **1.** book-keeping; accountancy; **tenir la c.,** to keep the books **2.** accounts department.

comptable [kɔ̃tabl] **1.** *a* book-keeping **2.** *nm* accountant; book-keeper; **expert c.** = chartered accountant.

comptant [kɔ̃tɑ̃] **1.** *a* **argent c.,** ready money **2.** *adv* **payer c.,** to pay (in) cash **3.** *nm* **vente au c.,** cash sale.

compte [kɔ̃t] *nm* (*a*) reckoning, calculation; **faire le c. des dépenses,** to add up expenses; **cela fait mon c.,** it's just the thing for me; **y trouver son c.,** to get sth out of it; **le c. y est,** it's the right amount, the right number; *F:* **il a son c.,** (i) he's done for (ii) he's drunk; **son c. est bon,** he's for it; **en fin de c., tout c. fait,** all things considered; after all; **tenir c. de qch,** to take sth into account; **ne tenir aucun c. de qch,** to ignore, to disregard, sth; **acheter qch à bon c.,** to buy sth cheap; **s'en tirer à bon c.,** to get off lightly (*b*) count; **c. à rebours,** countdown (*c*) account; **tenir les comptes,** to keep the accounts; *F:* **régler son c. à qn,** to settle s.o.'s hash; **c. en banque,** bank account; **c. chèque postal** = (National) Giro-bank account; **apprendre qch sur le c. de qn,** to learn sth about s.o.; **mettre qch sur le c. de qn,** to attribute sth to s.o.; **s'installer à son c.,** to set up one's own business; **prendre qch à son c.,** to accept responsibility for sth; **pour mon c.,** for my part (*d*) **rendre c. de qch,** to account for sth; **c. rendu,** report; review; **se rendre c. de qch,** to realize sth.

compte-gouttes [kɔ̃tgut] *nm inv Pharm: etc:* dropper, pipette; **au c.-g.,** sparingly.

compter [kɔ̃te] **1.** *vtr* (*a*) to count (up), reckon (up); **dix-neuf tous comptés,** nineteen in all, all told; **ses jours sont comptés,** his days are numbered; **sans c. que,** not to mention that; **il faut c. une heure,** it will take an hour; *Adm:* **à c. du 1er janvier,** with effect from 1st January (*b*) **c. cent francs à qn,** to pay s.o. a hundred francs (*c*) *Com:* to charge; **on ne compte pas l'emballage,** there is no charge for packing (*d*) to value; **c. sa vie pour rien,** to hold one's life of no account (*e*) **c. faire qch,** to intend to do sth; **c. sur moi,** to reckon on doing sth **2.** *vi* (*a*) **c. sur qn,** to count, depend, rely, on s.o.; **comptez sur moi,** you can depend on me; **j'y compte bien,** I hope so (*b*) **c. avec qn,** to reckon with s.o. (*c*) **c. parmi les meilleurs,** to rank among the best (*d*) to count; **cela ne compte pas,** that doesn't count; **ce qui compte c'est de réussir,** the main thing is to succeed.

compte-tours [kɔ̃ttur] *nm inv* revolution counter.

compteur [kɔ̃tœr] *nm* meter; **c. kilométrique** = mil(e)ometer; **c. de vitesse,** speedometer; **c. (de) Geiger,** Geiger counter.

comptoir [kɔ̃twar] *nm* **1.** *Com:* counter; bar; **garçon de c.,** bartender **2.** trading post **3.** branch (of bank).

compulser [kɔ̃pylse] *vtr* to examine, to inspect (documents).

computer [kɔ̃pyte] *vtr* to compute.

comte [kɔ̃t] *nm* count; (*in Eng*) earl.

comté [kɔ̃te] *nm* (*a*) *Hist:* earldom (*b*) county.

comtesse [kɔ̃tɛs] *nf* countess.

con, conne [kɔ̃, kɔn] *P:* **1.** *a* bloody stupid **2.** *n* bloody idiot; cretin; **faire le c.,** to fool about.

concassage [kɔ̃kasaʒ] *nm* crushing, grinding.

concasser [kɔ̃kase] *vtr* to crush, grind.

concasseur [kɔ̃kasœr] *nm* crusher.

concavité [kɔ̃kavite] *nf* (*a*) concavity (*b*) cavity. **concave** *a* concave.

concéder [kɔ̃sede] *vtr* (**je concède; je concéderai**) **1.** to concede, to grant (privilege) **2. c. qu'on a tort,** to admit that one is wrong.

concentration [kɔ̃sɑ̃trasjɔ̃] *nf* (*a*) concentration (*b*) **c. urbaine,** urban agglomeration (*c*) integration (of businesses) (*d*) concentration (of the mind).

concentrer [kɔ̃sɑ̃tre] **1.** *vtr* to concentrate; to focus (rays); to centre **2. se c. (sur),** to concentrate (on). **concentré 1.** *a* concentrated; condensed (milk); concentrating (mind) **2.** *nm* extract, concentrate; **c. de tomates,** tomato purée.

concentrique [kɔ̃sɑ̃trik] *a* concentric.

concept [kɔ̃sɛpt] *nm* concept.

conception [kɔ̃sɛpsjɔ̃] *nf* **1.** conception, conceiving **2.** (*a*) conception, idea (*b*) creation.

concerner [kɔ̃sɛrne] *vtr* (*used in third pers only*) to concern, affect; **en ce qui vous concerne,** as far as you are concerned; **est-ce que cela vous concerne?** is it any business of yours?

concert [kɔ̃sɛr] *nm* **1.** entente, agreement; **agir de c. avec qn,** to act in cooperation with s.o. **2.** (*a*) concert; **salle de c.,** concert hall (*b*) chorus (of approval).

concertation [kɔ̃sɛrtasjɔ̃] *nf Pol:* dialogue.

concerter [kɔ̃sɛrte] **1.** *vtr* to devise (plan) **2. se c. (avec qn),** to take counsel, to consult (with s.o.). **concerté** *a* concerted.

concertiste [kɔ̃sɛrtist] *n* concert performer.

concerto [kɔ̃sɛrto] *nm Mus:* concerto.

concession [kɔ̃sesjɔ̃] *nf* concession; plot (in cemetery).

concessionnaire [kɔ̃sesjɔnɛr] *nm Com:* agent, dealer.

concevoir [kɔ̃səvwar] *vtr* (*conj like* RECEVOIR) **1.** to conceive (child) **2.** (*a*) to conceive, imagine (idea); to form (plan); **c. de l'amitié pour qn,** to take a liking to s.o.; **la maison est bien conçue,** the house is well designed (*b*) to understand; **cela se conçoit facilement,** that's easily understood (*c*) **ainsi conçu,** (letter) worded as follows. **concevable** *a* conceivable.

concierge [kɔ̃sjɛrʒ] *n* (house) porter; caretaker (of flats).

concile [kɔ̃sil] *nm Ecc:* council.

conciliabule [kɔ̃siljabyl] *nm F:* confabulation.

conciliateur, -trice [kɔ̃siljatœr, -tris] *n* conciliator.

conciliation [kɔ̃siljasjɔ̃] *nf* conciliation; reconciliation.

concilier [kɔ̃silje] *vtr* (*impf & pr sub n.* **conciliions**) **1.** to conciliate, reconcile (two parties) **2.** (*a*) to win, gain (esteem) (*b*) **se c.,** to agree (avec, with); **se c. qn,** to gain s.o.'s goodwill. **conciliable** *a* reconcilable. **conciliant** *a* conciliating, conciliatory.

concision [kɔ̃sizjɔ̃] *nf* concision; conciseness. **concis** *a* concise, terse.

concitoyen, -enne [kɔ̃sitwajɛ̃, -ɛn] *n* fellow citizen.

conclave [kɔ̃klav] *nm Ecc:* conclave.

conclure [kɔ̃klyr] *v* (*pp* **conclu;** *pr ind* **je conclus;**

impf **je concluais) 1.** (*a*) *vtr* to conclude; to end, finish (*b*) *vtr* to arrive at (an understanding); **c. un marché,** to drive a bargain; **c'est une affaire conclue,** (i) that's settled (ii) it's a deal (*c*) *vi* to come to a conclusion **2.** (*a*) *vtr* to decide (*b*) *vi* **c. à qch,** to come to a conclusion about sth; **le jury a conclu au suicide,** the jury returned a verdict of suicide. **concluant** *a* conclusive, decisive.

conclusion [kɔ̃klyzjɔ̃] *nf* (*a*) conclusion; close (of speech); **en c.,** in short; to sum up (*b*) *Jur:* finding, decision; *pl* submissions.

concombre [kɔ̃kɔ̃br̩] *nm* cucumber.

concordance [kɔ̃kɔrdɑ̃s] *nf* concordance, agreement; *Gram:* sequence (of tenses). **concordant** *a* concordant, in agreement.

concordat [kɔ̃kɔrda] *nm Ecc:* concordat.

concorde [kɔ̃kɔrd] *nf* concord, harmony.

concorder [kɔ̃kɔrde] *vi* to agree, to tally (**avec,** with).

concourir [kɔ̃kurir] *vi* (*conj like* COURIR) **1.** (*of lines*) to converge, to concur **2.** to combine, unite; **c. à (faire) qch,** to work towards (doing) sth **3.** to compete.

concours [kɔ̃kur] *nm* **1.** (*a*) *A: & Lit:* concourse (of people) (*b*) coincidence (of events); **c. de circonstances,** combination of circumstances **2.** co-operation, help; (financial) aid; *Th: etc:* **avec le c. de,** those taking part were **3.** (*a*) competition; competitive exam; *Sp:* field events (*b*) **c. hippique,** horse show; **c. de beauté,** beauty contest.

concret, -ète [kɔ̃krɛ, -ɛt] *a* concrete, solid; **cas c.,** actual case, concrete example. **concrètement** *adv* in concrete terms.

concrétiser [kɔ̃kretize] *vtr* to put (idea) in concrete form; **se c.,** to take shape.

concubinage [kɔ̃kybinaʒ] *nm* cohabitation.

concupiscence [kɔ̃kypisɑ̃s] *nf* concupiscence.

concurremment [kɔ̃kyramɑ̃] *adv* concurrently, jointly.

concurrence [kɔ̃kyrɑ̃s] *nf* **1.** *Com: etc:* **jusqu'à c. de,** to the amount of, not exceeding **2.** competition, rivalry; **faire c.,** to compete (**à qn,** with s.o.).

concurrencer [kɔ̃kyrɑ̃se] *vtr* (**je concurrençai(s)**) to compete with (s.o., sth).

concurrent, -ente [kɔ̃kyrɑ̃, -ɑ̃t] *n* competitor; candidate. **concurrentiel, -ielle** *a* competitive.

condamnation [kɔ̃danasjɔ̃] *nf* **1.** *Jur:* conviction, judgment, sentence; **c. à mort,** death sentence **2.** condemnation; blame.

condamné, -ée [kɔ̃dane] *n* convict; sentenced, condemned, person.

condamner [kɔ̃dane] *vtr* **1.** (*a*) *Jur:* to convict, sentence; **c. qn à 10,000 francs d'amende,** to fine s.o. 10,000 francs; **le médecin l'a condamné,** the doctor has given up hope for him (*b*) to forbid (*c*) **c. une porte,** to block up a door (*d*) **c. sa porte,** to bar one's door to visitors **2.** to blame, censure, reprove (s.o.). **condamnable** *a* reprehensible.

condensateur [kɔ̃dɑ̃satœr] *nm* condenser.

condensation [kɔ̃dɑ̃sasjɔ̃] *nf* condensation.

condenser [kɔ̃dɑ̃se] *vtr & vpr* to condense. **condensé 1.** *a* condensed; **lait condensé,** condensed milk **2.** *nm* résumé; digest.

condescendance [kɔ̃desɑ̃dɑ̃s] *nf* condescension. **condescendant** *a* condescending.

condescendre [kɔ̃desɑ̃dr̩] *vi* to condescend (**à faire qch,** to do sth).

condiment [kɔ̃dimɑ̃] *nm* condiment, seasoning.

condisciple [kɔ̃disipl] *nm* fellow student, school mate.

condition [kɔ̃disjɔ̃] *nf* **1.** (*a*) condition; state; **en c.,** in good condition (*b*) *pl* conditions, circumstances; **dans ces conditions,** in that case (*c*) rank, station, position **2.** condition, stipulation; *pl* terms; **conditions de faveur,** preferential terms; **sans condition(s),** unconditional(ly); **acheter qch sous c.,** to buy on approval; **à c. de me prévenir,** provided (that) you let me know. **conditionnel, -elle** *a & nm* conditional. **conditionnellement** *adv* conditionally.

conditionnement [kɔ̃disjɔnmɑ̃] *nm* conditioning; *Com:* packaging.

conditionner [kɔ̃disjɔne] *vtr* **1.** to condition (air, textiles) **2.** to govern **3.** *Com:* to package.

condoléances [kɔ̃dɔleɑ̃s] *nfpl* condolences; **présenter ses c.,** to offer one's sympathy.

conducteur, -trice [kɔ̃dyktœr, -tris] **1.** *n* (*a*) leader, guide (*b*) driver (*c*) (machine) operator **2.** *a Ph: El:* conducting, conductive **3.** *nm El: Ph:* (*a*) conductor (of heat) (*b*) *El:* lead (wire); main.

conductibilité [kɔ̃dyktibilite] *nf Ph: El:* conductivity. **conductible** *a* conductive.

conduction [kɔ̃dyksjɔ̃] *nf Ph: etc:* conduction.

conduire [kɔ̃dɥir] *vtr* (*prp* **conduisant;** *pp* **conduit;** *ph* **je conduisis) 1.** (*a*) to conduct, escort (party); to lead; to guide; **c. qn à la gare,** to take, to drive, s.o. to the station; **c. qn à sa chambre,** to show s.o. to his room (*b*) **c. qn à faire qch,** to prevail on s.o. to do sth **2.** to drive (car); to steer (boat); *vi* **il conduit bien,** he's a good driver **3.** to convey, conduct (water, electricity) **4.** to conduct, manage, run (sth); **c. un orchestre,** to conduct an orchestra **5. se c.,** to behave; **se c. mal,** to behave badly.

conduit [kɔ̃dɥi] *nm* conduit, duct, passage, pipe; **c. d'aération,** air duct; **c. de ventilation,** ventilation shaft.

conduite [kɔ̃dɥit] *nf* **1.** (*a*) conducting, leading, escorting (of s.o.) (*b*) driving (of car); navigation (of boat); **c. à gauche,** left-hand drive; **leçon de c.,** driving lesson **2.** direction, management, control (of affairs); **sous la c. de qn,** under s.o.'s leadership **3.** conduct, behaviour; **c'est ma seule ligne de c.,** it's the only course open to me; **mauvaise c.,** misbehaviour **4.** pipe, conduit, duct; piping, tubing; **c. d'eau,** water main(s).

cône [kon] *nm* cone; **c. de pin,** pine cone.

confection [kɔ̃fɛksjɔ̃] *nf* **1.** making, preparation **2.** (*a*) ready-to-wear clothing industry (*b*) **robe de c.,** ready-made dress; **vêtements de c.,** off-the-peg clothes.

confectionner [kɔ̃fɛksjɔne] *vtr* to make (up) (dress); to prepare (dish).

confédération [kɔ̃federasjɔ̃] *nf* confederation, confederacy. **confédéré** *a & n* confederate.

conférence [kɔ̃ferɑ̃s] *nf* **1.** conference, discussion; **être en c.,** to be in a meeting **2.** lecture. **conférencier, -ière** [kɔ̃ferɑ̃sje, -jɛr] *n* lecturer.

conférer [kɔ̃fere] *v* (**je confère; je conférerai) 1.** *vtr* to confer, grant, award (privileges) **2.** *vi* to confer (**avec,** with).

confesse [kɔ̃fɛs] *nf* **aller à c.**, to go to confession.

confesser [kɔ̃fese] *vtr* **1.** to confess; to own (up) to (sth) **2.** to confess (one's sins) **3.** (*of priest*) to confess (penitent) **4. se c.**, to confess (one's sins)

confesseur [kɔ̃fesœr] *nm Ecc:* (father) confessor.

confession [kɔ̃fesjɔ̃] *nf* (*a*) confession (*b*) religious persuasion. **confessionnel, -elle** *a* denominational.

confessional, -aux [kɔ̃fesjɔnal, -o] *nm Ecc:* confessional.

confetti [kɔ̃feti] *nmpl* confetti.

confiance [kɔ̃fjɑ̃s] *nf* **1.** confidence, faith, trust; **avoir c. en qn, faire c. à qn**, to rely on s.o., to trust s.o.; **acheter qch de c.**, to buy sth. on trust; **digne de c.**, trustworthy; **maison de c.**, reliable firm; **avec c.**, (i) confidently (ii) trustingly; *Pol:* **vote de c.**, vote of confidence **2.** confidence, sense of security; **c. en soi**, self confidence, self assurance. **confiant** *a* **1.** confiding, trustful (**dans**, in) **2.** confident **3.** self-confident (manner).

confidence [kɔ̃fidɑ̃s] *nf* confidence; **faire une c. à qn**, to tell s.o. a secret; **faire c. de qch à qn**, to confide sth to s.o.; **en c.**, in confidence.

confident, -ente [kɔ̃fidɑ̃, -ɑ̃t] *n* confidant, *f* confidante. **confidentiel, -ielle** *a* confidential. **confidentiellement** *adv* confidentially.

confier [kɔ̃fje] *vtr* (*impf & pr sub* **n. confiions**) **1.** to trust, entrust (s.o. with sth) **2.** to confide, disclose; **c. qch à qn**, to tell s.o. sth in confidence **3. se c. à qn**, (i) to put one's trust in s.o. (ii) to confide in s.o.

configuration [kɔ̃figyrasjɔ̃] *nf* configuration; shape; lie (of the land).

confinement [kɔ̃finmɑ̃] *nm* confinement, confining.

confiner [kɔ̃fine] **1.** *vi* **c. à un pays**, to border on a country **2.** (*a*) *vtr* to confine (s.o.) (*b*) **se c. chez soi**, to live a retired life. **confiné** *a* enclosed (atmosphere); stale (air).

confins [kɔ̃fɛ̃] *nmpl* confines, borders (of country); limits (of science).

confire [kɔ̃fir] *vtr* (*pp* **confit**; *pr ind* **je confis**; *impf* **je confisais**) to preserve (fruit); to candy (peel); **c. au vinaigre**, to pickle.

confirmation [kɔ̃firmasjɔ̃] *nf* confirmation; **il m'en a donné c.**, he gave me confirmation of it.

confirmer [kɔ̃firme] *vtr* to confirm (news); to ratify (treaty); **le bruit ne s'est pas confirmé**, the news proved false.

confiscation [kɔ̃fiskasjɔ̃] *nf* confiscation.

confiserie [kɔ̃fizri] *nf* (*a*) confectioner's shop (*b*) confectionery, sweets, *NAm:* candy.

confiseur, -euse [kɔ̃fizœr, -øz] *n* = confectioner.

confit [kɔ̃fi] **1.** *a* crystallized (fruit) **2.** *nm* conserve (of goose).

confiture [kɔ̃fityr] *nf* jam; **c. d'oranges**, (orange) marmalade.

conflit [kɔ̃fli] *nm* conflict; clash (of interests); **entrer en c.**, to clash (**avec**, with).

confluent [kɔ̃flyɑ̃] *nm* confluence (of rivers).

confondre [kɔ̃fɔ̃dr] **1.** *vtr* (*a*) to confound; to mingle (*b*) to mistake, confuse; **je les confonds toujours**, I always mistake one for the other (*c*) to astound, stagger (s.o.) (*d*) to confound (criminal); **c. un menteur**, to show up a liar **2. se c.** (*a*) (*of colours*) to

blend (**en**, into) (*b*) (*of streams*) to intermingle (*c*) (*of interests*) to be identical (*d*) **se c. en excuses**, to apologize profusely. **confondu** *a* **1.** disconcerted **2.** dumbfounded, astounded (**de**, at).

conformation [kɔ̃fɔrmasjɔ̃] *nf* conformation. **conforme** *a* conformable, true (**à**, to); consistent (**à**, with); identical; **copie c. à l'original**, exact copy; *Adm:* **pour copie c.**, certified true copy; **il mène une vie c. à ses moyens**, he lives according to his means. **conformément** *adv* in accordance (**à**, with).

conformer [kɔ̃fɔrme] **1.** *vtr* to model (**à**, on); **c. sa vie à certains principes**, to shape one's life according to certain principles **2. se c. à qch**, to conform to sth; to comply with, to abide by, sth.

conformisme [kɔ̃fɔrmism] *nm* conformism, conformity.

conformiste [kɔ̃fɔrmist] *n* conformist.

conformité [kɔ̃fɔrmite] *nf* conformity, similarity; **en c. avec**, in accordance with.

confort [kɔ̃fɔr] *nm* comfort; **tout c. moderne**, all modern conveniences, *F:* all mod cons. **confortable** *a* comfortable, snug, cosy. **confortablement** *adv* comfortably; in comfort.

confrère [kɔ̃frɛr] *nm* colleague, fellow member (of profession, society).

confrérie [kɔ̃freri] *nf* (religious) brotherhood.

confrontation [kɔ̃frɔ̃tasjɔ̃] *nf* (*a*) confrontation (*b*) comparison.

confronter [kɔ̃frɔ̃te] *vtr* (*a*) to confront (**avec**, with) (*b*) to compare.

confusion [kɔ̃fyzjɔ̃] *nf* **1.** (*a*) confusion; disorder, muddle; **mettre la c. dans l'assemblée**, to throw the audience into confusion; *Med:* **c. mentale**, mental aberration (*b*) mistake, error; **c. de dates**, confusion of dates **2.** confusion, embarrassment. **confus** *a* **1.** confused, chaotic; indistinct (noise); obscure (style) **2.** embarrassed, ashamed. **confusément** *adv* confusedly; vaguely.

congé [kɔ̃ʒe] *nm* **1.** (*a*) **prendre c. de qn**, to take (one's) leave of s.o. (*b*) leave (of absence); **en c.**, on leave; **c. de maladie**, sick leave (*c*) holiday, *NAm:* vacation; **trois jours de c.**, three days off; **c. payé**, paid holiday **2.** (*a*) (notice of) dismissal; **donner son c. à qn**, to give s.o. his, her, notice; **demander son c.**, to give in one's notice (*b*) **donner c. à un locataire**, to give a tenant notice to quit **3.** authorization; release (of wine from bond); **c. de navigation**, clearance certificate.

congédier [kɔ̃ʒedje] *vtr* (*impf & pr sub* **n. congédiions**) to dismiss (s.o.).

congélateur [kɔ̃ʒelatœr] *nm* deep freeze; freezer (compartment).

congélation [kɔ̃ʒelasjɔ̃] *nf* freezing.

congeler [kɔ̃ʒle] (**il congèle**) to freeze (water); to deep-freeze (food); **viande congelée**, frozen meat **2. se c.**, to freeze.

congénère [kɔ̃ʒenɛr] *nm* fellow creature.

congénital, -aux [kɔ̃ʒenital, -o] *a* congenital.

congère [kɔ̃ʒɛr] *nf* snowdrift.

congestion [kɔ̃ʒɛstjɔ̃] *nf Med:* congestion; **c. cérébrale**, stroke; **c. pulmonaire**, pneumonia.

congestionner [kɔ̃ʒɛstjɔne] *vtr* **1.** to flush (face); **être congestionné**, to be flushed **2.** (*of cars*) to block (the street).

Congo [kɔ̃go] *Prnm Geog:* the Congo. **congolais, -aise** *a & n* Congolese.

congratuler [kɔ̃gratyle] *vtr Iron: F:* to congratulate.

congre [kɔ̃gr] *nm* conger (eel).

congrégation [kɔ̃gregasjɔ̃] *nf* congregation.

congrès [kɔ̃grɛ] *nm* congress.

congressiste [kɔ̃grɛsist] *n* participant at a congress.

conifère [kɔnifɛr] *nm Bot:* conifer.

conique [kɔnik] *a* cone-shaped, conical.

conjecture [kɔ̃ʒɛktyr] *nf* conjecture.

conjecturer [kɔ̃ʒɛktyre] *vtr* to conjecture.

conjoint [kɔ̃ʒwɛ̃] *a* 1. united, joint 2. married; *nm Jur:* **les conjoints,** husband and wife. **conjointement** *adv* (con)jointly.

conjonction [kɔ̃ʒɔ̃ksjɔ̃] *nf* conjunction. **conjonctif, -ive** *a* conjunctive.

conjoncture [kɔ̃ʒɔ̃ktyr] *nf* conjuncture; (combination of) circumstances.

conjugaison [kɔ̃ʒygɛzɔ̃] *nf* conjugation.

conjugal, -aux [kɔ̃ʒygal, -o] *a* conjugal; **vie conjugale,** married life. **conjugalement** *adv* **vivre c.,** to live as a married couple.

conjuguer [kɔ̃ʒyge] *vtr* 1. *Gram:* to conjugate 2. to combine (efforts).

conjuration [kɔ̃ʒyrasjɔ̃] *nf* conspiracy.

conjuré, -ée [kɔ̃ʒyre] *n* conspirator.

conjurer [kɔ̃ʒyre] *vtr & i* 1. (*a*) to exorcise (demon) (*b*) to ward off (danger) 2. **c. qn de faire qch,** to entreat, to beg, s.o. to do sth 3. **se c.,** to conspire (**contre,** against).

connaissance [kɔnɛsɑ̃s] *nf* 1. (*a*) acquaintance, knowledge; **prendre c. de qch,** to study, to enquire into, sth; **avoir c. de qch,** to be aware of sth; **pas à ma c.,** not to my knowledge; **en c. de cause,** with full knowledge of the facts (*b*) **une personne de ma c.,** someone I know; an acquaintance; **faire c. avec qn, faire la c. de qn,** to meet s.o.; **en pays de c.,** (i) among familiar faces (ii) on familiar ground (*c*) **c'est une de mes connaissances,** he is an acquaintance of mine 2. (*a*) knowledge, understanding; **avoir la c. de plusieurs langues,** to know several languages (*b*) *pl* learning, attainments; **il a des connaissances,** he's very knowledgeable 3. consciousness; **perdre c.,** to faint; **sans c.,** unconscious; **reprendre c.,** to regain consciousness, to come round.

connaissement [kɔnɛsmɑ̃] *nm Com:* bill of lading.

connaisseur, -euse [kɔnɛsœr, -øz] 1. *a* expert; critical 2. *n* expert, connoisseur.

connaître [kɔnɛtr] *vtr* (*prp* **connaissant;** *pp* **connu;** *pr ind* **je connais, il connaît;** *impf* **je connaissais;** *fu* **je connaîtrai**) 1. to know; to be acquainted with (sth); to be familiar with (sth); to be aware of (the circumstances); **il ne connaît pas l'amour,** he has no experience of love; **faire c. qch,** to bring sth to light; **cette région connaît actuellement une famine,** the region is now experiencing a famine; **connaissez-vous la nouvelle?** have you heard the news? **ni vu ni connu,** no one will be any the wiser; **il en connaît bien d'autres,** he has plenty more tricks up his sleeve 2. (*a*) to be acquainted with (s.o.); **c. qn de vue,** to know s.o. by sight; **c'est connu!** I've heard that one before! *F:* **ça me connaît, le foot,** I know all there is

to know about football (*b*) to make (s.o.'s) acquaintance; **ils se sont connus en 1970,** they met in 1970; **je vous le ferai c.,** I'll introduce him to you 3. to be versed in, to have a thorough knowledge of (sth); **il n'y connaît rien,** he doesn't know a thing about it, *F:* he hasn't a clue about it 4. (*a*) **se c. en qch,** to know all about sth; *F:* **il s'y connaît,** he's an expert (*b*) **il ne se connaît plus,** he has lost control of himself; **il ne se connaît plus de joie,** he is beside himself with joy.

connecter [kɔnɛkte] *vtr El:* to connect.

connerie [kɔnri] *nf P:* (piece of) damned stupidity.

connétable [kɔnetabl] *nm Hist:* High Constable.

connexion [kɔnɛksjɔ̃] *nf* connection.

connivence [kɔnivɑ̃s] *nf* connivance, complicity.

connu [kɔny] 1. *a* well-known; famous 2. *nm* **le c. et l'inconnu,** the known and the unknown.

conquérir [kɔ̃kerir] *vtr* (*conj like* ACQUÉRIR) (*a*) to conquer, subdue (country) (*b*) to win (over) (s.o.). **conquérant** *a* 1. conquering; swaggering (air) 2. *n* **Guillaume le C.,** William the Conqueror.

conquête [kɔ̃kɛt] *nf* 1. (act of) conquest; **faire la c. d'un pays,** to conquer a country; **faire la c. de qn,** to win s.o. over 2. conquered territory.

consacrer [kɔ̃sakre] *vtr* 1. (*a*) to consecrate (altar); to ordain (priest) (*b*) to dedicate (one's life to God); to devote (one's time); **combien de temps pouvez-vous me c.?** how much time can you spare me? 2. to establish, to sanction. **consacré** *a* sanctioned, established (custom); accepted (phrase).

conscience [kɔ̃sjɑ̃s] *nf* 1. consciousness; *Phil:* self-consciousness; **perdre c.,** to lose consciousness; **avoir c. de qch.,** to be aware of sth; **prendre c. de qch,** to realize sth 2. (*a*) conscience; **mauvaise c.,** guilty conscience; **avoir qch sur la c.,** to have sth on one's conscience; **faire qch par acquit de c.,** to do sth for conscience' sake (*b*) conscientiousness; **c. professionnelle,** professional integrity; **avec c.,** conscientiously. **consciencieux, -ieuse** *a* conscientious. **consciencieusement** *adv* conscientiously. **conscient** *a* conscious; (fully) aware (**de,** of). **consciemment** *adv* consciously, knowingly.

conscription [kɔ̃skripsjɔ̃] *nf Mil:* conscription, *NAm:* draft.

conscrit [kɔ̃skri] *nm Mil:* conscript, *NAm:* draftee.

consécration [kɔ̃sekrasjɔ̃] *nf* consecration; ratification; establishing (of custom).

consécutif, -ive [kɔ̃sekytif, -iv] *a* consecutive; **c. à,** following on. **consécutivement** *adv* consecutively.

conseil [kɔ̃sɛj] *nm* 1. counsel; (piece of) advice; **donner c. à qn,** to advise s.o.; **demander c. à qn,** to consult s.o.; **quelques conseils,** a few tips 2. **avocat-c.,** legal consultant; **ingénieur-c.,** consulting engineer 3. council, committee; **tenir c.,** to hold (a) council; **le c. des ministres,** the Cabinet; **c. municipal =** borough council; town council; *Com:* **c. d'administration,** board of directors; **c. de guerre,** (i) council of war (ii) court-martial; **c. de discipline,** disciplinary committee; **c. de sécurité,** Security Council.

conseiller[1] [kɔ̃seje] *vtr* to advise; to recommend; **il est conseillé de,** it is advisable to; **il est conseillé aux parents de,** parents are advised to.

conseiller[2], **-ère** [kɔ̃seje, -jɛr] *n* 1. counsellor, ad-

viser; **c. fiscal,** tax consultant **2. c. municipal,** town councillor; **c. général** = county councillor.
consentement [kɔ̃sɑ̃tmɑ̃] *nm* consent.
consentir [kɔ̃sɑ̃tir] *v (conj like* MENTIR) **1.** *vi* to consent, agree **2.** *vtr* **c. un prêt,** to grant a loan. **consentant** *a* consenting; agreeing; **elle est consentante,** she's willing.
conséquence [kɔ̃sekɑ̃s] *nf (a)* consequence, outcome, result; **qu'est-ce que cela aura pour c.?** what will be the effect of it? **cela ne tire pas à c.,** it's of no consequence; *adv phr* **en c.,** accordingly; *prep phr* **en c. de,** in consequence of *(b)* inference; **tirer une c. de qch,** to draw an inference from sth *(c)* importance; **personne sans c.,** person of no importance. **conséquent** *a* consistent; consequent; important; **par c.,** consequently, therefore.
conservateur, -trice [kɔ̃sɛrvatœr, -tris] **1.** *n (a)* keeper, warden; **c. d'un musée,** curator, keeper, of a museum; **c. de bibliothèque,** librarian *(b) Pol:* conservative **2.** *a (a)* conservative *(b)* preserving (process).
conservation [kɔ̃sɛrvasjɔ̃] *nf* **1.** *(a)* conserving; preserving *(b)* preservation (of buildings) **2. meubles d'une belle c.,** well preserved furniture.
conservatisme [kɔ̃sɛrvatism] *nm* conservatism.
conservatoire [kɔ̃sɛrvatwar] *nm* school, academy (of music, of drama); **le C. (de Paris),** the Paris conservatoire.
conserve [kɔ̃sɛrv] *nf* **1.** preserve; preserved, tinned, canned, food; **boîte de c.,** tin, can; **conserves au vinaigre,** pickles; **bœuf de c.,** corned beef; **mettre en c.,** to tin, to can **2.** *Nau:* consort; **naviguer de c.,** to sail in company.
conserver [kɔ̃sɛrve] *vtr* **1.** *(a)* to preserve, to conserve (fruit, meat) *(b)* to preserve (building) **2.** to keep, retain (rights); **c. sa tête,** to keep one's head, to remain cool **3. se c.,** *(of goods)* to keep.
conserverie [kɔ̃sɛrvəri] *nf* canning factory.
considérable [kɔ̃siderabl] *a* **1.** eminent **2.** considerable; extensive (property); significant (change). **considérablement** *adv* considerably, significantly.
considération [kɔ̃siderasjɔ̃] *nf* **1.** *(a)* consideration; attention, thought; **avec, sans, c.,** considerately, inconsiderately; **prendre qch en c.,** to take sth into consideration, into account; **en c. de,** on account of, because of; **sans c. de,** regardless of *(b) pl* réflexions **2.** reason, motive, consideration **3.** regard, esteem, consideration; *Corr:* **veuillez agréer l'assurance de ma haute c.,** I am yours very truly.
considérer [kɔ̃sidere] *vtr* **1.** *(je considère; je considérerai)* **1.** to consider; **tout bien considéré,** all things considered; **considérant que,** considering that **2.** to contemplate, gaze on **3.** to regard, to deem; **on le considère beaucoup,** he is highly thought of; **se c. comme responsable,** to hold oneself responsible.
consignataire [kɔ̃siɲater] *n Com:* consignee.
consigne [kɔ̃siɲ] *nf* **1.** order(s), instructions **2.** *Mil:* confinement (to barracks); *Sch:* detention **3.** left-luggage (office); **c. automatique,** left-luggage lockers **4.** deposit (on bottle).
consigner [kɔ̃siɲe] *vtr* **1.** to put a deposit (on a bottle) **2.** to record (fact) **3.** *(a)* to confine (soldier) to barracks; to keep in (pupil) *(b)* to refuse admittance to (s.o.); **c. sa porte à qn,** to bar one's door to s.o. **4.** to put (luggage) in the left-luggage office.

consistance [kɔ̃sistɑ̃s] *nf* **1.** *(a)* consistency; **prendre c.,** to thicken *(b)* stability (of mind); **sans c.,** spineless **2. bruit sans c.,** unfounded, groundless, rumour. **consistant** *a* firm; thick (paint); substantial (meal).
consister [kɔ̃siste] *vi* **c. en qch,** to consist of sth; **c. dans qch,** to consist in sth; **c. à faire qch,** to consist in doing sth.
consolation [kɔ̃sɔlasjɔ̃] *nf* consolation, comfort.
consoler [kɔ̃sɔle] *vtr* **1.** to console, comfort **2. se c. d'une perte,** to get over a loss. **consolant** *a* consoling, comforting.
consolidation [kɔ̃sɔlidasjɔ̃] *nf* consolidation, strengthening.
consolider [kɔ̃sɔlide] *vtr* **1.** to consolidate, strengthen **2.** to fund (debt) **3. se c.,** to consolidate, to strengthen.
consommateur, -trice [kɔ̃sɔmatœr, -tris] *n* consumer; customer (in café).
consommation [kɔ̃sɔmasjɔ̃] *nf* **1.** consummation (of work, marriage); perpetration (of crime) **2.** consumption (of petrol, electricity); use; **faire une grande c. de papier,** to go through a lot of paper; **société de c.,** consumer society **3.** drink (in café).
consommé [kɔ̃sɔme] **1.** *a* consummate (skill); accomplished (writer) **2.** *nm Cu:* clear soup, consommé.
consommer [kɔ̃sɔme] *vtr* **1.** to consummate, accomplish; to perpetrate (crime); to consummate (marriage) **2.** to consume, use up (petrol, electricity); to eat (food) **3.** *(a)* **voiture qui consomme,** car heavy on petrol *(b)* **vi c. au bar,** to have a drink in, at, the bar **4. ce plat se consomme froid,** this dish is eaten cold.
consonne [kɔ̃sɔn] *nf Ling:* consonant.
consortium [kɔ̃sɔrsjɔm] *nm* consortium.
conspiration [kɔ̃spirasjɔ̃] *nf* conspiracy, plot.
conspirer [kɔ̃spire] *vi* to conspire, plot (**contre,** against); **c. à faire qch,** to conspire to do sth. **conspirateur, -trice 1.** *a* conspiring, conspiratorial **2.** *n* conspirator, conspirer.
conspuer [kɔ̃spɥe] *vtr* to boo (play, speaker).
constance [kɔ̃stɑ̃s] *nf* constancy; steadfastness. **constant, -ante 1.** *a (a)* constant *(b)* firm, unshaken **2.** *nf Mth: etc:* constant. **constamment** *adv* constantly.
constat [kɔ̃sta] *nm* official statement; **c. à l'amiable,** unofficial account (of accident); **c. d'huissier,** affidavit (made by a process server).
constatation [kɔ̃statasjɔ̃] *nf* **1.** verification, establishment (of fact); noting; recording **2.** *pl* findings (of an enquiry).
constater [kɔ̃state] *vtr* **1.** to establish, note (fact); **c. une erreur,** to find a mistake; **vous pouvez c. vous-même,** you can see for yourself **2.** to state, record (sth); to certify (a death).
constellation [kɔ̃stɛlasjɔ̃] *nf* constellation. **constellé** *a* spangled, studded (**de,** with).
consternation [kɔ̃stɛrnasjɔ̃] *nf* consternation, dismay.
consterner [kɔ̃stɛrne] *vtr* to dismay; to fill with consternation.
constipation [kɔ̃stipasjɔ̃] *nf* constipation.
constiper [kɔ̃stipe] *vtr* to constipate. **constipé** *a (a) Med:* constipated *(b) F:* stiff, ill at ease.

constituer [kɔ̃stitɥe] *vtr* **1.** (*a*) to constitute; to form, make (up) (*b*) to set up, institute (committee); to incorporate (a society); to form (ministry) **2.** (*a*) to constitute, to appoint; **c. qn son héritier,** to make s.o. one's heir; **se c. prisonnier,** to give oneself up (to the police) (*b*) **c. une rente à qn,** to settle an annuity on s.o. **constituant** *a* constituent. **constitué** *a* **bien c.,** of sound constitution; healthy. **constitutif, -ive** *a* constituent, component.

constitution [kɔ̃stitysjɔ̃] *nf* **1.** constituting, establishing; forming (of committee); settlement (of dowry) **2.** *Med: Pol:* constitution **3.** composition (of air, water). **constitutionnel, -elle** *a* constitutional.

constructeur, -trice [kɔ̃stryktœr, -tris] *n* constructor, maker, engineer; builder; (car) manufacturer.

construction [kɔ̃stryksjɔ̃] *nf* **1.** construction; constructing, building, erecting; **matériaux de c.,** building materials; **c. navale,** shipbuilding **2.** building. **constructif, -ive** *a* constructive.

construire [kɔ̃strɥir] *vtr* (*conj like* CONDUIRE) **1.** to construct; to build; to make **2.** to assemble (machine); to construct (sentence); to build up (theory).

consul [kɔ̃syl] *nm* consul. **consulaire** *a* consular. **consulat** [kɔ̃syla] *nm* consulate.

consultation [kɔ̃syltasjɔ̃] *nf* (*a*) consultation, conference; **entrer en c. avec qn,** to consult with s.o. (*b*) advice, opinion (*c*) *Med:* visit to a doctor; **cabinet de c.,** consulting room, surgery; **heures de c.,** surgery hours. **consultatif, -ive** *a* consultative, advisory.

consulter [kɔ̃sylte] **1.** *vtr* to consult; **c. un médecin,** to take medical advice; **ils se sont consultés,** they put their heads together; **ouvrage à c.,** work of reference **2.** *vi Med:* to hold surgery.

consumer [kɔ̃syme] *vtr* **1.** to consume; to burn; **consumé par l'ambition,** eaten up with ambition **2.** to waste (time, fortune). **se c.,** to burn; to waste away.

contact [kɔ̃takt] *nm* **1.** contact, touch; **prendre c. avec qn,** to get in touch with s.o., to contact s.o.; **prise de c.,** preliminary contact; first meeting; **lentille, verre, de c.,** contact lens **2.** *El:* (*a*) connection, contact; *Aut:* **clef de c.,** ignition key; **mettre le c.,** to switch on; **couper le c.,** to switch off (*b*) switch. **contacter** [kɔ̃takte] *vtr* to contact (s.o.).

contagion [kɔ̃taʒjɔ̃] *nf* contagion; *Fig:* infectiousness (of laughter). **contagieux, -ieuse** *a* contagious; *Fig:* infectious (laugh).

contamination [kɔ̃taminasjɔ̃] *nf* contamination. **contaminer** [kɔ̃tamine] *vtr* to contaminate.

conte [kɔ̃t] *nm* story, tale; **c. de fées,** fairytale.

contemplation [kɔ̃tɑ̃plasjɔ̃] *nf* contemplation. **contemplatif, -ive** *a* contemplative.

contempler [kɔ̃tɑ̃ple] *vtr* to contemplate, to gaze at (sth).

contemporain, -aine [kɔ̃tɑ̃pɔrɛ̃, -ɛn] **1.** *a* (*a*) contemporary (*b*) contemporaneous (**de,** with) **2.** *n* contemporary.

contenance [kɔ̃tnɑ̃s] *nf* **1.** capacity, content (of bottle) **2.** countenance, bearing; **faire bonne c.,** to show a bold front; **perdre c.,** to lose face.

contenant [kɔ̃tnɑ̃] *nm,* **conteneur** [kɔ̃tnœr] *nm* container.

contenir [kɔ̃tnir] *vtr* (*conj like* TENIR) **1.** to contain; to hold (quantity, number); (*of theatre*) to seat; **lettre contenant chèque,** letter enclosing cheque **2.** to restrain; to hold (crowd) in check; to suppress (anger); to hold back (tears) **3.** **se c.,** to contain oneself; to control one's emotions.

content [kɔ̃tɑ̃] **1.** *a* (*a*) content (*b*) satisfied, pleased (**de,** with); **il est très c. ici,** he's very happy here (*c*) pleased; **je suis très c. de vous voir,** I am very pleased to see you; **il ne sera pas c.,** he won't like it (*d*) glad **2.** *nm* **manger tout son c.,** to eat one's fill.

contentement [kɔ̃tɑ̃tmɑ̃] *nm* (*a*) contentment (*b*) satisfaction (**de,** at, with).

contenter [kɔ̃tɑ̃te] **1.** *vtr* to content, satisfy (s.o.); to gratify (curiosity) **2.** **se c. de (faire) qch,** to be satisfied with (doing) sth.

contentieux, -ieuse [kɔ̃tɑ̃sjø, -jøz] **1.** *a* contentious **2.** *nm Adm:* (*a*) matters in dispute; litigation (*b*) legal department.

contenu [kɔ̃tny] **1.** *a* restrained, suppressed (passion, style) **2.** *nm* contents (of parcel); content (of letter).

conter [kɔ̃te] *vtr* to tell, relate; **en c. de belles à qn,** to take s.o. in; **elle ne s'en laisse pas c.,** you can't fool her.

contestation [kɔ̃tɛstasjɔ̃] *nf* **1.** contesting, dispute **2.** *Pol:* protest.

contester [kɔ̃tɛste] **1.** *vtr* to contest, dispute (point, right); **point contesté,** controversial point; **je lui conteste le droit,** I question his right **2.** *vi* to take issue (**sur,** over); *Pol:* to protest. **contestable** *a* debatable. **contestataire 1.** *a* contesting; anti-establishment **2.** *n* protester. **conteste** *adv phr* **sans c.,** indisputably, unquestionably.

conteur, -euse [kɔ̃tœr, -øz] *n* **1.** narrator **2.** storywriter.

contexte [kɔ̃tɛkst] *nm* context.

contiguïté [kɔ̃tigɥite] *nf* adjacency, proximity (of house). **contigu, -uë** *a* contiguous, adjacent; related (ideas).

continence [kɔ̃tinɑ̃s] *nf* continence. **continent¹** *a* continent.

continent² [kɔ̃tinɑ̃] *nm* **1.** continent **2.** mainland. **continental, -aux** *a* continental.

contingence [kɔ̃tɛ̃ʒɑ̃s] *nf Phil:* contingency. **contingent 1.** *a* contingent **2.** *nm* (*a*) *Mil:* contingent; **le c. annuel,** the annual intake (*b*) quota (*c*) share.

contingenter [kɔ̃tɛ̃ʒɑ̃te] *vtr* **1.** to fix quotas for (imports) **2.** to distribute (films) according to a quota.

continuation [kɔ̃tinɥasjɔ̃] *nf* continuation.

continuer [kɔ̃tinɥe] *vtr & i* (*a*) to continue; to carry on (tradition); to go on (doing sth); **c. sa route,** to continue on one's way; **continuez!** go on! (*b*) to extend. **continu** *a* continuous, unceasing. **continuel, -elle** *a* continual, unceasing. **continuellement** *adv* continually. **continûment** *adv* continuously.

continuité [kɔ̃tinɥite] *nf* continuity; continuation.

contorsion [kɔ̃tɔrsjɔ̃] *nf* contortion.

contorsionner (se) [səkɔ̃tɔrsjɔne] *vpr* to contort one's body.

contorsionniste [kɔ̃tɔrsjɔnist] *n* contortionist.

contour [kɔ̃tur] *nm* 1. outline 2. contour (line).

contourner [kɔ̃turne] *vtr* to pass round, skirt, bypass (hill, wood); **c. la loi**, to get round the law.

contraception [kɔ̃trasεpsjɔ̃] *nf* contraception. **contraceptif, -ive** 1. *a* contraceptive 2. *nm* contraceptive.

contracter[1] [kɔ̃trakte] *vtr* 1. (*a*) to contract (alliance) (*b*) to incur (debt) (*c*) **c. une assurance**, to take out an insurance policy 2. to acquire (habit); to catch (disease).

contracter[2] *vtr* 1. to contract, to draw together; **traits contractés par la douleur**, features drawn with pain 2. **se c.**, (*of heart*) to contract; (*of muscle*) to tense up, to contract. **contracté** *a* (*a*) *Gram:* contracted (*b*) tense (muscles).

contraction [kɔ̃traksjɔ̃] *nf* contraction.

contractuel, -elle [kɔ̃traktɥel] *n* contract employee; = traffic warden.

contradiction [kɔ̃tradiksjɔ̃] *nf* 1. contradiction; **être en c.**, to contradict; **esprit de c.**, contrariness 2. inconsistency, contradiction. **contradictoire** *a* contradictory (**à**, to); inconsistent (**à**, with); **débat c.**, debate.

contraindre [kɔ̃trɛ̃dr] *vtr* (*conj like* CRAINDRE) 1. to constrain; to restrain 2. to compel, to force, to constrain; **je fus contraint d'obéir**, I was obliged to obey 3. **se c.**, to restrain oneself. **contraignant** *a* restricting, constraining. **contraint** *a* constrained; forced (smile); stiff (manner); **c. et forcé**, under duress.

contrainte [kɔ̃trɛ̃t] *nf* 1. constraint; restraint; **parler sans c.**, to speak freely 2. compulsion, coercion; **agir sous la c.**, to act under duress.

contraire [kɔ̃trεr] 1. *a* contrary; opposite (direction); conflicting (interest); **sauf avis c.**, unless you hear to the contrary; **c. au règlement**, against the rule 2. *a* adverse; **le sort lui est c.**, fate is against him; **le climat lui est c.**, the climate does not agree with him 3. *nm* opposite, contrary; **c'est le c.**, it's the other way round; **je ne vous dis pas le c.**, I'm not denying it; **au c.**, on the contrary; **au c. des autres**, unlike the others. **contrairement** *adv* **c. à**, contrary to; unlike.

contrarier [kɔ̃trarje] *vtr* (*impf & pr sub* n. **contrariions**) 1. to thwart, oppose (plans) 2. to annoy, bother. **contrariant** *a* annoying.

contrariété [kɔ̃trarjete] *nf* annoyance.

contraste [kɔ̃trast] *nm* contrast; **mettre en c.**, to contrast; **en c. avec**, in contrast to.

contraster [kɔ̃traste] *vtr & i* to contrast. **contrasté** *a* contrasted, contrasting.

contrat [kɔ̃tra] *nm* contract, agreement; **c. de mariage**, marriage settlement.

contravention [kɔ̃travɑ̃sjɔ̃] *nf* (*a*) contravention, infringement (of law) (*b*) police offence (*c*) *Aut:* fine; (parking) ticket.

contre [kɔ̃tr] 1. *prep* (*a*) against; **se fâcher c. qn**, to get angry with s.o.; **c. son habitude**, contrary to his usual practice; **l'Angleterre c. l'Irlande**, England versus Ireland; **je n'ai rien c.**, I have nothing against it, him, etc (*b*) from; **s'abriter c. la pluie**, to shelter from the rain; **sirop c. la toux**, cough mixture (*c*) (in exchange) for; **livraison c. remboursement**, cash on delivery (*d*) to; **parier à cinq c. un**, to bet five to one

(*e*) close to, by; **s'appuyer c. un mur**, to lean against a wall; **sa maison est tout c. la mienne**, his house adjoins mine 2. *adv* against; **parler pour et c.**, to speak for and against; **la maison est tout c.**, the house is close by 3. *nm* (*a*) **disputer le pour et le c.**, to argue the pros and cons; *adv phr* **par c.**, on the other hand (*b*) *Cards:* double.

NOTE: *In the hyphenated nouns and adjectives below,* **contre** *remains inv; for irreg pl forms consult the second component.*

contre-allée [kɔ̃trale] *nf* side path; service road.

contre-amiral [kɔ̃tramiral] *nm* rear-admiral.

contre-attaque [kɔ̃tratak] *nf* counter attack.

contre-attaquer [kɔ̃tratake] *vtr & i* to counter-attack.

contrebalancer [kɔ̃trəbalɑ̃se] *vtr* (**n. contrebalançons**) to counterbalance, offset.

contrebande [kɔ̃trəbɑ̃d] *nf* 1. contraband, smuggling 2. contraband goods.

contrebandier, -ière [kɔ̃trəbɑ̃dje, -jεr] *n* smuggler.

contrebas (en) [ɑ̃kɔ̃trəba] *adv phr* (lower) down; below; **le café est en c. de la rue**, the café is below street level.

contrebasse[kɔ̃trəbas] *nf Mus:* (*a*) (double) bass (*b*) (double) bass player.

contrebasson [kɔ̃trəbasɔ̃] *nm Mus:* contrabassoon.

contrecarrer [kɔ̃trəkare] *vtr* to thwart (s.o.).

contrecœur (à) [akɔ̃trəkœr] *adv phr* unwillingly, reluctantly, grudgingly.

contrecoup [kɔ̃trəku] *nm* consequence (of action); repercussion.

contre-courant (à) [akɔ̃trəkurɑ̃] *adv phr* against the current.

contredire [kɔ̃trədir] *vtr* (*pr ind* v. **contredisez**; *otherwise like* DIRE) to contradict; to be at variance with.

contredit [kɔ̃trədi] *adv phr* **sans c.**, indisputably, unquestionably.

contrée [kɔ̃tre] *nf* (geographical) region.

contre-espionnage [kɔ̃trεspjɔnaʒ] *nm* counter-espionage.

contre-expertise [kɔ̃trεkspεrtiz] *nf* counter-valuation.

contrefaçon [kɔ̃trəfasɔ̃] *nf* 1. counterfeiting 2. counterfeit, forgery, fraudulent imitation.

contrefaire [kɔ̃trəfεr] *vtr* (*conj like* FAIRE) 1. (*a*) to imitate (*b*) *O:* to feign (*c*) to disguise (one's voice) 2. to counterfeit (coin).

contrefort [kɔ̃trəfɔr] *nm* 1. *Arch:* (close) buttress 2. *Geog:* spur (of mountain); *pl* foot-hills 3. stiffening (of shoe).

contre-haut (en) [ɑ̃kɔ̃trəo] *adv phr* higher up; above.

contre-indication [kɔ̃trɛ̃dikasjɔ̃] *nf Med:* contra-indication.

contre-indiquer [kɔ̃trɛ̃dike] *vtr Med:* to contra-indicate; **c'est contre-indiqué**, it's inadvisable.

contre-interrogatoire [kɔ̃trɛ̃terɔgatwar] *nm* cross-examination.

contre-jour (à) [akɔ̃trəʒur] *adv phr* against the light; **assis à c.-j.**, sitting with one's back to the light.

contremaître, -tresse [kɔ̃trəmɛtr̥, -trɛs] *n* foreman, forewoman.

contrepartie [kɔ̃trəparti] *nf* compensation; **en c.**, in return.

contre-performance [kɔ̃trəpɛrfɔrmɑ̃s] *nf* substandard performance.

contre-pied [kɔ̃trəpje] *nm* **1.** prendre le c.-p., to take the opposite course **(de,** to); **il prend toujours le c.-p. de ce qu'on lui dit,** he always does the opposite of what he's told **2.** *Sp:* prendre à c.-p., to wrong-foot (s.o.).

contre(-)plaqué [kɔ̃trəplake] *nm* plywood.

contrepoids [kɔ̃trəpwa] *nm* (a) counterbalance, counterweight (b) balancing pole (of rope dancer).

contre-poil (à) [akɔ̃trəpwal] *adv phr F:* **prendre qn à c.-p.,** to rub s.o. up the wrong way.

contrepoint [kɔ̃trəpwɛ̃] *nm Mus:* counterpoint.

contrepoison [kɔ̃trəpwazɔ̃] *nm* antidote.

contrer [kɔ̃tre] **1.** *vtr Box:* to counter (blow) **2.** *vtr & i Cards:* to double.

contre-révolution [kɔ̃trərevɔlysjɔ̃] *nf* counter-revolution.

contresens [kɔ̃trəsɑ̃s] *nm* **1.** misinterpretation; mistranslation **2.** wrong way (of material) **3.** à c., in the wrong way, direction; **à c. de,** in the opposite direction to.

contresigner [kɔ̃trəsiɲe] *vtr* to countersign.

contretemps [kɔ̃trətɑ̃] *nm* **1.** mishap, hitch **2.** *adv phr* arriver à c., to arrive at the wrong moment; **jouer à c.,** to play out of time.

contre-ut [kɔ̃tryt] *nm Mus:* top C.

contre-valeur [kɔ̃trəvalœr] *nf Fin:* exchange value.

contrevenant, -ante [kɔ̃trəvənɑ̃, -ɑ̃t] *n* offender.

contrevenir [kɔ̃trəvnir] *v ind tr (conj like* VENIR) to contravene, infringe.

contrevent [kɔ̃trəvɑ̃] *nm* (outside) shutter.

contre(-)vérité [kɔ̃trəverite] *nf* untruth, falsehood.

contre-visite [kɔ̃trəvizit] *nf* second (medical) opinion.

contribuable [kɔ̃tribɥabl] *n* taxpayer.

contribuer [kɔ̃tribɥe] *vi* **1.** to contribute **2.** to contribute, conduce.

contribution [kɔ̃tribysjɔ̃] *nf* **1.** tax; rate; **(bureau des) contributions,** tax office **2.** contribution, share.

contrit [kɔ̃tri] *a* contrite, penitent.

contrition [kɔ̃trisjɔ̃] *nf* contrition, penitence.

contrôle [kɔ̃trol] *nm* **1.** *Mil: etc:* roll, list, register **2.** (a) checking (of information) (b) *Adm:* inspection, supervision; *Th:* checking (of tickets) **3.** (a) authority (b) c. de soi-même, self-control (c) c. des naissances, birth control.

contrôler [kɔ̃trole] *vtr* **1.** to inspect (work); to check (tickets); to examine (passport); to verify, check (up) (information) **2.** (a) to control, supervise (operations) (b) to control (s.o.); **se c.,** to control oneself.

contrôleur, -euse [kɔ̃trolœr, -øz] *n* inspector.

contrordre [kɔ̃trɔrdr̥] *nm* counterorder.

controverse [kɔ̃trɔvɛrs] *nf* controversy. **controversé** *a* much debated.

contumace [kɔ̃tymas] *nf Jur:* condamné par c., sentenced in his absence.

contusion [kɔ̃tyzjɔ̃] *nf* contusion, bruise.

contusionner [kɔ̃tyzjɔne] *vtr* to bruise.

convaincre [kɔ̃vɛ̃kr̥] *vtr (conj like* VAINCRE) **1.** to convince **(de,** of); **se laisser c.,** to let oneself be persuaded **2.** to convict (s.o.), to prove (s.o.) guilty **(de,** of). **convaincant** *a* convincing. **convaincu** *a* convinced; **d'un ton c.,** with conviction.

convalescence [kɔ̃valesɑ̃s] *nf* convalescence; **être en c.,** to be convalescing; **maison de c.,** convalescent home. **convalescent, -ente** *a & n* convalescent.

convection [kɔ̃vɛksjɔ̃] *nf Ph:* convection.

convenable [kɔ̃vnabl] *a* **1.** suitable, fitting, appropriate, proper **2.** decent, respectable; **peu c.,** unacceptable **3.** *F:* adequate (salary). **convenablement** *adv* suitably, appropriately; correctly, properly; adequately.

convenance [kɔ̃vnɑ̃s] *nf* **1.** suitability, fitness; appropriateness; **mariage de c.,** marriage of convenience; **trouver qch à sa c.,** to find sth suitable **2.** les **convenances,** proprieties, etiquette.

convenir [kɔ̃vnir] *vi (conj like* VENIR) **1.** *(conj with* avoir) (a) to suit, fit; **si cela vous convient,** if that suits you; **c'est exactement ce qui me convient,** it's just what I need (b) *impers* il convient de, it is advisable to; **ce qu'il convient de faire,** the right thing to do **2.** *(conj with* avoir, *and with* être *to denote a state of agreement)* (a) to agree; **c. de qch,** to agree on, about, sth; **ils sont convenus,** they are agreed; *impers* il fut convenu que, it was agreed that; **comme convenu,** as agreed (b) **c. de qch,** to admit sth; **j'ai eu tort, j'en conviens,** I admit I was wrong. **convenu** *a* agreed (price); appointed (time); **c'est c.!** that's settled!

convention [kɔ̃vɑ̃sjɔ̃] *nf* **1.** convention; covenant, agreement; **c. collective** = collective bargaining **2.** les **conventions (sociales),** the social conventions; **de c.,** conventional. **conventionnel, -elle** *a* conventional.

convergence [kɔ̃vɛrʒɑ̃s] *nf* convergence. **convergent, -ente** *a* convergent.

converger [kɔ̃vɛrʒe] *vi* **(convergeant; ils convergeaient)** to converge.

conversation [kɔ̃vɛrsasjɔ̃] *nf* conversation, talk; **faire la c. à qn,** to chat with s.o.; **avoir de la c.,** to be a good conversationalist; **langage de la c.,** colloquial language.

converser [kɔ̃vɛrse] *vi* to converse **(avec,** with).

conversion [kɔ̃vɛrsjɔ̃] *nf* **1.** conversion (to a faith) **2.** conversion, change **(en,** into).

convertir [kɔ̃vɛrtir] *vtr* **1.** to convert **2.** to convert (sth into sth) **3. se c.,** to become converted (to a faith). **converti, -ie** **1.** *a* converted **2.** *n* convert. **convertible** **1.** *a* convertible **(en,** into) **2.** *nm* bed-settee.

convertisseur [kɔ̃vɛrtisœr] *nm El:* converter.

convexité [kɔ̃vɛksite] *nf* convexity. **convexe** *a* convex.

conviction [kɔ̃viksjɔ̃] *nf* conviction.

convier [kɔ̃vje] *vtr (impf & pr sub* n. **conviions)** to invite **(à,** to).

convive [kɔ̃viv] *n* guest (at table).

convocation [kɔ̃vɔkasjɔ̃] *nf* (a) convocation; inviting; convening (of assembly); *Jur:* summons (b) (letter of) notification to attend.

convoi [kɔ̃vwa] *nm* **1.** convoy **2. c. (funèbre),** funeral procession **3.** train, convoy; *Rail:* **c. de marchandises,** goods freight.

convoiter [kɔ̃vwate] *vtr* to covet, desire.

convoitise [kɔ̃vwatiz] *nf* covetousness; lust; **regard de c.,** covetous look.

convoquer [kɔ̃vɔke] *vtr* **1.** to summon, convoke (assembly); to convene (meeting) **2.** to invite (s.o.) to an interview; **le patron m'a convoqué dans son bureau,** the boss called me to his office.

convoyer [kɔ̃vwaje] *vtr* (je convoie, n. convoyons) to convoy, to escort (train, fleet).

convoyeur [kɔ̃vwajœr] *nm* (a) *Mil:* officer in charge of convoy; escort (b) escort, convoy (ship).

convulser [kɔ̃vylse] *vtr* to convulse. **convulsif, -ive** convulsive. **convulsivement** *adv* convulsively.

convulsion [kɔ̃vylsjɔ̃] *nf* convulsion.

convulsionner [kɔ̃vylsjɔne] *vtr* to convulse.

coopérateur, -trice [kɔɔperatœr, -tris] *n* cooperator.

coopération [kɔɔperasjɔ̃] *nf* (a) cooperation (b) = Voluntary Service Overseas.

coopérer [kɔɔpere] *vi* (je coopère; je coopérerai) to cooperate; to work together. **coopératif, -ive 1.** *a* cooperative **2.** *nf* cooperative (stores).

cooptation [kɔɔptasjɔ̃] *nf* co-option.

coopter [kɔɔpte] *vtr* to co-opt.

coordination [kɔɔrdinasjɔ̃] *nf* coordination.

coordonner [kɔɔrdɔne] *vtr* to coordinate. **coordonnateur, -trice 1.** *a* coordinating **2.** *n* (pers) coordinator. **coordonné, -ée 1.** *a* coordinated (movement); coordinate (clause) **2.** *nfpl* (a) *Mth:* coordinates (b) address and telephone number.

copain [kɔpɛ̃] *nm F:* friend, pal.

copeau [kɔpo] *nm* (wood) shaving; (metal) chip.

Copenhague [kɔpenag] *Prnf* Copenhagen.

copie [kɔpi] *nf* **1.** (a) copy; *Adm:* **pour c. conforme,** certified true copy (b) *Jour: Typ:* manuscript; copy (c) *Sch:* (i) fair copy (of exercise) (ii) (candidate's) paper (iii) double sheet (of paper) **2.** copy, reproduction (of picture); imitation (of style) **3.** *Cin:* (print) copy; print.

copier [kɔpje] *vtr* (*impf & pr sub* n. copiions) **1.** to copy, transcribe; **c. qch au propre,** to make a fair copy of sth **2.** to copy (picture); to imitate (style); *Sch:* to copy, to crib.

copieux, -ieuse [kɔpjø, -jøz] *a* copious; hearty (meal); generous (portion). **copieusement** *adv* copiously, heartily, generously.

copilote [kɔpilɔt] *nm Av:* copilot.

copine [kɔpin] *nf F:* (girl) friend; *cf* **copain.**

copiste [kɔpist] *n* copyist.

copropriété [kɔprɔpriete] *nf* joint ownership.

copulation [kɔpylasjɔ̃] *nf* copulation.

copuler [kɔpyle] *vtr* to copulate.

coq¹ [kɔk] *nm* (a) cock; **jeune c.,** cockerel; **le c. gaulois,** the French cockerel; **au chant du c.,** at cockcrow; **jambes de c.,** spindly legs; **vivre comme un c. en pâte,** to live in clover; **c. du village,** cock of the walk; *Box:* **poids c.,** bantam weight (b) cock, male (of birds); **c. faisan,** cock pheasant; **c. de bruyère,** capercaillie; wood grouse.

coq² *nm Nau:* **(maître-)c.,** (ship's) cook.

coq-à-l'âne [kɔkalɑn] *nm inv* sudden change of subject.

coque [kɔk] *nf* **1.** (a) shell (of egg); **œuf à la c.,** (soft-)boiled egg (b) shell, husk (of nut); **se renfermer dans sa c.,** to retire into one's shell (c) *Moll:* cockle **2.** hull (of ship); *Av:* fuselage; body (of car).

coquelet [kɔklɛ] *nm Cu:* cockerel.

coquelicot [kɔkliko] *nm Bot:* red poppy.

coqueluche [kɔklyʃ] *nf* whooping cough; **être la c. des femmes,** to be the ladies' idol.

coquet, -ette [kɔkɛ, -ɛt] **1.** *a* (a) coquettish, flirtatious (woman, smile) (b) smart, stylish (clothes); **elle est coquette,** (i) she likes pretty clothes (ii) she likes to look attractive; **fortune assez coquette,** tidy fortune **2.** *nf* **coquette,** flirt. **coquettement** *adv* smartly, stylishly (dressed).

coquetier [kɔktje] *nm* egg cup.

coquetterie [kɔketri] *nf* **1.** (a) coquetry, flirtatiousness (b) affectation (c) **avoir de la c. pour sa tenue,** to be fastidious about one's appearance **2.** smartness (of dress).

coquillage [kɔkijaʒ] *nm* **1.** shellfish **2.** (empty) shell (of shellfish).

coquille [kɔkij] *nf* **1.** shell (of snail, oyster) **2.** (a) **c. Saint-Jacques,** (i) scallop (ii) scallop shell (b) (scallop-shaped) dish **3.** (a) shell (of egg, nut); (of boat) **c. de noix,** cockleshell (b) **c. de beurre,** whorl of butter (c) *Typ:* misprint, literal (d) *Med:* spinal plaster.

coquillettes [kɔkijɛt] *nfpl* pasta shells.

coquin, -ine [kɔkɛ̃, -in] **1.** *n* rogue; *f* hussy; (in Provence) **c. de sort!** damn it! **petit c.! petite coquine!** you little rascal! **2.** *a* mischievous.

cor [kɔr] *nm* **1.** tine (of antler) **2.** (a) **c. (de chasse),** (hunting) horn; **réclamer qch à c. et à cri,** to clamour for sth (b) *Mus:* **c. d'harmonie,** French horn; **c. anglais,** cor anglais **3.** corn (on toe).

corail, *pl* **-aux** [kɔraj, -o] *nm* coral.

Coran (le) [ləkɔrã] *nm* The Koran.

corbeau, -eaux [kɔrbo] *nm Orn:* crow; **grand c.,** raven.

corbeille [kɔrbɛj] *nf* **1.** (open) basket; **c. à papier,** waste paper basket; **c. de mariage,** wedding presents **2.** *Th:* dress circle.

corbillard [kɔrbijar] *nm* hearse.

cordage [kɔrdaʒ] *nm* rope(s), gear, rigging.

corde [kɔrd] *nf* **1.** (a) rope, cord, line; **c. à linge,** clothes line; **c. raide,** tightrope; **c. à nœuds,** knotted climbing rope; **c. à sauter,** skipping rope; **sauter à la c.,** to skip; **trop tirer sur la c.,** to go too far; *F:* **il pleut des cordes,** it's raining cats and dogs (b) string; **c. à piano,** piano wire; **c. de boyau,** catgut; **instrument à cordes,** stringed instrument (c) halter, hangman's rope; **se mettre la c. au cou,** to put a noose round one's own neck (d) *Rac:* **la c.,** the rails; **tenir la c.,** to be on the inside (lane); *Aut:* **prendre un virage à la c.,** to cut a corner close; *Tex:* thread **2.** *Mth:* chord **3.** *Anat:* **cordes vocales,** vocal cords; **ce n'est pas dans mes cordes,** it's not in my line.

cordeau, -eaux [kɔrdo] *nm* **1.** line, string; **tiré au c.,** perfectly straight **2.** *Exp:* fuse, match.

cordée [kɔrde] *nf Mount:* roped party.

cordelette [kɔrdəlɛt] *nf* small cord.

cordialité [kɔrdjalite] *nf* cordiality. **cordial,** *pl*

-iaux 1. *nm* cordial; tonic **2.** *a* cordial, warm (welcome). **cordialement** *adv* cordially, warmly; *Corr:* **c. vôtre,** yours ever.

cordillère [kɔrdijɛr] *nf Geog:* cordillera.

cordon [kɔrdɔ̃] *nm* **1.** *(a)* cord; string; **c. de sonnette,** bellpull; **c. de chaussure,** shoelace *(b)* ribbon (of an order); **c.(-)bleu,** cordon bleu cook *(c)* **c. ombilical,** umbilical cord *(d) El:* cord, flex **2.** row, line; cordon (of police); **c. sanitaire,** sanitary cordon; quarantine line **3.** *Geog:* **c. littoral,** offshore bar.

cordonnerie [kɔrdɔnri] *nf (a)* shoemending *(b)* shoemender's shop.

cordonnier, -ière [kɔrdɔnje, -jɛr] *nm* shoemaker, cobbler.

Corée [kɔre] *Prnf* **C. (du Nord, du Sud),** (North, South) Korea. **coréen, -enne** *a & n* Korean.

coriace [kɔrjas] *a* tough (meat, person).

coriandre [kɔrjɑ̃dr̩] *nm Bot:* coriander.

Corinthe [kɔrɛ̃t] *Prnf Geog:* Corinth; **raisins de C.,** currants.

cormoran [kɔrmɔrɑ̃] *nm Orn:* cormorant.

corne [kɔrn] *nf* **1.** *(a)* horn; **à cornes,** horned; **donner un coup de c. à qn,** to gore s.o.; **faire les cornes à qn,** to jeer at s.o.; **c. à chaussure,** shoehorn *(b)* horn (of snail); (beetle's) antenna **2.** *(a)* **c. de brume,** foghorn *(b)* dog-ear (of page) **3. c. d'abondance,** cornucopia, horn of plenty.

cornée [kɔrne] *nf Anat:* cornea.

corneille [kɔrnɛj] *nf Orn:* crow; rook.

cornemuse [kɔrnəmyz] *nf Mus:* bagpipe(s).

corner [kɔrne] **1.** *vtr (a)* to blare (sth) out *(b)* to turn down the corner of (page); **page cornée,** dog-eared page **2.** *vi Aut:* to sound the horn; to hoot.

cornet [kɔrnɛ] *nm* **1.** *Mus:* (i) **c. à pistons,** cornet (ii) cornet stop (of organ) **2. c. acoustique,** ear trumpet; **c. à dés,** dice box; **c. de glace,** ice-cream cone.

corniaud [kɔrnjo] *nm* **1.** (mongrel) dog **2.** *F:* idiot, twit.

corniche [kɔrniʃ] *nf* **1.** cornice **2.** ledge (of rock); **(route en) c.,** corniche (road).

cornichon [kɔrniʃɔ̃] *nm* **1.** gherkin **2.** *F:* idiot, twit.

Cornouailles [kɔrnwaj] *Prnf Geog:* Cornwall.

cornue [kɔrny] *nf Ch:* retort.

corollaire [kɔrɔlɛr] *nm* corollary.

corolle [kɔrɔl] *nf Bot:* corolla.

coronaire [kɔrɔnɛr] *a* coronary.

corporation [kɔrpɔrasjɔ̃] *nf (a)* corporate body *(b) Hist:* (trade) guild. **corporatif, -ive** *a* corporate.

corporel, -elle [kɔrpɔrɛl] *a* corporeal (being); corporal (punishment); bodily (needs).

corps [kɔr] *nm* **1.** body; **c. robuste,** strong frame; **je me demande ce qu'il a dans le c.,** I wonder what stuff he's made of; **avoir le diable au c.,** (i) to be very excited (ii) to be angry; **prendre c.,** to take shape; **il n'a rien dans le c.,** (i) he hasn't eaten anything (ii) he has no energy; **gardes du c.,** bodyguards, lifeguards; *adv phr* **saisir qn à bras-le-c.,** to seize s.o. round the waist; **lutter c. à c.,** to fight hand to hand **2.** corpse, body **3.** *Ch:* body, substance; **c. simple,** element; **c. composé,** compound; *Med:* **c. étranger,** foreign body **4.** *(a)* main part (of sth); **faire c. avec qch,** to be an integral part of sth *(b) Nau:* **perdu c. et biens,** lost with all hands **5. le c. diplomatique,** the

diplomatic corps; **le c. enseignant, médical,** the teaching, the medical, profession; **c. d'armée,** (army) corps; **c. de garde,** guardroom.

corpulence [kɔrpylɑ̃s] *nf* stoutness, corpulence. **corpulent** *a* stout, corpulent.

corpuscule [kɔrpyskyl] *nm* corpuscle.

correct [kɔrɛkt] *a (a)* correct, proper (language); accurate (copy); *(of pers)* conventional *(b) F:* adequate, acceptable. **correctement** *adv* correctly; properly; accurately. **correcteur, -trice 1.** *a* correcting; corrective **2.** *n* marker (of exam papers); proofreader. **correctif, -ive 1.** *a* corrective **2.** *nm* qualifying statement.

correction [kɔrɛksjɔ̃] *nf* **1.** correction, correcting; proofreading; correction (of proofs); marking (of exam paper) **2.** punishment, thrashing **3.** correctness (of speech, dress); propriety (of behaviour). **correctionnel, -elle** *a* **tribunal c.,** *nf F:* **correctionnelle,** court of summary jurisdiction.

corrélation [kɔrelasjɔ̃] *nf* correlation.

correspondance [kɔrɛspɔ̃dɑ̃s] *nf* **1.** correspondence, agreement **2.** connection (between trains); *Av:* connecting flight; *(of train, boat)* **assurer la c.,** to connect with **3.** *(a)* (business) dealings *(b)* correspondence (by letter); **être en c. avec qn,** to be in correspondence with s.o.; **enseignement par c.,** correspondence course *(c)* mail.

correspondant, -ante [kɔrɛspɔ̃dɑ̃, -ɑ̃t] **1.** *a* corresponding (à, to, with) **2.** *n (a)* correspondent *(b)* penfriend.

correspondre [kɔrɛspɔ̃dr̩] *vi* **1.** to tally, agree, fit (à, with); to correspond (à, to, with) **2.** *(of rooms)* **(se) c.,** to communicate (with one another) **3. c. avec qn,** to correspond with s.o.

corrida [kɔrida] *nf* **1.** bullfight **2.** *F:* carry-on.

corridor [kɔridɔr] *nm* corridor, passage.

corrigé [kɔriʒe] *nm Sch:* fair copy (of work after correction); key.

corriger [kɔriʒe] *vtr* **(n. corrigeons) 1.** to correct, mark (exercise); to proofread; to correct (proofs); to rectify (mistake); **c. qn d'une habitude,** to cure s.o. of a habit **2.** to give (s.o.) a thrashing **3. se c.,** to mend one's ways; **se c. d'une habitude,** to break oneself of a habit.

corroborer [kɔrɔbɔre] *vtr* to corroborate.

corroder [kɔrɔde] *vtr* to corrode.

corrompre [kɔrɔ̃pr̩] *vtr* **1.** *(a)* to corrupt; to deprave; to debase (language) *(b)* to bribe (s.o.) *(c)* to taint (meat) **2. se c.** *(a)* to become corrupt *(b) (of meat)* to become tainted.

corrosion [kɔrozjɔ̃] *nf* corrosion. **corrosif, -ive** *a & nm* corrosive.

corruption [kɔrypsjɔ̃] *nf* corruption. **corrupteur, -trice 1.** *a* corrupt(ing) **2.** *n* corrupter, briber. **corruptible** *a* corruptible.

corsage [kɔrsaʒ] *nm (a)* bodice (of dress) *(b)* blouse, *NAm:* waist.

corsaire [kɔrsɛr] *nm Hist:* privateer.

Corse [kɔrs] *Prnf* Corsica. **corse** *a & n* Corsican.

corser [kɔrse] *vtr* to give body, flavour, to (sth); to strengthen (wine); to liven (sth) up; **l'affaire se corse,** (i) the plot thickens (ii) things are getting serious. **corsé** *a* full-bodied (wine); spicy (sauce, story).

corset [kɔrsɛ] *nm* corset.

corso [kɔrso] *nm* **c. (fleuri),** procession of floral floats; *pl corsi.*

cortège [kɔrtɛʒ] *nm* **1.** train, retinue **2.** procession.

corvée [kɔrve] *nf* **1.** *Mil: etc:* fatigue (duty); **être de c.,** to be on fatigue **2.** chore; **quelle c.!** what a drag!

corvette [kɔrvɛt] *nf Navy:* corvette.

coryza [kɔriza] *nm Med:* cold in the head.

cosaque [kɔzak] *nm* cossack.

cosmétique [kɔsmetik] **1.** *a* cosmetic **2.** *nm* hair oil.

cosmonaute [kɔsmɔnot] *n* cosmonaut.

cosmopolite [kɔsmɔpɔlit] *a* cosmopolitan.

cosmos [kɔsmɔs] *nm* cosmos; outer space. **cosmique** *a* cosmic.

cosse [kɔs] *nf* **1.** pod, husk **2.** *El:* cable terminal **3.** *P:* **avoir la c.,** to feel lazy.

cossu [kɔsy] *a* well-off (person).

costaud, -aude [kɔsto, -od] *a & n F:* strong, sturdy (person).

costume [kɔstym] *nm* (a) costume, dress; **c. de bain,** bathing costume (b) (man's) suit.

costumer [kɔstyme] *vtr* **1.** to dress (s.o.) (up) **2. se c.,** to dress up. **costumé** *a* **bal c.,** fancy-dress ball.

cotation [kɔtasjɔ̃] *nf Fin:* quotation.

cote [kɔt] *nf* **1.** (a) quota, share; **c. mal taillée,** rough and ready settlement (b) *Adm:* assessment **2.** (a) (indication of) dimensions (b) *Surv:* altitude; elevation (above sea level); **c. d'alerte,** (i) flood level (ii) danger point; *Mil:* **la c. 304,** hill 304 **3.** (classification) mark, number (of document); (library) shelf mark **4.** (a) *StExch: Com:* quotation; **c. des prix,** list of prices (b) quoted value (of secondhand car) (c) *F:* **avoir la c.,** to be popular (d) odds on (a horse) (e) *Sch:* mark (f) (film) rating.

côte [kot] *nf* **1.** rib; **se tenir les côtes,** to split one's sides laughing; **c. à c.,** side by side; *Cu:* **c. de bœuf,** rib of beef; **c. de porc,** pork chop; **c. première,** loin chop **2.** (a) slope (of hill); *CivE:* gradient; *Aut:* **démarrage en c.,** hill start (b) hill; **à mi-côte,** half-way up, down, the hill **3.** coast, coastline; **la c. d'Azur,** the (French) Riviera.

côté [kote] *nm* **1.** side; **assis à mes côtés,** sitting by my side **2.** (a) side (of mountain, road, table); **aller de l'autre c. de la rue,** to cross the street; **appartement c. jardin,** flat overlooking the garden; **pencher d'un c.,** to lean to one side, to lean sideways (b) **le c. scientifique,** the scientific aspect; **il a un c. méchant,** there's a mean streak in him; **le vent vient du bon c.,** the wind is in the right quarter; **prendre qch du bon c.,** to take sth well; **d'un c.,** on the one hand; **d'un autre c.,** on the other hand; **de mon c.,** for my part; **il n'y a rien à craindre de ce c.,** there's nothing to worry about on that score (c) side, direction, way; **de tous (les) côtés,** on all sides; **de c. et d'autre,** here and there; **du c. de Paris,** towards Paris; **il habite du c. de la rivière,** he lives near the river; **se mettre du c. du plus fort,** to take sides with the strongest; **de quel c.?** which way? (d) *F:* **(du) c. argent,** moneywise, as far as money is concerned **3.** *adv phr* (a) **de c.,** on one side; sideways; **mettre qch de c.,** to put sth aside; **regardée c.,** sidelong glance (b) **à c.,** to one side; near; **il habite à c.,** he lives next door; **tirer à c.,** to miss (the mark); **à c. de,** by the side of; next to; beside; **passer à c. de qch,** to avoid sth; **il n'est rien à c. de vous,** he's nothing compared to you.

coteau [kɔto] *nm* (a) hillside (b) hill.

côtelette [kotlɛt] *nf Cu:* cutlet; chop.

coter [kɔte] *vtr* **1.** *Surv: etc:* to mark the dimensions on (drawing); to put references on (map); **point coté,** spot height (on map) **2.** to classify, number (document) **3.** (a) *StExch: Com:* to quote (price); **ma voiture n'est pas cotée (à l'Argus),** my car is not listed in the car buyer's guide (b) **très coté,** (i) (of horse) well backed (ii) highly considered **4.** *Sch:* to mark (exercise).

coterie [kɔtri] *nf* (political, literary) set.

côtier, -ière [kotje, -jɛr] *a* coastal (trade); inshore (fishery).

cotisant, -ante [kɔtizɑ̃, -ɑ̃t] *n* subscriber; contributor.

cotisation [kɔtizasjɔ̃] *nf* (a) contribution (b) subscription.

cotiser [kɔtize] *vi* **1.** (a) to contribute (b) to subscribe **2. se c.,** to club together (to raise sum of money).

côtoiement [kotwamɑ̃] *nm* association (with others); encounter (with a situation).

coton [kɔtɔ̃] **1.** *nm* cotton; **fil de c.,** sewing cotton; **c. à repriser,** darning thread **2.** *nm* **c. (hydrophile),** cotton wool; *F:* **j'ai les jambes en c.,** my legs feel like jelly; **il a du c. dans les oreilles,** (i) he's deaf (ii) he doesn't want to hear **3.** *a F:* difficult. **cotonneux, -euse** *a* woolly (clouds); thick (fog).

cotonnade [kɔtɔnad] *nf* cotton fabric.

cotonnier, -ière [kɔtɔnje, -jɛr] **1.** *a* cotton (industry) **2.** *nm* cotton plant.

côtoyer [kotwaje] *vtr* **(je côtoie) 1.** to coast along, to keep close to (shore); to skirt (forest) **2.** to border on (river); **c. le ridicule,** to verge on the ridiculous.

cotte [kɔt] *nf Cl:* (a) *Mil:* **c. d'armes,** tunic (worn over armour); **c. de mailles,** coat of mail (b) overalls, dungarees.

cou [ku] *nm* neck; **la peau du c.,** the scruff of the neck; **se jeter au c. de qn,** to throw one's arms around s.o.'s neck; **endetté jusqu'au c.,** up to the eyes in debt; **prendre ses jambes à son c.,** to take to one's heels.

couac [kwak] *nm Mus:* squeak (on instrument); false note.

couchage [kuʃaʒ] *nm* **(matériel de) c.,** bedding; **sac de c.,** sleeping bag.

couchant [kuʃɑ̃] **1.** *a* **soleil c.,** setting sun **2.** *nm* (a) sunset (b) west.

couche [kuʃ] *nf* **1.** (a) *Lit:* bed (b) *usu pl* confinement, labour; **mourir en couches,** to die in childbi (h); **fausse c.,** miscarriage (c) **c. (de bébé),** (baby's) nappy, *NAm:* diaper **2.** (a) *Geol:* bed, layer (b) *Hort:* **c. de fumier,** hotbed (c) **couches sociales,** social strata (d) coat (of paint); layer (of dirt) (e) *P:* **il en tient une c.!** he's really thick!

coucher¹ [kuʃe] **1.** *vtr* (a) to put (child) to bed (b) to put (s.o.) up (for the night) (c) to lay (sth) down; **la pluie a couché les blés,** the rain has flattened the wheat; **c. un fusil en joue,** to aim a gun; **coucher en joue,** to aim at s.o. (d) to put (sth) down in writing **2.** *vi* (a) **c. à l'hôtel,** to sleep at the hotel (b) to sleep (avec, with) **3. se c.** (a) to go to bed (b) to lie down (c) (of sun) to set, go down (d) (of ship) to heel over.

coucher² *nm* 1. l'heure du c., bedtime 2. au c. du soleil, at sunset.

couchette [kuʃɛt] *nf* berth, bunk (on ship); couchette (on train).

coucou [kuku] *nm* 1. (a) *Orn:* cuckoo; (pendule à) c., cuckoo clock (b) *int* c.! (me voilà!), peek-a-boo! 2. *Bot:* cowslip 3. *P:* old plane, old crate.

coude [kud] *nm* 1. elbow; c. à c., side by side; shoulder to shoulder; **coup de c.**, nudge; **se serrer les coudes**, to stick together 2. (a) bend (in road) (b) bend, elbow (of pipe).

coudées [kude] *nfpl* avoir ses c. franches, (i) to have elbow room (ii) to have a free hand.

cou-de-pied [kudpje] *nm* instep; *pl* cous-de-pied.

coudoiement [kudwamɑ̃] *nm* contact, association.

coudoyer [kudwaje] *vtr* (je coudoie) to rub shoulders with (s.o.); to be in contact with (s.o.).

coudre [kudr] *vtr* (*prp* cousant; *pp* cousu; *pr ind* ils cousent; *impf* je cousais) to sew, stitch; to sew on (button); to sew up (wound); **machine à c.**, sewing machine.

coudrier [kudrije] *nm* hazel (tree).

couenne [kwan] *nf* (a) (thick) skin (b) (bacon) rind.

couette [kwɛt] *nf* duvet; continental quilt.

couiner [kwine] *vi* to squeak, to squeal.

coulée [kule] *nf* 1. running, flow(ing) (of liquid); c. de lave, lava flow; c. de boue, mud slide 2. *Metall:* casting.

couler [kule] 1. *vtr* (a) to run, pour (liquid) (b) to cast (molten metal) (c) *ICE:* c. une bielle, to burn out a connecting rod (d) to sink (a ship); c. qn, to discredit s.o.; **c. une vie heureuse**, to lead a happy life; *F:* se la c. douce, to have an easy time of it 2. *vi* (a) (of liquids) to flow, run; **faire c. l'eau**, to turn the water on; **faire c. un bain**, to run a bath; **faire c. le sang**, to shed blood (b) (of pen) to leak; (of nose) to run (c) (of ship) to sink 3. **se c.**, to glide, slip; **se c. entre les draps**, to slip into bed; **se c. le long du mur**, to hug the wall. **coulant** 1. *a* running, flowing (liquid); flowing (style); easy-going (pers) 2. *nm* sliding ring.

couleur [kulœr] *nf* 1. (a) colour; tint; **gens de c.**, coloured people, coloureds; **télévision en couleurs**, colour television; **sous c. de me rendre service**, under the pretext of helping me; *F:* il en a vu de toutes les couleurs, he's been through a lot (b) colour, complexion; **reprendre des couleurs**, to get back one's colour; **sans c.**, colourless (c) *pl Mil: etc:* colours, flag (d) c. paille, c. chair, straw coloured, flesh coloured 2. colour, paint; **boîte de couleurs**, box of paints 3. *Cards:* suit.

couleuvre [kulœvr] *nf* grass snake; **paresseux comme une c.**, bone-idle.

coulisse [kulis] *nf* 1. groove, runner; **porte à c.**, sliding door; **regard en c.**, sidelong glance 2. *Th:* les coulisses, the wings; **les coulisses de la politique**, behind the scenes in politics.

coulisser [kulise] *vi* to slide.

couloir [kulwar] *nm* 1. (a) corridor, passage (b) (athletics) lane 2. *Geog:* channel, gully; gorge.

coup [ku] *nm* 1. (a) knock, blow; rap, tap (on door); **donner de grands coups dans la porte**, to bang at the door; **se donner un c. à la tête**, to hit one's head; **c. de bec**, peck; **c. de bâton**, blow (with a stick); **c. de**

poing, c. de pied**, punch; kick; **c. bas**, hit below the belt; **c. de couteau**, stab; **ça m'a donné un c.!** it gave me a shock! *F:* tenir le c., to hold out; to stick it; **il tiendra le c.**, he'll make it; *F:* faire les quatre cents coups, to lead a reckless life; **corps couvert de coups**, body covered with bruises; **enfoncer un clou à coups de marteau**, to hammer a nail in (b) **c. de feu**, shot; **il fut tué d'un c. de fusil**, he was shot dead (c) **c. de vent**, gust of wind; **entrer en c. de vent**, to burst in; *Med:* **c. de froid**, chill, cold 2. (normal action of sth) (a) **c. d'aile**, stroke of the wing; **c. de dents**, bite; **boire qch à petits coups**, to sip sth; *F:* boire un c.**, to have a drink; **c. de crayon**, pencil stroke; **sur le c. de midi**, on the stroke of twelve; **c. de filet**, haul (of a net) (b) *Sp:* (i) stroke (ii) *Fb:* kick; **c. d'envoi**, kickoff; **c. franc**, free kick (iii) *Box:* blow, punch (iv) *Cards:* hand (v) *Chess:* move (c) **c. de chance**, stroke of luck; **c. d'État**, coup (d'état); **c. d'éclat**, distinguished action, glorious deed (d) **c. de tonnerre**, clap, peal, of thunder; **c. de sifflet**, (blast of a) whistle; **c. de sonnette**, ring of the bell; **c. de téléphone**, telephone call 3. influence; **agir sous le c. de la peur**, to act out of fear; **tomber sous le c. de la loi**, to come within the provisions of the law 4. (a) attempt; **c. d'essai**, trial shot; **marquer le c.**, to celebrate the occasion; *F:* ça vaut le c.**, it's worth it; **c. de tête**, impulsive act; **il prépare un mauvais c.**, he's up to no good; **sale c.**, dirty trick; *F:* il est dans le c.**, he's in on it (b) *adv phr* d'un seul c.**, at one go; **du premier c.**, at the first attempt; straight off; **du (même) c.**, (i) at the same time (ii) as a result; and so; **il fut tué sur le c.**, he was killed outright; **pour le c.**, this time; **après c.**, after the event; **tout à c.**, suddenly; **c. sur c.**, in rapid succession; **à c. sûr**, definitely.

coupable [kupabl] 1. *a* (a) guilty (person) (b) culpable (act) 2. *n* culprit.

coupage [kupaʒ] *nm* (a) blending (of wines) (b) diluting (of wine with water).

coupant [kupɑ̃] *a* cutting, sharp.

coupe¹ [kup] *nf* (a) cup; (contents) cup(ful); (champagne) glass; (fruit) dish, bowl (b) *Sp:* cup.

coupe² [kup] *nf* 1. (a) cutting (of hay); felling (of trees); cutting-out (of material); **c. de cheveux**, haircut; *F:* mettre qn en c. réglée, to exploit s.o.; **c. sombre**, drastic cut (b) cut (of a coat) (c) section 2. *Cards:* cut, cutting; **être sous la c. de qn**, to be under s.o.'s thumb.

coupé [kupe] *nm* *Aut:* coupé; *Danc:* coupée.

coupe-circuit [kupsirkɥi] *nm inv* *El:* circuit breaker.

coupe-coupe [kupkup] *nm inv* machete.

coupe-feu [kupfø] *nm inv* firebreak.

coupe-gorge [kupgɔrʒ] *nm inv* death trap.

coupe-papier [kuppapje] *nm inv* paper knife.

couper [kupe] *vtr & i* 1. (a) to cut; **c. (qch) en morceaux**, to cut (sth) up; **c. la tête à qn**, to cut off s.o.'s head; **c. bras et jambes à qn**, to discourage s.o.; **c. l'herbe sous les pieds de qn**, to cut the ground from under s.o.'s feet; **se faire c. les cheveux**, to get one's hair cut; **accent à c. au couteau**, accent you could cut with a knife; **c. une robe**, to cut out a dress (b) *Cards:* (i) to cut (ii) to trump 2. (a) to cut, to cross; **c. à travers champs**, to cut across country; **c.**

par le plus court, to take a short cut (b) *Aut:* **c. la route à qn,** to cut in 3. (a) to cut off, interrupt, stop; **c. l'appétit à qn,** to take s.o.'s appetite away; **c. la parole à qn,** to interrupt s.o.; **c. le souffle à qn,** to take s.o.'s breath away; *P:* **c. le sifflet à qn,** to shut s.o. up; *Tp:* **c. la communication,** to ring off; *abs* **ne coupez pas,** hold the line (b) **c. l'eau,** to turn off the water; *El:* **c. le courant,** to switch off the current; *Aut:* **c. le contact,** to switch off the ignition 4. **c. du vin,** (i) to blend (ii) to dilute, wine 5. *ind tr F:* **c. à une corvée,** to shirk an unpleasant job; **il n'y coupera pas,** he won't get out of it 6. **se c.** (a) to cut oneself; **se c. au doigt,** to cut one's finger (b) *F:* to give oneself away.

couperet [kupre] *nm* 1. meat cleaver 2. (guillotine) blade.

couple [kupl] *nm* 1. pair, (married) couple 2. *MecE: etc:* **c. moteur, c. (de torsion),** torque.

coupler [kuple] *vtr* to couple (together).

couplet [kuple] *nm* verse (of song).

coupole [kupɔl] *nf* cupola, dome.

coupon [kupɔ̃] *nm* 1. *Com:* remnant (of material) 2. *Fin:* coupon.

coupon-réponse [kupɔ̃repɔ̃s] *nm Post:* reply coupon; *pl* coupons-réponse.

coupure [kupyr] *nf* 1. cut (on finger) 2. (a) cutting, piece cut out; **c. de journal,** newspaper cutting (b) cut (in book, film) (c) *El:* **c. (de courant),** power cut (d) *Fig:* gap, gulf 3. *Fin:* (bank)note.

cour [kur] *nf* 1. (a) court; **à la c.,** at court; **être bien, mal, en c.,** to be in favour, out of favour (b) courtship; **faire la c. à une jeune fille,** to court a girl 2. **c. de justice,** court of justice 3. court, yard, courtyard; **c. de ferme,** farmyard; **c. de récréation,** school playground; schoolyard; *Mil:* **c. de quartier,** barrack square.

courage [kuraʒ] *nm* courage; bravery; **perdre, reprendre, c.,** to lose, to take, heart; **(du) c.!** (i) cheer up! (ii) keep it up! **il ne se sent pas le c.,** he doesn't feel up to it; **vous n'auriez pas le c. de les renvoyer!** you wouldn't have the heart to dismiss them! **courageux, -euse** *a* 1. courageous, brave 2. energetic. **courageusement** *adv* courageously, bravely; with energy.

couramment [kuramɑ̃] *adv* 1. easily, readily; fluently 2. generally, usually; **ce mot s'emploie c.,** this word is in current use.

courant, -ante [kurɑ̃, -ɑ̃t] 1. *a* (a) running; **chien c.,** hound (b) flowing; running (water) (c) current (account); **le cinq c.,** the fifth inst; **mot d'usage c.,** word in general use; **de taille courante,** of standard size 2. *nm* (a) current, stream; trend (of public opinion); **c. d'air,** draught (b) *El:* **c. (électrique),** electric current (c) course; **dans le c. de l'année,** in the course of the year; **être au c. de qch,** to know all about sth; **mettre qn au c. d'une décision,** to inform s.o. of a decision; **il est au c.,** he knows about it.

courbature [kurbatyr] *nf* stiffness, tiredness; **avoir une c.,** to be aching all over. **courbaturé** *a* aching.

courbe [kurb] 1. *a* curved 2. *nf* curve; graph; **c. de niveau,** contour (line); **c. de température,** temperature graph.

courber [kurbe] 1. *vtr* to bend, curve; **courbé par**

l'âge, bent with age; **c. la tête,** (i) to bow one's head (ii) to submit 2. *vi* to bend 3. **se c.,** to bow, bend, stoop.

courbette [kurbet] *nf* (low) bow; **faire des courbettes à qn,** to bow and scrape to s.o.

courbure [kurbyr] *nf* curve.

courette [kuret] *nf* small (court)yard.

coureur, -euse [kurœr, -øz] *n* 1. *nm* runner; racer; **c. de fond,** long-distance runner; **c. cycliste,** racing cyclist; **c. automobile,** racing driver 2. *nm* gadabout; **c'est un c. de cafés,** he's always in cafés; **c. (de filles),** womanizer; **c. de dot,** fortune hunter 3. *nf* man hunter.

courge [kurʒ] *nf Bot:* gourd; marrow; *NAm:* squash.

courgette [kurʒet] *nf* (small) marrow, courgette.

courir [kurir] *v* (*prp* courant; *pp* couru; *pr ind* je cours; *fu* je courrai; *the aux is* avoir) 1. *vi* (a) to run; **c. après qn,** to run after s.o.; **je cours l'appeler,** I'll run and get him; **arriver en courant,** to come running up; **faire qch en courant,** to do sth in a hurry; *F:* **tu peux toujours c.!** you can whistle for it! (b) *Sp:* to race; to run (in a race); **faire c. un cheval,** to race a horse (c) (*of ship*) to sail; **c. au large,** to stand out to sea; (d) to be current; **le bruit court que,** rumour has it that; **faire c. un bruit,** to spread a rumour (e) (*of blood*) to flow; (*of clouds*) to float; (*of water*) to rush (f) **par les temps qui courent,** nowadays; as things are at present; *Fin:* **intérêts qui courent,** accruing interest 2. *vtr* to run after (sth); to pursue, chase; to hunt (animal); **c. un risque,** to run a risk; **c. sa chance,** to try one's luck 3. *with cogn acc* (a) **c. une course,** to run a race (b) **c. le monde,** to roam the world; **c. les magasins,** to go round the shops; **c. les filles,** to chase girls.

couronne [kurɔn] *nf* 1. wreath (of flowers); **c. funéraire,** (funeral) wreath 2. (king's) crown; (ducal) coronet 3. ring; *Bot:* corona; *Anat:* crown (of tooth).

couronnement [kurɔnmɑ̃] *nm* (a) crowning, coronation (of king) (b) climax; crowning achievement.

couronner [kurɔne] *vtr* 1. to crown (s.o. king); to award a prize (to author, candidate); **efforts couronnés de succès,** efforts crowned with success 2. to crown (a tooth) 3. **se c. le genou,** to graze one's knee.

courrier [kurje] *nm* 1. (a) mail, post; **par retour du c.,** by return of post (b) (i) mail boat (ii) aircraft; *Mil:* courier 2. *Journ:* column; **c. des lecteurs,** letters to the Editor; **c. du cœur,** problem page; *F:* agony column.

courroie [kurwa] *nf* strap; *Tch:* belt.

courroucer [kuruse] *vtr Lit:* **(je courrouçai(s))** to anger, to incense (s.o.).

courroux [kuru] *nm Lit:* anger, wrath.

cours [kur] *nm* 1. (a) course (of river); course, path (of sun, moon); **c. d'eau,** river, waterway, stream; **donner libre c. à son imagination,** to give free rein to one's imagination; **année en c.,** current year; **travail en c.,** work in progress, on hand; **en c. de route,** during the journey; on the way; **au c. de,** in the course of (b) **voyage au long c.,** ocean voyage 2. circulation, currency (of money); **avoir c.,** (i) to be legal tender (ii) to be current 3. **c. du change,** rate of exchange **4.** (*a*) course (of lectures); lecture; lesson; **c. par correspondance,** correspondence course; **faire un c.,** to give a class (*b*) textbook, coursebook.

course [kurs] *nf* **1.** run, running; **au pas de c.,** at a run; **prendre sa c.,** to start running **2.** race, racing; **c. de fond,** long-distance (i) running (ii) race; **c. de vitesse,** sprint; **c. de taureaux,** bullfight; *F:* **être dans la c.,** to be in the know **3.** (*a*) excursion, outing; hike; climb (*b*) journey; (*in taxi*) **payer (le prix de) la c.,** to pay the fare (*c*) (business) errand; **faire des courses,** to go shopping **4.** (*a*) path, course (of planet); **poursuivre sa c.,** to go on one's way; *F:* **être à bout de c.,** to be exhausted, worn out (*b*) *MecE:* movement, travel (of tool); stroke (of piston).

coursier, -ière [kursje, -jɛr] **1.** *nm Lit:* steed, horse **2.** *n* messenger.

court¹ [kur] **1.** *a* (*a*) short; **avoir le souffle c.,** to be short of breath; **(le chemin) le plus c.,** the quickest way; **a short cut; 100 francs c'est un peu c.,** 100 francs is a bit mean (*b*) (*in time*) **c. intervalle,** short interval; **de courte durée,** short-lived **2.** *adv* short; **s'arrêter c.,** to stop suddenly; **couper c. à qn, à qch,** to cut s.o., sth, short **3.** (*a*) *adv phr* **tout c.,** simply, only (*b*) **prendre qn de c.,** to catch s.o. unawares (*c*) *prep phr* **à c. d'argent,** short of money; **être à c.,** to be at a loss for words, for sth to do.

court² *nm* (tennis) court.

courtaud, -aude [kurto, -od] *a* dumpy, squat.

court-bouillon [kurbujɔ̃] *nm Cu:* court-bouillon; *pl* **courts-bouillons.**

court-circuit [kursirkɥi] *nm El:* short circuit; *pl* **courts-circuits.**

court-circuiter [kursirkɥite] *vtr El:* to short-circuit (resistance).

courtier, -ière [kurtje, -jɛr] *n Com: Fin:* broker.

courtisan [kurtizɑ̃] *nm* (*a*) courtier (*b*) sycophant.

courtisane [kurtizan] *nf Hist:* courtesan.

courtiser [kurtize] *vtr* to pay court to (s.o.).

courtoisie [kurtwazi] *nf* courtesy. **courtois** *a* courteous. **courtoisement** *adv* courteously.

couru [kury] *a* **1.** sought after; popular (event) **2.** *F:* **c'est c. (d'avance),** it's a cert, a sure thing.

cousin¹, -ine [kuzɛ̃, -in] *n* cousin; **c. germain,** first cousin.

cousin² *nm Ent:* (*a*) gnat, midge (*b*) daddy-longlegs.

coussin [kusɛ̃] *nm* cushion.

coussinet [kusinɛ] *nm* **1.** small cushion; pad **2.** *MecE:* bearing.

cousu [kuzy] *a* sewn; **c. main,** hand sewn; *F:* **c'est du c. main,** it's first rate; **garder bouche cousue,** to keep one's mouth shut; **c. de fil blanc,** obvious.

coût [ku] *nm* cost; **c. de la vie,** cost of living. **coûtant** *a* **à prix c.,** at cost price.

couteau, -eaux [kuto] *nm* **1.** (*a*) knife; **c. de poche,** pocket knife; **c. à cran d'arrêt,** flick knife; **c. à découper,** carving knife; **coup de c.,** stab; **ils sont à couteaux tirés,** they are at daggers drawn; **mettre le c. sous la gorge à qn,** to hold a pistol to s.o.'s head (*b*) *Ph:* knife edge **2.** *Moll:* razor shell.

coutellerie [kutɛlri] *nf* **1.** (industry, wares) cutlery **2.** cutlery shop.

coûter [kute] *vi* **1.** to cost; **ça ne coûte rien,** it's free; **c. cher,** to be expensive; **cela vous coûtera cher,** you

shall pay dearly for this; **coûte que coûte,** at all costs; **cela lui a coûté la vie,** it cost him his life; *impers* **j'ai voulu l'aider; il m'en coûta,** I tried to help him, to my cost **2. ça ne coûte rien d'essayer,** there's no harm in trying; **cela m'en coûte de le dire,** it pains me to have to say this. **coûteux, -euse** *a* costly, expensive.

coutume [kutym] *nf* custom, habit; **avoir c. de faire qch,** to be in the habit of doing sth; **comme de c.,** as usual; **plus que de c.,** more than usual. **coutumier, -ière** *a* customary; usual; *Pej:* **il est c. du fait,** it's not the first time he's done that.

couture [kutyr] *nf* **1.** sewing, needlework; dressmaking; **maison de haute c.,** fashion house **2.** seam (in dress); **sans c.,** seamless; **sous toutes les coutures,** from every angle.

couturier, -ière [kutyrje, -jɛr] (*a*) *n* dressmaker, couturier, fashion designer (*b*) *nf* seamstress.

couvée [kuve] *nf* **1.** clutch (of eggs) **2.** brood (of chicks).

couvent [kuvɑ̃] *nm* (*a*) convent (*b*) convent school (*c*) monastery.

couver [kuve] **1.** *vtr* (*a*) (of hen) to sit on (eggs); *abs* to brood, to sit (*b*) to incubate, hatch (eggs) (*c*) to hatch (plot); to plot (vengeance); to be sickening for (an illness); **couver qn des yeux,** to look fondly at s.o. **2.** *vi* (of fire) to smoulder; (of riot) to brew.

couvercle [kuvɛrkl] *nm* lid, cover; cap, top (of jar).

couvert¹ [kuvɛr] *a* **1.** covered; **allée couverte,** shady walk; **ciel c.,** overcast sky **2. rester c.,** to keep one's hat on **3. chaudement c.,** warmly dressed.

couvert² *nm* **1.** cover(ing), shelter; **le vivre et le c.,** board and lodging; **être à c.,** to be under cover; **se mettre à c.,** to take cover; **à c. de la pluie,** sheltering from the rain; **mettre ses intérêts à c.,** to safeguard one's interests; **sous le c. de,** under the cover, the pretence, of **2.** (*a*) cutlery (for a place setting at table); **mettre, dresser, le c.,** to lay, set, the table; **mettre trois couverts,** to lay for three (*c*) (*in restaurant*) cover charge.

couverture [kuvɛrtyr] *nf* **1.** covering, cover; **c. de voyage,** (travelling) rug; **c. (de lit),** blanket; **tirer la c. à soi,** to take the lion's share; **c. d'un livre,** (dust) cover of a book **2.** roofing **3.** *Com: StExch:* cover.

couveuse [kuvøz] *nf Agr:* sitting hen; brooder; **c. (artificielle),** incubator.

couvre-feu [kuvrəfø] *nm inv* curfew.

couvre-lit [kuvrəli] *nm* bedspread; **c.-l. piqué,** quilt; *pl* **couvre-lits.**

couvre-pied(s) [kuvrəpje] *nm* coverlet; bedspread; *pl* **couvre-pieds.**

couvrir [kuvrir] *v* (*prp* **couvrant;** *pp* **couvert;** *pr ind* **je couvre**) **1.** *vtr* (*a*) to cover (sb, with); **mur couvert de lierre,** wall overgrown with ivy; **c. qn de cadeaux,** to shower s.o. with gifts; **c. qn,** to cover up for s.o.; *Ins:* **c. les risques,** to insure against risks; **c. la voix,** to drown the sound of voices; **c. son jeu,** to keep sth secret; **c. 50 kilomètres,** to cover 50 kilometres; **c. les frais,** to cover the cost (*b*) **c. un toit de tuiles, de chaume,** to tile, to thatch, a roof **2. se c.** (*a*) to put on one's (outdoor) clothes (*b*) to put on one's hat (*c*) to cover oneself (with glory, shame) (*d*) *Sp:* to cover, protect, oneself (*e*) (*of weather*) to become overcast (*f*) **se c. de taches,** to get covered in stains.

coyote [kɔjɔt] *nm Z:* coyote, prairie wolf.
crabe [krab] *nm* crab; **marcher en c.,** to walk crab-wise.
crac [krak] *int & nm* crack, snap, rip; bang.
crachat [kraʃa] *nm* spittle, spit.
crachement [kraʃmã] *nm* (a) spitting (b) crackle (of radio); shower (of sparks).
cracher [kraʃe] 1. *vi* (a) to spit; **il ne crache pas sur le champagne,** he doesn't turn up his nose at champagne (b) (of pen) to splutter (c) (of radio) to crackle 2. *vtr* (a) to spit (out); **c. des injures,** to hurl abuse; *F:* **j'ai dû c. mille francs,** I had to cough up a thousand francs (b) (of chimney, volcano) to belch out. **craché** *a* **c'est son père tout c.,** he's the spitting image of his father.
crachin [kraʃɛ̃] *nm* (fine) drizzle.
crack [krak] *nm* (a) crack horse (b) *F:* genius; ace.
Cracovie [krakɔvi] *Prnf Geog:* Cracow.
craie [krɛ] *nf* chalk.
craindre [krɛ̃dr] *vtr* (*prp* craignant; *pp* craint; *pr ind* je crains; *ph* je craignis) (a) to fear, dread; to be afraid of (sth); **ne craignez rien!** don't be alarmed! **je crains qu'il (ne) soit mort,** I am afraid he is dead; **il n'y a rien à c.,** there's nothing to fear; **c. pour qn,** to be anxious about s.o. (b) **c. le froid,** to be easily damaged by the cold; **je crains la chaleur,** I can't stand the heat; *Com:* **craint l'humidité,** to be kept in a dry place.
crainte [krɛ̃t] *nf* fear, dread; **de c. de tomber,** for fear of falling; **de c. qu'on ne l'entende,** for fear of his being overheard; **sans c.,** fearless(ly); **soyez sans c.,** have no fear. **craintif, -ive** *a* timid, timorous.
craintivement *adv* timidly, timorously.
cramoisi [kramwazi] *a & nm* crimson.
crampe [krãp] *nf Med:* cramp.
crampon [krãpɔ̃] *nm* 1. cramp (iron); clamp 2. climbing iron; stud (on boot); **c. à glace,** crampon 3. *F:* (of pers) leech.
cramponner (se) [səkrãpɔne] *vpr* **se c. à qch,** to hold on to sth; to cling to, to clutch, sth.
cran [krã] *nm* 1. (a) notch; tooth (of ratchet); cog (of wheel); **c. de sûreté,** safety catch; *F:* **être à c.,** to be very edgy (b) hole (in belt, in strap); **descendre d'un c.,** to come down a peg 2. *F:* **avoir du c.,** to have guts.
crâne [krɑn] 1. *nm* skull; head 2. *a* swaggering, jaunty (air). **crânien, -ienne** *a* cranial.
crâner [krɑne] *vi F:* to swagger; to show off.
crâneur, -euse [krɑnœr, -øz] *n F:* swanker, swaggerer.
crapaud [krapo] *nm* toad.
crapule [krapyl] *nf* scoundrel. **crapuleux, -euse** *a* sordid, loathsome.
craqueler [krakle] *vtr* (**je craquelle**) to crack; **se c.,** to crack.
craquelure [kraklyr] *nf* crack.
craquement [krakmã] *nm* cracking (sound); crack, snap; crackle, crunch; creak(ing), squeaking.
craquer [krake] 1. *vi* (a) to crack; to crackle; (of hard snow) to crunch (under the feet); (of shoes) to creak, to squeak (b) (of seam) to split; **son affaire craque,** his business is on the verge of collapse 2. *vtr* **c. une allumette,** to strike a match.
crasse [kras] 1. *af* crass (ignorance) 2. *nf* (a) (body)

dirt, filth; **vivre dans la c.,** to live in squalor (b) *F:* dirty trick. **crasseux, -euse** *a* grimy, filthy; squalid.
cratère [kratɛr] *nm* crater.
cravache [kravaʃ] *nf* riding whip; (hunting) crop.
cravacher [kravaʃe] (a) *vtr* to flog (horse); to horsewhip (pers) (b) *vi F:* to slog (to finish sth).
cravate [kravat] *nf* (a) (i) tie (ii) scarf, cravat (b) (decoration) ribbon.
cravater [kravate] *vtr* to put a tie on (s.o.); **se c.,** to put on one's tie. **cravaté** *a* wearing a tie.
crayeux, -euse [krɛjø, -øz] *a* chalky.
crayon [krɛjɔ̃] *nm* 1. (a) pencil; **c. de couleur,** coloured pencil, crayon; **écrit au c.,** pencilled; **c. à mine (de plomb),** lead pencil; **c. à bille,** ballpoint pen (b) pencil drawing, pencil sketch 2. *Toil:* **c. noir,** (i) eyebrow (ii) eye(liner), pencil.
crayonner [krɛjɔne] *vtr* 1. to make a pencil sketch of (sth) 2. to make a pencil note of (sth).
créance [kreɑ̃s] *nf* 1. belief, credence; **trouver c.,** to be believed 2. debt; *Jur:* claim.
créancier, -ière [kreɑ̃sje, -jɛr] *n* creditor.
créateur, -trice [kreatœr, -tris] 1. *a* creative (power) 2. *n* creator.
création [kreasjɔ̃] *nf* 1. (a) creation, creating (b) founding (of institution); creation (of work of art); *Com:* invention (of new product); *Th:* first production 2. *Com:* new product.
créativité [kreativite] *nf* creativity. **créatif, -ive** *a* creative.
créature [kreatyr] *nf* creature.
crécelle [kresɛl] *nf* (hand) rattle; **voix de c.,** rasping voice.
crèche [krɛʃ] *nf* 1. manger, crib 2. day nursery, crèche.
crédibilité [kredibilite] *nf* credibility.
crédit [kredi] *nm* 1. credit, repute, influence 2. *Fin: Com:* credit; **vendre qch à c.,** to sell sth (i) on credit (ii) on hire purchase; **faire c. à qn,** (i) to give s.o. credit (ii) to trust s.o.; **carte de c.,** credit card 3. credit side (of ledger); **porter une somme au c. de qn,** to credit s.o. with a sum.
créditer [kredite] *vtr* (a) **c. qn du montant d'une somme,** to credit s.o. with a sum (b) **c. qn de qch,** to give s.o. credit for sth.
créditeur, -trice [kreditœr, -tris] 1. *n* creditor 2. *a* having a credit; **solde c.,** credit balance.
credo [kredo] *nm inv* creed.
crédulité [kredylite] *nf* credulity. **crédule** *a* credulous.
créer [kree] *vtr* (a) to create; **se c. une clientèle,** to build up a clientele; **le pouvoir de c.,** the power of creation; **c. des ennuis,** to cause problems (b) *Th:* to create (role); to produce (a play) for the first time.
crémaillère [kremajɛr] *nf* 1. pothanger; trammel; **pendre la c.,** to give a house warming party 2. *Rail:* rack rail.
crémation [kremasjɔ̃] *nf* cremation. **crématoire** 1. *a* crematory 2. *n* crematorium.
crème [krɛm] *nf* 1. (a) cream; (on milk) skin; **c. fouettée, c. chantilly,** whipped cream; **gâteau à la c.,** cream cake; *nm* **un c.,** a white coffee (b) *F:* (pers) **la c.,** the cream (c) *Cu:* **c. anglaise,** (egg) custard; **c. pâtissière,** confectioner's custard; **c. glacée,** ice

cream 2. **c. de beauté,** face cream, beauty cream; **c. à raser,** shaving cream 3. *a inv* cream(-coloured). **crémeux, -euse** *a* creamy.

crémerie [kremri] *nf* creamery, dairy.

crémier, -ière [kremje, -jɛr] *n* dairyman, dairy-woman.

crémone [kremɔn] *nf* espagnolette (bolt).

créneau, -eaux [kreno] *nm* 1. *Fort:* crenel; **les créneaux,** the battlements 2. *(a)* gap, space; *Aut:* **faire un c.,** to reverse into a parking space *(b) Com:* gap, opening *(c) WTel: TV:* slot. **crénelé** *a* crenellated.

créole [kreɔl] *a & n Ethn:* Creole.

créosote [kreɔzɔt] *nf* creosote.

crêpe [krɛp] 1. *nf Cu:* pancake 2. *nm (a) Tex:* crape; **c. satin,** satin crêpe *(b)* black mourning crêpe *(c)* crêpe-rubber.

crêper [krepe] *vtr* to backcomb (hair); *F:* **se c. le chignon,** to fight, to have a set-to.

crêperie [krepri] *nf* pancake bar.

crépir [krepir] *vtr* to roughcast (wall). **crépi** *a & nm* roughcast.

crépissage [krepisaʒ] *nm* roughcasting.

crépitement [krepitmɑ̃] *nm* crackling; pattering; sputtering.

crépiter [krepite] *vi* to crackle; *(of rain)* to patter; *(of candle)* to sputter.

crépu [krepy] *a* frizzy (hair).

crépuscule [krepyskyl] *nm* twilight; dusk. **crépusculaire** *a* twilight (glow).

cresson [krɛsɔ̃] *nm Bot:* cress; **c. de fontaine,** water-cress.

Crète [krɛt] *Prnf Geog:* Crete.

crête [krɛt] *nf* 1. comb, crest (of bird); **c. de coq,** cockscomb 2. crest (of wave); crest, ridge (of mountain, roof) 3. *El:* peak.

crétin, -ine [kretɛ̃, -in] 1. *n (a) Med:* cretin *(b) F:* idiot, cretin 2. *a F:* idiotic, moronic.

crétinerie [kretinri] *nf* idiocy.

creusement [krøzmɑ̃] *nm* digging.

creuser [krøze] *vtr* 1. to hollow (out); to plough (a furrow); to dig; **front creusé de rides,** brow furrowed with wrinkles; **ça creuse l'estomac,** it whets the appetite 2. *(a)* to excavate; to dig (out) (trench); to cut (canal); to sink, to bore (well); *Fig:* **c. un abîme,** to create a gulf (between two people) *(b)* to examine (a problem); to go thoroughly into (a question) 3. **se c.,** to grow hollow; **se c. la tête,** to rack one's brains.

creuset [krøze] *nm* crucible, melting pot.

creux, -euse [krø, -øz] 1. *a* hollow; **yeux c.,** deep-set eyes; **voix creuse,** deep voice; **avoir l'estomac c.,** to be ravenous; **période creuse,** slack season; **heures creuses,** off-peak hours; **paroles creuses,** empty words 2. *adv* **sonner c.,** to sound hollow 3. *nm* hollow; hole; trough (of wave); belly (of sail); pit (of stomach); **le c. des reins,** the small of the back; **c. de la main,** hollow of one's hand; **avoir un c. dans l'estomac,** to be ravenous.

crevaison [krəvɛzɔ̃] *nf Aut:* puncture, *NAm:* flat.

crevasse [krəvas] *nf* crack (in skin); crevice (in wall); crevasse (in glacier).

crevasser (se) [səkrəvase] *vpr* to crack.

crève-cœur [krɛvkœr] *nm inv* heartbreak.

crève-la-faim [krɛvlafɛ̃] *nm inv* down-and-out.

crever [krəve] *v* (**je crève**) 1. *vi (a)* to burst, split; **mon pneu a crevé, j'ai crevé,** I've got a puncture, *NAm:* a flat; **c. d'orgueil,** to be bursting with pride; **c. de rire,** to split (one's sides) laughing *(b) (of animals), P: (of people)* to die; *F:* **c. de faim,** (i) to starve to death (ii) to be starving; **on crève de chaleur ici,** it's boiling in here 2. *vtr (a)* to burst (balloon, dam); to puncture (tyre); **c. le cœur à qn,** to break s.o.'s heart; **c. un œil à qn,** (i) to put out s.o.'s eye (ii) *(accidentally)* to blind s.o. in one eye; *F:* **ça vous crève les yeux,** it's staring you in the face *(b)* **c. qn,** to work s.o. to death; **se c. au travail,** to work oneself to death. **crevant** *a P:* killing; exhausting. **crevé** *a (a)* burst; punctured *(b) F:* dead *(c) P:* worn out.

crevette [krəvɛt] *nf* **c. grise,** shrimp; **c. (rose),** prawn.

cri [kri] *nm (a)* cry (of animal, person); squeal (of animal); chirp (of bird, insect) *(b)* shout, call; scream; **c. du cœur,** cri de cœur; **c. de guerre,** war cry; **c. d'horreur,** shriek of horror; **pousser un c. aigu,** to scream *(c) F:* **le dernier c.,** the latest fashion; the latest thing.

criailler [krijaje] *vi* 1. to cry out, bawl 2. to whine, complain, *F:* grouse; **c. après qn,** to nag s.o.

criailleries [krijajri] *nfpl* whining, *F:* grousing.

criard [kriar] *a (a)* squalling; scolding (woman) *(b)* **voix criarde,** shrill, piercing, voice; **couleur criarde,** loud colour.

criblage [kriblaʒ] *nm* sifting; riddling; screening.

crible [kribl] *nm* sieve, riddle; screen; **passer qch au c.,** (i) to screen sth (ii) to examine sth closely.

cribler [krible] *vtr* 1. to sift, riddle; to screen 2. **c. qn de balles,** to riddle s.o. with bullets; **c. qn de questions,** to bombard s.o. with questions. **criblé** *a* riddled (with holes); **c. de dettes,** up to one's eyes in debt.

cric [krik] *nm* (lifting) jack.

criée [krije] *nf* (**vente à la**) **c.,** (sale by) auction.

crier [krije] 1. *vi (a)* to cry; to call out, to shout; to scream, to shriek; to yell; **c. de douleur,** to cry out in pain; **c. après qn,** to rail against s.o.; **c. au secours,** to shout for help *(b) (of mouse)* to squeak; *(of cricket)* to chirp; *(of birds)* to call *(c) (of door)* to creak *(d) (of colours)* to clash 2. *vtr* to cry, hawk (vegetables); **c. qch sur les toits,** to cry sth from the house-tops; **c. un ordre,** to shout an order; **c. famine,** to cry famine; **c. vengeance,** to call for vengeance.

crieur, -euse [krijœr, -øz] *n* (street) hawker; **c. de journaux,** newspaper seller; *Hist:* **c. public,** town crier.

crime [krim] *nm (a)* crime; *Jur:* felony *(b)* murder *(c)* **ce n'est pas un c.!** it's not a crime!

Crimée [krime] *Prnf Geog:* Crimea.

criminalité [kriminalite] *nf* criminality. **criminel, -elle** 1. *a* criminal 2. *n* criminal; murderer; **voilà le c.,** there's the culprit. **criminellement** *adv* criminally.

crin [krɛ̃] *nm* horsehair; **les crins,** the mane and tail.

crinière [krinjɛr] *nf* mane; *(of pers)* mop of hair.

crique [krik] *nf* creek, cove.

crise [kriz] *nf* 1. crisis; emergency; **c. économique,** economic crisis; slump; **c. du logement,** housing shortage 2. *Med:* attack; (epileptic) fit; **c. de foie, c. cardiaque**, bilious attack; heart attack; **c. de nerfs**, fit of hysterics; **piquer une c.**, to throw a tantrum.

crispation [krispasjɔ̃] *nf* (*a*) tensing (of face) (*b*) nervous twitching; wince (of pain).

crisper [krispe] *vtr* (*a*) to contract; to clench; **visage crispé par la douleur**, face contorted with pain; **cela me crispe**, it gets on my nerves (*b*) **se c.**, to contract; to become tense; **ses mains se crispaient sur le volant**, his hands tightened on the wheel. **crispant** *a* irritating. **crispé** *a* nervous; tense.

crissement [krismɑ̃] *nm* grinding (of teeth); squeaking (of chalk); screeching (of brakes); crunching (of gravel).

crisser [krise] *vtr & i* to grate; to make a grinding sound; (*of brakes*) to screech; (*of gravel*) to crunch.

cristal, -aux [kristal, -o] *nm* **1.** crystal; **c. de roche**, rock crystal **2.** crystal (glass) **3.** **cristaux (de soude)**, washing soda. **cristallin, -ine 1.** *a* crystalline; crystal-clear **2.** *nm Anat:* crystalline lens.

cristallerie [kristalri] *nf* (crystal) glassworks.

cristallisation [kristalizasjɔ̃] *nf* crystallization.

cristalliser [kristalize] *vtr & i* to crystallize.

critère [kritɛr] *nm* criterion.

critérium [kriterjɔm] *nm Sp:* (eliminating) heat.

critique [kritik] **1.** *a* (*a*) critical; crucial (*b*) critical; **esprit c.**, critical mind **2.** *nm* critic; **c. d'art**, art critic **3.** *nf* (*a*) criticism (*b*) critical article; review; **faire la c. d'une pièce**, to review a play (*c*) censure.

critiquer [kritike] *vtr* (*a*) to criticize; to examine (sth) critically (*b*) to censure; to find fault with (s.o., sth). **critiquable** *a* open to criticism.

croassement [krɔasmɑ̃] *nm* caw(ing), croak(ing).

croasser [krɔase] *vi* to caw; to croak.

croc [kro] *nm* **1.** hook **2.** canine tooth; fang (of wolf); **montrer ses crocs**, to show one's teeth.

croc-en-jambe [krɔkɑ̃ʒɑ̃b] *nm* **faire un c.-en-j. à qn**, to trip s.o. up; *pl* **crocs-en-jambe**.

croche [krɔʃ] *nf Mus:* quaver; *NAm:* eighth note.

croche-pied [krɔʃpje] *nm* = **croc-en-jambe**; *pl* **croche-pieds**.

crochet [krɔʃɛ] *nm* **1.** (*a*) hook; **c. à boutons**, buttonhook; **vivre aux crochets de qn**, to live off s.o. (*b*) crochet hook; **faire qch au c.**, to crochet sth **2.** **c. de serrurier**, picklock **3.** (snake) fang **4.** *Typ:* square bracket **5.** **faire un c.**, (*of road*) to take a sudden turn; (*of pers*) to make a detour **6.** *Box:* hook **7.** **c. radiophonique**, talent contest.

crocheter [krɔʃte] *vtr* (**je crochète, n. crochetons**) to pick (lock).

crochu [krɔʃy] *a* hooked (nose); claw-like (fingers).

crocodile [krɔkɔdil] *nm* crocodile.

crocus [krɔkys] *nm Bot:* crocus.

croire [krwar] *v* (*prp* **croyant**; *pp* **cru**) **1.** *vtr* (*a*) **c. qch**, to believe sth; **il est à c. que** + *ind*, it is probable that; **tout porte à c. que**, there is every indication that; *F:* **faut pas c.!** don't you believe it! **je ne crois pas que cela suffise**, I don't think that will be enough; **je crois que oui**, I believe so; **n'en croyez rien!** don't you believe it! **à ce que je crois**, in my opinion; **on se croirait en octobre**, it feels like October; **je vous croyais anglais**, I thought you were English; **j'ai cru bien faire**, I thought I was doing the right thing; **il ne croyait pas si bien dire**, he didn't

know how right he was; **il se croit tout permis**, he thinks he can get away with anything; **il se croit malin**, he thinks he's clever (*b*) **c. qn**, to believe s.o.; **me croira qui voudra, mais**, believe me or not, but; *F:* **je te crois!** rather! of course! **vous pouvez m'en c.**, you can take it from me; **à l'en c., s'il faut l'en c., ce n'est pas difficile**, according to him, it's not difficult; **je ne pouvais en c. mes yeux**, I couldn't believe my eyes **2.** *vi* (*a*) to believe in (the existence of sth); **c'est à ne pas y c.**, it is beyond belief; it's unbelievable; **le médecin crut à une rougeole**, the doctor thought it was measles; *Corr:* **veuillez c. à mes sentiments distingués** = yours sincerely (*b*) to believe (in), have faith (in) (s.o.); **il ne croit plus**, he has lost his faith (in God).

croisade [krwazad] *nf Hist:* crusade.

croisé [krwaze] **1.** *a* (*a*) crossed; **mots croisés**, crossword; *Agr:* **race croisée**, crossbreed (*b*) double-breasted (coat) **2.** *nm* crusader.

croisée [krwaze] *nf* **1.** crossing; **à la c. de chemins**, at the crossroads, at the parting of the ways **2.** casement.

croisement [krwazmɑ̃] *nm* **1.** crossing, passing **2.** crossing (of roads); **c. (de routes)**, crossroads **3.** (*a*) crossbreeding (*b*) crossbreed; cross.

croiser [krwaze] **1.** *vtr* (*a*) to cross to intersect; **c. les bras**, (i) to fold one's arms (ii) to refuse to work; **c. qn dans l'escalier**, to pass s.o. on the stairs; **nos lettres se sont croisées**, our letters have crossed in the post (*b*) to interbreed, cross(breed) (animals, plants) **2.** *vi* (*a*) (*of garment*) to lap, fold over (*b*) *Nau:* to cruise **3.** **se c.** (*a*) to cross, to intersect; **leurs regards se sont croisés**, their eyes met (*b*) **le cheval peut se c. avec l'âne**, the horse can be crossed with the donkey.

croiseur [krwazœr] *nm Nau:* cruiser.

croisière [krwazjɛr] *nf* cruise.

croissance [krwasɑ̃s] *nf* growth, development.

croissant [krwasɑ̃] *nm* **1.** crescent (of moon) **2.** *Cu:* croissant.

croître [krwatr] *vi* (*prp* **croissant**; *pp* **crû**, *f* **crue**; *pr ind* **je crois, il croît**) to grow, increase (in size); (*of moon*) to wax; (*of river*) to rise; (*of heat*) to get more and more intense; (*of days*) to get longer.

croix [krwa] *nf* **1.** (*a*) cross; **la Sainte C.**, the Holy Cross; **mettre en c.**, to crucify; **mise en c.**, crucifixion; **faire le signe de (la) c.**, to cross oneself (*b*) **c'est la c. et la bannière**, it's the devil of a job; **la C. Rouge**, the Red Cross; *Mil:* **la C. de Guerre**, the Military Cross **2.** (*a*) **mettre les bras en c.**, to stretch one's arms out sideways; **marquer qch d'une c.**, to mark sth with a cross; *F:* **faire une c. sur qch**, to give sth up for good (*b*) **c. gammée**, swastika.

croque(-)mitaine [krɔkmitɛn] *nm* bogeyman; *pl* **croque(-)mitaines**.

croque-monsieur [krɔkməsjø] *nm inv* toasted cheese and ham sandwich.

croque-mort [krɔkmɔr] *nm* undertaker; *pl* **croque-morts**.

croquer [krɔke] **1.** *vi* (*a*) (*of fruit*) to crunch (between the teeth) (*b*) **c. dans une pomme**, to bite into an apple **2.** *vtr* (*a*) to crunch, munch; **chocolat à c.**, plain chocolate (*b*) to sketch; *F:* **elle est jolie à c.**, she's as pretty as a picture. **croquant** *a* crisp, crunchy.

croquet [krɔkɛ] *nm Games:* croquet.

croquette [krɔkɛt] *nf Cu:* rissole, croquette.

croquis [krɔki] *nm* sketch.

crosse [krɔs] *nf* 1. (bishop's) crook, crozier 2. *Sp:* (hockey) stick; (golf) club; *F:* **chercher des crosses à qn**, to pick a quarrel with s.o. 3. butt (of rifle); grip (of pistol).

crotale [krɔtal] *nm* rattlesnake.

crotte [krɔt] *nf (a)* dung; dropping; **c. de chien**, dog's dirt *(b)* **c. de chocolat**, chocolate *(c) O:* mud.

crotter [krɔte] *vtr* to dirty; to cover in mud. **crotté** *a* muddy.

crottin [krɔtɛ̃] *nm* (horse) dung, manure.

crouler [krule] *vi (a)* to totter *(b)* to collapse; *Th:* **faire c. la salle**, to bring the house down. **croulant** 1. *a* tumbledown, ramshackle (building); tottering (empire) 2. *nm P:* (of parents) **les croulants**, the old folk.

croup [krup] *nm Med:* croup.

croupe [krup] *nf* 1. croup, rump (of horse); **monter en c.**, to ride pillion 2. brow (of hill).

croupier [krupje] *nm* croupier (at casino).

croupir [krupir] *vi* 1. to wallow (in filth, in vice) 2. (of water) to stagnate. **croupi** *a* stagnant.

CROUS [krus] *abbr Centre régional des œuvres universitaires et scolaires.*

croustiller [krustije] *vi* (of food) to be crunchy; to be crisp, crusty. **croustillant** *a* crisp, crusty.

croûte [krut] *nf* 1. crust (of bread, pie); (cheese) rind; **la c. terrestre**, the earth's crust; **casser la c.**, to eat; *P:* **à la c.!** grub's up! 2. scab (on wound) 3. undressed leather; hide 4. *F:* daub.

croûton [krutɔ̃] *nm* 1. crust (of loaf) 2. *Cu:* croûton 3. *P:* old fossil.

croyance [krwajɑ̃s] *nf* belief (à, in). **croyable** *a* believable, credible; **pas c.**, unbelievable, incredible.

croyant, -ante [krwajɑ̃, -ɑ̃t] *n* believer.

CRS *abbr Compagnie républicaine de sûreté* = riot police.

cru[1] [kry] *a* raw, uncooked (food); raw (material); harsh, crude (colour); blunt (answer); crude, coarse (joke). **crûment** *adv* crudely; bluntly; coarsely.

cru[2] *nm* vineyard; **vin du c.**, local wine; **un grand c.**, a great wine; a vintage wine; **une histoire de son (propre) c.**, a story of his own invention.

cruauté [kryote] *nf* cruelty (**envers**, to).

cruche [kryʃ] *nf (a)* pitcher, jug *(b) F:* idiot, ass.

crucial, -iaux [krysjal, -jo] *a* crucial.

crucifier [krysifje] *vtr* to crucify.

crucifix [krysifi] *nm inv* crucifix.

crucifixion [krysifiksjɔ̃] *nf* crucifixion.

crudité [krydite] *nf* 1. **crudités**, raw vegetable hors d'œuvres 2. *(a)* crudity (of colours); glare (of light) *(b)* coarseness (of expression).

crue [kry] *nf* rising (of river); flood; **rivière en c.**, river in spate.

cruel, -elle [kryɛl] *a* cruel (**envers**, to); bitter (experience). **cruellement** *adv* cruelly; bitterly.

crûment [krymɑ̃] *adv see* **cru**[1].

crustacé [krystase] *nm* shellfish; **crustacés**, seafood, shellfish.

crypte [kript] *nf* crypt.

Cuba [kyba] *Prnf* Cuba. **cubain, -aine** *a & n* Cuban.

cube [kyb] 1. *nm (a) Mth:* cube; **élever au c.**, to cube (a number) *(b) Toys:* (wooden) brick 2. *a* **mètre c.**, cubic metre. **cubique** *a* cubic.

cuber [kybe] 1. *vtr Mth:* to cube (number) 2. *vi (a)* **c. 20 litres**, to have a cubic capacity of 20 litres *(b) F:* to mount up.

cubisme [kybism] *nm Art:* cubism. **cubiste** *a & n* cubist.

cubitus [kybitys] *nf Anat:* ulna.

cueillette [kœjɛt] *nf (a)* gathering, picking (of fruit, flowers) *(b)* crop, harvest.

cueillir [kœjir] *vtr (prp cueillant; pr ind je cueille; fu je cueillerai)* to pick, pluck, gather (flowers, fruit); to steal (a kiss); **c. des lauriers**, to win laurels; *F:* **c. qn**, (i) to pick s.o. up (ii) to arrest, nab, s.o.

cuiller, cuillère [kɥijɛr] *nf* 1. *(a)* spoon; **c. à soupe**, soup spoon; **c. à café**, (i) coffee spoon (ii) teaspoon *(b)* spoonful *(c) Fish:* spoon bait 2. *P:* hand, paw. **cuillerée** [kɥijre] *nf* spoonful.

cuir [kɥir] *nm* 1. *(a) Anat:* **c. chevelu**, scalp *(b)* hide 2. leather; **c. vert, brut**, raw hide; **c. verni**, patent leather.

cuirasse [kɥiras] *nf* 1. cuirass 2. armour (of warship, tank).

cuirassé [kɥirase] *nm* battleship.

cuirasser [kɥirase] *vtr* 1. to put a cuirass on (soldier); **se c. contre qch**, to steel oneself against sth 2. to armour(-plate) ship.

cuirassier [kɥirasje] *nm Mil:* cuirassier.

cuire [kɥir] *v (prp cuisant; pp cuit; pr ind je cuis, n. cuisons; fu je cuirai)* 1. *vtr (a)* to cook; **c. à l'eau**, to boil; **c. au four**, to bake, to roast *(b)* to fire (bricks) 2. *vi (a)* (of food) to cook; **c. à petit feu**, to cook slowly; to simmer; **chocolat à c.**, cooking chocolate; *F:* **on cuit dans cette salle**, the room's like an oven; **se c. au soleil**, to roast in the sun *(b)* to burn, smart; **les yeux me cuisent**, my eyes are smarting; *impers* **il vous en cuira**, you'll regret it.

cuisant [kɥizɑ̃] *a* smarting, burning (pain); biting (cold); caustic (remark); bitter (disappointment).

cuisine [kɥizin] *nf* 1. kitchen; **batterie de c.**, cooking utensils 2. *(a)* (art of) cooking; cookery; **faire la c.**, (i) to do the cooking (ii) to be cooking a meal *(b) F:* (dirty) tricks 3. (cooked) food.

cuisiner [kɥizine] 1. *vi* to cook 2. *vtr (a)* to cook (meat) *(b) F:* to grill (s.o.).

cuisinier, -ière [kɥizinje, -jɛr] 1. *n* cook 2. *nf* cooker, *NAm:* cookstove.

cuissardes [kɥisard] *nfpl* (i) thigh boots (ii) waders.

cuisse [kɥis] *nf* thigh; *Cu:* **c. de poulet**, chicken leg, *F:* drumstick; **se croire sorti de la c. de Jupiter**, to think a lot of oneself.

cuisson [kɥisɔ̃] *nf (a)* cooking *(b)* burning, firing (of bricks).

cuistot [kɥisto] *nm F:* cook.

cuit [kɥi] *a (a)* cooked; **bien c.**, well done; **c. à point**, done to a turn; **trop c.**, overdone, overcooked; **pas assez c.**, underdone *(b) F:* **il est c.**, he's had it *(c) F:* **c'est du tout c.**, it's a cinch.

cuite [kɥit] *nf F:* **prendre une c.**, to get drunk, plastered.

cuivre [kɥivr] *nm* **c. (rouge)**, copper; **c. jaune**, brass; *Mus:* **les cuivres**, the brass. **cuivré** *a* 1. copper

coloured; coppery; **teint c.**, bronzed complexion. 2.
Mus: **sons cuivrés**, brassy tones.

cul [ky] *nm* 1. (*a*) *P:* backside, bottom (of pers); *P:*
quel c.! a ce qu'il est c.! what a bloody fool! (*b*)
rump (of animal) 2. bottom, base (of bottle).

culasse [kylas] *nf* 1. breech (of gun) 2. *ICE:* cylinder
head.

culbute [kylbyt] *nf* (*a*) somersault (*b*) tumble; heavy
fall (*c*) *F:* **faire la c.**, (*of ministry*) to fall; (*of business*)
to collapse.

culbuter [kylbyte] 1. *vi* to turn a somersault; (*of
car*) to overturn; (*of thing*) to topple over 2. *vtr* to
knock over (sth); to overwhelm (enemy); to topple
(ministry).

cul-de-jatte [kydʒat] *nm* legless cripple; *pl culs-de-
jatte.*

cul-de-sac [kydsak] *nm* blind alley, cul-de-sac; *pl
culs-de-sac.*

culinaire [kyliner] *a* culinary.

culminer [kylmine] *vi* to culminate; to reach its peak.
culminant *a* **point c.**, highest point; height, climax.

culot [kylo] *nm* (*a*) *Sma:* base (of cartridge case,
shell); head (of cartridge); *El:* base (of bulb) (*b*) *F:*
cheek, nerve.

culotte [kylɔt] *nf* 1. *Cu:* rump (of beef) 2. (*a*) **une c.**,
knee breeches; **c. longue**, trousers; **c. de cheval**, riding
breeches; jodhpurs; **c. de golf**, plus fours; *F:* **c'est la
femme qui porte la c.**, it's the wife who wears the
trousers (*b*) (child's, woman's) panties, pants.

culotté [kylɔte] *a* 1. (*of pipe*) seasoned 2. *F:* full of
nerve; cheeky.

culpabilité [kylpabilite] *nf* culpability, guilt.

culte [kylt] *nm* 1. worship; **avoir le c. de l'argent**, to
worship money 2. form of worship; cult; religion;
liberté du c., freedom of worship.

cultivateur, -trice [kyltivatœr, -tris] *n* farmer.

cultiver [kyltive] *vtr* 1. to cultivate, farm (land) 2.
(*a*) to cultivate, grow (plants) (*b*) to cultivate (s.o.'s
friendship) 3. **se c.**, to broaden one's mind. **culti-
vable** *a* suitable for cultivation. **cultivé** *a* cultured, educated (pers).

culture [kyltyr] *nf* 1. (*a*) cultivation (of the soil); **c.
fruitière**, fruit farming (*b*) *pl* land under cultivation
2. cultivation (of plants) 3. culture; education; **c.
physique**, physical training. **culturel, -elle** *a* cultural; educational.

culturisme [kyltyrism] *nm* body building.

cumin [kymɛ̃] *nm Bot:* (*a*) cum(m)in (*b*) *Cu:* caraway
seeds.

cumul [kymyl] *nm* plurality (of offices); **c. des traitements**, concurrent drawing of salary.

cumuler [kymyle] *vtr & i* **c. des fonctions**, to hold a
plurality of offices; **c. deux traitements**, to draw two
(separate) salaries.

cupidité [kypidite] *nf* greed. **cupide** *a* greedy.

curage [kyraʒ] *nm* cleaning out.

cure [kyr] *nf* 1. care; *used only in* **n'avoir c. de qch**,
not to care about sth 2. *Ecc:* (*a*) office of parish
priest (*b*) parish (*c*) presbytery 3. *Med:* (course of)
treatment; cure; **c. d'amaigrissement**, slimming cure.
curable *a* curable. **curatif, -ive** curative.

curé [kyre] *nm* parish priest.

cure-dent(s) [kyrdɑ̃] *nm inv* toothpick; *pl cure-
dents.*

curée [kyre] *nf* (*a*) part of stag given to hounds (*b*)
scramble.

cure-pipe [kyrpip] *nm* pipe-cleaner; *pl cure-pipes.*

curer [kyre] *vtr* to clean out (drain, river); **se c. les
dents, les ongles**, to pick one's teeth; to clean one's
nails.

curieux, -ieuse [kyrjø, -jøz] *a* 1. (*a*) inquiring
(mind) (*b*) curious, interested; **je serai c. de voir cela**,
I shall be interested to see it (*c*) curious, inquisitive
(*d*) *n* inquisitive person; *F:* busybody; **attroupement
de c.**, crowd of bystanders, onlookers 2. (*a*) (*of
thing*) odd, peculiar, funny (*b*) *nm* **le c. dans cette
affaire**, the curious thing about this business.
curieusement *adv* curiously, strangely.

curiosité [kyrjozite] *nf* 1. (*a*) curiosity; interest (*b*)
inquisitiveness 2. curio; **curiosités d'une ville**, sights
of a town.

curiste [kyrist] *n* patient taking the waters at a spa.

cutané [kytane] *a* cutaneous; skin (disease).

cutiréaction [kytireaksjɔ̃] *nf Med:* skin test.

cuve [kyv] *nf* (*a*) vat (*b*) tank.

cuver [kyve] 1. *vi* (*of wine*) to ferment 2. *vtr F:* **c. son
vin**, to sleep it off.

cuvette [kyvɛt] *nf* 1. basin, bowl; **c. (de lavabo)**,
washbasin 2. pan (of WC) 3. *Geog:* basin.

cyanure [sjanyr] *nm Ch:* cyanide.

cyclamen [siklamɛn] *nm Bot:* cyclamen.

cycle [sik]] *nm* 1. cycle (of events); *Sch:* **premier c.,
second c.**, first, second, stage of (secondary) education 2. bicycle; cycle. **cyclique** *a* cyclical.

cyclisme [siklism] *nm* cycling. **cycliste** 1. *a* cycle
(race); **coureur c.**, racing cyclist 2. *n* cyclist.

cyclomoteur [siklomotœr] *nm* moped.

cyclomotoriste [siklomotorist] *n* moped rider.

cyclone [siklon] *nm* cyclone; *Fig:* whirlwind.

cyclope [siklɔp] *nm* cyclops.

cygne [siɲ] *nm* swan; **jeune c.**, cygnet.

cylindre [silɛ̃dr] *nm* (*a*) cylinder (*b*) roller. **cylindrique** *a* cylindrical.

cylindrée [silɛ̃dre] *nf Mch: ICE:* cubic capacity (of
cylinder, engine).

cymbale [sɛ̃bal] *nf Mus:* cymbal.

cynique [sinik] 1. *a* cynical 2. *nm* cynic. **cyniquement** *adv* cynically.

cynisme [sinism] *nm* cynicism.

cyprès [siprɛ] *nm Bot:* cypress.

cypriote [siprijɔt] *a & n Geog:* Cypriot.

cytise [sitiz] *nm Bot:* laburnum.

D

D¹, d [de] *nm* (the letter) D, d.

D² *abbr* (route) *départementale.*

DAB *abbr Distributeur automatique de billets,* cash dispenser.

dac, d'ac [dak] *int F:* OK.

dactylo [daktilo] *nf* (*a*) typist (*b*) typing.

dactylographie [daktilɔgrafi] *nf* typing.

dactylographier [daktilɔgrafje] *vtr* to type, to type out.

dada [dada] *nm F:* 1. (*child's language*) gee-gee 2. pet subject.

dadais [dadɛ] *nm F:* grand d., awkward boy.

dague [dag] *nf* dagger.

dahlia [dalja] *nm Bot:* dahlia.

daigner [dɛɲe] *vtr* to deign, condescend; elle n'a même pas daigné me voir, she wouldn't even see me.

daim [dɛ̃] *nm* (fallow) deer; buck; (**peau de) d.,** (i) buckskin (ii) suede.

daine [dɛn] *nf* doe.

dais [dɛ] *nm* canopy.

dallage [dalaʒ] *nm* paving; flagging.

dalle [dal] *nf* (*a*) flag(stone); paving stone (*b*) slab (of marble) (*c*) *P:* je n'y vois que d., I can't see a damned thing.

daller [dale] *vtr* to pave.

daltonisme [daltɔnism] *nm* colour blindness. **daltonien, -ienne** *a & n* colour blind (person).

dam [dɑ̃] *nm* au grand d. de qn, to s.o.'s great displeasure.

dame¹ [dam] *nf* 1. (*a*) lady (*b*) married woman; *P:* votre d., your missus (*c*) d. d'honneur, lady-in-waiting; d. de compagnie, lady's companion 2. (*a*) jeu de dames, (game of) draughts, *NAm:* checkers (*b*) (*at draughts*) king; *Chess: Cards:* queen; aller à d., (i) (*at draughts*) to make a king (ii) *Chess:* to queen (a pawn).

dame² *int A:* d. oui! well, yes! rather!

damer [dame] *vtr* 1. (*at draughts*) to crown (a piece); *Fig:* d. le pion à qn, to go one better than s.o. 2. to tamp (earth).

damier [damje] *nm* draughtboard, *NAm:* checkerboard; tissu en damier, chequered material.

damnation [dɑnasjɔ̃] *nf* damnation.

damner [dɑne] *vtr* to damn. **damné, -ée** *a & n* damned.

dancing [dɑ̃siŋ] *nm* dance hall.

dandinement [dɑ̃dinmɑ̃] *nm* waddle.

dandiner (se) [sədɑ̃dine] *vpr* to waddle.

Danemark [danmark] *Prnm Geog:* Denmark.

danger [dɑ̃ʒe] *nm* danger, peril; à l'abri du d., out of harm's way; courir un d., to be in danger; to run a risk; il n'y a pas de d., it's quite safe; mettre en d., to endanger; sans d., safe(ly); securely; *F:* pas de d.! not likely! no fear! *Med:* hors de d., off the danger list; d. public, public menace. **dangereux, -euse** *a* dangerous (**pour,** to, for). **dangereusement** *adv* dangerously.

danois, -oise [danwa, -waz] 1. *a* Danish 2. *n* (*cap* D) Dane; *Z:* grand D., Great Dane 3. *nm Ling:* Danish.

dans [dɑ̃] *prep* 1. (*of position*) (*a*) in; d. une boîte, in(side) a box; lire qch d. un journal, to read sth in the newspaper (*b*) within; d. un rayon de dix kilomètres, within a radius of ten kilometres (*c*) into; mettre qch d. une boîte, to put sth in(to) a box; tomber d. l'oubli, to sink into oblivion (*d*) out of; boire d. un verre, to drink out of a glass; copier qch d. un livre, to copy sth out of a book 2. (*of time*) (*a*) in, within; during; d. le temps, long ago, formerly; je serai prêt à partir d. cinq minutes, I shall be ready to go in five minutes; payer d. les dix jours, to pay within ten days (*b*) cela coûte d. les 10 francs, it costs about 10 francs 3. (*a*) être d. le commerce, to be in trade (*b*) d. les circonstances, in, under, the circumstances; être d. la nécessité de, to be obliged to; d. ce but, with this aim in view.

danse [dɑ̃s] *nf* dance, dancing; *Med:* d. de Saint-Guy, St Vitus's dance; professeur de d., dance teacher.

danser [dɑ̃se] *vi* to dance; faire d. qn, (i) to dance with s.o. (ii) *F:* to lead s.o. a dance. **dansant** *a* dancing; springy (step); lively (tune); soirée dansante, dance.

danseur, -euse [dɑ̃sœr, -øz] *n* (*a*) dancer (*b*) partner.

dard [dar] *nm* (*a*) sting (of insect) (*b*) tongue (of flame).

darder [darde] *vtr* 1. to hurl, dart (pointed object); to shoot forth; il a dardé sur moi un regard chargé de haine, he shot a glance of hatred at me 2. (*of thorn*) to point.

dare-dare [dardar] *adv* double-quick.

datation [datasjɔ̃] *nf* dating.

date [dat] *nf* date; sans d., undated; prendre d. pour qch, to fix a date for sth; (*of event*) faire d., to mark an epoch; être le premier en d., to come first; je le connais de longue d., I've known him for a long time; d. limite, deadline.

dater [date] 1. *vtr* to date (letter); non daté, undated 2. *vi* to date (**de,** from); à d. de ce jour, from today; de quand date votre dernier repas? when did you last eat? qui date, (i) memorable (event) (ii) dated, old-fashioned (dress).

datif, -ive [datif, -iv] *a & nm* dative (case).

datte [dat] *nf Bot:* date.

dattier [datje] *nm* date palm.

daube [dob] *nf* stew, casserole; bœuf en d., beef stew.

dauphin [dofɛ̃] *nm* 1. dolphin 2. (*a*) Dauphin (*b*) heir apparent.

davantage [davɑ̃taʒ] *adv* (*a*) more; il m'en faut d., I need still more; je n'en dis pas d., I shall say no more; nous ne resterons pas d., we will not stay any longer; se baisser d., to stoop lower; chaque jour d., more and more every day (b) **elle en a d. que lui**, she's got more than him.

DCA *abbr Défence contre avions.*

DDT *abbr dichloro-diphényl-trichloréthane.*

de [də] *(before vowels and h 'mute'* **d'**; **de** + *def art* **le**, **les**, *are contracted into* **du**, **des**) **1.** *prep (a)* from; **l'idée est de moi**, the idea is mine; **il l'a oublié? c'est bien de lui**, did he forget it? that's just like him; **du matin au soir**, from morning till night; **de vous à moi**, between ourselves; **de 20 à 30 personnes**, between 20 and 30 people; **de jour en jour**, from day to day (b) *(time)* **il partit de nuit**, he left by night; **de mon temps**, in my day *(c) (agent)* **accompagné de ses amis**, accompanied by his friends; **la statue est de Rodin**, the statue is by Rodin; **j'ai fait cela de ma propre main**, it's all my own work *(d) (manner)* **regarder qn d'un air amusé**, to look at s.o. with an amused expression *(e) (cause)* **sauter de joie**, to jump for joy; **tomber de fatigue**, to be ready to drop with exhaustion; **de soi-même**, of one's own accord *(f) (measure)* **âgé de seize ans**, sixteen years old; **ma montre retarde de dix minutes**, my watch is ten minutes slow; **la terrasse a 20 mètres de long**, the terrace is 20 metres long; **cheque de £10**, cheque for £10 *(g) (introducing complement of adj)* **digne d'éloges**, worthy of praise **2.** *prep (a)* **le livre de Pierre**, Peter's book; **le toit de la maison**, the roof of the house; **la conférence de Berlin**, the Berlin conference *(b) (material)* **un pont de fer**, an iron bridge *(c) (distinguishing mark)* **le professeur de français**, the French teacher; **le journal d'hier**, yesterday's paper *(d) (partitive)* **un verre de vin**, a glass of wine; **quelque chose de bon**, something good; **je ne l'ai pas vu de la soirée**, I haven't seen him all evening *(e) (forming compound prepositions)* **près de la maison**, near the house; **autour du jardin**, round the garden; **à partir de ce jour-là**, from that day onward *(f) (connecting vb and object)* **approcher de Paris**, to get near Paris; **manquer de courage**, to lack courage; **convenir d'une erreur**, to admit an error **3.** *serving as a link word (a)* **le mieux était de rire**, it was best to laugh; **je crains d'être en retard**, I'm afraid of being late *(b)* **la ville de Paris**, the city of Paris; **un drôle de type**, a funny chap; **il y eut trois hommes de tués**, three men were killed; *F:* **c'est d'un réussi!** it's *such* a success! **4.** *partitive article (used also as pl of* **un, une**) **n'avez-vous pas d'amis?** haven't you got any friends? **sans faire de fautes**, without making any mistakes; **donnez-nous de vos nouvelles**, let us hear from you; **avez-vous du pain?** have you any bread? *(intensive)* **mettre des heures à faire qch**, to spend hours over sth.

dé¹ [de] *nm (a) Gaming:* die; *pl* dice; **dés pipés**, loaded dice; **les dés sont jetés**, the die is cast *(b) Cu:* **couper en dés**, to dice (vegetables).

dé² *nm* **dé (à coudre)**, thimble.

DEA *abbr Diplôme d'études approfondies.*

déambuler [deãbyle] *vi* to stroll (about).

débâcle [debɑkl̩] *nf* **1.** break(ing) up (of drift ice) **2.** collapse (of a business) **3.** *Mil: etc:* rout.

déballage [debalaʒ] *nm (a)* unpacking *(b)* display (of goods).

déballer [debale] *vtr* to unpack (goods, cases).

débandade [debãdad] *nf* rout (of army); stampede (of horses); **à la d.**, in confusion.

débander [debãde] *vtr* **1.** to remove a bandage from (a wound) **2.** *Mil:* **se d.**, to break into a rout.

débaptiser [debatize] *vtr* to rename.

débarbouiller (se) [sədebarbuje] *vpr* to wash one's face.

débarcadère [debarkadɛr] *nm* landing stage, wharf.

débardeur [debardœr] *nm* **1.** docker **2.** *Cl:* tank top.

débarquement [debarkəmã] *nm* unloading (of cargo); landing (of passengers).

débarquer [debarke] **1.** *vtr* to unload (cargo); to disembark, land (passengers); to drop (pilot) **2.** *vi* to land, disembark (from boat); to alight (from train); *F:* **elle a débarqué hier soir**, she turned up last night.

débarras [debara] *nm (a)* riddance; **bon d.!** good riddance! *(b)* **(chambre de) d.**, boxroom.

débarrasser [debarase] *vtr* **1.** to disencumber; to clear (table); **d. qn de qch**, to relieve s.o. of sth; *F:* **d. le plancher**, to clear out **2.** **se d. de qch**, to get rid of sth; to extricate oneself from sth.

débat [deba] *nm* **1.** discussion; debate **2.** dispute.

débattre [debatr̩] *vtr (conj like* BATTRE*)* **1.** to debate, discuss; **prix à d.**, price by arrangement **2.** **se d.**, to struggle.

débauchage [deboʃaʒ] *nm* laying off (of workmen).

débauche [deboʃ] *nf* debauchery, dissolute living.

débauché, -ée 1. *a* debauched **2.** *n* debauchee.

débaucher [deboʃe] *vtr* **1.** *(a)* to lead (s.o.) astray; **d. la jeunesse**, to corrupt the young *(b) Ind:* to lay off (workers) **2.** **se d.**, to become corrupted.

débilité [debilite] *nf* debility; **d. mentale**, mental deficiency. **débile 1.** *a* weakly (child); weak, feeble **2.** *n* **un(e) d. mental(e)**, a mental defective.

débiliter [debilite] *vtr* to debilitate, weaken.

débiner [debine] *vtr F:* **1.** to run (s.o.) down **2.** **se d.**, to clear off.

débit¹ [debi] *nm* **1.** *(a)* (retail) sale *(b)* (retail) shop; *esp* **d. de tabac**, tobacconist's (shop); **d. de boissons**, bar; *F:* = pub **2.** *(a)* discharge (of pump); flow (of river) *(b) Ind:* output; *El:* power supplied **3.** delivery (of orator).

débit² *nm Com:* debit.

débitant, -ante [debitã, -ãt] *n* **d. de tabac**, tobacconist.

débiter¹ [debite] *vtr* **1.** to retail; to sell (goods) retail **2.** to cut up (meat) **3.** to discharge, to yield; *Ind:* to produce **4.** **d. des sottises**, to talk rubbish.

débiter² *vtr Com:* to debit.

débiteur, -trice [debitœr, -tris] **1.** *n* debtor **2.** *a* **compte d.**, debit account.

déblai [deblɛ] *nm* spoil earth.

déblaiement [deblɛmã] *nm* clearing (of ground).

déblayer [deblɛje] *vtr* **(je déblaye, je déblaie) 1.** to clear away (earth); to shovel away (snow) **2. d. un terrain**, (i) to clear a piece of ground (ii) to clear the way (for negotiations).

déblocage [debləkaʒ] *nm* freeing, releasing; unjamming; unfreezing (of prices).

débloquer [debləke] *vtr* **1.** to unjam (machine) **2.** to free, to release; *Fin:* to unfreeze (prices).

déboire [debwar] *nm* disappointment; setback.

déboisement [debwazmɑ̃] *nm* deforestation.

déboiser [debwaze] *vtr* to deforest (land).

déboîtement [debwatmɑ̃] *nm* dislocation (of limb).

déboîter [debwate] *vtr* 1. to disconnect (pipe) 2. to dislocate (joint); **se d. l'épaule,** to put one's shoulder out 3. *vi Aut:* to filter; to pull out.

débonnaire [debɔnɛr] *a* good-natured, easy-going.

débordement [debɔrdəmɑ̃] *nm* 1. (*a*) overflowing; **d. d'injures,** outburst, torrent, of abuse (*b*) *pl* excesses 2. *Mil:* outflanking (of enemy).

déborder [debɔrde] 1. *vtr & i* to overflow, run over; **plein à d.,** full to overflowing; **elle déborde de vie,** she's bubbling over with vitality 2. *vtr* (*a*) to project, stick out, beyond (sth); to overlap (sth) (*b*) *Mil:* to outflank (enemy) (*c*) to untuck (bed). **débordant** *a* 1. overflowing, brimming over; bursting (with health) 2. projecting; overlapping. **débordé** *a* 1. overflowing 2. snowed under (with work).

débouchage [debuʃaʒ] *nm* uncorking; unblocking.

débouché [debuʃe] *nm* 1. outlet (of passage) 2. opening; opportunity; *Com:* outlet.

déboucher¹ [debuʃe] *vtr* 1. to clear (choked pipe) 2. to uncork (bottle).

déboucher² *vi* to emerge, come out.

déboucler [debukle] *vtr* to unbuckle (belt).

débours [debur] *nm* disbursement; expenses; outlay.

débourser [deburse] *vtr* to spend, lay out (money).

debout [dəbu] *adv* (*a*) (*of thg*) upright, on end; (*of pers*) standing; **mettre qch d.,** to stand sth up; **tenir d.,** to be kept upright; **se tenir d.,** to stand; **places d. seulement,** standing room only; **ça ne tient pas d.,** that doesn't hold water; **se remettre d.,** to stand up; **rester d.,** to remain standing; **conte à dormir d.,** tall story (*b*) (*of pers*) **être d.,** to be up; **allons, d.! come on, get up!**

déboutonner [debutɔne] *vtr* 1. to unbutton 2. **se d.,** to unbutton oneself; (*of jacket*) to come undone.

débraillé [debraje] 1. *a* untidy, slovenly (person); sloppy (appearance); rude (manners) 2. *nm* untidiness, slovenliness.

débrancher [debrɑ̃ʃe] *vtr El: etc:* to disconnect; to unplug.

débrayage [debrɛjaʒ] *nm* 1. *Aut:* clutch 2. *F:* going on strike.

débrayer [debrɛje] *vi* (**je débraye, je débraie**) 1. *Aut:* to release the clutch 2. *Ind: F:* to go on strike.

débridé [debride] *a* unbridled.

débris [debri] *nmpl* remains, debris, fragments, scraps.

débrouiller [debruje] *vtr* 1. to unravel (thread); **d. une affaire,** to straighten out matters 2. **se d.,** to extricate oneself (from difficulties); to manage; **qu'il se débrouille,** he'll have to sort it out himself; **débrouillez-vous!** that's your lookout! **débrouillard, -arde** 1. *a* resourceful, smart 2. *n* resourceful person.

débroussailler [debrusaje] *vtr* 1. to clear (ground) of undergrowth 2. to clarify (matter).

débusquer [debyske] *vtr* to drive out (of ambush, of refuge).

début [deby] *nm* 1. first appearance (of actor); **faire son d.,** to make one's début; **société à ses débuts,** association in its infancy 2. beginning, start, outset; **dès le d.,** right at the start; **au d. des hostilités,** at the outbreak of hostilities; **appointements de d.,** starting salary.

débutant, -ante [debytɑ̃, -ɑ̃t] *n* beginner, novice; debutant actor, actress.

débuter [debyte] *vi* 1. to make one's first appearance, one's debut (on the stage) 2. to begin, start.

deçà [dəsa] (*a*) *adv A:* **d. et delà,** here and there (*b*) *prep phr* **en d. de qch,** (on) this side of sth; **rester en d. de la vérité,** to be short of the truth.

décachetage [dekaʃtaʒ] *nm* unsealing, opening.

décacheter [dekaʃte] *vtr* (*conj like* CACHETER) to unseal, break open (letter).

décade [dekad] *nf* (*a*) period of ten days (*b*) (*ten years*) decade.

décadence [dekadɑ̃s] *nf* decadence, decline. **décadent** *a* decadent; declining; *nm* decadent.

décaféiner [dekafeine] *vtr* to decaffeinate; **un café décaféine,** *n* **un décaféiné,** a (cup of) decaffeinated coffee.

décalage [dekalaʒ] *nm* (*a*) **d. horaire,** time difference, time lag (*b*) (amount of) shift.

décalaminer [dekalamine] *vtr ICE:* to decarbonize.

décalcomanie [dekalkɔmani] *nf* transfer (process, picture).

décaler [dekale] *vtr* 1. to unwedge 2. to move forward, to move back; to shift; **d. l'heure,** to alter the time.

décalque [dekalk] *nm* transfer; tracing.

décalquer [dekalke] *vtr* to transfer (design); to trace (drawing).

décamper [dekɑ̃pe] *vi F:* to clear off.

décanter [dekɑ̃te] *vtr* to decant, pour off.

décaper [dekape] *vtr* to scour, to clean (metal); to pickle (metal object); to scrub, to sand.

décapitation [dekapitasjɔ̃] *nf* beheading, decapitation.

décapiter [dekapite] *vtr* to decapitate, behead.

décapotable [dekapɔtabl] *a & nf Aut:* convertible.

décapsuler [dekapsyle] *vtr* to open, to take the top off (a bottle).

décapsuleur [dekapsylœr] *nm* bottle opener.

décarcasser (se) [sədekarkase] *vpr F:* to wear oneself out (doing sth).

décati [dekati] *a* (*of face*) wrinkled; **vieillard d.,** decrepit old man.

décéder [desede] *vi* (*conj like* CÉDER *aux* être) to die, decease. **décédé** *a* deceased.

déceler [desle] *vtr* (**je décèle**) to disclose (fraud); to divulge, betray (secret); to detect (sth).

décembre [desɑ̃br] *nm* December; **au mois de d., en d.,** in (the month of) December.

décence [desɑ̃s] *nf* (*a*) decency (*b*) propriety, decorum. **décent** *a* (*a*) decent (*b*) proper, seemly (behaviour). **décemment** *adv* decently.

décennie [deseni] *nf* decade.

décentralisation [desɑ̃tralizasjɔ̃] *nf* decentralization.

décentraliser [desɑ̃tralize] *vtr* to decentralize.

déception [desɛpsjɔ̃] *nf* disappointment.

décerner [deserne] *vtr* to award (a prize).

décès [desɛ] *nm* death.

décevoir [desəvwar] *vtr* (*conj like* RECEVOIR) to disappoint. **décevant** *a* disappointing.

déchaînement [deʃɛnmɑ̃] *nm* (*a*) breaking loose (*b*) outburst (of passion); (outburst of) fury.

déchaîner [deʃene] *vtr* 1. to unchain, to let loose 2. to unleash (passions, anger); to provoke (laughter) 3. (*a*) se d., to break out; la tempête s'est déchaînée, the storm broke (*b*) se d. contre qn, to fly into a rage against s.o.

déchanter [deʃɑ̃te] *vi* F: to come down a peg (or two).

décharge [deʃarʒ] *nf* 1. (*a*) unloading (of cart); unlading (of cargo) (*b*) discharge (of gunfire) (*c*) El: discharge; d. électrique, electric shock 2. (*a*) relief, easing (*b*) (tax) rebate (*c*) témoin à d., witness for the defence (*d*) release (of accused person) 3. discharge, outlet; tuyau de d., waste-pipe 4. d. publique, rubbish dump, rubbish tip.

déchargement [deʃarʒəmɑ̃] *nm* unloading; unlading; discharging.

décharger [deʃarʒe] *vtr* (**n. déchargeons**) 1. (*a*) to unload (cart); to unlade, to discharge (cargo) (*b*) to unload (firearm) (*c*) d. sa conscience, to ease one's mind (de, of) (*d*) d. son fusil sur qn, to fire one's gun at s.o. 2. (*a*) to lighten (ship) (*b*) d. qn d'une accusation, to acquit s.o. of a charge; d. qn d'une dette, to remit a debt 3. (*a*) se d., (*of gun*) to go off; (*of battery*) to run down; (*of anger*) to vent itself (sur, on) (*b*) d. qn, to relieve s.o. (of sth); se d. d'un fardeau, to put down a load; se d. de ses responsabilités, to pass off one's responsibilities (onto s.o.).

décharné [deʃarne] *a* emaciated (limbs); gaunt (face); bony (fingers).

déchausser [deʃose] *vtr* 1. to take off (s.o.'s) shoes 2. se d., to take off one's shoes; (*of teeth*) to get loose. **déchaussé** *a* barefoot(ed).

déchéance [deʃeɑ̃s] *nf* 1. downfall; decline 2. forfeiture (of rights); expiration (of insurance policy).

déchet [deʃɛ] *nm* (*a*) usu *pl* waste, refuse; déchets radioactifs, radioactive waste; déchets de viande, scraps (*b*) (*pers*) failure; (social) outcast.

déchiffrage [deʃifraʒ] *nm* sightreading (of music).

déchiffrement [deʃifrəmɑ̃] *nm* deciphering.

déchiffrer [deʃifre] *vtr* to decipher, make out (inscription); to decode (message); to sightread (music). **déchiffrable** *a* decipherable.

déchiqueter [deʃikte] *vtr* (je déchiquette) to cut, slash, tear, into strips, into shreds. **déchiqueté** *a* jagged (edge); cut to bits, to shreds.

déchirement [deʃirmɑ̃] *nm* tearing; d. de cœur, wrench, heartbreak.

déchirer [deʃire] *vtr* 1. to tear (garment); to tear up (paper); to tear open (envelope); sons qui déchirent l'oreille, ear-splitting sounds; cris qui déchiraient le cœur, heartrending cries; se d. un muscle, to tear a muscle 2. se d., to tear. **déchirant** *a* heartrending, harrowing.

déchirure [deʃiryr] *nf* tear, rent, slit, rip.

déchoir [deʃwar] *vi* (*pp* déchu; *pr ind* je déchois, n. déchoyons; *aux* être *or* avoir) to fall (from honour); sa popularité déchoit, his popularity is declining. **déchu** *a* fallen; dethroned (king); expired (policy).

décider [deside] *vtr* 1. (*a*) to decide, settle (question, dispute); voilà qui décide tout! that settles it! (*b*) l'assemblée décida la guerre, the assembly decided on

war 2. d. qn à faire qch, to persuade, induce, s.o. to do sth 3. *vi* (*a*) il faut que je décide, I must make a decision (*b*) d. de qch, to decide, to determine, sth 4. d. + *inf*, to decide (after deliberation) to (do sth); j'ai décidé de partir demain, I've decided to leave tomorrow; d. que + *ind*, to decide, settle, that 5. se d. (*a*) to make up one's mind; to come to a decision (*b*) je ne puis pas me d. à le faire, I cannot bring myself to do it; allons, décidez-vous, come on, make up your mind (*c*) se d. pour qn, to decide in favour of s.o. **décidé** *a* 1. settled (matter) 2. resolute, confident (person); determined (character); d'un ton d., decisively 3. être d. à faire qch, to be determined to do sth 4. avoir une supériorité décidée sur qn, to have a decided superiority over s.o. **décidément** *adv* decidedly, positively, definitely; d. je n'ai pas de chance! I really don't have much luck!

décimale [desimal] *nf* decimal. **décimal, -aux** *a* decimal.

décimation [desimasjɔ̃] *nf* decimation.

décimer [desime] *vtr* to decimate.

décision [desizjɔ̃] *nf* 1. (*a*) decision; forcer une d., to bring matters to a head (*b*) Jur: ruling; award 2. resolution, determination. **décisif, -ive** *a* 1. decisive (battle); conclusive (evidence); critical, crucial (moment) 2. peremptory (tone).

déclamation [deklamasjɔ̃] *nf* (*a*) declamation (*b*) ranting.

déclamer [deklame] 1. *vtr* to declaim (speech) 2. *vi* Pej: to rant; d. contre qn, to inveigh against s.o. **déclamatoire** *a* declamatory; ranting.

déclaration [deklarasjɔ̃] *nf* (*a*) declaration; proclamation, announcement (*b*) notification (of birth, death) (*c*) statement; d. sous serment, affidavit (*d*) d. (d'amour), declaration of love (*e*) d. en douane, customs declaration.

déclarer [deklare] *vtr* 1. (*a*) to declare, make known (one's intentions) (*b*) Cards: to declare, call, clubs 2. (*a*) to declare, proclaim, announce; déclarer coupable, found guilty (*b*) to notify (birth, death) (*c*) d. la guerre à qn, to declare war on s.o. (*d*) Cust: avez-vous quelque chose à d.? have you anything to declare? 3. se d., (i) to speak one's mind (ii) to declare one's love (iii) (*of fire, disease*) to break out; se d. pour qch, to declare for sth.

déclassement [deklasmɑ̃] *nm* change of class; Sp: relegation.

déclasser [deklase] *vtr* 1. to transfer (passengers) from one class to another 2. to lower the social position (of s.o.) 3. Sp: to relegate 4. to downgrade (hotel) 5. to put (files) out of order.

déclenchement [deklɑ̃ʃmɑ̃] *nm* 1. MecE: (*a*) releasing (of part) (*b*) trigger action; Phot: (shutter) release 2. starting; setting in motion.

déclencher [deklɑ̃ʃe] *vtr* 1. MecE: to release (part) 2. to set off (mechanism); to set (machine) in motion; to trigger off 3. se d., (*of mechanism*) to release itself; (*of bell*) to go off; (*of strike*) to start.

déclencheur [deklɑ̃ʃœr] *nm* Phot: shutter release.

déclic [deklik] *nm* 1. pawl, catch; trigger 2. click.

déclin [deklɛ̃] *nm* decline, close (of day); waning (of moon); falling off; au d. de sa vie, in his declining years.

déclinaison [deklinɛzɔ̃] *nf* 1. *Astr:* declination 2. *Gram:* declension.

décliner [dekline] 1. *vi (of moon)* to wane; *(of star)* to decline; *(of day)* to draw to a close 2. *vtr* to decline, refuse (offer) 3. *vtr (a) Gram:* to decline (noun) *(b)* to state, to give (one's name). **déclinable** *a Gram:* declinable.

déclivité [deklivite] *nf* declivity, slope, incline.

décocher [dekɔʃe] *vtr* to shoot (bolt); **d. un coup à qn,** to hit out at s.o.; **d. une remarque,** to fire a comment; **d. une œillade,** to flash a glance.

décoiffer [dekwafe] *vtr* 1. *(a)* to remove (s.o.'s) hat *(b)* to disarrange (s.o.'s) hair 2. **se d.** (i) to take off one's hat (ii) to disarrange one's hair.

décoincer [dekwɛ̃se] *vtr* to unjam, to unwedge.

décolérer [dekɔlere] *vi* (**je décolère; je décolérerai**) to calm down; *(used esp in the neg)* **il ne décolérait pas,** he was still fuming.

décollage [dekɔlaʒ] *nm Av:* takeoff.

décoller [dekɔle] 1. *vtr* to unstick, unglue 2. *vi (a) (of aircraft)* to take off *(b) F:* to budge 3. **se d.,** to come unstuck.

décolleté [dekɔlte] 1. *a* low-cut (dress); **d. dans le dos,** cut low at the back 2. *nm* neckline (of dress); **d. carré, en pointe,** square neck, V neck.

décolonisation [dekɔlɔnizasjɔ̃] *nf* decolonization.

décoloration [dekɔlɔrasjɔ̃] *nf* discolouration.

décolorer [dekɔlɔre] *vtr* 1. to discolour; to fade; to bleach (hair) 2. **se d.,** to lose colour, to fade, to bleach.

décombres [dekɔ̃br̩] *nmpl* rubbish, debris (of building); ruins.

décommander [dekɔmɑ̃de] *vtr* 1. to countermand; to cancel (meeting); to put off (guest); **d. une grève,** to call off a strike 2. **se d.,** to cancel an appointment.

décomposer [dekɔ̃poze] *vtr* 1. *Ph: Ch:* to decompose; to split (light) 2. to decompose, to rot (organic matter) 3. to contort, distort (features) 4. **se d.** *(a)* to decompose, to rot *(b) (of face)* to become contorted.

décomposition [dekɔ̃pozisjɔ̃] *nf* decomposition.

décompte [dekɔ̃t] *nm (a)* deduction *(b)* detailed account; breakdown.

décompter [dekɔ̃te] *vtr* to deduct.

déconcerter [dekɔ̃sɛrte] *vtr* to disconcert (s.o.).

déconfit [dekɔ̃fi] *a* crestfallen, discomfited.

déconfiture [dekɔ̃fityr] *nf* collapse, failure, downfall.

décongeler [dekɔ̃ʒle] *vtr* (**je décongèle**) to thaw, defrost, defreeze.

décongestionner [dekɔ̃ʒɛstjone] *vtr (a) Med:* to relieve congestion in (lungs) *(b)* to clear street (of traffic).

déconnecter [dekɔnɛkte] *vtr El:* to disconnect.

déconseiller [dekɔ̃seje] *vtr* **d. qch à qn,** to advise s.o. against sth; **c'est déconseillé, c'est à d.,** it's inadvisable; it's not recommended.

décontenancer [dekɔ̃tnɑ̃se] *vtr* (**n. décontenançons**) to put (s.o.) out of countenance; to disconcert.

décontracter (se) [sədekɔ̃trakte] *vpr* to relax.

décontraction [dekɔ̃traksjɔ̃] *nf* relaxation.

déconvenue [dekɔ̃vny] *nf* disappointment.

décor [dekɔr] *nm* 1. decoration (of house) 2. *Th: Cin: TV:* setting (of stage); set; *pl* scenery 3. *F: Aut:* **rentrer dans le d.,** to run off the road (into sth).

décorateur, -trice [dekɔratœr, -tris] *n (a)* interior decorator *(b)* stage designer.

décoration [dekɔrasjɔ̃] *nf* decoration. **décoratif, -ive** *a* decorative.

décorer [dekɔre] *vtr* 1. to decorate, ornament; to do up (house) 2. to decorate (s.o.).

décortiquer [dekɔrtike] *vtr* to husk (rice); to hull (barley); to shell (nuts).

décorum [dekɔrɔm] *nm* decorum.

découcher [dekuʃe] *vi* to stay out all night.

découdre [dekudr̩] *vtr (conj like* COUDRE) 1. *(a)* to unpick, unstitch (garment) *(b)* **en d.,** to fight 2. **se d.,** to come unstitched.

découler [dekule] *vi* to ensue, follow (**de,** from); **il en découle que,** it follows that.

découpage [dekupaʒ] *nm (a)* cutting up (of paper); carving (of meat); cutting out (of patterns) *(b)* cutout.

découper [dekupe] *vtr* 1. to cut up (paper); to carve (meat); **couteau à d.,** carving knife 2. to cut out (design); **d. un article dans un journal,** to cut an article out of a newspaper; **scie à d.,** fretsaw 3. **se d.,** to stand out, to show up (**sur,** on, against).

découpure [dekupyr] *nf* 1. *(a)* cutting out *(b)* fretwork 2. *(a)* piece cut out *(b)* cutting 3. indentation (in coastline).

découragement [dekuraʒmɑ̃] *nm* discouragement.

décourager [dekuraʒe] *vtr* (**n. décourageons**) 1. to discourage, dishearten; **d. qn de faire qch,** to deter s.o. from doing sth 2. **d. un projet,** to discourage a scheme 3. **se d.,** to become discouraged, disheartened; to lose heart. **décourageant** *a* discouraging, disheartening.

décousu [dekuzy] *a (a)* unsewn, unstitched (seam) *(b)* disconnected, disjointed (words, ideas); rambling (remarks, conversation).

découvert [dekuvɛr] 1. *a (a)* uncovered; bare (head) *(b)* open (country) *(c)* exposed, unprotected *(d)* overdrawn (account) 2. *nm* overdraft 3. *adv phr* **à d.,** uncovered, unprotected; **parler à d.,** to speak openly; **mettre qch à d.,** to expose sth to view; **compte à d.,** overdrawn account; **tirer à d.,** to overdraw (one's account).

découverte [dekuvɛrt] *nf* 1. discovery (of land); **aller à la d.,** to explore 2. *(a)* discovery, exposure (of plot) *(b)* (scientific) discovery.

découvrir [dekuvrir] *vtr (conj like* COUVRIR) 1. *(a)* to uncover *(b)* to expose, to lay bare; to unveil (statue); to disclose, reveal (secret); **se d. la tête,** to bare one's head; **d. ses dents,** to show one's teeth 2. to perceive, discern 3. *(a)* to discover (plot); to detect (error, criminal); to find out (sth) *(b)* to discover (a virus) 4. **se d.** *(a)* to take off one's hat; to take off one's clothes *(b) (of sky)* to clear (up) *(c)* to come to light; **la vérité se découvre toujours,** truth will out.

décrassage [dekrasaʒ] *nm* cleaning, scouring.

décrasser [dekrase] *vtr* to clean, scour; to scale (boiler); **se d.,** to clean oneself up.

décrépitude [dekrepityd] *nf* decrepitude, decay. **décrépit** *a* decrepit, senile; dilapidated.

décret [dekrɛ] *nm* decree.

décréter [dekrete] *vtr* (**je décrète; je décréterai**) to decree; to enact (law).

décrier [dekrie] *vtr* to disparage, discredit (s.o.); to run (s.o., sth) down.

décrire [dekrir] *vtr* (*conj like* ÉCRIRE) **1.** to describe, to depict (sth) **2.** to describe (curve, circle).

décrocher [dekrɔʃe] **1.** *vtr* to unhook, to take down (coat from peg); to disconnect (railway carriages); *Tp:* to pick up, lift (receiver); (*to stop it from ringing*) to take (the phone) off the hook; **se d. la mâchoire,** to dislocate one's jaw; **d. le grand succès,** to make a big hit **2.** *vi* (*a*) *Mil:* to withdraw (*b*) *Av:* to stall (*c*) *F:* to give up, to drop out.

décroiser [dekrwaze] *vtr* to uncross.

décroissance [dekrwasɑ̃s] *nf* decrease; diminution; decline; **être en d.,** to decrease.

décroître [dekrwatr] *vi* (*conj like* CROÎTRE, *except pp* **décru**) to decrease, decline, diminish; (*of moon*) to wane; (*of days*) to get shorter; **aller (en) décroissant,** to decrease.

décrotter [dekrɔte] *vtr* to remove mud from (boots).

décrue [dekry] *nf* fall, subsidence (of river).

déçu [desy] *a* disappointed.

décupler [dekyple] *vtr & i* to increase tenfold.

dédaigner [dedɛɲe] *vtr* to scorn, disdain; **cette offre n'est pas à d.,** this offer is not to be sneezed at. **dédaigneux, -euse** *a* disdainful; scornful. **dédaigneusement** *adv* disdainfully, scornfully.

dédain [dedɛ̃] *nm* disdain, scorn; **avec d.,** disdainfully; **avoir le d. de qch,** to have a contempt for sth.

dédale [dedal] *nm* maze (of streets).

dedans [dədɑ̃] **1.** *adv* inside; within; in (it); *F:* **mettre qn d.,** to put s.o. inside; **donner d.,** to fall into the trap; **en d.,** (on the) inside; within; **il est calme en d.,** inwardly he is calm; **en d. de,** within **2.** *nm* inside, interior (of house); **au d.,** (on the) inside; within; **au d. de,** inside, within.

dédicace [dedikas] *nf* dedication.

dédicacer [dedikase] *vtr* (**je dédicaçai(s)**) to dedicate (book); to autograph (book).

dédier [dedje] *vtr* to dedicate.

dédire (se) [sədedir] *vpr* (*conj like* DIRE, *except pr ind* **v. v. dédisez**) to retract (a statement); **se d. d'une promesse,** to go back on one's word.

dédit [dedi] *nm* **1.** retraction, withdrawal **2.** breaking (of promise) **3.** forfeit, penalty (for breaking contract).

dédommagement [dedɔmaʒmɑ̃] *nm* indemnity, compensation, damages.

dédommager [dedɔmaʒe] *vtr* (**n. dédommageons**) to indemnify, compensate (s.o.); **se faire d.,** to receive compensation.

dédouanement [dedwanmɑ̃] *nm* customs clearance.

dédouaner [dedwane] *vtr* to clear (goods) through customs.

dédoublement [dedubləmɑ̃] *nm* **d. de la personnalité,** split personality.

dédoubler [deduble] *vtr* **1.** (*a*) to divide into two (*b*) to run (train) in two portions **2. se d.,** to suffer from split personality.

déduction [dedyksjɔ̃] *nf* **1.** deduction, inference **2.**

Com: deduction, allowance; **sans d.,** terms net cash. **déductif, -ive** *a* deductive (reasoning).

déduire [dedɥir] *vtr* (*conj like* CONDUIRE) **1.** to deduce, infer **2.** to deduct.

déesse [deɛs] *nf* goddess.

défaillance [defajɑ̃s] *nf* (*a*) (moral, physical) lapse; failing; failure (to do sth); **sans d.,** without flinching; **moment de d.,** weak moment; **d. de mémoire,** lapse of memory; **d. cardiaque,** heart failure (*b*) fainting fit; blackout; **tomber en d.,** to faint. **défaillant, -ante** *a* (*a*) failing; declining; weak (heart) (*b*) **d. de fatigue,** exhausted (*c*) (*pers*) faint.

défaillir [defajir] *vi* (*prp* **défaillant;** *pr ind* **je défaille**) (*a*) to lose strength; **sa mémoire commence à d.,** his memory is beginning to fail (*b*) to flinch; **sans d.,** without flinching (*c*) to faint.

défaire [defɛr] *vtr* (*conj like* FAIRE) **1.** to demolish (wall) **2.** (*a*) to undo; to untie; to unwrap; to unpack; to unpick (seam); to undo, unzip (dress); to strip (bed); **d. ses cheveux,** to let one's hair down; **d. la table,** to clear the table (*b*) *A: & Lit:* **d. qn de qn,** to rid s.o. of s.o. **3.** to defeat (army) **4. se d.** (*a*) to come undone; to come apart; (*of hair*) to come down (*b*) **se d. de qn,** to get rid of s.o., *F:* to bump s.o off; (*c*) **se d. de qch,** to get rid of sth; **je ne veux pas m'en d.,** I don't want to part with it. **défait** *a* (*a*) drawn (features) (*b*) dishevelled (hair) (*c*) defeated (army).

défaite [defɛt] *nf* defeat.

défaitisme [defɛtism] *nm* defeatism. **défaitiste** *a & n* defeatist.

défalcation [defalkasjɔ̃] *nf* deduction.

défalquer [defalke] *vtr* to deduct.

défaut [defo] *nm* **1.** (*a*) absence, (total) lack (of sth); **d. de paiement,** non-payment; **le temps me fait d.,** I can't spare the time; **les provisions font d.,** there's a shortage of supplies; **la mémoire lui fait d.,** his memory fails him; **à d. de qch,** for lack of, failing, sth (*b*) **le d. de l'armure,** the joint in the harness; *Fig:* the vulnerable point (*c*) *Jur:* default; **faire d.,** to fail to appear; **jugement par d.,** judgment by default **2.** (*a*) fault, shortcoming; **c'est là son moindre d.,** that is the last thing one can reproach him with (*b*) defect, flaw; **sans d.,** faultless, flawless (*c*) **mettre qn en d.,** to put s.o. on the wrong track; **prendre qn en d.,** to catch s.o. out.

défaveur [defavœr] *nf* disfavour, discredit. **défavorable** *a* unfavourable (à, to). **défavorablement** *adv* unfavourably.

défavoriser [defavorize] *vtr* to be unfair to (s.o.); **candidat défavorisé,** candidate put at an unfair disadvantage.

défectif, -ive [defɛktif, -iv] *a* defective (verb).

défection [defɛksjɔ̃] *nf* defection from, desertion of, a cause; **faire d.,** to desert, *F:* to rat.

défectuosité [defɛktɥozite] *nf* (*a*) defectiveness (*b*) defect, flaw. **défectueux, -euse** *a* defective, faulty.

défendable [defɑ̃dabl] *a* defensible.

défendeur, -eresse [defɑ̃dœr, -(ə)rɛs] *n* *Jur:* defendant.

défendre [defɑ̃dr] *vtr* **1.** (*a*) to defend (s.o., cause); to champion (cause); to maintain, to uphold (right); to stand up for (one's friends) (**contre,** against) (*b*) to protect (**contre,** against, from) **2.** to forbid, prohibit; **d. qch à qn**, to forbid s.o. sth; **il m'est défendu de fumer**, I'm not allowed to smoke 3. **se d.** (a) to defend oneself; **il se défend bien en affaires**, he's a good businessman; **comment ça va?—je me défends**, how's it going?—I'm holding my own (b) **se d. d'avoir fait qch**, to deny having done sth (c) **se d. de, contre, qch**, to protect oneself from sth (d) **il ne put se d. de sourire**, he could not refrain from smiling.

défense [defɑ̃s] nf 1. Mil: Jur: defence; **prendre la d. de qn**, to stand up for s.o.; **sans d.**, unprotected, defenceless 2. tusk (of elephant) 3. prohibition; PN: **d. d'entrer, de fumer**, no admittance, no smoking; **faire d. à qn de faire qch**, to forbid s.o. to do sth.

défenseur [defɑ̃sœr] nm 1. (a) protector, defender (b) supporter, upholder (of a cause) 2. Jur: counsel for the defence.

défensif, -ive [defɑ̃sif, -iv] 1. a defensive 2. nf **se tenir sur la défensive**, to be on the defensive.

déférence [deferɑ̃s] nf deference, respect. **déférent, -ente** a deferential.

déférer [defere] v (**je défère; je déférerai**) 1. vtr (a) Jur: to refer (a case to a court) (b) **d. qn à la justice**, to hand s.o. over to justice 2. vi **d. à qn**, to defer to s.o.

déferlement [defɛrləmɑ̃] nm breaking (of waves); flood (of tourists, cars); wave (of enthusiasm).

déferler [defɛrle] 1. vtr Nau: to unfurl (sail) 2. vi (of waves) to break; **la foule déferle dans la rue**, the crowd is surging down the street.

défi [defi] nm (a) challenge; **relever un d.**, to take up a challenge (b) defiance; **d'un air de d.**, defiantly.

défiance [defjɑ̃s] nf 1. mistrust, distrust, suspicion 2. **d. de soi-même**, diffidence. **défiant** a mistrustful, distrustful.

déficience [defisjɑ̃s] nf deficiency. **déficient** a deficient; **enfant d.**, mentally deficient child.

déficit [defisit] nm deficit; shortage. **déficitaire** a (budget) showing a deficit; **récolte d.**, short crop.

défier [defje] vtr 1. (a) to challenge (b) to defy (s.o., sth) (c) to brave, to face (danger) 2. **se d. de qn**, to mistrust, distrust, s.o.

défigurer [defigyre] vtr to disfigure (s.o., sth); to deface (statue); to distort (the truth).

défilé [defile] nm 1. (mountain) pass 2. procession; Mil: march past; Av: flypast; **d. de modes**, fashion parade; **d. de visiteurs**, stream of visitors.

défiler [defile] vi 1. (a) Mil: to march past (b) to walk in procession (c) **les voitures défilent vers la côte**, the cars are streaming towards the coast 2. F: **se d.**, to slip off on the quiet.

définir [definir] vtr to define. **défini** a definite. **définissable** a definable.

définitif, -ive [definitif, -iv] a definitive; final; permanent; adv phr **en définitive**, finally, when all is said and done. **définitivement** adv definitely; for good.

définition [definisjɔ̃] nf 1. definition; **par d.**, by that very fact; logically 2. clue (of crossword).

déflagration [deflagrasjɔ̃] nf (a) combustion (b) explosion.

déflation [deflasjɔ̃] nf deflation.

défoncer [defɔ̃se] vtr (**n. défonçons**) 1. to stave in (boat); to smash in (box); to knock down (wall) 2. to break (sth) up 3. **se d.**, to get high (on drug).

déformation [deformasjɔ̃] nf 1. (a) deformation; **d. professionnelle**, professional idiosyncrasy, vocational bias (b) Phot: distortion (of image) 2. warping.

déformer [deforme] vtr 1. to deform; to put (sth) out of shape; Phot: to distort (image); PN: **chaussée déformée**, uneven road surface 2. to warp 3. **se d.**, to get out of shape, to warp.

défoulement [defulmɑ̃] nm release (from pent-up feelings).

défouler (se) [sədefule] vpr to unwind, F: to let off steam.

défraîchir (se) [sədefrɛʃir] vpr to lose its freshness; to fade. **défraîchi** a (shop)soiled (goods); faded (flowers).

défrayer [defreje] vtr (**je défraie, je défraye**) 1. **d. qn**, to pay s.o.'s expenses 2. **d. la chronique**, to be in the news.

défrichage [defriʃaʒ] nm clearing (of land).

défricher [defriʃe] vtr to clear, reclaim (land for cultivation); to break (new ground); **d. un sujet**, to do pioneer work in a subject.

défroisser [defrwase] vtr to take the creases out of (dress).

défunt, -unte [defœ̃, -œ̃t] 1. a defunct; **mon d. père**, my late father 2. n deceased.

dégagé [degaʒe] a free (movements); **allure dégagée**, swinging stride (b) free and easy (manner) (c) clear (road, sky); **vue dégagée**, open view.

dégagement [degaʒmɑ̃] nm 1. redemption (of pledge) 2. (a) release (b) relieving of congestion; clearing (of road); **voie de d.**, slip road; **porte de d.**, (side) exit (c) private passage (in suite of rooms) (d) Fb: clearance 3. (a) escape, release (of steam, gas) (b) emission (of heat, smell) 4. clearing (in front of house).

dégager [degaʒe] vtr (**n. dégageons**) 1. to redeem (pledge); to release (securities); to take (sth) out of pawn 2. (a) to disengage; to release; **d. qn d'une promesse**, to release s.o. from a promise; **d. sa responsabilité d'une affaire**, to disclaim responsibility in a matter (b) to relieve the congestion; to clear (road); **dégagez, s'il vous plaît!** gangway, clear the way, please! (c) **robe qui dégage les épaules**, dress that leaves the shoulders bare (d) to draw (conclusion); to bring out (sense); to derive (idea) (e) to loosen, to slacken (sth) (f) Fb: to clear (ball) 3. to emit, to give off (vapour, smell); to give out (heat) 4. **se d.** (a) to free oneself, to get free; to get clear (**de**, of); to break loose (**de**, from); **le ciel se d.**, the sky is clearing; **se d. d'une promesse**, to go back on a promise (b) (of gas, smell) to be given off (**de**, by), to escape; **il se dégage de l'oxygène**, oxygen is given off (c) to emerge, come out.

dégainer [degene] vtr to draw (sword, gun).

dégarnir [degarnir] vtr 1. to dismantle (room); to take the trimmings off (dress); to strip (bed); to withdraw troops from (town) 2. **se d.** (a) to become bald; (of tree) to lose its leaves (b) (of room) to empty (c) F: to run short of ready money. **dégarni** a empty; stripped; bare; bald.

dégât [dega] nm usu pl damage.

dégel [deʒɛl] nm thaw.

dégeler [deʒle] vtr & i, v impers (**il dégèle**) 1. to thaw;

to unfreeze (assets); to warm up (audience) **2. se d.,** to thaw (out).

dégénérer [deʒenere] *vi* (**je dégénère; je dégénérerai**) to degenerate (**de,** from; **en,** into). **dégénéré** *a* & *n* degenerate.

dégénérescence [deʒeneresãs] *nf* degeneration.

dégingandé [deʒɛ̃gãde] *a* F: (*pers*) gangling.

dégivrage [deʒivraʒ] *nm* de-icing; defrosting.

dégivrer [deʒivre] *vtr Aut: Av:* to de-ice; *DomEc:* to defrost.

déglinguer [deglɛ̃ge] *vtr F:* to smash up; **ma bicyclette est toute déglinguée,** my bicycle is falling to pieces.

dégonflement [degɔ̃fləmã] *nm* deflating; deflation.

dégonfler [degɔ̃fle] *vtr* **1.** to deflate (balloon, tyre) **2.** to reduce (swelling) **3.** *F:* to debunk (hero) **4. se d.** (*a*) (*of tyre, balloon*) to collapse, to go flat (*b*) (*of swelling*) to subside, to go down (*c*) *F:* to chicken out.

dégorger [degɔrʒe] *v* (**n. dégorgeons**) **1.** *vtr* (*a*) to disgorge, to pour out (*b*) to clear (pipe) **2.** *vi* & *pr* (*a*) (*of pond*) to flow out, to discharge (**dans,** into); (*of stream*) to overflow (*b*) *Cu:* **faire d. des concombres,** to salt cucumbers (to make them sweat).

dégouliner [deguline] *vi* (*of water*) to trickle, to drip.

dégourdir [degurdir] *vtr* **1.** to remove stiffness from (the limbs); to revive (by warmth, movement); **se d. les jambes,** to stretch one's legs a bit; **Paris l'a dégourdi,** Paris has taught him a thing or two **2. se d.** (*a*) to restore the circulation; to lose one's numb, stiff, feeling; to stretch one's limbs (*b*) to grow more alert. **dégourdi, -ie** *a* smart, bright (pers).

dégoût [degu] *nm* disgust, distaste, dislike.

dégoûter [degute] *vtr* (*a*) to disgust; **d. qn de qch,** to put s.o. off sth; **tout cela me dégoûte,** I'm sick of it all (*b*) **se d. de qch,** to take a dislike to sth; to get sick of sth. **dégoûtant** *a* disgusting, revolting. **dégoûté** *a* disgusted (**de,** with); sick (**de,** of); *F:* fed up.

dégoutter [degute] *vi* to drip, trickle.

dégradation [degradasjɔ̃] *nf* degradation; deterioration; dilapidation.

dégradé [degrade] *nm* (*colours*) gradation.

dégrader [degrade] *vtr* **1.** to degrade (s.o.) (from rank) **2.** to debase, to degrade (s.o.) **3.** to deface, damage (sth) **4. se d.** (*a*) to degrade, to demean, oneself (*b*) to fall into disrepair; to deteriorate. **dégradant** *a* degrading, lowering.

dégrafer [degrafe] *vtr* to unfasten, undo (dress); **se d.,** to come undone.

dégraisser [degrese] *vtr* **1.** to remove the fat from (meat); to skim the fat off (stock) **2.** to remove grease marks from (garment).

degré [dəgre] *nm* **1.** (*a*) step (of stair, ladder); degree (of musical scale) (*b*) degree (of heat) (*c*) proof (of alcoholic drink) **2.** degree (of relationship); **cousins au second d.,** second cousins; **d. de parenté,** degree of kinship; *Med:* **brûlure du troisième d.,** third degree burn; *Sch:* **enseignement du premier, second, d.,** primary, secondary, education; **au plus haut d.,** in the extreme; **par degré(s),** by degrees, gradually; *Mth:* **équation du second d.,** quadratic equation.

dégressif, -ive [degresif, -iv] *a* degressive.

dégrèvement [degrɛvmã] *nm* reduction (of tax).

dégrever [degrəve] *vtr* (**je dégrève**) to reduce (tax); to grant tax relief.

dégringolade [degrɛ̃gɔlad] *nf* (*a*) tumble (*b*) collapse.

dégringoler [degrɛ̃gɔle] *vtr* & *i F:* (*a*) to tumble down; **d. l'escalier,** to rush down the stairs (*b*) (*of business*) to collapse.

dégriser (se) [sədegrize] *vpr* to sober up.

dégrossir [degrosir] *vtr* to trim (timber); to roughhew (stone); to rough out (design); *F:* **d. qn,** to lick s.o. into shape; **il est mal dégrossi,** he's unrefined.

déguenillé [degnije] *a* ragged, tattered.

déguerpir [degerpir] *vi* to clear out, decamp.

déguisement [degizmã] *nm* (*a*) disguise (*b*) fancy dress.

déguiser [degize] *vtr* **1.** to disguise; to dress (s.o.) up (**en,** as sth) **2.** to disguise, conceal (truth); **parler sans rien d.,** to speak openly **3. se d.** (*a*) to disguise oneself (*b*) to dress up.

dégustateur, -trice [degystatœr, -tris] *n* wine taster.

dégustation [degystasjɔ̃] *nf* tasting, sampling (of wine, food).

déguster [degyste] *vtr* **1.** to taste, to sample (wine, food); to enjoy, savour (meal) **2.** to enjoy one's food. **3.** *P:* **qu'est-ce qu'on a dégusté!** we didn't half catch it!

dehors [dəɔr] **1.** *adv* (*a*) out, outside; **coucher d.,** to sleep (i) out of doors (ii) away from home; **mettre qn d.,** to throw s.o. out (*b*) **de d.,** from outside; **en d.,** (on the) outside; **en d. du sujet,** beside the question; **cela s'est fait en d. de moi,** (i) it was done without my knowledge (ii) without my participation (*c*) **au d.,** on the outside; **ne pas se pencher au d.!** do not lean out of the window! **2.** *nm* (*a*) outside, exterior (*b*) *usu pl* (outward) appearance.

déifier [deifje] *vtr* to deify.

déité [deite] *nf* deity.

déjà [deʒa] *adv* **1.** already; **il est d. parti,** he has already left; **d. en 1900,** as early as 1900 **2.** before, previously; **je vous ai d. vu,** I have seen you before **3.** yet; **faut-il d. partir?** need we go just yet? **d. trop de travail,** too much work as it is; **qu'est-ce que vous faites d.?** what did you say your job was?

déjeuner [deʒœne] **1.** *vi* (*a*) to (have) breakfast (*b*) to (have) lunch **2.** *nm* (*a*) lunch; **petit d.,** breakfast; **d. sur l'herbe,** picnic (lunch) (*b*) breakfast cup and saucer.

déjouer [deʒwe] *vtr* to thwart, to foil; to spoil (plan).

déjuger (se) [sədeʒyʒe] *vpr* (*conj like* JUGER) to reverse one's decision.

delà [d(ə)la] **1.** *prep phr* **par d. les mers,** beyond the seas **2.** *adv* **au-d.,** beyond; *nm* **l'au-d.,** the next world; *prep phr* **au d. de,** beyond; **n'allez pas au d. de 300 francs,** don't go above 300 francs; **il est allé au d. de ses promesses,** he was better than his word.

délabrement [delabrəmã] *nm* dilapidation; disrepair, decay.

délabrer [delabre] *vtr* to wreck, ruin (house, fortune, health) **2. se d.,** (*of house*) to become dilapidated; to fall into decay; (*of health*) to become impaired.

délabré *a* dilapidated; broken down; impaired (health).

délacer [delase] *vtr* (**n. délaçons**) to unlace; **se d.,** to come unlaced, undone.

délai [delɛ] *nm* **1.** delay; **sans d.,** without delay; immediately **2.** respite, time allowed; **à court d.,** at short notice; **dans le d. prescrit,** within the allotted time; **dans le plus bref d.,** as soon as possible; *Com:* **d. de paiement,** term of payment; **dans un d. de 3 jours,** within a period of 3 days; at 3 days' notice.

délaissement [delɛsmɑ̃] *nm* desertion, abandonment, neglect; loneliness.

délaisser [delɛse] *vtr* to forsake, desert, abandon.

délassement [delɑsmɑ̃] *nm* relaxation.

délasser [delɑse] *vtr* **1.** to rest, refresh (s.o.) **2. se d.,** to relax.

délateur, -trice [delatœr, -tris] *n* informer.

délation [delasjɔ̃] *nf* informing; denouncement.

délavé [delave] *a* (*a*) washed out, faded (colour) (*b*) waterlogged, sodden (earth).

délayage [delɛjaʒ] *nm* thinning out; mixing.

délayer [delɛje] *vtr* (**je délaie, délaye**) to add water to (a powder); to thin out; to mix; to water (liquid); **d. un discours,** to pad a speech.

Delco [delko] *nm Aut: Rtm:* distributor.

délecter (se) [sədelɛkte] *vpr* to take delight in, to revel in (sth). **délectable** *a* delectable.

délégation [delegasjɔ̃] *nf* delegation.

délégué, -ée [delege] *a & n* (*a*) delegate (*b*) deputy.

déléguer [delege] *vtr* (**je délègue; je déléguerai**) **1. d. qn pour faire qch,** to delegate s.o. to do sth **2.** to delegate (powers).

délestage [delɛstaʒ] *nm* (*a*) unballasting (*b*) *El:* power cut.

délester [delɛste] *vtr* (*a*) to unballast (ship) (*b*) *El:* to cut off the power (*c*) **se d. de qch,** to jettison sth; to unload sth.

délétère [deletɛr] *a* deleterious.

délibération [deliberasjɔ̃] *nf* **1.** deliberation, discussion **2.** reflection; consideration **3.** resolution, decision.

délibérer [delibere] *vi* **1.** to deliberate, to confer; **d. sur qch,** to discuss a matter; **le jury s'est retiré pour d.,** the jury retired to consider its verdict **2. d. de qch,** to deliberate sth. **délibéré** *a* deliberate; resolute; intentional. **délibérément** *adv* deliberately.

délicat [delika] *a* **1.** delicate; gentle (touch); refined, discerning (taste, person); tactful (behaviour) **2.** sensitive; delicate (health) **3.** difficult, ticklish (problem); tricky (job); delicate (situation) **4.** scrupulous, particular (conscience); **d. sur la nourriture,** fussy about food. **délicatement** *adv* delicately; tactfully.

delicatesse [delikatɛs] *nf* **1.** delicacy; softness (of texture, colouring) **2.** (*a*) gentleness (of touch) (*b*) refinement (of taste); tactfulness (of behaviour); **avec d.,** tactfully **3.** fragility; tenderness (of skin) **4.** difficulty, awkwardness (of situation) **5.** consideration (for s.o.); **avoir des délicatesses pour qn,** to treat s.o. considerately.

délice [delis] *nm* delight; **faire les délices de qn,** to delight s.o. **délicieux, -euse** *a* delicious; delightful. **délicieusement** *adv* deliciously; delightfully.

délier [delje] *vtr* to untie, undo; **le vin délie la langue,** wine loosens the tongue; **d. qn de qch,** to release s.o. from sth. **délié 1.** *a* slender, fine; nimble, agile (fingers); **avoir la langue déliée,** to be talkative **2.** *nm Typ:* thin stroke.

délimiter [delimite] *vtr* to delimit, demarcate (territory); to define (powers).

délinquance [delɛ̃kɑ̃s] *nf* delinquency; **d. juvénile,** juvenile delinquency. **délinquant, -ante** *a & n* deliquent; **d. primaire,** first offender.

déliquescence [delikesɑ̃s] *nf* deliquescence; *Fig:* decay. **déliquescent** *a* deliquescent; *Fig:* decaying.

délire [delir] *nm* **1.** delirium **2.** frenzy; **foule en d.,** ecstatic crowd.

délirer [delire] *vi* to be delirious; to rave.

délit [deli] *nm* offence.

délivrance [delivrɑ̃s] *nf* **1.** deliverance, rescue, release **2.** delivery; issue (of tickets).

délivrer [delivre] *vtr* **1.** to deliver; to rescue (captive); to release (prisoner) **2.** to deliver (goods); to issue (tickets) **3. se d. de qch,** to get rid of sth.

déloger [deloʒe] *v* (*conj like* LOGER) **1.** *vi* to go off, move away **2.** *vtr* to evict (tenant); to drive (s.o.) out.

déloyauté [delwajote] *nf* disloyalty, perfidy. **déloyal, pl -aux** *a* disloyal (friend); unfair (practice); *Sp:* **jeu d.,** foul play. **déloyalement** *adv* disloyally.

delta [dɛlta] *nm* delta.

déluge [delyʒ] *nm* (*a*) deluge, flood; torrent (of abuse); **cela remonte au d.,** it's as old as the hills (*b*) downpour (of rain).

déluré [delyre] *a* smart, sharp (pers).

démagogie [demagɔʒi] *nf* demagogy. **démagogique** *a* demagogic.

démagogue [demagɔg] *nm* demagogue.

démailler (se) [sədemaje] *vpr* (*of tights*) to ladder, to run.

demain [dəmɛ̃] *adv & nm* tomorrow; **à d.!** see you tomorrow! *F:* **c'est pas d. la veille,** it's not for a long time yet; **d. il fera jour,** tomorrow is another day.

demande [dəmɑ̃d] *nf* **1.** (*a*) request, application; **faire la d. de qch,** to ask for sth; **d. (en mariage),** proposal (of marriage); **sur la d. de qn,** at s.o.'s request; **d. de remboursement,** claim; **il faut faire une d.,** you must fill in an application form (*b*) *Com:* demand; **l'offre et la d.,** supply and demand (*c*) **d. en divorce,** divorce petition **2.** question, enquiry.

demander [dəmɑ̃de] *vtr* **1.** (*a*) to ask (for), to request; to claim (damages); **je vous demande pardon,** I beg your pardon; **d. qn en mariage,** to propose to s.o., to ask for s.o.'s hand; **on vous demande,** you're wanted; somebody wants to see you; **d. qch à qn,** to ask s.o. for sth; **combien demandez-vous de l'heure?** how much do you charge an hour? (*b*) **je demande à parler,** please let me speak **2.** to desire, want, need, require; **c'est très demandé,** it's in great demand; **le voyage demande 3 heures,** the journey takes 3 hours **3.** to demand, expect; **ne lui en demandez pas trop,** don't expect too much from him **4.** to ask, enquire; **d. à qn son avis,** to ask s.o.'s opinion; *F:* **je ne t'ai rien demandé!** mind your own business! **je vous demande un peu!** I ask you! **5. se d.,** to ask oneself, to wonder; **je me demande pourquoi,** I wonder why.

demandeur¹, -deresse [dəmãdœr, -drɛs] *n Jur:* plaintiff.

demandeur², -euse [dəmãdœr, -øz] *n (a) Com:* buyer (*b*) **d. d'emploi,** job seeker.

démangeaison [demãʒɛzɔ̃] *nf* itching; **j'ai une d.,** I've got an itch; **d. de faire qch,** urge, longing, to do sth.

démanger [demãʒe] *vi* (**il démangea(it);** *usu with dative of person*) to itch; **l'épaule me démange,** my shoulder's itching; **la main lui démange,** he's itching for a fight.

démantèlement [demãtɛlmã] *nm* demolition; breaking up; bringing down.

démanteler [demãtle] *vtr* (**je démantèle**) to demolish (fortifications); to break up (organization); to bring down (empire).

démantibuler [demãtibyle] *vtr F:* (*a*) to break up, demolish (*b*) **se d.,** to come to pieces.

démaquillage [demakijaʒ] *nm Toil:* removal of makeup.

démaquillant [demakijã] *nm* makeup remover.

démaquiller [demakije] *vtr* to remove makeup; **se d.,** to remove one's makeup.

démarcation [demarkasjɔ̃] *nf* demarcation; **ligne de d.,** dividing line.

démarche [demarʃ] *nf* 1. gait, walk 2. step; **faire une d. auprès de qn,** to approach s.o.; **faire les démarches nécessaires,** to take the necessary steps.

démarcheur, -euse [demarʃœr, -øz] *n* door-to-door salesman, saleswoman.

démarquer [demarke] *vtr* 1. *Com:* to mark down (goods) 2. to plagiarize (book) 3. *Sp:* to leave opponent unmarked 4. **se d. de,** to dissociate oneself from. **démarqué** *a Sp:* unmarked.

démarrage [demaraʒ] *nm* (*a*) starting (of engine); moving off (of car); start (of business); **d. en côte,** hill start (*b*) *Sp:* (sudden) spurt.

démarrer [demare] 1. *vtr* to start (car) 2. *vi* (*a*) (*of vehicle*) to start, to move off; (*of ship*) to cast off; (*of pers*) to drive off; **faire d.,** to start (car) (*b*) (*of business*) to begin to get going (*c*) *Sp:* to put on a spurt.

démarreur [demarœr] *nm Aut:* starter (motor).

démasquer [demaske] *vtr* (*a*) to unmask; to expose (*b*) *Fig:* **se d.,** to drop the mask.

démêlé [demele] *nm usu pl* contention; **il a eu des démêlés avec la police,** he's been in trouble with the police.

démêler [demele] *vtr* (*a*) to disentangle, unravel (string); to untangle (hair); to sort out (problem); to clear up (misunderstanding) (*b*) **se d.,** to extricate oneself (from difficulty).

demembrer [demãbre] *vtr* to dismember; to carve up (estate).

déménagement [demenaʒmã] *nm* moving (house); move; removal.

déménager [demenaʒe] *vtr & i* (n. **déménageons**) **d. (ses meubles),** to remove (one's furniture); to move (house); *F:* **d. à la cloche de bois,** to do a moonlight flit; **il déménage,** he's off his rocker! *F:* **allez! déménagez!** scram!

déménageur [demenaʒœr] *nm* removal man; furniture remover.

démence [demãs] *nf* insanity, madness. **dément,**

-ente *a* insane, mad; **c'est d.!** it's unbelievable! **démentiel, -elle** *a* insane.

démener (se) [sədəmne] *vpr (conj like* MENER*)* 1. to thrash about; to struggle 2. to exert oneself; to make a great effort.

démenti [demãti] *nm* denial, contradiction; refutation.

démentir [demãtir] *vtr (conj like* MENTIR*)* 1. to contradict (s.o.); to deny, refute (fact) 2. to belie; (*hopes*) to disappoint 3. **se d.,** to contradict oneself; to go back on one's word.

démesure [deməzyr] *nf* disproportion, excessiveness. **démesuré** *a* inordinate; beyond measure; unbounded; excessive. **démesurément** *adv* enormously; inordinately.

démettre [demɛtr̩] *vtr (conj like* METTRE*)* 1. to dislocate; **se d. l'épaule,** to put one's shoulder out (of joint) 2. (*a*) **d. qn de ses fonctions,** to deprive s.o. of his office (*b*) **se d. de ses fonctions,** to resign office.

demeure [dəmœr] *nf* 1. (*a*) **mettre qn en d. de payer,** to give s.o. notice to pay (*b*) stay; **à d.,** fixed, permanent, permanently 2. (place of) residence.

demeurer [dəmœre] *vi* 1. (*aux* être) to remain; to stay (in a place); **demeurons-en là,** let's leave it at that; **ne pouvoir d. en place,** to be unable to keep still 2. (*aux* avoir) to live, reside. **demeuré, -ée** 1. *a* halfwitted 2. *n* halfwit.

demi [dəmi] 1. *a* (*a*) half; **deux heures et demie,** (i) two and a half hours (ii) half past two; **une d.-heure,** half an hour (*b*) semi-; **d.-cercle,** semicircle (*c*) demi-; **d.-dieu,** demigod (*d*) **d.-cuit,** half cooked 2. *nm* (*a*) **un d.,** a half; (*beer*) **un d.,** = half a pint; a half (*b*) *Sp:* **les demis,** the half-backs (*c*) **à d.,** half; **à d. mort,** half-dead; **faire les choses à d.,** to do things by halves; **à d. transparent,** semi-transparent 3. *nf* **demie,** half hour; **il est la demie,** its half past. NOTE: *In all the following compounds* DEMI *is inv; the second component takes the plural.*

demi-cercle [-sɛrkl̩] *nm* semicircle, half circle.

demi-circulaire [-sirkyler] *a* semicircular.

demi-douzaine [-duzɛn] *nf* half dozen.

demi-finale [-final] *nf Sp:* semifinal.

demi-fond [-fɔ̃] *nm inv Sp:* (**course de) d.-f.,** middle distance race.

demi-frère [-frɛr] *nm* half brother.

demi-gros [-gro] *nm Com:* wholesale trade (in small quantities); cash and carry.

demi-heure [-dəmiœr] *nf* **une d.-h.,** half an hour.

démilitarisation [demilitarizasjɔ̃] *nf* demilitarization.

demilitariser [demilitarize] *vtr* to demilitarize.

demi-mal [-mal] *nm* **il n'y a que d.-m.,** it might have been worse.

demi-mot (à) [ad(ə)mimo] *adv phr* **entendre (qn) à d.-m.,** to (know how to) take a hint.

demi-pension [-pãsjɔ̃] *nf* half board.

demi-pensionnaire [-pãsjoner] *n* half boarder; *Sch:* day boarder.

demi-saison [-sɛzɔ̃] *nf* mid season.

demi-sel [-sɛl] 1. *nm* (slightly salted) cream cheese 2. *a inv* slightly salted (butter).

demi-sœur [-sœr] *nf* half sister.

démission [demisjɔ̃] *nf* resignation; **donner sa d.,** to tender one's resignation.

démissionner [demisjɔne] *vi* to resign; *F:* to give up.

demi-tarif [-tarif] *nm* half price; **billet (à) d.-t.**, half fare (ticket).

demi-ton [-tɔ̃] *nm Mus:* semitone.

demi-tour [-tur] *nm* half turn; about turn; *Aut:* U turn; **faire d.-t.**, to go back.

demi-voix (à) [ad(ə)miwwa] *adv phr* in an undertone; under one's breath.

démobilisation [demɔbilizasjɔ̃] *nf* demobilization.

démobiliser [demɔbilize] *vtr* to demobilize.

démocrate [demɔkrat] 1. *a* democratic 2. *n* democrat.

démocratie [demɔkrasi] *nf* democracy. **démocratique** *a* democratic. **démocratiquement** *adv* democratically.

démoder (se) [sədemɔde] *vpr* to go out of fashion, to become old fashioned. **démodé** *a* old-fashioned, out of date.

démographie [demɔgrafi] *nf* demography. **démographique** *a* demographic; **poussée d.**, population growth.

demoiselle [dəmwazɛl] *nf* 1. (*a*) spinster; single woman (*b*) **d. d'honneur**, (i) maid of honour (ii) bridesmaid 2. young lady 3. dragon fly.

démolir [demɔlir] *vtr* 1. to demolish, pull down (building) 2. to overthrow (authority); to demolish (argument); to ruin (reputation) 3. *F:* to beat (s.o.) up, to bash (s.o.) about.

démolisseur [demɔlisœr] *nm* demolition worker; demolition contractor.

démolition [demɔlisjɔ̃] *nf* demolition.

démon [demɔ̃] *nm* 1. *Myth:* genius 2. demon, devil, fiend; **le d.**, the Devil; **cette femme est un d.**, she's a wicked woman; **cet enfant est un d.**, that child is a little devil. **démoniaque** *a* demoniacal.

démonstrateur, -trice [demɔ̃stratœr, -tris] *n* demonstrator.

démonstration [demɔ̃strasjɔ̃] *nf* 1. demonstration; proof (of theorem); *Com:* demonstration (of article); **appareil de d.**, demonstration model 2. show (of friendship). **démonstratif, -ive** *a* demonstrative.

démonte-pneu [demɔ̃tpnø] *nm* tyre lever; *pl* **démonte-pneus.**

démonter [demɔ̃te] *vtr* 1. to throw off (rider) 2. **se laisser d.**, to get upset; **la nouvelle m'a démonté**, I was put out by the news 3. to take down, to take apart, to dismantle; to remove (tyre) 4. **se d.** (*a*) (*of mechanism*) to come apart (*b*) *F:* **il ne se démonte pas pour si peu**, he's not so easily put out. **démonté** *a* stormy, raging (sea); (*of pers*) disconcerted.

démontrer [demɔ̃tre] *vtr* 1. to demonstrate, to prove (sth) 2. to indicate, show (sth) clearly. **démontrable** *a* demonstrable.

démoralisation [demɔralizasjɔ̃] *nf* demoralization.

démoraliser [demɔralize] *vtr* to demoralize; to dishearten; **se d.**, to become demoralized. **démoralisant** *a* demoralizing.

démordre [demɔrdr̩] *vi* (*usu with neg*) **ne pas d. de ses opinions**, to stick to one's opinions; **il ne veut pas en d.**, he's sticking to his guns.

démoulage [demulaʒ] *nm* removal (of cast) from mould; turning out.

démouler [demule] *vtr* to remove (cast) from mould; to turn out (cake).

démultiplication [demyltiplikasjɔ̃] *nf MecE:* (*a*) reduction (*b*) reduction ratio.

démultiplier [demyltiplije] *vtr MecE:* to reduce the gear ratio, to gear down.

démunir [demynir] *vtr* 1. to deprive (s.o. of sth) 2. **se d. de qch**, to part with sth. **démuni** *a* unprovided (**de**, with); **d. d'argent**, penniless; *Com:* **être d. de qch**, to be sold out of sth.

démystifier [demistifje] *vtr* (*impf & pr sub* **n. démystifiions**) to undeceive, to disabuse.

dénatalité [denatalite] *nf* fall in the birthrate.

dénaturer [denatyre] *vtr* (*a*) to denature (alcohol) (*b*) to misrepresent, distort (words); **d. les faits**, to garble the facts. **dénaturé** *a* unnatural.

dénégation [denegasjɔ̃] *nf* denial.

déni [deni] *nm* **d. de justice**, denial of justice.

dénicher [denife] *vtr* (*a*) to find, discover, unearth; **comment m'avez-vous déniché?** how did you discover my whereabouts? (*b*) to drive (animal) out of hiding.

denier [dənje] *nm* 1. (*a*) (*Roman*) denarius (*b*) *A:* (*Fr*) denier 2. money, funds; **de mes deniers**, out of my own pocket; **pas un d.**, not a farthing 3. (*hosiery*) denier.

dénier [denje] *vtr* to deny (crime); to disclaim (responsibility); **d. qch à qn**, to refuse s.o. sth.

dénigrement [denigrəmɑ̃] *nm* denigration.

dénigrer [denigre] *vtr* to disparage.

dénivellation [denivɛlasjɔ̃] *nf* difference in level; **dénivellations d'une route**, (i) unevenness (ii) gradients, of a road.

dénombrement [denɔ̃brəmɑ̃] *nm* counting; census.

dénombrer [denɔ̃bre] *vtr* to count; to take a census of.

dénominateur [denɔminatœr] *nm* denominator.

dénomination [denɔminasjɔ̃] *nf* denomination, designation, name.

dénommer [denɔme] *vtr* to name; *F:* **un dénommé Charles**, a man called Charles.

dénoncer [denɔ̃se] *vtr* (**n. dénonçons**) 1. to indicate, to reveal 2. (*a*) to denounce (s.o.); to inform against (s.o.); **se d.**, to give oneself up (*b*) to expose (crime).

dénonciation [denɔ̃sjasjɔ̃] *nf* denunciation; information (**de qn**, against s.o.). **dénonciateur, -trice** 1. *n* denouncer, informer; exposer 2. *a* accusatory.

dénoter [denɔte] *vtr* to denote.

dénouement [denumɑ̃] *nm* result, outcome; *Th:* dénouement.

dénouer [denwe] *vtr* 1. to unknot; to untie, undo; **d. une intrigue**, to unravel a plot 2. **se d.** (*a*) to come undone (*b*) (*of plot*) to be resolved.

dénoyauter [denwajote] *vtr* to stone, *NAm:* to pit (fruit).

denrée [dɑ̃re] *nf usu pl* commodity; *esp* foodstuff, produce; **denrées alimentaires**, food products.

densité [dɑ̃site] *nf* denseness, density. **dense** *a* dense, crowded; thick; condensed.

dent [dɑ̃] *nf* 1. tooth; **d. de lait, de sagesse**, milk tooth; wisdom tooth; **faire, percer, ses dents**, to cut one's teeth; to teethe; **rage de dents**, toothache; **n'avoir**

rien à se mettre sous la d., to have nothing to eat; manger du bout des dents, to pick at one's food; rire du bout des dents, to force a laugh; avoir les dents longues, (i) to be very hungry (ii) to be grasping; garder une d. contre qn, to have a grudge against s.o.; être sur les dents, (i) to be worn out (ii) to be overworked 2. tooth (of comb, saw); cog (of wheel); prong (of fork); (jagged) peak (of mountain); en dents de scie, serrated, jagged. **dentaire** a dental. **denté** a cogged, toothed (wheel); dentate (leaf).

dentelé [dɑ̃tle] a jagged; serrated; perforated (stamp).

dentelle [dɑ̃tɛl] nf lace.

dentellière [dɑ̃teljɛr] nf (a) lacemaker (b) lace-making machine.

dentelure [dɑ̃tlyr] nf jagged outline (of coast); serration; perforation (on stamp).

dentier [dɑ̃tje] nm set of false teeth, denture.

dentifrice [dɑ̃tifris] nm toothpaste, toothpowder.

dentiste [dɑ̃tist] n dentist.

dentition [dɑ̃tisjɔ̃] nf dentition.

denture [dɑ̃tyr] nf set of (natural) teeth.

dénuder [denyde] vtr 1. to denude, to lay bare, strip 2. se d., to become bare; (of pers) to strip (naked). **dénudé** a bare; bald (head).

dénué [denɥe] a d. d'argent, without money; d. de sens, senseless; d. d'intelligence, unintelligent.

dénuement [denymɑ̃] nm destitution, penury; être dans le d., to be destitute.

déodorant [deɔdɔrɑ̃] a & nm Toil: deodorant.

dépannage [depanaʒ] nm (a) repairing; (emergency) repairs; **service de d.**, breakdown service (b) helping out.

dépanner [depane] vtr (a) to repair, to do running repairs on (car) (b) to help (s.o.) out.

dépanneur [depanœr] nm breakdown mechanic.

dépanneuse [depanøz] nf breakdown van, truck.

dépareillé [depareje] a odd, incomplete; **articles dépareillés**, oddments.

départ [depar] nm departure; start (of race); **dès son d.**, as soon as he had gone; **point de d.**, starting point; être sur le d., to be on the point of leaving; **produit de d.**, original material; **excursions au d. de Chamonix**, trips (leaving) from Chamonix; Sp: **faux d.**, false start; **donner le d.**, to start the race; Com: **prix d. usine**, price ex works.

départager [departaʒe] vtr (conj like PARTAGER) to decide between (opinions); **d. les votes**, to give the casting vote.

département [departəmɑ̃] nm Adm: department. **departemental, -aux** a departmental; **route départementale**, secondary road.

dépassé [depase] a out-of-date.

dépassement [depasmɑ̃] nm (a) surpassing (of oneself) (b) Aut: overtaking.

dépasser [depase] vtr 1. (a) to pass, to go beyond; **d. le but**, to overshoot the mark; **d. les bornes**, (i) to overstep the bounds (ii) to be beyond all bounds; **d. la trentaine**, to be over thirty (b) Aut: to overtake; **il est interdit de d.**, to top sth; **d. qn en hauteur**, to top sth; **d. qn de la tête**, to stand a head taller than s.o.; **son jupon dépasse**, her petticoat is showing; **cela dépasse ma compétence**, it's outside my competence; **cela me dépasse**, it's beyond me; **je suis**

dépassé par les événements, things are getting too much for me 3. to exceed; **d. la limite de vitesse**, to exceed the speed limit.

dépaysement [depeizmɑ̃] nm disorientation.

dépayser [depeize] vtr to disorientate. **dépaysé** a out of one's element; **je me sens d.**, I don't feel at home.

dépeçage [depəsaʒ] nm cutting up; jointing; carving (up).

dépecer [depəse] vtr (je dépèce) to cut up (carcass); to joint; to carve (meat).

dépêche [depɛʃ] nf (a) (official) despatch (b) d. (télégraphique), telegram.

dépêcher [depɛʃe] vtr 1. to dispatch 2. se d., to hurry, to be quick; **dépêchez-vous!** hurry up! get a move on! **se d. de faire qch**, to hurry to do sth.

dépeigner [depeɲe] vtr to make (s.o.'s) hair untidy; **dépeigné**, with uncombed hair.

dépeindre [depɛ̃dr] vtr (conj like PEINDRE) to depict, picture, describe (s.o., sth).

dépenaillé [depnaje] a ragged, tattered.

dépendance [depɑ̃dɑ̃s] nf 1. dependence 2. (a) dependency (of a country) (b) pl outbuildings 3. subjection; **être sous la d. de qn**, to be under s.o.'s domination. **dépendant** a dependent.

dépendre[1] [depɑ̃dr] vtr to take down (hanging object).

dépendre[2] vi 1. to depend (de, on); **ça ne dépend pas de nous**, it's not within our control; **il dépend de vous de le faire**, it rests with you to do it; **cela dépend**, that depends; we shall see 2. (of land) to belong to 3. to be subordinate (de, to); **ne d. que de soi**, to be one's own boss.

dépens [depɑ̃] nmpl 1. Jur: costs; Com: cost, expenses 2. prep phr **aux d. de qn**, at s.o.'s expense; **il apprit à ses d. que**, he learnt to his cost that.

dépense [depɑ̃s] nf 1. expenditure, outlay, expense; **dépenses courantes**, current expenditures, expenses; **je n'aurai pas dû faire cette d.**, I shouldn't have spent that money; **dépenses publiques**, public spending 2. (petrol, electricity) consumption.

dépenser [depɑ̃se] vtr 1. to spend, to lay out (money); **d. sans compter**, to be free with one's money 2. to spend, consume (energy) 3. se d., to exert oneself. **dépensier, -ière** 1. a extravagant 2. n spendthrift.

déperdition [deperdisjɔ̃] nf waste, wastage; loss (of heat, energy).

dépérir [deperir] vi to waste away; (of plant) to wither; (of business) to go downhill.

dépérissement [deperismɑ̃] nm wasting away; withering; decline.

dépêtrer [depetre] vtr 1. to extricate (s.o.) 2. se d., to get out of a scrape.

dépeuplement [depœpləmɑ̃] nm depopulation (of country).

dépeupler [depœple] vtr to depopulate (country).

dépilatoire [depilatwar] a depilatory; hair removing (cream).

dépistage [depistaʒ] nm tracking down (of criminal); (early) detection, screening (of disease).

dépister [depiste] vtr 1. to track down; to detect (disease) 2. to put (s.o.) off the scent.

dépit [depi] nm 1. spite, resentment; **par d.**, out of

déraciner [derasine] *vtr* **1.** to uproot (tree, pers) **2.** to eradicate (fault).

déraillement [derɑjmɑ̃] *nm* Rail: derailment.

dérailler [derɑje] *vi* (a) (*of train*) to become derailed (b) F: (*of machine*) to be on the blink (c) F: (*of pers*) to rave.

dérailleur [derɑjœr] *nm* Cy: derailleur (gears).

déraisonner [derɛzɔne] *vi* to talk nonsense. **déraisonnable** *a* unreasonable.

dérangement [derɑ̃ʒmɑ̃] *nm* (a) disturbance, trouble (b) disorder; (mental) derangement (c) **en d.,** out of order.

déranger [derɑ̃ʒe] *vtr* (**n. dérangeons**) **1.** (a) to disarrange (papers) (b) to disturb, trouble; **si cela ne vous dérange pas,** if it's no trouble to you (c) to upset (plans, s.o.) **2. se d.,** to move; **ne vous dérangez pas,** (i) please don't move (ii) please don't put yourself out on my account.

dérapage [derapaʒ] *nm* Aut: skid.

déraper [derape] *vi* Aut: to skid.

déréglement [deregləmɑ̃] *nm* **1.** disordered, unsettled, state; irregularity (of pulse) **2.** dissoluteness.

dérégler [deregle] *vtr* (**je dérègle; je déréglerai**) **1.** to upset; to unsettle **2. se d.,** (*of clock*) to go out of order; (*of pulse*) to become irregular. **déréglé** *a* out of order; upset; unsettled; dissolute (life).

dérider (se) [səderide] *vpr* F: (*of pers*) to brighten up, to cheer up.

dérision [derizjɔ̃] *nf* derision, mockery; **par d.,** derisively, mockingly; **tourner en d.,** to ridicule.

dérisoire [derizwar] *a* derisory, ridiculous, laughable (offer); absurdly low (price).

dérivatif, -ive [derivatif, -iv] **1.** *a* derivative **2.** *nm* distraction.

dérivation [derivasjɔ̃] *nf* **1.** diversion (of watercourse) **2.** Mth: Ling: derivation **3.** El: shunt **4.** Nau: Av: drift.

dérive [deriv] *nf* (a) Nau: leeway, drift; **à la d.,** adrift; **aller à la d.,** to drift (b) (**quille de) d.,** (i) centre board (ii) Av: fin.

dériver [derive] **1.** *vtr* (a) to divert (stream); El: to shunt (current) (b) Mth: Ling: to derive **2.** *vi* to be derived (from a source) **3.** *vi* Nau: to drift. **dérivé, -ée 1.** *a* derived **2.** (a) *nm* Ling: Ch: derivative; by-product (b) *nf* Mth: derivative.

dermatologie [dɛrmatɔlɔʒi] *nf* dermatology.

dermatologue [dɛrmatɔlɔg] *n* dermatologist.

dernier, -ière [dɛrnje, -jɛr] *a & n* **1.** (a) last, latest; **faire un d.** effort, to make a final effort; **mettre la dernière main,** to put the finishing touches (to sth); **jusqu'à sa dernière heure,** to his dying day; **il est arrivé bon d., le d.,** he arrived last; **au cours des dernières années,** over the past few years; **dernières nouvelles,** latest news; F: **vous connaissez la dernière?** have you heard the latest? **la dernière mode, le d. cri,** the latest fashion (b) **le mois d.,** last month; **ces derniers temps,** lately; **c'est notre petit d.,** he's our youngest (child); **le d. élève de la classe,** the bottom pupil in the form; **venir en d.,** to come last (c) **ce d. répondit,** the latter answered **2.** (a) utmost, highest; **au d. degré,** to the highest degree; **dans la dernière misère,** in utmost, in dire, poverty (b) lowest, worst; **de d. ordre,** very inferior; **le d. de mes soucis,** the least of my worries; **on le traite comme le d. des**

derniers, they treat him like dirt. **dernièrement** *adv* lately, of late, recently.

dernier-né [dɛrnjene] *nm* last-born child; *pl* **derniers-nés.**

dérobade [derɔbad] *nf* (a) evasion (b) swerve (of horse).

dérober [derɔbe] *vtr* **1.** (a) to steal, to make away with (sth) (b) **d. qn au danger,** to save s.o. from danger **2.** to hide, conceal **3. se d.** (a) to escape, steal away, slip away (à, from); **se d. aux regards,** to avoid notice; **je lui ai demandé, mais il s'est dérobé,** I asked him but he avoided the issue (b) (*of horse*) to swerve; to refuse (c) to give way (**sous,** under). **dérobé** *a* hidden, concealed; *adv phr* **à la dérobée,** stealthily, secretly.

dérogation [derɔgasjɔ̃] *nf* derogation (**à une loi,** of a law). **dérogatoire** *a* derogatory (clause).

déroger [derɔʒe] *vi* (**je dérogeai(s)**) (a) **d. à une loi,** to depart from the law (b) **d. à son rang,** to demean oneself.

déroulement [derulmɑ̃] *nm* (a) unrolling; unwinding, uncoiling (b) unfolding, development (of plot, events).

dérouler [derule] *vtr* **1.** to unroll; to unwind, to uncoil **2. se d.** (a) to unroll, to uncoil (b) to unfold; **le paysage se déroule devant nous,** the landscape stretches out before us; **les événements qui se déroulent,** the events which are taking place.

déroute [derut] *nf* rout; **en d.,** in (full) flight, routed.

dérouter [derute] *vtr* **1.** (a) to lead (s.o.) astray; **d. les soupçons,** to throw people off the scent (b) to divert, to reroute (ship, aircraft) **2.** to confuse, to disconcert. **déroutant** *a* disconcerting.

derrière [dɛrjɛr] **1.** *prep* (a) behind, at the back of (sth); **il faut toujours être d. elle,** you always have to keep an eye on her; **je suis d. vous,** I'll back you up (b) Nau: (i) abaft (ii) astern **2.** *adv* (a) behind, at the back, in the rear; **attaquer qn par d.,** to attack s.o. from behind; **passer par d.,** to go round the back; **pattes de d.,** hind legs (b) Nau: (i) aft (ii) astern **3.** *nm* (a) back, rear (of building) (b) behind, backside, bottom; (*of animal*) hindquarters.

derviche [dɛrviʃ] *nm* dervish; **d. tourneur,** whirling dervish.

des [de, dɛ] = **de les;** *see* **de** *and* **le.**

DES *abbr Diplôme d'études supérieures.*

dès [dɛ] *prep* since, from; as early as; **d. sa jeunesse,** from childhood; **d. l'abord,** from the outset; **d. maintenant,** from now on; **d. 1840,** as far back as 1840; **d. le matin,** first thing in the morning; **d. mon retour,** immediately on my return; *conj phr* **d. que +** *ind* as soon as; *adv phr* **d. lors,** (i) ever since (then) (ii) consequently, therefore; **d. lors que,** since, seeing that.

désabusé [dezabyze] *a* disillusioned, disenchanted.

désaccord [dezakɔr] *nm* (a) disagreement, dissension; **être en d.,** to disagree; **sujet de d.,** bone of contention (b) clash (of interests); **d. entre la théorie et les faits,** discrepancy between the theory and the facts.

désaccordé [dezakɔrde] *a* out of tune.

désaccoutumer [dezakutyme] *vtr* to get (s.o.) out of the habit (of sth); **se d. de qch,** to lose the habit of sth.

désaffectation [dezafεktasjɔ̃] *nf* closing down (of building).

désaffecter [dezafεkte] *vtr* to close down (building). **désaffecté** *a* disused.

désagréable [dezagreabl] *a* disagreeable, unpleasant. **désagréablement** *adv* disagreeably, unpleasantly.

désagrégation [dezagregasjɔ̃] *nf* disintegration; breaking up.

désagréger [dezagreʒe] *vtr* (je **désagrège**, n. désagrégeons; je **désagrégerai**) to disintegrate; to break up.

désagrément [dezagremɑ̃] *nm* (source of) annoyance; unpleasant occurrence; trouble.

désaltérer [dezaltere] *vtr* (je **désaltère**) to quench (s.o.'s) thirst; **se d.**, to quench one's thirst. **désaltérant** *a* thirst-quenching.

désamorcer [dezamɔrse] *vtr* (je **désamorçai(s)**) to unprime (fuse, cartridge); to defuse (bomb); to drain (pump); *Fig:* to render (sth) harmless.

désappointement [dezapwɛ̃tmɑ̃] *nm* disappointment.

désappointer [dezapwɛ̃te] *vtr* to disappoint.

désapprobation [dezaprɔbasjɔ̃] *nf* disapproval, disapprobation. **désapprobateur, -trice** *a* disapproving.

désapprouver [dezapruve] *vtr* to disapprove of, object to (sth).

désarçonner [dezarsɔne] *vtr* 1. (*of horse*) to unseat (rider) 2. *F:* to floor s.o.

désargenté [dezarʒɑ̃te] *a F:* broke.

désarmement [dezarməmɑ̃] *nm* disarming; disarmament; laying up (of ship).

désarmer [dezarme] 1. *vtr* (*a*) to disarm (s.o.) (*b*) to unload (gun) (*c*) to lay up (ship) 2. *vi* (*a*) to disarm (*b*) to relent. **désarmant** *a* disarming. **désarmé** *a* (*a*) disarmed (*b*) unarmed; defenceless.

désarroi [dezarwa] *nm* disarray; confusion.

désastre [dezastr] *nm* disaster, calamity. **désastreux, -euse** *a* disastrous, calamitous.

désavantage [dezavɑ̃taʒ] *nm* disadvantage, drawback; handicap; **avoir un d. sur qn**, to be at a disadvantage in comparison with s.o. **désavantageux, -euse** *a* disadvantageous, unfavourable. **désavantageusement** *adv* disadvantageously, unfavourably.

désavantager [dezavɑ̃taʒe] *vtr* (je **désavantageai(s)**) to put (s.o.) at a disadvantage (**par rapport à qn**, by comparison with s.o.); to penalize (s.o.).

désaveu [dezavø] *nm* disavowal, denial; repudiation.

désavouer [dezavwe] *vtr* to disavow, disown; to repudiate, deny; **se d.**, to retract.

désaxer [dezakse] *vtr* to unbalance, unhinge (mind).

desceller [desele] *vtr* to loosen, to pull free (stone).

descendance [desɑ̃dɑ̃s] *nf* (*a*) descent (*b*) descendants.

descendant, -ante [desɑ̃dɑ̃, -ɑ̃t] 1. *a* (*a*) descending; downward (motion) (*b*) (*of train, line*) down (*c*) *Mus:* descending (scale) 2. *n* descendant.

descendre [desɑ̃dr] 1. *vi* (*aux* être, *occ* avoir) (*a*) to descend; to come, go, down; **d. d'un arbre**, to come down from a tree; **d. en glissant**, to slide down; **la marée descend**, the tide is going out; **le**

baromètre descend, the glass is falling; **la police est descendue dans l'immeuble**, the police raided the building (*b*) to come, go, downstairs; **il n'est pas encore descendu**, he is not down yet; **faites le d.**, (i) send him down (ii) call him down; *Fig:* **d. dans la rue**, to go on a demonstration (*c*) to condescend; **d. jusqu'au mensonge**, to stoop to lying (*d*) to alight; to get off (bus, train); **d. de cheval**, to dismount; **tout le monde descend!** all change! (*e*) **d. à un hôtel**, to stay at a hotel (*f*) to extend downwards; (*of road*) to go downhill; **ses cheveux descendent jusqu'à la taille**, her hair comes down to her waist (*g*) (*of family*) to be descended (from) 2. *vtr* (*aux* avoir) (*a*) **d. les marches, la rue**, to go down the steps, the street (*b*) to take, bring, (sth) down; **d. les bagages**, to bring down the luggage (*c*) *F:* to shoot down, kill (partridge, man); **il s'est fait d. par la police**, he was shot down by the police (*d*) to put down, to drop (passengers).

descente [desɑ̃t] *nf* 1. (*a*) descent; coming down, going down (from height); *Ski:* run; **d. de cheval**, dismounting; **d. en parachute**, parachute drop (*b*) **accueillir qn à la d. du train**, to meet s.o. off the train (*c*) raid; incursion; *Jur:* **d. sur les lieux**, visit to the scene (of a crime); **d. de police**, police raid 2. taking down, letting down, lowering; *Art:* **D. de Croix**, Deposition 3. (*a*) slope; **d. rapide**, steep slope; **d. dangereuse**, dangerous hill (*b*) **d. de lit**, bedside rug.

description [dɛskripsjɔ̃] *nf* description; **faire la d. de qch**, to describe sth. **descriptif, -ive** *a* descriptive.

désembuer [dezɑ̃bɥe] *vtr* to demist.

désemparé [dezɑ̃pare] *a* (*a*) (ship) in distress (*b*) distraught, bewildered.

désemparer [dezɑ̃pare] *vi* **sans d.**, without stopping.

désemplir [dezɑ̃plir] *vi & pr usu in neg* **son magasin ne (se) désemplit pas**, his shop is always full.

désenchantement [dezɑ̃ʃɑ̃tmɑ̃] *nm* disenchantment; disillusion. **désenchanté** *a* disenchanted; disillusioned.

désenfler [dezɑ̃fle] *vi & pr* to become less swollen.

déséquilibre [dezekilibr] *nm* (*a*) *Ph:* imbalance (*b*) *Psy:* unbalance.

déséquilibrer [dezekilibre] *vtr* to unbalance; to throw off balance. **déséquilibré, -ée** 1. *a* unbalanced 2. *n* unbalanced person.

désert [dezɛr] 1. *a* deserted; uninhabited (place); lonely (spot) 2. *nm* desert. **désertique** *a* desert (region).

déserter [dezɛrte] *vtr* to desert.

déserteur [dezɛrtœr] *nm* deserter.

désertion [dezɛrsjɔ̃] *nf* desertion.

désespérer [dezɛspere] (je **désespère**; je **désespérerai**) 1. *vi* to despair; to lose hope; **d. de qn**, to despair of s.o. 2. *vtr* to drive (s.o.) to despair 3. **se d.**, to be in despair. **désespérant** *a* appalling; maddening; heartbreaking. **désespéré, -ée** 1. *a* desperate; hopeless 2. *n* (*a*) desperate person (*b*) (*pers*) suicide. **désespérément** *adv* despairingly; desperately.

désespoir [dezɛspwar] *nm* 1. despair; **être au d.**, to be in despair; **faire le d. de qn**, to be the despair of s.o., to drive s.o. to despair **2.** desperation; **en d. de cause,** in desperation.

déshabillé [dezabije] *nm Cl:* negligé(e); housecoat.

déshabiller [dezabije] *vtr* to undress (s.o.); **se d.,** to undress; to take off one's coat.

déshabituer [dezabitɥe] *vtr (a)* **d. qn de qch,** to break s.o. of the habit of sth *(b)* **se d.,** to lose the habit **(de,** of).

désherbage [dezɛrbaʒ] *nm* weeding.

désherbant [dezɛrbã] *nm* weedkiller.

désherber [dezɛrbe] *vtr* to weed.

déshériter [dezerite] *vtr* to disinherit (s.o.).

déshonneur [dezɔnœr] *nm* dishonour, disgrace.

déshonorer [dezɔnɔre] *vtr* to dishonour, to disgrace. **déshonorant** *a* dishonourable, discreditable.

déshydratation [dezidratasjɔ̃] *nf* dehydration.

déshydrater [dezidrate] *vtr* to dehydrate.

désignation [deziɲasjɔ̃] *nf* designation.

désigner [deziɲe] *vtr* **1.** to designate, show, indicate, point out; **d. qn par son nom,** to refer to s.o. by name **2.** *(a)* to appoint, fix (day, date); **être désigné pour faire qch,** to be cut out for sth *(b)* **d. qn à, pour, un poste,** to appoint s.o. to a post; **il a été désigné pour nous représenter,** he was chosen to represent us.

désillusion [dezilyzjɔ̃] *nf* disillusion.

désillusionner [dezilyzjɔne] *vtr* to disillusion.

désinfecter [dezɛ̃fɛkte] *vtr* to disinfect. **désinfectant** *a & nm* disinfectant.

désinfection [dezɛ̃fɛksjɔ̃] *nf* disinfection.

désintégration [dezɛ̃tegrasjɔ̃] *nf* disintegration, breaking up; splitting (of the atom).

désintégrer [dezɛ̃tegre] *vtr* **(je désintègre) 1.** to disintegrate; to split (the atom) **2. se d.,** to disintegrate; *(of atom)* to split.

désintéressement [dezɛ̃teresmã] *nm* **1.** disinterestedness **2.** paying off (of creditor).

désintéresser [dezɛ̃terese] *vtr* **1.** to pay off (creditor) **2. se d. de qch,** to take (i) no further interest (ii) no part, in sth. **désintéressé** *a* disinterested.

désintoxication [dezɛ̃tɔksikasjɔ̃] *nf Med:* treatment for alcoholism, for drug addiction.

désintoxiquer [dezɛ̃tɔksike] *vtr Med:* to treat for alcoholism, for drug addiction.

désinvolture [dezɛ̃vɔltyr] *nf* free and easy manner; **avec d.,** in an offhand way. **désinvolte** *a* casual, offhand, airy.

désir [dezir] *nm* desire **(de,** for); wish; **d. ardent,** craving; **prendre ses désirs pour des réalités,** to indulge in wishful thinking.

désirer [dezire] *vtr* to desire, want; to wish for (sth); **je désire qu'il vienne,** I would like him to come; **cela laisse à d.,** it's not satisfactory; there's room for improvement; **que désirez-vous?** what would you like? what can I do for you? **désirable** *a* desirable; **peu d.,** undesirable. **désireux, -euse** *a* anxious **(de,** to).

désistement [dezistəmã] *nm* withdrawal.

désister (se) [sədeziste] *vpr* to withdraw.

désobéir [dezɔbeir] *vi* **d. (à qn, à un ordre),** to disobey (s.o., an order).

désobéissance [dezɔbeisãs] *nf* disobedience. **désobéissant** *a* disobedient.

désobliger [dezɔbliʒe] *vtr* **(n. désobligeons)** to offend. **désobligeant** *a* disagreeable, offensive.

désodoriser [dezɔdɔrize] *vtr* to deodorize. **désodorisant** *a & nm* deodorant.

désœuvré [dezœvre] *a (of pers)* unoccupied, idle; at a loose end.

désœuvrement [dezœvrəmã] *nm* idleness; **par d.,** to kill time, for want of something to do.

désolation [dezɔlasjɔ̃] *nf (a)* desolation, devastation *(b)* grief, distress.

désoler [dezɔle] *vtr* **1.** to distress, upset (s.o.) **2. se d.,** to be upset. **désolant** *a* distressing, disappointing. **désolé** *a (a)* desolate (region) *(b)* distressed; **je suis désolé de vous avoir fait attendre,** I am so sorry to have kept you waiting.

désolidariser (se) [sədesɔlidarize] *vpr* **se d. de,** to dissociate from, to break one's ties with.

désopilant [dezɔpilã] *a* hilarious.

désordonné [dezɔrdɔne] *a (a)* disordered; disorganized, disorderly (life); uncoordinated (movements) *(b)* untidy (room) *(c) (pers)* (i) disorganized (ii) untidy.

désordre [dezɔrdr̩] *nm* **1.** *(a)* disorder, confusion; untidiness; chaos; **quel d.!** what a mess! **cheveux en d.,** untidy hair *(b) Med:* **d. nerveux,** nervous disorder **2.** disorderliness **3.** *pl* disturbances, riots.

désorganisation [dezɔrganizasjɔ̃] *nf* disorganization.

désorganiser [dezɔrganize] *vtr* to disorganize.

désorienter [dezɔrjãte] *vtr* to disorientate. **désorienté** *a* bewildered; **je suis tout d.,** I don't know where I am.

désormais [dezɔrmɛ] *adv* henceforth; from now on; in future.

désosser [dezɔse] *vtr* to bone (meat).

despote [dɛspɔt] *nm* despot. **despotique** *a* despotic.

despotisme [dɛspɔtism] *nm* despotism.

desquels, desquelles [dekɛl] *see* **lequel.**

dessaisir [desezir] *vtr* **1. d. un tribunal d'une affaire,** to remove a case from a court **2. se d. de qch,** to part with sth.

dessaler [desale] *vtr* **1.** to put (meat, fish) to soak (to remove salt) **2.** *F:* **d. qn,** to sharpen s.o.'s wits.

dessécher [deseʃe] *vtr* **(je dessèche; je dessécherai) 1.** to dry up **2.** to season (wood) **3.** *(a)* to wither (plant); to dry (skin) *(b)* to harden (brake); **d. son étreinte, d. son cœur,** to sharpen s.o.'s heart) **4. se d.** *(a)* to dry up *(b)* to become parched *(c)* to wither.

dessein [desɛ̃] *nm* **1.** design, plan, project **2.** intention, purpose; **dans ce d.,** with this intention; **à d.,** on purpose, intentionally; deliberately.

desseller [desele] *vtr* to unsaddle (horse).

desserrer [desere] *vtr* **1.** to loosen (screw); to slacken (belt, knot); to unscrew (nut); to unclench (fist, teeth); to release (brake); **je n'ai pas desserré les dents,** I didn't open my mouth **2. se d.,** to work loose; *(of grip)* to relax.

dessert [desɛr] *nm* dessert.

desserte [desɛrt] *nf* **1.** *Trans:* service; **d. d'un port par voie ferrée,** railway service to a port **2.** sideboard.

desservir¹ [desɛrvir] *vtr (conj like* SERVIR*) (a) (of* *railway*) to serve; **ce train ne dessert pas toutes les gares,** this train does not stop at every station (*b*) to lead into (a room).

desservir² *vtr* (*conj like* SERVIR) **1.** to clear (the table); *vi* to clear away **2. d. qn,** to be a bad friend to s.o.; to do s.o. a disservice.

dessin [desɛ̃] *nm* **1.** (*a*) (art of) drawing, sketching (*b*) drawing, sketch; **d. à la plume,** pen-and-ink sketch; *Cin:* **dessin(s) animé(s),** motion-picture cartoon; **d. humoristique,** cartoon **2.** design, pattern; **d. de mode,** fashion design **3.** draughtsmanship **4.** outline.

dessinateur, -trice [desinatœr, -tris] *n* **1.** (*a*) sketcher, drawer (*b*) cartoonist **2.** designer; dress designer, fashion designer **3.** draughtsman, draughtswoman.

dessiner [desine] *vtr* **1.** to draw, sketch; **d. qch d'après nature,** to draw sth from nature; **d. à l'encre,** to draw in ink **2.** to design (wallpaper, material) **3.** to show, outline (sth); **robe qui dessine la taille,** dress that shows off the figure; **visage bien dessiné,** finely chiselled face **4. se d.,** to stand out, take form; to be outlined.

dessoûler [desule] *vtr & i* to sober up.

dessous [dəsu] **1.** *adv* under(neath), below, beneath; **marcher bras dessus bras d.,** to walk arm in arm; **en d.,** underneath; **regarder qn en d.,** to give s.o. a shifty look; **agir en d.,** to act in an underhand way **2.** *nm* (*a*) lower part; underside, bottom; **les gens du d.,** the people on the floor below (us); **d. de bouteille,** coaster; **d. de table,** under the counter payment; **avoir le d.,** to get the worst of it; *Cl:* **d. de robe,** slip; petticoat (*b*) **les d. de la politique,** the shady side of politics.

dessous-de-plat [d(ə)sudpla] *nm inv* table mat.

dessus [dəsy] **1.** *adv* above, over; (up)on (it, them); **il a marché d.,** he trod on it; **j'ai failli lui tirer d.,** I nearly shot him; **mettre la main d.,** to lay hands on it, on them; **en d.,** on top; above **2.** *nm* (*a*) top, upper part; **d. de cheminée,** mantelpiece; **le d. du panier,** (i) the pick of the bunch (ii) the upper crust (*b*) **avoir le d.,** to have the upper hand; **reprendre le d.,** to get over it **3. de d.,** from, off; **tomber de d. sa chaise,** to fall off one's chair.

dessus-de-lit [dəsydli] *nm inv* bedspread.

destin [dɛstɛ̃] *nm* fate, destiny.

destinataire [dɛstinatɛr] *n* addressee (of letter); consignee (of goods); payee (of money order).

destination [dɛstinasjɔ̃] *nf* **1.** destination; **trains à d. de Paris,** trains for Paris; **passagers à d. de Londres,** passengers travelling to London **2.** purpose.

destinée [dɛstine] *nf* destiny; fate.

destiner [dɛstine] *vtr* **1.** to destine **2.** (*a*) **d. qch à qn,** to intend, mean, sth for s.o.; **la balle lui était destinée,** the bullet was aimed at him (*b*) **d. une somme d'argent à un achat,** to allot a sum of money to a purchase **3. il se destine à la médecine,** he intends to be a doctor.

destituer [dɛstitɥe] *vtr* to dismiss, discharge (s.o.); to remove (official) from office.

destitution [dɛstitɥsjɔ̃] *nf* dismissal.

destruction [dɛstryksjɔ̃] *nf* destruction; extermination (of rats). **destructeur, -trice 1.** *a* de-

structive **2.** *n* destroyer. **destructible** *a* destructible. **destructif, -ive** *a* destructive.

désuet, -ète [desɥɛ, -ɛt] *a* obsolete (word); out-of-date (theory).

désuétude [desɥetyd] *nf* disuse; **tomber en d.,** to fall into disuse; (*of law*) to fall into abeyance; **mot tombé en d.,** obsolete word.

désunion [dezynjɔ̃] *nf* disunity, disunion.

désunir [dezynir] *vtr* to disunite, divide.

détachage [detaʃaʒ] *nm* removal of stains.

détachant [detaʃɑ̃] *nm* stain remover.

détachement [detaʃmɑ̃] *nm* **1.** detachment; indifference (**de,** to) **2.** (*a*) secondment (*b*) *Mil:* detachment.

détacher¹ [detaʃe] *vtr* **1.** (*a*) to detach; to loose, unfasten, untie; to unhook (curtain); **il ne peut pas en d. ses yeux,** he can't take his eyes off it (*b*) to separate; to cut off, pull off, break off, tear off (*c*) **d. qn de qch,** to turn s.o. away from sth (*d*) *Mil: etc:* to detach, second (*e*) to bring out; *Mus:* to detach (the notes) **2. se d.** (*a*) (*of knot*) to come undone (*b*) to break loose (*c*) to break off; to separate; to come apart; (*of paint*) to flake off; **un bouton s'est détaché,** a button has come off (*d*) **se d. de la famille,** to break away from the family (*e*) **se d. sur le fond,** to stand out against the background. **détaché** *a* **1.** loose, detached; **pièces détachées,** spare parts **2.** indifferent, detached.

détacher² *vtr* to remove stains from (sth).

détail [detaj] *nm* **1.** *Com:* retail; **marchand au d.,** retailer; **vendre au d.,** to sell retail; **prix de d.,** retail price **2.** detail; **donner tous les détails,** to go into all the details; **raconter qch en d.,** to give a detailed account of sth; **c'est un d.,** it's not important; **d. d'une facture,** breakdown of an invoice.

détaillant, -ante [detajɑ̃, -ɑ̃t] *n* retailer.

détailler [detaje] *vtr* **1.** *Com:* to retail **2.** to relate (sth) in detail; to itemize (account). **détaillé** *a* detailed.

détaler [detale] *vi* (*of animal*) to bolt; *F:* (*of pers*) to beat it.

détartrer [detartre] *vtr* to descale (boiler); to scale (teeth).

détaxe [detaks] *nf* **1.** tax rebate **2.** decontrolling.

détaxer [detakse] *vtr* to remove the tax on; to reduce the tax.

détecter [detɛkte] *vtr* to detect. **détecteur, -trice 1.** *a* detecting **2.** *nm* detector.

détection [detɛksjɔ̃] *nf* detection.

détective [detɛktiv] *nm* detective; **d. privé,** private detective; *F:* private eye.

déteindre [detɛ̃dr] (*conj like* TEINDRE) **1.** *vtr* to take the colour out of (sth) **2.** *vi* (*a*) to fade, to lose colour (*b*) (*of colour*) to run; **d. sur,** to come off on (*c*) *Fig:* **cela déteint sur eux,** it rubs off on them.

dételer [detle] *vtr* (**je dételle, n. dételons**) (*a*) to unharness (*b*) to unhitch (horse(s)) (*c*) *vi F:* to ease off (work).

détendre [detɑ̃dr] *vtr* **1.** to slacken, relax; to relax (the mind); to steady (the nerves) **2. se d.,** to slacken, relax; **se d. pendant une heure,** to relax for an hour; **la situation se détend,** the situation is easing. **détendu** *a* slack; relaxed.

détenir [detnir] *vtr* (*conj like* TENIR) **1.** to hold, to be in possession of; **d. le record,** to hold the record **2.** to detain (s.o.); to keep (s.o.) prisoner.

détente [detɑ̃t] *nf* **1.** (*a*) relaxation, slackening (*b*) easing (of situation); détente (*c*) relaxation **2.** trigger (of gun).

détenteur, -trice [detɑ̃tœr, -tris] *n* holder; owner.

détention [detɑ̃sjɔ̃] *nf* (*a*) holding (of securities); possession (of firearms) (*b*) detention; imprisonment.

détenu, -e [detny] *n* prisoner.

détergent [detɛrʒɑ̃] *a & nm* detergent.

détérioration [deterjɔrasjɔ̃] *nf* deterioration; damage.

détériorer [deterjɔre] *vtr* **1.** to spoil, damage **2. se d.,** to deteriorate.

détermination [detɛrminasjɔ̃] *nf* determination; resolution; resolve.

déterminer [detɛrmine] *vtr* **1.** to determine (value, area); to fix (meeting place) **2.** to cause; to give rise to (sth); to determine (one's actions) **3. d. qn à faire qch,** to induce s.o. to do sth; **qu'est-ce qui vous a déterminé à partir?** what made you leave? **déterminant** *a* determining. **déterminé** *a* determined, resolute; definite, well-defined (purpose); specific (quantity, aim).

déterrer [detɛre] *vtr* to dig up, unearth; to disinter; **avoir une mine de déterré,** to look like death warmed up.

détersif, -ive [detɛrsif, -iv] *a & nm* detergent.

détester [detɛste] *vtr* to detest, hate; **je déteste être dérangé,** I hate to be disturbed; **il ne déteste pas les bonbons,** he rather likes sweets. **détestable** *a* awful, hateful, execrable; foul, ghastly. **détestablement** *adv* appallingly.

détonateur [detɔnatœr] *nm* detonator.

détonation [detɔnasjɔ̃] *nf* detonation, explosion; bang (of firearm).

détoner [detɔne] *vi* to detonate, explode.

détour [detur] *nm* **1.** detour, deviation; **faire un long d.,** to go a long way round **2. répondre sans d.,** to give a straightforward answer **3.** turn, curve, bend (in road, river).

détournement [deturnəmɑ̃] *nm* **1.** diversion (of river, of traffic); **d. d'avion,** hijacking **2.** (*a*) misappropriation (of funds) (*b*) **d. de mineur,** seduction of a minor.

détourner [deturne] *vtr* **1.** (*a*) to divert (traffic, river); to turn (weapon) aside; to distract (s.o.'s attention); **d. la conversation,** to change the conversation; **d. les soupçons,** to avert suspicion (*b*) to turn away; to avert (one's eyes) **2.** to misappropriate, embezzle (funds) **3. d. un avion,** to hijack a plane **4. se d.,** to turn away, aside. **détourné** *a* roundabout (route).

détraquement [detrakmɑ̃] *nm* breakdown (of mechanism, health).

détraquer [detrake] *vtr* (*a*) to put (machine) out of order; **son intervention a tout détraqué,** his intervention has upset everything; *F:* **il a le cerveau détraqué,** his mind is unhinged; **se d. l'estomac, les nerfs,** to wreck one's digestion, one's nerves (*b*) **se d.,** (*of mechanism*) to go out of order; (*of health*) to break down; (*of nerves*) to be upset.

détremper [detrɑ̃pe] *vtr* to moisten, soak; **champ détrempé,** sodden, waterlogged, field.

détresse [detrɛs] *nf* **1.** distress; grief, anguish **2.** (*a*) (financial) straits, difficulties (*b*) *esp Nau:* danger; **navire en d.,** ship in distress; **signal de d.,** distress signal; SOS.

détriment [detrimɑ̃] *nm* detriment, loss; **au d. de,** to the detriment of.

détritus [detritys] *nm* rubbish; refuse.

détroit [detrwa] *nm Geog:* strait(s).

détromper [detrɔ̃pe] *vtr* to undeceive.

détrôner [detrone] *vtr* to dethrone.

détruire [detrɥir] *vtr* (*prp* **détruisant;** *pp* **détruit;** *ind* **je détruis**) **1.** to demolish (building) **2.** to destroy, ruin; to dash (s.o.'s hopes) **3. critiques qui se détruisent,** criticisms that cancel each other out.

dette [dɛt] *nf* debt; **faire des dettes,** to run into debt; **avoir des dettes,** to be in debt; **être en d. envers qn,** to be indebted to s.o.

DEUG [dœg] *abbr Diplôme d'études universitaires générales.*

deuil [dœj] *nm* **1.** (*a*) mourning, sorrow (*b*) bereavement **2.** mourning (clothes); **grand d.,** deep mourning; **porter le d., être en d.,** to be in mourning.

deux [dø; *before a vowel sound in the same word group,* døz] *num a inv & nm* (*a*) two; **d. enfants** [døzɑ̃fɑ̃] two children; **Charles D.,** Charles the Second (*b*) **chapitre d.,** chapter two; **c'est clair comme d. et d. font quatre,** it's clear as daylight; **d. fois,** twice; **tous (les) d.,** both; **tous les d. jours,** every other day; **entre d. âges,** middle-aged; *Ten:* **à d.,** deuce. **deuxième** *num a & n* second; **appartement au d. (étage),** flat on the second, *NAm:* third, floor. **deuxièmement** *adv* secondly.

deux-pièces [døpjɛs] *nm inv* **1.** (*a*) two-piece swimsuit; bikini (*b*) two-piece (suit) **2.** two-roomed flat.

deux-points [døpwɛ̃] *nm Typ:* colon.

deux-roues [døru] *nm inv* two-wheeled vehicle.

dévaler [devale] **1.** *vi* to descend, go down; (*of stream*) to rush down; (*of garden*) to slope down **2.** *vtr* **d. l'escalier,** to rush down the stairs.

dévaliser [devalize] *vtr* to rob (s.o.); to burgle (a house).

dévalorisation [devalɔrizasjɔ̃] *nf* depreciation.

dévaloriser [devalɔrize] *vtr* to depreciate.

dévaluation [devalɥasjɔ̃] *nf* devaluation.

dévaluer [devalɥe] *vtr* to devalue (currency).

devancer [dəvɑ̃se] *vtr* (**n. devançons**) **1.** to precede **2.** to leave behind; to overtake; to outstrip; to forestall **3. d. les désirs de qn,** to anticipate s.o.'s wishes.

devancier, -ière [dəvɑ̃sje, -jɛr] *n* precursor.

devant [dəvɑ̃] **1.** *prep* before, in front of; **marchez tout droit d. vous,** go straight ahead, straight on; **d. un verre de vin,** over a glass of wine; **d. le danger,** in the face of danger; **égaux d. la loi,** equal in the eyes of the law; **d. votre silence,** in view of your silence **2.** *adv* before, in front; **aller d.,** to go in front; **sens d. derrière,** back to front; **ça se boutonne (par-)d.,** it buttons up at the front **3.** *nm* front (part), forepart; **d. (de chemise),** (shirt) front; **chambre sur le d.,** front room; **pattes de d.,** forelegs, front paws; **prendre les devants,** to make the first move; **gagner les devants,** to take the lead.

devanture [dəvɑ̃tyr] *nf* (*a*) front (of building) (*b*) **d. de magasin,** shopfront, shop window.

dévastation [devastasjɔ̃] *nf* devastation.

dévaster [devaste] *vtr* to devastate. **dévastateur, -trice** *a* devastating.

déveine [devɛn] *nf F:* (run of) bad luck.

développement [devlɔpmɑ̃] *nm* development; expansion; growth; **pays en voie de d.**, developing countries.

développer [devlɔpe] *vtr* 1. to develop (muscles); to evolve (theory); **d. ses dons naturels**, to improve one's natural gifts; **d. un projet**, to work out a plan 2. **se d.** (*a*) to spread out, to expand (*b*) to develop.

devenir [dəvnir] *v pred* (*conj like* VENIR; *aux* être) (*a*) to become; **qu'est-il devenu?** what has become of him? **que devient votre fils?** how is your son getting on? (*b*) to grow into; **d. homme**, to grow into a man (*c*) **d. grand**, (i) to grow tall (ii) to grow up; **d. vieux**, to grow old; **c'est à d. fou!** it is enough to drive one mad!

dévergonder (se) [sədevɛrgɔ̃de] *vpr* to fall into dissolute ways. **dévergondé** *a* shameless.

déverser [devɛrse] 1. *vtr* to pour (water); to tip, to dump (rubbish); **le train les déversa sur le quai**, the train deposited them on the platform 2. *vi & pr* (*of river*) to flow (**dans**, into).

dévêtir (se) [sədevetir] *vpr* (*conj like* VÊTIR) to undress.

déviation [devjasjɔ̃] *nf* deviation; curvature (of spine); *Aut:* diversion.

dévider [devide] *vtr* to unwind (spool); *F:* to reel off (story).

dévidoir [devidwar] *nm* reel.

dévier [devje] *v* (*pr sub & impf n.* **déviions**) 1. *vi* to deviate, swerve, diverge; to veer (off course); **faire d. une balle**, to deflect a bullet; **d. de ses principes**, to depart from one's principles 2. *vtr* to divert; to deflect.

devin, devineresse [dəvɛ̃, dəvinrɛs] *n* soothsayer; *F:* **je ne suis pas d.**, I can't see into the future.

deviner [d(ə)vine] *vtr* to guess; to predict (the future).

devinette [dəvinɛt] *nf* riddle.

devis [dəvi] *nm* estimate; quotation.

dévisager [devizaʒe] *vtr* (**n. dévisageons**) to stare, look hard, at (s.o.).

devise [dəviz] *nf* 1. (*a*) motto (*b*) slogan 2. *Fin:* currency; **devises étrangères**, foreign currency.

dévisser [devise] *vtr* to unscrew.

dévoiler [devwale] *vtr* 1. to unveil 2. to reveal, disclose (secret).

devoir¹ [dəvwar] *vtr* (*prp* **devant**; *pp* **dû**, *f* **due**; *pr ind* **je dois, ils doivent**; *ph* **je dus**; *fu* **je devrai**) 1. (*duty*) should, ought (*a*) (*general precept*) **tu dois honorer tes parents**, you should honour your parents (*b*) (*command*) **vous devez vous trouver à votre poste à trois heures**, you must be at your post at three o'clock (*c*) **je ne savais pas ce que je devais faire**, I didn't know what (I ought) to do; **il aurait dû m'avertir**, he should have warned me; **il a cru d. refuser**, he thought it advisable to refuse 2. (*compulsion*) must, have to; **enfin j'ai dû céder**, finally I had to give in 3. (*futurity*) (*a*) **je dois partir demain**, I am to, I have to, leave tomorrow; **je devais le recontrer à Paris**, I was to meet him in Paris; **le train doit arriver à midi**, the train is due to arrive at twelve o'clock (*b*) **il ne devait plus les revoir**, he was

(destined) never to see them again; **ça devait arriver!** it was bound to happen! 4. (*opinion expressed*) must; **vous devez avoir faim**, you must be hungry; **il ne doit pas avoir plus de 40 ans**, he can't be more than 40 5. **d. qch à qn**, to owe s.o. sth; **vous me devez 1000 francs**, you owe me 1000 francs; **je lui dois la vie**, I owe my life to him; **je lui dois bien cela**, it's the least I can do for him; **la réussite est due à ses parents**, it's thanks to his parents that he's so successful 6. (*a*) **se d. à qch**, to have to devote oneself to sth (*b*) **comme il se doit**, as is right and proper.

devoir² *nm* 1. (*a*) duty; **manquer à son d.**, to fail in one's duty; **se faire un d. de**, to make a point of; **se mettre en d. de faire qch**, to prepare to do sth; **il est de mon d. de vous le dire**, it is my duty to tell you; **faire qch par d.**, to do sth from a sense of duty (*b*) obligation (*c*) *Sch:* exercise; *pl* homework, prep 2. *pl* **rendre ses devoirs à qn**, to pay one's respects to s.o.

dévolu [devɔly] *a Jur:* (*of inheritance*) devolved; devolving (**à**, to, upon).

dévorer [devɔre] *vtr* to devour; **d. qn des yeux**, to gaze intently on s.o.; **d. sa fortune**, to squander one's fortune; **dévoré par les moustiques**, eaten alive by mosquitoes; **dévoré par l'angoisse**, sick with worry; **d. la route**, to eat up the miles. **dévorant** *a* (*a*) ravenous; gnawing (hunger) (*b*) consuming (fire); devouring (passion).

dévot, -ote [devo, -ɔt] 1. *a* devout, religious 2. *a & n* sanctimonious (person); *Pej:* bigot. **dévotement** *adv* devoutly.

dévotion [devɔsjɔ̃] *nf* devotion; devoutness, piety.

dévouement [devumɑ̃] *nm* self-sacrifice; devotion (to duty); dedication; **avec d.**, devotedly.

dévouer (se) [sədevwe] *vpr* 1. to devote oneself (to a cause) 2. **se d. pour qn**, to sacrifice oneself for s.o. **dévoué** *a* devoted, loyal; *Corr:* **votre tout d.** = yours sincerely.

dévoyer [devwaje] *vtr* (**je dévoie, n. dévoyons**; **je dévoierai**) 1. to lead astray 2. **se d.**, to go astray. **dévoyé, -ée** *a & n* delinquent.

dextérité [dɛksterite] *nf* dexterity, skill.

diabète [djabɛt] *nm Med:* diabetes. **diabétique** *a & n* diabetic.

diable [djɑbl] *nm* 1. devil; **tirer le d. par la queue**, to be hard up; **c'est bien le d. si**, it would be most surprising if; **que le d. l'emporte!** the devil take him! **au d. vauvert, au d. vert**, miles from anywhere, at the back of beyond; **ce n'est pas le d.**, (i) it's not so very difficult (ii) it's nothing to worry about; **où d. est-il allé**, where the devil has he gone? *int* **d.!** heavens! **bruit de tous les diables**, hell of a din; **pauvre d.!** poor beggar! **un grand d.**, a big fellow; **c'est un bon d.**, he's not a bad type; **un d. de temps, un temps du d.**, wretched weather; *a* **il est très d.**, he's a real little devil 2. (*a*) (two-wheeled) trolley (*b*) (*toy*) Jack-in-the-box. **diablement** *adv F:* devilish(ly), hellishly.

diabolique [djabɔlik] *a* diabolical, fiendish. **diaboliquement** *adv* diabolically, fiendishly.

diabolo [djabɔlo] *nm* 1. *Games:* diabolo 2. **d. menthe**, mint and lemonade.

diacre [djakr] *nm Ecc:* deacon.

diadème [djadɛm] *nm* diadem; tiara.

diagnostic [djagnɔstik] *nm Med:* diagnosis.

diagnostiquer [djagnɔstike] *vtr Med:* to diagnose.

diagonal, *pl* -**aux** [djagɔnal, -o] 1. *a* diagonal 2. *nf* **diagonale**, diagonal (line); **en diagonale**, diagonally.

diagramme [djagram] *nm* diagram; chart; graph.

dialecte [djalɛkt] *nm* dialect. **dialectique** 1. *a* dialectic 2. *nf* dialectics.

dialogue [djalɔg] *nm* dialogue; *Pol:* talks; **c'est un d. de sourds**, they're not on the same wavelength.

dialoguer [djalɔge] *vi* to hold a dialogue, to converse.

diamant [djamɑ̃] *nm* diamond.

diamantaire [djamɑ̃tɛr] *nm* diamond (i) cutter (ii) merchant.

diamètre [djamɛtr] *nm* diameter. **diamétralement** *adv* diametrically.

diantre [djɑ̃tr] *int A: & Lit:* **que d. veut-il?** what the devil does he want? **d.!** hell!

diapason [djapazɔ̃] *nm Mus:* 1. diapason, pitch 2. tuning fork.

diaphane [djafan] *a* diaphanous; translucent.

diaphragme [djafragm] *nm* diaphragm.

diapositive, *F:* **diapo** [djapozitiv, djapo] *nf Phot:* slide.

diarrhée [djare] *nf Med:* diarrhoea.

diatribe [djatrib] *nf* diatribe.

dichotomie [dikɔtɔmi] *nf* dichotomy.

dictateur [diktatœr] *nm* dictator. **dictatorial**, -**aux** *a* dictatorial.

dictature [diktatyr] *nf* dictatorship.

dictée [dikte] *nf* dictation; **écrire sous la d. de qn**, to take down s.o.'s dictation.

dicter [dikte] *vtr* to dictate; to impose (one's will).

diction [diksjɔ̃] *nf* diction; **professeur de d.**, elocution teacher.

dictionnaire [diksjɔnɛr] *nm* dictionary.

dicton [diktɔ̃] *nm* (common) saying, dictum.

dièse [djɛz] *nm Mus:* sharp; **fa d.**, F sharp.

diesel [djezɛl] *nm* diesel.

diète [djɛt] *nf* diet.

diététicien, -**ienne** [djetetisjɛ̃, -jɛn] *n* dietician.

diététique [djetetik] 1. *a* dietetic 2. *nf* dietetics.

dieu, -**ieux** [djø] *nm* 1. god; **grands dieux!** heavens! 2. (a) God; **un homme de D.**, a holy man; **D. merci!** thank god! **le bon D.**, God; **on lui donnerait le bon D. sans confession**, he looks as if butter wouldn't melt in his mouth (c) **D. merci!** thank goodness! **pour l'amour de D.**, for goodness' sake; **D. sait si j'ai travaillé**, heaven knows, God knows, I've worked hard enough 3. (a) *int* **mon D.!** good heavens! heavens above! (b) (*profane*) **nom de D.!** (sacré) **nom de D.!** for Christ's sake! God almighty!

diffamateur, -**trice** [difamatœr, -tris] *n* slanderer, libeller.

diffamation [difamasjɔ̃] *nf* slander, libel. **diffamatoire** *a* slanderous, libellous.

diffamer [difame] *vtr* to slander, libel.

différé [difere] *a WTel: TV:* **en d.**, (pre-)recorded.

différemment [diferamɑ̃] *adv* differently.

différence [diferɑ̃s] *nf* difference; **il n'y a pas de d. entre eux**, there's nothing to choose between them; **quelle d. avec l'autre!** what a difference from the other one! **à la d. de**, unlike; **à la d. que**, with this difference that. **différent** *a* (a) different; unlike

(b) various; different; **à différentes reprises**, at various times.

différenciation [diferɑ̃sjasjɔ̃] *nf* differentiation.

différencier [diferɑ̃sje] *vtr* 1. to differentiate (**de**, from); to distinguish (**entre ... et ...**, between ... and ...) 2. **se d.** (a) to differ (b) to differentiate oneself (**de**, from).

différend [diferɑ̃] *nm* difference, dispute, disagreement (**entre**, between).

différentiel, -**elle** [diferɑ̃sjɛl] *a & nm & f* differential.

différer [difere] *v* (je **diffère**; je **différerai**) 1. *vtr* to defer; to postpone; to put off (payment) 2. *vi* to differ; to be different (**de**, from; **en**, **par**, in); **d. d'opinion**, to differ in opinion.

difficile [difisil] *a* 1. difficult; hard; **circonstances difficiles**, trying circumstances; **les temps sont difficiles**, times are hard 2. difficult to get on with; particular, choosy; **enfant d.**, problem child; **d. sur la nourriture**, fussy about food; *n* **faire le d.**, to be hard to please. **difficilement** *adv* with difficulty.

difficulté [difikylte] *nf* difficulty; **être en d.**, to be in trouble; **faire**, **élever**, **des difficultés**, to raise objections, to make difficulties.

difformité [difɔrmite] *nf* deformity. **difforme** *a* deformed, misshapen.

diffuser [difyze] *vtr* 1. to diffuse (light) 2. (a) *Rad:* to broadcast (programme) (b) to distribute (news). **diffus** *a* diffuse.

diffuseur [difyzœr] *nm* distributor (of books).

diffusion [difyzjɔ̃] *nf* (a) diffusion (b) broadcasting (c) distribution.

digérer [diʒere] *vtr* (je **digère**; je **digérerai**) to digest; *F:* to stomach, to put up with (insult); **je digère mal**, I have a bad digestion.

digestion [diʒɛstjɔ̃] *nf* digestion. **digeste** *a* easily digestible. **digestif**, -**ive** 1. *a* digestive; **tube d.**, alimentary canal 2. *nm* liqueur.

digital, -**aux** [diʒital, -o] 1. *a* digital; **empreinte digitale**, fingerprint 2. *nf Bot:* **digitale**, digitalis.

digne [diɲ] *a* 1. deserving, worthy (**de**, of); **d. d'éloges**, praiseworthy; **il n'est pas d. de vivre**, he is not fit to live 2. dignified. **dignement** *adv* with dignity.

dignitaire [diɲitɛr] *nm* dignitary.

dignité [diɲite] *nf* 1. dignity; **air de d.**, dignified air 2. high position; dignity.

digression [digresjɔ̃] *nf* digression; **faire une d.**, to digress.

digue [dig] *nf* (a) dike, dam; embankment (of waterway) (b) breakwater; sea wall.

dilapidation [dilapidasjɔ̃] *nf* wasting, squandering.

dilapider [dilapide] *vtr* to waste, squander.

dilatation [dilatasjɔ̃] *nf* dilation, expansion.

dilater [dilate] *vtr* to dilate, to expand; **se d.**, to dilate, to expand.

dilemme [dilɛm] *nm* dilemma.

dilettante [diletɑ̃t] *n* dilettante, amateur.

diligence [diliʒɑ̃s] *nf* 1. (a) diligence, application (b) haste, dispatch 2. (stage)coach. **diligent** *a* diligent; speedy, prompt.

diluer [dilɥe] *vtr* to dilute (**de**, with); to thin down (paint).

dilution [dilysjɔ̃] *nf* dilution; thinning down.

diluvienne [dilyvjɛn] *af* **pluie d.**, torrential rain.

dimanche [dimɑ̃ʃ] *nm* Sunday; **d. de Pâques**, Easter Sunday; **il vient le d.**, he comes on Sundays; **F: chauffeur du d.**, Sunday driver.

dîme [dim] *nf Hist:* tithe.

dimension [dimɑ̃sjɔ̃] *nf* dimension, size; **à deux, à trois, dimensions**, two-dimensional, three-dimensional; **prendre les dimensions de qch**, to take the measurements of sth; **ce travail n'est pas à la d. de son talent**, this work is not equal to his talent.

diminué [diminɥe] *a* 1. *Mus:* diminished (interval) 2. **bas d.**, fully-fashioned stocking 3. tapering (column) 4. *nm* **un d. physique**, a physically handicapped person.

diminuer [diminɥe] 1. *vtr* to lessen; to diminish; to reduce; to shorten; to decrease; **cela vous diminuerait aux yeux du public**, it would lower you in the eyes of the public 2. *vi* to diminish, decrease, lessen; (*of fever*) to abate; (*of prices*) to fall; **d. de vitesse**, to slow down; **ses forces ont diminué**, his strength has declined. **diminutif, -ive** *a & nm* diminutive.

diminution [diminysjɔ̃] *nf* diminution, reduction, decrease, lowering, lessening; abatement.

dinde [dɛ̃d] *nf* turkey hen.

dindon [dɛ̃dɔ̃] *nm* turkey (cock); **être le d. de la farce**, to be made a fool of.

dindonneau, -eaux [dɛ̃dɔno] *nm* young turkey.

dîner [dine] 1. *vi* to dine, to have dinner; **avoir qn à d.**, to have s.o. to dinner 2. *nm* dinner; dinner party.

dînette [dinɛt] *nf* (*a*) doll's tea party (*b*) informal meal (between friends).

dîneur, -euse [dinœr, -øz] *n* diner.

dingue [dɛ̃g] *F:* (*a*) *a* crazy, nuts (*b*) *n* idiot, nutcase, loony.

dinosaure [dinɔsɔr] *nm* dinosaur.

diocèse [djɔsɛz] *nm Ecc:* diocese.

diphtérie [difteri] *nf Med:* diphtheria. **diphtérique** *a* diphtherial.

diphtongue [diftɔ̃g] *nf Ling:* diphthong.

diplomate [diplɔmat] *nm* 1. diplomat; diplomatist; *a* diplomatic 2. *Cu:* = trifle.

diplomatie [diplɔmasi] *nf* 1. diplomacy; **user de d.**, to be diplomatic 2. **entrer dans la d.**, to enter the diplomatic service. **diplomatique** *a* diplomatic.

diplôme [diplom] *nm* diploma. **diplômé, -ée** 1. *a* qualified 2. *n* = graduate; holder of diploma.

dire¹ [dir] *vtr* (*prp* **disant**; *pp* **dit**; *pr ind* **vous dites, ils disent**) 1. (*a*) to say, tell; **d. qch à qn**, to tell s.o. sth; to say sth to s.o.; **vous ne m'en avez jamais rien dit**, you never mentioned it (to me); **envoyer d. à qn que**, to send word to s.o. that; **ceci dit**, having said that; **qu'en dira-t-on?** what will people say? **d. ce qu'on pense**, to speak one's mind; **je vous l'avais bien dit!** what did I tell you! I told you so! **d. bonjour**, to say hello; **comme on dit**, as the saying goes; **cela ne se dit pas**, that isn't said; **qui vous dit qu'il viendra?** how do you know he'll come? *F:* **à qui le dites-vous?** you're telling me! **dites toujours!** go on! say it! **je ne sais comment d.**, I don't know how to put it; **je me disais que tout était fini**, I thought it was all over; **qu'en dites-vous?** what do you think of it? **à vrai d.**, to tell the truth; **pour ainsi d.**, so to speak; *F:* **vous l'avez dit**, exactly! you've said it! **cela va sans d.**,

that goes without saying; **on dit que c'est lui le coupable**, he is said to be the culprit; **on dirait qu'il va pleuvoir**, it looks like rain; **on aurait dit que**, it seemed as though; **il n'y a pas à d.**, there's no denying it; **dites donc**, look here, I say! *P:* **non, mais dis!** do you mind? **d. qu'il n'a que 20 ans!** to think he's only 20! **c'est beaucoup d.**, that's going rather far; **on dirait du Mozart**, it sounds like Mozart (*b*) **on le dit mort**, he is reported (to be) dead 2. (*a*) **d. à qn de faire qch**, to tell s.o. to do sth; **dites lui d'entrer**, ask him to come in (*b*) **dites qu'on le fasse entrer**, tell them to show him in 3. **d. des vers**, to recite poetry; **d. son chapelet**, to tell one's beads 4. (*a*) to show, express; **d. l'heure**, to tell the time; **cela en dit long sur son courage**, it speaks volumes for his courage; **ce nom ne me dit rien**, the name doesn't ring a bell; **ça ne me dit rien de bon**, I don't like the look of it (*b*) to suit, to appeal to (s.o.); **cette musique ne me dit rien**, I don't care for this music; **si cela te dit**, if you feel like it 5. (*a*) **vouloir d.**, to mean (*b*) **qu'est-ce à d.?** what does this mean? (*c*) **je lui ai fait d. de venir**, I sent for him; **il ne se le fit pas d. deux fois**, he didn't wait to be told twice (*d*) *F:* **je ne vous le fais pas d.**, I'm not telling you anything you don't know (already) (*e*) **faire d. qch par qn**, to send word of sth through s.o. (*f*) *with inf* **vous m'avez dit adorer la musique**, you told me you loved music.

dire² *nm* statement; assertion; **selon son d.**, according to him.

direct [dirɛkt] (*a*) *a* direct, straight; **personne directe**, straightforward person; **être en rapport d. avec qn**, to be in direct contact with s.o.; *Rail:* **train d.**, fast train (*b*) *nm* **émission en d.**, live broadcast. **directement** *adv* direct(ly), straight; **il est venu d. vers nous**, he came straight towards us; **d. contraire**, completely contrary.

directeur, -trice [dirɛktœr, -tris] 1. *n* director, manager, manageress; headmaster, -mistress, principal (of school); editor (of paper); head (of firm); **(président-)d. général**, general manager; **d. gérant**, managing director 2. *a* directing, controlling; guiding (principle).

direction [dirɛksjɔ̃] *nf* 1. (*a*) guidance, direction; management (of firm); editorship (of newspaper); headship (of school); leadership (of party) (*b*) (i) board of directors (ii) administrative staff; management (*c*) (i) manager's office (ii) head office (of firm) 2. direction, driving; *Aut: Nau:* steering; **d. assistée**, power (assisted) steering 3. direction, course; **quelle d. ont-ils prise?** which way did they go? **train en d. de Bordeaux**, train for Bordeaux 4. advice; guidance. **directorial, -aux** *a* directorial, managerial.

directive [dirɛktiv] *nf* directive.

dirigeable [diriʒabl] 1. *a* dirigible 2. *nm* airship.

diriger [diriʒe] *vtr* (**n. dirigeons**) 1. to direct, control, manage; to run (business, school); to edit (newspaper); to conduct (orchestra, proceedings) 2. (*a*) to direct, guide, lead (sth, s.o.); to steer (car, ship) (*b*) **d. ses pas vers**, to go, to move, towards; **d. son attention sur qch**, to turn one's attention to sth (*c*) to aim (gun) (**sur**, at); to level, point (telescope) (**sur**, at) 3. **se d.** (*a*) **se d. au radar**, to navigate by radar (*b*) **se diriger vers un endroit**, to make one's way towards a place; to head for a place (*c*) **se d. vers**

qn, to go up to s.o. **dirigeant, -ante** 1. *a* directing, guiding (power, principle); ruling (class) 2. *n* leader; ruler. **dirigé** *a* controlled; planned (economy).

discernement [disɛrnəmã] *nm* 1. perception; discrimination; distinguishing 2. discernment; **sans d.**, without proper judgment.

discerner [disɛrne] *vtr* (*a*) to discern, distinguish, make out (sth) (*b*) to discriminate (between sth and sth); **d. le bien du mal**, to tell right from wrong. **discernable** *a* discernible, visible.

disciple [disipl] *nm* disciple; follower.

discipline [disiplin] *nf* (*a*) discipline (*b*) subject.

discipliner [disipline] *vtr* to discipline; to control; **se d.**, to discipline oneself. **disciplinaire** *a* disciplinary. **discipliné** *a* disciplined.

discontinuer [diskɔ̃tinɥe] *vi* **sans d.**, without stopping. **discontinu** *a* discontinuous.

discontinuité [diskɔ̃tinɥite] *nf* discontinuity.

disconvenir [diskɔ̃vnir] *vi* (*conj like* VENIR; *aux* avoir) **je n'en disconviens pas**, I don't deny it.

discordance [diskɔrdɑ̃s] *nf* discordance, dissonance (of sounds); clash(ing) (of colours); conflict (of opinions); clash (of personalities). **discordant** *a* discordant, dissonant (sound); clashing (colours); conflicting (opinions).

discorde [diskɔrd] *nf* discord, dissension; **semer la d.**, to make trouble.

discothèque [diskɔtɛk] *nf* (*a*) record library (*b*) record collection (*c*) record cabinet (*d*) discothèque, F: disco.

discourir [diskurir] *vi* (*conj like* COURIR) *usu Pej:* to discourse; to hold forth (**sur, de,** on).

discours [diskur] *nm* 1. talk 2. discourse 3. speech, address 4. *Gram:* **parties du d.**, parts of speech.

discourtois [diskurtwa] *a* discourteous.

discrédit [diskredi] *nm* discredit; disrepute.

discréditer [diskredite] *vtr* 1. to disparage; to discredit 2. **se d.**, to discredit oneself.

discret, -ète [diskrɛ, -ɛt] *a* (*a*) discreet, cautious; *Post:* **sous pli d.**, under plain cover (*b*) quiet, unobtrusive, unassuming; simple, plain (clothes); modest (request); quiet, secluded (place). **discrètement** *adv* discreetly; quietly, unobtrusively.

discrétion [diskresjɔ̃] *nf* 1. discretion; **avoir de la d.**, to be discreet 2. *adv phr* **à d.**, (i) at one's own discretion (ii) unconditionally; **pain à d.**, unlimited (amounts of) bread.

discrimination [diskriminasjɔ̃] *nf* discrimination. **discriminatoire** *a* discriminatory.

discriminer [diskrimine] *vtr* to discriminate.

disculper [diskylpe] 1. *vtr* to exonerate (**de,** from) 2. **se d.**, to exonerate oneself (**de,** from).

discussion [diskysjɔ̃] *nf* discussion, debate; **la question en d.**, the question at issue; **sans d. possible**, indisputably; **entrer en d. avec qn**, to enter into an argument with s.o.

discuter [diskyte] 1. *vtr* (*a*) to discuss, debate; to examine (a problem); **discutons la chose**, let's talk it over; *F:* **d. le coup**, to have a chat (**sur, de,** on), dispute 2. *vi* **d. avec qn**, to argue with s.o.; **d. politique**, to discuss politics. **discutable** *a* debatable, questionable.

disette [dizɛt] *nf* scarcity, dearth; shortage.

diseur, -euse [dizœr, -øz] *n* **d., diseuse, de bonne aventure**, fortune teller.

disgrâce [disgrɑs] *nf* disfavour, disgrace.

disgracier [disgrasje] *vtr* to dismiss from favour. **disgracié** *a* out of favour.

disgracieux, -euse [disgrasjø, -øz] *a* 1. awkward, ungraceful 2. ungracious 3. plain (face).

disjoindre [disʒwɛ̃dr] *vtr* (*conj like* JOINDRE) 1. to disjoint, separate, take apart 2. **se d.**, to come apart.

disjoncteur [disʒɔ̃ktœr] *nm El:* circuit breaker.

dislocation [dislɔkasjɔ̃] *nf* dislocation.

disloquer [dislɔke] 1. *vtr* to dislocate; to break up (machine) 2. **se d.**, to break up, to come apart; **son bras s'est disloqué**, he's dislocated his arm.

disparaître [disparɛtr] *vi* (*conj like* CONNAÎTRE) to disappear; to vanish; **le soleil a disparu à l'horizon**, the sun sank below the horizon; **faire d. une tache**, to remove a stain; **faire d. la douleur**, to relieve the pain; **cette mode disparaît**, this fashion is going out.

disparate [disparat] *a* (*a*) dissimilar (*b*) ill-matched; clashing (colours).

disparité [disparite] *nf* disparity.

disparition [disparisjɔ̃] *nf* disappearance.

disparu, -ue [dispary] 1. *a* (*a*) missing; **être porté d.**, to be reported missing; **marin d. en mer**, sailor lost at sea (*b*) vanished (race); vanished (world) 2. *n* dead person; missing person; **notre cher d.**, our dear departed.

dispensaire [dispɑ̃sɛr] *nm* = outpatients' department; health centre.

dispense [dispɑ̃s] *nf* (*a*) exemption (*b*) *Ecc:* dispensation.

dispenser [dispɑ̃se] *vtr* 1. to exempt (s.o. from sth); **dispensez-moi de ce voyage**, spare me this journey 2. to dispense, distribute 3. **se d. de qch, de faire qch**, to get out of (doing) sth.

disperser [dispɛrse] *vtr* 1. to disperse, scatter; to spread; to break up (crowd) 2. **se d.**, to disperse, scatter; (*of clouds, crowd*) to break up. **dispersé** *a* scattered (leaves); disorganized (work).

dispersion [dispɛrsjɔ̃] *nf* dispersion, scattering; breaking up.

disponibilité [disponibilite] *nf* 1. availability (of seats) 2. *pl* (*a*) available time (*b*) *Fin:* liquid assets. **disponible** *a* available; at (s.o.'s) disposal; **êtes-vous d. ce soir?** are you free tonight?

dispos [dispo] *am* fit, well, in good form; **esprit d.**, fresh mind.

disposer [dispoze] 1. *vtr* (*a*) to dispose, arrange (*b*) **d. qn à faire qch**, to dispose, incline, s.o. to do sth 2. *vi* **d. de qch**, to dispose of sth; **disposez de moi**, I am at your service; **les renseignements dont je dispose**, the information in my possession; **vous pouvez en d.**, you may use it; **vous pouvez z.**, you may go 3. **se d. à faire qch**, to get ready to do sth.

dispositif [dispozitif] *nm* 1. *Jur:* purview, enacting terms 2. plan of action; **d. de défence**, defence system 3. apparatus, device, mechanism; **d. de sûreté**, safety device.

disposition [dispozisjɔ̃] *nf* 1. disposition; arrangement (of house); layout (of garden); **d. du terrain**, lie of the land 2. (*a*) state (of mind); frame of mind; **être en bonne d. pour faire qch**, to be in the mood to do sth; **être dans de bonnes dispositions à l'égard de**

qn, to be favourably disposed towards s.o. (b) predisposition, tendency (c) *pl* natural aptitude; **cet enfant a des dispositions**, he, she, is a (naturally) gifted child 3. *pl* (a) arrangements; **prendre des dispositions**, to make arrangements (b) provisions (of will); clauses (of law) 4. disposal; **libre d. de soi-même**, self-determination; **fonds à ma d.**, funds at my disposal; **je suis à votre d.**, I am at your service.

disproportion [disprɔprɔsjɔ̃] *nf* disproportion. **disproportionné** *a* disproportionate (à, avec, to); out of proportion (à, avec, with).

dispute [dispyt] *nf* quarrel, argument.

disputer [dispyte] *vtr* 1. (a) **d. qch**, to dispute, contest, sth; **d. un match**, to play a match (b) F: **d. qn**, to tell s.o. off; **se faire d.**, to get told off 2. **se d.**, to quarrel, argue (**pour**, over, about; **avec**, with).

disquaire [diskɛr] *nm* record dealer.

disqualification [diskalifikasjɔ̃] *nf* disqualification.

disqualifier [diskalifje] *vtr* (a) Sp: to disqualify (b) to discredit (s.o.).

disque [disk] *nm* 1. Sp: discus 2. (a) Tchn: disc, plate (b) Rec: record; **d. microsillon, de longue durée**, long-playing record, F: LP (c) Anat: **d. intervertébral**, (intervertebral) disc.

dissection [diseksjɔ̃] *nf* dissection.

dissemblance [disãblãs] *nf* dissimilarity. **dissemblable** *a* dissimilar.

dissémination [diseminasjɔ̃] *nf* scattering, spreading, dissemination.

disséminer [disemine] *vtr* to scatter (seeds); to spread (germs); to disseminate (ideas).

dissension [disãsjɔ̃] *nf* dissension, discord.

dissentiment [disãtimã] *nm* disagreement.

disséquer [diseke] *vtr* (**je dissèque; je disséquerai**) to dissect.

dissertation [disɛrtasjɔ̃] *nf* Sch: essay.

disserter [disɛrte] *vi* to discourse (on a subject); to talk at length, F: to hold forth.

dissidence [disidãs] *nf* dissidence; dissent. **dissident, -ente** 1. *a* dissident, dissenting 2. *n* Pol: dissident; Ecc: dissenter.

dissimilitude [disimilityd] *nf* dissimilarity.

dissimulation [disimylasjɔ̃] *nf* dissimulation; concealment. **dissimulateur, -trice** 1. *a* dissembling 2. *n* dissembler.

dissimuler [disimyle] *vtr* 1. to dissemble, dissimulate, conceal (feelings); **je ne vous dissimule pas qu'il en est ainsi**, I cannot hide the fact that it is like this 2. **se d.**, to hide. **dissimulé** *a* secretive.

dissipation [disipasjɔ̃] *nf* 1. (a) dissipation, dispersion (of clouds) (b) wasting (of time), squandering (of money) 2. (a) dissipation, dissolute living (b) misbehaviour, inattention (in school).

dissiper [disipe] *vtr* 1. (a) to dissipate, disperse, scatter (clouds); to clear up (misunderstanding); to dispel (fears) (b) to waste (time); to squander (money); to ruin (health) 2. **se d.** (a) (of suspicions) to vanish; (of fog) to lift, to clear; (of doubts) to fade (b) to be inattentive, to misbehave (in school). **dissipé** *a* (a) dissolute (b) inattentive.

dissociation [disɔsjasjɔ̃] *nf* dissociation.

dissocier [disɔsje] *vtr* to dissociate; to separate. **dissociable** *a* dissociable, separable.

dissolu [disɔly] *a* dissolute.

dissolution [disɔlysjɔ̃] *nf* 1. disintegration, dissolution 2. dissolving 3. dissolution (of parliament); breaking up (of meeting).

dissolvant [disɔlvã] *a & nm* solvent; **d. (pour ongles)**, nail varnish remover.

dissonance [disɔnãs] *nf* 1. dissonance 2. Mus: discord. **dissonant** *a* dissonant, discordant.

dissoudre [disudr] *vtr* (prp **dissolvant**; pp **dissous**, f **dissoute**; pr ind **je dissous, il dissout**; impf **je dissolvais**) 1. to dissolve; to melt (substance) in a liquid 2. to dissolve (parliament); to break up; to dissolve (partnership) 3. **se d.** (a) **se d. dans l'eau**, to dissolve in water (b) (of assembly) to break up.

dissuader [disɥade] *vtr* **d. qn de qch, de faire qch**, to dissuade s.o. from (doing) sth.

dissuasion [disɥazjɔ̃] *nf* dissuasion.

dissymétrie [disimetri] *nf* dissymmetry. **dissymétrique** *a* dissymetrical.

distance [distãs] *nf* distance; **suivre qn à d.**, to follow s.o. at a distance; **à quelle d. sommes-nous de la ville?** how far are we from the town? **à une courte d.**, within easy reach (**de**, of); **à une grande d.**, a long way off (**de**, from); **à dix ans de d. il s'en souvient encore**, ten years later he can still remember it; **de d. en d.**, at intervals; **tenir qn à d.**, to keep s.o. at a distance; **garder ses distances, se tenir à d.**, to keep one's distance; to keep aloof; **d. focale**, focal length. **distant** *a* (a) distant; **maisons distantes d'un kilomètre**, houses one kilometre apart (b) distant, aloof.

distancer [distãse] *vtr* (**n. distançons**) to outdistance, outrun, outstrip; **se laisser d.**, to fall behind.

distendre [distãdr] *vtr* 1. to distend 2. to strain (muscle) 3. **se d.**, to become distended; to slacken.

distension [distãsjɔ̃] *nf* distension; slackening.

distillateur [distilatœr] *nm* distiller.

distillation [distilasjɔ̃] *nf* distillation, distilling.

distiller [distile] *vtr* 1. to exude (poison, moisture, anger) 2. to distil (spirits).

distillerie [distilri] *nf* (a) distillery (b) distilling.

distinction [distɛ̃ksjɔ̃] *nf* 1. distinction; **faire une d. entre deux choses**, to make a distinction between two things; **sans d.**, indiscriminately 2. (a) distinction, honour (b) decoration 3. distinction, eminence. **distinct** *a* distinct, separate. **distinctement** *adv* distinctly. **distinctif, -ive** *a* distinctive.

distinguer [distɛ̃ge] *vtr* 1. to distinguish; to mark (off), characterize 2. to honour 3. **d. entre deux choses**, to distinguish between two things; **d. qch de qch**, to distinguish, to tell, sth from sth 4. to discern; to make out (features); **il fait trop noir pour bien d.**, it's too dark to see clearly 5. **se d.** (a) to distinguish oneself (b) **se d. des autres**, to be distinguishable from others (c) to be noticeable, conspicuous; to stand out. **distinguable** *a* distinguishable. **distingué** *a* distinguished; Corr: **veuiller agréer mes sentiments distingués**, yours faithfully.

distordre (se) [sədistɔrdr] *vpr* to become twisted.

distorsion [distɔrsjɔ̃] *nf* distortion; imbalance.

distraction [distraksjɔ̃] *nf* 1. absentmindedness 2. diversion, amusement, distraction, recreation.

distraire [distrɛr] *vtr* (conj like TRAIRE) 1. to distract, divert (s.o.'s attention) 2. to divert, entertain, amuse 3. **se d.**, to amuse oneself, to enjoy oneself. **distrait**

a absent-minded; inattentive, abstracted. **dis-traitement** *adv* absentmindedly, abstractedly. **distrayant** *a* entertaining.

distribuer [distribɥe] *vtr* to distribute, hand out (orders, prizes); to issue (provisions); to deal (out) (cards); to deliver (letters); *Th:* **d. les rôles,** to assign, cast, the parts in a play); to cast a play.

distributeur, -trice [distribytœr, -tris] **1.** *n* distributor **2.** *nm Tchn:* distributor; *Aut:* alternator; **d. automatique,** slot machine; **d. de billets,** (i) ticket machine (ii) cash dispenser.

distribution [distribysjɔ̃] *nf* (a) distribution; allotment (of duties); issue (of rations); delivery (of letters); arrangement (of furniture); *Com:* handling; *ICE: Aut:* distribution; *Sch:* **d. des prix,** prize giving (b) *Th:* cast; casting (c) **d. des eaux,** water supply.

district [distrik(t)] *nm* district.

dit [di] *a* (a) settled, fixed; **prendre qch pour d.,** to take sth for granted; **à l'heure dite,** at the appointed time (b) (so-)called; **la zone dite tempérée,** the so-called temperate zone.

dithyrambique [ditirãbik] *a* eulogistic.

diurétique [djyretik] *a & nm Med:* diuretic.

diurne [djyrn] *a* diurnal.

divagation [divagasjɔ̃] *nf* raving, rambling.

divaguer [divage] *vi* to rave, to ramble.

divan [divã] *nm* divan; couch.

divergence [diverʒãs] *nf* divergence. **divergent** *a* divergent.

diverger [diverʒe] *vi* (**n. divergeons**) to diverge (**de,** from).

divers [diver] *a pl* (a) diverse, varied; **opinions très diverses,** very different opinions; **(frais) d.,** sundry expenses; *Journ:* **faits d.,** news items (b) *indef adj always preceding the n* various; sundry; **en diverses occasions,** on various occasions. **diversement** *adv* in various ways.

diversifier [diversifje] (*pr sub & impf* **n. diversifiions**) *vtr* **1.** to diversify, vary **2. se d.,** to change; to vary.

diversion [diversjɔ̃] *nf* diversion; change.

diversité [diversite] *nf* diversity; variety.

divertir [divertir] *vtr* **1.** (*a*) *A:* to divert (attention) (*b*) to misappropriate (funds) **2.** to divert, entertain, amuse **3. se d.,** to amuse oneself, to enjoy oneself. **divertissant** *a* entertaining.

divertissement [divertismã] *nm* **1.** misappropriation (of funds) **2.** (a) entertainment, amusement; recreation (b) *Mus:* divertimento.

dividende [dividãd] *nm* dividend.

divinité [divinite] *nf* divinity. **divin** *a* divine; holy; sacred. **divinement** *adv* divinely.

diviser [divize] *vtr* **1.** to divide; to share (out); to part, separate; **d. pour régner,** divide and rule **2. se d.,** to divide, to break up (**en, into**).

diviseur [divizœr] *nm Mth:* divisor.

division [divizjɔ̃] *nf* **1.** division; partition; *Mth:* division; **d. du travail,** division of labour **2.** discord; disagreement.

divorce [divors] *nm* divorce.

divorcer [divorse] *vi* (**je divorçai(s)**) to get divorced; **d. d'avec qn,** to divorce s.o. **divorcé, -ée 1.** *a* divorced **2.** *n* divorcee.

divulguer [divylge] *vtr* to divulge, disclose, reveal.

dix [di, dis, diz] *num a inv & nm inv* **1.** card *a* (*at the end of the word group* [dis]; *before n or adj beginning with a vowel sound* [diz]; *before n or adj beginning with a consonant* [di]) ten; **il est dix heures** [dizœr], it's ten o'clock; **j'en ai dix** [dis], I have ten **2.** *nm inv* (*usu* [dis]) (*a*) **dix et demi,** ten and a half (*b*) (*ordinal uses*) **le d. mai** [ledime] the tenth of May; **le numéro d.,** number ten. **dixième** *num a & nm & f* tenth.

dix-huit [dizɥi(t)] *num a & nm inv* **1.** eighteen **2. le dix-huit mai,** the eighteenth of May. **dix-huitième** *num a & nm & f* eighteenth.

dix-neuf [diznœf] *num a & nm inv* **1.** nineteen **2. le dix-neuf mai,** the nineteenth of May. **dix-neuvième** *num a & nm & f* nineteenth.

dix-sept [dis(s)ɛt] *num a & nm inv* **1.** seventeen **2. le dix-sept mai,** the seventeenth of May. **dix-septième** *num a & nm & f* seventeenth.

dizaine [dizɛn] *nf* (about) ten; **une d. de personnes,** ten or a dozen people.

do [do] *nf inv Mus:* **1.** (*the note*) C **2.** (*in tonic sol-fa*) doh.

docilité [dosilite] *nf* docility. **docile** *a* docile. **docilement** *adv* with docility.

dock [dɔk] *nm* (*a*) *Nau:* dock; dockyard (*b*) *Com:* warehouse.

docker [dɔkɛr] *nm* docker.

docteur [dɔktœr] *nm* **1. d.** (**en médecine**), doctor (of medicine), MD; **leur fille est d.,** their daughter is a doctor; **le d. Thomas,** Dr Thomas **2.** *Sch:* **d. ès lettres** = Doctor of Literature.

doctoresse [dɔktɔrɛs] *nf* woman doctor.

doctrine [dɔktrin] *nf* doctrine, tenet. **doctrinaire 1.** *a* doctrinaire, pedantic **2.** *nm* doctrinarian. **doctrinal, -aux** *a* doctrinal.

document [dɔkymã] *nm* document. **documentaire 1.** *a* documentary **2.** *nm Cin:* documentary.

documenter [dɔkymãte] *vtr* **1. d. qn,** to brief s.o. **2. se d.,** to gather material (for book). **documenté** *a* well-informed, well-documented.

dodeliner [dɔdline] *vi* **d. de la tête,** to nod one's head.

dodo [dodo] *nm* (*nursery language*) bye-byes; **aller au d.,** to go to bye-byes.

dodu [dɔdy] *a* plump; chubby.

doge [dɔʒ] *nm Hist:* doge.

dogme [dɔgm] *nm* dogma. **dogmatique** *a* dogmatic.

dogue [dɔg] *nm* mastiff.

doigt [dwa] *nm* (*a*) finger; *Anat: Z:* digit; **mon petit d. me l'a dit,** a little bird told me so; **il n'a pas levé le d.,** he didn't lift a finger; **promener ses doigts sur qch,** to finger, feel, sth; **avoir des doigts de fée,** to have nimble fingers; **montrer du d.,** to point; **mettre le d. dans l'engrenage,** to get involved in sth; **vous avez mis le d. dessus,** you've hit the nail on the head (*b*) finger's breadth; **un d. de cognac,** a spot of brandy; **être à deux doigts de la mort,** to be within an ace of death (*c*) **d. de pied,** toe (*d*) finger (of glove).

doigté [dwate] *nm* **1.** *Mus:* fingering **2.** touch **3.** tact.

doigtier [dwatje] *nm* fingerstall.

doléances [dɔleãs] *nfpl* complaints; grievances.

dolent [dɔlã] *a* doleful.

dollar 124 **dorer**

dollar [dɔlar] *nm* dollar.

domaine [dɔmɛn] *nm* **1.** domain; (real) estate, property; **d. public,** public property **2.** field, scope, sphere.

dôme [dom] *nm* (*a*) *Arch:* dome, cupola (*b*) *Lit:* canopy (of trees).

domesticité [dɔmɛstisite] *nf coll* domestic staff; household. **domestique 1.** *a* domestic; household **2.** *n* (domestic) servant.

domestiquer [dɔmɛstike] *vtr* to domesticate (animal); to harness (atomic energy).

domicile [dɔmisil] *nm* (place of) residence; home; *Jur:* domicile; **sans d. fixe,** of no fixed address; **à d.,** at one's (private) house; at home; **franco à d.,** carriage paid.

domiciliation [dɔmisiljasjɔ̃] *nf Com:* domiciliation.

domicilier [dɔmisilje] *vtr* (*pr sub & impf n.* **dom-iciliions**) *Com:* to domicile (bill at bank). **domi-cilié** *a* resident, domiciled (**à,** at).

domination [dɔminasjɔ̃] *nf* domination, rule; (moral) influence; **d. de soi-même,** self control. **domi-nateur, -trice** *a* dominating, ruling; domineer-ing.

dominer [dɔmine] **1.** *vi* to rule (**sur,** over); to domin-ate; to prevail **2.** *vtr* (*a*) to dominate; to rule; to master, overcome (shyness); **sa voix dominait toutes les autres,** his voice rose above all others; *Sp:* **d. la partie,** to have the best of the game (*b*) to tower above (sth); to overlook **3.** **se d.,** to control one's feelings. **dominant 1.** *a* dominating, dominant, ruling; prevailing; outstanding **2.** *nf* **dominante** (*a*) *Mus:* dominant (*b*) chief characteristic.

dominicain, -aine [dɔminikɛ̃, -ɛn] *a & n* **1.** *Ecc:* dominican **2.** *Geog:* Dominican; **la République Dominicaine,** the Dominican Republic.

dominical, -aux [dɔminikal, -o] *a* **l'oraison dom-inicale,** the Lord's prayer; **repos d.,** Sunday rest.

domino [dɔmino] *nm* domino.

dommage [dɔmaʒ] *nm* **1.** (*a*) damage, injury (*b*) *F:* **quel d.!** what a pity! what a shame! **2.** *usu pl* (*a*) damage (to property) (*b*) *Jur:* **dommages et intérêts, dommages-intérêts,** damages.

domptage [dɔ̃taʒ] *nm* taming (of animals).

dompter [dɔ̃te] *vtr* to tame (animal); to break in (horse); to subdue, overcome (one's feelings). **domptable** *a* tamable.

dompteur, -euse [dɔ̃tœr, -øz] *n* tamer, trainer; **d. de chevaux,** horsebreaker.

DOM(TOM) [dɔm(tɔm)] *abbr Départements (et territoires) d'outre-mer.*

don [dɔ̃] *nm* **1.** giving **2.** (*a*) gift, present; donation (*b*) gift, talent.

donataire [dɔnatɛr] *n Jur:* donee.

donateur, -trice [dɔnatœr, -tris] *n* donor.

donation [dɔnasjɔ̃] *nf* donation, gift.

donc 1. *conj* [dɔ̃k] therefore, hence, consequently, so **2.** *adv* [dɔ̃, *but in oratory often* dɔ̃k] (*a*) (*emphatic*) **te voilà d. de retour,** so you're back; **mais taisez-vous d.!** do be quiet! **allons d.!** nonsense! come on! **com-ment d.?** how do you mean? **pensez d.!** (i) just think! (ii) that's what you think! (*b*) (*after interruption or digression*) **d.** [dɔ̃k] **pour en revenir à notre sujet,** so, to come back to our subject.

donjon [dɔ̃ʒɔ̃] *nm* keep (of castle).

donnant [dɔnɑ̃] *a* **d. d.,** give and take; tit for tat.

donne [dɔn] *nf Cards:* deal; **fausse d.,** misdeal.

donnée [dɔne] *nf* **1.** datum, given information **2.** *pl* data; facts.

donner [dɔne] **1.** *vtr* (*a*) to give; **d. un bal,** to give a ball; *abs* **d. aux pauvres,** to give to the poor; **d. des conseils,** to give advice; **d. à boire à qn,** to give s.o. something to drink; **cela me donne à croire que,** it leads me to believe that; **je vous le donne en mille,** you'll never guess; **s'en d.** (à cœur joie), to have a good time; **il n'est pas donné à tout le monde d'être écrivain,** not everyone can be a writer; **d. du sang,** give blood (*b*) **d. à qn qch à garder,** to entrust s.o. with sth; **d. la main à qn,** to shake hands with s.o. (*c*) **d. les cartes,** to deal the cards (*d*) to provide, furnish; (*of crops*) to yield; to furnish (proof); **d. du souci,** to cause anxiety; **cela donne à réfléchir,** this gives food for thought; **d. un bon exemple,** to set a good example; **qu'est-ce qu'on donne au cinéma?** what's on at the cinema? *F:* **ça n'a rien donné,** nothing came of it; it didn't work out (*e*) **d. faim à qn,** to make s.o. hungry (*f*) to attribute (sth to s.o.); **je lui donne trente ans,** I reckon she's about thirty; **d. raison à qn,** to agree with s.o. **2.** *vi* (*a*) **fenêtre qui donne sur la cour,** window that looks out on the yard; **la porte donne sur le jardin,** the door leads out into the garden; **le soleil donne dans la pièce,** the sun is shining into the room (*b*) **d. de la tête contre qch,** to knock one's head against sth; *F:* **il ne sait pas où d. de la tête,** he doesn't know which way to turn; **d. dans le piège,** *F:* **dans le panneau,** to fall into the trap (*c*) (*of material*) to stretch; to give **3.** **se d.** (*a*) to devote oneself (to a cause); **se d. des airs,** to give oneself airs (*b*) *Hamlet* **se donne ce soir,** they are playing *Hamlet* tonight (*c*) **se d. du tourment,** to worry; **se d. du mal,** (i) to work hard (ii) to take (great) trouble (over sth). **donné** *a & pp* given; fixed; **étant d. la situation,** in view of, considering, the situation; **étant d. qu'il est mineur,** since he is under age.

donneur, -euse [dɔnœr, -øz] *n* (*a*) giver; donor; *Med:* **d. de sang,** blood-donor; **d. de conseils,** busy-body, *NAm: F:* wise guy (*b*) *Cards:* dealer (*c*) *P:* (police) informer; squealer.

dont [dɔ̃] *rel pron* (= **de qui, duquel, desquels,** etc) (*a*) from, by, with, whom or which; **la famille d. je suis descendu,** the family from which I am de-scended; **la femme d. il est amoureux,** the woman he is in love with; **la façon d. il me regardait,** the way he looked at me (*b*) whom, which; **le livre d. j'ai besoin,** the book (that) I want; **voici ce d. il s'agit,** this is what it's all about (*c*) whose; **la dame d. je connais le fils,** the lady whose son I know; **la chambre d. la porte est fermée,** the room with the closed door (*d*) **quelques-uns étaient là, d. votre frère,** there were a few people there, including your brother.

dopage [dɔpaʒ] *nm* doping.

doper [dɔpe] *vtr* **1.** to dope (racehorse) **2.** **se d.,** to dope oneself.

dorénavant [dɔrenavɑ̃] *adv* henceforward, from now on.

dorer [dɔre] *vtr* **1.** to gild; *Fig:* **d. la pilule,** to sugar the pill **2.** *Cu:* to glaze (cake); to brown (meat) **3.** **se**

d. au soleil, to sunbathe. doré a gilded; gilt; golden (hair).

dorique [dɔrik] a Arch: Doric.

dorloter [dɔrlɔte] vtr to fondle; to pamper.

dormeur, -euse [dɔrmœr, -øz] n sleeper.

dormir [dɔrmir] vi (prp dormant; pr ind je dors) 1. to sleep; to be asleep; d. profondément, to be fast asleep; d. d'un sommeil léger, to be a light sleeper; le café m'empêche de d., coffee keeps me awake; d. trop longtemps, to oversleep; d. comme un loir, to sleep like a log; ne d. que d'un œil, to sleep with one eye open; vous pouvez d. sur les deux oreilles, (you can) rest assured; avoir envie de d., to feel sleepy; il dort debout, he can't keep his eyes open; une histoire à d. debout, a cock-and-bull story 2. to remain inactive; to lie dormant; eau qui dort, stagnant, still, water. dormant 1. a still (water); fixed (frame) 2. nm frame (of door, window).

dorsal, -aux [dɔrsal, -o] a dorsal.

dortoir [dɔrtwar] nm dormitory; cité-d., dormitory town.

dorure [dɔryr] nf 1. gilding 2. gilt, gilding.

doryphore [dɔrifɔr] nm Ent: Colorado beetle.

dos [do] nm 1. back; avoir le d. voûté, to be round-shouldered; vu de d., seen from behind, from the back; robe décolletée dans le d., low-backed dress; il me tombe toujours sur le d., he's always jumping down my throat; (of cat) faire le gros d., to arch its back; voyager à d. d'âne, to travel on a donkey; d. à d., back to back; je n'ai rien à me mettre sur le d., I haven't a thing to wear; F: avoir qn sur le d., to be saddled with s.o.; il a bon d., he can take the strain; F: j'en ai plein le d., I'm fed up with it 2. back (of chair); voir au d., (please) turn over.

dosage [dozaʒ] nm measuring out; quantity determination; proportioning.

dose [doz] nf dose (of medicine); par petites doses, in small quantities; forcer la d., to overdo it.

doser [doze] vtr 1. to determine the quantity of; to proportion 2. to measure out dose (of medicine).

doseur [dozœr] nm measure.

dossier [dosje] nm 1. back (of seat) 2. (a) documents, file; record (b) folder, file.

dot [dɔt] nf dowry.

dotation [dɔtasjɔ̃] nf endowment.

doter [dɔte] vtr (a) to provide with a dowry (b) to endow (hospital) (c) Ind: d. une usine d'un matériel neuf, to equip a factory with new plant.

douairière [dwɛrjɛr] nf dowager.

douane [dwan] nf Adm: customs; passer à la d., to go through customs; marchandises en d., bonded goods; (bureau de) d., customs house. douanier, -ière 1. a tarif d., customs tariff; union douanière, customs union 2. nm customs officer.

doublage [dublaʒ] nm doubling; Cin: dubbing.

double [dubl] 1. a double, twofold; valise à d. fond, suitcase with a false bottom; mot à d. sens, ambiguous word; jouer un d. jeu, to play a double game; faire qch en d. exemplaire, to make two copies of sth; faire coup d., to kill two birds with one stone; le prix est d. de ce qu'il était, the price is twice what it was; fermer à d. tour, to double-lock; à d. usage, dual-purpose 2. adv voir d., to see double 3. nm (a) double; ça ma couté le d., it cost me twice as much;

Ten: d. mixte, mixed doubles (b) duplicate, counterpart; copy. doublement 1. adv doubly 2. nm doubling; Aut: overtaking.

double-commande [dublkɔmɑ̃d] nf Av: Aut: dual controls; pl doubles-commandes.

double-décimètre [dubldesimɛtr] nm = ruler, foot rule; pl doubles-décimètres.

doubler [duble] 1. vtr (a) to double (size, amount) (b) to fold in two; to double; Nau: d. un cap, to weather a cape; Th: d. un rôle, to understudy a part; Cin: to stand in for (s.o.); d. le pas, to quicken one's pace; d. une voiture, vi d., to overtake (a car); Aut: défense de d., no overtaking, NAm: no passing (c) to line (coat) (d) Cin: to dub (film) 2. vi to double, to increase twofold.

doublure [dublyr] nf 1. lining (of garment) 2. Th: understudy; Cin: stand-in; occ stuntman.

douce see doux.

douceur [dusœr] nf 1. (a) sweetness (of honey) (b) pl sweet things, sweets; aimer les douceurs, to have a sweet tooth 2. softness; mildness (of climate) 3. pleasantness; les douceurs de l'amitié, the pleasures of friendship 4. gentleness; sweetness (of smile); en d., gently; démarrer en d., to start smoothly. douceâtre a sickly sweet. doucereux, -euse a sickly (sweet); smooth(-tongued) (pers); sugary (voice).

douche [duʃ] nf (a) shower; pl les douches, the shower room; d. écossaise, succession of good and bad news; ups and downs (b) soaking, drenching; d. (froide), let-down (c) shower unit.

doucher [duʃe] vtr to give (s.o.) a shower; se d., to take a shower.

doué [dwe] a gifted; être d. pour, to have a gift for.

douille [duj] nf (a) lamp socket (of electric lightbulb) (b) case (of cartridge).

douillet, -ette [duje, -jɛt] a (a) cosy (bed) (b) (pers) soft; over-sensitive. douillettement adv softly, delicately; élever d., to coddle (s.o.).

douleur [dulœr] nf 1. pain, ache 2. sorrow, grief. douloureux, -euse a 1. painful; aching; sore 2. sad, distressing. douloureusement adv painfully; distressingly.

doute [dut] nm doubt, uncertainty, misgiving; mettre en d., to challenge, to question; être dans le d., to be doubtful (sur, about); cela ne fait plus aucun d., there is no longer any doubt about it; sans d., no doubt, probably; sans aucun d., without a doubt.

douter [dute] 1. vi to doubt; d. du zèle de qn, to doubt, to question, s.o.'s enthusiasm; j'en doute, I doubt it; je ne doute pas qu'il vienne, I am confident he will come 2. se d. de qch, to suspect sth; je m'en doutais (bien), I thought as much; je m'en doute, I can well believe it; je ne me doutais pas qu'il fût là, I had no idea that he was there. douteux, -euse a doubtful, uncertain, questionable; dubious (company).

douves [duv] nfpl moat (of castle).

Douvres [duvr] Prnf Geog: Dover.

doux, douce [du, dus] a (a) sweet; smooth, soft; eau douce, (i) fresh (ii) soft, water (b) pleasant, agreeable (c) gentle; mild (climate); soft (light); gentle (slope) (d) gentle; meek (nature) (e) adv tout d.! gently! F: filer d., to give in; en douce, discreetly, on the quiet. **doucement** adv gently, softly; smoothly; **allez-y d.!** gently does it!

douzaine [duzɛn] nf dozen; **une d. de personnes,** about a dozen people; **à la d.,** by the dozen.

douze [duz] num a inv & nm inv twelve; **le d. mai,** the twelfth of May. **douzième** num a & n twelfth. **douzièmement** adv twelfthly, in the twelfth place.

doyen, -enne [dwajɛ̃, -ɛn] n 1. (a) Ecc: Sch: dean (b) doyen (of diplomatic corps) 2. senior; **d. d'âge,** oldest member.

Dr abbr Docteur.

draconien, -ienne [drakɔnjɛ̃, -jɛn] a Draconian, harsh.

dragée [draʒe] nf sugar(ed) almond. **dragéifié** a sugar-coated.

dragon [dragɔ̃] nm 1. dragon 2. Mil: dragoon.

drague [drag] nf dredger; Fish: dredge, dragnet.

draguer [drage] vtr 1. to dredge 2. to drag (pond); to sweep (channel) 3. vtr & i P: to chat up (girls).

dragueur [dragœr] nm 1. dredger; **d. de mines,** minesweeper 2. P: (pers) skirt chaser.

drain [drɛ̃] nm drain(pipe).

drainage [drɛnaʒ] nm drainage.

drainer [drene] vtr to drain (soil, abscess).

dramatisation [dramatizasjɔ̃] nf dramatization.

dramatiser [dramatize] vtr to dramatize.

dramaturge [dramatyrʒ] n dramatist, playwright.

drame [dram] nm 1. (a) (literary genre) drama (b) play (of a serious nature); tragedy 2. tragedy; **il ne faut pas en faire un d.,** there's no need to dramatize it. **dramatique** 1. a dramatic; tragic; **auteur d.,** playwright 2. nf television play. **dramatiquement** adv dramatically; tragically.

drap [dra] nm 1. cloth 2. d. (de lit), sheet; **être dans de beaux draps,** to be in a fine mess.

drapeau, -eaux [drapo] nm flag; Mil: colour; **être sous les drapeaux,** to serve in the (armed) forces.

draper [drape] vtr to drape; **se d.,** to drape oneself (**dans, de,** in); **se d. dans sa dignité,** to stand on one's dignity.

draperie [drapri] nf drapery.

drapier, -ière [drapje, -jɛr] n draper; cloth manufacturer.

dressage [drɛsaʒ] nm training; breaking in.

dresser [drɛse] vtr 1. to erect, put up (monument); to put up (ladder); to set (trap); to pitch (tent); **d. les oreilles,** to prick up one's ears 2. to prepare, to draw up (plan, report, list) 3. **d. qn contre qn,** to set s.o. against s.o. 4. (a) to train (animal); to break in (horse) (b) F: to discipline (s.o.); **ça le dressera!** that'll teach him! 5. **se d.** (a) to stand up, rise; to sit up, straighten up; **se d. sur la pointe des pieds,** to stand on tiptoe; **ses cheveux se dressaient,** his hair stood on end (b) **se d. contre qch,** to rise up against sth.

dresseur, -euse [drɛsœr, -øz] n trainer; **d. de fauves,** wild animal tamer.

dressoir [drɛswar] nm dresser, sideboard.

dribbler [drible] vtr Fb: to dribble.

dribbleur [driblœr] nm Fb: dribbler.

drille [drij] nm F: O: **un joyeux d.,** a cheerful character.

drogue [drɔg] nf (a) drug (b) F: drug(s), narcotic.

drogué, -ée [drɔge] n drug addict.

droguer [drɔge] vtr 1. (a) to dose (with medicine) (b) to drug (victim) 2. **se d.,** to take drugs; **il se drogue,** he's a drug addict.

droguerie [drɔgri] nf (a) = hardware store (b) = hardware trade.

droguiste [drɔgist] nm = ironmonger (dealing in paints, cleaning materials).

droit¹, droite [drwa, drwat] 1. a (a) straight, upright; **se tenir d.,** to stand up straight, to sit up straight; **angle d.,** right angle (b) direct, straight; **ligne droite,** nf droite, straight line; **en ligne droite,** as the crow flies (c) upright, honest (pers) (d) right (hand, side); **être le bras d. de qn,** to be s.o.'s right-hand man 2. adv (in a) straight (line), directly; **c'est d. devant vous, c'est tout d.,** it's straight ahead (of you) 3. nf **la droite,** the right, the right(-hand) side; Aut: **rouler à d.,** to drive on the right; **tenir la droite,** to keep to the right.

droit² nm 1. right; **droits civils,** civil rights; **d. d'aînesse,** birthright; **d. d'auteur,** copyright; **avoir d. à qch,** to have a right to sth; F: Iron: **il a eu d. à une bonne fessée,** he earned himself a good spanking; **avoir le d. de faire qch,** to be entitled to do sth; to be allowed to do sth; **à bon d.,** with good reason; **de quel d. est-il entré?** what right had he to come in? 2. charge, fee, due; **droits d'auteur,** royalties; **d. de douane,** duty 3. law; **faire son d.,** to study law.

droiture [drwatyr] nf uprightness.

drôle [drol] a (a) funny, amusing (b) strange, funny, odd; F: **se sentir tout d.,** to feel peculiar (c) F: **un d. de garçon,** a queer fish; **quelle d. d'idée!** what a funny idea! (intensive) **il faut une d. de patience,** it needs a hell of a lot of patience (d) adv P: **ça m'a fait tout d.,** it gave me an odd feeling. **drôlement** adv funnily; strangely; F: excessively, awfully; **il fait d. froid,** it's terribly cold.

drôlerie [drolri] nf funny remark.

dromadaire [drɔmadɛr] nm Z: dromedary.

dru [dry] 1. a thick, dense (grass, hair); heavy (rain) 2. adv thickly, heavily; **tomber d.,** to fall thick and fast.

druide [drɥid] nm druid.

du [dy] = de le; see de and le.

dû, due [dy] 1. a (a) due; owing; **en port dû,** carriage forward (b) proper; **en bonne et due forme,** in due form 2. nm due; **à chacun son dû,** give the devil his due. **dûment** adv duly.

dualité [dɥalite] nf duality.

duc [dyk] nm duke. **ducal, -aux** a ducal.

duché [dyʃe] nm duchy, dukedom.

duchesse [dyʃɛs] nf duchess.

duel [dɥɛl] nm duel; **se battre en d.,** to fight a duel.

duelliste [dɥelist] nm duellist.

dune [dyn] nf dune, sandhill.

Dunkerque [dœ̃kɛrk] Prnf Geog: Dunkirk.

duo [dɥo] nm Mus: duet.

duodénum [dɥɔdenɔm] nm Anat: duodenum.

dupe [dyp] nf dupe, F: sucker; a **je ne suis pas d.,** I'm not taken in by it.

duper [dype] vtr to dupe, to deceive, to fool (s.o.); **se d.,** to deceive oneself.

duperie [dypri] nf deception.

duplex [dyplɛks] (a) a inv & nm WTel: TV: (**émission**

en) **d.**, link-up (b) nm maison(n)ette, NAm: duplex (apartment).

duplicata [dyplikata] nm inv duplicate (copy).

duplicateur [dyplikatœr] nm duplicator.

duplicité [dyplisite] nf duplicity.

dur [dyr] a **1.** hard; tough (meat, wood); **œuf d.**, hard-boiled egg; (of pers) **être d. à cuire**, to be a tough nut **2.** hard, difficult; **rendre la vie dure à qn**, to make s.o.'s life a misery **3.** (a) **être d. d'oreille**, to be hard of hearing (b) hard, harsh; **avoir le cœur d.**, to be hard-hearted; **être d. avec qn**, to be hard on s.o.; **hiver d.**, hard winter **4.** adv **travailler d.**, to work hard; **élevé à la dure**, brought up the hard way **5.** nm P: tough guy, a hard nut; **un d. à cuire**, a hard nut to crack **6.** nf (a) **coucher sur la dure**, to sleep rough (b) F: **en voir de dures**, to have a hard time of it. **durement** adv hard, vigorously; severely; harshly.

durabilité [dyrabilite] nf durability. **durable** a durable, lasting. **durablement** adv durably.

durant [dyrã] prep during; **toute sa vie d.**, throughout his life; **parler des heures d.**, to talk for hours on end; **d. quelques instants**, for a few moments.

durcir [dyrsir] **1.** vtr to harden **2.** vi & pr to grow hard, to harden.

durcissement [dyrsismã] nm hardening.

durée [dyre] nf **1.** lasting quality; wear; life (of light bulb) **2.** duration; **de courte d.**, short; short-lived; **de longue d.**, long-lasting.

durer [dyre] vi to last; to continue; **voilà 3 ans que ça dure**, it's been going on for 3 years; **ça ne peut pas d.**, this (i) can't go on (ii) can't last long.

dureté [dyrte] nf **1.** hardness; toughness **2.** difficulty (of task) **3.** harshness, callousness; severity; **d. de cœur**, hard-heartedness.

durillon [dyrijõ] nm callosity, callus; corn (on foot).

duvet [dyvɛ] nm **1.** down (on chin, young bird, peach); **d. du cygne**, swansdown **2.** sleeping bag. **duveteux, -euse** a downy.

dynamique [dinamik] **1.** a dynamic. **2.** nf dynamics.

dynamisme [dinamism] nm dynamism.

dynamite [dinamit] nf dynamite.

dynamiter [dinamite] vtr to dynamite.

dynamo [dinamo] nf El: dynamo.

dysnastie [dinasti] nf dynasty. **dynastique** a dynastic.

dysenterie [disãtri] nf Med: dysentery.

dyslexie [dislɛksi] nf Med: dyslexia. **dyslexique** a dyslexic, dyslectic.

dyspepsie [dispɛpsi] nf Med: dyspepsia.

E

E, e [ə] *nm* (the letter) E, e.
E. *abbr* est.
eau [o] *nf* 1. water; **e. douce,** (i) fresh (ii) soft, water; **passer à l'e.,** to rinse; **e. grasse,** washing-up water; **mettre de l'e. dans son vin,** (i) to reduce one's expenses (ii) to draw in one's horns; **ville d'eau(x),** spa; **prendre les eaux,** to take, drink, the waters 2. (*a*) **e. de pluie,** rainwater (*b*) **cours d'e.,** waterway; stream; river; **jet d'e.,** fountain; **pièce d'e.,** (ornamental) lake; **tomber à l'e.,** (i) to fall into the water (ii) (*of plan*) to fall through (*c*) (*of ship*) **faire e.,** to (spring a) leak; **chaussures qui prennent l'e.,** shoes that let in the water (*d*) **service des eaux,** water supply; **château d'e.,** water tower; **conduite d'e.,** water mains; **e. courante,** running water 3. (*a*) **j'en avais l'e. à la bouche,** it made my mouth water (*b*) **diamant de la première e.,** diamond of the first water 4. **e. de Cologne,** eau de cologne; **e. de toilette,** toilet water; **e. oxygénée,** hydrogen peroxide; **e. de Javel,** = bleach; *AtomPh:* **e. lourde,** heavy water.
eau-de-vie [odvi] *nf* (plum, etc) brandy; *pl eaux-de-vie.*
eau-forte [ofɔrt] *nf* 1. *Ch:* nitric acid 2. etching; *pl eaux-fortes.*
ébahir [ebair] *vtr* to amaze, astound.
ébahissement [ebaismɑ̃] *nm* amazement, astonishment.
ébats [eba] *nmpl* revels, frolics.
ébattre (s') [sebatr] *vpr* (*conj like* BATTRE) to gambol; to frolic.
ébauchage [eboʃaʒ] *nm* roughing out; sketching out; outlining.
ébauche [eboʃ] *nf* rough sketch (of picture); outline (of a novel); **é. d'un sourire,** ghost of a smile.
ébaucher [eboʃe] *vtr* to rough out; to sketch out, outline (plan); **é. un sourire,** to give a faint smile.
ébène [ebɛn] *nf* ebony; (**d'un noir**) **d'é.,** jet-black.
ébéniste [ebenist] *nm* cabinet maker.
ébénisterie [ebenist(ə)ri] *nf* (*a*) cabinet making (*b*) cabinet work.
éberluer [eberlɥe] *vtr* to astound.
éblouir [ebluir] *vtr* to dazzle.
éblouissement [ebluismɑ̃] *nm* 1. (*a*) dazzle, glare (*b*) *Med:* (fit of) dizziness 2. dazzling sight.
éborgner [ebɔrɲe] *vtr* **é. qn,** to blind s.o. in one eye, to put s.o.'s eye out.
éboueur [ebuœr] *nm* dustman, *NAm:* garbage collector.
ébouillanter [ebujɑ̃te] *vtr* to scald.
éboulement [ebulmɑ̃] *nm* 1. falling in, crumbling; caving in, collapsing 2. rock fall; fallen rock. **é. de terre,** landslide, landslip.
ébouler (s') [sebule] *vpr* to crumble, cave in, collapse.
éboulis [ebuli] *nm* mass of fallen earth; debris; scree.

ébouriffer [eburife] *vtr* 1. to dishevel, ruffle (s.o.'s hair) 2. *F:* to amaze (s.o.). **ébouriffant** *a F:* breathtaking, startling.
ébranlement [ebrɑ̃lmɑ̃] *nm* shaking; shock.
ébranler [ebrɑ̃le] *vtr* 1. to shake; to loosen; to rock (building) 2. **s'é.,** to start (moving); (*of train*) to start; (*of procession*) to move off.
ébrécher [ebreʃe] *vtr* (**j'ébrèche; j'ébrécherai**) to notch; to make a notch in (sth); to chip (a plate); to break (a tooth); to make a hole in (one's capital).
ébréchure [ebreʃyr] *nf* nick, chip.
ébriété [ebriete] *nf* inebriation, intoxication.
ébrouer (s') [sebrue] *vpr* (*of horse*) to snort; (*of dog, pers*) to shake oneself.
ébruitement [ebrɥitmɑ̃] *nm* spreading (of rumour).
ébruiter [ebrɥite] *vtr* 1. to spread (rumour) 2. (*of news, rumour*) **s'é.,** to spread, *F:* to get around; to become known, to spread.
ébullition [ebylisjɔ̃] *nf* (*a*) boiling; **porter à l'é.,** to bring to the boil; *F:* **être en é.,** to be seething with rage (*b*) turmoil.
écaille [ekaj] *nf* 1. (*a*) scale (of fish) (*b*) flake (of paint); chip (of enamel); splinter (of wood) 2. shell (of tortoise); **lunettes à monture d'é.,** tortoiseshell-rimmed spectacles.
écailler [ekaje] *vtr* 1. (*a*) to scale (fish) (*b*) to flake off (paint) 2. **s'é.,** to flake off.
écarlate [ekarlat] *nf & a* scarlet.
écarquiller [ekarkije] *vtr* **é. les yeux,** to open one's eyes wide; to stare.
écart [ekar] *nm* 1. (*a*) distance apart, gap; **é. entre le prix de vente et le coût,** margin between selling price and cost price; **é. entre deux lectures,** difference between readings (*b*) separation, spreading out; **faire le grand é.,** to do the splits 2. (*a*) deviation; **faire un é.,** to step aside; (*of horse*) to shy; **écarts de jeunesse,** youthful indiscretions (*b*) digression (in speech) 3. **à l'é.,** aside, on one side, apart; **se tenir à l'é.,** to keep in the background, to keep oneself apart, aloof; **mettre à l'é. tout sentiment personnel,** to set aside any personal feeling.
écarteler [ekartəle] *vtr* (**j'écartèle**) to quarter (criminal).
écartement [ekartəmɑ̃] *nm* space, gap; *Rail:* gauge (of track).
écarter [ekarte] *vtr* 1. (*a*) to separate, part; to draw aside (curtains); to open (one's arms); to spread (one's legs) (*b*) to move (s.o., sth) aside; to brush aside (obstacles); **é. un coup, un danger,** to ward off a blow, a danger (*c*) to divert (suspicion) 2. **s'é.** (*a*) to move, step, stand, aside (*b*) to move apart, diverge (*c*) to deviate, stray (**de,** from); **s'é. du sujet,** to wander from the subject. **écarté** *a* 1. isolated, remote (house, spot) 2. (far) apart; **se tenir les jambes écartées,** to stand with one's legs apart.

ecchymose [ekimoz] *nf* bruise.

ecclésiastique [eklezjastik] **1.** *a* ecclesiastical; clerical **2.** *nm* ecclesiastic, clergyman.

écervelé [esεrvəle] **1.** *a* scatterbrained **2.** *n* scatter-brain.

échafaud [eʃafo] *nm* scaffold.

échafaudage [eʃafodaʒ] *nm* **1.** building up, construction **2.** (*a*) scaffolding (*b*) pile (of objects).

échafauder [eʃafode] *vtr* (*a*) to pile up (objects) (*b*) to build up, construct (argument, plan).

échalote [eʃalɔt] *nf Bot:* shallot.

échancrure [eʃɑ̃kryr] *nf* opening (in neckline); notch, nick (in wood); indentation (in coastline). **échancré** *a* scooped (neckline); indented (plank, coastline).

échange [eʃɑ̃ʒ] *nm* exchange; **faire un é. de qch pour, contre, qch,** to exchange, to swap, sth for sth.

échanger [eʃɑ̃ʒe] *vtr* (*n.* **échangeons**) to exchange, to swap (sth for sth).

échangeur [eʃɑ̃ʒœr] *nm* (*on motorway*) intersection.

échantillon [eʃɑ̃tijɔ̃] *nm* sample; specimen.

échantillonnage [eʃɑ̃tijɔnaʒ] *nm* sampling.

échappatoire [eʃapatwar] *nf* way out, loophole.

échappée [eʃape] *nf* **1.** *Sp:* sudden spurt (in race) **2.** space, interval; **é. (de vue),** vista (**sur,** over); **é. de soleil,** burst of sunshine.

échappement [eʃapmɑ̃] *nm* **1.** escape, leakage (of gas, water); (**tuyau d'**)**é.,** *Aut:* exhaust (pipe); **pot d'é.,** silencer, *NAm:* muffler; **é. libre,** cutout (to silencer) **2.** (*of clock*) escapement.

échapper [eʃape] *vi* **1.** (*aux* **être** *or* **avoir**) (*a*) to escape; **é. à qn,** to escape to s.o.; **il nous a échappé,** he got away; **ce propos m'a échappé,** I failed to hear this remark; **la vérité lui échappe parfois,** he sometimes blurts out the truth; **son nom m'échappe,** I can't remember his name; **é. à toute définition,** to defy definition (*b*) (*aux* **avoir**) *F:* **vous l'avez échappé belle,** you may have had a narrow escape (*c*) **laisser é.,** to let (s.o., sth) escape; to set free; to let out (secret); to let fall (a tear); **laisser é. l'occasion,** to let the opportunity slip (*d*) to escape (**de,** from, out of); **é. d'une maladie,** to survive an illness **2. s'é.,** to escape; to break free; (*of gas*) to leak; **un cri s'échappa de ses lèvres,** a cry burst from his lips.

écharde [eʃard] *nf* splinter, thorn.

écharpe [eʃarp] *nf* (*a*) sash (*b*) scarf (*c*) (arm) sling; **bras en é.,** arm in a sling.

écharper [eʃarpe] *vtr* to hack up; to tear to pieces.

échasse [eʃas] *nf* stilt.

échassier [eʃasje] *nm Orn:* wader.

échauder [eʃode] *vtr* to scald.

échauffement [eʃofmɑ̃] *nm* **1.** overheating (of engine) **2.** (over)excitement **3.** *Sp:* warm-up.

échauffer [eʃofe] *vtr* **1.** to overheat; **é. les oreilles de qn,** to irritate s.o. **2. s'é.** (*a*) to become overheated; **ne vous échauffez pas,** don't get excited; **la dispute s'échauffait,** feelings were beginning to run high (*b*) (*of athlete*) to warm up.

échauffourée [eʃofure] *nf* scuffle; clash; *Mil:* skirmish.

échéance [eʃeɑ̃s] *nf* **1.** (*a*) falling due (of bill); date of payment; expiry date; **venir à é.,** to fall due; **à trois mois d'é.,** at three months' date; **billet à longue, à courte, é.,** long-dated, short-dated, bill; **à longue**

é., in the long run (*b*) bill (falling due); **faire face à une é.,** to meet a bill **2.** expiry (of tenancy).

échec [eʃεk] *nm* **1.** (*a*) *Chess:* check; **é. et mat,** checkmate; **tenir qn en é.,** to hold s.o. in check (*b*) failure, setback; **faire é. à qn,** to frustrate s.o.'s plans; **voué à l'é.,** bound to fail **2.** *pl* chess; **partie d'échecs,** game of chess; **jeu d'échecs,** (i) chessboard (ii) chessmen.

échelle [eʃεl] *nf* **1.** (*a*) ladder; **é. d'incendie, é. de sauvetage,** fire escape; **faire la courte é. à qn,** to give s.o. (i) a leg up (ii) a helping hand; **il faut, il n'y a plus qu', tirer l'é.,** we may as well give up (*b*) ladder, run (in tights) **2.** (*a*) **é. sociale,** social scale (*b*) **é. des traitements,** salary scale; **é. mobile,** sliding scale (of prices) **3.** scale (of map, plan); **à petite, à grande, é.,** small-scale, large-scale.

échelon [eʃlɔ̃] *nm* (*a*) rung (of ladder) (*b*) step, grade, echelon; **monter par échelons,** to rise by degrees; **à l'é. ministériel,** at ministerial level.

échelonnement [eʃlɔnmɑ̃] *nm* spreading out (of payments); staggering (of holidays).

échelonner [eʃlɔne] *vtr* to space out (objects); to spread out (payments); to stagger (holidays).

écheveau, -eaux [eʃvo] *nm* (*a*) hank, skein (of yarn) (*b*) maze (of streets); intricacies (of plot).

échevelé [eʃəvle] *a* (*a*) dishevelled (pers); tousled (hair) (*b*) wild, frenzied (dance, rhythm).

échine [eʃin] *nf* **1.** spine, backbone; **courber l'é.,** to kowtow **2.** *Cu:* loin (of pork).

échiner (s') [seʃine] *vpr* to tire oneself out (doing sth); to slog (at sth).

échiquier [eʃikje] *nm* **1.** chessboard; **en é.,** chequered **2.** (*in Eng*) **l'É.,** the Exchequer.

écho [eko] *nm* **1.** echo; **se faire l'é. des opinions de qn,** to echo, to repeat, s.o.'s opinions **2.** *Journ:* **échos,** news items; gossip column.

échographe [ekograf] *nm* (ultrasound) scanner.

échographie [ekografi] *nf* (ultrasound) scan(ning).

échoir [eʃwar] *vi* (*prp* **échéant;** *pp* **échu;** *pr ind* **il échoit, ils échoient;** *impf* **il échoyait;** *fu* **il échoira;** *aux usu* **être**) **1. é. (en partage) à qn,** to fall to s.o.'s lot; **le cas échéant,** should the occasion arise **2.** (*a*) *Fin:* to mature, to fall due (*b*) (*of tenancy*) to expire.

échouer [eʃwe] *vi* **1.** *Nau:* to run aground, to ground; **échoué à sec,** high and dry (*b*) to fail; **le projet a échoué,** the plan fell through; **é. à un examen,** to fail an exam; **faire é. un projet,** to wreck a plan **2. s'é.,** to run aground.

éclabousser [eklabuse] *vtr* (*a*) to splash, spatter (**de,** with) (*b*) to damage, to smear, (s.o.'s) reputation.

éclaboussure [eklabusyr] *nf* (*a*) splash, spatter (of mud) (*b*) blot, smear (on reputation).

éclair [eklεr] *nm* **1.** flash of lightning; *pl* lightning; **rapide comme l'é.,** quick as lightning, as a flash; **passer comme un é.,** to flash by **2.** flash (of gun); flash, spark (of genius) **3.** *Cu:* éclair.

éclairage [eklεraʒ] *nm* (*a*) lighting; illumination; **é. par projecteurs,** floodlighting; **heure d'é.,** lighting-up time (*b*) light.

éclairagiste [eklεraʒist] *nm* lighting technician.

éclaircie [eklεrsi] *nf* **1.** break (in clouds); *Meteor:* bright interval **2.** clearing (in forest).

éclaircir [eklεrsir] *vtr* **1.** (*a*) to clear (fog); **s'é. la voix,** to clear one's throat (*b*) to lighten; to (make) clear (*c*) to throw light on, to clear up, to solve (mystery); to clarify (situation) (d) to thin (forest, sauce); to thin out (plants) **2. s'é.** (a) (of the weather) to clear (up); (of complexion, voice) to become clearer, to clear; **sa figure s'éclaircit**, his face lit up (b) **s'é.**, to get clear (sur qch, on sth) (c) (of hair, plant) to become thin, to thin (out).

éclaircissement [eklɛrsismɑ̃] nm (a) enlightenment, elucidation (b) **demander des éclaircissements**, to ask for an explanation.

éclairé [eklere] a (a) lit, illuminated (b) enlightened; well-informed.

éclairer [eklere] **1.** vtr (a) to light, illuminate; to light the way for (s.o.) (b) to shed, to throw, light on (sth) (c) to enlighten; **éclairez-moi sur ce sujet**, tell me what it's all about (d) Mil: **é. le terrain**, to reconnoitre the ground **2.** vi **cette lampe éclaire mal**, this lamp gives a poor light **3. s'é.**, (of street) to be lit; (of face) to light up, to brighten; (of situation) to become clearer. **éclairant** a lighting, illuminating. **éclairé** a enlightened (pers).

éclaireur, -euse [eklærœr, -øz] (a) nm Mil: scout (b) n (boy) scout; (girl) guide.

éclat [ekla] nm **1.** splinter, chip; **voler en éclats**, to fly into pieces; **briser qch en éclats**, to smash sth to pieces; **éclats de verre**, (i) broken glass (ii) flying glass **2.** burst (of noise, laughter); **éclats de voix**, shouts; **rire aux éclats**, to burst out laughing; **faire (de l'é.)**, to create a stir; **sans é.**, quietly **3.** (a) flash (of light); (b) glare (of the sun); glitter; brilliancy; **l'é. de ses yeux**, the sparkle in her eyes; **l'é. de jeunesse**, the bloom of youth (c) brilliance (of style); glamour; **aimer l'é.**, to be fond of show.

éclatement [eklatmɑ̃] nm bursting, explosion (of shell, gun); blow-out (of tyre); shattering (of glass).

éclater [eklate] **1.** vtr to split (branch); to burst (tyre) **2.** vi (a) to burst, explode; to blow up; (of glass) to shatter (b) (of war, epidemic) to break out; (of storm) to break; (of anger) to burst out; **quand la guerre a éclaté**, at the outbreak of war; **é. de rire**, to burst out laughing; **é. en sanglots**, to burst into tears; **é. de colère**, to fly into a rage **3.** vi (of jewels) to sparkle; **l'indignation éclate dans ses yeux**, his eyes are blazing with indignation. **éclatant** a **1.** loud, ringing (sound, laughter); piercing (shriek) **2.** glaring, dazzling (light, colour); sparkling (jewels).

éclectique [eklɛktik] a eclectic.

éclipse [eklips] nf eclipse.

éclipser [eklipse] vtr to eclipse; **s'é.**, to disappear, vanish.

éclopé, -ée [eklɔpe] **1.** a lame **2.** n slightly injured person.

éclore [eklɔr] vi def (pp **éclos**; pr ind **il éclot, ils éclosent**; impf **il éclosait**; no ph; aux usu être, occ avoir) **1.** (of eggs, chicks) to hatch (out) **2.** (of flowers) to open; (of day) to dawn.

éclosion [eklozjɔ̃] nf **1.** hatching (of eggs, chicks) **2.** opening, blossoming (of flowers).

écluse [eklyz] nf (canal) lock; **(porte d')é.**, sluice(gate).

éclusier, -ière [eklyzje, -jɛr] n lock keeper.

écœurement [ekœrmɑ̃] nm (a) nausea (b) disgust (c) discouragement.

écœurer [ekœre] vtr (a) to nauseate; to disgust (b)

to dishearten. **écœurant** a (a) nauseating, disgusting (b) disheartening.

école [ekɔl] nf (a) school; **é. maternelle**, nursery school, kindergarten; **é. primaire**, primary school; **é. libre** = independent school; **é. mixte**, co-educational school; **vous êtes à bonne é.**, you're in good hands (b) **les grandes écoles**, colleges of university level specializing in professional training; **é. normale**, college of education; = teacher training college (c) **é. d'équitation**, riding school.

écolier, -ière [ekɔlje, -jɛr] n (a) (primary) schoolboy, schoolgirl (b) novice.

écologie [ekɔlɔʒi] nf ecology.

écologiste [ekɔlɔʒist] n ecologist.

éconduire [ekɔ̃dɥir] vtr (conj like CONDUIRE) to show (s.o.) the door; to get rid of (s.o.) (politely); to dismiss (s.o.).

économat [ekɔnɔma] nm (a) bursarship (b) bursar's office (c) staff (discount) store.

économe [ekɔnɔm] **1.** n bursar (of college); steward **2.** a economical, thrifty, sparing.

économie [ekɔnɔmi] nf **1.** economy; **é. politique**, political economy **2.** economy, thrift; **faire une é. de temps**, to save time **3.** pl savings; **faire des économies**, to save money; **économies de bouts de chandelles**, cheeseparing. **économique** a **1.** economic (doctrine); **sciences économiques**, economics **2.** economical, inexpensive. **économiquement** adv economically; **les é. faibles**, the underprivileged.

économiser [ekɔnɔmize] vtr & i to economize, save (sur, on).

économiste [ekɔnɔmist] n economist.

écope [ekɔp] nf Nau: bailer.

écoper [ekɔpe] **1.** vtr Nau: to bail (out) **2.** vi F: to catch it, cop it; to get the blame.

écorce [ekɔrs] nf bark (of tree); rind, peel (of orange); **l'é. terrestre**, the earth's crust.

écorcher [ekɔrʃe] vtr **1.** to flay, to skin; F: **é. une langue**, to murder a language; **é. le client**, to fleece the customer **2.** (a) to graze, chafe (the skin) (b) to scrape; **son qui écorche l'oreille**, sound that grates on the ear.

écorchure [ekɔrʃyr] nf scratch, graze.

écorner [ekɔrne] vtr (a) to break the corner(s) off (sth); **livre écorné**, dog-eared book (b) **é. son capital**, to break into one's capital.

Écosse [ekɔs] Prnf Geog: Scotland. **écossais, -aise 1.** a Scottish, Scots **2.** n Scot; Scotsman, Scotswoman **3.** a & nm (tissu) **é.**, tartan **4.** nm Ling: Scots.

écosser [ekɔse] vtr to shell (peas).

écot [eko] nm **payer son é.**, to pay one's share.

écoulement [ekulmɑ̃] nm **1.** (a) (out)flow; drainage; **fossé d'é.**, drain; **(tube d')é.**, waste pipe (b) Med: discharge (c) dispersal (of crowd); flow (of traffic) **2.** sale (of goods).

écouler [ekule] vtr **1.** to sell (off) (goods); to utter (forged notes) **2. s'é.** (a) (of liquid) to flow out, run out; (of crowd) to disperse; (of money) to melt away (b) (of time) to pass, to slip away.

écourter [ekurte] vtr to shorten; to cut short (visit); to cut down (text).

écoute [ekut] nf **1. être aux écoutes**, (i) to eavesdrop (ii) to keep one's ears open **2.** Tp: WTel: listening-in; **é. de contrôle,** monitoring; **heures de grande é.,** peak listening time; *TV:* peak viewing time; *Tp:* **restez à l'é.,** hold the line, please; **écoutes téléphoniques,** (phone) tapping.

écouter [ekute] *vtr* 1. (*a*) to listen to (s.o., sth); **é. qn jusqu'au bout,** to hear s.o. out; **se faire é.,** to get a hearing; **é. aux portes,** to eavesdrop; **écoutez!** look (here)! (*b*) *WTel: Tp:* to listen in 2. to pay attention to (s.o.); **ne les écoutez pas!** don't mind them! **il s'écoute trop,** he coddles himself.

écouteur, -euse [ekutœr, -øz] *n* 1. (*a*) listener; **é. (aux portes),** eavesdropper (*b*) *WTel: Tp:* listener-in 2. *nm* (i) *Tp:* receiver (ii) *WTel:* earphone, headphone.

écrabouiller [ekrabuje] *vtr F:* to crush; to squash.

écran [ekrɑ̃] *nm* screen; *Cin:* **é. (de projection),** screen; **l'é.,** the cinéma; **porter à l'é.,** to film (sth); **le petit é.,** television.

écrasement [ekrazmɑ̃] *nm* crushing, squashing.

écraser [ekraze] 1. *vtr* (*a*) to crush; to squash; to flatten out; to swat (fly); **se faire é.,** to get run over; **écrasé d'impôts,** overburdened with taxes; **écrasé de travail,** overwhelmed with work (*b*) *P:* **en é.,** to sleep like a log 2. *vi* **écrase!** shut up! 3. **s'é.,** to collapse, crumple up; **s'é. sur le sol,** (*of pers*) to crash, to fall, to the ground; (*of aircraft*) to crash; **s'é. contre un arbre,** to crash into a tree. **écrasant** *a* crushing (defeat); overwhelming (proof, majority). **écrasé** *a* crushed, squashed; flat (nose).

écrémer [ekreme] *vtr* (**j'écrème; j'écrémerai**) to skim (milk).

écrevisse [ekrəvis] *nf* (freshwater) crayfish.

écrier (s') [sekrije] *vpr* to cry (out); to exclaim.

écrin [ekrɛ̃] *nm* (jewel) case.

écrire [ekrir] *vtr* (*prp* écrivant; *pp* écrit; *pr ind* j'écris, n. écrivons; *fu* j'écrirai, *ph* j'écrivis) (*a*) to write; **il écrit bien,** (i) he has good (hand)writing (ii) he's a good writer; **machine à é.,** typewriter; **é. une lettre à la machine,** to type a letter; **é. un mot à qn,** to scribble a note to s.o.; to send s.o. a line (*b*) to write (sth) down; *F:* **il est écrit que je n'irai pas,** I am fated not to go there; **c'est écrit,** it is, was, bound to happen (*c*) to write (book, song).

écrit [ekri] *nm* (*a*) writing; **par é.,** in writing (*b*) written document (*c*) *pl* works (of an author) (*d*) *Sch:* written exam(ination).

écriteau, -eaux [ekrito] *nm* placard; notice, sign.

écriture [ekrityr] *nf* 1. (*a*) writing script (*b*) (hand)writing; **é. à la machine,** typing 2. (*a*) *pl* (legal, commercial) papers, documents (*b*) *Book-k:* entry, item; **tenir les écritures,** to keep the accounts (*c*) **l'É. sainte,** Holy Scripture.

écrivain [ekrivɛ̃] *nm* author, writer; **femme é.,** woman writer; authoress.

écrou [ekru] *nm* (screw)nut.

écrouer [ekrue] *vtr* to consign (s.o.) to prison.

écroulement [ekrulmɑ̃] *nm* collapse, downfall.

écrouler (s') [sekrule] *vpr* to collapse, give way, fall in; (*of pers*) (i) to collapse (ii) to break down; *F:* **s'é. sur une chaise,** to drop onto a chair.

écru [ekry] *a* (*of material*) unbleached, natural-coloured; **soie écrue,** raw silk.

écu [eky] *nm* 1. shield 2. *Num: A:* crown.

écueil [ekœj] *nm* (*a*) reef, shelf; (*of ship*) **donner sur** les écueils, to strike the rocks (*b*) *Fig:* snag, stumbling block.

écuelle [ekɥɛl] *nf* bowl.

éculé [ekyle] *a* (*a*) (*of shoe*) down-at-heel (*b*) well worn (trick).

écume [ekym] *nf* 1. (*a*) froth; foam (*b*) scum (on jam); **é. de la société,** dregs of society 2. **é. (de mer),** meerschaum. **écumeux, -euse** *a* foamy.

écumer [ekyme] 1. *vtr* (*a*) to skim (soup) (*b*) to scour, pillage (countryside); **é. les mers,** to scour the seas 2. *vi* to foam, froth; **é. (de rage),** to foam with rage.

écumoire [ekymwar] *nf* skimmer, skimming ladle.

écureuil [ekyrœj] *nm* squirrel.

écurie [ekyri] *nf* stable; **mettre un cheval à l'é.,** to stable a horse; **é. (de courses),** (racing) stable.

écusson [ekysɔ̃] *nm* 1. shield, coat of arms 2. badge.

écuyer, -ère [ekɥije, -ɛr] *n* 1. *nm* (*a*) squire (*b*) equerry 2. *n* rider, horseman, horsewoman.

eczéma [ɛgzema] *nm* eczema.

édicter [edikte] *vtr* to decree.

édification [edifikasjɔ̃] *nf* 1. erection (of monument) 2. edification, moral improvement.

édifice [edifis] *nm* building, edifice; structure, fabric (of society).

édifier [edifje] *vtr* 1. to erect, build 2. (*a*) to edify (*b*) to enlighten, instruct (s.o.).

Édimbourg [edɛ̃bur] *Prnm Geog:* Edinburgh.

édit [edi] *nm* edict.

éditer [edite] *vtr* 1. to edit (text) 2. to publish (book).

éditeur, -trice [editœr, -tris] *n* (chief) editor; publisher.

édition [edisjɔ̃] *nf* 1. edition 2. publishing; **maison d'é.,** publishing firm.

éditorial, -aux [editorjal, -o] 1. *a* editorial 2. *nm* leading article, leader; editorial.

éditorialiste [editorjalist] *n* (*a*) leader writer (*b*) *WTel:* programme editor.

édredon [edrədɔ̃] *nm* eiderdown.

éducation [edykasjɔ̃] *nf* (*a*) education; **faire l'é. de qn,** to educate s.o.; **é. physique,** physical training (*b*) training (of animals) (*c*) upbringing, breeding; **sans é.,** ill bred; **il manque d'é.,** he has no manners. **éducateur, -trice** 1. *a* educational 2. *n* educator. **éducatif, -ive** *a* educative, educational.

édulcorer [edylkɔre] *vtr* 1. to sweeten (medicine) 2. to tone down, water down (report).

éduquer [edyke] *vtr* to bring up, to educate (child); **mal éduqué,** ill-bred.

effacement [efasmɑ̃] *nm* 1. obliteration (of word); wearing away (of inscription) 2. unobtrusiveness, self effacement.

effacer [efase] *vtr* (**n. effaçons**) 1. (*a*) to efface, obliterate, delete, erase; **e. un mot,** to rub out a word; **e. une tache,** to wash out, wipe out, a stain; **e. des imperfections,** to smooth out imperfections; **e. qch de sa mémoire,** to blot sth out of one's memory (*b*) **e. le corps,** to stand sideways; **e. les épaules,** to throw back the shoulders 2. **s'e.** (*a*) to become obliterated; to wear away; to fade (away); **s'e. à l'eau,** to wash off (*b*) to stand aside; to keep in the background. **effacé** *a* unobtrusive; retiring (pers, manner).

effarement [efarmɑ̃] *nm* fright; dismay.

effarer [efare] *vtr* to frighten, scare (s.o.); to dismay; to bewilder. **effarant** *a* bewildering.

effaroucher [efaruʃe] *vtr* **1.** to startle, scare away **2.** s'e. (*a*) to be frightened away (**de**, at, by); to take fright (**de**, at) (*b*) (*of pers*) to be shocked.

effectif, -ive [efɛktif, -iv] **1.** *a* (*a*) effective, efficacious (*b*) effective, actual; **valeur effective,** real value **2.** *nm* (*a*) *Mil:* strength; manpower; **à e. réduit,** under strength; *Sch:* **réduire l'e. des classes à 25,** to reduce the size of classes to 25 (*b*) *Mil:* **les effectifs,** the total strength; **crise d'effectifs,** shortage of manpower. **effectivement** *adv* **1.** effectively **2.** actually, in reality, really **3.** (*as answer*) that is so.

effectuer [efɛktɥe] *vtr* **1.** to effect, carry out, accomplish; to execute (operation); to make (payment); to accomplish (journey) **2.** s'e., to be made; (*of journey*) to take place.

efféminé [efemine] *a* effeminate.

effervescence [efɛrvesɑ̃s] *nf* **1.** effervescence **2.** agitation; **être en e.,** to be seething with excitement. **effervescent** *a* effervescent.

effet [efɛ] *nm* **1.** effect, result; **faire de l'e.,** to be effective; **à cet e.,** for this purpose; with this end in view; **sans e.,** ineffective, ineffectual **2.** (*a*) action, operation, working; **mettre un projet à l'e.,** en e., to put a plan into action; (*of law*) **prendre e.,** to become operative (*b*) *Cr: Ten:* spin, break (*c*) *MecE:* e. utile, efficiency; **à simple, à double,** e., single-action, double-action (*d*) **en e.,** as a matter of fact; indeed; **vous oubliez vos paquets!—en e.!** you are forgetting your parcels!—so I am! **3.** (*a*) impression; **voilà l'e. que cela m'a produit,** that is how it struck me; *F:* **ça m'a fait un e.,** it gave me quite a turn; **faire de l'e.,** to attract attention; **cela fait bon e.,** it looks well; **manquer son e.,** to fall flat; to misfire (*b*) *Art:* e. de lune, moonlight effect; *Cin: etc:* **effets sonores,** sound effects **4.** *Com:* e. de commerce, bill (of exchange); **e. à vue,** sight draft; **effets publics,** government stock, securities **5.** *pl* possessions, belongings; clothes, things; **effets mobiliers,** personal effects.

efficacité [efikasite] *nf* effectiveness; efficiency; efficacy. **efficace** *a* efficacious; effective; efficient. **efficacement** *adv* efficaciously; effectively; efficiently.

effigie [efiʒi] *nf* effigy.

effiler [efile] *vtr* **1.** *Tex:* to unravel, to fray **2.** to taper **3.** s'e. (*a*) to fray (*b*) to taper. **effilé** *a* **1.** frayed **2.** tapered; tapering (fingers), slender (figure).

effilocher (s') [sefiloʃe] *vpr* to fray.

efflanqué [eflɑ̃ke] *a* raw-boned (animal); skinny (pers).

effleurement [eflœrmɑ̃] *nm* (light) touch; skimming.

effleurer [eflœre] *vtr* to touch lightly; to skim; to graze (skin); **e. un sujet,** to touch on a subject; **quelques soupçons l'avaient effleuré,** some misgivings had crossed his mind.

effluve [eflyv] *nm* emanation.

effondrement [efɔ̃drəmɑ̃] *nm* breaking down; collapse; slump (in prices); **il est dans un état d'e. complet,** he's in a state of total collapse.

effondrer (s') [sefɔ̃dre] *vpr* to fall in; to break down; to collapse; (*of prices*) to slump; s'e. **dans un fauteuil,** to sink into an armchair.

efforcer (s') [seforse] *vpr* (*n. n.* **efforçons**) s'e. de faire qch, to strive, to do one's best, to make every effort, to do sth.

effort [efor] *nm* **1.** effort, exertion; **faire un e. sur soi-même,** to exercise self-control; **faire tous ses efforts,** to do one's utmost; **e. financier,** financial outlay; **sans e.,** effortlessly, easily; **faire des efforts de mémoire,** to rack one's brains **2.** *Mec:* strain, stress.

effraction [efraksjɔ̃] *nf Jur:* break-in; house breaking; **vol avec e.,** burglary.

effranger [efrɑ̃ʒe] *vtr* to fray (out) (edges of material).

effrayer [efreje] *vtr* (**j'effraie, j'effraye**) **1.** (*a*) to frighten, scare, startle (s.o.) (*b*) to appal **2.** s'e., to take fright; to get frightened. **effrayant** *a* (*a*) terrifying, frightening, appalling (*b*) *F:* tremendous; terrific (heat, appetite).

effréné [efrene] *a* unbridled; frantic.

effritement [efritmɑ̃] *nm* crumbling (away), disintegration.

effriter [efrite] *vtr* **1.** to cause to crumble, to disintegrate **2.** s'e., to crumble (away).

effroi [efrwa] *nm* fright, terror, fear, dread.

effronté [efrɔ̃te] *a* shameless, brazen; impudent; cheeky. **effrontément** *adv* shamelessly, brazenly, impudently; cheekily.

effronterie [efrɔ̃tri] *nf* effrontery, insolence, impudence; cheek.

effroyable [efrwajabl] *a* frightful, dreadful, appalling. **effroyablement** *adv* appallingly; *F:* tremendously.

effusion [efyzjɔ̃] *nf* **1.** effusion, outpouring; e. de sang, bloodshed **2.** effusiveness; **avec e.,** effusively.

égal, -aux [egal, -o] *a* **1.** (*a*) equal; **de force égale,** evenly matched; **à écartement é., à égale distance,** equidistant; *n* **traiter qn d'é. à é.,** to treat s.o. as an equal; **sans é.,** matchless; **à l'é. de,** as much as, equally with (*b*) level, even; steady (pace); **d'humeur égale,** even-tempered **2.** (all) the same; **cela m'est (bien) é.,** it's all the same to me; I don't mind; I don't care; **c'est é., il aurait pu venir,** all the same, he could have come. **également** *adv* equally; also; **j'en veux é.,** I want some too.

égaler [egale] *vtr* **1.** to equalize; to make (s.o., sth) equal **2.** to equal, to be equal to (sth); **deux et deux égalent quatre,** two and two make four **3.** s'é., to equal, be equal to.

égalisation [egalizasjɔ̃] *nf* **1.** equalization **2.** levelling. **égalisateur, -trice** *a* equalizing.

égaliser [egalize] *vtr* **1.** to equalize **2.** to level.

égalité [egalite] *nf* **1.** equality; **sur un pied d'é.,** on an equal footing, on equal terms; *Sp:* **é. de points, tie; à é.,** (*of result*) level; (*of teams*) drawn, tied; *Ten:* **é. à 40,** deuce **2.** evenness, regularity (of surface, breathing). **égalitaire** *a & n* egalitarian.

égard [egar] *nm* (*a*) consideration, respect; **avoir é. à qch,** to allow for sth; to take sth into consideration; **eu é. à,** in consideration of; **sans é. à,** regardless of, irrespective of; **à tous les égards,** in every respect; **n'ayez aucune crainte à cet é.,** don't worry about that; **à l'é. de,** with reference to, with respect to; **être injuste à l'é. de qn,** to be unjust to(wards) s.o. (*b*) **faire qch par é. pour qn,** to do sth (i) out of consideration for s.o. (ii) for s.o.'s sake; **sans é. pour qn,** with no consideration for s.o.

égarement [egarmã] *nm* 1. (*a*) mislaying (of object) (*b*) bewilderment; **é. (d'esprit)**, (mental) aberration 2. deviation; **il est revenu de ses égarements**, he has seen the error of his ways.

égarer [egare] *vtr* 1. (*a*) to lead (s.o.) astray; to mislead, misguide (s.o.) (*b*) to mislay, lose (sth) (*c*) to bewilder (s.o.) 2. **s'é.** (*a*) to lose one's way; to go astray; **colis qui s'est égaré**, parcel that has got lost (*b*) **son esprit s'égare**, his mind is wandering. **égaré** *a* lost; stray (bullet); remote (village); distraught (mind).

égayer [egɛje] *vtr* (**j'égaie, j'égaye; j'égaierai, j'égayerai**) 1. to enliven; to cheer (s.o.) up; to brighten (up) 2. **s'é.**, to be amused; **s'é. aux dépens de qn**, to make fun of s.o.

égide [eʒid] *nf* **sous l'é. de**, under the aegis, the care of.

églantier [eglãtje] *nm* wild rose, dog rose (bush).

églantine [eglãtin] *nf* wild rose, dog rose (flower).

église [egliz] *nf* church.

égoïsme [egɔism] *nm* selfishness. **égoïste** 1. *n* egoist 2. *a* selfish, egoistic. **égoïstement** *adv* selfishly, egoistically.

égorger [egɔrʒe] *vtr* (**n. égorgeons**) 1. to cut the throat of (s.o., animal) 2. to butcher, massacre, slaughter (persons).

égout [egu] *nm* sewer; drain; **eaux d'é.**, sewerage.

égoutier [egutje] *nm* sewerman, sewer worker.

égoutter [egute] 1. *vtr* to drain (cheese, lettuce); to strain (vegetables) 2. *vi* **faire é.**, to drain off (water); to hang up (washing) to drip 3. **s'é.**, to drain, drip.

égouttoir [egutwar] *nm* (*a*) draining board (*b*) draining rack, drainer.

égratigner [egratiɲe] *vtr* 1. to scratch 2. to nettle, ruffle (s.o.).

égratignure [egratiɲyr] *nf* 1. scratch 2. gibe; dig (at s.o.).

égrener [egrəne] *vtr* (**j'égrène, n. égrenons**) 1. (*a*) to shell (peas); to pick off (grapes from the bunch); to gin (cotton) (*b*) **é. son chapelet**, to tell one's beads 2. **s'é.** (*a*) (*of seed, berries*) to fall; to drop (from the bunch) (*b*) **des lumières s'égrènent le long du quai**, a string of lights stretches along the quay.

égrillard [egrijar] *a* ribald.

Égypte [eʒipt] *Prnf Geog:* Egypt. **égyptien, -ienne** *a & n* Egyptian.

eh [e] *int* hey! **eh bien!** well! now then!

éhonté [eõte] *a* shameless.

éjecter [eʒɛkte] *vtr* to eject; *F:* to throw (s.o.) out.

éjection [eʒɛksjõ] *nf* ejection; *F:* expulsion (of s.o.).

élaboration [elabɔrasjõ] *nf* elaboration.

élaborer [elabɔre] *vtr* to elaborate; to work out (plan).

élagage [elagaʒ] *nm* pruning (of tree).

élaguer [elage] *vtr* to prune (tree).

élagueur [elagœr] *nm* pruner.

élan¹ [elã] *nm* 1. (*a*) spring, bound, dash; (*when jumping*) **prendre son é.**, to take off; **saut sans é.**, avec é., standing jump, running jump (*b*) **travailler avec é.**, to work enthusiastically (*c*) impetus; **perdre son é.**, to lose momentum 2. burst, outburst (of feeling); impulse.

élan² *nm Z:* (*a*) (Scandinavian) elk (*b*) **é. du Canada**, moose.

élancé [elãse] *a* tall and slim; slender.

élancement [elãsmã] *nm* shooting pain.

élancer [elãse] *v* (**j'élançai(s), n. élançons**) 1. *vi* (*of finger*) to throb, to shoot (with pain) 2. (*a*) **s'é. en avant**, to spring forward; **s'é. sur qn**, to rush at s.o.; *F:* to go for s.o.; **s'é. à l'assaut**, to throw oneself into the fray (*b*) (*of child, plant*) to shoot up (*c*) **s'é. vers le ciel**, to soar skyward.

élargir [elarʒir] *vtr* 1. (*a*) to widen (road); to stretch (shoes); to let out (dress); to enlarge (hole) (*b*) to enlarge, extend (one's ideas, one's property); to widen (horizon) (*c*) to set (prisoner) free 2. **s'é.** (*a*) to widen (out); to broaden (out); (*of shoes*) to stretch (*b*) (*of ideas*) to grow, extend.

élargissement [elarʒismã] *nm* 1. widening, broadening 2. release (of prisoner).

élasticité [elastisite] *nf* elasticity; springiness; resilience (of pers). **élastique** 1. *a* (*a*) elastic; (made of) rubber (*b*) resilient, springy; **d'un pas é.**, with a springy step 2. *nm* (*a*) elastic; **en é.**, elastic(ated) (*b*) elastic band, rubber band.

Elbe [elb] *Geog:* 1. *Prnf* (the island of) Elba 2. *Prnm* **l'E.**, (the river) Elbe.

électeur, -trice [elɛktœr, -tris] *n* 1. *Hist:* Elector, Electress 2. elector, voter; **mes électeurs**, my constituents.

élection [elɛksjõ] *nf* 1. election, polling; **élections législatives**, (parliamentary) elections); **é. partielle**, by-election 2. election, choice, preference; **mon pays d'é.**, the country of my choice. **électoral, -aux** *a* electoral; election (committee).

électorat [elɛktɔra] *nm* electorate.

électricien [elɛktrisjẽ] *nm* electrician.

électricité [elɛktrisite] *nf* electricity.

électrification [elɛktrifikasjõ] *nf* electrification.

électrifier [elɛktrifje] *vtr* to electrify.

électrique [elɛktrik] *a* electric; electrical (unit, industry). **électriquement** *adv* electrically.

électriser [elɛktrize] *vtr* to electrify.

électro-aimant [elɛktroɛmã] *nm* electromagnet; *pl* **électro-aimants**.

électrocardiogramme [elɛktrokardjogram] *nm* electrocardiogram.

électrochoc [elɛktroʃɔk] *nm* **traitement par électrochocs**, electric shock treatment.

électrocuter [elɛktrokyte] *vtr* to electrocute.

électrocution [elɛktrokysjõ] *nf* electrocution.

électrode [elɛktrɔd] *nf* electrode.

électroménager [elɛktromenaʒe] *a* (domestic) electrical; *nm* **l'électroménager**, electric household appliances.

électron [elɛktrõ] *nm Ph:* electron.

électronicien, -ienne [elɛktrɔnisjẽ, -jɛn] *n* electronics engineer.

électronique [elɛktrɔnik] 1. *a* electronic 2. *nf* electronics.

électrophone [elɛktrofɔn] *nm* record player.

élégance [elegãs] *nf* elegance. **élégant** *a* elegant; smart, fashionable. **élégamment** *adv* elegantly.

élégie [eleʒi] *nf* elegy.

élément [elemã] *nm* 1. *Ch: Ph: etc:* element 2. (*a*) component; ingredient (of medicine); **é. décisif**, deciding factor; *Tchn:* **é. chauffant**, heating element; **éléments de cuisine**, kitchen units (*b*) *El:* cell (of battery) **3.** *pl* (*a*) rudiments, first principles (of a science) (*b*) data (of problem). **élémentaire** *a* elementary; rudimentary.

éléphant [elefɑ̃] *nm* elephant.

élevage [elvaʒ] *nm* **1.** breeding (of stock); stock farming; **faire de l'é.**, to breed; **poulet d'é.**, battery chicken **2.** (stock) farm; *NAm:* ranch.

élévation [elevasjɔ̃] *nf* **1.** (*a*) elevation, lifting, raising; *Ecc:* elevation (*b*) erection, setting up (of statue) **2.** rise (in temperature, price) **3.** grandeur (of style) **4.** *Arch:* elevation, vertical section **5.** rise in the ground; height.

élève [elɛv] *n* pupil; student; **é. pilote**, student pilot.

élever [elve] *vtr* (**j'élève**, **n. élevons**) **1.** (*a*) to raise (height, temperature, one's voice, prices); to lift up (load) (*b*) to promote (employee) (*c*) to elevate (the mind) **2.** (*a*) to erect, set up (machine, statue) (*b*) to raise (objection) **3.** to bring up, rear (child); to rear (stock); to breed (cattle, horses); to keep (bees); to grow (plants); **bébé élevé au biberon**, bottle-fed baby **4.** **s'é.** (*a*) to rise (up); **le château s'élève sur la colline**, the castle stands on the hill (*b*) (*of doubts, objection*) to arise (*c*) **le vent s'élève**, the wind is rising (*d*) **s'é. contre qch**, to protest, to make a stand, against sth (*e*) to raise oneself; (*of bird*) to rise up (*f*) (*in society*) to rise; **s'é. à force de travail**, to work one's way up (*g*) (*of temperature, prices*) to rise; **le compte s'élève à mille francs**, the bill comes, amounts, to a thousand francs. **élevé** *a* **1.** high (mountain, price); noble, elevated (style, mind); exalted (position) **2.** **bien é.**, well brought up, well-mannered; **mal é.**, ill-mannered; rude.

éleveur, -euse [elvœr, -øz] *n* stockbreeder.

elfe [ɛlf] *nm* elf.

éligibilité [eliʒibilite] *nf* eligibility. **éligible** *a* eligible.

élimer [elime] *vtr* to wear the nap off (material).

élimination [eliminasjɔ̃] *nf* elimination. **éliminatoire** *a* eliminatory; *Sp:* **épreuve é.**, *nf* é., (eliminating) heat.

éliminer [elimine] *vtr* to eliminate (candidate, suspect); to get rid of (body wastes); to rule out (theory); *Sp:* **être éliminé**, to be knocked out (in a tournament).

élire [elir] *vtr* (*conj like* LIRE) to elect, choose.

élite [elit] *nf* élite; first-class; **régiment d'é.**, crack regiment.

élitisme [elitism] *nm* elitism.

élixir [eliksir] *nm* elixir.

elle, elles [ɛl] *pers pron f* **1.** (*unstressed*) (*of pers*) she, they; (*of thg*) it, they; **qu'elle est jolie, cette broche!** how pretty that brooch is! **2.** (*stressed*) (*a*) (*subject*) she, it, they; **c'est elle, ce sont elles**, it is she, they; *F:* it's her, it's them; **je fais comme e.**, I do what she does; **e.-même**, herself (*b*) (*object*) her, it; them; **je suis content d'e.**, I'm pleased with her; **il aimait sa patrie et mourut pour e.**, he loved his country and died for it; **la voiture est à e.**, the car belongs to her, is hers; **e. ne pense qu'à e.**, she thinks only of herself.

élocution [elɔkysjɔ̃] *nf* elocution.

éloge [elɔʒ] *nm* **1.** culogy; **é. funèbre**, funeral oration **2.** praise; **faire l'é. de qn**, to speak highly of s.o., to

praise s.o. **élogieux, -euse** *a* eulogistic, laudatory.

éloigné [elwaɲe] *a* far (away), distant, remote (place, time); **é. de 5 km**, 5 km away; **maison éloignée de la gare**, house a long way from the station; **date plus éloignée**, later date; **parent é.**, distant relative; **rien n'est plus é. de ma pensée**, nothing is further from my thoughts; **se tenir é.**, to hold (oneself) aloof.

éloignement [elwaɲmɑ̃] *nm* **1.** removal; postponement; deferment (of payment) **2.** (*a*) absence (*b*) distance, remoteness.

éloigner [elwaɲe] *vtr* **1.** (*a*) to (re)move, to move away (s.o., sth) to a distance, further off; to get (sth) out of the way; **ils sont éloignés d'un kilomètre**, they are one kilometre apart; **é. une pensée**, to dismiss a thought (*b*) to postpone, put off (departure), to defer (payment) (*c*) to alienate, to estrange (s.o.) **2.** **s'é.** (*a*) to move off, withdraw; **ne vous éloignez pas!** don't go away! **s'é. du sujet**, to wander from the subject (*b*) **éloignez-vous un peu**, stand further back.

élongation [elɔ̃gasjɔ̃] *nf* pulled muscle.

éloquence [elɔkɑ̃s] *nf* eloquence. **éloquent** *a* eloquent; **ces chiffres sont éloquents**, these figures speak volumes. **éloquemment** *adv* eloquently.

élu, -e [ely] **1.** *a* chosen; elected; successful (candidate) **2.** *n* (*a*) *Ecc:* **les élus**, the elect (*b*) elected member.

élucidation [elysidasjɔ̃] *nf* elucidation.

élucider [elyside] *vtr* to elucidate, to clear up.

éluder [elyde] *vtr* to elude, evade; to dodge (question).

émaciation [emasjasjɔ̃] *nf* emaciation. **émacié** *a* emaciated.

émail, émaux [emaj, emo] *nm* enamel.

émailler [emaje] *vtr* **1.** to enamel **2.** *Cer:* to glaze **3.** (*of flowers*) to fleck, spangle (the fields); to pepper (text) (with mistakes).

émanation [emanasjɔ̃] *nf* emanation.

émancipation [emɑ̃sipasjɔ̃] *nf* emancipation.

émanciper [emɑ̃sipe] *vtr* **1.** to emancipate **2.** **s'é.**, to become liberated, independent.

émaner [emane] *vi* (*a*) (*of fumes*) to emanate (**de**, **from**) (*b*) **ordres émanant de qn**, orders (coming) from s.o.

émargement [emarʒəmɑ̃] *nm* initialling in the margin; **feuille d'é.**, pay sheet.

émarger [emarʒe] *vtr* (**j'émargeai(s)**) (*a*) **é. un compte**, to initial an account (in the margin) (*b*) *vi* to sign for, to draw, one's salary.

emballage [ɑ̃balaʒ] *nm* (*a*) packing, wrapping (of parcels) (*b*) packing material; boxes, crates; package.

emballement [ɑ̃balmɑ̃] *nm* **1.** (*of engine*) racing **2.** (*a*) excitement; burst of enthusiasm (*b*) angry outburst.

emballer [ɑ̃bale] *vtr* **1.** (*a*) to pack (goods); to wrap (sth) up; *P:* **e. qn**, to run s.o. in (*b*) (i) to race (the engine) (ii) *vi Sp:* to put on a spurt (*c*) *F:* to excite (s.o.); **être emballé par qch**, to be (mad) keen on sth **2.** **s'e.** (*a*) (*of horse*) to bolt (*b*) (*of engine*) to race (*c*) *F:* to be carried away (by enthusiasm); **ne vous emballez pas!** keep your head! keep cool!

embarcadère [ɑ̃barkadɛr] *nm* landing stage; wharf, quay.

embarcation [ābarkasjō] *nf* boat; small craft.

embardée [ābarde] *nf Nau:* yaw, lurch; *Aut:* swerve; **faire une e.,** to swerve (across the road).

embargo [ābargo] *nm* embargo.

embarquement [ābarkəmā] *nm* 1. embarcation (of passengers); loading (of goods) 2. boarding (ship, aircraft).

embarquer [ābarke] 1. *vtr* to embark (passengers); to put (passengers) on (train, bus); to ship (goods); *Fig:* **e. qn dans un procès,** to involve s.o. in a lawsuit; *P:* **e. un voleur,** to run in a thief 2. *vi & pr* (*a*) to embark; (**s'**)**e.** (**sur un navire**), to board (ship) (*b*) **s'e. dans une entreprise,** to embark on an undertaking.

embarras [ābara] *nm* 1. (*a*) **e. de voitures,** traffic block (*b*) **e. gastrique,** stomach upset; bilious attack 2. (*a*) difficulty, trouble; **se trouver dans l'e.,** to be in (financial) difficulties; **tirer qn d'e.,** to help s.o. out of a difficulty (*b*) *F:* **faire des e.,** to make a fuss 3. (*a*) embarrassment; hesitation; **n'avoir que l'e. du choix,** to have too much to choose from; **je suis dans l'e.,** I'm in a fix (*b*) embarrassment, confusion.

embarrassant [ābarasā] *a* 1. cumbersome 2. (*a*) perplexing (*b*) embarrassing, awkward.

embarrasser [ābarase] *vtr* 1. (*a*) to encumber, hamper (s.o.); to obstruct; **est-ce que ma valise vous embarrasse?** is my case in your, in the, way? (*b*) to embarrass; (i) to trouble, bother (s.o.) (ii) to perplex, puzzle (s.o.) (iii) to make (s.o.) feel awkward 2. **s'e.** (*a*) to burden, encumber, oneself (with sth) (*b*) (i) to trouble oneself (about sth) (ii) to feel embarrassed.

embarrassant *a* 1. cumbersome; awkward 2. (*a*) puzzling (*b*) embarrassing. **embarrassé** *a* 1. hampered (movements); **avoir les mains embarrassées,** to have one's hands full; **avoir l'estomac embarrassé,** to have an upset stomach 2. (*a*) puzzled (*b*) embarrassed.

embauchage [āboʃaʒ] *nm* engaging, taking on, hiring (of workmen).

embauche [āboʃ] *nf* 1. = embauchage 2. **chercher de l'e.,** to look for a job.

embaucher [āboʃe] *vtr* to engage, take on, sign on, (workers); to hire (farm hands).

embaumement [ābommā] *nm* embalming.

embaumer [ābome] *vtr* 1. to embalm (corpse) 2. (*a*) to perfume, scent; **air embaumé,** balmy air (*b*) *vi* to be fragrant (*c*) to smell of (sth); **l'église embaume l'encens,** the church is heavy with incense.

embellir [ābelir] 1. *vtr* to embellish; to improve (s.o.'s) looks 2. *vi* to improve (in looks).

embellissement [ābelismā] *nm* 1. embellishing, improving 2. improvement (in looks) 3. embellishment.

embêtement [ābetmā] *nm F:* annoyance; **j'ai des embêtements,** I'm in difficulties.

embêter [ābete] *vtr F:* 1. to annoy; **ça m'embête d'y aller,** (i) I can't be bothered to go there (ii) I wish I didn't have to go there 2. **s'e.,** to be, to get, bored. **embêtant** *a F:* (*a*) annoying (*b*) tiresome; boring.

emblée (d') [dāble] *adv phr* directly; right away; straight off.

emblème [āblɛm] *nm* 1. (*a*) emblem, device (*b*) badge, crest 2. symbol, sign.

emboîter [ābwate] *vtr* (*a*) to encase (*b*) to pack in tins, boxes (*c*) to fit (things) together; to joint; **les**

pièces s'emboîtent, the pieces interlock (*d*) **e. le pas à qn,** (i) to follow in, to dog, s.o.'s footsteps (ii) to follow suit.

embonpoint [ābōpwɛ] *nm* stoutness; **prendre de l'e.,** to get fat.

embouchure [ābuʃyr] *nf* 1. *Mus:* mouthpiece 2. mouth (of river).

embourber (s') [sāburbe] *vpr* to stick, to get stuck, in the mud.

embourgeoiser (s') [sāburʒwaze] *vpr* to become middle class.

embout [ābu] *nm* tip (of umbrella, stick); nozzle (of hose).

embouteillage [ābutɛjaʒ] *nm* (*a*) bottleneck (in street) (*b*) traffic jam; congestion (of traffic); hold up.

embouteiller [ābutɛje] *vtr* to block, to jam (traffic); **circulation embouteillée,** congested traffic.

emboutir [ābutir] *vtr* 1. to stamp (metal); to emboss 2. to bash (sth) in; **e. un arbre,** to crash (one's car) into a tree.

embranchement [ābrāʃmā] *nm* 1. branching (off) 2. (road) junction 3. (*a*) side road (*b*) *Rail:* branch line (*c*) *NatHist:* sub-kingdom.

embraser [ābraze] *vtr* 1. (*a*) to set (sth) ablaze (*b*) (*of sun*) to scorch (ground) (*c*) (*of sunset*) to set aglow 2. **s'e.** (*a*) to catch fire (*b*) to glow.

embrassade [ābrasad] *nf* embrace; hug.

embrasser [ābrase] *vtr* 1. (*a*) to embrace (s.o.); to hug (s.o.) (*b*) to kiss; **ils se sont embrassés,** they kissed; *Corr:* **je t'embrasse de tout mon cœur,** with much love (*c*) to take up (career); to seize (opportunity) 2. to contain, include, take in; to cover (facts of a case).

embrasure [ābrazyr] *nf* embrasure; window, door, recess.

embrayage [ābrɛjaʒ] *nm* 1. engaging (of the clutch) 2. clutch.

embrayer [ābrɛje] *vtr* (**j'embraie, j'embraye**) *MecE:* to connect, couple, engage; *vi* (i) to engage the gear (ii) *Aut:* to let in the clutch.

embrigader [ābrigade] *vtr* to enrol, to dragoon (a group of workers).

embrocher [ābroʃe] *vtr Cu:* to spit (meat).

embrouillement [ābrujmā] *nm* 1. entanglement 2. confusion (of ideas); jumbled state (of things).

embrouiller [ābruje] *vtr* 1. (*a*) to tangle (thread) (*b*) to confuse, muddle; **e. la question,** to cloud, confuse, the issue 2. **s'e.** (*a*) (*of threads*) to get tangled (*b*) (*of pers*) to get muddled, confused.

embroussaillé [ābrusaje] *a* covered with bushes; *F:* tousled (hair).

embrumer [ābryme] *vtr* 1. to cover (landscape) with mist, haze, fog 2. **s'e.,** to mist over. **embrumé** *a* misty; clouded.

embrun [ābrœ̃] *nm usu pl* spray, spindrift.

embryon [ābriō] *nm Biol:* embryo. **embryonnaire** *a* embryonic.

embûche [ābyʃ] *nf usu pl* plot (against s.o.); trap.

embuer [ābɥe] *vtr* (*of steam*) to mist up, over; to cloud (glass).

embuscade [ābyskad] *nf* ambush; **se tenir en e.,** to lie in ambush.

embusquer (s') [sābyske] *vpr* to lie in ambush.

éméché [emeʃe] a F: (slightly) tipsy; (a bit) screwed.

émeraude [ɛmrod] 1. nf emerald 2. a inv & nf emerald green.

émergence [emɛrʒɑ̃s] nf emergence.

émerger [emɛrʒe] vi (n. émergeons) 1. to emerge 2. to come into view; (from background) to come to light.

émeri [emri] nm emery; **toile (d')é.**, emery paper.

émerveillement [emɛrvɛjmɑ̃] nm (i) amazement (ii) wonder; **c'était un é.**, it was wonderful.

émerveiller [emɛrvɛje] vtr 1. to amaze; to fill (s.o.) with (i) wonder (ii) admiration. **s'é.**, to be filled, struck, with (i) amazement (ii) admiration.

émétique [emetik] a & nm emetic.

émetteur, -trice [emɛtœr, -tris] 1. a (a) issuing (banker) (b) WTel: **poste é.**, (i) transmitting (ii) broadcasting, station 2. nm WTel: transmitter.

émetteur-récepteur [emɛtœreseptœr] nm WTel: transmitter-receiver; pl émetteurs-récepteurs.

émettre [emɛtr] vtr (conj like METTRE) 1. (a) to emit (sound, heat); to give off (fumes); to give out (heat) (b) to express (opinion, wishes) (c) WTel: (i) to send out, transmit (ii) vtr & i to broadcast 2. to issue (cheque, banknotes).

émeute [emøt] nf riot; **faire é.**, to riot; **chef d'é.**, ringleader.

émeutier, -ière [emøtje, -jɛr] n rioter.

émietter [emjete] vtr 1. (a) to crumb (bread); to crumble (up) biscuit (b) to fritter away (a fortune) 2. **s'é.**, (of biscuit) to crumble; (of empire) to disintegrate, break up.

émigrant, -ante [emigrɑ̃, -ɑ̃t] 1. a emigrating 2. n emigrant.

émigration [emigrasjɔ̃] nf emigration.

émigré, -ée [emigre] n (a) Hist: émigré (b) (political) exile, refugee.

émigrer [emigre] vi to emigrate.

émincer [emɛ̃se] vtr (j'émincai(s)) to slice finely, thinly; to shred (vegetables).

éminence [eminɑ̃s] nf (a) rise, hill, height (b) eminence, distinction; Ecc: (cardinal) Eminence; **l'É. grise**, the power behind the throne. **éminent** a eminent; distinguished. **éminemment** adv eminently.

émissaire [emisɛr] nm emissary; a **bouc é.**, scapegoat.

émission [emisjɔ̃] nf 1. (a) emission; utterance (of sound); sending out (of signals) (b) WTel: (i) transmission (ii) broadcasting 2. issue (of tickets, banknotes) 3. broadcast.

emmagasinage [ɑ̃magazinaʒ] nm storage; accumulation.

emmagasiner [ɑ̃magazine] vtr 1. to store, warehouse 2. to accumulate (energy).

emmailloter [ɑ̃majote] vtr to swaddle (baby); to bind up, wrap up (limb).

emmêlement [ɑ̃mɛlmɑ̃] nm 1. tangling 2. tangle, muddle.

emmêler [ɑ̃mɛle] vtr 1. (a) to tangle (b) to mix up (facts); to muddle (story) 2. **s'e.**, to become tangled, mixed up; to get into a tangle, a muddle.

emménagement [ɑ̃menaʒmɑ̃] nm moving in.

emménager [ɑ̃menaʒe] vi (j'emménageai(s)) to move in.

emmener [ɑ̃mne] vtr (j'emmène) to take (s.o.) away, out; **je vous emmène avec moi**, I am taking you with me; **emmenez-le!** take him away! **e. qn au théâtre**, to take s.o. to the theatre.

emmerder [ɑ̃mɛrde] vtr P: (a) to annoy, bug (s.o.); **tu m'emmerdes**, you're a pain in the neck (b) **je l'emmerde**, he can go and get stuffed.

emmitoufler [ɑ̃mitufle] vtr to wrap (s.o.) up; **s'e.**, to muffle (oneself) up.

emmurer [ɑ̃myre] vtr to immure, wall in.

émoi [emwa] nm emotion, agitation; **en é.**, in a state of excitement; **toute la ville était en é.**, the whole town was in a commotion.

émoluments [emɔlymɑ̃] nmpl emoluments, salary.

émotion [emosjɔ̃] nf emotion; **vive é.**, excitement; thrill; **j'ai eu une é.**, I've had a shock. **émotif, -ive** a emotive. **émotionnel, -elle** a emotional.

émotionner [emosjone] vtr to touch, move, upset, s.o.; **s'é.**, to get excited.

émotivité [emotivite] nf emotionalism.

émoulu [emuly] a F: **frais é. (du collège)**, fresh from school.

émousser [emuse] vtr (a) to blunt (edge, pencil) (b) to dull, deaden (senses); to take the edge off (appetite).

émoustiller [emustije] vtr to exhilarate.

émouvoir [emuvwar] vtr (pp **ému**; otherwise conj like MOUVOIR) 1. (a) to excite, stir up, rouse (b) to affect, touch; **facile à é.**, emotional 2. **s'é.** (a) to get excited (b) to be touched, moved; **sans s'é.**, calmly. **émouvant** a moving, touching.

empailler [ɑ̃paje] vtr to stuff (animal).

empailleur, -euse [ɑ̃pajœr, -øz] n taxidermist.

empaqueter [ɑ̃pakte] vtr (j'empaquette) to pack (sth) up; to wrap (sth) up.

emparer (s') [sɑ̃pare] vpr s'e. de qch., to take hold of, lay hands on, seize, take possession of, get hold of, sth.

empâter [ɑ̃pate] vtr 1. to coat (palate) 2. **s'e.**, to thicken out.

empêchement [ɑ̃peʃmɑ̃] nm obstacle, hindrance; hitch; **je n'ai pas pu venir car j'ai eu un e.**, I couldn't come as something turned up (at the last minute).

empêcher [ɑ̃peʃe] vtr 1. to prevent, hinder, impede; **e. qn de faire qch**, to prevent s.o. from doing sth; impers: **(il) n'empêche que cela nous a coûté cher**, all the same, it has cost us a lot; F: **n'empêche**, (i) all the same (ii) so what? 2. **s'e.**, (usu neg) to refrain (de, from); **je ne pouvais m'e. de rire**, I couldn't help laughing. **empêché** a puzzled, at a loss; embarrassed.

empereur [ɑ̃prœr] nm emperor.

empeser [ɑ̃pəze] vtr (j'empèse) to starch (linen). **empesé** a starched (collar); stiff, starchy, formal (manner, style).

empester [ɑ̃peste] 1. vtr to make (place) stink; **air empesté par le tabac**, air reeking of tobacco 2. vi to stink.

empêtrer (s') [sɑ̃petre] vpr to become entangled, to get tangled up; **s'e. dans une mauvaise affaire**, to get mixed up in a bad business.

emphase [ɑ̃faz] nf bombast; pomposity. **emphatique** a bombastic; pompous.

empiétement [ɑ̃pjɛtmɑ̃] *nm* encroachment, trespass (**sur**, on).

empiéter [ɑ̃pjete] *vi* (**j'empiète; j'empiéterai**) e. **sur le terrain de qn**, to encroach (up)on s.o.'s land; e. **sur les droits de qn**, to infringe s.o.'s rights; e. **sur le domaine de qn**, to trespass on s.o.'s domain.

empiffrer (s') [sɑ̃pifre] *vpr P:* to stuff, gorge, oneself.

empilement [ɑ̃pilmɑ̃] *nm* (*a*) stacking, piling (up) (*b*) stack, pile.

empiler [ɑ̃pile] *vtr* 1. to stack, to pile (up) 2. (*of books*) **s'e.**, to pile up.

empire [ɑ̃pir] *nm* 1. (*a*) dominion; sway; **sous l'e. d'un tyran**, under the rule of a tyrant (*b*) influence, control; e. **sur soi-même**, self-control; **sous l'e. de la colère**, in a fit of anger 2. empire.

empirer [ɑ̃pire] 1. *vtr* to worsen; to make (sth) worse 2. *vi* to grow worse, to worsen.

empirisme [ɑ̃pirism] *nm* empiricism. **empirique** *a* empirical; rule-of-thumb.

emplacement [ɑ̃plasmɑ̃] *nm* site, location.

emplâtre [ɑ̃plɑtr] *nm* 1. (*a*) *Pharm:* plaster (*b*) *F:* **c'est un e.**, he's completely spineless 2. gaiter (for repairing tyre).

emplette [ɑ̃plɛt] *nf* purchase; **aller faire ses emplettes**, to go shopping.

emplir [ɑ̃plir] *vtr* 1. to fill (up) 2. **s'e.**, to fill up.

emploi [ɑ̃plwa] *nm* 1. use, employment (of sth); usage (of word); **mode d'e.**, directions for use; e. **du temps**, timetable (of work) 2. employment, post; job; **être sans e.**, to be unemployed.

employé, -ée [ɑ̃plwaje] *n* employee; e. **de magasin**, shop assistant; e. **de banque**, bank clerk; e. **(de bureau)**, office worker.

employer [ɑ̃plwaje] *vtr* (**j'emploie**) 1. (*a*) to employ, use (sth); **bien e. son temps**, to make the most of one's time; **ne savoir à quoi e. son temps**, to have no idea how to spend one's time (*b*) (i) to employ (workmen, staff) (ii) e. **qn**, to make use of s.o.'s services 2. (*a*) **s'e. à faire qch**, to occupy oneself, to spend one's time, (in) doing sth (*b*) **mot qui s'emploie au figuré**, word used in the figurative.

employeur, -euse [ɑ̃plwajœr, -øz] *n* employer.

empocher [ɑ̃pɔʃe] *vtr* to pocket (money).

empoignade [ɑ̃pwanad] *nf* quarrel, row.

empoigner [ɑ̃pwane] *vtr* 1. (*a*) to grasp, seize, grip (*b*) **ils se sont empoignés**, they had a set-to 2. to thrill, grip (reader).

empoisonnement [ɑ̃pwazɔnmɑ̃] *nm* (*a*) poisoning (*b*) *F:* **quel e.!** what a nuisance!

empoisonner [ɑ̃pwazɔne] *vtr* 1. to poison (s.o.); *vi* (*of plant*) to be poisonous 2. to poison (food); to infect (the air) 3. *F:* to bore (s.o.) stiff; to pester (s.o.) 4. **s'e.** (*a*) to take poison; to get food poisoning (*b*) *F:* to get bored. **empoisonnant** *a F:* annoying.

emporté [ɑ̃pɔrte] *a* quick-tempered, hot-headed.

emportement [ɑ̃pɔrtmɑ̃] *nm* (fit of) anger; **répondre avec e.**, to reply angrily.

emporte-pièce [ɑ̃pɔrtəpjɛs] *nm inv Tls:* punch; **mots à l'e.-p.**, biting, cutting, words.

emporter [ɑ̃pɔrte] *vtr* 1. to carry, take, away; **ils ont emporté de quoi manger**, they took some food with them; **mets à e.**, take-away food 2. (*a*) to carry, tear, sweep (s.o., sth) away; (*of illness*) to carry off; **le vent emporta son chapeau**, the wind blew off his hat; **cette moutarde vous emporte la bouche**, this mustard takes the roof off your mouth (*b*) to take (a fort) (by assault); e. **la journée**, to win the day 3. **se laisser e. par la colère**, to give way to anger 4. **l'e. sur qn**, to get the better of s.o. 5. **s'e.** (*a*) to lose one's temper (*b*) (*of horse*) to bolt.

empoté [ɑ̃pɔte] *a & n F:* awkward, clumsy (person).

empourprer (s') [sɑ̃purpre] *vpr* to flush; to turn crimson.

empreindre [ɑ̃prɛ̃dr] *vtr* (*conj like* PEINDRE) to impress, stamp; **visage empreint de terreur**, face full of terror.

empreinte [ɑ̃prɛ̃t] *nf* impression, (im)print, stamp; e. **des roues**, track of the wheels; e. **de pas**, footprint; e. **digitale**, fingerprint; e. **du génie**, mark, stamp, of genius.

empressement [ɑ̃prɛsmɑ̃] *nm* (*a*) eagerness, readiness, willingness; **mettre beaucoup d'e. à faire qch**, to show great keenness in doing sth (*b*) **témoigner de l'e. auprès de qn**, to pay marked attention to s.o.

empresser (s') [sɑ̃prese] *vpr* 1. to hurry; **il s'empressa de répondre à ma lettre**, he lost no time in answering my letter 2. **s'e. à faire qch**, to show eagerness, zeal, in doing sth; **s'e. auprès de qn**, (i) to dance attendance on s.o. (ii) to pay marked attention to s.o. **empressé** *a* eager, zealous; assiduous; attentive; *n* **faire l'e. auprès de qn**, to dance attendance on s.o.

emprise [ɑ̃priz] *nf* ascendancy (over person, mind); hold (on s.o.); **sous l'e. (de qn, qch)**, under the influence (of s.o., sth).

emprisonnement [ɑ̃prizɔnmɑ̃] *nm* imprisonment; **5 ans d'e.**, 5 years in prison.

emprisonner [ɑ̃prizɔne] *vtr* to imprison; to confine.

emprunt [ɑ̃prœ̃] *nm* 1. borrowing; **faire un e. à qn**, to borrow (money) from s.o.; **nom d'e.**, assumed name 2. loan.

emprunter [ɑ̃prœ̃te] *vtr* to borrow (à, from); e. **un nom**, to assume a name; **le cortège emprunta la rue de Rivoli**, the procession took, went down, the Rue de Rivoli. **emprunté** *a* selfconscious, stiff (manner).

emprunteur, -euse [ɑ̃prœ̃tœr, -øz] *n* borrower.

empuantir [ɑ̃pɥɑtir] *vtr* to infect (the air); to make (sth) stink.

ému [emy] *a* moved, touched; **il était tout é.**, he was quite overcome; **se sentir un peu é.**, to feel a bit nervous.

émulation [emylasjɔ̃] *nf* emulation, rivalry.

émule [emyl] *n* emulator, rival.

émulsion [emylsjɔ̃] *nf* emulsion.

en¹ [ɑ̃] *prep* 1. (*place*) (*a*) (*without def art*) **aller en ville**, to go (in)to town; **en ville**, in town; **partir en mer**, to go to sea; **venir en avion**, to come by air; **en tête**, at the head; **la suite en quatrième page**, continued on page four; (*with f names of countries*) **aller en France**, to go to France (*b*) (*with pers pron*) **il y a quelque chose en lui que j'admire**, there is something I admire about him; **un homme en qui j'ai confiance**, a man whom I trust (*c*) **en votre honneur**, in your honour; **regarder en l'air**, to look up at the sky; **le**

mariage aura lieu en l'église Saint-Jean, the marriage will be celebrated at St John's church 2. (*time*) (*a*) **en été**, in summer; **né en 1945**, born in 1945; **d'aujourd'hui en huit**, today week (*b*) **on peut y aller en 5 heures**, you can get there in 5 hours (*c*) **en l'an 1800**, in (the year) 1800; **en ce temps-là**, in those days; **en son absence**, during his absence 3. (*a*) (*state*) **être en deuil**, to be in mourning; **en vacances**, on holiday; **peindre qch en bleu**, to paint sth blue; **en réparation**, under repair (*b*) (*material*) **montre en or**, gold watch (*c*) (*manner*) **escalier en spirale**, spiral staircase; **docteur en médecine**, doctor of medicine; **fort en maths**, good at maths (*d*) (*change, division*) into; **briser qch en morceaux**, to break sth (in)to bits; **traduire une lettre en français**, to translate a letter into French (*e*) **de mal en pis**, from bad to worse; **d'année en année**, year by year 4. **envoyer qch en cadeau**, to send sth as a present; **agir en honnête homme**, to act like an honest man; **prendre la chose en philosophe**, to take the thing philosophically 5. (*with gerund*) **il marchait en lisant son journal**, he walked along reading his paper; **il répondit en riant**, he answered with a laugh; **elle sortit en dansant**, she danced out of the room; **en arrivant à Paris**, on arriving in Paris; **en attendant**, in the meantime.

en² *unstressed adv and pron* 1. *adv* (*a*) from there; **vous avez été à Londres?—oui, j'en arrive**, you've been to London?—yes, I've just come from there (*b*) on that account; **si vous étiez riche, en seriez-vous plus heureux?** if you were rich, would you be happier for it, any the happier? 2. *pron inv* (*a*) (*standing for n governed by* **de**) of (from, by, with, about) him, her, it, them; **j'aime mieux n'en pas parler**, I would rather not talk about it; **les rues en sont pleines**, the streets are full of it, of them; **qu'en pensez-vous?** what do you think about it, them? (*b*) (*quantity*) **combien avez-vous de chevaux?—j'en ai trois**, how many horses have you got?—I have three; **combien en voulez-vous?** how many, much, do you want? (*c*) (*replacing the possessive, of thgs*) **j'ai la valise, mais je n'en ai pas la clef**, I have the suitcase but I haven't got the key for it (*d*) (*standing for a clause*) **il ne l'a pas fait, mais il en est capable**, he didn't do it but he's quite capable of it (*e*) some, any; **j'en ai**, I have some; **je n'en ai pas**, I have none, I haven't any (*f*) (*indeterminate use*) **si le cœur vous en dit**, if you feel so inclined; **il en est ainsi**, that's the way it is (*g*) (*after imperative*) **prenez-en dix**, take ten (of them); **va-t'en**, go away.

ENA [ena] *abbr École nationale d'administration.*

enamourer (s') [sănamure] *vpr* to fall in love (**de**, with).

encadrement [ăkadrəmă] *nm* 1. framing 2. framework; frame; **dans l'e. de la porte**, in the doorway.

encadrer [ăkadre] *vtr* to frame (picture); to surround; **prévenu encadré par deux gendarmes**, accused man flanked by two policemen; *F:* **il a encadré un arbre**, he wrapped his car round a tree.

encaissement [ăkɛsmã] *nm* cashing (of cheque); receipt, collection (of money).

encaisser [ăkɛse] *vtr* (*a*) to cash; to receive, collect (money) (*b*) *F:* **en un coup**, to take a blow; **il sait e.**, he can take it; **je ne peux pas l'e.**, I can't stand him. **encaissé** *a* boxed in; deeply embanked (river); sunken (road).

encaisseur [ăkɛsœr] *nm* collector (of money); payee (of cheque); (bank) cashier.

encan [ăkã] *nm* (public) auction.

en-cas [ăka] *nm inv* emergency supply; snack; meal.

encastrer [ăkastre] *vtr* 1. to embed; to fit (**dans**, into) 2. **s'e.**, to fit (**dans**, into).

encaustique [ăkɔstik] *nf* wax, polish.

encaustiquer [ăkɔstike] *vtr* to wax, to polish.

enceindre [ăsɛ̃dṛ] *vtr* (*conj like* PEINDRE) to surround, encircle.

enceinte¹ [ăsɛ̃t] *nf* 1. surrounding wall; fence 2. enclosure 3. e. (acoustique), loudspeaker.

enceinte² *af* pregnant; **e. de 5 mois**, 5 months pregnant.

encens [ăsã] *nm* incense.

encenser [ăsãse] *vtr* to cense (altar); to burn incense to (idol).

encensoir [ăsãswar] *nm Ecc:* censer.

encerclement [ăsɛrkləmã] *nm* encircling.

encercler [ăsɛrkle] *vtr* to encircle; to shut in.

enchaînement [ăʃɛnmã] *nm* chain, series, train (of ideas, events).

enchaîner [ăʃɛne] *vtr* 1. to chain up (s.o., dog); *Fig:* to curb (passions) 2. (*a*) to link (up), connect (machinery, ideas); **e. la conversation**, to resume the conversation (*b*) *vi* (*in conversation*) to carry on, resume (*c*) *Cin:* to fade in 3. **s'e.**, to link up.

enchantement [ăʃătmã] *nm* 1. enchantment; **comme par e.**, as if by magic 2. delight.

enchanter [ăʃăte] *vtr* 1. to enchant, bewitch 2. to charm, delight; **cette idée ne l'enchante pas**, he's not taken with the idea. **enchanté** *a* 1. enchanted, bewitched 2. delighted (**de**, with); **e. de faire votre connaissance**, (i) delighted to meet you (ii) = how do you do?

enchanteur, -eresse [ăʃătœr, -rɛs] 1. *n* enchanter, enchantress 2. *a* bewitching; enchanting.

enchère [ăʃɛr] *nf* une **e.**, a bid; **les enchères, l'e.**, the bidding; **vente aux enchères**, sale by auction.

enchérir [ăʃerir] *vi* to make a higher bid; **e. sur qn**, (i) to outbid s.o. (ii) to go one better than s.o.

enchevêtrement [ăʃ(ə)vɛtrəmã] *nm* (*a*) entanglement (*b*) tangle.

enchevêtrer [ăʃvɛtre] *vtr* 1. to mix up, confuse, tangle (up) 2. **s'e.**, to get tangled up, mixed up.

enclave [ăklav] *nf* enclave.

enclaver [ăklave] *vtr* to enclose.

enclencher [ăklăʃe] *vtr MecE:* to engage; to throw into gear; *Fig:* to set in motion.

enclin [ăklɛ̃] *a* inclined, disposed; prone.

enclore [ăklɔr] *vtr* (*conj like* CLORE) to enclose, fence in.

enclos [ăklo] *nm* enclosure; paddock.

enclume [ăklym] *nf* anvil; **être entre l'e. et le marteau**, to be between the devil and the deep blue sea.

encoche [ăkɔʃ] *nf* notch, nick.

encoignure [ăkɔɲyr] *nf* corner, angle (of room).

encoller [ăkɔle] *vtr* to paste (paper); to glue (wood).

encolure [ăkɔlyr] *nf* 1. neck 2. collar size.

encombre [ăkɔ̃bṛ] *nm* **sans e.**, without mishap, without difficulty.

encombrement [ăkɔ̃brəmã] *nm* (*a*) congestion;

traffic jam; blocking (of telephone lines) (b) space (required); bulk.

encombrer [ãkõbre] vtr **1.** to encumber; to clutter up; to congest (the streets); **table encombrée de papiers,** table littered with papers; **e. le marché,** to glut the market **2. s'e.,** to burden oneself, to saddle oneself (**de,** with). **encombrant** a cumbersome; bulky; **il est e.,** he's always in the way.

encontre (à l') [alãkõtr] prep phr **à l'e. de,** against; in opposition to, contrary to; **aller à l'e. de la loi,** to run counter to the law.

encore [ãkɔr] adv **1.** (a) still; **il court e.,** he's still at large (b) yet; **pas e.,** not yet; **un homme que je n'avais e. jamais vu,** a man I had never seen before (c) more, again; **e. une tasse de café,** another cup of coffee; **quoi e.?** what else? **pendant e. trois mois,** for three months longer; **réduire e. le prix,** to reduce the price still further; **e. une fois,** once more; **e. autant,** as much again; **e. pire,** still worse; **e. vous!** (what,) you again! **2.** moreover, furthermore; **non seulement stupide, mais e. têtu,** not only stupid, but also pigheaded **3.** (restrictive) (a) **hier e.,** only yesterday; **e. si on pouvait lui parler,** if only one could speak to him (b) (with inversion) **je n'ai qu'un ciseau, e. est-il émoussé,** I have only one chisel and even that is blunt; **e. vous aurait-il fallu me prévenir,** all the same you should have let me know (c) **il vous en donnera 10 francs, et e.!** he'll give you 10 francs for it, if that! (d) conj phr **e. (bien) que** + sub, (al)though; **temps agréable e. qu'un peu froid,** pleasant weather if rather cold.

encouragement [ãkuraʒmã] nm encouragement.

encourager [ãkuraʒe] vtr (**n. encourageons**) to encourage. **encourageant** a encouraging.

encourir [ãkurir] vtr (conj like COURIR) to incur; to bring (punishment) upon oneself.

encrassement [ãkrasmã] nm dirtying; fouling, sooting (up); clogging.

encrasser (s') [sãkrase] vpr to get dirty, greasy; to foul up; to get clogged up; to soot up.

encre [ãkr] nf ink; **e. de Chine,** Indian ink; **écrit à l'e.,** written in ink.

encrier [ãkrije] nm inkpot; inkstand; inkwell.

encroûter (s') [sãkrute] vpr (a) to become encrusted (b) Fig: to get into a rut; to become fossilized.

encyclique [ãsiklik] a & nf encyclical (letter).

encyclopédie [ãsiklɔpedi] nf encyclop(a)edia. **encyclopédique** a encyclop(a)edic.

endémique [ãdemik] a endemic (disease).

endettement [ãdɛtmã] nm running into debt.

endetter (s') [sãdɛte] vpr to get, run, into debt. **endetté** a in debt.

endeuiller [ãdœje] vtr to plunge into mourning; to cast gloom over (event).

endiablé [ãdjable] a reckless, devil-may-care; wild, frenzied (music).

endiguer [ãdige] vtr **1.** to dam up (river) **2.** to (em)bank (river); to dyke (land) **3.** to hold back, contain (invasion).

endimancher (s') [sãdimãʃe] vpr to put on one's Sunday best.

endive [ãdiv] nf chicory.

endoctrinement [ãdɔktrinmã] nm indoctrination.

endoctriner [ãdɔktrine] vtr to indoctrinate.

endolori [ãdɔlɔri] a painful, sore; tender.

endommagement [ãdɔmaʒmã] nm damage, injury (**de,** to).

endommager [ãdɔmaʒe] vtr (**n. endommageons**) to damage, injure.

endormir [ãdɔrmir] vtr (conj like DORMIR) **1.** (a) to put, send, (s.o.) to sleep; to anaesthetize (patient); to bore (s.o.) (b) to deaden (pain) (c) **e. les soupçons,** to allay suspicion **2. s'e.,** to fall asleep. **endormant** a F: boring. **endormi** a **1.** (a) asleep, sleeping (b) sleepy **2.** (of limb) numb.

endossement [ãdosmã] nm (a) endorsing (b) endorsement.

endosser [ãdose] vtr **1.** to put on (clothes); **e. une responsabilité,** to shoulder, to assume, a responsibility **2.** to endorse (cheque).

endroit [ãdrwa] nm **1.** place, spot; **par endroits,** here and there, in places; **à quel e.?** where? whereabouts? **il s'est arrêté de lire à cet e.,** he stopped reading at that point **2.** right side (of material); **à l'e.,** right way round, right way up; Knit: **une maille à l'e.,** knit one.

enduire [ãdɥir] vtr (pp **enduit**; pr ind **j'enduis**; impf **j'enduisais**; fu **j'enduirai**) to smear, cover, coat (surface).

enduit [ãdɥi] nm coat, coating.

endurance [ãdyrãs] nf endurance. **endurant** a resistant; tough.

endurcir [ãdyrsir] vtr **1.** to harden; **être endurci à la fatigue,** to be inured to fatigue **2. s'e.** (a) to harden; to become hard (b) to become hardened, fit, tough. **endurci** a hardened (criminal); confirmed (bachelor).

endurcissement [ãdyrsismã] nm hardening; toughening (up); hardness, toughness.

endurer [ãdyre] vtr to endure, bear.

énergétique [enɛrʒetik] a (a) energizing (b) **dépense é.,** expenditure of energy.

énergie [enɛrʒi] nf **1.** energy; force, vigour; **avec é.,** energetically; **sans é.,** listless(ly) **2.** (a) **é. atomique,** atomic energy, nuclear power (b) Ind: energy, (fuel and) power. **énergique** a (a) energetic (b) strong, drastic (measures); emphatic (gesture); forceful (kick). **énergiquement** adv energetically; forcefully; **s'y mettre é.,** to put one's back into it.

énergumène [enɛrgymɛn] nm F: fanatic; ranter.

énervement [enɛrvəmã] nm nervous irritation; restiveness.

énerver [enɛrve] vtr **1.** (a) to enervate, weaken (b) **é. qn,** to get on s.o.'s nerves; to irritate s.o. **2. s'é.,** to become irritable, fidgety, nervy; to get worked up. **énervant** a irritating; nerve-racking; F: annoying, aggravating. **énervé** a irritated; fidgety, nervy; nervous.

enfance [ãfãs] nf **1.** (a) childhood; Fig: infancy; **première e.,** infancy; **c'est l'e. de l'art,** it's child's play (b) boyhood; girlhood **2.** childishness; **retomber en e.,** to sink into one's second childhood, one's dotage.

enfant [ãfã] n **1.** (a) child; boy; girl; **e. trouvé,** foundling; **faire l'e.,** to behave childishly (b) a childlike; babyish (smile) (c) F: lad, fellow; **allons-y, mes enfants!** come on folks! (d) **manière bon e.,** good-natured manner **2.** (a) offspring; F: **c'est son e.,** it's his baby, his brainchild (b) **un e. de Paris,** a native of Paris. **enfantin** a **1.** childish **2.** elementary; **c'est e.,** it's child's play.

enfantement [ãfãtmã] nm **1.** childbirth **2.** giving birth (to literary work).

enfanter [ãfãte] vtr & i (a) to give birth (to).

enfantillage [ãfãtijaʒ] nm childishness.

enfer [ãfɛr] nm hell; F: **aller un train d'e.,** to go hell for leather; **bruit d'e.,** hellish noise.

enfermer [ãfɛrme] vtr **1.** (a) to shut (sth, s.o.) up; **e. qn à clef,** to lock s.o. up; **tenir qn enfermé,** to keep s.o. in confinement; F: **il est bon à e.,** he ought to be locked up (b) to shut, hem, in; to enclose **2.** **s'e.,** to lock oneself in; **s'e. dans ses pensées,** to wrap oneself in one's thoughts.

enfiévrer [ãfievre] vtr (**j'enfièvre; j'enfiévrerai**) (a) to make (s.o.) feverish (b) to excite, fire (s.o.).

enfilade [ãfilad] nf **1.** succession (of doors); **maisons en e.,** row of houses **2.** Mil: enfilade.

enfiler [ãfile] vtr **1.** (a) to thread (needle); to string (beads) (b) to go along (a street) (c) to slip on (clothes); to pull on (trousers, tights) **2.** **s'e.** (a) **s'e. dans un couloir,** to disappear down a passage (b) F: to down (a drink, food) (c) F: to be stuck with (a task).

enfin [ãfɛ̃] **1.** adv (a) finally, lastly, after all; **e. et surtout,** last but not least (b) in fact, in a word, in short (c) at last **2.** int (a) that's that! (b) **mais e., s'il acceptait!** but still, if he did accept! (c) **e.! ce qui est fait est fait,** anyhow, what's done is done.

enflammer [ãflame] vtr **1.** (a) to inflame; to ignite; to set (sth) on fire (b) to inflame (wound) (c) to excite, fire (s.o.). **2.** **s'e.** (a) to catch fire (b) (of wound) to become inflamed (c) (of pers) to be stirred up, to get excited; **s'e. de colère,** to flare up. **enflammé** a burning, blazing; fiery; glowing (cheeks); inflamed (wound); impassioned (speech).

enflé [ãfle] nm F: idiot, twit.

enfler [ãfle] **1.** vtr to swell; **e. les joues,** to puff out one's cheeks **2.** vi & pr to swell; (of river) to rise.

enflure [ãflyr] nf swelling.

enfoncement [ãfɔ̃smã] nm **1.** driving in (of nail); breaking down (of door); sinking (in) **2.** hollow, depression; Arch: alcove, recess.

enfoncer [ãfɔ̃se] v (n. **enfonçons**) **1.** vtr (a) to drive (in) (nail); **e. la main dans sa poche,** to thrust one's hand into one's pocket; **e. son chapeau sur la tête,** to cram one's hat on one's head; F: **je ne peux pas lui e. ça dans la tête,** I can't get that into his head (b) to break open, break down (a door); Fig: **e. une porte ouverte,** to flog a dead horse (c) F: to get the better of s.o. **2.** vi to sink into (mud) **3.** **s'e.** (a) to penetrate, go deep (into sth); (of floor) to subside; to give way; **s'e. sous les couvertures,** to snuggle down under the bedclothes; **s'e. dans le crime,** to sink deeper into crime (b) **s'e. une aiguille dans le doigt,** to stick a needle in one's finger. **enfoncé** a sunken, deep (cavity); deep-set (eyes).

enfouir [ãfwir] vtr **1.** to hide (sth) in the ground; to bury (treasure) **2.** **s'e.,** to hide oneself; to bury oneself.

enfouissement [ãfwismã] nm burying.

enfourcher [ãfurʃe] vtr to mount (horse, bicycle).

enfourchure [ãfurʃyr] nf fork; crotch (of tree).

enfourner [ãfurne] vtr to put (bread) in an oven, (pottery) in a kiln; F: to gobble (sth) up.

enfreindre [ãfrɛ̃dr] vtr (conj like PEINDRE) to infringe.

enfuir (s') [sãfɥir] vpr (conj like FUIR) **1.** to flee, fly; to run away; to escape **2.** (of liquid) to run out.

enfumer [ãfyme] vtr to fill (room) with smoke; to smoke out (bees); **pièce enfumée,** smoky room.

engagé [ãgaʒe] **1.** a (of writer) committed **2.** n Mil: **e. (volontaire),** volunteer.

engagement [ãgaʒmã] nm **1.** (a) pawning (of object) (b) tying up (of capital) **2.** (a) promise, contract; commitment; **tenir ses engagements,** to meet one's obligations; **prendre un e.,** to enter into an engagement; **sans e.,** without obligation (b) engagement, appointment (of employee) (c) Sp: (i) entry (for event) (to), (ii) fixture **3.** Mil: engagement **4.** commitment (to), alignment (with) (a cause).

engager [ãgaʒe] vtr (n. **engageons**) **1.** to pawn; **e. sa parole,** to pledge one's word **2.** to engage (worker, artiste) **3.** (a) to catch, entangle (rope); **e. qn dans une querelle,** to involve s.o. in a quarrel (b) to tie up (money) (c) to put (machinery) into gear (d) **e. la clef dans la serrure,** to put, insert, the key in the lock **4.** to begin, start; to open (conversation); to enter (negotiations); **e. le combat,** to join battle; to engage **5.** **e. qn à faire qch,** to invite, urge, s.o. to do sth; **le beau temps nous engage à sortir,** the good weather makes us go out **6.** vi (of machinery) to come into gear. **s'engager** vpr **1.** **s'e. à faire qch,** to undertake, commit oneself, to do sth; **je suis trop engagé pour reculer,** I have gone too far to draw back **2.** (a) **s'e. chez qn,** to enter s.o.'s service (b) Mil: to enlist, to join up (c) **s'e. pour une course,** to enter for a race **3.** (of rope) to foul **4.** (a) **le tube s'engage dans l'ouverture,** the tube fits into the opening (b) **s'e. dans une rue,** to turn into a street (c) (of battle) to begin. **engageant** a engaging, prepossessing (manner).

engelure [ãʒlyr] nf chilblain.

engendrer [ãʒãdre] vtr **1.** to beget, father (child) **2.** to engender (strife); to generate (heat); to breed (disease).

engin [ãʒɛ̃] nm **1.** engine, machine; device; **engins de pêche,** fishing tackle **2.** **e. amphibie,** amphibious craft; **e. balistique, téléguidé,** ballistic, guided, missile.

englober [ãglɔbe] vtr to include; to take in.

engloutir [ãglutir] vtr **1.** (a) to swallow, to gulp down (food) (b) to engulf; to swallow up (ship, fortune) **2.** (of ship) **s'e.,** to be engulfed.

engloutissement [ãglutismã] nm swallowing; gulping down; engulfing.

engorgement [ãgɔrʒmã] nm (a) choking, blocking (b) obstruction.

engorger [ãgɔrʒe] vtr (n. **engorgeons**) to choke (up), stop (up); to block, clog.

engouement [ãgumã] nm infatuation, craze (**pour qn, qch,** for s.o., sth).

engouer (s') [sãgwe] vpr **s'e. de qn, de qch,** to become infatuated with s.o., to go crazy over sth.

engouffrer [ãgufre] vtr **1.** to engulf, swallow up **2.** **s'e.,** to be engulfed, swallowed up; **le train s'engouffra dans le tunnel,** the train plunged into the tunnel.

engourdir [ãgurdir] *vtr* 1. to numb (limb) 2. s'e. (*a*) (*of limb*) to grow numb; to go to sleep (*b*) (*of mind*) to become dull.

engourdissement [ãgurdismã] *nm* numbness; dullness, sluggishness.

engrais [ãgrɛ] *nm* (*a*) *Husb:* fattening food; **mettre à l'e.,** to fatten up (cattle) (*b*) manure; **e. chimique,** (chemical) fertilizer.

engraissement [ãgrɛsmã] *nm* fattening (of animals).

engraisser [ãgrɛse] 1. *vtr* (*a*) to fatten (*b*) to fertilize (land) 2. *vi* to grow stout; to put on weight.

engrenage [ãgrǝnaʒ] *nm* gearing; gear; mesh (of circumstances); **être pris dans l'e.,** to get caught up in the system.

engueulade [ãgœlad] *nf P:* slanging; blowing up; row.

engueuler [ãgœle] *vtr P:* to abuse, slang (s.o.); to blow (s.o.) up; **ils se sont engueulés,** they had a row.

enguirlander [ãgirlãde] *vtr F:* to tell (s.o.) off.

enhardir [ãardir] *vtr* (*a*) to make bolder; to give (s.o.) courage (*b*) s'e., to pluck up courage.

énigme [enigm] *nf* enigma, riddle. **énigmatique** *a* enigmatic. **énigmatiquement** *adv* enigmatically.

enivrement [ãnivrǝmã] *nm* intoxication, inebriation.

enivrer [ãnivre] *vtr* to intoxicate; to inebriate; to make (s.o.) drunk. **enivrant** *a* intoxicating.

enjambée [ãʒãbe] *nf* stride.

enjamber [ãʒãbe] *vtr* to step over, stride over (obstacle); (*of bridge*) to span (river).

enjeu, -eux [ãʒø] *nm Gaming:* stake.

enjoindre [ãʒwɛ̃dṛ] *vtr* (*conj like* JOINDRE) to enjoin (à qn de faire qch, s.o. to do sth).

enjôler [ãʒole] *vtr* to coax, wheedle. **enjôleur, -euse** 1. *a* coaxing, wheedling 2. *n* coaxer, wheedler.

enjoliver [ãʒolive] *vtr* to beautify, embellish; to embroider (story).

enjoliveur [ãʒolivœr] *nm Aut:* hub cap.

enjoué [ãʒwe] *a* lively, sprightly.

enjouement [ãʒumã] *nm* sprightliness.

enlacement [ãlasmã] *nm* 1. intertwining 2. embracing, clasping.

enlacer [ãlase] *vtr* (**n. enlaçons**) 1. to intertwine 2. to clasp (s.o.) in one's arms; to embrace, to hug (s.o.).

enlaidir [ãledir] 1. *vtr* to make (s.o.) ugly; to disfigure (landscape) 2. *vi* to grow ugly.

enlèvement [ãlɛvmã] *nm* 1. removal; carrying away; clearing away 2. kidnapping; carrying off; *Jur:* abduction 3. *Mil:* storming (of position).

enlever [ãlve] *vtr* (**j'enlève**) 1. (*a*) to remove; to take off (clothes); to carry, take (away); **e. le couvert,** to clear the table; **e. une tache,** to remove, take out, a stain; **enlevé par la mer,** carried away, washed away, by the sea; **la mort l'a enlevé à 20 ans,** death carried him off at 20 (*b*) **e. qch à qn,** to take sth (away) from s.o. (*c*) to carry off; to kidnap; to abduct; (*of girl*) **se faire e.,** to elope; **e. une course,** to win a race (*d*) *Mil:* to storm (position) (*e*) to raise; **e. le couvercle,** to lift the lid 2. **s'e.** (*a*) (*of paint*) to come off, to peel off (*b*) (*of goods*) to sell quickly, to be snapped up. **enlevé** *a* (*of sketch, music*) lively.

enlisement [ãlizmã] *nm* sinking (into quicksand).

enliser [ãlize] *vtr* 1. (*of quicksand, mud*) to suck in, swallow up 2. s'e., to sink (into quicksand, bog); **s'e. dans les détails,** to get bogged down in details.

enneigement [ãnɛʒmã] *nm* snowing up; **bulletin d'e.,** snow report. **enneigé** *a* snow-covered.

ennemi [ɛnmi] 1. *n* enemy; **se faire un e. de qn,** to make an enemy of s.o.; **être e. de qch,** to be opposed to sth 2. *a* enemy (country); hostile (**de,** to).

ennui [ãnɥi] *nm* 1. worry, anxiety; **avoir des ennuis,** to have problems; **créer des ennuis à qn,** to make trouble for s.o.; **quel e.!** what a nuisance! 2. boredom, tedium.

ennuyer [ãnɥije] *vtr* (**j'ennuie**) 1. (*a*) to annoy, worry (s.o.); **cela vous ennuierait-il d'attendre?** would you mind waiting? (*b*) to bore (s.o.) 2. **s'e.** (*a*) to be bored (*b*) **s'e. de qn,** to miss s.o. **ennuyeux, -euse** *a* (*a*) boring, tedious, tiresome, dull (*b*) annoying; **comme c'est e.!** what a nuisance!

énoncé [enõse] *nm* statement (of facts); terms (of a problem); text, wording (of an act).

énoncer [enõse] *vtr* (**n. énonçons**) to state (opinion, fact); to express (ideas).

énonciation [enõsjasjõ] *nf* stating, statement (of fact).

enorgueillir (s') [sãnɔrgœjir] *vpr* **s'e. de qch,** to pride oneself on sth.

énormité [enɔrmite] *nf* 1. (*a*) enormity; outrageousness (of demand); (*b*) enormousness, vastness, hugeness 2. *F:* **commettre une é.,** to put one's foot in it badly; **dire des énormités,** to say the most awful things. **énorme** *a* enormous, huge; tremendous; outrageous; **ça m'a fait un bien é.,** it did me a power of good. **énormément** *adv* 1. enormously, hugely; tremendously 2. **é. de bien,** an enormous amount of good; **é. de gens,** a great many people.

enquérir (s') [sãkerir] *vpr* (*conj like* ACQUÉRIR) to enquire, make enquiries (**de,** after); **s'e. du prix,** to ask the price.

enquête [ãkɛt] *nf* inquiry, investigation; (coroner's) inquest; **e. par sondage,** sample survey.

enquêter [ãkete] *vi* to hold an inquiry, to make investigations; **e. sur une affaire,** to inquire into a matter.

enquêteur, -euse [ãketœr, -øz] 1. *a Jur:* **commissaire e.,** investigating commissioner 2. *n* investigator; *Journ:* interviewer.

enquiquiner [ãkikine] *vtr F:* to infuriate, annoy.

enraciner [ãrasine] *vtr* 1. to root (tree); to establish (principles) 2. s'e. to take root; (*of habit*) to become established. **enraciné** *a* deep-rooted, deep-seated.

enrager [ãraʒe] (**n. enrageons**) *vi* to fume; to be furious; **faire e. qn,** to make s.o. wild. **enragé** 1. *a* (*a*) mad, rabid (dog) (*b*) rabid (socialist); keen (angler) 2. *n* **un e. de motos,** a motorbike fanatic.

enrayer [ãreje] *vtr* 1. (*a*) to arrest, stop (disease) (*b*) to jam (machine) 2. s'e., to jam.

enrégimenter [ãreʒimãte] *vtr* (*a*) to enrol (helpers) (*b*) to regiment (staff).

enregistrement [ãr(ǝ)ʒistrǝmã] *nm* 1. registration; registry; recording; entering (up) (of an order); **bureau d'e.,** (i) registry office (ii) booking office (for luggage) 2. (sound) recording; **e. sur bande,** tape recording.

enregistrer [ãr(ǝ)ʒistre] *vtr* 1. (*a*) to record (facts);

to register (a birth); to enter (up) (an order); to register, to check in (luggage) (b) F: to record (for sound reproduction); **e. sur bande,** to tape, to record on tape. **enregistreur, -euse 1.** a recording (device) **2.** nm recorder; recording machine, instrument.

enrhumer [ɑ̃ryme] vtr **1.** to give (s.o.) a cold; **être enrhumé,** to have a cold **2.** s'e., to catch (a) cold.

enrichir [ɑ̃riʃir] vtr **1.** to enrich **2.** s'e. (a) to grow rich (b) to grow, become, richer (**de,** with; **en,** in).

enrichissement [ɑ̃riʃismɑ̃] nm enriching; enrichment.

enrobage [ɑ̃rɔbaʒ] nm Cu: coating, covering.

enrober [ɑ̃rɔbe] vtr Cu: to coat, cover.

enrôlement [ɑ̃rolmɑ̃] nm enrolment; enlistment.

enrôler [ɑ̃role] vtr to enrol; to enlist.

enrouement [ɑ̃rumɑ̃] nm hoarseness, huskiness.

enrouer [ɑ̃rwe] vtr **1.** to make hoarse **2.** s'e., to get hoarse; **s'e. à force de crier,** to shout oneself hoarse. **enroué** a hoarse.

enrouler [ɑ̃rule] vtr **1.** (a) to roll up (map); to wind (cable) (b) to wrap (sth) up (**dans,** in) **2.** s'e., to wind, coil; to be wound (**autour de,** round).

ensabler (s') [sɑ̃sable] vpr (of harbour, river) to silt up; (of car) to get stuck in the sand.

ENSAM abbr École nationale supérieure d'arts et métiers.

ensanglanter [ɑ̃sɑ̃glɑ̃te] vtr to cover with blood; **mains ensanglantées,** bloodstained hands.

enseignant, -ante [ɑ̃sɛɲɑ̃, -ɑ̃t] **1.** a teaching **2.** n teacher.

enseigne [ɑ̃sɛɲ] **1.** nf (a) sign, token (of quality) (b) sign(board), shop sign; **e. du néon, lumineuse,** neon sign; F: **nous sommes tous logés à la même e.,** we're all in the same boat (c) Mil: ensign, colour **2.** nm (a) Mil: Hist: ensign (b) Navy: **e. (de vaisseau),** sublieutenant.

enseignement [ɑ̃sɛɲmɑ̃] nm (a) teaching; **il est dans l'e.,** he's a teacher; he teaches (b) **e. supérieur,** higher education; **e. par correspondance,** postal tuition.

enseigner [ɑ̃sɛɲe] vtr (a) to teach; **e. à qn à faire qch,** to teach s.o. to do sth; **e. l'anglais,** to teach English (b) **e. les enfants,** to teach children; **il enseigne,** he's a teacher.

ensemble [ɑ̃sɑ̃bl] **1.** adv (a) together; in company; **vivre e.,** to live together; **être bien e.,** to be good friends; **le tout e.,** the general effect; **agir d'e.,** to act in concert, as a body (b) at the same time, at once **2.** nm (a) whole, entirety; **l'e. du travail,** the work as a whole; **vue d'e.,** general view; overall picture; **dans l'e.,** on the whole, by and large (b) cohesion, unity; **avec e.,** harmoniously; as one (c) **e. vocal,** vocal ensemble; **e. de couleurs,** harmonious (group of) colours (d) set (of tools); suite (of furniture); Cl: suit, outfit; **grand e.,** new residential estate.

ensemblier [ɑ̃sɑ̃blije] nm interior decorator.

ensemencement [ɑ̃smɑ̃smɑ̃] nm sowing.

ensemencer [ɑ̃smɑ̃se] vtr (j'ensemençai(s)) to sow (field).

ensevelir [ɑ̃səvlir] vtr to bury; to shroud (corpse).

ensevelissement [ɑ̃səvlismɑ̃] nm burial; shrouding (of corpse).

ensoleiller [ɑ̃sɔleje] vtr (a) to give sunlight to (sth);

to shine on (sth) (b) to brighten (s.o.'s life). **ensoleillé** a sunny.

ensommeillé [ɑ̃sɔmeje] a sleepy, drowsy.

ensorceler [ɑ̃sɔrsəle] vtr (j'ensorcelle) (a) to bewitch (b) to captivate (s.o.).

ensuite [ɑ̃sɥit] adv after(wards), then; next, after that; **et e.?** what then? what next? **e. de quoi,** after which.

ensuivre (s') [sɑ̃sɥivr] vpr (conj like SUIVRE; used only in the third pers) to follow, ensue, result; **il s'ensuit que,** it follows that; F: **et tout ce qui s'ensuit,** and what not, and whatever, and all the rest of it.

entaille [ɑ̃taj] nf (a) notch, nick; groove; slot; **à entailles,** notched (b) gash, cut, slash.

entailler [ɑ̃taje] vtr (a) to notch, nick; to groove; to slot (b) to gash, cut, slash.

entame [ɑ̃tam] nf first cut, first slice.

entamer [ɑ̃tame] vtr **1.** to cut into (loaf); to open (bottle); **e. son capital,** to break into one's capital **2.** to begin, start (conversation); **e. des relations avec qn,** to enter into relations with s.o.; **e. un sujet,** to broach a subject; Cards: **e. trèfles,** to open clubs.

entartrage [ɑ̃tartraʒ] nm furring, scaling (of boiler).

entartrer (s') [sɑ̃tartre] vpr (of boiler) to fur, to scale.

entassement [ɑ̃tɑsmɑ̃] nm **1.** piling (up); crowding (in); packing together, cramming **2.** pile, heap.

entasser [ɑ̃tɑse] vtr **1.** (a) to accumulate; to pile, heap, (up); to stack (up) (cases); to amass (money) (b) to pack, crowd, cram (passengers, cattle) together **2.** s'e. (a) (of thgs) to accumulate (b) (of people) to crowd together.

entendement [ɑ̃tɑ̃dmɑ̃] nm understanding.

entendeur [ɑ̃tɑ̃dœr] nm used only in the phr **à bon e. salut!** a word to the wise is enough.

entendre [ɑ̃tɑ̃dr] vtr **1.** to intend, mean; **e. faire qch,** to intend, mean, to do sth; **qu'entendez-vous par là?** what do you mean by that? **faites comme vous l'entendez,** do as you think best **2.** (a) to hear; **on l'entend à peine,** he's scarcely audible; **je pouvais à peine me faire e.,** I could scarcely make myself heard; **on ne s'entend plus ici,** one can't hear oneself speak here; **e. parler de qch,** to hear of sth; **je ne veux plus e. parler de lui,** I don't want to hear him mentioned again; **e. dire que + ind,** to hear it said that; to be rumoured that; **e. dire qch à qn,** to hear s.o. say sth; vi **il entend mal,** he is hard of hearing (b) to listen to (s.o., sth); **à vous e.,** judging from what you say; according to you; **il n'a rien voulu e.,** he would not listen **3.** (a) to understand; **il ne l'entend pas ainsi,** he doesn't see it that way; **donner à e. à qn,** (i) to lead s.o. to believe sth (ii) to give s.o. to understand sth; **laisser e. qch,** to imply, insinuate, sth; **il n'entend pas la plaisanterie,** he can't take a joke; **c'est entendu,** agreed; all right; **bien entendu!** of course! **entendu!** all right! OK! (b) to know all about (sth); **je n'y entends rien,** I don't know the first thing about it. **s'entendre** vpr **1.** to agree; to understand one another; **ils s'entendent bien,** they get on (well); **ils ne sont pas fait pour s'e.,** they are not suited to each other; **ils s'entendent comme larrons en foire,** they are as thick as thieves **2.** to be skilled (**à,** in); **s'e. aux affaires,** to be a good businessman.

entente [ātāt] *nf* 1. (*a*) understanding (**de, of**) (*b*) **mot à double e.**, word with a double meaning 2. agreement, understanding (**entre,** between); **e. cordiale,** friendly understanding.

entériner [āterine] *vtr Jur:* to ratify, confirm.

entérite [āterit] *nf Med:* enteritis.

enterrement [ātɛrmā] *nm* (*a*) burial (*b*) funeral; *F:* **figure d'e.,** gloomy, funereal, expression.

enterrer [ātɛre] *vtr* to bury; **elle désire e. cette affaire,** she wants the whole thing buried and forgotten; *F:* **il nous enterrera tous,** he will outlive us all.

en-tête [ātɛt] *nm* (*a*) heading (of letter); **papier à entête,** headed notepaper (*b*) *Typ:* headline (of page), *NAm:* caption; *pl* **en-têtes.**

entêtement [ātɛtmā] *nm* obstinacy, stubbornness.

entêter [ātɛte] *vtr* 1. (*of smell*) to give (s.o.) a headache; **ces louanges l'entêtaient,** this praise went to his head 2. **s'e. dans une opinion,** to persist in an opinion. **entêté** *a* stubborn, obstinate.

enthousiasme [ātuzjasm] *nm* enthusiasm.

enthousiasmer [ātuzjasme] *vtr* 1. to fire (s.o.) with enthusiasm 2. **s'e.,** to become enthusiastic; **s'e. pour, de, sur, qn,** to be enthusiastic over s.o. **enthousiaste** *a* enthusiastic.

enticher (s') [sātiʃe] *vpr* **s'e. de qn, de qch,** to become infatuated with s.o., sth; to have a passion for s.o., sth.

entier, -ière [ātje, -jɛr] *a* 1. entire, whole; **lait e.,** full-cream milk; **la France entière,** the whole of France; **pendant des heures entières,** for hours on end; **nombre e., nm e.,** integer, whole number; **payer place entière,** to pay full fare 2. complete, full (authority); **l'entière direction de qch,** the sole management of sth; **elle est toute entière à ce qu'elle fait,** she is intent on what she is doing 3. *nm* entirety; **en e.,** entirely, in full, fully. **entièrement** *adv* entirely, wholly.

entité [ātite] *nf* entity.

entomologie [ātɔmɔlɔʒi] *nf* entomology. **entomologique** *a* entomological.

entonner [ātɔne] *vtr* to strike up (song); **e. les louanges de qn,** to sing s.o.'s praises.

entonnoir [ātɔnwar] *nm* funnel; **en (forme d')e.,** funnel-shaped.

entorse [ātɔrs] *nf* sprain, wrench, strain (*esp* of the ankle); **faire une e. à la loi,** to stretch the law; **donner une e. à la vérité,** to twist the truth.

entortiller [ātɔrtije] *vtr* (*a*) **e. qch dans qch,** to wind, twist, wrap, sth in sth, sth round sth (*b*) to wheedle; to get round (s.o.).

entour [ātur] *nm* **à l'e.,** around, round about; **à l'e. de,** round (about) (town).

entourage [āturaʒ] *nm* 1. setting, framework 2. set, circle (of friends); attendants; entourage (of monarch).

entourer [āture] *vtr* to surround (**de,** with); to fence in (field); to encircle (army); **s'e. d'amis,** to surround oneself with friends; **il était très entouré,** he was the centre of attraction; **e. qn de soins,** to lavish attention on s.o.

entracte [ātrakt] *nm Th:* 1. interval; intermission 2. interlude.

entraide [ātrɛd] *nf* (*no pl*) mutual aid.

entraider (s') [sātrede] *vpr* to help one another.

entrailles [ātraj] *nfpl* 1. entrails; bowels (of the earth) 2. compassion; **être sans e.,** to be heartless.

entrain [ātrɛ̃] *nm* liveliness, briskness; high spirits; drive; **manger avec e.,** to eat with gusto; **travailler avec e.,** to work with a will; **faire qch sans e.,** to do sth half-heartedly.

entraînement [ātrɛnmā] *nm* 1. (*a*) dragging (*b*) drive (of machine) 2. training; coaching (of team); **être à l'e.,** to be in training.

entraîner [ātrene] *vtr* 1. (*a*) to drag, carry, along; (*of river*) to carry away; **il m'a entraîné chez lui,** he took me along to his home; **entraîné par le courant,** swept along by the current (*b*) to drive (part of machine) 2. to seduce, inveigle (s.o.); **être entraîné dans un piège,** to be lured into a trap; **se laisser e.,** to allow oneself to be led astray 3. to result in (sth); to entail, involve; **cela peut e. des inconvénients,** this could land one in difficulties 4. *Sp:* to train (horse, athlete); to coach (team) 5. **s'e.,** to train (**à, pour, for**); **s'e. à faire qch,** to practise doing sth.

entraîneur [ātrɛnœr] *nm* trainer; coach.

entrave [ātrav] *nf* 1. shackle, fetter 2. hindrance, impediment (**à,** to).

entraver [ātrave] *vtr* 1. to shackle, fetter 2. to hinder, impede; **e. la circulation,** to hold up the traffic.

entre [ātr] *prep* 1. between; **e. les arbres,** (in) between the trees; **e. les deux,** betwixt and between 2. (*a*) among(st); **nous dînerons e. nous,** there won't be anyone else at dinner; **un homme dangereux e. tous,** a most dangerous man; **il l'admirait e. tous,** he admired him above all others; **ce jour e. tous,** this day of all days (*b*) **tomber e. les mains de l'ennemi,** to fall into the enemy's hands; **tenir qch e. les mains,** to hold sth in one's hands (*c*) **d'e.,** (from) among; **l'un d'e. eux,** one of them 3. **ils s'accordent e. eux,** they agree among themselves.

entrebâillement [ātrəbajmā] *nm* narrow opening, chink (of door).

entrebâiller [ātrəbaje] *vtr* to half-open (door); **la porte était entrebâillée,** the door was ajar.

entrechoquer (s') [sātrəʃɔke] *vpr* (*a*) to collide (*b*) to knock against one another; (*of glasses*) to chink.

entrecôte [ātrəkot] *nf Cu:* steak cut from ribs; entrecote steak, rib steak.

entrecouper [ātrəkupe] *vtr* 1. to intersect 2. to interrupt; **d'une voix entrecoupée,** with a catch in one's voice 3. (*of lines*) **s'e.,** to cut across each other.

entrecroiser [ātrəkrwaze] *vtr* 1. to intersect, cross (lines) 2. **s'e.,** to intersect, interlace; to criss-cross.

entrée [ātre] *nf* 1. entry, entering; **faire son e.,** to make one's entrance 2. (*a*) admission, admittance (to club); **avoir son e., ses entrées, dans un lieu,** to have the run of a place; **e. interdite,** no admittance; **e. libre,** open to the public; *Com:* no obligation to buy (*b*) *Com:* import; *Cust:* entry; **droit d'e.,** import duty 3. (*a*) way in; entrance; (entrance) hall; lobby (*b*) *Mch:* admission, inlet; *ICE:* **e. d'air,** air intake 4. *Cu:* entrée 5. headword (in dictionary).

entrefaite [ātrəfɛt] *nf* **sur ces entrefaites,** meanwhile, while all this was going on.

entrejambe [ɑ̃trəʒɑ̃b] nm Tail: (a) crutch (b) **(longueur d')e.**, inside leg length.

entrelacement [ɑ̃trəlasmɑ̃] nm intertwining, interlacing; network (of branches).

entrelacer [ɑ̃trəlase] vtr (conj like LACER) to intertwine, interlace; **mains entrelacées**, hand in hand.

entremêler [ɑ̃trəmɛle] vtr 1. to (inter)mix, (inter)mingle; to blend (colours) 2. s'e., to (inter)mix, (inter)mingle.

entremets [ɑ̃trəmɛ] nm e. **(sucré)**, sweet, dessert (as dinner course).

entremetteur, -euse [ɑ̃trəmɛtœr, -øz] n go-between; mediator.

entremettre (s') [sɑ̃trəmɛtr] vpr (conj like METTRE) to intervene; to act as go-between.

entremise [ɑ̃trəmiz] nf (a) intervention (b) mediation; **agir par l'e. de qn**, to act through s.o.

entreposer [ɑ̃trəpoze] vtr to warehouse, to store.

entrepôt [ɑ̃trəpo] nm warehouse, store.

entreprenant [ɑ̃trəprənɑ̃] a enterprising.

entreprendre [ɑ̃trəprɑ̃dr] vtr (conj like PRENDRE) 1. to undertake; to take (sth) in hand 2. to contract for (piece of work).

entrepreneur [ɑ̃trəprənœr] n contractor; e. **(en bâtiments)**, building contractor; e. **de transports**, carrier, forwarding agent; e. **de pompes funèbres**, undertaker.

entreprise [ɑ̃trəpriz] nf 1. (a) enterprise; undertaking; venture (b) Com: Ind: firm; e. **commerciale**, business corporation 2. contracting; **travail à l'e.**, work on, by, contract.

entrer [ɑ̃tre] vi (aux être) 1. (a) to enter; to go in, to come in; **entrez!** come in! PN: **défense d'e.**, no admittance; **faire e. qn**, (i) to show s.o. in (ii) to call s.o. in; e. **en passant**, to drop in (on s.o.); **je ne fais qu'e. et sortir**, I just dropped in for a moment; **empêcher qn d'e.**, to keep s.o. out; **faire e. qch dans qch**, to insert sth in sth; Th: **Hamlet entre**, enter Hamlet; e. **en courant**, to run in (b) e. **dans l'armée, dans une carrière**, to join the army, to take up a career; e. **en fonction**, to take up one's duties (c) e. **en colère**, to get angry; e. **en ébullition**, to come to the boil 2. to enter into, take part in (sth); **je n'entrerai pas dans l'affaire**, I will have nothing to do with the matter; e. **dans les idées de qn**, to agree with s.o.; e. **dans une catégorie**, to fall into a category 3. vtr (aux **avoir**) to bring, let, put (sth) in; to smuggle in (goods).

entresol [ɑ̃trəsɔl] nm mezzanine (floor).

entre-temps [ɑ̃trətɑ̃] adv meanwhile, in the meantime.

entretenir [ɑ̃trətnir] vtr (conj like TENIR) 1. to maintain; to keep (sth) up; e. **une route**, to keep a road in repair; e. **son français**, to keep up one's French; e. **le feu**, to keep the fire going 2. (a) to maintain, support (family) (b) e. **des soupçons**, to entertain, harbour, suspicions 3. e. **qn (de qch)**, to talk to s.o. (about sth) 4. s'e., to talk, converse (**avec, de**, about). **entretenu** a 1. kept (woman) 2. **jardin bien e.**, well-kept garden.

entretien [ɑ̃trətjɛ̃] nm 1. upkeep, maintenance; servicing (of car, radio); **manuel d'e.**, service manual; **produits d'e.**, (household) cleaning materials 2. support, maintenance (of family) 3. conversation;

interview; **j'ai eu un e. avec lui**, I had a talk with him.

entre-tuer (s') [sɑ̃trətɥe] vpr to kill one another.

entrevoir [ɑ̃trəvwar] vtr (conj like VOIR) to catch sight, catch a glimpse, of (s.o., sth); **j'entrevois des difficultés**, I foresee difficulties.

entrevue [ɑ̃trəvy] nf interview.

entrouvert [ɑ̃truvɛr] a half-open (window); **laissez la porte entrouverte**, leave the door ajar.

entrouvrir [ɑ̃truvrir] vtr (conj like OUVRIR) 1. to half-open; to set (door) ajar 2. s'e., to half-open.

énumérer [enymere] vtr (j'énumère; j'énumérerai) to count up.

envahir [ɑ̃vair] vtr 1. to invade, to overrun (country); **envahi par les mauvaises herbes**, overgrown with weeds; **quand le doute nous envahit**, when we are seized with doubt 2. to encroach on (s.o.'s territory). **envahissant** a intruding; invasive.

envahissement [ɑ̃vaismɑ̃] nm invasion; encroachment.

envahisseur, -euse [ɑ̃vaisœr, -øz] n invader.

enveloppe [ɑ̃vlɔp] nf 1. (a) wrapper, wrapping (of parcel) (b) envelope; **envoyer qch sous e.**, to send sth under cover 2. exterior, external appearance 3. sheathing, casing, jacket (of boiler); outer cover (of tyre).

envelopper [ɑ̃vlɔpe] vtr (a) to envelop; to wrap (sth) up; **enveloppé de brume, de mystère**, shrouded in mist, in mystery (b) to cover; to jacket, lag (boiler) (c) to surround; **la nuit nous enveloppa**, darkness closed in on us.

envenimer [ɑ̃vnime] vtr 1. (a) to poison (b) to aggravate, to inflame (quarrel) 2. (of wound) s'e., to fester; **la discussion s'envenimait**, the discussion was growing acrimonious.

envergure [ɑ̃vergyr] nf spread, breadth, span; wingspan (of bird, aircraft); **de grande e.**, far-reaching; on a large scale.

envers¹ [ɑ̃ver] nm wrong side, reverse, back (of material); **l'e. du décor**, the other side of the picture; **à l'e.**, (i) inside out (ii) wrong way up, upside down (iii) back to front.

envers² prep to, towards; e. **et contre tous**, in spite of all opposition.

envie [ɑ̃vi] nf 1. desire, longing; **avoir e. de qch**, to want sth; **j'avais e. de dormir**, I felt sleepy; **avec e.**, longingly 2. envy; **faire e. à qn**, to make s.o. envious 3. (a) hangnail (b) birthmark. **enviable** a enviable.

envier [ɑ̃vje] vtr (impf & pr sub n. **enviions**) 1. to covet, hanker after (sth); to wish for (sth) 2. to envy; to be envious of (s.o.). **envieux, -euse** a envious (**de**, of). **envieusement** adv enviously.

environ [ɑ̃virɔ̃] 1. adv about 2. nmpl surroundings, outskirts, neighbourhood; **habiter aux environs de Paris**, to live near Paris.

environnement [ɑ̃virɔnmɑ̃] nm surroundings; environment.

environner [ɑ̃virɔne] vtr to surround. **environnant** a surrounding (country).

envisager [ɑ̃vizaʒe] vtr (n. **envisageons**) to envisage, to consider, to contemplate (possibility); e. **l'avenir**, to look to the future; **il n'envisageait pas de partir**, he wasn't thinking of leaving.

envoi [ãvwa] *nm* 1. sending, dispatch, consignment (of goods); **e. par mer**, shipment; **e. de fonds**, remittance of funds; *Fb:* **coup d'e.**, kick-off 2. consignment, parcel.

envol [ãvɔl] *nm* (a) (*of birds*) taking flight (b) (*of aircraft*) takeoff; **piste d'e.**, runway; **pont d'e.**, flight deck.

envolée [ãvɔle] *nf* **e. d'éloquence**, flight of oratory.

envoler (s') [sãvɔle] *vpr* (a) (*of bird*) to fly away, to fly off; to take flight (b) (*of aircraft*) to take off (c) (*of hat*) to blow off; (*of papers*) to blow away.

envoûtement [ãvutmã] *nm* sympathetic magic; hoodoo.

envoûter [ãvute] *vtr* to practise sympathetic magic on (s.o.); **envoûté**, spellbound.

envoyé [ãvwaje] *nm* messenger, representative; (government) envoy; *Journ:* correspondent.

envoyer [ãvwaje] *vtr* (**j'envoie; n. envoyons;** *fu* **j'enverrai**) 1. to send; to despatch (goods); **envoyez-moi un petit mot**, drop me a line; **e. un baiser à qn**, to blow s.o. a kiss; **e. chercher qn**, to send for s.o.; *F:* **je ne le lui ai pas envoyé dire**, I told him straight; *F:* **e. promener qn**, to send s.o. packing 2. *P:* **s'e. un verre de vin**, to knock back a glass of wine; **s'e. une corvée**, to take on a tedious job.

envoyeur, -euse [ãvwajœr, -øz] *n* sender.

épagneul, -eule [epaɲœl] *n* spaniel.

épais, -aisse [epɛ, -ɛs] 1. *a* thick (hair, wall); dense (foliage); bulky (book); **e. de deux metres**, two metres thick; **avoir l'esprit é.**, to be thick(headed), dense 2. *adv* thick(ly); **semer é.**, to sow thick.

épaisseur [epesœr] *nf* 1. thickness; depth; **avoir deux mètres d'é.**, to be two metres thick 2. density, thickness (of fog, foliage).

épaissir [epesir] *vtr* 1. to thicken 2. **s'é.**, to thicken, become thick; (*of pers*) to put on weight; (*of darkness*) to deepen.

épaississement [epesismã] *nm* thickening.

épanchement [epãʃmã] *nm* effusion (of blood); outpouring (of feelings).

épancher [epãʃe] *vtr* 1. to pour out (liquid, one's heart) 2. **s'é.** (a) (*of blood*) to effuse (b) to pour out one's heart.

épandre [epãdr̩] *vtr* 1. to spread 2. **s'é.**, to spread.

épanouir (s') [sepanwir] *vpr* 1. (*of flower*) to open out, bloom 2. (*of face*) to beam, to light up. **épanoui** *a* in full bloom; full-blown (rose); beaming (face).

épanouissement [epanwismã] *nm* 1. (a) opening out, blooming (of flowers) (b) brightening up (of face) 2. (full) bloom.

épargnant, -ante [eparɲã, -ãt] *n* saver.

épargne [eparɲ] *nf* saving, economy; **vivre de ses épargnes**, to live on one's savings; **caisse d'é.**, savings bank.

épargner [eparɲe] *vtr* 1. to save (up), to put by (money, provisions); to economize; to be sparing with (sth) 2. to save (energy, time) 3. to spare, have mercy on (prisoner).

éparpillement [eparpijmã] *nm* scattering, dispersal.

éparpiller [eparpije] *vtr* 1. to disperse, scatter 2. (*of crowd*) **s'é.**, to scatter, disperse.

épars [epar] *a* scattered (houses); straggly (hair).

épatant [epatã] *a F:* wonderful; stunning; fine; splendid; **c'est un type é.**, he's a great chap.

épaté [epate] *a* flat (nose).

épater [epate] *vtr F:* to astound, flabbergast, amaze; to bowl (s.o.) over; to impress.

épaule [epol] *nf* shoulder.

épauler [epole] *vtr* 1. to bring (gun) to the shoulder; *vi* to take aim 2. to back (s.o.) up.

épaulette [epolɛt] *nf Cl:* (a) shoulder strap (b) *Mil:* epaulette.

épave [epav] *nf Nau:* wreck; **épaves d'un naufrage**, wreckage.

épée [epe] *nf* sword; rapier; **coup d'é.**, swordthrust; **coup d'é. dans l'eau**, wasted effort.

épeler [eple] *vtr* (**j'épelle**) to spell; to spell out (text).

épépiner [epepine] *vtr* to remove seeds, pips, from (fruit).

éperdu [epɛrdy] *a* distracted, bewildered; desperate (resistance); **é. de joie**, wild with delight. **éperdument** *adv* distractedly, madly; **je m'en moque é.**, I couldn't care less.

éperon [eprɔ̃] *nm* spur.

éperonner [eprɔne] *vtr* (a) to spur (horse); to urge (s.o.) on (b) to ram (enemy ship).

épervier [epɛrvje] *nm* 1. *Orn:* sparrowhawk 2. *Fish:* castnet.

éphémère [efemɛr] 1. *a* ephemeral, fleeting, short-lived 2. *nm Ent:* mayfly.

épi [epi] *nm* ear (of grain); spike (of flower).

épice [epis] *nf* spice; **pain d'é.**, gingerbread.

épicer [epise] *vtr* (**n. épiçons**) to spice. **épicé** *a* highly spiced; hot (seasoning).

épicerie [episri] *nf* (a) groceries (b) grocer's shop; grocery; **é. fine**, delicatessen.

épicier, -ière [episje, -jɛr] *n* grocer.

épidémie [epidemi] *nf* epidemic. **épidémique** *a* epidemic.

épiderme [epidɛrm] *nm* epidermis, skin. **épidermique** *a* epidermal, epidermic.

épier [epje] *vtr* (*impf & pr sub* **n. épiions**) 1. to watch; to spy on (s.o.) 2. to be on the lookout for (opportunity).

épilation [epilasjɔ̃] *nf* depilation; plucking (of eyebrows).

épilepsie [epilɛpsi] *nf* epilepsy. **épileptique** *a & n* epileptic.

épiler [epile] *vtr* to depilate; to pluck (eyebrows).

épilogue [epilɔg] *nm* epilogue.

épinard [epinar] *nm* **épinard(s)**, spinach.

épine [epin] *nf* 1. thornbush; **é. blanche**, hawthorn 2. (a) thorn, prickle; **tirer à qn une é. du pied**, to get s.o. out of a mess (b) spine (of hedgehog) 3. **é. dorsale**, backbone. **épineux, -euse** *a* thorny, prickly; **situation épineuse**, ticklish situation.

épingle [epɛ̃gl] *nf* pin; **é. de sûreté, é. de nourrice, é. anglaise**, safety pin; **é. à cheveux**, hairpin; **tiré à quatre épingles**, spick and span; **tirer son é. du jeu**, to get out of a ticklish situation; **coups d'é.**, pinpricks, petty annoyances.

épingler [epɛ̃gle] *vtr* 1. to pin; to pin (up) 2. *F:* to arrest, to nick (s.o.).

Épiphanie [epifani] *nf* Epiphany, Twelfth Night.

épique [epik] *a* epic.

épiscopat [episkɔpa] *nm* episcopate. **épiscopal, -aux** *a* episcopal.

épisode [epizɔd] *nm* episode; instalment; **film à épisodes**, serial. **épisodique** *a* episodic, occasional.

épitaphe [epitaf] *nf* epitaph.

épithète [epitɛt] *nf* epithet.

épître [epitr] *nf* epistle.

éploré [eplɔre] *a* tearful, weeping.

épluchage [eplyʃaʒ] *nm* 1. cleaning; picking (over); peeling 2. examination (of work).

éplucher [eplyʃe] *vtr* 1. to clean, pick (salad); to peel (potatoes) 2. to examine (work) in detail.

épluchure [eplyʃyr] *nf usu pl* peeling(s); refuse.

éponge [epɔ̃ʒ] *nf* sponge; **é. métallique**, (pot) scourer; **passons l'é. là-dessus**, let's forget it.

éponger [epɔ̃ʒe] *vtr* (**n. épongeons**) to sponge up, mop up (liquid); to sponge, mop (surface); **s'é. le front**, to mop one's brow.

épopée [epope] *nf* epic (poem).

époque [epɔk] *nf* 1. epoch, era, age; **faire é.**, to mark an epoch; **meubles d'é.**, period, (genuine) antique, furniture 2. date, period; **à l'é. de sa naissance**, at the time of his birth.

époumoner (s') [sepumɔne] *vpr* to shout oneself hoarse.

épouse [epuz] *nf see* **époux.**

épouser [epuze] *vtr* 1. to marry, wed 2. to take up, adopt (cause) 3. **é. la forme de qch**, to take the exact shape of sth; to fit exactly.

épousseter [epuste] *vtr* (**j'époussette**) to dust (furniture).

époustoufler [epustufle] *vtr F:* to astound, to flabbergast.

épouvantail, -ails [epuvɑ̃taj] *nm* 1. scarecrow 2. bugbear, bogy.

épouvante [epuvɑ̃t] *nf* terror, fright; **saisi d'é.**, terror-stricken; **film d'é.**, horror film.

épouvanter [epuvɑ̃te] *vtr* to terrify. **épouvantable** *a* dreadful, frightful; appalling. **épouvantablement** *adv* dreadfully, frightfully; appallingly.

époux, -ouse [epu, -uz] *n* husband, wife; **les é.**, the husband and wife.

éprendre (s') [seprɑ̃dr] *vpr* (*conj. like* PRENDRE) to fall in love (**de qn**, with s.o.); to take a fancy (**de qch**, to sth).

épreuve [eprœv] *nf* 1. (*a*) proof, test, trial; **mettre qch à l'é.**, to test sth; to put sth to the test; **à l'é. du feu**, fireproof; **bonté à toute é.**, never-failing kindness (*b*) *Sch:* (examination) paper (*c*) *Sp:* event; **é. (éliminatoire)**, (preliminary) heat 2. trial, affliction, ordeal 3. *Typ:* proof; *Phot:* print.

épris [epri] *a* in love (**de**, with).

éprouver [epruve] *vtr* 1. to test, try (sth); to put (sth) to the test 2. (*a*) to feel, experience (sensation) (*b*) to sustain, suffer (a loss); to meet with (difficulties). **éprouvant** *a* trying, testing. **éprouvé** *a* tried, tested, well-tried; stricken (area).

éprouvette [epruvɛt] *nf* test tube; **bébé é.**, test tube baby.

épuisement [epɥizmɑ̃] *nm* 1. exhausting; *Com:* **jusqu'à é. des stocks**, as long as supplies last 2. exhaustion.

épuiser [epɥize] *vtr* (*a*) to exhaust; to use up, consume; to drain, empty (tank) (*b*) to exhaust (s.o.); to wear, tire, (s.o.) out 2. **s'é.** (*a*) to become ex-

hausted; (*of spring*) to run dry, to dry up; (*of stock, money*) (i) to run out (ii) to run low (*b*) to wear, tire, oneself out. **épuisant** *a* exhausting. **épuisé** *a* exhausted; (*of edition*) out of print; (*of article*) sold out.

épuisette [epɥizɛt] *nf Fish:* landing net.

épuration [epyrasjɔ̃] *nf* (*a*) purification, purging (*b*) *Pol:* purge.

épurer [epyre] *vtr* to purify; *Pol:* to purge.

équateur [ekwatœr] 1. *nm* equator; **sous l'é.**, at the equator 2. *Prnm Geog:* É., Ecuador. **équatorial, -aux** *a* equatorial.

équation [ekwasjɔ̃] *nf Mth:* equation.

équerre [ekɛr] *nf* 1. *Tls:* square; **é. à dessin**, set square 2. **en é.**, **d'é.**, at right angles; **mettre d'é.**, to square.

équestre [ekɛstr] *a* equestrian (statue).

équeuter [ekøte] *vtr* to stalk, tail (fruit).

équidistant [ekɥidistɑ̃] *a* equidistant.

équilibrage [ekilibraʒ] *nm* counterbalancing; balancing.

équilibre [ekilibr] *nm* balance, equilibrium; stability; **mettre qch en é.**, to balance sth; **budget en é.**, balanced budget; **perdre l'é.**, to lose one's balance; **é. (mental)**, (mental) equilibrium.

équilibrer [ekilibre] *vtr* 1. to balance; to counterbalance 2. **s'é.**, to counterbalance each other. **équilibré** *a* balanced; **esprit bien é.**, well-balanced mind.

équilibriste [ekilibrist] *n* tightrope walker.

équinoxe [ekinɔks] *nm* equinox.

équipage [ekipaʒ] *nm* 1. *Nau:* crew; ship's company; *Av:* aircrew 2. equipage; retinue 3. pack of hounds; hunt; **maître d'é.**, master of hounds.

équipe [ekip] *nf* 1. gang (of workmen); *Mil:* working party; **é. de nuit**, night shift; **travailler par équipes**, to work in shifts; **chef d'é.**, foreman; **é. de secours**, rescue squad; **faire é. avec**, to team up with 2. *Sp:* team; side.

équipée [ekipe] *nf* 1. jaunt, walk 2. escapade, lark.

équipement [ekipmɑ̃] *nm* 1. (*a*) equipment; fitting out (*b*) **é. électrique**, electrical fittings 2. outfit, gear; equipment, kit.

équiper [ekipe] *vtr* to equip; to fit out (**de**, with).

équipier, -ière [ekipje, -jɛr] *n* team member, team mate.

équitable [ekitabl] *a* (*a*) equitable, fair (*b*) impartial, fair-minded (pers). **équitablement** *adv* equitably, fairly, impartially.

équitation [ekitasjɔ̃] *nf* (horse)riding; **école d'é.**, riding school.

équité [ekite] *nf* equity, fairness.

équivalence [ekivalɑ̃s] *nf* equivalence. **équivalent** *a & nm* equivalent (**à**, to).

équivaloir [ekivalwar] *vi* (*conj like* VALOIR) to be equivalent, equal in value (**à**, to); **cela équivaut à un refus**, that amounts to a refusal.

équivoque [ekivɔk] 1. *a* (*a*) equivocal, ambiguous (words) (*b*) questionable, dubious (conduct) 2. *nf* (*a*) ambiguity (of expression); **sans é.**, un equivocal(ly) (*b*) misunderstanding.

érable [erabl] *nm Bot:* maple (tree, wood).

érafler [erafle] *vtr* to scratch, graze.

éraflure [eraflyr] *nf* scratch, graze.

éraillé [eraje] *a* scratched (surface); raucous (voice).

ère [ɛr] *nf* era; epoch; **en l'an 1550 de notre è.**, in 1550 AD.

érection [erɛksjɔ̃] *nf* erection; setting up.

éreintement [erɛ̃tmɑ̃] *nm* 1. exhaustion 2. savage criticism.

éreinter [erɛ̃te] *vtr* 1. to exhaust; to tire (s.o.) out 2. to criticize (author) unmercifully; to pull to pieces. **éreintant** *a* exhausting, back-breaking. **éreinté** *a* exhausted, worn out, whacked.

ergot [ɛrgo] *nm* 1. spur (of cock) 2. *Agr:* ergot.

ergotage [ɛrgɔtaʒ] *nm* quibbling.

ergoter [ɛrgɔte] *vi* to quibble (sur, about).

ergoteur, -euse [ɛrgɔtœr, -øz] *n* quibbler.

ériger [eriʒe] *vtr* **n. (érigeons)** 1. to erect, set up, raise (statue) 2. to establish, set up (office, tribunal) 3. to elevate.

ermitage [ɛrmitaʒ] *nm* hermitage.

ermite [ɛrmit] *nm* hermit.

éroder [erɔde] *vtr* to erode, wear away; to eat away, corrode (metal).

érosion [erozjɔ̃] *nf* erosion; wearing away.

érotisme [erɔtism] *nm* eroticism. **érotique** *a* erotic.

errer [ɛre] *vi* 1. to roam, rove, wander (about); **laisser e. ses pensées**, to let one's thoughts wander 2. to err. **errant** *a* roaming, roving, wandering; **chien e.**, stray dog.

erreur [ɛrœr] *nf* 1. error; mistake, blunder; **e. judiciaire**, miscarriage of justice; **e. typographique**, misprint; **e. de sens**, wrong meaning; **par e.**, by mistake; **sauf e.**, if I am not mistaken; **faire e.**, to be mistaken 2. error; delusion; **induire qn en e.**, to mislead s.o. 3. **erreurs de jeunesse**, errors of youth.

erroné [ɛrɔne] *a* erroneous, wrong, mistaken.

ersatz [ɛrzats] *nm inv* substitute; **e. de café**, ersatz coffee.

érudit, -te [erydi, -it] 1. *a* erudite, scholarly 2. *n* scholar.

érudition [erydisjɔ̃] *nf* erudition, scholarship.

éruption [erypsjɔ̃] *nf* eruption; **entrer en e.**, to erupt.

ès [ɛs] *contracted article* = **en les**; **licencié(e) ès lettres** = Bachelor of Arts (BA).

escabeau, -eaux [ɛskabo] *nm* 1. (wooden) stool 2. stepladder.

escadre [ɛskadṛ] *nf Nau:* squadron; *Av:* wing.

escadrille [ɛskadrij] *nf Nau:* flotilla; *Av:* flight.

escadron [ɛskadrɔ̃] *nm* (*a*) *Mil:* squadron; *Av:* squadron (*b*) group, crowd.

escalade [ɛskalad] *nf* 1. (*a*) scaling, climbing (*b*) climb 2. *Pol:* escalation.

escalader [ɛskalade] *vtr* to scale, climb (wall).

escale [ɛskal] *nf* 1. *Nau:* port of call 2. call; *Av:* stop(over); **faire e.**, (i) *Nau:* to put into port (ii) *Av:* to touch down; **vol sans e.**, non-stop flight.

escalier [ɛskalje] *nm* staircase; (flight of) stairs; **e. de service**, backstairs; **e. de secours**, fire escape; **e. roulant**, escalator.

escalope [ɛskalɔp] *nf* escalope (of veal).

escamotage [ɛskamɔtaʒ] *nm* (*a*) conjuring (*b*) *Av:* retraction (of undercarriage).

escamoter [ɛskamɔte] *vtr* (*a*) to conjure (sth) away; to make (sth) vanish (*b*) to skip (job); to dodge (the issue) (*c*) *Av:* to retract (undercarriage) (*d*) to steal, pinch. **escamotable** *a* retractable (undercarriage); fold-away (bed).

escamoteur [ɛskamɔtœr] *nm* conjuror, conjurer.

escapade [ɛskapad] *nf* escapade; prank.

escargot [ɛskargo] *nm* snail.

escarmouche [ɛskarmuʃ] *nf* skirmish.

escarpement [ɛskarpəmɑ̃] *nm* steep slope; *Geog:* escarpment. **escarpé** *a* steep; precipitous, abrupt (slope); sheer (cliff).

escarpin [ɛskarpɛ̃] *nm* (*a*) dancing shoe (*b*) court shoe.

escient [ɛsjɑ̃] *nm* knowledge; *used in* **à bon e.**, deliberately, wittingly.

esclaffer (s') [sɛsklafe] *vpr* to burst out laughing; to roar with laughter; to guffaw.

esclandre [ɛsklɑ̃dṛ] *nm* scandal, scene.

esclavage [ɛsklavaʒ] *nm* slavery.

esclavagiste [ɛsklavaʒist] *nm NAm: Hist:* advocate of negro slavery.

esclave [ɛsklav] *n* slave; **vendu comme e.**, sold into slavery.

escompte [ɛskɔ̃t] *nm Com:* discount; *Fin:* **taux de l'e.**, minimum lending rate.

escompter [ɛskɔ̃te] *vtr* 1. *Com:* to discount (bill) 2. **e. un succès**, to anticipate success.

escorte [ɛskɔrt] *nf* escort; **faire e.**, to escort.

escorter [ɛskɔrte] *vtr* to escort; to convoy.

escouade [ɛskwad] *nf* squad, gang (of workmen).

escrime [ɛskrim] *nf* fencing; **faire de l'e.**, to fence.

escrimer (s') [sɛskrime] *vpr* to fight, struggle; **s'e. à faire qch**, to try hard to do sth.

escrimeur [ɛskrimœr] *nm* fencer.

escroc [ɛskro] *nm* swindler, sharper; crook.

escroquer [ɛskrɔke] *vtr* 1. **e. qch à qn**, to cheat s.o. of sth 2. **e. qn**, to swindle s.o.

escroquerie [ɛskrɔkri] *nf* swindling; swindle, fraud.

ésotérique [ezɔterik] *a* esoteric.

espace [ɛspas] *nm* 1. (*a*) space; room; *TownP:* **espaces verts**, open spaces (*b*) **un e. de deux mètres entre deux choses**, a distance of two metres between two things (*c*) **e. de temps**, space of time; **en l'e. d'un an**, within a year 2. (*void*) **regarder dans l'e.**, to stare into space; **e. atmosphérique**, outer space; **vol dans l'e.**, space flight.

espacement [ɛspasmɑ̃] *nm* spacing (out).

espacer [ɛspase] *vtr* (**n. espaçons**) 1. to space (out) 2. **s'e.**, to become less frequent. **espacé** *a* far between, far apart; at wide intervals.

espace-temps [ɛspastɑ̃] *nm inv Mth: Ph:* spacetime.

espadon [ɛspadɔ̃] *nm Ich:* swordfish.

espadrille [ɛspadrij] *nf* rope-soled sandal, shoe.

Espagne [ɛspaŋ] *Prnf Geog:* Spain. **espagnol, -ole** 1. *a* Spanish 2. *n* Spaniard 3. *nm Ling:* Spanish.

espèce [ɛspɛs] *nf* 1. (*a*) kind, sort; **de toute e.**, of every description; *F:* **cet e. d'idiot, cette e. d'idiote**, that silly fool (*b*) *pl* specie, coin; **payer en espèces**, to pay in cash 2. species (of plant, animal); **l'e. humaine**, mankind.

espérance [ɛsperɑ̃s] *nf* hope; **vivre dans l'e.**, to live in hope; **l'affaire n'a pas répondu à nos espérances**, the business did not come up to our expectations; **e. de vie**, expectation of life; life expectancy.

espérer [ɛspere] *vtr* (**j'espère; j'espérerai**) **1.** to hope; **j'espère vous revoir,** I hope I'll see you again; *vi* **e. en Dieu,** to trust in God **2.** to expect (s.o., sth); **je ne vous espérais plus,** I had given you up.

espièglerie [ɛspjɛgləri] *nf* **1.** mischievousness **2.** prank. **espiègle** *a & n* mischievous, roguish (child).

espion, -onne [ɛspjɔ̃, -ɔn] *n* spy.

espionnage [ɛspjɔnaʒ] *nm* espionage, spying; **film d'e.,** spy film.

espionner [ɛspjɔne] *vtr* to spy on; *vi* to spy.

esplanade [ɛsplanad] *nf* esplanade.

espoir [ɛspwar] *nm* hope; **dans l'e. de vous revoir,** in the hope of seeing you again; **avoir bon e.,** to be full of hope; **cas sans e.,** hopeless case.

esprit [ɛspri] *nm* **1.** (*a*) **le Saint-E.,** the Holy Ghost; **rendre l'e.,** to give up the ghost; **l'E. malin,** the Evil One (*b*) ghost, phantom; spirit (of the dead) (*c*) sprite **2.** (*a*) vital spirit; **perdre ses esprits,** to lose consciousness (*b*) *Ch:* (volatile) spirit; **e. de vin,** spirit(s) of wine **3.** (*a*) mind; **d'e. lent,** slow-witted; **avoir l'e. tranquille,** to be easy in one's mind; **perdre l'e.,** to go out of one's mind; **elle avait l'e. ailleurs,** her thoughts were elsewhere; **où aviez-vous l'e.?** what were you thinking of? **présence d'e.,** presence of mind; **une pareille idée ne me serait jamais venue à l'e.,** such an idea would never have occurred to me (*b*) wit; **traits d'e.,** witty remarks **4.** spirit, feeling; **e. de famille,** family feeling **5.** **e. fort,** freethinker; **un e. dangereux,** a dangerous man.

Esquimau, -aude, -aux [ɛskimo, -od, -o] *n & a* (*occ inv in f*) **1.** (*a*) Eskimo (*b*) **chien e.,** husky **2.** *nm* chocolate ice (stick); *F:* choc-ice.

esquinter [ɛskɛ̃te] *vtr F:* **1.** to exhaust, to tire (s.o.) out **2.** to spoil, damage (sth); to ruin (one's health).

esquisse [ɛskis] *nf* sketch; draft; outline; rough plan.

esquisser [ɛskise] *vtr* to sketch, outline; **e. un sourire,** to give the ghost of a smile.

esquive [ɛskiv] *nf* dodge; evasion.

esquiver [ɛskive] *vtr* **1.** to avoid, dodge, evade (blow); *vi Box:* **e. de la tête,** to duck **2.** **s'e.,** to slip away; to make oneself scarce.

essai [ɛsɛ] *nm* **1.** (*a*) trial, test(ing); **faire l'e. de qch,** to test sth, to try sth out; **prendre qch à l'e.,** to take sth on trial, on approval; **à titre d'e.,** experimentally; **pilote d'e.,** test pilot; **e. de vitesse,** speed trial (*b*) *Metall:* assay(ing) (of ore) **2.** (*a*) attempt, try; **coup d'e.,** trial shot (*b*) *Lit:* essay (*c*) *Rugby Fb:* try.

essaim [ɛsɛ̃] *nm* swarm (of bees).

essaimer [ɛsɛme] *vi* (*of bees*) to swarm; (*of population*) to hive off.

essayage [ɛsɛjaʒ] *nm* trying on, fitting (of clothes).

essayer [ɛsɛje] *vtr* (**j'essaie, j'essaye**) **1.** (*a*) to test, try; to try on (garment); *Metall:* to assay (*b*) **e. de qch,** to try, taste, sth (*c*) **e. de faire qch,** to try to do sth; **laissez-moi e.,** let me have a try **2.** **s'e. à faire qch,** to try one's hand at doing sth.

essence [ɛsɑ̃s] *nf* **1.** (*a*) petrol, *NAm:* gas(oline); **poste d'e.,** petrol pump; filling, petrol, *NAm:* gas, station (*b*) essence, extract **2.** nature, spirit, natural quality; **l'e. de l'affaire,** the gist of the matter.

essentiel, -elle [ɛsɑ̃sjɛl] **1.** *a* (*a*) essential; vital (organ) (*b*) essential, necessary **2.** *nm* **l'e.,** the essential thing, the main point. **essentiellement** *adv* (*a*) essentially (*b*) primarily.

essieu, -ieux [ɛsjø] *nm* axle(-tree).

essor [ɛsɔr] *nm* flight (of bird); **prendre son e.,** (i) to take wing, to soar (ii) to spring into life; **e. d'une industrie,** rise of an industry.

essorage [ɛsɔraʒ] *nm* wringing; spin drying.

essorer [ɛsɔre] *vtr* to wring (washing) dry, to spin dry.

essoreuse [ɛsɔrøz] *nf* spin drier.

essoufflement [ɛsufləmɑ̃] *nm* shortness of breath; breathlessness.

essouffler [ɛsufle] *vtr* **1.** to wind (horse, man) **2.** **s'e.,** to get out of breath. **essoufflé** *a* out of breath, *F:* puffed.

essuie-glace [ɛsɥiglas] *nm Aut:* windscreen, *NAm:* windshield, wiper; *pl* essuie-glaces.

essuie-main(s) [ɛsɥimɛ̃] *nm inv* hand towel.

essuyer [ɛsɥije] *vtr* (**j'essuie**) **1.** to wipe, dry (dishes); to wipe (sth) clean; to wipe up **2.** to suffer, endure (defeat, insult); **e. un refus,** to meet with a refusal.

est¹ [ɛ] *see* **être.**

est² [ɛst] **1.** *nm no pl* east; **vent d'e.,** (i) easterly wind (ii) east wind; **à l'e.,** eastwards, to the east (**de,** of) **2.** *a inv* **les régions e. de la France,** the eastern parts of France.

estafette [ɛstafɛt] *nf Mil:* liaison officer; dispatch rider.

estafilade [ɛstafilad] *nf* gash (in the face).

estaminet [ɛstaminɛ] *nm* (*esp in N Fr*) (small) public house; *F:* pub.

estampe [ɛstɑ̃p] *nf* **1.** *Tls:* punch **2.** print, engraving.

estamper [ɛstɑ̃pe] *vtr* **1.** to stamp, emboss (silver, coin) **2.** *F:* to swindle (s.o.).

estampille [ɛstɑ̃pij] *nf* (official) stamp.

esthète [ɛstɛt] *n* (a)esthete.

esthéticien, -ienne [ɛstetisjɛ̃, -jɛn] *n* beautician.

esthétisme [ɛstetism] *nm* (a)estheticism. **esthétique** **1.** *a* (a)esthetic; **chirurgie e.,** plastic surgery **2.** *nf* (a)esthetics. **esthétiquement** *adv* (a)esthetically.

estimation [ɛstimasjɔ̃] *nf* (*a*) estimation; valuing, appraising; assessment (*b*) estimate, valuation.

estime [ɛstim] *nf* **1.** guesswork; *Nau:* reckoning; **à l'e.,** by guesswork; *Nau:* by dead-reckoning **2.** (*a*) estimation, opinion (*b*) esteem, regard; **témoigner de l'e. pour qn,** to show regard for s.o.

estimer [ɛstime] *vtr* **1.** (*a*) to estimate; to value, to appraise (goods); to assess (damage) (*b*) to calculate (distance); *Nau:* to reckon **2.** (*a*) to consider; **s'e. heureux,** to count oneself lucky (*b*) to have a high opinion of (s.o.); to prize (sth). **estimable** *a* **1.** estimable **2.** fairly good.

estivant, -ante [ɛstivɑ̃, -ɑ̃t] *n* summer visitor; (summer) holiday maker. **estival, -aux** *a* summer.

estomac [ɛstɔma] *nm* stomach; **avoir de l'e.,** to have plenty of (i) pluck (ii) cheek.

estomaquer [ɛstɔmake] *vtr F:* to stagger, astound.

estomper [ɛstɔ̃pe] *vtr* **1.** to shade off (drawing); to blur (landscape) **2.** **s'e.,** to become blurred.

estourbir [ɛsturbir] *vtr F:* (*a*) to kill (s.o.), to do (s.o.) in (*b*) to knock (s.o.) flat.

estrade [ɛstrad] *nf* platform; rostrum; stage.

estragon [ɛstragɔ̃] *nm* Bot: tarragon.

estropier [ɛstrɔpje] *vtr* (*impf & pr sub* n. **estropiions**) (*a*) to cripple, maim (*b*) to murder (music); to mutilate (text). **estropié, -ée** 1. *a* crippled, maimed 2. *n* **les estropiés**, the maimed.

estuaire [ɛstɥɛr] *nm* estuary.

estudiantin [ɛstydjɑ̃tɛ̃] *a* student (life).

esturgeon [ɛstyrʒɔ̃] *nm* Ich: sturgeon.

et [e] 1. *conj* and; **et son frère et sa sœur**, both his brother and his sister; **j'aime le café; et vous?** I like coffee; do you? (NOTE: *there is no 'liaison' with* **et**: **j'ai écrit et écrit** [ʒeekrieekri]) 2. *nm* **et commercial**, ampersand.

étable [etabl] *nf* cowshed.

établi [etabli] *nm* (work)bench.

établir [etablir] *vtr* 1. (*a*) to establish (business, peace); to set up (agency); to fix, settle (place of residence); to quote, fix (price); to pitch (a camp); **é. un record**, to set a record (*b*) to establish, prove (fact); to substantiate (charge) (*c*) to work out, to draw up (plan); **é. un devis**, to make an estimate; **é. un compte**, to draw up an account (*d*) to institute, create (tribunal); to lay down (rule); to set (s.o.) up in business 2. **s'é.** (*a*) to settle (in a place); to set up (house) (*b*) **s'é. épicier**, to set up as a grocer (*c*) (*of custom*) to become established.

établissement [etablismɑ̃] *nm* 1. (*a*) establishment; setting up, putting up, fixing; building up (*b*) establishment, proving (of innocence) 2. working out; drawing up 3. instituting, forming (of government); laying down (of rules); founding (of industry) 4. establishment; setting up (of business); **frais d'é.**, initial outlay 5. (*a*) institution; **é. scolaire**, educational establishment (*b*) Hist: (colonial) trading centre; settlement (*c*) factory; business; firm; **les établissements Martin**, Martin & Co.

étage [etaʒ] *nm* 1. stor(e)y, floor (of building); **à deux étages**, two-storeyed; **au troisième é.**, on the third floor; *NAm:* on the fourth story 2. tier, step; *F:* **menton à deux étages**, double chin.

étagement [etaʒmɑ̃] *nm* terracing (of vines on hillsides).

étager [etaʒe] *vtr* (**j'étageai(s)**) to lay out in tiers.

étagère [etaʒɛr] *nf* (*a*) rack; shelf; (set of) shelves (*b*) shelf.

étai[1] [etɛ] *nm* Nau: stay.

étai[2] *nm* stay, prop.

étain [etɛ̃] *nm* 1. tin 2. pewter; **vaisselle d'é.**, pewter (plate).

étal, -aux, *occ* **-als** [etal, -o] *nm* stall.

étalage [etalaʒ] *nm* (*a*) display, show (of goods); **mettre qch à l'é.**, (i) to display sth for sale (ii) to put sth in the window; **article qui a fait l'é.**, shop-soiled article (*b*) showing off; **faire é. de ses bijoux**, to show off one's jewels.

étalagiste [etalaʒist] *n* window dresser.

étale [etal] *a* slack (sea, tide).

étalement [etalmɑ̃] *nm* (*a*) displaying (of goods) (*b*) spreading (out) (*c*) staggering (of holidays).

étaler [etale] *vtr* 1. (*a*) to display (goods) (*b*) to spread out (linen to dry); to spread (butter) (*c*) to flaunt, show off (one's wealth) (*d*) to stagger (holidays, payments) 2. **s'é.** (*a*) (*of village*) to spread out

(*b*) to stretch oneself out; to sprawl; **s'é. par terre**, (i) to lie down (full length) on the ground (ii) to come a cropper; to fall flat on one's face.

étalon[1] [etalɔ̃] *nm* stallion.

étalon[2] *nm* standard (of measures); **l'é. or**, the gold standard.

étamine [etamin] *nf* Bot: stamen.

étampe [etɑ̃p] *nf* 1. stamp, die 2. Tls: punch.

étanchéité [etɑ̃ʃeite] *nf* é. à l'eau, watertightness, airtightness. **étanche** *a* tight, impervious; **é. à l'eau, à l'air**, watertight, airtight.

étancher [etɑ̃ʃe] *vtr* 1. (*a*) to check the flow of (liquid); to sta(u)nch (blood); to stop (a leak) (*b*) to quench, slake (one's thirst) 2. to make (container) airtight, watertight.

étang [etɑ̃] *nm* pond, pool.

étape [etap] *nf* (*a*) stopping place; **faire é.**, to stop (*b*) day's run, march; **à, par, petites étapes**, by easy stages; **nous avons fait une é. de 500 kilomètres**, we covered 500 kilometres (*c*) **d'é. en é.**, stage by stage.

état [eta] *nm* 1. state, condition; **dans l'é. actuel des choses**, in the present circumstances; **mettre ses affaires en é.**, to put one's affairs in order; **en bon é.**, in good condition; undamaged; (*house*) in good repair; **en mauvais é., hors d'é.**, out of order; in need of repair; in poor condition; **remettre en é.**, to overhaul, to recondition; **en é. d'ivresse**, in a drunken state; **é. d'esprit**, state, frame, of mind; **être en é. de faire qch**, (i) to be in a fit state to do sth (ii) to be able, in a position, to do sth; **hors d'é. de nuire**, harmless; *F:* **être dans tous ses états**, to be upset 2. (*a*) statement, report, return; **é. néant**, nil return; **é. de compte**, statement of account; **é. des lieux**, inventory of fixtures (in rented premises); **é. périodique**, progress report (*b*) **faire é. de qch**, to take sth into account; **faire grand é. de qn**, to think highly of s.o. (*c*) Adm: **é. civil**, (i) civil status (ii) registry office 3. profession, trade; **épicier de son é.**, grocer by trade 4. Pol: (*a*) estate (of the realm) (*b*) state, body politic, (form of) government; **homme d'É.**, statesman.

étatiser [etatize] *vtr* to establish state control; to nationalize. **étatisé** *a* state-controlled.

étatisme [etatism] *nm* state control; state socialism.

état-major [etamaʒɔr] *nm* 1. (*a*) (general) staff; **officier d'é.-m.**, staff officer; **carte d'é.-m.** = ordnance survey map (*b*) headquarters 2. management (of firm); *pl* **états-majors**.

États-Unis [etazyni] *Prnm pl* **É.-U. (d'Amérique)**, the United States (of America); *F:* the States.

étau, -aux [eto] *nm* Tls: vice.

étayer [eteje] *vtr* (**j'étaie, j'étaye**) to stay, shore up, prop (up); to support (statement).

été [ete] *nm* summer; **en é.**, in summer; **é. de la Saint-Martin**, Indian Summer.

éteindre [etɛ̃dr] *vtr* (*conj like* TEINDRE) 1. (*a*) to extinguish, put out (fire); to turn off (gas); to switch off (light); **laisser é. le feu**, to let the fire go out; *vi* **éteignez**, switch off the light (*b*) to kill (ambition, desire); to quench (thirst); to subdue (passions) 2. **s'é.** (*a*) (*of fire*) to die out, to go out (*b*) (*of colour*) to fade; (*of sound*) to die away (*c*) (*of pers*) to die; (*of race, family*) to die out. **éteint** *a* (*a*) extinguished; **le feu est é.**, the fire is out (*b*) extinct (race, volcano) (*c*) dull (colour); faint (voice).

étendard [etɑ̃dar] *nm* standard.

étendre [etɑ̃dr̩] *vtr* **1.** (*a*) to spread, extend; to stretch; to lay (tablecloth); to spread (butter on bread); to hang out (washing); **é. le bras,** to stretch out one's arm; **é. qn (par terre),** to knock s.o. down; *F:* **se faire é. à un examen,** to fail an exam (*b*) to stretch (sth) out; **é. la pâte,** to roll out the dough; **é. ses connaissances,** to extend one's knowledge (*c*) to dilute (wine) **2. s'é.** (*a*) to stretch oneself out, to lie down (at full length); **s'é. sur un sujet,** to dwell, enlarge, on a subject (*b*) to extend, stretch; **la ligne s'étend jusqu'à Charenton,** the line stretches to Charenton (*c*) to expand, grow larger. **étendu,** *-ue* **1.** *a* (*a*) extensive (knowledge); far-reaching (influence); wide (plain) (*b*) outstretched (hands) **2.** *nf* **étendue,** extent, size, dimensions, area; scale (of disaster); stretch (of water); sweep (of country); expanse (of sea); range (of voice); extent (of knowledge).

éternel, -elle [etɛrnɛl] *a* (*a*) eternal; everlasting (*b*) perpetual, endless; **fumant son éternelle cigarette,** always smoking a cigarette. **éternellement** *adv* eternally; everlastingly; perpetually, endlessly.

éterniser [etɛrnize] *vtr* **1.** to eternalize; to drag on (discussion) **2. s'é.,** to last for ever; to drag on; (*of visitor*) to outstay his welcome; **on ne peut pas s'é. ici,** we can't stay here for ever.

éternité [etɛrnite] *nf* eternity; **de toute é.,** from time immemorial; **il y a une é. que je ne t'ai vu,** I haven't seen you for ages.

éternuement [etɛrnymɑ̃] *nm* **1.** sneezing **2.** sneeze.

éternuer [etɛrnɥe] *vi* to sneeze.

éther [etɛr] *nm Ch: Med:* ether.

Éthiopie [etjɔpi] *Prnf Geog:* Ethiopia. **éthiopien, -ienne** *a & n* Ethiopian.

éthique [etik] **1.** *a* ethical **2.** *nf* ethics.

ethnie [etni] *nf* ethnic group. **ethnique** *a* ethnic.

ethnologie [etnɔlɔʒi] *nf* ethnology. **ethnologique** *a* ethnological.

ethnologue [etnɔlɔg] *n* ethnologist.

étinceler [etɛ̃sle] *vi* (**il étincelle**) **1.** to throw out sparks **2.** (*of diamond, stars*) to sparkle, glitter, gleam; **ses yeux étincelaient de colère,** his eyes flashed with anger.

étincelle [etɛ̃sɛl] *nf* spark; **jeter, lancer, des étincelles,** to throw out sparks, to sparkle; **é. de génie,** flash of genius.

étiolement [etjɔlmɑ̃] *nm* (*a*) *Bot: Med:* chlorosis; *Hort:* blanching (*b*) atrophy (of the mind); weakening (of the intellect).

étioler [etjɔle] *vtr* **1.** (*a*) to blanch (*b*) to enfeeble (s.o.) **2. s'é.** (*a*) to blanch (*b*) (*of mind*) to become atrophied.

étiquetage [etiktaʒ] *nm* labelling.

étiqueter [etikte] *vtr* (**j'étiquète**) to label (luggage).

étiquette [etikɛt] *nf* **1.** label **2.** etiquette.

étirer [etire] *vtr* **1.** to stretch; to draw out; to draw (wire) **2. s'é.** (*a*) to stretch (oneself, one's limbs) (*b*) (*of jumper*) to stretch.

étoffe [etɔf] *nf* material; fabric; **avoir de l'é.,** to have plenty of grit; **il a l'é. d'un bon chef,** he has the makings of a good leader.

étoffer [etɔfe] *vtr* **1.** to use ample material in making

(sth); **é. un discours,** to give substance to a speech **2.** (*of pers*) **s'é.,** to fill out.

étoile [etwal] *nf* **1.** star; **é. filante,** shooting star; **coucher à la belle é.,** to sleep in the open; **né sous une bonne, une mauvaise, é.,** born under a lucky, an unlucky, star **2.** (*a*) star (of a decoration) (*b*) *Typ:* asterisk, star; **hôtel à cinq étoiles,** five-star hotel (*c*) **é. de mer,** starfish **3.** (film) star. **étoilé** *a* starry, starlit (sky); **la Bannière étoilée,** the Star-spangled Banner.

étole [etɔl] *nf Ecc:* stole.

étonnement [etɔnmɑ̃] *nm* astonishment, surprise; wonder, amazement.

étonner [etɔne] *vtr* **1.** to astonish, amaze, surprise; **cela ne m'étonnerait pas,** I shouldn't be surprised **2. s'é.,** to be astonished, surprised, to wonder (**de, at**); **je m'étonne qu'il ne voie pas le danger,** it amazes me that he does not see the danger. **étonnant** *a* astonishing, surprising; **rien d'é. (à cela),** (that's) no wonder; *F:* **vous êtes é.!** you're the limit! *n* **l'é. est qu'il soit venu,** the surprising thing is that he came. **étonnamment** *adv* astonishingly, surprisingly.

étouffée [etufe] *nf Cu:* **cuire à l'é.,** to steam (vegetables); to braise (meat).

étouffement [etufmɑ̃] *nm* **1.** suffocation, stifling (of s.o.); smothering (of fire); hushing-up (of scandal) **2.** choking sensation.

étouffer [etufe] **1.** *vtr* (*a*) to suffocate, smother (s.o.) (*b*) to stifle (cry); to smother (fire); to suppress (revolt); to muffle (sound); **é. une affaire,** to hush up a matter; **é. un sanglot,** to choke back a sob **2.** *vi & pr* (*a*) to suffocate, choke (*b*) **on étouffe ici,** it's stifling in here. **étouffant** *a* stifling, suffocating, stuffy; oppressive (heat).

étoupe [etup] *nf* **é. blanche,** tow; **e. noire,** oakum.

étourderie [eturdəri] *nf* **1.** thoughtlessness; **par é.,** inadvertently **2.** thoughtless action; careless mistake.

étourdir [eturdir] *vtr* **1.** (*a*) to stun, daze; to make (s.o.) dizzy (*b*) to ease, to deaden (pain) **2. s'é.,** to try to forget; **s'é. dans la boisson,** to drown one's sorrows. **étourdi, -ie 1.** *a* thoughtless, scatterbrained; foolish **2.** *n* scatterbrain. **étourdiment** *adv* thoughtlessly. **étourdissant** *a* deafening (noise); staggering, astounding (news).

étourdissement [eturdismɑ̃] *nm* giddiness, dizziness; **avoir un é.,** to feel giddy; **cela me donne des étourdissements,** it makes my head swim.

étourneau, -eaux [eturno] *nm* **1.** *Orn:* starling **2.** *F:* scatterbrain.

étrange [etrɑ̃ʒ] *a* strange, peculiar, odd; **chose é., il est revenu,** strange to say, he came back. **étrangement** *adv* strangely, oddly, peculiarly; **cela ressemble é. à la rougeole,** it looks suspiciously like measles.

étranger, -ère [etrɑ̃ʒe, -ɛr] **1.** (*a*) *a* foreign (*b*) *n* foreigner, alien (*c*) *nm* **vivre à l'é.,** to live abroad **2.** (*a*) *a* strange, unknown; **sa voix m'est étrangère,** I've never heard his voice (*b*) *n* stranger; **société fermée aux étrangers,** society not open to outsiders **3.** *a* extraneous, foreign; not belonging (to sth); irrelevant (**à, to**); **c'est é. à la question,** it's beside the point; **il est é. à la musique,** he has no knowledge of music.

étrangeté [etrɑ̃ʒte] *nf* strangeness, peculiarity, oddness (of conduct, style).

étranglement [etrɑ̃gləmɑ̃] *nm* **1.** (a) strangling, strangulation (of s.o.) (b) constriction; *Mch:* throttling **2.** bottleneck (in road); narrows (of river).

étrangler [etrɑ̃gle] *vtr* **1.** (a) to strangle, throttle (s.o.); **sa cravate l'étrangle,** his tie is choking him; *vi* **é. de soif,** to be parched with thirst (b) to constrict, compress; to throttle (steam) **2. s'é.,** to choke, suffocate; **s'é. avec une arête de poisson,** to choke on a fishbone; **s'é. de rire,** to choke with laughter.

étrangleur, -euse [etrɑ̃glœr, -øz] *n* strangler.

être¹ [ɛtr] *vi & pred (prp* **étant;** *pp* **été;** *pr ind* **je suis, tu es, il est, n. sommes, v. êtes, ils sont;** *pr sub* **je sois, n. soyons, ils soient;** *imp* **sois, soyons;** *impf* **j'étais;** *ph* **je fus;** *fu* **je serai) 1.** to be, to exist; **je pense, donc je suis,** I think, therefore I am; **elle n'est plus,** she is no more, she is dead; **cela étant,** that being the case; **eh bien, soit!** well, so be it! **ainsi soit-il,** so be it; *Ecc:* amen; **on ne peut pas ê. et avoir été,** you can't have your cake and eat it **2.** (a) **il est chef de gare,** he is a stationmaster; **c'est le chef de gare,** he's the stationmaster; **soit un triangle ABC,** given a triangle ABC (b) **l'homme est mortel,** man is mortal; **nous étions trois,** there were three of us (c) **ê. bien avec qn,** to be on good terms with s.o.; **nous sommes le dix,** it's the tenth (today) (d) **ê. à l'agonie,** to be dying; **il est tout à son travail,** he is entirely engrossed in his work (e) **ce tableau est de Gauguin,** this picture is by Gauguin; **il est de Londres,** he is from London; **il n'est pas des nôtres,** he isn't a member of our party; he isn't one of us; **être de service,** to be on duty (f) **j'étais là à l'attendre,** I was there waiting for her (g) *(with* ce *as neuter subject)* **je sais ce qui est arrivé,** I know what happened; **est-ce vrai?** is it true? **vous venez, n'est-ce pas?** you're coming aren't you? **n'est-ce pas qu'il a de la chance?** isn't he lucky? (h) *impers uses* (i) **il est midi,** it is twelve o'clock; **comme si de rien n'était,** as if nothing had happened; **soit dit sans offense,** if you don't mind my saying so (ii) **il était une fois,** once upon a time (i) *(with indeterminate* en) (i) **où en sommes-nous?** how far have we got? where are we? **vous n'en êtes pas encore là!** you haven't come to that yet! **je ne sais plus où j'en suis,** I don't know where I'm doing (ii) **j'en suis pour mon argent,** I've spent my money to no purpose (iii) **il en est pour le changement,** he's all for change (iv) **j'en suis!** count me in! I'm on! (v) **c'en est trop!** this is too much! (vi) *(impers)* **puisqu'il en est ainsi,** since that is how things are; **il n'en est rien!** nothing of the kind! (j) *(with indeterminate* y) **il y est pour quelque chose,** he's got something to do with it; **ça y est!** that's it! **vous y êtes?** are you with me? have you got it? **3.** (a) **ê. à qn,** to belong to s.o.; **je suis à vous dans un instant,** I'll be with you in a moment (b) **c'est à vous de jouer,** it's your turn to play **4.** *(aux use)* (a) *(with vi denoting change of place or state)* **il est arrivé,** he has arrived; **elle est née en 1950,** she was born in 1950 (b) *(with vpr)* **nous nous sommes trompés,** we (have) made a mistake **5.** *(as aux of the passive voice)* **il fut puni par son père,** he was punished by his father; **j'entends ê. obéi,** I mean to be obeyed **6.** (a) = **aller** *(in compound tenses and ph)* **j'avais été à Paris,** I had been to Paris (b) =

s'en aller *(in ph only)* **il s'en fut ouvrir la porte,** he went off to open the door.

être² *nm* (a) being, existence (b) being, individual; **ê. humain,** human being; **un ê. cher,** a loved one.

étreindre [etrɛ̃dr] *vtr (conj like* PEINDRE) to embrace, hug; to clasp (s.o.) in one's arms; **é. la main de qn,** to wring s.o.'s hand; **la peur l'étreignait,** he was in the grip of fear.

étreinte [etrɛ̃t] *nf* (a) embrace, hug; clutch; grasp, grip (b) (exertion of) pressure.

étrenne [etrɛn] *nf usu pl* New Year's gift; **les étrennes du facteur** = the postman's Christmas box.

étrenner [etrene] **1.** *vtr* to use (sth), to wear (dress), for the first time; to christen (object) **2.** *vi P:* **tu vas é.!** you're going to catch it!

étrier [etrije] *nm* stirrup; **vider les étriers,** to fall off (a horse).

étriqué [etrike] *a* (a) skimpy, tight (garment) (b) narrow, limited (outlook, life).

étroit [etrwa] *a* **1.** narrow; confined (space); **à l'esprit é.,** narrow-minded **2.** tight, close (knot, bond); tight(-fitting) (coat); **le sens é. d'un mot,** the strict meaning of a word **3.** *adv phr* **être à l'é.,** to be cramped for room.

étroitement *adv* tightly, closely; **ils sont é. liés d'amitié,** they are close friends.

étroitesse [etrwates] *nf* **1.** narrowness; **é. d'esprit,** narrow-mindedness **2.** tightness, closeness.

étude [etyd] *nf* **1.** (a) study, studying; **programme d'études,** curriculum; syllabus; **faire des études de français,** to study French; **faire ses études à,** to be educated at; *Sch:* **l'é. du soir,** (evening) prep; **(salle d')é.,** prep room (b) research (work); *CivE:* survey; **bureau d'études,** research department; **é. d'un canal,** project for a canal; **ingénieur d'études,** design engineer; **comité d'é.,** committee of enquiry; **mettre une question à l'é.,** to study a question **2.** *Mus:* study **3.** (a) office (of solicitor) (b) chambers (of barrister); (lawyer's) practice.

étudiant, -ante [etydjɑ̃, -ɑ̃t] *n* student; undergraduate; **é. en médecine,** medical student; **é. de première année,** freshman.

étudier [etydje] *(impf & pr sub* n. **étudiions)** *vtr* (a) to study; to prepare (lessons); to read (law); **é. son piano,** to practise the piano (b) to investigate, look into (a question); to devise (process); to design (machine) (c) to study (gestures). **étudié** *a* studied (calm), elaborate, deliberate (effect); keen (prices); **machine très étudiée,** carefully designed machine.

étui [etɥi] *nm* case, box; **é. à lunettes,** spectacle case; **é. de revolver,** holster.

étuve [etyv] *nf* **1.** steam room **2.** *Ch: Ind:* drying oven; *Med:* sterilizer; *F:* **quelle é.!** what an oven!

étuvée [etyve] *nf Cu:* **à l'é.,** steamed (vegetables); braised (meat).

étymologie [etimɔlɔʒi] *nf* etymology. **étymologique** *a* etymological.

eucalyptus [økaliptys] *nm* eucalyptus.

Eucharistie [økaristi] *nf Ecc:* Eucharist.

euh [ø] *int* er!

eunuque [ønyk] *nm* eunuch.

euphémisme [øfemism] *nm* euphemism. **euphémique** *a* euphemistic.

euphorie [øfɔri] *nf* euphoria. **euphorique** *a* euphoric.

euphorisant [øfɔrizɑ̃] *nm* euphoriant (drug).
eurodollar [ørɔdɔlar] *nm* Eurodollar.
Europe [ørɔp] *Prnf Geog:* Europe. **européen, -enne** *a & n* European.
européaniser [ørɔpeanize] *vtr* to Europeanize.
Eurovision [ørɔviziɔ̃] *Prnf* Eurovision.
euthanasie [øtanazi] *nf* euthanasia.
eux [ø] *see* **lui²**.
évacuation [evakɥasjɔ̃] *nf* evacuation.
évacué, -ée [evakɥe] *n* evacuee.
évacuer [evakɥe] *vtr* to evacuate.
évadé, -ée [evade] *n* escaped prisoner.
évader (s') [sevade] *vpr* to escape (**de,** from).
évaluation [evalɥasjɔ̃] *nf* valuation, appraisement; assessment; estimate.
évaluer [evalɥe] *vtr* to value, appraise; to assess; to estimate.
évangéliser [evɑ̃ʒelize] *vtr* to evangelize. **évangélique** *a* evangelical.
évangéliste [evɑ̃ʒelist] *nm* evangelist.
évangile [evɑ̃ʒil] *nm* **l'É.,** the Gospel; **prendre qch pour parole d'é.,** to take sth for gospel (truth).
évanouir (s') [sevanwir] *vpr* **1.** to vanish, disappear; *(of sound)* to die away **2.** to faint.
évanouissement [evanwismɑ̃] *nm* **1.** vanishing, disappearance; dying away (of sound) **2.** fainting fit; faint.
évaporation [evaporasjɔ̃] *nf* evaporation.
évaporer(s') [sevapore] *vpr* *(a)* to evaporate; **faire é. un liquide,** to evaporate a liquid *(b)* to vanish (into thin air). **évaporé, -ée 1.** *a* featherbrained **2.** *n* featherbrain.
évasement [evazmɑ̃] *nm* widening out, splaying; flare.
évaser(s') [sevaze] *vpr* to widen, open out; to flare out.
évasif, -ive [evazif, -iv] *a* evasive. **évasivement** *adv* evasively.
évasion [evazjɔ̃] *nf* **1.** escape (from prison); **é. des capitaux,** flight of capital; **é. fiscale,** tax avoidance **2.** escapism.
évêché [eveʃe] *nm* **1.** bishopric, see; diocese **2.** bishop's palace.
éveil [evɛj] *nm* **1.** *(a)* awakening *(b)* **être en é.,** to be wide awake; to be on the alert **2.** warning; **donner l'é.,** to raise the alarm.
éveiller [eveje] *vtr* **1.** to awake(n); to wake (s.o.) up; to arouse (curiosity, suspicion) **2. s'é.,** to wake (up); to awaken; *(of curiosity)* to be aroused. **éveillé** *a* **1.** awake **2.** wide awake; alert.
événement [evenmɑ̃] *nm* **1.** event **2.** occurrence, incident; **faire é.,** to cause a stir; **semaine pleine d'événements,** eventful week.
éventail, -ails [evɑ̃taj] *nm* **1.** fan; **en é.,** fan-shaped **2.** range (of goods).
éventaire [evɑ̃tɛr] *nm* *(a)* hawker's tray *(b)* (street) stall.
éventer [evɑ̃te] *vtr* **1.** *(a)* to air *(b)* to fan (s.o.) **2. s'é.,** *(of food)* to spoil; *(of beer)* to go flat, stale.
éventrer [evɑ̃tre] *vtr* to disembowel; to rip open, to slit open.
éventualité [evɑ̃tɥalite] *nf* possibility, eventuality, contingency. **éventuel, -elle 1.** *a* *(a)* possible; **à titre é.,** as a possible event; **client é.,** potential

customer *(b)* eventual (profits) **2.** *nm* eventuality, contingency. **éventuellement** *adv* possible; if necessary; should the occasion arise.
évêque [evɛk] *nm* bishop.
évertuer (s') [severtɥe] *vpr* to do one's utmost; to exert oneself.
éviction [eviksjɔ̃] *nf* eviction.
évidence [evidɑ̃s] *nf* *(a)* obviousness, clearness (of fact); **se rendre à l'é.,** to yield to the facts; **se refuser à l'é.,** to deny the facts; **de toute é.,** clearly, obviously *(b)* conspicuousness; **être en é.,** to be in a prominent position; **mettre en é.,** to bring to the fore; to put in a prominent position. **évident** *a* evident, obvious, clear, plain; **c'est é.,** it stands to reason. **évidemment** *adv* obviously; of course, certainly; naturally.
évider [evide] *vtr* to hollow out.
évier [evje] *nm* (kitchen) sink.
évincer [evɛ̃se] *vtr* (**n. évinçons**) **1.** to evict **2.** to oust, supplant.
évitement [evitmɑ̃] *nm* **1.** avoidance (of s.o., sth) **2.** *(a) Rail:* shunting (of train); **voie, gare, d'é.,** siding *(b)* **route d'é.,** bypass.
éviter [evite] *vtr* *(a)* to avoid, shun; to keep out of (s.o.'s) way; **é. un coup,** to dodge a blow; **é. de la tête,** to duck; **é. de faire qch,** to avoid doing sth *(b)* **é. une peine à qn,** to spare s.o. trouble. **évitable** *a* avoidable, preventable.
évocation [evɔkasjɔ̃] *nf* evocation. **évocateur, -trice** *a* evocative.
évoluer [evɔlɥe] *vi* **1.** *(a)* *(of troops)* to manoeuvre *(b)* (i) to move around (ii) to move in society **2.** to evolve, develop; *(of science)* to advance; *(of illness)* to make progress. **évolué** *a* (highly) developed, advanced; mature, broadminded (person).
évolution [evɔlysjɔ̃] *nf* **1.** *(a)* manoeuvre (of troops) *(b)* movement **2.** evolution; development; evolvement (of plan); course (of disease).
évoquer [evɔke] *vtr* *(a)* to evoke; to conjure up *(b)* to call to mind, to recall.
ex. *abbr exemple.*
exacerber [ɛgzasɛrbe] *vtr* to exacerbate, aggravate.
exact [ɛgzakt] *a* *(a)* exact; accurate, true, right, correct; **c'est e.,** it's quite true; it's a fact *(b)* strict; rigorous *(c)* punctual. **exactement** *adv* *(a)* exactly; accurately, correctly; just, precisely; **effet e. contraire,** directly opposite effect *(b)* punctually.
exaction [ɛgzaksjɔ̃] *nf* **1.** exaction **2.** extortion.
exactitude [ɛgzaktityd] *nf* *(a)* exactness, accuracy, exactitude *(b)* punctuality.
ex aequo [ɛgzeko] *Lt adj phr* of equal merit; **classés ex ae.,** placed equal.
exagération [ɛgzaʒerasjɔ̃] *nf* exaggeration.
exagérer [ɛgzaʒere] *vtr* (**j'exagère**) to exaggerate (danger); to overstate (truth); to overestimate, overrate (qualities); **tu exagères!** you're going too far! **exagéré** *a* exaggerated; excessive. **exagérément** *adv* exaggeratedly.
exaltation [ɛgzaltasjɔ̃] *nf* **1.** exaltation; exalting, extolling **2.** *(a)* exaltation, elation *(b) Med:* overexcitement.
exalter [ɛgzalte] *vtr* **1.** *(a)* to exalt, glorify, extol *(b)* to excite, inflame (imagination) *(c)* to exalt, dignify **2. s'e.,** to grow excited; to enthuse. **exaltant** *a*

exciting, stirring. **exalté, -ée 1.** *a* excited, impassioned; hotheaded (pers); uplifted (state of mind) **2.** *n* hothead; fanatic.

examen [ɛgzamɛ̃] *nm* (*a*) examination; investigation; inspection (of accounts); **e. attentif,** careful scrutiny; **e. de la vue,** sight testing; **question à l'e.,** matter under consideration; **e. de conscience,** self examination (*b*) *Sch:* exam(ination); **être reçu, refusé, à un e.,** to pass, to fail, an exam; **e. pour permis de conduire,** driving test; **jury d'e.,** the examiners.

examinateur, -trice [ɛgzaminatœr, -tris] *n* examiner.

examiner [ɛgzamine] *vtr* to examine; to scrutinize, study carefully; to investigate; to inspect; **se faire e. par un médecin,** to have oneself examined by a doctor; **e. une question,** to look into a question; **s'e. dans un miroir,** to examine oneself in a mirror.

exaspération [ɛgzasperasjɔ̃] *nf* exasperation.

exaspérer [ɛgzaspere] *vt* (**j'exaspère; j'exaspérerai**) **1.** to aggravate (pain) **2.** to exasperate, irritate.

exaucement [ɛgzosmɑ̃] *nm* granting, fulfilment (of wish).

exaucer [ɛgzose] *vtr* (**n. exauçons**) to grant, fulfil (wish).

excavation [ɛkskavasjɔ̃] *nf* **1.** excavation, excavating **2.** excavation, hollow, pit.

excédent [ɛksedɑ̃] *nm* excess, surplus; **e. de poids,** excess weight. **excédentaire** *a* excess, surplus.

excéder [ɛksede] *vtr* (**j'excède; j'excéderai**) **1.** to exceed, go beyond **2.** (*a*) to tire (s.o.) out; **excédé de fatigue,** worn out (*b*) to exasperate (s.o.).

excellence [ɛksɛlɑ̃s] *nf* **1.** excellence, pre-eminence; **par e.,** (i) par excellence, pre-eminently (ii) supremely, above all **2. votre E.,** your Excellency. **excellent** *a* excellent. **excellemment** *adv* excellently.

exceller [ɛksele] *vi* to excel (**à faire qch,** in doing sth).

excentricité [ɛksɑ̃trisite] *nf* eccentricity. **excentrique 1.** *a* (*a*) eccentric (*b*) outlying (suburb) (*c*) eccentric, odd (person) **2.** *n* eccentric.

excepter [ɛksɛpte] *vtr* to except, exclude (s.o., sth) (**de,** from); **les femmes exceptées,** apart from, except, the women. **excepté** *prep* except(ing), besides, but, with the exception of.

exception [ɛksɛpsjɔ̃] *nf* exception; **faire e. à une règle,** to be an exception to a rule; **tous à l'e. du docteur, e. faite du docteur,** all except the doctor. **exceptionnel, -elle** *a* exceptional; (i) special (leave) (ii) uncommon, out of the ordinary; outstanding (talent). **exceptionnellement** *adv* exceptionally.

excès [ɛksɛ] *nm* (*a*) excess; **pécher par e. de zèle,** to be overzealous; *Aut:* **e. de vitesse,** exceeding the speed limit; **manger avec e.,** to eat too much; **(jusqu')à l'e.,** to excess; too much; **scrupuleux à l'e.,** scrupulous to a fault; over-scrupulous (*b*) *pl* **commettre des e.,** to go too far; **e. de table,** overeating. **excessif, -ive** *a* excessive, extreme; **être e.,** to go to extremes. **excessivement** *adv* excessively.

excitation [ɛksitasjɔ̃] *nf* **1.** excitation (of the senses); **e. à la révolte,** incitement to rebellion **2.** (state of) excitement.

exciter [ɛksite] *vtr* **1.** (*a*) to excite; to arouse, stir up;

e. la pitié de qn, to move s.o. to pity (*b*) to urge (s.o.) on; to incite (s.o.) (to revolt); **e. qn contre qn,** to set s.o. against s.o. (*c*) to stimulate (nerve) **2. s'e.,** to get excited, worked up. **excitable** *a* excitable. **excitant 1.** *a* exciting **2.** *nm* stimulant. **excité, -ée 1.** *a* excited **2.** *n* hothead.

exclamation [ɛksklamasjɔ̃] *nf* exclamation.

exclamer (s') [sɛksklame] *vpr* to exclaim.

exclure [ɛksklyr] *vtr* (*ph* **j'exclus**) (*a*) to exclude, shut out, leave out; **candidat exclu,** unsuccessful candidate; **le mois d'août jusqu'au 31 exclu,** the month of August excluding 31st (*b*) **deux choses qui s'excluent,** two things that are mutually exclusive.

exclusion [ɛksklyzjɔ̃] *nf* exclusion; **à l'e. de,** to the exclusion of.

exclusivité [ɛksklyzivite] *nf* sole, exclusive, rights; **film en e.,** exclusive film; **article en e.,** exclusive. **exclusif, -ive** *a* exclusive, sole (rights, agent). **exclusivement** *adv* exclusively, solely; **depuis lundi jusqu'à vendredi e.,** from Monday to Friday exclusive.

excommunication [ɛkskɔmynikasjɔ̃] *nf* excommunication.

excommunier [ɛkskɔmynje] *vtr* (*impf & pr sub* **n. excomuniions**) to excommunicate.

excrément [ɛkskremɑ̃] *nm often pl* **excrément(s),** excrement.

excrétion [ɛkskresjɔ̃] *nf* excretion.

excroissance [ɛkskrwasɑ̃s] *nf* excrescence.

excursion [ɛkskyrsjɔ̃] *nf* excursion; tour; trip; outing; **e. à pied,** walking tour; hike.

excursionniste [ɛkskyrsjɔnist] *n* excursionist; tourist, tripper; hiker.

excuse [ɛkskyz] *nf* **1.** excuse **2.** *pl* apology; **faire ses excuses à qn,** to apologize to s.o.

excuser [ɛkskyze] *vtr* **1.** (*a*) to make excuses, apologize, for (s.o.) (*b*) to excuse, pardon (s.o.); **e. qn de faire qch,** to excuse s.o. (i) for doing sth (ii) from doing sth; **l'ignorance n'excuse personne,** ignorance is no excuse **2. s'e.,** to apologize; **s'e. auprès de qn,** to send one's apologies to s.o.; *F:* **je m'excuse,** excuse me. **excusable** *a* excusable, pardonable.

exécration [ɛgzekrasjɔ̃, ɛks-] *nf* execration, loathing.

exécrer [ɛgzekre, ɛks-] *vtr* (**j'exècre; j'exécrerai**) to execrate, loathe, detest. **execrable** *a* execrable, loathsome, abominable. **exécrablement** *adv* execrably, abominably.

exécutant, -ante [ɛgzekytɑ̃, -ɑ̃t] *n* executant; *Mus:* performer.

exécuter [ɛgzekyte] *vtr* **1.** (*a*) to execute; to carry out, achieve (plan); to perform, fulfill (promise); to play (piece of music); to perform (dance) (*b*) (i) to execute; to put to death (ii) *Jur:* to distrain upon (debtor) **2. s'e.,** to submit, to comply; **il faudra bien vous e.,** you'll have to bring yourself to do it. **exécutif, -ive** *a* executive; **le pouvoir e.,** *nm* **l'e.,** the Executive.

exécuteur, -trice [ɛgzekytœr, -tris] *n* **e. testamentaire,** executor, -trix.

exécution [ɛgzekysjɔ̃] *nf* **1.** execution, performance; carrying out (of plan); fulfilment (of promise); enforcement (of law); performance (of piece of music); **mettre un projet à e.,** to put a plan into execution;

en voie d'e., in progress 2. (a) **e. capitale,** execution; **ordre d'e.,** death warrant (b) Jur: distraint.

exemplaire [εgzãplεr] 1. a exemplary 2. nm (a) specimen (of work) (b) copy (of book); **en double e.,** in duplicate.

exemple [εgzãpl] nm 1. example; **donner l'e.,** to set an example; **prendre e. sur qn,** to follow s.o.'s example 2. lesson, warning; **faire un e. de qn,** to make an example of s.o. 3. instance, precedent; **par e.,** for instance; **par e.!** well! who'd have thought it! **ah non, par e.!** I should think not!

exemplifier [εgzãplifje] vtr to exemplify.

exempter [εgzãte] vtr e. **qn (de qch),** to exempt, excuse, s.o. (from sth).

exemption [εgzãpsjõ] nf exemption (de, from); freedom (from anxiety). **exempt** a exempt, free; e. **de soucis,** carefree; e. **de droits,** duty-free.

exercer [εgzεrse] vtr (n. exerçons) 1. (a) (i) to exercise (ii) Mil: to drill; e. **qn à faire qch,** to train s.o. to do sth (b) to exercise; e. **son influence sur qn,** to exert one's influence on s.o.; e. **une pression sur qch,** to exert pressure on sth (c) **médicament qui exerce une action sur le foie,** medicine that acts upon the liver (d) to exercise, practise (profession); to carry on (business, trade); vi **notre médecin n'exerce plus,** our doctor is no longer in practice 2. **s'e.** (a) to drill; to do exercises (b) to practise; **s'e. à qch,** to practise sth.' **exercé** a experienced, practised, trained.

exercice [εgzεrsis] nm 1. (a) exercise; **prendre de l'e.,** to take exercise (b) Mil: drill(ing), training (c) (school) exercises 2. (a) exercise (of power, privilege); practice (of profession); **dans l'e. de ses fonctions,** exercising one's duties; **avocat en e.,** practising barrister (b) **l'e. du culte,** public worship 3. financial year; year's trading.

exhalaison [εgzalεzõ] nf exhalation.

exhaler [εgzale] vtr 1. to exhale, emit (smell); to breathe (a sigh) 2. (of gas, vapour) to be given off.

exhaustif, -ive [εgzostif, -iv] a exhaustive. **exhaustivement** adv exhaustively.

exhiber [εgzibe] vtr 1. (a) to produce (documents); to present, show (passport) (b) to show, exhibit (animals); to display, show off (knowledge) 2. **s'e.,** to make an exhibition of oneself.

exhibitionnisme [εgzibisjɔnism] nm exhibitionism.

exhibitionniste [εgzibisjɔnist] n exhibitionist.

exhortation [εgzɔrtasjõ] nf exhortation.

exhorter [εgzɔrte] vtr to exhort, urge.

exhumation [εgzymasjõ] nf exhumation, disinterment; unearthing (of old documents).

exhumer [εgzyme] vtr (a) to exhume, disinter (b) to unearth, bring to light (old documents).

exigeant [εgziʒã] a exacting; hard to please.

exigence [εgziʒãs] nf 1. **elle est d'une e. insupportable,** she's intolerably demanding 2. (a) (unreasonable) demand (b) requirement, demand.

exiger [εgziʒe] vtr (n. exigeons) 1. to exact; to demand, require (de, from); to insist on (sth) 2. to require, call for, necessitate (care). **exigeant** a exacting, demanding; **être trop e.,** to expect too much.

exigible [εgziʒibl] a exactable; (payment) due.

exiguïté [εgzigɥite] nf exiguity, smallness; scantiness;

slenderness (of income). **exigu, -uë** a exiguous, tiny (flat); scanty (resources); slender (income).

exil [εgzil] nm exile, banishment.

exilé, -ée [εgzile] n exile.

exiler [εgzile] vtr 1. to exile, banish 2. **s'e.,** to go into (voluntary) exile; **s'e. du monde,** to withdraw from the world.

existence [εgzistãs] nf (a) existence (b) life.

exister [εgziste] vi to exist, be; to live; **la maison existe toujours,** the house is still standing; **rien n'existe pour lui que l'art,** nothing but art matters to him. **existant** a existing.

exode [εgzɔd] nm exodus; e. **rural,** rural depopulation.

exonération [εgzɔnerasjõ] nf exoneration; exemption; e. **d'impôts,** tax relief.

exonérer [εgzɔnere] vtr (j'exonère; j'exonérerai) to exonerate; to exempt (s.o. from income tax).

exorbitant [εgzɔrbitã] a exorbitant.

exorciser [εgzɔrsize] vtr to exorcise.

exorcisme [εgzɔrsism] nm exorcism.

exorciste [εgzɔrsist] n exorcist.

exotisme [εgzɔtism] nm exoticism. **exotique** a exotic.

expansion [εkspãsjõ] nf 1. (a) expansion; **en e.,** booming; (fast) expanding (b) spread (of ideas); **taux d'e. économique,** economic growth rate 2. expansiveness; **avec e.,** effusively.

expansivité [εkspãsivite] nf expansiveness. **expansif, -ive** a expansive; (of pers) effusive.

expatriation [εkspatrijasjõ] nf expatriation.

expatrié, -ée [εkspatrije] n expatriate.

expatrier [εkspatrije] vtr (impf & pr sub n. expatriions) 1. to expatriate 2. **s'e.,** to settle abroad.

expectative [εkspεktativ] nf expectation, expectancy; **rester dans l'e.,** to wait and see.

expectoration [εkspεktɔrasjõ] nf expectoration.

expectorer [εkspεktɔre] vtr to expectorate.

expédient [εkspedjã] 1. a expedient 2. nm expedient, device; **vivre d'expédients,** to live by one's wits.

expédier [εkspedje] vtr (impf & pr sub n. expédiions) 1. to dispatch; to get rid of, dispose of (s.o.) 2. (a) to dispatch; to expedite, hurry along (business); e. **son déjeuner,** to polish off one's lunch (b) Cust: to clear (goods) 3. Jur: to draw up (contract) 4. to dispatch; to forward, send off (letter); to ship (goods); e. **par la poste,** to post, to mail. **expéditeur, -trice** 1. n sender 2. a dispatching. **expéditif, -ive** a expeditious.

expédition [εkspedisjõ] nf 1. (a) expedition, dispatch (b) (customs) clearance 2. (a) dispatch(ing), forwarding, sending (b) consignment 3. (military, scientific) expedition. **expéditionnaire** 1. a expeditionary (force) 2. n shipping clerk.

expérience [εksperjãs] nf 1. experience; **avoir l'e. de qch,** to be experienced in sth; **faire l'e. de qch,** to experience sth; **connaître qch par e.,** to know sth from experience; **sans e.,** inexperienced (in) 2. experiment, test; **faire une e.,** to carry out an experiment.

expérimentateur, -trice [εksperimãtatœr, -tris] n experimenter.

expérimentation [εksperimãtasjõ] nf experimentation, experimenting.

expérimenter [εksperimãte] *vtr* to test, try (remedy); *abs* to make experiments. **expérimental, -aux** *a* experimental. **expérimentalement** *adv* experimentally. **expérimenté** *a* experienced; skilled.

expert, -erte [εkspεr, -εrt] **1.** *a* expert, skilled (**en, dans,** in) **2.** *nm* (*a*) expert; connoisseur (*b*) valuer, appraiser. **expertement** *adv* expertly.

expert-comptable [εkspεrkɔ̃tabl] *nm* = chartered accountant; *pl experts-comptables.*

expertise [εkspεrtiz] *nf* **1.** expert appraisement; valuation **2.** expert's report.

expertiser [εkspεrtize] *vtr* to value, estimate, appraise, assess; **faire e. qch,** to have sth valued.

expiation [εkspjasjɔ̃] *nf* expiation; atonement.

expier [εkspje] *vtr (impf & pr sub* **n. expiions)** to expiate, atone for (sin).

expiration [εkspirasjɔ̃] *nf* **1.** expiration; breathing out **2.** expiry, termination, end (of lease).

expirer [εkspire] **1.** *vtr* to expire; to breathe out (air) **2.** *vi* (*a*) to die (*b*) to come to an end; (*of lease*) to run out.

explétif, -ive [εkspletif, -iv] *a & nm* expletive.

explication [εksplikasjɔ̃] *nf* explanation; **donner l'e. de qch,** to explain sth; *Sch:* **e. de textes,** literary appreciation (of texts).

expliciter [εksplisite] *vtr* to clarify, to make explicit. **explicite** *a* explicit, clear, plain. **explicitement** *adv* explicitly, clearly, plainly.

expliquer [εksplike] *vtr* **1.** (*a*) to explain, make clear (*b*) to explain, expound, elucidate (doctrine); to account for (action); **je ne m'explique pas pourquoi,** I can't understand why **2.** **s'e.,** to explain oneself; **je m'explique,** this is what I mean; **s'e. avec qn,** to have it out with s.o. **explicable** *a* explicable, explainable. **explicatif, -ive** *a* explanatory.

exploit [εksplwa] *nm* exploit; feat; achievement.

exploitant [εksplwatã] *nm* farmer.

exploitation [εksplwatasjɔ̃] *nf* **1.** (*a*) exploitation; working (of mine); running (of railway, newspaper); utilization (of invention); tapping (of natural resources); **société d'e.,** development company; **e. agricole,** farming (*b*) exploitation, taking advantage of (tourists) **2.** (*a*) mine; works (*b*) farm (estate); holding.

exploiter [εksplwate] *vtr* to exploit; to work (mine); to operate (railway); to farm (land); to run (farm).

exploiteur, -euse [εksplwatœr, -øz] *n* exploiter.

explorateur, -trice [εksplɔratœr, -tris] *n* explorer.

exploration [εksplɔrasjɔ̃] *nf* exploration.

explorer [εksplɔre] *vtr* to explore.

exploser [εksploze] *vi* to explode, to blow up; (*of anger*) to burst out, to explode. **explosif, -ive** *a & nm* explosive.

explosion [εksplozjɔ̃] *nf* explosion; outburst (of fury); **faire e.,** to explode, blow up.

exportation [εksportasjɔ̃] *nf* export. **exportateur, -trice 1.** *a* exporting **2.** *n* exporter.

exporter [εksporte] *vtr* to export. **exportable** *a* exportable.

exposant, -ante [εkspozã, -ãt] **1.** *n* exhibitor **2.** *nm Mth:* exponent.

exposé [εkspoze] *nm* statement, account, report, exposition (of facts); **faire un e.,** to read a paper.

exposer [εkspoze] *vtr* **1.** (*a*) to exhibit, show, display (goods, works of art); **objet exposé,** exhibit (*b*) to set out (plans); **je leur ai exposé ma situation,** I explained to them how I was placed **2.** to expose; to lay open; **maison exposée au nord,** house facing north; **e. sa vie,** to imperil one's life; **s'e. à des critiques,** to lay oneself open to criticism.

exposition [εkspozisjɔ̃] *nf* **1.** (*a*) exhibition, show (*b*) exposure (to danger) (*c*) exposition, statement; *Lit:* introduction (*d*) *Mus:* exposition **2.** aspect, exposure (of house) **3.** *Phot:* exposure.

exprès¹, -esse [εkspres] **1.** *a* express, explicit (order); **défense expresse de fumer,** smoking strictly prohibited **2.** *a inv & nm* express (letter). **expressément** *adv* **1.** expressly, explicitly **2.** especially, on purpose.

exprès² [εksprε] *adv* designedly, on purpose, intentionally, deliberately; **je ne l'ai pas fait e.,** I didn't do it on purpose.

express [εkspres] *a & nm* **1.** express (train) **2.** espresso (coffee).

expression [εkspresjɔ̃] *nf* **1.** expression; voicing; show (of feelings); **au delà de toute e.,** inexpressible; **sans e.,** expressionless **2.** expression, term, phrase. **expressif, -ive** *a* expressive. **expressivement** *adv* expressively.

exprimer [εksprime] *vtr* **1.** (*a*) to express; to squeeze out (juice) (*b*) to express, to voice, to convey (feelings); (*of looks, gestures*) to show, manifest (pain, pleasure) **2.** **s'e.,** to express oneself; **si je peux m'e. ainsi,** if I may say so. **exprimable** *a* expressible.

expropriation [εksprɔprijasjɔ̃] *nf* expropriation.

exproprier [εksprɔprije] *vtr (impf & pr sub* **n. expropriions)** to expropriate.

expulser [εkspylse] *vtr* to expel; to eject; to turn (s.o.) out; to evict (tenant); to deport (alien); to expel (pupil).

expulsion [εkspylsjɔ̃] *nf* expulsion; deportation; ejection, eviction.

expurger [εkspyrʒe] *vtr* **(j'expurgeai(s))** to expurgate.

exquis [εkski] *a* exquisite.

extase [εkstaz] *nf* ecstasy; rapture; **être en e. devant qch,** to be in ectsasies over sth. **extatique** *a* ecstatic.

extasier (s') [sεkstazje] *vpr (impf & pr sub* **n. n. extasiions)** to go into ecstasies.

extensible [εkstãsibl] *a* extending; expanding (bracelet).

extension [εkstãsjɔ̃] *nf* **1.** (*a*) extension; stretching (*b*) spreading, enlargement; spread (of disease); **prendre de l'e.,** to spread **2.** extended meaning (of word); **par e.,** in a wider sense. **extensible** *a* extensible; extending (table); expanding (bracelet). **extensif, -ive** *a* extensive.

exténuer [εkstenye] *vtr* **1.** to exhaust; **être exténué,** to be tired out **2.** **s'e.,** to tire oneself out.

extérieur [εksterjœr] **1.** *a* (*a*) exterior, outer, external; outside (staircase, interests); **le monde e.,** the outside world (*b*) foreign (trade) **2.** *nm* (*a*) exterior, outside; **vu de l'e.,** seen from the outside; **à l'e.** (i) out of doors (ii) (on the) outside (iii) abroad (b) abroad (c) (outward) appearance; looks (d) *Cin:* location shot. **extérieurement** *adv* 1. externally, on the outside, outwardly 2. on the surface, in appearance.

extérioriser [ɛksterjɔrize] *vtr* to show (one's feelings).

extermination [ɛkstɛrminasjɔ̃] *nf* extermination.

exterminer [ɛkstɛrmine] *vtr* to exterminate.

externat [ɛkstɛrna] *nm* 1. day school 2. *Med:* nonresident medical studentship. **externe** 1. *a* (a) external, outside, outer; **angle e.**, exterior angle; *Pharm:* **pour l'usage e.**, for external use (b) **élève e.**, day pupil 2. *n* (a) day pupil (b) non-resident medical student.

extincteur [ɛkstɛ̃ktœr] *nm* fire extinguisher.

extinction [ɛkstɛ̃ksjɔ̃] *nf* 1. (a) extinction; extinguishing, putting out (b) abolition; paying off (of debt) 2. (a) extinction, dying out (of species) (b) e. de voix, loss of voice.

extirpation [ɛkstirpasjɔ̃] *nf* eradication.

extirper [ɛkstirpe] *vtr* to eradicate, to root out; *F:* e. qn de son lit, to drag s.o. out of bed.

extorquer [ɛkstɔrke] *vtr* to extort, wring (money, promise) (à qn, from s.o.).

extorqueur, -euse [ɛkstɔrkœr, -øz] *n* extortioner.

extorsion [ɛkstɔrsjɔ̃] *nf* extortion.

extra [ɛkstra] 1. *nm inv* (a) something extra; extra dish; **faire un e.**, to do something special (b) occasional job; extra help 2. *a inv* extra-special; first-class 3. *adv* extra-.

extraction [ɛkstraksjɔ̃] *nf* 1. extraction; extracting, mining, quarrying 2. extraction, birth.

extrader [ɛkstrade] *vtr Jur:* to extradite.

extradition [ɛkstradisjɔ̃] *nf* extradition.

extra-fin [ɛkstrafɛ̃] *a* superfine.

extraire [ɛkstrɛr] *vtr* (*conj like* TRAIRE) to extract, draw out, take out, pull out; to extract (tooth, coal);

s'e. d'une situation difficile, to get out of an awkward situation.

extrait [ɛkstrɛ] *nm* 1. extract; e. de viande, meat extract 2. extract, excerpt (from book); abstract (from deed, account); e. de naissance, birth certificate.

extraordinaire [ɛkstraɔrdinɛr] 1. *a* (a) extraordinary; special (messenger) (b) extraordinary, unusual; cela n'a rien d'e., that's nothing out of the ordinary (c) remarkable, outstanding 2. *adv phr* par e., exceptionally; strange to say; strangely enough. **extraordinairement** *adv* extraordinarily.

extra-scolaire [ɛkstraskɔlɛr] *a* out-of-school (activities).

extravagance [ɛkstravagɑ̃s] *nf* extravagance; absurdity; exorbitance (of price). **extravagant** *a* extravagant; absurd; wild (idea); exorbitant (demand, price).

extrême [ɛkstrɛm] 1. *a* (a) extreme; farthest, utmost (point) (b) intense, excessive (cold) (c) drastic, severe (measure) 2. *nm* extreme limit; pousser les choses à l'e., to carry matters to extremes. **extrêmement** *adv* extremely, exceedingly.

extrême-onction [ɛkstrɛmɔ̃ksjɔ̃] *nf Ecc:* extreme unction.

Extrême-Orient [ɛkstrɛmɔrjɑ̃] *Prnm Geog:* Far East.

extrémisme [ɛkstremism] *nm* extremism.

extrémiste [ɛkstremist] *n* extremist.

extrémité [ɛkstremite] *nf* (a) extremity, end; tip, point; *Anat:* les extrémités, the extremities (b) extremity, extreme (of misery); pousser qch à l'e., to carry sth to extremes; réduit à l'e., in dire distress.

exubérance [ɛgzyberɑ̃s] *nf* exuberance. **exubérant** *a* exuberant.

exultation [ɛgzyltasjɔ̃] *nf* exultation.

exulter [ɛgzylte] *vi* to exult, rejoice.

exutoire [ɛgzytwar] *nm* outlet (for anger).

ex-voto [ɛksvɔto] *nm inv* ex-voto; votive offering.

F

F¹, f [ɛf] *nm & f* (the letter) F, f.
F² *abbr Franc(s).*
fa [fa] *nm inv Mus:* 1. (the note) F; **clef de fa,** bass clef 2. (*in the Fixed Do system*) fa.
fable [fabl] *nf* (*a*) fable (*b*) story; invention; **être la f. de toute la ville,** to be the laughing stock of the town.
fabricant, -ante [fabrikã, -ãt] *n* maker, manufacturer.
fabrication [fabrikasjɔ̃] *nf* 1. manufacture, making; **article de f. française,** article made in France 2. forging.
fabrique [fabrik] *nf* 1. manufacture; **prix de f.,** manufacturer's price; **marque de f.,** trademark 2. factory, works; **f. de papier,** paper mill.
fabriquer [fabrike] *vtr* 1. to manufacture; **qu'est-ce que vous fabriquez?** (i) what are you making? (ii) *F:* what on earth are you up to? 2. to fabricate (story).
fabuleux, -euse [fabylø, -øz] *a* 1. fabulous 2. incredible; prodigious; **une somme fabuleuse,** a mint of money. **fabuleusement** *adv* fabulously.
fac [fak] *nf F:* (**faculté**) university.
façade [fasad] *nf* façade, front(age) (of house); **patriotisme de f.,** sham patriotism; *F:* **refaire sa f.,** to make up one's face.
face [fas] *nf* 1. face; **sauver, perdre, la f.,** to save, lose, face 2. flat (of sword blade); side (of lens, gramophone record); head side (of coin); **f. avant, arrière,** front, back 3. (*a*) **sa maison fait f. à l'église,** his house faces the church; **faire f. à des difficultés, à qn,** to cope with difficulties, with s.o. (*b*) **portrait de f.,** full-face portrait; **vue de f.,** front view; **la maison (d')en f.,** the house opposite; **regarder qn (bien) en f.,** to look s.o. full in the face; **regarder les choses en f.,** to face facts; **f. à f.,** face to face (**avec,** with) 4. *prep phr* **f. à,** facing; **en f. de,** opposite; **en f. l'un de l'autre,** opposite each other.
facétie [fasesi] *nf* facetious remark; **dire des facéties,** to crack jokes. **facétieux, -euse** *a* facetious.
facette [fasɛt] *nf* facet.
fâcher [fɑʃe] *vtr* 1. (*a*) to grieve (*b*) to anger; to make (s.o.) angry; to annoy 2. **se f.** (*a*) to get angry; to lose one's temper; to take offence (*b*) **se f. avec qn,** to quarrel with s.o.; **fâché** *a* 1. sorry 2. angry; **être f. contre qn,** to be annoyed with s.o. 3. **être f. avec qn,** to have fallen out with s.o.
fâcherie [fɑʃri] *nf* quarrel.
fâcheux, -euse [fɑʃø, -øz] *a* troublesome, tiresome, annoying; awkward (position); distressing (news). **fâcheusement** *adv* annoyingly; awkwardly.
facile [fasil] *a* 1. (*a*) easy; **c'est f. à dire,** it's more easily said than done (*b*) (i) easy-going; **homme f. à vivre,** man easy to get on with (ii) pliable, easily influenced 2. facile; fluent (style); ready, quick (writer); **je n'ai pas la parole f.,** words don't come easily to me; **elle a les larmes faciles,** she is easily moved to tears. **facilement** *adv* easily, readily.

facilité [fasilite] *nf* 1. (*a*) easiness (of task); **avec f.,** with ease, easily (*b*) **avoir la f. de faire qch.,** to enjoy the opportunity of doing sth; **facilités de paiement,** easy terms; *Bank:* **facilités de caisse,** overdraft facilities 2. aptitude, talent (**pour qch,** for sth); **f. de parole,** fluency 3. pliancy.
faciliter [fasilite] *vtr* to facilitate; to make (sth) easier, easy.
façon [fasɔ̃] *nf* 1. (*a*) (i) making, fashioning; workmanship (ii) style; **f. d'un manteau,** (i) making (up) (ii) cut, of a coat; **tailleur à f.,** bespoke tailor; **on travaille à f.,** customers' own materials made up (*b*) **cuir f. porc,** imitation pigskin 2. (*a*) manner, mode, way; **vivre à la f. des sauvages,** to live like savages; **je le ferai à ma f.,** I shall do it (in) my own way; **f. de parler,** manner of speaking; **de la bonne f.,** properly (*b*) *pl* manners; **en voilà des façons!** what a way to behave! (*c*) **sans façons** (i) (*of pers*) free-and-easy; uneremonious (ii) (*of manners*) rough and ready; **traiter qn sans f.,** to treat s.o. in an offhand manner; **sans plus de façons,** without any more ado (*d*) **de cette f.,** thus, in this way; **de f. ou d'autre,** (i) in one way or another (ii) by hook or by crook; **de toute f. j'irai,** anyhow, I shall go; **en aucune f.!** by no means! 3. **de f. à,** so as to; **de (telle) f. que,** so that; **parler de f. qu'on vous comprenne,** speak so as to be understood.
faconde [fakɔ̃d] *nf* fluency (of speech); *F:* gift of the gab.
façonner [fasɔne] *vtr* to work, shape; to make (up) (dress).
fac-similé [faksimile] *nm* facsimile; exact copy; *pl* **fac-similés.**
facteur, -trice [faktœr, -tris] *n* 1. (musical) instrument maker 2. postman, *f* postwoman 3. *Com:* agent, middleman 4. *nm Mth:* factor; **le f. humain,** the human factor.
factice [faktis] *a* artificial, imitation; dummy (parcel); feigned (emotion).
factieux, -euse [faksjø, -jøz] 1. *a* factious 2. *n* troublemaker.
faction [faksjɔ̃] *nf* 1. sentry duty, guard; **être de, en, f.,** to be on guard 2. faction; factious party.
factionnaire [faksjɔnɛr] *nm* (*a*) sentry (*b*) *Ind:* picket.
facture [faktyr] *nf* invoice; bill (of sale).
facturer [faktyre] *vtr* to invoice.
facultatif, -ive [fakyltatif, -iv] *a* optional; **arrêt f.,** request stop.
faculté [fakylte] *nf* 1. (*a*) option, right (*b*) faculty, ability; **facultés de l'esprit,** intellectual faculties (*c*) *pl* resources, means 2. *Sch:* faculty (of arts, law, medicine).
fadaise [fadɛz] *nf* (piece of) nonsense; **débiter des fadaises,** to talk rot.
fadeur [fadœr] *nf* insipidity; tastelessness; dullness (of colour); **dire des fadeurs,** to make uninspired re-

marks. **fade** *a* insipid; tasteless; dull, drab (colour); tame (joke).

fading [fɛdiŋ] *nm WTel:* fading (effect).

fagot [fago] *nm* faggot; bundle of firewood.

fagoter [fagɔte] *vtr F:* **1.** to rig (s.o.) out; **mal fagoté,** dowdy **2. se f.,** to rig oneself out.

faible [fɛbl] **1.** *a* (*a*) feeble, weak; **f. d'esprit,** feeble-minded; **points faibles,** shortcomings (**chez qn,** in s.o.); **c'est là son point f.,** that's his weakness (*b*) weak, thin (coffee, wine); faint (sound, smell); weak (voice); poor, slender (chance); **prix f.,** low price; **boisson f. en alcool,** drink with a low alcoholic content; **f. quantité,** small quantity (*c*) **élève f. en chimie,** pupil weak in chemistry **2.** *nm* (*a*) weakness, failing; **avoir un f. pour qch, pour qn,** to have a weakness, a soft spot, for sth, s.o. (*b*) **les faibles d'esprit,** the feeble-minded. **faiblement** *adv* feebly, weakly.

faiblesse [fɛblɛs] *nf* **1.** (*a*) feebleness, weakness; **tomber de f.,** to drop with exhaustion (*b*) faintness (*c*) **la f. humaine,** human frailty (*d*) smallness (of sum) **2.** **je l'aime avec toutes ses faiblesses,** I love him in spite of all his failings.

faiblir [fɛblir] *vi* to weaken; to grow weak(er); (*of sight*) to fail; (*of wind*) to drop; (*of courage*) to fail.

faïence [fajɑ̃s] *nf* crockery; earthenware.

faille [faj] *nf* (*a*) *Geol:* break (in lode) (*b*) flaw (in argument).

faillible [fajibl] *a* fallible.

faillir [fajir] *vi* (*prp* **faillant;** *pp* **failli;** *pr ind* **je faux, n. faillons;** *ph* **je faillis**) *used mostly in ph and compound tenses*) **1.** to fail; **f. à une promesse,** to fail to keep a promise **2. j'ai failli manquer le train,** I nearly missed the train. **failli, -ie** *a & n* bankrupt.

faillite [fajit] *nf Com:* failure, bankruptcy, insolvency; **faire f.,** to go bankrupt.

faim [fɛ̃] *nf* hunger; **avoir f.,** to be hungry; **avoir une f. de loup,** to be ravenous; **manger à sa f.,** to eat one's fill; **avoir f. de gloire,** to hunger for glory.

fainéanter [fɛneɑ̃te] *vi* to idle about. **fainéant, -ante 1.** *a* idle, lazy **2.** *n* idler, lazybones.

fainéantise [fɛneɑ̃tiz] *nf* idleness, laziness.

faire [fɛr] *vtr* (*prp* **faisant** [fəzɑ̃]; *pp* **fait** [fɛ]; *pr ind* **je fais; n. faisons** [fəzɔ̃], **v. faites** [fɛt], **ils font;** *pr sub* **je fasse;** *imp* **fais, faisons, faites;** *ph* **je fis;** *fu* **je ferai**) **1.** to make (*a*) **Dieu a fait l'homme à son image,** God created man in his own image; **comment est-il fait?** (i) what is he like? (ii) what does he look like? **il n'est pas fait pour cela,** he is not the man, he is not cut out, for that; **jambe bien faite,** shapely leg (*b*) **f. un gâteau,** to make, bake, a cake; **statue faite en, de, marbre,** statue made of marble; **vêtements tout faits,** ready-made clothes; **phrases toutes faites,** set phrases; **f. un tableau,** to paint a picture; **f. un chèque,** to write a cheque; **f. la guerre,** to wage war; **f. un miracle,** to work a miracle; **ferme où on fait de la betterave,** farm that grows beet (*c*) **f. un geste,** to make a gesture; **f. de l'œil à qn,** to ogle s.o. (*d*) **f. sa fortune,** to make one's fortune; **se f. des amis,** to make friends (*e*) **f. des provisions,** to lay in provisions (*f*) *P:* **on vous a fait,** you've been had; **tu es fait, mon vieux,** you've had it, chum! **2.** to do (*a*) **qu'est-que vous faites?** what are you doing? **il n'y a rien à f.,** there's nothing to be done; **je n'ai rien à f. avec eux,** I have nothing to do with them; **il n'a rien à f. ici,** he has no business (being) here; **que**

f.? what's to be done? what can I, we, do? **je le regardais f.,** I watched him at it; **faites vite!** look sharp! **avoir fort à f.,** to be hard put to it; **vous allez avoir de quoi f.,** you have your work cut out; **c'est bien fait!** it serves you right! **voilà qui est fait,** that's settled (*b*) to say; **'vous partez demain!' fit-il,** 'you leave tomorrow!' he said (*c*) **f. la ronde,** to go one's rounds; **f. son devoir,** to do one's duty; **f. ses besoins,** to relieve oneself; to go to the toilet (*d*) **f. un métier,** to practise a trade; **f. la laine,** to deal in wool (*e*) **f. du sport,** to go in for sport; **il fait son droit,** he's reading law; **f. son apprentissage,** to serve one's apprenticeship; **f. les magasins,** to go round the shops (*f*) **f. une promenade,** to go for a walk; *F:* **f. 100 à l'heure,** to do 100 kilometres an hour (*g*) **f. pitié, peur,** to arouse pity; to frighten (*h*) to amount to; **combien cela fait-il?** how much does that come to? **deux et deux font quatre,** two and two are four; **ça fait trois jours qu'il est parti,** it's three days since he left; **ce poulet fait trois kilos,** this chicken weighs three kilos (*i*) to be, constitute; **f. l'admiration de tous,** to be the admiration of all; **cela fera mon affaire,** (i) that will suit me (ii) that's just what I'm looking for; **quel taquin vous faites!** what a tease you are! (*j*) to matter; **qu'est-ce que ça fait?** what does it matter? **si cela ne vous fait rien,** if you don't mind; **cela ne fait rien,** never mind, it doesn't matter (*k*) **pourquoi agir comme vous le faites?** why do you act as you do? **3.** (*a*) to form; **ce professeur fait de bons élèves,** this master turns out good pupils; **se f. une opinion sur qch,** to form an opinion on sth (*b*) to arrange; **f. la chambre,** to clean, do, the bedroom; **f. sa valise,** to pack one's suitcase; **f. ses ongles,** to do one's nails; **f. les cartes,** to deal the cards; **à qui de f.?** whose deal is it? (*c*) **qu'allez-vous f. de votre fils?** what are you going to do with your son? **je n'ai que f. de ça,** I have no use for this; **f. ça fait riche,** it looks expensive; **il ne fait pas quarante ans,** he doesn't look forty (*d*) **f. le malade,** to sham illness, to pretend to be ill; **f. l'imbécile,** to play the fool **4. en f.** (*a*) **il n'en fait qu'à sa tête,** he does (just) what he likes; **n'en faites rien,** do no such thing (*b*) **c'en est fait de lui,** it's all up with him; he's done for (*c*) *P:* **(ne) t'en fais pas,** don't worry (*d*) **y f.; rien n'y fit,** it was all to no avail; **que voulez-vous que j'y fasse?** how can I help it? (*e*) *F:* **la f. à qn,** to take s.o. in; **on ne me la fait pas!** nothing doing! I'm not going to be had! **5.** *v impers* (*a*) **quel temps fait-il?** what is the weather like? **il fait du soleil,** it's sunny; **par le froid qu'il fait,** in this cold weather (*b*) **il fait mauvais voyager par ces routes,** it is hard travelling on these roads **6.** (*syntactical constructions*) (*a*) **il ne fait que lire toute la journée,** he does nothing but read all day; **je n'ai fait que le toucher,** I only touched it (*b*) **je ne fais que d'arriver,** I have only just arrived (*c*) **vous n'aviez que f. de parler,** you had no business to speak (*d*) **c'est ce qui fait que je suis venu si vite,** that's why I came so quickly (*e*) **faites qu'il vienne demain,** see to it that he comes tomorrow **7.** *causative* (*the noun or pron object is the subject of the inf*) (*a*) **je le fis chanter,** I made him sing; **il nous a fait venir,** he sent for us; **faites-le entrer,** show him in; **f. attendre qn,** to keep s.o. waiting (*b*) *with vpr* (i) (*reflexive pron omitted*) **f. asseoir qn,** to make s.o. sit down (ii) (*reflexive pron retained*) **je le fis s'arrêter,** I made him stop (*c*) (*the noun or pron is the object of the inf*) (i) **f. f. deux exemplaires,** to have two copies made (ii) **se f. +** *inf*; **un bruit se fit entendre,** a noise was heard; **il ne se le fit pas dire deux fois,** he didn't need to be told twice (d) **f. f. qch à qn,** to cause, get, s.o. to do sth; **faites-lui lire cette lettre,** get him to read this letter; **faites-lui comprendre que,** make him understand that **8. se f.** (a) to become; to develop, mature; **son style se fait,** his style is forming; **ce fromage se fera,** this cheese will ripen (b) to become; **se f. vieux,** to grow old; **se f. soldat,** to become a soldier (c) to adapt oneself; **se f. à qch,** to get used to sth (d) *impers* (i) **il se fait tard,** it is getting late (ii) **il se fit un long silence,** a long silence followed; **comment se fait-il que vous soyez en retard?** how come you're late? (e) **le miracle s'est fait tout seul,** the miracle came about by itself; **le mariage ne se fera pas,** the marriage will not take place.

faire-part [fɛrpar] *nm inv* card, notice (announcing birth, death, marriage); **f.-p. de mariage,** wedding card.

faisable [fəzabl] *a* feasible, practicable.

faisan [fəzɑ̃] *nm* (**coq**) f., (cock) pheasant. **faisandé** *a* (a) high, gamy (meat) (b) F: decadent.

faisceau, -eaux [fɛso] *nm* **1.** bundle (of sticks); **f. de preuves,** body of proof **2.** beam, searchlight; **f. hertzien,** radio beam; *TV:* **f. cathodique explorateur,** scanning electron beam; **f. électronique,** electron beam; **f. de lumière,** pencil of rays.

fait¹ [fɛ] *a* fully developed; **homme f.,** (i) grown man (ii) experienced man; **fromage f.,** ripe cheese.

fait² [fɛ *and sometimes* fɛt] *nm* (a) act, deed, feat; **faits et dits,** sayings and doings; **prendre qn sur le f.,** to catch s.o. in the act; **dire son f. à qn,** to talk straight to s.o. (b) fact; **f. accompli,** accomplished fact; **fait accompli; prendre f. et cause pour qn,** to stand up for s.o.; **aller droit au f.,** to go straight to the point; **en venir au f.,** to come to the point; **être au f. de la question,** to know how things stand; **mettre qn au f.,** to make s.o. acquainted with the facts; **au f., que venez-vous faire ici?** by the way, what have you come here for? **en f.,** as a matter of fact; in actual fact; actually; **de ce f.,** thereby, on that account; **du f., par le f., qu'il boite,** because he's lame; **en f., de,** as regards; **qu'est-ce que vous avez en f. de rôti?** what have you in the way of a joint? (c) occurrence, happening; *Journ:* **faits divers,** news in brief; **f. divers,** news item.

faîte [fɛt] *nm* **1.** *Const:* ridge (of roof) **2.** top (of tree, house); pinnacle (of glory).

faitout [fɛtu] *nm* stewpan.

falaise [falɛz] *nf* cliff.

fallacieux, -euse [falasjø, -øz] *a* fallacious, deceptive, misleading. **fallacieusement** *adv* fallaciously.

falloir [falwar] *v impers def* (*no prp; pp* **fallu;** *pr ind* **il faut;** *pr sub* **il faille;** *impf* **il fallait;** *fu* **il faudra**) **1.** (a) to be necessary, required; **il lui faut un nouveau pardessus,** he needs a new overcoat; **avez-vous tout ce qu'il (vous) faut?** have you everything you need? **c'est juste ce qu'il faut,** that's just the right thing; **il m'a fallu trois jours pour le faire,** it took me three days to do it (b) **s'en f.,** to be lacking, wanting; **je ne suis pas satisfait, tant s'en faut,** I am not satisfied, far from it; **peu s'en faut,** very nearly; **100 francs ou peu s'en faut,** the best part of 100 francs; **il s'en faut de peu qu'il accepte,** he is more than half inclined to accept (c)

comme il faut, proper(ly); **se conduire comme il faut,** to behave in a civilized manner; **ce sont des gens très comme il faut,** they are very decent people **2.** (a) to be necessary; **il faut partir,** I, we, you, etc must go; **il faut dire que,** I am bound to say that; **il nous faut le voir, il faut que nous le voyions,** we must see him; **il faudra marcher plus vite,** we shall have to walk faster; **il fallait le dire!** why didn't you say so! *F:* **c'est ce qu'il faudra voir!** we must see about that! *P:* **faut voir!** you should see it! **c'est simple mais il fallait y penser,** it's simple once you've thought of it; **il a fallu qu'elle le lui dise!** she *had* to tell him, she *would* tell him! (b) (*with* **le =** *noun clause*) **il viendra s'il le faut,** he will come if necessary; **vous êtes revenu à pied?—il (l') a bien fallu,** you walked back?—there was nothing else for it.

falot¹ [falo] *nm* (hand) lantern.

falot², -otte [falo, -ɔt] *a* insignificant, dim (pers).

falsification [falsifikasjɔ̃] *nf* falsification; forgery, faking.

falsifier [falsifje] *vtr* to falsify; to forge, fake (document); to adulterate (wine).

famélique [famelik] *a* famished; half-starved.

fameux, -euse [famø, -øz] *a* **1.** famous **2.** *F:* **fameuse idée,** splendid idea; **vous êtes un f. menteur!** you're a heck of a liar! **ce n'est pas f.,** it isn't up to much. **fameusement** *adv* famously; splendidly.

familial, -aux [familjal, -o] *a* **1.** family (life); **pot f.,** family-size jar; **allocation familiale,** family allowance **2.** *Aut:* *nf* **familiale,** estate car, *NAm:* station wagon.

familiariser [familjarize] *vtr* **1.** to familiarize **2. se f.** (a) to familiarize oneself (**avec,** with); to get accustomed (**avec,** to) (b) to grow familiar (in manner).

familiarité [familjarite] *nf* familiarity.

familier, -ère [familje, -ɛr] *a* **1.** domestic **2.** (a) familiar; **être f. avec qn,** to be on familiar terms with s.o.; **expression familière,** colloquialism; colloquial expression; **animal f.,** pet; *nm* **un des familiers de la maison,** a friend of the family (b) **visage qui lui est f.,** face which is well-known to him; **le mensonge lui est f.,** he is a habitual liar. **familièrement** *adv* familiarly.

famille [famij] *nf* family; household; **chef de f.,** (i) head of the family (ii) householder; **dîner en f.,** to dine at home with one's family; **avec eux je me sens en f.,** I feel quite at home with them; **cela tient de f.,** it runs in the family; **j'ai de la f. à Paris,** I have relatives in Paris.

famine [famin] *nf* famine, starvation.

fan [fã] *nm* *F:* fan.

fanal, -aux [fanal, -o] *nm* lantern, lamp; *Rail:* headlight; (ship's) navigation light.

fanatisme [fanatism] *nm* fanaticism. **fanatique 1.** *a* fanatic(al) **2.** *n* fanatic. **fanatiquement** *adv* fanatically.

fane [fan] *nf* haulm (of potatoes); (turnip) top.

faner [fane] **1.** *vi* to make hay **2.** *vtr* (a) to toss (hay) (b) to fade **3. se f.,** to wilt, to fade.

fanfare [fɑ̃far] *nf* **1.** flourish, fanfare (of trumpets) **2.** brass band.

fanfaronnade [fɑ̃faronad] *nf* boasting, bragging.

fanfaronner [fɑ̃farone] *vi* to boast, brag. **fanfaron, -onne 1.** *a* boasting, bragging **2.** *n* boaster.

fange [fɑ̃ʒ] *nf* mud, mire.

fanion [fanjɔ̃] *nm* lance pennon.

fantaisie [fɑ̃tezi] *nf* **1.** (a) imagination, fancy, fantasy; **de f.**, imaginary (b) *Mus:* fantasia 2. (a) fancy, desire; **il lui a pris la f. de se baigner**, he had a sudden idea he'd like a swim; **chacun s'amusait à sa f.**, everyone amused himself as he pleased; **articles de f.**, fancy goods; **bijoux de f.**, costume jewellery (b) whim.

fantaisiste 1. a whimsical, fanciful; eccentric 2. n entertainer; cabaret artiste.

fantasme [fɑ̃tasm] nm fantasy.

fantasque [fɑ̃task] a odd, whimsical.

fantassin [fɑ̃tasɛ̃] nm foot soldier, infantryman.

fantastique [fɑ̃tastik] a fantastic; fanciful; weird; **histoire f.**, incredible story. **fantastiquement** adv fantastically.

fantoche [fɑ̃tɔʃ] nm puppet; a **gouvernement f.**, puppet government.

fantôme [fɑ̃tom] nm phantom, ghost; **gouvernement f.**, shadow cabinet.

faon [fɑ̃] nm Z: fawn.

faramineux, -euse [faraminø, -øz] a F: phenomenal, colossal; astronomical.

farce [fars] nf 1. Cu: stuffing 2. (a) Th: farce (b) practical joke; Com: **farces et attrapes**, tricks and jokes.

farceur, -euse [farsœr, -øz] n 1. practical joker 2. joker, wag.

farcir [farsir] vtr 1. Cu: to stuff (poultry) 2. to cram; **farci de fautes**, crammed with mistakes 3. P: **se f. qch**, (i) to treat oneself to sth (ii) to put up with sth.

fard [far] nm makeup; rouge; greasepaint; **la vérité sans f.**, the plain unvarnished truth.

fardeau, -eaux [fardo] nm burden, load.

farder [farde] vtr 1. to paint; to make (s.o., one's face) up; to gloss over (the truth) 2. **se f.**, to make up, put on one's makeup.

farfelu, -ue [farfəly] a & n odd, scatty, eccentric (person).

farfouiller [farfuje] vi to rummage (about).

farine [farin] nf flour, meal; **f. de maïs**, cornflour; **f. d'avoine**, oatmeal. **farineux, -euse** 1. a floury, powdery, mealy 2. nm farinaceous, starchy, food.

fariner [farine] vtr Cu: to coat (sth) with flour; to flour.

farouche [faruʃ] a 1. fierce, untamed (animal); cruel (enemy) 2. (a) shy, timid (b) unsociable. **farouchement** adv fiercely.

fart [far(t)] nm wax (for skis).

farter [farte] vtr to wax (skis).

fascicule [fasikyl] nm instalment, part (of publication).

fascination [fasinasjɔ̃] nf fascination; charm.

fasciner [fasine] vtr to fascinate; to entrance, bewitch.

fascisme [faʃism] nm Pol: fascism. **fasciste** n fascist.

faste¹ [fast] nm no pl ostentation, display.

faste² à jour f., lucky day.

fastidieux, -euse [fastidjø, -øz] a dull, tedious, boring. **fastidieusement** adv tediously, boringly.

fastueux, -euse [fastɥø, -øz] a ostentatious; sumptuous. **fastueusement** adv ostentatiously.

fatal, -als [fatal] a 1. fatal; **coup f.**, fatal blow; **f. à qn**, fatal to s.o. 2. fated, inevitable; **c'était f.**, it was bound to happen. **fatalement** adv fatally; inevitably.

fatalisme [fatalism] nm fatalism. **fataliste** 1. n fatalist 2. a fatalistic.

fatalité [fatalite] nf 1. fate, fatality 2. mischance, misfortune.

fatigant [fatigɑ̃] a 1. tiring, fatiguing 2. tiresome; tedious, boring.

fatigue [fatig] nf (a) fatigue, tiredness, weariness; **tomber de f.**, to be tired out; **la f. des affaires**, the strain of business (b) (metal) fatigue (c) wear and tear (of machine, clothes).

fatiguer [fatige] 1. vtr (a) to tire (s.o.); **se f. les yeux**, to strain one's eyes; F: **il me fatigue!** he bores me! (b) to overwork (animal); to impose a strain on (machine); O: **f. la salade**, to mix the salad 2. vi (of engine) to labour 3. **se f.**, to tire; to get tired. **fatigué** a tired; jaded; weary; strained (heart); **f. par le voyage**, travel worn.

fatras [fatra] nm (a) jumble (b) rubbish.

fatuité [fatɥite] nf self-conceit, self-complacency.

faubourg [fobur] nm suburb. **faubourien, -ienne** a suburban; working-class (accent).

fauchaison [foʃɛzɔ̃] nf mowing, reaping.

fauche [foʃ] nf P: petty theft; pinching.

faucher [foʃe] vtr 1. (a) to mow, cut, reap (grass); **la voiture a fauché le poteau télégraphique**, the car knocked down the telegraph pole (b) P: to steal, pinch (sth) 2. to mow down (troops).

faucheur, -euse [foʃœr, -øz] n 1. (pers) mower, reaper 2. nf (mechanical) reaper.

faucille [fosij] nf sickle.

faucon [fokɔ̃] nm Orn: falcon, hawk.

faufiler [fofile] vtr 1. to tack, baste (seam) 2. **se f.**, to thread, pick, one's way; **il s'est faufilé avec les invités**, he sneaked in among the guests; **se f. entre les voitures**, to nip in and out of the traffic.

faune¹ [fon] nm Myth: faun.

faune² nf fauna, animal life; **la f. des boîtes de nuit**, the regular night club set.

faussaire [fosɛr] n forger.

faussement [fosmɑ̃] see **faux¹**.

fausser [fose] vtr 1. to falsify; to pervert (truth); distort (meaning); to alter (facts); **esprit faussé**, warped mind; **f. compagnie à qn**, to give s.o. the slip 2. to force (lock); to bend, to buckle; to wrench (key).

fausseté [foste] nf 1. falseness, falsity 2. falsehood, untruth 3. duplicity; **f. de conduite**, double dealing.

faute [fot] nf 1. lack, need, want; **faire f.**, to be lacking; **ne se faire f. de rien**, to deny oneself nothing; **sans f.**, without fail; **f. de**, for want of; failing; **f. de quoi**, failing which; otherwise; **f. de paiement**, non-payment 2. (a) fault, mistake; **prendre qn en f.**, to catch s.o. out; **ce n'est pas (de) ma f.**, it's not my fault; **à qui la f.?** whose fault is it? **c'est un peu de ma f.**, I'm partly to blame; **f. d'orthographe**, spelling mistake; **f. d'impression**, misprint (b) misconduct; transgression, offence (c) Fb: foul; Ten: fault.

fauteuil [fotœj] nm 1. armchair, easy chair; **f. à bascule**, rocking chair; **f. roulant**, wheelchair; Th: **f. d'orchestre**, orchestra stall; **arriver dans un f.**, to win hands down; Jur: **f. électrique**, electric chair 2. (a) chair (at meeting); **occuper le f.**, to be in the chair (b) seat (in the French Academy).

fauteur, -trice [fotœr, -tris] n instigator (of rising); **f. de troubles**, (political) agitator; troublemaker.

fautif, -ive [fotif, -iv] *a* **1.** faulty, incorrect; defective (memory); **calcul f.,** miscalculation **2.** offending, at fault; (*child*) naughty; *n* **c'est moi le f.,** I'm the culprit. **fautivement** *adv* incorrectly, by mistake.

fauve [fov] **1.** *a* fawn-coloured, tawny **2.** *nm* (*a*) fawn (colour) (*b*) **les (grands) fauves,** big game.

fauvette [fovɛt] *nf Orn:* warbler.

faux¹, fausse [fo, fos] *a* **1.** (*a*) false; untrue (*b*) not genuine; false (hair, teeth, jewellery); **f. témoin,** false, lying, witness; **fausse monnaie,** counterfeit coin(age); **fausse clef,** skeleton key; **fausse fenêtre,** blind window; **f. chèque,** forged cheque; *Anat:* **fausses côtes,** floating ribs (*c*) treacherous; **il est f. comme un jeton,** he's a hypocrite, *F:* a phoney (*d*) wrong, mistaken; **fausse date,** wrong date; **raisonnement f.,** unsound reasoning; **présenter la conduite de qn sous un f. jour,** to misrepresent s.o.'s conduct; **faire un f. pas,** to blunder; **faire fausse route,** to be on the wrong track; **f. calcul,** miscalculation; *Mus:* **fausse note,** wrong note **2.** (*a*) *adv* falsely, wrongly; **chanter f.,** to sing out of tune; **cela sonne f.,** that doesn't sound right; **rire qui sonne f.,** hollow laughter (*b*) *adv phr* **à f.,** wrongly; **accuser qn à f.,** to make a false accusation against s.o.; **porter à f.,** to be out of true. **3.** *nm* (*a*) **le f.,** the false; **distinguer le vrai du f.,** to distinguish truth from falsehood (*b*) (**bijouterie en**) **f.,** costume jewellery (*c*) forgery. **faussement** *adv* falsely, wrongly.

faux² *nf* scythe.

faux-filet [fofilɛ] *nm Cu:* sirloin; *pl faux-filets.*

faux-fuyant [fofɥijɑ̃] *nm* subterfuge, evasion, dodge; **chercher des f.-fuyants,** to hedge.

faux-monnayeur [fomɔnɛjœr] *nm* coiner; counterfeiter; *pl faux-monnayeurs.*

faveur [favœr] *nf* **1.** (*a*) favour; **gagner la f. de qn,** to win s.o.'s favour; **perdre la f. de qn,** to fall out of favour with s.o.; **prix de f.,** preferential price; **billet de f.,** complimentary ticket; **à la f. de,** by the help of; **à la f. de la nuit,** under cover of darkness; **plaider en f. de qn,** to plead in s.o.'s behalf; **en f. de,** (i) in aid of (ii) in consideration of (*b*) **faire une f. à qn,** to do s.o. a kindness **2.** ribbon. **favorable** *a* **1.** favourable; **être f. à,** to be in favour of **2.** favourable, propitious; auspicious (occasion). **favorablement** *adv* favourably.

favoriser [favɔrize] *vtr* to favour, to be partial to (s.o., sth); **f. les arts,** to patronize the arts; **les événements l'ont favorisé,** events were in his favour. **favori, -ite** **1.** *a & n* favourite **2.** *nmpl* side whiskers.

favoritisme [favɔritism] *nm* favouritism.

fayot [fajo] *nm P:* kidney bean.

FB *abbr* Franc belge.

fébrilité [febrilite] *nf* feverishness. **fébrile** *a* feverish. **fébrilement** *adv* feverishly.

fécondation [fekɔ̃dasjɔ̃] *nf Biol:* fertilization; impregnation.

féconder [fekɔ̃de] *vtr* to fertilize; to impregnate. **fécond** *a* fertile; fruitful (earth); fertile, rich (imagination); prolific (author).

fécondité [fekɔ̃dite] *nf* **1.** fruitfulness **2.** fertility.

fécule [fekyl] *nf* starch. **féculent** **1.** *a* starchy **2.** *nm* starchy food.

fédéraliser [federalize] *vtr* to federalize. **fédéral, -aux** *a* federal.

fédéralisme [federalism] *nm* federalism. **fédéra-**

liste *a & n* federalist.

fédération [federasjɔ̃] *nf* federation.

fée [fe] *nf* fairy; **conte de fées,** fairy tale.

feeder [fidœr] *nm* (gas) pipeline.

féerie [fe(ə)ri] *nf* **1.** enchantment **2.** fairyland **3.** *Th:* fairy play. **féerique** *a* (*a*) fairy, magic (castle) (*b*) fairylike, enchanting.

feindre [fɛ̃dr] *vtr & i* (*conj like* ATTEINDRE) to feign, simulate, sham; **f. de faire qch,** to pretend to do sth; **f. la maladie,** to malinger, to pretend to be ill. **feint** *a* feigned.

feinte [fɛ̃t] *nf* (*a*) feint, sham, pretence (*b*) *Box:* feint.

feinter [fɛ̃te] **1.** *vi Box:* to feint **2.** *vtr* to deceive (s.o.).

fêler [fele] *vtr* **1.** to crack (glass, china) **2. se f.,** to crack.

félicitations [felisitasjɔ̃] *nfpl* congratulations.

félicité [felisite] *nf* felicity, bliss(fulness); happiness, joy.

féliciter [felisite] *vtr* **1.** to congratulate (s.o.) **2. se f. de qch,** to be pleased with sth.

félin, -ine [felɛ̃, -in] *a* (*a*) feline; cat (family); *n* **les grands félins,** the big cats (*b*) catlike.

félonie [felɔni] *nf A:* disloyalty.

fêlure [felyr] *nf* crack (in china); split (in wood).

femelle [fəmɛl] **1.** *a* female (animal); she (animal); cow (elephant); hen (bird) **2.** *nf* female.

féminin [feminɛ̃] **1.** *a* feminine; **le sexe f.,** the female sex; **vêtements féminins,** women's clothes **2.** *nm Gram:* feminine (gender).

féminisme [feminism] *nm* feminism. **féministe** *a & n* feminist.

féminité [feminite] *nf* femininity.

femme [fam] *nf* **1.** woman; **elle est très f.,** she's very feminine; **f. auteur,** authoress; woman author; **f. médecin,** woman doctor; **f. d'affaires,** businesswoman **2.** wife **3. f. de chambre,** (i) housemaid (ii) chambermaid; **f. de ménage,** daily help, cleaning lady; **f. de charge,** housekeeper **4. remèdes de bonne f.,** old wives remedies.

fémur [femyr] *nm Anat:* femur, thighbone.

FEN *abbr* Fédération de l'éducation nationale.

fenaison [fənɛzɔ̃] *nf* **1.** haymaking; hay-harvest **2.** haymaking season.

fendiller (se) [səfɑ̃dije] *vpr* (*of wood, paint*) to crack.

fendre [fɑ̃dr] *vtr* **1.** (*a*) to split (*b*) to fissure; to crack; **f. l'air,** to cleave the air; **f. la foule,** to force one's way through the crowd; **il gèle à pierre f.,** it is freezing hard; **c'était à f. l'âme,** it was heartrending; **bruit à vous f. les oreilles,** ear-splitting noise **2. se f.** (*a*) (*of wood*) to split, crack (*b*) *Fenc:* to lunge.

fenêtre [f(ə)nɛtr] *nf* window; **f. à guillotine,** sash window; **f. à battants,** casement window; **regarder par la f.,** to look out of the window.

fenouil [fənuj] *nm Bot:* fennel.

fente [fɑ̃t] *nf* (*a*) crack, crevice, slit, chink (*b*) slot; **f. de poche,** pocket hole.

féodalisme [feɔdalism] *nm* feudalism. **féodal, -aux** *a* feudal.

fer [fɛr] *nm* **1.** iron; **f. forgé,** wrought iron **2.** (*a*) head (of axe, arrow); **f. de lance,** spearhead; **f. de rabot,** plane iron (*b*) sword; **croiser le f. avec qn,** to cross swords with s.o. **3. f. à souder,** soldering iron; **marquer au f. rouge,** to brand; **f. à repasser,** iron; **f. à friser,** curling tongs **4.** *pl* (*a*) irons, chains, fetters; **être aux fers,** to be in irons (*b*) *Obst:* forceps **5. f. à cheval,** horseshoe; *F:*

(of pers) **tomber les quatre fers en l'air,** to go sprawling.

fer-blanc [fɛrblã] *nm* tinplate; **boîte en f.-b.,** tin, (tin) can; *pl* fers-blancs.

férié [ferje] *a* **jour f.,** (public) holiday; *Adm:* bank holiday.

ferme¹ [fɛrm] **1.** *a (a)* firm, steady; **terre f.,** (i) firm ground (ii) mainland, terra firma; **répondre d'une voix f.,** to reply in a firm voice; **le marché reste très f.,** the market continues very strong; **attendre qn de pied f.,** to be quite ready for s.o. *(b)* **offre f.,** firm, definite, offer **2.** *adv* firmly; **frapper f.,** to hit hard; **tenir f.,** (i) to stand fast (ii) *(of nail)* to hold fast; **j'y travaille f.,** I am hard at it. **fermement** *adv* firmly, steadily.

ferme² *nf* farm; farmhouse.

ferment [fɛrmã] *nm* ferment,

fermentation [fɛrmãtasjɔ̃] *nf* fermentation; agitation, ferment.

fermenter [fɛrmãte] *vi* to ferment; *F:* to work; *(of dough)* to rise.

fermer [fɛrme] **1.** *vtr (a)* to close, shut; **f. violemment la porte,** to slam the door; **f. sa porte à qn,** to close one's door to s.o.; **f. à clef,** to lock (a door); **f. les rideaux,** to draw the curtains; **f. boutique,** to shut up shop; **on ferme!** closing time! **f. un trou,** to block up a hole; **f. un robinet,** to turn off a tap; **f. l'électricité,** to switch off the light; *P:* **ferme ta gueule! ferme-la!** shut up! shut your trap! *(b)* **f. la marche,** to bring up the rear **2.** *vi (of door)* to close, shut **3.** **se f.,** *(of door)* to close, shut; *(of eyes)* to close; *(of wound)* to heal, to close up. **fermé** *a* **1.** closed; **les yeux fermés,** blindfold, with eyes shut; **il a l'esprit fermé aux mathématiques,** mathematics are a closed book to him **2.** irresponsive; impassive (expression) **3.** exclusive (society).

fermeté [fɛrməte] *nf* firmness; steadfastness; strength (of mind).

fermette [fɛrmɛt] *nf (small farm) (b)* (country) weekend cottage.

fermeture [fɛrmətyr] *nf* **1.** closing, shutting; closure; **f. à clef,** locking; **f. de la pêche,** close of the fishing season; **heure de f.,** (i) closing time (ii) knocking-off time; **f. d'un compte,** closing of an account **2.** **f. éclair** *(Rtm),* **à glissière,** zip (fastener); zipper.

fermier, -ière [fɛrmje, -jɛr] *n* farmer; *f* (woman) farmer; farmer's wife; *a* **poulet f.,** farm, free-range, chicken.

fermoir [fɛrmwar] *nm* clasp, catch, fastener.

férocité [ferɔsite] *nf* ferocity, ferociousness; savagery. **féroce** *a* ferocious, savage, fierce; ravenous (appetite). **férocement** *adv* ferociously, savagely.

ferraille [fɛrɑj] *nf (a)* old iron, scrap iron; **mettre qch à la f.,** to put sth on the scrap heap, to scrap sth; **faire un bruit de f.,** to rattle, to clank *(b) F:* small change.

ferrailleur [fɛrɑjœr] *nm* scrap merchant.

ferrer [fɛre] *vtr* **1.** to fit, mount, (sth) with iron; to shoe (horse) **2.** to strike (fish). **ferré** *a* iron-shod; **souliers ferrés,** hob-nailed shoes; **voie ferrée** (i) (railway) track (ii) railway (line); *F:* **être f. sur un sujet,** to be well up in a subject.

ferreux, -euse [fɛrø, -øz] *a* ferrous.

ferronnerie [fɛrɔnri] *nf* **1.** ironworks **2.** ironmongery; ironwork; **f. (d'art),** art metalwork.

ferronnier, -ière [fɛrɔnje, -jɛr] *n* **1.** ironworker; **f. (d'art),** art metalworker **2.** ironmonger.

ferroviaire [fɛrɔvjɛr] *a* **trafic f.,** rail(way) traffic; *NAm:* railroad traffic.

ferrugineux, -euse [fɛryʒinø, -øz] *a* ferruginous.

ferry-boat [fɛribot] *nm* train ferry, car ferry; *pl* ferry-boats.

fertile [fɛrtil] *a* fertile, fruitful.

fertilisation [fɛrtilizasjɔ̃] *nf* fertilization.

fertiliser [fɛrtilize] *vtr* to fertilize.

fertilité [fɛrtilite] *nf* fertility.

fervent, -ente [fɛrvã, -ãt] **1.** *a* fervent; enthusiastic **2.** *n* enthusiast; *F:* fan.

ferveur [fɛrvœr] *nf* fervour.

fesse [fɛs] *nf* buttock; **les fesses,** the bottom, backside.

fessée [fɛse] *nf* spanking.

fesser [fɛse] *vtr* to spank (s.o.).

festin [fɛstɛ̃] *nm* feast, banquet.

festival, -als [fɛstival] *nm* festival.

festivités [fɛstivite] *nfpl* festivities.

festoyer [fɛstwaje] *vi* (**je festoie**) to feast.

fêtard, -arde [fɛtar, -ard] *n F:* reveller, roisterer.

fête [fɛt] *nf* **1.** *(a)* feast, festival; **f. légale** = bank holiday; **ce n'est pas tous les jours f.,** Christmas comes but once a year *(b)* **c'est demain ma f.,** it's my name day tomorrow; **f. des Mères,** Mother's Day; **souhaiter une bonne f. à qn,** to wish s.o. many happy returns **2.** *(a)* fête, fete; fair; **f. foraine,** fun fair; **f. de charité,** charity bazaar; **f. d'aviation,** air display, show *(b)* entertainment; **une petite f.,** a party **3.** festivity; **le village était en f.,** the village was on holiday; **air de f.,** festive air; **faire la f.,** to live it up; **faire f. à qn,** to welcome s.o. with open arms; **être de la f.,** to be one of the party; **se faire une f. de faire qch,** to look forward to doing sth.

Fête-Dieu [fɛtdjø] *nf Ecc:* Corpus Christi; *pl* Fêtes-Dieu.

fêter [fɛte] *vtr* **1.** **f. la naissance de qn,** to celebrate s.o.'s birthday **2.** **f. qn,** to entertain s.o.

fétiche [fetiʃ] *nm* fetish; *Aut:* mascot.

fétichisme [fetiʃism] *nm* fetishism. **fétichiste** *a* & *n* fetichist.

fétide [fetid] *a* fetid, stinking.

fétu [fety] *nm* straw.

feu¹, feux [fø] *nm* **1.** *(a)* fire; **il fait f. de tout bois,** he can turn anything to account; *F:* **avoir le f. au derrière,** to be in a tearing hurry; **mettre le f. à qch,** to set fire to sth, to set sth on fire; **en f.,** on fire; **le visage en f.,** flushed face; **prendre f.,** (i) to catch fire (ii) to fly into a rage; **au f.!** fire! *F:* **il n'y a pas le f. (à la maison),** there's no panic; **est-ce que vous avez du f.?** have you got a light, a match? *a inv* **rouge f.,** flame-coloured *(b)* heat, ardour; **tout f. tout flamme,** heart and soul **2.** *(a)* fire; **faire du f.,** to light a fire; **f. d'artifice,** fireworks; **f. de joie,** bonfire; **ça ne fera pas long f.,** it won't last long *(b)* **j'en mettrais la main au f.,** I would swear to it; **faire mourir qn à petit f.,** (i) to kill s.o. by inches (ii) to keep s.o. on tenterhooks *(c) Cu:* **faire cuire à f. doux, à petit f.,** to cook gently, over a slow heat, in a slow oven; **à f. vif,** over a strong heat, in a hot oven; **cuisinière à quatre feux,** four-burner, four-ring, cooker **3.** **armes à f.,** firearms; **faire f. sur qn,** to fire on s.o.; **ouvrir le f.,** to open fire; **f.! fire!** *(of plan)* **faire long f.,** to hang fire **4.** *(a) Nau:* light (of lighthouse); **feux de route,** navigation lights *(b) Av:* **feux de balisage,** boundary lights; *Av:* **feux de bord,** navigation lights *(c) Adm:*

feux de circulation, F: f. **rouge,** traffic lights; **donner le f. vert à qn,** to give s.o. the green light, the go-ahead; *Aut:* **feux de position, de stationnement,** sidelights, parking lights; **feux de route,** headlights; **feux de croisement,** dipped headlights (*d*) sparkle (of diamond); **n'y voir que du f.,** (i) to be dazzled (ii) to make neither head nor tail of sth.

feu[2] *a* (*inv if preceding article or poss adj*) late; **la feue reine, f. la reine,** the late queen.

feuillage [fœjaʒ] *nm* foliage.

feuille [fœj] *nf* 1. leaf (of plant); f. **de chou,** (i) cabbage leaf (ii) F: (*newspaper*) rag 2. f. **de métal,** sheet of metal 3. sheet (of paper); f. **de route,** *Mil:* travel warrant; f. (**quotidienne**), daily paper; *Adm:* f. **d'impôt,** (i) tax return (sheet) (ii) notice of assessment; f. **de paie,** pay slip; f. **de température,** temperature chart.

feuillet [fœjɛ] *nm* leaf (of book).

feuilleter [fœjte] *vtr* (**je feuillette**) (*a*) to turn over, flip through, the pages of (a book) (*b*) *Cu:* **pâte feuilletée,** flaky pastry.

feuilleton [fœjtɔ̃] *nm Journ: WTel: TV:* (i) instalment (of serial) (ii) serial (story).

feuillu [fœjy] *a* leafy; broad-leaved (tree).

feutre [føtr] *nm* 1. felt 2. (*a*) felt hat (*b*) felt(-tip) pen. **feutré** *a* lined with felt; muffled (sound); **à pas feutrés,** with noiseless tread.

fève [fɛv] *nf* bean; f. (**des marais**), broad bean.

février [fevrije] *nm* February; **au mois de f.,** en f., in (the month of) February; **le sept f.,** (on) the seventh of February.

FF *abbr* 1. *frères* 2. *Franc français.*

fi [fi] *int* (*a*) *O:* fie! for shame (*b*) **faire fi de qch,** to despise, scorn, sth.

fiabilité [fjabilite] *nf* reliability. **fiable** *a* reliable.

fiacre [fjakr] *nm* hackney carriage.

fiançailles [f(i)jãsaj] *nfpl* engagement.

fiancer (se) [səfjãse] *vpr* to become, to get, engaged.

fiasco [fjasko] *nm inv* fiasco; **faire f.,** (*of plan*) to come to nothing; (*of film*) to be a flop.

fibre [fibr] *nf* (*a*) fibre; grain (of wood); f. **de verre,** glass fibre, fibreglass (*b*) **avoir la f. sensible,** to be susceptible. **fibreux, -euse** *a* fibrous; stringy (meat).

ficeler [fisle] *vtr* (**je ficelle**) to tie up, do up (with string).

ficelle [fisɛl] *nf* 1. (i) string, twine (ii) pack thread; **tirer les ficelles,** to pull the strings; **connaître les ficelles,** to know the ropes 2. thin stick of French bread.

fiche [fiʃ] *nf* 1. (*a*) peg, pin (*b*) *El:* plug 2. (*a*) slip (of paper); memorandum slip; voucher; f. **scolaire,** school record chart; f. **dentaire,** dental chart; *Ind:* f. **de contrôle,** docket (*b*) (index) card; **jeu de fiches,** card index (*c*) tie-on label.

ficher [fiʃe] *vtr* 1. to drive in (nail); f. **une épingle dans qch,** to stick a pin into sth 2. to card-index 3. *F:* (*pp* **fichu;** *inf usu* **fiche**) (*a*) (= **mettre**) **fiche(r) qn à la porte,** to throw s.o. out (*b*) (= **faire**) **il n'a rien fichu de la journée,** he hasn't done a stroke all day (*c*) (= **donner**) **fichez-moi la paix!** shut up! (*d*) **fichez(-moi) moi va te faire fiche!** get to hell out of here! scram! 3. **se f.** *F:* (*a*) **se f. par terre,** to fall (*b*) **se f. dedans,** to make a mistake; to put one's foot in it (*c*) **se f. de qn,** to make

fun of s.o. (*d*) **je m'en fiche (pas mal)!** I couldn't care less!

fichier [fiʃje] *nm* (*a*) card-index; *Cmptr:* file (*b*) card-index cabinet.

fichu[1] [fiʃy] *a F:* 1. rotten, awful 2. **il est f.,** it's all up with him, he's had it; **ma robe est fichue,** my dress is ruined 3. **être bien f.,** to be well dressed; **être mal f.,** to be off colour 4. **il n'est pas f. de le faire,** he's not capable of doing it.

fichu[2] *nm* small shawl; headscarf.

fiction [fiksjɔ̃] *nf* fiction. **fictif, -ive** *a* fictitious, imaginary. **fictivement** *adv* fictitiously.

fidélité [fidelite] *nf* (*a*) fidelity; faithfulness; **serment de f.,** oath of allegiance (*b*) accuracy (of translation); reliability; *Rec:* **haute f.,** high fidelity, hi-fi. **fidèle** 1. *a* (*a*) faithful, loyal; staunch; **rester f. à une promesse,** to stand by a promise (*b*) accurate (copy); reliable (memory) 2. *n* (loyal) supporter; regular customer; *Ecc:* **les fidèles,** (i) the faithful (ii) the congregation. **fidèlement** *adv* faithfully; loyally; accurately.

fief [fjɛf] *nm* (*a*) *Jur: A:* fief (*b*) f. **électoral,** (loyal) constituency.

fiel [fjɛl] *nm* (*a*) gall (*b*) bitterness, malice.

fier[1], **-ère** [fjɛr] *a* 1. proud, haughty; **il n'y a pas là de quoi être f.,** that's nothing to boast about; f. **comme Artaban,** as proud as a peacock 3. *F:* **tu m'as fait une fière peur,** a fine fright you gave me; **je te dois une fière chandelle,** I owe you more than I can repay. **fièrement** *adv* proudly.

fier[2] **(se)** [səfje] *vpr* (*impf & pr sub* **n. n. fiions**) to trust; **se f. à qn,** to rely on s.o.; **fiez-vous à moi,** leave it to me; **ne vous y fiez pas,** (i) beware! (ii) don't count on it.

fierté [fjɛrte] *nf* 1. pride, self-respect 2. pride, haughtiness.

fièvre [fjɛvr] *nf* 1. fever; **avoir une f. de cheval,** to have a raging fever; **avoir (de) la f.,** to have a temperature 2. excitement, restlessness; **dans la f. de la campagne électorale,** in the heat of the election campaign. **fiévreux, -euse** *a* feverish. **fiévreusement** *adv* feverishly.

fifre [fifr] *nm* 1. fife 2. fife player.

figer [fiʒe] *vtr* (**figeant, il figeait**) 1. to coagulate, congeal; **figé sur place,** rooted to the spot 2. **se f.,** to coagulate, congeal; to clot; (*of features*) to set; **son sang se figea,** his blood ran cold.

fignoler [fiɲɔle] *vtr F:* to fiddle, to be finicky, over (a job).

figue [fig] *nf* (*a*) fig (*b*) f. **de Barbarie,** prickly pear.

figuier [figje] *nm* (*a*) fig tree (*b*) f. **de Barbarie,** prickly pear (tree).

figurant, -ante [figyrã, -ãt] *n Th: Cin:* walker-on, extra; **rôle de f.,** walk-on part.

figuratif, -ive [figyratif, -iv] *a* figurative; representational (art).

figuration [figyrasjɔ̃] *nf* 1. figuration, representation 2. *Th: Cin:* walkers-on, extras.

figure [figyr] *nf* 1. (*a*) figure; **figures de cire,** waxworks; f. **de proue,** figurehead (of ship); *Cards:* **les figures,** the court cards; **prendre f.,** to take shape; **faire piètre f.,** to look a sorry sight; **faire grande f. dans une entreprise,** to play an important role in a business (*b*) (geometrical) figure 2. face; **faire bonne f. à qn,** to give s.o. a warm welcome; **faire longue f.,** to pull a long face.

figurer [figyre] **1.** *vtr* to represent **2.** *vi* to appear, figure; *Th:* **f. sur la scène**, to walk on in **3. se f. qch**, to imagine sth; **figurez-vous la situation**, picture the situation to yourself; **figure-toi que**, would you believe that. **figuré** *a* figurative; **au f.**, in the figurative sense; figuratively.

figurine [figyrin] *nf* figurine.

fil [fil] *nm* **1.** (a) thread; **f. à coudre**, sewing thread; cotton; **de f. en aiguille**, little by little; gradually; **brouiller les fils**, to muddle things up (b) strand (of cable, rope); **sa vie ne tenait qu'à un f.**, his life hung by a thread; *F:* **avoir un f. à la patte**, to be tied up (with s.o.) **2. f. de fer**, wire; *F:* **il n'a pas inventé le f. à couper le beurre** = he'll never set the Thames on fire; *Tp:* **donner**, *F:* **passer**, **un coup de f. à qn**, to ring s.o. up; to call s.o.; **être au bout du f.**, to be on the phone, on the line (c) **haricots sans fils**, stringless beans **3.** grain (of wood) **4.** (a) **au f. de l'eau**, with the current; downstream; **au f. des jours**, day after day (b) **perdre le f. de la conversation**, to lose the thread of the conversation **5.** edge (of knife, razor).

filament [filamã] *nm* filament; fibre (of plant).

filandreux, -euse [filãdrø, -øz] *a* fibrous; stringy (meat).

filasse [filas] *nf* tow; **aux cheveux blond f.**, tow-headed.

filature [filatyr] *nf* **1.** spinning **2.** (spinning) mill **3.** shadowing (by detective).

file [fil] *nf* file (of soldiers); **entrer à la f.**, to file in; **en f. indienne**, in single file; **deux heures à la f.**, two hours on end; **prendre la f.**, to queue up; **se garer en double f.**, to double-park; **f. de voitures**, line of cars.

filer [file] **1.** *vtr* (a) to spin (cotton) (b) *Nau:* to pay out (cable) (c) to prolong, spin out (story) (d) (of detective) to shadow, tail (s.o.) (e) *F:* **f. qch à qn**, to slip s.o. sth **2.** *vi* (a) to flow smoothly (b) *F:* **f. doux**, to sing small (b) (of stitch) to run; (of stockings) to ladder (d) to slip by; **le temps file**, time flies; **f. à toute vitesse**, to rush along at full speed; **les voitures filaient sur la route**, cars were speeding along the road (e) **il a filé**, he made a bolt for it; **f. (en vitesse)**, to cut and run; **allez, filez!** buzz off! scram! **f. à l'anglaise**, to take French leave.

filet¹ [filɛ] *nm* **1.** (a) fine thread; thin streak (of light); thin trickle (of water) (b) **ajoutez un f. de citron**, add a dash of lemon **2.** *Cu:* fillet (of beef, fish).

filet² *nm* net(ting); (in circus) safety net; (trap) snare; **f. de pêche**, fishing net; **f. (à provisions)**, string bag; **f. (à cheveux)**, hairnet; *Rail:* **f. à bagages**, luggage rack.

filial, -aux [filjal, -o] **1.** *a* filial **2.** *nf* **filiale** (a) *Com:* subsidiary company (b) provincial branch (of association).

filière [filjɛr] *nf* **f. administrative**, official channels; **il a passé par la f.**, he's worked his way up.

filiforme [filiform] *a* threadlike.

filigrane [filigran] *nm* **1.** filigree (work) **2.** watermark (of banknotes).

filin [filɛ̃] *nm* rope.

fille [fij] *nf* **1.** daughter **2.** (a) girl; **jeune f.**, girl; young woman; **nom de jeune f.**, maiden name; **vieille f.**, old maid, spinster; **rester f.**, to remain single (b) **f. d'honneur**, maid of honour (c) **f. de joie**, *F:* **f.**, prostitute **3. f. de cuisine**, kitchen maid; **f. de salle**, waitress; **f. de comptoir**, barmaid.

fille-mère [fijmɛr] *nf O:* unmarried mother; *pl* **filles-mères**.

fillette [fijɛt] *nf* little girl.

filleul, -eule [fijœl] *n* godchild; godson, goddaughter.

film [film] *nm Phot:* film; *Cin:* film, *NAm:* movie; **f. d'actualité**, news film, newsreel; **f. annonce**, trailer.

filmer [filme] *vtr Cin:* to film, shoot (scene).

filmothèque [filmɔtɛk] *nf* film library.

filon [filɔ̃] *nm* (a) *Min:* vein (of metal) (b) *P:* cushy job; **il a trouvé le bon f.**, he's struck it rich.

filou, -ous [filu] *nm* (a) pickpocket, thief (b) rogue, swindler.

filouter [filute] *vtr* to swindle, cheat (s.o.).

fils [fis] *nm* son; **f. à papa**, daddy's boy; **c'est bien le f. de son père**, he's a chip off the old block; **être le f. de ses œuvres**, to be a self-made man; **M. Duval f.**, Mr Duval junior; **le f. Duval**, young Duval.

filtrage [filtraʒ] *nm* filtering, straining.

filtre [filtr] *nm* filter; strainer; (bout) **f.**, filter tip (of cigarette); **f. à café**, coffee filter; (**café**) **f.**, filter coffee; **papier f.**, filter paper.

filtrer [filtre] **1.** *vtr* to filter, strain **2.** *vi & pr* (se) **f.**, to filter, percolate (à travers, through). **filtrant** *a* filtering.

fin¹ [fɛ̃] *nf* **1.** end, close, termination; expiration (of contract); close (of day); **f. de semaine**, weekend; *Com:* **f. de mois**, monthly statement; **en f. de soirée**, towards the end of the evening; **il est venu vers la f. de l'après-midi**, he came late in the afternoon; **tirer à sa f.**, to draw to a close; **à la f. du livre**, at the back of the book; **vis sans f.**, endless screw; **il parle sans f.**, he never stops talking; **f. prématurée**, untimely death; **mettre f. à qch**, to put an end to, to stop, sth; **prendre f.**, to come to an end; **mener qch à bonne f.**, to bring sth to a successful conclusion; **à la f. il répondit**, in the end, finally, at last, he answered; *F:* **tu es stupide à la f.!** you really are very stupid! **en f. de compte**, in the end; to sum up; *F:* **à la f. des fins**, when all is said and done **2.** end, aim, purpose; **la f. justifie les moyens**, the end justifies the means; **en venir à ses fins**, to achieve one's aim(s); to get what one wants; **à quelle f.?** for what purpose? **à deux fins**, dual-purpose; **à toutes fins utiles**, (i) for whatever purpose it may serve (ii) to whom it may concern. **final, -als 1.** *a* final; last **2.** (a) *nf Sp:* **finale**, final (b) *nm Mus:* finale (of opera).

finalement *adv* finally, in the end.

fin², **fine** [fɛ̃, fin] **1.** *a* **dans le f. fond du panier**, right at the bottom of the basket; **au f. fond de la campagne**, in the depths of the country **2.** *a* (a) fine, first-class; **vins fins**, choice wines (b) fine, subtle; **f. tireur**, crack shot; **avoir l'oreille fine**, to have an acute ear; **f. comme l'ambre**, sharp as a needle; **bien f. qui le prendra**, it would take a smart person to catch him (c) fine, small, slender; **traits fins**, delicate features **3.** *nm* (a) **le f. de l'affaire**, the crux of the matter; **le f. du f.**, the ultimate (b) **jouer au plus f.**, to have a battle of wits **4.** *nf* **fine**, liqueur brandy **5.** *adv* finely; **café moulu f.**, finely ground coffee. **finement** *adv* **1.** finely, delicately (executed) **2.** smartly, subtly.

finaliste [finalist] *n Sp:* finalist.

finalité [finalite] *nf* finality.

finance [finãs] *nf* **1.** finance; **la haute f.**, (i) high finance (ii) the financiers **2.** *pl* **finances**, resources;

ministre des Finances = Chancellor of the Exchequer; **le Ministère des Finances** = the Treasury. **financier, -ière 1.** a financial **2.** nm financier. **financièrement** adv financially.

financement [finãsmã] nm financing.

financer [finãse] vtr (**n. finançons**) to finance (undertaking).

finesse [fines] nf **1.** fineness (of material); delicacy (of execution) **2.** (a) subtlety, shrewdness; **f. d'ouïe,** acuteness of hearing; **f. d'esprit,** shrewdness; **finesses d'une langue,** niceties of a language (b) cunning, guile (c) trick **3.** fineness (of dust); slimness (of waist); sharpness (of point).

fini [fini] **1.** a (a) finished, over, done with; F: **il est f.,** he's done for (b) accomplished (actor); well finished (piece of work); complete (idiot); utter (crook) (c) finite (space, tense) **2.** nm finish.

finir [finir] **1.** vtr to finish, end **2.** vi to come to an end, finish; **il finira mal,** he'll come to a bad end; **en f. avec qch,** to have done with sth; **je voudrais en f.,** I want to get it over with; **cela n'en finit pas,** there is no end to it; **pour en f.,** to cut the matter short; **la justice finit par triompher,** justice triumphs in the end.

finish [finiʃ] nm Sp: finish.

finition [finisjɔ̃] nf finish; finishing.

Finlande [fɛ̃lãd] Prnf Geog: Finland. **finlandais, -aise 1.** a Finnish **2.** n Finn. **finnois, -oise 1.** a Finnish **2.** nm Ling: Finnish.

fiole [fjɔl] nf phial.

fioriture [fjɔrityr] nf flourish, embellishment.

firmament [firmamã] nm firmament, sky.

firme [firm] nf firm.

fisc [fisk] nm (a) the Treasury, the Exchequer (b) the Inland Revenue. **fiscal, -aux** a fiscal; tax.

fission [fisjɔ̃] nf splitting, fission; **f. de l'atome,** nuclear fission.

fissure [fisyr] nf fissure, crack.

fissurer [fisyre] vtr to fissure, to crack.

fiston [fistɔ̃] nm F: son; **viens, f.,** come along, lad.

fixateur [fiksatœr] nm fixer (for dyes); Phot: fixing solution.

fixation [fiksasjɔ̃] nf **1.** fixing; attaching; Ch: fixation (of nitrogen) **2.** attachment; (ski) binding.

fixe [fiks] a **1.** fixed, firm; stationary; **idée f.,** obsession; **regard f.,** intent gaze **2.** fixed, regular, settled; **traitement f.,** nm f., fixed salary; **beau (temps) f.,** set fair; PN: **arrêt f.,** all buses stop here. **fixement** adv fixedly; **regarder f. qch,** to stare at sth.

fixer [fikse] vtr **1.** (a) to fix; to make (sth) firm, fast; to fasten; **f. l'attention de qn,** to hold s.o.'s attention; **f. qn,** to stare at s.o. (b) to fix, determine; to set, to appoint (time); to lay down (conditions, rules) **2. se f.,** to settle (down).

fixité [fiksite] nf fixity; steadiness (of gaze).

fjord [fjɔr] nm Geog: fjord.

flac [flak] nm & int plop, splash.

flacon [flakɔ̃] nm bottle; flask.

flageller [flaʒele] vtr to scourge, flog.

flageoler [flaʒɔle] vi (of legs) to shake, tremble, give way.

flageolet [flaʒɔlɛ] nm Hort: Cu: flageolet, (small) kidney bean.

flagrant [flagrã] a flagrant, glaring; **pris en f. délit,** caught in the act, red-handed.

flair [flɛr] nm (a) (of dogs) scent, (sense of) smell (b) (of pers) flair, intuition.

flairer [flɛre] vtr (a) (of dog) to scent, to nose out (game); **f. le danger,** to smell danger (b) to smell, sniff (at) (flower).

flamand, -ande [flamã, -ãd] **1.** a Flemish **2.** n Fleming **3.** nm Ling: Flemish.

flamant [flamã] nm Orn: flamingo.

flambant [flãbã] adv **f. neuf,** brand new.

flambeau, -eaux [flãbo] nm **1.** torch; **retraite aux flambeaux,** torchlight tattoo **2.** candlestick.

flamber [flãbe] **1.** vi to flame, blaze **2.** vtr to singe (fowl, hair); Cu: to flambé (pancake). **flambé 1.** a (a) Cu: flambé (b) F: **il est f.,** he's done for **2.** nf **flambée** (a) blaze (b) outbreak (of violence); rocketing (of prices).

flamboiement [flãbwamã] nm flaming; blazing; blaze.

flamboyer [flãbwaje] vi (**il flamboie**) to blaze; (of eyes) **f. de colère,** to flash with anger. **flamboyant** a Arch: flamboyant.

flamme [flam] nf **1.** (a) flame; **en flammes,** on fire, ablaze; **par le fer et la f.,** with fire and sword (b) fire, enthusiasm **2.** pennant, streamer.

flan [flã] nm Cu: baked custard (tart).

flanc [flã] nm flank, side; **f. de coteau,** hillside; **battre des flancs,** to heave, pant; **prêter le f. à la critique,** to lay oneself open to criticism; Mil: **tirer au f.,** to malinger.

flancher [flãʃe] vi F: **1.** (a) to flinch, give in; (of heart) to pack up (b) to quit **2. j'ai flanché en histoire,** I did badly in history.

Flandre [flãdr] Prnf Geog: Flanders.

flanelle [flanɛl] nf flannel; **f. de coton,** flannelette.

flâner [flane] vi to stroll; to dawdle; to saunter; F: to hang about.

flânerie [flanri] nf dawdling, strolling; idling.

flâneur, -euse [flanœr, -øz] n stroller; idler.

flanquer [flãke] vtr **1.** to flank (building, the enemy) **2.** F: to throw, chuck; **f. un coup de pied à qn,** to land s.o. a kick; **f. qn à la porte,** to throw s.o. out **3. se f. par terre,** to fall flat on one's face.

flaque [flak] nf puddle, pool.

flash [flaʃ] nm **1.** Phot: flash **2.** newsflash; pl **flashes.**

flasque [flask] a flaccid (flesh); flabby (hand); **se sentir f.,** to feel limp.

flatter [flate] vtr **1.** (a) to stroke, caress, pat (an animal) (b) to delight; **spectacle qui flatte les yeux,** sight that is pleasant to the eyes; **f. les caprices de qn,** to humour s.o.'s fancies (c) to flatter **2. se f.,** to flatter oneself, delude oneself; **se f. d'avoir fait qch,** to take the credit for having done sth.

flatterie [flatri] nf flattery. **flatteur, -euse 1.** a flattering **2.** n flatterer.

flatulence [flatylãs] nf Med: flatulence, F: wind.

fléau, -aux [fleo] nm **1.** flail **2.** scourge; curse; plague **3.** beam, arm (of balance).

flèche [flɛʃ] nf **1.** (a) arrow; **partir comme une f.,** to shoot off; **monter en f.,** (of aircraft) to shoot (straight) up; (of prices) to rocket (b) direction sign, arrow **2.** spire (of church).

flécher [fleʃe] vtr to arrow (route, direction).

fléchette [fleʃɛt] nf Games: dart.

fléchir [fleʃir] **1.** vtr (a) to bend, flex (b) to move (s.o.)

(to pity); **se laisser f.**, to let oneself be swayed 2. *vi (a)* to give way; to sag *(b)* to grow weaker.

fléchissement [fleʃismɑ̃] *nm* bending; falling (of prices).

flegme [flɛgm] *nm* phlegm; imperturbability. **flegmatique** *a* phlegmatic, imperturbable, stolid. **flegmatiquement** *adv* phlegmatically, imperturbably.

flemme [flɛm] *nf F:* laziness; **j'ai la f. de le faire,** I can't be bothered to do it. **flemmard, -arde** *F:* 1. *a* idle, lazy 2. *n* idler, slacker, lazybones.

flétan [fletɑ̃] *nm Ich:* halibut.

flétrir¹ [fletrir] *vtr* 1. to fade, wilt; to wither (up) (plants) 2. **se f.**, *(of colours)* to fade; *(of flowers)* to wither.

flétrir² *vtr* to stain, to cast a slur on (s.o.'s character).

fleur [flœr] *nf* 1. *(a)* flower; blossom, bloom; **arbre en fleur(s),** tree in flower; **faire une f. à qn,** to do s.o. a favour *(b)* **dans la f. de l'âge,** in the prime of life *(c)* bloom˙(on peach) 2. **à f. de,** on the surface of; **à f. d'eau,** at water level; **voler à f. d'eau,** to skim the water; **émotions à f. de peau,** skin-deep emotions; **avoir les nerfs à f. de peau,** to be on edge.

fleuret [flœrɛ] *nm* (fencing) foil.

fleurir [flœrir] 1. *vi (a) (of plants)* to flower, bloom, blossom *(b) (prp* **florissant)** to flourish, prosper 2. *vtr* to decorate (table) with flowers; to deck with flowers. **fleuri** *a* 1. in bloom, in flower 2. flowery (path); florid (complexion).

fleuriste [flœrist] *n* florist; florist's shop.

fleuron [flœrɔ̃] *nm* 1. *Bot:* floret 2. rosette; *Arch:* finial.

fleuve [flœv] *nm* river (as opposed to **tributary**); *a* **roman f.**, saga (novel); **discours f.**, lengthy speech.

flexibilité [flɛksibilite] *nf* flexibility. **flexible** 1. *a* flexible, pliable; adaptable (mind) 2. *nm* flexible lead, flex.

flexion [flɛksjɔ̃] *nf* 1. flexion, bending 2. *Ling:* inflexion (of word).

flibustier [flibystje] *nm (a) A:* freebooter *(b)* privateer *(c)* gun runner.

flic [flik] *nm F:* policeman, cop.

flic flac [flikflak] *int* splash! plop!

flingue [flɛ̃g] *nm P:* gun.

flinguer [flɛ̃ge] *vtr P:* to gun (s.o.) down.

flipper [flipœr] *nm* pin-ball machine.

flirt [flœrt] *nm F:* 1. flirtation, flirting 2. **mon f.**, my boyfriend, my girlfriend.

flirter [flœrte] *vi* to flirt.

floc [flɔk] *int* plop! flop!

flocon [flɔkɔ̃] *nm* flake (of snow, foam, cereal); flock (of wool, cotton). **floconneux, -euse** *a* fleecy, fluffy.

floraison [flɔrɛzɔ̃] *nf* flowering; blossoming (time).

floral, -aux [flɔral, -o] *a* floral; flower (show).

floralies [flɔrali] *nfpl* flower show.

flore [flɔr] *nf Bot:* flora.

florilège [flɔrilɛʒ] *nm* anthology of verse.

florissant [flɔrisɑ̃] *a* flourishing, prosperous.

flot [flo] *nm* 1. *(a)* wave *(b)* floods (of tears); torrent, stream (of abuse); crowd (of people); **entrer à flots,** to stream in; **couler à flots,** to pour out 2. *(of ship)* **à f.**, afloat; *(of pers)* solvent; **mettre à f.**, to launch (ship);

remettre à f., to refloat (ship); **remettre qn à f.**, to make s.o. solvent.

flottaison [flɔtɛzɔ̃] *nf* **(ligne de) f.**, waterline.

flotte¹ [flɔt] *nf* 1. fleet 2. *F:* water, rain.

flotte² *nf* float (of net).

flottement [flɔtmɑ̃] *nm* wavering, swaying; flapping (of flag); fluctuation (of floating currency); hesitation.

flotter [flɔte] 1. *vi (a)* to float *(b)* to wave (in the wind); *(of hair, clothes)* to hang loosely *(c)* to waver, hesitate; *(of thoughts)* to wander; *(of prices)* to fluctuate *(d) F:* **il flotte,** it's raining 2. *vtr* **f. du bois,** to float timber.

flotteur [flɔtœr] *nm* 1. float (of fishing line) 2. ball (of ball tap); **robinet à f.**, ballcock.

flottille [flɔtij] *nf Nau:* flotilla.

flou [flu] 1. *a* blurred (outline); fuzzy (image); hazy (horizon); vague (idea); fluffy (hair) 2. *nm* blur, fuzziness, softness, fluffiness.

fluctuation [flyktɥasjɔ̃] *nf* fluctuation.

fluctuer [flyktɥe] *vi* to fluctuate.

fluet, -ette [flyɛ, -ɛt] *a* thin, slender.

fluidité [flɥidite] *nf* fluidity; steady flow (of traffic). **fluide** 1. *a* fluid; **la circulation était f.**, the traffic kept moving 2. *nm* fluid.

fluor [flyɔr] *nm Ch:* fluorine.

fluorescence [flyɔrɛsɑ̃s] *nf* fluorescence. **fluorescent** *a* fluorescent; **éclairage f.**, strip lighting.

flûte [flyt] *nf* 1. flute; **petite f.**, piccolo; **f. à bec,** recorder 2. *(a)* long thin loaf (of French bread) *(b)* tall champagne glass; flute 3. *int F:* damn!

flutiste [flytist] *n* flautist, *esp NAm:* flutist.

fluvial, -aux [flyvjal, -o] *a* fluvial; river (police); **voie fluviale,** waterway.

flux [fly] *nm (a)* flow; flood; **le f. et reflux,** the ebb and flow *(b). Med: Ph:* flux.

fluxion [flyksjɔ̃] *nf Med:* inflammation; **f. de la gencive,** gumboil; **f. de poitrine,** pneumonia.

FMI *abbr Fonds monétaire international.*

FNAC [fnak] *abbr Fédération nationale des associations de cadres.*

FO *abbr Force ouvrière.*

foc [fɔk] *nm Nau:* jib.

focal, -aux [fɔkal, -o] *a* focal.

fœtus [fetys] *nm* f(o)etus.

foi [fwa] *nf* 1. faith; **il est de bonne f.**, he is completely sincere; **mauvaise f.**, dishonesty; **manque de f.**, breach of faith; **ma f., well; ma f., oui!** yes indeed! **f. d'honnête homme,** on my word as a gentleman 2. belief, trust; **avoir f. en qn,** to have faith in s.o.; **texte qui fait f.**, authentic text 3. (religious) faith, belief; **il n'a ni f. ni loi,** he fears neither God nor man.

foie [fwa] *nm* liver.

foin [fwɛ̃] *nm* 1. hay; **faire les foins,** to make hay; **tas de f.**, haycock; **rhume des foins,** hay fever 2. choke (of artichoke).

foire [fwar] *nf* fair; fun fair; **champ de f.**, fairground; **c'est une f. ici,** this place is a bear garden.

foirer [fware] *vi* 1. *P:* to fail, to flop 2. *(a) (of screw)* to slip *(b) Artil: (of fuse)* to hang fire.

fois [fwa] *nf* 1. time, occasion; **une f.**, once; **deux f.**, twice; **encore une f.**, once more; **une (bonne) f. pour toutes,** once (and) for all; **en une f.**, at one go; **pour une f. tu as raison,** you're right for once; **à la f.**, at one and the same time 2. *P:* **des f.**, sometimes, now and then;

des f. qu'il viendrait, in case he should come; **non, mais des f.!** that's a bit thick!

foison [fwazɔ̃] *nf* à f., plentifully; in abundance; **des pommes à f.,** plenty of apples.

foisonner [fwazɔne] *vi* to abound (**de,** in, with).
  foisonnant *a* teeming (with ideas).

folâtrer [fɔlɑtre] *vi* to romp, to frolic. **folâtre** *a* playful, frisky.

folie [fɔli] *nf* 1. madness; **être pris de f.,** to go mad; **aimer qn à la f.,** to be madly in love with s.o.; **aimer qch à la f.,** to have a mania for sth 2. folly; **dire des folies,** to talk wildly; **faire des folies,** (i) to act irrationally (ii) to be extravagant; **il a eu la f. de céder,** he was mad enough to give in.

folklore [fɔlklɔr] *nm* folklore. **folklorique** *a* traditional (costume); folk (dancing).

folle [fɔl] *see* **fou.**

follement [fɔlmɑ̃] *adv* 1. madly; foolishly, rashly 2. extravagantly; **on s'est f. amusé,** we had a fantastic time.

fomenter [fɔmɑ̃te] *vtr* to foment; to stir up (trouble).

foncer [fɔ̃se] *v* (**n. fonçons**) 1. *vtr* to deepen, darken (the colour of sth) 2. *vi (a)* **f. sur qn,** to rush at, swoop (down) on, s.o.; (*of bull, footballer*) to charge s.o. *(b) F:* to speed along; to forge ahead *(c)* to darken (colour). **foncé** *a* dark (colour); **bleu f.,** dark blue.

foncier, -ière [fɔ̃sje, -jɛr] *a* 1. of the land; **propriété foncière,** landed property; **impôt f.,** land tax 2. fundamental (commonsense). **foncièrement** *adv* fundamentally.

fonction [fɔ̃ksjɔ̃] *nf* 1. (*a*) function, office; **entrer en fonctions,** to take up one's duties; **faire f. de gérant,** to act as manager (*b*) **fonctions de l'estomac, du cœur,** functions of the stomach, of the heart 2. *Mth: etc:* function; **les prix varient en f. de la demande,** prices may vary in accordance with demand. **fonctionnel** *a* functional.

fonctionnaire [fɔ̃ksjɔnɛr] *nm* official, *esp* civil servant.

fonctionnement [fɔ̃ksjɔnmɑ̃] *nm* functioning (of government, plan); operation, running, working (of machine); **en (bon) état de f.,** in (good) working order; **mauvais f. du moteur,** fault in the engine.

fonctionner [fɔ̃ksjɔne] *vi* 1. to function 2. to act, work; **les trains ne fonctionnent plus,** the trains are no longer running; **faire f. une machine,** to operate a machine.

fond [fɔ̃] *nm* 1. (*a*) bottom; seat (of trousers, chair); heart (of artichoke); back (of the throat); **f. de cale,** bilge; **f. de bouteille,** dregs; **au f. il était très flatté,** in his heart of hearts he was extremely gratified (*b*) bottom, bed (of the ocean); **grands fonds,** ocean deeps; **hauts, petits, fonds,** shallows; **le grand, le petit, f.,** the deep, the shallow, end (of swimming pool); **à f.,** thoroughly; **visser une pièce à f.,** to screw a piece home; **connaître un sujet à f.,** to have a thorough knowledge of a subject; **à f. (de train),** at top speed 2. foundation; **rebâtir une maison de f. en comble,** to rebuild a house from top to bottom; **f. de teint,** (makeup) foundation cream; **accusation sans f.,** unfounded accusation; **faire f. sur qch,** to rely on sth; **cheval qui a du f.,** horse with staying power; **course de f.,** long-distance race; *Ski:* cross-country race; **cou-**

reur de f., long-distance runner; *Journ:* **article de f.,** leading article; **bruit de f.,** background noise; **au f., dans le f.,** basically, fundamentally; at bottom 3. back, far end; background (of picture); **fonds de boutique,** oddments; old stock; **au fin f. du désert,** in the heart of the desert.

fondamental, -aux [fɔ̃damɑ̃tal, -o] *a* fundamental; basic; **couleurs fondamentales,** primary colours. **fondamentalement** *adv* fundamentally, basically.

fondateur, -trice [fɔ̃datœr, -tris] *n* founder.

fondation [fɔ̃dasjɔ̃] *nf* 1. founding, foundation 2. *Const:* foundation (of house).

fondement [fɔ̃dmɑ̃] *nm* foundation; **soupçons sans f.,** groundless, unfounded, suspicions.

fonder [fɔ̃de] *vtr* 1. to found (business); to start, set up (newspaper, business); to float (company); to base, build (one's hopes) (**sur,** on) 2. **se f. sur qch,** to place one's reliance on sth; **je me fonde sur ce que vous venez de me dire,** I'm basing myself on what you've just told me. **fondé** 1. *a* founded, grounded, justified; **mal f.,** groundless, unjustified (suspicions) 2. *nm* **f. de pouvoir,** (i) *Jur:* proxy (ii) manager.

fonderie [fɔ̃dri] *nf* (*a*) smelting works (*b*) foundry.

fondre [fɔ̃dr] 1. *vtr* (*a*) to smelt (ore) (*b*) to melt (snow, wax); to melt down (metal) (*c*) to cast (bell) (*d*) to dissolve, melt (sugar) (*e*) to blend (colours) 2. *vi* (*a*) to melt, dissolve; **l'argent lui fond entre les mains,** he spends money like water (*b*) (*of sugar*) to melt, dissolve; **f. en larmes,** to dissolve in(to) tears 3. *vi* to swoop down (upon the prey) 4. **se f.,** to merge; (*of companies*) to amalgamate.

fondrière [fɔ̃drijɛr] *nf* (*a*) bog, quagmire (*b*) muddy hole (in road).

fonds [fɔ̃] *nm* 1. (*a*) **f. de commerce,** business (*b*) stock (-in-trade) 2. (*a*) funds; **mise de f.,** (i) putting up of capital (ii) paid-in capital; **rentrer dans ses f.,** to recover one's outlay; to get one's money back (*b*) fund (for special purpose); **f. commun,** pool; **F. monétaire international,** International Monetary Fund (*c*) means, resources; cash; **placer son argent à f. perdu,** to purchase a life annuity; **prêter à f. perdu,** to lend money without security; **être en f.,** to be in funds (*d*) *Fin:* stocks, securities.

fondu [fɔ̃dy] 1. *a* melted (butter); molten (lead) 2. *nf Cu:* **fondue,** (cheese) fondue; **f. bourguignonne,** meat fondue.

fontaine [fɔ̃tɛn] *nf* 1. spring; pool (of running water) 2. fountain.

fonte [fɔ̃t] *nf* 1. melting; thawing (of snow) 2. (*a*) smelting (of ore) (*b*) casting, founding 3. cast iron; **poêle en f.,** cast-iron stove.

fonts [fɔ̃] *nmpl Ecc:* **f. (baptismaux),** font.

football, *F:* **foot** [fut(bol)] *nm* (association) football, *F:* soccer.

footballeur [futbolœr] *nm* footballer.

footing [futiŋ] *nm* walking (for exercise).

forage [fɔraʒ] *nm* 1. drilling, boring; sinking (of well) 2. borehole; drill hole.

forain [fɔrɛ̃] *a & n* itinerant; **spectacle f.,** travelling show; (**marchand**) **f.,** stallkeeper (at fair); **fête foraine,** funfair.

forban [fɔrbɑ̃] *nm* corsair, pirate; *Fig:* rogue, shark.

forçat [fɔrsa] *nm* 1. *A:* galley slave 2. convict.

force [fɔrs] *nf* 1. (*a*) strength, force, vigour; **dans la f.**

de l'âge, in the prime of life; **être à bout de f.**, to be exhausted; **elle n'avait plus la f. de répondre**, she had no strength to answer; **tour de f.**, feat of strength, of skill; **travailleur de f.**, heavy worker (b) **ils sont de f. (égale)**, they are well matched; **je ne me sens pas de f. à faire cela**, I don't feel up to (doing) it (c) force, violence; **f. majeure**, circumstances outside one's control; **entrer de f. dans une maison**, to force one's way into a house; **f. lui fut d'obéir**, he had no alternative, no option, but to obey; **de gré ou de f.**, willy-nilly; **de toute f. il nous faut y assister**, we absolutely must be present; **à toute f.**, in spite of all opposition; **il veut à toute f. entrer**, he's determined to get in 2. (a) force (of blow, wind, argument); **par la f. des choses**, through the force of circumstances (b) **f. motrice**, motive power (c) **f. (électrique)**, electric power 3. **la f. armée**, the military; the troops; **les forces armées**, the armed forces; **f. d'intervention**, task force; **nous étions là en force(s)**, we turned out in (full) force 4. a inv A: & Lit: **f. gens**, many people 5. **à f. de**, by (dint of), by means of; **à f. de volonté**, by sheer force of will; **à f. de répéter**, by constant repetition.

forcé [fɔrse] a 1. forced; compulsory; Av: **atterrissage f.**, forced landing 2. forced, unnatural (laugh) 3. F: **c'est f.!** it's inevitable! **forcément** adv inevitably; **pas f.**, not necessarily.

forcené, -ée [fɔrsəne] 1. a frantic, mad, frenzied 2. n madman, madwoman.

forceps [fɔrsɛps] nm forceps.

forcer [fɔrse] vtr (n. **forçons**) 1. (a) to force, to compel; **être forcé de faire qch**, to be forced to do sth (b) **f. qn, qch**, to deal violently with s.o., to do violence to sth; **f. la consigne**, to force one's way in; **f. une serrure**, to force a lock; **f. la caisse**, to break into the till; **f. une porte**, to break open a door; **f. sa prison**, to break jail (c) to force (voice, pace); to force (plants); F: **f. la note**, to overdo it (d) **f. la dose d'un médicament**, to take, give, too large a dose of medicine 2. vi to strain; to overdo it; to force it 3. **se f.**, to force oneself (**pour faire qch**, to do sth).

forcing [fɔrsiŋ] nm sustained pressure.

forcir [fɔrsir] vi to get fat; to fill out.

forer [fɔre] vtr to drill, bore; to sink (a well).

foret [fɔrɛ] nm Tls: drill.

forêt [fɔrɛ] nf forest. **forestier, -ière** 1. a forest (region); forested (area); **exploitation forestière**, lumbering 2. nm forester.

forfait¹ [fɔrfɛ] nm heinous crime.

forfait² nm (contract for a) fixed price; flat rate; lump sum; **travail à f.**, (i) contract work (ii) job work; **voyage à f.**, (all-)inclusive, package, holiday, tour; **vente à f.**, outright sale. **forfaitaire** a prix f., fixed price; flat rate; contract price; **voyage à prix f.**, package holiday, tour.

forfait³ nm Sp: etc: **déclarer f.**, to scratch (a horse from a race), to withdraw from a competition.

forge [fɔrʒ] nm 1. smithy, forge 2. usu pl ironworks.

forger [fɔrʒe] vtr (n. **forgeons**) 1. to forge; **fer forgé**, wrought iron 2. to fabricate (story); to make up (excuse); to coin (word); to conjure up (vision).

forgeron [fɔrʒərɔ̃] nm blacksmith.

formaliser [fɔrmalize] vtr 1. to formalize 2. **se f.**, to take offence (**de**, at).

formalisme [fɔrmalism] nm formalism. **forma-liste** 1. a formalistic, punctilious 2. n formalist.

formalité [fɔrmalite] nf 1. formality; **sans autre f.**, without further ado 2. **sans formalité(s)**, without ceremony.

format [fɔrma] nm format (of book); **f. de poche**, pocket size.

formation [fɔrmasjɔ̃] nf 1. (a) formation, forming (b) education, training 2. (a) makeup; structure; formation (b) Mus: group. **formateur, -trice** a formative.

forme [fɔrm] nf 1. form, shape; (of pers) build, figure; **en f. d'œuf**, egg-shaped; **sans f.**, shapeless; **prendre f.**, to take shape; to materialize 2. (a) form; method of procedure; **quittance en bonne (et due) f.**, receipt in order; **faire qch dans les formes**, to do sth in the accepted way; **pour la f.**, as a matter of form; **de pure f.**, purely formal (b) pl manners; tact (c) **être en f.**, to be on form, to be fit 3. Ind: mould; Bootm: last; Hatm: block; Typ: form(e).

formel, -elle [fɔrmɛl] a 1. formal, express, precise (order); flat, categorical (denial); absolute (veto); strict (prohibition) 2. formal. **formellement** adv formally; strictly, expressly.

former [fɔrme] vtr 1. (a) to form; to make, create; to draw up (plan); to raise (objections) (b) to shape, fashion (c) to school (horse, child); to train (pilot); to mould (s.o.'s character) 2. **se f.**, to form, develop; (of plan) to take shape; **se f. aux affaires**, to acquire a business training.

formidable [fɔrmidabl] a (a) fearsome, formidable (b) F: tremendous, wonderful, terrific, fantastic. **formidablement** adv F: tremendously, fantastically.

formol [fɔrmɔl] nm Ch: formalin.

formulaire [fɔrmylɛr] nm (printed) form.

formulation [fɔrmylasjɔ̃] nf formulation; expression.

formule [fɔrmyl] nf 1. (a) formula (b) (set) form of words; Corr: **f. de politesse**, letter ending, formal ending 2. Adm: (printed) form.

formuler [fɔrmyle] vtr to formulate; to draw up (document); to express (wish).

fornication [fɔrnikasjɔ̃] nf fornication.

fort¹ [fɔr] 1. a (a) strong; **trouver plus f. que soi**, to meet one's match; **c'est une forte tête**, (i) he has a good head on his shoulders (ii) he is very independent; **être f. en maths**, to be good at maths (b) strong (rope, drink); high (fever, wind); intense (heat); heavy (rain); loud (voice); **c'est plus f. que moi!** I can't help it! **c'est trop f.!** that's a bit thick!; **ce qu'il y a de plus f.**, **c'est que**, the worst of it is that (c) ville, place, **forte**, fortified town (d) **se faire f. de faire qch**, to undertake to do sth (e) large, stout (pers); **elle est forte des hanches**, she's big round the hips; **forte somme**, large sum of money; **forte pente**, steep gradient; Com: **prix f.**, full price 2. adv (a) strongly; **frapper f.**, to strike hard; **y aller f.**, (i) to go hard at it (ii) to exaggerate; **crier f.**, to shout at the top of one's voice; **sentir f.**, to smell strong (b) very, extremely; **j'ai f. à faire**, I have a great deal to do.

fort² nm 1. strong part; **au f. de l'hiver**, in the depth of winter; **au (plus) f. du combat**, in the thick of the fight; **ce n'est pas son f.**, it's not his strong point, his forte 2. strong man 3. fort, stronghold.

forteresse [fɔrtərɛs] *nf* fortress; stronghold.

fortification [fɔrtifikasjɔ̃] *nf* fortification.

fortifier [fɔrtifje] *vtr* to fortify; to strengthen. **fortifiant** 1. *a* fortifying; invigorating, bracing 2. *nm* tonic.

fortuit [fɔrtɥi] *a* fortuitous; chance, casual (meeting); **cas f.**, accident. **fortuitement** *adv* fortuitously, by chance.

fortune [fɔrtyn] *nf* 1. fortune, chance, luck; **venez dîner à la f. du pot**, come and take pot luck; **de f.**, makeshift 2. *(a)* **il n'a pas de f.**, he's unlucky *(b)* **mauvaise f.**, misfortune; **avoir la bonne f. de rencontrer qn**, to have the good luck to meet s.o. 3. fortune, wealth; **faire f.**, to make one's, a, fortune; **avoir de la f.**, to be well off. **fortuné** *a* *(a)* A: fortunate *(b)* wealthy, well off.

forum [fɔrɔm] *nm* forum.

fosse [fos] *nf* 1. pit, hole; *Sp:* (jumping) pit; *Aut:* **f. (de réparation)**, inspection pit; **f. d'aisances**, cesspool; **f. septique**, septic tank; **f. d'orchestre**, orchestra pit; **f. aux lions**, lion's den 2. grave.

fossé [fose] *nm* ditch, trench; *Fig:* rift.

fossette [fosɛt] *nf* dimple.

fossile [fosil] *a* & *nm* fossil.

fossiliser (se) [səfɔsilize] *vpr* to fossilize.

fossoyeur [foswajœr] *nm* gravedigger.

fou, fol, folle [fu, fɔl] *(the form* **fol**, *used in the m before a vowel or* h *mute)* 1. *a* *(a)* mad, insane; **f. à lier**, raving mad; **il y a de quoi devenir f.**, it's enough to drive you mad; **f. de joie**, beside oneself with joy; **être f. de qn**, to be madly in love with s.o. *(b)* foolish, silly; **un fol espoir**, a mad hope *(c)* excessive, enormous; **succès f.**, tremendous success; **il gagne un argent f.**, he makes a mint, a fortune; **à une allure folle**, at breakneck speed; **il y avait un monde f.**, there was an enormous crowd; **prix f.**, exorbitant price; *F:* **c'est f. ce que c'est cher!** it's madly expensive! *(d)* out of control; loose (lock of hair); **f. rire**, uncontrollable laughter; **herbes folles**, rank weeds; *Bot:* **folle avoine**, wild oats 2. *n* *(a)* madman, madwoman; lunatic; **f. furieux**, raving lunatic; *F:* **maison de fous**, madhouse *(b)* fool; jester; **plus on est de fous plus on rit**, the more the merrier 3. *nm* *Chess:* bishop.

foudre [fudr] 1. *nf* thunderbolt, lightning; **coup de f.**, (i) *A:* unexpected event; bolt from the blue (ii) love at first sight 2. *nmpl* wrath.

foudroyer [fudrwaje] *vtr* (**je foudroie**) to strike (down) (by lightning); to blast; to crush (one's opponents); **arbre foudroyé**, blasted tree; **cette nouvelle m'a foudroyé**, I was thunderstruck at the news; **elle le foudroya du regard**, she gave him a withering look; she looked daggers at him. **foudroyant** *a* crushing (attack, news); withering (look); staggering (success); lightning (speed).

fouet [fwɛ] *nm* *(a)* whip; **coup de f.**, (i) cut (of whip); (ii) stimulus; **collision de plein f.**, head-on collision *(b)* *DomEc:* whisk.

fouetter [fwɛte] *(a)* *vtr* to whip, flog; to spank (child); to whisk, beat (eggs); to whip (cream); **il n'y a pas là de quoi f. un chat**, there's nothing to make such a fuss about; **avoir d'autres chats à f.**, to have other fish to fry *(b)* *vtr* & *i* **la pluie fouette (contre) les vitres**, the rain is lashing against the panes.

fougère [fuʒɛr] *nf* *Bot:* fern; bracken.

fougue [fug] *nf* fire, ardour, spirit; **plein de f.**, fiery. **fougueux, -euse** *a* fiery, ardent, spirited. **fougueusement** *adv* ardently.

fouille [fuj] *nf* 1. *(a)* excavation *(b) usu pl Archeol:* dig, excavations 2. search(ing) (of suspect).

fouiller [fuje] 1. *vtr* *(a)* to dig, excavate *(b)* to search (house, luggage); to search, frisk (suspect); **f. un tiroir**, to ransack a drawer 2. *vi* **f. dans une armoire**, to rummage in a cupboard; **f. dans le passé**, to rake up the past 3. **se f.**, to go through one's pockets. **fouillé** *a* well researched (work).

fouillis [fuji] *nm* jumble, mess, muddle.

fouine [fwin] *nf* Z: stone marten; **à tête de f.**, weasel-faced. **fouineur, -euse** 1. *a* inquisitive, nosy 2. *n* snooper, nosy parker.

fouiner [fwine] *vi* F: to ferret, to nose about.

fouir [fwir] *vtr* to dig (underground).

foulant [fulɑ̃] *a* P: exhausting, killing.

foulard [fular] *nm* 1. *Tex:* foulard 2. silk scarf; headscarf.

foule [ful] *nf* crowd; host (of ideas); **entrer en f.**, to crowd in, to come crowding in; **ils sont venus en f. pour voir la reine**, they flocked to see the queen.

foulée [fule] *nf usu pl* stride; *Rac:* **rester dans la f. d'un concurrent**, to follow close behind another competitor.

fouler [fule] *vtr* 1. to trample (down) (grass); to press, tread, crush (grapes); **f. qch aux pieds**, to trample sth underfoot 2. *(a)* **se f. la cheville**, to sprain, twist, one's ankle *(b)* *F:* **se f. (la rate)**, (i) to take a lot of trouble (ii) to flog oneself to death; **ne pas se f. (la rate)**, to take it easy.

four [fur] *nm* 1. *(a)* oven; **faire cuire au f.**, to bake; to roast (meat); **plat allant au f.**, ovenproof dish *(b)* *Cu:* **petits fours**, petits fours 2. kiln, furnace 3. *Th:* **faire (un) f.**, to be a flop.

fourberie [furbəri] *nf* deceit, cheating. **fourbe** *a* deceitful, cheating.

fourbi [furbi] *nm* F: kit, gear; paraphernalia; **tout le f.**, the whole caboodle.

fourbu [furby] *a* tired out, dead beat.

fourche [furʃ] *nf* 1. pitchfork; (garden) fork 2. fork(ing) (of road); **la route fait une f.**, the road forks. **fourchu** *a* forked; **pied f.**, cloven hoof.

fourcher [furʃe] *vi* **la langue lui a fourché**, he made a slip of the tongue.

fourchette [furʃɛt] *nf* (table) fork; *Stat:* bracket.

fourgon [furgɔ̃] *nm* van, wag(g)on; **f. mortuaire**, hearse.

fourgonnette [furgɔnɛt] *nf* Aut: small van.

fourmi [furmi] *nf* Ent: ant; **avoir des fourmis dans les jambes**, to have pins and needles in one's legs.

fourmilière [furmiljɛr] *nf* anthill, ant's nest.

fourmillement [furmijmɑ̃] *nm* 1. swarming (of ants) 2. pricking, tingling, sensation; pins and needles.

fourmiller [furmije] *vi* 1. to swarm; to teem 2. **le pied me fourmille**, I've got pins and needles in my foot.

fournaise [furnɛz] *nf* furnace; **cette chambre est une f.**, this room's like an oven.

fourneau, -eaux [furno] *nm* *(a)* furnace (of boiler); bowl (of pipe) *(b)* **f. de cuisine**, (kitchen) range; **f. à gaz**, gas stove, cooker *(c)* **haut f.**, blast furnace.

fournée [furne] *nf* batch (of loaves, *F:* of tourists).

fournil [furni] *nm* bakehouse.

fournir [furnir] *vtr* **1.** (*a*) to supply, furnish, provide; **magasin bien fourni**, well stocked shop (*b*) to yield, produce **2.** *v ind tr* **f. aux dépenses**, to defray the expenses; **f. aux besoins de qn**, to supply s.o.'s wants **3.** **se f.**, to provide oneself (**de**, with); to get supplies (**chez**, from). **fourni** *a* **1.** well stocked (shop) **2.** thick (hair).

fournisseur, -euse [furnisœr, -øz] *n* (*a*) supplier, stockist (*b*) **les fournisseurs**, tradesmen.

fourniture [furnityr] *nf* **1.** supplying, providing **2.** *pl* supplies; **fournitures de bureau**, office equipment, supplies; stationery.

fourrage [furaʒ] *nm* forage, fodder.

fourrager [furaʒe] *vi* to forage, rummage.

fourré¹ [fure] *nm* thicket.

fourreau, -eaux [furo] *nm* sheath, cover, case; scabbard (of sword); *MecE:* sleeve.

fourrer [fure] *vtr* **1.** (*a*) to cover, line, with fur (*b*) *F:* to stuff, cram; **f. ses mains dans ses poches**, to stuff one's hands in one's pockets; **f. son nez partout**, to poke one's nose into everything **2. se f. dans un coin**, to hide in a corner; **où est-il allé se f.?** where on earth has he hidden himself? **il ne sait plus où se f.**, he doesn't know where to put himself. **fourré²** *a* lined; fur-lined; **chocolats fourrés à la crème**, chocolate creams; **bonbon f.**, sweet with a soft centre.

fourre-tout [furtu] *nm inv* **1.** lumber room **2.** holdall.

fourreur [furœr] *nm* furrier.

fourrière [furjɛr] *nf* (animal, car) pound; **mettre une voiture en f.**, to impound, tow away, a car.

fourrure [furyr] *nf* (*a*) fur, skin; **manteau de f.**, fur coat (*b*) hair, coat (of animal).

fourvoyer [furvwaje] *vtr* (**je fourvoie**) **1.** to mislead (s.o.) **2. se f.**, to lose one's way, to go astray.

foutaise [futɛz] *nf P:* rubbish, rot.

foutre [futr] *vtr* (*pp* **foutu**; *pr ind* **je fous, n. foutons**) *P:* **1.** (*a*) **f. qch par terre**, to fling, chuck, sth on the ground (*b*) **il ne fout rien**, he does damn all; **fous le camp! fous-moi la paix!** clear off, bugger off! **2.** (*a*) **se f. de qn, qch**, to take the mickey out of s.o., sth; **je m'en fous**, I don't give a damn (*b*) **se f. dedans**, to boob. **foutu** *a* (*a*) bloody awful (*b*) ruined, done for; **il est f.**, he's had it (*c*) (*of machine, device*) **mal f.**, hopeless; **je me sens mal f.**, I feel terrible.

fox(-terrier) [fɔks(terje)] *nm* fox terrier.

foyer [fwaje] *nm* **1.** fire(place), hearth, grate **2.** source (of heat); centre (of learning, infection) **3.** (*a*) hearth, home; **f. d'étudiants**, students' union, club (*b*) *Th:* foyer; **f. des artistes**, green room **4.** focus (of lens); **verres à double f.**, bifocal lenses, bifocals.

FR3 *abbr TV: France Régions 3.*

fracas [fraka] *nm* din; crash.

fracasser [frakase] *vtr* to smash (sth) to pieces; to shatter (sth).

fraction [fraksjɔ̃] *nf* (*a*) fraction (*b*) part, portion.

fractionnement [fraksjɔnmɑ̃] *nm* dividing up, splitting up.

fractionner [fraksjɔne] *vtr* to divide up, to split up.

fracture [fraktyr] *nf Geol: Med:* fracture.

fracturer [fraktyre] *vtr* **1.** to force (lock) **2.** to fracture (bone).

fragilité [fraʒilite] *nf* **1.** fragility; brittleness **2.** frailty,

weakness. **fragile** *a* **1.** fragile; brittle **2.** frail; weak; precarious.

fragment [fragmɑ̃] *nm* fragment; chip (of stone); snatch (of conversation, song); extract (from book).

fragmentaire *a* fragmentary.

fragmentation [fragmɑ̃tasjɔ̃] *nf* fragmentation.

fragmenter [fragmɑ̃te] *vtr* to fragment, split up.

fraîchement [frɛʃmɑ̃] *adv* **1.** coolly **2.** freshly, recently.

fraîcheur [frɛʃœr] *nf* **1.** freshness, coolness, chilliness; **la f. du soir**, the cool of the evening **2.** freshness; bloom (of youth).

frais¹, fraîche [frɛ, frɛʃ] **1.** *a* (*a*) fresh; cool; chilly (breeze, reception); **il fait f.**, it's cool (*b*) new, recent; **œufs f.**, new-laid eggs; **peinture fraîche**, wet paint (*c*) **teint f.**, fresh complexion; **f. et dispos**, ready for anything; *P:* **me voilà f.!** I'm in a nice mess now! **2.** (*a*) *nm* **prendre le f.**, to take the air; **à mettre au f.**, to be kept in a cool place; **peint de f.**, freshly painted (*b*) *nf* **à la fraîche**, in the cool of the day).

frais² *nmpl* expenses, cost; **faux f.**, incidental expenses; **faire les f. de qch**, to bear the cost of sth; **faire qch à ses f.**, to do sth at one's own expense; **rentrer dans ses f.**, to get one's money back; **faire les f. de la conversation**, to keep the conversation going; **à grands f., à peu de f.**, at great, at little, cost; **se mettre en f. pour qn**, to put oneself out for s.o.; **j'en suis pour mes f.**, I've had all my trouble for nothing; I've wasted my time; **f. généraux**, overheads; *F:* **aux f. de la princesse**, at the government's, the firm's, expense.

fraise [frɛz] *nf* **1.** strawberry; **f. de bois**, wild strawberry **2.** *MecE:* (*a*) milling cutter (*b*) *Dent:* drill.

fraiser [freze] *vtr* (*a*) *MecE:* (i) to mill (ii) to countersink (hole) (*b*) *Dent:* to drill.

fraisier [frezje] *nm* strawberry plant.

framboise [frãbwaz] *nf* raspberry.

framboisier [frãbwazje] *nm* raspberry cane, bush.

franc¹ [frã] *nm* franc.

franc², franche [frã, frãʃ] *a* **1.** free; **f. de port**, postfree; carriage paid; *Fb:* **coup f.**, free kick **2.** (*a*) frank, open, candid; **avoir son f. parler**, to speak one's mind; **y aller de f. jeu**, to be quite straightforward about it; **jouer f. jeu (avec qn)**, (i) to play a straightforward game (ii) to play fair (with s.o.); *adv* **pour parler f.**, frankly speaking (*b*) real, true; pure (colour, wine); downright (scoundrel); **terre franche**, loam (*c*) **huits jours francs**, eight clear days. **franchement** *adv* **1.** frankly, candidly, openly **2.** really, quite; **c'était f. stupide**, it was sheer stupidity; **f.! really! honestly! c'est f. laid**, it's plain ugly.

France [frãs] *Prnf Geog:* France; **en F.**, in France; **les vins de F.**, French wines. **français, -aise** *1. a* French **2.** *n* Frenchman, -woman; **les F.**, the French **3.** *nm Ling:* French.

Francfort [frãkfɔr] *Prn Geog:* Frankfurt; **saucisse de F.**, frankfurter.

franchir [frãʃir] *vtr* (*a*) to clear (obstacle); to jump (over); to get over (*b*) to pass through; to cross (river, threshold); **f. le mur du son**, to break the sound barrier.

franchise [frãʃiz] *nf* **1.** (*a*) *Hist:* **charte de f.**, charter (of freedom) (of city) (*b*) exemption; **en f.**, (to import sth) duty free; **bagages en f.**, baggage allowance; **en f. (postale)** = OHMS, official paid (*c*) *Ins:*

accidental damage excess **2.** frankness, candour.

franchissement [frãʃismã] *nm* clearing (of obstacle); crossing (of river).

franc-maçon [frãmasɔ̃] *nm* freemason; *pl francs-maçons.*

franc-maçonnerie [frãmasɔnri] *nf* freemasonry.

franco [frãko] *adv* (a) free, carriage free; **f. (de port),** carriage paid (b) *F:* readily; **vas-y f.!** go ahead!

franco-canadien [frãkokanadjɛ̃] *a & nm* French Canadian.

francophile [frãkofil] *a & n* francophile.

francophobie [frãkofɔbi] *nf* francophobia. **francophobe** *a & n* francophobe.

francophone [frãkofon] *a* French-speaking; *n* French speaker.

franc-parler [frãparle] *nm* frankness, candour; plain speaking; outspokenness.

franc-tireur [frãtirœr] *nm Mil:* irregular (soldier); *Fig:* freelance; *pl francs-tireurs.*

frange [frãʒ] *nf* fringe.

franger [frãʒe] *vtr* to fringe.

frangin, -ine [frãʒɛ̃, -in] *n P:* brother, sister.

franquette [frãkɛt] *nf used only in* **à la bonne f.,** simply, without ceremony.

frappant [frapã] *a* striking (likeness).

frappe [frap] *nf* (a) striking (of coins) (b) *Typew:* striking (of keys); **faute de f.,** typing error.

frapper [frape] **1.** *vtr* (a) to strike, hit; **f. légèrement,** to tap; **f. la table du poing,** to bang one's fist on the table; **f. un coup,** to strike a blow; **f. des marchandises d'un droit,** to impose a duty on goods; **être frappé d'une maladie,** to be struck down by an illness; **ce qui m'a frappé le plus c'était son sang-froid,** what impressed me most was his coolness (b) to stamp; to strike coin (c) to type (letter) (d) to ice; to chill (wine); **whisky frappé,** whisky on the rocks **2.** *vi* **f. à la porte,** to knock at the door; **on frappe,** there's a knock (at the door); **f. du pied,** to stamp (one's foot) **3.** *F:* **se f.,** to get demoralized; to get panicky.

frasque [frask] *nf* prank, escapade.

fraternel, -elle [fratɛrnɛl] *a* fraternal, brotherly. **fraternellement** *adv* fraternally.

fraternisation [fratɛrnizasjɔ̃] *nf* fraternization.

fraterniser [fratɛrnize] *vi* to fraternize.

fraternité [fratɛrnite] *nf* fraternity, brotherhood.

fraude [frod] *nf* **1.** fraud, deception; **f. fiscale,** tax evasion; **passer qch en f.,** to smuggle sth through the customs **2.** fraudulence, deceit; **par f.,** under false pretences.

frauder [frode] **1.** *vtr* to defraud, cheat **2.** *vi* to cheat.

fraudeur, -euse [frodœr, -øz] *n* defrauder, cheat; smuggler.

frauduleux, -euse [frodylø, -øz] *a* fraudulent. **frauduleusement** *adv* fraudulently.

frayer [freje] *vtr* (je fraye, je fraie) **f. un chemin,** to clear a path; **se f. un passage,** to clear a way (for oneself); **se f. un chemin dans la foule,** to elbow one's way through the crowd.

frayeur [frejœr] *nf* fright; fear, dread.

fredaine [frədɛn] *nf* prank, escapade.

fredonner [frədɔne] *vtr* to hum (tune).

frégate [fregat] *nf* frigate; **capitaine de f.,** commander.

frein [frɛ̃] *nm* **1.** (horse's) bit; **mettre un f. aux désirs de** qn, to curb s.o.'s desires; **curiosité sans f.,** unbridled curiosity **2.** brake; *Aut:* **f. à main,** handbrake; **f. à disque,** disc brake; **mettre le f.,** to apply the brake(s); to brake.

freinage [frɛnaʒ] *nm* braking.

freiner [frɛne] **1.** *vtr* (a) to brake (vehicle) (b) to curb (inflation); to check (production) **2.** *vi* to brake, to apply the brake(s).

frelater [frəlate] *vtr* to adulterate (food).

frêle [frɛl] *a* frail, weak.

frelon [frəlɔ̃] *nm Ent:* hornet.

frémir [fremir] *vi* **1.** to vibrate, to quiver; (*of leaves*) to rustle; (*of hot water*) to simmer **2.** to tremble, shake, shudder.

frémissement [fremismã] *nm* **1.** rustle (of leaves); simmering (of water) **2.** (a) shuddering, quivering (b) shudder, tremor, quiver.

frêne [frɛn] *nm* ash (tree, timber).

frénésie [frenezi] *nf* frenzy, agitation; **applaudir avec f.,** to applaud frantically. **frénétique** *a* frantic, frenzied. **frénétiquement** *adv* frantically, frenetically.

fréquence [frekãs] *nf* frequency; *Med:* **f. du pouls,** pulse rate; *Ph: WTel:* **haute, basse, f.,** high, low frequency, current. **fréquent** *a* frequent. **fréquemment** *adv* frequently.

fréquentation [frekãtasjɔ̃] *nf* (a) frequenting (b) association (de, with); **mauvaises fréquentations,** bad company.

fréquenter [frekãte] *vtr* (a) to frequent; to visit (place) frequently (b) **f. qn,** (i) to associate with s.o. (ii) to see s.o. regularly; **quels gens fréquente-t-il?** what company does he keep? who does he go around with? **fréquenté** *a* much visited; popular (place); **endroit mal f.,** place with a bad reputation.

frère [frɛr] *nm* **1.** brother; **frères d'armes,** brothers-in-arms; *F:* **vieux f.,** old chap **2.** *Ecc:* friar; **f. lai,** lay brother.

fresque [frɛsk] *nf Art:* fresco.

fret [frɛ] *nm* **1.** freight; freightage **2.** chartering **3.** load, cargo; freight.

fréter [frete] *vtr* (je frète) **1.** to freight (out) (ship) **2.** to fit out, equip (ship).

frétillement [fretijmã] *nm* **1.** wriggling (of fish) **2.** quivering, fidgeting.

frétiller [fretije] *vi* (*of fish*) to wriggle; (*of dog*) **f. la queue,** to wag its tail; **f. d'impatience,** to quiver with impatience.

friable [frijabl] *a* friable, crumbly.

friandise [frijãdiz] *nf* delicacy, titbit. **friand, -ande** *a* fond of delicacies; **être f. de sucreries,** to have a sweet tooth.

fric [frik] *nm P:* cash, dough, lolly.

fric-frac [frikfrak] *nm P:* burglary, break-in; *pl fric-frac(s).*

friche [friʃ] *nf* waste land; fallow land; **être en f.,** to lie fallow.

fricot [friko] *nm F:* made-up dish; stew; **faire le f.,** to do the cooking.

fricoter [frikɔte] *vtr F:* **1.** to stew; to cook **2.** to plot; **je me demande ce qu'il fricote,** I wonder what he's up to.

friction [friksjɔ̃] *nf* friction; *Sp:* rub down; *Hairdr:* scalp massage.

frictionner [friksjɔne] *vtr* to rub.

frigidaire [frizidɛr] *nm Rtm:* refrigerator, fridge.

frigo [frigo] *nm F:* fridge.

frigorifier [frigɔrifje] *vtr* to refrigerate. **frigorifié** *a F:* (*pers*) frozen stiff. **frigorifique** *a* refrigerating; **wagon f.**, refrigerator van.

frileux, -euse [frilø, -øz] *a* sensitive to the cold; chilly (pers). **frileusement** *adv* with a shiver.

frime [frim] *nf F:* sham, pretence; **tout ça c'est de la f.**, it's all eyewash.

frimousse [frimus] *nf F:* (sweet, pretty little) face.

fringale [frɛ̃gal] *nf F:* hunger; **avoir la f.**, to be ravenous.

fringant [frɛ̃gɑ̃] *a* spirited, frisky (horse); dashing (pers).

fringuer (se) [səfrɛ̃ge] *vpr* to get dressed.

fringues [frɛ̃g] *nfpl P:* clothes, togs.

friper(se) [səfripe] *vpr* (*of garment*) to crumple, to get crumpled.

friperie [fripri] *nf* (*a*) secondhand clothes (*b*) rubbish, frippery.

fripier, -ière [fripje, -jɛr] *n* secondhand clothes dealer.

fripon, -onne [fripɔ̃, -ɔn] 1. *a* roguish 2. *n* rogue, rascal.

fripouille [fripuj] *nf F:* rogue; cad.

frire [frir] *vtr & i def* (*pp* **frit;** *for the vtr the parts wanting are supplied by* **faire f.**) to fry; **je fais f. des pommes de terre,** I'm frying potatoes.

frise [friz] *nf Arch:* frieze.

friser [frize] 1. (*a*) *vtr* to curl, wave; **fer à f.**, curling tongs (*b*) *vi* (*of hair*) to curl 2. *vtr* to touch, skim; **f. la soixantaine,** to be close on sixty. **frisé** *a* curly; **laitue frisée,** curly lettuce.

frisette [frizɛt] *nf* ringlet, small curl.

frisquet [friskɛ] *a F:* chilly.

frisson [frisɔ̃] *nm* (*a*) shiver (from cold) (*b*) shudder, thrill (of fear, pleasure); **j'en ai le f.**, it gives me the shudders.

frissonnement [frisɔnmɑ̃] *nm* 1. shivering, shuddering 2. shiver, shudder.

frissonner [frisɔne] *vi* (*a*) to shiver, shudder (*b*) to be thrilled (with delight); to quiver (with impatience) (*c*) (*of leaves*) to quiver.

frit [fri] *a* fried; **pommes de terre frites,** *nfpl* **frites,** chips; French fried potatoes.

friteuse [fritøz] *nf DomEc:* deep fryer; chip pan.

friture [frityr] *nf* 1. (*a*) frying (*b*) *WTel:* crackling (noise) 2. fried food, *esp* fried fish 3. *Cu:* (deep) fat.

frivolité [frivɔlite] *nf* frivolity. **frivole** *a* frivolous. **frivolement** *adv* frivolously.

froc [frɔk] *nm* (*a*) (monk's) frock, gown (*b*) *P:* trousers.

froid [frwa] 1. *a* (*a*) cold; **chambre froide,** cold room (*b*) cold (person); chilly (manner); **être f. avec qn,** to treat s.o. coldly; **garder la tête froide,** to keep cool (and collected) 2. *adv phr* **à f.**, in the cold state; *Aut:* **démarrer à f.**, to start from cold 3. *nm* (*a*) cold; **coup de f.**, cold snap; *Med:* chill; **prendre f.**, to catch a chill; **il fait f.**, it's cold; **il fait un f. de loup**, it's bitterly cold; **avoir f. aux mains,** to have cold hands; **ça m'a fait f. dans le dos,** it sent cold shivers down my spine; **elle n'a pas f. aux yeux,** she's very determined; she's got plenty of nerve (*b*) **l'industrie du f.,** (the) refrigerating (industry) (*c*) coldness; **ils sont en f.,** there is a coolness between them. **froidement** *adv* coldly; coolly.

froideur [frwadœr] *nf* coldness; **avec f.**, coldly.

froissement [frwasmɑ̃] *nm* (*a*) crumpling, creasing (*b*) rustle, rustling (of silk).

froisser [frwase] *vtr* 1. (*a*) to crease; to crumple (*b*) **f. qn,** to offend, to give offence to, s.o. 2. **se f.**, to take offence.

frôlement [frolmɑ̃] *nm* (*a*) slight rubbing, brushing (contre, against) (*b*) rustle (of silk).

frôler [frole] *vtr* to touch lightly; to brush; to skim (tree tops); **il a frôlé la mort,** he came close to death.

fromage [frɔmaʒ] *nm* 1. cheese; **f. blanc,** (sort of) cream cheese; **un gentil petit f.**, a nice easy job 2. *Cu:* **f. de tête,** brawn. **fromager, -ère** 1. *a* cheese 2. *n* cheesemonger.

fromagerie [frɔmaʒri] *nf* cheese dairy.

froment [frɔmɑ̃] *nm* wheat.

froncement [frɔ̃smɑ̃] *nm* **f. de(s) sourcils,** frown.

froncer [frɔ̃se] *vtr* (*n.* **fronçons**) 1. **f. les sourcils,** to knit one's brows; to frown 2. (*needlework*) to gather.

fronde [frɔ̃d] *nf* (*a*) sling (*b*) (toy) catapult. **frondeur, -euse** *a* critical (of the authorities).

front [frɔ̃] *nm* 1. forehead, brow; **marcher le f. haut,** to walk with one's head up high; **et vous avez le f. de me dire cela!** you have the face, the impudence, to tell me that! 2. face, front (of building); **f. de bataille,** battle front; **le f.**, the front (line); **f. de mer,** sea front; **faire f. à qch,** to face sth; **faire f.**, to stand fast 3. (*a*) **de f.**, abreast (*b*) **attaque de f.**, frontal attack; **heurter qch de f.**, to run headlong into sth. **frontal, -aux** *a* frontal, front.

frontière [frɔ̃tjɛr] *nf* frontier (line); border (line); boundary. **frontalier, -ière** 1. *a* border, frontier (region) 2. *n* inhabitant of frontier zone.

frontispice [frɔ̃tispis] *nm* frontispiece.

fronton [frɔ̃tɔ̃] *nm Arch:* pediment.

frottement [frɔtmɑ̃] *nm* (*a*) rubbing (*b*) friction.

frotter [frɔte] 1. *vtr* to rub; **se f. les mains,** to rub one's hands; **f. le parquet,** to polish the floor; **f. une allumette,** to strike a match 2. *vi* to rub 3. (*a*) **se f. contre qch,** to rub against sth (*b*) **se f. à qn, qch,** to come up against s.o., sth.

froussard, -arde [frusar, -ard] *n P:* coward, chicken.

frousse [frus] *nf P:* funk, fear, fright; **avoir la f.**, to be scared stiff.

fructifier [fryktifje] *vi* to bear fruit; *Fin:* to yield a profit.

fructueux, -euse [fryktɥø, -øz] *a* fruitful; profitable. **fructueusement** *adv* fruitfully, profitably.

frugalité [frygalite] *nf* frugality. **frugal, -aux** *a* frugal. **frugalement** *adv* frugally.

fruit [frɥi] *nm* fruit; **porter (ses) fruits,** to bear fruit; **étudier avec f.**, to study to good purpose; **sans f.**, fruitlessly; **fruits de mer** = seafood. **fruité** *a* fruity. **fruitier, -ière** 1. *a* fruit 2. *n* fruiterer, greengrocer.

frusques [frysk] *nfpl P:* clothes, togs.

fruste [fryst] *a* worn (coin); rough, coarse, unrefined (style, manners).

frustration [frystrasjɔ̃] *nf* frustration.

frustrer [frystre] *vtr* 1. to frustrate, disappoint 2. to defraud (s.o.) (**de qch,** of sth).

FS *abbr Franc suisse.*

fuel(-oil) [fjul(ɔjl)] *nm* fuel oil.

fugitif, -ive [fyʒitif, -iv] **1.** *a & n* fugitive, runaway **2.** *a* fleeting, transitory; passing (desire).

fugue [fyg] *nf* **1.** *Mus:* fugue **2. faire une f.,** to run away.

fuir [fɥir] *v (prp* **fuyant**) **1.** *vi (a)* to flee, run away; **faire f.,** to put to flight; **le temps fuit,** time flies, is slipping by *(b) (of horizon, forehead)* to recede *(c) (of tap)* to leak; *(of water)* to escape **2.** *vtr* to shun, avoid (s.o., sth).

fuite [fɥit] *nf* **1.** *(a)* flight, running away; **prendre la f.,** to take to flight; **être en f.,** to be on the run; **voleur en f.,** runaway thief *(b)* passage (of time) **2.** leak; escape (of gas); leakage.

fulgurant [fylgyrɑ̃] *a* lightning (speed, remark); searing (pain); **lancer un regard f. à qn,** to look daggers at s.o.

fulminer [fylmine] *vi* **f. contre qn,** to fulminate against s.o.

fume-cigarette [fymsigaret] *nm inv* cigarette holder.

fumée [fyme] *nf (a)* smoke; **rideau de f.,** smokescreen; **la f. vous gêne-t-elle?** do you mind my smoking? **sans f.,** smokeless; **partir en f.,** to go up in smoke; *Prov:* **il n'y a pas de f. sans feu,** there's no smoke without fire *(b)* steam (of soup); fumes (of wine).

fumer¹ [fyme] *vtr* to manure (land).

fumer² **1.** *vi (a)* to smoke; *(b) (of soup)* to steam; **f. de colère,** to fume, to rage **2.** *vtr (a)* to smoke; to smoke-cure (fish) *(b)* to smoke (a cigarette, a pipe); **défense de f.,** no smoking. **fumeux, -euse¹** *a* smoky, smoking; hazy (sky).

fumet [fymɛ] *nm* aroma; (pleasant) smell (of cooked food).

fumeur, -euse² [fymœr, -øz] *n* smoker.

fumier [fymje] *nm* **1.** manure, dung **2.** dunghill; manure heap **3.** *P:* bastard.

fumiste [fymist] *nm* **1.** heating engineer **2.** *F: (a)* practical joker *(b)* humbug, fraud, phoney.

fumisterie [fymistəri] *nf F:* hoax; fraud.

fumure [fymyr] *nf* manuring (of field).

funambule [fynãbyl] *n* tightrope walker.

funèbre [fynɛbr] *a* **1.** funeral (ceremony); **marche f.,** funeral march **2.** funereal, gloomy.

funérailles [fyneraj] *nfpl* funeral (ceremony).

funéraire [fynerɛr] *a* funeral, funerary; **pierre f.,** tombstone.

funeste [fynɛst] *a (a) Lit:* deadly, fatal *(b)* fatal, catastrophic; **influence f.,** disastrous influence.

funiculaire [fynikylɛr] *a & nm* funicular (railway).

fur [fyr] *nm used in the adv phr* **au f. et à mesure,** (in proportion) as, progressively; **au f. et à mesure des besoins,** as and when required; **payer qn au f. et à mesure,** to pay s.o. by instalments (as the work proceeds).

furax [fyraks] *a inv F:* hopping mad.

furet [fyrɛ] *nm (a) Z:* ferret; **jeu du f.,** hunt-the-slipper *(b)* inquisitive person, nosy parker.

fureter [fyrte] *vi (je* **furette)** *(a)* to ferret, go ferreting *(b)* to pry, to nose about. **fureteur, -euse** *a*

prying, *F:* nosy.

fureur [fyrœr] *nf* **1.** fury, rage, wrath **2.** fury, passion; **aimer qch avec f.,** to be passionately fond of sth; **avoir la f. de bâtir,** to have a craze for building; **chanson qui fait f.,** song that's all the rage; hit.

furibond [fyribɔ̃] *a* furious; full of fury.

furie [fyri] *nf* **1.** *Myth:* **les Furies,** the Furies; **c'est une f.,** she's a termagant **2.** fury, rage; **avec f.,** furiously; **en f.,** infuriated; **se mettre en f.,** to fly into a rage. **furieux, -euse** *a (a)* furious; in a passion; **rendre qn f.,** to enrage s.o. *(b) F:* tremendous (desire). **furieusement** *adv* furiously; tremendously.

furoncle [fyrɔ̃kl] *nm Med:* boil.

furtif, -ive [fyrtif, -iv] *a* furtive, stealthy. **furtivement** *adv* furtively, stealthily.

fusain [fyzɛ̃] *nm* **1.** spindle tree **2.** *(a)* charcoal pencil *(b)* charcoal drawing.

fuseau, -eaux [fyzo] *nm* **1.** spindle; **en f.,** tapered, tapering; **jambes en f.,** spindly legs **2. f. horaire,** time zone **3.** *Cl:* **(pantalon) f.,** fuseaux, tapered trousers, *esp* ski slacks.

fusée [fyze] *nf (a)* rocket; **f. éclairante,** flare; **f. spatiale,** space rocket; **avion (à) f.,** rocket-propelled aircraft *(b)* fuse (of bomb).

fuselage [fyzlaʒ] *nm Av:* fuselage.

fuselé [fyzle] *a* tapering; *Aut:* streamlined.

fuser [fyze] *vi* **1.** *(of colours)* to spread, run; *(of light)* to stream in, out **2.** *(a)* to fuse, melt *(b) Ch:* to crackle **3.** *Pyr: (of fuse)* to burn slowly.

fusible [fyzibl] *nm El:* fuse.

fusil [fyzi] *nm (a)* gun; **f. de chasse,** shotgun; **f. à air comprimé,** air gun; **f. harpon,** harpoon gun; **f. rayé,** rifle; **coup de f.,** gun shot, rifle shot; *Fig:* **changer son f. d'épaule,** to change one's opinions *(b)* **un bon f.,** a good shot.

fusilier [fyzilje] *nm* fusilier; **f. marin** = marine.

fusillade [fyzijad] *nf* fusillade, rifle fire.

fusiller [fyzije] *vtr (a)* to execute (by shooting); to shoot; **f. qn du regard,** to look daggers at s.o. *(b) P:* to mess up, ruin (sth).

fusil-mitrailleur [fyzimitrajœr] *nm* automatic rifle; light machine gun; *pl* **fusils-mitrailleurs.**

fusion [fyzjɔ̃] *nf* **1.** fusion, melting **2.** coalescing (of ideas); merger, merging (of companies).

fusionner [fyzjone] *vtr & i Com: (of companies)* to amalgamate, merge.

fût [fy] *nm* **1.** stock (of rifle) **2.** *(a)* shaft (of column) *(b)* bole (of tree) **3.** cask, barrel.

futaie [fytɛ] *nf* wood, forest; **arbre de haute f.,** timber tree.

futé [fyte] *a* sharp, smart, acute, crafty.

futilité [fytilite] *nf* futility; *pl* **futilités,** trivialities. **futile** *a* futile, trifling; frivolous (pers); idle (pretext).

futur [fytyr] **1.** *a* future; **future maman,** mother-to-be **2.** *n* **mon f., ma future,** my fiancé(e), my husband, wife, to be **3.** *nm Gram:* future.

fuyant [fɥijã] *a* **1.** fleeing; fleeting (moment) **2.** receding (forehead) **3.** *(of pers)* evasive; shifty (eyes).

fuyard, -arde [fɥijar, -ard] *n* fugitive; runaway.

G

G, g [ʒe] *nm* (the letter) G, g.

g *abbr* gramme(s).

gabardine [gabardin] *nf* 1. *Tex:* gabardine 2. (gabardine) raincoat.

gabarit [gabari] *nm* 1. (a) model (of ship); mould (of ship's part) (b) outline (of building) 2. (a) *MecE:* template (b) *Rail:* clearance (under bridge) 3. size, dimension.

Gabon [gabɔ̃] *Prnm Geog:* le G., the Gabon. **gabonais, -aise** *a & n* Gabonese.

gâcher [gɑʃe] *vtr* 1. to mix, temper (mortar) 2. (a) to spoil (sheet of paper); to bungle, botch, mess up (job) (b) to waste; **g. sa vie**, (i) to waste (ii) to make a mess of, one's life. **gâcheur, -euse** 1. *a* (a) wasteful (b) bungling 2. *n* (a) wasteful person (b) bungler.

gâchette [gɑʃɛt] *nf* trigger; *F:* **avoir la g. facile**, to be trigger-happy.

gâchis [gɑʃi] *nm F:* **quel g.!** what a (i) waste (ii) mess!

gadget [gadʒɛt] *m F:* gadget, thingummy; gimmick.

gadoue [gadu] *nf* mud, slush, slime.

gaffe [gaf] *nf* 1. (a) boathook (b) *Fish:* gaff 2. *F:* blunder; **faire une g.**, to put one's foot in it 3. *P:* **faire g.**, to be careful, to watch out.

gaffer [gafe] 1. *vtr* (a) to hook (b) to gaff (salmon) 2. *vi F:* to blunder; to put one's foot in it.

gaffeur, -euse [gafœr, -øz] *n F:* blunderer.

gag [gag] *nm Th: Cin:* gag.

gaga [gaga] *a F:* gaga, senile.

gage [gaʒ] *nm* 1. pledge, security; **mettre qch en g.**, to pawn sth; **prêteur sur gages**, pawnbroker 2. token sign 3. forfeit 4. *pl* wages, pay; **tueur à gages**, hired killer.

gager [gaʒe] *vtr* (n. **gageons**) 1. *Lit:* to wager, bet 2. to guarantee, secure (a loan).

gageure [gaʒœr] *nf* wager.

gagne-pain [gaɲpɛ̃] *nm inv* (means of) living, livelihood.

gagner [gaɲe] *vtr* 1. (a) to earn; **g. de l'argent**, to make money; **g. sa vie**, to earn, make, one's living (b) to gain; to benefit, profit (**à, by**); **g. du temps**, (i) to save time (ii) to gain time; **c'est toujours ça de gagné**, it is so much to the good; **et moi, qu'est-ce que j'y gagne?** and what do I get out of it? what's in it for me? **il gagne à être connu**, he improves on acquaintance 2. (a) to win, gain (a victory) (b) **g. la partie**, to win the game; *vi* **tu as gagné!** you've won! (c) **g. la confiance de qn**, to win s.o.'s confidence (d) to catch (cold) 3. to reach, arrive at (a place) 4. to gain on, overtake; *vi* (*of fire*) to spread; **g. du terrain**, to gain ground; **gagné par le sommeil**, overcome by sleep 5. *vi Med:* (*of disease*) to spread. **gagnant, -ante** 1. *a* winning (ticket) 2. *n* winner.

gaieté [gete] *nf* gaiety, cheerfulness; **de g. de cœur**, lightheartedly.

gaillard, -arde [gajar, -ard] 1. *a* (a) strong, vigorous (b) spicy (story) 2. *nm* **grand g.**, (great) strapping fellow 3. *nm Nau:* **g. d'avant**, forecastle; **g. d'arrière**,

poop. **gaillardement** *adv* boldly, bravely; vigorously.

gain [gɛ̃] *nm* 1. (a) gain, profit (b) earnings 2. (a) winning (of contest); **avoir g. de cause**, to win one's case (b) winnings.

gaine [gɛn] *nf* (a) casing (b) *Anat: Bot:* sheath (c) *Cl:* girdle, roll-on (d) (ventilation) shaft.

galanterie [galɑ̃tri] *nf usu pl* compliments. **galant** 1. *a* (a) attentive to women; gallant (b) **g. homme**, man of honour, gentleman 2. *nm* ladies' man. **galamment** *adv* gallantly; courteously.

galaxie [galaksi] *nf* galaxy; the Milky Way.

galbe [galb] *nm* curve (of furniture); curve(s), contour (of human figure). **galbé** *a* curved; shapely.

gale [gal] *nf Med:* scabies; *Vet:* mange. **galeux, -euse** *a* (*pers*) affected with scabies; (*dog*) mangy.

galère [galɛr] *nf Nau:* galley; *F:* **mais qu'allait-il faire dans cette g.?** but what the hell was he doing there?

galerie [galri] *nf* 1. (a) gallery; **g. de portraits**, portrait gallery (b) **g. marchande**, shopping arcade 2. *Th:* balcony, gallery; **première g.**, dress circle; **seconde g.**, upper circle; **troisième g.**, gallery; *F:* the gods; **jouer pour la g.**, to play to the gallery 3. *Min:* gallery 4. *Aut:* roof rack.

galérien [galerjɛ̃] *nm* galley slave.

galet [galɛ] *nm* (a) pebble (b) *pl* shingle; **plage de galets**, shingle beach.

galette [galɛt] *nf* (a) girdle cake; **g. des Rois**, Twelfth Night cake (b) buckwheat pancake (c) *P:* money, dough, bread.

galimatias [galimatja] *nm* gibberish.

galipette [galipɛt] *nf F:* somersault.

Galles [gal] *Prnf Geog:* **le pays de G.**, Wales. **gallois, -oise** 1. *a* Welsh 2. *n* Welshman, -woman; **les G.**, the Welsh 3. *nm Ling:* Welsh.

gallicisme [galisism] *nm Ling:* gallicism.

gallon [galɔ̃] *nm Meas:* gallon.

gallo-romain [galɔrɔmɛ̃] *a* Gallo-Roman.

galoche [galɔʃ] *nf* (a) clog (b) overshoe.

galon [galɔ̃] *nm* 1. braid 2. *pl* (NCO's) stripes; (officer's) gold braid; *F:* **prendre du g.**, to get promoted.

galop [galo] *nm* gallop; **petit g.**, canter; **prendre le g.**, to break into a gallop.

galopade [galɔpad] *nf* galloping, gallop; *Fig:* rush.

galoper [galɔpe] *vi* to gallop; to rush around; (*of child*) to run. **galopant** *a* galloping (inflation).

galopin [galɔpɛ̃] *nm* urchin; young scamp.

galvanisation [galvanizasjɔ̃] *nf* galvanization.

galvaniser [galvanize] *vtr* 1. to galvanize; to stimulate (s.o., a crowd) 2. *Metall:* to galvanize.

galvanomètre [galvanɔmɛtr] *nm El:* galvanometer.

galvauder [galvode] *vtr* 1. to bring into disrepute; to prostitute (one's talents) 2. **se g.**, to damage one's reputation.

gambade [gɑ̃bad] *nf* leap, gambol, caper.

gambader [gɑ̃bade] *vi* to leap; to gambol, caper.
Gambie [gɑ̃bi] *Prnf Geog:* the Gambia.
gamelle [gamɛl] *nf* **1.** mess tin, mess kettle **2.** *P:* ramasser une g., to come a cropper.
gaminerie [gaminri] *nf* childish prank; childish behaviour. **gamin, -ine 1.** *n* child, *F:* kid **2.** *a* (*a*) lively, mischievous (*b*) elle est encore gamine, she's still just a child.
gamme [gam] *nf* **1.** *Mus:* scale; faire des gammes, to practise scales **2.** range, series (of colours); gamut.
Gand [gɑ̃] *Prnm Geog:* Ghent.
gang [gɑ̃g] *nm* gang.
ganglion [gɑ̃gliɔ̃] *nm Anat:* ganglion.
gangrène [gɑ̃grɛn] *nf* **1.** gangrene **2.** corruption.
gangster [gɑ̃gstɛr] *nm* gangster; crook.
gant [gɑ̃] *nm* (*a*) glove; cela vous va comme un g., it fits you like a glove; il faut prendre des gants pour l'approcher, one has to handle him with kid gloves; jeter le g. à qn, to throw down the gauntlet; relever le g., to accept the challenge (*b*) g. de toilette = (face-)flannel.
ganter [gɑ̃te] *vtr* **1.** to glove; g. du sept, to take sevens in gloves **2.** se g., to put on one's gloves.
garage [garaʒ] *nm* **1.** *Rail:* shunting; voie de g., siding **2.** (*a*) garage; g. de canots, boathouse; g. d'avions, hangar (*b*) passing place (on narrow road).
garagiste [garaʒist] *nm Aut:* (*a*) garage owner, proprietor (*b*) garage mechanic.
garant, -ante [garɑ̃, -ɑ̃t] *n* (*a*) guarantor, surety, bail; se porter g. de qn, (i) to answer for s.o. (ii) to go, stand, bail for s.o.; je m'en porte g., I can vouch for it (*b*) *nm* authority, guarantee.
garantie [garɑ̃ti] *nf* (*a*) guarantee, safeguard (contre, against) (*b*) guarantee, pledge; guaranty (of payment); verser une somme en g., to leave a deposit; donner une g. pour qn, to stand security for s.o. (*c*) *Com:* warranty, guarantee.
garantir [garɑ̃tir] *vtr* **1.** to warrant, guarantee; g. un fait, to vouch for a fact; je vous garantis qu'il viendra, I'm sure he'll come **2.** to shelter, protect **3.** *Jur:* g. qn contre qch, to indemnify s.o. from, against, sth.
garçon [garsɔ̃] *nm* **1.** (*a*) boy; école de garçons, boys' school; c'est un g. manqué, she's a tomboy (*b*) son **2.** young man; g. d'honneur, best man; brave g., bon g., decent chap; beau g., handsome young man **3.** bachelor; vieux g., confirmed bachelor **4.** g. de bureau, office boy, messenger; g. de courses, errand boy, messenger; g. (de café, de restaurant), waiter; g. d'écurie, groom; g. d'étage, floor waiter.
garçonnière [garsɔnjɛr] *nf* bachelor flat; small one-bedroomed flat.
garde¹ [gard] *n* (*a*) keeper; *Adm:* G. des Sceaux, Lord Chancellor (*b*) guard; watchman; g. champêtre, rural policeman; g. forestier, ranger, forest warden; g. du corps, bodyguard (*c*) *nf* nurse; g. d'enfant, child minder (*d*) *Mil:* guardsman.
garde² *nf* **1.** (*a*) guardianship, care, custody; chien de g., watchdog; être sous bonne g., to be in safe custody, safe keeping; avoir qch en g., to have charge of sth; *Jur:* g. des enfants, custody of the children (after divorce) (*b*) guarding, protection **2.** (*a*) watch(ing); faire la g., to keep watch (*b*) care, guard; en g.! on guard! être, se tenir, sur ses gardes, to be on one's guard **3.** (*a*) prendre g. à qch, to beware of sth; prenez

g.! look out! (*b*) prendre g. à qch, to attend to sth; faire qch sans y prendre g., to do sth without meaning to, inadvertently (*c*) prendre g. à faire qch, to be careful to do sth; prenez g. de ne pas vous perdre, mind you don't get lost (*d*) prendre g. de faire qch, to be careful not to do sth; prenez g. de tomber, mind you don't fall (*e*) prendre g. que . . . (ne) + *sub*, to be careful that (sth does not happen); prenez g. qu'il ne vous voie, take care he doesn't see you **4.** guard (*a*) être de g., to be on guard (*b*) la g., the Guards (*c*) (salle de) g., guardroom **5.** hilt (of sword); jusqu'à la g., up to the hilt **6.** page de g., endpaper.
garde-à-vous [gardavu] *nm inv Mil:* attention; être au g.-à-v., to stand to attention; g.-à-v.! attention!
garde-barrière [gardbarjɛr] *n* gate-keeper (at level-crossing); *pl gardes-barrière(s)*.
garde-boue [gard(ə)bu] *nm inv* mudguard.
garde-chasse [gardʃas] *nm* gamekeeper; *pl gardes-chasse(s)*.
garde-chiourme [gard(ɛ)ʃjurm] *nm* martinet, slave-driver; *pl garde(s)-chiourme(s)*.
garde-côte [gard(ə)kot] *nm* **1.** coastguard **2.** (*a*) coastguard vessel (*b*) coast-defence ship; *pl garde-côte(s)*.
garde-feu [gard(ə)fø] *nm inv* (*a*) fender (*b*) fireguard (*c*) fire screen (*d*) *For:* tranchée g.-f., firebreak.
garde-fou [gard(ə)fu] *nm* **1.** parapet **2.** railing, handrail (of bridge); *pl garde-fous*.
garde-malade [gardmalad] *n* nurse; *pl gardes-malade(s)*.
garde-manger [gardmɑ̃ʒe] *nm inv* larder, pantry; (meat) safe.
garde-meuble [gard(ə)mœbl] *nm* furniture store; *pl garde-meuble(s)*.
garde-pêche [gard(ə)pɛʃ] *nm* **1.** water bailiff; *pl gardes-pêche* **2.** *inv* fishery protection vessel.
garder [garde] *vtr* **1.** to guard, protect; to keep watch over (s.o., sth); g. les enfants, la boutique, to mind the children, the shop; g. qn à vue, to keep a close watch on s.o. **2.** (*a*) to keep, to retain; g. un vêtement, (i) to keep a garment (ii) to keep on a garment; g. qn en otage, to detain, keep, s.o. as hostage (*b*) to preserve; g. une poire pour la soif, to put something by for a rainy day; g. les apparences, to keep up appearances; g. son sang-froid, to keep cool, calm; g. rancune à qn, to harbour resentment against s.o.; g. son sérieux, to keep a straight face; viande qui ne se garde pas bien, meat that does not keep well **3.** to remain in (a place); g. le lit, la chambre, to be laid up, to stay in bed, in one's room **4.** to observe, respect; g. un secret, sa parole, to keep a secret, one's word; il n'a pas gardé sa parole, he has broken his word **5.** se g. (*a*) to protect oneself; garde-toi! look out (for yourself)! (*b*) se g. de qch, to beware of sth (*c*) se g. de faire qch, to take care not to do sth; je m'en garderai bien! I shall do no such thing!
garderie [gard(ə)ri] *nf* g. (d'enfants), day nursery.
garde-robe [gard(ə)rɔb] *nf* wardrobe; *pl garde-robes*.
gardien, -ienne [gardjɛ̃, -jɛn] *n* guardian, keeper; watchman; caretaker; (museum) warder, warden; (car park) attendant; (prison) warder; g. de la paix, policeman; *Sp:* g. (de but), goalkeeper.

gare¹ [gar] *int* look out! out of the way! mind yourself!
g. à lui si, woe betide him if.

gare² *nf* (railway) station; **g. maritime,** harbour station; **g. de marchandises,** goods station, depot; **g. de
triage,** marshalling yard; **g. routière,** bus, coach,
station; **g. aérienne,** air terminal.

garenne [garɛn] *nf* (rabbit) warren; **lapin de g.,** wild
rabbit.

garer [gare] *vtr* 1. to shunt (train) 2. (*a*) to garage (car)
(*b*) to park (car) 3. **se g.** (*a*) to park (a car); **j'ai eu du
mal à me g.,** I've had trouble parking (*b*) **se g. de qch,**
to get out of the way of sth.

gargariser (se) [səgargarize] *vpr* to gargle.

gargarisme [gargarism] *nm* (*a*) gargle (*b*) gargling.

gargote [gargɔt] *nf* cheap restaurant.

gargouille [garguj] *nf* (*a*) (water)spout (of roof
gutter) (*b*) *Arch:* gargoyle.

gargouillement [gargujmɑ̃] *nm* gurgling; rumbling
(of stomach).

gargouiller [garguje] *vi* to gurgle; (*of stomach*) to
rumble.

gargouillis [garguji] *nm*=**gargouillement**.

garnement [garnəmɑ̃] *nm* (**mauvais**) **g.,** scamp; rascal.

garnir [garnir] *vtr* 1. to furnish, provide (**de,** with); **g.
qch à l'intérieur,** to line sth 2. to trim (dress, hat); to
garnish (a dish) 3. to pack (piston); to line (brake);
Fish: to bait (hook). **garni** 1. *a* well-lined (purse);
(*dish*) garnished; *Cu:* **plat g.,** meat with vegetables 2.
nm O: furnished room(s).

garnison [garnizɔ̃] *nf* garrison; **ville de g.,** garrison
town; **être en g. dans une ville,** to be garrisoned in a
town.

garniture [garnityr] *nf* 1. fittings; **g. de lit,** bedding; **g.
intérieure d'une voiture,** upholstery of a car 2.
trimming(s) 3. set; **g. de bureau,** desk set; **g. de toilette,**
toilet set 4. *Cu:* garnish(ing) (of dish) 5. (*a*) packing,
stuffing (*b*) (brake) lining.

garrot [garo] *nm* 1. *Med:* tourniquet 2. gar(r)otte 3.
withers (of horse).

garrotter [garɔte] *vtr* to tie up (prisoner).

gars [gɑ] *nm F:* boy; (young) man; **allons-y, les g.!**
come on, boys!

Gascogne (la) [lagaskɔɲ] *Prnf Geog:* Gascony; **le
Golfe de G.,** the Bay of Biscay. **gascon, -onne** *a &
n* Gascon.

gas(-)oil [gazwal, -ɔjl] *nm* diesel oil.

gaspillage [gaspijaʒ] *nm* squandering, wasting.

gaspiller [gaspije] *vtr* to squander; to waste.
gaspilleur, -euse 1. *a* wasteful 2. *n* waster,
squanderer.

gastrite [gastrit] *nf Med:* gastritis. **gastrique** *a*
gastric.

gastronome [gastrɔnɔm] *nm* gastronome.

gastronomie [gastrɔnɔmi] *nf* gastronomy.
gastronomique *a* gastronomic.

gâteau, -eaux [gato] *nm* 1. cake; (open) tart; **g. sec,**
(i) (sweet) biscuit (ii) plain cake; **g. de riz**=rice
pudding; *F:* **papa g.,** (i) indulgent father (ii) sugar
daddy; *F:* **c'est du g.,** it's a piece of cake; **partager le g.,**
to share the profit, to have one's slice of the cake 2. **g.
de miel,** honeycomb.

gâter [gate] *vtr* 1. (*a*) to spoil; to damage; **cela ne gâte
rien,** that won't do any harm (*b*) to pamper, spoil
(child) 2. **se g.,** to deteriorate; **les affaires se gâtent,**
things are going wrong; **le temps se gâte,** the weather's
breaking up. **gâté** *a* spoilt; tainted (meat); rotten
(fruit); decayed (teeth); **enfant g.,** spoilt child.

gâterie [gatri] *nf* treat; *pl* goodies.

gâteux, -euse [gatø, -øz] 1. *a* senile, gaga 2. *n*
dotard.

gâtisme [gatism] *nm* senility.

gauche [goʃ] *a* 1. warped; crooked 2. awkward,
clumsy 3. (*a*) **main g.,** left hand; **rive g.,** left bank (of
river) (*b*) *nf* **assis à ma g.,** seated on my left; **tiroir de g.,**
left-hand drawer (*c*) *nm Box:* left (*d*) *nf Pol:* **la g.,** the
left 4. **à gauche,** on the left(hand side), to the left;
tournez à g., turn left. **gauchement** *adv* awkwardly, clumsily. **gaucher, -ère** *a* left-handed.

gaucherie [goʃri] *nf* 1. left-handedness 2. awkwardness, clumsiness.

gauchir [goʃir] 1. *vpr & i* (*of wood*) to warp 2. *vtr* to
camber (sth).

gauchisme [goʃism] *nm Pol:* leftism. **gauchiste** *a
& n* leftist.

gauchissement [goʃismɑ̃] *nm* warping.

gaufre [gofr] *nf* 1. **g. de miel,** honeycomb 2. *Cu:* waffle;
moule à gaufres, waffle iron.

gaufrette [gofrɛt] *nf Cu:* wafer (biscuit).

gaufrier [gofrije] *nm Cu:* waffle iron.

gaule [gol] *nf* (long thin) pole.

gaullisme [golism] *nm Hist: Pol:* Gaullism.
gaulliste *a & n* Gaullist.

gaulois, -oise [golwa, -waz] 1. *a* Gallic, of Gaul;
esprit g., (broad) Gallic humour 2. *n* **les G.,** the Gauls
3. *nf Rtm:* **Gauloise,** popular brand of cigarette.

gavage [gavaʒ] *nm* cramming, force-feeding (of
geese).

gaver [gave] *vtr* 1. to cram, force-feed (geese) 2. **se g.,**
to gorge oneself.

gaz [gɑz] *nm* gas; **g. de ville,** town gas; **faire la cuisine au
g.,** to cook with gas; **g. toxique,** poison gas; **g.
lacrymogène,** tear gas; *F:* **mettre les g.,** to put one's
foot down, to step on the gas; **à pleins g.,** flat out; **g.
d'échappement,** exhaust fumes; *Med:* **avoir des g.,** to
have wind. **gazeux, -euse** *a* (*a*) gaseous (*b*) fizzy
(drink).

gaze [gɑz] *nf* gauze; **g. métallique,** wire gauze.

gazelle [gazɛl] *nf Z:* gazelle.

gazer [gaze] 1. *vtr Mil:* to gas 2. *vi F:* **ça gaze!**
everything's OK! **ça gaze?** how's things, OK?

gazoduc [gazɔdyk] *nm* gas pipeline.

gazogène [gazɔʒɛn] *nm* gas producer.

gazole [gazɔl] *nm* diesel oil.

gazomètre [gazɔmɛtr] *nm* gasometer.

gazon [gazɔ̃] *nm* (*a*) (short) grass; turf (*b*) lawn (*c*)
motte de g., sod.

gazouillement [gazujmɑ̃] *nm* twittering, chirping;
babbling.

gazouiller [gazuje] *vi* (*of bird*) to twitter, to chirp; (*of
child*) to babble.

gazouillis [gazuji] *nm*=**gazouillement**.

GDF *abbr* Gaz de France.

geai [ʒɛ] *nm Orn:* jay.

géant, -ante [ʒeɑ̃, -ɑ̃t] 1. *n* giant, *f* giantess 2. *a*
gigantic; *Com:* giant (size).

geignard, -arde [ʒɛɲar, -ard] *n* moaner, whiner.

geignement [ʒɛɲəmɑ̃] *nm* moaning, whining.

geindre [ʒɛdɼ] *vi* (*conj like* ATTEINDRE) to moan, whine.

gel [ʒɛl] *nm* (*a*) frost, freezing (*b*) *Ch:* gel.

gélatine [ʒelatin] *nf* gelatin(e). **gélatineux, -euse** *a* gelatinous.

gelée [ʒ(ə)le] *nf* 1. frost; **g. blanche**, hoar frost 2. *Cu:* jelly.

geler [ʒ(ə)le] *v* (**je gèle**) 1. *vtr* to freeze 2. *vi* (*a*) to become frozen; to freeze; **l'étang a gelé**, the pond has frozen over; **on gèle ici**, it's freezing in here (*b*) *impers* **il gèle à pierre fendre**, it's freezing hard. **gelé** *a* 1. frozen 2. frost-bitten.

gélule [ʒelyl] *nf Pharm:* capsule.

gelure [ʒəlyr] *nf Med:* frostbite.

Gémeaux [ʒemo] *npl Astr:* Gemini.

gémir [ʒemir] *vi* to groan; moan; to wail.

gémissement [ʒemismɑ̃] *nm* groan(ing), moan(ing); wail(ing).

gemme [ʒɛm] *nf* 1. (*a*) gem; precious stone (*b*) **a sel g.**, rock salt 2. pine resin.

gencive [ʒɑ̃siv] *nf Anat:* gum.

gendarme [ʒɑ̃darm] *nm* gendarme, policeman.

gendarmerie [ʒɑ̃darməri] *nf* 1. (*a*) (*in Fr*) state police force (*b*) **la G. royale du Canada**, the Royal Canadian Mounted Police 2. = police headquarters.

gendre [ʒɑ̃dɼ] *nm* son-in-law.

gène [ʒɛn] *nm Biol:* gene.

gêne [ʒɛn] *nf* 1. discomfort, embarrassment; **sans g.**, free and easy 2. **être dans la g.**, to be hard up, badly off. **gênant** *a* 1. cumbersome; in the way 2. embarrassing, awkward; (*of pers*) annoying.

généalogie [ʒenealɔʒi] *nf* genealogy; pedigree. **généalogique** *a* genealogical; **arbre g.**, family tree; pedigree.

gêner [ʒene] *vtr* 1. to constrict, cramp; **mes souliers me gênent**, my shoes pinch, are too tight 2. to hinder, obstruct, impede; to be in (s.o.'s) way; **g. la circulation**, to hold up the traffic 3. to inconvenience, embarrass; **cela vous gênerait-il que je revienne demain?** do you mind, will it bother you, if I come back tomorrow? **la fumée ne vous gêne pas?** do you mind my smoking? 4. **se g.**, (*a*) to put oneself out; **je ne me suis pas gêné pour le lui dire,** I made no bones about telling him so; **il ne se gêne pas avec nous,** he doesn't stand on ceremony with us, he makes himself at home (*b*) *Fig:* to tighten one's belt. **gêné** *a* (*a*) embarrassed, ill at ease (*b*) hard up, short of money.

général, -aux [ʒeneral, -o] 1. *a* general; **en règle générale,** as a general rule; **d'une façon générale,** broadly speaking; *Th:* **répétition générale,** *nf* **générale,** dress rehearsal; **quartier g.,** headquarters; **en g.,** in general; generally (speaking) 2. *nm Mil:* general; **g. de brigade,** brigadier 3. *nf* (*a*) **madame la générale,** the general's wife (*b*) alarm call (*c*) *Th:* dress rehearsal. **généralement** *adv* generally; **g. parlant,** generally, broadly speaking.

généralisation [ʒeneralizasjɔ̃] *nf* generalization.

généraliser [ʒeneralize] *vtr* 1. to generalize 2. **se g.,** to become widespread.

généraliste [ʒeneralist] *n Med:* general practitioner, GP.

généralité [ʒeneralite] *nf* generality; **dans la g. des cas,** in the majority of, in most, cases.

générateur, -trice [ʒeneratœr, -tris] 1. *a* generat-ing, generative; producing, inducing 2. *nm* generator.

génération [ʒenerasjɔ̃] *nf* generation.

générer [ʒenere] *vtr* (**je génère; je générerai**) to generate.

généreux, -euse [ʒenerø, -øz] *a* (*a*) noble, generous (soul); warm (heart) (*b*) generous, openhanded. **généreusement** *adv* generously.

générique [ʒenerik] 1. *a* a generic (term) 2. *nm Cin:* credit titles, credits.

générosité [ʒenerozite] *nf* (*a*) generosity (*b*) acts of generosity.

Gênes [ʒɛn] *Prnf Geog:* Genoa.

genèse [ʒɔnɛz] *nf* genesis, origin; *B:* **la G.,** (the Book of) Genesis.

genêt [ʒ(ə)nɛ] *nm Bot:* broom.

génétique [ʒenetik] (*a*) *a* genetic (*b*) *nf* genetics.

gêneur, -euse [ʒɛnœr, -øz] *n* intruder; spoilsport.

Genève [ʒ(ə)nɛv] *Prnf Geog:* Geneva.

genévrier [ʒ(ə)nevrije] *nm Bot:* juniper (tree).

génial, -aux [ʒenjal, -o] *a* full of genius; inspired; **idée géniale,** brilliant idea. **génialement** *adv* brilliantly.

génie [ʒeni] *nm* 1. (*a*) (guardian) spirit; (presiding) genius (*b*) genie, jinn 2. (*a*) (*quality*) genius; **homme de g.,** man of genius (*b*) (*pers*) genius (*c*) **g. d'une langue,** essence, spirit, of a language 3. (*a*) **g. civil,** (i) civil engineering (ii) civil engineers (as a body) (*b*) *Mil:* **le G. =** the (Royal) Engineers.

genièvre [ʒ(ə)njɛvɼ] *nm* 1. *Bot:* (*a*) juniper berry (*b*) juniper (tree) 2. gin.

génisse [ʒenis] *nf* heifer.

génital, -aux [ʒenital, -o] *a* genital; **organes génitaux,** genital organs, genitals.

génitif [ʒenitif] *nm Gram:* genitive (case).

génocide [ʒenɔsid] *nm* genocide.

génois, -oise [ʒenwa, -waz] 1. *a & n* Genoese 2. *nf* **génoise,** Genoese cake.

genou, -oux [ʒ(ə)nu] *nm* knee; **enfoncé jusqu'aux genoux dans la boue,** knee-deep in mud; **se mettre à genoux,** to kneel (down); **à genou(x),** kneeling, on one's knees; **demander qch à genoux,** to ask for sth on bended knee; **tenir qn sur ses genoux,** to hold s.o. on one's lap.

genre [ʒɑ̃r] *nm* 1. genus, kind; **le g. humain,** the human race, mankind 2. kind, sort; type; manner, way; **c'est plus dans son g.,** that's more in his line; **c'est un artiste dans son g.,** he is an artist in his way; **c'est dans le g. de,** it's like; **ce n'est pas mon g.,** (i) he, she, is not my type; it's not the sort of thing I like (ii) it's just not me; **ce n'est pas son g.,** that's not like him, her 3. (artistic) style, manner 4. manners, taste; **cela fait bon, mauvais, g.,** it's good, bad, form; it's in good, bad, taste 5. *Gram:* gender.

gens [ʒɑ̃] *nmpl* (*was originally feminine and most attrib adjectives preceding* **gens** *take the feminine form, but the word group is felt as masculine;* **ces bonnes gens sont venus me trouver; quels sont ces gens? quels or quelles sont ces bonnes gens? tout** *varies according as the attrib adjective has a distinctive feminine ending or not:* **toutes ces bonnes gens,** *but* **tous ces pauvres gens.**) 1. people, folk, men and women; **peu de g.,** few people; **qui sont ces g.-là?** who are these people? 2. (*a*) **jeunes g.,** (i) young people (ii) young men (*b*) **g. du**

monde, society people; **les g. du pays,** the locals (c) O: servants.

gentilhomme [ʒãtijɔm] nm man of gentle birth; gentleman; pl gentilshommes [ʒãtizɔm].

gentilhommière [ʒãtijɔmjɛr] nf manor house.

gentillesse [ʒãtijɛs] nf 1. (a) graciousness, engaging manner (b) kindness; **auriez-vous la g. de,** would you be so very kind as to 2. pl **dire des gentillesses,** to say nice things. **gentil, -ille** a (a) pleasing, nice; **c'est g. à vous de m'écrire,** it is very kind of you to write to me (b) nice; **sois gentil(le),** be a good boy, a good girl; (to adult) be an angel, be a dear. **gentiment** adv nicely; kindly.

génuflexion [ʒenyflɛksjɔ̃] nf genuflexion.

géodésie [ʒeɔdezi] nf geodesy, surveying.

géographe [ʒeɔgraf] n geographer.

géographie [ʒeɔgrafi] nf geography. **géographique** a geographic(al).

geôle [ʒol] nf A: & Lit: gaol, jail.

geôlier, -ière [ʒolje, -jɛr] n A: & Lit: gaoler, jailer.

géologie [ʒeɔlɔʒi] nf geology. **géologique** a geological.

géologue [ʒeɔlɔg] n geologist.

géométrie [ʒeɔmetri] nf geometry; **g. plane,** plane geometry; **g. dans l'espace,** solid geometry. **géométrique** a geometric(al).

géothermique [ʒeɔtɛrmik] a geothermal.

gérance [ʒerãs] nf management; **mettre qch en g.,** to appoint a manager for sth.

géranium [ʒeranjɔm] nm Bot: geranium.

gérant, -ante [ʒerã, -ãt] n manager, f manageress; director; **g. d'immeuble,** landlord's agent; a Journ: **rédacteur g.,** managing editor.

gerbe [ʒɛrb] nf sheaf (of wheat); **g. de fleurs,** spray of flowers; **g. d'étincelles,** shower of sparks; **g. d'eau,** spray of water.

gercer [ʒɛrse] vtr & i (il gerçait; il gerça) to crack (soil); to chap (hands).

gerçure [ʒɛrsyr] nf crack, cleft; chap (in skin).

gérer [ʒere] vtr (**je gère;** fu **je gérerai)** to manage, run (business, hotel); **mal g.,** to mismanage.

gériatrie [ʒerjatri] nf Med: geriatrics.

germain, -aine [ʒɛrmɛ̃, -ɛn] a **cousin g.,** first cousin.

germe [ʒɛrm] nm Biol: germ; eye (of potato); **pousser des germes,** to sprout; **les germes de la corruption,** the seeds of corruption.

germer [ʒɛrme] vi to germinate; to shoot; to sprout.

germination [ʒɛrminasjɔ̃] nf germination.

gérondif [ʒerɔ̃dif] nm Gram: 1. gerund 2. gerundive.

gérontologie [ʒerɔ̃tɔlɔʒi] nf Med: gerontology. **gérontologique** a gerontological.

gésier [ʒezje] nm gizzard.

gésir [ʒezir] vi def (used only in the following forms: prp **gisant;** pr ind **il gît, n. gisons)** to lie; (on gravestones) **ci-gît,** here lies.

gestation [ʒɛstasjɔ̃] nf (period of) gestation; pregnancy.

geste [ʒɛst] nm gesture, motion, movement; **d'un g. de la main,** with a wave of the hand; **écarter qn d'un g.,** to wave s.o. aside; **faire un g.,** to make a gesture; **joindre le g. à la parole,** to suit the action to the word.

gesticulation [ʒɛstikylasjɔ̃] nf gesticulating, gesticulation.

gesticuler [ʒɛstikyle] vi to gesticulate.

gestion [ʒɛstjɔ̃] nf management (of business, factory); administration, control; **mauvaise g.,** maladministration, mismanagement. **gestionnaire** 1. a administrative; **compte g.,** management account 2. n administrator; manager.

geyser [ʒezɛr] nm Geol: geyser.

Ghana [gana] Prnm Geog: Ghana. **ghanéen, -éenne** a & n Ghanaian.

ghetto [gɛto] nm ghetto.

gibecière [ʒibsjɛr] nf game bag; shoulder bag.

gibet [ʒibɛ] nm gibbet, gallows.

gibier [ʒibje] nm game (= wild animals); **gros g.,** big game; **g. à poil,** game animals; **g. à plumes,** game birds; **g. d'eau,** wildfowl; **g. de potence,** gallows bird.

giboulée [ʒibule] nf sudden shower (usu with snow or hail); **g. de mars** = April shower.

giboyeux, -euse [ʒibwajø, -øz] a well stocked with game.

giclée [ʒikle] nf spurt (of water, blood).

gicler [ʒikle] vi to squirt out; (of water, blood) to spurt (out); to splash up.

gicleur [ʒiklœr] nm ICE: jet.

gifle [ʒifl] nm slap in the face.

gifler [ʒifle] vtr to slap, smack (s.o.'s) face.

gigantesque [ʒigãtɛsk] a gigantic; huge.

gigolo [ʒigolo] nm gigolo.

gigot [ʒigo] nm Cu: leg of lamb.

gigoter [ʒigote] vi F: to wriggle, fidget.

gilet [ʒilɛ] nm (a) waistcoat, NAm: vèst (b) **g. de sauvetage,** life jacket (c) **g. (de corps),** singlet, vest, NAm: undershirt (d) cardigan.

gin [dʒin, ʒin] nm gin.

gingembre [ʒɛ̃ʒãbr] nm ginger.

girafe [ʒiraf] nm (a) Z: giraffe (b) (pers) beanpole.

giration [ʒirasjɔ̃] nf gyration. **giratoire** a gyratory; gyrating; **sens g.,** roundabout.

girl [gœrl] nf chorus girl; showgirl.

girofle [ʒirɔfl] nm Bot: clove; **clou de g.,** clove.

giroflée [ʒirɔfle] nf Bot: stock; **g. des murailles,** wallflower.

girolle [ʒirɔl] nf Fung: chanterelle (mushroom).

giron [ʒirɔ̃] nm lap; bosom.

girouette [ʒirwɛt] nf weathercock; vane.

gisement [ʒizmã] nm (a) Geol: layer, bed; deposit; **g. pétrolifère,** oilfield (b) Min: lode, vein (c) **g. préhistorique,** prehistoric site.

gîte [ʒit] nm 1. (a) resting place; lodging (b) form (of hare) 2. stratum, deposit (of ore) 3. leg of beef; **g. à la noix,** silverside.

givre [ʒivr̩] nm hoarfrost, rime.

givrer [ʒivre] 1. vtr (a) to cover with hoarfrost (b) to frost (cake) 2. vtr & pr Av: to ice up. **givré** a 1. frosty 2. (of cake) frosted; **orange givrée,** orange filled with sorbet 3. P: (a) drunk, canned (b) nuts.

glace [glas] nf 1. ice; **g. flottante,** drift ice; **retenu, pris, par les glaces,** icebound; **un accueil de g.,** an icy reception 2. (a) (plate) glass (b) (looking) glass, mirror; **g. à main,** hand mirror (c) Aut: etc: window 3. Cu: ice cream.

glacer [glase] vtr (n. **glaçons)** 1. (a) to freeze; **cela me glace le sang,** it makes my blood run cold (b) to ice (water) (c) to ice (cake) (d) to glaze (pastry); to surface (paper) 2. (of water) **se g.,** to freeze (over). **glacé** a 1. (a) frozen (river) (b) freezing, icy, cold; **j'ai**

les pieds glacés, my feet are cold as ice; **g. jusqu'aux os,** chilled to the bone (c) iced (coffee) **2.** glazed, glossy (paper); *Cu:* **cerises glacées,** glacé cherries.

glaciaire [glasjɛr] *a Geol:* glacial (erosion); **période g.,** ice age.

glacial, -als, *or* **-aux** [glasjal, -o] (*pl rarely used) a* icy; frosty; **zone glaciale,** arctic region; **accueil g.,** icy welcome. **glacialement** *adv* icily; frostily.

glaciation [glasjasjɔ̃] *nf* glaciation.

glacier¹ [glasje] *nm Geol:* glacier.

glacier² *nm* ice cream (i) manufacturer (ii) man.

glacière [glasjɛr] *nf* (a) ice box (b) *F:* refrigerator, fridge (c) insulated picnic box.

glaçon [glasɔ̃] *nm* (a) block of ice; ice floe (b) icicle (c) ice cube; **whisky aux glaçons,** whisky on the rocks (d) *F:* **c'est un g.!** he's a cold fish!

gladiateur [gladjatœr] *nm* gladiator.

glaïeul [glajœl] *nm Bot:* gladiolus.

glaire [glɛr] *nf* (a) white of an egg, egg white (b) mucus, phlegm.

glaise [glɛz] *nf* **(terre) g.,** clay. **glaiseux, -euse** *a* clayey.

gland [glɑ̃] *nm* **1.** acorn **2.** tassel.

glande [glɑ̃d] *nf* gland. **glandulaire** *a* glandular.

glaner [glane] *vtr* to glean.

glaneur, -euse [glanœr, -øz] *n* gleaner.

glapir [glapir] *vi* to yelp, yap; (of fox) to bark.

glapissement [glapismɑ̃] *nm* yapping, yelping; barking (of fox).

glas [glɑ] *nm* knell; **sonner le g.,** to toll the knell.

glissade [glisad] *nf* **1.** slip; *Av:* **g. sur l'aile, sur la queue,** side slip, tail dive **2.** (a) sliding; **faire une g.,** to slide (b) *Danc:* glissade **3.** slide, skid (on ice).

glissement [glismɑ̃] *nm* **g. de terrain,** landslide; **g. de sens,** shift in meaning; *Pol:* **g. à gauche,** swing to the left.

glisser [glise] **1.** *vi* (a) to slip; **le couteau lui a glissé des mains,** the knife slipped from his hands (b) (of wheel) to skid; *Av:* **g. sur l'aile,** to sideslip (c) to slide (on ice); **se laisser g. le long d'une corde,** to slide down a rope (d) to glide (over the water) (e) **g. sur qch,** (i) to make little impression on sth (ii) to touch lightly on (a subject) **2.** *vtr* (a) **g. qch dans la poche de qn,** to slip sth into s.o.'s pocket; **g. un mot à l'oreille de qn,** to drop a word in s.o.'s ear (b) *Knit:* to slip (a stitch) **3.** **se g.,** to creep, steal (**dans,** into); **se g. dans son lit,** to slip into bed. **glissant** *a* slippery.

glissière [glisjɛr] *nf* (a) groove; **porte à glissières,** sliding door (b) crash barrier.

global, -aux [glɔbal, -o] *a* total, aggregate, inclusive, gross, global; lump (payment). **globalement** *adv* globally; in the aggregate.

globe [glɔb] *nm* **1.** globe, sphere; **le g. terrestre,** the globe **2.** *Anat:* **g. de l'œil,** eyeball. **globuleux, -euse** *a* globular; **yeux g.,** protruding eyes.

globulaire [glɔbylɛr] *a* (a) globular (b) *Med:* **numération g.,** blood count.

globule [glɔbyl] *nf* (a) globule (b) (blood) corpuscle; **g. blanc, rouge,** white, red, corpuscle.

gloire [glwar] *nf* **1.** glory; **g. à Dieu!** glory (be) to God! **se couvrir de g.,** to cover oneself with glory; **pour la g.,** for the glory of it **2.** boast, pride; **s'attribuer toute la g. de qch,** to take all the credit for sth; **se faire g. de qch,** to glory in sth, to pride oneself on sth.

glorieux, -euse *a* **1.** glorious **2.** proud. **glorieusement** *adv* gloriously.

glorification [glɔrifikasjɔ̃] *nf* glorification.

glorifier [glɔrifje] (*impf & pr sub n.* **glorifiions**) *vtr* **1.** to praise, glorify **2. se g.,** to boast; **se g. de qch,** to take pride in sth.

gloriole [glɔrjɔl] *nf* vainglory.

glose [gloz] *nf* **1.** gloss, commentary **2.** comment, criticism.

glossaire [glɔsɛr] *nm* **1.** glossary **2.** vocabulary.

glotte [glɔt] *nf Anat:* glottis; *Ling:* **coup de g.,** glottal stop.

glouglou [gluglu] *nm* **1.** gurgle, gurgling **2.** gobble (of turkey).

gloussement [glusmɑ̃] *nm* clucking, cluck (of hen); gobble (of turkey); chuckle, chortle (of pers).

glousser [gluse] *vi* (of hen) to cluck; (of turkey) to gobble; (of pers) to chuckle, chortle.

gloutonnerie [glutɔnri] *nf* gluttony. **glouton, -onne 1.** *a* greedy, gluttonous **2.** *n* glutton. **gloutonnement** *adv* greedily, ravenously, gluttonously.

glu [gly] *nf* (a) birdlime (b) gum, glue. **gluant** *a* sticky, gummy, gluey.

glucose [glykoz] *nm* glucose; **g. sanguin,** blood sugar.

glutineux, -euse [glytinø, -øz] *a* glutinous.

glycérine [gliserin] *nf* glycerin(e).

glycine [glisin] *nf Bot:* wisteria.

gnangnan [nɑ̃nɑ̃] *F:* **1.** *a* flabby, wet **2.** *n* (pers) drip, wet.

gnognot(te) [nɔnɔt] *nf F:* **c'est de la g.,** it's rubbish.

gniole, gnôle [nol] *nf P:* brandy, rotgut, hooch.

gnome [gnom] *nm* gnome.

gnon [nɔ̃] *nm P:* blow, punch.

go [go] *used in the adv phr F:* **tout de go,** (i) easily, without a hitch (ii) all of a sudden.

GO *abbr WTel: Grandes ondes.*

goal [gol] *nm Fb:* goalkeeper.

gobelet [gɔblɛ] *nm* goblet, cup; beaker; **(verre) g.,** tumbler.

gober [gɔbe] *vtr* to swallow, gulp down; *F:* **g. des mouches,** to stand gaping; **il gobe tout ce qu'on lui dit,** he believes everything he's told.

godasse [gɔdas] *nf P:* shoe.

godet [gɔde] *nm* pot; (drinking) cup.

godiche [gɔdiʃ] *F:* **1.** *a* silly; clumsy **2.** *n* clot, dope; lump.

godille [gɔdij] *nf* stern oar; scull; **(faire qch) à la g.,** (to do sth) without rhyme or reason.

godillot [gɔdijo] *nm* (military) boot.

goéland [gɔelɑ̃] *nm Orn:* (sea)gull.

goélette [gɔelɛt] *nf* schooner.

goémon [gɔemɔ̃] *nm* seaweed; wrack.

gogo¹ (à) [agogo] *adv phr F:* **avoir de l'argent a g.,** to have money to burn.

gogo² *nm F:* easy dupe, sucker.

goguenard, -arde [gɔgnar, -ard] **1.** *a* mocking; bantering, jeering, sarcastic **2.** *n* joker; facetious, sarcastic, person.

goinfre [gwɛ̃fr] *nm F:* guzzler, greedyguts.

goinfrer (se) [səgwɛ̃fre] *vpr F:* to guzzle; to make a pig of oneself.

goitre [gwatr] *nm* goitre.

golden [gɔldɛn] *nf inv* Golden Delicious (apple).

golf [gɔlf] *nm* golf; **terrain de g.**, golf links, golf course.

golfe [gɔlf] *nm* gulf, bay; **le Courant du G.**, the Gulf Stream.

gomme [gɔm] *nf* 1. (a) gum; **g. arabique**, gum arabic; **g. laque**, shellac (b) *Comest:* **boule de g.**, gum; **g. à mâcher**, chewing gum 2. (a) g. (à effacer), (india) rubber, eraser (b) F: **à la g.**, useless, pointless 3. F: **mettre la g.**, to go all out; *Aut:* to put one's foot down.

gommer [gɔme] *vtr* 1. to gum 2. to erase, to rub out 3. *vi MecE:* to stick, jam; **piston gommé**, gummed piston.

gond [gɔ̃] *nm* hinge (pin) (of door); F: **sortir de ses gonds**, to lose one's temper.

gondole [gɔ̃dɔl] *nf* gondola.

gondoler [gɔ̃dɔle] 1. *vi & pr* (*of wood*) to warp; (*of paper*) to curl; (*of sheet iron*) to buckle 2. F: **se g.**, to split one's sides laughing. **gondolant** *a* F: side-splitting, hilarious.

gondolier, -ière [gɔ̃dɔlje, -jɛr] *n* gondolier.

gonflage [gɔ̃flaʒ] *nm Aut:* inflation.

gonflement [gɔ̃fləmɑ̃] *nm* inflating, inflation; distension (of stomach); swelling.

gonfler [gɔ̃fle] 1. *vtr* (a) to inflate, distend; to blow up, pump up (tyre); to puff out (one's cheeks); **le vent gonfle les voiles**, the wind fills the sails (b) to swell (c) F: to hot up, soup up (car engine) 2. *vi & pr* to become inflated; to swell; (*of stomach*) to become distended. **gonflé** *q* 1. (*of sail*) full 2. swollen, puffy (eyes); puffed (rice); **g. d'orgueil**, puffed up with pride; **avoir le cœur g.**, to be sad 3. sure, full, of oneself; F: **t'es g.**, you've got a nerve; **g. à bloc**, keyed up; raring to go.

gonfleur [gɔ̃flœr] *nm* (air) pump; *Aut:* (tyre) inflator.

gong [gɔ̃(g)] *nm* 1. gong 2. *Box:* bell.

gorge [gɔrʒ] *nf* 1. (a) throat, neck (b) bosom, bust (of woman); breast (of pigeon) 2. throat; **avoir mal à la g.**, to have a sore throat; **avoir la g. serrée**, to have a lump in one's throat; **crier à pleine g.**, to shout at the top of one's voice; **rire à g. déployée**, to roar with laughter 3. *Geog:* gorge 4. *Techn:* groove; tumbler (of lock).

gorgée [gɔrʒe] *nf* mouthful; gulp; **boire à petites gorgées**, to sip; **avaler d'une g.**, to gulp.

gorger [gɔrʒe] *vtr* (**n. gorgeons**) 1. to stuff, gorge; **gorgé d'eau**, saturated with water 2. **se g. (de qch)**, to stuff oneself (full of sth).

gorille [gɔrij] *nm* (a) *Z:* gorilla (b) F: bodyguard.

gosier [gozje] *nm* throat; gullet.

gosse [gɔs] *n* F: youngster, kid.

gothique [gɔtik] *a* Gothic.

gouache [gwaʃ] *nf Art:* gouache.

goudron [gudrɔ̃] *nm* tar.

goudronner [gudrɔne] *vtr* to tar.

gouffre [gufr] *nm* gulf, pit, abyss; *Geol:* swallow hole.

goujat [guʒa] *nm* boor, lout.

goujaterie [guʒatri] *nf* boorishness.

goujon [guʒɔ̃] *nm Ich: Const:* gudgeon.

goulée [gule] *nf* gulp.

goulet [gulɛ] *nm* gully (in mountains); *Nau:* narrows.

goulot [gulo] *nm* neck (of bottle); **boire au g.**, to drink (straight) from the bottle.

goulu, -ue [guly] 1. *a* greedy; gluttonous 2. *n* glutton. **goulûment** *adv* greedily.

goupille [gupij] *nf* (linch)pin.

goupiller [gupije] *vtr* 1. *Tchn:* to pin, key 2. F: to contrive, wangle (sth).

goupillon [gupijɔ̃] *nm* 1. sprinkler (for holy water) 2. brush (for gum, bottle).

gourde [gurd] *nf* (a) *Bot:* gourd (b) calabash, water bottle, flask (c) F: idiot, dimwit, dope 2. *a* F: thick.

gourdin [gurdɛ̃] *nm* club, cudgel.

gourer (se) [səgure] *vpr* P: to make a mistake, to boob.

gourmandise [gurmɑ̃diz] *nf* 1. greediness, gluttony; **manger avec g.**, to eat greedily 2. *pl* sweetmeats, dainties. **gourmand, -ande** 1. *a* greedy 2. *n* (a) gourmand, glutton (b) *nm Hort:* sucker.

gourmet [gurmɛ] *nm* gourmet, epicure.

gourmette [gurmɛt] *nf* chain bracelet.

gousse [gus] *nf* pod, shell, husk (of peas, beans); **g. d'ail**, clove of garlic.

gousset [gusɛ] *nm* (a) gusset (b) fob (pocket); waistcoat pocket.

goût [gu] *nm* 1. (sense of) taste 2. flavour, taste; bouquet (of wine); **g. du terroir**, local flavour, native tang; **cela a le g. de**, it tastes like; **sans g.**, tasteless(ly) 3. liking, preference, taste; **le g. des affaires**, a liking for business; **avoir du g. pour qch**, to have a taste for sth; **chacun (à) son g., à chacun son g.**, everyone to his taste; **une maison à mon g.**, a house to my liking; **ce n'est pas à mon g.**, I don't care for it; **prendre g. à qch**, to develop a taste for sth 4. **avoir du g.**, to have good taste; **mauvais g.**, (i) bad taste (ii) lack of taste; **s'habiller avec g.**, to dress well 5. style, manner; **quelque chose dans ce g.-là**, something of that sort.

goûter¹ [gute] *vtr* 1. (a) to taste (food) (b) to try, sample, taste (food) 2. **g. de qch**, (i) to taste sth (for the first time) (ii) to enjoy (s.o.'s hospitality) 3. **g. à qch**, to take a little of sth, to taste sth 4. *vi* to have tea.

goûter² *nm* = (afternoon) tea; tea party.

goutte [gut] *nf* 1. drop (of liquid); **tomber g. à g.**, to drip; **il suait à grosses gouttes**, sweat was pouring off him; **il tombait quelques gouttes**, it was spitting with rain; F: **avoir la g. au nez**, to have a runny nose 2. spot, splash (of colour); speck; fleck 3. small quantity; **une g. de bouillon**, a sip, a mouthful, of soup; **g. de cognac**, dash, nip, spot, of brandy; **encore une g. de café?** a drop more coffee? F: **prendre la g.**, to have a nip 4. *adv phr A: & Hum:* **je n'y vois g.**, (i) I can't see a thing (ii) I can't make anything of it 5. *Med:* gout.

goutte-à-goutte [gutagut] *nm inv Med:* drip.

gouttelette [gutlɛt] *nf* droplet.

goutter [gute] *vi* to drip.

gouttière [gutjɛr] *nf* 1. *Const:* gutter, guttering 2. spout, rainpipe 3. *Med:* cradle, splint.

gouvernail [guvɛrnaj] *nm Nau:* rudder, helm.

gouvernante [guvɛrnɑ̃t] *nf* 1. housekeeper 2. governess.

gouvernants [guvɛrnɑ̃] *nmpl* the party in power; the executive.

gouverne [guvɛrn] *nf* **pour votre g.**, for your guidance.

gouvernement [guvɛrnəmɑ̃] *nm* 1. (a) government, management (b) governorship (c) steering, handling (of boat) 2. (the) government; (the) Cabinet. **gouvernemental, -aux** *a* governmental; governing; **le parti g.**, the party in office.

gouverner [guvɛrne] *vtr* 1. *Nau:* to steer (ship) 2. (a) to govern, rule, control, direct (b) to manage, administer; **bien g. ses resources,** to make the most of one's resources (c) to govern (country) 3. *Gram:* to govern, to take.

gouverneur [guvɛrnœr] *nm* governor.

grabat [graba] *nm* litter (of straw); pallet.

grabuge [grabyʒ] *nm F:* quarrel, row, rumpus; **il y aura du g.,** there'll be ructions.

grâce [grɑs] *nf* 1. (a) grace, charm; **avoir de la g.,** to be graceful; **avec g.,** gracefully (b) **de bonne g.,** willingly; **de mauvaise g.,** unwillingly; **il serait de mauvaise g. de refuser,** it would be in bad taste to refuse 2. favour; **se mettre dans les bonnes grâces de qn,** to get into s.o.'s favour, into s.o.'s good books; **de g.!** for pity's sake! **g.!** mercy! 3. (act of) grace; **coup de g.,** finishing stroke, coup de grâce; **demander une g. à qn,** to ask a favour of s.o.; **c'est trop de grâces que vous me faites!** you really are too kind! 4. (a) *Jur:* free pardon; **je vous fais g. cette fois-ci,** I'll let you off this time (b) **demander g.,** to cry for mercy; **je vous fais g. du reste,** (i) you needn't do any more (ii) I'll spare you the rest 5. (a) thanks; (at meal) **dire les grâces,** to say grace; *pl* **action de grâces,** thanksgiving (b) **g. à,** thanks to, owing to.

gracier [grasje] *vtr (impf & pr sub* n. **graciions)** to pardon, reprieve.

gracieux, -euse [grasjø, -øz] *a* 1. graceful 2. (a) gracious (b) à titre g., as a favour; gratis; free of charge; **exemplaire envoyé à titre g.,** complimentary copy. **gracieusement** *adv* 1. gracefully 2. graciously, kindly 3. gratuitously, free of charge.

gracile [grasil] *a* slender.

gradation [gradasjɔ̃] *nf* gradation.

grade [grad] *nm* 1. rank; dignity; grade 2. (university) degree 3. *Mil:* rank; **monter en g.,** to be promoted; *F:* **en prendre pour son g.,** to be hauled over the coals 4. *Mth:* grade.

gradé [grade] *nm Mil:* non-commissioned officer, NCO; **tous les gradés,** all ranks (commissioned and non-commissioned).

gradin [gradɛ̃] *nm* step, tier.

graduation [graduasjɔ̃] *nf* 1. graduation 2. scale.

graduel, -elle [graduɛl] *a* gradual, progressive. **graduellement** *adv* gradually.

graduer [gradue] *vtr* 1. to graduate (thermometer) 2. to grade (studies). **gradué** *a* (a) graduated; **verre g.,** measuring glass (b) graded, progressive (exercises).

graffiti [grafiti] *nmpl* graffiti.

grain¹ [grɛ̃] *nm* 1. (a) grain; **g. de blé,** grain of wheat (b) cereals, grain, corn 2. **g. de café,** coffee bean; **g. de poivre,** peppercorn; **g. de raisin,** grape; **g. de beauté,** beauty spot; mole 3. (a) particle, atom; grain (of salt); speck (of dust) (b) **g. de jalousie,** hint of jealousy; **pas un g. de bon sens,** not an ounce of common sense; **il a un g.,** he's a bit touched, he's not all there 4. bead 5. grain, texture (of wood, leather); **contre le g.,** against the grain; **à gros grains,** coarse-grained.

grain² *nm* squall; gust of wind.

graine [grɛn] *nf* seed; **g. de lin,** linseed; **monter en g.,** to run to seed.

graineterie [grɛntri] *nf* seed trade, shop.

grainetier, -ière [grɛntje, -jɛr] *n* seed merchant.

graissage [grɛsaʒ] *nm* greasing, oiling, lubrication.

graisse [grɛs] *nf* (a) grease, fat; **g. de rôti,** dripping; **g. de porc,** lard (b) grease, lubricant.

graisser [grɛse] *vtr* to grease, oil, lubricate; **g. la patte à qn,** to grease s.o.'s palm. **graisseux, -euse** *a* greasy; fatty.

grammaire [gramɛr] *nf* grammar; **faute de g.,** grammatical error; **(livre de) g.,** grammar book. **grammatical, -aux** *a* grammatical. **grammaticalement** *adv* grammatically.

grammairien, -ienne [gramɛrjɛ̃, -jɛn] *n* grammarian.

gramme [gram] *nm Meas:* gram(me).

grand, grande [grɑ̃, grɑ̃d] *a* 1. (a) tall (in stature); large, big (in size); **homme g.,** tall man; **pas plus g. que ça,** only so high; **grands bras,** long arms; **grands pieds,** big feet; **grande distance,** great distance; **plus g. que nature,** larger than life; *Opt:* **objectif g. angle,** wide angle lens; **g. A.,** capital A (b) chief, main; **g. chemin,** main road; *Nau:* **le g. mât,** the mainmast; **g. ressort,** mainspring; **les grandes vacances,** the summer holidays, the long vacation (c) **quand tu seras g.,** when you are grown up; **elle se fait grande,** (i) she's growing up (ii) she's growing tall; **les grandes personnes,** the grown-ups; *Sch:* **les grandes classes,** the upper forms (d) *adv* **voir g.,** to have big ideas; **ouvrir la fenêtre toute grande,** to open the window wide; **porte grande ouverte,** wide-open door; *adv phr* **en g.,** (i) on a large scale (ii) full size; **reproduction en g.,** enlarged copy; **ouvrir un robinet en g.,** to turn a tap full on 2. **pas g. monde,** not many people; **le g. public,** the general public; **en grande partie,** to a great extent 3. **les grands hommes,** great men; **le g. monde,** (high) society; **grands vins,** vintage wines; **se donner de grands airs,** to give oneself airs 4. **grandes pensées,** great, noble, thoughts 5. great; **ce sont de grands amis,** they are great friends; **avec le plus g. plaisir,** with the greatest pleasure; **g. froid,** severe cold; **il fait g. jour,** it is broad daylight; **il est g. temps de partir,** it is high time we left; **g. bruit,** loud noise; **les grands blessés,** the seriously wounded; *Tex:* **couleur g. teint,** fast dye 6. *nm* (a) **grands et petits,** old and young; *Sch:* **les grand(e)s,** the senior boys, girls (b) **les grands de la terre,** the great of this world (c) *Pol:* **les Grands,** the Great Powers; **les Quatre Grands,** the Big Four. **grandement** *adv* 1. grandly, nobly 2. greatly, largely; **se tromper g.,** to be greatly mistaken; **il est g. temps de partir,** it's high time we left.

grand-chose [grɑ̃ʃoz] *indef pron m inv (usu coupled with* pas) **ça ne vaut pas g.-c.,** it's not worth much; **il ne fait pas g.-c.,** he doesn't do much; **il ne fera jamais g.-c.,** he'll never amount to much.

grand-duc [grɑ̃dyk] *nm* 1. grand duke 2. *Orn:* eagle owl; *pl* **grands-ducs.**

Grande-Bretagne [grɑ̃dbrətaɲ] *Prnf Geog:* Great Britain.

grandeur [grɑ̃dœr] *nf* 1. (a) size; height (of tree); **échelle de grandeurs,** scale of sizes; **g. nature,** full-size(d); life-size(d) (b) extent; scale 2. greatness (a) importance; magnitude; grandeur (b) majesty, splendour (c) nobility.

grandiloquent [grɑ̃dilɔkɑ̃] *a* grandiloquent.

grandiose [grɑ̃djoz] *a* grand, imposing; grandiose.

grandir [grɑ̃dir] 1. *vi* (a) (i) to grow tall (ii) to grow up; **il a grandi,** he is taller (b) **son influence grandit,** his influence is increasing 2. *vtr* (*a*) to make (sth) greater; to increase; **ses talons la grandissent,** her heels make her look taller (*b*) to magnify, to exaggerate (an incident).

grand(-)livre [grɑ̃livr̩] *nm* Com: ledger; *pl grands-livres.*

grand-maman [grɑ̃mamɑ̃] *nf* F: grandma, granny; *pl grand(s)-mamans.*

grand-mère [grɑ̃mɛr] *nf* (*a*) grandmother (*b*) F: old woman, granny; *pl grand(s)-mères.*

grand-messe [grɑ̃mɛs] *nf* Ecc: high mass; *pl grand(s)-messes.*

grand-oncle [grɑ̃tɔ̃kl̩] *nm* great uncle; *pl grands-oncles.*

grand-papa [grɑ̃papa] *nm* F: grandpa, grandad; *pl grands-papas.*

grand-peine (à) [agrɑ̃pɛn] *adv phr* with great difficulty.

grand-père [grɑ̃pɛr] *nm* grandfather; *pl grands-pères.*

grand-route [grɑ̃rut] *nf* highway, high road, main road; *pl grand-routes.*

grand-rue [grɑ̃ry] *nf* high street, main street; *pl grand-rues.*

grands-parents [grɑ̃parɑ̃] *nmpl* grandparents.

grand-tante [grɑ̃tɑ̃t] *nf* great-aunt; *pl grand(s)-tantes.*

grand-voile [grɑ̃vwal] *nf* Nau: mainsail; *pl grand(s)-voiles.*

grange [grɑ̃ʒ] *nf* barn.

granit(e) [granit] *nm* granite.

granulé [granyle] *nm* granule. **granuleux, -euse** *a* granulous, granular.

granuler [granyle] *vtr* to granulate.

graphique [grafik] 1. *a* graphic (sign, method) 2. *nm* diagram, graph.

graphite [grafit] *nm* graphite.

graphologie [grafɔlɔʒi] *nf* graphology.

grappe [grap] *nf* cluster, bunch (of grapes).

grappin [grapɛ̃] *nm* Nau: grapnel, hook; F: **mettre le g. sur qch,** to get hold of, to grab, sth.

gras, grasse [grɑ, grɑs] *a* 1. (*a*) fat; fatty; **matières grasses,** fats (*b*) rich (food); **faire g.,** to eat meat (*esp* on a fast day); **fromage g.,** full cream cheese (*c*) *nm* fat (of meat) 2. (*a*) fat, stout (pers) (*b*) fatted, fat (animal); plump (chicken) 3. greasy, oil (rag, hair); **eaux grasses,** swill 4. (*a*) thick; **boue grasse,** thick, slimy, mud; **toux grasse,** loose cough; **voix grasse,** oily voice (*b*) **plante grasse,** succulent (plant); Typ: **caractères g.,** heavy, bold, type; P: **il n'y en a pas g.,** there's not much of it; **le g. de la jambe,** the calf of the leg. **grassement** *adv* 1. **rire g.,** to give a deep chuckle 2. **récompenser qn g.,** to reward s.o. handsomely, generously. **grassouillet, -ette** *a* plump, chubby.

gras-double [grɑdubl̩] *nm* Cu: tripe.

gratification [gratifikasjɔ̃] *nf* (*a*) gratuity; tip (*b*) bonus.

gratifier [gratifje] *vtr* (*impf & pr sub* n. **gratifiions**) to present (qn de qch, s.o. with sth); Iron: **être gratifié d'une amende,** to be landed with a fine.

gratin [gratɛ̃] *nm* 1. Cu: (*a*) cheese topping; **au g.,** (cooked) with grated cheese (*b*) dish cooked *au gratin* 2. F: upper crust (of society).

gratiner [gratine] *vtr* Cu: to cook (sth) *au gratin.*

gratiné, -ée 1. *a* (*a*) Cu: au gratin (*b*) F: addition **gratinée,** enormous bill 2. *nf* Cu: onion soup *au gratin.*

gratis [gratis] 1. *adv* gratis; free of charge 2. *a* free.

gratitude [gratityd] *nf* gratitude, gratefulness.

gratte [grat] *nf* F: pickings, perks, rake-off.

gratte-ciel [gratsjɛl] *nm inv* skyscraper.

grattement [gratmɑ̃] *nm* scratching.

gratte-papier [gratpapje] *nm inv* Pej: penpusher.

gratte-pieds [gratpje] *nm inv* (metal) doormat.

gratter [grate] 1. *vtr* (*a*) to scrape, scratch; se **g. l'oreille,** to scratch one's ear; F: **ça me gratte terriblement,** it makes me itch like mad; F: g. **les fonds de tiroir,** to scrape the (bottom of the) barrel (*b*) to erase (a word) 2. *vi* (*a*) g. **à la porte,** to scratch at the door (*b*) g. **du violon,** to scrape on the fiddle (*c*) **plume qui gratte,** scratchy nib.

grattoir [gratwar] *nm* scraper.

gratuité [gratɥite] *nf* (*a*) **la g. de l'enseignement,** free education (*b*) gratuitousness. **gratuit** *a* (*a*) free (of charge) (*b*) gratuitous (insult). **gratuitement** *adv* (*a*) free of charge (*b*) gratuitously.

gravats [grava] *nmpl* rubble.

grave [grav] *a* 1. (*a*) grave, serious (mistake); grave, solemn (tone); sober (expression) (*b*) important (business) (*c*) severe, serious (illness, wound) 2. deep (voice); **sons graves,** bass tones 3. Gram: **accent g.,** grave accent. **gravement** *adv* gravely, solemnly, seriously.

graver [grave] *vtr* to engrave, carve; to cut (record); g. **à l'eau-forte,** to etch; **c'est gravé dans ma mémoire,** I'll never forget it.

graveur [gravœr] *nm* engraver; carver; g. **à l'eau-forte,** etcher.

gravier [gravje] *nm* gravel, grit.

gravillon [gravijɔ̃] *nm* fine gravel; PN: **gravillons,** loose chippings.

gravir [gravir] *vtr* to climb (mountain).

gravité [gravite] *nf* 1. Ph: gravity 2. gravity, seriousness, severity; **blessure sans g.,** slight wound.

graviter [gravite] *vi* 1. to gravitate 2. to revolve; (*of planet*) to orbit.

gravure [gravyr] *nf* 1. engraving; g. **sur bois,** woodcutting; g. **à l'eau-forte,** etching 2. print; engraving; etching; g. **en couleurs,** colour print; g. **hors texte,** full-page plate 3. carving (of stone) 4. cutting (of record).

gré [gre] *nm* 1. liking, taste; **à mon g.,** to my taste; **une chambre à mon g.,** a room that I like, that suits me 2. will, pleasure; **contre le g. de qn,** against s.o.'s wishes; **de mon plein g.,** of my own free will, my own accord; **de bon g.,** willingly; **bon g. mal g.,** whether we like it or not; willy-nilly; **de g. ou de force,** by fair means or foul; **au g. des flots,** at the mercy of the waves 3. **savoir (bon) g. à qn de qch,** to be grateful to s.o. for sth.

Grèce [grɛs] *Prnf Geog:* Greece. **grec, grecque** 1. *a* Greek; Grecian 2. *n* Greek 3. *nm* Ling: Greek.

gredin [grədɛ̃] *n* rogue; rascal.

gréement [gremɑ̃] *nm* Nau: rigging.

gréer [gree] *vtr* Nau: to rig.

greffage [grɛfaʒ] *nm* grafting.

greffe¹ [grɛf] *nm* 1. Hort: graft, slip; Surg: graft; transplant (of organ); g. **du cœur,** heart transplant 2. grafting.

greffe² *nf* Jur: office of the clerk of the court.

greffer [grefe] *vtr Hort: Surg:* to graft; *Surg:* to transplant (organ).

greffier [grefje] *nm* 1. *Jur:* clerk (of the court) 2. *Adm:* registrar.

greffon [grefɔ̃] *nm Hort:* graft; *Surg:* transplant, graft.

grégaire [gregɛr] *a* gregarious.

grêle[1] [grɛl] *a* slender, thin (leg); high-pitched (voice).

grêle[2] *nf* hail; **averse de g.**, hailstorm; **g. de coups**, shower of blows.

grêler [grele] 1. *v impers* **il grêle**, it's hailing 2. *vtr* to damage (crops) by hail.

grêlon [grɛlɔ̃] *nm* hailstone.

grelot [grəlo] *nm* (small round) bell; sleigh bell.

grelotter [grələte] *vi* to tremble, shake, shiver (with cold, fear).

grenade [grənad] *nf* 1. *Bot:* pomegranate 2. *Mil:* (a) grenade (b) **g. sous-marine**, depth charge.

grenadine [grənadin] *nf* pomegranate (syrup); grenadine.

grenat [grəna] 1. *nm* garnet 2. *a inv* garnet-red.

grenier [grənje] *nm* 1. granary, storehouse; **g. à foin**, hay loft 2. attic, garret.

grenouille[grənuj] *nf* 1. frog; *F:* **g. de bénitier**, church hen 2. *F:* = piggybank.

grès [grɛ] *nm* 1. sandstone 2. **poterie de g.**, stoneware; **pot de g.**, stone(ware) pot.

grésil [grezi(l)] *nm* sleet; hail; frozen rain.

grésillement [grezijmɑ̃] *nm* crackling (of fire); sizzling (of frying pan).

grésiller [grezije] *vi* to crackle; (*of frying pan*) to sizzle.

grève [grɛv] *nf* 1. (a) (sea)shore; (sandy) beach (b) (sand)bank 2. strike; walkout; **se mettre en g.**, to go, to come out, on strike; to strike; to take strike action; **g. perlée**, go-slow; **g. sauvage**, wildcat strike; **g. du zèle**, work(ing) to rule; **g. de la faim**, hunger strike.

grever [grəve] *vtr* (**je grève, n. grevons**) to burden (estate); **grevé d'impôts**, crippled by taxes.

gréviste [grevist] *n* striker.

gribouillage [gribujaʒ] *nm* scrawl, scribble; doodle.

gribouiller [gribuje] *vtr & i* to scrawl, scribble; to doodle.

gribouilleur, -euse [gribujœr, -øz] *n* scribbler.

gribouillis [gribuji] *nm* = **gribouillage**.

grief [gri(j)ɛf] *nm* grievance; **faire g. à qn de qch**, to hold sth against s.o.

grièvement [grijɛvmɑ̃] *adv* seriously, severely (wounded).

griffe [grif] *nf* 1. claw; talon (of hawk); (*of cat*) **faire ses griffes**, to sharpen its claws; **coup de g.**, scratch; **tomber sous les griffes de qn**, to fall into s.o.'s clutches 2. (a) stamped signature (b) (signature) stamp (c) (*on clothes*) label.

griffer [grife] *vtr* to scratch; to claw.

griffonnage [grifɔnaʒ] *nm* scribble, scrawl; doodle.

griffonner [grifɔne] *vtr & i* to scrawl, scribble (off) (letter); to scrawl; to doodle.

grignotement [griɲɔtmɑ̃] *nm* nibbling.

grignoter [griɲɔte] *vtr* to nibble (sth); to pick at (food); to eat away at (sth).

gril [gri(l)] *nm Cu:* grid(iron), grill; *F:* **être sur le g.**, to be on tenterhooks.

grillade [grijad] *nf* grill, grilled meat.

grillage [grijaʒ] *nm* (metal) grating; wire netting.

grillager [grijaʒe] *vtr* (**je grillageai(s)**) to surround (sth) with wire netting, wire fencing.

grille [grij] *nf* (a) (iron) bars; grille (of convent parlour); grating, grid; screen; (prison) bars (b) iron gate (c) railings (d) fire grate (e) (crossword) grid (f) scale (of salaries); timetable, schedule.

grille-pain [grijpɛ̃] *nm inv* toaster.

griller [grije] 1. *vtr* to grill (meat); to toast (bread); to roast (coffee) 2. *vtr* (a) to burn, scorch; to singe (one's hair); *F:* **g. une cigarette**, to smoke a cigarette (b) *El:* to burn out (bulb) (c) (*of sun, frost*) to scorch (vegetation); *Sp: F:* **g. un concurrent**, to race past a competitor; *Aut:* **g. un feu rouge**, to jump the lights; **g. une étape**, to miss out a stop 3. *vi* (a) *Cu:* (*of meat*) to grill; (*of bread*) to toast; (*of coffee*) to roast (b) **g. d'impatience**, to be burning with impatience; **g. d'envie de faire qch**, to be itching to do sth.

grillon [grijɔ̃] *nm Ent:* cricket.

grimace [grimas] *nf* grimace, wry face; **faire la g.**, to pull a face; **faire une g. de douleur**, to wince; **faire des grimaces**, to put on airs.

grimacer [grimase] *vi* (**n. grimaçons**) to grimace; to make faces; to pull a face; **g. de douleur**, to wince.

grimer [grime] *vtr & pr Th:* to make up.

grimoire [grimwar] *nm* 1. wizard's book of spells 2. illegible scrawl.

grimper [grɛ̃pe] (a) *vi* to climb (up) (b) *vtr* to climb (a mountain); **g. l'escalier**, to go up the stairs. **grimpant** *a* climbing (plant, animal).

grimpette [grɛ̃pet] *nf F:* steep climb.

grincement [grɛ̃smɑ̃] *nm* grinding; creaking; grating.

grincer [grɛ̃se] *vi* (**n. grinçons**) to grate; to grind; to creak; **g. des dents**, to grind, grit, one's teeth; **cela fait g. les dents**, it sets one's teeth on edge. **grinçant** *a* grating, creaking.

grincheux, -euse [grɛ̃ʃø, -øz] 1. *a* grumpy, bad-tempered 2. *n* grumbler, grouser.

grippe [grip] *nf* 1. **prendre qn en g.**, to take a dislike to s.o. 2. *Med:* influenza, *F:* flu; **g. gastro-intestinale**, gastric flu. **grippé** *a* suffering from flu.

gripper [gripe] *vtr & i MecE:* to seize up.

gris [gri] 1. *a* (a) grey; **g. perle**, pearl grey; **g.-bleu**, blue grey; **aux cheveux g.**, grey-haired (b) cloudy, dull (weather) (c) **faire grise mine**, to look anything but pleased; **faire g. mine à qn**, to give s.o. the cold shoulder (d) *F:* (slightly) drunk, tipsy 2. *nm* (a) grey (colour) (b) (= **tabac g.**) = shag. **grisâtre** *a* greyish.

griser [grize] *vtr* 1. to make (s.o.) tipsy; **grisé par le succès**, intoxicated with success 2. **se g.**, to get drunk, tipsy.

griserie [grizri] *nf* 1. tipsiness 2. intoxication, exhilaration.

grisonner [grizɔne] *vi* (*of pers, hair*) to go, to be going, grey.

grisou [grizu] *nm Min:* firedamp.

grive [griv] *nf Orn:* thrush.

grivoiserie [grivwazri] *nf* risqué joke; licentious story. **grivois, -oise** *a* risqué, licentious, rude.

Groenland [grɔɛnlɑ̃(d)] *Prnm Geog:* Greenland.

grog [grɔg] *nm* grog; toddy.

grognement [grɔɲmɑ̃] *nm* grunt; growl; snort.

grogner [grɔɲe] *vi* 1. to grunt; to growl; to snort 2. (*of* *pers)* to grumble; to grouse. **grognon 1.** *n* grumbler, grouser **2.** *s* (*f* **grognon** *or* **grognonne**), grumbling, peevish.

groin [grwɛ̃] *nm* snout (of pig).

grommeler [grɔmle] **1.** *vi* (**je gromelle**) to grumble, mutter **2.** *vtr* to mutter (an oath).

grommellement [grɔmɛlmɑ̃] *nm* grumbling, muttering.

grondement [grɔ̃dmɑ̃] *nm* **1.** growl(ing), snarling (of dog) **2.** rumble, rumbling (of thunder); roar (of torrent, engine); booming (of waves, guns).

gronder [grɔ̃de] **1.** *vi (a)* to growl, snarl *(b)* to rumble; *(of waves)* to roar; *(of guns)* to boom *(c) Lit:* **g. contre qn,** to g..umble at s.o. **2.** *vtr* to scold (s.o.), to tell (s.o.) off. **grondeur, -euse** *a* grumbling.

gronderie [grɔ̃dri] *nf* scolding.

groom [grum] *nm (in hotel)* bellboy.

gros, grosse [gro, gros] **1.** *(a)* a big, bulky, large; stout; **grosse corde,** thick rope; **g. pullover,** chunky sweater; **g. bout,** thick end (of stick); **grosse toile,** coarse linen; **g. sel,** cooking salt; **c'est un peu g.!** that's a bit much! **g. rire** (i) loud (ii) coarse, laugh; **grosse voix,** gruff voice; **g. mot,** coarse expression, swearword; **grosse somme,** large sum (of money); **ce n'est pas une grosse affaire,** (i) it's only a small business (ii) it's not very difficult; *Cards: etc:* **jouer g. (jeu),** to play for high stakes; **g. mangeur,** big eater; **g. buveur,** heavy, hard, drinker; **g. rhume,** heavy cold; **grosse fièvre,** high fever; **grosse faute,** serious mistake; **grosse mer,** heavy sea; **g. temps,** stormy, bad, weather; *F:* **les g. bonnets,** the bigwigs; **avoir le cœur g.,** to be sad at heart; *(of woman)* **grosse de trois mois,** three months pregnant *(b)* *adv* **gagner g.,** to earn a great deal; **il y a g. à parier que,** a hundred to one (that) **2.** *n* large, fat, person **3.** *nm (a)* bulk, chief part; **le plus g. est fait,** the hardest part of the job is done; **g. de l'été,** height of summer *(b)* **en g.,** roughly, broadly; on the whole; **évaluation en g.,** rough estimate *(c) Com:* wholesale trade; **acheter en g.,** to buy (i) wholesale (ii) in bulk; **boucher en g.,** wholesale butcher **4.** *nf Com:* **grosse,** gross; twelve dozen.

groseille [grozɛj] *nf* **1. g. (rouge),** redcurrant **2. g. à maquereau,** gooseberry.

groseillier [grozeje] *nm* **1.** (red)currant bush **2. g. à maquereau,** gooseberry bush.

grossesse [grosɛs] *nf* pregnancy; **robe de g.,** maternity dress.

grosseur [grosœr] *nf* **1.** size, bulk, volume; weight, fatness (of pers) **2.** *Med:* swelling, growth.

grossièreté [grosjɛrte] *nf (a)* coarseness, roughness (of object) *(b)* rudeness, vulgarity, coarseness (of manner); **dire des grossièretés,** to say rude things, to use coarse language *(c)* grossness (of mistake).

grossier, -ière *a (a)* coarse, rough *(b)* **ignorance grossière,** crass ignorance; **faute grossière,** blunder *(c)* rude, unmannerly *(envers, to)*; vulgar, coarse; ill-mannered, rude. **grossièrement** *adv* roughly, coarsely; crudely; rudely.

grossir [grosir] **1.** *vtr* to enlarge, to swell, to magnify; **torrent grossi par les pluies,** torrent swollen by the rain; **grossi trois fois,** magnified three times; **g. sa voix,** to raise one's voice **2.** *vi* to increase, swell; to grow bigger, larger; *(of pers)* to put on weight.

grossissement [grosismɑ̃] *nm* **1.** increase (in size) **2.**

(a) magnifying, enlargement *(b)* magnification.

grossiste [grosist] *nm* wholesaler.

grosso modo [grosomɔdo] *adv* roughly (speaking).

grotesque [grɔtɛsk] *a (a)* grotesque *(b)* ludicrous, absurd.

grotte [grɔt] *nf* (underground) cave; grotto.

grouillement [grujmɑ̃] *nm* swarming, crawling.

grouiller [gruje] *vi* **1.** to crawl, swarm **(de,** with) **2.** *P:* **se g.,** to get a move on.

groupe [grup] *nm* **1.** *(a)* group (of people); clump (of trees); cluster (of stars); party (of people); **par groupes de deux ou trois,** in twos and threes; **g. de travail,** working party; *Pol:* **g. de pression,** pressure group; *Med:* **g. sanguin,** blood group *(b)* **g. scolaire,** (multilateral) school block **2.** *El:* set; **g. électrogène,** generating set **3.** *Mil: etc:* **g. de combat,** squad; **g. d'artillerie,** battery; **g. d'aviation,** squadron.

groupement [grupmɑ̃] *nm* **1.** grouping **2.** group.

grouper [grupe] *vtr* **1.** to group; to arrange (in groups); *Com:* to bulk (parcels) **2. se g.,** to form a group; **se g. autour du feu,** to gather round the fire.

gruau [gryo] *nm* **1. (farine de) g.,** (finest) wheat flour **2.** *Cu:* gruel.

grue [gry] *nf* **1.** *Orn:* crane; **faire le pied de g.,** to cool one's heels **2.** *P:* prostitute, tart **3.** *MecE:* crane.

grumeau, -eaux [grymo] *nm* lump (in sauce).

gruyère [gryjɛr] *nm* gruyere (cheese).

gué [ge] *nm* ford; **passer une rivière à g.,** to ford a river. **guéable** *a* fordable.

guenille [gənij] *nf* tattered garment, old rag; **en guenilles,** in rags (and tatters).

guenon [gənɔ̃] *nf* she-monkey.

guépard [gepar] *nm Z:* cheetah.

guêpe [gɛp] *nf Ent:* wasp.

guêpier [gepje] *nm* **1.** wasps' nest; **tomber dans un g.,** to stir up a hornets' nest **2.** *Orn:* bee eater.

guère [gɛr] *adv (always with neg expressed or understood)* hardly (any), not much, not many, only a little, only a few; **je ne l'aime g.,** I don't much care for him; **cet appel n'a eu g. de succès,** the appeal met with very little success; **il ne mange g. que du pain,** he eats hardly anything but bread; **il ne tardera g. à venir,** he won't be long in coming; **il n'y a g. plus de six ans,** hardly more than six years ago; **il ne s'en faut (de) g.,** it's not far short.

guéridon [geridɔ̃] *nm* pedestal table.

guérilla [gerija] *nf* **1.** guer(r)illa warfare **2.** band of guer(r)illas.

guérillero [gerijero] *nm* guer(r)illa.

guérir [gerir] **1.** *vtr* to cure (pers, illness); heal (wound) **2.** *vi (a)* to be cured; to recover *(b) (of wound)* to heal **3. se g.,** to get better, to be cured; **se g. d'une habitude,** to break a habit. **guérissable** *a* curable.

guérison [gerizɔ̃] *nf* **1.** recovery **2.** *(a)* cure (of disease) *(b)* healing (of wound).

guérisseur, -euse [gerisœr, -øz] *n (a)* healer *(b)* quack (doctor) *(c)* faith healer.

guérite [gerit] *nf* **1.** sentry box **2.** cabin, shelter (for watchman).

Guernesey [gɛrnəzɛ] *Prnm Geog:* Guernsey.

guerre [gɛr] *nf* **1.** *(a)* war, warfare; **g. sur mer,** naval warfare; **g. atomique,** atomic warfare; **g. froide,** cold war; **se mettre en g.,** to go to war; **en temps de g.,** in wartime; **faire la g. à un pays,** to wage war on a country; **faire la g. avec qn,** to be in the war with s.o.; **à la g. comme à la g.,** one must take the rough with the smooth (*b*) **la première, seconde, g. mondiale,** the first, second, world war; **la drôle de g.,** the phoney war 2. strife, feud; **être en g. ouverte avec qn,** to be openly at war with s.o.; **de g. lasse,** for the sake of peace and quiet. **guerrier, -ière** 1. *a* warlike; war (dance) 2. *nm* warrior.

guet [gɛ] *nm* 1. watch(ing); lookout; **avoir l'œil au ḡ.,** to keep a sharp lookout 2. *Hist:* watch.

guet-apens [gɛtapã] *nm* ambush, snare; *pl* **guets-apens.**

guêtre [gɛtr̩] *nf* gaiter.

guetter [gete] *vtr* to lie in wait for, to be on the lookout for, to watch for (s.o.).

guetteur [gɛtœr] *nm Mil:* lookout (man).

gueule [gœl] *nf* 1. (*a*) mouth (of carnivorous animal (*b*) *P:* mouth (of pers); **(ferme) ta g.!** shut up! **avoir la g. de bois,** to have a hangover (*c*) *P:* face, mug; **avoir une sale g.,** to look nasty; **faire la g.,** to sulk, to look sulky (*d*) *F:* **ça a une drôle de g.,** it looks weird 2. mouth (of tunnel); muzzle (of gun).

gueule-de-loup [gœldəlu] *nf Bot:* snapdragon; *pl* **gueules-de-loup.**

gueulement [gœlmã] *nm F:* shout, yell.

gueuler [gœle] *vtr & i P:* to bawl, shout; to bawl out (song); to get stroppy; **faire g. la radio,** to turn the radio on full blast.

gueuleton [gœltõ] *nm P:* blowout.

gueux, -euse [gø, -øz] *n* (*a*) beggar; tramp (*b*) rascal, rogue.

gui [gi] *nm Bot:* mistletoe.

guibol(l)e [gibɔl] *nf P:* leg, pin.

guichet [giʃɛ] *nm* 1. (*a*) wicket (gate) (*b*) spy hole, grille, grating (in door); (service) hatch (in restaurant) 2. (*a*) *Bank: Post:* position; **g. fermé,** position closed (*b*) booking office; *Th:* box office.

guichetier, -ière [giʃtje, -jɛr] *nm* booking clerk; counter clerk.

guidage [gidaʒ] *nm* guiding; *Av:* guidance.

guide¹ [gid] *nm* 1. (*a*) (tourist, museum) guide; conductor (*b*) *nf* (girl) guide 2. guide (book).

guide² *nf* rein.

guider [gide] *vtr* to guide, conduct, direct, lead; **g. un élève dans le choix d'une carrière,** to advise a pupil in the choice of a career.

guidon [gidõ] *nm* handlebar(s) (of bicycle).

guigne [giɲ] *nf F:* bad luck; **avoir la g.,** to be out of luck.

guigner [giɲe] *vtr* to give a surreptitious glance at, to eye (sth).

guignol [giɲɔl] *nm* (*a*) = Punch; **faire le g.,** to act the fool (*b*) = Punch and Judy show; puppet show.

guillemets [gijmɛ] *nmpl* inverted commas, quotation marks; (*when dictating*) **ouvrez, fermez, les g.,** quote; unquote.

guilleret, -ette [gijrɛ, -ɛt] *a* lively (pers); brisk (tune); risqué (joke).

guillotine [gijɔtin] *nf* guillotine; **fenêtre à g.,** sash window.

guillotiner [gijɔtine] *vtr* to guillotine.

guimauve [gimov] *nf Comest:* marshmallow.

guimbarde [gɛbard] *nf* 1. Jew's harp 2. old banger; jalopy.

guindé [gɛde] *a* stiff, stilted; starchy (person); stilted (style).

Guinée [gine] *Prnf Geog:* Guinea.

guingois [gɛgwa] *adv phr* **de g.,** askew, lopsided.

guinguette [gɛgɛt] *nf* (suburban) café (with music and dancing, *usu* in the open).

guirlande [girlãd] *nf* garland, wreath, festoon.

guise [giz] *nf* manner, way, fashion; **faire à sa g.,** to do as one pleases; **en g. de,** (i) by way of (ii) instead of.

guitare [gitar] *nf Mus:* guitar.

guitariste [gitarist] *n* guitarist.

guitoune [gitun] *nf F:* tent; **coucher sous la g.,** to sleep under canvas.

guttural, -aux [gytyral, -o] 1. *a* guttural; throaty 2. *nf Ling:* **gutturale,** guttural.

Guyane [gɥijan] *Prnf Geog: Pol:* Guyana; **G. française,** French Guiana.

gym [ʒim] *nf* gym, *F:* PE.

gymkhana [ʒimkana] *nm* gymkhana.

gymnase [ʒimnaz] *nm* gymnasium.

gymnaste [ʒimnast] *n* gymnast.

gymnastique [ʒimnastik] 1. *a* gymnastic 2. *nf* gymnastics; **g. corrective,** remedial gymnastics; **g. intellectuelle,** mental gymnastics; *F:* **g. matinale,** morning exercises.

gynécologie [ʒinekɔlɔʒi] *nf* gyn(a)ecology. **gynécologique** *a* gyn(a)ecological.

gynécologue [ʒinekɔlɔg] *n* gyn(a)ecologist.

gyroscope [ʒirɔskɔp] *nm* gyroscope.

gyrostat [ʒirɔsta] *nm* gyrostat.

H

Words beginning with an aspirate h are shown by an asterisk.

H, h [aʃ] *nm & f* (the letter) H, h; **h muet(te), aspiré(e)**, mute h, aspirate h.
ha *abbr* hectare.
habileté [abilte] *nf* (*a*) ability, skill, skilfulness (*b*) cleverness, smartness. **habile** *a* clever, skilful, able, capable (workman); cunning, artful (politician); **mains habiles**, skilled hands; **h. à faire qch**, clever at doing sth. **habilement** *adv* cleverly, skilfully.
habillement [abijmã] *nm* 1. clothing, dressing 2. clothes, dress.
habiller [abije] *vtr* 1. (*a*) to dress (s.o.) (*b*) to clothe, to provide (s.o.) with clothes (*c*) to cover (furniture) 2. **s'h.**, (*a*) to dress (oneself); to get dressed; **s'h. en femme**, to dress up as a woman; **elle ne sait pas s'h.**, she has no taste in clothes (*b*) **s'h. chez un tailleur**, to get one's clothes made by a tailor. **habillé** *a* 1. dressed 2. (*of clothes*) smart, dressy.
habit [abi] *nm* 1. dress, costume; *pl* clothes; **h. du dimanche**, Sunday best; **h. de cour**, court dress 2. (*a*) *A:* coat (*b*) tails; **être en h.**, to be in evening dress 3. (monk's, nun's) habit.
habitable [abitabl̥] *a* (in)habitable, fit for habitation.
habitacle [abitakl̥] *nm Nau:* binnacle; *Av:* cockpit.
habitant, -ante [abitã, -ãt] *n* (*a*) inhabitant; resident (*b*) occupier, occupant (of flat, house) (*c*) inmate (of house).
habitat [abita] *nm* habitat (of animal, plant).
habitation [abitasjɔ̃] *nf* 1. habitation; inhabiting 2. dwelling (place), residence; house; **h. à loyer modéré (HLM)** = council house, council flat.
habiter [abite] 1. *vtr* (*a*) to inhabit, to live in (a place); **cette pièce n'a jamais été habitée**, this room has never been lived in (*b*) to occupy (house) 2. *vi* to live, reside.
habitude [abityd] *nf* (*a*) habit, custom; **prendre l'h. de faire qch**, to get into the habit of doing sth; **se faire une h. de**, to make it one's practice to; **avoir l'h. de faire qch**, to be in the habit of doing sth; **mauvaises habitudes**, bad habits; **il a l'h.**, he's used to it; **faire perdre une h. à qn**, to break s.o. of a habit; **d'h.**, usually, ordinarily; **comme d'h.**, as usual (*b*) knack; **je n'en ai plus l'h.**, I'm out of practice.
habitué, -ée [abitɥe] *n* frequenter; regular visitor, customer; habitué.
habituer [abitɥe] *vtr* 1. to accustom, make familiar; **h. qn à qch**, to get s.o. used to sth 2. **s'h.**, to get used to, get accustomed (**à**, to). **habituel, -elle** *a* usual, customary, regular; habitual. **habituellement** *adv* habitually, usually, regularly.
*****hache** [aʃ] *nf* axe; **h. de guerre**, tomahawk; *Fig:* **enterrer la h. de guerre**, to bury the hatchet.

*****hache-légumes** [aʃlegym] *nm inv Cu:* vegetable cutter, chopper.
*****hacher** [aʃe] *vtr* (*a*) to chop (up); to mince (meat); **h. menu**, to mince finely, to chop finely; **se faire h.**, to be cut to pieces (*b*) to hack (up), mangle; to interrupt (speech). **haché** 1. *a* (*a*) minced, chopped (*b*) jerky, staccato (style) 2. *nm Cu:* minced meat, minced beef.
*****hachette** [aʃɛt] *nf* hatchet.
*****hache-viande** [aʃvjãd] *nm inv Cu:* mincer.
*****hachis** [aʃi] *nm Cu:* minced meat; mince; **h. Parmentier** = cottage pie, shepherd's pie.
*****hachisch** [aʃiʃ] *nm* hashish.
*****hachoir** [aʃwar] *nm* 1. (*a*) chopper (*b*) chopping board 2. mincer, mincing machine.
*****haddock** [adɔk] *nm* smoked haddock.
*****hagard** [agar] *a* haggard, wild(-looking); drawn (face).
*****haie** [ɛ] *nf* (*a*) hedge; **h. vive**, quickset hedge (*b*) *Sp:* hurdle; *Turf:* fence; **course de haies**, (i) hurdle race (ii) steeplechase; **400 mètres haies**, 400 metres hurdles (*c*) line, row (of trees, people).
*****haillon** [ajɔ̃] *nm* rag (of clothing); **en haillons**, in rags and tatters.
*****haine** [ɛn] *nf* hatred; hate; **avoir de la h. pour qch, qn**, to hate, detest, sth, s.o. **haineux, -euse** *a* full of hatred, hate. **haineusement** *adv* with hatred.
*****haïr** [air] *vtr* (**je hais, n. haïssons**) *imp* hais) to hate, detest, loathe. **haïssable** *a* hateful, detestable.
*****halage** [alaʒ] *nm* towing; **chemin de h.**, towpath.
*****hâle** [ɑl] *nm* (sun)tan, sunburn. **hâlé** *a* (sun)tanned, sunburnt.
haleine [alɛn] *nf* breath; **avoir mauvaise h.**, to have bad breath; **perdre h.**, to get out of breath; **courir à perdre h.**, to run until one is out of breath; **discuter à perdre h.**, to argue nonstop; **hors d'h.**, out of breath; **travail de longue h.**, long and exacting task; **tenir qn en h.**, to keep s.o. in suspense.
*****haler** [ale] *vtr* to tow; to haul (in).
*****hâler** [ale] *vtr* (*of sun*) to tan, burn, brown.
*****halètement** [alɛtmã] *nm* panting; gasping (for breath); puffing.
*****haleter** [alte] *vi* (**je halète**) to pant; to gasp (for breath); to puff. **haletant** *a* panting, breathless, out of breath; gasping (for breath).
*****hall** [ɔl] *nm* entrance hall; (hotel) foyer; **h. de gare**, arrival, departure, hall.
*****halle** [al] *nf* (covered) market; **les Halles (centrales)**, the Central Market (of Paris).
*****hallier** [alje] *nm* thicket, copse, brake.
hallucination [alysinasjɔ̃] *nf* hallucination, delusion. **hallucinant** *a* staggering.
*****halo** [alo] *nm* 1. *Meteor:* halo 2. *Phot:* halation.
*****halte** [alt] *nf* 1. stop, halt; **faire h.**, to make a halt, to

(come to a) stop **2.** stopping place, resting place; *Rail:* halt.

haltère [altɛr] *nm* dumbbell; barbell; **faire des haltères,** to do weightlifting.

haltérophilie [alterɔfili] *nf* weightlifting.

*****hamac** [amak] *nm* hammock.

*****Hambourg** [ãbur] *Prnm Geog:* Hamburg. ***hambourgeois, -oise** *a & n* native, inhabitant, of Hamburg; Hamburger.

*****hameau, -eaux** [amo], *nm* hamlet.

hameçon [amsɔ̃] *nm* (fish) hook; **mordre à l'h.,** to rise to the bait.

*****hampe** [ãp] *nf* **1.** staff, pole (of flag); shaft (of spear) **2.** *Cu:* (a) thin flank (of beef) (b) breast (of venison).

*****hamster** [amster] *nm Z:* hamster.

*****hanche** [ãʃ] *nf* **1.** hip; **les (deux) poings sur les hanches,** with arms akimbo **2.** haunch (of horse); *pl* hindquarters.

*****handicap** [ãdikap] *nm* handicap.

*****handicaper** [ãdikape] *vtr* to handicap. **handicapé, -ée** *a & n* handicapped (person); **les handicapés,** the disabled.

*****hangar** [ãgar] *nm* **1.** (open) shed; shelter; depot; **h. à bateaux,** boathouse **2.** *Av:* hangar.

*****hanneton** [antɔ̃] *nm Ent:* cockchafer, maybug.

*****hanter** [ãte] *vtr* (*of ghost*) to haunt; **être hanté par une idée,** to be obsessed by an idea.

*****hantise** [ãtiz] *nf* haunting memory; obsession.

*****happer** [ape] *vtr* (*of birds*) to snap up, snatch, seize, catch (insects); **la voiture a été happée par un train,** the car was hit by a train.

*****harangue** [arãg] *nf* harangue, speech.

*****haranguer** [arãge] *vtr* (a) to harangue (b) to lecture (s.o.).

*****haras** [ara] *nm* stud farm.

*****harassement** [arasmã] *nm* fatigue, exhaustion.

*****harasser** [arase] *vtr* to tire (out), exhaust.

*****harcèlement** [arsɛlmã] *nm* harassing, tormenting.

*****harceler** [arsəle] *vtr* (**je harcèle**) to harass, torment; **h. qn de questions,** to pester, plague, s.o. with questions.

*****hardes** [ard] *nfpl* (worn) clothes.

*****hardiesse** [ardjɛs] *nf* (a) boldness, daring (b) impudence, effrontery; **il a eu la h. de me tourner le dos,** he had the audacity, the cheek, to turn his back on me. **hardi** *a* (a) bold; daring, fearless (b) rash (c) impudent (d) **h. les gars!** come on lads! **hardiment** *adv* boldly; daringly; rashly; impudently.

*****harem** [arɛm] *nm* harem.

*****hareng** [arã] *nm* herring; **h. bouffi,** bloater; **h. saur,** smoked herring; **h. (salé et) fumé,** kipper.

*****hargne** [arɲ] *nf* bad temper, surliness; aggressiveness. **hargneux, -euse** *a* snarling (dog); bad tempered, cantankerous, aggressive (person). **hargneusement** *adv* viciously, aggressively.

*****haricot** [ariko] *nm* **1.** *Cu:* **h. de mouton,** Irish stew **2. h. blanc,** haricot bean; **h. vert,** French bean; **h. à rames,** runner bean; *P:* **c'est la fin des haricots,** it's the bloody limit.

harmonica [armɔnika] *nm Mus:* harmonica, mouth organ.

harmonie [armɔni] *nf* **1.** (a) harmony; agreement; **en h. avec,** in keeping with; **vivre en h.,** to get on well (**avec,** with) (b) harmoniousness **2.** *Mus:* harmony.

harmonieux, -euse *a* (a) harmonious, tuneful (sound) (b) harmonious (family); (*of colours*) well matched. **harmonieusement** *adv* harmoniously.

harmonisation [armɔnizasjɔ̃] *nf* harmonization.

harmoniser [armɔnize] *vtr* **1.** to harmonize; to match (colours) **2. s'h.,** to harmonize, agree (**avec,** with); (*of colours*) to tone in (**avec,** with), to match.

harmonium [armɔnjɔm] *nm Mus:* harmonium.

*****harnachement** [arnaʃmã] *nm* **1.** harnessing (of horse) **2.** (a) harness (b) saddlery **3.** *F:* rig-out.

*****harnacher** [arnaʃe] *vtr* to harness; *F:* to rig (s.o.) out.

*****harnais** [arnɛ] *nm* (a) harness (b) saddlery.

*****harpe** [arp] *nf Mus:* harp.

*****harpie** [arpi] *nf Myth: Fig:* harpy.

*****harpiste** [arpist] *n* harpist.

*****harpon** [arpɔ̃] *nm* harpoon; **pêche au h.,** spear fishing.

*****harponner** [arpɔne] *vtr* **1.** to harpoon **2.** *P:* (a) to arrest, collar (s.o.) (b) to stop, corner (s.o.).

*****hasard** [azar] *nm* (a) chance, luck, accident; **coup de h.,** (i) stroke of luck (ii) fluke; **jeu de h.,** game of chance; **ne rien laisser au h.,** to leave nothing to chance; **le h. a voulu que,** as luck would have it; **au h.,** haphazardly, at random; **par h.,** by accident, by chance; **si par h. vous le voyez,** if you happen to see him (b) risk, danger; **à tout h.,** on the off chance; just in case; **les hasards de la guerre,** the hazards of war.

*****hasarder** [azarde] *vtr* **1.** to risk; to venture, hazard (one's life, a guess) **2.** to take risks; **se h. à faire qch,** to venture to do sth. **hasardeux, -euse** *a* hazardous, perilous, risky, rash.

*****hâte** [at] *nf* haste, hurry; **avoir h. de faire qch.,** (i) to be in a hurry to do sth (ii) to be eager, to long, to do sth; **à la h.,** in haste, hastily; **en toute h.,** with all possible speed, posthaste; **sans h.,** deliberately, in a leisurely way.

*****hâter** [ate] *vtr* **1.** to hasten; to hurry (sth) on; to accelerate (proceedings); **h. le pas,** to quicken one's pace **2. se h.,** to hasten, hurry. **hâtif, -ive** *a* (a) forward, early (spring, fruit); premature (decision); precocious (fruit) (b) hasty, hurried, ill-considered (plan). **hâtivement** *adv* hastily, hurriedly.

*****hausse** [os] *nf* rise, rising; increase (in prices); **être en h.,** to be going up (in price); *Fig:* **les affaires sont en h.,** things are looking up.

*****haussement** [osmã] *nm* **h. d'épaules,** shrug.

*****hausser** [ose] *vtr* **1.** to raise, lift; to heighten (wall); **h. les épaules,** to shrug (one's shoulders) **2. se h. sur la pointe des pieds,** to stand on tiptoe; **se h. jusqu'à qn,** to raise oneself to s.o.'s level.

*****haut** [o] **1.** *a* (a) high; tall (grass); lofty (building); **homme de haute taille,** tall man; **mur h. de six mètres,** wall six metres high; **haute mer,** high seas, open sea; **à mer haute,** at high tide (b) important, great; **de h. rang,** of high rank; **h. fonctionnaire,** high-ranking official; **haute finance,** high finance; **haute cuisine,** haute cuisine (c) raised; **marcher la tête haute,** to carry one's head high; **voix haute,** (i) loud voice (ii) high(-pitched) voice; **lire à haute voix,** to read aloud (d) **haute trahison,** high treason; **être h. en couleur,** (i) to have a high colour (ii) to be colourful; *WTel:* **haute fréquence,** high frequency (e) upper, higher; **le plus h. étage,** the top floor; **la plus haute branche,** the topmost branch; **les hautes classes,** (i) the upper classes (ii) *Sch:* the upper forms; *P:* **la haute,** the upper crust; *Geog:* **le h. Rhin,** the upper Rhine 2. *adv* (*a*) high (up), above, up; **h. les mains!** hands up! **parler h.,** to speak loudly; **parlez plus h.!** speak up! **penser tout h.,** to think aloud, out loud; **viser h.,** to aim high; **h. placé,** in a high position; in high places (*b*) back; **voir plus h.,** see above; **remonter plus h.,** to go further back (in time) 3. *nm* (*a*) height; **avoir deux mètres de h.,** to be two metres tall, high; **tomber de h.,** (i) to fall from one's high position (ii) to be taken aback (*b*) top; upper part; **h. de la table,** head of the table; **les hauts et les bas,** the ups and downs (of life); **l'étage du h.,** the top floor; **du h. de la falaise,** down from the cliff; **de h. en bas,** (i) downwards (ii) from top to bottom; **regarder qn de h. en bas,** to look s.o. up and down; **traiter qn de h.,** to patronize s.o.; to look down on s.o.; **du h. en bas,** from top to bottom; **en h.,** (i) above (ii) upstairs; **au h., en h., d'une échelle,** at the top of a ladder; **d'en h.,** (i) from above (ii) from upstairs. **hautement** *adv* (*a*) highly (esteemed) (*b*) openly, boldly.

****hautain** [otɛ̃] *a* haughty.

****hautbois** [obwa] *nm Mus:* oboe.

****haut-de-forme** [odfɔrm] *nm* top hat; *pl* **hauts-de-forme.**

****hauteur** [otœr] *nf* 1. (*a*) height, elevation; altitude; *Av:* **prendre de la h.,** to climb; **à la h. de qch,** abreast of, level with, sth; **arriver à la h. de qch,** to draw level with sth; **à la h. des yeux,** at eye level; **être, se montrer, à la h. d'une tâche,** to be equal to a task; *F:* **être à la h.,** to be up to it; *Sp:* **saut en h.,** high jump (*b*) depth; **h. libre, de passage,** headroom (of bridge); clearance (*c*) *Mus:* pitch (of note) (*d*) loftiness (of ideas) 2. haughtiness 3. height; hilltop.

****haut-fond** [ofɔ̃] *nm* shoal, shallow (in sea, river); *pl* **hauts-fonds.**

****haut(-)fourneau** [ofurno] *nm* blast furnace; *pl* **hauts-fourneaux.**

****haut-le-cœur** [olkœr] *nm inv* heave (of stomach); **avoir un h.-le-c.,** to retch.

****haut-le-corps** [olkɔr] *nm inv* sudden start, jump.

****haut-parleur** [oparlœr] *nm WTel:* (loud)speaker; *pl* **haut-parleurs.**

****Havane** [avan] 1. *prnf Geog:* Havana 2. *nm* Havana (cigar).

****hâve** [ɑv] *a* haggard, gaunt; sunken (cheeks).

****havre** [ɑvr] *nm Lit:* haven, port; harbour.

****havresac** [avrəsak] *nm* haversack; (workman's) tool bag.

Hawaï [awaj(i)] *Prnm Geog:* Hawaii. **hawaïen, -ïenne** *a & n Geog:* Hawaiian.

****Haye (la)** [laɛ] *Prnf Geog:* the Hague.

****hayon** [ajɔ̃] *nm* (*a*) rear door (of van) (*b*) hatchback (of car).

****hé** [e] *int* 1. (*to call attention*) hey! 2. well! **hé oui!** yes indeed!

hebdomadaire [ɛbdɔmadɛr] *a & nm* weekly.

hébergement [ebɛrʒəmɑ̃] *nm* lodging, sheltering; putting up, taking-in.

héberger [ebɛrʒe] *vtr* (**n. hébergeons**) to lodge, shelter; to put (s.o.) up, to take (s.o.) in.

hébétement [ebɛtmɑ̃] *nm* stupefaction.

hébéter [ebete] *vtr* **j'hébète; j'hébéterai**) to stupefy; to daze. **hébété** *a* dazed, vacant, bewildered.

hébraïque [ebraik] *a* Hebraic, Hebrew.

hébreu, -eux [ebrø] 1. *a m & nm* (**hébraïque** *is used for the f*) Hebrew 2. *nm Ling:* Hebrew; *F:* **c'est de l'h. pour moi,** it's all Greek to me.

H EC *abbr Hautes études commerciales.*

hécatombe [ekatɔ̃b] *nf* slaughter.

hectare [ɛktar] *nm* hectare (= 2.47 acres).

hectolitre [ɛktɔlitr] *nm* hectolitre.

hectomètre [ɛktɔmɛtr] *nm* hectometre.

****hein** [ɛ̃] *int* (*a*) eh? what? (*b*) **il fait beau aujourd'hui, h.?** fine day. isn't it?

hélas [elɑs] *int* alas! **h. non,** I'm afraid not.

****héler** [ele] *vtr* (**je hèle; jé hèlerai**) to hail, call (a taxi); to hail (a ship).

hélice [elis] *nf Nau: Av:* propeller, screw.

hélicoptère [elikɔptɛr] *nm* helicopter.

héligare [eligar] *nf* heliport.

héliport [elipɔr] *nm* heliport. **héliporté** *a* transported by helicopter.

hélium [eljɔm] *nm Ch:* helium.

hellénique [elenik] *a* Hellenic.

helvétique [ɛlvetik] *a* Swiss.

****hem** [ɛm] *int* (a)hem! hm!

hématie [emati] *nf* red blood corpuscle.

hématome [ematom] *nm Med:* h(a)ematoma, bruise.

hémicycle [emisikl] *nm Arch:* hemicycle; **l'h. de la Chambre,** the floor of the Chamber (of Deputies).

hémisphère [emisfɛr] *nm* hemisphere; **l'h. nord, sud,** the northern, southern, hemisphere. **hémisphérique** *a* hemispheric(al).

hémoglobine [emɔɡlɔbin] *nf* h(a)emoglobin.

hémophilie [emɔfili] *nf Med:* h(a)emophilia. **hémophile** 1. *a* h(a)emophilic 2. *n* h(a)emophiliac.

hémorragie [emɔraʒi] *nf Med:* h(a)emorrhage; bleeding.

hémorroïdes [emɔrɔid] *nfpl Med:* h(a)emorrhoids, piles.

hémostatique [emɔstatik] *a & nm* h(a)emostatic.

****hennir** [ɛnir] *vi* to whinny; to neigh.

hennissement [ɛnismɑ̃] *nm* whinny(ing), neigh(ing).

****hep** [ɛp] *int* hey (there)!

hépatite [epatit] *nf Med:* hepatitis. **hépatique** 1. *a* hepatic 2. *n* person suffering from a liver complaint.

héraldique [eraldik] 1. *a* heraldic 2. *nf* heraldry.

****héraut** [ero] *nm Hist: Fig:* herald.

herbacé [ɛrbase] *a Bot:* herbaceous.

herbage [ɛrbaʒ] *nm* 1. grassland; pasture 2. grass, herbage.

herbe [ɛrb] *nf* 1. herb, plant; **fines herbes,** herbs (for seasoning); mixed herbs; **mauvaise h.,** weed 2. grass; **couper l'h. sous le pied de qn,** to cut the ground from under s.o.'s feet 3. **en h.,** (i) unripe (wheat) (ii) budding (poet). **herbeux, -euse** *a* grassy. **herbivore** *Z:* 1. *a* herbivorous 2. *nm* herbivore.

herbicide [ɛrbisid] *nm* weed killer.

herbier [ɛrbje] *nm* herbarium.

herboriste [ɛrbɔrist] *n* herbalist.

herboristerie [ɛrbɔristəri] *nf* 1. herbalist's shop 2. herb trade.

Hercule [ɛryl] *Prnm* Hercules; **travail d'H.,** Herculean task. **herculéen, -enne** *a* Herculean.

hérédité [eredite] nf 1. Biol: heredity 2. Jur: right of inheritance. **héréditaire** a hereditary.

hérésie [erezi] nf heresy. **hérétique** 1. a heretical 2. n heretic.

*****hérisser** [erise] vtr 1. (a) to bristle (up); (of bird) to ruffle (feathers) (b) to make (sth) bristle; to cover with spikes; to make hair stand on end; **planche hérissée de clous**, plank spiked with nails; **h. un texte de citations**, to fill a text with quotations; **h. qn**, to get s.o.'s back up 2. **se h.**, to bristle (up); (of hair) to stand on end; (of pers) to get one's back up. **hérissé** a 1. bristling (de, with) 2. (of hair) standing on end; spiky, bristly; prickly.

*****hérisson** [erisɔ̃] nm Z: hedgehog.

héritage [eritaʒ] nm inheritance, heritage; **faire un h.**, to receive a legacy; **laisser qch en h. à qn**, to leave sth to s.o.

hériter [erite] 1. vi **h. d'une fortune**, to inherit a fortune 2. vtr **h. qch de qn**, to inherit sth from s.o.

héritier, -ière [eritje, -jɛr] n heir, f heiress.

hermétisme [ɛrmetism] nm 1. hermetism 2. abstruseness, obscurity (of text). **hermétique** a 1. tight (closed), hermetically sealed; hermetic (seal); airtight, watertight (joint) 2. abstruse, obscure (text). **hermétiquement** adv hermetically.

hermine [ɛrmin] nf 1. Z: stoat, ermine 2. Com: ermine (fur).

*****hernie** [ɛrni] nf 1. Med: hernia, rupture; **h. discale**, slipped disc 2. Aut: bulge, swelling (in tyre).

héroïne[1] [erɔin] nf heroine.

héroïne[2] nf Ch: heroin.

héroïsme [erɔism] nm heroism. **héroïque** a heroic. **héroïquement** adv heroically.

*****héron** [erɔ̃] nm Orn: heron.

*****héros** [ero] nm hero.

herpès [ɛrpɛs] nm Med: herpes.

*****herse** [ɛrs] nf 1. Agr: harrow 2. portcullis.

*****herser** [ɛrse] vtr Agr: to harrow.

hertz [ɛrts] nm El: hertz. **hertzien, -ienne** a Hertzian.

hésitation [ezitasjɔ̃] nf hesitation; **parler avec h.**, to speak hesitatingly; **sans h.**, unhesitatingly, without faltering.

hésiter [ezite] vi 1. to hesitate, waver; **h. à faire qch**, to be reluctant to do sth; **il n'y a pas à h.**, there's no time for hesitation 2. to falter (in speaking). **hésitant** a hesitant, wavering, faltering.

hétéroclite [eterɔklit] a heterogeneous, ill-assorted (collection).

hétérogène [eterɔʒɛn] a (a) heterogeneous, dissimilar (b) incongruous (collection); mixed (society).

*****hêtre** [ɛtr] nm beech (tree, wood).

heure [œr] nf (a) hour; **heures d'affluence, de pointe**, rush hour, peak period; **heures creuses**, off-peak hours; Journ: **(la) dernière h.**, stop press (news); **cent kilomètres à l'h.**, a hundred kilometres an hour; **payé à l'h.**, paid by the hour; **30 francs l'h.**, F: de l'h., 30 francs an hour; **semaine de 40 heures**, 40-hour week; **heures supplémentaires**, overtime (b) (time of day) **h. légale**, standard time; **h. d'été**, summer time; **quelle h. est-il?** what time is it? **quelle h. avez-vous?** what time do you make it? **cinq heures moins dix**, ten (minutes) to five; **dix-huit heures**, eighteen hundred (hours); six p.m.; **le train de neuf heures**, the nine o'clock train;

à une h. avancée, late in the day; **mettre sa montre à l'h.**, to set one's watch (right) (c) (appointed time) **l'heure d'aller se coucher**, bedtime; **h. d'éclairage**, lighting-up time; **à l'h. dite**, at the appointed time; **être à l'h.**, to be punctual, on time; **à ses heures, il était charmant**, when he felt like it he could be charming; **il est, c'est, l'h.**, (i) it's time (ii) time is up (d) (present time) **question de l'h.**, for the present; for the time being; **la question de l'h.**, the question of the moment; **à l'h. qu'il est**, (i) by this time, by now (ii) nowadays; now; currently (e) time, period; Sch: **h. de cours**, period; **cette mode a eu son h.**, this fashion has had its day; **j'attends mon h.**, I'm biding my time (f) **de bonne h.**, early; **de meilleure h.**, earlier; **faire qch sur l'h.**, to do sth right away; **à toute h.**, at any time; at all hours of the day; **tout à l'h.**, (i) just now, a few minutes ago (ii) soon, presently, directly; **à tout à l'h.!** so long! see you later! (g) int **à la bonne h.!** well done! good (for you)! fine!

heureux, -euse [œrø, -øz] a 1. happy; **h. comme un poisson dans l'eau**, (as) happy as a sandboy; **vivre h.**, to live happily; **je suis très h. de ce cadeau**, I'm very pleased with this present; **nous serions h. que vous acceptiez**, we should be glad if you would accept 2. (a) successful; **l'issue heureuse des négociations**, the happy outcome of the negotiations (b) fortunate (pers); **h. au jeu**, lucky at cards 3. (a) favourable; lucky, fortunate; **par un h. hasard**, by a fortunate coincidence; Iron: **c'est encore h.!** thank goodness for that! it's just as well! (b) **début h.**, auspicious beginning 4. felicitous, happy, apt (phrase). **heureusement** adv happily; successfully; luckily, fortunately; **il est venu, h.!** thank goodness he came!

*****heurt** [œr] nm shock, knock; collision; clash; **tout s'est fait sans h.**, everything went smoothly.

*****heurter** [œrte] vtr & i 1. (a) to knock (against), run into, bump into, bang into (s.o., sth); to collide with (s.o.) (b) **h. à la porte**, to knock on the door (c) to shock, offend (s.o.'s feelings); to go against (conventions) 2. **se h.** (a) **se h. à, contre, qch**, to run into, to collide with, sth; **se h. la tête contre qch**, to bump, bang, one's head against sth; **se h. à une difficulté**, to come up against a difficulty (b) (of vehicles) to collide; (of colours) to clash. **heurté** a clashing (colours); jerky (style).

hexagone [ɛgzagon] nm (a) hexagon (b) **l'H. (français)**, France. **hexagonal, -aux** a hexagonal.

HF abbr haute fréquence.

hibernation [ibɛrnasjɔ̃] nf hibernation.

hiberner [ibɛrne] vi to hibernate.

*****hibou, -oux** [ibu] nm Orn: owl; **jeune h.**, owlet.

*****hic** [ik] nm F: **voilà le h.**, that's the snag.

*****hideur** [idœr] nf hideousness; hideous sight. **hideux, -euse** a hideous. **hideusement** adv hideously.

hier [jɛr] 1. adv yesterday; **h. (au) soir**, last night; F: **je ne suis pas né d'h.**, I wasn't born yesterday 2. nm toute **la journée d'h.**, all day yesterday.

*****hiérarchie** [jerarʃi] nf hierarchy. **hiérarchique** a hierarchical; **par (la) voie h.**, through (the) official channels. **hiérarchiquement** adv hierarchically.

*****hiéroglyphe** [jerɔglif] nm hieroglyph.

*****hi-fi** [ifi] a & nf WTel: etc: F: hi-fi, high-fidelity.

hilarité [ilarite] nf hilarity, mirth, laughter. hilare a mirthful, hilarious.

hindouisme [ɛ̃duism] nm Hinduism. hindou, -e a & n Hindu.

*hippie [ipi] a & n F: hippie, hippy.

hippique [ipik] a concours h., horse show; sport h., equestrian sport.

hippocampe [ipokɑ̃p] nm Ich: sea horse.

hippodrome [ipɔdrom] nm racecourse.

hippopotame [ipɔpɔtam] nm Z: hippopotamus.

hirondelle [irɔ̃dɛl] nf Orn: swallow; h. de fenêtre, house martin.

hirsute [irsyt] a hairy, shaggy.

hispanique [ispanik] a Hispanic.

*hisser [ise] vtr 1. to hoist (up), pull up 2. se h. jusqu'à la fenêtre, to pull oneself up to the window; se h. sur la pointe des pieds, to stand on tiptoe.

histoire [istwar] nf 1. (a) history; l'H. sainte, Bible history; la petite h., sidelights on history (b) h. naturelle, natural history (c) Sch: history book 2. story, tale; livre d'histoires, story book; h. de fous, shaggy dog story; c'est toujours la même h., it's always the same old story; F: il est sorti, h. de prendre l'air, he went out just to get some air; F: en voilà une h.! what a lot of fuss! c'est toute une h., (i) it's a long story (ii) it's no end of a job 3. F: fib, story; tout ça c'est des histoires, that's all bunkum 4. F: faire des histoires, to make a fuss; il faut éviter d'avoir des histoires, we must keep out of trouble; pas d'histoires! no fuss! 5. F: thing(ummy). historique 1. a historic(al); monument h., ancient monument 2. nm historical record; history; faire l'h. des événements, to give a chronological account of events. historiquement adv historically.

historien, -ienne [istɔrjɛ̃, -jɛn] n historian.

hiver [ivɛr] nm winter; en h., in winter; temps d'h., wintry weather; vêtements, sports, d'h., winter clothes, sports.

hivernage [ivɛrnaʒ] nm 1. wintering (of cattle) 2. winter season.

hiverner [ivɛrne] vi to winter. hivernal, -aux a winter (cold); wintry (weather).

HLM abbr Habitation à loyer modéré.

*hochement [ɔʃmɑ̃] nm h. de tête, (i) shake of the head (ii) nod.

*hocher [ɔʃe] vtr & i h. la tête, (i) to shake one's head (ii) to nod.

*hochet [ɔʃɛ] nm (child's) rattle.

*hockey [ɔkɛ] nm Sp: hockey; h. sur glace, ice hockey.

*holà [ola] int 1. hallo! 2. stop! hold on! whoa! mettre le h. à qch, to put a stop to sth.

*holding [ɔldiŋ] nm Fin: holding company.

*hold-up [ɔldœp] nm inv F: hold-up.

*Hollande [ɔlɑ̃d] 1. Prnf Geog: Holland 2. nm (fromage de) h., Dutch cheese. hollandais, -aise 1. a Dutch 2. n Dutchman, -woman; les H., the Dutch 3. nm Ling: Dutch.

holocauste [ɔlɔkost] nm holocaust.

*homard [ɔmar] nm lobster.

homélie [ɔmeli] nf homily.

homéopathe [ɔmeɔpat] n hom(o)eopath.

homéopathie [ɔmeɔpati] nf hom(o)eopathy. homéopathique a hom(o)eopathic.

homérique [ɔmerik] a Homeric.

homicide [ɔmisid] nm homicide; h. volontaire, murder; h. involontaire, par imprudence, manslaughter.

hommage [ɔmaʒ] nm 1. homage; rendre h. à qn, to pay homage, tribute, to s.o. 2. pl respects, compliments; présenter ses hommages à une dame, to pay one's respects to a lady 3. tribute, token (of respect); h. de l'éditeur, complimentary copy; h. de l'auteur, with the author's compliments.

homme [ɔm] nm (a) man; mankind; de mémoire d'h., within living memory; les droits de l'h., human rights (b) (as opposed to woman or boy) parler à qn d'h. à h., to speak to s.o. man to man; P: mon h., my husband; h. à femmes, ladykiller; Com: rayon hommes, menswear (department), men's department (c) (individual) ce n'est pas l'h., qu'il me faut, he is not the man for me; trouver son h., to meet one's match; h. d'État, statesman; h. d'affaires, businessman; h. de peine, labourer; work hand; Nau: h. d'équipage, member of a ship's crew (d) l'abominable h. des neiges, the abominable snowman.

homme-grenouille [ɔmɡrənuj] nm Nau: frogman; pl hommes-grenouilles.

homme-orchestre [ɔmɔrkɛstr] nm one-man band; pl hommes-orchestres.

homme-sandwich [ɔmsɑ̃dwitʃ] nm sandwich-man; pl hommes-sandwich(e)s.

homogène [ɔmɔʒɛn] a homogeneous.

homogénéisation [ɔmɔʒeneizasjɔ̃] nf homogenization.

homogénéiser [ɔmɔʒeneize] vtr to homogenize.

homogénéité [ɔmɔʒeneite] nf homogeneity.

homologation [ɔmɔlɔgasjɔ̃] nf (official) approval (of appliance); Sp: ratification (of record).

homologue [ɔmɔlɔg] 1. a homologous 2. (a) nm homologue (b) n opposite number.

homologuer [ɔmɔlɔge] vtr 1. (a) Jur: to confirm, endorse (deed); ratify (decision); to grant probate of (will) (b) to approve (appliance) 2. (a) Jur: to prove (will) (b) prix homologués, authorized charges 3. Sp: to ratify (record); record homologué, official record.

homonyme [ɔmɔnim] 1. a homonymous 2. nm (a) homonym (b) namesake.

homosexualité [ɔmɔsɛksɥalite] nf homosexuality. homosexuel, -elle a homosexual.

*Hongrie [ɔ̃gri] Prnf Geog: Hungary. hongrois, -oise a & n Hungarian.

honnêteté [ɔnɛte] nf 1. honesty, integrity 2. courtesy 3. decency 4. fairness. honnête a 1. honest, honourable, upright 2. courteous (envers, to); h. homme, gentleman 3. decent, becoming 4. reasonable, fair. honnêtement adv honestly; courteously; decently; fairly.

honneur [ɔnœr] nm 1. honour; mettre son h. à faire qch, to be in honour bound, to make it a point of honour, to do sth; (ma) parole d'h.! (on) my word of honour! se faire h. de qch, to be proud of sth; cour d'h., main quadrangle 2. (a) réception en l'h. de qn, reception in honour of s.o.; invité d'h., guest of honour; président d'h., honorary president; faire h. au dîner, to do justice to the dinner; à qui ai-je l'h. (de parler)? to whom do I have the honour of speaking? j'ai l'h. de vous faire savoir que, I beg to inform you that; Games: à vous l'h., after you; jouer pour l'h., to play for love (b) credit; **faire h. à son pays,** to be a credit to one's country **3.** *pl (marks of esteem)* **rendre les derniers honneurs à qn,** to pay the last tribute to s.o.; **faire (à qn) les honneurs de la maison,** to do (s.o.) the honours of the house **4. faire h. à sa signature,** to honour one's signature **5.** *Cards:* **les honneurs,** honours.

honorabilité [ɔnɔrabilite] *nf (a)* honourable character *(b)* respectability. **honorable** *a (a)* honourable; **vieillesse h.,** respected old age *(b)* respectable; reputable; creditable (performance). **honorablement** *adv* honourably; creditably.

honoraire [ɔnɔrɛr] **1.** *a* honorary; **professeur h.,** emeritus professor **2.** *nmpl* fee(s) (of professional man); honorarium; (lawyer's) retainer.

honorer [ɔnɔre] *vtr* **1.** *(a)* to honour; to respect; **mon honoré confrère,** my respected colleague *(b)* to do honour to (s.o.); **h. une cérémonie de sa présence,** to grace a ceremony with one's presence *(c) Com:* to honour, meet (bill) *(d)* to do credit to (s.o.) **2. s'h.** *(a)* to gain distinction *(b)* **s'h. de qch,** to be proud of sth.

honorifique [ɔnɔrifik] *a* honorary (title, rank).

***honte** [ɔ̃t] *nf* **1.** *(a)* (sense of) shame; **sans h.,** shamelessly; **à ma grande h.,** to my shame; **avoir h.,** to be ashamed (of oneself); **faire h. à qn,** to put s.o. to shame *(b)* **fausse h.,** bashfulness, self-consciousness **2.** (cause of) shame, disgrace; **couvrir qn de h.,** to bring shame, disgrace, on s.o.; **quelle h.! c'est une h.!** what a disgrace! it's disgraceful! **honteux, -euse** *a* **1.** ashamed **2.** bashful, shamefaced **3.** shameful, disgraceful; **c'est h.!** it's disgraceful! **honteusement** *adv* shamefully, disgracefully.

hôpital, -aux [ɔpital, -o] *nm* hospital, infirmary; **salle d'h.,** ward.

***hoquet** [ɔkɛ] *nm* hiccup, hiccough; **avoir le h.,** to have (the) hiccups.

***hoqueter** [ɔkte] *vi* **(je hoquette, n. hoquetons)** to hiccup, hiccough.

horaire [ɔrɛr] **1.** *a (a)* **signal h.,** time signal *(b)* hourly; **débit h.,** output per hour **2.** *nm* timetable; schedule.

***horde** [ɔrd] *nf* horde.

horizon [ɔrizɔ̃] *nm* horizon, skyline; **la ligne d'h.,** the horizon; **à l'h.,** (i) on the horizon (ii) below the horizon; **tour d'h. politique,** political survey. **horizontal, -aux 1.** *a* horizontal **2.** *nf* **horizontale** *(a)* horizontal; **à l'h.,** in the horizontal position *(b)* horizontal line. **horizontalement** *adv* horizontally.

horloge [ɔrlɔʒ] *nf* clock; **h. normande,** grandfather clock; **l'h. parlante,** the speaking clock; **il est deux heures à l'h.,** it's two by the clock. **horloger, -ère 1.** *a* watchmaking (industry) **2.** *n* clock and watchmaker.

horlogerie [ɔrlɔʒri] *nf* **1.** clockmaking; watchmaking; **mouvement d'h.,** clockwork **2.** watchmaker's, clockmaker's (shop).

***hormis** [ɔrmi] *prep* except, save.

hormone [ɔrmɔn] *nf* hormone. **hormonal, -aux** *a* hormonal, hormone.

hormonothérapie [ɔrmɔnɔterapi] *nf* hormonotherapy, hormone treatment.

horoscope [ɔrɔskɔp] *nm* horoscope.

horreur [ɔrœr] *nf* **1.** horror; **frappé d'h.,** horror-stricken **2.** horror, repugnance, disgust; **faire h. à qn,** to horrify s.o.; **avoir qch en h.,** to have a horror of sth; to loathe, detest, sth **3.** horror, awfulness **4.** *(a)* horror, hideousness; **quelle h.!** (i) how revolting! (ii) what a frightful object! *(b)* **les horreurs de la guerre,** the horrors of war; **commettre des horreurs,** to commit atrocities.

horrible [ɔribl] *a* horrible, awful; dreadful; horrid; hideous (sight). **horriblement** *adv* horribly, awfully, dreadfully.

horrifier [ɔrifje] *vtr (imp & pr sub n. horrifiions, v. horrifiiez)* to horrify. **horrifique** *adv* horrific, hair-raising.

horripilant [ɔripilɑ̃] *a* exasperating, maddening.

***hors** [ɔr] *prep (liaison with r:* **hors elle** [ɔrɛl]) **1. longueur h. tout,** overall length; **h. taxe,** exclusive of tax; tax free; duty-free; **h. d'usage,** out of action, unserviceable **2. h. de,** out of, outside (of); **h. d'ici!** get out (of here)! **être h. d'affaire,** to have got through one's difficulties; *(of sick pers)* to be out of danger; **h. de portée,** out of reach; **h. de là,** apart from that, otherwise; **il est h. de lui,** he's beside himself; **c'est h. de prix,** it's prohibitive, exorbitant.

***hors-bord** [ɔrbɔr] *nm inv* (outboard) motor boat; speedboat.

***hors-concours** [ɔrkɔ̃kur] **1.** *adv* not competing, hors concours **2.** *a inv* ineligible to compete.

***hors-d'œuvre** [ɔrdœvr] *nm inv Cu:* hors d'œuvre; starter.

***hors-jeu** [ɔrʒø] *a & nm inv Sp:* offside.

***hors-la-loi** [ɔrlalwa] *nm inv* outlaw.

***hors-texte** [ɔrtɛkst] *nm inv* (inset) plate (in book).

hortensia [ɔrtɑ̃sja] *nm Bot:* hydrangea.

horticulteur [ɔrtikyltœr] *nm* horticulturist.

horticulture [ɔrtikyltyr] *nf* horticulture; gardening. **horticole** *a* horticultural.

hospice [ɔspis] *nm* **1.** hospice **2.** old people's home; children's home.

hospitalier, -ière [ɔspitalje, -jɛr] *a* **1.** hospitable **2. personnel h.,** hospital staff.

hospitalisation [ɔspitalizasjɔ̃] *nf* hospitalization.

hospitaliser [ɔspitalize] *vtr* to send (s.o.) to hospital; to hospitalize (s.o.).

hospitalité [ɔspitalite] *nf* hospitality.

hostie [ɔsti] *nf* (eucharistic) host.

hostilité [ɔstilite] *nf* **1.** hostility **(contre, envers, to(wards))**; enmity, ill-will **2.** *pl* hostilities. **hostile** *a* hostile; unfriendly.

hôte, hôtesse [ot, otɛs] *n* **1.** host, *f* hostess; landlord, landlady (of tavern); **hôtesse de l'air,** air hostess **2.** *(f* hôte*)* guest, visitor; **h. payant,** paying guest.

hôtel [otɛl] *nm* **1. h. (particulier),** mansion, town house **2. h. de ville,** town hall; **l'h. des Monnaies** = the Mint; **l'H. des ventes,** salesrooms (in Paris) **3.** *(a)* hotel *(b)* **h. meublé,** residential hotel (providing lodging but not board). **hôtelier, -ière 1.** *n* innkeeper; hotel keeper **2.** *a* **l'industrie hôtelière,** the hotel trade.

hôtellerie [otɛlri] *nf (a)* hostelry, inn, hotel *(b)* **l'h.,** the hotel trade.

hôtesse *see* **hôte.**

***hotte** [ɔt] *nf* **1.** basket (carried on back); (bricklayer's) hod **2.** (cooker) hood.

hou [u] *int* **1.** boo! **2. h. la vilaine!** tut-tut, you naughty girl!

*houblon [ublɔ̃] *nm Bot:* hop(s).

*houe [u] *nf Tls:* hoe.

*houille [uj] *nf* 1. coal 2. h. blanche, hydroelectric power. houiller, -ère 1. *a* coal; coal-bearing 2. *nf* houillère, coalmine; colliery.

*houle [ul] *nf* swell, surge (of sea); grosse h., heavy swell. houleux, -euse *a* heavy, swelling (sea); tumultuous (crowd); réunion houleuse, stormy meeting.

*houppe [up] *nf* (*a*) tuft; pompon (*b*) tassel (*c*) tuft (of hair).

*houppette [upɛt] *nf* powder puff.

*hourra [ura] *int & nm* hurrah(!).

*houspiller [uspije] *vtr* to scold (s.o.), to tell (s.o.) off.

*housse [us] *nf* (*a*) loose cover; *Aut:* seat cover; drap h., fitted sheet (*b*) dust sheet.

*houx [u] *nm Bot:* holly.

HT *abbr* 1. *El:* haute tension 2. hors taxe.

*hublot [yblo] *nm Nau:* porthole, scuttle.

*huche [yʃ] *nf* (*a*) bin; h. à pain, bread bin (*b*) hopper (of flour mill).

*hue [y] *int* (*to horse*) gee up!

*huée [ɥe] *nf* 1. boo, hoot 2. *pl* booing; jeering, jeers.

*huer [ɥe] 1. *vi* (*of owl*) to hoot 2. *vtr* to boo (actor).

huile [ɥil] *nf* oil; h. comestible, de table, edible oil, salad oil; h. de tournesol, sunflower (seed) oil; h. de lin, linseed oil; h. de foie de morue, cod liver oil; h. solaire, suntan oil; h. minérale, mineral oil; peinture à l'h., oil painting; portrait à l'h., portrait in oils; jeter de l'h. sur le feu, to add fuel to the fire; *P:* les huiles, the big shots.

huiler [ɥile] *vtr* to oil; to lubricate, grease. huileux, -euse *a* oily, greasy.

huis [ɥi] *nm A:* door; *Jur:* à h. clos, in camera.

huissier [ɥisje] *nm Jur:* (*a*) process server; = bailiff (*b*) h. audiencier, court usher.

*huit [ɥit] *num a inv & nm inv* (*as card adj before n or adj beginning with a consonant sound* [ɥi]) eight; h. jours, a week; (d')aujourd'hui en h., today week; donner ses h. jours à qn, to give s.o. (a week's) notice. huitième *num a & n* eighth. huitièmement *adv* eighthly.

*huitaine [ɥitɛn] *nf* 1. (about) eight 2. week; dans une h. (de jours), in a week or so.

*huitante [ɥitɑ̃t] *num a inv SwFr:* eighty.

huître [ɥitr] *nf* oyster.

*hululement [ylylmɑ̃] *nm* hoot(ing) (of owl).

*hululer [ylyle] *vi* (*of owl*) to hoot.

humain [ymɛ̃] 1. *a & nm* human; le genre h., human beings; mankind 2. *a* humane. humainement *adv* 1. humanly 2. humanely.

humaniser [ymanize] *vtr* to humanize; to make (s.o.) more humane.

humanisme [ymanism] *nm* humanism. humaniste 1. *a* humanistic 2. *n* humanist.

humanitaire [ymanitɛr] *a* humanitarian.

humanité [ymanite] *nf* (*a*) humanity; human nature (*b*) mankind (*c*) humaneness.

humble [œ̃bl] *a* humble. humblement *adv* humbly.

humecter [ymɛkte] *vtr* to damp(en), moisten.

*humer [yme] *vtr* h. le parfum d'une fleur, to smell a flower; h. l'air frais, to inhale, breathe in, the fresh air.

humérus [ymerys] *nm Anat:* humerus.

humeur [ymœr] *nf* 1. *Anat:* h. aqueuse, aqueous humour (of the eye) 2. (*a*) humour, mood; être de bonne h., to be in a good mood, in high spirits; de mauvaise h., in a bad mood; de méchante h., in a (bad) temper (*b*) temper; temperament; avoir l'h. vive, to be quick-tempered (*c*) *Lit:* bad mood; mouvement d'h., outburst of temper; avec h., irritably.

humide [ymid] *a* damp, moist, humid; wet; dank (cellar); temps h. et chaud, muggy weather; temps h. et froid, raw weather.

humidificateur [ymidifikatœr] *nm* humidifier.

humidification [ymidifikasjɔ̃] *nf* humidification.

humidifier [ymidifje] *vtr* to humidify; to dampen, moisten.

humidité [ymidite] *nf* humidity, damp(ness), moisture; craint l'h., to be kept dry; keep in a dry place; taches d'h., damp patches.

humiliation [ymiljasjɔ̃] *nf* humiliation.

humilier [ymilje] *vtr* 1. to humiliate 2. s'h., to humble oneself. humiliant *a* humiliating.

humilité [ymilite] *nf* humility.

humoriste [ymɔrist] *n* humorist. humoristique *a* humorous; dessin h., cartoon.

humour [ymur] *nm* humour; avoir (le sens) de l'h., to have a (good) sense of humour; h. noir, sick humour.

humus [ymys] *nm* humus.

*hune [yn] *nf Nau:* top.

*huppe [yp] *nf* tuft, crest (of bird).

*huppé [ype] *a F:* smart; high-class, posh.

*hurlement [yrləmɑ̃] *nm* howl(ing); yell(ing); roar(ing).

*hurler [yrle] 1. *vi* to howl; to roar; to yell; h. de douleur, to scream with pain 2. *vtr* to bawl out (song).

hurluberlu [yrlybɛrly] *nm* eccentric, crank.

*hutte [yt] *nf* hut, shed, shanty.

hybridation [ibridasjɔ̃] *nf Biol:* hybridization.

hybrider [ibride] *vtr Biol:* to hybridize, to cross.

hybridité [ibridite] *nf* hybridity.

hydratation [idratasjɔ̃] *nf Ch:* hydration.

hydrate [idrat] *nm Ch:* hydrate; h. de carbone, carbohydrate.

hydrater [idrate] *vtr Ch:* to hydrate, to moisturize. hydratant 1. *a* moisturizing 2. *nm* moisturizer.

hydraulique [idrolik] 1. *a* hydraulic; énergie h., hydroelectric power 2. *nf* (*a*) hydraulics (*b*) hydraulic engineering.

hydravion [idravjɔ̃] *nm* seaplane, hydroplane.

hydrocarbure [idrɔkarbyr] *nm Ch:* hydrocarbon.

hydro-électricité [idrɔelɛktrisite] *nf* hydroelectricity. hydro-électrique *a* hydroelectric.

hydrofoil [idrɔfɔil] *nm Nau:* hydrofoil.

hydrogène [idrɔʒɛn] *nm Ch:* hydrogen.

hydroglisseur [idrɔglisœr] *nm* hydroplane (speedboat).

hydrolyse [idrɔliz] *nf Ch:* hydrolysis.

hydromel [idrɔmɛl] *nm* mead.

hydrophile [idrɔfil] *a* absorbent (cotton wool).

hydropisie [idrɔpizi] *nf Med:* dropsy.

hydroxyde [idrɔksid] *nm Ch:* hydroxide.

hyène [jɛn] *nf Z:* hyena.

hygiène [iʒjɛn] *nf* hygiene; h. publique, public health. hygiénique *a* hygienic; healthy; sanitary; papier h., toilet paper; serviette h., sanitary towel.

hymne [imn] **1.** *nm* patriotic song; **h. national,** national anthem **2.** *nm & f Ecc:* hymn.
hyperbole [ipɛrbɔl] *nf* **1.** hyperbole **2.** *Mth:* hyperbola.
hypercritique [ipɛrkritik] *a* hypercritical, overcritical.
hyperémotivité [ipɛremɔtivite] *nf* hyperemotivity.
hyperfréquence [ipɛrfrekɑ̃s] *nf* ultra high frequency, UHF.
hypermarché [ipɛrmarʃe] *nm* hypermarket.
hypermétropie [ipɛrmetrɔpi] *nf* long-sightedness. **hypermétrope** *a* long-sighted.
hypernerveux, -euse [ipɛrnɛrvø, -øz] *a* highly strung.
hypersensible [ipɛrsɑ̃sibl̩] *a* hypersensitive.
hypertension [ipɛrtɑ̃sjɔ̃] *nf* hypertension, high blood pressure. **hypertendu** *a* suffering from high blood pressure.
hypnose [ipnoz] *nf* hypnosis.

hypnotiser [ipnɔtize] *vtr* to hypnotize. **hypnotique** *a* hypnotic.
hypnotiseur [ipnɔtizœr] *nm* hypnotist.
hypnotisme [ipnɔtism] *nm* hypnotism.
hypocrisie [ipɔkrizi] *nf* hypocrisy. **hypocrite 1.** *a* hypocritical **2.** *n* hypocrite. **hypocritement** *adv* hypocritically.
hypodermique [ipɔdɛrmik] *a* hypodermic.
hypotension [ipɔtɑ̃sjɔ̃] *nf* low blood pressure.
hypoténuse [ipɔtenyz] *nf* hypotenuse.
hypothèque [ipɔtɛk] *nf* mortgage. **hypothécaire** *a* **prêt h.,** mortgage (loan).
hypothéquer [ipɔteke] *vtr* **(j'hypothèque; j'hypothéquerai)** to mortgage; to secure (debt) by mortgage.
hypothèse [ipɔtez] *nf* hypothesis. **hypothétique** *a* hypothetical.
hystérie [isteri] *nf Med:* hysteria. **hystérique 1.** *a* hysterical **2.** *n* hysteric; hysterical person.

I

I, i [i] nm 1. (the letter) I, i 2. i grec, (the letter) Y, y.

ibérique [iberik] a Geog: Iberian; la péninsule i., the Iberian peninsula.

iceberg [isbɛrg] nm iceberg.

ici [isi] adv 1. here; les gens d'i., the local people, the locals; je ne suis pas d'i., I'm a stranger here; i.-bas, here below, on earth; il y a 20 kilomètres d'i. à Paris, it's 20 kilometres from here to Paris; passez par i., this way please; c'est i., this is the place; it's here; Tp: i. Jean, John speaking 2. jusqu'i., until now; up to now; d'i. lundi, between now and Monday, by Monday; d'i. là, by that time, by then; d'i. peu, before long.

icône [ikon] nf icon.

idéal, -als, -aux [ideal, -o] a & nm ideal; le beau i., the ideal of beauty. idéalement adv ideally.

idéaliser [idealize] vtr to idealize.

idéalisme [idealism] nm idealism. idéaliste 1. a idealistic 2. n idealist.

idée [ide] nf 1. (a) idea; notion; je n'en ai pas la moindre i., I haven't the faintest idea; I haven't a clue; on n'a pas i. de cela, you can't imagine it; quelle i.! what an idea! i. de génie, i. lumineuse, brainwave; j'ai i. que, I have an idea, a feeling, that (b) imagination; se faire des idées, to imagine things; i. fixe, obsession (c) view, opinion; (en) faire à son i., to do just what one likes; changer d'i., to change one's mind (d) whim, fancy; comme l'i. m'en prend, just as the fancy takes me; avoir des idées noires, to be worried, depressed 2. mind; j'ai dans l'i. que, I have a notion that; il me vient à l'i. que, it occurs to me that; cela m'est sorti de l'i., it's gone clean out of my head.

identification [idãtifikasjɔ̃] nf identification.

identifier [idãtifje] vtr 1. to identify 2. s'i., to identify (oneself), to become identified (à, avec, with). identifiable a identifiable. identique a identical (à, with). identiquement adv identically.

identité [idãtite] nf identity.

idéologie [ideɔlɔʒi] nf ideology. idéologique a ideological.

idiome [idjom] nm idiom. idiomatique a idiomatic; expression i., idiom.

idiotie [idjɔsi] nf 1. Med: (a) idiocy, imbecility (b) mental deficiency 2. stupidity; faire une i., to do sth stupid. idiot, -ote 1. a (a) Med: idiot (child) (b) idiotic, absurd; senseless (joke); stupid (pers). 2. n (a) Med: idiot, imbecile (b) idiot, fool; faire l'i., (i) to be an idiot (ii) to play the fool. idiotement adv idiotically, stupidly.

idiotisme [idjɔtism] nm idiom; idiomatic expression.

idolâtrer [idɔlatre] vtr to idolize.

idolâtrie [idɔlatri] nf idolatry. idolâtre a idolatrous.

idole [idɔl] nf idol, image; faire une i. de qn, to idolize s.o.

idylle [idil] nf idyll; romance. idyllique a idyllic.

if [if] nm yew (tree).

IFOP [ifɔp] abbr Institut français de l'opinion publique.

igloo, iglou [iglu] nm igloo.

ignare [iɲar] 1. a ignorant 2. n ignoramus.

ignifuger [iɲifyʒe] vtr (j'ignifugeai(s); n. ignifugeons) to fireproof. ignifuge 1. a fireproof 2. nm fireproof(ing) material.

ignoble [iɲɔbl] a (a) base; vile, ignoble; disgraceful (b) wretched, sordid (dwelling).

ignominie [iɲɔmini] nf ignominy, shame; disgrace. ignominieux, -euse a ignominious, shameful, disgraceful.

ignorance [iɲɔrãs] nf ignorance; tenir qn dans l'i. de qch, to keep s.o. in the dark about sth; dans l'i. de, ignorant of. ignorant, -ante. a (a) ignorant (b) ignorant, unaware (de, of) 2. n ignoramus. ignoré a unknown.

ignorer [iɲɔre] vtr 1. (a) not to know (about) (sth); to be ignorant, unaware, of (sth); je n'ignore pas les difficultés, I am aware of the difficulties; il ignore qui je suis, he doesn't know who I am (b) to ignore (s.o.) (c) i. que + sub or ind, not to know, to be unaware, that 2. s'i., not to know oneself; charme qui s'ignore, unconscious charm.

iguane [igwan] nm Rept: iguana.

il, ils [il] 1. pers pron nom m (of pers) he, they; (of thg) it, they; il est écrivain, he's a writer 2. inv it, there (a) il est vrai que j'étais là, it's true that I was there; il est six heures, it's six o'clock; il était une fois, once upon a time (b) (with impers vbs) il pleut, it's raining; il faut partir, we must go; you must go; il y a quelqu'un à la porte, there's someone at the door.

île [il] nf island, isle; habiter dans une î., to live on an island; Cu: î. flottante, floating island.

illégal, -aux [ilegal] a illegal; unlawful. illégalité [ilegalite] nf illegality. illégalement adv illegally, unlawfully.

illégitimité [ileʒitimite] nf illegitimacy (of child); unlawfulness (of marriage). illégitime a illegitimate; unlawful. illégitimement adv illegitimately; unlawfully.

illettré [iletre] a & n illiterate.

illicite [ilisit] a illicit, unlawful. illicitement adv illicitly, unlawfully.

illico [iliko] adv F: at once; pronto.

illimité [ilimite] a unlimited, boundless.

illisibilité [ilizibilite] nf illegibility. illisible a illegible, unreadable. illisiblement adv illegibly.

illogisme [ilɔʒism] nm illogicality. illogique a illogical. illogiquement adv illogically.

illumination [ilyminasjɔ̃] nf 1. (a) illumination; lighting; i. (par projecteurs), floodlighting (b) pl illuminations, lights 2. inspiration.

illuminé [ilymine] n visionary, crank.

illuminer [ilymine] vtr 1. to illuminate; to light up 2. s'i., to light up (de, with).

illusion [ilyzjɔ̃] nf 1. illusion; i. d'optique, optical

illusion; **se faire des illusions,** to delude oneself 2. delusion; **se faire i.,** to labour under a delusion. **illusoire** *a* illusory.

illusionner (s') [silyzjɔne] *vpr* to delude oneself.

illusionniste [ilyzjɔnist] *n* conjurer.

illustrateur [ilystratœr] *nm* illustrator.

illustration [ilystrasjɔ̃] *nf* illustration; picture.

illustre [ilystr] *a* illustrious, famous, renowned.

illustrer [ilystre] *vtr* to illustrate (book). **illustré** 1. *a* illustrated 2. *nm* illustrated magazine.

ilot [ilo] *nm* 1. islet, small island 2. (*a*) block (of houses) (*b*) **i. de résistance,** pocket of resistance.

image [imaʒ] *nf* 1. (*a*) reflection (*b*) *Cin: TV:* frame; **i. de télévision,** television picture 2. (*a*) **l'i. de son père,** the image of his father (*b*) picture, figure; **livre d'images,** picture book 3. (*a*) mental picture, impression (*b*) **i. de marque,** (i) brand image (of product) (ii) (public) image (of politician) 4. *Lit:* image; simile, metaphor; *pl* imagery. **imagé** *a* (*of style*) vivid; full of imagery.

imagerie [imaʒri] *nf Lit:* imagery.

imagination [imaʒinasjɔ̃] *nf* (*a*) imagination; **voir qch en i.,** to see sth in one's mind's eye (*b*) invention, fancy; **de pure i.,** unfounded.

imaginer [imaʒine] *vtr* 1. (*a*) to imagine; to conceive, invent, devise; **i. un projet,** to think out a plan; **bien imaginé,** well thought out (*b*) to picture; **imaginez un peu,** just imagine; **tout ce qu'on peut i. de plus beau,** the finest thing imaginable; **vous plaisantez, j'imagine,** you must be joking 2. **s'i.** (*a*) to delude oneself (with the thought) (that); **elle s'imagine que tout le monde l'admire,** she thinks everyone admires her (*b*) to imagine, picture. **imaginable** *a* imaginable, conceivable. **imaginaire** *a* imaginary; make-believe. **imaginatif, -ive** *a* imaginative.

imbattable [ɛ̃batabl] *a* unbeatable (prices).

imbécillité [ɛ̃besilite] *nf* 1. (*a*) imbecility (*b*) silliness, stupidity 2. silly, idiotic thing; **dire des imbécillités,** to talk nonsense. **imbécile** 1. *a* (*a*) *Med:* imbecile (*b*) silly, idiotic 2. *n* (*a*) *Med:* imbecile (*b*) idiot, fool; **faire l'i.,** to play the fool.

imberbe [ɛ̃bɛrb] *a* beardless.

imbiber [ɛ̃bibe] *vtr* 1. **i. qch de qch,** to soak sth in sth; to saturate, moisten, sth (with sth); **imbibé d'eau,** waterlogged, wet; saturated (with water) 2. **s'i.** (*a*) to become saturated (**de,** with); to absorb (*b*) to become absorbed; to sink in.

imbrication [ɛ̃brikasjɔ̃] *nf* overlap(ping) (of tiles).

imbriquer (s') [sɛ̃brike] *vpr* to overlap, fit in.

imbroglio [ɛ̃brɔljo] *nm* imbroglio.

imbu [ɛ̃by] *a* **i. de,** full of, steeped in.

imbuvable [ɛ̃byvabl] *a* (*a*) undrinkable (*b*) *F:* (*of pers*) insufferable.

imitation [imitasjɔ̃] *nf* 1. (*a*) imitation (*b*) mimicry; *Th:* impersonation (*c*) forgery 2. copy; **manteau en i. cuir,** imitation leather coat.

imiter [imite] *vtr* (*a*) to imitate; to copy; to model (**de,** on); **il leva son verre et tout le monde l'imita,** he raised his glass and everyone followed suit (*b*) to mimic; to take (s.o.) off; *Th:* to impersonate (s.o.) (*c*) to forge (signature). **imitateur, -trice** 1. *a* imitative 2. *n* imitator; *Th:* impersonator. **imitatif, -ive** *a* imitative.

immaculé [imakyle] *a* immaculate; spotless.

immangeable [ɛ̃mɑ̃ʒabl] *a* uneatable; inedible.

immanquable [ɛ̃mɑ̃kabl] *a* (target) that cannot be missed; certain, inevitable (event). **immanquablement** *adv* inevitably.

immatérialité [imaterjalite] *nf* immateriality. **immatériel, -ielle** *a* 1. immaterial, unsubstantial 2. intangible (assets).

immatriculation [imatrikylasjɔ̃] *nf* registration; *Aut:* **plaque, numéro, d'i.,** number, *NAm:* license, plate; registration, *NAm:* license, number.

immatriculer [imatrikyle] *vtr* to register (s.o., car, document); **voiture immatriculée SPF 342T,** car with registration, *NAm:* license, number SPF 342T; **se faire i.,** to register.

immaturité [imatyrite] *nf* immaturity.

immédiat [imedja(t)] 1. *a* (*a*) immediate, direct (cause) (*b*) immediate; close (proximity); near 2. *a* without delay; **changement i.,** instant change 3. *nm* **dans l'i.,** in the immediate future, for the time being. **immédiatement** *adv* immediately.

immémorial, -iaux [imemɔrjal, -jo] *a* immemorial; **de temps i.,** from time immemorial.

immensité [imɑ̃site] *nf* immensity; hugeness. **immense** *a* immeasurable, boundless; immense, vast, huge. **immensément** *adv* immensely.

immensurable [imɑ̃syrabl] *a* immeasurable.

immerger [imɛrʒe] *vtr* (**n. immergeons**) (*a*) to immerse, plunge, dip; to submerge; to lay (cable) underwater; to dump (waste) in sea (*b*) to bury (s.o.) at sea.

immérité [imerite] *a* unmerited, undeserved.

immersion [imɛrsjɔ̃] *nf* (*a*) immersion; laying (of cable) underwater; dumping (of waste) in the sea (*b*) submersion (*c*) burial at sea.

immettable [ɛ̃mɛtabl] *a* unwearable.

immeuble [imœbl] *nm* (*a*) real estate, landed property (*b*) block of flats, *NAm:* apartment building; office block.

immigration [imigrasjɔ̃] *nf* immigration. **immigrant, -ante** *a* & *n* immigrant. **immigré, -ée** *a* & *n* immigrant.

immigrer [imigre] *vi* to immigrate.

imminence [iminɑ̃s] *nf* imminence. **imminent, -ente** *a* imminent, impending.

immiscer (s') [simise] *vpr* (**n. n. immisçons**) to interfere, meddle (**dans,** in).

immixtion [imikstjɔ̃] *nf* interference, meddling.

immobile [imɔbil] *a* 1. motionless, still, unmoved; set (face); **rester i.,** to stand still 2. immovable; firm.

immobilier, -ière [imɔbilje, -jɛr] *a* **biens immobiliers,** *nm* immobilier, real estate; **société immobilière,** building society; **agence immobilière,** estate agency; **agent i.,** estate agent, *NAm:* realtor.

immobilisation [imɔbilizasjɔ̃] *nf* immobilization; standstill.

immobiliser [imɔbilize] *vtr* 1. (*a*) to immobilize, bring to a standstill (*b*) to fix (sth) in position; (*pers*) **immobilisé à domicile,** housebound 2. **s'i.,** to come to a standstill; to stop.

immobilité [imɔbilite] *nf* immobility; motionlessness; fixity; **i. politique,** political inertia.

immodéré [imɔdere] *a* immoderate, inordinate. **immodérément** *adv* immoderately, inordinately.

immolation [imɔlasjɔ̃] *nf* immolation, sacrifice.

immoler [imɔle] *vtr* to immolate, sacrifice.
immondices [imɔ̃dis] *nfpl* refuse; rubbish.
immonde *a* filthy; squalid; vile.
immoralité [imɔralite] *nf* immorality. **immoral,
-aux** *a* immoral.
immortaliser [imɔrtalize] *vtr* **1.** to immortalize **2.**
s'i., to win everlasting fame.
immortalité [imɔrtalite] *nf* immortality.
immortel, -elle 1. *a* immortal; undying **2.** *nm*
immortal, *esp* member of the Académie Française **3.**
nf immortelle, everlasting flower.
immotivé [imɔtive] *a* unmotivated, groundless.
immuable [imɥabl] *a* immutable, unalterable; fixed,
unchanging. **immuablement** *adv* immutably.
immunisation [imynizasjɔ̃] *nf Med:* immunization.
immuniser [imynize] *vtr Med:* to immunize; **être
immunisé contre qch,** (i) *Med:* to be immunized
against sth (ii) to be immune to sth.
immunité [imynite] *nf* immunity; **i. parlementaire,**
parliamentary privilege.
immutabilité [imytabilite] *nf* immutability.
impact [ɛ̃pakt] *nm* impact, shock.
impair [ɛ̃pɛr] **1.** *a* odd, uneven (number) **2.** *nm*
blunder; **commettre un i.,** to drop a brick.
impalpable [ɛ̃palpabl] *a* impalpable, intangible.
imparable [ɛ̃parabl] *a* unstoppable.
impardonnable [ɛ̃pardɔnabl] *a* unpardonable, unforgivable.
imparfait [ɛ̃parfɛ] **1.** *a* (*a*) unfinished, uncompleted
(*b*) imperfect, defective **2.** *nm Gram:* imperfect
(tense). **imparfaitement** *adv* imperfectly.
impartialité [ɛparsjalite] *nf* impartiality.
impartial, -aux *a* impartial, unbiased.
impartialement *adv* impartially.
impasse [ɛ̃pɑs] *nf* **1.** blind alley, dead end; cul-de-sac;
PN: no through road **2.** deadlock; **se trouver dans une
i.,** to find oneself in a dilemma, *F:* in a fix; **i.
budgétaire,** budget deficit **3.** *Cards:* finesse.
impassibilité [ɛ̃pasibilite] *nf* impassiveness.
impassible *a* impassive. **impassiblement** *adv*
impassively.
impatience [ɛ̃pasjɑ̃s] *nf* impatience; **être dans l'i. de
faire qch,** to be eager to do sth. **impatient** *a*
impatient; **être i. de faire qch,** to be eager to do sth.
impatiemment *adv* impatiently.
impatienter [ɛ̃pasjɑ̃te] *vtr* **1.** to annoy, provoke
(s.o.) **2. s'i.,** to lose patience, to get impatient.
impayable [ɛ̃pejabl] *a F:* priceless; killingly funny.
impayé [ɛ̃peje] *a* unpaid.
impeccable [ɛ̃pekabl] *a* impeccable. **impeccablement** *adv* impeccably.
impénétrabilité [ɛ̃penetrabilite] *nf* **1.** impenetra-
bility **2.** inscrutability. **impénétrable** *a* impenetrable, inscrutable.
impénitent [ɛ̃penitɑ̃] *a* unrepentant.
impensable [ɛ̃pɑ̃sabl] *a* unthinkable.
imper [ɛ̃pɛr] *nm Cl: F:* mac.
impératif, -ive [ɛ̃peratif, -iv] **1.** *a* imperious, imperative; peremptory (tone) **2.** *nm* (*a*) imperative;
requirement (*b*) *Gram:* imperative (mood).
impérativement *adv* imperatively.
impératrice [ɛ̃peratris] *nf* empress.
imperceptible [ɛ̃pɛrsɛptibl] *a* imperceptible.
imperceptiblement *adv* imperceptibly.

imperfection [ɛ̃pɛrfɛksjɔ̃] *nf* imperfection; defect,
flaw.
impérial, -aux [ɛ̃perjal, -o] **1.** *a* imperial **2.** *nf*
impériale, top (deck) (of bus); **autobus à i.,** double-
decker (bus).
impérialisme [ɛ̃perjalism] *nm* imperialism.
impérialiste *a & n* imperialist.
impérieux, -euse [ɛ̃perjø, -øz] *a* (*a*) imperious (*b*)
urgent, pressing. **impérieusement** *adv* im-
periously; urgently.
impérissable [ɛ̃perisabl] *a* imperishable, undying.
imperméabiliser [ɛ̃pɛrmeabilize] *vtr* to
(water)proof (cloth). **imperméable 1.** *a* impervious (à, to); impermeable; **i. à l'eau,** waterproof,
watertight; **i. à l'air,** airtight **2.** *nm Cl:* raincoat.
imperméabilité [ɛ̃pɛrmeabilite] *nf* impermeability.
impersonnel, -elle [ɛ̃pɛrsɔnɛl] *a* impersonal.
impertinence [ɛ̃pɛrtinɑ̃s] *nf* impertinence; rudeness. **impertinent** *a* impertinent; rude.
imperturbabilité [ɛ̃pɛrtyrbabilite] *nf* imperturbability. **imperturbable** *a* imperturbable.
imperturbablement *adv* imperturbably.
impétigo [ɛ̃petigo] *nm Med:* impetigo.
impétuosité [ɛ̃petɥozite] *nf* impetuosity; impulsive-
ness. **impétueux, -euse** *a* impetuous; impulsive;
raging (torrent). **impétueusement** *adv* im-
petuously.
impiété [ɛ̃pjete] *nf* impiety, ungodliness. **impie** *a*
impious; ungodly.
impitoyable [ɛ̃pitwajabl] *a* (*a*) pitiless (à, envers,
towards); merciless (*b*) relentless. **impitoyablement** *adv* pitilessly, mercilessly; relentlessly.
implacabilité [ɛ̃plakabilite] *nf* implacability.
implacable *a* implacable. **implacablement**
adv implacably.
implant [ɛ̃plɑ̃] *nm Med:* implant.
implantation [ɛ̃plɑ̃tasjɔ̃] *nf* implantation; introduction; settling, establishment.
implanter [ɛ̃plɑ̃te] *vtr* **1.** to plant; to introduce,
establish; to implant (idea) **2. s'i.,** to take root; to be
established; to settle.
implication [ɛ̃plikasjɔ̃] *nf* (*a*) implication (*b*) involve-
ment.
implicite [ɛ̃plisit] *a* implicit, implied.
implicitement *adv* implicitly.
impliquer [ɛ̃plike] *vtr* **1.** to implicate, involve **2. i.
(que),** to imply (that).
imploration [ɛ̃plɔrasjɔ̃] *nf* entreaty.
implorer [ɛ̃plɔre] *vtr* to implore, beseech, entreat
(s.o.).
impolitesse [ɛ̃pɔlites] *nf* **1.** impoliteness; rudeness **2.**
act of rudeness; impolite remark. **impoli** *a* impolite,
rude (envers, avec, to). **impoliment** *adv* impolitely,
rudely.
impolitique [ɛ̃pɔlitik] *a* impolitic, ill-advised.
impondérable [ɛ̃pɔ̃derabl] *a* imponderable.
impopularité [ɛ̃pɔpylarite] *nf* unpopularity.
impopulaire *a* unpopular.
importance [ɛ̃pɔrtɑ̃s] *nf* (*a*) importance; consequence, moment; **affaire d'i.,** important matter;
sans i., unimportant; **avoir de l'i.,** to be important;
cela n'a aucune i., it doesn't matter a bit; **prendre de
l'i.,** to gain ground (*b*) size (of town); extent (of
damage); gravity (of wound) (*c*) social importance,

position (d) se donner de l'i., to put on self-important airs. **important, -ante** 1. a (a) important, significant; **peu i.**, unimportant (b) large (town); considerable (sum, delay) 2. a & n self-important (person); **faire l'i.**, to put on airs 3. nm **l'i.**, the important thing.
importation [ɛ̃portasjɔ̃] nf 1. importation; **articles d'i.**, imports 2. (thg) import.
importer¹ [ɛ̃porte] vtr to import (goods). **importateur, -trice** 1. a importing (firm) 2. n importer.
importer² vi (used only in the third pers, participles and inf) 1. to be of importance; to matter; **les choses qui importent**, (the) things that matter 2. impers **il importe que** + sub, it is essential that; **peu importe que**, it doesn't matter much whether; **peu m'importe**, I don't mind; **n'importe**, never mind; **qu'importe?** what does it matter? **que m'importe?** what do I care? **n'importe comment, où, quand**, anyhow, anywhere, any time; **n'importe qui, quoi**, anyone, anything; **venez n'importe quel jour**, come any day; F: **ce n'est pas n'importe qui**, he isn't just anybody.
importun, -une [ɛ̃portœ̃, -yn] 1. a importunate; tiresome; unwelcome; ill-timed, inopportune; **je crains de vous être i.**, I'm afraid I'm disturbing you 2. n intruder; nuisance. **importunément** adv importunately.
importuner [ɛ̃portyne] vtr (a) to importune; to bother (b) to annoy, disturb.
importunité [ɛ̃portynite] nf importunity.
imposer [ɛ̃poze] 1. vtr (a) to impose, prescribe; to set (task); to dictate (terms); **i. une règle**, to lay down a rule; **i. (le) silence à qn**, to enjoin silence on s.o.; **i. le respect**, to command respect (b) Adm: **i. des droits sur qch**, to tax sth; **i. qn**, to tax s.o. 2. vi **en i.**, to inspire respect; **en i. à qn**, to impress s.o. 3. **s'i.** (a) to assert oneself (b) **s'i. à qn**, to foist, thrust, oneself on s.o.; to impose on s.o. (c) to be indispensable; **une visite au Louvre s'impose**, we, you, must visit the Louvre. **imposable** a taxable. **imposant** imposing; commanding, dignified. **imposé, -ée** 1. a Com: **prix i.**, fixed price 2. n taxpayer.
imposition [ɛ̃pozisjɔ̃] nf 1. Ecc: laying on (of hands) 2. imposing (of conditions) 3. imposition (of tax).
impossibilité [ɛ̃posibilite] nf 1. impossibility; **être dans l'i. de faire qch**, to find it impossible, to be unable, to do sth 2. **se heurter à des impossibilités**, to come up against unsurmountable obstacles. **impossible** a impossible; **i. m'est i. de le faire**, I can't (possibly) do it; **il a fait l'i. pour nous aider**, he did his utmost to help us; F: **il a fallu nous lever à une heure i.**, we had to get up at an unearthly hour.
imposteur [ɛ̃postœr] nm impostor.
imposture [ɛ̃postyr] nf imposture; deception, trickery.
impôt [ɛ̃po] nm 1. tax; **impôts locaux**, rates; **i. sur le revenu**, income tax; **i. sur les plus-values**, capital gains tax 2. taxes, taxation.
impotence [ɛ̃potɑ̃s] nf disability, infirmity. **impotent, -ente** 1. a disabled; crippled 2. n invalid; cripple.
impraticable [ɛ̃pratikabl] a 1. impracticable, unworkable 2. (a) (road) impassable (b) Sp: (of ground) unfit for play.
imprécation [ɛ̃prekasjɔ̃] nf imprecation, curse.

imprécision [ɛ̃presizjɔ̃] nf imprecision; inaccuracy (of fire). **imprécis** a vague, imprecise, indefinite; inaccurate (fire).
imprégnation [ɛ̃preɲasjɔ̃] nf impregnation; permeation.
imprégner [ɛ̃preɲe] vtr (j'imprègne; j'imprégnerai) 1. to impregnate (de, with); to permeate 2. **s'i.**, to become impregnated (de, with); **s'i. d'eau**, to become soaked with water.
imprenable [ɛ̃prənabl] a impregnable; **vue i.**, view that cannot be obstructed.
imprésario [ɛ̃presarjo] nm Th: etc: impresario; (business) manager.
impression [ɛ̃prɛsjɔ̃] nf 1. (a) Typ: printing; **faute d'i.**, misprint; **i. en couleurs**, colour printing (b) Phot: exposure 2. (a) impression (b) impression (of book) (c) priming coat, undercoat (of paint) (d) pattern (of material) 3. (mental) impression; **avoir l'i. que**, to have the feeling that; **faire i.**, to create a sensation.
impressionner [ɛ̃prɛsjɔne] vtr 1. to impress, affect; to make an impression on (s.o.); to upset 2. Phot: to produce an image on (sensitized paper); to expose (film). **impressionnable** a impressionable. **impressionnant** a impressive; upsetting.
imprévisibilité [ɛ̃previzibilite] nf unpredictability. **imprévisible** a unpredictable.
imprévoyance [ɛ̃prevwajɑ̃s] nf lack of foresight; improvidence. **imprévoyant** a lacking in foresight; improvident.
imprévu [ɛ̃prevy] 1. a unforeseen, unexpected (event) 2. nm (a) unexpected character (of event) (b) unforeseen event; **sauf i.**, barring accidents; **en cas d'i.**, in case of an emergency; unless something unforeseen happens; **plein d'i.**, full of surprises.
imprimer [ɛ̃prime] vtr 1. **i. un mouvement à un corps**, to transmit motion to a body 2. (a) to imprint, stamp (sth on sth) (b) Tex: to print (material) 3. (a) Typ: to print (b) to publish (book). **imprimé** 1. a printed 2. nm printed paper, book; (printed) form; Post: **imprimés**, printed matter 3. nm Tex: print.
imprimerie [ɛ̃primri] nf 1. printing 2. printing house, printing works; NAm: printery.
imprimeur [ɛ̃primœr] nm printer.
improbabilité [ɛ̃probabilite] nf improbability, unlikelihood. **improbable** a improbable, unlikely.
improductif, -ive [ɛ̃prodyktif, -iv] a unproductive.
impromptu [ɛ̃prɔ̃pty] 1. adv without preparation; impromptu 2. a unpremeditated; impromptu; extempore, off the cuff (speech) 3. nm Mus: impromptu.
imprononçable [ɛ̃prɔnɔ̃sabl] a unpronounceable.
impropriété [ɛ̃proprijete] nf impropriety; incorrectness (of word). **impropre** a (a) inappropriate, incorrect (term) (b) **i. à qch**, unsuitable for sth; **i. à la consommation**, unfit for human consumption.
improvisation [ɛ̃provizasjɔ̃] nf improvisation.
improviser [ɛ̃provize] vtr 1. to improvise; **discours improvisé**, impromptu speech 2. **s'i. cuisinier**, to act as cook.
improviste (à l') [alɛ̃provist] adv phr unexpectedly, without warning; **prendre qn à l'i.**, to take s.o. unawares.
imprudence [ɛ̃prydɑ̃s] nf imprudence; carelessness;

rashness. **imprudent, -ente 1.** *a* imprudent, careless, rash; unwise (action) **2.** *n* imprudent, careless, person. **imprudemment** *adv* imprudently, carelessly, rashly, unwisely.
impudence [ɛ̃pydɑ̃s] *nf* **1.** impudence **2.** impudent action. **impudent** *a* impudent.
impudeur [ɛ̃pydœr] *nf* immodesty. **impudique** *a* shameless, immodest.
impuissance [ɛ̃pцisɑ̃s] *nf* **1.** impotence, powerlessness, helplessness **2.** *Med:* (sexual) impotence. **impuissant** *a* impotent, helpless.
impulsion [ɛ̃pylsjɔ̃] *nf* **1.** (*a*) *Mec:* impulse; **i. de courant,** current impulse (*b*) impetus, impulse, boost; **les affaires ont reçu une nouvelle i.,** business shows renewed activity **2. sous l'i. du moment,** on the spur of the moment. **impulsif, -ive** *a* impulsive.
impunité [ɛ̃pynite] *nf* impunity. **impuni** *a* unpunished. **impunément** *adv* with impunity.
impureté [ɛ̃pyrte] *nf* impurity. **impur** *a* impure.
imputation [ɛ̃pytasjɔ̃] *nf* **1.** imputation, charge **2.** *Com:* charging (of expenses); **i. des charges,** cost allocation.
imputer [ɛ̃pyte] *vtr* **1.** to impute, attribute (crime) (à, to) **2.** *Com:* **i. des frais sur un compte,** to charge expenses to an account. **imputable** *a* **1.** attributable (à, to) **2.** *Com:* **frais i. sur un compte,** expenses chargeable to an account.
inabordable. [inabɔrdabl] *a* unapproachable, inaccessible; prohibitive (price).
inaccentué [inaksɑ̃tɥe] *a* unstressed (syllable).
inacceptable [inaksɛptabl] *a* unacceptable, inadmissible.
inaccessible [inaksɛsibl] *a* inaccessible; **région i.,** out-of-the-way place; **i. à la flatterie,** impervious to flattery.
inaccoutumé [inakutyme] *a* **1.** unaccustomed; unused (à, to) **2.** unusual.
inachèvement [inaʃɛvmɑ̃] *nm* incompletion. **inachevé** *a* unfinished, uncompleted.
inaction [inaksjɔ̃] *nf* inaction, idleness.
inactivité [inaktivite] *nf* inactivity. **inactif, -ive** *a* inactive; idle.
inadaptation [inadaptasjɔ̃] *nf* maladjustment. **inadapté, -ée** *a* & *n* maladjusted (person); **il est i.,** he's a (social) misfit; **vie inadaptée à ses besoins,** life unsuited to one's needs.
inadéquat [inadekwa] *a* inadequate.
inadmissible [inadmisibl] *a* inadmissible (request).
inadvertance [inadvɛrtɑ̃s] *nf* inadvertency; **par i.,** inadvertently.
inaliénable [inaljenabl] *a Jur:* inalienable.
inaltérable [inalterabl] *a* **1.** that does not deteriorate; permanent (ink); **i. à l'air,** unaffected by air **2.** (*a*) unalterable (*b*) unfailing, unvarying (good humour).
inamical, -aux [inamikal, -o] *a* unfriendly.
inamovible [inamɔvibl] *a* (*a*) non-removable; fixed; permanent (fixture) (*b*) (post) held for life.
inanimé [inanime] *a* (*a*) inanimate, lifeless (*b*) senseless, unconscious.
inanité [inanite] *nf* inanity, futility.
inanition [inanisjɔ̃] *nf* starvation; **tomber d'i.,** to faint with hunger.

inapaisable [inapɛzabl] *a* inappeasable. **inapaisé** *a* unappeased.
inaperçu [inapɛrsy] *a* unseen, unperceived, unobserved; unnoticed; **passer i.,** to go unnoticed.
inapplicable [inaplikabl] *a* inapplicable.
inapplication [inaplikasjɔ̃] *nf* lack of application. **inappliqué** *a* lacking in application, careless (pers.).
inappréciable [inapresjabl] *a* **1.** inappreciable; imperceptible **2.** inestimable, invaluable. **inapprécié** *a* unappreciated.
inaptitude [inaptityd] *nf* inaptitude; unfitness (à, for); incapacity (for work). **inapte** *a* inapt; unfit (à, for); unsuited (à, to); unfit (for military service).
inarticulé [inartikyle] *a* inarticulate.
inassouvi [inasuvi] *a* unappeased (hunger); unquenched (thirst).
inattaquable [inatakabl] *a* unassailable (position); unquestionable (right); irrefutable (proof); **i. par les acides,** acid-proof.
inattendu [inatɑ̃dy] *a* unexpected, unforeseen.
inattention [inatɑ̃sjɔ̃] *nf* inattention (à, to); carelessness; negligence (à, of); **faute d'i.,** careless mistake. **inattentif, -ive** *a* inattentive (à, to); unobservant (à, of).
inaudible [inodibl] *a* inaudible.
inauguration [inogyrasjɔ̃] *nf* inauguration; opening; unveiling; **discours d'i.,** inaugural speech. **inaugural, -aux** *a* inaugural; **voyage i.,** maiden voyage.
inaugurer [inogyre] *vtr* to inaugurate; to open (fête); to unveil (statue).
inavouable [inavwabl] *a* shameful. **inavoué** *a* unconfessed.
incalculable [ɛ̃kalkylabl] *a* incalculable.
incandescence [ɛ̃kɑ̃desɑ̃s] *nf* incandescence. **incandescent** *a* incandescent.
incantation [ɛ̃kɑ̃tasjɔ̃] *nf* incantation. **incantatoire** *a* incantatory.
incapable [ɛ̃kapabl] **1.** *a* & *n* incapable, inefficient, incompetent (person); **c'est un i.,** he's useless **2.** *a* **i. de faire qch,** (i) incapable (ii) unable, to do sth.
incapacité [ɛ̃kapasite] *nf* **1.** incapacity, inefficiency, incompetence (of pers); **i. de faire qch,** (i) incapability (ii) inability, to do sth **2.** disability; *Adm:* **i. permanente,** permanent disablement; **i. de travail,** industrial disablement.
incarcération [ɛ̃karserasjɔ̃] *nf* incarceration.
incarcérer [ɛ̃karsere] *vtr* (**j'incarcère; j'incarcérerai**) to incarcerate (s.o.).
incarnation [ɛ̃karnasjɔ̃] *nf* incarnation; embodiment.
incarner [ɛ̃karne] *vtr* **1.** to incarnate, embody; *Th:* to play the part of (a character) **2.** s'i. (*a*) to become incarnate (*b*) *Med:* (of nail) to become ingrown. **incarné** *a* **1.** *Theol:* incarnate (*b*) **la vertu incarnée,** virtue personified **2.** *Med:* ingrowing (nail).
incartade [ɛ̃kartad] *nf* prank.
incassable [ɛ̃kasabl] *a* unbreakable.
incendie [ɛ̃sɑ̃di] *nm* (outbreak of) fire; **i. de forêt,** forest fire; **pompe à i.,** fire engine; **i. volontaire,** arson.
incendier [ɛ̃sɑ̃dje] *vtr* (*impf & pr sub* **n. incendiions**) (*a*) to set (house, forest) on fire; to set fire to (sth); to burn (sth) down (*b*) to fire imagination (*c*) *P:* to tell

s.o. off. **incendiaire 1.** *a* incendiary (bomb); inflammatory (speech) **2.** *n* arsonist.

incertain [ɛ̃sɛrtɛ̃] *a* uncertain, doubtful; unsettled (weather); unreliable (memory); **i. de qch,** (i) unsure (ii) undecided, about sth.

incertitude [ɛ̃sɛrtityd] *nf* uncertainty; doubt; **être dans l'i.,** to be in a state of uncertainty.

incessamment [ɛ̃sesamɑ̃] *adv* immediately, without delay, shortly; **il arrivera i.,** he'll be arriving (at) any moment.

incessant [ɛ̃sesɑ̃] *a* unceasing, incessant; ceaseless; unremitting.

inceste [ɛ̃sɛst] *nm* incest. **incestueux, -euse** *a* incestuous.

inchangeable [ɛ̃ʃɑ̃ʒabl] *a* unchangeable. **inchangé** *a* unchanged.

incidemment [ɛ̃sidamɑ̃] *adv* incidentally.

incidence [ɛ̃sidɑ̃s] *nf* **1.** *Tchn:* incidence **2.** effect, impact.

incident [ɛ̃sidɑ̃] *nm* (*a*) incident; occurrence, happening; **arriver sans i.,** to arrive without mishap (*b*) difficulty, hitch; **i. de parcours,** setback; **i. technique,** technical hitch.

incinérateur [ɛ̃sineratœr] *nm* incinerator.

incinération [ɛ̃sinerasjɔ̃] *nf* (*a*) incineration (*b*) cremation.

incinérer [ɛ̃sinere] *vtr* (**j'incinère; j'incinérerai**) (*a*) to incinerate (*b*) to cremate.

inciser [ɛ̃size] *vtr* to incise. **incisif, -ive 1.** *a* incisive, sharp, cutting (remark) **2.** *nf* **incisive,** incisor.

incision [ɛ̃sizjɔ̃] *nf* incision.

incitation [ɛ̃sitasjɔ̃] *nf* incitement (à, to).

inciter [ɛ̃site] *vtr* to incite; to urge (on).

incivilité [ɛ̃sivilite] *nf* **1.** incivility, rudeness **2.** rude remark. **incivil** *a* uncivil, rude.

inclassable [ɛ̃klasabl] *a* unclassifiable.

inclinaison [ɛ̃klinɛzɔ̃] *nf* incline, gradient, slope; pitch, slant (of roof); tilt (of head, hat); list (of ship); angle (of trajectory); **comble à forte, à faible, i.,** high-pitched, low-pitched, roof.

inclination [ɛ̃klinasjɔ̃] *nf* **1.** inclination; bending, bow(ing) (of body); nod (of head) **2.** (*a*) tendency; bent; propensity; **avoir de l'i. à faire qch,** to be inclined to do sth; **avoir de l'i. pour qch,** to have a liking for sth (*b*) **mariage d'i.,** love match.

incliner [ɛ̃kline] **1.** *vtr* (*a*) to incline; to slant, slope (*b*) to tip up; to tilt (*c*) to bend, bow, incline (the head); **i. la tête,** to nod (one's head) (*d*) **i. qn à faire qch,** to influence, predispose, s.o. in favour of doing sth **2.** *vi* (*a*) (*of wall*) to lean, slope; (*of ship*) to list (*b*) **i. à la pitié,** to incline, be disposed, to pity **3.** **s'i.** (*a*) to slant, slope; (*of ship*) to heel (over) (*b*) to bend over, down (*c*) to bow (down) (**devant,** before); **s'i. devant qn,** to yield to s.o.; **j'ai dû m'i.,** I had to give in. **incliné** *a* **1.** sloping, tilting, tilted; **plan i.,** inclined plane **2. i. à qch,** inclined, disposed, to sth.

inclure [ɛ̃klyr] *vtr* (*conj like* CONCLURE except *pp* **inclus**) to enclose; to include. **inclus** *a* (*a*) enclosed (in letter) (*b*) included; **jusqu'à la page 5 incluse,** up to and including page 5. **inclusif, -ive** *a* inclusive.

inclusivement *adv* inclusively; **du vendredi au mardi i.,** from Friday to Tuesday inclusive.

inclusion [ɛ̃klyzjɔ̃] *nf* (*a*) enclosing (of document in a letter) (*b*) inclusion.

incognito [ɛ̃kɔnito] **1.** *adv* incognito **2.** *nm* **garder l'i.,** to remain incognito.

incohérence [ɛ̃koerɑ̃s] *nf* incoherence; inconsistency. **incohérent** *a* incoherent; inconsistent.

incolore [ɛ̃kɔlɔr] *a* colourless.

incomber [ɛ̃kɔ̃be] *vi* (*used only in third pers*) **i. à qn,** to be incumbent on, to devolve on, s.o.; **il nous incombe de,** it falls to us to; **la responsabilité incombe à l'auteur,** the responsibility lies with the author.

incombustible [ɛ̃kɔ̃bystibl] *a* incombustible; fire-proof.

incommoder [ɛ̃kɔmode] *vtr* **1.** to inconvenience, incommode, disturb, s.o. **2.** (*of food*) to upset (s.o.). **incommodant** *a* unpleasant, disagreeable, annoying. **incommodé** *a* ill at ease; **être i. par la chaleur,** to feel the heat.

incommodité [ɛ̃kɔmodite] *nf* (*a*) inconvenience (*b*) discomfort; awkwardness (of situation). **incommode** *a* inconvenient; uncomfortable; awkward (tool). **incommodément** *adv* inconveniently; uncomfortably; awkwardly.

incomparable [ɛ̃kɔ̃parabl] *a* incomparable, unrivalled, matchless. **incomparablement** *adv* incomparably.

incompatibilité [ɛ̃kɔ̃patibilite] *nf* incompatibility. **incompatible** *a* incompatible (**avec,** with).

incompétence [ɛ̃kɔ̃petɑ̃s] *nf* incompetence. **incompétent** *a* incompetent.

incomplet, -ète [ɛ̃kɔ̃plɛ, -ɛt] *a* incomplete. **incomplètement** *adv* incompletely.

incompréhension [ɛ̃kɔ̃preɑ̃sjɔ̃] *nf* incomprehension, lack of understanding; obtuseness. **incompréhensible** *a* incomprehensible. **incompréhensif, -ive** *a* uncomprehending; unsympathetic.

incompris [ɛ̃kɔ̃pri] *a* (*of pers*) misunderstood; unappreciated.

inconcevable [ɛ̃kɔ̃svabl] *a* inconceivable, unthinkable, unimaginable.

inconciliable [ɛ̃kɔ̃siljabl] *a* irreconcilable, incompatible (**avec,** with).

inconditionnel, -elle [ɛ̃kɔ̃disjɔnɛl] *a* unconditional; unquestioning (obedience).

inconduite [ɛ̃kɔ̃dɥit] *nf* loose living; *Jur:* misconduct.

inconfort [ɛ̃kɔ̃fɔr] *nm* discomfort. **inconfortable** *a* uncomfortable.

incongruité [ɛ̃kɔ̃grɥite] *nf* (*a*) incongruity, absurdity (*b*) impropriety (of behaviour) (*c*) improper remark, action. **incongru** *a* (*a*) incongruous; out of place (*b*) improper (question).

inconnu, -ue [ɛ̃kɔny] **1.** *a* unknown (**de, à,** to); **il m'était i.,** I didn't know him; **visages inconnus,** strange faces **2.** *n* (*a*) unknown person (i) stranger (ii) (mere) nobody (*b*) *nm* **l'i.,** the unknown; **saut dans l'i.,** leap in the dark **3.** *nf* *Mth:* **inconnue,** unknown (quantity).

inconscience [ɛ̃kɔ̃sjɑ̃s] *nf* **1.** unconsciousness **2.** unawareness; **c'est de l'i. pure,** it's sheer thoughtlessness, madness. **inconscient 1.** *a* (*a*) unconscious (act); automatic (movement) (*b*) thoughtless; oblivious, unaware (of things around one) **2.** *nm* *Psy:* **l'i.,** the unconscious. **inconsciemment** *adv* unconsciously, unknowingly; thoughtlessly.

inconséquence[ɛ̃kɔ̃sekãs] *nf* inconsistency, inconsequence, irrelevance. **inconséquent** *a* (*a*) inconsistent, inconsequent(ial) (*b*) irresponsible, rash (words).

inconsidéré[ɛ̃kɔ̃sidere] *a* ill considered, rash (act). **inconsidérément** *adv* inconsiderately, thoughtlessly, rashly.

inconsistance[ɛ̃kɔ̃sistãs] *nf* 1. insubstantiality; looseness (of soil); weakness (of nature) 2. inconsistency (of pers, act). **inconsistant** *a* inconsistent; fickle, erratic; runny (cream).

inconsolable[ɛ̃kɔ̃sɔlabl] *a* inconsolable.

inconstance[ɛ̃kɔ̃stãs] *nf* inconstancy, inconsistency; fickleness. **inconstant** *a* inconstant, inconsistent; fickle.

inconstitutionnel, -elle[ɛ̃kɔ̃stitysjɔnɛl] *a* unconstitutional.

incontestable[ɛ̃kɔ̃tɛstabl] *a* incontestable, indisputable; undeniable. **incontestablement** *adv* incontestably, indisputably; undeniably. **incontesté** *a* uncontested, undisputed.

incontinence[ɛ̃kɔ̃tinãs] *nf* incontinence. **incontinent** *a* incontinent.

incontrôlable[ɛ̃kɔ̃trolabl] *a* unverifiable; uncontrollable. **incontrôlé** *a* unverified; uncontrolled.

inconvenance[ɛ̃kɔ̃vnãs] *nf* (*a*) impropriety, unseemliness (*b*) **dire des inconvenances,** to make indiscreet remarks. **inconvenant** *a* improper, unseemly; ill-mannered; indiscreet (remarks).

inconvénient[ɛ̃kɔ̃venjã] *nm* disadvantage, drawback; inconvenience; **je n'y vois pas d'i.,** I can't see any objection(s) (to it); I've got nothing against it; **peut-on le faire sans i.?** is there a risk in doing it?

incorporation[ɛ̃kɔrpɔrasjɔ̃] *nf* (*a*) incorporation, blending (*b*) *Mil:* conscription.

incorporer[ɛ̃kɔrpɔre] *vtr* (*a*) **i. qch à qch,** to blend, mix, sth with sth (*b*) *Mil:* to draft (troops).

incorrection[ɛ̃kɔrɛksjɔ̃] *nf* 1. (*a*) incorrectness, inaccuracy (*b*) incorrectness, slovenliness; unsuitability (of clothes) (*c*) impoliteness, rudeness 2. impolite action, rude remark. **incorrect** *a* (*a*) incorrect; inaccurate, wrong (*b*) defective, faulty (*c*) **tenue incorrecte,** (i) slovenly (ii) unsuitable, clothes (*d*) (*of pers*) impolite, rude. **incorrectement** *adv* (*a*) incorrectly; inaccurately, wrongly (*b*) defectively (*c*) in a slovenly manner; unsuitably (dressed) (*d*) impolitely, rudely.

incorrigible[ɛ̃kɔriʒibl] *a* incorrigible.

incorruptible[ɛ̃kɔryptibl] *a* incorruptible.

incrédibilité[ɛ̃kredibilite] *nf* incredibility.

incrédulité[ɛ̃kredylite] *nf* incredulity. **incrédule 1.** *a* incredulous (**à l'égard de,** of); *Theol:* unbelieving **2.** *n* unbeliever.

increvable[ɛ̃krəvabl] *a* puncture-proof (tyre); *P:* tireless (pers).

incriminer[ɛ̃krimine] *vtr* to incriminate, accuse, indict (s.o.).

incrochetable[ɛ̃krɔʃtabl] *a* burglar-proof.

incroyable[ɛ̃krwajabl] *a* incredible, unbelievable. **incroyablement** *adv* incredibly, unbelievably.

incroyance[ɛ̃krwajãs] *nf* unbelief. **incroyant, -ante 1.** *a* unbelieving **2.** *n* non-believer.

incrustation[ɛ̃krystasjɔ̃] *nf* 1. encrusting; furring up (of boiler) **2.** (*a*) inlay; inlaid work (*b*) encrustation; fur, scale (in boiler).

incruster[ɛ̃kryste] *vtr* **1.** (*a*) to encrust; to scale, fur (up) (pipes) (*b*) to inlay (**de,** with) **2. s'i.** (*a*) to become encrusted; (*of boiler*) to fur up (*b*) **quand on l'invite, il s'incruste,** once you invite him you can't get rid of him.

incubateur[ɛ̃kybatœr] *nm* incubator.

incubation[ɛ̃kybasjɔ̃] *nf* incubation.

incuber[ɛ̃kybe] *vtr* to incubate.

inculpation[ɛ̃kylpasjɔ̃] *nf* indictment, charge.

inculpé, -ée[ɛ̃kylpe] *n* l'i., the accused.

inculper[ɛ̃kylpe] *vtr* to indict, charge.

inculquer[ɛ̃kylke] *vtr* to inculcate (**à,** in); to instil (**à,** into).

inculte[ɛ̃kylt] *a* uncultivated, wild; waste (land); unkempt (beard); uneducated (pers).

incurable[ɛ̃kyrabl] *a* & *n* incurable.

incursion[ɛ̃kyrsjɔ̃] *nf* inroad, foray, incursion.

incurver (s')[(s)ɛ̃kyrve] *vtr* & *pr* to bend, curve.

Inde[ɛ̃d] *Prnf Geog:* (*a*) India (*b*) **les Indes,** the Indies.

indécence[ɛ̃desãs] *nf* indecency. **indécent** *a* indecent. **indécemment** *adv* indecently.

indéchiffrable[ɛ̃deʃifrabl] *a* (*a*) indecipherable (*b*) illegible (writing) (*c*) unintelligible, incomprehensible; (*of pers*) inscrutable.

indéchirable[ɛ̃deʃirabl] *a* tearproof.

indécision[ɛ̃desizjɔ̃] *nf* indecision, indecisiveness. **indécis** *a* **1.** unsettled, undecided (question); indecisive, doubtful; vague **2.** (*of pers*) (*a*) undecided, in two minds (*b*) indecisive, irresolute.

indéfendable[ɛ̃defãdabl] *a* indefensible.

indéfini[ɛ̃defini] *a* **1.** indefinite; *Gram:* **pronom i.,** indefinite pronoun **2.** undefined. **indéfiniment** *adv* indefinitely. **indéfinissable** *a* indefinable.

indélébile[ɛ̃delebil] *a* indelible.

indélicatesse[ɛ̃delikatɛs] *nf* (*a*) indelicacy, tactlessness (*b*) unscrupulousness. **indélicat** *a* (*a*) indelicate, coarse; tactless (*b*) dishonest, unscrupulous. **indélicatement** *adv* (*a*) indelicately (*b*) unscrupulously.

indémaillable[ɛ̃demajabl] *a* ladderproof, run-resist (tights).

indemne[ɛ̃dɛmn] *a* undamaged; uninjured, unharmed, unscathed.

indemnisation[ɛ̃dɛmnizasjɔ̃] *nf* indemnification; compensation; indemnity.

indemniser[ɛ̃dɛmnize] *vtr* to indemnify; compensate (**de,** for).

indemnité[ɛ̃dɛmnite] *nf* (*a*) indemnity, indemnification, compensation (*b*) penalty (for delay) (*c*) allowance, grant; **i. de déplacement,** travelling expenses; **i. parlementaire** = MP's salary.

indéniable[ɛ̃denjabl] *a* undeniable. **indéniablement** *adv* undeniably.

indépendance[ɛ̃depãdãs] *nf* independence. **indépendant** *a* (*a*) independent (**de,** of); **circonstances indépendantes de ma volonté,** circumstances beyond my control (*b*) self-contained (flat). **indépendamment** *adv* independently (**de,** of); **i. de cela,** apart from that.

indescriptible[ɛ̃dɛskriptibl] *a* indescribable.

indésirable[ɛ̃dezirabl] *a* & *n* undesirable.

indestructible[ɛ̃dɛstryktibl] *a* indestructible.

indétermination [ɛ̃detɛrminasjɔ̃] *nf* vagueness; indecision, irresolution. **indéterminé** *a* 1. undetermined; indeterminate, indefinite, vague (ideas) 2. (*of pers*) irresolute, undecided.

index [ɛ̃dɛks] *nm inv* 1. (*a*) forefinger; index finger (*b*) pointer (of balance); indicator 2. index (of book).

indexation [ɛ̃dɛksasjɔ̃] *nf* (*a*) indexing (*b*) *PolEc:* index linking.

indexer [ɛ̃dɛkse] *vtr* 1. to index 2. to index-link, peg (prices).

indicateur, -trice [ɛ̃dikatœr, -tris] 1. *a* indicatory; **poteau i.**, signpost; **panneau i. (de route)**, road sign 2. *nm* (police) informer 3. *nm* (railway) timetable; (street) directory 4. *nm* indicator; gauge; **i. de vitesse**, *Aut:* speedometer; *Av:* airspeed indicator; **i. d'altitude**, altimeter.

indicatif, -ive [ɛ̃dikatif, -iv] 1. *a* indicative (**de**, of) 2. *a & nm Gram:* indicative (mood) 3. *nm* (*a*) *Tp:* dialling code (*b*) *WTel: etc:* **i. d'appel**, call sign; **i. (musical)**, signature tune, theme tune.

indication [ɛ̃dikasjɔ̃] *nf* 1. indication; indicating 2. (*a*) (piece of) information (*b*) sign, token; clue (*c*) notice 3. *esp pl* instruction(s); **indications du mode d'emploi**, directions for use; **sauf i. contraire**, unless otherwise stated; *Th:* **indications scéniques**, stage directions.

indice [ɛ̃dis] *nm* 1. indication, sign; mark, token 2. *Mth: etc:* (i) index (number) (ii) factor; **i. inférieur**, subscript; **i. du coût de la vie**, cost of living index; **i. des prix**, price index.

indicible [ɛ̃disibl] *a* (*a*) inexpressible, unutterable; unspeakable (*b*) indescribable.

indien, -ienne [ɛ̃djɛ̃, -jɛn] 1. *a* (*a*) *a & n* Indian (of India, America) (*b*) **a en file indienne**, in single file 2. *nf Tex:* **indienne**, printed calico, cotton print.

indifférence [ɛ̃diferɑ̃s] *nf* indifference (**envers**, to(wards)). **indifférent** *a* 1. indifferent (**à**, to); unconcerned 2. immaterial, unimportant; **cela m'est i.**, it's all the same to me; **parler de choses indifférentes**, to chat, talk, of this and that. **indifféremment** *adv* (*a*) indifferently (*b*) equally, indiscriminately.

indifférer [ɛ̃difere] *vtr def used in 3rd pers sing & pl with pronoun complement only* (**il indiffère, il indifférera**) **cela m'indiffère**, I'm indifferent, I couldn't care less about it.

indigence [ɛ̃diʒɑ̃s] *nf* poverty; destitution. **indigent** 1. *a* poor, destitute 2. *n* pauper.

indigène [ɛ̃diʒɛn] 1. *a* indigenous (**à**, to); native (population) 2. *n* native.

indigestion [ɛ̃diʒɛstjɔ̃] *nf* indigestion; **avoir une i.**, to have an attack of indigestion; *F:* **j'en ai une i.**, I'm sick of it. **indigeste** *a* 1. indigestible; stodgy (food) 2. undigested; confused, heavy (book).

indignation [ɛ̃diɲasjɔ̃] *nf* indignation; **avec i.**, indignantly.

indigner [ɛ̃diɲe] *vtr* 1. to make (s.o.) indignant 2. **s'i.**, to become, to be, indignant. **indigné** *a* indignant (**de**, for).

indignité [ɛ̃diɲite] *nf* 1. (*a*) unworthiness (*b*) baseness (of an action) 2. **souffrir des indignités**, to suffer indignities, humiliations. **indigne** *a* 1. (*a*) unworthy; undeserving (*b*) **ce travail est i. de lui**, this work is not good enough for him 2. shameful (action,

conduct). **indignement** *adv* 1. unworthily 2. shamefully.

indigo [ɛ̃digo] *nm & a inv* indigo(-blue).

indiquer [ɛ̃dike] *vtr* (*a*) to indicate; to point (out); **i. qch du doigt**, to point to sth, to point sth out (with one's finger); **i. le chemin à qn**, to show s.o. the way (*b*) to show, mark, indicate; **le compteur indique cent**, the meter reads one hundred; **la somme indiquée sur la facture**, the sum mentioned on the invoice (*c*) to show, tell; **i. un médecin à qn**, to tell s.o. of a doctor (*d*) to point to, to show (*e*) to appoint, name (a day); **à l'heure indiquée**, at the appointed time (*f*) to draw up (procedure); to prescribe (line of action); **c'était indiqué**, it was the obvious thing to do; **il est tout à fait indiqué pour ce poste**, he's just the man for the job; **ce n'est pas très indiqué**, it's not very advisable, suitable.

indirect [ɛ̃dirɛkt] *a* (*a*) indirect; roundabout (way); **éclairage i.**, concealed lighting; **contributions indirectes**, excise revenue (*b*) *Jur:* circumstantial (evidence). **indirectement** *adv* indirectly; in a roundabout way.

indiscipline [ɛ̃disiplin] *nf* lack of discipline. **indiscipliné** *a* undisciplined, unruly.

indiscrétion [ɛ̃diskresjɔ̃] *nf* (*a*) indiscretion; indiscreetness; **sans i.**, without being indiscreet (*b*) indiscreet action, remark; indiscretion. **indiscret, -ète** 1. *a* indiscreet, tactless (pers); **à l'abri des regards indiscrets**, safe from prying eyes 2. *n* indiscreet person. **indiscrètement** *adv* indiscreetly.

indiscutable [ɛ̃diskytabl] *a* indisputable, unquestionable. **indiscutablement** *adv* indisputably, unquestionably. **indiscuté** *a* undisputed, unquestioned.

indispensable [ɛ̃dispɑ̃sabl] 1. *a* indispensable (**à qn**, to s.o., **à**, **pour**, **qch**, for sth); essential (**à**, for, to); absolutely necessary; **il nous est i.**, we can't do without him, spare him 2. *nm* **ne prenez que l'i.**, don't take more than is absolutely necessary.

indisponible [ɛ̃dispɔnibl] *a* unavailable.

indisposer [ɛ̃dispoze] *vtr* 1. to make (s.o.) unwell; (*of food*) to upset, disagree with (s.o.) 2. to antagonize (s.o.). **indisposé** *a* (*a*) indisposed, unwell (*b*) (*of woman*) **être indisposée**, to have one's period.

indisposition [ɛ̃dispozisjɔ̃] *nf* (*a*) indisposition, (slight) illness (*b*) (*of woman*) (monthly) period.

indissociable [ɛ̃disɔsjabl] *a* indissociable.

indissoluble [ɛ̃disɔlybl] *a* indissoluble (bond, friendship).

indistinct [ɛ̃distɛ̃(kt)] *a* indistinct; hazy, vague, blurred; confused; faint. **indistinctement** *adv* (*a*) indiscriminately, indistinctly (*b*) indistinctly, hazily, vaguely; confusedly; faintly.

individu [ɛ̃dividy] *nm* 1. individual 2. *usu Pej:* person, individual; **quel est cet i.?** who's that fellow? **i. louche**, shady customer.

individualiser [ɛ̃dividɥalize] *vtr* 1. to individualize; to specify, particularize (case) 2. **s'i.**, to take on individual characteristics.

individualisme [ɛ̃dividɥalism] *nm* individualism. **individualiste** 1. *a* individualistic 2. *n* individualist.

individualité [ɛ̃dividɥalite] *nf* individuality. **individuel, -elle** *a* individual; personal (liberty);

private (fortune). **individuellement** *adv* individually, personally.

indivisibilité [ɛ̃divizibilite] *nf* indivisibility. **indivisible** *a* indivisible.

Indochine [ɛ̃dɔʃin] *Prn Geog: Hist:* Indochina.

indo-européen, -enne [ɛ̃doørɔpeɛ̃, -ɛn] *a* & *n Ethn: Ling:* Indo-European; *pl indo-européens, -ennes.*

indolence [ɛ̃dɔlɑ̃s] *nf* indolence; apathy, lethargy. **indolent** *a* indolent; apathetic, lethargic.

indolore [ɛ̃dɔlɔr] *a* painless.

indomptable [ɛ̃dɔ̃tabl] *a* unconquerable; untam(e)able; unmanageable; indomitable. **indompté** *a* unconquered; untamed.

Indonésie [ɛ̃dɔnezi] *Prnf Geog:* Indonesia. **indonésien, -ienne** *a* & *n* Indonesian.

indou, -oue [ɛ̃du] *a* & *n Ethn: Rel:* Hindu.

indu [ɛ̃dy] *a* undue; unwarranted; **à une heure indue,** at an ungodly hour. **indûment** *adv* unduly, improperly.

indubitable [ɛ̃dybitabl] *a* beyond doubt, indubitable. **indubitablement** *adv* indubitably, undoubtedly.

induction [ɛ̃dyksjɔ̃] *nf* induction; *El:* **courant d'i.,** induced current; **bobine d'i.,** induction coil.

induire [ɛ̃dɥir] *vtr* (*pr* **j'induis, n. induisons; ph j'induisis;** *pp* **induit**) 1. **i. qn en erreur,** to lead s.o. astray, to mislead s.o. 2. to infer, induce (conclusion).

indulgence [ɛ̃dylʒɑ̃s] *nf* indulgence, leniency. **indulgent** *a* indulgent, lenient.

industrialisation [ɛ̃dystrijalizasjɔ̃] *nf* industrialization.

industrialiser [ɛ̃dystrijalize] *vtr* 1. to industrialize 2. **s'i.,** to become industrialized.

industrie [ɛ̃dystri] *nf* 1. (*a*) activity; industry (*b*) ingenuity 2. industry, manufacturing; **l'i. automobile,** the motor industry; **l'i. du bâtiment,** the building trade; **l'i. du spectacle,** showbusiness. **industriel, -elle** 1. *a* industrial 2. *nm* manufacturer, industrialist. **industriellement** *adv* industrially.

industrieux, -euse [ɛ̃dystrijø, -øz] *a* busy, industrious.

inébranlable [inebrɑ̃labl] *a* unshak(e)able (*a*) immovable, firm (*b*) steadfast, unwavering.

inédit [inedi] *a* 1. unpublished (book) 2. new, original (plan).

ineffable [inefabl] *a* ineffable, unutterable.

ineffaçable [inefasabl] *a* ineffaceable (memory); indelible (stain); non-erasable.

inefficace [inefikas] *a* ineffective, ineffectual; inefficient.

inégalité [inegalite] *nf* 1. inequality, disparity (**entre,** between) 2. unevenness (of ground); **les inégalités du chemin,** the bumps in the road. **inégal, -aux** *a* 1. unequal 2. uneven; irregular. **inégalable** *a* matchless, incomparable. **inégalement** *adv* 1. unequally 2. unevenly. **inégalé** *a* unequalled.

inélégant [inelegɑ̃] *a* inelegant. **inélégamment** *adv* inelegantly.

inéligibilité [ineliʒibilite] *nf* ineligibility. **inéligible** *a* ineligible.

inéluctable [inelyktabl] *a* inescapable. **inéluctablement** *adv* inescapably.

inénarrable [inenarabl] *a* comical; priceless.

ineptie [inɛpsi] *nf* ineptitude; **dire des inepties,** to talk nonsense. **inepte** *a* inept, foolish.

inépuisable [inepɥizabl] *a* inexhaustible; unfailing (patience).

inéquitable [inekitabl] *a* inequitable, unfair.

inertie [inɛrsi] *nf* (*a*) inertia (*b*) sluggishness; passivity. **inerte** *a* inert; sluggish (nature); dull (intelligence); passive (pers).

inespéré [inɛspere] *a* unhoped-for, unexpected.

inestimable [inɛstimabl] *a* inestimable, invaluable.

inévitable [inevitabl] *a* unavoidable; inevitable, inescapable; **c'est i.,** it's bound to happen. **inévitablement** *adv* inevitably.

inexactitude [inɛgzaktityd] *nf* 1. inaccuracy, inexactitude; mistake 2. unpunctuality. **inexact** *a* 1. inexact, inaccurate, incorrect; wrong 2. unpunctual.

inexcusable [inɛkskyzabl] *a* inexcusable.

inexistant [inɛgzistɑ̃] *a* non-existent.

inexorable [inɛgzɔrabl] *a* inexorable, unrelenting. **inexorablement** *adv* inexorably.

inexpérience [inɛksperjɑ̃s] *nf* inexperience. **inexpérimenté** *a* 1. inexperienced; inexpert; unskilled 2. untested (process).

inexplicable [inɛksplikabl] *a* inexplicable. **inexplicablement** *adv* inexplicably. **inexpliqué** *a* unexplained.

inexploitable [inɛksplwatabl] *a* unexploitable; unworkable (mine). **inexploité** *a* unexploited; unworked (mine).

inexploré [inɛksplɔre] *a* unexplored.

inexpressif, -ive [inɛksprɛsif, -iv] *a* inexpressive; expressionless (face).

inexprimable [inɛksprimabl] *a* inexpressible.

inextinguible [inɛkstɛ̃g(ɥ)ibl] *a* inextinguishable; unquenchable (fire, thirst).

in extremis [inɛkstremis] 1. *adv phr* in extremis, at the last minute 2. *adj phr* last-minute (will).

inextricable [inɛkstrikabl] *a* inextricable. **inextricablement** *adv* inextricably.

infaillibilité [ɛ̃fajibilite] *nf* infallibility. **infaillible** *a* 1. infallible; unerring 2. certain, unfailing, infallible (remedy). **infailliblement** *adv* infallibly.

infaisable [ɛ̃fəzabl] *a* impracticable; **c'est i.,** it can't be done.

infamie [ɛ̃fami] *nf* 1. infamy 2. infamous action; foul deed; **dire des infamies à qn,** to slander s.o. **infamant** *a* 1. defamatory 2. infamous. **infâme** *a* infamous; foul (deed); unspeakable (crime).

infanterie [ɛ̃fɑ̃tri] *nf* infantry.

infantilisme [ɛ̃fɑ̃tilism] *nm* (*a*) *Med:* infantilism; retarded development (*b*) **c'est de l'i.,** how infantile, childish! **infantile** *a* (*a*) infantile; **psychiatrie i.,** child psychiatry (*b*) infantile, childish.

infarctus [ɛ̃farktys] *nm Med:* **i. (du myocarde),** coronary thrombosis.

infatigable [ɛ̃fatigabl] *a* indefatigable, untiring, tireless. **infatigablement** *adv* indefatigably, untiringly, tirelessly.

infatuation [ɛ̃fatɥasjɔ̃] *nf* self-conceit.

infatuer (s') [sɛ̃fatɥe] *vpr* **s'i. de qn, qch,** to become infatuated with s.o., sth. **infatué** *a* conceited; **i. de soi-même,** full of one's own importance.

infect [ɛ̃fɛkt] *a* (*a*) stinking; foul; **odeur infecte,** stench

(b) filthy (hovel); **temps i.,** filthy, foul, weather; **repas i.,** revolting meal.

infecter [ɛ̃fɛkte] *vtr* **1.** (a) to infect (**de,** with) (b) to poison (atmosphere); to contaminate (water) **2. s'i.,** to go septic.

infection [ɛ̃fɛksjɔ̃] *nf* **1.** infection **2.** stench. **infectieux, -euse** *a* infectious.

inférer [ɛ̃fere] *vtr* (**j'infère;** *fu* **j'inférerai**) to infer, gather (**de,** from).

infériorité [ɛ̃ferjɔrite] *nf* inferiority; **i. en nombre,** inferiority in numbers; *Psy:* **complexe d'i.,** inferiority complex. **inférieur, -eure** *a* **1.** inferior; lower; **lèvre inférieure,** lower, bottom, lip; (*of temperature*) **i. à la normale,** below normal **2.** (a) inferior; **d'un rang i.,** lower in rank (b) inferior, poor (quality) (c) **6 est i. à 8,** 6 is less than 8 **3.** *n* inferior.

infernal, -aux [ɛ̃fɛrnal, -o] *a* infernal; **c'est i.!** it's sheer hell!

infertile [ɛ̃fɛrtil] *a* infertile.

infester [ɛ̃feste] *vtr* to infest, overrun.

infidélité [ɛ̃fidelite] *nf* (a) infidelity, unfaithfulness, disloyalty (**à,** to) (b) inaccuracy (of translation). **infidèle 1.** *a* (a) unfaithful, faithless, disloyal (**à,** to) (b) inaccurate; unreliable (memory) **2.** *a & n Rel:* infidel.

infiltration [ɛ̃filtrasjɔ̃] *nf* infiltration; percolation.

infiltrer (s') [sɛ̃filtre] *vpr* **1.** to infiltrate, percolate, seep (**dans,** into; **à travers,** through); to filter, soak, in, through **2.** to infiltrate (**dans un pays,** in a country).

infime [ɛ̃fim] *a* tiny, minute.

infini [ɛ̃finite] *nf* (a) *Mth: etc:* infinity (b) **l'i. de l'espace,** the boundlessness of space; **une i. de raisons,** an infinite number of reasons; endless reasons. **infini 1.** *a* infinite; boundless, immeasurable (space); never-ending, endless; innumerable **2.** *nm* **l'i.,** the infinite; *Phot:* **mettre au point sur l'i.,** to focus on infinity; **à l'i.,** to infinity, ad infinitum. **infiniment** *adv* infinitely; **se donner i. de peine,** to give oneself no end of trouble, an infinite amount of trouble; **je regrette i.,** I'm terribly sorry. **infinitésimal, -aux** *a* infinitesimal.

infinitif, -ive [ɛ̃finitif, -iv] *a & nm Gram:* infinitive (mood).

infirmer [ɛ̃firme] *vtr* to invalidate.

infirmerie [ɛ̃firməri] *nf* infirmary; (*school, ship*) sick bay.

infirmier, -ière [ɛ̃firmje, -jɛr] **1.** *nm* male nurse **2.** *nf* nurse.

infirmité [ɛ̃firmite] *nf* (a) infirmity (b) physical disability. **infirme 1.** *a* (a) infirm (b) disabled, crippled **2.** *n* (a) invalid (b) cripple; disabled person.

inflammable [ɛ̃flamabl] *a* inflammable; *Tchn: & NAm:* flammable.

inflammation [ɛ̃flamasjɔ̃] *nf Med:* inflammation. **inflammatoire** *a* inflammatory.

inflation [ɛ̃flasjɔ̃] *nf PolEc:* inflation. **inflationniste 1.** *a* inflationary **2.** *n* inflationist.

infléchir [ɛ̃fleʃir] *vtr* **1.** to bend, inflect (ray) **2. s'i.** (a) to bend, curve; (*of ray*) to be inflected (b) (*of structure*) to cave in.

inflexibilité [ɛ̃flɛksibilite] *nf* inflexibility. **inflexible** *a* inflexible, unbending; unyielding, rigid.

inflexion [ɛ̃flɛksjɔ̃] *nf* **1.** (a) inflexion; bend(ing) (b)

bending (of body); nod (of head); **légère i. du corps,** slight bow **2.** inflexion, modulation (of voice).

infliger [ɛ̃fliʒe] *vtr* (**n. infligeons**) to inflict; to impose (penalty).

influence [ɛ̃flyɑ̃s] *nf* influence; **il a beaucoup d'i.,** he's very influential; **avoir une i. néfaste sur,** to have a harmful effect on. **influençable** *a* easily influenced. **influent** *a* influential.

influencer [ɛ̃flyɑ̃se] *vtr* (**n. influençons**) to influence, to have an influence on (s.o.).

influer [ɛ̃flye] *vi* **i. sur qn,** to influence, to have an influence on (s.o.).

influx [ɛ̃fly] *nm* **i. nerveux,** nerve impulse.

informateur, -trice [ɛ̃fɔrmatœr, -tris] *n* informant.

informaticien, -ienne [ɛ̃fɔrmatisjɛ̃, -jɛn] *n* computer scientist.

information [ɛ̃fɔrmasjɔ̃] *nf* (a) inquiry; *Jur:* **ouvrir une i.,** to begin legal proceedings (b) information; news (item); **prendre des informations (sur qn),** to make inquiries (about s.o.); **je vous envoie, pour votre i.,** I am sending you for your information; *WTel: TV: Journ:* **informations,** news (bulletin) (c) *Cmptr:* data; **traitement de l'i.,** data processing.

informatique [ɛ̃fɔrmatik] **1.** *nf* data processing; computer science; **le monde de l'i.,** the computer world **2.** *a* **réseau i.,** computer network, information network.

informe [ɛ̃fɔrm] *a* (a) formless, shapeless (b) ill-formed; misshapen.

informer [ɛ̃fɔrme] **1.** *vtr* **i. qn de qch,** to inform s.o. of sth; **veuillez m'en i.,** please let me know; **mal informé,** misinformed **2.** *vi Jur:* (a) **i. sur un crime,** to investigate a crime (b) **i. contre qn,** to inform against s.o. **3. s'i.,** to make inquiries; **s'i. de qch,** to ask about sth; to find out about sth. **informatif, -ive** *a* informative.

infortune [ɛ̃fɔrtyn] *nf* misfortune. **infortuné, -ée** **1.** *a* unfortunate, ill fated **2.** *n* wretched person; poor wretch.

infraction [ɛ̃fraksjɔ̃] *nf* **1.** infringement **2.** offence; breach (of law); **commettre une i.,** to be committing an offence.

infranchissable [ɛ̃frɑ̃ʃisabl] *a* impassable, insurmountable, insuperable (difficulty).

infrarouge [ɛ̃fraruʒ] *a & nm* infrared.

infrastructure [ɛ̃frastryktyr] *nf CivE:* substructure; *Tchn:* infrastructure.

infroissable [ɛ̃frwasabl] *a Tex: etc:* crease-resisting; uncrushable.

infructueux, -euse [ɛ̃fryktɥø, -øz] *a* unfruitful; fruitless.

infuser [ɛ̃fyze] **1.** *vtr* (a) to instil (**à,** into) (b) to steep, macerate (herbs) **2.** *vi* **faire i. le thé,** to infuse, brew, the tea.

infusion [ɛ̃fyzjɔ̃] *nf* infusion; herb tea; **i. de tilleul,** lime tea.

ingénierie [ɛ̃ʒeniri] *nf* engineering.

ingénier (s') [sɛ̃ʒenje] *vpr* **s'i. à faire qch,** to contrive, make an effort, to do sth.

ingénieur [ɛ̃ʒenjœr] *nm* engineer; **i. (des travaux publics),** civil engineer; **i. du son,** sound engineer.

ingéniosité [ɛ̃ʒenjozite] *nf* ingenuity; cleverness.

ingénieux, -euse *a* ingenious, clever.
ingénieusement *adv* ingeniously, cleverly.
ingénuité [ε̃ʒenɥite] *nf* ingenuousness, artlessness, naïvety, simplicity. **ingénu** *a* & *n* ingenuous, artless, naïve (person); **faire l'i.,** to affect simplicity.
ingénument *adv* ingenuously, artlessly, naïvely.
ingérer [ε̃ʒere] *vtr* (**je m'ingère, n.n. ingérons**) 1. to ingest (food) 2. **s'i. dans une affaire,** to interfere in, meddle with, a matter.
ingouvernable [ε̃guvεrnabl] *a* ungovernable.
ingratitude [ε̃gratityd] *nf* ingratitude, ungratefulness. **ingrat, -ate** 1. *a* (*a*) ungrateful (**envers,** towards) (*b*) unproductive, unprofitable (soil); thankless (task) (*c*) disagreeable, repellent (work) (*d*) unattractive (appearance); **l'âge i.,** the awkward age 2. *n* ungrateful, heartless, person.
ingrédient [ε̃gredjã] *nm* ingredient.
inguérissable [ε̃gerisabl] *a* (*a*) incurable (*b*) inconsolable (grief).
ingurgiter [ε̃gyrʒite] *vtr* to ingurgitate, swallow.
inhabileté [inabilte] *nf* lack of skill; clumsiness. **inhabile** *a* unskilled, clumsy; incompetent.
inhabilité [inabilite] *nf Jur:* incapacity, disability.
inhabitable [inabitabl] *a* uninhabitable. **inhabité** *a* uninhabited.
inhabituel, -elle [inabitɥεl] *a* unusual.
inhalation [inalasjɔ̃] *nf* inhalation.
inhaler [inale] *vtr* to inhale.
inhérent [inerã] *a* inherent (**à,** in).
inhiber [inibe] *vtr* to inhibit.
inhibition [inibisjɔ̃] *nf* inhibition.
inhospitalier, -ière [inɔspitalje, -jεr] *a* inhospitable.
inhumain [inymε̃] *a* inhuman; unfeeling.
inhumation [inymasjɔ̃] *nf* interment.
inhumer [inyme] *vtr* to inter.
inimaginable [inimaʒinabl] *a* unimaginable; unthinkable.
inimitable [inimitabl] *a* inimitable.
inimitié [inimitje] *nf* enmity, hostility, ill-feeling.
ininflammable [inε̃flamabl] *a* non-(in)flammable.
inintelligent [inε̃teliʒã] *a* unintelligent.
inintelligibilité [inε̃teliʒibilite] *nf* unintelligibility. **inintelligible** *a* unintelligible.
inintéressant [inε̃teresã] *a* uninteresting.
ininterrompu [inε̃terɔ̃py] *a* uninterrupted; unbroken; steady (progress).
iniquité [inikite] *nf* iniquity. **inique** *a* iniquitous.
initial, -aux [inisjal, -o] 1. *a* initial (letter); starting (price) 2. *nf* initial (letter). **initialement** *adv* initially.
initiation [inisjasjɔ̃] *nf* (*a*) initiation (**à,** into); **i. à la musique,** introduction to music (*b*) **i. à la gestion des stocks,** inventory control primer. **initiateur, -trice** 1. *a* initiatory 2. *n* initiator; pioneer (of scheme).
initiative [inisjativ] *nf* initiative; **prendre l'i. de faire qch,** to take the initiative in doing sth; **il n'a aucune i.,** he has no initiative; **syndicat d'i.,** tourist information bureau.
initier [inisje] *vtr* 1. to initiate (s.o.) (**à,** in); to introduce (s.o.) (to sth) 2. **s'i. à qch,** to learn sth; to get to know sth. **initié, -ée** 1. *a* initiated 2. *n* initiate.

injecter [ε̃ʒεkte] *vtr* 1. to inject 2. (*of eyes*) **s'i.,** to become bloodshot. **injectable** *a* injectable.
injection [ε̃ʒεksjɔ̃] *nf* injection; **moteur à i.,** injection engine.
injonction [ε̃ʒɔ̃ksjɔ̃] *nf* injunction; *Jur:* order.
injure [ε̃ʒyr] *nf* (*a*) insult; *pl* abuse (*b*) **faire i. à qn,** to insult s.o.
injurier [ε̃ʒyrje] *vtr* to abuse, insult (s.o.). **injurieux, -euse** *a* abusive, insulting. **injurieusement** *adv* abusively, insultingly.
injustice [ε̃ʒystis] *nf* (*a*) injustice, unfairness (**envers,** towards) (*b*) (*action*) injustice. **injuste** *a* unjust, unfair. **injustement** *adv* unjustly.
injustifiable [ε̃ʒystifjabl] *a* unjustifiable. **injustifié** *a* unjustified, unwarranted.
inlassable [ε̃lɑsabl] *a* untiring, unflagging; tireless (person). **inlassablement** *adv* untiringly, tirelessly; unflaggingly.
inné [ine] *a* innate, inborn.
innocence [inɔsɑ̃s] *nf* innocence (*a*) guiltlessness (*b*) naïvety (*c*) harmlessness. **innocent, -ente** 1. *a* (*a*) innocent (*b*) pure, innocent (*c*) naïve (*d*) harmless 2. *n* innocent; simpleton; **l'i. du village,** the village idiot. **innocemment** *adv* innocently.
innocenter [inɔsɑ̃te] *vtr* **i. qn (d'une accusation),** to clear s.o. (of a charge).
innombrable [inɔ̃brabl] *a* innumerable, countless; vast (crowd).
innommable [inɔmabl] *a* unspeakable (behaviour).
innovation [inɔvasjɔ̃] *nf* innovation. **innovateur, -trice** 1. *a* innovative 2. *n* innovator.
innover [inɔve] *vi* to innovate; to break new ground 2. *vtr* to introduce, invent (sth new).
inoccupé [inɔkype] *a* 1. unoccupied; idle 2. unoccupied; vacant (seat); uninhabited (house).
inoculation [inɔkylasjɔ̃] *nf* inoculation.
inoculer [inɔkyle] *vtr* (*a*) **i. une maladie à qn,** to infect s.o. with a disease; **elle nous a inoculé sa gaieté,** we were swept away by her gaiety (*b*) **i. qn,** to inoculate s.o. (**contre,** against).
inodore [inɔdɔr] *a* odourless; scentless.
inoffensif, -ive [inɔfɑ̃sif, -iv] *a* inoffensive; harmless, innocuous.
inondation [inɔ̃dasjɔ̃] *nf* (*a*) inundation, flooding (*b*) flood; deluge (of questions).
inonder [inɔ̃de] *vtr* (*a*) to inundate, flood (fields); to glut (market) (*b*) to soak, drench.
inopérable [inɔperabl] *a* inoperable.
inopiné [inɔpine] *a* sudden, unexpected. **inopinément** *adv* unexpected.
inopportun, -une [inɔpɔrtœ̃, -yn] *a* inopportune; untimely; unseasonable, ill-timed. **inopportunément** *adv* inopportunely.
inorganique [inɔrganik] *a* inorganic.
inorganisé [inɔrganize] *a* unorganized.
inoubliable [inublijabl] *a* unforgettable.
inouï [inui, inwi] *a* unheard of; extraordinary, outrageous; *F:* **il est i.,** he's incredible.
inox [inɔks] *a* & *nm F:* (**acier**) **i.,** stainless (steel).
inoxydable [inɔksidabl] *a* rustproof; **acier i.,** *nm* **i.,** stainless steel.
inqualifiable [ε̃kalifjabl] *a* unspeakable (behaviour).
inquiéter [ε̃kjete] *vtr* (**j'inquiète; j'inquiéterai**) 1. to

worry, disturb (s.o.); to harass (enemy); **sa santé m'inquiète,** I'm anxious about his health **2. s'i.,** to become anxious, to get worried; **ne vous inquiétez pas de cela,** don't bother about that. **inquiet, -iète 1.** *a* (*a*) restless; **sommeil i.,** troubled sleep (*b*) anxious; uneasy; worried **2.** *n* worrier. **inquiétant** *a* disturbing, worrying.

inquiétude [ɛ̃kjetyd] *nf* anxiety; concern, uneasiness; disquiet; **soyez sans i.,** don't worry.

inquisition [ɛ̃kizisjɔ̃] *nf* inquisition. **inquisiteur, -trice 1.** *a* inquisitive **2.** *n* inquisitor.

insaisissable [ɛ̃sɛzisabl̩] *a* (*a*) elusive (*b*) imperceptible.

insalubre [ɛ̃salybr] *a* insalubrious; unhealthy.

insanité [ɛ̃sanite] *nf* insanity; madness.

insatiable [ɛ̃sasjabl̩] *a* insatiable. **insatiablement** *adv* insatiably.

insatisfaction [ɛ̃satisfaksjɔ̃] *nf* dissatisfaction. **insatisfait** *a* (*a*) dissatisfied (*b*) unsatisfied (desire).

inscription [ɛ̃skripsjɔ̃] *nf* **1.** (*a*) entering, recording (in diary) (*b*) registration, enrolment; **feuille d'i.,** entry form; **prendre son i.,** to enter one's name **2.** (*a*) inscription (on tomb); entry (in account book) (*b*) directions (on signpost); notice.

inscrire [ɛ̃skrir] *vtr* (*prp* **inscrivant;** *pp* **inscrit;** *pr ind* **j'inscris,** n. **inscrivons;** *ph* **j'inscrivis;** *fu* **j'inscrirai**) **1.** (*a*) to inscribe, write down; to enter, take down, note (down) (details) (*b*) to register (marriage); to enrol (s.o.); to enter (s.o.'s) name; **se faire i. à un cours,** to put one's name down for a course; to enrol on a course (*c*) to inscribe, engrave (epitaph) **2. s'i.** (*a*) to put one's name down; to register, enrol (*b*) *Jur:* **s'i. en faux contre qch,** to deny sth (*c*) **ça s'inscrit dans le cadre de,** it's in keeping with.

insecte [ɛ̃sɛkt] *nm* insect.

insecticide [ɛ̃sɛktisid] *nm* insecticide.

insécurité [ɛ̃sekyrite] *nf* insecurity.

INSEE [inse] *abbr Institut national de la statistique et des études économiques.*

insémination [ɛ̃seminasjɔ̃] *nf* insemination.

inséminer [ɛ̃semine] *vtr* to inseminate.

insensé, -ée [ɛ̃sɑ̃se] *a* (*a*) mad, insane; *n* madman, -woman (*b*) senseless, foolish (*c*) extravagant, wild (scheme).

insensibilisation [ɛ̃sɑ̃sibilizasjɔ̃] *nf* anaesthetization.

insensibiliser [ɛ̃sɑ̃sibilize] *vtr Med:* to anaesthetize.

insensibilité [ɛ̃sɑ̃sibilite] *nf* insensitiveness, insensitivity; insensibility. **insensible** (*a*) insensitive; indifferent; insensible (*b*) imperceptible. **insensiblement** *adv* imperceptibly.

inséparable [ɛ̃separabl̩] **1.** *a* inseparable **2.** *nmpl Orn:* lovebirds.

insérer [ɛ̃sere] *vtr* (**j'insère; j'insérerai**) **1.** to insert **2. s'i.,** to fit (**dans,** into).

insertion [ɛ̃sɛrsjɔ̃] *nf* insertion.

insidieux, -euse [ɛ̃sidjø, -øz] *a* insidious. **insidieusement** *adv* insidiously.

insigne[1] [ɛ̃siɲ] *a* **1.** distinguished, remarkable (**par,** for); **faveur i.,** signal favour **2.** *Pej:* notorious; arrant (liar).

insigne[2] *nm* distinguishing mark; badge; *pl* insignia.

insignifiance [ɛ̃siɲifjɑ̃s] *nf* insignificance,

unimportance. **insignifiant** *a* insignificant, trifling.

insinuation [ɛ̃sinɥasjɔ̃] *nf* insinuation; innuendo.

insinuer [ɛ̃sinɥe] *vtr* **1.** to insinuate; to suggest, hint at (sth); **que voulez-vous i.?** what are you hinting, getting, at? **2. s'i.,** to penetrate; to creep (in); to worm one's way (into).

insipide [ɛ̃sipid] *a* (*a*) insipid; tasteless (*b*) dull, flat; tame (story).

insistance [ɛ̃sistɑ̃s] *nf* insistance (**à faire qch,** on doing sth); insistency.

insister [ɛ̃siste] *vi* to insist; **i. sur un fait,** to dwell, lay stress, on a fact; **i. pour faire qch,** to insist on doing sth; **n'insistez pas trop,** (i) don't put too much emphasis on that (ii) don't be too insistent. **insistant** *a* insistent.

insociable [ɛ̃sɔsjabl̩] *a* unsociable.

insolation [ɛ̃sɔlasjɔ̃] *nf* (*a*) exposure (to the sun) (*b*) sunstroke.

insolence [ɛ̃sɔlɑ̃s] *nf* (*a*) insolence, impertinence (*b*) insolent remark. **insolent** *a* (*a*) insolent, impertinent (*b*) extraordinary (success); **luxe i.,** unashamed luxury. **insolemment** *adv* insolently.

insolite [ɛ̃sɔlit] *a* unusual; strange, odd.

insoluble [ɛ̃sɔlybl̩] *a* insoluble (substance); insoluble, insolvable (problem).

insolvabilité [ɛ̃sɔlvabilite] *nf Com:* insolvency. **insolvable** *a* insolvent.

insomniaque [ɛ̃sɔmnjak] *n* insomniac.

insomnie [ɛ̃sɔmni] *nf* insomnia, sleeplessness; **nuit d'i.,** sleepless night.

insondable [ɛ̃sɔ̃dabl̩] *a* unfathomable.

insonorisation [ɛ̃sɔnɔrizasjɔ̃] *nf* soundproofing. **insonore** *a* soundproof.

insonoriser [ɛ̃sɔnɔrize] *vtr* to soundproof.

insouciance [ɛ̃susjɑ̃s] *nf* (*a*) unconcern; lack of concern (*b*) thoughtlessness. **insouciant** *a* (*a*) unconcerned (*b*) thoughtless; happy-go-lucky. **insoucieux, -euse** *a* carefree; heedless (**de,** of).

insoumission [ɛ̃sumisjɔ̃] *nf* rebelliousness; *Mil:* failure to rejoin one's unit. **insoumis, -ise 1.** *a* unsubdued **2.** *a & n* unruly, rebellious (person) **3.** *a & nm Mil:* absentee (soldier).

insoupçonnable [ɛ̃supsɔnabl̩] *a* above suspicion. **insoupçonné** *a* unsuspected (**de,** by).

insoutenable [ɛ̃sutnabl̩] *a* **1.** untenable (opinion) **2.** unbearable (pain).

inspecter [ɛ̃spɛkte] *vtr* to inspect.

inspecteur, -trice [ɛ̃spɛktœr, -tris] *n* inspector; overseer (of works); surveyor (of mines); **i. de la sûreté,** detective inspector.

inspection [ɛ̃spɛksjɔ̃] *nf* **1.** inspection; **faire l'i. de,** to inspect **2.** inspectorship, inspectorate.

inspirateur, -trice [ɛ̃spiratœr, -tris] *n* inspirer; instigator (of plot).

inspiration [ɛ̃spirasjɔ̃] *nf* **1.** *Physiol:* inspiration; breathing in **2.** (*a*) prompting; **sous l'i. de qn,** at s.o.'s instigation (*b*) inspiration; **i. soudaine,** brainwave.

inspirer [ɛ̃spire] *vtr* **1.** (*a*) **i. le respect,** to inspire respect; **inspiré par la jalousie,** prompted by jealousy (*b*) to inhale, to breathe in **2. s'i. de qn, de qch,** to draw one's inspiration from, to be inspired by, s.o., sth.

instabilité [ɛ̃stabilite] *nf* instability; unsteadiness.

instable a unstable; shaky; unsteady; unreliable; changeable (weather).

installateur [ɛ̃stalatœr] nm fitter, installer.

installation [ɛ̃stalasjɔ̃] nf 1. installation; installing; setting up (of machine, house); fitting out (of workshop); fixing (of curtains) 2. (a) arrangements (of house); fittings, equipment; i. **électrique,** wiring (b) Ind: plant.

installer [ɛ̃stale] vtr 1. (a) to install; i. **qn dans un fauteuil,** to make s.o. comfortable in an armchair (b) to set up (machine); to fit up, equip (factory, kitchen); to fix (curtains) (c) to establish, settle (one's family) 2. s'i., to install oneself; to settle (down); to make oneself at home; s'i. **à la campagne,** to settle in the country; **elle s'est installée chez moi,** she moved in with me.

instamment [ɛ̃stamɑ̃] adv insistently, earnestly.

instance [ɛ̃stɑ̃s] nf 1. (a) **demander qch avec i.,** to beg s.o. for sth (b) pl requests, entreaties (c) Jur: process, suit; **introduire une i. (en) justice,** to institute an action; **ils sont en i. de divorce,** their divorce proceedings are taking place; **tribunal d'i.** = magistrate's court; **tribunal de grande i.** = county court; **en seconde i.,** on appeal (d) authority 2. **être en i. de départ,** to be about to leave.

instant[1] [ɛ̃stɑ̃] a pressing, urgent.

instant[2] nm moment, instant; **à chaque i., à tout i.,** continually; at any moment, minute; **par instants,** now and then; **un i.!** wait a moment! **à l'i.,** (i) a moment ago (ii) immediately; **pour l'i.,** for the time being; **en un i.,** in no time; **soin de tous les instants,** ceaseless care.

instantané [ɛ̃stɑ̃tane] 1. a instantaneous 2. nm Phot: snapshot. **instantanément** adv instantaneously.

instauration [ɛ̃stɔrasjɔ̃] nf founding, institution.

instaurer [ɛ̃stɔre] vtr to found, institute.

instigateur, -trice [ɛ̃stigatœr, -tris] n instigator.

instigation [ɛ̃stigasjɔ̃] nf instigation.

instinct [ɛ̃stɛ̃] nm instinct; **d'i.,** instinctively. **instinctif, -ive** a instinctive. **instinctivement** adv instinctively.

instituer [ɛ̃stitɥe] vtr (a) to institute; to establish, set up, found (an institution) (b) to appoint (official).

institut [ɛ̃stity] nm 1. institute, institution; **l'I. (de France),** the Institute (composed of the five Academies) 2. (a) institute, college (b) i. **de beauté,** beauty salon.

instituteur, -trice [ɛ̃stitytœr, -tris] n (primary school) teacher.

institution [ɛ̃stitysjɔ̃] nf (a) institution (b) (educational) establishment; independent school. **institutionnel, -elle** a institutional.

instructeur [ɛ̃stryktœr] nm instructor.

instruction [ɛ̃stryksjɔ̃] nf 1. pl instructions, directions, orders 2. education; schooling; instruction; i. **professionnelle,** vocational training; **avoir de l'i.,** to be well educated 3. Jur: preliminary investigation (of case); **juge d'i.,** examining magistrate 4. (official) memo, circular.

instruire [ɛ̃strɥir] vtr (prp **instruisant;** pp **instruit;** pr ind **j'instruis;** ph **j'instruisis**) 1. (a) i. **qn de qch,** to inform s.o. of sth (b) to teach, educate, instruct (c) to train, drill (troops) (d) Jur: to examine (case) 2. s'i. (a)

to educate oneself (b) s'i. **de qch,** to get information about sth. **instruit** a educated; well-read.

instrument [ɛ̃strymɑ̃] nm (a) instrument, implement; i. **de travail,** tool; **être l'i. de qn,** to be s.o.'s tool (b) (musical) instrument (c) (legal) instrument. **instrumental, -aux** a instrumental.

instrumentation [ɛ̃strymɑ̃tasjɔ̃] nf Mus: scoring, instrumentation, orchestration.

instrumenter [ɛ̃strymɑ̃te] vtr Mus: to score, orchestrate (opera).

instrumentiste [ɛ̃strymɑ̃tist] n instrumentalist.

insu [ɛ̃sy] nm used in the phr **à l'i. de qn,** without s.o.'s knowledge, without s.o. knowing; **à mon i.,** without my knowing.

insubmersible [ɛ̃sybmɛrsibl] a unsinkable.

insubordination [ɛ̃sybɔrdinasjɔ̃] nf insubordination. **insubordonné** a insubordinate.

insuccès [ɛ̃syksɛ] nm failure.

insuffisance [ɛ̃syfizɑ̃s] nf 1. insufficiency, deficiency; shortage (of staff); inadequacy (of means) 2. incompetence, inefficiency. **insuffisant** a 1. insufficient; inadequate; **c'est i.,** it's not enough 2. incompetent.

insuffler [ɛ̃syfle] vtr to blow (into sth).

insulaire [ɛ̃syler] 1. a insular 2. n islander.

insuline [ɛ̃sylin] nf insulin.

insulte [ɛ̃sylt] nf insult.

insulter [ɛ̃sylte] vtr to insult, affront (s.o.). **insultant** a insulting, offensive.

insupportable [ɛ̃sypɔrtabl] a unbearable; intolerable; insufferable; **il est i.!** he's the limit!

insurger (s') [sɛsyrʒe] vpr (n. n. **insurgeons**) to rise (in rebellion); to revolt. **insurgé, -ée** a & n insurgent, rebel.

insurmontable [ɛ̃syrmɔ̃tabl] a insurmountable, insuperable (obstacle); unconquerable (aversion).

insurrection [ɛ̃syrɛksjɔ̃] nf insurrection, (up)rising, revolt. **insurrectionnel, -elle** a insurrectional, insurrectionary.

intact [ɛ̃takt] a (a) intact; untouched; undamaged (b) unsullied (reputation).

intangibilité [ɛ̃tɑ̃ʒibilite] nf (a) intangibility (b) inviolability. **intangible** a (a) intangible (b) inviolable.

intarissable [ɛ̃tarisabl] a inexhaustible. **intarissablement** adv inexhaustibly.

intégralité [ɛ̃tegralite] nf **l'i.,** the whole; **dans son i.,** in its entirety. **intégral, -als, -aux** 1. a (a) entire, complete, whole; **paiement i.,** payment in full; **texte i.,** full text; **édition intégrale,** unabridged edition (b) Mth: **calcul i.,** integral calculus 2. nf (a) Mth: integral (b) complete works. **intégralement** adv wholly, entirely. in full.

intégration [ɛ̃tegrasjɔ̃] nf integration.

intégrer [ɛ̃tegre] vtr (**j'intègre; j'intégrerai**) 1. to integrate (**à, dans,** into) 2. s'i., to become integrated (**à, dans,** into, with). **intégrant** a integral (part); **faire partie intégrante de,** to be part and parcel of.

intégrité [ɛ̃tegrite] nf integrity; uprightness, honesty. **intègre** [ɛ̃tegr] a upright, honest.

intellect [ɛ̃telɛkt] nm intellect. **intellectuel, -elle** 1. a intellectual; mental (fatigue) 2. n intellectual; Pej: highbrow. **intellectuellement** adv intellectually.

intelligence [ɛ̃teliʒɑ̃s] *nf* 1. understanding, comprehension; **avoir l'i. des affaires,** to have a good knowledge of, a good head for, business 2. intelligence, intellect 3. (a) **vivre en bonne i. avec qn,** to be on good terms with s.o.; **être d'i. avec qn,** to have an understanding with s.o., to be in collusion with s.o. (b) *pl* **avoir des intelligences avec l'ennemi,** to have secret dealings with the enemy. **intelligent** *a* intelligent; clever, bright. **intelligemment** *adv* intelligently; cleverly.

intelligibilité [ɛ̃teliʒibilite] *nf* intelligibility. **intelligible** *a* (a) intelligible, understandable (b) clear, distinct. **intelligiblement** *adv* intelligibly.

intempérance [ɛ̃tɑ̃perɑ̃s] *nf* intemperance. **intempérant** *a* intemperate.

intempéries [ɛ̃tɑ̃peri] *nfpl* bad weather.

intempestif, -ive [ɛ̃tɑ̃pestif, -iv] *a* untimely; inopportune (remark).

intemporel, -elle [ɛ̃tɑ̃pɔrɛl] *a* (a) timeless (b) immaterial.

intenable [ɛ̃tnabl] *a* (a) untenable (b) intolerable, unbearable.

intendance [ɛ̃tɑ̃dɑ̃s] *nf* 1. *Sch:* bursary 2. *Mil:* the Commissariat.

intendant, -ente [ɛ̃tɑ̃dɑ̃, -ɑ̃t] 1. *nm* (a) *Sch:* bursar (b) *Mil:* senior Commissariat officer (c) steward 2. *nf* (a) *Sch:* (woman) bursar (b) steward.

intensifier [ɛ̃tɑ̃sifje] *vtr* (*impf & pr sub* **n. intensifiions**), to intensify.

intensité [ɛ̃tɑ̃site] *nf* intensity; force (of wind); depth (of colour); severity (of cold); strength (of current). **intense** *a* intense; severe (pain, cold); deep (colour); heavy (traffic). **intensément** *adv* intensely. **intensif, -ive** *a* intensive.

intention [ɛ̃tɑ̃sjɔ̃] *nf* (a) intention; purpose, design; **sans mauvaise i.,** with no ill intent; **avoir l'i. de faire qch,** to intend to do sth; **avoir de bonnes intentions,** to mean well; **dans l'i. de,** with a view to (b) will, wish; **à l'i. de,** in honour of; for the sake of; in aid of; **je l'ai acheté à votre i.,** I bought it especially for you. **intentionné** *a* (a) **bien i., mal i.,** well, ill, disposed (envers qn, towards s.o.) (b) **personne bien intentionnée,** well intentioned, well meaning, person. **intentionnel, -elle** *a* intentional, deliberate. **intentionnellement** *adv* intentionally.

inter [ɛ̃tɛr] *nm* 1. *Tp:* trunk (line) 2. *Sp: F:* **i. droit, gauche,** inside right, left.

interaction [ɛ̃tɛraksjɔ̃] *nf* interaction.

interallié [ɛ̃tɛralje] *a* interallied.

interarmes [ɛ̃tɛrarm] *a inv Mil:* combined (staff, operations).

interastral, -aux [ɛ̃tɛrastral, -o] *a* interstellar (space).

intercaler [ɛ̃tɛrkale] *vtr* to insert, inset; to intersperse. **intercalaire** *a* **feuillet i.,** inset.

intercéder [ɛ̃tɛrsede] *vi* (**j'intercède**) to intercede (**auprès de,** with).

intercepter [ɛ̃tɛrsɛpte] *vtr* to intercept; to cut, to shut, off.

interception [ɛ̃tɛrsɛpsjɔ̃] *nf* interception; *WTel:* **i. des émissions,** monitoring.

interchangeable [ɛ̃tɛrʃɑ̃ʒabl] *a* interchangeable.

interclasse [ɛ̃tɛrklas] *nm Sch:* (short) break (between classes).

intercontinental, -aux [ɛ̃tɛrkɔ̃tinɑ̃tal, -o] *a* intercontinental.

interdépendance [ɛ̃tɛrdepɑ̃dɑ̃s] *nf* interdependance. **interdépendant** *a* interdependant.

interdiction [ɛ̃tɛrdiksjɔ̃] *nf* prohibition; forbidding; ban (**de, on**); **i. de fumer,** no smoking; smoking prohibited.

interdire [ɛ̃tɛrdir] *vtr* (*conj like* DIRE, *except pr ind and imp* **interdisez**) 1. (a) to forbid, prohibit; **la passerelle est interdite aux voyageurs,** passengers are not allowed on the bridge; **il est interdit de fumer,** no smoking; *PN:* **entrée interdite (au public),** no entry, no admittance; **passage interdit,** no thoroughfare; **i. à qn de faire qch,** to forbid s.o. to do sth (b) to suspend (s.o.) 2. **s'i. qch,** to give sth up; to refrain from sth; **il s'interdit d'y penser,** he doesn't let himself think about it. **interdit, -ite** 1. *a* disconcerted; bewildered; taken aback 2. *nm Ecc:* interdict.

intéressement [ɛ̃tɛrɛsmɑ̃] *nm Com:* profit (-)sharing scheme.

intéresser [ɛ̃tɛrese] *vtr* 1. (a) **i. qn dans son commerce,** to give s.o. a financial interest in the business (b) to affect, concern, interest (c) to interest, to be interesting to (s.o.); **ceci peut vous i.,** this may be of, prove of, interest to you (d) **i. qn à une cause,** to interest s.o. in a cause 2. **s'i.** (a) to put money (**dans,** into) (b) **s'i. à qn, qch,** to take an interest in s.o., sth. **intéressant** *a* interesting; **prix intéressant,** attractive price; **il cherche à se rendre i.,** he's drawing attention to himself. **intéressé** *a* 1. interested, concerned; **le premier i.,** the (person) most closely concerned, affected 2. selfish, self-interested.

intérêt [ɛ̃tɛrɛ] *nm* 1. interest; share, stake (in business) 2. advantage, benefit; **il y a i. à,** it is desirable to; **j'ai i. à le faire,** it's in my interest to do it; **agir dans son i.,** to act in one's own interest; **il sait où se trouve son i.,** he knows which side his bread is buttered; *Rail:* **ligne d'i. local,** branch line 3. (feeling of) interest; **prendre de l'i. à qn,** to take an interest in sth; **livre sans i.,** uninteresting book 4. *Fin:* **i. composé,** compound interest; **12% d'i.,** 12% interest.

interférence [ɛ̃tɛrferɑ̃s] *nf* interference; intrusion. **interférer** [ɛ̃tɛrfere] *vi* (**il interfère**) to interfere; to intrude.

intérieur [ɛ̃terjœr] 1. *a* (a) interior; inner (room); inside (pocket); internal (part); inland (sea) (b) inward (feelings) (c) domestic (administration); **commerce i.,** home trade 2. *nm* (a) interior, inside; **à l'i.,** inside, on the inside; indoors; **la porte était verrouillée à, de, l'i.,** the door was locked from the inside; **dans l'i. du pays,** inland (b) home, house; **vie d'i.,** home, domestic, life; **femme d'i.,** domesticated woman; **vêtements d'i.,** indoor clothes (c) *Adm:* **le Ministère de l'I.** = the Home Office (d) *Sp:* **i. droit, gauche,** inside right, left. **intérieurement** *adv* inwardly; inside, within; **rire i.,** to laugh to oneself.

intérim [ɛ̃terim] *nm* interim; **dans l'i.,** in the meantime; **secrétaire par i.,** interim secretary; **assurer l'i. (de qn),** to deputize, stand in (for s.o.); to act as locum (tenens). **intérimaire** 1. *a* temporary, provisional; interim; **directeur i.,** acting manager 2. *n* deputy; locum (tenens); temporary secretary, *F:* temp.

intérioriser [ɛterjɔrize] *vtr Psy:* to internalize. **interjection** [ɛ̃tɛrʒɛksjɔ̃] *nf* interjection.

interligne [ɛ̃tɛrliɲ] nm space between two lines; *Typewr:* spacing; **double i.**, double spacing.

interlocuteur, -trice [ɛ̃tɛrlɔkytœr, -tris] n speaker (in a conversation); **mon i.**, the person I was speaking to.

interlope [ɛ̃tɛrlɔp] a (a) illegal (b) suspect, shady.

interloquer [ɛ̃tɛrlɔke] vtr to disconcert (s.o.), to take (s.o.) aback.

interlude [ɛ̃tɛrlyd] nm Mus: Th: interlude.

intermède [ɛ̃tɛrmɛd] nm 1. interruption, interval 2. Th: interlude.

intermédiaire [ɛ̃tɛrmedjɛr] 1. a intermediate, intermediary, intervening (state, time) 2. n agent, intermediary; go-between; Com: middleman 3. nm intermediary, agency; **par l'i. de la presse**, through the medium of the press; **sans i.**, directly.

interminable [ɛ̃tɛrminabl] a interminable; endless, never-ending. **interminablement** adv endlessly, interminably.

intermittence [ɛ̃tɛrmitãs] nf intermittence. **intermittent** a intermittent; irregular (pulse); casual (work).

internat [ɛ̃tɛrna] nm 1. (a) living-in (system, period); Sch: boarding (b) resident medical studentship 2. boarding school.

international, -aux [ɛ̃tɛrnasjɔnal, -o] 1. a international 2. n Sp: international (player).

interne [ɛ̃tɛrn] 1. a internal; inner (ear); interior (angle) 2. n (a) Sch: boarder (b) = house physician, houseman, NAm: intern.

internement [ɛ̃tɛrnəmɑ̃] nm internment; confinement (of the mentally ill).

interner [ɛ̃tɛrne] vtr to intern; to confine (the mentally ill).

interpellation [ɛ̃tɛrpelasjɔ̃] nf questioning; heckling.

interpeller [ɛ̃tɛrpele] vtr to call on (s.o.); to call out to (s.o.); to question (s.o.); to challenge (s.o.); to heckle (s.o.).

interphone [ɛ̃tɛrfɔn] nm intercom.

interplanétaire [ɛ̃tɛrplanetɛr] a interplanetary; **voyage i.**, space flight.

interpoler [ɛ̃tɛrpole] vtr to interpolate.

interposer [ɛ̃tɛrpoze] vtr 1. to interpose 2. **s'i.**, to intervene.

interprétariat [ɛ̃tɛrpretarja] nm interpretership.

interprétation [ɛ̃tɛrpretasjɔ̃] nf interpretation.

interprète [ɛ̃tɛrprɛt] n 1. interpreter 2. Mus: Th: interpreter, performer.

interpréter [ɛ̃tɛrprete] vtr (**j'interprète; j'interpréterai**) (a) to interpret; to explain; **mal i.**, to misinterpret (b) Mus: Th: to interpret, perform, play, sing.

interrogation [ɛ̃tɛrɔgasjɔ̃] nf 1. interrogation; questioning; **point d'i.**, question mark 2. question, query; **i. orale, écrite**, oral, written, test. **interrogateur, -trice** 1. a interrogatory, questioning, inquiring 2. n interrogator, questioner; Sch: (oral) examiner. **interrogatif, -ive** 1. a inquiring, questioning 2. a & n Gram: interrogative.

interrogatoire [ɛ̃tɛrɔgatwar] nm (a) interrogation; cross-examination (b) questioning.

interroger [ɛ̃tɛrɔʒe] vtr (**n. interrogeons**) 1. (a) to cross-examine, interrogate, question (witness); to

examine (candidate); **i. qn du regard**, to look at s.o. inquiringly (b) to consult (history book); to sound (one's conscience) 2. **s'i.**, to question oneself; to wonder (**sur**, about; **si**, whether, if).

interrompre [ɛ̃tɛrɔ̃pr] vtr (conj like ROMPRE) 1. (a) to interrupt; to cut in, break in (on conversation) (b) to intercept, interrupt (c) to stop, suspend (traffic); to cut (s.o.) short; to break off (negotiations); to break (journey) 2. **s'i.**, to break off; to stop (talking). **interrompu** a interrupted; **sommeil i.**, broken sleep.

interrupteur [ɛ̃tɛryptœr] nm El: switch.

interruption [ɛ̃tɛrypsjɔ̃] nf (a) interruption (b) stoppage; break; breaking off (of negotiations); El: disconnection; **sans i.**, unceasingly, uninterruptedly (c) termination (of pregnancy).

intersection [ɛ̃tɛrsɛksjɔ̃] nf intersection.

interstice [ɛ̃tɛrstis] nm interstice; chink.

interurbain [ɛ̃tɛryrbɛ̃] Tp: 1. a long distance (call) 2. nm **appeler l'i.**, to make a long distance call.

intervalle [ɛ̃tɛrval] nm 1. distance, gap, space (**entre**, between) 2. interval; period (of time); **par intervalles**, now and then; **dans l'i.**, in the meantime.

intervenir [ɛ̃tɛrvənir] vi (conj like TENIR; aux être) 1. (a) to intervene; to interpose, to step in; **faire i. la force armée**, to bring in the army (b) to interfere 2. to happen, occur, arise; **un changement est intervenu**, a change has taken place 3. Med: to operate.

intervention [ɛ̃tɛrvɑ̃sjɔ̃] nf 1. intervening, intervention; Med: **i. chirurgicale**, surgical operation; **offre d'i.**, offer of mediation 2. interference.

intervertir [ɛ̃tɛrvertir] vtr to invert.

interview [ɛ̃tɛrvju] nf interview.

interviewé, -ée [ɛ̃tɛrvjuve] n interviewee.

interviewe(u)r [ɛ̃tɛrvjuvœr] nm interviewer.

intestin [ɛ̃tɛstɛ̃] nm Anat: **intestin(s)**, intestine(s); bowel(s). **intestinal, -aux** a intestinal.

intime [ɛ̃tim] 1. a (a) intimate; inward; deep-seated (fears); innermost (feelings) (b) close (friend); cosy (room); **dîner i.**, quiet dinner 2. n intimate friend, close friend. **intimement** adv intimately.

intimer [ɛ̃time] vtr 1. **i. à qn l'ordre de partir**, to give s.o. notice to go, to order s.o. to go 2. Jur: **i. qn**, to summons s.o.

intimidation [ɛ̃timidasjɔ̃] nf intimidation.

intimider [ɛ̃timide] vtr to intimidate; **nullement intimidé**, nothing daunted. **intimidant** a intimidating. **intimidateur, -trice** a intimidating.

intimité [ɛ̃timite] nf (a) intimacy; closeness (of friendship) (b) privacy; **dans l'i.**, in private (life); **le mariage a été célébré dans l'i.**, it was a quiet wedding.

intituler [ɛ̃tityle] vtr 1. to entitle, to give a title to; **article intitulé**, article headed 2. **s'i.**, to be called, entitled; often Pej: to call oneself.

intolérable [ɛ̃tɔlerabl] a intolerable, unbearable. **intolérablement** adv intolerably, unbearably.

intolérance [ɛ̃tɔlerɑ̃s] nf intolerance. **intolérant** a intolerant (**de**, of).

intonation [ɛ̃tɔnasjɔ̃] nf intonation.

intouchable [ɛ̃tuʃabl] a untouchable.

intoxication [ɛ̃tɔksikasjɔ̃] nf Med: intoxication, poisoning; **i. alimentaire**, food poisoning.

intoxiqué, -ée [ɛ̃tɔksike] n drug addict; alcoholic.

intoxiquer [ɛ̃tɔksike] *vtr* **1.** *Med:* to poison; *Pol:* brainwash **2. s'i.,** to poison oneself.

intraduisible [ɛ̃tradɥizibl] *a* untranslatable.

intraitable [ɛ̃trɛtabl] *a* intractable; obstinate, uncompromising, inflexible.

intramusculaire [ɛ̃tramyskylɛr] *a* intramuscular.

intransigeance [ɛ̃trɑ̃ziʒɑ̃s] *nf* intransigence. **intransigeant** *a* intransigent; uncompromising, strict (moral code); **sur ce point il est i.,** on this point he's adamant **2.** *n Pol:* intransigent.

intransitif, -ive [ɛ̃trɑ̃zitif, -iv] *a & nm Gram:* intransitive.

intransportable [ɛ̃trɑ̃spɔrtabl] *a* (*a*) untransportable (*b*) (*of patient*) unfit to travel.

intraveineux, -euse [ɛ̃travɛnø, -øz] *Med:* **1.** *a* intravenous **2.** *nf* intravenous injection.

intrépidité [ɛ̃trepidite] *nf* intrepidity, dauntlessness, fearlessness. **intrépide** *a* intrepid, dauntless, fearless; barefaced.

intrigue [ɛ̃trig] *nf* **1.** (*a*) intrigue; plot, scheme (*b*) (love) affair **2.** plot (of play).

intriguer [ɛ̃trige] **1.** *vtr* to puzzle, intrigue **2.** *vi* to scheme, plot, intrigue. **intrigant 1.** *a* scheming **2.** *n* schemer.

intrinsèque [ɛ̃trɛ̃sɛk] *a* intrinsic. **intrinsèquement** *adv* intrinsically.

introduction [ɛ̃trɔdyksjɔ̃] *nf* **1.** introduction; **lettre d'i.,** letter of introduction **2.** introductory chapter; **après quelques mots d'i.,** after a few introductory words.

introduire [ɛ̃trɔdɥir] *vtr* (*prp* **introduisant;** *pp* **introduit;** *ph* **j'introduisis**) **1.** (*a*) to introduce; to insert (key in lock) (*b*) to bring in; to admit, let in; to launch (a fashion) (*c*) to usher (s.o.) in, show (s.o.) in **2. s'i.,** to get in, enter; **s'i. dans qch,** to work, worm, one's way into sth; **l'eau s'introduit partout,** water gets in everywhere.

introniser [ɛ̃trɔnize] *vtr* to enthrone (king, bishop).

introuvable [ɛ̃truvabl] *a* not to be found; unobtainable; untraceable.

introverti, -ie [ɛ̃trɔvɛrti] **1.** *a* introverted **2.** *n* introvert.

intrus, -use [ɛ̃try, -yz] *n* intruder, *F:* gatecrasher.

intrusion [ɛ̃tryzjɔ̃] *nf* intrusion.

intuition [ɛ̃tɥisjɔ̃] *nf* intuition; **par i.,** intuitively. **intuitif, -ive** *a* intuitive. **intuitivement** *adv* intuitively.

inusable [inyzabl] *a* hard-wearing; everlasting.

inusité [inyzite] *a* (*a*) unusual (*b*) not in common use.

inutilisable [inytilizabl] *a* unusable. **inutilisé** *a* unused.

inutilité [inytilite] *nf* (*a*) uselessness (*b*) needlessness. **inutile** *a* (*a*) useless, unavailing; vain (*b*) needless, unnecessary; **c'est i.!** (i) it's no good! (ii) you needn't bother! **i. de dire que,** needless to say. **inutilement** *adv* (*a*) uselessly; in vain (*b*) needlessly, unnecessarily.

invaincu [ɛ̃vɛ̃ky] *a* unconquered; unbeaten.

invalider [ɛ̃valide] *vtr Jur:* to invalidate (will, election); to quash (election); to **unseat (elected member).**

invalidité [ɛ̃validite] *nf* (*a*) disablement, disability (*b*) chronic ill health. **invalide 1.** *a* invalid, infirm; disabled **2.** *n* invalid; disabled person.

invariable [ɛ̃varjabl] *a* invariably. **invariablement** *adv* invariably.

invasion [ɛ̃vazjɔ̃] *nf* invasion.

invective [ɛ̃vɛktiv] *nf* (*a*) invective (*b*) *pl* abuse.

invectiver [ɛ̃vɛktive] **1.** *vi* **i. contre qn,** to inveigh, rail, against s.o. **2.** *vtr* to abuse, to hurl abuse at (s.o.).

invendable [ɛ̃vɑ̃dabl] *a* unsaleable, unmarketable. **invendu 1.** *a* unsold **2.** *nmpl* **invendus,** unsold goods, articles.

inventaire [ɛ̃vɑ̃tɛr] *nm* (*a*) inventory; **faire, dresser, un i.,** to draw up an inventory (*b*) *Com:* stock list; stocktaking; **faire, dresser, l'i.,** to take stock (*c*) survey.

inventer [ɛ̃vɑ̃te] *vtr* (*a*) to find out, discover; **il n'a pas inventé la poudre,** he'll never set the Thames on fire (*b*) to invent; to devise; to dream up, to make up (story); **i. de faire qch,** to hit on the idea of doing sth. **inventif, -ive** *a* inventive.

inventeur, -trice [ɛ̃vɑ̃tœr, -tris] *n* inventor.

invention [ɛ̃vɑ̃sjɔ̃] *nf* **1.** (*a*) invention, inventing (*b*) imagination, inventiveness **2.** (*a*) (*thg invented*) invention; creation (*b*) **brevet d'i.,** patent (*c*) fabrication, lie; **pure i. tout cela!** that's sheer invention!

inventorier [ɛ̃vɑ̃tɔrje] *vtr* to make an inventory; to take stock.

invérifiable [ɛ̃verifjabl] *a* unverifiable.

inverser [ɛ̃vɛrse] *vtr* to reverse (current); to invert (order). **inverse 1.** *a* inverse, inverted, opposite; **en sens i.,** in the opposite direction **2.** *nm* opposite, reverse; **à l'i. du bon sens,** unreasonably. **inversement** *adv* inversely; conversely. **inversé** *a* reversed; inverted.

inversion [ɛ̃vɛrsjɔ̃] *nf* **1.** inversion **2.** reversal (of electric current).

invertébré [ɛ̃vɛrtebre] *a & nm* invertebrate.

investigateur, -trice [ɛ̃vɛstigatœr, -tris] **1.** *a* investigative **2.** *n* investigator.

investigation [ɛ̃vɛstigasjɔ̃] *nf* investigation.

investir [ɛ̃vɛstir] *vtr* **1. i. qn d'une fonction,** to invest, vest, s.o. with an office; **i. qn d'une mission,** to entrust s.o. with a mission **2.** *Mil:* to besiege (town) **3.** to invest (money).

investissement [ɛ̃vɛstismɑ̃] *nm* **1.** *Fin:* investment; investing **2.** *Mil:* besieging.

invétéré [ɛ̃vetere] *a* inveterate.

invincible [ɛ̃vɛ̃sibl] *a* invincible, unconquerable. **invinciblement** *adv* invincibly.

inviolable [ɛ̃vjɔlabl] *a* inviolable; sacred.

invisibilité [ɛ̃vizibilite] *nf* invisibility. **invisible** *a* invisible; unseen; **il restait i.,** he was nowhere to be found. **invisiblement** *adv* invisibly.

invitation [ɛ̃vitasjɔ̃] *nf* invitation; **venir sur l'i. de qn,** to come at s.o.'s invitation, request.

invite [ɛ̃vit] *nf* invitation, inducement.

inviter [ɛ̃vite] *vtr* **1.** to invite; **i. qn à entrer,** to ask s.o. in; **i. qn à dîner,** to invite s.o. to dinner **2.** (*a*) **i. le désastre,** to court disaster (*b*) **i. qn à faire qch,** (i) to invite, request, s.o. to do sth (ii) to tempt s.o. to do sth.

invivable [ɛ̃vivabl] *a* unbearable; *F:* (*of pers*) impossible to live with.

invocation [ɛ̃vɔkasjɔ̃] *nf* invocation.

involontaire [ɛ̃vɔlɔ̃tɛr] *a* involuntary, unintentional. **involontairement** *adv* involuntarily, unintentionally.

invoquer [ɛ̃vɔke] *vtr* **1.** to call upon, to invoke (the

Deity); **i. l'aide de la justice,** to appeal to the law **2.** to call for, refer to (documents); **i. une raison,** to put forward a reason.

invraisemblance [ɛ̃vrɛsɑ̃blɑ̃s] *nf* **1.** unlikeliness, improbability **2.** implausibility. **invraisemblable** *a* improbable; implausible; **histoire i.,** tall story; **chapeau i.,** incredible hat.

invulnérabilité [ɛ̃vylnerabilite] *nf* invulnerability. **invulnérable** *a* invulnerable.

iode [jɔd] *nm* iodine.

iodler [jɔdle] *vtr & i* to yodel.

iodure [jɔdyr] *nm Ch:* iodide.

ion [jɔ̃] *nm Ph: Chem:* ion. **ionique** *a* ionic.

ionisation [jɔnizasjɔ̃] *nf* ionization.

ioniser [jɔnize] *vtr* to ionize.

IPES [ipɛs] *abbr Institut préparatoire à l'enseignement secondaire.*

Irak [irak] *Prnm Geog:* Irak, Iraq. **irakien, -ienne** *a & n* Iraqi.

Iran [irɑ̃] *Prnm Geog:* Iran. **iranien, -ienne** *a & n* Iranian.

Iraq [irak] *Prnm Geog:* Iraq. **iraquien, -ienne** *a & n* Iraqi.

irascibilité [irasibilite] *nf* irascibility; quick temper. **irascible** *a* irascible.

iris [iris] *nm* **1.** iris (of eye) **2.** *Bot:* iris.

Irlande [irlɑ̃d] *Prnf Geog:* Ireland; **I. du Nord,** Northern Ireland. **irlandais, -aise** **1.** *a* Irish **2.** *n* Irishman; Irishwoman **3.** *nm Ling:* Irish, Erse.

ironie [irɔni] *nf* irony. **ironique** *a* ironic(al). **ironiquement** *adv* ironically.

ironiser [irɔnize] *vi* to be ironical (**sur,** about).

irradier [iradje] **1.** *vi* to radiate; (*of pain*) to spread **2.** *vtr* to irradiate.

irraisonné [irɛzɔne] *a* unreasoned.

irrationalité [irasjɔnalite] *nf* irrationality. **irrationnel, -elle** *a* irrational. **irrationnellement** *adv* irrationally.

irréalisable [irealizabl] *a* unrealizable; impracticable, unworkable.

irrecevable [irəsəvabl] *a* inadmissible (evidence); unacceptable (theory).

irréconciliable [irekɔ̃siljabl] *a* irreconcilable.

irrécouvrable [irekuvrabl] *a* irrecoverable.

irrécupérable [irekyperabl] *a* irreparable (loss); irretrievable; non-retrievable; irredeemable.

irrécusable [irekyzabl] *a* unimpeachable, irrecusable (evidence).

irréductible [iredyktibl] *a* **1.** irreducible **2.** indomitable; relentless (opposition).

irréel, -elle [ireɛl] *a* unreal.

irréfléchi [irefleʃi] *a* **1.** unconsidered, thoughtless **2.** hasty, rash.

irréflexion [ireflɛksjɔ̃] *nf* thoughtlessness.

irréfutable [irefytabl] *a* irrefutable. **irréfutablement** *adv* irrefutably.

irrégularité [iregylarite] *nf* irregularity. **irrégulier, -ière** *a* irregular; uneven (ground); fitful (sleep); erratic (pulse, life). **irrégulièrement** *adv* irregularly; unevenly; fitfully; erratically.

irrémédiable [iremedjabl] *a* irremediable; incurable (disease); irreparable (injury). **irrémédiablement** *adv* irremediably; incurably; irreparably.

irremplaçable [irɑ̃plasabl] *a* irreplaceable.

irréparable [ireparabl] *a* irreparable; beyond repair.

irrépressible [irepresibl] *a* irrepressible.

irréprochable [irepro ʃabl] *a* irreproachable; faultless.

irrésistible [irezistibl] *a* irresistible. **irrésistiblement** *adv* irresistibly.

irrésolution [irezɔlysjɔ̃] *nf* irresolution, irresoluteness, indecision. **irrésolu** *a* **1.** irresolute, indecisive (nature); faltering (steps) **2.** unsolved (problem). **irrésolument** *adv* irresolutely.

irrespectueux, -euse [irɛspɛktɥø, -øz] *a* disrespectful.

irrespirable [irɛspirabl] *a* unbreathable.

irresponsabilité [irɛspɔ̃sabilite] *nf* irresponsibility. **irresponsable** *a* irresponsible.

irrévérence [ireverɑ̃s] *nf* irreverence. **irrévérencieux, -ieuse** *a* irreverent.

irréversible [ireversibl] *a* irreversible.

irrévocable [irevɔkabl] *a* irrevocable. **irrévocablement** *adv* irrevocably.

irrigation [irigasjɔ̃] *nf Agr: Med:* irrigation.

irriguer [irige] *vtr Agr: Med:* to irrigate.

irritabilité [iritabilite] *nf* irritability. **irritable** *a* irritable.

irritation [iritasjɔ̃] *nf* irritation.

irriter [irite] *vtr* **1.** (*a*) to irritate, annoy (*b*) *Med:* to irritate **2. s'i.** (*a*) to get angry, annoyed (with s.o., sth) (*b*) (*of sore*) to become irritated, inflamed.

irruption [irypsjɔ̃] *nf* irruption; **faire i. dans une salle,** to burst into a room.

Islam [islam] *nm Rel:* Islam. **islamique** *a* Islamic.

Islande [islɑ̃d] *Prnf Geog:* Iceland. **islandais, -aise** **1.** *a* Icelandic **2.** *n* Icelander **3.** *nm Ling:* Icelandic.

isocèle [izosɛl] *a Mth:* isosceles (triangle).

isolation [izɔlasjɔ̃] *nf* insulation; **i. acoustique,** soundproofing.

isolationnisme [izɔlasjɔnism] *nm* isolationism. **isolationniste** *a & n* isolationist.

isolement [izɔlmɑ̃] *nm* **1.** isolation **2.** *El:* insulation.

isoler [izɔle] *vtr* **1.** (*a*) to isolate (**de,** from) (*b*) *El:* to insulate (*c*) to soundproof **2. s'i.** (*a*) to become isolated (*b*) to live apart (from society). **isolant 1.** *a* (*a*) isolating (*b*) insulating; **bouteille isolante,** vacuum flask; **cabine isolante,** soundproof box **2.** *nm* insulator. **isolé** *a* **1.** isolated **2.** *El:* insulated. **isolément** *adv* separately; individually; in isolation.

isoloir [izɔlwar] *nm* polling booth.

Isorel [izɔrɛl] *nm Rtm:* hardboard.

isotherme [izɔtɛrm] *a* isothermal; refrigerated (lorry).

isotope [izɔtɔp] *nm Ch:* isotope.

Israël [israɛl] *Prnm Geog:* Israel. **israélien, -ienne** *a & n* Israeli. **Israélite 1.** *a* Jewish; *BHist:* Israelite **2.** *n* Jew, *f* Jewess; *BHist:* Israelite.

issu [isy] *a* descended (**de,** from); born (**de,** of); **être i. de,** to stem from.

issue [isy] *nf* **1.** exit, way out; outlet; **i. de secours,** emergency exit; **voie sans i.,** cul-de-sac, dead end; *PN:* no through road; **se ménager une i.,** to find a way out **2.** issue, conclusion, outcome; solution; end, close (of meeting).

isthme [ism] *nm Geog: Anat:* isthmus.

Italie [itali] *Prnf Geog:* Italy. **italien, -ienne 1.** *a &*
n Italian **2.** *nm Ling:* Italian.

italique [italik] *a & nm Typ:* italic (type); italics; **en**
italique(s), in italics.

itinéraire [itinerɛr] *nm* (*a*) itinerary; route, way (*b*)
guide (book).

itinérant [itinerã] *a* itinerant; **ambassadeur i.,** roving,
peripatetic, ambassador.

IVG *abbr interruption volontaire de grossesse,* termination of pregnancy.

IUT *abbr Institut universitaire de technologie*
= Polytechnic.

ivoire [ivwar] *nm* ivory.

ivresse [ivrɛs] *nf* (*a*) drunkenness; intoxication (*b*)
rapture, ecstasy. **ivre** *a* drunk, intoxicated; **i. de joie,**
mad with joy.

ivrogne [ivrɔɲ] *nm* drunkard.

ivrognerie [ivrɔɲri] *nf* drunkenness.

J

J, j [ʒi] *nm* (the letter) J, j; *Mil: etc:* **le jour J,** D day.

jabot [ʒabo] *nm* **1.** crop (of bird) **2.** *Cl:* frill, ruffle, jabot.

jacassement [ʒakasmɑ̃] *nm* chatter(ing), jabber(ing).

jacasser [ʒakase] *vi* to chatter, jabber.

jachère [ʒaʃɛr] *nf* **terre en j.,** fallow land.

jacinthe [ʒasɛ̃t] *nf Bot:* hyacinth; **j. des bois,** bluebell.

Jacques [ʒɑk] *Prnm* James; *F:* **faire le J.,** to act dumb.

jacquet [ʒakɛ] *nm Games:* backgammon.

Jacquot [ʒako] **1.** *Prnm F:* Jim, Jimmy **2.** *nm* West African grey parrot, *F:* Poll (parrot), Polly.

jade [ʒad] *nm Miner:* jade.

jadis [ʒadis] *adv Lit:* formerly, once; **au temps j.,** in the olden days.

jaguar [ʒagwar] *nm Z:* jaguar.

jaillir [ʒajir] *vi* to spring (up); to shoot (out); to gush (out); to squirt (out); *(of blood)* to spurt; *(of sparks)* to fly.

jaillissement [ʒajismɑ̃] *nm* gush(ing), spouting, spurt(ing).

jais [ʒɛ] *nm Miner:* jet.

jalon [ʒalɔ̃] *nm* (range) pole; *Fig:* **poser des jalons,** to pave the way; to blaze a trail.

jalonnement [ʒalɔnmɑ̃] *nm* marking out, off.

jalonner [ʒalɔne] *vtr* to stake out, mark out; *Fig:* to blaze (a trail).

jalouser [ʒaluze] *vtr* to envy (s.o.); to be jealous of (s.o.).

jalousie [ʒaluzi] *nf* **1.** jealousy; envy **2.** Venetian blind. **jaloux, -ouse** *a* (a) jealous (b) careful; **j. de sa réputation,** careful of one's reputation. **jalousement** *adv* jealously.

Jamaïque [ʒamaik] *Prnf Geog:* Jamaica. **jamaïquain, -aine** *a & n* Jamaican.

jamais [ʒamɛ] **1.** *adv* ever; **si j. il revenait,** if he ever came back; **à j., pour j.,** for ever; **à tout j.,** for ever and ever; for evermore **2.** *adv* (*with 'neg expressed or understood*) never; **sans j. y avoir pensé,** without ever having thought of it; **c'est le cas ou j.,** now or never; **j. de la vie!** never! out of the question! *F:* not on your life! **3.** *nm* **j., au grand j.,** never, (repeat) never.

jambe [ʒɑ̃b] *nf* **1.** leg; **avoir de bonnes jambes,** to be a good walker; **aux longues jambes,** long-legged; **se sauver à toutes jambes,** to run off at full speed; *F:* **prendre ses jambes à son cou,** to take to one's heels; **ça me fera une belle j.!** a fat lot of good that'll do me! **avoir les jambes rompues,** to be worn out; **n'avoir plus de jambes,** to be tired out; **je n'ai plus mes jambes de vingt ans,** I'm not as young as I was **2. j. de force,** strut, prop, brace.

jambon [ʒɑ̃bɔ̃] *nm* ham; **j. de pays, fumé,** smoked ham; **j. blanc,** boiled ham.

jambonneau, -eaux [ʒɑ̃bɔno] *nm* knuckle of ham.

jante [ʒɑ̃t] *nf* rim (of wheel).

janvier [ʒɑ̃vje] *nm* January; **au mois de j., en j.,** in (the month of) January; **le premier, le sept, j.,** (on) the first, the seventh, of January.

Japon [ʒapɔ̃] *Prnm Geog:* Japan; **au J.,** in, to, Japan. **japonais, -aise** *a & n* Japanese.

jappement [ʒapmɑ̃] *nm* yelp(ing), yap(ping).

japper [ʒape] *vi* (*of dog*) to yelp, yap.

jaquette [ʒakɛt] *nf* (a) (man's) morning coat (b) (woman's) jacket (c) (dust) jacket (of book).

jardin [ʒardɛ̃] *nm* garden; **j. potager,** kitchen garden, vegetable garden; **j. d'agrément,** pleasure garden; **j. des plantes,** botanical garden; *Sch:* **j. d'enfants,** nursery school, kindergarten. **jardinier, -ière 1.** *a* **plantes jardinières,** garden plants **2.** *n* gardener **3.** *nf* **jardinière,** (i) window box (ii) jardinière; *Cu:* **jardinière (de légumes),** mixed vegetables; *Sch:* **jardinière d'enfants,** nursery school, kindergarten, mistress.

jardinage [ʒardinaʒ] *nm* gardening.

jardiner [ʒardine] *vi* to garden.

jardinet [ʒardinɛ] *nm* small garden.

jargon [ʒargɔ̃] *nm* (a) jargon (b) slang (c) gibberish.

jarret [ʒarɛ] *nm* **1.** bend of the knee; ham (in man); hock (of horse); **avoir le j. solide,** to have a good pair of legs **2.** *Cu:* knuckle (of veal); shin (of beef).

jarretelle [ʒartɛl] *nf Cl:* suspender; *NAm:* garter.

jarretière [ʒartjɛr] *nf* garter; **Ordre de la J.,** Order of the Garter.

jars [ʒar] *nm Orn:* gander.

jaser [ʒaze] *vi* (a) to chatter (de, about); to gossip; **j. comme une pie (borgne),** to talk nineteen to the dozen (b) to blab; to tell tales. **jaseur, -euse 1.** *a* talkative **2.** *n* chatterbox; gossip.

jasmin [ʒasmɛ̃] *nm Bot:* jasmine.

jatte [ʒat] *nf* bowl; (milk) pan.

jauge [ʒoʒ] *nf* **1.** (a) gauge; capacity (of cask) (b) *Nau:* tonnage (of ship) **2.** *Tchn:* gauge; *Aut:* **j. de niveau d'huile,** dipstick.

jauger [ʒoʒe] *vtr* (*n. jaugeons*) **1.** to gauge, measure, the capacity of (a cask), the tonnage of (a ship); **j. un homme,** to size up a man **2.** (*of ship*) **j. 300 tonneaux,** to be of 300 tons burden.

jaune [ʒon] **1.** *a* (a) yellow (b) *a inv* **j. citron,** lemon yellow; *adv* **rire j.,** to give a sickly smile **2.** *nm* (a) yellow (colour); **ocre j.,** yellow ochre (b) **j. d'œuf,** yolk (of egg) (c) *Ind: F:* blackleg, scab. **jaunâtre** *a* yellowish; sallow (complexion).

jaunir [ʒonir] *vi & tr* to grow, turn, yellow; to fade.

jaunisse [ʒonis] *nf Med:* jaundice; *F:* **il en ferait une j.,** he would be mad with jealousy, green with envy.

java [ʒava] *nf Danc:* Javanaise; *P:* **faire la j.,** to live it up.

Javel [ʒavɛl] *nm DomEc:* **eau de J.** =bleach.

javelliser [ʒavelize] *vtr* to chlorinate.

javelot [ʒavlo] *nm* javelin.

jazz [dʒaz] *nm Mus:* jazz.

J-C *abbr Jésus Christ.*

je, *before vowel* **j'** [ʒ(ə)] *pers pron nom* I.

Jean¹ [ʒɑ̃] *Prnm* John; **la Saint-J.**, Midsummer Day.

jean² [dʒin] *nm Cl:* jeans.

jeep [(d)ʒip] *nf Aut:* jeep.

je-m'en-fichisme [ʒmɑ̃fiʃism] *nm P:* couldn't-care-less attitude.

je(-)ne(-)sais(-)quoi [ʒɔnsɛkwa] *nm inv* **un je-ne-s.-q.**, an indefinable something.

jérémiades [ʒeremjad] *nfpl* whining, complaining.

jerrycan [ʒerikan] *nm* jerrycan.

Jersey [ʒɛrzɛ] **1.** *Prnm Geog:* (Island of) Jersey **2.** *nm Cl:* **j.**, jersey; *Knit:* **point (de) j.**, stocking stitch.

jésuite [ʒezɥit] *nm Ecc:* Jesuit.

Jésus [ʒezy] *(a) Prnm* Jesus; **J.-Christ**, Jesus Christ; **l'an 44 avant J.-C., après J.-C.**, the year 44 BC, AD *(b) nm* statue of the infant Jesus *(c) F:* **mon j.**, my little pet.

jet¹ [ʒɛ] *nm* **1.** *(a)* throw, cast; **à un j. de pierre**, within a stone's throw; *Art: Lit:* **premier j.**, first sketch *(b) Metall:* cast, casting; **faire qch d'un seul j.**, to do sth at one go **2.** *(a)* jet, gush (of liquid); spurt (of blood); flash (of light); **j. d'eau**, fountain; spray *(b)* young shoot (of tree) **3.** jet (of nozzle); spout (of pump, watering can).

jet² [dʒɛt] *nm Av:* jet (aircraft).

jetée [ʒəte] *nf* jetty, pier; breakwater.

jeter [ʒəte] *vtr* **(je jette, n. jetons) 1.** to throw, fling; to throw away; **j. son argent par les fenêtres**, to throw one's money down the drain; **j. qch par terre**, to throw sth down; **j. ses armes**, to throw down one's arms; **à j.**, (i) to be thrown away (ii) disposable; **le sort en est jeté**, the die is cast; **j. un cri**, to utter a cry; **j. un regard (sur qn)**, to cast a glance (at s.o.); **j. les fondements d'un édifice**, to lay the foundations of a building; *Nau:* **j. la sonde**, to heave the lead; **j. l'ancre**, to cast anchor; *Fig:* **j. l'éponge**, to throw in the sponge **2.** **se j. par la fenêtre**, to throw oneself out of the window; **se j. sur qn**, to attack s.o.; **se j. à l'eau**, (i) to jump into the water (ii) to take the plunge; **se j. à corps perdu dans une entreprise**, to fling oneself into an undertaking.

jeton [ʒətɔ̃] *nm (a) Cards: etc:* counter; chip; *Tp:* token *(b)* **j. de présence**, director's fees *(c) P:* punch, blow; **avoir les jetons**, to have the jitters.

jeu, jeux [ʒø] *nm* **1.** *(a)* play; **salle de jeux**, playroom; **j. de mots**, play on words; pun; **j. d'esprit**, witticism; **j. de main**, horseplay; **c'est un j. d'enfant**, it's child's play; **se faire (un) j. de qch**, to make light of sth *(b)* (manner of) playing; acting (of actor); playing (of musician); **j. muet**, dumb show **2.** *(a)* **jeux d'adresse**, games of skill; **jeux olympiques**, Olympic games; **terrain de jeux**, sports ground; **ce n'est pas du j.**, that's not fair; **jouer beau j., jouer le j.**, to play fair; **où en est le j.?** what's the score? *Cards:* **avoir un beau j.**, to have a good hand; *Ten:* **j. et partie**, game and set; **mettre la balle en j.**, to bring the ball into play *(b) (place)* **j. de boules**, bowling green; **j. de quilles**, skittle alley **3.** set; **j. d'échecs**, chess set; **j. de cartes**, pack, *NAm:* deck, of cards; **j. d'outils**, set of tools **4.** gaming, gambling; **maison de j.**, gaming house; **jouer gros j.**, to play for high stakes; **faites vos jeux!** place your bets! **mettre tout en j.**, to stake one's all; to risk everything; **les intérêts en j.**, the interests at issue, at stake; **montrer, cacher, son j.**, to show, hide, one's hand **5.** *(activity, action)* **les forces en j.**, the forces at work; **mettre qch**

en **j.**, to bring sth into play; **j. d'un piston**, length of stroke of a piston; **j. d'une serrure**, action of a lock **6.** *MecE:* clearance, play; **trop de j.**, too much play; **prendre du j.**, to work loose.

jeudi [ʒødi] *nm* Thursday; **j. saint**, Maundy Thursday.

jeun (à) [aʒœ̃] *adj phr* **1.** fasting; *Med:* **à prendre à j.**, to be taken on an empty stomach **2.** sober.

jeune [ʒœn] **1.** *a (a)* young; youthful; **j. homme**, young man; **j. fille**, (young) girl, young woman; **jeunes gens**, (i) young people (ii) young men; **j. détenu**, young offender *(b)* younger; **M. Dupont J.**, Mr Dupont junior *(c)* **vin j.**, new wine **2.** *n* **les jeunes**, young people; the younger generation.

jeûne [ʒøn] *nm* fast(ing).

jeûner [ʒøne] *vi* to fast.

jeunesse [ʒœnɛs] *nf (a)* youth; boyhood, girlhood; **dans sa première j.**, in his, her, early youth; **erreurs de j.**, youthful indiscretions *(b)* **avoir un air de j.**, to look young *(c)* **la j.**, young people; **livres pour la j.**, children's books.

JO *abbr Journal officiel.*

joaillerie [ʒɔajri] *nf* **1.** jeweller's shop **2.** jewellery **3.** jewellery trade.

joaillier, -ière [ʒɔaje, -jɛr] *n* jeweller.

jobard, -arde [ʒɔbar, -ard] **1.** *a* gullible **2.** *n* mug, sucker.

jockey [ʒɔkɛ] *nm* jockey.

joggeur [dʒɔgœr] *nm* jogger.

jogging [dʒɔgiŋ] *nm* **faire du j.**, to go jogging.

joie [ʒwa] *nf* **1.** joy; delight; gladness; **sauter de j.**, to jump for joy; **à ma grande j.**, to my great delight; **faire la j. de qn**, to make s.o. happy; **se faire une j. de faire qch**, to (take a) delight in doing sth; **feu de j.**, bonfire; **j. de vivre**, joy of living; **il se faisait une j. de vous voir**, he was looking forward (so much) to seeing you; **à cœur j.**, to one's heart's content **2.** **fille de j.**, prostitute.

joindre [ʒwɛ̃dr] *v (prp* joignant; *pp* joint; *pr ind* je joins, il joint, n. joignons; *ph* je joignis) **1.** *vtr (a)* to join; to bring together; **j. les deux bouts**, to make (both) ends meet *(b)* to add (à, to); **j. le geste à la parole**, to suit the action to the word; **j. l'utile à l'agréable**, to combine business with pleasure; **j. sa voix aux protestations**, to join in the protests *(c)* to join (one's regiment) *(d)* (= rejoindre) to meet, join (s.o.); **comment puis-je vous j.?** how can I get in touch with you? **2.** *vi & pr (of boards)* to fit, to meet **3.** **se j.**, to join, unite; **voulez-vous vous j. à nous?** would you like to join us? **joint 1.** *a* joined, united; **pieds joints**, feet close together; **à mains jointes**, with clasped hands; *Com:* **pièces jointes**, enclosures **2.** *nm (a)* joint, join; washer (of tap); **trouver le j.**, to find a way; **j. de cardan**, universal joint; **j. à rotule**, ball(-and-socket) joint *(b) P: (drugs)* joint.

jointure [ʒwɛ̃tyr] *nf Anat: Tchn:* joint, join; **jointures (des doigts)**, knuckles.

joker [ʒɔkɛr] *nm Cards:* joker.

joli [ʒɔli] **1.** *a* pretty; good-looking (girl); **jolie à croquer**, pretty as a picture; **il a une jolie fortune**, he has a tidy fortune **2.** *nm* **voilà du j.!** here's a fine mess! **le j. de l'affaire c'est que**, the best of it is that.

joliment [ʒɔlimɑ̃] *adv* pleasantly; nicely, attractively; **j. dit**, neatly put; *F:* **j. en retard**, awfully late.

jonc [ʒɔ̃] *nm (a) Bot:* rush *(b)* **(canne de) j.**, Malacca cane; **j. d'Inde**, rattan.

joncher [ʒɔ̃ʃe] *vtr* **j. la terre de fleurs,** to strew the ground with flowers.

jonction [ʒɔ̃ksjɔ̃] *nf* junction, joining; **point de j.,** meeting point.

jongler [ʒɔ̃gle] *vi* to juggle (**avec,** with).

jonglerie [ʒɔ̃gləri] *nf* juggling.

jongleur, -euse [ʒɔ̃glœr, -øz] *n* juggler.

jonque [ʒɔ̃k] *nf* (Chinese) junk.

jonquille [ʒɔ̃kij] *nf Bot:* (a) jonquil (b) daffodil.

Jordanie [ʒɔrdani] *Prnf Geog:* Jordan. **jordanien, -ienne** *a & n* Jordanian.

joue [ʒu] *nf* cheek; **j. contre j.,** cheek to cheek; **coucher, mettre, qn en j.,** to aim (a gun) at s.o.

jouer [ʒwe] *v* **1.** *vi* (a) to play; **j. avec qn, avec qch,** to play with s.o.; to play, fiddle, with sth (b) **j. aux cartes, au tennis,** to play cards, tennis; **j. aux soldats,** to play (at) soldiers; **c'est à qui de j.?** whose turn is it (to play)? (*at draughts, chess*) whose move is it? (c) **j. du piano,** to play the piano; **j. des coudes,** to elbow one's way (through a crowd) (d) to gamble; **j. aux courses,** to back horses (e) *Fin:* to speculate (f) *Th:* to act; **faire j. (qch),** to bring (sth) into action; **faire j. un ressort,** to release a spring (g) to be(come) operative; to operate (h) (*of wood*) to warp (i) (*of part*) to fit loosely **2.** *vtr* (a) to stake; **j. gros jeu,** to play for high stakes (b) to play (card) (c) to act, play, perform (role); **j. un air au piano,** to play a tune on the piano; **qu'est-ce qui se joue actuellement?** what's on at the moment? **j. la surprise,** to feign surprise (d) to trick, fool (s.o.) **3. se j.** (a) **faire qch en se jouant,** to do sth easily (b) **se j. de qn,** to trifle with, to make fun of, s.o.

jouet [ʒwɛ] *nm* toy, plaything; **être le j. d'une illusion,** to be the victim of an illusion.

joueur, -euse [ʒwœr, -øz] *n* **1.** (a) player; **j. de golf,** golfer; **être beau j.,** to be a good loser; **a enfant j.,** playful child (b) *Mus:* performer, player **2.** gambler.

joufflu [ʒufly] *a* chubby(-cheeked).

joug [ʒu(g)] *nm* **1.** yoke **2.** beam (of balance).

jouir [ʒwir] *vi* (a) **j. de la vie,** to enjoy life (b) **j. de toutes ses facultés,** to be in full possession of all one's faculties; **j. d'une bonne réputation,** to have a good reputation.

jouissance [ʒwisɑ̃s] *nf* (a) pleasure, enjoyment (b) possession; use.

joujou, -oux [ʒuʒu] *nm F:* toy; **faire j. avec une poupée,** to play with a doll.

jour [ʒur] *nm* **1.** (a) (day)light; **le petit j.,** the morning twilight; **il fait j.,** it's (getting) light; **en plein j.,** (i) in broad daylight (ii) publicly; **voyager de j.,** to travel by day, in the day(time); **c'est le j. et la nuit,** they're as different as chalk and cheese (b) **donner le j. à un enfant,** to give birth to a child; **mettre qch au j.,** to bring sth to light; to publish (fact) (c) light(ing); **voir qch sous son vrai j.,** to see sth in its true light **2.** (a) aperture, opening; well of (staircase); **jours entre les planches,** gaps, chinks, between the planks (b) *Needlew:* **à j.,** hemstitched (c) (*of facts*) **se faire j.,** to come out; **la vérité se fait j. dans son esprit,** the truth is dawning on him **3.** (a) day; **huit jours, quinze jours,** a week, a fortnight; **quel j. sommes-nous?** what day is it (today)? (b) *Com:* **à ce j.,** to date; **je l'ai vu l'autre j.,** I saw him the other day; **un j. ou l'autre,** one day; **d'un j. à l'autre,** day by day; **nous l'attendons d'un j. à l'autre,**

we're expecting him any day (now); **vêtements de tous les jours,** everyday clothes; **au j. le j.,** from day to day; **mettre (qch) à j.,** to bring (sth) up to date; to update (sth); **un de ces jours,** one of these days; *F:* **à un de ces jours!** I'll be seeing you! (c) *Mil: etc:* **service de j.,** day duty; **être de j.,** to be on (day) duty (d) **de nos jours,** nowadays; these days; (*in restaurant*) **plat du j.,** dish of the day, *F:* today's special; **vieux jours,** old age.

journal, -aux [ʒurnal, -o] *nm* **1.** journal, diary, record; *Nau:* **j. de bord,** log book **2.** (news)paper; **les journaux,** the Press; **j. parlé, télévisé,** radio, television, news. **journalier, -ière 1.** *a* daily (task); everyday (occurrence) **2.** *nm* day labourer.

journalisme [ʒurnalism] *nm* journalism; **faire du j.,** to be a journalist.

journaliste [ʒurnalist] *n* journalist; reporter. **journalistique** *a* journalistic.

journée [ʒurne] *nf* **1.** day(time); **dans, pendant, la j.,** during the day; **toute la j.,** all day (long), the whole day; **à longueur de j.,** for days on end; **faire la j. continue,** to work through lunch; **il ne fait rien de la j.,** he does nothing all day long **2.** (a) day's work; **travailler à la j.,** to work by the day; **femme de j.,** daily help, char(woman); *F:* daily; **aller en j.,** to do daily work (for s.o.) (b) day's wages (c) day's march (d) of battle; **gagner la j.,** to win the day.

journellement [ʒurnɛlmɑ̃] *adv* daily; every day.

joute [ʒut] *nf* (a) *Hist:* joust (b) **j. sur l'eau,** water tournament.

jouter [ʒute] *vi Hist:* to joust.

jovialité [ʒɔvjalite] *nf* joviality, jollity. **jovial, -aux** *a* jovial, jolly, merry. **jovialement** *adv* jovially.

joyau, -aux [ʒwajo] *nm* jewel; gem; **les joyaux de la Couronne,** the regalia, the Crown jewels.

joyeux, -euse [ʒwajø, -øz] *a* happy, joyful; merry, joyous; cheerful; **j. Noël!** merry Christmas! **joyeusement** *adv* joyfully, merrily, cheerfully.

jubilation [ʒybilasjɔ̃] *nf* jubilation.

jubilé [ʒybile] *nm* jubilee.

jubiler [ʒybile] *vi F:* to rejoice; to gloat.

jucher (se) [səʒyʃe] *vpr* (*of birds*) to roost; to perch.

juchoir [ʒyʃwar] *nm* perch; hen roost.

judaïsme [ʒydaism] *nm* Judaism. **judaïque** *a* Judaic (law); Jewish.

judiciaire [ʒydisjɛr] *a* judicial, legal (inquiry, error).

judicieux, -euse [ʒydisjø, -øz] *a* judicious, discerning; **peu j.,** injudicious. **judicieusement** *adv* judiciously.

judo [ʒydo] *nm* judo.

juge [ʒyʒ] *nm* judge; **j. d'instruction,** examining magistrate; **j. d'instance,** police court magistrate; **les juges** = the bench; *Fb:* **j. de touche,** linesman; **je vous en fais j.,** judge for yourself.

jugé [ʒyʒe] *nm* guesswork; **tirer au j.,** to fire blind.

jugement [ʒyʒmɑ̃] *nm* **1.** *Jur:* (a) trial (of case); **mettre, faire passer, qn en j.,** to bring s.o. to trial; **passer en j.,** to stand trial; **j. par défaut,** judgement by default; **le j. dernier,** the Last Judgment (b) decision, award; (*in criminal cases*) sentence **2.** opinion, estimation; verdict; **porter un j. sur qch,** to pass judgement on sth **3.** discernment, discrimination; **montrer du j.,** to show good sense; **erreur de j.,** error of judgment.

jugeote [ʒyʒɔt] *nf F:* common sense, gumption.

juger¹ [ʒyʒe] *vtr* (**n. jugeons**) **1.** (*a*) to judge; to try (cases, prisoner); to pass sentence on; to adjudicate (claim) (*b*) to pass judgment on; to criticize **2.** (*a to*) think, believe; **on le jugeait fou**, people thought he was mad (*b*) **jugez de ma surprise**, imagine my surprise; **à en juger par**, judging by; **à vous de j.**, it's up to you to draw your own conclusions.

juger² *nm* = **jugé**.

jugulaire [ʒygylɛr] **1.** *a & nf* jugular (vein). **2.** *nf* chin strap (of helmet).

juguler [ʒygyle] *vtr* to suppress, stifle (revolt); to arrest (disease).

juif, juive [ʒɥif, ʒɥiv] **1.** *a* Jewish **2.** *n* Jew, *f* Jewess; *F:* **le petit j.**, the funnybone.

juillet [ʒɥijɛ] *nm* July; **au mois de j., en j.**, in (the month of) July; **le premier, le sept, j.**, (on) the first, the seventh, of July.

juin [ʒɥɛ̃] *nm* June; **au mois de j.**, in (the month of) June; **le premier, le sept, j.**, (on) the first, the seventh, of June.

jumeau, -elle, *pl* **-eaux** [ʒymo, -ɛl] **1.** *a & n* twin; **frères jumeaux, sœurs jumelles,** twin brothers, twin sisters; **maisons jumelles,** semidetached houses; **lits jumeaux,** twin beds **2.** *nfpl* binoculars; **jumelles de théâtre,** opera glasses.

jumelage [ʒymlaʒ] *nm* twinning.

jumeler [ʒymle] *vtr* (**je jumelle, n. jumelons**) to pair; to arrange in pairs; to twin (towns). **jumelé** *a* arranged in pairs; *Aut:* **pneus jumelés,** dual tyres; **textes jumelés,** bilingual texts; **villes jumelées,** twin(ned) towns.

jument [ʒymɑ̃] *nf* mare.

jungle [ʒɔ̃gl, ʒœ̃gl] *nf* jungle.

junior [ʒynjɔr] *a & n* junior.

jupe [ʒyp] *nf* skirt; **pendu aux jupes de sa mère,** tied to his mother's apron strings.

jupon [ʒypɔ̃] *nm* (*a*) waist petticoat, underskirt; slip (*b*) *P:* girl, woman, *P:* (bit of) skirt; **courir le j.,** to chase the girls.

jurer [ʒyre] **1.** *vtr* (*a*) **j. sa foi,** to pledge one's word (*b*) (*to promise*) to vow; **j. la fidélité à qn,** to swear, pledge, fidelity to s.o.; **faire j. le secret à qn,** to swear s.o. to secrecy; **j. de se venger,** to swear revenge (*c*) (*to assert*) **j'en jurerais,** I would swear to it **2.** *vi* (*a*) to swear (profanely); to curse (*b*) (*of colours*) to clash. **juré, -ée 1.** *a* sworn **2.** *n* juror; juryman, jurywoman; **les jurés,** the jury.

juridiction [ʒyridiksjɔ̃] *nf* jurisdiction.

juridique [ʒyridik] *a* judicial; legal; **conseiller j.,** legal adviser. **juridiquement** *adv* legally.

juriste [ʒyrist] *nm* jurist; legal expert.

juron [ʒyrɔ̃] *nm* oath; curse; swearword.

jury [ʒyri] *nm* **1.** *Jur:* jury; **chef, membre, du j.,** foreman, member, of the jury **2.** selection committee; panel of judges; **j. d'examen,** board of examiners.

jus [ʒy] *nm* **1.** juice; **j. de fruit,** fruit juice **2.** *Cu:* juice (of meat); gravy **3.** *P:* (*a*) water (*b*) coffee (*c*) electric current.

jusant [ʒyzɑ̃] *nm* ebb (tide).

jusque [ʒysk(ə)] *prep* **1.** as far as; up to; **jusqu'ici,** up to here; so far; **j.-là,** thus far; up to there; **jusqu'ici c'est très bien,** so far so good; **jusqu'où?** how far? **depuis Londres jusqu'à Paris,** all the way from London to

Paris; **jusqu'à un certain point,** up to a certain point; **j. chez lui,** right up to his door; **compter jusqu'à dix,** to count up to ten **2.** (*a*) till, until; **jusqu'ici,** until now; to date; **jusqu'à présent,** till now; **jusqu'à mon dernier jour,** to my dying day; **jusqu'au jour où,** (i) until (such time as) (ii) until the time when (*b*) **remonter jusqu'en 1800,** to go back as far as 1800 **3.** (*intensive*) **il sait jusqu'à nos pensées,** he knows our very thoughts; **sévère jusqu'à mériter le reproche d'être cruel,** severe to the point of cruelty **4.** *conj phr* **jusqu'à ce que** *usu* + *sub,* till, until.

juste [ʒyst] **1.** *a* (*a*) just, right, fair; **rien de plus j.,** nothing could be fairer (*b*) **être j. envers qn,** to be fair to s.o.; *n* **les justes,** the just, the righteous **2.** *a* (*a*) right, exact, accurate; **le mot j.,** the exact word, the right word; **raisonnement j.,** sound reasoning; **avoir l'oreille j.,** to have a good ear (for music); **le piano n'est pas j.,** the piano is out of tune; **j. milieu,** happy medium; **votre réponse n'est pas j.,** you've given the wrong answer; **ma montre est j.,** my watch is right; **c'est j.,** that's so! that's right! **rien de plus j.,** you're perfectly right (*b*) scanty, bare (allowance); tight (shoes); tightfitting (dress); **c'est bien j.,** there's barely enough (food, etc) to go round; **c'est tout j. s'il sait lire,** he can barely read **3.** *adv* (*a*) rightly; **frapper j.,** to strike home; **chanter j.,** to sing in tune (*b*) exactly, precisely, just; **à dix heures j.,** at ten o'clock sharp; **j. à temps,** just in time; **c'est j. ce qu'il faut,** it's the very thing (*c*) barely; **vous avez tout j. le temps,** you have barely the time; you haven't a moment to lose; **échapper tout j.,** to escape by the skin of one's teeth; **je ne sais pas au juste si,** I don't exactly know whether; **comme de j.,** as is only fair. **justement** *adv* justly, rightly, deservedly; precisely, exactly; **voici j. la lettre que j'attendais,** here's the very letter I was waiting for.

justesse [ʒystɛs] *nf* **1.** exactness, precision, accuracy; **raisonner avec j.,** to argue soundly **2.** **de j.,** just; by the skin of one's teeth.

justice [ʒystis] *nf* **1.** justice; **c'est j. que** + *sub,* it is only right that; **en toute j.,** by rights; in all fairness; **avec j.,** justly; **rendre j. à qn,** (i) to do justice to s.o.(ii) to deal with s.o. according to his deserts; **ce n'est que j.,** it's only fair; **se faire j.,** (i) to take the law into one's own hands (ii) to commit suicide **2.** law, legal proceedings; **aller en j.,** to go to law; **poursuivre qn en j.,** to take legal action against s.o.

justification [ʒystifikasjɔ̃] *nf* justification; proof. **justificatif, -ive** *a* justificatory; **pièce justificative,** written proof, evidence.

justifier [ʒystifje] *v* (*impf & pr sub* **n. justifiions**) **1.** *vtr* (*a*) to justify, vindicate (s.o.'s conduct); to bear out (statement); to warrant (action, expenditure) (*b*) to prove, make good (assertion) **2.** *v ind tr* **j. de,** to prove **3.** **se j.,** to clear oneself; to justify oneself.

jute [ʒyt] *nm Tex:* jute; **toile de j.,** hessian.

juteux, -euse [ʒytø, -øz] *a* juicy.

juvénile [ʒyvenil] *a* juvenile; youthful; *Jur:* **délinquence j.,** juvenile delinquency.

juxtaposer [ʒykstapoze] *vtr* to place side by side, to juxtapose.

juxtaposition [ʒykstapozisjɔ̃] *nf* juxtaposition.

K

K, k [kɑ] *nm* (the letter) K, k.

k. *abbr kilo.*

kaki¹ [kaki] *nm & a inv* khaki.

kaki² *nm Bot:* persimmon.

kaléidoscope [kaleidɔskɔp] *nm* kaleidoscope.

kamikaze [kamikaze] *nm* kamikaze.

kangourou [kãguru] *nm Z:* kangaroo.

kaolin [kaɔlɛ̃] *nm* kaolin.

kapok [kapɔk] *nm* kapok.

karaté [karate] *nm Sp:* karate.

kayac, kayak [kajak] *nm* kayak; canoe.

képi [kepi] *nm* kepi; peaked cap.

kermesse [kɛrmɛs] *nf (a)* village fair *(b)* (charity) fête; bazaar.

kérosène [kerɔzɛn] *nm* paraffin (oil); kerosene.

kg. *abbr kilogramme.*

kidnapper [kidnape] *vtr* to kidnap.

kidnappeur, -euse [kidnapœr, -øz] *n* kidnapper.

kif-kif [kifkif] *a inv F:* same, likewise; **c'est k.-k.,** c'est du kif, it's all the same.

kilo(gramme) [kilo, kilɔgram] *nm* kilogram(me).

kilométrage [kilɔmetraʒ] *nm* =mileage length in kilometres.

kilomètre [kilɔmɛtr] *nm* kilometre. **kilométrique** *a* **borne k.** = milestone.

kilowatt [kilɔwat] *nm* kilowatt.

kilowattheure [kilɔwatœr] *nm* kilowatt-hour.

kimono [kimɔnɔ] *nm Cl:* kimono.

kinésithérapeute [kineziterapøt] *n* physiotherapist.

kinésithérapie [kineziterapi] *nf* physiotherapy.

kiosque [kjɔsk] *nm* **1.** *(a)* kiosk; **k. à musique,** bandstand; **k. de jardin,** pavilion *(b)* **k. à journaux,** newspaper stall **2.** *Nau:* conning tower (of submarine).

kirsch [kirʃ] *nm* kirsch.

kiwi [kiwi] *nm Orn:* kiwi.

klaxon [klaksɔ̃] *nm Aut: Rtm:* hooter, horn.

klaxonner [klaksɔne] *vi Aut:* to hoot, sound one's horn.

kleptomanie [klɛptɔmani] *nf* kleptomania. **kleptomane** *a & n* kleptomaniac.

knock-out [knɔkut, nɔkaut] **1.** *a inv Sp:* **mettre (qn) k.-o.,** to knock (s.o.) out; **être k.-o.,** to be knocked out **2.** *nm* knockout.

ko *abbr Box:* knock-out.

koala [kɔala] *nm Z:* koala (bear).

krach [krak] *nm* (financial) crash.

kyrielle [kirjɛl] *nf* long string (of words); stream (of requests).

kyste [kist] *nm Med:* cyst.

L

L, l [ɛl] *nm or f* (the letter) L.

l. *abbr* litre.

l', la[1] [la] *def art & pron f see* **le**[1·2].

la[2] *sm inv Mus:* 1. (the note) A; **donner le la,** (i) to give an A (ii) *Fig:* to set the tone 2. la(h) (in tonic sol-fa).

là [la] *adv* 1. (*of place*) there (*a*) **là où vous êtes,** where you are; **quand il n'est pas là,** when he's away; **est-ce qu'il est là?** is he in? **les choses en sont là,** this is the state of things at the moment; **la question n'est pas là,** that's not the point; **loin de là,** far from it; **à cinq pas de là,** five paces away; *F:* **ôtez-vous de là!** get out of there! **passez par là,** go that way; **viens là!** come here! **il est là,** he's here; *F:* **elle a 35 ans, par là,** she's about 35 (*b*) (*emphatic use*) **c'est là qu'il habite,** that's where he lives; **c'est là qu'elle a été interrompue,** it was at that moment that she was interrupted; **que dites-vous là?** what's that you're saying? **il est bête à ce point-là?** is he (really) that stupid? *see also* **ce**[1] 1., **ce**[2] 5.; **celui-là, celle-là,** *see* **celui** 4. (*c*) **comme menteur il est un peu là!** he's a pretty good liar! 2. (*of time*) then; **d'ici là,** between now and then; in the meantime 3. **qu'entendez-vous par là?** what do you mean by that? **de là on peut conclure que,** from this one can conclude that 4. *int* **là! voilà qui est fait,** there now! that's done; **hé là!** doucement! gently does it! **là, là,** there now, there, there; **oh là là!** oh dear!; **alors là, ce n'est pas étonnant!** well, *that's* not surprising! 5. **là-bas,** over there; **là-dedans,** in there; inside; in this; **là-dessous,** under that, under there, underneath; **là-dessus,** on that, on it; about that; **là-dessus, il est sorti,** with that, he went out; **là-haut,** up there, upstairs.

label [label] *nm Com:* stamp; seal (of approval).

labeur [labœr] *nm* labour, toil, hard work.

labo [labo] *nm F:* lab.

laborantin, -ine [labɔrɑ̃tɛ̃, -in] *n* laboratory, *F:* lab, assistant.

laboratoire [labɔratwar] *nm* laboratory, *F:* lab.

laborieux, -euse [labɔrjø, -øz] *a* 1. arduous, hard (work); laboured (style); *F:* **il n'a pas encore fini? c'est l.!** hasn't he finished yet? it's taking a long time! 2. (*pers*) laborious, hard-working; **les classes laborieuses,** the working classes. **laborieusement** *adv* laboriously; hard.

labour [labur] *nm* ploughing, *NAm:* plowing; digging; **(terre de) l.,** ploughed land.

labourage [labura3] *nm* ploughing, *NAm:* plowing; digging.

labourer [labure] *vtr* (*a*) to plough, *NAm:* to plow; **l. à la bêche,** to dig (*b*) **se l. les mains,** to lacerate one's hands; **visage labouré de rides,** face furrowed with wrinkles.

laboureur [laburœr] *nm* ploughman, *NAm:* plowman.

labrador [labradɔr] *nm Z:* Labrador (retriever).

labyrinthe [labirɛ̃t] *nm* labyrinth, maze.

lac [lak] *nm* lake; *F:* (*of project*) **c'est dans le l.,** it's fallen through.

lacer [lase] *vtr* (**n. laçons**) to lace (up), tie (up).

lacération [laserasjɔ̃] *nf* laceration; tearing up, ripping (up).

lacérer [lasere] *vtr* (**je lacère; je lacérerai**) to tear, lacerate; to rip to pieces.

lacet [lasɛ] *nm* 1. (shoe)lace; lace (of corset); **chaussures à lacets,** lace-up shoes, *F:* lace-ups 2. (hairpin) bend; **sentier en lacets,** zigzag path; **la route monte en lacets,** the road winds steeply up 3. noose, snare (for rabbits).

lâche [laʃ] 1. *a* (*a*) loose, slack; loosely fitting (clothes); lax (discipline) (*b*) cowardly; (*of behaviour*) low, despicable 2. *n* coward. **lâchement** *adv* (*a*) loosely, slackly (*b*) in a cowardly manner.

lâcher [laʃe] 1. *vtr.* (*a*) to release; to slacken, loosen (spring); **l. un coup de fusil,** to fire a shot (*b*) to let go; to release, to drop (bomb, parachutist); **lâchez-moi!** let me go! **l. ses études,** to give up one's studies; **l. pied,** to give way; to give in; **l. prise,** (i) to let go (ii) to give up; *F:* **l. qn,** to drop, ditch, s.o.; **il ne m'a pas lâché d'une semelle,** he stuck to me like a leech; *P:* **l. les sous, les l.,** to fork out, pay up (*c*) to set free; **l. un chien,** to let a dog loose; **l. un chien contre qn,** to set a dog on s.o.; *P:* **l. le paquet, le morceau,** to tell the truth, come clean 2. *vi* to get loose; (*of spring*) to slacken; (*of rope*) to slip; **mes freins ont lâché,** my brakes failed; **ses nerfs ont lâché,** she lost her nerve.

lâcheté [laʃte] *nf* 1. (*a*) cowardice (*b*) act of cowardice 2. (*a*) despicableness; baseness (*b*) low, despicable, action.

lâcheur, -euse [laʃœr, -øz] *n F:* unreliable person.

laconisme [lakɔnism] *nm* laconism. **laconique** *a* laconic. **laconiquement** *adv* laconically.

lacrymogène [lakrimɔ3ɛn] *a* gaz l., tear gas.

lacté [lakte] *a* milky; **régime l.,** milk diet.

lacune [lakyn] *nf* lacuna, gap; blank (in memory).

là-dedans, la-dessous, etc *see* **là** 5.

ladite [ladit] *see* **ledit**.

lagon [lagɔ̃] *nm,* **lagune** [lagyn] *nf* lagoon.

lai, -e [lɛ] *a Ecc:* lay; **frère l.,** lay brother.

laïciser [laisize] *vtr* to secularize.

laïcité [laisite] *nf* secularity.

laideron [lɛdrɔ̃] *nm* ugly girl, woman.

laideur [lɛdœr] *nf* 1. ugliness; unattractiveness; plainness 2. meanness, lowness; **les laideurs de la vie,** the ugly side of life. **laid** *a* (*a*) ugly; unsightly; unattractive; (*of face*) plain; **l. comme un pou,** as ugly as sin (*b*) mean, low (action); ugly (vice).

lainage [lɛna3] *nm* (*a*) woollen fabric (*b*) woollen garment, article; *pl* woollens.

laine [lɛn] *nf* wool; **l. peignée,** worsted; **jupe en, de,**

l., woollen skirt; l. de verre, glass wool. laineux, -euse a fleecy, woolly. lainier, -ière a woollen (trade); wool (industry).

laïque [laik] 1. a laic; secular (education); lay (dress); école l. = state school 2. n layman, laywoman; les laïques, the laity.

laisse [lɛs] nf leash, lead; tenir en l., to keep on a leash.

laissé-pour-compte [lesepurkɔ̃t] 1. a rejected (pers, article) 2. (a) nm Com: reject, unsold article (b) n unwanted person; misfit; pl laissé(e)s-pour-compte.

laisser [lɛse] vtr 1. to let, allow; je les ai laissés dire, I let them talk; l. voir qch., to show, to reveal, sth; l. tomber qch, to drop sth; se l. aller, to let oneself go; F: laissez-moi rire! don't make me laugh! ne vous laissez pas aller comme ça! pull yourself together! F: ce vin se laisse boire, this wine is quite drinkable; se l. emporter par la colère, to give way to anger; laisse faire, never mind; leave it; laissez-le faire! leave it to him! il s'est laissé faire, he offered no resistance; allons, laisse-toi faire! go on, be a devil! 2. (a) to leave (sth, s.o., somewhere); allons, je vous laisse, right, I'm going, I'm off; partir sans l. d'adresse, to go away without leaving one's address; l. qch de côté, to leave sth out; to put sth aside; c'est à prendre ou à l., take it or leave it (b) l. la fenêtre ouverte, to keep the window open; je vous laisse libre d'agir, I leave you free to act; laissez-moi (tranquille)! leave me alone! laissez, c'est moi qui paie, leave that, I'm paying; laissez donc! don't bother! don't worry! vous pouvez nous l., you may leave us (c) cela nous laisse le temps de, that leaves us time to; laissez-moi vos clefs, leave me your keys; je vous le laisserai à bon compte, I will let you have it cheap; cela laisse (beaucoup) à désirer, it leaves much to be desired (d) Lit: ne pas l. de faire qch., not to fail to do sth; cela ne laisse pas de m'inquiéter, I feel anxious all the same.

laisser-aller [lɛseale] nm inv 1. casualness 2. carelessness.

laisser-faire [lɛsefɛr] nm non-interference; laissez-faire.

laisser-passer [lɛsepɑse] nm inv pass, permit.

lait [lɛ] nm 1. milk; l. entier, whole milk; l. écrémé, skimmed milk; petit l., whey; l. caillé, curds; l. concentré, evaporated milk; l. en poudre, dried milk, powdered milk; café au l., white coffee; chocolat au l., milk chocolate; l. de poule, egg nog (without alcohol); vache à l., milch cow; l. maternel, mother's milk; frère, sœur, de l., foster brother, sister; cochon de l., suck(l)ing pig 2. (a) l. de coco, coconut milk; l. de chaux, limewater (b) Toil: l. démaquillant, cleansing milk. laiteux, -euse a milky. laitier, -ière 1. a l'industrie laitière, the milk industry; produits laitiers, dairy produce; vache laitière, nf laitière, milch cow; milker 2. n (a) milkman; milkwoman (b) dairyman; dairywoman.

laitage [lɛtaʒ] nm dairy produce.

laitance [lɛtɑ̃s] nf Ich: milt; Cu: soft roe.

laiterie [lɛtri] nf (a) dairy (b) dairy farming.

laiton [lɛtɔ̃] nm brass.

laitue [lɛty] nf lettuce; l. romaine, cos lettuce.

lama [lama] nm 1. (Buddhist) lama 2. Z: llama.

lambeau, -eaux [lɑ̃bo] nm scrap, bit, shred (of cloth, paper, flesh); vêtements en lambeaux, clothes in tatters; mettre en lambeaux, to tear to shreds.

lambiner [lɑ̃bine] vi F: to dawdle. lambin, -ine F: 1. a dawdling, slow 2. n dawdler, slowcoach.

lambris [lɑ̃bri] nm panelling; (on wall) wainscoting.

lame [lam] nf 1. (a) lamina, thin plate, strip (of metal); leaf (of spring); (microscope) slide; slat (of Venetian blind); l. de parquet, floorboard (b) blade (of sword, knife); l. de rasoir, razor blade (c) Lit: (i) sword (ii) swordsman 2. wave; l. de fond, ground swell; l. de houle, roller. lamé a & nm lamé.

amelle [lamɛl] nf (a) (thin) strip; slat (of blind); gill (of mushroom) (b) (microscope) slide.

lamentable [lamɑ̃tabl] a (a) lamentable, deplorable (accident); sort l., terrible fate (b) mournful (voice) (c) (of result) shockingly bad; awful, appalling; orateur l., pitiful speaker. lamentablement adv lamentably.

lamentation [lamɑ̃tasjɔ̃] nf lamentation; wailing; lament; moaning.

lamenter (se) [səlamɑ̃te] vpr se l. sur son sort, to bemoan, lament, one's fate; se l. sur son propre sort, to feel sorry for oneself.

laminage [laminaʒ] nm lamination.

laminer [lamine] vtr to laminate (metal, plastic).

laminoir [laminwar] nm rolling mill.

lampadaire [lɑ̃padɛr] nm (a) standard lamp (b) street lamp.

lampe [lɑ̃p] nf (a) lamp; l. à huile, oil lamp (b) l. de bureau, reading lamp, desk light; l. de chevet, bedside light; l. de poche, (electric) torch; NAm: flashlight; l. à alcool, spirit lamp; l. à souder, blowlamp (b) (radio) valve.

lampion [lɑ̃pjɔ̃] nm (a) fairylight (for illuminations) (b) Chinese lantern.

lance [lɑ̃s] nf 1. (a) spear (b) lance 2. l. d'incendie, fire-hose nozzle.

lance-bombes [lɑ̃sbɔ̃b] nm inv Av: bomb thrower.

lancée [lɑ̃se] nf momentum, impetus; continuer sur sa l., to keep going.

lance-flammes [lɑ̃sflam] nm inv Mil: flame-thrower.

lance-fusée [lɑ̃sfyze] nm inv Mil: rocket launcher.

lance-grenades [lɑ̃sgrənad] nm inv Mil: grenade launcher.

lancement [lɑ̃smɑ̃] nm (a) throwing; l. du disque, throwing the discus; l. du poids, putting the shot (b) launching (of missile, rocket, ship, new product); Com: floating (of company).

lance-missiles [lɑ̃smisil] nm inv Mil: missile launcher.

lance-pierre(s) [lɑ̃spjɛr] nm inv catapult.

lancer [lɑ̃se] vtr (n. lançons) 1. (a) to throw, fling, hurl; to shoot (an arrow); to send up (a rocket); l. des pierres à qn, to throw stones at s.o.; l. des bombes, to throw bombs; l. des étincelles, to shoot out sparks; l. qch en l'air, to toss sth in the air; l. un coup d'œil à qn, to dart a glance at s.o. (b) Sp: to throw (a ball); l. le disque, to throw the discus; l. le poids, to put the shot 2. to start, set (s.o., sth) going (a) l. un cheval, to start a horse off at full gallop; l. un chien contre qn, to set a dog on s.o.; si vous le lancez sur ce sujet il ne s'arrêtera plus, if you start him on this subject he will never stop (b) to launch (ship, scheme, attack); to release (bomb); to float (company); to bring out (actor); to launch (new product); to launch, set (fashion); to start (up) (engine); **l. qn (dans les affaires)**, to set s.o. up (in business); **cet acteur est lancé**, this actor has made a name for himself **3. se l. en avant**, to rush forward; **se l. à la poursuite de qn**, to dash off in pursuit of s.o.; **se l. dans les affaires**, to launch out into business; **elle veut se l.**, she wants to make a name for herself.

lance-torpilles [lɑ̃stɔrpij] nm inv Navy: **(tube) l.-t.**, torpedo tube.

lanceur, -euse [lɑ̃sœr, -øz] n (a) Sp: thrower; Cr: bowler (b) launcher (of spacecraft) (c) promoter (of company).

lanciner [lɑ̃sine] **1.** vi (of pain) to shoot; (of finger) to throb **2.** vtr to harass, trouble, torment. **lancinant** a shooting, throbbing (pain); haunting (memory); insistent (tune).

landau [lɑ̃do] nm **1.** Veh: landau **2.** pram; NAm: baby carriage.

lande [lɑ̃d] nf (sandy) moor; heath; waste; NAm: barren.

langage [lɑ̃gaʒ] nm language; speech (of the individual); **tenir un l. grossier à qn**, to speak rudely to s.o.; **changer de l.**, to change one's tune; **en voilà un l.!** that's no way to talk! **l. argotique**, slang; **l. chiffré**, cipher, code. **langagier, -ière** a linguistic.

lange [lɑ̃ʒ] nm (a) pl A: swaddling clothes (b) baby's flannel blanket.

langer [lɑ̃ʒe] vtr A: to wrap (a baby) in swaddling clothes.

langoureux, -euse [lɑ̃gurø, -øz] a languorous.

langouste [lɑ̃gust] nf Crust: spiny lobster; crawfish, crayfish.

langoustine [lɑ̃gustin] nf (a) Norway lobster (b) Dublin Bay prawn; Cu: pl scampi.

langue [lɑ̃g] nf **l.** tongue; **tirer la l.**, (i) to put out one's tongue (ii) F: to be very thirsty (iii) F: to have one's tongue hanging out (for sth); **avoir la l. bien pendue**, to have a ready tongue; **elle a la l. trop longue**, she talks too much; (with reference to riddle) **donner sa l. au chat**, to give up; **mauvaise l.**, backbiter; **l. de vipère**, spiteful gossip; F: **avoir un cheveu sur la l.**, to lisp **2. langues de feu**, tongues of flame; **l. de terre**, spit of land **3.** language (of a people); **professeur de langues vivantes**, modern language teacher; **pays de l. anglaise**, English-speaking country; **avoir le don des langues**, to be a good linguist; **l. verte**, slang.

langue-de-chat [lɑ̃gdəʃa] nf Cu: (flat) finger biscuit; pl langues-de-chat.

languette [lɑ̃gɛt] nf small tongue (of wood); strip (of tinfoil); tongue (of shoe).

langueur [lɑ̃gœr] nf listlessness, languor.

languir [lɑ̃gir] vi to languish; to pine; Lit: to waste away; (of plant) to wilt; **l. d'amour**, to be lovesick; **l. après qch**, to long, pine, for sth; **ne nous faites pas l.**, don't keep us on tenterhooks; **la conversation languit**, the conversation is flagging. **languissant** a (a) languid, listless (b) languishing.

lanière [lɑnjɛr] nf strip (of material); thin strap; thong; lash (of whip).

lanterne [lɑ̃tɛrn] nf (a) lantern; **l. vénitienne**, Chinese lantern; **l. magique**, magic lantern (b) Aut: sidelight.

laper [lape] vtr & i (of dog) to lap (up) (water, milk).

lapider [lapide] vtr to stone (s.o.) (to death).

lapin, -ine [lapɛ̃, -in] n (buck) rabbit, f doe; **l. de**

garenne, wild rabbit; **l. domestique**, tame rabbit; Com: **peau de l.**, cony (skin); P: **poser un l. à qn**, to stand s.o. up; **mon petit l.**, my darling, my lamb.

Laponie [laponi] Prnf Geog: Lapland. **lapon, -one** **1.** a Lapp, Lappish **2.** (a) n Lapp, Laplander (b) nm Ling: Lapp(ish).

laps [laps] nm **un l. de temps**, a lapse of time.

laquais [lakɛ] nm footman; Pej: flunkey.

laque [lak] **1.** nf (a) Paint: lake; **l. en écailles**, shellac (b) (hair) lacquer; hair spray **2.** nm lacquer; **l. de Chine**, japan.

laquelle [lakɛl] see **lequel**.

laquer [lake] vtr to lacquer; to japan.

larbin [larbɛ̃] nm F: Pej: flunkey.

larcin [larsɛ̃] nm (a) Jur: larceny; petty theft (b) loot.

lard [lar] nm (a) fat (esp of pig) (b) bacon; **l. maigre**, streaky bacon; P: **gros l.**, fat slob; **tête de l.**, pigheaded idiot.

larder [larde] vtr to lard (piece of meat); **l. qn de coups de couteau**, to stab s.o. (all over) with a knife.

lardon [lardɔ̃] nm Cu: piece of larding bacon; lardon.

large [larʒ] **1.** a (a) broad, wide; **l. d'épaules**, broad-shouldered; **route l. de dix mètres**, road ten metres wide; **vêtements larges**, loose-fitting clothes; **d'un geste l.**, with a sweeping gesture; **dans un sens l.**, in a broad sense; **avoir l'esprit l.**, to be broad-minded; **il n'est pas très l.**, he's not very generous (b) large, big, ample **2.** nm (a) Nau: open sea; **brise du l.**, sea breeze; F: **prendre le l.**, to clear off, to beat it; **au l. de Cherbourg**, off Cherbourg (b) breadth; **dix mètres de l.**, ten metres wide; **se promener de long en l.**, to walk up and down, to and fro **3.** adv **calculer l.**, to allow a wide margin of error; **voir l.**, (i) to be broad-minded (ii) to think big. **largement** adv (a) broadly, widely; **services l. rétribués**, highly paid services (b) amply; **avoir l. le temps**, to have plenty of time; **il en a eu l.** (assez), he's had more than enough.

largesse [larʒɛs] nf liberality; generosity; generous gift.

largeur [larʒœr] nf breadth, width; **avoir 3 mètres de l.**, to be three metres wide; **en l., dans la l.**, widthwise; **distance en l.**, distance across; **l. d'esprit**, broad-mindedness.

larguer [large] vtr (a) Nau: to loose (rope); **l. les amarres**, to cast off the mooring ropes (b) to drop (parachutist) (c) F: to chuck (s.o.).

larme [larm] nf tear; **fondre en larmes**, to burst into tears; **pleurer à chaudes larmes**, to weep bitterly; **larmes de crocodile**, crocodile tears; F: **une l. de rhum**, a drop of rum.

larmoyer [larmwaje] vi (**je larmoie**) (of the eyes) to water; (of pers) to weep, to snivel. **larmoyant** a tearful; maudlin.

larron [larɔ̃] nm A: thief; F: **s'entendre comme larrons en foire**, to be as thick as thieves.

larve [larv] nf larva; grub (of insect); Fig: worm.

laryngite [larɛ̃ʒit] nf Med: laryngitis.

laryngologiste [larɛ̃gɔlɔʒist] n Med: throat specialist.

larynx [larɛ̃ks] nm Anat: larynx.

las, lasse [lɑ, lɑs] a tired, weary.

lascar [laskar] nm F: (smart) character; rogue.

lasciveté [lasivte] nf lasciviousness. **lascif, -ive** a lascivious.

laser [lazɛr] *nm Ph:* laser.

lasser [lase] *vtr* **1.** to tire, weary; to exhaust (s.o.'s patience) **2. se l.,** to get tired of (s.o., sth); **on ne se lasse pas de l'écouter,** one is never tired of listening to him. **lassant** *a* wearisome, tedious.

lassitude [lasityd] *nf* lassitude, weariness.

lasso [laso] *nm* lasso; **prendre au l.,** to lasso.

latence [latɑ̃s] *nf* latency. **latent** *a* latent (disease); hidden, concealed.

latéral, -aux [lateral, -o] *a* lateral: **rue latérale,** side street. **latéralement** *adv* laterally; on, at, the side.

latex [latɛks] *nm inv* latex.

latin, -ine [latɛ̃, -in] **1.** *a & nm* Latin; **le Quartier l.,** the Latin Quarter; **Amérique latine,** Latin America; **les Latins,** the Latin races **2.** *nm Ling:* Latin; *F:* **l. de cuisine,** dog Latin; **j'y perds mon l.,** I can't make head or tail of it. **latino-américain, -aine** *a & n* Latin-American; *pl latino-américain(e)s.*

latitude [latityd] *nf* (a) latitude; scope, freedom (b) *Geog:* latitude; **à 30° de l. nord,** at latitude 30° North.

latte [lat] *nf* lath, batten, slat.

lauréat, -ate [lɔrea, -at] **1.** *a* prizewinning **2.** *n* laureate, prizewinner.

laurier [lɔrje] *nm Bot:* (bay) laurel; *Cu:* **feuille de l.,** bay leaf.

laurier-rose [lɔrjeroz] *nm Bot:* oleander; *pl lauriers-roses.*

laurier-sauce [lɔrjesos] *nm Bot: Cu:* bay (tree); *pl lauriers-sauce.*

lavabo [lavabo] *nm* (a) washbasin (b) (*place for washing*) *pl* toilets.

lavage [lavaʒ] *nm* washing; wash; bathing (of wound); *Med:* **l. d'estomac,** stomach wash; **l. de cerveau,** brainwashing.

lavande [lavɑ̃d] *nf Bot:* lavender.

lavandière [lavɑ̃djɛr] *nf* **1.** washerwoman; laundress **2.** *Orn:* wagtail.

lavasse [lavas] *nf F:* dishwater.

lave [lav] *nf Geol:* lava.

lave-glace [lavglas] *nm Aut:* windscreen, *NAm:* windshield, washer; *pl lave-glaces.*

laver [lave] *vtr* to wash; **l. à grande eau,** to swill down; **se l.,** to wash, to have a wash; **se l. les dents,** to clean one's teeth; *F:* **l. la tête à qn,** to haul s.o. over the coals; **se l. les mains,** to wash one's hands; **je m'en lave les mains,** I wash my hands of this affair; **l. la vaisselle,** to wash up, to do the washing-up; to wash the dishes; **ce tissu ne se lave pas,** this material isn't washable; **l. une plaie,** to bathe a wound. **lavable** *a* washable.

laverie [lavri] *nf* **l. automatique,** launderette.

lavette [lavɛt] *nf* (a) (dish)mop; dishcloth (b) *P:* (*pers*) drip.

laveur, -euse [lavœr, -øz] *n* washer; **laveuse,** washer-woman; **l. de carreaux, de vitres,** window cleaner.

lave-vaisselle [lavvɛsɛl] *nm inv* (a) dishwasher, washing-up machine (b) washing-up liquid.

lavoir [lavwar] *nm* (a) **l. (public),** (public) wash-house (b) washtub.

laxatif, -ive [laksatif, -iv] *a & nm Med:* laxative.

laxisme [laksism] *nm* laxity.

layette [lɛjɛt] *nf* (set of) baby clothes; layette; **rayon l.,** babywear department.

le¹, la¹, les¹ [lə, la, le] *def art* (**le** and **la** are elided to **l'** before a vowel or h mute; **le** and **les** contract with **à, de,**

into **au, aux; du, des**) the (a) (*particularizing*) **ouvrez la porte,** open the door; **il est venu la semaine dernière,** he came last week; **j'apprends le français,** I am learning French; **l'un ... l'autre,** (the) one ... the other; **mon livre et le tiens,** my book and yours; **il est arrivé le lundi 12,** he arrived on Monday the 12th; **oh! le beau chat!** what a beautiful cat! **debout, les enfants!** time to get up children! **la France,** France; **les Alpes,** the Alps; **le roi Édouard,** King Edward; **le cardinal Richelieu,** Cardinal Richelieu; **le Dante,** Dante; **la Callas,** Callas; (*place names*) **le Caire,** Cairo; **je vais au Caire,** I'm going to Cairo; (*with most feast days*) **la Toussaint,** All Saints' Day; **à la Noël,** at Christmas; (*parts of the body*) **hausser les épaules,** to shrug one's shoulders; **elle ferma les yeux,** she closed her eyes; **il s'est pincé le doigt,** he pinched his finger (b) (*forming superlatives*) **le meilleur vin de sa cave,** the best wine in his cellar; **mon ami le plus intime,** my most intimate friend; **c'est elle qui travaille le mieux,** she's the one who works best (c) (*generalizing*) **je préfère le café au thé,** I prefer coffee to tea (d) (*distributive*) **trois fois l'an,** three times a year; **cinq francs la livre,** five francs a pound; **il vient le jeudi,** he comes on Thursdays (e) (*rendered by indef art in Eng*) **donner l'exemple,** to set an example; **demander le divorce,** to sue for a divorce; **la belle excuse!** a fine excuse! **il n'a pas le sou,** he hasn't a penny.

le², la², les² *pers pron* **1.** (*replacing n*) him, her, it, them (a) **je ne le lui ai pas donné,** I did not give it to him; **tu le sais aussi bien que moi,** you know it as well as I do; **les voilà!** there they are! **ne l'abîmez pas,** don't spoil it (b) (*following the vb*) **donnez-le-lui,** give it to him; **regardez-les,** look at them **2.** *neut pron* **le** (a) (*replacing an adj or n used as an adj*) **son frère est médecin, il voudrait l'être aussi,** his brother is a doctor, he would like to be one too (b) (*replacing a clause*) **il me l'a dit,** he told me so; **est-il parti? — je me le demande,** has he gone? — that's what I'm wondering; **vous le devriez,** you ought to.

lèche [lɛʃ] *nf P:* bootlicking; **faire de la l.,** to be a bootlicker.

lèche-bottes [lɛʃbɔt] *n inv P:* bootlicker.

lécher [leʃe] *vtr* (**je lèche; je lécherai**) to lick; **se l. les doigts,** to lick one's fingers; *F:* **il s'en léchait les babines,** he licked his chops over it; **l. les bottes de qn,** to lick s.o.'s boots; **l. les vitrines,** to go window shopping.

lécheur, -euse [leʃœr, -øz] *n P:* bootlicker.

lèche-vitrines [lɛʃvitrin] *nm inv F:* window shopping.

leçon [ləsɔ̃] *nf* lesson; **leçons particulières,** private lessons, tuition; **que cela vous serve de l.,** let that be a lesson to you; **faire la l. à qn,** (i) to give s.o. instructions (ii) to give s.o. a lecture.

lecteur, -trice [lɛktœr, -tris] **1.** *n* (a) reader; **le nombre de lecteurs,** the readership (b) foreign language assistant (at university) **2.** *nm* **l. de cassettes,** cassette player.

lectorat [lɛktɔra] *nm* readership (of a newspaper).

lecture [lɛktyr] *nf* reading; **il m'a apporté de la l.,** he brought me something to read; **l. à haute voix,** reading aloud; **faire la l. à qn,** to read aloud to s.o.; **l. pour la jeunesse,** children's books, books for children.

ledit, ladite, *pl* **lesdits, lesdites** [lədi, ladit, ledi, ledit] (*contracted with* **à** *and* **de** *to* **audit, auxdit(e)s, dudit, desdit(e)s** *a* the (afore)said, the aforementioned.

légalisation [legalizasjɔ̃] *nf* legalization. **légal, -aux** *a* legal; **fête légale,** statutory holiday. **légalement** *adv* legally.

légaliser [legalize] *vtr* 1. to legalize 2. to attest, certify (signature).

légalité [legalite] *nf* legality; **rester dans la l.,** to keep within the law.

légat [lega] *nm* **l. (du Pape),** (papal) legate.

légataire [legatɛr] *n Jur:* legatee, heir; **l. universel,** sole legatee.

légation [legasjɔ̃] *nf* legation.

légende [leʒɑ̃d] *nf* (*a*) (*story*) legend (*b*) inscription (on coin); caption (of illustration); list of references; key, legend (to diagram, map). **légendaire** *a* legendary.

légèreté [leʒɛrte] *nf* lightness; slightness (of injury); mildness; flightiness (of conduct); fickleness. **léger, -ère** 1. *a* (*a*) light; **avoir le sommeil l.,** to be a light sleeper; **avoir la main légère,** to be (i) gentle (ii) clever, with one's hands; *Fig:* to rule with a light hand; **conduite légère,** flightly conduct; **femme légère,** woman of easy virtue; **propos légers,** idle talk; **repas l.,** light meal (*b*) slight (pain); gentle (breeze); faint (sound); mild (tobacco); light (wine); weak (tea); mild (injury); trivial (loss) 2. *adv phr* **à la légère,** lightly; **parler à la l.,** to speak thoughtlessly; **traiter une affaire à la l.,** to make light of a matter.

légion [leʒjɔ̃] *nf* legion; **la L. (étrangère),** the Foreign Legion; **L. d'honneur,** Legion of Honour; **ils sont l.,** they are legion.

légionnaire [leʒjɔnɛr] *nm* (*a*) *Hist:* legionary (*b*) legionnaire (*c*) member of the Legion of Honour.

législateur, -trice [leʒislatœr, -tris] *n* legislator.

législation [leʒislasjɔ̃] *nf* legislation. **législatif, -ive** *a* legislative; **élection législative,** parliamentary election; **le pouvoir l.,** the legislature.

législature [leʒislatyr] *nf* 1. legislature 2. term of office.

légiste [leʒist] *nm* legist, jurist; **médecin l.,** forensic pathologist.

légitimer [leʒitime] *vtr* 1. to legitimate, legitim(at)ize (child) 2. to justify (action, claim) 3. to recognize (title). **légitime** *a* 1. legitimate, lawful 2. rightful (claim); justifiable; well-founded (fears); *Jur:* **l. défense,** self-defence. **légitimement** *adv* legitimately, lawfully, justifiably, rightfully.

légitimité [leʒitimite] *nf* legitimacy.

legs [lɛ, lɛg] *nm* legacy, bequest; **faire un l. à qn,** to leave s.o. a legacy.

léguer [lege] *vtr* (**je lègue; je léguerai**) to bequeath; to hand down, pass on (tradition).

légume [legym] 1. *nm* vegetable; **légumes verts,** greens; **légumes secs,** dried vegetables 2. *nf P:* **grosse l.,** big shot, bigwig.

légumier [legymje] *nm* vegetable dish.

légumineuse [legyminøz] *nf* leguminous plant.

Léman [lemɑ̃] *Prnm Geog:* **le lac L.,** Lake Geneva.

L. en D. *abbr Licencié en Droit.*

lendemain [lɑ̃dmɛ̃] *nm* next day; **le l. matin,** the next morning, the morning after; **penser au l.,** to think of the future; **il est devenu célèbre du jour au l.,** he became famous overnight; **au l. de son départ,** in the days following his departure; **des succès sans l.,** short-lived successes.

lenteur [lɑ̃tœr] *nf* (*a*) slowness (*b*) *pl* slow progress. **lent, lente**[1] *a* slow; slow-acting (poison); **avoir l'esprit l.,** to be slow-witted. **lentement** *adv* slowly.

lente[2] *nf Ent:* nit.

lentille [lɑ̃tij] *nf* 1. *Cu:* lentil 2. *Opt:* lens; **l. (cornéenne),** contact lens.

léopard [leɔpar] *nm* (*a*) *Z:* leopard (*b*) (*fur*) leopardskin.

lèpre [lɛpr] *nf Med:* leprosy. **lépreux, -euse** 1. *a* (*a*) leprous (*b*) peeling, scaly (wall) 2. *n* leper.

léproserie [leprozri] *nf* leper hospital.

lequel, laquelle, lesquels, lesquelles [ləkɛl, lakɛl, lekɛl] *pron* (*contracted with* **à** *and* **de** *to* **auquel, auxquel(le)s; duquel, desquel(le)s**) 1. *rel pron* who, whom; which (*a*) (*of thgs after prep*) **l'adresse à laquelle il devait m'écrire,** the address at which he had to write to me; **décision par laquelle,** decision whereby (*b*) (*of pers*) **la dame avec laquelle elle était sortie,** the lady with whom she had gone out; **le monsieur chez lequel je vous ai rencontré,** the gentleman at whose house I met you (*c*) (*to avoid ambiguity*) **le père de cette jeune fille, lequel est très riche,** the girl's father, who is very rich (*d*) (*adjectival*) **voici cent francs, laquelle somme vous étais due,** here's a hundred francs, (which was) the sum owed to you; **il écrira peut-être, auquel cas,** perhaps he will write, in which case 2. *interr pron* which (one)? **lequel (de ces chapeaux) préférez-vous?** which (of these hats) do you prefer? **lequel d'entre nous?** which one of us?

les *see* **le**[1,2].

lesbienne [lɛzbjɛn] *nf* lesbian.

lèse-majesté [lɛzmaʒɛste] *nf* high treason, lesemajesty.

léser [leze] *vtr* (**je lèse, n. lésons; je léserai**) to wrong (s.o.); to injure (s.o.); to encroach upon (s.o.'s rights); (*of action*) to endanger (s.o.'s interests); *Med:* to injure (organ).

lésiner [lezine] *vi* to be stingy; to skim (**sur,** over); to haggle (**sur,** over).

lésinerie [lezinri] *nf* stinginess.

lésineur, -euse [lezinœr, -øz] *n* haggler.

lésion [lezjɔ̃] *nf Med: Jur:* lesion.

L. ès L. *abbr Licencié ès Lettres.*

lessivage [lesivaʒ] *nm* washing.

lessive [lesiv] *nf* (*a*) detergent; washing powder (*b*) (household) washing; wash; **faire la l.,** to do the washing.

lessiver [lesive] *vtr* 1. (*a*) *Lit:* to wash (linen) (*b*) to scrub (floor) 2. *P:* (*at cards*) **se faire l.,** to be cleaned out (*b*) to lick (s.o.). **lessivé** *a P:* (*of pers*) exhausted, washed out.

lessiveuse [lesivøz] *nf* copper; (laundry) boiler.

lest [lɛst] *nm* (*no pl*) ballast.

leste [lɛst] *a* (*a*) light; nimble, agile; **avoir la main l.,** to be quick with one's hands (*b*) risqué (joke). **lestement** *adv* lightly; nimbly.

lester [leste] *vtr* (*a*) to ballast (*b*) *F:* to cram (pocket).

léthargie [letarʒi] *nf* lethargy; inactivity. **léthargique** *a* lethargic.

lettre [lɛtr] *nf* (*a*) letter; **écrire qch en toutes lettres,** to write sth out in full; **c'est écrit en toutes lettres,** it's all there in black and white; **à la l.**, to the letter; **au pied de la l.**, literally; **l. morte**, dead letter; **ce document est resté l. morte**, this document is now worthless (b) letter; *pl* **lettres**, mail, letters; **l. recommandée**, (i) recorded delivery letter (ii) registered letter; *F:* **c'est passé comme une l. à la poste**, it went off without a hitch; **lettres de noblesse**, letters patent of nobility (c) *pl* literature; humanities; **homme de lettres**, man of letters; **lettres modernes**, French language and literature; **lettres classiques**, classics; *Sch:* **faculté des lettres**, faculty of arts. **lettré** *a* well-read.

leucémie [løsemi] *nf Med:* leuk(a)emia. **leucémique** 1. *a* leuk(a)emic 2. *n* leuk(a)emia sufferer.

leur[1] [lœr] 1. *poss a* their; **un de leurs amis**, a friend of theirs; **leurs père et mère**, their father and mother 2. (a) *poss pron* **le leur, la leur, les leurs**, theirs (b) *nm* **ils n'y mettent pas du leur**, they don't pull their weight; **les leurs**, their own family, friends, etc; **j'étais des leurs**, I was with them; **ils ont encore fait des leurs**, they've been up to their old tricks again.

leur[2] *pers pron see* **lui**[1].

leurre [lœr] *nm* (a) lure; bait; decoy (b) delusion; deception.

leurrer [lœre] *vtr* (a) to lure (b) to deceive, delude; **se l.**, to delude oneself.

levage [ləvaʒ] *nm* lifting, hoisting.

levain [ləvɛ̃] *nm* leaven; **sans l.**, unleavened.

levant [ləvɑ̃] 1. *a* **soleil l.**, rising sun; **au soleil l.**, at sunrise 2. *nm* (a) **le l.**, the east (b) *Geog:* **le L.**, the Levant.

levée [ləve] *nf* (a) raising, lifting; lifting (of embargo); closing (of meeting); gathering (of crops); collection (of letters) (b) mail collected (c) embankment, sea wall (d) *Cards:* trick; **faire une l.**, to take a trick.

lever[1] [ləve] *vtr* (**je lève, n. levons; je lèverai**) 1. (a) to raise, to lift (up); to put up, to hold up; **l. les bras au ciel**, to throw up one's hands (in astonishment); **il ne veut pas l. le petit doigt**, he won't lift a finger; **l. la tête**, (i) to hold up one's head (ii) to raise one's head, to look up; **l. un enfant**, to help a child get up and dress; **l. les yeux**, to look up; **l. son verre**, to raise one's glass; to drink a toast; **l. l'ancre**, (i) to weigh anchor (ii) *F:* to leave; **l. un lièvre**, to start a hare (b) to raise (siege); to break (camp); to lift (embargo); to close (meeting) (c) **l. une difficulté**, to remove a difficulty 2. to levy (troops, tax); to collect (letters); *Cards:* **l. (les cartes)**, to pick up a trick 3. **l. un plan**, to draw, get out, a plan 4. *vi* (*of dough*) to rise; (*of plants*) to shoot 5. **se l.**, to rise, to get up (*of hands, curtain*) to go up (b) to stand up; **se l. de table**, to leave the table (c) to get up (from bed); **se l. du pied gauche**, to get out of bed on the wrong side (d) **le jour se lève**, day is breaking, dawning; **le soleil se lève**, the sun is rising; **le vent se lève**, the wind is rising, is getting up. **levé** 1. *a* (a) raised; **dessin à main levée**, freehand drawing; **voter à main levée**, to vote by a show of hands (*of pers*) up; out of bed 2. *nm* plan, survey (of a piece of land).

lever[2] *nm* 1. (a) rising, getting up (from bed) (b) levee (c) **l. du soleil**, sunrise, *NAm:* sun-up; **l. du jour**, daybreak 2. *Th:* raising (of the curtain); **un l. de rideau**, a curtain raiser.

lève-tard [lɛvtar] *nm inv F:* late riser.

lève-tôt [lɛvto] *nm inv F:* early riser.

levier [ləvje] *nm* 1. (a) lever; **force de l.**, leverage (b) *Tls:* crowbar 2. lever, handle; *Aut:* **l. (de changement) de vitesse**, gear lever, gear stick; **être aux leviers de commande**, to be in control, in command.

levraut [ləvro] *nm* leveret; young hare.

lèvre [lɛvr̩] *nf* lip; rim (of crater); **j'ai le mot sur les lèvres**, I have the word on the tip of my tongue; **manger du bout des lèvres**, to pick at one's food; **rire du bout des lèvres**, to force a laugh; **pincer les lèvres**, to purse one's lips.

lévrier [levrije] *nm Z:* greyhound.

levure [ləvyr] *nf* yeast.

lexicographie [lɛksikɔgrafi] *nf* lexicography.

lexique [lɛksik] *nm* (a) lexicon (b) vocabulary; glossary.

lézard [lezar] *nm* (a) lizard; **faire le l.**, to bask in the sun (b) lizard skin.

lézarde [lezard] *nf* crevice, crack.

lézarder (se) [səlezarde] *vpr* (*of wall*) to crack. **lézardé** *a* (*of wall*) cracked, full of cracks.

liaison [ljɛzɔ̃] *nf* 1. (a) joining, binding; bonding (of bricks) (b) *Ling:* liaison (c) *Cu:* thickening (for sauce) (d) *Mil:* liaison, intercommunications; **être en l. avec**, to be in touch with; **établir une l. radio**, to establish radio contact (e) (air, sea, road, rail) link 2. (a) (close) contact, relationship; **l. d'affaires**, business connection; **travailler en l. étroite avec qn**, to work in close collaboration with s.o. (b) **l. (amoureuse)**, (love) affair.

liane [ljan] *nf Bot:* liana.

liant [ljɑ̃] *a* sociable; friendly.

liasse [ljas] *nf* bundle (of letters); wad (of banknotes); file (of papers).

Liban [libɑ̃] *Prnm Geog:* Lebanon. **libanais, -aise** *a & n* Lebanese.

libellé [libele] *nm* wording.

libeller [libele] *vtr* to draw up (document); to word (letter); to make out (cheque).

libellule [libɛlyl] *nf* dragonfly.

libéralisation [liberalizasjɔ̃] *nf* liberalization.

libéraliser [liberalize] *vtr* to liberalize.

libéralisme [liberalism] *nm* liberalism.

libéralité [liberalite] *nf* liberality; (generous) gift. **libéral, -aux** *a & n* liberal. **libéralement** *adv* liberally.

libération [liberasjɔ̃] *nf* liberation; freeing; releasing; discharge, release.

libérer [libere] *vtr* (**je libère; je libérerai**) 1. to liberate, release; to set (s.o.) free, to free (s.o.); to discharge (prisoner); *Com:* to ease (restrictions); to free (s.o., an institution, of debt); **l. le passage**, to unblock, to free, the way 2. **se l.**, to free oneself; **se l. (d'une dette)**, to redeem a debt; **se l. pour deux jours**, to (arrange to) take two days off.

liberté [liberte] *nf* liberty, freedom; **animaux en l.**, animals in the wild; **mettre en l.**, to set free; to discharge (prisoner); **l'assassin est toujours en l.**, the murderer is still at large; *Jur:* **(mise en) l. provisoire, sous caution**, (release on) bail; **avoir pleine l. d'action**, to have a free hand; **parler en toute l.**, to speak freely; **mon jour de l.**, my day off; **j'ai pris la l. de dire**, I took the liberty of saying; **prendre des libertés avec qn**, to take liberties with s.o.

libertin, -ine [libɛrtɛ̃, -in] *a & n* libertine.
libraire [librɛr] *n* bookseller.
librairie [librɛri] *nf* (*a*) bookselling, book trade (*b*) bookshop.
libre [libr̩] *a* 1. (*a*) free; **je suis l. de onze heures à midi,** I'm free between eleven and twelve; **être l. de faire qch,** to be free to do sth; **laisser qn l. d'agir,** to give s.o. a free hand; **l. à vous de le faire,** you are quite at liberty to do it; **l. à vous d'essayer,** you are welcome to try; **l. penseur,** freethinker; **école l.,** independent (Catholic) school (*b*) (*of movement*) unrestrained; **elle a les cheveux libres,** she wears her hair loose (*c*) **l. de soucis,** carefree (*d*) **être l. avec qn,** to treat s.o. in a familiar way; **manières libres,** free and easy manner 2. (*a*) clear, open (space); vacant (seat); **avoir du temps l.,** to have some free, spare, time; **le lundi est mon jour l.,** Monday is my day off; **je vous laisse le champ l.,** I'll leave you to it; **la voie est l.,** the coast is clear; *Tp:* **la ligne n'est pas l.,** the line is engaged; (*taxi sign*) **l.,** for hire; **à l'air l.,** in the open air (*b*) *Aut: Cy:* **roue l.,** free wheel; **descendre une côte en roue l.,** to freewheel down a hill (*c*) *Sp:* **aile l.,** hang gliding. **librement** *adv* freely.
libre-échange [libreʃɑ̃ʒ] *nm* free trade.
libre-service [librəsɛrvis] *nm* self-service (shop, restaurant); *pl* libres-services.
libriste [librist] *n Sp:* hang glider.
Libye [libi] *Prnf Geog:* Libya. **libyen, -enne** *a & n* Libyan.
licence [lisɑ̃s] *nf* 1. (*a*) leave, permission; *Adm:* **l. d'importation,** import licence (*b*) *Sp:* permit (*c*) *Sch:* bachelor's degree; **l. ès lettres, ès sciences,** bachelor's degree in arts, in science; **passer sa l.,** to take one's degree 2. (*a*) licence, abuse of liberty; **l. poétique,** poetic licence (*b*) licentiousness.
licencié, -iée [lisɑ̃sje] *n* (*a*) *Sch:* **l. ès lettres, ès sciences,** bachelor of arts, of science (*b*) *Sp:* permit holder.
licenciement [lisɑ̃simɑ̃] *nm* dismissal (of employee); **il y a eu beaucoup de licenciements,** there were many redundancies.
licencier [lisɑ̃sje] *vtr* (*pr sub & impf* **n. licenciions**) to dismiss (employee); to make (workers) redundant.
licencieux, -euse [lisɑ̃sjø, -øz] *a* licentious.
lichen [likɛn] *nm Bot:* lichen.
lichette [liʃɛt] *nf P:* small slice, nibble (of bread, cheese).
licite [lisit] *a* licit, lawful; permissible.
licorne [likɔrn] *nf* unicorn.
licou [liku] *nm* halter.
lie [li] *nf* dregs; **l. (de vin),** lees, sediment, of wine; **la l. de la société,** the dregs of society; *a inv* **l.(-)de(-)vin,** wine-coloured.
liège [ljɛʒ] *nm* cork.
lien [ljɛ̃] *nm* (*a*) tie, bond; **l. de parenté,** family relationship; **liens de famille,** family ties; **l. d'amitié,** bond of friendship (*b*) link, connection.
lier [lje] *vtr* (*pr sub & impf* **n. liions**) 1. (*a*) to bind, fasten, tie, tie up; **on l'a lié à un arbre,** he was tied to a tree; **ce contrat vous lie,** you are bound by this agreement; **l'intérêt nous lie,** we have common interests; **l. des idées,** to link ideas; *Mus:* **l. deux notes,** (i) to slur (ii) to tie, two notes (*b*) *Cu:* **l. une sauce,** to thicken a sauce (*c*) **l. amitié, conversation, avec qn,** to strike up a friendship with s.o.; to enter into conversation with s.o. 2. (*a*) **se l. (d'amitié) avec qn,** to form a friendship with s.o.; to make friends with s.o.; **ils sont très liés,** they are very close friends (*b*) **le lait et le jaune d'œuf se lient facilement,** milk and egg yolk blend easily.
lierre [ljɛr] *nm Bot:* ivy.
lieu, -eux [ljø] *nm* 1. (*a*) place; locality; spot; **mettre qch en l.,** to put sth in a safe place; **en haut l.,** in high circles, places; **le l. du crime,** the scene of the crime; **en tous lieux,** everywhere; **j'étais sur les lieux,** I was on the spot; **l. de rendez-vous,** meeting place; **l. commun,** commonplace; **en premier l.,** in the first place, first of all; **en dernier l.,** last of all, lastly, finally; **en son l.,** in due course (*b*) *pl* premises 2. (*a*) **avoir l.,** to take place; **la réunion aura l. le 10,** the meeting will be held on the 10th (*b*) ground(s), cause; **il y a (tout) l. de supposer que + *ind*,** there is (every) reason to suppose, for supposing, that; **je vous écrirai s'il y a l.,** I shall write to you if necessary; **tout donne l. à croire que,** everything leads one to believe that; **son retour a donné l. à une réunion de famille,** his return was the occasion for a family gathering (*c*) **tenir l. de qch.,** to take the place of sth; **au l. de,** instead of; **au l. que + *ind*,** whereas.
lieu(-)dit [ljødi] *nm* locality; *pl* lieux(-)dits.
lieue [ljø] *nf* league (=4 kilometres); **j'étais à cent lieues de penser que,** I should never have dreamt that.
lieuse [ljøz] *nf Agr:* (mechanical) sheaf binder.
lieutenant [ljøtnɑ̃] *nm Mil:* lieutenant; *Merchant Navy:* mate; *Navy:* **l. de vaisseau,** lieutenant; *Av:* **l. (aviateur),** flying officer.
lieutenant-colonel [ljøtnɑ̃kɔlɔnɛl] *nm Mil:* lieutenant colonel; *Av:* wing commander; *pl* lieutenants-colonels.
lièvre [ljɛvr̩] *nm Z:* hare; **mémoire de l.,** memory like a sieve.
liftier [liftje] *nm* lift attendant, *NAm:* elevator operator.
lifting [liftiŋ] *nm Surg:* facelift.
ligament [ligamɑ̃] *nm* ligament.
ligature [ligatyr] *nf* ligature.
ligaturer [ligatyre] *vtr* to ligature.
ligne [liɲ] *nf* 1. (*a*) line; cord; **l. de pêche,** fishing line; **l. de fond,** ledger line (*b*) **l. droite,** straight line; **l. brisée,** broken line; *Fb:* **l. de touche,** touchline; *Ten:* **l. de fond,** base line; *Aut:* **l. blanche,** white line (*c*) (out)line; **l. élégante d'une voiture,** good line of a car; **grandes lignes d'une œuvre,** broad outline of a work; **soigner sa l.,** to watch one's figure, one's waistline (*d*) **l. de flottaison,** waterline (of ship); **l. de mire,** line of sight; **l. de tir,** line of fire; **descendre en l. directe de,** to be lineally descended from (*e*) **l. de maisons,** row of houses; **se mettre en l.,** to line up; **question qui vient en première l.,** question of primary importance; **hors l.,** out of the ordinary; unrivalled, outstanding (artist); **sur toute la l.,** completely, absolutely (*f*) **écris-moi deux lignes,** drop me a line; (*in dictating*) **à la l.,** new paragraph 2. (*a*) *Rail:* line; **l. aérienne, maritime,** airline, shipping line; **l. d'autobus,** bus (i) service (ii) route (*b*) *El:* (power) line; **l. à haute tension,** high tension wire, line; **l. téléphonique,** telephone line; **la l. est occupée,** the line is engaged, *NAm:* busy.
lignée [liɲe] *nf* (line of) descendants; line, lineage.

ligoter [ligɔte] *vtr* to tie (s.o.) up; to bind (s.o.) hand and foot.

ligue [lig] *nf* league, confederacy.

liguer [lige] *vtr* 1. to bond (nations) together; **être ligué avec qn**, to be in league with s.o. 2. **se l.**, to form a league (**avec, contre**, with, against).

lilas [lila] 1. *nm Bot:* lilac 2. *a inv* lilac.

limace [limas] *nf* 1. (*a*) slug (*b*) *P:* slowcoach 2. *P:* shirt.

limaçon [limasɔ̃] *nm O:* snail; **escalier en l.**, spiral staircase.

limande [limɑ̃d] *nf Ich:* dab; **l.-sole**, lemon sole.

lime [lim] *nf* file; **l. à ongles**, nail file.

limer [lime] *vtr* to file; to file down, off.

limier [limje] *nm* bloodhound; *Fig:* sleuth.

limitation [limitasjɔ̃] *nf* limitation, restriction; **l. des naissances**, birth control; **l. des salaires**, wage restraint; **l. de vitesse**, speed limit; **il n'y a pas de l. de temps**, there's no time limit.

limite [limit] *nf* 1. boundary; limit; **l. d'âge**, age limit; **dépasser les limites**, to go too far; **dans une certaine l.**, up to a point; **à la l. j'accepterais de le voir**, if I have to, I'll (agree to) see him; **il est à la l. de ses forces**, he's completely exhausted; **sans limites**, boundless, limitless; **ma patience a des limites!** my patience is wearing thin! 2. **cas l.**, borderline case; **vitesse l.**, maximum speed; **date l.**, closing date, deadline.

limiter [limite] *vtr* (*a*) to bound, to mark the bounds of (countries, property) (*b*) to limit; to restrict; to set bounds, limits, to (s.o.'s powers, rights); **se l. à**, to limit oneself to. **limitatif, -ive** *a* limiting, restrictive, restricting.

limitrophe [limitrɔf] *a* adjacent (**de**, to); bordering (**de**, on).

limoger [limɔʒe] *vtr F:* to dismiss (s.o.).

limon¹ [limɔ̃] *nm* mud, silt.

limon² *nm Veh:* shaft.

limonade [limɔnad] *nf* (fizzy) lemonade.

limpidité [lɛ̃pidite] *nf* limpidity, clarity, clearness. **limpide** *a* limpid, clear.

lin [lɛ̃] *nm* (*a*) flax; **graine de l.**, linseed; **huile de l.**, linseed oil (*b*) (**toile de**) **l.**, linen.

linceul [lɛ̃sœl] *nm* shroud.

linéaire [lineɛr] *a* linear; **dessin l.**, geometrical drawing.

linge [lɛ̃ʒ] *nm* (*a*) linen; **gros l.**, household linen; **l. de table**, table linen; **l. (de corps)**, underwear (*b*) washing; **corde à l.**, clothesline (*c*) piece of linen; **essuyer qch avec un l.**, to wipe sth with a cloth.

lingerie [lɛ̃ʒri] *nf* 1. underwear; (*women's*) lingerie 2. linen room.

lingot [lɛ̃go] *nm* ingot; **or, argent, en lingots**, bullion.

linguiste [lɛ̃gɥist] *n* linguist. **linguistique** 1. *a* linguistic 2. *nf* linguistics.

lino [lino] *nm F:* (= linoléum) lino.

linoléum [linɔleɔm] *nm* linoleum.

linotte [linɔt] *nf Orn:* linnet; *F:* **tête de l.**, scatterbrain.

linteau, -eaux [lɛ̃to] *nm Const:* lintel.

lion, -onne [ljɔ̃, -ɔn] *n* 1. lion, lioness 2. *Astr:* **le L.**, Leo.

lionceau, -eaux [ljɔ̃so] *nm* lion cub.

lippe [lip] *nf* (thick) lower lip. **lippu** *a* thick-lipped.

liquéfaction [likefaksjɔ̃] *nf* liquefaction.

liquéfier [likefje] (*pr sub & impf* n. **liquéfiions**) *vtr* to liquefy.

liqueur [likœr] *nf* 1. liqueur; **vin de l.**, dessert wine 2. *Ch:* solution; **l. titrée**, standard solution.

liquidation [likidasjɔ̃] *nf* liquidation; clearing (of accounts); settlement; **entrer en l.**, to go into liquidation.

liquide [likid] 1. *a* liquid; **la soupe est trop l.**, the soup is too watery, too thin; **argent l.**, cash; ready money 2. *nm* (*a*) liquid, fluid (*b*) *F:* (alcoholic) drink (*c*) (ready) cash, ready money.

liquider [likide] *vtr* (*a*) to liquidate; to wind up (a business); to settle (account); *F:* to liquidate, eliminate (s.o.); **c'est liquidé**, it's (all) over (*b*) to sell off (stock).

liquidité [likidite] *nf* liquidity; **liquidités**, liquid assets.

liquoreux, -euse [likɔrø, -øz] *a* liqueur-like, syrupy (wine).

lire¹ [lir] *vtr* (*prp* **lisant**; *pp* **lu**; *pr ind* **je lis, il lit**; *impf* **je lisais;** *fu* **je lirai**) to read; **l. tout haut, à haute voix**, to read aloud; **l. une carte**, to read a map; *Mus:* **l. à première vue**, to sightread; **avoir beaucoup lu**, to be well read; **l. dans la pensée de qn**, to read s.o.'s thoughts; **il l'a lu dans un livre**, he read about it in a book; **l. dans le jeu de qn**, to know s.o.'s game; **elle a voulu me l. les lignes de la main**, she wanted to read my hand; **la peur se lisait sur son visage**, fear was written on her face; *Corr:* **dans l'attente de vous l.**, hoping to hear, looking forward to hearing, from you.

lire² *nf* lira.

lis [lis] *nm* lily.

Lisbonne [lizbɔn] *Prnf Geog:* Lisbon.

liseron [lizrɔ̃] *nm Bot:* bindweed, convolvulus.

liseur, -euse [lizœr, -øz] 1. *n* reader 2. *nf* bed jacket.

lisibilité [lizibilite] *nf* legibility. **lisible** *a* (*a*) legible (writing) (*b*) readable (book). **lisiblement** *adv* legibly.

lisière [lizjɛr] *nf* 1. selvage, selvedge (of cloth) 2. edge, border (of field, forest).

lisser [lise] *vtr* to smooth, polish (stone); to smooth down (hair); to smooth out (crease); (*of bird*) **se l. les plumes**, to preen its feathers. **lisse** *a* smooth, polished; sleek.

liste [list] *nf* list, roll; *Mil:* roster; **l. électorale**, electoral roll; **l. noire**, blacklist; **faire une l.**, to draw up, to make, a list.

lit [li] *nm* 1. bed; **l. pour deux personnes, grand l.**, double bed; **lits jumeaux**, twin beds; **l. de camp**, camp bed; **l. d'enfant**, cot, *NAm:* crib; **au l. les enfants!** time for bed, children! **aller au l.**, to go to bed; **se mettre au l.**, to get into bed; **être au l., garder le l.**, to be, to stay, in bed; to be laid up; **cloué au l.**, bedridden; **faire les lits**, to make the beds; **faire l. à part**, to sleep apart, in separate beds; **l. de mort**, deathbed; **enfant du second l.**, child of the second marriage 2. bed, layer (of soil, sand); bed (of river) 3. set (of the tide); **être dans le l. de la marée**, to be in the tideway; **dans le l. du vent**, in the wind's eye.

litanie [litani] *nf* litany; **c'est toujours la même l.**, it's the same old story.

literie [litri] *nf* bedding.

lithographie [litɔgrafi] *nf* (*a*) lithography (*b*) lithograph.

litière [litjɛr] nf (stable) litter.

litige [litiʒ] nm Jur: litigation; dispute; lawsuit; objet en l., subject of the action; Fig: bone of contention. litigieux, -euse a litigious; contentious.

litre [litr] nm (a) Meas: litre (b) litre bottle.

littéraire [literɛr] a literary.

littéral, -aux [literal, -o] a literal. littéralement adv literally.

littérateur [literatœr] nm literary man; man of letters.

littérature [literatyr] nf literature; (profession) writing.

littoral, -aux [litɔral, -o] 1. a littoral, coastal (region) 2. nm coast(line); littoral.

liturgie [lityrʒi] nf liturgy. liturgique a liturgical.

livide [livid] a (a) livid (b) pallid; ghastly (pale).

livraison [livrɛzɔ̃] nf delivery (of goods); l. franco, delivered free; payable à la l., payable on delivery; prendre l. de qch, to take delivery of sth; PN: Com: l. à domicile, we deliver (anywhere).

livre¹ [livr] nf 1. (weight) = pound; half a kilo 2. (money) l. (sterling), pound (sterling).

livre² nm book; le l., the book trade, industry; l. de classe, schoolbook; Pol: l. blanc = blue book; l. de poche, paperback; l. d'or, visitors' book; tenir les livres, to keep the accounts; tenue des livres, bookkeeping.

livrée [livre] nf livery.

livrer [livre] vtr 1. (a) to deliver, surrender; to give (s.o., sth) up; Com: to deliver (goods); l. qn à la justice, to hand s.o. over to justice; l. qn à la mort, to send s.o. to his death; livré à soi-même, left to oneself; l. un secret, to betray a secret; l. ses secrets à qn, to confide one's secrets to s.o.; l. passage à qn, to let s.o. pass (b) l. bataille, to join battle (à, with) 2. se l. (a) se l. à la justice, to surrender to justice; to give oneself up; se l. à qn, se l., to confide in s.o. (b) se l. à la boisson, to take to drink, to indulge in drink; se l. au désespoir, to give way to despair (c) to be engaged in (an occupation); to hold (an enquiry); se l. à l'étude, to devote oneself to study; se l. à un sport, to practise a sport.

livret [livre] nm 1. small book; handbook; Fin: passbook, bank book; Adm: l. de famille, family record book; l. scolaire, school report book 2. Mus: libretto.

livreur, -euse [livrœr, -øz] n delivery man, boy; delivery woman, girl.

lobe [lɔb] nm Anat: Bot: lobe.

local, -aux [lɔkal, -o] 1. a local (authority, disease) 2. nm premises, building; room; l. d'habitation, dwelling; locaux, offices. localement adv locally.

localisation [lɔkalizazjɔ̃] nf localization.

localiser [lɔkalize] vtr to localize; to confine (epidemic); to locate (noise).

localité [lɔkalite] nf locality.

locataire [lɔkatɛr] n (a) tenant (b) lodger.

location [lɔkasjɔ̃] nf (a) hire; (i) hiring (ii) letting out on hire; prendre qch en l., to rent (a house); to hire (a car; donner qch en l., to rent (out), to let (a house); to hire out (a car) (b) i) renting, tenancy (ii) letting (of house); prix de l., rent (c) Th: (bureau de) l., box office, booking office. locatif, -ive a valeur locative,

rental (value); réparations locatives, repairs incumbent upon the tenant.

lock-out [lɔkaut] nm inv Ind: lockout.

lock(-)outer [lɔkaute] vtr Ind: to lock out (the personnel).

locomotion [lɔkɔmɔsjɔ̃] nf locomotion.

locomotive [lɔkɔmɔtiv] nf Rail: locomotive, engine.

locution [lɔkysjɔ̃] nf expression, phrase; l. figée, set phrase.

logarithme [lɔgaritm] nm logarithm.

loge [lɔʒ] nf 1. (porter's, freemason's) lodge 2. Th: (a) box; être aux premières loges, to have a ringside seat (b) (artist's) dressing room.

logement [lɔʒmɑ̃] nm 1. lodging, housing; quartering, billeting (of troops); crise du l., housing shortage 2. (a) accommodation; lodgings; F: digs; l. meublé, furnished rooms, flat (b) Mil: quarters; (in private house) billet.

loger [lɔʒe] v (n. logeons) 1. vi to lodge, live; (of troops) to be quartered, billeted; Mil: l. chez l'habitant, to be billeted (in private house); l. à un hôtel, to put up, stay, at a hotel; être logé et nourri, to have board and lodging 2. vtr (a) to lodge, house (s.o.); to put (s.o.) up; to quarter, billet (troops) (b) to place, put; l. une balle dans qch, to lodge a bullet in sth 3. se l. (a) to find accommodation, a house; nous avons trouvé à nous l., we've found somewhere to live (b) (of ball) to get stuck (in a tree, on the roof); la balle s'est logée dans le mur, the bullet lodged itself in the wall. logeable a (of house) habitable.

logeur, -euse [lɔʒœr, -øz] n landlord, landlady.

loggia [lɔdʒja] nf loggia.

logiciel [lɔʒisjɛl] nm Cmptr: software.

logique [lɔʒik] 1. a logical 2. nf logic; vous manquez de l., you're not being very logical. logiquement adv logically.

logis [lɔʒi] nm Lit: home, house, dwelling; corps de l., main building.

logistique [lɔʒistik] 1. a logistic 2. nf logistics.

loi [lwa] nf (a) law; homme de l., lawyer; faire la l. à qn, to lay down the law to s.o.; se faire une l. de faire qch, to make a rule of doing sth; mettre (qn) hors la l., to outlaw (s.o.) (b) act (of Parliament); law, statute; projet de l., bill (c) law (of nature); les lois de la pesanteur, the laws of gravity.

loin [lwɛ̃] adv 1. (a) (of place) far; plus l., farther (on); further; moins l., less far; est-ce l. d'ici? is it far from here? la poste est l., the post office is a long way off; il ira l., he'll go far; l. derrière lui, far behind him; il y a l. d'ici à Paris, it's a long way to Paris; ne pas être l. d'une découverte, to be on the brink of a discovery; je ne suis pas fâché, l. de là! I'm not angry, far from it! (b) de l., (i) by far (ii) from afar; il est de l. plus intelligent que moi, he is far more intelligent than I am (c) je l'ai reconnu de l., I recognized him from a distance; nm au l., in the distance; apercevoir qn au l., to see s.o. a long way away 2. (of time) (a) la famille remonte l., the family goes back a long way; (in text) voir plus l., see later, see following pages; il n'est pas l. de midi, it's getting on for twelve o'clock; ce jour est encore l., that day is still far off (b) voir l., (i) to be shrewd (ii) to be far-sighted (c) de l. en l., at long intervals, now and then.

lointain [lwɛ̃tɛ̃] 1. a distant, remote (country, period);

faraway (look) **2.** *nm* **dans le l.,** in the distance, in the background.

loir [lwar] *nm Z:* dormouse.

loisible [lwazibl] *a* permissible; **il lui est l. de refuser,** it is open to him to refuse.

loisir [lwazir] *nm* leisure; **avoir des loisirs,** to have some spare time; **laisser à qn le l. de,** to give s.o. the opportunity to; **à l.,** at leisure.

Londres [lɔ̃dr] *Prn usu f Geog:* London. **londonien, -ienne 1.** *a* of London **2.** *n* Londoner.

long, longue [lɔ̃, lɔ̃g] **1.** *a* long (*a*) (*of space*) **corde longue de cinq mètres,** rope five metres long; **le chemin le plus l.,** the longest way (round) (*b*) time-consuming; **l. discours,** lengthy speech; **je trouve le temps l.,** time seems to drag; **je ne serai pas l.,** I won't be long; **l. soupir,** long-drawn sigh; **c'est un travail l. à faire,** it's slow work; **elle fut longue à s'en remettre,** she was a long time getting over it; **projet à longue échéance,** long-term project; **disque (de) longue durée,** long-playing record; **à la longue,** in the long run, in the end **2.** *nm* (*a*) (*of space*) length; **table qui a 2 mètres de l.,** table 2 metres in length, 2 metres long; **en l.,** lengthwise; **de l. en large,** up and down, to and fro; **expliquer qch en l. et en large,** to explain sth in great detail; **étendu de tout son l.,** stretched out at full length; **tout le l. du rivage,** all along the shore; **tomber de tout son l.,** to fall flat on one's face; **le l. de,** along, alongside; **se faufiler le l. du mur,** to creep along the wall (*b*) (*of time*) **tout le l. du jour,** all day long **3.** *adv* (*a*) (*of amount*) **inutile d'en dire plus l.,** I need say no more; **regard qui en dit l.,** meaningful, eloquent, look; **cette action en dit l. sur,** this action speaks volumes for; **en savoir l.,** to know a lot (*b*) **s'habiller l.,** to wear long clothes. **longuement** *adv* for a long time; at (great) length. **longuet, -ette** *a F:* rather long.

long-courrier [lɔ̃kurje] *a & nm Nau: Av:* ocean-going (ship); ocean liner; *Av:* long-haul, long-range (aircraft); *pl* long-courriers.

longe [lɔ̃ʒ] *nf* leading rein, halter, tether.

longer [lɔ̃ʒe] *vtr* (n. longeons) to pass, go, along(side) (road); (*of path*) to border; **la route longe un bois,** the road skirts a wood; **l. la côte,** to hug the coast.

longévité [lɔ̃ʒevite] *nf* longevity, long life.

longitude [lɔ̃ʒityd] *nf* longitude; **par 10° de l. ouest,** at 10° longitude west. **longitudinal, -aux** *a* longitudinal.

longtemps [lɔ̃tɑ̃] **1.** *adv* long; a long time; **attendre l.,** to wait for a long time; **cela ne pouvait durer l.,** it couldn't last long **2.** *nm* **il y a l.,** long ago; **il y a l. que je ne l'ai vu,** it's a long time since I last saw him; **depuis l.,** for a long time; **l. avant, après, long before, after; pendant l.,** for a long time; **avant l.,** before long; **je n'en ai pas pour l.,** it won't take me long; *F:* **il n'en a plus pour l.,** he hasn't much longer to live.

longueur [lɔ̃gœr] *nf* length; **jardin qui a cent mètres de l.,** garden a hundred metres long; **couper qch en l., dans le sens de la l.,** to cut sth lengthwise; (*of speech*) **traîner en l.,** to drag (on); **à l. de journée,** throughout the day; all day; **à l. de journées,** for days on end; **roman plein de longueurs,** novel full of tedious passages; *Sp:* **gagner d'une l.,** to win by a length.

longue-vue [lɔ̃gvy] *nf* telescope; *pl* longues-vues.

lopin [lɔpɛ̃] *nm* **l. de terre,** patch, plot of ground.

loquace [lɔkas] *a* talkative; garrulous.

loque [lɔk] *nf* rag; **être en loques,** to be in rags, in tatters; **tomber en loques,** to fall to pieces; **une l. humaine,** a human wreck.

loquet [lɔke] *nm* latch (of door).

lorgner [lɔrɲe] *vtr* to eye, peer at (sth); to have one's eye on (money, inheritance).

lorgnette [lɔrɲɛt] *nf* (pair of) opera glasses; spyglass.

lorgnon [lɔrɲɔ̃] *nm* pince-nez.

lors [lɔr] *adv* (*a*) **depuis l.,** ever since then (*b*) **l. ... que,** when; **l. de sa naissance,** when he was born.

lorsque [lɔrsk(ə)] *conj* (becomes **lorsqu'** *before a vowel*) (at the moment, at the time) when; **lorsqu'il sera parti,** when he's gone.

losange [lɔzɑ̃ʒ] *nm* (*a*) **en l.,** diamond-shaped (*b*) *Mth:* rhomb(us).

lot [lo] *nm* (*a*) share; portion; **l. (de terre),** plot (of land) (*b*) prize (at a lottery); **gros l.,** first prize; jackpot (*c*) batch (of goods); set (of towels); (*at auction*) lot.

loterie [lɔtri] *nf* (*a*) lottery (*b*) raffle, draw.

lotion [losjɔ̃] *nf* lotion.

lotir [lɔtir] *vtr* **1.** to divide (sth) into lots, plots, batches; to parcel out (estate, into building lots) **2. l. qn de qch,** to allot sth to s.o.; **être bien loti, mal loti,** to be well off, badly off.

lotissement [lɔtismɑ̃] *nm* **1.** (*a*) division (of goods) into lots; parcelling out (of land) (*b*) sale (by lots) **2.** (*a*) (building) plot (*b*) housing development.

loto [lɔto] *nm Games:* (*a*) lotto (*b*) = bingo (*c*) lotto set.

lotus [lɔtys] *nm Bot:* lotus.

louable [lwabl] *a* laudable, praiseworthy.

louage [lwaʒ] *nm* **contrat de l.,** rental agreement, contract; **voiture de l.,** rented, hire, car.

louange [lwɑ̃ʒ] *nf* praise; **à la l. de qn,** in s.o.'s praise.

loubar(d) [lubar] *nm F:* yob; lout.

louche¹ [luʃ] *a* shady, suspicious, fishy; **c'est l.,** it's odd, strange; *nm* **il y a du l.,** there's something peculiar going on.

louche² *nf* (soup) ladle.

loucher [luʃe] *vi* to squint; **l. de l'œil gauche,** to have a squint in the left eye.

louer¹ [lwe] *vtr* **1.** to hire, rent, let (out) (à, to); **maison à l.,** house to let **2.** to rent (house) (à, from); to reserve, book (seat).

louer² *vtr* **1.** to praise, commend; **l. qn de, pour, qch,** to praise s.o. for sth; **Dieu soit loué!** thank God! **2. se l. de qch,** to be pleased with sth; **se l. d'avoir fait qch,** to congratulate oneself on having done sth.

loueur, -euse [lwœr, -øz] *n* hirer.

loufoque [lufɔk] *F:* (*a*) *a* crazy, barmy (*b*) *n* crackpot, *NAm:* screwball.

loup [lu] *nm* (*a*) wolf; **marcher à pas de l.,** to walk stealthily; **avoir une faim de l.,** to be ravenously hungry; **il fait un froid de l.,** it's bitterly cold; *F:* (*term of affection*) **mon petit l.,** my darling, my pet; *Ich:* **l. (de mer),** sea perch; *F:* **l. de mer,** (i) (*sailor*) old salt (ii) striped tee-shirt (*b*) black velvet mask (worn at masked ball).

loupe [lup] *nf* magnifying glass.

louper [lupe] *v F:* **1.** *vi* **ça n'a pas loupé,** that's what happened, sure enough **2.** *vtr* to botch, bungle; to make a mess of (sth); to miss (train); to fail (exam); **la soirée est loupée,** the party's a flop.

loup-garou [lugaru] *nm* (a) werewolf (b) bogeyman; *pl* loups-garous.

lourdeur [lurdœr] *nf* heaviness; **l. d'esprit**, slow-wittedness; **j'ai des lourdeurs d'estomac**, I feel bloated.

lourd, lourde *a* (a) heavy; ungainly; **yeux lourds de fatigue**, eyes heavy with tiredness; **j'ai la tête lourde**, I feel headachy; **avoir l'estomac l.**, to feel bloated; **avoir la main lourde**, to be heavy-handed; *adv* **peser l.**, to weigh, to be, heavy (b) clumsy; **avoir l'esprit l.**, to be slow-witted; **lourde erreur**, serious mistake; **incident l. de conséquences**, incident fraught with consequences; **silence l. de menaces**, ominous silence (c) close, sultry (weather) (d) *F:* **il n'en reste pas l.**, there isn't much left; **il n'en fait pas l.**, he doesn't exactly overwork. **lourdaud, -aude 1.** *a* clumsy, oafish **2.** *n* oaf. **lourdement** *adv* heavily; **se tromper l.**, to make a serious mistake.

loustic [lustik] *nm F:* joker; **c'est un drôle de l.**, he's a strange bloke.

loutre [lutr] *nf* (a) *Z:* otter (b) otterskin.

louve [luv] *nf Z:* she-wolf.

louveteau, -eaux [luvto] *nm Z:* wolf-cub; *Scout:* cub (scout).

louvoyer [luvwaje] *vi* (**je louvoie**) (a) *Nau:* to tack (b) to evade; to dodge the issue.

loyauté [lwajote] *nf* (a) honesty, fairness; **manque de l.**, dishonesty, unfairness (b) loyalty, fidelity. **loyal, -aux** *a* **1.** honest, fair; **jeu l.**, fair play **2.** loyal, faithful; true (friend). **loyalement** *adv* (a) honestly, fairly (b) loyally, faithfully.

loyer [lwaje] *nm* rent.

LSD *abbr acide lysergique synthétique diéthylamide.*

lubie [lybi] *nf* whim, fad, craze; **encore une de ses lubies!** another of his crazy ideas!

lubrification [lybrifikasjɔ̃] *nf* lubrication.

lubrifier [lybrifje] *vtr* to lubricate; to grease, oil. **lubrifiant** *a & nm* lubricant.

lubrique [lybrik] *a* lewd.

lucarne [lykarn] *nf* (a) dormer window, attic window (b) skylight.

lucidité [lysidite] *nf* lucidity, clearness; clear-headedness; consciousness. **lucide** *a* lucid, clear (mind); clear-headed (person); conscious. **lucidement** *adv* lucidly, clearly.

lucratif, -ive [lykratif, -iv] *a* lucrative, profitable; **à but l.**, profit-making; **à but non l.**, non-profit-making. **lucrativement** *adv* lucratively, profitably.

lueur [lyœr] *nf* gleam, glimmer; **à la l. d'une bougie**, by candlelight; **les premières lueurs de l'aube**, the first light of dawn.

luge [ly3] *nf* toboggan, sledge; **faire de la l.**, to sledge.

lugubre [lygybr] *a* lugubrious, dismal, gloomy.

lui¹, *pl* **leur** [lɥi, lœr] *pers pron m & f* (to) him, her, it, them (a) (*unstressed*) **je le lui donne**, I give it (to) him, (to) her; **donnez-lui-en**, give him some; **cette maison leur appartient**, this house belongs to them; **je lui ai serré la main**, I shook his, her, hand; **il leur jeta une pierre**, he threw a stone at them (b) (*stressed in imp*) **montrez-le-leur**, show it to them.

lui², *pl* **eux** [lɥi, ø] *stressed pers pron m* (a) (*subject*) he, it, they; **c'est lui**, it's him; **ce sont eux**, *F:* **c'est eux**, it's them; **il a raison, lui**, he's the one who's right; **qu'est-ce qu'il a dit?—lui? rien**, what did he say?—him? nothing; **c'est lui-même qui me l'a dit**, he told me so himself; **eux deux**, the two of them (b) (*object*) him, it, them; **lui, je le connais**, I know *him*; **ce livre est à eux**, this book is theirs; **voilà une photo de lui**, here's a photograph of him; **j'ai confiance en lui**, I trust him; **ne fais pas comme lui**, don't do what he did; **un ami à lui**, a friend of his (c) (*refl*) him(self), it(self), them(selves); **ils ne pensent qu'à eux**, they think only of themselves.

luire [lɥir] *vi* (*prp* **luisant**; *pp* **lui** (*no f*); *pr ind* **il luit**; *fu* **il luira**) to shine; gleam, glow, glisten; (*of stars*) to glimmer. **luisant, -ante** *a* shining, bright; shiny, glossy; gleaming (eyes); glowing (embers) **2.** *nm* gloss, sheen.

lumbago [lɔ̃bago] *nm Med:* lumbago.

lumière [lymjɛr] *nf* light; **l. (du jour)**, **l. du soleil**, **l. électrique**, daylight, sunlight, electric light; **donner de la l.**, to turn on the light, to switch the light on; **mettre qch en l.**, to bring sth to light; **faire (toute) la l. sur qch**, to clarify sth; *F:* **ce n'est pas une lumière**, he's not very bright; **avoir des lumières sur qch**, to have some knowledge about sth.

luminaire [lyminɛr] *nm* (a) light; candle (in church); lamp (b) *coll* lights, lighting.

luminosité [lyminozite] *nf* luminosity, brightness. **lumineux, -euse** *a* luminous; **rayon l.**, ray of light; **idée lumineuse**, brilliant idea.

lunch [lœ̃ʃ] *nm* buffet lunch; *pl* lunch(e)s.

lundi [lœ̃di] *nm* Monday.

lune [lyn] *nf* moon; **pleine l.**, **nouvelle l.**, full moon, new moon; **l. de miel**, honeymoon; **demander la l.**, to ask for the moon; **être dans la l.**, to be in the clouds; **en forme de l.**, crescent-shaped; **pierre de l.**, moonstone. **lunaire** *a* lunar. **lunatique** *a* quirky, temperamental. **luné** *a* **être bien, mal, l.**, to be in a good, bad, mood.

lunette [lynɛt] *nf* **1. l. d'approche**, telescope **2.** *pl* (**paire de) lunettes**, (pair of) glasses, spectacles; **lunettes de soleil**, sunglasses; **lunettes de protection**, goggles **3.** *Aut:* **l. arrière**, rear window.

luron [lyrɔ̃] *nm F:* lad; **un gai l.**, a bit of a lad.

lustre [lystr] *nm* **1.** lustre, polish, gloss **2.** chandelier. **lustrer** [lystre] *vtr* to glaze, polish (up), lustre. **lustré** *a* glossy; shiny (with wear).

luth [lyt] *nm Mus:* lute.

lutin [lytɛ̃] *nm* imp, elf.

lutrin [lytrɛ̃] *nm Ecc:* lectern.

lutte [lyt] *nf* **1.** wrestling; **l. libre**, all-in wrestling **2.** (a) fight; struggle, tussle; conflict; **l. à mort**, life and death struggle; **l. contre l'alcoolisme**, campaign against alcoholism; **l. d'intérêts**, clash of interests (b) strife; **la l. des classes**, the class struggle.

lutter [lyte] *vi* **1.** to wrestle **2.** to struggle, fight, compete; **l. contre la maladie**, to fight against, to combat, disease; **l. contre le vent**, to battle with the wind; **l. contre un incendie**, to fight a fire; **l. de vitesse avec qn**, to race s.o.

lutteur, -euse [lytœr, -øz] *n* (a) wrestler (b) fighter.

luxation [lyksasjɔ̃] *nf Med:* dislocation (of joint).

luxe [lyks] *nm* (a) luxury; luxuriousness (of house); **se payer le l. d'un cigare**, to indulge in a cigar; **articles de l.**, luxury goods; **édition de l.**, de luxe edition; **gros l.**, ostentation (b) abundance (of food); wealth (of details). **luxueux, -euse** *a* luxurious. **luxueusement** *adv* luxuriously.

Luxembourg [lyksâbur] *Prnm Geog:* Luxemburg. **luxembourgeois, -oise** *a & n* (native, inhabitant) of Luxemburg.

luxer [lykse] *vtr* to dislocate (joint); **se l. l'épaule,** to dislocate one's shoulder.

luxure [lyksyr] *nf* lust.

luxuriance [lyksyriãs] *nf* luxuriance. **luxuriant** *a* luxuriant.

luzerne [lyzɛrn] *nf* lucern(e), alfalfa.

lycée [lise] *nm* = grammar school, high school, secondary school; **l. technique,** technical high school.

lycéen, -enne [liseɛ̃, -ɛn] *n* grammar school, high school, secondary school, pupil.

lymphe [lɛ̃f] *nf* lymph. **lymphatique** *a* lymphatic; lethargic, sluggish.

lyncher [lɛ̃ʃe] *vtr* to lynch.

lynx [lɛ̃ks] *nm* lynx.

lyophilisé [ljɔfilize] *a* freeze-dried (coffee).

lyre [lir] *nf Mus:* lyre.

lyrisme [lirism] *nm* lyricism. **lyrique** *a* lyric(al) (poem); **poète l.,** lyric poet; **drame l.,** opera.

lysergique [lisɛrʒik] *a* lysergic.

M

M, m [ɛm] *nm or f* (the letter) M, m.

M. *abbr* Monsieur.

m' *see* **me.**

ma [ma] *poss af see* **mon.**

macabre [makabr̩] *a* macabre; gruesome (discovery); grim (humour).

macadam [makadam] *nm* 1. macadam; **m. goudronné,** tarmac(adam) 2. road.

macadamiser [makadamize] *vtr* to macadamize, to tarmac.

macaron [makarɔ̃] *nm* 1. *Cu:* macaroon 2. (*a*) (round) motif; badge (*b*) *F:* rosette (of decoration).

macaroni [makarɔni] *nm Cu:* macaroni.

macchabée [makabe] *nm P:* corpse, stiff.

macédoine [masedwan] *nf* (*a*) **m. de fruits,** fruit salad; **m. de légumes,** mixed vegetables (*b*) medley; hotchpotch.

macération [maserasjɔ̃] *nf* maceration.

macérer [masere] *vtr* (**je macère; je macérerai**) to macerate.

Mach [mak] *nm Av:* (**nombre de) M.,** Mach number.

mâche [maʃ] *nf* corn salad, lamb's lettuce.

mâchefer [maʃfɛr] *nm* clinker, slag.

mâcher [maʃe] *vtr* to chew, masticate; **m. le mors,** *F:* (*of pers*) **m. son frein,** to champ at the bit; **je ne vais pas lui m. les mots,** I won't mince words with him; **m. le travail à qn,** to do half the work for s.o.

machiavélique [makjavelik] *a* Machiavellian.

machin [maʃɛ̃] *n F:* 1. **monsieur M.,** Mr What's his name 2. *nm* thing(ummy); whatsit; **passe-moi le m.,** pass me the what's its name; **qu'est-ce que c'est que ce m.-là?** what's that gadget?

machination [maʃinasjɔ̃] *nf* plot.

machine [maʃin] *nf* 1. (*a*) machine; **m. à coudre,** sewing machine; **m. à laver,** washing machine; **m. à laver la vaisselle,** dishwasher; **m. à écrire,** typewriter; **écrit à la m.,** typed, typewritten; **m. à calculer,** calculating machine, adding machine; **m. à sous,** (i) slot machine (ii) fruit machine; *Ind:* **les machines,** the machinery; **les grosses machines,** the heavy plant; **machines agricoles,** agricultural machinery; **fait à la m.,** machine-made; **la m. administrative,** the bureaucratic machinery (*b*) *F:* = (*vehicle, bicycle, motorcycle*) machine; **m. volante,** flying machine 2. (*a*) engine; **m. à vapeur,** steam engine; **m. à pétrole, à gaz,** oil, gas, engine (*b*) *Rail:* locomotive. **machinal, -aux** *a* mechanical, unconscious (action). **machinalement** *adv* mechanically.

machine-outil [maʃinuti] *nf* machine-tool; *pl* **machines-outils.**

machiner [maʃine] *vtr* to scheme, plot; **affaire machinée d'avance,** put-up job.

machinisme [maʃinism] *nm* mechanization.

machiniste [maʃinist] *nm* 1. driver (of bus) 2. *Th:* stagehand.

mâchoire [maʃwar] *nf* 1. jaw 2. **mâchoires d'un étau,** jaws of a vice.

mâchonner [maʃɔne], *F:* **mâchouiller** [maʃuje] *vtr* to chew (away) (at sth).

maçon [masɔ̃] *nm* (*a*) (stone)mason; bricklayer (*b*) (free)mason.

maçonnerie [masɔnri] *nf* 1. masonry; stonework; brickwork 2. (free)masonry.

macrobiotique [makrɔbjɔtik] *a* macrobiotic.

maculer [makyle] *vtr* to stain, spot.

Madame, *pl* **Mesdames** [mådam, medam] *nf* 1. (*à*) **M., Mme, Dupont, Mrs Dupont; Mesdames, Mmes, Dupont,** the Mrs Dupont; **M. la marquise de X,** the Marchioness of X; **m. la directrice,** the manageress, the headmistress; **comment va m. votre mère?** how is your mother? (*b*) (*used alone*) (*pl* **ces dames**) **voici le chapeau de m.,** here is your hat, madam; **M. se plaint que,** this lady is complaining that 2. (*a*) (*in address*) Madam; **entrez, mesdames,** please come in, ladies (*b*) *Corr:* (*always written in full*) **Madame,** (Dear) Madam; **Chère Madame,** Dear Mrs X.

Mademoiselle, *pl* **Mesdemoiselles** [madmwazɛl, medmwazɛl] *nf* 1. Miss; **Mademoiselle, Mlle, Smith,** Miss Smith; **Mesdemoiselles Smith,** the Misses Smith; **voici le chapeau de m.,** here's Miss X's hat; **comment va m. votre cousine?** how is your cousin? **voici m. la directrice,** here's the manageress, the headmistress 2. (*a*) (*in address*) **merci, m.,** thank you, Miss (X) (*b*) (*pl* **ces demoiselles**) **m. est servie,** dinner is served, madam; **que prendront ces demoiselles?** what can I offer you, ladies? (*c*) *Corr:* (*always written in full*) **Mademoiselle,** (Dear) Madam; **Chère Mademoiselle,** Dear Miss X.

Madère [madɛr] 1. *Prnf Geog:* Madeira 2. *nm* Madeira (wine).

madone [madɔn] *nf* madonna.

madrier [madrije] *nm* (piece of) timber; beam; thick board, plank.

magasin [magazɛ̃] *nm* 1. (*a*) shop, store; **grand m.,** department store; **m. à libre service,** self-service store; **m. à succursales multiples,** chain store; **employé(e) de m.,** shop assistant; **courir, faire, les magasins,** to go shopping (*b*) store, warehouse 2. magazine (of rifle, projector).

magasinage [magazinaʒ] *nm* warehousing, storing.

magasinier [magazinje] *nm* warehouseman, storekeeper.

magazine [magazin] *nm* (illustrated) magazine.

mage [maʒ] *nm* magus.

magicien, -ienne [maʒisjɛ̃, -jɛn] *n* magician, wizard; *f* sorceress.

magie [maʒi] *nf* magic. **magique** *a* magical. **magiquement** *adv* magically.

magistrat [maʒistra] *nm* magistrate; judge; **il est m.,** he sits on the Bench. **magistral, -aux** magisterial, authoritative; masterful (manner); masterly (work). **magistralement** *adv* authoritatively.

magistrature [maʒistratyr] *nf* magistrature; **la m. assise,** the judges, the Bench.

magnanimité [maɲanimite] *nf* magnanimity. **magnanime** *a* magnanimous.

magnat [magna] *nm* magnate, tycoon.

magner (se) [səmaɲe] *vpr P:* to get a move on.

magnésie [maɲezi] *nf Ch: Pharm:* 1. magnesia 2. **sulfate de m.**, Epsom salts.

magnésium [maɲezjɔm] *nm Ch:* magnesium.

magnétisation [maɲetizasjɔ̃] *nf* 1. magnetisation 2. mesmerizing, hypnotizing.

magnétiser [maɲetize] *vtr* 1. to magnetize 2. to mesmerize, to hypnotize. **magnétique** *a* magnetic.

magnétiseur, -euse [maɲetizœr, -øz] *n* mesmerizer, hypnotizer.

magnétisme [maɲetism] *nm* 1. magnetism 2. mesmerism, hypnotism.

magnéto [maɲeto] *nf ICE:* magneto.

magnétophone [maɲetofɔn] *nm* tape recorder.

magnétoscope [maɲetɔskɔp] *nm* video tape recorder.

magnificence [maɲifisɑ̃s] *nf* magnificence. **magnifique** *a* magnificent; grand; superb; glorious, wonderful. **magnifiquement** *adv* magnificently.

magot¹ [mago] *nm F:* hoard (of money); pile.

magot² *nm* 1. *Z:* Barbary ape 2. Chinese grotesque porcelain figure.

mai [mɛ] *nm* 1. May; **au mois de m., en m.,** in (the month of) May; **le premier m.,** (on) the first of May, (on) May day; **le sept m.,** (on) the seventh of May 2. maypole.

MAIF [maif] *abbr Mutuelle assurance des instituteurs de France.*

maigreur [mɛgrœr] *nf* 1. thinness, leanness 2. poorness, meagreness. **maigre** *1. a (a)* thin, skinny, lean; **m. comme un clou,** as thin as a rake; **homme grand et m.,** *n* **un grand m.,** a tall, thin man *(b)* lean (meat); scanty (vegetation); small (crop); poor (land); **m. repas,** frugal meal; **jour m.,** day of abstinence 2. *nm* lean (part of meat). **maigrement** *adv* meagrely; poorly.

maigrir [mɛgrir] 1. *vi* to get thin(ner); to lose weight; **elle essaie de m.,** she's slimming, dieting; **j'ai maigri de dix kilos,** I have lost ten kilos 2. *vtr (a) (of illness)* to make (s.o.) thin(ner) *(b) (of dress)* to make (s.o.) look thin(ner).

mail [maj] *nm* 1. avenue, promenade 2. sledgehammer.

maille [mɑj] *nf* 1. *(a)* stitch (in knitting); **m. à l'endroit,** plain (stitch); knit; **m. à l'envers,** purl (stitch) *(b)* link (of chain) 2. mesh (of net).

maillet [majɛ] *nm (a) Tls:* mallet; maul; beetle *(b)* croquet mallet.

mailloche [majɔʃ] *nf Tls:* beetle.

maillon [majɔ̃] *nm* link (of a chain).

maillot [majo] *nm Cl: (a)* **m. de corps,** vest *(b)* **m. de bain,** swimming costume, swimsuit *(c) Sp:* jersey; singlet *(d) Th: etc:* tights; leotard.

main [mɛ̃] *nf* 1. *(a)* hand; **serrer la m. à (qn),** to shake hands with (s.o.); **se donner la m.,** to hold hands; **la m. dans la m.,** hand in hand; **porter la m. sur qn,** to strike s.o.; **donner un coup de m. à (qn),** to lend (s.o.) a (helping) hand; **en venir aux mains,** to come to blows; **je n'en mettrais pas la m. au feu,** I shouldn't like to swear to it; **ne pas y aller de m. morte,** (i) to put one's back into it (ii) to exaggerate; **faire m. basse sur qch,** to help oneself to sth, to pinch sth; **haut les mains!** hands

up! **à bas les mains!** hands off! **sous la m.,** within reach; to hand; *F:* **passer la m. dans le dos à qn,** to flatter s.o.; **avoir le cœur sur la m.,** to be very generous, open-handed *(b)* **prendre un plateau, son courage, à deux mains,** to take a tray, one's courage, in both hands; **attaque à m. armée,** armed attack; **donner de l'argent à pleine(s) main(s),** to dish out money by the handful; **tenir le succès entre ses mains,** to have success within one's grasp; **passer aux mains de, tomber dans les mains de, qn,** to fall into s.o.'s hands; **être en bonne mains,** to be in good hands; **prendre une affaire en m.,** to take a matter in hand; **mettre la m. sur qch.,** to lay hands on sth; **article de seconde m.,** secondhand article; **renseignement de première m.,** firsthand information *(c)* **à la m.,** by hand; **écrit à la m.,** handwritten; **mettre la dernière m. à qch,** to put the finishing touches to sth; **se faire la m.,** to get one's hand in; **il a perdu la m.,** he's out of practice; **avoir le coup de m.,** to have the knack; **fait (à la) m.,** handmade *(d)* **avoir sa voiture bien en m.,** to have the feel of one's car; **tenez-vous en m.,** control yourself; **avoir la haute m. dans une affaire,** to be in control of a matter; **gagner haut la m.,** to win hands down *(e) adv phr* **de longue main,** for a long time (past); (friend) of long standing 2. *(a)* hand(writing) *(b)* **m. courante,** handrail 3. *Cards:* hand 4. **m. de papier,** = approx quire of paper.

main-d'œuvre [mɛ̃dœvr] *nf* 1. labour; manpower; **embaucher de la m.-d'œ.,** to take on hands 2. cost of labour; *pl* **mains-d'œuvre.**

mainmise [mɛ̃miz] *nf* seizure (sur, of).

maint [mɛ̃] *a Lit:* many; **m. auteur,** many an author; **maintes et maintes fois,** time and (time) again.

maintenant [mɛ̃tnɑ̃] *adv* now; **vous devriez être prêt m.,** you ought to be ready by now; **à vous m.,** your turn (next).

maintenir [mɛ̃tnir] *vtr (conj like* TENIR*)* 1. *(a)* to maintain; to keep, hold, (sth) in position; **m. la foule,** to hold back the crowd *(b)* to uphold, keep (the law); to preserve (peace); **m. sa position,** to hold one's own 2. **se m.** *(a)* to last *(b)* to hold on; **les prix se maintiennent,** prices remain steady *(c)* to be maintained, to continue; **le temps se maintient,** the weather's holding.

maintien [mɛ̃tjɛ̃] *nm* 1. maintenance, upholding, keeping (of law, order) 2. bearing, carriage; **leçons de m.,** lessons in deportment.

maire [mɛr] *nm* mayor.

mairie [mɛri] *nf (a)* town hall; municipal buildings *(b)* town council.

mais [mɛ] 1. *adv (emphatic)* **m. oui!** why, certainly! *NAm:* sure! **m. non!** not at all! **m. qu'avez-vous donc?** whatever's the matter? **m. c'est vrai!** it really is true! **m. enfin!** well really! 2. *conj* but 3. *nm* **il y a un m.,** there's one snag; **il n'y a pas de m.,** there's no buts about it.

maïs [mais] *nm* maize, *NAm:* corn; **farine de m.,** cornflour.

maison [mɛzɔ̃] *nf* 1. *(a)* house; **m. de ville, de campagne,** town, country, house; **m. de rapport,** (block of) flats, apartment house *(b)* home; **à la m.,** at home; **dans la m.,** in the house, indoors; **dépenses de la m.,** household expenses 2. *(a)* **m. d'arrêt,** prison; **m. de santé,** (i) nursing home (ii) mental home; **m. de repos,** rest home, convalescent home; **m. de retraite,** old people's home; **m. des jeunes,** youth centre; **m.**

religieuse, convent (b) firm; **m. de commerce,** business company; **m. mère,** head office 3. (a) family; **être de la m.,** to be one of the family; **le fils de la m.,** the son of the house (b) **la m. des Bourbons,** the House of Bourbon (c) household, staff; **gens de m.,** domestic staff 4. (a) (on menu) **pâté m.,** home-made pâté (b) F: first-rate, excellent.

maisonnée [mɛzɔne] nf household, family.

maisonnette [mɛzɔnɛt] nf small house.

maître, -esse [mɛtr̩, mɛtrɛs] n 1. (a) master, f mistress; **maîtresse de maison,** mistress of the house; hostess; **parler en m.,** to speak authoritatively; **être m. de la situation,** to be master of the situation; **être m., maîtresse, de soi(-même),** to be self-possessed; **être m. de sa voiture,** to be in control of one's car; **se rendre m., maîtresse, de qch,** (i) to take possession of sth (ii) to gain control of sth (b) (school)teacher; **m., maîtresse, d'école,** primary school teacher; **m. assistant=**assistant lecturer (at university); **m. de chapelle,** choirmaster; **m. nageur,** swimming instructor (c) **m. charpentier,** master carpenter; **c'est fait de main de m.,** it is a masterpiece; **coup de m.,** master stroke; **m. d'œuvre,** foreman; **m. clerc,** clerk (in barrister's chambers); Nau: **m. d'équipage,** boatswain; **m. d'hôtel,** (i) butler (ii) head waiter (iii) Nau: chief steward (d) (title given to member of legal profession) Maître 2. attrib (a) **maîtresse femme,** capable woman; **m. filou,** arrant scoundrel (b) chief, principal; **maîtresse poutre,** main girder 3. nf **maîtresse,** mistress.

maîtrise [mɛtriz] nf 1. (a) Sch: = master's degree (b) choir school (attached to a cathedral) 2. mastery; **m. de soi,** self-control.

maîtriser [mɛtrize] vtr 1. to master; to subdue; to control; to overcome (fears); to overpower (s.o.) 2. **se m.,** to control oneself; **ne pas savoir se m.,** to have no self-control. **maîtrisable** a controllable.

majesté [maʒɛste] nf 1. majesty; **sa M.,** His, Her, Majesty 2. (a) stateliness (b) grandeur. **majestueux, -euse** a majestic; imposing. **majestueusement** adv majestically.

majeur [maʒœr] 1. a (a) major, greater; **en majeure partie,** for the most part; Geog: **le lac M.,** Lake Maggiore (b) **être absent pour raison majeure,** to be unavoidably absent; **affaire majeure,** matter of great importance; **cas de force majeure,** case of absolute necessity (c) **devenir m.,** to come of age (d) Mus: major 2. (a) n (pers) major (b) nm middle finger.

major [maʒɔr] nm 1. Mil: (**médecin) m.,** medical officer 2. Sch: candidate who came first in the entrance exam for admission to a Grande École.

majoration [maʒɔrasjɔ̃] nf (a) surcharge (b) increase (in price).

majorer [maʒɔre] vtr 1. to make an additional charge on (bill); **m. une facture de 10%,** to put (a) 10% (surcharge) on an invoice 2. to raise, increase, the price of (sth).

majorette [maʒɔrɛt] nf (drum-)majorette.

majorité [maʒɔrite] nf 1. majority; **élu à la m. de dix,** elected by a majority of ten; **être en m., avoir la m.,** to be in a, in the, majority; **dans la m. des cas,** in most cases 2. Jur: majority, coming of age; **atteindre sa m.,** to come of age. **majoritaire** a **vote m.,** majority vote.

Majorque [maʒɔrk] Prnf Geog: Majorca.

majuscule[maʒyskyl] 1. a capital (letter) 2. nf capital letter; Typ: upper case letter.

mal[1], maux [mal, mo] nm 1. (a) evil; hurt, harm; **faire du m.,** to do harm; **il fait plus de bruit que de m.,** his bark is worse than his bite; **s'en tirer sans aucun m.,** to escape uninjured, unhurt; **je ne lui veux pas de m.,** I mean him no harm; **il n'y a pas grand m.!** there's no great harm done! (b) **dire du m. de qn,** to speak ill of s.o.; **prendre qch en m.,** to take sth amiss; **tourner qch en m.,** to put the worst interpretation on sth (c) wrong(doing); **le bien et le m.,** right and wrong, good and evil; **il ne pense pas à m.,** he doesn't mean any harm 2. (a) disorder; disease; ailment; pain; **prendre (du) m.,** to be taken ill; **m. de tête,** headache; **m. de dents,** toothache; **m. de gorge,** sore throat; **m. de cœur,** sickness, nausea; **m. de mer,** seasickness; **m. du siècle,** worldweariness; **où avez-vous m.?** where is the pain? where does it hurt? **vous me faites (du) m.,** you're hurting me; **mon genou me fait m.,** my knee's hurting; **avoir le m. du pays,** to be homesick (b) **non sans m.,** not without difficulty; **se donner du m. pour faire qch,** to take pains to do sth; **avoir du m. à faire qch,** to have difficulty in doing sth.

mal[2] adv 1. (a) badly, ill; **m. à l'aise,** ill at ease; **m. agir,** to do wrong; **faire qch tant bien que m.,** to do sth after a fashion; **de m. en pis,** from bad to worse; **s'y m. prendre,** to go the wrong way about it; **m. comprendre,** to misunderstand; **on voit m.,** you can't see properly; **vous ne feriez pas m. de,** it wouldn't be a bad plan to (b) **aller, se porter, m.,** to be ill; **comment allez-vous?—pas m.!** how are you?—not bad! pretty well! **être au plus m.,** to be dangerously ill (c) F: **pas m. (de qch),** a fair amount (of sth); **pas m. de temps,** quite a (long) time; **pas m. de gens,** a good many people 2. (with adj function) (a) not right; **c'est très m. à lui,** it's very unkind of him (b) uncomfortable, badly off; **nous ne sommes pas m. ici,** we are quite comfortable here (c) **ils sont m. ensemble,** they are on bad terms (d) **se sentir m.,** to feel ill, sick, faint; **se trouver m.,** to faint (e) **pas m.,** not bad, quite good; **il n'est pas m.,** he's quite good-looking.

maladie [maladi] nf illness, sickness; disease; complaint; **faire une m.,** to be ill; F: **il en fait une m.,** he's making a song and dance about it; **m. de peau,** skin disease; **m. de foie, de cœur,** liver, heart, complaint; **m. mentale,** mental illness; Vet: **m. des chiens, de Carré,** distemper. **malade** 1. a (a) ill, sick, unwell; **tomber m.,** to fall ill; **dent m.,** aching tooth; **jambe m.,** bad leg; **m. d'inquiétude,** sick with worry; **être m. du cœur,** to have heart trouble; **esprit m.,** disordered mind (b) mad, crazy 2. n sick person; invalid; Med: patient; **les malades,** the sick. **maladif, -ive** a sickly; morbid, unhealthy.

maladresse [maladrɛs] nf 1. (a) clumsiness, awkwardness (b) tactlessness 2. blunder. **maladroit, -oite** 1. a (a) unskilled, clumsy, awkward (b) blundering; tactless 2. n clumsy person. **maladroitement** adv clumsily.

malaise[1] [malɛz] nm 1. uneasiness, discomfort 2. indisposition; **avoir un m.,** to feel faint.

malaisé [malɛze] a difficult. **malaisément** adv with difficulty.

Malaisie [malɛzi] Prnf Geog: Malaysia, Malaya.

malais, -aise² *a & n* Malay(an); Malaysian.

malappris, -ise [malapri, -iz] **1.** *a* uncouth, ill-bred **2.** *n* lout; **c'est un m.,** he has no manners.

malavisé [malavize] *a* ill-advised; injudicious.

malaxer [malakse] *vtr* **1.** to knead (dough); to work (butter); to mix (cement) **2.** to massage (leg).

malchance [malʃɑ̃s] *nf* **1.** bad luck; **par m.,** as ill luck would have it **2.** mishap, misfortune. **malchanceux, -euse** *a* unlucky.

malcommode [malkɔmɔd] *a* inconvenient; awkward.

mâle [mɑl] *a & nm* **1.** male; cock (bird); buck (rabbit); dog (fox); bull (elephant); **un ours m.,** a he-bear; **héritier m.,** male heir **2.** manly (courage); virile (style).

malédiction [malediksjɔ̃] *nf* curse.

maléfice [malefis] *nm* evil spell. **maléfique** *a* evil.

malencontreux, -euse [malɑ̃kɔ̃trø, -øz] *a* awkward, unfortunate, untoward (event). **malencontreusement** *adv* unfortunately.

malentendu [malɑ̃tɑ̃dy] *nm* misunderstanding.

malfaçon [malfasɔ̃] *nf* bad work(manship); defect.

malfaisant [malfəzɑ̃] *a* evil-minded; evil; harmful.

malfaiteur, -trice [malfɛtœr, -tris] *n* criminal; lawbreaker.

malformation [malfɔrmasjɔ̃] *nf* malformation.

malgache [malgaʃ] *a & n* Malagasy, Madagascan.

malgré [malgre] *prep* in spite of; notwithstanding; **m. cela, m. tout,** for all that, nevertheless; **je l'ai fait m. moi,** I did it in spite of myself.

malhabile [malabil] *a* unskilful; clumsy, awkward. **malhabilement** *adv* clumsily.

malheur [malœr] *nm* **1.** (*a*) misfortune; calamity; accident; **un m. n'arrive jamais seul,** it never rains but it pours; **quel m.!** what a tragedy! (*b*) *F:* **faire un m.,** (i) to do something desperate (ii) to make a hit **2.** misfortune, unhappiness; **il fait le m. de ses parents,** he brings sorrow to his parents **3.** (*a*) bad luck; **quel m.!** what a pity! **par m.,** unfortunately; **ça porte m.,** it's bad luck; **j'ai le m. de le connaître,** I am unfortunate enough to know him; **jouer de m.,** to be unlucky; *F:* **ces lettres de m.!** these blasted letters! (*b*) *int* hell! **malheureux, -euse** *a* (*a*) unfortunate, unhappy, wretched (pers, business); poor, badly off (pers); sad, miserable (expression); *n* **les m.,** the unfortunate, the needy; **le m.!** poor man! (*b*) unlucky; **candidat m.,** unsuccessful candidate; **c'est bien m. pour vous!** it's hard luck on you! **il est bien m. que** + *sub,* it's a great pity that; **le voilà enfin, ce n'est pas m.!** here he comes at last, and a good job too! (*c*) *F:* paltry, wretched; **une malheureuse pièce de cinq francs,** a miserable five-franc piece. **malheureusement** *adv* unfortunately.

malhonnêteté [malɔnɛtte] *nf* **1.** dishonesty **2.** rudeness. **malhonnête** *a* (*a*) dishonest; crooked (*b*) rude, impolite. **malhonnêtement** *adv* (*a*) dishonestly (*b*) rudely.

malice [malis] *nf* **1.** (*a*) malice, maliciousness, spitefulness; **ne pas entendre m. à qch,** to see no harm in sth (*b*) mischievousness, naughtiness **2.** (*a*) *O:* smart remark (*b*) **boîte à m.,** box of tricks. **malicieux, -ieuse** *a* (*a*) mischievous, naughty (*b*) mocking (smile); joking, bantering (remark). **malicieusement** *adv* mischievously.

malin, -igne [malɛ̃, -iɲ] *a* **1.** (*a*) *nm* **le M.,** the Devil

(*b*) malicious (*c*) **tumeur maligne,** malignant tumour **2.** (*a*) shrewd, cunning; **il est plus m. que ça,** he knows better; **elle n'est pas maligne,** she's not very bright (*b*) *n* **c'est un m.,** he knows a thing or two; **faire le m.,** to show off, to try to be smart (*c*) *F:* **c'est pas bien m.,** it's not very difficult.

malingre [malɛ̃gr] *a* sickly, puny.

malintentionné [malɛ̃tɑ̃sjɔne] *a & n* ill-intentioned, spiteful (person).

malle [mal] *nf* (*a*) trunk, box (*b*) *Aut:* boot, *NAm:* trunk.

malléabilité [maleabilite] *nf* malleability. **malléable** *a* malleable.

mallette [malɛt] *nf* small (suit)case.

malmener [malməne] *vtr* (**je malmène**) (*a*) to ill-treat; to mishandle, misuse (sth) (*b*) to abuse (s.o.).

malnutrition [malnytrisjɔ̃] *nf* malnutrition.

malodorant [malɔdɔrɑ̃] *a* evil-smelling, smelly, stinking.

malotru, -ue [malɔtry] *n* boor; uncouth person.

malpoli [malpɔli] *a* impolite.

malpropreté [malprɔprəte] *nf* dirtiness. **malpropre** *a* (*a*) dirty, grubby; slovenly, untidy (*b*) smutty, indecent (story); unsavoury (business). **malproprement** *adv* in a slovenly manner.

malsain, -aine [malsɛ̃, -ɛn] *a* **1.** unhealthy **2.** unwholesome.

malséant [malseɑ̃] *a* unseemly; unbecoming.

Malte [malt] *Prnf Geog:* Malta. **maltais, -aise** *a & n* Maltese.

maltraiter [maltrete] *vtr* to ill-treat, ill-use; to handle (s.o., sth) roughly; to manhandle (s.o.).

malveillance [malvɛjɑ̃s] *nf* malevolence; **avec m.,** malevolently. **malveillant** *a* (*a*) malevolent; malicious (*b*) spiteful.

maman [mamɑ̃] *nf* mummy, mum.

mamelle [mamɛl] *nf* breast; *Z:* udder; teat, dug.

mamelon [maml̃ɔ] *nm* **1.** *Anat:* nipple, teat **2.** *Geog:* hillock; knoll.

mamie [mami] *nf F:* granny, gran.

mammaire [mamɛr] *a Anat:* mammary.

mammifère [mamifɛr] *nm* mammal.

mammouth [mamut] *nm* mammoth.

manche¹ [mɑ̃ʃ] *nf* **1.** (*a*) sleeve; **robe sans manches,** sleeveless dress; **avoir qn dans sa m.,** to have s.o. in one's pocket; *F:* **ça, c'est une autre paire de manches,** that's quite another matter (*b*) **m. à incendie,** fire hose; **m. à air,** (i) *Nau:* ventilator (ii) *Av:* wind sock **2.** (*a*) *Cards:* hand (played); single game (*b*) *Sp:* heat (*c*) *Ten:* set **3.** *Geog:* **la M.,** the (English) Channel.

manche² *nm* (*a*) handle; shaft; **m. à balai,** (i) broomstick (ii) *Av:* joystick (*b*) *F:* idiot, clot.

manchette [mɑ̃ʃɛt] *nf* **1.** (*a*) cuff (*b*) oversleeve (*c*) *Wr:* forearm smash **2.** (newspaper) headline.

manchon [mɑ̃ʃɔ̃] *nm* **1.** muff **2.** *MecE:* casing, sleeve; **m. d'accouplement,** coupling sleeve; *Aut:* **m. d'embrayage,** clutch.

manchot, -ote [mɑ̃ʃo, -ɔt] **1.** *a & n* one-armed, one-handed (person); *F:* **il n'est pas m.,** he's clever with his hands **2.** *nm Orn:* penguin.

mandarin [mɑ̃darɛ̃] *nm Hist:* mandarin; *Pej:* pedant.

mandarine [mɑ̃darin] *nf* mandarin(e) (orange); tangerine.

mandat [mɑ̃da] *nm* **1.** (*a*) mandate; commission;

territoire sous m., mandated territory (b) Pol: (electoral) mandate (c) Jur: power of attorney; proxy **2.** Jur: warrant; **m. de perquisition,** search warrant; **m. d'arrêt,** warrant for arrest; **m. de comparution,** summons (to appear); **m. de dépôt,** committal (of prisoner) **3.** order (to pay); money order; draft; **m. postal** = postal order.

mandataire [mɑ̃datɛr] n **1.** mandatory (of electors) **2.** (pers) proxy; representative **3.** Jur: authorized agent; attorney **4.** trustee.

mandater [mɑ̃date] vtr **1.** to elect, commission (representative) **2. m. des frais,** to pay expenses by money order, by draft.

mandat-poste [mɑ̃dapɔst] nm = postal order, money order; pl mandats-poste.

mandoline [mɑ̃dɔlin] nf Mus: mandolin(e).

manège [manɛʒ] nm **1.** (a) horsemanship, riding (b) **(salle de) m.,** riding school (c) **m. (de chevaux de bois),** merry-go-round; roundabout **2.** stratagem, trick; **j'observais leur m.,** I was watching their little game.

manette [manɛt] nf handle, hand lever.

mangeaille [mɑ̃ʒɑj] nf F: food, grub.

mangeoire [mɑ̃ʒwar] nf manger; (feeding) trough.

manger¹ [mɑ̃ʒe] vtr (n. mangeons) (a) to eat; **il mange de tout,** he'll eat anything; **m. dans une assiette,** to eat off a plate; **salle à m.,** dining room; **m. au restaurant,** to eat out; **donner à m. à qn, aux poules,** to give s.o. sth to eat; to feed the hens; **m. comme quatre,** to eat like a horse; **m. à sa faim,** to eat one's fill; **nous avons bien mangé,** we had a very good meal (b) **mangé par les mites,** motheaten; **m. ses mots,** to mumble; P: **m. le morceau,** to let out a secret; to spill the beans (c) **m. son argent,** to squander one's money. **mangeable** a edible, eatable.

manger² nm food.

mange-tout [mɑ̃ʒtu] a inv & nm inv Hort: (a) **(pois) m.-t.,** sugar-pea (b) **(haricot) m.-t.,** French bean, NAm: string bean.

mangeur, -euse [mɑ̃ʒœr, -øz] n eater.

mangue [mɑ̃g] nf mango (fruit).

maniabilité [manjabilite] nf handiness (of tool); manoeuvrability. **maniable** a manageable; easy to handle; handy (tool).

maniaque [manjak] a & n **1.** maniac; raving lunatic **2.** finicky, faddy (pers); n fusspot, crank.

manie [mani] nf (a) Psy: mania, obsession; **m. de la persécution,** persecution mania (b) mania, craze; **avoir la m. de la propreté,** to be obsessed with cleanliness; **il a ses petites manies,** he has his little fads.

maniement [manimɑ̃] nm handling; Mil: **m. d'armes,** drill; arms' manual.

manier [manje] vtr (impf & pr sub n. maniions) **1.** to handle (tool) **2.** to handle, manage, control (horse, business); **m. les avirons,** to ply the oars.

manière [manjɛr] nf **1.** (a) manner, way; **c'est sa m. d'être,** that's the way he is; **laissez-moi faire à ma m.,** let me do it my own way; **de cette m.,** thus; in this way; **de m. ou d'autre, d'une m. ou d'une autre,** somehow or other; **en quelque m.,** in a way; **d'une m. générale,** generally speaking; **en aucune m.,** under no circumstances; **de toute m.,** in any case; **de (telle) m. que,** so that (b) Art: style, manner **2.** pl manners; F: **qu'est-ce que c'est que ces manières?** that's no way to behave! F: **faire des manières,** (i) to be affected (ii) to affect

reluctance. **maniéré** a affected (pers, behaviour).

maniérisme [manjerism] nm **1.** mannerism **2.** affectation.

manif [manif] nf F: (= manifestation) demo.

manifestant, -ante [manifɛstɑ̃, -ɑ̃t] n demonstrator.

manifestation [manifɛstasjɔ̃] nf (a) manifestation (of feeling) (b) demonstration (c) revelation (d) **m. sportive,** sporting event.

manifeste¹ [manifɛst] a manifest, obvious, evident. **manifestement** adv manifestly, obviously, evidently.

manifeste² nm **1.** manifesto, proclamation **2.** (ship's) manifest.

manifester [manifɛste] **1.** vtr to manifest; to reveal; to evince (opinion); to show, express (joy, grief); **m. sa volonté,** to make one's wishes clear **2.** vi to demonstrate **3. se m.,** to appear; to show itself.

manigance [manigɑ̃s] nf intrigue; pl underhand practices; fiddling, wire-pulling.

manigancer [manigɑ̃se] vtr (n. manigançons) to scheme, to plot; **qu'est-ce qu'ils manigancent?** what are they up to?

manipulateur, -trice [manipylatœr, -tris] n operator; technician.

manipulation [manipylasjɔ̃] nf **1.** (a) manipulation, handling (b) Med: manipulation **2.** Sch: practical work; Ch: Ph: experiment.

manipuler [manipyle] vtr **1.** to manipulate; to handle, operate (apparatus) **2.** to rig (accounts, election).

manivelle [manivɛl] nf crank; Aut: (starting) handle.

manne [man] nf manna.

mannequin [mankɛ̃] nm **1.** (a) (anatomical) manikin (b) Dressm: dummy **2.** (pers) model.

manœuvre [manœvr̩] **1.** nf (a) working, driving (of machine); manœuvring (b) Nau: handling (of ship); seamanship; **maître de m.,** boatswain (c) Mil: etc: (i) drill, exercise (ii) tactical exercise; manoeuvre; **grandes manœuvres,** army manoeuvres, exercises; **terrain de m.,** drill ground, parade ground (d) Mil: **m. d'encerclement,** encircling movement (e) Rail: shunting (f) scheme, manoeuvre, intrigue (g) pl scheming; **manœuvres frauduleuses,** swindling **2.** nm (unskilled) worker; labourer.

manœuvrer [manœvre] **1.** vtr (a) to work, operate (machine) (b) to manoeuvre, handle (vehicle) (c) Rail: to shunt **2.** vi to manoeuvre.

manoir [manwar] nm manor house.

manomètre [manɔmɛtr̩] nm manometer, pressure gauge.

manque [mɑ̃k] nm (a) lack; deficiency; shortage; **m. de parole,** breach of faith; **m. de crédit,** credibility gap; **par m. de,** through lack of; **m. de chance!** bad luck! Med: **(crise de) m.,** withdrawal (symptoms) (b) pl shortcomings.

manquement [mɑ̃kmɑ̃] nm **m. à une règle,** violation of a rule; **m. à la discipline,** breach of discipline.

manquer [mɑ̃ke] **1.** vi (a) **m. de qch,** to lack, to be short of, to be out of, sth; **m. de politesse,** to be impolite; **m. de courage,** to lack courage; **je ne manque de rien,** I have all I need (b) **il a manqué (de) tomber,** he nearly fell (c) impers **il s'en manque de beaucoup,** far from it (d) to be lacking, in short supply; **les mots me**

manquent, words fail me; les vivres commencent à m., provisions are running short; la place me manque, I haven't any room; *impers* il ne manque pas de, there's no shortage of; il me manquait plus que cela! that's the last straw! il manque quelques pages, there are a few pages missing; il lui manque un bras, he has lost an arm; il me manque 10 francs, I'm 10 francs short (*e*) to give way; le cœur lui manque, his heart failed him (*f*) to be absent, missing; m. à un rendez-vous, to fail to keep an appointment; m. à l'appel, to be absent from rollcall; m. à qn, to be missed by s.o.; ça me manque, I miss it (*g*) to fall short; m. à son devoir, to fail in one's duty; m. à sa parole, to break one's word; m. à une règle, to violate a rule; le coup a manqué, the attempt failed (*h*) ne manquez pas de nous écrire, be sure to write to us 2. *vtr* (*a*) to miss (target, train); m. une occasion, to lose, miss, an opportunity; m. un coup, to make an abortive attempt; to fail; *F:* il n'en manque pas une, he's always putting his foot in it (*b*) to be absent from, to miss (meeting) (*c*) m. sa vie, to make a mess of one's life. manquant *a* missing. manqué *a* missed (opportunity); unsuccessful, abortive (attempt); coup m., (i) miss (ii) failure; garçon m., tomboy.

mansarde [mɑ̃sard] *nf* Arch: (toit en) m., mansard roof 2. attic.

mansuétude [mɑ̃sɥetyd] *nf* leniency.

manteau, -eaux [mɑ̃to] *nm* 1. coat; m. de pluie, raincoat; sous le m. de la nuit, under cover of darkness 2. m. de cheminée, mantelpiece.

mantille [mɑ̃tij] *nf Cl:* mantilla.

manucure [manykyr] *n* manicurist.

manuel, -elle [manɥɛl] 1. *a* manual (work) 2. *nm* manual, handbook.

manufacture [manyfaktyr] *nf* 1. manufacture 2. factory.

manufacturer [manyfaktyre] *vtr* to manufacture.

manuscrit [manyskri] *a & nm* manuscript; lettre manuscrite, handwritten letter; m. (dactylographié), typescript.

manutention [manytɑ̃sjɔ̃] *nf* (*a*) handling (of goods) (*b*) storehouse; stores.

manutentionnaire [manytɑ̃sjɔnɛr] *n* warehouse-man; packer.

mappemonde [mapmɔ̃d] *nf* map of the world in two hemispheres; m. céleste, planisphere.

maquereau, -eaux [makro] *nm* 1. Ich: mackerel 2. *P:* pimp.

maquette [makɛt] *nf* scale model.

maquettist [makɛtist] *n* model maker.

maquillage [makijaʒ] *nm* 1. (*a*) making up (of face) (*b*) faking (of pictures) 2. makeup.

maquiller [makije] *vtr* to make up (s.o.'s face) (*b*) to fake (pictures) 2. se m., to make up (one's face).

maquis [maki] *nm* (*a*) Geog: maquis; scrub, bush (*b*) (1939–45 war) maquis; underground forces; prendre le m., to go underground.

maquisard [makizar] *nm* (1939–45 war) maquis.

maraîchage [marɛʒaʒ] *nm* market gardening. maraîcher, -ère [marɛʃɛr] (*a*) a jardin m., market garden; produits maraîchers, market garden produce (*b*) *n* market-gardener, NAm: truck farmer.

marais [marɛ] *nm* marsh(land); bog, fen; swamp; m. salant, saltmarsh.

marasme [marasm] *nm* (*a*) stagnation, slackness, slump (*b*) depression, dejection.

marathon [maratɔ̃] *nm Sp:* marathon.

marâtre [marɑtr] *nf* cruel (step)mother.

maraude [marod] *nf* (*a*) pilfering, petty thieving (*b*) taxi en m., cruising taxi.

marauder [marode] *vi* to thieve, pilfer.

maraudeur, -euse [marodœr, -øz] *n* (*a*) marauder (*b*) petty thief; prowler.

marbre [marbr] *nm* 1. (*a*) marble (*b*) marble (statue) (*c*) marble top 2. Typ: press stone. marbré *a* marbled; mottled; veined.

marbrier [marbrije] *nm* monumental mason.

marbrure [marbryr] *nf* marbling, veining; mottling.

marc [mar] *nm* 1. marc (of grapes); (eau de vie de) m., marc (brandy) 2. m. de café, coffee grounds.

marcassin [markasɛ̃] *nm* young wild boar.

marchand, -ande [marʃɑ̃, -ɑ̃d] 1. *n* merchant; dealer; shopkeeper; tradesman; m. en gros, en détail, wholesaler, retailer; m. de légumes, greengrocer; m. de poisson, fishmonger; m. de tabac, tobacconist; m. ambulant, hawker; m. de quatre saisons, costermonger 2. *a* (*a*) commercial; saleable, marketable (article); market (price) (*b*) marine marchande, merchant navy.

marchandage [marʃɑ̃daʒ] *nm* bargaining, haggling.

marchander [marʃɑ̃de] *vtr* (*a*) to haggle, to bargain, over (sth) (*b*) il ne marchande pas sa peine, he spares no efforts (to do sth).

marchandise [marʃɑ̃diz] *nf* merchandise, goods; commodity; Nau: cargo; train de marchandises, freight train; étaler sa m., to make the most of oneself.

marche [marʃ] *nf* 1. step, stair 2. (*a*) walking; aimer la m., to be fond of walking; ralentir sa m., to slacken one's pace; se mettre en m., to set out, start off; deux heures de m., two hours' walk (*b*) Mil: etc: march; ordres de m., marching orders; ouvrir la m., to lead the way; fermer la m., to bring up the rear (*c*) Mus: m. funèbre, funeral march 3. (*a*) running (of trains); sailing (of ships); mettre en m. un service, to start, run, a service (*b*) en m., moving; m. arrière, reversing (of car); entrer dans le garage en m. arrière, to back into the garage 4. (*a*) running, working (of machine); (of machine) être en m., to be running, working; mettre en m., to start (a machine) (*b*) course (of events); march (of time).

marché [marʃe] *nm* 1. (*a*) dealing, buying; m. noir, black market; faire son m., to do one's shopping (*b*) deal, bargain; conclure un m., to strike a bargain; c'est m. conclu, it's a bargain; *F:* done! par-dessus le m., into the bargain (*c*) acheter qch (à) bon m., to buy sth cheap(ly); à meilleur m., cheaper; articles bon m., low-priced goods; bargains 2. market; m. aux puces, flea market; lancer un article sur le m., to market an article; le M. commun, the Common Market.

marchepied [marʃəpje] *nm* (*a*) steps (of train) (*b*) Aut: runningboard.

marcher [marʃe] *vi* 1. to tread; m. sur les pieds de qn, to tread on s.o.'s toes; ne marchez pas sur les pelouses, keep off the grass 2. (*a*) to walk, go; boiter en marchant, to limp; deux choses qui marchent toujours ensemble, two things that always go together; façon de m., gait (*b*) *F:* to obey orders; faire m. qn, (i) to order s.o. about (ii) to pull s.o.'s leg; il marchera, he'll do it; **je ne marche pas!** nothing doing! (*c*) *Mil: etc:* to march; **en avant, marche!** quick march! **3.** (*a*) (*of trains*) to move, travel, go; (*of ships*) to sail; (*of plans*) to progress; **le temps marche,** time goes on; **les affaires marchent,** business is brisk; **est-ce que ça marche?** are you getting on all right? **la répétition a bien marché,** the rehearsal went well (*b*) (*of machine*) to work, run, go; **ma montre ne marche plus,** my watch won't go.

marcheur, -euse [marʃœr, -øz] *n* walker.

mardi [mardi] *nm* Tuesday; **m. gras,** Shrove Tuesday.

mare [mar] *nf* (stagnant) pool; pond; **m. de sang,** pool of blood.

marécage [mareka3] *nm* marsh; bog, swamp. **marécageux, -euse** *a* marshy, boggy, swampy.

maréchal, -aux [mareʃal, -o] *nm* **1.** **m.-ferrant,** blacksmith; farrier **2.** marshal (of royal household) **3.** *Mil:* (*a*) **m. (de France)** = field marshal (*b*) **m. des logis,** sergeant (in mounted arms).

marée [mare] *nf* **1.** tide; **m. haute, basse,** high, low, water; high, low, tide; **m. montante, descendante,** flood tide, ebb tide; **port de m.,** tidal harbour; **m. humaine,** flood of people; **m. noire,** oil slick **2.** fresh (seawater) fish; **train de m.,** fish train; **arriver comme m. en carême,** to be inevitable.

marelle [marɛl] *nf* hopscotch.

margarine [margarin] *nf* margarine.

marge [mar3] *nf* **1.** (*a*) border, edge (of ditch, road); **vivre en m. (de la société),** (i) to lead a quiet life (ii) to live on the fringe of society (*b*) margin (of book); **note en m.,** marginal note **2. m. de sécurité,** safety margin; **m. d'erreur,** margin of error; **avoir de la m.,** to have plenty of (i) time (ii) scope; *Com:* **m. bénéficiaire,** profit margin. **marginal, -aux 1.** *a* marginal **2.** *nmpl PolEc:* **les marginaux,** the fringe.

marguerite [margərit] *nf Bot:* **(petite) m.,** daisy; **grande m.,** oxeye daisy, marguerite.

mari [mari] *nm* husband.

mariage [marja3] *nm* (*a*) marriage; matrimony; **m. d'amour,** love match (*b*) wedding; **m. religieux,** church wedding; **m. civil,** civil marriage = register office; **acte de m.,** marriage certificate; **demande en m.,** proposal (of marriage) (*c*) marriage, blend (of colours).

marié, -ée [marje] *a & n* married (person); **nouveau m., nouvelle mariée, le, la, marié(e),** (the) bridegroom, (the) bride; **nouveaux mariés,** newlyweds; **robe de mariée,** wedding dress.

marier [marje] *vtr* (*impf & pr sub* **n. mariions**) **1.** (*a*) (*of priest*) to marry (a couple) (*b*) to marry off (daughter); **fille à m.,** marriageable daughter (*c*) to join, unite; to blend (colours) **2. se m.,** to marry, to get married; **se m. avec qn,** to marry s.o.; (*of colour*) **se m. avec qch,** to blend with sth.

marihuana [mariɥana], **marijuana** [mari3ɥana] *nf* marihuana.

marin, -ine¹ [marɛ̃, -in] **1.** *a* marine (plant, engine); **carte marine,** sea chart; **mille m.,** nautical mile; **costume m.,** sailor suit; **avoir le pied m.,** to be a good sailor **2.** *nm* sailor, seaman; **se faire m.,** to go to sea; **m. d'eau douce,** landlubber.

marinade [marinad] *nf Cu:* (*a*) pickle (*b*) marinade.

marine² [marin] *nf* **1.** seamanship; **terme de m.,** nautical term **2.** the sea service; **la m. marchande,** the merchant navy; **la m. de guerre,** the navy; **officier de**

m., naval officer **3.** *a inv* navy-blue **4.** *nm* (Royal) Marine.

mariner [marine] *vtr* (*a*) to pickle; to salt; to souse (*b*) *Cu:* to marinate, to marinade.

marionnette [marjɔnɛt] *nf* puppet; **m. à gaine,** glove puppet; **m. (à fil),** marionette; **(spectacle de) marionnettes,** puppet show.

marionnettiste [marjɔnɛtist] *n* puppeteer.

marital, -aux [marital, -o] *a* marital; husband's (authority). **maritalement** *adv* maritally; **vivre m.,** to cohabit.

maritime [maritim] *a* maritime; **ville m.,** seaboard town; **commerce m.,** seaborne trade; **assurance m.,** marine insurance; **agent m.,** shipping agent; **arsenal m.,** naval dockyard; *Rail:* **gare m.,** harbour station.

marjolaine [mar3olɛn] *nf Bot:* (sweet) marjoram.

marmaille [marmaj] *nf coll F:* children; kids, brats.

marmelade [marməlad] *nf* (*a*) compote (of fruit); **m. de pommes,** stewed apples (*b*) **m. (d'oranges),** (orange) marmalade (*c*) *F:* **mettre en m.,** to reduce to a pulp.

marmite [marmit] *nf* (*a*) (cooking) pot; (stew)pan; **m. à conserves,** preserving pan; **m. autoclave,** pressure cooker (*b*) *Mil:* dixie, camp kettle.

marmonnement [marmɔnmɑ̃] *nm* mumbling, muttering.

marmonner [marmɔne] *vtr* to mumble, mutter.

marmot [marmo] *nm F:* child, brat.

marmotte [marmɔt] *nf Z:* marmot.

marmotter [marmɔte] *vtr* to mumble, mutter.

Maroc [marɔk] *Prnm Geog:* Morocco. **marocain, -aine** *a & n* Moroccan.

maroquin [marɔkɛ̃] *nm* (*a*) morocco (leather) (*b*) minister's portfolio.

maroquinerie [marɔkinri] *nf Com:* (*a*) fancy leather work (*b*) morocco-leather goods trade (*c*) (fancy) leather shop.

maroquinier [marɔkinje] *nm* dealer in fancy leather goods.

marotte [marɔt] *nf* fad, hobby.

marque [mark] *nf* **1.** mark; **m. (de fabrique),** trademark; brand; **m. déposée,** registered trademark; **produits de m.,** branded goods; **m. courante,** standard make; **personnage de m.,** distinguished, prominent, person; **porter la m. du génie,** to bear the stamp of genius; **marques d'amitié,** tokens of friendship **2.** marker, marking tool **3.** (*a*) *Games:* score (*b*) *Games:* counter (*c*) *Sp:* **à vos marques! prêts! partez!** on your marks! get set! go!

marquer [marke] **1.** *vtr* (*a*) to mark; to put a mark on (sth); *Com:* **prix marqué,** list price (*b*) to record, note; *Games:* **m. un but,** to score a goal; **m. les points,** to keep the score (*c*) to indicate, show; **la pendule marque dix heures,** the clock says ten o'clock; **m. le pas,** to mark time **2.** *vi* (*a*) (*of pencil*) to write (*b*) to stand out, make a mark; **notre famille n'a jamais marqué,** our family has never been outstanding. **marquant** *a* prominent, outstanding (incident, personality). **marqué** *a* marked, unmistakable (difference); pronounced (features); distinct (inclination).

marqueur [markœr] *nm* (felt-tip) marker (pen).

marquis [marki] *nm* marquis, marquess.

marquise [markiz] *nf* **1.** marchioness **2.** (*a*) awning (*b*) canopy; glass porch.

marraine [marɛn] *nf* godmother; sponsor (at baptism); christener (of ship).

marre [mar] *adv P:* **avoir m. de qch, de qn,** to be fed up with sth, s.o.; **j'en ai m.,** I've had enough.

marrer (se) [səmare] *vpr P:* to laugh, to kill oneself laughing; **tu me fais m.,** you make me laugh. **marrant** *a* (*a*) (screamingly) funny (*b*) odd, strange, funny; **vous êtes m., vous alors!** you're the limit!

marron [marɔ̃] **1.** *nm* (*a*) (edible) chestnut; **m. glacé,** glacé chestnut (*b*) **m. d'Inde,** horse chestnut (*c*) *P:* blow, thump, clout **2.** *a inv & nm* chestnut (brown).

marronnier [marɔnje] *nm* chestnut tree; **m. d'Inde,** horse-chestnut tree.

Mars [mars] **1.** *Prnm Myth: Astr:* Mars **2.** *nm* **au mois de m., en m.,** in (the month of) March; **le premier m.,** (on) the first of March; **le sept m.,** (on) the seventh of March; **blé de m.,** spring wheat.

Marseille [marsɛj] *Prn Geog:* Marseille(s). **marseillais, -aise** *a & n Geog:* Marseillais; **la Marseillaise,** the Marseillaise.

marsouin [marswɛ̃] *nm Z:* porpoise.

marteau, -eaux [marto] **1.** *nm* (*a*) hammer; **m. pneumatique,** pneumatic drill; **m.-piqueur,** hammer drill; **entre l'enclume et le m.,** between the devil and the deep blue sea (*b*) (door) knocker; striker (of clock) **2.** *a F:* crazy, round the bend.

marteau-pilon [martopilɔ̃] *nm* power hammer; *pl* **marteaux-pilons.**

martèlement [martɛlmɑ̃] *nm* hammering.

marteler [martəle] *vtr* (**je martèle**) to hammer; **m. à froid,** to cold-hammer; **m. ses mots,** to hammer out one's words.

martial, -aux [marsjal, -o] *a* martial; warlike; soldierly (bearing); **loi martiale,** martial law; **cour martiale,** court martial.

martien, -ienne [marsjɛ̃, -jɛn] *a & n* Martian.

martinet [martinɛ] *nm* **1.** strap **2.** *Orn:* swift.

martin-pêcheur [martɛ̃peʃœr] *nm Orn:* kingfisher; *pl* **martins-pêcheurs.**

martre [martr] *nf Z:* marten; **m. zibeline,** sable; **m. du Canada,** mink.

martyre[1] [martir] *nm* martyrdom; **souffrir le m.,** to suffer agonies; **mettre qn au m.,** to torture s.o. **martyr, -yre[2]** *a & n* martyr; **peuple m.,** martyred people.

martyriser [martirize] *vtr* **1.** to martyr (s.o.) **2.** to martyrize, to torture; to make a martyr of (s.o.).

marxisme [marksism] *nm Pol:* Marxism. **marxiste** *a & n* Marxist.

mascarade [maskarad] *nf* masquerade.

mascaret [maskarɛ] *nm* bore, tidal wave (in estuary).

mascotte [maskɔt] *nf* mascot; charm.

masculin [maskylɛ̃] **1.** *a* (*a*) male (*b*) masculine **2.** *a & nm Gram:* masculine (gender); **au m.,** in the masculine.

masochisme [mazɔʃism] *nm* masochism. **masochiste 1.** *a* masochistic **2.** *n* masochist.

masque [mask] *nm* mask; **m. à gaz,** gas mask; **m. à oxygène,** oxygen mask; **m. sous-marin,** (skin-diver's) mask; **m. (antirides, facial),** face pack; **m. mortuaire,** death mask.

masquer [maske] *vtr* **1.** (*a*) to mask; to put a mask on (s.o.); **bal masqué,** masked ball (*b*) to hide, screen, conceal (sth); to shade (light); to disguise (smell);

Aut: **virage masqué,** blind corner **2. se m.,** to hide, conceal.

massacre [masakr] *nm* massacre, slaughter; butchery.

massacrer [masakre] *vtr* **1.** to massacre, slaughter, butcher **2.** *F:* to bungle, spoil (work); to murder (music); to ruin (clothes). **massacrante** *af* (*used in phr*) **être d'une humeur m.,** to be in a vile temper.

massacreur, -euse [masakrœr, -øz] *n F:* bungler.

massage [masaʒ] *nm* massage.

masse[1] [mas] *nf* **1.** (*a*) mass; **tomber comme une m.,** to fall heavily; **en m.,** (i) en masse (ii) as a whole; **exécutions en m.,** mass executions; *F:* **avoir des livres en m.,** to have masses of books; **taillé dans la m.,** carved in the block (*b*) mass, crowd; **les masses, la m.,** the masses; **la m. de,** the majority of; *F:* **il n'y en a pas des masses,** there aren't an awful lot **2.** *Fin:* **m. monétaire,** money supply **3.** *El:* earth; **mettre le courant à la m.,** to earth the current; *AtomPh:* **m. critique,** critical mass.

masse[2] *nf* **1.** sledgehammer **2.** (*a*) *AArms:* **m. (d'armes),** mace (*b*) (ceremonial) mace.

massepain [maspɛ̃] *nm* marzipan.

masser[1] [mase] *vtr* **1.** to mass (crowds) **2. se m.,** to mass; to form a crowd.

masser[2] *vtr* to massage.

masseur, -euse [masœr, -øz] *n* masseur, masseuse.

massif, -ive [masif, -iv] **1.** *a* (*a*) massive, bulky (*b*) solid (silver) (*c*) *action* massive, mass attack; **dose massive,** massive dose **2.** *nm* (*a*) clump (of shrubs) (*b*) *Geog:* mountain mass; massif. **massivement** *adv* en masse, in a body.

mass(-)media [masmedja] *nmpl* mass media.

massue [masy] *nf* club, bludgeon; **coup de m.,** staggering blow

mastic [mastik] *nm* **1.** (*a*) mastic (resin) (*b*) cement, mastic compound; (*for windows*) putty; (*for wood*) filler **2.** *a inv* putty-coloured.

mastiquer [mastike] *vtr* **1.** to cement; to fill in (cracks); to putty (window) **2.** to masticate, chew.

mastodonte [mastɔdɔ̃t] *nm* **1.** *Paleont:* mastodon **2.** (*pers*) colossus.

masure [mazyr] *nf* hovel, shanty.

mat[1] [mat] *a* mat(t), unpolished, dull; **son m.,** dull sound; thud.

mat[2] *Chess:* **1.** *a inv* checkmated **2.** *nm* (check)mate.

mât [mɑ] *nm* (*a*) mast, pole; **m. d'artimon,** mizzenmast; **m. de misaine,** foremast; **m. de charge,** cargo boom; derrick (*b*) **m. de tente,** tent pole; **m. de cocagne,** greasy pole.

match [matʃ] *nm Sp:* match; **m. prévu,** fixture; **faire m. nul,** to tie, draw; *pl* **matchs, matches** [matʃ].

matelas [matla] *nm* mattress; **m. pneumatique,** inflatable mattress; air mattress.

matelasser [matlase] *vtr* to pad, quilt, cushion, stuff (chair); mattress-maker.

matelot [matlo] *nm* sailor, seaman.

mater [mate] *vtr* (*a*) *Chess:* to (check)mate (*b*) to subdue, tame (s.o.); to bring (s.o.) to heel.

matérialisation [materjalizasjɔ̃] *nf* materialization.

matérialiser [materjalize] *vtr & pr* to materialize.

matérialisme [materjalism] *nm* materialism. **matérialiste 1.** *a* materialistic **2.** *n* materialist.

matériau [materjo] *nm CivE:* (building) material.

matériaux [materjo] *nmpl* material(s).

matériel, -elle [materjɛl] **1.** *a* (*a*) material, physical (body) (*b*) materialistic, sensual (pleasures, mind) (*c*) **besoins matériels,** bodily needs **2.** *nm* (*a*) equipment; material; plant; **m. agricole,** farm machinery, implements; *Rail:* **m. roulant,** rolling-stock; **m. de camping,** camping equipment; **m. scolaire,** school equipment (*b*) *Cmptr:* hardware. **matériellement** *adv* materially.

maternité [matɛrnite] *nf* **1.** (*a*) maternity, motherhood (*b*) pregnancy **2.** maternity hospital. **maternel, -elle** *a* **1.** maternal; motherly (care); **école maternelle,** *n/*la maternelle, nursery school **2.** (*a*) aïeul **m.,** maternal grandfather (*b*) **langue maternelle,** mother tongue. **maternellement** *adv* maternally.

math(s) [mat] *nfpl Sch: F:* maths; **fort en m.,** good at maths.

mathématicien, -ienne [matematisjɛ̃, -jɛn] *n* mathematician.

mathématique [matematik] **1.** *a* mathematical **2.** *nfpl* mathematics. **matheux, -euse** *n F:* maths fiend.

matière [matjɛr] *nf* **1.** matter, material, substance; **matière(s) première(s),** raw material(s); **m. grasse,** fat; **m. plastique,** plastic **2.** subject (matter); (school) subject; topic, theme; **table des matières,** (table of) contents (of book); **entrer en m.,** to broach the subject; **il n'y a pas m. à rire,** it's no laughing matter; **en m. de musique,** as far as music is concerned.

matin [matɛ̃] *nm* morning; **quatre heures du m.,** four o'clock in the morning; **de grand m.,** early in the morning; **rentrer au petit m.,** to come home very early in the morning; **un de ces (quatre) matins,** one of these (fine) days. **matinal, -aux** *a* **1.** morning (breeze); **à cette heure matinale,** at this early hour **2.** **comme tu es m.!** you're up early!

matinée [matine] *nf* **1.** morning; **dans la m.,** in (the course of) the morning; **faire (la) grasse m.,** to sleep late, *F:* to have a lie in **2.** *Th: etc:* matinée, afternoon performance.

matois, -oise [matwa, -waz] **1.** *a* sly, cunning, crafty **2.** *n* crafty person; **fin m.,** sly devil.

matou [matu] *nm* tom(cat).

matraquage [matrakaʒ] *nm* bludgeoning, beating up.

matraque [matrak] *nf* bludgeon, truncheon, *F:* cosh; *F:* **coup de m.,** overcharging (in restaurant).

matraquer [matrake] *vtr* to bludgeon, *F:* cosh, s.o.

matrice [matris] *nf* (*a*) *Anat:* womb (*b*) *Metalw:* die; mould (*c*) *Mth:* matrix.

matricule [matrikyl] *a & nm* (**numéro**) **m.,** (regimental, administrative) number.

matriculer [matrikyle] *vtr* **1.** to enter (s.o.'s) name on a register; to enrol (s.o.) **2.** to stamp with a number.

matrimonial, -aux [matrimɔnjal, -o] *a* matrimonial.

matrone [matrɔn] *nf* matron; *Pej:* **vieille m.,** old bag.

mâture [matyr] *nf* masts; masts and spars; **dans la m.,** aloft.

maturité [matyrite] *nf* maturity; ripeness; **venir à m.,** to come to maturity.

maudire [modir] *vtr* (*prp* **maudissant;** *pp* **maudit;** *pr sub* **je maudisse;** *ph* **je maudis**) to curse. **maudit 1.** *a* (*a*) (ac)cursed (*b*) **quel m. temps!** what bloody awful

weather! **2.** *n* **le M.,** the Devil; **les maudits,** the damned.

maugréer [mogree] *vi* to curse, fume; to grumble (**contre,** at).

Maurice [mɔris] *Prnm* Maurice; *Geog:* **l'île M.,** Mauritius.

mausolée [mozɔle] *nm* mausoleum.

maussade [mosad] *a* (*a*) surly, sullen; sulky; disgruntled (*b*) **temps m.,** dull, gloomy, weather.

mauvais [mɔvɛ] *a* (*a*) evil, ill; wicked (person); **mauvaise action,** wrong(doing); **de plus en plus m.,** worse and worse; **le plus m.,** the worst; **avoir l'air m.,** to look (i) wicked (ii) vicious; **c'est un m. sujet,** he's a bad lot (*b*) ill-natured; **c'est une mauvaise langue,** she's a gossip (*c*) nasty, unpleasant; bad (breath, dream); rough (sea); **m. temps,** bad weather; **m. pas,** tight spot; **trouver qch m.,** to dislike sth; **prendre qch en mauvaise part,** to take offence at sth; *adv* **sentir m.,** to smell bad; **il fait m.,** the weather is bad (*d*) **m. pour la santé,** bad for the health (*e*) imperfect, inadequate; **mauvaise santé,** poor health; **il a fait une mauvaise bronchite,** he's had a bad attack of bronchitis; **faire de mauvaises affaires,** to be doing badly (in business); **m. frein,** defective brake (*f*) wrong; **c'est la mauvaise clef,** it's the wrong key; **rire au m. endroit,** to laugh in the wrong place.

mauve [mov] **1.** *nf Bot:* mallow **2.** *a & nm* mauve.

mauviette [movjɛt] *nf* frail, puny, person; weakling.

maxillaire [maksilɛr] *a Anat:* maxillary; *a & nm* (**os**) **m.,** jawbone.

maximum [maksimɔm] **1.** *nm* maximum; **porter la production au m.,** to raise production to a maximum; *pl* **maximums, maxima 2.** *a usu inv* **rendement m.,** maximum output. **maximal, -aux** *a* maximal; maximum (effect).

mayonnaise [majɔnɛz] *nf Cu:* mayonnaise.

mazout [mazut] *nm* (fuel) oil; **chauffage central au m.,** oil-fired central heating.

Mᵉ *abbr Jur:* Maître.

me [m(ə)] *before a vowel sound* **m',** *pers pron* (*a*) (*acc*) me; **il m'aime,** he loves me; **me voici,** here I am (*b*) (*with pr vbs*) myself; **je me suis dit que,** I said to myself that.

méandre [meɑ̃dr] *nm* meander (of river); winding (of road).

mec [mɛk] *nm P:* chap, guy, bloke.

mécanicien, -ienne [mekanisjɛ̃, -jɛn] **1.** *n* (*a*) (garage) mechanic; **m. dentiste,** dental mechanic (*b*) *Nau:* engineer; *Rail:* engine driver, *NAm:* engineer; *Av:* **m. de bord, m. navigant,** flight engineer **2.** *nf* **mécanicienne,** machinist (on sewing machine). **mécanique 1.** *a* mechanical; clockwork (toy); **industries mécaniques,** mechanical engineering industries **2.** *nf* (*a*) mechanics (*b*) engineering (*c*) mechanism, piece of machinery. **mécaniquement** *adv* mechanically.

mécanisation [mekanizasjɔ̃] *nf* mechanization.

mécaniser [mekanize] *vtr* to mechanize.

mécanisme [mekanism] *nm* **1.** mechanism, machinery; works **2.** working; technique.

mécanographie [mekanɔgrafi] *nf* (*a*) data processing (*b*) data processing department.

méchanceté [meʃɑ̃ste] *nf* **1.** (*a*) wickedness, mischievousness (*b*) unkindness, spitefulness; **faire qch par m.,** to do sth out of spite **2.** spiteful act, remark;

quelle m.! what a nasty thing to do, to say! **méchant, -ante** *a* (*a*) unpleasant, disagreeable; **être de méchante humeur**, to be in a (bad) temper (*b*) spiteful, malicious, unkind (pers) (*c*) (*of pers*) wicked, evil; (*of child*) naughty, mischievous; *n* **petit m.!** you naughty boy! **les méchants**, the wicked; (*in films*) the bad guys (*d*) vicious (animal); *PN*: **chien m.** = beware of the dog. **méchamment** *adv* (*a*) spitefully, maliciously (*b*) mischievously.

mèche [mɛʃ] *nf* **1.** (*a*) wick (*b*) fuse (of mine); *F*: **vendre la m.**, to give the game away **2.** lock (of hair); **m. postiche**, hairpiece **3.** *Tls*: bit, drill.

mécompte [mekɔ̃t] *nm* **1.** miscalculation; error **2.** mistaken judgment; disappointment; **il a eu un grave m.**, he's been badly let down.

méconnaissance [mekɔnɛsɑ̃s] *nf* failure to recognize (s.o.'s talent); misreading (of the facts); ignoring (one's obligations).

méconnaître [mekɔnɛtr] *vtr* (*conj like* CONNAÎTRE) to fail to recognize; to fail to appreciate (s.o.'s talent); to disregard (duty); **m. les faits**, to ignore the facts. **méconnaissable** *a* hardly recognizable, unrecognizable. **méconnu** *a* unrecognized, unappreciated; misunderstood.

mécontentement [mekɔ̃tɑ̃tmɑ̃] *nm* dissatisfaction (**de**, with); displeasure (**de**, at); discontent; annoyance. **mécontent, -ente 1.** *a* discontented, dissatisfied (**de**, with); **il est m. de ce que vous avez dit**, he's annoyed with what you said **2.** *n* malcontent.

mécontenter [mekɔ̃tɑ̃te] *vtr* to dissatisfy, displease, annoy (s.o.).

Mecque (la) [lamɛk] *Prnf Geog:* Mecca.

médaille [medaj] *nf* **1.** medal; **le revers de la m.**, the other side of the picture **2.** (official) badge. **médaillé, -ée 1.** *a* holding a medal **2.** *n* medal-holder.

médaillon [medajɔ̃] *nm* medallion; locket.

médecin [medsɛ̃] *nm* doctor, physician; **femme m.**, woman doctor; **m. généraliste**, general practitioner; GP; **m. consultant**, consultant; **m. légiste**, forensic pathologist; **m. militaire**, army medical officer.

médecine [medsin] *nf* (art of) medicine; **m. générale**, general practice; **m. légale**, forensic medicine; **m. du travail**, industrial medicine.

media [medja] *nmpl* media.

médiateur, -trice [medjatœr, -tris] *n* mediator; intermediary.

médiation [medjasjɔ̃] *nf* mediation.

médical, -aux [medikal, -o] *a* medical. **médicalement** *adv* medically.

médicament [medikamɑ̃] *nm* medicine, drug.

médicinal, -aux [medisinal, -o] *a* medicinal.

médiéval, -aux [medjeval, -o] *a* medi(a)eval.

médiocrité [medjɔkrite] *nf* mediocrity; **les médiocrités**, second-raters. **médiocre** *a* mediocre; second-rate, moderate (ability); **vin m.**, poor wine. **médiocrement** *adv* indifferently, poorly.

médire [medir] *vi* (*conj like* DIRE, *except pr ind and imp* **médisez**) **m. de qn**, to speak ill of s.o.; to slander s.o.; to run s.o. down.

médisance [medizɑ̃s] *nf* (*a*) slander; scandalmongering (*b*) (piece of) scandal, slander. **médisant, -ante 1.** *a* slanderous **2.** *n* slanderer, scandalmonger.

méditation [meditasjɔ̃] *nf* meditation; **plongé dans la m.**, lost in thought. **méditatif, -ive** *a* meditative, thoughtful.

méditer [medite] **1.** *vi* to meditate, to muse **2.** *vtr* to contemplate, meditate (on) (sth); to have (an idea) in mind.

Méditerranée (la mer) [lamɛrmediterane] *Prnf Geog:* the Mediterranean (Sea). **méditerranéen, -enne** *a* Mediterranean.

médium [medjɔm] *nm Psychics:* medium.

méduse [medyz] *nf* jellyfish.

méduser [medyze] *vtr F:* to petrify; to paralyse, stupefy.

meeting [mitiŋ] *nm Pol: Sp:* meeting, rally; **m. d'aviation**, air show.

méfait [mefɛ] *nm* misdeed; misdemeanour; **méfaits d'un orage**, storm damage.

méfiance [mefjɑ̃s] *nf* distrust; mistrust; suspicion; **avec m.**, distrustfully; **sans m.**, unsuspectingly. **méfiant, -ante** *a* distrustful, suspicious.

méfier (se) [səmefje] *vpr* (*impf & pr sub* **n. n. méfiions**) (*a*) **se m. de qn**, to distrust, mistrust, s.o.; **méfiez-vous des voleurs**, beware of pickpockets (*b*) to be on one's guard.

mégalomanie [megalɔmani] *nf* megalomania. **mégalomane** *a & n* megalomaniac.

mégarde (par) [parmegard] *adv phr* inadvertently; accidentally; by mistake.

mégère [meʒɛr] *nf* shrew, termagant.

mégot [mego] *nm F:* cigarette end; fag end; butt (of cigar).

meilleur [mɛjœr] *a* **1.** (*comp of* **bon**) better; **rendre qch m.**, to improve sth; **je ne connais rien de m.**, I don't know anything better; **de meilleure heure**, earlier; **m. marché**, cheaper; *adv* **il fait m.**, the weather's better **2.** (*sup of* **bon**) (*a*) **le meilleur**, (i) the better (of two) (ii) the best; **m. ami**, best friend (*b*) *n* **que le m. gagne**, may the best man win; **pour le m. et pour le pire**, for better (or) for worse; *Sp*: **prendre le m. sur qn**, to get the better of s.o.

mélancolie [melɑ̃kɔli] *nf* melancholy, dejection, gloom. **mélancolique** *a* melancholy, gloomy.

mélange [melɑ̃ʒ] *nm* **1.** mixing; blending (of tea); crossing (of breeds) **2.** mixture; blend; cross (of breeds); miscellany; mix (of cement); **sans m.**, unmixed, unadulterated; **m. détonant**, explosive mixture.

mélanger [melɑ̃ʒe] *vtr* (**n. mélangeons**) **1.** to mix, to mingle; to blend (teas); **m. tous les dossiers**, to mix up all the files **2. se m.**, to mix, mingle, blend.

mélasse [melas] *nf* molasses, treacle; **m. raffinée**, golden syrup; *F*: **être dans la m.**, to be in the soup, in a mess.

mêlée [mele] *nf* (*a*) conflict; fray, mêlée (*b*) *F:* scuffle, tussle, free-for-all (*c*) *Rugby Fb:* scrum.

mêler [mele] *vtr* **1.** (*a*) to mix, mingle, blend; **il est mêlé à tout**, he's got a finger in every pie (*b*) to mix up; jumble up, muddle (up) (papers); to tangle (hair); to confuse; to shuffle (cards); *F:* **vous avez bien mêlé les cartes!** a nice mess you've made of it! (*c*) **m. qn à qch**, to involve s.o. in sth; **m. qn à la conversation**, to bring s.o. into the conversation **2. se m.**, to mix, mingle, blend; **se m. à la foule**, to lose oneself in the crowd; **se m. à la conversation**, to join in the conversation; **mêlez-vous de ce qui vous regarde**, mind your own business; **se m. de politique,** to dabble in politics.

nélèze [melɛz] *nm* larch (tree).

néli-mélo [melimelo] *nm F:* muddle; jumble; hotchpotch.

nélodie [melɔdi] *nf* melody, tune. **mélodieux, -euse** *a* melodious, tuneful. **mélodieusement** *adv* melodiously, tunefully. **mélodique** *a* melodic.

nélodrame [melɔdram] *nm* melodrama. **mélodramatique** *a* melodramatic.

nélomane [melɔman] *n* music lover; **être m.,** to be music-mad.

nelon [məlɔ̃] *nm* **1.** *Bot:* melon **2. (chapeau) m.,** bowler (hat).

nembrane [mãbran] *nf* **1.** *Anat:* membrane **2.** *Rec:* diaphragm.

nembre [mãbr] *nm* **1.** (*a*) limb; member (*b*) member (of a club, a society, a family); *pl* membership **2.** *Ling: Mth:* member.

nembrure [mãbryr] *nf* (*a*) *coll* limbs; **homme à forte m.,** powerfully built man (*b*) frame(work) (of building).

nême [mɛm] **1.** *a* (*a*) same; **être du m. âge,** to be of the same age; **ce m. jour,** that same day; **en m. lieu,** in the same place; **en m. temps,** at the same time; **cela revient au m.,** it comes to the same thing (*b*) (*following the noun*) very; **aujourd'hui m.,** this very day; **c'est cela m.,** that's the very thing (*c*) self; **elle est la bonté m.,** she's kindness itself; **moi-m.,** myself; **lui-m.,** himself, itself; **elle-m.,** herself, itself; **vous-m.,** yourself; **vous-mêmes,** yourselves; **eux-mêmes, elles-mêmes,** themselves **2.** *adv* even; **m. si je le savais,** even if I knew **3. de m.,** in the same way; **faire de m.,** to do likewise; **il en est de m. des autres,** the same holds good for the others; **de m. que,** (just) as, like; **tout de m.,** all the same; for all that; **boire à m. la bouteille,** to drink straight out of the bottle; **des maisons bâties à m. le trottoir,** houses built flush with the pavement; **couché à m. la terre,** lying on the bare ground; **taillé à m. la pierre,** cut out of solid rock; **à m. la peau,** next to the skin; **être à m. de faire qch,** to be able to do sth; to be in a position to do sth; **il n'est pas à m. de faire ce voyage,** he's not up to making the journey.

némé [meme] *nf F:* grandma, gran(ny).

némère [memɛr] *nf F:* **1.** grandma, gran(ny) **2.** *Pej:* (blousy) middle-aged woman.

némoire¹ [memwar] *nf* (*a*) memory; **il n'a pas de m.,** he's got a bad memory; **si j'ai bonne m.,** if I remember rightly (*b*) recollection, remembrance; **garder la m. de qch,** to keep sth in mind; **rappeler qch à la m. de qn,** to remind s.o. of sth; **j'ai eu un trou de m.,** my mind went blank; **réciter qch de m.,** to recite sth from memory; **de m. d'homme,** within living memory.

némoire² *nm* **1.** (*a*) memorial; (written) statement; report (*b*) paper, thesis **2.** (contractor's) account; bill (of costs) **3.** *pl* (autobiographical) memoirs.

némorable [memɔrabl̩] *a* memorable; eventful (year).

némorandum [memɔrãdɔm] *nm* **1.** memorandum, note **2.** notebook.

némoriser [memɔrize] *vtr* to memorize.

nenace [mənas] *nf* threat, menace.

nenacer [mənase] *vtr* (**n. menaçons**) to threaten, menace; **m. qn du poing,** to shake one's fist at s.o.; **m. de faire qch,** to threaten to do sth; **la tempête menace,** a storm is brewing. **menaçant** *a* threatening, menacing.

ménage [menaʒ] *nm* **1.** (*a*) housekeeping; **tenir le m.,** to keep house; **pain de m.,** large (homemade) loaf (*b*) **faire le m.,** to do the housework; **faire des ménages,** to go out cleaning; **femme de m.,** cleaner, daily (help) **2.** **monter son m.,** to furnish one's house **3.** household, family; **jeune m.,** young (married) couple; **se mettre en m.,** to set up house; **faire bon, mauvais, m. (ensemble),** to live happily, unhappily, together; **scènes de m.,** domestic rows.

ménagement [menaʒmã] *nm* caution, care; consideration; **avec ménagement(s),** carefully, cautiously; tactfully; **parler sans ménagement(s),** to speak bluntly, tactlessly.

ménager¹ [menaʒe] *vtr* (**n. ménageons**) **1.** (*a*) to save; to economize on (sth); to use (sth) sparingly; **m. sa santé,** to take care of one's health; **m. qn,** to deal tactfully with s.o.; **ne le ménagez pas,** don't spare him; **sans m. ses paroles,** without mincing one's words (*b*) to contrive, arrange; **m. une surprise à qn,** to prepare a surprise for s.o.; **m. une sortie,** to provide an exit **2. se m.,** to spare oneself, to take care of oneself.

ménager², -ère [menaʒe, -ɛr] **1.** *a* (*a*) household (equipment); **travaux ménagers,** housework; **arts ménagers,** domestic science; **eaux ménagères,** waste water; **Salon des Arts ménagers** = Ideal Home Exhibition (*b*) housewifely (virtues, duties) **2.** *nf* (*a*) housewife; **elle est bonne ménagère,** she's a good housekeeper (*b*) canteen of cutlery.

ménagerie [menaʒri] *nf* menagerie.

mendiant, -ante [mãdjã, -ãt] *n* beggar.

mendicité [mãdisite] *nf* begging.

mendier [mãdje] *v* (*impf & pr sub* **n. mendiions**) **1.** *vi* to beg **2.** *vtr* to beg (for) (sth).

menée [məne] *nf* intrigue; *pl* (political) schemings; **déjouer les menées de qn,** to outwit s.o.

mener [məne] *vtr* (**je mène**) **1.** (*a*) to lead; **m. qn à sa chambre,** to take, show, s.o. to his room (*b*) to be, go, ahead (of); *Fig:* **m. la danse,** to call the tune; **m. le deuil,** to be chief mourner; *Games:* **m. par huit points,** to lead by eight points (*c*) **cela ne mène à rien,** this is getting us nowhere; **cela nous mène à croire que,** that leads us to believe that (*d*) to control, manage; **mari mené par sa femme,** henpecked husband **2.** to drive (horse); to steer (boat) **3.** to manage, conduct (business); **m. une campagne,** to conduct a campaign (**contre,** against); **m. qch à bien,** to bring sth to a successful conclusion; **m. une vie tranquille,** to lead a quiet life.

ménestrel [menɛstrɛl] *nm* minstrel.

meneur, -euse [mənœr, -øz] *n* (*a*) leader; **m. du jeu,** (i) moving spirit (ii) *TV:* quiz master; compère (*b*) ringleader; agitator.

menhir [menir] *nm* menhir; standing stone.

méninge [menɛ̃ʒ] *nf Anat:* meninx, *pl* meninges; *F:* **se creuser les méninges,** to rack one's brains.

méningite [menɛ̃ʒit] *nf Med:* meningitis.

ménopause [menɔpoz] *nf* menopause.

menotte [mənɔt] *nf* **1.** (*child's language*) little hand; handy **2.** *pl* handcuffs.

mensonge [mãsɔ̃ʒ] *nm* (*a*) lie; *F:* fib; **petit m., m. innocent,** white lie (*b*) lying. **mensonger, -ère** *a* lying; untrue, false; deceitful.

menstruation [mɑ̃stryasjɔ̃] *nf* menstruation.

mensualiser [mɑ̃sɥalize] *vtr* to pay (staff) monthly.

mensualité [mɑ̃sɥalite] *nf* monthly payment. mensuel, -elle 1. *a* monthly 2. *nm* (*a*) monthly magazine (*b*) employee paid monthly. mensuellement *adv* monthly.

mensuration [mɑ̃syrasjɔ̃] *nf* measurement; measuring; *F:* (*of woman*) mensurations, vital statistics.

mentalité [mɑ̃talite] *nf* mentality. mental, -aux *a* mental. mentalement *adv* mentally.

menteur, -euse [mɑ̃tœr, -øz] 1. *a* (*a*) lying (person) (*b*) false, deceptive (appearance) 2. *n* liar.

menthe [mɑ̃t] *nf Bot:* mint; m. verte, spearmint, garden mint; m. anglaise, poivrée, peppermint; pastilles de m., (pepper)mints.

mention [mɑ̃sjɔ̃] *nf* (*a*) mention; faire m. de qn, to refer to, to mention, s.o.; *Sch:* reçu avec m. = passed with distinction (*b*) *Post:* endorsement; m. *inconnu*, endorsed *not known* (*c*) reference (at head of letter).

mentionner [mɑ̃sjɔne] *vtr* to mention.

mentir [mɑ̃tir] *vi* (*prp* mentant; *pr ind* je mens) to lie; to tell lies; sans m.! honestly! m. à sa réputation, to belie one's reputation.

menton [mɑ̃tɔ̃] *nm* chin.

menu [məny] 1. *a* (*a*) small; fine (gravel); slender, slight (figure); tiny; menue monnaie, small change (*b*) trifling; petty; menus détails, minute, small, details; menus frais, minor expenses 2. *adv* small, fine; hacher m., to chop up small; to mince; écrire m., to write small 3. *nm* (*a*) raconter qch par le m., to relate sth in detail (*b*) (*in restaurant*) menu.

menuiserie [mənɥizri] *nf* 1. joinery, woodwork, carpentry 2. joiner's shop.

menuisier [mənɥizje] *nm* joiner; m. en meubles, cabinet maker; m. en bâtiments, carpenter.

méprendre (se) [səmeprɑ̃dr] *vpr* (*conj like* PRENDRE) to be mistaken, to make a mistake (sur, quant à, about); il n'y a pas à s'y m., there can be no mistake about it.

mépris [mepri] *nm* contempt, scorn; avoir du m. pour qn, to despise s.o.; au m. de qch, in defiance of sth; avec m., scornfully, contemptuously.

méprise [mepriz] *nf* mistake, misapprehension.

mépriser [meprize] *vtr* to despise, scorn; to hold (s.o., sth) in contempt. méprisable *a* contemptible, despicable. méprisant *a* contemptuous, scornful.

mer [mɛr] *nf* (*a*) sea; la haute m., the open sea; en haute m., en pleine m., out at sea; m. d'huile, sea as smooth as a millpond; au bord de la m., at the seaside; gens de m., seamen; partir à la m., to go to the seaside; partir en m., to go to sea; mal de m., seasickness; grosse m., heavy sea; un homme à la m.! man overboard! sur m., afloat; prendre la m., to put (out) to sea; mettre une embarcation à la m., to lower a boat; *F:* ce n'est pas la m. à boire, it's quite easy (*b*) basse m., low water; m. haute, high tide.

mercenaire [mɛrsənɛr] *a* & *n* mercenary.

mercerie [mɛrsəri] *nf* (*a*) haberdashery, *NAm:* notions (*b*) haberdasher's shop, *NAm:* notions store.

merci [mɛrsi] 1. *adv* (*a*) m. (bien, beaucoup), thank you (very much) (*b*) no thank you; prenez-vous du thé?—(non) m.! will you have some tea?—no, thank you 2. *nm* thank(-)you 3. *nf* mercy; à la m. de qn, at s.o.'s mercy; sans m., merciless(ly).

mercier, -ière [mɛrsje, -jɛr] *n* haberdasher.

mercredi [mɛrkrədi] *nm* Wednesday; le m. des Cendres, Ash Wednesday.

mercure [mɛrkyr] *nm Ch:* mercury.

merde [mɛrd] *nf P:* 1. shit; il est dans la m., he's in hell of a mess 2. *int* shit! bloody hell!

mère [mɛr] *nf* 1. (*a*) mother; m. de famille, mother, housewife; m. célibataire, unmarried mother (*b*) *F:* m. Dupont, old Mrs Dupont (*c*) *Ecc:* M. supérieu, Mother Superior 2. (*a*) la reine m., the Queen Moth (*b*) *Com:* maison m., parent company.

mère-patrie [mɛrpatri] *nf* mother country; *pl* mère patries.

méridien, -ienne [meridjɛ̃, -jɛn] *a* & *nm* meridia

méridional, -aux [meridjɔnal, -o] 1. *a* south(ern) *n* southerner; southern Frenchman.

meringue [mərɛ̃g] *nf Cu:* meringue.

mérinos [merinos] *nm* merino (sheep, cloth).

merise [məriz] *nf* wild cherry.

merisier [mərizje] *nm* wild cherry (tree).

mérite [merit] *nm* (*a*) merit; worth; chose de peu de m thing of little worth, value; s'attribuer le m. de qch, take the credit for sth (*b*) excellence, talent; homme m., man of talent, of ability.

mériter [merite] *vtr* 1. to deserve, merit; il n'a q ce qu'il mérite, he's got what he deserves; it serv him right; cela mérite d'être vu, it's worth seeing voilà ce qui lui a mérité cette renommée, that is wh earned him this fame. méritoire *a* meritorio deserving.

merlan [mɛrlɑ̃] *nm Ich:* whiting.

merle [mɛrl] *nm Orn:* blackbird.

merlu(s) [mɛrly] *nm Ich:* hake.

merluche [mɛrlyʃ] *nf* 1. *Ich:* hake 2. *Cu:* dri (unsalted) cod.

merveille [mɛrvɛj] *nf* marvel, wonder; faire m., d merveilles, to work wonders; à m., excellently; porter à m., to be in excellent health. merveilleu -euse 1. *a* marvellous, wonderful 2. *nm* le m., supernatural. merveilleusement *adv* marv lously, wonderfully.

mes *see* mon.

mésalliance [mezaljɑ̃s] *nf* misalliance; faire une n to marry beneath oneself.

mésange [mezɑ̃ʒ] *nf Orn:* tit; m. bleue, bluetit.

mésaventure [mezavɑ̃tyr] *nf* misadventure, misha

mesdames, -demoiselles *see* madame, m demoiselle.

mésentente [mezɑ̃tɑ̃t] *nf* misunderstanding, d agreement.

mésestimer [mezɛstime] *vtr* 1. to underestima undervalue, underrate 2. to have a poor opinion (s.o.).

mesquinerie [mɛskinri] *nf* 1. meanness (*a*) pettin (*b*) niggardliness 2. mean trick. mesquin *a* mean, shabby (appearance); paltry, petty (excuse) (*of pers*) mean, stingy. mesquinement *a* meanly.

mess [mɛs] *nm Mil:* mess.

message [mesaʒ] *nm* message.

messager, -ère [mesaʒe, -ɛr] *n* messenger.

messagerie [mesaʒri] *nf* carrying trade; messager maritimes, (i) sea transport of goods (ii) shipping lin

messe [mɛs] *nf Ecc:* mass.

messeigneurs *see* monseigneur.
Messie [mesi] *Prnm* Messiah.
messieurs *see* monsieur.
mesure [məzyr] *nf* 1. (a) prendre les mesures de qn, to take s.o.'s measurements; prendre la m. de qn, to size s.o. up; donner sa m., to show what one is capable of; être à la m. de qn, to measure up to s.o.; dans une certaine m., to a certain degree; dans la m. où, insofar as; dans la m. du possible, de mes moyens, as far as possible, as best I can; (au fur et) à m., in proportion; successively; one by one; à m. que, (in proportion) as; à m. que je reculais il s'avançait, as (fast as) I retreated he advanced (b) prendre des mesures, to take action; prendre des mesures contre qch, to make provision against sth; prendre ses mesures, to make one's arrangements; par m. d'économie, as a measure of economy 2. (a) gauge, standard; m. de longueur, measure of length; poids et mesures, weights and measures (b) (*quantity measured out*) une m. de vin, a measure of wine 3. required size, amount; dépasser la m., to overstep the mark; rester dans la juste m., to keep within bounds; être en m. de faire qch, to be in a position to do sth 4. *Mus:* (a) bar (b) time; battre la m., to beat time; en m., in (strict) time. mesurable *a* measurable. mesuré *a* measured (tread); temperate, restrained, moderate (language).

mesurer [məzyre] *vtr* 1. (a) to measure (dimensions, quantity); to measure out (wheat); to measure up (land); to measure off (cloth); m. qn des yeux, to take a customer's measurements; m. qn des yeux, to look s.o. up and down (b) (*of pers*) m. deux mètres, to be two metres tall; la colonne mesure dix mètres, the column is ten metres high (c) m. la nourriture à qn, to ration s.o.'s food (d) to calculate; to weigh (one's words); to size (s.o.) up; m. la distance, to judge, estimate, the distance 2. se m. avec, à, qn, to measure one's strength against s.o.; to pit oneself against s.o.

métabolisme [metabolism] *nm* metabolism.
métairie [meteri] *nf* small farm (held on a sharecropping agreement).
métal, -aux [metal, -o] *nm* metal. métallique *a* metallic. métallisé *a* metallic (paint).
métallurgie [metalyrʒi] *nf* metallurgy. métallurgique *a* metallurgic.
métallurgiste [metalyrʒist] *nm* (a) metallurgist (b) metalworker.
métamorphose [metamɔrfoz] *nf* metamorphosis.
métamorphoser [metamɔrfoze] *vtr* 1. to metamorphose, transform 2. se m., to change completely; to be transformed.
métaphore [metafɔr] *nf* metaphor; figure of speech. métaphorique *a* metaphorical. métaphoriquement *adv* metaphorically.
métayage [metɛjaʒ] *nm Agr:* sharecropping.
météo [meteo] *F:* 1. *nf* (a) weather forecast, report (b) met(eorological) office 2. *nm* Monsieur M., the weather man.
météore [meteɔr] *nm* meteor. météorique *a* meteoric.
météorite [meteɔrit] *nm or f* meteorite.
météorologie [meteɔrɔlɔʒi] *nf* meteorology. météorologique *a* meteorological; bulletin m., weather report, forecast; station, navire, m., weather station, ship.

météorologiste [meteɔrɔlɔʒist], météorologue [meteɔrɔlɔg] *n* meteorologist.
métèque [metɛk] *nm F: Pej:* foreigner; dago, wog.
méthane [metan] *nm Ch:* methane.
méthode [metɔd] *nf* 1. method, system, way; elle a sa m., she has her own way of doing things; il a beaucoup de m., he's very methodical; avec, sans, m., methodical(ly), unmethodical(ly) 2. primer; m. de piano, piano tutor. méthodique *a* methodical, systematic. méthodiquement *adv* methodically, systematically.
méticuleux, -euse [metikylø, -øz] *a* meticulous, punctilious; scrupulous (care). méticuleusement *adv* meticulously.
métier [metje] *nm* 1. trade, profession, craft, occupation, business; quel est votre m.? what do you do (for a living)? what's your job? gens de m., professionals, experts; il est charpentier de son m., he's a carpenter by trade; tours de m., tricks of the trade; parler m., to talk shop; terme de m., technical term; risques de m., occupational hazards; *F:* quel m.! what a life! 2. *Tex:* (a) m. à tisser, loom (b) m. à tapisserie, à broder, tapestry frame, embroidery frame.
métis, -isse [metis] 1. *a* (*of pers*) halfcaste; *Pej:* halfbred; (*of animal*) crossbred; mongrel (dog); hybrid (plant) 2. *n* (*of pers*) halfcaste; (*animal*) crossbreed; mongrel 3. *a & nm* (*tissu*) m., linen-cotton mixture.
métrage [metraʒ] *nm* 1. measurement 2. (metric) length; *Cin:* footage, length (of film).
mètre[1] [mɛtr] *nm Pros:* metre.
mètre[2] *nm* 1. *Meas:* metre; m. carré, cube, square, cubic, metre 2. (metre) rule; m. pliant, folding rule; m. à ruban, tape measure. métrique *a* metric.
métrer [metre] *vtr* (je mètre) 1. to measure (by the metre) 2. *Const:* to survey (for quantities).
métreur, -euse [metrœr, -øz] *n* quantity surveyor.
métro [metro] *nm* underground (railway); *NAm:* subway; le m. de Londres, the underground, *F:* the tube.
métronome [metronɔm] *nm Mus:* metronome.
métropole [metrɔpɔl] *nf* (a) capital city (b) mother country (c) (archbishop's) see.
mets [mɛ] *nm* dish (of food).
mettable [mɛtabl] *a* (*of clothes*) wearable.
metteur [mɛtœr] *nm* m. en scène, (i) *Th:* producer (ii) *Cin:* director; *WTel:* m. en ondes, producer.
mettre [mɛtr] *vtr* (*pp* mis; *pr ind* je mets, il met; *ph* je mis; *fu* je mettrai) 1. (a) to put, lay, place, set; m. la table, le couvert, to lay the table; m. qn à la porte, (i) to throw s.o. out (ii) to sack s.o.; *Games:* m. un enjeu, to lay a stake; m. dans le mille, to get a bull's eye; qu'est-ce qui vous a mis cela dans la tête? what put that into your head? m. le feu à qch, to set sth on fire; j'y mettrai tous mes soins, I will give the matter my full attention; m. du temps à faire qch, to take time over sth (b) to put on (clothes); qu'est-ce que je vais m.? what shall I wear? je n'ai rien à me m., I haven't got anything to wear; j'ai du mal à m. mes chaussures, I find it difficult to get my shoes on (c) m. du linge à sécher, to hang the washing out to dry; m. de l'eau à chauffer, to put some water on to heat 2. to set, put (in a condition); to put on, turn on (gas, television); m. une machine en mouvement, to set a machine going; m. la télé plus

fort, to turn up the telly; **m. en vente une maison,** to put a house up for sale; **m. le réveil à cinq heures,** to set the alarm for five o'clock; *Nau:* **m. à la voile,** to set sail **3.** *(a)* to admit, grant; **mettons que vous ayez raison,** suppose you're right; **mettons cent francs,** let's call it a hundred francs *(b)* **mettez que je n'ai rien dit,** consider that unsaid **4. se m.** *(a)* to go, get; **se m. au lit,** to go to, to get into, bed; **se m. à table,** to sit down at (the) table; **mettez-vous près du feu,** sit down by the fire; **je ne savais où me m.,** I didn't know where to (i) go, stand, sit (ii) *Fig:* put myself *(b)* to begin, start, set about (sth); **se m. au travail,** to set to work; **il est temps de s'y m.,** we'd better get down to it, get on with it; **se m. à rire,** to start laughing; **il s'est mis à boire,** he's taken to drink; **il s'est mis à pleuvoir,** it began to rain *(c)* to dress; **se m. en smoking,** to put on a dinner jacket *(d)* **se m. en rage,** to get into a rage; **se m. en route,** to set off *(e)* **le temps se met au beau, à la pluie,** the weather is turning out fine; it's turning to rain.

meuble [mœbl] **1.** *a (a)* movable *(b)* terre **m.,** light, loose, soil **2.** *nm* piece of furniture; *pl* furniture; **être dans ses meubles,** to have a home of one's own.

meubler [mœble] *vtr* **1.** to furnish; to stock (farm, cellar) (de, with); **m. ses loisirs,** to occupy, fill up, one's free time; **m. la conversation,** to stimulate the conversation **2. se m.,** to furnish one's home. **meublé 1.** *a* furnished (room); **non m.,** unfurnished; **cave bien meublée,** well stocked cellar **2.** *nm* furnished room, flat, apartment(s); **habiter en m.,** to live in a furnished flat.

meuglement [mœgləmɑ̃] *nm* mooing (of cow).
meugler [mœgle] *vi (of cow)* to moo.

meule [mœl] *nf* **1.** *(a)* millstone *(b)* **m. à aiguiser,** grindstone; **m. à polir,** buff(ing) wheel *(c)* **m. de fromage,** round cheese **2.** stack, rick (of hay); **m. de foin,** haystack.

meunier, -ière [mønje, -jɛr] **1.** *nm* miller **2.** *nf* miller's wife **3.** *a* milling (plant).

meurtre [mœrtr̩] *nm Jur:* murder; **au m.!** murder! **meurtrier, -ière 1.** *a* murderous; deadly (weapon) **2.** *n* murderer, *f* murderess **3.** *nf Fort:* meurtrière, loophole.

meurtrir [mœrtrir] *vtr* to bruise; **être tout meurtri,** to be black and blue all over.

meurtrissure [mœrtrisyr] *nf* bruise.

meute [møt] *nf (a)* pack (of hounds) *(b)* mob (of pursuers).

Mexico [mɛksiko] *Prn Geog:* Mexico City.
Mexique [mɛksik] *Prnm Geog:* Mexico (state). **mexicain, -aine** *a & n Geog:* Mexican.

Mgr *abbr Monseigneur.*

mi¹ [mi] *adv* half, mid-, semi-; **la mi-avril,** mid-April; **à mi-hauteur,** halfway up, down.

mi² *nm inv Mus:* (a) (the note) E *(b)* mi (in the Fixed Do system).

miaou [mjau] *nm* miaow, mew (of cat).

miaulement [mjolmɑ̃] *nm* mewing, miaowing; caterwauling.

miauler [mjole] *vi* to mew, to miaow; to caterwaul.

mica [mika] *nm* mica.

mi-carême [mikarɛm] *nf* mid-Lent; *pl mi-carêmes.*

miche [miʃ] *nf* round loaf, cob loaf.

micheline [miʃlin] *nf* railcar.

mi-chemin (à) [amiʃmɛ̃] *adv phr* halfway, midway.

mi-clos [miklo] *adv* half-closed, half-shut (eyes, shutters); *pl mi-clos(es).*

micmac [mikmak] *nm F:* (a) scheming; intrigue *(b)* fuss, carry-on.

mi-corps (à) [amikɔr] *adv phr* to the waist; **saisi à mi-c.,** caught round the waist; **portrait à mi-c.,** half-length portrait.

mi-côte (à) [amikot] *adv phr* halfway up, down, the hill.

micro [mikro] *nm F:* microphone, mike.

microbe [mikrɔb] *nm* microbe, germ. **microbien, -ienne** *a* microbial, microbic.

microbiologie [mikrɔbjɔlɔʒi] *nf* microbiology.

microcosme [mikrɔkɔsm] *nm* microcosm.

micro-électronique [mikrɔelɛktrɔnik] *nf* micro-electronics.

microfilm [mikrɔfilm] *nm Phot:* microfilm.

microfilmer [mikrɔfilme] *vtr* to microfilm.

microphone [mikrɔfɔn] *nm* microphone, *F:* mike; transmitter, mouthpiece (of telephone); **m. caché,** *F:* bug.

microphotographie [mikrɔfɔtɔgrafi] *nf* **1.** microphotography **2.** microphotograph.

micropoint [mikrɔpwɛ̃] *nm* microdot.

microprocesseur [mikrɔprɔsɛsœr] *nm* microprocessor.

microscope [mikrɔskɔp] *nm* microscope.

microscopie [mikrɔskɔpi] *nf* microscopy. **microscopique** *a* microscopic.

microsillon [mikrɔsijɔ̃] *nm Rec:* **1.** microgroove **2.** (disque) **m.,** long-playing record, L.P.

midi [midi] *nm no pl* **1.** midday, noon, twelve o'clock; **sur le m.,** *F:* **sur les m.,** about noon; **avant m.,** before noon; a.m.; **après m.,** after twelve; p.m.; **m. et demi,** half-past twelve; **chercher m. à quatorze heures,** to look for difficulties where there aren't any **2.** *(a)* south; **chambre au m.,** room facing south *(b)* southern part, south (of country); *esp* **le M. (de la France),** the South of France.

mi-distance (à) [amidistɑ̃s] *adv phr* halfway, midway.

mie [mi] *nf* crumb (of loaf, as opposed to crust).

miel [mjɛl] *nm* honey; **elle était tout sucre et tout m.,** she was all sweet and sugary; **paroles de m.,** honeyed words; **lune de m.,** honeymoon. **mielleux, -euse** *a Pej:* honeyed, sugary (words); bland (smile), unctuous (pers). **mielleusement** *adv* unctuously.

mien, mienne [mjɛ̃, mjɛn] *(a) poss pron* **le m., la mienne, les miens, les miennes,** mine; **un de vos amis et des miens,** a friend of yours and mine *(b) nm* (i) my own (property); mine; **le m. et le tien,** mine and your(s) (ii) *nmpl* **j'ai été renié par les miens,** I have been disowned by my own people.

miette [mjɛt] *nf (a)* crumb (of broken bread) *(b)* morsel, scrap; **mettre un vase en miettes,** to smash a vase to smithereens.

mieux [mjø] *adv* **1.** *comp (a)* better; **il faut m. les surveiller,** you must watch them more closely; **vous feriez m. de m'écouter,** you'd do better to listen to me; *Prov:* **m. vaut tard que jamais,** better late than never; **ça va m.,** things are improving; **pour m. dire,** to be more exact; **pour ne pas dire m.,** to say the least (of it); **de m. en m.,** better and better; **(faire qch) à qui m. m.,** to vie with one another (in doing sth) *(b) (with a)* *function*) (i) **c'est on ne peut m.**, it couldn't be better (ii) **vous serez m. dans ce fauteuil**, you will be more comfortable in this armchair (iii) **il est m.**, he's (feeling) better (iv) **il est m. que son frère**, he's better-looking than his brother (c) *nm* (i) **le m. est l'ennemi du bien**, leave well alone; **faute de m.**, for want of something better; **je ne demande pas m.**, I shall be delighted; **j'avais espéré m.**, I had hoped for better things (ii) *Med:* **un m.**, an improvement 2. *sup* (a) **le m.**, (the) best; **la femme le m. habillée de Paris**, the best-dressed woman in Paris (b) (*with adj function*) (i) **ce qu'il y a de m. à faire, c'est de**, the best thing to do is to; **c'est tout ce qu'il y a de m.**, there's absolutely nothing better (ii) **être le m. du monde avec qn**, to be on the best of terms with s.o. (c) *nm* **agir pour le m.**, to act for the best; **au m.**, at best; **faire de son m.**, to do one's best.

mièvrerie [mjɛvrəri] *nf* (insipid) charm, prettiness. **mièvre** *a* (insipidly) pretty; pretty-pretty.

mignard [miɲar] *a* affected.

mignon, -onne [miɲɔ̃, -ɔn] 1. *a* dainty, delicate; sweet, adorable 2. *n* pet, darling.

migraine [migrɛn] *nf* migraine.

migration [migrasjɔ̃] *nf* migration. **migrateur, -trice** *a* migrating; migrant. **migratoire** *a* migratory.

mijaurée [miʒɔre] *nf* conceited, affected, woman.

mijoter [miʒɔte] 1. *vtr Cu:* to simmer (sth), to let (sth) simmer; **m. un projet**, to turn a scheme over in one's mind; **m. un complot**, to hatch a plot 2. *vi Cu:* to simmer.

mil [mil] *a* (*used only in writing out dates* A.D.) thousand; **l'an mil neuf cent trente**, the year 1930.

milice [milis] *nf* militia.

milicien, -ienne [milisjɛ̃, -jɛn] *n* member of a militia; *m* militiaman.

milieu, -eux [miljø] *nm* 1. middle; **au m. de**, in the middle of; *Lit:* amid(st); **au beau m. de la rue**, right in the middle of the street; **au m. du courant**, in midstream; **au m. de la nuit**, at dead of night; **la table du m.**, the middle table 2. (a) *Ph:* medium (b) surroundings, environment; (social) sphere; **les gens de mon m.**, people in my set; **les milieux bien informés**, well informed people, quarters (c) **le m.**, **les gens du m.**, the underworld 3. middle course; mean; **le juste m.**, the happy medium.

militaire [militɛr] 1. *a* military; **service m.**, military service; **camion m.**, army lorry, *NAm:* truck 2. *nm* soldier; **les militaires**, the military, the armed forces.

militarisation [militarizasjɔ̃] *nf* militarization.

militariser [militarize] *vtr* to militarize.

militer [milite] *vi* to militate (**pour**, in favour of; **contre**, against); **cela milite en sa faveur**, that tells in his favour. **militant, -ante** *a & n* militant.

mille¹ [mil] 1. *num a & n & inv inv* (a) thousand; **m. hommes**, a thousand men; **deux m.**, two thousand; **m. un**, a thousand and one (b) countless, many; **je vous l'ai m. dit fois**, I've told you a thousand times; *F:* **il a des m. et des cents**, he has pots of money 2. *nm* bull's eye.

mille² *nm* (a) mile (= 1.609m) (b) **m. (marin)**, nautical mile.

mille(-)feuille [milfœj] *nm Cu:* millefeuille.

millénaire [milenɛr] 1. *a* millennial 2. *nm* millenium.

mille-pattes [milpat] *nm inv* centipede, millipede.

millésime [milezim] *nm* (a) date (on coin) (b) *Ind:* year of manufacture; (*of wine*) year, vintage.

millet [mijɛ] *nm Bot:* millet; **(grains de) m.**, birdseed.

milliard [miljar] *nm* one thousand million, *NAm:* billion. **milliardaire** *a & n* multi-millionaire. **milliardième** *num a & n* one thousand millionth, *NAm:* billionth.

millième [miljɛm] *num a & n* thousandth.

millier [milje] *nm* (about a) thousand; a thousand or so; **des milliers**, thousands.

million [miljɔ̃] *nm* million; **il est riche à millions**, he's a millionaire. **millionième** *num a & n* millionth. **millionnaire** *a & n* millionaire.

mime [mim] *nm* 1. *Th:* mime 2. *n* (*pers*) (a) mime (b) mimic.

mimer [mime] *vtr* 1. *Th:* to mime (a scene) 2. to mimic, to ape (s.o.).

mimique [mimik] *nf* (a) mimicry (b) mime; sign language.

mimosa [mimɔza] *nm* mimosa.

minable [minabl] *a F:* seedy-looking (person); shabby (appearance); **un salaire m.**, miserable, pathetic, salary.

minauder [minode] *vi* to simper, mince.

minauderies [minodri] *nfpl* simpering manner.

minceur [mɛ̃sœr] *nf* thinness; slenderness, slimness; scantiness (of income). **mince** 1. *a* thin; slender, slim (person); scanty (income) 2. *int P:* **m. alors!** (i) well! good heavens! (ii) blast (it)! 3. *adv* thinly.

mine¹ [min] *nf* 1. mine; **m. de houille, de charbon**, coalmine; colliery; pit; **m. d'or**, goldmine; **m. à ciel ouvert**, opencast mine; **ingénieur des Mines**, mining engineer 2. **m. de plomb**, graphite, blacklead; **m. (de crayon)**, (pencil) lead 3. *Mil:* mine; **champ de mines**, minefield.

mine² *nf* 1. appearance, look; **juger les gens sur la m.**, to judge people by appearances; **ça ne paie pas de m.**, it isn't much to look at; **il ne paie pas de m.**, his appearance goes against him; **faire m. d'être fâché**, to pretend to be angry; *F: Iron:* **nous avons bonne m. maintenant!** we *do* look silly! *P:* **m. de rien**, as if nothing had happened 2. (*facial expression*) (a) **avoir bonne, mauvaise, m.**, to look well, ill; **vous avez meilleure m.**, you're looking better; **il a une sale m.**, he *does* look ill; **faire la m.**, to look sulky; **faire grise m. à qn**, to greet s.o. coldly (b) *pl* gestures, expressions (of a baby); *Pej:* **faire des mines**, to simper.

miner [mine] *vtr* 1. to mine, undermine; **miné par l'envie**, consumed with envy 2. to mine (road).

minerai [minrɛ] *nm* ore.

minéral, -aux [mineral, -o] 1. *a* mineral; *Ch:* inorganic; **source minérale**, spa 2. *nm* mineral.

minéralogie [mineralɔʒi] *nf* mineralogy.

minéralogique [mineralɔʒik] *a* 1. mineralogical 2. *Adm:* **numéro m.**, registration number, *NAm:* licence number (of car); **plaque m.**, number plate, *NAm:* licence plate (of car).

minéralogiste [mineralɔʒist] *n* mineralogist.

minet, -ette [minɛ, -ɛt] *n F:* (a) pussy (cat) (b) fashionable young man, young woman.

mineur¹ [minœr] *nm* (a) miner; **m. de houille**, coalminer; **m. de fond**, pitface worker (b) *Mil:* sapper.

mineur², -eure 1. *a* (a) minor, lesser (b) *Jur:* under age (c) *Mus:* minor (key); **en ut m.**, in C minor **2.** *n* minor **3.** *nm Mus:* minor key.

mini [mini] *nf* **1.** *Cl: F:* mini(skirt) **2.** *Aut: Rtm* mini.

miniature [minjatyr] *nf* miniature; **en m.**, in miniature, on a small scale; **golf m.**, miniature golf.

miniaturiste [minjatyrist] *n* miniaturist.

minier, -ière [minje, -jɛr] *a* mining (industry, district).

minimum [minimɔm] **1.** *nm* **réduire les frais au m.**, to reduce expenses to a minimum; **m. vital**, minimum living wage; **thermomètre à minima**, minimum thermometer; *pl* **minima, minimums 2.** *a* **la largeur, les largeurs, minimum(s), minima**, the minimum width(s); **vitesse m.**, minimum speed. **minime** *a* small; trivial; trifling. **minimal, -aux** *a* minimal, minimum (effect).

ministère [minister] *nm* **1.** (a) *A: & Lit:* agency (b) *Ecc:* **le saint m.**, the ministry **2.** *Adm:* (a) ministry; office; **entrer au m.**, to take office (b) **former un m.**, to form a government (c) government department; **M. de l'Intérieur** = Home Office; **M. des Affaires étrangères** = Foreign Office, *U.S:* State Department (d) *Jur:* **le M. public** = the Director of Public Prosecutions. **ministériel, -elle** *a* ministerial; **crise ministérielle**, cabinet crisis.

ministre [ministr] *nm* **1.** (a) *A: & Lit:* servant, agent (b) *Ecc:* minister; clergyman **2.** minister; secretary (of State); **Premier M.**, Prime Minister; **M. de l'Intérieur** = Home Secretary; **M. des Affaires étrangères** = Foreign Secretary, *U.S:* Secretary of State; **M. des Finances** = Chancellor of the Exchequer.

minium [minjɔm] *nm* red lead paint.

minois [minwa] *nm* (pretty) face (of child).

minoration [minɔrasjɔ̃] *nf* decrease.

minorer [minɔre] *vtr* to decrease; to lower, reduce (figure).

minorité [minɔrite] *nf* **1.** *Jur:* minority **2. être er. m.**, to be in the minority; **mettre en m.**, to defeat. **minoritaire 1.** *a* minority (party) **2.** *n* member of a minority.

Minorque [minɔrk] *Prnf Geog:* Minorca.

minoterie [minɔtri] *nf* **1.** (large) flour mill **2.** flour-milling.

minotier [minɔtje] *nm* (flour) miller.

minou [minu] *nm F:* pussy (cat).

minuit [minɥi] *nm* midnight; **m. et demi**, half-past twelve at night.

minus [minys] *nm inv F:* half-wit, moron.

minuscule [minyskyl] *a* (a) small, minute, tiny, minuscule (b) **lettre m.**, *nf* **m.**, small letter.

minutage [minytaʒ] *nm* timing.

minute [minyt] *nf* **1.** minute (of hour, degree); **faire qch à la m.**, to do sth at a moment's notice; **réparations à la m.**, repairs while you wait; *F:* **m. (papillon)!** just a minute! hold on! **2.** *Adm:* minute, draft; record (of deed).

minuter [minyte] *vtr* **1.** to minute, draft (agreement); to record (deed) **2.** to time; **sa journée est soigneusement minutée**, his day is run on a tight schedule.

minuterie [minytri] *nf* (a) **m. d'enregistrement**, counting mechanism (of meter) (b) timer, automatic timeswitch.

minutie [minysi] *nf* **1.** meticulousness; attention to

detail **2.** *pl* trifles, minutiae. **minutieux, -ieuse** scrupulously careful, meticulous (person); minute detailed (inspection, work). **minutieusemen** *adv* minutely; meticulously.

mioche [mjɔʃ] *n F:* child; kid, brat.

mi-pente (à) [amipɑ̃t] *adv phr* halfway up, down the hill.

mirabelle [mirabɛl] *nf* cherry plum.

miracle [mirɑkl] *nm* miracle; **faire un m.**, to perform work, a miracle; **cela tient du m.**, it's miraculous; **pa m.**, miraculously; *a inv* **produit m.**, miracle product **miraculé, -ée** *a & n* miraculously cured (person) **miraculeux, -euse** *a* miraculous; wonderfu **remède m.**, wonder drug. **miraculeusement** *ad* miraculously.

mirador [miradɔr] *nm* **1.** *Mil:* observation post **2** watchtower (of prison camp).

mirage [miraʒ] *nm* mirage.

mire [mir] *nf* **1. ligne de m.**, line of sight; *Sma:* **point d m.**, aim **2.** *TV:* test card.

mirer (se) [səmire] *vpr* to look at, admire oneself; **le arbres se mirent dans l'eau**, the trees are reflected in the water.

mirobolant [mirɔbɔlɑ̃] *a F:* wonderful, fabulous staggering.

miroir [mirwar] *nm* mirror, (looking) glass; **m. au alouettes**, (i) *Ven:* lark mirror (ii) *Fig:* snare.

miroitement [mirwatmɑ̃] *nm* flashing, gleam(ing) glistening; shimmer.

miroiter [mirwate] *vi* to flash; to gleam, to glisten; (o water) to shimmer; (of jewel, lights) to sparkle.

miroiterie [mirwatri] *nf* mirror factory, trade, shop

mis, mise[1] [mi, miz] *a* **bien m.**, well dressed.

misaine [mizɛn] *nf Nau:* **(voile de) m.**, (square foresail.

misanthropie [mizɑ̃trɔpi] *nf* misanthropy. **misanthrope 1.** nm misanthrope **2.** a misanthropic

mise[2] [miz] *nf* **1.** (a) placing; putting; **m. à l'eau** launching (of ship); **m. en bouteilles**, bottling (o wine); **m. à terre**, landing (of goods) (b) **m. er pratique**, carrying out; putting into practice; **m. à jour**, updating; **m. à mort**, kill(ing); **m. en liberté** release; **m. en retraite**, pensioning (off); **m. en garde** warning, caution; **m. en marche**, starting (of engine) *WTel:* **m. en ondes**, production; **m. en plis**, setting (o hair) **2.** dress; **soigner sa m.**, to dress with care **3.** (c *Gaming:* stake (b) bid (at auction); **m. à prix**, reserve price; upset price (c) **m. de fonds**, putting up o money; capital outlay.

miser [mize] *vtr* (a) to stake (**sur**, on); to back (a horse (b) *F:* to bank, count (**sur**, on).

misère [mizɛr] *nf* **1.** (a) misery (b) trouble; **misère domestiques**, domestic worries; **faire des misères à qn** to tease s.o. unmercifully **2.** extreme poverty; destitution; **dans la m.**, poverty-stricken; **crier m.**, to plead poverty **3.** trifle; **cent francs? une m.!** a hundre francs? a mere nothing! **misérable 1.** *a* (a) miserable; unhappy; wretched; poor; **quartier m.**, poverty stricken district (b) wretched, worthless; **pour un m franc**, for a wretched franc **2.** *n* (a) poor wretch (b) *O* scoundrel, wretch. **misérablement** *adv* miserably. **miséreux, -euse 1.** *a* poverty-stricken destitute **2.** *n* down-and-out.

miséricorde [mizerikɔrd] *nf* mercy; **crier m.**, to cry for mercy. **miséricordieux, -ieuse** *a* merciful.

misogynie [mizɔʒini] *nf* misogyny. **misogyne** 1. *a* misogynous 2. *n* misogynist.

miss [mis] *nf F:* beauty queen; **Miss France,** Miss France; *pl* **miss**(es).

missile [misil] *nm* (guided) missile.

mission [misjɔ̃] *nf* mission; **avoir m. de faire qch,** to be commissioned to do sth; *Mil:* **en m.,** on detached service; *Ecc:* **missions étrangères,** foreign missions. **missionnaire** *a & n* missionary.

missive [misiv] *nf* missive, letter.

mistral [mistral] *nm Meteor: (in S.E. France)* mistral.

mite [mit] *nf* 1. mite; **m. du fromage,** cheese mite 2. clothes moth. **mité** *a* motheaten.

mi-temps [mitɑ̃] *nf inv* 1. *Fb: etc:* half-time 2. **emploi à mi-t.,** part-time job.

miteux, -euse [mitø, -øz] 1. *a F:* shabby, tatty (clothes) 2. *n F:* down-at-heel person.

mitigé [mitiʒe] *a* mitigated, modified; *Jur:* **peine mitigée,** reduced sentence.

mitonner [mitone] 1. *vtr* to simmer (soup) 2. *vi (of soup)* to simmer.

mitoyen, -enne [mitwajɛ̃, -jɛn] *a* **mur m.,** party wall.

mitraille [mitraj] *nf (a) AMil:* grapeshot *(b)* hail of bullets.

mitrailler [mitraje] *vtr (a)* to machine-gun *(b)* **m. qn de questions,** to fire questions at s.o.

mitraillette [mitrajɛt] *nf* submachine-gun.

mitrailleuse [mitrajøz] *nf* machine gun.

mitre [mitr] *nf* mitre.

mitron [mitrɔ̃] *nm* baker's boy.

mi-vitesse (à) [amivites] *adv phr* at half speed.

mi-voix (à) [amivwa] *adv phr* in an undertone, under one's breath, in a subdued voice.

mixage [miksaʒ] *nm Cin: etc:* (sound) mixing.

mixe(u)r [miksœr] *nm DomEc:* 1. mixer 2. liquidizer.

mixité [miksite] *nf* co-education.

mixte [mikst] *a* 1. mixed (race, bathing); **commission m.,** joint commission; **école m.,** co-educational school; *nm Ten:* **double m.,** mixed doubles 2. dual-purpose; **train m.,** composite train (goods and passengers); **billet m.,** combined rail and road ticket.

mixture [mikstyr] *nf* mixture; concoction.

MLF *abbr Mouvement de libération de la femme.*

Mlle *abbr Mademoiselle.*

Mme *abbr Madame.*

mobile [mɔbil] 1. *a (a)* mobile, movable *(b) O:* unstable, changeable, fickle (nature) *(c)* detachable; **album à feuilles mobiles,** loose-leaf album *(d)* moving (target); changing (expression); mobile (features) 2. *nm (a)* moving body; body in motion *(b)* driving power; motive (of a crime) *(c) Art:* mobile.

mobilier, -ière [mɔbilje, -jɛr] 1. *a Jur:* movable, personal; **biens mobiliers,** personal estate; *Fin:* **valeurs mobilières,** stocks and shares 2. *nm (a)* furniture *(b)* suite of furniture.

mobilisation [mɔbilizasjɔ̃] *nf* mobilization.

mobiliser [mɔbilize] *vtr* to mobilize (troops); to liberate (capital); **m. toute son énergie,** to summon up all one's strength.

mobilité [mɔbilite] *nf* mobility.

mobylette [mɔbilɛt] *nf Rtm:* moped.

mocassin [mɔkasɛ̃] *nm* moccasin.

mocheté [mɔʃte] *nf F: (a)* ugliness *(b) (pers)* fright; *(object)* eyesore. **moche** *a F:* rotten, lousy (treatment); poor, shoddy (work); ugly (person).

mode¹ [mɔd] *nf* 1. fashion; **être à la m.,** to be in fashion, in vogue; **c'est la m. des chapeaux,** hats are in fashion; **à la m. de,** after the style of; **passé de m.,** out of fashion, out of date; **jupe très m.,** fashionable skirt; **la (haute) m.,** the fashion trade 2. *pl Com: (a)* fashions *(b)* **(articles de) modes,** millinery.

mode² *nm* 1. *Gram:* mood 2. *Mus:* mode 3. method, mode; **m. d'emploi,** directions for use; **m. de vie,** way of life.

modelage [mɔdlaʒ] *nm* 1. modelling 2. model.

modèle [mɔdɛl] 1. *nm (a)* model, pattern; **bâti sur le même m.,** built to one pattern, on the same lines; **m. déposé,** registered pattern; **m. réduit,** scale model; **prendre qn pour m.,** to take s.o.'s model; to model oneself on s.o.; **m. de vertu,** paragon of vertu *(b) Cl:* model dress, hat *(c)* (artist's) model; **servir de m. à un artiste,** to sit for an artist 2. *a* **époux m.,** model, exemplary, husband.

modelé [mɔdle] *nm (a)* relief *(b)* contour (of body).

modeler [mɔdle] *vtr* 1. **(je modèle)** to model; to mould; to shape (s.o.'s destiny) 2. **se m. sur qn,** to model oneself on s.o.

modération [mɔderasjɔ̃] *nf* 1. moderation, restraint 2. reduction (in price). **modérateur, -trice** 1. *a* moderating, restraining 2. *n* moderator 3. *nm* regulator.

modérer [mɔdere] *vtr* **(je modère; je modérerai)** 1. to moderate, restrain; to reduce (speed); to curb (one's impatience) 2. to reduce (price) 3. **se m.,** to control oneself, to keep calm. **modéré** *a* moderate, restrained. **modérément** *adv* moderately, in moderation.

modernisation [mɔdɛrnizasjɔ̃] *nf* modernization.

moderniser [mɔdɛrnize] *vtr* to modernize. **moderne** *a* modern.

modernisme [mɔdɛrnism] *nm* modernism. **moderniste** *a & n* modernist.

modestie [mɔdɛsti] *nf* modesty. **modeste** *a* modest, unassuming; simple, unpretentious; **d'origine m.,** of humble origin; *n* **ne faites pas le m.,** don't be (so) modest. **modestement** *adv* modestly.

modification [mɔdifikasjɔ̃] *nf* modification, alteration.

modifier [mɔdifje] *vtr (pr sub & impf* n. **modifiions)** 1. to modify (statement, penalty); to alter, change (plan) 2. **se m.,** to be modified, to alter.

modique [mɔdik] *a* moderate, reasonable (cost); slender (income).

modiste [mɔdist] *nf* milliner.

modulation [mɔdylasjɔ̃] *nf* modulation; *WTel:* **m. de fréquence,** frequency modulation.

module [mɔdyl] *nm* 1. *Mth:* modulus 2. *Space:* module.

moduler [mɔdyle] *vtr & i* to modulate.

moelle [mwal] *nf* 1. marrow (of bone); **m. épinière,** spinal cord; **corrompu jusqu'à la m.,** rotten to the core 2. *Bot:* pith.

moelleux, -euse [mwalø, -øz] *a* 1. soft, velvety (to the touch); mellow (wine, voice); **tapis m.,** springy carpet; **couverture moelleuse,** luxurious blanket 2. *nm* softness; mellowness (of voice). **moelleusement** *adv* softly, luxuriously.

mœurs [mœr(s)] *nfpl* morals, manners (of people); customs (of country); habits (of animals); **gens sans m.,** unprincipled people; *Adm:* **la police des m.** = the vice squad; **femme de m. légères,** woman of easy virtue.

moi [mwa] **1.** *stressed pers pron* (*a*) (*subject*) I; **c'est m.,** it is I; it's me; **il est plus âgé que m.,** he is older than me; **elle est invitée et m. aussi,** she is invited and so am I; **m., je veux bien,** for my part, I'm willing; **je l'ai fait m.- même,** I did it myself (*b*) (*object*) me; **à m.!** help! **ce livre est à m.,** this book is mine; **un ami à m.,** a friend of mine (*c*) (*after imp*) (i) *acc* **laissez-m. tranquille,** leave me alone (ii) *dat* **donnez-le-m.,** give it (to) me **2.** *nm* ego, self; **le culte du m.,** egoism.

moignon [mwaɲɔ̃] *nm* stump (of amputated limb, sawn-off branch).

moi-même [mwamɛm] *pers pron* myself; *see* **moi** *and* **même** **1.** (*c*).

moindre [mwɛ̃dr] *a* **1.** *comp* less(er); lower (price); *n* **de deux maux choisir le m.,** to choose the lesser of two evils **2.** *sup* **le, la, m.,** the least; **pas la m. chance,** not the slightest, remotest, chance; **c'est la m. des choses,** it's the least I can do. **moindrement** *adv* **sans être le m. intéressé,** without being in the least bit interested.

moine [mwan] *nm* monk, friar.

moineau, -eaux [mwano] *nm Orn:* sparrow.

moins [mwɛ̃] **1.** *adv* (*a*) *comp* less; **m. encore,** still less, even less; **elle est m. jolie que sa sœur,** she's not as pretty as her sister; **beaucoup m. long,** much shorter; **m. d'argent,** less money; **m. d'hommes,** fewer men; **plus on le punit m. il travaille,** the more he's punished the less he works; **de m. en m.,** less and less; **m. de dix francs,** less than ten francs; **en m. de dix minutes,** within, under, in less than, ten minutes; **en m. de rien,** in less than no time; **dix francs de m.,** (i) ten francs less (ii) ten francs short; **20% de visiteurs en m.,** 20% fewer visitors; **à moins de,** unless, barring; **à m. d'avis contraire,** unless I hear to the contrary; **à m. que + *sub*,** unless; **à m. que vous (ne) l'ordonniez,** unless you order it; **rien m. que,** (i) anything but (ii) nothing less than; **non m. que,** as well as; quite as much as (*b*) *sup* least; **les élèves les m. appliqués,** the least industrious pupils; **le m. de gens possible,** as few people as possible; **pas le m. du monde,** not in the least (degree); by no means; not in the slightest; *n* **c'est (bien) le m. (qu'il puisse faire),** it's the least he can do; **du m** , at least, that is to say, at all events; **au m.,** at least (= not less than); *F:* **tu as fait ton travail, au m.?** you've done your work I hope? **vous compterez cela en m.,** you may deduct that **2.** (*a*) *prep* minus, less; **six m. quatre égale deux,** six minus four, take away four, equals two; **une heure m. cinq,** five (minutes) to one; **il fait m. dix (degrés)** (−10°), it's minus ten (degrees) (*b*) *nm Mth:* minus (sign).

moire [mwar] *nf Tex:* moire, moiré. **moiré** *a Tex:* watered, moiré (silk).

mois [mwa] *nm* (*a*) month; **le m. en cours,** the current month; **louer qch au m.,** to hire sth by the month; **cent francs par m.,** a hundred francs a, per, month (*b*) month's wages, salary.

Moïse [mɔiz] **1.** *Prnm BHist:* Moses **2.** *nm* (*a*) wicker cradle; Moses basket (*b*) carrycot.

moisir [mwazir] **1.** *vtr* to mildew **2.** *vi* to mould; to go mouldy. **moisi 1.** *a* mouldy, mildewy, mildewed; musty **2.** *nm* mould, mildew; **sentir le m.,** to smell musty.

moisissure [mwazisyr] *nf* **1.** mildew, mould **2.** mouldiness.

moisson [mwasɔ̃] *nf* **1.** (*a*) harvest(ing) (of cereals); **faire la m.,** to harvest **2.** (cereal) crop; **rentrer la m.,** to gather in the crops, the harvest.

moissonner [mwasɔne] *vtr* to reap; to harvest, gather (crops).

moissonneur, -euse [mwasɔnœr, -øz] **1.** *n* (*pers*) harvester, reaper **2.** *nf* **moissonneuse,** reaping machine; harvester.

moissonneuse-batteuse [mwasɔnøzbatøz] *nf* combine-harvester; *pl* **moissonneuses-batteuses.**

moiteur [mwatœr] *nf* moistness, sweatiness; **m. froide,** clamminess. **moite** *a* moist, sweaty (hands); muggy (weather); **(froid et) m.,** clammy.

moitié [mwatje] **1.** *nf* half; **la m. du temps,** half the time; **la bouteille était à m. pleine,** the bottle was half full; **couper qch par (la) m.,** to cut sth in half; **à m. prix,** at half price; **s'arrêter à m. chemin,** to stop halfway; **m. plus,** half as much again; **m.-m.,** fifty-fifty; half and half; **être de m. avec qn dans qch,** to share and share alike; **à m., half; à m. mort,** half-dead; **à m. cuit,** half-cooked; **faire les choses à m.,** to do things by halves **2.** *adv* **m. riant, m. pleurant,** half laughing, half crying; **m. l'un, m. l'autre,** half and half.

moka [mɔka] *nm* (*a*) mocha (coffee) (*b*) *Cu:* mocha cake.

mol *see* **mou¹.**

molaire [mɔlɛr] *nf* molar (tooth).

môle [mol] *nm* mole; (harbour) breakwater.

molécule [mɔlekyl] *nf* molecule. **moléculaire** *a* molecular.

molester [mɔlɛste] *vtr* to treat (s.o.) roughly, to manhandle (s.o.).

molette [mɔlɛt] *nf* serrated roller, wheel; knurl; **clef à m.,** adjustable spanner; monkey wrench.

molle *see* **mou¹.**

mollement [mɔlmɑ̃] *adv* (*a*) softly (*b*) slackly, feebly; weakly, indolently.

mollesse [mɔlɛs] *nf* (*a*) softness (of cushion); flabbiness (*b*) weakness, lifelessness; laxity; **sans m.,** briskly.

mollet [mɔlɛ] **1.** *a* softish; **œuf m.,** soft-boiled egg **2.** *nm* calf (of leg).

molleton [mɔltɔ̃] *nm* (*a*) soft thick flannel (*b*) fleece (*c*) table felt.

molletonner [mɔltɔne] *vtr* to line with fleece.

mollir [mɔlir] *vi* (*a*) to soften; to become soft (*b*) (of effort) to slacken; (of wind) to die down, to abate; **mes jambes mollissent,** my legs are giving way.

mollusque [mɔlysk] *nm* **1.** mollusc **2.** *F:* (*pers*) great lump.

molosse [mɔlɔs] *nm* mastiff.

môme [mom] **1.** *n F:* child, kid, brat **2.** *nf P:* woman, bird.

moment [mɔmɑ̃] *nm* **1.** (*a*) moment; **le m. venu,** when the time had come; **à ce m.-là,** at that moment, time; in those days; **à un m. donné,** at a given time; **au m. donné,** at the appointed time; **c'est le bon m. pour,** now is the time to; **un m.!** just a moment! **sur le m. je n'ai pas su que faire,** for a moment I was at a loss; **arriver au**

bon m., to arrive in the nick of time; **par moments,** at times, now and again; **à tout m., à tous moments,** constantly; **au m. de partir,** just as I was leaving, was about to leave; **du m. que,** seeing that (b) stage, point 2. *Mec:* moment (of force, inertia); momentum.

momentané a momentary (effort); temporary (absence). **momentanément** adv momentarily; temporarily.

momie [mɔmi] nf mummy.

momifier [mɔmifje] vtr (impf & pr sub **n. momifiions**) to mummify.

mon, ma, mes [mɔ̃, ma, mɛ] poss a (**mon** is used instead of **ma** before f words beginning with vowel or h mute) my; **mon ami, mon amie,** my friend; **un de mes amis,** a friend of mine; **c'est mon affaire à moi,** it's my own business; **non, mon colonel,** no, sir.

monarchie [mɔnarʃi] nf monarchy. **monarchique** a monarchical. **monarchiste** a & n monarchist.

monarque [mɔnark] nm monarch.

monastère [mɔnastɛr] nm monastery. **monastique** a monastic.

monceau, -eaux [mɔ̃so] nm heap, pile.

mondain, -aine [mɔ̃dɛ̃, -ɛn] 1. a (a) mundane, worldly (pleasures) (b) fashionable (resort); **réunion mondaine,** society gathering (c) **la police mondaine** = the vice squad 2. n socialite; society man, woman.

mondanités [mɔ̃danite] nfpl social events.

monde [mɔ̃d] nm 1. world; **le m. entier,** the whole world; **dans le m. entier,** all over the world; **le Nouveau M.,** the New World; **le tiers m.,** the third world; **mettre un enfant au m.,** to give birth to a child; **venir au m.,** to be born; **être seul au m.,** to be alone in the world; **il est encore de ce m.,** he's still alive; **pour rien au m.,** not for the world, not on any account; **personne au m.,** no man alive; **le meilleur du m.,** the best in the world; **vieux comme le m.,** (as) old as the hills; **le bout du m.,** the ends of the earth; the back of beyond; **ainsi va le m.,** it's the way of the world 2. (a) **le (beau) m.,** (fashionable) society; **le grand m.,** high society; **aller beaucoup dans le m.,** to move in fashionable circles; **homme du m.,** man of the world (b) milieu; **le m. de la haute finance,** the financial world 3. people; **peu de m.,** not many people, not a large crowd; **avoir du m. à dîner,** to have people to dinner; **il connaît son m.,** he knows the people he has to deal with; **tout le m.,** everybody. **mondial, -aux** a worldwide; **guerre mondiale,** global warfare; **la première, deuxième, guerre mondiale,** World War One, Two, the First, Second, World War. **mondialement** adv throughout the world; universally.

monégasque [mɔnegask] a & n (native) of Monaco.

monétaire [mɔnetɛr] a monetary; **unité m. d'un pays,** currency of a country.

mongolisme [mɔ̃gɔlism] nm Med: mongolism. **mongolien, -ienne** a & n mongol.

moniteur, -trice [mɔnitœr, -tris] n instructor, instructress; *Sp:* coach; *Aut:* driving instructor; assistant (in holiday camp), *NAm:* (camp) counselor.

monnaie [mɔnɛ] nf 1. money; **pièce de m.,** coin; **m. légale,** legal tender; **(l'hôtel de) la M.** = the Mint; **payer qn en m. de singe,** to fob s.o. off with empty promises 2. change; **petite m.,** small change; **rendre à**

qn la m. de sa pièce, to pay s.o. back in his own coin.

monnayer [mɔnɛje] vtr (**je monnaie**) to coin, mint (money).

monnayeur [mɔnɛjœr] nm minter; **faux m.,** counterfeiter.

monochrome [mɔnɔkrom] a monochrome.

monocle [mɔnɔkl̩] nm monocle.

monocoque [mɔnɔkɔk] a *Aut:* monoshell.

monocorde [mɔnɔkɔrd] a monotonous (sound).

monoculture [mɔnɔkyltyr] nf *Agr:* monoculture.

monogramme [mɔnɔgram] nm monogram.

monographie [mɔnɔgrafi] nf monograph.

monokini [mɔnɔkini] nm topless bathing suit.

monolingue [mɔnɔlɛ̃g] a monolingual.

monolithe [mɔnɔlit] 1. n monolith 2. a monolithic.

monologue [mɔnɔlɔg] nm monologue, soliloquy.

monologuer [mɔnɔlɔge] vi to soliloquize.

monomanie [mɔnɔmani] nf monomania.

monôme [mɔnom] nm 1. *Mth:* monomial 2. students' rag parade.

monomoteur [mɔnɔmɔtœr] 1. a single-engined 2. nm single-engined aircraft.

monophonique [mɔnɔfɔnik] a monophonic.

monoplace [mɔnɔplas] a & n single-seater (car, aircraft).

monopole [mɔnɔpɔl] nm monopoly.

monopolisation [mɔnɔpɔlizasjɔ̃] nf monopolization.

monopoliser [mɔnɔpɔlize] vtr to monopolize.

monorail [mɔnɔraj] a & nm monorail.

monosyllabe [mɔnɔsilab] 1. a monosyllabic 2. nm monosyllable. **monosyllabique** a monosyllabic.

monotonie [mɔnɔtɔni] nf monotony. **monotone** a monotonous; dull, humdrum (life).

monseigneur [mɔ̃sɛɲœr] nm (a) (referring to prince) His Royal Highness; (to cardinal) his Eminence; (to duke, archbishop) his Grace; (to bishop) his Lordship; pl nosseigneurs (b) (when speaking) your Royal Highness; your Eminence; your Grace; your Lordship; pl messeigneurs.

monsieur, pl **messieurs** [mɔsjø, mɛsjø] nm 1. (a) **M. Robert Martin,** Mr Robert Martin; **Messieurs, MM., Durand et Cie,** Messrs Durand and Co.; **m. le duc,** (i) the Duke (of) (ii) his, your, Grace (b) **m. Jean,** (of adult) Mr John, (of small boy) Master John (c) (used alone) **voici le chapeau de m.,** here is Mr X's hat; **m. n'est pas là,** Mr X is out 2. (a) (in address) sir; **bonsoir, messieurs,** good evening, gentlemen; **m. a sonné?** did you ring, sir? **que prendront ces messieurs?** what will you have, gentlemen? (b) Corr: (always written in full) (i) (to stranger) **Monsieur,** Dear Sir (ii) (implying previous acquaintance) **Cher Monsieur,** Dear Mr X 3. (gentle)man; **le m. qui vient de sortir,** the (gentle)man who has just gone out.

monstre [mɔ̃str̩] 1. nm (a) monster, monstrosity (b) monster; **les monstres marins,** the monsters of the deep; *F:* **cet enfant est un petit m.!** this child's a little devil! 2. a huge; colossal; monster. **monstrueux, -euse** a monstrous; unnatural; colossal; shocking, scandalous. **monstrueusement** adv monstrously.

monstruosité [mɔ̃stryozite] nf 1. monstrousness 2. monstrosity.

mont [mɔ̃] nm mount, mountain; **il est toujours par**

monts et par vaux, he's always on the move; **promettre monts et merveilles à qn,** to promise s.o. the earth.

montage [mɔ̃taʒ] *nm* setting (of jewel); mounting (of photograph); assembling (of apparatus); *Cin:* editing; *Ind:* **chaîne de m.,** assembly line.

montagne [mɔ̃taɲ] *nf* (a) mountain; **une m. de,** mountains of, a heap of; (*at fair*) **montagnes russes,** switchback, big dipper, roller coaster (b) mountain region; **à la m.,** in the mountains. **montagnard, -arde** (a) *n* mountain dweller; highlander (b) *a* mountain, highland (people). **montagneux, -euse** *a* mountainous (country).

montant [mɔ̃tɑ̃] 1. *a* rising, ascending; **chemin m.,** uphill road; **marée montante,** rising tide; **col m.,** stand-up collar; *Rail:* **train m.,** up train 2. *nm* (a) upright (of ladder); post, pillar; *Fb:* **les montants,** the goal-posts (b) total amount (of account); **j'ignore le m. de mes dettes,** I don't know what my debts amount to.

mont-de-piété [mɔ̃d(ə)pjete] *nm A:* pawnshop; *pl* **monts-de-piété.**

monté [mɔ̃te] *a* 1. mounted (man) 2. **il était m., il avait la tête montée,** his blood was up, he was worked up 3. set (jewel); **pièce mal montée,** badly produced play; **coup m.,** put-up job; frame-up.

monte-charge [mɔ̃tʃarʒ] *nm inv* hoist, goods lift, *NAm:* goods elevator.

montée [mɔ̃te] *nf* 1. (a) rise, rising; **tuyau de m.,** uptake pipe (b) uphill pull, climb; *Aut:* **essai de m.,** climbing test; **vitesse en m.,** climbing speed 2. gradient, slope (up).

monte-plats [mɔ̃tpla] *nm inv* service lift; hoist; dumb waiter.

monter [mɔ̃te] 1. *vi* (*aux usu* être, *occ* avoir) (a) to go up; to climb (up), mount, ascend; to go upstairs; **m. une échelle,** to climb, go up, a ladder; **m. se coucher,** to go (up) to bed; **montez chez moi,** come up to my room (b) to climb on, into (sth); **m. à cheval,** (i) to mount (ii) to ride; **m. à bicyclette,** to ride a bicycle; **m. en voiture,** to get into a car; **m. à bord,** to go on board (ship) (c) to rise, to go up; **la somme monte à cent francs,** the total amounts to, comes to, a hundred francs; **faire m. les prix,** to raise prices; **le sang lui monte à la tête,** the blood rushes to his head; **faire m. les larmes aux yeux de qn,** to bring tears to s.o.'s eyes; **m. comme une soupe au lait,** to flare up, to go off the deep end (d) (*of road*) to climb (e) (*of pers*) **m. dans l'estime de qn,** to rise in s.o.'s estimation 2. *vtr* (a) to mount; to climb (up), go up, come up (hill, stairs); **m. la rue en courant,** to run up the street (b) *Mil:* **m. la garde,** to mount guard (c) to ride (horse) (d) to command (ship); to man (boat) (e) to raise, carry up, take up; **m. du vin de la cave,** to bring up, fetch, wine from the cellar (f) **se m. la tête,** to get excited; **m. qn contre qn,** to set s.o. against s.o. (g) to set, mount (jewel); to mount (photo); to fit on (tyre); to erect (apparatus); to equip (workshop); to assemble (machine); *Th:* to set (scene); to stage (play); *Cin:* to edit (film); **m. un magasin,** to open a shop; **m. un coup,** to hatch a plot; to plan a job; *Knit:* **m. les mailles,** to cast on 3. **se m.** (a) to amount, to add up, to come (à, to) (b) to equip oneself, to fit oneself out (en, with) (c) *F:* to lose one's temper.

monteur, -euse [mɔ̃tœr, -øz] *n Cin:* editor; *MecE: etc:* fitter.

monticule [mɔ̃tikyl] *nm* hillock, mound.

montre [mɔ̃tr] *nf* 1. (a) show, display; **faire m. d'un grand courage,** to display great courage (b) shop window; showcase 2. watch; **m.(-bracelet),** wrist-watch; **à ma m. il est midi,** by my watch it's midday; **cela lui a pris dix minutes m. en main,** it took him ten minutes by the clock; **contre la m.,** against the clock; against time.

montrer [mɔ̃tre] *vtr* 1. (a) to show; to display, exhibit (b) to point out; **m. qn du doigt,** to point s.o. out (with one's finger); **m. le chemin à qn,** to show s.o. the way (c) **m. à qn comment faire qch,** to show s.o. how to do sth 2. **se m.** (a) to appear; to show oneself (b) **il se montra prudent,** he showed prudence; **il s'est montré très courageux,** he displayed great courage.

monture [mɔ̃tyr] *nf* 1. mount; (saddle) horse 2. setting (of jewel); mount(ing) (of picture); frame (of spectacles); **lunettes sans m.,** rimless spectacles.

monument [mɔnymɑ̃] *nm* 1. monument, memorial; **m. funéraire,** monument (over a tomb); **m. aux morts,** war memorial 2. public, historic, building. **monumental, -aux** *a* monumental.

moquer (se) [səmɔke] *vpr* **se m. de qn,** to make fun of s.o.; **vous vous moquez,** you're joking; **je m'en moque comme de l'an quarante,** I couldn't give a damn; **c'est se m. du monde!** it's the height of impertinence!

moquerie [mɔkri] *nf* mockery, jeering, scoffing; derision. **moqueur, -euse** *a* mocking.

moqueusement *adv* mockingly.

moquette [mɔkɛt] *nf* fitted carpet.

moral, -aux [mɔral, -o] 1. *a* (a) moral; ethical (b) mental, intellectual; **courage m.,** moral courage 2. *nm* (state of) mind; morale; **remonter le m. de, à, qn,** to raise s.o.'s spirits; *F:* **avoir le m. à zéro,** to be down in the dumps.

morale [mɔral] *nf* 1. (a) morals; **contraire à la m.,** immoral (b) ethics; moral science; **faire la m. à qn,** to lecture s.o. 2. moral (of story). **moralement** *adv* morally.

moraliser [mɔralize] 1. *vi* to moralize 2. *vtr* to lecture (s.o.). **moralisateur, -trice** 1. *a* moralizing; edifying 2. *n* moralizer. **moraliste** 1. *a* moralistic 2. *n* moralist.

moralité [mɔralite] *nf* 1. (a) morality; (good) moral conduct (b) morals; honesty 2. moral lesson; moral (of a story).

morbidité [mɔrbidite] *nf* morbidity, morbidness. **morbide** *a* morbid.

morceau, -eaux [mɔrso] *nm* 1. piece, bit (of food); **aimer les bons morceaux,** to like good things (to eat); *F:* **manger un m.,** to have a bite to eat, a snack; **lâcher le m.,** to give the game away 2. piece (of soap, cloth, music); bit; scrap; lump (of sugar); patch (of land); **mettre qch en morceaux,** to pull sth to pieces, to bits; *Lit:* **morceaux choisis,** selected passages, extracts.

morceler [mɔrsəle] *vtr* (**je morcelle**) to cut up (sth) into small pieces; **m. une propriété,** to break up, to divide, an estate.

morcellement [mɔrsɛlmɑ̃] *nm* breaking up, division.

mordiller [mɔrdije] *vtr & i* to nibble.

mordoré [mɔrdɔre] *a & nm* bronze (colour).

mordre [mɔrdr] *vtr & ind tr* (a) to bite; **se m. la langue,** to bite one's tongue; **il s'en mord les lèvres,** he bitterly regrets it; **m. la poussière,** to bite the dust (b) **lime qui mord,** file that bites; **acide qui mord (sur) les métaux,** acid that eats away metals; **m. dans une pomme,** to take a bite out of an apple; **m. sur qch,** to encroach on sth; **m. à l'hameçon,** to rise to the bait; *F:* **il mord au latin,** he's taken to latin; *Fish:* **ça mord,** I've got a bite (c) *(of cogwheels)* to catch, engage. **mordant** 1. *a (a)* mordant, biting, caustic, cutting (remark) (b) piercing (sound); biting (cold) **2.** *nm (a)* bite (of file) (b) mordancy; keenness, punch. **mordu, -e** 1. *a (a)* bitten (b) *F:* madly in love **2.** *n* fan; *F:* **les mordus du football,** football fans.

morfondre (se) [sǝmɔrfɔ̃dr] *vpr* to be bored to death; to mope.

morgue [mɔrg] *nf* **1.** pride, arrogance **2.** mortuary, morgue.

moribond, -onde [mɔribɔ̃, -ɔ̃d] *a* moribund, dying, at death's door; *n* **un m.,** a dying man.

morille [mɔrij] *nf Fung: Cu:* morel.

morne [mɔrn] *a* dejected; gloomy; dull (weather); dreary, dismal.

morosité [mɔrozite] *nf* moroseness, sullenness, gloominess. **morose** *a* morose, sullen, gloomy.

morphine [mɔrfin] *nf* morphine.

morphinomane [mɔrfinɔman] *n* morphine addict.

morphologie [mɔrfɔlɔʒi] *nf* morphology. **morphologique** *a* morphological.

morpion [mɔrpjɔ̃] *nm P:* crab (louse).

mors [mɔr] *nm* **1.** *Tls:* jaw (of vice) **2.** *Harn:* bit; **prendre le m. aux dents,** (i) *(of horse)* to take the bit between its teeth (ii) to take the bit between one's teeth.

morse [mɔrs] *nm* **1.** *Z:* walrus **2. M.,** Morse (code).

morsure [mɔrsyr] *nf* bite.

mort[1], **morte** [mɔr, mɔrt] **1.** *a (a)* dead (pers, language); **m. et enterré,** dead and buried; **il est m.,** he's dead; **m. de peur,** frightened to death; **plus m. que vif,** half dead with fright (b) **temps m.,** (i) *Sp:* stoppage (in match) (ii) period of inactivity; *Mec:* **point m.,** neutral position (of lever); *Aut:* neutral gear (c) **eau morte,** stagnant water; *Art:* **nature morte,** still life (d) **balle morte,** spent bullet **2.** *n* dead person; **les morts,** the dead, the departed; *Ecc:* **jour, fête, des morts,** All Souls' day; **l'office des morts,** the burial service; **tête de m.,** skull; **faire le m.,** (i) to pretend to be dead (ii) to lie low; *Aut: F:* **la place du m.,** the front passenger seat **3.** *nm Cards:* dummy.

mort[2] *nf* death; **mettre qn à m.,** to put s.o. to death; **condamner à m.,** to condemn, *Jur:* to sentence, to death; **arrêt de m.,** death sentence; **à m. les traîtres!** death to the traitors! **blessé à m.,** mortally wounded; *F:* **freiner à m.,** to jam on the brakes; **se donner la m.,** to take one's own life; **mourir de sa belle m.,** to die a natural death; **être à l'article de la m.,** to be at death's door; **haïr qn à m.,** to hate s.o. like poison; **silence de m.,** dead silence; **il avait la m. dans l'âme,** he was sick at heart; **je m'en souviendrai jusqu'à la m.,** I'll remember it to my dying day.

mortadelle [mɔrtadɛl] *nf Comest:* mortadella.

mortalité [mɔrtalite] *nf* mortality; death rate; **m. infantile,** infant mortality.

mort-aux-rats [mɔrora] *nf inv* rat poison.

mortel, -elle [mɔrtɛl] *a (a)* mortal; destined to die; *n* **un m., une mortelle,** a mortal (b) fatal (wound); **coup**

m., mortal blow, death blow; **il a fait une chute mortelle,** he fell to his death (c) *F:* deadly dull; **je l'ai attendu deux mortelles heures,** I waited two solid hours for him (d) deadly; **ennemi m.,** mortal enemy; **d'une pâleur mortelle,** deathly pale. **mortellement** *adv* mortally, fatally; **m. pâle,** deathly pale; **m. ennuyeux,** deadly dull.

morte-saison [mɔrtsɛzɔ̃] *nf* slack period, off season; *pl* **mortes-saisons.**

mortier [mɔrtje] *nm* **1.** *(a)* mortar; **pilon et m.,** pestle and mortar (b) *Artil:* mortar **2.** *Const:* **m. ordinaire,** lime mortar.

mortification [mɔrtifikasjɔ̃] *nf* mortification; humiliation.

mortifier [mɔrtifje] *vtr (impf & pr sub* **n. mortifiions)** *(a)* to mortify (flesh, passions) (b) to mortify (s.o.); to hurt (s.o.'s) feelings.

mort-né, -née [mɔrne] *a & n* stillborn (child); **projet m.-né,** abortive plan; *pl* **mort-nés, -nées.**

mortuaire [mɔrtɥɛr] *a* mortuary (urn); **drap m.,** pall; **chambre m.,** death chamber; **la maison m.,** the house of the deceased.

morue [mɔry] *nf Ich:* (i) cod (ii) **m. (séchée),** salted (and dried) cod.

mosaïque [mɔzaik] *nf Art:* mosaic.

Moscou [mɔsku] *Prn Geog:* Moscow. **moscovite** *a & n Geog:* Muscovite.

mosquée [mɔske] *nf* mosque.

mot [mo] *nm* word; **m. pour m.,** word for word; **prendre qn au m.,** to take s.o. at his word; **faire du m. à m.** [motamo] to translate word for word; **sans m. dire,** without (saying) a word; **dire deux mots à qn,** to have a word with s.o.; **avoir le dernier m.,** to have the last word; **ignorer le premier m., ne pas savoir un (traître) m., de la chimie,** not to know the first thing about chemistry; **à ces mots,** (i) so saying (ii) at these words; **en un m., en quelques mots,** briefly, in a word; **au bas m.,** at the lowest estimate; **gros m.,** coarse expression; swear word; **le m. de l'énigme,** the key to the enigma; **voilà le fin m. de l'affaire!** so that's what's at the bottom of it! **faire comprendre qch à qn à mots couverts,** to give s.o. a hint of sth; **m. de passe,** password; **m. d'ordre,** watchword; **mots croisés,** crossword (puzzle); **écrire un m. à qn,** to drop s.o. a line; **placer un m., avoir son m. à dire,** to have one's say; **bon m.,** witty remark, witticism; **avoir toujours le m. pour rire,** to be always ready for a joke.

motard [mɔtar] *nm F: (a)* motorcyclist (b) motorcycle policeman; speed cop; **m. d'escorte,** police outrider.

motel [mɔtɛl] *nm* motel.

moteur, -trice [mɔtœr, -tris] **1.** *a* motive, propulsive, driving (power); *Cy:* **roue motrice,** back wheel; **voiture à roues avant motrices,** car with front-wheel drive; **force motrice,** driving force **2.** *nm* motor, engine; **m. à combustion interne, à explosion,** internal combustion engine; **m. à deux, à quatre temps,** two-stroke, four-stroke, engine; **m. électrique,** electric motor; **m. à avion; m. d'avion,** aero-engine **3.** *nf Rail:* **motrice,** motor coach.

motif [mɔtif] *nm (a)* motive, incentive; reason; **soupçons sans m.,** groundless suspicions (b) *Art:* motif; design; *Mus:* theme.

motion [mɔsjɔ̃] *nf* motion, proposal; **m. de censure,** motion of censure.

motivation [mɔtivasjɔ̃] *nf* motivation.

motiver [mɔtive] *vtr* (*a*) to motivate (an action) (*b*) to justify, warrant; to state the reason for. **motivé** *a* (*a*) motivated (*b*) justified; **refus m.**, justifiable refusal.

moto [mɔto] *nf F:* motorbike.

motocross [mɔtɔkrɔs] *nm Sp:* motorcycle scramble; motocross.

motoculteur [mɔtɔkyltœr] *nm Agr:* motor cultivator.

motocyclette [mɔtɔsiklɛt] *nf* motorcycle, *F:* motorbike.

motocycliste [mɔtɔsiklist] *nm* motorcyclist.

motonautisme [mɔtɔnotism] *nm* motorboating.

motopompe [mɔtɔpɔ̃p] *nf* motor(-driven) pump.

motorisation [mɔtɔrizasjɔ̃] *nf* motorization.

motoriser [mɔtɔrize] *vtr* to motorize.

motrice *see* **moteur.**

motte [mɔt] *nf* clod, lump (of earth); **m. de gazon**, sod, turf; **m. de beurre**, pat, block, of butter.

motus [mɔtys] *int* mum's the word!

mou¹ mol, *f* **molle** [mu, mɔl] **1.** *a* (*the masc form* **mol** *is used before vowel or* h *mute*) soft; slack; weak, lifeless, spineless (pers); flabby (flesh); feeble (attempt); lax (government); **m. au toucher**, soft to the touch **2.** *nm* slack (of rope); **donner du m. à un cordage**, to slacken a rope.

mou² *nm* lights, lungs (of slaughtered animal).

mouchard [muʃar] *nm F:* (*a*) informer; police spy; grass; *Sch:* sneak (*b*) (mechanical) speed check (on vehicles) (*c*) watchman's clock (*d*) *Av:* observation plane.

moucharder [muʃarde] *vtr F:* to inform, grass, on (s.o.); *Sch:* to sneak on (s.o.).

mouche [muʃ] *nf* **1.** fly; **m. domestique**, housefly; **m. bleue**, bluebottle; **prendre la m.**, to take offence; **quelle m. vous pique?** what's the matter with you? *F:* **c'est une fine m.**, he's a sharp customer; *Box:* **poids m.**, flyweight **2.** bull's eye (of target); **faire m.**, to hit the bull's eye; to score a bull.

moucher [muʃe] *vtr* **1.** (*a*) to wipe, blow (child's) nose (*b*) *F:* to snub (s.o.), to tell (s.o.) off **2.** **se m.**, to wipe, blow, one's nose.

moucheron [muʃrɔ̃] *nm* midge; gnat.

moucheté [muʃte] *a* (*a*) spotty, speckled, flecked (*b*) *Fenc:* buttoned (sword).

mouchoir [muʃwar] *nm* handkerchief; **m. (de tête)**, headscarf; **jardin grand comme un m. de poche**, garden as big as a pocket handkerchief.

moudre [mudr] *vtr* (*prp* **moulant;** *pp* **moulu;** *pr ind* **je mouds, n. moulons**) to grind.

moue [mu] *nf* pout; **faire la m.**, to purse one's lips, to pout, to look sulky; to pull a face.

mouette [mwɛt] *nf Orn:* (sea)gull.

mouffette [mufɛt] *nf Z:* skunk.

moufle [mufl] *nf* mitten.

mouillage [mujaʒ] *nm* anchorage, moorage.

mouiller [muje] *vtr* **1.** (*a*) to wet, moisten, damp; **se m. les pieds**, to get one's feet wet (*b*) to dilute, water down (wine) (*c*) to cast, drop (anchor); to bring (ship) to anchor (*d*) *Nau:* to lay (mine) (*e*) to palatalize (consonant) **2.** *vi Nau:* to lie at anchor **3.** **se m.** (*a*) to get wet; (*of eyes*) to fill with tears (*b*) *F:* to get involved (in crime). **mouillé** *a* **1.** moist, damp, wet; **m.**

jusqu'aux os, wet through; *F:* **poule mouillée**, drip, wet **2.** (*of ship*) at anchor; moored.

moulage [mulaʒ] *nm* **1.** casting, moulding **2.** cast.

moule¹ [mul] *nm* mould; matrix; **m. à gâteaux**, cake tin; **m. à tarte**, flan case.

moule² *nf* **1.** mussel **2.** (*pers*) drip, wet; fool.

mouler [mule] *vtr* (*a*) to cast (statue) (*b*) to mould; **robe qui moule la taille**, tight-fitting dress; **se m. sur qn**, to model oneself on s.o.

moulin [mulɛ̃] *nm* (*a*) mill; **m. à eau**, watermill; **m. à vent**, windmill; *F:* **faire venir l'eau au m.**, to bring grist to the mill; **on y entre comme dans un m.**, anybody can go in (*b*) **m. à légumes**, mill; **m. à poivre**, pepper mill; **m. à café**, coffee grinder.

mouliner [muline] *vtr* **1.** *Fish:* to reel in (the line) **2.** *Cu:* to pass through a food mill.

moulinet [mulinɛ] *nm* **1.** (*a*) *Fish:* reel (*b*) turnstile **2. faire des moulinets (avec sa canne)**, to twirl one's stick.

Moulinette [mulinɛt] *nf Rtm:* food mill.

moulu [muly] *a* (*a*) ground, powdered (*b*) dead-beat, *F:* fagged out; **m. (de coups)**, black and blue; aching all over.

moulure [mulyr] *nf* (ornamental) moulding.

mourir [murir] *vi* (*prp* **mourant;** *pp* **mort;** *pr ind* **je meurs, ils meurent;** *pr sub* **je meure, nous mourions;** *ph* **il mourut;** *fu* **je mourrai;** *aux* **être**) (*a*) to die; **il est mort hier**, he died yesterday; **m. de faim**, (i) to die of starvation (ii) to be starving; **elle l'aimait à en m.**, she was desperately in love with him; **faire m. qn**, to put s.o. to death; *F:* **il me fera m.**, he will be the death of me; **m. d'envie de faire qch.**, to be dying to do sth; **m. de peur**, to be scared to death; **s'ennuyer à m.**, to be bored to death; **je mourais de rire**, I nearly died laughing; **c'est à m. de rire**, it's simply killing (*b*) (*of fire*) to die out; (*of voice*) to trail off. **mourant, -ante 1.** *a* dying; faint (voice) **2.** *n* dying man, woman.

mousquetaire [muskətɛr] *nm Hist:* musketeer.

mousse¹ [mus] *nf* **1.** moss; **couvert de m.**, moss-grown, mossy **2.** (*a*) froth, foam (of sea); head (on beer); lather (of soap); *F:* **se faire de la m.**, to fret, worry (*b*) *Cu:* mousse; **m. au chocolat**, chocolate mousse **3.** *Ind:* **m. de caoutchouc, caoutchouc m.**, foam rubber **4.** *Knit:* **point m.**, knit stitch.

mousse² *nm* ship's boy.

mousseline [muslin] *nf* (*a*) *Tex:* muslin; **m. de soie**, chiffon (*b*) **pommes (de terre) m.**, creamed potatoes.

mousser [muse] *vi* to froth, foam; to lather; (*of wine*) to sparkle, to fizz. **mousseux, -euse** *a* (*a*) mossy (*b*) foaming (*c*) *a & nm* sparkling (wine).

mousson [musɔ̃] *nf* monsoon.

moustache [mustaʃ] *nf* (*a*) moustache (*b*) whiskers (of cat).

moustiquaire [mustikɛr] *nf* mosquito net.

moustique [mustik] *nm* **1.** *Ent:* (*a*) mosquito (*b*) gnat **2.** *F:* child, brat.

moutard [mutar] *nm P:* urchin; brat.

moutarde [mutard] *nf* mustard; **la m. lui monta au nez**, he lost his temper, he flared up.

moutardier [mutardje] *nm* mustard pot.

mouton [mutɔ̃] *nm* **1.** (*a*) sheep; **éleveur de moutons**, (i) sheep farmer (ii) wool grower; *Equit:* **saut de m.**, buck; *Fig:* **revenons à nos moutons**, let's get back to the point (b) Cu: mutton; **ragoût de m.**, mutton stew (c) (**peau de**) m., sheepskin (d) pl white horses (on waves) (e) pl fluff (under bed) **2.** CivE: ram.

moutonner [mutɔne] vi **1.** (of sea) to break into white horses; to froth **2.** (of sky) **se m.**, to become covered with fleecy clouds. **moutonneux, -euse** a (of sea) flecked with white horses; (of sky) covered with fleecy clouds.

mouvement [muvmã] nm **1.** movement; motion; **sans m.**, motionless; **faire un m.**, to move; **mettre qch en m.**, to put, set, sth in motion; **se mettre en m.**, to start off; to get going; **être toujours en m.**, to be always on the move; **le m. d'une grande ville**, the bustle of a large town; **ville sans m.**, lifeless, dull, town; Mec: **pièces en m.**, moving parts (of machine); **m. perpétuel**, perpetual motion; Mus: (i) movement (of symphony) (ii) **presser le m.**, to quicken the time **2.** (a) change, modification; Geog: fall, rise (in sea level); **m. de terrain**, undulation, **m. de personnel**, staff changes; **être dans le m.**, to be in the swim, up to date (b) **premier m.**, first impulse; **m. d'humeur**, outburst of temper; **de son propre m.**, of one's own accord; **m. de plaisir**, thrill of pleasure (c) Pol: etc: movement; **m. insurrectionnel**, uprising **3.** traffic; Rail: **mouvements des trains**, train arrivals and departures; Journ: **mouvements des navires**, shipping intelligence **4.** works, action, movement; **m. d'horlogerie**, clockwork. **mouvementé** a **1.** animated, lively; thrilling; full of incident; busy (street); eventful (life) **2.** **terrain m.**, undulating ground.

mouvoir [muvwar] v (prp **mouvant**; pp **mû, mue**; pr ind **je meus, ils meuvent**; pr sub **je meuve, n. mouvions, ils meuvent**; fu **je mouvrai**) **1.** to drive (machinery); to propel (ship); **mû à la vapeur**, steam-driven; **mû par la colère, l'intérêt**, moved by anger, prompted by interest **2. se m.**, to move, stir. **mouvant** a moving, mobile; unstable, changeable; **sables mouvants**, quicksand.

moyen¹ -enne [mwajɛ̃, -ɛn] **1.** a (a) middle; **les classes moyennes**, the middle class(es); **le m. âge** [mwajɛnaʒ] the Middle Ages; Sch: **cours m.**, intermediate class (b) average, mean (speed, level, price); **le Français m.**, the average Frenchman; the man in the street (c) medium; **de taille moyenne**, medium-sized, middle-sized **2.** nf **moyenne** (a) Mth: mean (b) average; **en moyenne**, on (an) average (c) Sch: passmark. **moyennement** adv moderately, fairly; fairly well.

moyen² nm (a) means; **par tous les moyens**, by fair means or foul; **employer les grands moyens**, to take extreme measures; **au m. de**, with the help of; **y a-t-il m. de le faire?** is it possible to do it? **il n'y a pas m.**, it can't be done; it's impossible; F: **pas m.!** no way! **trouver le m. de faire qch**, to find a way of doing sth; **faire qch par ses propres moyens**, to do sth on one's own; **dans la (pleine) mesure de mes moyens**, to the best, utmost, of my ability; **enfant qui a des moyens**, talented child; **enlever les moyens à qn**, to cramp s.o.'s style (b) **vivre au-dessus de ses moyens**, to live beyond one's means; **je n'en ai pas les moyens**, I can't afford it. **moyennant** prep on (a certain) condition; **faire qch m. finance**, to do sth for a consideration; **m. paiement de dix francs**, on payment of ten francs; **m. quoi**, in consideration of which.

moyenâgeux, -euse [mwajɛnaʒø, -øz] a (a) medi(a)eval (b) oldfashioned.

moyen-courrier [mwajɛ̃kurje] nm medium-range aircraft; pl **moyens-courriers**.

Moyen-Orient [mwajɛ̃ɔrjɑ̃] Prnm Geog: (the) Middle East.

moyeu, -eux [mwajø] nm hub (of wheel).

mû see **mouvoir**.

mue [my] nf **1.** (a) moulting (of birds); shedding of the antlers; sloughing (of reptiles) (b) moulting season (c) feathers moulted; antlers, etc, shed; slough (of reptiles) **2.** breaking of the voice (at puberty).

muer [mɥe] vi **1.** (a) (of bird) to moult; (of stag) to shed its antlers; (of reptile) to slough; to cast its skin (b) (of voice) to break (at puberty) **2. se m. (en)**, to change (oneself) (into).

muet, -ette [mɥɛ, -ɛt] **1.** a (a) dumb (b) **j'écoutais, m. d'étonnement**, I listened in mute astonishment; **m. de colère**, speechless with anger (c) dumb, mute; **rester m.**, to remain silent (d) silent (film); Th: **rôle m.**, silent part (e) Ling: silent (letter); **h m., muette**, mute h **2.** (a) n dumb person (b) nm **le m.**, silent films, cinema.

mufle [myfl] nm **1.** muzzle (of ox) **2.** F: lout, boor.

muflerie [myfləri] nf boorishness.

muflier [myflije] nm Bot: antirrhinum, snapdragon.

mugir [myʒir] vi (a) (of cow) to low, moo; to bellow (b) (of sea, wind) to roar; to boom; (of wind) to howl.

mugissement [myʒismã] nm (a) lowing, mooing (of cow); bellowing (b) roaring, booming (of sea, wind); howling (of wind).

muguet [mygɛ] nm Bot: lily of the valley.

mulâtre [mylɑtr] a & n mulatto, half-caste.

mule¹ [myl] nf (she-)mule.

mule² nf (slipper) mule.

mulet¹ [mylɛ] nm (he-)mule. **muletier, -ière 1.** a mule (track) **2.** nm mule driver.

mulet² nm Ich: grey mullet.

mulot [mylo] nm field mouse.

multicolore [myltikɔlɔr] a multicoloured.

multimillionnaire [myltimiljɔnɛr] a & n multimillionaire.

multinational, -aux [myltinasjɔnal, -o] a multinational.

multiple [myltipl] **1.** a multiple, manifold; multifarious (duties); **maison à succursales multiples**, chain store **2.** nm Mth: multiple.

multiplication [myltiplikasjɔ̃] nf multiplication; increase (in the number of).

multiplicité [myltiplisite] nf multiplicity.

multiplier [myltiplije] vtr (impf & pr sub n. **multiplions**) **1.** to multiply (**par**, by) **2. se m.** (a) to multiply; **les crimes se multiplient**, crime is on the increase (b) to be in half a dozen places at once; to do one's utmost (to help s.o.).

multirisque [myltirisk] a multiple risk.

multitude [myltityd] nf multitude (**de**, of); crowd; multiplicity.

municipalité [mynisipalite] nf **1.** municipality (a) local administrative area (b) local council **2.** town hall. **municipal, -aux** a municipal; **conseil m.**, local council.

munir [mynir] vtr **1.** supply, furnish, equip, provide (**de**, with) **2. se m.**, to provide oneself (**de**, with).

munitions [mynisjɔ̃] nfpl ammunition.

muqueuse [mykøz] *nf* mucous membrane.

mur [myr] *nm* wall; **aux murs de briques**, brick(-built); **mettre qn au pied du m.**, to drive s.o. into a corner; **se taper la tête contre les murs**, to hit one's head against a brick wall; **m. du son**, sound barrier. **mural, -aux** *a* mural; wall.

mûr [myr] *a* ripe (fruit); mellow (wine); mature (mind, age); **après mûre réflexion**, after mature consideration; **m. pour qch**, ready for sth.

muraille [myrɑj] *nf* (high defensive) wall.

mûre [myr] *nf* 1. mulberry 2. m. (sauvage, de ronce), blackberry.

murer [myre] *vtr* 1. to wall in; to wall up, brick up (doorway) 2. se m., to shut oneself away.

mûrier [myrje] *nm* (a) mulberry (tree, bush) (b) m. (sauvage), blackberry bush; bramble.

mûrir [myrir] *vtr & i* to ripen, mature.

murmure [myrmyr] *nm* murmur, murmuring; *pl* muttering; grumbling.

murmurer [myrmyre] *vtr & i* to murmur; to grumble, complain; **m. entre ses dents**, to mutter.

musaraigne [myzarɛɲ] *nf Z:* shrew.

muscade [myskad] *nf* (noix) m., nutmeg.

muscadier [myskadje] *nm* nutmeg tree.

muscat [myska] *a & nm Vit:* (raisin) m., muscat grape, muscatel (grape); (vin) m., muscatel (wine).

muscle [myskl] *nm* muscle. **musclé** *a* muscular; brawny. **musculaire** *a* muscular (system).

musculature [myskylatyr] *nf* musculature.

muse [myz] *nf* Muse.

museau, -eaux [myzo] *nm* (a) muzzle, snout (of animal) (b) F: face; **vilain m.**, ugly mug.

musée [myze] *nm* (a) museum (b) m. (de peinture, d'art), art gallery.

museler [myzle] *vtr* (je muselle) to muzzle (dog, the press).

muselière [myzəljer] *nf* muzzle.

muséum [myzeɔm] *nm* natural history museum.

musicalité [myzikalite] *nf* musicality; musical quality. **musical, -aux** *a* musical. **musicalement** *adv* musically.

music-hall [myzikol] *nm* music hall; **numéros de m.-h.**, variety turns; *pl* music-halls.

musicien, -ienne [myzisjɛ̃, -jɛn] *a & n* 1. musician; **elle est bonne musicienne**, (i) she's very musical (ii) she's a good musician 2. member of a band, an orchestra; *Mil:* bandsman.

musique [myzik] *nf* 1. (a) music; **mettre des paroles en m.**, to set words to music; **instrument de m.**, musical instrument; **m. de chambre**, chamber music; **m. d'ambiance, de fond**, background music; **faire de la m.**, (i) to make music (ii) to be a musician (b) F: **il connaît la m.**, he knows what's what 2. band; **chef de m.**, bandmaster.

musulman, -ane [myzylmɑ̃, -an] *a & n* Moslem, Muslim.

mutation [mytasjɔ̃] *nf* (a) change, alteration; *Biol: Mus:* mutation (b) transfer (of personnel).

muter [myte] *vtr* to transfer (personnel).

mutilation [mytilasjɔ̃] *nf* mutilation.

mutiler [mytile] *vtr* (a) to mutilate, maim (b) to deface. **mutilé, -ée** *a & n* mutilated, maimed (pers); **m. de la face**, disfigured (person); **m. de guerre**, disabled ex-serviceman.

mutiner (se) [səmytine] *vpr* to rise in revolt; to rebel; to mutiny.

mutinerie [mytinri] *nf* rebellion; mutiny. **mutin, -ine** 1. *a & n* mischievous (child) 2. *nm* mutineer. **mutiné** 1. *a* rebellious 2. *nm* mutineer.

mutisme [mytism] *nm* dumbness, muteness; **se renfermer dans le m.**, to maintain a stubborn silence.

mutualité [mytɥalite] *nf* 1. reciprocity 2. mutual insurance; **société de m.**, friendly society. **mutuel, -elle** *a & nf* mutual; (société d'assurance) mutuelle, mutual insurance company. **mutuellement** *adv* mutually; **s'aider m.**, to help one another.

myopie [mjɔpi] *nf* myopia; short-sightedness. **myope** *a & n* myopic; shortsighted (person).

myosotis [mjɔɔtis] *nm Bot:* forget-me-not.

myriade [mirjad] *nf* myriad.

myrte [mirt] *nm Bot:* myrtle.

myrtille [mirtij] *nf Bot:* bilberry.

mystère [mister] *nm* mystery. **mystérieux, -euse** *a* mysterious. **mystérieusement** *adv* mysteriously.

mysticisme [mistisism] *nm* mysticism. **mystique** 1. *a* mystic(al) 2. *n* mystic.

mystification [mistifikasjɔ̃] *nf* (a) mystification (b) hoax.

mystifier [mistifje] *vtr* (impf & pr sub n. mystifiions) (a) to mystify (b) to hoax; to pull (s.o.'s) leg. **mystificateur, -trice** 1. *a* mystifying 2. *n* hoaxer.

mythe [mit] *nm* myth, legend. **mythique** *a* mythical. **mythomane** *a & n* mythomaniac.

mythologie [mitɔlɔʒi] *nf* mythology. **mythologique** *a* mythological.

myxomatose [miksɔmatoz] *nf* myxomatosis.

N

N, n [ɛn] *nm* (the letter) N, n.

N *abbr* **1.** *nord* **2.** (*route*) *nationale*.

nacelle [nasɛl] *nf* basket, nacelle (of balloon); nacelle, gondola (of airship).

nacre [nakṛ] *nf* mother of pearl.

nacré [nakre] *a* (lustre).

nage [naʒ] *nf* **1.** rowing; **chef de n.,** stroke (oarsman) **2.** (*a*) swimming; **traverser une rivière à la n.,** to swim across a river (*b*) stroke (in swimming); **n. libre,** freestyle (*c*) **être en n.,** to be bathed in sweat.

nageoire [naʒwar] *nf* fin (of fish); flipper.

nager [naʒe] *vi* (**n. nageons**) **1.** to row **2.** (*a*) to swim; (*with cogn acc*) **n. la brasse,** to swim (the) breast-stroke; **n. entre deux eaux,** to swim under water (*b*) to float; to be submerged (in liquid); **le bois nage sur l'eau,** wood floats on water; **la viande nage dans la graisse,** the meat is swimming in fat; **il nage dans ses vêtements,** his clothes are far too big for him; *F:* **je nage complètement,** I'm all at sea, I'm lost; **n. dans l'opulence,** to be rolling in money.

nageur, -euse [naʒœr, -øz] *n* (*a*) swimmer (*b*) oarsman.

naguère [nagɛr] *adv* not long since, a short time ago; formerly.

naïf, -ïve [naif, -iv] *a* **1.** ingenuous, naïve **2.** credulous, gullible; *n* **un naïf,** a gullible fool. **naïvement** *adv* naïvely.

nain, naine [nɛ̃, nɛn] **1.** *n* dwarf, midget **2.** *a* dwarf(ish) (person, plant).

naissance [nɛsɑ̃s] *nf* (*a*) birth; **à la n.,** at birth; **de n.,** (blind, deaf) from birth; **lieu de n.,** birthplace; **donner n. à un enfant, une rumeur,** to give birth to a child, to give rise to a rumour; **contrôle, limitation, des naissances,** birth control; *Adm:* **extrait de n.,** birth certificate; **être français de n.,** to be French by birth (*b*) root (of nail, hair); base (of neck); source (of river); **prendre n.,** to originate, take form.

naissant [nɛsɑ̃] *a* nascent.

naître [nɛtṛ] *vi* (*prp* **naissant**; *pp* **né**; *pr ind* **je nais, ils naissent;** *ph* **je naquis;** *aux* **être**) (*a*) to be born; **il est né en 1880,** he was born in 1880; **il est né aveugle,** he was born blind; *F:* **je ne suis pas né d'hier,** I wasn't born yesterday; *impers* **il naît moins de garçons que de filles,** there are fewer boys born than girls; **Mme Long, née Thomas,** Mrs Long, née Thomas; **il est né de parents allemands,** he was born of German parents (*b*) (*of hopes, fears*) to be born, to spring up; (*of day*) to dawn, break (*c*) (*of plant*) to spring up, come up (*d*) (*of plan, of river*) to originate, rise, arise; **faire n.,** to awaken, arouse (suspicion, etc.).

naïveté [naivte] *nf* naïvety.

nana [nana] *nf P:* woman, bird, chick.

nantir [nɑ̃tir] *vtr* (*a*) *Jur:* to give security to, to secure (creditor) (*b*) **se n. de qch,** to provide oneself with sth.

napalm [napalm] *nm* napalm.

naphtaline [naftalin] *nf* **(boules de) n.,** mothballs.

naphte [naft] *nm* naphtha; mineral oil.

nappe [nap] *nf* **1.** (*a*) tablecloth (*b*) cloth, cover; **n. d'autel,** altar cloth **2.** sheet (of ice, flame); layer (of petrol); blanket (of fog); **n. de mazout,** oil slick.

napper [nape] *vtr Cu:* to coat (**de,** with).

napperon [naprɔ̃] *nm* (small linen) cloth, mat.

narcisse [narsis] *nm Bot:* narcissus.

narcotique [narkɔtik] *a & nm* narcotic.

narguer [narge] *vtr* to flout, scoff at (sth, s.o.).

narine [narin] *nf* nostril.

narquois, -oise [narkwa, -waz] *a* mocking bantering (tone, smile). **narquoisement** *adv* mockingly.

narrateur, -trice [naratœr, -tris] *n* narrator.

narration [narasjɔ̃] *nf* **1.** narrating, narration **2.** (*a*) narrative (*b*) *Sch:* essay. **narratif, -ive** *a* narrative.

nasal, -aux [nazal, -o] *a* nasal.

naseau, -eaux [nazo] *nm* nostril (of horse).

nasillement [nazijmɑ̃] *nm* (nasal) twang.

nasiller [nazije] *vi* to speak through the nose. **nasillard** *a* nasal (tone).

nasse [nas] *nf* eel pot, lobster pot; hoop net.

natal, -als [natal] *a* (*rarely used in the pl*) native (land); **ville natale,** birthplace.

natalité [natalite] *nf* birthrate.

natation [natasjɔ̃] *nf* swimming.

natif, -ive [natif, -iv] **1.** *a* (*a*) native (*b*) natural, inborn **2.** *n* native.

nation [nasjɔ̃] *nf* nation; **l'Organisation des Nations Unies,** the United Nations Organization.

national, -aux [nasjɔnal, -o] **1.** *a* national; state (education) **2.** *nmpl* **nationaux,** nationals (of a country) **3.** *nf* **nationale,** main road = A road; *NAm:* state highway.

nationalisation [nasjɔnalizasjɔ̃] *nf* nationalization.

nationaliser [nasjɔnalize] *vtr* to nationalize.

nationalisme [nasjɔnalism] *nm* nationalism. **nationaliste** *a & n* nationalist.

nationalité [nasjɔnalite] *nf* nationality.

natte [nat] *nf* **1.** (straw) mat, matting **2.** (*hair*) plait, pigtail.

naturalisation [natyralizasjɔ̃] *nf* naturalization.

naturaliser [natyralize] *vtr Adm: etc:* to naturalize; **se faire n. français(e),** to become a naturalized Frenchman, Frenchwoman.

nature [natyr] *nf* **1.** nature; **plus grand que n.,** larger than life; **n. morte,** still life (painting); **d'après n.,** (to paint) from life; *F:* **il a disparu dans la n.,** he's vanished into thin air **2.** (*a*) kind, character; **c'est, ce n'est pas, de n. à,** it's likely, not likely, to; **ce n'est pas dans sa n.,** it's not in his nature (*b*) character, disposition, temperament; **il est timide de n.,** he is naturally shy; **une n. violente,** a naturally violent person 3. **payer en n.**, to pay in kind 4. *a inv Cu:* plain; **café n.**, black coffee; **whisky n.**, neat whisky.

naturel, -elle [natyrɛl] 1. *a (a)* natural; bodily (needs); **enfant n.**, illegitimate child; **c'est n. chez elle**, it comes naturally to her; **mais c'est tout n.**, it was a pleasure; *esp NAm:* you're welcome *(b)* natural (gift); natural, unaffected (person); **soie naturelle**, pure silk 2. *nm (a)* native (of country) *(b)* nature, disposition *(c)* naturalness *(d) Cu:* **au n.**, (served) plain. **naturellement** *adv* naturally; of course.

naufrage [nofraʒ] *nm* (ship)wreck.

naufragé, -ée [nofraʒe] 1. *a* (ship)wrecked 2. *n* shipwrecked person; castaway.

nauséabond [nozeabɔ̃] *a* nauseating (smell).

nausée [noze] *nf (a)* nausea; **avoir la n., des nausées**, to feel sick *(b)* disgust; **ça me donne la n., j'en ai la n.**, it makes me sick.

nautique [notik] *a* nautical; **sports nautiques**, water sports; **fête n.**, water festival; **carte n.**, (sea) chart.

naval, -als [naval] *a* naval, nautical (terms); **construction navale**, shipbuilding; **chantier n.**, shipyard.

navarin [navarɛ̃] *nm Cu:* lamb stew, casserole.

navet [navɛ] *nm* 1. turnip 2. *F:* third-rate film, novel.

navette [navɛt] *nf (a)* shuttle; **faire la n.**, *(of vehicle)* to run a shuttle service, *(of pers)* to commute, *(of ship)* to ply (**entre**, between) *(b) Tex:* shuttle.

navigabilité [navigabilite] *nf* 1. navigability (of river) 2. seaworthiness; airworthiness. **navigable** *a* navigable (river).

navigant [navigɑ̃] *a* **personnel n.**, *nmpl* **les navigants**, (i) *Nau:* sea-going personnel (ii) *Av:* flying personnel.

navigateur [navigatœr] *nm* navigator.

navigation [navigasjɔ̃] *nf* navigation; sailing; **compagnie de n.**, shipping company; **compagnie de n. aérienne**, airline.

naviguer [navige] *vi* to sail; to navigate; *Av:* to fly; *F:* **il a beaucoup navigué**, he's been around a lot.

navire [navir] *nm* ship, vessel; **n. de guerre**, warship; **n. de commerce**, merchant ship.

navire-citerne [navirsitɛrn] *nm Nau:* tanker; *pl* navires-citernes.

navrer [navre] *vtr (a)* to grieve (s.o.) deeply; to distress, upset (s.o.) *(b)* to annoy (s.o.). **navrant** *a* distressing, upsetting. **navré** *a* sorry (**de**, to); distressed.

nazisme [nazism] *nm Pol:* nazism. **nazi, -ie** *a & n Pol:* Nazi.

ne, n' [n(ə)] *neg adv* 1. not; *(forming neg verb with* **pas**) **je ne le connais pas**, I do not, I don't, know him; **il n'a pas d'argent**, he hasn't any money 2. *used alone (ie with omission of* **pas**) *with* **cesser, oser, pouvoir, savoir, importer; je n'ose lui parler**, I dare not speak to him; **je ne saurais vous le dire**, I can't tell you; *always used without* **pas** *in the phr* **n'importe**, never mind, it doesn't matter 3. *in the following constructions: (a)* **que ne ferait-il pour vous?** what would he not do for you? *(b)* **il n'a confiance qu'en elle**, he trusts only her; **il n'y a pas que ça!** that's not all! *(c)* **si je ne me trompe**, unless I am mistaken; **voilà six mois que je ne l'ai vu**, it is now six months since I (last) saw him; **qu'à cela ne tienne!** by all means! **je n'ai que faire de son aide**, I don't need his help 4. *used with a vague negative connotation (a) (expressions of fear)* **je crains qu'il ne prenne froid**,

I'm afraid he may catch cold *(b)* **évitez qu'on ne vous voie**, take care not to be seen; **à moins qu'on ne vous appelle**, unless they call you *(c) (comparison)* **il est plus fort qu'on ne pense**, he is stronger than you think.

né [ne] *a* born.

néanmoins [neɑ̃mwɛ̃] *adv* nevertheless, yet.

néant [neɑ̃] *nm (a)* nothingness; **réduire qch à n.**, to annihilate sth, to wipe sth out *(b) (on form)* none; nil.

nébuleux, -euse [nebylø, -øz] *a (a)* cloudy (sky) *(b)* obscure, nebulous (ideas).

nécessaire [neseser] 1. *a* necessary; *(of pers)* indispensable (**à**, to); **choses qu'il est n. de savoir**, things one should know; **il est n. qu'on en parle**, we must talk about it 2. *nm (a)* necessities; **le strict n.**, the bare essentials; **je ferai le n.**, I'll see to it *(b)* **n. à couture**, sewing kit; **n. à ongles**, manicure set; **n. de toilette, de voyage**, toilet bag; grip. **nécessairement** *adv* necessarily; **doit-il n. partir?** must he go?

nécessité [nesesite] *nf (a)* necessity; **ce voyage est une n.**, this journey is essential; **être dans la n. de faire qch**, to be compelled to do sth *(b) pl* necessities (of life); requirements (of job); **de première n.**, indispensable.

nécessiter [nesesite] *vtr* to necessitate, require (sth).

nécessiteux, -euse *a* needy.

nécrologie [nekrɔlɔʒi] *nf* obituary notice; *Journ:* deaths.

nécropole [nekrɔpɔl] *nf* necropolis.

nectar [nɛktar] *nm* nectar.

néerlandais, -aise [neɛrlɑ̃dɛ, -ɛz] 1. *a* Dutch 2. *(a) n* Dutchman, -woman *(b) nm Ling:* Dutch.

nef [nɛf] *nf* nave; **n. latérale**, side aisle.

néfaste [nefast] *a* ill-fated, unlucky; harmful (**à**, to); **influence n.**, pernicious influence.

négatif, -ive [negatif, -iv] 1. *a* negative (answer, quantity); *Phot:* **épreuve négative**, *nm* **n.**, negative 2. *nf* négative, negative; **dans la n.**, (to answer) in the negative. **négativement** *adv* negatively.

négation [negasjɔ̃] *nf* 1. negation, denial 2. *Gram:* negative.

négligé [negliʒe] 1. *a (a)* neglected (wife) *(b)* slovenly (appearance); slipshod (work) 2. *nm (a)* slovenliness *(b) Cl:* négligé, negligee.

négligence [negliʒɑ̃s] *nf* negligence, carelessness.

négliger [negliʒe] *vtr* (**n. négligeons**) 1. to neglect (one's health, duty); to be careless about (one's appearance); **se n.**, to neglect oneself 2. *(a)* to disregard (advice) *(b)* **n. de faire qch**, to leave sth undone. **négligeable** *a* negligible; insignificant. **négligent** *a* negligent, careless; casual. **négligemment** *adv* carelessly.

négoce [negos] *nm* trade, business.

négociant, -ante [negɔsjɑ̃, -ɑ̃t] *n* merchant dealer; **n. en gros**, wholesaler.

négociateur, -trice [negɔsjatœr, -tris] *n* negociator.

négociation [negɔsjasjɔ̃] *nf* negotiation.

négocier [negɔsje] *vtr* to negotiate. **négociable** *a* negotiable.

nègre, négresse [negr, negrɛs] 1. *n (a)* negro, negress; *Pej:* nigger *(b) F:* ghost writer 2. *a (f* **nègre**) **la race nègre**, the negro race.·

neige [nɛʒ] *nf* snow; **n. fondue**, (i) sleet (ii) slush; **boule de n.**, snowball; **train de n.**, winter sports train; *Ind:* **n. carbonique**, dry ice; *Cu:* **blancs d'œufs battus en n.**, beaten egg whites.

neiger [neʒe] *v impers* (**il neigeait**) to snow. **neigeux, -euse** *a* snowy, snow-covered.

nénuphar [nenyfar] *nm Bot:* water lily.

néo-gallois, -oise [neogalwa, -waz] *a & n* (native, inhabitant) of New South Wales; *pl* **néo-gallois, -oises.**

néolithique [neɔlitik] *a* neolithic.

néologisme [neɔlɔʒism] *nm* neologism.

néon [neɔ̃] *nm Ch:* neon.

néophyte [neɔfit] *nm* (a) neophyte (b) beginner.

néo-zélandais, -aise [neozelɑ̃dɛ, -ɛz] **1.** *a* New Zealand (government, butter) **2.** *n* New Zealander; *pl* **néo-zélandais, -aises.**

nerf [nɛr] *nm* (a) *Anat:* nerve; **elle a les nerfs malades**, she suffers from nerves; **porter sur les nerfs à qn**, to get on s.o.'s nerves; **avoir les nerfs en boule**, to be on edge, to be nervy; **être sur les nerfs**, to be tense; **avoir ses nerfs**, to have a fit of nerves (b) **avoir du n.**, to have stamina; **mets-y du n.!** [nɛrf] put some guts into it! **allons, du n.!** come on, buck up!

nerveux, -euse [nɛrvø, -øz] *a* **1.** nervous (system, illness) nerve (centre) **2.** sinewy (hand); wiry (body); stringy (meat); **moteur n.**, responsive engine **3.** nervous, tense, highly strung, *F:* nervy (person). **nerveusement** *adv* nervously, tensely.

nervosité [nɛrvozite] *nf* nervousness, tension; irritability, edginess.

nervure [nɛrvyr] *nf* (a) nervure, vein (of leaf) (b) *Arch:* rib (of vault).

n'est-ce pas [nɛspɑ] *adv phr* (*inviting assent*) **vous venez, n'est-ce pas?** you're coming, aren't you? **il fait chaud, n'est-ce pas?** it's hot, isn't it? **il ne comprend pas, n'est-ce pas?** he doesn't understand, does he?

net, nette [nɛt] *a* **1.** clean; neat, tidy (house); clear (conscience); **n. d'impôt**, tax free; *nm* **mettre qch au n.**, to make a fair copy of sth **2.** (a) clear (idea); plain, straight (answer); distinct, marked (difference); **contours nets**, sharp outlines; *Phot:* **image nette**, sharp image (b) net (weight, price); net, clear (profit) **3.** *adv* plainly, outright; **refuser n.**, to refuse flatly; **parler n.**, to speak bluntly, frankly; **s'arrêter n.**, to stop dead; **se casser n.**, to break clean through.

nettement *adv* clearly, distinctly; plainly, flatly; **parler n.**, to speak bluntly.

netteté [nɛt(ə)te] *nf* **1.** cleanness (of break) **2.** neatness (of appearance, work); clearness, clarity (of thought); sharpness (of image).

nettoyage [nɛtwajaʒ] *nm* cleaning; *Mil:* mopping up; **n. à sec**, dry cleaning; **le grand n.**, spring cleaning.

nettoyer [nɛtwaje] *vtr* (**je nettoie**) (a) to clean; **n. au chiffon**, to dust; **n. à sec**, to dry-clean (b) *Mil:* to mop up (c) *P:* to finish (s.o.) off; (of burglar) to strip (house).

neuf¹ [nœf, nœv] *num a inv & nm inv* nine **1. card a** (at the end of the word-group [nœf]; before **ans** and **heures** [nœv]; otherwise before vowel sounds [nœf]; before a noun and adjective beginning with a consonant usu [nœ]; often [nœf]) **j'en ai n.** [nœf] I have nine; **il a n. ans** [nœvɑ̃] he's nine years old **2.** ordinal and other

uses (always [nœf]) **le n. mai**, the ninth of May; **Louis N.**, Louis the Ninth.

neuf², neuve [nœf, nœv] **1.** *a* (a) new; fresh (idea); **à l'état n.**, as (good as) new (b) *F:* **quoi de n.?** what's new? **2.** *nm* **habillé de n.**, dressed in new clothes; **il y a du n.**, I have news for you; *adv phr* **remettre qch à n.**, to renovate sth, to do sth up (like new).

neurasthénie [nørasteni] *nf* depression. **neurasthénique** *a* depressive.

neurologie [nørɔlɔʒi] *nf Med:* neurology.

neurologue [nørɔlɔg] *n* neurologist.

neutralisation [nøtralizasjɔ̃] *nf* neutralization.

neutraliser [nøtralize] *vtr* to neutralize.

neutralité [nøtralite] *nf* neutrality.

neutre [nøtr] *a* **1.** neuter; *nm Ling:* **au n.**, in the neuter **2.** neutral.

neutron [nøtrɔ̃] *nm* neutron.

neuvième [nœvjɛm] **1.** *num a & n* ninth **2.** *nm* ninth (part). **neuvièmement** *adv* ninthly.

neveu, -eux [nəvø] *nm* nephew.

névralgie [nevralʒi] *nf* neuralgia. **névralgique** *a* neuralgic.

névrose [nevroz] *nf* neurosis. **névrosé, -ée** *a & n* neurotic (patient).

nez [ne] *nm* **1.** (a) nose; **parler du n.**, to speak through one's nose; **faire un pied de n. à qn**, to cock a snook at s.o. (b) **mettre le n. à la fenêtre**, to show one's face at the window; **n. à n.**, face to face; **baisser le n.**, to look ashamed; **faire un long n.**, to pull a face; **ça lui a passé sous le n.**, it slipped through his fingers; **fermer la porte au n. de qn**, to shut the door in s.o.'s face; **rire au n. de qn**, to laugh in s.o.'s face (c) **avoir du n.**, to have flair (d) **au n. et à la barbe de qn**, right under s.o.'s nose; *F:* **je l'ai dans le n.**, I can't stand him; **se bouffer le n.**, to quarrel **2.** bow (of ship); nose (of aircraft).

NF *abbr normes françaises* = British Standards.

ni [ni] *conj* (**ne** *is either expressed or implied*) (a) nor, or; **ni moi (non plus)**, neither do I; **sans argent ni bagages**, without money or luggage (b) **sans manger ni boire**, without (either) eating or drinking; **il ne peut ni ne veut accepter**, he neither can nor wants to accept (c) **ni . . . ni**, neither . . . nor; **ni l'un ni l'autre**, neither (of them); **ni vu ni connu**, no one will know.

niais, -aise [njɛ, -ɛz] **1.** *a* simple, foolish (person); inane (laugh) **2.** *n* fool, simpleton. **niaisement** *adv* foolishly, inanely.

niaiserie [njɛzri] *nf* silliness, foolishness; **dire des niaiseries**, to talk nonsense.

niche [niʃ] *nf* **1.** niche, recess **2.** (dog) kennel, *NAm:* doghouse **3.** trick, prank.

nichée [niʃe] *nf* brood (of birds, children); litter (of puppies).

nicher [niʃe] **1.** *vi* (of bird) to build a nest; to nest; *F:* (of pers) to hang out **2. se n.**, (of bird) to nest; (of village) to nestle; **niché dans un fauteuil**, curled up in an armchair.

nickel [nikɛl] **1.** *nm* nickel **2.** *a P:* spick and span; neat.

nickeler [nikle] *vtr* (**je nickelle**) to nickel-plate.

niçois, -oise [niswa, -waz] *a & n* (native) of Nice.

nicotine [nikɔtin] *nf* nicotine.

nid [ni] *nm* (a) nest; **n. de brigands**, robber's den; **n. à poussière**, dust trap; **n. de poule**, pothole (in road)

(b) n. de mitrailleuses, nest of machine-guns; n. de résistance, centre of resistance.

nièce [njɛs] *nf* niece.

nier [nje] *vtr* (*impf & pr sub* n. niions) to deny (fact); *abs* l'accusé nie, the accused denies the charge.

nigaud, -aude [nigo, -od] (*a*) *n* simpleton, *F:* twit (*b*) *a* silly, simple.

Niger [niʒɛr] *Prnm Geog:* (*a*) the (river) Niger (*b*) (*state*) Niger. **Nigérien, -ienne** *a & n* (native, inhabitant) of Niger.

Nigéria [niʒerja] *Prnm Geog:* Nigeria. **Nigérian, -ianne** *a & n* Nigerian.

Nil [nil] *Prnm* the (river) Nile; (*colour*) (vert de) N., eau-de-nil.

nippes [nip] *nfpl F:* clothes, togs.

nipper [nipe] *vtr F:* to tog out; se n., to get togged out.

nippon, -one [nipɔ̃, -ɔn] *a & n* Nipponese, Japanese.

nitrate [nitrat] *nm Ch:* nitrate. **nitrique** *a* nitric.

nitroglycérine [nitrogliserin] *nf* nitroglycerine.

niveau, -eaux [nivo] *nm* 1. (*instruments*) n. à bulle d'air, spirit level; n. d'huile, d'essence, oil, petrol, gauge 2. (*a*) n. de bruit, noise level (*b*) (ground, sea) level; l'eau arrivait au n. des genoux, the water was knee-deep; *Rail:* passage à n., level, *NAm:* grade, crossing; être au même n. que, de n. avec, qch, to be level with sth (*c*) n. de vie, standard of living; n. social, social standing; au n., up to standard; être au n. de qch, to be on a par with sth.

nivelage [nivlaʒ] *nm,* **nivellement** [nivɛlmã] *nm* levelling.

niveler [nivle] *vtr* (je nivelle) to level; n. au plus bas, to level down.

noble [nɔbl] 1. *a* noble 2. *n* noble(man), noblewoman; les nobles, the nobility. **noblement** *adv* nobly.

noblesse [nɔblɛs] *nf* nobility; petite n., gentry.

noce [nɔs] *nf* 1. (*a*) wedding (*b*) wedding party (*c*) voyage de noces, honeymoon (trip); noces d'or, golden wedding; épouser qn en secondes noces, to marry for the second time 2. *F:* faire la n., to live it up; je n'étais pas à la n., I was having a bad time.

noceur, -euse [nɔsœr, -øz] *n* reveller.

nocivité [nɔsivite] *nf* noxiousness, harmfulness. **nocif, -ive** *a* harmful, noxious (à, to).

noctambule [nɔktãbyl] *n F:* night owl.

nocturne [nɔktyrn] 1. *a* nocturnal; night (attack); (*of shop*) n. le vendredi, late night opening on Fridays 2. *nm* (*a*) night bird (*b*) *Mus:* nocturne 3. *nm or f Sp:* evening fixture.

Noël [nɔɛl] *nm* 1. Christmas; la nuit de N., Christmas Eve; le Père N., Father Christmas 2. (*a*) Christmas carol (*b*) Christmas present.

nœud [nø] *nm* 1. (*a*) knot; faire son n. de cravate, to knot one's tie; les nœuds de l'amitié, the bonds of friendship (*b*) crux (of problem) (*c*) *Cost:* bow; faire un n., to tie a bow; n. papillon, bow tie 2. (*a*) knot (in timber) (*b*) *Ph:* node 3. n. ferroviaire, railway junction 4. *NauMeas:* knot.

noir, noire [nwar] 1. *a* (*a*) black; dark (eyes, hair); race noire, negro race (*b*) dark, swarthy (complexion); être n. de coups, to be black and blue (*c*) dark (night); gloomy (thoughts); utter (poverty);

black (mood, humour); macabre (film); il faisait n., nuit noire, it was pitch-dark; ma bête noire, my pet aversion (*d*) dirty, grimy (hands) (*e*) regarder qn d'un œil n., to give s.o. a black look (*f*) *P:* drunk, tight 2. *n* black (man, woman) 3. *nm* (*a*) black; c'était écrit n. sur blanc, it was there in black and white; voir tout en n., to look at the dark side of everything; être en n., to wear black; to be in mourning (*b*) mascara; eyeliner (*c*) bull's eye (of target) (*d*) dark, darkness; j'ai peur du n., dans le n., I'm afraid of the dark (*e*) acheter au n., to buy on the black market; travail (au) n., moonlighting 4. *nf Mus:* noire, crochet. **noirâtre** *a* blackish, darkish. **noiraud, -aude** *a & n* swarthy (man, woman).

noirceur [nwarsœr] *nf* (*a*) blackness, darkness (*b*) base action.

noircir [nwarsir] 1. *vi* to become black; to darken; (*of skin*) to tan 2. *vtr* to blacken; n. du papier, to scribble; n. la réputation de qn, to blacken s.o.'s character 3. se n., to grow black; (*of sky*) to darken. **noircissement** [nwarsismã] *nm* blackening. **noircissure** [nwarsisyr] *nf* black spot, mark.

noise [nwaz] *nf* chercher n. à qn, to try to pick a quarrel with s.o.

noisetier [nwaztje] *nm* hazel tree.

noisette [nwazɛt] 1. *nf* hazelnut; n. de beurre, knob of butter 2. *a inv* (*colour*) hazel.

noix [nwa] *nf* 1. walnut; n. de beurre, knob of butter 2. nut; n. de coco, coconut; n. d'acajou, cashew nut 3. *P:* à la n., useless; rubbishy.

nom [nɔ̃] *nm* 1. name; traiter qn de tous les noms, to call s.o. names; n. de famille, surname; n. de guerre, assumed name; n. de théâtre, stage name; n. et prénoms, full name; surname and given names; crime sans n., unspeakable crime; n. de n.! n. d'une pipe! hell! au n. du ciel! in heaven's name! *Com:* n. déposé, registered (trade) name; se faire un n., to make a name for oneself; connaître qn de n., to know s.o. by name; au n. de la loi, in the name of the law; faire qch au n. de qn, to do sth on s.o.'s behalf 2. *Gram:* noun; n. propre, proper noun.

nomade [nɔmad] 1. *a* nomadic 2. *n* nomad.

nombre [nɔ̃br] *nm* 1. number; (un) bon n. de gens, a good many people; le plus grand n., the majority; venir en n., to come in large numbers; faire n., to make up the numbers; ils ont vaincu par le n., they conquered by force of numbers; surpasser en n., to outnumber; ils sont au n. de huit, there are eight of them; mettre qn au n. de ses amis, to number s.o. among one's friends 2. *Gram:* number. **nombreux, -euse** *a* (*a*) numerous; (large) family; réunion peu nombreuse, small gathering (*b*) many (objects); peu n., few.

nombril [nɔ̃bri] *nm* navel.

nomenclature [nɔmãklatyr] *nf* nomenclature; list.

nominal, -aux [nɔminal, -o] *a* nominal; appel n., roll call; valeur nominale, face value. **nominalement** *adv* nominally.

nominatif, -ive [nɔminatif, -iv] 1. *a* nominal; état n., list of names; *Fin:* titres nominatifs, registered securities 2. *nm Gram:* nominative (case).

nomination [nɔminasjɔ̃] *nf* 1. nomination (for a post) 2. appointment; recevoir sa n., to be appointed.

nommer [nɔme] *vtr* 1. (*a*) to name (s.o.) (*b*) to mention by name; **qn que je ne nommerai pas,** s.o. who shall be nameless; **n. un jour,** to appoint a day (*c*) to appoint (to a post); to nominate (candidate); **être nommé au grade supérieur,** to be promoted 2. **se n.** (*a*) to give one's name (*b*) to be called, named.

non [nɔ̃] *adv* (*no liaison with the following word except in compounds*) 1. no, not; **le voulez-vous?**—**n.,** do you want it?—no (I don't); **répondre (par) n.,** to answer no; **c'est dégoûtant, n.?** it's disgusting isn't it? **mais n.!** oh no! **je pense que n.,** I don't think so; **faire signe que n.,** to shake one's head; **qu'il vienne ou n.,** whether he comes or not; **n. (pas) que je le craigne,** not that I fear him; *nm inv* les **n. l'emportent,** the noes have it 2. **n. loin de la ville,** not far from the town; **n. sans raison,** not without reason; **n. seulement il pleut mais encore il fait froid,** not only is it raining but it's also cold.

non-agression [nɔnagresjɔ̃, nɔ̃-] *nf* non-aggression.

non-alcoolisé [nɔnalkɔlize, nɔ̃-] *a* non-alcoholic.

non-alignement [nɔnaliɲmɑ̃, nɔ̃-] *a Pol:* non-alignment.

nonante [nɔnɑ̃t] *num a* & *nm inv Belg: SwFr:* ninety.

non-assistance [nɔnasistɑ̃s, nɔ̃-] *nf* **n.-a. à personne en danger,** failure to assist s.o. in danger.

nonce [nɔ̃s] *nm* **n. du Pape,** Papal Nuncio.

nonchalance [nɔ̃ʃalɑ̃s] *nf* nonchalance; indifference. **nonchalant** *a* nonchalant. **nonchalamment** *adv* nonchalantly.

non-combattant [nɔ̃kɔ̃batɑ̃] *a* & *nm* non-combatant; *pl* non-combattants.

non-conformisme [nɔ̃kɔ̃fɔrmizm] *nm* non-conformism.

non-existant [nɔnegzistɑ̃, nɔ̃-] *a* non-existent.

non-ferreux, -euse [nɔfɛrø, -øz] *a* non-ferrous.

non-intervention [nɔnɛ̃tervɑ̃sjɔ̃] *nf* non-intervention.

non-livraison [nɔ̃livrɛzɔ̃] *nf Com:* non-delivery.

non-paiement [nɔ̃pemɑ̃] *nm* non-payment.

non-retour [nɔ̃rətur] *nm* **point de n.-r.,** point of no return.

non-sens [nɔ̃sɑ̃s] *nm inv* **c'est un n.-s.,** it's nonsense, meaningless.

non-valable [nɔ̃valabl] *a* 1. *Jur:* invalid (clause) 2. (*of ticket, passport*) not valid.

non-valeur [nɔ̃valœr] *nf* bad debt; worthless security; *pl* non-valeurs.

nord [nɔr] 1. *nm no pl* north; **au n. de,** (to the) north of; **vent du n.,** north, northerly, wind; **la mer du N.,** the North Sea; **l'Amérique du N.,** North America; *F:* **perdre le n.,** to lose one's head 2. *a inv* north; **le Pôle N.,** the North Pole.

nord-africain, -aine [nɔrafrikɛ̃, -ɛn] *a* & *n* North African; *pl* nord-africain(e)s.

nord-américain, -aine [nɔramerikɛ̃, -ɛn] *a* & *n* North American; *pl* nord-américain(e)s.

nord-est [nɔrɛst] *nm* north-east.

nordique [nɔrdik] 1. *a* Nordic 2. *n* Scandinavian.

nordiste [nɔrdist] 1. *a* northern 2. *Hist:* Yankee.

nord-ouest [nɔrwɛst] *nm* north-west.

normal, -aux [nɔrmal, -o] 1. *a* (*a*) normal; **c'est tout à fait n.!** it's quite usual, natural! **elle n'est pas nor-** **male,** there's sth wrong with her; **école normale,** college of education (*b*) standard (weight, size) 2. *nf* **la normale,** the normal, the norm; **revenir à la n.,** to return to normality; **au-dessus de la n.,** above average. **normalement** *adv* normally, usually.

normaliser [nɔrmalize] *vtr* to normalize; to standardize.

Normandie [nɔrmɑ̃di] *Prnf Geog:* Normandy. **normand, -ande** *a* & *n* Norman; *F:* **réponse normande,** non-committal answer.

norme [nɔrm] *nf* norm, standard; **conforme à la n.,** up to standard.

Norvège [nɔrvɛʒ] *Prnf Geog:* Norway. **norvégien, -ienne** 1. *a* & *n* Norwegian 2. *nm Ling:* Norwegian.

nostalgie [nɔstalʒi] *nf* nostalgia; homesickness. **nostalgique** *a* nostalgic, homesick.

notabilité [nɔtabilite] *nf* notability. **notable** *a* notable. **notablement** *adv* notably.

notaire [nɔtɛr] *nm* notary; *Scot:* notary public.

notamment [nɔtamɑ̃] *adv* notably; especially, in particular.

notation [nɔtasjɔ̃] *nf* notation; marking (of work).

note [nɔt] *nf* 1. (*a*) note; **prendre des notes,** to take notes; **prendre n. de qch,** to make a note of sth; **n. de service,** memo(randum) (*b*) annotation; **n. en bas de page,** footnote 2. *Sch:* mark; **bonne, mauvaise, n.,** good, bad, mark 3. *Mus:* note; **cette remarque était dans la n.,** that remark struck the right note; **n. d'originalité,** touch of originality 4. bill.

noter [nɔte] *vtr* 1. to note; to take notice of (sth); **notez (bien) qu'il n'a rien dit,** he didn't say anything, mind you 2. (*a*) to write, jot, down; **notez-le,** make a note of it (*b*) to mark (passage) (*c*) *Sch:* to mark (work).

notice [nɔtis] *nf* 1. note 2. instructions, directions; **n. d'emploi,** directions for use; **n. publicitaire,** advertisement.

notification [nɔtifikasjɔ̃] *nf* notification.

notifier [nɔtifje] *vtr* (*impf* & *pr sub* **n. notifiions**) to notify.

notion [nɔsjɔ̃] *nf* notion, idea; **perdre la n. du temps,** to lose all sense of time; **il a des notions de chimie,** he has a smattering of chemistry.

notoire [nɔtwar] *a* well-known (fact); notorious (criminal); **c'est n.,** it's common knowledge. **notoirement** *adv* notoriously.

notoriété [nɔtɔrjete] *nf* notoriety (of fact); fame; reputation (of pers).

notre, *pl* **nos** [nɔtr, no] *poss a* our; **nos père et mère,** our father and mother.

nôtre [notr] 1. *poss a* ours; **sa maison est n.,** his house is ours 2. **le n., la n., les nôtres,** (*a*) *poss pron* ours; our own (*b*) *nm* (i) **le n.,** our own; **il faut y mettre du n.,** we must do our bit (ii) **les nôtres,** our own (friends); our family; **est-il des nôtres?** is he joining us?

nouba [nuba] *nf P:* **faire la n.,** to live it up.

nouer [nwe, nue] *vtr* 1. (*a*) to tie, knot, fasten; to tie up, do up (parcel) (*b*) **avoir la gorge nouée,** to have a lump in one's throat (*c*) **n. conversation avec qn,** to start a conversation with s.o. 2. **se n.** (*of cord*) to become knotty; (*of hands*) to join together. **noueux, -euse** *a* knotty, gnarled.

nougat [nuga] *nm Comest:* nougat.

nouille [nuj] *nf* 1. *pl Cu:* noodles 2. *F:* idiot, noodle; **c'est une n.,** he's a drip.

nounou [nunu] *nf* nanny.

nounours [nunurs] *nm* teddy (bear).

nourri [nuri] *a* 1. nourished, fed; **bien n.,** well fed; **mal n.,** underfed 2. heavy (fire); lively, sustained (conversation).

nourrice [nuris] *nf (a)* (wet) nurse; **mettre un enfant en n.,** to put out a child to nurse *(b) Aut:* spare can, jerrycan (of petrol).

nourrir [nurir] *vtr* 1. to nurse (infant) 2. to feed (people, animals, fire); to keep (one's family); **ça ne nourrit pas son homme,** it doesn't provide a living; **le lait nourrit,** milk is nourishing 3. to foster (hatred); to harbour (thoughts); to cherish (hope) 4. **se n. de (qch),** to eat, feed on, live on (sth). **nourrissant** *a* nourishing.

nourrisson [nurisõ] *nm* infant.

nourriture [nurityr] *nf* food; **n. saine,** healthy diet.

nous [nu] *pers pron* 1. *(a) (subject)* we *(b) (object)* us; to us; **il n. en a parlé,** he spoke to us about it *(c) (reflexive)* **n. n. chauffons,** we are warming ourselves; **n. n. connaissons,** we know each other 2. **n. tous,** all of us; us all; **un ami à n.,** a friend of ours; **n. l'avons fait n.-mêmes,** we did it ourselves; **ce livre est à n.,** that book belongs to us.

nouveau, -el, -elle¹, -eaux [nuvo, -el] *a* (**nouvel** *is used before m sing nouns beginning with a vowel or* **h** *'mute')* 1. new *(a) (usu follows noun)* **pommes de terre nouvelles,** new potatoes *(b)* **il n'y a rien de n.,** there's nothing new; *nm* **j'ai appris du n.,** I have some news; **c'est du n.,** that's news to me 2. *(usu precedes noun)* new, fresh, another; **une nouvelle raison,** a further reason; **la nouvelle génération,** the rising generation; **jusqu'à nouvel ordre,** until further notice; **le nouvel an,** the new year; *nmpl* **les nouveaux,** the newcomers; *Sch:* the new boys, girls 3. *(with adv function)* **le n. venu,** the newcomer 4. **de n.,** again; **à n.,** afresh, (all over) again; *Book-k:* **solde à n.,** balance brought forward.

nouveau-né, -née [nuvone] *a & n* new-born (child); *pl nouveau-nés, -nées.*

nouveauté [nuvote] *nf* 1. novelty 2. change, innovation; **c'est une n.!** that's new! 3. new thing; new invention, new publication 4. *pl* **magasin de nouveautés,** fashion shop; **nouveautés de printemps,** (new) spring fashions.

nouvelle² *nf* 1. *usu in pl (a)* (piece of) news; *Journ:* **dernières nouvelles,** late news *(b) pl* news (of, about, s.o., sth); **avez-vous de ses nouvelles?** have you heard from him? **prendre des nouvelles de qn,** to ask about s.o.; **goûtez ça, vous m'en direz des nouvelles,** taste this, I'm sure you'll like it; **vous aurez de mes nouvelles!** I'll give you what for! 2. short story.

Nouvelle-Angleterre [nuvelãgləter] *Prnf Geog:* New England.

Nouvelle-Calédonie [nuvelkaledɔni] *Prnf Geog:* New Caledonia.

Nouvelle-Écosse [nuvelekɔs] *Prnf Geog:* Nova Scotia.

Nouvelle-Guinée [nuvelgine] *Prnf Geog:* New Guinea.

nouvellement [nuvelmã] *adv* newly, lately, recently.

Nouvelle-Orléans [nuvelɔrleã] *Prnf Geog:* New Orleans.

Nouvelle-Zélande [nuvelzelãd] *Prnf Geog:* New Zealand.

novembre [nɔvãbr̩] *nm* November; **au mois de n., en n.,** in (the month of) November.

novice [nɔvis] 1. *n Rel:* novice; probationer (in profession); beginner, novice 2. *a* inexperienced (**dans,** in).

noyade [nwajad] *nf* drowning (accident).

noyau, -aux [nwajo] *nm* 1. stone, pit (of fruit) 2. nucleus (of atom, cell); core (of the earth); group, circle (of people); **n. de résistance,** hard core of resistance.

noyé, -ée [nwaje] 1. *a.* drowned; drowning; **être n.,** to be all at sea 2. *n* drowned man, woman.

noyer¹ [nwaje] *nm* walnut (tree, wood).

noyer² (je noie, n. noyons) 1. *vtr (a)* to drown; to swamp, inundate (earth); **yeux noyés de larmes,** eyes brimming with tears; **noyé dans la foule,** lost in the crowd; **noyé dans l'obscurité,** shrouded in darkness *(b)* to flood (engine) *(c)* to countersink (screw) 2. **se n.,** to drown; to drown oneself; **se n. dans les détails,** to get bogged down in details; **se n. dans un verre d'eau,** to make a mountain out of a molehill.

nu [ny] 1. *a (a)* naked; bare; *Art:* nude; **nu comme un ver,** stark naked. NOTE: **nu** *before the noun it qualifies is invariable and is joined by a hyphen to the noun;* **aller pieds nus, aller nu-pieds,** to go barefoot(ed); *nmpl* **nu-pieds,** flip-flops, *NAm:* thongs *(b)* uncovered, undisguised; **la vérité nue,** the plain, naked, truth *(c)* bare (room) 2. *nm Art:* nude 3. **à nu,** bare, naked; **mettre à nu,** to lay bare, expose; to strip (wire); to lay bare (one's heart).

NU *abbr* Nations Unies.

nuage [nɥaʒ] *nm (a)* cloud; **ciel couvert de nuages,** overcast sky; **sans nuages,** cloudless; unclouded (future) *(b)* gloom, shadow *(c)* **être dans les nuages,** to have one's head in the clouds. **nuageux, -euse** *a* cloudy, overcast (sky).

nuance [nɥãs] *nf* shade (of colour); hue, tinge (of bitterness); **je ne saisis pas la n.,** I don't see the difference.

nucléaire [nykleer] *a* nuclear.

nudisme [nydism] *nm* nudism.

nudiste [nydist] *n* nudist.

nudité [nydite] *nf (a)* nudity, nakedness *(b)* bareness (of wall).

nues [ny] *nfpl* skies; **porter qn aux n.,** to praise s.o. to the skies; **tomber des n.,** to be thunderstruck.

nuire [nɥir] *v ind tr (pp* **nui,** *otherwise conj like* CONDUIRE) 1. **n. à qn,** to be harmful to s.o.; to harm s.o.; **cela nuira à sa réputation,** it will injure his reputation 2. **se n.,** to do oneself a lot of harm.

nuisible [nɥizibl] *a* harmful, injurious (**à,** to); **animaux nuisibles,** pests.

nuit [nɥi] *nf (a)* night; **cette n.,** (i) tonight (ii) last night; **dans la n. de lundi,** during Monday night; **voyager de n., la n.,** to travel at night; **être de n.,** to be on night shift; **je n'ai pas dormi de la n.,** I didn't sleep a wink all night *(b)* darkness; **il se fait n.,** it's getting dark; **à la n. tombante,** at nightfall; **avant la**

n., before dark; **dans la n. des temps,** in the mists of time.

nul, nulle [nyl] **1.** (*with* **ne** *expressed or understood*) (*a*) *indef a* no; not one; **n. espoir,** no hope; **sans n. doute,** without any doubt (*b*) *indef pron* no one; nobody; **n. d'entre nous,** none of us **2.** *a* (*a*) worthless; useless; **il est n. en maths,** he's hopeless at maths (*b*) (*of result*) nil; (*of election*) null and void; *Jur:* **n. et non avenu,** null and void; *Sp:* **course nulle,** dead heat; **le score est n.,** it's a nil draw (*c*) non-existent (funds). **nullement** *adv* (*with* **ne,** *expressed or understood*) not at all, not in the least.

nullité [nulite] *nf* **1.** nullity, invalidity (of deed) **2.** incompetence; uselessness **3.** (*of pers.*) nonentity; *F:* wash-out.

numérique [nymerik] *a* numerical. **numérique-ment** *adv* numerically.

numéraire [nymerɛr] *nm* metallic currency; cash.

numéro [nymero] *nm* (*a*) number; **j'habite au n. 10,** I live at number 10; **n. d'appel,** telephone number (*b*) number, issue (of periodical); **ancien n.,** back number (*c*) *Th:* number, turn; **il a fait son petit n.,** he put on his little act (*d*) (*of pers*) **quel n.!** what a character! **numéral, -aux** *a & nm* numeral.

numéroter [nymerɔte] *vtr* to number (street); to paginate (book).

nuptial, -aux [nypsjal, -o] *a* nuptial, bridal; **cérémonie nuptiale,** wedding.

nuque [nyk] *nf* nape (of the neck).

nutrition [nytrisjɔ̃] *nf* nutrition. **nutritif, -ive** *a* nourishing, nutritious; nutritive; **valeur nutritive,** food value.

nylon [nilɔ̃] *nm Rtm:* nylon; **bas (de) n.,** nylon stockings, nylons.

nymphe [nɛ̃f] *nf* **1.** nymph **2.** *Biol:* pupa, chrysalis.

O

O, o [o] *nm* (the letter) O, o.

oasis [ɔazis] *nf* oasis.

obéir [ɔbeir] *v ind tr* (*a*) to obey; **o. à qn**, to obey s.o.; **se faire o.**, to enforce obedience; **o. à un ordre**, to comply with an order; **o. à une impulsion**, to act on an impulse. **obéissant** *a* obedient.

obéissance [ɔbeisɑ̃s] *nf* obedience (à, to).

obélisque [ɔbelisk] *nm* obelisk.

obésité [ɔbezite] *nf* obesity, corpulence. **obèse** *a* obese, fat (person).

objecter [ɔbʒɛkte] *vtr* to raise (sth) as an objection; **il n'a rien à o.**, he has no objection (to make); **o. la fatigue**, to plead tiredness; **on lui objecta son âge**, they took exception to his age.

objecteur [ɔbʒɛktœr] *nm* **o. de conscience**, conscientious objector.

objectif, -ive [ɔbʒɛktif, -iv] **1.** *a* objective; unbiased **2.** *nm* aim, object(ive), end **3.** *nm Phot:* (i) lens (ii) camera. **objectivement** *adv* objectively.

objection [ɔbʒɛksjɔ̃] *nf* objection; **faire une o.**, to object.

objet [ɔbʒɛ] *nm* **1.** (*a*) object, thing; **objets trouvés**, lost property (*b*) *Gram: Phil:* object **2.** (*a*) subject (of conversation); **o. de pitié**, object of pity; **faire, être, l'o. de**, to be the subject of (*b*) object, purpose (of action); **remplir son o.**, to attain one's end; **sans o.**, pointless.

obligation [ɔbligasjɔ̃] *nf* **1.** (moral) obligation; duty; **se voir dans l'o. de faire qch**, to be under an obligation to do sth **2.** *Jur:* obligation, bond **3.** *Com: Fin:* bond, debenture.

obligatoire [ɔbligatwar] *a.* obligatory; compulsory; *F:* **c'était o.!** it *had* to happen! **obligatoirement** *adv* compulsorily; *F:* inevitably.

obligé, -ée [ɔbliʒe] **1.** *a* (*a*) obliged, compelled (**de faire qch**, to do sth) (*b*) inevitable; **c'est o. qu'il rate son examen**, he's bound to fail his exam (*c*) obliged, grateful (**de**, for) **2.** *n* person under obligation; *Jur:* obligee.

obligeance [ɔbliʒɑ̃s] *nf* **il a eu l'o. de m'accompagner**, he was kind enough to accompany me.

obliger [ɔbliʒe] *vtr* (**n. obligeons**) **1.** to oblige, compel; **mon devoir m'y oblige**, I am in duty bound to do it; **o. qn à faire qch**, to force s.o. to do sth; **être obligé de faire qch**, to be obliged to do sth **2. o. qn**, to oblige s.o., to do s.o. a favour. **obligeant** *a* obliging, kind. **obligeamment** *adv* obligingly.

oblique [ɔblik] **1.** *a* oblique (line); **regard o.**, sidelong glance **2.** *nf* oblique line. **obliquement** *adv* obliquely.

obliquer [ɔblike] *vi* to take an oblique direction.

oblitération [ɔbliterasjɔ̃] *nf* cancellation (of stamp).

oblitérer [ɔblitere] *vtr* (**j'oblitère; j'oblitérerai**) to cancel (stamp).

oblong, -ongue [ɔblɔ̃, -ɔ̃g] *a* oblong.

obole [ɔbɔl] *nf* small offering.

obscénité [ɔpsenite] *nf* obscenity. **obscène** *a* obscene.

obscur [ɔpskyr] *a* **1.** dark; gloomy **2.** (*a*) obscure; difficult to understand; abstruse (subject) (*b*) vague, dim (foreboding); obscure, humble (birth); unknown (writer). **obscurément** *adv* obscurely.

obscurcir [ɔpskyrsir] **1.** *vtr* to obscure; to darken, cloud **2. s'o.**, to darken; to grow dark; (*of subject*) to become obscure.

obscurcissement [ɔpskyrsismɑ̃] *nm* obscuring, darkening.

obscurité [ɔpskyrite] *nf* darkness; obscurity; **dans l'o.**, in the dark.

obsédé, -ée [ɔpsede] *n* **o. sexuel**, sex maniac.

obséder [ɔpsede] *vtr* (**j'obsède; j'obséderai**) to obsess, to haunt; **obsédé par une idée**, obsessed by an idea. **obsédant** *a* obsessive, haunting.

obsèques [ɔpsɛk] *nfpl* funeral.

obséquieux, -euse [ɔpsekjø, -øz] *a* obsequious.

observance [ɔpsɛrvɑ̃s] *nf* observance (of rule).

observateur, -trice [ɔpsɛrvatœr, -tris] **1.** *n* observer; *Mil: etc:* spotter **2.** *a* observant, observing.

observation [ɔpsɛrvasjɔ̃] *nf* **1.** observance **2.** observation; **malade en o.**, patient under observation **3.** observation, remark; comment; **faire une o. à qn**, to criticize s.o.

observatoire [ɔpsɛrvatwar] *nm* (*a*) *Astr:* observatory (*b*) observation post.

observer [ɔpsɛrve] **1.** *vtr* (*a*) to observe, to keep (to) (rules, laws) (*b*) to watch (s.o., sth); **on nous observe**, we're being watched (*c*) to observe (stars); to examine (under microscope) (*d*) to note, notice; to point out (detail); **faire o. qch à qn**, to draw s.o.'s attention to sth **2. s'o.**, to watch oneself, to be careful.

obsession [ɔpsɛsjɔ̃] *nf* obsession. **obsessionnel** *a* obsessional.

obstacle [ɔpstakl] *nm* obstacle (à, to); *Equit:* jump, fence; **faire o. à qch**, to obstruct sth, to hinder sth.

obstétrique [ɔpstetrik] *nf* obstetrics.

obstination [ɔpstinasjɔ̃] *nf* obstinacy, stubbornness. **obstiné** *a* stubborn, obstinate. **obstinément** *adv* obstinately, stubbornly.

s'obstiner [sɔpstine] *vpr* **s'o. à qch, à faire qch**, to persist in sth, in doing sth; **s'o. au silence**, to remain obstinately silent.

obstruction [ɔpstryksjɔ̃] *nf* obstruction; blockage; **faire de l'o.**, to obstruct.

obstruer [ɔpstrye] *vtr* to obstruct, to block.

obtenir [ɔptənir] *vtr* (*conj like* TENIR) to obtain, get (permission); to achieve (result); **j'ai obtenu de le voir**, I managed to see him.

obtention [ɔptɑ̃sjɔ̃] *nf* obtaining; **pour l'o. de qch**, to obtain sth.

obturateur [ɔptyratœr] *nm* obturator; *Phot:* shutter.

obturation [ɔptyrasjɔ̃] *nf* sealing; filling (of tooth); *Phot:* **vitesse d'o.,** shutter speed.

obturer [ɔptyre] *vtr* to seal; to fill (tooth).

obtus, -use [ɔpty, -yz] *a* obtuse.

obus [ɔby] *nm Artil:* shell.

OC *Ondes courtes.*

occasion [ɔkazjɔ̃] *nf* (*a*) opportunity, occasion, chance; **saisir une o.,** to seize an opportunity; **avoir l'o. de faire qch,** to have the chance to do sth; **à l'o.,** when the opportunity presents itself (*b*) bargain; **voiture d'o.,** secondhand car (*c*) **à l'o. de son mariage,** on the occasion of his marriage; **dans les grandes occasions,** on special occasions. **occasionnel, -elle** *a* occasional; chance (meeting); casual (help). **occasionnellement** *adv* occasionally.

occasionner [ɔkazjɔne] *vtr* to cause (delay); to bring about, give rise to (unpleasantness).

occident [ɔksidɑ̃] *nm* west. **occidental, -ale, -aux** 1. *a* west(ern) 2. *n* Westerner.

occulte [ɔkylt] *a* occult (science).

occupant, -ante [ɔkypɑ̃, -ɑ̃t] (*a*) *a* occupying (forces) (*b*) *n* occupier; occupant; *Mil:* **l'o.,** the occupying power.

occupation [ɔkypasjɔ̃] *nf* 1. occupation; occupancy (of house); occupation (of country) 2. occupation, work, employment, job; **avoir de l'o.,** to be busy. **occupé** *a* (*of pers*) busy; (*of toilet, telephone*) engaged; (*of seat*) taken; (*of zone*) occupied.

occuper [ɔkype] *vtr* 1. (*a*) to live in (house) (*b*) to occupy, fill, take up (time, space) (*c*) to hold, to have (job) (*d*) to give occupation to (s.o.); to employ (workmen); **son travail l'occupe beaucoup,** his work keeps him very busy (*e*) to occupy (country) 2. **s'o.** (*a*) to keep oneself busy; **s'o. à faire qch,** to busy oneself with sth (*b*) **s'o. de,** to deal with; to be in charge of; to attend to; to be interested in; **je m'en occuperai,** I shall see to it; **occupe-toi de ce qui te regarde!** mind your own business! *Com:* **est-ce qu'on s'occupe de vous?** are you being served?

occurrence [ɔkyrɑ̃s] *nf* occurrence; instance; **en l'o.,** in this case; as it is.

OCDE *abbr Organisation de coopération et de développement économique.*

océan [ɔseɑ̃] *nm* ocean. **océanique** *a* oceanic.

Océanie [ɔseani] *Prnf Geog:* Oceania.

ocre [ɔkr] *nf* ochre.

octane [ɔktan] *nm Ch:* octane.

octante [ɔktɑ̃t] *num a A: & Dial:* eighty.

octave [ɔktav] *nf Mus: etc:* octave.

octobre [ɔktɔbr] *nm* October; **au mois d'o., en o.,** in (the month of) October.

octogénaire [ɔktɔʒenɛr] *a & n* octogenarian.

octogone [ɔktɔgɔn] *nm* octagon. **octogonal, -aux** *a* octagonal, eight-sided.

octroi [ɔktrwa] *nm* (*a*) concession, grant(ing) (*b*) *Hist:* city toll.

octroyer [ɔktrwaje] *vtr* (**j'octroie**) to grant, concede (**à,** to); **s'o.,** to allow oneself (sth).

oculaire [ɔkylɛr] 1. *a* ocular; **témoin o.,** eyewitness. 2. *nm Opt:* eyepiece.

oculiste [ɔkylist] *nm* oculist.

ode [ɔd] *nf Lit:* ode.

odeur [ɔdœr] *nf* odour, *NAm:* odor; smell, scent;

mauvaise o., bad smell; **ça a une bonne o.,** it smells nice; **sans o.,** odourless; **être en o. de sainteté,** to be in favour.

odieux, -euse [ɔdjø, -øz] *a* odious; abominable (crime); obnoxious (behaviour); **cet enfant est o.,** this child is unbearable. **odieusement** *adv* odiously.

odorant [ɔdɔrɑ̃] *a* sweet-smelling.

odorat [ɔdɔra] *nm* sense of smell.

œil, *pl* **yeux** [œj, jø] *nm* 1. eye; **il a les yeux bleus,** he has blue eyes; **visible à l'o. nu,** visible to the naked eye; **je n'ai pas fermé l'o. de la nuit,** I didn't sleep a wink all night; **faire qch les yeux fermés,** to do sth with one's eyes shut; **risquer un o.,** to take a peep; **ouvrir de grands yeux,** to open one's eyes wide; *P:* **mon o.!** my foot! **regarder qn dans les yeux,** to look s.o. straight in the eye; **d'un o. critique,** with a critical eye; **cela saute aux yeux,** it's obvious; **coûter les yeux de la tête,** to cost the earth; *F:* **à l'o.,** free, gratis 2. sight; **avoir de bons, mauvais, yeux,** to have good, bad, eyesight; **d'un o. malin,** with a mischievous look; **chercher qn des yeux,** to look around for s.o.; **il n'a d'yeux que pour elle,** he has eyes only for her; **avoir l'o.,** to be observant, sharp-eyed; **avoir qn à l'o.,** to keep an eye on s.o.; **coup d'o.,** (i) view (ii) glance; **regarder qn d'un bon o.,** to look favourably on s.o.; **voir du même o. que qn,** to see eye to eye with s.o.; *F:* **faire de l'o. à qn,** to make eyes at s.o. 3. (*a*) eye (of needle) (*b*) hole (in gruyère cheese); globule of fat (on soup) (*c*) eye (of cyclone).

œillade [œjad] *nf* glance; wink; **lancer des œillades à qn,** to make eyes at s.o.

œillère [œjɛr] *nf* (*on horse*) blinker; (*of pers*) **avoir des œillères,** to be narrow-minded.

œillet [œjɛ] *nm Bot:* carnation; **o. mignardise,** pink; **o. de poète,** sweet william; **o. d'Inde,** French marigold.

œsophage [ezɔfaʒ] *nm Anat:* oesophagus.

œuf, *pl* **œufs** [œf, ø] *nm* (*a*) egg; **o. frais,** new-laid egg; *Cu:* **o. à la coque,** boiled egg; **o. dur,** hard-boiled egg; **o. sur le plat, au plat,** fried egg; **œufs brouillés,** scrambled eggs; **marcher sur des œufs,** to tread on thin ice; **tuer qch dans l'o.,** to nip sth in the bud (*b*) *Biol:* ovum; *pl* spawn (of frog, fish); hard roe (of fish) (*c*) *F:* idiot, blockhead.

œuvre [œvr] *nf* 1. (*a*) work; **se mettre à l'o.,** to get down to work; **mettre en o.,** to implement (sth); **j'ai tout mis en o.,** I've done everything possible; **faire de bonnes œuvres,** to do charitable work; **faire o. utile,** to do useful work; **l'incendie avait fait son o.,** the fire had done the damage (*b*) **o. de bienfaisance,** charitable institution (*c*) (finished) work, production; **œuvres complètes,** complete works 2. *nm* **l'o. de Molière,** the works of Molière.

offense [ɔfɑ̃s] *nf* 1. offence, *NAm:* offense; insult 2. trespass, offence; *Ecc:* **pardonne-nous nos offenses,** forgive us our trespasses 3. libel (against head of State).

offenser [ɔfɑ̃se] *vtr* 1. (*a*) to offend, to give offence to (s.o.) (*b*) to offend against (good taste) 2. **s'o.,** to take offence (**de,** at). **offensant, -ante** *a* offensive, insulting.

offensif, -ive [ɔfɑ̃sif, -iv] 1. *a* offensive (war, weapon) 2. *nf* offensive; **passer à l'offensive,** to go

into the offensive; **offensive de l'hiver,** onset of winter.
office [ɔfis] 1. *nm* (*a*) office, function, duty; **faire o. de secrétaire,** to act as secretary; **remplir son o.,** to fulfill its function; *adv phr* **d'o.** (i) officially (ii) automatically (*b*) service, (good) turn (*c*) *Ecc:* service (*d*) office, bureau; **o. de publicité,** advertising agency 2. *nf* pantry.
officiel, -elle [ɔfisjɛl] 1. *a* official (statement); formal (call) 2. *n* official. **officiellement** *adv* officially.
officier[1] [ɔfisje] *vi* (*impf & pr sub* **n. officiions**) to officiate.
officier[2] *nm* officer; **o. de marine,** naval officer; **o. ministériel,** member of the legal profession; **o. de l'état civil** = registrar.
officieux, -euse [ɔfisjø, -øz] *a* unofficial. **officieusement** *adv* unofficially.
offrande [ɔfrɑ̃d] *nf* offering.
offrant [ɔfrɑ̃] *nm* **le plus o.,** the highest bidder.
offre [ɔfr] *nf* offer, proposal; (*at auction*) bid; *PolEc:* **l'o. et la demande,** supply and demand; *Fin:* **o. publique d'achat,** takeover bid; *Journ:* **offres d'emploi,** situations vacant; *F:* job ads.
offrir [ɔfrir] *vtr* (**j'offre; j'offrirai**) (*a*) to give (present); **c'est pour o.,** it's for a present; **s'o. qch,** to treat oneself to sth; **o. un déjeuner à qn,** to invite s.o. to lunch; **on lui a offert un emploi,** he was offered a job; **o. de faire qch,** to offer to do sth (*b*) to present (advantage); to provide (explanation) 2. **s'o.** (*a*) to offer oneself; **s'o. à faire qch,** to offer to do sth (*b*) (*of opportunity*) to present itself.
offusquer [ɔfyske] 1. *vtr* to offend, shock (s.o.) 2. **s'o.,** to take offence (**de,** at).
ogive [ɔʒiv] *nf* 1. *Arch:* rib; **voûtes d'ogives,** ribbed vault 2. nose cone (of rocket); **o. nucléaire,** nuclear warhead.
ogre, ogresse [ɔgr, ɔgrɛs] *n* ogre, ogress; **manger comme un o.,** to eat like a horse.
oie [wa] *nf* (*a*) goose (*b*) (*pers*) silly goose.
oignon [ɔɲɔ̃] *nm* 1. (*a*) onion; **petits oignons,** pickling onions; *F:* **occupe-toi de tes oignons,** mind your own business (*b*) *Bot:* bulb 2. *Med:* bunion.
oiseau, -eaux [wazo] *nm* 1. bird; **oiseaux domestiques, de basse-cour,** poultry; **c'est l'o. rare,** he's one in a million; **drôle d'o.,** queer customer 2. (bricklayer's) hod.
oiseau-mouche [wazomuʃ] *nm Orn:* hummingbird; *pl* **oiseaux-mouches.**
oiseleur [wazlœr] *nm* bird catcher.
oiselier, -ière [wazəlje, -jɛr] *n* bird seller.
oisellerie [wazɛlri] *nf* bird shop.
oiseux, -euse [wazø, -øz] *a* trivial, trifling (question); pointless (remark). **oiseusement** *adv* idly, unnecessarily.
oisif, -ive [wazif, -iv] 1. *a* idle 2. *n* (*a*) idler (*b*) person of leisure. **oisivement** *adv* idly, lazily.
oisiveté [wazivte] *nf* idleness.
oisillon [wazijɔ̃] *nm* fledgling.
oison [wazɔ̃] *nm* gosling.
oléagineux, -euse [ɔleaʒinø, -øz] 1. *a* oleaginous 2. *n* oleaginous plant.
oléoduc [ɔleɔdyk] *nm* (oil) pipeline.
olivâtre [ɔlivatr] *a* olive(-coloured); sallow (complexion).

olive [ɔliv] (*a*) *nf* olive; **huile d'o.,** olive oil (*b*) *a inv* olive-green.
oliveraie [ɔlivrɛ] *nf* olive grove.
olivier [ɔlivje] *nm* (*a*) olive tree (*b*) olive (wood).
olympiade [ɔlɛ̃pjad] *nf Sp:* Olympiad.
olympique [ɔlɛ̃pik] *a* olympic (games).
ombrage [ɔ̃braʒ] *nm* shade (of trees); **prendre o. de qch,** to take umbrage at sth.
ombrager [ɔ̃braʒe] *vtr* (**il ombrageait**) to shade. **ombragé** *a* shaded, shady.
ombrageux, -euse [ɔ̃braʒø, -øz] *a* 1. nervous, shy (horse) 2. (*of pers*) easily offended; touchy.
ombre [ɔ̃br] *nf* 1. shadow; **ombres chinoises,** shadowgraph; shadow play 2. shade; **se reposer à l'o.,** to rest in the shade; **30° à l'o.,** 30° in the shade; **tu me fais de l'o.,** you're in my light; **jeter une o. sur qch,** to cast a gloom over sth; *F:* **mettre qn à l'o.,** to put s.o. behind bars 3. darkness; obscurity; **laisser dans l'o.,** to leave in the dark; **rester dans l'o.,** to remain in the background 4. (*a*) ghost, shade, shadowy figure; **n'être plus que l'o. de soi-même,** to be a mere shadow of one's former self (*b*) **vous n'avez pas l'o. d'une chance,** you haven't the ghost of a chance 5. *Art:* **l'o. et la lumière,** light and shade; **il y a une o. au tableau,** there's a fly in the ointment 6. **o. à paupières,** eye shadow.
ombrelle [ɔ̃brɛl] *nf* parasol, sunshade.
omelette [ɔmlɛt] *nf Cu:* omelet(te).
omettre [ɔmɛtr] *vtr* (*conj. like* METTRE) to omit; to leave out; **o. de faire qch,** to fail to do sth.
omission [ɔmisjɔ̃] *nf* omission; oversight.
omnibus [ɔmnibys] 1. *nm Hist:* omnibus 2. *a inv* **train o.,** slow, stopping, train.
omnipotence [ɔmnipotɑ̃s] *nf* omnipotence. **omnipotent** *a* omnipotent.
omniprésent [ɔmniprezɑ̃] *a* omnipresent.
omniscient [ɔmnisjɑ̃] *a* omniscient.
omnivore [ɔmnivɔr] *a* omnivorous.
omoplate [ɔmoplat] *nf* shoulder blade.
OMS *abbr Organisation mondiale de la santé.*
on [ɔ̃] *indef pron nom* (*occ becomes* **l'on,** *esp after vowel sound*) 1. (*indeterminate*) **on ne sait jamais,** one never knows; **on n'en sait rien,** nobody knows anything about it; **on dit qu'elle était folle,** they say she was mad; **on frappe,** someone's knocking; **on demande une bonne cuisinière,** wanted, a good cook 2. (*specific pers or people; a following adj n or pp is masc, fem or pl as the sense requires*) **on parlait très peu,** we didn't talk much; **où va-t-on?** where are we going? **nous, on est tous égaux,** we're all equal.
once [ɔ̃s] *nf Meas:* ounce.
oncle [ɔ̃kl] *nm* uncle.
onctueux, -euse [ɔ̃ktɥø, -øz] *a* (*a*) creamy (*b*) *Fig:* unctuous, oily, smooth. **onctueusement** *adv* unctuously.
onde [ɔ̃d] *nf* 1. *Lit:* wave; water 2. *Ph:* (*a*) wave; *WTel:* **ondes moyennes, petites ondes,** medium waves; **ondes courtes,** short waves (*b*) **sur les ondes,** on the radio, on the air; **mettre en ondes,** to produce for radio; to adapt for broadcasting.
ondée [ɔ̃de] *nf* heavy shower.
on-dit [ɔ̃di] *nm inv* rumour, hearsay.
ondoyer [ɔ̃dwaje] *vi* (**j'ondoie**) to undulate, wave,

ripple; to float on the breeze. **ondoyant** *a* undulating, wavy.

ondulation [ɔ̃dylasjɔ̃] *nf* undulation; (*in hair*) wave.

onduler [ɔ̃dyle] **1.** *vi* to undulate, ripple; (*of road*) to roll up and down; (*of hair*) to be wavy **2.** *vtr* to wave (the hair). **ondulant** *a* undulating, waving. **onduleux, -euse** *a* undulating; wavy (line); swaying (motion).

onéreux, -euse [ɔnerø, -øz] *a* costly; heavy (expenditure); **à titre o.**, subject to payment.

ongle [ɔ̃gl] *nm* (finger)nail; claw (of animal); **ongles des orteils**, toenails; **se faire les ongles**, to cut, to file, one's nails; **se ronger les ongles**, to bite one's nails.

ONU [ony] *abbr Organisation des Nations Unies.*

onyx [ɔniks] *nm* onyx.

onze [ɔ̃z] *num a inv & nm inv* (*the e of* le, de, *is not, as a rule, elided before* onze *and its derivatives*) (*a*) eleven; **nous n'étions que o.** [kɛ̃ɔz], qu'o., there were only eleven of us; **le onze avril**, the eleventh of April (*b*) *Sp:* **le o. de France**, the French eleven, the French team.

onzième [ɔ̃zjɛm] *num a & n* eleventh. **onzièmement** *adv* in the eleventh place.

opacité [ɔpasite] *nf* opacity; opaqueness.

opale [ɔpal] *nf* opal. **opalin, -ine** *a* opalescent, opaline.

opaque [ɔpak] *a* opaque; thick (fog).

OPEP *abbr Organisation des pays exportateurs de pétrole.*

opéra [ɔpera] *nm* **1.** opera; **o. bouffe**, comic opera; **o. comique**, light opera **2.** opera house.

opérateur, -trice [ɔperatœr, -tris] *n* (machine) operator; *Cin:* cameraman.

opération [ɔperasjɔ̃] *nf* **1.** operation; process; *Iron:* **par l'o. du Saint-Esprit**, by magic **2.** *Mil: Surg:* operation; **salle d'o.**, operating theatre **3.** (financial) deal; **opérations de Bourse**, Stock Exchange transactions. **opérationnel, -elle** *a* operational.

opératoire [ɔperatwar] *a Surg:* operative.

opéré, -ée [ɔpere] *n Med:* patient who has had an operation.

opérer [ɔpere] (**j'opère; j'opérerai**) **1.** (*a*) *vtr* to bring about, to effect; **o. des miracles**, to work wonders (*b*) to operate on (patient) (**de**, for); **se faire o.**, to have an operation **2.** *vi* to act, to proceed; **comment faut-il o.?** what's the procedure? **3.** **s'o.**, to come about, to take place. **opérable** *a* operable.

opérette [ɔperɛt] *nf* operetta; light opera.

ophtalmologie [ɔftalmɔlɔʒi] *nf* ophthalmology. **ophthmologique** *a* ophthalmological.

ophtalmologiste [ɔftalmɔlɔʒist] *n* ophthalmologist.

opiniâtreté [ɔpinjatrəte] *nf* obstinacy; perseverance. **opiniâtre** *a* obstinate; headstrong (person); unrelenting (hatred); persistent (efforts).

opinion [ɔpinjɔ̃] *nf* opinion (**de**, of; **sur**, on, about); view; **je partage votre o.**, I agree with you.

opium [ɔpjɔm] *nm* opium.

opportun, -une [ɔpɔrtœ̃, -yn] *a* (*a*) opportune, timely, convenient; **au moment o.**, at the right moment (*b*) advisable (decision). **opportunément** *adv* opportunely.

opportunisme [ɔpɔrtynism] *nm* opportunism. **opportuniste** *a & n* opportunist.

opportunité [ɔpɔrtynite] *nf* (*a*) opportuneness,

timeliness (*b*) advisability.

opposé [ɔpoze] **1.** *a* opposing (armies); opposite (side); conflicting (interests); contrasting (colours); **o. à**, opposed to, against **2.** *nm* (*a*) the reverse, the opposite (of sth); **à l'o. de**, contrary to (*b*) **à l'o.**, on the opposite side.

opposer [ɔpoze] *vtr* **1.** (*a*) to oppose; to bring (rivals) into conflict; to bring together (teams); **o. qch à qch**, to set sth against sth; **je n'ai rien à o. à cela**, I have no objection to this (*b*) to put forward (arguments); to put up (resistance); **o. son refus**, to protest (*c*) to compare, to contrast (**à**, with) **2.** (*a*) **s'o. à**, to oppose (sth); to be opposed (to sth); to rebel against (parents); **rien ne s'o. à votre succès**, nothing stands between you and success (*b*) (*of rivals*) to clash; (*of teams*) to meet; **couleurs qui s'opposent**, contrasting colours.

opposition [ɔpozisjɔ̃] *nf* **1.** opposition; **mettre o. à qch**, to oppose sth; *Pol:* **l'o.**, the Opposition; *Com:* **faire o. à un chèque**, to stop (payment of) a cheque **2.** contrast; conflict (of ideas); **par o. à qch**, as opposed to sth.

opprimer [ɔprime] *vtr* to oppress; to cause (s.o.) difficulty in breathing; (*of guilt*) to weigh (s.o.) down. **oppressif, -ive** *a* oppressive.

oppresseur [ɔprescœr] *nm* oppressor.

oppression [ɔpresjɔ̃] *nf* oppression; difficulty in breathing.

opprimer [ɔprime] *vtr* (*a*) to oppress, crush (a people) (down); to suppress, stifle (opinion) (*b*) (*of heat*) to oppress.

opprobre [ɔprɔbr] *nm Lit:* shame, disgrace.

opter [ɔpte] *vi* **o. pour qch**, to opt for, decide on, sth.

opticien, -ienne [ɔptisje, -jɛn] *n* optician.

optimisme [ɔptimism] *nm* optimism. **optimiste 1.** *a* optimistic **2.** *n* optimist.

optimum [ɔptimɔm] *a & nm* optimum. **optimal** *a* optimum, optimal.

option [ɔpsjɔ̃] *nf* option, choice (**entre**, between); **o. d'achat**, option of purchase; *Sch:* **matière à o.**, optional subject.

optique [ɔptik] **1.** *a* optic (nerve); optical **2.** (*a*) *nf* optics; **instruments d'o.**, optical instruments (*b*) point of view.

opulence [ɔpylɑ̃s] *nf* opulence, wealth. **opulent** *a* opulent; rich, wealthy.

opuscule [ɔpyskyl] *nm* opuscule, pamphlet.

or [ɔr] *nm* **1.** gold; **or noir**, oil; **montre en or**, gold watch; **j'ai une femme en or**, I have a wonderful wife; **affaire en or**, excellent bargain; **affaire d'or**, gold mine **2.** gold (colour); **chevelure d'or**, golden hair.

or *conj.* now; but, yet.

oracle [ɔrakl] *nm* oracle.

orage [ɔraʒ] *nm* (thunder)storm; (political) row; **le temps est à l'o.**, there's thunder in the air. **orageux, -euse** *a* **1.** stormy (sky, life) **2.** thundery (weather, sky).

oraison [ɔrɛzɔ̃] *nf* **1.** **o. funèbre**, funeral oration **2.** prayer.

oral, -aux [ɔral, -o] **1.** *a.* oral **2.** *nm* oral (examination). **oralement** *adv* orally.

orange [ɔrɑ̃ʒ] **1.** *nf* orange; **o. sanguine**, blood orange **2.** *nm* (*colour*) orange; *a inv* orange(-coloured).

orangeade [ɔrɑ̃ʒad] *nf* orangeade.

oranger [ɔrɑ̃ʒe] *nm* orange tree.

orangeraie [ɔrɑ̃ʒrɛ] *nf* orange grove.

orangerie [ɔrɑ̃ʒri] *nf* orangery.

orateur,-trice [ɔratœr, -tris] *nm* orator, speaker.

oratoire [ɔratwar] **1.** *a.* oratorical **2.** *nm* oratory.

oratorio [ɔratɔrjo] *nm Mus:* oratorio.

orbite [ɔrbit] *nf* **1.** *Anat:* (eye) socket **2.** (*a*) orbit (of planet); **mettre sur o., en o.,** to put into orbit (*b*) sphere of influence. **orbital, -aux** *a* orbital.

Orcades [ɔrkad] *Pr nfpl* the Orkneys.

orchestration [ɔrkɛstrasjɔ̃] *nf* orchestration.

orchestre [ɔrkɛstr̩] *nm* (*a*) orchestra; (dance) band; **chef d'o.,** conductor (*b*) *Th:* (orchestra) stalls. **orchestral, -aux** *a* orchestral.

orchidée [ɔrkide] *nf* orchid.

ordinaire [ɔrdinɛr] **1.** *a* ordinary, usual, common; everyday (clothes); standard (quality); **vin o.,** table wine; **peu o.,** unusual; *F:* incredible; *Fin:* **actions ordinaires,** ordinary shares **2.** *nm* (*a*) custom, usual practice; **d'o.,** usually, as a rule; **comme d'o.,** as usual (*b*) **cela sort de l'o.,** it's out of the ordinary. **ordinairement** *adv* usually, as a rule.

ordinal, -aux [ɔrdinal, -o] **1.** *a* ordinal **2.** *nm* ordinal number.

ordinateur [ɔrdinatœr] *nm* computer.

ordonnance [ɔrdɔnɑ̃s] *nf* **1.** order; disposition (of picture); layout (of building) *Jur:* statute, order **3.** *Mil:* **officier d'o.,** aide-de-camp; *Navy:* flag-lieutenant **4.** *Med:* prescription.

ordonné [ɔrdɔne] **1.** *a.* orderly, well-ordered (life); tidy (person) **2.** *nf Mth:* ordinate.

ordonner [ɔrdɔne] *vtr* **1.** to arrange (sth.) **2.** to order, command; **o. à qn de faire qch,** to order s.o. to do sth; **o. à qn de se taire,** to tell s.o. to be quiet; **o. un traitement à qn,** to prescribe a treatment for s.o. **3.** to ordain (priest).

ordre [ɔrdr̩] *nm* **1.** order; **o. alphabétique,** alphabetical order; **numéro d'o.,** serial number; **c'est dans l'o. des choses,** it's in the nature of things; **avoir de l'o.,** to be tidy; to be methodical; **sans o.,** untidy, untidily; **mettre de l'o. dans qch,** to put sth in order; to tidy up (room); **mettre ses affaires en o.,** to settle one's affairs; to set one's house in order; **en o. de marche,** in working order **2.** order, discipline; **o. public,** law and order; **service d'o.,** police patrol **3.** **o. du jour,** (i) agenda (of meeting) (ii) *Mil:* order of the day; *Mil:* **cité à l'o. (du jour)** = mentioned in despatches; **être à l'o. du jour,** to be topical **4.** (*a*) *Arch: Biol:* order; class, division, category; **de premier o.,** first-rate; first class; **d'o. privé,** of a private nature; **de l'o. de 3 millions,** of the order of 3 million; **dans le même o. d'idées,** in the same line of thought (*b*) order; **entrer dans les ordres,** to take holy orders; **o. des avocats** = the Bar; **o. de la Légion d'honneur,** Order of the Legion of Honour **5.** (*a*) order; command; **par o., sur l'o., de qn,** by order of s.o.; **être aux ordres de qn,** to be at s.o.'s disposal; **sous les ordres de qn,** under s.o.'s command; **jusqu'à nouvel o.,** until further notice (*b*) *Com:* **payez à l'o. de,** pay to the order of; **billet à o.,** bill of exchange payable to order.

ordure [ɔrdyr] *nf* **1.** (*a*) dirt, filth (*b*) excrement, dung (*c*) filth; **écrire des ordures,** to write obscenities **2.** *pl* rubbish, refuse, *NAm:* garbage; **jette ça aux ordures,** throw that in the dustbin. **ordurier, -ière** *a* filthy; obscene.

orée [ɔre] *nf* edge (of forest).

oreille [ɔrɛj] *nf* **1.** ear; **avoir mal à l'o., aux oreilles,** to have earache; **avoir l'o. basse,** to be crestfallen; **tirer les oreilles à qn,** to tweak s.o.'s ears; **ils s'est fait tirer l'o.,** he took a lot of coaxing **2.** **n'écouter que d'une o.,** to listen with half an ear; **j'en ai les oreilles rebattues,** I'm sick of hearing it; **souffler qch à l'o. de qn,** to whisper sth to s.o.; **dresser l'o.,** to prick up one's ears; **faire la sourde o.,** to turn a deaf ear; **avoir de l'o.,** to have a good ear for music.

oreiller [ɔreje] *nm* pillow.

oreillons [ɔrejɔ̃] *nmpl Med:* mumps.

orfèvre [ɔrfɛvr̩] *nm* goldsmith, silversmith; **être o. en la matière,** to be an expert on the subject.

orfèvrerie [ɔrfɛvrəri] *nf* (*a*) goldsmith's, silversmith's, trade; goldsmith's, silversmith's, shop (*b*) (gold, silver) plate.

organe [ɔrgan] *nm* **1.** *Anat:* organ **2.** part (of machine); **organes de transmission,** transmission gear **3.** (*a*) *Lit:* voice (*b*) spokesman (*c*) instrument (of government).

organique [ɔrganik] *a Ch: Med: Jur:* organic.

organisateur, -trice [ɔrganizatœr, -tris] **1.** *a* organizing **2.** *n* organizer.

organisation [ɔrganizasjɔ̃] *nf* organization; arrangement.

organiser [ɔrganize] **1.** *vtr* to organize; to arrange **2.** **s'o.,** to get organized.

organisme [ɔrganism] *nm* **1.** *Biol:* organism; *Anat:* **l'o.,** the system **2.** *Adm:* organization, body.

organiste [ɔrganist] *n Mus:* organist.

orgasme [ɔrgasm] *nm* orgasm, climax.

orge [ɔrʒ] *nf* barley.

orgelet [ɔrʒəlɛ] *nm* stye (on the eye).

orgie [ɔrʒi] *nf* orgy.

orgue [ɔrg] *nm* (*Ecc: nfpl* **orgues**) *Mus:* organ; **o. de Barbarie,** barrel organ.

orgueil [ɔrgœj] *nm* pride, arrogance. **orgueilleux, -euse** *a* arrogant, proud. **orgueilleusement** *adv* proudly, arrogantly.

orient [ɔrjɑ̃] *nm* orient; **l'O.,** the East; **le proche O.,** the Near East; **le moyen O.,** the Middle East; **l'extrême O.,** the Far East. **oriental, -aux 1.** *a* eastern; oriental **2.** *n* Oriental.

orientation [ɔrjɑ̃tasjɔ̃] *nf* **1.** (*a*) orientation; **table d'o.,** panoramic table; **sens de l'o.,** sense of direction (*b*) *Sch:* **o. professionnelle,** careers advice (*c*) positioning (of aerial) **2.** (*a*) aspect (of house) (*b*) trend (of politics).

orienter [ɔrjɑ̃te] *vtr* **1.** (*a*) to orient(ate) (building); **terrasse orientée au sud,** terrace facing south (*b*) to turn, direct (aerial) (*c*) to guide (student); to direct (traveller); **o. la conversation vers un autre sujet,** to turn the conversation (onto another subject) (*d*) to set (map) by compass **2.** **s'o.,** to find one's bearings; **s'o. vers qch,** to turn towards sth; to lean towards sth. **orientable** *a* adjustable; directional.

orifice [ɔrifis] *nm* opening, orifice; mouth.

originaire [ɔriʒinɛr] *a.* (*a*) originating (**de,** from, in); native (**de,** of) (*b*) original, first (owner). **originairement** *adv* originally.

original, -aux [ɔriʒinal, -o] a & n **1.** original (text); Typew: top copy **2.** (a) original, fresh (idea) (b) odd, eccentric; **c'est un o.**, he's an odd character. **originalement** adv originally.

originalité [ɔriʒinalite] nf (a) originality (b) eccentricity, oddity (c) original feature.

origine [ɔriʒin] nf **1.** origin, beginning; **à l'o.**, originally; **dès l'o.**, from the outset **2.** extraction, birth; **d'o. anglaise**, of English extraction **3.** source; derivation (of word); origin (of custom); **avoir son o. dans**, to originate in; **bureau d'o.**, office of dispatch; **pneus d'o.**, original tyres. **originel, -elle** a original. **originellement** adv originally; from the outset.

orme [ɔrm] nm elm (tree, wood).

orné [ɔrne] a ornate, florid (style).

ornement [ɔrnəmɑ̃] nm ornament, adornment, embellishment; **sans o.**, unadorned, plain; **d'o.**, ornamental.

ornementation [ɔrnəmɑ̃tasjɔ̃] nf ornamentation.

ornementer [ɔrnəmɑ̃te] vtr to ornament, to decorate. **ornemental, -aux** a ornamental, decorative.

orner [ɔrne] vtr to ornament, decorate; **robe ornée de dentelle**, dress trimmed with lace.

ornière [ɔrnjɛr] nf rut; **sortir de l'o.**, (i) to get out of the rut (ii) to get out of trouble.

ornithologie [ɔrnitɔlɔʒi] nf ornithology. **ornithologique** a ornithological.

ornithologiste [ɔnitɔlɔʒist], **ornithologue** [ɔrnitɔlɔg] n ornithologist.

orphelin, -ine [ɔrfəlɛ̃, -in] n orphan; a orphan(ed); **o. de père, de mère**, fatherless, motherless.

orphelinat [ɔrfəlina] nm orphanage.

orteil [ɔrtɛj] nm toe; **gros o.**, big toe.

orthodoxie [ɔrtɔdɔksi] nf orthodoxy. **orthodoxe** a & n orthodox.

orthographe [ɔrtɔgraf] nf spelling. **orthographique** a orthographic(al).

orthographier [ɔrtɔgrafje] vtr to spell.

orthopédie [ɔrtɔpedi] nf orthop(a)edics. **orthopédique** a orthop(a)edic.

orthopédiste [ɔrtɔpedist] n orthop(a)edist.

ortie [ɔrti] nf (stinging) nettle; **o. blanche**, dead nettle.

os [ɔs; pl o] nm bone; **trempé jusqu'aux os**, soaked to the skin; **os à moelle**, marrow bone; **viande sans os**, boned meat; F: **il y a un os**, there's a snag, a hitch.

OS abbr ouvrier spécialisé.

oscillation [ɔsilasjɔ̃] nf oscillation; swing.

osciller [ɔsile] vi **1.** to oscillate; (of pendulum) to swing; (of boat) to rock; (of flame) to flicker **2.** to waver; (of market) to fluctuate. **oscillatoire** a oscillatory.

osé [oze] a bold, daring (attempt); risqué (joke); **être trop o.**, to go too far.

oseille [ozɛj] nf (a) Bot: sorrel (b) P: money, dough.

oser [oze] vtr to dare; **je n'ose pas le faire**, I daren't do it; **si j'ose dire**, if I may say so; **j'ose le croire**, I like to think so.

osier [ozje] nm (a) osier, willow (b) wicker(work); **panier d'o.**, wicker basket.

ossature [ɔsatyr] nf **1.** Anat: frame, bone structure **2.** frame(work) (of building); structure (of society).

osselet [ɔslɛ] nm knucklebone.

ossements [ɔsmɑ̃] nmpl bones (of dead men, animals).

osseux, -euse [ɔsø, -øz] a bony (hand); bone (structure).

ostensible [ɔstɑ̃sibl] a conspicuous. **ostensiblement** adv conspicuously.

ostentation [ɔstɑ̃tasjɔ̃] nf ostentation; **avec o.**, ostentatiously.

ostracisme [ɔstrasism] nm ostracism.

otage [ɔtaʒ] nm hostage.

OTAN [ɔtɑ̃] abbr Organisation du traité de l'Atlantique Nord.

otarie [ɔtari] nf sealion.

ôter [ote] **1.** vtr to remove; to take away; to take off (clothes); to take out (stain); **ô. qch à qn**, to take sth away from s.o.; **ô. ses forces à qn**, to deprive s.o. of his strength; **je ne peux pas me l'ô. de l'idée**, I can't get it out of my mind **2.** **s'ô.**, to move away; **ôtez-vous de là!** get out of here! **ô. le couvert**, to clear the table.

otite [ɔtit] nf Med: ear infection.

oto-rhino-laryngologie [ɔtɔrinɔlarɛ̃gɔlɔʒi] nf oto(rhino)laryngology.

oto-rhino-laryngologiste [ɔtɔrinɔlarɛ̃gɔlɔʒist] n ear, nose and throat specialist.

ou [u] conj or; **voulez-vous du bœuf ou du jambon?** would you like beef or ham? **qu'il le veuille ou non**, whether he likes it or not; **entrez ou sortez**, either come in or go out; **ou vous obéirez ou (bien) vous serez puni**, either you obey or (else) you will be punished.

où [u] adv **1.** interr where? **où en êtes-vous?** how far have you got (with it)? **par où?** which way? **d'où vient-il?** where does he come from? **jusqu'où?** how far? **déposez-le n'importe où**, put it down anywhere **2.** rel. (a) where; **partout où il va**, wherever he goes; **c'est là où je l'ai laissé**, it's where I left it; **d'où on conclut qu'il est coupable**, from which one concludes that he is guilty (b) when; **le jour où je l'ai vu**, the day I saw him (c) in which, at which; **la maison où il demeure**, the house he lives in; **dans l'état où elle est**, in the state she's in **3.** (concessive) **où que vous soyez**, wherever you may be.

ouate [wat] nf (usu **la ouate**, occ **l'ouate**) (a) padding (b) cotton wool. **ouaté 1.** padded; quilted **2.** muffled (sound).

ouater [wate] vtr to pad; to quilt.

oubli [ubli] nm **1.** (a) forgetting, neglect (of duty) (b) forgetfulness; **o. de soi(-même)**, self-effacement (c) oblivion **2.** omission, oversight.

oublier [ublije] **1.** vtr (a) to forget; **o. de faire qch**, to forget to do sth; **se faire o.**, to keep out of the limelight; **on ne nous le laissera pas o.**, we shall never hear the last of it (b) to overlook; to neglect (duty); to leave (sth) out **2.** **s'o.**, to forget oneself; **ça ne s'oublie pas**, it's not easily forgotten.

ouest [wɛst] **1.** nm no pl west; **vent d'o.**, westerly wind; **à l'o.**, in the west; westwards; **à l'o. de qch**, (to the) west of sth **2.** a inv west (coast); westerly (wind); western (province).

ouf [uf] int phew! **il n'a pas eu le temps de dire o.**, he couldn't say a word.

Ouganda [ugɑ̃da] Prnm Geog: Uganda.

oui [wi] **1.** *adv* yes; **je crois que o.**, *F:* **qu'o.**, I think so; **faire signe que o.**, to nod in agreement; **vient-il?—o.**, is he coming?—yes (he is); **mais o.**, (yes) of course; **tu viens, o. ou non?** are you coming or not? **2.** *nm inv* **deux cents oui**, two hundred ayes.

oui-dire [widir] *nm inv* hearsay.

ouïe [wi] *nf* **1.** (sense of) hearing; **avoir l'o.** fine, to have sharp ears **2.** *pl* (a) sound holes (of violin) (b) gills (of fish).

ouille [uj] *int* ouch!

ouïr [wir] *vtr* (*pp* **ouï**) *Lit: Jur:* to hear.

ouragan [uragɑ̃] *nm* hurricane; (political) storm; **entrer en o. dans une pièce**, to burst into a room.

ourler [urle] *vtr Needlew:* to hem.

ourlet [urle] *nm Needlew:* hem.

ours, -e [urs] *n* (a) *Z:* bear; she bear; **o. blanc, o. polaire**, polar bear; **o. brun**, brown bear (b) (*pers.*) boor; **o. mal léché**, lout.

oursin [ursɛ̃] *nm* sea-urchin.

ourson [ursɔ̃] *nm Z:* bearcub.

oust(e) [ust] *int F:* **(allez) o.!** beat it! hop it!

outil [uti] *nm* tool; implement.

outillage [utijaʒ] *nm* (a) set of tools; kit (b) (factory) equipment.

outiller [utije] *vtr* to equip, supply (workman) with tools; to fit out (workshop).

outrage [utraʒ] *nm* outrage; flagrant insult; **faire o. à qch**, to insult, offend, sth; **o. à agent**, insulting a police officer; *Jur:* **o. à magistrat**, contempt of court; **o. à le pudeur**, indecent behaviour.

outrager [utraʒe] *vtr* (n. **outrageons**) **1.** to insult, to offend **2.** to outrage, violate (the truth, morals). **outrageant** *a* insulting; offensive. **outrageux, -euse** *a Lit:* outrageous, excessive. **outrageusement** *adv* outrageously, excessively.

outrance [utrɑ̃s] *nf* excess; **à o.**, to the utmost; in the extreme. **outrancier, -ière** *a* extreme.

outre [utr] **1.** *prep* (a) (*in a few set phrases*) beyond; **o. mesure**, to excess; overmuch; **se fatiguer o. mesure**, to overtire oneself (b) in addition to; **o. cela**, in addition to that; furthermore **2.** *adv* further, beyond; **passer o.**, to go on; **passer o. à qch**, to disregard sth; **en o.**, besides, moreover; **o. qu'il est riche**, apart from being rich.

outré [utre] *a.* (a) exaggerated, excessive (praise) (b) indignant, outraged.

outre-Atlantique [utratlɑ̃tik] *adv phr* across the Atlantic.

outre-Manche [utrəmɑ̃ʃ] *adv phr* across the Channel.

outremer [utrəmɛr] *nm* **1.** lapis lazuli **2.** **(bleu d')o.**, ultramarine (blue).

outre-mer [utrəmɛr] *adv* overseas.

outrepasser [utrəpase] *vtr* to go beyond (limits); to exceed (orders).

outrer [utre] *vtr* **1.** to exaggerate **2.** to outrage.

outre-tombe (d') [dutrɔtɔb] *adv phr* from beyond the grave.

ouvert [uvɛr] *a* (a) open; (of tap) on, running; (of collar) undone; **porte grande ouverte**, wide-open door; **plaie ouverte**, gaping wound; **à cœur o.**, open-heart (surgery); **à bras ouverts**, with open arms (b) **o. au public**, open to the public; **compte o.**, open account (d) **caractère o.**, frank, open, nature; **avoir l'esprit o.**, to be open-minded. **ouvertement** *adv* openly; overtly.

ouverture [uvertyr] *nf* **1.** (a) opening, unlocking (of door); opening (of account) (b) **faire des ouvertures à qn**, to make overtures to s.o. (c) *Mus:* overture (d) **heures d'o.**, business hours (of shop); visiting hours (of museum) **2.** opening (in wall); gap, break (in hedge); *Phot:* aperture; *Cards:* opening **3. o. d'esprit**, open-mindedness.

ouvrable [uvrabl] *a* **jour o.**, weekday, working day; **heures ouvrables**, business hours.

ouvrage [uvraʒ] *nm* **1.** (a) work; **se mettre à l'o.**, to set to work (b) workmanship **2.** piece of work; product; book; *CivE:* **ouvrages d'art**, construction works; **boîte à o.**, workbox.

ouvre-boîte(s) [uvrəbwat] *nm* tin opener; can opener; *pl* **ouvre-boîtes**.

ouvre-bouteille(s) [uvrəbutɛj] *nm* bottle opener; *pl* **ouvre-bouteilles**.

ouvreuse [uvrøz] *nf* usherette.

ouvrier, -ière [uvrije, -jɛr] **1.** *n* worker; workman; female worker; **o. agricole**, farm labourer; **o. qualifié**, skilled worker **2.** *a* working class; industrial, labour (unrest); **la classe ouvrière**, the working class; **syndicat o.**, trade union, *NAm:* labor union.

ouvrir [uvrir] *v* (*prp* **ouvrant**; *pp* **ouvert**; *pr ind* **j'ouvre**) **1.** *vtr* (a) to open (door, suitcase); to turn on (a tap); to switch on (electricity); **o. à qn**, to let s.o. in; **o. brusquement la porte**, to fling the door open; **va o.!** go and answer the door! **ça ouvre l'appétit**, it whets the appetite (b) to cut through, open up (canal, wall, mine); to cut open (stomach); to build (road); **s'o. un chemin à travers la foule**, to push one's way through the crowd (c) to begin; to open (ball); to open (up) (shop); **o. le feu**, to open fire; **o. le jeu**, to open play (d) to head (list); **o. la marche**, to lead the way, to take the lead **2.** *vi* to open (**sur**, on; **par**, with) **3.** **s'o.** (a) (of door, shop) to open; (of flower) to open out; **la porte s'ouvrit**, the door came open; **la vie qui s'ouvre devant moi**, the life opening before me (b) **s'o. à qn**, to open one's heart to s.o. (c) to gash (one's leg); **s'o. les veines**, to slash one's wrists.

ovaire [ɔvɛr] *nm* ovary.

ovale [ɔval] *a* oval, egg-shaped; *Sp: F:* **ballon o.**, (i) rugger ball (ii) rugger.

ovation [ɔvasjɔ̃] *nf* ovation.

OVNI [ɔvni] *abbr objet volant non identifié*, unidentified flying object, UFO.

ovin [ɔvɛ̃] **1.** *a* ovine **2.** *nmpl* **les ovins**, sheep.

ovulation [ɔvylasjɔ̃] *nf* ovulation.

ovule [ɔvyl] *nm* ovule, ovum.

oxydation [ɔksidasjɔ̃] *nf Ch:* oxid(iz)ation.

oxyde [ɔksid] *nm Ch:* oxide.

oxyder [ɔkside] *vtr Ch:* to oxidize; **s'o.**, to become oxidized.

oxygène [ɔksiʒɛn] *nm Ch:* oxygen.

oxygéner [ɔksiʒene] (**il oxygène**) **1.** *vtr* to oxygenate; **eau oxygénée**, hydrogen peroxide **2.** **s'o.**, to take a breath of fresh air.

ozone [ozɔn] *nm Ch:* ozone.

P

P, p [pe] *nm* (the letter) P, p.

p *abbr* page.

pacage [pakaʒ] *nm Agr:* pasture (land).

pacha [paʃa] *nm* pasha; **mener une vie de p.,** to live like a lord.

pachyderme [pakidɛrm] *nm* elephant.

pacification [pasifikasjɔ̃] *nf* pacification.

pacifier [pasifje] *vtr (impf & pr sub.* **n. pacifiions**) to pacify (country); to appease, calm. **pacificateur, -trice** 1. *a* pacifying 2. *n* peacemaker; pacifier. **pacifique** *a (a)* pacific; peaceable (person) *(b)* peaceful, quiet *(c)* **l'océan P., n le P.,** the Pacific (Ocean). **pacifiquement** *adv* peaceably; peacefully.

pacifisme [pasifism] *nm Pol:* pacifism. **pacifiste** *a & n Pol:* pacifist.

pacotille [pakɔtij] *nf* cheap and shoddy goods; **bijoux de p.,** paste jewelry.

pacte [pakt] *nm* pact, agreement.

pactiser [paktize] *vi* to take sides with (s.o.); to treat with (the enemy); to come to terms (with one's conscience).

pagaie [pagɛ] *nf* paddle (for canoe).

pagaïe, pagaille [pagaj] *nf* disorder, muddle; mess; **quelle p.!** what a shambles! **il y en a en p.,** there are masses of them.

paganisme [paganism] *nm* paganism.

pagayer [pagɛje] *vtr & i* **(je pagaie)** to paddle (a canoe).

pagayeur, -euse [pagɛjœr, -øz] *n* paddler.

page¹ [paʒ] *nf* page (of book); *Fig:* chapter (of history); *Typ:* **mettre en pages,** to make up (into pages); **être à la p.,** to be up to date; to keep in touch.

page² *nm* page (boy).

pagne [paɲ] *nm* loincloth.

pagode [pagɔd] *nf* pagoda.

paie [pɛ] *nf (a)* pay, wages; **feuille de p.,** payslip; *F:* **il y a une p. qu'on ne t'a pas vu,** we haven't seen you for ages *(b)* payment; **jour de p.,** pay day.

paiement [pɛmɑ̃] *nm* payment.

païen, -ïenne [pajɛ̃, -jɛn] *a & n* pagan, heathen.

paillasse [pajas] *nf* straw mattress.

paillasson [pajasɔ̃] *nm* doormat.

paille [pɑj] *nf* 1. *(a)* straw; **chapeau de p.,** straw hat; **être sur la p.,** to be destitute; **tirer à la courte p.,** to draw lots; *P:* **il en demande 1 million: une p.!** he wants £1000 for it: peanuts! *(b)* (drinking) straw *(c) a inv* straw-coloured 2. **p. de fer,** steel wool 3. flaw (in glass). **paillé** *a* straw-bottomed (chair).

pailleter [pajte] *vtr* **(je paillette)** to spangle. **pailleté** *a* sequined; spangled.

paillette [pajɛt] *nf (a)* sequin; spangle *(b)* **savon en paillettes,** soap flakes *(c)* speck (of gold).

pain [pɛ̃] *nm* 1. bread; **p. complet,** wholemeal bread; **p. frais, p. rassis,** fresh, stale, bread; **p. grillé,** toast; **p. d'épices =** gingerbread; **acheter qch pour une bou-**chée de p.,** to buy sth for a song; **avoir du p. sur la planche,** to have a lot on one's plate 2. *(a)* loaf; **p. de mie,** sandwich loaf; **p. de campagne,** farmhouse loaf; **petit p.,** roll; **ça se vend comme des petits pains,** its selling like hot cakes; *Cu:* **p. de poisson,** fish loaf *(b)* bar, cake (of soap).

pair [pɛr] 1. *a* even (number); **jours pairs,** even dates 2. *nm (a)* equal, peer; **de p. (avec),** on a par (with) *(b)* peer (of the realm) 3. *nm* (state of) equality; par; *Fin:* **remboursable au p.,** repayable at par; **travailler au p.,** to work in exchange for board and lodging; **jeune fille au p.,** au pair girl.

paire [pɛr] *nf* pair; brace (of birds); yoke (of oxen); **ça, c'est une autre p. de manches,** that's another story; **les deux font la p.,** they're two of a kind.

pairesse [pɛrɛs] *nf* peeress.

pairie [peri] *nf* peerage.

paisible [pɛzibl] *a* peaceful, quiet, peaceable. **paisiblement** *adv* peacefully, quietly; peaceably.

paître [pɛtr] *v. (prp* **paissant;** *pr ind* **je pais, il paît)** 1. *vtr* **p. l'herbe,** to graze 2. *vi* to graze; *F:* **je l'ai envoyé p.,** I sent him packing.

paix [pɛ] *nf (a)* peace; **faire la p. avec qn,** to make it up with s.o.; **signer la p.,** to sign a peace treaty; **en temps de p.,** in peacetime *(b)* peace, quiet; **avoir la p.,** to have a bit of peace and quiet; **dormir en p.,** to sleep peacefully; *P:* **fiche-moi la p.!** leave me alone! **la p.!** shut up!

Pakistan [pakistɑ̃] *Prnm Geog:* Pakistan. **Pakistanais, -aise** *a & n* Pakistani.

palace [palas] *nm* luxury hotel.

palais¹ [palɛ] *nm* 1. palace 2. **P. de justice,** law courts; **p. des sports,** sports centre.

palais² *nm (a)* palate *(b)* (sense of) taste.

palan [palɑ̃] *nm* hoist.

pale [pal] *nf* blade (of oar); paddle (of water wheel).

pâle [pɑl] *a* pale; pallid; wan (smile); faint (light); poor (imitation); **p. comme un linge,** as white as a sheet.

palefrenier [palfrənje] *nm* groom, ostler.

paletot [palto] *nm* (short) jacket, overcoat.

palette [palɛt] *nf* 1. paddle (of water wheel) 2. (painter's) palette.

pâleur [pɑlœr] *nf* pallor, paleness.

palier [palje] *nm* 1. *(a)* landing (of stairs); **nous sommes voisins de p.,** we live on the same floor *(b)* stage; **l'inflation a atteint un nouveau p.,** inflation has reached a new level 2. *Aut:* level stretch 3. *MecE:* bearing.

pâlir [pɑlir] 1. *vi* to (become, grow) pale; *(of star)* to grow dim; *(of light, colour)* to fade; **faire p. qn (d'envie),** to make s.o. green with envy 2. *vtr* to turn (s.o.) pale. **pâlissant** *a* fading.

palissade [palisad] *nf* fence; hoarding.

pallier [palje] *vtr (impf & pres sub* **n. palliions**) to palliate; to alleviate (pain); to extenuate (offence); to make up for (lack of sth). **palliatif, -ive** *a & nm* palliative.

palmarès [palmarɛs] *nm Sch:* prize list; *Sp:* (list of) medal winners; **le p. (de la chanson)**, the charts, the top thirty, the hit parade.

palme [palm] *nf* 1. palm (leaf); (*symbol*) palm, victory; **vin de p.**, palm wine; **palmes (académiques)**, decoration given by the Ministry of Education 2. *Sp: etc:* flipper (of frogman). **palmé** *a* 1. *Bot:* palmate (leaf) 2. *Orn:* webfooted; **pied p.**, webbed foot.

palmeraie [palmərɛ] *nf* palm grove.

palmier [palmje] *nm* 1. palm tree; **cœur de p.**, palm tree heart 2. *Cu:* biscuit shaped like a palm leaf.

palombe [palɔ̃b] *nf* ringdove, wood pigeon.

pâlot, -otte [pɑlo, -ɔt] *a* pale, peaky.

palourde [palurd] *nf* clam.

palper [palpe] *vtr* to feel; to finger (sth); *Med:* to palpate; *F:* to make (money). **palpable** *a* palpable; tangible.

palpitation [palpitasjɔ̃] *nf* palpitation; quivering, fluttering; pounding (of heart).

palpiter [palpite] *vi* to palpitate; (*of pulse, eyelid*) to flutter, to quiver; (*of heart*) to pound. **palpitant** *a* thrilling, exciting (film, novel).

paludisme [palydism] *nm Med:* malaria.

pamphlet [pɑ̃flɛ] *nm* satirical tract; lampoon.

pamplemousse [pɑ̃pləmus] *nm* grapefruit.

pan¹ [pɑ̃] *nm* 1. skirt, flap (of garment); tail (of shirt) 2. section, piece; **p. de mur**, (section of) wall; **p. de bois**, timber framing; **p. de ciel**, patch of sky 3. face, side (of angular building).

pan² *int* 1. bang! wham! 2. *F:* (*to child*) **attention, p. p.!** watch it or you'll get a smacking!

panacée [panase] *nf* panacea.

panache [panaʃ] *nm* (*a*) plume; **p. de fumée**, trail of smoke; (*b*) dashing air; **il a du p.**, he has an air about him.

panaché [panaʃe] 1. *a.* variegated, multicoloured; motley (crowd); **glace panachée**, mixed(-flavour) ice cream 2. *nm* shandy.

panais [panɛ] *nm* parsnip.

Panama [panama] 1. *Prnm* Panama 2. *nm* panama hat.

panard [panar] *nm P:* foot, hoof.

panaris [panari] *nm Med:* whitlow.

pancarte [pɑ̃kart] *nf* sign, notice; placard.

pancréas [pɑ̃kreas] *nm Anat:* pancreas.

paner [pane] *vtr Cu:* to coat (meat, fish) with breadcrumbs.

panier [panje] *nm* (*a*) basket; **jeter qch au p.**, to throw sth out, away; **p. à provisions**, shopping basket; **p. à salade**, (i) salad shaker (ii) *F:* Black Maria; **p. à bouteilles**, bottle carrier; *F:* **p. percé**, spendthrift (*b*) basket(ful) (of fruit); **le dessus du p.**, the pick of the bunch (*c*) *Sp:* (*basketball*) basket.

panique [panik] *nf* panic, scare; **pris de p.**, panic-stricken.

paniquer [panike] 1. *vtr* to get (s.o.) into a panic 2. *vi* to panic 3. *F:* **se p.**, to panic.

panne [pan] *nf* (*a*) (mechanical) breakdown; (electrical) failure, *NAm:* outage; **en p.**, out of order; **p. de courant**, power cut; **p. de moteur**, engine failure; **tomber en p. sèche**, to run out of petrol; **tomber en p.**, to break down (*b*) (*of pers*) **rester en p. devant une difficulté**, to be stuck over a difficulty; **laisser qn en p.**, to let s.o. down.

panneau, -eaux [pano] *nm* 1. panel, *pl* panelling;

p. vitré, glass panel 2. board; **p. d'affichage**, (i) noticeboard (ii) (advertisement) hoarding; *Aut:* **p. indicateur**, signpost; **p. de signalisation (routière)**, roadsign; **tomber dans le p.**, to fall into the trap.

panonceau, -eaux [panɔ̃so] *nm* (*a*) plaque (*b*) sign.

panorama [panorama] *nm* panorama. **panoramique** *a* panoramic.

pansage [pɑ̃saʒ] *nm* grooming (of horse).

panse [pɑ̃s] *nf* (*a*) *F:* paunch, belly (*b*) first stomach (of ruminant).

pansement [pɑ̃smɑ̃] *nm* dressing; bandage; **p. (adhésif)**, (sticking) plaster; **faire un p.**, to dress a wound.

panser [pɑ̃se] *vtr* 1. to groom (horse) 2. to dress (wound); to bandage (limb).

pantalon [pɑ̃talɔ̃] *nm* (pair of) trousers, *NAm:* pants.

pantelant [pɑ̃tlɑ̃] *a* panting; heaving.

panthéon [pɑ̃teɔ̃] *nm* pantheon.

panthère [pɑ̃tɛr] *nf Z:* panther.

pantin [pɑ̃tɛ̃] *nm* (*a*) *Toys:* jumping jack (*b*) (*pers*) puppet, stooge.

pantomime [pɑ̃tɔmim] *nf* 1. *Th:* (*a*) mime (*b*) mime show 2. scene, fuss.

pantouflard, -arde [pɑ̃tuflar, -ard] *a & n F:* stay-at-home.

pantoufle [pɑ̃tufl] *nf* slipper.

paon [pɑ̃] *nm* peacock.

papa [papa] *nm F:* dad(dy); pa, *NAm:* pop; *F:* **aller à la p.**, to potter, tootle, along; **musique de p.**, old-fashioned music.

papal, -aux [papal, -o] *a* papal.

papauté [papote] *nf* papacy.

pape [pap] *nm Ecc:* pope.

papelard [paplar] *nm F:* (piece of) paper.

paperasse [papras] *nf Pej:* (*usu pl*) papers; forms.

paperasserie [paprasri] *nf* 1. (accumulation of) papers; forms; *F:* bumf 2. red tape; **il y a trop de p.**, there's too much paperwork.

papeterie [papɛtri] *nf* 1. (*a*) paper manufacturing (*b*) paper mill 2. (*a*) stationer's shop (*b*) stationery.

papetier, -ière [paptje, -jɛr] *n* (*a*) paper manufacturer (*b*) stationer.

papier [papje] *nm* 1. (*a*) paper; **p. journal**, newsprint; **p. parcheminé**, greaseproof paper; **p. à cigarettes**, cigarette paper; *Phot:* **p. sensible**, sensitized paper; **p. calque**, tracing paper; **p. à lettres**, writing paper, notepaper; **p. machine**, typing paper; **p. brouillon**, scrap paper; **p. à dessin**, drawing paper; **p. d'emballage**, wrapping paper; **p. hygiénique**, toilet paper, *F:* loo paper (*b*) **un p.**, a sheet of paper (*c*) **p. mâché**, papier-mâché; **avoir une mine de p. mâché**, to look washed out 2. (*a*) document, paper; **être dans les petits papiers de qn**, to be in s.o.'s good books; *F:* **rayez cela de vos papiers!** (you can) forget it! (*b*) *Jur:* **p. timbré**, official paper (*c*) *Fin:* bill(s); **p.-monnaie**, paper money (*d*) *pl Adm:* **papiers (d'identité)**, (identity) papers (*e*) *Journ:* article 3. **p. d'aluminium**, **d'argent**, aluminium foil, silver foil; tinfoil.

papillon [papijɔ̃] *nm* 1. butterfly; **p. de nuit**, moth; *Swim:* **brasse p.**, butterfly stroke 2. (*a*) inset (in book) (*b*) sticker (*c*) *Aut:* (parking) ticket (*d*) *Tchn:* wing nut.

papillote [papijɔt] *nf* 1. *A:* curlpaper (for hair) 2. sweet paper; frill (for meat).

papillotement [papijɔtmɑ̃] *nm* twinking; flickering; blinking.

papilloter [papijɔte] *vi (of eyes)* to blink; *(of light)* to twinkle; *Cin:* to flicker.

papoter [papɔte] *vi* to chatter.

paquebot [pakbo] *nm Nau:* liner.

pâquerette [pɑkrɛt] *nf Bot:* daisy.

Pâques [pɑk] **1.** *nfpl* Easter; **joyeuses P.,** happy Easter; **faire ses P.,** to take the sacrament at Easter **2.** *nm (contraction of* jour de Pâques, *used without article)* Easter; **remettre qch à P. ou à la Trinité,** to put sth off indefinitely.

paquet [pakɛ] *nm (a)* parcel, packet; package; bundle; **faire un p.,** to make up a parcel; **p. de café,** bag of coffee; **faire ses paquets,** to pack one's bags *(b)* heap (of snow); sheet (of rain); **p. de mer,** heavy sea *(c)* wad (of notes); *F:* **il a touché un joli p.,** he made a fat sum; **mettre le p.,** to go all out *(d) Rugby:* **p. (d'avants),** pack.

par [par] *prep* **1.** *(a) (of place)* by; through; **regarder p. la fenêtre,** to look out of the window; **p. monts et p. vaux,** over hill and dale; **il court p. les rues,** he runs through the streets; **p. tout le pays,** throughout the country; **p. 10° de latitude nord,** at a latitude of 10° North; **passer p. Calais,** to go via Calais; **venez p. ici,** come this way *(b) (of time)* on; in; **p. le passé,** in the past; **p. un jour d'hiver,** on a winter's day; **p. cette chaleur,** in this heat **2.** *(a) (showing the agent)* **il a été puni p. son père,** he was punished by his father; **faire qch p. soi-même,** to do sth unaided; **je l'ai appris p. les Martin,** I heard of it through, from, the Martins *(b) (showing the means, instrument)* **prendre qn p. la main,** to take s.o. by the hand; **envoyer qch p. la poste,** to send sth by post; **elle est remarquable p. sa beauté,** she is remarkable for her beauty *(c) (emphatic)* **vous êtes p. trop aimable,** you are far too kind. **3.** *(cause, motive)* **j'ai fait cela p. amitié,** I did it out of friendship; **p. pitié!** for pity's sake! **4.** *(distributive)* **p. ordre alphabétique,** in alphabetical order; **trois fois p. jour,** three times a day; **1,000 francs p. semaine,** 1,000 francs per week **5.** *p. + inf;* **commencer p. faire qch,** to begin by doing sth; **commencez p. le commencement,** begin at the beginning; **tu vas finir p. m'agacer!** I've had enough of you! **6.** *adv phr* **p.-ci, p.-là,** hither and thither; here and there **7.** *prep phr (a)* **de p. le monde,** throughout the world *(b)* **de p. qn,** by order of s.o.; in the name of s.o.

para [para] *nm F:* para.

parabole [parabɔl] *nf* **1.** parable **2.** *Mth:* parabola. **parabolique** *a Mth:* parabolic; **radiateur p.,** *nm* **p.,** electric fire.

parachèvement [paraʃɛvmɑ̃] *nm* completion; perfection.

parachever [paraʃve] *vtr (conj like* ACHEVER) to complete; to finish (sth) off; to perfect.

parachutage [paraʃytaʒ] *nm* parachuting.

parachute [paraʃyt] *nm* parachute.

parachuter [paraʃyte] *(a) vtr & i* to parachute *(b) vtr* to pitchfork (s.o. into a job).

parachutisme [paraʃytism] *nm* parachuting.

parachutiste [paraʃytist] *nm* parachutist; *Mil:* paratrooper.

parade [parad] *nf* **1.** *Mil:* parade **2.** parade, show;

faire p. de ses bijoux, to show off one's jewels; **habits de p.,** ceremonial clothes **3.** *Fenc: Box:* parry.

parader [parade] *vi* to make a display; to show off.

paradis [paradi] *nm* paradise; **le p. terrestre,** the garden of Eden; *Fig:* heaven on earth; *Orn:* **oiseau de p.,** bird of paradise.

paradoxe [paradɔks] *nm* paradox. **paradoxal, -aux** *a* paradoxical. **paradoxalement** *adv* paradoxically.

paraffine [parafin] *nf* paraffin (wax).

parages [paraʒ] *nmpl (a) Nau:* sea area; waters; region(s) *(b)* **dans les p.,** in the vicinity, near; **que faites-vous dans ces p.?** what are you doing in this neck of the woods?

paragraphe [paragraf] *nm* paragraph.

Paraguay [paragwɛ] *Prnm* Paraguay. **Paraguayen, -enne** *a & n* Paraguayan.

paraître [parɛtr] *vi* (je parais, il paraît, n. paraissons) **1.** *(a)* to appear; to make one's appearance; **elle n'a pas paru de la journée,** she hasn't been seen all day *(b) (of book)* to appear, to come out; *(of periodical)* to appear, to come out **2.** *(a)* to be visible, apparent; **cette tache paraît à peine,** the stain hardly shows; **laisser p. ses sentiments,** to show one's feelings *(b)* **p. en public,** to appear in public; **chercher à p.,** to show off *(c) impers* **je suis très mal.—il n'y paraît pas,** I'm very ill.—you don't look it **3.** *(a)* to seem, to look; **il paraît triste,** he looks sad; **il paraissait furieux,** he sounded furious *(b) impers* **il paraît qu'elle s'en va,** apparently, she's leaving; **à ce qu'il paraît,** apparently; it would seem so; **il paraît que si, que non,** so it appears; it seems not.

parallèle [paralɛl] **1.** *a (a)* parallel (à, to, with) *(b)* similar *(c)* unofficial **2.** *nf Mth:* parallel (line) **3.** *nm (a)* parallel, comparison; **mettre qch en p. avec qch,** to compare sth with sth *(b) Geog:* parallel (of latitude). **parallèlement** *adv* parallel (à, to, with); concurrently.

parallélisme [paralelism] parallelism; *Aut:* (wheel) alignment.

parallélogramme [paralelɔgram] *nm* parallelogram.

paralyser [paralize] *vtr* to paralyse.

paralysie [paralizi] *nf* paralysis.

paralytique [paralitik] *a & n* paralytic.

paramètre [paramɛtr] *nm* parameter.

paranoïaque [paranɔjak] *a & n* paranoiac.

parapet [parapɛ] *nm* parapet.

paraphe [paraf] *nm (a)* flourish (after signature) *(b)* initials (of one's name).

parapher [parafe] *vtr* to initial.

paraphrase [parafraz] *nf* paraphrase.

paraphraser [parafraze] *vtr* to paraphrase.

parapluie [paraplɥi] *nm* umbrella.

parasite [parazit] **1.** *nm (a) Biol:* parasite *(b)* hanger-on, sponger *(c) pl WTel: TV:* interference, atmospherics **2.** *a* parasitic; **bruits parasites,** interference.

parasol [parasɔl] *nm* parasol, sunshade; beach umbrella.

paratonnerre [paratɔnɛr] *nm* lightning conductor.

paravent [paravɑ̃] *nm* (draught) screen.

parc [park] *nm* **1.** park; grounds (of castle); **p. naturel,** nature reserve **2.** *(a)* **p. de stationnement,** car park,

NAm: parking lot; **p. d'attractions,** amusement park; **p. (pour enfants),** playpen; **p. à moutons,** sheepfold; **p. à huîtres,** oyster-bed (*b*) *Mil:* depot **3.** fleet (of buses, cars); **p. automobile,** number of vehicles on the road.

parcelle [parsɛl] *nf* fragment; particle (of gold); parcel (of land); grain (of truth).

parce que [pars(ə)kə] *conj phr* because.

parchemin [parʃəmɛ̃] *nm* parchment; vellum.

parcimonie [parsimɔni] *nf* parcimony. **parcimonieux, -euse** *a* parcimonious. **parcimonieusement** *adv* parcimoniously.

par-ci par-là [parsiparla] *adv* here and there; now and then.

parcmètre [parkmɛtr] *nm* parking meter.

parcourir [parkurir] *vtr* (*conj like* COURIR) **1.** to travel through, go over (country); **p. plusieurs kilomètres,** to cover several kilometres; **p. les mers,** to sail the seas; **un frisson me parcourut,** a shiver went through me **2.** to examine (cursorily); **p. qch des yeux,** to glance at, over, sth; **p. un livre,** to skim through a book.

parcours [parkur] *nm* **1.** (*a*) distance covered; journey, run; **payer le p.,** to pay the fare (*b*) route (of bus); course (of river) (*c*) *Sp:* course.

par-delà [pardəla] *adv & prep* beyond.

par-dessous [pardəsu] *prep & adv* under, beneath, underneath.

pardessus [pardəsy] *nm* overcoat.

par-dessus [pardəsy] *prep & adv* over (the top of); **p.-d. bord,** overboard; **par-d. le marché,** into the bargain; **j'en ai p.-d. la tête,** I've had enough.

par-devant [pardəvɑ̃] *adv & prep* in front of; round the front; at the front; **p.-d. notaire,** in the presence of a lawyer.

pardon [pardɔ̃] *nm* (*a*) pardon; forgiveness (of an offence); *Jur:* (free) pardon; **(je vous demande) p.,** I beg your pardon; (I'm) sorry; **p. Monsieur, vous avez l'heure?** excuse me Sir, have you got the time? *F:* **et puis p.! elle ne fiche rien,** she doesn't do a thing I can tell you (*b*) *Ecc:* (*in Brittany*) religious festival.

pardonner [pardɔne] *vtr* to pardon, forgive; **p. (à) qn,** to forgive s.o.; **pardonnez-moi,** excuse me; **je ne me le pardonnerai jamais,** I'll never forgive myself; **maladie qui ne pardonne pas,** fatal illness. **pardonnable** *a* forgivable.

paré [pare] *a* ready; prepared (**contre,** for); **vous voilà p.!** you're all set!

pare-boue [parbu] *nm inv* mudflap (of car, bicycle).

pare-brise [parbriz] *nm inv Aut: etc:* windscreen, *NAm:* windshield.

pare-chocs [parʃɔk] *nm inv Aut:* bumper.

pareil, -eille [parɛj] **1.** *a.* (*a*) like, alike; similar; **p. à,** the same as, just like (*b*) same, identical; **l'an dernier à pareille époque,** this time last year (*c*) such; like that; **en p. cas,** in such cases; **comment a-t-il pu faire une chose pareille!** how could he do such a thing! **2.** *n* (*a*) **lui et ses pareils,** he and people like him; **mes pareils,** my equals; people in my position (*b*) equal, fellow, match; **il n'a pas son p.,** he's second to none; **sans p.,** unequalled, unparalleled; *P:* **c'est du p. au même,** it comes to the same thing **3.** *nf* **rendre la pareille à qn,** to give s.o. tit for tat **4.** *adv F:* **faire p.,** to do the same (thing). **pareillement** *adv* in the same way; also, likewise; **à vous p.!** the same to you!

parent, -ente [parɑ̃, -ɑ̃t] **1.** *nmpl* (*a*) parents; father and mother (*b*) *Lit:* forefathers **2.** *n* (*a*) (blood) relation, relàtive; **être p. avec, de, qn,** to be related to s.o.; **p. pauvre,** poor relation (*b*) *Biol:* parent **3.** *a* related; similar.

parenté [parɑ̃te] *nf* **1.** relationship; kinship; **il n'y a pas de p. entre eux,** they're not related **2.** *coll.* relatives, relations.

parenthèse [parɑ̃tɛz] *nf* parenthesis, digression; *Typ:* bracket; **entre parenthèses,** (i) in brackets (ii) incidentally, by the way.

parer¹ [pare] *vtr* **1.** (*a*) to dress, trim (meat, leather, timber) (*b*) to adorn (s.o.) (**de,** with) **2. se p.,** to deck oneself out; to adorn oneself (**de,** with); to assume (false title).

parer² **1.** *vtr* (*a*) to avoid, ward off; fend off (*b*) *Box: Fenc:* to parry, ward off (blow) **2.** *vi* **p. à** (**qch**), to provide, guard, against (sth); **p. à toute éventualité,** to be prepared for anything; **p. au plus pressé,** to attend to the most urgent things first.

pare-soleil [parsɔlɛj] *nm inv Aut:* sun visor.

paresse [parɛs] *nf* (*a*) laziness, idleness (*b*) sluggishness (of mind).

paresser [parese] *vi* to laze about, around. **paresseux, -euse** **1.** *a* (*a*) lazy, idle; **p. comme une couleuvre,** bone idle (*b*) sluggish (stomach, mind) **2.** *n.* lazy person, *F:* lazybones **3.** *nm Z:* sloth. **paresseusement** *adv* lazily.

parfaire [parfɛr] *vtr* (*conj like* FAIRE) to perfect.

parfait [parfɛ] **1.** *a.* (*a*) perfect; faultless; flawless; **en ordre p.,** in perfect order; **vous avez été p.,** you were wonderful; **(c'est) p.!** (that's) perfect; *F:* great! (*b*) complete, total; utter, downright (fool) **2.** *nm* (*a*) *Gram:* perfect (tense) (*b*) *Cu:* parfait. **parfaitement** *adv* perfectly; completely; totally; utterly; **tu l'as vu?—p.,** did you see him?—I certainly did.

parfois [parfwa] *adv* sometimes, at times.

parfum [parfœ̃] *nm* **1.** fragrance, scent (of flower); bouquet (of wine); aroma (of coffee) **2.** *Toil:* scent, perfume **3.** flavour (of ice cream).

parfumer [parfyme] *vtr* **1.** (*a*) to scent, to perfume (*b*) *Cu:* to flavour (**à,** with) **2. se p.,** to use scent; **elle se parfume trop,** she wears too much scent. **parfumé, -ée** *a* scented; fragrant; **p. à la vanille,** vanilla-flavoured.

parfumerie [parfymri] *nf* perfumery; perfume shop.

parfumeur, -euse [parfymœr, -øz] *n* perfumer.

pari [pari] *nm* **1.** bet, wager; **les paris sont ouverts,** it's anyone's guess **2.** betting.

parier [parje] *vtr* (*impf & pr sub* **n. pariions**) to bet, to wager; to lay, stake (money); **je te parie qu'il est là,** I bet you he's there; **p. sur un cheval,** to back a horse; **il y a gros à p. qu'il ne viendra pas,** the odds are (that) he won't come; **je l'aurais parié,** I might have known it.

parisien, -ienne [parizjɛ̃, -jɛn] *a & n* Parisian.

paritaire [pariter] *a* equal (representation); joint (commission).

parité [parite] *nf* parity.

parjure [parʒyr] **1.** (*a*) *nm* perjury (*b*) *n* perjurer **2.** *a* false (oath); faithless (person).

parjurer (se) [səparʒyre] *vpr* to perjure oneself; to commit perjury.

parking [parkiŋ] *nm* (a) parking (b) carpark, *NAm:* parking lot.

parlant [parlɑ̃] *a* speaking; talking; lifelike (portrait); meaningful (gesture); vivid (description); *Tp:* **l'horloge parlante**, the speaking clock.

parlement [parləmɑ̃] *nm* parliament. **parlementaire 1.** *a* parliamentary **2.** *n* member of Parliament.

parlementer [parləmɑ̃te] *vi* to parley; to negotiate.

parler¹ [parle] **1.** (a) *vi* to speak, talk; **p. haut, p. bas**, to speak loudly; to speak in a low voice; **parlez plus fort!** speak up! **p. par gestes**, to use sign language (b) **parlez-vous sérieusement?** are you serious? do you really mean it? **laissez-le p.**, let him have his say; **p. pour ne rien dire**, to talk for the sake of talking; to make small talk; **je ne peux pas le faire p.**, I can't get a word out of him; **c'est une façon de p.**, (i) it's a way of speaking (ii) don't take it literally; **voilà qui est bien parlé!** well said! *P:* **tu parles!** (i) you're telling me! you bet! (ii) you must be joking! no way! (c) **p. à qn**, to talk to s.o.; **elle a trouvé à qui p.**, she has met her match; **nous ne nous parlons pas**, we're not on speaking terms (d) **p. de qn, de qch**, to mention, to speak of, s.o.; **il n'en parle jamais**, he never talks about it; **n'en parlons plus**, let's drop the subject; **cela ne vaut pas la peine d'en p.**, it isn't worth mentioning; **il ne veut pas en entendre p.**, he won't hear of it; **p. mal de qn**, to speak ill of s.o.; **faire p. de soi**, to get talked about; **tout le monde en parle**, it's the talk of the town; **de quoi parle ce livre?** what's this book about? *P:* **tu parles d'un idiot!** talk about an idiot! (e) **p. à l'imagination**, to fire the imagination **2. p. (le) français**, to speak French; **p. affaires**, to talk business; to talk shop.

parler² *nm* (a) speech (b) dialect.

parleur, -euse [parlœr, -øz] *n* talker.

parloir [parlwar] *nm* parlour; visiting room (of school, convent).

parmi [parmi] *prep* among, amongst; **p. nous**, with us.

parodie [parɔdi] *nf* parody; mockery.

parodier [parɔdje] *vtr* (*impf & pr sub* **n. parodiions**) to parody.

paroi [parwa] *nf* **1.** (a) partition (between rooms) (b) wall (of rock); (rock) face **2.** side (of car, ship); lining (of stomach).

paroisse [parwas] *nf* parish. **paroissial, -aux** *a* parish (hall).

paroissien, -ienne [parwasjɛ̃, -jɛn] *n* parishioner.

parole [parɔl] *nf* **1.** (spoken) word; *pl* lyrics (of song); **p. blessante**, hurtful remark; *Iron:* **belles paroles**, fine words **2.** promise, word; **tenir p.**, to keep one's word; **manquer à sa p.**, to break one's word; **je l'ai cru sur p.**, I took his word for it; **p. d'honneur!** you have my word (of honour)! **3.** (a) speech, speaking; delivery; **avoir la p. facile**, to be a fluent speaker; **perdre la p.**, to lose the power of speech (b) **adresser la p. à qn**, to speak to s.o.; **prendre la p.**, (to begin) to speak.

paroxysme [parɔksism] *nm* (a) *Med:* crisis (point) (b) paroxysm (of anger, pain); **être au p. de la joie**,

to be ecstatically happy; **atteindre son p.**, to reach its highest point.

parpaing [parpɛ̃] *nm* bondstone; breezeblock.

parquer [parke] *vtr* **1.** to pen (cattle); to park (cars) **2. se p.**, to park.

parquet [parke] *nm* **1.** *Jur:* public prosecutor's room **2.** (wooden, parquet) floor, flooring.

parrain [parɛ̃] *nm* godfather; sponsor.

parrainage [parɛnaʒ] *nm* sponsorship.

parrainer [parene] *vtr* to sponsor.

parsemer [parsəme] *vtr* (**je parsème, n. parsemons**) to strew, sprinkle, scatter (**de**, with); **ciel parsemé d'étoiles**, sky studded with stars; **parsemé de difficultés**, riddled with difficulties.

part [par] *nf* **1.** (a) share, part, portion; **diviser qch en parts**, to divide sth into portions; **la p. du lion**, the lion's share (b) **pour ma p.**, as for me; (speaking) for myself (c) **prendre qch en bonne, en mauvaise, p.**, to take sth in good part; to take offense at sth **2.** share, participation; **prendre p. à qch**, to take part in, to share in, sth; to join in (sth); **faire p. de qch. à qn**, to inform s.o. of sth; **faire la p. de qch**, to take sth into consideration **3.** (a) **nulle p.**, nowhere; **autre p.**, elsewhere, somewhere else; **de p. et d'autre**, on both sides; **de toute(s) part(s)**, on all sides; **de p. en p.**, through and through, right through; **d'autre p.**, moreover; **d'une p., d'autre part**, on the one hand, on the other hand (b) **de la p. de**, from; on behalf of; *Tp:* **c'est de la p. de qui?** who's speaking? **cela m'étonne de sa p.**, that surprises me, coming from him **4. à p.**, apart, separately; **prendre qn à p.**, to take s.o. aside; **plaisanterie à p.**, joking apart; **un cas à p.**, a special case; **une femme à p.**, an exceptional woman; **à p. quelques exceptions**, with a few exceptions.

partage [partaʒ] *nm* **1.** (a) division, dividing, sharing (out); **faire le p. de qch**, to divide sth up (b) **il y a p. d'opinions**, opinions are divided; **sans p.**, undivided; *Geog:* **ligne de p. des eaux**, watershed, *NAm:* divide **2.** share, portion, lot; **recevoir qch en p.**, to receive sth in a will.

partager [partaʒe] *vtr* (**n. partageons**) **1.** (a) to divide (into shares); to share (out); to divide (one's time) (b) to divide (into groups, sections, portions); **les avis sont partagés**, opinions are divided **2.** to share; to agree with; **p. l'avis de qn**, to share s.o.'s opinion **3. se p.**, to divide, to be divided; **ils se sont partagé les bénéfices**, they shared the profits between them. **partagé** *a* divided; shared; **amour p.**, mutual love.

partance [partɑ̃s] *nf* **en p.**, (of train) due to leave; (of aircraft) outward bound; (of ship) (just) sailing; **en p. pour Londres**, (bound) for London.

partant [partɑ̃] **1.** *a* departing **2.** *nm* person leaving; departing traveller; *Sp: Turf:* starter; runner; **non p.**, non-runner.

partenaire [partənɛr] *n* partner.

parterre [partɛr] *nm* **1.** flower bed, border **2.** *Th:* (a) (the) pit (b) audience.

parti [parti] *nm* **1.** (political) party; **prendre le p. de qn, prendre p. pour qn**, to stand up for s.o.; to take sides with s.o. **2.** (marriageable person) match **3.** decision, choice; course (of action); **prendre le p. de faire qch**, to make up one's mind to do sth; **prendre son p. de qch**, to make the best of it; **p. pris**, prejudice, bias; **sans p. pris,** unbiased; objective **4.** advantage, profit; **tirer p. de qch,** to take advantage of sth; to turn sth to (good) account.

partialité [parsjalite] *nf* partiality (**envers,** for, to); bias (**contre,** against). **partial, -aux** *a* partial; bias. **partialement** *adv* in a biased way.

participant, -ante [partisipã, -ãt] **1.** *a* participating **2.** *n* participant; member; competitor; **les participants à la manifestation,** those taking part in the demonstration.

participation [partisipasjõ] *nf* **1.** participation (**à,** in); (*in show*) appearance; **p. au frais,** cost sharing **2.** *Com:* share, interest; **p. aux bénéfices,** profit sharing; **p. ouvrière,** worker participation.

participe [partisip] *nm Gram:* participle.

participer [partisipe] *vi* **1. p. à** (*a*) to take part in (meeting, game); to participate in (discussion); (*of actor*) to appear in (show); to be involved in (plot); **p. à la joie de qn,** to share s.o.'s joy (*b*) to contribute (money); to share in (profits) **2.** *Lit:* **p. de,** to partake of (sth).

particulariser [partikylarize] *vtr* (*a*) to particularize (a case) (*b*) **se p.,** to be distinguished (**par,** by).

particularité [partikylarite] *nf* particularity; distinctive feature.

particule [partikyl] *nf* **1.** particle **2.** *Gram:* particle; **avoir un nom à p.,** to belong to the nobility.

particulier, -ière [partikylje, -jɛr] **1.** *a* (*a*) particular, special (*b*) peculiar, characteristic (*c*) unusual, uncommon; peculiar; **faire qch avec un soin p.,** to do sth with particular care (*d*) private; personal (account); **leçons particulières,** private lessons, private tuition **2.** *n* private person; private individual; **simple p.,** ordinary person; **que nous veut ce p.?** what does that character want? **3.** *nm* (*a*) **du p. au général,** from the specific to the general (*b*) *adv phr* **en p.,** in particular; **recevoir qn en p.,** to receive s.o. privately. **particulièrement** *adv* particularly, especially.

partie [parti] *nf* **1.** (*a*) part (of a whole); **les parties du corps,** the parts of the body; **parties génitales,** genitals; private parts; *Gram:* **parties du discours,** parts of speech; **en grande p.,** to a great extent; **faire p. de,** to be part of; to belong to (club); to be among (the winners) (*b*) **comptabilité en p. simple, double,** single entry, double entry, book-keeping (*c*) field, subject; **je ne suis pas de la p.,** that's not (in) my line (*d*) *Mus:* part **2.** (*a*) party; **p. de chasse,** shooting party; **p. de campagne,** outing (in the country); **ce n'est pas une p. de plaisir!** it's no picnic! **voulez-vous être de la p.?** will you join us? (*b*) game (of cards, of chess); **la p. se trouve égale,** it's a close match **3.** *Jur:* party (to dispute); **avoir affaire à forte p.,** to have a powerful opponent to deal with; **prendre qn à p.,** to take s.o. to task; **p. civile,** plaintiff claiming damages (in criminal case).

partiel, -elle [parsjɛl] **1.** *a* partial; **paiment p.,** part payment **2.** *nm Sch:* class exam. **partiellement** *adv* partially, partly.

partir [partir] *vi* (*conj like* MENTIR, *aux* être) **1.** (*a*) to depart, leave, start; to set out, off; to go (away, off); (*of ship*) to sail; (*of aircraft*) to take off; **je pars à huit heures,** I'm leaving at eight o'clock; **p. pour, à, Paris,** to leave for, to set out for, Paris; **p. en**

vacances, to go on holiday; **partez!** (i) get out! (ii) *Sp:* go! **p. comme une flèche,** to be off like a shot; *P:* **c'est parti mon kiki!** off we go! **le moteur est parti,** the engine started; **le fusil est parti,** the gun went off; **p. d'un éclat de rire,** to burst out laughing; **l'affaire est mal partie,** the business has got off to a bad start (*b*) to go; to give way; to break; (*of button*) to come off; (*of stain*) to come off (*c*) to emanate, spring (from); (*of road*) to start (from); **ça part du cœur,** it comes from the heart; **en partant du principe qu'il a raison,** assuming that he's right (*d*) **à p. d'aujourd'hui,** from today (onwards); **à p. du 15,** on and after the 15th; **robes à p. de 200 francs,** dresses from 200 francs (upwards) **2. faire p.,** to remove (stain); to fire (gun); to let off (fireworks); to start (engine); **faire p. qn,** to send s.o. away.

partisan, -ane [partizã, -an] **1.** *n* partisan, follower **2.** *Mil:* guer(r)illa (soldier), partisan **3.** *a* (*a*) party, sectarian (*b*) **être p. de (faire) qch,** to be in favour of (doing) sth.

partitif, -ive [partitif, -iv] *a & nn Gram:* partitive.

partition [partisjõ] *nf* **1.** partition, division **2.** *Mus:* score.

partout [partu] *adv* (*a*) everywhere; **p. où,** wherever; **j'ai mal p.,** I ache all over; **un peu p.,** all over the place (*b*) all; *Ten:* **30 p.,** 30 all; **40 p.,** deuce.

partouze [partuz] *nf P:* orgy.

parure [paryr] *nf* (*a*) costume, finery (*b*) jewels; set (of jewellery); **p. de table,** table linen.

parvenir [parvənir] *vi* (*conj like* VENIR, *aux* être) **1. p. à un endroit,** to reach a place; **votre lettre m'est parvenue,** I received your letter; **faire p. qch à qn,** to send sth to s.o. **2.** (*a*) to reach (a great age); to succeed; to achieve (one's purpose); **p. à faire qch,** to manage to do sth (*b*) *abs* to succeed in life.

parvenu [parvəny] *n* parvenu, upstart.

parvis [parvi] *nm* square (in front of church).

pas¹ [pa] *nm* **1.** (*a*) step, pace, stride; footstep; **p. à p.,** step by step; little by little; **allonger le p.,** to step out; **marcher à grands p.,** to stride along; **d'un p. lourd,** with a heavy tread; **faire un p. en avant,** to step forward; **faux p.,** (i) slip, stumble (ii) (social) blunder; **j'y vais de ce p.,** I'm going at once; **c'est à deux p. d'ici,** it's just a stone's throw from here (*b*) pace; *Mil: Danc:* step; **au p.,** (i) at a walking pace (ii) *Aut:* dead slow; **mettre son cheval au p.,** to walk one's horse; **p. cadencé,** quick time; **p. de gymnastique,** jog trot; **p. de l'oie,** goose step (*c*) precedence; **avoir le p. sur qn,** to rank before s.o. **2.** footprint, tracks; **arriver sur les p. de qn,** to follow close on s.o.'s heels **3.** **p. de la porte,** doorstep, doorway; **p. de porte,** key money **4.** passage; (mountain) pass; strait; **le P. de Calais,** the Straits of Dover; **sauter le p.,** to take the plunge **5.** *Tchn:* thread (of screw).

pas² *neg adv* **1.** (*a*) not; no; **je ne sais p.,** I don't know; **p. du tout,** not at all; **p. encore,** not yet; **qui l'a vu?—p. moi,** who saw him?—not me; I didn't; **tu es contente, p. vrai?** you're pleased, aren't you? (*b*) *F:* **c'est p. vrai!** you're kidding! **p. possible!** no! incredible! **2.** (*a*) **p. un mot ne fut dit,** not a word was spoken (*b*) **fier comme p. un,** proud as anything.

passable [pasabl] *a* passable, tolerable; reasonable; *Sch:* **mention p.** = pass(mark). **passablement** *adv* tolerably, reasonably; rather (long); quite a lot.

passade [pasad] *nf* passing fancy.

passage [pasaʒ] *nm* **1.** (*a*) crossing (of sth); passing over, through, across; going past (a place); **guetter le p. de qn**, to watch for s.o.; **j'attend le p. de l'autobus**, I'm waiting for the bus to come; **on sourit sur son p.**, people smile as he goes by; **livrer p.**, to make way; **il est de p. à Paris**, (i) he's passing through Paris; (ii) he's in Paris for a few days (only); **il m'a saisi au p.**, he caught me as I went past; *PN:* **p. interdit**, no entry (*b*) *Nau:* **payer son p.**, to pay for one's passage (*c*) transition; **p. du jour à la nuit**, change from day to night **2.** (*a*) way, way through; alley(way); passage(way); **barrer le p. à qn**, to block s.o.'s way (*b*) *Rail:* **p. à niveau**, level crossing; **p. souterrain**, subway; *NAm:* underground passage; **p. clouté**, pedestrian crossing **3.** passage (in book, music).

passager, -ère [pasaʒe, -ɛr] **1.** *a* (*a*) fleeting, transitory (beauty); momentary (pain); intermittent (showers) (*c*) busy (street) **2.** *n* passenger; **p. clandestin**, stowaway. **passagèrement** *adv* temporarily.

passant, -ante [pasɑ̃, -ɑ̃t] **1.** *a* busy (street) **2.** *n* passer-by **3.** *nm Harn:* keeper.

passe [pas] **1.** *nf* (*a*) *Fb: etc:* pass; **p. en avant**, forward pass (*a*) *Fenc:* pass, thrust; **p. d'armes**, heated exchange (*c*) **mot de p.**, password (*d*) (*at roulette*) any number above 18 (*e*) *Nau:* pass; channel; **être en p. de faire qch**, to be on the way to doing sth; **être dans une mauvaise p.**, to be in a tight corner **2.** *nm F:* master key, pass key, skeleton key.

passé, -ée [pase] **1.** *a* (*a*) past, gone by; **la semaine passée**, last week; **il est quatre heures passées**, it's after four (*b*) over; **l'orage est p.**, the storm's over (*c*) faded (colour) **2.** *nm* (*a*) past; **comme par le p.**, as in the past (*b*) *Gram:* past (tense); **p. composé**, perfect (tense) **3.** *prep.* beyond; **p. cette date**, after this date.

passe-droit [pasdrwa] *nm* (undeserved) privilege; *pl* **passe-droits**.

passe-montagne [pasmɔ̃taɲ] *nm* balaclava; *pl* **passe-montagnes**.

passe-partout [paspartu] *nm inv* masterkey, pass key, skeleton key; *a inv* all-purpose (phrase).

passe-passe [paspas] *nm no pl* **tour de p.-p.**, conjuring trick.

passe-plat [paspla] *nm inv* serving hatch.

passeport [paspɔr] *nm* passport.

passer [pase] **1.** *vi* (*aux avoir or* être) to pass; to go (on, by, along); to proceed; **p. sur un pont**, to cross (over) a bridge; **p. par-dessus, par-dessous, qch**, to get over, under, sth; **faire p. le plat**, to hand the dish round; **par où est-il, a-t-il, passé?** which way did he go? **je ne peux pas p.**, I can't get by; **laisser p.**, to let in (light, air); to let through (s.o.); to overlook (mistake); **p. à l'ennemi**, to go over to the enemy; *Sch:* **p. dans la classe supérieure**, to be moved up (a form); **en passant**, by the way; **soit dit en passant**, by the way (*b*) *Aut:* **p. en seconde**, to go, to change, into second (gear) (*c*) **le mot est passé dans l'usage**, the word is in common use (*d*) **la route passe par le village**, the road runs through the village (*e*) to go through; **passez par la fenêtre**, go through the window (*f*) (*of film*) to be showing; (*of programme*)

to be on (*g*) **p. son chemin**, to go one's way; (*aux* être) **p. chez qn**, to call on s.o.; **en passant, je suis entré dire bonjour**, I just dropped in on my way by; **est-ce que le facteur est passé?** has the postman been? (*h*) (*aux avoir*) to undergo, pass through (sorrow, sickness); **j'ai passé par là**, I've been through it; **tout le monde y passe**, it happens to us all; *F:* **il a failli y p.**, he nearly died (*i*) (*aux avoir*) to disappear, to cease; **la douleur a passé**, the pain has gone; **le vert est passé de mode**, green is out of fashion; **le plus dur est passé**, the worst is over; **ça lui passera**, he'll grow out of it; **couleurs qui passent**, colours that fade (*j*) (*of time*) to elapse, to go by; **comme le temps passe (vite)!** how time flies! **faire p. le temps**, to pass the time (*k*) (*aux avoir or* être) to become; **p. capitaine**, to be promoted (to) captain; (*l*) (*aux avoir*) **p. pour riche**, to be considered rich; **se faire p. pour**, to pass oneself off as (*m*) (*aux avoir*) to be accepted; **qu'il revienne demain, passe encore**, if he returns tomorrow, well and good; **ça ne passe pas**, that won't do; it won't wash **2.** *vtr* (*a*) to pass, cross, go over (bridge, sea); to go, pass, through (gate); to clear (customs); to cross (frontier); **p. une maison**, to go past a house (*b*) to carry across; to ferry (goods) over; **p. des marchandises en fraude**, to smuggle goods (*c*) **p. qch à qn**, to hand sth to s.o.; **il m'a passé son rhume**, I caught his cold; **p. une commande**, to place an order (**de qch**, for sth); *Tp:* **passez-moi M. X**, put me through to Mr X; **passe-moi un coup de fil**, give me a call; **p. sa colère sur qn**, to vent one's anger on s.o. (*d*) **p. le balai, le chiffon**, to sweep up; to dust; (**se**) **p. la main dans les cheveux**, to run one's fingers through one's hair; **p. sa tête par la fenêtre**, to put one's head out of the window; **p. une chemise**, to slip on a shirt; *Aut:* **p. la seconde**, to change into second (gear) (*e*) to show (film); to play (record) (*f*) to pass, spend (time) (*g*) to pass, exceed, go beyond; **il a passé la soixantaine**, he's over sixty; **cela passe les bornes**, that's going too far (*h*) to pass over; to excuse (fault); **on ne lui passe rien**, he doesn't get away with anything (*i*) to omit, leave out; **p. qch sous silence**, to keep quiet about sth; **et j'en passe!** and that's not all! (*j*) **p. une loi**, to pass a law (*k*) **p. un examen**, to sit (for) an exam(ination); to take an exam(ination) (*l*) to strain (liquid); to sift (flour); **p. le café**, to filter the coffee **3.** **se p.** (*a*) to happen; to take place; **que se passe-t-il?** what's going on? **tout s'est bien passé**, everything went (off) smoothly; *F:* **ça ne se passera pas comme ça**, I won't stand for it (*b*) to pass away, to cease; (*of time*) to elapse, to go by; (*of pain*) to pass off (*c*) **se p. de qch**, to do without sth; **ces faits se passent de commentaires**, these facts need no comment.

passerelle [pasrɛl] *nf* **1.** footbridge **2.** (*a*) *Nau:* bridge (*b*) *Nau: Av:* gangway.

passe-temps [pastɑ̃] *nm inv* pastime.

passe-thé [paste] *nm inv* tea strainer.

passeur, -euse [pasœr, -øz] *n* (*a*) ferryman, -woman (*b*) *Pol:* frontier runner.

passible [pasibl] *a* liable (**de**, to, for).

passif, -ive [pasif, -iv] **1.** *a* (*a*) passive (obedience); *Gram:* **forme passive**, passive (*b*) *Com:* **dettes passives**, liabilities **2.** *nm* (*a*) *Gram:* passive (*b*) *Com:* debt. **passivement** *adv* passively.

passion [pasjɔ̃] *nf* 1. la P., the Passion 2. passion; **avoir la p. des voitures,** to have a passion for cars; **parler avec, sans, p.,** to speak passionately, dispassionately.

passionnant [pasjɔnɑ̃] *a* exciting, fascinating, gripping (story).

passionné, -ée [pasjɔne] (*a*) *a* passionate; impassioned; **p. de qch,** passionately fond of sth (*b*) *n* enthusiast, fanatic. **passionnément** *adv* passionately.

passionnel, -elle [pasjɔnɛl] *a* passional; **crime p.,** crime of passion.

passionner [pasjɔne] *vtr* 1. to impassion; to fascinate, to grip; to intrigue; **le sport le passionne,** sport is his passion 2. **se p. de, pour, qch,** to become enthusiastic about sth; to conceive a passion for sth.

passoire [paswar] *nf Cu:* strainer; sieve; **p. à légumes,** colander.

pastel [pastɛl] *nm Art:* pastel.

pastèque [pastɛk] *nf* watermelon.

pasteur [pastœr] *nm* 1. shepherd 2. *Ecc:* pastor; (Protestant) minister.

pasteurisation [pastœrizasjɔ̃] *nf* pasteurization.

pasteuriser [pastœrize] *vtr* to pasteurize.

pastiche [pastiʃ] *nm* pastiche.

pasticher [pastiʃe] *vtr* to do a pastiche of.

pastille [pastij] *nf* lozenge; **p. contre la toux,** cough drop, cough pastille; **p. de menthe,** mint.

pastis [pastis] *nm* aniseed aperitif.

pastoral, -aux [pastɔral, -o] 1. *a* pastoral 2. *nf* **pastorale,** *Lit:* pastoral; *Mus:* pastoral(e).

patate [patat] *nf* 1. sweet potato 2. *F:* (*a*) potato, spud (*b*) idiot, fathead.

patati [patati] *int F:* **et p. et patata,** and so on and so forth.

patatras [patatra] *int F:* crash!

pataud, -aude [pato, -od] *a F:* lumpish, clumsy (pers).

patauger [patɔʒe] *vi* (**n. pataugeons**) (*a*) to wade, squelch (in the mud); to paddle (in the water) (*b*) to flounder.

pâte [pɑt] *nf* 1. (*a*) *Cu:* pastry; (cake) mixture; **p. à pain,** dough; **p. brisée,** short(crust) pastry; **p. feuilletée,** flaky pastry; **p. à frire,** batter; **pâtes (alimentaires),** pasta, noodles (*b*) (fruit) jelly; (almond) paste (*c*) (paper) pulp; **p. dentifrice,** toothpaste; **p. à modeler,** modelling clay.

pâté [pate] *nm* 1. (*a*) *Cu:* **p. en croûte,** (meat) pie (*b*) pâté; **p. de foie,** liver pâté (*c*) sand castle 2. block (of houses) 3. ink blot.

pâtée [pate] *nf* (*a*) mash, feed (*b*) *F:* thrashing.

patelin [patlɛ̃] *nm F:* village.

patent [patɑ̃] *a* obvious, evident.

patente [patɑ̃t] *nf* (trading) licence.

patère [patɛr] *nf* hat peg, coat peg.

paternalisme [paternalism] *nm* paternalism. **paternaliste** *a* paternalistic.

paternel, -elle [paternɛl] *a* paternal; fatherly; **le domicile p.,** (the family) home; **du côté p.,** on the father's side. **paternellement** *adv* paternally, in a fatherly way.

paternité [paternite] *nf* paternity.

pâteux, -euse [patø, -øz] *a* (*a*) pasty; doughy (bread); coated (tongue) (*b*) thick (voice).

pathétique [patetik] 1. *a* pathetic, moving; *Anat:* pathetic (muscle) 2. *nm* pathos.

pathologie [patɔlɔʒi] *nf* pathology. **pathologique** *a* pathological.

patibulaire [patibylɛr] *a* **une mine p.,** a sinister look.

patience [pasjɑ̃s] *nf* (*a*) patience; **prendre p.,** to be patient; **je suis à bout de p.,** my patience is exhausted (*b*) jeu de p., jigsaw (puzzle).

patient, -ente [pasjɑ̃, -ɑ̃t] 1. *a* patient 2. *n Med:* patient. **patiemment** *adv* patiently.

patienter [pasjɑ̃te] *vi* to exercise patience; **p. un instant,** to wait a moment.

patin [patɛ̃] *nm* (*a*) cloth pad (for parquet floors) (*b*) skate; **patins à glace, à roulettes,** ice skates, roller skates (*c*) runner (of sledge); **p. (de frein),** brake block.

patinage [patinaʒ] *nm* skating; **p. artistique,** figure skating.

patine [patin] *nf* patina, sheen.

patiner [patine] *vi* 1. to skate 2. (*of wheel*) to spin; (*of clutch*) to slip 3. to give a patina, a sheen, to.

patineur, -euse [patinœr, -øz] *n* skater.

patinoire [patinwar] *nf* skating rink, ice ring.

pâtisserie [patisri] *nf* 1. pastry; (small) cake; *Com:* confectionery 2. pastry making 3. cake shop; confectioner's.

patissier, -ière [patisje, -jɛr] *n* pastrycook; confectioner.

patois [patwa] *nm* patois.

patraque [patrak] *a F:* out of sorts, peaky.

patriarche [patriarʃ] *nm* patriarch.

patricien, -ienne [patrisjɛ̃, -jɛn] *a & n* patrician.

patrie [patri] *nf* homeland; fatherland.

patrimoine [patrimwan] *nm* patrimony; heritage.

patriote [patriot] 1. *a* patriotic. 2. *n* patriot. **patriotique** *a* patriotic.

patriotisme [patriɔtism] *nm* patriotism.

patron, -onne [patrɔ̃, -ɔn] *n* 1. patron; patron saint. 2. (*a*) employer; head (of firm); proprietor; owner, *F:* boss (*b*) *Nau:* skipper 3. *nm* (sewing, knitting) pattern. **patronal, -aux** *a* of employers; employer's.

patronage [patrɔnaʒ] *nm* 1. patronage 2. youth club.

patronat [patrɔna] *nm* (body of) employers.

patronner [patrɔne] *vtr* to support, to sponsor (s.o.).

patrouille [patruj] *nf* patrol.

patrouiller [patruje] *vi* to patrol, to be on patrol.

patrouilleur [patrujœr] *nm* (*a*) *Mil:* patroller (*b*) patrol boat.

patte [pat] *nf* 1. paw; foot (of bird); leg (of insect); *F:* (*of pers*) hand, paw; **pattes de mouche,** spidery handwriting; **pattes (de lapin),** sideburns; **marcher à quatre pattes,** to go on all fours; **court sur pattes,** short-legged; **pattes de devant, de derrière,** forelegs, forefeet; hind legs, hind feet; (*of cat*) **faire p. de velours,** to draw in its claws; **tomber dans les pattes de qn,** to fall into s.o.'s clutches 2. flap (of pocket); tongue (of shoe); fluke (of anchor); strap (on garment).

patte-d'oie [patdwa] *nf* 1. crossroads 2. (*wrinkle*) crow's-foot; *pl* **pattes-d'oie.**

pâturage [pɑtyraʒ] *nm* (*a*) grazing (*b*) pasture.

pâture [pɑtyr] *nf* **1.** food, fodder (of animals) **2.** pasture.

pâturer [pɑtyre] *vi* (*of cattle, etc*) to graze, to feed.

paume [pom] *nf* palm (of hand).

paumer [pome] *P:* **1.** *vtr* to lose **2. se p.,** to get lost. **paumé, -ée** **1.** *a F:* lost; **il est p.,** he doesn't know where he is **2.** *n P:* (*pers*) wreck; bum.

paupière [popjɛr] *nf* eyelid.

paupiette [popjɛt] *nf Cu:* (meat) olive.

pause [poz] *nf* **1.** pause; *Fb: etc:* half time; *Ind: etc:* meal break; **p. café,** coffee break, (=) tea break **2.** *Mus:* semibreve rest.

pauvre [povr̩] **1.** *a* (*a*) poor; **p. d'esprit,** half-witted; **minerai p. en métal,** ore with a low metal content (*b*) poor, unfortunate; **le p. homme!** poor fellow! **p. de moi!** poor me! (*c*) shabby (dress, furniture); paltry (excuse); weak (argument); *F:* **c'est un p. type,** he's pathetic; **p. idiot!** silly fool! *n* **le p.!** poor chap! **mon p.,** my dear (friend) **2.** *n* poor man, poor woman; **les pauvres,** the poor. **pauvrement** *adv* poorly; **p. vêtu,** shabbily dressed.

pauvreté [povrəte] *nf* poverty; shabbiness.

pavage [pavaʒ] *nm* paving, cobblestones.

pavaner (se) [səpavane] *vpr* to strut (about).

pavé [pave] *nm* **1.** (*a*) paving stone, paving block; cobblestone; **un p. dans la mare,** a (nice) bit of scandal (*b*) **p. de viande,** thick piece of meat **2.** pavement; paving (*b*) the streets; **battre le p.,** to loaf about the streets; **être sur le p.,** (i) to be homeless (ii) to be out of a job; **mettre qn sur le p.,** to throw s.o. out.

paver [pave] *vtr* to pave; to cobble (street).

pavillon [pavijɔ̃] *nm* **1.** detached house; **p. de banlieue,** suburban house; **p. de jardin,** summerhouse; **p. de chasse,** shooting lodge **2.** horn (of hooter); bell (of brass instrument); pavilion (of ear) **3.** *Nau:* flag, colours; **p. de départ,** Blue Peter.

pavoiser [pavwaze] **1.** *vtr* (*a*) *Nau:* to dress (ship) (*b*) to deck with flags **2.** *vi* (*a*) *Nau:* to dress ship (*b*) to put out the flags (*c*) to rejoice.

pavot [pavo] *nm Bot:* poppy.

payer [peje] **1.** *vtr* (**je paye, je paie**) (*a*) **p. qn,** to pay s.o.; **combien vous a-t-il fait p.?** how much did he charge you? **bien, mal, payé,** well, badly, paid; **p. qn de paroles,** to put s.o. off with fine words (*b*) to pay, settle (debt); *Com:* **p. un effet,** to honour a bill (*c*) to pay for (sth); **p. qch à qn,** to pay s.o. for sth; **p. le dîner à qn,** to treat s.o. to dinner (*d*) **il l'a payé de sa vie,** it cost him his life; **vous me le paierez!** you'll pay for this! *F:* **je suis payé pour le savoir,** I've learnt it the hard way **2.** *vi* (*a*) **p. de sa personne,** to risk one's own skin; **p. d'audace,** to take the risk (*b*) (*of crime, business*) to pay **3. se p.** (*a*) **je me suis payé une glace,** I treated myself to an ice cream; **se p. le tête de qn,** to make fun of s.o. (*b*) **cela ne se paie pas,** it's something money can't buy.

pays [pe(j)i] *nm* (*a*) country; land; **p. étranger,** foreign country; **voir du p.,** to travel around (a lot), to see the world (*b*) region, district, locality; **vous n'êtes pas de ce pays?** you don't belong to these parts? **être en p. de connaissance,** (i) to be among friends (ii) to be on home ground; **vin du p., de p.,** local wine (*c*) **p. de montagne(s),** hill country; *pl* **p. bas,** lowlands (*d*) native land; home; **avoir le mal du p.,** to be homesick.

paysage [peizaʒ] *nm* landscape; scenery.

paysagiste [peizaʒist] landscape painter; (**jardinier**) **p.,** landscape gardener.

paysan, -anne [peizɑ̃, -an] *n & a* peasant; rustic; country(man), country(woman).

Pays-Bas [peiba] *Pr nmpl* the Netherlands.

PC *abbr* **1.** *Parti communiste* **2.** *Poste de commandement.*

PCC *abbr Pour copie conforme.*

PCV *abbr Tp: paiement contre vérification,* transfer(red) charge.

P-DG *abbr président-directeur général.*

péage [peaʒ] *nm* **1.** toll; **autoroute à p.,** toll motorway **2.** toll house.

peau, -eaux [po] *nf* **1.** skin; **à fleur de p.,** skin-deep; **il n'a que la p. et les os,** he's nothing but skin and bones; **prendre qn par la p. du cou,** to take s.o. by the scruff of the neck; **faire p. neuve,** to turn over a new leaf; **risquer sa p.,** to risk one's neck; **sauver sa p.,** to save one's skin; *F:* **avoir qn dans la p.,** to be crazy about s.o.; **se sentir mal dans sa p.,** to feel uncomfortable; *P:* **j'aurai sa p.!** I'll get him! **2.** pelt, fur; hide, leather; **p. de mouton,** sheepskin; *P:* **p. de vache,** (*man*) bastard; (*woman*) cow **3.** peel (of fruit); rind (of cheese).

Peau-Rouge [poruʒ] *a & n* Red Indian; redskin; *pl Peaux-Rouges.*

pébroque [pebrɔk] *nm P:* umbrella, brolly.

peccadille [pekadij] *nf* peccadillo.

pêche¹ [pɛʃ] *nf* peach.

pêche² *nf* **1.** fishing; **p.** (**à la ligne**), angling; (*in sea*) line fishing; **p. à la mouche,** fly fishing; **aller à la p.,** to go fishing **2.** catch.

péché [peʃe] *nm* sin; transgression; **p. mortel,** mortal sin; **les septs péchés capitaux,** the seven deadly sins; **son p. mignon,** his weakness; **péchés de jeunesse,** youthful indiscretions.

pécher [peʃe] *vi* (**je pèche; je pécherai**) to sin; **p. par orgueil,** to commit the sin of pride; **p. par excès,** to exceed what is required.

pêcher¹ [peʃe] *nm* peach tree.

pêcher² *vtr* **1.** to fish for (trout); to catch (fish); to gather (mussels); **p. à la ligne,** to angle; **p. à la mouche,** to fly fish; **p. la baleine,** to go whaling **2.** *F:* **où avez-vous pêché cela?** where did you get hold of that?

pêcheur, pêcheresse [peʃœr, peʃrɛs] *n* sinner.

pêcheur, -euse [pɛʃœr, -øz] *n* fisher; fisherman, -woman; **p. à la ligne,** angler; **p. de perles,** pearl diver; *a* **bateau p.,** fishing smack.

pécule [pekyl] *nm* savings; earnings of convict (paid on discharge); *Mil: Navy:* gratuity (on discharge).

pécuniaire [pekynjɛr] *a* financial.

pédagogie [pedagɔʒi] *nf* pedagogy; education. **pédagogique** *a* pedagogic(al); educational.

pédagogue [pedagɔg] *n* educationalist.

pédale [pedal] *nf* pedal; treadle (of lathe).

pédaler [pedale] *vi* to pedal.

pédalier [pedalje] *nm* crank gear.

pédalo [pedalo] *nm* pedal boat.

pédant, -ante [pedɑ̃, -ɑ̃t] **1.** *n* pedant **2.** *a* pedantic.

pédantisme [pedɑ̃tism] *nm* pedantry.

pédéraste [pederast] *nm* pederast, homosexual.

pédiatre [pedjatr̩] *n* paediatrician.

pédiatrie [pedjatri] *nf Med:* paediatrics.

pédicure [pedikyr] *n* chiropodist.

pedigree [pedigre] *nm* pedigree.

pègre [pɛgr̩] *nf* the underworld.

peigne [pɛɲ] *nm* comb; *Tex:* card; **passer qch au p. fin**, to go through sth with a fine toothcomb.

peigner [peɲe] *vtr* 1. (*a*) to comb (out) (hair); **mal peigné**, unkempt; tousled (hair) (*b*) *Tex:* to card (wool) 2. **se p.**, to comb one's hair.

peignoir [pɛɲwar] *nm* dressing gown; bath robe.

peinard [penar] *a P:* cushy; **rester p.**, to take things easy.

peindre [pɛ̃dr̩] *vtr* (*prp* **peignant**; *pp* **peint**; *pr ind* **je peins**; *ph* **je peignis**) 1. to paint; **p. qch en vert**, to paint sth green; **papier peint**, wallpaper 2. to paint, portray, depict; **se faire p.**, to have one's portrait painted; **p. à l'huile, à l'aquarelle**, to paint in oils, in water colours; **l'innocence est peinte sur son visage**, innocence is written on his face.

peine [pɛn] *nf* 1. punishment, penalty; **p. capitale**, capital punishment; **sous p. de mort**, on pain of death; **défense d'entrer sous p. d'amende**, trespassers will be prosecuted 2. (*a*) sorrow, affliction; **avoir de la p.**, to feel sad; **faire de la p. à qn**, to grieve, distress, s.o.; **cela fait p. à voir**, it's painful to see (*b*) **être dans la p.**, to be in distress, in trouble 3. pains, trouble; **se donner de la p. pour faire qch**, to take trouble to do sth; **donnez-vous la p. de vous asseoir**, please take a seat; **c'est p. perdue**, it's a waste of effort, of time; **ça ne vaut pas la p.**, it's not worth the trouble; **ce n'est pas la p.**, don't bother; **c'était bien la p. de venir!** we might as well have stayed at home! **homme de p.**, odd-job man 4. difficulty; **avoir de la p. à faire qch**, to find it difficult to do sth; **il n'est jamais en p. de trouver une excuse**, he's never at a loss for an excuse; *adv phr* **avec p.**, **à grand-p.**, with (great) difficulty; **sans p.**, easily 5. *adv phr* **à p.**, hardly, barely, scarcely; **il est à p. 3 heures**, it's only just 3 o'clock; **j'étais à p. sorti qu'il se mit à pleuvoir**, I had only just gone out when it started to rain.

peiner [pene] 1. *vtr* to pain, distress, upset (s.o.) 2. *vi* to toil, labour; **il peinait sur son travail**, he was struggling with his work; *Aut:* **le moteur peine**, the engine's labouring.

peintre [pɛ̃tr̩] *nm* painter; **(artiste) p.**, artist; **p. en bâtiment(s)**, house painter.

peinture [pɛ̃tyr̩] *nf* 1. (*a*) painting; **faire de la p.**, to paint; **p. à l'huile, à l'eau**, oil painting; water colour (*b*) **p. au pistolet**, spray painting 2. picture, painting 3. paint; *PN:* **attention à la p.!** wet paint.

péjoratif, -ive [peʒɔratif, -iv] *a* pejorative.

Pékin [pekɛ̃] *Prnm Geog:* Peking. **pékinois, -oise** (*a*) *a & n* Pekinese (*b*) *nm* (dog) pekinese, *F:* peke.

pelage [pǝlaʒ] *nm* coat, wool, fur (of animal).

pelé [pǝle] (*a*) *a* bald; hairless (skin); bare (countryside); threadbare (material) (*b*) *nm F:* **il n'y avait que trois pelés et un tondu**, there was hardly anyone there.

pêle-mêle [pɛlmɛl] *adv* higgledy-piggledy.

peler [p(ǝ)le] (**je pèle**) 1. *vtr* to peel, skin (fruit) 2 *vi* (of skin) to peel.

pèlerin [pɛlrɛ̃] *n* pilgrim.

pèlerinage [pɛlrinaʒ] *nm* pilgrimage.

pèlerine [pɛlrin] *nf Cl:* cape.

pélican [pelikɑ̃] *nm Orn:* pelican.

pelle [pɛl] *nf* 1. shovel; **p. à ordures**, dustpan; **p. à tarte**, tart slice; **ramasser l'argent à la p.**, to be raking it in; *F:* **ramasser une p.**, to fall flat on one's face 2. (child's) spade.

pelletée [pɛlte] *nf* shovelful, spadeful.

pelleteuse [pɛltøz] *nf* mechanical shovel.

pellicule [pelikyl] *nf* 1. *Phot:* film 2. *pl* dandruff.

pelote [p(ǝ)lɔt] *nf* 1. ball (of wool, string); **p. à épingles**, pincushion; *F:* **faire sa p.**, to feather one's nest 2. *Sp:* **p. basque**, pelota.

peloter [p(ǝ)lɔte] *vtr P:* to pet, to paw.

peloton [p(ǝ)lɔtɔ̃] *nm* 1. group (of people); *Sp:* **le p.**, the main body (of runners) 2. *Mil:* (*a*) platoon (*b*) class, party; **p. d'exécution**, firing squad.

pelouse [p(ǝ)luz] *nf* lawn; *Sp:* green.

peluche [p(ǝ)lyʃ] *nf* (*a*) *Tex:* plush; **jouet en p.**, soft toy (*b*) (bit of) fluff.

pelure [p(ǝ)lyr] *nf* (*a*) peel, skin (of apple, onion); peeling (of vegetables); **p. d'oignon**, dark rosé wine (*b*) *F:* (over)coat.

pénal, -aux [penal, -o] *a* penal (code).

pénaliser [penalize] *vtr Sp: Games:* to penalize (a competitor, a player).

pénalité [penalite] *nf Jur: Sp:* penalty.

penalty [penalti] *nm Fb:* penalty (kick); *pl* **penalties**.

penaud [pǝno] *a* sheepish.

penchant [pɑ̃ʃɑ̃] *nm* propensity, tendency; leaning (towards sth); fondness (for sth); **avoir un p. pour la boisson**, to be partial to drink.

pencher [pɑ̃ʃe] 1. *vtr* to bend, lean; **p. la tête en avant**, to lean forward 2. *vi* (*a*) to lean (over); to tip (to one side); **faire p. la balance**, to tip the scales (*b*) **p. pour qch**, to incline towards, to prefer, sth 3. **se p.** (*a*) to bend, stoop, lean; **se p. (en, au) dehors**, to lean out (*b*) **se p. sur un problème**, to look into a problem; **se p. sur qn**, to take care of s.o. **penché** *a* leaning; slanting; tilting; **p. sur ses livres**, bent over one's books.

pendaison [pɑ̃dɛzɔ̃] *nf* hanging; **p. de la crémaillère**, housewarming (party).

pendant¹ [pɑ̃dɑ̃] 1. *a* (*a*) hanging, pendent; dangling (legs); drooping (branch); **oreilles pendantes**, flap ears, lop ears (*b*) pending (lawsuit); outstanding (question) 2. *nm* (*a*) pendant; **p. (d'oreille)**, drop earring (*b*) counterpart, match (of picture); **ces deux tableaux (se) font p.**, these two pictures make a pair.

pendant² *prep* during; **p. l'été**, in summer; during the summer; **p. trois jours**, for three days; **p. ce temps**, meanwhile, in the meantime; *conj phr* **p. que**, while, whilst; **p. que vous y êtes**, while you're about it.

pendentif [pɑ̃dɑ̃tif] *nm Jewel:* pendant.

penderie [pɑ̃dri] *nf* (hanging) cupboard, wardrobe.

pendre [pɑ̃dr̩] 1. *vtr* (*a*) to hang (sth) (up); **p. le linge**, to hang out the washing; **p. la crémaillère**, to give a housewarming party (*b*) to hang (on the gallows); *F:* **qu'il aille se faire p. ailleurs**, let him go hang 2. *vi* to hang (down); (of legs) to dangle; (of cheeks) to sag; *F:* **ça lui pend au nez**, he's got it coming to him 3. **se p.**, to hang oneself; **se p. à qch**, to hang on, cling on, to sth; **se p. au cou de qn**, to hang round s.o.'s neck.

pendu [pãdy] **1.** *a* hanged, hung; hanging; **p. aux jupes de sa mère,** clinging to his mother's skirts; **avoir la langue bien pendue,** to be a great talker **2.** *n* hanged man, hanged woman.

pendule [pãdyl] **1.** *nm* pendulum **2.** *nf* clock.

pendulette [pãdylɛt] *nf* small (travelling) clock.

pénétration [penetrasjɔ̃] *nf* penetration.

pénétrer [penetre] *v* (**je pénètre; je pénétrerai**) **1.** *vi* to penetrate; to enter; **l'eau avait pénétré partout,** the water had got in everywhere **2.** *vtr* (*a*) **la balle a pénétré l'os,** the bullet penetrated, pierced, the bone; **p. la pensée de qn,** to see through s.o.; **p. un secret,** to fathom a secret (*b*) **être pénétré d'un sentiment,** to be imbued with a feeling **3.** **se p. d'une idée,** to let an idea sink in. **pénétrable** *a* penetrable. **pénétrant** *a* penetrating; sharp (object); piercing (cold); drenching (rain). **pénétré** *a* penetrated, imbued (**de,** with); earnest (tone, air).

pénible [penibl] *a* **1.** laborious, hard (task); difficult (life); tedious, tiresome (work) **2.** painful, distressing (sight, news); **ça m'est trop p.,** I can't bear it; *F:* **il est vraiment p.,** he's really impossible! **péniblement** *adv* laboriously; with difficulty.

péniche [peniʃ] *nf* barge.

pénicilline [penisilin] *nf Med:* penicillin.

péninsule [penɛ̃syl] *nf* peninsula.

pénitence [penitãs] *nf* **1.** penitence, repentance **2.** (*a*) penance (*b*) punishment; **mettre un enfant en p.,** to put a child in the corner. **pénitent, -ente** *a* penitent.

pénitencier [penitãsje] *nm* penitentiary.

Pennsylvanie [pãsilvani, pɛ̃-] *Prnf Geog:* Pennsylvania.

pénombre [penɔ̃br] *nf* half light, semi-darkness.

pensée¹ [pãse] *nf Bot:* pansy.

pensée² *nf* thought; **venir à la p. de qn,** to occur to s.o.; **saisir la p. de qn,** to grasp s.o.'s meaning; **libre p.,** free thinking.

penser [pãse] *v* **1.** *v ind tr* to think; **p. à qn, à qch,** to think of s.o., sth; **je l'ai fait sans y p.,** I did it without thinking; **pensez-vous!** don't you believe it! **vous n'y pensez pas!** you don't mean it! **ah, j'y pense!** by the way! **rien que d'y p.,** the mere thought (of it); **p. à faire qch,** to remember to do sth; **il me fait p. à mon frère,** he reminds me of my brother **2.** *vi* to think; **je pense comme vous,** I agree with you; **voilà ma façon de p.,** that's the way I see it; **pensez donc!** just fancy! **3.** *vtr* (*a*) **je le pensais bien,** I thought as much; **je pense que oui, que non,** I think so, I think not; **pensez si j'étais furieux,** you can imagine how angry I was (*b*) **je le pense fou,** I think he's mad (*c*) **p. du bien de qn,** to think well of s.o. (*d*) **p. faire qch,** to expect to do sth; to consider doing sth; **je pense le voir demain,** I hope to see him tomorrow; **j'ai pensé mourir de rire,** I nearly died laughing. **pensant** *a* thinking (man, woman); **bien pensant,** orthodox, right-thinking. **pensif, -ive** *a* pensive, thoughtful. **pensivement** *adv* thoughtfully.

penseur, -euse [pãsœr, -øz] *n* thinker.

pension [pãsjɔ̃] *nf* **1.** pension, allowance; **p. de retraite,** retirement, old age, pension; **p. alimentaire,** (i) living allowance (ii) maintenance allowance; alimony **2.** (*a*) (*payment for board and lodging*) **être en p. chez qn,** to board with s.o.; **p. complète,** full

board; **demi-p.,** half board (*b*) **p. de famille,** boarding house **3.** (private) boarding school.

pensionnaire [pãsjɔnɛr] *n* boarder; lodger; resident (in hotel).

pensionnat [pãsjɔna] *nm* boarding school.

pensionné, -ée [pãsjɔne] *n* pensioner.

pensionner [pãsjɔne] *vtr* to pension (s.o.).

pentagone [pɛ̃tagɔn] *nm* pentagon.

pente [pãt] *nf* (*a*) slope, incline, gradient; **en p.,** sloping, shelving; **rue en p.,** steep street; *Fig:* **être sur une mauvaise p.,** to be going downhill; **remonter la p.,** to get back on one's feet (*b*) camber (of road); pitch (of roof).

Pentecôte [pãtkot] *nf* Whitsun; **dimanche de la P.,** Whit Sunday.

pénurie [penyri] *nf* scarcity, shortage.

pépé [pepe] *nm F:* grandad, grandpa.

pépée [pepe] *nf P:* girl, bird, chick.

pépère [pepɛr] **1.** *nm* (*a*) **gros p.,** old fatty (*b*) grandad, granpa **2.** *a* quiet (spot); cushy (job).

pépiement [pepimã] *nm* cheep(ing), chirp(ing), tweet(ing).

pépier [pepje] *vi* to cheep, chirp.

pépin¹ [pepɛ̃] *nm* **1.** pip (of apple, grape); **sans pépins,** seedless **2.** *F:* hitch; **avoir un p.,** to hit a snag.

pépin² *nm F:* umbrella, brolly.

pépinière [pepinjɛr] *nf* **1.** *Hort:* nursery (garden) **2.** nest.

pépiniériste [pepinjerist] *n* nursery gardener.

perçant [pɛrsã] *a* piercing; keen, sharp (eyes); shrill (voice).

perce [pɛrs] *nf* **mettre en p.,** to broach, tap (wine).

percée [pɛrse] *nf* **1.** (*a*) opening; glade, clearing (in forest) (*b*) breach, gap (in wall) **2.** *Mil: Sp:* breakthrough.

percement [pɛrsəmã] *nm* piercing; boring (of hole); opening (of street); driving (of tunnel); cutting (of canal).

perce-neige [pɛrsənɛʒ] *nm or f inv Bot:* snowdrop.

perce-oreille [pɛrsɔrɛj] *nm Ent:* earwig; *pl* **perceoreilles.**

percepteur [pɛrsɛptœr] *nm* tax collector.

perceptible [pɛrsɛptibl] *a* **1.** perceptible (**à,** by, to) **2.** collectable (tax).

perceptif, -ive [pɛrsɛptif, -iv] *a* perceptive.

perception [pɛrsɛpsjɔ̃] *nf* **1.** perception **2.** collection (of taxes); (**bureau de) p.,** tax (collector's) office.

percer [pɛrse] *v* (**je perçais(s); n. perçons**) **1.** *vtr* (*a*) to pierce, to go through (sth); to wear a hole in (sth); **p. un abcès,** to lance an abscess; **p. qch à jour,** to find sth out (*b*) to perforate; to make a hole in (sth); to drill, bore (hole); to drive (tunnel); to cut (canal); **p. une porte dans un mur,** to make a door in a wall; **se faire p. les oreilles,** to have one's ears pierced **2.** *vi* to pierce; to come, break, through; (*of emotion*) to show; (*of author*) to start to make a name; **ses dents percent,** he's cutting his teeth.

perceuse [pɛrsøz] *nf* drill.

percevoir [pɛrsəvwar] *vtr* (*conj like* RECEVOIR) **1.** to perceive, discern **2.** to collect (taxes) **3.** to receive (interest). **percevable** *a* perceivable; collectable (tax).

perche [pɛrʃ] *nf* **1.** (*a*) (thin) pole; *Sp:* **saut à la p.,** pole vaulting (*b*) *F:* (*pers*) beanpole **2.** *Ich:* perch.

percher [pɛrʃe] **1.** *vi* (*of birds*) to perch, roost; *F:* to live **2.** *vtr F:* to put, stick (sth somewhere) **3.** (*of bird*) **se p. sur une branche,** to perch on a branch.

perchoir [pɛrʃwar] *nm* perch.

percolateur [pɛrkɔlatœr] *nm* (coffee) percolator.

percussion [pɛrkysjɔ̃] *nf* percussion.

percussionniste [pɛrkysjɔnist] *n* percussionist.

percuter [pɛrkyte] **1.** *vtr* to strike (sth) sharply **2.** *vi* **la voiture a percuté contre un arbre,** the car crashed into a tree. **percutant** *a* forceful (speech).

percuteur [pɛrkytœr] *nm* firing pin.

perdant, -ante [pɛrdɑ̃, -ɑ̃t] **1.** *a* losing; **billet p.,** blank (ticket at lottery) **2.** *n* loser.

perdition [pɛrdisjɔ̃] *nf* (*a*) *Rel:* perdition; **lieu de p.,** den of iniquity (*b*) *Nau:* **en p.,** (i) in distress (ii) sinking.

perdre [pɛrdr̩] *vtr* **1.** to ruin, destroy; **le jeu l'a perdu,** gambling was his undoing **2.** to lose; **p. son père,** to lose one's father; **p. la partie,** to lose the game; **p. haleine,** to get out of breath; **tu ne perds rien pour attendre!** just you wait! **p. son temps,** to waste (one's) time; **p. qn de vue,** to lose sight of s.o. **3.** *vi* (*a*) **le fût perd,** the cask is leaking (*b*) **vous n'y perdez rien,** you haven't missed anything (by it) **4. se p.** (*a*) to be lost; **se p. dans la foule,** to vanish in the crowd (*b*) (*of power*) to be wasted; (*of food*) to go bad (*c*) to lose one's way; *F:* **je m'y perds,** I can't make head or tail of it; **il y a des fessées qui se perdent,** he, she, deserves a good spanking.

perdreau, -eaux [pɛrdro] *nm* young partridge.

perdrix [pɛrdri] *nf* partridge.

perdu [pɛrdy] *a* **1.** ruined, (*of patient*) done for; **âme perdue,** lost soul **2.** (*a*) lost; **à mes moments perdus,** in my spare time; **il habite un trou p.,** he lives at the back of beyond; **c'est peine perdue,** it's a waste of time (*b*) *Com:* non-returnable (packing) **3. à corps p.,** recklessly.

père [pɛr] *nm* **1.** father; **de p. en fils,** from father to son; **M. Martin p.,** Mr Martin senior; **le p. Jean,** old John; **p. de famille,** father; **nos pères,** our forefathers **2.** *Ecc:* father; **le (révérend) P. X,** Father X; (*form of address*) **mon p.,** father **3.** *Breed:* sire.

péremptoire [perɑ̃ptwar] *a* peremptory.

perfection [pɛrfɛksjɔ̃] *nf* perfection; **à la p.,** to perfection, perfectly.

perfectionnement [pɛrfɛksjɔnmɑ̃] *nm* perfecting (de, of); improving; **cours de p.,** refresher course.

perfectionner [pɛrfɛksjɔne] **1.** *vtr a* to perfect (*b*) to improve (machine, method) **2. se p.,** to improve; to increase one's knowledge; **se p. en allemand,** to improve one's German. **perfectionné** *a* sophisticated.

perfide [pɛrfid] *a* treacherous; perfidious.

perfidie [pɛrfidi] *nf* perfidy; treacherous act.

perforateur, -trice [pɛrfɔratœr, -tris] **1.** (*a*) *nm* perforator; punch; *Cmptr:* card punch (*b*) *n* punch card operator.

perforation [pɛrfɔrasjɔ̃] *nf* perforation; *Cmptr:* punch (hole).

perforer [pɛrfɔre] *vtr* to perforate; to bore (through), to drill; to punch; **carte perforée,** punch(ed) card; **bande perforée,** punch(ed) tape.

performance [pɛrfɔrmɑ̃s] *nf Sp: etc:* performance.

perfusion [pɛrfyzjɔ̃] *nf Med:* perfusion.

péricliter [periklite] *vi* (*of business*) to collapse.

péril [peril] *nm* peril, danger; **mettre qch en p.,** to endanger sth; **au p. de sa vie,** at the risk of one's life.

périlleux, -euse [perijø, -øz] *a* perilous, dangerous; **saut p.,** somersault.

périmé [perime] *a* out-of-date; expired (passport); (ticket) no longer valid.

périmètre [perimɛtr̩] *nm* perimeter; area.

période [perjɔd] *nf* period; age, era; **p. de beau temps,** spell of fine weather; **p. électorale,** election time. **périodique 1.** *a* periodical, recurrent, intermittent **2.** *nm* periodical. **périodiquement** *adv* periodically.

péripétie [peripesi] *nf* event; *pl* turns; ups and downs (of life); adventures.

périphérie [periferi] *nf* **1.** periphery **2.** outskirts (of town). **périphérique** *a* peripheral; **boulevard p.,** *nm* **p.,** ring road; *US:* circular route.

périphrase [perifraz] *nf* circumlocution.

périple [peripl̩] *nm* (*a*) sea voyage (*b*) journey.

périr [perir] *vi* to perish; to be destroyed; to die; **p. noyé,** to drown. **périssable** *a* perishable.

périscope [periskɔp] *nm* periscope.

péritonite [peritɔnit] *nf Med:* peritonitis.

perle [pɛrl] *nf* **1.** (*a*) pearl; **p. fine, de culture,** real, cultured, pearl (*b*) *Fig:* gem, treasure (*c*) *F:* howler **2.** bead (of glass, metal).

permanence [pɛrmanɑ̃s] *nf* **1.** permanence; **en p.,** permanently; continuously **2. être de p.,** to be on duty, on call; **la p. est assurée le dimanche,** there's someone on duty on Sundays **3.** (duty) office; *Sch:* = prep. room.

permanent [pɛrmanɑ̃] **1.** *a* permanent (court); standing (committee); continuous (performances); *Cin:* **p. de 2 heures à 11 heures,** continuous showings from 2 till 11 o'clock **2.** *nf Hairdr:* **permanente,** permanent wave, *F:* perm **3.** *nm Pol:* official.

permettre [pɛrmɛtr̩] *vtr* (*conj like* METTRE) to permit, allow; to enable; **p. qch à qn,** to allow s.o. sth; **p. à qn de faire qch,** to let s.o. do sth, to allow s.o. to do sth; **est-il permis d'entrer?** may I come in? **il se croit tout permis,** he thinks he can do anything he likes; **permettez-moi de vous dire,** may I say; **permettez!** excuse me! if you don't mind! **vous permettez?** may I? **2. se p. de faire qch,** to take the liberty of doing sth; **se p. un verre de vin,** to indulge in a glass of wine.

permis [pɛrmi] **1.** *a* allowed, permitted, lawful, permissible **2.** *nm Adm:* permit, licence; **p. de séjour,** residence permit; **p. d'inhumer,** burial certificate; **p. de construire,** planning permission; *Aut:* **p. (de conduire),** (i) driving licence (ii) driving test.

permission [pɛrmisjɔ̃] *nf* (*a*) permission; **demander la p.,** to ask permission (*b*) *Mil: etc:* leave (of absence); (*certificate*) pass; **en p.,** on leave.

permissionnaire [pɛrmisjɔnɛr] *nm* soldier on leave.

permutation [pɛrmytasjɔ̃] *nf* permutation.

permuter [pɛrmyte] **1.** *vtr* to permutate **2.** *vi* to change, to swop (jobs).

pernicieux, -ieuse [pɛrnisjø, -jøz] *a* pernicious.

pérorer [perɔre] *vi* to hold forth; to speechify, to spout.

Pérou [peru] *Prnm Geog:* Peru; *F:* **ce n'est pas le P.,** it's no great catch.

perpendiculaire [pɛrpɑ̃dikylɛr] *a & nf* perpendicular (à, to). **perpendiculairement** *adv* perpendicularly; **p. à,** perpendicular to.

perpétrer [pɛrpetre] *vtr* (**je perpètre; je perpétrerai**) to perpetrate (a crime).

perpétuer [pɛrpetɥe] **1.** *vtr* to perpetuate; to carry on (name) **2. se p.,** to remain, to survive. **perpétuel, -elle** *a* perpetual; permanent. **perpétuellement** *adv* perpetually.

perpétuité [pɛrpetɥite] *nf* perpetuity; **à p.,** in perpetuity; (sentenced) for life.

perplexe [pɛrplɛks] *a* perplexed, puzzled.

perplexité [pɛrplɛksite] *nf* perplexity.

perquisition [pɛrkizisjɔ̃] *nf* (police) search or inquiry; **mandat de p.,** search warrant.

perquisitionner [pɛrkizisjɔne] *vi Jur:* to carry out a search; **p. au domicile de qn,** to search s.o.'s house.

perron [pɛrɔ̃] *nm* steps (leading to entrance).

perroquet [pɛrɔkɛ] *nm Orn:* parrot.

perruche [peryʃ] *nf Orn:* (a) budgerigar, *F:* budgie (b) (*woman*) chatterbox.

perruque [peryk] *nf* wig.

persécuter [pɛrsekyte] *vtr* to persecute.

persécuteur, -trice [pɛrsekytœr, -tris] *n* persecutor.

persécution [pɛrsekysjɔ̃] *nf* persecution.

persévérer [pɛrsevere] *vi* (**je persévère; je persévérerai**) to persevere (**dans,** in). **persévérant** *a* persevering.

persienne [pɛrsjɛn] *nf* (slatted) shutter.

persiflage [pɛrsiflaʒ] *nm* banter.

persil [pɛrsi] *nm Bot:* parsley.

persistance [pɛrsistɑ̃s] *nf* persistence; **avec p.,** persistently.

persister [pɛrsiste] *vi* to persist; **p. à faire qch,** to persist in doing sth. **persistant** *a* persistent.

personnage [pɛrsɔnaʒ] *nm* (a) personage; (very) important person; **p. connu,** celebrity (b) person; individual (c) character (in play, novel) (d) figure (in painting).

personnalité [pɛrsɔnalite] *nf* **1.** personality; individuality **2.** personage; **c'est une p.,** he's an important person.

personne [pɛrsɔn] **1.** *nf* (a) person; individual; **300 personnes,** 300 people; **une tierce p.,** a third party; **100 francs par p.,** 100 francs a head; **grande p.,** grown-up, adult; **p. à charge,** dependant (b) en p., in person; personally; **il est la bonté en p.,** he is kindness itself (c) **elle est bien de sa p.,** she's very attractive, good-looking; **exposer sa p.,** to expose oneself to danger (d) *Gram:* **à la troisième p.,** in the third person **2.** *pron indef m inv* (a) anyone, anybody; **il le sait mieux que p.,** nobody knows it better than he does; **je ne dois rien à p.,** I don't owe anything to anyone (b) (*with ne expressed or understood*) no one; nobody; **qui est là?—p.,** who's there?—nobody; **il n'y a p. de blessé,** nobody's been injured; **je n'ai vu p.,** I didn't see anyone; **sans nommer p.,** without naming anybody, naming no names.

personnel, -elle [pɛrsɔnɛl] **1.** *a* personal (letter, business, pronoun); not transferable (ticket); private (income) **2.** *nm* (a) personnel, staff; employees; **faire partie du p.,** to be on the staff (b) *Mil: etc:* manpower. **personnellement** *adv* personally.

personnification [pɛrsɔnifikasjɔ̃] *nf* personification.

personnifier [pɛrsɔnifje] *vtr* (*impf & pr sub* n. **personnifiions**) to personify; **elle est la bonté personnifiée,** she is goodness itself.

perspective [pɛrspɛktiv] *nf* (a) *Art:* perspective (b) outlook, view, prospect; **avoir qch en p.,** to have sth in view (c) viewpoint.

perspicacité [pɛrspikasite] *nf* shrewdness, insight. **perspicace** *a* shrewd.

persuader [pɛrsɥade] *vtr* to persuade, convince (**qn de qch,** s.o. of sth); **j'en suis persuadé,** I'm sure of it; **se p. de qch,** to convince oneself of sth.

persuasion [pɛrsɥazjɔ̃] *nf* **1.** persuasion **2.** conviction, belief. **persuasif, -ive** *a* persuasive, convincing.

perte [pɛrt] *nf* **1.** ruin, destruction; **il court à sa p.,** he's heading for disaster **2.** loss; **vendre à p.,** to sell at a loss; **p. sèche,** dead loss; **à p. de vue,** as far as the eye can see; **p. de temps,** waste of time **3.** loss, leakage (of heat).

pertinence [pɛrtinɑ̃s] *nf* pertinence, relevance.

pertinent [pɛrtinɑ̃] *a* pertinent; relevant (à, to). **pertinemment** *adv* pertinently; to the point; **je le sais p.,** I know it for a fact.

perturbation [pɛrtyrbasjɔ̃] *nf* perturbation; disruption; disturbance; **p. (atmosphérique),** (atmospheric) disturbance.

perturber [pɛrtyrbe] *vtr* to disrupt (public services); to disturb (s.o.). **perturbateur, -trice** (*a*) *a* disturbing, upsetting (*b*) *n* troublemaker.

pervers, -erse [pɛrvɛr, -ɛrs] **1.** *a* perverse, perverted, depraved **2.** *n* depraved person; pervert.

perversion [pɛrvɛrsjɔ̃] *nf* perversion.

perversité [pɛrvɛrsite] *nf* perversity.

pervertir [pɛrvɛrtir] *vtr* to pervert; **se p.,** to become depraved.

pesant [pəzɑ̃] **1.** *a* heavy, weighty; ponderous, clumsy (style, writer); deep (sleep) **2.** *nm* **ça vaut son p. d'or,** it's worth its weight in gold. **pesamment** *adv* heavily.

pesanteur [pəzɑ̃tœr] *nf* **1.** weight; *Ph:* gravity **2.** heaviness; weightiness.

pèse-bébé [pɛzbebe] *nm* baby scales; *pl* **pèse-bébés.**

pesée [pəze] *nf* (a) weighing (b) force, effort.

pèse-lettre(s) [pɛzlɛtr] *nm* letter scales; *pl* **pèse-lettres.**

pèse-personne [pɛzpɛrsɔn] *nm* (bathroom) scales; *pl* **pèse-personnes.**

peser [pəze] *v* (**je pèse, nous pesons**) **1.** *vtr* to weigh (parcel, one's words); **réponse bien pesée,** considered answer; **se p.,** to weigh oneself **2.** *vi* to weigh; to be heavy; **p. sur,** to lie heavy on (stomach, conscience); **le temps lui pèse,** time hangs heavy on his hands; **la responsabilité pèse sur lui,** the responsibility rests on his shoulders.

pessimisme [pesimism] *nm* pessimism. **pessimiste 1.** *a* pessimistic **2.** *n* pessimist.

peste [pɛst] *nf* (a) plague, pestilence; **fuir qch comme la p.,** to avoid sth like plague (b) (*of child*) pest, nuisance.

pester [pɛste] *vi* p. contre le mauvais temps, to curse the (bad) weather.

pestilence [pɛstilɑ̃s] *nf* stench, stink. **pestilentiel, -elle** *a* stinking.

pétale [petal] *nm Bot:* petal.

pétanque [petɑ̃k] *nf (in the Midi)* game of bowls.

pétard [petar] *nm* 1. (a) *Rail:* detonator, fog signal (b) *(firework)* firecracker, banger (c) *P:* revolver, gat 2. *F:* (a) din, racket; **faire du p.,** to raise a stink (b) **être en p.,** to be in a flaming temper 3. *P:* backside, bum.

péter [pete] *v* (je pète, n. pétons) 1. *vi P:* to fart (b) *(of burning wood)* to crackle; *(of string)* to snap; *(of balloon)* to burst 2. *vtr F:* to break, bust (sth); **p. la santé,** to be bursting with health.

pétillement [petijmɑ̃] *nm* crackling; bubbling; sparkling.

pétiller [petije] *vi (of burning wood)* to crackle; *(of drink)* to sparkle, fizz, bubble; *(of eyes)* to sparkle. **pétillant** *a* bubbly, fizzy; sparkling.

petit, -ite [pəti, -it] *a & n* 1. *a* (a) small; little; **un p. homme,** a little man; **c'est un homme p.,** he's short; **une toute petite maison,** a tiny little house; **p. bois,** kindling wood; **en p.,** on a small scale, in miniature; **p. à p.,** little by little, gradually; *F:* **le p. coin,** the toilet, the loo; *NAm:* the john (b) **un p. coup de rouge,** a nice drop of red wine; **ma petite Louise,** my dear Louise; **p. ami, petite amie,** boyfriend, girlfriend (c) lesser, minor; **petite industrie,** light industry; *Com:* **petite caisse,** petty cash; **petits pois,** (garden) peas; **p. salé** = streaky bacon 2. *a* (a) insignificant, petty; **p. commerçant,** small shopkeeper; **p. cousin,** second cousin (b) delicate; **il a une petite santé,** he's never really well 3. mean, ungenerous; **c'est un p. esprit,** he's got a small mind 4. (a) *a* **p. enfant,** little child; **les petits Anglais,** English children (b) *n* little boy; little girl; **pauvre petit(e),** poor little things; *(term of affection)* **bonjour, mon p.,** hello, my dear (c) *nm* young (of animal); **faire des petits,** to have young. **petitement** *adv* poorly; meanly, pettily; **être p. logé,** to live in cramped accommodation.

petite-fille [p(ə)titfij] *nf* grand-daughter; *pl* petites-filles.

petite-nièce [p(ə)titnjɛs] *nf* great-niece; *pl* petites-nièces.

petitesse [pətites] *nf* (a) smallness, small size (of an object); slenderness (b) meanness, pettiness.

petit-fils [p(ə)tifis] *nm* grandson; *pl* petits-fils.

pétition [petisjɔ̃] *nf* petition; **adresser une p. à qn,** to petition s.o.

pétitionner [petisjone] *vi* to petition.

pétitionnaire [petisjonɛr] *n* petitioner.

petit-neveu [p(ə)tinvø] *nm* great nephew; *pl* petits-neveux.

petits-enfants [p(ə)tizɑ̃fɑ̃] *nmpl* grand-children.

pétrification [petrifikasjɔ̃] *nf* petrification.

pétrifier [petrifje] *vtr* to petrify; **pétrifié de, par la, peur,** paralysed with fear.

pétrin [petrɛ̃] *nm* kneading trough; *F:* être dans le p., to be in a fix, in a jam.

pétrir [petrir] *vtr* to knead (dough).

pétrole [petrɔl] *nm* petroleum; (mineral) oil; **p. lampant,** paraffin oil, *NAm:* kerosene.

pétrolier, -ière [petrɔlje, -jɛr] 1. *a* l'industrie pétrolière, the petroleum, oil, industry 2. *nm* (a) (oil) tanker (b) oil magnate.

pétrolifère [petrɔlifɛr] *a* oil-bearing; **gisement p.,** oilfield.

P et T [peete] *abbr Postes et Télécommunications.*

peu [pø] 1. *adv* (a) little; **p. ou point,** little or none, or nothing; **ce n'est pas p. dire,** that's saying a good deal; **quelque p. surpris,** somewhat surprised; **p. de chose,** (very) little; not much; **pour si p. de chose,** for so small a matter (b) few; **p. de gens,** few people; **p. d'entre eux,** few of them (c) not very; un-; **p. utile,** not very useful; useless; **p. intelligent,** unintelligent; **p. honnête,** dishonest; **p. profond,** shallow 2. *nm* (a) little, bit; **son p. d'éducation,** (i) what little education he's had (ii) his lack of education; **un p. de vin,** a little wine; **un tout petit p.,** a tiny bit, a tiny drop; **encore un p.?** a little more? *F:* **ça, c'est un p. fort!** that's a bit much! **pour un p. je l'aurais jeté dehors,** I all but threw him out; **écoutez un p.,** just listen; *F:* **je vous demande un p.!** I ask you! **p. à p.,** gradually; little by little (b) **après,** shortly after(wards); not long after; **avant p., d'ici p., sous p.,** before long; **depuis p.,** lately; **il l'a manqué de peu,** he just missed it; **à p. près,** about; roughly.

peuple [pœpl] *nm* 1. people; nation 2. (a) **le p.,** the masses; **les gens du p.,** the lower classes (b) crowd.

peuplement [pœpləmɑ̃] *nm* populating (of region); stocking; planting (with trees).

peupler [pœple] 1. *vtr* to populate (country); to stock (fish pond); to plant (with trees); **rue peuplée de gens,** crowded street; **pays très peuplé,** densely populated country 2. **se p.,** to become populated; *(of street)* to fill (up), to be filled (with).

peuplier [pœplije] *nm* poplar.

peur [pœr] *nf* 1. fear, fright; **avoir p.,** to be frightened; **n'ayez pas p.!** don't be afraid; **j'ai p. qu'il (ne) soit en retard,** I'm afraid he may be late; **prendre p.,** to take fright; *F:* **avoir une p. bleue,** to be scared to death; **faire p. à qn,** to frighten, to scare, s.o.; *F:* **il m'a fait une de ces peurs!** he gave me such a fright! **laid à faire p.,** frightfully ugly; **sans p.,** fearless; fearlessly 2. *prep phr* **de p. de,** for fear of (sth).

peureux, -euse [pœrø, -øz] *a* fearful. **peureusement** *adv* in fear.

peut-être [pøtɛtr] *adv* perhaps, maybe, possibly; **il est p.-ê. rentré chez lui,** he may have gone home; **p.-ê. bien qu'il viendra,** he might well come; *Iron:* **tu le sais mieux que moi, p.-ê.?** you think you know better, do you?

phalange [falɑ̃ʒ] *nf* phalanx.

pharaon [faraɔ̃] *nm Hist:* Pharaoh.

phare [far] *nm* 1. lighthouse; *Av:* beacon; **p. d'atterrissage,** landing light 2. *Aut:* headlight; **phares code,** dipped headlights; **rouler pleins phares,** to drive on full beam; **p. anti-brouillard,** foglamp; **p. de recul,** reversing light.

pharmacie [farmasi] *nf* 1. (a) *(science)* pharmacy (b) pharmacy, chemist's shop, *NAm:* drugstore (c) pharmaceuticals; medicines (d) (armoire à) p., medicine cabinet; **p. portative,** first-aid kit. **pharmaceutique** *a* pharmaceutical.

pharmacien, -ienne [farmasjɛ̃, -jɛn] *n* (dispensing) chemist, pharmacist, *NAm:* druggist.

pharynx [farɛ̃ks] *nm* pharynx.
phase [fɑz] *nf* phase.
phénol [fenɔl] *nm* phenol.
phénomène [fenɔmɛn] *nm* (*a*) phenomenon (*b*) (*pers*) character; (*abnormal*) freak. **phénoménal, -aux** *a* phenomenal. **phénoménalement** *adv* phenomenally.
philanthrope [filɑ̃trɔp] *n* philanthropist.
philanthropie [filɑ̃trɔpi] *nf* philanthropy. **philanthropique** *a* philanthropic.
philatélie [filateli] *nf* stamp collecting, philately. **philatélique** *a* philatelic.
philatéliste [filatelist] *n* philatelist, stamp collector.
philharmonique [filarmɔnik] *a* philharmonic.
philosophe [filɔzɔf] 1. *n* philosopher 2. *a* philosophical.
philosophie [filɔzɔfi] *nf* phylosophy. **philosophique** *a* philosophical. **philosophiquement** *adv* philosophically.
phlébite [flebit] *nf Med:* phlebitis.
phobie [fɔbi] *nf* phobia.
phonétique [fɔnetik] 1. *a* phonetic 2. *nf* phonetics. **phonétiquement** *adv* phonetically.
phonique [fɔnik] *a* phonic.
phonographe [fɔnɔgraf] *nm* gramophone; record player; *NAm:* phonograph.
phonothèque [fɔnɔtɛk] *nf* sound archives.
phoque [fɔk] *nm* (*a*) *Z:* seal (*b*) *Com:* sealskin.
phosphate [fɔsfat] *nm Ch:* phosphate.
photo [fɔto] *nf* photograph, photo; **prendre qn en p.**, to take a photograph of s.o.
photocopie [fɔtɔkɔpi] *nf* photocopy.
photocopier [fɔtɔkɔpje] *vtr* to photocopy.
photocopieur [fɔtɔkɔpjœr] *nm* photocopier.
photo-électrique [fɔtɔelɛktrik] *a* photoelectric.
photographe [fɔtɔgraf] *n* (*a*) photographer (*b*) camera dealer.
photographie [fɔtɔgrafi] *nf* 1. photography; **faire de la p.**, to take photographs 2. photograph. **photographique** *a* photographic.
photographier [fɔtɔgrafje] *vtr* to photograph; **se faire p.**, to have one's photograph taken.
photo-robot [fɔtɔrɔbo] *nm* identikit (picture); *pl* **photos-robots**.
phrase [frɑz] *nf* 1. sentence; **p. toute faite**, stock phrase; **faire des phrases**, to speak in flowery language 2. *Mus:* phrase.
physicien, -ienne [fizisjɛ̃, -jɛn] *n* physicist.
physiologie [fizjɔlɔʒi] *nf* physiology. **physiologique** *a* physiological.
physiologiste [fizjɔlɔʒist] *n* physiologist.
physionomie [fizjɔnɔmi] *nf* physiognomy; face; **il manque de p.**, his face lacks character.
physionomiste [fizjɔnɔmist] *n* **je ne suis pas p.**, I have no memory for faces.
physique [fizik] 1. *a* physical; **douleur p.**, bodily pain; **culture p.**, physical training 2. *nf* physics 3. *nm* physique (of pers); **au p.**, physically; **il a le p. de l'emploi**, he looks the part. **physiquement** *adv* physically.
piaffer [pjafe] *vi* (of horse) to paw the ground; **p. d'impatience**, to fidget.
piaillement [pjajmɑ̃] *nm* squawking.

piailler [pjaje] *vi* to squawk, to squeak.
pianiste [pjanist] *n* pianist.
piano [pjano] 1. *nm* piano; **p. à queue**, grand piano; **p. droit**, upright piano 2. *adv Mus:* piano, softly.
pic¹ [pik] *nm* 1. pick, pickaxe, *NAm:* pickax 2. (mountain) peak; *adv phr* **à p.**, sheer; **sentier à p.**, precipitous, steep, path; **couler à p.**, to sink like a stone; **arriver à p.**, to turn up in the nick of time.
pic² *nm Orn:* woodpecker; **pic vert** [pivɛr] green woodpecker.
pichet [piʃe] *nm* (small) jug; pitcher.
picoler [pikɔle] *vi P:* to tipple, to booze.
picorer [pikɔre] *vtr & i* (of bird) to peck.
picotement [pikɔtmɑ̃] *nm* pricking, tingling, smarting.
picoter [pikɔte] 1. *vtr* (*a*) to prick (holes) (*b*) (of bird) to peck (at) (food) (*c*) to tickle (throat); to prickle (skin); **la fumée me picotait les yeux**, the smoke made my eyes sting, smart 2. *vi* (of eyes) to sting, smart; (of throat) to tickle; (of skin) to prickle.
pie [pi] 1. *nf* (*a*) *Orn:* magpie (*b*) *F:* chatterbox 2. *a inv* piebald (horse); **vache p.**, black and white cow.
pièce [pjɛs] *nf* 1. (*a*) piece; **p. de bétail**, head of cattle; **p. de musée**, museum piece; **p. de blé**, wheatfield; **p. de vin**, cask of wine; *Cu:* **p. montée**, tiered cake; **p. d'eau**, ornamental lake; **p. (de monnaie)**, coin; **p. de dix francs**, ten-franc piece; **ils se vendent à la p.**, they are sold separately; **ils coûtent dix francs p.**, they cost ten francs each; **donner la p. à qn**, to give s.o. a tip; **travail à la p., aux pièces**, piecework (*b*) *Jur: Adm:* document, paper; **p. à conviction**, exhibit (in criminal case) (*c*) *Mus: Lit:* piece; **p. (de théâtre)**, play 2. (*a*) piece; **p. de bœuf**, joint of beef; **histoire inventée de toutes pièces**, complete fabrication (*b*) *MecE:* part (of machine); component part; **pièces de rechange, pièces détachées**, replacement parts, spare parts; spares (*c*) *Needlw:* patch (*d*) room (in house); **un (appartement de) trois pièces**, a three-roomed flat, *NAm:* apartment (*e*) *Games:* (chess) piece; draughts(man), *NAm:* checker 3. fragment, bit; **mettre qch en pièces**, to break sth to pieces, to bits; to tear sth to pieces.
pied [pje] *nm* 1. (*a*) foot; **p. plat**, flat foot; *F:* **être bête comme ses pieds**, to be unbelievably stupid; **avoir bon p. bon œil**, to be hale and hearty; **faire qch au p. levé**, to do sth at a moment's notice; **faire du p. à qn**, to give s.o. a kick (as a warning); **se lever du p. gauche**, to get out of bed on the wrong side; **de la tête aux pieds**, from head to foot; **faire des pieds et des mains pour faire qch**, to move heaven and earth to do sth; *F:* **ça lui fera les pieds!** that'll serve him right! *P:* **il me casse les pieds**, he gets on my nerves; **mettre p. à terre**, to dismount; **mettre les pieds chez qn**, to set foot in s.o.'s house; *F:* **mettre les pieds dans le plat**, to put one's foot in it; **marcher sur les pieds de qn**, to tread on s.o.'s toes; **frapper du pied**, to stamp one's foot (*b*) **coup de p.**, kick; **à p.**, on foot; **aller à p.**, to walk; **mettre une affaire sur p.**, to set up, to start, a business; **remettre qn sur p.**, to set s.o. on his feet again (*c*) *Cu:* (calf's) foot; (pig's) trotter (*d*) *P:* fool, idiot; **conduire comme un p.**, to be a lousy driver 2. (*a*) footing, foothold; **avoir le p. marin**, to be a good sailor; **perdre p.**, to get out of

one's depth; **prendre p.,** to get a foothold, a footing; *P:* **c'est le p.!** it's great! **sur un p. d'égalité,** on an equal footing; **vivre sur un grand p.,** to live on a grand scale 3. (*a*) foot (of stocking, bed, mountain); base (of wall); *CivE:* **à p. d'œuvre,** on site (*b*) leg (of chair); stem, foot (of glass); **p. de lampe,** lampstand (*c*) stalk (of plant); **p. de céleri,** head of celery (*d*) stand, rest; tripod 4. *Meas:* foot; **p. à p.,** step by step 5. *Pros:* (metrical) foot.

pied-à-terre [pjetatɛr] *nm inv* pied-à-terre; small flat.

pied-d'alouette [pjedalwɛt] *nm* larkspur; *pl pieds-d'alouette.*

pied-de-poule [pjedpul] *a & nm Tex:* broken check, houndstooth (material); *pl pieds-de-poule.*

piédestal, -aux [pjedestal, -o] *nm* pedestal.

pied-noir [pjenwar] *n F:* Algerian-born Frenchman, -woman; *pl pieds-noirs.*

piège [pjeʒ] *nm* trap, snare; **p. à loups,** mantrap; **tendre un p.,** to set a trap (à, for); **être pris à son propre p.,** to be caught in one's own trap; **dictée pleines de pièges,** dictation full of pitfalls.

piéger [pjeʒe] *vtr* (**je piège, n. piégeons**) 1. to trap (animal, s.o.) 2. (*a*) to set a trap in (sth) (*b*) to booby-trap.

pierraille [pjeraj] *nf* loose stones; ballast.

pierre [pjɛr] *nf* (*a*) stone; **p. d'achoppement,** stumbling block; **cœur de p.,** heart of stone; *Prov:* **p. qui roule n'amasse pas mousse,** a rolling stone gathers no moss; **c'est une p. dans votre jardin,** that's a dig at you; **faire d'une p. deux coups,** to kill two birds with one stone (*b*) *Const:* **p. de taille,** ashlar, free-stone; **poser la première p.,** to lay the foundation stone (*c*) gem; **p. précieuse,** precious stone (*d*) **p. à aiguiser,** whetstone; **p. à briquet,** (lighter) flint. **pierreux, -euse** *a* stony.

pierreries [pjer(ə)ri] *nfpl* precious stones, gems.

Pierrot [pjero] *nm* (*a*) *Th:* Pierrot, clown (*b*) *Orn: F:* sparrow.

piété [pjete] *nf* piety; **articles de p.,** devotional objects.

piétinement [pjetinmɑ̃] *nm* (*a*) stamping, trampling (with the feet) (*b*) lack of progress.

piétiner [pjetine] 1. *vtr* to trample, stamp, on (sth); to tread (sth) under foot 2. *vi* **p. d'impatience,** to stamp (one's feet) with impatience; **p. sur place,** to mark time; **cette affaire piétine,** this business is making no headway.

piéton [pjetɔ̃] *nm* pedestrian. **piéton, -onne, piétonnier, -ière** *a* pedestrian; **rue piétonne, piétonnière,** pedestrian precinct.

piètre [pjɛtr] *a* wretched, poor; paltry (excuse); **p. consolation,** cold comfort; **il a p. allure,** he's a sorry sight.

pieu, pl -eux [pjø] *nm* (*a*) stake, post; *CivE:* pile (*b*) *P:* bed; **se mettre au p.,** to hit the sack.

pieuvre [pjœvr] *nf* octopus.

pieux, -euse [pjø, -øz] *a* pious, devout; **p. mensonge,** white lie. **pieusement** *adv* piously.

pif [pif] *nm P:* (*a*) nose, conk (*b*) **au p.,** at a rough guess.

pigeon, -onne [piʒɔ̃, -ɔn] *n* 1. pigeon; **p. voyageur,** carrier pigeon, homing pigeon; **p. ramier,** wood pigeon 2. *F:* (*pers*) sucker; mug.

pigeonnier [piʒɔnje] *nm* dovecote.

piger [piʒe] *vtr* (**je pigeai(s); n. pigeons**) *P:* to understand, to twig; *vi* **tu piges?** get it?

pigment [pigmɑ̃] *nm* pigment.

pigmentation [pigmɑ̃tasjɔ̃] *nf* pigmentation.

pigmenter [pigmɑ̃te] *vtr* to pigment.

pignon [piɲɔ̃] *nm* 1. gable (end) 2. *MecE:* pinion; gear.

pile¹ [pil] *nf* 1. pile; heap, stack 2. pier (of bridge) 3. *El:* battery; **p. de rechange,** spare battery; *AtomPh:* **p. atomique,** nuclear reactor.

pile² 1. *nf* reverse (of coin); **p. ou face,** heads or tails. 2. *adv F:* **s'arrêter p.,** to stop dead; **ça tombe p.,** that is just what I need; **à six heures p.,** at six on the dot.

piler [pile] *vtr* (*a*) to pound; to crush (*b*) *F:* to thrash (s.o.).

pilier [pilje] *nm* pillar, column; *Rugby Fb:* prop forward.

pillage [pijaʒ] *nm* looting, pillaging, ransacking; plagiarizing.

pillard, -arde [pijar, -ard] 1. *a* pillaging, looting 2. *n* looter.

piller [pije] *vtr* to pillage, loot, ransack; **p. un auteur,** to plagiarize an author.

pilon [pilɔ̃] *nm* (*a*) pestle (*b*) (chicken) drumstick (*c*) wooden leg.

pilonnage [pilɔnaʒ] *nm* pounding; *Mil:* shelling, bombardment.

pilonner [pilɔne] *vtr* to pound; *Mil:* to shell, to bombard.

pilori [pilɔri] *nm* pillory; **mettre qn au p.,** to pillory s.o.

pilotage [pilɔtaʒ] *nm Nau:* pilotage, piloting; *Av:* piloting, flying.

pilote [pilɔt] *nm* (*a*) *Nau:* pilot (*b*) *Av:* pilot; **p. de ligne,** airline pilot; **p. d'essai,** test pilot; **p. automatique,** automatic pilot (*c*) driver, pilot (of racing car).

piloter [pilɔte] *vtr* to pilot (ship, aircraft); to drive (racing car); **p. qn,** to show s.o. round.

pilotis [pilɔti] *nm CivE:* piling; pile.

pilule [pilyl] *nf Pharm:* pill; **prendre la p.,** to be on the pill; *Fig:* **avaler la p.,** to swallow the pill.

piment [pimɑ̃] *nm Bot:* pepper, capsicum; *Cu:* **p. rouge** (i) red pepper (ii) chilli, pimento; **avoir du p.,** to be spicy. **pimenté** *a* hot; spicy.

pimpant [pɛ̃pɑ̃] *a* smart, spruce.

pin [pɛ̃] *nm* (*a*) pine (tree); **p. d'Écosse,** Scotch fir; **pomme de p.,** pine cone; fir cone (*b*) pine(wood).

pinard [pinar] *nm P:* (cheap) wine; plonk.

pince [pɛ̃s] *nf* 1 (*a*) pincers, pliers; tongs; *Surg:* forceps; **p. à épiler,** tweezers; **p. à sucre,** sugar tongs (*b*) clip; **p. à linge,** clothes peg (*c*) crowbar 2. (*a*) claw (of crab); *P:* hand, paw (*b*) *P:* **aller à pinces,** to foot it 3. *Dressm:* pleat; dart.

pincé [pɛ̃se] *a* affected; prim, stiff; **sourire p.,** wry smile.

pinceau, -eaux [pɛ̃so] *nm* (*a*) (paint)brush (*b*) *P:* foot (*c*) **p. de lumière,** pencil of light.

pincée [pɛ̃se] *nf* pinch (of salt).

pincement [pɛ̃smɑ̃] *nm* pinching; pang, twinge (of regret).

pince-monseigneur [pɛ̃smɔ̃seɲœr] *nf* jemmy; *pl pinces-monseigneur.*

pincer [pɛ̃se] *vtr* (**n. pinçons**) 1. (*a*) to pinch, nip; **se p.**

le doigt dans la porte, to catch one's finger in the door; **p. les lèvres**, to purse one's lips; **se p. le nez**, to hold one's nose; *abs F:* **ça pince dur!** it's freezing (cold)! (b) *Hort:* to nip off (buds) (c) *Mus:* to pluck (string) (d) *Dressm:* to put darts in **2.** to grip, hold fast; *F:* to catch, cop (thief); **en p. pour qn**, to be crazy about s.o.

pince-sans-rire [pɛ̃ssɑrir] *nm inv* person of dry (and ironical) humour.

pincettes [pɛ̃sɛt] *nfpl* (a) tweezers (b) (fire)tongs; **il n'est pas à prendre avec des p.**, (i) he's filthy dirty (ii) he's like a bear with a sore head.

pinède [pinɛd] *nf* (*in S. of France*) pine forest.

pingouin [pɛ̃gwɛ̃] *nm Orn:* (a) auk (b) penguin.

ping-pong [piŋpɔ̃g] *nm Rtm:* table tennis.

pingre [pɛ̃gr] *F:* **1.** *a* mean, stingy. **2.** *nm & f* miser, skinflint.

pinson [pɛ̃sɔ̃] *nm Orn:* finch; chaffinch.

pintade [pɛ̃tad] *nf* guinea fowl.

pioche [pjɔʃ] *nf* pickaxe, pick, mattock.

piocher [pjɔʃe] **1.** *vtr* (a) to dig (with a pick) (b) *F:* to grind at, to swot up (sth); **p. son anglais**, to swot up one's English **2.** *vi Cards:* to draw from the stock.

piolet [pjɔlɛ] *nm* ice axe.

pion [pjɔ̃] *nm* **1.** *Sch: F:* = prefect (paid to supervise pupils) **2.** (a) *Chess:* pawn (b) *Draughts:* piece, draughts(man), *NAm:* checker.

pioncer [pjɔ̃se] *vi* (**je pionçai(s)**) *P:* to sleep, to have a snooze.

pionnier [pjɔnje] *nm* pioneer.

pipe [pip] *nf* pipe; **p. de bruyère**, briar pipe.

pipeau, -eaux [pipo] *nm Mus:* (reed)pipe.

pipe(-)line [piplin] *nm* pipeline; *pl* pipe(-)lines.

pipi [pipi] *nm F:* pee; wee(-wee); **aller faire p.**, to go to the loo.

piquant, -ante [pikɑ̃, -ɑ̃t] **1.** *a* (a) prickly; thorny (plant) (b) prickly (beard); biting (wind) (c) pungent (taste); hot (mustard); tart, sour (wine); *Cu:* **sauce piquante**, piquant sauce (d) cutting (remarks) **2.** *nm* (a) prickle, thorn; spine (of porcupine); barb (of barbed wire) (b) piquancy; **le changement donne du p. à la vie**, variety is the spice of life.

pique¹ [pik] *nm Cards:* spade(s).

pique² *nf* spiteful remark.

piqué [pike] *a* **1.** (a) quilted (coverlet); **p. à la machine**, machine-stitched (b) *nm* quilting; piqué **2.** (a) wormeaten (wood); damp-spotted (mirror); fly-spotted (b) *F:* barmy, loony **3.** sour (wine) **4.** *nm Av:* **descente en p.**, nose dive.

pique-assiette [pikasjɛt] *nm & f inv F:* scrounger, sponger.

pique-nique [piknik] *nm* picnic; *pl* pique-niques.

pique-niquer [piknike] *vi* to (have a) picnic.

piquer [pike] *vtr* **1.** (a) to prick, sting; (*of flea*) to bite; *abs* **ça pique**, it stings; (*of beard*) it's bristly; **moutarde qui pique**, hot mustard; **la fumée pique les yeux**, smoke makes the eyes smart (b) *Med:* to give (s.o.) an injection; **se faire p.**, to have an injection; **p. un chien**, to put a dog down (c) to pique, offend (s.o.) (d) to arouse (curiosity) **2.** to eat into, to pit (surface); to spot, to mark (sth); *P:* **se p. le nez**, to booze **3.** (a) to prick, puncture (sth); **p. (à la machine)**, to (machine) stitch; **p. la viande**, to prick meat (b) *F:*

to pinch, to swipe (**qch à qn**, sth from s.o.) **4.** to stick, insert (sth into sth); **p. une photo au mur**, to pin a photograph on the wall **5.** (a) **p. une tête**, to take a header, to dive (b) *vi Av:* to dive **6.** *F:* **p. un cent mètres**, to go into a sprint; **p. une crise**, to throw a fit; **p. une crise de larmes**, to burst into tears **7. se p.** (a) to prick oneself; to give oneself an injection (b) to take offence (c) **se p. de qch, de faire qch**, to pride oneself on sth, on doing sth (d) **se p. au jeu**, to get excited over a game (e) to become spotted (with rust); (*of metal*) to pit (f) (*of wine*) to turn sour.

piquet [pikɛ] *nm* **1.** stake, post; (tent) peg **2. p. de grève**, strike picket; *Sch:* **être au p.**, to stand in the corner.

piqueter [pikte] *vtr* (**je piquette; n. piquetons**) to spot, dot (**de**, with).

piquette [pikɛt] *nf* **1.** vinegary wine; plonk **2.** *P:* **prendre une p.**, to get a hammering.

piqûre [pikyr] *nf* **1.** (a) prick, sting, bite (of insect) (b) *Med:* injection, *F:* shot **2.** (a) puncture; small hole; pit (in metal); wormhole (in wood) (b) stitching; quilting.

pirate [pirat] *nm* (a) pirate; **p. de l'air**, hijacker, sky-jacker (b) pirate, shark.

pirater [pirate] *vt* to pirate.

piraterie [piratri] *nf* (act of) piracy; **p. aérienne**, hijacking, skyjacking.

pire [pir] **1.** *comp a* worse; **cent fois p.**, a hundred times worse; **le remède est p. que le mal**, the cure is worse than the complaint **2.** *sup a* **le p., la p., les pires**, the worst (a) **nos pires erreurs**, our worst mistakes (b) **n le p. c'est que**, the worst is that; **s'attendre au p.**, to expect the worst.

pirogue [pirɔg] *nf* (dugout) canoe.

pis¹ [pi] *nm* udder (of cow).

pis² *adv* (*chiefly in certain set phrases; usu form is* **plus mal**) **1.** *comp* worse; **aller de mal en p.**, to go from bad to worse; **tant p.!** never mind! **2.** *sup* **le p.**, (the) worst; *nm* **en mettant les choses au p.**, if the worst comes to the worst.

pis(-)aller [pizale] *nm inv* last resort; stopgap; makeshift.

pisciculture [pisikyltyr] *nf* fish breeding.

piscine [pisin] *nf* swimming pool.

pisse [pis] *nf P:* pee.

pissenlit [pisɑ̃li] *nm Bot:* dandelion.

pisser [pise] *vi P:* (a) to pee (b) to gush out (c) (*with cogn acc*) **p. du sang** (i) to pass blood with the urine (ii) to bleed profusely.

pistache [pistaʃ] *nf* pistachio (nut).

piste [pist] *nf* **1.** track, trail; (*police*) lead; **suivre une fausse p.**, to be on the wrong track **2.** *Sp: etc:* (a) racecourse (i) running track; racetrack; **tour de p.**, lap (b) (circus) ring; (skating) rink; (ski) run, piste; (dance) floor (c) *Av:* runway; **p. d'envol**, take-off strip; **p. d'atterrissage**, landing strip **3.** *Rec:* track; *Cin:* **p. sonore**, soundtrack.

pister [piste] *vtr* to track, to trail.

pistolet [pistɔlɛ] *nm* pistol, gun; **p. (à peinture)**, spray gun; **p.-mitrailleur**, submachine gun.

piston [pistɔ̃] *nm* **1.** (a) *MecE:* piston (of machine, pump) (b) string-pulling **2.** *Mus:* valve (of cornet); **cornet à pistons**, cornet.

pistonner [pistɔne] *vtr* to pull strings for (s.o.).

piteux, -euse [pitø, -øz] *a* piteous, pitiable, miserable; **en p. état,** in a sorry state. **piteusement** *adv* piteously.

pitié [pitje] *nf* pity, compassion; **avoir p. de qn,** to have pity, mercy, on s.o.; **sans p.,** pitiless(ly), merciless(ly), ruthlessly; **il me faisait p.,** I felt sorry for him; **c'est à faire p.!** it's pitiful! it's pathetic!

piton [pitɔ̃] *nm* **1.** eye (bolt); piton, peg; **p. à vis,** screw eye **2.** peak (of mountain).

pitoyable [pitwajabl̩] *a* pitiable, pitiful.

pitre [pitr̩] *nm* (circus) clown; buffoon; **faire le p.,** to fool about.

pitrerie [pitrəri] *nf* clowning.

pittoresque [pitɔresk] **1.** *a* picturesque; colourful (description, style) **2.** *nm* picturesqueness, vividness (of style).

pivert [pivɛr] *nm Orn:* green woodpecker.

pivoine [pivwan] *nf Bot:* peony.

pivot [pivo] *nm* pivot; pin, axis; *Dent:* post. **pivotant** *a* pivoting, revolving; swivel (chair).

pivoter [pivɔte] *vi* to pivot; to swivel, revolve; **p. sur ses talons,** to swing round on one's heels.

PJ *abbr Police judiciaire.*

placage [plakaʒ] *nm* veneering (of wood); facing (of stone).

placard [plakar] *nm* **1.** (wall) cupboard **2.** poster; placard; notice; **p. publicitaire,** advertisement (in newspaper) **3.** *F:* thick layer.

placarder [plakarde] *vtr* to stick, put up (poster) (on wall); **p. un mur,** to placard a wall with posters.

place [plas] *nf* **1.** (*a*) place; position; **changer sa chaise de p.,** to shift one's chair; **remettre qch à sa p.,** to put sth away; **remettre qn à sa p.,** to put s.o. in his place; **à vos places!** take your seats! **il ne peut pas rester en p.,** he can't keep still (*b*) stead; **je viens à la p. de mon père,** I've come instead of my father; **à votre p.,** if I were you (*c*) **faire p. à qn,** to make way for s.o.; **occuper beaucoup de p.,** to take up a great deal of room; **(faites) p.!** stand aside! **2.** (*a*) seat; **louer deux places au théâtre,** to book two seats at the theatre; **voiture à deux, à quatre, places,** twoseater, four-seater; **prix des places** (i) fares (ii) prices of admission; **payer p. entière,** to pay (i) full fare (ii) full price (*b*) situation, office, post; **perdre sa p.,** to lose one's job **3.** (*a*) locality, spot; square; **p. du marché,** market square; **sur p.,** on the spot; **faire du sur p.,** to mark time; **rester sur p.,** to stay put (*b*) **achats sur p.,** local purchases (*c*) *Mil:* **p. (forte),** fortified town.

placement [plasmɑ̃] *nm* **1. bureau de p.** (i) employment bureau, agency (ii) job centre **2.** investment.

placer [plase] *vtr* (**je plaçai(s); n. plaçons**) **1.** (*a*) to place; to put, set (in a certain place); to find a place for (a guest, a spectator); *Th: etc:* **p. qn,** to show s.o. to his seat; **vous êtes bien placé pour le savoir,** you're in a position to know; **je n'ai pas pu p. un mot,** I couldn't get a word in edgeways; **maison bien placée,** well situated house (*b*) to find a post, a job, for (s.o.); **p. un apprenti chez qn,** to apprentice s.o. to s.o.; **il a placé sa fille,** he's married off his daughter (*c*) to invest (money) (*d*) to sell (goods); **valeurs difficiles à p.,** shares difficult to negotiate **2. se p.** (*a*) to take one's seat, one's place (*b*) to obtain a situation, to find a job.

placide [plasid] *a* placid; calm.

plafond [plafɔ̃] *nm* **1.** ceiling; roof (of car) **2. prix p.,** maximum price; ceiling (price).

plafonner [plafɔne] **1.** *vtr* to put a ceiling in (room) **2.** *vi* (*of price*) to reach a ceiling, a maximum.

plafonnier [plafɔnje] *nm* ceiling light; *Aut:* courtesy light.

plage [plaʒ] *nf* **1.** (*a*) beach (*b*) seaside resort **2. p. arrière** (i) *Navy:* quarter deck (ii) *Aut:* window shelf **3.** (*a*) area (*b*) **p. de prix,** price range (*c*) track (of gramophone record).

plagiat [plaʒja] *nm* plagiarism.

plagier [plaʒje] *vtr* to plagiarize.

plaider [plede] **1.** *vtr* to plead (a cause); **p. la folie,** to plead insanity; **la cause s'est plaidée hier,** the case was heard yesterday **2.** *vi* to plead (**pour,** for); to go to court; **p. pour qn,** to speak for s.o.

plaideur, -euse [plɛdœr, -øz] *n* litigant.

plaidoirie [plɛdwari] *nf* counsel's speech.

plaidoyer [plɛdwaje] *nm* speech for the defence; defence, plea (for s.o., sth).

plaie [ple] *nf* (*a*) wound, sore; cut; **remuer le fer dans la p.,** to turn the knife in the wound (*b*) scourge (*c*) *F:* (*of pers*) **quelle p.!** what a pest!

plaignant, -ante [plɛɲɑ̃, -ɑ̃t] *a & n Jur:* plaintiff.

plaindre [plɛ̃dr̩] (**je plains; n. plaignons; je plaindrai**) **1.** *vtr* (*a*) to pity; **elle n'est pas à p.,** (i) she has nothing to worry about (ii) she doesn't deserve any sympathy (*b*) *F:* to begrudge **2. se p.,** to complain; to moan, groan; **se p. de qch, de qn,** to complain of, about, s.o., sth.

plaine [plen] *nf* plain.

plain-pied [plɛ̃pje] *adv phr* **de p.-p.,** on one floor, on a level (**avec,** with).

plainte [plɛ̃t] *nf* **1.** moan, groan **2.** (*a*) complaint (*b*) *Jur:* indictment, complaint; **porter p. contre qn,** to lodge a complaint against s.o. **plaintif, -ive** *a* plaintive (tone). **plaintivement** *adv* plaintively.

plaire [plɛr] **1.** *v ind tr* (*prp* **plaisant;** *pp* **plu;** *pr ind* **il plaît**) **p. à qn,** to please s.o.; **ça me plaît,** I like it, I enjoy it; **ça devrait lui p.,** it should appeal to him; **chercher à p. à qn,** to try to please s.o.; **elle ne lui plaît pas,** he's not attracted to her; **je fais ce qui me plaît,** I do as I like; **quand ça me plaît,** when it suits me; when I feel like it; *impers* **s'il vous plaît,** please; **plaît-il?** I beg your pardon? **comme il vous plaira,** (just) as you like **2. se p.** à **faire qch,** to enjoy doing sth; **je me plais beaucoup à Paris,** I love being in Paris; **la vigne se plaît sur les coteaux,** the vine thrives, does well, on hillsides.

plaisance [plɛzɑ̃s] *nf* **bateau de p.,** pleasure boat; **maison de p.,** country house; **navigation de p.,** yachting, sailing.

plaisancier [plɛzɑ̃sje] *nm* yachtsman.

plaisant [plɛzɑ̃] **1.** *a* (*a*) pleasant, agreeable (*b*) funny, amusing (*c*) (*always before the noun*) ridiculous, absurd. **plaisamment** *adv* pleasantly; amusingly; ridiculously.

plaisanter [plɛzɑ̃te] **1.** *vi* to joke, jest; **je ne plaisante pas,** I'm serious; **dire qch en plaisantant,** to say sth as a joke; **vous plaisantez!** you're joking! you don't mean it! **il ne plaisante pas là-dessus,** he takes this seriously **2.** *vtr* to tease (**qn sur qch,** so about sth).

plaisanterie [plɛzɑ̃tri] *nf* joke; joking; prank, practical joke; **mauvaise p.,** nasty trick.

plaisantin [plɛzɑ̃tɛ̃] *nm* practical joker.

plaisir [plɛzir] *nm* 1. pleasure; delight; **faire p. à qn,** to please s.o.; **cela me fait grand p. de vous voir,** I'm delighted to see you; **cela fait p. à voir,** it's a pleasure to see; **faire à qn le p. de,** to do s.o. the favour of; **voulez-vous me faire le p. de vous taire!** will you *please* be quiet! **au p. de vous revoir,** good-bye; I hope we'll meet again; **j'ai le p. de vous dire que,** I am pleased to be able to tell you that; **prendre p. à faire qch,** to enjoy doing sth 2. amusement, enjoyment; **partie de p.,** picnic, outing.

plan¹ [plɑ̃] 1. *a* even, level, flat, plane (surface) 2. *nm* (*a*) *Mth: etc:* plane; **p. d'eau,** stretch of water (*b*) *Art: etc:* **premier p.,** foreground; **second p.,** middle ground; **au second p.,** in the middle distance; **reléguer qn au second p.,** to push s.o. into the background; **sur le p. politique,** in the political sphere (*c*) *Cin:* shot (*d*) *DomEc:* **p. de travail,** worktop.

plan² *nm* (*a*) plan; drawing; draft; **lever les plans d'une région,** to survey an area; **p. cadastral,** survey map (*b*) scheme, project; **p. de travail,** plan of work (*c*) *F:* **laisser qch, qn, en p.,** to abandon, to ditch, sth; to leave s.o. in the lurch.

planche [plɑ̃ʃ] *nf* 1. (*a*) board, plank; shelf; **p. à dessin,** drawing board; **p. de salut,** last hope; **faire la p.,** to float on one's back (*b*) **p. à pain,** bread board; **p. à repasser,** ironing board (*c*) *Nau:* gangplank (*d*) *Th:* **monter sur les planches,** to go on the stage 2. *Art:* (printed) plate, engraving 3. *Hort:* (flower) bed.

plancher [plɑ̃ʃe] *nm* floor; **prix p.,** bottom price.

plancton [plɑ̃ktɔ̃] *nm Biol:* plankton.

planer [plane] *vi* 1. (*a*) (*of bird*) to soar; to hover (*b*) *Av:* to glide; **vol plané,** gliding 2. **p. sur qch,** to hang over sth.

planétarium [planetarjɔm] *nm* planetarium.

planète [planɛt] *nf Astr:* planet. **planétaire** *a.* planetary.

planeur [planœr] *nm* glider.

planification [planifikasjɔ̃] *nf PolEc:* planning.

planifier [planifje] *vi Adm:* to plan.

planning [planiŋ] *nm* (*a*) *Ind:* work schedule (*b*) **p. familial,** family planning.

planque [plɑ̃k] *nf P:* (*a*) hideout (*b*) cushy job.

planquer [plɑ̃ke] *P:* 1. to hide, to stash, away 2. **se p.,** to hide, to take cover.

plant [plɑ̃] *nm* (*a*) seedling (*b*) plantation.

plantation [plɑ̃tasjɔ̃] *nf* 1. planting (of trees, seeds) 2. (tea, coffee) plantation; **p. d'oranges,** orange grove.

plante¹ [plɑ̃t] *nf* sole (of the foot).

plante² *nf* plant; **p. potagère,** vegetable; **p. à fleurs,** flowering plant; **p. d'appartement,** house plant; **p. de serre,** hothouse plant.

planter [plɑ̃te] *vtr* 1. (*a*) to plant, set (seeds) (*b*) to fix, set (up); **p. un pieu,** to drive in a stake; **p. une échelle contre un mur,** to stand a ladder against a wall; **p. une tente,** to pitch a tent; **p. un baiser sur la joue de qn,** to plant a kiss on s.o.'s cheek; *F:* **p. là qn,** to leave s.o. in the lurch 2. **se p.,** to stand, take one's stand; **se p. devant qn,** to stand squarely in front of s.o.

planteur [plɑ̃tœr] *nm* planter.

plantoir [plɑ̃twar] *nm Hort:* dibble.

planton [plɑ̃tɔ̃] *nm Mil:* orderly; *F:* **faire le p.,** to hang around.

plantureux, -euse [plɑ̃tyrø, -øz] *a* 1. copious (meal) 2. rich, fertile (countryside).

plaque [plak] *nf* 1. (*a*) plate, sheet (of metal); slab (of marble); block (of chocolate); patch (of ice) (*b*) *Rail:* **p. tournante,** turntable (*c*) *El:* plate (*d*) **p. photographique,** photographic plate 2. (ornamental) plaque; **p. de porte,** door plate, name plate; **p. commémorative,** commemorative tablet 3. badge; **p. d'identité,** identity disc; *Aut:* **p. minéralogique,** number plate, *NAm:* license plate.

plaqué [plake] *a & nm* 1. (**métal**) **p.,** plated metal; (electro)plate 2. (**bois**) **p.,** veneered wood.

plaquer [plake] *vtr* 1. (*a*) to veneer (wood); to plate (metal); to plaster down (hair); **les épaules plaquées au mur,** shoulders pinned to the wall (*b*) *Rugby Fb:* to tackle (opponent) (*c*) *Mus:* to strike (and hold) a chord (*d*) *P:* to abandon, ditch, chuck (s.o.); **tout p.,** to chuck everything up 2. **se p. au sol,** to lie flat on the ground.

plastic [plastik] *nm* plastic explosive.

plasticage [plastikaʒ] *nm* plastic bomb attack.

plastifier [plastifje] *vtr* to plasticize.

plastique [plastik] 1. *a* plastic; **matière p.,** plastic 2. *nf* plastic art 3. *nm Ind:* plastic.

plastron [plastrɔ̃] *nm* 1. (fencer's) plastron 2. shirt front.

plastronner [plastrɔne] *vi* to strut, to swagger.

plat [pla] 1. *a* (*a*) flat, level; **cheveux plats,** straight hair; **chaussure à talon p.,** flat(-heeled) shoe; **mer plate,** smooth sea (*b*) flat, dull, insipid; **style p.,** commonplace style; **vin p.,** dull, flat, wine (*c*) *adv phr* **à p.,** flat; (*of joke*) **tomber à p.,** to fall flat; **tomber à p. ventre,** to fall flat on one's face; **être à p. ventre devant qn,** to grovel to s.o.; **pneu à p.,** flat tyre, *NAm:* tire; *F:* **être à p.,** (i) to be exhausted, all in (ii) *Aut:* to have a flat tyre 2. *nm* (*a*) flat (part); *Sp:* **le p.,** flat racing; *F:* **faire du p. à qn,** (i) to grovel to s.o. (ii) to make advances to s.o. (*b*) *Cu:* (*container or contents*) dish; *F:* **mettre les petits plats dans les grands,** to lay on a great meal; **en faire tout un p.,** to make a great fuss about sth (*c*) *Cu:* course (at dinner); **p. de résistance,** main course, main dish.

platane [platan] *nm Bot:* plane tree.

plateau, -eaux [plato] *nm* 1. (*a*) tray; **p. à, de, fromages,** cheeseboard (*b*) pan, scale (of balance); shelf (of oven); top (of table) 2. *Geog:* plateau 3. (*a*) platform; *Th:* floor (of the stage); *Cin:* set (*b*) *Rail:* flat truck 4. (*a*) *Tchn:* disc, plate (*b*) turntable (of record deck).

plate-bande [platbɑ̃d] *nf* flower bed; *F:* **ne marchez pas sur mes plates-bandes,** mind your own business.

plate-forme [platfɔrm] *nf* platform; *Rail:* flat truck; *pl* **plates-formes.**

platine [platin] 1. *nm* platinum 2. *nf Rec:* turntable, deck.

platitude [platityd] *nf* 1. dullness (of character, style) 2. platitude.

plâtras [platra] *nm* rubble.

plâtre [platr] *nm* (*a*) plaster (*b*) *pl* plasterwork (*c*) plaster cast.

plâtrer [plɑtre] *vtr* to plaster (wall, ceiling); *Med:* to set (leg) in plaster.

plâtrier [plɑtrije] *nm* plasterer.

plausible [plozibl] *a* plausible.

plébiscite [plebisit] *nm* plebiscite.

plébisciter [plebisite] *vtr* to vote for (s.o.) by plebiscite.

plein [plɛ̃] 1. *a* (*a*) full (**de**, of); filled, replete (**de**, with); **bouteille pleine**, full bottle; **pleine bouteille**, bottleful; **salle pleine à craquer**, room full to bursting; *F:* **être p.**, to be drunk; **les doigts pleins d'encre**, fingers covered in ink (*b*) (*of animal*) pregnant; with lamb, in calf (*c*) complete, entire, whole; **pleine lune**, full moon; **p. pouvoir**, full power; **p. sud**, due south; **pleine mer**, (i) high tide (ii) the open sea; **de son p. gré**, of one's own free will (*c*) solid (tyre); continuous (line) (*d*) **en p. visage**, full in the face; **en p. hiver**, in the middle of winter; **en p. air**, in the open (air); **en p. jour**, (i) in broad daylight (ii) publicly; **en p. milieu**, right in the middle; **en pleine saison**, at the height of the season; **en p. travail**, hard at work (*e*) **respirer à pleins poumons**, to breathe deep(ly); **travailler à p. temps**, to work full time (*f*) *adv* **il avait des larmes p. les yeux**, his eyes were full of tears; *F:* **il y avait p. de gens**, there were lots of people 2. *nm* (*a*) *Aut:* **faire le p. (d'essence)**, to fill up (with petrol); **le p. s'il vous plaît**, fill her up please! (*b*) full (extent); **la saison bat son p.**, the season is in full swing (*c*) **en p. dans le centre**, right in the middle. **pleinement** *adv* fully, entirely; wholly; to the full.

plein-emploi [plɛnɑ̃plwa] *nm inv Pol: Ind:* full employment.

plénipotentiaire [plenipɔtɑ̃sjɛr] *a* & *nm* plenipotentiary.

pléonasme [pleonasm] *nm* pleonasm.

pléthore [pletɔr] *nf* plethora. **pléthorique** *a* plethoric; superabundant.

pleurer [plœre] 1. *vtr* to weep for, mourn (for) (s.o.); to bemoan; **p. des larmes de joie**, to weep tears of joy; **p. toutes les larmes de ses yeux**, to cry one's eyes out 2. *vi* (*a*) to cry, weep, shed tears (**sur**, over; **pour**, for); **p. de joie**, to weep for joy; **triste à p.**, terribly sad (*b*) (*of eyes*) to water, to run.

pleurésie [plœrezi] *nf Med:* pleurisy.

pleurnicher [plœrniʃe] *vi* to whine, snivel. **pleurnicherie** [plœrniʃri] *nf* snivelling, whining.

pleurnicheur, -euse [plœrniʃœr, -øz] 1. *n* whiner, sniveller, crybaby 2. *a* whining, snivelling.

pleuvoir [pløvwar] *v* (*pp* **plu**; *pr ind* **il pleut, ils pleuvent**; *fu* **il pleuvra**) 1. *v impers* to rain; **il pleut à petites gouttes**, it's drizzling; **il pleut à verse**, it's pouring (with rain) 2. *vi* & *tr* (*of blows*) to rain down; **les invitations pleuvent sur lui**, invitations are pouring in on him.

pleuvoter [pløvɔte] *v impers* to drizzle.

pli [pli] *nm* 1. (*a*) pleat; fold (in curtains); *Hairdr:* **mise en plis**, set (*b*) wrinkle, pucker; *Geol:* fold (*c*) crease (in trousers); **faux p.**, crease (*d*) habit; **prendre le p. de faire qch**, to get into the habit of doing sth 2. bend (of the arm, leg) 3. cover, envelope (of letter); **sous p. séparé**, under separate cover 4. *Cards:* trick; **faire un p.**, to take a trick.

plie [pli] *nf Ich:* plaice.

plier [plije] 1. *vtr* (*impf* & *pr sub* **n. pliions**) (*a*) to fold (up); to turn down (page) (*b*) to bend (bough, knee); **plié en deux**, doubled up (with laughter, pain); **p. qn à la discipline**, to bring s.o. under discipline 2. *vi* (*a*) to bend (over) (*b*) to submit, yield; (*of army*) to give way 3. **se p.**, to fold up; **se p. aux circonstances**, to yield, to submit, to circumstances. **pliable** *a* foldable, flexible. **pliant** 1. *a* folding (chair); collapsible (table) 2. *nm* folding chair; campstool.

plinthe [plɛ̃t] *nf* skirting (board).

plissement [plismɑ̃] *nm* pleating (of material); creasing; *Geol:* fold.

plisser [plise] 1. *vtr* (*a*) to pleat (skirt) (*b*) to crease, crumple (face); to wrinkle (face); to pucker (lips); **p. les yeux**, to screw up one's eyes 2. *vi* & *pr* to crease, crumple; to wrinkle, pucker. **plissé** *a* pleated.

plissure [plisyr] *nf* pleats.

pliure [plijyr] *nf* fold; bend (of arm, leg).

plomb [plɔ̃] *nm* 1. (*a*) lead; **de p.**, lead (pipe); leaden (sky); blazing (sun); deep (sleep); **n'avoir pas de p. dans la tête**, to be scatter-brained (*b*) *Typ:* type 2. shot 3. lead (weight); **fil à p.**, plumb line; **à p.**, upright, vertical(ly) 4. *El:* fuse, cut-out; **faire sauter les plombs**, to blow the fuses.

plombage [plɔ̃baʒ] *nm Dent:* filling.

plomber [plɔ̃be] *vtr* (*a*) to cover (sth) with lead (*b*) to weight with lead (*c*) *Dent:* to fill (tooth) (*d*) to seal (parcel) (with lead).

plomberie [plɔ̃bri] *nf* (*a*) plumbing (*b*) plumber's shop.

plombier [plɔ̃bje] *nm* plumber.

plonge [plɔ̃ʒ] *nf* washing up (in restaurant).

plongée [plɔ̃ʒe] *nf* (*a*) plunge, dive; **p. sous-marine**, skin diving (*b*) (*submarine*) submersion.

plongeoir [plɔ̃ʒwar] *nm* diving board.

plongeon [plɔ̃ʒɔ̃] *nm* dive.

plonger [plɔ̃ʒe] *v* (**je plongeai(s); n. plongeons**) 1. *vi* (*a*) to dive; to plunge down (*b*) (*of submarine*) to submerge 2. *vtr* to plunge, immerse (s.o., sth, in sth); **p. la main dans sa poche**, to thrust one's hand into one's pocket; **plongé dans ses pensées**, lost in thought 3. **se p. dans**, to immerse oneself in.

plongeur, -euse [plɔ̃ʒœr, -øz] *n* (*a*) diver; **p. sous-marin**, skin diver (*b*) washer-up (in restaurant).

plouf [pluf] *int* plop! splash!

ployer [plwaje] *v* (**je ploie**) 1. *vtr Lit:* to bend 2. *vi* to bend, to sag; (*of army*) to yield.

pluie [plɥi] *nf* (*a*) rain, shower; **p. battante**, pouring rain, downpour; **p. fine**, drizzle; **temps de p.**, wet weather; **le temps est à la p.**, it looks like rain; **parler de la p. et du beau temps**, to talk about the weather; to make conversation; *F:* **il n'est pas tombé de la dernière p.**, he's no fool; **faire la p. et le beau temps**, to rule the roost (*b*) shower (of blows); hail (of bullets).

plumage [plymaʒ] *nm* plumage, feathers.

plumard [plymar] *nm P:* bed.

plume [plym] *nf* 1. feather; **gibier à plumes**, game birds; *F:* **il y a laissé des plumes**, he didn't get away unscathed; **léger comme une p.**, as light as a feather 2. (pen) nib; **dessin à la p.**, pen and ink drawing; **prendre la p.**, to put pen to paper.

plumeau [plymo] *nm* feather duster.

plumer [plyme] *vtr* to pluck (poultry); *F:* to fleece (s.o.).

plumet [plymɛ] *nm* plume.

plumier [plymje] *nm* pencil box, pencil case.

plupart (la) [laplypar] *nf* most; the greater, greatest, part; **la p. des hommes,** the majority of (the) men, most (of the) men; **la p. d'entre eux,** most of them; **la p. du temps,** most of the time; **pour la p.,** mostly.

pluriel, -elle [plyrjɛl] *a & nm Gram:* plural.

plus [ply] *(often* [plys] *at the end of a word group;* [plyz] *before a vowel)* **1.** *adv* (*a*) more; **il est p. grand que moi,** he is taller than I (am), than me; **deux fois p. grand,** twice as big; **p. d'une fois,** more than once; **p. de dix hommes,** more than ten men; **il a p. de vingt ans,** he's over twenty; **p. loin,** farther on; **p. tôt,** sooner; **et qui p. est** [plyze], and what is more; moreover; **p. on est de fous, p. on rit,** the more the merrier; **trois fois p.,** three times as much; **il y en a tant et p.,** there's an awful lot (of it, of them) (*b*) **(le) p.,** most; **la p. longue rue, la rue la p. longue,** de la ville, the longest street in the town; **le p. de fautes,** the most mistakes; **(tout) au p.,** at the (very) most; at best; **c'est tout ce qu'il y a de p.** simple, nothing could be simpler (*c*) **je ne veux p. de cela,** I don't want any more of that; **p. jamais,** never again; **sans p. attendre,** without waiting any longer; **p. de doute,** there is no more doubt about it; **il n'y en a p.,** there's none left; **p. rien,** nothing more; **p. que dix minutes!** only ten minutes left! (*d*) **non p.,** (not) either; **ni moi non p.,** neither do I, neither did I, I don't, I didn't either (*e*) [plys] plus, also, besides, in addition; **p. 20 degrés,** plus 20 (degrees); **500 francs d'amende, p. les frais,** 500 francs fine with, plus, costs (*f*) **de p.,** more; **rien de p., merci,** nothing else, thank you; **de p. en p.,** more and more; **de p. en p. froid,** colder and colder; **en p.,** in addition ((i) into the bargain (ii) extra); **le vin est en p.,** wine is extra; **p. ou moins** [plyzumwɛ̃], more or less; **ni p. ni moins,** neither more nor less **2.** *nm* (*a*) more; **sans p.,** (just that and) nothing more (*b*) *Mth:* plus (sign).

plusieurs [plyzjœr] *a & pron* several; **p. personnes,** a number of people.

plus-que-parfait [plyskəparfɛ] *nm Gram:* pluperfect (tense); *pl* **plus-que-parfaits.**

plus-value [plyvaly] *nf* (*a*) increase in value; appreciation (of property); **impôt sur les p.-values,** capital gains tax (*b*) surplus; profit; *pl* **plus-values.**

plutonium [plytɔnjɔm] *nm* plutonium.

plutôt [plyto] *adv* (*a*) rather, sooner; **p. souffrir que mourir,** it is better to suffer than to die; **prend celui-là p. que l'autre,** take this one instead of that one (*b*) rather; quite; on the whole; **il faisait p. froid,** the weather was rather cold; **p. long,** on the long side.

pluvieux, -ieuse [plyvjø, -jøz] *a* rainy (season); wet (weather).

PME *abbr Petites et moyennes entreprises.*

PMI *abbr Petites et moyennes industries.*

PMU *abbr Pari mutuel urbain.*

PNB *abbr Produit national brut.*

pneu, *pl* **pneus** [pnø] *nm* tyre, *NAm:* tire. **pneumatique 1.** *a* pneumatic; air (pump); inflatable (mattress); **canot à p.,** rubber dinghy **2.** *nm* (*a*) = PNEU (*b*) (*in Paris*) express letter.

pneumonie [pnømɔni] *nf* pneumonia.

PO *abbr WTel: petites ondes.*

poche [pɔʃ] *nf* **1.** pocket; **p. intérieure, p. revolver,** inside (breast) pocket; hip pocket; **livre de p.,** paperback; **argent de p.,** pocket money; **j'en suis de ma p.,** I am out of pocket by it; **payer de sa p.,** to pay out of one's own money; **j'ai 100 francs en p.,** I've got 100 francs on me; **connaître qch comme sa p.,** to know sth like the back of one's hand; *F:* **faire les poches à qn,** to go through s.o.'s pockets; **c'est dans la p.,** it's in the bag **2.** (*a*) bag; **p. d'air,** (i) *Av:* air pocket (ii) airlock (*b*) (kangaroo) pouch (*c*) *Biol:* sac **3.** (*a*) (*of trousers*) **faire des poches,** to go baggy (at the knees) (*b*) bags (under the eyes).

pocher [pɔʃe] *vtr* Cu: to poach (eggs); *F:* **p. un œil à qn,** to give s.o. a black eye.

pochette [pɔʃɛt] *nf* (*a*) pouch; envelope (for papers); case (of instruments) (*b*) pocket handkerchief (*c*) **p. d'allumettes,** book of matches (*d*) sleeve (of record).

poêle¹ [pwal] *nf* frying pan.

poêle² *nm* stove.

poème [pɔɛm] *nm* poem; *F:* **c'est tout un p.,** it defies description.

poésie [pɔezi] *nf* **1.** poetry **2.** poem.

poète [pɔɛt] **1.** *nm* poet **2.** *a* poetic; **être p.,** to be a poet. **poétique** *a* poetic(al). **poétiquement** *adv* poetically.

poétesse [pɔetɛs] *nf* poetess.

pognon [pɔɲɔ̃] *nm P:* money, dough.

poids [pwa] *nm* **1.** (*a*) weight; heaviness; **perdre du p.,** to lose weight; **vendre au p.,** to sell by weight; **il ne fait pas le p.,** he's not up to the job; **p. lourd,** heavyweight (*b*) importance; **son opinion a du p.,** his opinion carries weight **2.** weight (in clock); *Sp:* **lancer le p.,** to put the shot **3.** load, burden; **p. utile,** live weight; *Av:* payload; **p. mort,** dead weight; *Aut:* **p. lourd,** heavy goods vehicle.

poignant [pwaɲɑ̃] *a* poignant; harrowing (experience).

poignard [pwaɲar] *nm* dagger; **coup de p.,** stab.

poignarder [pwaɲarde] *vtr* to stab, to knife (s.o.).

poigne [pwaɲ] *nf* grip, grasp; **avoir de la p.,** to be forceful, firm.

poignée [pwaɲe] *nf* **1.** (*a*) handful; fistful; **à poignées,** in handfuls; by the handful (*b*) **p. de main,** handshake; **donner une p. de main à qn,** to shake hands with s.o. **2.** handle (of door); hilt (of sword); haft (of tool).

poignet [pwaɲɛ] *nm* **1.** wrist **2.** *Cl:* cuff.

poil [pwal] *nm* **1.** (*a*) (*of animal*) hair, fur; **à p. long,** long-haired, shaggy (*b*) coat (of animals); **cheval d'un beau p.,** sleek horse; **chien au p., à p. dur,** wire-haired, rough-coated dog (*c*) nap (of cloth); pile (of velvet, of carpet) (*d*) bristle (of brush) **2.** (*of pers*) hair (on the body); *F:* **à p.,** naked; **se mettre à p.,** to strip off; **avoir un p. dans la main,** to be workshy; **être de mauvais, de bon, p.,** to be in a bad, a good, mood **3.** *F:* **à un p. près,** as near as dammit; **un p. plus vite,** a fraction faster; **au p.!** (i) great! fantastic! (ii) perfect! **poilu 1.** *a* hairy, shaggy **2.** *nm F:* French soldier (1914–18).

poinçon [pwɛ̃sɔ̃] *nm* **1.** (*a*) (engraver's) point (*b*) awl **2.** (*a*) (perforating) punch (*b*) die, stamp (*c*) **p. de contrôle,** hallmark.

poinçonner [pwɛ̃sɔne] *vtr* **1.** to prick, bore; to punch **2.** (*a*) to punch, clip (ticket) (*b*) to stamp, hallmark.

poinçonneur, -euse [pwɛ̃sɔnœr, -øz] **1.** n (*pers*) ticket puncher **2.** nf **poinçonneuse,** punching machine.

poindre [pwɛ̃dṛ] vi (**il point; il poignait; il poindra;** *used esp in 3rd pers and in inf*) (*of daylight*) to dawn, break; (*of plants*) to come up, come out.

poing [pwɛ̃] nm fist; **serrer les poings,** to clench one's fists; **menacer qn du p.,** to shake one's fist at s.o.; **coup de p.,** punch; **donner un coup de p. à qn,** to punch s.o.; **dormir à poings fermés,** to sleep soundly.

point¹ [pwɛ̃] nm **1.** (a) *Needlew:* stitch; **faire un p. à qch,** to put a few stitches in sth (b) **p. de côté,** stitch (in the side); **avoir un p. au dos,** to have a stabbing pain in one's back **2.** (a) (*in time*) **le p. du jour,** daybreak; **être sur le p. de faire qch,** to be about to do sth; **arriver juste à p.,** to arrive in the nick of time (b) (*in space*) **p. de départ,** starting point, place; **p. de vue,** (i) (*panorama*) view(point) (ii) point of view, viewpoint; **à tous les points de vue,** in every respect; **du, au, p. de vue international,** from the international point of view; *Mec:* **p. d'appui,** fulcrum (of lever); **p. chaud,** hot spot; **p. mort,** neutral (gear); *Com:* **p. de vente,** stockist; **faire le p. (d'une question)**, to take stock (of a question); **mettre (qch) au p.,** to focus, adjust (sth); to perfect (design); to tune (engine); to finalize (arrangements); **recherche et mise au p.,** research and development **3.** (a) point, dot; punctuation mark; **p. (final),** full stop, *NAm:* period; **deux points,** colon; **p. d'exclamation,** exclamation mark, *NAm:* exclamation point; *F:* **un p., c'est tout!** and that's that! (b) *Games:* point, score; **marquer les points,** to keep the score (c) *Sch:* mark (d) speck, spot, dot **4.** (a) point, stage, degree; **p. d'ébullition,** boiling point; **jusqu'à un certain p.,** to a certain extent; **à tel p. que,** so much so that; **vous n'êtes pas malade à ce p.-là,** you're not as ill as all that (b) **mal en p.,** in a bad way; ill (c) **à point,** in the right condition; *Cu:* done to a turn; (*of steak*) well done **5.** point, particular; **p. de droit,** point of law; **p. d'honneur,** point of honour; **n'ayez aucune crainte sur ce p.,** don't worry on that score; **en tout p.,** in every respect.

point² adv A: *Lit:* = PAS².

pointage [pwɛ̃taʒ] nm (a) checking, ticking off (names on list) (b) *Ind:* clocking in, out (c) aiming (of gun).

pointe [pwɛ̃t] nf **1.** (a) point (of pin); tip, head (of arrow); toe (of shoe); peak (of roof); **coup de p.,** thrust; **p. d'asperge,** asparagus tip; **en p.,** pointed; tapering; **sur la p. des pieds,** on tiptoe; *Danc:* **faire des pointes,** to dance on point(s) (b) peak; **heures de p.,** rush hour(s); peak period (c) *Mil:* point (of advanced guard); **nous avons fait une p. jusqu'à Paris,** we pressed on as far as Paris (d) **p. du jour,** daybreak; **p. d'ironie,** touch of irony; **p. d'ail,** touch of garlic; *Sp:* **p. de vitesse,** spurt, sprint **2.** *Geog:* **p. (de terre),** spit (of land) **3.** (a) *Tls:* point (b) nail, tack (c) *Sp:* spike (on shoe).

pointer¹ [pwɛ̃te] **1.** vtr (a) to check, tick off (names on list); *Nau:* to plot (position) (on the map) (b) to point, level (telescope); to aim (gun); to train (searchlight) (**sur,** on) **2.** vi & pr (a) *Ind:* (**se) p.** (à

l'arrivée, à la sortie), to clock in, out (b) *F:* **se p.,** to turn up.

pointer² **1.** vtr (a) to thrust, stab; to prick (b) (*of horse, dog*) **p. les oreilles,** to prick up its ears **2.** vi to appear; (*of plant*) to sprout; (*of day*) to dawn.

pointillé [pwɛ̃tije] **1.** a dotted (line) **2.** nm dotted line.

pointilleux, -euse [pwɛ̃tijø, -øz] a particular; fastidious; finicky, pernickety (person).

pointu [pwɛ̃ty] a (sharp-)pointed.

pointure [pwɛ̃tyr] nf size (in shoes, gloves).

poire [pwar] nf **1.** pear; **couper la p. en deux,** to split the difference **2.** *El:* (pear-shaped) switch **3.** *P:* (a) face, mug (b) mug, sucker.

poireau, -eaux [pwaro] nm leek; *F:* **faire le p.,** to kick one's heels.

poireauter [pwarote] vi *F:* to kick one's heels.

poirier [pwarje] nm pear tree; **faire le p.,** to do a headstand.

pois [pwa] nm **1.** pea; **p. chiche,** chickpea; **p. de senteur,** sweet pea **2.** *Cu:* **petits p.,** garden peas; **p. cassés,** split peas **3.** **tissu à p.,** spotted, polka dot, material.

poison [pwazɔ̃] nm poison; *F:* (*pers*) **quel p.!** what a pest!

poisse [pwas] nf *F:* bad luck; **c'est la p.!** just my luck!

poisser [pwase] vtr (a) to make (hands) sticky (b) *P:* to catch, nab (s.o.). **poisseux, -euse** a sticky.

poisson [pwasɔ̃] nm fish; **p. rouge,** goldfish; **p. d'avril!** April fool! **être comme un p. dans l'eau,** to be in one's element; *Astr:* **Poissons,** Pisces. **poissonneux, -euse** a (*of lake*) full of fish.

poissonnerie [pwasɔnri] nf fishmonger's (shop).

poissonnier, -ière [pwasɔnje, -jɛr] n fishmonger.

poitrine [pwatrin] nf (a) chest; **rhume de p.,** cold on the chest (b) breast; bosom; **tour de p.,** (i) chest measurement (ii) (*of woman*) bust measurement (c) *Cu:* breast (of veal); belly (of pork); **p. fumée** = streaky bacon.

poivre [pwavṛ] nm pepper; **grain de p.,** peppercorn; **p. et sel,** pepper-and-salt (colour).

poivrer [pwavre] vtr to pepper (food). **poivré** a peppery (food); spicy (story).

poivrier [pwavrije] nm **1.** pepper plant **2.** pepper pot.

poivron [pwavrɔ̃] nm sweet pepper; capsicum; **p. vert, rouge,** green, red, pepper.

poivrot, -ote [pwavro, -ɔt] n *P:* drunkard.

poix [pwa] nf pitch.

poker [pɔker] nm *Cards:* poker.

polaire [pɔlɛr] a polar; **l'étoile p.,** n **la p.,** the pole star.

polariser [polarize] vtr to polarize; to focus (attention).

pôle [pol] nm (a) pole; **p. nord, sud,** north, south, pole (b) centre (of attention).

polémique [polemik] **1.** a controversial **2.** nf polemic, controversy.

poli [pɔli] **1.** a (a) polished; bright (metal) (b) polite, courteous (person, manners); **sois p.!** don't be rude! **2.** nm polish, gloss. **poliment** adv politely.

police¹ [pɔlis] nf **1.** policing; **faire la p.,** to maintain law and order; **numéro de p. d'un véhicule,** registration number of a vehicle. **2.** police (force); **p. de la route,** traffic police; **p. judiciaire (PJ)** = Criminal Investigations Department (CID); **p. des mœurs** = vice squad; **appeler p. secours,** to dial 999 (for the police); **être dans, de, la p.,** to be in the police; **agent de p.,** police constable, policeman; **remettre qn entre les mains de la p.,** to give s.o. in charge. **policier, -ière 1.** *a* **chien p.,** police dog; **roman p.,** detective novel **2.** *nm* police officer; detective.

police² *nf* (insurance) policy; **p. d'assurance vie,** life insurance policy.

polichinelle [polifinɛl] *nm* **1.** Punch **2.** buffoon.

polio(myélite) [poljo(mjelit)] *nf* *Med:* polio(myelitis).

polir [polir] *vtr* **1.** to polish; to burnish (metal) **2.** to polish (up) (style); to refine manners.

polisson, -onne [polisɔ̃, -ɔn] **1.** *n* naughty child; (little) devil **2.** *a* naughty (child); dirty (story).

polissonnerie [polisɔnri] *nf* naughty trick.

politesse [polites] *nf* politeness; good manners; courtesy.

politicien, -ienne [politisjɛ̃, -jɛn] *n* often Pej: politician.

politique [politik] **1.** *a* (*a*) political; **(homme) p.,** politician; **économie p.,** economics (*b*) politic; diplomatic (answer) **2.** *nf* (*a*) policy; **p. extérieure,** foreign policy (*b*) politics. **politiquement** *adv* politically.

polka [polka] *nf* *Danc: Mus:* polka.

pollen [polɛn] *nm* *Bot:* pollen.

polluer [polɥe] *vtr* to pollute (atmosphere). **polluant 1.** *a* polluting **2.** *nm* pollutant.

pollution [polysjɔ̃] *nf* pollution.

polo [polo] *nm* **1.** *Sp:* polo **2.** *Cl:* sweat shirt.

polochon [polɔʃɔ̃] *nm* *P:* bolster.

Pologne [polɔɲ] *Prnf Geog:* Poland. **polonais, -aise 1.** (*a*) *a* Polish (*b*) *n* Pole **2.** *nm* *Ling:* Polish **3.** *nf* *Danc: Mus:* **polonaise,** polonaise.

poltronnerie [poltrɔnri] *nf* cowardice. **poltron, -onne 1.** *a* cowardly **2.** *n* coward.

polychrome [polikrom] *a* polychrome, polychrom(at)ic.

polyclinique [poliklinik] *nf* polyclinic.

polycopier [polikɔpje] *vtr* to duplicate, to stencil.

polyculture [polikyltyr] *nf* mixed farming.

polyester [poliɛstɛr] *nm* polyester.

polyéthylène [polietilɛn] *nm* polythene.

polygamie [poligami] *nf* polygamy. **polygame 1.** *a* polygamous **2.** *n* polygamist.

polyglotte [poliglɔt] *a* & *n* polyglot.

polygone [poligɔn] *nm* (*a*) *Mth:* polygon (*b*) *Mil:* shooting range.

Polynésie [polinezi] *Prnf Geog:* Polynesia. **polynésien, -ienne** *a* & *n* Polynesian.

polysyllabe [polisilab] *nm* polysyllable. **polysyllabique** *a* polysyllabic.

polyvalent [polivalɑ̃] *a* (*a*) *Ch:* polyvalent (*b*) versatile, general-purpose (tool).

pommade [pɔmad] *nf* pomade, cream (for hair); ointment (for skin); **passer de la p. à qn,** to butter s.o. up.

pomme [pɔm] *nf* **1.** (*a*) apple; **p. à cidre,** cider apple; *Anat:* **p. d'Adam,** Adam's apple (*b*) **p. de terre,** potato; **pommes frites,** chips, *NAm:* French fries;

pommes chips, potato crisps; *F:* **tomber dans les pommes,** to pass out, to faint (*c*) **p. de pin,** fir cone, pine cone **2.** knob (of walking stick); heart (of lettuce); rose (of watering can)

pommeau, -eaux [pɔmo] *nm* pommel (of sword); knob (of walking stick).

pommelé [pɔmle] *a* dappled, mottled; mackerel (sky); **gris p.,** dapple-grey.

pommette [pɔmɛt] *nf* cheekbone.

pommier [pɔmje] *nm* apple tree.

pompe¹ [pɔ̃p] *nf* pomp, ceremony; **entrepreneur de pompes funèbres,** undertaker, *NAm:* mortician.

pompe² *nf* **1.** pump; **p. à incendie,** fire engine; *Aut:* **p. à air,** air pump; **p. à essence,** (i) petrol pump, *NAm:* gas pump (ii) petrol station, *NAm:* gas station **2.** *P:* shoe.

pomper [pɔ̃pe] *vtr* (*a*) to pump; to suck up (liquid) (*b*) *Sch:* F: to copy (sth) (**sur** from) (*c*) *P:* to drink, to knock back (*d*) to exhaust (s.o.).

pompeux, -euse [pɔ̃pø, -øz] *a* pompous. **pompeusement** *adv* pompously.

pompier [pɔ̃pje] *nm* fireman; *pl* fire brigade.

pompiste [pɔ̃pist] *n* *Aut:* petrol, *NAm:* gas, pump attendant.

pompon [pɔ̃pɔ̃] *nm* pompon; bobble; **c'est le p.!** that's the limit!

pomponner (se) [səpɔ̃pɔne] *vpr* to doll oneself up.

ponçage [pɔ̃saʒ] *nm* sanding, rubbing down.

ponce [pɔ̃s] *nf* **(pierre) p.,** pumice (stone).

poncer [pɔ̃se] *vtr* (**je ponçai(s)**) to sand, to rub down. **ponceuse** [pɔ̃søz] *nf* sander.

ponction [pɔ̃ksjɔ̃] *nf* *Med:* puncture; tapping (of lung).

ponctualité [pɔ̃ktɥalite] *nf* punctuality. **ponctuel, -elle** *a* punctual. **ponctuellement** *adv* punctually.

ponctuation [pɔ̃ktɥasjɔ̃] *nf* punctuation.

ponctuer [pɔ̃ktɥe] *vtr* to punctuate.

pondération [pɔ̃derasjɔ̃] *nf* levelheadedness; weighting.

pondérer [pɔ̃dere] *vtr* (**je pondère**) to balance (powers); to weight. **pondéré** *a* (*pers*) levelheaded.

pondre [pɔ̃dr] *vtr* (*a*) to lay (eggs); *abs* to lay; **œuf frais pondu,** new-laid egg (*b*) *F:* to produce (novel).

poney [pɔnɛ] *nm* pony.

pont [pɔ̃] *nm* **1.** (*a*) bridge; **p. tournant, basculant, suspendu,** swingbridge, bascule bridge, suspension bridge; *Adm:* **les ponts et chaussées** = the department of civil engineering; *F:* **faire le p.,** to make a long weekend of it; **faire un p. d'or à qn,** to offer s.o. a fortune to take on a job; **vivre sous les ponts,** to be a tramp (*b*) *Ind:* platform, stage, bridge; (*in garage*) **p. élévateur,** (repair) ramp; **p. roulant,** overhead crane (*c*) *Av:* **p. aérien,** airlift **2.** deck (of ship) **3.** *MecE:* live axle; *Aut:* **p. arrière,** back axle.

ponte¹ [pɔ̃t] *nf* (*a*) laying (of eggs) (*b*) eggs (laid).

ponte² *nm* *F:* big shot.

pontife [pɔ̃tif] *nm* pontiff. **pontifical, -aux** *a* pontifical.

pontifier [pɔ̃tifje] *vi* to pontificate.

pont-levis [pɔ̃l(ə)vi] *nm* drawbridge; *pl* **ponts-levis.**

ponton [pɔ̃tɔ̃] *nm* **1.** *Mil:* pontoon **2.** landing stage.

pop [pɔp] *a inv* pop (music, art).

pope [pɔp] *nm* pope (of Orthodox church).

popeline [pɔplin] *nf Tex:* poplin.

popote [pɔpɔt] 1. *nf F:* **faire la p.**, to do the cooking 2. *a inv* stay-at-home (person).

populace [pɔpylas] *nf Pej:* rabble.

populaire [pɔpylɛr] *a* (a) popular; *Pol:* of, for, the people; **manifestation p.**, mass demonstration (b) **expression p.**, slang expression; **chanson p.**, (i) folk song (ii) popular song; **quartier p.**, working class district (c) **se rendre p.**, to make oneself popular.

populariser [pɔpylarize] *vtr* to popularize.

popularité [pɔpylarite] *nf* popularity.

population [pɔpylasjɔ̃] *nf* population. **populeux, -euse** *a* densely populated; crowded.

porc [pɔr] *nm* 1. (a) pig, *NAm:* hog (b) pigskin (c) *F:* (*pers*) swine 2. *Cu:* pork.

porcelaine [pɔrsəlɛn] *nf* porcelain, china.

porcelet [pɔrsəlɛ] *nm* piglet.

porc-épic [pɔrkepik] *nm* porcupine.

porche [pɔrʃ] *nm* porch.

porcherie [pɔrʃəri] *nf* pigsty.

pore [pɔr] *nm* pore. **poreux, -euse** *a* porous.

pornographie [pɔrnɔgrafi] *nf* pornography. **pornographique** *a* pornographic.

port[1] [pɔr] *nm* harbour, port; **arriver à bon p.**, to come safe into port; to arrive safe and sound; **droits de p.**, harbour dues; **p. maritime**, seaport; **p. militaire**, naval base; **p. de pêche**, fishing port; **p. d'attache**, home port.

port[2] *nm* 1. (act of) carrying; **p. d'armes**, carrying of firearms (b) wearing (of uniform, of beard) 2. cost of transport; postage; **franc(o) de p.**, carriage paid; **en p. dû**, carriage forward 3. bearing, carriage (of person).

portail, -ails [pɔrtaj] *nm* portal; gate.

portant [pɔrtɑ̃] *a* **être bien, mal, p.**, to be in good, poor, health; to be fit, to be unwell.

portatif, -ive [pɔrtatif, -iv] *a* portable.

porte [pɔrt] *nf* 1. (a) gateway, doorway, entrance; **p. cochère**, carriage entrance; (*in airport*) **p. d'embarquement**, departure gate (b) *Ski:* gate 2. door; doorstep; **p. d'entrée**, front door; **p. de sortie**, (*also Fig:*) way out; **p. de service**, tradesmen's entrance; **à my p.**, on my doorstep; **p. tournante**, revolving door; *F:* **je lui ai parlé entre deux portes**, I spoke to him briefly; **mettre qn à la p.**, (i) to throw s.o. out (ii) to sack s.o.; *nm* **faire du p.-à-p.**, to sell, to canvass, (from) door to door; **écouter aux portes**, to eavesdrop 3. eye (of hook and eye).

porte-avions [pɔrtavjɔ̃] *nm inv* aircraft carrier.

porte-bagages [pɔrtbagaʒ] *nm inv* (a) luggage-rack (b) *Aut:* roofrack.

porte-bonheur [pɔrtbɔnœr] *nm inv* (lucky) charm, mascot.

porteclefs [pɔrt(ə)kle] *nm inv* key ring.

porte-couteau [pɔrt(ə)kuto] *nm* knife rest; *pl* *porte-couteaux.*

porte-documents [pɔrtdɔkymɑ̃] *nm inv* briefcase.

porte-drapeau [pɔrtdrapo] *nm* standard bearer; *pl* *porte-drapeau(x).*

portée [pɔrte] *nf* 1. span (of roof, bridge); bearing (of beam) 2. (a) litter (of animals) (b) *Mus:* stave; staff 3. (a) reach (of arm); range, scope; compass (of voice); **canon à longue p.**, **à courte p.**, long-range, short-range, gun; **à p. de voix**, within call; **à p. d'oreille**, within earshot; **à p. de (la) vue**, within sight; **hors de p.**, out of, beyond, reach; **à la p. de tout le monde**, (i) available to everybody (ii) that everyone can understand (b) bearing, (full) significance; implication (of words).

porte-fenêtre [pɔrt(ə)fənɛtr] *nf* French window; *pl* *portes-fenêtres.*

portefeuille [pɔrtəfœj] *nm* (a) portfolio (b) wallet, *NAm:* billfold; **lit en p.**, apple pie bed; **jupe p.**, wrap-over skirt (c) *Fin:* **effets en p.**, bills in hand.

portemanteau, -eaux [pɔrtmɑ̃to] *nm* coat rack, coat stand; hat stand.

porte(-)mine [pɔrt(ə)min] *nm* propelling pencil; *pl* *porte-mine(s).*

porte-monnaie [pɔrtmɔnɛ] *nm inv* purse.

porte-parole [pɔrtparɔl] *nm inv* spokesman, spokeswoman; mouthpiece.

porte-parapluies [pɔrtparaplɥi] *nm inv* umbrella stand.

porte-plume [pɔrtəplym] *nm inv* penholder.

porter [pɔrte] 1. *vtr* (a) to carry; to bear (burden); **p. qn dans son cœur**, to have a great affection for s.o. (b) to produce; to bear (fruit); **cela vous portera bonheur**, that will bring you luck (c) to carry (sth) habitually; **p. du noir, une bague**, to wear black, a ring; **le bleu se porte beaucoup**, blue is very fashionable; **p. la tête haute**, to hold one's head high (d) to carry, convey, take (sth somewhere); **portez-lui ce livre**, take him this book; **il porta le verre à ses lèvres**, he raised the glass to his lips (e) **p. un coup à qn**, to strike s.o.; **p. ses regards sur qn**, to look at s.o.; **p. une accusation contre qn**, to bring a charge against s.o. (f) to inscribe, enter; **p. une somme au crédit de qn**, to credit a sum to s.o.; **se faire p. malade**, to report sick (g) to induce, incline, prompt; **tout me porte à croire que**, everything leads me to believe that (h) to raise, carry; **p. la température à 100°**, to raise the temperature to 100° (i) to show (interest, affection, for s.o., sth); **par la tendresse que je vous porte**, by the love I bear you (j) to declare, state; **la loi porte que**, the law provides that; **p. témoignage**, to bear witness 2. *vi* (a) to rest, bear; (*discussion*) to turn on; (*action*) to focus on; **la perte a porté sur nous**, we had to stand the loss (b) to hit, reach; **aucun des coups n'a porté**, none of the blows took effect; **chaque mot a porté**, every word went home; **son discours a porté sur ses auditeurs**, his speech made an impact on his audience; **sa voix porte bien**, his voice carries well; **sa tête a porté sur le trottoir**, his head hit the pavement 3. **se p.** (a) to go, proceed (to a place); (*of look, choice, suspicion*) **se p. sur**, to fall on; **se p. au secours de qn**, to go to s.o.'s help (b) **se p. bien, mal**, to be well, unwell (c) **se p. caution, candidat**, to stand as surety, as candidate.

porte-revues [pɔrtravy] *nm inv* magazine rack.

porte-savon [pɔrtsavɔ̃] *nm* soapdish; *pl* *porte-savons.*

porte-serviettes [pɔrtsɛrvjɛt] *nm inv* towel rail.

porteur, -euse [pɔrtœr, -øz] 1. *n* (a) carrier, bearer (of message); **par p.**, by messenger (b) (railway) porter; **p. d'eau**, water carrier; **p. de germes**, (germ) carrier (c) *Fin:* payee (of cheque); **p. d'actions**, shareholder; **payable au p.,** payable to bearer **2.** *a* (*a*) bearing (axle); **câble p.,** suspension cable (*b*) *El:* carrier (wave, frequency).

porte-voix [pɔrtəvwa] *nm inv* loudhailer; megaphone.

portier, -ière² [pɔrtje, -jɛr] *n* porter; commissionaire; janitor.

portière² *nf Rail: Aut:* door.

portillon [pɔrtijɔ̃] *nm* gate.

portion [pɔrsjɔ̃] *nf* portion, share, part; helping (of food); stretch (of road).

portique [pɔrtik] *nm* (*a*) portico, porch (*b*) *Gym:* crossbeam.

Porto [pɔrto] **1.** *Prnm Geog:* Oporto **2.** *nm* (*wine*) port.

portrait [pɔrtrɛ] *nm* portrait; likeness; **faire le p. de qn,** to paint s.o.'s portrait; **c'est le p. vivant de son père,** he's the living image of his father.

portraitiste [pɔrtretist] *n* portrait painter.

portrait-robot [pɔrtrɛrɔbo] *nm* identikit (picture); *pl* **portraits-robots.**

portuaire [pɔrtyɛr] *a* harbour, port (installations).

Portugal [pɔrtygal] *Prnm Geog:* Portugal. **portugais, -aise 1.** *a & n* Portuguese **2.** *nm Ling:* Portuguese.

pose [poz] *nf* **1.** placing; hanging (of curtain, picture); laying (of bricks, carpet); installation (of electricity); fitting (of lock); **p. de câbles,** cable laying **2.** (*a*) pose, posture; attitude; **prendre une p.,** to strike a pose (*b*) posing, affectation **3.** *Phot:* (*a*) exposure (*b*) time exposure.

posé [poze] *a* calm, sedate (person); steady (bearing); sober (appearance). **posément** *adv* calmly, sedately.

poser [poze] **1.** *vi* (*a*) (*of beam*) to rest, lie (on sth) (*b*) to pose (as artist's model); to sit (for one's portrait) (*c*) to show off; to strike an attitude **2.** *vtr* (*a*) to place, put, lay, set, (down) (sth somewhere); **posele sur la table,** put it (down) on the table; **p. un avion,** to land an aircraft; **p. sa candidature,** to stand (as a candidate); to apply (for a job); **p. une question à qn,** to put a question to s.o.; to ask s.o. a question; **p. un problème à qn,** to set s.o. a problem; *Mth:* **p. un chiffre,** to put down a number (*b*) to put up, hang (curtain, picture); to lay (bricks, carpet); to install (electricity); to fit (lock) (*c*) to establish (s.o.'s reputation) (*d*) **posons que,** let's suppose, supposing, that **3. se p.** (*a*) (*of bird*) to settle, alight; (*of aircraft*) to land (*b*) **un problème se pose,** we are faced with a problem; **se p. des questions,** to wonder (*c*) **se p. comme prêtre,** to pose as a priest.

poseur, -euse [pozœr, -øz] **1.** *n Tchn:* layer (of pipes, cables); *Rail:* **p. de voie,** platelayer; *Navy:* **p. de mines,** minelayer **2.** *a & n* affected (person); showoff, poseur.

positif, -ive [pozitif, -iv] (*a*) *a* positive (*b*) *nm Phot:* positive (print). **positivement** *adv* positively.

position [pozisjɔ̃] *nf* **1.** (*a*) position (of ship, aircraft); *Aut:* **feux de p.,** sidelights; **prendre p.,** to take a stand (*b*) *Mil: etc:* **p. de repli,** position to fall back on **2.** posture, attitude **3.** (*a*) condition, circumstances; **p. gênante,** embarrassing situation; **p. sociale,** social standing (*b*) *Fin:* **demander sa p.,** to ask for the balance of one's account.

posologie [pozɔlɔʒi] *nf Med:* dosage.

possédant, -ante [pɔsedɑ̃, -ɑ̃t] *a & n* propertied; **les possédants,** the wealthy.

possédé, -ée [pɔsede] **1.** *a* possessed (**de,** by, of); dominated (by passion) **2.** *n* person possessed; madman, madwoman, maniac.

posséder [pɔsede] *v* (**je possède; je posséderai**) **1.** *vtr* (*a*) to be in possession of (sth); to possess, own; to have (property); **p. un titre,** to hold a title (*b*) to have a thorough knowledge of (a language); to be master of (a subject) (*c*) (*of demon*) to possess (s.o.) (*d*) *F:* to fool (s.o.); **je me suis fait p.,** I've been had **2. se p.,** to control oneself, one's temper; **il ne se possédait plus de joie,** he was beside himself with joy.

possesseur [pɔsesœr] *nm* possessor, owner.

possession [pɔsesjɔ̃] *nf* **1.** possession; ownership; **être en p. de qch.,** to be in possession of sth; *Com:* to be in receipt of sth; **avoir qch en sa p.,** to have sth in one's possession **2.** possession (by evil spirit); **p. de soi-même,** self-control. **possessif, -ive** *a & nm* possessive.

possibilité [pɔsibilite] *nf* possibility; feasibility; **si j'ai la p. de lui écrire,** if it's possible for me to write to him.

possible [pɔsibl] **1.** *a* possible; feasible; **c'est (bien) p.,** it's (quite) possible; it's quite likely; **ce n'est pas p.! F: pas p.!** it's not possible! you can't mean it! **est-il p. de faire des fautes pareilles?** how can people make such mistakes? **il ne m'est pas p. de le faire,** I can't possibly do it; **aussitôt que, dès que, p.,** as soon as possible; **si (c'est) p.,** if possible; **la boîte la plus grande p.,** the largest possible box **2.** *nm* **dans la mesure du p.,** as far as possible; **faire tout son p. pour,** to do one's utmost to; **il s'est montré aimable au p.,** he couldn't have been nicer.

post- [pɔst] *pref* post-.

postdater [pɔstdate] *vtr* to postdate (letter).

poste¹ [pɔst] *nf* (*a*) post, mail; **les Postes et Télécommunications,** the postal services = the Post Office; **p. aérienne,** airmail; **mettre une lettre à la p.,** to post, mail, a letter (*b*) (**bureau de**) **p.,** post office; **grande p.,** head, main, post office. **postal, -aux** *a* postal (service).

poste² *nm* **1.** (*a*) post, station; **être à son p.,** to be at one's post; **à vos postes!** to your posts! **p. de commandement,** headquarters; *Navy:* **p. d'équipage,** crew's quarters (*b*) **p. d'incendie,** fire station; **p. de police,** police station; **p. d'essence,** petrol station, *NAm:* gas station; **p. de contrôle,** checkpoint; *Av:* **p. de pilotage,** cockpit; *Rail:* **p. d'aiguillage,** signal box (*c*) (radio, television) set; **p. émetteur, récepteur,** transmitter, receiver (*d*) telephone; **p. 35,** extension 35 **2.** (*a*) post, appointment, job (*b*) *Ind:* shift **3.** *Book-k:* entry, item.

poster¹ [pɔste] **1.** *vtr* (*a*) to post, mail (letter) (*b*) to post (sentry); to station (men) **2. se p.,** to position oneself.

poster² [pɔstɛr] *nm* poster.

postérieur [pɔsterjœr] **1.** *a* (*a*) (*of time*) posterior; subsequent (**à,** to), later (*b*) (*of place*) hind, back **2.** *nm F:* posterior, behind. **postérieurement** *adv* subsequently; at a later date.

postérité [pɔsterite] *nf* posterity.

posthume [pɔstym] *a* posthumous.

postiche [pɔstiʃ] **1.** *a* false (hair) **2.** *nm* hairpiece.

postier, -ière [pɔstje, -jɛr] *n* post office employee.

postillon [pɔstijɔ̃] *nm Hist:* postilion.

postopératoire [pɔstɔperatwar] *a Med:* postoperative (care).

postscolaire [pɔstskɔlɛr] *a Sch:* continuation (classes); **enseignement p.,** further education.

post-scriptum [pɔstskriptɔm] *nm inv* postscript.

postsynchroniser [pɔstsɛ̃krɔnize] *vtr Cin:* to dub (film).

postulant, -ante [pɔstylɑ̃, -ɑ̃t] *n* (a) applicant (b) *Ecc:* postulant.

postuler [pɔstyle] *vtr* (a) to apply for (post) (b) to postulate (principle).

posture [pɔstyr] *nf* **1.** posture, attitude (of the body) **2.** position (in society, business); **être en bonne, en mauvaise, p.,** to be well, badly, placed.

pot [po] *nm* **1.** pot, jug, can, jar; **p. de chambre,** chamber pot; *(for child)* **(petit) p.,** potty; **p. de fleurs,** pot of flowers; **p. à fleurs,** flowerpot; **p. à eau** [potao] water jug; **p. à lait,** milk can, jug; *F:* **prendre un p.,** to have a drink; **avoir du p.,** to be lucky; **coup de p.,** stroke of luck; **manque de p.,** hard luck; **payer les pots cassés,** to carry the can 2. *Aut:* **p. d'échappement,** exhaust (pipe, system); silencer, *NAm:* muffler.

potable [pɔtabl] *a* **1.** drinkable; **eau p.,** drinking water **2.** *F:* fair; good enough.

potage [pɔtaʒ] *nm* soup.

potager, -ère [pɔtaʒe, -ɛr] **1.** *a Cu:* **herbes potagères,** pot herbs; **plante potagère,** vegetable **2.** *a & nm* **(jardin) p.,** kitchen garden.

pot-au-feu [pɔtofø] *nm inv* (a) boiled beef with vegetables (b) stewing beef.

pot-de-vin [pɔdvɛ̃] *nm* **1.** tip **2.** bribe; *pl* pots-de-vin.

poteau, -eaux [pɔto] *nm* (a) post, pole, stake; *Sp:* goalpost; **p. indicateur,** signpost; **p. télégraphique,** telegraph pole; *Sp:* **p. de départ, d'arrivée,** starting post, finishing post (b) **p. (d'exécution),** execution post; **au p.!** down with him!

potelé [pɔtle] *a* plump and dimpled; chubby (child).

potence [pɔtɑ̃s] *nf* **1.** gallows, gibbet **2.** support, arm, crosspiece, bracket.

potentiel, -elle [pɔtɑ̃sjɛl] *a & nm* potential. **potentiellement** *adv* potentially.

poterie [pɔtri] *nf* **1.** pottery (works) **2.** (piece of) pottery; **p. (de terre),** earthenware.

potiche [pɔtiʃ] *nf* (large) oriental vase.

potier [pɔtje] *nm* potter.

potin [pɔtɛ̃] *nm F:* **1.** gossip **2.** noise, row, racket.

potion [posjɔ̃] *nf* potion.

potiron [pɔtirɔ̃] *nm* pumpkin.

pot-pourri [popuri] *nm Mus: etc:* pot pourri, medley; *pl* pots-pourris.

pou, *pl* **poux** [pu] *nm* louse; *pl* lice.

pouah [pwa] *int* ugh!

poubelle [pubɛl] *nf* dustbin, *NAm:* garbage can, trash can.

pouce [pus] *nm* **1.** (a) thumb; *F:* **donner un coup de p. à qn,** to pull strings for s.o.; **manger sur le p.,** to have a (quick) snack; **se tourner les pouces,** to twiddle one's thumbs; *Sch: P:* **p.!** pax! (b) *occ* big toe **2.** *Meas:* inch.

poudre [pudr] *nf* **1.** (a) powder; **réduire qch en p.,** to grind sth to a powder; **p. d'or,** gold dust; **p. dentifrice,** tooth powder; **p. à récurer,** scouring powder; **sucre en p.,** caster sugar; **lait en p.,** powdered milk, dried milk (b) face powder **2.** (explosive) powder; **p. à canon,** gunpowder; **la nouvelle s'est répandue comme une traînée de p.,** the news spread like wildfire.

poudrer [pudre] *vtr* to powder; to sprinkle with powder; **se p.,** to powder (one's face). **poudreux, -euse** *a* powdery; dusty; **neige poudreuse,** powdered snow.

poudrerie [pudrari] *nf* (gun)powder factory.

poudrier [pudrije] *nm Toil:* (powder) compact.

poudrière [pudrijɛr] *nf* powder magazine.

pouf [puf] **1.** *int* (a) wallop! bump! (b) phew! **2.** *nm Furn:* pouf(fe).

pouffer [pufe] *vi* **p. (de rire),** to burst out laughing, to guffaw.

pouilleux, -euse [pujø, -øz] **1.** *a* lousy, verminous; filthy (person); squalid, seedy (part of town) **2.** *n* tramp.

poulailler [pulaje] *nm* (a) hen house (b) *Th: F:* the gallery; the gods.

poulain [pulɛ̃] *nm* colt, foal; *Sp:* trainee; protégé.

poularde [pulard] *nf Cu:* fattened pullet.

poule [pul] *nf* (a) hen; *Cu:* (boiling) fowl; **p. au pot,** boiled chicken; **ma (petite) p.!** my pet! **lait de p.,** (non-alcoholic) egg flip, egg nog; **quand les poules auront des dents,** when pigs can fly (b) **p. d'eau,** moorhen; **p. faisane,** hen pheasant (c) *P:* (fast young) woman; bird, *NAm:* broad.

poulet [pulɛ] *nm* (a) chicken (b) *F:* cop.

pouliche [puliʃ] *nf* filly.

poulie [puli] *nf* **1.** pulley; (i) sheave (ii) block **2.** (belt) pulley; driving wheel.

poulpe [pulp] *nm* octopus.

pouls [pu] *nm Med:* pulse; **prendre le p. à qn,** to take s.o.'s pulse.

poumon [pumɔ̃] *nm* lung; **p. d'acier,** iron lung; **respirer à pleins poumons,** to take a deep breath.

poupe [pup] *nf Nau:* stern, poop.

poupée [pupe] *nf* **1.** (a) doll; dolly (b) *F:* girl, bird, doll **2.** finger bandage.

poupon [pupɔ̃] *n* (tiny) baby.

pouponner [pupɔne] *vi* to play the doting mother.

pouponnière [pupɔnjɛr] *nf* day nursery, crèche.

pour[1] [pur] *prep.* **1.** (a) for; instead of; **allez-y p. moi,** go in my place; **mot p. mot,** word for word; **agir p. qn,** to act on s.o.'s behalf (b) **prendre qn p. un autre,** to take s.o. for someone else; **laisser qn p. mort,** to leave s.o. for dead; *F:* **c'est p. de vrai,** I mean it, I'm serious (c) *(direction)* **je pars p. la France,** I'm leaving for France; **le train p. Paris,** the Paris train (d) *(time)* **p. quinze jours,** for a fortnight; **p. toujours,** for ever; **p. le moment,** for the time being; **il sera ici p. quatre heures,** he'll be here (i) for four hours (ii) by four o'clock; **j'en ai p. une heure,** it'll take me an hour; **donnez-moi p. 100 francs d'essence,** give me 100 francs' worth of petrol; **être p. beaucoup,** to count for much (e) *(purpose)* **je suis ici p. affaires,** I'm here on business; **vêtements pour hommes,** clothes for men; **c'est p. cela qu'il est venu,** that's why he came; **il est venu p. le compteur,** he came about the meter (f) because of; **faites-le p. moi,** do it for my sake; **j'avais peur p. lui,** I was nervous on his account; **p. la forme,** for form's sake (g) **parler p. qn,** to speak in favour of s.o.; *adv F:* **moi, je suis p.,** I'm in favour of it (h) **p. mon compte,** as far as I'm concerned; **il est grand p. son âge,** he's tall for his age; **p. ce qui est de nos vacances,** as for our holidays; **p. moi,** for my part; **p. moi c'est absurde,** in my opinion it's ridiculous; *F:* **p. de la chance, c'est de la chance,** you're in luck and no mistake! (i) **dix p. cent,** ten per cent (j) **être bon p. les animaux,** to be kind to animals 2. **p. + inf** (a) (in order) to; **il faut manger p. vivre,** one must eat to live; **p. ainsi dire,** so to speak (b) **p. ne pas être en retard,** so as not to be late; **être trop faible p. marcher,** to be too weak to walk (c) although; **p. être petit il n'en est pas moins brave,** though small he is none the less brave (d) because of; **être puni p. avoir désobéi,** to be punished for disobeying; **je le sais p. l'avoir vu,** I know it from having seen it (e) of a nature to; **cela n'est pas p. me surprendre,** that does not come as a surprise to me (f) *F:* **être p. partir,** to be about to leave (g) **mourir p. mourir,** if we must die 3. (a) **p. que + sub** in order that; **il est trop tard p. qu'elle sorte,** it is too late for her to go out (b) **p.** (+ *adj or n*) **que + sub** however, although; **cette situation, p. terrible qu'elle soit,** this situation, terrible though it may be (c) **p. peu que + sub,** if only, if ever; **p. peu que vous hésitiez, vous êtes fichu,** if you hesitate at all, you've had it.

pour² *nm* **peser le p. et le contre,** to weigh the pros and cons.

pourboire [purbwar] *nm* tip.

pourcentage [pursɑ̃taʒ] *nm* percentage; rate (of interest); commission.

pourchasser [purʃase] *vtr* to pursue; to hound (debtor); to hunt down (criminal).

pourparlers [purparle] *nmpl* talks; **entrer en p.,** to begin negotiations (**avec,** with).

pourpre [purpr] 1. *nf* purple (dye) (of the ancients) 2. *nm* crimson 3. *a* crimson; (*of pers*) purple (with rage).

pourquoi [purkwa] 1. *adv & conj* why; **p. faire?** what for? **p. cela?** why? **mais p. donc?** what on earth for? **voilà p.,** that's why; **p. pas?** why not? 2. *nm inv* reason; **les p. et les comment,** the whys and wherefores.

pourrir [purir] 1. *vi* to rot, decay; to go rotten, to go bad; **p. en prison,** to rot in prison; **laisser p. la situation,** to let the situation deteriorate 2. *vtr* to rot. **pourri** 1. *a* rotten (fruit, wood); bad (meat); wet (weather); corrupt (society) 2. *nm* (a) rotten, bad, part (of fruit); **sentir le p.,** to smell of decay (b) *P:* (*pers*) swine.

pourrissement [purismɑ̃] *nm* deterioration.

pourriture [purityr] *nf* 1. (a) rotting, rot (b) rottenness (of society) 2. *F:* (*pers*) swine.

poursuite [pursɥit] *nf* 1. (a) pursuit; chase; **se lancer à la p. de qn,** to set off in pursuit of s.o. (b) carrying out of (piece of work); *Com:* **p. du client,** follow-up system. 2. *usu pl Jur:* **poursuites judiciaires,** legal proceedings; **engager des poursuites contre qn,** to take legal action against s.o.

poursuivant, -ante [pursɥivɑ̃, -ɑ̃t] *n* pursuer.

poursuivre [pursɥivr] *v* (*conj like* SUIVRE) 1. *vtr* (a) to pursue; to go after, to chase, to hunt (s.o., animal); to hound (s.o.); **poursuivi par la guigne,** dogged by bad luck (b) **p. qn (en justice),** to prosecute s.o. (c) to pursue, continue, go on with (work, a story); **p. un but,** to work towards an end; **p. un avantage,** to follow up an advantage 2. *vi* **poursuivez,** go on; continue (your story) 3. **se p.,** to continue, to go on.

pourtant [purtɑ̃] *adv* nevertheless, however, still, (and) yet.

pourtour [purtur] *nm* periphery, circumference (of building); precincts (of a cathedral); **mur de p.,** enclosure wall.

pourvoir [purvwar] *v* (*prp* **pourvoyant;** *pp* **pourvu;** *pr ind* **je pourvois;** *pr sub* **je pourvoie**) 1. *v ind tr* to provide; **p. aux besoins de qn,** to cater for, to attend to, s.o.'s needs; **p. aux frais,** to defray the cost; **p. à un emploi,** to fill a job 2. *vtr* (a) **p. qn de qch,** to supply s.o. with sth (b) to equip, fit (**de,** with) 3. **se p.,** to provide oneself (**de,** with).

pourvoyeur, -euse [purvwajœr -øz] *n* supplier.

pourvu que [purvykə] *conj phr* provided (that); so long as; **p. qu'il ne fasse pas de gaffes!** let's hope he doesn't put his foot in it!

pousse [pus] *nf* 1. growth (of hair, leaves, feathers) 2. (young) shoot, sprout.

poussé [puse] *a* advanced (studies); *Aut:* **moteur p.,** souped-up engine.

pousse-café [puskafe] *nm inv F:* (after dinner) liqueur.

poussée [puse] *nf* 1. thrust; **centre de p.,** aerodynamic centre; **force de p.,** upward thrust; **p. du vent,** wind pressure 2. pushing, pressure (of crowd) 3. push, shove 4. (a) growth; eruption, outbreak (of pimples); **p. de fièvre,** sudden rise in temperature (b) bulge (in profits).

pousser [puse] 1. *vtr* (a) to push, shove, thrust; to wheel (bicycle); to slide (bolt); **p. qn du coude,** to nudge s.o.; **p. la porte,** (i) to push the door to (ii) to push the door open (b) to drive (on), impel, urge; **p. qn à faire qch.,** to push s.o. into doing sth (c) to push on; to pursue (studies); to urge on (horse); to drive (engine) hard; to push (pupil); **p. la plaisanterie un peu loin,** to carry a joke too far; **p. la vente,** to push the sale (d) to put forth, shoot out (leaves) (e) to utter (cry); to heave (sigh); to give (cheer); **p. un cri,** to shout, to scream 2. *vi* (a) to push; **p. à la roue,** to put one's shoulder to the wheel (b) to push on, make one's way (to a place) (c) (*of plants*) to grow; (*of teeth*) to come through; **ses dents commencent à p.,** he's beginning to cut his teeth; **laisser p. sa barbe,** to grow a beard 3. **se p.,** to move.

poussette [puset] *nf* pushchair.

poussière [pusjer] *nf* (a) dust; **couvert de p.,** dusty; **tomber en p.,** to crumble into dust (b) speck of dust; *F:* **10 francs et des poussières,** 10 francs plus (a bit). **poussiéreux, -euse** *a* dusty.

poussif, -ive [pusif, -iv] *a* short-winded (person); puffing (engine).

poussin [pusɛ̃] *nm* (a) chick (b) *Cu:* spring chicken (c) *F:* **mon p.,** pet.

poussoir [puswar] *nm* (push) button.

poutre [putr] *nf* 1. (wooden) beam 2. (metal) girder.

poutrelle [putrɛl] *nf* small beam; girder.

pouvoir¹ [puvwar] *vtr* (*prp* **pouvant;** *pp* **pu;** *pr ind* **je peux, je puis** (*always* **puis-je), tu peux, il peut, ils peuvent;** *pr sub* **je puisse;** *fu* **je pourrai) 1.** to be able; can; **je ne peux (pas) le faire,** I can't do it; **cela ne peut (pas) se faire,** it cannot, it can't, be done; **comment a-t-il pu dire cela?** how could he say that? **il aurait pu le faire s'il avait voulu,** he could have done it if he had wanted to; **faire tout ce qu'on peut,** to do one's (level) best; **on n'y peut rien,** it can't be helped; **il travaille on ne peut mieux,** he couldn't work better; **il n'en peut plus (de fatigue),** he's worn out, tired out; **sauve qui peut,** every man for himself; **qu'est-ce qu'il peut bien me vouloir?** whatever can he want (from me)? **la loi ne peut rien contre lui,** the law can't touch him **2.** (*a*) to be allowed; may; **vous pouvez partir,** you may go; **puis-je entrer?** may I, can I, come in? (*b*) **puissiez-vous dire vrai!** let's hope you're right! **3.** to be possible, probable; *vpr* **cela se peut (bien),** it may be; it could well be; **la porte a pu se fermer seule,** the door could have closed on its own; **il pouvait avoir dix ans,** he may, might, have been ten; **advienne que pourra,** come what may; **il se peut qu'il vienne,** he may come.

pouvoir² *nm* **1.** power; force, means; **il n'est pas en mon p. de,** it is not within my power to **2.** influence, power; **être au p. de qn,** to be in s.o.'s power **3.** (*a*) **p. paternel,** paternal authority (*b*) competence, power; **abuser de ses pouvoirs,** to abuse one's authority (*c*) **p. politique,** political power; **prendre le p.,** to come into office; (*illegally*) to seize power; **le parti au p.,** the party in power; **les pouvoirs publics,** the authorities **4.** *Jur:* power of attorney; **avoir plein(s) pouvoir(s) pour agir,** to have full powers to act.

prairie [preri] *nf* meadow; grassland, *NAm:* prairie.

praline [pralin] *nf* praline; sugared almond. **praliné** *a* praline-flavoured.

practicable [pratikabl] *a* practicable; feasible (plan); passable, negotiable (road, ford).

practicien, -ienne [pratisjɛ̃, -jɛn] *n* (legal, medical) practitioner.

pratique [pratik] **1.** *nf* (*a*) practice; application (of theory); **mettre qch en p.,** to put sth into practice; **en p.,** in practice (*b*) practice, experience; **p. d'un sport,** practice of a sport; **perdre la p. de qch.,** to lose the knack of sth, to get out of practice; **avoir une longue p. de qch,** to have a long practical experience of sth (*c*) *Jur:* practice (of the law); **terme de p.,** legal term (*d*) **pratiques religieuses,** religious observances **2.** *a* practical, useful (method); handy (gadget); convenient (time); **sens p.,** practical common sense. **pratiquement** *adv* in practice; practically.

pratiquer [pratike] *vtr* **1.** to practise (rules, virtues); to employ, use; **il pratique le football,** he plays football; **elle pratique la natation,** she's a (keen) swimmer; *Med:* **p. une intervention,** to carry out an operation; *abs* **il ne p. pas,** (i) he doesn't go to church (ii) *Med:* he is not in practice; *Com:* **prix pratiqués,** current prices **2.** to make (opening); to bore (hole); to open (road). **pratiquant, -ante 1.** *a* practising **2.** *n* follower (of faith); regular churchgoer.

pré [pre] *nm* meadow.

préalable [prealabl] **1.** *a* (*a*) previous, prior (**à,** to) (*b*) preliminary (agreement) **2.** *nm* prerequisite, condition; **au p.,** first; beforehand. **préalablement** *adv* first (of all); beforehand; **p. à,** prior to.

préambule [preãbyl] *nm* preamble (**de,** to); prelude.

préau, -aux [preo] *nm* (court)yard (of prison); (covered) playground.

préavis [preavi] *nm* (advance) notice; **sans p.,** without warning.

précaire [preker] *a* precarious (tenure); delicate (health).

précaution [prekosjɔ̃] *nf* **1.** precaution; **prendre des précautions,** to take precautions; **par p.,** as a precaution **2.** caution, care; **avec p.,** cautiously.

précédent [presedã] **1.** *a* preceding, previous, former; **le jour p.,** the day before **2.** *nm* precedent; **sans p.,** unprecedented. **précédemment** *adv* previously, before.

précéder [presede] *vtr* (**je précède, n. précédons; je précéderai**) (*a*) to precede; to go, to come, before; *abs* **la page qui précède,** the preceding page (*b*) to precede, get ahead of (s.o.).

précepte [presɛpt] *nm* precept.

précepteur [preseptœr] *n* tutor; (private) teacher.

prêcher [prefe] **1.** *vtr & i* to preach (gospel) (**à,** to); **p. l'économie,** to preach economy; **p. d'exemple,** to practise what one preaches **2.** *vtr* to preach to (s.o.); to lecture (s.o.).

précieux, -euse [presjø, -øz] *a* (*a*) precious; valuable; invaluable (*b*) precious; affected (style). **précieusement** *adv* very carefully.

précipice [presipis] *nm* chasm; abyss; precipice.

précipitation [presipitasjɔ̃] *nf* great haste; precipitation.

précipiter [presipite] **1.** *vtr* (*a*) to throw down, hurl down; **p. qn dans le désespoir,** to plunge s.o. into despair (*b*) to hurry, hasten, rush; to precipitate (events); **il ne faut rien p.,** we mustn't rush things **2.** *vi Ch:* to precipitate **3. se p.** (*a*) to dash, to rush (headlong); to make a rush (**sur,** at, upon) (*b*) to speed up; (*of pulse*) to quicken; **l'action se précipite,** the action is moving faster. **précipitamment** *adv* hastily; **sortir p.,** to rush out. **précipité 1.** *a* hasty, hurried; headlong (flight); racing (pulse) **2.** *nm Ch:* precipitate.

précis [presi] **1.** *a* precise, exact, accurate, definite; **à deux heures précises,** at two o'clock sharp; **en termes p.,** in distinct terms; **sans raison précise,** for no particular reason **2.** *nm* abstract, summary; précis (of document). **précisément** *adv* (*a*) precisely, exactly (*b*) as a matter of fact.

préciser [presize] **1.** *vtr* to specify; to state precisely; **p. les détails,** to go into further detail; **je tiens à p. que,** I wish to make it clear that; **p. la date,** to give the exact date **2.** *vi* to be precise, explicit **3.** (*of ideas*) **se p.,** to become clear; to take shape.

précision [presizjɔ̃] *nf* **1.** precision, exactness, accuracy; **instruments de p.,** precision instruments **2.** *pl* precise details; **demander des précisions sur qch,** to ask for more information about sth.

précoce [prekɔs] *a* precocious; early (fruit); premature (senility). **précocement** *adv* precociously.

préconçu [prekɔ̃sy] *a* preconceived.

préconiser [prekɔnize] *vtr* to recommend, advocate.

précurseur [prekyrsœr] **1.** *nm* precursor, forerunner **2.** *am* precursory.

prédécesseur [predesɛsœr] *nm* predecessor.

prédestination [predɛstinasjɔ̃] *nf* predestination.

prédestiner [predɛstine] *vtr* to predestine (à, to).

prédiction [prediksjɔ̃] *nf* prediction.

prédilection [predilɛksjɔ̃] *nf* predilection, partiality; **de p.,** favourite.

prédire [predir] *vtr* (*conj. like* DIRE *except pr ind & imp* v. **prédisez**) to predict, foretell.

prédisposer [predispoze] *vtr* to predispose (à, to).

prédisposition [predispozisjɔ̃] *nf* predisposition (à, to).

prédominance [predɔminɑ̃s] *nf* predominance.

prédominer [predɔmine] *vi* to predominate. **prédominant** *a* predominant.

prééminence [preeminɑ̃s] *nf* pre-eminence (sur, over). **prééminent** *a* pre-eminent.

préexistence [preɛgzistɑ̃s] *nf* pre-existence.

préexister [preɛgziste] *vi* to pre-exist. **préexistant** *a* pre-existent.

préfabriqué [prefabrike] 1. *a* prefabricated 2. *nm* prefabricated house, material; prefab.

préface [prefas] *nf* preface, foreword.

préfecture [prefɛktyr] *nf Fr Adm:* prefecture; **P. de police,** Paris police headquarters. **préfectoral, -aux** *a* prefectural.

préférable [preferabl] *a* preferable (à, to); **il serait p. d'y aller,** it would be better to go there. **préférablement** *adv* preferably.

préférence [preferɑ̃s] *nf* preference; **de p.,** preferably; **de p. à,** in preference to; **il n'a pas de p.,** it's all the same to him. **préférentiel, -elle** *a* preferential.

préférer [prefere] *vtr* (je **préfère**; je **préférerai**) to prefer (à, to); to like better; **je préfère du thé,** I'd rather have tea. **préféré, -ée** *a & n* favourite.

préfet [prefɛ] *nm* prefect.

préfigurer [prefigyre] *vtr* to foreshadow.

préfixe [prefiks] *nm* prefix.

préhistoire [preistwar] *nf* prehistory. **préhistorique** *a* prehistoric.

préjudice [preʒydis] *nm* prejudice, detriment; (moral) injury; wrong, damage; **porter p. à qn,** to inflict injury, loss, on s.o. **préjudiciable** *a* prejudicial, detrimental, harmful.

préjugé [preʒyʒe] *nm* prejudice, preconception; **avoir un p. contre,** to be prejudiced, biased, against (sth).

préjuger [preʒyʒe] *vtr* (*conj like* JUGER) **p. de qch,** to prejudge sth.

prélasser (se) [səprelase] *vpr* to lounge; to bask (in the sun).

prélat [prela] *nm* prelate.

prélèvement [prelɛvmɑ̃] *nm* 1. deduction in advance; levying (of tax) 2. (*a*) sample; **faire un p. de sang,** to take a sample of blood (*b*) amount deducted; *Bank:* = standing order.

prélever [prelve] *vtr* (*conj like* LEVER) to deduct in advance; to levy (tax).

préliminaire [preliminɛr] 1. *a* preliminary 2. *nmpl* preliminaries.

prélude [prelyd] *nm* prelude (de, à, to).

préluder [prelyde] *vi* **p. à qch,** to be a prelude to sth.

prématuré, -ée [prematyre] 1. *a* premature; untimely 2. *n* premature baby. **prématurément** *adv* prematurely.

préméditation [premeditasjɔ̃] *nf* premeditation; **avec p.,** deliberately.

préméditer [premedite] *vtr* to premeditate; **p. de faire qch,** to plan to do sth; **insulte préméditée,** deliberate insult.

premier, -ière [prəmje, -jɛr] *a & n* 1. (*a*) first; **le p. janvier,** the first of January; **le p. de l'an,** New Year's day; **premières difficultés,** initial difficulties; **dans les premiers temps,** at first; **en p.** (lieu), in the first place; firstly; **du, au, p. coup,** at the first attempt; **arriver le p., en p.,** to arrive first; **ce n'est pas le p. venu,** he isn't just anybody; *Aut:* **première (vitesse),** first (gear) (*b*) **sens p. d'un mot,** original meaning of a word; **vérité première,** basic truth; *Ind:* **matières premières,** raw materials 2. **habiter au p.** (étage), to live on the first floor, *NAm:* the second floor; **p. plan,** foreground; *Fig:* forefront; **première marche,** bottom stair 3. **au p. rang,** in the first rank; **le tout p.,** the foremost; **p. ministre,** Prime Minister, Premier; **p. choix,** best quality; **de première importance,** of the highest importance; **de première nécessité,** essential; *Rail:* **voyager en première,** to travel first class; *Mth:* **nombres premiers,** prime numbers; *Th:* **p. rôle,** leading part, lead; *Sch:* (classe de) **première** = lower sixth (form); **il est le p. de sa classe,** he's top of his form; *P:* **de première,** first-class 4. *.nf* (*a*) *Th:* **première,** first night; **première** (*b*) *Mount:* first ascent. **premièrement** *adv* first(ly), in the first place; for a start.

premier-né, première-née [prəmjene, prəmjerne] *a & n* firstborn; *pl* **premiers-nés, premières-nées.**

prémonition [premɔnisjɔ̃] *nf* premonition.

prémunir [premynir] 1. *vtr* **p. qn contre qch,** to caution s.o. against sth 2. **se p. contre qch,** to protect oneself against sth.

prenant [prənɑ̃] *a* engaging (voice); fascinating (book); engrossing (film).

prendre [prɑ̃dr] *v* (*prp* **prenant;** *pp* **pris;** *pr ind* **ils prennent;** *pr sub* **je prenne;** *ph* **je pris;** *fu* **je prendrai**) 1. *vtr* (*a*) to take (up), to take hold of (sth); **p. qn par les cheveux,** to grab s.o. by the hair; **aller p. son parapluie,** to get one's umbrella; **je sais comment le p.,** I know how to handle him; **p. qch sur la table, dans un tiroir,** to take sth from the table, out of a drawer; **où avez-vous pris cela?** (i) where did you get that from? (ii) where did you get that idea? (*b*) to take (in) (lodgers); **p. qch sur soi,** to take responsibility for sth; **il a très mal pris la chose,** he took it very badly (*c*) **p. qch à qn,** to take sth from s.o.; **cela me prend tout mon temps,** it takes up all my time (*d*) *F:* **il prend cher,** he charges a lot; **c'est à p. ou à laisser,** take it or leave it; **à tout p.,** on the whole; all in all; **à bien p. les choses,** rightly speaking (*e*) to take, capture; **p. un poisson,** to catch a fish; **se faire p.,** to get caught; **se laisser p.,** to let oneself be taken in; **p. qn à voler,** to catch s.o. stealing; **p. qn sur le fait,** to catch s.o. in the act; **que je vous y prenne!** let me catch you (at it)! **on ne m'y prendra pas!** I know better! **être pris,** to be stuck; **se p. le pied dans une racine,** to catch one's foot on a root (*f*) **l'envie lui a pris de partir,** he was seized with a desire to go away; **qu'est-ce qui lui prend?** what's come over him? **bien lui en a pris,** it was lucky for him that he did (*g*) to call for, collect (s.o.); (*of* *taxi*) to pick (s.o.) up; (*of boat*) to take in (cargo) (*h*) to buy, book (tickets); **p. une chambre,** to take a room; **p. des vacances,** to take a holiday; **p. des renseignements,** to make enquiries; **p. des notes,** to take notes (*i*) to engage (staff); **p. qn comme exemple,** to take s.o. as an example (*j*) **p. qn pour,** to (mis)take s.o. for; **se faire p. pour,** to pass oneself off as (*k*) to take, eat (food); **qu'est-ce que vous pren(dr)ez?** what will you have (to drink)? *F:* **qu'est-ce que tu vas p.!** you're for it! (*l*) to acquire (habit); **p. froid,** to catch cold (*m*) to take on, assume (appearance); **p. un air innocent,** to put on an innocent air; **p. du poids,** to put on weight (*n*) to take, go, by (train, bus); **p. à travers champs,** to strike across country; *Aut:* **p. un virage,** to take a bend; *Nau:* **p. le large,** to take to the open sea **2.** *vi* (*a*) (*of cement, jelly*) to set; (*of engine*) to seize (up); (*of food*) to catch, to stick (in the pan) (*b*) (*of plant*) to take root; (*of fire*) to take, to catch; **le vaccin a pris,** the vaccine has taken (effect); **cette mode ne prendra pas,** this fashion won't catch on; **ça ne prend pas!** it won't wash! (*c*) **p. à gauche,** to bear (to the) left, to fork left **3. se p.** (*a*) to catch, to be caught; **son manteau s'est pris à un clou,** her coat (got) caught on a nail (*b*) **il se prend pour un héros,** he thinks he's a hero (*c*) **se p. d'amitié pour qn,** to take a liking to s.o. (*d*) to attack s.o.; **s'en p. à qn,** to lay the blame on s.o. (*e*) **il sait comment s'y p.,** he knows how to set about it; **vous vous y prenez mal,** you're going the wrong way about it; **s'y p. à deux fois,** to have two goes (at sth).

preneur, -euse [prənœr, -øz] *n* taker; *Fin: Com:* buyer; *Jur:* lessee.

prénom [prenɔ̃] *nm* Christian name; first name, *NAm:* given name.

prénommer [prenɔme] **1.** *vtr* to name (s.o.); **le prénommé Victor,** the man called Victor **2. se p.,** to be called, named.

préoccupation [preɔkypasjɔ̃] *nf* (*a*) preoccupation (**de,** with); concern (**de,** about); anxiety, worry.

préoccuper [preɔkype] **1.** *vtr* to preoccupy, engross (s.o.); **elle a l'air préoccupé,** she has something on her mind; **sa santé me préoccupe,** I'm anxious about his health **2. se p. de qch,** to concern oneself with sth; to worry about sth. **préoccupant** *a* worrying.

préparateur, -trice [preparatœr, -tris] *n* (laboratory) assistant.

préparatifs [preparatif] *nmpl* preparations (**de,** for).

préparation [preparasjɔ̃] *nf* preparation; preparing; training; **annoncer qch sans p.,** to announce sth abruptly.

préparer [prepare] **1.** *vtr* (*a*) to prepare; to get ready; to make preparations for; to arrange (meeting); **elle prépare le déjeuner,** she's cooking, *NAm:* fixing, the lunch (*b*) **p. qn à qch,** (i) to prepare s.o. for sth (ii) to train s.o. for sth (*c*) to prepare, to study, for (exam) **2. se p.** (*a*) **un orage se prépare,** a storm is brewing; **il se prépare quelque chose,** there's something brewing, afoot (*b*) **se p. à qch, à faire qch,** to get ready for sth, to do sth. **préparatoire** *a* preparatory.

prépondérance [prepɔ̃derɑ̃s] *nf* preponderance (**sur,** over). **prépondérant** *a* preponderant.

préposé, -ée [prepoze] *n Adm:* official; attendant; **p. (des postes),** postman; **p. des douanes,** customs officer.

préposer [prepoze] *vtr* to appoint (s.o.) (**à,** to).

préposition [prepozisjɔ̃] *nf Gram:* preposition.

préretraite [prerətrɛt] *nf* early retirement.

prérogative [prerɔgativ] *nf* prerogative.

près [prɛ] **1.** *adv* near; **tout p.,** nearby, close by; **plus p.,** nearer **2.** *adv phr* **à cela p.,** except on that point, with that one exception; **à cela p. que,** except that; **à 5 centimètres p.,** to within 5 centimetres; **à peu p.,** nearly, about; **il était à peu p. certain,** it was fairly certain; **ce n'est pas à beaucoup p. la somme qu'il me faut,** it's nowhere near the amount I need; **de p.,** close, near; (from) close to; **tirer de p.,** to fire at close range; **suivre qn de p.,** to follow s.o. closely **3.** *prep phr* **p. de qn,** near (to), close to, s.o.; **il est p. de midi,** it's nearly, almost twelve (o'clock); **p. de pleurer,** on the verge of tears; **p. de partir,** about to leave; **je ne suis pas p. de le revoir,** it will be a long time before I see him again; *adv phr F:* **être p. de ses sous,** to be tight-fisted.

présage [prezaʒ] *nm* portent, sign; **mauvais p.,** bad omen.

présager [prezaʒe] *vtr* (**n. présageons**) **1.** to (fore)bode, to portend **2.** to predict; to foresee, to foretell.

presbyte [prɛzbit] *a* long-sighted (person).

presbytère [prɛzbitɛr] *nm RCCh:* presbytery.

presbytie [prɛsbisi] *nf* long-sightedness.

prescience [presjɑ̃s] *nf* prescience, foreknowledge (**de,** of).

prescription [prɛskripsjɔ̃] *nf* prescription; stipulation.

prescrire [prɛskrir] *vtr* (*conj like* ÉCRIRE) to prescribe, lay down; to stipulate (quality); to prescribe (remedy).

préséance [preseɑ̃s] *nf* precedence (**sur,** over).

présélection [preselɛksjɔ̃] *nf* preselection; shortlisting (for job).

présélectionner [preselɛksjone] *vtr* (*a*) *Tch:* to preselect (*b*) to short-list (candidate).

présence [prezɑ̃s] *nf* **1. avoir de la p.,** to have an imposing presence **2.** presence, attendance; *Sch:* régularité de p.,** regular attendance; *Ind:* **feuille de p.,** time card; **en p.,** face to face; **mettre deux personnes en p.,** to bring two people together; **en p. de ces faits,** faced with these facts; **en ma p.,** in my presence; **p. d'esprit,** presence of mind.

présent¹ [prezɑ̃] *a & n* (*a*) present; **les personnes présentes,** those present; **être p. à une cérémonie,** to attend a ceremony; **cela m'est toujours p. à l'esprit,** I never forget it; **le (temps) p.,** the present (time); *Gram:* the present (tense); **à p.,** just now; **jusqu'à p.,** until now, as yet; **dès à p.,** from now on; **à p. que,** now that.

présent² *nm Lit:* present, gift.

présentation [prezɑ̃tasjɔ̃] *nf* **1.** (*a*) presentation; *Com:* **payable à p.,** payable on demand (*b*) appearance **2.** introduction (**à qn,** to s.o.); **p. de collections,** fashion show.

présenter [prezɑ̃te] **1.** *vtr* (*a*) to present, offer; **p. la main,** to hold out one's hand; **p. une excuse à qn,** to offer an apology to s.o.; **p. ses hommages à qn,** to pay one's respects to s.o.; **p. son passeport,** to show one's passport; *Mil:* **présentez armes!** present arms! *(b)* to table (motion); to put (resolution); *TV:* to compere (show); **p. les faits,** to present the facts; **son travail est bien présenté,** his work is well set out *(c)* **p. qn à qn,** to introduce s.o. to s.o.; **p. qn comme candidat,** to put s.o. up as candidate **2.** *vi F:* **il présente bien,** he's a man of impressive appearance **3.** **se p.** *(a)* **une occasion se présente,** an opportunity presents itself; **si le cas se présente,** if the case arises; **attendre que qch se présente,** to wait for sth to turn up; **la chose se présente bien,** the matter looks promising; **se p. sous un jour nouveau,** to appear in a new light *(b)* to present oneself; to stand for, *NAm:* run for (elections); **se p. à qn,** to introduce oneself to s.o.; **se p. à un examen,** to sit (for) an exam.

préservation [prezɛrvasjɔ̃] *nf* preservation, protection.

préserver [prezɛrve] *vtr* to preserve, to protect **(de,** from). **préservatif, -ive 1.** *a & nm* preservative; protective **2.** *nm* (contraceptive) sheath.

présidence [prezidɑ̃s] *nf (a)* presidency; chairmanship *(b)* presidential residence.

président, -ente [prezidɑ̃, -ɑ̃t] *n* **1.** *(a)* president (of republic); **la Présidente,** the president's wife **2.** *(a)* chairman, chairwoman (of meeting) *(b) PolHist:* **p. du Conseil** = Prime Minister *(c)* **p. du jury,** (i) *Jur:* foreman of the jury (ii) *Sch:* chief examiner *(d)* **p.-directeur général,** chairman and managing director. **présidentiel, -elle** *a* presidential.

présider [prezide] *vtr & i (a)* to preside over (council); to chair (meeting) *(b)* to preside, to be in the chair; **p. à qch,** to govern sth.

présomption [prezɔ̃psjɔ̃] *nf (a)* presumption *(b)* presumptuousness. **présomptueux, -euse** *a* presumptuous.

presque [prɛsk] *adv* **1.** almost, nearly; **c'est p. de la folie,** it's little short of madness **2.** *(with negative)* scarcely, hardly; **p. jamais,** hardly ever; **p. rien,** next to nothing.

presqu'île [prɛskil] *nf* peninsula.

pressant [prɛsɑ̃] *a* pressing, urgent (need, danger); insistent (creditor).

presse [prɛs] *nf* **1.** press, pressing-machine; **p. à imprimer,** printing press; *(book)* **mettre sous p.,** to send to press **2.** press; newspapers; magazines; **service de p.,** publicity department **3.** urgency; **il n'y a pas de p.,** there's no hurry.

pressé [prɛse] *a* **1.** *(a)* pressed, compressed; **citron p.,** fresh lemon juice *(b)* crowded, close together **2.** in a hurry; **p. de partir,** in a hurry to go; **ce n'est pas p.,** it's not urgent; *nm* **parer au plus p.,** to attend to the most urgent things (first).

presse-citron [prɛssitrɔ̃] *nm inv* lemon squeezer.

pressentiment [prɛsɑ̃timɑ̃] *nm* presentiment; premonition; **avoir un p. que,** to have a feeling that.

pressentir [prɛsɑ̃tir] *vtr (conj like* MENTIR*)* **1.** to have a presentiment, a foreboding, of (sth); to sense (sth); **laisser p. qch,** to forewarn sth **2.** **p. qn sur qch,** to approach s.o. about sth, to broach a matter with s.o.

presse-papier(s) [prɛspapje] *nm inv* paperweight.

presse-purée [prɛspyre] *nm inv* potato masher.

presser [prɛse] **1.** *vtr (a)* to press; to squeeze (lemon,

sponge); to press (record, grapes); **p. qn contre soi,** to clasp s.o. in one's arms *(b)* to press, push (button) *(c)* **pressé par ses créanciers,** hard pressed by his creditors; **p. qn de questions,** to ply s.o. with questions; **p. qn,** to urge s.o. *(d)* to hurry (s.o.) (up, on); to speed up (work); **p. le pas,** to quicken one's pace; **qu'est-ce qui vous presse?** why are you in such a hurry? **2.** *vi* **le temps presse,** time is short; **l'affaire presse,** the matter is urgent; **rien ne presse,** there's no hurry **3.** **se p.** *(a)* to crowd, to throng; to crush *(b)* **se p. contre qn,** to snuggle (up) against s.o. *(c)* to hurry (up); **sans se p.,** without hurrying.

pressing [prɛsiŋ] *nm Com:* *(a)* steam pressing *(b)* dry-cleaners.

pression [prɛsjɔ̃] *nf* **1.** *(a)* pressure; **p. atmosphérique,** atmospheric pressure; **p. artérielle,** blood pressure; **bière (à la) p.,** draught beer; *Av:* **cabine sous p.,** pressurized cabin *(b)* **exercer une p. sur qn,** to put pressure on s.o. **2.** **bouton (à) p., un, une, p.,** press stud, snap fastener.

pressoir [prɛswar] *nm (a)* (wine, oil) press *(b)* press house.

pressurisation [prɛsyrizasjɔ̃] *nf* pressurization.

pressuriser [prɛsyrize] *vtr* to pressurize.

prestance [prɛstɑ̃s] *nf* imposing bearing.

prestation [prɛstasjɔ̃] *nf* **1.** benefit; allowance; **prestations sociales,** national insurance benefits **2.** fee; service **3.** *(of sportsman, artiste)* performance.

preste [prɛst] *a* quick, sharp, nimble; alert.

prestidigitateur, -trice [prɛstidiʒitatœr, -tris] *n* conjurer.

prestidigitation [prɛstidiʒitasjɔ̃] *nf* conjuring.

prestige [prɛstiʒ] *nm* prestige; glamour; **sans p.,** undistinguished; **publicité de p.,** prestige advertising. **prestigieux, -euse** *a* prestigious.

présumer [prezyme] *vtr* **1.** to presume; **p. qn innocent,** to assume s.o. to be innocent **2.** **p. de faire qch,** to presume to do sth; **trop p.,** to overestimate.

présupposer [presypoze] *vtr* to presuppose.

prêt¹ [prɛ] *a* ready, prepared; **être p. à tout,** (i) to be game for anything (ii) to be prepared to do anything; **p. à rendre service,** willing to help.

prêt² *nm* **1.** lending; loan; **p. à court terme,** short-(-term) loan; **p. hypothécaire,** mortgage loan **2.** advance (on wages).

prêt-à-porter [prɛtaporte] *nm coll* ready-to-wear clothes.

prétendant, -ante [pretɑ̃dɑ̃, -ɑ̃t] **1.** *n* applicant; candidate; pretender **2.** *nm* suitor.

prétendre [pretɑ̃dr] *vtr* **1.** to claim (as a right); to require **2.** to maintain, to assert; to claim; **je prétends que c'est faux,** I maintain that it's a lie; **on prétend que,** people say that; it is said that **3.** *v ind tr* **p. à qch,** to lay claim to, to aspire to sth.

prétendu, -ue [pretɑ̃dy] *a* alleged, would-be. **prétendument** *adv* allegedly.

prétention [pretɑ̃sjɔ̃] *nf (a)* pretension, claim **(à,** to) *(b)* prententiousness; **sans prétention(s),** unpretentious, simple. **prétentieux, -euse** *a* pretentious. **prétentieusement** *adv* pretentiously.

prêter [prete] **1.** *vtr (a)* to lend; *esp NAm:* to loan; **p. qch à qn,** to lend sth to s.o.; **p. sur gage(s),** to lend against security *(b)* to give, lend (support); **p. attention,** to pay attention; **p. l'oreille,** to listen; **p. ser-**

ment, to take an oath (c) to attribute, ascribe (à, to); **p. de généreux sentiments à qn**, to credit s.o. with generous feelings (d) *vi* **p. à qch**, to give rise to sth; **privilège qui prête aux abus**, privilege that lends itself to abuses 2. **se p.**, to lend oneself, to be a party (à, to); to consent to (arrangement). **prêteur, -euse** *a* ready, willing, to lend; **il n'est pas p.**, he doesn't believe in lending.

prétérit [preterit] *nm* preterite (tense).

prétexte [pretɛkst] *nm* pretext, excuse; **sous p. de**, on the pretext of; **sous aucun p.**, on no account.

prétexter [pretɛkste] *vtr* to allege as a pretext; **p. la fatigue**, to plead fatigue.

prêtre [prɛtṛ] *nm* priest.

prêtresse [prɛtrɛs] *nf* priestess.

prêtrise [prɛtriz] *nf* priesthood.

preuve [prœv] *nf* proof, evidence; **faire p. d'intelligence**, to show intelligence; **faire ses preuves**, to prove oneself; *(of technique)* to be well tried; **il a fait ses preuves**, he's experienced.

prévaloir [prevalwar] *(conj. like* VALOIR, *except pr sub* **je prévale**) 1. *vi* to prevail (sur, contre, over, against); **faire p. son droit**, to insist upon one's rights; **faire p. son opinion**, to win acceptance for one's opinion 2. **se p. (de qch)**, to take advantage of sth; to presume on (one's birth).

prévenance [prevnɑ̃s] *nf* attention; kindness; thoughtfulness. **prévenant** *a* kind, attentive, considerate (**envers**, to); thoughtful.

prévenir [prevnir] *vtr (conj like* VENIR *but with aux* AVOIR) 1. (*a*) to forestall, anticipate (s.o., s.o.'s wishes) (*b*) to prevent, ward off (illness, danger); **to avert** (accident); *Prov:* **mieux vaut p. que guérir**, prevention is better than cure 2. to predispose, to bias (s.o. in favour of s.o.); **p. qn contre qn**, to prejudice s.o. against s.o. 3. to inform, forewarn (s.o. of sth); **vous auriez dû p. me**, you should have told me.

préventif, -ive [prevɑ̃tif, -iv] *a* 1. preventive (medicine); **à titre p.**, as a preventive 2. *Jur:* **détention préventive**, detention awaiting trial. **préventivement** *adv* as a preventive.

prévention [prevɑ̃sjɔ̃] *nf* 1. predisposition (**en faveur de**, in favour of); prejudice, bias (**contre**, against); **observateur sans p.**, unbias(s)ed observer 2. *Jur:* **être en état de p.**, to be in custody 3. prevention (of disease); **p. routière**, road safety.

prévenu, -ue [prevny] 1. *a* (*a*) prejudiced; bias(s)ed (*b*) charged (**de**, with) 2. *n Jur:* accused (person).

prévision [previzjɔ̃] *nf* anticipation; expectation; **en p. de qch.**, in expectation of sth; **p. du temps**, weather forecasting; **prévisions météorologiques**, weather forecast; *Fin:* **prévisions budgétaires**, budget estimates. **prévisible** *a* foreseeable.

prévoir [prevwar] *vtr (conj like* VOIR *except fu and condit* **je prévoirai, je prévoirais**) 1. to foresee, forecast, anticipate (events); **tout laisse p.**, all signs point to; **rien ne fait p. un changement**, there is no prospect of a change 2. to take measures beforehand; to provide for (sth); to make provision for (sth); **la réunion est prévue pour demain**, the meeting is scheduled for tomorrow; **on ne peut pas tout p.**, one can't think of everything; **comme prévu**, as planned.

prévoyance [prevwajɑ̃s] *nf* foresight, forethought;

precaution; **société de p.**, provident society. **prévoyant** *a* provident; far-sighted.

prier [prije] *(impf & pr sub)* n. **priions**, v. **priiez**) 1. *vtr* (*a*) to pray to (God) (*b*) to beg, beseech, entreat; **se faire p.**, to require a great deal of persuasion; **sans se faire p.**, willingly (*c*) to ask, request; **p. qn d'entrer**, to ask s.o. (to come) in; **je vous en prie**, (i) please do! (ii) please don't! (iii) *(when thanked for sth)* it's a pleasure 2. *vi* to pray (**pour**, for).

prière [prijɛr] *nf* 1. prayer; **être en prières**, to be praying 2. request, entreaty; **à la p. de qn**, at s.o.'s request; **p. de ne pas fumer**, no smoking please.

primaire [primɛr] 1. *a* (*a*) primary (school) (*b*) *Pej:* (*of pers*) of limited outlook 2. *nm* (*a*) *Sch:* primary education (*b*) *Geol:* primary era.

prime¹ [prim] *a Lit:* **de p. abord**, to begin with; at first.

prime² *nf* 1. *Fin: Ins:* premium 2. *Com: Adm:* (*a*) subsidy, grant; bonus; **p. de rendement**, productivity bonus (*b*) free gift.

primer [prime] 1. *vtr & i* to take precedence over (s.o., sth); to be of prime importance 2. *vtr* to award a prize to (s.o., sth).

primesautier, -ière [primsotje, -jɛr] *a* spontaneous, impulsive.

primeur [primœr] *nf* 1. **avoir la p. d'une nouvelle**, to be the first to hear a piece of news 2. **cultiver des primeurs**, to grow early vegetables, fruit; **marchand de primeurs**, greengrocer.

primevère [primvɛr] *nf Bot:* primula; **p. à grandes fleurs**, primrose.

primitif, -ive [primitif, -iv] *a* (*a*) primitive, primeval, original, earliest; **couleurs primitives**, primary colours; *nm Art:* **les primitifs**, the primitives (*b*) first, original (*c*) primitive, crude (customs). **primitivement** *adv* originally.

primo [primo] *adv* firstly, first (of all).

primordial, -aux [primɔrdjal, -o] *a* essential, of prime necessity.

prince [prɛ̃s] *nm* prince; **p. héritier**, crown prince; **être bon p.**, to be generous. **princier, -ière** *a* princely.

princesse [prɛ̃sɛs] *nf* princess; *F:* **aux frais de la p.**, at the government's, at the firm's, expense; on the house.

principal, -aux [prɛ̃sipal, -o] 1. *a* principal, chief, leading (person, thing); main (object); major (role); **associé p.**, senior partner 2. *nm* (*a*) principal, chief; head(master); head clerk (*b*) principal thing, main point; **c'est le p.**, that's the main thing (*c*) *Com:* principal; capital sum. **principalement** *adv* principally, chiefly.

principauté [prɛ̃sipote] *nf* principality.

principe [prɛ̃sip] *nm* principle; **par p.**, on principle; **en p.**, as a rule; in principle; **avoir pour p. de**, to make it a matter of principle to; **partir du p. que**, to work on the assumption that.

printemps [prɛ̃tɑ̃] *nm* spring, springtime; **au p.**, in (the) spring. **printanier, -ière** *a* spring; springlike.

priorité [prijɔrite] *nf* priority; *Aut:* **p. (de passage)**, right of way; *PN:* **p. à droite** = give way (to vehicles coming from the right); **route à p.**, major road. **prioritaire** *a* having priority; *Aut:* having right of way.

pris [pri] a 1. (a) (of seat) occupied; taken; **tout est pris,** everything is booked; **avoir les mains prises,** to have one's hands full (b) (of pers) busy, occupied 2. (a) p. de peur, panic-stricken; p. de boisson, under the influence of drink (b) blocked (nose); sore (throat) 3. (of jelly) set; (of river) frozen over.

prise [priz] nf 1. (a) hold, grasp, grip; (to lift) purchase; **avoir p. sur qn,** to have a hold over s.o.; **lâcher p.,** to let go; **donner p. aux reproches,** to lay oneself open to reproaches (b) **être aux prises avec qn,** to grapple with s.o.; **en p.,** in gear; Aut: **en p. (directe),** in top gear; **p. directe,** direct drive 2. congealing, setting 3. taking; capture; **la p. de la Bastille,** the fall of the Bastille; **p. d'otages,** taking of hostages; **p. de vues,** taking of photographs; Cin: TV: shooting; Cin: TV: **p. de vue,** shot; take; **p. de son,** sound recording 4. (thing taken) catch (of fish); dose (of medicine); sample (of ore); Med: **p. de sang,** blood sample 5. Mch: etc: **p. d'air,** air inlet, air intake; **p. d'eau,** intake of water; El: **p. de courant,** plug; (power) point; **p. de terre,** earth, NAm: ground.

priser [prize] 1. vtr & i to take snuff 2 vtr to prize, to value (sth).

prisme [prism] nm prism.

prison [prizɔ̃] nf 1. prison, jail; **aller en p.,** to go to prison, to jail 2. imprisonment; **faire de la p.,** to serve a prison sentence. **prisonnier, -ière** [prizɔnje, -jɛr] n prisoner.

privation [privasjɔ̃] nf 1. deprivation; **p. de la vue,** loss of sight 2. privation, hardship.

privautés [privote] nfpl liberties.

privé [prive] 1. (a) private (person, enterprise); inside (information); unofficial (visit) 2. nm private life; Ind: **le p.,** the private sector; **en p.,** in private; **dans le p.,** (i) in private life (ii) in a private firm.

priver [prive] 1. vtr to deprive (s.o. of sth); **je ne vous en prive pas?** can you spare it? 2. **se p. de qch,** to do without, to go without, sth; to deprive oneself of sth; to deny oneself sth.

privilège [privilɛʒ] nm (a) privilege; prerogative (b) licence, grant; (bank) charter. **privilégié** a (a) privileged (b) licensed; Fin: **banque privilégiée,** chartered bank; **action privilégiée,** preference share.

privilégier [privileʒje] vtr (pr sub & impf n. privilégiions) to privilege.

prix [pri] nm 1. (a) value, worth, cost; **à tout p.,** at all costs; **faire qch. à p. d'argent,** to do sth for money; **se vendre à p. d'or,** to fetch huge prices; **à aucun p.,** not at any price; **au p. de,** at the expense of (b) price; **p. courant,** market price; **p. de revient,** cost price; **je vous ferai un p. (d'ami),** I'll let you have it cheap; **repas à p. fixe,** set price meal; **articles de p.,** expensive goods; **c'est hors de p.,** the price is prohibitive; **ça n'a pas de p.,** it's priceless; **mettre à p. la tête de qn,** to put a price on s.o.'s head; (at auction) **mise à p.,** reserve price (c) charge; **p. du voyage,** fare 2. (a) reward, prize; **le p. Nobel,** the Nobel Prize (b) (pers) prizewinner (c) prizewinning book (d) Sp: race; Aut: **grand p. (automobile),** grand prix.

probabilité [prɔbabilite] nf probability, likelihood.

probable [prɔbabl] a probable, likely; **peu p.,** unlikely. **probablement** adv probably.

probant [prɔbɑ̃] a convincing.

probité [prɔbite] nf probity, integrity.

problème [prɔblɛm] nm problem; issue; Mth: problem, sum; F: **il n'y a pas de p.,** (i) no problem (ii) naturally! of course! **problématique** a problematical.

procédé [prɔsede] nm 1. proceeding, dealing, conduct; **procédés honnêtes,** (i) courteous behaviour (ii) square dealing 2. process; method (of working); **p. de fabrication,** manufacturing process.

procéder [prɔsede] v (je procède, n. procédons) 1. vi (a) to proceed (de, from); to originate (de, in) (b) to proceed, act 2. v ind tr **p. à une enquête,** to conduct an enquiry.

procédure [prɔsedyr] nf Jur: procedure; proceedings.

procès [prɔsɛ] nm (legal) proceedings; action; **p. civil,** lawsuit; **p. criminel,** (criminal) trial; **intenter un p. à qn,** (i) to bring an action against s.o.; to sue s.o. (ii) to prosecute s.o.; **gagner, perdre, son p.,** to win, to lose, one's case; **faire le p. de qn,** to criticize s.o.

procession [prɔsesjɔ̃] nf procession.

processus [prɔsesys] nm process; method.

procès-verbal [prɔseverbal] nm 1. (official) report; minute(s) (of meeting); record (of evidence) 2. policeman's report (about an offence); **dresser un p.-v. contre qn,** to book s.o.; pl procès-verbaux.

prochain [prɔʃɛ̃] 1. a (a) nearest (village) (b) next; **dimanche p.,** next Sunday; **le mois p.,** next month; **la p. fois,** next time; **au revoir, à une prochaine fois!** goodbye, see you (some time)! (c) near; immediate; **dans un avenir p.,** in the near future 2. nm neighbour, fellow being. **prochainement** adv soon, shortly.

proche [prɔʃ] 1. adv **tout p.,** close by, nearby; close at hand; **de p. en p.,** gradually; step by step; **p. de la ruine,** on the verge of ruin 2. a near (de, to); neighbouring; **la ville la plus p.,** the nearest town; **ses proches (parents),** his close relations; **ils sont proches parents,** they are closely related.

Proche-Orient [prɔʃɔrjɑ̃] Prnm Geog: (the) Near East.

proclamation [prɔklamasjɔ̃] nf proclamation; declaration.

proclamer [prɔklame] vtr to proclaim, declare, publish; to announce (results).

procréer [prɔkree] vtr to procreate.

procuration [prɔkyrasjɔ̃] nf Com: Fin: Jur: procuration, proxy, power of attorney.

procurer [prɔkyre] vtr & pr **p. qch à qn,** to procure, obtain, get, sth for s.o.; **se p. de l'argent,** to raise, obtain, money; **où peut-on se p. ce livre?** where can one buy this book?

procureur [prɔkyrœr] nm **p. de la République** = public prosecutor; **p. général** = Attorney General.

prodigalité [prɔdigalite] nf prodigality; extravagance.

prodige [prɔdiʒ] 1. nm prodigy, wonder, marvel; **faire des prodiges,** to work wonders; **tenir du p.,** to have a miraculous quality; **c'est un p.,** (i) he's a prodigy (ii) it's prodigious 2. a **enfant p.,** infant prodigy. **prodigieux, -euse** a prodigious, extraordinary; phenomenal, stupendous. **prodigieusement** adv prodigiously; stupendously.

prodigue [prɔdig] 1. a prodigal, wasteful (de, of);

être p. de son argent, to be free with one's money; *B:* l'enfant p., the prodigal son 2. *n* spendthrift.

prodiguer [prodige] *vtr* (*a*) to be prodigal, lavish, of (sth); p. qch à qn, to lavish sth on s.o. (*b*) to waste, squander.

producteur, -trice [prodyktœr, -tris] 1. *a* productive (de, of); producing; pays p. de blé, wheat-growing country 2. *n* producer.

production [prodyksjɔ̃] *nf* 1. (*a*) production; exhibition (of documents) (*b*) producing; production; generation (of electricity); augmenter la p., to increase the output; *Cin:* directeur de p., producer 2. (*a*) product; p. littéraire, literary output (*b*) yield (of mine).

productivité [prodyktivite] *nf* productivity.

produire [produir] (*conj like* CONDUIRE) 1. *vtr* (*a*) to produce, bring forward (evidence) (*b*) to produce, yield; to bring forth (offspring); to generate (heat) (*c*) to produce, bring about (result, effect) (*d*) to produce (film) 2. se p. (*a*) to occur, happen; to take place (*b*) (*of actor*) to appear.

produit [produi] *nm* 1. (*a*) product; produits agricoles, farm produce; produits chimiques, chemicals; produits de beauté, cosmetics; *PolEc:* p. national brut, gross national product (*b*) yield; p. d'une vente, proceeds of a sale; p. de la journée, day's takings; le p. de 10 ans de travail, the result of 10 years' work 2. *Mth:* product.

proéminent [proeminɑ̃] *a* prominent.

prof [prof] *n F:* = PROFESSEUR.

profanateur, -trice [profanatœr, -tris] *n* profaner.

profanation [profanasjɔ̃] *nf* profanation; desecration. **profane** 1. *a* profane; secular (music); unhallowed 2. *n* uninitiated person; layman.

profaner [profane] *vtr* 1. to profane; to desecrate (church); to violate (grave) 2. to misuse, degrade (talent).

proférer [profere] *vtr* (je profère; je proférerai) to utter.

professer [profese] *vtr* 1. to profess (opinion, religion); to hold (views) 2. to teach; to be a professor of, a lecturer in (a subject).

professeur [profesœr] *nm* (school)teacher; (school)-master, -mistress; (*at univérsity*) (i) professor (ii) lecturer; p. de piano, piano teacher.

profession [profesjɔ̃] *nf* 1. profession (of faith); faire p. de qch, to profess sth 2. profession, occupation; business, trade. **professionnel, -elle** 1. *a* professional; vocational (training); occupational (disease) 2. *n* professional.

professorat [profesora] *nm* 1. teaching post; professorship 2. *coll* teaching (profession). **professoral, -aux** *a* professorial.

profil [profil] *nm* 1. profile; de p., in profile 2. profile, contour, outline; section; p. en travers, cross section.

profiler [profile] 1. *vtr* (*a*) to profile; to draw (sth) in section (*b*) to shape (a piece) (*c*) to streamline (car) 2. se p., to be outlined, silhouetted (à, sur, contre, on, against).

profit [profi] *nm* profit, benefit; vendre à p., to sell at a profit; mettre qch à p., to turn sth to good account; tirer p. de qch, (i) to take advantage of sth

(ii) to make use of sth; au p. des pauvres, in aid of the poor.

profiter [profite] *vi* 1. p. de qch, to take advantage of sth; to turn sth to good account; p. de l'occasion, to seize the opportunity 2. p. à qn, to benefit s.o. 3. (*of child, plant*) to thrive, grow. **profitable** *a* profitable; beneficial. **profitablement** *adv* profitably.

profiteur, -euse [profitœr, -øz] *n* profiteer.

profond [profɔ̃] 1. *a* (*a*) deep (well, lake; voice); peu p., shallow (*b*) deep-seated, underlying (cause) (*c*) profound; thorough (knowledge); deep (sleep); heavy (sigh) 2. *adv* creuser p., to dig deep 3. *nm* au plus p. de mon cœur, in my heart of hearts; au plus p. de la nuit, at dead of night. **profondément** *a* deeply, profoundly; dormir p., to sleep soundly; s'incliner p., to make a low bow.

profondeur [profɔ̃dœr] *nf* 1. depth (of water); en p., in depth; peu de p., shallowness 2. profoundness, profundity; depth (of feeling).

profusion [profyzjɔ̃] *nf* profusion; abundance; wealth (of ideas); des bouteilles à p., bottles galore.

progéniture [progenityr] *nf* offspring.

programmation [programasjɔ̃] *nf Cmptr:* programming.

programmeur, -euse [programœr, -øz] *n* (*pers*) (computer) programmer.

programme [program] *nm* (*a*) programme (*b*) *Sch:* p. (d'études), curriculum; syllabus; les auteurs au p., the set books (*c*) *Cmptr:* program(me).

programmer [programe] *vtr Cmptr: TV: etc:* to program(me).

progrès [progre] *nm* progress; improvement; faire des p., to improve.

progresser [progrese] *vi* to progress, advance; to make headway (*b*) to improve; to gain ground. **progressif, -ive** *a* progressive. **progressivement** *adv* progressively.

progression [progresjɔ̃] *nf* progress(ion); advance(ment).

prohiber [proibe] *vtr* to prohibit, forbid. **prohibitif, -ive** *a* prohibitory (law); prohibitive (price).

prohibition [proibisjɔ̃] *nf* prohibition.

proie [prwa] *nf* prey; *Ven:* quarry; oiseau de p., bird of prey; être la p. de qn, de qch, to fall prey to s.o., to sth; être en p. aux remords, to be tormented by remorse.

projecteur [projɛktœr] *nm* (*a*) (film) projector (*b*) searchlight; floodlight; *Th:* spotlight.

projectile [projɛktil] *nm* projectile; missile.

projection [projɛksjɔ̃] *nf* 1. (*a*) projection; throwing forward, up, out (*b*) *Cin: etc:* projection; appareil de p., (slide, film) projector; cabine de p., projection room; conférence avec projections, lecture (illustrated) with slides 2. *Mth: Arch:* projection, plan; p. horizontale, ground plan.

projectionniste [projɛksjɔnist] *n Cin:* projectionist.

projet [proje] *nm* (*a*) plan, project; scheme; former le p. de, to plan to (*b*) plan (of building); draft (of novel); p. de loi, bill; en p., at the planning stage.

projeter [proj(ə)te] *v* (je projette, n. projetons) 1. *vtr* (*a*) to project; to throw, to cast (shadow); to throw up, throw off; to send out (smoke) (*b*) to show, screen (film) (e) to plan (journey) **2. se p.,** to project, stand out; (of shadow) to fall, to be cast (**sur,** on).

prolétaire [prɔleter] a & nm proletarian.

prolétariat [prɔletarja] nm proletariat. **prolétarien, -ienne** a proletarian.

prolifération [prɔliferasjɔ̃] nf proliferation. **prolifique** a prolific.

proliférer [prɔlifere] vi (**il prolifère**) to proliferate.

prologue [prɔlɔg] nm prologue (**de,** to).

prolongation [prɔlɔ̃gasjɔ̃] nf prolongation (in time); lengthening (of stay); extension (of leave); *Fb:* **prolongations,** extra time.

prolongement [prɔlɔ̃ʒmɑ̃] nm (a) continuation; extension (of wall) (b) pl developments (of action).

prolonger [prɔlɔ̃ʒe] v (**n. prolongeons**) **1.** vtr to prolong, extend; to protract, draw out, spin out (argument); **visite très prolongée,** protracted visit; *Mth:* **p. une droite,** to continue a line **2. se p.,** to be prolonged; to continue, extend. **prolongé** a prolonged.

promenade [prɔmnad] nf **1.** (a) walking (b) walk; stroll; outing (in car); **faire une p. (à pied),** to go for a walk; **faire une p. à cheval,** to go riding; **p. en vélo,** cycle ride; **p. en bateau,** row, sail; **une p. en voiture,** to go for a drive **2.** promenade, (public) walk; parade.

promener [prɔmne] v (**je promène**) **1.** vtr (a) to take (s.o.) (out) for a walk, a drive (b) to take, lead, (s.o.) about; to take (dog) for a walk; to exercise (horse); **cela vous promènera un peu,** that will get you out a bit (c) **p. sa main sur qch,** to pass, run, one's hand over sth; **p. ses yeux sur qch,** to run one's eye(s) over sth **2. se p.** (a) to walk; to go for a walk, for a drive; *F:* **envoyer p. qn,** to send s.o. packing (b) (of eyes, thoughts) to wander.

promeneur, -euse [prɔmnœr, -øz] n walker, stroller.

promesse [prɔmɛs] nf **1.** promise; **faire une p.,** to make a promise; **plein de promesses,** very promising **2.** *Com:* **p. d'achat,** undertaking to buy.

promettre [prɔmɛtr] v (conj like METTRE) **1.** vtr (a) to promise; **p. qch à qn,** to promise s.o. to do sth; *F:* **je vous promets qu'on s'est amusé,** we had a great time (b) **le temps promet de la chaleur,** it looks as though it will be hot (c) vi **enfant qui promet,** child who shows promise; *F:* **ça promet!** that's a good start! **2 se p. qch,** to promise oneself sth; **se p. de travailler,** to resolve to work.

promontoire [prɔmɔ̃twar] nm *Geog:* promontory; headland, cape.

promoteur, -trice [prɔmɔtœr, -tris] n (a) promoter, originator (**de,** of) (b) *Sp:* promoter, organizer (c) **p. (de construction),** property developer.

promotion [prɔmɔsjɔ̃] nf **1.** promotion; **p. à l'ancienneté,** promotion by seniority **2.** coll *Sch:* (students of the same) year; *NAm:* = class **3.** *Com:* (**article en) p.,** (item on) special offer. **promotionnel, -elle** a promotional; on (special) offer.

promouvoir [prɔmuvwar] vtr (conj like MOUVOIR) to promote (**à,** to).

prompt [prɔ̃] a prompt, quick, ready; swift; hasty. **promptement** adv promptly, quickly.

promptitude [prɔ̃tityd] nf promptness; quickness; swiftness.

promu, -ue [prɔmy] a & n (person) who has been promoted.

promulguer [prɔmylge] vtr to promulgate.

prôner [prone] vtr (a) to extol (b) to recommend (sth).

pronom [prɔnɔ̃] nm *Gram:* pronoun. **pronominal, -aux** a pronominal.

prononcé [prɔnɔ̃se] a pronounced, marked (taste, feature); **nez p.,** large nose; **accent p.,** strong accent; **peu p.,** faint.

prononcer [prɔnɔ̃se] vtr (**je prononçai(s); n. prononçons**) **1.** vtr (a) to utter, say (word); **il ne faut jamais p. son nom,** you must never mention his name; **sans p. un mot,** without (saying) a word (b) to deliver, make (speech); *Jur:* to pronounce (sentence) (c) to pronounce (word; **mal p. un mot,** to mispronounce a word **3. se p.,** to express one's opinion; to make a decision.

prononciation [prɔnɔ̃sjasjɔ̃] nf pronunciation; **défaut de p.,** speech defect.

pronostic [prɔnɔstik] nm forecast.

pronostiquer [prɔnɔstike] vtr to forecast.

propagande [prɔpagɑ̃d] nf propaganda; publicity; *Com:* **faire de la p.,** to advertise.

propagateur, -trice [prɔpagatœr, -tris] n propagator; spreader.

propagation [prɔpagasjɔ̃] nf propagation.

propager [prɔpaʒe] v (**n. propageons**) **1.** vtr to propagate; to spread (abroad). **2. se p** (a) (of disease) to spread (b) (of light, sound) to be propagated (c) (of plant) to propagate, reproduce.

propane [prɔpan] nm propane.

propension [prɔpɑ̃sjɔ̃] nf propensity, tendency, inclination (**à,** to).

propergol [prɔpergɔl] nm (rocket) propellant.

prophète, prophétesse [prɔfɛt, prɔfetɛs] n prophet, seer, f prophetess.

prophétie [prɔfesi] nf prophesy.

prophétiser [prɔfetize] vtr to prophesy; to foretell. **prophétique** a prophetic. **prophétiquement** adv prophetically.

propice [prɔpis] a propitious (**à,** to); auspicious; favourable.

proportion [prɔpɔrsjɔ̃] nf **1.** proportion, ratio; **p. d'alcool dans un vin,** percentage of alcohol in a wine; **hors de p. avec,** out of proportion to **2.** pl size; **salle de vastes proportions,** hall of vast dimensions. **proportionnel, -elle** a proportional (**à,** to). **proportionnellement** adv proportionally, proportionately (**à,** to).

proportionné [prɔpɔrsjɔne] a **1. bien p.,** well-proportioned (body) **2.** proportionate, suited (**à,** to).

proportionner [prɔpɔrsjɔne] to proportion.

propos [prɔpo] nm **1.** purpose; intention; **de p. délibéré,** deliberately, on purpose **2.** subject, matter; **à (ce) p.,** in connection with that; while we're on the subject; **à tout p.,** at every turn; **dire qch. à p.,** to say sth to the point; **arriver fort à p.,** to arrive at just the right moment; **à p. de,** in connection with, on the subject of; **à quel p.?** in what connection? what about? **juger à p. de,** to see fit to; **à p., où est-il?** by the way, where is he? **3.** remark; pl talk.

proposer [prɔpoze] vtr **1.** to propose (plan); to propound (theory); to put forward (amendment); **p. de**

l'argent à qn, to offer s.o. money; **être proposé pour un emploi**, to be recommended for a job; **p. un candidat**, to put forward a candidate; **je lui ai proposé de le faire**, I suggested that he should do it 2. **se p.** (*a*) to offer one's services, to come forward (*b*) **se p. qch**, to have sth in view.

proposition [prɔpozisjɔ̃] *nf* 1. proposal, proposition 2. *Mth:* proposition; *Gram:* clause.

propre [prɔpr] 1. *a* (*a*) proper (meaning); *Gram:* **nom p.**, proper noun; **ce sont ses propres paroles**, those are his very words (*b*) peculiar (**à**, to); **une façon de marcher à lui propre**, his own special way of walking (*c*) with; **de mes propres yeux**, with my own eyes; **ses idées lui sont propres**, his ideas are his own; **remettre qch en main(s) propre(s)**, to deliver sth personally (*d*) appropriate, suitable, proper; **p. à qch**, adapted, fitted, suited, to sth; **p. à tout**, fit for anything (*e*) clean; neat; **p. comme un sou neuf**, as clean as a new pin; *F:* **nous voilà propres!** we're in a nice mess! **c'est du p.!** what a mess! *nm* **recopier au p.**, to make a fair copy 2. *nm* (*a*) property, attribute, nature, characteristic (of nation, pers) (*b*) **au p.**, in the literal sense, literally (*c*) **avoir qch en p.**, to possess sth in one's own right. **proprement** *adv* 1. properly; in fact; *F:* well and truly; **à p. parler**, strictly speaking; **p. dit**, actual 2. (*a*) cleanly; neatly (*b*) *F:* well; **assez p.**, tolerably well.

propre(-)à(-)rien [prɔprarjɛ̃] *n* good-for-nothing; *pl* **propres(-)à(-)rien.**

propreté [prɔprǝte] *nf* cleanliness; cleanness; neatness, tidiness.

propriétaire [prɔprieter] *n* 1. proprietor; owner; landowner 2. landlord, landlady.

propriété [prɔpriete] *nf* 1. (*a*) ownership; **p. privée**, private property; **p. littéraire**, copyright; **p. industrielle**, patent rights (*b*) property, estate; **propriétés immobilières**, real estate 2. property, characteristic (of metal, plant) 3. propriety, correctness (of language).

propulser [prɔpylse] *vtr* to propel.

propulseur [prɔpylsœr] 1. *a* propellant, propulsive 2. *nm* propeller.

propulsion [prɔpylsjɔ̃] *nf* propulsion; **à p. nucléaire**, nuclear-powered.

pro rata [prɔrata] *nm inv* **au p. de qch**, in proportion to sth.

prorogation [prɔrɔgasjɔ̃] *nf* prorogation; extension.

proroger [prɔrɔʒe] *vtr* (**n. prorogeons**) to prorogue (Parliament); to extend (time limit).

prosaïque [prɔzaik] *a* prosaic, commonplace.

prosaïquement *adv* prosaically.

proscription [prɔskripsjɔ̃] *nf* proscription, banishment; prohibition; banning.

proscrire [prɔskrir] *vtr* (*conj like* ÉCRIRE) (*a*) to proscribe, outlaw, banish (s.o.) (*b*) to prohibit, to ban.

proscrit, -ite [prɔskri, -it] *n* outlaw.

prose [proz] *nf* prose.

prospecter [prɔspɛkte] *vtr* 1. *Min:* to prospect 2. *Com:* to canvass.

prospecteur, -trice [prɔspɛktœr, -tris] *n* 1. prospector 2. canvasser.

prospection [prɔspɛksjɔ̃] *nf* 1. *Min:* prospecting 2. *Com:* canvassing.

prospectus [prɔspɛktys] *nm* 1. prospectus 2. handbill; leaflet; brochure.

prospère [prɔspɛr] *a* prosperous, thriving, flourishing.

prospérer [prɔspere] *vi* (**je prospère; je prospérerai**) to prosper, thrive.

prospérité [prɔsperite] *nf* prosperity.

prostate [prɔstat] *nf* prostate (gland).

prosterner [prɔstɛrne] 1. *vtr Lit:* to bow (head) 2. **se p.** (*a*) to prostrate oneself; to bow down (**devant**, before) (*b*) to grovel (**devant**, to). **prosterné** *a* prostrate.

prostituée [prɔstitɥe] *nf* prostitute.

prostituer [prɔstitɥe] 1. *vtr* to prostitute 2. **se p.**, to prostitute oneself.

prostitution [prɔstitysjɔ̃] *nf* prostitution.

prostration [prɔstrasjɔ̃] *nf* prostration. **prostré** *a* prostrate(d).

protecteur, -trice [prɔtɛktœr, -tris] 1. *n* (*a*) protector; guardian (*b*) patron, patroness 2. *a* (*a*) protecting (*b*) patronizing (tone).

protection [prɔtɛksjɔ̃] *nf* 1. protection (**contre**, from, against); preservation (of the environment) 2. patronage.

protectorat [prɔtɛktɔra] *nm* protectorate.

protégé, -ée [prɔteʒe] *n* favourite; protégé, *f* protégée.

protège-cahier [prɔtɛʒkaje] *nm* exercise-book cover; *pl* **protège-cahiers.**

protéger [prɔteʒe] *vtr* (**je protège, n. protégeons; je protégerai**) 1. to protect; to shelter, shield, guard (**contre**, against, from); **se p. de qch**, to protect oneself from sth 2. to patronize.

protéine [prɔtein] *nf* protein.

protestant, -ante [prɔtɛstɑ̃, -ɑ̃t] *a & n* Protestant.

protestantisme [prɔtɛstɑ̃tism] *nm* Protestantism.

protestataire [prɔtɛstater] 1. *a* (letter) of protest 2. protester.

protestation [prɔtɛstasjɔ̃] *nf* 1. protestation; declaration 2. protest.

protester [prɔtɛste] 1. *vtr* (*a*) to protest, to declare (*b*) *Com:* to protest (bill) 2. *vi* **p. de son innocence**, to protest one's innocence; **p. contre qch**, to protest against sth, to challenge sth.

prothèse [prɔtɛz] *nf* prosthesis, artificial limb; **p. dentaire**, false teeth, denture(s).

protocole [prɔtɔkɔl] *nm* protocol; etiquette; formalities. **protocolaire** *a* formal.

prototype [prɔtɔtip] *nm* prototype.

protubérance [prɔtyberɑ̃s] *nf* protuberance; bulge. **protubérant** *a* protruding, bulging.

proue [pru] *nf* prow, stem, bow(s) (of ship).

prouesse [prues] *nf* 1. *Lit:* valour 2. feat, achievement (in sport).

prouver [pruve] *vtr* 1. to prove (fact) 2. **p. sa capacité**, to give proof of (one's) capacity.

provenance [prɔvnɑ̃s] *nf* source, origin; **train en p. de Lille**, train from Lille.

provençal, -aux [prɔvɑ̃sal, -o] 1. *a & n* Provençal; of Provence 2. *nm Ling:* Provençal.

provenir [prɔvnir] *vi* (*conj like* VENIR) to proceed, arise, result, come (**de**, from); to originate (**de**, in).

proverbe [prɔvɛrb] *nm* proverb. **proverbial, -aux** *a* proverbial.

providence [prɔvidɑ̃s] *nf* providence; *Fig:* guardian angel. **providentiel, -elle** *a* providential. **providentiellement** *adv* providentially.

province [prɔvɛ̃s] *nf* 1. province 2. **la p.,** the provinces, the country; **vivre en p.,** to live in the provinces; **vie de p.,** provincial life. **provincial, -aux** *a* provincial.

proviseur [prɔvizœr] *nm Sch:* head(master) (of a *lycée*).

provision [prɔvizjɔ̃] *nf* 1. provision, store, stock, supply; **faire p. de,** to stock up with; **faire ses provisions,** to go shopping; **sac à provisions,** shopping bag 2. *Com:* funds, reserve; **chèque sans p.,** cheque without cover, *F:* dud cheque.

provisoire [prɔvizwar] 1. *a* provisional; acting (manager); temporary; **à titre p.,** provisionally; **dividende p.,** interim dividend 2. *nm* sth temporary; **s'installer dans le p.,** to treat sth temporary as permanent. **provisoirement** *adv* provisionally, temporarily.

provocateur, -trice [prɔvɔkatœr, -tris] 1. *a* provocative 2. *n* instigator.

provocation [prɔvɔkasjɔ̃] *nf* provocation.

provoquer [prɔvɔke] *vtr* 1. to provoke (s.o.) 2. to induce, instigate; **p. qn au crime,** to incite s.o. to crime 3. to cause, bring about (desired result); to give rise to (comment); to produce (response); **p. la curiosité,** to arouse curiosity; **p. le sommeil,** to induce sleep. **provocant** *a* provocative.

proxénète [prɔksenet] *nm* procurer, pimp.

proximité [prɔksimite] *nf* proximity; nearness, closeness; **à p.,** near at hand, close by; **à p. de,** close to.

prude [pryd] 1. *a* prudish 2. *nf* prude.

prudence [prydɑ̃s] *nf* prudence; carefulness; caution; wisdom; **par p.,** as a precaution. **prudent** *a* prudent; careful, cautious; wise (decision); advisable. **prudemment** *adv* prudently; carefully, cautiously.

prune [pryn] 1. *nf* plum; **p. de damas,** damson; **verre de p.,** glass of plum brandy; *P:* **pour des prunes,** for nothing; **des prunes!** no fear! not likely! 2. *a inv* plum-coloured.

pruneau, -eaux [pryno] *nm* 1. prune 2. *P:* (rifle) bullet.

prunelle [prynɛl] *nf* 1. *Bot:* sloe; **(liqueur de) p.,** sloe gin 2. pupil (of the eye); **comme la p. de ses yeux,** like the apple of one's eye.

prunellier [prynelje] *nm* blackthorn.

prunier [prynje] *nm* plum tree.

PS *abbr* 1. *post scriptum* 2. *Pol:* Parti socialiste.

psalmodier [psalmɔdje] *vi* (*pr sub & impf* n. **psalmodiions**) to chant.

psaume [psom] *nm* psalm.

pseudonyme [psødɔnim] *nm* assumed name; pen name; stage name.

psychanalyse [psikanaliz] *nf* psychoanalysis. **psychanalytique** *a* psychoanalytic.

psychanalyser [psikanalize] *vtr* to psychoanalyse.

psychanalyste [psikanalist] *n* psychoanalyst.

psychiatre [psikjatr] *n* psychiatrist.

psychiatrie [psikjatri] *nf* psychiatry. **psychiatrique** *a* psychiatric; mental (hospital).

psychique [psiʃik] *a* psychic(al).

psychologie [psikɔlɔʒi] *nf* psychology. **psychologique** *a* psychological. **psychologiquement** *adv* psychologically.

psychologue [psikɔlɔg] *n* psychologist.

psychose [psikoz] *nf* 1. *Med:* psychosis 2. obsession; obsessive fear.

puant [pɥɑ̃] *a* (*a*) stinking, foul-smelling (*b*) obnoxious (pers).

puanteur [pɥɑ̃tœr] *nf* stench; stink.

public, -ique [pyblik] 1. *a* public; open (meeting); *Adm:* **ministère p.** = public prosecutor 2. *nm* **le p.,** the public; the audience; **le grand p.,** the general public; the consumer; **en p.,** in public. **publiquement** *adv* publicly.

publication [pyblikasjɔ̃] *nf* publication.

publicité [pyblisite] *nf* (*a*) publicity; advertising; **faire de la p.,** to advertise (*b*) advertisement, *F:* ad(vert); *TV:* commercial. **publicitaire** *a* publicity, advertising; **vente p.,** promotional sale.

publier [pyblije] *vtr* (*pr sub & impf* n. **publiions**) (*a*) to publish; proclaim; (*b*) to publish (book).

puce [pys] *nf* flea; **marché aux puces, les puces,** flea market; **mettre la p. à l'oreille à qn,** to arouse s.o.'s suspicions; **jeu de puces,** tiddlywinks.

puceron [pysrɔ̃] *nm* greenfly.

pudeur [pydœr] *nf* modesty; sense of decency; **sans p.,** shameless(ly); **rougir de p.,** to blush for shame.

pudibond [pydibɔ̃] *a* easily shocked; prudish.

pudique [pydik] *a* modest; chaste. **pudiquement** *adv* modestly.

puer [pɥe] *vi* to stink, smell; **p. l'ail,** to smell of garlic.

puéricultrice [pɥerikyltris] *nf* paediatric nurse.

puériculture [pɥerikyltyr] *nf* paediatric nursing; child care.

puérilité [pɥerilite] *nf* puerility, childishness. **puéril** *a* puerile, childish.

pugilat [pyʒila] *nm* fight, brawl.

puis [pɥi] *adv* then, afterwards, next; **et p.,** and besides; **et p. c'est tout,** and that's all (there is to it); **et p. après?** (i) what then? (ii) *F:* so what?

puisard [pɥizar] *nm* cesspool.

puiser [pɥize] *vtr* to draw (water) (**à, dans,** from); **p. dans son sac,** to dip into one's bag.

puisque [pɥisk(ə)] *conj* since, as, seeing that; **p. je te dis que je l'ai vu!** but I tell you I saw it!

puissance [pɥisɑ̃s] *nf* 1. power; force (of habit); strength (of wind); power (of engine); **p. en chevaux,** horsepower; *Aut:* **p. fiscale,** engine rating 2. *Mth:* **10 (à la) p. 4,** 10 to the power of 4, 10 to the 4th 3. **avoir qn en sa p.,** to have s.o. in one's power; **p. paternelle,** parental authority 4. *Pol:* **les grandes puissances,** the great powers 5. **en p.,** potential(ly). **puissant** 1. *a* powerful, strong 2. *nm* **les puissants,** the mighty.

puits [pɥi] *nm* 1. well; hole; **p. à ciel ouvert,** open well; **p. de science,** mine of information 2. shaft, pit (of mine); **p. d'aération,** ventilation shaft.

pull(-over) [pul(ɔvɛr)] *nm Cl:* pullover, jersçy; *pl* pull-overs.

pulluler [pylyle] *vi* (*a*) to multiply rapidly (*b*) to abound; to swarm.

pulmonaire [pylmɔnɛr] *a* pulmonary; **congestion p.,** congestion of the lungs.

pulpe [pylp] *nf* pulp.

pulsation [pylsasjɔ̃] *nf* (*a*) throbbing; beating (*b*) throb; (heart)beat.

pulsion [pylsjɔ̃] *nf Psy:* impulse; drive, urge.

pulvérisateur [pylverizatœr] *nm* spray; vaporizer.

pulvérisation [pylverizasjɔ̃] *nf* (*a*) pulverization (*b*) spray(ing), vaporizing.

pulvériser [pylverize] *vtr* (*a*) to pulverize; to grind (sth) to powder (*b*) to spray, vaporize (liquid).

puma [pyma] *nm Z:* puma.

punaise [pynɛz] *nf* 1. *Ent:* bug 2. drawing pin; *NAm:* thumbtack.

punir [pynir] *vtr* to punish; **puni par la loi;** punishable by law. **punissable** *a* punishable. **punitif, -ive** *a* punitive.

punition [pynisjɔ̃] *nf* punishment.

pupille¹ [pypil] *nm* & *f Jur:* ward; **p. de la Nation,** war orphan.

pupille² *nf* pupil (of the eye).

pupitre [pypitr] *nm* 1. desk; **p. à musique,** music stand 2. *Mus:* group (of instruments); **chef de p.,** leader (of a group).

pur [pyr] *a* 1. pure; indiluted (wine); neat, straight (whisky); **la pure vérité,** the plain, the simple, truth; **p. hasard,** mere chance; **c'est de la folie p.,** it's sheer madness; **en p. perte,** for nothing 2. pure (air); **ciel p.,** clear sky. **purement** *adv* purely.

purée [pyre] *nf Cu:* **p. (de pommes de terre),** mashed potatoes; **p. de tomates,** tomato purée; *F:* **être dans la p.,** to be in the soup.

pureté [pyrte] *nf* purity; pureness; clearness (of the sky).

purgatoire [pyrgatwar] *nm Theol:* purgatory.

purge [pyrʒ] *nf Med: Pol:* purge.

purger [pyrʒe] *v* (**n. purgeons**) 1. *vtr* (*a*) to purge, cleanse, clear (*b*) *Jur:* to serve (sentence) (*c*) *MecE:* to drain (cylinder); to bleed (pipe) 2. **se p.,** to take a purgative. **purgatif, -ive** *a* & *nm* purgative.

purification [pyrifikasjɔ̃] *nf* purification; cleansing.

purifier [pyrifje] *v* (*pr sub & impf* **n. purifiions**) 1. *vtr* to purify, cleanse; to refine (metal) 2. **se p.,** to become pure; to cleanse oneself.

purin [pyrɛ̃] *nm* liquid manure.

puritain, -aine [pyritɛ̃, -ɛn] 1. *n* puritan 2. *a* puritan(ical).

puritanisme [pyritanism] *nm* puritanism.

pur-sang [pyrsɑ̃] *nm inv* thoroughbred.

pus [py] *nm Med:* pus.

pustule [pystyl] *nf* pustule.

putain [pytɛ̃] *nf P:* whore; **p. de voiture!** bloody car!

putois [pytwa] *nm* polecat; **p. d'Amérique,** skunk.

putréfaction [pytrefaksjɔ̃] *nf* putrefaction.

putréfier (se) [səpytrefje] to putrefy.

PV *abbr procès-verbal.*

puzzle [pœzl] *nm* jigsaw (puzzle).

pygmée [pigme] *nm* pygmy, pigmy.

pyjama [piʒama] *nm* pyjamas, *NAm:* pajamas; **un p.,** a pair of pyjamas.

pylône [pilon] *nm* pylon.

pyramide [piramid] *nf* pyramid.

Pyrénées (les) [lepirene] *Prnfpl Geog:* the Pyrenees. **pyrénéen, -enne** *a* Pyrenean.

pyromane [piroman] *n* pyromaniac.

python [pitɔ̃] *nm Rept:* python.

Q

Q, q [ky] *nm* (the letter) Q, q.
QG *abbr Mil:* quartier général.
QI *abbr* quotient intellectuel.
qu' = **que** before a vowel or **h** mute.
quadragénaire [kwadraʒenɛr] *a & n* quadragenarian, forty-year-old (pers).
quadrangulaire [kwadrɑ̃gylɛr] *a* quadrangular, four-cornered (building).
quadrilatère [k(w)adrilatɛr] *nm* quadrilateral.
quadrillage [kadrijaʒ] *nm* (a) square pattern, grid pattern (b) *Mil: etc:* covering (of zone).
quadriller [kadrije] *vtr* (a) to rule in squares (b) to cover, to control (zone). **quadrillé** *a* squared.
quadrimoteur, -trice [k(w)adrimɔtœr, -tris] *a & nm Av:* four-engined (aircraft).
quadripartite [kwadripartit] *a* four-power (conference).
quadriréacteur [kwadrireaktœr] *nm Av:* four-engined jet aircraft.
quadrupède [k(w)adrypɛd] *a & nm* quadruped.
quadruple [k(w)adrypl] *a & nm* quadruple, fourfold; **être payé au q.**, to be repaid fourfold; **payer le q. du prix**, to pay four times the price.
quadrupler [k(w)adryple] *vtr & i* to quadruple, to increase fourfold.
quadruplés, -ées [k(w)adryple] *npl* quadruplets, *F:* quads.
quai [ke] *nm* (a) quay, warf; pier; **à q.**, alongside the quay (b) (river) embankment (c) *Rail:* platform; **le train est à q.**, the train's in; *P.N:* **accès aux quais** = to the trains.
qualification [kalifikasjɔ̃] *nf* (a) designation, title (b) qualification; *Sp:* **obtenir sa q.**, to qualify.
qualifier [kalifje] *v* (*impf & pr sub* **n. qualifiions**) 1. *vtr* (a) to style, term, qualify; **acte qualifié de crime**, action termed a crime; **q. qn de menteur**, to call s.o. a liar (b) *Gram:* to qualify (c) **q. qn à faire qch**, to qualify s.o. to do sth 2. **se q.** (a) **se q. colonel**, to call oneself colonel (b) *Sp:* to qualify (**pour**, for). **qualificatif, -ive** *Gram:* 1. *a* qualifying 2. *nm* qualifier. **qualifié** *a* (a) qualified; skilled (worker); **non q.**, unskilled (b) *Jur:* aggravated (offense).
qualité [kalite] *nf* 1. (a) quality; **de bonne q.**, of good quality (b) (good) quality; **produit de q.**, high-quality product 2. quality, property (of sth) 3. qualification, capacity; profession, occupation; *Adm:* **nom, prénom et q.**, surname, first name and occupation or description; **agir en q. d'avocat**, to act (in one's capacity) as a barrister; **avoir les qualités requises pour un emploi**, to have the necessary qualifications for a job; **avoir q. pour agir**, to have authority to act. **qualitatif, -ive** *a* qualitative.
quand [kɑ̃] 1. *conj* (a) when; **je lui en parlerai q. je le verrai**, I'll mention it to him when I see him; *F:* **q. je vous le disais!** didn't I tell you so! (b) **q. (même)**, even if, even though, although; **q. bien même**, even

if; **je le ferai q. même**, I'll do it all the same 2. *adv* **q. viendra-t-il?** when will he come? **à q. le mariage?** when will the wedding be? **depuis q. êtes-vous à Paris?** how long, since when, have you been in Paris? **de q. est ce journal?** what is the date of this paper? **c'est pour q.?** when is it for?
quant à [kɑ̃ta] *adv phr* **q. à moi**, as for me; **q. à cela**, as to that; for that matter; **q. à l'avenir**, as for the future.
quantité [kɑ̃tite] *nf* quantity, amount; **en q.**, in bulk; **des fruits en q.**, plenty of fruit; **en grande q., en q. industrielle**, in large quantities; **q., des quantités, de gens**, a great many, a great number, a lot of people. **quantitatif, -ive** *a* quantitative.
quarantaine [karɑ̃tɛn] *nf* 1. (about) forty, some forty; **approcher de la q.**, to be getting on for forty 2. quarantine; **mettre en q.**, (i) to quarantine (ii) to send (s.o.) to Coventry.
quarante [karɑ̃t] *num a inv & nm inv* forty; *F:* **je m'en fiche comme de l'an q.**, I don't care a damn. **quarantième** *num a & n* fortieth.
quart [kar] *nm* 1. (a) quarter, fourth part; **donner un q. de tour à une vis**, to give a screw a quarter turn; *Aut:* **partir au q. de tour**, to start first time; *Com:* **remise du q.**, 25% discount; **q. d'heure**, quarter of an hour; **passer un mauvais q. d'heure**, to have a bad time of it; **il est deux heures et q., un q.**, it's a quarter past two; **trois quarts**, three quarters; **cinq heures moins le q.**, a quarter to five; *Sp:* **q. de finale**, quarter final (b) **un q. de beurre**, a quarter of a kilo of butter (c) quarter litre, *NAm:* liter, bottle; *Mil:* quarter litre mug 2. *Nau:* watch; **être de q.**, to be on watch.
quartette [kwartɛt] *nm* jazz quartet(te).
quartier [kartje] *nm* 1. quarter, fourth part; *Cu:* quarter (of lamb, beef) 2. part, piece, portion; segment (of orange); plot (of land); **mettre qch en quartiers**, to tear sth to pieces 3. (a) district, neighbourhood; **q. des spectacles**, theatreland; **je ne suis pas du q.**, I don't live round here; **de q.**, local (b) *Mil:* **rentrer au q.**, to return to quarters, barracks; **Q. général**, headquarters 4. **faire q. à qn**, to give s.o. quarter.
quartz [kwarts] *nm* quartz, rock crystal.
quasi [kazi] *adv* quasi, almost; **q. aveugle**, almost blind; **j'en ai la q.-certitude**, I'm practically certain of it.
quatorze [katɔrz] *num a inv & nm inv* fourteen; **le q. juillet**, the fourteenth of July. **quatorzième** *num a & n* fourteenth.
quatrain [katrɛ̃] *nm* quatrain.
quatre [katr] *num a inv & nm inv* four; **le q. août**, the fourth of August; **habiter au (numéro) q.**, to live at number four; **monter l'escalier q. à q.**, to rush upstairs four at a time; **un de ces q. matins**, *F:* **un de ces q.**, one of these days; **il se mettrait en q. pour vous**, he would do anything for you. **quatrième** 1. *num a & n* fourth; **habiter au q. (étage)**, to live on

the fourth, *NAm:* fifth, floor **2.** *nf Aut:* fourth gear; *Sch:* = *approx* third form (of secondary school).

Quatre-Cantons [katr(ə)kɑ̃tɔ̃] *Prnmpl Geog:* **lac des Q.-C.,** Lake Lucerne.

quatre-vingt-dix [katrəvɛ̃dis] *num inv a & nm inv* ninety. **quatre-vingt-dixième** *num a & n* ninetieth.

quatre-vingts [katrəvɛ̃] *num a & nm* (*omits the final* **s** *when followed by a num a or when used as an ordinal*) eighty; **page q.-vingt,** page eighty; **quatre-vingt-un,** eighty-one. **quatre-vingtième** *num a & n* eightieth.

quatuor [kwatyɔr] *nm Mus:* quartet(te).

que[1] [k(ə)] *rel pron* **1.** (*of pers*) that, whom; (*of thg*) that, which; (*neut*) which, what; (*in Eng often omitted*) (*subject*) **advienne q. pourra,** come what may **2.** (*attrib*) **menteur q. tu es!** you liar! **coavert qu'il était de poussière,** covered with dust as he was; **purs mensonges q. tout cela!** that's all a pack of lies! **c'est une belle maison q. la vôtre,** yours is a beautiful house **3.** (*object*) **l'homme q. vous voyez,** the man (that) you see; **les livres q. vous avez achetés,** the books you have bought; **il n'est venu personne, q. je sache,** nobody came as far as I know **4.** **les jours qu'il fait chaud,** on hot days; **depuis 3 mois q. j'habite Paris,** for the three months I have been living in Paris.

que[2] *interr pron neut* **1.** what? **q. voulez-vous?** what do you want? **q. faire?** what's to be done? what could one do? **q. dire?** what could I say? **2.** **qu'est-il arrivé? q. s'est-il passé?** what (has) happened? **3.** (*a*) (*interr*) **que ne le disiez-vous?** why didn't you say so? (*b*) (*exclamatory*) **qu'il est beau!** how handsome he is! **que de gens!** what a lot of people!

que[3] *conj* **1.** that (*often omitted in Eng*); **je désire qu'il vienne,** I want him to come; **je pense q. non,** I think not **2.** (*a*) (*imp or optative*) **qu'elle entre!** let her come in! **q. je vous y reprenne!** just let me catch you at it again! (*b*) (*hypothetical*) **qu'il pleuve ou qu'il fasse du vent,** whether it rains or blows; **q. tu le veuilles ou non,** whether you wish it or not **3.** **il l'affirmerait q. je ne le croirais pas,** even if he said it was true, I would not believe it **4.** (*a*) **approchez qu'on vous entende,** come nearer so that we can hear you; **à peine était-il rentré q. le téléphone a sonné,** he had scarcely come in when the telephone rang; **il y a trois jours q. je ne l'ai vu,** it is three days since I saw him (*b*) **quand il entrera et qu'il vous trouvera ici,** when he comes in and finds you here **5.** (*in comparison*) **aussi grand q. moi,** as tall as I (am); **tout autre q. moi,** anyone but me **6.** **ne ... que,** only; **il n'a qu'une jambe,** he has only one leg; **il ne fait qu'entrer et sortir,** he just slipped in and out again; **il n'y a pas q. lui qui le sache,** he's not the only one who knows it; **il ne me reste plus q. vingt francs,** I have only twenty francs left; **je ne bois jamais q. de l'eau,** I never drink anything but water **7.** *F:* (*a*) **q. non! q. si! q. oui!** surely not! yes indeed! (*b*) **qu'il dit!** so he says, that's what he says!

Québec [kebɛk] *Prnm* Quebec. **québécois, -oise** *a & n* Quebecer; of Quebec.

quel, quelle [kɛl] *a & pron* **1.** what, which; **q. que soit le résultat,** whatever the result may be; **quels que soient ces hommes,** whoever these men may be;

à n'importe quelle heure, at any time **2.** (*interrogative*) **quelle heure est-il?** what's the time? **q. livre lisez-vous?** which book are you reading? **de ces deux projets q. est le plus sûr?** which is the safer of these two plans? **3.** (*exclamatory*) **q. homme! what a man!**

quelconque [kɛlkɔ̃k] *a* **1.** any (whatever); **trois points quelconques,** any three points **2.** **répondre d'une façon q.,** to make some sort of reply **3.** ordinary, commonplace; poor, indifferent; **il est très q.,** he's a very ordinary sort of man; **son travail est q.,** his work is mediocre.

quelque [kɛlk(ə)] **1.** *a* (*a*) some, any; **adressez-vous à q. autre,** apply to someone else (*b*) some, a few; **il y a quelques jours,** a few days ago; **cent et quelques mètres,** a hundred metres, *NAm:* meters, plus; **quarante et quelques,** forty odd (*c*) (*correlative to* **qui, que** + *sub*) **q. ambition qui l'agite,** whatever ambition moves him; **de q. côté que vous regardiez,** whichever way you look **2.** *adv* (*a*) some, about; **q. dix ans,** some ten years (*b*) (*correlative to* **que** + *sub*) **q. grandes que soient ses fautes,** however great his faults may be.

quelque chose [kɛlkəʃoz] *indef pron m inv* something, anything; **q. c. de nouveau,** something new; **il y a q. c.,** there's something the matter; **ça m'a fait q. c.,** I felt it a good deal; *F:* **ça alors, c'est q. c.!** that's really a bit much!

quelquefois [kɛlkəfwa] *adv* sometimes; occasionally; now and then.

quelque part [kɛlkəpar] *adv* somewhere.

quelqu'un, quelqu'une [kɛlkœ̃, kɛlkyn] *pl* **quelques-uns, -unes** [kɛlkəzœ̃, -yn] *indef pron* **1.** *m & f* one (or other); **quelques-uns des magasins,** some of the shops; **quelques-un(e)s d'entre nous,** a few of us, some of us **2.** *m* someone, somebody; anyone, anybody; **q. me l'a dit,** someone told me; **q. de trop,** one too many; **q. d'autre,** someone else; *F:* **est-il q.?** is he anybody important?

quémander [kemɑ̃de] *vtr* to beg for (sth).

qu'en-dira-ton [kɑ̃diratɔ̃] *nm inv* gossip.

quenelle [kənɛl] *nf Cu:* quenelle.

querelle [kərɛl] *nf* quarrel; **querelles de famille,** family squabbles; **q. d'amoureux,** lovers' tiff.

quereller [kərɛle] **1.** *vtr* to quarrel with (s.o.) **2.** **se q.,** to quarrel. **querelleur, -euse** *a* quarrelsome.

qu'est-ce que [kɛskə] *interr pron* what? **q. q. vous voulez?** what do you want? **q. q. c'est que ça?** what's that?

qu'est-ce qui [kɛski] *interr pron* what? **q. q. est arrivé?** what's happened?

question [kɛstjɔ̃] *nf* (*a*) question, query; **poser une q. à qn,** to ask s.o. a question; **mettre qch en q.,** to question sth; to challenge (a statement) (*b*) question, matter, point, issue; **questions d'actualité,** topics of the day; **la personne en q.,** the person in question; **la q. n'est pas là,** that's not the point; **de quoi est-il q.?** what is it all about? **il est q. de lui élever une statue,** there's some talk of putting up a statue to him.

questionnaire [kɛstjɔner] *nm* questionnaire.

questionner [kɛstjɔne] *vtr* to question (s.o.); to ask (s.o.) questions.

quête [kɛt] *nf* **1.** quest, search; **se mettre en q. de qch,**

to go in search of sth **2.** collection; **faire la q.,** to take the collection; to make a collection (for sth).

quêter [kete] *vtr* to take the collection; to collect (money).

quêteur, -euse [kɛtœr, -øz] *n* collector.

queue [kø] *nf* **1.** tail; **q. de renard,** fox's brush; **q. de cheval,** pony tail; **finir en q. de poisson,** to fizzle out; *Aut:* **faire une q. de poisson à qn,** to cut in front of s.o. **2.** tail (of comet); handle (of pan); stalk (of fruit, flower); pigtail; **habit à q.,** tail coat **3.** (tail) end (of procession); rear (of train); **venir en q.,** to bring up the rear; **être à la q. de la classe,** to be at the bottom of the class; **histoire sans q. ni tête,** cock-and-bull story **4.** queue, *NAm:* line; **faire (la) q.,** to queue up; *NAm:* to stand in line **5.** (billiard) cue.

queue-de-pie [kødpi] *nf* tail coat, *F:* tails; *pl* **queues-de-pie.**

qui¹ [ki] *rel pron m & f sg & pl* **1.** *(subject)* who, that; *(of thg)* which, that; **phrase q. n'est pas française,** sentence that is not French; **vous q. êtes libres,** you who are free; **je le vois q. vient,** I see him coming **2.** *(a)* (= *celui qui*) **sauve q. peut,** every man for himself; **adressez-vous à q. vous voudrez,** apply to anyone you like *(b)* (= *ce qui*) **voilà q. me plaît,** that's what I like; *see also* **ce¹ 3.** *(after prep)* whom, *occ* which; *(may be omitted in Eng)* **voilà l'homme à q. je pensais,** there is the man of whom I was thinking, there is the man I was thinking about **4.** *indef* **on se dispersa q. d'un côté, q. d'un autre,** we scattered, some going one way, some another **5. q. que,** who(so)ever, whom(so)ever; **q. que ce soit,** anyone (whatever).

qui² *interr pron m sg* who? whom? **q. a dit cela?** who said that? **q. désirez-vous voir?** who(m) do you wish to see? **à q. est ce couteau?** whose knife is this? **q. d'autre?** who else? **de q. parlez-vous?** who are you talking about? **c'est à q. rentrera le premier,** it's a question of who will get back first; *F:* **il est là—q.? ça? q. donc?** he's there—who? **q. des deux a raison?** which of the two is right?

quiconque [kikɔ̃k] *indef pron m sg* **1.** who(so)ever; anyone who **2.** (= **qui que ce soit**) anyone (else); anybody (else).

qui est-ce que [kiɛskə] *interr pron m sg* whom? **qui est-ce que vous désirez voir?** who(m) do you wish to see?

qui est-ce qui [kiɛski] *interr pron m sg* who?

quiétude [kjetyd] *nf* peace (of mind); **en toute q.,** with an easy mind.

quille¹ [kij] *nf (a)* ninepin, skittle; **jeu de quilles,** (i) set of skittles (ii) skittle alley *(b) P:* leg, pin.

quille² *nf* keel (of ship).

quincaillerie [kɛ̃kajri] *nf* **1.** hardware, iron-mongery **2.** hardware business; ironmonger's.

quincaillier, -ière [kɛ̃kaje, -jɛr] *n* ironmonger.

quinine [kinin] *nf* quinine.

quinquagénaire [kɛ̃kaʒenɛr] *a & n* quinquagen-arian, fifty-year-old (pers).

quinquennal, -aux [kɛ̃kɛnal, -o] *a* quinquennial; five-year (plan).

quintal, -aux [kɛ̃tal, -o] *nm Meas:* quintal (= 100 kg).

quinte [kɛ̃t] *nf* **1.** *Mus:* fifth **2.** *Cards:* quint **3.** *Fenc:* quinte **4. q. de toux,** fit of coughing.

quintessence [kɛ̃tɛsɑ̃s] *nf* quintessence.

quintette [kɛ̃tɛt] *nm* quintet(te).

quintuple [kɛ̃typl] *a & nm* quintuple; fivefold.

quintuplés, -ées [kɛ̃typle] *npl* quintuplets, *F:* quins.

quintupler [kɛ̃typle] *vtr & i* to quintuple, to in-crease fivefold.

quinzaine [kɛ̃zɛn] *nf* **1.** (about) fifteen, some fifteen **2.** fortnight, two weeks.

quinze [kɛ̃z] *num a inv & nm inv* **1.** fifteen; **Louis Q.,** Louis the Fifteenth; **le q. mai,** (on) the fifteenth of May; **habiter au (numéro) q.,** to live at number fifteen; *Ten:* **q. partout,** fifteen all; *Rugby Fb:* **le q. de France,** the French fifteen **2. q. jours,** a fortnight; **aujourd'hui en q.,** a fortnight (from) today; **tous les q. jours,** once a fortnight, once every two weeks.

quinzième *num a & n* fifteenth.

quiproquo [kiprɔko] *nm (taking of one thing for another)* mistake, misunderstanding.

quittance [kitɑ̃s] *nf* receipt.

quitte [kit] *a* **1.** free, quit, rid **(de,** of); **être q. de dettes,** to be out of debt; **nous sommes quittes,** we're quits; **tenir qn q. de qch,** to let s.o. off sth; **il en a été q. pour la peur,** he got off with nothing more than a fright; **q. ou double,** double or quits **2.** *inv* **je le ferai, q. à être grondé,** I'll do it even if I'm told off.

quitter [kite] *vtr* **1. q. la partie,** to give up; to throw up the sponge **2.** to leave (place, person); to take off (one's clothes); **ne le quittez pas des yeux,** don't let him out of your sight; *Tp:* **ne quittez pas!** hold the line!

qui-vive [kiviv] *nm inv* **être sur le q.-v.,** to be on the alert.

quoi¹ [kwa] *rel pron* **1.** what; **c'est en q. vous vous trompez,** that is where you are wrong; **après q.,** after which; **sans q.,** otherwise **2. il a bien autre chose à q. penser!** he has something else to think about! **il a de q. vivre,** he has enough to live on; *F:* **il a de q.,** he's well off; **il y a de q. vous faire enrager,** it's enough to drive you mad; **il n'y a pas de q. être fier,** there's nothing to be proud of; **il n'y a pas de q.,** don't mention it; not at all; *NAm:* you're welcome! **avez-vous de q. écrire?** have you (got) anything to write with? **3.** *(correlative to* **qui, que** + *sub) (a)* **q. qu'il arrive,** whatever happens; **q. qu'il en soit,** be that as it may *(b)* **q. que ce soit,** anything (whatever).

quoi² *interr pron* what? **q. d'autre?** what else? **q. de nouveau?** what news? **eh bien! q.?** well, what about it? **de q. parlez-vous?** what are you talking about? **en q. puis-je vous être utile?** can I help you? **c'est en q.?** what is it made of? **et puis q. encore!** what next!

quoique [kwak(ə)] *conj usu* + *sub* (al)though; **quoi-qu'il soit pauvre,** although he's poor.

quolibet [kɔlibɛ] *nm* gibe, jeer.

quote-part [kɔtpar] *nf* share, quota, portion; *pl* **quotes-parts.**

quotidien, -ienne [kɔtidjɛ̃, -jɛn] **1.** *a* daily, every-day; **la vie quotidienne,** everyday life **2.** *nm* daily (paper). **quotidiennement** *adv* daily, every day.

quotient [kɔsjɑ̃] *nm* **1.** *Mth:* quotient **2. q. intellec-tuel,** intelligence quotient, I.Q.

R

R, r [ɛr] *nm* (the letter) R, r.

rabâcher [rabɑʃe] **1.** *vi* to keep repeating oneself **2.** *vtr* **ils rabâchent toujours la même chose,** they're always harping on the same string.

rabâcheur, -euse [rabɑʃœr, -øz] *n* repetitive person.

rabais [rabɛ] *nm* reduction (in price); rebate, discount; **vendre qch au r.,** to sell sth at a discount; *F:* **travail au r.,** badly paid job.

rabaisser [rabese] *vtr* **1.** (*a*) to lower (sth); to reduce (price) (*b*) to disparage, belittle (s.o., sth) **2. se r.,** to lower, disparage, oneself.

rabat [raba] *nm* flap (of table, pocket).

rabat-joie [rabaʒwa] *nm inv* killjoy, spoilsport.

rabattage [rabataʒ] *nm* beating (for game).

rabatteur, -euse [rabatœr, -øz] *n* (*a*) beater (*b*) tout.

rabattre [rabatr] *v* (*conj like* BATTRE) **1.** *vtr* (*a*) to fold back; to shut down (lid); to lower (blind); to turn down (collar); to press down (seam); **porte rabattue contre le mur,** door folded back to the wall; **le vent rabat la fumée,** the wind drives down the smoke (*b*) to reduce, lessen; **r. 100 francs du prix,** to take 100 francs off the price; **r. l'orgueil de qn,** to humble s.o.'s pride; *Knit:* **r. les mailles,** to cast off (*c*) to drive (game) **2. se r.** (*a*) (*of table*) to fold (*b*) **se r. sur,** to fall back on (*c*) *Aut:* to cut in (after overtaking). **rabattable** *a* **siège r.,** folding seat.

rabbin [rabɛ̃] *nm Rel:* rabbi.

rabiot [rabjo] *nm P:* (*a*) extra food (*b*) extra time.

râblé [rable] *a* broad-backed.

rabot [rabo] *nm Tls:* plane.

raboter [rabote] *vtr* (*a*) to plane (wood) (*b*) to scrape (surface). **raboteux, -euse** *a* rough, uneven (surface).

rabougri [rabugri] *a* stunted (person, plant); shrivelled.

rabrouer [rabrue] *vtr* to snub (s.o.), to brush (s.o.) off.

racaille [rakaj] *nf* rabble, riff-raff.

raccommodage [rakɔmɔdaʒ] *nm* (*a*) mending, repairing; darning (*b*) mend, repair; darn.

raccommoder [rakɔmɔde] *vtr* **1.** to mend, repair; to darn (sock) **2.** to reconcile (two persons); **ils se sont raccommodés,** they made it up.

raccord [rakɔr] *nm* **1.** join; **faire des raccords (de peinture),** to touch up (the paintwork) **2.** (*a*) connection, coupling; joint (*b*) *Cin:* link scene.

raccordement [rakɔrdəmɑ̃] *nm* joining; linking up; connecting.

raccorder [rakɔrde] *vtr* to join (up), to connect; to link up.

raccourci [rakursi] *nm* (*a*) abridgement (*b*) **en r.,** (i) briefly (ii) in miniature (*c*) short cut.

raccourcir [rakursir] **1.** *vtr* (*a*) to shorten; to take up (sleeve) (*b*) to abridge, curtail; to cut short **2.** *vi*

& *pr* to grow shorter; to shrink.

raccourcissement [rakursismɑ̃] *nm* shortening.

raccrocher [rakrɔʃe] **1.** *vtr* (*a*) to hook up, to hang (sth) up, again; *vi Tp:* to hang up, to ring off (*b*) *F:* to get hold of (sth, s.o.) **2. se r. à qch,** to catch hold of, to grab hold of, sth; to cling to, to hang on to (pers, hope).

race [ras] *nf* **1.** race; descent, ancestry; **de r. noble,** of noble blood **2.** race, stock, breed; **chien de r.,** pedigree dog; **cheval de r.,** thoroughbred horse; (*of pers*) **avoir de la r.,** to be distinguished, aristocratic. **racé** *a* pure bred, thoroughbred; aristocratic (pers).

rachat [raʃa] *nm* (*a*) repurchase, buying back (*b*) *Ins:* surrender (of policy) (*c*) atonement (for a sin).

racheter [raʃte] *v* (*conj like* ACHETER) **1.** *vtr* (*a*) to repurchase; to buy back; to buy in (*b*) to redeem (debt, pledge); to ransom (prisoner); to redeem; to atone (for one's sins) (*c*) *Ins:* to surrender (policy) (*d*) to buy some more of (sth) **2. se r.,** to redeem oneself; to make amends.

rachitisme [raʃitism] *nm Med:* rickets. **rachitique** *a* rickety.

racial, -aux [rasjal, -o] *a* racial.

racine [rasin] *nf* (*a*) root; **prendre r.,** to take root (*b*) *Mth:* **r. carrée,** square root.

racisme [rasism] *nm* racialism. **raciste** *a* & *n* rac(ial)ist.

raclée [rakle] *nf F:* hiding, thrashing, licking.

racler [rakle] *vtr* to scrape (away, off); **se r. la gorge,** to clear one's throat.

racolage [rakɔlaʒ] *nm* soliciting.

racoler [rakɔle] *vtr* to solicit.

racontar [rakɔ̃tar] *nm F:* story, piece of gossip.

raconter [rakɔ̃te] *vtr* to tell, relate, recount; **qu'est-ce qu'il raconte?** what's he talking about, what's he saying?

racorni [rakɔrni] *a* hardened; shrivelled.

radar [radar] *nm* radar.

rade [rad] *nf Nau:* roadstead, roads; **navire en r.,** ship in harbour; **mettre qn en r., qch en r.,** to leave s.o. in the lurch; to shelve (sth).

radeau, -eaux [rado] *nm* raft.

radiateur [radjatœr] *nm* (*a*) radiator; **r. électrique,** electric fire; **r. soufflant,** fan heater (*b*) *Aut: etc:* radiator.

radiation [radjasjɔ̃] *nf* **1.** *Ph:* radiation **2.** crossing out, crossing off; striking off.

radical, -aux [radikal, -o] *a* & *nm* radical. **radicalement** *adv* radically.

radier [radje] *vtr* (*impf* & *pr sub* **n. radiions**) to cross off, strike off (a list).

radieux, -euse [radjø, -øz] *a* radiant; beaming; dazzling (sky); brilliant (sunshine).

radin [radɛ̃] *a* & *nm P:* mean, stingy (person).

radio [radjo] *F:* **1.** *nm* (*a*) radio(gram) (*b*) radio operator **2.** *nf* (*a*) radio, wireless; **à la r.,** on the radio;

passer à la r., to broadcast; to go on the air, on the radio (b) radiotelegraphy (c) radio (set) (d) X-ray photograph; **passer à la r., passer une r.,** to be X-rayed.

radioactivité [radjoaktivite] *nf* radioactivity. **radioactif, -ive** *a* radioactive.

radiodiffuser [radjodifyze] *vtr WTel:* to broadcast.

radiodiffusion [radjodifysjɔ̃] *nf WTel:* broadcasting.

radioélectricien, -ienne [radjoelɛktrisjɛ̃, -jɛn] *n* radio (and television) technician.

radiogramme [radjogram] *nm* radiogram.

radiographie [radjografi] *nf* (a) radiography; X-ray photography (b) X-ray photograph.

radiographier [radjografje] *vtr* (*impf & pr sub* **n. radiographiions**) to X-ray.

radioguidage [radjogidaʒ] *nm Av: Nau:* radio control.

radiologie [radjoloʒi] *nf* radiology.

radiologue [radjolog] *n* radiologist.

radiophonie [radjofoni] *nf* radiotelephony.

radioreportage [radjoreportaʒ] *nm WTel:* broadcasting (of news); running commentary.

radioreporter [radjoreporter] *nm WTel:* reporter, commentator.

radioscopie [radjoskopi] *nf* radioscopy.

radiotélévisé [radjotelevize] *a* broadcast on radio and television.

radis [radi] *nm* radish; *F:* **je n'ai pas un r.,** I haven't got a penny.

radium [radjom] *nm* radium.

radotage [radotaʒ] *nm* drivel.

radoter [radote] *vi* to (talk) drivel; to ramble on.

radoteur, -euse [radotœr, -øz] *n* dotard.

radoucir [radusir] 1. *vtr* to calm, soften; to smooth (s.o.) down; to mollify (s.o.) 2. **se r.,** to calm down; (*of weather*) to grow milder.

radoucissement [radysismɑ̃] *nm* (a) softening; calming down (b) milder spell (of weather).

rafale [rafal] *nf* (a) squall; strong gust (of wind) (b) burst (of gunfire).

raffermir [rafɛrmir] 1. *vtr* to strengthen; to steady (nerves) 2. **se r.,** to grow stronger; to grow steadier.

raffinage [rafinaʒ] *nm* (sugar, oil) refining.

raffinement [rafinmɑ̃] *nm* refinement; sophistication.

raffiner [rafine] *vtr* (a) to refine (sugar, oil) (b) to polish (style, manners).

raffinerie [rafinri] *nf* refinery.

raffineur, -euse [rafinœr, -øz] *n* (oil, sugar) refiner.

raffoler [rafole] *vi* **r. de qch,** to be excessively fond of, *F:* to adore, sth.

raffut [rafy] *nm F:* noise, row.

rafiot [rafjo] *nm Nau:* (old) tub.

rafistoler [rafistole] *vtr F:* to patch (sth) up.

rafle [rafl̩] *nf* (police) round-up, raid.

rafler [rafle] *vtr F:* to swipe.

rafraîchir [rafreʃir] 1. *vtr* (a) to cool, refresh (b) to freshen up, to revive (colour); to do up, renovate; **r. la mémoire à qn,** to refresh s.o.'s memory 2. *vi* **mettre le vin à r.,** to chill the wine 3. **se r.** (a) (*of weather*) to grow cooler (b) (i) to freshen oneself up (ii) to refresh oneself. **rafraîchissant** *a* refreshing; cooling.

rafraîchissement [rafreʃismɑ̃] *nm* (a) cooling (of liquid) (b) cold drink; *pl* refreshments.

ragaillardir [ragajardir] *vtr* to perk (s.o.) up; to cheer (s.o.) up.

rage [raʒ] *nf* 1. rabies 2. (a) rage, fury; **la tempête fait r.,** the storm is raging (b) passion, mania (for sth); **r. d'écrire,** mania for writing (c) **r. de dents,** raging toothache.

rager [raʒe] *vi* (**n. rageons**) *F:* to rage; to be in a rage; to fume; **ça me fait r. de voir ça!** it makes me wild, mad, to see it! **rageant** *a F:* maddening, infuriating. **rageur, -euse** *a* violent-tempered (person); infuriated (tone). **rageusement** *adv* furiously.

ragots [rago] *nmpl F:* gossip, tittle-tatle.

ragoût [ragu] *nm Cu:* stew, ragout. **ragoûtant** *a* **peu r.,** unpleasant; unappetizing.

raid [rɛd] *nm* 1. *Mil:* raid 2. *Sp:* long-distance rally.

raide [rɛd] 1. *a* (a) stiff (limb, joints); taut, tight (cable); **corde raide,** tightrope; **cheveux raides,** straight hair; *F:* **r. (comme un passe-lacet),** (stony) broke (b) stiff (manner); inflexible, unbending (character) (c) steep (slope) (d) *F:* **ça, c'est un peu r.!** that's a bit steep! **il en a vu de raides,** he's had some queer experiences (e) *P:* **boire du r.,** to drink raw spirits 2. *adv* (a) (to strike) hard (b) **ça monte r.,** it's a steep climb (c) **tomber r. mort,** to drop dead.

raideur [rɛdœr] *nf* 1. stiffness (of limb, joints); tightness (of cable) 2. stiffness (of manner); inflexibility 3. steepness (of slope).

raidillon [rɛdijɔ̃] *nm* (short and steep) rise.

raidir [rɛdir] 1. *vtr* (a) to stiffen; to tighten (b) to harden (resistance) 2. **se r.** (a) to stiffen, to grow stiff; to tighten; **il se raidit,** he grew tense (b) to take a hard line.

raidissement [rɛdismɑ̃] *nm* stiffening; tightening.

raie¹ [rɛ] *nf* 1. line, stroke 2. streak; stripe 3. parting (in hair).

raie² *nf Ich:* ray, skate.

raifort [rɛfor] *nm* horseradish.

rail [raj] *nm* (a) rail; **r. conducteur,** live rail; (*of train*) **quitter les raïls,** to jump the metals; to be derailed; **remettre l'économie sur les rails,** to put the economy back on its feet (b) railways, *NAm:* railroads.

railler [raje] *vtr* to laugh at, to make fun of (s.o.). **railleur, -euse** (i) *a* mocking, joking (ii) *n* scoffer; joker.

raillerie [rajri] *nf* joking; mocking.

rainure [rɛnyr] *nf* groove, channel; slot.

raisin [rɛzɛ̃] *nm* (**grain de**) **r.,** grape; **grappe de r.,** bunch of grapes; **raisins secs,** raisins; **raisins de Corinthe,** (dried) currants; **raisins de Smyrne,** sultanas.

raison [rɛzɔ̃] *nf* 1. reason, motive, ground (**de,** for); **ce n'est pas une r.!** that's no excuse! **pour quelle r.?** why? what for? **sans r.,** needlessly; **en r. de,** because of; **r. de plus,** all the more reason; **r. d'être,** raison d'être 2. (faculty of) reason; **il n'a pas toute sa r.,** he's not quite sane; **entendre r.,** to listen to reason 3. **donner r. à qn,** to admit that s.o. is right; **avoir r.,** to be right; **se faire une r.,** to accept the inevitable; **avec r.,** rightly; **boire plus que de r.,** to drink too much; **comme de r.,** as one might expect 4. satisfaction, reparation; **avoir r. de qn,** to get the better of s.o. 5 *Com:* **r. sociale,** name, style (of a firm) 6. *Mth:* **r. directe, indirecte,** direct, inverse; ratio; **à r.**

de, at the rate of; **en r. de,** according to. **raison-nable** a reasonable; sensible. **raisonnable-ment** adv reasonably; sensibly; moderately.
raisonnement [rɛzɔnmɑ̃] nm (a) reasoning (b) argument.
raisonner [rɛzɔne] **1.** vi to reason, to argue (**sur,** about) **2.** vtr (a) **r. ses actions,** to consider, justify, one's actions (b) to reason with (s.o.). **raisonné** a reasoned (argument). **raisonneur, -euse** (a) a reasoning, rational; argumentative (b) n reasoner; arguer.
rajeunir [raʒœnir] **1.** vtr (a) to rejuvenate (s.o.); to make (s.o.) look younger, feel younger (b) to reno-vate; to update, to modernize **2.** vi to grow young again **3. se r.,** to make oneself out to be younger than one is. **rajeunissant** a rejuvenating (cream).
rajeunissement [raʒœnismɑ̃] nm rejuvenation.
rajouter [raʒute] vtr to add (sth); to add more of (sth).
rajustement [raʒystəmɑ̃] nm readjustment.
rajuster [raʒyste] vtr to readjust (sth); to put (sth) straight; **se r.,** to tidy oneself up.
râle[1] [rɑl] nm rattle (in the throat); death rattle.
râle[2] nm Orn: rail.
ralenti [ralɑ̃ti] **1.** a slow(er); **au trot r.,** at a slow trot **2.** nm (a) slow motion; Cin: **scène au r.,** scene in slow motion (b) Ind: Mch: idling, slow running; (of engine) **tourner au r.,** to idle, to tick over.
ralentir [ralɑ̃tir] **1.** vtr & i to slow down; to slacken (speed); PN: r.! slow! **r. sa marche,** to reduce speed **2. se r.,** (of movement) to slow down; (of enthusiasm) to abate, to flag. **ralentissement** [ralɑ̃tismɑ̃] nm slowing down; flagging.
râler [rɑle] vi **1.** to give the death rattle **2.** F: to groan, to grouse; **r. en silence,** to fume; **faire r. qn,** to infuriate s.o.
râleur, -euse [rɑlœr, -øz] n F: grouser, grumbler.
ralliement [ralimɑ̃] nm (a) rally(ing) (b) winning over (of adherents).
rallier [ralje] v (pr sub & impf n. **ralliions**) **1.** vtr (a) to rally, assemble (troops) (b) to rejoin (unit) (c) to win (s.o.) over; to bring (s.o.) round (to an opinion) **2. se r.** (a) (of troops) to rally (b) **se r. à,** to join (party); to come round to (an opinion).
rallonge [ralɔ̃ʒ] nf (a) extension piece; extension cord; (extra) leaf (of table) (b) additional payment.
rallonger [ralɔ̃ʒe] (n. **rallongeons**) (a) vtr to lengthen; to make (sth) longer (b) vi F: **les jours rallongent,** the days are getting longer.
rallumer [ralyme] **1.** vtr to relight (lamp, fire); to rekindle (fire); to revive (anger, hope) **2. se r.,** to light up again; (of anger) to revive.
rallye [rali] nm Sp: (car) rally.
ramage [ramaʒ] nm (a) floral design (b) song (of birds).
ramassage [ramasaʒ] nm gathering, collecting, picking up; **r. à la pelle,** shovelling up; **r. scolaire,** school bus service.
ramasser [ramase] vtr **1.** (a) to gather (sth) together; **r. toutes ses forces,** to gather all one's strength (b) to collect, gather (several things); to gather (to-gether); F: **r. un procès-verbal,** to get a ticket (c) to pick up, take up; **r. à la pelle,** to shovel up; F: **r. une bûche,** to come a cropper **2. se r.** (a) to gather oneself (for an effort); (of tiger) to crouch (for a spring) (b) to pick oneself up (after a fall).

ramasseur, -euse [ramasœr, -øz] n collector; Ten: **r. de balles,** ballboy, ballgirl.
ramassis [ramasi] nm Pej: heap, pile (of thgs); bunch (of people).
rambarde [rɑ̃bard] nf Nau: etc: (guard) rail.
rame[1] [ram] nf Hort: stake, stick.
rame[2] nf oar.
rame[3] nf **1.** ream (of paper) **2.** made-up train; **la r. directe pour Tours,** the through coach(es) for Tours; **r. (de Métro),** underground train.
rameau, -eaux [ramo] nm (small) branch, bough, twig; **le dimanche des Rameaux,** Palm Sunday.
ramener [ramne] v (conj like MENER) **1.** vtr (a) to bring (s.o., sth) back (again); **r. qn en voiture,** to drive s.o. home; **r. qn à la vie,** to bring s.o. back to life (b) to pull (back) (blanket); to draw in (one's legs); **r. son chapeau sur ses yeux,** to pull down one's hat over one's eyes **2. se r.** (a) F: (of pers) to arrive, to roll up (b) **se r. à,** to come down to, to boil down to.
ramer [rame] vi to row.
rameur, -euse [ramœr, -øz] n rower; oarsman, oarswoman.
ramier [ramje] am & nm Orn: (pigeon) **r.,** wood pigeon.
ramification [ramifikasjɔ̃] nf ramification.
ramifier (se) [səramifje] vtr & pr to ramify, branch out.
ramollir [ramɔlir] **1.** vtr to soften **2. se r.,** to soften, to go soft. **ramolli** a F: soft(witted).
ramonage [ramɔnaʒ] nm chimney sweeping.
ramoner [ramɔne] vtr to sweep (chimney).
ramoneur [ramɔnœr] nm (chimney) sweep.
rampe [rɑ̃p] nf **1.** slope, rise, incline **2.** ramp; **r. de lancement,** launching pad **3.** banisters, handrail **4.** Th: footlights; **cette pièce ne passe pas la r.,** this play doesn't get across.
ramper [rɑ̃pe] vi to creep, to crawl; (of plant) to creep, to trail; **r. devant qn,** to grovel before s.o.
ramure [ramyr] nf (a) branches, foliage (b) antlers (of stag).
rancard [rɑ̃kar] nm P: (a) information, tip (b) date, rendezvous.
rancart [rɑ̃kar] nm **mettre qch au r.,** to discard (sth); to shelve (project).
rance [rɑ̃s] a rancid, rank.
rancir [rɑ̃sir] vi to go rancid.
rancœur [rɑ̃kœr] nf rancour; resentment.
rançon [rɑ̃sɔ̃] nf ransom; **la r. du progrès,** the price of progress.
rançonner [rɑ̃sɔne] vtr to hold (s.o.) to ransom; F: to fleece (customer).
rancune [rɑ̃kyn] nf rancour, spite; **garder r. à qn,** to bear s.o. a grudge; **sans r.!** no hard feelings! **ran-cunier, -ière** a vindictive, spiteful (person).
randonnée [rɑ̃dɔne] nf outing, run, trip, excursion; **r. à pied,** hike.
rang [rɑ̃] nm **1.** (a) row, line; row (of onions, knit-ting); **r. de perles,** string of pearls (b) Mil: rank; **en rangs serrés,** in close order; **se mettre en r. par 6,** to form rows of 6 **2.** rank, place; station; **avoir r. de colonel,** to hold the rank of colonel; **arriver au pre-mier r.,** to come to the front; **par r. d'âge,** according to age.

rangée [rɑ̃ʒe] *nf* row, line; tier (of seats).

rangement [rɑ̃ʒmɑ̃] *nm* (*a*) tidying (up), putting away; **volume de r.**, storage space (*b*) arrangement.

ranger [rɑ̃ʒe] *v* (**n. rangeons**) 1. *vtr* (*a*) to arrange (*b*) to put away; to tidy away, to put back in its place; **r. une voiture**, to pull in to the side (*c*) to arrange, tidy (room) (*d*) **r. qn parmi les meilleurs**, to rank, count, s.o. among the best 2. **se r.** (*a*) to draw up, line up (*b*) **se r. du côté de qn**, to side with s.o. (*c*) **se r.** (**de côté**), to get out of the way (*d*) **il s'est rangé**, he has settled down. **rangé** *a* (*a*) tidy, well-ordered (room) (*b*) settled (pers).

ranimer [ranime] 1. *vtr* to revive, to put new life into (s.o., sth); to bring (s.o.) back to life; to bring (s.o.) round; to stir up (fire); to rekindle (anger); to liven up (conversation) 2. **se r.**, to revive; (*of fire*) to burn up.

rapace [rapas] *a* 1. predatory; **oiseau r.**, *nm* **r.**, bird of prey 2. rapacious, grasping (person).

rapacité [rapasite] *nf* rapacity.

rapatrié, -iée [rapatrije] *n* repatriate.

rapatriement [rapatrimɑ̃] *nm* repatriation.

rapatrier [rapatrije] *vtr* (*pr sub & impf* **n. rapatriions**) to repatriate; to send (s.o.) home (from abroad).

râpe [rɑp] *nf* rasp; grater.

râper [rɑpe] *vtr* to rasp; to grate. **râpé** 1. *a* (*a*) grated (cheese) (*b*) threadbare (clothes) 2. *nm* grated cheese.

rapetisser [raptise] 1. *vtr* to make (sth) smaller; to reduce 2. *vi & pr* to shorten; to become shorter, smaller; to shrink.

râpeux, -euse [rɑpø, -øz] *a* rough (to the touch).

raphia [rafja] *nm* raffia.

rapiat, -ate [rapja, -at] 1. *a* stingy, miserly 2. *n* miser, skinflint.

rapide [rapid] 1. *a* (*a*) rapid, swift, fast; speedy (recovery) (*b*) steep (slope) 2. *nm* (*a*) rapid (in river); (*b*) express (train), fast train. **rapidement** *adv* (*a*) rapidly, swiftly (*b*) steeply.

rapidité [rapidite] *nf* (*a*) rapidity, swiftness, speed (*b*) steepness.

rapiécer [rapjese] *vtr* (**je rapièce; je rapiécerai**) to patch (garment).

rappel [rapɛl] *nm* 1. (*a*) recall (of ambassador) (*b*) **r. à l'ordre**, call(ing) to order (*c*) *Mil:* **r. sous les drapeaux**, recall to the colours (of reservists) (*d*) *Th:* curtain call 2. reminder; **lettre de r.**, (letter of) reminder; *Com:* **r. de traitement**, back pay 3. *Mec:* readjustment; **vis de r.**, adjusting screw 4. *Med:* (**piqûre de**) **r.**, booster (injection).

rappeler [raple] (*conj like* APPELER) 1. *vtr* (*a*) to call (s.o.) again; *Tp:* to call again, to call back (*b*) to recall (ambassador); to call (s.o.) back; **r. qn à l'ordre**, to call s.o. to order; **r. qn à la vie**, to bring s.o. back to life (*c*) to call (back) to mind; **vous me rappelez mon oncle**, you remind me of my uncle; *Com:* **prière de r. ce numéro**, in reply please quote this number 2. **se r. qch**, to recall, remember, sth; to call sth to mind.

rapport [rapɔr] *nm* 1. (*a*) return, yield; **immeuble de r.**, block of flats (for letting); **d'un bon r.**, profitable; that brings in a good return (*b*) account, report, statement (*c*) (official) report; return (of expenses) 2. (*a*) relation, connection (**avec**, with); **sans r. avec**

le sujet, without any bearing on the subject; **avoir r. à qch**, to relate to sth; **par r. à qch**, in comparison with sth; **sous tous les rapports**, in every respect (*b*) ratio, proportion; **r. de 1 à 3**, ratio of 1 to 3 (*c*) relations (between people); **mettre qn en r. avec qn**, to bring s.o. in contact, to put s.o. in touch, with s.o.; **avoir des rapports avec qn**, (i) to be in touch with s.o. (ii) to have sexual intercourse with s.o.

rapporter [rapɔrte] 1. *vtr* (*a*) to bring back; to return (sth) (*b*) to add, to join, to put in (pieces to build a machine) (*c*) to bring in, yield; **cela ne rapporte rien**, it doesn't pay; *vi* **affaire qui rapporte**, profitable business (*d*) (i) to report, to give an account of (sth) (ii) *vi* to sneak; to tell tales; **r. sur qn**, to tell on s.o., to sneak (*e*) **r. qch à une cause**, to attribute, ascribe, sth to a cause (*f*) *Jur:* to revoke (decree); to cancel (order); **r. un ordre de grève**, to call off a strike 2. **se r.** (*a*) to agree, tally (**avec**, with) (*b*) to refer, to relate (**à**, to) (*c*) **s'en r. à qn**, to rely on s.o.; **je m'en rapporte à vous**, (i) I take your word for it (ii) I leave it to you.

rapporteur, -euse [rapɔrtœr, -øz] *n* 1. telltale, sneak 2. *nm* reporter, recorder 3. *nm Mth:* protractor.

rapprochement [raprɔʃmɑ̃] *nm* (*a*) bringing together (*b*) linking, comparing (of ideas) (*c*) reconciliation.

rapprocher [raprɔʃe] *vtr* 1. (*a*) to bring (objects) nearer, closer together; **r. une chaise du feu**, to draw up a chair to the fire (*b*) to bring (two people) together; **un intérêt commun les rapproche**, a common interest brings, draws, them together (*c*) to put together, to compare (facts) 2. **se r.** (*a*) **se r. de qch**, to draw near(er) to sth (*b*) **se r. de la vérité**, to approximate to the truth (*c*) **se r. de qn**, to be reconciled, to make it up, with s.o. **rapproché** *a* near (in space, time) (**de**, to); close together; **yeux rapprochés**, close-set eyes.

rapsodie [rapsɔdi] *nf* rhapsody.

rapt [rapt] *nm Jur:* abduction; kidnapping.

raquette [rakɛt] *nf* 1. *Games:* racket; (table tennis) bat 2. snowshoe.

rare [rar] *a* 1. rare (book, insect); **les visites sont rares**, the visits are few and far between; **se faire r.**, to be seldom seen; **l'argent est r.**, money is scarce; **ça n'a rien de r.**, there's nothing unusual about it 2. rare, uncommon, exceptional (merit, beauty) 3. thin (hair); sparse (vegetation). **rarement** *adv* rarely, seldom.

raréfier (se) [sərarefje] *vpr* (*a*) (*of air*) to rarefy, to get thin (*b*) to become scarce.

rareté [rarte] *nf* 1. (*a*) rarity (*b*) scarcity, scarceness (of objects); infrequency (of visits) 2. (*a*) (*object*) rarity (*b*) rare occurence.

ras [rɑ] 1. *a* (*a*) close-cropped (hair); short-piled (carpet); **à poil r.**, short-haired (dog) (*b*) bare, blank; **en rase campagne**, in the open country; **faire table rase**, to make a clean sweep (*c*) **cuillerée rase**, level spoonful; **à r. bord**, to the brim (*d*) *F:* **en avoir r. le bol**, to be fed up to the back teeth 2. *prep phr* **au r. de**, (on a) level with, flush with; **voler au r. du sol**, to fly close to the ground.

rasade [razad] *nf* brim-full glass; bumper.

rasage [razaʒ] *nm* shaving, shave.

rase-mottes [razmɔt] *nm Av:* **vol en r.-m.,** hedge hopping; **faire du r.-m.,** to skim the ground.

raser [rɑze] **1.** *vtr* (*a*) to shave (off) (*b*) *F:* to bore (s.o.) (*c*) to raze (building) to the ground (*d*) to graze, brush, skim (over); **r. le mur,** to hug the wall **2. se r.** (*a*) to shave (*b*) *F:* to be bored. **rasant** *a F:* boring.

raseur, -euse [rɑzœr, -øz] *n F:* bore.

rasoir [rɑzwar] *nm* **1.** razor; **r. électrique,** electric shaver, razor **2.** *F:* (*pers*) bore.

rassasier [rɑsazje] *v* (*pr sub & impf* n. **rassasiions**) **1.** *vtr* (*a*) to satisfy (hunger); **être rassasié,** to have eaten one's fill (*b*) to sate, satiate, surfeit, cloy (**de,** with) **2. se r.,** to eat one's fill.

rassemblement [rɑsɑ̃bləmɑ̃] *nm* **1.** assembling, gathering; *Mil:* **r.!** fall in! **2.** crowd, gathering.

rassembler [rɑsɑ̃ble] **1.** *vtr* (*a*) to reassemble, to bring together again (*b*) to assemble; to gather together, collect together; to round up (cattle); to summon up (strength) **2. se r.,** to assemble, to gather.

rasseoir [rɑswar] *vtr* (*conj like* ASSEOIR) **1.** *vtr* to seat (s.o.) again; to replace (a statue) on its base **2. se r.,** to sit down again.

rasséréner (se) [sərɑserene] *vpr* (**je me rassérène**) (*of pers*) to recover one's peace of mind.

rassir [rɑsir] *vi & pr* (**se**) **r.,** to get stale. **rassis** *a* stale.

rassurer [rɑsyre] **1.** *vtr* to reassure (s.o.), to put (s.o.'s) mind at rest **2. se r.,** to feel reassured; **rassurez-vous,** put your mind at rest.

rat [ra] *nm* **1.** (*a*) rat; **mort aux rats,** rat poison; **être fait comme un r.,** to be caught out (*b*) **r. des champs,** fieldmouse; **r. musqué,** musk rat, musquash **2. r. d'hôtel,** hotel thief; **petit r.** (**de l'opéra**), young ballet pupil.

ratatiner [ratatine] **1.** *vtr & pr* to shrivel (up); to shrink; to dry up **2.** *vtr P:* (*a*) to bump (s.o.) off (*b*) to beat (s.o.) up.

rate [rat] *nf Anat:* spleen.

raté, -ée [rate] *n* **1.** (*pers*) failure **2.** *nm* misfire; *Aut:* **le moteur avait des ratés,** the engine was misfiring.

râteau, -eaux [rɑto] *nm* rake.

râtelier [rɑtəlje] *nm* **1.** rack (in stable) **2. r. à pipes, à outils,** pipe rack, tool rack **3.** *F:* set of false teeth; denture.

rater [rate] **1.** *vi* (*of gun, engine*) to misfire; (*of enterprise*) to fail; to miscarry **2.** *vtr* (*a*) **r. son coup,** to miss the mark (*b*) *F:* **r. un coup,** to fail in an attempt; **r. son train,** to miss one's train; **r. un examen,** to fail an exam; **j'ai raté l'occasion,** I missed the chance.

ratiboiser [ratibwaze] *vtr P:* **1. r. qch à qn,** to do s.o. out of sth **2.** to rook (s.o.).

ratification [ratifikɑsjɔ̃] *nf* ratification.

ratifier [ratifje] *vtr* to ratify.

ration [rɑsjɔ̃] *nf* ration(s).

rationaliser [rɑsjɔnalize] *vtr* to rationalize. **rationnel** *a* rational. **rationnellement** *adv* rationally.

rationnement [rɑsjɔnmɑ̃] *nm* rationing.

rationner [rɑsjɔne] *vtr* to ration.

ratissage [ratisaʒ] *nm* raking; combing.

ratisser [ratise] *vtr* **1.** to rake (path); to rake up

(leaves) **2.** *F:* (*a*) to rook, to fleece (s.o.) (*b*) to comb (district).

RATP *abbr Trans: Régie autonome des transports parisiens.*

raton [ratɔ̃] *nm* **r. laveur,** raccoon.

rattachement [rataʃmɑ̃] *nm* fastening, tying up; linking up.

rattacher [rataʃe] **1.** *vtr* (*a*) to fasten, to tie (up), (sth) again; to refasten (*b*) to bind (s.o. to his family) (*c*) **r. qch à qch,** to link up sth with sth **2. se r. à qch,** (i) to be fastened to sth (ii) to be connected with sth.

rattrapage [ratrapaʒ] *nm* making up (for lost time); *Sch:* **cours de r.,** remedial course (for backward children).

rattraper [ratrape] **1.** *vtr* (*a*) to recapture; to catch (s.o. sth) again; *F:* **on ne m'y rattrapera pas!** you won't catch me doing that again! (*b*) to overtake; to catch (s.o.) up (*c*) to recover (one's money); to make up for (lost time); to catch up on (sleep) (*d*) *Cu:* to retrieve (curdled mayonnaise) **2. se r.** (*a*) **se r. à une branche,** to save oneself by catching hold of a branch (*b*) **se r. de ses pertes,** to make good one's losses; to recoup oneself.

rature [ratyr] *nf* erasure; crossing out (of word); deletion.

raturer [ratyre] *vtr* to erase; to cross out (a word).

rauque [rok] *a* hoarse, raucous, harsh (voice).

ravage [ravaʒ] *nm usu pl* **faire des ravages,** to wreak havoc.

ravager [ravaʒe] *vtr* (**n. ravageons**) to ravage, devastate; to lay waste; (*of illness*) to ravage. **ravagé** *a F:* mad, nuts, bonkers. **ravageur, -euse** *a* devastating.

ravalement [ravalmɑ̃] *nm Const:* repointing, redressing (of stonework); rough casting.

ravaler [ravale] *vtr* (*a*) to swallow (sth) again; to choke back (sob) (*b*) to degrade, to lower (s.o.) (*c*) *Const:* (i) to repoint, re-dress (wall) (ii) to roughcast (wall).

ravauder [ravode] *vtr* to mend (clothes); to darn.

rave [rav] *nf Bot:* **1.** rape **2.** radish; **céleri r.,** celeriac.

ravi [ravi] *a* delighted (**de,** with).

ravier [ravje] *nm* hors-d'œuvre dish.

ravigoter [ravigɔte] *vtr F:* to buck (s.o.) up.

ravin [ravɛ̃] *nm* ravine, gully.

raviner [ravine] *vtr* to gully; to furrow.

ravir [ravir] *vtr* **1. r. qch à qn,** to rob s.o. of sth **2.** to delight (s.o.); **cela lui va à r.,** she looks charming in it.

raviser (se) [səravize] *vpr* to change one's mind; to think better of it.

ravissant [ravisɑ̃] *a* ravishing, delightful, lovely.

ravissement [ravismɑ̃] *nm* rapture.

ravisseur [ravisœr] *nm* abductor, kidnapper.

ravitaillement [ravitajmɑ̃] *nm* supplying; refuelling; supplies.

ravitailler [ravitaje] **1.** *vtr* to supply, provision (**en,** with); to feed (people); **r. un avion en vol,** to refuel an aircraft in flight **2. se r.,** to take in (fresh) supplies; to stock up; **se r. (en carburant),** to refuel.

raviver [ravive] *vtr* **1.** to revive (fire, memory) **2.** to brighten up (colour).

ravoir [ravwar] *vtr* (*only in inf*) **1.** to get (sth) back again **2.** *F:* (*in neg*) to get (sth) clean.

rayer [reje] *vtr* (**je raie, je raye**) **1.** (*a*) to scratch; to score (*b*) to rule, line (paper) (*c*) to stripe (fabric) **2.** to strike out, delete (name). **rayé** *a* striped.

rayon[1] [rɛjɔ̃] *nm* **1.** ray (of light, hope); beam (of light); **r. de soleil,** sunbeam; **rayons X,** X-rays **2.** (*a*) radius of (circle) (*b*) range; **dans un r. de 2 km,** within a radius of 2 km; **r. d'action,** range of action; scope; **à grand r. d'action,** long-range **3.** spoke (of wheel).

rayon[2] *nm* **1. r. de miel,** honeycomb **2.** (*a*) shelf (of cupboard); *pl* set of shelves (*b*) (*in shop*) (i) department (ii) counter; **ce n'est pas mon r.,** (i) that's not my concern (ii) that's not in my line; **c'est son r.,** that's right up his street.

rayonnage [rɛjɔnaʒ] *nm* shelving; set of shelves.

rayonne [rɛjɔn] *nf Tex:* rayon.

rayonnement [rɛjɔnmɑ̃] *nm* (*a*) *Ph:* radiation (*b*) radiance (*c*) (cultural) influence.

rayonner [rɛjɔne] *vi* (*a*) *Ph:* to radiate (*b*) to beam, shine; **il rayonnait de joie,** he was radiant, beaming, with joy (*c*) to radiate (from a centre); **r. autour d'Avignon,** to make Avignon the centre (for excursions). **rayonnant** *a* radiant.

rayure [rɛjyr] *nf* (*a*) stripe, streak; **à rayures,** striped (*b*) scratch.

raz [rɑ] *nm* strong current; race; **r. de marée,** (i) tidal wave (ii) *Pol:* landslide.

razzia [razja] *nf* raid; **faire (une) r. sur qch,** to plunder sth.

ré [re] *nm inv Mus:* **1.** (the note) D **2.** re (in the Fixed Do system).

RDA *abbr République Démocratique Allemande.*

réaccoutumer [reakutyme] *vtr* to re-accustom (**à,** to); **se r.,** to re-accustom oneself.

réacteur [reaktœr] *nm* **1.** *AtomPh:* (atomic, nuclear) reactor **2.** jet engine.

réaction [reaksjɔ̃] *nf* reaction; **r. en chaîne,** chain reaction; **avion à r.,** jet (aircraft).

réactionnaire [reaksjɔnɛr] *a & n* reactionary.

réadaptation [readaptasjɔ̃] *nf* **1.** rehabilitation; re-education **2.** readjustment.

réadapter [readapte] *vtr* **1.** to rehabilitate; to re-educate **2.** to readjust.

réaffirmer [reafirme] *vtr* to reaffirm.

réagir [reaʒir] *vi* to react.

réalisateur, -trice [realizatœr, -tris] *n Cin: TV: WTel:* producer; director (of play).

réalisation [realizasjɔ̃] *nf* (*a*) realization; carrying out (of plan); fulfilment, achievement (*b*) *Cin: TV: WTel:* production.

réaliser [realize] **1.** *vtr* (*a*) to realize; to achieve (ambition); to carry out (plan); to create (work of art); *Cin: etc:* to produce (film) (*b*) to convert (asset) into cash; to make (profit) (*c*) *F:* to understand (mistake) **2. se r.** (*a*) (*of projects*) to materialize; (*of prediction*) to come true (*b*) to fulfil oneself.

réalisme [realism] *nm* realism. **réaliste 1.** *a* realistic **2.** *n* realist.

réalité [realite] *nf* reality; **devenir une r.,** to come true; **en r.,** in (actual) fact, in reality.

réanimation [reanimasjɔ̃] *nf* resuscitation.

réanimer [reanime] *vtr* to resuscitate (s.o.).

réapparaître [reaparetr] *vi* (*conj like* APPARAÎTRE, *aux usu* **être**) to reappear.

réapparition [reaparisjɔ̃] *nf* reappearance.

réarmement [rearmǝmɑ̃] *nm* rearmament.

réarmer [rearme] *vtr* (*a*) to rearm (*b*) to recock (gun); to reset (camera shutter).

réassortir [reasɔrtir] *vtr* (*conj like* ASSORTIR) **1.** to match (up) (a set) **2.** to restock (shop); **se r.,** to restock.

rébarbatif, -ive [rebarbatif, -iv] *a* grim, forbidding, unprepossessing; repugnant.

rebâtir [rǝbɑtir] *vtr* to rebuild.

rebattre [rǝbatr] *vtr* (*conj like* BATTRE) (*a*) to re-shuffle (cards) (*b*) *F:* **r. les oreilles à qn** de qch, to din sth into s.o.'s ears. **rebattu** *a* hackneyed (story).

rebelle [rǝbɛl] **1.** *a* rebellious; stubborn, obstinate; unruly (hair); **r. à,** unamenable to **2.** *n* rebel.

rebeller (se) [sǝrǝbele] *vpr* to rebel, to revolt (**contre,** against).

rébellion [rebeljɔ̃] *nf* rebellion, revolt.

rebiffer (se) [sǝrǝbife] *vpr F:* to get one's back up.

reboiser [rǝbwaze] *vtr* to reafforest.

rebondir [rǝbɔ̃dir] *vi* (*a*) to rebound; to bounce (*b*) *Fig:* to start off, to start up, again. **rebondi** *a* rounded, chubby (cheeks); plump (person); fat (belly).

rebondissement [rǝbɔ̃dismɑ̃] *nm* new development (in a case).

rebord [rǝbɔr] *nm* edge, border, rim; **r. d'une fenêtre,** window sill.

reboucher [rǝbuʃe] *vtr* to stop, block, plug (sth) up again; to recork (bottle).

rebours [rǝbur] *nm* wrong way (of the grain), contrary, reverse; **à r.,** against the grain, the wrong way; **compter à r.,** to count backwards; **compte à r.,** countdown.

rebouteux, -euse [rǝbutø, -øz] *n* bonesetter.

reboutonner [rǝbutɔne] *vtr* to rebutton; to button up again.

rebrousse-poil (à) [arǝbruspwal] *adv phr* **brosser un chapeau à r.-p.,** to brush a hat the wrong way, against the nap; **prendre qn à r.-p.,** to rub s.o. up the wrong way.

rebrousser [rǝbruse] *vtr* **1.** to brush up (hair) **2. r. chemin,** to turn back; to retrace one's steps.

rebuffade [rǝbyfad] *nf* rebuff; snub.

rébus [reby] *nm* rebus.

rebut [rǝby] *nm* (**article de) r.,** reject; rubbish; *Ind:* **pièces de r.,** rejects; **mettre qch au r.,** to throw sth away; *Post:* **bureau des rebuts,** dead-letter office; *Pej:* **le r. de la société,** the dregs of society.

rebuter [rǝbyte] **1.** *vtr* (*a*) to rebuff, to repulse (s.o.) (*b*) to reject, discard (sth) (*c*) to dishearten, discourage (s.o.) (*d*) to shock, disgust (s.o.) **2. se r.,** to lose heart, to be discouraged. **rebutant** *a* irksome; disheartening; repellent.

récalcitrant [rekalsitrɑ̃] *a* recalcitrant.

recaler [rǝkale] *vtr F:* to fail (s.o. in an exam); **être recalé,** to fail.

récapitulation [rekapitylasjɔ̃] *nf* recapitulation, summing up. **récapitulatif, -ive** *a* summary.

récapituler [rekapityle] *vtr* to recapitulate; to sum up.

recel [rǝsɛl] *nm* receiving (and concealing) (of stolen goods).

receler [rəs(ə)le] *vtr* (**je recèle; je recèlerai**) *Jur:* to receive (stolen goods); to harbour (criminal); to conceal.

receleur, -euse [rəslœr, -øz] *n Jur:* receiver.

récemment [resamã] *adv* recently; lately.

recensement [rəsãsmã] *nm* (*a*) census; counting (of votes); registration (*b*) *Com:* new inventory.

recenser [rəsãse] *vtr* (*a*) to take the census; to register (*b*) to make an inventory of.

recenseur, -euse [rəsãsœr, -øz] *n* census taker.

récent [resã] *a* recent.

récépissé [resepise] *nm* receipt.

récepteur, -trice [reseptœr, -tris] **1.** *a* receiving (apparatus) **2.** *nm Tp:* receiver.

réception [resepsjɔ̃] *nf* **1.** (*a*) receipt (of letter) (*b*) taking delivery (of goods) **2.** (*a*) welcome; **faire une bonne r. à qn**, to welcome s.o. warmly (*b*) (official, court) reception; party; **salle de r.**, reception room (*c*) (hotel) reception desk, office; enquiry office **3.** *Tp: WTel: etc:* reception; **appareil, poste, de r.**, receiving set. **réceptif, -ive** *a* receptive.

réceptionnaire [resepsjɔnɛr] *n Com:* receiving clerk.

réceptionner [resepsjɔne] *vtr* to check and sign for (goods).

réceptionniste [resepsjɔnist] *n* receptionist.

réceptivité [reseptivite] *nf* receptivity.

récession [resesjɔ̃] *nf* recession. **récessif, -ive** *a* recessive.

recette [rəsɛt] *nf* **1.** receipts, returns; (*of film*) **faire r.**, to be a (box office) success **2.** (*a*) collection (of money due) (*b*) receiving; receipt (of stores) **3.** *Adm:* (tax) collector's office **4.** *Cu:* recipe; *Ch:* formula.

receveur, -euse [rəsəvœr, -øz] *n* **1.** receiver, recipient (of blood) **2.** (*a*) collector (of taxes); **r. des postes**, postmaster, postmistress; (*b*) (bus) conductor, conductress.

recevoir [rəsəvwar] *v* (*prp* **recevant**; *pp* **reçu**; *pr ind* **je reçois, ils reçoivent**; *pr sub* **je reçoive**; *fu* **je recevrai**) **1.** *vtr* (*a*) to receive, get (letter); **r. un prix**, to win a prize; *Com:* **nous avons bien reçu votre lettre**, we are in receipt of your letter (*b*) to receive (punishment); to incur (blame) (*b*) (*a*) to receive, welcome (s.o.) (*b*) to entertain (friends); **r. des amis à dîner**, to have friends to dinner; **le médecin reçoit à 6 heures**, the doctor's surgery is at 6 (*c*) to receive, admit; **elle reçoit des pensionnaires**, she takes in boarders; (*d*) **être reçu à un examen**, to pass an exam; **être reçu premier**, to come out top; **être reçu médecin**, to qualify as a doctor (*e*) to receive, catch (water) **3.** *Sp:* **se r.**, to land.

rechange [rəʃãʒ] *nm* replacement; **r. de vêtements**, change of clothes; spare set of clothes; *Aut: etc:* **pièces de r.**, spare parts, spares.

réchapper [reʃape] *vi* (*aux* **avoir** *or* **être**) to escape (**de**, from) (disaster, accident).

recharge [rəʃarʒ] *nf* refill (for ballpoint pen); reload (of firearm); recharging (of battery).

rechargement [rəʃarʒəmã] *nm* refilling; reloading; recharging.

recharger [rəʃarʒe] *vtr* (*conj like* **CHARGER**) (*a*) to recharge (battery) (*b*) to reload (lorry, camera, gun) (*c*) to refill (pen).

réchaud [reʃo] *nm* (*a*) stove; **r. à gaz**, gas ring (*b*) hot plate.

réchauffé [reʃofe] *nm* (*a*) warmed-up food (*b*) rehash; stale news, old joke.

réchauffer [reʃofe] **1.** *vtr* (*a*) to reheat; to warm (sth) up again; to warm up (food, s.o.) (*b*) **r. le courage de qn**, to rekindle s.o.'s courage; **r. le cœur à qn**, to put new heart into s.o. **2.** **se r.**, to get warm; to warm oneself (up).

rêche [rɛʃ] *a* harsh, rough.

recherche [rəʃɛrʃ] *nf* **1.** (*a*) search, quest, pursuit; **être à la r. de qn**, to be looking for, to be in search of, s.o.; **courir à la r. d'un médecin**, to run for a doctor (*b*) (scientific, medical) research; **faire des recherches sur qch**, (i) to do research on sth (ii) to enquire into sth **2.** affectation, studied elegance; meticulous care.

rechercher [rəʃɛrʃe] *vtr* (*a*) to search for, seek (s.o., sth); to inquire into (causes); **il est recherché par la police**, he's wanted by the police (*b*) to seek (after), to try to obtain (favours). **recherché** *a* **1.** sought after; in demand **2.** (*a*) choice; exquisite (*b*) affected.

rechigner [rəʃiɲe] *vi* to balk at, to jib at (work).

rechute [rəʃyt] *nf Med:* relapse.

rechuter [rəʃyte] *vi Med:* to have a relapse.

récidive [residiv] *nf* (*a*) repetition of an offence (*b*) recurrence (of a disease).

récidiver [residive] *vi* **1.** to repeat an offence. **2.** (*of disease*) to recur.

récidiviste [residivist] *n* recidivist.

récif [resif] *nm* reef.

récipient [resipjã] *nm* container, receptacle.

réciprocité [resiprosite] *nf* reciprocity.

réciproque [resiprok] **1.** *a* reciprocal, mutual (benefits, love) **2.** *nf* **rendre la r. à qn**, to get even with s.o. **réciproquement** *adv* **1.** **ils s'aident r.**, they help one another **2.** vice versa.

récit [resi] *nm* narrative; account; **faire le r. de**, to give an account of.

récital [resital] *nm* recital.

récitation [resitasjɔ̃] *nf* recitation; **apprendre une r.**, to learn a text by heart.

réciter [resite] *vtr* to recite (poem).

réclamation [reklamasjɔ̃] *nf* (*a*) complaint; objection (*b*) claim.

réclame [reklam] *nf* (*a*) advertising; **faire de la r.**, to advertise; **article (en) r.**, special offer (*b*) advertisement; **r. lumineuse**, illuminated sign.

réclamer [reklame] **1.** *vi* to complain; **r. contre qch**, to protest against, object to, sth **2.** *vtr* (*a*) to lay claim to, to claim (sth); to (re)claim (lost property); **r. son argent**, to ask for one's money back (*b*) to call for (s.o., sth); **r. qch à grands cris**, to clamour for sth; **plante qui réclame beaucoup de soins**, plant that demands constant care **3.** **se r. de qch**, to quote sth as one's authority.

reclasser [rəklase] *vtr* **1.** (*a*) to reclassify (*b*) to regrade (staff) **2.** to rehabilitate.

reclus, -use [rəkly, -yz] **1.** *a* secluded, cloistered **2.** *n* recluse.

réclusion [reklyzjɔ̃] *nf Jur:* imprisonment.

recoiffer [rəkwafe] *vtr* **r. qn**, to do s.o.'s hair (again); **se r.**, to do one's hair.

recoin [rəkwɛ̃] *nm* nook, recess.

récolte [rekɔlt] *nf* **1.** harvesting, gathering (of crops); vintaging (of grapes) **2.** harvest, crop(s); vintage.

récolter [rekɔlte] *vtr* (*a*) to harvest, to gather in (crop) (*b*) to collect (signatures).

recommandation [rəkɔmɑ̃dasjɔ̃] *nf* (*a*) recommendation; (**lettre de**) **r.,** (i) letter of introduction (ii) testimonial (*b*) *Post:* registration.

recommander [rəkɔmɑ̃de] **1.** *vtr* (*a*) to recommend (product, s.o.) (*b*) **r. la prudence à qn,** to advise s.o. to be careful; **je vous recommande de rester,** I strongly advise you to stay (*c*) *Post:* to register (letter) **2.** (*a*) **se r. de qn,** to give s.o.'s name as a reference (*b*) **se r. de qch,** to merit consideration for sth. **recommandable** *a* (*a*) commendable (*b*) advisable, recommendable. **recommandé** *a Post:* registered; *nm* **envoi en r., un r.,** registered letter, parcel.

recommencement [rəkɔmɑ̃smɑ̃] *nm* new beginning.

recommencer [rəkɔmɑ̃se] *v* (**n. recommençons**) **1.** *vtr* to begin, start (sth) (over) again; to repeat (mistake) **2.** *vi* to do it again; to start afresh; **le voilà qui recommence!** he's at it again!

récompense [rekɔ̃pɑ̃s] *nf* (*a*) reward; **en r. de,** as a reward for (*b*) award, prize.

récompenser [rekɔ̃pɑ̃se] *vtr* to reward (**qn de qch,** s.o. for sth).

recompter [rəkɔ̃te] *vtr* to recount, to count again.

réconciliation [rekɔ̃siljasjɔ̃] *nf* reconciliation.

réconcilier [rekɔ̃silje] *vtr* to reconcile (persons, inconsistencies); **se r. avec qn,** to make it up with s.o.

reconduction [rəkɔ̃dyksjɔ̃] *nf* renewal (of lease).

reconduire [rəkɔ̃dɥir] *vtr* (*conj like* CONDUIRE) (*a*) to see, to take, (s.o.) home; to take (s.o.) back (*b*) to see, to show, (s.o.) out (*c*) to renew (lease).

réconfort [rekɔ̃fɔr] *nm* consolation, comfort.

réconforter [rekɔ̃fɔrte] *vtr* **1.** to strengthen, to fortify (s.o.) **2.** to comfort (s.o.). **réconfortant** *a* strengthening; comforting.

reconnaissable [rəkɔnɛsabl] *a* recognizable (**à,** by, from, through).

reconnaissance [rəkɔnɛsɑ̃s] *nf* **1.** recognition (of s.o., sth) **2.** (*a*) recognition; acknowledgment; admission (*b*) **donner une r. à qn,** to give s.o. an i.o.u. **3.** *Mil:* reconnaissance; *F:* recce; **avion de r.,** reconnaissance aircraft **4.** gratitude.

reconnaissant [rəkɔnɛsɑ̃] *a* (*a*) grateful (**de,** for) (*b*) thankful (**de,** for).

reconnaître [rəkɔnɛtr] *vtr* (*conj like* CONNAÎTRE) **1.** (*a*) to recognize; to know (s.o.) again; to identify (sth); **r. qn à sa démarche,** to know, tell, s.o. by his walk; **je vous reconnais bien là!** that's just like you! **je n'arrive pas à les r.,** I can't tell them apart **2.** (*a*) to recognize, acknowledge (truth); to admit (a mistake); **r. qn pour chef,** to acknowledge s.o. as leader; **reconnu pour incorrect,** admittedly incorrect (*b*) to own, acknowledge (a child) **3.** to reconnoitre, explore **4.** **se r.** (*a*) **gaz qui se reconnaît à son odeur,** gas recognizable by its smell (*b*) **se r. vaincu,** to admit defeat (*c*) to get one's bearings; **je ne m'y reconnais plus,** I'm completely lost.

reconquérir [rəkɔ̃kerir] *vtr* (*conj like* CONQUÉRIR) to regain, recover, reconquer (province); to win back (freedom).

reconquête [rəkɔ̃kɛt] *nf* reconquest.

reconsidérer [rəkɔ̃sidere] *vtr* (*conj like* CONSIDÉRER) to reconsider.

reconstituer [rəkɔ̃stitɥe] *vtr* (*a*) to reconstitute; to reconstruct (a crime); to restore (damaged building); to piece together (facts). **reconstituant** *a & nm* tonic.

reconstitution [rəkɔ̃stitysjɔ̃] *nf* reconstitution, reconstruction; restoration (of building).

reconstruction [rəkɔ̃stryksjɔ̃] *nf* reconstruction.

reconstruire [rəkɔ̃strɥir] *vtr* (*conj like* CONSTRUIRE) to reconstruct, rebuild.

reconversion [rəkɔ̃vɛrsjɔ̃] *nf* (*a*) reconversion (*b*) redeployment (of workers).

reconvertir [rəkɔ̃vɛrtir] *vtr* (*a*) to reconvert (factory) (*b*) to redeploy (staff) (*c*) **se r.,** to change one's occupation.

recopier [rəkɔpje] *vtr* (*conj like* COPIER) to recopy, to copy out (again); to make a fair copy of (draft).

record [rəkɔr] *nm Sp: etc:* record; **en un temps r.,** in record time.

recordman [rəkɔr(d)man] *nm* record holder; *pl* recordmen.

recoucher [rəkuʃe] **1.** *vtr* to put (child) to bed again **2.** **se r.,** to go back to bed.

recouper [rəkupe] *vtr* (*a*) to cut again; to cut more (*b*) to confirm; **se r.,** to tally.

recourbé [rəkurbe] *a* bent, curved.

recourir [rəkurir] *vi* (*conj like* COURIR) **r. à qn, à l'aide de qn,** to call on s.o. for help; to turn to s.o.; **r. à la justice,** to take legal proceedings; **r. à la violence,** to resort to violence.

recours [rəkur] *nm* (*a*) recourse, resort, resource; **en dernier r.,** as a last resort; **avoir r. à qch,** to resort to sth (*b*) *Jur:* **r. en cassation,** appeal; **r. en grâce,** petition for reprieve.

recouvrement [rəkuvrəmɑ̃] *nm* recovery; collection (of debts, bill, tax).

recouvrer [rəkuvre] *vtr* **1.** to recover, retrieve, get back (one's property); to regain (strength, freedom) **2.** to recover, collect (debts, taxes).

recouvrir [rəkuvrir] *v* (*conj like* COUVRIR) **1.** *vtr* (*a*) to re-cover (*b*) to cover (over), to overlay (**de,** with); **fauteuil recouvert de velours,** armchair covered in velvet (*c*) to cover up, hide (faults) (*d*) to overlap (slates) **2.** (*of sky*) **se r.,** to cloud over (again).

récréation [rekreasjɔ̃] *nf* (*a*) recreation, relaxation (*b*) *Sch:* break, playtime; **cour de r.,** playground.

recréer [rəkree] *vtr* to recreate.

récrier (se) [sərekrije] *vpr* (*conj like* CRIER) to exclaim, cry out **2. se r. contre qch.,** to protest against sth.

récrimination [rekriminasjɔ̃] *nf* recrimination.

récriminer [rekrimine] *vi* to recriminate (**contre,** against).

récrire [rekrir] *vtr* (*conj like* ÉCRIRE) to rewrite; to write (sth) over again.

recroqueviller (se) [sərəkrɔkvije] *vpr* (*a*) to shrivel up, to curl up (*b*) to huddle up, to curl up (**dans un coin,** in a corner). **recroquevillé** *a* shrivelled, curled up.

recrudescence [rəkrydesɑ̃s] *nf* renewed outbreak, fresh outbreak.

recrue [rəkry] *nf* recruit.

recrutement [rəkrytmɑ̃] *nm* recruitment.

recruter [rəkryte] *vtr* to recruit.

rectangle [rɛktãgl] *nm* rectangle. **rectangulaire** *a* rectangular.

rectification [rɛktifikasjɔ̃] *nf* rectification; correction.

rectifier [rɛktifje] *vtr* (*pr sub & impf* n. **rectifiions**) (*a*) to rectify, correct (calculation, mistake); to amend (text, account) (*b*) to adjust (instrument) (*c*) to straighten (alignment).

rectiligne [rɛktiliɲ] *a* rectilinear.

rectitude [rɛktityd] *nf* **1.** straightness (of line) **2.** rectitude, uprightness, integrity.

reçu [rəsy] **1.** *a* received, accepted, recognized (opinion, custom **2.** *nm Com:* receipt.

recueil [rəkœj] *nm* collection (of poems); miscellany; anthology.

recueillement [rəkœjmã] *nm* self-communion, meditation, contemplation.

recueillir [rəkœjir] (*conj like* CUEILLIR) **1.** *vtr* (*a*) to collect, gather (anecdotes); to catch (rainwater); to pick up (information) (*b*) to gather, get in (crops); **r. un héritage,** to inherit (*c*) to take in, to shelter (s.o.) **2.** **se r.,** to collect oneself, one's thoughts; to meditate. **recueilli** *a* meditative.

recul [rəkyl] *nm* **1.** receding, recession; backward movement; retreat; **il eut un mouvement de r.,** he started back; *Aut:* **phare de r.,** reversing light. **2.** recoil (of cannon); kick (of rifle) **3.** room to move back; **prendre du r.,** to step back(wards).

reculade [rəkylad] *nf* retreat.

reculer [rəkyle] **1.** *vi* to move back, step back, draw back; to recede; to retreat; (*of car*) to back; (*of cannon*) to recoil; (*of rifle*) to kick; **faire r.,** to move back, to force back; **ne r. devant rien,** to shrink from nothing **2.** *vtr* (*a*) to move back; to back (horse) (*b*) to postpone, put off (decision) **3.** **se r.,** to draw back; to move back; to stand back. **reculé** *a* distant, remote.

reculons (à) [ar(ə)kylɔ̃] *adv phr* **marcher à r.,** to walk backwards; **sortir à r.,** to back out.

récupération [rekyperasjɔ̃] *nf* recovery; salvage; recuperation; rehabilitation.

récupérer [rekypere] *vtr* (**je récupère; je récupérerai**) **1.** to recover; to get (sth) back; to collect, to pick up (s.o.); **r. ses forces,** *vi* **r.,** to recuperate; to recover one's strength **2.** (*a*) to recover, salvage (waste material) (*b*) to rehabilitate (s.o.) **3.** to recoup (a loss); to make up (lost time).

récurer [rekyre] *vtr* to scour (pan).

récusation [rekyzasjɔ̃] *nf Jur:* challenge.

récuser [rekyze] *Jur:* **1.** *vtr* to challenge (witness) **2.** **se r.,** to decline to give an opinion.

recyclage [rəsiklaʒ] *nm* (*a*) reorientation (of student); retraining (of staff) (*b*) recycling.

recycler [rəsikle] *vtr* (*a*) to reorientate (student's studies); to retrain (staff) (*b*) to recycle.

rédacteur, -trice [redaktœr, -tris] *n* (*a*) writer, drafter (of document) (*b*) *Journ:* member of editorial staff; sub-editor; **r. en chef,** (chief) editor; **r. politique,** political correspondent; **r. aux actualités,** news editor.

rédaction [redaksjɔ̃] *nf* **1.** (*a*) drafting (of document) (*b*) editing **2.** (*a*) editorial staff (*b*) editorial offices **3.** *Sch:* essay.

reddition [redisjɔ̃] *nf Mil:* surrender.

redemander [rədmãde] *vtr* to ask for (sth) again; to ask for more of (sth).

rédemption [redãpsjɔ̃] *nf* redemption. **rédempteur, -trice 1.** *a* redeeming **2.** *n* redeemer.

redescendre [rədesãdr] **1.** *vi* to come, to go, down again **2.** *vtr* (*a*) to take (sth) down again (*b*) to come, to go, down (stairs) again.

redevable [rəd(ə)vabl] *a* **être r. de qch à qn,** to be indebted to s.o. for sth; to owe (one's life) to s.o.

redevance [rəd(ə)vãs] *nf* (*a*) dues; *Tp:* rental (*b*) royalties (*c*) (television) licence fee.

redevenir [rədəvnir] *vi* (*conj like* DEVENIR) **r. jeune,** to grow young again.

rédiger [rediʒe] *vtr* (n. **rédigeons**) **1.** to draw up, to draft (agreement); to write (article) **2.** to edit.

redire [rədir] *vtr* (*conj like* DIRE) **1.** to tell, say, (sth) again; to repeat **2. trouver à r. à qch,** to take exception to sth; to find fault with sth; **il n'y a rien à r. à cela,** there's nothing to be said against that.

redite [rədit] *nf* (useless) repetition.

redondance [rədɔ̃dãs] *nf* redundance. **redondant** *a* redundant.

redonner [rədɔne] *vtr* to give (sth) back; to return (sth); to give more of (sth).

redoublant, -ante [rədublã, -ãt] *n Sch:* pupil who is repeating a year.

redoublement [rədubləmã] *nm* redoubling; increase.

redoubler [rəduble] **1.** *vtr* to redouble, increase (dose, efforts); **r. ses cris,** to shout louder than ever; *Sch:* **r. une classe,** to repeat a year **2.** *vi* **la pluie redoubla,** the rain came on worse than ever; **r. d'efforts,** to redouble one's efforts.

redouter [rədute] *vtr* to dread, fear. **redoutable** *a* fearsome, formidable.

redoux [rədu] *nm Meteor:* rise in temperature.

redressement [rədrɛsmã] *nm* straightening; (economic) recovery; **r. fiscal,** back tax.

redresser [rədrɛse] **1.** *vtr* (*a*) to set (sth) upright again (*b*) to right (boat); to straighten up (aircraft) (*c*) *Opt:* to erect (inverted image) (*d*) to straighten (sth) (out) (*e*) **r. la tête,** to hold up one's head; to look up (*f*) *El:* to rectify (current) (*g*) to redress, to right (wrong, grievance); to rectify (mistake) **2.** **se r.** (*a*) to stand up (straight) again; **se r. sur son séant,** to sit up straight (again) (*b*) (*of economy*) to recover (*c*) to draw oneself up.

redresseur, -euse [rədrɛsœr, -øz] **1.** *n* righter (of wrongs) **2.** *nm El:* rectifier (of current).

réduction [redyksjɔ̃] *nf* **1.** (*a*) reduction; cutting down (of expenditure); stepping down (of voltage) (*b*) capture (of town) **2.** (*a*) **réductions de salaires,** wage cuts; **grandes réductions de prix,** great reductions (in price) (*b*) reduced copy, reduction.

réduire [reduir] *vtr* (*conj like* CONDUIRE) **1.** *vtr* (*a*) to reduce (pressure, amount, speed); to lower, to cut (price); to cut down (expenses); to step down (voltage); **billet à prix réduit,** cheap ticket; **édition réduite,** abridged edition; **modèle réduit,** scaled-down model; scale model (*b*) **r. qch en miettes,** to crumble sth up (*c*) *Cu:* **r. une sauce,** to reduce a sauce (*d*) *Ch:* to reduce (oxide) (*e*) **r. qn à la misère,** to reduce s.o. to poverty (*f*) to reduce (fracture) **2.** **se r.** (*a*) **se r. au**

strict **nécessaire**, to confine oneself to what is strictly necessary; **ses bagages se réduisent au strict minimum**, he packs only the bare essentials in his luggage (b) **les frais se réduisent à peu de chose**, the expenses come to very little; **se r. en poussière**, to crumble into dust.

réduit [redɥi] *nm* (a) small room; hovel (b) alcove, nook.

rééditer [reedite] *vtr* (a) to republish (book) (b) F: to repeat.

réédition [reedisjɔ̃] *nf* (a) new edition (b) F: repetition, repeat.

rééducation [reedykasjɔ̃] *nf Med:* re-education; rehabilitation; **r. de la parole**, speech therapy.

rééduquer [reedyke] *vtr Med:* to re-educate; to rehabilitate.

réel, -elle [reɛl] 1. *a* (a) real, actual (fact, person); **salaire r.**, net earnings (b) (before noun) real, great (pleasure) 2. *nm* **le r.**, reality. **réellement** *adv* really; in reality.

réélection [reelɛksjɔ̃] *nf* re-election.

réélire [reelir] *vtr (conj like* ÉLIRE) to re-elect.

réescompter [reeskɔ̃te] *vtr Fin:* to rediscount.

réévaluation [reevalɥasjɔ̃] *nf* revaluation.

réévaluer [reevalɥe] *vtr* to revalue.

réexpédier [reɛkspedje] *vtr (conj like* EXPÉDIER) (a) to forward (letters) (b) to send back.

refaire [rəfɛr] *(conj like* FAIRE) 1. *vtr* (a) to remake; to do again; **c'est à r.**, it will have to be done again (b) to repair; to do up (house); F: **elle se refait une beauté**, she's doing her face again (c) F: to diddle (s.o.); to take (s.o.) in; **on vous a refait**, you've been had 2. **se r.** (a) to recuperate; to recover one's health (b) to change one's ways (c) to retrieve one's losses.

réfection [refɛksjɔ̃] *nf* repairing; repairs.

réfectoire [refɛktwar] *nm* refectory, dining hall, canteen.

référence [referɑ̃s] *nf* (a) reference, referring; **livre de r.**, reference book; **faire r. à**, to refer to; **r. au bas de page**, footnote (b) reference (on letter) (c) *pl* (employer's) reference, testimonial.

référendum [referɛ̃dɔm] *nm* referendum.

référer [refere] *v* (**je réfère; je référerai**) 1. *vi* **en r. à qn**, to refer a matter to s.o. 2. **se r.** (a) **se r. à qch**, to refer to sth (b) **s'en r. à qn d'une question**, to refer the matter to s.o.

refermer [rəfɛrme] 1. *vtr* to shut, to close (up) again 2. **se r.** (of door) to close again; (of wound) to heal.

refiler [rəfile] *vtr P:* **r. qch à qn**, to palm sth off on s.o.; to pass on sth to s.o.

réfléchir [refleʃir] 1. *vtr* to reflect (light) 2. (a) *vi* **r. à, sur, qch**, to reflect, to ponder, on sth; **réfléchissez-y**, think it over; **donner à r. à qn**, to give s.o. food for thought; **parler sans r.**, to speak without thinking, hastily (b) **r. que**, to realize that 3. **se r.**, (of light, heat) to be reflected; (of sound) to reverberate. **réfléchi** *a* (a) reflective, thoughtful (person); deliberate (action); considered (opinion); **tout bien r.**, everything considered (b) reflexive (verb).

réflecteur, -trice [reflɛktœr, -tris] 1. *a* reflecting (mirror, panel) 2. *nm* reflector.

reflet [rəflɛ] *nm* reflection; reflected light, image; **r. des eaux**, gleam on the waters; **chevelure à reflets**

d'or, hair with glints of gold; **il n'est qu'un pâle r. de son père**, he's only a pale reflection of his father.

refléter [rəflete] *vtr* (**il reflète; il reflétera**) 1. to reflect (light) 2. **se r.**, to be reflected.

réflexe [reflɛks] 1. *a Ph: Physiol:* reflex (light, action) 2. *nm* (a) *Physiol:* reflex (b) reflex, reaction; **avoir de bons réflexes**, to react quickly.

réflexif, -ive [reflɛksif, -iv] *a Mth:* reflexive.

réflexion [reflɛksjɔ̃] *nf* 1. reflection, reflexion (of light) 2. reflection, thought; **agir sans r.**, to act without thinking; **(toute) r. faite**, everything considered; **à la r.**, when you think about it; on second thoughts 3. remark; **une r. désobligeante**, an unpleasant remark.

refluer [rəflye] *vi* to flow back; (of tide) to ebb; (of blood) to rush back; (of crowd) to surge back.

reflux [rəfly] *nm* flowing back; backward surge; ebb tide.

refondre [rəfɔ̃dr] *vtr* to recast (bell, text).

refonte [rəfɔ̃t] *nf* recasting; re-organization.

réformation [reformasjɔ̃] *nf* reform; RelH: **la R.**, the Reformation.

réforme [reform] *nf* 1. reform (of calendar); RelH: Reformation 2. *Mil:* discharge (for physical unfitness); invaliding out; *Ind:* **matériel en r.**, scrapped plant.

réformé, -ée [reforme] *a & n* 1. Protestant; *a* reformed (church) 2. (serviceman, -woman) discharged for unfitness.

reformer [rəforme] *vtr* to form again, to reform.

réformer [reforme] *vtr* 1. to reform (law) 2. (a) *Mil:* to discharge as unfit; to invalid out of service (b) *Ind:* to scrap (equipment). **réformateur, -trice** (a) *a* reforming (b) *n* reformer.

refoulement [rəfulmɑ̃] *nm* driving, forcing, back; *Psy:* repression.

refouler [rəfule] *vtr* to drive back, force back; to turn back (an alien); to suppress (feelings); to force back (tears); *Psy:* to repress (an instinct).

réfractaire [refrakter] 1. *a* (a) refractory, insubordinate (b) fireproof (clay, brick) (c) resistant; **r. aux acides**, acid-proof 2. *n* rebel; conscientious objector.

réfracter [refrakte] *vtr* to refract.

réfraction [refraksjɔ̃] *nf Ph:* refraction.

refrain [rəfrɛ̃] *nm* 1. refrain (of song); F: **c'est toujours le même r.**, it's always the same old story 2. **r. en chœur**, chorus.

réfréner [refrene] *vtr* (**je refrène; je refrénerai**) to curb, restrain.

réfrigérateur [refriʒeratœr] *nm* refrigerator, F: fridge.

réfrigération [refriʒerasjɔ̃] *nf* refrigeration.

réfrigérer [refriʒere] *vtr* (**je réfrigère; je réfrigérerai**) to refrigerate; **viande réfrigérée**, chilled meat. **réfrigérant** *a* refrigerating; frosty (reception).

refroidir [rəfrwadir] 1. *vtr* (a) to cool, chill (air, water) (b) to cool (engine); *Ind:* **refroidi par (l')air, par (l')eau**, air-cooled, water-cooled (c) to cool (friendship); to damp (sympathy); to cool (off) enthusiasm (d) *P:* to kill (s.o.); to bump (s.o.) off 2. *vi & pr* to grow cold; to cool down; **laisser r. son thé**, to let one's tea get cold; **le temps a refroidi, s'est refroidi**, it's turned colder; *Med:* **se r.**, to catch a chill.

refroidissement [rəfrwadismã] *nm* (*a*) cooling (*b*) *Med:* chill.

refuge [rəfyʒ] *nm* (*a*) refuge; shelter; (climber's) hut (*b*) traffic island.

réfugié, -ée [refyʒje] *n* refugee.

réfugier (se) [sərefyʒje] *vpr* to take refuge.

refus [rəfy] *nm* refusal; **ce n'est pas de r.**, I can't say no (to that).

refuser [rəfyze] **1.** *vtr* (*a*) to refuse, decline; to turn down (offer); **r. l'entrée à qn**, to deny s.o. entry; **r. toute qualité à qn**, to refuse to see any good in s.o.; **r. de faire qch**, to refuse to do sth (*b*) to reject (s.o.); to turn (s.o.) away; to fail (candidate); **être refusé**, to fail **2. se r. à qch**, to set one's face against sth; to shut one's eyes to sth; **se r. à faire qch**, to refuse to do sth.

réfutation [refytasjɔ̃] *nf* refutation.

réfuter [refyte] *vtr* to refute.

regagner [rəgaɲe] *vtr* **1.** to regain, recover, win back confidence; to get back (money); **r. le temps perdu**, to make up for lost time **2.** to get back to (a place).

regain [rəgɛ̃] *nm* **1.** second crop (of hay) **2.** renewal; revival.

régal -als [regal] *nm* (*a*) feast (*b*) treat.

régaler [regale] **1.** *vtr F:* to entertain, to treat (s.o.) to delicious meal **2. se r.**, *F:* to feast (**de**, on); to treat oneself (**de**, to); **on s'est bien régalé**, we had a slap-up meal.

regard [rəgar] *nm* **1.** (*a*) look, glance, gaze; **chercher qn du r.**, to look round for s.o.; **lancer un r. furieux à qn**, to glare at s.o.; **détourner le r.**, to look away; **attirer le(s) regard(s)**, to attract attention (*b*) **en r. de qch**, (i) opposite, facing, sth (ii) compared with sth; **texte avec photos en r.**, text with photographs on the opposite page; **au r. de qch**, with regard to sth **2.** manhole; peephole.

regarder [rəgarde] *vtr* **1.** (*a*) to regard, consider (*b*) **ne r. que ses intérêts**, to consider only one's own interests (*c*) *vi* **r. à qch**, to pay attention to sth; **sans r. à la dépense**, regardless of expense; **à y bien r.**, on thinking it over; **je ne regarde pas à 2 francs**, 2 francs more or less makes no difference; **je n'y regarde pas de si près**, I am not as particular, as fussy, as all that (*d*) to concern (s.o.); **cela ne vous regarde pas**, that's no concern of yours; that's none of your business; **en ce qui me regarde**, as far as I'm concerned **2.** (*a*) to look at; to watch (game); **r. qn fixement**, to stare at s.o.; **r. qn de travers**, to look askance at s.o.; **r. qn avec méfiance**, to eye s.o. suspiciously; **se faire r.**, to attract attention; **r. qn faire qch**, to watch s.o. do sth; *F:* **regardez-moi ça!** just look at that! **non, mais tu ne m'as pas regardé!** what do you take me for! (*b*) *vi* **r. à la fenêtre**, to look in at the window; **r. par la fenêtre**, to look out of the window; **puis-je r.?** may I have a look? **3.** to look on to; to face (sth). **regardant** *a* close(-fisted), stingy (person).

régate [regat] *nf* regatta.

régence [reʒɑ̃s] *nf* regency.

régénérer [reʒenere] *vtr* (**je régénère; je régénérerai**) **1.** to regenerate **2.** to reactivate.

régent [reʒɑ̃] *nm* regent.

régenter [reʒɑ̃te] *vtr* to domineer over, to dictate to (s.o.).

régie [reʒi] *nf* **1.** (*a*) administration; management, control (*b*) state-owned company **2.** *Th:* management; *Cin:* production; *TV:* central control room.

regimber [rəʒɛ̃be] *vi* to baulk, to jib (**contre**, at).

régime [reʒim] *nm* **1.** regime; form of government, of administration; **le r. du travail**, the organization of labour; **r. parlementaire**, parliamentary system **2. r. (nominal)**, rating (of engine); speed; **à plein r.**, (at) full speed; **3.** *Med:* diet; **être au r.**, to be on a diet **4.** *Gram:* object **5.** bunch (of bananas, dates).

régiment [reʒimɑ̃] *nm* regiment; *F:* **être au r.**, to do (one's) military service.

région [reʒjɔ̃] *nf* region, area. **régional, -aux** *a* regional; local.

régionalisme [reʒjonalism] *nm* regionalism. **régionaliste 1.** *a* regional **2.** *n* regionalist.

régir [reʒir] *vtr* to govern, rule.

régisseur [reʒisœr] *nm* manager; steward; *Th:* stage manager; *Cin:* assistant director.

registre [rəʒistr] *nm* **1.** register; record; account book; minute book; *Adm:* **les registres de l'état civil**, the registers of births, marriages and deaths **2.** *Mus:* register **3. r. de cheminée**, register, damper (of chimney).

réglable [reglabl] *a* adjustable.

réglage [reglaʒ] *nm* (*a*) regulating, adjusting, adjustment (of apparatus); tuning (of engine) (*b*) *WTel: etc:* control tuning.

règle [regl] *nf* **1.** rule, ruler; **r. à calcul**, slide rule **2.** rule (of conduct, art, grammar); **règles du jeu**, rules of the game; **en r.**, in order; according to the rules; **c'est de r.**, it's normal practice; **tout est en r.**, everything is in order; **bataille en r.**, proper fight; **en r. générale**, as a general rule; **dans les règles**, according to rule **3. prendre qn pour r.**, to take s.o. as an example **4.** *Physiol:* **avoir ses règles**, to have one's period.

réglé [regle] *a* ruled (paper); **papier non r.**, plain paper **2.** regular; well-ordered (life); steady, stable (person).

règlement [regləmɑ̃] *nm* **1.** settlement, adjustment (of difficulty, account); payment; **faire un r. par chèque**, to pay by cheque; **r. de compte(s)**, settling of scores **2.** regulation(s); rules (of society). **réglementaire** *a* regular, statutory; regulation (uniform); prescribed (time); **ce n'est pas r.**, it's against the rules.

réglementation [regləmɑ̃tasjɔ̃] *nf* **1.** regulation; control **2.** regulations, rules.

réglementer [regləmɑ̃te] *vtr* to regulate; to make rules for (sth); to control.

régler [regle] *vtr* (**je règle; je réglerai**) **1.** to rule (paper) **2.** (*a*) to regulate, order (one's life, conduct) (*b*) to regulate, adjust; **r. une montre**, to set a watch right; **r. le moteur**, to tune the engine **3.** (*a*) to settle (question); **r. ses affaires**, to put one's affairs in order (*b*) to settle (account); to pay (bill); **r. par chèque**, to pay by cheque; **r. un compte avec qn**, to settle a score with s.o.

réglisse [reglis] *nf* liquorice.

règne [rɛɲ] *nm* **1.** *Z: Bot:* kingdom **2.** reign; **sous le r. de Louis XIV**, in the reign of Louis XIV.

régner [reɲe] *vi* (**je règne; je régnerai**) (*of monarch*) to reign, rule; (*of conditions, opinion*) to prevail; to be prevalent; **faire r. l'ordre,** to maintain law and order.

regorger [rəgɔrʒe] *vi* **(je regorgeai(s); n. regorgeons)** *(a)* to overflow, run over *(b)* to abound **(de,** in); to be glutted **(de,** with); **les trains regorgent de gens,** the trains are packed (with people).

régresser [regrese] *vi* to regress.

régression [regresjɔ̃] *nf* regression; **en (voie de) r.,** on the decline. **régressif, -ive** *a* regressive.

regret [rəgrɛ] *nm* regret **(de,** for); **avoir r. d'avoir fait qch,** to regret having done sth; **j'ai le r. de vous annoncer que,** I am sorry to inform you that; **faire qch à r.,** to do sth reluctantly, regretfully.

regretter [rəgrɛte] *vtr* **1.** to regret (s.o., sth); **je regrette de vous avoir fait attendre,** I'm sorry I kept you waiting; **je regrette!** (I'm) sorry! **2.** to miss (s.o.). **regrettable** *a* regrettable; unfortunate (mistake).

regroupement [rəgrupmɑ̃] *nm* regrouping; round-up; amalgamation.

regrouper [rəgrupe] *vtr & pr (a)* to regroup; to gather together; to assemble *(b)* to amalgamate.

régularisation [regylarizasjɔ̃] *nf* regularization; putting in order; regulation.

régulariser [regylarize] *vtr (a)* to regularize (sth); to put (document) into proper form; to put in order *(b)* to regulate.

régularité [regylarite] *nf (a)* regularity *(b)* steadiness, evenness *(c)* equability *(d)* punctuality.

régulation [regylasjɔ̃] *nf* regulation; (traffic, birth) control. **régulateur, -trice** *(a) a* regulating *(b) nm Tchn:* regulator.

régulier, -ière [regylje, -jɛr] **1.** *a (a)* regular; valid (passport) *(b)* steady (pulse); even (motion); regular (service); ordered (life); steady (work); **humeur régulière,** even temper **2.** *a & nm* regular (soldier, priest). **régulièrement** *adv* regularly; steadily, evenly.

réhabilitation [reabilitasjɔ̃] *nf* rehabilitation; reinstatement; renovation.

réhabiliter [reabilite] *vtr* **1.** to rehabilitate (s.o.); to discharge (bankrupt); to reinstate (s.o. in his rights) **2.** to renovate (old building).

rehausser [rəose] *vtr* **1.** to raise, to heighten (wall); to make (sth) higher **2.** to enhance, set off (colour); to bring out, to emphasize (detail).

réimpression [reɛ̃presjɔ̃] *nf(a)* reprinting *(b)* reprint.

réimprimer [reɛ̃prime] *vtr* to reprint.

Reims [rɛ̃s] *Prnm Geog:* Rheims.

rein [rɛ̃] *nm* **1.** *Anat:* kidney; **r. artificiel,** kidney machine **2.** *pl* loins, back; **la chute des reins,** the small of the back; **mal aux reins,** backache; **il a les reins solides,** he's a man of substance; **casser les reins à qn,** to ruin s.o.

réincarnation [reɛ̃karnasjɔ̃] *nf* reincarnation.

réincarner (se) [səreɛ̃karne] *vpr* to be reincarnated.

reine [rɛn] *nf (a)* queen; **r. mère,** queen mother *(b)* queen (bee) *(c)* **r. de beauté,** beauty queen.

reine-claude [rɛnklod] *nf* greengage; *pl reines-claudes.*

reine-marguerite [rɛnmargərit] *nf Bot:* China aster; *pl reines-marguerites.*

reinette [rɛnɛt] *nf* pippin (apple); **r. grise,** russet.

réinscrire [reɛ̃skrir] *vtr (conj like* INSCRIRE) to write down again; to re-register; **se r.,** to re-enrol, re-register.

réinstaller [reɛ̃stale] *vtr* to reinstall; **se r.,** to settle down again.

réintégration [reɛ̃tegrasjɔ̃] *nf* reinstatement; return **(de,** to).

réintégrer [reɛ̃tegre] *vtr (conj like* INTÉGRER) **1. r. qn (dans ses fonctions),** to reinstate s.o. **2. r. son domicile,** to return to one's home.

réitérer [reitere] *vtr* **(je réitère; je réitérerai)** to reiterate, repeat.

rejaillir [rəʒajir] *vi (a)* to spurt back, to gush out; to splash up, out *(b)* **tout cela rejaillit sur moi,** all this is a reflection on me.

rejet [rəʒɛ] *nm* **1.** *(a)* throwing out, up *(b)* material thrown out; spoil (earth) **2.** rejection (of proposal, *Med:* of transplant); dismissal (of an appeal) **3.** *Hort:* shoot.

rejeter [rəʒte] *(conj like* JETER) **1.** *vtr (a)* to throw, fling, (sth) back; to return (ball); **r. son chapeau en arrière,** to tilt one's hat back *(b)* to throw up *(c)* to transfer; **r. la faute sur d'autres,** to lay the blame on others *(d)* to reject, to turn down (offer); **r. un projet de loi,** to throw out a bill *(e) Knit:* **r. les mailles,** to cast off **2. se r.,** to fall back **(sur,** on).

rejeton [rəʒtɔ̃] *nm* **1.** *Hort:* shoot, sucker **2.** offspring.

rejoindre [rəʒwɛ̃dr] *(conj like* ATTEINDRE) **1.** *vtr (a)* to rejoin, reunite, to join (together) again; to connect (streets); **sa pensée rejoint la mienne,** his ideas are akin to mine *(b)* **r. qn,** to rejoin s.o.; to overtake s.o.; to catch s.o. up (again); **il a évité de r. la route nationale,** he avoided joining the main road **2. se r.** *(a)* to meet *(b)* to meet again.

réjouir [reʒwir] *vtr* **1.** to delight, gladden, cheer (s.o.) **2. se r.** *(a)* to rejoice **(de,** at, in); to be glad **(de,** of); to be delighted **(de,** at); **je me réjouis de le revoir,** (i) I am looking forward to seeing him again (ii) I am delighted to see him again *(b)* to enjoy oneself. **réjoui** *a* jolly, cheerful.

réjouissance [reʒwisɑ̃s] *nf* rejoicing. **réjouissant** *a (a)* cheering, heartening *(b)* entertaining, amusing.

relâche [rəlɑʃ] **1.** *nm (a)* slackening (of rope) *(b)* relaxation, respite; rest; **travailler sans r.,** to work without a break *(c) Th:* closure; **faire r.,** to be closed **2.** *nf Nau: (a)* call; **faire r. dans un port,** to put into a port *(b)* port of call.

relâchement [rəlɑʃmɑ̃] *nm* relaxing, slackening; relaxation; laxity.

relâcher [rəlɑʃe] **1.** *vtr (a)* to loosen, slacken (cord); to relax (muscle, discipline) *(b)* to release, to let go (prisoner, caged bird) **2.** *vi Nau:* to put into port **3. se r.** *(a) (of rope)* to slacken; *(of muscle)* to relax; *(of pers)* to become slack; *(of zeal)* to flag; *(of discipline)* to get lax *(b) (of pers)* to relax, to take a rest.

relais [rəlɛ] *nm* **1.** *(a)* relay; *Ind:* shift; *Sp:* **course de r.,** relay race; **prendre le r.,** to take over **(de qn,** from s.o.) *(b)* coaching inn; post house; **r. gastronomique,** restaurant with a reputation for good food; *Aut:* **r. routier,** service station (with café) **2.** *MecE:* relay (unit); *El:* relay; **r. de radio-diffusion,** relay broadcasting station.

relance [rəlɑ̃s] *nf* boost; fresh start; revival (of economy).

relancer [rəlɑ̃se] *vtr* (*conj like* LANCER) 1. to throw (sth) back; *Ten:* to return (the ball) 2. (*a*) to boost (trade); to revive (economy) (*c*) to badger (s.o.); to harass (debtor).

relater [rəlate] *vtr* to relate, state (facts).

relatif, -ive [rəlatif, -iv] *a* (*a*) relative (position, value, *Gram:* pronoun) (*b*) **questions relatives à un sujet,** questions related to a subject (*c*) comparative. **relativement** *adv* relatively; in relation (à, to); comparatively.

relation [rəlasjɔ̃] *nf* 1. (*a*). relation, connection; **les relations humaines,** human relations; **se mettre en relations avec qn,** to get in touch with s.o.; **être en relations d'affaires avec qn,** to have business dealings with s.o.; **en relations d'amitié (avec qn,** on friendly terms (with s.o.); **r. étroite entre deux faits,** close connection between two facts (*b*) acquaintance; **avoir des relations,** (i) to be well connected (ii) to have influential friends 2. account, report.

relativité [rəlativite] *nf* relativity.

relaxation [rəlaksasjɔ̃] *nf* relaxation.

relax(e) [rəlaks] 1. *F:* (*a*) *a* relaxed; casual, informal; relaxing; **fauteuil relax(e),** reclining chair (*b*) *nm* relaxation, rest 2. *nf* **relaxe** (*a*) relaxation (*b*) release, discharge (of accused person).

relaxer (se) [sərəlakse] *vpr* to relax.

relayer [rəleje] (**je relaie, je relaye**) 1. *vtr* (*a*) to relay, relieve (s.o.), take turns with (s.o.); *Sp:* to take over from (s.o.) (*b*) to relay (broadcast) 2. **se r.,** to take turns (**pour faire,** to do); *Sp:* to take over from one another.

relayeur [rəlɛjœr] *nm Sp:* relay runner.

reléguer [rəlege] *vtr* (*conj like* LÉGUER) to relegate (à, to).

relent [rəlɑ̃] *nm* unpleasant smell, taste.

relève [rəlɛv] *nf* 1. *Mil:* relief (of sentry); changing (of the guard); **prendre la r.,** to take over (**de,** from) 2. relief (troops).

relevé [rəlve] 1. *a* (*a*) raised, erect (head); turned up (collar); **pantalon à bords relevés,** turn-up trousers; turn-ups (*b*) exalted (position); noble (sentiment) (*c*) highly seasoned (sauce) 2 *nm* (*a*) summary; (gas, electricity) meter reading; *Com:* **r. de compte,** statement (of account); bank statement (*b*) survey.

relèvement [rəlɛvmɑ̃] *nm* 1. recovery (of business); increase (in wages); raising (of tax) 2. *Nau:* bearing; position.

relever [rəlve] *v* (*conj like* LEVER) 1. *vtr* (*a*) (i) to raise, lift, set, up again; to set (s.o.) on his feet again; to rebuild (wall) (ii) to pick up (from the ground) (iii) to raise (higher); to turn up (collar); to roll up (sleeve); **r. la tête,** to hold up one's head; to look up; **r. les prix,** to increase prices (*b*) to call attention to (sth); to notice; to point out (defects); to pick up (mistake) (*c*) to enhance (colour); to season (sauce) (*d*) to relieve (sentry); to take (s.o.'s) place; **r. qn d'une promesse,** to release s.o. from a promise (*e*) to note; to take down (statement); to record (temperature); to make out (account); to read (meter) (*f*) *Nau:* take the bearing(s) of (a place); *Surv:* to survey, plot, (piece of land) 2. *vi* (*a*) **r. de maladie,** to be recovering from an illness (*b*) **r. de qn, de qch,** to be a matter for, to be the concern of, s.o., sth; to

come under s.o., sth 3. **se r.** (*a*) to rise to one's feet (again), to get up (again); to pick oneself up (*b*) (*of trade, courage*) to revive, to recover (*c*) **se r. de qch.,** to recover from sth; **il ne s'en relèvera pas,** he'll never get over it.

releveur, -euse [rəlvœr, -øz] *n* meter reader.

relief [rəljɛf] *nm* 1. *Art: Geog:* relief; **carte en r.,** relief map; **photo en r.,** 3-dimensional photograph; **mettre qch en r.,** to bring (sth) out; to set (sth) off; **position très en r.,** prominent position 2. *pl* scraps, leftovers.

relier [rəlje] *vtr* (*a*) to connect, link, join (*b*) to bind (book).

relieur [rəljœr] *nm* (book)binder.

religieux, -euse [rəliʒjø, -øz] 1. *a* religious; sacred (music); church (wedding); scrupulous (care) 2. *nm* monk; *nf* nun 3. *nf Cu:* cream éclair. **religieusement** *adv* religiously.

religion [rəliʒjɔ̃] *nf* (*a*) religion; (religious) faith; **entrer en r.,** to take the vows (*b*) **se faire une r. de qch,** to make a religion of sth.

reliquaire [rəlikɛr] *nm* reliquary.

reliquat [rəlika] *nm* remainder; balance (of account).

relique [rəlik] *nf* relic; **garder qch comme une r.,** to treasure sth.

relire [rəlir] *vtr* (*conj like* LIRE) to re-read; to read (over) again.

reliure [rəljyr] *nf* 1. bookbinding; **atelier de r.,** bindery 2. binding.

relogement [rəlɔʒmɑ̃] *nm* rehousing.

reloger [rəlɔʒe] *vtr* (*conj like* LOGER) to rehouse.

reluire [rəlɥir] *vi* (*conj like* LUIRE) to shine; to glitter, glisten, gleam; **faire r. qch,** to polish sth up. **reluisant** *a* shining, gleaming (**de,** with); *Pej:* **c'est peu r.,** it's not brilliant.

reluquer [rəlyke] *vtr F:* to eye (s.o.) (up).

remâcher [rəmɑʃe] *vtr* to ruminate on (sth); to brood over (sth).

remanger [rəmɑ̃ʒe] *vtr* (*conj like* MANGER) to eat again; to eat more of (sth).

remaniement [rəmanimɑ̃] *nm* altering; reshaping, recasting; modification; reshuffle.

remanier [rəmanje] *vtr* (*impf & pr sub*) n. **remaniions**) to recast, reshape, alter, adapt; to reshuffle (cabinet).

remarier (se) [sərəmarje] *vpr* to remarry.

remarquable [rəmarkabl] *a* (*a*) remarkable, noteworthy (**par,** for); distinguished (**par,** by); outstanding (event) (*b*) strange, astonishing; **il est r. qu'il n'ait rien entendu,** it's a wonder that he heard nothing. **remarquablement** *adv* remarkably.

remarque [rəmark] *nf* remark; comment; **faire une r.,** (i) to make a remark (ii) to make a critical observation.

remarquer [rəmarke] *vtr* (*a*) to remark, notice, observe; **ça ne se remarque pas,** it doesn't show; **faire r. qch à qn,** to point sth out to s.o.; **se faire r.,** to attract attention (*c*) to remark, observe, say.

remballer [rɑ̃bale] *vtr* to repack; to pack (up) again.

rembarquer [rɑ̃barke] 1. *vtr* to re-embark 2. *vi & pr* to re-embark.

rembarrer [rɑ̃bare] *vtr F:* to rebuff (s.o.).

remblai [rɑ̃blɛ] *nm* (a) filling material; earth; (**terre de**) **r.**, ballast (b) embankment, bank.

remblayer [rɑ̃bleje] *vtr* (**je remblaie, je remblaye**) (a) to fill (up) (b) to embank, to bank (up) (road, railway line).

rembobiner [rɑ̃bɔbine] *vtr* to rewind.

remboîter [rɑ̃bwate] *vtr* to reassemble; to fit together again.

rembourrage [rɑ̃buraʒ] *nm* stuffing, padding.

rembourrer [rɑ̃bure] *vtr* to stuff, to pad, to upholster (chair).

remboursement [rɑ̃bursəmɑ̃] *nm* repayment; reimbursement; refund.

rembourser [rɑ̃burse] *vtr* 1. to repay, refund (expenses); to pay off (annuity); to return (loan) 2. **r. qn de qch**, to reimburse s.o. for sth; **on m'a remboursé**, I got my money back. **remboursable** *a* (*of loan*) repayable; refundable.

rembrunir (se) [sərɑ̃brynir] *vpr* (*of sky*) to cloud over, to darken; (*of pers*) to become gloomy.

remède [rəmɛd] *nm* remedy, cure (**à, pour, contre**, for); **r. de bonne femme**, old wives' cure; **c'est sans r.**, it's beyond remedy.

remédier [rəmedje] *v ind tr* (*impf & pr sub* n. **remédiions**) **r. à qch**, to remedy, to cure, sth, to put sth right.

remembrement [rəmɑ̃brəmɑ̃] *nm* regrouping (of land).

remembrer [rəmɑ̃bre] *vtr Adm:* to regroup (land).

remerciement [rəmɛrsimɑ̃] *nm* thanks, acknowledgement; **lettre de r.**, thank-you letter.

remercier [rəmɛrsje] *vtr* (*impf & pr sub* n. **remerciions**) 1. to thank (**de, pour**, for); **il me remercia d'un sourire**, he smiled his thanks; **voulez-vous du café?—je vous remercie**, will you have some coffee?—no, thank you 2. to dismiss (employee).

remettre [rəmɛtr] *vtr* (*conj like* METTRE) 1. *vtr* (a) to put (sth) back (again); **r. son manteau**, to put one's coat on again; **r. qch à sa place**, to replace sth; **r. qn à sa place**, to put s.o. in his place; **r. un os**, to set a bone; **r. en état**, to repair; **r. en marche**, to restart (machine) (b) **r. qn (sur pied)**, to put s.o. back on his, on her, feet (c) (*see* r.), to recall s.o.; **je ne vous remets pas**, I don't remember you (d) to hand over, to deliver (letter); to turn (s.o.) over (to the police) (e) to postpone; **r. une affaire au lendemain**, to put off a matter till the next day (f) to remit (penalty); to pardon (offence) (g) *F:* **remettons ça!** let's do it again! let's have another drink! 2. **se r.** (a) **se r. au lit**, to go back to bed; **le temps se remet (au beau)**, the weather is clearing up (again) (b) **se r. au travail**, to start work again (c) **se r. d'une maladie**, to recover from an illness; **remettez-vous!** pull yourself together! (d) **s'en r. à qn**, to rely on s.o. for sth (e) **se r. avec qn**, to make it up with s.o.

réminiscence [reminisɑ̃s] *nf* 1. reminiscence 2. vague recollection.

remise [rəmiz] *nf* 1. (a) putting back (of sth, in its place) (b) **r. en état**, repairing; **r. en ordre**, putting in order; **r. en marche**, restarting 2. (a) delivery, handing over (of letter) (b) remission (of penalty, tax); **faire r. d'une dette**, to cancel a debt 3. (a) remittance (b) discount 4. shed, outhouse.

remiser [rəmize] *vtr* to garage (car); to put (sth) away.

rémission [remisjɔ̃] *nf* remission (of sin, of debt); **sans r.**, relentlessly; without a break.

remontage [rəmɔ̃taʒ] *nm* (a) winding up (of clock) (b) putting together, reassembling (of parts).

remontant [rəmɔ̃tɑ̃] 1. *a* (a) fortifying (drink) (b) perpetual (rose) 2. *nm* tonic; *F:* pick-me-up.

remontée [rəmɔ̃te] *nf* climb (after descent); *Sp:* **un belle r.**, a good recovery; **r. mécanique**, skilift.

remonte-pente [rəmɔ̃tpɑ̃t] *nm* skilift; *pl* **remonte-pentes.**

remonter [rəmɔ̃te] 1. *vi* (*aux usu* être, *occ* avoir) (a) to go up (again); (*of temperature*) to rise; (*of prices*) to go up; **r. en voiture**, to get into one's car again (b) (*of clothes*) to ride up (c) to go back (in time); **tout cela remonte loin**, all that goes back a long way (d) (*of tide*) to flow 2. *vtr* (a) to go up, to climb, up (hill, stairs) again; **r. la rue**, to go up the street; **r. la rivière**, to go, row, sail, swim, upstream (b) to take up (again); to pull up (socks); to hitch up (trousers); to heighten (wall) (c) to wind (up) (clock); **r. (les forces de) qn**, to put new life into s.o.; **un verre de vin vous remontera**, a glass of wine will do you good, will buck you up (d) to refit; to reassemble (parts) (e) to restock (shop); to replenish (one's wardrobe) 3. **se r.**, to recover one's strength; **prendre qch pour se r.**, to take a tonic.

remontoir [rəmɔ̃twar] *nm* winder.

remontrance [rəmɔ̃trɑ̃s] *nf* remonstrance; **faire des remontrances à qn**, to reprimand s.o.

remontrer [rəmɔ̃tre] *vtr* (a) to show, demonstrate, (sth) again (b) **il m'en a remontré**, he taught me a thing or two.

remords [rəmɔr] *nm* remorse, self reproach; **un r.**, a twinge of remorse; **avoir un, des, r.**, to be conscience-stricken.

remorquage [rəmɔrkaʒ] *nm* towing.

remorque [rəmɔrk] *nf* 1. towing; **prendre une voiture en r.**, to tow a car; *Fig:* **être à la r.**, to keep in tow 2. tow line. 3. (a) tow; vessel towed (b) *Aut:* trailer; **r. (de) camping**, caravan.

remorquer [rəmɔrke] *vtr* to tow; to haul.

remorqueur [rəmɔrkœr] *nm* tugboat.

remous [rəmu] *nm* (a) eddy; wash (of ship); swirl (of the tide); backwash; *Av:* **r. d'air**, (i) slip-stream (ii) eddy (b) disturbance; bustle (of crowd); **ce livre va provoquer des r.**, this book will cause a stir.

rempailler [rɑ̃paje] *vtr* to re-seat, re-bottom (chair).

rempart [rɑ̃par] *nm* rampart.

remplaçant, -ante [rɑ̃plasɑ̃, -ɑ̃t] *n* substitute; locum (tenens); supply teacher; *Sp:* reserve.

remplacement [rɑ̃plasmɑ̃] *nm* replacement; substitution; **en r. de qch**, instead of sth, as a replacement for sth; **faire des remplacements**, (i) to take temporary jobs (ii) to do supply teaching.

remplacer [rɑ̃plase] *vtr* (*conj like* PLACER) 1. to take the place of (s.o., sth); to deputize for (s.o.) 2. (a) to replace; **r. qch par qch**, to put sth in place of sth (b) to supersede (s.o.). **remplaçable** *a* replaceable.

remplir [rɑ̃plir] *vtr* 1. to fill up, to refill (glass) (**de**, with); to fill in (gap, space); to occupy, take up (time) 2. **r. de**; to fill; **r. l'air de ses cris**, to fill the air with one's cries 3. to fill in, *NAm:* fill out (a form) 4. to fulfil (promise, order); to perform (one's duty); *Th:* **r. un rôle**, to fill a part.

remplissage [rɑ̃plisaʒ] *nm* filling up; padding (of speech).

remplumer (se) [sərɑ̃plyme] *vpr F:* (a) to be in funds again (b) to put on weight again.

remporter [rɑ̃pɔrte] *vtr* 1. to take (sth) back, away 2. to carry off (prize); to achieve (success); to win (victory).

remue-ménage [rəmymenaʒ] *nm inv* stir, commotion; confusion, upset.

remuer [rəmɥe] 1. *vtr* to move; to shift; to stir (coffee); to turn over (the ground); to stir up (s.o.); **r. ciel et terre**, to move heaven and earth 2. *vi* to move, stir, *F:* budge; (to child) **ne remue pas tout le temps!** don't fidget! 3. **se r.**, to move, to stir; to be active; **remuez-vous un peu!** get a move on!

rémunération [remynerasjɔ̃] *nf* remuneration, payment (**de**, for).

rémunérer [remynere] *vtr* (**je rémunère; je rémunérerai**) to remunerate; to pay for (services). **rémunérateur, -trice** *a* remunerative; lucrative.

renâcler [rənɑkle] *vi* (a) (of animal) to snort; (of pers) to sniff (**à qch.**, at sth) (b) to show reluctance; to hang back; to jib (at a job).

renaissance [rənɛsɑ̃s] *nf* (a) rebirth (b) renewal (c) *Hist:* **la R.**, the Renaissance; *a inv* **mobilier R.**, Renaissance furniture.

renaître [rənɛtr] *vi* (conj like NAÎTRE) 1. to be born again; **r. à la vie**, to take on a new lease of life 2. to return, to reappear; (of plants) to grow, to spring up, again; (of day) to dawn; (of hope) to revive.

rénal, -aux [renal, -o] *a* renal; kidney (stone).

renard, -arde [rənar, -ard] *n* fox, vixen; **c'est un fin r.**, he's a sly (old) fox.

renchérir [rɑ̃ʃerir] *vi* (a) (of goods) to get dearer; to increase in price (b) **r. sur qn**, to outdo s.o.; to go one better than s.o.

renchérissement [rɑ̃ʃerismɑ̃] *nm* rise in price.

rencontre [rɑ̃kɔ̃tr] *nf* 1. meeting, encounter; **faire la r. de qn**, to meet s.o.; **aller à la r. de qn**, to go to meet s.o.; **faire une mauvaise r.**, to have an unpleasant encounter 2. *Sp:* match; *Box:* fight.

rencontrer [rɑ̃kɔ̃tre] 1. *vtr* (a) to meet; to come upon (sth); to encounter, meet with (difficulty, opposition); **la voiture a rencontré un autobus**, the car collided with a bus (b) to have a meeting with (s.o.); *Sp:* to meet, to play against (another team) 2. **se r.** (a) to meet (b) to collide (c) to occur; **comme cela se rencontre!** how lucky! 2. (of ideas) to agree.

rendement [rɑ̃dmɑ̃] *nm* (a) yield (of land); return (on investment) (b) output (of workers); output, production (of works) (c) efficiency, performance (of machine).

rendez-vous [rɑ̃devu] *nm inv* 1. rendezvous; appointment; **donner r.-v. à qn**, to arrange to meet s.o.; **j'ai r.-v. avec lui à 3 heures**, I'm meeting him at 3 o'clock; **r.-v. spatial**, docking in space 2. meeting place; **r.-v. de chasse**, meet.

rendormir [rɑ̃dɔrmir] (conj like DORMIR) 1. *vtr* to send, lull, (s.o.) to sleep again 2. **se r.**, to go to sleep again, to go back to sleep.

rendre [rɑ̃dr] 1. *vtr* (a) to give back, return, restore; to repay (money); **r. la santé à qn**, to restore s.o. to

health; **r. la monnaie à qn**, to give s.o. his change; **je le lui rendrai!** I'll be even with him! (b) to render; to pay (tribute); **r. grâce à qn**, to give thanks to s.o.; **r. service à qn**, to be of help to s.o.; **r. la justice**, to administer justice; **r. compte de qch**, to account for sth (c) to yield; to give, produce; **placement qui rend 10%**, investment that brings in 10%; **terre qui ne rend rien**, unproductive land; **le moteur rend bien**, the engine runs well (d) to convey, deliver (goods); **prix rendu**, delivery price (e) to bring up, throw up (food); *vi* to vomit, to be sick; **r. l'âme**, to give up the ghost (f) to give up, surrender (one's arms) (g) to issue, pronounce (decree); to deliver (judgment); to return (verdict) (h) to reproduce, render, express; **elle rend très bien Chopin**, she plays Chopin very well (i) **le homard me rend malade**, lobster makes me ill; **il se rend ridicule**, he is making himself ridiculous; **vous me rendez fou!** you're driving me mad! 2. **se r.** (a) **se r. dans un lieu**, to go to, make one's way to, a place; **se rendre chez qn**, to call on s.o. (b) to surrender; to give in; to give oneself up; **rendez-vous!** hands up! (c) **se r. compte de qch**, to realize sth.

rendu [rɑ̃dy] 1. *a* **r. (de fatigue)**, exhausted 2. *nm Com:* return.

rêne [rɛn] *nf usu pl* rein.

renégat, -ate [rənega, -at] *n* renegade.

renfermer [rɑ̃fɛrme] 1. *vtr* to contain, to hold, to enclose 2. **se r. en soi-même**, to withdraw into oneself. **renfermé** 1. *a* (of pers) withdrawn 2. *nm* **sentir le r.**, to smell stuffy, musty.

renflé [rɑ̃fle] *a* bulging.

renflement [rɑ̃fləmɑ̃] *nm* bulge.

renflouer [rɑ̃flue] *vtr* to refloat (ship); to set (business, s.o.) on its, on his, feet again.

renfoncement [rɑ̃fɔ̃smɑ̃] *nm* recess.

renforcer [rɑ̃fɔrse] (conj like FORCER) 1. *vtr* to reinforce; to strengthen (wall, position); to intensify (effort) to consolidate (peace); to confirm (statement 2. **se r.**, to strengthen, to intensify.

renfort [rɑ̃fɔr] *nm* 1. reinforcement(s); fresh supply; **envoyé en r.**, sent up to reinforce; **de r.**, strengthening; supporting; **à grand r. d'épingles**, with the help of lots of pins 2. strengthening piece; reinforcement.

renfrogner (se) [sərɑ̃frɔɲe] *vpr* to scowl. **renfrogné** *a* sullen.

rengager [rɑ̃gaʒe] (conj like ENGAGER) 1. *vtr* to re-engage; to renew (combat) 2. **se r.**, to re-enlist.

rengaine [rɑ̃gɛn] *nf* **vieille r.**, old refrain; **c'est toujours la même r.**, it's always the same old story.

rengainer [rɑ̃gene] *vtr* to sheathe, put up (sword); *F:* to withhold (compliment).

rengorger (se) [sərɑ̃gɔrʒe] *vpr* (of bird) to strut; (of pers) to swagger.

reniement [rənimɑ̃] *nm* disowning, renunciation; denial; repudiation.

renier [rənje] *vtr* (conj like NIER) 1. to disown, renounce (friend); to deny (Christ); to disavow (action) 2. to repudiate (opinion).

reniflement [rənifləmɑ̃] *nm* (a) sniffing (b) sniff.

renifler [rənifle] 1. *vi* to sniff; to snort 2. *vtr* (a) to sniff (up) (sth) (b) to sniff, smell (a flower).

renne [rɛn] *nm* reindeer.

renom [rənɔ̃] *nm* renown, fame; reputation; **de grand r., en r.**, famous.

renommé [rənɔme] *a* renowned, famous, well-known (**pour**, for).

renommée [rənɔme] *nf* (a) renown, fame (b) reputation (c) (public) report.

renoncement [rənɔ̃smã] *nm* renouncement (à, of); self denial, renunciation.

renoncer [rənɔ̃se] *v ind tr* (**n. renonçons**) r. à qch, to renounce, give up, sth; r. à qn, to drop s.o.; r. à faire qch, (i) to give up doing sth (ii) to drop the idea of doing sth.

renonciation [rənɔ̃sjasjɔ̃] *nf* renunciation.

renouer [rənwe] *vtr* (a) to tie (up), knot (sth) again (b) to renew, resume (correspondence); r. (amitié) avec qn, to renew one's friendship with s.o.

renouveau [rənuvo] *nm* revival; r. de vie, new lease of life.

renouveler [rənuvle] *vtr* (**je renouvelle, n. renouvelons**) 1. (a) to renew, to renovate; r. ses pneus, to get a new set of tyres (b) to change (method, staff) completely; r. la face du pays, to transform the country 2. to renew (promise, lease, passport); to revive (custom); to renew (acquaintance); *Com:* r. une commande, to repeat an order 3. se r. (a) to be renewed (b) to recur; to happen again. **renouvelable** *a* renewable.

renouvellement [rənuvɛlmã] *nm* (a) replacement (of stock) (b) renewal (of lease, passport) (c) revival (of custom).

rénovateur, -trice [renɔvatœr, -tris] 1. *a* renovating 2. *n* renovator, restorer.

rénovation [renɔvasjɔ̃] *nf* (a) renovation, restoration (b) renewal; revival.

rénover [renɔve] *vtr* (a) to renovate (house) (b) to renew; to revive.

renseignement [rɑ̃sɛɲmã] *nm* (a) (piece of) information; *Tp: etc:* renseignements, enquiries; donner des renseignements sur qch, to give information about sth; prendre des renseignements sur qn, to enquire about s.o.; bureau de renseignements, inquiry office (b) *Mil:* service de r., intelligence branch; agent de r., (intelligence) agent.

renseigner [rɑ̃sɛɲe] *vtr* 1. r. qn sur qch, to inform s.o., to give s.o. information about sth; on vous a mal renseigné, you have been misinformed 2. se r. sur qch, to find out about sth; to make enquiries about sth.

rentabilité [rɑ̃tabilite] *nf* profitability. **rentable** *a* profitable; ce n'est pas r., it doesn't pay.

rente [rɑ̃t] *nf* 1. annuity, pension, allowance; r. viagère, life annuity 2. *usu pl* (unearned) income; vivre de ses rentes, to live on one's private income 3. rentes (sur l'état), (government) stocks.

rentier, -ière [rɑ̃tje, -jɛr] *n* person of independent, of private means.

rentrant, -ante [rɑ̃trɑ̃, -ɑ̃t] *a* (a) *Mth:* angle r., reflex angle (b) *Av:* retractable (undercarriage).

rentrée [rɑ̃tre] *nf* 1. (a) return, home-coming; *Space:* r. atmosphérique, re-entry into the atmosphere (b) re-opening (of schools, theatres); re-assembly (of Parliament); *Sch:* la r. (des classes), the beginning of term 2. (a) taking in, receipt (of money) (b) bringing in (of crops).

rentrer [rɑ̃tre] 1. *vi* (aux être) (a) to re-enter; to come in; to go in, again; to return; r. dans sa chambre, to go back into one's room; r. dans ses droits, to recover one's rights; r. dans les bonnes grâces de qn, to regain favour with s.o.; r. dans ses frais, to be reimbursed; (of actor) r. en scène, to come on again (b) to return home, to come home; il est l'heure de r., it's time to go home; elle rentre de Paris, she's just home from Paris (c) (of schools, law courts) to re-open, to resume; (of Parliament) to reassemble; (of pupil) to go back to school (d) (of thgs) to go back (in); faire r. qch dans sa boîte, to put sth back in its box (e) (of money) to come in (f) to enter, go in; r. en soi-même, to retire within oneself; il lui est rentré dedans, he ran into him (g) cela ne rentre pas dans mes fonctions, that's not part of my job; r. dans une catégorie, to fall into a category (h) c'est rentré dans l'ordre, it's back to normal; order has been restored 2. *vtr* (aux avoir) to take in, bring in, get in, pull in; *Av:* to raise (landing gear); r. la récolte, to gather in the harvest; qui a rentré les chaises? who brought the chairs in? r. sa chemise, to tuck in one's shirt.

renverse [rɑ̃vɛrs] *nf* tomber à la r., (i) to fall backwards (ii) to be bowled over.

renversement [rɑ̃vɛrsəmã] *nm* reversal, inversion; overthrow.

renverser [rɑ̃vɛrse] 1. *vtr* (a) to reverse, invert (image, proposition, *Mus:* chord); r. la vapeur, (i) to reverse steam (ii) to go back on one's decision; r. les rôles, to turn the tables (on s.o.) (b) to turn (sth) upside down; ne pas r., this side up (c) to knock (sth) over; to overturn, upset; to spill (liquid); il a été renversé par une voiture, he was knocked down by a car (d) to overthrow (government) *F:* cela m'a renversé, I was astonished, staggered, by it 2. se r., to fall over, to fall down; to upset; to overturn; (of boat) to capsize; se r. sur sa chaise, to lean back in one's chair. **renversant** *a F:* astounding, staggering.

renvoi [rɑ̃vwa] *nm* 1. return(ing), sending back (of goods) 2. dismissal (of employee); discharge, expulsion 3. putting off, postponement 4. referring, reference (of a matter to an authority) 5. cross reference; footnote 6. burp, belch; (of food) donner des renvois, to repeat.

renvoyer [rɑ̃vwaje] *vtr* (conj like ENVOYER) 1. to send back; to return; to throw back (sound); to reflect (heat, light) 2. (a) to send (s.o.) away (b) to dismiss, *F:* sack (employee); to expel (pupil) 3. to put off, postpone (meeting) 4. to refer (s.o., sth, to an authority).

réorganisation [reɔrganizasjɔ̃] *nf* reorganization.

réorganiser [reɔrganize] *vtr* to reorganize.

réouverture [reuvɛrtyr] *nf* re-opening.

repaire [rəpɛr] *nm* den; lair; haunt (of criminals).

repaître (se) [sərəpɛtr] *vpr* (a) (of animal) to eat it's fill; (b) se r. de, to revel in (sth).

répandre [repɑ̃dr] 1. *vtr* (a) to pour out; to spill (salt, wine); to shed (blood) (b) to spread, diffuse, scatter; to give off, to give out (heat, scent); (to strew (flowers); to sprinkle (sand); to spread (terror); to spread (terror); r. des nouvelles, to spread, circulate, news 2. se r. (a) se r. dans le monde, to lead a social life; se r. en excuses, to be full of apologies; to apologize profusely (b) (*of liquid*) to spill; to run over; (*of smell, rumour*) to spread; **les touristes se répandent dans la ville**, tourists are invading the town; **la nouvelle s'est très vite répandue**, the news spread quickly. **répandu** *a* widespread, prevalent.

reparaître [rəparɛtr] *vi* (*conj like* PARAÎTRE; *aux usu* avoir) to reappear.

réparateur, -trice [reparatœr, -tris] **1.** *a* repairing, restoring **2.** *n* repairer, mender.

réparation [reparasjɔ̃] *nf* **1.** repair(ing); mending; restoration; **être en r.**, to be under repair; **faire des réparations**, to do some repairs **2.** reparation, amends; **r. civile**, compensation; **r. légale**, legal redress.

réparer [repare] *vtr* **1.** to repair, mend (shoe, machine); to restore; **r. ses pertes**, to make good one's losses **2.** to make amends for (misdeed); to rectify (mistake, omission); to redress (wrong); to make good (damage). **réparable** *a* repairable; which can be repaired.

reparler [rəparle] *vi* **r. de qch**, to speak about sth again, later; **r. à qn**, to speak to s.o. again.

repartie [rəparti] *nf* retort; **avoir l'esprit de r.**, to be quick at repartee.

repartir [rəpartir] *vi* (*conj like* MENTIR) (*aux* être) to set out again; **je repars pour Paris**, I'm off to Paris again; **r. à zéro**, to start from scratch.

répartir [repartir] *vtr* (**je répartis, n. répartissons**) **1.** to distribute, divide, share out (**entre**, among); to spread over (payments); **charge uniformément répartie**, evenly distributed load **2.** to apportion; to assess (taxes).

répartition [repartisjɔ̃] *nf* distribution; sharing out, dividing up; apportionment.

repas [rəpɑ] *nm* meal; **r. de noce** = wedding breakfast; **r. léger**, light meal; snack; **aux heures des r.**, at mealtime(s).

repassage [rəpɑsaʒ] *nm* (*a*) sharpening (of knife) (*b*) ironing (of clothes).

repasser [rəpɑse] **1.** *vi* (*aux usu* être) to pass by again, go by again; **r. chez qn**, to call on s.o. again; *F:* **tu peux toujours r.!** you've got another think coming! **2.** *vtr* (*a*) to pass over again; to cross (over) again (*b*) to go over, look over (again); to play back (tape); to show (film) again; to resit (exam); **r. qch dans son esprit**, to go over sth in one's mind (*c*) **repassez-moi du pain**, pass me some (more) bread; **repassez-moi cette lettre**, let me see that letter again (*d*) to sharpen, grind (knife, tool) (*e*) to iron (clothes); **fer à r.**, iron; **planche à r.**, ironing board.

repayer [rəpeje] *vtr* (*conj like* PAYER) to pay again.

repêchage [rəpeʃaʒ] *nm* (*a*) fishing out (*b*) helping out; *Sch:* **épreuve de r.**, exam to give candidates a second chance.

repêcher [rəpeʃe] *vtr* (*a*) to fish (sth) up (again), out (again) (*b*) to rescue; to save (drowning man); *Sch:* **r. un candidat**, to give a candidate a second chance (at an oral exam); **ceux qui ont échoué en juin peuvent se r. en octobre**, those who failed in June may sit the exam again in October.

repeindre [rəpɛ̃dr] *vtr* (*conj like* PEINDRE) to repaint.

repenser [rəpɑ̃se] **1.** *vi* to think again (**à**, about) (sth); **j'y repenserai**, I'll think it over; **je n'y ai pas repensé**, I didn't give it another thought **2.** *vtr* to reconsider (a problem).

repentir¹ (se) [sərəpɑ̃tir] **1.** *vpr* (**je me repens; pr sub je me repente**) to repent; **se r. de qch, d'avoir fait qch**, to be sorry for sth, for having done sth. **repentant** *a* repentant.

repentir² *nm* repentance; remorse.

répercussion [reperkysjɔ̃] *nf* repercussion.

répercuter [reperkyte] **1.** *vtr* (*a*) to reverberate, reflect back (sound); to reflect (light, heat) (*b*) to pass (price increase) **2.** **se r.**, to have repercussions (**sur**, on).

repère [rəpɛr] *nm* (reference) mark; line; marker; **point de r.**, landmark.

repérage [rəperaʒ] *nm* locating (of fault; target); **r. radio**, radio location.

repérer [rəpere] (**je repère; je repérerai**) **1.** *vtr* to locate (fault, target); to identify, *F:* to spot (aircraft); **r. qn dans la foule**, to spot s.o., to pick s.o. out, in the crowd; **se faire r.**, to attract attention **2.** **se r.**, to get one's bearings; to find one's way about.

répertoire [repertwar] *nm* **1.** index, list, catalogue; **r. d'adresses**, (i) directory (ii) address book **2.** repertory (of information) **3.** *Th:* repertoire, repertory; **pièce du r.**, stock play.

répertorier [repertorje] *vtr* (*impf & pr sub* **n. répertoriions**) to index, to list (item).

répéter [repete] (**je répète; je répéterai**) **1.** *vtr* (*a*) to repeat; to say, to do (sth) (over) again; **il ne se le fera pas r.**, he won't need to be told twice (*b*) *Th:* to rehearse; to learn (lesson); to practise (piano) **2.** **se r.**, (*of pers*) to repeat oneself; (*of event*) to recur, to happen again.

répétition [repetisjɔ̃] *nf* **1.** repetition; **fusil à r.**, repeating rifle; **montre à r.**, repeater (watch) **2.** *Th:* rehearsal; (choir) practice; **r. générale**, dress rehearsal.

repeuplement [rəpœpləmɑ̃] *nm* repopulation; restocking; replanting.

repeupler [rəpœple] *vtr* to repopulate (country); to restock (pond); to replant (forest); **se r.**, to become repopulated.

repiquage [rəpikaʒ] *nm* (*a*) planting out (of seedlings) (*b*) *Rec:* (re-)recording.

repiquer [rəpike] *vtr* (*a*) to prick, pierce (sth) again; (*b*) to plant out (seedlings); **plant à r.**, bedding plant (*c*) *Rec:* to (re-)record.

répit [repi] *nm* respite; breathing space; **sans r.**, without a break; continuously.

replacer [rəplase] *vtr* (**n. replaçons**) **1.** to replace; to put (sth) back in its place; to re-invest (funds) **2.** **r. qn**, to find a new job for s.o.

replanter [rəplɑ̃te] *vtr* to replant.

replâtrage [rəplɑtraʒ] *nm* (*a*) replastering (*b*) patching up (after quarrel).

replâtrer [rəplɑtre] *vtr* (*a*) to replaster (wall) (*b*) to patch up (quarrel).

replet, -ète [rəplɛ, -ɛt] *a* (*of pers*) podgy, dumpy.

repli [rəpli] *nm* **1.** fold, crease (in cloth); innermost recess (of conscience) **2.** winding, bend, meander; coil (of rope) **3.** *Mil:* withdrawal, falling back.

replier [rəplije] (*conj like* PLIER) **1.** *vtr* (*a*) to fold up (again); to coil up; to fold, bend, back; to turn in (edge); (*of bird*) to fold (wings) (*b*) to withdraw (troops) **2.** **se r.** (*a*) (*of thg*) to fold up, to fold back; (*of snake*) to coil up (*b*) (*of stream, path*) to wind, turn, bend, meander (c) **se r. sur soi-même,** to retire within oneself (d) *Mil:* to withdraw.

réplique [replik] *nf* 1. (a) retort, rejoinder; **argument sans r.,** unanswerable argument; *F:* **et pas de r.!** don't answer back! (b) *Th:* cue; **donner la r. à un acteur,** (i) to give an actor his cue (ii) to play opposite an actor 2. replica.

répliquer [replike] 1. *vtr* **r. qch à qn,** to say sth in answer to s.o. 2. *vi* to retort; to answer back.

répondant [repɔ̃dɑ̃] *nm* surety, guarantor.

répondeur [repɔ̃dœr] *nm* (telephone) answering machine.

répondre [repɔ̃dr̩] 1. *vtr* to answer; to reply; **r. qch,** to say sth in reply 2. *v ind tr* (a) **r. à qn, à qch,** to answer, to reply to, s.o.; to return (greeting); to comply with (request); **r. par écrit,** to reply in writing; **r. à l'appel,** to answer to one's name (b) to answer, to meet (requirements); to come up to (standard) 3. *vi* **r. de qn, de qch,** to answer for s.o., for sth; **je vous en réponds!** you can take my word for it.

réponse [repɔ̃s] *nf* 1. (a) answer, reply; **avoir r. à tout,** to have an answer for everything; **la lettre est restée sans r.,** the letter was left unanswered (b) response (to an appeal) 2. *Physiol:* response (to stimulus).

report [rəpɔr] *nm* 1. *Book-k:* (a) carrying forward (b) amount carried forward 2. postponement 3. *Phot:* transfer.

reportage [rəpɔrtaʒ] *nm Journ:* 1. reporting 2. (newspaper) report; **r. en exclusivité,** scoop 3. *WTel:* running commentary (on match).

reporter[1] [rəpɔrte] 1. *vtr* (a) to carry back; to take back; **r. un livre à qn,** to take a book back to s.o. (b) to postpone, to defer (sth) (à, until) (c) *Book-k:* to carry over (total) 2. **se r. à qch,** to refer to sth; **se r. au passé,** to look back to the past.

reporter[2] [rəpɔrter] *nm Journ:* reporter.

repos [rəpo] *nm* 1. (a) rest; **au r.,** at rest; **prendre du r.,** to take a rest; **jour de r.,** day off; *Mil:* **r.!** (stand) at ease! (b) pause, rest (in a verse) 2. peace, tranquillity (of mind); **de tout r.,** absolutely safe, reliable; **valeur de tout r.,** gilt-edged security.

repose-pied [rəpozpje] *nm inv* footrest.

reposer [rəpoze] 1. *vtr* (a) to put (sth) down (again); to replace (sth) (b) to rest; **r. sa tête sur un coussin,** to rest one's head on a cushion; **r. l'esprit,** to rest the mind (c) to restate (problem), to ask (question) again 2. *vi* to lie, to rest; **ici repose,** here lies (buried); **le commerce repose sur le crédit,** trade is based on credit 3. **se r.** (a) to rest, to take a rest; to relax (b) **se r. sur qn,** to rely on s.o. **reposant** *a* restful; refreshing (sleep); relaxing.

repose-tête [rəpoztɛt] *nm inv* headrest.

repousser [rəpuse] 1. *vtr* (a) to push back, to push away, to thrust aside; to repel (attack); to reject, to turn down (offer); **repoussé de tout le monde,** spurned by all (b) to postpone (event) (c) to be repellent to (s.o.); to repel (d) to emboss (leather); to chase (metal) 2. *vi* (of tree, plant) to shoot (up) again; (of hair) to grow again. **repoussant** *a* repulsive, repellent.

répréhensible [repreɑ̃sib]] *a* reprehensible.

reprendre [rəprɑ̃dr̩] *v* (*conj like* PRENDRE) 1. *vtr* (a) to retake, recapture (town, prisoner) (b) to take, to

pick up (sth) again; **r. sa place,** to resume one's seat; **r. du pain,** to take, have, some more bread; **je vous reprendrai en passant,** I'll pick you up again as I go by (c) **la fièvre l'a repris,** he's had another bout of fever; **sa timidité l'a repris,** his shyness got the better of him again; *F:* **on ne m'y reprendra plus,** I shan't be had another time; **que je ne t'y reprenne plus!** don't let me catch you at it again! (d) to take back (gift, unsold goods); to re-engage (employee); to retract (promise) (e) to resume, take up again (conversation, work); to recapitulate (facts); **r. du goût pour qch,** to recover one's taste for sth; **r. des forces,** to regain strength; **r. la parole,** to resume (talking); **oui, reprit-il,** yes, he replied (f) to repair, to mend; to take in (coat, dress) (g) to reprove, reprimand (**de,** for); to find fault with (s.o., sth) 2. *vi* (a) to recommence; (*of fashion*) to return; (*of patient, business*) to recover; **le froid a repris,** the cold weather has set in again (b) (*of plant*) to take root again. 3. **se r.** (a) to recover oneself, to pull oneself together; to collect one's thoughts (b) to correct oneself (in speaking) (c) **se r. à espérer,** to begin to hope again (d) **s'y r. à plusieurs fois,** to make several attempts (at sth, at doing sth).

représailles [rəprezaj] *npl* reprisals, retaliation; **en r. pour, de, qch,** as a reprisal for sth.

représentant, -ante [rəprezɑ̃tɑ̃, -ɑ̃t] *n* representative; *Com:* agent; representative, *F:* rep.

représentation [rəprezɑ̃tasjɔ̃] *nf* (a) representation (b) agency (c) *Th:* performance (d) **frais de r.,** entertainment allowance. **représentatif, -ive** *a* representative.

représenter [rəprezɑ̃te] *vtr* 1. to present (sth) again 2. (a) to represent; **tableau représentant un moulin,** picture of a mill; **représentez-vous mon étonnement,** just imagine my astonishment (b) to represent, stand for, act for (s.o.); **se faire r.,** to appoint a representative; **r. une maison de commerce,** to be the agent(s) for a firm; **r. qn en justice,** to appear for s.o. (c) to correspond to, to represent (an amount) 3. *Th:* (a) to perform, act (a play); to put on (a play) (b) to act (a part) 4. **r. qch à qn,** to represent, point out, sth to s.o. 5. *vi* **il ne représente pas au physique,** he's not very impressive physically 6. (a) **se r. à un examen,** to resit an exam (b) (*of opportunity*) to occur again.

répression [represjɔ̃] *nf* repression. **répressif, -ive** *a* repressive.

réprimande [reprimɑ̃d] *nf* reprimand, reproof.

réprimander [reprimɑ̃de] *vtr* to reprimand, reprove.

réprimer [reprime] *vtr* to suppress, to repress; to hold back (tears); to quell (revolt).

repris [rəpri] *nm* **r. de justice,** habitual criminal, old offender.

reprise [rəpriz] *nf* 1. (a) retaking, recapture (b) taking back (of unsold goods) (c) trade-in (allowance); part exchange 2. (a) resumption, renewal; return (of fashion); revival (of play); rerun (of film); *TV:* repeat (b) renewal (of activity); new spell of cold weather); recovery (of business) (c) **r. (de vitesse),** acceleration (of engine) (d) *Box:* round; *Fb:* second half (of match) (e) **faire qch à plusieurs reprises,** to do sth several times, on several occasions; **à 3 reprises,** 3 times over 3. *Needlew:* darn; mend.

repriser [rəprize] *vtr* to darn, to mend.

réprobation [reprɔbasjɔ̃] *nf* reprobation. **réprobateur, -trice** *a* reproachful, reproving.

reproche [rəprɔʃ] *nm* reproach; **faire des reproches à qn,** to blame s.o.; **ton de r.,** reproachful tone; **vie sans r.,** blameless life.

reprocher [rəprɔʃe] *vtr* to reproach; **je n'ai rien à me r.,** I have nothing to blame myself for; **qu'est-que vous reprochez à ce livre?** what do you find wrong with this book?

reproduction [rəprɔdyksjɔ̃] *nf* 1. (*a*) reproduction; **organes de r.,** reproductive organs (*b*) reproduction; duplication (of documents); *Publ:* **r. interdite,** all rights reserved 2. copy, reproduction. **reproducteur, -trice** *a* reproductive.

reproduire [rəprɔdɥir] (*conj like* CONDUIRE) 1. *vtr* to reproduce; to copy, to make a copy of (sth) 2. se r. (*a*) to reproduce, breed (*b*) (*of events*) to recur.

réprouvé, -ée [repruve] *n* reprobate.

réprouver [repruve] *vtr* 1. to condemn (crime); to disapprove of (s.o., sth) 2. *Theol:* to damn.

reptile [reptil] *nm* reptile.

repu [rəpy] *a* sat(iat)ed, full.

républicain, -aine [repyblikɛ̃, -ɛn] *a & n* republican.

république [repyblik] *nf* republic.

répudiation [repydjasjɔ̃] *nf* repudiation; renouncement.

répudier [repydje] *vtr* (*pr sub & impf* n. **répudiions**) 1. to repudiate (wife, opinion) 2. to renounce (succession).

répugnance [repynɑ̃s] *nf* 1. (*a*) repugnance; dislike (pour, à, of, for); aversion (**pour, à,** to, from, for) (*b*) loathing (**pour, à,** of, for) 2. r. **à faire qch,** reluctance to do sth; **avec r.,** reluctantly.

répugner [repyne] *vi* 1. r. **à qch, à faire qch,** to feel repugnance to sth, to doing sth; to be loath to do sth 2. r. **à qn,** to be repugnant to s.o.; *impers* il me **répugne de le faire,** I loathe doing it. **répugnant** *a* repugnant, loathsome; revolting.

répulsion [repylsjɔ̃] *nf* repulsion. **répulsif, -ive** *a* repulsive.

réputation [repytasjɔ̃] *nf* reputation; good name; **jouir d'une bonne r.,** to have a good reputation; **se faire une r.,** to make a name for oneself; **connaître qn de r.,** to know s.o. by repute; **il a la r. d'être cruel,** he is reputed to be cruel. **réputé** *a* reputable; **r. pour qch,** renowned, famous, for sth.

requérir [rəkerir] *vtr* (*conj like* ACQUÉRIR) 1. to solicit (favour); to request (s.o.'s presence) 2. to call for, to demand (sth).

requête [rəkɛt] *nf* request, petition; **adresser une r. à qn,** to petition s.o.; **à, sur, la r. de qn,** at s.o.'s request.

requiem [rekɥi(j)ɛm] *nm* requiem.

requin [rəkɛ̃] *nm Z: Fig:* shark.

requinquer [rəkɛ̃ke] *vtr F:* 1. to buck (s.o.) up 2. se r., to perk up.

requis [rəki] 1. *a* required, requisite 2. *nm* labour conscript.

réquisition [rekizisjɔ̃] *nf* (*a*) requisitioning; r. **civile,** conscription for a public service (*b*) requisition.

réquisitionner [rekizisjɔne] *vtr* to requisition; to commandeer (provisions); to conscript (manpower).

réquisitoire [rekizitwar] *nm Jur:* charge, indictment.

RER *abbr Trans: Réseau express régional.*

rescapé, -ée [rɛskape] *a & n* (person) rescued; survivor (of disaster).

réseau, -eaux [rezo] *nm* (*a*) network, system (of roads, rivers); *WTel: TV:* network; *El:* r. **national,** national grid system; r. **de distribution urbain,** town mains; *Tp:* r. **urbain,** local area (*b*) r. **d'espionnage,** spy ring; r. **d'intrigues,** web of intrigue.

réservation [rezɛrvasjɔ̃] *nf* (*a*) reservation; booking (*b*) (hotel) reservation.

réserve [rezɛrv] *nf* 1. reserve, reservation; **sous r.,** subject to; **sous toutes réserves,** with reservations; **sans r.,** unreserved(ly) (*b*) reserve, reticence; caution 2. (*a*) reserve (of provisions, equipment); *pl* reserves (of oil) (*b*) *Mil:* **armée de r.,** reserve army; **officier de r.,** officer of the Reserve (*c*) **mettre qch en r.,** to reserve sth; to put sth by; **tenir qch en r.,** to keep sth in reserve, in store 3. (*a*) (nature) reserve; (game) preserve; (Indian) reservation (*b*) store(house), storeroom (*c*) (*library*) reserve collection.

réserver [rezɛrve] *vtr* 1. (*a*) to reserve; to set aside, to put by; to save up; to keep back; r. **une place à qn,** to keep a seat for s.o.; r. **des places,** to book seats; **place réservée,** reserved seat; r. **du bois,** to store wood; **se r. le droit de,** to reserve the right to; **tous droits réservés,** all rights reserved; **je me réserve,** I'll wait and see; *PN:* **pêche réservée,** private fishing (*b*) to set apart, to earmark (money for a purpose). **réservé** *a* reserved; cautious; shy, reticent.

réserviste [rezɛrvist] *nm Mil:* reservist.

réservoir [rezɛrvwar] *nm* 1. (*a*) reservoir (*b*) fish pond 2. tank, container; r. **à gaz,** gas holder, gasometer.

résidence [rezidɑ̃s] *nf* (*a*) residence; **lieu de r.,** place of residence; **en r. surveillée,** under house arrest (*b*) home; r. **secondaire,** second home; weekend cottage; **changer de r.,** to move (house) (*c*) block of luxury flats.

résident, -ente [rezidɑ̃, -ɑ̃t] *n* (*a*) *Dipl:* resident (*b*) (alien) resident. **résidentiel, -elle** *a* residential.

résider [rezide] *vi* 1. to reside, live (**à, dans,** at, in) 2. **la difficulté réside en ceci,** the difficulty lies, resides, in this.

résidu [rezidy] *nm* (*a*) residue; remnants; (industrial) waste (*b*) *Mth:* remainder. **résiduel, -elle** *a* residual.

résignation [rezinasjɔ̃] *nf* resignation; **avec r.,** resignedly, with resignation.

résigner [rezine] 1. *vtr* to resign; to give (sth) up 2. **se r. à qch,** to resign oneself to sth. **résigné** *a* resigned (**à,** to).

résiliation [reziljasjɔ̃] *nf* termination (of contract).

résilier [rezilje] *vtr* to terminate (contract).

résine [rezin] *nf* resin. **résineux, -euse** *a* resinous; coniferous (tree); *nm* **un r.,** a conifer.

résistance [rezistɑ̃s] *nf* 1. (*a*) resistance, opposition (**à,** to); **n'offrir aucune r.,** to offer no resistance; *Hist:* **la R.,** the Resistance (movement) (*b*) resistance (to disease) (*c*) *El:* resistance; (*of heater*) element 2. (*a*) strength, toughness; **r. au choc**, impact resistance; **tissu qui n'a pas de r.**, flimsy material (*b*) resistance, stamina, endurance (*c*) **pièce de r.**, principal feature (of entertainment); *Cu:* **plat, pièce, de r.**, main course.

résister [reziste] *v ind tr* (*a*) to resist; **r. à qn**, to resist s.o., to offer resistance to s.o. (*b*) **r. à (qch)**, to resist (temptation); to hold out against (attack); to withstand (plant); **le plancher résiste au poids**, the floor supports the weight; **ces couleurs ne résistent pas**, these colours are not fast. **résistant 1.** *a* (*a*) resistant; strong, tough; fast (colour); hardy (plant); **r. à la chaleur**, heatproof (*b*) (*pers*) strong, tough **2.** *n* member of the Resistance movement.

résolu [rezɔly] *a* resolute, determined (person). **résolument** *adv* resolutely, determinedly.

résolution [rezɔlysjɔ̃] *nf* **1.** (*a*) solution (of problem) (*b*) termination (of agreement); cancellation (of sale) **2.** (*a*) resolution; resolve; **prendre la r. de faire qch**, to resolve, to determine, to do sth (*b*) resoluteness; **manquer de r.**, to lack determination (*c*) **prendre une r.**, to pass a resolution.

résonance [rezɔnɑ̃s] *nf* (*a*) resonance (*b*) *Fig:* echo.

résonateur [rezɔnatœr] *nm* resonator.

résonner [rezɔne] *vi* to resound, to reverberate, to resonate; **r. de**, to ring with. **résonnant** *a* resonant.

résorber [rezɔrbe] *vtr* to resorb; to absorb; to reduce, to curb.

résorption [rezɔrpsjɔ̃] *nf* resorption; absorption; reduction.

résoudre [rezudr] (*prp* **résolvant;** *pp* **résolu,** *occ* **résous, -oute;** *pr ind* **je résous;** *impf* **je résolvais;** *fu* **je résoudrai**) **1.** *vtr* (*a*) **r. qch en qch**, to resolve, break up, sth into sth (*b*) to annul, terminate (contract) (*c*) to resolve, clear up (difficulty); to solve (problem); to settle (question) (*d*) **r. qn à faire qch**, to persuade s.o. to do sth; **r. de partir**, to decide to go **2.** (*a*) **se r. en qch**, to resolve into rain (*b*) **se r. à faire qch**, to resolve, to make up one's mind, to do sth.

respect [rɛspɛ] *nm* respect, regard; **avec r.**, respectfully; **r. de soi**, self-respect; **faire qch par r. pour qn**, to do sth out of respect for s.o.; **tenir qn en r.**, to keep s.o. at a respectful distance; **présentez mes respects à votre mère**, give my regards to your mother. **respectabilité** [rɛspɛktabilite] *nf* respectability.

respecter [rɛspɛkte] *vtr* to respect, have regard for (s.o., sth); **r. la loi**, to abide by the law; **se faire r.**, to command respect; **se r.**, to respect oneself; **un homme qui se respecte**, any self-respecting man. **respectable** *a* respectable; fairly large, reasonably large. **respectablement** *adv* respectably.

respectif, -ive [rɛspɛktif, -iv] *a* respective. **respectivement** *adv* respectively.

respectueux, -euse [rɛspɛktɥø, -øz] *a* respectful; **r. de la loi**, law-abiding; **être r. des opinions d'autrui**, to show respect for the opinion of others; *Corr:* **veuillez agréer mes sentiments r.**, yours sincerely. **respectueusement** *adv* respectfully.

respiration [rɛspirasjɔ̃] *nf* breathing, respiration; **retenir sa r.**, to hold one's breath.

respirer [rɛspire] **1.** *vi* to breathe; **r. profondément**, to take a deep breath; **laissez-moi r.**, let me get my breath **2.** *vtr* (*a*) to breathe (in); to inhale; **aller r. un peu d'air**, to go out for a breather (*b*) to exude, to emanate (happiness); to radiate (peace). **respirable** *a* breathable. **respiratoire** *a* breathing, respiratory.

resplendir [rɛsplɑ̃dir] *vi* to shine, to gleam, to glitter. **resplendissant** *a* shining; glittering; **visage r. de santé**, face glowing with health.

responsabilité [rɛspɔ̃sabilite] *nf* responsibility (**de**, for); **avoir la r. de qch**, to be responsible for sth; **r. civile**, civil liability.

responsable [rɛspɔ̃sabl] *a* responsible, answerable, accountable (**de qch**, for sth); **être r. envers qn**, to be responsible to s.o.; **il l'a rendu r. de l'accident**, he blamed him for the accident; **être r. des dommages**, to be liable for damages.

resquiller [rɛskije] **1.** *vtr* to get (seat in theatre) without paying **2.** *vi* to avoid paying (for sth).

resquilleur, -euse [rɛskijœr, -øz] *n* (*a*) cheat (who has not paid); fare dodger (*b*) queue jumper (*c*) gate crasher.

ressac [rəsak] *nm* **1.** undertow **2.** surf.

ressaisir [rəsezir] **1.** *vtr* to recapture; (*fear*) to grip (again) **2.** **se r.**, to regain one's self-control; to pull oneself together.

ressasser [rəsase] *vtr* to turn (sth) over in one's mind; to keep trotting out (the same story).

ressemblance [rəsɑ̃blɑ̃s] *nf* resemblance, likeness; **avoir de la r. avec qn, avec qch**, to bear resemblance with s.o., with sth.

ressembler [rəsɑ̃ble] **1.** *v ind tr* **r. à qn, à qch**, to resemble, to be like, s.o., sth; *F:* **ça ne ressemble à rien**, (i) it's like nothing on earth (ii) it doesn't make sense; **ça ne lui ressemble pas de dire ça**, it's not like him to say that **2.** **se r.**, to be (a)like; **ils se ressemblent comme deux gouttes d'eau**, they're as like as two peas. **ressemblant, -ante** *a* like, alike.

ressemeler [rəsəmle] *vtr* (*conj like* SEMELER) to resole (shoes).

ressentiment [rəsɑ̃timɑ̃] *nm* resentment (**de**, at; **contre**, against).

ressentir [rəsɑ̃tir] (*conj like* MENTIR) **1.** *vtr* (*a*) to feel (pain, joy) (*b*) to feel, experience (shock) **2.** **se r. d'un accident**, to feel the effects of an accident.

resserre [rəsɛr] *nf* (*a*) tool shed (*b*) storeroom.

resserrement [rəsɛrmɑ̃] *nm* **1.** contraction, tightening; narrowing **2.** **r. du crédit**, credit squeeze.

resserrer [rəsere] **1.** (*a*) to contract; to narrow (*b*) to tie (up) again; to tighten **2.** **se r.** (*a*) to contract; to become narrower (*b*) to draw closer together. **resserré** *a* narrow; confined.

resservir [rəsɛrvir] (*conj like* MENTIR) **1.** *vtr* to serve again; **resservez-vous**, have another helping **2.** *vi* to be used again **3.** **se r.**, to help oneself again (to dish).

ressort [rəsɔr] *nm* **1.** (*a*) elasticity, springiness; **faire r.**, to spring back; **avoir du r.**, to be resilient (*b*) spring; **r. à boudin**, coil spring; **grand r.**, mainspring; **à r.**, spring-loaded; **l'intérêt est un puissant r.**, self-interest is a powerful motive **2.** *Jur:* province, scope, competence; **ce n'est pas de mon r.**, it's not my line of work.

ressortir [rəsɔrtir] *vi* (*conj like* MENTIR, *except in* 3) **1.** (*aux* **être**) to come, go, out again **2.** (*aux usu* **être**)

(a) to stand out, to be evident; **faire r. qch**, to bring out sth; **faire r. un fait**, to emphasize a fact (b) to result, follow (**de**, from); **le prix moyen ressort à 20 francs**, the average price works out at 20 francs 3. (*aux avoir*) (*prp* **ressortissant**; *pr ind* **il ressortit**; *impf* **il ressortissait**) **r. à qn, à qch**, to be under the jurisdiction of s.o., of sth.

ressortissant, -ante [rəsɔrtisã, -ãt] *n* national (of a country).

ressouder [rəsude] 1. *vtr* to resolder; to patch up (friendship) 2. (*of bone*) to knit, mend.

ressource [rəsurs] *nf* 1. (a) resource, resourcefulness; **personne de r.**, resourceful person (b) **ruiné sans r.**, irretrievably ruined 2. expedient, shift; **je n'avais d'autre r. que la fuite**, there was no course open to me but to flee; **dernière r.**, last resort 3. *pl* resources, means; **être à bout de ressources**, to have exhausted all the possibilities.

ressouvenir (se) [sərəsuvnir] *vpr* (*conj like* VENIR) **se r. de qch**, to remember, to recall, sth.

ressusciter [resysite] 1. *vtr* (a) to resuscitate (s.o.); to restore to life; to raise (the dead) (b) to revive (fashion) 2. *vi* to revive, to come back to life; to rise (from the dead).

restant, -ante [rɛstã, -ãt] 1. *a* (a) remaining, left (b) **poste restante**, poste restante 2. *nm* remainder, rest; **r. d'un compte**, balance of an account.

restaurant [rɛstɔrã] *nm* restaurant; **manger au r.**, to eat out; **r. libre-service**, (self-service) cafeteria; **r. universitaire**, university canteen.

restaurateur, -trice [rɛstɔratœr, -tris] *n* (a) restorer (b) restaurant owner, manager.

restauration [rɛstɔrasjɔ̃] *nf* (a) restoration; restoring (b) catering.

restaurer [rɛstɔre] 1. *vtr* (a) to restore (building, health); to re-establish (discipline) (b) to refresh (s.o.) 2. **se r.**, to have sth to eat.

reste [rɛst] *nm* 1. rest, remainder, remains; **avoir un r. d'espoir**, to have still some hope left; **il y a un r. de fromage**, there's some cheese left over; **ne pas demander son r.**, to have had enough of it; **et le r.**, and everything else; and everything that goes with it; and so on; **être en r.**, to be indebted (**avec qn**, to s.o.); **de r.**, (to) spare; left over; **au r., du r.**, besides, moreover 2. *pl* remnants, remains, leavings, scraps (of meal); leftovers (b) **restes mortels**, mortal remains.

rester [rɛste] *vi* (*aux être*) 1. to remain; to be left; **il me reste cinq francs**, I have five francs left; **(il) reste à savoir**, it remains to be seen 2. (a) to remain; to stay; **il est resté à travailler**, he stayed behind to work; **restez où vous êtes**, stay where you are; **r. assis**, to remain sitting; **r. ^à dîner**, to stay to dinner; **où en sommes-nous restés?** where did we leave off? **la chose en reste là**, there the matter rests; **que cela reste entre nous**, this is strictly between ourselves (b) **r. tranquille, calme**, to keep still; to remain calm (c) to last 3. to stay (in hotel).

restituer [rɛstitɥe] *vtr* 1. to restore (text) 2. to restore; to return, to hand (sth) back; to make restitution of (sth); to refund (money) 3. to release (energy); to reproduce (sound).

restitution [rɛstitysjɔ̃] *nf* restoration; restitution.

restreindre [rɛstrɛ̃dr] 1. *vtr* (*prp* **restreignant**; *pp* **restreint**; *pr ind* **je restreins**; *fu* **je restreindrai**) to restrict, to curb; to limit; to cut down (expenses) 2. **se r.**, to cut down expenses. **restreint** *a* restricted, limited (**à**, to).

restriction [rɛstriksjɔ̃] *nf* restriction, limitation; **r. mentale**, mental reservation; **sans r.**, unreservedly. **restrictif, -ive** *a* restrictive.

résultat [rezylta] *nm* result; outcome (of action); effect (of treatment); *pl* **résultats**, results (of exam, contest).

résulter [rezylte] *vi* (*used only in the third pers & prp; aux usu* être) to result, follow, arise (**de**, from); **qu'en est-il résulté?** what was the outcome? **résultant, -ante** 1. *a* resultant, resulting 2. *nf* résultante, consequence, result; resultant.

résumé [rezyme] *nm* summary, résumé; **en r.**, in short; to sum up.

résumer [rezyme] *vtr* to summarize; to sum up; **voilà à quoi ça se résume**, that's what it amounts to.

résurrection [rezyrɛksjɔ̃] *nf* 1. resurrection 2. revival (of the arts).

rétablir [retablir] 1. *vtr* (a) to re-establish; to restore (order); **r. sa santé**, to recover one's health (b) to reinstate (s.o. to his post) 2. **se r.** (a) to recover; to get well again (b) **l'ordre se rétablit**, order is being restored.

rétablissement [retablismã] *nm* 1. re-establishment; restoration 2. recovery (after illness) 3. *Gym:* pull-up; **faire un r.**, to heave oneself up.

rétamer [retame] *vtr* 1. to re-tin (pan) 2. *F:* **être rétamé**, (i) to be drunk (ii) to be fagged out (iii) to be broke.

retape [rətap] *nf F:* **faire la r.**, to solicit.

retaper [rətape] 1. *vtr* (a) *F:* to patch up, to do up; to fix up (car); **vieille maison à r.**, old house in need of modernisation; **ça vous retapera**, that will buck you up (b) to retype (letter) 2. **se r.**, to get back on one's feet; to pick up.

retapisser [rətapise] *vtr* to repaper (room).

retard [rətar] *nm* 1. (a) delay; **le train a du r.**, the train is (running) late; **votre montre a dix minutes de r.**, your watch is ten minutes slow; **être en r.**, (i) to be late (ii) to be behindhand; **compte en r.**, account outstanding (b) **élève en r. sur les autres**, backward pupil; **r. de croissance**, slow development; **en r. sur son siècle**, behind the times 2. lag (of tides); *Aut:* **r. à l'allumage**, retarded ignition.

retardataire [rətardatɛr] 1. *a* (a) late (b) backward 2. *n* latecomer.

retardement [rətardəmã] *nm* **à r.**, delayed action; self-timing (device); **bombe à r.**, time bomb.

retarder [rətarde] 1. *vtr* (a) to retard, delay, hold (s.o.) up; to make (s.o.) late (b) to delay, put off (event); to defer (payment) (c) to put back (clock) 2. *vi* (a) to be late, slow, behindhand; **ma montre retarde**, my watch is slow; **la pendule retarde de 10 minutes**, the clock is 10 minutes slow; **il retarde sur son siècle**, he's behind the times; **vous retardez**, you're not up to date (b) *Tchn:* to lag. **retardé** *a* backward (child).

retéléphoner [rətelefɔne] *vtr* to ring (s.o.) up, to phone (s.o.), again.

retenir [rət(ə)nir] (*conj like* TENIR) 1. *vtr* (a) to hold (s.o., sth) back; to detain; **r. l'attention**, to hold the attention; **r. qn à dîner**, to keep s.o. to dinner; **r. qn prisonnier**, to hold s.o. prisoner; **je ne vous retiens pas**, I mustn't keep you (*b*) to hold (sth) in position; to secure (sth); **r. l'eau**, to be watertight (*c*) to retain; **r. une somme sur le salaire de qn**, to deduct an amount from s.o's wages (*d*) to remember; **retenez ce numéro**, don't forget this number (*e*) to reserve, to book (seat, room, table); to engage (staff) (*f*) Mth: **je pose 2 et je retiens 5**, put down 2 and carry 5 (*g*) to restrain, curb (anger); to hold back (one's tears); to stifle (cry); **r. son souffle**, to hold one's breath **2. se r.** (*a*) **se r. à qch**, to cling to sth (*b*) to restrain, control, oneself; to hold oneself in; **se r. de faire qch**, to stop oneself from doing sth.

rétention [retɑ̃sjɔ̃] *nf Med: Jur:* retention.

retentir [rətɑ̃tir] *vi* to (re)sound, echo, ring, reverberate; (*of horn*) to sound; **r. de**, to resound with; **r. sur**, to have an effect upon. **retentissant** *a* resounding (voice, success); loud (noise); dismal (failure).

retentissement [rətɑ̃tismɑ̃] *nm* resounding noise; repercussions (of event); stir.

retenue [rət(ə)ny] *nf* **1.** (*a*) deduction, docking (of pay); **faire une r. de 5% sur les salaires**, to deduct 5% from the wages (*b*) sum kept back (*c*) *Mth:* carry over **2.** *Sch:* detention **3.** reserve, discretion; restraint; **sans r.**, unrestrainedly.

réticence [retisɑ̃s] *nf* reticence, reserve; **sans r.**, unreservedly. **réticent** *a* reticent; reluctant.

rétif, -ive [retif, -iv] *a* restive.

rétine [retin] *nf* retina.

retirer [rətire] **1.** *vtr* (*a*) to pull, draw, take, out; to withdraw (sth); to remove; **r. ses bagages**, to check out luggage; **r. son manteau**, to take off one's coat; **r. un bouchon**, to draw a cork (*b*) **r. un profit de qch**, to derive a profit from sth; **qu'est-ce que vous en avez retiré?** what did you get out of it? (*c*) to extract, obtain (oil) (*d*) **r. qch à qn**, to withdraw sth from s.o.; to take sth back from s.o; **r. sa main**, to draw one's hand away; **r. le permis de conduire à qn**, to disqualify s.o. from driving (*e*) to withdraw, take back (promise, remark); **r. sa candidature**, to stand down **2. se r.** (*a*) to retire, withdraw; **vous pouvez vous r.**, you may go; **se r. à la campagne**, to retire to the country; (*of candidate*) **se r. en faveur de qn**, to stand down in favour of s.o. (*b*) to retire (from business (*c*) (*of floods*) to subside; (*of sea*) to recede; (*of tide*) to ebb. **retiré** *a* secluded, remote (place); **vivre r.**, to live in seclusion.

retombée [rətɔ̃be] *nf* **1.** *Arch:* springing **2.** *pl* (*a*) (radioactive) fallout (*b*) repercussions.

retomber [rətɔ̃be] *vi* (*aux usu être*) **1.** to fall (down) again; **r. sur ses pieds**, to land on one's feet (again); **r. dans le chaos**, to fall back into chaos; **r. malade**, to fall ill again **2.** to sink (back), fall (back) (into an armchair); **laisser r. ses bras**, to drop one's arms; **faire r. la faute sur qn**, to lay the blame on s.o.; **la responsabilité retombe sur moi**, the responsibility falls on me **3.** (*of hair, draperies*) to hang down.

rétorquer [retɔrke] *vtr* to retort.

rétorsion [retɔrsjɔ̃] *nf Jur: Pol:* retortion, retaliation.

retouche [rətuʃ] *nf* (slight) alteration; touching up; *Phot:* retouching.

retoucher [rətuʃe] *vtr* to retouch, touch up (picture, photograph); to alter (dress).

retour [rətur] *nm* **1.** turn, vicissitude, reversal (of fortune, opinion); **r. de conscience**, qualms of conscience; **faire un r. sur le passé**, to look back on the past **2.** return; going back, coming back; **être de r.**, to be back (again); **à mon r.**, on my return; **dès mon r.**, as soon as I'm back; **partir sans r.**, to leave for ever; **être perdu sans r.**, to be irretrievably lost; **voyage de r.**, return journey; **billet de r.**, return ticket; **par r. (du courrier)**, by return (of post); **r. de maladie**, recurrence of disease; **r. de l'hiver**, return of winter; *Cin:* **r. en arrière**, flashback; **r. d'âge**, change of life **3.** backlash (of mechanism); *Aut:* **avoir des retours**, to backfire; **r. de manivelle**, backfire kick **4.** return (of goods, letter); **vendu avec faculté de r.**, on sale or return **5. payer de r.**, to requite s.o.

retourner [rəturne] **1.** *vtr* (*a*) to turn (sth) inside out; to turn out (pocket) (*b*) to turn (sth) over; to turn up, down, back; to turn over (soil); to turn (omelette); to turn up (card); **r. une pièce**, to ransack a room; **r. une question dans tous les sens**, to thrash out a question; *F:* **cela m'a tout retourné**, it gave me quite a turn (*c*) to turn (sth) round; **r. la tête**, to turn one's head; to look round; **r. une situation**, to reverse a situation (*d*) **r. qch à qn**, to return sth to s.o.; to give sth back to s.o. **2.** *vi* (*aux usu être*) (*a*) to return; to go back; **r. chez soi**, to go home; **r. sur le passé**, to revert to the past (*b*) (*of mistake, crime*) **r. sur qn**, to recoil on s.o. **3.** *impers.* **de quoi retourne-t-il?** *F:* what's it all about? what's going on? **3. se r.** (*a*) to turn (round); to turn over; **avoir le temps de se r.**, to have time to look round (*b*) to turn around, to look round, to look back; **se r. contre qn**, to turn against s.o., to round on s.o. (*c*) **s'en retourner**, to return, go back.

retracer [rətrase] *vtr* (*conj like* TRACER) **1.** to retrace, redraw (line) **2.** to relate, recount (event).

rétractation [retraktasjɔ̃] *nf* retraction.

rétracter [retrakte] **1.** *vtr* (*a*) to retract, to draw in (claws) (*b*) to withdraw; to go back on (one's word) **2. se r.** (*a*) (*of materials*) to shrink; (*of muscle*) to retract (*b*) retract, to back down.

rétraction [retraksjɔ̃] *nf* contraction; retraction. **rétractile** *a* retractile.

retrait [rətrɛ] *nm* **1.** withdrawal (of order, troops); cancelling (of licence) **2. r. de fonds**, withdrawal of money invested **3.** recess (in wall); **en r.**, recessed (shelves); sunk (panel); **maison en r.**, house set back (from the road); **rester en r.**, to stay in the background.

retraite [rətrɛt] *nf* **1.** *Mil: etc:* retreat, withdrawal **2.** tattoo; **battre la r.**, to beat, sound, the tattoo; **r. aux flambeaux**, torchlight tattoo **3.** (*a*) retirement; **caisse de r.**, pension fund; **être à la, en, r.**, to be retired; **mettre qn à la r.**, to pension s.o. off; **prendre sa r.**, to retire (*b*) retirement pension **4.** (*a*) **vivre dans la r.**, to live in retirement; **maison de r.**, old people's home (*b*) *Ecc:* retreat; **faire une r.**, to be in retreat **5.** (*a*) retreat; place of retirement (*b*) shelter; refuge; lair; (thieves') hideout.

retraité, -ée [rətrete] **1.** *a* retired **2** *n* pensioner.

retranchement [rətrɑ̃ʃmɑ̃] *nm Mil:* entrenchment; *Fig:* **forcer qn dans ses derniers retranchements**, to drive s.o. to the wall.

retrancher [rətrɑ̃ʃe] **1.** *vtr* (*a*) **r. qch de qch,** to cut off sth from sth; **r. un passage d'un livre,** to cut a passage out of a book; **r. qch sur une somme,** to deduct sth from a sum (*b*) **r. qch à qn,** to dock s.o. of sth **2. se r.** (*a*) to entrench oneself (*b*) **se r. dans le silence,** to take refuge in silence.

retransmettre [rətrɑ̃smetr] *vtr* (*conj like* METTRE) to broadcast, to relay.

retransmission [rətrɑ̃smisjɔ̃] *nf* broadcast.

rétrécir [retresir] **1.** *vtr* (*a*) to take in (garment) (*b*) to shrink (garment) (*c*) to narrow (street) **2.** *vi & pr* to contract; to narrow; (*of garment*) to shrink.

rétrécissement [retresismɑ̃] *nm* narrowing; contracting; shrinking.

rétribuer [retribɥe] *vtr* to pay (employee, service); **travail rétribué,** paid work.

rétribution [retribysjɔ̃] *nf* payment.

rétro [retro] *a inv* period (play); **la mode r.,** the Twenties fashion.

rétroactif, -ive [retrɔaktif, -iv] *a* retroactive, retrospective; **augmentation avec effet r. au 1er juillet,** pay rise backdated to 1st July. **rétroactivement** *a* retroactively, retrospectively.

rétroaction [retrɔaksjɔ̃] *nf*, **rétroactivité** [retrɔaktivite] *nf* retrospective effect.

rétrograde [retrɔgrad] *a* retrograde, backward (motion); reactionary.

rétrograder [retrɔgrade] **1.** *vi* to re(tro)gress; to move backwards; to go back; *Aut:* to change down **2.** *vtr* to reduce to a lower rank.

rétrospectif, -ive [retrɔspektif, -iv] *a* retrospective; in retrospect; *Art:* **nf rétrospective,** retrospective (exhibition). **rétrospectivement** *adv* retrospectively.

retrousser [rətruse] *vtr* to turn up, roll up (sleeves, trousers); to tuck up (skirt); to curl (up) (one's lip); **nez retroussé,** turned-up nose, snub nose.

retrouvailles [rətruvaij] *nfpl* reunion.

retrouver [rətruve] **1.** *vtr* (*a*) to find (s.o., sth) (again); to rediscover; **r. son chemin,** to find one's way again; **la clé a été retrouvée,** the key has been found; **r. sa santé, ses forces,** to recover one's health, strength (*b*) **aller r. qn,** to go and join s.o.; **je vous retrouverai ce soir,** I'll see you again this evening **2. se r.** (*a*) **se r. dans la même position,** to find oneself, to be, in the same position again; **se r. à Paris,** to be back in Paris to find one's bearings; **je ne m'y retrouve plus,** I can't make it out; *F:* **s'y r.,** to break even (*c*) to meet again; **comme on se retrouve!** fancy meeting you!

rétroviseur [retrɔvizœr] *nm Aut:* driving mirror, rearview mirror.

réunification [reynifikasjɔ̃] *nf Pol:* reunification.

réunion [reynjɔ̃] *nf* **1.** reunion; bringing together, reuniting; **r. d'une chose à une autre,** union of one thing with another **2.** (*a*) coming together; **salle de r.,** assembly room (*b*) assembly, gathering, meeting; **r. publique,** public meeting (*c*) social gathering, party.

Réunion (La) [lareynjɔ̃] *Prnf Geog:* Reunion.

réunir [reynir] **1.** *vtr* to unite; to join together; to bring (people) together; **r. une somme,** to collect a sum of money; **r. le comité,** to call a committee meeting **2. se r.** (*a*) to meet; to gather together (*b*)

réussir [reysir] **1.** *vi* (*a*) to turn out (well, badly); **le homard ne me réussit pas,** lobster doesn't agree with me (*b*) to succeed (**dans,** in); to be successful (**dans,** at); **r. à un examen,** to pass an exam; **r. à faire qch,** to manage to do sth; **il réussira,** he will do well (*c*) (*of play*) to be a success; (*of plant*) to thrive; (*of business*) to prosper **2.** *vtr* to make a success of (sth); to be successful with (s.o.); **la photo est réussie,** the photograph came out well; *F:* **r. son coup,** to pull it off. **réussi** *a* successful; well executed; **c'était très r.,** it was a great success.

réussite [reysit] *nf* **1.** success, successful result **2.** *Cards:* patience.

revaloir [rəvalwar] *vtr* (*conj like* VALOIR; *used chiefly in the fu*) to return, pay back, in kind; **je vous revaudrai cela!** (i) I'll get even with you! (ii) I'll repay you some day.

revaloriser [rəvalɔrize] *vtr* **1.** (*a*) to revalue (currency) (*b*) to give a new value to (idea) **2.** to reassess (prices) at a higher level.

revanche [rəvɑ̃ʃ] *nf* **1.** (*a*) revenge; **prendre sa r. sur qn,** to get even with s.o. (*b*) **jouer la r.,** to play the return game **2. en r.,** (i) in return, in compensation (ii) on the other hand.

rêvasser [rɛvase] *vi* to daydream.

rêvasserie [rɛvasri] *nf* daydreaming.

rêve [rɛv] *nm* **1.** dream; **faire un r.,** to (have a) dream **2.** daydream; **la maison de nos rêves,** our dream house; **c'est le r.!** it's ideal!

revêche [rəvɛʃ] *a* bad-tempered, cantankerous, sour.

réveil [revɛj] *nm* **1.** (*a*) waking, awakening; **à mon r.,** on waking (*b*) *Mil:* reveille **2.** alarm (clock).

réveille-matin [revɛjmatɛ̃] *nm inv* alarm clock.

réveiller [revɛje] **1.** *vtr* (*a*) to (a)wake (s.o.); to wake (s.o.) up; to rouse (s.o.) up; to stir (s.o.) up; to awaken (memory); to revive (courage) **2. se r.** (*a*) (*of pers*) to wake (up) (*b*) (*of feelings*) to be awakened, roused, stirred up; (*of nature*) to revive.

réveillon [revɛjɔ̃] *nm* midnight supper (*esp on* Christmas Eve or New Year's Eve).

réveillonner [revɛjɔne] *vi* to see Christmas, the New Year, in.

révélateur, -trice [revelatœr, -tris] **1.** *a* revealing **2.** *n* revealer **3.** *nm Phot:* developer.

révélation [revelasjɔ̃] *nf* revelation, disclosure; **c'est une r.!** it's an eye-opener! **la dernière r.,** the latest discovery.

révéler [revele] (**je révèle; je révélerai**) **1.** *vtr* (*a*) to reveal, disclose; to let out (secret) (*b*) to show (talent); to reveal (kindness, good humour); to betray (faults) **2. se r.** (*a*) to reveal oneself; **se r. difficile,** to prove difficult (*b*) (*of mystery*) to be revealed; (*of fact*) to come to light.

revenant [rəvnɑ̃] *nm* ghost; *F:* **quel r. vous faites!** you're quite a stranger!

revendeur, -euse [rəvɑ̃dœr, -øz] *n* (*a*) retailer (*b*) secondhand dealer.

revendication [rəvɑ̃dikasjɔ̃] *nf* (*a*) claiming (*b*) claim, demand. **revendicatif, -ive** *a* demanding; protest (movement).

revendiquer [rəvɑ̃dike] *vtr* to claim, demand; to assert (one's rights); to claim (responsibility).

revendre [rəvɑ̃dr] *vtr* to resell; to sell (again); **on en a à r.**, we've got loads of it; **avoir de l'énergie à r.**, to have too much energy.

revenir [rəv(ə)nir] *vi* (*conj like* VENIR *aux* être) 1. (*a*) to return; to come back; **en revenant de l'église**, on the way back from church; **je reviens dans une minute**, I'll be back in a minute; **r. sur ses pas**, to retrace one's steps; to turn back; **r. sur une promesse**, to go back on a promise; **r. sur le passé**, to rake up the past; **il n'y a pas à y r.**, there's no going back on it (*b*) (*of food*) to repeat 2. (*a*) to return, come back (**à qn**, to s.o.); **à chacun ce qui lui revient**, to each one his due (*b*) **cela me revient à la mémoire**, I'm beginning to remember it; it's coming back to me; **son nom ne me revient pas**, I can't think of his name (*c*) **son visage ne me revient pas**, I don't like the look of him 3. (*a*) **r. d'une maladie, de sa surprise**, to get over an illness, one's surprise; **r. de ses illusions**, to lose one's illusions; **r. d'une erreur**, to realize one's mistake; **je n'en reviens pas!** I can't get over it! **r. de loin**, to have been at death's door; **r. à soi**, to recover consciousness; to come to (*b*) *Cu:* **faire r.**, to brown 4. **en r. à qch**, **y r.**, to revert to sth; **pour en r. à la question**, to come back to the subject 5. (*a*) to cost; **cela me revient à 50 francs**, it's costing me 50 francs; **cela revient cher**, it's expensive (*b*) **cela revient au même**, it comes to the same thing 6. **s'en r.**, to return.

revente [rəvɑ̃t] *nf* resale.

revenu [rəv(ə)ny] *nm* income (of pers); (State) revenue; yield (of investment).

rêver [rɛve] 1. *vi* (*a*) to dream; **r. de qch.**, to dream about sth (*b*) **r. à qch**, to ponder over sth (*c*) **tu rêves!** you're imagining things! **on croirait r.**, one can hardly believe it 2. *vtr* to dream of (sth); **vous l'avez rêvé!** you must have dreamt it!

réverbération [reverberasjɔ̃] *nf* reverberation; reflection (of light, heat).

réverbère [reverber] *nm* street lamp, light.

réverbérer [reverbere] *vtr* (**il réverbère; il réverbérera**) to reverberate; (*of light, heat*) to reflect; (*of sound*) to send back.

révérence [reverɑ̃s] *nf* 1. reverence (**envers, pour,** for) 2. bow; curtsey; **tirer sa r.** (**à qn**), to take one's leave (of s.o.). **révérenciel, -ielle** *a* reverential.

révérend, -ende [reverɑ̃, -ɑ̃d] *a Ecc:* reverend.

révérer [revere] *vtr* (**je révère, je révérerai**) to revere.

rêverie [rɛvri] *nf* reverie; (day)dreaming.

revers [rəvɛr] *nm* 1. (*a*) reverse (of coin); wrong side (of material); other side (of page); back (of the hand); *Ten:* (**coup de**) **r.**, backhand (stroke) (*b*) facing, lapel (of coat); (trouser) turn-up; **bottes à r.**, top boots 2. reverse (of fortune); setback.

reverser [rəvɛrse] *vtr* to pour (sth) out again; to pour (sth) back.

réversion [reversjɔ̃] *nf Jur: Biol:* reversion. **réversible** *a* reversible; *Jur:* revertible.

revêtement [rəvɛtmɑ̃] *nm* 1. coating, covering; lining 2. (*a*) coat(ing) (*b*) facing (of wall); surface (of road).

revêtir [rəvɛtir] (*conj like* VÊTIR) 1. *vtr* (*a*) to clothe, dress; **r. qn de qch**, to dress s.o. in sth; **r. qn d'une**

dignité, to invest s.o. with a dignity; **pièce revêtue de votre signature**, document bearing your signature (*b*) to face, coat, cover, case, line (*c*) **r. un uniforme**, to put on a uniform; **r. la forme humaine**, to assume human shape 2. **se r. de qch**, to put on sth; to assume (a dignity); **se r. de neige**, to be covered with snow.

rêveur, -euse [rɛvœr, -øz] 1. *a* dreamy 2. *n* dreamer. **rêveusement** *adv* dreamily.

revigorer [rəvigɔre] *vtr* to invigorate.

revirement [rəvirmɑ̃] *nm* (sudden) change (of fortune); reversal (of feeling); change (of opinion).

réviser [revize] *vtr* 1. to revise (text); to audit (accounts); to review (case) 2. (*a*) *Sch:* to revise (*b*) to service (car, watch).

réviseur [revizœr] *nm* proofreader.

révision [revizjɔ̃] *nf* 1. revision; auditing (of accounts); review (of case) 2. (*a*) *Sch:* revision (*b*) servicing (of car, watch).

revivifier [rəvivifje] *vtr* (*impf & pr sub* **n. revivifiions**) to revive.

revivre [rəvivr] (*a*) *vi* (*conj like* VIVRE) to live again; to come to life again; **faire r. qn, qch**, to bring s.o. to life again; to revive sth.

révocation [revɔkasjɔ̃] *nf* 1. revocation, repeal (of order, edict) 2. removal, dismissal (of official). **révocable** *a* revocable; removable.

revoici [rəvwasi] *prep F:* **me r.!** here I am again!

revoilà [rəvwala] *prep F:* **le r.!** there he is again!

revoir [rəvwar] *vtr* (*conj like* VOIR) 1. to see again; to meet (s.o.) again; *nm inv* **au r.**, goodbye; **faire au r. de la main**, to wave goodbye 2. to revise (text); to re-examine (accounts); to read (proofs).

révolte [revɔlt] *nf* revolt, rebellion.

révolté, -ée [revɔlte] *n* rebel.

révolter [revɔlte] 1. *vtr* (*a*) to revolt, disgust, shock (s.o.) 2. **se r.** (*a*) to revolt, rebel (**contre**, against) (*b*) to be revolted, outraged (**contre**, by). **révoltant** *a* revolting; outrageous.

révolu [revɔly] *a* (*of time*) completed; **avoir quarante ans révolus**, to have completed one's fortieth year; **jours révolus**, bygone days.

révolution [revɔlysjɔ̃] *nf* (*a*) revolution (of a wheel) (*b*) *Pol:* revolution; **toute la ville est en r.**, the whole town is in an uproar.

révolutionnaire [revɔlysjɔnɛr] *a & n* revolutionary.

révolutionner [revɔlysjɔne] *vtr* (*a*) to revolutionize (*b*) to stir up.

revolver [revɔlvɛr] *nm* revolver; gun.

révoquer [revɔke] *vtr* 1. to revoke, repeal (decree); to countermand (order) 2. to dismiss (official).

revue [rəvy] *nf* 1. review; inspection; *Mil:* review; **passer en r.**, to be reviewed 2. (*a*) *Pub:* review, magazine; journal (*b*) *Th:* revue; variety show.

révulser (se) [sərevylse] *vpr* (*of eyes*) to roll upwards; (*of face*) to contort.

rez-de-chaussée [redʃose] *nm inv* (*a*) ground floor, *NAm:* first floor, main floor (*b*) ground floor flat.

RF *abbr* République française.

RFA *abbr* République Fédérale Allemande.

rhabiller [rabije] 1. *vtr* to dress (s.o.) again 2. **se r.** to get dressed again; *F:* **il peut aller se r.**, he's had it!

rhapsodie [rapsɔdi] *nf* rhapsody.

rhéostat [reɔsta] nm El: rheostat.

rhésus [rezys] nm rhesus (monkey, factor).

Rhin [rɛ̃] Prnm Geog: the Rhine.

rhinocéros [rinɔserɔs] nm rhinoceros.

rhododendron [rɔdɔdɛ̃drɔ̃] nm Bot: rhododendron.

rhubarbe [rybarb] nf Bot: rhubarb.

rhum [rɔm] nm rum.

rhumatisant, -ante [rymatizɑ̃, -ɑ̃t] a & n Med: rheumatic (pers).

rhumatisme [rymatism] nm Med: rheumatism. rhumatismal, -aux a rheumatic.

rhumatologie [rymatɔlɔʒi] nf Med: rheumatology. rhumatologue [rymatɔlɔg] n rheumatologist.

rhume [rym] nm Med: cold; r. de cerveau, head cold; r. des foins, hay fever.

riant [rijɑ̃] a 1. smiling (face, person) 2. cheerful, pleasant (prospect, atmosphere).

ribambelle [ribɑ̃bɛl] nf string (of names); swarm (of children).

ribouldingue [ribuldɛ̃g] nf P: spree, binge.

ricain, -aine [rikɛ̃, -ɛn] a & n F: American, Yank.

ricanement [rikanmɑ̃] nm sneering laugh.

ricaner [rikane] vi to laugh derisively.

richard, -arde [riʃar, -ard] n F: moneybags.

riche [riʃ] a 1. rich, wealthy, well-off; être r. à millions, to be worth millions; r. d'espérances, full of hope; r. en protéines, with a high protein content 2. valuable, handsome (gift); rich (harvest, ore); faire un r. mariage, to marry money 3. F: une r. idée, a splendid idea 4. n rich person; les riches, the wealthy. richement adv richly.

richesse [riʃɛs] nf 1. wealth; riches 2. musée plein de richesses, museum full of treasures 3. richness; fertility (of soil).

ricin [risɛ̃] nm castor oil plant; huile de r., castor oil.

ricocher [rikɔʃe] vi (a) to rebound; to glance off (b) (of bullet) to ricochet.

ricochet [rikɔʃɛ] nm (a) rebound; faire des ricochets, to play ducks and drakes (b) ricochet.

rictus [riktys] nm grin; grimace.

ride [rid] nf 1. wrinkle 2. ripple (on water); ridge (of sand).

rideau, -eaux [rido] nm 1. screen, curtain (of trees); r. de fumée, smoke screen 2. (a) curtain, NAm: drape; tirer les rideaux, to draw the curtains (b) Th: (drop) curtain (c) r. de fer, Iron curtain (d) blower (of fireplace).

rider [ride] 1. vtr (a) to wrinkle, line (forehead); to shrivel (skin) (b) to ripple (the water) 2. se r. (a) to wrinkle; to become lined (b) (of water) to ripple.

ridicule [ridikyl] 1. a ridiculous, ludicrous, absurd; se rendre r., to make a fool of oneself 2. nm (a) ridiculousness, absurdity; tomber dans le r., to become ridiculous (b) ridicule. ridiculement adv ridiculously.

ridiculiser [ridikylize] vtr to ridicule; to hold up to ridicule; se r., to make a fool of oneself.

rien [rjɛ̃] 1. pron indef m (a) anything; (in questions rien is preferred to quelque chose when a negative answer is expected) y a-t-il r. de plus triste? is there anything more depressing? (b) nothing, not anything; il n'y a r. à faire, there is nothing to be done; il ne faut r. lui dire, he must not be told anything; ne dites r., say nothing; il ne vous faut

r. d'autre? do you require anything else? ça ne fait r., it doesn't matter; si cela ne vous fait r., if you don't mind, comme si de r. n'était, as if nothing had happened; il n'en est r.! nothing of the kind! je n'en ferai r., I shall do nothing of the sort; elle n'a r. de son père, she doesn't take after her father in any way; il n'était pour r. dans l'affaire, he had no hand in the matter; F: r. de r., absolutely nothing (c) que faites-vous?— r., what are you doing?— nothing; r. du tout, nothing at all; parler pour r., to waste one's breath; merci beaucoup—de r., thank you very much—not at all, don't mention it; NAm: you're welcome; en moins de r., in less than no time; une affaire de r. (du tout), a trivial matter; un homme de r., a worthless man; trois fois r., next to nothing; Ten: quinze à r., fifteen love (d) il est inutile de r. dire, you needn't say anything; sans r. faire, without doing anything (e) r. que, nothing but; only, merely; je frémis r. que d'y songer, the mere thought of it makes me shudder; r. qu'à moi, to me alone; r. que cela? is that all? (f) on ne peut pas vivre de r., you can't live on nothing; ce n'est pas r.! that's something! ce n'est pas pour r. que, it's not without good reason that 2. nm (a) trifle; mere nothing; des riens, small talk, trivia (b) just a little; un r. d'ail, a touch of garlic; en un r. de temps, in no time (at all) (c) un r. bruyant, a bit noisy.

rieur, -euse [rijœr, -øz] 1. a laughing; cheerful 2. n laugher.

rigide [riʒid] a rigid; stiff; strict. rigidement adv rigidly.

rigidité [riʒidite] nf rigidity; stiffness; strictness.

rigolade [rigolad] nf F: fun; laugh, joke; c'est de la r., it's a farce.

rigole [rigɔl] nf (a) drain; channel (b) rivulet (of water).

rigoler [rigɔle] vi F: (a) to laugh; tu rigoles! you're joking! (b) to have fun, to enjoy oneself; on a bien rigolé, we had a good laugh. rigolo, -ote F: 1. a comic, funny; queer, odd 2. nm comic, wag.

rigoureux, -euse [riguro, -øz] a 1. rigorous; severe, harsh; hard (winter) 2. strict. rigoureusement adv rigorously; harshly; strictly.

rigueur [rigœr] nf 1. rigour, harshness, severity; tenir r. à qn, not to forgive s.o. 2. strictness; être de r., to be compulsory; ce n'est pas de r., it's optional; à la r., if need be, at a pinch.

rime [rim] nf rhyme; F: sans r. ni raison, without rhyme or reason.

rimer [rime] 1. vtr to versify; to put into rhyme 2. vi (a) to rhyme (avec, with); F: cela ne rime à rien, it doesn't make sense (b) to write verse.

rimmel [rimɛl] nm Rtm: mascara.

rinçage [rɛ̃saʒ] nm rinsing (out); rinse.

rince-doigts [rɛ̃sdwa] nm inv finger bowl.

rincer [rɛ̃se] vtr (n. rinçons) 1. to rinse (clothes); to rinse (out) (glass); se r. la bouche, to rinse (out) one's mouth; se r. l'œil, to get an eyeful 2. P: se faire r., to be cleaned out (gambling).

ring [riŋ] nm Box: ring.

riper [ripe] vi to slip, to skid.

riposte [ripɔst] nf 1. riposte; counterstroke; Box: counter, return 2. retort.

riposter [ripɔste] *vi* 1. *Box:* to riposte, to counter 2. to retort; to answer back.

riquiqui [rikiki] *a inv F:* mean, stingy; wretched (little).

rire¹ [rir] *vi* (*pp* ri; *pr ind* je ris, n. rions; *fu* je rirai) 1. to laugh; **se tenir les côtes de r.,** to be convulsed with laughter; **r. bruyamment,** to guffaw; **r. tout bas,** to chuckle; **r. bêtement,** to giggle; **c'était à mourir de r.,** it was killingly funny; **il n'y a pas de quoi r.,** it's no laughing matter; **r. de qn,** to laugh at s.o.; to make fun of s.o.; **laissez-moi r.!** don't make me laugh! 2. to joke; **vous voulez r.!** you're joking! **prendre qch en riant,** to laugh sth off; **pour r.,** for fun; **je l'ai fait, histoire de r.,** I did it for a joke 3. **se r. de qch,** to make light of sth.

rire² *nm* (*a*) laughter, laughing; **avoir un accès de fou r.,** to laugh uncontrollably (*b*) **un r.,** a laugh; **un gros r.,** a guffaw; **un petit r. bête,** a giggle, a titter; **r. moqueur,** sneer.

ris [ri] *nm Cu:* **r. (de veau),** (calf) sweetbread.

risée [rize] *nf* (*a*) derision; **s'exposer à la r. publique,** to expose oneself to public scorn (*b*) **être la r. de l'Europe,** to be the laughing stock of Europe.

risette [rizet] *nf* **fais (la) r. à papa!** smile for daddy!

risible [rizibl] *a* ludicrous, laughable.

risque [risk] *nm* risk; **à vos risques et périls,** at your own risk; **risques de métier,** occupational hazards; *Ins:* **police tous risques,** comprehensive, all-risks, policy; **r. d'incendie,** fire risk. **risqué** *a* risky, hazardous; risqué.

risquer [riske] 1. *vtr* to risk, venture, chance; **r. sa vie,** to risk one's life; **r. le coup,** to chance it; **je ne veux rien r.,** I'm not taking any chances; **la grève risque de durer longtemps,** the strike may (well) go on for a long time; *F:* **il risque de gagner,** he has a good chance of winning 2. **se r.,** to take a risk; **se r. à faire qch.,** to venture, to dare, to do sth.

risque-tout [riskətu] *nm inv* daredevil.

rissoler [risɔle] *vtr & i Cu:* to brown.

ristourne [risturn] *nf* refund, rebate; *Com:* discount.

ristourner [risturne] *vtr* to refund; to give a rebate.

rite [rit] *nm* rite; ritual (of everyday life).

ritournelle [riturnel] *nf Mus:* ritornello; *F:* **c'est toujours la même r.,** it's always the same old story.

rituel, -elle [rituɛl] 1. *a* ritual 2. *nm* ritual.

rivage [rivaʒ] *nm* bank (of river); shore.

rival, -aux [rival, -o] *a & n* rival; **sans r.,** unrivalled.

rivaliser [rivalize] *vi* **r. avec qn,** to rival s.o.; to compete, vie, with s.o.; **r. d'adresse avec qn,** to vie in skill with s.o.

rivalité [rivalite] *nf* rivalry, competition.

rive [riv] *nf* bank; shore.

river [rive] *vtr* (*a*) to rivet (*b*) to clinch (nail); *F:* **r. son clou à qn,** to shut s.o. up. **rivé** *a* riveted (à, to); **r. sur place,** rooted to the spot.

riverain, -aine [rivrɛ̃, -ɛn] 1. *a* (*a*) riverside, waterside (property) (*b*) bordering on a road; wayside (property) 2. *n* (*a*) riverside resident (*b*) resident (of street); *PN:* **route interdite sauf aux riverains,** access only.

rivet [rive] *nm* rivet.

rivetage [rivtaʒ] *nm* riveting.

riveter [rivte] *vtr* (**je rivette**) to rivet.

rivière [rivjɛr] *nf* (*a*) river, stream (*b*) *Sp:* water jump (*c*) **r. de diamants,** diamond rivière, diamond necklace.

rixe [riks] *nf* brawl, scuffle; row.

riz [ri] *nm* rice; **r. au lait,** rice pudding.

rizière [rizjɛr] *nf* paddy field(s), rice field(s).

RN *abbr Route nationale.*

robe [rɔb] *nf* (*a*) (woman's) dress; gown; **r. du soir,** evening dress (*b*) **r. d'intérieur,** housecoat; **r. de chambre,** dressing gown; *Cu:* **pommes de terre en r. de chambre, en r. des champs,** jacket potatoes (*c*) (long) robe, gown (of lawyer); **les gens de r.,** the legal profession.

robinet [rɔbine] *nm* tap, *NAm:* faucet.

robinetterie [rɔbinetri] *nf* taps, cocks and fittings.

robot [rɔbo] *nm* robot; **r. (ménager),** food processor; **avion r.,** pilotless aircraft.

robuste [rɔbyst] *a* robust (health, person); sturdy (person); hardy (plant); stout (faith).

robustesse [rɔbystes] *nf* robustness, sturdiness, hardiness.

roc [rɔk] *nm* rock.

rocade [rɔkad] *nf* bypass.

rocaille [rɔkaj] *nf* (*a*) **(jardin de) r.,** rockery; rock garden (*b*) rubble (*c*) stony ground. **rocailleux, -euse** *a* rocky, stony.

rocambolesque [rɔkɑ̃bɔlesk] *a* fantastic, incredible.

roche [rɔʃ] *nf* rock, boulder; **r. de fond,** bedrock; **eau de r.,** clear spring water.

rocher [rɔʃe] *nm* rock; crag. **rocheux, -euse** *a* rocky; **les (montagnes) Rocheuses,** the Rocky Mountains.

rodage [rɔdaʒ] *nm* grinding; *Aut:* running in.

roder [rɔde] *vtr* (*a*) to grind; to polish (gem); to grind in (valve) (*b*) *Aut:* to run in (new car); **être rodé,** (*of show*) to have got into its stride; (*of pers*) to have been broken in.

rôder [rode] *vi* to prowl; to lurk; to wander about (the streets).

rôdeur, -euse [roder, -øz] *n* prowler.

rogne [rɔɲ] *nf F:* bad temper; **se mettre en r.,** to get mad.

rogner [rɔɲe] *vtr* to clip, trim, cut down; **r. sur les dépenses,** to reduce expenses.

rognon [rɔɲɔ̃] *nm Cu:* kidney.

rognures [rɔɲyr] *nfpl* clippings, trimmings; scraps.

roi [rwa] *nm* (*a*) king; **les rois mages,** the Magi, the three kings; **jour, fête, des Rois,** Twelfth night (*b*) **r. des resquilleurs,** champion gatecrasher.

roitelet [rwatle] *nm* 1. petty king 2. *Orn:* wren.

rôle [rol] *nm* 1. list; register; roster; **à tour de r.,** in turns. 2. *Th:* part, role; **premier r.,** leading part; **distribution des rôles,** cast(ing); **jouer un r. secondaire,** to play second fiddle; **la radio a pour r. de,** the function of radio is to.

romain, -aine [rɔmɛ̃, -ɛn] 1. *a & n* Roman; **l'Empire r.,** the Roman Empire; **chiffres romains,** Roman numerals 2. *nf* **romaine,** cos lettuce 3. *nf* **romaine,** steelyard.

roman¹ [rɔmɑ̃] *nm* 1. (*a*) novel; **r. policier,** detective novel; **r. noir,** thriller; **r. d'amour,** love story; **r. feuilleton,** serial (story) (*b*) **le r.,** fiction (*c*) **l'histoire de sa vie est tout un r.,** the story of his life is quite a romance 2. *Lit:* romance.

roman², **-ane** [rɔmɑ̃, -an] *a & nm* **1.** *Ling:* Romance **2.** *Arch:* romanesque; (*in Eng*) Norman.

romance [rɔmɑ̃s] *nf Mus:* (sentimental) ballad, lovesong.

romancer [rɔmɑ̃se] *vtr* to fictionalize.

romancier, **-ière** [rɔmɑ̃sje, -jɛr] *n* novelist.

romand [rɔmɑ̃] *a Geog:* **la Suisse romande**, French (speaking) Switzerland.

romanesque [rɔmanɛsk] *a* romantic.

romanichel, **-elle** [rɔmaniʃel] *n* gipsy.

romantique [rɔmɑ̃tik] *a* romantic.

romantisme [rɔmɑ̃tism] *nm* romanticism.

romarin [rɔmarɛ̃] *nm Bot:* rosemary.

rompre [rɔ̃pr̩] (*pr ind* **il rompt**) **1.** *vtr* (*a*) to break (in two); to snap (stick); **se r. le cou**, to break one's neck (*b*) (*of stream*) **r. ses digues**, to burst its banks; *Mil:* **r. les rangs**, to dismiss (*c*) **r. le silence**, to break the silence (*d*) **r. un choc**, to deaden a shock (*e*) to break off (engagement, diplomatic relations) (*f*) **r. l'équilibre**, to upset the balance (*g*) **r. un cheval**, to break in a horse; **r. qn à la discipline**, to break s.o. in to discipline **2.** *vi* (*a*) to break (off, up, in two); to snap; **r. avec qn**, to break with s.o.; **r. avec une habitude**, to break (oneself of) a habit (*b*) **r. devant l'ennemi**, to break before the enemy **3.** **se r.**, to break (in two); (*of branch*) to snap, break off. **rompu** *a* (*a*) broken; **r. de fatigue**, worn out (*b*) broken in; **être r. aux affaires**, to be experienced in business.

romsteck [rɔmstɛk] *nm Cu:* rumpsteak.

ronce [rɔ̃s] *nf Bot:* bramble; blackberry bush.

ronchonnement [rɔ̃ʃɔnmɑ̃] *nm F:* grumbling, grousing.

ronchonner [rɔ̃ʃɔne] *vi F:* to grumble, grouse.

ronchonneur, **-euse** [rɔ̃ʃɔnœr, -øz] *n F:* grumbler, grouser.

rond, **ronde** [rɔ̃, rɔ̃d] **1.** *a* (*a*) round (ball, table); rounded; plump (figure) (*b*) **en chiffres ronds**, in round figures; **compte r.**, round sum (*c*) *P:* drunk, tight **2.** *adv* **tourner r.**, (i) to run true (ii) to run smoothly; *F:* **ça ne tourne pas r.**, it's not working properly; things aren't going well **3.** *nm* (*a*) round, circle; **tourner en r.**, (i) to go round in a circle (ii) to go round in circles; **r. de serviette**, napkin ring (*b*) disc; slice (of sausage); *P:* **il n'a pas un r.**, he hasn't a penny; he's broke **4.** *nf* **ronde** (*a*) round (dance); **faire la r.**, to dance in a ring (*b*) round(s); (*of policeman*) beat; **faire la ronde**, to go the rounds (*c*) roundhand (*d*) *Mus:* semibreve (*e*) *adv phr* **à la ronde**, around; **à des kilomètres à la ronde**, for miles around; **passer qch à la ronde**, to pass sth round. **rondement** *adv* briskly; bluntly.

rondelet, **-ette** [rɔ̃dlɛ, -ɛt] *a* roundish, plump (person); **somme rondelette**, tidy sum.

rondelle [rɔ̃dɛl] *nf* **1.** disc; slice (of sausage) **2.** (*a*) ring (*b*) washer.

rondeur [rɔ̃dœr] *nf* **1.** (*a*) roundness (*b*) *pl* rounded forms (*c*) (*of woman*) curves **2.** straightforwardness, frankness.

rondin [rɔ̃dɛ̃] *nm* log.

rondouillard [rɔ̃dujar] *a* plump, fat.

rond-point [rɔ̃pwɛ̃] *nm* roundabout, *NAm:* traffic circle; *pl* **ronds-points**.

ronflement [rɔ̃fləmɑ̃] *nm* (*a*) snoring, snore (*b*) roar(ing); hum(ming); purr(ing).

ronfler [rɔ̃fle] *vi* **1.** to snore **2.** (*of wind, fire*) to roar; (*of organ*) to boom; (*of top*) to hum; (*of engine*) to purr. **ronflant** *a* high-sounding, pompous (title).

ronfleur, **-euse** [rɔ̃flœr, -øz] *n* snorer.

ronger [rɔ̃ʒe] (**n. rongeons**) *vtr* (*a*) to gnaw; to nibble; **rongé par les vers**, wormeaten; **se r. les ongles**, to bite one's nails; **se r. les sangs**, to eat one's heart out (*b*) (*of acid, rust*) to corrode; to eat away; **rongé de chagrin**, consumed with grief.

rongeur, **-euse** [rɔ̃ʒœr, -øz] *a & nm* rodent.

ronronnement [rɔ̃rɔnmɑ̃] *nm* purr(ing); hum.

ronronner [rɔ̃rɔne] *vi* (*a*) to purr (*b*) *Mch:* to hum.

roquet [rɔkɛ] *nm* pug (dog).

roquette [rɔkɛt] *nf* rocket.

rosace [rozas] *nf* (*a*) rose (window) (*b*) (ceiling) rose.

rosaire [rozɛr] *nm Ecc:* rosary.

rosbif [rɔzbif] *nm* roast beef; **un r.**, a joint of beef.

rose [roz] **1.** *nf* (*a*) *Bot:* rose; **r. sauvage**, wild rose, dog rose; *F:* **roman à l'eau de r.**, sentimental novel; **pas de r. sans épines**, no rose without a thorn; **découvrir le pot aux roses**, to find out the secret (*b*) **r. trémière**, hollyhock **2.** (*a*) a pink; rosy; **tout n'est pas r.**, it's not all roses (*b*) *nm* pink; **voir la vie en r.**, to see everything through rose-coloured spectacles.

rosé [roze] *a* rosy, pale pink; **vin r.**, *nm* **r.**, rosé wine

roseau, **-eaux** [rozo] *nm Bot:* reed.

rosée [roze] *nf* dew.

roseraie [rozrɛ] *nf* rose garden.

rosette [rozɛt] *nf* (*a*) bow (of ribbon) (*b*) rosette (*esp* of the Legion of Honour).

rosier [rozje] *nm* rose tree, rose bush.

rosir [rozir] *vtr & i* to turn pink.

rosse [rɔs] **1.** *nf* (*a*) *F:* (*horse*) nag, screw (*b*) *P:* beast, swine; (*woman*) bitch **2.** *a P:* nasty, rotten (person).

rosser [rɔse] *vtr F:* to beat, thrash (s.o.).

rosserie [rɔsri] *nf F:* (*a*) nastiness (*b*) dirty trick (*c*) spiteful remark.

rossignol [rɔsiɲɔl] *nm* **1.** *Orn:* nightingale **2.** skeleton key **3.** unsaleable article.

rot [ro] *nm F:* belch, burp.

rotation [rɔtasjɔ̃] *nf* **1.** rotation; **movement de r.**, rotational motion **2.** (*a*) rotation (of crops) (*b*) turnround (of buses); turnover (of stocks). **rotatif**, **-ive 1.** *a* rotary **2.** *nf* **rotative**, rotary press. **rotatoire** *a* rotary.

roter [rɔte] *vi F:* to belch, to burp.

rôti [roti] *nm* roast (meat); **un r. de porc**, a joint of pork.

rotin [rɔtɛ̃] *nm Bot:* rattan; **chaise en r.**, cane chair.

rôtir [rotir] **1.** *vtr* (*a*) to roast (meat) (*b*) *F:* (*of sun*) to scorch; **se r. au soleil**, to bask in the sun **2.** *vi* to roast, to scorch.

rôtisserie [rotisri] *nf* steakhouse; grill room.

rôtisseur, **-euse** [rotisœr, -øz] *n* steakhouse proprietor.

rôtissoire [rotiswar] *nf* spit roaster.

rotonde [rotɔ̃d] *nf* rotunda.

rotor [rɔtɔr] *nm El:* rotor.

rotule [rɔtyl] *nf* kneecap; *F:* **être sur les rotules**, to be fagged out.

rouage [rwaʒ] *nm* **1.** wheels; works (of a watch); **les rouages de l'État**, the wheels of State **2.** (toothed) wheel, cog wheel.

roublard, -arde [rublar, -ard] *a & n F:* crafty, foxy, wily (person).

roucoulement [rukulmã] *nm* cooing.

roucouler [rukule] *vtr & i* to coo; to warble (a song).

roue [ru] *nf* (*a*) wheel; **véhicule à deux roues,** two-wheeled vehicle; **r. de secours,** spare wheel; **faire r. libre,** to freewheel; **faire la r.,** (i) (*of peacock*) to fan its tail (ii) to strut about (iii) to do a cartwheel (*b*) **r. dentée,** cogwheel; **r. d'engrenage,** gear(wheel).

roué [rwe] *a* cunning, sly.

rouer [rwe] *vtr* **r. qn de coups,** to beat s.o. black and blue.

rouet [rwɛ] *nm* spinning wheel.

rouge [ruʒ] **1.** *a* (*a*) red; **r. de colère, de honte,** flushed with anger, with shame; **devenir r. comme une pivoine, une tomate,** to turn as red as a beetroot; *adv* **voir r.,** to see red (*b*) (*inv in compounds*) **r. sang,** blood red **2.** *nm* (*a*) red; **porter le fer au r.,** to make the iron red-hot; *Pol:* **un r.,** a Red, a Commie (*b*) **rouge; r. à lèvres,** lipstick (*c*) red wine.

rougeâtre [ruʒɑtr] *a* reddish.

rougeaud, -eaude [ruʒo, -od] *a & n* red-faced (person).

rouge-gorge [ruʒgɔrʒ] *nm Orn:* robin (red-breast); *pl* **rouges-gorges.**

rougeole [ruʒɔl] *nf Med:* measles.

rougeoyer [ruʒwaje] *vi* (**il rougeoie**) (*of thgs*) (*a*) to turn red (*b*) to glow (red). **rougeoyant** *a* reddening; glowing.

rouget [ruʒɛ] *nm Ich:* red mullet; **r. grondin,** gurnard.

rougeur [ruʒœr] *nf* **1.** redness **2.** blush, flush **3.** red spot, blotch (on the skin).

rougir [ruʒir] **1.** *vtr* (*a*) to redden; to turn (sth) red (*b*) **fer rougi au feu,** iron heated red-hot (*c*) to flush (the face) **2.** *vi* (*a*) to redden, to turn red (*b*) (*of pers*) to turn, go, red; to blush, to flush (up); **faire r. qn,** to make s.o. blush; **r. jusqu'aux oreilles,** to go bright red; **r. de qch,** to be ashamed of sth. **rougissant** *a* blushing; reddening.

rougissement [ruʒismã] *nm* blush(ing).

rouille [ruj] **1.** *nf* rust **2.** *Agr:* mildew, blight **3.** *a inv* rust(-coloured).

rouiller [ruje] **1.** *vi* to rust **2.** *vtr* to rust; to make (iron) rusty **3.** **se r.** (*a*) to rust (up); to get rusty (*b*) **je me rouille,** I'm getting rusty (*c*) (*of muscles*) to get stiff. **rouillé** *a* rusty, rusted; (*of memory*) rusty; (*of muscles*) stiff.

roulade [rulad] *nf* **1.** roll (downhill) **2.** *Mus:* roulade, run **3.** *Cu:* meat olive.

roulant [rulã] **1.** *a* rolling; (*of furniture*) on wheels; sliding (door); moving (staircase); *Rail:* **matériel r.,** rolling stock; **personnel r.,** (train) crews **2.** *a F:* killing (joke) **3.** *nf F: Mil:* **roulante,** field kitchen.

roulé [rule] **1.** *a* rolled; **col r.,** polo neck **2.** *nm Cu:* (*a*) rolled joint (*b*) Swiss roll.

rouleau, -eaux [rulo] *nm* **1.** (*a*) roller; **r. compresseur,** road roller; **r. à vapeur,** steam roller; **r. à pâtisserie,** rolling pin; **passer le gazon au r.,** to roll the lawn (*b*) (hair) roller, curler; *Typew:* **r. porte-papier,** impression roller **2.** **r. à vapeur,** roll (of paper); spool (of film); **je suis au bout de mon r.,** I'm at the end of my tether **3.** *Sp:* roll.

roulement [rulmã] *nm* **1.** (*a*) rolling (of ball); **r.**

d'yeux, rolling of the eyes (*b*) rolling (of vehicle); **bande de r.,** tread (of tyre) (*c*) running (of machine) **2.** rumbling (of thunder); roll(ing) (of drum) **3.** *MecE:* **r. à billes,** ball bearing **4.** (*a*) *Com:* **r. de fonds,** circulation of capital (*b*) alternation, taking turns; rotation; **par r.,** in rotation.

rouler [rule] **1.** *vtr* (*a*) to roll (sth) (along); **r. un projet dans sa tête,** to turn over a plan in one's mind (*b*) *F:* **r. qn,** to con s.o.; to diddle s.o. (*c*) to roll up (map, sleeve); to roll (cigarette) (*d*) to roll (lawn) (*e*) **r. les r,** to roll one's r's (*f*) **r. qn dans une couverture,** to wrap s.o. up in a blanket **2.** *vi* (*a*) to roll (over, along, about); **r. (en voiture),** to drive; **nous avons roulé toute la nuit,** we travelled all night; **cette voiture a peu roulé,** this car has a low mileage; *Av:* **r. sur le sol,** to taxi; *F:* **ça roule,** everything's fine; **r. sur l'or,** to be rolling in money; **la conversation roulait sur le sport,** we were talking about sport (*b*) to roll; to rumble (*c*) *Nau:* (*of ship*) to roll **3.** **se r.** (*a*) to roll; to turn over and over (*b*) to roll up (into a ball) (*c*) *F:* **se r. par terre,** to fall about laughing.

roulette [rulɛt] *nf* **1.** (*a*) caster; roller; small wheel; **patins à roulettes,** roller skates; *F:* **ça marche comme sur des roulettes,** things are going like clockwork (*b*) dentist's drill **2.** (*game*) roulette; (*instrument*) roulette wheel; **r. russe,** Russian roulette.

roulis [ruli] *nm Nau: Av:* roll(ing); **coup de r.,** lurch.

roulotte [rulɔt] *nf* caravan; *NAm:* trailer.

Roumanie [rumani] *Prnf Geog:* Rumania, Ro(u)-mania. **roumain, -aine** *a & n* Rumanian, Ro(u)-manian.

roupie [rupi] *nf Num:* rupee.

roupiller [rupije] *vi F:* to snooze, to have a kip; to doze.

roupillon [rupijɔ̃] *nm F:* snooze, kip.

rouquin, -ine [rukɛ̃, -in] **1.** *a F:* red-haired; red, carroty (hair) **2.** *n* redhead.

rouspétance [ruspetãs] *nf F:* grousing.

rouspéter [ruspete] *vi* (**je rouspète**) *F:* to grumble, grouse.

rouspéteur, -euse [ruspetœr, -øz] **1.** *a* quarrel-some; grumbling **2.** *n* grumbler; grouser.

rousse [rus] *see* **roux.**

rousseur [rusœr] *nf* redness; **tache de r.,** freckle.

roussi [rusi] *nm* **ça sent le r.!** (i) there's a smell of burning (ii) there's trouble ahead.

roussir [rusir] **1.** *vtr* (*a*) to redden; *Cu:* to brown (meat) (*b*) to scorch, singe (linen) **2.** *vi* (*a*) to turn brown; to redden (*b*) *Cu:* **faire r.,** to brown (*c*) to singe; to get scorched.

route [rut] *nf* **1.** road; **r. nationale, grande r.,** main road; *NAm:* highway; = A road; **r. départementale,** secondary road; **prendre la r. de Paris,** to take the road to Paris **2.** (*a*) route; way; **se mettre en r.,** to set out; **en r.!** let's go! **faire r. ensemble,** to travel together; **frais de r.,** travel(ling) expenses; **montrer la r. à qn,** to show s.o. the way (*b*) *Nau:* course; **faire r. sur Calais,** to steer for Calais (*c*) **mettre le moteur en r.,** to start (up) the engine; **mettre des travaux en r.,** to start operations.

routier, -ière [rutje, -jɛr] *a & n* **1.** *a* **carte routière,** road map; **réseau r.,** road network; **transports routiers,** road transport; **gare routière,** bus, coach, station **2.** *nm* **gros r.,** heavy (goods) lorry, *NAm:*

heavy truck 3. (*pers*) long-distance lorry driver, *NAm:* truck driver; **restaurant des routiers,** *F:* **r.** = transport café.

routine [rutin] *nf* routine; **examen de r.,** routine examination. **routinier, -ière** *a* routine; humdrum.

rouvrir [ruvrir] *vtr & i & pr* (*conj like* COUVRIR) to reopen.

roux, rousse [ru, rus] **1.** (*a*) *a* (russet-)red, (reddish-) brown; (*of hair*) red; *Cu:* **beurre r.,** brown butter (*b*) *n* redhead **2.** *nm* (*a*) russet, reddish-brown (colour) (*b*) *Cu:* roux.

royal, -aux [rwajal, -o] *a* royal, regal, kingly. **royalement** *adv* royally; *F:* **je m'en fiche r.,** I couldn't care less about it.

royaliste [rwajalist] *a & n* royalist.

royaume [rwajom] *nm* kingdom, realm.

Royaume-Uni [rwajomyni] *Prnm* the United Kingdom.

royauté [rwajote] *nf* royalty; kingship.

RP *abbr Relations publiques.*

RSVP *abbr Répondez s'il vous plaît.*

ruade [rɥad] *nf* buck, kick (of horse); **lancer une r.,** to lash out (**à,** at).

ruban [rybã] *nm* **1.** (*a*) ribbon, band; **r. de chapeau,** hatband (*b*) **mètre à r.,** measuring tape; **r. adhésif,** adhesive tape, sticky tape; **r. magnétique,** magnetic, recording, tape **2. r. d'acier,** steel band.

rubéole [rybeɔl] *nf Med:* rubella; German measles.

rubis [rybi] *nm* ruby; **montre montée sur r.,** jewelled watch.

rubrique [rybrik] *nf* (*a*) rubric (*b*) *Journ:* heading; item; column.

ruche [ryʃ] *nf* (bee)hive.

rude [ryd] *a* **1.** (*a*) uncouth, unpolished (*b*) rough (skin); stiff, hard (brush); harsh (voice); rugged (path) **2.** (*a*) hard (winter); arduous (task); severe (blow); rude (shock); stiff (climb) (*b*) gruff, ungracious, brusque; **il a été à r. école,** he had a strict upbringing **3.** *F:* **r. appétit,** hearty appetite; **r. peur,** real fright. **rudement** *adv* (*a*) roughly, harshly (*b*) *F:* terribly, awfully; **je suis r. fatigué,** I'm terribly tired.

rudesse [rydɛs] *nf* roughness, ruggedness; coarseness; harshness; crudeness.

rudiments [rydimã] *nmpl* rudiments; smattering (of knowledge); principles (of theory). **rudimentaire** *a* rudimentary.

rudoyer [rydwaje] *vtr* (**je rudoie**) to treat roughly; to knock (s.o.) about.

rue [ry] *nf* street; **la grande r.,** the high street; **r. à sens unique,** one-way street; **être à la r.,** to be out on the street.

ruée [rɥe] *nf* rush; stampede, scramble; **la r. vers l'or,** the gold rush.

ruelle [rɥɛl] *nf* lane; alley.

ruer [rɥe] **1.** *vi* to kick, to lash out **2. se r. sur qn,** to hurl, fling, oneself at s.o.; **se r. à la porte,** to rush for the door.

rugby [rygbi] *nm* Rugby (football); *F:* rugger; **r. à quinze,** Rugby Union; **r. à treize,** Rugby League.

rugbyman, -men [rygbiman, -mɛn] *nm* rugby player.

rugir [ryʒir] *vi* to roar; to howl.

rugissement [ryʒismã] *nm* roar, howl.

rugosité [rygozite] *nf* ruggedness, roughness.

rugueux, -euse [rygø, -øz] *a* rugged, rough.

ruine [rɥin] *nf* ruin **1.** (*a*) downfall; decay (of building); **tomber en r.,** to fall in ruins (*b*) downfall (of pers, society); **ça sera sa r.,** it will be the ruin of him **2.** (*usu pl*) ruins.

ruiner [rɥine] *vtr* to ruin, destroy; **se r. la santé,** to ruin one's health. **ruineux, -euse** *a* ruinous; expensive.

ruisseau, -eaux [rɥiso] *nm* **1.** (*a*) brook; (small) stream (*b*) stream (of blood); flood (of tears) **2.** (street) gutter.

ruissellement [rɥisɛlmã] *nm* streaming, running (of water).

ruisseler [rɥisle] *vi* (**il ruisselle**) **1.** (*of water*) to stream, run, flow **2.** (*of surface*) to run, to drip; **r. de,** to drip with.

rumeur [rymœr] *nf* **1.** (*a*) distant murmur, hum (of traffic) (*b*) din, clamour (*c*) rumblings (of discontent) **2.** rumour.

ruminant [ryminã] *nm Z:* ruminant.

rumination [ryminasjõ] *nf* rumination.

ruminer [rymine] **1.** *vi* (*of animal*) to ruminate; to chew the cud **2.** *vtr* **r. une idée,** to ruminate on, over, an idea.

rumsteck [rɔmstɛk] *nm* rumpsteak.

rupin, -ine [rypɛ̃, -in] *a & n P:* stinking rich (person).

rupture [ryptyr] *nf* (*a*) bursting (of dam) (*b*) breaking (in two); rupture (of blood vessel); tearing (of ligament) (*c*) breaking off (of talks); calling off (of deal); breach (of contract); (*of relationship*) breakup, split.

rural, -aux [ryral, -o] **1.** *a* rural; **vie rurale,** country life **2.** *n* countryman, countrywoman.

ruse [ryz] *nf* ruse, trick; cunning; **r. de guerre,** stratagem.

ruser [ryze] *vi* to use cunning, trickery. **rusé** *a* crafty, sly, cunning.

Russie [rysi] *Prnf Geog:* Russia. **russe** *a & n* Russian.

rustaud, -aude [rysto, -od] **1.** *a* boorish, uncouth **2.** *nm* boor; country bumpkin, *NAm:* hick.

rustique [rystik] **1.** *a* (*a*) rustic; country (life) (*b*) hardy (plant) **2.** *nm* rustic style.

rustre [rystr] **1.** *a* boorish **2.** *nm* boor, lout.

rut [ryt] *nm* (*of animals*) rut(ting); **être en r.,** to be on heat.

rutabaga [rytabaga] *nm* swede; *NAm:* rutabaga.

rutilement [rytilmã] *nm* gleam(ing).

rutiler [rytile] *vi* to gleam. **rutilant** *a* gleaming.

rythme [ritm] *nm* rhythm; **r. respiratoire,** breathing rate; **r. de vie,** tempo of life; **suivre le r.,** to keep up (the pace); **au r. de,** at the rate of.

rythmer [ritme] *vtr* to put rhythm into, to give rhythm to (tune, sentence). **rythmé** *a* rhythmic(al). **rythmique 1.** *a* rhythmical **2.** *nf* rhythmics.

S

S, s [ɛs] *nm* (the letter) S, s; **faire des s,** to zigzag; **en S,** S-shaped; winding.

S *abbr* **1.** *sud* **2.** *Saint.*

sa [sa] *poss af see* **son¹.**

SA *abbr Société anonyme.*

sabbat [saba] *nm* **1.** (Jewish) Sabbath **2.** *F:* row, racket.

sable [sabl̩] *nm* **1.** sand; **sables mouvants,** quicksands; **tempête de s.,** sandstorm. **sablonneux, -euse** *a* sandy.

sablage [sablaʒ] *nm* (a) sanding (b) sandblasting.

sablé [sable] *nm Cu:* (kind of) shortbread.

sabler [sable] *vtr* **1.** to sand (path) **2.** *F:* **s. le champagne,** to celebrate with champagne **3.** to sandblast (cashing).

sablier [sablije] *nm* hourglass; egg timer.

sablière [sablijɛr] *nf* sandpit.

sabord [sabɔr] *nm Nau:* port(hole).

sabordage [sabɔrdaʒ] *nm* scuttling.

saborder [sabɔrde] *vtr* **1.** to scuttle (ship) **2.** to ruin, destroy (sth).

sabot [sabo] *nm* **1.** (a) clog, sabot (b) *P:* old, useless, article; old heap (c) *F:* like an old boot **2.** (horse's) hoof **3. s. de frein,** brake shoe.

sabotage [sabɔtaʒ] *nm* (a) botching (of work) (b) (act of) sabotage.

saboter [sabɔte] *vtr* to botch (a job); to sabotage (sth).

saboteur, -euse [sabɔtœr, -øz] *n* **1.** bungler, botcher **2.** saboteur.

sabre [sabr̩] *nm* sabre; **s. d'abordage,** cutlass; **s. au clair,** (with) drawn sword.

sabrer [sabre] *vtr* (a) to cut down with sword (b) *F:* to make cuts in (text) (c) *F:* to criticize, slate (s.o.).

sac¹ [sak] *nm* (a) sack, bag; **s. à main,** handbag, *NAm:* purse; **s. à outils,** toolbag; **s. de voyage,** travel bag, overnight bag; **s. de couchage,** sleeping bag; **s. à dos,** rucksack; **s. à provisions,** shopping bag; **l'affaire est dans le s.,** it's in the bag (b) *F:* ten francs.

sac² *nm* sacking, pillage; **mettre à s.,** to sack (town); to ransack (house).

saccade [sakad] *nf* jerk, jolt; **par saccades,** by fits and starts. **saccadé** *a* jerky, abrupt (movement, style); irregular (breathing); staccato (voice).

saccage [sakaʒ] *nm* havoc.

saccager [sakaʒe] *vtr* (**n. saccageons**) (a) to sack, pillage (town); to ransack (house) (b) to create havoc in, to wreck (garden); **ils ont tout saccagé,** they've turned everything upside down.

saccharine [sakarin] *nf* saccharin(e).

sachet [saʃɛ] *nm* sachet; bag; **s. de thé,** teabag.

sacoche [sakɔʃ] *nf* satchel; toolbag; saddlebag.

sacquer [sake] *vtr F:* to dismiss, to sack (s.o.).

sacraliser [sakralize] *vtr* to consider (sth) as sacred.

sacre [sakr̩] *nm* anointing (of king); consecration (of bishop).

sacrement [sakrəmɑ̃] *nm Ecc:* sacrament; **le saint S.,** the Blessed Sacrament.

sacrer [sakre] **1.** *vtr* to anoint (king); to consecrate (bishop) **2.** *vi F:* to curse and swear. **sacré** *a* (a) holy (scripture); sacred, consecrated (place) (b) *P:* damn(ed); bloody; **un s. menteur,** a hell of a liar.

sacrifice [sakrifis] *nm* sacrifice.

sacrifier [sakrifje] *vtr* (*pr sub & impf* n. **sacrifiions**) (a) to sacrifice (victim) (b) to sacrifice, give up (time, money) (**à,** to); **se s.,** to sacrifice oneself.

sacrilège [sakrilɛʒ] **1.** *a* sacrilegious (thought) **2.** (a) *nm* sacrilege (b) *n* sacrilegious person.

sacristain [sakristɛ̃] *nm* sacristan; sexton.

sacristie [sakristi] *nf Ecc:* sacristy, vestry.

sacro-saint [sakrosɛ̃] *a* sacrosanct.

sacrum [sakrɔm] *nm Anat:* sacrum.

sadisme [sadism] *nm* sadism. **sadique 1.** *a* sadistic **2.** *n* sadist.

safari [safari] *nm* safari; **faire un s.,** to go on safari.

safran [safrɑ̃] *nm* saffron.

sagacité [sagasite] *nf* sagacity, shrewdness. **sagace** *a* sagacious, shrewd.

sagaie [sagɛ] *nf* assegai.

sage [saʒ] *a* **1.** wise; *nm* sage; wise man **2.** prudent, wise (policy); sensible (person) **3.** well behaved; good (child); **s. comme une image,** as good as gold **4.** moderate. **sagement** (a) wisely, sensibly (b) properly; quietly.

sage-femme [saʒfam] *nf* midwife; *pl* sages-femmes.

sagesse [saʒɛs] *nf* **1.** (a) wisdom; (b) prudence, discretion; **agir avec s.,** to act wisely **2.** good behaviour **3.** moderation.

Sagittaire [saʒitɛr] *nm Astr:* Sagittarius.

sagouin [sagwɛ̃] *nm F:* dirty, filthy, man; slob.

saignée [seɲe] *nf* **1.** (a) *Med:* blood-letting; **faire une s. à qn,** to bleed s.o. (b) drain (on one's resources) **2.** bend of the arm **3.** (drainage) trench, ditch; hole (in wall, for pipe).

saignement [seɲmɑ̃] *nm* bleeding; **s. du nez,** nose-bleed.

saigner [seɲe] **1.** *vi* (*of wound, pers*) to bleed; **je saigne du nez,** my nose is bleeding **2.** *vtr Med: Fig:* to bleed (s.o.); **s. qn à blanc,** to bleed s.o. white; **se s. aux quatre veines,** to bleed oneself white. **saignant** *a* (a) bleeding (wound) (b) *Cu:* rare (meat).

saillie [saji] *nf* **1.** (a) *Breed:* covering (by male) (b) sally, flash of wit **2.** projection; **faire s.,** to project, jut out.

saillir [sajir] **1.** *vtr* (*prp* **saillissant;** *pp* **sailli;** *pr ind* je **saillis;** *fu* je **saillirai**) *Breed:* to cover (female) **2.** *vi* (*used only in prp* **saillant**) to jut out; to protrude; (*of eyes*) to bulge. **saillant** *a* (a) projecting, protruding; prominent; bulging (eyes) (b) salient, outstanding (feature).

sain, saine [sɛ̃, sɛn] *a* healthy (person); sound, sane (judgment); wholesome (food); **s. et sauf**, safe and sound; **s. de corps et d'esprit**, sound in body and mind. **sainement** *adv* healthily; soundly; sanely.

saindoux [sɛ̃du] *nm Cu:* lard.

saint, sainte [sɛ̃, sɛ̃t] 1. *a* (*a*) holy; **la Sainte Église**, the Holy Church; **le Vendredi S.**, Good Friday (*b*) saintly, godly (person) (*c*) sanctified, consecrated; **lieu s.**, holy place; *F:* **toute la sainte journée**, the whole blessed day (*d*) saint; **S. Pierre**, Saint Peter; **la S. Georges**, St George's day 2. *n* saint; (*woman*) **sainte nitouche**, pious hypocrite 3. *nm* **le S. des Saints**, the Holy of Holies.

saint-bernard [sɛ̃bɛrnar] *nm inv* St Bernard (dog); *Fig:* good samaritan.

Saint-Esprit [sɛ̃tɛspri] *Prnm* le S.-E., Holy Ghost, Spirit.

sainteté [sɛ̃təte] *nf* holiness, saintliness; sanctity; *Ecc:* **Sa Sainteté**, His Holiness (the Pope).

saint-frusquin [sɛ̃fryskɛ̃] *nm no pl P:* **tout le s.-f.**, the whole caboodle.

Saint-glinglin [sɛ̃glɛ̃glɛ̃] *nf no pl F:* **jusqu'à la S.-g.**, till the cows come home.

Saint-Laurent (le) [ləsɛ̃lɔrɑ̃] *Prnm Geog:* the Saint Lawrence (river).

Saint-Père [sɛ̃pɛr] *nm* Holy Father.

Saint-Siège (le) [ləsɛ̃sjɛʒ] *nm Ecc:* the Holy See.

Saint-Sylvestre (la) [lasɛ̃silvɛstr̩] *nf* New Year's Eve.

saisie [sezi] *nf* seizure (of goods).

saisir [sezir] 1. *vtr* (*a*) to seize; to grasp; to take hold, catch hold, of (sth); **s. l'occasion**, to jump at the opportunity; **être saisi (d'étonnement)**, to be startled (*b*) *Jur:* to seize (real estate) (*c*) to perceive, grasp (the truth, a meaning); **je ne saisis pas**, I don't understand; *F:* I don't get it; **il n'ai pas saisi son nom**, I didn't catch his name; **il saisit vite**, he's quick on the uptake 2. *Cu:* to seal (meat) 3. **se s. de qch**, to seize (on) sth. **saisissant, -ante** *a* striking (resemblance); gripping (words); thrilling (spectacle).

saisissement [sezismɑ̃] *nm* (*a*) sudden chill (*b*) access (of joy) (*c*) shock.

saison [sɛzɔ̃] *nf* season; **en cette s.**, at this time of year; **en toute(s) saison(s)**, all the year round; **la belle s.**, the summer months; **la haute s.**, the tourist season; **de s.**, in season; **hors de s.**, out of season. **saisonnier, -ière** (*a*) *a* seasonal (*b*) *n* seasonal worker.

salade [salad] *nf* 1. (*a*) salad; **s. de fruits**, fruit salad; **quelle s.!** what a shambles! (*b*) *pl P:* lies, stories 2. *Hort: Cu:* salad vegetable; lettuce, endive.

saladier [saladje] *nm* salad bowl.

salaire [salɛr] *nm* (*a*) wage(s), pay; salary (*b*) reward, retribution.

salaison [salɛzɔ̃] *nf* salting (of fish).

salamandre [salamɑ̃dr̩] *nf* 1. *Z:* salamander 2. slow-combustion stove.

salami [salami] *nm* salami (sausage).

salarié, -ée [salarje] 1. *a* (*a*) wage-earning; salaried (*b*) paid (work) 2. *n* wage earner.

salaud [salo] *n P:* (dirty) bastard, swine; **tour de s.**, dirty trick.

sale [sal] *a* dirty 1. (*a*) dirty, filthy (*b*) offensive, filthy (story, word) 2. *F:* (*always before the noun*) **s. type**, rotten bastard; **s. coup**, dirty trick; **s. temps**, foul

weather. **salement** *adv* (*a*) dirtily (*b*) *P:* damn, bloody (difficult).

saler [sale] *vtr* 1. (*a*) to salt; to season with salt (*b*) *F:* to overcharge; to fleece (customers); **s. la note**, to bump up the bill; **on l'a salé**, he got a tough sentence 2. to salt, cure (bacon). **salé** *a* 1. salt (fish); salted (butter, nuts); **c'est trop s.**, it's too salty; *nm* **du s.**, salt pork; **petit s.** = streaky bacon 2. (*a*) spicy, juicy (joke) (*b*) *F:* stiff (price).

saleté [salte] *nf* 1. (*a*) dirtiness, filthiness (of pers, street) (*b*) dirt, filth, mess (*c*) trashy goods; rubbish, junk 2. (*a*) nastiness, obscenity (*b*) nasty, coarse, remark (*c*) dirty trick.

salière [saljɛr] *nf* salt cellar.

saligaud, -aude [saligo, -od] *n P:* (*a*) filthy pig (*b*) bastard, swine; *f* bitch.

salin, -ine [salɛ̃, -in] *a* saline.

salir [salir] *vtr* 1. to dirty, soil; **s. sa réputation**, to tarnish one's reputation 2. **se s.**, to get dirty; to dirty one's clothes. **salissant** *a* (*a*) dirty (work) (*b*) easily soiled; which shows the dirt.

salive [saliv] *nf* saliva, spittle.

saliver [salive] *vi* to salivate.

salle [sal] *nf* 1. (*a*) hall; (large) room; **s. de séjour**, living room; **s. à manger**, (i) dining room (ii) dining room suite; **s. de bain(s)**, bathroom; **s. d'eau**, shower room; **s. de classe**, classroom; **s. des professeurs**, staff room (*b*) **s. des fêtes**, village hall (*c*) **s. d'attente**, waiting room; **s. de ventes**, sale room; **s. d'hôpital**, (hospital) ward; **s. d'opérations**, operating theatre 2. *Th:* auditorium, house; **s. pleine**, full house.

salon [salɔ̃] *nm* (*a*) drawing room; sitting room; lounge; **jeux de s.**, parlour games (*b*) saloon, cabin (in ship) (*c*) **s. de thé**, tea room(s); **s. de coiffure**, hairdressing salon (*d*) (art) exhibition; (motor, trade) show (*e*) *Lit:* salon.

salopard [salɔpar] *nm P:* bastard, swine.

salope [salɔp] *nf P:* (*a*) bitch (*b*) slut (*c*) tart.

saloper [salɔpe] *vtr P:* to botch, bungle (sth).

saloperie [salɔpri] *nf P:* (*a*) filth, muck (*b*) trash; rubbish (*c*) dirty trick (*d*) dirty, filthy, remark.

salopette [salɔpɛt] *nf* dungarees; overalls.

salpêtre [salpɛtr̩] *nm* saltpetre.

salsifis [salsifi] *nm Bot:* salsify.

saltimbanque [saltɛ̃bɑ̃k] *n* acrobat.

salubre [salybr̩] *a* healthy.

salubrité [salybrite] *nf* healthiness; **s. publique**, public health.

saluer [salɥe] *vtr* (*a*) to salute; to bow to (s.o.); **s. qn de la main**, to wave to s.o. (*b*) to greet, to hail (s.o.); **saluez-le de ma part**, give him my regards; **je vous salue, Marie**, hail, Mary.

salut [saly] *nm* 1. (*a*) safety; **port de s.**, haven of refuge (*b*) salvation; **l'Armée du S.**, the Salvation Army 2. (*a*) bow, greeting; *F:* **s.!** (i) hello, hi, there! (ii) (*on leaving*) see you! (*b*) *Mil:* salute.

salutaire [salytɛr] *a* salutary; beneficial.

salutation [salytasjɔ̃] *nf* salutation, greeting; *Corr:* **veuillez agréer mes salutations distinguées**, yours faithfully.

salve [salv] *nf* salvo; burst (of applause).

samedi [samdi] *nm* Saturday.

sanatorium [sanatɔrjɔm] *nm* sanatorium.

sanctification [sɑ̃ktifikasjɔ̃] *nf* sanctification.

sanctifier [sãktifje] *vtr* (*impf & pr sub* n. **sanctifiions**) to sanctify, to hallow.

sanction [sãksjɔ̃] *nf* **1.** sanction; approbation; assent **2.** (*a*) s. (**pénale**), penalty; punishment (*b*) *Pol:* **prendre des sanctions contre un pays,** to impose sanctions on a country.

sanctionner [sãksjɔne] *vtr* **1.** to sanction; to approve **2.** to penalize; to sanction.

sanctuaire [sãktɥɛr] *nm* sanctuary.

sandale [sãdal] *nf* sandal.

sandalette [sãdalɛt] *nf* light sandal.

sandow [sãdo] *nm Rtm:* **1.** *Gym:* chest expander **2.** luggage elastic.

sandwich [sãdwitʃ] *nm* sandwich; **pris en s.,** sandwiched, stuck (**entre**, between); *pl* **sandwich(e)s**.

sang [sã] *nm* **1.** blood; **à s. froid, à s. chaud,** cold-blooded, warm-blooded; **être en s.,** to be covered in blood; **avoir le s. chaud,** to be quick-tempered; **se faire du mauvais s.,** to worry; **mon s. n'a fait qu'un tour,** my heart missed a beat **2.** (*a*) blood, race, lineage; **cheval pur s.,** thoroughbred; **c'est dans le s.,** it's in the blood (*b*) blood, kinship.

sang-froid [sãfrwa] *nm no pl* coolness, composure; **perdre son s.-f.,** to lose one's self-control; *adv phr* **de s.-f.,** deliberately; in cold blood.

sanglant [sãglã] *a* **1.** (*a*) bloody (wound, battle); bloodstained (handkerchief) (*b*) blood-red **2.** cruel (reproach); scathing (criticism); **larmes sanglantes,** bitter tears.

sangle [sãgl] *nf* strap; *Harn:* girth; *Furn:* webbing; **lit de s.,** camp bed.

sangler [sãgle] *vtr* (*a*) to girth (horse) (*b*) to strap up.

sanglier [sãglije] *nm* (wild) boar.

sanglot [sãglo] *nm* sob.

sangloter [sãglɔte] *vi* to sob.

sangsue [sãsy] *nf* leech.

sanguin, -ine [sãgɛ̃, -in] **1.** *a Anat:* **groupe s.,** blood group; **transfusion sanguine,** blood transfusion (*b*) sanguine, fiery (temperament); ruddy (complexion) **2.** *nf* **sanguine** (*a*) red chalk drawing (*b*) blood orange.

sanguinaire [sãginɛr] *a* bloodthirsty (person); bloody (fight).

sanitaire [sanitɛr] **1.** *a* (*a*) medical (staff, equipment); health (measures) (*b*) *Plumb:* sanitary (equipment, engineering) **2.** *nm* **les s.,** *F:* **les sanitaires,** sanitary installations; (the) plumbing.

sans [sã] *prep* **1.** (*a*) without; **s. le sou,** without a penny; **s. faute,** without fail; **suffisant, s. plus,** adequate but no more (than that); **vous n'êtes pas s. le connaître,** you must know him; **non s. difficulté** not without difficulty; *F:* **que ferais-tu s.?** how would you manage without? *conj phr* **s. que nous le sachions,** without our knowing (*b*) -less, -lessly; -free; un-; **plaintes s. fin,** endless complaints; **être s. le sou,** to be penniless; **s. enfants,** childless; **s. sel,** salt-free; **s. hésiter,** unhesitatingly **2. s. vous, je ne l'aurais jamais fait,** but for you, I should never have done it; **s. cela, s. quoi,** otherwise.

sans-abri [sãzabri] *n inv* homeless.

sans-façon [sãfasɔ̃] **1.** *nm* (*a*) bluntness (of speech) (*b*) informality (*c*) offhand manner **2.** *a & n inv* (*a*) informal (person) (*b*) offhand (person).

sans-gêne [sãʒɛn] **1.** *nm* (offensive) offhandedness; over-familiarity **2.** *a inv* offhand (person).

sans-soin [sãswɛ̃] *n inv* careless person.

sans-souci [sãsusi] *a inv* happy-go-lucky.

sans-travail [sãtravaj] *n inv* unemployed person.

santé [sãte] *nf* (*a*) health; wellbeing; **être en bonne s.,** to be well; **avoir une s. fragile,** *F:* **une petite s.,** to be delicate; **boire à la s. de qn,** to drink s.o.'s health; **à votre s.!** your health! *F:* cheers! (*b*) **services de s.,** health services.

saoul *see* **soûl.**

sape [sap] *nf* **1.** (*a*) undermining (of wall); sapping (*b*) sap, trench **2.** *pl P:* clothes, gear.

saper [sape] *vtr* **1.** *Mil: & Fig:* to undermine **2.** *P:* to dress; **être bien sapé,** to be well turned out.

sapeur [sapœr] *nm Mil:* sapper.

sapeur-pompier [sapœrpɔ̃pje] *nm* fireman.

saphir [safir] *nm* sapphire.

sapin [sapɛ̃] *nm* (*a*) fir(tree) (*b*) (**bois de**) s., deal (*c*) **s. de Noël,** Christmas tree.

sapinière [sapinjɛr] *nf* fir plantation.

saquer [sake] *vtr F:* to dismiss, to sack (s.o.).

sarabande [sarabãd] *nf* (*a*) *Danc: Mus:* saraband (*b*) *F:* racket, bedlam.

sarbacane [sarbakan] *nf* blowpipe; (*toy*) pea-shooter.

sarcasme [sarkasm] *nm* sarcasm; sarcastic remark. **sarcastique** *a* sarcastic.

sarcler [sarkle] *vtr* to weed (garden); to hoe (crop).

sarcophage [sarkɔfaʒ] *nm* sarcophagus.

Sardaigne [sardɛɲ] *Prnf Geog:* Sardinia. **sarde** *a & n* Sardinian.

sardine [sardin] *nf* sardine.

sardonique [sardɔnik] *a* sardonic.

SARL *abbr Société anonyme à responsabilité limitée.*

sarment [sarmã] *nm* vine shoot.

sarrasin [sarazɛ̃] *nm* buckwheat.

sas [sɑ] *nm* **1.** sieve **2.** (*a*) *HydE:* lock chamber (*b*) *Nau: Space:* airlock.

Satan [satã] *Prnm* Satan. **satané** *a F:* confounded; **s. temps!** filthy weather! **satanique** *a* satanic.

satelliser [satelize] *vtr* (*a*) to put (satellite) into orbit (*b*) *Pol:* to make (country) into satellite.

satellite [satelit] *nm* satellite.

satiété [sasjete] *nf* satiety; surfeit; **à s.,** more than enough.

satin [satɛ̃] *nm Tex:* satin.

satiner [satine] *vtr* to give a satin finish to (material). **satiné** *a* satiny, satin-like.

satire [satir] *nf* satire. **satirique** *a* satirical. **satiriquement** *adv* satirically.

satiriser [satirize] *vtr* to satirize.

satisfaction [satisfaksjɔ̃] *nf* satisfaction, contentment; gratification; **donner de la s. à qn,** to give s.o. cause for satisfaction; **obtenir s.,** to get satisfaction (**de qch,** for sth).

satisfaire [satisfɛr] (*conj like* FAIRE) **1.** *vtr* (*a*) to satisfy, to please (s.o.); to gratify (s.o.'s wish); **s. l'attente de qn,** to come up to s.o.'s expectations (*b*) **se s. de peu,** to be content with very little (*c*) **se s.,** to relieve oneself **2.** *v ind tr* **s.** (**à qch**), to meet (demands, condition); to carry out (undertaking); to comply with (regulation). **satisfaisant** *a* satisfactory, satisfying (meal). **satisfait, -aite** *a*

satisfied; contented; **être s. de qch,** to be happy,
pleased, about sth.

saturation [satyrasjɔ̃] *nf* saturation.

saturer [satyre] *vtr* to saturate (**de,** with); **saturé
d'eau,** waterlogged.

Saturne [satyrn] *Prnm Astr:* Saturn.

satyre [satir] *nm* (*a*) *Myth:* satyr (*b*) *F:* sex maniac.

sauce [sos] *nf* (*a*) sauce; *occ* gravy; **à quelle s. sera-
t-il mangé?** how shall we deal with him? (*b*) *F:* (rain)
shower.

saucer [sose] *vtr* (**je sauçai(s)**) (*a*) to mop up the
sauce on one's plate (*b*) **se faire s.,** to get soaked,
drenched.

saucière [sosjɛr] *nf* sauceboat, gravy boat.

saucisse [sosis] *nf* sausage.

saucisson [sosisɔ̃] *nm* dried sausage.

sauf¹, sauve [sof, sov] *a* safe, unhurt, unharmed;
(*of honour*) intact.

sauf² *prep* save, but, except; **il n'a rien s. son salaire,**
he has nothing except his wages; **s. correction,** subject to correction; **s. avis contraire,** unless you hear
to the contrary; **s. erreur ou omission,** errors and
omissions excepted; **s. s'il pleut,** unless it rains, if it
doesn't rain.

sauf-conduit [sofkɔ̃dɥi] *nm* safe-conduct; pass; *pl
sauf-conduits.*

sauge [soʒ] *nf* (*a*) *Bot: Cu:* sage (*b*) *Bot:* salvia.

saugrenu [sogrəny] *a* absurd, preposterous.

saule [sol] *nm Bot:* willow; **s. pleureur,** weeping
willow.

saumâtre [somɑtr] *a* (*a*) briny (*b*) *F:* bitter, unpleasant.

saumon [somɔ̃] 1. *nm* salmon 2. *a inv* 2. salmon-
pink. **saumoné** *a* **truite saumonée,** salmon trout.

saumure [somyr] *nf* (pickling) brine.

sauna [sona] *nm* sauna.

saupoudrer [sopudre] *vtr* to sprinkle, dust, dredge
(**de,** with).

saur [sor] *am* **hareng s.,** red herring.

saut [so] *nm* 1. (*a*) leap, jump, vault; *Sp:* **s. en longueur, en hauteur,** long jump, high jump; **s. en parachute,** parachute drop; **au s. du lit,** on getting out
of bed; **s. périlleux,** somersault; **faire un s. en ville,**
to pop into town; **il n'y a qu'un s. d'ici là,** it's only a
stone's throw (away) (*b*) **s. de température,** sudden
rise in temperature 2. waterfall.

saut-de-mouton [sodmutɔ̃] *nm CivE:* flyover.

saute [sot] *nf* sudden change (of wind, mood); jump
(in price, temperature).

sauté [sote] *a* & *nm Cu:* sauté.

saute-mouton [sotmutɔ̃] *nm no pl* leapfrog.

sauter [sote] 1. *vi* (*aux avoir*) (*a*) to jump; to leap; **s.
à la perche,** to pole-vault; **s. à la corde,** to skip; **s. du
lit,** to leap out of bed; **s. à terre,** to jump down; **s.
en parachute,** to parachute; **s. à la gorge de qn,** to
fly at s.o.'s throat; **s. au cou de qn,** to fling one's
arms round s.o.'s neck; **ça saute aux yeux,** it's obvious; *F:* **et que ça saute!** and make it snappy! **s. en
l'air,** (i) to jump up (ii) *F:* to hit the roof; **s. sur une
occasion,** to jump at the chance (*b*) to explode; to
blow up; (*of business*) to collapse; (*of button*) to
come off, fly off; (*of fuse*) to blow, *F:* to go (*c*) **faire
s.,** to blast (rock); to blow up (bridge); to blow
(fuses); to pop (cork); to dandle (child); *Cu:* to sauté

(potatoes); to toss (pancake); **faire s. la banque,** to
break the bank; **se faire s. la cervelle,** to blow one's
brains out 2. *vtr* (*a*) to jump (over), leap over, clear
(ditch, fence); **s. le pas,** to take the plunge (*b*) to
skip (page); to drop (a stitch); **s. une classe,** to skip
a form; *F:* **je la saute!** I'm starving!

sauterelle [sotrɛl] *nf* grasshopper; *occ* locust.

sauterie [sotri] *nf* party.

sauteur, -euse [sotœr, -øz] 1. *n* jumper 2. *nf* **sau-
teuse,** frying pan.

sautillement [sotijmɑ̃] *nm* hopping.

sautiller [sotije] *vi* to hop (about); **s'en aller en sau-
tillant,** to skip off.

sautoir [sotwar] *nm Jewel:* chain; **porté en s.,** worn
on a chain, round the neck.

sauvage [sovaʒ] 1. *a* (*a*) wild (plant, animal); savage
(person); **chat s.,** wildcat (*b*) unsociable; shy; retiring
(*c*) unauthorized; unofficial; **grève s.,** wildcat strike
2. *n* (*f occ* **sauvagesse**) (*a*) savage; *FrC:* (American)
Indian (*b*) unsociable person. **sauvagement** *adv*
savagely.

sauvagerie [sovaʒri] *nf* savagery.

sauve *see* **sauf¹.**

sauvegarde [sovgard] *nf* safeguard; safe keeping;
sous la s. de qn, under s.o.'s protection.

sauvegarder [sovgarde] *vtr* to safeguard.

sauve-qui-peut [sovkipø] *nm inv* stampede, panic
flight.

sauver [sove] 1. *vtr* (*a*) to save, rescue (s.o.) (**de,**
from) (*b*) to salvage (ship, goods); *Fig:* **s. les
meubles,** to save sth from the wreckage 2. **se s.** (*a*)
to escape (**de,** from) (*b*) to run away; to be off (*c*)
(*of milk*) to boil over.

sauvetage [sovtaʒ] *nm* (*a*) life saving; rescue; **s.
aérien en mer,** air-sea rescue; **canot de s.,** lifeboat;
échelle de s., fire escape (*b*) salvage (of ship, goods).

sauveteur [sovtœr] *nm* rescuer.

sauvette (à la) [alasovet] *adv phr* hurriedly; **marchand à la s.,** illicit street vendor.

sauveur [sovœr] 1. *a* saving 2. *n* saviour.

savane [savan] *nf Geog:* savanna(h).

savant, -ante [savɑ̃, -ɑ̃t] 1. *a* (*a*) learned (**en,** in);
scholarly (*b*) skilful, clever; **chien s.,** performing
dog 2. *n* scientist; scholar. **savamment** *adv*
learnedly; skilfully, cleverly; **j'en parle s.,** I know
what I'm talking about.

savate [savat] *nf* worn-out old shoe.

saveur [savœr] *nf* savour, flavour.

Savoie [savwa] *Prnf Geog:* Savoy; *Cu:* **biscuit de S.**
= sponge cake.

savoir¹ [savwar] *vtr* (*prp* **sachant;** *pp* **su;** *pr ind* **je
sais, n. savons, ils savent;** *impf* **je savais;** *fu* **je saurai**)
1. to know; **s. une langue,** to know a language; **il en
sait des choses, plus d'une,** he knows a thing or two
2. (*a*) to be aware of (sth); **je ne savais pas cela,** I
didn't know, wasn't aware of, that; **elle est jolie, et
elle le sait bien,** she's pretty, and doesn't she know
it! **je n'en sais rien,** I know nothing about it; **peut-on
s.?** what's it about? *F:* **je ne veux pas le s.,** that's
nothing to do with me; **sans le s.,** unconsciously;
pas que je sache, not to my knowledge; **on ne sait
jamais,** you never can tell; **si j'avais su,** had I known
(*b*) to know of (s.o.) (*c*) **je me savais très malade,** I
knew I was very ill 3. to understand; **il sait ce qu'il**

veut, he knows his own mind; **ne s. que faire,** to be at a loss what to do; **je ne sais que penser,** I don't know what to think; **sachez que,** I would have you know that **4.** (a) **c'est à s.,** that remains to be seen; **je voudrais bien s. pourquoi,** I wonder why; **je crois s. qu'il est ici,** I understand he's here (b) **faire s. qch à qn,** to inform s.o., to let s.o. know, of sth (c) conj phr **à savoir,** namely, that is to say **5.** to know how, to be able; **savez-vous nager?** can you swim? **il saura le faire,** he can manage it; **je ne saurais vous le dire,** I'm afraid I can't tell you **6.** (a) pron phr **je ne sais qui,** somebody or other; **un je ne sais quoi de déplaisant,** something vaguely unpleasant; **un je sais tout,** a know-all; (b) adj phr **je ne sais quelle maladie,** some illness or other (c) adv phr **il y a je ne sais combien de temps,** heaven knows how long ago (d) **des robes, des chapeaux, que sais-je?** dresses, hats, and goodness knows what else! **Dieu sait! Heaven knows!**

savoir² nm knowledge, learning.

savoir-faire [savwarfɛr] nm inv savoir-faire; ability; know-how.

savoir-vivre [savwarvivr̩] nm inv savoir-vivre; good manners; tact.

savon [savɔ̃] nm soap; **(pain de) s.,** cake of soap; **s. de Marseille** = household soap; F: **passer un s. à qn,** to give s.o. a good ticking off.

savonnage [savɔnaʒ] nm soaping.

savonner [savɔne] vtr to (wash with) soap. **savonneux, -euse** a soapy.

savonnette [savɔnɛt] nf bar, cake, of soap.

savourer [savure] vtr to relish, savour. **savoureux, -euse** a savoury, tasty; spicy (story).

saxophone [saksɔfɔn] nm Mus: saxophone.

saxophoniste [saksɔfɔnist] n Mus: saxophonist.

sbire [sbir] nm F: Pej: (i) (officious) policeman (ii) thug.

scabreux, -euse [skabrø, -øz] a 1. difficult, tricky, risky **2.** indecent, shocking.

scandale [skɑ̃dal] nm scandal; **faire s.,** to provoke an uproar; **faire un s.,** to make a scene. **scandaleux, -euse** a scandalous, disgraceful; shocking. **scandaleusement** adv scandalously, disgracefully.

scandaliser [skɑ̃dalize] vtr to scandalize, to shock (s.o.); to be scandalized **(de,** by).

scander [skɑ̃de] vtr to scan (verse); to chant (slogan).

Scandinavie [skɑ̃dinavi] Prnf Geog: Scandinavia. **scandinave** a & n Scandinavian.

scaphandre [skafɑ̃dr̩] nm (a) diving suit (b) space suit.

scaphandrier [skafɑ̃drije] nm diver (in diving-suit).

scarabée [skarabe] nm beetle.

scarlatine [skarlatin] nf Med: scarlet fever.

scarole [skarɔl] nf Bot: curly endive.

sceau, sceaux [so] nm seal; stamp, mark (of genius); **sous le s. du secret,** under the seal of secrecy.

scélérat, -ate [selera, -at] A: & Lit: **1.** a wicked **2.** n scoundrel.

scellement [sɛlmɑ̃] nm Const: sealing; bedding.

sceller [sele] vtr **1.** (a) to seal (b) to ratify, confirm **2.** Const: to bed, fasten. **scellé 1.** a sealed **2.** nm seal.

scénario [senarjo] nm Th: scenario; Cin: film script.

scénariste [senarist] n scriptwriter.

scène [sɛn] nf **1.** (a) stage; **entrer en s.,** to appear, come on; **mettre en s.,** to stage, to direct (play); **metteur en s.,** producer; **mise en s.,** production (b) theatre, drama (c) **la s. politique,** the political scene **2.** (a) Th: scene; **la s. se passe à Paris,** the action takes place in Paris (b) **troisième s. du second acte,** act two, scene three (c) **c'était une s. pénible,** it was a painful scene (d) F: scene, row; **faire une s.,** to make a scene; **s. de ménage,** domestic squabble.

scénique [senik] a theatrical; stage (lighting); **indications scéniques,** stage directions.

scepticisme [sɛptisism] nm scepticism. **sceptique 1.** a sceptical **2.** n sceptic. **sceptiquement** adv sceptically.

sceptre [sɛptr̩] nm sceptre.

schéma [ʃema] nm (a) diagram; (sketch) plan (b) project, plan. **schématique** a diagrammatic; schematic; Pej: oversimplified.

schématiquement adv diagrammatically, schematically; in outline.

schématiser [ʃematize] vtr to schematize; to (over)-simplify.

schisme [ʃism] nm schism.

schiste [ʃist] nm Geol: schist.

schizophrénie [skizofreni] nf Psy: schizophrenia. **schizophrène** a & n Psy: schizophrenic.

schnoque [ʃnɔk] nm vieux s., old fool.

sciage [sjaʒ] nm sawing.

sciatique [sjatik] **1.** a sciatic **2.** nf Med: sciatica.

scie [si] nf **1.** saw; Tls: **s. à découper,** fretsaw; jigsaw; **s. à métaux,** hacksaw; **en dents de s.,** serrate(d) **2.** F: (a) (pers) bore (b) hit tune.

sciemment [sjamɑ̃] adv knowingly, wittingly.

science [sjɑ̃s] nf **1.** knowledge, learning; skill **2.** science; **sciences naturelles, appliquées,** natural, applied, science.

science-fiction [sjɑ̃sfiksjɔ̃] nf science fiction.

scientifique [sjɑ̃tifik] **1.** a scientific **2.** n scientist. **scientifiquement** adv scientifically.

scier [sje] vtr (pr sub & impf n. sciions) **1.** to saw (wood, stone); F: **s. qn,** to amaze s.o. **2.** to saw off (branch).

scierie [siri] nf sawmill.

scieur [sjœr] nm sawyer.

scinder [sɛ̃de] **1.** vtr to divide, split up **2. se s.,** to split up.

scintillement [sɛ̃tijmɑ̃] nm sparkling, twinkling; glittering.

scintiller [sɛ̃tije] vi to scintillate; to sparkle; to glitter; (of star) to twinkle.

scission [sisjɔ̃] nf scission, division, split; **faire s.,** to secede.

sciure [sjyr] nf **s. (de bois),** sawdust.

sclérose [skleroz] nf Med: sclerosis; Fig: ossification; **s. en plaques,** multiple sclerosis.

scléroser (se) [səskleroze] vpr Med: to sclerose, to harden; Fig: to become ossified.

scolaire [skɔlɛr] a scholastic; **année s.,** academic year; **livres scolaires,** school books, text books.

scolarisation [skɔlarizasjɔ̃] nf (a) school attendance (b) schooling.

scolariser [skɔlarize] vtr to provide schooling.

scolarité [skɔlarite] *nf Sch:* **s. obligatoire**, compulsory school attendance; **prolongation de la s.,** raising of the school-leaving age.

scoliose [skɔljoz] *nf Med:* scoliosis.

scooter [skuter] *nm* (motor) scooter.

scorbut [skɔrbyt] *nm Med:* scurvy.

score [skɔr] *nm Sp:* score.

scories [skɔri] *nfpl* (a) slag (b) *Geol:* (volcanic) slag; scoria.

scorpion [skɔrpjɔ̃] *nm* scorpion; *Astr:* **le S.,** Scorpio.

scotch [skɔtʃ] *nm* 1. scotch (whisky) 2. *Rtm:* Sellotape, Scotchtape.

scout [skut] *nm* (boy) scout.

scoutisme [skutizm] *nm* scouting.

scribe [skrib] *nm* scribe.

scribouillard, -arde [skribujar, -ard] *n F: Pej:* penpusher.

script [skript] *nm* **(écriture) s.,** script printing, writing.

script-girl [skriptgœrl] *nf Cin:* continuity girl.

scrupule [skrypyl] *nm* scruple, (conscientious) doubt (**sur**, about); **sans scrupules**, unscrupulous(ly); **avoir des scrupules à faire qch**, to have qualms about doing sth. **scrupuleux, -euse** *a* scrupulous (**sur**, about, over, as to); **peu s.,** unscrupulous. **scrupuleusement** *adv* scrupulously.

scrutateur, -trice [skrytatœr, -tris] 1. *a* searching (look) 2. *n* scrutineer, teller (of ballot).

scruter [skryte] *vtr* to scrutinize; to scan; to examine closely.

scrutin [skrytɛ̃] *nm* 1. poll; **dépouiller le s.,** to count the votes 2. **tour de s.,** ballot; **voter au s.,** to ballot 3. voting; (parliamentary) division; **procéder au s.,** to take the vote; (*in Eng Parliament*) to divide; **projet adopté sans s.,** bill passed without a division.

sculpter [skylte] *vtr* to sculpture, to sculpt; to carve; **bois sculpté,** carved wood.

sculpteur [skyltœr] *nm* sculptor; **femme s.,** sculptress; **s. sur bois,** woodcarver.

sculpture [skyltyr] *nf* sculpture; **s. sur bois,** woodcarving. **sculptural** *a* sculptural; statuesque (figure).

se [sə] *before a vowel sound* **s'**, *pers pron acc & dat* 1. (*a*) (*reflexive*) oneself; himself, herself, itself, themselves; **se flatter,** to flatter oneself; **elle s'est coupée au doigt, elle s'est coupé le doigt,** she has cut her finger (*b*) (*reciprocal*) each other, one another; **il est dur de se quitter,** it is hard to part 2. (*giving passive meaning to active verbs*) **la clef s'est retrouvée,** the key has been found; **cet article se vend partout,** this article is sold everywhere; **la porte s'est ouverte,** the door opened, came open 3. (*in purely pronom conjugation*) *see* **s'en aller, se dépêcher,** *etc Note:* se is *usu omitted before an infinitive dependent on* **faire, laisser, mener, envoyer, voir;** *e.g.* **se taire: faire taire les enfants.**

séance [seɑ̃s] *nf* 1. sitting, session, meeting; **la s. s'ouvrira, sera levée, à huit heures,** the meeting will open, adjourn, at eight; **s. d'information,** briefing 2. (cinema) performance; show; **s. de spiritisme,** seance 3. (*a*) sitting (for one's portrait) (*b*) period; **s. d'entraînement,** training session.

séant [seɑ̃] 1. (*a*) *a* sitting; in session (*b*) *A: & Lit:* becoming (**à**, to); fitting 2. *nm* **se mettre sur son s.,** to sit up (in bed).

seau, seaux [so] *nm* pail, bucket; **s. à charbon,** coal scuttle; **apporter un s. d'eau,** to bring a bucket(ful) of water.

sébile [sebil] *nf* wooden (begging) bowl.

sec, sèche [sɛk, sɛʃ] 1. *a* (*a*) dry (weather, ground); *F:* **j'ai la gorge sèche,** I'm parched (*b*) dried (fish, fruit); seasoned (wood); dry (wine); (*c*) **perte sèche,** dead loss; **en cinq s.,** in no time 2. (*a*) spare, gaunt (person); lean (figure); **s. comme un coup de trique,** as thin as a rake (*b*) sharp, dry, curt (remark); incisive (tone); sharp (blow); **casser qch d'un coup s.,** to snap sth off; **accueil très s.,** cool reception (*c*) unsympathetic, unfeeling (heart) (*d*) dry, bald (narrative) 3. *adv* (*a*) **boire s.,** to drink hard (*b*) hard; sharply; **virer s.,** to swing round sharply 4. *adv phr* (*a*) **à s.,** (i) dry (ii) dried up (iii) *F:* hard up; broke; **mettre une mare à s.,** to drain a pond; **navire à s.,** ship aground (*b*) *P:* **aussi s.,** straight away 5. *nm* **tenir au s.,** keep in a dry place 6. *nf P:* **sèche,** cigarette, fag. **sèchement** *adv* curtly, tartly.

SECAM [sekam] *abbr TV: système séquentiel à mémoire.*

sécateur [sekatœr] *nm* secateur(s); pruning shears.

sécession [sesɛsjɔ̃] *nf* secession; **faire s.,** to secede (**de**, from). **sécessionniste** *a & n* secessionist.

sèche-cheveux [sɛʃʃəvø] *nm inv* hair drier.

sèche-linge [sɛʃlɛ̃ʒ] *a inv* **armoire s.-l.,** drying, airing, cupboard.

sécher [seʃe] *v* (**je sèche; je sécherai**) 1. *vtr* (*a*) to dry (clothes, one's tears); to dry up; **se s. au soleil,** to dry oneself in the sun (*b*) *F: Sch:* to skip (a lecture) 2. (*a*) *vi* to (become) dry; to dry up, to dry out; **faire s. le linge,** to dry the linen (*b*) *F:* to dry up; *Sch:* to be stumped (by examiner).

sécheresse [seʃrɛs] *nf* 1. (*a*) dryness (of the air, ground) (*b*) drought 2. (*a*) curtness (of manner) (*b*) coldness (of heart).

séchoir [seʃwar] *nm* 1. drying room, ground 2. (*a*) drier, drying apparatus; **s. (à cheveux),** hairdrier (*b*) clothes horse.

second, -onde [səgɔ̃, -ɔ̃d] 1. *a* (*a*) second; **en s. lieu,** secondly, in the second place; *a & nm* **au s. (étage),** on the second, *NAm:* third, floor; **de seconde main,** secondhand; **au s. plan,** in the background; **le don de seconde vue,** the gift of second sight (*b*) *Com:* junior (partner); *Th:* supporting (role); **de s. choix,** second rate 2. *nm* principal assistant; second (in command); *Nau:* first mate 3. *nf* **seconde** (*a*) *Aut:* second (gear); *Rail:* **voyager en seconde,** to travel second (class); *Sch:* **(classe de) seconde** = fifth form (*b*) second (of time); **(attendez) une seconde!** just a second!

secondaire [səgɔ̃dɛr] *a* 1. secondary; **enseignement s.,** secondary education 2. subordinate; of minor importance; side (effect).

seconder [səgɔ̃de] *vtr* 1. to second, back (s.o.) up 2. to forward, promote (s.o.'s plans).

secouer [səkwe] 1. *vtr* (*a*) to shake (tree, one's head); to plump up (pillow); (*of shock*) to shake (s.o.); **on a été secoués,** (*in car*) we were shaken about; we had a rough ride; (*on ship*) we had a rough crossing (*b*) to shake up, rouse (s.o.); *F:* **secouez-vous!** pull yourself together! get a move on! *F:* **s. (les puces à) qn** (i) to tell s.o. off (ii) to rouse s.o. to action (c) to shake down (fruit); to shake off (yoke, dust) **2. se s.** (a) to shake oneself (b) to get a move on.

secourir [səkurir] *vtr (conj like* COURIR) to help, aid. **secourable** *a* helpful.

secourisme [səkurizm] *nm* first aid.

secouriste [səkurist] *n* first-aid worker.

secours [səkur] *nm* help, relief, aid; **crier au s.,** to shout for help; **au s.! help! porter s. à qn,** to help s.o.; *Med:* **premiers s.,** first aid; **s. en montagne,** mountain rescue (service); **cela m'a été d'un grand s.,** it has been a great help; **le s. aux enfants,** child welfare (work); **sortie de s.,** emergency exit; *Rail:* **convoi de s.,** breakdown train; *Aut:* **roue de s.,** spare wheel.

secousse [səkus] *nf* shake, shaking; jolt, jerk; shock; **s. sismique,** earth tremor; **se dégager d'une s.,** to wrench oneself free; **sans s.,** smoothly; **s. politique,** political upheaval; **se remettre d'une s.,** to recover from a shock.

secret, -ète [səkre, -ɛt] **1.** *a* (a) secret, hidden (b) reticent (person) **2.** *nm* (a) secret; **garder un s.,** to keep a secret; **être du s., dans le s.,** to be in the secret, *F:* in the know (b) secrecy; privacy; **en s.,** secretly; **abuser du s. professionnel,** to commit a breach of confidence (c) **au s.,** in solitary confinement. **secrètement** *adv* secretly.

secrétaire [səkreter] **1.** *n* secretary; **s. particulier,** private secretary; **s. général,** Secretary General; **s. de mairie** = town clerk **2.** *nm* writing desk.

secrétariat [səkretarja] *nm* **1.** secretaryship **2.** secretary's office; secretariat.

sécréter [sekrete] *vtr* **(il sécrète; il sécrétera)** (of gland) to secrete.

sécrétion [sekresjɔ̃] *nf* secretion.

sectaire [sekter] *a & n* sectarian.

sectarisme [sektarism] *nm* sectarianism.

secte [sekt] *nf* sect.

secteur [sektœr] *nm* **1.** *Mth:* sector **2.** (a) area, district; *Com:* **s. de vente,** sales area (b) *Mil:* sector (c) *El:* mains **3.** field (of activity); **le s. privé,** the private sector; private enterprise; *F:* **ce n'est pas mon s.,** that's not my line.

section [seksjɔ̃] *nf* **1.** section, cutting **2.** (a) section; *Adm:* branch (b) *Mil:* platoon **3.** *Mth:* (i) section (ii) intersection **4.** fare stage (on bus route).

sectionnement [seksjɔnmã] *nm* cutting, severing.

sectionner [seksjɔne] *vtr* to sever; **se s.,** to be severed.

séculaire [sekyler] *a* century-old; age-old.

séculier, -ière [sekylje, -jɛr] *a* (a) secular (b) laic; lay.

sécurité [sekyrite] *nf* **1.** security; **s. de l'emploi,** security of employment; *Adm:* **S. sociale** = National Health (Service); Social Security **2.** safety; **s. routière,** road safety; **règles de s.,** safety rules.

sédatif, -ive [sedatif, -iv] *a & nm Med:* sedative.

sédentaire [sedãter] *a* sedentary.

sédiment [sedimã] *nm* sediment. **sédimentaire** *a* sedimentary.

séditieux, -euse [sedisjø, -øz] **1.** *a* (a) seditious (b) mutinous; rebellious **2.** *n* rebel, mutineer.

sédition [sedisjɔ̃] *nf* sedition; mutiny.

séducteur, -trice [sedyktœr, -tris] **1.** *n* seducer, seductress **2.** *a* fascinating, beguiling.

séduction [sedyksjɔ̃] *nf* **1.** seduction **2.** charm; attraction.

séduire [seduir] *vtr (conj like* CONDUIRE) **1.** to seduce (s.o.) **2.** to fascinate, captivate, charm; to attract (s.o.). **séduisant** *a* attractive (person); appealing (idea).

segment [segmã] *nm* segment.

segmentation [segmãtasjɔ̃] *nf* segmentation.

segmenter [segmãte] *vtr* to segment.

ségrégation [segregasjɔ̃] *nf* segregation.

ségrégationnisme [segregasjɔnism] *nm* segregationism. **ségrégationniste** *a & n* segregationist.

seiche [sɛʃ] *nf Mol:* cuttlefish.

seigle [sɛgl] *nm* rye.

seigneur [sɛɲœr] *nm* **1.** lord **2. le S.,** the Lord. **seigneurial, -aux** *a* stately, lordly.

sein [sɛ̃] *nm* (a) breast; bosom; **donner le s. à un enfant,** to breastfeed (a child) (b) womb (c) **au s. de la famille,** in the bosom of the family; **au s. de la commission,** within the committee.

séisme [seism] *nm* earthquake.

SEITA [seita] *abbr Service d'exploitation industrielle des tabacs et allumettes.*

seize [sez] *num a inv* sixteen; **le s. mai,** (on) the sixteenth of May; **habiter au numéro s.,** to live at number sixteen. **seizième** *num a & n* sixteenth.

séjour [seʒur] *nm* **1.** (a) stay; **s. de quinze jours,** fortnight's stay (b) **(salle de) s.,** living room **2.** *Lit:* abode.

séjourner [seʒurne] *vi (of pers)* to stay; *(of snow)* to lie.

sel [sɛl] *nm* **1.** (a) salt; **s. fin,** table salt; **régime sans s.,** salt-free diet (b) **sels de bain,** bath salts **2.** piquancy; wit.

sélecteur [selektœr] *nm* selector; switch.

sélection [seleksjɔ̃] *nf* selection, choice; **s. professionnelle,** professional aptitude test; *Sp:* **match de s.,** trial game. **sélectif, -ive** *a* selective.

sélectionner [seleksjɔne] *vtr* to choose, select; to pick. **selectionné** *a & n* selected (player).

sélectionneur, -euse [seleksjɔnœr, -øz] *n Sp:* selector.

self(-service) [sɛlf(sɛrvis)] *nm* self-service (restaurant); *pl self-services.*

selle [sɛl] *nf* **1.** *Physiol:* stool; motion; **aller à la s.,** to have a motion **2.** saddle; **se mettre en s.,** to mount **3.** *Cu:* saddle (of mutton).

seller [sele] *vtr* to saddle (horse).

sellerie [sɛlri] *nf* saddlery; harness room.

sellette [sɛlɛt] *nf* (small) seat; stool; *Fig:* **mettre qn sur la s.,** to carpet s.o., to put s.o. on the carpet.

sellier [selje] *nm* saddler.

selon [s(ə)lɔ̃] *prep* according to; **s. moi,** in my opinion; **c'est s.,** it all depends; **s. que** + *ind,* depending on whether.

seltz [sɛls] *nm* **eau de s.,** soda (water).

semailles [səmaj] *nfpl* sowing; **le temps des s.,** sowing time.

semaine [səmɛn] *nf* (a) week; **deux fois par s.,** twice a week; **fin de s.,** weekend; *F:* **la s. des quatres jeudis,** never (in a month of Sundays) (b) working week; **faire**

la s. **anglaise**, to work a five-day week (c) week's pay.

sémantique [semãtik] 1. a semantic 2. nf semantics.

sémaphore [semafɔr] nm semaphore.

semblable [sãblabl] 1. a (a) alike; similar (à, to); s. à son père, like his father (b) such; **je n'ai rien dit de s.**, I said nothing of the sort 2. n (a) fellow; like, equal, counterpart; **vous et vos semblables**, you and people like you (b) **nos semblables**, our fellow men.

semblant [sãblã] nm semblance, appearance; **faux s.**, pretence; **un s. de résistance**, a show of resistance; **faire s. de faire qch**, to pretend to be doing sth.

sembler [sãble] vi (aux avoir) (a) to seem, to appear; **elle semblait heureuse**, she seemed happy (b) impers **il me semble l'entendre encore**, it's as though I can hear him still; **à ce qu'il me semble**, it seems to me that; I think; **faites comme bon vous semble(ra)**, do as you think best; **il semble que** + ind or sub, it seems that; it looks as if.

semelle [səmɛl] nf sole (of shoe); **s. intérieure**, insole; **s. compensée**, wedge heel; **il ne reculera pas d'une s.**, he won't give way an inch; **il ne me quitte pas d'une s.**, he's always at my heels.

semence [səmãs] nf 1. (a) seed; **blé de s.**, seed corn (b) Physiol: semen 2. (a) **s. de perles**, seed pearls (b) (tin)tack.

semer [səme] vtr (**je sème, n. semons**) 1. to sow (seeds, a field) 2. to strew, scatter (flowers); to spread (news, discord); **s. de l'argent**, to throw money about 3. F: (a) to shake off, get rid of (s.o.) (b) to lose (sth).

semestre [səmɛstr] nm 1. half-year 2. six-monthly payment 3. Sch: semester. **semestriel, -ielle** a half-yearly, six-monthly.

semeur, -euse [səmœr, -øz] n sower.

semi-automatique [səmiɔtɔmatik] a semi(-)automatic.

semi-circulaire [səmisirkylɛr] a semicircular.

semi-conducteur [səmikɔ̃dyktœr] nm El: semi(-)conductor.

sémillant [semijã] a lively, vivacious.

séminaire [seminɛr] sm (a) seminary (b) Sch: seminar.

séminariste [seminarist] nm seminarist.

semi-remorque [səmir(ə)mɔrk] nf trailer; semi-trailer; articulated lorry.

semis [səmi] nm 1. sowing 2. seedbed 3. seedlings.

sémitique [semitik] a Semitic.

semonce [səmɔ̃s] nf 1. Nau: **coup de s.**, warning shot 2. reprimand, scolding.

semoule [səmul] nf semolina.

sempiternel [sãpitɛrnɛl] a eternal, never-ending.

sénat [sena] nm 1. senate 2. senate house.

sénateur [senatœr] nm senator. **sénatorial, -aux** a senatorial.

Sénégal [senegal] Prnm Geog: Senegal. **sénégalais, -aise** a & n Senegalese.

sénilité [senilite] nf senility. **sénile** a senile.

sens [sãs] nm 1. sense (of touch, sight, time); **le sixième s.**, the sixth sense; **reprendre ses s.**, to regain consciousness; **s. moral**, conscience 2. sense, judgment; **s. commun**, common sense; **un homme de bon s.**, a sensible man; **ça n'a pas de s.**, it doesn't make

(any) sense; **à mon s.**, in my opinion 3. sense, meaning (of a word); **s. propre**, literal meaning; **dépourvu de s.**, meaningless; **en ce s. que**, in that 4. direction, way; **dans le mauvais s.**, the wrong way (up, round); **en s. inverse**, in the opposite direction; **dans le s. de la longueur**, lengthwise; **dans le s. (inverse) des aiguilles d'une montre**, (anti-)clockwise; **retourner qch dans tous les s.**, to turn sth over and over; PN: **s. unique**, one-way street; PN: **s. interdit**, no entry; Rail: **dans le s. de la marche**, facing the engine; adv phr **s. dessus dessous** (i) upside down (ii) in a mess.

sensation [sãsasjɔ̃] nf 1. sensation; feeling (of warmth, cold); **j'ai la s. de le connaître**, I have a feeling I know him 2. excitement; **roman à s.**, sensational novel; **faire s.**, to create a sensation; **la pièce a fait s.**, the play was a hit. **sensationnel, -elle** a sensational; F: superb, fantastic.

sensé [sãse] a sensible (person, action).

sensibilisation [sãsibilizasjɔ̃] nf sensitization; growing public awareness (à, of).

sensibiliser [sãsibilize] vtr to sensitize; to make (s.o.) sensitive to (sth).

sensibilité [sãsibilite] nf sensitivity, sensitiveness.

sensible [sãsibl] a 1. (a) sensitive (à, to; sur, about); susceptible (to pain, influence); **peu s.**, insensitive, F: thick-skinned; **être s. au froid**, to feel the cold; **toucher la note s.**, to appeal to the emotions (b) sympathetic; **cœur s.**, tender heart (c) sensitive (balance, thermometer) (d) painful, sore (when touched); sensitive, tender (tooth) 2. sensible; perceptible; **le monde s.**, the tangible world; **un vide s.**, a noticeable gap. **sensiblement** adv (a) approximately, more or less (b) appreciably, perceptibly.

sensiblerie [sãsibləri] nf sentimentality.

sensitif, -ive [sãsitif, -iv] 1. a Physiol: sensory 2. nf Bot: sensitive plant.

sensoriel, -ielle [sãsɔrjɛl] a sensory.

sensualité [sãsɥalite] nf sensuality.

sensuel, -elle [sãsɥɛl] a sensual; sensuous. **sensuellement** adv sensually; sensuously.

sentence [sãtãs] nf 1. maxim 2. (a) sentence, judgment (b) decision, award. **sentencieux, -ieuse** a sententious.

senteur [sãtœr] nf Lit: scent.

senti [sãti] a heartfelt; well chosen (words).

sentier [sãtje] nm (foot)path; **s. battu**, beaten track.

sentiment [sãtimã] nm 1. (a) sensation, feeling (of joy, hunger) (b) sense (of duty); consciousness; **avoir le s. que**, to have a feeling that, to be aware that 2. (a) sentiment, sensibility; **ses sentiments vis-à-vis de moi**, his feelings towards me; **faire du s.**, to sentimentalize (b) **avoir du s. pour qn**, to feel attracted to s.o. (c) Corr: **veuillez agréer mes sentiments distingués**, yours faithfully.

sentimentalité [sãtimãtalite] nf sentimentality. **sentimental, -aux** a sentimental. **sentimentalement** adv sentimentally.

sentinelle [sãtinɛl] nf Mil: sentry; **en s.**, on guard, on sentry duty.

sentir [sãtir] (conj like MENTIR) 1. vtr (a) to feel (pain, hunger, joy); **s. qch pour qn**, to feel affection for s.o. (b) to be conscious of; to be aware (of danger); **je sens que vous avez raison**, I have a feeling that you are right; **l'effet se fera s.**, the effect will be felt (c) to smell (odour, flower); F: **je ne peux pas le s.**, I can't stand him 2. vi (a) (with cogn acc) to taste of, smell of (sth); **ça sent le brûlé**, there's a smell of burning; **vin qui sent le bouchon**, corked wine; **la pièce sent l'humidité**, the room smells damp (b) **s. bon**, to smell good; **ça sent bon le café**, there's a delicious smell of coffee (c) F: to smell, to stink; **s. des pieds**, to have smelly feet 3. **se s.** (a) **je me sens fatigué(e)**, I feel tired; **se s. du courage**, to feel brave (b) **il ne se sent pas de joie**, he is beside himself with joy; F: **tu ne te sens plus?** have you gone mad?

seoir [swar] vi (used only in prp **seyant, séant**; pr ind **il sied**) to suit, become; **comme il sied**, as is fitting.

sépale [sepal] nm Bot: sepal.

séparation [separasjɔ̃] nf (a) separation; parting; **s. de corps**, legal separation (of husband and wife) (b) partition, division; **mur de s.**, dividing wall; **faire une s. entre**, to draw a dividing line between.

séparatisme [separatism] nm separatism. **séparatiste** a & n separatist.

séparer [separe] 1. vtr (a) to separate (**de**, from); **s. les bons d'avec les mauvais**, to separate the good from the bad; **s. qch en trois**, to divide sth in three; **personne ne peut nous s.**, no one can come between us (b) to divide, keep apart; to distinguish (sth from sth); **mur qui sépare deux champs**, wall dividing two fields 2. **se s.** (a) to separate, part (**de**, from); to part company; **se s. de sa femme**, to separate from one's wife (b) (of river, road) to divide, branch off (c) (of crowd, assembly) to break up, disperse. **séparable** a separable (**de**, from). **séparé** a 1. separate, distinct 2. separated, apart. **séparément** adv separately.

sépia [sepja] nf sepia.

sept [sɛt] num a inv & nm inv seven; **le s. mai**, (on) the seventh of May.

septante [sɛptɑ̃t] num a & nm inv Belg: SwFr: seventy.

septembre [sɛptɑ̃br] nm September; **en s.**, in September; **le premier s.**, (on) the first of September; **fin de s.**, late September.

septennat [sɛptɛna] nm seven-year term.

septentrional [sɛptɑ̃trijɔnal] a northern.

septicémie [sɛptisemi] nf blood poisoning, septicaemia.

septième [sɛtjɛm] num a & n seventh; **être au s. ciel**, to be in seventh heaven. **septièmement** adv in the seventh place.

septique [sɛptik] a Med: septic; Hyg: **fosse s.**, septic tank.

septuagénaire [sɛptчaʒenɛr] a & n septuagenarian.

sépulcre [sepylkr] nm sepulchre. **sépulchral, -aux** a sepulchral.

sépulture [sepyltyr] nf 1. burial, interment 2. burial place.

séquelles [sekɛl] nfpl aftermath; after-effects.

séquence [sekɑ̃s] nf sequence.

séquestration [sekɛstrasjɔ̃] nf sequestration; confinement (of s.o.).

séquestre [sekɛstr] nf **mettre sous s.**, to sequester (property).

séquestrer [sekɛstre] vtr to sequestrate, to sequester (property); to confine (s.o.) illegally.

sérail, -ails [seraj] nm seraglio.

séraphin [serafɛ̃] nm seraph.

serein [sərɛ̃] a serene, calm. **sereinement** adv serenely, calmly.

sérénade [serenad] nf serenade.

sérénité [serenite] nf serenity, calmness.

serf, serve [sɛrf, sɛrv] n Hist: serf.

serge [sɛrʒ] nm Tex: (woollen) serge.

sergent [sɛrʒɑ̃] nm Mil: sergeant; **s.-chef**, quartermaster sergeant; **s. instructeur**, drill sergeant; A: **s. de ville**, policeman.

série [seri] nf 1. (a) series; succession; TV: etc: **s. (d'émissions)**, series; **s. de jours chauds**, spell of hot weather; **s. noire**, chapter of accidents; run of bad luck (b) Bill: break; run (of cannons) (c) Sp: heat; **s. éliminatoire**, qualifying heat 2. (a) series (of stamps); set (of tools); range (of cars, samples) (b) Ind: Com: range, line (of goods); **fabrication en s.**, mass production; **article de s.**, standard article; **article hors s.**, custom-built article; **fins de s.**, remnants; Publ: remainders (c) group, category; Sp: rating.

sérieux, -euse [serjø, -øz] 1. a (a) serious, grave, sober; **s. comme un pape**, as solemn as a judge (b) serious-minded (person) (c) earnest, genuine; reliable, responsible (person); **êtes-vous s.?** do you mean it? **d'un air s.**, seriously; **offre sérieuse**, bona fide offer; **peu s.**, irresponsible (person) (d) important (matter); serious (illness); Com: **client s.**, good customer 2. nm seriousness, gravity; **garder son s.**, to keep a straight face; **se prendre au s.**, to take oneself seriously. **sérieusement** adv seriously; genuinely; gravely.

serin [sərɛ̃] nm Orn: canary.

seriner [sərine] vtr Pej: **s. qch à qn**, to drum sth into s.o.

seringue [sərɛ̃g] nf syringe.

seringuer [sərɛ̃ge] vtr to syringe.

serment [sɛrmɑ̃] nm (solemn) oath; **prêter s.**, to take an oath; **faire s. de faire qch**, to swear to do sth; **déclaration sous s.**, sworn statement; **faire un faux s.**, to commit perjury.

sermon [sɛrmɔ̃] nm sermon; Fig: lecture.

sermonner [sɛrmɔne] vtr to lecture (s.o.).

serpe [sɛrp] nf billhook.

serpent [sɛrpɑ̃] nm snake; serpent; **s. à sonnettes**, rattlesnake.

serpenter [sɛrpɑ̃te] vi (of river, road) to wind, to meander, to curve.

serpentin [sɛrpɑ̃tɛ̃] nm (a) coil (of tubing) (b) paper streamer.

serpillière [sɛrpijɛr] nf DomEc: floorcloth.

serpolet [sɛrpɔlɛ] nm Bot: wild thyme.

serrage [sɛraʒ] nm tightening (of screw); clamping (of joint).

serre [sɛr] nf 1. greenhouse; conservatory; glasshouse; **s. chaude**, hothouse; **sous s.**, under glass 2. pl claws, talons (of bird of prey).

serrement [sɛrmɑ̃] nm squeezing, pressure; **s. de main**, handshake; **s. de cœur**, pang.

serrer [sere] 1. vtr (a) to press, squeeze, clasp; **s. la main à qn**, to shake s.o.'s hand; **s. qn entre ses bras**, to hug s.o.; **s. le cou à qn**, to strangle s.o.; **s. qch dans sa main**, to grip sth; **sela me serre le cœur**, it wrings my heart (b) to tighten (knot, screw); to screw up (nut); to clench (fists, teeth); s. les freins, to put on the brakes (c) to close up; to press close together; Mil: to close (ranks) (d) to keep close to (s.o., sth); to hug (the shore, the kerb); s. qn de près, to follow s.o. closely; s. une question de près, to study a question closely; PN: serrez à droite! = keep to nearside (lane); F: se s. les coudes, to back one another up 2. se s. (a) to stand, sit, close together; to crowd; serrez-vous! sit closer! se s. les uns contre les autres, to huddle together; se s. contre qn, to snuggle up to s.o. (b) to tighten up; mon cœur se serra, my heart sank (c) Fig: to tighten one's belt. serré (a) a tight (boots, knot); compact, serried (ranks); narrow (pass); close (writing); les dents serrées, with clenched teeth; serrés comme des sardines, packed like sardines; avoir le cœur s., to have a heavy heart; surveillance serrée, close supervision; Sp: arrivée serrée, close finish (b) adv jouer s., to play a cautious game.

serrure [seryr] nf lock; s. de sûreté, safety lock; trou de (la) s., keyhole.

serrurerie [seryrri] nf (a) locksmith's trade (b) ironwork.

serrurier [seryrje] nm locksmith.

sertir [sertir] vtr to set (precious stone).

sérum [serɔm] nm serum.

servant, -ante [servɑ̃, -ɑ̃t] 1. a serving 2. nm (a) Artil: gunner (b) Ecc: s. (de messe), server 3. nf servante (a) maidservant (b) dinner waggon.

serveur, -euse [servœr, -øz] 1. barman, barmaid; waiter, waitress 2. Cards: dealer; Ten: server.

serviabilité [servjabilite] nf obligingness. serviable a obliging; helpful.

service [servis] nm 1. (a) service; être au s. de qn, to be in s.o.'s service; porte de s., tradesmen's entrance; escalier de s., backstairs (b) service (in hotel, restaurant); s. compris, service included; libre s., self-service (in shop); Com: s. après-vente, after-sales service (c) Adm: s. contractuel, contract service; Adm: Mil: états de s., service record; s. militaire, military service; faire son s., to do one's national service; apte au s., fit for service; libéré du s., discharged (d) Ten: service 2. duty; être de s., to be on duty; s. de garde, guard duty; officier de s., duty officer; s. de jour, de nuit, day, night, duty; tableau de s., duty roster 3. (a) branch, department, service; Adm: chef de s., head of department; s. de renseignements, enquiry office; Tp: directory enquiries; les services publics, public utilities; s. des eaux, water supply; s. postal, mail, postal, service (b) Mil: corps, service; s. des renseignements, intelligence (service) (c) (health, social) service; s. des contagieux, isolation ward (d) Com: (accounts, dispatch) department (of firm) 4. (a) running (of machine); s. manuel, manual operation (b) use (of machine); en s., in use, in operation; en état de s., in working order; hors (de) s., out of order (c) service (of train, aircraft); assurer le s. entre A et B, to run between A and B 5. rendre un bon, un mauvais, s. à qn, to do s.o. a good, a bad, turn; à votre s., at your service; ça m'a rendu grand s., it was very useful to me 6. Rel: service 7. (a) course (of a meal) (b) Rail: etc: premier s., first sitting (for lunch, dinner) 8. set (of utensils); s. de table, dinner service.

serviette [servjɛt] nf 1. (a) (table) napkin (b) s. (de toilette), (hand) towel; s. hygiénique, sanitary towel 2. briefcase.

serviette-éponge [servjɛtepɔ̃ʒ] nf (terry) towel; pl serviettes-éponges.

servile [servil] a servile (pers); slavish (imitation). servilement adv servilely; slavishly.

servilité [servilite] nf servility.

servir [servir] v (conj like MENTIR) 1. vi (a) to serve; to be useful (à qn, to/s.o.); to be in use; la machine peut s. encore, the machine is still fit for use; cela peut s. un jour, it may come in handy one day (b) s. à qch, to be useful for sth; cela ne sert à rien de pleurer, it's no good crying; ça ne servira pas à grand-chose, it won't be much use; à quoi sert d'y aller? what's the use of going there? (c) s. de, to serve as, be used as (sth); (of pers) to act as; s. de prétexte, to serve as a pretext; ça m'a servi de leçon, it was a lesson to me 2. vtr (a) to be a servant to (s.o.); to serve (s.o.) (b) vi to serve (in army) (c) to serve, attend to (customer); to wait on (diner); Madame est servie, dinner is served, madam; F: en fait de pluie nous sommes servis, we've had more than our share of rain (d) to serve (up), dish up (a meal); s. à boire à qn, to fill s.o.'s glass (e) to help, be of service to (s.o.) (f) s. la messe, to serve at mass (g) Ten: to serve; Cards: à vous de s., (it's) your deal 3. se s. (a) to serve oneself; s. d'un plat, to help oneself to a dish; servez-vous! help yourself! (b) se s. chez Martin, to shop at Martin's (c) se s. de qch, to use sth, to make use of sth.

serviteur [servitœr] nm servant.

servitude [servityd] nf (a) servitude (b) constraint.

servofrein [servofrɛ̃] nm Aut: etc: servobrake.

ses [se, se] poss a see SON[1].

session [sesjɔ̃] nf session, sitting.

seuil [sœj] nm 1. threshold; doorstep; Fig: brink (of death); s. de rentabilité, break-even point 2. Geog: shelf; HydE: sill (of lock).

seul [sœl] a 1. (preceding the n) (a) only, sole, single; comme un s. homme, as one man; son s. souci, his one, only, care; mon s. et unique stylo, my one and only pen; pas un s., not (a single) one; none whatever; il était le s. à le dire, he was the only one who said it (b) la seule pensée m'effraie, the mere thought frightens me 2. (following the n or used predicatively) alone, by oneself; on one's own; une femme seule, a single woman; se sentir très s., to feel very lonely; parler s. à qn, to have a private conversation with s.o.; je l'ai fait tout s., I did it (by) myself; parler tout s., to talk to oneself 3. seule la violence le contraindrait, nothing short of violence would compel him; s. un expert pourrait nous conseiller, only an expert could advise us; nous sommes seuls à le savoir, we're the only people who know of it.

seulement [sœlmɑ̃] adv 1. (a) only; nous sommes s. deux, there are only two of us; il vient s. de partir, he's only just gone (b) solely, merely 2. even; il ne m'a pas s. remercié, he didn't even thank me; si s., if only 3. je viendrais bien, s., I'd like to come, but.

sève [sɛv] nf sap (of plant).

sévère [sever] a 1. severe; stern, harsh; climat s., hard climate 2. strict (discipline). sévèrement adv severely; sternly, harshly; strictly.

sévérité [severite] *nf* severity; sternness, harshness.

sévices [sevis] *nmpl* brutality, cruelty.

sévir [sevir] *vi* 1. **s. contre qn,** to deal ruthlessly with s.o. 2. *(of epidemic, war)* to rage, to hold sway.

sevrage [səvraʒ] *nm* weaning.

sevrer [səvre] *vtr* (**je sèvre, n. sevrons**) to wean (child, lamb).

sexe [sɛks] *nm* 1. sex; **le s. faible,** the fair sex 2. sex organs.

sextant [sɛkstɑ̃] *nm Mth: Nau:* sextant.

sexualité [sɛksɥalite] *nf* sexuality. **sexuel, -elle** *a* sexual. **sexuellement** *adv* sexually.

sexy [sɛksi] *a P:* sexy.

seyant [sɛjɑ̃] *a* becoming (dress, colour).

SGDG *abbr sans garantie du gouvernement.*

shah [ʃa] *nm* shah.

shakespearien, -ienne [ʃɛkspirjɛ̃, -jɛn] *a* Shakespearian.

shampooing [ʃɑ̃pwɛ̃] *nm* shampoo; **faire un s. à qn,** to shampoo s.o.'s hair; **s. colorant,** rinse.

shérif [ʃerif] *nm* sheriff.

shoot [ʃut] *nm Fb:* shot.

shooter [ʃute] *vi Fb:* to shoot.

short [ʃɔrt] *nm Cl:* (pair of) shorts.

si¹ [si] *conj (by elision s' before il, ils)* 1. *(a)* if; **si on ne le surveille pas, il s'échappera,** unless he is watched he will escape; **si j'avais su,** had I but known, if I'd known; **si ce n'était mon rhumatisme,** if it weren't for my rheumatism; **si je ne me trompe,** if I'm not mistaken; **si seulement,** if only *(b)* **s'il est malheureux, c'est bien de sa faute,** if he's unhappy, it is his own fault; **c'est à peine s'il peut distinguer les chiffres,** he can hardly see the numbers 2. whether, if; **je me demande si c'est vrai,** I wonder whether it's true, if it's true; *F:* **vous connaissez Paris?—si je connais Paris!** you know Paris?—of course I know Paris! **si c'est malheureux de voir ça!** isn't it dreadful to see that! 3. how; how much; **pensez si j'étais furieux!** you can imagine how angry I was! 4. what if; suppose; **et si elle l'apprend?** and what if she hears of it? **et si on faisait une partie de bridge?** what about a game of bridge? 5. *nm* **tes si et tes mais,** your ifs and buts.

si² *adv* 1. *(a)* so; so much; **un si bon dîner,** such a good dinner; **ce n'est pas si facile,** it's not so easy *(b)* **il n'est pas si beau que vous,** he is not as handsome as you *(c)* **si bien que,** with the result that 2. **si jeune qu'il soit,** young as he is; **si peu que ce soit,** however little it may be 3. *(in answer to a neg question)* yes; **il n'est pas parti?—si,** he hasn't gone?—yes, he has; **il ne s'en remettra pas—mais si!** he won't get over it—of course he will!

si³ *nm inv Mus:* 1. (the note) B 2. ti (in fixed do system).

siamois, -oise [sjamwa, -waz] *a & n* Siamese; **(chat) s.,** Siamese cat; **frères s., sœurs siamoises,** Siamese twins.

Sibérie [siberi] *Prnf Geog:* Siberia. **sibérien, -ienne** *a & n* Siberian.

sibilant [sibilɑ̃] *a* sibilant, hissing (sound).

sic [sik] *adv* sic.

Sicile [sisil] *Prnf Geog:* Sicily. **sicilien, -ienne** *a & n* Sicilian.

sidéral, -aux [sideral, -o] *a* sidereal.

sidérer [sidere] *vtr* (**il sidère; il sidérera**) *F:* to flabbergast, to stagger s.o. **sidérant** *a* staggering. **sidéré** *a* flabbergasted, staggered.

sidérurgie [sideryrʒi] *nf* iron and steel metallurgy. **sidérurgique** *a* **industrie s.,** iron and steel industry.

sidérurgiste [sideryrʒist] *n* iron and steel metallurgist.

siècle [sjɛkl] *nm* 1. century 2. age, period (of time); **notre s.,** the age we live in; **être d'un autre s.,** to be behind the times; *F:* **il y a un s. que je ne vous ai vu,** I haven't seen you for ages.

siège [sjɛʒ] *nm* 1. *(a)* seat, centre (of learning, activity); **s. social,** registered offices (of a company) *(b) Ecc:* **s. épiscopal,** see 2. *Mil:* siege; **faire le s. de,** to lay siege to; **lever le s.,** (i) to raise the siege (ii) *Fig:* to get up and go 3. seat, chair; **s. à la Chambre,** seat (in parliament); **le s. du juge,** the judge's bench; **prenez un s.,** take a seat 4. seat (of chair); *Av:* **s. éjectable,** ejector seat.

siéger [sjeʒe] *vi* (**je siège, n. siégeons; je siégerai**) 1. *(of company)* to have its head office, headquarters; **c'est là que siège le mal,** that's where the trouble lies 2. *(of assembly)* to sit 3. **s. à la Chambre,** to have a seat in Parliament; *Jur:* **s. au tribunal,** to be on the bench.

sien, sienne [sjɛ̃, sjɛn] 1. *poss a* his, hers, its, one's; **adopter qch comme s.,** to adopt sth as one's own; **faire s.,** to accept as one's own 2. **le s., la sienne, les siens, les siennes** *(a) poss pron* **ma sœur est plus jolie que la sienne,** my sister is prettier than his, than hers; **il prit mes mains dans les deux siennes,** he took my hands in both of his *(b) nm* (i) **à chacun le s.,** to each his own; **y mettre du s.,** to contribute (to an undertaking) (ii) *pl* his own, her own, one's own (friends, family) (iii) *F:* **il a encore fait des siennes,** he's been up to his tricks again.

sieste [sjɛst] *nf* siesta, nap; **faire la s.,** to take a nap (after lunch).

sifflement [sifləmɑ̃] *nm* whistling, whistle; hiss(ing); wheezing.

siffler [sifle] 1. *vi (a)* to whistle; *(of snake, goose)* to hiss; *(of breathing)* to wheeze *(b)* to blow a whistle 2. *vtr (a)* to whistle (a tune); *Sp:* **s. une faute, la mi-temps,** to whistle for a foul, for half time *(b)* to whistle for, to whistle up (a taxi); to whistle for (a dog); *Aut: F:* **se faire s. (par la police),** to be pulled up (by the police); *F:* **s. une fille,** to wolf-whistle *(c) Th:* to hiss, to boo *(d) P:* to swig, to knock back (drink). **sifflant, ante** *a* whistling; hissing; wheezing.

sifflet [siflɛ] *nm* 1. whistle 2. catcall, boo, hiss.

siffleur, -euse [siflœr, -øz] 1. *a* whistling; hissing 2. *n* whistler; hisser, booer.

sifflotement [siflɔtmɑ̃] *nm* whistling.

siffloter [siflɔte] *vtr & i* to whistle.

sigle [sigl] *nm* abbreviation; acronym.

signal, -aux [siɲal, -o] *nm* signal; **faire des signaux,** to signal; *Fig:* **donner le s. de qch,** to be the signal for sth; *Adm:* **signaux lumineux,** traffic lights; **s. de détresse,** distress signal; **s. d'alarme,** alarm (signal).

signalement [siɲalmɑ̃] *nm* description; particulars.

signaler [siɲale] *vtr* 1. *(a)* to point out (**qch à qn,** s.o. to sth); to call, draw attention to (sth); to signal out; **s. un livre à qn,** to recommend a book to s.o. (b) to report; to notify; **rien à s.,** nothing to report (c) to signal (train, ship) **2. se s.,** to distinguish oneself (**par,** by); **se s. à l'attention de qn,** to catch s.o.'s eye.

signalisation [siɲalizasjɔ̃] *nf* **1.** signalling; signposting **2.** (road) signs; **s. routière,** road signs; **panneau de s.,** direction indicator; **poteau de s.,** signpost; **feux de s.,** traffic lights.

signaliser [siɲalize] *vtr* to signpost (road).

signataire [siɲatɛr] *n* signatory.

signature [siɲatyr] *nf* **1.** signing **2.** signature.

signe [siɲ] *nm* **1.** sign; indication; symptom (of illness); mark, token (of friendship); **ne pas donner s. de vie,** to show no sign of life; **c'est bon, c'est mauvais, s.,** it's a good, a bad, sign; **la réunion a eu lieu sous le s. de la cordialité,** cordiality was the keynote of the proceedings **2.** sign, symbol, mark; **signes de ponctuation,** punctuation marks; **s. du zodiaque,** sign of the zodiac **3.** *Adm:* **signes particuliers,** special peculiarities (of pers) **4.** sign, gesture, motion; **faire s. à qn,** (i) to make a sign to s.o. (ii) to get in touch with s.o.; **faire s. à qn de la main,** to wave to s.o.; **faire s. que oui,** to nod; **faire s. que non,** to shake one's head.

signer [siɲe] **1.** *vtr* to sign (a document); *F:* **c'est signé,** it's easy to guess who did that! **2. se s.,** to cross oneself.

signet [siɲɛ] *nm* bookmark.

signification [siɲifikasjɔ̃] *nf* meaning, significance, sense. **significatif, -ive** *a* significant.

signifier [siɲifje] *vtr* (*pr sub & impf* **n. signifiions**) **1.** to mean, signify; **que signifie ce mot?** what does this word mean? **cela ne signifie rien,** (i) it doesn't mean anything (ii) it's of no importance; (*denoting indignation*) **qu'est-ce que cela signifie?** what's the meaning of this? **2.** to notify (**qch à qn,** s.o. of sth); **s. son congé à qn,** to give s.o. notice.

silence [silɑ̃s] *nm* **1.** silence; **s. de mort,** deathly hush; **garder le s.,** to keep silent (**sur,** about); **s.!** silence! be quiet! **en s.,** in silence; **passer qch sous s.,** to hush sth up **2.** *Mus:* rest. **silencieux, -euse 1.** *a* silent; peaceful; quiet **2.** *nm Tchn:* silencer; *NAm:* muffler. **silencieusement** *adv* silently.

silex [silɛks] *nm* flint.

silhouette [silwɛt] *nf* (a) silhouette (b) (*of pers*) figure; (*of building*) outline (c) *Mil:* figure target.

silice [silis] *nf Ch:* silica.

silicium [silisjɔm] *nm Ch:* silicon.

silicone [silikɔn] *nf Ch:* silicone.

sillage [sijaʒ] *nm* (a) wake (of ship); **marcher dans son s.,** to follow in his wake (b) *Av:* slipstream.

sillon [sijɔ̃] *nm* (a) *Agr:* furrow (b) line (on the forehead) (c) track (of wheel); **s. de lumière,** streak of light (d) *Rec:* groove.

sillonner [sijɔne] *vtr* (a) to furrow; to cut across, to cross; **montagne sillonnée par les torrents,** mountain scored by torrents (b) (*of light*) to streak (the sky).

silo [silo] *nm Agr:* silo.

simagrées [simagre] *nfpl* affected airs; pointless formalities; **faire des s.,** to make a fuss.

similarité [similarite] *nf* similarity, likeness. **similaire** *a* similar (**à,** to); like.

similitude [similityd] *nf* similitude; resemblance; similarity.

simple [sɛ̃pl] *a* **1.** (a) simple; single (flower, ticket); *Ten:* **s. messieurs, dames,** men's, ladies', singles (b) (*not compound*) *Gram:* **passé s.,** past historic (tense); *Ch:* **corps s.,** element **2.** (a) ordinary, common; **un s. particular,** a private citizen; **s. soldat,** private (soldier) (b) **c'est une s. question de temps,** it's simply a matter of time; **de la folie pure et s.,** sheer madness; **croire qn sur sa s. parole,** to believe s.o. on his word alone (c) plain, simple (pers); simple (dress, food, truth); unaffected (modesty) (d) easy (method); **c'est s. comme bonjour,** it's as easy as pie **3.** (a) simpleminded; *nm* **un s. d'esprit,** a halfwit (b) ingenuous; credulous; *F:* green. **simplement** *adv* simply; plainly; unaffectedly; just, merely. **simplet, -ette** *a* simple, ingenuous.

simplicité [sɛ̃plisite] *nf* **1.** simplicity; unaffectedness **2.** artlessness, simpleness.

simplification [sɛ̃plifikasjɔ̃] *nf* simplification.

simplifier [sɛ̃plifje] *vtr* (*impf & pr sub* **n. simplifiions**) to simplify; **trop s.,** to oversimplify.

simulacre [simylakr] *nm* semblance, show; pretence; **s. de combat,** sham fight.

simulateur, -trice [simylatœr, -tris] (a) *n* pretender, malingerer (b) *nm Tchn:* **s. de vol,** flight simulator.

simulation [simylasjɔ̃] *nf* simulation; pretence.

simuler [simyle] *vtr* to simulate; to feign, sham; **s. une maladie,** to pretend to be ill; to malinger. **simulé** *a* feigned; sham.

simultané [simyltane] *a* simultaneous. **simultanément** *adv* simultaneously.

sinapisme [sinapism] *nm Med:* mustard plaster.

sincérité [sɛ̃serite] *nf* (a) sincerity, frankness, candour (b) genuineness. **sincère** *a* **1.** sincere, frank, candid (person) **2.** sincere, genuine. **sincèrement** *adv* sincerely; frankly; genuinely.

sinécure [sinekyr] *nf* sinecure; *F:* **ce n'est pas une s.,** it's not exactly a rest cure.

Singapour [sɛ̃gapur] *Prnm Geog:* Singapore.

singe [sɛ̃ʒ] *nm* (a) monkey, ape (b) *F:* ape, imitator (c) (*child*) monkey (d) *F:* ugly person; horror.

singer [sɛ̃ʒe] *vtr* (**n. singeons**) to ape, mimic (s.o.).

singeries [sɛ̃ʒri] *nfpl* (a) airs and graces (b) clowning; **faire des s.,** to clown about.

singulariser [sɛ̃gylarize] **1.** *vtr* to make (s.o.) conspicuous **2. se s.,** to attract attention, to make oneself conspicuous.

singularité [sɛ̃gylarite] *nf* singularity; peculiarity.

singulier, -ière [sɛ̃gylje, -jɛr] *a* **1.** (a) singular; **combat s.,** single combat; *nm Gram:* **au s.,** in the singular (b) peculiar (à, to) **2.** (a) peculiar, remarkable (merit, virtue) (b) odd, curious (person, custom, fact) (c) conspicuous. **singulièrement** *adv* singularly; peculiarly; oddly; conspicuously; particularly.

sinistre [sinistr] **1.** *a* sinister, ominous; **un s. menteur,** an awful liar **2.** *nm* (a) disaster, catastrophe (*esp* fire, earthquake, shipwreck) (b) loss, damage (through disaster). **sinistré, -ée 1.** *a* **bâtiment s.,** damaged building; **zone sinistrée,** disaster area **2.** *n* victim of a disaster.

sinon [sinɔ̃] *conj* **1.** otherwise, (or) else, if not **2.**

except; unless; **il ne fait rien s.** dormir, he does nothing except sleep; **s. que,** except that.

sinueux, -euse [sinɥø, -øz] *a* sinuous; winding (path); meandering (stream); tortuous (reasoning).

sinuosité [sinɥozite] *nf (a)* winding; meandering *(b)* bend (of river).

sinus [sinys] *nm Anat:* sinus.

sinusite [sinyzit] *nf Med:* sinusitis.

sionisme [sjɔnism] *nm* Zionism. **sioniste** *a & n* Zionist.

siphon [sifɔ̃] *nm (a)* siphon *(b)* trap (of sink pipe).

siphonner [sifɔne] *vtr* to siphon. **siphonné** *a F:* crazy, nuts.

sire [sir] *nm (a) A:* lord *(b) Pej:* **triste s.,** sad individual *(c) (to king)* Sire.

sirène [sirɛn] *nf* 1. siren, mermaid 2. *(a)* siren, hooter *(b)* foghorn.

sirop [siro] *nm* syrup; (fruit) cordial; *Med:* linctus; **s. contre la toux,** cough mixture.

siroter [sirɔte] *vtr F:* to sip.

sirupeux, -euse [sirypø, -øz] *a* syrupy.

sis [si] *a Jur:* located.

sismique [sismik] *a* seismic.

sismographe [sismɔgraf] *nm* seismograph.

site [sit] *nm (a)* beauty spot *(b)* (building) site.

sitôt [sito] *adv (a)* (= AUSSITÔT) as soon, so soon; **s. dit s. fait,** no sooner said than done; **s. que + ind,** as soon as; *Lit:* **s. après,** immediately after *(b)* **vous ne le reverrez pas de s.,** it will be a long time before you see him again.

situation [sitɥasjɔ̃] *nf* 1. situation, position, site (of town) 2. state, condition; (social, financial) position, standing; **être en s. de faire qch,** to be in a position to do sth; **exposer la s.,** to explain the state of affairs 3. job; **se faire une belle s.,** to work one's way up into a good position.

situer [sitɥe] *vtr* to place, situate, locate (a house); to place (sth in its context); *F:* **s. qn,** to size s.o. up; **l'action se situe à Rome,** the action takes place in Rome.

six *num a inv & nm (before noun beginning with consonant* [si]; *before noun beginning with a vowel sound* [siz]; *otherwise* [sis]) 1. *card a* six; **s. hommes** [sizɔm] six men; **s. petits enfants,** six little children; **à s. heures,** at six o'clock; **j'en ai s.,** I have six 2. *(ordinal use)* **le s. mai,** (on) the sixth of May; **Charles S.,** Charles the Sixth. **sixième** 1. *num a & n* sixth; **au s. (étage),** on the sixth floor, *NAm:* seventh floor 2. *nm* sixth (part) 3. *nf Sch:* = first form (of secondary school). **sixièmement** *adv* in the sixth place.

sketch [skɛtʃ] *nm Th:* sketch; *pl* sketches.

ski [ski] *nm* 1. ski 2. skiing; **faire du s.,** to ski; **chaussures de s.,** ski boots; **s. de fond,** cross-country skiing; **s. nautique,** water skiing.

skier [skje] *vi* to ski.

skieur, -euse [skjœr, -øz] *n* skier.

slalom [slalɔm] *nm* slalom; *F:* **faire du s.,** to zigzag.

slave [slav] 1. *a* Slav, Slavonic 2. *n* Slav.

slip [slip] *nm Cl:* briefs; (woman's) pants, knickers; (men's) underpants; **s. de bain,** swimming trunks.

slogan [slɔgɑ̃] *nm* slogan.

slow [slo] *nm* slow dance.

smala [smala] *nf F:* tribe.

SMIC *abbr salaire minimum interprofessionnel de croissance.*

smicard, -arde [smikar, -ard] *n* minimum wage earner.

smoking [smɔkiŋ] *nm* dinner jacket, *NAm:* tuxedo.

snack(-bar) [snak(bar)] *nm F:* snack bar; *pl* snack-bars, snacks.

SNCF *abbr Société nationale des chemins de fer français.*

snob [snɔb] 1. *nm* snob 2. *a (a)* snobbish, snobby *(b)* pretentious, posh.

snober [snɔbe] *vtr Pej:* to snub (s.o.); to treat (sth) contemptuously.

snobisme [snɔbism] *nm* snobbery.

sobre [sɔbṛ] *a* temperate, abstemious (person); sober (style); sparing (of words). **sobrement** *a* soberly; moderately.

sobriété [sɔbrijete] *nf* sobriety; moderation.

sobriquet [sɔbrikɛ] *nm* nickname.

sociabilité [sɔsjabilite] *nf* sociability. **sociable** *a* sociable.

social, -aux [sɔsjal, -o] *a (a)* social; **l'ordre s.,** the social order; **guerre sociale,** class war *(b) Com:* **raison sociale,** name, style, of the firm; **siège s.,** head office. **socialement** *adv* socially.

social-démocrate [sɔsjaldemɔkrat] *a & n Pol:* social democrat; *pl* sociaux-démocrates.

socialisation [sɔsjalizasjɔ̃] *nf PolEc:* socialization.

socialiser [sɔsjalize] *vtr PolEc:* to socialize.

socialisme [sɔsjalism] *nm* socialism. **socialiste** *a & n* socialist.

sociétaire [sɔsjetɛr] *n* member (of a society).

société [sɔsjete] *nf* 1. *(a)* society; community *(b)* company; gathering, group; **ça ne se fait pas dans la bonne s.,** it's not done in the best society 2. *(a)* society, association; *Sp:* club *(b) Com:* company, firm; partnership; **s. par actions,** joint-stock company; **s. anonyme,** public company; **s. à responsabilité limitée =** limited (liability) company 3. *(a)* company, companionship *(b)* (fashionable) society.

sociologie [sɔsjɔlɔʒi] *nf* sociology. **sociologique** *a* sociological.

sociologue [sɔsjɔlɔg] *n* sociologist.

socle [sɔkl] *nm* base, pedestal, plinth.

socquette [sɔkɛt] *nf* ankle sock, *NAm:* bobby sock.

soda [sɔda] *nm* **s. à l'orange,** orangeade.

sodium [sɔdjɔm] *nm Ch:* sodium.

sœur [sœr] *nf* 1. sister; *F:* **et ta s.!** get lost! 2. *Ecc:* sister, nun.

sofa [sɔfa] *nm* sofa, settee.

SOFRES [sɔfrɛs] *Société française d'enquêtes et de sondages.*

soi [swa] *pers pron (stressed, usu but not always, referring to an indef subject)* oneself; himself, herself, itself, etc.; **chacun pour s.,** everyone for himself; **en s.,** in itself; **il va de s. que,** it goes without saying that; **se parler à s.-même,** to talk to oneself; **petits services qu'on se rend entre s.,** small mutual services.

soi-disant [swadizɑ̃] 1. *a inv (a)* self-styled, would-be; **une s.-d. comtesse,** a self-styled countess *(b)* **les arts s.-d. libéraux,** the so-called liberal arts 2. *adv* supposedly; **il est parti s.-d. pour réfléchir,** he went away, ostensibly to think it over.

soie [swa] nf 1. bristle (of wild boar) 2. silk; **robe de s.**, silk dress; **papier de s.**, tissue paper.

soierie [swari] nf silk goods; silk trade.

soif [swaf] nf (a) thirst; **avoir s.**, to be thirsty; **boire à sa s.**, to drink one's fill; **ça me donne s.**, it makes me thirsty (b) craving (for power).

soigner [swaɲe] vtr (a) to look after, take care of (s.o., sth); to attend to (sth); to nurse, to look after; (of doctor) to attend (patient); to treat (illness); **se s.**, (i) to look after oneself (ii) F: to coddle oneself; **cette maladie ne se soigne pas**, this disease cannot be treated; **il faut te faire s.**, (i) you should see a doctor (ii) F: you need your head examining! (b) to take care over (sth); **s. sa popularité**, to nurse one's public; **s. sa ligne**, to watch one's figure. **soigné** a well finished, carefully done; neat; carefully prepared (meal); polished (style); groomed (appearance); well-kept (hands); **peu s.**, slovenly; P: **un rhume s.**, a stinker of a cold.

soigneur [swaɲœr] nm Sp: second; trainer.

soigneux, -euse [swaɲø, -øz] a careful; tidy (pers). **soigneusement** adv carefully.

soi-même [swamɛm] pers pron oneself; see **soi** and **même** 1(c).

soin [swɛ̃] nm (a) care; **le s. des enfants**, looking after children; **prendre s. de qn, qch**, to look after s.o., sth; Corr: **aux (bons) soins de**, care of; **soins du ménage**, housekeeping; **il prend peu de s. de sa personne**, he's very slovenly about his appearance (b) care, attention, trouble; **avoir s.**, to take care; **avoir s. que** + sub, to see that (sth is done); **je vous laisse le s. de décider**, I'll leave it to you to decide (c) **avoir beaucoup de s.**, to be very tidy; **avec s.**, carefully; with care; **manque de s.**, carelessness (d) pl care, attention; **soins médicaux**, medical care; **premiers soins**, first aid; **être aux petits soins pour qn**, to wait on s.o. hand and foot.

soir [swar] nm evening; **à dix heures du s.**, at ten (o'clock) in the evening; **hier, demain, (au) s.**, yesterday evening, tomorrow evening; **la veille au s.**, the previous evening; **du matin au s.**, from morning till night.

soirée [sware] nf 1. (duration of) evening 2. (a) (evening) party; **s. dansante**, dance; **tenue de s.**, evening dress (b) Th: **représentation de s.**, evening performance.

soit [swa, before a vowel or as int: swat] (third pers sing of pr sub of être) 1. (a) int **s.!** all right! O.K.! agreed! (b) suppose; if, for instance; **s. ABC un triangle**, given a triangle ABC (c) **trois objets à dix francs, s. trente francs**, three articles at ten francs, that is to say thirty francs 2. (a) conj **s. l'un, s. l'autre**, either one or the other (b) conj phr **s. qu'il vienne, s. qu'il ne vienne pas**, whether he comes or not.

soixantaine [swasɑ̃tɛn] nf about sixty, F: sixty odd; **il a passé la s.**, he's in his sixties.

soixante [swasɑ̃t] num a inv & nm inv sixty; **page s.**, page sixty; **s. et un**, sixty-one; **s. et onze**, seventy-one. **soixantième** num a & n sixtieth.

soixante-dix [swasɑ̃tdis] num a inv & nm inv seventy. **soixante-dixième** num a & n seventieth.

soja [sɔʒa] nm Bot: soya bean, soy.

sol¹ [sɔl] nm (a) ground, earth; **cloué au s.**, (i) Av: grounded (ii) rooted to the spot (b) Agr: soil (c) floor.

sol² nm inv Mus: 1. (the note) G 2. sol, soh (in fixed do system).

sol-air [sɔlɛr] a inv ground-to-air (missile).

solaire [sɔlɛr] a solar; sun (lotion).

soldat [sɔlda] nm (a) soldier; serviceman; **simple s.**, private; **le S. inconnu**, the Unknown Soldier; **se faire s.**, to join the army (b) **s. de plomb**, lead soldier.

solde¹ [sɔld] nf pay; demi-s., half pay; Pej: **être à la s. de qn**, to be in s.o.'s pay.

solde² nm Com: 1. balance; **s. débiteur, créditeur**, debit, credit, balance; **pour s. de tout compte**, in full settlement 2. (a) surplus stock; remnant; **soldes**, sale goods; bargains (b) sale; **prix de s.**, sale price; **en s.**, to clear; reduced.

solder [sɔlde] vtr 1. (a) Com: to balance (an account) (b) Com: to settle, to discharge (an account) (c) **se s. par un échec**, to end in failure 2. to sell off (surplus stock).

sole [sɔl] nf Ich: sole.

solécisme [sɔlesism] nm solecism.

soleil [sɔlɛj] nm 1. sun 2. sunshine; **il fait du s.**, the sun's shining, it's sunny; **prendre un bain de s.**, to sunbathe; **jour de s.**, sunny day; **sans s.**, sunless; **coup de s.**, (i) sunburn (ii) touch of sunstroke; **se faire une place au s.**, to have one's place in the sun 3. Bot: sunflower 4. Gym: **grand s.**, grand circle 5. Pyr: catherine wheel.

solennel, -elle [sɔlanɛl] a solemn; formal, official (occasion). **solennellement** adv solemnly.

solennité [sɔlanite] nf solemnity.

solfège [sɔlfɛʒ] nm Mus: solfa.

solidaire [sɔlider] a 1. Jur: joint and several; jointly liable; **obligation s.**, obligation binding on all parties 2. interdependent; **nous sommes solidaires**, we stand together; **être s. d'un mouvement**, to associate oneself with a movement. **solidairement** adv jointly.

solidariser (se) [sɔsɔlidarize] vpr to show solidarity (avec, with).

solidarité [sɔlidarite] nf 1. joint responsibility 2. (a) interdependence (b) solidarity; **grève de s.**, sympathy strike.

solide [sɔlid] 1. a (a) solid (body, food) (b) solid, strong; secure (foundation); sturdy (pers); solid (meal); sound (argument); Com: sound; **coup de poing s.**, hefty blow; **avoir la tête s.**, to have a hard head; **être s. sur ses jambes**, to be steady on one's legs 2. nm solid (body). **solidement** adv solidly, firmly, securely.

solidification [sɔlidifikasjɔ̃] nf solidification.

solidifier [sɔlidifje] vtr (pr sub & impf n. **solidifiions**) to solidify.

solidité [sɔlidite] nf solidity; soundness; strength.

soliloque [sɔlilɔk] nm soliloquy.

soliste [sɔlist] n soloist.

solitaire [sɔliter] 1. a solitary, lonely; deserted (spot); **pin s.**, lone pine 2. nm (a) (pers) (i) recluse (ii) lone wolf; **en s.**, alone (b) Games: solitaire (c) solitaire (diamond) (d) old boar.

solitude [sɔlityd] nf (a) solitude, loneliness (b) Lit: lonely spot.

solive [sɔliv] nf Const: joist.

sollicitation [sɔlisitasjɔ̃] nf 1. entreaty, appeal 2. call (of hunger, ambition).

solliciter [sɔlisite] *vtr* 1. to request, to beg for (interview); to apply (for a job); **s. des voix,** to canvas for votes; **il est sollicité de toutes parts,** he is very much in demand 2: to attract (attention); to appeal to (curiosity).

solliciteur, -euse [sɔlisitœr, -øz] *n* petitioner.

sollicitude [sɔlisityd] *nf* solicitude; concern (**pour,** for).

solo [sɔlo] *nm Mus:* solo.

sol-sol [sɔlsɔl] *a inv* ground-to-ground (missile).

solstice [sɔlstis] *nm* solstice.

solubilité [sɔlybilite] *nf* solubility. **soluble** *a* (*a*) soluble; **café s.,** instant coffee (*b*) solvable (problem).

solution [sɔlysijɔ̃] *nf* 1. *Ch: Ph: etc:* solution 2. solution, answer (to question, problem); **s. de facilité,** easy way out.

solvabilité [sɔlvabilite] *nf* solvency. **solvable** *a* (financially) solvent.

solvant [sɔlvɑ̃] *nm Ch:* solvent.

Somalie [sɔmali] *Prnf Geog:* **(République de) S.,** Somalia. **somali, -ie** *a & n* Somali; **Côte française des Somalis,** French Somaliland.

sombre [sɔ̃br] *a* (*a*) dark, sombre, gloomy; *inv* **bleu s.,** dark blue (*b*) dim (light); dull (sky) (*c*) dismal (thoughts); **une s. histoire,** a murky story; *F:* **un s. idiot,** a first-class idiot. **sombrement** *adv* sombrely, darkly, gloomily, dismally.

sombrer [sɔ̃bre] *vi* (*of ship*) sink; (*of empire*) to founder; **s. dans le désespoir,** to sink into despair.

sommaire [sɔmɛr] 1. *a* (*a*) summary, succinct, concise (*b*) hasty; improvised (*c*) *Jur:* summary (proceedings) 2. *nm* summary, synopsis. **sommairement** *adv* summarily; hastily; **vêtu s.,** scantily dressed.

sommation [sɔmasjɔ̃] *nf* 1. *Jur:* summons; demand 2. (sentry's) challenge.

somme[1] [sɔm] *nf* (*a*) sum, amount; **s. totale,** grand total, total sum (*b*) **en s.,** on the whole, in short; **s. toute,** when all's said and done (*c*) sum (of money).

somme[2] *nm* nap; *F:* snooze; **faire un s.,** to have a snooze.

sommeil [sɔmɛj] *nm* 1. sleep, slumber; **s. de plomb,** heavy sleep; **avoir le s. léger,** to be a light sleeper; **en s.,** (lying) dormant 2. drowsiness, sleepiness; **avoir s.,** to be sleepy.

sommeiller [sɔmeje] *vi* 1. to doze 2. *Fig:* to lie dormant.

sommelier [sɔməlje] *nm* wine waiter.

sommer [sɔme] *vtr* **s. qn de faire qch,** to call on s.o. to do sth.

sommet [sɔmɛ] *nm* top, summit (of hill); vertex (of angle, curve); crest (of wave); crown (of head); pinnacle (of power); *Pol:* **conférence au s.,** summit meeting.

sommier [sɔmje] *nm* base, springing (of bed).

sommité [sɔmite] *nf* leading light.

somnambule [sɔmnɑ̃byl] *n* somnambulist; sleepwalker.

somnambulisme [sɔmnɑ̃bylism] *nm* somnambulism, sleepwalking.

somnifère [sɔmnifɛr] *nm* 1. *a* soporific 2. *nm* soporific; sleeping pill.

somnolence [sɔmnɔlɑ̃s] *nf* somnolence; sleepiness, drowsiness. **somnolent** *a* somnolent; sleepy, drowsy.

somnoler [sɔmnɔle] *vi* to drowse, to doze.

somptueux, -euse [sɔ̃ptɥø, -øz] *a* sumptuous, magnificent. **somptueusement** *adv* sumptuously, magnificently.

somptuosité [sɔ̃ptɥozite] *nf* sumptuousness, magnificence.

son[1], **sa, ses** [sɔ̃, sa, se] *poss a* (son *is used instead of* sa *before fem nouns beginning with a vowel or* h *mute*) his, her, its, one's; **un s. ami,** a friend of his, of hers; **ses père et mère,** his, her, father and mother; **sa voiture à lui est sale,** his own car is dirty; **à sa vue,** at the sight of him, of her; *F:* **son imbécile de frère,** that stupid brother of his, of hers; **avoir son importance,** to have a certain importance.

son[2] *nm* (*a*) sound (of voice, instrument); ringing (of a bell); **s. du tambour, de la trompette,** beat of the drum, blare of the trumpet (*b*) *Ph: Mus:* sound, tone; *Av:* **mur du s.,** sound barrier; *Cin: Rec:* **enregistrement du s.,** sound recording; **prise de s.,** sound pick-up; **ingénieur du s.,** sound engineer; **(spectacle) de s. et lumière,** son et lumière.

son[3] *nm* bran.

sonate [sɔnat] *nf Mus:* sonata.

sondage [sɔ̃daʒ] *nm* (*a*) *Nau: Av: etc:* sounding; probe (*b*) *Min:* boring (*c*) *Med:* probing (of wound) (*d*) **s. d'opinion,** opinion poll.

sonde [sɔ̃d] *nf* 1. *Nau:* (*a*) sounding line, plummet (*b*) *Meteor: Av:* **s. spatiale,** space probe 2. *Med:* probe; **s. creuse,** catheter 3. *Min:* borer; drill.

sonder [sɔ̃de] *vtr* 1. (*a*) *Nau:* to sound; to fathom (a mystery) (*b*) *Meteor:* to probe (*c*) *Min:* **s. un terrain,** *vi* **s.,** to make borings 2. (*a*) to probe, examine; to investigate, test (*b*) to sound (s.o.) out; **s. le terrain,** to see how the land lies 3. *Med:* to probe (wound); to sound (patient).

songe [sɔ̃ʒ] *nm* dream; **faire un s.,** to dream.

songer [sɔ̃ʒe] *vi* (**n. songeons**) 1. (*a*) *Lit:* to dream (**de,** of) (*b*) to muse; to (day)dream; to think (**à faire qch,** of doing sth) 2. (*a*) **s. à qch,** to think of sth; **il ne faut pas y s.,** that's quite out of the question; **s. à l'avenir,** to plan for the future; **songez à ce que vous faites!** think what you're doing! (*b*) to imagine; **songez donc!** just think! just imagine! (*c*) to remember; **songez à lui,** bear him in mind. **songeur, -euse** *a* dreamy (pers); pensive, thoughtful.

songerie [sɔ̃ʒri] *nf* reverie.

sonique [sɔnik] *a* a sonic.

sonner [sɔne] 1. *vi* to sound; (*of clocks*) to strike; (*of bells*) to ring, to toll; (*of telephone*) to ring; (*of keys*) to jingle; **s. creux,** to sound hollow; **sa réponse sonne faux,** his reply does not ring true; **s. mal, bien,** to sound bad, good; **midi vient de s.,** it has just struck twelve; **son heure a sonné,** his hour has come 2. *vtr* (*a*) to sound; **s. la cloche,** to ring the bell; *vi* **on sonne,** there's a ring at the door; **l'horloge a sonné 2 heures,** the clock has struck 2 (o'clock); *v ind tr* **s. du clairon,** to sound the bugle; *F:* **il va se faire s. (les cloches)!** he'll catch it! (*b*) to ring for (s.o.); *P:* **on ne t'a pas sonné!** nobody asked you! (*c*) *P:* **s. qn,** to knock s.o. out; to stagger s.o. **sonnant** *a* striking (clock); **à dix heures sonnant(es),** on the stroke of ten. **sonné** *a* 1. **dix heures sonnées,** past ten (o'clock); **il a 40 ans sonnés,** he's on the wrong side of 40 2. *F:* (*a*) groggy (*b*) crazy, cracked.

sonnerie [sɔnri] *nf* **1.** ringing (of bells) **2.** (a) striking mechanism (of clock) (b) (electric, alarm) bell **3.** *Mil:* (bugle) call.

sonnette [sɔnɛt] *nf* **1.** (small) bell; (house) bell; **coup de s.,** ring (at the door) **2. serpent à sonnettes,** rattlesnake.

sonneur, -euse [sɔnœr, -øz] *n* bellringer.

sono [sɔno] *nf F:* P.A. system, sound system.

sonore [sɔnɔr] *a* (a) resonant; echoing (vault) (b) ringing (voice); clear-toned (bell); resounding (laughter) (c) acoustic(al); **onde sonore,** soundwave; *Cin:* **film s.,** sound film; **bande s.,** sound track.

sonorisation [sɔnɔrizasjɔ̃] *nf* wiring (of room) for sound; P.A. system.

sonoriser [sɔnɔrize] *vtr* to wire (a room) for sound.

sonorité [sɔnɔrite] *nf* (a) tone (b) resonance (c) accoustics.

sophistiqué [sɔfistike] *a* sophisticated.

soporifique [sɔpɔrifik] *a & nm* soporific.

soprano [sɔprano] *n* soprano.

sorbet [sɔrbɛ] *nm* sorbet; water ice.

sorbetière [sɔrbɔtjɛr] *nf* ice-cream freezer.

sorcellerie [sɔrsɛlri] *nf* witchcraft, sorcery; magic.

sorcier, -ière [sɔrsje, -jɛr] *n* sorcerer, sorceress; wizard, *f* witch; **vieille sorcière,** old hag; *F:* **ce n'est pas s.,** you couldn't call it difficult.

sordide [sɔrdid] *a* **1.** sordid, filthy; squalid (room) **2.** sordid (crime). **sordidement** *adv* sordidly; squalidly.

sornettes [sɔrnɛt] *nfpl* nonsense; twaddle.

sort [sɔr] *nm* **1.** lot, condition in life; *F:* **faire un s. à qch,** to polish off (the bottle, a dish) **2.** destiny, fate; **ironie du s.,** irony of fate **3.** chance, fortune, lot; **tirer au s.,** (i) to draw lots (ii) to toss, to spin, a coin; **le s. (en) est jeté,** the die is cast **4.** spell, charm; **jeter un s. à qn,** to cast a spell on s.o.

sortable [sɔrtabl] *a F:* presentable.

sorte [sɔrt] *nf* **1.** manner, way; **habillé de la s.,** dressed like that; *adv phr* **en quelque s.,** as it were, in a way; *conj phr* **parlez de (telle) s. qu'on vous comprenne,** speak so as to be understood; **faites en s. que tout soit prêt,** see to it that everything is ready **2.** sort, kind; **toute(s) sorte(s) de choses,** all kinds of things; **je n'ai rien dit de la s.,** I said no such thing, nothing of the kind.

sortie [sɔrti] *nf* **1.** (a) going out; coming out; departure; *Th:* exit; **c'est ma première s. depuis mon accident,** it's my first time out since my accident; **à la s. des classes,** after school (b) launching (of new model); release (of new record); appearance (of new book) (c) leaving (for good); retirement (of official); **à ma s. d'école,** when I left school (d) outflow (of liquid); **tuyaux de s.,** outgoing pipes (e) *Com:* export (of goods); **sorties de fonds,** expenses, outgoings **2.** trip, excursion; outing; leave; **jour de s.,** day out; day off **3.** (a) *Mil:* sally, sortie; *Fb:* run out (by goalkeeper) (b) outburst, tirade **4.** exit, way out; **s. de secours,** emergency exit; **sorties de Paris,** roads out of Paris **5. s. de bain,** bath-wrap.

sortilège [sɔrtilɛʒ] *nm* (magic) spell.

sortir¹ [sɔrtir] *v* (*conj like* MENTIR) **1.** *vi* (*aux* être) (a) to go, come, out; to leave the room, the house; **s. de la salle,** to go out of the room; **faites le s.,** get him out of here; **s. du lit,** to get out of bed; to get up;

Th: **Macbeth sort,** exit Macbeth; *F:* **d'où sortez-vous?** where have you been all this time? **s. d'un emploi,** to leave a job; **ça m'est sorti de la mémoire,** it's slipped my memory; **il n'en sortira pas grand-chose,** not much will come of it (b) (*of record, film*) to be released; (*of book*) to come out (c) **s. d'un emploi,** to leave a job; to go out (on foot); to drive out; to sail out; **s. en courant,** to run out (d) to have just come out; **je sors de table,** I have just got up from table; **on sortait de l'hiver,** winter was just over; **il sort d'ici,** he's just left (e) *P:* **je sors d'en prendre,** I've had enough (f) **s. de son sujet,** to wander from one's subject; **cela sort de l'ordinaire,** it's out of the ordinary; (*of train*) **s. des rails,** to jump the rails; **il ne sort pas de là,** he sticks to his point (g) to go out; **Madame est sortie,** Mrs X is out (h) to get out, extricate oneself (from difficulty, danger); **il n'y pas à s. de là,** there is no way out; *F:* **j'ai trop à faire, je n'en sors pas,** I've too much to do, I can't get through it (i) to come (from a good family); **s. de l'université,** to graduate (from university) (j) to stand out, stick out, project; to emerge (from obscurity); **yeux qui sortent de la tête,** protruding eyes; **faire s. un rôle,** to emphasize a part **2.** *vtr* (*aux* avoir) to take out, bring out, pull out; to take out (child, dog); **s. la voiture,** to get the car out; **le malade s'en sortira,** the patient will pull through; **s. un livre,** to publish a book; *F:* **il nous en a sorti une bonne,** he came out with a good one.

sortir² *nm* **au s. du théâtre,** on coming out of the theatre; **au s. de l'hiver,** at the end of winter.

sosie [sɔzi, so-] *nm* (*pers*) double.

sot, sotte [so, sɔt] **1.** *a* silly, stupid, foolish **2.** *n* fool, idiot, ass. **sottement** *adv* stupidly, foolishly.

sottise [sɔtiz] *nf* (a) stupidity, foolishness (b) foolish act; stupid remark.

sou [su] *nm A:* sou (= five centimes); (*still used, esp colloquially, although the coin has disappeared*) **être sans le s.,** to be penniless, *F:* broke; **être près de ses sous,** to be mean, *F:* stingy; **machine à sous,** slot machine; fruit machine, one-armed bandit; **pas ambitieux pour un s.,** not in the least ambitious; **il n'a pas pour deux sous de courage,** he hasn't an ounce of courage.

soubassement [subasmɑ̃] *nm* base (of building).

soubresaut [subraso] *nm* sudden start; jolt; **il a eu un s.,** he made a convulsive movement.

soubrette [subrɛt] *nf A:* maid.

souche [suʃ] *nf* **1.** stump (of tree); root stock (of iris); vine stock; **rester planté comme une s.,** to stand stock still **2.** (a) founder (of family); **de vieille s.,** of old stock (b) strain (of virus) **3.** *Com:* counterfoil, stub (of cheque, ticket).

souci¹ [susi] *nm Bot:* marigold.

souci² *nm* **1.** care; preoccupation; concern (**de,** for); **avoir le s. de la vérité,** to be meticulously truthful; **c'est le cadet de mes soucis,** that's the least of my worries **2.** anxiety, worry; **se faire du s.,** to worry; **sans s.,** free from anxiety; **soucis d'argent,** money worries.

soucier (se) [səsusje] *vpr* (*impf & pr sub* **n. n. soucions**) to be concerned, to worry (**de qn, qch,** about s.o., sth); **se s. des autres,** to worry about other people; *F:* **je m'en soucie comme de l'an quarante,** I don't care a damn about that. **soucieux, -euse** *a* (*a*) anxious, concerned (**de,** about); **peu s.,** unconcerned (*b*) anxious, worried.

soucoupe [sukup] *nf* saucer; **s. volante,** flying saucer.

soudain [sudɛ̃] **1.** *a* sudden, unexpected **2.** *adv* suddenly, all of a sudden. **soudainement** *adv* suddenly.

soudaineté [sudɛnte] *nf* suddenness.

Soudan [sudɑ̃] *Prnm Geog:* the Sudan.

soude [sud] *nf Ch: Ind:* soda; **cristaux de s.,** washing soda; **bicarbonate de s.,** bicarbonate of soda; **s. caustique,** caustic soda.

souder [sude] **1.** *vtr* (*a*) to solder (*b*) to weld; to join (fractured bone) **2. se s.** (*a*) to fuse together (*b*) (*of bone*) to knit (together).

soudeur, -euse [sudœr, -øz] *n* (*pers*) solderer; welder.

soudoir [sudwar] *nm* soldering iron.

soudure [sudyr] *nf* **1.** (*a*) soldering (*b*) soldered joint **2.** (*a*) welding (*b*) weld **3.** (*a*) join (of bones) (*b*) *PolEc:* **faire la s.,** to bridge the gap (before the next instalment of income is due).

souffle [sufl] *nm* **1.** (*a*) breath, puff, blast (of air, wind) (*b*) blast (of explosion) (*c*) *Av:* slipstream **2.** (*a*) respiration, breathing; **retenir son s.,** to hold one's breath; **avoir le s. coupé,** to be winded; *F:* **c'est à vous couper le s.,** it's breathtaking (*b*) *Med:* **s. (au cœur),** (heart, cardiac) murmur (*c*) breath, wind (of runner); **être à bout de s.,** to be out of breath; **reprendre son s.,** to get one's breath back.

soufflé [sufle] **1.** *a* (*a*) puffed up; **soufflé (omelette)** (*b*) *F:* flabbergasted, taken aback **2.** *nm Cu:* soufflé.

souffler [sufle] **1.** *vi* (*a*) to blow (*b*) to get one's breath back (*c*) to pant; to puff (*d*) **le vent souffle en tempête,** it's blowing a gale **2.** *vtr* (*a*) to blow (glass) (*b*) to blow off (dust); to blow out (candle) (*c*) to breathe, utter (a sound); to whisper; **ne pas s. mot de qch,** not to breathe a word about sth (*d*) to prompt (an actor) (*e*) *F:* to pinch, nick (sth from s.o.) (*f*) (*of explosion*) to blast (building); *F:* (*of event*) to take (s.o.) aback; to stagger (s.o.).

soufflerie [sufləri] *nf* **1.** bellows (of organ, forge) **2.** (*a*) blower (*b*) wind tunnel.

soufflet [suflɛ] *nm* **1.** (pair of) bellows **2.** (*a*) *Rail:* concertina vestibule (*b*) *Dressm:* gusset **3.** slap in the face.

souffleur, -euse [suflœr, -øz] *n* **1.** glass blower **2.** *Th:* prompter.

souffrance [sufrɑ̃s] *nf* **1. en s.,** (work) pending; (parcel) awaiting delivery **2.** suffering, pain.

souffre-douleur [sufrədulœr] *nm inv* butt (of one's jokes); scapegoat.

souffrir [sufrir] *v* (*prp* **souffrant;** *pp* **souffert;** *pr ind* **je souffre**) **1.** *vtr* (*a*) to suffer; to endure, undergo, put up with, bear (pain, fatigue, loss); *F:* **ils ne peuvent pas se s.,** they can't stand each other (*b*) to permit, allow; **souffrez que je vous dise la vérité,** allow me to tell you the truth **2.** *vi* (*a*) to feel pain; to suffer (from rheumatism, thirst); **souffre-t-il?** is he in pain? **mon bras me fait s.,** my arm is hurting (me); **je souffre de le voir si changé,** it pains, grieves, me to see him so changed; **s. de la guerre,** to be

hard hit by the war (*b*) to suffer injury; (*of thgs*) to be damaged (by sth); **les vignes ont souffert de la gelée,** the vines have suffered from the frost (*c*) (*of trade*) to be in a bad way. **souffrant** *a* suffering; unwell, poorly. **souffreteux, -euse** *a* sickly.

soufre [sufr] *nm* sulphur.

souhait [swɛ] *nm* wish, desire; **présenter ses souhaits à qn,** to offer s.o. one's good wishes; *adv phr* **à s.,** to one's liking; **réussir à s.,** to succeed to perfection; (*when sneezing*) **à vos souhaits!** (God) bless you!

souhaiter [swɛte] *vtr* (*a*) to wish; **s. les richesses,** to want to be rich; **je vous souhaite de réussir,** I hope you'll succeed (*b*) **je vous souhaite une bonne année,** I wish you a happy new year; **s. bon voyage à qn,** to wish s.o. a good journey. **souhaitable** *adv* desirable.

souiller [suje] *vtr* **1.** to soil, dirty (clothes) (**de,** with); **souillé de boue,** mudstained **2.** to pollute, to contaminate; **s. ses mains de sang,** to stain one's hands with blood **3.** to tarnish, dishonour (one's name).

souillon [sujɔ̃] *nf* slattern, slut.

souillure [sujyr] *nf* stain.

soûl [su] **1.** *a F:* drunk; **s. comme un Polonais,** drunk as a lord **2.** *nm* **manger, boire, tout son s.,** to eat, drink, one's fill; **rire tout son s.,** to laugh till one can laugh no more.

soulagement [sulaʒmɑ̃] *nm* relief.

soulager [sulaʒe] **1.** *vtr* (**n. soulageons**) to ease (pressure); to relieve, alleviate (pain, grief); to soothe, comfort (s.o.'s mind, s.o.'s sorrow); **ça me soulage l'esprit,** it's a great weight off my mind **2. se s.** (*a*) to relieve one's feelings, one's mind (*b*) *F:* to relieve oneself.

soûlard, -arde [sular, -ard] *n P:* drunkard, boozer.

soûler [sule] **1.** *vtr* to get, make (s.o.) drunk **2. se s.,** to get drunk; **se s. de qch,** to intoxicate oneself with sth.

soûlerie [sulri] *nf P:* booze-up; drunken binge.

soulèvement [sulɛvmɑ̃] *nm* (*a*) **s. de cœur,** nausea (*b*) *Geol:* upthrust (*c*) revolt, uprising.

soulever [sulve] *vtr* **1.** (*a*) to raise (*usu* with effort); to lift (up) (a weight) (*b*) to raise (sth) slightly (*c*) to raise (doubts, a question, an objection) (*d*) to rouse, stir up (people to revolt) (*e*) **ça soulève le cœur,** it's nauseating **2. se s.** (*a*) to rise; (*of sea*) to heave; (*of stomach*) to turn (*b*) to raise oneself up (*c*) to revolt; to rise (in rebellion).

soulier [sulje] *nm* shoe; *F:* **être dans ses petits souliers,** to be in an awkward situation.

souligner [suliɲe] *vtr* (*a*) to underline (word) (*b*) to emphasize (word, fact).

soumettre [sumɛtr] *vtr* (*conj like* METTRE) **1.** to subdue (people, passions) **2.** to submit, refer (a question) (**à qn,** to s.o.); to put (one's plans) before (s.o.) **3.** to subject (sth to an examination); **s. qn à une épreuve,** to put s.o. through a test; **être soumis à des règles,** to be bound by rules **4. se s.,** to submit (to authority); to comply (to s.o.'s wishes); to abide by (s.o.'s decision).

soumis [sumi] *a* **1.** submissive **2.** subject (to law, tax, authority).

soumission [sumisjɔ̃] *nf* (*a*) submission; **faire (sa) s.,** to surrender, yield (*b*) obedience, submissiveness (**à,** to).

soupape [supap] *nf Tchn:* valve; **s. de sûreté,** safety valve; **s. à flotteur,** ballcock.

soupçon [supsɔ̃] *nm* **1.** suspicion; **j'en avais le s.!** I suspected as much! **au-dessus de tout s.,** above suspicion **2.** suspicion, inkling; **je n'en avais pas le moindre s.,** I never suspected it for a moment **3.** *F:* dash, hint, soupçon (of vinegar, garlic); touch (of fever, irony); drop (of wine).

soupçonner [supsɔne] *vtr* to suspect; **je ne soupçonnais pas que,** I had no idea that. **soupçonneux, -euse** *a* suspicious.

soupe [sup] *nf* soup; **il est très s. au lait,** he flares up very easily; **s. à l'oignon,** onion soup; *F:* **à la s.!** grub's up!

soupente [supɑ̃t] *nf* closet (*esp* under stairs).

souper[1] [supe] *vi* to have supper; *F:* **j'en ai soupé,** I've had enough of it.

souper[2] *nm* supper.

soupeser [supəze] *vtr* (**je soupèse**) to feel the weight of (sth) (in the hand); to weigh up (a problem).

soupière [supjɛr] *nf* soup tureen.

soupir [supir] *nm* **1.** sigh; **s. de soulagement,** sigh of relief; **rendre le dernier s.,** to breathe one's last **2.** *Mus:* crochet rest.

soupirail, -aux [supiraj, -o] *nm* (small) basement window.

soupirer [supire] *vi* (*a*) to sigh (*b*) **s. après qch,** to long for sth.

souple [supl] *a* supple; flexible (branch, character); lithe (figure); **esprit s.,** versatile mind.

souplesse [suples] *nf* suppleness; flexibility; litheness; versatility.

source [surs] *nf* **1.** spring; source (of river); **eau de s.,** spring water; **s. thermale,** hot spring **2.** origin (of evil, wealth, news); **aller à la s. du mal,** to get to the root of the evil; **je le tiens de bonne s.,** I have it on good authority.

sourcil [sursi] *nm* eyebrow.

sourciller [sursije] *vi* to frown; **sans s.,** without turning a hair, without batting an eyelid. **sourcilleux, -euse** *a* finicky.

sourd, sourde [sur, surd] **1.** (*a*) *a* deaf; **s. comme un pot,** deaf as a post; **rester s. aux prières,** to turn a deaf ear to entreaties (*b*) *n* deaf person; **crier comme un s.,** to yell; **frapper comme un s.,** to hit out wildly **2.** *a* dull (tint, pain); dull, muffled (sound); hollow (voice); secret (desire); veiled (hostility). **sourdement** *adv* dully; secretly.

sourdine [surdin] *nf Mus:* mute; **en s.,** softly, quietly; **mettre une s. à qch,** to tone sth down.

sourd-muet, sourde-muette [surmɥe, surdmɥɛt] **1.** *a* deaf-and-dumb **2.** *n* deaf-mute; *pl* **sourd(e)s-muet(te)s.**

souriant [surjɑ̃] *a* smiling; pleasant (surroundings).

souricière [surisjɛr] *nf* (*a*) mousetrap (*b*) trap, *esp* police trap.

sourire[1] [surir] *vi* (*conj like* RIRE) **1.** to smile (à, to); **faire s.,** to provoke a smile **2.** (*a*) (*of thgs*) to please; to appeal (à qn, to s.o.) (*b*) **tout lui sourit,** he makes a success of everything.

sourire[2] *nm* smile; **adresser un s. à qn,** to give s.o. a smile; **gardez le s.!** keep smiling!

souris [suri] *nf* (*a*) mouse; **s. blanche,** white mouse (*b*) *P:* (*woman*) bird.

sournois, -oise [surnwa, -waz] *a* sly, crafty (person); shifty (look); underhand (method). **sournoisement** *adv* slyly.

sous [su] (*a*) *prep* **1.** under(neath), beneath, below; **s. un arbre,** under a tree; **s. terre,** underground, below ground; **s. clef,** under lock and key; **s. nos yeux,** before our eyes; **connu s. le nom de X,** known as X; **s. la pluie,** in the rain (*b*) **s. les tropiques,** in the tropics (*c*) **s. Louis XIV,** in the reign of Louis XIV; **s. peine de mort,** on pain of death; **s. un prétexte,** under a pretext **2.** within; **s. 3 jours,** within 3 days; **s. peu,** before long.

sous- [su] before vowel sound [suz] *comb fm* sub-; under-; assistant. NOTE: *in the plural of hyphenated words of which the first element is* sous-, sous- *remains invariable and the second element takes the pl form.*

sous-alimenté [suzalimɑ̃te] *a* underfed, undernourished.

sous-bois [subwa] *nm inv* undergrowth.

sous-chef [suʃɛf] *nm* **1.** deputy chief clerk **2.** assistant manager.

sous-couche [sukuʃ] *nf* substratum.

souscripteur, -trice [suskriptœr, -tris] *n* subscriber.

souscription [suskripsjɔ̃] *nf* **1.** *Fin: etc:* subscription, application (à des actions, for shares) **3.** subscription, contribution (of sum of money); **lancer une s.,** to start a fund.

souscrire [suskrir] *vtr* (*conj like* ÉCRIRE) **1.** *vtr* (*a*) to sign (*b*) to subscribe (money to a charity) (*c*) to take out (a subscription, *Ins:* a policy); to apply, subscribe, for (shares) **2.** *vi* (*a*) **s. à,** to subscribe for (sth); **s. pour,** to subscribe to (a charity) (*b*) **s. à une opinion,** to endorse an opinion.

sous-développé [sudevlɔpe] *a* under-developed.

sous-directeur, -trice [sudirɛktœr, -tris] *n* assistant manager(ess).

sous-entendre [suzɑ̃tɑ̃dr] *vtr* to understand; to imply.

sous-entendu [suzɑ̃tɑ̃dy] *nm* (*a*) thing understood (*b*) implication; insinuation.

sous-équipé [suzekipe] *a* underequipped.

sous-estimer [suzɛstime] *vtr* to under-estimate, undervalue, underrate.

sous-exposer [suzɛkspoze] *vtr Phot:* to underexpose.

sous-fifre [sufifr] *nm F:* dogsbody.

sous-jacent [suʒasɑ̃] *a* underlying.

sous-lieutenant [suljøtnɑ̃] *nm Mil:* second-lieutenant; *Navy:* sub-lieutenant; *Av:* pilot officer.

sous-locataire [sulɔkatɛr] *n* subtenant.

sous-location [sulɔkasjɔ̃] *nf* **1.** subletting **2.** sublease.

sous-louer [sulwe] *vtr* to sublet.

sous-main [sumɛ̃] *nm inv* blotting pad.

sous-marin [sumarɛ̃] **1.** *a* submarine (life); underwater (fishing) **2.** *nm* submarine.

sous-officier [suzɔfisje] *nm* **1.** non-commissioned officer **2.** *Navy:* petty officer.

sous-préfecture [suprefɛktyr] *nf* subprefecture.

sous-préfet [suprefɛ] *nm Adm:* sub-prefect.

sous-produit [suprɔdɥi] *nm Ind:* by-product.

sous-secrétaire [susəkretɛr] *n* undersecretary.

soussigné [susiɲe] *a & n* undersigned.

sous-sol [susɔl] *nm* 1. *Geol:* subsoil, substratum 2. *Const:* basement.

sous-titre [sutitʀ] *nm Cin:* subtitle.

sous-titrer [sutitʀe] *vtr Cin:* to subtitle; **film sous-titré,** film with subtitles.

soustraction [sustʀaksjɔ̃] *nf* (a) removal (b) *Mth:* substraction.

soustraire [sustʀɛʀ] *(conj like* TRAIRE*)* 1. *vtr* (a) to take away, remove (b) to protect, shield (s.o. from sth) (c) *Mth:* to subtract (**de,** from) 2. **se s. à qch,** to avoid, elude, sth; **se s. à un devoir,** to shirk a duty.

sous-vêtement [suvɛtmɑ̃] *nm* undergarment; *pl* underwear.

soutane [sutan] *nf* cassock, soutane.

soute [sut] *nf Nau:* store room; locker; **s. à charbon,** coal bunker; **s. à munitions,** magazine; **s. à bagages,** (i) luggage room (ii) *Av:* luggage compartment.

souteneur [sutnœʀ] *nm* procurer, pimp.

soutenir [sutniʀ] *(conj like* TENIR*)* 1. *vtr* (a) to support; to hold (s.o., sth) up; to sustain (s.o.) (b) to keep, maintain (family) (c) to back (up) (cause, person); to back (s.o. financially) (d) to maintain, uphold (opinion); to assert (fact); *Sch:* to defend (thesis) (e) to keep up, sustain, maintain (conversation, speed) (f) to bear (reproach, comparison); to hold out against (attack) 2. **se s.** (a) **se s. sur ses pieds,** to stand on one's feet; **je ne me soutiens plus,** I'm ready to drop (b) to last, continue; **l'intérêt se soutient,** the interest is kept up (c) (*of point of view*) to be tenable. **soutenu** *a* sustained (effort); unflagging (interest).

souterrain [sutɛʀɛ̃] 1. *a* underground, subterranean; **passage s.,** subway 2. *nm* underground passage; tunnel.

soutien [sutjɛ̃] *nm* (a) support; **il est sans s.,** he has nobody behind him (b) supporter; *Adm:* **s. de famille,** breadwinner.

soutien-gorge [sutjɛ̃gɔʀʒ] *nm Cl:* brassière, *F:* bra; *pl* **soutiens-gorge.**

soutirer [sutiʀe] *vtr* to draw off, to rack (wine); to extract (money from s.o.).

souvenir[1] [suvniʀ] *(conj like* VENIR*; aux* être*)* 1. *v impers Lit:* **il me souvient d'avoir dit,** I remember having said 2. **se s. de qch, de qn,** to remember, recall, sth, s.o.; **je m'en souviendrai!** I won't forget it! **faire s. qn de qch,** to remind s.o. of sth.

souvenir[2] *nm* 1. recollection, memory; **vague s.,** vague recollection; **avoir s. de qch,** to have a recollection of sth; **en s. de qn,** in memory of, in remembrance of s.o.; **veuillez me rappeler à son bon s.,** please remember me to him 2. keepsake, souvenir, memento; **magasin de souvenirs,** souvenir shop.

souvent [suvɑ̃] *adv* often; **le plus s.,** more often than not; **peu s.,** seldom.

souverain, -aine [suvʀɛ̃, -ɛn] 1. *a* sovereign (power, prince); supreme (happiness) 2 *n* sovereign. **souverainement** *adv* (a) supremely, intensely (b) with sovereign power.

souveraineté [suvʀɛ̃te] *nf* sovereignty.

soviet [sɔvjɛt] *nm* Soviet. **soviétique** *a & n* Soviet (citizen).

soya [sɔja] *nm Bot:* soya (bean).

soyeux, -euse [swajø, -øz] *a* silky.

SPA *abbr Société protectrice des animaux.*

spacieux, -euse [spasjø, -øz] *a* spacious (room); roomy (car).

sparadrap [spaʀadʀa] *nm* (adhesive, sticking) plaster.

spartiate [spaʀsjat] *a & n Geog:* & *Fig:* Spartan.

spasme [spasm] *nm* spasm. **spasmodique** *a* spasmodic.

spatial, -aux [spasjal, -o] *a* spacial; **engin s.,** spacecraft; **voyage s.,** space flight.

spatule [spatyl] *nf* spatula; **en s.,** spatulate.

speaker, speakerine [spikœʀ, spikʀin] *n WTel: TV:* announcer; (woman) announcer.

spécial, -aux [spesjal, -o] *a* (a) special; particular; *Journ:* **envoyé s.,** special correspondent (b) *F:* peculiar. **spécialement** *adv* (e)specially, particularly.

spécialisation [spesjalizasjɔ̃] *nf* specialization.

spécialiser (se) [səspesjalize] *vpr* to specialize (**dans,** in).

spécialiste [spesjalist] *n* specialist (**en,** in).

spécialité [spesjalite] *nf* speciality; special feature; special field; **il a la s. de me taper sur les nerfs,** he has a knack of getting on my nerves.

spécieux, -euse [spesjø, -øz] *a* specious; plausible.

spécification [spesifikasjɔ̃] *nf* specification.

spécifier [spesifje] *vtr* (*impf & pr sub* n. **spécifiions**) to specify; to state (definitely). **spécifique** *a* specific. **spécifiquement** *adv* specifically.

spécimen [spesimɛn] *nm* specimen; *Pub:* inspection copy.

spectacle [spɛktakl] *nm* 1. spectacle, sight, scene; **se donner en s.,** to make an exhibition of oneself 2. *Th:* play, entertainment, show; **le s.,** show business; **aller au s.,** to go to the theatre; **salle de s.,** (concert) hall; theatre; *Cin:* **film à grand s.,** epic. **spectaculaire** *a* spectacular; dramatic.

spectateur, -trice [spɛktatœʀ, -tʀis] *n* spectator; onlooker; witness (of accident); member of audience; **les spectateurs,** the audience.

spectre [spɛktʀ] *nm* 1. spectre, ghost 2. *Opt:* spectrum. **spectral, -aux** *a* spectral.

spéculateur, -trice [spekylatœʀ, -tʀis] *n* speculator.

spéculation [spekylasjɔ̃] *nf* speculation. **spéculatif, -ive** *a* speculative.

spéculer [spekyle] *vi* 1. to speculate (**sur,** on, about) 2. *Fin:* to speculate; *Fig:* **s. sur qch,** to bank on sth.

spéléologie [speleɔlɔʒi] *nf* speleology; potholing. **spéléologique** *a* speleological.

spéléologue [speleɔlɔg] *n* speleologist; potholer.

sperme [spɛʀm] *nm* sperm, semen.

sphère [sfɛʀ] *nf* 1. sphere; **s. terrestre,** globe 2. sphere (of activity, influence). **sphérique** *a* spherical.

sphincter [sfɛ̃ktɛʀ] *nm Anat:* sphincter.

sphinx [sfɛ̃ks] *nm inv* sphinx.

spiral, -aux [spiʀal, -o] 1. *a* spiral 2. *nf* **spirale,** spiral; **en spirale,** (i) *adv* in a spiral; spirally (ii) *a* spiral.

spirite [spiʀit] *n* spiritualist.

spiritisme [spiʀitism] *nm* spiritualism.

spiritualité [spiʀitɥalite] *nf* spirituality.

spirituel, -elle [spiʀitɥɛl] *a* 1. spiritual (power, life); **concert s.,** concert of sacred music 2. witty (person, answer). **spirituellement** adv 1. spiritually 2. wittily.

spiritueux, -euse [spirituø, -øz] nm Adm: spirituous liquor; **les s.,** spirits.

splendeur [splɑ̃dœr] nf splendour; **c'est une s.,** it's magnificent; **dans toute sa s.,** in all its glory. **splendide** a splendid, magnificent. **splendidement** adv splendidly.

spoliation [spɔljasjɔ̃] nf despoiling (of s.o.).

spolier [spɔlje] vtr (impf & pr sub **n. spoliions**) to despoil, rob (s.o.) **(de,** of).

spongieux, -euse [spɔ̃ʒjø, -jøz] a spongy.

spontanéité [spɔ̃taneite] nf spontaneity. **spontané** a spontaneous. **spontanément** adv spontaneously.

sporadique [spɔradik] a sporadic. **sporadiquement** adv sporadically.

spore [spɔr] nf spore.

sport [spɔr] 1. nm sport; games; **sports d'hiver,** winter sports; **chaussures de s.,** sports shoes; F: **vous allez voir du s.!** now you'll see some action! 2. a inv casual (clothes). **sportif, -ive** 1. a sporting; athletic 2. n sportsman, sportswoman; games player; athlete.

spot [spɔt] nm 1. Elcs: spot 2. Th: spot(light) 3. TV: **s. (publicitaire),** commercial, F: ad.

square [skwar] nm (public) square (with garden).

squelette [skəlɛt] nm Anat: & Fig: skeleton. **squelettique** a skeletal; **il est s.,** he's all skin and bone.

stabilisateur, -trice [stabilizatœr, -tris] 1. a stabilizing 2. nm (a) Aer: Nau: etc: stabilizer; Av: tailplane (b) Ch: stabilizer.

stabilisation [stabilizasjɔ̃] nf stabilization.

stabiliser [stabilize] vtr 1. to stabilize 2. **se s.,** to become stable.

stabilité [stabilite] nf stability. **stable** a stable; lasting (peace).

stade [stad] nm 1. stadium 2. stage (of development).

stage [staʒ] nm period of training; training course; (of teacher) teaching practice. **stagiaire** 1. a training (period) 2. n trainee.

stagnation [stagnasjɔ̃] nf stagnation.

stagner [stagne] vi to stagnate. **stagnant** a stagnant.

stalactite [stalaktit] nf Geol: stalactite.

stalagmite [stalagmite] nf Geol: stalagmite.

stalle [stal] nf 1. stall (in cathedral) 2. stall, box (in stable).

stand [stɑ̃d] nm 1. stand (on racecourse, at exhibition); stall (at fête) 2. **s. (de tir),** rifle range.

standard [stɑ̃dar] 1. nm (a) Tp: switchboard (b) **s. de vie,** standard of living 2. a inv standard.

standardisation [stɑ̃dardizasjɔ̃] nf standardization.

standardiser [stɑ̃dardize] vtr Ind: to standardize.

standardiste [stɑ̃dardist] n Tp: switchboard operator.

standing [stɑ̃diŋ] nm F: status, standing; **appartement de grand s.,** luxury flat.

star [star] nf Cin: (actress) star.

starlette [starlɛt] nf Cin: (young actress) starlet.

starter [starter] nm Aut: choke.

station [stasjɔ̃] nf 1. position; **s. debout,** standing, upright, position 2. break (in journey); halt, stop 3. (a) (bus) stop; Rail: halt; (small) station; (underground station); (taxi) rank (b) (ski, health) resort; **s. thermale,** spa (c) **s. radio,** radio station; **s. de télévision,** television broadcast station (d) El: **s. centrale,** power station. **stationnaire** a stationary.

stationnement [stasjɔnmɑ̃] nm stopping, parking; **s. interdit,** no parking; no waiting.

stationner [stasjɔne] vi to stop; (of car) to park; PN: **défense de s.,** no parking; no waiting.

station-service [stasjɔ̃sɛrvis] nf Aut: service, petrol, filling, NAm: gas, station; pl **stations-service.**

statique [statik] a static (electricity).

statisticien, -ienne [statistisjɛ̃, -jɛn] n statistician.

statistique [statistik] 1. a statistical 2. nf statistics; **les statistiques,** statistics.

statue [staty] nf statue.

statuer [statɥe] vi to give a ruling **(sur,** on).

statuette [statɥɛt] nf statuette.

statu quo [statykwo] nm status quo.

stature [statyr] nf stature, height.

statut [staty] nm (a) statute; regulation (b) status. **statutaire** a statutory.

stellaire [stelɛr] a stellar (light).

stencil [stɛnsil] nm stencil.

sténo(dactylo) [steno(daktilo)] 1. n shorthand typist 2. nf shorthand typing.

sténo(graphie) [steno(grafi)] nf shorthand. **sténographique** a shorthand.

sténographier [stenɔgrafje] vtr (impf & pr sub **n. sténographiions**) to take (sth) down in shorthand.

stentor [stɑ̃tɔr] nm **voix de s.,** stentorian voice.

steppe [stɛp] nf Geog: steppe.

stère [stɛr] nm Meas: stere.

stéréo [stereo] a inv & nf F: stereo.

stéréophonie [stereɔfɔni] nf stereophony. **stéréophonique** a stereophonic.

stéréotype [stereɔtip] nm stereotype; cliché. **stéréotypé** a stereotyped.

stérile [steril] a sterile; barren **(en,** of); fruitless (efforts).

sterilet [sterilɛ] nm Hyg: coil, loop.

stérilisateur [sterilizatœr] nm sterilizer.

stérilisation [sterilizasjɔ̃] nf sterilization.

stériliser [sterilize] vtr to sterilize.

stérilité [sterilite] nf sterility; barrenness.

sternum [stɛrnɔm] nm Anat: sternum, breastbone.

stéthoscope [stetɔskɔp] nm Med: stethoscope.

stigmate [stigmat] nm (a) mark (b) Rel: **stigmates,** stigmata.

stigmatiser [stigmatize] vtr to stigmatize.

stimulateur [stimylatœr] nm **s. cardiaque,** pacemaker.

stimulation [stimylasjɔ̃] nf stimulation.

stimuler [stimyle] vtr to stimulate. **stimulant** 1. a stimulating 2. nm (a) Med: stimulant (b) stimulus, incentive.

stimulus [stimylys] nm stimulus.

stipulation [stipylasjɔ̃] nf stipulation.

stipuler [stipyle] vtr to stipulate.

stock [stɔk] nm Com: stock (of goods).

stockage [stɔkaʒ] nm stocking (of goods).

stocker [stɔke] vtr (a) to stock goods (b) to stockpile.

stoïcisme [stɔisism] *nm* stoicism. **stoïque** *a* stoic, stoical. **stoïquement** *adv* stoically.

stop [stɔp] **1.** *int* stop! **2.** *nm Aut:* (*a*) brake light (*b*) stop sign; red light **3.** *nm F:* **faire du s.,** to hitch (-hike).

stoppage [stɔpaʒ] *nm* invisible mending.

stopper¹ [stɔpe] *vtr & i* to stop.

stopper² *vtr* to repair by invisible mending.

store [stɔr] *nm* (roller, Venetian) blind; shade; awning (of shop).

strabisme [strabism] *nm* squint(ing).

strapontin [strapɔ̃tɛ̃] *nm Aut: Th:* folding seat; tip-up seat.

stratagème [strataʒɛm] *nm* stratagem.

strate [strat] *nf Geol:* stratum.

stratège [stratɛʒ] *nm* strategist.

stratégie [strateʒi] *nf* strategy. **stratégique** *a* strategic.

stratification [stratifikasjɔ̃] *nf* stratification.

stratifier [stratifje] *vtr* to stratify.

stratosphère [stratɔsfer] *nf* stratosphere.

strict [strikt] *a* (*a*) strict; bare (essentials, minimum); plain (truth) (*b*) exact, strict (person) (**sur,** about) (*c*) severe (suit, hairstyle). **strictement** *adv* strictly; plainly.

strident [stridɑ̃] *a* strident, shrill.

strie [stri] *nf* **1.** *Geol: Anat:* stria **2.** (*a*) ridge (*b*) streak (of colour).

strier [strije] *vtr* (*impf & pr sub*) **n. striions) 1.** to striate, score **2.** (*a*) to ridge (*b*) to streak.

strophe [strɔf] *nf* stanza.

structure [stryktyr] *nf* structure. **structural, -aux** *a* structural. **structuralement** *adv* structurally. **structurel** *a* structural.

structurer [stryktyre] *vtr* to structure.

strychnine [striknin] *nf* strychnine.

stuc [styk] *nm Const:* stucco.

studieux, -ieuse [stydjø, -jøz] *a* studious. **studieusement** *adv* studiously.

studio [stydjo] *nm* **1.** (artist's, film, recording) studio **2.** one-roomed flat, studio apartment.

stupéfaction [stypefaksjɔ̃] *nf* stupefaction, amazement.

stupéfaire [stypefɛr] *vtr* to stun, to astound, to amaze. **stupéfait** *a* stunned, astounded, amazed.

stupéfier [stypefje] *vtr* (*impf & pr sub* **n. stupéfiions**) to astound, amaze, dumbfound. **stupéfiant 1.** *a* astounding, amazing **2.** *nm* narcotic; drug.

stupeur [stypœr] *nf* **1.** stupor **2.** amazement; **muet de s.,** dumbfounded.

stupide [stypid] *a* (*a*) *Lit:* stunned (*b*) stupid; silly; foolish. **stupidement** *adv* stupidly.

stupidité [stypidite] *nf* stupidity; stupid remark, action.

style [stil] *nm* **1.** stylus, style **2.** *Lit:* style; **dans le s. de,** in the style of; **robe, meubles, de s.,** period dress, furniture.

styler [stile] *vtr* to train.

stylisation [stilizasjɔ̃] *nf* stylization.

styliser [stilize] *vtr* to stylize.

stylo [stilo] *nm* (fountain, ballpoint) pen.

su [sy] *nm* knowledge; **à mon su,** to my knowledge.

suaire [sɥɛr] *nm* shroud.

suant [sɥɑ̃] *a P:* boring.

suave [sɥav] *a* (*a*) sweet, pleasant (music, scent) (*b*) suave, smooth (tone, manner). **suavement** *adv* suavely.

suavité [sɥavite] *nf* suavity; sweetness; smoothness.

subalterne [sybaltɛrn] **1.** *a* subordinate, minor (official, position); junior (employee) **2.** *nm* (*a*) subordinate (*b*) *Mil:* subaltern.

subconscient [sybkɔ̃sjɑ̃] *a & nm* subconscious.

subdiviser [sybdivize] *vtr* to subdivide.

subdivision [sybdivizjɔ̃] *nf* subdivision.

subir [sybir] *vtr* to undergo (trial, examination, change, torture); to serve (one's sentence); to be under (an influence); to suffer, sustain (defeat, loss); to submit to (punishment, fate); **faire s. qch à qn,** to subject s.o. to sth; to inflict sth on s.o.

subit [sybi] *a* sudden, unexpected. **subitement** *adv* suddenly; all of a sudden.

subjectivité [sybʒɛktivite] *nf* subjectivity.

subjectif, -ive *a* subjective. **subjectivement** *adv* subjectively.

subjonctif, -ive [sybʒɔ̃ktif, -iv] *a & nm Gram:* subjunctive (mood).

subjuguer [sybʒyge] *vtr* to subjugate, subdue; to captivate (hearts).

sublimation [syblimasjɔ̃] *nf Psy:* sublimation.

sublime [syblim] *a* sublime.

sublimer [syblime] *vtr Psy:* to sublimate.

submerger [sybmɛrʒe] *vtr* (**n. submergeons**) **1.** to submerge; to flood (field); to swamp (boat); to immerse (object) **2.** to overwhelm; **être submergé de travail,** to be snowed under with work.

submersion [sybmɛrsjɔ̃] *nf* submersion; flooding. **submersible 1.** *a* submersible **2.** *nm* submarine.

subordination [sybɔrdinasjɔ̃] *nf* subordination.

subordonner [sybɔrdɔne] *vtr* to subordinate (**à,** to); **le service est subordonné au nombre des voyageurs,** the service depends on the number of travellers. **subordonné 1.** *a* subordinate **2.** (*a*) *n* subordinate (*b*) *nf Gram:* subordinate clause.

suborner [sybɔrne] *vtr Jur:* to suborn; to bribe, to seduce (young girl).

subreptice [sybrɛptis] *a* surreptitious. **subrepticement** *adv* surreptitiously.

subséquent [sypsekɑ̃] *a* subsequent; ensuing; later (will).

subside [sypsid] *nm* subsidy; allowance.

subsidaire [sypsidjɛr] *a* subsidiary.

subsistance [sybzistɑ̃s] *nf* subsistence; livelihood; maintenance.

subsister [sybziste] *vi* **1.** to subsist; to (continue to) exist; to remain **2.** to live (**de,** on).

substance [sypstɑ̃s] *nf* **1.** substance; **en s.,** in substance **2.** matter, material, stuff. **substantiel, -elle** *a* substantial. **substantiellement** *adv* substantially.

substantif, -ive [sypstɑ̃tif, -iv] **1.** *a* substantive **2.** *nm Gram:* substantive, noun.

substituer [sypstitɥe] **1.** *vtr* to substitute (**à,** for) **2. se s. à qn,** to substitute for s.o., to take the place of s.o.

substitut [sypstity] *nm* assistant; *Jur:* deputy public prosecutor.

substitution [sypstitysjɔ̃] *nf* substitution.

subterfuge [syptɛrfyʒ] *nm* subterfuge.

subtil [syptil] *a* **1.** (*a*) subtle; discerning, shrewd (mind) (*b*) delicate, fine (distinction) (*c*) subtle (argument). **subtilement** *adv* subtly.

subtiliser [sybtilize] *vtr F:* to steal, sneak (sth).

subtilité [sybtilite] *nf* subtlety; fineness.

subvenir [sybvənir] *v ind tr* (*conj like* VENIR; *aux* **avoir**) **s. à,** to come to the aid of (s.o.); to provide for (s.o.'s needs); to meet (expenses).

subvention [sybvãsjõ] *nf* subsidy, grant.

subventionner [sybvãsjɔne] *vtr* to subsidize; to grant financial aid to (institution).

subversion [sybvɛrsjõ] *nf* subversion. **subversif, -ive** *a* subversive.

suc [syk] *nm* juice; *Bot:* sap.

succédané [syksedane] *nm* substitute (**de,** for).

succéder [syksede] *v ind tr* (**je succède; je succéderai**) **s. à qn,** to succeed, follow after, s.o.; **s. à une fortune,** to inherit a fortune; **se s.,** to follow, to succeed, one another.

succès [syksɛ] *nm* success; **avoir du s.,** (i) to turn out a success (ii) *Com:* to be a success, to catch on; **sans s.,** unsuccessful(ly); **livre à s.,** bestseller; **s. fou,** great success, *Th:* smash hit; **chanson à s.,** hit (song).

successeur [syksɛsœr] *nm* successor.

succession [syksesjɔ̃] *nf* **1.** (*a*) succession; series, sequence (of ideas, days) (*b*) succession (to the crown, the presidency); **prendre la s. de,** to succeed (s.o.); to take over (business) **2.** *Jur:* inheritance; estate. **successif, -ive** *a* successive. **successivement** *adv* successively.

succinct, -incte [syksɛ̃, syksɛ̃t] *a* succinct; frugal (meal). **succinctement** *adv* succintly; frugally.

succion [syksjõ] *nf* suction; sucking.

succomber [sykɔ̃be] *vi* **1.** to succumb; to sink (under the weight); **je succombe au sommeil,** I can't stay awake **2.** (*a*) to be overpowered (**sous le nombre,** by numbers) (*b*) to succumb (to temptation); to be overcome (by emotion) (*c*) to die; to succumb (to illness).

succulent [sykylã] *a* succulent, tasty.

succursale [sykyrsal] *nf Com:* branch.

sucer [syse] *vtr* (**n. suçons**) to suck.

sucette [sysɛt] *nf* (*a*) (baby's) dummy (*b*) lollipop.

sucre [sykr̩] *nm* sugar; **s. de canne,** cane sugar; **s. en poudre, s. semoule,** caster sugar; **s. cristallisé,** granulated sugar; **s. en morceaux,** lump sugar; **s. d'orge,** barley sugar; **il a été tout s. tout miel,** he was all sweetness and light.

sucrer [sykre] *vtr* to sugar; to sweeten; *F:* **s. les fraises,** to be an old dodderer; *P:* **se s.,** to line one's pockets. **sucré** *a* **1.** sugared, sweetened (tea); sweet (fruits); **trop s.,** too sweet; **non s.,** unsweetened **2.** sugary (words, manner).

sucrerie [sykrəri] *nf* **1.** sugar refinery **2.** *pl* sweets, confectionery; **aimer les sucreries,** to have a sweet tooth.

sucrier, -ière [sykrije, -jɛr] **1.** *a* (of) sugar; sugar-producing **2.** *n* sugar manufacturer **3.** *nm* sugar bowl, basin.

sud [syd] **1.** *nm no pl* south; **vent du s.,** south(erly) wind; **maison exposée au s.,** house facing south; **au s.,** in the south; **au s. de,** (to the) south of; **l'Amérique du S.,** South America; **vers le s.,** southward **2.** *a inv* south, southerly, southern.

sud-africain, -aine [sydafrikɛ̃, -ɛn] *a & n Geog:* South African; **la République sud-africaine,** the Republic of South Africa.

sud-est [sydɛst] **1.** *nm no pl* southeast **2.** *a inv* south-easterly; southeastern.

sudiste [sydist] *nm US: Hist:* Southerner; *a* Southern (army).

sud-ouest [sydwɛst] **1.** *nm no pl* southwest **2.** *a inv* southwesterly; southwestern.

Suède [sɥɛd] *Prnf Geog:* Sweden; **gants de s.,** suède gloves. **suédois, -oise 1.** *a* Swedish **2.** *n* Swede **3.** *nm Ling:* Swedish.

suédine [sɥedin] *nf Tex:* suedette.

suer [sɥe] **1.** *vi* (*a*) to sweat; to perspire; *F:* **tu me fais s.!** you're a pain in the neck! (*b*) (*of walls*) to ooze (*c*) to labour, to sweat **2** *vtr* to sweat (blood); to exude (poverty).

sueur [sɥœr] *nf* sweat, perspiration; **être en s.,** to be sweating; **avoir des sueurs froides,** to be in a cold sweat.

suffire [syfir] *vi* (*prp* **suffisant;** *pp* **suffi**) (*a*) to suffice; to be sufficient; to be enough; **cela ne me suffit pas (pour vivre),** that is not enough for me (to live on); **il suffit de l'écouter pour,** one only has to listen to him to; *F:* **ça suffit,** that'll do! that's enough! **il suffit d'une heure,** one hour is (long) enough (*b*) **s. à qch,** to be equal to sth; **il ne peut pas s. à tout,** he cannot cope with everything; (*of country*) **se s. (à soi-même),** to be self-supporting.

suffisance [syfizãs] *nf* **1.** sufficiency; **avoir qch en s.,** to have plenty of sth **2.** complacency; self-importance; conceit. **suffisant** *a* **1.** sufficient, adequate, enough; **c'est s. pour le voyage,** that's enough for the journey **2.** self-satisfied, self-important, conceited (air, tone); **faire le s.,** to give oneself airs. **suffisamment** *adv* sufficiently, enough, adequately.

suffixe [syfiks] *nm Gram:* suffix.

suffocant [syfɔkã] *a* (*a*) suffocating, stifling (*b*) staggering.

suffocation [syfɔkasjõ] *nf* suffocation; (fit of) choking.

suffoquer [syfɔke] **1.** *vtr* (*of smell*) to suffocate, stifle; (*of news*) to stagger (s.o.) **2.** *vi* to choke (**de,** with).

suffrage [syfraʒ] *nm* suffrage, vote; **s. universel,** universal franchise.

suggérer [syɡʒere] *vtr* (**je suggère; je suggérerai**) to suggest (**à,** to); **s. de faire qch,** to suggest doing sth.

suggestion [syɡʒɛstjõ] *nf* suggestion. **suggestif, -ive** *a* suggestive.

suicide [sɥisid] *nm* suicide. **suicidaire** *a* suicidal. **suicidé, -ée** [sɥiside] *n* (*pers*) suicide.

suicider (se) [səsɥiside] *vpr* to commit suicide.

suie [sɥi] *nf* soot.

suif [sɥif] *nm* tallow.

suintement [sɥɛ̃tmã] *nm* oozing.

suinter [sɥɛ̃te] *vi* to ooze.

Suisse¹ [sɥis] *Prnf Geog:* Switzerland; **la S. romande,** French-speaking Switzerland.

suisse² **1.** *a* Swiss **2.** *nm* (*a*) **un S.,** a Swiss (man) (*b*) *Ecc:* verger (*c*) **petit s.,** small cream cheese; petit suisse.

Suissesse [sɥisɛs] *nf often Pej:* Swiss (woman).

suite [sɥit] *nf* 1. (*a*) continuation; **faire s. à qch**, to follow sth; *Corr:* (**comme**) **s. à notre lettre**, further to our letter; *Com:* **donner s. à**, to deal with, to carry out (an order); to give effect to (a decision); (*of article*) **sans s.**, discontinued; **prendre la s. de**, to succeed to (a business); **à la s.**, one after the other; **se mettre à la s.**, to join (the back of) the queue; *adv phr* **de s.**, (i) in succession (ii) consecutively; **dix voitures de s.**, ten cars in a row; **dix heures de s.**, ten hours on end; **dix jours de s.**, ten days running; **et ainsi de s.**, and so on; *adv phr* **tout de s.**, *F:* **de s.**, at once, immediately; **dans la s.**, subsequently; **par la s.**, later on, afterwards, eventually (*b*) sequel (of book, film); *Jour:* **s. à la page 30**, continued on page 30 (*c*) coherence, consistency (in reasoning); **sans s.**, (i) disconnected (thoughts) (ii) incoherently; **s. dans les idées**, singleness of mind 2. suite, retinue 3. (*a*) series, sequence, succession (of events); **s. de malheurs**, run of misfortunes (*b*) *Mth:* series (*c*) *Mus:* (orchestral) suite 4. consequence, result; after effects (of illness); *adv phr* **par s.**, consequently; **par s. de**, in consequence of, on account of.

suivant¹ [sɥivɑ̃] 1. along (a line) 2. *prep* according to, in accordance with (instructions); **s. lui**, in his opinion; **s. que** + *ind*, depending on whether.

suivant² -**ante** [sɥivɑ̃, -ɑ̃t] *a* next, following (page, day); **le dimanche s.**, next Sunday; **notre méthode est la suivante**, our method is as follows; **au s.!** next (person) please!

suivi [sɥivi] *a* 1. connected (speech); sustained, coherent (reasoning); regular (correspondence); consistent (effort); unwavering (policy) 2. well attended, popular (lectures, classes).

suivre [sɥivr] *vtr* (*prp* **suivant**; *pp* **suivi**; *pr ind* **je suis**, **n. suivons**) 1. (*a*) to follow, to go behind, after (s.o., sth); **s. qn de près**, to follow close on s.o.'s heels; (*on letter*) (**prière de**) **faire s.**, please forward; **à s.**, to be continued; *Com:* **s. un article**, to (continue to) stock an article (*b*) to understand; **je ne vous suis pas**, I don't follow you; I'm not with you (*c*) to pursue (animal, enemy) (*d*) to be attentive to (sth); **suivez attentivement**, pay attention (*e*) to watch, observe (s.o.'s progress, course of events) (*f*) to follow up (a clue) 2. (*a*) to succeed; to come after; **ces deux mots se suivent**, these two words are consecutive; **événements qui se suivent**, events which follow each other (*b*) *impers* **il suit que**, it follows that; **comme suit**, as follows 3. (*a*) to go along, to follow (road, train of thought); **s. son chemin**, to go on one's way (*b*) to obey, conform to (fashion, law); to follow, to act upon (advice) 4. (*a*) to attend (course of lectures) (regularly); **s. un cours**, to take a course (of study) (*b*) to practise, exercise (profession, calling).

sujet¹ -**ette** [syʒɛ, -ɛt] 1. *a* subject; liable, prone, exposed (à, to); **s. à oublier**, apt to forget 2. *n* subject (of a state).

sujet² *nm* 1. (*a*) subject; cause, reason, ground (of complaint, anxiety); subject (of quarrel); **avoir s. de faire**, to have cause for doing; *prep phr* **au s. de qn, de qch**, relating to, concerning, s.o., sth; about s.o., sth (*b*) subject (matter); theme (of book, picture); topic (of conversation); **un beau s. de roman**, a fine subject for a novel (*c*) *Gram:* subject 2. individual, fellow; **mauvais s.**, bad lot; *Sch:* **bon s.**, good pupil.

sujétion [syʒesjɔ̃] *nf* 1. subjection (à, to) 2. constraint.

sulfamide [sylfamid] *nm Ch:* sulpha drug.

sulfate [sylfat] *nm Ch:* sulphate.

sulfure [sylfyr] *nm Ch:* sulphide. **sulfureux, -euse** *a* sulphurous. **sulfurique** *a* sulphuric. **sulfurisé** *a* **papier s.**, greaseproof paper.

sultan [syltɑ̃] *nm* sultan.

sultane [syltan] *nf* sultana.

summum [sɔmɔm] *nm* acme, summit.

super [sypɛr] *F:* 1. *a* super, great 2. *nm Aut:* = four-star, five-star, petrol.

superbe [sypɛrb] *a* (*a*) superb; stately (building) (*b*) magnificent (horse); marvellous (weather, show). **superbement** *adv* superbly, magnificently.

supercarburant [sypɛrkarbyrɑ̃] *nm* = four-star, five-star, petrol; high-grade petrol.

supercherie [sypɛrʃəri] *nf* swindle; hoax.

superficie [sypɛrfisi] *nf* (*a*) surface (*b*) area.

superficiel, -elle [sypɛrfisjɛl] *a* superficial; skin-deep (wound); shallow (mind); *Ph:* **tension superficielle**, surface tension. **superficiellement** *adv* superficially.

superflu [sypɛrfly] 1. *a* (*a*) superfluous, unnecessary (*b*) vain, useless (regrets) 2. *nm* superfluity; surplus.

supérieur, -eure [sypɛrjœr] 1. *a* (*a*) upper (storey, limb) (*b*) superior (à, to); **s. à la moyenne**, above average; **rester s. à la situation**, to remain master of the situation (*c*) higher, upper; **classes supérieures**, (i) upper classes (of society) (ii) *Sch:* upper forms; **enseignement s.**, higher, university, education; **animaux supérieurs**, higher animals (*d*) *Com:* of superior quality (*e*) superior (manner) 2. *n* (*a*) **il est votre s.**, (i) he's your superior (ii) he's a better man than you; **s. hiérarchique**, immediate superior (*b*) head of a convent, monastery; **la mère supérieure, la Supérieure**, the Mother Superior.

supériorité [sypɛrjorite] *nf* superiority; **s. d'âge**, seniority; **air de s.**, superior air.

superlatif, ive [sypɛrlatif, -iv] *a* superlative.

supermarché [sypɛrmarʃe] *nm Com:* supermarket.

superposer [sypɛrpoze] *vtr* to superpose, pile (à, on); to superimpose (images).

superposition [sypɛrpozisjɔ̃] *nf* superposition; superimposition.

superproduction [sypɛrprodyksjɔ̃] *nf Cin:* spectacular.

supersonique [sypɛrsonik] *a* supersonic.

superstition [sypɛrstisjɔ̃] *nf* superstition. **superstitieux, -euse** *a* superstitious. **superstitieusement** *adv* superstitiously.

superstructure [sypɛrstryktyr] *nf* superstructure.

superviser [sypɛrvize] *vtr* to supervise.

supplanter [syplɑ̃te] *vtr* to supplant.

suppléance [sypleɑ̃s] *nf* temporary post, supply post. **suppléant, -ante** *n* (*pers*) substitute (**de**, for); supply teacher; deputy; (doctor's) locum; *Th:* understudy 2. *a* temporary (official); **professeur s.**, (i) (assistant) lecturer (ii) supply teacher.

suppléer [syplee] 1. *vtr* to take the place of, to deputize for (s.o.); **se faire s.**, to find a substitute, a deputy 2. *vi* **s. à qch**, to make up for, to compensate for, sth; **s. à un poste vacant**, to fill a vacant post.

supplément [syplemɑ̃] *nm* (*a*) supplement, addition; **en s.**, additional; extra; supplementary (b) extra payment; *Rail:* excess fare (c) supplement (to book) (d) (*in restaurant*) extra charge. **supplé-mentaire** a supplementary; additional, extra, further; *Ind:* **une heure s.**, an hour's overtime; **train s.**, relief train.

suppliant, -ante [sypliɑ̃, -ɑ̃t] **1.** a imploring, pleading (look) **2.** n suppliant, supplicant.

supplication [syplikasjɔ̃] nf supplication; entreaty.

supplice [syplis] nm (a) (severe corporal) punishment; torture; **le dernier s.**, capital punishment; (b) torment, anguish, agony; **être au s.**, to be in agonies.

supplier [syplije] vtr (impf & pr sub n. **suppliions**) to beseech, to implore, to entreat; **taisez-vous, je vous en supplie**, be quiet, I beg you.

supplique [syplik] nf petition.

support [sypɔr] nm **1.** support, prop **2.** rest (for tools); stand (for lamp) **3.** *Com:* **s. publicitaire**, advertising medium.

supporter¹ [sypɔrte] vtr **1.** to support, prop, hold up, bear, carry (ceiling); to support, back up (person, theory) **2.** (a) to endure, bear; to withstand (pain, heat); to tolerate (drink); **il ne supporte pas les champignons**, mushrooms disagree with him (b) to tolerate, put up with (rudeness); **je ne peux pas le s.**, I can't stand him; **je ne supporte pas qu'il fasse cela**, I won't tolerate him doing that. **supportable** a bearable, tolerable; **pas s.**, intolerable.

supporter² [sypɔrter] nm Sp: supporter.

supposer [sypoze] vtr **1.** to suppose, assume, imagine; **en supposant que** + sub, **à s. que** + sub, **supposons que** + sub, suppose that; **on le suppose à Paris, on suppose qu'il est à Paris**, he's supposed to be in Paris **2.** to presuppose, imply; **cela lui suppose du courage**, it implies courage on his part. **supposé** a supposed, alleged (thief); assumed, false (name).

supposition [sypozisjɔ̃] nf supposition.

suppositoire [sypozitwar] nm Med: suppository.

suppression [sypresjɔ̃] nf suppression; discontinuance (of a service); removal; deletion (of word); cancellation (of train).

supprimer [syprime] vtr **1.** to suppress (newspaper, document); to abolish (law, tax); to withdraw (driving licence); to omit, delete (word); to cancel (train); to remove (difficulty); to quell (revolt); *F:* **s. qn**, to kill s.o.; **se s.**, to commit suicide **2.** **s. qch à qn**, to deprive s.o. of sth.

suppuration [sypyrasjɔ̃] nf Med: suppuration.

suppurer [sypyre] vi Med: to suppurate.

supputation [sypytasjɔ̃] nf calculation.

supputer [sypyte] vtr to calculate.

supranational, -aux [sypranasjɔnal, -o] a supranational.

suprématie [sypremasi] nf supremacy.

suprême [syprɛm] **1.** a (a) supreme; highest (degree); **pouvoir s.**, sovereignty (b) last (requests) **2.** nm Cu: (chicken) supreme. **suprêmement** adv supremely.

sur¹ [syr] prep **1.** (a) on, upon; **assis s. une chaise**, sitting on a chair; *PN:* **virages s. 2 kilomètres**, bends for 2 kilometres; **la clef s. la porte**, the key's in the door; **je n'ai pas d'argent s. moi**, I have no money on me; **page s. page**, page after page; **s. un ton de reproche**, in a reproachful tone (b) towards;

avancer s. qn, to advance on, against, s.o.; **le train s. Orléans**, the train for Orleans (c) over, above; **avoir autorité s. qn**, to have authority over s.o.; **s. toute(s) chose(s)**, above all (things); **un pont s. une rivière**, a bridge across a river (d) about, concerning **2.** (of time) (a) about (midday); towards (evening); **il va s. ses 18 ans**, he's getting on for 18 (b) **s. quoi**, whereupon; **s. ce, je vous quitte**, and now I must leave you; **il est s. son départ**, he's about to leave **3.** (a) out of; **un jour s. quatre**, one day out of four; **une fois s. deux**, every other time; **on paye les pompiers s. les fonds de la ville**, the firemen are paid out of the town funds (b) (in measurements) by; **huit mètres s. six**, eight metres by six.

sur² [syr] a sour (fruit); tart.

sûr [syr] a **1.** (a) sure; safe, secure (shelter, beach); **peu s.**, insecure, unsafe; **jouer au plus s.**, to play for safety; **le plus s. serait de**, the safest course would be to (b) trustworthy, reliable (person, memory); trusty, staunch (friend); **temps s.**, settled weather; **avoir le coup d'œil s.**, to have an accurate eye; **goût s.**, discerning taste; **avoir la main sûre, le pied s.**, to have a steady hand, to be surefooted; **mettre son argent en mains sûres**, to put one's money into safe hands **2.** sure, certain; infallible (remedy); **être s. de réussir**, to be sure of success; **je suis s. de lui**, I can depend on him; **s. de soi**, self-assured; **à coup s.**, for certain; without fail; *F:* **bien s.!** of course; *NAm:* sure! **bien s.?** you really mean it? **bien s. que non!** of course not! **3.** adv *F:* surely; **pas s.!** perhaps not! **sûrement** adv **1.** surely, certainly; **il va s. revenir**, he's sure to come back **2.** surely, securely, safely; reliably.

surabondance [syrabɔ̃dɑ̃s] nf superabundance. **surabondant** a superabundant.

surabonder [syrabɔ̃de] vi to superabound.

suranné [syrane] a outdated.

surcharge [syrʃarʒ] nf **1.** overloading **2.** (a) overload (b) excess weight (of luggage) **3.** additional charge; surcharge (on postage stamp).

surcharger [syrʃarʒe] vtr (n. **surchargeons**) to overburden, overload; **texte surchargé de corrections**, text covered with corrections.

surchauffer [syrʃofe] vtr (a) to overheat (b) *Ph:* to superheat.

surchoix [syrʃwa] nm finest quality; a inv top-quality.

surclasser [syrklase] vtr to outclass.

surcroît [syrkrwa] nm addition, increase; **s. de travail**, extra work; **par s.**, in addition; **pour s. de malheur**, to make matters worse.

surdité [syrdite] nf deafness.

sureau, -eaux [syro] nm elder (tree).

surélever [syrelve] vtr (conj like ÉLEVER) Const: etc: to raise, heighten.

surenchère [syrɑ̃ʃer] nf (a) higher bid; outbidding (b) **une s. de violence**, ever-increasing violence.

surenchérir [syrɑ̃ʃerir] vi to overbid; **s. (sur qn)**, to outbid (s.o.), to bid higher (than s.o.).

surestimation [syrestimasjɔ̃] nf overestimate, overvaluation.

surestimer [syrestime] vtr to overestimate, overvalue (price, cost); **s. qn**, to overrate s.o.

sûreté [syrte] nf **1.** (a) safety, security; **être en s.**, to be safe, in a safe place; **mettre en s.**, to put in a safe place; **serrure de s.**, safety lock (*b*) security, protection; (*police*) **agent de la s.**, detective; **la S.** = New Scotland Yard **2.** sureness (of hand, foot); soundness (of taste, judgment); **s. de soi**, self-confidence **3.** *Com:* surety, security, guarantee.

surévaluer [syrevalɥe] *vtr* to overestimate.

surexcitation [syrɛksitasjɔ̃] *nf* overexcitement.

surexciter [syrɛksite] *vtr* to overexcite. **surexcité** *a* overexcited.

surface [syrfas] *nf* (*a*) surface; **faire s., revenir en s.**, (i) (*of submarine*) to surface (ii) (*of pers*) *F:* to come to; **tout en s.**, superficial (*b*) area; **s. utile**, working surface; **s. couverte**, floor area.

surfait [syrfɛ] *a* overrated.

surfin [syrfɛ̃] *a Com:* superfine.

surgelé [syrʒəle] *a* deep-frozen; *a & nm* (**produits**) **surgelés**, (deep-)frozen foods.

surgir [syrʒir] *vi* (*aux avoir, occ être*) to rise; to come into view; to loom (up); **s. brusquement**, to appear suddenly; (*of plant*) to spring up; (*of difficulties*) to crop up.

surhomme [syrɔm] *nm* superman. **surhumain** *a* superhuman.

surimposer [syrɛ̃poze] *vtr* to increase the tax on (sth); to overtax.

surir [syrir] *vi* to turn sour.

sur-le-champ [syrləʃɑ̃] *adv* at once; on the spot; immediately.

surlendemain [syrlɑ̃dmɛ̃] *nm* **le s. de son départ**, two days after he left; **elle est partie le s.**, she left two days later.

surmenage [syrmənaʒ] *nm* overwork; **s. intellectuel**, mental fatigue.

surmener [syrməne] *vtr* (*conj like* MENER) to overwork; **se s.**, to overwork (oneself); to overdo it.

surmonter [syrmɔ̃te] **1.** *vtr* to overcome, surmount (obstacle); to master, get the better of (one's anger, grief) **2. se s.**, to control oneself, one's emotions.

surnager [syrnaʒe] *vi* (**n. surnageons**) (*a*) to float on the surface (*b*) to remain.

surnaturel, -elle [syrnatyrɛl] *a* (*a*) supernatural; *nm* **le s.**, the supernatural (*b*) inexplicable; uncanny.

surnom [syrnɔ̃] *nm* nickname.

surnombre [syrnɔ̃br] *nm* **en s.**, too many; **exemplaires en s.**, spare copies.

surnommer [syrnɔme] *vtr* **s. qn, qch**, to (nick)name s.o., sth.

surpasser [syrpase] *vtr* to surpass; to exceed (one's hopes); to outdo (a rival); to transcend (s.o.); **se s.**, to surpass oneself.

surpeuplement [syrpœpləmɑ̃] *nm* overpopulation. **surpeuplé** *a* overpopulated.

surplis [syrpli] *nm Ecc:* surplice.

surplomb [syrplɔ̃] *nm* overhang; **en s.**, overhanging.

surplomber [syrplɔ̃be] *vi & tr* to overhang.

surplus [syrply] *nm* surplus, excess; **payer le s.**, to pay the difference; **au s.**, besides, what's more; **marchandises en s.**, surplus goods.

surpopulation [syrpɔpylasjɔ̃] *nf* overpopulation.

surprenant [syrprənɑ̃] *a* surprising, astonishing.

surprendre [syrprɑ̃dr] *vtr* (*conj like* PRENDRE) **1.** (*a*) to surprise; to come upon (s.o.) unexpectedly; to catch (s.o.) unawares; **aller s. un ami chez lui**, to

drop in unexpectedly on a friend; **être surpris par la pluie**, to be caught in the rain; **je me surpris à pleurer**, I found myself crying (*b*) to intercept (glance); to overhear **2.** to astonish; **ça a l'air de vous s.**, you seem surprised. **surprenant** *a* surprising, astonishing. **surpris** *a* surprised.

surprise [syrpriz] *nf* surprise; **à sa grande s.**, much to his surprise; **par s.**, by surprise; **il m'a fait sa demande par s.**, he sprang his request on me; **quelle bonne s.!** what a pleasant surprise!

surprise-partie [syrprizparti] *nf* party; *pl* surprises-parties.

surproduction [syrprɔdyksjɔ̃] *nf* overproduction.

surréalisme [syrealism] *nm* surrealism. **surréaliste** *a & n* surrealist.

sursaut [syrso] *nm* (involuntary) start, jump; **s. d'énergie**, burst of energy; **se réveiller en s.**, to wake up with a start.

sursauter [syrsote] *vi* to start (involuntarily); to (give a) jump; **faire s. qn**, to startle s.o.

surseoir [syrswar] *v ind tr* (*pr p* **sursoyant**; *pr ind* **je sursois, n. sursoyons**) *Jur:* **s. à un jugement**, to suspend a judgment; **s. à l'exécution d'un condamné**, to reprieve a condemned man.

sursis [syrsi] *nm Jur:* delay; reprieve; **condamné à un an avec s.**, given a one-year suspended sentence. **sursitaire** *a & nm* provisionally exempted (conscript).

surtaxe [syrtaks] *nf* supertax, surtax.

surtaxer [syrtakse] *vtr* to surtax; to surcharge.

surtout [syrtu] *adv* particularly, especially; **s. n'oubliez pas de**, above all, don't forget to; *conj phr F:* **s. que**, especially as.

surveillance [syrvejɑ̃s] *nf* supervision, surveillance; *Sch:* invigilation.

surveillant, -ante [syrvejɑ̃, -ɑ̃t] *n* supervisor; overseer; shopwalker; *Sch:* invigilator.

surveiller [syrveje] **1.** *vtr* (*a*) to supervise (work); to tend (machine) (*b*) to watch (over), observe; to look after (s.o.); *Sch:* to invigilate; to keep an eye on (children) **2. se s.**, to keep a watch on oneself.

survenir [syrvənir] *vi* (*conj. like* VENIR; *aux être*) (*of events*) to happen, to occur; *F:* to crop up; (*of difficulty*) to arise; (*of pers*) to arrive unexpectedly.

survêtement [syrvɛtmɑ̃] *nm* tracksuit.

survie [syrvi] *nf* survival; *Rel:* afterlife.

survivance [syrvivɑ̃s] *nf* survival.

survivre [syrvivr] *v ind tr* (*conj like* VIVRE; *aux avoir*) to survive, outlive (**à qn, à qch**, s.o., sth); **se s.**, to live on (in one's works). **survivant, -ante 1.** *a* surviving **2.** *n* survivor.

survol [syrvɔl] *nm* (*a*) flight over (a place) (*b*) skimming (of problem).

survoler [syrvɔle] *vtr Av:* to fly over (mountain); **s. une question**, to get a general view of a problem.

survolté [syrvɔlte] *a* **1.** *El:* boosted **2.** *F:* excited, worked up.

sus [sy(s)] *adv* **en s. de**, in addition to.

susceptibilité [sysɛptibilite] *nf* susceptibility; sensitiveness.

susceptible [sysɛptibl] *a* **1. s. de**, susceptible (of proof); open to (improvement); **s. de faire qch**, capable of doing sth; liable, likely, to do sth **2.** susceptible, touchy, easily offended.

susciter [sys(s)ite] *vtr* to give rise to (difficulties); to cause (astonishment); to arouse (hostility).

suspect, -ecte [syspε(kt), -εkt] **1.** *a* suspicious, doubtful, suspect; **devenir s.** (à qn), to arouse (s.o.'s) suspicion; **cela m'est s.**, I don't like the look of it; **tenir qn pour s.**, to be suspicious of s.o. **2.** *n* suspect.

suspecter [syspεkte] *vtr* to suspect (s.o.); to doubt (sth); to cast suspicion on (s.o.'s good faith).

suspendre [syspɑ̃dr̩] **1.** *vtr* (*a*) to suspend; to hang up (clothes); to sling (hammock) (*b*) to defer, postpone; to suspend, stop (payment); to suspend (judgment); to adjourn (meeting) (*c*) to suspend (an official) **2.** **se s.**, to hang (à, from; **par,** by).

suspendu [syspɑ̃dy] *a* suspended; hanging; **pont s.**, suspension bridge; **voiture bien suspendue,** car with good suspension; **être s. aux lèvres de qn**, to be hanging on s.o.'s every word.

suspens [syspɑ̃] *nm* **en s.**, in suspense; (i) (*of pers*) in doubt (ii) (*of thg*) in abeyance; **tenir qn en s.**, to keep s.o. in suspense.

suspense [syspεns] *nm* suspense.

suspension [syspɑ̃sjɔ̃] *nf* **1.** (*a*) suspension; hanging (up) (*b*) *Ch:* suspension **2.** (*a*) (temporary) discontinuance, interruption; suspension (of hostilities, payment); adjournment; *Gram:* **points de s.**, suspension points (*b*) suspension (of an official) **3.** (*a*) light pendant; ceiling lamp (*b*) *Aut: etc:* suspension; springs, springing.

suspicion [syspisjɔ̃] *nf* suspicion.

susurrer [sysyre] *vi Lit:* to murmur, to whisper.

suture [sytyr] *nf Surg:* suture.

suturer [sytyre] *vtr Surg:* to suture, to stitch.

suzerain, -aine [syzrɛ̃, -ɛn] *a & n* suzerain.

suzeraineté [syzrɛnte] *nf* suzerainty.

svelte [svεlt] *a* slender.

sveltesse [svεltεs] *nf* slenderness.

SVP *abbr s'il vous plaît.*

sycomore [sikɔmɔr] *nm Bot:* sycamore.

syllable [silab] *nf* syllable. **syllabique** *a* syllabic.

syllogisme [silɔʒism] *nm* syllogism.

sylphe [silf] *nm*, **sylphide** [silfid] *nf* sylph; **taille de sylphide,** sylphlike waist.

sylvestre [silvεstr] *a* woodland (tree).

sylviculture [silvikyltyr] *nf* forestry.

symbole [sɛ̃bɔl] *nm* symbol. **symbolique** *a* symbolic. **symboliquement** *adv* sybolically.

symboliser [sɛ̃bɔlize] *vtr* to symbolize.

symbolisme [sɛ̃bɔlism] *nm* symbolism.

symétrie [simetri] *nf* symmetry. **symétrique** *a* symmetrical. **symétriquement** *adv* symmetrically.

sympa [sɛ̃pa] *a F:* likeable; nice.

sympathie [sɛ̃pati] *nf* (*a*) sympathy, instinctive attraction, liking; **avoir de la s. pour qn,** to like s.o.'s; **se prendre de s. pour qn,** to take a (liking) to s.o. (*b*) **idées qui ne sont pas en s.**, conflicting ideas. **sympathique** *a* **1.** sympathetic; in sympathy (with

s.o.'s ideas) **2.** likeable, attractive, nice (personality); congenial (surroundings); **il m'a été tout de suite s.**, I took to him at once **3.** *Anat:* sympathetic (nerve). **sympathiquement** *adv* in a friendly way.

sympathiser [sɛ̃patize] *vi* to get on well (together, with s.o.); to be friendly. **sympathisant, -ante** **1.** *a* sympathizing **2.** *n Pol:* sympathizer.

symphonie [sɛ̃fɔni] *nf Mus:* symphony. **symphonique** *a* symphonic.

symposium [sɛ̃pozjɔm] *nm* symposium.

symptôme [sɛ̃ptom] *nm* (*a*) symptom (*b*) sign, indication. **symptômatique** *a* symptomatic.

synagogue [sinagɔg] *nf* synagogue.

synchronisation [sɛ̃krɔnizasjɔ̃] *nf* synchronization.

synchroniser [sɛ̃krɔnize] *vtr* to synchronize. **synchronisé** *a* synchronized.

synchronisme [sɛ̃krɔnism] *nm* synchronism.

syncope [sɛ̃kɔp] *nf* **1.** *Med:* blackout, fainting fit; **tomber en s.**, to faint **2.** *Mus:* (*a*) syncopation (*b*) syncopated note.

syndic [sɛ̃dik] *nm* syndic; **s. de faillite,** official receiver.

syndicat [sɛ̃dika] *nm* syndicate; (trade, tenants') association; (employers') federation; **s. d'initiative,** tourist (information) office; **s. (ouvrier),** trade union. **syndical, -aux** *a* syndical; **mouvement s.,** trade union movement.

syndicalisme [sɛ̃dikalism] *nm* trade unionism. **syndicaliste** (*a*) *a* trade-union (*b*) *n* trade unionist.

syndiquer [sɛ̃dike] **1.** *vtr* to unionize **2.** **se s.**, to form a union; to join a union. **syndiqué, -ée 1.** *a* ouvrier s., trade unionist; **ouvriers non-syndiqués,** non-union workers **2.** *n* union member.

syndrome [sɛ̃drom] *nm Med:* syndrome.

synode [sinɔd] *nm Ecc:* synod.

synonymie [sinɔnimi] *nf* synonymy. **synonyme 1.** *a* synonymous (**de**, with) **2.** *nm* synonym.

syntaxe [sɛ̃taks] *nf Gram:* syntax. **syntactique, syntaxique** *a* syntactic(al).

synthèse [sɛ̃tεz] *nf* synthesis; recap, summary.

synthétique *a* synthetic. **synthétiquement** *adv* synthetically.

synthétiser [sɛ̃tetize] *vtr* to synthesize.

syphilis [sifilis] *nf Med:* syphilis. **syphilitique** *a & n* syphilitic.

Syrie [siri] *Prnf Geog:* Syria. **syrien, -ienne** *a & n* Syrian.

systématisation [sistematizasjɔ̃] *nf* systematization.

systématiser [sistematize] *vtr* to systematize.

système [sistεm] *nm* system; method, plan; **s. métrique,** metric system; **s. nerveux,** nervous system; **le s. D,** resourcefulness; *F:* **il me tape sur le s.,** he gets on my nerves. **systématique** *a* systematic; (*of pers*) dogmatic. **systématiquement** *adv* systematically.

T

T, t [te] *nm* (the letter) T, t (*a*) **t euphonique** *forms a link between verbal endings -a, -e and the pronouns* **il, elle, on; va-t-il? ira-t-elle? donne-t-on?** (*b*) **en T, T-shaped.**

t *abbr* **1.** *tour* **2.** *Meas:* tonne.

ta [ta] *see* **ton¹.**

tabac¹ [taba] *nm* **1.** *Bot:* tobacco (plant) **2.** tobacco; **t. à priser,** snuff; **(débit, bureau) de t.,** tobacconist's (shop); **c'est du même t.,** it's the same thing **3.** *a inv* tobacco-coloured.

tabac² *nm F:* **passer qn à t.,** to beat s.o. up.

tabasser [tabase] *vtr F:* to beat (s.o.) up.

tabatière [tabatjer] *nf* (*a*) snuffbox (*b*) *Const:* hinged skylight.

tabernacle [tabernakl] *nm* tabernacle.

table [tabl] *nf* **1.** (*a*) table; **t. pliante,** folding table; **t. roulante,** trolley; **t. d'opération,** operating table; **t. de nuit,** bedside table; *Pol:* **t. ronde,** round-table conference (*b*) **mettre la t.,** to lay, to set, the table; **la t. est bonne,** the food's good; **se mettre à t.** (i) to sit down to table (ii) *P:* to confess, to come clean; **à t.!** lunch, dinner, is ready! **être à t.,** to be having a meal **2.** *DomEc:* **t. de cuisson,** hob (unit) **3.** (*flat surface*) **t. de travail,** work(ing) surface, top **4.** list, catalogue; **t. des matières,** (table of) contents.

tableau, -eaux [tablo] *nm* **1.** (*a*) board; *Sch:* **t. (noir),** blackboard; **t. d'affichage,** notice board; **t. de bord,** (i) *Aut:* dashboard (ii) *Av:* instrument panel; *El:* **t. de distribution,** switchboard (*b*) (*in hotel*) key rack **2.** (*a*) picture, painting; **un magnifique t.,** a beautiful scene (*b*) *Th:* scene **3.** (*a*) list, table; chart; (duty) roster; *Rail:* timetable; *F:* **gagner sur les deux, sur tous, les tableaux,** to win on both, on all, counts (*b*) **être rayé du t.,** to be struck off the rolls (*c*) **t. d'honneur,** honours board, list **4.** *Ven:* bag.

tabler [table] *vi* **t. sur qch,** to count, to bank, on sth.

tablette [tablet] *nf* **1.** shelf (of bookcase); flap (of desk) **2.** *A:* writing tablet; *Fig:* **mettre qch sur ses tablettes,** to make a note of sth; bar (of chocolate); *Pharm:* tablet.

tablier [tablije] *nm* **1.** apron; pinafore; overall **2.** (*a*) *Aut:* dashboard (*b*) hood (of fireplace) **3.** (steel) shutter.

tabou [tabu] *a & nm* taboo.

tabouret [tabure] *nm* stool; footstool.

tac [tak] *nm* click; **répondre du t. au t.,** to give tit for tat.

tache [taʃ] *nf* (*a*) stain, spot; blob (of paint); flaw (in precious stone); bruise (on fruit); blot (of ink); stain (on reputation); **sans t.,** spotless (*b*) **t. de rousseur,** freckle.

tâche [taʃ] *nf* task; job; **travail à la t.,** piecework; **prendre à t. de faire qch,** to undertake to do sth.

tacher [taʃe] **1.** *vtr* to stain, spot (garment); to sully (reputation); **taché d'encre,** inkstained **2. se t.,** to get dirty (i) to soil one's clothes (ii) to stain.

tâcher [taʃe] *vi* to try, endeavour (**de,** to); **tâche de ne pas recommencer,** mind it doesn't happen again.

tacheté [taʃte] *a* spotted, speckled; mottled; tabby (cat).

tacite [tasit] *a* tacit; implied. **tacitement** *adv* tacitly.

taciturne [tasityrn] *a* taciturn, silent.

tacot [tako] *nm F:* (*car*) banger, crate.

tact [takt] *nm* tact; **avoir du t.,** to be tactful; **avec t., sans t.,** tactfully, tactlessly.

tactile [taktil] *a* tactile.

tactique [taktik] **1.** *a* tactical **2.** *nf* tactics.

taffetas [tafta] *nm Tex:* taffeta.

taie [te] *nf* **1. t. d'oreiller,** pillowcase, pillowslip **2.** *Med:* leucoma.

taillader [tajade] *vtr* to slash, gash.

taille [taj] *nf* **1.** cutting (of stone, gems, hair); *Hort:* pruning, trimming; **t. de cheveux,** haircut **2.** (*method of cutting*) cut **3.** edge (of sword) **4.** (*a*) stature, height (of pers); dimensions (of monument); **t. debout,** full height (of s.o.); **de grande t., de t. moyenne,** very tall, of medium height; **de petite t.,** small; *Com:* **quelle est votre t.?** what size do you take? *F:* **il est de t. à vous battre,** he's strong enough to beat you; **il n'est pas de t. à être chef,** he's not cut out to be a leader (*b*) waist; **tour de t.,** waist measurement; **elle a la t. mannequin,** she has a perfect figure; **prendre qn par la t.,** to put an arm round s.o.'s waist.

taille-crayon(s) [tajkrɛjɔ̃] *nm inv* pencil sharpener.

tailler [taje] **1.** *vtr* (*a*) to cut (stone, diamond, grass, hair); to prune (tree); to trim, clip (hedge, beard); to dress (vine); to sharpen (pencil); **se t. un chemin à travers la foule,** to carve one's way through the crowd (*b*) to cut out (a garment); **bien taillé,** well cut **2.** *vi* **t. dans la chair,** to cut into the flesh **3.** *P:* **se t.,** to leave, to buzz off. **taillé** *a* **bien t.,** well built; **t. pour commander,** cut out to be a leader.

tailleur, -euse [tajœr, -øz] *n* **1.** (*a*) (stone) cutter (*b*) tailor; **s'asseoir en t.,** to sit cross-legged **2.** *nm* (woman's tailored) suit.

taillis [taji] *nm* copse, coppice.

tain [tɛ̃] *nm* silvering (for mirrors); **miroir sans t.,** two-way mirror.

taire [ter] **1.** *vtr* (*prp* **taisant;** *pp* **tu**) to say nothing about (sth); **qn dont je tairai le nom,** s.o. who shall be nameless **2. se t.,** to hold one's tongue, to be(come) silent; **faire t. (qn),** to silence (s.o.), *F:* to shut (s.o.) up; **tais-toi!** be quiet! *F:* shut up!

talc [talk] *nm* talc; talcum powder.

talent [talɑ̃] *nm* talent, aptitude, gift; **avoir du t.,** to be talented; **il a le t. de se faire des ennemis,** he has a gift for making enemies. **talentueux, -euse** *a* talented.

taler [tale] *vtr* to bruise (fruit).

talisman [talismɑ̃] *nm* talisman.
taloche [talɔʃ] *nf F:* cuff, clout.
talocher [talɔʃe] *vtr F:* to hit, clout (s.o.).
talon [talɔ̃] *nm* **1.** heel; **être sur les talons de qn,** to be (hot) on s.o.'s heels; **tourner les talons,** to take to one's heels; **t. d'Achille,** Achilles' heel **2.** (*a*) (*at cards*) stock; talon (*b*) counterfoil, stub (of cheque).
talonner [talɔne] *vtr* (*a*) to follow (s.o.) closely; to hound (s.o.) (*b*) to spur on (horse) (*c*) *Rugby Fb:* to heel (out).
talonneur [talɔnœr] *nm Rugby Fb:* hooker.
talquer [talke] *vtr* to sprinkle with talc.
talus [taly] *nm* **1.** slope; **en t.,** sloping **2.** bank, embankment, ramp.
tambouille [tɑ̃buj] *nf P:* food, grub.
tambour [tɑ̃bur] *nm* **1.** drum; **bruit de t.,** drumming; **t. de basque,** tambourine; **sans t. ni trompette,** quietly, without fuss **2.** drummer; **t. de ville,** town crier **3.** (*a*) (*container*) barrel, cylinder, drum (*b*) revolving door (*c*) brake drum (*d*) drum (of washing machine) (*e*) (embroidery) frame.
tambourin [tɑ̃burɛ̃] *nm* tambourine.
tambouriner [tɑ̃burine] **1.** *vi* to drum (with the fingers) **2.** *vtr* to drum out (rhythm).
tambour-major [tɑ̃burmaʒɔr] *nm Mil:* drum major; *pl* tambours-majors.
tamis [tami] *nm* sieve, sifter; strainer; *Ind:* riddle, screen; **passer au t.,** (i) to sift (ii) to examine (sth) thoroughly.
tamisage [tamizaʒ] *nm* sieving; sifting; straining; filtering.
Tamise (la) [latamiz] *Prnf* the Thames.
tamiser [tamize] *vtr* to sieve; to sift, screen; to strain, filter.
tampon [tɑ̃pɔ̃] *nm* **1.** plug, stopper; waste plug (of bath) **2.** (*a*) (i) *Surg:* wad, swab (ii) **t. hygiénique, périodique,** tampon (*b*) (inking) pad (*c*) rubber stamp; postmark (*d*) **t. buvard,** blotter **3. t. de choc,** buffer; **état t.,** buffer state.
tamponner [tɑ̃pɔne] *vtr* **1.** to plug; to stop up; *Med:* to plug (wound) **2.** to dab; to rubberstamp; **se t. le front,** to mop one's brow. **3.** to run into, collide with (another car or train).
tam-tam [tamtam] *nm* (*a*) tomtom (*b*) *F:* fuss, ballyhoo.
tancer [tɑ̃se] *vtr* (**n. tançons**) *Lit:* to berate, to scold (s.o.).
tandem [tɑ̃dɛm] *nm* (*a*) tandem (bicycle) (*b*) pair, twosome.
tandis [tɑ̃di(s)] *conj phr* **t. que** (*a*) whereas (*b*) while, whilst.
tangage [tɑ̃gaʒ] *nm Nau: etc:* pitching.
tangent, -ente [tɑ̃ʒɑ̃, -ɑ̃t] **1.** *a Mth:* tangential, tangent (à, to); *P:* **c'est t.,** it's touch and go **2.** *n F:* borderline case **3.** *nf Mth* tangent; *F:* **prendre la t.,** (i) to dodge the question (ii) to slip away.
Tanger [tɑ̃ʒe] *Prn Geog:* Tangier(s).
tangible [tɑ̃ʒibl] *a* tangible.
tango [tɑ̃go] *nm* tango.
tanguer [tɑ̃ge] *vi* (*of ship*) to pitch; *Fig:* to reel.
tanière [tanjɛr] *nf* den, lair.
tank [tɑ̃k] *nm Mil:* tank.
tanker [tɑ̃kɛr] *nm Nau:* tanker.
tannage [tanaʒ] *nm* tanning (of hides).

tanner [tane] *vtr* **1.** to tan (hides) **2.** *P:* (*a*) to pester (s.o.) (*b*) **t. (le cuir à) qn,** to thrash s.o. **tannant** *a P:* boring, annoying.
tannerie [tanri] *nf* **1.** tannery **2.** tanning (of hides).
tanneur [tanœr] *nm* tanner.
tant [tɑ̃] *adv* **1.** (*a*) so much; **t. de bonté,** such kindness; *F:* **t. qu'à faire, j'aimerais autant y aller,** while I'm about it, if it comes to that, I'd just as soon go there; **t. pour cent,** so much per cent; **il a t. et plus d'argent,** he has any amount of money; **ils tiraient t. et plus,** they were pulling with all their strength; **faire t. et si bien que,** to work to such good purpose that; **t. s'en faut,** far from it; **t. soit peu,** a little; somewhat (*b*) so many; as many; **t. de fois,** so often; **t. d'amis,** so many friends (*c*) **t. que,** as much as, as many as; **t. que possible,** as much as possible (*d*) so; to such a degree; **n'aimer rien t. que le chocolat,** to like nothing so much as chocolate; **en t. que,** in so far as; (*e*) **t. aimable qu'il soit,** however pleasant he may be; (*f*) **t. mieux,** so much the better; good! **t. pis!** too bad! what a pity! never mind! **2.** (*a*) as much, as well (as); **j'ai couru t. que j'ai pu,** I ran as hard as I could; **t. en Inde qu'ailleurs,** both in India and elsewhere; **t. bien que mal,** somehow or other, after a fashion (*b*) as long, as far, (as); **t. que je vivrai,** as long as I live; **t. que la vue s'étend,** as far as the eye can see; **t. que vous y êtes,** while you're at it (*c*) so long (as); **t. qu'il n'est pas là,** so long as he isn't there.
tante [tɑ̃t] *nf* **1.** aunt; **t. à la mode de Bretagne** (i) first cousin once removed (ii) very distant relative **2.** *P:* homosexual, queer.
tantième [tɑ̃tjɛm] *nm Com:* percentage, quota (of profits).
tantinet [tɑ̃tinɛ] *nm F:* tiny bit; **un t. plus long,** a fraction longer.
tantôt [tɑ̃to] *adv* **1.** this afternoon; **t. triste, t. gai,** now sad, now happy; **t. à Paris, t. à Londres,** sometimes in Paris, sometimes in London.
taon [tɑ̃] *nm* gadfly, horsefly.
tapage [tapaʒ] *nm* (*a*) din; *F:* racket; **faire du t.,** to make a row (*b*) fuss, scandal. **tapageur, -euse** *a* (*a*) noisy; rowdy (party) (*b*) loud, flashy (clothes).
tapant [tapɑ̃] *a* **à 7 heures tapant(es),** on the stroke of 7, at 7 o'clock sharp.
tape [tap] *nf* slap; pat.
tape-à-l'œil [tapalœj] **1.** *a inv* loud, flashy **2.** *nm* show, flash.
taper [tape] **1.** *vtr* (*a*) to tap, smack, slap, hit; **t. une lettre,** to type a letter; *vi* **savoir t.,** to be able to type; **t. un air (au piano),** to thump out a tune (on the piano); *P:* **se t. qch,** (i) to treat oneself to sth (ii) to get landed with sth (*b*) *F:* **t. qn de mille francs,** to touch s.o. for a thousand francs **2.** *vi* to tap, rap (**sur,** on); **le soleil nous tapait sur la tête,** the sun was beating down on us; *F:* **ça tape,** it's pretty hot; **t. sur les nerfs de qn,** to get on s.o.'s nerves; **t. dans le tas,** (i) to pitch into the crowd (ii) (*meal*) to tuck in; **t. du pied,** to stamp one's foot.
tapette [tapɛt] *nf* **1.** (*a*) carpet beater (*b*) fly swatter (*c*) mousetrap (*d*) *P:* tongue; **il a une bonne t.!** he's a chatterbox **2.** *P:* homosexual, pansy.
tapeur, -euse [tapœr, -øz] *n F:* cadger.
tapin [tapɛ̃] *nm P:* **faire le t.,** to walk the streets.
tapinois [tapinwa] *adv phr* **en t.,** stealthily.

tapioca [tapjɔka] *nm* tapioca.

tapir (se) [sətapir] *vpr* to crouch; to cower; to hide.

tapis [tapi] *nm* 1. cloth, cover; **t. vert**, gaming table; **mettre qch sur le t.**, to bring sth up for discussion 2. carpet; **t. de pied**, rug 3. **t. roulant** (i) conveyor belt (ii) moving walkway 4. mat; **aller au t.**, to be knocked down.

tapisser [tapise] *vtr* (a) to hang (wall) with tapestry (b) to paper (room); **murs tapissés d'affiches**, walls covered with posters (c) to line (box) with paper.

tapisserie [tapisri] *nf* 1. tapestry making 2. tapestry; (*at dance*) **faire t.**, to be a wallflower 3. tapestry work 4. wallpaper.

tapissier, -ière [tapisje, -jɛr] *n* 1. tapestry maker 2. (a) (interior) decorator (b) upholsterer.

tapoter [tapɔte] *vtr* to pat (child's cheek).

taquin, -ine [takɛ̃, -in] 1. *a* (given to) teasing 2 *n* tease.

taquiner [takine] *vtr* to tease (s.o.); to bother, worry (s.o.).

taquinerie [takinri] *nf* teasing.

tarabiscoté [tarabiskɔte] *a* over-elaborate.

tarabuster [tarabyste] *vtr* (a) (*of pers*) to pester (s.o.) (b) (*of thg*) to bother, worry (s.o.).

taratata [taratata] *int* nonsense! rubbish!

tard [tar] (a) *adv* late; **plus t.**, later (on); **au plus t.**, at the latest; *impers* **il est t.**, **il se fait t.**, it's (getting) late; **pas plus t. qu'hier**, only yesterday (b) *nm* **sur le t.**, late (on) in life.

tarder [tarde] *vi* 1. (a) to delay; **sans t.**, without delay; **t. en chemin**, to loiter on the way; **t. à faire qch.**, to be slow in, to put off, doing sth (b) **il ne va pas t. (à venir)**, he won't be long (in coming) 2. *impers* **il lui tarde de partir**, he is longing to get away. **tardif, -ive** *a* belated (regrets); late (hour, fruit). **tardivement** *adv* belatedly.

tare [tar] *nf* 1. (a) *Com:* loss in value (due to damage, waste) (b) (physical, moral) defect 2. *Com:* tare; **faire la t.**, to allow for the tare. **taré, -ée** 1. *a* (a) depraved, corrupt (b) degenerate 2. *n* degenerate; *F:* cretin.

targette [tarʒɛt] *nf* (door) bolt.

targuer (se) [sətarge] *vpr* **se t. de qch**, to pride oneself on sth.

tarif [tarif] *nm* (a) tariff, price list (b) rate; tariff; scale of charges; **tarifs postaux**, postal rates; **plein t.**, (i) *Rail:* full fare (ii) full tariff (iii) *F:* maximum penalty. **tarifaire** *a* tariff (laws).

tarifer [tarife] *vtr* to fix the rate, the price, of (goods).

tarir [tarir] 1. *vtr* to dry up (spring, tears); **se t.**, to dry up 2. *vi* (*of waters*) to dry up, run dry; **une fois sur ce sujet il ne tarit pas**, once he is on the subject he never stops.

tarissement [tarismã] *nm* drying up.

tartare [tartar] 1. *a & n* Tartar 2. *a & nm Cu:* **sauce t.**, tartar(e) sauce; **(steak) t.**, steak tartare.

tarte [tart] 1. *nf Cu:* (open) tart; flan; *F:* **c'est de la t.**, it's easy, a piece of cake 2. *nf P:* slap 3. *a F:* (a) (*pers*) stupid, daft (b) (*thg*) ugly.

tartelette [tartəlɛt] *nf Cu:* tartlet, tart.

tartine [tartin] *nf* 1. slice of bread (and butter) 2. *F:* long-winded speech.

tartiner [tartine] *vtr* to spread (bread) with butter; to butter; **fromage à t.**, cheese spread.

tartre [tartr̩] *nm* tartar (on teeth); fur (in boiler).

tas [tɑ] *nm* 1. (a) heap, pile (of stones, wood); stook, shock (of wheat); **mettre des objets en t.**, to pile things up (b) mass (of things, people); **un t. de mensonges**, a pack of lies; **il y en a des t. (et des t.)**, there are heaps of them; *F: Pej:* **tout un t. de gens**, a whole gang of people; **t. d'imbéciles!** bunch of fools! (c) **tirer dans le t.**, to fire into the crowd 2. building site; **être sur le t.**, to be on the job; **formation sur le t.**, on-the-job training.

tasse [tɑs] *nf* (a) cup; **t. à café**, coffee cup; **t. de café**, cup of coffee (b) **boire la t.**, to get a mouthful (when swimming).

tassement [tasmã] *nm* compressing, packing; settling.

tasser [tɑse] 1. *vtr* to compress; to squeeze, (objects) together; to ram, pack (earth); to pack (passengers into vehicle) 2. **se t.** (a) (*of foundations*) (i) to settle, set (ii) to sink, subside; *F:* **ça se tassera**, things will settle down; **il se t.**, he is beginning to shrink (with age) (b) to crowd (up) together; **tassez-vous un peu**, squeeze up a bit.

tata [tata] *nf* 1. *F:* auntie 2. *P:* homosexual, pansy.

tâter [tɑte] *vtr* to feel, touch; to try, to test (s.o.'s courage); **t. le terrain**, to see how the land lies; **avancer en tâtant**, to grope one's way forward 2. *v ind tr* **t. de qch**, to try one's hand at sth; *F:* **il a tâté de la prison**, he's done time 3. **se t.** (a) to feel oneself (for injuries) (b) to think it over.

tatillon, -onne [tatijɔ̃, -ɔn] *a* finicky, fussy.

tâtonnement [tɑtɔnmã] *nm* **tâtonnements**, trial and error.

tâtonner [tɑtɔne] *vi* 1. to grope (in the dark); **marcher en tâtonnant**, to feel one's way 2. to proceed cautiously, tentatively.

tâtons (à) [atɑtɔ̃] *adv phr* **avancer à t.**, to grope one's way along; **chercher qch à t.**, to grope, feel, for sth.

tatouage [tatuaʒ] *nm* 1. tattooing 2. tattoo.

tatouer [tatwe] *vtr* to tattoo (the body).

taudis [todi] *nm* slum; hovel.

taule [tol] *nf P:* prison, nick; **faire de la t.**, to do time.

taupe [top] *nf* 1. (a) *Z:* mole (b) mole skin 2. **vieille t.**, old crone.

taupinière [topinjɛr] *nf* molehill.

taureau, -eaux [tɔro] *nm* bull; **course de taureaux**, bullfight; *Astr:* **le T.**, Taurus.

tautologie [totɔlɔʒi] *nf* tautology.

taux [to] *nm* (a) rate (of wages, of exchange); (established) price (of shares) (b) proportion, ratio (c) percentage; rate; degree (of invalidity); level (of cholesterol).

taverne [tavɛrn] *nf* inn, tavern.

taxation [taksasjɔ̃] *nf* 1. fixing of prices 2. taxation.

taxe [taks] *nf* 1. (a) fixed price; fixed rate (b) charge; rate; **t. postale**, postage 2. tax, duty; **t. à la valeur ajoutée**, value added tax.

taxer [takse] *vtr* 1. to regulate the price (of bread), the rate of (wages, postage); to surcharge (letter). 2. to tax, impose a tax on (s.o., sth) 3. to accuse (**de**, of). **taxable** *a* taxable.

taxi [taksi] *nm* (a) taxi (cab) (b) *F:* taxi driver.

taxidermie [taksidɛrmi] *nf* taxidermy.

taximètre [taksimɛtr̩] *nm* taximeter.

taxiphone [taksifɔn] *nm* public callbox, pay phone.

Tchad [tʃad] *Prnm Geog:* 1. Lake Chad. 2. **la République du T.,** the Republic of Chad.

Tchécoslovaquie [tʃekɔslɔvaki] *Prnf Geog:* Czechoslovakia. **tchécoslovaque** *a & n* Czech, Czechoslovak(ian). **tchèque** *a & n* Czech.

te, *before a vowel* **t'** [t(ə)] *pers pron, unstressed* (*a*) (*acc*) you (*b*) (*dat*) (to) you; (*c*) (*with vpr*) yourself.

technicien, -ienne [tɛknisjɛ̃, -jɛn] *n* technician.

technicité [tɛknisite] *nf* technical nature.

technique [tɛknik] 1. *a* technical 2. *nf* (*a*) technology; **t. de l'ingénieur,** engineering (*b*) technique. **techniquement** *adv* technically.

technocracie [tɛknɔkrasi] *nf* technocracy.

technologie [tɛknɔlɔʒi] *nf* technology. **technologique** *a* technological.

technologue [tɛknɔlɔg] *n* technologist.

teck [tɛk] *nm* teak.

teckel [tɛkɛl] *nm* dachshund.

TEE *abbr Trans-Europe-Express.*

teigne [tɛɲ] *nf* 1. *Med:* ringworm 2. *P:* unpleasant character.

teindre [tɛ̃dr̩] (*prp* teignant; *pp* teint; *pr ind* je teins, n. teignons; *impf* je teignais; *fu* je teindrai) to dye 2. **se t. (les cheveux),** to dye one's hair.

teint [tɛ̃] *nm* 1. dye, colour 2. complexion, colouring.

teinte [tɛ̃t] *nf* (*a*) tint, shade (*b*) touch, tinge (of malice, irony).

teinter [tɛ̃te] *vtr* to tint; **t. légèrement,** to tinge.

teinture [tɛ̃tyr] *nf* 1. dyeing 2. (*a*) dye (*b*) colour, tinge 3. *Pharm:* tincture.

teinturerie [tɛ̃tyr(ə)ri] *nf* 1. dyeing 2. dry cleaner's.

teinturier, -ière [tɛ̃tyrje, -jɛr] *n* 1. dyer 2. dry cleaner.

tel, telle [tɛl] *a* 1. (*a*) such; **un t. homme,** such a man; **de telles choses,** such things (*b*) **en t. lieu,** in such and such a place; **vous amènerez telle personne que vous voudrez,** you may bring anyone you like (*c*) **à t. point,** to such, to so great, an extent; **de telle sorte que,** (i) + *ind* (*result*) (ii) + *sub* (*purpose*), in such a way that, so that 2. (*a*) like; as; **t. père, t. fils,** like father like son (*b*) **t. que,** such as, like; **un homme t. que lui,** a man like him; **voir les choses telles qu'elles sont,** to look facts in the face; *F:* **t. que,** straight out (*c*) **rien de t. qu'un bon whisky,** there's nothing like a good whisky (*d*) **t. quel,** *P:* **t. que,** just as it is; **je vous achète la maison telle quelle,** I'll buy the house from you (just) as it stands 3. *pron* (*a*) such a one; **t. l'en blâmait, t. l'en excusait,** one would blame him, another would excuse him (*b*) **t. fut son langage,** such were his words; *n* **un t., une telle,** so-and-so; **monsieur un t., un T.,** Mr so-and-so.

télé [tele] *nf F:* telly, TV.

télécommande [telekɔmɑ̃d] *nf* remote control.

télécommander [telekɔmɑ̃de] *vtr* to operate by remote control.

télécommunication [telekɔmynikasjɔ̃] *nf* telecommunication.

téléférique [teleferik] *nm* (*a*) telpher (line) (*b*) cable car.

télégramme [telegram] *nm* telegram.

télégraphe [telegraf] *nm* telegraph.

télégraphie [telegrafi] *nf* telegraphy. **télégraphique** *a* telegraphic.

télégraphier [telegrafje] *vtr & i* to telegraph, to wire.

télégraphiste [telegrafist] *n* telegraphist.

téléguidage [telegidaʒ] *nm* radio control.

téléguider [telegide] *vtr* to radio-control.

téléimprimeur [teleɛ̃primœr] *nm* teleprinter.

téléobjectif [teleɔbʒɛktif] *nm Phot:* telephoto lens.

télépathie [telepati] *nf* telepathy. **télépathique** *a* telepathic.

téléphone [telefɔn] *nm* telephone, *F:* phone; **avoir le t.,** to be on the phone; **coup de t.,** telephone call; *Pol:* **t. rouge,** hot line; *F:* **t. arabe,** bush telegraph; grapevine.

téléphoner [telefɔne] *vtr & i* to telephone; **t. à qn,** to ring s.o. (up), to phone s.o., *esp NAm:* to call (s.o.); to give (s.o.) a call. **téléphonique** *a* telephone (booth, call).

téléphoniste [telefɔnist] *n* (telephone) operator.

télescopage [telɛskɔpaʒ] *nm* telescoping; *Aut:* **t. en série,** pile-up.

télescope [telɛskɔp] *nm* telescope. **télescopique** *a* telescopic.

télescoper [telɛskɔpe] *vi, tr & pr* (*of vehicle*) to telescope; to crumple up; to concertina.

téléscripteur [teleskriptœr] *nm* teleprinter.

télésiège [telesjɛʒ] *nm* chairlift.

téléski [teleski] *nm* ski tow, ski lift.

téléspectateur, -trice [telespɛktatœr, -tris] *n* (tele)viewer.

télétype [teletip] *nm* teleprinter.

téléviser [televize] *vtr* to televise.

téléviseur [televizœr] *nm* television set.

télévision [televizjɔ̃] *nf* television; **à la t.,** on television.

télex [telɛks] *nm* (*Rtm*) telex (machine).

tellement [tɛlmɑ̃] *adv* to such a degree; **c'est t. facile,** it's so easy; **t. de gens,** so many people; **ce n'est pas t. beau,** it's not all that beautiful.

téméraire [temerɛr] *a* rash, reckless. **témérairement** *adv* rashly, recklessly.

témérité [temerite] *nf* 1. temerity, rashness 2. reckless action.

témoignage [temwaɲaʒ] *nm* 1. (*a*) testimony, evidence (*b*) evidence, statement 2. token (of friendship).

témoigner [temwaɲe] 1. *vi* to testify; to give evidence 2. *vtr or ind tr* **t. (de),** to show, to give evidence of (good will); **t. de l'intérêt à qn,** to show an interest in s.o.; **t. que,** to show that.

témoin [temwɛ̃] *nm* 1. (*a*) witness; **être t. d'un accident,** to witness an accident; **t. à un acte,** witness to a signature (*b*) **t. à charge, à décharge,** witness for the prosecution, for the defence; **t. oculaire,** eyewitness; **prendre qn à t.,** to call s.o. to witness (*c*) second (in duel) 2. (*a*) sample (*b*) **lampe t.,** warning light (*c*) *Sp:* baton (*d*) **appartement t.,** show flat.

tempe [tɑ̃p] *nf Anat:* temple.

tempérament [tɑ̃peramɑ̃] *nm* 1. (*a*) (physical) constitution, temperament (*b*) (moral) temperament disposition (*c*) **avoir du t.,** to have character 2. *Com:* **à t.,** by instalments; **achat à t.,** credit purchase; **vente à t.,** sale on hire purchase.

tempérance [tɑ̃perɑ̃s] *nf* temperance. **tempérant** *a* temperate.

température [tɑ̃peratyr] *nf* temperature; **avoir de la t.,** to have a temperature; **prendre la t.,** (i) to take (ii) to gauge, the temperature; **t. d'ébullition,** boiling point.

tempérer [tɑ̃pere] *vtr* (**je tempère; je tempérerai**) to temper, moderate (heat, passions). **tempéré** *a* temperate (climate).

tempête [tɑ̃pɛt] *nf* storm; *Nau:* hurricane; **t. de neige,** blizzard, snowstorm; **le vent souffle en t.,** it's blowing a gale force wind; **une t. dans un verre d'eau,** a storm in a teacup; **t. d'applaudissements,** thunderous applause. **tempétueux, -euse** *a* tempestuous, stormy.

tempêter [tɑ̃pete] *vi* (*of pers*) to rage, to rant and rave.

temple [tɑ̃pl] *nm* temple; (protestant) church; chapel.

temporaire [tɑ̃pɔrɛr] *a* temporary; provisional. **temporairement** *adv* temporarily.

temporel, -elle [tɑ̃pɔrɛl] *a* (a) temporal; wordly (b) *Gram:* temporal (clause).

temporisateur, -trice [tɑ̃pɔrizatœr, -tris] **1.** *n* temporizer **2.** *a* temporizing.

temporisation [tɑ̃pɔrizasjɔ̃] *nf* temporizing; calculated delay.

temporiser [tɑ̃pɔrize] *vi* to temporize; to play for time.

temps [tɑ̃] *nm* **1** (a) time; **vous avez bien le t., vous avez tout le t.,** you have plenty of time; **cela prend du t.,** it takes time; **prendre son t.,** to take one's time; (**donnez-moi**) **le t. de m'habiller et j'arrive,** just give me time to get dressed and I'm coming; **nous n'avons pas le t.,** there's no time, we haven't time; **de t. en t.,** now and then; **travailler à plein t.,** to work full time (b) time, period; **dans quelque t.,** in a (little) while; **il y a peu de t.,** a little while ago; not long ago; **peu de t. après,** not long after; **entre t.,** meanwhile; **t. d'arrêt,** pause, halt; **marquer un t.,** to pause (c) term (of service); **faire son t.,** to serve one's time; (*of prisoner*) to do one's time (d) **t. mort,** idle time (of machine); dead time; **en t. réel,** real time (e) age, days, time(s); **le bon vieux t.,** the good old days; **dans le t.,** in the old days; at one time; **au t. de Napoléon,** in Napoleon's time; **par les t. qui courent,** these days; nowadays; **être de son t.,** to be up to date; **de mon t.,** in my day (f) hour, time; **arriver à t.,** to arrive on time; **en t. voulu, utile,** in due time; **il est grand t. que,** it's high time that; **il était t.!** it's not too soon! **il n'est plus t. de pleurer,** it's too late to cry now **2.** weather; **par tous les t.,** in all weathers; **quel t. fait-il?** what's the weather like? **si le t. le permet,** weather permitting; **beau t.,** fine weather **3.** *Gram:* tense. **4.** (a) *Mus:* measure, beat; **à deux t.,** in double time (b) **moteur à deux t.,** two-stroke engine.

tenable [tənabl] *a* (*usu with neg*) bearable; **par cette chaleur, le bureau n'est pas t.,** the office is unbearable in this heat.

tenace [tənas] *a* tenacious; obstinate (pers); stubborn (will); persistent (illness). **tenacement** *adv* stubbornly.

ténacité [tenasite] *nf* tenacity; stubbornness.

tenaille [tənaj] *nf* pincers; tongs.

tenailler [tənaje] *vtr* to torture; **tenaillé par la faim,** gnawed by hunger.

tenancier, -ière [tənɑ̃sje, -jɛr] *n* (bar, hotel) manager, manageress.

tenant, -ante [tənɑ̃, -ɑ̃t] **1.** *a* **séance tenante,** then and there **2.** *n* champion (of s.o.); defender (of an opinion); *Sp:* holder (of a title) **3.** *nm* (*of landed property*) **d'un seul t.,** all in one block; *Fig:* **les tenants et aboutissants de l'affaire,** the ins and outs of the case.

tendance [tɑ̃dɑ̃s] *nf* tendency, inclination; propensity; trend; **tendances vers le communisme,** communist leanings; **avoir t. à (faire) qch,** to be inclined to (do) sth; to have a tendency to (do) sth. **tendancieux, -ieuse** *a* tendentious.

tendon [tɑ̃dɔ̃] *nm* tendon, sinew; **t. d'Achille,** Achilles' tendon.

tendre¹ [tɑ̃dr] *a* (a) tender; soft; delicate (colour) (b) early (age); (c) fond, affectionate, loving. **tendrement** *adv* tenderly, fondly, lovingly.

tendre² **1.** *vtr* (a) to stretch, tighten (belt); to bend, draw (bow); to set (spring) (b) to pitch (tent); to spread (sail); to lay carpet); to hang (wallpaper) (c) to stretch out, hold out; **t. la main,** (i) to hold out one's hand (ii) to beg; **t. le cou,** to crane one's neck (d) to (over)strain, to stretch **2.** *vi* to tend, lead (à, to); **où tendent ces questions?** where are these questions leading? (*of thg*) **t. à sa fin,** to be near its end **3. se t.,** to become taut; to become strained.

tendresse [tɑ̃drɛs] *nf* (a) tenderness; fondness; love; **avec t.,** lovingly (b) *pl* tokens of affection.

tendreté [tɑ̃drəte] *nf* tenderness (of food).

tendu [tɑ̃dy] *a* (a) stretched, taut, tight; strained (relations); **avoir les nerfs tendus,** to be tense; **situation tendue,** tense situation (b) outstretched (hand).

ténèbres [tenɛbr] *nfpl* darkness, gloom. **ténébreux, -euse** *a* **1.** gloomy, dark, sombre (wood, prison) **2.** mysterious, sinister; obscure.

teneur [tənœr] *nf* **1.** tenor, terms (of document). **2.** *Tchn:* amount, content, percentage; **t. en eau,** water content, moisture content.

tenir [tənir] *v* (*prp* **tenant;** *pp* **tenu;** *pr ind* **je tiens, ils tiennent;** *pr sub* **je tienne;** *impf* **je tenais;** *ph* **je tins;** *fu* **je tiendrai**) **1.** *vtr* (a) to hold; **t. qch à la main,** to hold sth in one's hand; **se t. par la main,** to hold hands; *F:* **t. un rhume,** to have a cold; **je tiens mon homme,** I've got my man; *Prov:* **mieux vaut t. que courir,** a bird in the hand is worth two in the bush; **tiens! tenez! look! look here! tenez! c'est pour vous!** here you are! (b) to hold, contain; **voiture qui tient 6 personnes,** *vi* **voiture où l'on tient à 6,** car that takes 6 people; *vi* **tout ça tient en deux mots,** all that can be said in a couple of words (c) to retain; **baril qui tient l'eau,** barrel that holds water (d) **t. de,** to have, get, derive, (sth) from; **il tient sa timidité de sa mère,** he gets his shyness from his mother (e) to hold, stock (groceries) (f) to keep, to run (a shop, a school); to have charge of (the cash); **Mlle X tenait le piano,** Miss X was at the piano (g) to hold, maintain (opinion, line of conduct); to keep (one's word) (h) to deliver (speech) (i) **t. qn en mépris, grand respect,** to hold s.o. in contempt, great esteem (j) to hold back, restrain (one's tongue, one's impatience); to control (child) (k) to hold, keep (sth in a certain position); **t. qch en état,** to keep sth in good order; **t. qn à l'œil,** to keep an eye on s.o.; **tenez votre gauche,** keep to the left (*l*) to be confined to (one's room, one's bed (*m*) *Nau:* **t. la mer,** to be seaworthy; *Aut:* **t. la route,** to hold the road (*n*) to occupy, take up (space); **vous tenez trop de place,** you're taking up too much room (*o*) **t. les yeux fermés,** to keep one's eyes shut; **t. qn captif,** to hold s.o. prisoner; **t. qn pour intelligent,** to consider s.o. clever; **tenez-vous-le pour dit,** I shan't tell you again; take that as final. **2.** *vi (a)* to hold; to adhere; to hold on firmly; **clou qui tient bien,** nail that holds well; **la porte tient,** the door won't open *(b)* **sa terre tient à la mienne,** his estate borders on mine *(c)* to remain; **il ne tient pas en place,** he can't keep still; **il ne tient plus sur ses jambes,** he's ready to drop *(d)* **t. (bon),** to hold out, to stand fast; **tiens bon!** hold tight! **je n'y tiens plus,** I can't stand it any longer *(e)* to last, endure; **couleur qui tient bien,** fast colour; **le vent va t.,** the wind will last, keep up; **mon offre tient toujours,** my offer still stands *(f)* to sit, to be held, to take place *(g)* **t. pour,** to be for, be in favour of (s.o., sth) *(h)* **t. à qch,** (i) to value, prize, sth; **t. à faire qch,** to be bent on doing sth; **je n'y tiens pas,** I'd rather not (do it); I don't care for it; **je tiens beaucoup à ce qu'il vienne,** I'm very anxious, keen, that he should come (ii) to depend on, result from, sth; **à quoi cela tient-il?** what's the reason for it? *impers* **il ne tient qu'à vous de le faire,** it rests entirely with you to do it; **qu'à cela ne tienne,** never mind that (*i*) **t. de qn,** to take after s.o.; **cela tient du miracle,** it sounds like a miracle; **cela tient de (la) famille,** it runs in the family **3.** **se t.** *(a)* to keep, be, remain, stand, sit; **se t. chez soi,** to stay at home; **tenez-vous là!** stay where you are! **tenez-vous droit,** (i) sit up (ii) stand (up), straight; **se t. tranquille,** to keep quiet; **tiens-toi bien!** behave yourself! *(b)* **se t. à qch,** to hold on to sth *(c) (of facts)* to hold together *(d)* to contain oneself; **il ne se tenait pas de joie,** he couldn't contain himself for joy; **je ne pouvais me t. de rire,** I couldn't help laughing *(e)* **se, s'en, t. à (qch),** to keep to (sth); to abide by (sth); **s'en t. à qch,** to confine oneself to sth; to be satisfied, content, with sth; **je ne sais pas à quoi m'en t.,** I don't know what to believe, where I stand.

tennis [tenis] *nm* **1.** (lawn) tennis; **t. de table,** table tennis. **2.** (lawn) tennis court **3.** *pl* tennis shoes; gym shoes, *NAm:* sneakers.

tennisman, *pl* **-men** [tenisman, -mɛn] *nm* tennis player.

ténor [tenɔr] *nm (a) Mus:* tenor *(b) F: Pol: Sp:* star performer.

tension [tɑ̃sjɔ̃] *nf* **1.** *(a)* tension; stretching; tightening *(b) Mec:* **t. de rupture,** breaking strain, stress **2.** tightness (of rope); tenseness (of relations) **3.** *(a)* pressure (of steam); *Med:* **t. artérielle,** blood pressure; **avoir de la t.,** to suffer from high blood pressure *(b) El: Elcs:* voltage; tension; **haute t.,** high voltage; **fil sous t.,** live wire.

tentacule [tɑ̃takyl] *nm Z: Fig:* tentacle. **tentaculaire** *a* tentacular; sprawling (town).

tentateur, -trice [tɑ̃tatœr, -tris] **1.** *a* tempting **2.** *n* tempter, temptress.

tentation [tɑ̃tasjɔ̃] *nf* temptation.

tentative [tɑ̃tativ] *nf* attempt, endeavour; bid; **t. d'assassinat,** attempted murder.

tente [tɑ̃t] *nf* tent; **coucher sous la t.,** to sleep under canvas; *Med:* **t. à oxygène,** oxygen tent.

tenter [tɑ̃te] *vtr* **1.** **t. sa chance,** to try one's luck **2.** to tempt (s.o.); **se laisser t.,** to yield to temptation **3.** to attempt, try; **t. une expérience,** to try an experiment; **t. de faire qch,** to try to do sth. **tentant** *a* tempting, enticing; attractive (offer).

tenture [tɑ̃tyr] *nf (a)* hanging *(b) FrC:* curtain, *NAm:* drape *(c)* **(papier-)t.,** wallpaper.

tenu [təny] *a & pp (a)* **bien t.,** well kept; tidy (house); neat (garden); **mal t.,** badly kept, neglected (child, garden); untidy (house); *(b)* **être t. de, à, faire qch,** to be obliged to do sth; **être t. au secret professionnel,** to be bound by professional secrecy.

ténu [teny] *a* tenuous, thin; slender, fine; subtle (distinction).

tenue [təny] *nf* **1.** *(a)* sitting, session (of assembly) *(b)* keeping, managing, running (of shop, house); **t. des livres,** book-keeping **2.** *(a)* bearing, behaviour; **un peu de t.!** watch your manners! *(b)* standard, quality (of magazine) *(c) Aut:* **t. de route,** road-holding qualities **3.** dress; clothes; **t. de soirée,** evening dress; **en grande t.,** in full dress; **t. de ville,** (i) town clothes (ii) (man's) lounge suit; **t. de tous les jours,** casuals; **t. de combat,** battledress.

ter [tɛr] *Lt adv (in address)* **5 t.,** 5b, *occ* 5c.

térébenthine [terebɑ̃tin] *nf* turpentine.

tergal [tɛrgal] *nm Rtm:* Terylene.

tergiversation [tɛrʒiversasjɔ̃] *nf* tergiversation; beating about the bush.

tergiverser [tɛrʒiverse] *vi* to equivocate; to beat about the bush.

terme¹ [tɛrm] *nm* **1.** term, end, limit (of life, journey); **mettre un t. à qch,** to put a stop to sth; **mener qch à bon t.,** to bring sth to a successful conclusion **2.** (appointed) time; *(of pregnant woman)* **être à t.,** to have reached her time; **avant t.,** prematurely; **accouchement avant t.,** premature childbirth; *Ind: etc:* **prévisions à court t., à long t.,** short-range, long-range, forecasts **3.** *(a)* quarter (of rent); term *(b)* quarter's rent *(c)* quarter day.

terme² *nm* **1.** term, expression; **t. de métier,** technical term; **en d'autres termes,** in other words; **il m'a dit en termes propres,** he told me in so many words **2.** *pl* wording (of clause); terms, conditions **3.** *pl* terms, footing; **être en bons termes avec qn,** to be on good, friendly, terms with s.o.

terminaison [tɛrminɛzɔ̃] *nf* termination; ending.

terminer [tɛrmine] **1.** *vtr* to terminate; to end, finish; to conclude (bargain); to complete (job); to wind up (meeting) **(par,** with); to end (one's days); **en avoir terminé avec qch,** to have finished with sth **2.** **se t.,** to end; to come to an end; **se t. par, en,** to end with, in. **terminal, -ale, -aux** *a* terminal, final; *Sch:* **classe terminale,** *nf* **terminale** = upper sixth (form).

terminologie [tɛrminɔlɔʒi] *nf* terminology.

terminus [tɛrminys] *nm* (railway, coach) terminus.

termite [tɛrmit] *nf Ent:* termite, white ant.

termitière [tɛrmitjɛr] *nf Ent:* termitarium.

terne [tɛrn] *a* dull, lustreless; drab (clothes, life); lifeless (eyes); flat (voice).

ternir [tɛrnir] *vtr* to tarnish, dull; to tarnish (reputation); **se t.,** to become tarnished.

terrain [tɛrɛ̃] *nm* (a) (piece of) ground, plot of land; **t. à bâtir,** development site; **t. vague,** waste ground; (b) *Geog:* country, ground (c) ground, soil; **t. gras,** rich soil (d) (football, cricket) field; (golf) course, links; *Av:* **t. d'atterrissage,** landing strip, airstrip; *Mil: etc:* **gagner, céder, du t.,** to gain, lose, ground; **être sur son t.,** to be on familiar ground; **je ne suis plus sur mon t.,** I'm out of my depth; **préparer le t.,** to pave the way; *Ind: etc:* **sur le t.,** in the field.

terrasse [tɛras] *nf* (a) terrace; bank (b) pavement; **la t. (du café),** outside (the café) (c) *Const:* balcony, veranda, terrace; **(toit en) t.,** flat roof.

terrassement [tɛrasmɑ̃] *nm* (a) banking, digging (b) earthwork, embankment.

terrasser [tɛrase] *vtr* **1.** to work the soil of (vineyard) **2.** (a) to lay (s.o.) low; **t. un adversaire,** to bring down, to throw an opponent; (b) to overwhelm, crush (s.o.).

terrassier [tɛrasje] *nm* navvy.

terre [tɛr] *nf* **1.** (a) the earth; the world; **revenir sur t.,** to come down to earth; **il a les pieds sur t.,** he's down to earth (b) ground, land; **t. ferme,** continent, mainland; **dans les terres,** inland; **tremblement de t.,** earthquake; **à t., par t.,** on the ground; to the ground; **tomber par t.,** to fall down (from standing position); **politique de la t. brulée,** scorched earth policy; **sous t.,** underground; **être sous t., en t.,** to be in one's grave (c) *El:* earth; **mettre à la t.,** to earth; (*of ship*) **être à t.,** to be aground; **descendre à t.,** to land, go ashore; *adj phr* **t. à t.,** matter-of-fact, down-to-earth **2.** soil, ground; **t. grasse,** rich land **3.** (a) estate, property (b) territory; **terres étrangères,** foreign countries; **la T. Sainte,** the Holy Land **4.** loam, clay; **sol en t. battue,** mud floor; **t. cuite,** (i) baked clay (ii) terracotta.

terreau, -eaux [tɛro] *nm Hort:* compost.

Terre-Neuve [tɛrnœv] **1.** *Prnf Geog:* Newfoundland **2.** *nm inv* **un t.-n.,** a Newfoundland (dog). **terre-neuvien, -ienne** (a) *a* Newfoundland (b) *n* Newfoundlander; *pl* **terre-neuviens, -iennes.**

terre-plein [tɛrplɛ̃] *nm* earth platform; terrace; (*on road*) **t.-p. de stationnement,** layby; **t.-p. circulaire,** central island (of roundabout); *pl* **terre-pleins.**

terrer (se) [sətɛre] *vpr Ven: & Fig:* to go to earth; to hide away.

terrestre [tɛrɛstr] *a* (a) land (animal); worldly (thoughts); earthly (paradise).

terreur [tɛrœr] *nf* **1.** terror; dread; **fou de t.,** wild with fear **2.** *F:* gangster, thug.

terreux, -euse [tɛrø, -øz] *a* (a) earthly (taste, smell) (b) grubby (hands); muddy (complexion); gritty (lettuce).

terrible [tɛribl] *a* (a) terrible, dreadful; appalling, awful (b) *F:* terrific, great, incredible. **terriblement** *adv* terribly, dreadfully.

terrien, -ienne [tɛrjɛ̃, -jɛn] **1.** *a* (a) landed (proprietor) (b) country, rural **2.** *n* (a) landsman, -woman (b) countryman, -woman (c) earthman, -woman; earthling.

terrier[1] [tɛrje] *nm* burrow, hole (of rabbit); earth (of fox); set (of badger).

terrier[2] *a & n* **(chien) t.,** terrier.

terrifier [tɛrifje] *vtr* (*impf & pr sub* **n. terrifiions**) to terrify. **terrifiant** *a* terrifying.

terrine [tɛrin] *nf* (a) earthenware vessel; terrine (b) (*pâté*) terrine.

territoire [tɛritwar] *nm* territory; district, area, under jurisdiction. **territorial, -aux 1.** *a* territorial **2.** *nf* **la territoriale,** the territorial army.

terroir [tɛrwar] *nm Agr:* soil; **accent du t.,** local accent, rural accent.

terroriser [tɛrɔrize] *vtr* to terrorize.

terrorisme [tɛrɔrism] *nm* terrorism.

terroriste [tɛrɔrist] *n* terrorist.

tertiaire [tɛrsjɛr] *a* tertiary; **secteur t.,** service industries.

tertio [tɛrsjo] *adv* thirdly.

tertre [tɛrtr] *nm* hillock, mound.

tes [te, tɛ] *poss a pl see* **ton**[1].

tesson [tɛsɔ̃] *nm* potsherd; **t. de bouteille,** piece of broken bottle.

test [tɛst] *nm* test, trial.

testament[1] [tɛstamɑ̃] *nm* will, testament; **ceci est mon t.,** this is my last will and testament. **testamentaire** *a* disposition **t.,** clause (of a will).

testament[2] *nm B:* **l'ancien, le nouveau, T.,** the Old, the New, Testament.

testateur, -trice [tɛstatœr, -tris] *n* testator, testatrix.

tester[1] [tɛste] *vi* to make one's will.

tester[2] *vtr* to test.

testicule [tɛstikyl] *nm Anat:* testicle.

tétanos [tetanos] *nm Med:* tetanus, lockjaw.

têtard [tɛtar] *nm* tadpole.

tête [tɛt] *nf* **1.** (a) head; **de la t. aux pieds,** from head to foot; **t. nue,** bareheaded; *F:* **faire la t.,** to sulk; **tenir t. à qn,** to stand up to s.o.; **j'en ai par-dessus la t.,** I can't stand it any longer; **la t. la première,** head first; **ne (pas) savoir où donner de la t.,** not to know which way to turn; **100F par t.,** *F:* **par t. de pipe,** 100F per head; **dîner t. à t.,** to dine alone together; **j'en donnerais ma t. à couper,** I'd stake my life on it; **avoir mal à la t.,** to have a headache; **se laver la t.,** to wash one's hair; **signe de t.,** nod; *Fb:* **faire une t.,** to head the ball; *Swim:* **piquer une t.,** to dive (b) face, appearance; *F:* **faire une drôle de t.,** to pull a long face; **je connais cette t.-là,** I know that face **2.** headpiece, brains, mind; **se creuser la t.,** to rack one's brains; **c'est une femme de t.,** she is a capable woman; **avoir la t. dure,** to be thickheaded; **c'est une t. de mule,** he's pigheaded; *F:* **c'est une t. à claques,** he just asks for it; **se mettre qch dans la t.,** to set one's mind on sth; **forte t., mauvaise t.,** strong-minded, rebellious, person; **t. chaude,** hothead; **calcul de t.,** mental arithmetic; **il n'en fait qu'à sa t.,** he does exactly as he pleases; **où ai-je la t.!** what am I thinking about! **vous perdez la t.!** have you taken leave of your senses? **avoir toute sa t.,** to have one's wits about one; **à t. reposée,** at one's leisure **3.** (a) leader (b) summit, crown, top (of volcano, tree); head (of book); **t. de chapitre,** chapter heading (c) head (of nail, screw, pin) (d) *Elcs:* **t. d'enregistrement,** record(ing) head (of tape recorder); **t. de lecture,** tape reader (e) **t. nucléaire,** nuclear warhead; **t. chercheuse,** homing device (f) front place; *Rail:* **voiture de t.,** front carriage; **marcher en t.,** to lead the way; **prendre la t.**, to take the lead; **être à la t. de la classe**, to be top of the form; *Rail: etc:* **t. de ligne** (i) terminus (ii) railhead; *Mil:* **t. de pont**, (i) bridgehead (ii) beach head.

tête-à-queue [tɛtakø] *nm inv Aut:* spin.

tête-à-tête [tɛtatɛt] *nm inv* private interview; tête-à-tête; **en t.-à-t. avec**, alone with.

tête-bêche [tɛtbɛʃ] *adv* head to foot; head to tail.

tête-de-mort [tɛtdəmɔr] *nf* **1.** death's head; skull and crossbones **2.** Dutch cheese; *pl* têtes-de-mort.

tête-de-nègre [tɛtdənɛgr] *a & nm inv* dark brown.

tétée [tete] *nf (a)* sucking (by baby) *(b)* (milk taken by baby at one) feed *(c)* feeding time.

téter [tete] *vtr* (**il tète**) *(a) (of baby, of young)* to suck; **donner à t. à un enfant**, to feed a child *(b) F:* to suck on (pipe).

tétine [tetin] *nf (a)* teat *(b)* (rubber) teat; dummy, comforter, *NAm:* pacifier.

téton [tetɔ̃] *nm F:* (woman's) breast.

têtu [tety] *a* stubborn, pigheaded.

texte [tɛkst] *nm (a)* text (of author, book); (actor's) lines; **erreur de t.**, textual error *(b)* subject, topic. **textuel, -elle** *a* textual; literal, word-for-word. **textuellement** *adv* textually; literally, word-for-word.

textile [tɛkstil] **1.** *a* textile **2.** *nm (a)* textile *(b)* textile industry, textiles.

texture [tɛkstyr] *nf* texture.

TGV *abbr train grande vitesse.*

Thaïlande [tailɑ̃d] *Prnf Geog:* Thailand.

thé [te] *nm* **1.** tea; **t. au citron**, lemon tea; *a inv* rose t., tea rose **2.** tea party.

théâtre [teɑtr] *nm* **1.** *(a)* theatre, playhouse; **t. de verdure**, open-air theatre *(b)* theatre (of war) **2.** stage, scene; **mettre une pièce au t.**, to stage a play **3.** *(a)* dramatic art; **pièce de t.**, play; **faire du t.**, to be an actor; **coup de t.**, dramatic turn (of events) *(b)* plays, dramatic works; **le t. anglais**, English drama. **théâtral, -aux** *a* theatrical; dramatic (effect); stage (performance); *Pej:* stagy. **théâtralement** *adv* theatrically.

théière [tejɛr] *nf* teapot.

thème [tɛm] *nm (a)* theme, topic; subject *(b) Sch:* prose (composition).

théologie [teɔlɔʒi] *nf* theology. **théologique** *a* theological.

théologien [teɔlɔʒjɛ̃] *nm* theologian.

théorème [teɔrɛm] *nm* theorem.

théoricien, -ienne [teɔrisjɛ̃, -jɛn] *n* theor(et)ician, theorist.

théorie [teɔri] *nf* theory; **en t.**, in theory. **théorique** *a* theoretic(al). **théoriquement** *adv* theoretically.

thérapie [terapi] *nf Med:* therapy.

thermal, -aux [tɛrmal, -o] *a* thermal; **eaux thermales**, hot springs; **établissement t.**, hydropathic establishment; **station thermale**, spa.

thérapeuthique [terapøtik] **1.** *a* therapeutic **2.** *nf* therapeutics; therapy.

thermique [tɛrmik] *a Ph:* thermal, thermic; *El:* **centrale t.**, thermal power station.

thermoélectrique [tɛrmoelɛktrik] *a* thermoelectric(al).

thermomètre [tɛrmɔmɛtr] *nm* thermometer.

thermonucléaire [tɛrmɔnykleɛr] *a AtomPh:* thermonuclear.

Thermos [tɛrmɔs] *nm or f trademark applied to vacuum flasks and other articles manufactured by Thermos (1925) Ltd;* (**bouteille**) **T.**, Thermos flask.

thermostat [tɛrmɔsta] *nm* thermostat.

thermothérapie [tɛrmɔterapi] *nf Med:* thermotherapy; heat treatment.

thésauriser [tezorize] *vtr & i* to hoard (money).

thèse [tɛz] *nf* **1.** thesis, proposition, argument **2.** *Sch:* thesis (submitted for degree).

thon [tɔ̃] *nm Ich:* tunny(fish), tuna (fish).

thorax [tɔraks] *nm Anat:* thorax. **thoracique** *a* thoracic; **cage t.**, rib cage.

thrombose [trɔ̃boz] *nf Med:* thrombosis.

thym [tɛ̃] *nm Bot:* thyme.

thyroïde [tiroid] *a & nf Anat:* thyroid (gland). **thyroïdien, -ienne** *a* thyroid.

tiare [tjar] *nf* tiara.

Tibet [tibɛ] *Prnm Geog:* Tibet.

tibia [tibja] *nm Anat:* tibia, shinbone.

tic [tik] *nm (a) Med:* tic; twitch(ing) *(b) F:* (unconscious) habit; mannerism.

ticket [tikɛ] *nm (a)* ticket; numbered slip, check; **t. de quai**, platform ticket *(b)* **t. de pain**, bread coupon.

tic(-)tac [tiktak] *nm* tick-tock; **faire t.-t.**, to tick.

tiédeur [tjedœr] *nf* tepidness; lukewarmness; **avec t.**, halfheartedly. **tiède** *a* tepid; lukewarm (bath, friendship); *(of air)* mild; *adv* **boire qch t.**, to drink sth when it's lukewarm. **tièdement** *adv* lukewarmly; halfheartedly.

tiédir [tjedir] **1.** *vi* to become tepid, lukewarm *(of friendship)* to cool (off) **2.** *vtr* to make tepid, lukewarm.

tien, tienne [tjɛ̃, tjɛn] **1.** *poss a* yours; **mes intérêts sont tiens**, my interests are yours **2.** **le t., la tienne, les tiens, les tiennes** *(a) poss pron* **ses enfants ressemblent aux tiens**, his children are like yours *(b) nm* (i) your own (property); yours; **si tu veux du mien, donne-moi du t.**, if you want some of mine, give me some of yours; **y mettre du t.**, to contribute your share; to make concessions (ii) *pl* your own (people, friends) (iii) *F:* **tu as encore fait des tiennes**, you have been up to your old tricks again.

tiens [tjɛ̃] *int see* **tenir 1.** hello! hullo! **2.** look! hey! **3. t., t.!** indeed? well, well!

tiercé [tjɛrse] *nm Turf:* forecast of the first three horses.

tiers, f tierce [tjɛr, tjɛrs] **1.** *a* third; **une tierce personne**, a third party; **le t. état**, the third estate **2.** *nm (a)* third (part); **remise d'un t. (du prix)**, discount of a third; *F:* a third off; **perdre les deux t. de son argent**, to lose two thirds of one's money *(b)* third person, third party; **assurance au t.**, third party insurance **3.** *nf* tierce *(a) Mus:* third *(b) Cards:* tierce.

tiers-monde [tjɛrmɔ̃d] *nm Pol:* third world.

tifs, tiffes [tif] *nmpl P:* hair.

tige [tiʒ] *nf* **1.** *(a)* stem, stalk (of plant) *(b)* trunk, bole (of tree) **2.** *(a)* shaft (of column); shank (of key) *(b)* rod (of piston) *(c)* leg (of stocking).

tignasse [tiɲas] *nf* mop (of hair).

tigre, tigresse [tigr, tigrɛs] *n Z:* tiger, tigress. **tigré** *a* striped; spotted; streaked; tabby (cat).

tilleul [tijœl] *nm Bot:* lime (tree); **(infusion de)** t., lime(-blossom) tea.

timbale [tɛ̃bal] *nf* **1.** *Mus:* kettledrum; *(in orchestra)* **les timbales,** the timpani **2.** metal drinking cup **3.** *Cu:* timbale.

timbalier [tɛ̃balje] *nm Mus:* timpanist.

timbrage [tɛ̃braʒ] *nm* stamping; postmarking.

timbre [tɛ̃br̩] *nm* **1.** *(a)* bell; **t. électrique,** electric bell *(b)* timbre, quality in tone (of voice, instrument) **2.** *(a)* stamp (on document); **t. de la poste,** postmark *(b)* **t.(-poste),** (postage) stamp.

timbré [tɛ̃bre] *a F:* mad; cracked, dotty.

timbrer [tɛ̃bre] *vtr* to stamp (passport); to postmark (letter); to stick a stamp on (a letter).

timide [timid] *a (a)* timid; timorous *(b)* shy, bashful; diffident **(envers,** with). **timidement** *adv* timidly; timorously, shyly.

timidité [timidite] *nf (a)* timidity; timorousness *(b)* shyness, bashfulness, diffidence.

tintement [tɛ̃tmɑ̃] *nm* ringing; tinkling, tinkle; jingling, chinking.

tinter [tɛ̃te] **1.** *vtr* to ring, toll (bell) **2.** *vi (a) (of bell)* to ring, toll; *(of small bells)* to tinkle; *(of coins)* to chink; *(of keys)* to jingle; **faire t. les verres,** to clink glasses *(b) (of the ears)* to buzz, to ring; **les oreilles ont dû vous t. hier soir,** your ears must have been burning last night *(ie* you were being talked about).

tintin [tɛ̃tɛ̃] *int F:* no go! nothing doing!

tintouin [tɛ̃twɛ̃] *nm* trouble, bother.

tique [tik] *nf Arach:* tick.

tiquer [tike] *vi F:* to wince; to show sign(s) of emotion; **il n'a pas tiqué,** he didn't turn a hair.

tir [tir] *nm* **1.** shooting; gunnery **2.** *(a)* fire, firing; **champ de t.,** range; **t. au fusil,** rifle shooting *(b) Fb:* **t. au but,** shot (at goal) **3.** *(a)* rifle range *(b)* shooting gallery.

tirade [tirad] *nf* tirade.

tirage [tiraʒ] *nm* **1.** *(a)* pulling, hauling *(b) F:* trouble; friction (between two people) **2.** draught (of flue) **3.** drawing (of lottery) **4.** *Typ:* *(a)* printing (off) *(b)* number printed; printing, edition (of book, recording); **journal à gros t.,** paper with a wide circulation **5.** drawing (of cheque).

tiraillement [tirajmɑ̃] *nm* **1.** tugging (on rope) **2.** t. **d'estomac,** pangs of hunger **3.** *F:* wrangling, friction.

tirailler [tiraje] **1.** *vtr* to pull (s.o., sth) about; to tug at (s.o.); *F:* **tiraillé entre deux émotions,** torn between two opposing feelings **2.** *vi* to shoot aimlessly.

tirailleur [tirajœr] *nm Mil:* skirmisher.

tirant [tirɑ̃] *nm* t. **d'eau,** (ship's) draught; **avoir dix pieds de t. d'eau,** to draw ten feet of water.

tire [tir] *nf* **1.** **voleur à la t.,** pickpocket **2.** *P:* car.

tiré, -ée [tire] **1.** *a (a)* drawn, haggard, peaked (features); **aux cheveux tirés,** with one's hair scraped back *(b)* **tiré par les cheveux,** far-fetched **2.** *nf* tirée, *F: (a)* long distance, long haul *(b)* **une t. de,** loads of.

tire-au-flanc [tiroflɑ̃] *nm inv F:* skiver.

tire-bouchon [tirbuʃɔ̃] *nm* corkscrew; *pl tire-bouchons.*

tire-d'aile (à) [atirdɛl] *adv phr* **s'envoler à t.-d'a.,** to fly swiftly away.

tire-fesses [tirfɛs] *nm inv F:* ski tow, ski lift.

tire-larigot (à) [atirlarigo] *adv phr F:* (to drink) to one's heart's content.

tirelire [tirlir] *nf* **1.** money box; piggy bank **2.** *P:* face, mug.

tirer [tire] **1.** *vtr (a)* to pull out; to stretch; to pull up (socks); *F:* **encore une heure à t. avant le dîner!** still another hour to get through before dinner! *(b)* to pull, tug, draw; **t. les cheveux à qn,** to pull s.o.'s hair; **t. qn par la manche,** to tug at s.o.'s sleeve; **t. la jambe,** to limp; **t. les rideaux,** to draw the curtains *(c)* **t. son chapeau à qn,** to raise one's hat to s.o. *(d)* to pull out, draw out, take out, extract; to draw (wine, water); **t. un journal de sa poche,** to pull a paper out of one's pocket; **t. une dent à qn,** to pull out, draw, s.o.'s tooth; **t. plaisir de qch,** to derive pleasure from sth; **t. de l'argent de qch,** to make money from sth; **mot tiré du latin,** word derived from Latin; **t. qn d'un mauvais pas,** to get s.o. out of a difficulty; **t. qn du lit,** to drag s.o. out of bed; **t. qn du sommeil,** to arouse s.o. from sleep *(e)* to draw (a line); *(f)* to print (off) (proof); **t. une épreuve d'un cliché,** to take a print from a negative *(g) Com:* to draw (bill of exchange); **t. un chèque sur une banque,** to draw a cheque on a bank *(h)* to fire (shot); to shoot (arrow); to let off (fireworks); **t. un coup de revolver sur qn,** to shoot s.o. with a revolver *(i) vi* to shoot; *(of firearm)* to go off; **t. sur qn,** to fire at s.o. *(j)* **t. un lièvre,** to shoot a hare; *Nau:* **navire qui tire vingt pieds,** ship that draws twenty feet (of water) **2.** *vi (a)* to pull (on cable); **t. sur sa pipe,** to draw on one's pipe *(b)* to tend (to), to incline (to); to verge (on); **bleu tirant sur le vert,** blue verging on green; **le jour tire à sa fin,** the day is drawing to its close; **t. sur la soixantaine,** to be getting on for sixty *(c)* **t. sur la gauche,** to pull to the left *(d) (of chimney)* to draw **3.** **se t.** *(a)* **se t. d'un mauvais pas,** to get out of a fix; **s'en t. sans aucun mal,** to escape unharmed; **on s'en tire,** we just manage to make ends meet; we just get by *(b) F: (of pers)* to be off, to clear off.

tiret [tire] *nm Typ:* *(a)* hyphen *(b)* dash.

tireur, -euse [tirœr, -øz] *n* **1.** *Com:* drawer **2.** shooter; **t. d'élite,** marksman; sharpshooter; **t. embusqué,** sniper **3.** **t. de cartes,** fortune teller **4.** *nf* **tireuse,** bottle filler.

tiroir [tirwar] *nm* drawer.

tiroir-caisse [tirwarkɛs] *nm Com:* till; *pl tiroirs-caisses.*

tisane [tizan] *nf* infusion; (herb) tea; **t. de camomille,** camomile tea.

tison [tizɔ̃] *nf* (fire)brand.

tisonner [tizone] *vtr* to poke (the fire).

tisonnier [tizonje] *nm* poker.

tissage [tisaʒ] *nm Tex:* weaving.

tisser [tise] *vtr* to weave; *(of spider)* to spin.

tisserand, -ande [tisrɑ̃, -ɑ̃d], **tisseur, -euse** [tisœr, -øz] *n* weaver.

tissu [tisy] *nm (a)* texture *(b)* fabric, tissue, textile; material; **t. de mensonges,** string, tissue, of lies *(c) Biol:* tissue.

tissu-éponge [tisyepɔ̃ʒ] *nm* (terry) towelling.

titre [titr̩] *nm* **1.** *(a)* title (of nobility); official title; **se donner le t. de,** to style oneself *(b)* **sans t. officiel,** without any official status; *adj phr* **en t.,** titular; on the regular staff; **propriétaire en t.**, legal owner (c) *Sp:* title **2.** (a) diploma, certificate; **pourvu de tous ses titres,** fully qualified (b) voucher; **t. de transport,** ticket (c) title deed (d) *Fin:* warrant, bond, certificate; *pl* stocks and shares, securities **3.** title, claim, right; **à t. de,** by right of, by way of; **à t. de précaution,** just in case; **à t. d'ami,** as a friend; **à t. d'essai,** as a trial measure; experimentally; **à juste t.,** fairly, rightly; **à quel t.?** by what right? **à t. gratuit,** free of charge **4.** (a) title (of book) (b) heading (of chapter); **les gros titres,** (the) banner headlines **5.** title, titre (of solution, gold); grade (of ore); fineness (of coinage); **t. d'eau,** degree of humidity.

titrer [titre] *vtr* **1.** (a) to give a title to (s.o., sth) (b) *Journ:* to run as a headline **2.** *Ch:* to titrate. **titré** *a* **1.** titled (person) **2.** qualified (teacher) **3.** *Ch:* titrated (solution).

tituber [titybe] *vi* to reel (about); to lurch; to stagger, to totter.

titulaire [titylɛr] **1.** *a* titular (bishop, professor) **2.** *n* holder (of right, title, certificate); bearer (of passport).

TNP *abbr Théâtre national populaire.*

toast [tost] *nm* **1.** toast; **porter un t.,** to toast (s.o.) **2.** (piece of) toast.

toboggan [tɔbɔgã] *nm* (a) toboggan (b) chute (in swimming bath); (fairground) slide (c) flyover, overpass.

toc [tɔk] **1.** (a) *int* **t. t.!** tap, tap! (b) *nm* tap, rap (on door) **2.** *nm F:* **bijoux en t.,** imitation jewellery; **c'est du t.,** it's fake.

tocsin [tɔksɛ̃] *nm* tocsin; alarm bell.

toge [tɔʒ] *nf* (a) *Hist:* toga (b) *Jur: Sch:* gown.

Togo [tɔgo] *Prnm Geog:* Togo(land); **République du T.,** Republic of Togo. **togolais, -aise** *a & n Geog:* Togolese.

toi [twa] *stressed pers pron (subject or object)* you; **c'est t.,** it's you; **il est plus âgé que t.,** he is older than you; **tu as raison, t.,** you are right; **ce livre est à t.,** this book is yours; **tu le vois t.-même,** you can see it yourself; **tais-t.,** be quiet! *F:* shut up!

toile [twal] *nf* **1.** (a) linen, linen cloth; **t. à matelas,** tick(ing); **drap de t.,** linen sheet (b) cloth; **t. cirée,** (i) oilcloth (ii) *Nau:* oilskin (c) canvas (d) **t. émeri,** emery cloth; **t. d'amiante,** asbestos (e) **t. d'araignée,** cobweb; spider's web **2.** (a) oil painting; canvas (b) *Th:* curtain; **t. de fond,** back drop **3.** *Nau:* sail.

toilette [twalɛt] *nf* **1.** washstand **2.** (a) washing (and dressing); **faire sa t.,** to wash and dress; **faire un brin de t.,** to have a wash and brush up; to freshen up; **le chat fait sa t.,** the cat is washing itself; **cabinet de t.,** washroom; bathroom (b) *PN:* **toilettes,** toilet(s); public conveniences, lavatory **3.** (woman's) dress, clothes; **t. de bal,** ball dress.

toi-même [twamɛm] *pers pron* yourself.

toiser [twaze] *vtr* to eye (s.o.) scornfully (up and down).

toison [twazɔ̃] *nf* **1.** fleece **2.** *F:* mop (of hair).

toit [twa] *nm* roof; **habiter sous les toits,** to live in a garret; **crier qch sur les toits,** to proclaim sth from the rooftops; *Aut:* **t. ouvrant,** sunshine roof; **le t. paternel,** the home, the paternal roof.

toiture [twatyr] *nf* roofing, roof.

tôle [tol] *nf* sheet metal; **t. ondulée,** corrugated iron.

tolérance [tɔlerãs] *nf* tolerance; *Rel:* toleration; *Cust:* allowance; **il y a une t. d'un litre,** you are allowed to bring in a litre free of duty.

tolérer [tɔlere] *vtr* (**je tolère; je tolérerai**) (a) to tolerate (opinion, religion); to put up with (s.o., sth) (b) to allow tacitly, wink at (abuses) (c) *Med:* to tolerate (drug). **tolérable** *a* tolerable, bearable. **tolérant, -ante** *a* tolerant.

tôlerie [tolri] *nf* sheet-iron and steel-plate trade, works, goods.

tôlier [tolje] *nm* sheet-metal worker; *Aut:* panel beater.

tollé [tɔle] *nm* outcry (of indignation).

tomate [tɔmat] *nf* tomato; **sauce t.,** tomato sauce.

tombe [tɔ̃b] *nf* (a) tomb, grave (b) tombstone. **tombal, -aux** *a* **pierre tombale,** tombstone, gravestone.

tombeau, -eaux [tɔ̃bo] *nm* tomb; monument; **t. de famille,** family vault.

tombée [tɔ̃be] *nf* fall (of rain, snow); **à la t. de la nuit,** at nightfall.

tomber [tɔ̃be] *(aux être)* **1.** *vi* (a) to fall (down); *(of aircraft)* to crash; **ça tombe en poussière,** it's crumbling to dust; **impers il tombe de la neige,** it's snowing; **t. d'une échelle,** to fall off a ladder; **t. de cheval,** to fall off a horse; *F:* **t. dans les pommes,** to pass out, to faint; **je tombe de sommeil,** I'm ready to drop; **faire t. qch,** to knock sth over; **laisser t. qch,** to drop sth; **laisser t. qn,** (i) to drop s.o. (ii) to let s.o. down; **se laisser t. dans un fauteuil,** to sink, *F:* to flop, into an armchair; **t. à l'eau,** (i) to fall in (the water) (ii) *(of plan)* to fall through; **fruits tombés,** windfalls; *Journ:* **le journal est tombé,** the paper has gone to bed (b) *(of wind, anger, fever)* to drop, abate, subside, die down; *(of conversation)* to flag; **la nuit tombe,** night is falling; **le vent tombe,** the wind is dropping (c) **t. entre les mains de qn,** to fall into s.o.'s hands; **t. en disgrâce,** to fall into disgrace; **t. dans un piège,** to fall into a trap (d) **t. sur l'ennemi,** to attack, fall on, the enemy (e) **t. sur qn, qch,** to come across s.o., sth; **il va nous t. sur le dos d'un jour à l'autre,** he'll be landing in on us any day; **Noël tombe un jeudi,** Christmas is on a Thursday; **vous tombez bien,** you've come in the nick of time; **t. juste,** to come, to happen, at the right moment (f) to fail; *Th:* **la pièce est tombée (à plat),** the play flopped (g) to fall, hang down; **ses cheveux lui tombent dans le dos,** her hair hangs down her back; **jupe qui tombe bien,** skirt that hangs well (h) **t. amoureux de qn,** to fall in love with s.o.; **t. malade,** to fall ill **2.** *vtr (aux avoir) F:* **t. la veste,** to take off one's jacket. **tombant** *a* (a) falling; **la nuit tombante,** nightfall (b) flowing (hair); drooping (moustache); sloping (shoulders).

tombereau, -eaux [tɔ̃bro] *nm* (a) tipcart (b) cartload.

tombola [tɔ̃bɔla] *nf* tombola, raffle.

tome [tɔm] *nm* volume; tome.

ton¹, ta, tes [tɔ̃, ta, tɛ] *poss a* (**ton** *is used instead of* **ta** *before fem words beginning with a vowel or* **h** *mute; for use of* **ton,** *as opposed to* **votre,** *see* TU) your; **un de tes amis,** a friend of yours; **ton ami(e),** your friend; **c'est t. affaire à toi,** that's your business.

ton² *nm* **1.** (a) tone, intonation; **hausser le t.,** to raise (the tone of) one's voice; **forcer le t.,** to speak more loudly and more urgently; **faire baisser le t. à qn,** to take s.o. down a peg (or two); **elle le prend sur ce t.?** is that how she speaks to you? (*b*) tone, manners, breeding; **c'est de mauvais t.,** it's bad form, bad manners, vulgar 2. *Mus:* (*a*) **(hauteur du) t.,** pitch; **donner le t.,** (i) to give (an orchestra) the tuning A (ii) *F:* to set the fashion; **sortir du t.,** to be out of tune (*b*) key (*c*) **tons et demi-tons,** tones and semi-tones 3. *Ling:* pitch, accent 4. tone, tint, colour, shade; **être dans le t.,** to tone in, match in.

tonalité [tɔnalite] *nf Art: Mus:* tonality; tone; *Tp:* dialling tone.

tondeur, -euse [tɔ̃dœr, -øz] 1. *n* shearer (of sheep) 2. *nf* **tondeuse** (*a*) shears (for sheep); (hair) clippers (*b*) **tondeuse (à gazon),** lawnmower.

tondre [tɔ̃dr] *vtr* (*a*) to shear (sheep); to clip (hair, horse, hedge); to mow (lawn) (*b*) *F:* to fleece (s.o.).

tonifier [tɔnifje] *vtr* (*impf & pr sub* **n. tonifiions**) to tone up (the nervous system, a patient); to give tone to (the skin); to invigorate. **tonifiant** *a* bracing, tonic.

tonique [tɔnik] *a* 1. *Med:* (*a*) **médicament t.,** *nm* **t.,** tonic (*b*) stimulating, revivifying 2. *Ling:* tonic (accent); accented, stressed (syllable) 3. *Mus:* **note t.,** *nf* **t.,** keynote.

tonitruant [tɔnitryã] *a* thundering, booming.

tonnage [tɔnaʒ] *nm* tonnage.

tonne [tɔn] *nf Meas:* metric ton (= 1000 kilograms); tonne; *F:* **des tonnes de,** tons of.

tonnelier [tɔnəlje] *nm* (wet) cooper.

tonnelle [tɔnɛl] *nf* arbour, bower.

tonneau, -eaux [tɔno] *nm* 1. cask, barrel; **bière au t.,** draught beer 2. *Nau:* ton 3. *Av:* roll; *Aut:* somersault; **faire un t.,** to flip over.

tonner [tɔne] *vi* 1. to thunder; *impers* **il tonne,** it's thundering 2. (*of cannon*) to boom; *F:* **t. contre qn,** to rage against s.o. **tonnant** *a* thundering, booming.

tonnerre [tɔnɛr] *nm* (*a*) thunder; **t. d'applaudissements,** thunderous applause (*b*) *int* **t.!** heavens above! *F:* **du t.,** wonderful, terrific.

tonsure [tɔ̃syr] *nf* (*a*) tonsure (*b*) *F:* bald patch.

tonte [tɔ̃t] *nf* 1. (*a*) sheep shearing (*b*) clip (*c*) shearing time 2. mowing (of lawn).

tonton [tɔ̃tɔ̃] *nm F:* uncle.

tonus [tɔnys] *nm* (*a*) *Med:* tonicity (of muscle); tone (*b*) (*of pers*) energy, dynamism.

top [tɔp] *nm WTel: TV:* time signal; **les tops,** the pips; **au 4ème t.,** on the 4th stroke.

topaze [tɔpaz] *nf* topaz.

toper [tɔpe] *vi F:* to agree (**à qch,** to sth); **tope là!** done! agreed!

topinambour [tɔpinãbur] *nm Bot:* Jerusalem artichoke.

topographie [tɔpɔgrafi] *nf* topography. **topographique** *a* topographic(al).

toquade [tɔkad] *nf F:* craze (for sth); infatuation (with s.o.).

toque [tɔk] *nf* cap; (chef's) hat.

toqué, -ée [tɔke] *F:* 1. *a* (*a*) crazy, nuts (*b*) infatuated, madly in love (**de,** with) 2. *n* nutcase.

torche [tɔrʃ] *nf* torch; **t. électrique,** electric torch; *NAm:* flashlight.

torcher [tɔrʃe] *vtr* to wipe (sth) clean.

torchis [tɔrʃi] *nm Const:* cob, daub.

torchon [tɔrʃɔ̃] *nm* (*a*) (kitchen) cloth; floorcloth; dishcloth; tea towel; duster; **le t. brûle chez eux,** they're at daggers drawn (*b*) *F:* badly written article; (*newspaper*) rag.

tordant [tɔrdã] *a F:* screamingly funny.

tordre [tɔrdr] 1. *vtr* to twist; to wring (clothes, one's hands); **t. le cou à qn,** to wring s.o.'s neck; **t. la bouche,** to pull a face; **se t. le pied,** to twist one's ankle 2. **se t.** (*a*) to writhe, twist (with pain); *F:* **se t. (de rire),** to split one's sides laughing (*b*) to bend, to buckle, to twist. **tordu, -ue** *a* 1. twisted (limbs); buckled, bent (chassis) 2. (*a*) warped (mind) (*b*) *F:* mad, cracked, round the bend; *n* **c'est un t., une tordue,** he's, she's, a nutcase.

toréador [tɔreadɔr] *nm* toreador, bullfighter.

tornade [tɔrnad] *nf* tornado.

torpeur [tɔrpœr] *nf* torpor.

torpillage [tɔrpijaʒ] *nm* torpedoing.

torpille [tɔrpij] *nf* torpedo.

torpiller [tɔrpije] *vtr* to torpedo.

torpilleur [tɔrpijœr] *nm* torpedo boat.

torréfier [tɔrefje] *vtr* (*impf & pr sub* **n. torréfiions**) to roast (coffee).

torrent [tɔrã] *nm* torrent, mountain stream; **il pleut à torrents,** it's raining in torrents; **t. de larmes,** flood of tears. **torrentiel, -elle** *a* torrential.

torride [tɔrid] *a* torrid (zone); scorching (heat).

torsade [tɔrsad] *nf* twisted cord.

torsader [tɔrsade] *vtr* to twist (rope, cord).

torse [tɔrs] *nm* torso, trunk; **t. nu,** stripped to the waist; **bomber le t.,** to stick out one's chest.

torsion [tɔrsjɔ̃] *nf* torsion; twisting.

tort [tɔr] *nm* 1. wrong; error, fault; **avoir t., être dans son t.,** to be (in the) wrong; **donner t. à qn,** to lay the blame on s.o.; **à t. ou à raison,** rightly or wrongly; **à t. et à travers,** at random, without rhyme or reason 2. injury, harm, detriment; **la grêle a fait beaucoup de t.,** the hail has done a great deal of damage; **faire du t. à qn,** (i) to wrong s.o.; to do s.o. an injustice (ii) to damage s.o.'s cause, business, reputation.

torticolis [tɔrtikɔli] *nm* stiff neck; torticollis.

tortiller [tɔrtije] 1. *vtr* to twist (up) (paper, hair); to twirl (one's moustache) 2. *vi* (*a*) **t. des hanches,** to swing, to wiggle, the hips (*b*) *F:* to quibble 3. **se t.,** to wriggle; to writhe, squirm.

tortionnaire [tɔrsjɔnɛr] *nm* torturer.

tortue [tɔrty] *nf* tortoise; **t. de mer,** turtle; **marcher comme une t.,** to crawl along at a snail's pace.

tortueux, -euse [tɔrtɥø, -øz] *a* tortuous, winding (road); devious (conduct).

torture [tɔrtyr] *nf* torture.

torturer [tɔrtyre] *vtr* to torture (prisoner); **la jalousie le torturait,** he was tortured by jealousy; **se t. l'esprit,** to rack one's brains.

tôt [to] *adv* (*a*) soon; **mardi au plus t.,** (on) Tuesday at the earliest; **t. ou tard,** sooner or later; **nous n'étions pas plus t. rentrés que,** we had no sooner returned than; **revenez au plus t.,** come back as soon as possible (*b*) early; **se lever t.,** to rise early; **vous auriez dû me le dire plus t.,** you should have told me earlier, before; *a* **il est trop t.,** it's too early; *P:* **c'est pas trop t.!** and about time too!

total, -aux [tɔtal, -o] 1. *a* total, complete, whole 2. *nm* whole, total; **faire le t.,** to add up; **au t.,** all in all; *F:* **et t., il a tout perdu,** and to cut a long story short, he lost everything. **totalement** *adv* totally, completely.

totaliser [tɔtalize] *vtr* to total.

totalitarisme [tɔtalitarism] *nm* totalitarianism. **totalitaire** *a* totalitarian.

totalité [tɔtalite] *nf* totality, whole; **la t. de,** all of; **en t.,** wholly; all; **pris dans sa t.,** taken as a whole.

toubib [tubib] *nm F:* doctor, quack.

toucan [tukã] *nm Orn:* toucan.

touchant [tuʃã] 1. *a* touching, moving (sight, speech) 2 *prep* concerning, about.

touche [tuʃ] *nf* 1. (*a*) touch, touching; **pierre de t.,** touchstone (*b*) *Art:* (brush)stroke (*c*) *Fenc: Lit:* hit; *Fish:* bite; *F:* **faire une t.,** to make a hit (*d*) *Sp:* (i) touchline (ii) throw-in; **rester sur la t.,** to stay on the sidelines (*e*) *P:* **drôle de t.,** weird-looking guy 2. key (of typewriter, piano, computer).

touche-à-tout [tuʃatu] *n inv* meddler, busybody.

toucher¹ [tuʃe] 1. *vtr* (*a*) to touch (s.o., sth); *Fb:* to handle (the ball); *Fenc:* to hit (one's opponent); *F:* **touche du bois!** touch wood; (*to child*) **pas touche!** don't touch! **t. un chèque,** to cash a cheque; **t. son salaire,** *vi* **t.,** to get one's pay, to be paid (*b*) to move, touch (s.o.); **t. qn jusqu'aux larmes,** to move s.o. to tears (*c*) to concern, affect (s.o.); **en ce qui vous touche,** as far as you are concerned (*d*) *Nau:* **t. à un port,** to call at a port; **t. (le fond),** (i) to touch bottom (ii) to be aground (*e*) to get hold of (s.o.); (*of letter*) to reach (s.o.) (*h*) to touch on, deal with (fact, subject) 2. *v ind tr* to meddle, interfere (**à,** with); to touch, to tamper with (sth); **n'y touchez pas!** hands off! **n'avoir pas l'air d'y t.,** to look as if butter wouldn't melt in one's mouth 3. *vi* (*a*) **t. à qch,** to be in touch, in contact, with sth; to be near to sth; to border on sth; to adjoin sth; **l'année touche à sa fin,** the year is drawing to a close (*b*) **t. à,** to concern, to affect (*c*) **t. au plafond,** to touch, reach, the ceiling 4. **se t.,** to touch, to adjoin.

toucher² *nm* touch, feel; **chaud au t.,** hot to the touch.

touffe [tuf] *nf* tuft (of hair, straw); clump (of trees). **touffu** *a* bushy (beard); thick (wood); abstruse (book).

touiller [tuje] *vtr F:* to stir (up); to toss (salad).

toujours [tuʒur] *adv* 1. always, ever; **un ami de t.,** a lifelong friend; **pour t.,** for ever 2. still; **il fait t. aussi chaud,** it is as hot as ever; **cherchez t.,** go on looking 3. nevertheless, all the same; **je peux t. essayer,** I can at least try; **t. est-il que,** the fact remains that; **c'est t. ça,** it's always something.

toupet [tupɛ] *nm* 1. tuft of hair, quiff 2. *F:* cheek, sauce; nerve; **avoir du t.,** to have a nerve.

toupie [tupi] *nf* 1. top 2. **vieille t.,** old trout.

tour¹ [tur] *nf* 1. tower; tower block; *Av:* **t. de contrôle,** control tower 2. *Chess:* castle, rook.

tour² *nm* 1. (*a*) (turning) lathe (*b*) (potter's) wheel 2. (*a*) circumference, circuit; **faire le t. du monde,** to go round the world; **t. d'horizon,** general survey; *Sp:* **t. de piste,** lap; **faire le t. du cadran,** to sleep round the clock; **t. de taille,** waist measurement (*b*) turn (of phrase); course, direction (of business affair); **l'af-**

faire prend un mauvais t., the matter is taking a bad turn; **t. d'esprit,** turn of mind (*e*) **se donner un t. de reins,** to strain one's back 3. (*a*) round, revolution, turn (of wheel); **frapper à t. de bras,** to strike with all one's might; **donner un t. de clef,** to turn the key in, to lock, the door; *F:* **mon sang n'a fait qu'un t.,** my heart seemed to stop beating (*b*) stroll; **faire un t. de jardin,** to stroll round the garden (*c*) trip, tour 4. rotation, turn; **à qui le t.!** whose turn is it? **chacun (à) son t.,** each one in his turn; **t. à t.,** in turn; **à t. de rôle,** in turns 5. trick, feat; **jouer un mauvais t. à qn,** to play s.o. a nasty trick; **t. de main,** flick of the wrist; **je n'ai pas le t. de main,** I haven't the knack; **t. de force,** feat of strength; **il a plus d'un t. dans son sac,** he's got more than one trick up his sleeve.

tourbe [turb] *nf* peat, turf. **tourbeux, -euse** *a* peaty, boggy.

tourbière [turbjɛr] *nf* peat bog.

tourbillon [turbijɔ̃] *nm* 1. whirlwind; swirl (of dust); **t. de neige,** flurry of snow 2. (*a*) whirlpool (*b*) eddy (of water, wind) (*c*) whirl, hustle and bustle (of life, business).

tourbillonnement [turbijɔnmã] *nm* whirl(ing).

tourbillonner [turbijɔne] *vi* to whirl (round); to eddy, swirl.

tourelle [turɛl] *nf* turret; *Mil: etc:* (gun) turret.

tourisme [turism] *nm* tourism; touring; tourist trade; **agence, bureau, de t.,** travel agency; **voiture de t.,** private car.

touriste [turist] *n* tourist. **touristique** *a* tourist (guide).

tourment [turmã] *nm* torment; anguish.

tourmente [turmãt] *nf* (*a*) gale, storm; **t. de neige,** blizzard (*b*) (political) upheaval.

tourmenter [turmãte] *vtr* 1. (*a*) to torture, torment; to harass (*b*) to plague, pester (s.o.) 2. **se t.,** to be anxious, to worry. **tourmenté** *a* distorted (forms); tormented, tortured (mind); turbulent (life).

tournage [turnaʒ] *nm* (*a*) turning (on the lathe) (*b*) *Cin:* shooting.

tournant, -ante [turnã, -ãt] 1. *a* (*a*) turning; revolving; **fauteuil t.,** swivel chair; **pont t.,** swing bridge (*b*) winding (road); spiral (staircase) 2. *nm* (*a*) turning; bend; (street) corner; *F:* **je l'aurai au t.,** I'll get him yet! (*b*) turning point.

tournebouler [turnəbule] *vtr F:* to upset (s.o.).

tournebroche [turnəbrɔʃ] *nm* roasting jack; spit.

tourne-disque [turnədisk] *nm Rec:* record player; *pl* tourne-disques.

tournedos [turnədo] *nm Cu:* tournedos.

tournée [turne] *nf* 1. (official's, doctor's, postman's) round; *Th:* **en t.,** on tour; **faire la t. des magasins,** to go round the shops 2. round (of drinks).

tournemain [turnəmɛ̃] *nm* **en un t.,** in an instant.

tourner [turne] 1. *vtr* (*a*) to turn; to fashion, shape, on a lathe; to throw (a pot) (*b*) to revolve, turn round, rotate; to turn (key in lock); **t. la tête,** to turn one's head; **t. le dos à qn,** (i) to turn one's back on s.o. (ii) to have one's back turned to s.o.; *Cin:* **un film,** to make a film; **t. une scène,** to film a scene; *Cu:* **t. une crème,** to stir a custard; *Fb:* **t. la mêlée,** to wheel the scrum (*c*) to change, convert; **t. qch en plaisanterie,** to laugh sth off (*d*) to turn over (page);

to turn up (card); **t. et retourner qch,** to turn sth over and over (*e*) to get round (corner, obstacle); to evade (a difficulty, the law) (*f*) F: **t. le lait,** to turn the milk sour; **ça lui a tourné la tête,** it's gone to his head 2. *vi* (*a*) to revolve; to go round; (*of machine*) to turn; **t. autour de qn,** to hang, hover, round s.o.; **t. autour du pot,** to beat about the bush; **la tête lui tourne,** he feels giddy; **faire t. la clef dans la serrure,** to turn the key in the lock (*b*) to change direction; **tournez à gauche,** turn left; **t. court,** to come to a sudden end; **le temps tourne au froid,** it's turning cold (*c*) to turn out, result; **bien t.,** to turn out well; F: **ça va mal t.,** it will lead to trouble (*d*) to tend (**à,** to); **l'affaire tournait au tragique,** the affair was taking a tragic turn; **t. (à l'aigre),** to turn (sour) (*e*) Cin: **t. dans un film,** to act in a film 3. **se t.** (*a*) **se t. vers qn,** to turn towards s.o. (*b*) **se t. contre qn,** to turn against s.o. (*c*) to turn round. **tourné** *a* (*a*) turned (on a lathe); shaped, made; **elle est bien tournée,** she has a lovely figure; **mal t.,** badly made; (*of letter*) badly written; **avoir l'esprit mal t.,** to have a nasty turn of mind (*b*) sour (milk, wine).

tournesol [turnəsɔl] *nm Bot:* sunflower.

tourneur [turnœr] *nm* turner; thrower.

tournevis [turnəvis] *nm Tls:* screwdriver.

tourniquet [turnikɛ] *nm* 1. (*a*) turnstile (*b*) revolving stand 2. (*a*) *Pyr:* Catherine wheel (*b*) (garden) sprinkler 3. *Med:* tourniquet.

tournis [turni] *nm* **donner le t. à qn,** to make s.o. giddy.

tournoi [turnwa] *nm* tournament.

tournoiement [turnwamɑ̃] *nm* whirling; wheeling; eddying, swirling.

tournoyer [turnwaje] *vi* (**je tournoie, n. tournoyons**) to turn round and round; (*of birds*) to wheel; to spin; (*of water*) to eddy, swirl; **faire t. qch,** to whirl sth round.

tournure [turnyr] *nf* 1. turn, course (of events); **les affaires prennent une mauvaise t.,** things are taking a turn for the worse 2. shape, form, figure; **t. d'esprit,** turn of mind; **prendre t.,** to take shape.

tourte [turt] *nf* (*a*) round loaf (*b*) (meat) pie.

tourteau, -eaux [turto] *nm* edible crab.

tourterelle [turtərɛl] *nf* turtledove.

tous [tu(s)] *see* **tout.**

Toussaint (la) [latusɛ̃] *Prnf* All Saints' day.

tousser [tuse] *vi* to cough; (*of engine*) to splutter.

toussoter [tusɔte] *vi* to clear one's throat; to cough slightly; to have a slight cough.

tout, toute, *pl* **tous, toutes** [tu, tut, tu, tut] (*when* **tous** *is a pron it is pronounced* [tus]) 1. *a* (*a*) (*noun undetermined*) any, every, all; **pour toute réponse, il éclata de rire,** his only answer was to burst out laughing; **t. autre que vous,** anybody but you; **toute liberté d'agir,** full liberty to act; **j'ai toute raison de croire que,** I have every reason to believe that; **repas à toute heure,** meals served at any time (*b*) (*intensive*) **à la toute dernière minute,** at the very last minute; **de toute beauté,** most beautiful; **à toute vitesse,** at full speed; **de toute importance,** all-important; of the utmost importance; **t. à vous,** entirely yours (*c*) the whole; all; **t. le monde,** everybody, everyone; **toute la journée,** the whole day, all day long; **pendant t. l'hiver,** throughout the winter; **t.**

Paris, the whole of Paris (*d*) all, every; **tous les jours,** every day; **tous les invités,** all the guests; **de tous (les) côtés,** from all sides; **toutes proportions gardées,** making due allowance (*e*) **tous (les) deux,** both; **tous les deux jours,** every other day (*f*) **c'est toute une histoire,** (i) it's a long story (ii) it's quite a job 2. *pron* (*a*) *sg neut* all, everything; **c'est t.,** that's all; **t. ce qui vous plaira,** whatever you like; anything you like; F: **et t. et t.,** and all the rest of it; **t. est bien qui finit bien,** all's well that ends well; **il mange de t.,** he eats anything (and everything); **c'est t. ce qu'il y a de plus beau,** it is most beautiful; F: **il a t. du fonctionnaire,** he's the typical civil servant; **c'est t. dire,** I needn't say more; **à t. prendre,** all in all, all things considered; F: **drôle comme t.,** awfully funny (*b*) *pl* **une fois pour toutes,** once and for all; **tous** [tus] **à la fois,** all together; **le meilleur de tous,** the best of them all; F: **on l'aimait bien tous,** we were all very fond of him 3. *nm* **le t.,** the whole; the lot; **le t. est de réussir,** the main thing is to succeed; **jouer le t. pour le t.,** to stake everything; F: **ce n'est pas le t., ça!** that's not getting us very far! *adv phr* **du t. au t.,** entirely; **en t.,** in all; **(pas) du t.,** not at all 4. *adv* (*intensive*) (*before a fem adj beginning with a consonant or* h *aspirate* **tout** *becomes* **toute**) (*a*) quite, entirely; completely; very; **t. nouveau(x), toute(s) nouvelle(s),** quite new; **t. seul,** all, quite, alone; **toute vêtue de noir,** dressed all in black; **de t. premier ordre,** of the very first order; **t. droit,** bolt upright; **t. neuf,** brand new; **t. nu,** stark naked; **t. éveillé,** wide awake; **t. fait,** ready-made; **t. au bout,** right at the end; **c'est t. comme chez nous!** it's just like home! *adv phr* **t. à fait,** quite, entirely; **t. au plus, t. au moins,** at the very most, at the very least; **t. à vous,** yours ever (*b*) **t. en parlant,** while speaking (*c*) **t. ignorant qu'il est, qu'il soit,** ignorant though he is, though he may be (*d*) **être t. oreilles,** to be all ears.

tout-à-l'égout [tutalegu] *nm inv* main(s) drainage.

toutefois [tutfwa] *adv* yet, nevertheless, however.

toute-puissance [tutpɥisɑ̃s] *nf* omnipotence.

tout-puissant, toute-puissante *a* almighty, omnipotent; *nm* **le T.-P.,** the Almighty.

toutou, -tous [tutu] *nm* (*child's word*) doggie.

toux [tu] *nf* cough.

toxicologie [tɔksikɔlɔʒi] *nf* toxicology. **toxicologique** *a* toxicological.

toxicologue [tɔksikɔlɔg] *n* toxicologist.

toxicomane [tɔksikɔman] *n* drug addict.

toxicomanie [tɔksikɔmani] *nf* drug addiction.

toxine [tɔksin] *nf Physiol:* toxin.

toxique [tɔksik] 1. *a* toxic; **gaz t.,** poison gas 2. *nm* poison.

trac [trak] *nm F:* fright; funk; **avoir le t.,** to have the wind up; *Th:* to have stage fright.

tracas [traka] *nm* worry, trouble, bother.

tracasser [trakase] 1. *vtr* to worry, bother, plague (s.o.) 2. **se t.,** to worry.

trace [tras] *nf* (*a*) trace; trail, track, spoor; footprint(s) (of person); **être sur la t. de qn,** to be on s.o.'s tracks; **il suit les traces de son père,** he's following in his father's footsteps; **retrouver t. de qn, de qch,** to find a trace of s.o., of sth (*b*) scar, mark (of wound, burn) (*c*) (slight) trace (of poison, regret).

tracé [trase] *nm* 1. layout (of town); lie, alignment (of road) 2. (*a*) outline, sketch, diagram (*b*) graph (of curve); *Rad:* plot.

tracer [trase] *vtr* (**n. traçons**) to trace; to plot (curve); to lay out (road); to map out (route); to draw (a line); to outline (plan).

trachée [trake] *nf Anat:* trachea, windpipe.

tract [trakt] *nm* leaflet.

tracteur [traktœr] *nm* tractor.

traction [traksjɔ̃] *nf* traction; *Aut:* t. avant, front-wheel drive.

tradition [tradisjɔ̃] *nf* tradition; **de t.**, traditional. **traditionnel, -elle** *a* traditional; usual, habitual. **traditionnellement** *adv* traditionally.

traducteur, -trice [tradyktœr, -tris] *n* translator.

traduction [tradyksjɔ̃] *nf* 1. translating 2. translation.

traduire [tradɥir] *vtr* (*conj like* CONDUIRE) 1. t. qn en justice, to sue, prosecute, s.o. 2. (*a*) to translate (de, from; en, into) (*b*) to represent; to express (feeling, idea); **vous traduisez mal ma pensée**, you're misinterpreting my thoughts; **sa douleur se traduisit par les larmes**, his grief found expression in tears. **traduisible** *a* translatable.

trafic [trafik] *nm* 1. (*a*) trading, trade (*b*) *Pej:* traffic, illicit trading; **t. de la drogue**, drug trafficking; **t. d'armes**, arms dealing; *F:* **un drôle de t.**, suspicious goings-on 2. *Trans:* traffic.

trafiquant, -ante [trafikã, -ãt] *n Pej:* (drug) trafficker; **t. du marché noir**, black marketeer.

trafiquer [trafike] 1. *vi Pej:* t. de, en, qch, to traffic in sth; **t. de sa conscience**, to sell one's conscience 2. *vtr* to doctor (wine, engine).

tragédie [traʒedi] *nf* tragedy.

tragédien, -ienne [traʒedjɛ̃, -jɛn] *n* tragic actor, actress.

tragique [traʒik] 1. (*a*) *a* tragic (writer, play, role, event) (*b*) *nm* **cela tourne au t.**, the thing is becoming tragic; **prendre qch au t.**, to make a tragedy of sth 2. *n* writer of tragedies 3. *nm Th:* tragedy. **tragiquement** *adv* tragically.

trahir [trair] *vtr* 1. to betray; to reveal, give away (secret); **t. sa pensée**, to give oneself away 2. to betray (s.o.'s confidence); to deceive (s.o.); *F:* to let s.o. down; **ses jambes l'ont trahi**, his legs failed him.

trahison [traizɔ̃] *nf* treason; treachery; betrayal.

train [trɛ̃] *nm* 1. (*a*) train, string, line (of vehicles); series; set (of wheels, tyres); *Aut:* t. avant, arrière, front, rear, axle (assembly); **t. de pensées**, train of thought (*b*) *Rail:* train; **t. de voyageurs, de marchandises**, passenger, goods, train; **t. supplémentaire**, relief train; **t. auto-couchettes**, car-sleeper; **voyager en t., par le t.**, to travel by train (*c*) *Mil:* train (of transport) (*d*) quarters (of horse); **t. de derrière, de devant**, hindquarters, forequarters (*e*) **t. de roulement**, undercarriage (of wheeled vehicle); *Av:* t. (d'atterrissage), landing gear, undercarriage 2. (*a*) pace, rate; **aller bon t.**, to go at a good pace; **aller son petit t.**, to jog along; **à fond de t.**, at top speed; **au t. où vont les choses**, at *this* rate; **mise en t.**, warming-up (*b*) **mettre qch en t.**, to set sth going; **en t. de faire qch**, (busy) doing sth; **il est en t. de travailler**, he is busy working; **le t. ordinaire des jours**, the daily routine; **les choses vont leur t.**, things are going along

as usual (*c*) **t. de vie**, way of life, life style; **mener grand t.**, to live on a grand scale 3. mood; **être en t.**, to be in good form; **être mal en t.**, to be out of sorts.

traînard, -arde [trɛnar, -ard] *n* straggler; *F:* slow-coach.

traîne [trɛn] *nf* 1. **à la t.**, in tow; *Fig:* être à la t., to lag behind 2. train (of dress).

traîneau, -eaux [trɛno] *nm* sledge, sleigh.

traînée [trɛne, trene] *nf* trail (of smoke, blood); train (of gunpowder); **se répandre comme une t. de poudre**, to spread like wildfire.

traîner [trɛne, trene] 1. *vtr* to drag, pull, draw (sth) along; to drag out (a speech); to drawl (one's words); **t. la jambe**, to limp; **t. les pieds**, to shuffle; **t. le pied**, to lag behind 2. *vi* (*a*) to trail, drag (in the dust) (*b*) to lag, to trail, behind (*c*) to linger; to dawdle; **t. dans la rue**, to hang about the streets (*d*) to lie about; **laisser t. ses affaires**, to leave one's belongings lying about (*e*) to flag, droop, languish; (*of illness*) to drag on; **l'affaire traîne**, the matter is hanging fire; **t. en longueur**, to drag (on) 3. **se t.** (*a*) to crawl (along); **se t. aux pieds de qn**, to go on one's knees to s.o. (*b*) to drag oneself along, about; (*of time*) to drag on. **traînant** *a* dragging, trailing; drawling (voice).

train-train [trɛ̃trɛ̃] *nm F:* hundrum routine, daily round.

traire [trɛr] *vtr* (*prp* **trayant**; *pp* **trait**; *pr ind* **ils traient**; *no ph*) to milk (cow); to draw (milk).

trait [trɛ] *nm* 1. pulling; **tout d'un t.**, at one stretch; **cheval de t.**, draught horse 2. (*a*) arrow; **partir comme un t.**, to be off like a shot (*b*) beam (of light) (*d*) **t. d'esprit**, flash of wit 3. draught, gulp; **d'un (seul) t.**, at one gulp 4. (*a*) stroke, mark, line; **t. de crayon**, stroke of the pencil; **d'un t.**, with one stroke (*b*) **t. d'union**, (i) hyphen (ii) link 5. (*a*) feature (of face); **traits fins**, fine features (*b*) trait (of character) 6. act, deed (of courage, kindness); **t. de génie**, stroke of genius 7. reference (to sth), bearing (on sth); **avoir t. à qch**, to refer to sth.

traite [trɛt] *nf* 1. stretch (of road); **(tout) d'une t.**, at a stretch, without interruption 2. (*a*) *A:* transport (of goods); trading; (ivory, slave) trade (*b*) **t. des blanches**, white slave trade 3. *Fin:* (banker's) draft; bill (of exchange) 4. milking.

traité [trɛte] *nm* 1. treatise 2. *Pol:* treaty.

traitement [trɛtmã] *nm* 1. (*a*) treatment; *Med:* course of treatment; **mauvais t.**, illtreatment; *Med:* **premier t.**, first aid (*b*) processing (of raw materials) 2. salary.

traiter [trete] 1. *vtr* (*a*) to treat; to treat (s.o.) (well, badly); **t. qn en ami**, to treat s.o. like, as, a friend (*b*) **t. qn de lâche**, to call s.o. a coward (*c*) **t. un malade**, to treat a patient; **se faire t. pour un cancer**, to undergo treatment for cancer (*d*) *Ind:* to process; to treat, spray (vines) (*e*) *esp Lit:* to entertain 2. *vtr* (*a*) to negotiate; to handle (business) (*b*) to discuss, deal with (a subject) 3. *vi* (*a*) **t. de la paix**, to treat for peace (*b*) **t. d'un sujet**, to deal with a subject.

traiteur [trɛtœr] *nm* caterer.

traître, traîtresse [trɛtr, trɛtrɛs] 1. *a* treacherous; *F:* **pas un t. mot**, not a single word 2. *n* traitor, traitress; *Th:* villain; **en t.**, treacherously. **traîtreusement** *adv* treacherously.

traîtrise [tretriz] *nf* treachery; treacherousness.

trajectoire [traʒɛktwar] *nf* path (of star, aircraft); trajectory (of comet, satellite).

trajet [traʒe] *nm (a)* journey; ride, drive, flight, crossing; **j'ai fait une partie du t. en avion,** I flew part of the way *(b)* path (of projectile).

tralala [tralala] *nn inv F:* **en grand t.,** (i) with a lot of fuss (ii) all dressed up.

trame [tram] *nf* 1. *Tex:* woof, weft; *Fig:* thread (of existence); framework (of novel) 2. *TV:* raster.

tramer [trame] *vtr* to hatch (plot); **il se trame quelque chose,** there's something afoot.

tram(way) [tram(wɛ)] *nm* tram(car), *NAm:* street-car.

tranchant [trɑ̃ʃɑ̃] 1. *a (a)* cutting, sharp (tool, knife); keen (edge); *(b)* trenchant (words, opinion); peremptory (tone) 2. *nm* (cutting) edge (of knife).

tranche [trɑ̃ʃ] *nf* 1. slice (of bread, meat); rasher (of bacon); **t. de salaires,** wage bracket; **t. de vie,** slice, cross section, of life 2. slab (of marble) 3. *(a)* edge (of coin); (cut) edge (of book) *(b)* section.

tranchée [trɑ̃ʃe] *nf* trench; *Agr:* drain; cutting (through forest); **t. garde-feu,** fire break.

trancher [trɑ̃ʃe] 1. *vtr (a)* to slice (bread); to cut *(b)* to cut short (discussion); to settle (question, problem) once and for all; **t. le mot,** to speak plainly; *vi* **t. net,** to bring to a firm conclusion 2. *vi (of colours, characteristics)* to contrast strongly (**sur,** with); to stand out (against). **tranché** *a* distinct (colour); clear-cut (opinion).

tranquille [trɑ̃kil] *a (a)* tranquil; calm, still, quiet; **se tenir t.,** to keep (i) still (ii) quiet *(b)* quiet, peaceful (town) *(c)* undisturbed; easy (conscience); **laissez-moi t.,** leave me alone; **dormir t.,** to sleep in peace; **il n'a pas l'esprit t.,** he's uneasy in his mind; **soyez t.,** set your mind at rest; **sois t., il reviendra!** he'll come back, don't worry! **tranquillement** *adv* tranquilly, calmly, quietly.

tranquilliser [trɑ̃kilize] *vtr* to calm; to reassure; to set (mind) at rest **2. se t.** *(a) (of sea)* to become calm *(b)* to set one's mind at rest. **tranquillisant** 1. *a* reassuring (news); soothing (effect) 2. *nm Med:* tranquillizer.

tranquillité [trɑ̃kilite] *nf* tranquillity, calm(ness); quiet, stillness; **t. d'esprit,** peace of mind; **troubler la t. publique,** to disturb the peace; **en toute t.,** with an easy mind.

transaction [trɑ̃zaksjɔ̃] *nf Com:* transaction; *pl* dealings, deals.

transat [trɑ̃zat] *nm* deck chair.

transatlantique [trɑ̃zatlɑ̃tik] 1. *a* transatlantic 2. *nm (a)* (Atlantic) liner *(b)* deck chair.

transbahuter [trɑ̃sbayte] *vtr F:* to move, shift; to lug (sth) around.

transbordement [trɑ̃sbɔrdəmɑ̃] *nm* transhipment (of cargo); transfer.

transborder [trɑ̃sbɔrde] *vtr* to tranship; to transfer (passengers, goods). **transbordeur** *a & nm* (**pont**) **t.,** transporter bridge.

transcendance [trɑ̃sɑ̃dɑ̃s] *nf* transcendence. **transcendant, -ante** *a* transcendent; *Mth:* transcendental. **transcendantal, -aux** *a* transcendental.

transcender [trɑ̃sɑ̃de] *vtr* to transcend.

transcription [trɑ̃skripsjɔ̃] *nf (a)* transcription, transcribing *(b)* transcript, copy.

transcrire [trɑ̃skrir] *vtr (conj like* ÉCRIRE*)* 1. to transcribe; **t. une lettre à la machine,** to type out a letter 2. *Mus:* to transcribe.

transe [trɑ̃s] *nf* 1. *usu pl* fright, fear; **être dans les transes,** to be in agonies of anticipation 2. (hypnotic) trance.

transférer [trɑ̃sfere] *vtr* (**je transfère; je transférerai**) to transfer; to make over, assign (goods to s.o.).

transfert [trɑ̃sfɛr] *nm* transfer; *Psy:* transference.

transfiguration [trɑ̃sfigyrasjɔ̃] *nf* transfiguration.

transfigurer [trɑ̃sfigyre] *vtr* to transfigure.

transformateur [trɑ̃sfɔrmatœr] *nm El:* transformer.

transformation [trasfɔrmasjɔ̃] *nf* transformation (**en,** into); change; conversion; **industrie de t.,** processing industry.

transformer [trɑ̃sfɔrme] 1. *vtr* to transform, change (**en,** into); to convert (sth into sth); *Rugby Fb:* to convert (a try) **2. se t.,** to be transformed, to change, turn (**en,** into). **transformable** *a* convertible.

transfuge [trɑ̃sfyʒ] *n* renegade.

transfusion [trɑ̃sfyzjɔ̃] *nf* (blood) transfusion.

transgresser [trɑ̃sgrese] *vtr* to transgress; to disobey (orders); to infringe, to contravene (rules).

transgression [trɑ̃sgresjɔ̃] *nf* transgression.

transiger [trɑ̃ziʒe] *vi* (**n. transigeons**) to compromise.

transir [trɑ̃zir] *vtr (a)* to chill to the bone *(b)* to paralyze (with fear). **transi** *a* perished (with cold); paralyzed (with fear).

transistor [trɑ̃zistɔr] *nm* transistor.

transit [trɑ̃zit] *nm* transit; **en t.,** in transit; **marchandises de t.,** goods for transit.

transiter [trɑ̃zite] 1. *vtr* to forward (goods) 2. *vi (of goods)* to be in transit.

transitif, -ive [trɑ̃zitif, -iv] *a* transitive.

transition [trɑ̃zisjɔ̃] *nf* transition; **de t.,** transitional; **sans t.,** abruptly. **transitoire** *a* transitory, transient; transitional (period); temporary (measure).

translucide [trɑ̃slysid] *a* translucent.

transmetteur [trɑ̃smetœr] *nm* transmitter.

transmettre [trɑ̃smetr] *vtr (conj like* METTRE*)* to transmit (light, message); to pass on message, disease); to inpart (truth); *WTel:* to send (message); to broadcast (programme).

transmission [trɑ̃smisjɔ̃] *nf* 1. *(a)* transmission; passing on (of order); imparting (of truth); sending (of message); *WTel: TV:* **t. en direct,** live broadcast; **t. en différé,** recorded broadcast; *Mil:* **les transmissions,** signals *(b) MecE:* **la t.,** the transmission (gear) 2. *(a) Adm:* **t. des pouvoirs,** handing over *(b)* **t. de pensée,** thought transference.

transparaître [trɑ̃sparɛtr] *vi (conj like* PARAÎTRE*)* to show through.

transparence [trɑ̃sparɑ̃s] *nf* transparency. **transparent** *a* transparent; clear.

transpercer [trɑ̃spɛrse] *vtr* (**n. transperçons**) to transfix; to stab, to pierce (s.o., sth) through.

transpiration [trɑ̃spirasjɔ̃] *nf* perspiration, sweat.

transpirer [trɑ̃spire] *vi* 1. *(aux avoir)* to perspire, to sweat 2. *(aux avoir or* **être***)* to transpire; to come to light.

transplantation [trɑ̃splɑ̃tasjɔ̃] *nf* transplantation; *Surg:* **t. cardiaque,** heart transplant.

transplanter [trɑ̃splɑ̃te] *vtr* to transplant.

transport [trɑ̃spɔr] *nm* **1.** transport, carriage (of goods, passengers); haulage; **les transports en commun,** public transport; **frais de t.,** freight charges **2.** *Navy:* troopship **3.** transport, rapture; outburst of feeling.

transporter [trɑ̃spɔrte] *vtr* **1** to transport, carry (goods); **t. qn d'urgence à l'hôpital,** to rush s.o. to hospital; **se t. sur les lieux,** to visit the scene of the crime, of the accident **2.** to transport, to carry away; **cette nouvelle l'a transporté,** he was overjoyed by the news.

transporteur [trɑ̃spɔrtœr] *nm* (a) carrier, forwarding agent (b) *Ind:* conveyor.

transposer [trɑ̃spoze] *vtr* to transpose.

transposition [trɑ̃spozisjɔ̃] *nf* transposition.

transvaser [trɑ̃zvaze] *vtr* to decant (wine).

transversal, -aux [trɑ̃sversal, -o] *a* transverse, transversal; cross (section, gallery). **transversalement** *adv* transversely, crosswise.

trapèze [trapez] *nm* (a) *Mth:* trapezium, *NAm:* trapezoid (b) *Gym:* trapeze.

trapéziste [trapezist] *n* trapeze artist.

trappe [trap] *nf* **1.** *Ven:* trap, pitfall **2.** (a) trap (door) (b) hatch.

trappeur [trapœr] trapper (of wild animals).

trapu [trapy] *a* (a) thick-set, squat, stocky (man, horse) (b) *Sch: F:* brainy; stocky (problem).

traquenard [traknar] *nm Ven: & Fig:* trap, pitfall.

traquer [trake] *vtr* to track down, hunt down (animal, criminal).

travail, -aux [travaj, -o] *nm* **1.** *Med:* labour; **femme en t.,** woman in labour; **salle de t.,** labour room **2.** (a) work; **se mettre au t.,** to start, get down to work; **cesser le t.,** (i) to stop work; to knock off (for the day) (ii) to down tools; **vêtements de t.,** working clothes; **Ministère du T. =** Department of Employment (b) **t. de tête, t. intellectuel,** brainwork; **t. manuel,** manual labour; **t. en série,** mass production; **t. noir,** moonlighting; *Sch:* **travaux pratiques,** practical work (c) operation; working (of the digestion); fermenting (of wine) (d) exercise; practice (e) occupation, employment; **trouver du t.,** to find a job; **sans t.,** unemployed, *F:* jobless (f) (place of) work **3.** (a) piece of work; job (b) (literary) work; **auteur d'un t. sur les métaux,** author of a work on metals (c) *Adm:* **travaux publics,** public works; *PN:* **travaux,** road works (ahead) **4.** workmanship.

travailler [travaje] **1.** *vtr* (a) *esp Lit:* to torment, worry, obsess; **se t. l'esprit,** to worry (b) to work (up)on (s.o.); to bring pressure to bear (up)on (s.o.) (c) to work, fashion, shape (wood, metal); **t. la pâte,** to knead the dough; **t. son style,** to polish one's style (d) to work at, study (one's part, a subject) **2.** *vi* (a) to work, labour, toil; **t. ferme, dur,** to work hard; **je vais t. dans ma chambre,** I'm going to do some work in my room; **sa femme travaille,** his wife works, has a job; **le temps travaille pour nous,** time is on our side; **t. à faire qch,** to make an effort to do sth (b) (of wine) to ferment, to work; (of wood) to warp; (of imagination) to work. **travaillé** *a* worked, wrought (iron, stone); laboured, elaborate

(style). **travailleur, -euse 1.** *a* hard-working **2.** *n* worker; **les travailleurs,** the workers, the working people. **travailliste 1.** *n* member of the Labour party **2.** *a* Labour (member, Party).

travée [trave] *nf* **1.** *Const:* bay **2.** span (of bridge) **3.** bank (of seats).

travers [traver] *nm* **1.** (a) breadth; *adv phr:* **en t.,** across, crosswise; **profil en t.,** cross section; *prep phr* **en t. de,** across; **à t. qch, au t. de qch,** through sth; **à t. le monde,** throughout the world (b) *NAm:* **de t.,** **par le t.,** on the beam, abeam **2. de t.,** the wrong way; **tout va de t.,** everything is going wrong; **regarder qn de t.,** to look askance, to scowl, at s.o.; **il a la bouche de t.,** his mouth is crooked **3.** failing, bad habit, fault.

traverse [travers] *nf* **1. (chemin de) t.,** short cut **2. (barre de) t.,** cross bar, cross piece; *Rail:* sleeper.

traversée [traverse] *nf* (a) passage, (sea) crossing (b) **faire la t. d'une ville,** to cross, pass through, a town.

traverser [traverse] *vtr* to cross, to go across (street); to go, to pass, through (town, crisis); **t. la foule,** to make one's way through the crowd; **t. la rivière à la nage,** to swim across the river; **t. qch de part en part,** to go clean through sth; **une idée m'a traversé l'esprit,** an idea occurred to me.

traversin [traversɛ̃] *nm* bolster (for bed).

travesti, -ie [travesti] **1.** *nm* drag artist **2.** *nm* fancy dress **3.** *n* transvestite.

travestir [travestir] *vtr* **1.** to disguise (en, as) **2.** to travesty, parody (poem, play); to misrepresent (s.o.'s thoughts).

trébucher [trebyʃe] *vi* (aux avoir) to stumble; **faire t. qn,** to trip s.o. up.

trèfle [trefl] *nm* **1.** *Bot:* trefoil, clover **2.** *Arch:* trefoil **3.** *Cards:* clubs.

tréfonds [trefɔ̃] *nm* **dans le t. de mon cœur,** in my heart of hearts.

treillage [trejaʒ] *nm* trellis (work); lattice; trellis fence.

treille [trej] *nf* vine arbour; trellised vines.

trellis [treji] *nm* **1.** trellis (work); lattice; **t. métallique,** wire mesh **2.** (a) *Tex:* canvas (b) *pl Mil:* fatigue dress.

treize [trez] *num a inv & nm inv* thirteen; **Louis T.,** Louis the Thirteenth; **le t. mai,** (on) the thirteenth of May. **treizième** *num a & n* thirteenth. **treizièmement** *adv* in the thirteenth place.

tréma [trema] *nm* diaeresis.

tremble [trɑ̃bl] *nm Bot:* aspen.

tremblement [trɑ̃bləmɑ̃] *nm* **1.** trembling, quivering, shaking; quavering (of voice) **2.** tremor (of fear); **t. de terre,** earthquake; *F:* **et tout le t.,** and the whole caboodle.

trembler [trɑ̃ble] *vi* (a) to tremble, quiver; to quake; to shiver (with cold); to shake (with anger); (of light) to flicker; (of voice) to quaver; **faire t. les vitres,** to make the windows rattle (b) to tremble with fear; **en tremblant,** tremulously; **je tremble pour lui,** I fear for him.

tremblote [trɑ̃blɔt] *nf P:* **avoir la t.,** (i) to have the jitters (ii) to have the shivers.

tremblotement [trɑ̃blɔtmɑ̃] *nm* trembling.

trembloter [trɑ̃blɔte] *vi* to tremble (slightly); to quiver; (of voice) to quaver; (of light) to flicker.

trémolo [tremɔlo] *nm Mus:* tremolo; quaver (in voice).

trémousser (se) [sətremuse] *vpr (a)* to fidget *(b)* **marcher en se trémoussant,** to walk with a wiggle.

trempe [trɑ̃p] *nf* **1.** steeping, dipping, soaking **2.** *Metall:* hardening, quenching **3.** *(a)* temper (of steel) *(b)* quality; **un homme de sa t.,** a man of his calibre.

tremper [trɑ̃pe] **1.** *vtr (a)* to mix, dilute, with water *(b)* to soak, steep (in a liquid); to dip (bread in soup); **se t. dans l'eau,** to plunge into the water; **se faire t.,** to get drenched; **t. ses mains dans l'eau,** to dip one's hands in the water *(c) Metall:* to temper, quench (steel) **2.** *vi (a) (of dirty linen)* to (lie in) soak *(b)* **t. dans un complot,** to have a hand in a plot. **trempé** *a* wet, soaked, drenched; **t. de sueur,** bathed in sweat; **t. jusqu'aux os,** soaked to the skin.

trempette [trɑ̃pɛt] *nf F:* **faire t.,** (i) to dip bread (ii) to have a quick dip, a quick bathe.

tremplin [trɑ̃plɛ̃] *nm* springboard; diving board; ski jump; *Fig:* springboard.

trentaine [trɑ̃tɛn] *nf* (about) thirty, some thirty; thirty (francs) or so; **il approche de la t.,** he's getting on for thirty.

trente [trɑ̃t] *num a inv & nm inv* thirty; *F:* **se mettre sur son t. et un,** to dress smartly. **trentième** *num a & n inv* thirtieth.

trente-six [trɑ̃tsi, -is, -iz; *see also* **six**] *num a inv & nm inv* (i) thirty-six (ii) *F:* umpteen; **voir t.-s. chandelles,** to see stars (after a blow on the head).

trépan [trepɑ̃] *nm Surg:* trepan.

trépanation [trepanasjɔ̃] *nf Surg:* trepanning.

trépaner [trepane] *vtr Surg:* to trepan.

trépas [trepa] *nm Lit:* death.

trépasser [trepase] *vi (aux avoir, occ être) A: & Lit:* to die, to pass away. **trépassé, -eé** *a & n* deceased (person).

trépidation [trepidasjɔ̃] *nf* vibration.

trépider [trepide] *vi (of machines)* to vibrate. **trépidant** *a* vibrating.

trépied [trepje] *nm* tripod.

trépignement [trepiɲmɑ̃] *nm* stamping (of feet).

trépigner [trepiɲe] *vi* **t. de colère,** to stamp one's feet with rage.

très [trɛ] *adv* very, most; (very) much; **t. connu,** very well known; **t. estimé,** highly esteemed; **t. nécessaire,** most essential; **nous sommes t. amis,** we are great friends; **t. en avant,** a long way ahead; **t. bien,** very well.

trésor [trezɔr] *nm* **1.** *(a)* treasure; *F:* **mon t.,** my darling *(b)* treasure house **2.** *pl* riches; wealth **3.** **le T. (public),** the (French) Treasury **4.** **un t. de faits,** a mine of facts.

trésorerie [trezɔrri] *nf* **1.** treasury **2.** *(a)* treasurership *(b)* treasurer's office **3.** funds.

trésorier, -ière [trezɔrje, -jɛr] *n* treasurer; paymaster, paymistress.

tressaillement [tresajmɑ̃] *nm* start (of surprise); shudder (of fear); wince (of pain).

tressaillir [tresajir] *vi (conj like* CUEILLIR*)* to give a start; to shudder (with fear); to leap (with joy); **t. de douleur,** to wince.

tressauter [tresote] *vi* to start, jump (with fear, surprise); *(of thgs)* to be jolted about.

tressage [tresaʒ] *nm* plaiting, braiding, weaving.

tresse [trɛs] *nf* plait (of hair); braid.

tresser [trese] *vtr* to plait (hair, straw); to braid; to weave (basket).

tréteau, -eaux [treto] *nm* **1.** trestle, support, stand **2.** *pl Th:* stage, boards.

treuil [trœj] *nm* winch, windlass.

trêve [trɛv] *nf (a)* truce *(b)* respite; **t. de plaisanteries!** that's enough joking!

tri [tri] *nm* sorting (out); classifying; **faire le t. de,** to sort (out), to pick out; *Rail: etc:* **bureau de t.,** sorting office.

triage [triaʒ] *nm* sorting; *Rail:* **gare de t.,** marshalling yard.

triangle [triɑ̃gl] *nm* triangle. **triangulaire** *a* triangular; three-cornered (election, fight).

tribal, -aux [tribal, -o] *a* tribal.

tribord [tribɔr] *nm Nau:* starboard (side); **à t.,** to starboard.

tribu [triby] *nf* tribe.

tribulation [tribylasjɔ̃] *nf* tribulation; trouble.

tribunal, -aux [tribynal, -o] *nm* law court; **t. pour enfants,** juvenile court; **t. militaire,** military tribunal; **le t. de l'opinion publique,** the bar of public opinion.

tribune [tribyn] *nf* **1.** rostrum, (speaker's) platform **2.** *(a)* (public) gallery *(b) Sp:* (grand)stand **3.** forum, discussion, debate.

tributaire [tribytɛr] *a & nm* tributary; **être t. de,** to be dependent on.

tricentenaire [trisɑ̃tnɛr] *nm* tercentenary.

triche [triʃ] *nf F:* cheating.

tricher [triʃe] *vi & tr* to cheat (**sur,** over); to lie (**sur,** about).

tricherie [triʃri] *nf* cheating; **une t.,** a trick.

tricheur, -euse [triʃœr, -øz] *n* cheat.

tricolore [trikɔlɔr] *a* tricolour(ed); **le drapeau t.,** the French flag; *nmpl Sp: F:* **les Tricolores,** the French team.

tricot [triko] *nm* **1.** knitting; knitted fabric; *Com:* knitwear **2.** (knitted) jersey; jumper; **t. de corps,** vest.

tricoter [trikote] *vtr* to knit.

tricycle [trisikl] *nm* tricycle.

trident [tridɑ̃] *nm* trident.

trier [trie] *vtr (impf & pr sub* **n. triions**) *(a)* to sort *(b)* to pick out, sort out, choose (the best).

trieur, -euse [triœr, -øz] **1.** *n* sorter **2.** *nm Ind:* grader.

trilogie [trilɔʒi] *nf Lit:* trilogy.

trimbal(l)er [trɛ̃bale] *vtr F:* **1.** to drag, lug (parcels) about **2. se t.,** to trail along.

trimer [trime] *vi F:* to work hard, slave away (at sth); **faire t. qn,** to keep s.o. hard at it.

trimestre [trimɛstr] *nm* **1.** quarter; *Sch:* term; **par t.,** quarterly **2.** quarter's salary; quarter's rent; *Sch:* term's fees. **trimestriel, -elle** quarterly; *Sch:* end-of-term (report).

tringle [trɛ̃gl] *nf* rod; **t. de rideau,** curtain rod.

trinité [trinite] *nf Theol:* Trinity; **la T.,** Trinity Sunday.

trinquer [trɛ̃ke] *vi (a)* to clink glasses; **t. à qn, qch,** to drink to s.o., sth *(b) P:* to cop it.

triomphateur, -trice [triɔ̃fatœr, -tris] *n* triumphant victor.

triomphe [triɔ̃f] *nm* triumph; **en t.,** in triumph; **arc de t.,** triumphal arch. **triomphal, -aux** *a* triomphal, triomphant. **triomphalement** *adv* triumphantly.

triompher [triɔ̃fe] *vi* 1. to triumph 2. to exult, glory (in sth). **triomphant** *a* triumphant.

tripatouiller [tripatuje] *vtr F:* to tamper, to fiddle about, with (sth).

tripe [trip] *nf usu pl* (*a*) entrails (of animal); *Cu:* tripe (*b*) *P:* (*of pers*) guts; **rendre tripes et boyaux,** to be horribly sick.

triperie [tripri] *nf* tripe shop; tripe trade.

tripette [tripɛt] *nf F:* **ne pas valoir t.,** to be utterly worthless.

tripier, -ière [tripje, -jɛr] *n* tripe butcher.

triple [tripl] *a & nm* treble, threefold; *F:* **t. menton,** triple chin; **en t. exemplaire,** in triplicate; **un t. sot,** a prize idiot; **le t. de,** three times as much as. **triplement** 1. *adv* trebly, threefold 2. *nm* trebling, tripling.

triplé, -ée [triple] *n* triplet.

tripler [triple] *vtr & i* to treble, triple; to increase threefold.

triporteur [triportœr] *nn* carrier tricycle.

tripot [tripo] *nm* gambling den; *P:* dive.

tripotage [tripotaʒ] *nm F:* fiddling around.

tripotée [tripote] *nf P:* 1. thrashing 2. lots, loads (**de,** of).

tripoter [tripote] 1. *vi* (*a*) to fiddle about; mess about (in the water); (*b*) to rummage (in a drawer) (*b*) to engage in shady business; **t. dans la caisse,** to tamper with the cash 2. *vtr* (*a*) to finger, handle (s.o., sth); **se t. le nez,** to fiddle with one's nose (*b*) to meddle with (sth).

tripoteur, -euse [tripotœr, -øz] *n F:* schemer; shady dealer.

trique [trik] *nf F:* cudgel; **donner des coups de t.,** to cudgel.

triste [trist] *a* 1. (*a*) sad (**de,** at); sorrowful (person); woebegone (face, news); **tout t.,** very dejected; in low spirits (*b*) dreary, dismal (life, weather, room); **faire t. figure,** to pull a long face 2. unfortunate, painful (news, duty); sad (occasion); **c'est une t. affaire,** it's a bad business 3. poor, sorry, wretched (meal, excuse). **tristement** *adv* sadly, sorrowfully; wretchedly.

tristesse [tristɛs] *nf* (*a*) sadness; sorrow; **avec t.,** sadly (*b*) dullness, dreariness; bleakness.

triturer [trityre] *vtr* (*a*) to grind, to rub down (*b*) to knead (*c*) to manipulate.

trivialité [trivjalite] *nf* 1. vulgarity, coarseness 2. coarse expression. **trivial, -aux** *a* vulgar, coarse (expression). **trivialement** *adv* coarsely.

troc [trɔk] *nm* exchange (in kind); barter; **faire un t.,** to make an exchange.

troène [trɔɛn] *nm Bot:* privet.

troglodyte [trɔglɔdit] *nm* cave dweller.

trogne [trɔɲ] *nf F:* (boozy) face.

trognon [trɔɲɔ̃] *nm* (*a*) core (of apple); stump (of cabbage); *F:* **jusqu'au t.,** completely; to the (bitter) end (*b*) *F:* sweetie.

trois [trwa] *before a vowel sound in the same word group* [trwaz] *num a inv & nm* three; **à t. heures,** at three o'clock; **les t. quarts du temps,** most of the time; **couper qch en t.,** to cut sth in three; **entrer par t.,** to come in in threes, three at a time; **Henri T.,**

Henry the Third; **le t. mai,** (on) the third of May; **j'habite au t.,** I live at number three. **troisième** *num a & n* third; **personnes du t. âge,** retired people; senior citizens. **troisièmement** *adv* thirdly, in the third place.

trolleybus [trɔlɛbys] *nm* trolleybus.

trombe [trɔ̃b] *nf* 1. waterspout 2. **t. de vent,** whirlwind; **t. d'eau,** cloudburst; **entrer, sortir, en t.,** to burst in, out (like a whirlwind).

trombine [trɔ̃bin] *nf P:* (*a*) head, nut (*b*) face, mug.

trombone [trɔ̃bɔn] *nm* 1. *Mus:* (*a*) trombone (*b*) trombone player 2. *F:* (wire) paper clip.

trompe [trɔ̃p] *nf* 1. (*a*) horn (*b*) hooter 2. proboscis (of insect); trunk (of elephant) 3. *Anat:* (Fallopian) tube.

trompe-l'œil [trɔ̃plœj] *nm inv* 1. trompe-l'œil (painting) 2. *Pej:* illusion; eye-wash.

tromper [trɔ̃pe] *vtr* 1. (*a*) to deceive; to cheat; to take (s.o.) in (*b*) to betray, be unfaithful to (wife, husband) (*c*) to mislead; to disappoint (s.o.'s hopes) (*d*) to outwit, baffle, elude (s.o.) (*e*) to relieve (tedium); to while away (the time); **t. la faim,** to stave off one's hunger 2. **se t.,** to be mistaken; to be wrong; **si je ne me trompe,** if I'm not mistaken; **se t. dans son calcul,** to be out in one's reckoning; **se t. de direction,** to go the wrong way; **il n'y a pas à s'y t.,** there is no doubt about it. **trompeur, -euse** 1. *a* deceitful (person); deceptive (appearance) 2. *n* deceiver. **trompeusement** *adv* deceitfully; deceptively.

tromperie [trɔ̃pri] *nf* deceit, deception.

trompette [trɔ̃pɛt] 1. *nf* trumpet 2. *nm* trumpet player.

trompettiste [trɔ̃petist] *n* trumpet player.

tronc [trɔ̃] *nm* 1. (*a*) trunk (of tree, of body) (*b*) *Anat:* trunk, main stem (of artery) 2. collection box; poor box.

tronche [trɔ̃ʃ] *nf P:* head, nut.

tronçon [trɔ̃sɔ̃] *nm* section.

tronçonner [trɔ̃sɔne] *vtr* to cut into sections.

tronçonneuse [trɔ̃sɔnøz] *nf* chain saw.

trône [tron] *nm* throne.

trôner [trone] *vi* (*a*) to sit enthroned (*b*) *Pej:* to lord it.

tronquer [trɔ̃ke] *vtr* to truncate; to curtail, cut down (text).

trop [tro] 1. *adv* too (*a*) (*with adj*) too, over-; **c'est t. difficile,** it's too difficult; **vous êtes t. aimable** [trɔpɛmabl] you are most kind; **t. fatigué,** overtired; too tired (**pour,** to); **vous n'êtes pas t. en avance,** you are none too early (*b*) (*with vb*) too much, unduly, over-; **t. travailler,** to overwork, to work too hard; **on ne saurait t. le répéter,** it cannot be too often repeated; **je ne sais t. que dire,** I hardly know what to say 2. *nm* too much, too many; **j'ai une carte de t., en t.,** I have one card too many; **une fois de t.,** once too often; **être de t.,** to be in the way, unwelcome; *adv phr* **par t.,** (altogether) too (much); **par t. généreux,** far too generous; **c'est t. fort!** it's a bit much! **c'en est t.!** this really is the limit!

trophée [trofe] *nm* trophy.

tropique [trɔpik] *nm Geog:* tropic (of Cancer, Capricorn); *pl* **les tropiques,** the tropics. **tropical, -aux** *a* tropical.

trop-perçu [trɔpɛrsy] *nm* over-payment (of taxes); *pl* **trop-perçus**.

trop-plein [trɔplɛ̃] *nm* overflow; *pl* **trop-pleins**.

troquer [trɔke] *vtr* to exchange, barter, swap (**qch contre qch**, sth for sth).

troquet [trɔkɛ] *nm P:* small café; bar.

trot [tro] *nm* trot; **t. enlevé**, rising, *NAm:* posting, trot; **au petit, au grand, t.**, at a gentle, at a brisk, trot; **course de t.**, trotting race; *F:* **allez, au t.!** at the double!

trotte [trɔt] *nf* distance, run; **il y a une bonne t. d'ici là**, it's a fair distance from here.

trotter [trɔte] 1. *vi* (*of horse or rider*) to trot; (*of mice*) to scamper; *F:* **toujours à t.**, always on the go; **air qui vous trotte par la tête**, tune that keeps running through your head.

trotteur, -euse [trɔtœr, -øz] 1. *n* trotter, trotting horse 2. *nf* **trotteuse**, second hand (of watch).

trottiner [trɔtine] *vi* to trot (about, along).

trottinette [trɔtinɛt] *nf* (child's) scooter.

trottoir [trɔtwar] *nm* pavement, *NAm:* sidewalk; **t. roulant**, travelator; **faire le t.**, to walk the streets.

trou [tru] *nm* 1. (*a*) hole; eye (of needle); **t. de serrure**, keyhole; hole; *F:* **boire comme un t.**, to drink like a fish (*b*) gap (in hedge, in memory) 2. (*a*) hole; (*in road*) pothole; *Av:* **t. d'air**, air pocket; *Th:* **t. du souffleur**, prompter's box (*b*) *F:* place; dump, hole 3. *Mch: etc:* **t. d'aération**, air vent.

trouble¹ [trubl] *a* 1. cloudy (liquid); dim (light); murky, overcast (sky); confused (situation); **avoir la vue t.**, to be dimsighted; *adv* **voir t.**, to have blurred vision 2. confused (mind); uneasy (conscience).

trouble² *nm* (*a*) confusion, disorder; *Med:* **troubles de digestion**, digestive disorder (*b*) agitation, uneasiness; embarrassment (*c*) *pl* (public) disturbances.

trouble-fête [trubləfɛt] *nm inv* spoilsport.

troubler [truble] *vtr* 1. to make (liquid) cloudy, muddy; to cloud (s.o.'s mind); to dim (s.o.'s eyes) 2. to disturb (silence, meeting); to impede (progress); to spoil (happiness); to upset (digestion); **t. le repos**, to create a disturbance 3. (*a*) to perturb; to confuse, upset (s.o.) (*b*) to excite (s.o.); to stir (the senses) 4. **se t.** (*a*) (*of wine*) to get cloudy; (*of sky*) to become overcast; (*of vision*) to become blurred, to grow dim; (*of voice*) to break (with emotion) (*b*) to become confused, flustered; **sans se t.**, unruffled.

troublant *a* disturbing; disquieting, disconcerting.

trouée [true] *nf* gap, opening, breach.

trouer [true] *vtr* to make a hole, holes, in (a wall); to wear a hole in (garment); to perforate; **avoir les bas troués**, to have holes in one's stockings.

troufion [trufjɔ̃] *nm P:* soldier.

trouille [truj] *nf P:* **avoir la t.**, to be scared stiff; **flanquer la t. à qn**, to put the wind up s.o. **trouillard, -arde** *P:* 1. *a* cowardly, chicken 2. *n* coward, chicken.

troupe [trup] *nf* 1. (*a*) troop, band, group (of people); gang (of thieves) (*b*) *Th:* troupe, company (*c*) herd (of cattle); flock (of birds) 3. *Mil:* (*a*) troop; **officier de t.**, regimental officer (*b*) *pl* troops, forces.

troupeau, -eaux [trupo] *nm* herd, drove (of cattle); flock (of sheep, geese); herd, horde (of tourists).

trousse [trus] *nf* 1. *pl* **être aux trousses de qn**, to be

hot on s.o.'s heels 2. (first-aid, tool) kit; (instrument) case; **t. de toilette**, dressing case; toilet bag; **t. d'écolier**, pencil case.

trousseau, -eaux [truso] *nm* 1. bunch (of keys) 2. (*a*) outfit (of clothing) (*b*) (bride's) trousseau.

trouvaille [truvaj] *nf* (*a*) (lucky) find (*b*) brainwave.

trouver [truve] *vtr* 1. (*a*) to find; **je ne trouve pas mes clefs**, I can't find my keys; **aller t. qn**, to go and (i) find (ii) see, s.o. (*b*) to discover, invent (a process) 2. **t. (qch) par hasard**, to discover, come upon, come across (sth); **c'est bien trouvé!** good idea! **exemple mal trouvé**, badly chosen example; **t. la mort**, to meet one's death; **il trouve du plaisir à lire**, he enjoys reading 3. to think, consider; **je la trouve jolie**, I think she's pretty; **vous trouvez?** you think so? **comment as-tu trouvé ce livre?** how did you like the book? 4. **se t.** (*a*) to be; to find oneself (in a situation) (*b*) to feel; **je me trouve bien ici**, I'm very comfortable here; **se t. bien de qch**, to feel all the better for sth; **se t. mieux**, to feel better (*c*) to happen; to turn out; **il se trouve que**, it so happens that; *F:* **si ça se trouve, il est déjà rentré**, he's probably already returned.

truand [tryɑ̃] *n P:* gangster.

truander [tryɑ̃de] *vtr F:* to swindle (s.o.).

truc [tryk] *nm F:* 1. (*a*) knack; **trouver le t.**, to find a way (of doing sth) (*b*) trick, dodge; **les trucs du métier**, the tricks of the trade 2. (*a*) (**machin**)**-t.**, what's-his-name (*b*) thingummy, whatsit.

trucage [trukaʒ] *nm* 1. faking; cheating, fiddling 2. *pl Cin:* special effects.

truchement [tryʃmɑ̃] *nm* intermediary; **par le t. de qn**, through (the intervention of) s.o.

truculence [trykylɑ̃s] *nf* colourfulness. **truculent** *a* colourful.

truelle [tryɛl] *nf* 1. trowel 2. **t. à poisson**, fish slice.

truffe [tryf] *nf* (*a*) truffle (*b*) nose (of dog).

truffer [tryfe] *vtr* 1. *Cu:* to flavour with truffles 2. **truffé de**, riddled with (mistakes); peppered with (quotations).

truie [trɥi] *nf* sow.

truite [trɥit] *nf Ich:* trout.

truquage [trukaʒ] *nm =* TRUCAGE.

truquer [tryke] *vtr* to fake (antiques, photographs); to fix (match); *F:* to cook (accounts); to rig (an election).

TSF *abbr* Telegraphie sans fil.

TSVP *abbr Tournez s'il vous plaît.*

ttc *abbr* toutes taxes comprises.

tu [ty] *pers pron, subject of verb* (*a*) (*usual form of address to relations, close friends, children, animals*) you; **qui es-tu?** who are you? *F:* **être à tu et à toi avec qn**, to be on close terms with s.o. (*b*) *Rel:* Thou.

tuba [tyba] *nm* 1. *Mus:* tuba 2. snorkel.

tube [tyb] *nm* 1. (*a*) tube, pipe (*b*) *Anat:* **t. digestif**, digestive tract (*c*) *F:* hit song 2. (*container*) tube (of toothpaste, paint).

tubercule [tybɛrkyl] *nm* 1. *Bot:* tuber 2. *Med:* tubercle.

tuberculose [tybɛrkyloz] *nf Med:* tuberculosis. **tuberculeux, -euse** 1. *a Bot:* tubercular; *Med:* tuberculous 2. *n* tubercular patient; TB case.

tubulaire [tybylɛr] *a* tubular.

tuer [tɥe] *vtr* **1.** to kill; to slaughter, butcher (animals) **2.** (*a*) to kill (s.o.); **t. qn d'un coup de poignard,** to stab s.o. to death; **t. qn d'une balle,** to shoot s.o. dead; **se faire t.,** to get killed; **les tués,** the dead (*b*) **t. le temps,** to kill time **3. l'ennui le tue,** he's bored to death **4. se t.** (*a*) to kill oneself; to commit suicide (*b*) to get killed (*c*) **se t. à travailler,** to work oneself to death; **je me tue à vous le dire,** I'm sick and tired of telling you. **tuant** *a* (*a*) exhausting, backbreaking (*b*) exasperating, boring.

tuerie [tyri] *nf* slaughter, butchery.

tue-tête (à) [atytɛt] *adv phr* at the top of one's voice; **crier à t.-t.,** to bawl, yell.

tueur, -euse [tɥœr, -øz] (*a*) *n* killer, murderer; **t. à gages,** hired assassin (*b*) *nm* slaughterman, slaughterer.

tuile [tɥil] *nf* **1.** (*a*) (roofing) tile (*b*) *Cu:* (almond) slice **2.** *F:* (piece of) bad luck; **quelle t.!** what rotten luck!

tulipe [tylip] *nf Bot:* tulip.

tuméfié [tymefje] *a* swollen, puffed up.

tumeur [tymœr] *nf Med:* tumour.

tumulte [tymylt] *nm* tumult, hubbub, uproar, commotion; turmoil (of passions); hustle and bustle (of business). **tumultueux, -euse** *a* tumultuous, riotous (gathering); turbulent, stormy.

tunique [tynik] *nf Cl:* tunic.

Tunisie [tynizi] *Prnf Geog:* Tunisia. **tunisien, -ienne** *a & n* Tunisian.

turban [tyrbã] *nm* turban.

turbine [tyrbin] *nf* turbine.

turboréacteur [tyrbɔreaktœr] *nm* turbojet.

turbot [tyrbo] *nm Ich:* turbot.

turbulence [tyrbylãs] *nf* turbulence. **turbulent** *a* turbulent; boisterous (child).

turc, *f* turque [tyrk] *see* **Turquie.**

turf [tyrf] *nm* **1.** racecourse **2. le t.,** racing; the turf.

turfiste [tyrfist] *n* racegoer.

turlupiner [tyrlypine] *vtr F:* to worry, bother.

Turquie [tyrki] *Prnf Geog:* Turkey. **turc, *f* turque 1.** *a* Turkish **2.** *n* (*a*) Turk (*b*) *nm Ling:* Turkish.

turquoise [tyrkwaz] *a inv & nf* turquoise.

tutelle [tytɛl] *nf* **1.** *Jur:* tutelage, guardianship **2.** (*a*) *Pol:* trusteeship (*b*) protection; **prendre qn sous sa t.,** to take s.o. under one's wing.

tuteur, -trice [tytœr, -tris] **1.** *n* (*a*) guardian (*b*) protector **2.** *nm Hort:* support, stake.

tutoiement [tytwamã] *nm* use of the familiar **tu** and **toi.**

tutoyer [tytwaje] *vtr* (**je tutoie**) to address (s.o.) as **tu; ils se tutoyent,** they are on first-name terms.

tutu [tyty] *nm* ballet skirt, tutu.

tuyau, -aux [tɥijo] *nm* **1.** (*a*) pipe, tube; **t. d'eau, de gaz,** water pipe, gas pipe; **t. flexible, en caoutchouc,** (i) rubber tubing (ii) hosepipe; **t. d'incendie,** fire hose; **t. d'arrosage,** garden hose; **t. de cheminée,** chimney flue; **t. d'orgue,** organ pipe; *Aut:* **t. d'échappement,** exhaust pipe (*b*) stem (of tobacco pipe) **2.** *F:* tip; **avoir des tuyaux,** to be in the know.

tuyauter [tɥijote] *vtr F:* to give (s.o.) a tip, to put (s.o.) in the know.

tuyauterie [tɥijotri] *nf* pipes, piping.

TVA *abbr* Taxe à la valeur ajoutée, value added tax, VAT.

tympan [tẽpã] *nm Anat:* eardrum.

type [tip] *nm* **1.** type; standard model; *attrib* **maison t.,** show house; **exemple t.,** typical example **2.** *F:* character; **drôle de t.,** queer sort of chap; **t'es un chic t.!** you're a good sort!

typhoïde [tifɔid] *a* **fièvre t.,** *nf* **t.,** typhoid (fever).

typhon [tifɔ̃] *nm Meteor:* typhoon.

typhus [tifys] *nm Med:* typhus (fever).

typique [tipik] *a* **1.** symbolical **2.** typical, true to type. **typiquement** *adv* typically.

typographe [tipɔgraf] *nm* typographer.

typographie [tipɔgrafi] *nf* typography. **typographique** *a* typographic(al); **erreur t.,** misprint.

typologie [tipɔlɔʒi] *nf* typology.

tyran [tirã] *nm* tyrant.

tyrannie [tirani] *nf* tyranny. **tyrannique** *a* tyrannical.

tyranniser [tiranize] *vtr* to tyrannize (s.o.).

tyrolien, -ienne [tirɔljẽ, jɛn] *a & n* Tyrolese.

U

U, u [y] *nm* (the letter) U, u.
UDF *abbr* Union pour la démocracie française.
UER *abbr* Unité d'enseignement et de recherche.
ulcération [ylserasjɔ̃] *nf* ulceration.
ulcère [ylsɛr] *nm* ulcer. **ulcéreux, -euse** *a* ulcerous, ulcerated.
ulcérer [ylsere] (il **ulcère**; il **ulcérera**) **1.** *vtr* (*a*) Med: to ulcerate (*b*) to appal (s.o.) **2.** Med: s'u., to ulcerate.
ultérieur [ylterjœr] *a* ulterior; subsequent (à, to); later (date, meeting); Com: further (orders). **ultérieurement** *adv* later (on), subsequently.
ultimatum [yltimatɔm] *nm* ultimatum.
ultime [yltim] *a* ultimate, final, last.
ultra- [yltra] *pref* ultra-.
ultramoderne [yltramɔdɛrn] *a* ultramodern.
ultra(-)son [yltrasɔ̃] *nm* Ph: ultrasound; **ultra(-)sons**, ultrasonic waves. **ultrasonique** *a* ultrasonic.
ultra(-)violet, -ette [yltravjɔlɛ, -ɛt] *a & nm* ultraviolet.
un, une [œ̃, yn] **1.** *num a & n* (*a*) one; **il n'en reste qu'un**, there's only one left; **un à un, un par un**, one by one; **une heure**, one o'clock; **page un**, page one; Journ: **la une**, front page (of newspaper); F: **en savoir plus d'une**, to know a thing or two; F: **il était moins une**, that was a close thing, a close shave; **un jour sur deux**, every other day; **une, deux, trois, partez!** one, two, three, go! **il n'a fait ni une ni deux**, he didn't hesitate for a moment; **et d'un! et d'une!** that's that (for a start)! (*b*) one (and indivisible); **c'est tout un**, it's all one, all the same **2.** *indef pron* one; **un qui a de la chance**, a lucky one; (**l')un d'entre nous**, one of us; **les uns disent que**, some say that **3.** *indef art* (*a*) (*pl* **des**) a, an (*pl* some); **un jour, une pomme**, a day, an apple; **venez me voir un lundi**, come and see me one Monday; **pour une raison ou pour une autre**, for some reason or other (*b*) **ce sera un Einstein**, he'll be another Einstein (*c*) (*intensive*) **il a fait une de ces têtes!** you should have seen his face!
unanimité [ynanimite] *nf* unanimity; **à l'u.**, unanimously; **la proposition a fait l'u.**, the proposal was accepted unanimously. **unanime** *a* unanimous. **unanimement** *adv* unanimously.
UNEF *abbr* Union nationale des étudiants de France.
UNESCO [ynɛsko] *abbr* United Nations educational, scientific and cultural organisation.
uni [yni] *a* **1.** united, close (family) **2.** smooth, level, even (ground) **3.** plain (material, colour); self-coloured (material).
unième [ynjɛm] *num a* (*used only in compounds*) first; **trente et u.**, thirty-first.
unification [ynifikasjɔ̃] *nf* unification. **unificateur, -trice** *a* unifying.
unifier [ynifje] *vtr* (*impf & pr sub n.* **unifiions**)

to unify (ideas); to consolidate (loans); to standardize.
uniforme [ynifɔrm] **1.** *a.* uniform, unvarying; regular (life) **2.** *nm* Mil: etc: uniform; **endosser l'u.**, to join the forces; **quitter l'u.**, to leave the service. **uniformément** *adv* uniformly; evenly.
uniformisation [ynifɔrmizasjɔ̃] *nf* standardization.
uniformiser [ynifɔrmize] *vtr* to make uniform; to standardize.
uniformité [ynifɔrmite] *nf* uniformity.
unijambiste [yniʒɑ̃bist] *a & n* one-legged (person).
unilatéral, -aux [ynilateral, -o] *a* unilateral.
unilingue [ynilɛ̃g] *a* unilingual.
union [ynjɔ̃] *nf* **1.** union; coming together; combination; blending (of colours) **2.** union, society, association; **l'U. Soviétique**, the Soviet Union **3.** marriage **4.** unity, agreement; **l'u. fait la force**, unity is strength.
unique [ynik] *a* **1.** sole, only, single; **fils u.**, only son; **(rue à) sens u.**, one-way street; **voie u.**, single line traffic; **seul et u.**, one and only **2.** unique, unrivalled, unparalleled; F: **il est u.**, he's priceless! **uniquement** *adv* solely; only, merely; **u. pour vous voir**, especially to see you.
unir [ynir] **1.** *vtr* (*a*) to unite, join, combine, link; **u. le geste à la parole**, to suit the action to the word (*b*) to smooth, level (ground) **2.** s'u., to unite, join (together), combine; **s'u. à qn**, (i) to join forces with s.o. (ii) to marry s.o.
unisexe [ynisɛks] *a* unisex.
unisson [ynisɔ̃] *nm* Mus: unison; **à l'u.**, in unison.
unitaire [yniter] *a* **1.** Pol: unitarian **2.** unitary (system); **prix u.**, unit price.
unité [ynite] *nf* **1.** (*a*) unit (of measure) (*b*) Mth: unity, one; Com: **prix de l'u.**, unit price (*c*) Mil: unit; Navy: ship **2.** (*a*) unity; oneness (of God) (*b*) unity; uniformity (of action).
univers [yniver] *nm* universe. **universel, -elle** *a* universal; worldwide (reputation). **universellement** *adv* universally.
universalité [yniversalite] *nf* universality.
universitaire [yniversiter] **1.** *a* university (studies, town); **cité u. =** (students') hall(s) of residence **2.** *n* (*a*) member of the teaching profession (*b*) academic.
université [yniversite] *nf* university.
uranium [yranjɔm] *nm* Ch: uranium.
urbain [yrbɛ̃] *a* (*a*) urban; city (b) urbane.
urbanisation [yrbanizasjɔ̃] *nf* urbanization.
urbaniser [yrbanize] *vtr* to urbanize; **s'u.**, to become urbanized.
urbanisme [yrbanism] *nm* town planning. **urbaniste 1.** *a* urban **2.** *n* town planner.
urbanité [yrbanite] *nf* urbanity.
urée [yre] *nf* Ch: urea.
urémie [yremi] *nf* Med: uraemia.

urgence [yrʒɑ̃s] nf (a) urgency; **transporter qn d'u. à l'hôpital,** to rush s.o. to hospital; **en cas d'u.,** in case of emergency; **il a été appelé d'u.,** he received an urgent call (b) emergency; **salle des urgences,** emergency ward. **urgent** a urgent, pressing (matter, need); **rien d'u.,** nothing urgent.

urger [yrʒe] vi F: to be urgent.

urine [yrin] nf urine.

uriner [yrine] vi to urinate.

urinoir [yrinwar] nm (public) urinal.

urne [yrn] nf (a) urn (b) ballot box; **aller aux urnes,** to go to the polls.

URSS abbr Union des Républiques Socialistes Soviétiques.

urticaire [yrtikɛr] nf Med: urticaria, nettle-rash, hives.

us [ys] nmpl **les us et coutumes,** ways and customs.

USA abbr États-Unis d'Amérique.

usage [yzaʒ] nm 1. (a) use, using, employment; **faire u. de qch,** to use, to make use of, sth; **faire bon, mauvais, u. de qch,** to make good, bad, use of sth; Pharm: **à l'u. externe,** for external use; **article à mon u.,** article for my personal use; **article d'u.,** article for everyday use; **à usages multiples,** multi-purpose (equipment); **avoir l'u. de,** to have the use of (b) wear, service (of garments): **garanti à l'u.,** guaranteed to wear well 2. (a) usage; custom; practice; **d'u. courant,** in common, in everyday use; **les conditions d'u.,** the usual terms; **il est d'u. de** + inf, it is usual, customary, to (b) practice, experience; **l'u. du monde,** good breeding; **c'est l'u.,** it's the done thing. **usagé** a worn, used (article).

usager, -ère [yzaʒe, -ɛr] n user (of sth); **usagers de la route,** road users.

user [yze] 1. v ind tr **u. de qch.,** to use sth, make use of sth; **u. de son droit,** to exercise one's right 2. vtr (a) to use (up), consume (sth) (b) to wear (out, away, down) 3. **s'u.,** to wear (away); to wear out. **usé** a worn (out); threadbare; hackneyed, trite (subject); old (joke).

usine [yzin] nf factory; works; mill, plant; **u. à gaz,** gasworks.

usiner [yzine] vtr (a) to machine (castings) (b) to manufacture.

usité [yzite] a used; in use; current.

ustensile [ystɑ̃sil] nm utensil, implement; tool; **u. de cuisine,** kitchen utensil.

usuel, -elle [yzɥɛl] a usual, customary, habitual, common, ordinary; **le français u.,** everyday French.

usufruit [yzyfrɥi] nm Jur: usufruct; life interest. **usufruitier, -ière** a & n usufructuary.

usure¹ [yzyr] nf usury; **rendre un bienfait avec u.,** to repay a service with interest. **usuraire** a usurious.

usure² nf (a) wear (and tear); Mil: **guerre d'u.,** war of attrition; F: **je l'aurai à l'u.,** I'll wear him down (b) wearing away; erosion.

usurier, -ière [yzyrje, -jɛr] n usurer.

usurpateur, -trice [yzyrpatœr, -tris] 1. n usurper 2. a usurping.

usurpation [yzyrpasjɔ̃] nf usurpation.

usurper [yzyrpe] 1. vtr to usurp 2. vi **sur les droits de qn,** to encroach on s.o.'s rights.

ut [yt] nm inv Mus: (the note) C.

utérus [yterys] nm Anat: uterus; womb.

utile [ytil] a useful, serviceable; helpful; **en quoi puis-je vous être u.?** what can I do for you? **cela m'a été très u.,** it came in very handy; **en temps u.,** in (good) time; in due course; **est-il u. d'y aller?** is there any point in going? **livre u. à lire,** useful book to read; nm **joindre l'u. à l'agréable,** to combine business with pleasure. **utilement** adv usefully; profitably.

utilisateur, -trice [ytilizatœr, -tris] n user. **utilisation** [ytilizasjɔ̃] nf utilization, use.

utiliser [ytilize] vtr to use; to utilize; to make use of. **utilisable** a usable.

utilitaire [ytilitɛr] a & n utilitarian.

utilité [ytilite] nf utility, use(fulness); service; **ça peut avoir son u.,** it can come in useful; **n'être d'aucune u.,** to be of no earthly use.

utopie [ytɔpi] nf utopia. **utopique** a utopian.

V

V, v [ve] *nm* (the letter) V, v.
V *abbr El:* volt.

vacance [vakɑ̃s] *nf* 1. vacancy; vacant post 2. *pl*
holidays; *esp NAm:* vacation; (*of Parliament*) recess;
Sch: **les grandes vacances,** the summer holidays; the
long vacation; **vacances de neige,** winter (sports)
holiday(s); **être en vacances,** to be on holiday.

vacancier, -ière [vakɑ̃sje, -jɛr] *n* holidaymaker;
NAm: vacationist.

vacant [vakɑ̃] *a* vacant, unoccupied (house).

vacarme [vakarm] *nm* din, racket, row.

vaccin [vaksɛ̃] *nm Med:* vaccine.

vaccination [vaksinasjɔ̃] *nf Med:* vaccination; inoculation.

vacciner [vaksine] *vtr Med:* to vaccinate; to immunize; to inoculate; **se faire v.,** to get vaccinated,
inoculated.

vache [vaʃ] 1. *nf* (*a*) cow; **v. laitière,** dairy cow; *P:* **v.
à lait,** mug, sucker; *F:* **parler français comme une v.
espagnole,** to murder the French language; **manger
de la v. enragée,** to have a hard time of it; **coup en
v.,** dirty trick; *F:* **ah la v.!** hell! damn! (*b*) *P:* (*man*)
swine; (*woman*) bitch, cow (*c*) cowhide (*d*) **v. à eau,**
(canvas) water carrier 2. *a F:* rotten, mean. **vachement** *adv P:* **c'est v. dur,** it's damned hard; **c'est v.
bon,** it's bloody good.

vacher [vaʃe] *nm* cowherd.

vacherie [vaʃri] *nf P:* (*a*) meanness (*b*) dirty trick;
nasty remark.

vacillement [vasijmɑ̃] *nm* unsteadiness; wobbling;
flickering; faltering; wavering.

vaciller [vasije] *vi* 1. (*a*) to be unsteady; to sway, to
wobble; **v. sur ses jambes,** to be shaky on one's legs;
(*b*) (*of light*) to flicker 2. to vacillate, waver, falter.
vacillant *a* unsteady, wobbly; flickering, shaky;
wavering.

vadrouille [vadruj] *nf F:* **être en v.,** to roam, to rove
about.

vadrouiller [vadruje] *vi F:* to roam, to rove about.

va-et-vient [vaevjɛ̃] *nm inv* 1. (*a*) (i) backward and
forward motion (ii) see-saw motion; **faire le va-et-
v. entre A et B,** to go to and fro between A and B;
porte v.-et-v., swing door (*b*) comings and goings
(of people) 2. *El:* two-way switch.

vagabond, -onde [vagabɔ̃, -ɔ̃d] 1. *a* vagabond,
roaming, roving (life) 2. *n* vagabond; *Pej:* vagrant,
tramp.

vagabondage [vagabɔ̃daʒ] *nm* wandering; *Pej:*
vagrancy.

vagabonder [vagabɔ̃de] *vi* to rove, to wander
(about).

vagin [vaʒɛ̃] *nm Anat:* vagina.

vagir [vaʒir] *vi* (*of newborn baby*) to cry, wail.

vagissement [vaʒismɑ̃] *nm* cry, wail(ing) (of newborn baby).

vague¹ [vag] *nf* wave; **grosse v.,** billow; **v. de fond,**

blind roller; **v. de chaleur,** heatwave; **v. d'enthousiasme,** wave, surge, of enthusiasm.

vague² 1. *a* vague, indefinite; dim (recollection);
sketchy (knowledge); **un v. cousin,** a distant cousin
2. *nm* vagueness, indefiniteness; **avoir du v. à l'âme,**
to have vague yearnings. **vaguement** *adv* vaguely,
dimly.

vague³ 1. *a* **regarder qn d'un air v.,** to gaze vacantly
at s.o.; **terrain v.,** waste ground 2. *nm* space; **regard
perdu dans le v.,** abstracted look.

vaillance [vajɑ̃s] *nf* valour, bravery, courage, gallantry. **vaillant** *a* (*a*) *Lit:* valiant, brave, courag-
ous; stout (heart) (*b*) **être v.,** to be in good health; **je
ne suis pas v.,** I'm not up to the mark. **vaillamment** *adv* valiantly, bravely.

vain [vɛ̃] *a* 1. (*a*) vain; sham, unreal; **vaines paroles,**
empty words; **vaines promesses,** hollow promises (*b*)
ineffectual, vain, useless; **en v.,** in vain; vainly 2.
vain, conceited. **vainement** *adv* vainly, in vain.

vaincre [vɛ̃kr] *vtr* (*prp* vainquant; *pp* vaincu; *pr ind* il
vainc; *ph* je vainquis) 1. (*a*) to conquer, defeat, vanquish (adversary) (*b*) *Sp:* to beat (rival) 2. to overcome, conquer (disease, difficulties).

vainqueur [vɛ̃kœr] 1. *nm* (*a*) victor, conqueror (*b*)
Sp: winner 2. *am* conquering, victorious (hero).

vaisseau, -eaux [veso] *nm* 1. ship, vessel; **v. de
guerre,** warship; **v. amiral,** flagship; **v. spatial,**
spacecraft 2. *Anat:* vessel.

vaisselier [veseljie] *nm Furn:* dresser.

vaisselle [vesɛl] *nf* dishes; crockery; **faire, laver, la
v.,** to wash up, to do the washing up; to do the
dishes.

val [val] *nm* (narrow) valley; vale; *pl usu* **vals,** *except
in the phr* **par monts et par vaux** [vo], up hill and
down dale.

valable [valabl] *a* valid; **billet v. pour un mois,** ticket
valid for a month; **un roman v.,** a good novel. **va-
lablement** *adv* validly.

valdinguer [valdɛ̃ge] *vi P:* to come a cropper; **envoyer v. (qn),** to send (s.o.) spinning.

valet [valɛ] *nm* 1. *Cards:* jack, knave 2. **v. (de chambre),** manservant, valet; **v. de ferme,** farmhand; **v. de
pied,** footman 3. stand (of mirror).

valeur [valœr] *nf* 1. value, worth; **cela n'a pas
grande v.,** it's not worth much; **homme de v.,** man of
merit; **mettre une terre en v.,** to develop land; **v.
marchande,** market(able) value; **objets de v.,** valuables; **sans v.,** worthless, valueless (*b*) **boire la v. d'un
verre de vin,** to drink the equivalent of a glass of
wine (*c*) import, weight, value; **mettre qch en valeur,**
to show sth to an advantage; **mettre un mot en v.,** to
emphasize a word 2. *Fin:* (*a*) asset (*b*) *pl* bills, shares,
securities, stocks; **valeurs mobilières,** stocks and
shares.

valeureux, -euse [valœrø, -øz] *a* valorous. **valeu-
reusement** *adv* valorously.

validation [validasjɔ̃] *nf* validation; authentication.

valider [valide] *vtr* to validate (ticket); to authenticate (document). **valide** *a* (*a*) valid (contract, reason) (*b*) (*pers*) fit (for service); able-bodied.

validité [validite] *nf* validity.

valise [valiz] *nf* (*a*) suitcase; **faire ses valises,** to pack (one's bags) (*b*) **la v. (diplomatique),** the (diplomatic) bag.

vallée [vale] *nf* valley.

vallon [valɔ̃] *nm* small valley. **vallonné** *a* undulating (country).

valoir [valwar] *vtr & i* (*prp* **valant;** *pp* **valu;** *pr ind* je **vaux,** il **vaut;** *pr sub* je **vaille;** *impf* je **valais;** *fu.* je **vaudrai**) **1.** (*a*) to be worth; **maison qui vaut deux cent mille francs,** house worth two hundred thousand francs; **à v. sur (une somme),** on account of (a sum); **ne pas v. grand-chose,** not to be worth much; **cela ne vaut rien,** that's no good; **ce n'est rien qui vaille,** it isn't worth having (*b*) to be equivalent to; **un franc vaut cent centimes,** a franc is equal to a hundred centimes; **c'est une façon qui en vaut une autre,** it is as good a way as any (other); **il ne vaut pas mieux que son frère,** he's no better than his brother; *F:* **ça se vaut,** it's the same either way (*c*) *impers* **il vaudrait mieux rester ici,** it would be better to stay here; **il vaut mieux qu'il en soit ainsi,** (it is) better that it should be so; **mieux vaut tard que jamais,** better late than never; **autant vaut rester ici,** we may as well stay here (*d*) **faire v. qch,** to make the most of sth; **to bring sth out; to emphasize sth; faire v. ses droits,** to assert one's claims; **j'ai fait v. que,** I pointed out that; **se faire v.,** (i) to make the most of oneself (ii) to push oneself forward **2.** to be worth, to deserve, to merit (sth); **ça en vaut la peine,** it's worth it, it's worth the trouble; **ça ne vaut pas la peine d'y penser,** it's not worth a moment's thought; *F:* **ça vaut le coup,** it's worth a try **3. cela lui a valu une décoration,** it won him a decoration; **qu'est-ce qui me vaut cet honneur?** to what do I owe this honour?

valorisation [valɔrizasjɔ̃] *nf* valorization.

valoriser [valɔrize] *vtr* to valorize.

valse [vals] *nf* waltz.

valser [valse] *vi* to waltz; *F:* **faire v. qn,** to keep s.o. on the hop; **envoyer v. qn,** to send s.o. (i) flying (ii) packing; **faire v. l'argent,** to spend money like water.

valseur, -euse [valsœr, -øz] *n* waltzer.

valve [valv] *nf* valve.

vampire [vɑ̃pir] *nm* **1.** vampire **2.** *Z:* vampire bat.

vandale [vɑ̃dal] *nm* vandal.

vandalisme [vɑ̃dalism] *nm* vandalism.

vanille [vanij] *nf* vanilla.

vanité [vanite] *nf* **1.** vanity; futility, emptiness **2.** vanity, conceit; **tirer v. de qch,** to pride oneself on sth; **sans v.,** with all due modesty. **vaniteux, -euse** *a* vain, conceited. **vaniteusement** *adv* conceitedly.

vanne [van] *nf* sluice (gate), water (gate).

vanneau, -eaux [vano] *nm Orn:* lapwing, peewit; **œufs de v.,** plover's eggs.

vanner [vane] *vtr* **1.** to winnow **2.** *P:* to tire out, to exhaust; **être vanné,** to be dead beat.

vannerie [vanri] *nf* basketwork.

vannier [vanje] *nm* basket maker.

vantardise [vɑ̃tardiz] *nf* (*a*) boastfulness (*b*) boast.

vantard, -arde 1. *a* boasting, boastful, bragging **2.** *n* braggart, boaster.

vanter [vɑ̃te] **1.** *vtr* to praise (s.o., sth); to speak highly of (sth) **2. se v.,** to boast, brag; **il n'y a pas de quoi se v.,** there's nothing to boast about.

va-nu-pieds [vanypje] *n inv* (barefoot) tramp, beggar.

vapes [vap] *nfpl P:* **tomber dans les v.,** to pass out; **être dans les v.,** to be in a daze.

vapeur [vapœr] *nf* **1.** vapour; haze **2. v. (d'eau)** (i) (water) vapour (ii) steam; **machine à v.,** steam engine; **bateau à v.,** steamer, steamship; **à toute v.,** full steam ahead; **cuit à la v.,** steamed **3.** *AMed:* vapours.

vaporeux, -euse [vapɔrø, -øz] *a* (*a*) vaporous, steamy (*b*) filmy; hazy.

vaporisateur [vapɔrizatœr] *nm* spray.

vaporiser [vapɔrize] **1.** *vtr* to spray **2. se v.,** to vaporize.

vaquer [vake] *vi* **1.** *Adm:* to be on vacation **2. v. à qch,** to attend to sth; **v. au ménage,** to see to the housework; **v. à ses affaires,** to go about one's business.

varappe [varap] *nf* rock climbing.

varech [varɛk] *nm* wrack, seaweed; kelp.

vareuse [varøz] *nf Nau:* (*a*) (sailor's) jersey (*b*) pea jacket (*c*) *Mil:* tunic.

variante [varjɑ̃t] *nf* variant.

variation [varjasjɔ̃] *nf* variation, change (**de,** in).

varice [varis] *nf* varicose vein.

varicelle [varisɛl] *nf Med:* chickenpox.

varier [varje] *v.* (*impf & pr sub* n. **variions**) **1** *vtr* to vary; to diversify **2.** *vi* to vary, change; (*of markets*) to fluctuate. **variable 1.** *a* variable, changeable; unsettled (weather); **le baromètre est au v.,** the barometer is at change; **être v.,** to vary **2.** *nf Mth:* variable. **varié** *a* varied; varying, various (types).

variété [varjete] *nf* variety (**de,** of); diversity (of opinions); **(spectacle de) variétés,** variety show.

variole [varjɔl] *nf Med:* smallpox.

Varsovie [varsɔvi] *Prnf Geog:* Warsaw.

vase¹ [vaz] *nm* vase; **v. de nuit,** chamberpot; **en v. clos,** in isolation; *Ph:* **vases communicants,** communicating vessels.

vase² *nf* mud, silt, slime, sludge.

vaseline [vazlin] *nf Rtm:* vaseline.

vaseux, -euse [vazø, -øz] *a* **1.** muddy, slimy, sludgy **2.** *F:* (*of pers*) seedy, off colour; **il a l'air v.,** he looks a bit washed out; **excuse vaseuse,** lame excuse; **idées vaseuses,** woolly ideas.

vasistas [vazistɑs] *nm* fanlight (over door).

vasque [vask] *nf* **1.** basin (of fountain) **2.** (ornamental) bowl.

vassal, -ale, -aux [vasal, -o] *n* vassal.

vaste [vast] *a* vast, immense, spacious, huge; *F:* great (joke).

Vatican (le) [lǝvatikɑ̃] *nm* the Vatican.

va-tout [vatu] *nm inv* **jouer son va-t.,** to stake one's all.

vau (à) [avo] *adv phr* **à v.-l'eau,** with the stream; **tout va à v.-l'eau,** everything is going to rack and ruin.

vaudeville [vodvil] *nm Th:* vaudeville, light comedy.

vaurien, -ienne [vorjɛ̃, -jɛn] n good-for-nothing; **petit v.!** you little rascal!

vautour [votur] nm Orn: vulture.

vautrer (se) [səvotre] vpr (a) to wallow (in mud, in vice) (b) to sprawl (on grass, on a sofa).

va-vite (à la) [alavavit] adv phr in a rush, in a hurry; in a slap-dash way.

VDQS abbr vin délimité de qualité supérieure.

veau, veaux [vo] nm 1. (a) calf; **pleurer comme un v.,** to cry one's eyes out (b) v. **marin,** seal calf (c) F: lump, lout 2. Cu: veal; **côtelette de v.,** veal chop; **foie de v.,** calf's liver 3. calf (leather); calfskin.

vecteur [vɛktœr] nm Mth: vector.

vécu [veky] a real(-life); **choses vécues,** actual experiences.

vedette [vədɛt] nf 1. (a) Navy: vedette boat (b) Nau: small motorboat; launch 2. (a) **mots en v.,** words in bold type; (of actor) **avoir la v.,** to top the bill; **être en v.,** to be in the limelight; to hit the headlines; **mettre en v.,** to highlight (b) Th: Cin: star.

végétal, -aux [veʒetal, -o] 1. a plant (life); vegetable (oil) 2. nm vegetable, plant.

végétarien, -ienne [veʒetarjɛ̃, -jɛn] a & n vegetarian.

végétation [veʒetasjɔ̃] nf 1. vegetation 2. pl Med: **végétations,** adenoids. **végétatif, -ive** a vegetative.

végéter [veʒete] vi (**je végète; je végéterai**) (of pers) to vegetate.

véhémence [veemɑ̃s] nf vehemence. **véhément** a vehement.

véhicule [veikyl] nm vehicle; medium (of sound).

véhiculer [veikyle] vtr to transport, to convey.

veille [vɛj] nf 1. (a) sitting up, staying up (at night); watching (by night) (b) vigil (c) Mil: (night le) watch; Nau: lookout (d) wakefulness; **entre la v. et le sommeil,** between waking and sleeping 2. (a) eve; preceding day, previous day; **la v. de la bataille,** the day before the battle; **la v. de Noël,** Christmas Eve; **la v. au soir,** the evening before (b) **être à la v. de la ruine,** to be on the brink, on the verge, on the point, of ruin.

veillée [veje] nf 1. night nursing (of the sick); vigil (by dead body) 2. evening (spent with friends); **faire la v. chez des voisins,** to spend the evening with neighbours.

veiller [veje] 1. vi (a) to sit up, keep awake (b) to watch, be on the look-out; to stand by (c) v. **sur qn, qch,** to look after s.o., sth (d) v. **à qch,** to watch over, to see to, sth; v. **aux intérêts de qn,** to look after s.o.'s interests; Fig: v. **au grain,** to look out for squalls 2. vtr to sit up with, watch over (sick person, dead body).

veilleur, -euse [vejœr, -øz] 1. nm Mil: etc: lookout; v. **de nuit,** nightwatchman 2. nf **veilleuse** (a) night light; Fig: **mettre qch en v.,** to shelve sth, to put sth off (b) Aut: sidelight.

veinard, -arde [vɛnar, -ard] a & n F: lucky, jammy (person); v.! you lucky devil!

veine [vɛn] nf 1. Anat: Bot: vein 2. (a) Geol: vein; lode (of ore); seam (of coal) (b) vein, inspiration; **être en v. de faire qch,** to be in the mood to do sth (c) F: luck; **avoir de la v.,** to be lucky; **coup de v.** (i)

stroke of luck (ii) fluke; **pas de v.!** rotten luck! **c'est bien ma v.!** just my luck!

veiner [vene] vtr to vein, grain (door).

vêlage [vɛlaʒ] nm (of cow) calving.

vêler [vele] vi (of cow) to calve.

vélin [velɛ̃] nm vellum (parchment).

velléité [veleite] nf vague desire, vague inclination. **velléitaire** a (of pers) weak-willed; irresolute.

vélo [velo] nm F: bicycle, bike; **aller à, en, v.,** to cycle; **faire du v.,** to cycle, to do some cycling; **il va au bureau en v.,** he cycles to the office.

vélocité [velɔsite] nf speed, swiftness.

vélodrome [velɔdrom] nm cycle-racing track.

vélomoteur [velɔmotœr] nm moped.

velours [v(ə)lur] nm velvet; v. **côtelé,** corduroy.

velouté [v(ə)lute] 1. a velvety; soft as velvet; downy; mellow (wine) 2. nm (a) velvetiness, softness (of material); bloom (of peach) (b) Cu: cream soup; velouté sauce.

velu [vəly] a hairy.

venaison [vənɛzɔ̃] nf Cu: venison.

vénal, -als, -aux [venal, -o] a 1. venal; Com: **valeur vénale,** market value 2. Pej: venal, mercenary; corrupt (person, press).

vénalité [venalite] nf venality.

venant [vənɑ̃] nm **à tout v., à tous venants,** to all comers, to all and sundry.

vendable [vɑ̃dab(l)] a saleable, marketable.

vendange [vɑ̃dɑ̃ʒ] nf 1. (often in pl) vintage (season) 2. (a) vintage; grape gathering; wine harvest (b) the grapes.

vendanger [vɑ̃dɑ̃ʒe] vtr & i (n. **vendangeons**) to vintage; to gather (the grapes).

vendangeur, -euse [vɑ̃dɑ̃ʒœr, -øz] n grape picker.

vendetta [vɑ̃deta] nf vendetta.

vendeur, -euse [vɑ̃dœr, -øz] n (a) (in shop) salesman, saleswoman; (shop) assistant (b) Jur: vendor.

vendre [vɑ̃dr] vtr 1. to sell; v. **qch à qn,** to sell sth to s.o.; v. **à terme,** to sell on credit; v. **comptant,** to sell for cash; v. **moins cher que qn,** to undersell s.o.; v. **chèrement sa vie,** to sell one's life dearly; v. **un objet 50 francs,** to sell an object for 50 francs; **cela se vend comme des petits pains,** it's selling like hot cakes; **maison à v.,** house for sale 2. v. **qn,** to betray s.o.

vendredi [vɑ̃drədi] nm Friday; v. **saint,** Good Friday.

vendu [vɑ̃dy] nm traitor.

vénéneux, -euse [venenø, -øz] a poisonous.

vénération [venerasjɔ̃] nf veneration, reverence.

vénérer [venere] vtr (**je vénère; je vénérerai**) to venerate, reverence, revere; to worship (saint). **vénérable** a venerable.

vénerie [vɛnri] nf venery.

vénérien, -ienne [venerjɛ̃, -jɛn] a Med: venereal.

vengeance [vɑ̃ʒɑ̃s] nf 1. revenge; **par v.,** out of revenge 2. vengeance, retribution; **ce crime crie v.,** this crime cries for revenge.

venger [vɑ̃ʒe] (**nous vengeons**) 1. vtr to avenge 2. se v., to be revenged; to have one's revenge; **se v. sur qn (de qch),** to take revenge on s.o. (for sth). **vengeur, -eresse** 1. n avenger 2. a Lit: avenging, (re)vengeful.

véniel, -elle [venjɛl] *a* venial (sin).

venin [vənɛ̃] *nm* venom. **venimeux, -euse** *a* venomous.

venir [v(ə)nir] *vi* (*prp* venant; *pp* venu; *pr ind* je viens; ils viennent; *pr sub* je vienne; *impf* je venais; *ph* je vins; *fu* je viendrai; *aux* être) 1. (*a*) to come; je viens! I'm coming! je ne ferai qu'aller et v., I'll come straight back; mais venez donc! do come along! il est venu vers moi, he came up to me; v. au monde, to be born; l'année qui vient, the coming year; next year; dans les jours à v., in the days to come; faire v. qn, to send for, fetch, s.o.; faire v. ses robes de Paris, to get one's dresses from Paris; voir v. qn, to see s.o. coming; *F:* je vous vois v.! I see what you're getting at; *impers* est-il venu qn? has anyone called? (*b*) venez me trouver à quatre heures, come and see me at four o'clock (*c*) (*pr & impf only*) v. de faire qch, to have (only) just done sth; il vient de sortir, he has just gone out 2. (*denoting origin*) (*a*) il vient d'Amérique, he comes from America; mot qui vient du latin, word derived from Latin; tout cela vient de ce que, all this is the result of (*b*) *impers* d'où vient(-il) que? how is it that? 3. (*a*) to occur; le premier exemple venu, the first example that comes to mind; il me vient à l'esprit que, it occurs to me that; il ne m'est pas venu à l'idée que, it never entered my head that (*b*) v. à faire qch, to happen to do sth 4. (*a*) to attain, reach; l'eau leur venait aux genoux, the water came up to their knees (*b*) en v. à qch, à faire qch, to come to sth, to the point of doing sth; en v. aux coups, to come to blows; les choses en sont-elles venues là? have things come to such a point? où voulez-vous en v.? what are you driving at? 5. (*of plants, teeth, children*) to grow (up); il lui est venu des boutons, he developed spots 6 *A: & Lit:* s'en v., to come (along).

Venise [vəniz] *Prnf* Venice.

vénitien, -ienne [venisjɛ̃, -jɛn] *a & n* Venetian; store v., Venetian blind.

vent [vɑ̃] *nm* 1. (*a*) wind; v. du nord, north wind; v. frais, strong breeze; coup de v., gust of wind; squall; entrer, sortir, en coup de v., to dash in, out; il fait du v., it's windy (weather); *Fig:* il a le v. en poupe, he's on the road to success; aller v. arrière, to sail before the wind; sous le v., (to) leeward; au v., (to) windward; côté du v., weatherside; côté sous le v., leeside (*b*) aire de v., point of the compass; regarder d'où vient le v., to see which way the wind blows; quel bon v. vous amène? what lucky chance brings you here? *F:* être dans le v., to be trendy, with it (*c*) air; en plein v., in the open air; mettre qch au v., to hang sth out to dry (*d*) blast (of gun) (*e*) *Med:* wind, flatulence (*f*) ce n'est que du v., it's just hot air 2. *Ven:* scent; avoir v. de qch, to get wind of sth.

vente [vɑ̃t] *nf* sale; v. aux enchères, (sale by) auction; salle des ventes, auction rooms; v. de charité, (charity) bazaar; bureau de v., sales agency; en v., for sale, on sale.

venter [vɑ̃te] *v impers* to blow, to be windy. **venté** windy, windswept.

ventilateur [vɑ̃tilatœr] *nm* ventilator; fan.

ventilation [vɑ̃tilasjɔ̃] *nf* (*a*) ventilation (*b*) *Book-k:* apportionment, breakdown (of expenses).

ventiler [vɑ̃tile] *vtr* (*a*) to ventilate, air (room) (*b*) *Book-k:* to apportion, to break down (expenses).

ventouse [vɑ̃tuz] *nf* (*a*) *Med:* cupping glass (*b*) *Z:* sucker (*c*) suction pad; faire v., to adhere by suction.

ventre [vɑ̃tr] *nm* 1. (*a*) stomach; abdomen, belly; *F:* tummy; se coucher à plat v., to lie flat on one's stomach; v. à terre, at full speed; avoir mal au v., to have stomach ache; prendre du v., to be getting a paunch (*b*) stomach; n'avoir rien dans le v. (i) to be starving (ii) to have no guts (*c*) womb 2. *Tchn:* bulge, swell; belly (of ship, aircraft).

ventricule [vɑ̃trikyl] *nm Anat:* ventricle.

ventriloque [vɑ̃trilɔk] *n* ventriloquist.

ventru [vɑ̃try] *a* (*a*) (*of pers*) potbellied (*b*) bulbous (object).

venu, -ue[1] [v(ə)ny] 1. *a* (*a*) bien v., healthy, thriving; enfant mal v., sickly child (*b*) (*of remark*) bien v., mal v., appropriate; inappropriate; il serait mal v. d'insister, it would be ill mannered to insist 2 *n* le premier v. (i) the first to arrive (ii) anybody; ce n'est pas le premier v., he's not just anybody; le dernier v. (i) the last to arrive (ii) *Pej:* a (mere) nobody; un nouveau v., a newcomer.

venue[2] [v(ə)ny] *nf* coming, arrival (of s.o., sth); des allées et venues, comings and goings.

vêpres [vɛpr] *nfpl Ecc* vespers; evensong.

ver [vɛr] *nm* 1. worm; *Med:* v. solitaire, tapeworm; *F:* tirer les vers du nez à qn, to worm information out of s.o. 2 grub, larva, maggot; v. du bois, woodworm; v. luisant, glow worm; v. à soie, silkworm.

véracité [verasite] *nf* veracity; truthfulness.

véranda [verɑ̃da] *nf* veranda(h).

verbaliser [vɛrbalize] *vi* (*of policeman*) to charge s.o.

verbe [vɛrb] *nm* 1. tone of voice; speech; avoir le v. haut (i) to speak loudly (ii) to be dictatorial 2. *Theol:* le V., the Word 3. *Gram:* verb. **verbal, -aux** *a* verbal. **verbalement** *adv* verbally.

verbiage [vɛrbjaʒ] *nm* verbiage.

verdâtre [vɛrdɑtr] *a* greenish.

verdeur [vɛrdœr] *nf* 1. (*a*) tartness, acidity (of wine, fruit) (*b*) crudeness (of speech) 2. vigour; vitality.

verdict [vɛrdikt] *nm Jur:* verdict.

verdir [vɛrdir] *vtr & i* to turn green.

verdoyant [vɛrdwajɑ̃] *a* green; verdant.

verdure [vɛrdyr] *nf* 1. (*a*) greenness; (*b*) greenery; *Lit:* verdure 2. *Cu:* (green) salad vegetable.

véreux, -euse [verø, -øz] *a* 1. maggoty, wormeaten (fruit) 2. dubious; shady (dealings).

verge [vɛrʒ] *nf* (*a*) rod (*b*) *Anat:* penis.

verger [vɛrʒe] *nm* orchard.

verglas [vɛrgla] *nm* (*on roads*) black ice. **verglacé** *a* icy (road).

vergogne [vɛrgɔɲ] *nf sans v.,* shameless(ly).

vergue [vɛrg] *nf Nau:* yard.

véridique [veridik] *a* (*a*) truthful, veracious (*b*) authentic.

vérificateur, -trice [verifikatœr, -tris] 1. *a* appareil v., testing machine 2. *n* (*pers*) controller, inspector, examiner.

vérification [verifikasjɔ̃] *nf* verification; inspection, examination (of work); proof, confirmation; v. de comptes, audit(ing).

vérifier [verifje] (*impf & pr sub n.* vérifiions) 1. *vtr* (*a*) to verify; to inspect, examine, check (work); to audit (accounts) (*b*) to verify, prove, confirm 2. (*of* *statement*) **se v.**, to prove correct. **vérifiable** *a* verifiable, that can be checked.

vérin [verẽ] *nm Tchn:* jack.

véritable [veritabl] *a* **1.** true **2.** real, genuine; **un v. coquin**, a downright rogue; **c'est une v. folie**, it's sheer; madness. **véritablement** *adv* truly; really, genuinely.

vérité [verite] *nf* **1.** truth; **dire la v.**, to tell the truth; **à la v.**, to tell the truth; as a matter of fact; **en v.**, really, actually **2.** truth; **c'est la v.**, it's a fact; *F:* **c'est la v. vraie**, it's the honest truth; **dire à qn ses quatre vérités**, to tell s.o. a few home truths **3.** sincerity; truthfulness.

vermeil, -eille [vermɛj] **1.** *a* vermilion; bright red; ruby (lips); rosy (cheeks) **2.** *nm* silver gilt.

vermicelle [vermisɛl] *nm Cu:* vermicelli.

vermifuge [vermify3] *a & nm* vermifuge.

vermillon [vermijõ] *a inv & nm* vermilion; bright red.

vermine [vermin] *nf* vermin.

vermoulu [vermuly] *a* wormeaten.

vermout(h) [vermut] *nm* vermouth.

vernir [vernir] *vtr* to varnish; to French polish (mahogany); *Cer:* to glaze. **verni** *a* varnished; French polished; **chaussures vernies**, patent (leather) shoes; *F:* **être v.**, to be lucky.

vernis [verni] *nm* varnish, polish, glaze, gloss; **v. au tampon**, French polish; **v. à ongles**, nail varnish; **v. de politesse**, veneer of politeness.

vernissage [vernisa3] *nm* (*a*) varnishing; *Cer:* glazing (*b*) private view (at an exhibition).

vérole [verɔl] *nf Med:* **1. petite v.**, smallpox **2.** *P:* pox.

verre [vɛr] *nm* **1.** glass; **v. blanc**, plain glass; **v. dépoli**, frosted glass; **v. coloré**, stained glass; **papier de v.**, sandpaper; **articles de v.**, glassware; **sous v.**, under glass **2.** (*object made of glass*) glass; lens (of spectacles); **il porte des verres**, he wears glasses; **verres de contact**, contact lenses; **v. de montre**, watch glass; **v. grossissant**, magnifying glass **3.** (*a*) **v. (à boire)**, (drinking) glass; **v. à vin**, wineglass; **v. à dents**, tooth mug (*b*) **boire, prendre, un v.**, to have a drink; **prendre un v. de trop**, to have one too many **4. v. soluble**, waterglass.

verrerie [vɛr(ə)ri] *nf* (*a*) glassmaking (*b*) glassworks (*c*) glassware.

verrier [vɛrje] *nm* glassmaker.

verrière [vɛrjɛr] *nf* **1.** glass casing **2.** stained glass window **3.** glass roof.

verroterie [vɛrɔtri] *nf* small glassware.

verrou [vɛru] *nm* bolt, bar; **pousser, mettre, le v.**, to bolt the door; **mettre qn sous les verrous**, to put s.o. under lock and key; **être sous les verrous**, to be behind bars.

verrouillage [vɛruja3] *nm* (*a*) bolting, locking (*b*) locking mechanism.

verrouiller [vɛruje] *vtr* to bolt (door); to lock.

verrue [vɛry] *nf* wart; **v. plantaire**, verruca.

vers¹ [vɛr] *nm* verse, line (of poetry); **v. blancs, v. libres**, blank verse, free verse; **écrire des v.**, to write poetry.

vers² *prep* **1.** (*of place*) toward(s), to; **v. Pau**, near Pau, round about Pau **2.** (*of time*) (*a*) toward(s); **v. la fin du siècle**, towards the end of the century (*b*)

about; **venez v. (les) trois heures**, come (at) about three (o'clock).

versant [vɛrsã] *nm* slope, side (of mountain); **v. de colline**, hillside.

versatilité [vɛrsatilite] *nf* changeability, fickleness. **versatile** *a* changeable, fickle.

verse [vɛrs] *adv phr* **il pleut à v.**, it's pouring (down), bucketing down.

versé [vɛrse] *a* experienced, practised, (well) versed (**dans**, in).

Verseau [vɛrso] *Prnm Astr:* **le V.**, Aquarius.

versement [vɛrs(ə)mã] *nm* payment; paying in; **en plusieurs versements**, by instalments.

verser [vɛrse] **1.** *vtr* (*a*) to overturn, upset (sth) (*b*) to pour (out) (liquid); to tip (out, in); **se v. à boire**, to pour oneself a drink (*c*) to shed (tears); to spill (blood) (*d*) to pay (in), to deposit (money) (*e*) **v. un document au dossier**, to add a document to the file (*f*) **v. qn dans**, to assign s.o. to **2.** *vi* (*a*) (*of car*) to overturn (*b*) **v. dans**, to fall, to drift, into. **verseur, -euse 1.** *a* **bec v.**, spout; pouring lip **2.** *n* pourer.

verset [vɛrse] *nm* verse (of bible).

version [vɛrsjõ] *nf* **1.** (*a*) translation (into mother tongue); *Sch:* unseen (*b*) film en v. **originale**, film in the original language; **film en v. française**, film dubbed in French **2.** version, account (of event).

verso [vɛrso] *nm* verso, back (of sheet of paper); **voir au v.**, see overleaf.

vert [vɛr] **1.** *a* (*a*) green; *Aut:* **feu v.**, green light; **légumes verts**, green vegetables, *F:* greens; **plantes vertes**, evergreens (*b*) green (wood); unripe (fruit); young (wine) (*c*) (*of old pers*) hale and hearty; **verte vieillesse**, green old age (*d*) spicy, risqué (story); **il en a vu des vertes et des pas mûres**, he's been through a lot (*e*) sharp (reprimand) **2.** *nm* (*a*) green colour; **v. bouteille**, bottle green; **v. pomme**, apple green (*b*) **mettre un cheval au v.**, to turn a horse out to grass; *F:* **se mettre au v.**, to go to the country to recuperate. **vertement** *adv* (to reprimand) sharply.

vert-de-gris [vɛrdəgri] *nm inv* verdigris.

vertèbre [vɛrtɛbr] *nf Anat:* vertebra. **vertébral, -aux** *a* vertebral; **colonne vertébrale**, spine. **vertébré** *a & nm* vertebrate.

vertical, -ale, -aux [vɛrtikal, -o] **1.** *a* vertical; perpendicular; upright **2.** *nf* **verticale**, vertical; **à la verticale**, vertically. **verticalement** *adv* vertically; straight up, down.

vertige [vɛrti3] *nm* **1.** dizziness, giddiness; **avoir le v.**, to feel dizzy; **ça me donne le v.**, it makes me feel dizzy **2.** vertigo; fear of heights. **vertigineux, -euse** *a* vertiginous; dizzy, giddy (height); break-neck, breathtaking (speed); staggering (rise in prices). **vertigineusement** *adv* dizzily; breathtakingly (fast, high).

vertu [vɛrty] *nf* **1.** virtue **2.** quality, property, virtue (of remedy); **en v. de**, by virtue of; in accordance with. **vertueux, -euse** *a* virtuous. **vertueusement** *adv* virtuously.

verve [vɛrv] *nf* animation, verve.

vésicule [vezikyl] *nf Anat:* vesicle; **v. biliaire**, gall bladder.

vespasienne [vespazjɛn] *nf* street urinal.

vessie [vesi] *nf* bladder.

veste [vɛst] *nf Cl:* jacket; *F:* **retourner sa v.**, to be a turncoat; **remporter une v.**, to come a cropper.

vestiaire [vɛstjɛr] *nm (a) (in theatre)* cloakroom *(b) Sp: etc:* changing room, locker room.

vestibule [vɛstibyl] *nm* vestibule, (entrance) hall.

vestige [vɛstiʒ] *nm* vestige, trace, remains (of prehistoric man); remnant, relic (of the past).

vestimentaire [vɛstimɑ̃tɛr] *a* clothing (trade); **détail v.**, detail of one's dress.

veston [vɛstɔ̃] *nm* (man's) jacket; **complet-v.**, lounge suit.

vêtement [vɛtmɑ̃] *nm* garment; *pl* clothes, clothing; **industrie du v.**, clothing trade; **vêtements de sport, de plage**, sportswear, beachwear; **vêtements de dessous**, underwear, underclothes.

vétéran [veterɑ̃] *nm* veteran; old campaigner.

vétérinaire [veterinɛr] **1.** *a* veterinary **2.** *nm* veterinary surgeon, vet.

vétille [vetij] *nf* trifle; triviality.

vêtir [vetir] *(prp* **vêtant;** *pp* **vêtu;** *pr ind* **je vêts) 1.** *vtr* to clothe; to dress **2. se v.**, to dress (oneself). **vêtu** *a (of pers)* dressed; **v. de**, dressed in, wearing.

veto [veto] *nm* veto; **mettre, opposer, son v. à qch**, to veto sth.

vétusté [vetyste] *nf* decay, decrepitude. **vétuste** *a* decayed.

veuf, veuve [vœf, vœv] **1.** *a.* widowed (man, woman) **2.** *n* widower, *f* widow.

veuvage [vœvaʒ] *nm* widowhood.

vexation [vɛksasjɔ̃] *nf* humiliation.

vexer [vɛkse] **1.** *vtr* to annoy, offend, upset, hurt (s.o.) **2. se v. de qch**, to be upset, offended, about sth. **vexant** *a* annoying; hurtful.

via [vja] *prep* via.

viabilité [vjabilite] *nf* **1.** practicability (of road) **2.** development (of site ready for building) **3.** viability (of plan). **viable** *a* viable.

viaduc [vjadyk] *nm* viaduct.

viager, -ère [vjaʒe, -ɛr] **1.** *a* for life; **rente viagère**, life annuity **2.** *nm* life interest; **placer son argent en v.**, to invest one's money in an annuity.

viande [vjɑ̃d] *nf* meat; **v. de boucherie**, butcher's meat; **v. rouge, blanche**, red, white, meat; **v. de cheval**, horsemeat.

vibration [vibrasjɔ̃] *nf* vibration.

vibrer [vibre] *vi* to vibrate; **faire v. le cœur de qn**, to stir, to thrill, s.o.'s heart. **vibrant** *a* vibrating; vibrant; resonant (voice); stirring (speech). **vibratoire** *a* vibratory.

vicaire [vikɛr] *nm* curate (of parish); **v. général**, vicar-general.

vice [vis] *nm* **1.** *(a)* depravity, corruption *(b)* vice **2.** fault, defect; **v. de construction**, faulty construction; **v. de forme**, flaw (in a deed); faulty drafting.

vice-amiral [visamiral] *nm* vice-admiral; *pl* **vice-amiraux**.

vice-président, -ente [visprezidɑ̃, -ɑ̃t] *(a)* vice-president *(b)* vice-chairman; *pl* **vice-président(e)s**.

vice-roi [visrwa] *nm* viceroy; *pl* **vice-rois**.

vicier [visje] *vtr (impf & pr sub* **n. viciions)** to vitiate, corrupt, spoil; to pollute, contaminate (air). **vicié** *a* corrupt; tainted; polluted (air). **vicieux, -euse** *a* **1.** depraved, corrupt (pers) **2.** defective, faulty, imperfect; incorrect (pronunciation); **cercle v.**, vicious circle **3.** restive (horse). **vicieusement** *adv* pervertedly.

vicinal, -aux [visinal, -o] *a* **chemin v.**, local road.

vicomte [vikɔ̃t] *nm* viscount.

vicomtesse [vikɔ̃tɛs] *nf* viscountess.

victime [viktim] *nf* victim, sufferer; *(of accident)* casualty, victim; **être la v. d'une illusion**, to labour under an illusion.

victoire [viktwar] *nf* victory; **chanter, crier, v.**, to crow, to triumph. **victorieux, -ieuse** *a* victorious; triumphant. **victorieusement** *adv* victoriously.

victuailles [viktɥaj] *nfpl* food, provisions.

vidange [vidɑ̃ʒ] *nf (a)* draining, emptying (of cesspools) *(b) Aut:* oil change; **faire la v.**, to change the oil *(c)* **tuyau de v.**, wastepipe.

vidanger [vidɑ̃ʒe] *vtr* **(je vidangeai(s))** to empty (cesspool); to drain (tank).

vide [vid] **1.** *a* empty; blank (space); unoccupied, vacant (seat); **bouteilles vides**, empty bottles, *F:* empties; **v. de sens**, meaningless **2.** *nm (a)* empty space; void; blank; **combler les vides**, to fill (up) the gaps *(b) Ph:* vacuum; **emballé sous v.**, vacuum-packed *(c)* emptiness; **regarder dans le v.**, to stare into space; **camion revenant à v.**, lorry returning empty.

vidéo [video] *a & nf inv* video.

vidéocassette [videokasɛt] *nf* videocassette.

vide-ordures [vidɔrdyr] *nm inv* rubbish chute.

vide-poches [vidpɔʃ] *nm inv Aut:* glove compartment.

vider [vide] *vtr* **1** *(a)* to empty; to clear out (room, drawer); to drain (glass); **videz vos verres!** drink up! **v. les lieux**, to vacate the premises; to quit; *F:* **v. qn**, to wear s.o. out; *F:* **v. son sac**, to get sth off one's chest *(b) (of horse)* to throw (rider); *F:* to throw (s.o.) out *(c)* to clean (fish); to draw (fowl); to core (apple) *(d)* to settle (question) **2. se v.**, to (become) empty.

vie [vi] *nf* **1.** life; **être en v.**, to be alive; **avoir la v. dure**, to be hard to kill; to die hard; **donner la v. à un enfant**, to give birth to a child; **être entre la v. et la mort**, to hover between life and death; **il y va de la v.**, it's a case of life and death; **sans v.**, lifeless; unconscious; **musique pleine de v.**, lively music **2.** lifetime; **pour la v.**, for life; **jamais de la v.!** never! not on your life! **nommé à v.**, appointed for life **3.** existence, way of life; **c'est la v.!** such is life! **changer de v.**, to turn over a new leaf; **la v. Américaine**, the American way of life; *F:* **faire la v.**, (i) to lead a riotous life (ii) to kick up a row **4.** living, livelihood; **niveau de v.**, standard of living; **coût de la v.**, cost of living; **gagner sa v.**, to earn one's living.

vieil, vieille *see* **vieux**.

vieillard [vjejar] *nm (f usu* **vieille)** old man; **les vieillards**, old people; the elderly.

vieillerie [vjɛjri] *nf* oldfashioned thing.

vieillesse [vjɛjɛs] *nf* (old) age; **la v.**, the old, the elderly, the aged.

vieillir [vjejir] **1.** *vi (a)* to grow old *(b)* to age (in appearance); **il a vieilli**, he looks older; he's aged *(c)* to become obsolete, out of date; **ce mot a vieilli**, this word is obsolescent *(d) (of wine, cheese)* to mature **2.** *vtr* to age; to make (s.o.) look older; **ce chapeau**

la **vieillit**, that hat makes her look older 3. **se v.**, to make oneself look older. **vieillissant** *a* ageing. **vieillot, -otte** *a* antiquated, old-fashioned.

vieillissement [vjejismã] *nm* ageing, growing old; becoming outdated.

vierge [vjɛrʒ] 1. *nf* (*a*) virgin; **la (Sainte) V.**, the Blessed Virgin (Mary) (*b*) *Astr:* **la V.**, Virgo 2. *a* virgin, virginal; virgin (soil, forest); blank (page); pure (white); **réputation v.**, untarnished reputation.

Vietnam [vjɛtnam] *Prnm Geog:* Vietnam. **vietnamien, -ienne** *a & n* Vietnamese.

vieux, vieil, *f* **vieille** [vjø, vjɛj] *a* (*the form* **vieil** *is used before masc nouns beginning with a vowel or h mute, but* **vieux** *also occurs in this position*) 1. (*a*) old; **se faire v.**, to be getting on (in years); *n* **un v., une vieille**, an old man, an old woman; **les v.**, old people; the elderly; *F:* **mes v.**, my parents; *F:* **eh bien, mon v.!** well, old chap! *adv* **elle s'habille plus v. que son âge**, she dresses too old for her age (*b*) longstanding (friendship); **un vieil ami**, an old friend; **vieille fille**, old maid; spinster; **v. garçon**, (confirmed) bachelor; **il est v. dans ce métier**, he's an old hand at this job; *n F:* **un v. de la vieille**, a veteran 2. (*a*) old, ancient (building); worn, shabby (hat); stale (news); **v. papiers**, waste paper; **le bon v. temps**, the good old days; *adj phr inv* **v. jeu**, oldfashioned; out of date; **ça c'est v. jeu**, that's old hat (*b*) *inv* **des rubans vieil or**, old-gold ribbons.

vif, vive[1] [vif, viv] 1. *a* (*a*) alive, living; **être brûlé v.**, to be burnt alive; **de vive force**, by force; **de vive voix**, by word of mouth; **eau vive**, spring water; **marée de vive eau**, spring tide; **chaux vive**, quicklime (*b*) lively, animated; fast; hot (fire); (*of pers*) vivacious; **vive allure**, brisk pace; **avoir l'humeur un peu vive**, to be quick tempered (*c*) sharp (wind, retort); acute (pain); **l'air est v.**, there's a nip in the air; **arête vive**, sharp edge (*d*) keen, quick (wit); vivid (imagination); **vive satisfaction**, great satisfaction; **v. intérêt**, deep interest (*e*) bright, vivid, intense (colour); (*of complexion*) **couleur vive**, high colour 2. *nm Jur:* living person 3. (*a*) *nm* living flesh; quick; **blessé au v.**, stung to the quick; **j'ai les nerfs à v.**, my nerves are on edge; **entrer dans le v. du sujet**, to get to the heart of the matter (*b*) **pêcher au v.**, to fish with live bait.

vigie [viʒi] *nf Nau:* (*a*) lookout (*b*) watchtower.

vigilance [viʒilɑ̃s] *nf* vigilance; watchfulness. **vigilant** *a* watchful, alert; vigilant.

vigile [viʒil] *nm* (night)watchman.

vigne [viɲ] *nf* 1. *Vit:* (*a*) vine (*b*) vineyard 2. *Bot:* **v. vierge**, Virginia creeper.

vigneron, -onne [viɲrɔ̃, -ɔn] *n* vine grower; wine grower.

vignette [viɲɛt] *nf* (*a*) *Art:* vignette; illustration (*b*) *Com:* label; *Aut:* = (road) tax disc.

vignoble [viɲɔbl] *nm* vineyard.

vigoureux, -euse [viguRø, -øz] *a* vigorous, strong, sturdy; robust; powerful; strenuous (opposition). **vigoureusement** *adv* vigorously.

vigueur [vigœr] *nf* 1. vigour, strength; **sans v.**, (*of pers*) exhausted; **avec v.**, vigorously 2. (*of decree*) **en v.**, in force; **entrer en v.**, to come into effect; **cesser d'être en v.**, to lapse; to cease to apply.

vil [vil] *a* 1. **vendre qch à v. prix**, to sell sth at a low price, *F:* dirt cheap 2. *A:* & *Lit:* vile, base (pers).

vilain, -aine [vilɛ̃, -ɛn] 1. *n* (*a*) *F:* **oh, le v.!** oh, la **vilaine!** you naughty boy! you naughty girl! (*b*) *F:* trouble; **il y aura du v.**, there's going to be trouble 2. *a* (*a*) nasty, bad, unpleasant; **c'est un v. monsieur**, he's a nasty piece of work; **v. tour**, mean, dirty, trick (*b*) ugly (story); nasty (wound) (*c*) shabby (hat); sordid, wretched (street).

vilebrequin [vilbRəkɛ̃] *nm* (*a*) *Tls:* (bit) brace (*b*) *Med:* crankshaft.

villa [vila] *nf* house (in a residential area).

village [vilaʒ] *nm* village; **v. de toile**, camp site. **villageois, -oise** 1. *n* villager 2. *a* rustic; village (customs).

ville [vil] *nf* town; city; **v. d'eaux**, spa; **v. champignon**, mushroom town; **v. satellite**, satellite town; **en v.**, in town; in the town centre; **habiter à la v.**, to live in a town; **gens de la v.**, townspeople.

villégiature [vileʒjatyR] *nf* (*a*) holiday; *NAm:* vacation; **en v.**, on holiday (*b*) (holiday) resort.

vin [vɛ̃] *nm* wine; **les grands vins**, vintage wines; **v. ordinaire**, **v. de table**, table wine; **v. de Bordeaux**, claret; **v. de Bourgogne**, burgundy; **v. chaud**, mulled wine; **offrir un v. d'honneur à qn**, to hold a reception in honour of s.o.; **entre deux vins**, drunk, tight.

vinaigre [vinɛgR] *nm* vinegar.

vinaigrette [vinɛgRɛt] *nf Cu:* French dressing, vinaigrette.

vindicatif, -ive [vɛ̃dikatif, -iv] *a* vindictive.

vingt [vɛ̃] *num a inv & nm inv* twenty; **v. et un** [vɛ̃teœ̃] twenty-one; **v.-deux** [vɛ̃dø] twenty-two; **le v. juin** [ləvɛ̃ʒɥɛ̃] (on) the twentieth of June; **les années v.**, the twenties (1920–29); **les moins de v. ans**, teenagers; **je te l'ai dit v. fois**, I've told you a hundred times. **vingtième** *num a & n* twentieth. **vingtièmement** *adv* in the twentieth place.

vingtaine [vɛ̃tɛn] *nf* (about) twenty; a score; **une v. de gens**, some twenty people.

vinicole [vinikɔl] *a* wine(-growing), wine-producing (area).

vinyle [vinil] *nm* vinyl.

viol [vjɔl] *nm* 1. *Jur:* rape 2. violation (of a sanctuary).

violacé [vjɔlase] *a* purplish-blue.

violation [vjɔlasjɔ̃] *nf* violation, infringement, breach (of law).

violence [vjɔlɑ̃s] *nf* violence, force; **faire v. à qn**, to do violence to s.o.; **se faire v.**, to force oneself. **violent** *a* violent; high (wind); fierce (encounter); strenuous (effort). **violemment** *adv* violently.

violenter [vjɔlɑ̃te] *vtr* to rape (a woman).

violer [vjɔle] *vtr* 1. to violate; to break (law); to desecrate (grave) 2. to rape (a woman).

violet, -ette [vjɔlɛ, -ɛt] 1. *a* violet, purple 2. *nm* (the colour) purple 3. *nf Bot:* **violette**, violet.

violon [vjɔlɔ̃] *nm* 1. (*a*) violin; **c'est son v. d'Ingres**, it's his hobby (*b*) violin (player); **premier v.**, (i) first violin (ii) leader (of the orchestra) 2. *P:* **le v.**, the cells, the lockup.

violoncelle [vjɔlɔ̃sɛl] *nm Mus:* (*a*) cello (*b*) cello (player); cellist. **violoncelliste** [vjɔlɔ̃selist] *n* cellist, cello player.

violoniste [vjɔlɔnist] *n* violinist.

vipère [vipɛr] *nf* viper, adder; **langue de v.**, spiteful, venomous, tongue.

virage [viraʒ] *nm* **1.** turn; cornering (of car); *Av:* **v. sur l'aile,** bank(ing) **2.** *(a)* (sharp) turn, corner, bend; **v. en épingle à cheveux,** hairpin bend; **v. à la corde,** sharp turn *(b)* banked corner.

virée [vire] *nf F:* *(a)* trip, run, outing (in a car); walk *(b)* = pub crawl.

virement [virmɑ̃] *nm* **v. (bancaire),** (credit) transfer; **banque de v.,** clearing bank.

virer [vire] **1.** *vi (a)* to turn; to sweep round; *Aut:* to take a bend, a corner; to corner; **v. court,** to corner sharply *(b) Av:* to bank *(c)* to turn (round); to slew round, swing round *(d) Nau:* **v. de bord,** to tack *(e)* to change colour; **rouge qui vire à l'orange,** red which is turning orange *(f) Phot:* to tone *(g) Med: (of skin test)* to come up positive **2.** *vtr (a) Bank:* to transfer (a sum) *(b) Phot:* to tone (print) *(c) F:* to throw, chuck (s.o.) out *(d) Med: F:* **v. sa cuti,** to give a positive skin test.

virevolte [virvɔlt] *nf* half-turn (of dancer); twirl.

virevolter [virvɔlte] *vi (of pers)* to spin round.

virginité [virʒinite] *nf* virginity; maidenhood.

virgule [virgyl] *nf (a) Gram:* comma *(b) Mth:* decimal point; **trois v. cinq (3,5),** three point five (3·5) *(c) Elcs:* **v. flottante,** floating point.

viril [viril] *a (a)* virile, male *(b)* manly; **l'âge v.,** manhood. **virilement** *adv* in a manly way.

virilité [virilite] *nf* virility, manliness.

virtuel, -elle [virtɥɛl] *a* potential; *Phil:* virtual. **virtuellement** *adv* potentially; virtually.

virtuose [virtɥoz] *n* virtuoso.

virtuosité [virtɥozite] *nf* virtuosity.

virulence [virylɑ̃s] *nf* virulence. **virulent** *a* virulent.

virus [virys] *nm Med:* virus; **avoir le v. du ski,** to have a craze for skiing.

vis [vis] *nf* screw; **v. sans fin,** endless screw, worm (screw); **escalier à v.,** spiral staircase; *Aut:* **v. platinées,** (contact) points.

visa [viza] *nm* visa; stamp (on document); **v. de censure,** censor's certificate.

visage [vizaʒ] *nm (a)* face; **se faire le v.,** to make (one's face) up; **à deux visages,** two-faced; **avoir bon v.,** to look well; **faire bon v. à qn,** to be outwardly friendly to s.o.; **à v. découvert,** openly *(b)* **v. pâle,** paleface.

visagiste [vizaʒist] *n* beautician.

vis-à-vis [vizavi] **1.** *adv phr* opposite; face to face **2.** *prep phr* **v.-à-v. de** *(a)* opposite, facing *(b)* towards, in relation to, vis-à-vis (s.o., sth); **sincère v.-à-v. de soi-même,** sincere with oneself **3.** *nm* person opposite; *Cards:* partner; **nous avons le lac pour v.-à-v.,** we look out onto the lake.

viscères [viser] *nfpl Anat:* internal organs; viscera.

viscosité [viskozite] *nf* viscosity.

visée [vize] *nf* **1.** aim; sighting; **ligne de v.,** line of sight **2.** *usu pl* aims; plans; ambitions.

viser[1] [vize] **1.** *vi* to (take) aim (à, at, for); **v. à faire qch,** to aim at doing sth; **v. juste,** to aim straight; **v. haut,** to set one's sights high **2.** *vtr (a)* to aim, take aim, at (s.o., sth); *Golf:* **v. la balle,** to address the ball *(b)* to have (sth) in view; **je ne vise personne,** I am not alluding to anybody in particular **3.** *P:* to look, to have a look, at.

viser[2] *vtr Adm:* to visa; to countersign.

viseur, -euse [vizœr, -øz] **1.** *n* aimer **2.** *nm (a) Phot:* viewfinder *(b)* sighting tube; *Av:* **v. de lancement,** bomb sight(s).

visibilité [vizibilite] *nf* visibility; *Av:* **vols sans v.,** instrument flying.

visible [vizibl] *a* **1.** *(a)* visible, perceptible *(b)* obvious, evident, clear; **très v.,** conspicuous **2.** *(a)* ready to receive visitors; **je ne suis pas v.,** I'm not at home, not in; **je ne serai pas v. avant midi,** I can't see anybody before midday *(b) (of exhibition)* open to the public. **visiblement** *adv* obviously, evidently, clearly.

visière [vizjɛr] *nf (a)* visor (of helmet) *(b)* peak (of cap) *(c)* eyeshade.

vision [vizjɔ̃] *nf* **1.** *(a)* vision; (eye)sight *(b)* sight, view; **v. momentanée (de qch),** glimpse (of sth) **2.** vision; imagination (of poet) **3.** vision; **tu as des visions,** you're seeing things. **visionnaire** *a & n* visionary.

visionner [vizjɔne] *vtr* to view.

visionneuse [vizjɔnøz] *nf Cin: Phot:* viewer.

visite [vizit] *nf* **1.** *(a)* visit; (social) call; **faire une v., rendre v., à qn,** to call on s.o.; to visit s.o.; **v. officielle,** official visit; **carte de v.,** visiting card *(b)* visitor; caller; **nous attendons des visites, de la v.,** we're expecting visitors *(c)* **v. à domicile,** (house)call, visit **2.** *(a)* inspection, examination, survey; overhauling (of machinery); (medical) examination; **la v.,** (i) *(at doctor's)* surgery (ii) *Mil:* sick parade; **v. de douane,** customs examination *(b)* visit (to place of interest); **v. dirigée,** conducted tour.

visiter [vizite] *vtr* **1.** *(of doctor)* to visit (a patient); *Com:* to call on (a client) **2.** *(a)* to examine, inspect (building, machinery); to overhaul (machinery); to view (house for sale) *(b)* to visit, search (house); to examine (suitcase) *(c)* to visit (as tourist); **on nous a fait v. l'usine,** we were shown round the factory.

visiteur, -euse [viziter, -øz] *n* visitor.

vison [vizɔ̃] *nm Z:* mink; *Com:* mink coat.

visqueux, -euse [viskø, -øz] *a* viscous, sticky, gluey; tacky; thick (oil); slimy (secretion).

visser [vise] *vtr (a)* to screw (on, in, down, up); **être vissé sur sa chaise,** to be glued to one's chair *(b) F:* to treat (s.o.) severely; to crack down on (s.o.).

visuel, -elle [vizɥɛl] *a* visual; **champ v.,** field of vision. **visuellement** *adv* visually.

vital, -aux [vital, -o] *a* vital.

vitalité [vitalite] *nf* vitality.

vitamine [vitamin] *nf* vitamin. **vitaminé** *a* enriched with vitamins.

vite [vit] *adv* quickly, fast, rapidly, speedily; **le temps passe v.,** time flies; **ça ne va pas v.,** it's slow work; **il sera v. guéri,** he'll soon be better; **faites v.!** hurry up! **allons, et plus v. que ça!** now then, get a move on! **pas si v.!** not so fast! hold on! **au plus v.,** as quickly as possible; **il eut v. fait de s'habiller,** he was dressed in no time; **on a v. fait de dire,** it's easy to say.

vitesse [vites] *nf* **1.** speed, rapidity; quickness; **à la v. de,** at the rate of; **faire de la v.,** to speed (along); **en v.,** quickly, at speed; **partir en v.,** to rush off; **gagner qn de v.,** to outstrip s.o.; **prendre de la v.,** to gather speed; *Av:* **se mettre en perte de v.,** to stall; *Aut:* **indicateur de v.,** speedometer; **à toute v.,** at full, at top, speed; *F:* all out; **v. de croisière,** cruising speed

2. (a) velocity; **v. acquise,** impetus; momentum (b) *Aut:* gear; **changer de v.,** to change gear; *Aut:* **boîte de vitesses,** gearbox; **deuxième v.,** second gear; **filer en quatrième v.,** (i) to drive in top (gear) (ii) *F:* to disappear at top speed.

viticole [vitikɔl] *a* wine-producing, wine-growing (district); wine (industry).

viticulture [vitikyltyr] *nf* wine growing. **viticulteur** [vitikyltœr] *nm* wine grower.

vitrage [vitraʒ] *nm* (a) windows (of church) (b) glass partition.

vitrail, -aux [vitraj, -o] *nm* stained glass window.

vitre [vitṛ] *nf* pane (of glass); window (pane).

vitrer [vitre] *vtr* to glaze (window). **vitré** *a* glazed; **porte vitrée,** glass door. **vitreux, -euse** *a* vitreous (mass); glassy (appearance); glazed (eyes).

vitrerie [vitrəri] *nf* glaziery; glass industry.

vitrier [vitrije] *nm* glazier.

vitrification [vitrifikasjɔ̃] *nf* vitrification; glazing.

vitrifier [vitrifje] *vtr* (impf & pr sub **n. vitrifiions**) to vitrify; **brique vitrifiée,** glazed brick.

vitrine [vitrin] *nf* **1.** shop window; **en v.,** in the window **2.** glass case; display cabinet; showcase.

vitriol [vitri(j)ɔl] *nm* vitriol.

vitupération [vityperasjɔ̃] *nf* vituperation.

vitupérer [vitypere] *vi* (je **vitupère, n. vitupérons**) to vituperate, protest, storm (**contre qn, qch,** against s.o., sth).

vivable [vivabḷ] *a F:* (of house) livable (in); (of pers) livable with.

vivace [vivas] *a* (a) long-lived (b) *Bot:* hardy (c) *Bot:* perennial (d) undying, inveterate (hatred).

vivacité [vivasite] *nf* **1.** hastiness (of temper); petulance; **avec v.,** hastily **2.** (a) acuteness (of feeling); heat (of a discussion); intensity (of passion) (b) vividness, brilliance, brightness (of colour, light) **3.** vivacity, vivaciousness, liveliness; **v. d'esprit,** quick-wittedness.

vivant [vivɑ̃] **1.** *a* (a) alive, living; **il est encore v.,** he's still alive; **poisson v.,** live fish; **portrait v.,** lifelike portrait; **être le portrait v. de qn,** to be the living image of s.o.; **langue vivante,** modern language (b) lively, animated (street, scene); vivid (picture) **2.** *nm* living being; **bon v.,** (i) jovial fellow (ii) man who enjoys (the pleasures of) life **3.** *nm* **de son v.,** during his lifetime, in his day; **du v. de mon père,** when my father was alive.

vivats [viva] *nmpl* cheers.

vive² [viv] *exclam see* **vivre 1.** (a).

vivement [vivmɑ̃] *adv* **1.** (a) briskly, sharply, suddenly (b) *int* **v. les vacances!** roll on the holidays! (c) **répondre v.,** to answer sharply **2.** (a) vividly (b) keenly, deeply; acutely; **s'intéresser v. à qch,** to take a keen interest in sth.

viveur [vivœr] *nm* pleasure seeker; fast liver.

vivier [vivje] *nm* fishpond; fish tank.

vivifier [vivifje] *vtr* (impf & pr sub **n. vivifiions**) to vivify; to invigorate. **vivifiant** *a* invigorating, bracing.

vivisection [viviseksjɔ̃] *nf* vivisection.

vivoter [vivɔte] *vi* to rub along; to keep going (somehow).

vivre¹ [vivṛ] **1.** *vi* (pp **vécu;** pr ind **je vis**) (a) to live; to be alive; **cesser de v.,** to die; **cette robe a vécu,** this

dress is finished, has had its day; **vive le roi!** long live the King! *Mil:* **qui vive?** who goes there? (b) **il vécut vieux,** he lived to be an old man (c) to spend one's life; **v. à Paris,** to live in Paris; **v. avec qn,** to live with s.o.; **il a beaucoup vécu,** he's seen (a lot of) life; **être facile à v.,** to be easy to get on with; **savoir v.,** to know how to behave; **il fait bon v.,** life is pleasant (d) to subsist; **v. bien,** to live in comfort; **travailler pour v.,** to work for one's living; **avoir de quoi v.,** to have enough to live on **2.** *vtr* **v. sa vie,** to live one's own life; **les événements que nous avons vécus,** the events we lived through.

vivre² *nm* (a) **le v. et le couvert,** board and lodging (b) *pl* provisions, supplies.

vlan, v'lan [vlɑ̃] *int* wham! bang!

vocabulaire [vɔkabylɛr] *nm* vocabulary; *Pej:* **quel v.!** what language!

vocal, -aux [vɔkal, -o] *a* vocal. **vocalement** *adv* vocally.

vocation [vɔkasjɔ̃] *nf* **1.** vocation; (divine) call **2.** vocation; calling, bent, inclination; **avoir la v. de l'enseignement,** to be cut out for teaching.

vocifération [vɔsiferasjɔ̃] *nf* vociferation; *pl* shouts.

vociférer [vɔsifere] *vi* (je **vocifère; je vociférerai**) to vociferate (**contre,** against); to shout, hurl (insults).

vœu, -x [vø] *nm* **1.** vow; **faire (le) v. de faire qch,** to vow to do sth, to make a vow to do sth **2.** wish; **faire un v.,** to make a wish; **tous nos vœux de bonheur!** all good wishes for your happiness! **meilleurs vœux,** best wishes.

vogue [vɔg] *nf* fashion, vogue; **être en v.,** to be in fashion; **c'est la grande v.,** it's all the rage.

voici [vwasi] *prep* **1.** here is, are; **me v.,** here I am; **la v. qui vient,** here she comes; **v. ce dont il s'agit,** this is what it's all about; **mon ami que v. vous le dira,** my friend here will tell you; **la petite histoire que v.,** the following little story **2.** (= IL Y A) **je l'ai vu v. trois ans,** I saw him three years ago; **v. trois mois que j'habite ici,** I've been living here for the last three months.

voie [vwa] *nf* **1.** (a) way, road, route, track; *Adm:* *Aut:* traffic lane; **v. publique,** public highway; **route à quatre voies,** four-lane road, *NAm:* four-lane highway; *Astr:* **la V. lactée,** the Milky Way; **v. de communication,** road, thoroughfare; **v. sans issue,** no through road; **v. navigable,** waterway; **par v. de terre,** by land; **par la v. des airs,** by air (b) *Ven:* (often *pl*) tracks (of game); **mettre qn sur la v.,** to put s.o. on the right track (c) *Rail:* **v. ferrée,** railway, *NAm:* railroad, track; **v. de garage,** siding; **mettre un projet sur une v. de garage,** to shelve a plan; **v. étroite,** narrow-gauge line; **sur quelle v. arrive le train?** on which platform does the train come in? (d) *Nau:* **v. d'eau,** leak (e) *Anat:* passage, duct; **les voies digestives,** the digestive tract(s) **2.** way; **voies et moyens,** ways and means; **par (la) v. diplomatique,** through diplomatic channels; **une v. dangereuse,** a dangerous course; **affaire en bonne voie,** business that is going well; **en v. d'achèvement,** nearing completion; **en v. de construction,** under construction; **pays en v. de développement,** developing countries; **en v. de guérison,** getting better; **être en (bonne) v. de réussir,** to be on the road to success; *Jur:* **voies de**

fait, acts of violence; **se livrer à des voies de fait sur qn,** to assault s.o.

voilà [vwala] *prep* **1.** (*a*) there is, are; **le v.,** there he is; **la pendule que v.,** that clock (there); **en v. assez!** that's enough! that will do! **en v. une idée!** what an idea! **v. tout,** that's all; **le v. qui entre,** there he is coming in; **v. qui est curieux!** that's odd! **v. ce qu'il m'a dit,** that's what he told me; **v. comme elle est,** that's just like her; **v.! there you are! et v.! and that's that!** (*in restaurant*) **v., monsieur!** coming, sir! (*b*) (= **voici**) **me v.!** here I am! **2.** (= **il y a**) **en juin v. trois ans,** in June three years ago; **v. dix ans que je le connais,** I've known him for ten years.

voilage [vwalaʒ] *nm* (*a*) net (*b*) net curtain.

voile [vwal] **1.** *nf* sail; **faire v.,** to set sail (**pour,** for); **toutes voiles dehors,** in full sail; **faire de la v.,** to go sailing; *F:* **mettre les voiles,** to leave, to push off **2.** *nm* (*a*) veil; **prendre le v.,** to take the veil; **sous le v. de la religion,** under the cloak of religion (*b*) film, mist (before one's eyes) (*c*) *Tex:* voile (*d*) *Anat:* **v. du palais,** soft palate, velum (*e*) *Med:* shadow (on lung).

voiler [vwale] **1.** *vtr* (*a*) to veil (*b*) to veil, obscure, dim; to muffle **2.** (*a*) **se v. (le visage)** to wear a veil; *Fig:* **se v. la face,** to bury one's head in the sand (*b*) **se v.,** (i) (*of sky*) to become overcast, to cloud over (ii) (*of wheel*) to warp, to buckle. **voilé** *a* veiled; misty (light, sky); muffled (sound); husky (voice).

voilier [vwalje] *nm* sailing ship, sailing boat; windjammer.

voilure [vwalyr] *nf* (*a*) sails (of ship) (*b*) *Av:* wing(s), flying surface, aerofoil.

voir [vwar] *vtr* (*prp* **voyant;** *pp* **vu;** *pr ind* **ils voient;** *pr sub* **je voie;** *ph* **je vis;** *fu* **je verrai**) **1.** to see; to set eyes on (s.o., sth); to sight (ship); **détail vu de près,** close-up detail; *F:* **on aura tout vu!** wonders will never cease! **je l'ai vu de mes propres yeux,** I saw it with my own eyes; **il ne voit pas plus loin que le bout de son nez,** he can't see further than the end of his nose; **à le v.,** to judge by his looks; **on voit son jupon,** her slip is showing; **on n'y voit rien,** you can't see a thing (it's so dark); **v. rouge,** to see red; **voyez vous-même!** see for yourself! **voyez un peu!** just look at him, just look at it! **faire v. qch à qn,** to show sth to s.o.; **faites v.!** let me see it! **en faire v. à qn,** to make s.o.'s life a misery; *P:* **voyons v.,** let's see; let's have a look; **dites v.,** tell me; **essayez v.,** just have a try **2. v. + inf** (*a*) **v. venir qn,** to see s.o. coming; **je l'ai vu tomber,** I saw him fall (*b*) **v. faire qch,** to see sth done; **il l'a vu faire la vaisselle,** he saw him do the washing up (*c*) **se v. refuser qch,** to be refused sth (*d*) **je me suis vu forcé de partir,** I was forced to leave **3.** (*a*) to visit; **aller v. qn,** to go and see s.o.; **v. du pays,** to travel (*b*) **il ne voit personne,** he sees, he receives, no one; **on ne te voit plus!** you're quite a stranger; **je ne peux pas le v.,** I can't stand (the sight of) him **4.** (*a*) to understand; **je vois où vous voulez en venir,** I see what you're driving at; *F:* **ni vu, ni connu,** nobody's any the wiser for it (*b*) to perceive, observe; **cela se voit,** that's obvious; **la tache ne se voit pas,** you can't see the mark; the mark doesn't show; **vous voyez ça d'ici,** you can imagine what it's like; **je ne le vois pas marié,** I can't imagine him married **5.** (*a*) to look after, to see to, to see about

(sth); **v. une affaire à fond,** to examine a matter thoroughly; **je verrai,** I'll think about it; **c'est ce que nous verrons!** that remains to be seen; **il n'a rien à v. là-dedans,** it has nothing to do with him (*b*) **il va v. à nous loger,** he'll see that we have somewhere to stay; **c'est à vous de v. que rien ne vous manque,** it's up to you to see that you have everything you need (*c*) *int* **voyons!** (i) let's see (ii) come, now! **6.** to consider (sth in a particular way); **c'est sa façon de v. les choses,** it's his way of looking at things; **se faire bien v. de qn,** to get into s.o.'s good books; **être bien vu de tous,** to be well thought of by all; **mal vu,** poorly considered; disliked.

voire [vwar] *adv* indeed; **v. (même),** and even; or even.

voirie [vwari] *nf* **1.** administration of public thoroughfares; **le service de v.,** the highways department **2.** (*a*) refuse collection (*b*) refuse dump.

voisin, -ine [vwazɛ̃, -in] **1.** *a* neighbouring, adjoining; **la chambre voisine,** the next room; **il habite la maison voisine,** he lives next door; **émotion voisine de la terreur,** emotion akin to terror, bordering on terror **2.** *n* neighbour; **v. d'à côté,** next-door neighbour; **mon v. de table,** the person I was sitting next to (at table); **en bon v.,** in a neighbourly way.

voisinage [vwazinaʒ] *nm* **1.** vicinity; proximity, nearness **2.** neighbourhood, vicinity; **être en bon v. avec qn,** to be on neighbourly terms with s.o.

voisiner [vwazine] *vi* **v. avec qn, qch,** to be (placed) side by side with s.o., with sth; to adjoin sth.

voiture [vwatyr] *nf* (*a*) (horse-drawn) vehicle; (*for people*) carriage, coach; (*for goods*) cart (*b*) car, *NAm:* automobile; **v. de tourisme,** private car; **v. de sport,** sports car (*c*) *Rail:* coach, carriage, *NAm:* car; **en v.!** all aboard! (*d*) **v. d'enfant,** pram, *NAm:* baby carriage.

voix [vwa] *nf* **1.** voice; **parler à v. haute, à haute v.,** to speak (i) in a loud voice (ii) aloud; **parler à v. basse,** to speak in a low voice, in an undertone; (*of dogs*) **donner de la v.,** to bark, to bay; *Mus:* **chanter à plusieurs v.,** to sing in parts; **être en v.,** to be in voice **2.** **rester sans v.,** to remain speechless; **la v. de la conscience,** the dictates of conscience; **la v. de la nature,** the call of nature; **mettre une question aux v.,** to put a question to the vote; **la Chambre alla aux v.,** the House divided; **avoir v. au chapitre,** to have a say in the matter **3.** *Gram:* voice.

vol¹ [vɔl] *nm* **1.** (*a*) flying, flight; **prendre son v.,** to take wing; to take off; **au v.,** on the wing; **à v. d'oiseau,** as the crow flies; **vue à v. d'oiseau,** bird's-eye view; **attraper une balle au v.,** to catch a ball in mid air; **saisir une occasion au v.,** to grasp an opportunity (*b*) *Av:* **heures de v.,** flying time; **v. à voile,** gliding; **v. libre,** hang gliding **2.** flock, flight (of birds); covey (of game birds).

vol² *nm* theft; stealing, robbery; **v. avec effraction,** breaking and entering; **v. à la tire,** pickpocketing; **v. à main armée,** armed robbery; *F:* **c'est du v.!** it's daylight robbery!

volage [vɔlaʒ] *a* fickle, flighty.

volaille [vɔlaj] *nf* **1.** *coll* poultry; **une v.,** a fowl; **marchand de v.,** poulterer **2.** *Cu:* poultry, *esp* chicken; **foies de v.,** chicken livers.

volant [vɔlɑ̃] **1.** *a* (*a*) flying; fluttering; *Av:* **personnel**

v., flying staff (b) loose; movable; **feuille volante,** loose leaf 2. nm (a) Games: shuttlecock (b) fly-wheel (c) handwheel; Aut: (steering) wheel; **prendre le v.,** to take the wheel (d) Dressm: flounce.

volatil [vɔlatil] a Ch: etc: volatile.

volatile [vɔlatil] nm bird; esp fowl.

volatiliser [vɔlatilize] 1. vtr (a) Ch: to volatilize (b) to make (sth) disappear 2. se v., to vanish into thin air.

vol-au-vent [vɔlovɑ̃] nm inv Cu: vol-au-vent.

volcan [vɔlkɑ̃] nm (a) volcano (b) fiery, impetuous, person. **volcanique** a volcanic.

volée [vɔle] nf 1. flight (of bird, projectile); **prendre sa v.,** to take wing; **lancer qch à toute v.,** to hurl sth; **coup de v.,** Fb: punt; Ten: volley 2. flock, flight (of birds); band (of girls) 3. volley (of missiles); shower (of blows); **recevoir une bonne v.,** to get a sound thrashing; **sonner à toute v.,** (i) to set all the bells ringing (ii) (of bells) to ring in full peal 4. **v. d'escalier,** flight of stairs.

voler¹ [vɔle] vi to fly; **v. de ses propres ailes,** to fend for oneself; **on aurait entendu v. une mouche,** you could have heard a pin drop; **v. en éclats,** to fly into pieces.

voler² vtr 1. to steal; **v. qch à qn,** to steal sth from s.o.; **je me suis fait v. ma valise,** I've had my suitcase stolen; F: **il ne l'a pas volé,** it serves him right; he asked for it 2. (a) to rob (s.o.) (b) to swindle, cheat (s.o.).

volet [vɔlɛ] nm (a) shutter (of window); volet (of triptych) (b) ICE: throttle valve (of carburettor) (c) **carte à v.,** stub card (d) Av: flap (e) tear-off, detachable, section (of cheque).

voleter [vɔlte] vi (**il volette**) to flutter (about).

voleur, -euse [vɔlœr, -øz] 1. n thief; robber; (shop-keeper) swindler; **au v.!** stop thief! **v. de grand chemin,** highwayman 2. a être v., to be a thief.

volière [vɔljɛr] nf aviary.

volley-ball [vɔlɛbol] nm Sp: volleyball.

volleyeur, -euse [vɔlɛjœr, -øz] n volleyball player.

volontaire [vɔlɔ̃tɛr] 1. a (a) voluntary; Mil: **engagé v.,** volunteer (b) self-willed, headstrong, obstinate; **menton v.,** firm chin 2. n volunteer. **volontairement** adv voluntarily, willingly; deliberately, intentionally.

volonté [vɔlɔ̃te] nf 1. (a) will; **v. de fer,** iron will; **manque de v.,** lack of will(power); **avec la meilleure v. du monde,** with the best will in the world (b) **bonne v.,** goodwill; willingness; **mauvaise v.,** ill will; unwillingness; **faire qch de bonne v.,** to do sth willingly, with good grace (c) **en faire à sa v.,** to have one's own way; **à v.,** at will; ad lib; **du vin à v.,** as much wine as one likes; **sucrer à v.,** add sugar to taste 2. (a) **les dernières volontés (de qn),** (s.o.'s) last will and testament; (s.o.'s) last wishes (b) **elle fait ses quatre volontés,** she does just what she pleases.

volontiers [vɔlɔ̃tje] adv (a) willingly, gladly, with pleasure; **très v.,** I'd love to; **il cause v.,** he's fond of talking (b) readily; **on croit v. que,** we are apt to think that.

volt [vɔlt] nm El Meas: volt.

voltage [vɔltaʒ] nm El: voltage.

volte-face [vɔltəfas] nf inv (a) turning round (b)

Fig: volte-face; **faire v.-f.,** to reverse one's opinions, one's policy; to do a U turn.

voltige [vɔltiʒ] nf 1. Equit: (haute) v., trick riding 2. Av: aerobatics.

voltiger [vɔltiʒe] vi (n. **voltigeons**) (of bird, insect) to fly about; to flit; to flutter about.

volubilis [vɔlybilis] nm Bot: convolvulus; morning glory.

volubilité [vɔlybilite] nf volubility. **volubile** a voluble.

volume [vɔlym] nm 1. volume, tome 2. (a) volume, bulk, mass; **faire du v.,** to take up space (b) volume (of sound). **volumineux, -euse** a voluminous, bulky.

volupté [vɔlypte] nf (sensual) pleasure. **voluptueux, -euse** a voluptuous. **voluptueusement** adv voluptuously.

volute [vɔlyt] nf Arch: volute; curl (of smoke).

vomi [vɔmi] nm vomit.

vomir [vɔmir] vtr (a) to vomit; to bring up (food); vi to be sick, to throw up; **c'est à (faire) v.,** it's enough to make you sick (b) to belch forth (smoke) (c) to loathe, to abhor (s.o.).

vomissement [vɔmismɑ̃] nm vomiting.

voracité [vɔrasite] nf voracity.

vorace [vɔras] a voracious. **voracement** adv voraciously.

vos [vo] see **votre.**

votant, -ante [vɔtɑ̃, -ɑ̃t] n voter.

vote [vɔt] nm 1. (a) vote (b) voting, ballot(ing), poll; **droit de v.,** franchise; **accorder le droit de v. aux femmes,** to give women the vote 2. Pol: **v. d'une loi,** passing of a bill; **v. de confiance,** vote of confidence.

voter [vɔte] 1. vi to vote; **v. à main levée,** to vote by (a) show of hands; **v. communiste,** to vote communist 2. vtr (a) Pol: to pass, carry (a bill) (b) to vote (money).

votre, pl vos [vɔtr, vo] poss a your; **un de vos amis,** a friend of yours.

vôtre [vɔtr] **le vôtre, la vôtre, les vôtres;** (a) poss pron yours; your own; **sa mère et la v.,** his mother and yours; F: **à la v.!** cheers! (your) good health! (b) nm (i) **il faut y mettre du v.,** you must pull your weight (ii) pl your own (friends, family); **je serai des vôtres,** I'll be joining you.

vouer [vwe] vtr to vow, dedicate, consecrate; **se v. à l'étude,** to devote one's life to study; **voué à l'échec,** doomed to failure.

vouloir¹ [vulwar] vtr (prp **voulant;** pp **voulu;** pr ind **je veux, il veut, ils veulent;** pr sub **je veuille, n. voulions, ils veuillent;** imp in 1. **voulez,** otherwise **veuille, veuillez;** impf **je voulais;** fu **je voudrai**) 1. to will (sth); to be determined on (sth); **Dieu le veuille!** please God! Prov: **v., c'est pouvoir,** where there's a will there's a way; **vous l'avez voulu!** you have only yourself to blame! 2. (a) to want, to wish (for), to desire (sth); **il sait ce qu'il veut,** he knows his own mind; **faites comme vous voudrez,** do as you please; **qu'il le veuille ou non,** whether he likes it or not; **je ne veux pas!** I will not have it! **que voulez-vous!** (i) what do you want? (ii) what do you expect? **que voulez-vous que j'y fasse?** what do you want me to do about it? **que lui voulez-vous?** what do you want from him? **voulez-vous du thé?** would you like some tea? **ils ne veulent pas de moi,** they won't have me; **de l'argent en veux-tu (en voilà),** money galore (b) **v. qn pour roi,** to want s.o. as king (c) **je ne lui veux pas de mal,** I mean him no harm; **en v. à qn,** to bear s.o. a grudge; **ne m'en veuillez pas,** don't be cross with me; **à qui en voulez-vous?** what's the trouble now? **pourquoi lui en veux-tu?** what have you got against him? **s'en v.,** to be angry with oneself (**de qch,** about sth) 3. **v. + inf, v. que + sub** (a) to will, to require, to demand; **le mauvais sort voulut qu'il arrivât trop tard,** as ill luck would have it he arrived too late; **je veux être obéi,** I intend to be obeyed; **v. absolument faire qch,** to insist on doing sth; **le moteur ne veut pas démarrer,** the engine won't start (b) to want, wish; **il voulait me frapper,** he wanted to hit me; **je fais de lui ce que je veux,** I can do as I like with him; **je voudrais être à ta place,** I wish I were in your place; **voulez-vous que j'ouvre la fenêtre?** shall I open the window? **que voulez-vous que je fasse?** what do you expect me to do? **rentrons, voulez-vous?** let's go in, shall we? (c) to try to (do sth); **il voulut me frapper,** he made as if to strike me (d) to mean, intend; **je voulais écrire un livre sur ce sujet,** I meant to write a book on this subject; **faire qch sans le v.,** to do sth unintentionally (e) **v. (bien) faire qch,** to consent, be willing, to do sth; **je veux bien que vous veniez,** I'd like you to come; **veuillez vous asseoir,** will you please sit down; do (please) sit down; **je veux bien attendre,** I'm quite happy to wait; **si vous voulez,** if you like; **si vous (le) voulez bien,** if you don't mind (f) **(bien** used as an intensive) **voulez-vous bien vous taire!** will you be quiet! F: do shut up! 4. (a) to admit, to allow; **je veux bien que vous ayez raison,** (I grant you that) you may be right (b) to be convinced, to maintain; **il veut absolument que je me sois trompé,** he insists that I was mistaken 5. (of thg) to require, need, demand; **la vigne veut un terrain crayeux,** the vine requires a chalky soil.

vouloir[2] nm **bon, mauvais, v.,** goodwill, ill will (**pour, envers,** towards).

voulu [vuly] a 1. required, requisite (formalities); **j'agirai en temps v.,** I shall take action at the proper time 2. deliberate, intentional; **négligence voulue,** studied negligence.

vous [vu] pers pron sg & pl 1. (unstressed) (a) (subject) you (b) (object) you; to you; **je v. en ai parlé,** I've spoken to you about it (c) (refl) **v. allez v. faire du mal,** you'll hurt yourself, yourselves (d) (reciprocal) **v. v. connaissez,** you know one another, each other 2. (stressed) (a) (subject) you; **v. et votre femme,** you and your wife; **v. tous,** you all, all of you; **v. autres Anglais,** you English (b) (object) **c'est à v. que je parle,** it's you I'm talking to; **c'est à v. de jouer,** it is your turn to play; **ceci est à v.,** this is yours; **un ami à v.,** a friend of yours; **j'ai confiance en v.,** I trust you (c) (refl) **v. ne pensez qu'à v.(-même),** you think only of yourself.

vous-même(s) [vumɛm] pers pron yourself, pl yourselves.

voûte [vut] nf vault, arch; Lit: **la v. céleste,** the canopy of heaven; Anat: **v. plantaire,** arch of the foot.

voûter [vute] 1. vtr (a) to arch, vault (roof) (b) to make (s.o.) stooped 2. **se v.,** to become bent, round-

shouldered; to begin to stoop. **voûté** a vaulted, arched (roof); stooping, round-shouldered (person); bent (back).

vouvoiement [vuvwamã] nm addressing s.o. as **vous.**

vouvoyer [vuvwaje] vtr (**je vouvoie, n. vouvoyons**) to address (s.o.) as **vous.**

voyage [vwajaʒ] nm journey, trip; tour; (at sea) voyage; **aimer les voyages,** to be fond of travel; **v. d'affaires,** business trip; **v. organisé,** package tour, package holiday; **v. de noces,** honeymoon; **il est en v.,** he's away; **frais de v.,** travelling expenses; **compagnon de v.,** (i) travelling companion (ii) fellow passenger; **bon v.!** have a good trip!

voyager [vwajaʒe] vi (n. **voyageons**) (a) to travel; **v. par mer,** to travel by sea; **j'aime v.,** I love travelling (b) Com: to travel; **v. pour les vins,** to travel in wine.

voyageur, -euse [vwajaʒœr, -øz] 1. n (a) traveller; (in train) passenger (b) **v. de commerce,** commercial traveller 2. a travelling.

voyant, -ante [vwajã, -ãt] 1. n clairvoyant 2. a gaudy, loud, garish (colour); showy, conspicuous 3. nm Aut: **v. d'huile,** oil indicator light; warning light.

voyelle [vwajɛl] nf vowel.

voyeur, -euse [vwajœr, -øz] n voyeur, voyeuse; F: Peeping Tom.

voyou [vwaju] 1. nm (young) lout, layabout; hooligan 2. a loutish.

vrac [vrak] nm **en v.,** loose, in bulk; **marchandises en v.,** loose goods (not packed); **outils jetés en v. sur le plancher,** tools thrown higgledy piggledy on the floor.

vrai [vrɛ] 1. a (a) true, truthful; **c'est (bien) v.!** its true! F: **pour de v.,** really, seriously; NAm: for real; **c'est pour de v.,** I'm serious (b) true, real, genuine (c) downright, regular (liar); **c'est une vraie attrape,** it's a real swindle 2. adv truly, really, indeed; **dire v.,** to tell the truth; **à v. dire,** as a matter of fact; F: **tu m'aimes (pas) v.?** you do love me don't you? **v. de v.!** really and truly! **pas v.?** I'm right, aren't I? F: **c'est pas v.!** really? oh no! 3. nm truth; **il y a du v. là-dedans,** there's some truth in it. **vraiment** adv really, truly, in truth; **v.?** really?

vraisemblable [vrɛsãblabl] 1. a probable, likely; credible; plausible; conceivable; **excuse peu v.,** unconvincing excuse 2. nm what is probable, likely. **vraisemblablement** adv in all likelihood; probably, very likely; conceivably.

vraisemblance [vrɛsãblãs] nf probability, likelihood.

vrille [vrij] nf 1. Tls: gimlet 2. Av: spin; **descente en v.,** spinning dive.

vrombir [vrɔ̃bir] vi to buzz; to hum; to throb.

vrombissement [vrɔ̃bismã] nm buzz(ing); hum(ming); throb(bing).

vu, vue[1] [vy] 1. n **au vu de tous,** openly, publicly; **au vu et au su de tous,** as everyone knows; **c'est du déjà vu,** that's nothing new 2. prep considering, seeing; **vu la chaleur, je voyagerai de nuit,** in view of the heat I'll travel by night; conj phr F: **vu que + ind** seeing that.

vue[2] [vy] nf 1. (eye)sight; vision; **avoir la v. basse,** (i) to have poor eyesight (ii) to be shortsighted; **connaître qn de v.,** to know s.o. by sight; **perdre qn de v.,** (i) to lose sight of s.o. (ii) to lose touch with s.o.;

personnes les plus en v., people most in the public eye; **personnalité en v.,** prominent personality; **(bien) en v.,** conspicuous; **à perte de v.,** as far as the eye can see; **faire qch à la v. de tous,** to do sth in full view of everybody; **à v. d'œil,** visibly; before one's very eyes; *F:* **à v. de nez,** at a rough guess **2.** view; **échange de vues,** exchange of views **3. à première v.,** at first sight; *Com:* **payable à v.,** payable at sight **4.** *(a)* view; outlook; **chambre avec v. sur la mer,** room that looks out onto the sea *(b)* intention, purpose; **avoir qch en v.,** to have sth in mind; **en v. de,** with a view to; **travailler en v. de l'avenir,** to work with an eye to the future.

vulgaire [vylgɛr] *a* vulgar; common; coarse. **vulgairement** *adv* vulgarly; commonly; coarsely.

vulgarisation [vylgarizasjɔ̃] *nf* popularization.

vulgariser [vylgarize] *vtr* to popularize.

vulgarité [vylgarite] *nf* vulgarity.

vulnérabilité [vylnerabilite] *nf* vulnerability.

vulnérable *a* vulnerable.

vulve [vylv] *nf Anat:* vulva.

Vve *abbr* veuve, widow.

W

W, w [dubləve] *nm* (the letter) W, w.
wagon [vagɔ̃] *nm Rail:* carriage, coach, *NAm:* car (for passengers); wagon, truck, *NAm:* car (for goods); **monter en w.,** to board the train; **w. à bestiaux,** cattle truck; **w. frigorifique,** refrigerated van.
wagon-citerne [vagɔ̃sitɛrn] *nm* tank wagon; *pl wagons-citernes.*
wagon-lit [vagɔ̃li] *nm* sleeping-car, *F:* sleeper; *pl wagons-lits.*
wagon(n)et [vagɔnɛ] *nm* tip truck.
wagon-restaurant [vagɔ̃rɛstɔrɑ̃] *nm* restaurant-car; dining-car; *pl wagons-restaurants.*
wallon, -onne [valɔ̃, -ɔn; wa-] **1.** *a & n Geog:* Walloon. **2.** *nm Ling:* Walloon.
water-polo [watɛrpɔlo] *nm Sp:* water polo.
waters [watɛr] *nmpl F:* lavatory, loo, toilet; *NAm:* john.
watt [wat] *nm ElMeas:* watt, ampere-volt.
WC [vese] *abbr water closet.*
week-end [wikɛnd] *nm* weekend; *pl week-ends.*
western [wɛstɛrn] *nm Cin:* western.
whisky [wiski] *nm* whisky; *pl whiskys.*

X

X, x [iks] *nm* (the letter) X, x; **Monsieur X,** Mr X;
rayons X, x-rays; **je vous l'ai dit x fois,** I've told you
a thousand times.

xénophobie [ksenɔfɔbi] *nf* xenophobia. **xéno-**
phobe *a & n* xenophobe.

Xérès [kseres, gzeres] **1.** *Prn Geog:* Jerez **2.** *nm* (**vin**
de) X., sherry.

xylophone [ksilɔfɔn] *nm Mus:* xylophone.

Y

an asterisk (*) before a noun indicates that the def art is **le** *or* **la,** *not* **l'**

Y, y¹ [igrɛk] *nm* (the letter) Y, y.
y² [i] *adv & pron* **1.** *adv* there; here; **j'y suis, j'y reste!** here I am and here I stay! **je n'y suis pour personne,** I'm not at home to anybody; *F:* **ah, j'y suis!** ah, now I understand, I've got it! **vous n'y êtes pas du tout,** you're wide of the mark; **pendant que vous y êtes,** while you're at it **2.** *pron inv* (*a*) **j'y gagnerai,** I shall gain by it; **je m'y attendais,** I expected as much; **venez nous voir—je n'y manquerai pas,** come and see us—I certainly shall (*b*) (*standing for pers just mentioned*) **pensez-vous à lui?**—**oui, j'y pense,** are you thinking of him?—yes, I am **3.** (*indeterminate uses*) **je vous y prends!** I have caught you (in the act)! **ça y est!** [saje] (i) that's done! (ii) that's done it! I knew it! **il y est pour quelque chose,** he's got a hand in it;

he's got something to do with it **4. vas-y** [vazi] (i) go (there) (ii) get on with it! go on!
*yacht [jɔt] *nm Nau:* yacht.
*yachting [jɔtiŋ] *nm* yachting.
*yaourt [jaurt] *nm* yoghurt.
yeux [jø] *nmpl see* œil.
*yé-yé [jeje] **1.** *a inv* **chanson yé-yé,** pop song **2.** *n* pop fan.
*yoga [jɔga] *nm* yoga.
*yog(h)ourt [jogurt] *nm* = **yaourt**.
*Yougoslavie [jugɔslavi] *Prnf Geog:* Yugoslavia. ***yougoslave** *a & n* Yugoslav.
*youyou [juju] *nm Nau:* dinghy.
*yo-yo [jojo] *nm Rtm:* yo-yo.

Z

Z, z [zɛd] *nm* (the letter) Z, z.
Zaïre [zair] *Prnm* Zaire.
Zambie [zãbi] *Prnf Geog:* Zambia.
zèbre [zɛbr̩] *nm* 1. zebra; **courir comme un z.,** to run like a hare 2. *F:* individual, bod.
zébrer [zebre] *vtr* (**je zèbre**) to stripe; to streak. **zébré** *a* striped (**de,** with); stripy.
zébrure [zebryr] *nf* 1. stripe 2. stripes; zebra markings.
zébu [zeby] *nm Z:* zebu.
zèle [zɛl] *nm* zeal (**pour,** for); *Ind:* **grève du z.,** work to rule (strike); *F:* **faire du z.,** to be over-zealous. **zélé, -ée** *a & n* zealous (person).
zénith [zenit] *nm* zenith.
zéro [zero] *nm* 1. nought; *Tp:* **z. sept,** O [ou] seven; **c'est un z.,** he's a nonentity; *Sp:* **trois à z.,** three nil; *Ten:* **quinze à z.,** fifteen love 2. zero (of scale); **recommencer à z.,** to start from scratch; *Sch* **z. de conduite,** bad conduct mark; *F:* **avoir le moral à z.,** to be depressed; **mais en maths, z. (pour la question),** as far as maths goes, he's useless 3. *a* **z. faute,** no mistakes; **z. heure,** zero hour.
zeste [zɛst] *nm Cu:* peel, zest (of lemon, orange).
zézaiement [zezɛmã] *nm* lisp.
zézayer [zezeje] *vi & tr* (**je zézaie, je zézaye**) to lisp.
ZI *abbr* zone industrielle.
zibeline [ziblin] *nf* 1. *Z:* (**martre**) **z.,** sable 2. sable (fur).
zig [zig] *nm P:* bloke, guy.

zigomar [zigomar], **zigoto** [zigoto] *nm P:* bloke, guy; **un drôle de z.,** a queer customer.
zigouiller [ziguje] *vtr P:* to do (s.o.) in.
zigzag [zigzag] *nm* zigzag; **faire des zigzags,** to zigzag.
zigzaguer [zigzage] *vi* to zigzag.
zinc [zɛ̃g] *nm* 1 zinc 2. *F:* (zinc) counter; bar 3. *F:* aeroplane, crate.
zinzin [zɛ̃zɛ̃] *F:* 1. *a* cracked, nuts 2. *nm* thingummy.
zizanie [zizani] *nf* discord.
zizi [zizi] *nm F:* willy.
zodiaque [zodjak] *nm* zodiac.
zona [zona] *nm Med:* shingles.
zone [zon] *nf* (a) zone; *Geog:* **z. tempérée,** temperate zone; **z. houillère,** coal belt; *Meteor:* **z. de dépression,** trough (of low pressure) (b) *Adm:* **z. verte,** green belt; *Aut:* **z. bleue,** meter zone; **z. postale,** postal area; **la Z.,** slum area; *PolEc:* **z. franche,** free zone; **z. franc,** franc area; **z. dangereuse,** danger zone.
zoo [zo] *nm* zoo.
zoologie [zɔɔlɔʒi] *nf* zoology. **zoologique** *a* zoological.
zoologiste [zɔɔlɔʒist] *n* zoologist.
zoom [zum] *nm Cin:* zoom (lens).
zouave [zwav] *nm Mil:* zouave; *F:* **faire le z.,** to play the fool, to fool around.
zoulou, -ous [zulu] *a & n* Zulu.
zozoter [zɔzɔte] *vi F:* to lisp.
zut [zyt] *int F:* (a) damn! blast it! (b) go to hell! get stuffed! **avoir un œil qui dit z. à l'autre,** to squint.